T5-CVR-772

DIRECTORY OF AMERICAN SCHOLARS

DIRECTORY OF AMERICAN SCHOLARS

TENTH EDITION

VOLUME I

HISTORY, ARCHAEOLOGY, & AREA STUDIES

Caryn E. Klebba, Editor

GALE GROUP

THOMSON LEARNING™

Detroit • New York • San Diego • San Francisco
Boston • New Haven, Conn. • Waterville, Maine
London • Munich

Caryn E. Klebba, *Editor*

Jason B. Baldwin, *Assistant Editor*

Contributing Editors: Alex Alviar, Claire M. Campana, Eric Hoss, Chris Lopez, Christine Maurer, Jenai Mynatt, Jaime E. Noce, Kathleen E. Maki Potts, Amanda C. Quick

Lynne Maday, *Contributor*

Erin E. Braun, *Managing Editor*

Ralph Wiazowski, *Programmer/Analyst*
Venus Little, *Manager, Database Applications, Technical Support Services*

Dorothy Maki, *Manufacturing Manager*
Evi Seoud, *Production Manager*
NeKita McKee, *Buyer*

Data Capture Specialists: Nikkita Bankston, Cynthia A. Jones, Frances L. Monroe

Mike Logusz, *Graphic Artist*

ISBN: 0-7876-5008-0 (Volume 1)
ISBN: 0-7876-5009-9 (Volume 2)
ISBN: 0-7876-5010-2 (Volume 3)
ISBN: 0-7876-5011-0 (Volume 4)
ISBN: 0-7876-5012-9 (Volume 5)
ISBN: 0-7876-5013-7 (Volume 6)
ISBN: 0-7876-5007-2 (set)
ISSN: 0070-5101

Printed in the United States of America
Published in the United States by Gale Group

CONTENTS

MAJOR HUMANITIES & SOCIAL SCIENCE DISCIPLINES

Volume I: History, Archaeology, & Area Studies

Aesthetics
Architecture
Archaeology
Area Studies
Art
Art History
Assyriology
Community Studies
Community Planning
Demography
Geography
History
International Studies
Urban Studies
Western Civilization

Volume II: English, Speech, & Drama

Advertising
Audiology
Bibliography
Cinema
Classical Literature
Communications
Composition (Language Arts)
Creative Writing
Drama
English Literature
Film Studies
Journalism
Library Science
Literary Theory
Literature
Marketing
Mass Communication
Media Studies
Music
Music History
Musicology
Performing Arts
Poetry
Rhetoric
Speech Communication
Speech-Language Pathology
Theater Studies

Volume III: Foreign Languages, Linguistics, & Philology

Classical Languages
Comparative Literature
Foreign Languages
Foreign Literature Studies
Linguistics
Modern Languages
Philology
Romance Languages
Translation

Volume IV: Philosophy, Religion, & Law

Accounting
Business Administration
Corrections
Criminal Justice
Criminology
Economics
Epistemology
Ethics
Evangelism
Forensic Sciences
Government
Homiletics
International Relations
Missiology
Philosophy
Political Science
Public Affairs
Religious Studies
Statistics

Volume V: Psychology, Sociology, & Education

Adult Education
Anthropology
Behavioral Sciences
Child Development
Clinical Psychology
Counseling
Culture Studies
Education
Ethnology
Folklore
Gender Studies
Gerontology
Health Studies
Human Development
Language Education
Psychology
Social Work
Sociology
Women's Studies

metrop metropolitan
Mex Mexican, Mexicano, Mexico
mfg manufacturing
mfr manufacture, manufacturer
mgr manager(s)
mgt management
Mich Michigan
mid middle
mil military
Minn Minnesota
Miss Mississippi
mitt mitteilung
mkt market, marketing
MLA Modern Language Association of America
Mo Missouri
mod modern,moderna, moderne, moderno
monatsh monatsheft(e)
monatsschr monatsschrift
monogr monograph
Mont Montana
morphol morphologica, morphologie, morphology
mt mount, mountain(s)
munic municipal
mus museum(s)
musicol musicological, musicology

n north
nac nacional
NASA National Aeronautics & Space Administration
nat nationaal, national, nationale, nationalis, naturalized
NATO North Atlantic Treaty Organization
naz nazionale
NB New Brunswick
NC North Carolina
MCTE National Council of Teachers of English
NDak North Dakota
NDEA National Defense Education Act
NEA National Education Association
Nebr Nebraska
Ned Nederland, Nederlandsch
Nev Nevada
Neth Netherlands
Nfld Newfoundland
NH New Hampshire
NJ New Jersey
NMex New Mexico
no number
nonres nonresident
norm normal, normale
Norweg Norwegian
Nov November
NS Nova Scotia
NSW New South Wales
NT Northwest Territories
numis numismatic, numismatico, numismatique
NY New York
NZ New Zealand

occas occasional
occup occupation, occupational
Oct October
Ohio
OEEC Organization for European Economic Cooperation
off office, officer(s), official(s)
Okla Oklahoma
Ont Ontario
oper operation(s), operational, operative
ord ordnance
Ore Oregon
orgn organization, organizational
orient oriental, orientale, orientalist, orientalia
ornithol ornithological, ornithology

Pa Pennsylvania
Pac Pacific
paleontol paleontological, paleontology
PanAm Pan American
pedag pedagogia, pedagogic, pedagogical, pedagogico,
pedagogoie, pedagogik, pedagogique, pedagogy
Pei Prince Edward Island
penol penological, penology
phenomenol phenomenological, phenomenologie, phenomenology
philol philologica, philological, philologie, philologisch, philology
philos philosophia, philosophic, philosophical, philosophie,
philosophique, philosophisch, philosophical, philosohpy,
philosozophia
photog photographic, photography
photogr photographer(s)
phys physical
pkwy parkway
pl place
polit politica, political, politicas, politico, politics,
politek, politike, politique, politsch, politisk
polytech polytechnic
pop population
Pontif Pontifical
Port Portugal, Portuguese
postgrad postgraduate
PR Puerto Rico
pract practice
prehist prehistoric
prep preparation, preparatory
pres president
Presby Presbyterian
preserv preservation
prev prevention, preventive
prin principal(s)
prob problem(s)
probtn probation
proc proceding
prod production
prof professional, professor, professorial
prog program(s), programmed, programming
proj project, projective
prom promotion
prov province, provincial
psychiat psychiatria, psychiatric, psychiatrica, psychiatrie,
psychiatrique, psychiatrisch, psychiatry
psychol psychological
pt point
pub pub, publique
publ publication(s), published, publisher(s), publishing
pvt private

qm quartermaster
quad quaderni
qual qualitative, quality
quart quarterly
Que Quebec

rd road
RD Rural Delivery, Rural Free Delivery Rural Free Delivery
rec record(s), recording
rech recherche
redevelop redevelopment
ref reference
regist register, registered, registration
registr registrar
rehabil rehabilitation
rel(s) relacion, relation(s), relative, relazione
relig religion, religious
rep representative
repub republic
req requirement(s)
res research, reserve
rev review, revised, revista, revue
rhet rhetoric, rhetorical
RI Rhode Island
Rt Right
Rte Route
Russ Russian
rwy railway

s south
SAfrica South Africa
SAm South America, South American
Sask Saskatchewan
SC South Carolina
Scand Scandinavian
sch(s) school(s)
scholar scholarship
sci science(s), scientia, scientific, scientifico, scientifique,
scienza
SDak South Dakota
SEATO Southeast Asia Treaty Organization
sec secondary
sect section
secy secretary
sem seminaire, seminar, seminario, seminary
sen senator, sneatorial
Sept September
ser serial, series
serv service(s)
soc social, sociedad, sociedade, societa, societas, societate,
societe, societet, society(ies)
soc sci social science(s)
sociol sociological, sociology
Span Spanish
spec special
sq square
sr senior
sr sister
St Saint, Street
sta station
statist statistical, statistics
Ste Sainte, Suite
struct structural, structure(s)
subcomt subcommittee
subj subject
substa substa
super superieur, superior, superiore
suppl supplement, supplementary
supt superintendent
supv supervising, supervision
supvr supervisor
supvry supervisory
surg surgical, surgery
surv survey
Swed Swedish
Switz Switzerland
symp symposium
syst system, systematic

tech technic(s), technica, technical, technicky, techniczny,
techniek, technik, technika, technikum, technique, technisch
technol technologic, technological, technologicke,
technologico, technologiczny, technologie, technologika,

technologique, technologisch, technology
tecnol technologia, technologica, technologico
tel telegraph(s), telephone
temp temporary
Tenn Tennessee
Terr Terrace
teol teologia, teologico
Tex Texas
textbk textbook(s)
theol theological, theologie, theologique, theologisch, theology
theoret theoretic(al)
ther therapy
trans transactions
transp transportation
transl translation, translator(s)
treas treasurer, treasury
trop tropical
TV television
twp township

u und
UAR United Arab Republic
UK United Kingdom
UN United Nations
unemploy unemployment
UNESCO United Nations Educational, Scientific & Cultural Organization
UNICEF United Nations Children's Fund
univ(s) universidad, universite, university(ies)
UNRRA United Nations Relief & Rehabilitation Administration
UNRWA United Nations Relief & Works Agency
USA United States of America
US United States
USPHS United States Public Health Service
USSR Union of Soviet Socialist Republics
Utah

Va Virginia
var various
veg vegetable(s), vegetation
ver vereeniging, verein, vereingt, vereinigung
vet veteran, veterinarian, veterinary
VI Virgin Islands
vis visiting
voc vocational
vocab vocabulary
vol(s) volume(s), voluntary, volunteer(s)
vchmn vice chairman
vpres vice president
Vt Vermont

w west
Wash Washington
wetensch wetenschappelijk, wetenschappen
WHO World Health Organization
WI West Indies
wid widow, widowed, widower
Wis Wisconsin
wiss wissenschaft(en), wissenschaftliche(e)
WVa West Virginia
Wyo Wyoming

yearbk yearbook(s)
YMCA Young Men's Christian Association
YMHA Young Men's Hebrew Association
YWCA Young Women's Christian Association
YWHA Young Women's Hebrew Association

z zeitschrift

PREFACE

First published in 1942 under the auspices of the American Council of Learned Societies, the *Directory of American Scholars* remains the foremost biographical reference to American humanities scholars. With the tenth edition, the Gale Group has added social science scholars, recognizing the close relationship of the social sciences to the humanities.

The directory is arranged for convenient use in five subject volumes: Volume I: History, Archaeology, and Area Studies; Volume II: English, Speech, and Drama; Volume III: Foreign Languages, Linguistics, and Philology; Volume IV: Philosophy, Religion, and Law; Volume V: Psychology, Sociology, and Education. Each volume of biographical listings contains a geographic index. Volume VI contains an alphabetical index, a discipline index, an institutional index and a cumulative geographic index of scholars listed in the first five volumes.

The tenth edition of the *Directory of American Scholars* profiles more than 30,000 United States and Canadian scholars currently active in teaching, research, and/or publishing. The names of entrants were obtained from a variety of sources, including former entrants, academic deans, or citations in professional journals. In most cases, nominees received a questionnaire to complete, and selection for inclusion was made based on the following criteria:

1. Achievement, by reason of experience and training, of a stature in scholarly work equivalent to that associated with the doctoral degree, coupled with current activity in such work;

or

2. Achievement as evidenced by publication of scholarly works;

or

3. Attainment of a position of substantial responsibility by reason of achievement as outlined in (1) and (2).

Enhancements to the tenth edition include the addition of the fifth subject volume, Volume V: Psychology, Sociology, and Education, and the renaming of Volume I to better reflect the disciplines covered within. An outline of the major disciplines within the social sciences and humanities has been added to each volume to assist in locating scholars associated with disciplines related to, but not named outright in the titles of the individual volumes. Please see page ix for this information. Those individuals involved in multiple fields are listed in all appropriate volumes.

The tenth edition of the *Directory of American Scholars* is produced by fully automated methods. Limitations in the printing method have made it necessary to omit most diacritics.

Individual entries can include: place and year of birth, *primary discipline(s), vital statistics, education, honorary degrees, past and present professional experience, concurrent positions, *membership in international, national and regional societies, honors and awards, *research interest, *publications, postal mailing and electronic mailing addresses. Elements preceded by an asterisk are limited as to the number of items included. If an entrant exceeded these limitations, the editors selected the most recent information. Biographies received in the offices of the Gale Group after the editorial deadline were included in an abbreviated manner whenever possible.

The editors have made every effort to include material as accurately and completely as possible within the confines of format and scope. However, the publishers do not assume and hereby disclaim any liability to any party for any loss or damage caused by errors or omissions in the *Directory of American Scholars*, whether such errors or omissions result from negligence, accident, or any other cause.

Thanks are expressed to those who contributed information and submitted nominations for the new edition. Many societies provided membership lists for the research process and published announcements in their journals or newsletters, and their help is appreciated.

Comments and suggestions regarding any aspect of the tenth edition are invited and should be addressed to The Editors, *Directory of American Scholars*, Gale Group, 27500 Drake Road, Farmington Hills, MI 48333-3535.

ABBREVIATIONS

AAAS American Association for the Advancement of Science
AAUP American Association of University Professors
abnorm abnormal
acad academia, academic, academica, academie, academique, academy
accad accademia
acct account, accountant, accounting
acoust acoustical, accounstic(s)
adj adjunct, adjutant
actg acting
activ activities, activity
addn addition(s), additional
AID Agency for International Development
adjust adjust
admin administration, administrative
adminr administrator(s)
admis admissions
adv advisor(s), advisory
advan advance(d), advancement
advert advertisement, advertising
aerodyn aerodynamic(s)
aeronaut aeronautic(s), aeronautical
aesthet aesthetics
affil affiliate(s), affiliation
agr agricultural, agriculture
agt agent
AFB Air Force Base
AHA American Historical Association
akad akademi, akademia
Ala Alabama
Algem algemeen, algemen
allergol allergological, allergology
allgem allgemein, allgemeine, allgemeinen
Alta Alberta
Am America, Americain, American, Americana, Americano, Amerika, Amerikaansch, Amerikaner, Amerikanisch, Amerikansk
anal analysis, analytic, analytical
analog analogue
anat anatomic, anatomical, anatomy
ann annal(s)
anthrop anthropological, anthropology
anthropom anthropometric, anthropometrical, anthropometry
antiq antiquaire(s), antiquarian, antiquary(ies), antiquities
app appoint, appointed, appointment
appl applied
appln application
approx approximate, approximately
Apr April
apt apartment(s)
arbit arbitration
arch archiv, archiva, archive(s), archivio, archivo
archaeol archaeological, archaeology
archaol archaologie, archaologisch
archeol archeological, archeologie, archeologique, archeology
archit architectural, architecture
Arg Argentina, Argentine
Ariz Arizona
Ark Arkansas
asn association
asoc asociacion
assoc(s) associate(s), associated
asst assistant
Assyriol Assyriology
astrodyn astrodynamics
astron astronomical, astronomy
astronaut astronautical, astronautics
astronr astronomer
attend attendant, attending
atty attorney
audiol audiology
Aug August
auth author(s)
AV audiovisual
ave avenue

b born
BC British Columbia
bd board
behav behavior, behavioral, behaviour, behavioural
Bibl Biblical, Biblique
bibliog bibliografia, bibliographic, bibligraphical, bibliography(ies)
bibliogr bibliographer
bibliot biblioteca, bibliotec, bibliotek, bibliotheca, bibliothek, bibliothequeca
biog biographical, biography
biol biological, biology
bk(s) books
bldg building
blvd boulevard
bol boletim, boletin
boll bollettino
bor borough
bot botanical, botany
br branch
Brit Britain, British
Bro(s) Brother(s)
bull bulletin
bur bureau
bus business
BWI British West Indies

c children
Calif California
Can Canada, Canadian, Canadien, Canadienne
cand candidate
cartog cartografic, cartographical, cartography
cartogra cartographer
Cath Catholic, Catholique
CBS Columbia Broadcasting System
cent central
Cent Am Central America
cert certificat, certificate, certified
chap chapter
chem chermical, chemistry
chg charge
chemn chairman
Cie Compagnie
cient cientifica, cientifico
class classical
clin(s) clinic(s)
Co Companies, Company, County
coauth coauth
co-dir co-director
co-ed co-editor
co-educ co-educational
col(s) colegio, college(s), collegiate
collab collaboration, collaborative, collaborating, collaborator
Colo Colorado
Comdr Commander
com commerce, commercial
commun communication(s)
comn(s) commission(s)
comnr commissioner
comp comparative, comparee
compos composition(s)
comput computer, computing
comt committee
conf conference
cong congress
Conn Connecticut

conserv conservacion,conservation, conservatoire, conservatory
consol consolidated, consolidation
const constitution, constitutional
construct construction
consult consultant, consulting
contemp contemporary
contrib contribute, contribution
contribur contributor
conv convention
coop cooperation, cooperative
coord coordinating, coordination
coordr coordinator
corresp corresponding
Corp Corporation
coun council, counsel, counseling
counr councillor, counselor
criminol criminology
Ct Court
ctr center
cult cultra, cultural, culturale, culture
cur curator
curric curriculum
cybernet cybernetics
CZ Canal Zone
Czeck Czechoslovakia

DC District of Columbia
Dec December
Del Delaware
deleg delegate, delegations
demog demographic, demography
demonstr demonstrator
dent dental, dentistry
dep deputy
dept department
Deut Deutsch, Deutschland
develop development
diag diagnosis, diagnostic
dialectol dialectology
dig digest
dipl diploma, diploma, diplomate, diplome
dir director(s), directory
directory
Diss Abstr Dissertation Abstracts
dist district
distrib distributive
distribr distributors
div division, divorced
doc document, documentation
Dom Dominion
Dr Doctor, Drive
Drs Doctroandus

e east
ecol ecological, ecology
econ economic(s), economical, economy
ed edicion, edition, editor, editorial, edizione
educ education, educational
educr educator(s)
Egyptol Egyptology
elec electric, electrical, electricity
electrical
elem elementary
emer emeriti, emeritus
encour encouragement
encycl encyclopedia
employ employment
Eng England
environ environment, environmental
EPDA Education Professions Development Act
equip equipment
ERIC Educational Resources Information Center
ESEA Elementary & Secondary Education Act

espec especially
estab established, establishment
estud estudante, estudas, estudianet, estudio(s), estudo(s)
ethnog ethnographical, ethnography
ethnol ethnological, ethnology
Europ European
eval evaluation
evangel evangelical
eve evening
exam examination
examr examiner
except exceptional
exec executive(s)
exeg exegesis(es), exegetic, exegetical, exegetics
exhib exhibition(s)
exp experiment, experimental, experimentation
exped expedition(s)
explor exploration(s)
expos exposition
exten extension

fac faculties, faculty
facil facilities, facility
Feb February
fed federal
fedn federation
fel(s) fellow(s), fellowship(s)
filol filologia, filologico
filos filosofia, filosofico
Fla Florida
FLES Foreign Languages in the Elementary Schools
for foreign
forsch forschung, forschungen
found foundation
Fr Francais(s), French
Ft Fort

Ga Georgia
gen general, generale
geneal genealogical, genealogy
genoot genootschap
geod geodesy, geodetic
geog geografia, geografico, geographer(s), geographic,
geographie, geographical, geography
geogr geographer
geol geologic, geological, geology
geophys geophysical
Ger German, Germanic, Germanisch, Germany
Ges gesellschaft
gov governing, governors
govt government
grad graduate
Gr Brit Great Britain
guid guidance
gym gymnasium

handbk(s) handbooks
Hawaii
Hisp Hispanic, Hispanico, Hispano
hist historie, historia, historial, historic, historica,
historical, historique, historische, history
histol histology, histological
Hoshsch Hoshschule
hon honorable, honorary
hosp(s) hospital(s)
hq headquarters
HumRRO Human Resources Research Office
hwy highway

Ill Illinois

illum illuminating, illumination
illus illustrate, illustration
illusr illustrator
imp imperial
improv improvement
Inc Incorporated
incl include, included, includes, including
Ind Indiana
indust(s) industrial, industry(ies)
infor information
inst institut, instritute(s), institution(s), instituto
instnl institutional, institutionalized
instr instruction, instructor(s)
instruct instructional
int internacional, international, internazionale
intel intelligence
introd introduction
invest investigacion, investiganda, investigation,
investigative
investr investigator
ist istituto
Ital Italia, Italian, Italiana, Italiano, Italica, Italien,
Italienisch, Italienne, Italy

J Journal
Jan January
jour journal, journalism
jr junior
jurisp jurisprudence
juv juvenile(s)

Kans Kansas
Koninki koninklijk
Ky Kentucky

La Louisiana
lab laboratorie, laboratorio, laboratorium, laboratory(ies)
lang language(s)
lect lecture(s)
lectr lecturer
legis legislacion, legislatief, legislation, legislative,
legislativo, legislature, legislazione
lett letter(s), lettera, letteraria, letterature, lettere
lib liberal
libr libary(ies), librerio
librn librarian(s)
lic license, lecencia
ling linguistic(s), linguistica, linguistique
lit liteary, literatur, literatura, literature, littera,
literature
Ltd Limited

m married
mach machine(s), machinery
mag magazine
Man Manitoba
Mar March
Mariol Mariological, Mariology
Mass Massachusetts
mat matematica, matematiche, matematico, matematik
math mathematics, mathematical, mathematics, mathematik,
mathematique(s), mathematisch
Md Maryland
mech mechanical
med medical, medicine
Mediter Mediterranean
mem member, memoirs, memorial
ment mental, mentally

Biographies

A

AAGESON, JAMES W.
PERSONAL Born 11/24/1947, Havre, MT, m, 1970, 3 children **DISCIPLINE** NEW TESTAMENT STUDIES; HISTORY OF EARLY CHRISTIANITY **EDUCATION** MDiv, 76, MTh, 77, D Phil, 84. **CAREER** Prof Relig, Concordia,Col. **MEMBERSHIPS** Soc Bibl Lit; Cath Bibl Asn **RESEARCH** Pauline Studies; New Testament Socio-linguistics; Jewish-Christian relations. **SELECTED PUBLICATIONS** Auth, Written Also for Our Sake: Paul and the Art of Biblical Interpretation, John Knox Press, 93; Paul's Gospel and the Language of Control: A Summary, Teaching at Concordia, 93; Judaizing and Lectionary, Early Jewish, Anchor Bible Dictionary; Typology, Correspondence, and the Application of Scripture in Romans 9-11, The Pauline Writings: A Sheffield Reader, Sheffield Acad Press, 95; Control in Pauline Language and Culture: A Study of Rom 6; New Testament Studies, 96; A Theoretical Context for Understanding I Cor 1:18-2:16, Teaching at Concordia, 96; 2 Timothy and Its Theology: In Search of a Theological Pattern, Soc of Bibl Lit Sem Papers, 97; Paul and Judaism: The Apostle in the Context of Recent Interpretation, World and World, 00; In the Beginning: Critical Concepts for the Study of the Bible, Westview Pr, 01. **CONTACT ADDRESS** 901 S Eight St., Moorhead, MN 56562. **EMAIL** aageson@cord.edu

ABADIE, HUBERT DALE
PERSONAL Born 05/18/1935, Edgard, LA, m, 1964, 3 children **DISCIPLINE** MODERN BRITISH HISTORY **EDUCATION** Loyola Univ La, BS, 57; La State Univ, MA, 61; Univ Calif, Los Angeles, PhD(Hist), 71. **CAREER** Actg asst prof, 62-64, asst prof, 67-72, assoc prof, 72-80, prof Hist, Univ Miss, 80-98, assoc dean grad sch, 77-82; act dean, col Lib Arts, 82-84; assoc dean grad sch, 84; act assoc v chan Academic Affairs, 84-85; act dean, col Lib Arts, 85-86; dean, Col Lib Arts, 86-98; dean emer, Col of Lib Arts, prof emeritus Hist, 98; assoc dir, Croft Inst for Int Studies, 98-99. **RESEARCH** Modern British political history; liberal imperialism in Britain; Victorian nonconformists. **SELECTED PUBLICATIONS** Co-ed, Sir Roger Casement, Theodore Roosevelt, and Congo reform: an unpublished letter, Mid Am, 1/65; A Song of Huey Lang, Louisiana History, XI, 70, 271-273; auth, "Dismissals, Non-renewals, Terminations," Resource Handbook for Academic Deans, 113-115. **CONTACT ADDRESS** Croft Inst for Int Studies, Univ of Mississippi, General Delivery, University, MS 38677-9999. **EMAIL** dabadi@olemiss.edu

ABBOT, WILLIAM WRIGHT
PERSONAL Born 05/20/1922, Louisville, GA, m, 1958, 2 children **DISCIPLINE** AMERICAN HISTORY **EDUCATION** Univ Ga, AB, 43; Duke Univ, MA, 49, PhD (hist), 53. **CAREER** From asst prof to assoc prof hist, Col William & Mary, 53-58; assoc prof, Northwestern Univ, 58-59 & Rice Univ, 61-63; prof, Col William & Mary, 63-66; Prof Hist, Univ VA, 66-, Bk rev ed, William & Mary Quart, 55-61, ed, 63-66; assoc ed, J Southern Hist, 61-62, ed, 62-63; mem, Coun Inst Early Am Hist & Cult, 76-; ed, Papers of George Washington, 77- **MEMBERSHIPS** AHA; Orgn Am Historians; Southern Hist Asn. **RESEARCH** Eighteenth century America. **SELECTED PUBLICATIONS** Auth, The Royal Governors of Georgia, 1754-1775, Univ NC, 57; The Colonial Origins of the United States, 1607-1763, Wiley, 75. **CONTACT ADDRESS** Corcoran Dept of Hist, Univ of Virginia, Charlottesville, VA 22903.

ABBOTT, ALBERT
PERSONAL Born 03/31/1922, Philadelphia, PA, m, 1950, 2 children **DISCIPLINE** AMERICAN HISTORY **EDUCATION** John Carroll Univ, BS, 52, MA, 58; Georgetown Univ, PhD(hist), 62. **MEMBERSHIPS** Am Acad Polit & Soc Sci; Acad Polit Sci; AHA. **RESEARCH** American colonial and Negro history; American Civil War. **CONTACT ADDRESS** Dept of Hist, Fairfield Univ, Fairfield, CT 06430.

ABBOTT, CARL
PERSONAL Born 12/03/1944, Knoxville, TN **DISCIPLINE** HISTORY **EDUCATION** Swarthmore Col, BA, 66; Univ Chicago, MA, 67; PhD, 71. **CAREER** Visg asst prof, hist, Univ Denver, 71-72; asst to assoc prof, hist and urban studies, Old Dominion Univ, 72-78; assoc dir, grad prog, pub hist, Portland State Univ, 78-79; assoc prof, urban studies and planning, Portland State Univ, 79-83; Aspinall prof, hist, polit sci, and pub affairs, Mesa Col, 85; Banneker prof, Washington area studies, vis prof, urban and reg planning, George Washington Univ, 87; prof, urban studies and planning, Portland State Univ, 83. **HONORS AND AWARDS** Pres, Urban Hist Asn, 98. **RESEARCH** History of U.S. cities and city planning; Regional growth and planning in American West. **SELECTED PUBLICATIONS** Auth, "Political Terrain: Washington, DC, from Tidewater Turn to Global Metropolis," Chapel Hill, Univ North Carolina Press, 99; coauth, Planning a New West: The Columbia River Gorge National Scenic Area, with Sy Adler and Margery P. Abbott, Corvallis, Ore State Univ Press, 97; auth, Planning the Oregon Way: A Twenty Year Evaluation, ed with Deborah Howe and Sy Adler, Corvallils, Ore State Univ Press, 94; The Metropolitan Frontier: Cities in the Modern American West, Tucson, Univ Ariz Press, 93; Articles, The International Cities Hypothesis: An Approach to American Urban History, Jour of Urban Hist, 24, Nov, 97; Thinking about Cities: The Central Tradition in U.S. Urban Histoty, Jour of Urban Hist, 22, Sep, 96; The Internationalization of Washington, D.C., Urban Affairs Rev, 31, May, 96; Beautiful Downtown Burbank: Changing Metropolitan Geography in the Modern West, Jour of the West, 34, Jul, 95; Reading Urban History: Influential Books and Historians, Jour of Urban Hist, 21, Nov, 94; Metropolitan Portland: Reputation and Reality, Built Environ, 20, 1, 94; The Politics of Land Use Law in Oregon: Senate Bill 100, Twenty Years After, Ore Hist Quart, 94, Spr, 93. **CONTACT ADDRESS** School of Urban Studies and Planning, Portland State Univ, Portland, OR 97207. **EMAIL** abbottc@pdx.edu

ABBOTT, ELIZABETH
PERSONAL Born Ottawa, ON, Canada **DISCIPLINE** HISTORY **EDUCATION** Sir George Williams Univ, BA, 63; McGill Univ, MA, 66, PhD, 71. **CAREER** Res dir, Centre d'Etude Que, Concordia Univ, 66-84; prof hist, Dawson Col, 72-84; Reuters reporter, Haiti, 86-88; ed-in-chief, Chronicle Publ, 89-91; Dean Women, Trinity Col, Dean St Hilda's Col, Univ Toronto. **SELECTED PUBLICATIONS** Auth, Haiti: The Duvaliers and their Legacy, 88; ed, Racism or Responsible Government? The French Canadian Dilemma of the 1840's, 67; ed, Debates of the Legislative Assembly of United Canada 1841-1854, vols 1-19, 70-83; co-comp, Bibliographie pour Servir a l'Etude de l'Histoire du Canada Francais, 66; co-comp, L'inventaire de la Collection Louis-Hippolyte LaFontaine, 68. **CONTACT ADDRESS** 44 Devonshire Pl, Toronto, ON, Canada M5S 2E2. **EMAIL** abbott@trinity.utoronto.ca

ABBOTT, WILLIAM M.
PERSONAL Born 12/20/1951, Ridgewood, NJ, s **DISCIPLINE** HISTORY **EDUCATION** Univ Calif, AB, 74; Oxford Univ, DPhil, 82. **CAREER** Vis lecturer, Univ Calif, 82; res hist, Univ Calif, 84-85; asst prof, Fairfield Univ, 85-. **HONORS AND AWARDS** Teacher of the Year, Fairfield Univ, 89; Phi Beta Kappa. **MEMBERSHIPS** Phi Beta Kappa, Phi alpha Theta. **RESEARCH** Early Modern English History; Early Stuart Ecclesiastical History **SELECTED PUBLICATIONS** Auth, James Ussher and 'Ussherian' Episcopacy, 1640-1656: The Primate and his Reduction Manuscript, Albion, 90; auth, "History and Economics," College Teaching, (94): 22-26. **CONTACT ADDRESS** Dept History, Fairfield Univ, 1073 N Benson Rd, Fairfield, CT 06430-5171. **EMAIL** smabbott@fair1.fairfield.edu

ABBOUD, PETER FOUAD
PERSONAL Born 06/30/1931, Jaffa, Palestine, w, 1952, 1 child **DISCIPLINE** LINGUISTICS, ARABIC STUDIES **EDUCATION** Univ London, BS, 56; Am Univ Cairo, MA, 60; Univ Tex, Austin, PhD, 64. **CAREER** From asst instr to instr English, Am Univ Cairo, 57-61; asst prof, 64-68, assoc prof ling, 68-, prof Arabic, 84, Univ Tex, Austin; visit fac and sch, Georgetown Univ, 63, Univ of Mich, 65, 69, 70, 77, 78, 91, 94, Columbia Univ 66, Princeton Univ, 67, Univ Chicago, 94; dir, sch Arabic, Middlebury Col, 82-90; chmn, dept Mid Eastern Land and Cult, 94-98. **HONORS AND AWARDS** Am Res Ctr is Egypt fel, 71-72; Fulbright fel 75-76. **MEMBERSHIPS** Ling Soc Am; Am Orient Soc; Am Asn Teachers Arabic; Mid E Studies Asn N Am. **RESEARCH** Classical Arabic; Arabic dialectology; and Arabic language teaching. **SELECTED PUBLICATIONS** Coauth, Beginning Cairo Arabic, Univ Tex, 65; Elementary Modern Standard Arabic, Inter-Univ Comt Near Eastern Lang, 68; auth, The Teaching of Arabic in the United States: The State of the Art, ERIC Clearinghouse for Ling, 68; coauth, Modern Standard Arabic: Intermediate Level, Ctr Near Eastern & N African Studies, Mich, 71; auth, Spoken Arabic, In: Current Trends in Linguistics, Vol VI, Mouton, 71; On Ablaut in Cairo Arabic, Afro-Asiatic Ling, 76; auth, The Verb in Northern Najdi Arabic, Bull Sch Oriental and Afr Stu, 79; auth The Classical Arabic Jussive Forms and Their Reflexes in the Modern Arabic Dialects, Zeit Deutsch Morgenlanisch Gesellschaft, 82; auth, Some Grammatical(Morphological and Syntactic-Semantic) Considerations in Arabic-English Bilingual Dictionaries, The Arabic Dictionary to Non-Arabic Speakers, Arab League Education, Cultural, and Scientific Organization, 83; coauth, Computer Assisted Instruction Program for Vocabulary and Reading Comprehension for Modern Standard Arabic, Intermediate Level, 84; auth, "The Hal Construction and the Main Verb in the Sentence," The Fergusonian Impact, Vol I, Mouton, 86; auth, "Speech and Religious Affiliation in Egypt," Studies in Honor of Edgar C. Polome, Mouton, 88; auth, A Methodology for Teaching Grammar Functionally (in Arabic), Al-Arabiyya, 89; coauth, Come Let's Read with the Arabs, Beginning, Intermediate, Advanced Levels, Come Let's Listen with the Arabs, Beginning, Intermediate, Advanced Levels, and Come Let's Speak Fusha, Beginning, Intermediate, Advanced Levels, Sch of Arabic, Middlebury Col, 90; auth, The Teaching of Arabic in the United States: When and Whither, The Teaching of Arabic as a Foreign Language, Issues and Directions, Al-Arabiyya Monograph Series, No 2, 95. **CONTACT ADDRESS** Dept of Middle Eastern Lang and Cult, Univ of Texas, Austin, WMB 5.120, Austin, TX 78712.

ABDALLA, ISMAIL H.
PERSONAL Born 01/01/1939, Nuhudi, Sudan, m, 1971, 1 child **DISCIPLINE** HISTORY **EDUCATION** Khartown Univ, MA, 64; Univ Wis Madison, PhD, 81 **CAREER** Asst/Assoc Prof, Col of William and Mary, 82-. **HONORS AND AWARDS** Award for Outstanding Teaching, Col of William and Mary, 85. **MEMBERSHIPS** African Studies Asn, Middle E Studies Asn, Sudan Studies Asn. **RESEARCH** Islam in Africa, Traditional Medicine in Sub-Sahara. **SELECTED PUBLICATIONS** Co-ed, Healing Strategies in Africa, 85; ed, Challenges and Perspectives on Sudanese Studies, 93; auth, Islam, Medicine and Practitioners in Northern Nigeria, 97. **CONTACT ADDRESS** Dept Hist, Col of William and Mary, PO Box 8795, Williamsburg, VA 23187-8795. **EMAIL** ixabda@wm.edu

ABEL, ELIE
PERSONAL Born 10/17/1920, Montreal, PQ, Canada **DISCIPLINE** HISTORY **EDUCATION** McGill Univ, BA, 41, LLD, 71; Columbia Univ, MS, 42; Univ Western Ont, LLD, 76. **CAREER** Journalist, vars publs, 41-70; dean, sch jour, Columbia Univ, 70-79; prof comm, Stanford Univ, 79-91; Mary Lou and George Boone Centennial prof & dir, Stanford in Washington, 93-94. **SELECTED PUBLICATIONS** Auth, The Missile Crisis, 66; coauth, Special Envoy to Churchill and Stalin 1941-46; coauth, Roots of Involvement: The U.S. in Asia 1784-1971; coauth, The Shattered Bloc: Behind the Upheaval in Eastern Europe, 90; ed, What's News: The Media in American Society, 81; ed, Leaking: Who Does It? Who Benefits? At What Cost?, 87. **CONTACT ADDRESS** 4101 Cathedral Ave NW, Apt 904, Washington, DC 20016-3585.

ABEL, KERRY
DISCIPLINE SOCIAL AND CULTURAL HISTORY **EDUCATION** Queen's Univ, BA, PhD; Univ Manitoba, MA. **CAREER** Prof; Carleton Univ. **RESEARCH** Social and cultural history of the Canadian north. **SELECTED PUBLICATIONS** Ed, Aboriginal Resource Use in Canada: Historical and Legal Aspects, with Jean Friesen, Winnipeg: Univ of Manitoba Press, 91; auth, Colonies: A History of Canada before Confederation, with D.H. Adenson, P. Baskerville, Bercuson, J. Bumsted and J. Reid, Toronto: McGraw-Hill Ryerson, 92; auth, "Northern Athapaskan Oral Traditions and the White River Volcano," with D. Wayne Moodie and A.J.W. Catchpole, Ethnohistory 39/2, (92): 148-71; auth, Drum Songs: Glimpses of Dene History, Montreal and Kingston: McGill-Queen's Univ Press, 93; ed, "The Northwest and the North," in M. Brook Taylor, ed., Canadian History: A Reader's Guide, Vol. 1, Toronto: Univ of Toronto Press, (94): 325-55; ed, "Prophets, Priests and Preachers: Glimpses of Dene History," in K.S. Coates and Robin Fisher, eds., Out of the Background: Readings on Canadian Native History, Toronto: Copp Clark, (96): 118-149. **CONTACT ADDRESS** Dept of Hist, Carleton Univ, 1125 Colonel By Dr, Ottawa, ON, Canada K1S 5B6. **EMAIL** kabel@ccs.carleton.ca

ABELS, RICHARD
PERSONAL Born 10/31/1951, Brooklyn, NY, m, 1975, 2 children **DISCIPLINE** HISTORY **EDUCATION** Columbia Univ, BA, 73, MA, 75, MPhil, 76, PhD, 82. **CAREER** Asst prof, Cornell Col, 81-82; asst prof, USNA, 82-85; assoc prof, USNA 85-91; prof, USNA, 91-. **HONORS AND AWARDS** Teaching excellence award, USNA; Phi Beta Kappa; Magna Cum Laude, Columbia Univ. **MEMBERSHIPS** Charles Homer Haskins Soc for Anglo-Saxon, Norman, Angevin and Viking Hist; fel Royal Hist Soc; AHA; Medieval Academy. **RESEARCH** Anglo-Saxon hist; Anglo-Norman hist; medieval military hist; medieval heresy. **SELECTED PUBLICATIONS** Coauth, "The Participation of Women in Languedocian Catharism", in Mediaeval Studies 41, 97; auth, The Council of Whitby: A Study in Early Anglo Saxon Politics; auth, "the Devolution of Brookland in Ninth-Century Kent", in Archaeologia Cantiana 99, 83; auth, "Bookland and Fyrd Service in Late Saxon England", in Anglo-Norman Studies 7, 85; auth, Lordship and Military Obligation in Anglo-Saxon England, Univ Calif, 88; auth, Historical Introduction to Domesday Bedfordshire, Alecto Editions, 91; auth, "English Tactics and Strategy in the Late Tenth Century", in The Battle of Maldon A.D. 991, Oxford: Basil Blackwell, 91; auth, "King Alfred's Peace-Making Strategies with the Vikings", in The Haskins Society Journal: Studies in Medieval History 3, 92; auth, "English Logistics and Military Administration 871-1066: The Impact of the Viking Wars", in Military Aspects of Scandinavian Society in a European Perspective, AD 1-1300, 97; auth, "Sheriffs, Lord-Seeking and the Norman Settlement of the South-East Midlands", in Anglo-Norman Studies 19, 97; auth, Alfred the Great: War, Kingship and Culture in Ninth-Century England, Longman, 98. **CONTACT ADDRESS** History Dept, United States Naval Acad, Annapolis, MD 21402-5044. **EMAIL** abels@nadn.navy.mil

ABELSON, ELAINE S.
DISCIPLINE HISTORY **EDUCATION** NYork Univ, PhD, 86. **CAREER** Fac, Eugene Lang Col. **RESEARCH** Dimensions of inequality; gender, urban women, and homelessness in the Great Depression. **SELECTED PUBLICATIONS** Auth, When Ladies Go A-Thieving: Middle-Class Shoplifters in the Victorian Department Store, 90. **CONTACT ADDRESS** Eugene Lang Col, New Sch for Social Research, 66 West 12th St, New York, NY 10011.

ABOU-EL-HAJ, BARBARA
DISCIPLINE ART HISTORY **EDUCATION** UCLA, PhD, 75. **CAREER** Assoc prof/ch, SUNY Binghamton. **RESEARCH** Soc hist of medieval art and archit; monastic arts; political economy of building; cult of saints. **SELECTED PUBLICATIONS** Auth, The Medieval Cult of Saint in Formations and Transformations, Cambridge UP, 97; Artistic Integration Inside the Cathedrals, Social Consensus Outside? in Artistic Integration in Early Gothic Churches, Univ Toronto P, 95; Building and Decorating at Reims and Amiens in Europaische Skulptur im 12./13. Jahrhundert, Frankfurt am Main, 94. **CONTACT ADDRESS** SUNY, Binghamton, PO Box 6000, Binghamton, NY 13902-6000. **EMAIL** abouel@binghamton.edu

ABOU-EL-HAJ, RIFAAT ALI
PERSONAL Born 11/21/1933, Jerusalem, Palestine, m, 1967, 4 children **DISCIPLINE** EUROPEAN, NEAR EASTERN & COMPARATIVE HISTORY **EDUCATION** Washington & Lee Univ, AB, 56; Princeton Univ, MA, 59, PhD, 63. **CAREER** Asst instr, Princeton Univ, 60; from instr to asst prof, St Lawrence Univ, 62-64; from asst prof to assoc prof, 64-73, prof, Calif State Univ, Long Beach, 73-93; Prof, Binghamton Univ, Binghamton, 93-; Consult, Choice, 64; assoc ed, The Hist Teach, 80-90; Ahmet Ertegun Visiting Prof, Princeton Univ, 96-97. **RESEARCH** Ottoman Turkish history; Arab history; Modern European history; Comparative history. **SELECTED PUBLICATIONS** Auth, Closure of Ottoman Frontier in Europe: 1699-1703, 69 & Ottoman Vezir and Pasha households: 1683-1703, 74, J Am Oriental Soc; Ottoman attitudes toward negotiations, Der Islam, 74; The Narcissism of Mustafa II, 1695-1703, Studia Islamica, 74; The Rebellion of 1703 and the Structure of Ottoman Politics, The Formation of the Modern State: The Ottoman Empire from the 16th-18th Centuries, Albany, 92; auth & co-ed, The Ottoman City and Its Part: Urban Structure and Social Order, New Rochelle, 92; Theorizing beyond the nation-state: Ottoman society from 16th-19th Centuries, in Armagan: Festschrift fur Andreas Tietz, Prage, 95; Historiography in South West Asian and North African studies since Sa'id's Orientalism, in History after the Three Worlds: A Crisis in Historical Consciousness, 00; auth, Modern Devletin Dogusu: Osmanli Imparatorlogu (15-18. Yuzyillar), Ankara, 01. **CONTACT ADDRESS** Hist Dept, SUNY, Binghamton, Binghamton, NY 13902-6000. **EMAIL** rasultani@aol.com

ABRAMS, BRADLEY
DISCIPLINE RUSSIAN AND EAST CENTRAL EUROPEAN HISTORY **EDUCATION** Univ Tex, BA, 86; Stanford Univ, PhD, 97. **CAREER** Asst prof. **RESEARCH** Central and east central European history. **SELECTED PUBLICATIONS** Auth, Die Vertreibung der Sudetendeutschen und die tschechoslowakische Opposition in den 70er Jahren, Transit, 95; The Price of Retribution: The Trial of Jozef Tiso, E Europ Polit Soc, 96. **CONTACT ADDRESS** Dept of History, Columbia Col, New York, 2960 Broadway, New York, NY 10027-6902.

ABRAMS, DOUGLAS CARL
PERSONAL Born 01/07/1950, Tarboro, NC, m, 1980, 2 children **DISCIPLINE** HISTORY **EDUCATION** Bob Jones Univ, BA, 72; NC State Univ, MA, 74; Univ Md, PhD, 81. **CAREER** Prof, Bob Jones Univ, 74- ; ch, dept of soc studs educ, Bob Jones Univ, 92- . **HONORS AND AWARDS** NEH Summer seminars, 83, 86; Am Coun of Learned Soc Res Grant, 88; Hearst Fel. **MEMBERSHIPS** Southern Hist Asn, Org of Am Hist. **RESEARCH** 20th Century American social and political history. **SELECTED PUBLICATIONS** Auth, "A Progressive-Conservative Duel: The 1920 Democratic Gubernatorial Primaries in North Carolina," North Carolina Historical Review, (78): 421-443; auth, "Celebrating the Bicentennial of the Constitution," Balance, (87): 1-2,4; auth, "Robert Clive," in Great Lives from History: British and Commonwealth Series, (87): 611-616; auth, "Irony of Reform: North Carolina Blacks and the New Deal," North Carolina Historical Review, (89): 149-178; auth, "William Jennings Bryan: 'He Kept the Faith'," in Faith of Our Fathers: Scenes from American Church History, Bob Jones University Press, 91; auth, "Fundamentalism and Politics," in Political Parties and Elections in the United States: An Encyclopedia, Garland Press, 91; auth, Conservative Constraints: North Carolina and the New Deal, Univ Press of Miss, 92; auth, "Chapter 23: 'To the Present'" in World History for Christian Schools, Bob Jones Univ Press, 94; auth, "Agricultural Adjustment Administration," in Handbook of North Carolina History, forthcoming. **CONTACT ADDRESS** Dept of Soc Sci, Bob Jones Univ, 1700 Wade Hampton, Greenville, SC 29614-0001. **EMAIL** cabrams@bju.edu

ABRAMS, RICHARD M.
PERSONAL Born 07/12/1932, Brooklyn, NY, m, 1960, 3 children **DISCIPLINE** UNITED STATES HISTORY **EDUCATION** Columbia Univ, AB, 53, AM, 55 PhD, 62. **CAREER** Lectr hist, Columbia Univ, 57-60; from instr to assoc prof, 61-72, prof hist, Univ Calif, Berkeley, 72-, Soc Sci Res Coun fel, 64-65; Fulbright lectr, Inst of US Studies, Univ London, 68-69; NEH fel, 72; dir, summer sem col teachers, NEH, 77, 79, 81, & 84; vis prof hist, Normal Univ, Beijing, CHN, 85, 97; dist vis prof hist, Innsbruck, AUT, 88; dist Fulbright prof US hist, Moscow State Univ, 89; visiting prof, Fudeur Univ, Shenphai, 99; dir, International & Area Studies Teaching Program, U C Berkeley, 99-. **MEMBERSHIPS** AHA; Am Soc Legal Hist; Econ Hist Assn. **RESEARCH** History of business in American life; American business expansion abroad in the early 20th century; business and government relations in the United States since 1875. **SELECTED PUBLICATIONS** Auth, Conservatism in a progressive Era, Harvard, 62; auth, The failure of progressivism, In: The Shaping of 20th Century America, 2nd ed, Little, 71; co-ed, The Shaping of 20th Century America, 2nd ed, 71; Legal change and the legitimacy of the corporation in America, Stanford Law Rev, 4/72; coauth, The Unfinished Century, Little, 73; auth, The Burdens of Progress, Scott, 78; auth, The Reputation of Felix Frankfurter, The Am Bar Res Jour, Summer, 85; auth, The US Military & Higher Education, Annals, AAPSS, vol 502, 89; Business & Gout, Encycl of Am Pol Hist, ed by Jack Greene, Scribner's, 84; auth Not a Unity but a Miltiple: American Culture and the Modern Political (Dis)Order, Inst of Gov Stud, Berkeley, 94. **CONTACT ADDRESS** Dept of History, Univ of California, Berkeley, Berkeley, CA 94720-2550. **EMAIL** abramsr@socrates.berkeley.edu

ABRAMSON, DANIEL
DISCIPLINE ART HISTORY **EDUCATION** Princeton Univ, BA 86; Harvard Univ, MA 90, PhD 93. **CAREER** Connecticut Col, asst prof 93-98; Tufts Col, asst prof 98-. **CONTACT ADDRESS** Dept of Art and Art History, Tufts Univ, Medford, 11 Talbot Ave, Medford, MA 02155.

ABU-GHAZALEH, ADNAN M.
PERSONAL Born 07/22/1927, m, 1962, 3 children **DISCIPLINE** MIDDLE EAST HISTORY **EDUCATION** Univ London, BA, 58; NYork Univ, MA, 61, PhD(mod hist), 67. **CAREER** Lectr Europ hist, Col Educ, Jordan, 58-60 & 61-63; dir, Am-Jordanian Cult Rels, Ministry Educ, Jordan, 63-64; from asst prof to assoc prof Mid E hist, 64-72, prof Mid E Hist, State Univ NY Col Plattsburgh, 72-. **MEMBERSHIPS** Fel, Mid E Studies Asn NAm. **RESEARCH** Palestine problem; Arab nationalism; Ottoman European diplomacy 1875-1914. **SELECTED PUBLICATIONS** Auth, Usua al-Mujtama al-Arabi (basic features of Arab society), al-Nahda Press, Jordan, 60; Nationalism and Literary Writing in Mandatory Palestine, Islamic Rev & Arab Affairs, London, England, 5/70; Al-Muarrikhun al-Falastiniuun al-Arab fi Zaman al-Intidab al-Baritani (Palestinian Arab historian during the British mandate), Shuun Falastiniyyah, Beirut, Lebanon, 5/71; Arab Cultural Nationalism in Palestine during the British mandate, J Palestine Studies, Beirut, Lebanon, 4/72; Arab Cultural Nationalism in Palestine, 1919-1948, Inst Palestine Studies, Beirut, 73; American Missions in Syria, 88; Palestinian-Arab Culture 1919-1960, 91; History and Culture of the Ancient Middle East and North Africa, 93. **CONTACT ADDRESS** Dept of Hist, SUNY, Col at Plattsburgh, Plattsburgh, NY 12901.

ABZUG, ROBERT H.
PERSONAL Born 05/02/1945, New York, NY, m, 1980, 2 children **DISCIPLINE** HISTORY **EDUCATION** Harvard Univ, BA, 67; Univ Calif, PhD. **CAREER** Instr, Univ Calif, 76-77; Lectr, Univ Calif, 77-78; Vis Prof, Univ Munich, 90-91; From Asst Prof to Prof, Univ Tex, 78-; **HONORS AND AWARDS** Fred Crawford Mem Res Asn, Emory Univ, 83; Nat Endowment Humanities Fel for Independent Study, 83; Am Coun of Learned Soc, Grant-in-Aid, 84; Nat Endowment Humanities, Summer Stipend, 87; NEH Grant, 89; Frederick Binkard Artz Summer Res Grant, Oberlin Col, 93; German-Am Acad Coun Found Lectureship Grant, 98; John Simon Guggenheim Mem Found Fel, 00-01. **MEMBERSHIPS** AHA. Orgn of Am Historians, Soc for Historians of the Early Republic, Am Soc of Church Hist. **RESEARCH** American cultural and intellectual history, history of American religion, history of psychology, Holocaust studies. **SELECTED PUBLICATIONS** Auth, Passionate Liberator: Theodore Dwight Weld and the Dilemma of Reform, Oxford, 80; auth, Inside the Vicious Heart: Americans and the Liberation of Nazi Concentration Camps, Oxford, 85; co-ed, New Perspectives on Race and Slavery in America: Essays in Honor of Kenneth M. Stampp, Univ Ky Pr, 86; auth, Cosmos Crumbling: American Reform and the Religious Imagination, Oxford, 94; ; auth, America Views the Holocaust, 1933-1945: A Brief Documentary History, St Martins (Bedord), 99; auth, Faith, Anxiety and Existence: Rollo May and the Transformation of American Culture, forthcoming. **CONTACT ADDRESS** History Dept, Univ of Texas, Austin, Campus Mail Code B7000, Austin, TX 78712. **EMAIL** zug@mail.utexas.edu

ACCAD, EVELYNE
PERSONAL Born 10/06/1943, Beirut, Lebanon **DISCIPLINE** FRANCOPHONE STUDIES, AFRICAN STUDIES **EDUCATION** Anderson Col, BA, 67; Ball State Univ, MA, 68; Ind Univ, Bloomington, PhD(comp lit), 73. **CAREER** From teaching asst to instr French, Anderson Col, 65-68; teacher English & girl's counr, Int Col, Beirut, 68-70; teaching asst comp lit, Ind Univ, 71-73; asst prof, 71-80, Assoc Prof French, Univ Ill, 80-. **MEMBERSHIPS** African Lit Asn (pres, 78); African Studies Asn; MLA. **RESEARCH** Women in literature and society; African and Near Eastern literatures; 20th century French literature. **SELECTED PUBLICATIONS** Auth, Des Femmes, des Hommes et la Guerre: Fiction et realite au Proche-Orient, Paris: Study, 93; contribur, Bahithat: Women and Writing, v 2, 95-96; auth, Arab Women's Literary Inscriptions: A Note and Extended Bibliography, Col Lit, 95; auth, Truth Versus Loyalty, in Bell, ed, Radically Speaking: Feminism Reclaimed, Spinifex, 96; auth, Trois Chansons, in Ecritures de Femmes: Nouvelles Cartographies, Yale, 96; auth, Assia Djebar's Contribution to Arab Women's Literature: Rebellion, Maturity, Vision, World Lit Today, 96; auth, Wounding Words: A Woman's Journal in Tunisia, Heinemann, 96; auth, Saadawi's Woman at Point Zero, in, Oxford Companion to African Literature, Oxford, forthcoming; auth, Violence and Sexuality, in, Sexual Aggression: Key Research and Activism, Purdue, forthcoming; auth, Nawal El Saadawi, in, Fifty African and Caribbean Women Writers, Greenwood, forthcoming. **CONTACT ADDRESS** French Dept, Univ of Illinois, Urbana-Champaign, 707 S Mathews Ave, Urbana, IL 61801-3625. **EMAIL** evaccad@aol.com

ACCAMPO, ELINOR A.
DISCIPLINE HISTORY **EDUCATION** Univ Calif, Berkeley, PhD, 84. **CAREER** Assoc prof; Univ Southern Calif; prof, Colo Col, 79-81; prof, Denison Univ, 82-83; prof, USC, 83-; actg ch, Gender Stud Prog, USC, 88-89. **RESEARCH** Social and cultural history of modern France; history of gender; family, and sexuality. **SELECTED PUBLICATIONS** Auth, Industrialization, Family Life, and Class Relations: Saint Chamond, 1815-1914, Univ Calif Press, 89; The Rhetoric of Reproduction and the Reconfiguration of Womanhood in the French Birth Control Movement, 1890-1920, J Family Hist, Vol 21, 96; coauth, Gender and the Politics of Social Reform in France, 1870-1914, John Hopkins UP, 95. **CONTACT ADDRESS** Dept of History, Univ of So California, University Park Campus, Los Angeles, CA 90089. **EMAIL** accampo@usc.edu

ACHENBAUM, W. ANDREW
PERSONAL Born 03/02/1947, Philadelphia, PA, m, 1971, 2 children **DISCIPLINE** HISTORY; GERONTOLOGY **EDUCATION** Amherst Col, BA, 68; Univ Pa, MA, 70; Univ Mich, PhD, 76. **CAREER** Asst prof hist, Canisius Col, 76-80; asst res scientist, Inst Geront, Univ Mich, Ann Arbor, 78-80; Asst Prof Hist, Carnegie-Mellon Univ, 80-, Consult hist & humanities, Inst Gerontology, 77-78. **MEMBERSHIPS** Orgn Am Historians; Geront Soc; Soc Sci Hist Asn. **RESEARCH** United States social and cultural history; history of aging; social welfare. **SELECTED PUBLICATIONS** Auth, Old Age in The New Land: The American Experience Since 1790, Johns Hopkins Univ, 78; coauth, Old age and modernization, Gerontologist, 6/78; auth, From womb through bloom to tomb, Rev Am Hist, 6/78; coauth, Images of Old Age in America, 1790-Present, Inst of Gerontology, 78; auth, Modern Values and Aging America, Little Brown, 82. **CONTACT ADDRESS** Dept of Hist, Carnegie Mellon Univ, Pittsburgh, PA 15213.

ACHTENBERG, DEBORAH
DISCIPLINE HISTORY OF PHILOSOPHY, ANCIENT PHILOSOPHY **EDUCATION** New Schl for Soc Res, PhD, 82. **CAREER** Assoc prof, Univ Nev, Reno. **RESEARCH** Aristotle; ethics; political philosophy. **SELECTED PUBLICATIONS** Essays on Aristotle's ethics were recently published in Crossroads of Norm and Nature: Essays on Aristotle's 'Ethics' and 'Metaphysics' (Rowman & Littlefield Press), Essays in Ancient Greek Philosophy IV (SUNY) and Feminism and Ancient Philosophy (Routledge). **CONTACT ADDRESS** Univ of Nevada, Reno, Reno, NV 89557. **EMAIL** achten@scs.unr.edu

ACKERMAN, JAMES SLOSS
PERSONAL Born 11/08/1919, San Francisco, CA, m, 1947, 4 children **DISCIPLINE** HISTORY, ARCHITECTURE **EDUCATION** Yale Univ, BA, 41; NYork Univ, MA, 47, PhD, 52. **CAREER** Lectr hist art, 46 & 49, Yale Univ; from asst prof to prof hist art & archit, 52-60, Univ Calif, Berkeley; chmn dept, 63-68, prof, 60-, Harvard Univ;, chmn, 82-, ed-in-chief, Art Bull, 56-60; Coun Humanities fel, Princeton Univ, 60-61; mem, Coun Comt for Yale Art Gallery, 66-; Slade prof fine art, Cambridge Univ, 69-70; pres, Artists Found, 77-; mem, Coun Scholars, Libr Congr, 80-; Mellon Lectr, 85-, Natl Gallery of Art; Meyer Schapiro vis prof, Art Hist, 88. **HONORS AND AWARDS** Distinguished Teaching in Art Educ Medal, Nat Gallery Art, 66; Centennial Citation, Univ Calif, 67; Morey Awd, Col Art Assn Am; Hitchcock Prize, Soc Archit Hist; Grand Off Italian Republic,72; DFA, Col of Art, 84; Gold Medal, Istituto di Storia dell'Arte Lombarda: Inst Honors, Amer Inst Archit,87; DArch, Univ Venice,88; Gold Medal,Istituto di Storia dell'Arte Lombarda, 87; Col Art Ass of Amer, Dist Tchng Awd, 91; Premio Daria Borghese, 95; Paul Kristeller Career Achiev Awd, Renaissance Soc Am; Fel, Am Philosophical Soc; ma, harvard univ, 60; lhd, kenyon col, 61 & univ md baltimore county, 76; dfa, md inst col art, 72. **MEMBERSHIPS** Col Art Assn Am; Soc Archit Hist; Renaissance Soc Am; fel, Am Acad Rome; fel, Am Acad Arts & Sci. **RESEARCH** Italian renaissance art and architecture; history of architectural theory. **SELECTED PUBLICATIONS** Auth, Architecture of Michelangelo, Viking, 61; coauth, Seventeenth Century Science and the Arts, Princeton, 61; auth, Art and Archaeology, Englewood Cliffs, 63; auth, Palladio, Harmondsworth, 66; Palladio's Villas, Augustin, 67; coauth, Views of Florence, Walker, 67; auth, The Villa: Form and Ideology of Country Houses, Princeton & London, 90; auth, Distance Points; Studies in Theory and Renaissance Art and Architecture, Cambridge, 91; co-ed, Conventions of Architectural Drawing, Cambridge, 00. **CONTACT ADDRESS** Harvard Univ, Sackler Museum, Cambridge, MA 02138. **EMAIL** jsackerm@fas.harvard.edu

ADAMEC, LUDWIG W.
PERSONAL Born 03/10/1924, Vienna, Austria, m, 1958, 1 child **DISCIPLINE** NEAR & MIDDLE EASTERN STUDIES **EDUCATION** Univ Calif, Los Angeles, BA, 60, MA, 61, PhD, 66. **CAREER** Asst prof Near Eastern hist & Arabic, 67-70, assoc prof, 70-72, Prof Near Eastern Hist & Lang, Univ Ariz, 72-, Dir Near Eastern Ctr, 75-; assoc ed, Afghanistan J, 73-77. **HONORS AND AWARDS** Res grant, Univ Calif, Los Angeles, 66; Near Eastern hist & Ford Found fac res grant, 66-67; Fulbright res, Iran, 73-74; mem, bd dirs, Am Res Ctr in Egypt, 78- & Ctr Arabic Studies Abroad, 79-81; vpres, Am Inst Iranian Studies, 79-; trustee, Am Res Inst in Turkey, 79-; prof, Univ Baluchistan, Quetta, Pakistan, 81-82. **MEMBERSHIPS** Fel Mid E Studies Asn NAm; Mid E Inst. **RESEARCH** Afghanistan studies, diplomatic history, German-Afghan relations and politics; history and politics of the Islamic world; history and politics of the Near and Middle East, Iran Afghanistan, Pakistan, the Arabic world and Turkey. **SELECTED PUBLICATIONS** Auth, Afghanistan 1900-1923, A Diplomatic History, Univ Calif, 67; coauth, Afghanistan: Some New Approaches, Univ Mich, 69; ed, Historical and Political Gazetteer of Afghanistan, (6 vols), 72, 73, 75, 78 & 80, Akad Drucku-u, Graz; auth, Afghanistan's Foreign Affairs in the Mid-Twentieth Century: Relations with the USSR, Germany, and Britain, Univ Ariz, 73; ed, Historical and Political Who's Who of Afghanistan, 74 & Historical Gazetteer of Iran, (4 vols), 76 & 81, Akad Druck-u, Graz. **CONTACT ADDRESS** Dept of Near and Middle Eastern Studies, Univ of Arizona, 1 University of Az, Tucson, AZ 85721-0001.

ADAMS, GRAHAM, JR.
PERSONAL Born 03/04/1928, New York, NY **DISCIPLINE** HISTORY **EDUCATION** Williams Col, BA, 48; Columbia Univ, MA, 54, PhD, 62. **CAREER** Lectr, Univ Aberdeen (Scotland), 62-63; asst prof, Barnard Col, Columbia Univ, 63-64; asst prof, Univ Mo, 64-66; assoc prof, Wayne State Univ, 66-67; assoc prof to prof, 67-93, head hist dept, 67-75, ch Am stud, 67-93, PROF EMER HISTORY, MT ALLISON UNIV. **HONORS AND AWARDS** Am Philos Soc res grant, 66; Can Coun res grant, 75-76; SSHRC grant, 82-83; US Embassy grant res Am stud, 89-90. **MEMBERSHIPS** Am Hist Asn; Orgn Am Hist; Can Hist Asn. **SELECTED PUBLICATIONS** Auth, Age of Industrial Violence 1910-1915, 66, 71; ed consult, Harvard Bus Hist Rev; ed consult, Can Rev Am Stud. **CONTACT ADDRESS** Dept of History, Mount Allison Univ, 63D York St, Sackville, NB, Canada E4L 1G9.

ADAMS, HENRY
PERSONAL Born 05/12/1949, Boston, MA, m, 1989 **DISCIPLINE** AMERICAN ART OF THE 19TH CENTURY **EDUCATION** Harvard Univ, BA, 71; Yale Univ, PhD, 80. **CAREER** Prof, Case Western Reserve Univ; Curator, Am Painting, Cleveland Mus Art; Curator, Carnegie Mus of Art, Pittsburgh; Curator Am Art Nelson-Atkins Mus Art, Kansas City; Dir, Cummer Mus Art,Jacksonville; Fla; Interim dir,Kemper Mus Contemporary Art & Design,Kansas City. **HONORS AND AWARDS** Distinguished Service Medal, William Jewell Col, 89; Col Art Asn's Arthur Kingsley Porter Prize, 85; Frances Blanshard Prize. **SELECTED PUBLICATIONS** Auth, exhib cat, John La Farge, 87; Thomas Hart Benton: An American Original, 89; Thomas Hart Benton: Drawing from Life, 90; Albert Bloch: The American Blue Rider, 97; Dale Chihuly: Thirty Years in Glass, 97. **CONTACT ADDRESS** Case Western Reserve Univ, 10900 Euclid Ave, Cleveland, OH 44106. **EMAIL** adams@cma-oh.org

ADAMS, MARILYN M.
DISCIPLINE HISTORICAL THEOLOGY **EDUCATION** Univ Ill, AB, 64; Cornell Univ, PhD, 67; Princeton Theol Sem, ThM, 84; ThM, 85. **HONORS AND AWARDS** NEH, Younger Humanist fel, 74-75; Am Coun Learned Soc fel, 88-89; UC Pres Coun Hum fel, 88-89; Guggenheim fel, 89-90. **SELECTED PUBLICATIONS** Auth, Ockham's Treatise on Predestination, God's Foreknowledge, and Future Contingents, Century-Crofts, 69; Paul of Venice: On the Truth and Falsity of Propositions and On the Significatum of a Proposition, Oxford Univ Press, 77; William Ockham, Notre Dame Univ Press, 87; Ed, The Philosophical Theology of John Duns Scotus: A Collection of Essays by Allan B. Wolter, Oxford Univ Press, 90; Couth, The Problem of Evil, Oxford Univ Press, 90. **CONTACT ADDRESS** Yale Univ, 409 Prospect St., New Haven, CT 06511-2167.

ADAMS, MICHAEL CHARLES
PERSONAL Born 07/26/1945, Chesterfield, England, m, 1985, 2 children **DISCIPLINE** WAR STUDIES; HISTORY **EDUCATION** Univ Wales, BA, 66; Univ Sussex, PhD(Am studies), 73. **CAREER** Lectr English, North Nottinghamshire Col Further Educ, 70-71; asst prof hist, 72-77, asst to pres, 76-77, dir Grad Ctr, 77-78, assoc provost, 78-80, His & GEO Chair 81-85, 92-96; Regents Prof, 96-. **HONORS AND AWARDS** Jefferson Davis Book Prize, 78. **MEMBERSHIPS** Am His Asn; Org Am Hist, KY His Soc; Am Assoc Uni Admins; Southern His Assoc. **RESEARCH** United States and British cultural and military history; the Southern region of the United States; Victorian sexual attitudes. **SELECTED PUBLICATIONS** Auth, Our Masters the Rebels: A Speculation on Union Military Failure in the East 1861-1865, Harvard Univ, 78; auth, The Great Adventure: Male Desire and the Coming of World War One, IN Univ, 90; auth, Fighting for Defeat, NE Univ, 92; The Best War Ever: America and World War Two, Johns Hopkins Univ, 94. **CONTACT ADDRESS** Dept of Hist & Geog, No Kentucky Univ, Highland Heights, KY 41076. **EMAIL** adamsm@nku.edu

ADAMS, NICHOLAS
PERSONAL Born New York, NY, s, 1977 **DISCIPLINE** HISTORY **EDUCATION** Cornell Univ, AB, 70; NYork Univ, PhD, 77. **CAREER** Asst prof, 78-89, Lehigh Univ; Mary Conover Mellon Prof, 89-, Vassar Col. **RESEARCH** Architecture and Urbanism **CONTACT ADDRESS** Art Dept, Vassar Col, Poughkeepsie, NY 12604. **EMAIL** niadams@vassar.edu

ADAMS, RALPH JAMES QUINCY
PERSONAL Born 09/22/1943, Hammond, IN, m, 1979, 1 child **DISCIPLINE** MODERN BRITISH HISTORY **EDUCATION** Ind Univ, BS, 65; Valparaiso Univ, MA, 69; Univ Calif, Santa Barbara, PhD, 72. **CAREER** Lectr hist, Univ Calif, Santa Barbara, 71-73; asst prof, Bethany Col, WVa, 73-74; asst prof, 74-79; assoc prof hist, 79-87; prof hist, 87-, Tex A&M Univ; Res fel, St. Catherine's Col, Oxford, 93; Distinguished Fac fel, Queen Mary & Westfield Col, London, 99. **MEMBERSHIPS** Conf Brit Studies; Royal Historical Soc (fel); Western Conf Brit Studies (pres, 80, 99-00). **RESEARCH** British political history, military, and diplomatic history. **SELECTED PUBLICATIONS** Auth, Bonar Law, Cassell & Co. Ltd, London & Tex A&M Univ, 78; coauth, The Conscription Controversy in Great Britain, 1900-1918, Macmillan, London & Ohio State Univ, 87; coauth, Edwardian Conservatism, Croom Helm, London, 90; ed, The Great War: Essays on the Military, Political, and Social History of World War I, Macmillan, London & Tex A&M Univ, 90; auth, British Politics and Foreign Policy in the Age of Appeasement, 1935-1939, Macmillan, London & Stanford Univ, 93; ed, British Appeasement and the Origins of World War II, Houghton Mifflin, 94; auth Bonar Law, John Murray, London & Stanford Univ, 99; auth, Arthur James Balfour, First Earl of Balfour, John Murray, London (forthcoming). **CONTACT ADDRESS** Dept of Hist, Texas A&M Univ, Col Station, College Station, TX 77843-4236. **EMAIL** RJQA@TAMU.EDU

ADAMS, RICHARD E. W.
PERSONAL Born 07/17/1931, Kansas City, MO, m, 1955, 4 children **DISCIPLINE** ANTHROPOLOGY AND ARCHAEOLOGY **EDUCATION** BA, anthrop, Univ NMex, 53; MA, anthrop, Harvard Univ, 60; PhD, anthrop, 63. **CAREER** Asst prof to prof, anthrop, Univ Minn, 63-72; dean, humanities and social sci, Univ Tex San Antonio, 72-79; prof, anthrop, Univ Tex San Antonio, 80-. **HONORS AND AWARDS** Fulbright scholar, resident fel, Rochefeller Ctr, Bellagio, Italy, overseas fel, Churchill Col, Cambridge Univ, England; Nat Geographic Soc grant, 83-94; Nat Endowment for the Humanities grant, 85-94. **MEMBERSHIPS** Soc for Amer Archaeol; Registry of Prof Archaeol; Tex Archaeol Soc. **RESEARCH** New world archaeology; Primary ancient civilizations; Maya archaeology. **SELECTED PUBLICATIONS** Auth, Prehistoric Mesoamerica, Univ Ok Press, 92; coauth, "The Tombs of Rio Azul," National Geographic Res and Exploration (92); auth, The Ancient Civilizations of the New World, Westview Press, 97; auth, Rio Azul: An Ancient Maya City, Univ of Ok Press, 99; ed, The Origins of Maya Civilization; auth, Ancient Civilizations of the New World, Rio Azul. **CONTACT ADDRESS** Univ of Texas, San Antonio, 14070 Mint Tr., San Antonio, TX 78232-3509. **EMAIL** radams@utsa.edu

ADAMS, RUSSELL LEE
PERSONAL Born 08/13/1930, Baltimore, MD, m **DISCIPLINE** AFRICAN-AMERICAN STUDIES **EDUCATION** Morehouse Col, BA, 1952; University of Chicago, MA, 1954, PhD, 1971. **CAREER** Fed City College, assoc prof, 69-71; Howard Univ, assoc prof, 71-, chairman, Dept of Afro-American Studies, currently. **MEMBERSHIPS** Private consultant, Afro-American Studies Career Program In-Serv & Dept, Montgomery County Board of Education; consultant for numerous facilities including: University of Pittsburgh, Center for Deseg, 1976-, Wilmington DE Public Schools, 1977, Newark-New Castle-Marshalton McKean School District, Jackson Public Schools, 1969-70; lecturer/consultant, US Info Agency, 1977; chairman, committee on status of blacks in profession Amer Pol Sci Assn, 1974-77; NAACP, Curr Eval Pool, Prince Georges County Bd of Ed 1976-. **SELECTED PUBLICATIONS** Auth, Great Negroes Past & Present, 1963-69, 1972; Leading American Negroes, 1965; Perceptual Difficulties Dev Pol Sci Varia, Spring 1976; publisher, Black Studies Movement, Assessment Journal of Negro Education, 1977. **CONTACT ADDRESS** Dept of Afro-American Studies, Howard Univ, 2400 Sixth St NW, Washington, DC 20059-0002.

ADAMS, WILLIAM
PERSONAL Born 08/25/1946, New London, CT, m, 1969, 2 children **DISCIPLINE** HISTORY **EDUCATION** Cent Okla State Univ, BA, 66; Univ NDak, MA, 73; DA, 75; SUNY, MA, 78. **CAREER** Prof, Univ Tex, 89-. **SELECTED PUBLICATIONS** Auth, Portrait of a Border City: Brownsville, Texas, 97; auth, Valley Vets: World War II Veterans of the Rio Grande Valley, 99; auth, Remembering Xinxiang, 00. **CONTACT ADDRESS** Dept Hist, Univ of Texas, Brownsville, 80 Fort Brown St, Brownsville, TX 78520-4956. **EMAIL** wadams@utb1.utb.edu

ADAMS, WINTHROP LINDSAY
PERSONAL Born 03/09/1947, Newport News, VA, 1 child **DISCIPLINE** ANCIENT GREEK & ROMAN HISTORY **EDUCATION** Univ Va, BA, 69, PhD, 75. **CAREER** Instr hist, Univ Va, 74; vis asst prof, 74-75, asst prof, 75-82, Assoc Prof

Hist, Univ Utah, 82-; vis assoc prof, Univ Mich, 84. **HONORS AND AWARDS** Univ Utah Pres Teaching Scholar; Ramona Cauron Awd Teaching Excellence, Univ Utah. **MEMBERSHIPS** AHA; Am Philol Asn; Assoc Ancient Historians; Am Cath Hist Asn; Soc Ancient Military Hist **RESEARCH** Ancient Macedonia, Hellenistic Greek history, Roman Imperialism. **SELECTED PUBLICATIONS** Auth, The Dynamics of Internal Macedonian Politics in the Time of Cassander, Archaia Makedonia III, pages, 12-25; Cassander and the crossing of the Hellespont, Diordorus 17, 17, 4, Vol II, pages 111-115 & The royal Macedonian tomb at Vergina: An historical interpretation, Vol III, pages 67-72, Ancient World; co-ed, Philip II, Alexander the Great and the Macedonian Heritage, Univ Press Am, 4/82; Perseus and the Third Macedonian War, in Philip II, Alexander the Great and the Macedonian Heritage, Univ Press Am, 82; Macedonian Kingship and the Right of Petition, Archaia Makedonia, 86; Cassander, Alexander IV, and the Tombs at Vergina, Ancient World, 91; Philip V, Hannibal and the Origins of the First Macedonian War, Archaia Makedonia, 92; Cassander the the Greet City-States (319-317 B C), J Balkan Studies, 93; In the Wake of Alexander: Macedonia and the Agegean after the Death of Alexander the Great, Ancient World, 96; Historical Perspectives of Greco-Macedonian Ethnicity in the Hellenistic Age, Balkan Studies, 96; Philip II and the Thracian Frontier, in Proceedings of the II International Congress of Ancient Thrace, Komotini, Greece, 97; The Successors to Alexander, in The Greek World in the Fourth Century, Routlegde, 97; Philip II, the League of Corinth and the Governance of Greece, Archaia Makedonia, forthcoming. **CONTACT ADDRESS** Dept of Hist, Univ of Utah, 217 Carlson Hall, Salt Lake City, UT 84112-3124. **EMAIL** winthrop.adams@m.cc.utah.edu

ADAMSON, WALTER L.
PERSONAL Born 02/28/1946, Washington, DC, m, 1972, 2 children **DISCIPLINE** HISTORY **EDUCATION** Swarthmore Col, BA, 68; Univ Calif Berkeley, MA, 69; Brandeis Univ, PhD, 76. **CAREER** Whitman Col, asst prof 75-77; Harvard Univ, Mellon Fel, 77-78; Emory Univ, asst, assoc, prof, Dobbs Prof, 78 to 87-. **HONORS AND AWARDS** Marraro Prize (twice). **RESEARCH** Modern European intellectual and cultural history; modern Italian history. **SELECTED PUBLICATIONS** Auth, Avant-garde Florence: From Modernism to Fascism; Marx and the Disillusionment of Marxism; Hegemony and Revolution: Antonio Gramsci's Political and Cultural Theory. The first and third of these both received the as the best book in Italian history. **CONTACT ADDRESS** Dept History, Emory Univ, 221 Bowden Hall, 561 Kilgo Cir, Atlanta, GA 30322-1950. **EMAIL** wadamso@emory.edu

ADAMTHWAITE, ANTHONY
PERSONAL Born 10/30/1938, Leeds, England, m, 1967, 4 children **DISCIPLINE** HISTORY **EDUCATION** Univ Durham, BA, 61; Univ Leeds, PhD, 66. **CAREER** Lectr, Univ Col, 64-70; sen lectr, Univ Bradford, 70-78; prof, Loughborough Univ, 78-89; prof, Univ Calif Berkeley, 90-. **HONORS AND AWARDS** Fel, Royal Hist Soc. **MEMBERSHIPS** Am Hist Asn; Soc for French Hist Studies; Soc of Hist of Am For Relations; W Soc for French Hist. **RESEARCH** Twentieth Century French and British foreign policies; The European union; Treatment of prisoners of war. **SELECTED PUBLICATIONS** Auth, Grandeur and misery: France's bid for power in Europe, 1914-1940, 95. **CONTACT ADDRESS** Dept Hist, Univ of California, Berkeley, 3229 Dwinelle Hall, Berkeley, CA 94720. **EMAIL** Adamthwa@socrates.berkeley.edu

ADAS, MICHAEL PETER
PERSONAL Born 02/04/1943, Detroit, MI, m, 1967, 2 children **DISCIPLINE** COMPARATIVE COLONIAL HISTORY, 20TH CENTURY **EDUCATION** Western MI Univ, BA, 65; Univ Wis, MA, 66 & 67, PhD, 71. **CAREER** From asst prof to assoc prof, 74, chmn dept hist, 79-81, prof, 79; distinguished prof, 89; Bd of Governor's prof & Abraham Voorhees prof hist, Rugers Univ, New Brunswick, 97, Bd gov ch, 96-97; Carnegie Found res fel, 75. **HONORS AND AWARDS** Genevieve Gorst Herfurth Bk Award, Univ WI, 75; NJNEH Hum Bk Award, 90; Dexter Prize Hist Tech Soc, 91; Guggenheim Fel, 94-95. **MEMBERSHIPS** AHA, SHOT. **RESEARCH** Tech and western colonial domination; World War I as a global conflict **SELECTED PUBLICATIONS** Auth, The Burma Delta, Economic Development and Social Change on an Asian Rice Frontier, Univ Wis, 74; Prophets of Rebellion: Millenarian Protest against the European Colonial Order, Univ NC, 79, Cambridge, 86; Machines as the Measure of Men: Science, Technology and Western Dominance, Cornell Univ, 89, co-auth (with Peter Stearns and Stuart Schwartz), World Civilizations: The Global Experience, harperCollins, 92, and Turbulent Passage: A Global History of the Twentieth Century, HarperCollins, 93; ed, Islamic and European Expansion: The Forging of a Global Order, AHA/Temple, 93; ed, vol on Technology, In: An Expanding World, series, Variorum 96; State, Market and Peasant in South and Southeast Asian History, Variorum, 98; auth, World Civilizations: The Global Experience, 3rd. Edition, 00; ed, Agricultural and Pastoral Societies in Ancient and Classical History, AHA/Temple, 01. **CONTACT ADDRESS** Dept of Hist, Rutgers, The State Univ of New Jersey, New Brunswick, PO Box 5059, New Brunswick, NJ 08903-5059. **EMAIL** madas@rci.rutgers.edu

ADDINGTON, LARRY H.
PERSONAL Born 11/16/1932, Charlotte, NC, m, 1963, 1 child **DISCIPLINE** MILITARY & MODERN EUROPEAN HISTORY **EDUCATION** Univ NC, AB, 55, MA, 56; Duke Univ, PhD(hist), 62. **CAREER** Asst prof hist, San Jose State Col, 62-64; asst prof hist, The Citadel, 64-66, assoc prof Hist, The Citadel, 66-70, consult mil hist, US Army Combat Develop Command, 68-69; prof hist, Citadel, 70; visit prof hist, Duke Univ, 76-77; dept head, hist, Citadel, 89-94; retired 94. **HONORS AND AWARDS** Moncado Awd, Am Mil Inst, 68; Phi Beta Kappa, UNC, 55; Moncado Awd, Am Mil Int, 68; Distinguished Teaching Awd, Citadel, 71; Citadel Development Foundation Fellow, 82-89. **MEMBERSHIPS** AHA; AAUP; Southern Hist Asn. **RESEARCH** Nineteenth and twentieth century European political and Modern military history. **SELECTED PUBLICATIONS** Auth, From Moltke to Hitler:The Evolution of German Military Doctrine, 1865-1939, The Citadel, 66; Operation Sunflower, Rommel versus the General Staff, Mil Affairs, fall 67; auth, The Blitzreig Era and the German General Staff, 1865-1941, Rutgers Univ, 71; Antiaircraft Artillery versus the Fighter-Bomber: the Duel over North Vietnam, 1964-1968, Army Mag, 12/73; The Coast Artillery Corps and Artillery Organization, 1906-1950, Mil Affairs, 77; The Patterns of War since the 18th Century, Indiana Univ, 84; The Patterns of War to the 18th Century, Indiana Univ, 90; Military Science. The Academic Press Dictionary of Science and Technology, 92; The National Defense Act of 1920, The United States in the First World War: An Encyclopedia, Garland Pub, 95; America's War in Vietnam, A Short Narrative History, Indiana Univ, 00. **CONTACT ADDRESS** 1341 New Castle St., Charleston, SC 29407. **EMAIL** downfall@gateway.net

ADDISS, STEPHEN L.
PERSONAL Born 04/02/1935, New York, NY **DISCIPLINE** FINE ART **EDUCATION** Harvard Univ, BA, 57; Univ Mich, MA, 73; PhD, 77. **CAREER** Asst Prof to Prof, Prof, Univ Richmond, 92-. **HONORS AND AWARDS** Distinguished Educ Awd, Univ Richmond **SELECTED PUBLICATIONS** Auth, Tao Te Ching, Hackett Pub, 93; auth, Haiga: Takebe Socho and the Haiku-Painting Tradition, Univ of Hawaii Press, 95; auth, How to Look at Japanese Art, Harry N. Abrams, 96; co-auth, Haiku People, Weatherhill, 98; auth, The Resonance of the Qin in Far Eastern Art, China Inst, 99; auth, The Old Taoist: the Life, Painting, and Poetry of Kokojin, Columbia Univ Press, 00. **CONTACT ADDRESS** Dept Art & Art Hist, Univ of Richmond, 28 Westhampton Way, Richmond, VA 23173-0001. **EMAIL** saddiss@richmond.edu

ADELSON, FRED B.
DISCIPLINE ART HISTORY **EDUCATION** Univ Mass, BA 70; Columbia Univ, MA, 71; PhD, 82. **CAREER** Adj lectr, Upsala Col, 72; adj instr, St Peter's Col, 72-73; adj instr, Rutgers Univ, New Brunswick, 72-73; adj instr, Kean Col NJ, 73-74; vis lectr, Rutgers Univ, Camden, 86-87; prof, Rowan Univ, 74-. **HONORS AND AWARDS** Rockefeller Found fel, Columbia Univ, 78; res and develop grant, Glassboro State Col, 78; 83; 84; 87; 89; 91; fac fel prog, Princeton Univ, 89/90; arts rev, NJers Sect, NYork Times. **MEMBERSHIPS** Col Art Asn; Asn of Hist of Am Art ; Phi Kappa Phi. **SELECTED PUBLICATIONS** Auth, Architecture: Norman Jaffe, Archit Digest, 78; A New Look at Alvan Fisher, The Gilcrease Mag of Am Hist and Art, 84; An American Snowfall: Early Winter Scenes by Alvan Fisher, Arts in Va, 83-84; Art Under Cover: American Gift-Book Illustrations, The Mag ANTIQUES, 84; Con=struct=ures, Reading Pub Mus and Art Gallery, Reading, Pa, 85. Alvan Fisher in Maine: His Early Coastal Scenes, The Am Art J, 86; Home on La Grange: Alvan Fisher's Lithographs of Lafayette's Residence in France, The Mag ANTIQUES, 88; American Eclipse with Race Track, Masterworks of American Art from the Munson-Williams-Proctor Inst, Harry N. Abrams, 89; Dichotomy #18, The Painted Bride Art Ctr, Philadelphia, 89; Con=struct=ures, The Port of Hist Mus, Philadelphia, 93. Thomas Eakins and Walt Whitman, The Art of Thomas Eakins, Nat Portrait Gallery, London, Eng, 93. **CONTACT ADDRESS** Art Dept, Rowan Univ, Col of Fine & Peforming Arts, 201 Mullica Hill Rd, Glassboro, NJ 08027-1701. **EMAIL** adelson@rowan.edu

ADELSON, ROGER
PERSONAL Born 07/11/1942, Abilene, KS, d **DISCIPLINE** HISTORY **EDUCATION** George Wash Univ, BA, 64; Washington Univ, MA, 68; Oxford Univ, B.Litt, 70; Washington Univ, PhD, 72 **CAREER** Lectr, Harvard Univ, 74; from asst prof to prof, Ariz State Univ, 74-. **HONORS AND AWARDS** Alistair Horne Res Fel, 72-73; Senior Res Fel, St Antony Col, Oxford Univ, 72-73; Outstanding Teacher Awd, 79; Churchill Prize, 93; **MEMBERSHIPS** Amer Hist Assoc; North Amer Conf on Brit Studies; Council Foreign Relations; Middle East Studies Assoc; Conference Hist Jrn **RESEARCH** British and U.S. power in the Middle East in 20th Century; Comparative and Global History since 1500 **SELECTED PUBLICATIONS** Auth, Speaking of History: Conversations with Historians, East Lansing, 97; auth, London and the Invention of the Middle East: Money, Power and War, 1902-1922, New Haven, 95; auth, Mark Sykes: Portrait of an Amateur, London, 75 **CONTACT ADDRESS** Dept History, Arizona State Univ, PO Box 872501, Tempe, AZ 85287-2501. **EMAIL** adelsonr@asu.edu

ADLER, PHILIP JOSEPH
PERSONAL Born 03/30/1930, Philadelphia, PA, m, 1971, 1 child **DISCIPLINE** MODERN HISTORY **EDUCATION** Loyola Univ, Los Angeles, BA, 54; Univ Vienna, PhD(hist), 61. **CAREER** Foreign serv officer, US Dept State, 62-66; assoc prof, 66-75, Prof Hist E Carolina Univ, 75-, Lectr hist, Univ Md, 65-66; Fulbright-Hays fac res prog grant, 71-72; Nat Endowment for Humanities res fel, 76 & 79. **MEMBERSHIPS** AHA; Am Asn Advan Slavic Studies; Am Asn Southeastern Europ Studies. **RESEARCH** Ethnic culture in East Europe; Serbian history; Social Institutions. **SELECTED PUBLICATIONS** Auth, Notes on the beginning of modern Serbian literature, Southeastern Europe, Vol I, 74; Habsburg school reform among the Orthodox minorities, Slavic Rev, 74; German contractees in early 19th century Serbia, Sudost-Forsch Yearbk, 74; The introduction of public schooling for the Jews of Hungary (1849-1860), Jewish Social Studies, 74; Serbs, Magyars and Staatsinteresse in 18th century Austria, Austrian Hist Yearbk, 78; Nation and Nationalism Among the Serbs of Hungary, 1790-1870, E Europ Quart, 79; The South Slaves of the Habsburg Empire: An Annotated Bibliography, 1945-1980 (in prep); Broken Bonds- The Disintegration of Yugoslavia, Int Hist Rev, Vol 0016, 94; Bosnia-A Short History, Int Hist Rev, Vol 0018, 96. **CONTACT ADDRESS** Dept of Hist, East Carolina Univ, Greenville, NC 27834.

ADOLPHSON, MIKAEL
PERSONAL Born 03/10/1961, Norrkoping, Sweden **DISCIPLINE** HISTORY, JAPANESE HISTORY **EDUCATION** Univ Lund, Sweden, 85; Stanford Univ, MA, 92, PhD, 96. **CAREER** Asst prof, Univ Okla, 95-99; asst prof, Harvard Univ, 99-. **MEMBERSHIPS** Asn Asian Studies. **RESEARCH** Pre-1600 Japan. **SELECTED PUBLICATIONS** Auth, "Enryaku-ji--An Old Power in a New Era," in The Origins of Japan's Medieval World, ed J. P. Mass, Stanford Univ Press, 97; auth, The Gates of Power: Monks, Courtiers, and Warriors in Premodern Japan, Honolulu: Univ Haw Press, 2000. **CONTACT ADDRESS** Dept E Asian Lang, Harvard Univ, 2 Divinity Ave, Cambridge, MA 02138-2020.

AESCHBACHER, WILLIAM DRIVER
PERSONAL Born 01/12/1919, Tonganoxie, KS, m, 1944, 3 children **DISCIPLINE** AMERICAN HISTORY **EDUCATION** Univ Nebr, BS, 40, MA, 46, PhD(hist), 48. **CAREER** Assoc prof soc sci, Murray State Col, 48-56; dir, Nebr State Hist Soc & ed, Nebr Hist, 56-63; dir, Eisenhower Libr, 63-66; prof hist, Univ Utah, 66-68; Prof Hist, Univ Cincinnati, 68- **MEMBERSHIPS** Orgn Am Hist (secy-treas, 56-76); AHA; Southern Hist Asn; Western Hist Asn; Am Asn State & Local Hist. **RESEARCH** Western history; state and local history; agricultural history. **SELECTED PUBLICATIONS** Auth, Presidential libraries: New dimension in research facilities, Midwestern Quart, winter 65; The Mississippi Valley Historical Association 1870-1965, J Am Hist, 9/67; Allis-Chalmers - Farm Equipment 1914-1985, Jour of West, Vol 0035, 97. **CONTACT ADDRESS** Dept of Hist, Univ of Cincinnati, Cincinnati, OH 45221.

AFRICA, THOMAS WILSON
PERSONAL Born 12/24/1927, Portland, OR, m, 1952, 2 children **DISCIPLINE** ANCIENT HISTORY **EDUCATION** Univ Calif, Los Angeles, AB, 56, MA, 57, PhD, 59. **CAREER** Instr hist, Univ Calif, Santa Barbara, 59-60; asst prof, La State Univ, 60-61; from asst prof to prof, Univ Southern Calif, 61-69; prof hist, State Univ NY, Binghamton, 69-80, chmn dept, 76; Res & Writing, 80-, Res grant-in-aid, Am Coun Learned Soc, 60. **MEMBERSHIPS** AHA; Hist Sci Soc; Soc Promotion Hellenic Studies; Soc Prom Roman Studies. **RESEARCH** Historiography; Hellenistic age; effect of psychology in history. **SELECTED PUBLICATIONS** Auth, Phylarchus and the Spartan Revolution, Univ Calif, 61; Opium addiction of Marcus Aurelius, J Hist Ideas, 61; Rome of the Caesars, 65 & Science and the State in Greece and Rome, 67, Wiley; The Ancient World, Houghton, 69; The one-eyed man against Rome, Historia, 12/70; The Immense Majesty, Crowell, 74; Psychohistorical study of Brutus, J Interdisciplinary Hist, 78; The Owl at Dusk - 2 Centuries of Classical Scholarship, Jour of Hist of Ideas, Vol 0054, 93; The Wicked Knight and the Use of Anecdotes, Greece & Rome, Vol 0042, 95. **CONTACT ADDRESS** 421 African Rd, Vestal, NY 13850.

AGNEW, JOHN A.
PERSONAL Born 08/29/1949, Millom, England, d, 2 children **DISCIPLINE** GEOGRAPHY **EDUCATION** Univ Exeter, BA, 70; Univ Liverpool, Cert Ed, 71; Ohio State Univ, MA, 73; PhD, 76. **CAREER** Asst prof, Syracuse, 75-80; vis asst prof, Univ BC, 79; assoc prof to prof and prog dir, Syracuse Univ, 81-96; prof, UCLA, 96-. **HONORS AND AWARDS** Wasserstrom Award, Syracuse Univ, 95; Chancellor's Award for Distinguished Scholar, Syracuse Univ, 96; Fel, Royal Geog Soc, 94-. **MEMBERSHIPS** Royal Geog Soc; Asn of Am Geogr; Am Polit Sci Asn; coun for Europ Studies; Conf Group on Italian Polit and Soc; Soc for Italian Hist Studies. **RESEARCH** Political geography, particularly geopolitics and place and politics; Urban geography, particularly of Europe and Italy; International political economy. **SELECTED PUBLICATIONS** Auth, Mastering Space, 95; auth, Human Geography: An Essen-

tial Anthology, 96; auth, Geopolitics, 98; auth, reinventing Geopolitics, 01. **CONTACT ADDRESS** Dept Geog, Univ of California, Los Angeles, 1255 Bunche Hall, PO Box 951524, Los Angeles, CA 90095-1524. **EMAIL** jagnew@geog.ucla.edu

AHEARN, EDWARD J.
PERSONAL Born 10/31/1937, New York, NY, m, 1979, 2 children **DISCIPLINE** COMPARATIVE LITERATURE & FRENCH STUDIES **EDUCATION** Manhattan Col, BA, 59; Yale Univ, PhD, 63. **CAREER** Asst prof French, 63-68, assoc prof, 68-80, Prof, 80-95, Univ Prof, Comp Lit & Fr Studies, Brown Univ, 95-; Fel, Ctr Advan Studies, Univ Ill. **HONORS AND AWARDS** Harbison Awd for Gifted Teaching, Danforth Found, 70. **MEMBERSHIPS** MLA. **RESEARCH** Comparative literature of the 19th & 20th century. **SELECTED PUBLICATIONS** Auth, Rimbaud: Visions of Habitations, Univ Calif, 83; Marx & Modern Fiction, Yale, 91; Visionary Fictions: Apocalyptic Writing from Blake to the Modern Age, Yale, 96. **CONTACT ADDRESS** Dept of Comparative Lit, Brown Univ, Box E, Providence, RI 02912-9127. **EMAIL** Edward_Ahearn@brown.edu

AHERN, WILBERT H.
PERSONAL Born 07/12/1942, Greenville, IL, m, 1963, 2 children **DISCIPLINE** AMERICAN HISTORY **EDUCATION** Oberlin Col, BA, 63; Northwestern Univ, MA, 66, PhD, 68. **CAREER** From asst prof to Morse-Alumni Distinguished Teaching Prof Hist, Univ MN, Morris, 67-; co-dir, W Cent Minn Hist Res Ctr, 72-73, dir, 73-87, 96-; actg acad dean, Univ MN, Morris, 78-79; coordr, Freshman Sem Prog, Univ Minn, Morris, 81-87; Danforth assoc, 81-86; chr, div of Soc Sci, 87-95. **HONORS AND AWARDS** Resident res fel, Newberry Libr, 74-75; Horace T. Morse-Amoco Awd for Outstanding Contributions to Undergrad Educ, Univ Minn, 84; Solon J. Buck Awd for Best Article, Minnesota History 84; Academy of Distinguished Teachers, Univ Minnesota, 99-. **MEMBERSHIPS** AAUP; Orgn Am Historians; AHA. **RESEARCH** United States, 1850-1917; race and nationality in America; social and intellectual history. **SELECTED PUBLICATIONS** Auth, "The Cox Plan of Reconstruction: A Case Study in Ideology and Race Relations," Civil War History, 70; "Assimilationist Racism: The Case of the Friends of the Indian," Journal of Ethnic Studies, summer 76; Laissiz Faire vs. Equal Rights: Liberal Republicans and Limits to Reconstruction," Phylon, 3/79; "The Returned Indians': Hampton Institute and Its Indian Alumni, 1878-1893," Journal of Ethnic Studies, 82; "Indian Education and Bureaucracy: The School at Morris," Minnesota History, 84; To Kill the Indian and Save the Man: The Boarding Scholar in American Indian Education, 86; "Enhancing the Faculty Development at Tribal College," Tribal College Journal, 96; "An Experiment Aborted: Returned Indian Students and the Indian School Service," Ethnohistory, 97. **CONTACT ADDRESS** Div of Soc Sci, Univ of Minnesota, Morris, 600 E 4th St, Morris, MN 56267-2134. **EMAIL** ahernwh@cda.umn.mrs.edu

AHMADI, SHAHWALI
PERSONAL Born 12/06/1964, Kabul, Afghanistan, m, 1999 **DISCIPLINE** LITERATURE, PERSIAN, NEAR EASTERN STUDIES **EDUCATION** Calif State Univ Hayward, BA, 87; Univ Calif Los Angeles, MA, 91; PhD, 97. **CAREER** Lectr, Univ Vir, 96-00; asst prof, Univ Calif Berkeley, 00-. **HONORS AND AWARDS** FLAS Fel; Chancellor's Awd. **MEMBERSHIPS** MLA; MESA. **RESEARCH** Literary theory and criticism. **SELECTED PUBLICATIONS** Ed, Critique and Vision: An Afghan Journal of Culture, Politics and History. **CONTACT ADDRESS** English Dept, Univ of California, Berkeley, 250 Barrows Hall, Berkeley, CA 94720-0001. **EMAIL** ahmadi@socrates.berkeley.edu

AIKIN, ROGER
DISCIPLINE ART HISTORY **EDUCATION** Univ Calif, Berkeley, PhD. **CAREER** Assoc prof & dept ch; Creighton Univ, 80-; stud photog in Oregon and Calif; work rep in Ansel Adams coll in the Ctr for Creative Photog in Tucson. **SELECTED PUBLICATIONS** Publ on, Calif art and photography of the 20th century; Renaissance and Baroque Art. **CONTACT ADDRESS** Dept of Fine and Performing Arts, Creighton Univ, 2500 California Plaza, Omaha, NE 68178. **EMAIL** leca@creighton.edu

AINLEY, MARIANNE G.
PERSONAL Born Budapest, Hungary **DISCIPLINE** HISTORY OF SCIENCE, WOMEN'S STUDIES **EDUCATION** Sir George Williams Univ, BA, 64; Univ Montreal, MS, 80; McGill Univ, PhD, 85. **CAREER** Independent scholar, SSHRCC Can Strategic Grants Div, 86-87, 89-91; prin, Simone de Beauvoir Inst & Dir Women's Studs, Concordia Univ, 91-95; prof & ch, Women's Studies, Univ Northern BC, 95-. **MEMBERSHIPS** McGill Ctr Tchr Women; Soc Can Ornithol; Can Hist Educ Soc; Can Women's Stud Asn; Can Sci Tech Hist Asn; Can Res Inst Advan Women; Hist Sci Soc Am. **RESEARCH** Hist of Canaadian women and scientific work, feminist scientific biography, First Nations women and environmental knowledge, the hist of ornithology, and Candian environmental hist. **SELECTED PUBLICATIONS** Auth, Restless Energy: A Biography of Wiliam Rowan, 1891-1957, 93; auth, Louise de Kiriline Lawrence & the World of Nature: A Trubute in the Can Field Naturalist, 94; auth, Canadian Women's Contributions to Chemistry, 1900-1970, in Can Chem News, 94; auth, Despite the Odds, Essays on Canadian Women and Science, The Emergence of Canadian Ornithoogy - AN Historical Overview to 1950, in Contributions to the History of North American Ornithology, 95. **CONTACT ADDRESS** Women's Stud Prog, Univ of British Columbia, 3333 University Way, Prince George, BC, Canada V2N 4ZN. **EMAIL** ainley@unbc.ca

AJOOTIAN, AILEEN
DISCIPLINE ANCIENT ART, CLASSICAL ARCHAEOLOGY **EDUCATION** SUNY, Oswego, BA; Univ OR, MA; Byrn Mawr Col, MA, PhD. **CAREER** Instr, Cleveland State Univ, Univ OR, McMaster Univ, Ontario; asst prof Classics and Art, Univ MS, 96-. **HONORS AND AWARDS** Anna C and Oliver C Colburn fel, Archaeological Institute of Am; fel, Whiting, Kress, Oscar Broneer, Bryne Rubel, Am Numis Soc. **RESEARCH** Sculptures and sculptors on the Pnyx. **SELECTED PUBLICATIONS** Among her many publ are those about Sparta and Praxiteles. **CONTACT ADDRESS** Univ of Mississippi, Oxford, MS 38677.

AKEHURST, F. R. P.
DISCIPLINE OLD FRENCH AND THE HISTORY OF FRENCH **EDUCATION** Univ Colo, PhD; Univ Minn, JD. **CAREER** Instr, Univ Minn, Twin Cities. **RESEARCH** Medieval French law. **SELECTED PUBLICATIONS** Ed, Handbook of the Troubadours, Univ Calif Press, 95; transl, "Coutumes de Beauvasis" of Philippe de Beaumanoir, Univ Pa Press, 92; published on the troubadours, the trouveres, and the fabliaux. **CONTACT ADDRESS** Univ of Minnesota, Twin Cities, 9 Pleasant St. SE, 260 Folwell Hall, Minneapolis, MN 55455.

AKENSON, DONALD
PERSONAL Born 05/22/1941, Minneapolis, MN, d, 2 children **DISCIPLINE** HISTORY **EDUCATION** Yale Col, BA, 62; Harvard Univ, EdM, 63; PhD, 67. **CAREER** Asst prof, Yale Col, 67-70; assoc prof to prof, Queen's Univ, 70-. **HONORS AND AWARDS** Chauncey Brewster Tinker Mem Prize, Yale, 61; Phi Beta Kappa, 61; Fel, Royal Soc of Can, 76; Chalmers Prize, 85; Landon Prize, 87; Fel, Royal Hist Soc, UK, 88; Grawemeyer Awd; 93; DLitt, McMaster Univ, 95; Trillium Prize, 95; Medal, Univ of BC, 95; Molson Prize Laureate, 96; DHum, Lethbridge Univ, 96; DLitt, Univ of Guelph, 00. **RESEARCH** Irish History, Biblical History. **SELECTED PUBLICATIONS** Auth, A Mirror to Kathleen's Face: Education in Independent Ireland, 1922-60, McGill-Queen's Univ Pr, (Montreal, Kingston), 75; auth, Between Two Revolutions: Islandmagee, Co. Antrim, 1798-1920, PD Meany Co, Hamden, (Toronto, Hamden), 79; auth, The Irish in Ontario: A Study in Rural History, McGill-Queen's Univ Pr, (Montreal, Kingston), 84; auth, Small Differences: Irish Caths and Irisih Protestants, 1815-1921, An International Perspective, McGill-Queen's Univ Pr, (Montral, Kingston), 88; auth, God's Peoples: Covenant and Land in South Africa, Isreael and Ulster, Cornell Univ Pri, McGill-Queen's Univ Pr, (Ithaca, Monteal, Kingston), 92; auth, The Irish Diaspora, A Primer, Inst of Irish Studies, Queens Univ of Belfast and PD Meany, (Toronto), 93; auth, Conor: A Biography of Conor Cruise O'Brien, McGill-Queen's Univ Pr, Cornell Univ Pr, (Montreal, Kingston, Ithaca), 94; auth, If the Irish Ran the World. Montserrat, 1630-1730, Liverpool Univ Pr, Univ of the W Indies Pr, McGill-Queen's Univ Pr, (Liverpool, Mona, Montreal), 97; auth, Surpassing Wonder. The Invention of the Bible and the Talmuds, Harcourt, Brace, McGill-Queen's Univ Pr, (NY, Montreal, Kingston), 98; auth, Saint Saul. A Skeleton Key to the Historical Jesus, Oxford Univ Pr, McGill-Queen's Univ Pr, (NY, Montreal, Kingston), 00. **CONTACT ADDRESS** Dept Hist, Queen's Univ at Kingston, Kingston, ON, Canada K7L 3N6.

AKIN, WILLIAM ERNEST
PERSONAL Born 12/15/1936, Chambers County, AL, m, 1971, 4 children **DISCIPLINE** HISTORY **EDUCATION** Univ of MD BA 61, Univ of MD MA 63, Univ of Rochester PhD 71. **CAREER** Instr SUNY Binghamton 66-69, Asst Prof Loyola College of Monteral 69-74, Assoc Prof and Dean of Hum Concordia Univ Montreal 74-79, Prof and Academic Vice Pres Ursinus College Collegeville PA 79-. **HONORS AND AWARDS** LLD Tohoko Gakuin Univ Sendai Japan. **MEMBERSHIPS** Soc for Baseball Res, Soc for Sports Hist, AHA. **RESEARCH** US Soc Hist, Sports Hist **SELECTED PUBLICATIONS** Technocracy and the American Dream 1900-1941, 77; Faculty Development in Liberal Arts Colleges, 85; History of the Town of Brighton NY:1814-1964, 64. **CONTACT ADDRESS** Ursinus Col, PO Box 1000, Collegeville, PA 19426. **EMAIL** wakin@ursinus.edu

AKSAN, VIRGINIA
DISCIPLINE HISTORY **EDUCATION** Allegheny Col, BA; Berkley Col, MLS; Univ Toronto, MA, PhD. **HONORS AND AWARDS** SSHRC grant **MEMBERSHIPS** Turkish Studies Asn. **RESEARCH** 18th century Ottoman history. **SELECTED PUBLICATIONS** Auth, An Ottoman Statesman in War and Peace: Ahmed Resmi Efendi 1700-1783; art, The One-Eyed Fighting the Blind: Mobilization, Supply and Command in the Russo-Turkish War of 1768-74, Int Hist Rev; auth, "Whatever Happended to the Janissaries?" in War in Hist, 98; auth, Locating the Ottomans amongh Early Modern Empires," in J Of Early Modern Hist, 99. **CONTACT ADDRESS** History Dept, McMaster Univ, 1280 Main St W, Hamilton, ON, Canada L8S 4L9. **EMAIL** vaksan@mcmaster.ca

ALAIMO, KATHLEEN
PERSONAL Born 12/21/1956, Brooklyn, NY, m, 1983, 2 children **DISCIPLINE** HISTORY, POLITICAL SCIENCE **EDUCATION** Brooklyn Col, BA, 78; Univ Chicago, MA, 79; Univ Wis, PhD, 89. **CAREER** Asst Prof, Xavier Univ, 87-92; From Asst Prof to Assoc Prof, St Xavier Univ, 93-. **HONORS AND AWARDS** Summer Inst Grant, Nat Endowment Humanities, 91; Writing Coun Grant, St Xavier Univ, 93; Excellence in Teaching Awd, St Xavier Univ, 95, 97; Fac Develop Grant, St Xavier Univ, 96; Who's Who in America's Teachers, 99; Res Sabbatical, St Xavier Univ, 00. **MEMBERSHIPS** AHA, SFHS, Coord Coun for Women in Hist, WHA, HES, AAUP. **RESEARCH** European social history, women's history, history of adolescence, history of child rights. **SELECTED PUBLICATIONS** Rev, "Childhood and Adolescence in Modern European History," J of Soc Hist 24:3 (91): 591-602; auth, "Shaping Adolescence in the Popular Milieu: Social Policy, Reformers and French Youth 1870-1920," J of Family Hist 17:4 (92): 419-438; auth, "Adolescence, Gender and Class in Education Reform in France: The Development of Enseignement Primaire Superieur 1880-1910," Fr Hist Studies 18:4 (94): 1025-1055; co-ed, Children as Equals: Exploring the Rights of the Child, UP of Am, forthcoming; auth, "Juvenile Delinquency and Hooliganism in Europe from the Renaissance to the Present," in The Encycl of European Soc Hist (Scribners, forthcoming). **CONTACT ADDRESS** Dept Hist & Polit Sci, Saint Xavier Univ, 3700 W 103rd St, Chicago, IL 60655-3105. **EMAIL** alaimo@sxu.edu

ALBALA, KENNETH
PERSONAL Born 11/03/1964, Brooklyn, NY, m, 2 children **DISCIPLINE** HISTORY **EDUCATION** George Washington Univ, BA, 86; Yale Univ, MA, 87; Columbia Univ, PhD, 93. **CAREER** From asst prof to assoc prof, Univ of the Pacific, 94-. **MEMBERSHIPS** Renaissance Soc, Sixteenth-Century Studies, Oxford Symposium. **RESEARCH** Food and Medicine. **SELECTED PUBLICATIONS** Auth, Food and Nutrition in the Renaissance, UC Press, in press. **CONTACT ADDRESS** Dept Hist, Univ of the Pacific, Stockton, 3601 Pacific Ave, Stockton, CA 95211-0110. **EMAIL** kalbala@uop.edu

ALBERT, PETER J.
PERSONAL Born 07/24/1946, Racine, WI, m, 1991, 2 children **DISCIPLINE** AMERICAN HISTORY; LABOR HISTORY; THE AMERICAN REVOLUTION **EDUCATION** St. John's Univ, BA, 67; Univ of Wis at Madison, MA, 69; Univ of Md at Col Park, PhD, 76. **CAREER** Asst ed, 74-76, assic ed, 76-85, co-ed, Samuel Gompers Papers, Univ Md, Col Park, 85-. **SELECTED PUBLICATIONS** Co-ed, Samuel Gompers Papers-7 volumes-; co-ed, Perspectives on the American Revolution-14 volumes-. **CONTACT ADDRESS** History Dept, Univ of Maryland, Col Park, Room M2198, McKeldin Libr, College Park, MD 20742-7315. **EMAIL** pa3@umail.umd.edu

ALBIN, THOMAS R.
PERSONAL Born 05/10/1951, Wakeeney, KS, m, 1971, 3 children **DISCIPLINE** CHURCH HISTORY **EDUCATION** Oral Roberts Univ, BA, 73, MA, 76; Fuller Theol Sem, MA, 77; Univ Cambridge, PhD, 00. **CAREER** Vis lect, 87-88, Boston Univ School of Theol, adj fac, 89; asst prof, 88-92, Univ Dubuque Theol Sem, dir, contextual ed & instr in spiritual formation, 92-99, Univ Dubuque Theol Sem. **HONORS AND AWARDS** BA, magna cum laude, 73; MA, 78; G. Lemuel Fenn Ministerial Scholar; John Wesley Fel, a Fund for Theol Ed, ATFE, 78-82; Bethune-Baker grant, fac of Div, Cambridge Univ; Pasadena Methodist Found Scholar; Charis Awd for Excel in Tchng, UDTS, 90-91, 92-93. **MEMBERSHIPS** Am Academy of Relig; Charles Wesley Soc; Oxford Inst for Methodist Theol Stud: Spiritual Dirs Int; Wesley Hist Soc, Eng. **RESEARCH** Wesleyan Hist & Spiritual Formation. **SELECTED PUBLICATIONS** Auth, Spiritual Formation and Contextual Education, in the Report of the Proceedings of the Asn of Theol Field Ed, 93; auth, John and Charles Wesley, The Dict of Christian Ethics & Pastoral Theol, IVP, 95; auth, What We Believe and Why We Believe It: Understanding Our Doctrinal Standards and Our Theological Task, a 6 wk stud, pvtly printed, local United Methodist Churches, 96; rev, Of Laughter in the Amen Corner: The Life of Evangelist Sam Jones by Kathleen Minnix, 93, pub in Missiology: An Int Rev, vol XXV, no 2, 97; auth, One week of devotions in Disciplines 1999, Upper Room, 98; auth, The Charles Wesley Family in Bristol, Proceed of the Charles Wesley Soc, vol 4, 97, 98; auth, The Role of Small Groups in Early Methodist Spiritual Formation, in The Role of the Heart in N Amer Methodism, Scarecrow Press. **CONTACT ADDRESS** 4116 Helena Bay Ct., Hermitage, TN 37076-3105. **EMAIL** talbin@univ.dbq.edu

ALBISETTI, JAMES C.
PERSONAL Born 03/03/1949, Wilmington, DE, d **DISCIPLINE** HISTORY **EDUCATION** Amherst Col, BA, 71; Yale Univ, PhD, 76. **CAREER** Lectr, Yale Univ, 77-78; vis asst prof, Hamilton Col, 78-79; asst prof to prof, Univ of Ky, 79-.

HONORS AND AWARDS Ger Studies Assoc Book Prize, 85; Univ of Ky Res Prof, 89-90. **MEMBERSHIPS** AHA; Hist of Educ Soc; Conf Group on Central Europ Hist; Europ Sect, S Hist Assoc; Ger Studies Assoc; Int Standing Conf for the Hist of Educ. **RESEARCH** 19th-century Germany, educational history, women's history. **SELECTED PUBLICATIONS** Auth, Secondary School Reform in Imperial Germany, Princeton Univ Pr, 83; auth, Schooling German Girls and Women, Princeton Univ Pr, 89. **CONTACT ADDRESS** Dept Hist, Univ of Kentucky, 500 S Limestone St, Lexington, KY 40506-0001. **EMAIL** jcalbi01@pop.uky.edu

ALBRECHT, CATHERINE
DISCIPLINE HISTORY **EDUCATION** Indiana Univ, PhD. **CAREER** Asst prof, Univ Baltimore, 90-94; Assoc prof, Univ Baltimore, 94-. **MEMBERSHIPS** Am Hist Asn; Am Asn Advancement Slavic Studies. **SELECTED PUBLICATIONS** Auth, The Czech Economics Profession before 1914, Duncker und Humbolt, 95; auth, Two Czech Economists: Albin Braf and Josef Kaizl, E Central Europe, 92; auth, National Economy or Economic Nationalism in the Bohemian Crownlands, 1848-1914, Labyrinth of Nationalism/Complexities of Diplomacy: Essays in Honor of Barbara and Charles Jelavich, Slavica, 92; auth, Pride in Protection: The Jubilee Exhibition of 1891 and Economic Competition between Czechs and Germans in Bohemia, Austrian Hist Yearbook, 93; auth, Economic Nationalism Among German Bohemians, Nationalities Papers, 96. **CONTACT ADDRESS** Univ of Baltimore, 1420 N. Charles Street, Baltimore, MD 21201.

ALDEN, DAURIL
PERSONAL Born 12/01/1926, San Francisco, CA, m, 1979, 2 children **DISCIPLINE** HISTORY **EDUCATION** Univ Calif, AB, 50; MA, 52; PhD, 59. **CAREER** Instr to prof, Univ Wash, 59-; vis asst prof, Univ Calif, 62-63; vis assoc prof, Columbia Univ, 67. **HONORS AND AWARDS** Guggenheim, 76-77; Mellon, 80; Nat Endowment for the Humanities, 76,86,95; Gulbenkian Foundation, 69; Joh Gilmary Shea Prize; Am Cath Hist Asn, 98; Joao de Castro Prize, Comissao Nacional para as comemoracoes dos descobrimentos Portugueses, 97; Conf on Latin Am Hist, Distinguished Service Awd, 99. **MEMBERSHIPS** Am Hist Asn, Cof on Latin Am Hist. **RESEARCH** Colonial Brazil, Portuguese Empire, Comparative Colonialism, History of the society of Jesus, 16th to 19th centuries, especially Portuguese Assistancy. **SELECTED PUBLICATIONS** Auth, The Making of an Enterprise: the Role of the Jesuits in Portugal, its Empire, and Beyond, 1540-1750, Stanford Univ Press, 96; auth, "Serafim Leite, S.J. Premier Historian of Colonial Brazil," in Jesuit Encounters in the New World 1549-1767, Institutum Historicum: Rome, (97): 21-35; auth, "Some Reflections Concerning Enigmas of Padre Antonio Vieira," Actas do congresso internacional do III centenario do Padre Antonio Vieira, Braga, (99): 645-651; auth, "West Approaches the East: The Portuguese Advance in Eastern Lands and Seas, 1498-1549," in The Encounter between Europe and Asia during the Period of the Great Navigations, Sophia Univ: Tokyo, 35-46; auth, "The Suppression of the Society of Jesus in the Portuguese Assistancy in Asia: The fate of Survivors, 1760-1777," Papers of the Vasco da Gama Quincentenary Coference, Melbourne and Perth, 21-29 June 1997, Oxford Univ Press, 00; auth, An Uncommon Life: C.R. Boxer, Soldier, Historian, Teacher, Collector, Traveler, Lisbon, (in press). **CONTACT ADDRESS** Dept Hist, Univ of Washington, PO Box 353560, Seattle, WA 98195-3560.

ALDRED, LISA
PERSONAL Born 03/06/1960, s **DISCIPLINE** NATIVE AMERICAN STUDIES **EDUCATION** Duke Univ, BA, 81; Univ NC Sch Law, JD, 85; Univ NC Chapel Hill, PhD, 99. **CAREER** Law clerk, McCain & Essen, 84; law assoc, McCain & Essen, 85-86; staff legal researcher, Big Mountain Legal Offense/Defense Comt, 86; adj prof, Univ of NC School of Law, 89; asst ed, Dialectical Anthrop, 91-92; asst prof, Mont State Univ Center for Native Am Studies, 94-97; instr, Montana State Univ Center for Native Am Studies, 97-. **HONORS AND AWARDS** Lawyer's Co-operative Awd, 84; NSF Grad Fel, 91-94; John Honigmann Awd for Outstanding Grad Student, 91 & 97; Steven Polgan Awd for Applied Anthrop, 93; Carolina Soc of Fel, Univ of NC Chapel Hill, 96-97. **MEMBERSHIPS** Am Anthrop Asn, Soc for Cultural Anthrop. **RESEARCH** New age commodification of Native American spirituality, sacred land in Native American religion. **SELECTED PUBLICATIONS** Coauth, "The American Medical Association v. the American Tort System," Campbell Law Rev 241 (86); auth, "Family Law in Orange County," Orange County Women's Center in Chapel Hill, NC (90); auth, " No More cigar Store Indians': Ethnographic Representations By and Of The Waccamaw-Siouan Peoples and Their Socioeconomic, Legal and Political Consequences," Dialectical Anthrop 18, Chelsea House Pub (New York), 90; auth, "Changing Woman and Her Children: The Enmeshment of Navajo Religion in Their Homelands," The European Rev of Native Am Studies 14,1 (forthcoming); auth, "Biligaana in Dine' Bi Keyah: Conflicting Views of Land, Religion and Law in the Big mountain Dine' Relocation Case," Ayaangwaamizin: International J of Indigenous Philos, 2, 2 (forthcoming). **CONTACT ADDRESS** Center Native Am Studies, Montana State Univ, Bozeman, W Kagy Ave, Bozeman, MT 59717-0001.

ALDRETE, GREGORY S.
PERSONAL Born 09/08/1966, MN, s **DISCIPLINE** ANCIENT HISTORY **EDUCATION** Princeton, AB, 88; Univ Mich, PhD, 95. **CAREER** Asst Prof, Univ Wisc, 95-. **HONORS AND AWARDS** Cic Minority fel, 88-90; Inst Hum Summer fel, 90; Mich Minority Merit fel, 90-91; Rackham Merit fel, 93-95; NEH fel, 96; Wisc Tchg fel, 97-98; Teaching at its Best Awd, 99; NEH Fel, 00. **MEMBERSHIPS** Am Philol Asn; Am Hist Asn; Asn Ancient Hist **RESEARCH** Roman history; Rhetoric and oratory; Social and economic history. **SELECTED PUBLICATIONS** co-auth, Feeding the City: The Organization, Operation, and Scale of the Supply System for Rome, Life, Death, and Entertainment in the Roman Empire, Univ Mich Press, 98; auth, Making History Come Alive in the Classroom Through the Use of Role-Playing, Teaching Forum, 98; rev, Controlling Laughter: Political Humor in the Late Roman Republic, Hist Rev, 98; auth, Gestures and Acclamations in Ancient Rome, Johns Hopkins Univ Press, 99. **CONTACT ADDRESS** Univ of Wisconsin, Green Bay, 2420 Nicolet Dr., Theatre Ha, Green Bay, WI 54311. **EMAIL** aldreteg@uwgb.edu

ALDRICH, MARK
PERSONAL Born 10/16/1941, Northhampton, MA, m, 1965 **DISCIPLINE** ECONOMIC HISTORY **EDUCATION** Middlebury Col, BA 63; Univ Calif Berk, MA 64; Univ Texas, PhD 69. **CAREER** Smith Col, asst prof, assoc prof, prof, 68 to 83-, Marilyn Carlson Nelson Prof of Econ, 95-. **MEMBERSHIPS** EHA; SHT. **RESEARCH** History of workplace safety. **SELECTED PUBLICATIONS** Auth, Safety First: Technology Business and Labor in the Transformation of Work Safety in America, Bal, John Hopkins Univ Press, 97; auth, The Peril of the Broken Rail: the Carriers the Steel Companies and Rail Technology, 1900-1945, Technology and Culture, forthcoming; Energy Conservation on Steam Railroads: Institutions Markets Technology, 1889-1943, Railroad History, 97; auth, The Perils of Mining Authracite: Regulation Technology and Safety, 1870-1945, Penn History, 97; auth, The Cherry Mine Disaster of 1909: The Rest of the Story as told by George S. Rice, Mining History Jour, 97; auth, The Last Run of Engineer Peake: Work safety on the Rio Grande Southern Around the Time of World War I, Jour of the West, 97; Locomotive Inspection Materials at the National Archives, Railroad History, 96; auth, Preventing the Needless Peril of the Coal Miner: The Bureau of Mines and the Campaign to Prevent Coal Mine Explosions, Technology and Culture, 95; auth, Does Comparable Worth Correct for Discrimination?, David Saunders, ed, New Approaches to Employee Management, Greenwich CT, JAI, 94. **CONTACT ADDRESS** Smith Col, 10 Prospect St, Northampton, CT 01063. **EMAIL** maldrich@smith.edu

ALDRICH, MICHELE
PERSONAL Born 10/06/1942, Seattle, WA, m, 1965 **DISCIPLINE** HISTORY AND GEOLOGY **EDUCATION** Univ Calif Berkeley, BA, geol, 64; Univ Tex Austin, PhD, hist, 74. **CAREER** Lectr, hist dept, Smith Col, 69-70; archiv, Valley Women's Ctr, 70-73; asst ed, Joseph Henry Papers, Smithsonian Inst, 74-75; consult, Aaron Burr Papers, NY Hist Soc, 75-76; fieldworker, Women's Hist Sources Survey, Univ Minn, 76-77; project dir, Women in Sci, AAAS, 77-83; dir, info svc, AAAS, 90-94; archiv, AAAS, 83-85, 95; visiting fel, dept of sci and tech studies, Cornell Univ, 96-; consult archiv, Winthrop Grp, 98-. **HONORS AND AWARDS** Geol Soc of Amer Hist of Geol award, 92. **MEMBERSHIPS** Orgn of Amer Hist; Hist of Sci Soc; New England Archiv. **RESEARCH** History of American Science. **SELECTED PUBLICATIONS** Co-ed, Theodore Hittell's California Academy of Sciences 1853-1906: A Narrative History, 97; auth, Scientific Association Records Programs: A Beginner's Guide AAAS: 95; co-ed, Directory of Historians of American Science, Forum for the History of America Science, 93; co-auth, Fishes of the Old Red Sandstone: Blossburg, Pennsylvania, 1830-1900, Earth Sci Hist, vol 11, 21-29, 92; auth, Women in Geology, Women of Science: Righting the Record, Ind Univ Press, 42-71, 90. **CONTACT ADDRESS** 24 Elm St., Hatfield, MA 01038. **EMAIL** 73061.2420@compuserve.com

ALEXANDER, CHARLES C.
PERSONAL Born 10/24/1935, Cass Co, TX, m, 1960, 1 child **DISCIPLINE** UNITED STATES HISTORY **EDUCATION** Lamar Univ, BA, 58; Univ Tex, MA, 59; PhD, 62. **CAREER** From instr to asst prof hist, Univ Houston, 62-66; assoc prof, Univ Ga, 66-70; Vis assoc prof, Univ Tex, 68-69; from prof to Distinguished Prof Hist, Ohio Univ, 70-. **HONORS AND AWARDS** LR Bryan Jr Awd, Tex Gulf Coast Hist Asn, 62. **MEMBERSHIPS** Orgn Am Hist; Southern Hist Asn. **RESEARCH** American society, thought, and culture in the 20th century. **SELECTED PUBLICATIONS** Auth, Crusade for Conformity: The Ku Klux Klan in Texas, 1920-1930, Tex Gulf Coast Hist Asn, 62; The Ku Klux Klan in the Southwest, Univ Ky, 65; coauth, This New Ocean: A History of Project Mercury, US Govt Printing Off, 66; auth, Nationalism in American Thought, 1930-1945, Rand McNally, 69; Holding the Line: The Eisenhower Era, 1952-1961, Ind Univ, 75; Here the Country Lies: Nationalism and the Arts in Twentieth-Century America, Ind Univ Press, 80; Ty Cobb, Oxford Univ Press, 84; John McGraw, Viking, 88; Our Game: An American Baseball History, Holt, 91; Rogers Hornsby, Holt, 95. **CONTACT ADDRESS** Dept of Hist, Ohio Univ, Athens, OH 45701-2942. **EMAIL** alexande@ohio.edu

ALEXANDER, JOHN T.
PERSONAL Born 01/18/1940, Cooperstown, NY, m, 1964, 2 children **DISCIPLINE** MODERN RUSSIAN HISTORY **EDUCATION** Wesleyan Univ, AB, 61; Ind Univ, AM, 63, PhD(hist), 66. **CAREER** From asst prof to prof hist, Univ Kansas, 66-. **HONORS AND AWARDS** Int Res & Exchange Bd exchange fel to USSR, 71 & 75; prin investr res grant, Nat Libr, Med, US Publ Health Serv, 72-73 & 75; vis fel, Kennan Inst Adv Russ Study, 81; Byron Caldwell Smith Awd, for best work by Kans auth in all fields, 89; Balfour Jeffrey Higuchi Endowment Awd for research achievement in the humanities, 92. **MEMBERSHIPS** Am Asn Advan Slavic Studies; Cent States Slavic Conf; Rocky Mountain Asn Slavic Studies; Brit Study Group 18 century Russia. **RESEARCH** Eighteenth century Russian society; early modern Russia; Russian medical history. **SELECTED PUBLICATIONS** Auth, Autocratic Politics in a National Crisis: The Imperial Russian Government and Pugachev's Revolt, 1773-1775, Ind Univ, 69; ed, S F Platonov, The Time of Troubles, Univ Kans, 70; auth, Western views of the Pugachev rebellion, Slavonic & E Europ Rev, 70; Emperor of the Cossacks: Pugachev and the Frontier Jacquerie of 1773-1775, Coronado, 73; S F Platonov: eminence and obscurity, introd to Rex Pyles transl, S F Platonov, Boris Godunov, Acad Int, 73; Cath II, Bubonic Plague and industry in Moscow, Am Hist Rev, 74; Bubonic Plague in Early Modern Russia, Johns Hopkins, 80; Catherine the Great and Public Health, J Hist Med, 81; Catherine the Great: Life and Legend, Oxford, 89; transl, E.V. Anisimov, The Reforms of Peter the Great, Sharpe, 93; auth, Anisimov, Empress Elizabeth, Acad Int, 95; Aeromania, Fire Balloons, and Catherine the Great's Ban of 1783, The Hist, 96; The Petrine Era and After, In: Freeze, Russia, A History, Oxford, 97; Ivan Shuvalov and Russian Court Politics, In: Literature, Lives, Astra, 94. **CONTACT ADDRESS** Dept of Hist, Univ of Kansas, Lawrence, Lawrence, KS 66045-0001. **EMAIL** jatalex@falcon.cc.ukans.edu

ALEXANDER, JON
PERSONAL Born 03/31/1943, Harrisburg, PA **DISCIPLINE** HISTORY **EDUCATION** Temple Univ, PhD, 71; Harvard Univ, MTS, 74. **CAREER** Assoc Prof, 98-, Providence College; Asst Prof, 75-78, Aquiwas Inst; Asst Prof, 70-71, Jackson State Univ. **MEMBERSHIPS** AAR; AHA. **RESEARCH** US Religious Autobiography and Biography. **SELECTED PUBLICATIONS** Auth, American Personal Religious Accounts 1600-1980: Toward an Inner History of America's Faiths, NY, Edward Mellen Press, 83; William Porcher DuBose: Selected Writings, Mahwah, Paulist Press, 88; Job Considered as a Conversion Account, Spirituality Today, 90. **CONTACT ADDRESS** History Dept, Providence Col, Providence, RI 02918-0001.

ALEXANDER, MICHAEL C.
PERSONAL Born 01/28/1947, Geneva, NY, m, 1968, 2 children **DISCIPLINE** ANCIENT HISTORY **EDUCATION** Swarthmore Col, BA, 68; U of Toronto, MA, 70, PhD, 77. **CAREER** Univ of Alberta, sess lecrt, 74-75; Swarthmore Col, inst, 75-76; Univ of Ill, Chicago, asst prof, assoc prof, 76-. **HONORS AND AWARDS** NEH Fell, NHC Fell, U of Ill Fel. **MEMBERSHIPS** APA, AHA, ASLH **RESEARCH** Roman repub hist and law. **SELECTED PUBLICATIONS** Auth, Trials in the Late Roman Republic, 146 BC to 50 BC, U of T Press, 90; Hortensius' Speech in Defence of Verres, in: Phoenix, 76; The legatio Asiatica of Scaurus: Did It Take Place?, in: Trans of APA, 81; Repetition of Prosecution, and the Scope of Prosecution, in the Standing Criminal Courts of the Late Republic, in: Classical Antiquity, 82. **CONTACT ADDRESS** Dept of History, Univ of Illinois, Chicago, M/C 198, Chicago, IL 60607-7109. **EMAIL** micalexa@uic.edu

ALEXANDER, RALPH H.
PERSONAL Born 09/03/1936, Tyler, TX, m, 1964, 3 children **DISCIPLINE** SEMITICS AND OLD TESTAMENT; ARCHAEOLOGY **EDUCATION** Rice Univ, AB, 59; Dallas Theol Sem, ThM, 63, ThD, 68. **CAREER** Instr, S Bible Training School, 63-64, 65-66; asst prof of Bible and Archaeology, Wheaton Col, 66-72; prof Hebrew Scripture, dir summer quart Israel Prog, 74 & 78, W Baptist Sem, 73-87; assoc archaeologist, Albright Inst Archaeology, 77-78; dir, Advan Trng Studies Coordr Old Testament Concentration Bibl Educ Exten Int Austria, 87-95; dir, educ develop & advan trng studies, cis, bibl educ exten int, Moscow, 95-. **HONORS AND AWARDS** US Govt Fulbright grant, Israel, 64-65; Henry Thiessen Awd New Testament; Outstanding Young Men Amer, 70; Outstanding Educ Amer; Who's Who Relig. **MEMBERSHIPS** Amer Schools Oriental Res; Archeol Inst Amer; Evangel Theol Soc; Fel Evangel Europ Tchrs; Inst Bibl Res; Israel Explor Soc; Nat Asn Hebrew Prof; Near East Archeol Soc; Soc Bibl Lit. **RESEARCH** Psalms; Old Testament Archaeology; Old Testament Law & Prophets. **SELECTED PUBLICATIONS** Contribur, New Commentary on the Whole Bible, Tyndale, 94; auth, Marriage and Divorce, Dictionary of Old Testament Ethics, Baker, 96; A New Covenant and An Eternal People, Israel: The Land and the People, Kregel, 98. **CONTACT ADDRESS** Box 3366, Gresham, OR 97030. **EMAIL** ralphmyrna@earthlink.net

ALEXANDER, RONALD R.
PERSONAL Born 01/03/1942, London, WV, m, 1964, 3 children **DISCIPLINE** HISTORY **EDUCATION** WVa Inst Technol, BA, 64; Univ Ky, MA, 67, PhD, 76. **CAREER** Prof hist, WVA Inst Technology, 66-. **RESEARCH** American Civil War period; history of West Virginia Institute of Technology; First World War period. **SELECTED PUBLICATIONS** Auth, To hell with the Hapsburgs and Hohenzollerns, J WVa Hist Assn, spring 77; auth, West Virginia Tech, a History, Pictrial Histories Pub Co, Charleston, WV, 92. **CONTACT ADDRESS** Dept of History, West Virginia Univ Inst of Tech, 405 Fayette Pike, Montgomery, WV 25136-2436. **EMAIL** dsoliv@wvit.wvnet.edu

ALEXANDER, THOMAS G.
PERSONAL Born 08/08/1935, Logan, UT, m, 1959, 5 children **DISCIPLINE** HISTORY **EDUCATION** Weber State Univ, AS 55; Utah State Univ, BS 60, MS 61; Univ Cal Berk, PhD 65. **CAREER** Brigham Young Univ, Lemuel Hardison Redd Jr Prof, prof, assoc prof, asst prof, 64-00; SO IL Univ, adj assoc prof, 70-71; Univ Nebraska, vis lectr, 66. **HONORS AND AWARDS** AASLH Awd of Merit; NSDAR Amer Hist Medal Awd; Grace Arrington Awd; David W Beatrice C Evans Awd; NHPRC Fel; USHS Fel; USHS dist Awd. **MEMBERSHIPS** AHA; OAH, WHA; ASEH; MHA; USHS **RESEARCH** Auth, Western history; Amer environ history; Utah history; Latter-day Saint history **SELECTED PUBLICATIONS** Auth, Things in Heaven and Earth: The Life and Times of Wilford Woodruff, A Mormon Prophet (Salt Lake City: Signature Books, 91) 2nd ed revised, 93; auth, Utah, The Right Place: The Official Centennial History, (Layton, UT: Gibbs Smith, 95) 2nd ed revised, 96; auth, From Arms to Aircraft: A Brief History of Hill Air Force Base, with Doug McChristian, (Hill Air Force Base, UT: Hill Air Force Base, 96); Keeping Company with Wilford Woodruff, Jour of Morm Hist, 97; Reflections On Utah's Kingdom, Colony and Commonwealth, Rough Draft, 97; The Transformation of Utah from a Colony of Wall Street to Colony of Washington, The Thetean, 96; Utah's Constitution: A Reflection of the Territorial Experience, UT Hist Quart, 96; auth, "Sylvester Q. Cannon and the Revival of Environmental Consciousness in the Mormon Community," Environmental History 3 (98): 488-507; auth, "The Progressive Struggle to Reform the American Democratic Republic," in Gary Daynes, ed, Fulfilling the Founding: A Reader for American Heritage (Needham Heights, MA: Pearson Custom Publishing, (99): 165-184; auth, "Nineteen Years Later," Sunstone 22 (99): 24-27; auth, "Wilford Woodruff and Zion's Camp: Baptism by Fire and theSpiritual Confirmation of a Future Prophe," BYU Studies 39 (00): 130-146. **CONTACT ADDRESS** Dept of History, Brigham Young Univ, Provo, UT 84602-4446. **EMAIL** Thomas_Alexander@BYU.EDU

ALFORD, TERRY L.
PERSONAL Born 10/07/1945, Mobile, AL, s, 3 children **DISCIPLINE** AMERICAN HISTORY **EDUCATION** MS State Univ, BA, 66, MA 67, PhD, 70. **CAREER** Prof hist, Northern VA Community Col, 72-, Nat Endowment for Hum fel hist, 78-79. **MEMBERSHIPS** Surratt Soc; Lincoln grp of DC; Lincoln Inst of mid-Atlantic. **RESEARCH** Old South; Civil War; John Wilkes Booth; Lincoln Assassination. **SELECTED PUBLICATIONS** Auth, Prince Among Slaves, Harcourt Brace Jovanovich, 77; ed, John Wilkes Booth: A Sisters Memoir, univ Pres of MS, 96; ed board, Lincoln Herald; consul to Time Life Books, ABC News. **CONTACT ADDRESS** Dept of Hist, No Virginia Comm Col, 8333 Little River Tp, Annandale, VA 22003-3743. **EMAIL** talford@nv.va.cc.us

ALLAN, SARAH K. M.
PERSONAL Born 02/20/1945, m, 1963 **DISCIPLINE** ASIAN STUDIES **EDUCATION** UCLA, BA, 66; Univ Calif Berkeley, MA 69; PhD, 74. **CAREER** Univ of London, 72-95; Burlington Northern Found Prof of Asian Studies, Dartmouth Col, 95-. **RESEARCH** Early China. **SELECTED PUBLICATIONS** Coauth, China, Cassells, (London), 80; auth, The Heir and the Sage: Dynastic Legend in Early China, CMC (San Francisco), 81; auth, "The Myth of the Xia Dynasty", J of the Royal Asiatic Soc 2, (84): 242-256; coauth, "Oracle Bone Collections in Great Britain, Beijing, 85; auth, The Shape of the Turtle: Myth, Art and Cosmos in Early China, SUNY Pr, (Albany), 91; coauth, Chinese Bronzes: A Selection from European Collections, Wenwu Pr, (Beijing), 95; auth, The Way of Water and Sprouts of Virtue, SUNY Pr, (Albany), 97; auth, "Tian as Sky: the Conceptual Implications" En Suivant La Voie Royale: Melanges en hommage a Leon Vandermeersch, ed Jacques Gernet and Marc Kalinowski, Ecole Francaise D'Extreme-Orient, (Paris, 97): 225-30; auth, Early Chinese History, Thought and Culture, Liaoning Jaioyu Pr, (Shenyang), 99; coauth, Oracle Bone Inscriptions in the Museum of Far Eastern Antiquities, Stockholm, Sweden, Zhonghau Shuju, (China), 99. **CONTACT ADDRESS** Dept Asian Studies, Dartmouth Col, 6191 Bartlett Hall, Hanover, NH 03755-3530.

ALLEE, MARK
DISCIPLINE HISTORY **EDUCATION** Univ Pa, PhD, 87. **CAREER** Hist, Loyola Univ. **RESEARCH** Early modern 16th-19th centuries history; soc history; local history; law and society. **SELECTED PUBLICATIONS** Auth, Law and Society in Late Imperial China: Northern Taiwan in the Nineteenth Century, Stanford UP, 94; Code, Culture, Custom: Foundations of Civil Case Verdicts in a Nineteenth Century Court, In Civil Law in Chinese History, Stanford UP, 94. **CONTACT ADDRESS** Fine Arts Dept, Loyola Univ, Chicago, 6525 N. Sheridan Rd., Chicago, IL 60626. **EMAIL** mallee@orion.it.luc.edu

ALLEN, BERNARD LEE
PERSONAL Born 07/19/1937, Weston, WV, m, 1964, 2 children **DISCIPLINE** HISTORY, PHILOSOPHY **EDUCATION** WVa Univ, BS, 59; Southern Ill Univ, MA, 64; WVa Univ, PhD(hist), 71. **CAREER** Instr hist & philos, WVa Univ, Parkersburg, 66-68 & WVa Univ, 70-71; asst prof hist & philos, 71-74, actg asst dean arts & sci, 75-76; assoc prof, 74-81, dean arts & sci & actg dean occup tech, 76, asst dean instr, 79-80, Prof Hist & Philos, Parkersburg Community Col;adj instr, Wheeling Jesuit Univ, 93-98; adj instr, Washington St Comm Coll, 93-98. **HONORS AND AWARDS** Bd of Dir, WV Hum Fnd, Outstand Svc to Higher Edu, WV Prof of the Yr. **MEMBERSHIPS** Appalachian Stud Assn, WV Hist Assn of Col and Univ Tchrs of Hist; Oil, Gas, and Indus Hist Assn. **RESEARCH** John Dewey's philosophy of history; mid-Ohio valley; women of the Ohio valley; U.S. social and ideological history; the Virginias and the Carolinas. **SELECTED PUBLICATIONS** Auth, John Dewey's Views on History, 1859-1971, Univ Microfilms, 71; Oarkersburg: A Bicentennial History, Parkersburg Bicentennial Commission, 85; Lessons, Data Day, 90; Compassion: A History of the Harry Logan Children's Home, Harry Logan Children's Home Fnd, 92; co-auth, Where It All Began, 94. **CONTACT ADDRESS** Dept of Hist, West Virginia Univ, Parkersburg, 300 Campus Dr, Parkersburg, WV 26101. **EMAIL** BALLEN@ALPHA.WVUP.WVNET.EDU

ALLEN, GARLAND E.
PERSONAL Born 02/13/1936, Louisville, KY, d, 2 children **DISCIPLINE** HISTORY OF SCIENCE **EDUCATION** Univ Louisville, BA, 57. **CAREER** Instr 65-76, Harvard Univ; Asst Prof, Assoc Prof, 67-, Washington Univ; vis Prof, 89-91, Harvard Univ. **HONORS AND AWARDS** Warren Cen Fel; Sigma Xi Ntl Lectr, Sigma Xi Bicentenn Lectr, Marine Biol Lab Trustee; George Sarton Awd. **MEMBERSHIPS** HSS; ISH; PSSB; BSHS. **RESEARCH** History of Genetics in 20th Century; Eugenics in the US. **SELECTED PUBLICATIONS** Auth, T.H. Morgan, The Man & His Science, Princeton Univ Pr (Princeton), 78; auth, Life Science in the Twentieth Century, Cambridge Univ Pr (NYork), 78; Genetics and Behavior, in: Encyc of Applied Ethics, NY, Academic Press, 97; The social economic origins of genetic determination: a case history of the American Eugenics Movement, 1900-1940 and its lessons for today, Genetica, 97; The Double-Edged Sword of Genetic Determinism: Social and Political Agendas in Genetic Studies of Homosexuality, 1940-1994, in: Vernon A Rosario ed, Science and Homosexualities, NY, Routledge, 97; rev, Biologists Under Hitler, by Ute Deichmann, trans by T Dunlap, Endeavor, 98. **CONTACT ADDRESS** Biology Dept, Washington Univ, Saint Louis, MO 63130. **EMAIL** allen@brodec.wustl.edu

ALLEN, HOWARD W.
PERSONAL Born 05/17/1931, Dahlgren, IL, m, 1983, 3 children **DISCIPLINE** HISTORY **EDUCATION** Univ Chicago, BA, 52; MA, 55; Univ Wash, PhD, 59. **CAREER** Asst prof, Univ of Akron, 61-62; Southern Ill Univ, 62-97; chair, Southern Ill Univ, 83-88. **HONORS AND AWARDS** Vis Scholar, Univ of Mich, 76-77; Queen Awd for Excellence in Teaching, Ill Univ, 97. **MEMBERSHIPS** AHA, Soc Sci Hist Assoc. **RESEARCH** Capital Punishment in American History, Twentieth Century Political History. **SELECTED PUBLICATIONS** Coauth, "Computers and Historical Studies," Jour of Am Hist LIV, (67): 599-607; coauth, "The Cities and the Election of 1928," Am Hist Rev 74, (69): 1205-1220; coed, Electoral Change and Stability in American Political History, Free Pr, (NY), 71; coauth, "From the Populist Era to the New Deal: A Study of Partisan Realignment in Washington State, 1889-1950," Soc Sci His III, (79): 115-143; coauth, "Vote Fraud and Data Validity," Analyzing Electoral History, ed Jerome M. Clubb, W.H. Flanigan, N. Zingale, (Sage Publ, 81): 153-193; auth, Poindexter of Washington: A Study of Progressive Politics, S Ill Univ Pr, (Carbondale, IL), 81; coauth, "Congress in Crisis: Changes in Personnel and the Legislative Agenda in the U.S. Congress in the 1890s," Soc Sci Hist 16, (92): 401-420; coed, Illinois Elections, 1818-1990: Candidates and County Returns for President, Governor, Senate and the House of Representatives, SIU Pr, (Carbondale, IL), 92. **CONTACT ADDRESS** Dept Hist, So Illinois Univ, Carbondale, MC 4519, Carbondale, IL 62901. **EMAIL** hwallen@siu.edu

ALLEN, JACK
PERSONAL Born 06/18/1914, Prestonsburg, KY, m, 1941, 3 children **DISCIPLINE** HISTORY **EDUCATION** Eastern Ky State Teachers Col, AB, 35; George Peabody Col, AM, 38, PhD, 41. **CAREER** Asst prof hist, Eastern Ky State Teachers Col, 40-46; assoc prof, 46-54, chmn dept hist & polit sci, 56-74, chmn div soc sci, 63-74, actg exec dean acad affairs, 74-75, dir prog educ policy specialists, 74-77, prof, 54-80, Emer Prof Hist, George Peabody Col, 80-, Vis prof, Univ Colo, 59; consult, pub sch, Phoenix, Ariz, 60, Nova Sch, Ft Lauderdale, Fla, 63-67, pub sch, Oak Ridge, Tenn, 65-67 & Tri-Univ proj elem educ, 67-68; social studies specialist, Repub of Korea, 61 & 69; evaluator, title XI Insts Hist, 65; ad hoc comt soc sci/social studies, US Off Educ, 65-66; mem coun, Thirteen Original States Fund, 78-. **HONORS AND AWARDS** Am Asn State & Local Hist Awd, 61. **MEMBERSHIPS** Nat Coun Social Studies (pres, 58); Am Coun Educ; Orgn Am Historians; Am Studies Asn. **RESEARCH** Recent American history; social education. **SELECTED PUBLICATIONS** Coauth, Nations Around the Globe, 66 & The Earth and Our States, 66, Prentice-Hall; History: USA, 67 & 76, auth, Documents: USA, 67, coauth, USA: History With Documents, Vols I & II, 71, auth, American Society in Civic Issues, 73, American Society, 78 & Americans, 79, Am Bk Co; Education in the 80's: Social Studies, Nat Educ Asn, 81. **CONTACT ADDRESS** 3705 Hilldale Dr, Nashville, TN 37215.

ALLEN, LEE NORCROSS
PERSONAL Born 04/16/1926, Valley, AL, m, 1963, 2 children **DISCIPLINE** HISTORY **EDUCATION** Auburn Univ, BS, 48, MS, 49; Univ Penn, PhD, 55. **CAREER** Instr to prof, 52-61, Eastern Col; prof, 61, dean, grad schl, 65-86, dean, arts & sci, 75-90, Samford Univ; Univ Historian, 90-01; Prof Emeritus, 01. **HONORS AND AWARDS** Certificate of Merit, Am Asn of State and Local Hist, 70; Distinguished Service Awd, Southern Baptist Hist Soc, 92. **MEMBERSHIPS** Am, Southern Ala, Birmingham-Jefferson hist societies/associations; Whitsitt, Southern, Ala Baptist hist association/societies; Shades Valley Rotary Club, Mountain Brook Baptist Church. **RESEARCH** Baptist hist, local hist, political hist of 1920's in USA. **SELECTED PUBLICATIONS** Auth, The Woman Suffrage Movement in Alabama, 58; auth, The 1924 Underwood Campaign in Alabama, 62; auth, The McAdoo Campaign. . . in 1924, 63; auth, Born for Missions, 84; auth, Courage to Care: Ida V. Moffett, 88; auth, Notable Past, Bright Future, 94; auth, Outward Focus, 94; coauth, The Life of Paul P. Piper, 98; coauth, The Boaz Heritage, 98; auth, Ralph W. Beeson, 01. **CONTACT ADDRESS** 5025 Wendover Dr., Birmingham, AL 35223-1631. **EMAIL** catherinballen@ca.com

ALLEN, MICHAEL
PERSONAL m, 3 children **DISCIPLINE** HISTORY **EDUCATION** Central State Wash Col, BA, 74; Univ Montana, MA, 77; Univ Wash, Seattle, PhD, 85. **CAREER** Asst Prof, Tenn Tech Univ, 85-88; Asst Prof, Deep Spring Col, 88-89; Asst Prof, Eastern Montana Col, 89-90; Asst to Full Prof, Univ Wash Tacoma, 90-. **HONORS AND AWARDS** Phi Alpha Theta Book Prize, 90. **MEMBERSHIPS** The Hist Soc, Nat Asn of Scholars, Rodeo Hist Soc. **RESEARCH** Early America, Frontier, Pacific Northwest, American Studies (Literature and Folklore), American Social. **SELECTED PUBLICATIONS** Auth, Western Rivermen, 1763-1861: Ohio and Mississippi Boatmen and the Myth of the Alligator Horse, La State Univ Press (Baton Rouge), 90; auth, "Rise and Decline of the Early Rodeo Cowgirl: The Career of Mable Strickland, 1916-1941," Pac Northwest Quart 83 (Oct 92): 122-127; auth, "'Row Boatmen Row!,': Songs of the Early Ohio and Mississippi Boatmen," Gateway Heritage, Miss Hist Soc 14 (Winter 93-94): 93-94; auth, "The 'New' Western History Stillborn," The Historian (Fall 94): 201-208; auth, "'When the Cowboys Are Indians and the Indians Are Cowboys': Plains and Plateau Indian Rodeo Riders in Literature," Pac Northwest Forum (Fall-Winter 96): 94-111; auth, "Who Was David Crockett?," in Tennessee in American History, ed. Whiteaker and Dickinson (96); auth, "Real Cowboys? The Origins and Evolution of North American Rodeo," J of the W 37 (Jan 98): 69-79; auth, "Yakima Canutt: From Colfax to Hollywood," Columbia Magazine of Northwest Hist (Summer 98); auth, Rodeo Cowboys in the North American Imagination, Univ of Nev Press (Reno), 98; co-ed, Frontiers of Western History: Origins, Evolution, and Future of Western History, Simon and Schuster Custom Press (Meedham, MA), 99. **CONTACT ADDRESS** Dept Lib Arts, Univ of Washington-Tacoma, 1900 Commerce St, Tacoma, WA 98402-3106. **EMAIL** magician@u.washington.edu

ALLEN, MICHAEL I.
DISCIPLINE MEDIEVAL HISTORY **EDUCATION** Tufts Univ, BA, 85; Yale Univ, MA, 86; Univ Toronto, PhD, 94. **CAREER** Asst prof, Univ Chicago. **HONORS AND AWARDS** Phi Beta Kappa, Tufts Univ, 84; Seymour Simches Scholar, Tufts Univ, 85; University Fel, Yale Univ, 85-86; Jr Fel, Massey Col, 88-91; Open Fel, Univ of Toronto, 88-91; Doctoral Fel, 91-92; Borsa di studio, Settimana internazionale di studio, Centro Italiano di studi sull'Alto Medioevo, Spoleto, Italy, 91; Queen Elizabeth II Ontario Fel, 92-93; Postdoctoral Fel, 93-95; George C. Metcalf Fel, 94-95; Res Fel in the Michigan Soc of Fellows, Univ of Mich, 95-98. **RESEARCH** Early medieval cultures, literatrures and societies; medieval historical writing; books, script, and learning in medieval Europe; role of women in medieval education; Latin paleography. **SELECTED PUBLICATIONS** Coed, "Bede and Frechulf at Medieval St. Gallen," In Beda Venerabilis: Historian, Monk and Northumbrian, Groningen: Egbert Forsten, 96; transl, "Addenda and Corrigenda to 'Flavius Renatus Vegetius,' CTC, VI, 175-184," vol 8, Washington, D.C.: Catholic Univ of Am Press, (in press); auth, "The Metrical Passio Crispini et Crispiniani of Henry of Avranches," Analecta Bollandiana 108, (90): 357-86; rev, James C. Russell, The Germanization of Early Medieval Christianity: A Sociohistorical Approach to Religious Transformation, (Ox-

ford, 93), In Catholic Historical Rev 81, (95): 416-17; auth, M.M. Hildebrandt, The External School in Carolingian Soc, (Leiden: Birll, 92), In Speculum 69, (94): 173-74; auth, Pierre Riche, The Carolingians: A Family Who Forged Europe, Philadelphia: Univ of Pennsylvania Press, (93): 398; Georg Holzherr, Einsiedeln: The Monastery and Church of Our Lady of the Hermits, Munich: Schnell und Steiner, (88): 104. **CONTACT ADDRESS** Dept of Classics, Univ of Chicago, 1010 E 50th St, Chicago, IL 60637. **EMAIL** frechulf@uchicago.edu

ALLEN, ROBERT L.
PERSONAL Born 05/29/1942, Atlanta, GA, m, 1995 **DISCIPLINE** AFRICAN-AMERICAN STUDIES **EDUCATION** Attended Univ of Vienna, 1961-62; Morehouse Col, BS, 1963; attended Columbia Univ, 1963-64; New School for Social Research, NYork, MA, 1967; Univ of California, San Francisco, PhD, 1983. **CAREER** Guardian Newsweekly NYC, staff reporter 1967-69; San Jose State Coll, asst prof new coll & black studies dept 1969-72; The Black Scholar Mag, editor; Mills College, Oakland CA, began as lecturer, became asst prof of ethnic studies, 73-84; Wild Trees Press, gen mgr, 84-90; The Black Scholar, Senior Ed, 90-; African-American & Ethnic Studies, Uiversity Of California-Berkeley, Visiting Prof, 94-. **HONORS AND AWARDS** Guggenheim fellowship, 1978; Winner American Book Awd, 1995. **MEMBERSHIPS** Pres, Black World Foundation; mem, American Sociological Assn; mem, American Historical and Cultural Society; mem, Association of Black Sociologists; mem, Pacific Sociological Assn; mem, Council for Black Studies; Bay Area Black Journalists; bd mem, Oakland Men's Project; bd mem, San Francisco Book Council. **SELECTED PUBLICATIONS** Auth, "Black Awakening in Capitalist Amer" Doubleday, 1969, "Reluctant Reformers, The Impact of Racism on Amer Social Reform Movements" Howard Univ Press, 1974; contributor to periodicals; author, The Port Chicago Mutiny, Amistad Books, 1989; coeditor Brotherman Ballantine, 1995. **CONTACT ADDRESS** Black Scholar, PO Box 2869, Oakland, CA 94618.

ALLEN, WILLIAM SHERIDAN
PERSONAL Born 10/05/1932, Evanston, IL, m, 1982, 4 children **DISCIPLINE** MODERN GERMAN HISTORY **EDUCATION** Univ Mich, AB, 55; Univ Conn, MA, 56; Univ Minn, PhD(Ger hist), 62. **CAREER** Instr Hist, Bay City Jr Col, 58-59 & Mass Inst Technol, 60-61; from asst prof to assoc prof, Univ Mo, 61-67; assoc prof, Wayne State Univ, 67-70; Prof Hist to Prof Emer, SUNY, Buffalo, 74-. **HONORS AND AWARDS** Chancellors Awd Excellence Teaching, State Univ NY, 76; Univ Mo res coun grant, 63; Am Philos Soc grants, 63-64 & 65-66; Alexander von Humboldt Found fel, 65-66; res grants res coun, State Univ NY, 71-72 & 72-73; mem, Conf Group German Polit; mem, Nat Arch Liaison Comt, 69-78; Nat Endowment for the Humanities summer fel, 79. **MEMBERSHIPS** Am Conf for Irish Stud; AHA; Conf Group Cent Europ Hist. **RESEARCH** Socialist underground in Nazi Germany; social history of Weimar and Nazi Germany; nineteenth century Irish nationalism. **SELECTED PUBLICATIONS** Auth, The Nazi Seizure of Power, Quadrangle, 65; contribr, Widerstand, Verfolgung, Emigration, Bod Godesberg, 67; The German Church Struggle and the Holocaust, Wayne Univ, 73; Reappraisals of Fascism, Franklin Watts, 75; auth, The Infancy of Nazism, Franklin Watts, 76; contribr, Totalitarianism Reconsidered, Nat Univ Publ, 81; Die Reihen fast Geschlossen, Hammer, 81. **CONTACT ADDRESS** Dept of History, SUNY, Buffalo, 581 Park Hall, Buffalo, NY 14260-4130.

ALLINSON, GARY
PERSONAL Born 08/12/1942, Williams, IA, m, 1965, 1 child **DISCIPLINE** HISTORY **EDUCATION** Stanford Univ, BA, 64; MA, 66; PhD, 71. **CAREER** Asst prof to full prof, Univ Pitts, 71-83; Ellen Bayard Weedon Prof, Univ Vir, 83-. **HONORS AND AWARDS** Phi Eta Sigma; Phi Beta Kappa; For Area Train Fel; Woodrow Wilson Fel; Fulbright Fel; Japan Found Fel; SSRF Grant. **MEMBERSHIPS** AAS. **RESEARCH** Modern Japanese history: social, economic, urban, political and cultural. **SELECTED PUBLICATIONS** Auth, Japanese Urbanism, Univ Cal Press, 75; auth, Suburban Tokyo, Univ Cal Press, 79; auth, Political Dynamics in Contemporary Japan, Cornell Univ Press, 93; auth, Japan's Postwar History, Cornell Univ Press, 97; auth, The Columbia Guide to Modern Japanese History, Columbia Univ Press, 99. **CONTACT ADDRESS** Dept History, Univ of Virginia, Randall Hall, Charlottesville, VA 22903-3244.

ALLISON, ROBERT
PERSONAL Born 04/21/1957, East Orange, NJ, m, 1985, 2 children **DISCIPLINE** HISTORY **EDUCATION** Harvard Univ, ALB, 86; AM, 88; PhD, 92. **CAREER** Prof, Suffolk Univ, 92-. **HONORS AND AWARDS** Petra T. Shattuck Distinguished Teaching Awd, Harvard Univ, 97; William T. Lothrop Prize runner-up, Am Neptune, 97; Harvard Merit Fel, 90-91; Robert Middlekauff Fel, 91; NEH, Young Scholars Awd, 86. **MEMBERSHIPS** Am Hist Asn; Boston Athenaeum; Bostonian Soc; Colonial Soc of MA; U.S.S. Constitution Museum Brd of Overseers; Omohundru Inst of Early Am Hist and Culture; Org of Am Hist; Phi Alpha Theta. **SELECTED PUBLICATIONS** Auth, The Crescent Obscured: The United States and the Muslim World, 1776-1815, Oxford Univ Press, 95; ed, The Interesting Narrative of Olaudah Equiano, or Gustavus Vassa, the African, Bedford Books, 95; ed, American Eras: Development of a Nation, 1783-1815, Gale Research, 97; auth, "Sailing to Algiers: American Sailors encounter the Muslim World," American Neptune, 97; auth, "Olaudah Equiano," in The Human Tradition in U.S. History, Scholarly Res, 98; ed, American Eras: Revolutionary Era, 1754-1783, Gale Research, 98; auth, "Americans and the Muslim World: First Encounters," in The Middle East and the United States: A Historical and Political Reassessment, Westview, 99; ed, History in Dispute: American Political and Social Movements, 1945 - Present: The Pursuit of Liberty, St. James Press, 00; ed, History in Dispute: American Political and Social Movements, 1900-1945: The Pursuit of Progress, St. James Press, 00. **CONTACT ADDRESS** Dept Hist, Suffolk Univ, 8 Ashburton Pl, Boston, MA 02108-2701. **EMAIL** ballison@acad.suffolk.edu

ALLITT, PATRICK
PERSONAL Born 08/26/1956, Birmingham, England, m, 1984, 1 child **DISCIPLINE** HISTORY **EDUCATION** Oxford Univ, BA; Univ of Calif at Berkeley, MA; PhD. **CAREER** From asst prof to full prof, Emory Univ, 88-. **HONORS AND AWARDS** Henry Luce Post Doctoral Fel, Harvard Divinity Sch, 85-88; Fel, Princeton Univ Center for the Study of Am Relig, 92-93; Excellence in Soc Sci Teaching Awd, Emory Univ, 99-00. **MEMBERSHIPS** Am Historical Asn, Catholic Historical Asn. **RESEARCH** American religious, intellectual, and environmental history. **SELECTED PUBLICATIONS** Auth, Catholic Intellectuals and Conservative Politics in America, Cornell Univ Press, 93; auth, Catholic Converts: British and American Intellectuals Turn To Rome, Cornell Univ Press, 97; auth, Major Problems in American Religious History, Houghton-Mifflin, 00). **CONTACT ADDRESS** Dept Hist, Emory Univ, 1364 Clifton Rd NE, Atlanta, GA 30322-1061. **EMAIL** pallitt@emory.edu

ALLMAN, JEAN M.
DISCIPLINE HISTORY **EDUCATION** Northwestern Univ, PhD, 87. **CAREER** Prof of hist, Univ of Illinois. **RESEARCH** West African history. **SELECTED PUBLICATIONS** Auth, The Quills of the Porcupine: Asante Nationalism in An Emergent Ghana, 93; Making Mothers: Missionaries, Medical Officers and Women's Work in Colonial Asante, Hist Workshop, 94; Hewers of Wood, Carriers of Water: Islam, Class and Politics on the Eve of Ghana's Independence, African Studies Rev, 91; Of Spinsters, Concubines and Wicked Women: Reflections on Gender and Social Change in Colonial Asante, Gender Hist, 91; The Youngmen and the Porcupine: Class, Nationalism and Asante's Struggle for Self-Determination, J African Hist, 90; co-ed, Social History of Africa, Heinemann; ed, "Becoming Asante/ Becoming Akan: thoughts on Gender, Identity and the Colonial Encounter," in C. Lentz and P. Nugent, Ethnicity in Ghana: The Limits of Invention, London: MacMillan, (00): 97-118; auth, I Will Not Eat Strone: A Women's History of Colonial Asante, with V. Tashjian, Heinemann, 00; ed, Our Days Dwindle: Memories of my Childhood Days in Asante, by T.E. Kyei, Heinemann, 01. **CONTACT ADDRESS** History Dept, Univ of Minnesota, Twin Cities, 614 Social Sciences Tower, 267 19th Ave. S, Minneapolis, MN 55455. **EMAIL** jallman@uiuc.edu

ALLMENDINGER, DAVID F.
PERSONAL Born 05/13/1938, Wooster, OH, m, 1965, 2 children **DISCIPLINE** HISTORY **EDUCATION** Univ Missouri, BA, 61; Univ Wis, Madison, MS, 62; PhD, 68. **CAREER** Asst prof, Reed Col, 67-69; asst prof, Smith Col, 69-72; vis assoc prof, Univ Mich, 73-74; assoc prof to prof, Univ Delaware, 74-. **HONORS AND AWARDS** Lindhack Found Dist Teach Awd; Rachal VHS Awd; Phi Beta Kappa. **MEMBERSHIPS** OAH; WSHS; VHS. **RESEARCH** US History; Early National and Antebellum Periods, (1787-1861). **SELECTED PUBLICATIONS** Auth, Ruffin: Family and Reform in the Old South, Oxford Univ Press (NY), 90; auth, Paupers and Scholars: The Transformation of Student Life in Nineteenth-Century New England, St Martin's Press (NY), 75; ed, Edmund Ruffin, Incidents of My Life: Edmund Ruffin's Autobiographical Essay's, vol 17, Virginia Hist Soc Documents (Charlottesville: Univ Press Vir, 90); ed, The American People in the Antebellum North (West Haven, CT: Pendulum Press, 73). **CONTACT ADDRESS** Dept History, Univ of Delaware, 15 Orchard Ave, Newark, DE 19716-2555. **EMAIL** dfa@udel.edu

ALOFSIN, ANTHONY
DISCIPLINE ART HISTORY, ARCHITECTURAL HISTORY, MODERN ARCHITECTURE **EDUCATION** Philips Acad, dipl, 67; Harvard Col, AB, 71; Harvard Grad School Design, M archit, 81; Columbia Univ, M philos, 83; Columbia Univ PhD, 87. **CAREER** Adj prof Art History, Coll Fine Arts, Roland Roessner Centennial prof, School Archit, Univ Tex Austin, 87-. **HONORS AND AWARDS** Vasari Awdard, Univ Tex Austin, 90; Fac Research Awdard, Univ Research Inst, 93-4, Int Assoc Art Critics, Best Archit Show, 93-94; Book Awdard, Am Inst Archit, 94; Fac Research Awdard, Univ Research Inst, 95; Competitive Awd, Univ Tex Austin, 97-98. **MEMBERSHIPS** Am Inst Archit; Coll Art Assoc; Hist Ger Cent Europ Art Archit; Soc Archit Hist; Soc Hist E Europ Russ Art Archit. **RESEARCH** Modernism; Historiography; modern European, Central European and American Architecture. **SELECTED PUBLICATIONS** Ed, Frank Lloyd Wright: An Index to the Taliesin Correspondence, 88; auth, Frank Lloyd Wright: The Lost Years, 1910-1922, 93; co-ed, center, A J for Archit , Am, 93; contrubur, American National Biography, 94; introd to Studies and Executed Buildings, 98; Frank Lloyd Wright: Europe and Beyond, 99. **CONTACT ADDRESS** School of Archit, Univ of Texas, Austin, Goldsmith Hall, Austin, TX 78712. **EMAIL** alofsin@mail.utexas.edu

ALPERN ENGEL, BARBARA
PERSONAL Born 06/28/1943, New York, NY **DISCIPLINE** HISTORY **EDUCATION** City Col NYork, BA, 65; Harvard Univ, MA, 67; Columbia Univ, PhD, 74. **CAREER** Asst prof, 76-92, assoc prof, 82-92, prof, 92-, dir, Central and Eastern European Stu, 93-95, dept ch, 95-. **SELECTED PUBLICATIONS** Auth, Between the Fields and the City: Women, Work and Family in Russia, 1861-1914, Cambridge, 94; Women, Men and the Languages of Peasant Resistance, 1870-1917, Princeton, 94; auth, "Women in Imperial, Soviet and Post-Soviet Russia," Washington, D.C., Am Historical Asn, 99. **CONTACT ADDRESS** History Dept, Univ of Colorado, Boulder, Boulder, CO 80309. **EMAIL** barbara.engel@colorado.edu

ALPERS, EDWARD A.
PERSONAL Born 04/23/1941, Philadelphia, PA, m, 1963, 2 children **DISCIPLINE** HISTORY **EDUCATION** Harvard Col, AB, 63; Univ London, PhD, 63. **CAREER** Lectr, Workers Educ Asn, 65; lectr, Univ E Africa, 66-68; asst prof to prof and dean, UCLA, 66-; Assoc, Univ Eduardo Mondlane Mozambique, 76; lectr, Somali Nat Univ, 80. **HONORS AND AWARDS** Harvard Scholar, 63; Travel Grant, Univ London, 64; Fel, Univ Calif, 70; Res Fel, UCLA, 72-73; Res Grant, Fundacao Calouste Glubenkian, 75; Res Fel, NEH, 78-79; Fulbright Sen Fel, 80; Travel Grant, James S. Coleman African Studies Ctr, 83, 94. 97; Travel Grant, UCLA, 81; Phi Beta Kappa, 95; Boniface I. Obichere Lifetime Achievement Awd, Calif State Univ, 99. **MEMBERSHIPS** African Studies Asn; Am Hist Asn; Asn of Concerned Africa Scholars; Can African Studies Asn. **RESEARCH** Eastern Africa and the Indian Ocean; The African Diaspora; Islam in Mozambique. **SELECTED PUBLICATIONS** Auth, "The Story of Swema: Female Vulnerability in Nineteenth-Century East Africa," in Women and Slavery in Africa, Heinemann, 97; auth, "The African Diaspora in the Northwestern Indian Ocean: reconsideration of an old problem, new directions for research," Comparative Studies of south Asia, Africa & the Middle East, (97): 62-81; auth, "East Central Africa," in The History of Islam in Africa, (Ohio Univ Press, 00), 83-99; co-ed, History, Memory and Identity: The Origins of Mauritian Slaves, Univ Mauritius, 01. **CONTACT ADDRESS** Dept Hist, Univ of California, Los Angeles, 6265 Bunche, Box 951473, Los Angeles, CA 90095-1473. **EMAIL** alpers@history.ucla.edu

ALSOP, JAMES
DISCIPLINE HISTORY **EDUCATION** Winnipeg Univ, BA; Univ Western Ontario, MA; Cambridge Univ, PhD. **RESEARCH** English taxation **SELECTED PUBLICATIONS** Co-auth, English Seamen and Trader in Guinea 1553-1565, 92. **CONTACT ADDRESS** History Dept, McMaster Univ, 1280 Main St W, Hamilton, ON, Canada L8S 4L9. **EMAIL** alsopj@mcmaster.ca

ALTER, GEORGE
PERSONAL Born 03/02/1949, Boston, MA, m, 1992, 1 child **DISCIPLINE** HISTORY **EDUCATION** Univ Penn, BA, 71; Univ Penn, PhD, hist, 78; Univ Mich, MA, applied econ, 78. **CAREER** Asst prof, dept of hist, Ind Univ, 79-87; assoc prof, dept of hist, Ind Univ, 87-; acting dir, Population Inst for Res and Training, Ind Univ, 87-88; dir, undergrad studies, dept of hist, Ind Univ, 96-98; dir, Population Inst for Res and Training, Ind Univ, 91-. **HONORS AND AWARDS** Internal Acad Residential fel, Ind Univ Inst for Adv Study, 95; Ind Univ summer facul fel, 95; Nat Res Svc award, Nat Inst on Aging, 89; Ind Heritage Res grant, 88; Ind Univ summer facul fel, 86; Nat Endow for the Humanities fel at Newberry Libr, 85; Lilly postdoctoral teaching fel, 82-83; Ind Univ summer facul fel, 80; post-doctoral fel, econ demography, Population Studies Ctr, Univ Mich, 77-78, 78-79; Penfield fel, 75-76; teaching asst, Univ Penn, 74-75; Univ Penn pre-doctoral fel, 71-75. **MEMBERSHIPS** Soc Sci Hist Asn; Population Asn of Amer; Econ Hist Asn; Cliometrics Soc; Soc de Demographi Hist. **RESEARCH** Historical demography; Family history; Economic history. **SELECTED PUBLICATIONS** Article, co-auth, Mortality and Economic Stress: Individual and Household Reponses in a Nineteenth-Century Belgian Village, Population and Economy: From Hunger to Modern Economic Growth, Oxford Univ Press, 98; article, co-auth, The sick and the well: adult health in Britain during the health transition, Health Trans Rev, suppl to vol 6, 19-44, 96; article, The European Marriage Pattern as Solution and Problem: Households of the Elderly in Verviers Belgium, 1831, Intl Jour of Family Hist, 1, 123-138, 96; article, Infant and Child Mortality in the United States and Canada, Infant and Child Mortality in the Past, Oxford, Clarendon Press, 91-108, 97; article, co-auth, Household Patterns of the Elderly and the Proximity of Children in a Nineteenth-Century City, Verviers, Belgium, 1831-1846, Aging and Generational Rela-

tions, Walter de Gruyter, 30-52, 96; article, Trends in United States Old Age Mortality, 1900-1935: Evidence from Railroad Pensions, Aging in the Past: Society, Demography, and Old Age, 328-59, Univ Calif Press, 95; article, co-auth, The Savings of Ordinary Americans: The Philadelphia Saving Fund Society in the Mid-nineteenth Century, Jour of Econ Hist, 54, 735-67, 94. **CONTACT ADDRESS** Dept of History, Indiana Univ, Bloomington, 1020 E Kirkwood Ave, Ballantine Hall 742, Bloomington, IN 47405. **EMAIL** alter@indiana.edu

ALTHERR, THOMAS L.
PERSONAL Born 04/26/1948, Buffalo, NY, d **DISCIPLINE** HISTORY **EDUCATION** SUNY BA, 70; Ohio State Univ, MA, 71; PhD, 76. **CAREER** Res Asst, Ohio Legislative Service Commission, 76-77; Teacher, Woodstock Country School, 77-78; Asst Prof to Prof, Metropolitan state Col of Denver, 79-. **HONORS AND AWARDS** Scholar Awd, Golden Key Nat Honor Soc, 99; CHOICE Outstanding Academic Book Awd, 98; Res Grant, Early Am Industries Asn, 98; Winterthur Fel, Winterthur Library, 97-98; Mellon Fel, Va Hist Soc, 94; Weston A Cate Res Fel, Va Hist Soc, 92; Leland D Case 14th Annual Western Hist Writing Contest, Second Prize, 88; Smithsonian Inst Res Grant, 87; Prof Development Grant, Metropolitan State Col of Denver, 86-present, Fulbright-Hays Jun Lectureship, Spain, 85; NEH Summer Seminar, 83, 80. **MEMBERSHIPS** Am Asn for the Hist of Medicine, Am Literature Asn, Am soc for Environmental Hist, Am Studies Asn, Colo Vintage Baseball Asn, Early am Industries Asn, Forest Hist Soc, N Eng Am studies Asn, N Am Soc for Sport Hist, NE Popular Culture Asn, Ohio/Ind/Mich Am Studies Asn, Org of Am Hist, Popular Culture/Am Culture Asn, Rocky Mountain Am Studies Asn, Rutland Hist Soc, Soc for Am Baseball Res, Vt Hist Soc. **SELECTED PUBLICATIONS** Auth, "Will's Panther club: Rev. William J Ballou, the Irrepressible and Uncompromising Order of Pantherites and the Catamount-sighting controversy in Chester, Vermont, 1934-1936," Vermont History, (98): 5-30; auth, "Academic Historians and Hunting: A Call for More and Better Scholarship," Environmental History Review, (95): 39-56; auth, Sports in North America: A documentary History, Vol I, Parts I and II, Early American Sports to 1820, Academic Intl Press, 97; ed, Procreation or Pleasure? Sexual Attitudes in American History, Robert E Krieger Pub, 83; auth, "Let 'Er Rip: Popular Cultural Images of the American West in Wild West Shows, rodeos, and Rendezvous," in Wanted Dead or Alive: The American West in Popular Culture, Univ Ill Press, 96; auth, "Tombochiqui, or, The American savage: John Cleland's Noble Savage Satire," American Indian Quarterly, (85): 411-420; auth, "A place level enough to play Ball" baseball and Baseball-Type Games in the colonial era, Revolutionary War and Early American Republic," NINE, forthcoming; auth, "Drunk with the Chase: The Influence of Francis Parkman's The California and Oregon Trail on Herman Melville's Moby Dick or The Whale," Journal of the American Studies Asn of Tex, (90): 1-14; auth, "The Fanatics in Grand conclave: The Rutland, Vermont free or reform Convention of 1858,: Rutland Hist Soc Quarterly, (99): 33-48; auth, "Maine in 1797: remarks by an Anonymous Resident of New Gloucester," Maine Hist Soc Quarterly, forthcoming; **CONTACT ADDRESS** Dept Hist, Metropolitan State Col of Denver, PO Box 173362, Denver, CO 80217-3362.

ALTHOLZ, JOSEF L.
PERSONAL Born 07/14/1933, Bronx, NY, d **DISCIPLINE** HISTORY **EDUCATION** Cornell Univ, BA, 54; Columbia Univ, MA, 55; PhD, 60. **CAREER** Instr, to prof, Univ of Minn 59-; vis prof, Univ of Wis, 70-71; vis prof, Univ of Leicester, 76. **HONORS AND AWARDS** Guggenheim Fel, 64-65; Fel, Royal Hist Soc, 73. **MEMBERSHIPS** AHA; Am Cath Hist Assoc; N Am Conf on Brit Studies; Am Soc of Church Hist; Res Soc for Victorian Periodicals; Am conf for Irish Studies. **RESEARCH** Brit history, church history of 18th and 19th-centuries, Victorian periodicals **SELECTED PUBLICATIONS** Auth, The Liberal Catholic Movement in England, Burns & Cates, (London), 62; auth, The Churches in the Nineteenth-Century, Bobbs-Merrill (Indianapolis), 67; ed, Victorian England 1837-1901, Cambridge Univ Pr, (Cambridge), 70; coed, the Correspondence of Lord Acton and Richard Simpson, 3 vols, Cambridge Univ Pr (Cambridge), 71-75; ed, The Mind and Art of Victorian England, Univ of Minn Pr, (Minneapolis), 76; auth, The Religious Press in Britain, 1760-1900, Greenwood Pr, (Westport, CT), 89, auth, Anatomy of a Controversy, Scholar Pr, (aldershot), 94; auth, "Lord Acton and the Plan of the Cambridge Modern History", Hist J,39, (96): 723-736; ed, Selected Documents in Irish History, M.E. Sharpe, (Armonk, NY), 00. **CONTACT ADDRESS** Dept Hist, Univ of Minnesota, Twin Cities, 267 19th Ave S, Minneapolis, MN 55455-0499. **EMAIL** altho001@tc.umn.edu

ALTMAN, IDA
PERSONAL Born 04/30/1950, Washington, DC, s **DISCIPLINE** HISTORY **EDUCATION** Univ Mich, BA, 71; Univ Tex, MA, 72; Johns Hopkins Univ, PhD, 81. **CAREER** Instr, 82-, prof, Dept of History, 93-, Univ of New Orleans. **HONORS AND AWARDS** Herbert E Bolton Prize; Spain and America in the Quincentennial of the Discovery Prize, both for book Emigrants and Society. **MEMBERSHIPS** Amer Hist Asn; Conference on Latin Amer History; Soc for Spanish and Portuguese Historical Soc. **RESEARCH** Colonial Spanish Amer; Mexico; early modern Spain; emigration. **SELECTED PUBLICATIONS** Coauth, To Make America, European Emigration in the Early Modern Period, Univ of CA Press, 91; art, Spanish Society in Mexico City after Conquest, Hispanic Amer Hist Rev 71:3, 91; coauth, The Contact of Cultures Perspectives on the Quincentenary, Amer Hist Rev 99, 94. **CONTACT ADDRESS** Dept of History, Univ of New Orleans, New Orleans, LA 70148. **EMAIL** ixahi@uno.edu

ALTSTADT, AUDREY L.
DISCIPLINE HISTORY **EDUCATION** Univ Chicago, PhD, 83. **CAREER** Assoc prof, Univ MA Amherst. **HONORS AND AWARDS** Honorary doctorate from Khazar Univ (Baker), 00. **RESEARCH** Soviet hist; Azerbarjan & Caucases. **SELECTED PUBLICATIONS** Auth, The Azerbaijani Turks, Stanford, 92; auth, "O Patria Mia: Nation Conflict in Mountainous Korabagh," in W.R. Dunan & G.P. Holman, eds Ethnic Nationalism and Regional Conflict (Westview, 94); auth, "Azerbaijan's Struggle toward Democracy," in K. Dawisha & B. Parrott, eds, Conflict, Cleavage & Change in Central Asia and The Caucasus (Cambridge Press, 97). **CONTACT ADDRESS** Dept of Hist, Univ of Massachusetts, Amherst, Herter Hall, Amherst, MA 01003.

ALVAREZ, JOSE E.
PERSONAL Born 02/23/1955, Marianao, Cuba, m, 1991 **DISCIPLINE** HISTORY **EDUCATION** Flor Atlan Univ, BA, 77; MA, 81; Flor State Univ, PhD, 95. **CAREER** Asst prof, Univ Houston, 96-. **HONORS AND AWARDS** Cult Coop Prog; West Pt Sum Sem. **MEMBERSHIPS** SMH; SSPHS; WW2SA; WHAT. **RESEARCH** The Spanish Foreign Legion; Spanish Colonialism in Morocco. **SELECTED PUBLICATIONS** Auth, "Tank Warfare During the Rif Rebellion, 1921-1927," ARMOR (97); auth, "Between Gallipoli and D-Day: Alhucemas, 1925," J Mil Hist (99); auth, The Betrothed of Death: The Spanish Foreign Legion During the Rif Rebellion, 1920-1927, Greenwood Press (00). **CONTACT ADDRESS** Dept Social Science, Univ of Houston, 1 Main St, Houston, TX 77002-1014. **EMAIL** alvarezj@zeus.dt.uh.edu

ALVES, ABEL A.
PERSONAL Born 03/21/1962, New Bedford, MA, m, 1988 **DISCIPLINE** HISTORY **EDUCATION** Southeastern Mass Univ, BA, 82; Univ Mass Amherst, MA, 84; PhD, 90. **CAREER** Vis instr, Allegheny col, 88-90; asst prof to assoc prof, Ball State Univ, 90-. **HONORS AND AWARDS** Miriam Chrisman Awd, 89; NEH Scholar, 92; Hurley goodall Awd, 97. **RESEARCH** History and Ethology, Mexican History, Early Modern History, World History. **SELECTED PUBLICATIONS** Auth, "Sor Juana Ines de la Cruz", "Estevan", "Richelieu", "Hernan Cortes", Historic World Leaders, eds Anne Commire and Deborah Klezmer, Gale Res, (94); auth, "Of Peanuts and Bread: Images of the Raw and the Refined in the Sixteenth-Century Conquest of New Spain", Coded Encounters: Writing, Gender and Ethnicity in Colonial Latin America, eds F. Javier Cevallos-Candau, Jeffrey A. Cole, Nina M. Scott and Nicomedes Suarez-Arauz, Univ of Mass Pr, (Amherst, 94): 62-72; auth, Brutality and Benevolence: Human Ethnology, Culture and the Birth of Mexico, Greenwood Pr, (Westport, CT and London), 96; coauth, Grain: Its Effect on Civilization and Health (forthcoming); auth, "Madame Roland", "Catherine de Medici", Gluckel of Hameln", "Jane Goodall", Women in World History, Eds, Anne Commire and Deborah Klezmer, Gale Res, (Detroit), (forthcoming); auth, "The Alpha Factor and the Conquest of Mexico: A Study in Ethnological History", Int J of Anthrop (forthcoming). **CONTACT ADDRESS** Dept History, Ball State Univ, 2000 W University Ave, Muncie, IN 47306-1022. **EMAIL** 00aaalves@bsu.edu

AMAN, MOHAMMED M.
PERSONAL Born 01/03/1940, Alexandria, Egypt, m, 1972, 1 child **DISCIPLINE** MIDDLE EASTERN STUDIES **EDUCATION** Cairo Univ Egypt, BA (with honors), 1961; Columbia Univ , NYork, MS, 1965; Univ of Pittsburgh, PhD, 1968; New York Univ, postdoctoral studies in Comp Sci, 1970-71. **CAREER** Univ of Pittsburgh, research asst, 65-66; Duquesne Univ Pittsburgh, reference librarian, 66-68; Pratt Inst NY, asst prof; St Johns Univ NY, asst and assoc prof, 69-73, dir and prof 73-76; Long Island Univ, Greenvale Long Island NY, dean & prof, 76-79; Univ of Wisconsin-Milwaukee, dean and prof, 79-. **HONORS AND AWARDS** Beta Phi Mu Intl Lib & Info Sci Honor Soc; award of appreciation from the Black Caucus of the Amer Library Assn, 1986; Awd of Serv, Assn for Library and Information Science Educ, 1988; UNESCO consultant on the Revival of the Alexandrian Library Project, 1988-; John Ames Humphry/OCLC-Forest Press Awd for Outstanding Contributions to Intl Librarianship, Amer Library Assn, 1989; Black Caucus of the Amer Library Assn (BCALA), Leadership Awd, 1994; the WLA Special Service Awd, 1992; Black Caucus of The ALA Awd of Excellence, 1995; Prof Kaula Medal & Citation, 1996; WLA, Librarian of the Year, 1998. **MEMBERSHIPS** Info mgmt consultant UNIDO 1978-; UNESCO 1982-, US-AID 1984-96; chmn Intl Relations Comm Amer Lib Assn 1984-86, Assn Lib & Info Sci Ed 1985-86; Amer Soc for Info Science Intl Rel Comm; chair, Intl Issues in Information Special Interest Group; life mem, founding exec bd mem, NAACP 1984-; mem Amer Arab Affairs Council 1983-; mem Egyptian Amer Scholars Assn 1971-; bd member, A Wisconsin African Relief Effort (AWARE), 1986-89; bd member, Wisconsin African Historical Society/Museum, 1988-, member, Audience Development Committee, Milwaukee Art Museum; founder, Milwaukee Leader's Forum. **SELECTED PUBLICATIONS** Auth, contrib consult, Intl Library Review, 1969-91; ed-in-chief, Digest of Middle East Studies (DOMES), Arab Serials & Periodicals, 1979; Cataloging & Classification of Non-Western Library Material, 1980; Librarianship in the Third World, 1976, Developing Computer Based Library Sys 1984, Online Access to Database 1984, Information Services 1986; Urban Library Management, 1990. **CONTACT ADDRESS** Sch Libr & Info Sci, Univ of Wisconsin, Milwaukee, PO Box 413, Enderis Hall, Milwaukee, WI 53201. **EMAIL** aman@slis.uwm.edu

AMANAT, ABBAS
PERSONAL Born Tehran, Iran, m, 1947 **DISCIPLINE** HISTORY **EDUCATION** Tehran Univ, BA, 71; Oxford Univ, DPhil, 81. **CAREER** Prof, Yale Univ, 83-. **HONORS AND AWARDS** Ed, Encycl Iranica, 85; Ed in Chief, J of Iranian Studies, 91-98. **MEMBERSHIPS** Mid E Studies Assoc, Soc for Iranian Studies. **RESEARCH** History of modern Middle East, Iran, Islam and Shi'ism. **SELECTED PUBLICATIONS** Auth, Resurrection and Renewal: The Making of the Babi Movement in Iran, Cornell Univ Pr (Ithaca, NY), 89; ed, Crowning Anguish: Memoirs of a Persian Princess from the Harem to Modernity, Magi Publ (Wash, DC), 95; auth, Pivot of the Universe: Hasir al-Din Shah Aajar and the Iranian Monarchy, Calif Univ Pr (Berkeley, CA), 97; auth, In Search of Modern Iran: Authority, Nationhood and Culture from the Rise of Sofan'd Shi'ism to the Shaping of the Islamic Republic 1501-1989, Yale Univ Pr (New Haven, CT), forthcoming. **CONTACT ADDRESS** Dept Hist, Yale Univ, PO Box 208324, New Haven, CT 06520-8324. **EMAIL** abbas.amanat@yale.edu

AMAR, JOSEPH P.
PERSONAL Born 12/29/1946, Grand Rapids, MI, s **DISCIPLINE** SEMITIC LANGUAGES; HISTORY **EDUCATION** The Catholic Univ of America, PhD, 88. **CAREER** Prof, Univ NortreDane, 88-, Chair, Classics Dept, 97-. **MEMBERSHIPS** North Amer Patristics Soc (NAPS); Middle East Studies Assoc (MESA). **RESEARCH** Cultural/linguistic interplay; Syriac language & lit; medieval Christian Arabic; Islamic history. **CONTACT ADDRESS** Dept of Classics, Univ of Notre Dame, 304 O'Shaughnessy Hall, Notre Dame, IN 46556. **EMAIL** Joseph.P.Amar.1@nd.edu

AMBLER, EFFIE
DISCIPLINE EUROPEAN AND RUSSIAN HISTORY **EDUCATION** Bryn Mawr Col, AB, 58; Ind Univ, Bloomington, PhD, 68. **CAREER** Asst prof hist, 65-66, Hollins Col; instr, 66-68, asst prof, 68-, assoc prof, 78-, Wayne St Univ. **MEMBERSHIPS** AAUP; Assn Advan Slavic Studies; AHA. **RESEARCH** Social and cultural history of the Russian Empire. **SELECTED PUBLICATIONS** Auth, Russian Journalism and Politics, 1861-81, The Career of Aleksei S Suvorin, Wayne State Univ, 72. **CONTACT ADDRESS** Dept of History, Wayne State Univ, 3094 FAB, Detroit, MI 48202-3919.

AMBROSE, LINDA M.
PERSONAL m, 2 children **DISCIPLINE** HISTORY **EDUCATION** Univ Waterloo, BA, MA, PhD. **CAREER** Asst prof, Laurentian Univ. **SELECTED PUBLICATIONS** Auth, For Home and Country, the Centennial His of the Women's Institutes in ontario, Boston Mills, 96. **CONTACT ADDRESS** Dept of History, Laurentian Univ, 935 Ramsey Lake Rd, Sudbury, ON, Canada P3E 2C6.

AMBROSIUS, LLOYD
PERSONAL m, 1963, 2 children **DISCIPLINE** U.S. DIPLOMATIC HISTORY **EDUCATION** Univ Ill, Urbana-Champaign, PhD, 67. **CAREER** Mary Ball Washington Prof, Univ Col Dublin, 77-78; Prof, ch, dept Hist, Univ Nebr, Lincoln, 93-97. **HONORS AND AWARDS** Fulbright Fel, Univ Cologne, 72-73, Fulbright fel, Univ Heidelberg, Ger, 96. **RESEARCH** Diplomatic relations between the U S and the Weimar Republic. **SELECTED PUBLICATIONS** Auth, Woodrow Wilson and the American Diplomatic Tradition: The Treaty Fight in Perspective, Cambridge UP, 87; Wilsonian Statecraft: Theory and Practice of Liberal Internationalism during World War I, Scholarly Resrcs, 91. **CONTACT ADDRESS** Univ of Nebraska, Lincoln, 618 Oldfather Hall, Lincoln, NE 68588-0327. **EMAIL** lambrosius1@unl.edu

AMDUR, KATHRYN E.
DISCIPLINE HISTORY **EDUCATION** Cornell Univ, BA, 69; Stanford Univ, MA, 71, PhD, 78. **CAREER** Assoc prof **RESEARCH** Modern European social and political history, especially the history of labor movements in twentieth-century France; French trade unionism and industrial transformation in the 1930s through the 1950s. **SELECTED PUBLICATIONS** Auth, Syndicalist Legacy: Trade Unions and Politics in Two French Cities in the Era of World War I. **CONTACT ADDRESS** Dept History, Emory Univ, 221 Bowden Hall, 561 Kilgo Cir, Atlanta, GA 30322-1950. **EMAIL** kamdur@emory.edu

AMIJI, HATIM M.
PERSONAL Born 06/11/1939, Zanzibar **DISCIPLINE** HISTORY **EDUCATION** London, BA (Hons) 1964; Princeton Univ, MA, PhD. **CAREER** Univ of MA Dept of History, assoc prof. **HONORS AND AWARDS** E African Railways & Harbours Rsch Awd 1963; Rockefeller Found Fellow 1965-67; Princeton Univ Fellow 1969-70; Zanzibar Govt Scholar 1961-64; Superior Merit Awd Univ of MA. **MEMBERSHIPS** Sec gen Zanzibar Youth League 1960; lecturer Trinity Coll Nabingo Uganda 1964; lecturer Princeton Univ 1969-70; rsch assoc Dept of History Univ of Nairobi Kenya 1967-68; lecturer Dept of History & Centre for African Studies Boston Univ 1972; dir African Studies Workshop World Affairs Council Boston 1972; mem Middle Eastern Studies Assoc; fellow E African Acad; mem African Studies Assoc of USA; ed bd Gemini Review; founder mem Pan-African Univ Org. **CONTACT ADDRESS** Dept History, Univ of Massachusetts, Boston, Harbor Campus Univ of MA, Boston, MA 02125.

AMMON, THEODORE G.
DISCIPLINE HISTORY OF PHILOSOPHY, EPISTEMOLOGY, PHILOSOPHY AND LITERATURE **EDUCATION** Miss State Univ, BA; Wash Univ, MA, PhD. **CAREER** Dept Philos, Millsaps Col **SELECTED PUBLICATIONS** Publ on, ethical duties of teachers; philos underpinnings of lit of Jorge Luis Borges; teaching strategies for moral develop. **CONTACT ADDRESS** Dept of Philosophy, Millsaps Col, 1701 N State St, Jackson, MS 39210. **EMAIL** ammontg@okra.millsaps.edu

AMUSSEN, SUSAN
DISCIPLINE HISTORY **EDUCATION** Princeton Univ, BA; Brown Univ, MA, PhD. **CAREER** Prof. **RESEARCH** Literature and history; women's studies; history of Christianity; feminist theology; feminist and critical pedagogy. **SELECTED PUBLICATIONS** Auth, Crime, loi, et justice rurale en Angleterre a l'epoque moderne, Etudes Rurales, 86; An Ordered Society: Gender and Class in Early Modern England, 88; Elizabeth I and Alice Balstone: Gender, Class, and the Exceptional Woman in Early Modern England, 94; Being Stirred To Much Unquietness: Violence and Domestic Violence in Early Modern England, J Women's Hist, 94; Discipline and Punish: The Uses and Meaning of Violence in Early Modern England, J British Studies, 95. **CONTACT ADDRESS** History Dept, Union Inst, 440 E McMillan St, Cincinnati, OH 45206-1925.

ANCTIL, PIERRE
PERSONAL Born 07/28/1952, Quebec, PQ, Canada **DISCIPLINE** HISTORY **EDUCATION** Univ Laval, BA, 73, MA, 75; New Sch Soc Res (NY), PhD, 80. **CAREER** Res, Inst quebcois de recherche sur la culture, 80-88; dir, Fr Can stud & asst prof, Jewish stud, McGill Univ, 88-91; conseiller en services aux communautes culturelles, Min Educ, Govt Que, 91-93; Conseiller EN Relations Interculturelles, Min Des Relations Avec Les Citoyens Et De L'Immigration, Govt Que, 93-. **HONORS AND AWARDS** Can res fel, SSHRCC, 88-91. **MEMBERSHIPS** Asn Can Jewish Stud; Inst quebecois d'etudes sur la culture juive; Can Ethnic Studies Asn; vice pres, Can Multicultur Adv Comt, 90-91; mem bd govs, Montreal Holocaust Mem Ctr, 90-91. **RESEARCH** Canadian-Jewish studies; French Canadian studies. **SELECTED PUBLICATIONS** Auth, Le Rendez-vous manque les Juifs de Montreal face au Quebec de l'entre-deux-guerres, 88; auth, Le Devoir, les Juifs et l'immigration: De Bourassa a Laurendeau, 88; ed, Juifs et realites juives au Quebec, 84; ed, Un Homme Grand: Jack Kerouac at the Crossroads of Many Cultures, 90; ed, An Everyday Miracle, Yiddish Culture in Montreal, 90; ed, If One Were to Write a History.. Selected Writings by Robert F. Harney, 91; transl, Poemes yiddish (J.I. Segal), 92; transl, Le Montreal juif d'autrefois (Israel Medresh), 97. **CONTACT ADDRESS** 360 McGill St, Montreal, QC, Canada H2Y 2E9.

ANDERSON, BETTY S.
PERSONAL Born 04/02/1965, Hyannis, MA **DISCIPLINE** HISTORY **EDUCATION** Trinity Col, BA, 87; UCLA, MA, 91; PhD, 97. **CAREER** Asst Prof, Boston Univ, 99-. **HONORS AND AWARDS** Fulbright Fel, 93-94; Fel, USIA/ACOR in Jordan, 94-95, 00; Fulbright Hayes Group Study Abroad Awd, 93. **MEMBERSHIPS** MESA; AHA; WHA. **RESEARCH** Modern Middle East (Fertile Crescent); Jordan; Nationalism; Political Parties. **SELECTED PUBLICATIONS** Auth, "The Status of 'Democracy' in Jorday," Critique, (97): 55-76; auth, "Liberalization in Jordan in the 1950s and 1990s: Similarities or Differences?" Jordanies, (97): 207-217; auth, "Jordanian Political Parties of the 1950s: Social Transformatin and the Dynamic Role of Nationalist Ideology," in Social Identities, Development Policies and the State in Jordan, 1946-1996, Darthala Pub, forthcoming; auth, "Domestic Influences on Policy-Making: the History of the Jordanian National Movement, 946-1957," forthcoming. **CONTACT ADDRESS** Dept Hist, Boston Univ, 226 Bay State Rd, Boston, MA 02215. **EMAIL** banderso@bu.edu

ANDERSON, CHARLES SAMUEL
PERSONAL Born 03/04/1930, Madison, WI, m, 1951, 2 children **DISCIPLINE** HISTORICAL THEOLOGY **EDUCATION** St Olaf Col, BA, 51; Univ Wis, MA, 54; Luther Theol Sem, BD, 57; Union Theol Sem, NYork, PhD (Hist Theol & Reformation Studies), 62. **CAREER** Teaching asst English, Univ Wis, 53-54; from asst prof to prof Hist Theol, Luther Theol Sem, 61-77, dir Grad Studies, 68-72, vpres Acad Affairs & dean, 77-80, pres, Augsburg Col, 80-97, clergyman, Am Lutheran Church, 57-; mem, Rockefeller Scholar Area Selection Comt, 63, 69; comn Inter Church Affairs, Am Lutheran Church, 64; vis lectr, Northwestern Lutheran Theol Sem, 64; Am Asn Theol Sch sabbatical studies grant, 67-68; vis lectr, Concordia Theol Sem, 68; Bush Found fel, 71-; chmn div Theol Studies, Lutheran Coun USA, 72-. **HONORS AND AWARDS** Phi Betta Kappa, Rockefeller & Martin Luther fell; Bush Leadership fell. **MEMBERSHIPS** Am Soc Church Hist; Renaissance Soc Am; Soc Reformation Res. **RESEARCH** Reformation theology; the military aspects of the Reformation; improvement of education for ministry. **SELECTED PUBLICATIONS** Auth, International Luther studies, Ecumenist, 66; Will the real Luther please stand up, Dialog, 67; The Reformation Then and Now, 67; The Augsburg Historical Atlas of Christianity in the Middle Ages and Reformation, 67, 72 & ed, Readings in Luther for Laymen, 67, Augsburg; auth, Robert Barnes, In: Interpretors of Luther, 68 & ed, Facet Books Reformation Series, 69-, Fortress; auth, Faith and Freedom: The Christian Faith According to the Lutheran Confessions, Augsburg, 78. **CONTACT ADDRESS** 1377 Grantham St, Saint Paul, MN 55108. **EMAIL** andersoc@visi.com

ANDERSON, DAVID L.
PERSONAL Born 08/10/1946, Pampa, TX, m, 1973, 1 child **DISCIPLINE** HISTORY **EDUCATION** Rice Univ, BA, 68; Univ Va, MA, 71; PhD, 74. **CAREER** Vis Asst Prof, Univ Mont, 74-75; Vis Asst Prof, Tex Technol Univ, 75-76; Vis Asst Prof, Univ Mont, 76-77; Vis Asst Prof, Sam Houston St Univ, 77-80; Lectr, Calif Polytech St Univ, 80-81; From Asst Prof to Prof, Univ Indianapolis, 90-; Vis Prof, Anhui Normal Univ, People's Republic of China, 94. **HONORS AND AWARDS** Robert H Ferrell Book Prize, Soc for Historians of Am For Rels, 91; Ind Prof of the Year, Coun for Advan and Support of Educ, 92. **MEMBERSHIPS** Soc for Historians of Am for Rels, AHA, Orgn of Am Historians. **SELECTED PUBLICATIONS** Auth, Trapped by Success: The Eisenhower Administration and Vietnam 1953-1961, Columbia UP (New York, NY), 91; auth, Shadow on the White House: Presidents and the Vietnam War 1945-1975, UP Kan (Lawrence, KS), 93; auth, "The United States and Vietnam," in The Vietnam War (London: Macmillan, 98), 95-114; auth, "The Vietnam War (1960-1975): Military and Diplomatic Course," in The Oxford Companion to Am Military Hist (New York, NY: Oxford UP, 99), 759-763. **CONTACT ADDRESS** Dept Hist, Univ of Indianapolis, E Hanna Ave, Indianapolis, IN 46227-3697. **EMAIL** anderson@uindy.edu

ANDERSON, FRED
DISCIPLINE HISTORY **EDUCATION** Colo State Univ, BA, 71; Harvard Univ, MA, 73; PhD, 81. **CAREER** Lec, Harvard, 81-83; asst prof, 83-89, assoc prof, Univ Colo, 89-. **SELECTED PUBLICATIONS** Auth, A People's Army: Massachusetts Soldiers and Society in the Seven Years' Warm Univ NC, 84; Why Did Colonial New Englanders Make Bad Soldiers? Contractual Principles and Military Conduct during the Seven Years' War, 81; A People's Army: Provincial Military Service in Massachusetts during the Seven Years' War, William Mary Quarterly, 83; Bringing the War Home: The Revolutionary Experience of Newport and New York, Rev Am Hist, 87; The Colonial Background to the American Victory, Greenwood, 88; co-auth, The Problem of Fragmentation and the Prospects for Synthesis in Early American Social History, William Mary Quarterly, 93. **CONTACT ADDRESS** History Dept, Univ of Colorado, Boulder, Boulder, CO 80309. **EMAIL** andersof@spot.colorado.edu

ANDERSON, GERALD D.
PERSONAL Born 11/14/1944, Hitterdahl, MN, m, 1978, 3 children **DISCIPLINE** HISTORY, BRITISH AND MODERN EUROPEAN HISTORY **EDUCATION** Concordia Col, BA, 65; NDak State Univ, MA, 66; Univ Iowa, PhD, 73. **CAREER** Waldorf Col, Forest City, Iowa, 66-70; Drake Univ, Des Moines, Iowa, 73; asst prof, Luther Col, 79-85; NDak State Univ, Fargo, 85-. **HONORS AND AWARDS** Who's Who in Am, since 78; Fulbright grant for study in the Netherlands, summer 91; Outstanding Teacher Awd, HSS, NDak State Univ, 92. **MEMBERSHIPS** Northern Great Plains Hist Conf, Governor's Coun, Am Hist Soc, Am Cultural Soc. **RESEARCH** Britiain in the Interwar years, British Civil liberties, The Cold War, Scandinavians in America. **SELECTED PUBLICATIONS** Auth, "Pacifists, Communists, and the National Government," Columbia, Mo: Univ of Mo Press (83); auth, "Prairie Voices: An Oral History of Scandinavian Americans in the Upper Midwest," Hamar, Norway, accepted for pub by Norsk Utvandrermuseum; auth, "The Uffda Trial," Hatsings, MN: Martin House (94); auth, "The Western Perspective Study Guide," Vol I and II, Fort Worth: Harcourt Brace (99). **CONTACT ADDRESS** Dept Hist, No Dakota State Univ, PO Box 5075, Fargo, ND 58105-5075.

ANDERSON, GORDON A.
PERSONAL Born 01/16/1947, Rockford, IL, m, 1970, 3 children **DISCIPLINE** LIBRARY SCIENCE, EUROPEAN STUDIES **EDUCATION** Iowa, BA, 70; Univ S Calif, MA, 75; Iowa, MLS, 80; Kansas, MA, 81. **CAREER** Slavic and Ger lang Cataloger, Univ of Nebr Libr, Lincoln, 81-84; Head, Slavic Dept, Univ of Kans Libr, Lawrence, 85-93; Ref Librn and Europe Studies Bibliogr, Univ of Kans Libr, Lawrence, 94-. **MEMBERSHIPS** Am Asn for Advancement of Slavic Studies, Western Europ Studies Sect, Asn od Col and Res Libr, Am Libr Asn. **RESEARCH** Central European Publishing, European History. **CONTACT ADDRESS** Univ of Kansas, Lawrence, 350 Watson Library, Lawrence, KS 66045-2800. **EMAIL** ganderson@ukans.edu

ANDERSON, GREG
PERSONAL Born 10/24/1962, Weston Super Mare, England **DISCIPLINE** CLASSICS; HISTORY **EDUCATION** Univ of Newcastle UK, BA, 86; Univ of London UK, MA, 88; Yale Univ PhD, 97. **CAREER** Asst Prof, 97-98, Elmira College; Asst Prof, 98-, Univ of IL, Chicago. **MEMBERSHIPS** APA **RESEARCH** Ancient Grecian to ancient greek political & cultural history, sports history, nationalism. **SELECTED PUBLICATIONS** Auth, The Athenian Experiment: Building a New Kind of Political Community in Ancient Attica, 508-490 B.C.", Ann Arbor, Univ of Mich Press, forthcoming; Alcmeonid Homelands Political Exile and the Unification of Attica, in: Historia, forthcoming; Games for Heros, Greek Athletics and the Invention of the Olympic Tradition, in: Report of the Yale-Smithsonian Annual Seminar on Material Culture, 97. **CONTACT ADDRESS** Dept of History, Univ of Illinois, Chicago, 601 S Morgan St, Chicago, IL 60607-7109. **EMAIL** gregand@uic.edu

ANDERSON, JAMES D.
DISCIPLINE HISTORY **EDUCATION** Univ Ill, PhD, 73. **CAREER** Prof, Univ Ill Urbana Champaign **RESEARCH** History American education; history of African-American educatio; race in American life and culture. **SELECTED PUBLICATIONS** Auth, Race, Meritocracy, and the American Academy During the Immediate Post World War II Era, Hist Edu Quarterly, 93; How We Learn About Race Through History, Univ Minn, 94; Literacy and Education in the African American Experience, Hampton, 95. **CONTACT ADDRESS** History Dept, Univ of Illinois, Urbana-Champaign, 52 E Gregory Dr, Champaign, IL 61820. **EMAIL** janders@uiuc.edu

ANDERSON, JANET A.
PERSONAL Born 03/29/1934, Washington, DC, s **DISCIPLINE** ART HISTORY **EDUCATION** Pa State Univ, BA, 57, MA, 59; Univ Mich, PhD, 70. **CAREER** Penn Hall Jr Col, 59-67; Univ of Wisc-Whitewater, 69-. **RESEARCH** Women artists; 17th century art. **SELECTED PUBLICATIONS** Women in the Fine Arts: A Bibliography and Illustration Guide, 90; auth, articles in Dictionary of Women Artists, 97; Pedro de Mena: 17th Century Spanish Sculptor, Edwin Meller Press, 98. **CONTACT ADDRESS** N7750 Engel Rd, Rte 3, Whitewater, WI 53190.

ANDERSON, MARGARET LAVINIA
PERSONAL Born 10/18/1941, Washington, DC, m, 1989, 1 child **DISCIPLINE** HISTORY **EDUCATION** Swarthmore Col, BA, 63; Brown Univ, PhD, 71. **CAREER** Asst prof to prof, Swarthmore Col, 70-90; assoc prof to prof, Univ of Calif Berkeley, 90. **HONORS AND AWARDS** Flack fac Awd for teaching, 85; best article Awd, Confr Group on Central European Hist, 84 & 87; first prize for best syllabus in Ger studies, DAAD, 93; NEH summer stipend, 72 & 93; NEH fel, 94-95; Judith Lee Ridge Article Prize, Western Asn of Women Historians, 95. **MEMBERSHIPS** Am Hist Asn, Ger Studies Asn, Catholic Hist Asn, Western Asn of Women Historians. **RESEARCH** Germany between 1850-1925, history of Catholicism 1830-1918, history of elections, political parties, and parliaments, history of Germans in the Ottoman Empire. **SELECTED PUBLICATIONS** Auth, "History in the Comic Mode: Jonathan Sperber's 1848," Central European Hist vol 25, 3 (92): 333-342; auth, "Voter, Junker, Landraat, Priest: The Old Authorities and the new Franchise in Imperial Germany, 1871-1914," Am Hist Rev 98, 5 (93): 1448-1474; auth, "The Limits of Secularization: On the Problem of the Catholic Revival in 19th Century Germany," Hist J, 38, 3 (95): 647-670; auth, "Clerical Election Influence and Communal Solidarity: Catholic Political Culture in the German Empire, 1871-1914," Elections before Democracy. Essays on the Electoral History of Latin America and Europe, Macmillan (NY, New York and London, Eng), 96; auth, Practicing Democracy: Elections and Political Culture in Imperial Germany, Princeton Univ Press, 00; auth, "The Divisions of the Pope: The Catholic Revival and Europe's Transition to Democracy," Rivals and Revivals: Religion and politics in Nineteenth-Century Spanish America and Europe, forthcoming. **CONTACT ADDRESS** Dept Hist, Univ of California, Berkeley, 3229 Dwinelle Hall, Berkeley, CA 94720-2550.

ANDERSON, MARK
DISCIPLINE AMERICAN HISTORY **EDUCATION** Univ Calif, PhD, 95. **CAREER** Asst prof. **RESEARCH** Role of the mass media in the Mexican Revolution. **SELECTED PUBLICATIONS** Pub(s), nineteenth-century Amer lit; auth, Revolution by Headlines: Mass Media in the Mexican Revolution, Uni-

versity of Oklahoma Press, forthcoming **CONTACT ADDRESS** Dept of Hist, Brock Univ, 500 Glenridge Ave., Saint Catharines, ON, Canada L2S 3A1. **EMAIL** manderso@spartan.ac.brocku.ca

ANDERSON, NANCY FIX
PERSONAL Born 08/23/1941, Dallas, TX **DISCIPLINE** HISTORY **EDUCATION** Stanford Univ, BA, 65; Univ Calif Irvine, MA, 67; Tulane Univ, 73. **CAREER** Loyola Univ New Orleans, assoc prof history, 87-97, prof history, 97-. **HONORS AND AWARDS** Dux Academicas Awd, Loyola Univ, 94. **MEMBERSHIPS** Amer Historical Assn; Southern Conf on British Studies; Southern Assn of Women Historians. **RESEARCH** Victorian English women and the family; Annie Besant. **SELECTED PUBLICATIONS** Auth, Woman against Women in Victorian England: A Life of Eliza Lynn Linton, 87; "Bridging Cross-Cultural Feminisms: Annie Besant and Women's Rights in England and India, 1874-1933," Women's History Review, no. 3, 94; "Not a Fit and Proper Person: Annie Besant's Struggle for Child Custody, 1878-9," in Maternal Instincts: Visions of Motherhood and Sexuality in Britain, 1875-1925, 97. **CONTACT ADDRESS** Dept of History, Loyola Univ, New Orleans, 6363 St Charles Ave, Box 65, New Orleans, LA 70118. **EMAIL** anderson@loyno.edu

ANDERSON, ROBERT MAPES
PERSONAL Born 04/06/1929, New York, NY **DISCIPLINE** AMERICAN SOCIAL HISTORY & AMERICAN RELIGIOUS HISTORY **EDUCATION** Wagner Col, BA, 59; Columbia Univ, MA, 62, PhD, 69. **CAREER** Hist ed, Monarch Press, New York, 62-64; lectr hist, 64-65, from instr to assoc prof, 65-77, chmn, Dept Hist & Polit Sci, 70-75, prof hist, Wagner Col, 77-. **MEMBERSHIPS** AHA; Orgn Am Historians; AAUP. **RESEARCH** American religious history. **SELECTED PUBLICATIONS** Ed, United States Since 1865, Monarch, 63; Vision of the Disinherited: The Making of American Pentecostalism, Oxford Univ Press, 79, 2nd ed, Hendrickson Press, 92. **CONTACT ADDRESS** Wagner Col, 631 Howard Ave, Staten Island, NY 10301-4428. **EMAIL** rmander877@aol.com

ANDERSON, STANFORD OWEN
PERSONAL Born 11/13/1934, Redwood Falls, MN, M **DISCIPLINE** HISTORY OF ARCHITECTURE AND CITIES **EDUCATION** Univ Minn, Minneapolis, BA, 57; Univ Calif, Berkeley, MA (Archit), 58; Columbia Univ, PhD(hist art & archit), 68. **CAREER** Unit master archit design, Archit Asn, London, 62-63; asst prof, 63-68, assoc prof, 68-71, prof hist of archit & archit, Mass Inst Technol, 71-, Dept Hd, Architecture, MIT, 91-; proj res dir, Inst Archit & Urban Studies, New York, 70-72; vis lectr, Archit Asn, London, 74-78; comnr, Boston Landmarks Comn, 80-87; Board of Dir, Fulbright Assn, 98-. **HONORS AND AWARDS** Fulbright (Germany), 61-62; Guggenheim, 69-70; ACLS, 77-78. **MEMBERSHIPS** Asn Col Schs Archit; Brit Soc Philos Sci; Col Art Asn Am; Soc Archit Historians; Bd Dir, Fulbright Assoc, 98-. **RESEARCH** History of modern architecture and urbanism; analysis and design of urban space; historiography. **SELECTED PUBLICATIONS** Modern architecture and industry: Peter Behrens, Oppositions, winter 77, summer 80 & winter 81; ed, On Streets, MIT Press, 78 & G Gili, Barcelona, 81; auth, The plan of Savannah: city plan as resource, Harvard Archit Rev 2, 81; Types and conventions in time, Perspecta 18, 82; Architectural Design as a System of Research Programmes, Design Stud, vol V, 146-150; Peter Behren's Highest Kultursymbol, the Theater, Perspecta 26, 103-134; Hermann Muthesius: Style-Architecture and Building Art, Getty Center, Santa Monica, CA, 94; Memory in Architecture/Erinnerung in der Architektur, Daidalos, 58, 95; The New Empiricism-Bay Region-Axis': Kay Fisker and Postwar Debates on Functionalism, Regionalism, and Monumentality, J Archit Educ, L, 3, 203-213; Peter Behrens and a New Architecture for the Twentieth Century, MIT Press, 00. **CONTACT ADDRESS** Dept of Archit, Massachusetts Institute of Technology, 77 Massachusetts Ave, Cambridge, MA 02139-4307. **EMAIL** soa@mit.edu

ANDERSON, TERRY HOWARD
PERSONAL Born 12/08/1946, Kankakee, IL **DISCIPLINE** AMERICAN HISTORY **EDUCATION** Univ MN, BA, 71; Univ MO, MA, 73; Ind Univ, PhD, 78. **CAREER** Assoc Instr Am hist and Asst Oral Historian, IN Univ, 74-76; asst prof, VA Polytech Inst & State Univ, 78-79; from Asst Prof to Prof Recent Am Hist, TX A&M Univ, 79, Oral Historian, 79-88, Systems Asst Prof, TX A&M System, Prairie View A&M, 81, TX A&M-Koriyama, Japan, 91. **HONORS AND AWARDS** Fulbright Lectr, China, 94-95. **MEMBERSHIPS** Orgn Am Historians; Oral Hist Asn; Soc Historians Am For Rels; Am Hist Asn. **RESEARCH** Cold War; sixty's--soc movements of 1960's and early 1970's; oral hist. **SELECTED PUBLICATIONS** Auth, Becoming sane with psychohistory, Historian, 11/78; The United States, Great Britain, and the Cold War, 1944-1947, Univ Mo Press, 81; A guide to the oral history collection of Texas A&M, Sterling Evans Libr, 81; coauth, A Flying Tiger's Diary, Tex A&M Univ Press, 84; auth, The Movement and the Sixties, Oxford Univ Press, 95; The Sixties, Addison Wesley Longman, 98. **CONTACT ADDRESS** Dept Hist, Texas A&M Univ, Col Station, College Station, TX 77843. **EMAIL** tha@tamu.edu

ANDERSON, THOMAS H.
PERSONAL Born 10/18/1942, Washington, PA, m, 2 children **DISCIPLINE** GEOLOGY **EDUCATION** Franklin & Marshall Col, BA, 64; Univ Tex, MA, 67; PhD, 69. **CAREER** Asst Prof to full prof, Univ Pittsburgh, 74-. **MEMBERSHIPS** Res Assoc, Carnegie Museum of Nat Hist, GSA Fel, Sigma Xi, Phi Kappa Phi, AGU, AAPG, Appalachian Geol Soc, Pgh Geol Soc, PAPG. **CONTACT ADDRESS** Dept Geol & Planet Sci, Univ of Pittsburgh, 321 Old Engineering, Pittsburgh, PA 15260. **EMAIL** taco@pitt.edu

ANDERSON, WILLIAM L.
DISCIPLINE CHEROKEE HISTORY **EDUCATION** Univ AL, PhD. **CAREER** Hist Dept, Western Carolina Univ **RESEARCH** Cherokee history. **SELECTED PUBLICATIONS** Auth, Guide to Cherokee Documents in Foreign Archives, 83; auth, Cherokee Removal: Before and After, 91. **CONTACT ADDRESS** Western Carolina Univ, Cullowhee, NC 28723.

ANDREA, ALFRED J.
PERSONAL Born 11/18/1941, Boston, MA, m, 1965, 2 children **DISCIPLINE** HISTORY **EDUCATION** Boston Col, AB (magna cum laude), 63; Cornell Univ, PhD, 69. **CAREER** Instr, 67-69, Asst Prof, 69-75, Assoc Prof, 75-82, Dir, Medieval-Renaissance prog, Living/Learning Center, 75-77, Co-dir & Assoc Prof in Italy, 78-79; Eli Lilly Exchange prof, univ of Puget Sound, 78-79; Dir of Grad studies, Dept of Hist, 92-94, Prof, 82-01; Dir of Undergrad studies, Dept of Hist, Unvi of VT, 96-01; Prof Emer, 01. **HONORS AND AWARDS** Fourth Annual Donald B. hoffman Fac Advisor Awd, Alexander von Humboldt Fel, 65-; Phi Alpha Theta Int Honor Soc in Hist, 91; Distinguished Scholar-in-Residence, Univ of Lousiville, 02. **MEMBERSHIPS** World Hist Asn; Medieval Acad of Am; New England Medieval Confr; Am Soc of Church Hist; Phil Alpha Theta Honor Soc in Hist; New England Regional World Hist Asn; Soc for the Study of the Crusades and the Latin East. **RESEARCH** Medieval Europe, 300-1500; Global History to 1700; Medieval Ecclesiastical History; Papal-Byzantine Relations, 330-1453; The Crusades; Long-distance trade and travel, 200 B.C.E-1500 C.E. **SELECTED PUBLICATIONS** The Sources for the Fourth Crusade, An Appendix to Donald E. Queller and The Devastatio Constantinopolitana, A Special Perspective on the Fourth Crusade: An Analysis, new Edition, and Translation, Historical Reflections/Reflexions Historiques, 93; Thomas Madden, the Fourth Crusade, Univ of Pa Press, 96; The Anonymous Chronicler of Halberstadt's Account of the Fourth Crusade: Popular Religiosity in the Early Thirteenth Century, Historical Reflections/Reflexions Historiques, 96; auth, The Capture of Constantinople, Univ Penn Press, 97; contribur, Using the Human Record: Suggestions from the Editors, a new manual on tchg global history to accompany The Human Record, 98; Auth, The Medieval Record: Sources of Medieval European History, Houghton Mifflin Co., 98; auth, The Human record, vol 1, 4th ed, Houghton Mifflin, 00; auth, Using the Human Record: Suggestions From the Ed, 4th ed, Houghton Mifflin, 00. **CONTACT ADDRESS** Dept of Hist, Univ of Vermont, Burlington, VT 05405. **EMAIL** aandrea@zoo.uvm.edu

ANDREW, JOHN ALFRED
PERSONAL Born 01/16/1943, Boston, MA, m, 1966, 2 children **DISCIPLINE** HISTORY **EDUCATION** Univ NH, BA, 65, MA, 67; Univ Tex, PhD, 73. **CAREER** Prof, Franklin & Marshall Coll. **HONORS AND AWARDS** Ford Found Schol, 61-66; John Pine Grad Stud Schol Awd, 71-72; Phi Alpha Theta; Pi Sigma Alpha; Pi Gamma Mu; American Philosophical Soc Res Gra, 75; Moody Gra, LBJ Found, 93, 97. **MEMBERSHIPS** Org of Amer Historians, Penn Hist Assn, Amer Studies Assn, Soc for Historian of the Early Amer Republic. **RESEARCH** Social and political history **SELECTED PUBLICATIONS** Auth, Rebuilding the Christian Commonwealth: New England Congregationalists and Foreign Missions, 1800-1830, Univ Ky, 76; auth, From Revivals to Removal: Jeremiah Evarts, the Cherokee Nation and the Search for the Soul of America, Univ Ga, 92; auth, The Other Side of the Sixties: Young Americans for Freedom and the Rise of Conservative Politics, Rutgers Univ, 97; auth, Lyndon Johnson and the Great Society, Ivan R Dee, 98; auth, Betsey Stockton: Strangers in a Strange Land, J of Presbyterian Hist, 74; auth, AD Recalls: Betsey Stockton, in AD, 76; auth, Educating the Heathen: The Foreign Mission School Controversy and American Ideals, in J Amer Studies, 78; auth, Dear Prexy: Letters from the War Years, in F&M Today, 82; auth, Impending Crises of the 1960's: National Goals and National Purpose, in Viet Nam Generation, 94; auth, Struggle for the Republican Party in 1960, in Historian, 97; auth, Cracks in the Consensus: The Rockefeller Brothers Fund Special Studies Project and Eisenhower America, in Presidential Studies Quart, 98; auth, Pro-War and Anti-Draft: Young Americans for Freedom and the War in Viet Nam, in The Viet Nam War on Campus: Other Voices, More Distant Drums, forthcoming. **CONTACT ADDRESS** Dept of History, Franklin and Marshall Col, Lancaster, PA 17604. **EMAIL** j_andrew@acad.fandm.edu

ANDREWS, ANTHONY P.
PERSONAL Born 08/23/1949, Washington, DC, m, 1989, 2 children **DISCIPLINE** ANTHROPOLOGY, ARCHAEOLOGY **EDUCATION** Harvard Univ, BA, 72; Univ Arizona, MA, 76; Univ Arizona, PhD, 80. **CAREER** Asst prof Anthro, Hamilton Col, 80-81; asst prof Anthro, New Col of USF, 81-85; assoc prof Anthro, New Col of USF, 85-89; prof Anthro, New Col of USF, 89-; Chair, Div of Soc Sci, New Col of USF, 89-95. **HONORS AND AWARDS** Magna Cum Laude, 72; multiple res grants; State of Florida Teaching Awd. **MEMBERSHIPS** Soc Am Archeol; Am Anthro Asn; Sociedad Mexicana de Antropologia; Sociedad Espanola de Estudios Mayas. **RESEARCH** Prehispanic and historical archaeology and ethnohistory of eastern Mesoamerica; historical cartography and history of Yucatan. **SELECTED PUBLICATIONS** Auth, A Preliminary Study of the Ruins of Xcaret, Quintano Roo, Mexico, Tulane Univ, 75; auth, Ecab: Poblado y Provincia del Siglo XVI en Yucatan, Instituto Nacional de Antropologia e Historia, Mexico, 79; auth, Arqueologia Historica en el Area Maya, Sociedad Mexicana de Antropologia, Mexico, 85; auth, Instituto Nacional de Antropologia e Historia, Mexico, 86; First Cities, St Remy/Smithsonian, 95; "A Brief History of Underwater Archaelogy in the Maya Area." Ancient Mesoamerica; "Late Postclassic Lowland Maya Archaeology." Jrnl World Prehistory. **CONTACT ADDRESS** Division of Soc Sci, New Col of the Univ of So Florida, Sarasota, FL 34243. **EMAIL** andrews@sar.usf.edu

ANDREWS, AVERY D.
PERSONAL Born 09/06/1927, New York, NY **DISCIPLINE** HISTORY **EDUCATION** Harvard Univ, AB, 50; Univ Pa, LLB, 53, MA, 58, PhD, 62. **CAREER** Instr, 61-62, Haverford Col, Bryn Mawr Col; instr, 62-63, Univ Del; instr, 63, Univ Pa; Asst prof to assoc prof, 65-77; asst dean arts and sci, 75-94, George Washington Univ; acad admin, Columbian Sch of Arts & Sci, 92-95. **MEMBERSHIPS** Amer Hist Assoc; Medieval Acad of Amer, Renaissance Soc of Amer. **RESEARCH** Italian states, commerce and individuals in the eastern Mediterranean; 14th & 15th cent, & its effects on western culture, soc & politics **SELECTED PUBLICATIONS** Coauth, The Lost Fifth Book of the Life of Pope Paul II, Stud in the Renaissance, 70; art, Caffa, Pera, Dictionary of the Middle Ages, New York, 82-89. **CONTACT ADDRESS** Dept of History, The George Washington Univ, Washington, DC 20052. **EMAIL** aandrews@gwu.edu

ANDREWS, GEORGE REID
PERSONAL Born 04/10/1951, New Haven, CT, m, 1974, 3 children **DISCIPLINE** LATIN AMERICAN HISTORY **EDUCATION** Dartmouth Col, BA, 72; Univ Wis-Madison, MA, 74, PhD(hist), 78. **CAREER** Librn, Shattuck Libr, 77-78; staff assoc, Social Sci Res Coun, 78-81; asst prof to prof hist, Univ Pittsburgh, 81-. **HONORS AND AWARDS** Herfurth Awd, Univ WI-Madison, 81; Whitaker Prize, Middle Atlantic Coun on Latin Am Studies, 93; Guggenheim fel, 96. **MEMBERSHIPS** Latin Am Studies Asn; Conf Latin Am Hist; AHA. **RESEARCH** Race and class relations; Spanish American independence movements; urbanization. **SELECTED PUBLICATIONS** Auth, Toward a Re-evaluation of the Latin American Family Firm, Inter-Am Econ Affairs, 76; Race Versus Class Association: The Afro-Argentines of Buenos Aires, 1850-1900, J Latin Am Studies, 79; The Afro-Argentine Officers of Buenos Aires Province, 1800-1860, J of Negro Hist, 79; The Afro-Argentines of Buenos Aires, 1800-1900, Univ WI Press, 80; Spanish American Independence: A Structural Analysis, Latin Am Perspectives, 85; Latin American Workers, J of Soc Hist, 87; Comparing the Comparers: White Supremacy in the United States and South Africa, J of Soc Hist, 87; Black and White Workers: Sao Paulo, Brazil, 1888-1928, Hispanic Am Hist Rev, 88; coauth, The Abolition of Slavery and the Aftermath of Emancipation in Brazil, Duke Univ Press, 88, auth, Blacks and Whites in Sao Paulo, Brazil, 1888-1988, Univ WI Press, 91; Black Political Protest in Sao Paulo, Brazil, 1888-1988, J of Latin Am Studies, 92; Racial Inequality in Brazil and the United States: A Statistical Comparison, J of Soc Hist, 92; co-ed, The Social Construction of Democracy, 1870-1990, NY Univ Press, 95; auth, Brazilian Racial Democracy: An American Counterpoint, J of Contemp Hist, 96; Black Workers in the Export Years: Latin American, 1880-1930, Int Labor and Working- Class Hist, 97. **CONTACT ADDRESS** Dept Hist, Univ of Pittsburgh, 3p38 Forbes Quad, Pittsburgh, PA 15260-0001. **EMAIL** reid1@pitt.edu

ANDRIEN, KENNETH JAMES
PERSONAL Born 03/15/1951, Upper Darby, PA, m, 2 children **DISCIPLINE** LATIN AMERICAN HISTORY, SPANISH HISTORY **EDUCATION** Trinity Col, BA, 73; Duke Univ, MA, 75, PhD(hist), 77. **CAREER** Asst prof Hist, 78-84, assoc prof , 85-94, prof hist, OH State Univ, 95-. **HONORS AND AWARDS** Phi Beta Kappa. **MEMBERSHIPS** AHA; Latin Am Studies Asn; Conf Latin Am Hist. **RESEARCH** Political, social and economic history of the Andean Region, 16th-19th centuries. **SELECTED PUBLICATIONS** Auth, Crisis and Decline: The Viceroyalty of Peru in the Seventeenth Century, Univ NM Press, 85; The Kingdom of Quito, 1690-1830: The State and Regional Development, Cambridge Univ Press, 95; co-ed, with Rolena Adorno, Transatlantic Encounters: Europeans and Andeans in the Sixteenth century, Univ CA Press, 91; with Lyman L. Johnson, The Political Economy of Spanish America in the Age of Revolution, 1750-1850, Univ NM Press, 94; and articles in Past and Present, Hispanic Am Hist Rev, J Latin Am Studies, and The Americas. **CONTACT ADDRESS**

Dept Hist, Ohio State Univ, Columbus, 230 W 17th Ave, Columbus, OH 43210-1367. **EMAIL** andrien.1@osu.edu

ANDRONIKOV, SERGEI V.
PERSONAL Born 09/25/1957, Moscow, Russia, m, 1982, 1 child **DISCIPLINE** GEOGRAPHY **EDUCATION** Moscow State Univ, MSc, 80; Dokuchaev Soil Inst, Russia, PhD, 87. **CAREER** Sr. Researcher, Dokuchaev Soil Inst Russia, 90-98; NATO Royal Soc Res Fel, Stirling Univ UK, 96-98; Asst Prof, Univ of Central Ark, 98-. **MEMBERSHIPS** AAG, Ark Geog Soc. **RESEARCH** GIS, Remote Sensing, Environmental Geography. **SELECTED PUBLICATIONS** Auth, "The influence of human activity on ecological processes in landscapes and on the peculiarities of soil formation in the irrigated zone," in Agroecology and fertility of soils, (Leningrad, 86); auth, "Environmental impact on landscapes in irrigated zone of Turkmenia," in Agroecology and fertility of soils, (Leningrad, 86); coauth, "Microscopic fungi in the tropical soils of Laos," Eurasian Soil Sci 26 (94); auth, Agroecological peculiarities of soils in dry subtropics, (Moscow), 88; auth, "The application of Remote Sensing data, obtained from the system 'Fragment' for soil-ecological monitoring," Results of explorations of V. V. Dokuchaev Soil Inst 43, (87); auth, "The utilization of Remote Sensing information of different resolution for ecological and agricultural purposes," Results of explorations of V. V. Dokuchaev Soil Inst 44, (88); auth, "Application computer system 'ALES' for determining soil-terrain, biophysical conditions due to current and future climate in the basin of the river Rhine," Comput Appln for determinational ecol suitability for different land-use types in the Rhine Basin, Wageningen (94); coauth, Soils of humid tropics of Laos and their rational Land Use, (Moscow), 96; coauth, "A geostatical basis for spatial variability of heavy metals on contaminated lands," in Air, Water and Soil Pollution (in press); coauth, "Spatial analysis of heavy metal behaviors at contaminated sites," in Environmental Management (in press). **CONTACT ADDRESS** Dept Polit Sci and Geog, Univ of Central Arkansas, 201 Donaghey Ave, Conway, AR 72035-5003. **EMAIL** sergeia@mail.uca.edu

ANGEL, MARC D.
PERSONAL Born 07/25/1945, Seattle, WA, m, 1967, 3 children **DISCIPLINE** HISTORY **EDUCATION** Yeshiva Col BA 67; Yeshiva Univ Grad Sch, MS 70, PhD 75; City Col NYork, MA 70. **CAREER** Shearith Israel NYC, rabbi 69-. **HONORS AND AWARDS** Nat Jewish Book Awd **MEMBERSHIPS** RCA **RESEARCH** Hist and culture of Jews, Spanish and Portuguese backgrounds. **SELECTED PUBLICATIONS** Auth,"LaAmerica: The Sephandic Experience in the U.S.," Jewik Publication Society, Philadelphia, 82; auth, Voices in Exile: A Study in Sephardic Intellectual History, Hoboken NJ, KTAV pub 91; The Essential Pele Yoetz, condensed/trans, NY, Sepher-Hermon Press 91; auth, Seeking Good Speaking Peace: Collected Essays of Rabbi Marc D. Angel, ed, Hayyim J. Angel, Hoboken NJ, KTAV Pub 94; auth, Rhythms of Jewish Living, Northvale NJ, Jason Aronson Pub 97; The Orphaned Adult, NV NJ, Jason Aronson Pub 97; Exploring the Thought of Rabbi Joseph B. Soloveitchik, ed, Hoboken NJ, 97; auth, "The Jews of Rhods," Sephr-Herman Press, 78, 80, 98; auth, "Living Truth and Peace: The Grand Religious Worldview of Rassi Benzio Uziel, NV, NJ, Jason Aronson, 99. **CONTACT ADDRESS** Shearith Israel, 8 West 70th Street, New York, NY 10023.

ANGELOU, MAYA
PERSONAL Born 04/04/1928, St. Louis, MO, d **DISCIPLINE** LITERATURE, HISTORY **CAREER** Author, poet, playwright, stage and screen producer, director, actress, 54-; Southern Christian Leadership Conference, coordinator, 59-60; Arab Observer Egypt, associate editor, 61-62; University of Ghana, asst administrator, 63-66; African Review, editor, 64-66; California State University, Wichita State University, visiting professor; Wake Forest Univ, Department of Humanities, Reynolds Prof of Am Studies, 74-. **HONORS AND AWARDS** 32 Honorary Degrees; Pulitzer Prize Nomination, "Just Give Me A Cool Drink of Water 'fore I Diiie," 1972; Tony Awd Nomination, "Look Away," 1975; Ladies Home Journal, one of the Women of the Year in Communications, 1976; Emmy Awd Nomination, Performance, "Roots," 1977; Distinguished Woman of North Carolina, 1992; Essence Magazine, Woman of the Year, 1992; Horatio Alger Awd, 1992; Women In Film, Crystal Awd, 1992; American Academy of Achievement, Golden Plate Awd, 1990; Horatio Alger Awds Dinner Chairman, 1993; National Society for the Prevention of Cruelty to Children, London, England, NSPCC Maya Angelou CPT and Family Centre, London, England, center dedication, June 20, 1991; NAACP, Image Awd, Literary Work, Nonfiction, 1998. **MEMBERSHIPS** American Federation of Television & Radio Artists; board of trustees, American Film Institute, 1975-; Directors Guild; Actors' Equity; Women's Prison Assn. **SELECTED PUBLICATIONS** Author, works include: I Know Why the Caged Bird Sings, 1970; Just Give Me A Cool Drink of Water 'Fore I Die, 1971; Gather Together in My Name, 1974; Oh Pray My Wings Are Gonna Fit Me Well, 1975; Singin & Swingin & Getting Merry Like Christmas, 1976; And Still I Rise, 1978; The Heart of a Woman, 1981; Shaker, Why Don't You Sing? 1983; All God's Children Need Traveling Shoes, 1986; Mrs Flowers: A Moment of Friendship, 1986; Wouldn't Take Nothing for My Journey Now, Random, 1993; poems: Maya Angelou, 1986; Now Sheba Sings the Song, 1987; I Shall Not Be Moved, Random House, 1990; plays include: Cabraret for Freedom, 1960; The Least of These, 1966; Ajax, 1974; And Still I Rise, 1976; screenplays include: Georgia Georgia, 1972; All Day Long, 1974; PBS-TV Documentaries: "Who Cares About Kids" "Kindred Spirits," KERA-TV, Dallas, TX; "Rainbow In The Clouds," series, host, writer, WTVS-TV, Detroit, MI; "To The Contrary," Maryland Public Television; lecturer: Nancy Hanks Lecture, American Council for the Arts, 1990; contributing writer: "Brewster Place," mini-series, HARPO Productions; panelist: Institute for the Study of Human Systems, Zermatt, Switzerland, 1990; lyricist: "King Now," theatrical project, London, England; has appeared in numerous plays and TV productions as both an actress and singer; wrote and presented a poem for President Clinton's Swearing-In Ceremonies, 1993; Down in the Delta, director; named UNICEF National Ambassador, 1996. **CONTACT ADDRESS** Dept of Humanities, Wake Forest Univ, PO Box 7314, Winston-Salem, NC 27109.

ANGLIN, DOUGLAS G.
PERSONAL Born 12/16/1923, Toronto, ON, Canada **DISCIPLINE** POLITICAL SCIENCE, HISTORY **EDUCATION** Univ Toronto, BA, 48; Corpus Christi Col & Nuffield Col, Univ Oxford, BA, 50, MA, 54, DPhil, 56. **CAREER** Asst to assoc prof polit sci, Univ Man, 51-58; assoc prof to prof, 58-89, PROF EMER, CARLETON UNIV, 93-; assoc res fel, Nigerian Inst Soc Econ Res, Univ Ibadan, 62-63; vice chancellor, Univ Zambia, 65-69; res assoc, Ctr Int Stud, Princeton Univ, 69-70. **MEMBERSHIPS** African Stud Asn (US); Can Inst Int Affairs; Can Polit Sci Asn; Can Asn African Stud (pres 73-74). **SELECTED PUBLICATIONS** Auth, The St Pierre and Miquelon Affaire of 1941, 66; auth, Zambia Crisis Behaviour: Confronting Rhodesia's Unilateral Declaration of Independence 1965-1966, 94; coauth, Zambia's Foreign Policy: Studies in Diplomacy and Dependence, 79; co-ed, Africa: The Political Pattern, 61; co-ed, Canada, Scandinavia and Southern Africa, 79; co-ed, Conflict and Change in Southern Africa, 79. **CONTACT ADDRESS** Dept of Political Science, Carleton Univ, 1125 Colonel By Dr, Ottawa, ON, Canada K1S 5B6. **EMAIL** d_anglin@carleton.ca

ANGUS, MARGARET
PERSONAL Born 05/23/1908, Chinook, MT **DISCIPLINE** HISTORY **EDUCATION** Univ Mont, BA, 30; Queen's Univ, LLD, 73. **CAREER** Dir radio, Queen's Univ, 57-68; mus cur, 68-85; dir, Ont Hist Stud Ser, 72-88; pres, Frontenac Hist Found, 73-76, 79-81; gov, Heritage Can, 74-79; dir, Ont Heritage Found, 75-81. **MEMBERSHIPS** Ont Hist Soc (pres 69-71); Archit Conservancy Ont; Kingston Hist Soc (pres 72-74); Cataraqui Archaeol Res Found (dir 83-84). **SELECTED PUBLICATIONS** Auth, The Old Stones of Kingston, 66; auth, The Story of Bellevue House, 67; auth, History of Kingston General Hospital, vol I, 72, vol II, 94; contribur, Oliver Mowat's Ontario, 72; contribur, Kingston 300, 73; contribur, John A. Lived Here, 84; contribur, Queen's History in Names, 91; contribur, Summerhill, Queen's University at Kingston, 97; ser ed, Buildings of Architectural and Historic Significance in Kingston. **CONTACT ADDRESS** 1201-322 Brock St, Kingston, ON, Canada K7L 1S9.

ANKENY, RACHEL A.
PERSONAL Born 04/13/1967, Detroit, IL **DISCIPLINE** HISTORY, PHILOSOPHY **EDUCATION** St. John's Col, BA, 88; Univ Pittsburgh, MA, 95; MA, 96; PhD, 97. **CAREER** Asst prof, Univ of Pittsburgh, 97-98; asst prof, Connecticut Col, 98-. **HONORS AND AWARDS** Javits Fel, 92-96; Mellon Fel, 96-97; Davis Ctr Fel, Princeton Univ, 99-00. **MEMBERSHIPS** Am Philos Assoc; Philos of Sci Assoc; Hist of Sci Soc; Am Soc of Bioethics and Humanities; Sigma Xi. **RESEARCH** History and Philosophy of biomedical sciences, bioethics. **CONTACT ADDRESS** History and Philosophy of Science, Connecticut Col, 270 Mohegan Ave, Box 5548, New London, CT 06320. **EMAIL** raank@conncoll.edu

ANNA, TIMOTHY
PERSONAL Born 11/03/1944, Lexington, KY **DISCIPLINE** HISTORY **EDUCATION** Duke Univ, BA, 66, MA, 68, PhD, 69. **CAREER** Asst prof to prof, 69-97, DISTINGUISHED PROF HISTORY, UNIV MANITOBA, 97-. **HONORS AND AWARDS** Rh Inst res award hum, 84; Killam res fel, 94-96; fel, Royal Soc Can, 95. **RESEARCH** Latin American history, 19th and 20th centuries; Mexico, Peru, Spain. **SELECTED PUBLICATIONS** Auth, The Fall of the Royal Government in Mexico City, 78; auth, The Fall of the Royal Government in Peru, 79; auth, Spain and the Loss of America, 83; auth, The Mexican Empire of Iturbide, 90; auth, Forging Mexico 1821-1835, 98. **CONTACT ADDRESS** Dept of History, Univ of Manitoba, 28 Trueman Walk, Winnipeg, MB, Canada R3T 5V5. **EMAIL** anna@cc.umanitoba.ca

ANNIS, JAMES L.
PERSONAL Born 05/13/1957, Rockledge, FL, s **DISCIPLINE** HISTORY **EDUCATION** Hanover Col, BA, 78; Ball State Univ, MA, 80, PhD, 85. **CAREER** Assoc prof of Hist, Montgomery Col, 86-. **MEMBERSHIPS** Org of Am Hists, Southern Hist Asn. **RESEARCH** 20th century South and American political history. **SELECTED PUBLICATIONS** Auth, Howard Baker: Conciliation in an Age of Crisis; coauth with Sen William H. Frist, Tennessee Senators, 1911-2001: Portraits of Leadership in a Century of Change. **CONTACT ADDRESS** Dept Hist & Pol Sci, Montgomery Col, Rockville, 51 Mannakee St, Rockville, MD 20850-1101. **EMAIL** jannis@mc.cc.md.us

ANTHONY, DAVID HENRY, III
PERSONAL Born 04/28/1952, Brooklyn, NY, m **DISCIPLINE** HISTORY **EDUCATION** NYork Univ, AB 1968-72; Univ of Wis-Madison, MA History 1975, DPhil History 1983. **CAREER** Fulbright Fellow Dept of State, rsch assoc 1976-77; Univ of Dar es Salaam Tanzania, rsch assoc 1976-77; Clark Univ, visiting prof 1979; Coppin State Coll, instructor of history 1980-84; Univ of Oregon, Eugene, OR, assistant professor of history, 84-88; Univ of California, Oakes College, Santa Cruz, assistant professor, currently. **HONORS AND AWARDS** Fulbright Hays Awd Fulbright Found Dept of State 1976-77; President's Humanities Fellowship, University of California, 1990-91. **MEMBERSHIPS** Curr spec Madison Metro Sch Dist 1977-78; consul Swahili Anteiro Pietila Helen Winternitz 1980; rsch affiliate Univ of FL Ctr for African studies 1982; visiting prof History Dept Towson State Univ 1982-83; judge Gr Baltimore History Fair 1982-84; mem Phi Alpha Theta 1983-; mem Fulbright Alumni Assn 1981-. **CONTACT ADDRESS** Univ of California, Santa Cruz, 1156 High St, Santa Cruz, CA 95064.

ANTLIFF, MARK
DISCIPLINE ART HISTORY **EDUCATION** Yale Univ, PhD. **CAREER** Assoc prof, Duke Univ. **RESEARCH** Art in Europe before 1945; interrelation of art and philos. **SELECTED PUBLICATIONS** Auth, Inventing Bergson: Cultural Politics and the Parisian Avant-Garde; co-auth, Fascist Visions: Art and Ideology in France and Italy. **CONTACT ADDRESS** Dept of Art and Art Hist, Duke Univ, East Duke Building, Durham, NC 27706. **EMAIL** antliff@duke.edu

ANTON, HARLEY F.
PERSONAL Born 06/26/1951, McComb, MS, m, 1985 **DISCIPLINE** HISTORY, EDUCATION **EDUCATION** Samford, Univ, BA, 73; Louisiana State Univ, MA, 76. **CAREER** Instr, Louisiana State Univ, 80-87; asst prof, Middle Tenn State Univ, 88-. **HONORS AND AWARDS** Tenn Dev Educator of the Year, 97. **MEMBERSHIPS** NADE. **RESEARCH** Standardized testing, cognitive processing. **SELECTED PUBLICATIONS** Coauth, Key to Better College Reading, Townsend Pr, 96; coauth, Improving Reading Comprehension Skills, Townsend Pr, 94. **CONTACT ADDRESS** Dept Dev Studies, Middle Tennessee State Univ, 1301 E Main St, Murfreesboro, TN 37132-0001. **EMAIL** hanton@mtsu.edu

APENA, IGHO ADELINE
PERSONAL Born 06/21/1950, Nigeria, m, 1999 **DISCIPLINE** HISTORY **EDUCATION** Ibadan, Nigeria, BA; Univ London, MA; Univ Lagos, Nigeria, PhD. **CAREER** Lib officer, Kings Col, Univ of Aberdeen Scotland; Off, Dept of Hea and Soc Security, London; Lib Off, Brit Coun, London; Off, Greater London Coun; Manager Crothal and Co, London; Vis Prof, African Hist/Women Stud, Unif Guyana,; Consult, Women non-governmental organizations, Georgetown Guyana; Lect/Res fel, Oral Hist Proj, Univ of the West Indies, Jamaica; Consult, African Caribbean Inst of Jamaica; assoc prof, Hist/women studs, Sage Cols. **HONORS AND AWARDS** Spec Female Awd (Nigeria); British Coun Overseas Awd; McCllelan Fel, Humanities; dist person award, Isoko Women Asn. **MEMBERSHIPS** African Stud Asn of the US; Soc for the Comp Stud of Civilization; Third World Stud Asn; NYork State African Stud Asn; African Women Scholars; Am Hist Asn. **RESEARCH** Human rights of women global context; women sexuality and global change; women in the African experience; women in developing world; women in developing countries; the African Caribbean hist/culture. **SELECTED PUBLICATIONS** Auth, Guyanese Women's Reactions to Structural Adjustment Program, 95; auth, Colinization, Commerce and Entrepreneurship in Nigeria. The Western Delta 1914-1960, 97; coauth, African and Its Peoples, 98. **CONTACT ADDRESS** Russell Sage Col, Troy, NY 12180. **EMAIL** apenaa@sage.edu

APONIUK, NATALIA
PERSONAL Born Gronlid, SK, Canada **DISCIPLINE** UKRAINIAN CANADIAN STUDIES **EDUCATION** Univ Sask, BA, 62; Univ Toronto. MA, 63, PhD, 74. **CAREER** Tchg asst, Slavic Langs, Univ Toronto, 63-65, 66-67, 73-74; asst prof, Reed Col, 67-72; lectr, Univ Alta, 74-75; instr, ESL, 75-77; asst prof, 77-86, Dir, Ctr Ukranian Can Studs 82-93, Assoc Prof, German & Slavic Studs, Univ Manitoba, 86-. **HONORS AND AWARDS** Hantelman Postgrad Fel, Univ Sask, 62-63; Prov Ont Govt Fel, 63-67; Taras Schevchenko Memorial Scholar, 64-65; Ukrainian Woman of Year, Winnipeg, 86; Univ Man Outreach Awd, 92; Univ Man Awd Serv, 93. **MEMBERSHIPS** Conf Ukrainian Studs; Can Asn Slavists; Can Women's Studs Asn. **SELECTED PUBLICATIONS** Auth, Perspectives on an Ethnic Bestseller: All of Baba's Children, in Can Ethnic Studs, 10, 78; auth, Some Images of Ukrainian Women in Canadian Literature, in J Ukrainian Studs, 8, 83; auth, Ukrainian Canadian Heritage Studies, in Horizons, 1, 92. **CONTACT AD-**

DRESS Dept of German & Slavic Stud, Univ of Manitoba, Winnipeg, MB, Canada R3T 2N2. **EMAIL** aponiuk@cc.UManitoba.CA

APOSTOLOS-CAPPADONA, DIANE
PERSONAL Born 05/10/1948, Trenton, NJ **DISCIPLINE** AMERICAN CULTURAL HISTORY; RELIGION AND CULTURE **EDUCATION** Cath Univ of Amer, MA, 79; George Wash Univ, BA, 70, MA, 73, PhD, 88. **CAREER** Lectr, relig, Mt Vernon Col, 80-85; lectr, relig, George Wash Univ, 81-86; adj facul, christ and art, Pacific Sch of Relig, 85-86, 88-92; adj prof, art and culture, Liberal Studies prog, Georgetown Univ, 85-; adj prof, Ctr for Muslim-Christian understanding, Georgetown Univ, 96-. **HONORS AND AWARDS** Sr fel, Ctr for the Study of World Relig, Harvard Univ, 96-97; res grant, Amer Acad of Relig; res grant, Amer Coun of Learned Soc; NEH grant; Award for excellence in the Arts, The Newington-Cropsey Foundation, 00. **MEMBERSHIPS** Amer Acad of Relig; Amer Asn of Mus; Amer Asn of Univ Women; Amer Studies Asn; Col Art Asn; Col Theol Soc; Congress on Res in Dance; Soc for Art, Relig, and Contemporary Culture. **RESEARCH** Images of women in religious art; Iconography of the Black Madonna; Relationship between art, gender, religion and culture; Iconography of Mary Magdalene. **SELECTED PUBLICATIONS** Auth, The Spirit and the Vision: The Influence of Christian Romanticism on the Development of 19th-century American Art, Scholar's Press, 95; co-ed, Women, Creativity and the Arts, Contiuum Publ, 95; auth, Encyclopedia of Women in Religious Art, Continuum Publ, 96; auth, Picasso's Guernica as Mythic Iconoclasm: An Eliadean Reading of Modern Art, Myth and Method, Univ Va Press, 96; auth, Picturing Devotion: Rogier's Saint Luke Drawing the Virgin and Child, Saint Luke Drawing the Virgin and Child: Essays in Context, Brepols, 97; entries, The Dictionary of Art and The New Catholic Encyclopedia, vol 19: suppl, 96; auth, Dictionary of Women in Religious Art, Oxford Univ Press, 98; auth, Dictionary of Christian Art, Continuum Publ, 98; auth, Beyond Belief: The Artistic Journey and two entries in Beyond Belief: Modern Art and the Religious Imagination, The Nat Gallery of Victoria, Melbourne, 98; entries, Encycl of Comparative Iconography, 98. **CONTACT ADDRESS** Center for Muslim-Christian Understanding, Georgetown Univ, ICC #260, Washington, DC 20057-1052. **EMAIL** apostold@georgetown.edu

APPEL, SUSAN K.
PERSONAL Born 07/07/1946, Toledo, OH **DISCIPLINE** ART HISTORY **EDUCATION** BFA, Bowling Green State Univ, 68; MA, art hist, Univ Iowa, Iowa City, 72; PhD, art history, Univ Ill at Urbana-Champaign, 90. **CAREER** Tchg asst, Univ Iowa, Iowa City, Iowa, 69-72; photographer and archit surv, Iowa State Hist Preserv Prog ,Iowa City, Iowa, 74; cons archit hist, City of Muscatine, Iowa, 74; cons archit hist, Environ Res Ctr, Iowa City, Iowa, 74-77; instr, art, Augustana Col, Rock Island, Ill, 74-76; asst prof, art, Phillips Univ, Enid, Okla, 76-79; visiting lectr, 82-83, course coord, 81-82, tchg asst, 79-81, Univ of Ill at Urbana-Champaign, 79-83; cons archit hist, The Urbana Grp, Urbana, Ill, 92; assoc chair for curric, 99-01, acting assoc chair, 98-99, assoc prof, art hist, 92-, asst prof, art hist, 89-92, lectr and instr, 83-89, Ill State Univ, Normal, Ill. **HONORS AND AWARDS** Univ Large Grant, Ill State Univ, 99-00; Univ Small Grant, Ill State Univ, 98; Reader, Advan Placement Test in Art Hist, Educ Testing Svc, Trenton, NJ State Col, 94-98, 99-; Preserv Svc Heritage Awd, Preserv and Conserv Asn of Champaign, 97; Appointed Mem of the City of Champaign, Ill, Hist Preserv Comn, 97-; nominee outstanding tchr, Dept of Art as Col of Fine Arts, 96; Appointed mem of the Ill Hist Sites Adv Coun, 93-96, 99-01; Univ Tchg Initiative Awd, Ill State Univ, 95; Col Outstanding Res Awd, Col of Fine Arts, Ill State Univ, 94; Soc for Indust Archaeol/Hist Amer Eng Record Fel, 92-93; Univ Res Grant and Small Grant, Ill State Univ, 92-93; Univ Res Grant, Ill State Univ, 90-91; Col of Fine Arts Facul Res Initiative, Ill State Univ, 88; Computerized Instr Rev Grant, Col of Fine Arts, Ill State Univ, summer, 86; Rosann S. Berry Fel, Soc of Archit Hist, 85; Res Travel Grants, Sch of Art and Design, Univ Ill, 84, 85; Dissertation Res Grant, Grad Col, Univ Ill, summer 83; Allerton Amer Traveling Scholar, Sch of Archit, Univ Ill, summer, 80; Victorian Soc in Amer Scholar to its summer sem in Victorian archit, Boston, 80; Honor Soc of Phi Kappa Phi, Univ Ill, Univ fel and res asst, Univ Ill, 81-82; participant, NEH Summer Sem for Col Tchrs, Urban Hist of the Mediterranean and Near East, Univ Calif Berkeley, summer, 78; Univ Iowa scholar, Delta Phi Delta, Nat Art Hon, Bowling Green State Univ; Two-Dimensional Design and Life Drawing awards, Bowling Green State Univ. **MEMBERSHIPS** Col Art Asn; Landmarks Preserv Coun of Ill; Midwest Art Hist Soc; Nat Trust for Hist Preserv; Soc for Indust Arheol; Soc of Archit Hist; Vernacular Archit Forum; Victorian Soc in Amer; Women's Caucus for Art. **RESEARCH** Architectural development of pre-Prohibition American breweries; American architectural history, including vernacular architecture; Historic preservation issues related to American architecture. **SELECTED PUBLICATIONS** Auth, Historic Breweries in the Contemporary Landscape, From Industry to Industrial Heritage, Proceedings of the Ninth International Conference on the Conservation of the Industrial Heritage in Montreal/Ottawa, Canada, May 29-June 2, 1994, 99-110, Ottawa, Can Soc for Indust Heritage, 98; Chicago and the Rise of Brewery Architecture, Chicago Hist, Mag of the Chicago Hist Soc, XXIV, 1, 4-19, spring, 95; Building Milwaukee's Breweries: an Overview of Pre-Prohibition Brewery Architecture in the Cream City, Wisc Mag of Hist, 78, 3, 163-199, spring, 95; book rev, Breweries of Wisconsin, by Jerry Apps, Madison, Univ Wisc Press, 1992, in Monatshefte fur deutschen Unterricht, deutsche Sprache und Litatur, LXXXVI, 2, 262-264, summer 94; contrib, Chicago: An Industrial Guide, Chicago, Pub Works Hist Soc, 91. **CONTACT ADDRESS** 307 N. Garfield Av., Champaign, IL 61821-2615. **EMAIL** skappel@ilstu.edu

APPIAH, KWAME ANTHONY
DISCIPLINE AFRO-AMERICAN STUDIES AND PHILOSOPHY **EDUCATION** Cambridge Univ, England, BA, PhD. **CAREER** Prof. **MEMBERSHIPS** Past pres, Socr African Philos in NAm & is an ed of Transition. **RESEARCH** Epistemology and philosophy of language; African philosophy; philosophical problems of race and racism; Afro-American and African literature and literary theory. **SELECTED PUBLICATIONS** Auth, My Father's House: Africa in the Philosophy of Culture, 92 & Color Conscious: The Political Morality of Race, 96. **CONTACT ADDRESS** Dept of Philosophy, Harvard Univ, 8 Garden St, Cambridge, MA 02138. **EMAIL** appiah@fas.harvard.edu

APPLEBAUM, DAVID
DISCIPLINE MODERN EUROPEAN HISTORY **EDUCATION** Brooklyn Col, BA; Univ Wis, PhD, 73. **CAREER** Instr, coordr, semester abroad prog, Rowan Col of NJ. **RESEARCH** French cultural, social, and legal history. **SELECTED PUBLICATIONS** Published a number of articles in French cultural, social, and legal history. **CONTACT ADDRESS** Rowan Univ, Glassboro, NJ 08028-1701.

APPLEBY, JOYCE
PERSONAL Born 04/09/1929, Omaha, NE, w, 3 children **DISCIPLINE** HISTORY **EDUCATION** Stanford Univ, BA, 50; Univ CA, MA, 59; PhD, 66, Claremont Graduate Sch. **CAREER** Asst prof, 67-70, assoc prof, 70-73, assoc dean, coll of arts and letters, 74-75, prof, 73-81 San Diego State Univ; chair of the dept of hist, 87-88, UCLA; harmsworth prof, 90-91, prof, 81-, Oxford. **MEMBERSHIPS** Elected member, Amer Philosophical Soc, 93; UCLA Coll of Letters and Sci distinguished Prof Award, 93; Council of the Smithsonian Institution, 94-98; delegate, Amer Council of Learned Societies, 94-98; John Simon Guggenheim Memorial Found Fel, 94-95; council, Amer Historical Assn, 96-99; Pres, Amer Historical Assn, 97. **RESEARCH** Early modern England, France, US. **SELECTED PUBLICATIONS** Ed, The Popular Sources of American Capitalism, Studiesin American Political Development, 96;Recollections of the Early Republic: Selected Autobiographies, 97; auth, The Personal Roots of the First American Temperance Movement, American Philosophical Society Proceedings for 1997; The Power of History, American Historical Review, 98; Ed with Terence Ball, The Political Writings of Thomas Jefferson; auth, Inheriting the Revolution: The First Generation of Americans; auth, Telling the Truth About History; auth, Liberalism and Republicanism in the Historical Imagination. **CONTACT ADDRESS** 615 Westholme Ave., Los Angeles, CA 90024. **EMAIL** appleby@history.ucla.edu

APPLETON, THOMAS H., JR.
PERSONAL Born 01/15/1950, Memphis, TN **DISCIPLINE** HISTORY **EDUCATION** Univ Memphis, BA, 71; Univ Ky, MA, 73; PhD, 81. **CAREER** asst ed, Ky Hist Soc, 79-81; managing ed, Ky Hist Soc, 81-90; ed in chief, Ky Hist Soc, 90-00; prof, Eastern Ky Univ, 00-. **HONORS AND AWARDS** Phi Beta Kappa. **MEMBERSHIPS** Southern Hist Asn, Southern Asn for Women Historians, Ky Asn of Teachers of Hist. **RESEARCH** Kentucky, the United States. **SELECTED PUBLICATIONS** Co-ed, A Mythic Land Apart: Reassessing Southerners and Their History, Greenwood Press, 97; co-ed, Negotiating the Boundaries of Southern Womanhood, Univ Mo Press, 00. **CONTACT ADDRESS** Hist Dept, Eastern Kentucky Univ, Keith Hall 323, Richmond, KY 40475-3102.

ARBAGI, MARTIN GEORGE
PERSONAL Born 02/16/1940, Brooklyn, NY, m, 1971, 3 children **DISCIPLINE** BYZANTINE HISTORY, EARLY MEDIEVAL HISTORY **EDUCATION** Georgetown Univ, BA, 61; Rutgers Univ, New Brunswick, MA, 63, PhD(hist), 69. **CAREER** Asst prof hist, Univ Maine, Orono, 67-69; asst prof, 69-85, assoc prof, Wright State Univ, 85-, Mem exec comt, Conf Greek, Roman & Byzantine Studies, 75-77, 80- **MEMBERSHIPS** Mediaeval Acad Am, Nat Assoc of Schol, Ohio Class Conf. **RESEARCH** Byzantine East and Latin West to 1100. **SELECTED PUBLICATIONS** Auth, A Tenth-Century Emperor Michael of Constantinople, Speculum, 7/73; The Celibacy of Basil II, Byzantine Studies, 7/75; Byzantium, Germany, the Regnum Italicum and the Magyars in the Tenth-Century, Byzantine Studies, 1/79; Urbs Regia, Continuity, #10, 85. **CONTACT ADDRESS** Dept of Hist, Wright State Univ, Dayton, 3640 Colonel Glenn Hwy, Allyn Hall, Dayton, OH 45435-0002. **EMAIL** arbagi@gemair.com

ARBINO, GARY P.
PERSONAL Born 01/16/1960, North Hollywood, CA, m **DISCIPLINE** ARCHAEOLOGY, OLD TESTAMENT INTERPRETATION **EDUCATION** Humboldt State Univ, BA; Golden Gate Baptist Theol Sem, MDiv, PhD. **CAREER** Asst curator, design dir, Marian Eakins Archaeol Col, 91-98, Curator, 98-; from adj prof to assoc prof, Golden Gate Baptist Theol Sem, 92-. **HONORS AND AWARDS** Will Edd Langford Memorial scholar, 92; Who's Who Among Students In Amer Univ(s) and Col(s), 89, 92; Broadman Seminarian Awd, 89; National Dean's List, 87, 92; supvr, sem library's audio-visual dept and video production studio, 90-96; lib circulation svc, 94-96. **MEMBERSHIPS** Mem, Am Sch(s) of Oriental Res; Soc Biblical Lit; member adv bd, Nat Asn prof(s)of Hebrew; Am Inst of Archaeol. **RESEARCH** Tel Miqne/Ekron Excavations; Bet Shemesh Excavations; Tel Rehov. **SELECTED PUBLICATIONS** Auth, New Eerdmans Dictionary of the Bible, 00. **CONTACT ADDRESS** Golden Gate Baptist Theol Sem, 201 Sem Dr, Mill Valley, CA 94941-3197. **EMAIL** garyarbino@ggbts.edu

ARBURY, STEVE
DISCIPLINE ART HISTORY **EDUCATION** Albion Col, BA magna cum laude, 75; Rutgers Univ, MA, 78, PhD, 92. **CAREER** Librn asst, Albion Col Libr, 74-75; intern/asst to the cur, The Jewish Mus, NY, 76; librn asst, Art Libr, 75-76, instr, 78-80, asst tchr, 79, cofounder/ed, Rutgers Art Rev, 79-81, curatorial asst, Fine Arts Coll, Rutgers Univ, 80-81; instr, Univ Urbino, Italy, 81; adj prof, 84-88, hd, Fine Arts Libr, 84-88, instr, Roanoke Mus Fine Arts, 85; gallery dir, Roanoke Col, 86-88; prof, 88-, cur, Art Hist Vis Rsrc Ctr, 88-98; Dir, RU Art Mus, 98-. **HONORS AND AWARDS** Phi Beta Kappa, Albion Col, 75; Mary Bartlett Cowdrey fel, Rutgers Univ, 79-80; NJ State Grant, Rutgers Univ, 79-80, 80-81; Louis Bevier grad fel, Rutgers Univ, 80-81; Fulbright scholar/Span Govt grant, 81-82, 82-83; Outstanding Young Men of Am Awd, 85; Distinguished Leadership Awd, 86; Men of Achievement Awd, 87; grant, Radford Univ, 93; fac prof develop leave, Radford Univ, 97; Awd of Excellence, The Kemper A. Dobbins Annual Art Exhib, Va Mus of Transp, 97. **MEMBERSHIPS** Col Art Asn of Am; Midwest Art Hist Soc; Southeastern Col Art Conf; Am Soc for Hisp Art Hist Stud; Am Acad of Res Hist of Medieval Spain; Vis Rsrcs Asn; 16th Century Stud Conf; Am Asn of Mus; AAUP. **SELECTED PUBLICATIONS** Auth, Gifford Beal, Arthur B. Frost, Jr, Samuel Halpert, Marsden Hartley, Kinetic Art, Jonas Lie, Joseph Pickett, Joshua Shaw, Maurice Sterne, in ed Matthew Baigell, Dictionary of American Art, Harper & Row, 79; Slide Computerization with FileMaker II Software and the Apple Macintosh SE, Vis Rsrc Assn Bull 17, no 1, 90; Slide Computerization with FileMaker Plus and the Apple Macintosh SE, Southeastern Col Art Conf Rev XI, no 5, 90; Spanish Catafalques of the Golden Age, Rutgers Art Rev 12/13, 91-92; ASA Slide Classification System and Computerized Cataloging: Reference Manual, Newly rev ed, 95; Catafalque, Alonso de Mena, in The Dictionary of Art, 34 vols, MacMillan, 96; auth, "Abduction," "Judgment," "Laughter," in The Encyclopedia of Comparative Iconography, 2 vols. Fitzroy Dearborn, 98; auth, Catalog, Selections from the Permanent Collection, RU Art Museum, 99. **CONTACT ADDRESS** Art Dept, Radford Univ, PO Box 6965, Radford, VA 24142. **EMAIL** sarbury@runet.edu

ARCHDEACON, THOMAS JOHN
PERSONAL Born 07/05/1942, New York, NY, m, 1968, 3 children **DISCIPLINE** HISTORY **EDUCATION** Fordham Univ, BA, 64; Columbia Univ, MA, 65, PhD, 71. **CAREER** Capt, asst prof, 69-72, US Military Acad; asst prof, 72-76, assoc prof, 76-82, prof, 82-, Univ Wisc-Madison. **MEMBERSHIPS** Amer Hist Assn; Org of Amer Hist; Irish Amer Cult Inst; Amer Conf for Irish Stud; Ctr for Migration Stud. **RESEARCH** Immigration. **SELECTED PUBLICATIONS** Auth, Correlation and Regression Analysis: A Historian's Guide, Univ Wisc Press, 94; auth, Becoming American: An Ethnic History, Free Press, 83; auth, New York City, 1664-1710: Conquest and Change, Cornell Univ Press, 76. **CONTACT ADDRESS** Dept of History, Univ of Wisconsin, Madison, 455 N Park St, Madison, WI 53706. **EMAIL** tjarchde@facstaff.wisc.edu

ARCISZEWSKA, BARBARA
DISCIPLINE ART HISTORY **EDUCATION** Courtauld Inst, London, MA, 86; Univ Toronto, PhD, 94. **CAREER** Postdoctoral fel, Univ Toronto, 94-96; Yale Ctr for British Art, 96; Canadian Ctr for Archit, 97-. **HONORS AND AWARDS** SSHRC post-doctoral fel, 94-96; res fel, Yale Univ Mellon Ctr for British Art, 96. **MEMBERSHIPS** Col Art Assoc; Soc of Archit Hist; Soc for Eighteenth Century Stud. **RESEARCH** Art and architectural history from the Renaissance to the eighteenth century. **SELECTED PUBLICATIONS** Auth, A Villa Fit for A King: The Role of Palladian Architecture in the Ascending of the House of Hanover under George I, in Mandel, ed, Artas Propagande, RACAR, 92; auth, the Church of Sint Jan in Hertogenbosch: Defining the Boundaries of Patronage in Late Medieval Methelandith Architecture, in Wilkins, ed, The Search for a Patron in the Middle Ages and Renaissance, Mellen, 96. **CONTACT ADDRESS** 162-4020 Dundas St West, Toronto, ON, Canada M6S 4W6. **EMAIL** arciszew@chass.utoronto.ca

ARGEN, RALPH J., III
PERSONAL Born 07/26/1958, Buffalo, NY, m, 1983, 3 children **DISCIPLINE** GEOLOGY; LAW; PHILOSOPHY **EDUCATION** Syracuse Univ, BS, 81; State Univ NYork Buffalo, MS, 88, MA, 89, JD, 93, PhD, 94. **CAREER** Construction mgt, Claims Consultant. **MEMBERSHIPS** PA Bar Asn; Wash DC Bar Asn. **RESEARCH** Construction law; Ethics; Environmental Ethics and Value Theory. **SELECTED PUBLICATIONS** Auth, The Commensurability of Environmental Geology and Petroleum Geology, AAPG Bulletin, vol 74, 600, May 90. **CONTACT ADDRESS** 17711 Crystal Cove Pl, Tampa, FL 33549. **EMAIL** rargenl@tampabay.rr.com

ARGERSINGER, JO ANN E.
PERSONAL Born 02/16/1953, Birmingham, AL, m, 1973 **DISCIPLINE** HISTORY **EDUCATION** Univ Md, BA, 74; George Wash Univ, MA, 76; PhD, 80. **CAREER** Instr to Asst Prof, Dickinson Col, 78-83; Asst Prof to Prof and Provost, 83-98; Prof and Chancellor, S Ill Univ, 98-. **HONORS AND AWARDS** Fel, Rockefeller, 88; Henry Kaiser Res Grant, 88; NEH Summer Seminar, 86; Distinguished Alumna of the Year, 95; Dean's Merit Awd, 00; Dickinson Col Parents' Prize for Dissertation, 80. **MEMBERSHIPS** Am Hist Asn; Org of Am Hist; Soc Sci Hist; S Hist. **RESEARCH** U.S. Labor, Economic, Gender and the history of higher education. **SELECTED PUBLICATIONS** Co-auth, The American Journey, Prentice-Hall, 98; auth, Making the Amalgamated, Johns Hopkins Univ Press, 99. **CONTACT ADDRESS** Dept Hist, So Illinois Univ, Carbondale, 285 Lake Indian Hills Dr, Carbondale, IL 62901. **EMAIL** jarger@siu.edu

ARGERSINGER, PETER
PERSONAL Born 10/28/1944, Dayton, OH, m, 1973 **DISCIPLINE** HISTORY **EDUCATION** Univ Kans, AB, 65; Univ Wisc, MA, 66; PhD, 70. **CAREER** Instr, W Tex State Univ, 70-71; asst prof to prof, Univ Md, 71-98; prof, S Ill Univ, 98-. **HONORS AND AWARDS** Binkley-Stephenson Award, Org of Am Hist, 90; Woodrow Wilson Fel, 90-91; Andrew Mellon Fel, Mass Hist Soc, 91-92. **MEMBERSHIPS** Am Hist Asn; Org of Am Hist; Agricultural Hist Soc; Soc Sci Hist Asn; Soc for the Hist of the Gilded Age and Progressive Era; W Hist Asn. **RESEARCH** American Political History; American Rural History. **SELECTED PUBLICATIONS** Auth, Structure, Process, and Party: Essays in American Political History, London, 91; ed, Populism: Its Rise and Fall, Univ Press of Kans, 92; auth, The Limits of Agrarian Radicalism: American Politics and Western Populism, Univ Press of Kans, 95; auth, The American Journey : A History of the United States, Prentice Hall, 98. **CONTACT ADDRESS** Dept Hist, So Illinois Univ, Carbondale, MC 4519, Carbondale, IL 62901. **EMAIL** parger@siu.edu

ARIETI, JAMES ALEXANDER
PERSONAL Born 05/12/1948, New York, NY, m, 1976, 2 children **DISCIPLINE** CLASSICS, HISTORY **EDUCATION** Grinnell Col, BA, 69; Stanford Univ, MA, 72, PhD(classics), 72. **CAREER** Asst prof classics, Stanford Univ, 73-74; asst prof, Pa State Univ, 74-75; asst prof classics & hist, Cornell Col, 75-77; asst prof, 78-81, assoc prof, 81-88, prof classics, Hampden-Sydney Col, 88-95, Thompson Prof Classics, 95-; asst bibliographer ling, MLA, 74-75; NEH fel, classics, 77-78; chemn bd & sr fel, Hesperis Inst for Humanistic Studies, 77-. **HONORS AND AWARDS** Phi Beta Kappa, 69; Woodrow Wilson fel, 69; Mettauer Reseach Award, 86, 97; John Templeton Prize for Science & Religion, 96. **MEMBERSHIPS** Am Philol Asn; Class Asn of Middle West & South; VA Classical Asn. **RESEARCH** Ancient historiography and philosophy; ancient literary criticism; Septuagint. **SELECTED PUBLICATIONS** Auth, The Vocabulary of Septuagint Amos, J Biblical Lit, 74; Nudity in Greek Athletics, Class World, 75; coauth, The Dating of Longinus, Studia Classica, 75; co-ed, MLA Int Bibliography, In; 1974 Vol III, MLA, 76; contrib, Two Studies in Latin Phonology, Studia Ling et Philol, 76; coauth, Love Can Be Found, Harcourt Brace Jovanovich, 77; auth, Empedocles in Rome: Rape and the Roman Ethos, Clio, 81; A Herodotean Source for Rasselas, Note & Queries, 81; coauth, Longinus on the Sublime, Edwin Meller pub, 85; co-ed, Hamartia: The Concept of Error in the Western Tradition, Edwin Mellen Pub, 83; auth, Interpreting Plato: The Dialogues as Drama, Rowman & Littlefield, 91; Discourses on the First Book of Herodotus, Littlefield Adams Books, 95; numerous articles and reviews. **CONTACT ADDRESS** Dept of Classics, Hampden-Sydney Col, Hampden-Sydney, VA 23943. **EMAIL** jarieti@email.hsc.edu

ARMBRECHT, THOMAS J. D.
PERSONAL Born 04/09/1970, ME **DISCIPLINE** FRENCH STUDIES **EDUCATION** Middlebury Col, BA, 92; Brown Univ, MA, 95; PhD, 99. **CAREER** For asst, Lycee Fenelon, France, 95-96; TA, Brown Univ, 93-99; instr, Antink Lang, Turkey, 99; asst prof, Colby Col, 00; asst prof, Col of William & Mary, 00-. **HONORS AND AWARDS** Phi Beta Kappa, Middlebury Col, 92; Gay Scholar Awd, Johnson and Wales Univ, 95. **MEMBERSHIPS** MLA, Centre de Documentation Professionale Marguerite Yourcenar. **RESEARCH** 20th-century French Literature, French Theatre, Queer Studies, Minority Literature. **SELECTED PUBLICATIONS** Auth, "Paradox and Perversions: the Intersection of Catholicism and Queer Culture," Univ of Mass Pr, forthcoming. **CONTACT ADDRESS** Col of William and Mary, PO Box 1852, Williamsburg, VA 23187-1852. **EMAIL** txarmb@wm.edu

ARMFIELD, FELIX L.
PERSONAL Born 08/27/1962, NC, s **DISCIPLINE** HISTORY **EDUCATION** N C Central Univ, BA, 84; MA, 89; Mich State Univ, PhD, 97. **CAREER** Asst Prof, Western Ill Univ, 95-. **HONORS AND AWARDS** Distinguished service Awd, Intl Friendship Club, Western Ill Univ, 98; NEH Fel, Duke Univ, 94. **MEMBERSHIPS** Org of Am Hist, Asn for the Study of African Am Life and Hist, Soc of Hist of the gilded age and Progressive era, Il State Hist soc, Western Ill Univ Black Caucus, Affirmative acting and Equity Coun. **RESEARCH** Black social reform(ers)) of the twentieth century; local black history and preservation. **SELECTED PUBLICATIONS** Auth, "Fire on the Prairies: First Illinois Race Riot, Spring Valley 1895," The Journal of Illinois History, forthcoming; rev, of "Reaping the Whirlwind: The civil rights Movement in Tuskegee," by Robert J Norrell, Arkansas Review, (98): 259-260; auth, "Black Life in West Central Illinois, 1818-1918," Illinois alive, 1818-1918!, 99; auth, "Jewel Eugene Kinckle Jones & The Development of Early African American Social Work," The Sphinx, (99): 21-25; auth, "Carrie Bullock" & "Frances Elliott Davis," in Black Women in America: An Historical Encyclopedia, Carlson Pub, 92; auth, "Eugene Kinckle Jones and the rise of Professional Black Social Workers, 1910-1940," forthcoming; auth, "Earl E Thorpe, Psychohistory and Historiography," contours, forthcoming; auth, "Eugene Kinckle Jones: A statesman for the times," in African American Leadership in Social Welfare History: An empowerment tradition, Nat Asn of Soc Work Press, forthcoming; auth, "The social Work Club" & "The National Association of black Social Workers," in encyclopedia of African American Association, Garland Pub, forthcoming. **CONTACT ADDRESS** Dept Hist, Western Illinois Univ, 1 Univ Circle, Macomb, IL 61455-1367. **EMAIL** felix.armfield@ccmail.wiu.edu

ARMITAGE, DAVID
PERSONAL m, 2000 **DISCIPLINE** HISTORY **EDUCATION** Cambridge, PhD, 92. **CAREER** Res fel, Emmanuel Col, Cambridge, 90-93; asst prof Hist, 93-97, assoc prof Hist, Columbia Univ, 97-. **HONORS AND AWARDS** Irene Samuel Memorial Awd of the Milton Soc of Am, 95; Phillip and Ruth Hettleman Awd for Jr Fac, Columbia Univ, 96, 98; fel, Nat Humanities Center, 96-97; Georges Lurcy Jr Fac fel, 96-97; fel, Royal Hist Soc, 97-, Charles Warren Center for Am Hist, Fel; Harvard Univ, Fel, 00-01, Longman/Hist Today Book of the Year Awd, 01. **MEMBERSHIPS** Hakluyt Soc; Am Hist Asn; North Am Conference on British Studies; Assocs of the John Carter Brown Library; Assocs of the Omohundro Inst of Early Am Hist and Culture; Eighteenth-Century Scottish Studies Soc; Forum for European Expansion and Global Interaction. **RESEARCH** Early modern British hist; hist of the first British Empire; history of political thought. **SELECTED PUBLICATIONS** Co-ed, Milton and Republicanism, Cambridge, 95, paperback, 98; auth, John Robertson, ed, A Union for Empire, 95; Past and Present, 97; Journal of British Studies, 97; and Nicholas Canny, ed, The Oxford History of the British Empire, vol 1, 98; auth, American Historical Review, 99; auth, Journal of the History of Ideas, 00; auth, The Ideological Origins of the British Empire, Cambridge, 00. **CONTACT ADDRESS** Dept of History, Columbia Univ, Fayerweather Hall, New York, NY 10027. **EMAIL** da56@columbia.edu

ARMITAGE, SUSAN
PERSONAL Born 05/17/1937 **DISCIPLINE** US WOMEN'S HISTORY **EDUCATION** Univ London, PhD, 68. **CAREER** Prof, Washington State Univ. **HONORS AND AWARDS** Dist Fulbright Scholar, Moscow State Univ, 95. **RESEARCH** Women in the U.S. West. **SELECTED PUBLICATIONS** Coauth, Out of Many, Prentice Hall, 94; co-ed, The Women's West, 87; So Much To Be Done: Women Settlers on the Mining and Ranching Frontier, 90; Writing the Range: Race, Class, and Culture in the Women's West, 98. **CONTACT ADDRESS** Dept of History, Washington State Univ, 301 Wilson Hall, PO Box 644030, Pullman, WA 99164-4030. **EMAIL** armitage@wsu.edu

ARMSTRONG, BRIAN G.
PERSONAL Born 08/01/1936, Titusville, PA, m, 1959, 2 children **DISCIPLINE** HISTORY **EDUCATION** Houghton Col, AB, 58; Gordon Div Sch, BD, 61; Princeton Theol Sem, ThM, 62, OhD, 67. **CAREER** Tch fel, Princeton Theol Sem, 65-67; asst prof, 67-70, assoc prof, Ga State Univ, 70-89; vis ACLS schol Univ Geneva, 72-73; actg ch, hist, 73-74, asst dean, 74-75, actg ch, For Lang, 79-80, ch, hon prg cmt, 80-84, ch bach of interdisc stu cmt, 84-86, grad dir, coll of arts & scis, 84-85, prof to prof emer, Ga State Univ, 91-. **MEMBERSHIPS** AHA, ASCH, ASRR, Calvin Stu Soc, ICCR, NAS, RSA, SCSC, SHA **RESEARCH** History of reference; early modern France; Calvin and Calvinism, 17th century France. **SELECTED PUBLICATIONS** Auth, Calvinism and the Amyraut Heresy, Univ Wis, 69; auth, Bibliographia Molinaei: An Alphabetical and Descriptive Bibliography: The Works of Pierre du Moulin, 94. **CONTACT ADDRESS** Dept of Hist, Georgia State Univ, 38 Peachtree Center Ave, 805 General Classroom Bldg, Atlanta, GA 30303-3083. **EMAIL** hisbga@panther.gsu.edu

ARMSTRONG, CHARLES
PERSONAL Born 02/11/1962, Taegu, Korea, m, 1986, 2 children **DISCIPLINE** MODERN KOREAN AND EAST ASIAN HISTORY **EDUCATION** Yale Univ, BA, 84, London Sch of Economics, M.Sc., 88; Univ Chicago, PhD, 94 **CAREER** Asst prof. **HONORS AND AWARDS** Fulbright Senior Scholar Fel, Korea, 00-01. **MEMBERSHIPS** Asn of Asian Studies; Am Hist Asn. **RESEARCH** Modern East Asia; International history, World history. **SELECTED PUBLICATIONS** Auth, Surveillance and Punishment in Post-Liberation North Korea, Positions, East Asia Cult Critique 3:3, 96; A Socialism of Our Style: North Korean Idology in a Post-Communist Era, North Korean Foreign Policy in the Post-Cold War Era, 97; ed, Korean Society, Routledge, 01. **CONTACT ADDRESS** Dept of Hist, Columbia Col, New York, 2960 Broadway, New York, NY 10027-6902. **EMAIL** cra10@columbia.edu

ARMSTRONG, FREDERICK H.
PERSONAL Born 03/27/1926, Toronto, ON, Canada **DISCIPLINE** HISTORY **EDUCATION** Univ Toronto, BA, 49, MA, 51, PhD, 65. **CAREER** Instr, Univ Toronto, 62-63; fac mem, 63-75, prof, 75-89, res prof, 89-91, PROF EMER HISTORY, UNIV WESTERN ONTARIO, 91-. **HONORS AND AWARDS** Univ Western Ont Pres Medal, 79; Am Soc State Local Hist Awd Merit, 84. **MEMBERSHIPS** Champlain Soc (coun 74-, vice pres 80-88, pres 88-91); Ont Hist Soc (dir 63-65, 72-80, pres 77-79); Royal Hist Soc. **SELECTED PUBLICATIONS** Auth, Handbook of Upper Canadian Chronology, 67, 2nd ed, 85; auth, Organizing for Preservation, 78; auth, Toronto: The Place of Meeting, 83; auth, The Forest City: An Illustrated History of London, Canada, 86; auth, A City in the Making, 89; coauth, Reflections on London's Past, 75. **CONTACT ADDRESS** Dept of History, Univ of Western Ontario, London, ON, Canada N6A 5C2.

ARMSTRONG, JOE C. W.
PERSONAL Born 01/30/1934, Toronto, ON, Canada **DISCIPLINE** HISTORY, CARTOGRAPHY **EDUCATION** Bishop's Univ, BA, 58. **CAREER** Sr Indust Develop Off, Govt Can, 72-96; Prop, Canadiana Collection, Art & Discovery Maps of Canada, 78-93. **HONORS AND AWARDS** Fel, Royal Geog Soc (UK), 80; fel, Royal Geog Soc (Can), 81; Hon dir, Can Inst Surveyors, 83. **MEMBERSHIPS** Champlain Soc. **SELECTED PUBLICATIONS** Auth, From Sea Unto Sea/Art & Discovery Maps of Canada, 82; auth, Champlain, Eng ed 87, Fr ed 88; auth, Farewell the Peaceful Kingdom: The Seduction and Rape of Canada 1963-1994, 95. **CONTACT ADDRESS** 347 Keewatin Ave, Toronto, ON, Canada M4P 2A4.

ARMSTRONG, PAT
DISCIPLINE CANADIAN STUDIES **EDUCATION** Carleton Univ, PhD. **CAREER** Prof, dir, Can Stud, Carleton Univ; Prof, York Univ. **RESEARCH** Transformations in the Canadian social security system; changes in the organization and structure of work. **SELECTED PUBLICATIONS** Co-auth, Wasting Away: Warning Signals for Canadian Health Care, Garamond, 97; Take Care: Warning Signals for the Canadian Health System, Garamond, 94; The Double Ghetto: Canadian Women and Their Segregated Work, McClelland and Stewart, 94; auth, Restructuring Pay Equity for a Restructured Workforce: Canadian Perspectives, Gender Work and Organisations 4, 96; From Caring and Sharing to Greedy and Mean, Language, Culture and Value at the Dawn of the 21st Century, Carleton UP, 96; Unravelling the Safety Net: Transformations in Health Care and Their Impact on Women, Women and Canadian Public Policy, Harcourt Brace, 96; Women and Health: Challenges and Changes, Feminist Issues: Race, Class and Sexuality, Prentice-Hall, 95; Caring and Women's Women's Work, Health and Can Soc, 94; Caring and Women's Work, Health and Can Soc, 94; Gender Relations, The Social World, McGraw-Hill Ryerson, 94. **CONTACT ADDRESS** Dept of Sociol, York Univ, 4700 Keele St, 2148 Vari Hall, Toronto, ON, Canada M3J 1P3.

ARMUS, SETH
PERSONAL Born 10/29/1966, Toledo, OH, s **DISCIPLINE** HISTORY **EDUCATION** Univ Minn, BA, 90; SUNY at Stonybrook, MA, 91; PhD, 98. **CAREER** Asst Prof, St Joseph's Col, 97-. **MEMBERSHIPS** Soc for French Hist Studies, Am Hist Asn, Western Soc for French History, MLA. **RESEARCH** 20th Century France, Intellectual History of Modern Europe. **SELECTED PUBLICATIONS** Auth, "The American Menace in the Horelleberg Affair," French Polit and Soc (Spring 99). **CONTACT ADDRESS** Dept Hist, St. Joseph's Col, Suffolk, 155 W Roe Blvd, Patchogue, NY 11772-2325. **EMAIL** setharmus@aol.com

ARN, MARY-JO
PERSONAL Born, OH **DISCIPLINE** MEDIEVAL STUDIES **EDUCATION** SUNY Binghamton, Medieval Cert, 75; PhD, 75. **CAREER** Wetenschappelijk medewerker, Rijks Univ, 80-87; vis scholar, Univ Pa, 88-91; adj prof, Rutgers Univ, 90-91; assoc prof, Bloomsburg Univ, 91-98; vis scholar, Harvard Univ, 98-00. **HONORS AND AWARDS** R. H. Robbins Res Fel, 84; NEH Fel, 89; Pa State Sys Higher Educ Res Grant, 97. **MEMBERSHIPS** MAA; ICMA; ICLS; APICES; NCS; EBS. **RESEARCH** The nature of lyric; late medieval transchannel culture; the poetry of Charles d'Orleans; manuscripts and their

contexts. **SELECTED PUBLICATIONS** Auth, "Three Ovidian Women in Chaucer's 'Troilus:' Medea, Helen, Oenone," Chaucer Rev (81); auth, "The Triumph of Grace in 'Dobest,'" English Studies (82); auth, "Fragment of an Abraham-and-Sarah Play," Comp Drama (84); ed, Historical and Editorial Studies, Wolters/Noordhoff, 85; auth, "Poetic Form as a Mirror of Meaning in the English Poems of Charles of Orleans," Philol Quart (90); ed, Medieval Food and Drink, Cemers (NYork), 90; auth, "Charles of Orleans and the Poems of BL MS, Harley 682," English Studies, 74 (93): 222-35; ed, Fortunes Stabilnes: Charles of Orleans's English Book of Love, Medieval/ Renaissance Texts/Studies (NYork), 95; ed, Charles d'Orleans in England, 1415-1440, D.S. Brewer (Woodbridge, Suff/ Rochester, NYork), 00. **CONTACT ADDRESS** 379 Broadway, Apt 6, Somerville, MA 02138. **EMAIL** arn@karolus.net

ARNOLD, BILL T.
PERSONAL Born 09/01/1955, Lancaster, KY, m, 1977, 3 children **DISCIPLINE** OLD TESTAMENT AND ANCIENT NEAR EASTERN STUDIES **EDUCATION** Asbury Col, BA, 77; Asbury Theol Sem, M Div, 80; Hebrew Union Col, PhD, 85. **CAREER** Assoc prof, old testament and bibl lang, Wesley Bibl Sem, 85-89; prof, old testament and bibl lang, Wesley Bible Sem, 89-91; assoc prof, old testament and semitic lang, Ashland Theol Sem, 91-93; prof, old testament and semitic lang, Ashland Theol Sem, 93-95; prof, old testament and semitic lang, Asbury Theol Sem, 95-. **HONORS AND AWARDS** Lykins Found Scholar, 77-78; Magee Christ Educ Found Scholar, 73-79; Intl Hon Soc of Theta Phi, 79; Joseph and Helen Regenstein Found fel, 80-81; S. H. and Helen R. Scheuer grad fel, 82-84; Nat Endow for the Humanities, summer stipend, 88; Eta Beta Rho, Nat Hon Soc of Students of Hebrew Lang and Culture, 92. **MEMBERSHIPS** Amer Oriental Soc; Amer Sch of Orient Res; Inst for Bibl Res; Nat Asn of the Prof of Hebrew; Soc of Bibl Lit; Wesleyan Theol Soc. **RESEARCH** Genesis; History of Israelite religion; Israelite historiography. **SELECTED PUBLICATIONS** Auth, What Has Nebuchadnezzar to do with David? On the Neo-Babylonian Period and Early Israel, Syria-Mesopotamia and the Bible, Sheffield Acad Press, 98; articles, The New Intl Dict of Old Testament Theol and Exegesis, Zondervan Publ House, 97; auth, The Use of Aramaic in the Hebrew Bible: Another Look at Bilingualism in Ezra and Daniel, Jour of Northwest Semitic Lang, 22, 2, 1-16, 96; auth, Luke's Characterizing Use of the Old Testament in the Book of Acts, 300-323, Hist, Lit, and Soc in the Book of Acts, Cambridge Univ Press, 96; auth, Age, Old (the Aged), Daniel, Theology of Manna Vision, Evang Dict of Bibl Theol, Baker Book House, 96; auth, Forms of Prophetic Speech in the Old Testament: A Summary of Claus Westermann's Contributions, Ashland Theol Jour, 27, 30-40, 95; auth, Babylonians, 43-75, Peoples of the Old Testament World, Baker Book House, 94; auth, The Weidner Chronicle and the Idea of History is Israel and Mesopotamia, 129-148, Faith, Tradition, and History: Old Testament Historiography in Its Near Eastern Context, Eisenbrauns, 94. **CONTACT ADDRESS** Asbury Theol Sem, 204 N Lexington Ave, Wilmore, KY 40390-1199. **EMAIL** Bill_Arnold@ats.wilmore.ky.us

ARNOLD, ERIC ANDERSON
PERSONAL Born 12/04/1939, Cleveland, OH, 3 children **DISCIPLINE** MODERN EUROPEAN & FRENCH HISTORY **EDUCATION** Oberlin Col, AB, 61; Columbia Univ, MA, 63, PhD(hist), 69. **CAREER** Lectr Europ hist, Newark England Col, 64-65; instr hist, Ohio State Univ, 65-69; asst prof, 69-80, assoc prof French & Europ Hist, Univ Denver, 80-. **MEMBERSHIPS** AHA; Western Soc Fr Hist; Soc Fr Hist Studies. **RESEARCH** Revolutionary and Napoleonic France. **SELECTED PUBLICATIONS** Auth, Some Observations on the French Opposition to Napoleonic Conscription, 1804-1806, Fr Hist Studies; Administrative Leadership in a Dictatorship: The Position of Joseph Fouche in the Napoleonic Police, 1800-1810, Rocky Mountain Soc Sci J, spring 74; Rouget de Lisle and the Maiseillaise, In: Western Society for French History, Vol 5, spring 78; Fouche, Napoleon and the General Police, Univ Press Am, 79; Some observations on the interdisciplinary teaching of eighteenth century French civilization, Teaching Hist: J Methods, fall 79; articles, in An Historical Dictionary of the French Revolution (in prep), An Historical Dictionary of Napoleonic France (in prep) & An Historical Dictionary of the French Second Empire (in prep), Greenwood Press; ed and trans, A Documentary Sruvey of Napoleonic France, Lanham, Md, 94 and A Documentary Survey of Napoleonic France: Supplement, Lanham, MD, 96. **CONTACT ADDRESS** Dept of History, Univ of Denver, 2199 S University, Denver, CO 80210-4711. **EMAIL** earnold@du.edu

ARNOLD, JOSEPH L.
PERSONAL Born 06/21/1937, Chicago, IL, m, 3 children **DISCIPLINE** HISTORY **EDUCATION** OH State Univ, PhD. **CAREER** Prof, Univ MD Baltimore County. **RESEARCH** Am urban hist. **SELECTED PUBLICATIONS** Auth, The New Deal in the Suburbs: A History of the Greenbelt Town Program; Maryland: Old Line to New Prosperity; pubs on flood control and the Army Corps of Engineers. **CONTACT ADDRESS** Dept of Hist, Univ of Maryland, Baltimore, 1000 Hilltop Circle, Baltimore, MD 21250. **EMAIL** arnold@umbc.edu

ARNOULT, SHARON L.
PERSONAL Born 05/26/1954, San Antonio, TX, m, 1978 **DISCIPLINE** HISTORY **EDUCATION** Univ Tx Austin, BS, 76, BA, 84, MA, 91, PhD, 97 **CAREER** Instr, 83-90, Austin Comm Col; teaching asst, 87-93, Univ Tx Austin; instr to asst prof, 91-, SWest Tex St Univ; asst prof, Midwestern State Univ. **HONORS AND AWARDS** Meadows Fel in Fine Arts, S Methodist Univ, 79-80, 80-81; Dora Bonham Grad Scholar, 85; Sheffield Fund Awd for Europ Hist, 91; Jr Fel, Univ Tx Austin, 97. **MEMBERSHIPS** Amer Hist Assoc; Church of England Record Soc; Hist Soc of the Episcopal Church, N Amer Conf on British Stud; Sixteenth Century Stud Conf; Soc for Reformation Res. **RESEARCH** Liturgy & identity in English church; sixteenth & seventeenth centuries; English reformation; women & relig; image of Charles I. **SELECTED PUBLICATIONS** Auth, The Sovereignties of Body and Soul: Women's Political and Religious Actions in the English Civil war, Women and Sovereignty, Edinburgh Univ Press, 91; art, Spiritual and Sacred Publique Actions: The Book of Common Prayer and the Understanding of Worship in the Elizabethan and Jacobean Church of England, Religion and the English People, 1500-1640: New Voices, New Perspectives, Sixteenth Century Stud, 98; rev, Katherine L French's, The Parish in English Life, 1400-1600, Sixteenth Century J, 98. **CONTACT ADDRESS** Dept of History, Midwestern State Univ, 3410 Taft Blvd, Wichita Falls, TX 76308-2099. **EMAIL** sharon.arnoult@nexus.mwsu.edu

ARTHUR, ALAN
DISCIPLINE HISTORY OF MEDIEVAL AND REFORMATION EUROPE **EDUCATION** Alberta Univ, BA; Univ Toronto, MA; Emory Univ, PhD. **CAREER** Assoc prof. **RESEARCH** Early modern France. **SELECTED PUBLICATIONS** Auth, Popular Religion in France, Encycl of the Reformation, Oxford UP, 95. **CONTACT ADDRESS** Dept of Hist, Brock Univ, 500 Glenridge Ave, Saint Catharines, ON, Canada L2S 3A1. **EMAIL** aarthur@spartan.ac.BrockU.CA

ARTIBISE, ALAN F. J.
PERSONAL Born 01/23/1946, Dauphin, MB, Canada **DISCIPLINE** URBAN AND SOCIAL HISTORY **EDUCATION** Univ Man, BA, 67; Univ BC, PhD, 72. **CAREER** Lectr, hist & Can stud, Cariboo Col(Kamloops), 71, chmn soc sci & coordr Can stud prog, 73-75; head, W Can sect hist div, Can Mus Civilization, 75-76; fac mem to prof hist, Univ Victoria, 76-82; prof hist & dir, Inst Urban Stud, Univ Winnipeg, 83-88; sch dir, 88-93, Prof Community & Regional Planning, Univ BC, 88-00; Exec Dir, Public Policy Res Ctr, Univ Missouri, St. Louis, 00; prof, Hist and Public Policy; E. Des Lee Endowed prof of Community Collaboration and Public Policy. **HONORS AND AWARDS** Man Hist Soc Medal; Awd Merit Can Hist Asn; Awd Merit Am Asn State & Local Hist; Awd Merit Asn Can Stud USA; Excellence Planning Awd, Planning Inst BC; Media Club Can Awd; Marie Tremaine Medal Bibliog Soc Can. **MEMBERSHIPS** Asn Can Stud (pres, 82-86); Pacific Rim Coun Urban Develop; Can Reg Sci Asn; Can Hist Asn; Can Fedn Hum; Urban Affairs Asn; Am Planning Asn; Urban Land Institute. **SELECTED PUBLICATIONS** Auth, Winnipeg: A Social History of Urban Growth, 75; auth, Winnipeg: An Illustrated History, 77; auth, The Canadian City: Essays in Social and Urban History, 77, 2nd ed, 84; auth, Western Canada Since 1870: A Bibliography and Guide, 78; auth, The Usable Urban Past, 79; auth, Town and City: Aspects of Western Canadian Urban Development, 81; auth, Canada's Urban Past: A Bibliography and Guide to Urban Studies, 81; auth, Shaping the Canadian Urban Landscape, 82; auth, Power and Place: Canadian Urban Development in the North American Context, 86; auth, Canadian Regional Development: The Urban Dimension, 89; auth, The Pacific Fraser Region: Towards 2010, 91; ed-in-chief, Urban Hist Rev/Revue d'histoire urbaine, 75-88; assoc ed, Prairie Forum; assoc ed, America: Hist & Life; assoc ed, Urban Affairs Quart; assoc ed, Public Works Mgt & Policy; assoc ed, Can J Urban Res; assoc ed, J Urban Affairs; gen ed, Hist Can Cities series. **CONTACT ADDRESS** Univ of Missouri, St. Louis, 8001 Natural Bridge Rd., Saint Louis, MO, Canada 63121. **EMAIL** artibise@umsl.edu

ARYEETEY-ATTOH, SAMUEL
PERSONAL Born Accra, Ghana, m, 4 children **DISCIPLINE** GEOGRAPHY **EDUCATION** Univ Ghana, BA, 77; Carleton Univ, MA, 80; Boston Univ, PhD, 88. **CAREER** Lecturer to Instructor, Boston Univ, 84-87; Asst Prof to Full Prof and Dept Chair, Univ Toledo, 87-. **HONORS AND AWARDS** Fel, Boston Univ, 80-84; Director of Latin Am Scholars; 500 Leaders of Influence, 95; Who's Who in the Midwest; who's Who in the World; Who's Who in America; Intl Man of the Year, Cambridge, 95-96; Outstanding Advisor Awd, Univ Toledo, 92; special Dean's Merit Awd, 93, 94, 96; Outstanding contribution Awd, African People's Asn;, 96; master Teacher Awd, 93-95, 95-97; **MEMBERSHIPS** Asn Am Geog; Am Inst of Cert Planners; Urban Land Inst; Am Planners Asn; Grad Fac Asn. **SELECTED PUBLICATIONS** Auth, "Legacy of continuity and Change," in World Regional Geography: A Developmental Approach, Prentice Hall, 98; auth, "West, Central, East Africa: Diversity in Development," in World Regional Geography: A Developmental Approach, Prentice Hall, 98; auth, "Southern Africa: Development in Transition," in World Regional Geography: A Developmental Approach, Prentice Hall, 98; co-auth, "Angola," in The Columbia Gazetteer of the World, Columbia Univ Press, 98; co-auth, "Central Africa Republic," in The Columbia Gazetteer of the World, Columbia Univ Press, 98; co-auth, "Kenya," in The Columbia Gazetteer of the World, Columbia Univ Press, 98; co-auth, "Uganda," in The Columbia Gazetteer of the World, Columbia Univ Press, 98; co-auth, "Central City Distress in Ohio's elastic Cities: Regional and Local Responses," Urban Geography, (98): 735-756; co-auth, "The Drivers of Greenhouse Gas emissions: what do we learn from local cast studies?," Local Environment, (98): 263-277; co-auth, "The Spatial Dynamics of Greenhouse Gas Emissions in Northwest Ohio," Applied Geography Proceedings, (98): 128-136. **CONTACT ADDRESS** Dept Geog, Univ of Toledo, 2801 W Bancroft St, Toledo, OH 43606. **EMAIL** sattoh@uoft02@utoledo.edu

ASANTE, MOLEFI KETE
PERSONAL Born 08/14/1942, Valdosta, GA, m **DISCIPLINE** AFRICAN-AMERICAN STUDIES **EDUCATION** Southwestern Christian Col, AA 1962; Oklahoma Christian Col, BA 1964; Pepperdine Univ, MA 1965; UCLA, PhD 1968. **CAREER** CA State Polytechnic Coll, instr, 67; CA State Univ Northridge, instr, 68; Purdue Univ, asst prof, 68-69; Pepperdine Univ, visit prof, 69; Univ of CA LA, asst prof, 69-71; CA State Univ, visit prof, 71; Univ of CA LA, dir Center for Afro-Amer Studies, 70-73, assoc prof speech, 71-73; FL State Univ Tallahassee, visit assoc prof, 72; State Univ of NY Buffalo, prof communication dept; Center for Positive Thought Buffalo, curator; Univ of Ibadan, Univ of Nairobi, external examiner, 76-80; Zimbabwe Inst of Mass Communications, fulbright prof; Howard Univ, visiting prof, 79-80; Temple Univ Dept of African-American Studies, prof, currently. **HONORS AND AWARDS** Doctor of Humane Letetrs, Univ of New Haven, New Haven CT, 76; Dr of Humane Letters, Sojourner-Douglass Col, Baltimore MD, 91; Morgan State Univ, Col of Arts and Sciences Awd for Distinguished Academic Service, 95; Walter Annenberg Ch for Distinguished Scholard, Howard Univ, 95. **MEMBERSHIPS** Spec in Black Rhetoric County Probation Dept LA 1969-; mem Intl Soc for Gen Semantics; Intl Assn for Symbolic Analysis; Intl Comm Assn; Western Speech Assn; Central State Speech Assn; So Speech Assn; Natl Assn for Dramatic & Speech Arts; ed bds Nigerian Journal of Political Economy, Afrodiaspora, Afrique Histoire, Africa and the World, Urban African Quarterly, Journal of African Civilization; contributing writer for Buffalo Challenger, Philadelphia New Observer, Philadelphia Tribune; UNESCO reviewer for scholarly books 1985; consultant Zimbabwe Ministry of Information and Telecommunications; Intl Scientific Comm of FESPAC 1986-87 Senegal; chairperson, IMHOTEP 1987-; president, Natl Council for Black Studies, 1988-; vice president, African Heritage Studies Assn 1989-. **SELECTED PUBLICATIONS** Auth, Afrocentricity: The Theory of Social Change, Buffalo: Amulefi Publishing Co., 80; auth, Kemet, Afrocentricity and Knowledge, Trenton: Africa World Press, 90; auth, The Book of African Names, Trenton, Africa World Press, 91; auth, Malcolm X as Cultural Hero and Other Afrocentric Essays, Trenton: Africa World Press, 95; auth, Love Dance: Poetry and Illustrations, Princeton: Sungai Press, 96; ed, African Intellectual Heritage, with Abu Abarry, Philadelphia: Temple Univ Press, 96; auth, The Afrocentric Idea, Revised and Expanded Edition, Philadelphia: Temple Univ Press, 98; auth, African American Atlas, New York: Macmillan, 99. **CONTACT ADDRESS** Dept African-Am Studies, Temple Univ, Gladfelter Hall 025-26, 1115 W Berks St, Philadelphia, PA 19122.

ASH, STEPHEN V.
PERSONAL Born 11/22/1948, El Centro, CA, m, 1970 **DISCIPLINE** HISTORY **EDUCATION** Gettysburg Col, BA, 70; Univ Tenn, MA, 74; PhD, 83. **CAREER** Asst prof, Univ Tenn, 95-98; assoc prof, Univ Tenn, 98-. **HONORS AND AWARDS** NAA Outstand Teach Awd; ACLS Fel; THC/TLA Bk Awd; Choice Awd, Outstand Bk; Phi Kappa Phi. **MEMBERSHIPS** OAH; SHA; THS; ETHS; VHS. **RESEARCH** History; United States. **SELECTED PUBLICATIONS** Auth, Middle Tennessee Society Transformed, 1860-'1870: War and Peace in the Upper South, La St UP, 88; auth, When the Yankees Came: Conflict and Chaos in the Occupied South, 1861-1865, Univ NC Press, 95, ppbk, 99; auth, Secessionists and Other Scoundrels: Selections from Parson Brownlow's Book, La St Univ Press, 99; coauth, Tennesseans and Their History, Univ Tenn Press, 99. **CONTACT ADDRESS** Dept Hist, Univ of Tennessee, Knoxville, 915 Volunteer Blvd, 6th Fl, Dunford Hall, Knoxville, TN 37996-4065. **EMAIL** sash@utk.edu

ASHANIN, CHARLES B.
PERSONAL Born 11/15/1920, Montenegro, Yugoslavia, m, 1953, 4 children **DISCIPLINE** RELIGION HISTORY **EDUCATION** Church Col, Yugoslavia, AB, 43; Univ Glasgow, BD, 52, PhD, 55. **CAREER** Asst prof relig, Univ Col Ghana, 55-60; from assoc prof to prof relig & philos, Allen Univ, 60-65; prof, Claflin Univ, 65-67; assoc prof early church hist, 67-76, Prof Early Church Hist, Christian Theol Sem, 76-; Guest scholar, Princeton Theol Sem, 57; vis scholar & Lilly fel, Harvard Divinity Sch, 64-65; assoc ed, The Logas, 68-; fel, Woodbrooke Col, Eng, 73-74; mem, Patristic Cong Am Acad Relig. **MEMBERSHIPS** Am Soc Church Hist; Orthodox Theol Soc Am. **RESEARCH** Roman Empire and Christian Church in the IV century; history of Christian humanism from the beginning until AD 1536; philosophy of religion; religion and culture;

Emperor Constantine and his age. **SELECTED PUBLICATIONS** **CONTACT ADDRESS** Christian Theol Sem, 1000 W 42nd St, Indianapolis, IN 46208.

ASHBY, LEROY
PERSONAL Born 11/19/1937, Grand Junction, CO, m, 1958, 2 children **DISCIPLINE** TWENTIETH CENTURY AMERICAN HISTORY **EDUCATION** Univ Md, PhD, 66. **CAREER** Prof, Washington State Univ; Johnson Distinguished Prof of History. **HONORS AND AWARDS** WSU President's Fac Excellence Awd in Instruction, 83; CASE prof of the Yr for the State of Wash, 90 & 93. **MEMBERSHIPS** AHA, OAH, ASA, WHA. **RESEARCH** Child welfare, Popular Cultures, 20th Century Politics. **SELECTED PUBLICATIONS** Auth, The Spearless Leader: Senator Borah and the Progressive Movement in the 1920's, Univ Ill Press, 72; Saving the Waifs: Reformers and Dependent Children, Temple UP, 84; William Jennings Bryan: Champion of Democracy, Twayne, 87; Fighting the Odds: The Life of Senator Frank Church, WSU Press, 94 & Endangered Children: Dependency, Neglect and Abuse in American History, Twayne, 97. **CONTACT ADDRESS** Dept of History, Washington State Univ, 301 Wilson Hall, PO Box 644030, Pullman, WA 99164-4030. **EMAIL** ashby@wsu.edu

ASHER, ROBERT
PERSONAL Born 10/01/1944, New York, NY, m, 1968, 1 child **DISCIPLINE** LABOR & SOCIAL HISTORY **EDUCATION** City Col NYork, BA, 66; Harvard Univ, AM, 67; Univ Minn, PhD(hist), 71. **CAREER** Asst prof, 71-77, Assoc Prof Hist, Univ CT, 77-. **MEMBERSHIPS** Orgn Am Historians; Labor Historians. **RESEARCH** Early Welfare state in United States and Great Britain; automation in meatpacking, 1950-1965; production standard bargaining, 1938-1965; technological change and work skills since 1960. **SELECTED PUBLICATIONS** Auth, "Union Nativism and the Immigrant Response," Labor History, 23, (82): 325-328; auth, Connecticut Workers and Technological Change, Storrs: Center for Oral History, 83; ed, "Industrial Safety and Labor Relations in the United States, 1865-1917," in Charles Stephenson and Robert Asher, ed., Life and Labor: Dimensions of American Working-Class History, Albany: State Univ of New York Press, (86): 115-130; auth, Labor Divided: Race and Ethnicity in United States Labor Sturggles, 1930-1960, Albany: State Univ of New York Press, 90; ed, Autowork, ed. with R. Edsforth, Albany: State Univ of New York Press, 95; ed, The American Artisan: Crafting Social Identity, 1750-1850, ed. with H. Rock and P. Gilje, Baltimore: Johns Hopkins Univ Press, 95; auth, Concepts in American History, New York: HarperCollins, 95. **CONTACT ADDRESS** Dept Hist, Univ of Connecticut, Storrs, Storrs, CT 06268. **EMAIL** asher@uconnvm.uconn.edu

ASHLEY, SUSAN A.
PERSONAL Born 09/27/1943, Portland, OR, m, 1967, 2 children **DISCIPLINE** MODERN EUROPEAN HISTORY **EDUCATION** Carleton Col, BA, summa cum laude, 65; Columbia Univ, MA, 67, PhD, Columbia Univ, 73; Europ Inst, cert, 73. **CAREER** Instr, Hist, 70-73; vist asst Prof, Denver Univ, Grad School of Intl Studies, 73; asst prof hist, CO Col, 73-79, assoc prof hist, CO Col, 79-86; Academic Director, Assoc Col of the Midwest Florence and London-Florence Progs, Florence Italy, 84-85, Visiting Prof, 91-92; Ch, Hist dept, CO Col, 88-97; Prof of Hist, CO Col, 86-; Carlton Prof of the Soc Sci, CO Col, 94-97; William R. Hochman Prof of History, 00-. **HONORS AND AWARDS** Phi Beta Kappa; Best Unpubl Manuscript Awd, Society for Italian Hist Studies, 73; Carlton Prof Soc Sci, 94-97; School Dist Exemplary Awd, 93, 95, 97; Awd of Merit, Western Society for French Hist, 90; Mellon Faculty Develop Grants, CO Col, 79, 81, 83, 84, 87, 98; Research Grant, CO Col, 71, 79, 88, 90, 97; Ford For Area Fellow, 68-71; President's Fellow, CO Univ, 66-67; Woodrow Wilson Fellow, 65-66; William R. Hochman Prof of History, 00-. **MEMBERSHIPS** AHA; FHS; SIHS; CONGRIP; Soc Ital Hist Studies; Pres, Western Society for French Hist, 97-98; Vice Pres and Pres Elect, Western Society for French Hist, 96-97; Governing Council and Sect, Western Society for french Hist, 86-96. **RESEARCH** Definitions of marginality in late 19th-20th century France and Italy **SELECTED PUBLICATIONS** Auth, The Parliamentary Politics of the French Right, Proc Soc Fr Hist, fall 74; The Failure of Gambetta's Grand Ministere, Fr Hist Studies, spring 75; Ministries and Majorities: France, 1879-1902, Proceedings of the Western Society for French Hist, IX, 82; End of the Century Crises, Proceedings of the Western Society for French Hist, X, 83; The Radical Left in Parliament, 1879-1902, IX, 84; Allain-Targe, Brisson, Dupuy, Casimir-Perier, Scheurer-Kestner, Deputies of the Third Republic, Dict of the Third Republic, Greenwood Press, 85; auth, "The mechanics of social reform: accident insurance in France and Italy" in Proceedings of the Annual Meeting of the Western Society for French History, vol 18, 91; "Marginal people: degeneration and genius," in Proceedings of the Western Society for for French History: Selected Papers of the Annual Meeting," vol. 24, 97; ed, "Vacher the Ripper of the Southwest," in Vincent, K. Steven and Alison Klairmont-Longo, eds., The Human Tradition in Modern France, Wilmington, Delaware: Scholarly Resources, 00. **CONTACT ADDRESS** Dept Hist, Colorado Col, 14 E Cache La Poudre, Colorado Springs, CO 80903-3294. **EMAIL** sashley@ColoradoCollege.edu

ASKEW, THOMAS A.
PERSONAL Born 10/08/1931, Lorain, OH, m, 1953, 3 children **DISCIPLINE** HISTORY **EDUCATION** Wheaton Col, BA, 53; MA, 58; Northwestern Univ, MA, 62; PhD, 69. **CAREER** Asst prof, Wheaton Col, 60-68; prof, Nat Col Edu, 68-72; vis fac, Univ Ill, 69-72; prof, Gordon Col, 72-96; dept chair, 76-98; East-West Inst dir, prof, 96-. **HONORS AND AWARDS** Danforth Fel, 63, 64, 65; Excel Teach Awd, Sr Fac, Gordon Coll; Pres, Con Faith and Hist; Publisher, Christ Schl Rev; Bd Trust, Essex Inst Museum; Ed Bd, Fides et Historia, Christ Hist. **MEMBERSHIPS** AHA; Con Faith and Hist. **RESEARCH** American religious and educational history; World Christianity and Mission; Colonial New England. **SELECTED PUBLICATIONS** Coauth, The Churches and the American Experience (84); co-ed, Liberty and Law: Reflections on the Constitution (87); coauth, A Centennial History of Gordon College (88). **CONTACT ADDRESS** Dept History, Gordon Col, Massachusetts, 255 Grapevine Rd, Wenham, MA 01984-1813. **EMAIL** jethaskew@aol.com

ASSELIN, OLIVIER
DISCIPLINE MODERN AND CONTEMPORARY ART **EDUCATION** Univ de Montreal, Univ de Paris VIII, MA, 83; doctorate, 86; McGill Univ, PhD, 86-90. **CAREER** Dept Art Hist, Concordia Univ. **RESEARCH** Canadian contemporary art and in XVIIIth-century aesthetics and art theory. **SELECTED PUBLICATIONS** Pub(s), articles and rev(s), periodicals (Parachute, Protee, Trois, La recherche photographique, 24 images, Jeu; co-ed, Fictions supremes. La question du site dans l'esthetique de Diderot; De la curiosite. Petite anatomie d'un regard; auth, L'art philosophique, Definitions de la culture visuelle III, Proc of the conf Art et philos, Montreal, Musee d'art contemporain, 98; The Sublime: the Limits of Vision and the Inflation of Commentary, Theory Rules: Art as Theory, Theory and Art, Toronto, YYZ Bk(s), Univ Toronto Press, 96. **CONTACT ADDRESS** Dept Art Hist, VA-432, Concordia Univ, Montreal, 1455 de Maisonneuve W, Montreal, QC, Canada H3G 1M8. **EMAIL** oasselin@alcor.comcordia.ca

AST, THERESA
PERSONAL Born 08/11/1954, Harlingen, TX, d, 3 children **DISCIPLINE** HISTORY **EDUCATION** Kennesaw State Univ, BA, 88; Emory Univ, MA, 92; PhD, 00. **CAREER** Instr, State Univ W Ga, 94-97; instr, Reinhardt Col, 98-00. **HONORS AND AWARDS** Teacher of the Year, State Univ W Ga Hist Dept, 96-97; Teacher of the Year, Reinhardt Col, 99-00. **MEMBERSHIPS** AHA, SAWH, AAUP, OAH, SAH. **RESEARCH** World War II Veterans, Nazi Germany. **CONTACT ADDRESS** Dept Soc Sci, Reinhardt Col, 7300 Reinhardt College Cr, Waleska, GA 30183. **EMAIL** tla@mail.reinhardt.edu

ASTER, SIDNEY
PERSONAL Born 05/24/1942, Montreal, PQ, Canada **DISCIPLINE** HISTORY **EDUCATION** McGill Univ, BA, 63, MA, 65; London Sch Econ, Univ London, PhD, 69. **CAREER** Lectr, Univ Glasgow, 69-70; prin res asst to Sir Martin Gilbert, Winston Churchill Official Biogr, 69-70; prin res asst to former Romanian min, V.V. Tilea, 70-73; prin res asst to Baron Salter of Kidlington, 72-75; vis assoc prof, Concordia Univ, 75; asst prof, 76-80, assoc prof, 80-91, PROF HISTORY, UNIV TORONTO, 91-, acting assoc dean hum, 96-97. **HONORS AND AWARDS** Lt Gov Gold Medal Hist (Que), 63; Que govt fels, 64-68; Leverhulme Trust fel, 73; Twenty-Seven Fedn Awd, 76. **SELECTED PUBLICATIONS** Auth, 1939: The Making of the Second World War, 73; auth, Les Origines de la Seconde Guerre Mondiale, 74; auth, Anthony Eden, 76; auth, British Foreign Policy 1918-1945: A Guide TO Research Materials, 91; ed, A.P. Young, The 'X' Documents, The Secret History of Foreign Office Contacts with the German Resistance 1937-1939, 74; ed, The Second World War as a National Experience, 81; ed, A.P. Young, Die X-Dokumente: Die geheimen Kontakte Carl Goerdelers mit der britischen Regierung, 1938/1939, 89. **CONTACT ADDRESS** Erindale Col, Univ of Toronto, Mississauga, ON, Canada L5L 1C6. **EMAIL** saster@credit.erin.utoronto.ca

ASTOUR, MICHAEL CZERNICHOW
PERSONAL Born 12/17/1916, Kharkov, Russia, m, 1952 **DISCIPLINE** ANCIENT HISTORY **EDUCATION** Univ Paris, Lic es Lett, 37; Brandeis Univ, PhD(Mediter studies), 62. **CAREER** Asst prof Europ lang, Brandeis Univ, 60-65, Mediter studies, 63-65; assoc prof, 65-69, Prof Ancient Hist, Southern IL Univ, Edwardsville, 69-, Vis prof, Univ NC, Chapel Hill, 69-70; Am Philos Soc grant, 72; assoc fel, Am Res Inst, Turkey, 72. **MEMBERSHIPS** Corresp mem Inst Antiq & Christianity; Am Name Soc; AHA; Am Orient Soc; Soc Bibl Lit. **RESEARCH** History, geography and civilization of the ancient Near East; western Semitic lit and mythology; Greco-Semitic connections. **SELECTED PUBLICATIONS** Auth, Place Names, In: Ras Shamra Parallels, vol 2, Pont Bibl Inst, Rome, 75; Continuite et changement dans la toponymie de la Syrie du Nord, In: La Toponymie Antique, Univ Strasbourg & E J Brill, Leiden, 77; Tall-Al-Hamidya, vol 2, with S. Eichler and M. Wafler, and D. Warburton, J of the Am Oriental Soc, vol 113, 93; The Hurrians, with G. Wilhelm, J of Near Eastern Studies, vol 53, 94; The Cities of Seleukid Syria, with J. D. Granger, J of the Am Oriental Soc, vol 114, 94; Place-Names from the Elba Tablets (Italian), with A. Archi, P. Piacentini, and F. Pomponio, J of the Am Oriental Soc, vol 117, 97. **CONTACT ADDRESS** Dept of Hist Studies, So Illinois Univ, Edwardsville, Edwardsville, IL 62026.

ATHANASSOGLOU-KALLMYER, NINA MARIA
PERSONAL Born Athens, Greece, d, 1 child **DISCIPLINE** EIGHTEENTH AND NINETEENTH CENTURY EUROPEAN ART **EDUCATION** Univ Paris, BA; Univ Thessaloniki, Phd; Princeton, MFA, PhD. **CAREER** Prof, art hist. **HONORS AND AWARDS** Mellon fel; Getty fel; J.S. Guggenheim Fel; Inst for Advanced Study, Princeton; A. Kingsley Porter prize; CINOA int competition, first runner-up. **MEMBERSHIPS** CAA; AHNCA: EC/ASECS; Amis de Gericault. **RESEARCH** Eighteenth and nineteenth-century art and culture. **SELECTED PUBLICATIONS** Auth, French Images from the Greek War of Independence: Art and Politics under the Restoration, Yale Univ Press, 89; Eugene Delacroix Prints, Politics and Satire, Yale Univ Press, 92; auth, Cezanne and the Land: Regionalism and Modernism in Late Nineteenth Century France, forthcoming. **CONTACT ADDRESS** Dept of Art Hist, Univ of Delaware, Newark, DE 19716. **EMAIL** nina@udel.edu

ATKESON, EDWARD B.
PERSONAL Born 12/06/1929, Newport News, VA, m, 1954 **DISCIPLINE** MILITARY STRATEGY **EDUCATION** US Military Acad, BS 51; Syracuse Univ, MEA 64; US Army Comm Gen Staff Col, 63; US Army War Col, 69; Luton Univ (UK), PhD, 00. **CAREER** US Army 51-84; Harvard Univ Cen Intl Affs, Fell 73-74; US Army War College, Dep Comm 75-76; US Army Europe, Dep Ch of Staff Intell, 78-80; Nat Intell coun, mem 82-84. **HONORS AND AWARDS** Beta Gamma Sigma Sch Awd; Us Army Dist Ser Medal; CIA Dist Ser Medal; many other Milt Awds. **MEMBERSHIPS** IISS; ACUS; ASSOC US ARMY; ASSOC FORMER INTELL OFFICERS. **RESEARCH** Foreign Military forces and strategy **SELECTED PUBLICATIONS** Auth, The Final Argument of Kings: Reflections on the Art of War, Hero Books 88; The Powder Keg: An Intelligence Officers Guide to Military Forces in the Middle East 1996-2000, Nova Pub, 96, auth, "A Tale of Three Wars," Army War College Fnd Press (98); over 100 articles in journals and newspapers. **CONTACT ADDRESS** 202 Vassar Place, Alexandria, VA 22314. **EMAIL** ebatkeson@aol.com

ATKIN, MURIEL ANN
PERSONAL Born New York, NY **DISCIPLINE** RUSSIAN & IRANIAN HISTORY **EDUCATION** Sarah Lawrence Col, BA, 67; Yale Univ, MPhil, 71, PhD(hist), 76. **CAREER** Asst prof, Univ TX, San Antonio, 76-80; Assoc Prof Hist, George Washington Univ, 80-83. **MEMBERSHIPS** Am Asn Advan Slavic Studies; Middle East Studies Asn; Soc Iranian Studies. **RESEARCH** Russo-Iranian relations; Russia's empire; Central Asia. **SELECTED PUBLICATIONS** Auth, Russia and Iran 1780-1828, Univ MN Press, 80; auth, "The Subtlest Battle: Islam in Soviet Tajckistan, Foreign Policy Researc Institute, 89;auth, "Islamas Faith, Politics, and Bogeyman in Tajikistan, The Politics of Religon in Russia and the New States of Eurasia, ed. M. Bourdeaux, M.E. Sharpe, 95; auth, "Thwarted Democratization in Tajikistan, Conflict, cleavage, and change in Central Asia, eds. "K. Dawisha and B. Parrott," Cambridge Univ Press, 97; auth, "Tajikistan: Reform, Reaction, and Civil War, New States, New Politics, eds, "I. Bremmer and R. Taras," Cambridge Univ Press, 97; auth, "The Rhetoric of Islamophobia, Central Asia and the Caucasus, no. 1, 00. **CONTACT ADDRESS** Hist Dept, The George Washington Univ, Washington, DC 20052-0001. **EMAIL** matkin@gwu.edu

ATKINS, E. TAYLOR
PERSONAL Born 05/04/1967, Murray, KY, m, 1991, 1 child **DISCIPLINE** HISTORY **EDUCATION** Univ Ark, BA, 89; Univ Ill at Urbana-Champaign, AM, 92; PhD, 97. **CAREER** Affiliate prof, Univ Ark, 96 & 97; vis asst prof, Univ Iowa, 97; asst prof, Northern Ill Univ, 97-. **HONORS AND AWARDS** Andrew W. Mellon Fel in the Humanities, 90; Fulbright Fel, 93-95; Northeast Asia Coun Short-term Res Grant, 98. **MEMBERSHIPS** Am Hist Asn, Asn for Asian Studies, Soc for Japanese Studies, Soc for Transnational Cultural Studies. **RESEARCH** Transnational Popular Culture, Comparative Musicology, Authenticity and Cultural Ownership, Modern Japanese History and Culture, Aesthetic Systems. **SELECTED PUBLICATIONS** Auth, Blue Nippon: Authenticating Jazz in Japan, Duke Univ Press, forthcoming. **CONTACT ADDRESS** Dept Hist, No Illinois Univ, 1425 W Lincoln Hwy, Dekalb, IL 60115-2828. **EMAIL** etatkins@niu.edu

ATTREED, LORRAINE C.
PERSONAL Born 12/28/1954, Kingston, NY, m, 1988 **DISCIPLINE** HISTORY **EDUCATION** Univ NMex, Albuquerque, BA, 76; Univ York, Eng, MA, 80; Harvard Univ, AM, 81, PhD, 84. **CAREER** Assoc prof, 92- & asst prof, 86-92, Holy Cross Col; lectr, 84-85 & tchg fel/tchg asst, 81-86, Harvard Univ; freelance consult on acquisition of rare manuscripts, private NY collectors, 81-87. **HONORS AND AWARDS** Fac fel, 97; Hewlett-Mellon grant, 96; res and publ grant, Rome, Italy; elected fel, Royal Hist Soc Eng, 95; 8 res and publ grants, Holy Cross Col, 87-93; Nat Endowment for the Humanities Travel to Collections grant, 92; Batchelor Ford Summer fac fel, Holy

Cross Col, 88; American Bar Foundation and National Endowment for the Humanities fel, 86; Krupp Found fel, 82; Sheldon Memorial Trust awd, Univ York, 79; Marshall Scholar to Univ York, 77, 2 yrs; Phi Beta Kappa, Univ NMex chap, 76 & Phi Alpha Theta, honor soc hist, 75. **MEMBERSHIPS** Elected gen sec, New Eng Medieval Conf, 97-98, 5 year term; mem, plan comt and session ch for conf Pages Past and Present: Commun Arts from the Middle Ages to the Internet, Higgins Armory Mus, Worcester, 98; mem, selection comt, William Schallek Mem Grad Fel, 91-; elected pres, New Eng Medieval Conf, 95-96, 94-95; mem, plan comt, Medievalism conf 10th annual meeting, Higgins Armory Mus, 95; elected VP, New Eng Medieval Conf, and co-organizer 94 21st annual meeting, Higgins Armory Mus, 93-94; mem, Best Book in Non-N Amer Urban Hist prize comt, Urban Hist Asn, 93-94; reader medieval entries, David Pinkney Prize of the Soc for Fr Hist Stud, Best Bk publ 91, 92-93; treas, New Eng Hist Asn, 91-92; mem, Urban Hist Asn comt to awd prize for best article in urban hist publ 90, 91-92. **RESEARCH** Medieval Europe, 500-1500; England, medieval and early modern; Renaissance Europe; Medieval France; all in fields of political, social, institutional, urban and constitutional. **SELECTED PUBLICATIONS** Auth, An Indenture between Richard Duke of Gloucester and the Scrope Family of Masham and Upsall, Yorkshire, Speculum, 83; auth, Medieval Bureaucracy in Fifteenth-Century York, York Historian, 85; auth, A New Source for Perkin Warbeck's Invasion of 1497, Mediaeval Studies, 86; auth, England's Official Rose: Tudor Concepts of the Middle Ages, in Hermeneutics and Medieval Culture (Albany), SUNY Press, 89; auth, The York House Books, 1461-1490 (London & Gloucester, England), Alan Suttong Publishing, 91; auth, Arbitration and the Growth of Urban Liberties in Late Medieval England, Journal of British Studies, 92; The Politics of Welcome--Ceremonies and Constitutional Development in Later Medieval English Towns, in City and Spectacle in Medieval Europe (Minneapolis), Univ of Minnesota Press, 94; auth, Poverty, Payments, and Fiscal Policies in English Provincial Towns, in Portraits of Medieval Living: Essays in Memory of David Herlihy (Ann Arbor), Univ of MI Press, 96; auth, Friends in Need or in Deed?: Anglo-Portuguese Relations in the Fifteenth Century, Mediterranean Studies, 00; auth, The King's Towns: Identity and Survival in Late Medieval English Boroughs (NY and London), Peter Lang, 01. **CONTACT ADDRESS** Dept of History, Col of the Holy Cross, Worcester, MA 01610-2395. **EMAIL** lattreed@holycross.edu

ATTREP, ABRAHAM M.
DISCIPLINE HISTORY **EDUCATION** La Col, BA, 55; Tulane Univ, MA, 58; Univ GA, PhD, 72. **CAREER** Tchr, Sulphur High Sch, 58-59; hist instr, Millsaps Col, 59-61; instr, Bolton High Sch, 61-62; instr, 62-66, asst prof hist, 68-72, assoc prof hist, 72-78, prof hist, La Tech Univ, 78-; tchg asst, Univ GA, 66-68. **HONORS AND AWARDS** Tchg Awd, Amoco Found, 86-87; appointed William Y. Thompson Prof of Hist, 95; Participant in Nat Endowment for the Humanities Summer Seminars and Institute Program, "Islamic Origins," Univ of Chicago, 00. **RESEARCH** Medieval hist, Renaissance and Reformation, Europ soc and intellectual hist. **SELECTED PUBLICATIONS** Auth, Muslim World, 67; auth, Eastern Orthodoxy Language and Love, The Living Church, 74; The White Lie, Southern Federation of Syrian-Lebanese American Clubs, 76; auth, A Lenten Incident, The Orthodox Observer, 76; auth, 'A State of Wretchedness and Impotence': A British View of Constantinople, Int Jour Mid East Studies, 78; ; auth, The Teacher and His Teachings Chrysostom's Homeletic Approach as seen in Commentaries on the Johannine Gospel, St Vladimir's Theol Quart, 94; auth, St. Ephrem the Syrian (306 A.D.--373 A.D.) A Voice for Our Times?, Jour Orthodox Life and Thought, 95; auth, From the Old to the New: Some of St. Gregoy of Nyssa's Teachings and the Modern Era, The Greek Orthodox Theological Review, 97. **CONTACT ADDRESS** Dept of Hist, Louisiana Tech Univ, PO Box 3178, Ruston, LA 71272.

AUCOIN, BRENT J.
DISCIPLINE HISTORY **EDUCATION** Univ Ark, PhD, 99; Miami Univ, MA, 93; Louisiana State Univ, BA, 91. **CAREER** Asst Prof and Chair, Williams Baptist Col 99-00; instr, St. Persburg State Univ, 98-99; Teacher, St. Petersburg Christian School, 98-99; Graduate Asst, Lecturer, Univ of Arkansas, 96-98; Graduate Asst, Discussion Group Leader, Univ of Arkansas, 94-95. **HONORS AND AWARDS** Fulbright College of Arts and Sciences Dissertation Research Grant, 97; Mary D. Hudgins Fel, 97; Nominee, Excellence in Teaching for Graduate Assistants Awd, 94; Best Paper Delivered at Phi Alpha Theta Arkansas Regional Meeting, 94; The Univ of Arkansas Press Daisy Bates Awd, 94; Mary D. Hudgins Research Grant, 94; Miami Univ Master's Thesis Research Grant, 93. **MEMBERSHIPS** Phi Alpha Theta History Honor Society; Southern Historical Assoc; The Historical Society; Amer Historical Assoc; Arkansas Historical Assoc. **SELECTED PUBLICATIONS** Auth, "Thomas Goode Jones: A Conservative Democrat's Crusade Against Lynching, 1890-1914," The Ozark Historical Review, XXIV, (Spring 95): 30-36; auth, "The Southern Manifesto and Southern White Resistance to Desegregation," The Arkansas Historical Quarterly, LV, Summer 96: 173-198; auth, "Thomas Goode Jones and African American Civil Rights in the New South," The Historian, LX, (Winter 98): 257-271; auth, "My Life and an Era: The Autobiography of Buck Colbert Franklin," by Franklin, John Hope and John Whittington franklin, eds, (Baton Rouge: Louisiana State Univ Press, 97), American Journal of Legal History, Forthcoming; auth, "John Archibald Campbell, Southern Moderate, 1811-1889," by Saunders, Robert, Jr. (Tuscaloosa: The Univ of Alabama Press, 97), Journal of Mississippi History, LX (Summer 98): 173-74; auth, "From Demagogue to Dixiecrat: Horace Wilkinson and the Politics of Race," (Lanham, Md." Univ Press of America, 95), Georgia Historical Quarterly, LXXXI, (Winter 98): 1048-50. **CONTACT ADDRESS** Dept History, Williams Baptist Col, PO Box 3547, Walnut Ridge, AR 72476. **EMAIL** baucoin@wbcoll.edu

AUERBACH, JEROLD
PERSONAL Born 05/07/1936, Philadelphia, PA, m, 1982, 4 children **DISCIPLINE** HISTORY **EDUCATION** Oberlin Col, BA, 57; Columbia Univ, PhD, 65. **CAREER** Lecturer, Queens College, CUNY, 64-65; Asst Prof, Brandeis Univ, 65-71; Asst Prof-Prof, Wellesley College, 71-. **HONORS AND AWARDS** Pelzer Awd, OAH, 64; Liberal Arts Fellow; Harvard Law School, 69-70; Guggenheim Fellow, 74-75; Visiting Scholar, Harvard Law School 78-85; NEH College Teachers Fellowship, 86-87; 91-92; Grants from ACCS, 66; SSRC, 69-10; NSF, 79-81; Littauer Foundation, 86, 99. **RESEARCH** Modern Amer History; legal history; Jewish history. **SELECTED PUBLICATIONS** Auth, "Labor and Liberty," 66; auth, "Unequal Justice," 76; "Justice Without Law?", 83; "Rabbis and Lawyers," 90; "Jacob's Voices," 96. **CONTACT ADDRESS** Dept History, Wellesley Col, 106 Central St., Wellesley Hills, MA 02481-8268. **EMAIL** jsauerbach@aol.com

AUGER, REGINALD
PERSONAL Born 04/03/1955, Quebec, PQ, Canada **DISCIPLINE** ARCHAEOLOGY, HISTORY **EDUCATION** Univ Montreal, BS, 78; Memorial Univ Nfld, MA, 83; Univ Calgary, PhD, 89. **CAREER** PROF ARCHAEOLOGY, LAVAL UNIV. **MEMBERSHIPS** CELAT (Interdisc stud); Can Archaeol Asn; Soc Am Archaeol; Soc Hist Archaeol; Asn canadienne francaise pour l'avancement des sciences. **RESEARCH** Arctic prehistory; contact between Inuit & Europeans in Labrador. **SELECTED PUBLICATIONS** Auth, Labrador Inuit and Europeans in the Strait of Belle isle, 91; co-ed, Ethnicity and Culture, 87. **CONTACT ADDRESS** Dept of History, Univ of Laval, Ste. Foy, QC, Canada G1K 7P4. **EMAIL** reginald.auger@celat.ulaval.ca

AUGUST, ANDREW
PERSONAL Born 10/12/1962, Detroit, MI, m, 1 child **DISCIPLINE** HISTORY **EDUCATION** Univ Mich, BA, 84; Columbia Univ, MA, 85; Mphil, 87; PhD, 93. **CAREER** Adj Asst Prof, New York Univ; Adj Asst Prof, Drew Univ; Asst Prof, Pa State Univ, 95-. **HONORS AND AWARDS** Phi Beta Kappa Soc. **MEMBERSHIPS** North Am Council on Brit Studies. **RESEARCH** British social history of the nineteenth and twentieth centuries. **SELECTED PUBLICATIONS** Auth, Poor Women's Lives: Gender, Work and Poverty in Late-Victorian London, Fairleigh Diehinson Univ Pr, 99. **CONTACT ADDRESS** Dept Hist, Pennsylvania State Univ, Abington-Ogontz, 1600 Woodland Rd, Abington, PA 19001-3918. **EMAIL** axa24@psu.edu

AUGUSTINE, DOLORES L.
PERSONAL Born 04/01/1955, Washington, DC, m, 1993, 2 children **DISCIPLINE** HISTORY **EDUCATION** Georgetown Univ, BS, 76; Frele Universitat, MA, 84; PhD, 91. **CAREER** Vis Instr, Sweet Briar Col, 89-90; Instr to assoc Prof, St John's Univ, 90-. **HONORS AND AWARDS** Stipendium nach dem Nachwuchsforderungsgesetz, 85-86; IRES, 86; Berlin Airlift Foundation, 88-89; DAAD, 94; Nat Sci Foundation grant, 97-99; NEH summer grant, 98. **MEMBERSHIPS** Am Hist Asn, German Studies Asn, AAUP. **RESEARCH** German bourgeoisie/wealthy business families; Social history of East German engineering profession, (since 1945). **SELECTED PUBLICATIONS** Auth, Patricians and Parvenus: Wealth and High Society in Wilhelmine Germany, Berg Pub, 94; auth, "Berufliches Selbstbld, Arbeitshabitus und Mentalitatsstrukturen von software-Experten der DDR," in eliten im Sozialismus. Studien zur Sozialgeschichte der DDR, 99; auth, "The socialist 'Silicon Ceiling': East German Women in computer Science," in 1999 symposium on Technology and Society. Women and Technology: Historical, Societal, and Professional perspectives, 99; auth, "Frustrated Technocrats: Engineers in the Ulbricht Era," in Science under socialism. East Germany in comparative Perspective, 99; auth, Zwischen pribilegierung und entmachtung: Ingenieure in der Ulbricht-Ara," in Naturwissenschaft und Technik in der DDR, 97; auth, "The Banking families in Berline and vienna around 1900," in Cities of finance, 96; auth, "frustrierte Technokraten. Zur sozialgeschichte des Ingenieruberufs in der Ulbicht-Ara," in die Grenzen der Kidtatur. Staat und Gesellschaft in der DDR, 96 **CONTACT ADDRESS** Dept Hist, St. John's Univ, 8150 Utopia Pkwy, Jamaica, NY 11439-0001. **EMAIL** augustid@stjohns.edu

AUGUSTINOS, GERASIMOS
PERSONAL Born 10/18/1939, Syracuse, NY, m, 1966, 2 children **DISCIPLINE** EASTERN EUROPEAN HISTORY **EDUCATION** Syracuse Univ, AB, 62; Ind Univ, Bloomington, MA, 64, PhD(hist), 71. **CAREER** Asst prof, 71-76, Assoc Prof Hist, Univ SC, 77-92; Prof, 92-. **MEMBERSHIPS** Am Asn Advan Slavic Studies; Mod Greek Studies Asn. **RESEARCH** Southeast Europe and Eastern Mediterranean; comparative nationalism; modern Greece. **SELECTED PUBLICATIONS** Auth, Consciousness and history: Nationalist critics of Greek Society, 77, East Europ Monographs; auth, Diverse Paths to Modernith in Southeastern Europe: Essays in National Development, Greenwood Press, 91; auth, The Greeks of Asia Minor: Confession, Community and Ethnicity in the 19th Century, Kent State Univ Press, 92; auth, The National Idea in Eastern Europe: The Politics of Ethnic and Civic Community, Houghton Mifflin, 96. **CONTACT ADDRESS** Dept of Hist, Univ of So Carolina, Columbia, Columbia, SC 29208. **EMAIL** augustinos@sc.edu

AULT, BRADLEY A.
PERSONAL Born 09/22/1961, Seymour, IN, m, 1983, 1 child **DISCIPLINE** CLASSICAL ARCHAEOLOGY **EDUCATION** IN Univ, BA; MA; 2nd MA; PhD. **CAREER** Asst prof, present, SUNY Buffalo. **HONORS AND AWARDS** Commr Inst Coop Scholar, Traveling Scholar; Univ MN; Horstmann fellow, Freie Universitat Berlin; Fulbright fellow, Am Schl Class Studies Athens; blegen res fellow, vassar col. **MEMBERSHIPS** Archaeological Inst of America. **RESEARCH** Class archaeol, Ancient-Medieval art hist. **SELECTED PUBLICATIONS** Auth, publ about ancient Greek agricultural practice and Roman metalwork. **CONTACT ADDRESS** Dept Classics, SUNY, Buffalo, 712 Clemens Hall, Buffalo, NY 14261. **EMAIL** clarbrad@acsu.buffalo.edu

AURAND, HAROLD, JR.
PERSONAL Born 11/29/1963, Bellefonte, PA, s **DISCIPLINE** HISTORY **EDUCATION** Penn St Univ, BA, 86; Univ Minn, MA, 89, PhD, 98. **CAREER** Instr, 92-97, asst prof, Pa State Univ, 92-. **RESEARCH** Early Amer politics, sports hist. **CONTACT ADDRESS** 119 North St, Apt 1A, Port Carbon, PA 17965.

AURAND, HAROLD WILSON
PERSONAL Born 06/24/1940, Danville, PA, m, 1962, 2 children **DISCIPLINE** AMERICAN LABOR HISTORY **EDUCATION** Franklin & Marshall Col, BA, 62; Pa State Univ, University Park, MA, 63, PhD(Hist), 69. **CAREER** From instr to asst prof, 64-72, assoc prof Hist, PA State Univ, Hazelton, 72-. **HONORS AND AWARDS** Amoco Found Outstanding Teaching Awd, 80. **MEMBERSHIPS** Orgn Am Historians. **RESEARCH** American labor history, 1867 to 1920. **SELECTED PUBLICATIONS** Auth, the Workingmen's Benevolent Association, Labor Hist, 66; The Anthracite Strike of 1887, Pa Hist, 68; Diversifying the Economy of the Anthracite Regions, 1880-1900, Pa Mag Hist & Biog, 70; From the Molly Maguires to the United Mine Workers, Temple Univ, 71; Social Motivation of the Anthracite Mine Workers: 1901-1920, Labor Hist, Summer 77; The Anthracite Miner; An Occupational Analyis, Pa Mag Hist & Biog, 80. **CONTACT ADDRESS** Pennsylvania State Univ, Hazleton, Hazleton, PA 18201-1202. **EMAIL** hwa1@psu.edu

AUSMUS, HARRY JACK
PERSONAL Born 06/14/1937, Lafollette, TN, m, 1963, 2 children **DISCIPLINE** EUROPEAN INTELLECTUAL HISTORY, HISTORIOGRAPHY **EDUCATION** E Tenn State Univ, BA, 59, MA, 63; Drew Univ, BD, 63; Oh State Univ, PhD(hist), 69. **CAREER** Prof Hist, Southern CT State Col, 67-. **MEMBERSHIPS** AHA; Soc Reformation Res. **RESEARCH** Modern European intellectual history; historigraphy; philosophy of history. **SELECTED PUBLICATIONS** Auth, Schelling on History, 1841, CT Rev, 72; Schopenhauer and Christianity, IL Quart, 74; Schopenhauer's View of History: A Note, Hist & Theory, 76; Schopenhauer's Philosophy of Language, Midwest Quart, 77; Nietzsche and Eschatology, J Relig, 10/78; The Polite Escape: On the Myth of Secularyation, OH Univ Press, 82; Nothing But History-Reconstruction and Extremity After Metaphysics, with D. D. Roberts, Am Hist Rev, Vol 102, 97. **CONTACT ADDRESS** Dept of Hist, So Connecticut State Univ, 501 Crescent St, New Haven, CT 06515-1330.

AUSTEN, RALPH ALBERT
PERSONAL Born 01/09/1937, Leipzig, Germany, m, 1967, 2 children **DISCIPLINE** AFRICAN & COLONIAL HISTORY **EDUCATION** Harvard Univ, AB, 58; PhD(hist), 66; Univ Calif, Berkeley, MA, 60. **CAREER** Tutor, Dept of Hist, Harvard Univ, 64-65; asst prof hist, NY Univ, 65-67; asst prof hist, Univ Chicago, 67-74, chairman, Comm on African Studies, 74-79, assoc dir, Civilization Course Mat Prog, 77-80, assoc prof Hist, Univ Chicago, 74-85, prof hist, Univ Chicago, 85-, Dir, Master Arts Prog Social Sci, 78-84, 87-90, assoc dir, Center for Middle Eastern Studies, 91-95, cochair, comm on African and African-American Studies, 86-90, 92-, chair, Comm on Int Relations, 97-99; Rockefeller Found exchange fel, Univ Ibadan, 69-70; Fulbright prof, Univ Yaounde, 72-73; Soc Sci Res Coun fel, Europe, Cameroon, 72-73; NSF fel, 75; vis fel, Harry S. Truman Inst, Hebrew Univ, Jerusalem, 84; Fulbright Res Scholar, Europe, Cameroon, 87; vis prof, hist, Univ of Cape Town, South Africa, 91, 94; vis Directeur d'Etudes, Centre d'Etudes Africaines, Ecole des Hautes Etudes en Science Sociales, Paris, 91; vis fel, Forchungsschwerpunk Modrner Orient, berlin, 95. **HONORS AND AWARDS** Woodrow Wilson Fel, Univ of

Calif, 58-59; Foreign Area Fel Found, Harvard Univ, 60-62; Foreign Area Fel Found, England and East Africa, 62-64; teaching fel, Harvard Univ, 64-65; NEH grant for res on the oral epic of Jeki la Njambe in Cameroon, 91. **MEMBERSHIPS** Tanzania Hist Soc; Hist Soc Nigeria; AHA; African Studies Asn; Int African Inst. **SELECTED PUBLICATIONS** Auth, "'Africanist' Historiography and its Critics: Can There be an Autonomous African History?," in African Historiography: Essays in Honour of Ade Ajayi, ed. Toyin Falola (Lagos, London, Longman, 93; auth, "The Moral Economy of Witchcraft: an Essay in Comparative History," in Modernity and its Malcontents, ed. J. and J. L. Comaroff (Univ of Chicago, 93); auth (review), "The Uncomfortable Relationship: African Enslavement in the Common History of Blacks and Jews," Tikkun 9.2 (94): 65-68; auth, The Elusive Epic: The Narrative of Jeki la Njambe in the Historical Culture of the Cameroon Coast, African Studies Asn Press (Atlanta), 96; coauth, "History, Oral Tradition and Structure in Ibn Khaldun's Chronology of Mali Rulers," History of Africa 22 (96): 17-28; auth, "Orality, Literacy and Literature: A Comparison of Three West African Heroic Narratives," in A Cloth of Many Silks: a Fetschrift for Ivor Wilks (Evanston, Northwestern Univ Press, 97); ed, In Search of Sunjata: The Mande Epic as History, Literature, and Performance, Indiana Univ Press, 99; coauth, Middlemen of the Cameroon Rivers: the Duala and Their Hinterland, ca. 1600-ca. 1960, Cambridge Univ Press, 99; auth, "Teaching Africa as a Space of Historical Cultures: Dilemmas and Solutions," in Great Ideas for Teaching about Africa, ed. Jane Parpart and Misty L. Bastian (Boulder, Lynn Reiner, 99); auth, "Coming of Age Through Colonial Education: African Autobiography as Reluctant Bildungsroman (the Case of Camara Laye)," Boston Univ Discussion Papers in the African Humanities. **CONTACT ADDRESS** Univ of Chicago, 5828 S University Ave, Chicago, IL 60637-1539. **EMAIL** wwb3@midway.uchicago.edu

AUSTENSEN, ROY ALLEN
PERSONAL Born 05/31/1942, Berwyn, IL, m, 1966, 3 children **DISCIPLINE** MODERN HISTORY **EDUCATION** Concordia Col, Ill, BS, 63; Univ Ill, Urbana, MA, 64, PhD(hist), 69. **CAREER** Instr hist, Univ IL, Urbana, 68-69; asst prof, 69-75, Assoc Prof Hist, IL State Univ, 75-, Nat Endowment for Humanities fel, 82-83. **HONORS AND AWARDS** Best Article award, Conf Group Cent Europ Hist, 80; W Dee Halverson Prize, Western Asn Ger Studies, 81. **MEMBERSHIPS** AHA; Conf Group Cent Europ Hist; Soc Hist Educ; Western Asn Ger Studies. **RESEARCH** European diplomatic history; Austrian history. **SELECTED PUBLICATIONS** Auth, Count Buol and the Metternich Tradition, In: Austrian History Yearbook, 73-74; History and the Humanities: An Integrative Approach, In: The Social Studies, 9-10/75; Felix Schwarzenberg: Realpolitiker or Metternichian?, In: Mitteilugen des Osterreichischen Staatsarchivs, 77; Austria and the Stuggle for Supremacy in Germany, 1848-1864, J Modern Hist, 6/80; Mother-Tongue and Fatherland-Language and Politics in German, with M. Townson, German Studies Rev, Vol 17, 94; From the Aehrenthal Legacy-Letters and Documents on Austrian-Hungarian Domestic and Foreign-Policy 1885-1912, German, with S. Wank and F. Fellner, Slavic Rev, Vol 55, 96. **CONTACT ADDRESS** Valparaiso Univ, 651 College Ave., Valparaiso, IN 46383-6493.

AUSTIN, GAYLE M.
DISCIPLINE THEATRE HISTORY **EDUCATION** CUNY, PhD. **CAREER** Instr, Hunter Col; instr, Univ SC; assoc prof, Ga State Univ; exec dir, Southeast Playwrights Proj, 87-89. **SELECTED PUBLICATIONS** Auth, The Madwoman in the Spotlight: Plays of Maria Irene Fornes, in Making a Spectacle, Univ Mich Press, 89; The Exchange of Women and Male Homosocial Desire in Miller's 'Death of a Salesman' and Hellman's 'Another Part of the Forest,' in Feminist Rereadings of Modern American Drama, Fairleigh Dickinson UP, 89; Feminist Theories for Dramatic Criticism, Univ Mich Press, 90; Resisting the Birth Mark: Subverting Hawthorne in a Feminist Theory Play, in Upstaging Big Daddy: Directing Theater as if Gender and Race Matter, Univ Mich Press, 93. **CONTACT ADDRESS** Georgia State Univ, Atlanta, GA 30303. **EMAIL** jougma@panther.gsu.edu

AUSTIN, JUDITH
PERSONAL Born 06/18/1940, San Diego, CA **DISCIPLINE** UNITED STATES HISTORY **EDUCATION** Duke Univ, BA, 61; Columbia Univ, MA, 63. **CAREER** Ed, Teachers Col Press, Columbia Univ, 62-66; Res Historian & Archivist, ID State Hist Soc, 67-, Ed, ID Yesterdays, 76-. **MEMBERSHIPS** Western Hist Asn; Orgn Am Historians; Forest Hist Soc; Am Asn State & Local Hist; AHA. **RESEARCH** Western United States; United States political and social. **SELECTED PUBLICATIONS** Auth, Joseph Thing, In: Mountain Men and Fur Trade of the Far West, Vol 9, Arthur Clark; coauth, Case Study of Federal Expenditures on a Water and Related Land Resources Project: Boise Project, Idaho and Oregon, Idaho Water Resource Bd and Idaho Water Resources Res Inst, 74; Desert, Sagebrush, and the Pacific Northwest, In: The Pacific Northwest: A Region in Myth and Reality, OR State Univ (in prep). **CONTACT ADDRESS** 1621 Martha St, Boise, ID 83706.

AUTEN, ARTHUR
DISCIPLINE HISTORY **EDUCATION** Case Western Reserve Univ, BA, MA, PhD. **CAREER** Prof, Hartford Univ. **SELECTED PUBLICATIONS** Auth, Western Civilization, 97; American History, 97; ed, Readings in Western Civilization, 96. **CONTACT ADDRESS** History Dept, Univ of Hartford, 200 Bloomfield Ave, West Hartford, CT 06117.

AVAKUMOVIC, IVAN
PERSONAL Born 08/22/1926, Belgrade, Yugoslavia, m, 1957, 1 child **DISCIPLINE** MODERN HISTORY, POLITICAL SCIENCE **EDUCATION** Cambridge Univ, BA, 47, MA, 52; Univ London, MA, 54; Oxford Univ, DPhil(soc sci), 58. **CAREER** Asst lectr polit, Aberdeen Univ, 57-58; from asst prof to assoc prof polit sci & int rels, Univ Man, 58-63; from assoc prof to prof polit sci, 63-69, Prof Hist, Univ BC, 69-, Can Coun leave fel, 68-69; Killam Sr Fel, Killam Found, 76-77. **MEMBERSHIPS** AHA; Am Asn Advan Slavic Studies; Am Polit Sci Asn; Can Hist Asn. **RESEARCH** Movements of social dissent; East European politics and history; international relations. **SELECTED PUBLICATIONS** Coauth, The Anarchist Prince--A Biographical Study of Peter Kropotkin, Boardman, London & NY, 50; auth, The Communist Party in Canada: a history, by Ivan Avakumovic; coauth, Peter Kropotkin: From Prince to Rebel, by George Woodcock, Ivan Avakumovic, 90. **CONTACT ADDRESS** Dept of Hist, Univ of British Columbia, 1873 E Mall, Ste 1297, Vancouver, BC, Canada V6T 1Z1.

AVERY, KEVIN J.
PERSONAL Born 09/19/1950, Jersey City, NJ, s, 2 children **DISCIPLINE** HISTORY OF NINETEENTH-CENTURY AMERICAN ART **EDUCATION** Columbia Univ, PhD, 95. **CAREER** Assoc Curator, Dept of Am Paintings and Sculpture, Metropolitan Museum of Art; adjunct asst prof, Dept of Art, Hunter Col, CUNY. **HONORS AND AWARDS** Chester Dale Fel, Metropolitan Museum of Art, 83-84; Andrew Mellon Fel, MMA, 84-85; Whiting Fel, Columbia Univ, 87-88. **MEMBERSHIPS** Col Art Asn; Historians of Nineteenth-Century Art. **RESEARCH** Hudson River School landscape painting; Frederic E. Church; Sanford R. Gifford; Thomas Cole; panorama painting. **SELECTED PUBLICATIONS** Auth, American Drawings in the Metropolitan Museum of Art, Volume I: Catalogue of Works by Artists born between 1738 and 1835, Metropolitan Museum of Art, forthcoming; American Tonalism, Am Tonalism from the Metropolitan Museum of Art, Montclair Art Museum, 99; Movies for Manifest Destiny: The Moving Panorama Phenomenon in America, Panorama of Bunyan's Pilgrim's Progress, Montclair Art Museum, 99; Church's Great Picture: The Heart of the Andes, Metropolitan Museum of Art, 93; Picturing the Frontier: the Panorama Phenomenon in America, Sehsuct [The Desire to See], Kunst-und Ausstellungshalle der Bundesrepublik Deutschland, 93. **CONTACT ADDRESS** Dept of Am Paintings and Sculpture, Metropolitan Mus of Art, 1000 Fifth Ave, New York, NY 10028. **EMAIL** kevin.avery@mermuseum.org

AVRICH, PAUL HENRY
PERSONAL Born 08/04/1931, Brooklyn, NY, m, 1954, 2 children **DISCIPLINE** HISTORY **EDUCATION** Cornell Univ, AB, 52; Columbia Univ, AM, 59, PhD, 61. **CAREER** Vis asst Prof, 61-62 & 63-64, Wesleyan Univ; vis assoc prof, 66, vis prof, 81, Columbia Univ; instr to assoc prof, 60-70, prof, 70-82, dist prof hist, 82-, Queens Col, NY. **HONORS AND AWARDS** Amer Coun of Learned Socs and Soc Sci Res Coun Slavic Stud Grant 62; Amer Philos Soc res grant, 64; Guggenheim fel, 67-68; NEH sr fel, 72-73; Amer Coun of Learned Soc Fel, 82-83; co-win Philip Taft Labor Hist Awd 84; NEH fel, 89-90. **MEMBERSHIPS** AHA; Am Assn Advan Slavic Studies; Orgn Am Historians. **RESEARCH** Modern Russian history; anarchism; revolutionary movements. **SELECTED PUBLICATIONS** Auth, The Russian Anarchists, Princeton, 67; auth, "Kronstadt 1921," Princeton, 70; auth, Russian Rebels 1600-1800, Schocken, 72; ed, The Anarchists in the Russian Revolution, Cornell Univ, 73; auth, An American Anarchist: The Life of Voltairine de Cleyre, The Modern School Movement, Princeton, 78; auth, The Haymarket Tragedy, Princeton, 84; auth, Anarchist Portraits, Princeton, 88; auth, Sacco and Vanzetti: The Anarchist Background, Princeton, 91; auth, Anarchist Voices: An Oral History of Anarchism in America, Princeton, 95. **CONTACT ADDRESS** 425 Riverside Dr, New York, NY 10025. **EMAIL** paulavr@aol.com

AXELRAD, ALLAN M.
PERSONAL Born 07/15/1941, Washington, DC, 2 children **DISCIPLINE** AMERICAN STUDIES, HISTORY **EDUCATION** Univ Calif, Riverside, BA, 65, MA, 65; Univ Pa, MA, 69, PhD(Am civilization), 74. **CAREER** Lectr Am studies, Skidmore Col, 72-73; asst prof Am studies, Sacred Heart Col, 73-75; lectr hist, Calif Polytech State Univ, San Luis Obispo, 75-76; lectr, 76-80, Prof Am Studies, CA State Univ, Fullerton, 76-. **MEMBERSHIPS** Am Studies Asn; Orgn Am Historians; ALA. **RESEARCH** Pretwentieth-century American cultural history, James Geuimore Cooper. **SELECTED PUBLICATIONS** Auth, Ideology and Utopia in the Works of Ignatius Donnelly, Am Studies, 71; History and Utopia: A Study of the World View of James Fenimore Cooper, Norwood, 78; The Protagonist of the Protestant Ethic: Max Weber's Ben Franklin, Rendezvous, 78; The Order of the Leatherstocking Tales: D H Lawrence, David Noble, and the Iron Trap of History, Am Lit, 82; auth, Wish Fulfillment in the Wilderness: D H Lawrence and the Leatherstocking Tales, American Quarterly, 87. **CONTACT ADDRESS** Dept of Am Studies, California State Univ, Fullerton, Fullerton, CA 92834. **EMAIL** aaxelrad@fullerton.edu

AXTELL, JAMES LEWIS
PERSONAL Born 12/20/1941, Endicott, NY, m, 1963, 2 children **DISCIPLINE** HISTORY **EDUCATION** Yale Univ, BA, 63; Cambridge Univ, PhD(hist), 67. **CAREER** Asst prof hist, Yale Univ, 66-72; assoc prof, Sarah Lawrence Col, 72-75; vis prof, Northwestern Univ, Ill, 77-78; Prof Hist, Col William & Mary, 78-, Kenan prof hum, 86-; Res fel hist, Social Sci Res Coun, 65-66; Morse Jr Fac res fel, Yale Univ, 69-70; res fel, Nat Endowment Humanities, 75-77, 86, 92; res fel, J S Guggenheim Found, 81-82; res fel Am Coun Learned Socs, 87. **HONORS AND AWARDS** Outstanding Fac, Va State Counc High Educ, 88; Loyola-Mellon Hum Aw, 92; Fleming Lecturer Southern Hist, LSU, 96. **MEMBERSHIPS** AHA; Orgn Am Historians; Am Soc Ethnohistory; Champlain Soc; Haklyut Soc; Colonial Soc Mass; Mass His Soc; Soc Am Historians; French Colonial His Soc; Soc for the Hist of Discoveries. **RESEARCH** History of Colonial North America; ethnohistory of Indian-white relations; history of Am higher education. **SELECTED PUBLICATIONS** Auth, The Educational Writings of John Locke: A Critical Edition with Introduction and Notes, Cambridge Univ Press, 68; auth, The School upon a Hill: Education and Society in Colonial New England, Yale Univ Press, 74; auth, Indian Missions: A Critical Bibliography, Newberry Libr Ctr Hist Am Indian, 78; auth, The Indian Peoples of Eastern America: A Documentary History of the Sexes, Oxford Univ Press, 81; auth, The European and the Indian: Essays in the Ethnohistory of Colonial North America, Oxford Univ Press, 81; auth, The Invasion Within: The Contact of Cultures in Colonial North America, Oxford Univ Press, 85; auth, After Columbus: Essays in the Ethnohistory of Colonial North America, Oxford Univ Press, 88; auth, Beyond 1492: Encounters in Colonial North America, Oxford Univ Press, 92; auth, The Indians' New South: Cultural Change in the Colonial Southeast, LSU, 97; auth, The Pleasures of Academia: A Celebration and Defense of Higher Education, Nebraska Univ Press, 98; auth, Natives and Newcomers: the Cultural Origisn of North Am, Oxford Univ Pr, 00. **CONTACT ADDRESS** Dept of Hist, Col of William and Mary, Williamsburg, VA 23187-8795. **EMAIL** jlaxte@wm.edu

B

BAACKMANN, SUSANNE
PERSONAL Born 10/14/1958, Gladbeck, Germany, m, 1993, 1 child **DISCIPLINE** GERMAN STUDIES **EDUCATION** Univ Duisburg, MA; Univ Calif Berkeley, PhD. **CAREER** Assoc prof, Univ NMex, 93-. **HONORS AND AWARDS** Fulbright Fel, 86; Outstanding Teaching Awd, 89. **MEMBERSHIPS** MLA; AATG. **RESEARCH** Contemporary German culture; women's literature. **SELECTED PUBLICATIONS** Auth, Erular Mirliebe Chamburg: Argument, 95; auth, Conquering Women: Women, War and Sexuality in the German Cultural Imagination, Univ Calif Pr, 00. **CONTACT ADDRESS** 4050 Anderson Ave SE, Albuquerque, NM 87108-4309. **EMAIL** theodo@unm.edu

BABCOCK, ROBERT HARPER
PERSONAL Born 12/19/1931, Cincinnati, OH, m, 1955, 6 children **DISCIPLINE** AMERICAN & CANADIAN HISTORY **EDUCATION** State Univ NYork, Albany, AB, 53; MA, 57; Duke Univ, PhD, 70. **CAREER** Teacher Am hist, Guilderland Sr High Sch, 57-66; instr, Duke Univ, 68-69; from asst prof to assoc prof hist, Wells Col, 69-75, chmn dept, 72-74; actg chmn, 79, assoc prof to prof to prof emeritus, hist, Univ ME, Orono, 75-, Consult, Nat Endowment for Humanities, 75-. **HONORS AND AWARDS** Albert B Corey Prize, Can & Am Hist Asns, 76. **MEMBERSHIPS** AHA; Can Hist Asn; Orgn Am Historians; Asn Can Studies US; Atlantic Asn Historians. **RESEARCH** Late 19th & 20th century American history; Canadian social and economic history; Canadian-American relations. **SELECTED PUBLICATIONS** Contrib, The Influence of the United States on Canadian Development: Eleven Case Studies, Duke Univ, 72; auth, Gompers in Canada, Univ Toronto, 74; Economic Development in Portland and Saint John During the Age of Iron and Steam, 1850-1914, Am Rev Can Studies, spring 79; Samuel Gompers et les travailleurs quebecois, 1900-1914, In: Le mouvement ouvrier au Quebec, Boreal Press, 80; Will You Walk-Yes, Well Walk- Popular Support for a Street Railway Strike in Portland, Maine, Labor Hist, Vol 35, 94; Dictionary of Canadian Biography, Vol 13, with R. Cook, Acadiensis, Vol 25, 95; Where the Fraser-River Flows-The Industrial Workers of the World in British-Columbia, with M. Leier, Labor Hist, Vol 36, 95. **CONTACT ADDRESS** Dept of Hist, Univ of Maine, Orono, ME 04473. **EMAIL** babcock@maine.edu

BABCOCK, WILLIAM SUMMER
PERSONAL Born 06/18/1939, Boston, MA, m, 1960, 2 children **DISCIPLINE** CHURCH HISTORY **EDUCATION** Brown Univ, AB, 61; Yale Univ, MA, 65, PhD(relig studies), 71. **CAREER** From instr to asst prof, 67-91; Am Coun Learned Socs studies fel, 73-74; Dir, graduate program in religious studies, 90-; Assoc Prof Church Hist, Perkins Sch Theol, Southern Methodist Univ, 91-; Provost ad interim and VP for Academic Affairs, 95-96. **MEMBERSHIPS** Am Soc Church Hist; Mediaeval Acad Am; NAm Patristics Soc; Am Cath Hist Asn. **RESEARCH** Augustine; Latin Patristics; history of Christian theology. **SELECTED PUBLICATIONS** Auth, Grace, Freedom and Justice: Augustine and the Christian Tradition, summer 73 & Patterns of Roman Selfbood: Marcus Aurelius and Augustine of Hippo, fall 74, Perkins Sch Theol J; Augustine's Interpretation of Romans (AD 394-396), Augustinian Studies 19, 79; Agustin y Ticonio: sobre la appropriacion latina de Pablo, Augustinus, 7-12/81; Art and Architecture, Christian, In: Abingdon Dict of Living Religions, 81; auth, Augustine on Sin and Moral Agency, J Religious Ethics 16, 88; Tyconius: The Book of Rules, 89; ed, Paul and the Legacies of Paul, 90; auth, Cupiditas and Caritas: The Early Augustine on Love and Human Fulfillment, In: The Ethics of st. Augustine, 91; auth, Augustine and the Spirituality of Desire, Augustinian Studies 25 (94); Is There Only One True Religion or Are There Many, with S. M. Ogden, Theology Today, Vol 50, 94; auth, Sin and Punishment: The early Augustine on Evil, In: Augustine: Presbyter Factus Sum, 94. **CONTACT ADDRESS** Perkins Sch of Theol, So Methodist Univ, Dallas, TX 75275. **EMAIL** wbabcock@mail.smu.edu

BABSON, JANE F.
PERSONAL Born 08/17/1925, Leitchfield, KY, m, 1954, 2 children **DISCIPLINE** ART & ART HISTORY **EDUCATION** Mt Holyoke, BA (art hist); Univ IL, Champaign, MFA. **CAREER** Former member of the staff of the Corcoran Gallery of Art, Washington, DC; Professional Printmeaker, Artitist and Photographer; founder, The Winstead Press LTD, 86-. **MEMBERSHIPS** Soc of Architectural Hist; Nat Trust for Historic Preservation; The Ephemera Soc, London; IL Hist Soc; Am Crafts Coun. **RESEARCH** A.. of Sir Jacob Epstein and his art; Am Colonial forts; res on early colonial America. **SELECTED PUBLICATIONS** Auth, The Architecture of Early Illinois Forts, IL Hist Soc J, spring 68, from book Some Early Types in the Northwest Territory, 1679-1832, IL Hist Soc Lib, 67; The Epsteins, A Family Album, Taylor-Hall Pub, 84. **CONTACT ADDRESS** 202 Slice Dr, Stamford, CT 06907. **EMAIL** winstead.press@gte.net

BACCHIOCCHI, SAMUELE
PERSONAL Born Rome, Italy **DISCIPLINE** THEOLOGY AND CHURCH HISTORY **EDUCATION** Newbold Col, Eng, BA; Andrews Univ, BD, MA; Pontifical Gregorian Univ, Ital, PhD, summa cum laude, 74. **CAREER** Prof, Andrews Univ. **HONORS AND AWARDS** Gold medal, Pope Paul VI. **SELECTED PUBLICATIONS** Auth, Immortality or Resurrection? A Biblical Study on Human Nature and Destiny; From Sabbath to Sunday: A Historical Investigation of the Rise of Sunday Observance in Early Christianity; Divine Rest for Human Restlessness: A Theological Study of the Good News of the Sabbath for Today; The Sabbath in the New Testament. Answers to Questions; God's Festivals in Scripture and History, Vol I: The Spring Festivals; God's Festivals in Scripture and History, Vol 2: The Fall Festivals; Wine in the Bible: A Biblical Study on the Use of Alcoholic Beverages; The Advent Hope for Human Hopelessness. A Theological Study of the Meaning of the Second Advent for Today; Women in the Church: A Biblical Study on the Role of Women in the Church; Christian Dress and Adornment; Hal Lindsey's Prophetic Jigsaw Puzzle: Five Predictions that Failed!; The Time of the Crucifixion and the Resurrection; The Marriage Covenant: A Biblical Study on Marriage, Divorce, and Remarriage. **CONTACT ADDRESS** Andrews Univ, Berrien Springs, MI 49104-0180.

BACHARACH, JERE L.
PERSONAL Born 11/18/1938, New York, NY, m, 1962, 2 children **DISCIPLINE** ISLAMIC HISTORY **EDUCATION** Trinity Col, CT, BA, 60; Harvard Univ, MA, 62; Univ Mich, PhD(hist), 67. **CAREER** Asst prof, 67-73, assoc prof, 73-82, Prof Hist, Univ WA, 82-, Chmn res & training comt, Mid E Studies Asn, 77-; prin investigator, NEH Mus & Hist Orgn award, 77-79; ed, MESA Bull, 78-. **MEMBERSHIPS** AHA; Am Orient Soc; Mediaeval Acad Am; Am Numis Soc; Mid E Studies Asn N Am. **RESEARCH** Medieval Islamic political, economic and numismatic history. **SELECTED PUBLICATIONS** Auth, A Near East Studies Handbook, Univ Wash, rev ed, 76; co-ed, The Warp and Weft of Islam, Henry Art Gallery, 78; Symbols of Islam, 82. **CONTACT ADDRESS** Dept of Hist, Univ of Washington, Seattle, WA 98105.

BACHRACH, BERNARD S.
PERSONAL Born 05/14/1939, New York, NY **DISCIPLINE** MEDIEVAL HISTORY **EDUCATION** Queens Col, NYork, BA, 61; Univ Calif, Berkeley, MA, 62, PhD, 66. **CAREER** Lectr Hist, Queens Col, NY, 66-67; from asst prof to assoc prof, 67-75, assoc dir, Prog Jewish Studies, 76-80, Prof Hist, Univ MN, Minneapolis, 76-, Adj Prof Ancient Studies & Relig Studies, 80-, McKnight award Europ hist, 68; Am Coun Learned Socs res grant, 73-74; co-ed, Medieval Prospography. **HONORS AND AWARDS** Fel, Medieval Academy of Am, 93; CEE Distinguished Teaching Awd by the Univ of Minn, 93; Institute for Advanced Study, Princeton, 97-98. **MEMBERSHIPS** AHA; Mediaeval Acad Am; Soc Antiquaires de l'Ouest; Asn Medieval Historians of Mid-West. **RESEARCH** Medieval Europe. **SELECTED PUBLICATIONS** Auth, Montjoie-et-Saint-Denis-Paris and St-Denis as the Origins of the Spiritual Center of Gaul (French), with A. Lombardjourdan, Speculum-A J of Medieval Studies, Vol 67, 92; Sociobiology and Human Social Behavior-Reply, J of Interdisciplinary Hist, Vol 23, 93; auth, Fulk Nerra-the Neo Roman Consul: A Political Biography of the Angevin Count (Berkeley: University of Calif Pr, 93), 987-1040; Anthropologists and Early-Medieval History-Some Problems, Cithara-Essays in the Judeo-Christian Tradition, Vol 33, 94; Terrence J. Daly Comment on Medieval Seige Warfare-Reply, J of Military Hist, Vol 58, 94; auth, State-Building in Medieval France: Studies Early Angevin History, London: Variorum, 95; Feifs and Vassals-The Medieval Evedence Reinterpreted, with S. Reynolds, Albion, Vol 27, 95; Roman Defeat, Christian Response, and the Literary Construction of the Jew, with D. M. Olster, Speculum-A J of Medieval Studies, Vol 71, 96; Medieval Source Identification and Citations (French), J. Berlioz, Speculum- A J of Medieval Studies, Vol 71, 96; Medieval Diplomatics (French), with O. Guyotjeannin, J. Pycke, and B. M. Tock, Speculum-A J of Medieval Studies, Vol 71, 96; Arms, Armies and Fortifications in the 100 Years War, with A. Curry and M. Hughes, Historian, Vol 59, 96; Phantoms of Remembrance-Memory and Oblivion at the End of the First Millennium, with P. J. Geary, J of Interdisciplinary Hist, Vol 27, 96; Warfare Under the Anglo-Norman Kings, 1066-1135, with S. Morillo, Int Hist Rev, Vol 18, 96; Knights and Warhorses-Military Service and the English Aristocracy Under Edward III, with A. Ayton, J of Military Hist, Vol 60, 96; Family Power in Southern Italy-The Duchy-og-Gaeta and Its Neighbors, 850-1139, with P. Skinner, J of Interdisciplinary Hist, Vol 27, 97; King Alfred the Great, with A. P. Smith, J of Military Hist, Vol 61, 97; Neglected Heroes-Leadership and War in the Early-Medieval Period, with T. L. Gore, Speculum-A J of Medieval Studies, Vol 72, 97; Medieval Warfare Source Book, Vol 1, Warfare in Western Christendom, with D. Nicolle, Int Hist Rev, Vol 19, 97; ed, Medieval Prosopography; ed, Res Mitiraris; auth, "Pirenne and Charlemagne," in After Rome's Fall: Narrators and Sources of Early Medieval History , ed Alexander C. Murray (Toronto: Univ of Toronto Pr, 98), 214-231. **CONTACT ADDRESS** 614 Soc Sci, Univ of Minnesota, Twin Cities, 267 19th Ave S, 614 Soc Sci, Minneapolis, MN 55455. **EMAIL** bachr001@umn.edu

BADASH, LAWRENCE
PERSONAL Born 05/08/1934, Brooklyn, NY, 2 children **DISCIPLINE** HISTORY OF SCIENCE **EDUCATION** Rensselaer Polytech Inst, BS (physics), 56; Yale Univ, PhD(hist of sci), 64. **CAREER** Instr Hist of Sci, Yale Univ, 64-65, res assoc, 65-66; asst prof, 66-73, assoc prof, 73-79, prof Hist of Sci, Univ Calif, Santa Barbara, 79-, consult, Am Chem Soc, 61, Time-Life Publ, Inc, 63 & Gen Res Corp, 68; NATO fel, 65-66; NSF res grants, 65-66 & 69-72; mem adv bd, Reactor Hist Proj, Rand Corp, 75-77; mem adv bd, inst Appropriate Technol, Univ Calif, 77-79; dir summer seminar on Global Security and Arms Control, Univ Calif, 83, 86; instr, Cen of Postgrad Studies, Dubrovnik, 86, 87, 96; vis prof Meiji Gakuin Univ, Yokohama, 93. **HONORS AND AWARDS** Fel, US European Summer School on Global Security and Arms Control. Univ Sussex, 87; fell, Amer Assoc for the Advancement of Sciences (AAAS), 84; fell, John Simon Memorial Foundation, 84-85; fell, Amer Physical Soc, 87; fell, Summer Seminar on East-West Sec Probs, Moscow State Institute of International Affairs, 89. **MEMBERSHIPS** Hist Sci Soc; AAAS; Fedn Am Sci; WCoast Hist of Sci Soc. **RESEARCH** History of modern physics, especially radioactivity and nuclear physics; development of military and civilian uses of nuclear energy. **SELECTED PUBLICATIONS** Auth, Radioactivity before the Curies, Am J Physics, 2/65; How the newer alchemy was received, Sci Am, 8/66; Rutherford, Boltwood, and the age of the earth: The origin of radioactive dating techniques, Proc Am Philos Soc, 6/68; ed, Rutherford and Boltwood, Letters on Radioactivity, Yale Univ, 69; Rutherford Correspondence Catalog, Am Inst Physics, 74; auth, The completeness of 19th century science, Isis, 3/72; Radioactivity in America: Growth and decay of a science, Johns Hopkins, 79; ed, Reminiscences of Los Alamos, 1943-1945, Reidel, 80; Kapitza, Rutherford, and the Kremlin, Yale Univ, 85; Scientists and the Development of Nuclear Weapons, Humanities Press, 95. **CONTACT ADDRESS** Dept of History, Univ of California, Santa Barbara, Santa Barbara, CA 93106-0001. **EMAIL** badash@humanitas.ucsb.edu

BADGER, REID
PERSONAL Born 07/31/1942, Salt Lake City, UT, m, 1965, 2 children **DISCIPLINE** AMERICAN STUDIES **EDUCATION** US Naval Acad, BS, 64; Syracuse Univ, MSS, 74, PhD, 75. **CAREER** Prof, 74-98 dir, program in Amer Studies, 75-80, asst dean, Coll of Arts and Sci, 80-83, 98- prof emeritus of American Studies, Univ of AL. **MEMBERSHIPS** Amer Studies Assoc; Amer Historical Assn; Organization of Amer Historians; Ctr for Black Music Research **RESEARCH** American Culture **SELECTED PUBLICATIONS** Auth, A Life in Ragtime: A Biography of James Reese Europe, Oxford Univ Press, 95; auth, Pride without Prejudice: The Day New York Drew No Color Line, Prospects: A Journ of Amer Cultural Studies, 91; A Military Band Whose Exotic Beat Led Them All, New York Newsday, May 15, 95; The Jazz King, The Baltimore Sun, Feb 1, 98. **CONTACT ADDRESS** Amer Studies Program, Univ of Alabama, Tuscaloosa, University, AL 35486. **EMAIL** rbadger@tenhoor.as.ua.edu

BADIAN, ERNST
PERSONAL Born 08/08/1925, Vienna, Austria, m, 1950, 2 children **DISCIPLINE** HISTORY, CLASSICAL STUDIES **EDUCATION** Univ NZ, BA, 45; MA, 46; Oxford Univ, BA, 50; MA, 54; DPhil, 56; Victoria Univ, Wellington, LitD, 62. **CAREER** Jr lectr classics, Victoria Univ Wellington, 47-48; asst lectr classics & ancient hist, Univ Sheffield, 52-54; lectr classics, Univ Durham, 54-65; prof ancient hist, Univ Leeds, 65-69; prof classics & hist, SUNY Buffalo, 69-71; prof hist, Harvard Univ, 71-82; John Moors Cabot Prof Hist, Harvard Univ, 82-98; John Moors Cabot Prof Hist Emer, Harvard Univ, 98-. **HONORS AND AWARDS** Conington Prize, Oxford Univ, 59, for Foreign Clientelae; Fel Brit Acad, Am Acad Arts & Scis, Am Numismatic Soc; corresp mem, Austrian Acad Scis, German Archaeol Inst; for mem, Finnish Acad Scis; hon mem, Soc Prom Roman Studies; hon Fel, Univ Col, Oxford; Austrian Cross of Hon in Sci & Art, 99; fel, Am Coun Learned Socs 72, 82; Leverhulme Fel, 73; Guggenheim Fel, 84; vis mem, Inst Adv Study, Princeton, fall 80, fall 92; fel, Nat Hum Ctr, 88; Hon LitD, Macquarie Univ, 93, Univ Canterbury, 99. **MEMBERSHIPS** Mem, Am Philol Asn, Asn Ancient Historians, Class Asn Can, UK Class Asn, Soc Prom Hellenic Studies, Virgil Soc. **RESEARCH** Alexander the Great; Roman Republic; Achaemenid Persia. **SELECTED PUBLICATIONS** Auth, Foreign Clientelae 264-270 BC, 58; auth, Studies in Greek and Roman History, 64; ed, Polybius, 66; ed, Ancient Society and Institutions, 66; auth, Roman Imperialism in the Late Republic, 67; auth Publicans and Sinners, 72; ed, "Sir Ronald Syme," Roman Papers Vols 1-2 (79); auth, From Plataea to Potidaea, 93; auth, Zoellner und Suender, 97; Ed, Am J Ancient Hist, 76-00. **CONTACT ADDRESS** Dept of Hist, Harvard Univ, Robinson Hall, Cambridge, MA 02138.

BAER, JOACHIM THEODOR
PERSONAL Born 11/11/1933, Essen, Germany, 2 children **DISCIPLINE** RUSSIAN STUDIES, POLISH STUDIES **EDUCATION** Ind Univ, AB, 57; Harvard Univ, PhD, 63. **CAREER** Asst prof Russ, Vanderbilt Univ, 62-66; asst prof Slavic lang & lit & Jonathan Dickinson Bicentennial preceptor, Princeton Univ, 66-71; asst prof Russ & Polish lang & lit, NY Univ, 71-73; assoc prof Slavic lang & lit, 73-76, prof, Univ NC, Greensboro, 76-, NDEA-Fulbright Hays award, Poland, 65-66 & res scholar, Inst Lit Studies, Polish Acad Sci, 69-70; Ger Acad Exchange Serv res awards, 74 & 78. **HONORS AND AWARDS** Distinguished Service Awd, Polish Am Club, 93; Phi Beta Kappa, Ind Univ, 57. **MEMBERSHIPS** Am Asn Advan Slavic Studies; Am Asn Teachers Slavic & East Europ Lang; Int Asn Slavic Lang & Lit; AAUP; Schopenhauer Ges. **RESEARCH** Nineteenth and early 20th century Russian literature; late 19th and early 20th century Polish literature; Russian and Polish. **SELECTED PUBLICATIONS** Auth, Dal' und Leskov als Vertreter des Kunstlerischen Philologismus, Z Slavische Philol, Vol XXXVII, No 1; Nietzsche's Influence in the Early Work of Waclaw Berent, Scando-Slavica, 71; Philologism and Conservatism in Nineteenth-Century Russian Literature, Slavic Studies, Hokkaido Univ, 72; Vladimir Ivanovic Dal' as a Belletrist, Mouton, The Hague, 72; co-ed, Mnemozina: Studia Litteraria Russica in Honorem Vsevolod Setchkarev, Fink, Munich, 74; auth, Waclaw Berent, His Life and Work, Institutum Historicum Polonicum, Rome, 74, Ex Antemurale, XVIII: 75-239; Arthur Schopenhauer und die russische Literatur des spaten 19 und fruhen 20 Jahrhundert, Sagner, Munich, 80; Schopenhauer und Afanasij Fet, 61 Schopenhauer Jahrbuch fur das Jahr 1980, KrAm, Frankfurt, 80. **CONTACT ADDRESS** Dept of Ger & Russ, Univ of No Carolina, Greensboro, 1000 Spring Garden, Greensboro, NC 27412-0001. **EMAIL** jtbaer@fagan.uncg.edu

BAEZ, ANGEL DAVID CRUZ
PERSONAL Born 01/19/1948, Cayey, PR, m, 1965, 3 children **DISCIPLINE** GEOGRAPHY **EDUCATION** Univ Puerto Rico, Ba, 69; Univ Wis, MS, 71; PhD, 77. **CAREER** Full prof, Univ Puerto Rico, 72-. **HONORS AND AWARDS** Ford Fel, 70-72; NASA Fel, 88,89. **MEMBERSHIPS** Asn of Am Geogr, N Am Cartographic Information Soc, Am Soc of Photogrammetry and remote sensing. **RESEARCH** Geographic information systems, Remote sensing, Computer Cartography. **SELECTED PUBLICATIONS** Auth, "Housing Preferences and Attitudes of Blacks Toward Housing discrimination in Metropolitan Miami," Urban Geography, 98; auth, "Poblacion de Puerto Rico" in the Enciclopedia Puertorriquenia Siglo XXI, 98; auth, Atlas of Puerto Rico, Cuban American National Council, 97; auth, "Residential Segregation by socioeconomic Class in Metropolitan Miami: 1990," Urban Geography, (97): 474-496; auth, "Esta la Agricultura de Puerto Rico lista para la Globalizacion?," Globalization in America, A Geographical Approach, 96. **CONTACT ADDRESS** Dept Geog, Univ of Puerto Rico, Rio Piedras, PO Box 22515, Rio Piedras, PR 00931-2515. **EMAIL** acruz@upracd.upr.clu.edu

BAGBY, WESLEY MARVIN
PERSONAL Born 06/15/1922, Albany, GA, m, 1969, 2 children **DISCIPLINE** HISTORY **EDUCATION** Univ NC, AB, 43; MA, 45; Columbia Univ, PhD, 53. **CAREER** Instr hist, Pfeiffer Jr Col, 45-46, Wake Forest Col, 46-48, Univ Tenn, 49-51, Univ Md, 51-52; from assoc prof to prof hist, WVa Univ, 56-. **HONORS AND AWARDS** Fulbright Lectr, Tamkang Col & Fu Jen Univ, 75-76; Fulbright Lectr, Nankai Univ, 82-83; Benedum Distinguished Scholar Awd, 92; Golden Apple Awd, Golden Key Nat Hon Soc, 92. **MEMBERSHIPS** AHA; AAUP; Soc Historians of Am Foreign Rels. **RESEARCH** Recent American history; American diplomatic history. **SELECTED PUBLICATIONS** Auth, The Road to Normalcy: The Presidential Campaign and Election of 1920, Johns Hopkins Press (Baltimore, MD), 62; auth, "The Harding Election: Wilson Repudiated," in History of the First World War, ed. Peter Young (London: Purnell, 71); auth, "An Identification and Classification of America's Historic Foreign Policies," Tamkang J (76): 55-67; auth, Contemporary American Economic and Political Problems, Nelson-Hall (Chicago, IL), 81; auth, Contemporary American Social Problems, Nelson-Hall (Chicago, IL), 82; auth, Contemporary International Problems, Nelson-Hall (Chicago, IL), 83; auth, Introduction to Social Science, Nelson-Hall (Chicago, IL), 87; auth, The Eagle-Dragon Alliance: America's Relations with China in World War II, Univ Del Press (Wilmington, DE), 92; auth, "Iraq and the United States," Encycl of Contemp Soc Issues (97); auth, America's International Relations Since World War I, Oxford (New York, NY), 99. **CONTACT ADDRESS** Dept of Hist, West Virginia Univ, Morgantown, P O Box 6303, Morgantown, WV 26506-6303. **EMAIL** wbagby@wvu.edu

BAGLEY, ROBERT W.
PERSONAL Born 04/10/1947, Ann Arbor, MI **DISCIPLINE** ARCHAEOLOGY **EDUCATION** Harvard Univ, AB, 67; Univ Chicago, MS, 70; Harvard Univ, MA, 71; PhD, 81. **CAREER** Asst Prof, Harvard Univ, 81-85; Asst Prof, Princeton Univ, 85-. **HONORS AND AWARDS** Who's Who in the East. **RESEARCH** Chinese Archaeology. **SELECTED PUBLICATIONS** Co-auth, The Great Bronze Age of China, 80; auth, Shang Ritual Bronzes, 87. **CONTACT ADDRESS** Dept Art & Archaeol, Princeton Univ, McCormick Hall, Princeton, NJ 08544-0001.

BAGNALL, ROGER SHALER
PERSONAL Born 08/19/1947, Seattle, WA, m, 1969, 2 children **DISCIPLINE** GREEK PAPYROLOGY, ANCIENT HISTORY **EDUCATION** Yale Univ, BA, 68; Univ Toronto, MA, 69, PHD(class studies), 72. **CAREER** Asst prof classics, Fla State Univ, 72-74; asst prof Greek & Latin, 74-79, assoc prof to prof Classics & Hist, Columbia Univ, 74-; mem bd, Scholars Press, 77-85; pres, Egyptological Sem of NY, 81-83; vis prof, Univ Florence, 81. **HONORS AND AWARDS** Am Coun Learned Soc grant-in-aid, 75; Am Coun Learned Soc study fel, 76-77; Am Philos Soc grant-in-aid, 80; Guggenheim fel, 90-91; Fel, Am Numismatic Soc; Assoc Academie Royale des Sciences; des Lettres et des Beaux-Arts de Relgique; Member, American Academy of Arts and Sciences. **MEMBERSHIPS** Am Soc Papyrologists (secy-treas, 74-79); Am Philol Asn (secy-treas, 79-85); Asn pour les Etudes Grecques; Egypt Exploration Soc; Asn Ancient Historians. **RESEARCH** Greek papyri; social and economic history of the late Roman Egypt; Hellenistic social and economic history. **SELECTED PUBLICATIONS** Coauth, Ostraka in the Royal Ontario Museum (2 vols), Samuel Stevens, Toronto, 71-76; auth, Ptolemaic Foreign Correspondence in Tebtunis Papyrus 8, J Egyptian Archaeol, 75; The Administration of the Ptolemaic Possessions, Brill, Leiden, 76; coauth, Ostraka in Amsterdam Collections, Terra, Zutphen, 76; auth, The Florida Ostraka: Documents from the Roman Army in Upper Egypt, Duke Univ, 76; Bullion Purchases and Landholding in the Fourth Century, Chronique d'Egypt, 77; coauth, The Chronological Systems of Byzantine Egypt, Terra, Zutphen, 78; Columbia Papyri VII, Scholars Press, 78; auth, Egypt in Late Antiquity, Princeton, 93; coauth, Demography of Roman Egypt, Cambridge, 94; auth, Reading Papyri, Writing Ancient History, Routledge, 95. **CONTACT ADDRESS** Columbia Univ, 1130 Amsterdam Ave, Rm 606, New York, NY 10027-6900. **EMAIL** bagnall@atscolumbia.edu

BAIGELL, MATTHEW
DISCIPLINE AMERICAN ART **EDUCATION** Univ Pa, PhD. **CAREER** Prof II, Rutgers, The State Univ NJ, Univ Col-Camden. **RESEARCH** American art. **SELECTED PUBLICATIONS** Auth, Jewish-American Artists and the Holocaust, Rutgers UP, 97; coauth, Soviet Dissident Art: Interviews after Perestroika, Rutgers UP, 95; auth, Artist and Identity in 20th Century America, Cambridge Univ Pr, 00; coed, Confilcted Identities: Jewish Artists and Modern Art, Rutgers Univ Pr, 00. **CONTACT ADDRESS** Dept of Art Hist, Rutgers, The State Univ of New Jersey, New Brunswick, Voorhees Hall, 71 Hamilton St, New Brunswick, NJ 08903. **EMAIL** baigell@rci.rutgers.edu

BAILEY, ANNE J.
PERSONAL Born 08/07/1944, Cleburne, TX, d, 2 children **DISCIPLINE** HISTORY **EDUCATION** Univ Tex, BA, 82; Tex Christian Univ, MA, 84; PhD, 87. **CAREER** Tarrant County Jr Col, 84-87; Texas Tech Univ, 87-88; Ga Southern Univ, 88-93; Univ of Ark, 93-97; Ga Col and State Univ, 97-. **HONORS AND AWARDS** Barnett Fel, 86-87; Grant, Ga Southern Col, 88, 93-94; Andrew J. Mellon Res Stipend, 95. **MEMBERSHIPS** Ga Hist Assoc; Hist Soc; Soc of Civil War Hist; Soc of Mil Hist; Ark Hist Assoc; E Tex Hist Assoc; Ga Assoc of Hist; Southern Hist Assoc; St. George Tucker Soc; Southern Assoc of Women Hist. **RESEARCH** American Civil War; Military History. **SELECTED PUBLICATIONS** Auth, Between the Enemy and Texas: Parson's Texas Cavalry in the Civil War, Tex Christian Univ Pr, (Fort Worth), 89; auth, "Georgia", A Nation of Sovereign States: Secession and War in the Confederacy; J of Confederate Hist 10, (94): 69-81; auth, Texans in the Confederate Cavalry, Ryan Place Pub, (Fort Worth), 95; coauth, Portraits of Conflict: A Photographic History of Georgia in the Civil War, Univ of Ark Pr, (Fayetteville), 96; auth, "The Defenders: The Nancy Harts", Valor and Lace: The Roles of Confederate Women 1861-1865: J of Confederate Hist 15 (96): 35-55; coauth, "The History and Historians of Civil War Arkansas", Ark Hist Quarterly LVIII (99): 233-263; coed, Civil War Arkansas: Beyond Battles and Leaders, Univ of Ark Pr, (Fayetteville), 00; auth, The Chessboard of War: Sherman and Hood in the Autumn Campaigns of 1864, Univ of Nebr Pr, (Lincoln), 00; auth, "In the Far Corner of the Confederacy: A Question of Conscience for German-Speaking Texans", Families at War: Loyalty and Conflict in the Civil War South, Oxford Univ Pr, (NY), 00; auth, "Defiant Unionists: Militant Germans in Confederate Texas", Southern Unionists: Kinship, Community and Conflicting Loyalties in the Civil War South, Univ of Ga Pr, (Athens), (forthcoming). **CONTACT ADDRESS** Dept Hist and Geog, Ga Col and State Univ, Box 49, Milledgeville, GA 31061-0490. **EMAIL** abailey@mail.gcsu.edu

BAILEY, BETH
DISCIPLINE AMERICAN STUDIES **EDUCATION** Univ Chicago, PhD, 86. **CAREER** Assoc Prof, Univ NMex; Bd Od eds, Am Stud and Pacific Hist Rev. **HONORS AND AWARDS** Grant, ACLS, NEH, Ann Whitney Olin Scholar, Columbia Univ, 91-94, Sr Fulbright Lectureship, Indonesia, 96. **RESEARCH** American Cultural History, Popular Culture. **SELECTED PUBLICATIONS** Auth, From Front Porch to Back Seat: Courtship in 20th Century America, 88; coauth, The First Strange Place: The Alchemy of Race and Sex in WWII Hawaii, 92; auth, Sex in the Heartland, 99; auth, The Columbia Companion to America in the 1960's, 99. **CONTACT ADDRESS** Univ of New Mexico, Albuquerque, Albuquerque, NM 87131. **EMAIL** blbailey@unm.edu

BAILEY, CHARLES E.
PERSONAL Born 09/29/1940, Logan, WV, m, 1968, 3 children **DISCIPLINE** HISTORY, RELIGION **EDUCATION** Bob Jones Univ, BA, 62; MA, 63; Roosevelt Univ, MA, 69; Univ Va, PhD, 78. **CAREER** Teacher, Adirondack Col, 72-; adj prof, Plattsburgh Univ at ACC, 76-. **HONORS AND AWARDS** Listed in Who's Who Among Scholars in Am Community, Technical and Junior Colleges, 86-; Phi Alpha Theta; President's Awd for Excellence, Adirondack Col, 89; Distinguished Prof, Adirondack Col, 90. **RESEARCH** World War I. **SELECTED PUBLICATIONS** Auth, "The British Protestant Theologians and the First World War," Harvard Theol Rev 77.2 (84): 195-221; auth, "The Verdict of French Protestantism Against Germany in the First World War," Church Hist 58.1 (89): 66-82; auth, "Nietzsche: Moralist or Immoralist?--The Verdict of the European Theologians," Hist of European Ideas (89): 799-814. **CONTACT ADDRESS** Dept Soc Sci, Adirondack Comm Col, 439 Bay Rd, Queensbury, NY 12804-1408.

BAILEY, CHARLES RANDALL
PERSONAL Born 02/07/1938, Plain City, OH, m, 1970, 2 children **DISCIPLINE** MODERN EUROPEAN HISTORY & HISTORY OF EDUCATION **EDUCATION** Oh Univ, BA, 60; Univ Chicago, MA, 62, PhD(hist), 68. **CAREER** Instr hist, Juniata Col, 62-63; asst prof, 67-78, Assoc Prof Hist, State Univ NY Col Geneseo, 78-, Nat Endowment for Humanities fel, Univ NC, Chapel Hill, 78-79. **MEMBERSHIPS** AHA; Soc Fr Hist Studies. **RESEARCH** Eighteenth-century French education. **SELECTED PUBLICATIONS** Auth, French Secondary Education, 1763-1790: The Secularization of Ex-Jesuit Colleges, Am Philos Soc, 78; Municipal colleges: Small-town secondary schools in France prior to the revolution, Fr Hist Studies, 82. **CONTACT ADDRESS** Dept of Hist, SUNY, Col at Geneseo, 1 College Cir, Geneseo, NY 14454-1401.

BAILEY, DONALD ATHOLL
PERSONAL Born 02/24/1940, Rochester, MN, m, 1963, 2 children **DISCIPLINE** EUROPEAN HISTORY **EDUCATION** Univ Sask, BA, 62; Oxford Univ, Hons, 64, MA, 68; Univ MM, Minneapolis, PhD(hist), 73. **CAREER** Instr hist, Univ Sask, 64-65; lectr, Carleton Col, 66-67; from instr to asst prof, 69-77, Assoc Prof Hist, Univ Winnipeg, 77-, Part-time instr, Mennonite Brethren Col Arts, 81. **MEMBERSHIPS** Soc Fr Hist Studies; Can Hist Asn; Western Soc Fr Hist. **RESEARCH** France at the time of Cardinal Richelieu; life of Michel de Marillac, 1563-1632. **CONTACT ADDRESS** Dept of Hist, Univ of Winnipeg, 515 Portage Ave, Winnipeg, MB, Canada R3B 2E9. **EMAIL** don.bailey@uwinnipeg.ca

BAILEY, JOHN WENDELL
PERSONAL Born 04/02/1934, Richmond, VA, m, 1959, 2 children **DISCIPLINE** AMERICAN HISTORY **EDUCATION** Hampden Sydney Col, BS, 59; Univ MD, MA, 61; Marquette Univ, PhD(hist), 74. **CAREER** Asst prof hist, Allegany Col, 61-66; asst prof, 67-74, Assoc Prof 75-81; Prof Hist 82-, Carthage Col, 74-, Chairperson Dept, 77-. **MEMBERSHIPS** Western Hist Asn; Orgn Am Historians; AHA; Southern Hist Asn; Western Am Lit Asn. **RESEARCH** Western military frontier; Western American literature. **SELECTED PUBLICATIONS** Auth, The McNeill Rangers and the capture of General Crook and Kelley, Md Hist Mag, 67; The presidential election of 1900 in Nebraska: McKinley over Bryan, Nebr Hist, 73; contribr, Kenosha County in the 20th Century, Kenosha County Bicentennial Comn, 76; auth, General Alfred Terry and the Decline of the Sioux, 1866-1890, Greenwood, 79; contribr, Kenosha retrospective, Kenosha County Bicentennial Comn, 81; ed., "Issues in American History," American Heritage, 91; auth, Kenosha Comets," Bager, 97; contrib, "The Military and Conflict Between Cultures," Tex A&M, 97; auth, "The Life and Works of General Charles King," Edwin Mellen, 98. **CONTACT ADDRESS** Dept of Hist, Carthage Col, 2001 Alford Park Dr, Kenosha, WI 53140-1994. **EMAIL** bailey1@carthage.edu

BAILEY, STEPHEN
PERSONAL Born 04/04/1939, Chicago, IL, m, 1966, 3 children **DISCIPLINE** MODERN EUROPEAN HISTORY **EDUCATION** Univ Chicago, BA, 60, PhD, 66. **CAREER** Asst prof, 65-71, assoc prof, 71-79, prof hist, 79-, Dir, Florence Prog, Assoc Cols of Midwest, 77-78, assoc dean, Knox Coll, 85-. **MEMBERSHIPS** AHA. **RESEARCH** Germany during World War I; literature and politics under Napoleon III. **SELECTED PUBLICATIONS** Art, The Berlin Strike of January 1918, Central European History, Vol XII, Vol 2, 6/80. **CONTACT ADDRESS** Dept of History, Knox Col, Illinois, 2 E South St, Galesburg, IL 61401-4938. **EMAIL** sbailey@knox.edu

BAILEY, VICTOR
PERSONAL Born 08/14/1948, Keighley, United Kingdom, m, 1999 **DISCIPLINE** HISTORY, BRITISH **EDUCATION** Univ Warwick, BA, 69; Univ Cambridge, Mphilo, 70; Univ Warwick, PhD, 75. **CAREER** Cen Crimino Res, Oxford res off; Worcester Col, Oxford univ, fel, 78; Univ Hull, lectr, 83; Univ Kansas, prof, 88-. **HONORS AND AWARDS** Hon Res fel, Univ Hull; Kemper Fellowship for Teaching Excellence; Love Prize of the North Am Conf. Brit Stud for best published article in 97. **MEMBERSHIPS** AHA; North Am Conf Brit Stud. **RESEARCH** Hist Mod Brit; Hist Eng Crim Law Admin. **SELECTED PUBLICATIONS** English Prisons, Penal Culture and the Abatement of Imprisonment, 1895-1922, J Brit Stud, 97; The Fabrication of Deviance, Dangerous Classes and Criminal Classes in Vict England, in: R Malcolmson and J Rule, eds, Protest and Survival: The Historical Experience, Essays for E P Thompson, The New Press, 93; This Rash Act: Suicide Across the Life Cycle In the Victorian City, Stanford Univ Press, 98. **CONTACT ADDRESS** Dept Hist, Univ of Kansas, Lawrence, 3001 Wescoe Hall, Lawrence, KS 66045. **EMAIL** vbailey@ukans.edu

BAILY, SAMUEL LONGSTRETH
PERSONAL Born 05/09/1936, Philadelphia, PA, m, 1960, 3 children **DISCIPLINE** LATIN AMERICAN HISTORY **EDUCATION** Harvard Univ, BA, 58; Columbia Univ, MA, 63; Univ Pa, PhD(Latin Am hist), 64. **CAREER** Asst prof hist, 64-68, assoc dir, Latin Am Inst, 67-70, grad adv hist, 70-71, dir, Rutgers Jr Yr Mex, 74-75, assoc prof hist, 68-78, Prof Hist, Rutgers Univ, 78-, Chmn Undergrad Educ, Dept Hist, 81-, Am Friends Serv, Mex, 58-59; prog dir, Cambridge Neighborhood House, 59-60; dir, NDEA Summer Inst, Latin Am Hist, Rutgers Univ, 67, Soc Sci Res Coun fel, 68; Am Philos Soc grant, 73 & 80; chmn, Chile-Rio Plata Group, Conf Latin Am Hist, 77-78. **MEMBERSHIPS** AHA; Latin Am Studies Asn; Am Ital Hist Asn. **RESEARCH** Twentieth century Argentina; Italian immigration in the Western Hemisphere; labor history in Latin America. **SELECTED PUBLICATIONS** Auth, The Italians and Organized Labor in the United States and Argentina: 1880-1910, Int Migration Rev, summer 67; The Italians and the Development of Organized Labor in Argentina, Brazil and the United States, 1880-1914, J Social Hist, winter 69; ed, Nationalism in Latin America, Knopf, 71; co-ed, Perspective on Latin America, Macmillan, 74; auth, The United States and the Development of South America, Watts, 76; Role of the Press and the Assimilation of Italians in Buenos Aires and Sao Paulo, Int Migration Rev, fall 78; Marriage Patterns and Immigrant Assimilation in Buenos Aires, Hisp Am Hist Rev, 2/80; Chain Migration of Italians to Argentina, Studi Emigrazione, spring 82. **CONTACT ADDRESS** Dept of Hist, Rutgers, The State Univ of New Jersey, New Brunswick, P O Box 5059, New Brunswick, NJ 08903-5059.

BAILYN, BERNARD
PERSONAL Born 09/10/1922, Hartford, CT, m, 1952 **DISCIPLINE** HISTORY **EDUCATION** Williams Col, MA, BA, 45; Harvard Univ, MA, 47, PhD(hist), 53. **CAREER** Instr educ, 53-54, from asst prof to prof hist, 54-66, ed-in-chief, John Harvard Libr, 62-70, Winthrop prof hist, 66-81, Adams Univ Prof & James Duncan Phillips Prof Emer, Harvard Univ, 81-, Co-ed,

Perspectives Am Hist, 67-77; Trevelyan lectr, Cambridge, 71. **HONORS AND AWARDS** Robert H Lord Awd, 67; Bancroft & Pulitzer Prizes in Hist, 68; Nat Bk Awd in Hist, 75; Thomas Jefferson Medal, 93; Henry Allen Moe Prize, Am Philos Soc, 94; Bruce Catton Prize, Soc of Am Hist, 00; lhd, lawrence univ, 67, bard col, 68, clark univ, 75, yale univ, 76 & grinnell col, 79; littd, williams col, mass, 69, rutgers univ & fordham univ, 76. **MEMBERSHIPS** Am Hist Soc (pres, 81); Nat Acad Educ; Royal Hist Soc; Am Philos Soc; Am Acad Arts & Sci. **SELECTED PUBLICATIONS** Auth, The Ideological Origins of the American Revolution, 67; auth, The Ordeal of Thomas Hutchinson, 74; auth, Voyagers to the West, 86; auth, Faces of Revolution, 90; auth, On the Teaching and Writing of History, 94. **CONTACT ADDRESS** Dept Hist, Harvard Univ, Cambridge, MA 02138.

BAIRD, BRUCE C.
PERSONAL Born 11/22/1956, New Orleans, LA, m, 1987 **DISCIPLINE** HISTORY **EDUCATION** Texas A & M Univ, BS, 77; Col Wm & Mary, MA, 90; Univ Fla, PhD, 95. **CAREER** Adj asst prof, Univ Fla, 95-96; ASST PROF HIST, UNIV ALA, HUNTSVILLE, 97-; H-SHEAR book rev ed, 97-. **HONORS AND AWARDS** Ohio State Univ fel 96-97; Jacob K. Javits fel, 94-95. **MEMBERSHIPS** AHA; So Hist Asn; Soc Historians Early Am Rep. **RESEARCH** Early Am South **SELECTED PUBLICATIONS** Auth, Necessity and the Perverse Supply of Labor in Pre- Clasical British Political Economy, Hist Pol Econ 29.3, fall 97; auth, The Social Origins of Dueling in Virginia, In Lethal Imagination: Violence and Brutality in American History, NY Univ Press, forthcoming. **CONTACT ADDRESS** Dept of History, Univ of Alabama, Huntsville, 409 Roberts Hall, Huntsville, AL 35899. **EMAIL** bairdb@email.uah.edu

BAIRD, DAVID
PERSONAL Born 07/08/1939, Oklahoma City, OK, m, 1961, 2 children **DISCIPLINE** AMERICAN HISTORY **EDUCATION** George Wash Univ, AA, 59; Univ Cent Okla, BA, 61; Univ Okla, MA, 65, PhD, 69. **CAREER** Tchg asst, Univ OK, 66-68; asst, assoc prof, Univ AR, 68-78; prof, prof, dept hd, OK State Univ, 78-84; prof, OK State Univ, 84-88; Howard A. White prof, Pepperdine, 88-; Fulbright lectr, Univ Canterbury, New Zealand, 91; vis prof, Ger, 92-93 ch, Adv Coun Am Hist Assn, 92-93; ch, 94-. **HONORS AND AWARDS** Cert Merit, OK State Hist Preservation Off, 91; grant, OK Found Hum, 97. **MEMBERSHIPS** Mem, Prog Commun, 86-87; Mem Commun, 92-93; Commun on Ethnicity, 97-. **SELECTED PUBLICATIONS** Auth, The Quapaw Indians: A History of the Downstream People, Norman: Univ Okla P, 80; A Creek Warrior for the Confederacy: The Autobiography of Chief G. W. Grayson, Norman: Univ Okla Press, 88; The Quapaws, Chelsea House, 89; co-auth,The Story of Oklahoma, Univ Okla Press, 94; Oklahoma: The Stories of the State and Its People, Univ OK Press, 98. **CONTACT ADDRESS** Dept of Hum and Tchr Educ, Pepperdine Univ, 24255 Pacific Coast Hwy, Malibu, CA 90263. **EMAIL** dbaird@pepperdine.edu

BAIRD, JAY WARREN
PERSONAL Born 07/01/1936, Toledo, OH, m, 1958, 3 children **DISCIPLINE** MODERN EUROPEAN & GERMAN HISTORY **EDUCATION** Denison Univ, BA, 58; Columbia Univ, MA & PhD(mod hist), 66. **CAREER** Instr hist western civilization, Stanford Univ, 63-65; asst prof mod Europe, Pomona Col, 65-67; from asst prof to assoc prof, 67-75, Prof Mod Europe & Ger, Miami Univ, 75-, Nat Endowment for Humanities fel, 69-70; Am Philos Soc grant, 71; ed consult, Can Rev Hist Nationalism, 73-; mem nat screening bd, Fulbright-Hays Fel, Ger, 75-77; consult, Nat Endowment for Humanities, 76-, Nat Found Jewish Cult, 81. **MEMBERSHIPS** AHA; Conf Group Cent Europe Hist; Conf Group on German Politics; Am Asn Advan Humanities. **RESEARCH** Third Reich; Nazi propaganda; German film. **SELECTED PUBLICATIONS** Auth, The Nazi propaganda campaign of 1945, J Hist Deuxieme Guerre Mondiale, 69; The myth of Stalingrad, J Contemp Hist, London, 70; ed, From Nurenberg to My Lai, Heath, 72; auth, The Mythical World of Nazi War Propaganda: 1939-1945, Univ Minn, 74; L'expert en Bolshevisme du Dr Goebbels, J Hist Deuxieme Mondiale, 10/74; The World of Charlemagne, Forum Press, 77; Das Politische Testament Julius Streichers, Vierteljahrshefte fur Zeitgeschichte, 78; Nazi film propaganda and the Soviet Union, Film & Hist, 81. **CONTACT ADDRESS** Dept of Hist, Miami Univ, 500 E High St, Oxford, OH 45056-1602.

BAIRD, KEITH E.
PERSONAL Born 01/20/1923 **DISCIPLINE** AFRICAN-AMERICAN STUDIES **EDUCATION** Columbia University, BS, 1952; Union Graduate School, PhD, 1982. **CAREER** Hunter College, professor/director, Afro-American studies, 69-70; Hofstra University, professor of humanities, 70-73; SUNY at Old Westbury, professor of humanities, 73-75; SUNY at Buffalo, assoc prof of anthropology, 75-; Clark Atlanta University, Dept of Social Sciences, professor, currently. **HONORS AND AWARDS** Travel Seminar Grant, Ford Foundation, 1969; publication, Names from Africa, Johnson Publishing Co, 1972; Summer Scholarship Grant, US GOR Friendship Comm, University of Jena, 1981. **MEMBERSHIPS** Assoc fellow, Center for Afro-American Studies, Atlanta University, 1973-; SUNY Chancellor's Task Force on Afro Studies, 1984; consult on Gullah Lang, Sea Island Center, 1977; pres emeritus, New York African Studies Assn; assoc ed, Freedomways; ed bd, Journal of Black Studies, African Urban Quarterly. **CONTACT ADDRESS** Dept of Social Sciences, Clark Atlanta Univ, 223 James Brawley SW, Atlanta, GA 30314-4358.

BAJPAI, SHIVA GOPAL
PERSONAL Born 07/02/1923, Balhemau, India, m, 1967, 1 child **DISCIPLINE** SOUTH ASIAN HISTORY **EDUCATION** Banaras Hindu Univ, BA, 55, MA, 57; Univ London, PhD(Indian Hist), 67. **CAREER** Asst prof Hist, Hindu Degree Col, Gorakhpur Univ, 57-58; lectr, Banaras Hindu Univ, 58-68; res assoc Hist Geog & Cult, S Asia Hist Atlas Proj, Univ Minn, Minneapolis, 67-70; asst prof, 70-74, assoc prof, 74-78, prof Hist, Calif State Univ, Northridge, 78-, dir coord Asian Studies Prog, 73-, ed consult, Can Rev Study Nationalism, Univ of PEI, 73. **MEMBERSHIPS** Asn Asian Studies; Am Orient Soc. **RESEARCH** Intellectual history of classical and medieval South Asia; political idealogies and practices; regions and regionalism in ancient and early medieval history of South Asia; India's cultural relations with China and Southeast Asia in the classical period. **SELECTED PUBLICATIONS** Auth, Chingiz Khan, the Mongol World Conqueror, 66, Chiang Kai Shek, 66 & Jonaraja, The Poet-Historian of Medieval Kashmir, 67, Hindi Encycl, Vols IV & V; Concept of neutrality and non-alignment in the post-Kautiliyan political thought in India, Actes XXIX Cong Int des Orientalists, L'Asiatheque, Paris, 76; coauth, A Historical Atlas of South Asia, Univ Chicago, 78. **CONTACT ADDRESS** Dept of History, California State Univ, Northridge, 18111 Nordhoff St, Northridge, CA 91330-8200. **EMAIL** sbajpai@csun.edu

BAK, JANOS M.
PERSONAL Born 04/25/1929, Budapest, Hungary, m, 1951, 3 children **DISCIPLINE** MEDIEVAL HISTORY **EDUCATION** Eotvos Lorand Univ, Budapest, MA, 50; Univ Gottingen, Dr Phil(hist), 60. **CAREER** Instr hist, Acad Commerce, Budapest, 53-56; Brit Coun scholar, St Anthony's Col, Oxford, 60-62; asst, Univ Marburg, 63-66; asst prof, Univ Del, 66-68; Assoc Prof Hist, Univ BC, 68-, Ger Res Asn res scholar, 62-64; vis prof, Univ Kassel, 80. **MEMBERSHIPS** Am Asn Study Hungarian Hist; Conf Group Social & Admin Hist: Mediaeval Acad Am; Mediaeval Asn Pac; Int Comt Hist Paul Asn; Int Asn Hungarian Studies. **RESEARCH** Medieval central Europe; constitutional history; social history. **SELECTED PUBLICATIONS** Auth, Konigtum und Stande in Ungarn im 14-16, Jahrhundert, Steiner Verlag, Wiesbaden, 73; Medieval symbology of the state: P E Schramm's contribution, Viator, 4: 33-63, 73; ed, The German Peasant War of 1525, F Cass, Eng, 77; auth, Serfs and Serfdom: Words and Things, Rev of the F Braudel Ctr, 4: 3-18; co-ed (with Bela K Kiraly), From Hunyadi to Rakoczi: War and Society in Late Medieval and Early Modern Hungary, Brooklyn, NY, 82; co-ed (with Gy Litran), Socialism and Social Science: Selected Works of Ervin Szabo, Routledge & Kegan Paul; London, 82; Decreta Regni Hungariae-Laws and Decrees of Hungary, 1458-1490 (Latin and German), F. Dory, ed, Hisorisches Jahrbuch, Vol 113, 93; The 2 Cities-Medieval Europe, 1050-1320, with M. Barber, Histoire Sociale, Vol 27, 94; East-Central Europe in the Middle Ages, 1000-1500, with J. W. Sedlar, Speculum-A J of Medieval Studies, Vol 71, 96. **CONTACT ADDRESS** Dept of Hist, Univ of British Columbia, Vancouver, BC, Canada V6T 1W5.

BAKER, DONALD G.
PERSONAL Born 02/16/1932, Elgin, IL, d, 1 child **DISCIPLINE** AMERICAN STUDIES **EDUCATION** Univ Denver, BA, 53; Syracuse Univ, MA, 58, PhD, 61. **CAREER** Asst prof Am studies & govt & dir Am studies prog, Skidmore Col, 59-64; dir soc sci div, 64-71, assoc prof, 64-68, prof polit sci & am studies, Southampton Col, Long Island Univ, 68-; Ford grant fac supvr, NY State Grad Legis Internship Prog, Columbia Univ, Hunter Col & Syracuse Univ, 60-64; adj prof polit sci, Grad Sch Pub Affairs, State Univ NY, 62-63; lectr progs, Peace Corps, 63-66, consult, 64-65; sr res fel race rels, Ctr Inter-Racial Studies, Univ Rhodesia, Salisbury, 75-76; sr res fel develop studies, Ctr Applied Soc Sci, Univ Zimbabwe, Salisbury, 80, sr assoc mem, St. Antony's Coll, Oxford Univ, 79-80 and 85-86; assoc res fel, Southern African res prog, Yale Univ, 92-93; vis res fel, sociol, Victoria Univ, New Zealand, 93. **MEMBERSHIPS** Am Studies Assn; Am Polit Sci Assn; Can Assn Am Studies; Assn Can Studies US. **RESEARCH** Comparative studies of race and ethnicity; problems of development in Third World countries; politics and literature. **SELECTED PUBLICATIONS** Co-ed, The Autobiography of James Monroe, Syracuse Univ, 59; co-ed, Postwar America: The Search for Identity, Glencoe, 69; ed, Politics of Race: Comparative Studies, Saxon House/Heath, Eng, 75; auth, Race, Ethnicity and Power: A Comparative Study, Routledge & Kegan Paul, 83. **CONTACT ADDRESS** Div of Soc Sci, Long Island Univ, Southampton Col, 239 Montauk Hwy, Southampton, NY 11968-4198. **EMAIL** dbaker@southampton.liunet.edu

BAKER, JAMES FRANKLIN
PERSONAL Born 05/17/1943, Houston, TX, m, 1963, 2 children **DISCIPLINE** UNITED STATES HISTORY **EDUCATION** Univ Houston, BA, 65; Tulane Univ, MA, 67, PhD, 70. **CAREER** Instr Hist, Xavier Univ La, 69-70; asst prof, 70-76, assoc prof, 76-80, prof Hist, Univ Central Okla, 80-. **MEMBERSHIPS** Soc Historians Am Foreign Rels. **RESEARCH** United States foreign relations; United States 20th century. **CONTACT ADDRESS** Dept of History & Geography, Univ of Central Oklahoma, 100 N University Dr, Edmond, OK 73034-5209.

BAKER, JEAN HARVEY
PERSONAL Born 02/09/1933, Baltimore, MD, m, 1953, 4 children **DISCIPLINE** AMERICAN HISTORY **EDUCATION** Goucher Col, AB, 61; Johns Hopkins Univ, MA, 64, PhD, 71. **CAREER** Instr hist, Col Notre Dame, Md, 65-69; asst prof, 69-76, assoc prof hist, Goucher Col, 76, Prof of Am Coun Learned Socs Fel, 77-78. **HONORS AND AWARDS** Willie Lee Rose Prize, Berkshire History Prize. **MEMBERSHIPS** Orgn Am Historians; Women Historians. **RESEARCH** Am polit hist; Civil War and Reconstruction; women's hist. **SELECTED PUBLICATIONS** Auth, Politics of Continuity, 73 & Ambivalent Americans, 77, Johns Hopkins Univ; Affairs of Party, Cornell Univ Press, 82; Mary Todd Lincoln: A Biography, W.W. Norton, 87; The Stevensons: Biography of an American Family, W.W. Norton, 95. **CONTACT ADDRESS** Dept of Hist, Goucher Col, 1021 Dulaney Vlly Rd, Baltimore, MD 21204-2780. **EMAIL** jbaker@goucher.edu

BAKER, JOSEPH WAYNE
PERSONAL Born 06/26/1934, Zion, IL **DISCIPLINE** REFORMATION & RENAISSANCE HISTORY **EDUCATION** Western Baptist Col, BA, 57; Talbot Theol Sem, BD, 61; Pepperdine Col, BA, 62; Univ IA, MA, 64, PhD(hist), 70. **CAREER** Instr hist, OH State Univ, 65-68; from instr to asst prof, 68-76, Assoc Prof Hist, Univ Akron, 76-, Am Philos Soc grant, 72. **MEMBERSHIPS** Am Soc Reformation Res; AHA; Sixteenth Century Studies Conf (treas, 76-77); Am Soc Church Hist. **RESEARCH** The Reformation; the Reformed tradition; Puritanism. **SELECTED PUBLICATIONS** Auth, Church, State and Dissent: The Crisis of the Swiss Reformation, 1531-1536, Church History 57, 88; auth, Christian Discipline and the Early Reformaed Tradition: Bullinger and Calvin, In Calviniana: Ideas and Influence of Jean Calvin, ed. Robert V. Schnucker, Sixteenth Century Essays and Studies 10, Kirksville, MO: Sixteenth Century Publishers, Inc, 88; co-auth with Charles S. McCoy, Fountainhead of Federalism: Heinrich Bullinger and the Convenantal Tradition. With a Traslation of De testamento seu foedere Dei unico et aeterno (1534) by Heinrich Bullinger, Louisville, KY: Westminster/John Knox Press, 91; auth, The Reformation at Zurich in the Thought and Theology of Huldrych Zwingli and Heinrich Bullinger, in Reformation Europe: A Guide to Research II, ed, William S. Maltby, Reformation Guides to Research 3, St. Louis: Center for Reformation Research, 92; auth, Christian Discipline, Church and State, and Toleration: Bullinger, Calvin and Basel 1530-1555, in Reformiertes Erbe. Festschrift fur Gottfried W. Locher zu seinem 80. Geburstag, Volume One, ed, Heiko A. Oberman, et al, Zurich, 92; auth, Church, State and Toleration: John Locke and Calvin's Heirs in England, 1644-1689, In Later Calvinism: International Perspectives, ed, W. Fred Graham, Kirksville, MO: Sixteenth Century Publishers, Inc, 93; auth, The Covenantal Basis for the Development of Swiss Political Federalism: 1291-1848, in Publius: The Journal of Federalism 23, 93; auth, University Business Partnerships, Roman-Littlefield, 93; co-ed, Ethical Theory and Business, Prentice Hall, 97; auth, Heinrich Bullinger, the Covenant, and the Reformed Tradition in Retrospect, Sixteenth Century Journal 29, 98; auth, Business Ethics: A Kantian Perspective, Blackwell, 99. **CONTACT ADDRESS** Dept of Hist, Univ of Akron, 635 Shady Ledge Dr, Akron, OH 44313. **EMAIL** jwayne@neo.rr.com

BAKER, KEITH M.
PERSONAL Born 08/07/1938, Swindon, England, d, 2 children **DISCIPLINE** HISTORY **EDUCATION** Cambridge Univ, BA, 60; MA, 63; Univ of London, PhD, 64. **CAREER** Instr, Reed Col, 64-65; asst prof to prof, Univ of Chicago, 65-89; prof, Stanford Univ, 88-; Dean, 00-. **HONORS AND AWARDS** NEH Fel, 67-68; ACSL Fel, 72-73; Univ of Chicago Press Laing Prize, 75; Guggenheim Fel, 79; Chevalier dans L'Ordre des Palmes Academiques, 88-; JE Wallace Sterling Prof, 92-; Anthony P Meier Familu Prof, 95-00. **MEMBERSHIPS** AHA; Am Soc for Eighteenth-Century Studies; Soc for Fr Hist Studies. **RESEARCH** Early modern intellectual history, the French Enlightenment, political culture of the Old Regime and the French Revolution. **SELECTED PUBLICATIONS** Auth, Condorcet. From Natural Philosophy to Social Mathematics, Univ of Chicago Pr, 75; coed, The Old Regime and the French Revolution, Univ of Chicago Pr, 87; ed, The French Revolution and the Creation of Modern Political Culture, Vol 1, The Political Culture of the Old Regime, Pergamon Pr, (Oxford), 87; auth, Inventing the French Revolution. Essays on French Political Culture in the Eighteenth Century, Cambridge Univ Pr, (Cambridge), 90; ed, The French Revolution and the Creation of Modern Political Culture, vol 4, The Terror, Pergamon Pr, (Oxford), 94. **CONTACT ADDRESS** Dept Hist, Stanford Univ, Stanford, CA 94305-2024. **EMAIL** kbaker@stanford.edu

BAKER, MELVA JOYCE
PERSONAL Born 11/17/1939, Baca County, CO **DISCIPLINE** UNITED STATES & WOMEN'S HISTORY **EDUCATION** Univ Colo, Boulder, BA, 61; Univ Calif, Santa Barbara, MA, 70, PhD(hist), 78. **CAREER** Teacher hist & English, Boulder, CO & Ventura, CA, 61-68; res asst & reader, Univ CA, Santa Barbara, 68-69, teaching asst hist, 70-74, lectr, 75-77; vis asst prof, KS State Univ, 79-80; Dir Educ Serv, Info Serv, ABC-CLIO, 80-, Proj coordr, Neighborhood Youth Corps, Dept Labor, 70-71; instr, Santa Barbara City Col, 77-78. **MEMBERSHIPS** Am Hist Asn; Orgn Am Historians; Western Asn Women Historians; Asn Bibliog Hist. **RESEARCH** American popular culture; American women's history; research methodologies. **SELECTED PUBLICATIONS** Auth, Images of Women in Film: The War Years, 1941-1945, Univ Microfilms Int Res Press, 81. **CONTACT ADDRESS** PO Box 621, Summerland, CA 93067.

BAKER, PAUL R.
PERSONAL Born 09/28/1927, Everett, WA, m, 1972, 1 child **DISCIPLINE** AMERICAN STUDIES & HISTORY **EDUCATION** Stanford Univ, AB, 49; Columbia Univ, MA, 51; Harvard Univ, PhD, 60. **CAREER** Instr hist, CA Inst Technol, 60-62, asst prof hum, 62-63; lectr hist, Univ CA, Riverside, 63-64; lectr, Univ OR, 64-65; from assoc prof to prof emeritus, NYork Univ, 65-; dir, grad prog Am Civilization, NYork Univ, 72-92; Consult & panelist, Nat Endowment for Hum, 74. **HONORS AND AWARDS** Mary C. Turpie Prize of the Am Studies Asn for excellence in tchg, administration, and Advisement; NJ Literary Hall of Fame; res grant, NYork Univ, 66, 74, 75. **MEMBERSHIPS** Am Studies Asn; Orgn Am Historians; Soc Archit Historians; Victorian Soc Am. **RESEARCH** Am intellectual hist; Am painting and archit; Am cult hist. **SELECTED PUBLICATIONS** Ed, Views of Society and Manners in America, Harvard Univ, 63; auth, Lord Byron and the American in Italy, Keats-Shelley J, winter 64; The Fortunate Pilgrims: Americans in Italy, 1800-1860, Harvard Univ, 64; ed, The Atomic Bomb: The Great Decision, Holt, 68, Holt-Dryden, 2nd rev ed, 76; gen ed, American Problem Studies Series, Holt-Dryden, 41 Vols, 69-; coauth, The American Experience, Sadlier (5 vols), 76-79; auth, Richard Morris Hunt, Mass Inst Technol, 80; Auth, Stanny: The Gilded Life of Stanford White, Free Pr, 89. **CONTACT ADDRESS** Dept of Hist, New York Univ, 53 Washington Sq, New York, NY 10012. **EMAIL** prbaker2@aol.com

BAKER, RICHARD ALLAN
PERSONAL Born 03/18/1940, Stoneham, MA, m, 1963, 2 children **DISCIPLINE** POLITICAL HISTORY **EDUCATION** Univ Mass, Amherst, BA, 62; Mich State Univ, MA, 65; Columbia Univ, MS, 68; Univ Maryland, PhD, 82. **CAREER** Instr hist, Holy Apostles Sem, Cromwell, Conn, 65-67; ref lib Amer hist, Lib Cong, Wash, DC, 68-70; dir res US Govt policy, Govt Res Corp, 70-75; dir, Senate Hist off, US Senate, Wash, DC, 75-. **HONORS AND AWARDS** Beta Phi Mu; Phi Kappa Phi, Joseph Towne Wheeler Awd, 68; Ralph W Hidy Awd, 86. **MEMBERSHIPS** Orgn Am Hist; AHA; APSA; Natl Coun of Pub Hist; Soc for Hist in Fed Govt **RESEARCH** United States Congressional history; American political history; historical bibliography. **SELECTED PUBLICATIONS** Ed, Proceedings, Conference on the Research Use and Disposition of Senators' Papers, 78, Govt Printing Off, OAH Mag of Hist, sum, 98; auth, Managing Congressional Papers: A Senate View, Am Archivist, 7/78; The Records of Congress: Opportunities and Obstacles in the Senate, Pub Hist, sum 80; auth, Conservation Politics: The Senate Career of Clinton P. Anderson, NMex, 85; auth, The Senate of the United States: A Bicentennial History, Krieger, 88; auth, Exploring Legislative Ethics, Plenum, 85; auth, The United States Senate, Readers' Comp to Amer Hist, Houghton Mifflin, 91; auth, Research Opportunities in the Records of the United States Senate, Western Hist Q 24, 93; auth, Legislative Power over Appointments and Confirmations, Encycl of Amer Legislative Sys 3, Scribners, 94; auth, The United States Congress Responds to Judicial Review, Constitutional Justice Under Old Constitutions, Kluwer Law, 95 **CONTACT ADDRESS** US Senate, Hist Office, Washington, DC 20510-7108. **EMAIL** Richard_Baker@sec.senate.gov

BAKER, THOMAS H.
PERSONAL Born 10/14/1933, Houston, TX, m, 1955, 2 children **DISCIPLINE** AMERICAN HISTORY **EDUCATION** TX A&M Univ, BA, 55; Univ TX, MA, 63, PhD(hist), 65. **CAREER** Assoc prof hist, MS State Col Women, 63-68; spec res assoc, Oral Hist Prog, Univ TX, Austin, 68-69; assoc prof, 69-76, assoc vice chancellor, 73-81, Prof Hist, Univ AR, Little Rock, 76-, Mem bd dir, Inst Politics & Govt, 73-77. **MEMBERSHIPS** Orgn Am Historians; Southern Hist Asn; Ark Hist Asn (pres, 81-82). **RESEARCH** History of American South; 20th century United States history. **SELECTED PUBLICATIONS** Auth, The Early Newspaper of Memphis, Tennessee, 1827-1860, W Tenn Hist Soc Papers, 63; Refugee Newspaper: the Memphis Daily Appeal, 1862-1865, J Southern Hist, 8/63; Yellowjack: the Yellow Fever Epidemic of 1878 in Memphis, Tennessee, Bull Hist Med, 68; The Memphis Commercial Appeal: The History of a Southern Newspaper, LA State Univ, 71; 1st Movers and the Growth of Small Industry in Northeastern Italy, Comparative Studies in Society and History, Vol 36, 94; Fulbright-A Biography, with R. B. Woods, AR Hist Quart, Vol 55, 96; A Matter of Black-and-White-The Autobiography of Ada Louise Sipuelfisher, with Al Sipuelfisher and D. Goble, AR Hist Quart, Vol 55, 96; Beyond Batholomew-The Portland Area History, with R. Dearmondhuskey, AR Hist Quart, Vol 56, 97. **CONTACT ADDRESS** Dept of Hist, Univ of Arkansas, Little Rock, Little Rock, AR 72204.

BAKER, THOMAS LINDSAY
PERSONAL Born 04/22/1947, Cleburne, TX, m, 1990, 2 children **DISCIPLINE** HISTORY **EDUCATION** Texas Tech Univ, BA, 69, MA, 72, PhD, 77. **CAREER** Res assoc, Hist of Engineering Prog, Texas Technol Univ, 70-75, 77; Fulbright lectr Tech Univ Wroclaw Poland, 75-77; cur of Agr & Technol, Panhandle-Plains Hist Mus, 78-87; cur of Hist, Fort Worth Mus Sci & Hist, 87-89; asst prof, Dept Mus Studies, Baylor Univ, 89-97; dir, Texas Heritage Mus, Hill Col, 97-. **HONORS AND AWARDS** Coral H Tullis, 80; Kate Broocks Bates Awd, 80; Ralph Coats Roe Medal, 87; Cert Commendation Am Asn State & Loc Hist, 93; Glenda Morgan Awd for Museum Excellence, Texas Historical Commission, 99. **MEMBERSHIPS** Orgn Am Hist; Am Asn of Mus; Int Molinological Soc; W Hist Asn; Texas State Hist Asn; Nat Trust for Hist Preserv; Soc SW Arch; W Writers of Am. **RESEARCH** History of Texas and the American West; History of engineering and technology; Social and cultural history of the United States. **SELECTED PUBLICATIONS** Auth The First Polish Americans: Silesian Settlements in Texas, Texas A & M Univ Press, 79; A Field Guide to American Windmills, Univ Okla Press, 85; Adobe Walls: The History and Archeology of the 1874 Trading Post, Texas A & M Univ Press, 86; Lighthouses of Texas, Texas A & M Univ Press, 91; auth, Till Freedom Cried Out, Texas A & M Univ Press, 97; The WPA Oklahoma Slave Narratives, Univ Okla Press, 98; auth, North American Windmill Manufacturers' Trade Literature, Univ of Okla Pr, 98; auth, The Texas Red River Country, Texas A & M Univ Pr, 98; auth, The 702 Model Windmill, American Wind Power Center, 99. **CONTACT ADDRESS** PO Box 507, Rio Vista, TX 76093. **EMAIL** TLBAKER@hillcollege.hill-college.cc.tx.us

BAKER, WILLIAM JOSEPH
PERSONAL Born 01/28/1938, Chattanooga, TN, m, 1961, 2 children **DISCIPLINE** ENGLISH & INTELLECTUAL HISTORY **EDUCATION** Furman Univ, BA, 60; Southeast Sem, BD, 63; Cambridge Univ, PhD(hist), 67. **CAREER** Asst prof hist, Eastern TN State Univ, 66-67; asst prof hist & chmn dept hist & polit sci, Tusculum Col, 67-69; Bailey lectr hist, Univ NC, Charlotte, 70; asst prof, 70-73, assoc prof, 73-82, Prof Hist, Univ ME, Orono, 82-, Am Philos Soc res grant, 69-70 & 77; lectr, Duke Univ, 81. **MEMBERSHIPS** AHA; Conf Brit Studies; NAm Soc Sport Hist. **RESEARCH** Victorian England; Anglo-American history; sports history. **SELECTED PUBLICATIONS** Auth, Hurrell Froude and the Reformers, J Ecclesiastical Hist, 7/70; Charles Kingsley on the Crimean War: A Study in Chauvinism, Southern Humanities Rev, summer 70; Julius Charles Hake: A Victorian Interpreter of Luther, S Atlantic Quart, winter 71; ed, America Perceived: A View from Abroad in the 19th Century, Pendulum, 74; auth, Historical Meaning in Mother Goose, J Popular Cult, winter 76; The Making of a Working-Class Football Culture in Victorian England, J Social Hist, winter 79; Beyond Port and Prejudice: Charles Lloyd of Oxford, 1784-1829, Univ Maine, 81; ed (with John M Carroll), Sports in Modern America, River City. **CONTACT ADDRESS** 42 Grant St, Bangor, ME 04401.

BAKEWELL, PETER
DISCIPLINE HISTORY **EDUCATION** Cambridge Univ, BA, 65, MA, 68, PhD, 69. **CAREER** Prof and dir, Latin Am and Caribbean Studies Prog, Emory Univ. **HONORS AND AWARDS** Herbert Eugene Bolton Prize, Conf Lat Am Hist, 73; Mexican Reg Hist Medal, Banco Nacional de Mexico, 88. **RESEARCH** Spanish American colonial history. **SELECTED PUBLICATIONS** Auth, Silver Mining and Society in Colonial Mexico: Zacatecas, 1546-1700; Miners of the Red Mountain: Indian Labor in Potosi, 1545-1650; Silver and Entrepreneurship in Seventeenth-Century Potosi: The Life and Times of Antonio Lopez de Quiroga; A History of Latin America: Empires and Sequels, 1450-1930. **CONTACT ADDRESS** Dept History, Emory Univ, 222 Bowden Hall, Atlanta, GA 30322-1950. **EMAIL** pbakewe@emory.edu

BAKKEN, GORDON MORRIS
PERSONAL Born 01/10/1943, Madison, WI, d, 1964, 2 children **DISCIPLINE** AMERICAN HISTORY, LAW **EDUCATION** Univ Wis-Madison, BS, 66, MS, 67, PhD(Am hist), 70, JD, 73. **CAREER** From asst prof to assoc prof Am hist, 69-76, Prof Hist, CA State Univ, Fullerton, 76-, Dir Fac Affairs & Records, 74- . **HONORS AND AWARDS** Penrose Fund/Am Philos Soc fel, 74 **MEMBERSHIPS** AHA; Orgn Am Historians; Western Hist Asn. **RESEARCH** American legal history. **SELECTED PUBLICATIONS** Auth, The Development of Law on the Rocky Moutain Frontier, 1850-1912, Westport CT, Greenwood Press, 83; auth, The Development of Law in Frontier California: Civil Law and Society, 1850-1890, Westport, CT, Greenwood Press, 85; auth, Rocky Mountain Constitution Making, 1850-1912, Westport CT, Greenwood Press, 87; auth, California Legal History Manuscripts in the Huntington Library: A Guide, San Marino, CA, Huntington Library Publications, 89; auth, Practicing Law in Frontier California, Lincoln, Nebraska, Univ of Nebraska Press, 91; auth, Surviving the North Dakota Depression, Pasadena, CA, Wood & Jones, 92; coauth, Learning California History , Wheaton, IL, Harlan Davidson, Inc, 99; ed, Law in the Western United States, Norman: Univ of Oklahoma Press, in press, 00; coauth, The American West, six volumes, Garland Publishing, Inc, New York, 01; auth, ed, California History: A Topical Approach, Harlan Davidson, Inc, est, 01. **CONTACT ADDRESS** Dept of Hist, California State Univ, Fullerton, Fullerton, CA 92834-6846. **EMAIL** gbakken@fullerton.edu

BALCER, JACK MARTIN
PERSONAL Born 11/09/1935, Newark, NJ **DISCIPLINE** ANCIENT HISTORY & ARCHEOLOGY **EDUCATION** Montclair State Col, BA, 57; Univ Mich, MA, 58, PhD, 64. **CAREER** Asst prof hist, Denison Univ, 64-65; asst prof hist, Ind Univ, Bloomington, 65-71; assoc prof, 71-80, prof hist, 80-, Ohio State Univ; numismatist, Archaeological Expedition, Malyan, Iran, 76. **HONORS AND AWARDS** NEH grant, 67; Danforth teaching associateship, 68-70. **MEMBERSHIPS** Am Numis Soc; Archaeol Inst Am; Assn Ancient Historians. **RESEARCH** Athenian and Persian Empires; Greek history, archaeology and numismatics. **SELECTED PUBLICATIONS** Art, Erich Friedrich Schmidt, Achaemenid History, 91; art, ancient Epic Conventions in the Bisitun Text, Achaemenid History, 94; art, Herodotus, The Early State, Lydia, Historia, 94; art, The Liberation of Ionia: 478 B C, Historia, 97. **CONTACT ADDRESS** Dept of History, Ohio State Univ, Columbus, 230 W 17th Ave, Columbus, OH 43210-1361. **EMAIL** balcer.1@osu.edu

BALDWIN, JOHN WESLEY
PERSONAL Born 07/13/1929, Chicago, IL, m, 1954, 3 children **DISCIPLINE** HISTORY **EDUCATION** Wheaton Col, BA, 50; Pa State Univ, MA, 51; Johns Hopkins Univ, PhD(hist), 56. **CAREER** From instr to asst prof hist, Univ MI, 56-61; assoc prof medieval hist, 61-66, Prof Hist, Johns Hopkins Univ, 66-, Charles Homer Prof of Hist, 86-, emeritus, 01-. **HONORS AND AWARDS** Pres and fel of the Medieval Acad of Am, Foreign mem of the Royal Danish Acad of Sciences and Letters, fel at the Am Acad of Science and Letters; Corresponding fel of the British Acad, Correspondant e'tranger de l'Acadeunie des Inscriptious et Belles Lettres (France); Chevalier de l'ordre des Arts et des Lettres (France); Commissiou Internatiouale de Diplomatique, Guggenheim fel, 60, 83; Charles Howreu Haskins Medal, 90, Medieval Acad. **MEMBERSHIPS** AHA; Medieval Acad Am; Soc Fr Hist Studies. **RESEARCH** Medieval history; medieval France; intellectual history of the 12th and 13th centuries. **SELECTED PUBLICATIONS** Auth, "Medieval Theories of the Just Price," Am Philos Soc (59); auth, Masters, Princes, and Merchants: The Social Views of Peter the Chanter and His Circle (2 vols), Princeton Univ, 70; auth, The Scholastic Culture of the Middle Ages, 1000-1300, Heath, 71; auth, The Government of Philip Augustus: Foundations of French Royal Power in the Middle Ages, Univ of Calif, 86; auth, Les Registres de Philippe Auguste, Academie des Inscriptious, 92; auth, The Language of Sex: Five Voices from Northern France Around 1200, Fayard 94; auth, Aristocratic Life in Medieval France: The Romances of Jean Reuart and Gerbert de Moutreuil, Johns Hopkins Univ, 00. **CONTACT ADDRESS** Dept of Hist, Johns Hopkins Univ, Baltimore, 3400 N Charles St, Baltimore, MD 21218-2680.

BALDWIN, PETER
PERSONAL Born 12/22/1956, Ann Arbor, MI, 2 children **DISCIPLINE** HISTORY **EDUCATION** Yale Univ, BA, 78; Harvard Univ, MA, 80; PhD, 86. **CAREER** Asst prof, Harvard Univ, 86-90; asst prof to prof, UCLA, 90-. **RESEARCH** Comparative history of modern Europe. **SELECTED PUBLICATIONS** Auth, The Politics of Social Solidarity: Class Bases of the European Welfare State, Cambridge Univ Press, 90; auth, Contagion and the State in Europe, 1830-1930, Cambridge Univ Press, 99. **CONTACT ADDRESS** Dept Hist, Univ of California, Los Angeles, 6265 Bunche, Box 951473, Los Angeles, CA 90095-1473. **EMAIL** pbaldwin@ucla.edu

BALJON, NEIL
PERSONAL Born 09/08/1949, Oeastgeest, Netherlands, m, 1989, 3 children **DISCIPLINE** ARCHITECTURE **EDUCATION** Delft Tech Univ, MA, 75, PhD, 93. **CAREER** Urban designer, 77-82; systems analyst, 82-89; writer, 89- . **MEMBERSHIPS** Soc Archit Historians; Am Soc Aesthet. **RESEARCH** Eighteenth and nineteenth century architectural writings; design theory; architectural aesthetics. **SELECTED PUBLICATIONS** Auth, The Structure of Architectural Theory: A Study of Some Writings by Gottfried Semper, John Ruskin, and Christopher Alexander, Delft Technical, 93; auth, Design Justifications as an Instance of Modal Logic, or of Rhetoric, in Design Stud, 96; auth, Interpreting Ruskin: The Argument of The Seven Lamps of Architecture and The Stones of Venice, in J of Aesthet and Art Criticism, 97; auth, As Architecture, in Architecture and Civilization, Rodopi, 99. **CONTACT ADDRESS** 17207 Merlot Pl, Poway, CA 92064-1102. **EMAIL** ARB20@cornell.edu

BALL, LARRY D., SR
PERSONAL Born 06/24/1940, Wynne, AR, m, 1959, 1 child **DISCIPLINE** HISTORY **EDUCATION** Ark State Univ, BA, 61; MA, 63; Univ Col, PhD, 70. **CAREER** Instr, Ark State Univ, 70-71; asst prof, 71-76; assoc prof, 76-83; prof, 83-. **HONORS AND AWARDS** SHSM Auth Awd, 87; AHA, Violet B Gingles Awd, 88; AHS, Leland Sonnichsen Awd, 98. **MEMBERSHIPS** AHA; WHA. **RESEARCH** History of the American West (Frontier Law Enforcement Institutions). **SELECTED PUBLICATIONS** Auth, The United States Marshalls of New Mexico and Arizona Territories, 1846-1912, Univ New Mex Press (Albuquerque), 78; coauth, Voices from State: An Oral History of Arkansas State University, Ark State Univ Press (State Coll, AR), 84; auth Desert Lawmen: The High Sheriffs of New Mexico and Arizona, 1846-1912, Univ New Mex Press (Albuquerque), 92; auth, Elfego Baca in Life and Legend, Tex West Press (El Paso), 92. **CONTACT ADDRESS** Dept History, Arkansas State Univ, PO Box 1690, State University, AR 72467-1690.

BALL, SUSAN
PERSONAL Born 05/25/1947, Pasadena, CA, m, 1983, 1 child **DISCIPLINE** ART AND ARCHITECTURAL HISTORY **EDUCATION** Yale Univ, PhD, 78. **CAREER** Asst prof, Univ Delaware, 78-81; asst treas Chase Manhattan Bank, 82-85; dir, Govt & Found Affairs, Art Inst Chicago, 85-86; exec dir, Col Art Asn, 86- . **MEMBERSHIPS** Coll Art Asn; Am Asn of Mus. **RESEARCH** Late nineteenth, early twentieth century European art and architecture. **SELECTED PUBLICATIONS** Auth, Rossetti and the Double Work of Art, 79; Andre Derain, 80; Ozenfaut and Purism, 81. **CONTACT ADDRESS** Col Art Association, 275 7th Ave, New York, NY 10001. **EMAIL** sball@collegeart.org

BALLARD, ALLEN BUTLER, JR.
PERSONAL Born 11/01/1930, Philadelphia, PA, d **DISCIPLINE** HISTORY **EDUCATION** Kenyon Clg, BA 1952; Harvard Univ, MA, PhD 1961. **CAREER** City Coll of NY, asst prof, assoc prof, 61-69; City Univ of NY, dean of faculty, 69-76; professor emeritus, 86, prof of history, SUNY-Albany, 86-. **HONORS AND AWARDS** Ford Fndtn, Natl Humanities Cntr, Moton Ctr Grants; Fulbright Schlr; Phi Beta Kappa 1952. **SELECTED PUBLICATIONS** "The Education of Black Folk" Harper & Row, 1974; "One More Days Journey" McGraw-Hill 1984. **CONTACT ADDRESS** History, SUNY, Albany, 1400 Washington Ave, Albany, NY 12222.

BALTAKIS, ANTHONY
PERSONAL Born 12/19/1944, NJ, m, 1972, 2 children **DISCIPLINE** HISTORY **EDUCATION** John Carroll Univ, BA, 67; Univ S Fla, MA, 92; Univ Akron, PhD, 97. **CAREER** Instr, Univ Akron, 92-97; Res consultant, AFL/CIO Union Summer Project, 96; Assoc Prof, La State Univ, 97. **HONORS AND AWARDS** Outstanding Teacher of the Year, La State Univ, 00; Gander Res Grant, Univ Akron, 96; Martin Fel, Univ Akron, 95; Kennedy Foundation Res Grant, 95-96. **MEMBERSHIPS** Phi Alpha Theta, Am Hist Asn, LA Hist Asn. **RESEARCH** McClellan "Rackets" Committee 1957-1959 (including JFK, RFK, Hoffa, Walter Reuther); 20th Century History; Civil War; American Popular Culture. **SELECTED PUBLICATIONS** Auth, "Michigan Historical Review," 99; auth, "On the Defensive: Walter Reuther's testimony before the McClellan Larson Rackets Committee; auth, "Don't Knock the Rock: A Cultural Study," Pompa, 98; auth, "Politics and Policies of JFK and RFK: The McClellan Committee Investigation of Organized Labor Leads to Organized Crime, 1957-1960, JFK Assassination Chronicles, 98; rev, of "Eleanor Roosevelt," Library of America Biography Series; rev, of "The Betrayal of Local 14," Journal of Labor Research. **CONTACT ADDRESS** Dept Liberal Arts, Louisiana State Univ, Eunice, PO Box 1129, Eunice, LA 70535-1129.

BALTZER, REBECCA
DISCIPLINE MEDIEVAL MUSIC **EDUCATION** Boston Univ, PhD. **CAREER** Prof; act, Medieval Stud prog; vis prof, Princeton Univ, 96. **MEMBERSHIPS** Current treas & past VP, Amer Musicol Soc. **RESEARCH** Medieval music, espec that of the Notre-Dame School and Ars Antiqua; notation; hist of theory; codicology; liturgy and liturgical books of medieval Paris. **SELECTED PUBLICATIONS** Ed, vol 5, critical edition of the Magnus liber organi, Monaco, 95; co-ed, The Union of Words and Music in Medieval Poetry, Tex, 91 & The Divine Office in the Latin Middle Ages, Oxford, 98. **CONTACT ADDRESS** School of Music, Univ of Texas, Austin, 2613 Wichita St, Austin, TX 78705.

BAMBACH, CHARLES
DISCIPLINE HISTORY **EDUCATION** Univ Mich, PhD, 87. **CAREER** Assoc prof. **RESEARCH** Hermeneutics; contemporary continental philosophy; 19th and 20th century European intellectual history and philosophy. **SELECTED PUBLICATIONS** Auth, Heidegger, Dilthey, and the Crisis of Historicism, Cornell, 95; The Genesis of Heidegger's Being and Time, Am Cath Philos Quart, 95; Phenomenological Res as Destruktion: The Early Heidegger's Reading of Dilthey, Philos Today, 93; The Six Great Themes in Western Metaphysics, Mod Age, 95; Hermeneutics and the Life World, Psychohis Rev, 92. **CONTACT ADDRESS** Dept of History, Univ of Texas, Dallas, Richardson, TX 75083-0688. **EMAIL** cbambach@utdallas.edu

BANES, RUTH A.
PERSONAL Born 07/07/1950, Rochester, NY, m, 1975 **DISCIPLINE** AMERICAN STUDIES **EDUCATION** Univ NMex, BA, 72, PhD, 78. **CAREER** Asst prof English, Elon Col, NC, 78-79; from vis asst prof to assoc prof of Am Studies, Univ S Fla, 79-; grad dir, Am Studies, Univ S Fla, 90-; grad dir, Master of Lib Arts, Univ S Fla, 99-. **HONORS AND AWARDS** NEH Summer Sem, 80, 83, 87; Outstanding Undergraduate Teaching Awd, Univ S Fla, 91; Undergraduate Teaching Incentive Awd, Univ S Fla, 94. **MEMBERSHIPS** Am Studies Asn; Am Cult Asn; Can Asn for Am Studies; Pop Cult Asn; Rocky Mt Am Studies Asn; S Am Studies Asn. **RESEARCH** American autobiography; culture studies; popular music (country and blues); women's studies; approaches to American Studies; regionalism in American culture. **SELECTED PUBLICATIONS** Auth, "Doris Ulmann and Her Mountain Folk," J Am Cult (85); auth, "Southerners Up North: Autobiographical Indications of Southern Ethnicity," Perspectives on the Am S (85); auth, "Counterculture Politics in Popular Culture Studies," Can Rev of Am Studies (86); auth, "Caught in the Web," Women's Rev of Bks (86); auth, "The Dark Side: Southern Gothic in Country Music," in Developing Dixie: Modernization in a Traditional Society (88); auth, "Florida Bound Blues," Popluar Music and Soc (88); contribur, "Loretta Lynn, Dolly Parton, Blues Singing Women," in Encycl of S Cult (89); contribur, "Southern Autobiography," in Encycl of S Cult (89); auth, "Relentlessly Writing the Weary Song: Blues Legacies in Literature," Can Rev of Am Studies (90); auth, "Dixie's Daughters: The Country Music Female," in You Wrote My Life: Lyrical Themes in Country Music (92). **CONTACT ADDRESS** Dept of Am Studies, Univ of So Florida, 4202 Fowler Ave, Tampa, FL 33620-9951. **EMAIL** banes@luna.cas.usf.edu

BANKER, JAMES RODERICK
PERSONAL Born 04/29/1938, Plattsburgh, NY, m, 1961, 2 children **DISCIPLINE** ITALIAN RENAISSANCE, HISTORY OF THE MIDDLE AGES **EDUCATION** Taylor Univ, AB, 61; Boston Univ, MA, 62; Univ Rochester, PhD(Ital Renaissance hist), 71. **CAREER** From instr to asst prof, 67-76, Assoc Prof Ital Hist, NC State Univ, 86-, Nat Endowment for Humanities scholar death in Mid Ages, 76-77; summer school, Florence Italy, Duke univ, 88-89, 95-97. **HONORS AND AWARDS** Villa I Tatti, Harvard Univ Center for Italian Renaissance Studies, research in Florence, 92-93; Appointment to Comitato Scientifico della Fondazione Piero della Francesca, 94; Honorary Citizenship in the city of Borgo San Spolcro, 95. **MEMBERSHIPS** AHA; Renaissance Soc Am; Triangle renaissance group; Triangle intellectual hist group **RESEARCH** Death in the Middle Ages and Renaissance; Medieval and Renaissance rhetoric; grief and consolation in the Italian Renaissance; Piero della Francesca, Relationship between society and cultute. **SELECTED PUBLICATIONS** Auth, Giovanni di Bonandrea and Civic Society, Manuscripta, 74; Ars Dictaminis and Rhetorical Textbooks at the Bolognese University, Medievali & Humanistica, 74; Mourning a Son: Childhood and Paternal Love in the Consolateria of G Manetti, Hist Childhood Quart, 76; Albertanus of Brescia-The Pursuit of Happiness in the Early 13th-Century, with J. M. Powell, Cath Hist Rev, Vol 79, 93; A Legal and Humanistic Library in Borgo-San-Sepolcro in the Middle of the 15th-Century, Rinascimento, Vol 33, 93; Episcopal Power and Florentine Society, AD 1000-1320, with G. W. Dameron, Speculum-A J of Medieval Studies, Vol 68, 93; The Cult of Remembrance and the Black Death-6 Renaissance Cities in Central Italy, with S. K. Cohn, Cath Hist Rev, Vol 79, 93; The Formation of a Medieval Church-Ecclesiastical Change in Verona 9509-1150, with M. C. Miller, Speculum-A J of Medieval Studies, Vol 70, 95; A New World in a Small Place-Church and Religion in the Diocese of Rieti, 1188-1378, with R. Brentano, Am Hist Rev, Vol 100, 95; A Moral Art-Grammar, Society, and Culture in Trecento Florence, with P. F. Gehl, Cath Hist Rev, Vol 82, 96; Piety and Charity in Late Medieval Florence, with J. Henderson, Cath Hist Rev, Vol 82, 96. **CONTACT ADDRESS** Dept of Hist, No Carolina State Univ, Raleigh, NC 27695-8108. **EMAIL** james_banker@ncsu.edu

BANKER, MARK T.
PERSONAL Born 02/04/1951, OakRidge, TN, m, 1976, 1 child **DISCIPLINE** HISTORY **EDUCATION** Warren Wilson Col, NC, BA hist, 73; Univ VA, MAT hist, 75; Univ New Mexico, PhD, 87. **CAREER** Warren Wilson Col, teaching intern, 74-76; Menaul School, NM, teacher us hist, dean stud, 76-83; Univ NM, instr, 86, grad asst 83-86; Albuquerque Academy, NM, teacher us hist, 86-87; Webb Sch Knoxville, TN, hist teacher, 87-. **HONORS AND AWARDS** Warren Wilson Col Schs Medal 70, 71, 72, 73; Who's Who in Am Col Univ; Warren Wilson Cll Awd for excell in Hist Pol Sci; Magna Cum Laude, Warren Wilson; Dorothy Woodward Found Gnt; Webb Sch Most Influential Teacher, 90, 91, 92, 94, 98; Nat Endow for the Humanities/Readers Digest Awd; Distg Ser Awd, Warren Wilson Alumni Asn. **MEMBERSHIPS** OAH; WHA; Presby Hist Soc; East TN Hist Soc; Appalachian Stud Asn. **SELECTED PUBLICATIONS** Of Missionaries Multiculturalism and Mainstream Malaise: Historical Insights into the Presbyterian Predicament, 97; Beyond the Melting Pot & Multiculturalism: Insights into Am Culture Politics from Southern Appalachian Studies Conference, Boone NC, 98; Mountain Vistas: Insights into the Rural-urban Encounter and Am culture Politics form Southern Appalachia and Hispanic New Mexico, 97; Warren Wilson College: A Centennial Portrait, with Reuben A Holden, NC 94, numerous articles and pub. **CONTACT ADDRESS** Webb Sch, Knoxville, 9800 Webb School Dr, Knoxville, TN 37923. **EMAIL** mark_banker@awebbschool.org

BANNER, LOIS W.
PERSONAL Born Los Angeles, CA, M, 2 children **DISCIPLINE** HISTORY **EDUCATION** Columbia, PhD, 70. **CAREER** Prof; past ch, Prog for the Study of Women and Men; past ch, Dept Hist, Univ Southern Calif. **HONORS AND AWARDS** Best book on Women's Issues, Independent Publishers 1999 Book Awds; Humanities Fellow, Rockefeller Foundation, 78-9; Fellow, Radcliffe Institute, 74-5; NEH Summer Seminars for College Teachers, 84; 92. **MEMBERSHIPS** Pres, Conf Gp in Women's Hist, 79-81; pres, Amer Stud Asn, 86-88; pres, Pacific Coast Branch, AHA, 91-93. **RESEARCH** Women and Gender; Social; Popular Culture. **SELECTED PUBLICATIONS** Auth, In Full Flower: Aging Women, Power and Sexuality, Knopf, 92; American Beauty, Knopf, 83, paperback Univ Chicago; Elizabeth Cady Stanton: A Radical for Woman's Rights, Little, Brown, 79; Women in Modern America: A Brief History, Harcourt Brace, 74; co-ed, Clio's Consciousness Raised: New Perspectives on the History of Women, Harper and Row, 74; auth, Finding Fran: History and Memory in the Lives of two Women, Columbia University Press, 98. **CONTACT ADDRESS** Dept of History, Univ of So California, University Park Campus, Los Angeles, CA 90089. **EMAIL** lbanner@usc.edu

BANNING, LANCE
PERSONAL Born 01/24/1942, Kansas City, MO, m, 1964, 1 child **DISCIPLINE** HISTORY **EDUCATION** Univ of Miss, BA, 64; Wash Univ, MA; PhD, 71. **CAREER** Lectr, Brown Univ, 71-73; asst prof to prof, Univ of Ky, 73-. **HONORS AND AWARDS** NEH fel, 74-75; Guggenheim fel, 79-80; Univ Res prof, 84-85; Nat Hums Ctr fel, 86-87, Ctr for the Hist of Freedom fel, 91, Fulbright Disting Ch Awd, 97; Phi Alpha Theta Int Book Awd; Merle Curti Awd, OAH. **SELECTED PUBLICATIONS** Auth, The Jeffersonian Persuasion: Evolution of a Party Ideology, Cornell Univ Pr, 78; auth, After the Constitution: Party Conflict in the New Republic, Wadsworth, 89; auth, "The Republican Interpretation: Retrospect and Prospect", The Republican Synthesis Revisited: Essays in Honor of George Athan Billias, ed Milton M. Klein, Univ Pr of Va, (92): 91-117; auth, "The Jeffersonians: First Principles", Democrats and the American Idea: a Bicentennial Appraisal, ed Peter B. Kovler, Center for Nat Policy Pr, (92): 1-27; auth, "Political Economy and the Creation of the Federal Republic", Devising Liberty: Preserving and Creating Freedom in the New American Republic, ed David Thomas Konig, Stanford Univ Pr, (95): 11-49; auth, The Sacred Fire of Liberty: James Madison and the Founding of the Federal Republic, Cornell Univ Pr, 95; auth, Jefferson and Madison: Three Conversations from the Founding, Madison House, 95; **CONTACT ADDRESS** Dept Hist, Univ of Kentucky, 500 S Limestone St, Lexington, KY 40506-0001. **EMAIL** Lancebanning@yahoo.com

BARAHONA, RENATO
PERSONAL Born 11/17/1966, Mexico, m, 1983, 1 child **DISCIPLINE** HISTORY **EDUCATION** The Johns Hopkins Univ, BA, 66; Ecol Practique des Hautes Etudies, Vleme Section, Paris, Diplome, 71; Princeton Univ, PhD, 79. **CAREER** Lectr, Univ Ill, Chicago, 75-79, asst prof, 79-85, assoc prof, 85-, assoc dean for Undergrad Educ, 88-91, assoc chair, 97-98. **MEMBERSHIPS** Am Hist Asn, Renaissance Soc, Sixteenth Century Studies Conf, Soc for Spanish and Portuguese Hist Studies. **SELECTED PUBLICATIONS** Auth, Vizcaya on the Eve of Carlism: Politics and Society, 1800-1833, Reno: Univ Nevado Press (89); auth, "The Basques and the Loss of the American Colonies (1810-1840): Approach to a Problem," Revista Internacional de Estudios Vascos, Tomo XXXVI, No 1 (91); auth, "Courtship, Seduction and Abandonment in Early Modern Spain. The Example of Vizcaya, 1500-1700," in Sex and Love in Golden Age Spain,, Alain Saint-Saens, ed, New Orleans: Univ Press of the South (96); auth, "Origins and Causes of Carlism in Vizcaya, 1759-1833," chapter in Identidad y nacialismo en la Espana contemporanea: El Carlismo, 1833-1975, Stanley G,. Payne, dir, Madrid: Actas Ed, Coleccion Luis Hernando de Larramendi (96); auth, "Mujeres vascas, sexualidad y la ley en la Espana moderna, siglos XVI y XVII," in Historia silenciada de la mujer. La mujer espanola desde la epoca medieval hasta la contemporanes, Alain sint-Saens, dir, Madrid: Ed Complutense (96); auth, "Coaccion consentimiento en las relaciones sexuales modernas, siglo 16 a 18," Meridies (in press). **CONTACT ADDRESS** Dept Hist, Univ of Illinois, Chicago, 851 S Morgan St # 723, Chicago, IL 60607-7042. **EMAIL** barahona@uic.edu

BARANY, GEORGE
PERSONAL Born 04/12/1922, Budapest, Hungary, m, 1981 **DISCIPLINE** HISTORY **EDUCATION** Univ Colo, MA, 58, PhD, 60. **CAREER** Dept of Hist, Univ of Denver Colorado, 60-92; Prof Emer, 92-. **HONORS AND AWARDS** Fel, Am Coun-

cil of Learned Soc, 64, 67, 72; fel, Am Philos Soc, 61, 82; Fulbright-Hays Fac Res Abroad Prog, U.S. Dept of Educ, 81, 84, 88; Fulbright Award, Hungary, 86, 89. **MEMBERSHIPS** AHA; Am Asn Advan Slavic Studies; Am Asn Study Hungarian Hist; Western Slavic Asn. **RESEARCH** History of the Austro-Hungarian Empire; Hungarian-American relations; East European history. **SELECTED PUBLICATIONS** Auth, Stephen Szechenyi and the Awakening of Hungarian Nationalism, 1791-1841, Princeton Univ Press, 68; auth, "Native Fascism in the Successor States, 1918-1945," in The Dragon's Teeth: The Roots of Hungarian Fasicsm, ed. Peter F. Sugar (ABC Clio Press, 71), 73-82; auth, "Jews and Non-Jews in Eastern Europe," in Chapter on the Assimilation of Jews in Hungary, (Jerusalem, 74), 51-99; auth, "Die Habsburgermonarchie 1848-1918," in Ungarns Verwaltung, ed. Adam Wandruszka and Peter Urbanitsch (75), 306-468; auth, "Hungarian History-World History," in Indiana University Studies on Hungary, ed. Gyorgy Ranki (Hungarian Acad of Sci, Budapest, 84), 59-83; auth, The Anglo-Russian Entente Cordiale of 1697-1698: Peter I and William III at Utrecht, E Europ Monogr, 86; auth, "Szechenyi Istvan nacionalizmusa," in Europa vonzasaban, ed. Ferenc Glatz (Budapest, 93), 139-154; auth, "A Wallenbergkutatas idoszeru problemai es feladatai," in The Holocaust in Hungary: Fifty Years Later, ed. Randolph L. Braham and Attila Pok (NY: Holocaust Series and E Europ Monogr, 97), 567-598; auth, "Jozsef Eotvos," in Encyclopedia of Modern East Central Europe 1815-1989, ed. Richard Frucht (NYork and London, 00). **CONTACT ADDRESS** Dept Hist, Univ of Denver, Denver, CO 80210.

BARBER, ELIZABETH J. WAYLAND
PERSONAL Born 12/02/1940, Pasadena, CA, m, 1965 **DISCIPLINE** ARCHAEOLOGY, LINGUISTICS **EDUCATION** Bryn Mawr Col, BA, 62; Yale Univ, PhD, 68. **CAREER** Res assoc, Princeton Univ, 68-89; LECTR TO FULL PROF, OCCIDENTAL COL, 70-. **HONORS AND AWARDS** NEH Grants, 72, 74, & 93; J Guggenheim Memorial Fel, 79-80; Wenner-Gren ACLS Haynes grants; book prizes from Amer Hist Asn, 93, Costume Soc, 92, 95 & 00. **MEMBERSHIPS** Archaeol Inst of Am; Linguistic Soc of Am; Textile Soc of Am; Costume Soc of Am; CIETA. **RESEARCH** Prehistoric archaeology and languages of Southern & Eastern Europe; decipherment; ancient textiles, costumes, & rituals. **SELECTED PUBLICATIONS** Auth, The Mummies of Urumchi, W.W. Norton, 99; auth, Women's Work-The First 20,000 Years, W.W. Norton, 94; auth, Prehistoric Textiles, Princeton Univ Press, 91; auth, Archaeological Decipherment, Princeton Univ Press, 74; auth, On the Origins of the Vily/Rusalki, Varia on the Indo-European Past, 97; auth, Minoan Women and the Challenge of Weaving for Home, Trade, and Shrine, TEXNH: Craftsmen, Craftswomen and Craftsmanship in the Aegean Bronze Age, 97; auth, Textiles of the Neolithic through Iron Ages, The Oxford Encycl of Archaeol in the Near East, 97; auth, On the Antiquity of East European Bridal Clothing, Dress, 94; auth, The Peplos of Athena, Goddess and Polis: The Panathenaic Festival in Ancient Athens, Princeton, 92. **CONTACT ADDRESS** Language Dept, Occidental Col, 1126 N. Chester Ave., Los Angeles, CA 90041. **EMAIL** barber@oxy.edu

BARBER, MARYLIN J.
DISCIPLINE HISTORY **EDUCATION** Queen's Univ, BA, MA; Univ London, PhD. **CAREER** Assoc prof, Carleton Univ. **RESEARCH** Female immigration to Canada; imperialism and relig. **SELECTED PUBLICATIONS** Auth, "Immigrant Domestic Servants in Canada," Can Hist Assn Booklet, Canada's Ethnic Groups Series, 91; The Servant Problem in Manitoba, 1896-1930, First Days, Fighting Days: Women in Manitoba Hist, Can Plains Res Ctr, 87; Domestic Servants in the 20th Century Ontario Kitchen, Consuming Passions, The Ontario Hist Soc, 90; The Fellowship of the Maple Leaf Teachers, The Anglican Church and the World of W Can 1820-1970, Can Plains Res Ctr, 91; The Motor Caravan Mission: Anglican Women Workers in the New Era, Women Within the Christian Church in Canada , Univ Toronto Press, 95. **CONTACT ADDRESS** Dept of Hist, Carleton Univ, 1125 Colonel By Dr, Ottawa, ON, Canada K1S 5B6. **EMAIL** marilyn_barber@carleton.ca

BARBOUR, HUGH
PERSONAL Born 08/07/1921, Peking, China, m, 1959, 3 children **DISCIPLINE** CHURCH HISTORY **EDUCATION** Harbard Univ, AB, 42; Union Theol Sem, NYork, BD, 45; Yale Univ, PhD(relig), 52. **CAREER** Pastor, Congregational Church, Coventry, CT, 45-47; instr Bible & relig, Syracuse Univ, 47-49; instr Bible, Wellesley Col, 50-53; from asst prof to assoc prof relig, 53-67, Prof Relig, Earlham Col, 67-, Mem gov bd, Nat Coun Churches, 72-. **MEMBERSHIPS** Soc Bibl Theol; Soc Bibl Lit. **RESEARCH** Theological writings of William Penn. **SELECTED PUBLICATIONS** Auth, The Quakers in Puritan England, Yale Univ, 64; Step by Step in Reading the Old Testament, Asn Press, 64; Programmed teaching for Old Testament, Relig Educ, 11-12/67; Protestant Quakerism, 71 & The God of peace, 72, Quaker Relig Thought; co-ed, Early Quaker Writings, 1650-1700, Eerdmans, 73; Margaret Fell and the Rise of Quakerism, with B. Y. Kunze, J of Relig, Vol 76, 96; Gentle Invaders-Quaker Women Educators and Racial Issues During the Civil-War and Reconstruction, with L. B. Selleck, Church History, Vol 66, 97. **CONTACT ADDRESS** 1840 SW E St., Richmond, IN 47374.

BARDAGLIO, PETER W.
PERSONAL Born 04/25/1953, Hartford, CT, m, 1983, 3 children **DISCIPLINE** HISTORY **EDUCATION** Brown Univ, AB, 75; Stanford Univ, MA, 78; Stanford Univ, PhD, 87. **CAREER** Visiting lectr, Univ Md at Col Pk, fall 95, 81-83; visiting prof in Amer studies, Univ Exeter, 94-95; instr, 83-87, asst prof, 87-93, assoc prof, 93-99, Prof 99-, Goucher Col. **HONORS AND AWARDS** Who's Who in Am, 00; Who's Who in the East, 99-00; Outstanding Educ of the Year, Md Asn of Higher Educ, May, 98; James Rawley prize, Orgn of Amer Hist, 96; Who's Who Among America's Teachers, 96, 98; Caroline Doebler Bruckerl Awd for Outstanding Teaching, may, 94; Nat Endow for the Humanities summer stipend, 92; Littleton-Griswold Res grant, Amer Hist Asn, 89-90; Awd for outstanding teaching in soc sci, May, 88; Elizabeth Conolly Todd Distinguished Prof, 95-00, Goucher Col; Jesse Ball duPont Fellow, Nat Humanities Ctr, 99-00. **MEMBERSHIPS** Amer Hist Asn; Orgn of Amer Hist; Southern Hist Asn; Amer Soc for Legal Hist; Amer Studies Asn; Southern Asn for Women Hist. **RESEARCH** Race, gender, and the law in the 19th century South; History of childhood. **SELECTED PUBLICATIONS** Auth, Shameful Matches: The Regulation of Interracial Sex and Marriage in The South before 1900, Sex, Love, Race: Crossing Boundaries in North American History, NY, NY Univ Press (99):112-38; auth, Reconstructing the Household: Families, Sex and the Law in the Nineteenth-Century South, Chapel Hill, Univ NC Press, 95; article, Shameful Matches: The Regulation of Interracial Sex and Marriage in the South before 1900; Sex, Love, Race: Crossing Boundaries in North American History, NY, NY Univ Pr, n-2-38, 99; article, Rape and the Law in the Old South: Calculated to Excite Indignation in Every Heart, Jour of Southern Hist, 60, 749-72, nov, 94; article, The Children of Jubilee: African-American Childhood in Wartime, Divided Houses: Gender and the Civil War, NY, Oxford Univ Press, 213-29, 92; article, An Outrage Upon Nature: Incest and the Law in the Nineteenth-Century South, In Joy and in Sorrow: Women, Family and Marriage in the Victorian South, 1830-1900, NY, Oxford Univ Press, 32-51, 91. **CONTACT ADDRESS** Goucher Col, 1021 Dulaney Valley Rd., Baltimore, MD 21204. **EMAIL** pbardagi@goucher.edu

BARKAN, ELLIOTT ROBERT
PERSONAL Born 12/15/1940, Brooklyn, NY, m, 1994, 3 children **DISCIPLINE** AMERICAN HISTORY, ETHNIC STUDIES **EDUCATION** Queens Col, NYork, BA, 62; Harvard Univ, MA, 64, PhD(hist), 69. **CAREER** Instr hist, Pace Col, 64-68; from asst prof to prof, 68-74, Full Prof Hist, CA State Col, San Bernardino, 74-, Consult, Los Angeles City Sch Syst, 73-74; Calif State Univ Soc Sci Res Council's Field Inst fel, 82-83; vis prof, Summer Inst, Amerika House, Falkenstein, West Germany, 78; VP/Pres. Elect of the I&EHS, Fulbrights & India, 83, England, 87-8; & Norway 93. **MEMBERSHIPS** AHA; Orgn Am Historians; Immigration & Ethnic Hist Soc. **RESEARCH** Comparative American ethnic history & contemporary immigration. **SELECTED PUBLICATIONS** ed, Edmund Burke on the American Revolution, Harper, 66; auth, The Emergence of a Whig Persuasion: Conservatism, Democratism, and the New York State Whigs, NY Hist, 10-71; James Barbour (1775-1842), In: Encyclopedia of Southern History, 76; Proximity and Commuting Immigration, In: American Ethnic Revival, 77; French Canadian Americans, In: Harvard Encyclopedia of American Ethnic Groups, 80; The Price of Equality: Comparative American Ethnic History, Prentice-Hall; coauth (with Nikolas Khokhlov), Socio Economic Data Indices of Naturalization Patterns in the United States, A Theory Revisited, Ethnicity, 6/80; auth, Asian & Pacific Migration, Greenwood, 92; Race, Religion, and Nationality in American Society-A Model of Ethnicity-From Contact to Assimilation-Response, J of Am Ethnic Hist, Vol 14, 95; The White Peril-Foreign Relations and Asian Immigration to Australia and North-America, 1919-1978, with S. Brawley, J of Am Hist, Vol 82, 95; And Still They Come, Harland Davidson, 96; Peopling Indiana-The Ethnic Experience, with R. M. Taylor and C. A. McBirney, J of Am Hist, Vol 84, 97; ed., A Nation of Peoples, Greenwood, 99; co-ed, U.S. Immigration & Naturalization Laws and Issues, Greenwood, 99; ed., Making It in America, forthcoming 00, ABC-Clio. **CONTACT ADDRESS** Dept of Hist, California State Univ, San Bernardino, 5500 University Pky, San Bernardino, CA 92407-7500. **EMAIL** ebarkan@csusb.edu

BARKER, JOHN W.
PERSONAL Born 10/07/1933, Brooklyn, NY, m, 1998, 2 children **DISCIPLINE** MEDIEVAL HISTORY **EDUCATION** Brooklyn Col, BA, 55; Rutgers Univ, MA, 56, PhD, 61. **CAREER** Teaching asst, Rutgers Univ, 57-59; instr, Brooklyn Col, 58-59; jr fel, Dumbarton Oaks, 59-62; vis prof, Inst for Res in the Humanities, Univ of Wis, 64-65; vis prof, Inst for Advanced Study, Princeton Univ, 78-79; asst to assoc prof, 67; prof of hist, 70-96, Prof Emeritus, Univ of Wis, 96-. **HONORS AND AWARDS** Phi Beta Kappa, 55; prize for Outstanding Lit Achievement, Coun for Wis Writers, 67; Guggenheim Fel, 74-75. **MEMBERSHIPS** Medieval Academy; Byzantine Studies Conf; Midwest Medieval Conf; Soc for the Study of the Crusades and the Latin East. **RESEARCH** Byzantine history & civilization; Venetian history & civilization; crusades; music & western cultural history. **SELECTED PUBLICATIONS** Auth, Justinian and the Later Roman Empire, Univ of Wis Press, 66; Manuel II Palaeologus (1391-1425): A Study in Late Byzantine Statesmanship, Rutgers Univ Press, 69; The Monody of Demetrios Kydones on the Zealot Rising of 1345 in Thessaloniki, Essays in Memory of Basil Laourdas, Thessaloniki, 75; Miscellaneous Genoese Documents on the Levantine World of the Late Fourteenth and Early Fifteenth Centuries, Essays in Honor of Peter Charanis, 79; Byzantium and the Display of War Trophies: Between Antiquity and the Venetians, TO EAA, 93. **CONTACT ADDRESS** History Dept, Univ of Wisconsin, Madison, Humanities Bldg, Madison, WI 53706. **EMAIL** jwbarker@facstaff.wisc.edu

BARKER, NANCY NICHOLS
PERSONAL Born 12/26/1925, Mt Vernon, NY, m, 1950 **DISCIPLINE** MODERN EUROPEAN HISTORY **EDUCATION** Vassar Col, BA, 46; Univ PA, MA, 47, PhD, 55. **CAREER** Asst instr, Univ PA, 48-49; instr, Univ DE, 49-50; lectr mod Europ hist, 55-67, from asst prof to assoc prof hist, 67-72, Prof Hist, Univ TX, Austin, 72-, TX Res Inst res grant, 67-68. **HONORS AND AWARDS** Gilbert Chinard Prize for Bk on Franco-Am Rels, 72; Summerfield G Roberts Awd for Bk on Repub of Tex, 72. **MEMBERSHIPS** AHA; Soc Fr Hist Studies. **RESEARCH** Nineteenth century Europe; France in the New World; French Revolution. **SELECTED PUBLICATIONS** Auth, France, Austria and the Mexican Venture, 1861-1864, Fr Hist Studies, fall 63; Austria, France and the Venetian Question, J Mod Hist, 6/64; Distaff Diplomacy: The Empress Eugenie and the Foreign Policy of the Second Empire, Univ TX, Austin & London, 67; co-ed & contribr, Diplomacy in an Age of Nationalism: Essays in Honor of Lynn Marshall Case, Martinus Nijhoff, The Hague, 71; ed & transl, Recognition, Rupture and Reconciliation, Vol I, In: The French Legation in Texas, TX Hist Asn, 71; auth, From Texas to Mexico: An Affairiste at Work, Southwestern Hist Quart, 7/71; ed & transl, Mission Miscarried, Vol II, In: The French Legation in Texas, TX Hist Asn, 73; Let Them Eat Cake-The Mythical Marie Antoinette and the French Revolution, Historian, Vol 55, 93. **CONTACT ADDRESS** Dept of Hist, Univ of Texas, Austin, Austin, TX 78712.

BARKER, ROSANNE M.
DISCIPLINE HISTORY **EDUCATION** Univ Calif, Santa Barbara, BA, MA, PhD. **CAREER** Asst prof to assoc prof, Sam Houston State Univ, 92-. **RESEARCH** History of women, native americans, colonial america. **SELECTED PUBLICATIONS** Auth, Small Town Progressivism: Pearl Chase and Female Activism in Conservation in Santa Barbara, California, Southern Calif Quart. **CONTACT ADDRESS** Dept of History, Sam Houston State Univ, 1903 University Ave, Suite 314, PO Box 2239, Huntsville, TX 77341. **EMAIL** his_rmb@shsu.edu

BARKER, THOMAS M.
PERSONAL Born 08/26/1929, Minneapolis, MN, m, 1955, 2 children **DISCIPLINE** MODERN HISTORY **EDUCATION** Carleton Col, BA, 51; Harvard Univ, AM, 52; Univ Minn, PhD, 57. **CAREER** Asst prof hist, Glassboro State Col, 58-62; asst prof, Western IL Univ, 62-63; assoc prof, 63-68, Prof Hist, State Univ NY Albany, 68-, State Univ NY Res Found fels & grants, 64-67; Am Philos Soc grants, 68, 75; Int Res & Exchange Bd grants, 70-71 & 76-77; Nat Endowment Humanities transl prog, 79. **MEMBERSHIPS** Inter-univ Sem Armed Forces & Soc; War & Soc East Cent Europe Res Proj; Soc For Slovene Studies; Inter-univ Ctr Europ Studies; Am Asn Study Hungarian Hist. **RESEARCH** German and Austrian history, 17th-20th centuries, especially social and military history. **SELECTED PUBLICATIONS** Auth, Double Eagle and Crescent: Vienna's Second Turkish Siege and its Historical Setting, State Univ NY, 67; ed, transl, Frederick the Great and the Making of Prussia, Holt, 71; auth, The Military Intellectual and Battle: Raimondo Montecuccoli and the Thirty Years War, State Univ NY, 74; The Slovene Minority of Carinthia, 82 & Army, Aristocracy, Monarchy: Essays on War, Society and Government in Austria, 1618-1780, In: Social Science Monographs, 82, Columbia; Oss and the Yugoslav Resistance, 1943-1945, with K. Ford, J of Military Hist, Vol 57, 93; The Uskoks of Senj-Piracy, Banditry and the Holy War in the 16th-Century Adriatic, with C. W. Bracewell, J of Military Hist, Vol 57, 93; Kirk Ford Comment on Thomas M. Barker, Book Review-Reply, J of Military Hist, Vol 58, 94; Gubbins and Soe, with P. Wilkinson and J. B. Ashley, J of Military Hist, Vol 58, 94; Cambridge Illustrated History of Warfare, with G. Parker, J of Military Hist, Vol 60, 96; The Military Revolution-Military Innovation and the Rise of the West, 1500-1800, with G. Parker, J of Military Hist, Vol 61, 97. **CONTACT ADDRESS** Dept of Hist, SUNY, Albany, 1400 Washington Ave, Albany, NY 12222.

BARKER, WILLIAM SHIRMER, II
PERSONAL Born 12/15/1934, St. Louis, MO, m, 1957, 2 children **DISCIPLINE** CHURCH HISTORY **EDUCATION** Princeton Univ, BA, 56; Cornell Univ, MA, 59; Covenant Theol Sem, BD, 60; Vanderbilt Univ, PhD, 70. **CAREER** Instr, Covenant Col, 58-64; asst prof, 64-70; assoc prof, dean of fac, 70-72; assoc prof, dean of fac, Covenant Theol Sem, 72-77; assoc prof, pres, 77-84; prof, Westminster Theol Sem, 87-, vice pres for acad affairs, 91-00. **HONORS AND AWARDS** Phi Beta Kappa. **MEMBERSHIPS** Am Soc of Ch Hist; Ev Theol Soc; Coal on Faith and Hist; 16th-Cent Soc. **RESEARCH** American Presbyterianism; English Puritans. **SELECTED**

PUBLICATIONS Ed, Presbyterian Jour, 84-87; auth, Puritan Profiles: 54 Influential Puritans at the Time When the Westminster Confession of Faith Was Written; The Hemphill Case, Benjamin Franklin, and Subscription to the Westminster Confession, Amer Presbyterians, 91. **CONTACT ADDRESS** 508 Sunnyside Ave., Webster Groves, MO 63119.

BARKER-BENFIELD, GRAHAM JOHN
PERSONAL Born 05/28/1941, London, England, 1 child **DISCIPLINE** HISTORY **EDUCATION** Trinity Col, BA Hons, 63; Univ CA, Los Angeles, PhD, 68. **CAREER** Asst prof hist, Am Univ, 69-72; vis asst prof, Lewis & Clark Col, 72-74; asst prof Am studies, 74-75, asst prof, 75-78, Assoc to Full Prof Hist, State Univ NY, Albany, 78-, NEH & Shelby Cullom Davis Ctr fel hist, Princeton Univ, 77-78. **HONORS AND AWARDS** Univ Awd for Excellence in Teaching, State Univ NY, Albany, 92; The Chancellor's Awd for Excellence in Teaching, SUNY, 92; ma, trinity col. **MEMBERSHIPS** AHA; Orgn Am Historians; Brit Soc 18th Century Studies. **RESEARCH** American social hist, hist of sex roles, British hist of sex roles. **SELECTED PUBLICATIONS** Sexual Surgery in Late Nineteenth Century America, Int J Health Serv, 75 & Random, In: Seizing Our Bodies, 78; The Horrors of the Half Known Life: Male Attitudes Toward Women and Sexuality in Nineteenth Century America, Harper & Row, 76, 2nd ed. Routledge, 00; Female Circumcision, Women & Health, spring 76; Mother-Emancipator: The Meaning of Jane Addam's Sickness and Cure, J Family Hist, winter 79; Weir Mitchell and the Woman Question: Gender and Therapy, Quart J Ideology, fall 81; Mary Wollstonecraft's Depression and Diagnosis: The Relation Between Sensibility and Women's Susceptibility to Nervous Disorders, Psychohistory Rev, 85; Mary Wollstonecraft: Eighteenth Century Common Wealth Woman, J of the Hist of Ideas, 89; The Culture of Sensibility: Sex and Society in Eighteenth-Century Britain, Univ of Chicago Press, 92; Portraits of American Women, ed with C. Clinton,. St. Martin's, 91, rev ed Oxford Univ Press, 98; Sex and Sensibility, in The Age of Romanticism and Revolution: An Oxford Companion to British Culture, ed 1, McCalman, Oxford Univ Press, 99; Sensibility, An Oxford Companion is the Romantic Age, British Culture, 1776-1832, Oxford Univ Pr, 99; The Anglo American Origins of Sensibility, Small Change? The Strange Career of American Philanthropy, Cambridge Univ Pr, 01. **CONTACT ADDRESS** Dept of Hist, SUNY, Albany, 1400 Washington Ave, Albany, NY 12222-1000.

BARKIN, KENNETH
PERSONAL Born 07/16/1939, Brooklyn, NY, 3 children **DISCIPLINE** MODERN GERMAN HISTORY **EDUCATION** Brooklyn Col, BA, 60; Brown Univ, PhD, 66. **CAREER** Asst prof mod hist, Brandeis Univ, 65-68; from asst prof to assoc prof, 68-76, prof mod hist, Univ of Calif, Riverside, 76-; Mem adv comt, Coun Int Educ, 76-79; Ed, Central Europ Hist, 91-. **HONORS AND AWARDS** Biannual Prize for Best Article, Conf Group Cent Europ Hist, 69-70, 82-83. **MEMBERSHIPS** AHA; Conf Group Cent Europ. **RESEARCH** Economic and educational history of nineteenth century Germany. **SELECTED PUBLICATIONS** Auth, The Controversy Over German Industrialization, Univ Chicago, 70; A case study in comparative history: Populism in Germany and America, in The State of American History, Quadrangle, 70; Conflict and concord in Wilhelmian social thought, Cent Europ Hist, 3/72; Germany's Path to Industrial Maturity, Laurentian Univ Rev, 6/73; Autobiography and history, Societas, spring 76; Amerikanische ver offentlichungen zur modernen deutschen sozial-und Wirtschaftsgeschichte, Geschichte und Gesellschaft, 78; From uniformity to pluralism: German historical writing since World War I, Ger Life & Lett, winter 81; Preussens Schulen sind besser, in Hilfe, Schule, Berlin, 81. **CONTACT ADDRESS** Dept of Hist, Univ of California, Riverside, 900 University Ave, Riverside, CA 92521-0001. **EMAIL** barkin@ucracl.ucr.edu

BARLOW, K. RENEE
DISCIPLINE ANTHROPOLOGY, ARCHAEOLOGY, BEHAVIORAL ECOLOGY **EDUCATION** Brigham Young Univ, BS, 84; Univ Utak, MA, 93, PhD, 97, **CAREER** Mus asst, Brigham Young Univ Mus Peoples and Cultures, 81- 83; Archaeologist, Salt Lake City, 85-90; archaeologist, Northwest Archaeol Consult, Seattle, 96; adj instr, Univ Utah/princ investigator, Univ Archeol Ctr, 93-98; cur collect, Edge of the Cedars Mus, Utah State Div Pks & Rec, 98-. **CONTACT ADDRESS** Edge of the Cedars State Park, 4159 S 570 E, Apt I, Salt Lake City, UT 84107-2043. **EMAIL** NRDPR.rbarlow@state.ut.us

BARMAN, JEAN
PERSONAL Born 08/01/1939 **DISCIPLINE** HISTORY, EDUCATION **EDUCATION** Macalester Col, BA, 61; Harvard Univ, MA, 63; Univ Calif Berkeley, MLS, 70; Univ BC, EdD, 82. **CAREER** Prof, Educational Studies, Univ BC **HONORS AND AWARDS** Can Hist Educ Asn Founders' Prize, 89, 92-93; Can Hist Asn Reg Hist Prize, 92; UBC Alumni Prize Soc Sci, 92; Killam res fel, 92-93; UBC Killam Tchg Prize, 96. **MEMBERSHIPS** Can Hist Asn. **RESEARCH** Canadian Educational and Social History; British Columbia History; Private Education and Canada; Aboriginal Schooling; Qualitative Research Methodology. **SELECTED PUBLICATIONS** Auth, "British Columbia Local Histories: A Bibliography," Victoria: British Columbia Heritage Trust, (91), 196; auth, "The West beyond the West: A History of British Columbia," University of Toronto Press, (91), 429; auth, "History of Canadian Childhood and Youth: A Bibliography," Westport, CT: Greenwood Press, (92), 492; auth, "Contemporary Canadian Childhood and Youth: A Bibliography," Westport, CT: Greenwood Press, (92), 486; auth, "First Nations Eduation in Canada: The Circle Unfolds," Vancouver; UBC Pres, (95), 355; auth, "Children, Teachers and Schools in the History of British Columbia," ed. Barman, J., Sutherland, N. and Wilson, J.D. Calgary: Detselig, (95), 426; auth, "Writing the History of Northern British Columbia," (Lakehead University, 96), 298-335; auth, "I walk my own track in life & no mere male can bump me off it': Constance Lindsay Skinner and the Work of History," in Creating Historical Memory: English-Canadian Women and the Work of History," ed. Beverly Boutilier and Alison, (Prentice Vancouver: UBC Press, 97); auth, "British Columbia: Historical Interpretations," ed. Barman J., McDonald, R.A.J., and Wade J., Burnaby: Open Learning Agency, 97; auth, "Families vs. Schools: Children of Aboriginal Descent in British Columbia Classrooms of the Late Nineteenth Century," ed. Edgar-Andre Montigny and Lori Chambers, Family Matters: Papers in Post-Confederation Canadian Family History, (Toronto: Canadian Scholars' Press, 98), 73-89. **CONTACT ADDRESS** Educ Studies Dept, Univ of British Columbia, Vancouver, BC, Canada V6T 1Z4. **EMAIL** jean.barman@ubc.ca

BARMAN, RODERICK JAMES
PERSONAL Born 01/16/1937, Radlett, England, m, 1963, 2 children **DISCIPLINE** LATIN AMERICAN HISTORY **EDUCATION** Cambridge Univ, BA, 59; Univ Calif, Berkeley, MA, 65, PhD(hist), 70. **CAREER** Vis asst prof hist, State Univ NY Albany, 70-71; asst prof Hisp & Ital studies, 71-78, Assoc Prof Hist, Univ BC, 78-, Can Coun res grant, 73-78; contrib ed, Handbk of Latin Am Studies, 76-. **HONORS AND AWARDS** Conf on Latin Am Hist prize, 77. **MEMBERSHIPS** Soc Latin Am Studies, England; Can Asn Latin Am Studies; AHA; Conf Latin Am Hist; Latin Am Studies Asn. **RESEARCH** Social and political structure of 19th century Brazil; education in the Empire of Brazil; history of packing in BC and of Latin Am who settled in the province 1858-1920. **SELECTED PUBLICATIONS** Auth, "Justiniano Jose da Rocha e a Conciliacao: como se escreveu Acao; reacao; transacao," Revista do Instituto Historico e Geografico Brasileiro, 301, Barman, R.J., (73): 3-32; auth, "The Role of the Law Graduate in the Political Elite of Imperial Brazil," Journal of InterAmerican Studies and World Affairs, Barman, R.J., and Barman, J., 18, No 4, (74): 423-50; auth, "Politics on the Stage: the Late Brazilian Empire as Dramatized by Franca Juniro," Luso-Brazilian Review, 13, No 2, Barman, R.J., (76): 244-66; auth, "The Brazilian Peasantry Reexamined: the Implications of the Quebra-Quilo Revolt, 1874-1875," Hispanic American Historical Review, Barman, R.J., 57, No 3, (77): 402-24; auth, "Business and Government in imperial Brazil: the Experience of Viscount Maua," Journal of Latin American Studies, Barman, R.J., 13, Pt 2, (81): 239-64; auth, Brazil: The Forging of a Nation, 1798-1852, Barman, R.J., Stanford CA: Stanford Univ Press, (88): 334; auth, "Brazil and Its Historians in North America: the last Forty Years," The Americas, 46, No 3, Barman, R.J., (90): 373-99; auth, Citizen Emperor: Pedro II of Brazil, 1825-1891, Barman, R.J., Stanford CA: Stanford Univ Press, (99): 546. **CONTACT ADDRESS** Dept of Hist, Univ of British Columbia, 1873 E Mall, Ste 1297, Vancouver, BC, Canada V6T 1Z1. **EMAIL** rbarman@interchange.ubc.ca

BARMANN, LAWRENCE F.
PERSONAL Born 06/09/1932, s **DISCIPLINE** HISTORY, HISTORICAL THEOLOGY **EDUCATION** St Louis Univ, BA, 54; PhL, 57; STL, 64; Fordham Univ, MA, 60; Cambridge Univ, ENG, PhD, 70. **CAREER** Teach, St Louis Univ HS, 57-59; from asst prof to prof, St Louis Univ, 70-. **HONORS AND AWARDS** Nancy McNair Ring Awd, SLU, 75; Outstand Teach, Human, SLU, 98; Outstand Teach, Emerson Elec Awd, 99. **MEMBERSHIPS** AAR; ACHA. **RESEARCH** Baron Friedrich von Hugel; Roman Catholic Modernism; Nineteenth Century and Early Twentieth Century European (esp English) Religious History. **SELECTED PUBLICATIONS** Auth, Baron Friedrich von Hugel and the Modernist Crisis in England, Cambridge Univ Press (72); auth, the Letters of Baron Friedrich von Hugel and Professor Norman Kemp Smith, Fordham Univ Press (81); auth, "Confronting Secularization: Origins of the London Society for the Study of Religion," Church Hist (93): 22-40; auth, "Theological Inquiry in an Authoritarian Church: Newman and Modernism," in Discourse and Context: An Interdisciplinary Study of John Henry Newman, ed. Gerard Magill (SW Univ Press, 93), 181-206; auth, "The Modernist As Mystic: Baron Friedrich von Hugel," Zeitschrift fur Neuere Theologicgeschichte (97): 221-250; co-ed, Sanctity and Secularity During the Modernist Period, Soc Bollandistes (Brussels), 99. **CONTACT ADDRESS** Dept American Studies, Saint Louis Univ, 221 N Grand Blvd, Saint Louis, MO 63103. **EMAIL** barmann@slu.edu

BARNARD, VIRGIL JOHN
PERSONAL Born 11/05/1932, Wichita, KS, m, 1954, 3 children **DISCIPLINE** HISTORY **EDUCATION** Oberlin Coll, BA, 55; Univ Chicago, MA, 57; PhD, 64. **CAREER** Instr, Hist, Ohio State Univ, 60-64; asst prof, Oakland Univ, 64-67; assoc prof, Oakland Univ, 67-71; prof, Oakland Univ, 71-97; Prof Emer, Hist, Oakland Univ, 97-. **MEMBERSHIPS** Am Hist Asn; Org Am Hist; AAUP **RESEARCH** US History, 1945-present; US labor history. **SELECTED PUBLICATIONS** Walter Reuther and the Rise of Auto Workers; From Evangelicalism to Progressivism at Oberlin College; assoc edr, Children and Youth in America: A Documentary History. **CONTACT ADDRESS** Dept Hist, Oakland Univ, Rochester, MI 48309-4401. **EMAIL** Barnard@oakland.edu

BARNES, ANDREW E.
PERSONAL Born 03/05/1953, St Louis, MO, m, 1999, 1 child **DISCIPLINE** HISTORY **EDUCATION** Wesleyan Univ, BA, 75; Princeton Univ, MA, 78; PhD, 83. **CAREER** Instr, asst prof, assoc prof, Carnegie Mellon Univ, 81-96; assoc prof, Ariz State Univ, 96-. **HONORS AND AWARDS** Fulbright Grnt, 92; OMSC res Grnt, 98. **MEMBERSHIPS** ASA. **RESEARCH** History of Christianity; history of western civilization; history of race relations; history of cultural contact social history. **SELECTED PUBLICATIONS** Auth, Social History and Issues in Human Consciousness: Some Interdisciplinary Connections, NY UP, 89; auth, The Social Dimension of Piety: Associative Life and Religious Change in the Penitent Confraternities of Marseille 1499-1792, Paulist Press, 94; auth, "Cliques and Participation in a Pre? Modem French Voluntary Association: The Penitents Bourras of Marseille in the Eighteenth Century," J Interdis Hist (88); auth, "Religious Anxiety and Devotional Change in Sixteenth Century French Penitential Confratemities," 16th-Cen J (88); auth, "On the Necessity of Shaping Men before Forming Christians: The Institutionalization of Catholicism in Early Modem Europe and Modem Africa," Hist Reflect (89); auth, "Blaspheming like Brute Beasts: Multiculturalism from a Historical Perspective," Contention (92); auth, "The Social Transformation of the French Parish Clergy, 1500-1800," Soc Ident Mod Euro (93); auth, "Evangelization Where it is Not Wanted': Colonial Administrators and Missionaries in Northern Nigeria 1900-1933," J Relig Africa (95); auth, "Aryanizing Projects: African Collaborators and Colonial Transcripts," Comp Stud (98); auth, "Church and Society" Encycl Euro Soc Hist, 01. **CONTACT ADDRESS** Dept Hist, Arizona State Univ, Tempe, AZ 85224. **EMAIL** andrew.barnes@asu.edu

BARNES, JAMES JOHN
PERSONAL Born 11/16/1931, St. Paul, MN, m, 1955, 2 children **DISCIPLINE** ENGLISH & MODERN EUROPEAN HISTORY **EDUCATION** Amherst Col, BA, 54; Oxford Univ, BA, 56, MA 61; Harvard Univ, PhD, 60. **CAREER** Instr hist, Amherst Col, 59-62; from asst prof to assoc prof, 62-76, prof hist, Wabash Col, 76-, Soc Sci Res Coun res grant-in-aid, 62-63 & 70; Am Coun Learned Soc res grant, 64-65; Am Philos Soc res grant 64-65. **HONORS AND AWARDS** Phi Beta Kappa, 54; Rhodes Scholar, 54-56; Amherst Col res grant, 61-62; Woodrow Wilson Fel, 56-67; D H L Col of Wooster, 76; Fulbright Scholar, 78; Distinguished Alumni, St Paul Acad & Summit Sch, 89; Hon Alumnus, Wabash Col, 94; DHL Amherst Col, 99. **MEMBERSHIPS** AHA; Conf Brit Studies; Southern Historians Asn; Bibli Soc Engl. **RESEARCH** Eng and mod Europ soc and economic hist; lit taste since 1800; nineteenth century Anglo-Am rel. **SELECTED PUBLICATIONS** Auth, Free Trade in Books: A Study of the London Book Trade Since 1800, Clarendon, Oxford, 64; Edward Lytton Bulwer and the publishing firm of Harper and Brothers, Am Lit, 3/66; Clio's blind disciples: Parkman, Prescott and Thierry, Am Oxonian, 4/69; Galignani and the publication of English books in France, Bibliog Soc England, 12/70; Authors, Publishers, and Politicians: The Quest for an Anglo-American Copyright Agreement, 1815-1854, Routledge Univ, London, 74 & Ohio State Univ, 74; Mein Kampf in Britain 1930-39, Weiner Libr Bull, Vol XXVII, 74; co-auth, Hitler's Mein Kampf in Britain & America, 1930-39; Cambridge Univ Press, 80; co-auth, James Vincent Murphy, Translator and Interpreter of Fascist Europe, 1880-1946, Univ Press Am, 87; co-auth, Private & Confidential: Letters from British Ministers in Washington to Their Foreign Secretaries in London, 1845-47, Susquehanna Univ Press, 93. **CONTACT ADDRESS** Dept of Hist, Wabash Col, PO Box 352, Crawfordsville, IN 47933-0352. **EMAIL** barnesj@wabash.edu

BARNES, KENNETH C.
PERSONAL Born 04/24/1956, Conway, AR, m, 1978, 2 children **DISCIPLINE** HISTORY **EDUCATION** Duke Univ, PhD, 85. **CAREER** Prof, 92-, Univ Cen AR; Asst Prof, 91-92, Univ S MS; Asst, Assoc Prof, 82-91, Concordia Univ IL. **HONORS AND AWARDS** Fulbright Fel; NEH Fel; DAAD. **SELECTED PUBLICATIONS** Auth, Who Killed John Clayton?: Political Violence and the Emergence of the New South 1861-1893, Durham NC, Duke Univ Press, 98; Nazism Liberalism and Christianity: Protestant Social Thought in Germany and Great Britain 1925-1937, Lexington KY, Univ Press of KY, 91. **CONTACT ADDRESS** Dept History, Univ of Central Arkansas, 210 Donaghey Rd, Conway, AR 72035. **EMAIL** kennethb@mail.uca.edu

BARNES, THOMAS GARDEN
PERSONAL Born 04/29/1930, Pittsburgh, PA, m, 1955, 4 children **DISCIPLINE** HISTORY **EDUCATION** Harvard Univ, AB, 52; Oxford Univ, DPhil, 55. **CAREER** From asst prof to assoc prof hist, Lycoming Col, 56-60; lectr, 60-61, from asst

prof to prof hist, 61-74, Prof Hist & Law, Univ Calif, Berkeley, 74-, Am Acad Arts & Sci grant, 58; Huntington Libr grant, 60; Am Coun Learned Soc fel, 62; ed, Pub Rec Off, 63-; proj dir, Am Bar Found Anglo-Am Legal Hist Proj, 65-86; Guggenheim fel, 71; historian, Centennial Hist Hastings Col Law, 73-78; co-chair, Canadian stu prog, Univ of Calif, Berkeley 82-; chair, ed board, Legal Class Lib, 82-. **HONORS AND AWARDS** Alexander Prize, Royal Hist Soc, 58. **MEMBERSHIPS** Selden Soc; fel Royal Hist Soc. **RESEARCH** English legal history; Tudor-Stuart England; Court of Star Chamber, 1596-1641; early Canadian legal history. **SELECTED PUBLICATIONS** Auth, Somerset assize orders, 1629-1640, Somerset Rec Soc, 59; auth, Clerk of the Peace in Caroline Somerset, 61; auth, Somerset 1625-1640, 61; coauth, The European World: A History, 66; co-ed, A Documentary History of Europe, 72; auth, Hastings College of the Law: The First Century, 78. **CONTACT ADDRESS** Sch of Law, Univ of California, Berkeley, 454 Boalt Hall, Berkeley, CA 94720-7200. **EMAIL** Garnest@law.berkeley.edu

BARNES, TIMOTHY DAVID

PERSONAL Born 03/13/1942, Yorkshire, England, m, 1965, 3 children **DISCIPLINE** CLASSICS, HISTORY **EDUCATION** Oxford Univ, BA, 64, MA, 67, DPhil, 70. **CAREER** Jr res fel classics, Queen's Col, Oxford, 66-70; from asst prof to assoc prof, Univ Col, Toronto, 70-76; assoc chmn grad studies, 79-83, Prof Classics Univ Toronto, 76-. **HONORS AND AWARDS** Conington Prize, Oxford Univ, 74. **MEMBERSHIPS** Am Philol Asn; Can Class Asn; Am Soc Papyrologists; Am Asn Ancient Historians; Soc Promotion Roman Studies. **RESEARCH** Hist, lit, culture and religions of Roman Empire from Augustus to the sixth century, Theodosian Code, Early Christian Hagiography. **SELECTED PUBLICATIONS** Auth, Athanasius and Constantius, Theology and Politics in the Constantinian Empire, Harvard UP, 93; auth, From Eusebius to Augustine, Selected papers 1982-1993, Aldershot: Varorium Reprints, 94; auth, "The Sources of the Historia Augusta 1967-1992," Historae Augustae Colloquium Maceratense, (95): 1-28; auth, "Statistics and the Conversion of the Roman Aristocracy," Journal of Roman Studies 85, (95): 135-147; auth, "Emperors, Panegyrics, Prefects, Provinces and Palaces," Journal of Roman Archaeology 9, 96; auth, Representation and Reality in Ammianus Marcellinus, book being prepared for submission to Cornell UP. **CONTACT ADDRESS** Dept of Classics, Univ of Toronto, 97 St George St, Toronto, ON, Canada M5S 2E8. **EMAIL** tbarnes@chass.utoronto.ca

BARNES, TIMOTHY MARK

PERSONAL Born 04/27/1942, Los Angeles, CA, 2 children **DISCIPLINE** EARLY AMERICAN HISTORY **EDUCATION** Univ NMex, BA, 65, MA, 66, PhD(Hist), 69. **CAREER** Asst Am Hist, Univ NMex, 65-67; asst prof, Univ Albuquerque, 68; assoc prof, 69-80, prof Am Hist, Calif Poly State Univ, San Luis Obispo, 80-, Distinguished teacher, Calif Poly State Univ, 77-78. **MEMBERSHIPS** Orgn Am Historians. **RESEARCH** Loyalists of the American Revolution. **SELECTED PUBLICATIONS** Auth, Loyalist newspapers of the American Revolution: Bibliography and biography, Proc Am Antiquarian Soc, 4/74; Moral Allegiance: John Witherspoon & Loyalist Recautatise in Loyalist Community in North American, Greenwood Press, 90; Loyalist Discourse and the Moderation of the American Revolution in Stephen Lucus, ed, Discourse in and Revolutionary Era, Michigan State University Press, 98. **CONTACT ADDRESS** Dept of History, California Polytech State Univ, San Luis Obispo, 1 Grand Ave, San Luis Obispo, CA 93407-0001. **EMAIL** tbarnes@calpoly.edu

BARNETT, RICHARD CHAMBERS

PERSONAL Born 04/27/1932, Davenport, FL, m, 1957, 2 children **DISCIPLINE** MODERN HISTORY **EDUCATION** Wake Forest Col, BA, 53; Univ NC, PhD, 63. **CAREER** Instr social studies, Gardner-Webb Col, 56-68; from instr to assoc prof, 61-76, chmn dept, 68-75, prof hist, Wake Forest Univ, 76-94, Prof Emer, 94-. **MEMBERSHIPS** Conf Brit Studies; AHA. **RESEARCH** Sixteenth century English administrative history. **SELECTED PUBLICATIONS** Auth, Place, Profit, and Power: The Household of William Cecil, Lord Burghley, Univ NC, 69. **CONTACT ADDRESS** 2130 Royall Dr, Winston-Salem, NC 27106. **EMAIL** barnetrc@WFU.edu

BARNETT, SUZANNE WILSON

PERSONAL Born 06/01/1940, Columbus, OH, m, 1969 **DISCIPLINE** CHINESE HISTORY **EDUCATION** Muskingum Col, BA, 61; Harvard Univ, AM, 63, PhD(hist, E Asian lang), 73. **CAREER** Vis asst prof hist, Univ VA, 73; asst prof, 74-79, assoc prof, 79-85, prof hist, Univ Puget Sound, 85-, Robert G Albertson Prof, 98-03; dir, Henry Luce Found Proj on Chinese-Am Interaction, Harvard Univ, 77-79. **MEMBERSHIPS** AHA (coun, 92-95, local arrangements 97-98) ; Asn Asian Studies (bd dir, 79-82). **RESEARCH** Conceptual change in late imperial China; Protestant missions in China; educational innovation. **SELECTED PUBLICATIONS** Auth, Silent Evangelism: Presbyterians and the Mission Press in China, J Presbyterian Hist, winter 71; Protestant expansion and Chinese views of the West, Mod Asian Studies, 4/72; contrib, article, In: Reform in Nineteenth Century China, Harvard Univ, 76; co-ed and contrib, chapter in Christianity in China: Early Protestant Missionary Writings, Harvard Univ, 85; Foochow's Academics: Public Ordering and Expanding Education in the Late Nineteenth Century, Bull Inst Med Hist, June 87; co-ed, Asia in the Undergraduatge Curriculum, ME Sharpe, 00. **CONTACT ADDRESS** Dept Hist, Univ of Puget Sound, 1500 N Warner St, Tacoma, WA 98416-0033. **EMAIL** sbarnett@ups.edu

BARNEY, WILLIAM LESKO

PERSONAL Born 02/02/1943, Kingston, PA, m, 1967, 2 children **DISCIPLINE** AMERICAN HISTORY **EDUCATION** Cornell Univ, BA, 64; Columbia Univ, MA, 65, PhD(Am hist), 71. **CAREER** Asst prof US hist, 71-75, Trenton St Col; assoc prof, 75-82, prof, 82-, Univ NC Chapel Hill. **HONORS AND AWARDS** NEH fel, 77; Fulbright Sr Lectr Univ Genva, 87. **MEMBERSHIPS** AHA; Orgn Amer Hist; Southern Hist Assn. **RESEARCH** Antebellum South; Civil War. **SELECTED PUBLICATIONS** Auth, Road to Secession, Praeger, 72; auth, The Secessionist Impulse, Princeton Univ, 74; auth, Flawed Victory: A New Perspective on the Civil War, Praeger, 75 & Univ Press Am, 80; auth, Passage of the Republic, CD Health, 87; coauth, The American Journey, Prentice Hall, 97. **CONTACT ADDRESS** 407 Westwood Dr, Chapel Hill, NC 27516. **EMAIL** wbarney@email.uhc.edu

BARNHART, MICHAEL

PERSONAL Born 06/08/1951, Hanover, PA, m, 1988, 1 child **DISCIPLINE** HISTORY **EDUCATION** Northwestern Univ, BS, 73; Harvard Univ, AM, 74; PhD, 80. **CAREER** Prof, SUNY SB, 80-. **HONORS AND AWARDS** Chancellor Awd, Excel Teach. **MEMBERSHIPS** AHA; AAS; SHAFR. **RESEARCH** US-Japan relations; 20th century. **SELECTED PUBLICATIONS** Auth, Japan Prepares for Total War, Cornell, 87; auth, Japan and the World Since 1868, Edward Arnold Ltd, 95. **CONTACT ADDRESS** Dept History, SUNY, Stony Brook, 100Nicholls Rd, Stony Brook, NY 11794-0001. **EMAIL** micheal.barnhart@sunysb.edu

BARNHILL, GEORGIA BRADY

PERSONAL Born 12/08/1944, Mount Kisco, NY, m, 1987 **DISCIPLINE** HISTORY **EDUCATION** Wellesley Col, BA, art hist, 66. **CAREER** Readers Svcs Dept, 68-69, Amer Antiq Soc; Andrew W. Mellon Curator, Graphic Arts, 69-, Amer Antiq Soc. **HONORS AND AWARDS** APS fels, 86; Bibl Soc Amer, 86; Huntington Lib Soc, 93; Maurice Rickards Awd Ephemera Soc. **MEMBERSHIPS** AAS; Print Coun of Amer; Colonial Soc of Mass; Grolier Club; Amer Hist Print Collectors Soc; Sonneck Soc; Amer Printing Hist Assn, Col Art Assn, ARLIS. **RESEARCH** History of Amer prints & illustrated bks. **SELECTED PUBLICATIONS** Ed, Prints of New England, Worcester: Amer Antiq Soc, 91; auth, Political Cartoons of New England 1812-1861, Amer Antiq Soc, 91; auth, FOC Darley's Illustrations for Southern Humor, Graphic Arts & the South, Univ Ark Press, 93; auth, Political Cartoons at the American Antiquarian Society, Inks, vol 2, 95; auth, Pictorial Histories of the United States, Visual Rsrcs, vol 11, 95; auth, Wild Impressions: The Adirondackson Paper, Adirondack Mus, 95; auth, Extracts from the Journals of Ethan A Greenwood': Portrait Painter and Museum Proprietor, Proc of Amer Antiq Soc, vol 103, 93; coauth, Early American Lithography: Images to 1830, Boston Athenaeum, 97; co-ed, The Cultivation of Artists in Nineteenth-Century America, Amer Antiq Soc, 97; auth, Illustrations of the Adirondacks in the Popular Press, Adirondack Prints & Printmakers, Adirondack Mus & Syracuse Univ Press, 98; auth, "The Catalogue of Am Engravings: A Manual for Users," Am Antiquarian Soc, vol 108, 98; auth, "Depictions of the White Mountains in the Popular Pr," Historical New Hampshire 54 (99); auth, "The Market for Images from 1670 to 1790 in Am," Imprint 25 (00). **CONTACT ADDRESS** Am Antiquarian Soc, 185 Salisbury St., Worcester, MA 01609. **EMAIL** gbarnhill@mwa.org

BARNHILL, JOHN HERSCHEL

PERSONAL Born 03/02/1947, Walnut Ridge, AR, d, 1 child **DISCIPLINE** HISTORY **EDUCATION** Okla St Univ, PhD, 81. **CAREER** Instr, 77-81, Okla St Univ; asst dir, 81-82, 45th Infantry Div Mus, OK; videotape archiv, 82-84, OK Dept of Lib; hist, engg & instl div, 84-85, Tinker AFB; prog analysts, OK City, 85-, DISA Area Command, OK City. **HONORS AND AWARDS** Phi Alpha Theta, 73-74; Phi Theta Kappa, 77-81; Phi Kappa Phi, 81-; LeRoy Fischer Awd, 81; Outstanding Young Men of Amer, 81; Dist Alumnus, Corpus Christi St Univ, 83; Air Force Org Excel Awds, 84-85, 86-87, 88-89, 90, 92-93; Who's Who in South & Southwest, 91; Air Force Assn Beacon of Freedom Awd, 91; Who's Who in World, 94; Joint Meritorious Unit Awd, 96. **RESEARCH** Non-mainstream relig movements; roles of minority groups in Amer society. **SELECTED PUBLICATIONS** Art, Civil Rights in Utah: The Mormon Way, J of West XXV, 86; art, Triumph of Will: The Coal Strike of 1899-1903 in Indian Territory, Chronicles of OK, LXI, 83; art, Civil Rights in the 1940's: The Fair Employment Practices Commission, Brooks Hays, and the Arkansas Plan, Negro Hist Bull, LV, 82; art, The Way West: The California Road, Red River Valley Hist Rev, VI, 81; art, Digging Coal: Conflict or Conciliation? The English Strike of 1893 and the American Strike of 1894, OK St Hist Rev, II, 81; art, With 'All' Deliberate Speed: Desegregation of the Public Schools in Oklahoma City and Tulsa, 1954-1972, Red River Valley Hist Rev, VI, 81; art, The Punitive Expedition Against Pancho Villa: The Forced Motorization of the American Army, Mil Hist of Texas & The Southwest XIV, 78; auth, From Surplus to Substitution: Energy in Texas, Amer Press, 83; art, :Morris Dees," Encycl of Civil Rights, forthcoming; art, "Red Scare," Encycl of Immigration, forthcoming; art, "The Irish," Encycl of Immigration, forthcoming; art, "The British Isles," Encycl of Immigration, forthcoming; art "Political, Ethnic, and Religious Persecution," Encycl of Immigration, forthcoming; art, "Immigration," History Behind the Headlines, forthcoming. **CONTACT ADDRESS** DISA Enterprise Computing Center, 8705 Industrial Blvd, Tinker AFB, OK 73145. **EMAIL** jbarnhil@okc.disa.mil

BAROLSKY, PAUL

PERSONAL Born 07/13/1941, Paterson, NJ, m, 1966, 2 children **DISCIPLINE** ART HISTORY, LITERARY CRITICISM **EDUCATION** Middlebury Col, BA, 63; Harvard Univ, MA, 64, PhD(Art hist), 69. **CAREER** Asst prof, Cornell Univ, 68-69; Commonwealth Prof Art Hist, Univ VA, 69-. **RESEARCH** Italian Renaissance art and literature. **SELECTED PUBLICATIONS** Michelanglo's Nose, Penn State, 90; Why Mona Lisa Smiles, Penn State, 91; Giotto's Father, Penn State, 92; The Faun in the Garden, Penn State, 94; Fables of Art, VA Quart Rev, Vol 71, 95; A Very Brief History of Art From Narcissus to Picasso, Classical J, Vol 90, 95; The Visionary Experience of Renaissance Art, Word & Image, Vol 11, 95; Johannes Vermeer, with A. K. Wheelock, VA Quart Rev, Vol 72, 96; Flesh and the Ideal-Winckelman and the Origins of Art History, with A. Potts, Classical J, Vol 91, 96; The Fable of Failure in Modern Art, VA Quart Rev, Vol 73, 97. **CONTACT ADDRESS** Dept of Art, Univ of Virginia, 102 Fayerweather, Charlottesville, VA 22903. **EMAIL** pb4r@virginia.edu

BARON, SAMUEL HASKELL

PERSONAL Born 05/24/1921, New York, NY, m, 1949, 3 children **DISCIPLINE** HISTORY **EDUCATION** Cornell Univ, BS, 42; Columbia Univ, MA, 48, PhD, 52. **CAREER** Instr hist, Univ TN, 48-53; vis lectr, Northwest Univ, 53-54; vis asst prof, Univ MO, 54-55 & Univ NE, 55-56; from asst prof to prof, Grinnell Col, 56-66; prof, Univ CA, San Diego, 66-72; Alumni Distinguished Prof Hist, Univ NC, Chapel Hill, 72-91, Fel E Asian Studies, Harvard Univ, 58-59; Am Philos Soc res grant, 63; Inter-Univ travel grant fel, 63-64; Am Coun Learned Soc fels, 64-71; Int Res & Exchange Bd fel, 70; Guggenheim Mem Found fel, 70-71; pres, Conf Slavic & East Europ Studies, 75; Nat Endowment for Humanities fel, 76. **MEMBERSHIPS** AHA; Am Asn Advan Slavic Studies; AAUP. **RESEARCH** Russian social and intellectual history. **SELECTED PUBLICATIONS** Auth, Plekhanov: The Father of Russian Marxism, 63 & The Travels of Olearius in Seventeenth Century Russia, 67, Stanford Univ; contribr, Revisionism: Essays in the History of Marxist Ideas, Allen & Unwin, 62; co-ed, Windows on the Russian Past, Essays on Soviet Historiography Since Stalin, Am Asn Advan Slavic Studies, 77; auth, Muscovite Russia: Collected Essays, Variorum, 80; auth, Explorations in Muscovite History, Variorum, 91; auth, Plekhaner in Russian History and Soviet Historiography, Univ Pittsburgh, 95. **CONTACT ADDRESS** Dept of Hist, Univ of No Carolina, Chapel Hill, Chapel Hill, NC 27514.

BARR, ALWYN

PERSONAL Born 01/18/1938, Austin, TX, m, 1961, 2 children **DISCIPLINE** HISTORY **EDUCATION** Univ of Tex, BA, 59; MA, 61; PhD, 66. **CAREER** Asst prof, Purdue Univ, 66-69; from assoc prof to prof, Tex Tech Univ, 69-, chair, Dept of Hist, 78-85. **HONORS AND AWARDS** Tullis Prize, 71, fel, 72, Tex State Hist Asn; Pres Excellence in Teaching Awd, 87; Pres Acad Ach Awd, 92. **MEMBERSHIPS** Am Hist Asn; Orgn Am Hist; S Hist Asn; Texas State His Asn. **RESEARCH** African American history, Civil War, Southern history. **SELECTED PUBLICATIONS** Auth, Texans in Revolt: The Battle for San Antonio, 1835, 90; auth, Black Texans: A History of African Americans in Texas, 1528-1995, 96; auth, Polignac's Texas Brigade, 98; auth, Reconstruction to Reform: Texas Politics, 1876-1906, 00. **CONTACT ADDRESS** Dept of Hist, Texas Tech Univ, Lubbock, TX 79409-1013. **EMAIL** jbarr@ttacs.ttu.edu

BARR, DAVID LAWRENCE

PERSONAL Born 04/24/1942, Belding, MI, m, 1966, 3 children **DISCIPLINE** BIBLICAL STUDIES, HISTORY OF RELIGIONS **EDUCATION** Ft Wayne Bible Col, BA, 65; FL State Univ, MA, 69, PhD, 74. **CAREER** Consult relig pub educ, Relig Instr Asn, 67-71; instr relig, FL A&M Univ, 72-74; asst prof, Univ Northern IA, 74-75; asst prof, 75-80, assoc prof, 80-88, prof relig, Wright State Univ, 88, Chmn, Relig Dept, Wright State Univ, 80-86, Dir, Honors Prog 87-94. **HONORS AND AWARDS** Pres, Eastern Grt Lakes Bible Soc; Pres, Mideast Honors Asn; Phi Kappa Phi; Pres Fac. **MEMBERSHIPS** Soc Bibl Lit; Cath Bibl Asn, Am Acad Relig. **RESEARCH** Apocalypse of John; Narrative analysis; Soc world of early Christianity. **SELECTED PUBLICATIONS** Co-ed (with Nicholas Piediscalzi), The Bible in American Education, a centennial volume prepared for the Soc of Bibl Lit, Fortress Press and Scholars Press, 82; New Testament Story: An Introduction, Wadsworth Publ Co, 87, 2nd ed, 95; Co-ed (with Linda Bennett Elder and Elizabeth Struthers Malbon), Biblical and Humane:

A Festschrift for John Priest; Tales of the End: A Narrative Commentary on the Book of Revelation, Polebridge Press, 98. **CONTACT ADDRESS** Dept of Relig, Wright State Univ, Dayton, 3640 Colonel Glenn, Dayton, OH 45435-0002. **EMAIL** david.barr@wright.edu

BARRETT, DAVID P.
DISCIPLINE HISTORY **EDUCATION** Univ Toronto, BA, MA, MP; London Univ, PhD. **RESEARCH** Republican China **SELECTED PUBLICATIONS** Auth, Ideological Foundations of the Wang Jingwei Regime: Rural Pacification, the New Citizens' Movement, and the Great East Asia War, 93. **CONTACT ADDRESS** History Dept, McMaster Univ, 1280 Main St W, Hamilton, ON, Canada L8S 4L9. **EMAIL** barrett@mcmaster.ca

BARRETT, JAMES R.
PERSONAL Born 06/14/1950, Chicago, IL, M, 1 child **DISCIPLINE** HISTORY **EDUCATION** Univ Ill Chicago, AB; Univ Warwick, England, MAUniv; Pittsburgh, PhD, 81. **CAREER** Part-time Instr, Univ of Pittsburgh, 76-81; asst prof, NC State Univ, 81-84; visiting asst prof, Univ of NC, 83-84; assoc ch and dir, Univ of Illinois, 84-; fac, Univ of Illinois, 95-; ch, Univ of Illinois, 97-. **HONORS AND AWARDS** Richard G. and Carole J. Cline Univ Scholar, 90-93; Lloyd Lewis Fel in Am hist, 90-91; Beckman Res Awd, 87, 92; Fac, Fel, 94; IREX Short-term Res Grant, 94; Carlton Qualey Article Awd, Immigration and Ethnic Hist Soc, 99; **MEMBERSHIPS** Illinois State Hist Soc; U.S. Women's Hist Search Committee, 87-88; US Cultural and Intellectual Hist Search Committee, 92-93; General Council, Women's Studies, 94-; Task Force to Establish a Humanities Institute at the Univ of Illinois, 94-95; Diaspora Course Dev Committee, Afro-Am Studies Program, 96-97; Humanities Council, 97-. **RESEARCH** U.S.,comparative working-class history and class; race; ethnicity in twentieth-century U.S. social history; Current research interests focus on the social and ideological bases of labor radicalism and the mentalities of immigrant workers. **SELECTED PUBLICATIONS** Auth, The Jungle, Upton Sinclair, Univ of Illinois Press, 88; auth, Steve Nelson, American Radical, Steve Nelson, James R. Barrett and Rob Ruck, Univ of Pittsburgh Press, 81, 92; auth, Work and Community in 'The Jungle': Chicago's Packing House Workers, 1894-1922; James R. Barrett, Univ of Illinois Press, 87, 90; auth, William Z. Foster and the Tragedy of American Radicalism, James R. Barrett, Univ of Illinois Press, (forthcoming, 00); auth, "The Rise of the Working Class in Illinois History, (92); auth, "Americanization from The Bottom Up: Immigration and the Remaking of the American Working Class, 1880-1930," Journal of American History, 79, (92): 996-1020; auth, "William Z. Foster" in Marijo Buhle, Paul Buhle, Harvey Kaye, eds, The American Radical, Routledge, (94); auth, "Boring from Within and Without: William Z. Foster, the Trade Union Educational League, and American Communism in the 1920's," in Arnesen, Greene, and Laurie, eds, Labor Histories: Class, Politics, and the Working Class Experience, Univ of Illinois Press, 98; auth, "How White People Became White," in Richard Delgado and Jean Stefancic, eds, Critical White Studies: Looking Behind the Mirror, Temple Univ Press, (97): 402-406; auth, "In Between Peoples: Race, Nationality and the "New Immigrant' Working Class," David Roediger, Journal of American Ethnic History, 16, (97): 3-44. **CONTACT ADDRESS** History Dept, Univ of Illinois, Urbana-Champaign, 309 gregory hall, mc 466, 810 s wright, Urbana, IL 61801. **EMAIL** jrbarret@staff.uiuc.edu

BARRETT, MICHAEL BAKER
PERSONAL Born 10/12/1946, Honululu, HI, m, 1969, 1 child **DISCIPLINE** MODERN GERMAN & MILITARY HISTORY **EDUCATION** The Citadel, BA, 68; Univ MA, MA, 69, PhD, 77. **CAREER** Lectr, Univ MA, 75-76; instr, 76-78, asst prof, 78-82, Assoc Prof Hist, The Citadel, 82-; Dean Graduate School, 85-90. **MEMBERSHIPS** AHA; Conf Group Cent Europ Hist; Am Mil Inst; Southern Hist Asn. **RESEARCH** Weimar Republic-Third Reich military; Weimar Republic police. **SELECTED PUBLICATIONS** Ed, Proc of The Citadel Symposium on Hitler and the National Socialist Era, 82. **CONTACT ADDRESS** Hist Dept, The Citadel, The Military Col of So Carolina, 171 Moultrie St, Charleston, SC 29409-0002. **EMAIL** barrettm@citadel.edu

BARRON, HAL S.
PERSONAL Born 12/29/1951, Louisville, KY, m, 1977, 1 child **DISCIPLINE** AMERICAN HISTORY **EDUCATION** Oberlin Col, AB, 73; Univ Pa, MA, 76, PhD(Hist), 80. **CAREER** Instr, 799-80; asst prof, 80-85; assoc prof, 85-91; full prof History, Harvey Mudd Col, 91-; dept chmn, 93-98; mem grad fac History, Claremont Grad Univ, 81-; visit assoc prof Waseda Univ, Tokyo, Japan, 89-90; NEH sen fell, 93; Newberry Library, NEH fel, 86-87; NEH Sum Stipend, 92; Huntington Library, Haynes Found fell, 88; Haynes Found Sum res fell, 86; NEH Sum Stipend, 82. **HONORS AND AWARDS** Carstensen Awd agr hist, 81; Arnold & Lois S Graves Awd, 82. **MEMBERSHIPS** Am Hist Assoc. Orgn Am Historians; Social Sci Hist Asn, Exec Comm, 97-99; convener Rural History network 80-92, prog comm, 87; Agr Hist Soc, exec comm, 94-97 nominating com. 00-. **RESEARCH** Rural history; social history. **SELECTED PUBLICATIONS** Auth, The impact of rural depopulation on the local economy: Chelsea, Vt, 1840-1900, Agr Hist, 80; auth, Listening to the Silent Majority: Te New Rural History of the Nineteenth-Century North, in Ferleger, auth, Those Who Stayed Behind: Rural Society in Nineteenth-Century New England, NY, Cambridge U. Press, 84, 87 paperback; ed., Agricultural and National Development: Views on the Nineteenth Century, Ames, Iowa State U. Press, 90; Mixed Harvest: The Second Great Transformation in the Rural North, 1870-1930, Chapel Hill, UNC Press, dual edition, 97. **CONTACT ADDRESS** Dept of Humanities & Social Sci, Harvey Mudd Col, 301 E 12th St, Claremont, CA 91711-5990. **EMAIL** hal_barron@hmc.edu

BARROWS, FLOYD DELL
PERSONAL Born 12/05/1927, Ft Collins, CO, m, 1953, 2 children **DISCIPLINE** ENGLISH HISTORY **EDUCATION** Univ Calif, Los Angeles, BA, 56, PhD(English hist), 67. **CAREER** Teaching asst, Univ Calif, Los Angeles, 57-59; instr humanities, Northwest Mo State Col, 60-63; asst prof hist, 63-66; from instr to assoc prof, 66-78, prof humanities & asst chmn dept, Mich State Univ, 78-. **MEMBERSHIPS** AHA, Orgn Am Historians; Soc Hist Educ. **RESEARCH** Late Stuart and Hanoverian periods of English history; American history, Civil War period; war and peace: its influence on Western culture and the arts. **CONTACT ADDRESS** Dept Humanities, Michigan State Univ, East Lansing, MI 48824.

BARROWS, ROBERT
PERSONAL Born 11/06/1946, Rutland, VT, m, 1989 **DISCIPLINE** US HISTORY **EDUCATION** Muskingum Col, BA, 68; Indiana Univ, MA, 72; PhD, 77. **CAREER** Hist ed, Ind Hist Bureau, 77-89; asst prof to assoc prof, Indiana Univ, 89- . **MEMBERSHIPS** Ogn Am Hist; Urban Hist Asn; Soc Hist Gilded Age and Prog Era, Ind Hist Soc. **RESEARCH** Indiana/ Indianapolis (esp 1900-1945). **SELECTED PUBLICATIONS** Auth, "Beyond the Tenement: Patterns of American Urban Housing, 1870-1930," J Urban Hist, 9, pp 395-420, (83); auth, "Indianapolis: Silver Buckle on the Rust Belt" Snowbelt Cities: Metropolitan Politics in the NE & MidW since WW II, Ind Univ Press, pp 137-157, (90); auth, "'Building Up the State': Women Reformers and Child Welfare Work in Indiana during WW I," Mid-American, pp 267-283, (95); co-ed, The Encyclopedia of Indianapolis (Bloomington and Indianapolis, Ind Univ Press, (94); auth, "Urbanizing American, The Gilded Age: Essays on the Origins of Modern America, Schol Resources, pp 91-110, (96). **CONTACT ADDRESS** Dept Hist, Indiana Univ-Purdue Univ, Indianapolis, 425 Univ Blvd, Indianapolis, IN 46202. **EMAIL** rbarrows@iupui.edu

BARSTOW, ANNE LLEWELLYN
PERSONAL Born 06/22/1929, Jacksonville, FL, m, 1952, 3 children **DISCIPLINE** MEDIEVAL & WOMEN'S HISTORY **EDUCATION** Univ Fla, BA, 49; Columbia Univ, MA, 64, PhD(medieval hist), 78. **CAREER** Asst prof, 70-79, Assoc Prof Medieval Hist, State Univ NY, Col Old Westbury, 79-, Lectr, Relig Dept, NY Univ, 70-73 & Episcopal Divinity Sch, 78. **MEMBERSHIPS** Am Acad Relig; AHA; Inst Res Hist; Feminist Theol Inst. **RESEARCH** Late medieval radical female mysticism: Joan of Arc; history of compulsory celebacy laws for priesthood; the churches' attitudes towards clergy wives. **SELECTED PUBLICATIONS** Auth, Early Goddess Religions, In: An Introductin to the Religion of the Goddess, Seabury Press, 82; Anglican Clergy Wives after the Reformation, In: Women in New Worlds, Vol II, Abingdon Press, 82; Married Priests and the Reforming Papacy: The Eleventh-Century Debates, 82 & Joan of Arc and Radical Mysticism, Edwin Mellen Press; Womens Lives in Medieval Europe-A Sourcebook, E. Amt, ed, Church Hist, Vol 63, 94; The Albigensian Crusades, with J. R. Strayer and C. Lansing, Church Hist, Vol 63, 94; Ways of Lying-Dissimulation, Persecution, and Conformity in Early Modern Europe, with P. Zagorin, Am Hist Rev, Vol 99, 94; Backlash & Excerpts From the Speeches to 1992 Republican National Convention on the Nature, Manifestations and Effects of the Feminist Movement in the Last 30 Years, J of Feminist Studies in Religion, Vol 10, 94; Confession and Community in 17th-Century France-Catholic and Protestant Coexistence in Aquitaine, with G. Hanlon, Church Hist, Vol 64, 95; Women Religious-The Founding of English Nunneries After the Norman Conquest, with S. Thompson, Church Hist, Vol 64, 95; The Oldest Vocation-Christian Motherhood in the Middle Ages, with C. W. Atkinson, Church Hist, Vol 64, 95; Growing Up in Medieval London-The Experience of Childhood in History, with B. A. Hanawalt, Church Hist, Vol 64, 95; From Virile Woman to Womanchrist-Studies in Medieval Religion and Literature, with B. Newman, Church Hist, Vol 65, 96; The Law of the Father-Patriarchy in the Transition From Feudalism to Capitalism, with M. Murray, Am Hist Rev, Vol 102, 97. **CONTACT ADDRESS** 606 W 122 St, New York, NY 10027.

BARTELIK, MAREK
PERSONAL Born 10/13/1956, Olsztyn, Poland, s **DISCIPLINE** FINE ARTS **EDUCATION** Tech and Agricultural Acad Poland, BS, 81; Columbia Univ, MS, 87. **CAREER** Instructor, Hunter Col, 95; Adj Instructor, Fairfield Univ, 96; Grad Teaching Fel, Col of Staten Island, 98-99; Adj Prof, Cooper Union, 96-. **HONORS AND AWARDS** Judith Rothschild Foundation Awd, New York, 97; Fel, State Univ NJ, 97; Dissertation Year Fel, CUNY, 97-98; Grad Teach Fel, CUNY, 97. **MEMBERSHIPS** Col Art Asn; Intl Asn of Art Critics; Hist of German and Cent European Art and Architecture; Soc of Hist of E European and Russian art and Architecture. **SELECTED PUBLICATIONS** Co-auth, The sculpture of Ursula von Rydingsvard, Hudson Hills Press, 96; auth, to Invent a Garden: The Life and art of Adja Yunkers, Hudson Hills Press, 00. **CONTACT ADDRESS** Dept Humanities & Soc Sci, Cooper Union for the Advancement of Science and Art, 41 Cooper Sq, New York, NY 10003-7136. **EMAIL** marekbl@ibm.net

BARTH, GUNTHER
PERSONAL Born 01/10/1925, Duesseldorf, Germany, m, 1960, 4 children **DISCIPLINE** AMERICAN & URBAN HISTORY **EDUCATION** Univ OR, BA, 55, MA, 57; Harvard Univ, PhD(hist), 62. **CAREER** Tutor hist, Harvard Col, 60-62; from instr to assoc prof, 62-71, Prof Hist, Univ Calif, Berkeley, 71-, Guggenheim fel, 68-69; Fulbright prof, Univ Cologne, 70-71, Univ Salzburg, 84-85. **MEMBERSHIPS** AHA; Orgn Am Historians. **RESEARCH** Social and cultural history; urban society in comparative perspective; immigration. **SELECTED PUBLICATIONS** Auth, All Quiet in the Yamhill, Univ Ore, 59; Bitter Strength, Harvard Univ, 64; "Metropolism and Urban Elites in the Far West," in The Age of Industrialism in America, Free Press, 68; Instant Cities, 75 & City People, 80, Oxford Univ; auth, Fleeting Moments: Nature and Culture in American History, Oxford Univ, 90; auth, The Lewis and Clark Expedition: Selections from the Journals Arranged by Topics, St Martin's Press, 98; auth, "Strategies for Finding the Northwest Passage: The Rules of Alexander Mackenzie and Meriwether Lewis," in Memoirs of the American Philosophical Society, vol 231, 99. **CONTACT ADDRESS** Dept of Hist, Univ of California, Berkeley, Berkeley, CA 94720. **EMAIL** barth@socrates.berkeley.edu

BARTHOLOMEW, JAMES RICHARD
PERSONAL Born 06/30/1941, Hot Springs, SD **DISCIPLINE** JAPANESE HISTORY; HISTORY OF SCIENCE **EDUCATION** Stanford Univ, BA, 63, MA, 64, PhD(hist), 72. **CAREER** Asst prof, 71-77, from assoc prof to prof Japanese Hist, Ohio State Univ, 77-91; Nat Endowment for Humanities fel, 76-77; Nat Science Found, 85-86; vis fel, Sch Hist Studies, Inst Advan Study, Princeton, NJ, 76-; Fulbright Fel, 95-96. **MEMBERSHIPS** AHA; Asn Asian Studies; Hist Sci Soc. **RESEARCH** Modern Japanese history; history of Japanese science. **SELECTED PUBLICATIONS** Japanese culture and the problem of modern science, In: Science and Values, Humanities, 74; Why was there no scientific revolution in Tokugawa Japan? Japanese Studies Hist Sci, No 15, 76; Japanese modernization and the Imperial Universities, 1870-1920, J Asian Studies, 78; Science, Bureaucracy and Freedom in Meiji and Talsho Japan, In: Dimensions of Conflict in Modern Japan, 82; The formation of Science in Japan: Building a Research Tradition, Yale Univ Press, 1989, paperback, 93. **CONTACT ADDRESS** Dept of History, Ohio State Univ, Columbus, 230 W 17th Ave, Columbus, OH 43210-1361. **EMAIL** bartholomew.5@osu.edu

BARTLETT, BEATRICE S.
PERSONAL Born New Haven, CT, s **DISCIPLINE** HISTORY **EDUCATION** Yale Univ, PhD, 80. **CAREER** Asst prof, Yale Univ, 83-89, assoc prof, 89-93, prof, 93-. **HONORS AND AWARDS** Year's stay in Beijing in order to use materials in the Number One Historical Archives, under the auspices of the Comt on Scholar Commun with China, 80-81; two-year post-doctoral association with the Fairbank Ctr for East Asian Res, Harvard Univ, 81-83; invited State Guest at State Archives Bd Conf in China, 85; Fulbright-Hays for travel and research in China, CSC Fel for living expenses, 91. **MEMBERSHIPS** Asn for Asian Studies, Soc for Ch'ing Studies, Comt on East Asian Libraries. **RESEARCH** Qing communication systems, archives, historical writing from those archives, and central government decision-making. **SELECTED PUBLICATIONS** Ed, Teaching about Asia at the Secondary Level: Report of the Fifteenth Yale Conference on the Teaching of Social Studies, New Haven: Yale Univ (69); ed, Guide to the Study of United States History outside the U.S. 1945-1980, ed Lewis Hanke, 5 vols, New York: Kraus Int (85); collaborator, Reading Documents: The Rebellion of Chung Jen-chieh, by Philip A. Kuhn and John King Fairbank, also Chian Yung-chen, 2 vols, Cambridge, MA: Harvard Univ John King Fairbank Center for East Asian Res (86, revised, 93); auth, Monarchs and Ministers: The Grand Council in Mid-Ch'ing China, 1723-1820, Berkeley: Univ Calif Press (91, paperback, 94); auth, "Remembrance of John King Fairbank in Fairbank Remembered, comp. Paul A. Cohen and Merle Goldman, Cambridge: Harvard Univ Press (92); auth, "Court and Countryside: the Traditional Chinese New Year's Dragon Dance," The Yale-China Rev, 3.1 (winter 95); auth, "Archival Management in the Late Imperial Era: Possibilities for Using Ming-Ch'ing Archivists' Tracking Methods for our own Purposes," Chin-tai Chung-kuo li-shih tang-an yen-t'ao hui lun-wen chi, Taipei: Academia Historica (98): 273-298; auth, "Answering the Qjanlong Emperor's Questions: The State History Office Explanations of Revising the Official Biographies," in Qingzhu Wang Zhonghan jiaoshou bashiwu, Wei Qingyuan jiaoshou qishi shouzhen xueshu lunwen ji," Hefei: Huangshan Shushe (99); auth, "From Closed to Open Doors: A Foreigner's View of the Qing Central Government Archives," Janus (forth-

coming). **CONTACT ADDRESS** Dept Hist, Yale Univ, PO Box 208324, New Haven, CT 06520-8324. **EMAIL** beatrice.bartlett@yale.edu

BARTLETT, IRVING HENRY
PERSONAL Born 02/02/1923, Springfield, MA, m, 1944 **DISCIPLINE** AMERICAN SOCIAL & INTELLECTUAL HISTORY **EDUCATION** Ohio Wesleyan Univ, BA, 48; Brown Univ, MA, 49, PhD(Am civilization), 52. **CAREER** Lectr Am Civilization, US Info Serv, Pakistan, 52-53; asst prof, RI Col Educ, 53-54 & Mass Inst Technol, 54-60; pres, Cape Cod Community Col, 60-64; prof hist, Carnegie-Mellon Univ, 64-80; Kennedy prof am Civilization, 80-93, Emer Prof Am Stud, 94-, Univ Mass. **HONORS AND AWARDS** Vchm bd trustees, Community Col, Allegheny County, 64-71; Guggenheim fel, 66-67; Dorrance vis prof hist, Trinity Col, Conn, 71-72; Charles Warren Fel, Charles Warren Ctr Studies Am Hist, Harvard Univ, 78-79. **MEMBERSHIPS** AHA; Am Studies Asn. **RESEARCH** American social and intellectual history; biography. **SELECTED PUBLICATIONS** Auth, From Slave to Citizen: The Story of the Negro in Rhode Island, Providence Urban League, 53; Bushnell, Cousin and Comprehensive Christianity, J Relig, 4/57; ed, William Ellery Channing: Unitarian Christianity and Other Essays, Bobbs, 57; auth, Wendell Phillips, Brahmin Radical, Beacon, 61; The American Mind at the Mid-Nineteenth Century, Crowell, 67; coauth, New History of the United States, Holt, 69; Daniel Webster, 78 & Wendell and Ann Phillips, 80, Norton; auth, John C. Calhoun, 93. **CONTACT ADDRESS** 47 Bradley Hill Rd, Hingham, MA 02043. **EMAIL** vkbihb@aol.com

BARTLETT, KENNETH ROY
PERSONAL Born 11/28/1948, Toronto, ON, Canada, m, 1971 **DISCIPLINE** RENAISSANCE & MEDIEVAL EUROPEAN HISTORY **EDUCATION** Univ Toronto, BA, 71, MA, 72, PhD(medieval studies), 78. **CAREER** Asst to the pres, 79-80, Asst Prof Hist, Univ Toronto, 78-, Exec Asst to Vice pres Inst Rel, 80-, Chmn, Toronto Renaissance & Reformation Colloquium, 81. **HONORS AND AWARDS** President of the Canadian Soc for Renaissance Studies, 82-84; Victoria Univ Excellence in Teaching Awd. **MEMBERSHIPS** Can Soc Renaissance Studies (secy-treas, 80-82 & pres, 82-84); Renaissance Soc Am; Medieval Acad Am; AHA; Can Soc Ital Studies. **RESEARCH** Cultural and intellectual relations between England and Italy in the 16th century; English travellers and residents in Italy during the Renaissance; espionage and secret operatives in the 16th century. **SELECTED PUBLICATIONS** Auth, The English in Italy 1525-1558: A Study in Culture and Politics, 91; Auth, The Civilization of the Italian Renaissance, 92; Coauth, Giovanni Della Casa's Galateo, 3rd ed, 94; ed, Renaissance and Reformation/Renaissance et Reforme, 85-90. **CONTACT ADDRESS** Dept of Hist, Univ of Toronto, 100 St George St, Sidney Smith Hall, Rm 2074, Toronto, ON, Canada M5S 3G3. **EMAIL** bartlett@artsci.utoronto.ca

BARTLETT, RICHARD ADAMS
PERSONAL Born 11/23/1920, m, 1945, 4 children **DISCIPLINE** UNITED STATES HISTORY **EDUCATION** Univ Colo, BA, 42, PhD, 53; Univ Chicago, MA, 47. **CAREER** Instr hist, Agr & Mech Col, TX, 45-52; info librn, legis ref serv, Libr Cong, 53-55; dir FL State Univ Col Prog, Tyndall Air Force Base, 55-57; from asst prof to assoc prof, 57-67, Prof Hist, FL State Univ, 67-, Assoc ed, J Libr Hist, 66-74; sr historian, hist Great Plains, Univ Mid-Am, 76. **HONORS AND AWARDS** Spur Awd, Western Writers Am, 62. **MEMBERSHIPS** AHA, Orgn Am Historians; Western Hist Asn; Southern Hist Asn. **RESEARCH** The westward movement; conservation. **SELECTED PUBLICATIONS** Auth, Great Surveys of the American West, Univ OK, 62; ed, The Gilded Age: America, 1865-1900, Addison-Wesley, 69; auth, Nature's Yellowstone, Univ NM, 74; The New Country, Oxford Univ, 74; contribr, The Great Plains Experience: A Cultural History, Univ Mid-Am, 78; coauth, Freedom's Trail, Houghton; Josiah Royce From Grass Valley to Harvard, with R. V. Hine, Montana-The Magazine of Western History, Vol 43, 93; Creating the West-Historical Interpretations, 1890-1990, with G. D. Nash, J of the West, Vol 33, 94; George Montague Wheeler-The Man and the Myth, with D. O. Dawdy, Montana-The Magazine of Western Hist, Vol 45, 95; Death in Yellowstone-Accidents and Foolhardiness in the First National Park, with L. H. Whittlesey, J of the West, Vol 35, 96; Yellowstone Ski Pioneers-Peril and Heroism on the Winter Trail, with P. Schullery, J of the West, Vol 36, 97; Kinship With the Land-Regionalist Thought in Iowa, 1894-1942, with E. B. Burns, Pacific Hist Rev, Vol 66, 97; Wind Energy in America-A History, with R. W. Righter, Pacific Hist Rev, Vol 66, 97; Ghost Grizzlies-Does the Great Bear Still Haunt Colorado, with D. Petersen, J of the west, Vol 36, 97. **CONTACT ADDRESS** Dept of Hist, Florida State Univ, Tallahassee, FL 32306.

BARTLETT, SANDRA
PERSONAL Born 06/30/1947, Ft Lee, VA, m, 1969, 2 children **DISCIPLINE** GEOGRAPHY **EDUCATION** Miss State Univ, BA, 80; MSS, 83. **CAREER** Instr, Miss State Univ, 87-91; Instr, Miss State Univ, 91-. **HONORS AND AWARDS** Who's Who Among Am Teachers, 94, 96, 97, 98. **MEMBERSHIPS** Miss Geog Soc, Miss Coun for the Soc Studies. **RESEARCH** World demography. **SELECTED PUBLICATIONS** Auth, "World Population Growth and the Demographic Transition," Miss J for the Soc Studies (96):14-16; auth, "The Geography of France," Splendors of Versailles: Teacher's Guide (97). **CONTACT ADDRESS** Dept Humanities, Mississippi Univ for Women, 1100 College St, Box W1634, Columbus, MS 39701-5800. **EMAIL** sbart@muw.edu

BARTLEY, ABEL A.
PERSONAL Born 02/11/1965, Jacksonville, FL, m, 1994, 1 child **DISCIPLINE** HISTORY **EDUCATION** Fla State Univ, BA, 87; MA, 90, PhD, 94. **MEMBERSHIPS** AHA; S Conf on African Am Studies; Fla Hist Soc. **RESEARCH** Southern urban political development, 20th century U.S. **SELECTED PUBLICATIONS** Auth, Keeping the Faith: Race, Politics and Social Development. **CONTACT ADDRESS** Dept Hist, Univ of Akron, 302 Buchtel Mall, Akron, OH 44325-0001. **EMAIL** abel@uakron.edu

BARTLEY, NUMAN V.
PERSONAL Born 10/29/1934, Ladonia, TX, m, 1968 **DISCIPLINE** AMERICAN HISTORY **EDUCATION** E Tex State Col, BS, 55; N Tex State Univ, MA, 61; Vanderbilt Univ, PhD(recent Am hist), 68. **CAREER** From instr to assoc prof hist, GA Inst Technol, 64-72; assoc prof, 72-76, Prof Hist, Univ GA, 76-, Consult & area studies dir, Westinghouse VISTA Training Prog, 67-69; sr res fel, Inst Southern Hist, Johns Hopkins Univ, 69-70; vis scholar, Inter-Univ Consortium Polit Res, Univ MI, 71; fel, Woodrow Wilson Int Ctr Scholars, Washington, DC, 72. **HONORS AND AWARDS** Chastain Awd, Southern Polit Sci Asn, 76. **MEMBERSHIPS** Orgn Am Historians; Southern Hist Asn; Southern Polit Sci Asn. **RESEARCH** South; Recent United States. **SELECTED PUBLICATIONS** Auth, The Rise of Massive Resistance: Race and Politics in the South During the 1950's, LA State Univ, 69; From Thurmond to Wallace: Political Tendencies in Georgia, 1948-1968, Johns Hopkins, 70; coauth, Southern Politics and the Second Reconstruction, Johns Hopkins, 75; auth, Voters and Party Systems, Hist Teacher, 75; The South and Sectionalism in American Politics, J Politics, 76; coauth, A History of Georgia, Univ GA, 77; co-ed, Southern Elections: County and Precinct Data, 1950-1972, LA State Univ, 78; The Creation of Modern Georgia, Univ GA, 82; Politics in the New South-Republicanism, Race, and Leadership in the 20th-Century, with R. K. Scher, Am Hist Rev, Vol 98, 93; Agenda for Reform-Winthrop Rockefeller as Governor of Arkansas, 1967-71, with C. K. Urwin, Southwestern Hist Quart, Vol 97, 93; Strom Thurmond and the Politics of Southern Change, with N. Cohodas, Am Hist Rev, Vol 99, 94; Social-Change and Sectional Identity, J of Southern Hist, Vol 61, 95; Conflict of Interests-Organized Labor and the Civil Rights Movement in the South, 1954-1968, with A. Draper, J of Am Hist, Vol 82, 95. **CONTACT ADDRESS** Dept of Hist, Univ of Georgia, Athens, GA 30602.

BARTLEY, RUSSELL HOWARD
PERSONAL Born 03/03/1939, Glen Ridge, NJ, m, 1963, 1 child **DISCIPLINE** MODERN HISTORY **EDUCATION** Colgate Univ, BA, 61; Middlebury Col, MA, 62; Stanford Univ, MA, 65, PhD(hist), 71. **CAREER** Instr, 69-71, Asst Prof Hist, Univ WI-Milwaukee, 71-, Nat Endowment for Humanities fel, 73. **MEMBERSHIPS** AHA; Am Asn Advan Slavic Studies; Conf Latin Am Hist; MLA. **RESEARCH** Modern Latin American history; Soviet historiography of Latin America. **SELECTED PUBLICATIONS** Auth, On scholarly dialogue: The case of United States and Soviet Latin Americanists, Latin Am Res Rev, 70; A decade of Soviet scholarship in Brazilian history: 1958-1968, Hist Am Hist Rev, 70; coauth, Latin America in Basic Historical Collections: A Working Guide, Hoover Inst, 72. **CONTACT ADDRESS** Dept of Hist, Univ of Wisconsin, Milwaukee, Milwaukee, WI 53201.

BARTON, CARLIN
DISCIPLINE HISTORY **EDUCATION** Univ CA, PhD, 84. **CAREER** Assoc prof, Univ MA Amherst. **RESEARCH** Ancient hist. **SELECTED PUBLICATIONS** Auth, Roman The Sorrows of the Ancient Romans; The Gladiator and the Monster, Princeton, 93; Savage Miracles, The Redemption of Lost Honor and the Sacramentum of the Gladiator and the Martyr, Representations, 94; All Things Beseem the Victor, Gender Rhet, 94. **CONTACT ADDRESS** Dept of Hist, Univ of Massachusetts, Amherst, Mass Ave, Amherst, MA 01003.

BARTON, H. ARNOLD
PERSONAL Born 11/30/1929, Los Angeles, CA, m, 1960 **DISCIPLINE** EUROPEAN HISTORY **EDUCATION** Pomona Col, BA, 53; Princeton Univ, PhD(hist), 62. **CAREER** Lectr hist, Univ Alta, 60-61, asst prof, 61-63; asst prof, Univ CA, Santa Barbara, 63-70; assoc prof, 70-75, Prof Hist, Southern IL Univ, Carbondale, 75-, Publ grant, Swed State Humanistic Res Coun, 73; ed, Swed Pioneer Hist Quart, 74-; Nat Endowment for Humanities fel, 76; Elected mem, Royal Soc Humanistic Studies as Uppsala, Sweden. **HONORS AND AWARDS** Distinguished hist "Swedish-Am of the Year". **MEMBERSHIPS** AHA; Soc Advan Scand Studies; Swed Pioneer Hist Soc; Swed Emigrant Inst. **RESEARCH** 18th century Europe, Scandinavia, France, and American immigration. **SELECTED PUBLICATIONS** Auth, Letters from the Promised Land: Swedes in America, 1840-1914, 75; auth, Count Axel von Fersen: Aristocrat in an Age of Revolution, 75; auth, The Search for Ancestors: A Swedish-American Family Saga, 79; auth, Scandinavia in the Revolutionary Era, 1760-1815, 86; auth, A Folk Divided: Homeland Swedes and Swedish Americans, 94. **CONTACT ADDRESS** Dept of Hist, So Illinois Univ, Carbondale, Carbondale, IL 62901-4300. **EMAIL** habarton@siu.edu

BARTON, MARCELLA BIRO
PERSONAL Born 08/24/1936, Bedford, OH, d, 2 children **DISCIPLINE** INTELLECTUAL AND RELIGIOUS HISTORY **EDUCATION** Univ Calif, BA, 70; Univ Akron, MA, 73; Univ Chicago, PhD(hist), 81. **CAREER** Prof Hist, Univ of Rio Grande, OH, 80-. **HONORS AND AWARDS** Edwin A Jones, Excellence in Teaching Awd, Univ, of Rio Grande 86; National Endowment for the Humanities Summer grant, Harvard Univ, 88; Honors Students Distinguished Teaching Awd, Univ of Rio Grande, 96; Distinguished Service Awd, Gallipolis of Rio Grande, 93; Distinguished Service Awd, Welsh-American Heritage Museum, 99-00; Ohio Academy of History Distinguished Service Awd, 00. **MEMBERSHIPS** AHA; Am Soc Church Hist; Am Cath Hist Asn; OH Acad Hist. **RESEARCH** Intellectual and religious history with an emphasis on Britain, Europe, and America. **SELECTED PUBLICATIONS** Rev, Calvinists Incorporated: Welsh Immigrants on Ohio's Industrial Frontier, by Anne Kelly Knowles, The Historian Vol 60, no 4, (98): 866-867; review, Dublins Merchant-Quaker: Anthony Sharp and the Community of Friends, 1643-1707, Richard L Greaves, Church History, vol 68 no 1, (99), 189-191; auth, "Rio Grande Univ in Ohio site of Welsh music premiere," Y Drych, April 98, p 17; auth, " Hillary Tann's 'The Moor' Premiers at Rio Grande," Ninnau, 98; auth, " Saint Theresa of Avila: Did She Have Epilepsy?" The Catholic Historical Review, Vol 68. No 4, 82; " The Welsh Errand Into the Wilderness," Pathways to Savoring the Past and Shaping the Future: An Ohio Appalachia Source book, (97), 56-63; auth, " The Welsh Errand Into the Wilderness," Ninnau, vol 22 no 3, (97): 2-3; ed and intro, Catalogue of Books, Welsh-American Heritage Museum Oak Hill; ed and intro, Welsh-Americans, The Manuscript Collection the Historical Society of Pennsylvania; gen ed, Welsh-American Reference Series, The Madog Center for Welsh Studies, The Univ of Rio Grande and Univ Press of American, New York, **CONTACT ADDRESS** Univ of Rio Grande, 4201 Springdale Rd, Rio Grande, OH 45674. **EMAIL** mbarton@rio.edu

BARTON, MIKE ALAN
PERSONAL Born 09/30/1940, Wichita, KS, m, 1964, 1 child **DISCIPLINE** THEATRE HISTORY, DRAMATIC LITERATURE **EDUCATION** Kans State Teachers Col, BA, 61, MS, 66; Ind Univ, PhD(theatre hist), 71. **CAREER** Prof actor, New York City, 61-62; instr speech, Kans State Teachers Col, 65-66; instr theatre, Univ Omaha, 66-68; asst, Ind Univ, Bloomington, 68-71; prof Theatre, Drake Univ, 71-. **RESEARCH** Nineteenth century theatre history; film history. **SELECTED PUBLICATIONS** Auth, Silent films: High camp or genuine art, Advance, 11/72; Aline Bernstein, In: Notable American Women, Harvard Univ, 78. **CONTACT ADDRESS** Dept of Theatre Arts, Drake Univ, 2507 University Ave, Des Moines, IA 50311-4505. **EMAIL** mike.barton@drake.edu

BARUA, PRADEEP P.
DISCIPLINE SOUTH HISTORY **EDUCATION** Univ Ill, Urbana-Champaign, PhD, 95. **CAREER** Olin Post-Doctoral fel & lectr, Yale Univ, 95-96; instr, Univ Nebr, Kearney. **RESEARCH** Comparative colonialism. **SELECTED PUBLICATIONS** Auth, Ethnic Conflict in the Military of Developing Nations a Comparative of India and Nigeria, Armed Forces & Soc, Vol 19, No 1, 92; Inventing Race: The British and the Martial Races of India, The Historian, Vol 58, No 1, 95. **CONTACT ADDRESS** Univ of Nebraska, Kearney, Kearney, NE 68849. **EMAIL** BARUAP@UNK.EDU

BARZUN, JACQUES
PERSONAL Born 11/30/1907, Creteil, France **DISCIPLINE** HISTORY **EDUCATION** Columbia Univ, AB, 27, MA, 28, PhD, 32. **CAREER** From instr to prof hist, Columbia Univ, 29-67, dean grad faculties, 55-58, dean faculties & provost, 58-67, Univ prof & adv arts, 67-75; Lit Adv, Scribner's, 75-, Fel, Coun Learned Soc, 33-34; extraordinary fel, Churchill Col, Cambridge; Mellon lectr, Nat Gallery Art, 73; dir, Macmillan Co, Peabody Inst Music & Art & Coun Basic Educ. **HONORS AND AWARDS** Silver Medal, Royal Soc Arts, 72; French Legion of Honor. **MEMBERSHIPS** Am Inst Arts & Lett (pres, 72-75 & 77-78); fel Royal Soc Arts; AHA. **RESEARCH** History of modern European thought and culture; the French race. **SELECTED PUBLICATIONS** Auth, Classic, Romantic and Modern, 61; Science: The Glorious Entertainment, 64, The American University, 68 & coauth, A Catalogue of Crime, 71, Harper; auth, Berlioz and the Roman Century, Columbia Univ, 69; coauth, The Modern Researcher, Harcourt, 70; auth, On Writing, Editing and Publishing, 71 & ed, Hector Berlioz: Evenings With the Orchestra, 73, Univ Chicago; The Press and the Prose & Content, Grammar and Linguistics of Broadcast News, Am Scholar, Vol 63, 94; Psychotherapy Awry & Response to Paul McHugh Article on the Lozano-Beanbayog Case, Am Scholar, Vol 63, 94; Attitudes and Assumptions & A Reply to Benjamin Fortson Commentary on the Article, The Press and

the Prose, Am Scholar, Vol 64, 95; Is Music Unspeakable & The Fear of Talking About a Musical Performance, Am Scholar, Vol 65, 96. **CONTACT ADDRESS** 597 Fifth Ave, New York, NY 10017.

BASCH, NORMA
PERSONAL Born Norwich, CT **DISCIPLINE** AMERICAN HISTORY, LAW **EDUCATION** Columbia Univ, BA, 56; NYork Univ, PhD(Am civilization), 79. **CAREER** Prof Hist, Rutgers Univ, 79-. **HONORS AND AWARDS** NEH Res fel, 85-86; ACLS fel, 88-89; Am Antiquarian fel, 91; Berkshire Article Prize, 94; Binkley Stevenson Prize, 98; Scribes Bk award for legal writing, 00. **MEMBERSHIPS** AHA; Orgn Am Historians; Am Studies Asn; Soc Historians Early Am Repub. **RESEARCH** Women's history; cultural history; legal history. **SELECTED PUBLICATIONS** Auth, "Invisible Women: The Legal Fiction of Marital Unity in Antebellum America," Feminist Studies (79); auth, In the Eyes of the Law: Women, Marriage and Property in 19th Century New York, Cornell Univ Press, 82; auth, "Marriage, Morals, and Politics in the Election of 1828," J of Am Hist 80 (93); auth, "Equity is Equality: Emerging Concepts of Women's Political Status in the Age of Jackson," Journal of the Early Republic (83): 297; auth, "Relief in the Premises: Divorce as a Women's Remedy, 1815-1870," Lawaud History Review 8 (90): 1; auth, Framing American Divorce: From the Revolutionary Generation to the Victorians, Univ of Calif Press, 99. **CONTACT ADDRESS** Dept of Hist, Rutgers, The State Univ of New Jersey, Newark, Newark, NJ 07102. **EMAIL** nbasch@mindspring.com

BASHIRI, IRAJ
PERSONAL Born 07/31/1940, Behbahan, Iran, m, 1968, 3 children **DISCIPLINE** CENTRAL ASIAN AND IRANIAN LANGUAGES, LITERATURES, AND CULTURES **EDUCATION** Pahlavi Univ, BA, 63; Univ Mich, Ann Arbor, MA, 68, PhD, 72. **CAREER** Lectr, Pahlavi Univ & British Coun, Shiraz, Iran, 63-64; instr, Imperial Iranian Air Forces, 65; lectr, Univ of Mich, 67-72; vis asst prof, 72-73, asst prof, 73-78, assoc prof, 78-96, prof, Univ Minn, Minneapolis, 96-, assoc chemn, 81-83, acting chemn, 83-84, 89-91, assoc chemn, 87-89, chemn, 97-98; IREX Res Resident Scholar for Tajikistan, 93-94. **HONORS AND AWARDS** Col of Liberal Arts Distinguished Teacher Awd, 80; honorary doctorate in History and Culture, Tajikistan State Univ, 96; honorary Academician, Acad of Scis of Tajikistan, 97. **MEMBERSHIPS** Soc for Iranian Studies, Middle East Studies Asn of North Am, Asn for the Advancement of Central Asian Res, Asn for Central Asian Studies. **RESEARCH** Central Asian and Iranian languages, literatures and cultures; Islam and communism; identity. **SELECTED PUBLICATIONS** Auth, Persian for Beginners (72); auth, To Be as the Origin of Syntax: A Persian Framework, Bibliotheca Islamica (73); auth, Hedayat's Ivory Tower: Structural Analysis of the Blind Owl, Manor House (74); auth, Hafiz' Shirazi Turk: A Structuralist's Point of View, Muslim World, 7 & 8 (79); auth, "Hafiz and the Sufic Ghazal," Studies in Islam (Jan 79); auth, Persian for Beginners: Pronunciation and Writing (80), Tape Manual with Notes on Grammar (80), Reading Texts (81), Persian Syntax (91), Burgess Pub Co; auth, The Fiction of Sadeq Hedayat, Amir Kabir Inst of Iranian Studies, Mazda Pubs (84); ed and contribur, The Pearl Canon, Mazda Pubs Bilingual Series (86); auth, Firdowsi's Shahname: 1000 Years After, Acad of Scis of Tajikistan, Dunshanbe (94); auth, Kamal Khujandi: Epoch and Its Importance in the History of Central Asian Civilization, Tehran-Dushanbe (96); transl, The History of a National Catastrophe by Rahim Masov (96); auth, The Samanids and the Revival of the Civilization of the Iranian Peoples, Acad of Scis of Tajikistan, Dunshanbe (99). **CONTACT ADDRESS** Dept Slavic & Central Asian Langs & Lits, Univ of Minnesota, Twin Cities, 211 Nolte Center, 315 Pillsbury Dr SE, Minneapolis, MN 55455. **EMAIL** bashi001@maroon.tc.umn.edu

BASIL, JOHN DURYEA
PERSONAL Born 01/19/1934 **DISCIPLINE** MODERN RUSSIAN HISTORY **EDUCATION** Univ Wash, PhD(Russ hist), 66. **CAREER** Asst prof hist, LA State Univ, New Orleans, 66-68; Assoc Prof Hist, Univ SC, 68-. **HONORS AND AWARDS** Distinguished Prof, Hist, Univ SC, 93. **MEMBERSHIPS** Am Asn Advan Slavic Studies. **RESEARCH** Russian Revolution of 1917; Russian church history. **SELECTED PUBLICATIONS** Auth, Russia and the Bolshevik Revolution, Russ Rev, 1/68; Orthodox Church in 1917, Church Hist, 12/78; Pobedonostsev, Konstantin, Petrovich & An Examination of the Changing Political and Religious Relationships Between Church and State in Late Imperial Russia-An Argument for a Russian State Church, Church Hist, Vol 64, 95; Swiss Theologians in Czarist Russia 1700-1917-Emigration and the Everyday Life in Russia of Clergymen and Their Wives (German), with H. Schneider, Slavic Rev, Vol 55, 96; The Price of Prophecy-Orthodox Churches on Peace, Freedom, and Security, with A. F. C. Webster, Church Hist, Vol 65, 96; The Mershoviksiu 1917, (Slavica); Church-State Relations ai Late Imperial Russia. **CONTACT ADDRESS** Dept of Hist, Univ of So Carolina, Columbia, Columbia, SC 29208. **EMAIL** basil@gwm.sc.edu

BASS, GEORGE FLETCHER
PERSONAL Born 12/09/1932, Columbia, SC, m, 1960, 2 children **DISCIPLINE** CLASSICAL & NAUTICAL ARCHEOLOGY **EDUCATION** Johns Hopkins Univ, MA, 55; Univ Pa, PhD(class archaeol), 64. **CAREER** Res asst class archaeol, univ mus, 62-62, res assoc, 63-64, asst prof, univ, 64-68, Assoc Prof Class Archaeol, Univ PA, 68-80, Vis scholar archaeol, St John's Col, Cambridge, 69-70; pres to Archaeol dir, Inst Nautical Archaeol, 73-; dist prof anthrop, TX A&M Univ, 80-. **HONORS AND AWARDS** John Oliver La Gorce gold medal, Nat Geog Soc. **MEMBERSHIPS** Archaeol Inst Am. **SELECTED PUBLICATIONS** Auth, Mycenaean and Protogeometric Tmbs in the Halicarnassos Peninsula, Am J Archaeol, 67: 353-361; ed, Underwater Ecavations at Yassi Ada: A Byzantine Shipwreck, Archaologischer Anzeiger, 62; Smithsonian Twentieth-Century Treasury of Science, Simon & Schuster, 66; auth, Archaeology Under Water, Praeger, New York & Thames & Hudson, London, 66; Cape Gelidonya: A Bronze Age Shipwreck, Am Philos Soc, 67; ed, A History of Seafaring Based on Underwater Archaeology, Thamas & Hudson, London & Walker, New York, 72; auth, Archaeology Beneath the Sea, Walker, 76. **CONTACT ADDRESS** Dept of Anthrop, Texas A&M Univ, Col Station, College Station, TX 77843. **EMAIL** gfbass@tamu.edu

BASSETT, CHARLES WALKER
PERSONAL Born 07/07/1932, Aberdeen, SD, m, 1956, 2 children **DISCIPLINE** AMERICAN LITERATURE & STUDIES **EDUCATION** Univ SDak, AB, 54, MA, 56; Univ Kans, PhD(English), 64. **CAREER** From instr to asst prof English, Univ Pa, 64-69; asst prof, 69-74, assoc prof, 74-80, prof English, Colby Col, 80-, chrm, dept of English, 87-89, Colby Col, dir AM studies, 71-96, Univ Pa fac res grant, 68; humanities grants, Colby Col, 78 & 79, Mellon grant, 79 & 83. **HONORS AND AWARDS** Mary C. Turpie Awd, Am Stud Asn; Senior Class Teaching Awd, 93, 97. **MEMBERSHIPS** Am Studies Asn; MLA. **RESEARCH** American fiction; American history. **SELECTED PUBLICATIONS** Auth, Katahdin, Wachusett, and Kilimanjaro: The symbolic mountains of Thoreau and Hemingway, Thoreau J, 4/71; O'Hara's roots (43 part ser), weekly in Pottsville Republican, Pa, 71-72; Undergraduate and graduate American studies programs in the US: A survey, Am Quart, 8/75; Naturalism revisited: The case of John O'Hara, Colby Libr Quart, 12/75; John O'Hara and The Noble Experiment: The use of alcohol in Appointment in Samarra, winter 78-79, John O'Hara: Irishman and American, 8/79 & O'Hara and history, 12/81, John O'Hara J; John O'Hara, In: Vol IX, Part 2, Dict of Literary Biography, 81. **CONTACT ADDRESS** Dept of English, Colby Col, 150 Mayflower Hill, Waterville, ME 04901-4799. **EMAIL** cwbasset@colby.edu

BASSETT, WILLIAM W.
PERSONAL Born 12/18/1932, Peoria, IL, m, 1973, 3 children **DISCIPLINE** LAW; LEGAL HISTORY **EDUCATION** S. T.L. St. Mary of the Lake (IL), MA, 58; Gregorian Univ (Rome), JCD, 65; Cath Univ Am (Wash), JD, 72. **CAREER** Asst to assoc prof, 67-73, Cath Univ Am, 67-73; scholar in res, 73-74, Ludwig-Maximilians Universitat (Munich); vis prof 82-83, Univ Calif; Prof Law, 74-, Univ San Francisco, 74-. **MEMBERSHIPS** Seldon Soc; Canon Law Soc Am; Asn Iuris Canonici Int; Am Soc Legal Hist **RESEARCH** Law of Religious Organizations; Legal History. **SELECTED PUBLICATIONS** California Commmunity Property Law, Bancroft Whitney, 95; Religious Organizations and the Law, West, 98. **CONTACT ADDRESS** School of Law, Univ of San Francisco, 2150 Fulton St., San Francisco, CA 94117. **EMAIL** Bassettw@usfca.edu

BAST, ROBERT
DISCIPLINE HISTORY **EDUCATION** W Theol Sem, MDiv, 84; Univ Ariz, PhD, 93. **CAREER** Assoc prof, hist, Univ Tenn. **MEMBERSHIPS** AHA; Sixteenth Century Studies Conf, Fruhe Neuzeit Interdisziplinar. **RESEARCH** Early modern Europe; early modern Germany; history of the Reformation. **SELECTED PUBLICATIONS** Auth, Honor your Fathers: Catechisms and the Emergence of Patriarchal Ideology in Germany C. 1400-1600, 97; auth, Continuity and Change, The Harvest of Late Medieval and Reformation History, coed. Robert J. Bast, Brill Academic Publishers, 00. **CONTACT ADDRESS** Dept Hist, Univ of Tennessee, Knoxville, 915 Volunteer Blvd, 6th Fl, Dunford Hall, Knoxville, TN 37996-4065. **EMAIL** rbast@utk.edu

BATALDEN, STEPHEN KALMAR
PERSONAL Born 05/23/1945, Minneapolis, MN, m, 1970, 2 children **DISCIPLINE** HISTORY **EDUCATION** Augsburg Col, BA, 67; Univ Minn, MA, 72, PhD(Russian hist), 75. **CAREER** Instr hist, Augsburg Col, 69-70; asst prof, Grambling State Univ, 75-76; asst prof, 76-81; assoc prof Hist, Az State Univ, 81-; prof. **HONORS AND AWARDS** Grants from the International Res and Exchanges Bd and Fulbright fel. **MEMBERSHIPS** AHA; Am Asn Advan Slavic Studies; Modern Greek Studies Asn. **RESEARCH** Relig and cultural hist of modern Russia and the Balkans. **SELECTED PUBLICATIONS** Auth, Catherine II's Greek Prelate: Eugenois Voulgaris in Russia, 1771-1806, (Boulder/New York: East European Quarterly/Columbia Univ Press, 82); ed, Seeking God: The Recovery of Religious Identity in Orthodox Russia, Ukraine, and Georgia, DeKalb: Northern Illinois Univ Press, 93; coauth, The Newly Independent States of Eurasia: Handbook of Former Soviet Republics, Phoenix: Oryx Press, 97; auth, Preispituvanje na tradicijata: Esei za istorijata na pravoslavieto, The Reexamination of Tradition: Essays on the History of Eastern Orthodoxy, Skopje: Kultura, 97. **CONTACT ADDRESS** Dept Hist, Arizona State Univ, Tempe, AZ 85281. **EMAIL** stephen.batalden@asu.edu

BATES, DONALD G.
PERSONAL Born 03/18/1933, Windsor, ON, Canada **DISCIPLINE** HISTORY OF MEDICINE **EDUCATION** Univ Western Ont, MD, 58, BA, 60; Johns Hopkins Univ, PhD, 75. **CAREER** Intern, Victoria Hosp, 58-60; NIH fel, Inst Hist Med, Johns Hopkins Univ, 60-62; instr to assoc prof, 62-75, ch, 66-82, 87-88, COTTON-HANNAH PROF HIST MED, DEPT SOCIAL STUD MED, McGILL UNIV, 75-. **MEMBERSHIPS** Am Asn Hist Med; Am Asn Advan Sci; Can Soc Hist Med; Soc Social Hist Med. **SELECTED PUBLICATIONS** Auth, Thoughts on Peace and Security, 85-87; ed, Knowledge and the Scholarly Medical Traditions, 95. **CONTACT ADDRESS** Dept of Social Stud Med, McGill Univ, 3655 Drummond St, Rm 416, Montreal, QC, Canada H3G 1Y6. **EMAIL** md65@musica.mcgill.ca

BATINSKI, EMILY E.
DISCIPLINE LATIN EPIC, ROMAN HISTORIANS, SILVER AGE LITERATURE **EDUCATION** Univ Colo, PhD, 83. **CAREER** Assoc prof Classics, dept chair, univ fac senate, univ coun on acad prog abroad, La State Univ. **RESEARCH** Silver Age Roman epic; Latin lyric; Roman historians; genre theory. **SELECTED PUBLICATIONS** Auth, Lucan's Catalogue of Caesar's Troops: Paradox and Convention, in Class J; Word-patterning in the Latin Hendecasyllable, in Latomus. **CONTACT ADDRESS** Dept of For Lang and Lit, Louisiana State Univ, 222 Prescott Hall, Baton Rouge, LA 70803. **EMAIL** slbati@lsu.edu

BAUER, ARNOLD JACOB
PERSONAL Born 04/11/1931, 1 child **DISCIPLINE** HISTORY **EDUCATION** Univ Americas, BA, 56; Univ Calif, Berkeley, PhD(hist), 69. **CAREER** Prof Hist, Univ CA, Davis, 70-. **RESEARCH** History of Spanish America; Chile; rural history. **SELECTED PUBLICATIONS** Auth, The Church and Spanish American Agrarian Structure, Americas, 71; Chilean Rural Labor in the 19th Century, Am Hist Rev, 71; Chilean Rural Society from the Spanish Conquest to 1930, Cambridge Univ, 75. **CONTACT ADDRESS** Dept Hist, Univ of California, Davis, Davis, CA 95616-5200.

BAUER, CRAIG A.
PERSONAL Born 05/20/1947, New Orleans, LA, m, 1 child **DISCIPLINE** HISTORY **EDUCATION** SE La Univ, BA, 70; MA, 73; Univ S Miss, PhD, 89. **CAREER** Supvr of educ, Jefferson Parish, La Dept of Jus Serv, 82-95; instr, Our Lady of the Holy Cross Col, 90-98; prin, St Charles Borromeo Sch, 97-98; assoc prof, Our Lady of the Holy Cross Col, 98-. **HONORS AND AWARDS** Phi Alpha Theta, Nat Hist Honor Soc; Pi Gamma Mu, Nat Soc Sci Honor Soc; Kappa Gamma Pi, Nat Cath Grad Honor Soc. **MEMBERSHIPS** Orgn of Am Historians, S Hist Asn, La Hist Asn, Jefferson Hist Soc of La. **RESEARCH** The South, Civil War, Louisiana history **SELECTED PUBLICATIONS** Auth, A Leader Among Peers: The Life and Times of Duncan F, Kenna, Univ of La-LaFayette, 93. **CONTACT ADDRESS** Dept Natural & Soc Sci, Our Lady of the Holy Cross Col, 4123 Woodland Dr, New Orleans, LA 70131-7337. **EMAIL** cbauer@olhcc.edu

BAUGH, DANIEL ALBERT
PERSONAL Born 07/10/1931, Philadelphia, PA, m, 1955, 3 children **DISCIPLINE** BRITISH HISTORY **EDUCATION** Univ Pa, AB, 53, AM, 57; Cambridge Univ, PhD, 61. **CAREER** From instr to asst prof hist, Princeton Univ, 61-69; assoc prof, 69-82, Prof Hist, Cornell Univ, 82-98, prof emer, 98-, Soc Sci Res Coun grant-in-aid, 66-67; NEH fel, 77-78. **MEMBERSHIPS** Fel Royal Hist Soc; AHA; Econ Hist Soc; Soc Nautical Res; Mid Atlantic Conf Brit Studies (pres, 92-94); Navy Records Soc (vice pres, 99-); Am Friends of the Inst of Hist Res (pres). **RESEARCH** British administrative history; British social and economic history 1660-1890; British naval history; European maritime history. **SELECTED PUBLICATIONS** Auth, British Naval Administration in the Age of Walpole, Princeton, 65; The cost of poor relief in Southeast England, 1790-1834, Econ Hist Rev, 75; Naval Administration 1715-1750, Navy Record Soc, 77; Great Britain's Blue-Water Policy, 1689-1815, Intl Hist Rev, 88; Maritime Strength and Atlantic Commerce: the Uses of a Grand Marine Empire, in An Imperial State at War, 94; The Eighteenth Century Navy as a National Institution, 1690-1815, in Oxford Illustrated History of the Royal Navy; auth, Withdrawing from Europe: Anglo-French Maritime Geopolitics, 1750-1800, Intl Hist Rev, 98. **CONTACT ADDRESS** History Dept, Cornell Univ, Mcgraw Hall, Ithaca, NY 14853-4601.

BAUGHMAN, T. H.
DISCIPLINE HISTORY **EDUCATION** Stetson Univ, BA, 68; Ohio Univ, MA, 69; Fla State Univ, PhD, 90. **CAREER** Chair, Benedictine Col; Dean Univ Central Okla. **MEMBER-**

SHIPS AHA, Royal Geog Soc, The Explorer's Club. **RESEARCH** History of Polar Region, Edwardian Education. **SELECTED PUBLICATIONS** auth, Pilgrims on the Ice, Univ Neb Press, 99; auth, Before the Heroes Come, Univ Neb Press, 94. **CONTACT ADDRESS** Dept Hist, Univ of Central Oklahoma, Edmond, OK 73034-5209.

BAUM, DALE
PERSONAL Born 03/14/1943, Jersey City, NJ **DISCIPLINE** UNITED STATES & LATIN AMERICAN HISTORY **EDUCATION** Georgetown Univ, BA, 65; Univ Minn, MA, 72, PhD(hist), 78. **CAREER** Teaching asst, Univ of Minnesota, 72-73; res asst, Univ of Minnesota, 73-75; asst prof, Texas A&M Univ, 78-84; assoc porf, Texas A&M Univ, 85-98; prof, Texas A&M Univ, 99-. **HONORS AND AWARDS** Fac Acad Study Leave, Tex A&M Univ, 87, 99; Col of Liberal Arts Summer Res Grant, Texas A&M Univ, 82; Col of Liberal Arts Summer Res Grant, Texas A&M Univ, 79; Grad Sch Doctoral Dissertation Fel, Univ of Minn, 77-78. **MEMBERSHIPS** Am Hist Asn; Organization of Am Hist; Phi Alpha Theta; Social Science Hist Asn; Southern Historical Asn; Texas State Hist Asn. **RESEARCH** Civil War and reconstruction; American voting behavior. **SELECTED PUBLICATIONS** Auth, The Civil War Party System: The Case of Massachusetts, 1848-1876, Chapel Hill and London: Univ of North Carolina Press, 84; auth, "The Massachusetts Voter: Party Loyalty in the Gilded Age, 1872-1896," in Jack Tager and John Ifkovic, eds, Massachusetts in the Gilded Age: Selected Essays, Amherst: Univ of Massachusetts Press, 85; auth, "The Texas Voter and the Crisis of the Union, 1859-1861," Journal of Southern History 53, 87; auth, "Texas Patrons of Husbandry: Geography, Social Contexts, and Voting Behavior," Agricultural History 63, 89; auth, "Pinpointing Apparent Fraud in the 1861 Texas Secession Referendum," Journal of Interdisciplinary History 22, 91; auth, "Chicanery and Intimidation in the 1869 Texas Gubernatorial Race," Southwestern Historical Quarterly, 97, (93): 37-54; auth, "Ethnic Conflict and Machine Politics in San Antonio, 1892-1899," Journal of Urban History, (93): 63-84; auth, "Lyndon Johnson's Victory in the 1948 Texas Senate Race: A Reappraisal," Political Science Quarterly, 109, No 3, (94): 1-19; auth, "Female Ballots: The Impact of the Adoption of the Nineteenth Amendment," Journal of Interdisciplinary History, 85, Reprinted in Nancy F. Cott, ed., History of Women in the United States: Historical Articles on Women's Lives and Activities, Munich, New Providence, London, and Paris: K.G. Saur, 94; auth, The Shattering of Texas Unionism: Politics in the Lone Star during the Civil War Era, Louisiana State Univ Press, 98. **CONTACT ADDRESS** Dept of Hist, Texas A&M Univ, Col Station, College Station, TX 77843. **EMAIL** d-baum@tamu.edu

BAUMLER, ALAN
DISCIPLINE HISTORY **EDUCATION** N Ill Univ; BA, 87; Univ Ill, MA, 90, PhD, 97. **CAREER** Lectr, Univ Ill, 93; Sangamon State Univ, 95; asst prof, Piedmont Col, 95-. **HONORS AND AWARDS** Ill-Tamkang fel, 89, 92-93; FLAS, 90-92; resident scholar, nanking, china, 1994; internet proj reviewer, longman press; ed, neh journey to the west website. **RESEARCH** China, Japan, early modern Europe. **SELECTED PUBLICATIONS** Rev, Edward L. Dreyer, China at War 1901-1949, China Infor, 96; auth, Playing with Fire: The Nationalist Government and Popular Anti-Opium Agitation in 1927-1928, Republican China 21:1, 95. **CONTACT ADDRESS** Dept of Hist, Piedmont Col, 165 Central Ave., PO Box 10, Demorest, GA 30535. **EMAIL** dprice@piedmont.edu

BAUSUM, HENRY S.
PERSONAL Born 02/19/1924, Annapolis, MD, m, 1947, 2 children **DISCIPLINE** HISTORY **EDUCATION** Univ MD, BA, 49; Boston Univ, AM, 51; Univ Chicago, PhD(hist), 63. **CAREER** Assoc prof hist, Carson-Newman Col, 56-64; assoc prof, 64-80, Prof Hist, VA Mil Inst, 80-, Vis assoc prof, Univ VA, 67-68. **MEMBERSHIPS** AAUP; AHA; Va Soc Hist Teachers (pres-elect, 77-79); Va Soc Sci Asn. **RESEARCH** Historiography; early modern European history; contemporary world history. **SELECTED PUBLICATIONS** Auth, Alternative to Pax Americana, World Affairs, 9/67; Edenic Images of the Western World: A Reappraisal, SAtlantic Quart, autumn 68; co-ed, Teaching History Today, Monthly Column in AHA Newsletter, 74-; The History of War & Symposium, Panel 1, Intro, J of Military Hist, Vol 57, 93; The 'Bombing of Auschwitz Re-Examined'-Comment, J of Military Hist, Vol 61, 97. **CONTACT ADDRESS** George C. Marshall Lib, Virginia Military Inst, Lexington, VA 24450.

BAXTER, COLIN FRANK
PERSONAL Born 02/17/1942, Harrow, England, m, 1972, 1 child **DISCIPLINE** BRITISH & MODERN MILITARY HISTORY **EDUCATION** E Tenn State Univ, BSc, 61; Univ Ga, MA, 63, PhD(hist), 65. **CAREER** Asst prof hist, Furman Univ, 65-71; Prof Hist 90-. **MEMBERSHIPS** Soc for Mil. Hist. **RESEARCH** British History. **SELECTED PUBLICATIONS** Auth, Lord Palmerston: Panic-monger or Naval Peacemaker, Soc Sci, autumn 72; The Duke of Somerset and the Creation of the British Ironclad Navy, 1859-66, Mariner's Mirror, 8/77; Hidden Ally-The French Resistance, Special Operations, and the Landings in Southern France, 1944, with A. L. Funk, Am Hist Rev, Vol 100, 95; The Hardest Victory-RAF Bomber Command in the Second World War, with D. Richards, Historian, Vol 59, 97; auth, "The Normandy Campaign, 1944: A Selected Bibliography," Greenwood, 92, coeditor; auth, "The American Military Tradition From Colonial Times to the Present," Scholarly Resource, 93; auth, "The War in North Africa, 1940-1943: A Selected Biography," Greenwood, 96; auth, "Field Marshal Bernard Law Montgomery, 1887-1976: A Selected Bibliography," Greenwood, 99. **CONTACT ADDRESS** Dept of Hist, East Tennessee State Univ, Johnson City, TN 37614. **EMAIL** baxterc@etsu.edu

BAXTER, DOUGLAS CLARK
PERSONAL Born 09/20/1942, Flint, MI, m, 1977, 1 child **DISCIPLINE** EARLY MODERN EUROPEAN & FRENCH HISTORY **EDUCATION** Wayne State Univ, AB, 64; Univ Wis, MA, 66; Univ MN, PhD, 71. **CAREER** From instr to asst prof, 69-76, assoc prof hist, OH Univ, 76. **HONORS AND AWARDS** Phi Beta Kappa, 64. **MEMBERSHIPS** AHA; Soc Fr Hist Studies; Western Soc Fr Hist. **RESEARCH** Seventeenth & eighteenth century French hist; soc-institutional hist; mil hist. **SELECTED PUBLICATIONS** Auth Louvois, Francois-Michel Le Tellier, Encycl Britannica, 73; Servants of the Sword: French Intendants of the Army, 1630-70, Univ Ill, 76; Pension Expectations of the French Military Commis, In: Adapting to Condition. War and Society in the Eighteenth Century, Univ Ala, 86; First Encounters, Bourbon Princes Meet Their Brides: Ceremony, Gender, and Monarchy, Proceedings of the Western Soc for Fr Hist, vol 22, Univ Calif-Riverside, 95; articles on Asiento, Madame de Maintenon, Philip V, and Princesse des Ursins, In: The Treaties of the War of Spanish Succession: An Historical and Critical Dictionary, Greenwood, 95; auth, "Royal Expectations: Gendered Visions of Bourbon Brides, 1680-1773," Women In French Studies, 98; auth, "Note Josephine and : The Contesse de porvened and it Campaign to Marry Her Sister to the Conte d'Artois, 1772-1773," Dalhoisie French Studies, in press (Spring 01). **CONTACT ADDRESS** Dept of Hist, Ohio Univ, Athens, OH 45701-2979. **EMAIL** baxter2@ohio.edu

BAXTER, STEPHEN BARTOW
PERSONAL Born 03/08/1929, Boston, MA, m, 1953, 6 children **DISCIPLINE** HISTORY **EDUCATION** Harvard Univ, BA, 50; Cambridge Univ, PhD, 55. **CAREER** Instr hist, Dartmouth Col, 54-57; vis asst prof, Univ MO, 57-58; from asst prof to assoc prof, 58-66, prof, 66-74, alumni distinguished prof, 68-69, Kenan Prof Hist, Univ NC, Chapel Hill, 75-, Guggenheim fels, 59-60 & 73-74; sr ed, Studies in Brit Hist & Cult, 75-; Clark Libr Prof, Univ CA, Los Angeles, 77-78; dir, Nat Endowment for Humanities postdoctoral sem, 78-79. **MEMBERSHIPS** AHA; fel Royal Hist Soc; Mediaeval Acad Am; Conf Brit Studies. **RESEARCH** English administrative and constitutional history. **SELECTED PUBLICATIONS** Auth, Development of the Treasury, 1660-1702, Harvard Univ, 57; The Struggle for a New Order in England: Cromwell's Search for Lawful Government, 1647-58, In: Major Crises in Western Civilization, Harcourt, 65; Recent writings on William III, J Mod Hist, 9/66; William III, Longmans, Green, 66; Basic Documents of English History, Houghton, 69; The Age of Personal Monarchy in England, In: Eighteenth Century Studies Presented to Arthur M Wilson, Univ Press New Eng, 72; A Comment on Clayton Roberts Perspective, Albion, Vol 25, 93; The Augustan Court-Queen Anne and the Decline of Court Culture, with R. O. Bucholz, Am Hist Rev, Vol 100, 95; Holland and the Dutch-Republic in the 17th-Century-The Politics of Particularism, J. L. Price, Am Hist Rev, Vol 101, 96. **CONTACT ADDRESS** Dept of Hist, Univ of No Carolina, Chapel Hill, Chapel Hill, NC 27514.

BAYLEY, C. C.
PERSONAL Born 03/05/1907, Congleton, England, m, 1936, 2 children **DISCIPLINE** HISTORY **EDUCATION** Univ Manchester, BA, 28, MA, 29; Univ Chicago, PhD, 38. **CAREER** Lectr, Univ Toronto, 31; asst prof, Colorado Col, 32; univ fel, Univ Chicago, 35; fac mem, 35, Emer Kingsford Prof & Prof History, McGill Univ. **HONORS AND AWARDS** Guggenheim fel, 48; Can Coun sr fel, 66; Killam fel, 70; fel, Royal Soc Can, 61. **SELECTED PUBLICATIONS** Auth, The Formation of the German College of Electors, 49; auth, War and Society in Renaissance Florence, 61; auth, Mercenaries for the Crimea: The German, Swiss and Italian Legions in British Service 1854-1856, 77. **CONTACT ADDRESS** 3610 McTavish St, No 34, Montreal, QC, Canada H3A 1Y2.

BAYLOR, MICHAEL G.
DISCIPLINE EARLY MODERN EUROPEAN HISTORY **EDUCATION** PhD; Stanford Univ. **CAREER** Prof, Lehigh Univ **HONORS AND AWARDS** Dir, Sci and Technol Soc Prog. **RESEARCH** Social and cultural history of Reformation Germany. **SELECTED PUBLICATIONS** Co-auth, Technology and Values in American Civilization, in Context: History and the History of Technology; New Worlds, New Technologies, New Issues; ed, The Radical Reformation; ed., Revelation and Revolution: Basic Writings of Thomas Muntzer. **CONTACT ADDRESS** Dept Hist, Lehigh Univ, Bethlehem, PA 18015. **EMAIL** mgb2@lehigh.edu

BAYNTON, DOUGLAS C.
PERSONAL Born 04/26/1953, NJ, m, 1997 **DISCIPLINE** HISTORY **EDUCATION** W Or Univ, BS, 86; Univ Iowa, PhD, 93. **CAREER** Vis asst prof to asst prof, 94-, Univ Iowa. **HONORS AND AWARDS** Smithsonian Inst Postdoctoral Fel, Nat Museum of Amer Hist, 97-98; Obermann Center for Adv Stud, Univ Iowa, Res Seminar Fel, 97; Irving T Zola Emerging Scholar Awd, Soc for Disabilities Stud, 96. **MEMBERSHIPS** Amer Hist Assoc; Amer Stud Assoc; Org of Amer Hist; Soc for Disability Stud; Amer Sign Lang Teachers Assoc. **RESEARCH** Amer cultural hist; hist of disability. **SELECTED PUBLICATIONS** Auth, Forbidden Signs: American Culture and the Campaign Against Sign Language, Univ Chicago Press, 96; art, Out of Sight: The Suppression of American Sign Language, Multilingual America: Transnationalism, Ethnicity, and the Languages of American Literature, NYU Press, 98; art, Disability: A Useful Category of Historical Analysis, Disability Stud Quart, 97; art, A Silent Exile on this Earth: The Metaphorical Construction of Deafness in the Nineteenth Century, The Disability Stud Reader, 97; "Evolutionary Theory and the Campaign Against Sign Language," Anthropology and Human Movement II: Searching for Origins, Scarecrow Pr, 99; "Bodies and Environments: The Cultural Construction of Disability," in Employment, Disability and the Americans with Disabilities Act: Issues in Law, Public Policy and Res, ed. Peter Blanck (Northwester Univ Pr, 00); "Disability and the Justification of Inequality in Am Hist," The New Disability Hist: Am Perspectives, ed. Paul Longmore and Lauri Umansky (New York Univ Pr, 00). **CONTACT ADDRESS** Dept of History, Univ of Iowa, 280 SH, Iowa City, IA 52242. **EMAIL** douglas-baynton@uiowa.edu

BAYOR, RONALD HOWARD
PERSONAL Born 03/14/1944, New York, NY, m, 1966, 2 children **DISCIPLINE** AMERICAN HISTORY, URBAN-ETHNIC STUDIES **EDUCATION** City Col New York, BA, 65; Syracuse Univ, MA, 66; Univ PA, PhD(hist), 70. **CAREER** Grad asst hist, Syracuse Univ, 66; grad asst hist, Univ PA, 66-69; from instr to asst prof Am hist, St John's Univ, 69-73; asst prof, 73-77, assoc prof, 77-82, prof hist, Ga Inst Technol, 83-, Vis asst prof, NY Univ, 72 & Lehman Col, 73; consult, Urban Inst, 73-74; consult, New York Ctr Visual Hist, 79; ed, J Am Ethnic Hist, 80-; consultant, conference, "First Generation Immigrants," East Carolina Univ, 88; consultant, museum exhibit, Creating Community: The Jews of Atlanta, 92-95; consultant, museum exhibit, "Hist of the Irish in New York," Museum of the City of New York, 92-95; senior advisor/editor, Greenwood Press Series, The New Americans. 94-; special ed, Transaction Publishers Book Series on Ethnic Studies, 94-. **HONORS AND AWARDS** Outstanding Academic Book, for Choice, for Neighbors in Conflict, 78; GA Tech Outstanding Teacher of the Year Awd, 83; Am Hist Asn Albert J. Beveridge Grant for Research in the History of the Western Hemisphere, 86; GA Tech School of Social Science, Excellence in Teaching Awd, 90; Distinguished Service Awd, Immigration History Soc, 92; Nat Endowment for the Humanities Fellowship, 92-93; John S. Donnelly, Sr Prize for best book in history and social sciences, Am Conference for Irish Studies, 97 for co-edited book The New York Irish; Outstanding Book Awd, Gustavus Myers Center for the Study of Human Rights in North America, for Race and the Shaping of Twentieth-Century Atlanta. **MEMBERSHIPS** AHA; Orgn Am Historians; Am Ital Hist Asn; Immigration Hist Soc; Am Jewish Hist Soc; Urban Hist Asn; H-Ethnic; H-Urban; Southern Hist Asn. **RESEARCH** History of cities; ethnic and racial groups in cities. **SELECTED PUBLICATIONS** Auth, Italians, Jews and Ethnic Conflict, Int Migration Rev, winter 72; The Transplanted Americans, Immigrants in an Urban World & The Darker Side of Urban Life, Slums in the City, In: Cities in Transition, Nelson-Hall, 74; Italians and Jews in New York: The La Guardia Elections, Proc Am Ital Hist Asn, 74; Neighbors in Conflict: The Irish, Germans, Jews and Italians of New York City, 1929-1941, Johns Hopkins Univ, 78; Ethnic Residential Patterns in Atlanta, 1880-1940, Ga Hist Quart, winter 79; auth, "Ethnicity in Urban Am," J Urban Hist 7 (81); ed, Neighborhoods in Urban America, Kennikat Press, 82; auth, "A City Too Busy to Hate: Atlanta's Business Community and Civil Rights," in Business an dIts Environment, ed. Harold Sharlin (Greenwood Pr, 83); co-auth, Engineering the New South: Georgia Tech, 1885-1985, Univ GA Press, 85; auth, "Klans, Coughlinites, and Aryan Nations: Patterns of Am Anti-Semitism in the Twentieth Century," Am Jewish Hist 76 (86); Changing Neighborhoods: Ethnic and Racial Succession in the Urban North and South, in From Melting Pot to Multiculturalism, ed, Valeria Lerda, Bulzione Editore, 90; Reform Mayors and Urban Politics: New York and Chicago, a review essay, J of Urban Hist, Nov 91; The Twentieth-Century Urban South and the Atlanta Experience, GA Hist Quart, 75, fall 91; auth, "Reform Mayors and Urban Politics: New York and Chicago," J of Urban Hist, 91; Race and City Services: The Shaping of Atlanta's Police and Fire Departments, Atlanta Hist, 36, fall 92; The Civil Rights Movement as Urban Reform: Atlanta's Black Neighborhoods and a New Progressivism, GA Hist Quart 77, summer 93; Fiorello LaGuardia: Ethnicity and Reform, Harlan-Davidson, 93; Historical Encounters: Intergroup Relations in a Nation of Nations, The Annals of the Am Academy of Political and Social Sciences, Nov 93; co-ed, The New York Irish, Johns Hopkins Univ Press, 96; Race and the Shaping of Twentieth-Century Atlanta, Univ of NC Press, 96; The Changing South, J of Policy Hist, 9, 2, 97; auth, "Irish-Jewish Relations," in En-

cyclopedia of the Irish in Am, ed. Michael Glazier (Univ Notre Dame Pr, 99). **CONTACT ADDRESS** School of History, Technology, and Society, Georgia Inst of Tech, 685 Cherry St., Atlanta, GA 30332. **EMAIL** RB2@prism.gatech.edu

BAYS, BRAD A.
PERSONAL Born 09/21/1966, Ponca City, OK, m, 1988, 1 child **DISCIPLINE** GEOGRAPHY **EDUCATION** Okla State Univ, BA, 89; Univ Tenn-Knoxville, MS, 91; Univ Nebr-Lincoln, PhD, 96. **CAREER** Asst prof, Northwestern State Univ of La, 94-95; vis asst prof, Okla State Univ, 95-96, asst prof, 96-. **HONORS AND AWARDS** Andrew Hill Clark Awd, 94; OSU Arts and Sci Fac Coun Jr Fac Awd for Scholarly Excellence (99); expertise on the historical geography of Native Am resettlement and land issues, especially in Indian Territory and Okla; professional interests in outdoor recreation, especially environmental impacts of hunting and sportfishing. **MEMBERSHIPS** Asn Am Geogs. **RESEARCH** Cultural and historical geography. **SELECTED PUBLICATIONS** Auth, Townsite Settlements and Dispossession in the Cherokee Nation, 1866-1907, New York: Garland (98); various articles and book chapters. **CONTACT ADDRESS** Dept Geography, Oklahoma State Univ, Stillwater, Stillwater, OK 74078-0001. **EMAIL** bbays@okstate.edu

BAYS, DANIEL HENRY
PERSONAL Born 03/27/1942, Berrien Springs, MI, m, 1967, 2 children **DISCIPLINE** MODERN CHINESE & EAST ASIAN HISTORY **EDUCATION** Stanford Univ, AB, 64; Univ Mich, Ann Arbor, MA, 67, PhD(hist), 71. **CAREER** Asst prof, 71-76, Assoc Prof Hist, Univ KS, 76-, Nat Endowment for Humanities fel, 73; Fulbright res fel, Repub China, 77-78. **MEMBERSHIPS** AHA; Asn Asian Studies; Soc Ch'ing Studies; Soc Study Chinese Relig. **RESEARCH** Chinese politics, 1895-1911; early 20th century Sino-foreign relations; Christianity in China, 1860-1915. **SELECTED PUBLICATIONS** Auth, Agrarian reform in Kwangtung, 1950-1953, Mich Papers in Chinese Studies, 69; The nature of provincial political authority in Late Ch'ing times, Mod Asian Studies, 70; The Chinese Government and the revolutionary students in Japan after 1900, J Asian Hist, 73; Missionaries and reform institutions in Modern China, Mod Asian Studies, 75; contribr, Chang Chih-tung after the 100 days, In: Reform in Nineteenth Century China, Harvard Univ, 76; auth, China Enters the Twentieth Century, Univ Mich, 78; Christianity and the Chinese Sectarian Tradition, Ch'ing-shih wen-t'i, 82; Popular Religious Movements in China and US in the 19th Century, Fides et Historia, 82. **CONTACT ADDRESS** Dept of Hist, Univ of Kansas, Lawrence, Lawrence, KS 66045-0001.

BAZILLION, RICHARD J.
PERSONAL Born 02/25/1943, Saint John, NB, Canada, m, 1965, 2 children **DISCIPLINE** MODERN EUROPEAN HISTORY **EDUCATION** Boston Univ, BA, 96; Harvard Univ, MAT, 66, PhD, 70, MALS, 78. **CAREER** Librn, Algoma Univ Col, 80-90; dir libr svc, Brandon Univ, 90-95; prof, dean libr & Infor svc, Winona St Univ, 95- . **HONORS AND AWARDS** Dankstipendium, 68-69. **MEMBERSHIPS** Amer Libr Assoc; Assoc of Col & Res Libr. **RESEARCH** Industrialization in nineteenth century kingdom of Saxony; architecture of acad libr bdlg; German History Society. **SELECTED PUBLICATIONS** Auth, State Bureaucracy and the Modernization Process in the Kingdom of Saxony, 1840-1861, German Hist, UK, 95; Building Virtual and Spatial Libraries for Distance Learning, Cause/Effect, 95; Teaching on the Web and in the Studio Classroom, Syllabus, 98; coauth, Academic Libraries as High-Tech Gateways: A Guide to Design and Space Decisions, Amer Libr Assoc, 2000. **CONTACT ADDRESS** Library, Winona State Univ, PO Box 5838, Winona, MN 55987. **EMAIL** rbazillion@winona.msus.edu

BEALE, DAVID OTIS
PERSONAL Born, VA, m, 3 children **DISCIPLINE** CHURCH HISTORY, THEOLOGY **EDUCATION** Bob Jones Univ, BA, 73, MA, 75, PhD(church hist), 80. **CAREER** Grad asst hist & church hist, 73-78, prof Church Hist, Theology & Bible, Bob Jones Univ, 78-. **HONORS AND AWARDS** Certificate of Award, Society for the Advancement and Preservation of Fundamental Studies of the Christian Faith, 95. **MEMBERSHIPS** Society for the Advancement and Preservation of Fundamental Studies. **RESEARCH** Historical Theology; Church Fathers; Colonial American churches; American Christianity since 1800; Baptist History; continued on-site research in British Isles and Holland tracing roots of Puritans, Pilgrims, Methodists, and Baptists. **SELECTED PUBLICATIONS** Auth, A Pictorial History of Our English Bible, Bob Jones Univ Press, 82; In Pursuit of Purity: American Fundamentalism Since 1950, Bob Jones Univ Press, 86; Ancient Attitudes towards Abortion, 1/82; A Family Travel and Tour Guide: Role of Protestant Churches in Early American History, 7-8/82; Fundamentalism: Past and Present, 10/82; The Purgatory Myth, 1/83; Francis Makemie: Champion of Religious Liberty, 5-6/83; Peter Muhlenberg: from the Pulpit to the Battlefield, 7-8/83; Lessons from the Catacombs, 12/83; The Pilgroms and God's Providence, 11/84; The Log College, 3/85; Faith for Family; The Revelation of Jesus Christ, Rev 19:1-21, Bibl Viewpoint, 11/82; auth, The Mayflower Pilgrims: Roots of Puritan, Presbyterian, Congregationalist, and Baptist Heritage (Belfast, Northern Ireland and Greenville, SC: Ambassador-Emerald International, 00). **CONTACT ADDRESS** Relig Dept, Bob Jones Univ, 1700 Wade Hampton, Greenville, SC 29614-0001. **EMAIL** davidbeale@home.com

BEAME, EDMOND MORTON
PERSONAL Born 05/05/1931, New York, NY, m, 1952, 2 children **DISCIPLINE** RENAISSANCE & REFORMATION HISTORY **EDUCATION** Cornell Univ, BA, 52; Univ Ill, PhD(hist), 57. **CAREER** Lectr hist, Univ Toronto, 58-62; asst prof, 62-66, Assoc Prof Hist, McMaster Univ, 66-. **MEMBERSHIPS** AHA; Renaissance Soc Am; Am Soc Reformation Res. **RESEARCH** Reformation religious thought and political theory; Italian Renaissance theatre. **SELECTED PUBLICATIONS** Auth, The Limits of Toleration in Sixteenth Century France, Studies Renaissance, 67; co-ed, The Comedies of Ariosto, Univ Chicago, 75; The Politiques and the Historians, J of the History of Ideas, Vol 54, 93. **CONTACT ADDRESS** Dept of Hist, McMaster Univ, 1280 Main St W, Hamilton, ON, Canada L8S 4L9.

BEAN, JONATHAN J.
PERSONAL Born 10/02/1962, Burlington, VT, m, 1992, 2 children **DISCIPLINE** HISTORY **EDUCATION** St. Michael's Col, BA; Univ Vermont, 90; Ohio State Univ, PhD, 94. **CAREER** Lecturer, St. Michael's Col, fall 94; vis Asst Prof, Juaniata Col, Spring 95; Asst Prof, Southern Illinois Univ Carbondale, fall 95-Spring 99; Assoc Prof, Southern Illinois Univ Carbondale, fall 99-. **HONORS AND AWARDS** Henry Adams Prize (Best Book), Society for History in the Federal government, 97; Hermann E. Krooss Prize (Best Dissertation), Business History Conference 95; Queen Awd for Excellence in History Teaching, Southern Illinois Univ Carbondale, 98; Visiting Scholar social Philosophy and Policy Ctr, Summer 99; Social Change Research Grant, Institute for Humane Studies, 97-98; Fac Fellowship Grant, Earhart Foundation, 97-98; John E. Rovensky Fel, Univ of Illinois Foundation, 93-94; Misc minor grants. **MEMBERSHIPS** Business History Conference; Economic and Business Historical Society; The Historical Society; Society for History in the Federal government; National Assoc of Scholars. **RESEARCH** U.S. Business-Governement Relations; policy history. **SELECTED PUBLICATIONS** Auth, "Coping with Crisis: Independent Tire Dealers and the Politics of Radical Conservatism, 1942-1946," National Social Science Perspectives Journal 4, no. 3, 94: 16-26; auth, "An Old Story of High Purposes But Inadequate Means: The Small Defense Plants Administration and the Politics of Small Business, 1951-1953," Essays in Economic and Business History 12, 94: 95-105; auth, "Marketing the Great American commodity: Nathaniel Massie and Land Speculation on the Ohio Frontier, 1780-1815," Ohio History 103, Summer-Autumn, 94: 152-69; auth, "World War II and the Crisis of Small Business: The Smaller War Plants Corporation, 1942-1946," Journal of Policy History, vol. 6, no. 3 Summer, 94: 215-43; auth, "Beyond the Broker State: A History of the Federal Government's Policies Toward Small Business, 1936-1961," Business and Economic History 24, no 1, fall 95: 9-12; auth, "Nikolai Bukharin and the New Economic Policy: A Middle Way?" The Independent Review: A Journal of Political Economy 2, no. 1 Summer 97: 79-97; auth, "Statism and Entrepreneurship: Russian Economic History, 1890-1997," Continuity, no. 22 Spring 98: 95-108; auth, "The Conservative View in U.S. History," The Good Society 9, no. 1, 99; auth, "Burn, Baby, Burn: Small Business in the Urban Riots of the 1960s," The Independent Review: A Journal of Political Economy, forthcoming, Fall 2000; auth, "Beyond the Broker State: Federal Policies Toward Small Business, 1936-1961, Univ of North Carolina Press, 96. **CONTACT ADDRESS** Dept History, So Illinois Univ, Carbondale, Southern Illinois Union, Carbondale, IL 62901. **EMAIL** jonbean@siu.edu

BEANBLOSSOM, RONALD EDWIN
PERSONAL Born 11/24/1941, Des Moines, IA, m, 1998, 2 children **DISCIPLINE** HISTORY OF MODERN PHILOSOPHY **EDUCATION** Morningside Col, BA, 64; Union Theol Sem, NYork, BD, 67; Univ Rochester, PhD(philos), 71. **CAREER** Asst prof philos, Northern Ill Univ, 70-77; Univ Chaplain, Ohio Northern Univ, 79-; assoc prof Philos & relig, Ohio Northern Univ, 82-87; chemn dept Philos & relig, 88-91; prof Philos & relig, 87-. **HONORS AND AWARDS** Sara A Ridenour Endowed Chair for Humanities, 89-90. **MEMBERSHIPS** Am Philos Asn. **RESEARCH** British empiricism; theories of perception; problems of knowledge; Quarterly, 88; Natural Reason: Essays in Honor of Joseph Norio Uemura, Hamline, 92; Reid and Hume, On the Nature of Belief, Reid Studies, 98. **SELECTED PUBLICATIONS** Auth, Walton on rational action, Mind, 71; Thomas Reid's Inquiry & Essays, LLA, 75; Russel's indebtedness to Reid, Monist, 78; A new foundation for human scepticism, Philos Studies, 76. **CONTACT ADDRESS** Dept of Philos & Relig, Ohio No Univ, 525 S Main St, Ada, OH 45810-1555.

BEARDSLEY, EDWARD HENRY
PERSONAL Born 05/18/1935, Jacksonville, FL, m, 1960, 3 children **DISCIPLINE** UNITED STATES HISTORY, HISTORY OF SCIENCE & MEDICINE **EDUCATION** Univ Fla, BChE, 53; Univ Wis, MS, 63, PhD(hist), 66. **CAREER** Tech sales, Rohm & Haas Co, 58-60; asst prof Am hist, 66-70, dean freshmen, 73-75, Assoc Prof Am Hist, Univ SC, 70-. **HONORS AND AWARDS** Willia, B Hesseltine Awd, WI Mag Hist, 67; Distinguished Teaching Awd, Univ SC, 70. **MEMBERSHIPS** Orgn Am Historians. **RESEARCH** History of American medicine and public health; history of American science. **SELECTED PUBLICATIONS** Auth, The Rise of the American Chemistry Profession, Univ Fla, 64; An industry revitalized, Wis Mag Hist, 65; Hrry L Russell and Agricultural Science in Wisconsin, Univ Wis, 69; The American scientist as social activist, Isis, 73; Allied against sin: American and British responses to VD, Med Hist, 76; Doctors to the barricades, Bull Hist Med, 77; Secrets between friends, Social Studies Sci, 77; Medical research exchange between Russia and West in WWII, Med Hist, 78; The History of American Sci & Med, Info Sources Hist Sci & Med, 82. **CONTACT ADDRESS** Dept of Hist, Univ of So Carolina, Columbia, Columbia, SC 29208.

BEARDSMORE, BARRY
DISCIPLINE HISTORY OF THE FRENCH LANGUAGE **EDUCATION** Univ Brit Columbia, PhD. **RESEARCH** Old and Middle French romance. **SELECTED PUBLICATIONS** Auth, Ysaie le Triste: a Tale of Two Heroes, Zeitschrift fur romanische Philologie, 89; About the Seventieth of the Cent Nouvelles Nouvelles, Romania 110, 89; Les elements epiques dans le roman, Ysaie le Triste, Memorias de la Real Academia de Buenas Letras de Barcelona, 90. **CONTACT ADDRESS** Dept of French, Univ of Victoria, PO Box 3045 STN CSC, Victoria, BC, Canada V8W 3P4. **EMAIL** bfb@uvvm.uvic.ca

BEARSS, EDWIN COLE
PERSONAL Born 06/26/1923, Billings, MT, m, 1958, 3 children **DISCIPLINE** AMERICAN MILITARY HISTORY **EDUCATION** Georgetown Univ, BS, 49; Ind Univ, MA, 55. **CAREER** Historian, Vicksburg Nat Mil Park, 55-58; regional res historian, 58-66, historian, Div Hist, 66-72, Survry Historian Hist Preserv, East Denver Serv Ctr, Southeast Region, Nat Park Serv, 72-, Mem, Civil War Centennial Comn, 58-60. **HONORS AND AWARDS** Super Performance Awds, Nat Park Serv, 58, 66 & 67; Harry S Truman Awd, Kansas City Civil War Round Table, 61. **MEMBERSHIPS** Fel Col Mil Hist. **RESEARCH** American Civil War; American revolution; recent presidents, especially Hoover, Eisenhower and Johnson. **SELECTED PUBLICATIONS** Coauth, Fort Smith: Little Gibraltar on the Arkansas, Univ OK, 69; ed, A Southern Record, 70 & Memoirs of the First Missouri Confederate Brigade: Anderson, 72, Morningside; A Louisiana Confederate: Diary of Felix Pierre Poche, LA State Univ, 72; auth, General John Hunt Morgan's second Kentucky raid, Register, 4/73; contribr, A History of Mississippi, Univ & Col MS, 73; auth, The Battle of Brice's Crossroads, Morningside, 79; coauth (with A M Gibson), Fort Smith: Little Gibraltar on the Arkansas, 79; The Civil War in the American West, with A. M. Josephy, Pacific Hist Rev, Vol 62, 93; Pea Ridge-Civil War Campaign in the West, with W. L. Shea and E. J. Hess, J of Am Hist, Vol 81, 94; auth, Vicksburg Campaign, Vol I, Vicksburg is the Key, Morningside, 91; auth, Vicksburg Campaign, Vol II, Grant Strikes the Fatal Blow, Morningside, 91; auth, Vicksburg Campaign, Vol III, Unvexed to the Sea, Morningside, 91; auth, River of Lost Opportunities, 95. **CONTACT ADDRESS** 1126 17th St S, Arlington, VA 22202.

BEATTY, EDWARD N.
PERSONAL Born 12/14/1960, Philadelphia, PA **DISCIPLINE** HISTORY **EDUCATION** Univ New Mex, MA, 92; Stan Univ, PhD, 96. **CAREER** Asst prof, Duqu Univ, 97-. **RESEARCH** Mexico; Latin America; economic history. **SELECTED PUBLICATIONS** Auth, "Invencion e innovacion: ley de patentes y tecnologia en el Mexico del siglo xix," Hist Mex 45 (96): 567-619; auth, "The Political Basis of Industrialization in Mexico Before 1911," J Econ Hist 58 (98): 525-528; auth, "Commercial Policy in Porfirian Mexico: The Structure of Protection," in Institutional Change and Economic Performance in Mexico, eds. Stephen Haber, Jeffery Bortz (Stan Univ Press, 00); auth, "The Impact of Foreign Trade on the Mexican Economy: Terms of Trade and the Rise of Industry, 1880-1923," J Latin Am Stud 32 (00); Auth, Institutions and Investment: The Political Basis of Industrialization in Mexico before 1911, Stan Univ Press, forthcoming. **CONTACT ADDRESS** Dept History, Duquesne Univ, 600 Forbes Ave, Pittsburgh, PA 15282-0001.

BEAUDOIN-ROSS, JACQUELINE
PERSONAL Born 08/15/1931, Montreal, PQ, Canada **DISCIPLINE** HISTORY **EDUCATION** McGill Univ, BA, 52, MA, 75. **CAREER** Curator, Costume & Textiles, McCord Museum Canadian History, 79-; lectr, Concordia Univ, 80-81; lectr, McGill Univ, 86. **SELECTED PUBLICATIONS** Coauth, Costume in Canada: An Annotated Bibliography, 84; coauth, Costume in Canada: The Sequel, 91; coauth, Form and Fashion: Nineteenth Century Montreal Dress, 92; coauth, Daring Deco-Styles and Lifestyles, 95; contribur, The Canadian Encyclopedia, 85; contribur, Encyclopedia of the North American Colonies, 93. **CONTACT ADDRESS** McCord Mus, 690 Sherbrooke St W, Montreal, QC, Canada H3A 1E9.

BEAUDRY, MARY CAROLYN
PERSONAL Born 11/25/1950, Great Lakes, IL **DISCIPLINE** HISTORICAL ARCHAEOLOGY, ANTHROPOLOGY, MATERIAL CULTURE STUDIES **EDUCATION** Col William & Mary, BA, 73; Brown Univ, MA, 75; PhD, 80. **CAREER** Assoc Prof Archaeol, Boston Univ, 90-; Dir, Spencer-Peirce Little Archaeol Proj, Newbury, MA, 86. **HONORS AND AWARDS** Recipient of three grants for the Nat Endowment for the Humanities; NEH fel for Advanced Study at Winterthur Mus and Libr, 94-95. **MEMBERSHIPS** Council for Northeast Hist Archaeol; Soc Hist Archaeol (pres, 89); Soc Indus Archaeol; Soc Post-Medieval Archaeol; Registry of Prof Archaeol; World Archaeol Congress. **RESEARCH** Historical archaeol of landscapes and households; comparative colonialism; culture contact; minorities and women; ceramic analysis and typologies; foodways; method and theory; public outreach. **SELECTED PUBLICATIONS** Coauth, Living on the Boott: Historical Archaeology at the Boott Mills Boardinghouses, Lowell, Massachusetts, Univ MA Press, 86; ed, Documentary Archaeology in the New World, Cambridge Univ Press, 88; coed, The Art and Mystery of Historical Archaeology, CRC Press, 92. **CONTACT ADDRESS** Dept of Archaeol, Boston Univ, Boston, MA 02215. **EMAIL** beaudry@bu.edu

BEAUMONT, DANIEL E.
PERSONAL Born Seattle, WA **DISCIPLINE** NEAR EASTERN STUDIES **EDUCATION** Univ Wash, BA, 75, MA, 86; Princeton Univ, PhD, 91 **CAREER** Tchg asst, 88-89; lectr, 91-92, Princeton Univ; Asst Prof to Assoc Prof of Arabic, Univ of Rochester, 92-. **HONORS AND AWARDS** Fulbright grant, 89; Princeton fel, 90; and numerous fellowships and grants. **MEMBERSHIPS** MESA. **RESEARCH** Literature; Narrative; Psychoanalysis. **SELECTED PUBLICATIONS** Auth, A Mighty and Never Ending Affair, Jour Arabic Lit, 93; The Trickster and Rhetoric in the Maqamat, Edebiyat, 94; Parody and Lying in Medieval Islam: Jahiz's Book of Misers, Studia Islamica, 94; Hard-boiled: Narrative Discourse in Early Muslim Traditions, Studia Islamica, 96; The Modality of Narrative, Jour Am Acad Relig, 97; In the Second Degree: Fictional Technique in Tanukhi's Al-Faraj ba'd ash-shidda, Jour Arabic & Mid E Lit, 98; King, Queen, Master, Slave: The Master/Slave Dialectic and The One Thousand and One Nights, Neophilologus, 98; Peut-on tuer avec des noyaux de dattes?: Intertextuality and Dream-work in The Thousand and One Nights and Genesis, Comp Lit, 98. **CONTACT ADDRESS** Dept Relig & Classics, Univ of Rochester, Rochester, NY 14627. **EMAIL** dano@troi.cc.rochester.edu

BEAUMONT, ROGER A.
PERSONAL Born 10/02/1935, Milwaukee, WI, m, 1974, 2 children **DISCIPLINE** HISTORY **EDUCATION** Univ Wis, BS, 57, MS, 60; KS State Univ, PhD(hist), 73. **CAREER** Asst to dir, Ctr Advan Study Orgn Sci, Univ WI-Milwaukee, 65-67; instr hist, Univ WI-Oshkosh, 68-69; from asst prof to assoc prof, Ctr Advan Study Orgn Sci, Univ WI-Milwaukee, 70-74; assoc prof, 74-79, prof hist, Tex A&M Univ, 79-. **MEMBERSHIPS** Am Mil Inst; Inter-Univ Sem Armed Forces & Soc; US Naval Inst; Science Fiction & Fantasy Writers of Am. **RESEARCH** Modern military history. **SELECTED PUBLICATIONS** Auth, Military Elites, Bobbs-Merrill, 74; co-ed, War in the Next Decade, Univ Ky & Macmillan, UK, 74; auth, Sword of the Raj, Bobbs-Merrill, 77; Nerves of War, AFCEA Press, 86; Elite Forces and Special Operations, Greenwood, 88; Joint Military Operations, Greenwood, 94; War Chaos and History, Praeger, 95; four res monographs, 85 book chapters and articles. **CONTACT ADDRESS** Dept Hist, Texas A&M Univ, Col Station, College Station, TX 77843. **EMAIL** rabeaum@acs.tamu.edu

BEAVER, DANIEL R.
PERSONAL Born 09/23/1928, Hamilton, OH, m, 1972, 3 children **DISCIPLINE** AMERICAN HISTORY **EDUCATION** Heidelberg Col, AB, 51; Univ Cincinnati, MA, 54; Northwestern Univ, PhD, 62. **CAREER** From instr to assoc prof, 58-70, prof Hist, Univ Cinncinati, 70-, Mershon fel, 64-65; lect, 71-73, Harold K Johnson prof, US Army Mil Hist Inst, US Army War Col, 83-84; Distinguished Vis Scholar, US Army Ctr Mil Hist, 85-87. **MEMBERSHIPS** AHA; Orgn Am Hist; Asn Mil Hist. **RESEARCH** Diplomatic and military history. **SELECTED PUBLICATIONS** Auth, Newton D Baker and the American War Effort 1917-1919, Univ Nebr, 66; Some Pathways in Modern History, Wayne State Univ, 68; War and Society in the Seventeenth Century, Some Dimensions of Military History, US Army War Col, 72; The Problem of Military Supply, War Business and American Society, Kennikat, 77; Ideas and Policy: The War Department Wheeled Vehicle Program 1920-1940, Mil Aff Fall 83; Logistics in John E Vessup (ed) Encycl of the Am Mil, Scribner's, 94. **CONTACT ADDRESS** Dept Hist, Univ of Cincinnati, PO Box 210373, Cincinnati, OH 45221-0373. **EMAIL** beaverd8@email.uc.edu

BEAVER, DONALD DE BLASIIS
PERSONAL Born 07/16/1936, New York, NY, m, 1962, 2 children **DISCIPLINE** HISTORY OF SCIENCE **EDUCATION** Harvard Col, AB, 58; Yale Univ, PhD(hist of sci), 66. **CAREER** Asst prof hist of sci & phys sci, Univ Mo, Kansas City, 66-70,; asst prof hist of sci, Franklin & Marshall Col, 70-71; assoc prof, 71-84, Prof Hist of Sci, Williams Col, 85-, Univ Mo, Kansas City fac res grant, 67-68 & asst prof res grant, 68; vis fel hist sci, Yale Univ, 77-78; visiting fel, STS, MIT 84-85. **MEMBERSHIPS** AAAS; Hist Sci Soc; Midwest Junto Hist Sci; Soc Social Study Sci **RESEARCH** History of science in America; social history of science; Sarah Bowdich Lee (1791-1856). **SELECTED PUBLICATIONS** Coauth, Collaboration in an invisible college, Am Psychologist, 11/66; auth, Altruism, patriotism, and science: Scientific journals in the early republic, Am Studies, spring 71; The Smithsonian origin of the Royal Society Catalogue of Scientific Papers, Sci Studies, 72; Reflections on the natural history of eponymy and scientific law, Social Studies Sci, No 6, 2/76; Studies in Scientific Collaboration: Vol I, The Professional Origins of Scientific Co-Authorship, Vol II, Scientific Co-Authorship, Research Productivity and Visibility in the French Elite, 1799-1830, Vol III, Professionalization and the Natural History of Modern Scientific Co-Authorship, Scientometrics 1, 78-79; auth, "Marketin gthe Monster: Advertising Computer Technology," with William Aspray, Annals of the Hsitory of Computing 8:2, (86): 127-143; auth, "Textbooks of Natural Philosophy: The Beatification of Technology," in From Ancient Omens to Statistical Mechanics, Acta Historica Scientiarum Naturalium et Medicinalium, 39, (87): 203-213; auth, Science at Wililams: The First Two Hundred Yeard, A Bicentennial Overview, ed. With Aaron D. Jorgenson and Alexia L. Rosoff, Williams Col, Williamstown, Mass., 96; auth, "Writing natural history for survival, 1820-1856: the case of Sarah Bowdich, later Sarah Lee," Archives of Natural History, 26:1, (99): 19-31. **CONTACT ADDRESS** Dept of the Hist of Sci, Williams Col, 117 Bronfman Science Center, 18 Hoxsey St, Williamstown, MA 01267-2600. **EMAIL** dbeaver@williams.edu

BECK, GUY
PERSONAL Born 08/03/1948, New York, NY, m, 1979 **DISCIPLINE** HISTORY OF RELIGION **EDUCATION** Syracuse Univ, PhD, MA; Univ FL, MA. **CAREER** Asst Prof, 95-97, Loyola Univ; Act Asst Prof, 90-95, LSU; Vis Asst Prof, 97-99, College of Charleston; ; **HONORS AND AWARDS** Fulbright Schshp; AIIS SR Res Fel. **MEMBERSHIPS** AAR; SE. **RESEARCH** Sacred sound, Hindu Music; Phenomenology of Ethno musicology. **SELECTED PUBLICATIONS** Auth, Seven entries for Encarta Encyclopedia on CD-ROM by Microsoft Inc, including, Om, Bhagavata Purana, Sutra, Mudra, Prayer Wheel, Satori, Ahura Mazda; auth, Religious Music of Northern Areas, in: Garland Encyc of World Music: South Asia Volume, Alison Arnold, ed; Bhajan/Devotional Music, Music Festivals and Music Academies, for the Encyc of Hinduism; auth, Devotional Hymns from Sanskrit, in: Religions In India, DS Lopez Jr ed, Princeton Univ Press, 95; Fire in the Atman: Repentance in Hinduism, in: Repentance: A Comparative Perspective, Amitai Etzioni, David Carney, ed, Lanham MD, Rowman and Littlefield, 97. **CONTACT ADDRESS** Liberal Arts & Sciences, Tulane Univ, 200 Gibson Hall, New Orleans, LA 70118. **EMAIL** beckg@tulane.edu

BECK, HERMAN
PERSONAL Born 01/30/1955, Mannheim, Germany, s **DISCIPLINE** HISTORY **EDUCATION** Univ Freiburg, MA, 81; Univ Calif, PhD, 89. **CAREER** Vis Asst Prof, Bowdoin Col, 89-90; From Asst Prof to Assoc Prof, Univ Miami, 96-. **HONORS AND AWARDS** Fel, Berlin Hist Kommission, 93; Fel, Princeton Univ, 97-98; Excellence in Teach Awd, Univ Miami, 96. **MEMBERSHIPS** AHA, Ger Studies Asn, HS, GHS, London Sch of Econ Soc. **RESEARCH** Modern German history, 19th-Century Prussian history, the Weimar Republic and Nazi Germany. **SELECTED PUBLICATIONS** Auth, "The Social Policies of Prussian Officials: The Bureaucracy in a New Light," in J of Mod Hist 64 (92), 263-298; auth, "The Origins of the Authoritarian Welfare State in Prussia: Conservatives, Bureaucracy and the Social Question 1815-1870," Univ Mich Pr (Ann Arbor, MI), 95. **CONTACT ADDRESS** Dept Hist, Univ of Miami, PO Box 248107, Miami, FL 33124-8107. **EMAIL** hbeck@miami.edu

BECK, JAMES HENRY
PERSONAL Born 05/14/1930, New York, NY, m, 1956, 1 child **DISCIPLINE** HISTORY OF ART **EDUCATION** Oberlin Col, BA, 52; NYork Univ, MA, 54; Columbia Univ, PhD (art hist), 63. **CAREER** Asst prof art hist, Univ AL, Tuscaloosa, 58-59 & AZ State Univ, 59-60; from instr to assoc prof, 61-71, Prof Art Hist, Columbia Univ, 71-, Fels, Instr Advan Studies, 67, Villa I Tatti, Harvard Univ, 67-68 & 72, Guggenheim Found, 73-74 & Nat Endowment for Hum, 81-82. **MEMBERSHIPS** Col Art Asn; Medieval Soc Am; Renaissance Soc Am. **RESEARCH** Italian art of the 14th, 15th and 16th centuries. **SELECTED PUBLICATIONS** Auth, Mariano di Jacopo detto il Taccola, Il Polifilo, Milan, 69; Jacopo della Quercia e suo portale a Bologna, Edizioni Alfa, Bologna, 70; Michelangelo: A Lesson in Anatomy, Viking, 75; Raphael Library of Great Painters, Abrams, 76; Masaccio: The Documents, Villa I Tatti, 78; Leonardo's Rules of Painting, Viking Press, 79; Italian Renaissance Painting, Harper, 81. **CONTACT ADDRESS** Dept of Art History, Columbia Univ, 2960 Broadway, New York, NY 10027-6900. **EMAIL** JHB3@Columbia.edu

BECKER, LLOYD GEORGE
PERSONAL Born 12/07/1942, Brooklyn, NY, m, 1995, 2 children **DISCIPLINE** AMERICAN LITERATURE & STUDIES **EDUCATION** Col William & Mary, AB, 64; State Univ NYork Buffalo, MA, 68, PhD, 80. **CAREER** Instr, 67-69, asst prof, 69-73, assoc prof, 73-78, prof eng, Suffolk County Community Col, 78. **HONORS AND AWARDS** NEH Summer Res Grant, 92. **MEMBERSHIPS** Am Lit Asn; Asn Lit Scholars & Critics; Western Lit Asn; Ralph Waldo Emerson Soc; Melville Soc; Mark Twain Circle; Jack London Soc. **RESEARCH** 19th Century Lit & Painting; Western Am Lit, esp. contemp fiction; Mythology. **SELECTED PUBLICATIONS** Auth, William Sidney Mount's Transparent Summer Morning, In: Paumanok Rising, Street Press, 80; Scenes of the Familiar, Emblems of the Eternal: Cultural Contexts of Shepherd Alonzo Mount, The Long Island Hist Jour, fall 90; Ken Nunn's Pomsra Queen, Western Am Lit, Aug. 94. **CONTACT ADDRESS** 533 College Rd, Selden, NY 11784. **EMAIL** beckerl@sunysuffolk.edu

BECKER, MARJORIE R.
PERSONAL Born 11/19/1952, Macon, GA, d **DISCIPLINE** LATIN AMERICAN HISTORY **EDUCATION** Duke, BA, 74, MA, 80; Yale Univ, MA, 82, MPhil, 83, PhD, 88. **CAREER** Prof, Univ Southern Calif, 87-. **HONORS AND AWARDS** Ahmanson Awd, Hewlitt Foundation Awd, Ph Kappi Phi recognition, Setting the Virgin on Fire, vis res fel, ct for U S Mexican Studies, Fac Fulbright res fel, Am Coun of Learned Societies grant-in-aid, Nat Endowment for the Humanities summer stipend, Charlotte NewCombe Doctorial Dissertation Fel, Inter-Am Found fel, Doherty fel, Tinker Found res grant, NDFL fel, Am Assoc of Univ Women fel, Yale Univ fel, Yale Hist Dept res fel. **RESEARCH** Cultural invention, race; gender; ethnicity,;class; spiritual life; socialism; liberalism; national states. **SELECTED PUBLICATIONS** Auth, Setting the Virgin on Fire: Lazaro Cardenas, Michoacan Peasants, and the Redemption of the Mexican Revolution, Berkeley, 95, rep, 96; Torching La Purisima, Dancing at the Altar: The Construction of Hegemony in Revolutionary Michoacan, 1934-1940, in Joseph &Nugent, Everyday Forms of State Formation: Revolution & the Negotiation of Rule in Modern Mexico, Duke, 94; Cardenistas, Campesinos and The Weapons of the Weak: The Limits of Everyday Resistance in Michoacan, Mexico, 1934-1940, in Peasant Stud 16, 89; Black & White and Color: Cardenismo & the Search for a Campesino Ideology, in comp Stud Soc and Hist 29, 87; Lazaro Cardenas & the Mexican Counter-Revolution: The Struggle over Culture in Michoacan, 1934-1940; auth, " When I was a Child, I Danced as a Child, But Not that I am Old , I Think about Salvation: Concepcion Gonzalez an a past that would not stay put," Rethinking History 1:3, 97. **CONTACT ADDRESS** Dept of History, Univ of So California, University Park Campus, Los Angeles, CA 90089. **EMAIL** mbecker@rcf.usc.edu

BECKER, MARVIN BURTON
PERSONAL Born 07/20/1922, Philadelphia, PA, m, 1944, 2 children **DISCIPLINE** MEDIEVAL & RENAISSANCE HISTORY **EDUCATION** Univ PA, BS, 46, Am, 47, PhD, 50. **CAREER** Teacher hist, Lincoln Prep Sch, 45-50; asst prof medieval hist, Univ AR, 50-52; asst prof hist, Baldwin-Wallace Col, 52-57; assoc prof hist, Western Reserve Univ, 57-63; prof, Univ Rochester, 63-73; chemn dept, 77-79, prof hist, Univ Mich, Ann Arbor, 73-; asst, Univ PA, 47-48; Fulbright res fel, Italy, 53-55 & Guggenheim mem fel, 56-57; Am Philos Soc fels, 61-62; Am Coun Learned Soc fel, Harvard Ctr Renaissance Studies, Florence, Italy, 63-64; prof, Johns Hopkins Univ, 66-67, sr fel, Inst Humanities, 66-67; fel, Inst Advan Studies, Princeton Univ, 68-69; vis prof hist, Univ Toronto, 71; vis prof hist, Univ AZ, 80. **HONORS AND AWARDS** Deputazione de Storia Patria per la Toscana. **MEMBERSHIPS** AHA; Mediaeval Acad Am; Renaissance Soc Am. **RESEARCH** Social, economic, cultural hist Italy. **SELECTED PUBLICATIONS** Auth, Church and State in Florence on the Eve of the Renaissance, Mediaeval Acad; Florence in Transition, Johns Hopkins Univ, Vol I, 67, Vol II, 68; An Essay on the Novi Cives and Florentine Politics, Mediaeval Studies, 62; Florentine Popular Government, 1343-48, Proc Am Philos Soc, 62; Medieval Italy, IN Univ, 81; Civility and Society in Western Europe, 1300-1600, IN Univ, 88; The Emergence of Civil Society in the 18th Century, IN Univ, 94. **CONTACT ADDRESS** Dept Hist, Univ of Michigan, Ann Arbor, 435 S State St, Ann Arbor, MI 48109-1003.

BECKER, PETER WOLFGANG
PERSONAL Born 09/06/1929, Munich, Germany **DISCIPLINE** MODERN EUROPEAN HISTORY **EDUCATION** N Tex State Univ, BA, 60; Stanford Univ, MA, 61, PhD(hist), 71. **CAREER** Instr hist, San Jose State Col, 65-66; from instr to asst prof, 66-76, asst chmn, 76-78, Assoc Prof Hist, Univ SC, 76-, Asst Chmn, 82-. **MEMBERSHIPS** AHA; Southern Hist Asn. **RESEARCH** Modern German history. **SELECTED PUBLICATIONS** Transl, Franzen, History of the Church, Herder, 69; History of the Church, Vol V: Reformation and Counter Reformation, 80, History of the Church, Vol VII: Church Between Revolution and Restoration, 81 & History of the Church, Vol VIII: Church in the Age of Liberalism, 81, Seabury; The Politics of Progressive Education-The Odenwaldschule in Nazi Germany, with D. Shirley, J of Interdiciplinary Hist, Vol, 25, 95. **CONTACT ADDRESS** Dept of Hist, Univ of So Carolina, Columbia, Columbia, SC 29208.

BECKER, ROBERT ARTHUR
PERSONAL Born 06/09/1943, Brooklyn, NY, 3 children **DISCIPLINE** AMERICAN HISTORY **EDUCATION** St Lawrence Univ, BA, 65; Univ Wis-Madison, MA, 67, PhD, 71. **CAREER** Vis lectr Am Hist, Univ Ill, Urbana-Champaign, 70-71; asst prof, 71-80, assoc prof Am Hist, LA State Univ, Baton Rouge, 80-. **HONORS AND AWARDS** Phi Beta Kappa. **MEMBERSHIPS** Orgn Am Historians. **RESEARCH** American revolution, 1763-1789; American Colonial South. **SELECTED PUBLICATIONS** Asst ed, Documentary History of the First Federal Elections, I Univ Wis, 74; auth, Revolution and reform: an interpretation of Southern taxation, 1763-1783, William & Mary Quart, 7/75; Salvs populi suprema lex: Public order and South Carolinas' debtor laws, 1783-1787, SC Hist Mag, 1/79; Revolution, Reform and the Politics of American Taxation, 1763-1783, La State Univ Press, 80. **CONTACT ADDRESS** Dept of History, Louisiana State Univ and A&M Col, Baton Rouge, LA 70803-0001. **EMAIL** rbecke2@isu.edu

BECKER, SEYMOUR
PERSONAL Born 09/15/1934, Rochester, NY, m, 1981, 2 children **DISCIPLINE** MODERN HISTORY **EDUCATION** Williams Col, AB, 56; Harvard Univ, AM, 58, PhD(Russ Hist), 63. **CAREER** From instr to assoc prof, 62-86, prof Hist, Rutgers Univ, 86-, exchange scholar, Moscow State Univ, 67-68; Russian Academy of Sciences, 84, 88. **MEMBERSHIPS** AHA; Am Asn Advan Slavic Studies; Assn for Study of Nationalities. **RESEARCH** Social and political hist of Russia, 1861-1917; Russian imperial policy, 1861-1917. **SELECTED PUBLICATIONS** Auth, Russia's Protectorates in Central Asia: Bukhara and Khiva, 1865-1924, Harvard Univ, 68; contribr, The Nationality Question in Soviet Central Asia, Praeger, 73; auth, Nobility nd Privilege in Late Imperial Russia, Northern Illinois Univ, 85; contrib, Russian colonial Expansion to 1917, Mansell Publ. Ltd, 88; Central Asia: Its Strategic Importance and Future Prospects, St Martin's, 94. **CONTACT ADDRESS** Dept of History, Rutgers, The State Univ of New Jersey, New Brunswick, 16 Seminary Place, New Brunswick, NJ 08901-1108. **EMAIL** sbecker@nyc.rr.com

BECKER, SUSAN D.
PERSONAL Born 04/30/1938, Cleveland, OH, d **DISCIPLINE** HISTORY **EDUCATION** Case Western Reserve, PhD. **CAREER** Assoc prof to prof emer, Univ Tenn. **HONORS AND AWARDS** Phi Alpha Thetz, Phi Beta Kappa. **MEMBERSHIPS** OAH, AHA. **RESEARCH** Am women, historography, methodology. **SELECTED PUBLICATIONS** Auth, The Origins of the Equal Rights Amendment: American Feminism Between the Wars, Greenwood; coauth, Discovering the American Past: A Look at the Evidence, Houghton Mifflin. **CONTACT ADDRESS** Dept of History, Univ of Tennessee, Knoxville, 915 Volunteer Blvd, 6th Fl, Dunford Hall, Knoxville, TN 37996-4065. **EMAIL** sbecker1@utk.edu

BECKER, WILLIAM HENRY
PERSONAL Born 03/28/1943, New York, NY, m, 1965, 2 children **DISCIPLINE** AMERICAN BUSINESS & ECONOMIC HISTORY **EDUCATION** Muhlenberg Col, BA, 64; Johns Hopkins Univ, PhD, 69. **CAREER** Asst prof, Univ MD Baltimore County, 69-73, assoc prof, 73-80; vis assoc prof, 80-82, assoc prof, 82-83, prof hist, George Washington Univ, 83-; Vis Prof Hist, Johns Hopkins Univ, 96 & Nat Univ Singapore, 98. **HONORS AND AWARDS** Newcomen Awd, Outstanding Bk Bus Hist, 79-82. **MEMBERSHIPS** AHA; Orgn Am Historians; Econ Hist Asn; Econ Hist Asn; Bus Hist Conf. **RESEARCH** Hist of business; comp business hist; business-government rel. **SELECTED PUBLICATIONS** Auth, The Dynamics of Business-Government Relations: Industry and Exports, 1893-1921, Univ Chicago Press, 82; co-ed (with Samuel F Wells), Economics and Diplomacy: An Assessment of American Diplomacy Since 1789, Columbia Univ Press, 84; gen ed, The Encyclopedia of American Business History & Biography, 9 vol, Broccoli Clark Layman, 86-92. **CONTACT ADDRESS** Dept of Hist, The George Washington Univ, 2035 H St N W, Washington, DC 20052. **EMAIL** whbecker@gwu.edu

BECKHAM, STEPHEN DOW
PERSONAL Born 08/31/1941, Coos Bay, OR, m, 1967, 2 children **DISCIPLINE** AMERICAN WEST, NATIVE AMERICANS, UNTED STATES HISTORY **EDUCATION** Univ Ore, BA, 64; Univ Calif, Los Angeles, MA, 66, PhD(hist), 69. **CAREER** Lectr hist, Long Beach State Univ, 68-69; assoc prof, Linfield Col, 69-76; assoc prof, 77-81, prof hist, Lewis & Clark Col, 81-92, Pamplin Prof Hist, Lewis & Clark Col, 92-; Nat Endowment for Humanities res grant to write & narrate six TV progs for CBS & Ore Educ Broadcasting, 71-72; consult, US Forest Serv, US Bur Land Mgt, US Army Corps Engineers, US Coast Guard, Ore Dept Transp, Ore State Parks; expert witness, US Dept of Justice, Ore Dept of Justice, Karuk Tribe of Calif, Cow Creek Band of Umpqua Tribe of Indians, Chinook Indian Tribe, Cowlitz Indian Tribe; adv Comt Hist Preserv, State of Ore, 77-85; bd adv, Nat Trust Hist Preserv, Washington, DC, 77-85, bd, John & LaRee Caughey Found, 79-, bd, Ore Hist Soc, 94-. **HONORS AND AWARDS** Asher Distinguished Teaching Awd, Am Hist Asn, 95; Ore Prof of the Year, Counc Advance and Support of Higher Educ, 92-93; Sears-Roebuck Found Teaching Excellence and Campus Leadership Awd, Lewis & Clark Col, 90. **MEMBERSHIPS** AHA; Western Hist Asn **RESEARCH** Indian-white relations; history of Pacific Northwest and Calif **SELECTED PUBLICATIONS** Auth, Requiem for a People: The Rogue Indians and the Frontiersmen, Univ Okla, 71, Ore State Univ Press, 91; The Simpsons of Shore Acres, Arago, 71; Coos Bay: The Pioneer Period, 1851-1890, Arago, 73; The Indians of Western Oregon: This Land Was Theirs, Arago, 77; You May Have Someting There: Identifying Historical Cultural Resources in the Pacific Northwest, USDA Forest Service, 78; Land of the Umpqua: A History of Douglas County, Oregon, Doug Co Comnr, 87; Lewis & Clark College, Trustees of Lewis & Clark Col, 91; Many Faces: An Anthology of Ore Autobiography, Ore State Univ Press, 93; Seventy-Five Years at Building: Hoffman Construction Company, Hoffman Corp, 95; Hist of Western Ore Since 1846, vol 7, Northwest Coast, Handbook of North Am Indians, Smithsonian Inst, 90; History Since 1846, vol 12, Plateau, Handbookd of North Am Indians, Smithsonian Inst, 98. **CONTACT ADDRESS** Dept of Hist, Lewis and Clark Col, 0615 SW Palatine Hill Rd, Portland, OR 97219-7879. **EMAIL** beckham@lclark.edu

BECKLEY, WILLIAM
PERSONAL Born 02/11/1946, Hamburg, PA, m, 1987, 2 children **DISCIPLINE** FINE ART **EDUCATION** Kutztown State Univ, BFA, 68; Tyler Sch Art, MFA, 70. **CAREER** Instructor, Sch of Visual Arts, 70-. **HONORS AND AWARDS** Pollock-Krasner Grant, 97; NY Coun of the Arts, 86, 76, 73; NEH, 79. **SELECTED PUBLICATIONS** Auth, "Romanticism: An Outline (I'm Sitting by the Sea)," Flash Art, (79): 26-27; Co-ed, Uncontrollable Beauty, Toward a New Aesthetics,98; auth, "Introduction," in The End of the Art World, 98; auth, "Introduction," in Sculpture in the Age of Doubt, 99; auth, "Introduction," in Beauty and the Contemporary Sublime, 99; **CONTACT ADDRESS** Dept Humanities & Sci, Sch of Visual Arts, New York, 209 E 23rd St, New York, NY 10010-3901.

BECKMAN, GARY M.
PERSONAL Born 08/22/1948, Pittsburgh, PA, m, 1985 **DISCIPLINE** HISTORY **EDUCATION** Pomona Col, BA, 70; Yale Univ, PhD, 77. **CAREER** Asst Prof, Yale Univ, 78-88; assoc prof, Yale Babylonian, 88-92; vis assoc prof to prof, Univ Mich, 92-. **HONORS AND AWARDS** Deutsche Akademische Austauschdrenst Stipendiat, 75-77; Fel Univ Penn, 97-98. **MEMBERSHIPS** Am Oriental Soc, Am Schools of Oriental Res. **RESEARCH** History and Culture of Mesopotamia and Anatlia in the Second Millennium, History of Assyriology **SELECTED PUBLICATIONS** Auth, Hittite Birth Rituals, 83; auth, Hittite Diplomatic Texts, 96; ed, Catalogue of the Babylonian Collections at Yale,Vol 2, 95; ed, Catalogue of the Babylonian Collections at Yale, Vol 4, 00. **CONTACT ADDRESS** Univ of Michigan, Ann Arbor, 105 South State St, Ann Arbor, MI 48109-1285. **EMAIL** sidd@umich.edu

BECKWITH, JOHN
PERSONAL Born 03/09/1927, Victoria, BC, Canada **DISCIPLINE** HISTORY OF MUSIC **EDUCATION** Victoria Col, 44-45; Royal Conserv Music, 45-50; Univ Toronto, MusB, 47, MusM, 61. **CAREER** Lectr, 55-61, asst prof 61-66, assoc prof, 66-70, dean, 70-77, Prof Music, Univ Toronto (RETIRED), 70-90; dir, Inst Can Music, 84-90; assoc ed, Can Music J, 57-62. **HONORS AND AWARDS** Can Music Coun Annual medal, 72; MusD (honoris causa), Mt Allison Univ, 74; Univ Toronto Sesquicentennial Awd, 77; MusD (honoris causa), McGill Univ, 78; Can Music Coun Composer Year, 85; mem, Order Can, 87; Richard S. Hill Awd, US Music Libr Asn, 90; Toronto Arts Awd, 94; Mus D (honoris causa), Univ Guelph, 95; diplome d'honneur, Can Conf Arts, 96. **MEMBERSHIPS** Can Musical Heritage Soc; Toronto Musicians Asn; Can League Composers; Sonneck Soc Am Music. **SELECTED PUBLICATIONS** Auth, Music Papers, 97; ed, Canadian Composers study ser, 75-90; ed, The Canadian Musical Heritage, vol 5, Hymn Tunes, 86, vol 18, Oratoria and Cantata Excerpts, 95; co-ed, The Modern Composer and His World, 61; co-ed, Contemporary Canadian Composers, 75; co-ed, Musical Canada, 88; contribur, Dictionary of Contemporary Music, 74; Can consult & contribur, The New Grove, 80; contribur & exec bd mem, Encyclopedia of Music in Canada, 81, 93. **CONTACT ADDRESS** Fac of Music, Univ of Toronto, Toronto, ON, Canada M5S 1A1.

BEDESKI, ROBERT E.
PERSONAL Born 11/03/1937, Detroit, MI **DISCIPLINE** POLITICAL SCIENCE, ASIAN STUDIES, HISTORY **EDUCATION** Univ Calif Berkeley, BA, 64, MA, 65, PhD, 69. **CAREER** Asst prof, Ohio State Univ, 69-73; asst prof, 73-75, assoc prof, Carleton Univ, 75-89; prof Political Science, Univ Victoria, 89-; vis prof, Meiji Univ (Tokyo), 93-94. **HONORS AND AWARDS** Nat Defense Foreign Lang fel in Japanese, 65-67; sr res fel, Ctr Chinese Stud, Univ Calif Berkeley, 67-69; Social Sci Res Coun grant contemporary China, 71-72; SSHRC leave grant, 80-81; Japan Found res fel, 80-81; Pacific Cultur Found grant 82-83; Bilateral Exchange Grant SSHRC & Chinese Acad Soc Sci, 83-84, 86; res fel, Kyungnam Univ Inst Far Eastern Stud (Korea), 88; res fel, Int Cultur Soc Korea, 90; Japan Found fel, 93-94. **MEMBERSHIPS** Can Soc Chinese Stud (bd dir); Can Polit Sci Asn; Can Asian Stud Asn; Int Polit Sci Asn; Can Inst Strategic Stud; Japanese Stud Asn Can (pres 95-96). **SELECTED PUBLICATIONS** Auth, State-Building in Modern China: The Kuomintang in the Prewar Period, 81; auth, The Fragile Entente: the 1978 Japan-China Peace Treaty in a Global Context, 83; auth, The Transformation of South Korea: Reform and Reconstitution in the Sixth Republic Under Roh Tae Woo 1987-93, 94; ed, Confidence Building in the North Pacific: New Approaches to the Korean Peninsula, 96. **CONTACT ADDRESS** Dept of Political Science, Univ of Victoria, Victoria, BC, Canada V8W 3P5. **EMAIL** rbedeski@uvic.ca

BEDFORD, DAVID
PERSONAL Born 07/24/1949, Fort Worth, TX, m, 1977, 3 children **DISCIPLINE** SPANISH AND LATIN AMERICAN STUDIES **EDUCATION** Texas Tech Univ, BA, 70; MA, 73, Univ Tex at Austin, PhD, 76; SW Baptist Theol Sem, MA, 94. **CAREER** Linguist, Missionary Orient Center, 75-83; Dir, S Ill Univ at Carbondale, 84-88; Dir, Port Lang School, Brazil, 88-94; Instr, Texas Christian Univ, 96-. **MEMBERSHIPS** AATSP; ACTFL. **RESEARCH** Argentine fantastic literature, contemporary Argentine authors, culture studies. **SELECTED PUBLICATIONS** Auth, "Afro-Brazilian Spritist Christology: the Attraction and challenge of Umbaude", Boletin Teologizo 2 (97):29-95; auth, Myths of Buenos Aires by Alejandro Polina", Hispania 81 (98):519-29. **CONTACT ADDRESS** Dept Spanish, Texas Christian Univ, Fort Worth, TX 76129. **EMAIL** d.bedford@tcu.edu

BEDFORD, HAROLD
PERSONAL Born 10/31/1929, Toronto, ON, Canada **DISCIPLINE** RUSSIAN & EAST EUROPEAN STUDIES **EDUCATION** Univ Toronto, BA, 51, MA, 52; Univ London, PhD, 56. **CAREER** Lectr, 55-59, asst prof, 59-64, assoc prof, 64-75, prof Slavic lang & lit, ctr Russian & E European stud, 75-95, prof emer, Univ Toronto, 95-. **MEMBERSHIPS** Can Friends Finland. **SELECTED PUBLICATIONS** Auth, The Seeker: D.S. Merezhkovskiy, 75; auth, "Tragedy as Ideology; D.S. Merezhkovsky's Paul I," in E.N. Burstynsky and R.Lindheim, eds., Working Order, (Edmonton, 90): 241-48. **CONTACT ADDRESS** Ctr Russian & East European Studies, Univ of Toronto, Toronto, ON, Canada M5S 1A1.

BEDFORD, HENRY F.
PERSONAL Born 06/21/1931, Oskaloosa, IA, m, 1952, 4 children **DISCIPLINE** AMERICAN HISTORY **EDUCATION** Amherst Col, BA, 52; Univ Wis, MA, 53; Univ MA, PhD(hist), 65. **CAREER** Chmn dept hist, 66-69, dean fac, 69-73, vprin, 79-82, Mem Fac Hist, Phillips Exeter Acad, 57-, Nat comt, Scholastic Aptitude Test, 77-81. **MEMBERSHIPS** AHA; Orgn Am Historians; New Eng Hist Asn. **RESEARCH** American socialism; American labor history; nineteenth century American history. **SELECTED PUBLICATIONS** Auth, The Union Divides, 63 & From Versailles to Nuremberg, 69, Macmillan; Socialism and the Workers in Massachusetts, 1886-1913, Univ MA, 66; coauth, The Americans: A Brief History, 72, 76 & 80 & Trouble Downtown, 78, Harcourt Brace Jovanovich; Wolf Creek Station-Kansas Gas and Electric Company in the Nuclear Era, with C. Miner, J of Am Hist, Vol 81, 95. **CONTACT ADDRESS** Dept of Hist, Phillips Exeter Acad, Exeter, NH 03833.

BEDFORD, STEVEN M.
PERSONAL Born 10/03/1953, Norfolk, VA, m, 1986, 2 children **DISCIPLINE** HISTORY **EDUCATION** Columbia Univ PhD 94. **CAREER** Fitzgerald Halliday Inc, principle planner 98-; TAMS Consultants Inc, assoc 95-98; Trinity Col, freelance vis and adj positions, 85-93. **MEMBERSHIPS** SAH; US/ICOMOS: Ntl Council **RESEARCH** Architectural history, military and coldwar. **SELECTED PUBLICATIONS** Auth, The Dictionary of Art, forthcoming; John Russell Pope, Architect of Empire, NY Rizzoli 98; John Russell Pope Christopher Grant Lafarge and Palmer and Hornbostel IN: Mackay, Baker, Traynor eds, Long Island Country Houses and Their Architects, 1860-1940, NY Norton 97; Managing Travel in Connecticut: 100 Years of Progress, CT Dept of Trans 95. **CONTACT ADDRESS** Dept of History, Fordham Univ, 409 Sand Brook Rd, PO Box 7, Middlebury, CT 06762. **EMAIL** bedford@aol.com

BEDNAREK, JANET
PERSONAL Born 10/14/1959, Omaha, NE, m, 1991 **DISCIPLINE** HISTORY **EDUCATION** Creignton Univ, BA, 81; MA, 83; Univ Pittsburgh, PhD, 87. **CAREER** Historian, US Air Force, 89-92; Asst to Assoc Prof, Univ of Dayton, 92-; Hist Dept Chair, Univ of Dayton, 99-. **HONORS AND AWARDS** Andrew Mellon Pre-Doctoral Fel, Univ of Pittsburgh 85-87; Summer Res Fel, Univ of Dayton, 93, 94, 97. **MEMBERSHIPS** Urban Hist Asn, Soc for the Hist of Technology, Orgn of Am Historians, Am Hist Asn. **RESEARCH** US urban, Municipal airports. **SELECTED PUBLICATIONS** Auth, The Changing Image of the City: Planning for Downtown Omaha, 1945-1973 (Lincoln, NE: Univ of Nebr Press, 92); ed, The Enlisted Experience: A Conversation with the Chief Master Sergeants of the Air Force (Wash, DC: Air Force Hist and Mus Prog, 95); auth, "'Damned Fool Idea': The American Combat Glider Program, 1941-1947," Air Power Hist 46-4 (96): 38-49; auth, "From the Baysdorfers to Strategic Air Command: Avia-

tion Dreams in Omaha, Nebraska, 1908-1948," J of the W 34-3 (July 97): 39-43; auth, "False Beacon: Regional Planning and the Location of Dayton's Municipal Airport," Ohio Hist 106 (Summer/Autumn 97): 124-125; auth, "Innovation in America's Aviation Support Infrastructure: The Evolving Relationship between Airports, Cities and Industry," in Innovation and the Development of Flight, ed. Roger D. Launius (College Station, TX: Tex A&M Univ Press, 99), 52-79; co-ed, Proceedings of the National Aerospace Conference, Wright State Univ Press (Dayton, OH), 99. **CONTACT ADDRESS** Dept Hist, Univ of Dayton, 300 College Pk, Dayton, OH 45469-0001. **EMAIL** janet.bednarek@notes.udayton.edu

BEDOS-REZAK, BRIGITTE
PERSONAL Born 06/03/1953, Paris, France, m, 1980 **DISCIPLINE** HISTORY **EDUCATION** Ecole nationale de Chartes, Paris, Sorbonne, 77 **CAREER** Curator, Ctr Dept Seals, Nat Archive France, 77-80; vis curator/Mellon fel, dept Medieval art, Metrop Mus Art, 82-87; adj assoc prof, State Univ NY, Stony Brook, 85-87; dir, summer sem col teach, NEH, 87; vis assoc prof, 87-89, assoc prof, 89-94, dir grad stud, 90-93, PROF HIST, UNIV MD, COL PK, 94; aff prof, Jos & Rebecca Meyerhoff Ctr Jewish Stud, Univ Md, 95-; vis prof, Ecole Hautes Etudes Scis Soc, Paris, 95; mem Sch Hist Stud, Inst Adv Stud, Princeton, 96-97. **HONORS AND AWARDS** Univ Md, Col Pk, grad res bd, summer res award; NEH fel Ind Study, Res. **MEMBERSHIPS** NEH grant rev; ed bd, Historical Reflections/Reflexions historiques, 93-; rev, Cornell Univ Press; Medieval Acad Am; AHA; Apices; Asn Archivistes France; Columbia Univ Sem Medieval Stud; Int Ctr Medieval Art; Majestas; Medieval Acad Am; Soc l'Ecole Chartes; Soc Fr Hist Stud; Soc fr d'heraldique, sigillographic; Soc Nat Antiquaires France. **RESEARCH** Medieval civilization; hist anthro Middle Ages; medieval pol hist; medieval Fr soc, cult hist; medieval diplomatics, sigillography; Latin, old Fr paleography; women's stud medieval hist. **SELECTED PUBLICATIONS** Ed, contr, Polity and Place: Regionalism in Medieval France, Historical Reflection/Reflexions historiques, 19:2, 93; auth, Form and Order in Medieval France, Studies in Social and Quantitative Sigillography, Various, 93; Elements de semiotique medievale. Le cas des sceaux, L'Atelier du medieviste, forthcoming; auth, Form as Social Process, and Towards a Cultural Biography of the Gothic Cathedral: Reflections on History and Art History, in Artistic Integration in Gothic Buildings, Univ Toronto Press, 95; auth, Seals and Sigillography, Medieval France: An Encyclopedia, Garland, 95; auth, Montmorency, Lexicon des Mittelalters, vol 6, Artemis and Winkler, 93; auth, Secular Administration, Medieval Latin Studies: An Introduction and Bibliographical Guide, and Anthology of Medieval Latin, Catholic Univ Am Press, 97. **CONTACT ADDRESS** Dept of History, Univ of Maryland, Col Park, College Park, MD 20742. **EMAIL** bb54@umail.umd.edu

BEEBE, RALPH KENNETH
PERSONAL Born 02/14/1932, Caldwell, ID, m, 1953, 3 children **DISCIPLINE** AMERICAN HISTORY **EDUCATION** George Fox Col, AB, 54; Linfield Col, MEd, 55; Univ OR, MA, 69, PhD(curric & instr), 72. **CAREER** Dean of men, George Fox Univ, 55-57; teacher hist, Willamette High Sch, Eugene, OR, 57-66 & Churchill High Sch, Eugene, OR, 66-74; assoc prof, 74-80, prof 80-97, prof hist emer, George Fox Univ, 97-. **HONORS AND AWARDS** John Hay Fellow, summer 62; NEH Summer Seminars for Col Teachers, 76, 81; Christian Col Consortium travel/study grants, 86, 87; Northwest Yearly Meeting of Friends Church Social Service Awd, 96; George Fox Univ John Woolman Peacemaking Awd, 97. **MEMBERSHIPS** NEA; Orgn Am Historians; Friends Hist Asn; Conference on Faith and History; Asn for Preservation of Civil War Sites; Nat Museum of Civil War Medicine. **RESEARCH** 19th Century United States; inquiry teaching of history; Quaker history; Middle East. **SELECTED PUBLICATIONS** Auth, A Garden of the Lord: A History of Oregon Yearly Meeting of Friends Church, Barclay, 68; The Worker and Social Change: The Pullman Strike of 1894, Heath, 70; Thomas Jefferson, the Embargo and the Decision for Peace, Addison-Wesley, 72; coauth, Waging Peace, A study in Biblical Pacifism, Barclay Press, 80, 81; War Tax Concerns, 1986: Blessed are the Peacemakers, A Palestinian Christian in the Occupied West Bank, 90; auth, A History of George Fox College, Barclay, 91. **CONTACT ADDRESS** George Fox Univ, 414 N Meridan St, Newberg, OR 97132-2625. **EMAIL** rbeebe@georgefox.edu

BEECHER, JONATHAN F.
PERSONAL Born 04/26/1937, Boston, MA, m, 1974, 2 children **DISCIPLINE** HISTORY **EDUCATION** Harvard Col, AB, 59; Harvard Univ, PhD, 68. **CAREER** Instr, Harvard Univ, 67-69; asst prof to prof, Univ of Calif Santa Cruz, 70-; Chair, 89-92. **HONORS AND AWARDS** Phi Beta Kappa, 59; Bowdoin Prize, 59; Fulbright Fel, 59-60; Fr Govt Grants, 62-64; ACLS Fel, 76-77; Am Philos Soc Res Grant, 86; VCSC Distinguished Teaching Awd, 88; Guggenheim Fel, 88-89, Univ of Calif Pres Res Fel, 89; Univ Calif Pres Awd, 96; Chevalier dans l'Order des Palmes Academiques, Fr, 98. **MEMBERSHIPS** AHA; Assoc d'Etudes Fourieristics; Melville Soc; Soc d'histoire de la Revolution de 1848. **RESEARCH** History of Utopian Thought, 19th Century French Utopian Socialism, Revolution of 1848, Herman Melville, 19th Century Russian Intellectual History. **SELECTED PUBLICATIONS** Cotransl, coed, The Utopian Vision of Charles Fourier, 71; auth, Charles Fourier: The Visionary and his World, 87; auth, Victor Considerant and the Rise and Fall of French Romantic Socialism, 00. **CONTACT ADDRESS** Dept Hist, Univ of California, Santa Cruz, 1156 High St, Santa Cruz, CA 95064-1077. **EMAIL** jbeecher@cats.ucsc.edu

BEECHER, MAUREEN URSENBACH
PERSONAL Born 03/19/1935, Calgary, AB, Canada **DISCIPLINE** COMPARATIVE LITERATURE, WESTERN HISTORY **EDUCATION** Brigham Young Univ, BSc, 58; Univ UT, MA, 66, PhD(comp lit), 73. **CAREER** Res historian & ed western hist, Church of Jesus Christ Latter-Day Saints, 72-80; Assoc Prof to Prof Emer English & Res Historian, Brigham Young Univ, Provo, UT, 80-. **HONORS AND AWARDS** John Whitmer Hist Asn Awd, 78. **MEMBERSHIPS** AHA; Western Hist Asn; Mormon Hist Asn; Asn for Mormon Lett. **RESEARCH** History of women in America; history of Mormon women; literature of the Mormon movement. **SELECTED PUBLICATIONS** Auth, Three Women and the Life of the Mind, UT Hist Quart, winter 75; Letters From the Frontier: Commerce, Nauvoo and Salt Lake City, J of Mormon Hist, 75; Past and Present: Some Thoughts on Being a Mormon Woman, Sunstone, 76; Under the Sunbonnets: Mormon Women with Faces, BYU Studies, summer 76; contribr, The Oft-crossed Border: Canadians in Utah, In: The Peoples of Utah, Utah State His Soc, 76; contribr, Eliza R Snow, In: Mormon Sisters, Emmeline, 77; auth, The Eliza Enigma: The Life and Legend of Eliza R Snow, Dialogue: J Mormon Thought, reprinted in, Sister Saints, spring 78; contribr, Women in Twentieth Century Utah, In: Utah's History, Brigham Young Univ, 78. **CONTACT ADDRESS** Dept of English, Brigham Young Univ, Provo, UT 84602. **EMAIL** maureen_beecher@byu.edu

BEECHERT, EDWARD D.
PERSONAL Born 06/10/1920, Hawthorne, CA, m, 1950, 3 children **DISCIPLINE** UNITED STATES ECONOMIC HISTORY, LATIN AMERICAN DEVELOPMENT **EDUCATION** Univ Calif, Berkeley, MA, 50, PhD, 57. **CAREER** Instr hist, MX City Col, 53; instr hist & econ, Modesto Jr Col, 55-57; instr hist, Ventura Col, 57-60; asst prof soc sci, Sacramento State Col, 60-63; from asst prof to assoc prof hist, Univ HI, Hilo Campus, 63-66; assoc prof, St Mary's Col, CA, 66-68; assoc prof, 68-73, Prof Hist, Univ HI, 73-, Coordr, Pac Regional Oral Hist Prog, 70-, Grant archaeol of Dos Pueblos, Samuel Mosher Found, 56-57; grant, Inst Am Hist, 64; staff mem Negro in Am econ, Inst Am Hist, Univ Calif, 65; grant for Hutchison Plantation Paper, Nat Arch, 76; Nat Endowment for Humanities grant, 77-78. **MEMBERSHIPS** Econ Hist Asn; Orgn Am Historians; Oral Hist Asn. **RESEARCH** Industrialization in developing areas; trade unions and economic development. **SELECTED PUBLICATIONS** Auth, The Gap Between Planning Goals and Achievements, Inter-Am Econ Rev, 6/66; Writing the History of Hawaiian Trade Unions, 67, coauth, American Trade Union Movement, 70, ed, History of the Honolulu Typographical Union, 70 & auth, A History of Local 5 (hotel workers), 70, Univ HI; Racial Divisions and Labor Organizing in Hawaii, Southwest Labor Hist Conf, 3/77; Labor Relations in Hawaii, 1850-1937, Univ CA, 80; The Filipino in the ILWU Philippines Study Association, Univ MI; Organizing Asian-American Labor-The Pacific Coast Canned Salmon Industry, 1870-1942, with C. Friday, Pacific Hist Rev, Vol 64, 95. **CONTACT ADDRESS** Dept of Hist, Univ of Hawaii, Manoa, Honolulu, HI 96822.

BEELER, JOHN F.
PERSONAL Born 10/03/1936, Greensboro, NC, m, 1995 **DISCIPLINE** MODERN BRITISH HISTORY, NAVAL MILITARY HISTORY **EDUCATION** Guilford Col, AB, 74; Univ North Carolina Greensboro, MA, 86; Univ Illinois, Urbana, PhD, 91. **CAREER** Vis instr, Univ Illinois, Urbana, 89; Macarthur Scholar, 89-90; post doc fel, Yale Univ, 91-92; vis asst prof, Eastern Illinois Univ, 92-93; asst prof, assoc prof, prof, Univ Alabama, 93-99-. **HONORS AND AWARDS** Paul W. Birdsall Prize, 98; Outstand Commit Teach Awd, AAA, 99. **RESEARCH** British National Security Policy, 1850-1914. **SELECTED PUBLICATIONS** Auth, British Naval Policy in the Gladstone-Disraeli Era, 1866-1880 (Stanford Univ Press, 97). **CONTACT ADDRESS** Dept History, Univ of Alabama, Tuscaloosa, PO Box 870212, Tuscaloosa, AL 35487-0154.

BEER, BARRETT L.
PERSONAL Born 07/04/1936, Goshen, IN, m, 1965, 2 children **DISCIPLINE** ENGLISH HISTORY **EDUCATION** DePauw Univ, BA, 58; Univ Cincinnati, MA, 59; Northwestern Univ, PhD, 65. **CAREER** Instr hist, Kent State Univ, 62-65; asst prof, Univ NM, 65-68, asst dean col art & sci, 66-68; assoc prof, 68-76, Prof Hist, Kent State Univ, 76-, Res grants, Am Philos Soc, 66 & Univ NM, 66-68; vis assoc prof, Northwestern Univ, 69; res fel, Kent State Univ, 73 & 77. **MEMBERSHIPS** AHA; Conf Brit Studies. **RESEARCH** Early modern England. **SELECTED PUBLICATIONS** Auth, The Rise of John Dudley, Hist Today, 4/65; A Critique of the Protectorate, Huntington Libr Quart, 5/71; London and Rebellions of 1548-1549, J Brit Studies, 11/72; Northumberland: The Political Career of John Dudley, Duke of Northumberland, Kent State Univ, 73; co-ed, The Letters of William, Lord Paget of Beaudesert, 1547-1563, Camden Miscellany Vol XXV, Royal Hist Soc, London, 74; The Commoyson in Norfolk, 1549: A Narrative of Popular Rebellion in Sixteenth Century England, J Medieval & Renaissance Studies, spring 76; Hugh Latimer and the Lusty Knave of Kent: The Commonwealth Movement of 1549, Bull Inst Hist Res, 11/79; Rebellion and Riot: Popular Disorder in England during the Reign of Edward VI, Kent State Univ Press, 82; auth, Tudor England Observed: The World of John Stow, Sutton, 98. **CONTACT ADDRESS** Kent State Univ, Kent, OH 44242. **EMAIL** bbeer@kent.edu

BEERS, BURTON FLOYD
PERSONAL Born 09/13/1927, Chemung, NY, m, 1952, 2 children **DISCIPLINE** MODERN HISTORY **EDUCATION** Hobart Col, AB, 50; Duke Univ, MA, 52, PhD, 56. **CAREER** From instr to assoc prof, 55-66, Prof Hist, NC State Univ, 66-96, Fel, East Asian Studies, Harvard Univ, 59-60; Fulbright vis lect, Nat Taiwan Univ, 66-67; mem, Nat Adv Bd, China Coun, 78-81; Chief Exec ed, NC State Hum Pubs, 93-96; Prof Emer, 97-. **HONORS AND AWARDS** Phi Beta Kappa, Phi Kappa Phi, Alumni Distinguished Prof, NC State Univ, 70; Alexander Quarles Holladay Medal for Excellence, NC State Univ, 92; Medal for Excellence, Hobart, 94; NC Council for Soc Stud, 97; Watauga Medal, 98. **MEMBERSHIPS** AHA; Asn Asian Studies; Southern His Asn; Soc Hist Am For Rels, NC Literary and Hist Asn; World Hist Asn. **RESEARCH** Amer Far East policy; mod E Asia; world hist and geog. **SELECTED PUBLICATIONS** Auth, Vain Endeavor: Robert Lansing's Attempts to End the American Japanese Rivalry, Duke Univ, 62; China in Old Photographs, Scribner's, 78; coauth, The Far East: A History of the Western Impact and the Eastern Response, 1830-1965, 66-75; The Far East: A History of Western Impacts and Eastern Responses, 1830-1975, Prentice-Hall, 75; contribr, American East Asian Relations, Harvard Univ, 72;World History: Patterns of Civilization 1st-6th eds, 83-93; Chiliying: Life on a Chinese Commune, NCSU Col of Ed, 79; NCSU: A Pictorial history, 86; Teaching History and the Social Studies, Greenwood Publishing Group, 93; contribr, North Carolina Biographical Dictionary, UNC Press, 94; co-auth, Japan and Korea: Regional Studies Series, Globe Books, 93; Globe Fearon Historical Case Studies: The Vietnam War, 97. **CONTACT ADDRESS** 629 S Lakeshore Dr, Raleigh, NC 27607. **EMAIL** Burtbeers@aol.com

BEETH, HOWARD
PERSONAL Born 02/05/1942, Petersburg, VA, s, 1 child **DISCIPLINE** U.S. HISTORY **EDUCATION** Temple Univ, BA, 66, MA, 68; Univ Houston, PhD, 84. **CAREER** Prof, hist, Tex Southern Univ, Houston, 88-01. **HONORS AND AWARDS** Scholar-of-the-Year Awd, Tex Southern Univ, 92 **MEMBERSHIPS** SWestern Hist Asn (pres 95-96); Am Hist Asn; Friends Hist Asn; NC Friends Hist Soc. **RESEARCH** Southern history; African-American history; urban history. **SELECTED PUBLICATIONS** Co-ed, Black Dixie: Afro-Texan History and Culture in Houston, Tex A&M Univ Press, 92; auth, Historiographical Developments in Early North American Quaker Studies, The Southern Friend, 91; auth, A Black Elite Agenda in the Urban South: The Call for Political Change and Racial Economic Solidarity in Houston during the 1920's, Essays in Econ and Business Hist 10, 92; auth, How to Resist? Reformism vs. Communism in Houston's Black Press during the 1920s, Bringing the World Together: Proceedings of the Nat Asn African Am Studies, 96. **CONTACT ADDRESS** Dept Hist, Texas So Univ, 3100 Cleburne Ave, Houston, TX 77004. **EMAIL** beeth.howard@excite.com

BEHROOZ, MAZIAR
PERSONAL Born 03/20/1959, Tehran, Iran **DISCIPLINE** HISTORY, NEAR EAST **EDUCATION** St Mary's Col, CA, BA, 82; San Francisco State Univ, MA, 86; Univ Cal, LA, PhD, 93. **CAREER** Lectr, Univ Cal, Berkeley, 95-98; instr, San Francisco State Univ, 95-. **MEMBERSHIPS** MESA; Iranian Studies. **RESEARCH** Middle East; Iran. **SELECTED PUBLICATIONS** Auth, Rebels With a Cause: The Failure of the Left in Iran (London, I B Tauns, 99). **CONTACT ADDRESS** Dept History, San Francisco State Univ, 1600 Holloway Ave, San Francisco, CA 94132-1722. **EMAIL** mroozbeh@sfsu.edu

BEIDLER, PETER GRANT
PERSONAL Born 03/13/1940, Bethlehem, PA, m, 1963, 4 children **DISCIPLINE** ENGLISH & AMERICAN LITERATURE, AMERICAN INDIAN STUDIES **EDUCATION** Earlham Col, BA, 62; Lehigh Univ, MA, 65, PhD(English), 68. **CAREER** From asst prof to prof, 68-78, Lucy G Moses Dist Prof English, Lehigh Univ, 78-; NEH fel anthrop, Univ AZ, 73-74. **HONORS AND AWARDS** CASE Nat Prof of the Year, 83; Lindback Teaching Awd, 71, 94. **MEMBERSHIPS** MLA; Asn Study of Am Indian Lit. **RESEARCH** Chaucer; American Indian literature; Medieval literature. **SELECTED PUBLICATIONS** Auth, Fig Tree John, An Indian in Fact and Fiction, Univ AZ Press, 77; with Marion F Egge, The American Indian in Short Fiction: An Annotated Bibliography, Scarecrow Press, 79; John Gower's Literary Transformations in the Confessio Amantis, Univ Press Am, 82; Distinguished Teachers on Effective Teaching: Observations on Effective Teaching by College Professors Recognized by the Council for Advancment and Support of Education, Jossey-Bass, Pubs, 86; Ghosts, Demons,

and Henry James: The Turn of the Screw at the Turn of the Century, Univ MO Press, 89; Writing Matters, McGraw-Hill, 90, Macmillan, 92; Henry James, The Turn of the Screw: Text and Five Contemporary Critical Essays, Bedford Books of St Martin's Press, 95; Geoffrey Chaucer, The Wife of Bath: Complete, Authoritative Text with Biographical and Historical Contexts, Critical History, and Essays from Five Contemporary Critical Perspectives, Bedford Books of St Martin's Press, 96; The Wife of Bath's Prologue and Tale: An Annotated Bibliography, with Elizabeth M. Biebel, Univ Toronto Press, 98; Masculinities in Chaucer, Boydell & Brewer, 98; auth, A Reader's Guide to the Novels of Louise Erdrich, with Gay Barton, Univ of MO Press, 99; auth, The Native American in Short Ficiton in the Saturday Evening Post, with Marion F. Egge, Scarecrow Press of the Univ Press of America, 00. **CONTACT ADDRESS** Dept English, Lehigh Univ, 35 Sayre Dr, Bethlehem, PA 18015-3076. **EMAIL** pgb1@lehigh.edu

BEIK, WILLIAM
DISCIPLINE HISTORY **EDUCATION** Haverford Col, BA, 63; Harvard Univ, MA, 66; PhD, 69. **CAREER** Prof **HONORS AND AWARDS** Herbert Baxter Adams Prize, Am Hist Assn. **RESEARCH** Early modern French social and institutional history. **SELECTED PUBLICATIONS** Auth, Absolutism and Society in Seventeenth-Century France: State Power and Provincial Aristocracy in Languedoc; Urban Protest in Seventeenth-Century France: the Culture of Retribution; co-ed, New Approaches to European History (series), Cambridge UP; auth, Louis XIV and Absolutism: A Study with Documents. **CONTACT ADDRESS** Dept History, Emory Univ, 221 Bowden Hall, 561 Kilgo Cir, Atlanta, GA 30322-1950. **EMAIL** wbeik@emory.edu

BEINFELD, SOLON
PERSONAL Born 07/20/1934, New York, NY **DISCIPLINE** MODERN EUROPEAN HISTORY **EDUCATION** NYork Univ, AB, 54; Harvard Univ, AM, 56, PhD(hist), 61. **CAREER** Asst prof, 61-70, Assoc Prof Hist, Wash Univ, 70-. **MEMBERSHIPS** AHA. **RESEARCH** Modern European history, especially France, Germany and diplomacy. **SELECTED PUBLICATIONS** Auth, Dimensions of the Holocaust-The Number of Jewish Victims Under National-Socialism (German), with W. Benz, Jahrbucher Fur Geschite Osteuropas, Vol 41, 93. **CONTACT ADDRESS** Washington Univ, Saint Louis, MO 63130.

BEIRIGER, EUGENE
DISCIPLINE HISTORY **EDUCATION** Northwestern Univ, BA, 80; Univ Ill, MA, 81; Univ Ill at Chicago, PhD, 92. **CAREER** From instr to assoc prof, Barat Col, 85-; dir of hist & int studies, Barat Col. **HONORS AND AWARDS** Board of Trustees Prof of the Year; listed in Who's Who Among America's Teachers. **MEMBERSHIPS** Am Hist Asn, N Am Confr on British Studies, Am Asn of Univ Professors, Chicago Coun on For Relations. **RESEARCH** Twentieth-century British and European Political/Diplomatic History, Anglo-German Relations, Anglo-American Relations. **SELECTED PUBLICATIONS** Auth, Churchill, Munitions and Mechanical Warfare: Politics of Supply and Strategy. **CONTACT ADDRESS** Dept Humanities, Barat Col, 700 E Westleigh Rd, Lake Forest, IL 60045-3263. **EMAIL** beiriger@barat.edu

BEISNER, ROBERT L.
PERSONAL Born 03/08/1936, Lexington, NE, m, 1976, 2 children **DISCIPLINE** AMERICAN HISTORY **EDUCATION** Univ Chicago, MA, 60, PhD(hist), 65. **CAREER** Instr soc sci, Univ Chicago, 62-63; instr hist, Colgate Univ, 63-65; from asst prof to assoc prof, 65-71, Prof Hist, American Univ, 71-98, Chmn, 81-90, EMERITUS, 98-; Nat Endowment for Humanities Younger Scholar's fel, 68-69. **HONORS AND AWARDS** Nevins Prize, Soc Am Historians, 66; John H Dunning Prize, AHA, 68. **MEMBERSHIPS** Orgn Am Historians; Soc Am Historians; Soc Historians of Am Foreign Rels. **RESEARCH** United States diplomatic history; Dean Acheson. **SELECTED PUBLICATIONS** Auth, Twelve Against Empire: The Anti-Imperialists, 1898-1900, McGraw, 68; From the Old Diplomacy to the New, 1865-1900, Am Hist Ser, Harlan Davidson, Inc, 75, 2nd ed, 86; History and Henry Kissinger, Diplomatic History, fall 90; Patterns of Peril: Dean Acheson Joins the Cold Warriors, 1945-46, Diplomatic Hist, summer 96; Dean Acheson's Alger Hiss, Weekly Standard, 12/2/96. **CONTACT ADDRESS** 3851 Newark St, NW, Washington, DC 20016-3026. **EMAIL** huskerindc@rcn.com

BEITO, DAVID T.
PERSONAL Born 03/08/1956, Minneapolis, MN, m, 1997, 2 children **DISCIPLINE** HISTORY **EDUCATION** Univ Minn, BA, 80; Univ Wisc, MA, 83; PhD, 86. **CAREER** Dir, Inst for Humane Studies George Mason Univ, 86-88; rrban studies fel, Pac Inst for Public Policy Res, 88-89; lectr, Univ Nev Las Vegas, 89-93; asst prof to assoc prof, 94-. **HONORS AND AWARDS** Urban Hist Asn Awd, 91; Ellis Hawley Prize, 95; Vis Scholar, Bowling Green State Univ, 99. **MEMBERSHIPS** Am Hist Asn; Hist Soc; Urban Hist Asn. **RESEARCH** The history of American mutual aid and self-help; Civil rights; Housing regulation. **SELECTED PUBLICATIONS** Co-auth, "Rival Road Builders: Private Toll Roads in Nevada, 1852-1880," Nev Hist Soc Quart, (98): 71-91; co-auth, "God Democrats and the Decline of Classical Liberalism, 1896-1900," Independent Rev, 00; auth, From Mutual Aid to the Welfare State: Fraternal Societies and Social Services, 1890-1967, Univ NC Press, 00. **CONTACT ADDRESS** Dept Hist, Univ of Alabama, Tuscaloosa, Box 870212, Tuscaloosa, AL 35487-0212. **EMAIL** dbeito@history.as.ua.edu

BELISLE, JEAN
DISCIPLINE ART HISTORY **EDUCATION** Univ de Paris IV, PhD, 83. **CAREER** Dept Art Hist, Concordia Univ **HONORS AND AWARDS** Awd, Quebec Sci Tchr(s) Assn. **RESEARCH** Canadian art, industrial archaeology and sculpture. **SELECTED PUBLICATIONS** Co-auth, La sculpture traditionelle au Quebec, Di L'omme, 96; auth, A propos d'un bateau a vapeur, HMH, 94. **CONTACT ADDRESS** Dept Art Hist, VA-432, Concordia Univ, Montreal, 1455 de Maisonneuve W, Montreal, QC, Canada H3G 1M8.

BELL, ANDREW J. E.
DISCIPLINE HISTORY **EDUCATION** Stanford Univ, PhD, 94. **CAREER** Asst prof,Columbia Col Columbia. **SELECTED PUBLICATIONS** Auth, pubs on Ancient Greece and Rome, and Ancient Mediterranean. **CONTACT ADDRESS** History Dept, Univ of Nevada, Las Vegas, 4505 Md Pky, Las Vegas, NV 89154.

BELL, JAMES BRUGLER
PERSONAL Born 04/17/1932, St. Paul, MN, m, 1957, 4 children **DISCIPLINE** HISTORY **EDUCATION** Univ Minn, Minneapolis, BA, 55; Episcopal Theol Sch, MDiv, 61; Balliol Col, Oxford, DPhil (mod hist), 64. **CAREER** Instr hist, OH State Univ, 64-67; vis lectr, Col Wooster, 67; res fel & lectr, Princeton Univ, 67-69; Dir & Librn, New Eng Hist Geneal Soc, 73-, Nat Hist Publ Comn fel, 67-68; chmn, Commonwealth MA Arch Adv Comn, 74-; comnr, MA Hist Comn, 74-78. **MEMBERSHIPS** Orgn Am Historians; AHA; fel Soc Antiquaries; Am Antiquarian Soc. **RESEARCH** Eighteenth century American and English history. **SELECTED PUBLICATIONS** Contribr, Charles P McIlvaine, In: For the Union: Ohio Leaders in the Civil War, OH State Univ, 68; Anglican Clergy in Colonial America Ordained by Bishops of London, Proc Am Antiq Soc, 73; Anglican Quilldrivers in Eighteenth Century America, Hist Mag Protestant Episcopal Church, 74; auth, Portraits at the New England Historic Genealogical Society, 11/76 & Furniture at the New England Historic Genealogical Society, 5/78, Antiques Mag; contribr, Richard Rush: Spokesman for the Administration, July 4, 1812, Colonial Soc Mass, 78; Searching for Your Ancestors, Family Hist Rec Bk, 81; Waiting for Mario, The Espositos, Joyce, and Beckett, Eire-Ireland, Vol 30, 95. **CONTACT ADDRESS** New England Historical Genealogical Society, Newbury St, Boston, MA 02116.

BELL, JOHN D.
DISCIPLINE HISTORY **EDUCATION** Princeton Univ, PhD. **CAREER** Prof, Univ MD Baltimore County . **RESEARCH** Russ and East Europ hist. **SELECTED PUBLICATIONS** Auth, Peasants in Power and The Bulgarian Communist Party from Blagoev to Zhivkov; pubs on Bulgaria and its history; co-auth, Bulgaria's Road from Dictatorship to Democracy. **CONTACT ADDRESS** Dept of Hist, Univ of Maryland, Baltimore, Hilltop Circle, PO Box 1000, Baltimore, MD 21250. **EMAIL** bell@umbc2.umbc.edu

BELL, JOHN P.
DISCIPLINE HISTORY **EDUCATION** Tulane Univ, PhD, 68. **CAREER** Prof emer, Ind Univ-Purdue Univ, Ft Wayne. **SELECTED PUBLICATIONS** Auth, Crisis in Costa Rica: the 1948 Revolution. **CONTACT ADDRESS** Dept of History, Indiana Univ-Purdue Univ, Fort Wayne, 2101 E Coliseum Blvd, Fort Wayne, IN 46805-1499.

BELL, LELAND V.
PERSONAL Born 03/02/1934, Johnson City, NY, m, 1961, 2 children **DISCIPLINE** AMERICAN CIVILIZATION, MODERN EUROPEAN HISTORY **EDUCATION** Wayne State Univ, AB, 58; Pa State Univ, AM, 61; WVa Univ, PhD(hist), 68. **CAREER** Instr hist, Jr Col Kansas City, 62-64; asst prof, West Liberty State Col, 64-66; instr, WV Univ, 67-68; Prof Hist, Cent State Univ, OH, 68-, Adj prof, Sch Community Educ, Wittenberg Univ, 70-71, Wright State Univ, 73, Union Grad Sch, 73, Univ Dayton, 76 & Antioch Col, 76; proj dir, OH Prog Humanities, 79-80. **HONORS AND AWARDS** Outstanding Educr of Am, 74-75. **MEMBERSHIPS** AHA; Am Asn Hist Med; Cheiron; Orgn Am Historians. **RESEARCH** Intellectual history; history of mental health, history of technology. **SELECTED PUBLICATIONS** In Hitler's Shadow, The Anatomy of American Nazism, Kennikat, 73; The Failure of Nazism in America: the German American Bund, 1936-1941, Polit Sci Quart, 70; Death in the Technocracy, J Human Rels, 70; Violence in Contemporary American Art, IL Quart, 73; Treating the Mentally Ill, From Colonial Times to the Present, Praeger, 80 Colonial Psychiatry and the African Mind, with J. McCullock, Int J of African Historical Studies, Vol 29, 97. **CONTACT ADDRESS** Center for African Studies, Central State Univ, 1400 Brush Row Road, Wilberforce, OH 45384.

BELL, RUDOLPH MARK
PERSONAL Born 11/05/1942, New York, NY, m, 1964, 2 children **DISCIPLINE** HISTORY **EDUCATION** Queens Col, BA, 63; City Univ of NYork, PhD, 69. **CAREER** Instr to prof, Rutgers, 68-, chair 89-94; vis prof, Univ of Ariz, spring 79. **HONORS AND AWARDS** Fulbright-Hays Scholar, 71-72; Rutgers Univ Bd of Trustees Awd for Excellence in Research, 88; Study Abroad Dir, Italy, 76-77, 81-83, 86-87, 94-95; Study Abroad Dir, Ireland and UK, 95-96. **RESEARCH** Italian civilization and culture from the Middle Ages to the present. **SELECTED PUBLICATIONS** Auth, Holy Anorexia, Chicago: Univ of Chicago Press (85, paperback, 86); auth, La santa anoressia: digiuno e misticismo dal medioevo a oggi, Roma e Bari: Laterza & Figli (87, edizione economico 97), Milano: Mondadori (94), Italian transl by Anna Casini Paszkowski; auth, Santa Anorexia: vrouwelijle wegen naar heiligheid Italia 1200-1800, Amsterdam: Wereldbibliotheek (90), Dutch transl by Roland Fagel; auth, "Telling Her Sins: Male Confessors and Female Penitents in Catholic Reformation in Italy," in Lynda L. Coon, et al, eds, That Gentle Strength: Historical Perspectives on Women in Christianity, Charlottesville (90): 118-33; auth, "The Medieval and Early Modern Data Bank in Europe and North America," in Rainer Metz, et al, eds, Historical Information Systems, Leuven (90): 67-76; auth, L'anorexie sainte: jeuner et mysticism du Moyen Age a nos jours, Paris: Presses Universitaires de France (94), French transl by Caroline Ragon-Ganovelli; auth, How to Do It: Guides to Good Living for Renaissance Italians, Chicago: Univ of Chicago Press (99). **CONTACT ADDRESS** Dept Hist, Rutgers, The State Univ of New Jersey, New Brunswick, PO Box 5059, New Brunswick, NJ 08903-5059. **EMAIL** rbell@rci.rutgers.edu

BELL, SUSAN GROAG
PERSONAL Born, Czechoslovakia **DISCIPLINE** HISTORY OF WOMEN **EDUCATION** Stanford Univ, AB, 64; Univ Santa Clara, MA, 70. **CAREER** Adj lectr, Univ Santa Clara, 71-81; Lectr Hist, Stanford Univ, 82-, Senior scholar, Instr, Res on Women & Gender, Stanford Univ, 78-. **MEMBERSHIPS** AHA; Conf British Studies; Coord Comt Women in the Hist Profession; Western Asn Women Historians; Garden Hist Soc. **RESEARCH** European and British women's intellectual history; history of women as gardeners; history of women and literacy. **SELECTED PUBLICATIONS** Auth, Christine de Pizan, 1364-1430: Humanism and the Problem of a Studious Woman, Feminist Studies, 76; Lady Warwick: Aristocrat, Socialist Gardener, San Jose Studies, 82; Medieval Women Bookowners: Arbiters of Lay Piety and Ambassadors of Culture, Signs: J of Women in Culture and Soc, 82; coauth, Women, the Family and Freedom: 1750-1950; The Debate in Documents, 2 Vols, Stanford Univ Press; coauth, Revealing Lives: Autobiography, Biography and Gender, Albany, NY, State Univ of New York press, 90;' auth, Between Worlds, In Cxechoslovakia, England and Americ: A Memoir, New York, E P Dutton/William Abrahams 91; auth, " A Lost Tapestry: Margaret of Savoy's "Cite Des Dames," Une Femme de Lettres au Moven Age: Etudes autour de Christine De Pizan, Orleans , France, Editions paradigme, 95; auth, "A New Approach to the Influence of Christine de Pizan: The Lost Tapestries of "The City of Ladies," Actes du colloque d' Orleans, Juillet 1995, Etudes christiniennes, vol 3, Paris, Honore Champion, (98): 7-11; auth, "Vanessa's Garden," Singular Continuities, Stanford Univ Press, 00. **CONTACT ADDRESS** Inst for Research on Women and Gender, Stanford Univ, Stanford, CA 94305-8640. **EMAIL** groagbel@stanford.edu

BELL, WILLIAM DUDLEY
PERSONAL Born 03/13/1931, Macon, MS, m, 1960, 2 children **DISCIPLINE** UNITED STATES HISTORY **EDUCATION** Miss State Univ, BA, 53, BS, 58, MA, 62; La State Univ, PhD(hist), 73. **CAREER** Assoc prof hist, Athens Col, 65-73; asst prof, 73-76, Assoc Prof Hist, Meridian Br, MI State Univ, 76-, Coord Lib Arts Prog, 73-, Adv, Ala Hist Comn, 66-. **MEMBERSHIPS** Southern Hist Asn; Am Asn State & Local Hist. **RESEARCH** United States 19th century; Civil War and Reconstruction; Ku Klux Klan; Mississippi military history. **SELECTED PUBLICATIONS** Auth, Edward James, Smithsonian, Vol 25, 94. **CONTACT ADDRESS** Dept of Hist, Mississippi State Univ, Hwy 19 N, Meridian, MS 39301.

BELL, WILLIAM GARDNER
PERSONAL Born 10/29/1914, New York, NY, m, 1947, 1 child **DISCIPLINE** MILITARY HISTORY **CAREER** Assoc ed, Armored Cavalry J, 47-50; ed, Armor Mag, 50-53; mil historian, Off Chief Mil Hist, US Dept Army, 56-59, br & div chief, 59-62; Mil Historian, US Army Ctr Mil Hist, 63-, Ed, Dept Army Hist Summary, 69-74, contribr, 75-78. **MEMBERSHIPS** AHA, Western Hist Asn; Western Lit Asn; US Comn Mil Hist; Soc Hist in Fed Govt. **RESEARCH** Army-Indian frontier campaigns; Snake River Basin; Western art. **SELECTED PUBLICATIONS** Auth, Society and Journal of the Mounted Arm, Armor Mag, 58; Frontier Lawman, Am West, 64; The Snake: A Noble and Various River, Potomac Corral, Westerners, 69; contribr, American Military History, Off Chief Mil Hist, US Army, 69; John Gregory Bourke: A Soldier-Scientist on the Frontier, Potomac Corral, Westerners, 78; Quarters One: The United States Army Chief of Staff's Residence, Fort Myer, Va, US Army Ctr Mil Hist, 81; A Rebirth of Classic Western Art, Southwest Art, 82; Secretaries of War and Secretaries of

the Army: Portraits and Biographical Sketches, US Army Ctr Mil Hist, 82; Commanding Generals and Chiefs of Staff: Portraits and Biographical Sketches, US Army Ctr Mil Hist; My Interest Lays Toward the Horse-Canadian-Born Author, Artist, and Horseman, Will James Changed His Name, His Country, and His Language to Follow His Dream of Becoming a Genuine American Cowboy, Am Hist, Vol 31, 96. **CONTACT ADDRESS** US Army Ctr of Mil Hist, 1000 Independence Ave SW, Washington, DC 20314.

BELLAMY, DONNIE DUGLIE
PERSONAL Born 09/13/1938, Jacksonville, NC, m, 1959, 2 children **DISCIPLINE** POLITICAL SCIENCE, AMERICAN HISTORY **EDUCATION** NC Cent Univ, AB, 62, MA, 64; Univ Mo-Columbia, PhD, 70. **CAREER** Instr soc sci, Lincoln Univ, Mo, 63-64; instr soc sci, 64-67, from asst prof to assoc prof hist, 67-75, chmn dept hist, 73-, chmn div soc sci, 74-, prof hist, 75, Regents prof hist, 81-, Fort Valley State Col. **HONORS AND AWARDS** Ford Found fel hist, 68-70. **MEMBERSHIPS** Southern Hist Assn; Assn Study Afro-Am Life & Hist; Gd Assn of Historians. **RESEARCH** Education of Blacks; slavery; Antebellum. **SELECTED PUBLICATIONS** Art, Legal Status of Black Georgians during the Colonial and Revolutionary Eras, Journal of Negro History; auth, Light in the Valley: A Pictorial History of Fort Valley State College Since 1985, Donning Company Publishers, 96; auth, From Slavery to Freedom: A Pictorial History of Shish Missionary Baptist Church Since 1863, Donning Company Publishers, 98. **CONTACT ADDRESS** Fort Valley State Univ, 1005 State Univ Dr, Box 4456, Fort Valley, GA 31030-3298.

BELLEGARDE-SMITH, PATRICK
PERSONAL Born 08/08/1947, Spokane, WA **DISCIPLINE** AFRICAN HISTORY **EDUCATION** Syracuse Univ, BA 1968; The Amer Univ, MA, PhD 1977. **CAREER** Howard Univ Dept of Romance Languages, lecturer 77; Bradley Univ Inst of Intl Studies, assoc prof, 78-86; The Univ of WI-Milwaukee, prof of Dept of Africology, 86-. **MEMBERSHIPS** Amer Association of University Professors; African Studies Association, Association of Caribbean Studies; National Council for Black Studies; National Conf of Black Political Scientists; Association of Caribbean Historians; Latin Amer Studies Assn. **SELECTED PUBLICATIONS** Auth, "In the Shadow of Powers, Dantes Bellegarde in Haitian Social Thought" Atlantic Highlands, Humanities Press 1985; "Haiti: The Breached Citadel," Westview Press 1990; "Fragments of Bone: African Religions in the Americas," Univ Press of Florida, 1999. **CONTACT ADDRESS** Dept of Africology, Univ of Wisconsin, Milwaukee, PO Box 413, Milwaukee, WI 53201. **EMAIL** pbs@uwm.edu

BELLESILES, MICHAEL A.
DISCIPLINE HISTORY **EDUCATION** Univ Calif Santa Cruz, BA, 75; Univ Calif Irvine, PhD, 86. **CAREER** Assoc prof, Emory Univ. **HONORS AND AWARDS** Fel, Stanford Humanities Ctr, 98-99. **RESEARCH** Early American history, focusing on the Revolution; the early Republic; constitutional law; origins of American gun culture. **SELECTED PUBLICATIONS** Auth, Revolutionary Outlaws: Ethan Allen and the Struggle for Independence on the Early American Frontier; Lethal Imagination, NYork Univ Press; BiblioBase, Houghton Mifflin; Arming America, Knopf. **CONTACT ADDRESS** Dept History, Emory Univ, Bowden 222, Atlanta, GA 30322-1950. **EMAIL** mbelles@emory.edu

BELLINZONI, ARTHUR J.
PERSONAL Born 02/21/1936, Brooklyn, NY, s **DISCIPLINE** HISTORY AND PHILOSOPHY OF RELIGION **EDUCATION** Princeton Univ, AB; Harvard Univ, MA, PhD. **CAREER** PROF RELIG, DIR PLANNED AND LEADERSHIP GIVING, WELLS COL **HONORS AND AWARDS** Exxon Educational Found Travel Grant for study in Israel; Ruth and Albert Koch Prof of Humananities, Wells Coll **MEMBERSHIPS** Soc Bibl Lit; Am Acad Relig; Am School Orient Res; Novi Testamenti Studiorum Soc. **RESEARCH** Old Testament; New Testament; Second Century Christianity; Middle East; Major Gift Fund Development. **SELECTED PUBLICATIONS** The Sayings of Jesus in the Writings of Justin Martyr, Brill; Intellectual Honesty and Religious Commitment, Fortress Press; The Two Source Hypothesis: A Critical Appraisal, Mercer University Press; The Influence of the Gospel of Matthew on Christian Literature Before Saint Irenaeus, Mercer Univ Press; "The Source of the Agraphon in Justin Martyr's Dialogue with Trypho 47:5," in Virgilae Christianae. **CONTACT ADDRESS** PO Box 5, Aurora, NY 13026. **EMAIL** ajb@wells.edu

BELLOT, LELAND JOSEPH
PERSONAL Born 12/10/1936, Port Arthur, TX, m, 1958, 2 children **DISCIPLINE** HISTORY **EDUCATION** Lamar State Univ, BA, 58; Rice Univ, MA, 60; Univ Tex, Austin, PhD, 67. **CAREER** Acting Dean, 74-75, Dean, Sch of Humanities and Soc Sci, 75-79, Acting Vice Pres, Acad Affairs, 79-80, from asst prof to full prof, Calif State Univ, Fullerton, 64-. **MEMBERSHIPS** AHA; Conf Brit Stud; Phi Kappa Phi; Phi Alpha Theta; Am Soc for Eighteenth-Century Studies; Am Friends of the Inst for Hist Res. **RESEARCH** Modern British history, 18th century; Anglo Am history; comparative slavery. **SELECTED PUBLICATIONS** Auth, "The Evangelical Defense of Slavery in Britain's Old Colonial Empire," The J of S Hist, 1 (71): 19-40; auth, William Knox: The Life and Thought of an Eighteenth-Century Imperialist, Univ Tex Press, 77; ed, "William Knox Asks What Is Fit To Be Done With America?," in Sources of American Independence, (IL: Univ Chicago Press, 78); rev, of "Proslavery: A History of the Defense of Slavery in America, 1701-1840," by Larry E. Tise, The J of S Hist, 3 (Aug, 89): 482-483; auth, "Wild Hares and Red Herrings: A Case-Study of Estate Management, Game Laws and Property Rights in Eighteenth-Century English Countryside," The Huntington Libr Quart (Winter, 93): 15-39; auth, Richard Grenville, Earl Temple, 1711-1779, forthcoming. **CONTACT ADDRESS** Dept of Hist, California State Univ, Fullerton, Fullerton, CA 92634. **EMAIL** lbellot@fullerton.edu

BELLUSH, BERNARD
PERSONAL Born 11/15/1917, New York, NY, m, 1947, 2 children **DISCIPLINE** HISTORY **EDUCATION** City Col NYork, BSS, 41; Columbia Univ, MA, 43, PhD(hist), 51. **CAREER** Tutor, Hunter Col, 46-49; asst prof, 51-61, assoc prof & sub-chmn dept, 61-68, Prof Hist, City Col New York, 68-, Lectr, Ballard Sch, YWCA, 50-53; Am Philos Soc grants, 59-60 & 62; lectr, Teachers Col, Columbia Univ, 60, vis assoc prof, 64-66; lectr, Cooper Union, 61; Fulbright prof, State Univ Utrecht, 66-67 & 70-71; mem nat bd, Am for Democratic Action, 71-, NY State chmn, 71-73. **MEMBERSHIPS** AHA; Orgn Am Historians; Am Civil Liberties Union. **RESEARCH** Franklin D Roosevelt and the New Deal area; John G Winant, governor of New Hampshire; Robert P Bass and the Progressive Era. **SELECTED PUBLICATIONS** Auth, Goy Vey Response to Simurda,Stephen Article on Handler, Evelyn, Lingua Fr, Vol 0003, 93. **CONTACT ADDRESS** Dept of Hist, City Col, CUNY, Convent Ave at 138th St, New York, NY 10031.

BELOHLAVEK, JOHN M.
PERSONAL Born 12/03/1943, Avalon, PA, m, 1982 **DISCIPLINE** HISTORY **EDUCATION** Thiel Col, BA, 65; Univ Nebr, MA, 67; Univ Nebr, PhD, 70. **CAREER** From asst prof to prof, Univ S Fla, 70-. **HONORS AND AWARDS** Fulbright Fel to the USSR, 80-81; Undergrad Teaching Awd, Univ S Fla, 92. **MEMBERSHIPS** Soc for Historians of the Early Am Republic, Southern Hist Asn, Orgn of Am Historians. **RESEARCH** Nineteenth-Century U.S. History, Biography. **SELECTED PUBLICATIONS** Auth, George M. Dallas, Jacksonian Patrician, Penn State Press, 77; auth, Let the Eagle Soar: The Foreign Policy of Andrew Jackson, 85. **CONTACT ADDRESS** Dept Hist, Univ of So Florida, 4202 E Fowler Ave, Tampa, FL 33620-9951. **EMAIL** belohlav@chuma1.cas.usf.edu

BELTMAN, BRIAN W.
PERSONAL Born 10/05/1945, Orange City, IA, m, 1983, 2 children **DISCIPLINE** AMERICAN HISTORY **EDUCATION** Northwestern Col, BA, 67; Univ of Wis Madison, MA, 68; PhD, 74. **CAREER** Asst prof, Univ of SC, Univ of Mid-Am, Ariz State Univ, Dartmouth Col, Hamilton Col, 75-80; adj prof, Univ of SC, 80-. **HONORS AND AWARDS** Nat Defense Educ Fel. **RESEARCH** Dutch-American Ethnic studies, American West - immigration and settlement process, Military history - Vietnam War. **SELECTED PUBLICATIONS** Auth, "Territorial Commands of the Army: The System Refined But Not Perfected, 1815-1821", J of the Early Republic 11, (91): 185-218; auth, "A Dutch Family and Its Iowa roots", Origins 10, (92): 27-34; auth, "Ethnic Persistence and Change: The Experience of a Dutch-American Family in Rural Iowa", Annals of Iowa 52, (93): 1-49; auth, "Frisian Farmer in the Missouri Valley: A Selected Portion of the Life and Letters of Ulbe Eringa, Proceedings of the Tenth Viennial Conf of the Assoc for the Advan of Dutch-Am Studies, Northwestern Col, 95; auth, "Ethnic Territoriality and the Persistence of Identity: Dutch Settlers in Northwest Iowa", 1869-1880", Annals of Iowa 55, (96): 101-137; auth, "Dutch Farmer in the Missouri Valley: The Life and Letters of Ulbe Eringa, 1866-1950", Univ of IL Pr, (Urbana and Chicago), 96. **CONTACT ADDRESS** Dept Hist, Univ of So Carolina, Columbia, Columbia, SC 29225. **EMAIL** bbeltman@scana.com

BELZ, HERMAN JULIUS
PERSONAL Born 09/13/1937, Camden, NJ, m, 1961, 2 children **DISCIPLINE** AMERICAN NINETEENTH CENTURY & CONSTITUTIONAL HISTORY **EDUCATION** Princeton Univ, AB, 59; Univ Wash, MA, 63, PhD(hist), 66. **CAREER** From asst prof to assoc prof, 66-77, univ res bd grant, 68, prof Hist, Univ MD, Col Park, 77-; Am Philos Soc grant, 72; Am Bar Found legal hist merit res fel, 72-73; Guggenheim fel, 80-81; Project 87 fel, 80-81; academic advisor, James Madison Memorial Fel Found. **HONORS AND AWARDS** Beveridge Awd, AHA, 66. **MEMBERSHIPS** AHA; Orgn Am Historians; Am Soc Legal Hist; Southern Hist Asn. **RESEARCH** Constitutionalism and political action; the legitimacy of Supreme Court decision making; secession, revolution, and social contract theory in Am political thought. **SELECTED PUBLICATIONS** Auth, Changing Conceptions of Constitutionalism in the Era of World War Two and the Cold War, J Am Hist, 12/72; The New Orthodoxy in Reconstruction Historiography, Rev Am Hist, 3/73; New Left Reverberations in the Academy: The Anti-pluralist Critique of Constitutionalism, Rev Polit, 4/74; The Freedmen's Bureau Act of 1865 and the Principle of No Discrimination According to Color, Civil War Hist, 9/75; Protection of Personal Liberty in Republican Emancipation Legislation of 1862, J Southern Hist, 8/76; Race, Law, and Politics in the Struggle for Equal Pay during the Civil War, Civil War Hist, 9/76; A New Birth of Freedom: The Republican Party and Freedmen's Rights 1861-1866, Greenwood, 76; Emancipation and Equal Rights: Politics and Constitutionalism in the Civil War Era, Norton, 78; coauth, The American Constitution: Its Origins and Development, W. W. Norton, 91; Equality Transformed: A Quarter Century of Affirmative Action, Transaction Pubs, 91; Abraham Lincoln, Constitutionalism and Equal Rights in the Civil War Era, Fordham Univ Press, 98. **CONTACT ADDRESS** Dept of Hist, Univ of Maryland, Col Park, College Park, MD 20742-0001. **EMAIL** hb5@umail.umd.edu

BEN-AMOS, DAN
PERSONAL Born 09/03/1934, Tel Aviv, Israel, m, 1984, 3 children **DISCIPLINE** ASIAN STUDIES **EDUCATION** Hebrew Univ Jerusalem, BA, 61; Ind Univ, MA, 64; PhD, 67. **CAREER** Asst prof, Univ of Calif, LA, 66-67; prof, Univ of Pa, 67- **HONORS AND AWARDS** Fel, Am council for Learned Soc,72-73; Guggenheim Fel, 75-76; NEH Fel, 80-81. **MEMBERSHIPS** Am Folklore Soc; Am Anthrop Assoc; World Union of Jewish Studies; Assoc of Jewish Studies, Folklore Fel Int of the Finnish Acad of Sciences and Letters. **RESEARCH** Folklore, Jewish folklore, African folklore. **SELECTED PUBLICATIONS** Coed, cotransl, of "In Praise of the Baal Shem Tov", (Bloomington: Indiana Univ Pr), 70; coed, Folklore: Performance and Communication, Approaches to Semiotics, 40 (The Hague: Mouton Pr, 75); ed, New Theories in Oral Literature: Literary Forms in Social Context (Tel-Aviv: Tel-Aviv Univ) 75; auth, Sweet Words: Storytelling Events in Benin, Inst for the Study of Human Issues (Philadelphia), 75; ed, Folklore Genres, Am Folklore Soc Bibliogr and Special Series, Vol 26 (Tex: Univ of Tex Pr), 76; auth Folklore in Context: Essays, (New Delhi, Madras: S Asian Pub), 82; coed, Mimekor Yisrael: Classical Jewish Folktales: Abridged and Annotated Edition by Micha Joseph bin Gorion, Ind Univ Pr, 90; coed, Cultural Memory and the Construction of Identity, (Detroit: Wayne State Univ Pr), 99. **CONTACT ADDRESS** Asian and Middle East Studies, Univ of Pennsylvania, 847 Williams Hall, 6305, Philadelphia, PA 19104-3325. **EMAIL** dbamos@sas.upenn.edu

BEN-ATAR, DORON
DISCIPLINE AMERICAN HISTORY **EDUCATION** Columbia Univ, PhD. **CAREER** Assoc prof, Fordham Univ. **RESEARCH** Psychohistory. **SELECTED PUBLICATIONS** Auth, The Origins of Jeffersonian Commercial Policy and Diplomacy, 93; Alexander Hamilton's Alternative Technology Piracy and the Report on Manufactures, William and Mary Quart 52, 95; Private Friendship and Political Harmony?, Rev(s) Amer Hist, 96. **CONTACT ADDRESS** Dept of Hist, Fordham Univ, 113 W 60th St, New York, NY 10023.

BEN-GHIAT, RUTH
PERSONAL Born 05/17/1960, Evanston, IL, m, 1999, 1 child **DISCIPLINE** HISTORY **EDUCATION** Univ Calif Los Angeles, BA, 81; Brandeis Univ, PhD, 91. **CAREER** Asst prof, Univ NCar, Charlotte, 91-95; asst prof, Fordham Univ, 95-99; assoc prof, NYork Univ, 00-. **HONORS AND AWARDS** Fulbright Res Fel (Italy); postdoctoral fel, Getty Res Inst; fel, Am Philos Soc; Mellon For Area Fel, Libr Cong. **MEMBERSHIPS** AHA; AAIS; Soc for Ital Hist Studies; Soc for Cinema Studies; MLA. **RESEARCH** Twentieth century Italian culture and politics, Italian film, fascism and its memory. **SELECTED PUBLICATIONS** Auth, "Fascism, Writing, and Memory," J of Mod Hist, 95; auth, "Envisioning Modernity: Desire and Discipline in the Italian Fascist Film," Critical Inquiry, 96; auth, "Liberation: Film and the Flight from the Italian Past," in Italian Fascism: History, Memory, and Representation, ed. Richard Bosworth and Patrizia Dogliani (St Martins, 99); auth, La cultura fascista, Mulino, 00; auth, Fascist Modernities: Italy, 1922-1945, Univ Calif Press, 01; auth, "The Secret Histories of Roberto Benigni's 'Life is Beautiful,'" Yale J of Criticism, 01. **CONTACT ADDRESS** Dept of Ital Studies, New York Univ, 24 W Twelfth St, New York, NY 10011. **EMAIL** ruth.benghiat@nyu.edu

BENDER, MELVIN E.
PERSONAL Born 03/15/1953, Elgin, IL, m, 1975, 6 children **DISCIPLINE** HISTORY **EDUCATION** Central Baptist Col, AA, 77; Univ Central Ark, MA, 86; BSE, 79; Univ Memphis, PhD, 97. **CAREER** From asst prof to prof, 79-, Central Baptist Col; adj prof, 96-, Univ Central Ark. **HONORS AND AWARDS** Who's Who Among Am Teachers, 95, 97; Academic Excellence Awd, 89, 99, Central Baptist Col; Awd for Best Church Hist, 95, Ark Hist Asn. **MEMBERSHIPS** Ark Hist Asn, Ark Asn of Col Hist Teachers; Phi Alpha Theta; Friends of Nat Hist Day; Civil War Trust. **RESEARCH** Modern North Africa; Jehovah Witnesses in Hitler's Holocaust; American Higher Education in the South. **SELECTED PUBLICATIONS** Auth, Prison Experiences and Treatment of Officers Captured at Arkansas Post, 81; auth, History in the Bible College Curriculum, 89; auth, Founding of Central Baptist College, 95; auth, A Small School with a Big Heart, 92. **CONTACT ADDRESS** 1501 College Ave, Conway, AR 72032. **EMAIL** dbender@admin.cbc.edu

BENDER, THOMAS
PERSONAL Born 04/18/1944, San Mateo, CA, m **DISCIPLINE** HISTORY **EDUCATION** Univ Santa Clara, BA, 66; Univ Calif, Davis, MA, 67, PhD, 71. **CAREER** Asst prof, Univ Wisc-Green Bay, 71-74; asst prof, 74-76, assoc prof, 76-77, prof, 77-, New York Univ, Samuel Rudin Prof of the Humanities, 77-82, Univ Prof of the Humanities, 82-. **HONORS AND AWARDS** Frederick Jackson Turner Prize, 75; Guggenheim fel, 80-81; Rockefeller Humanities fel, 84-85; Getty Scholar, 92-93; Fel, Am Acad of Arts and Scis, 94-; Fel, Soc of Am Hists, 83-. **MEMBERSHIPS** AHA, OAH, ASA, PEN Writers Guild, New York Councill for the Humanities, 89-96; chair, 93-95. **RESEARCH** US cultural history, cities, intellectuals, historiography. **SELECTED PUBLICATIONS** Auth, Toward an Urban Visions: Ideas and Institutions in Nineteenth Century America (75); auth, Community and Social Change in America (78); coauth, New Directions in American Intellectual History, 79; auth, New York Intellect: A History of Intellectual Life in New York City, from 1750 to the Beginnings of Our Own Time (87); coauth, Historical Literacy, 89; ed, The Anti-Slavery Debate: Capitalism and Abolitionism as a Problem in Historical Interpretation (92); auth, Intellect and Public Life: Essays on the Social History of Academic Intellectuals in the United States (93); co-ed, Budapest and New York (94); coauth, The New American History, 97; coauth, Histoire comparee des intellectuals, 97; co-ed, American Academic Culture in Transformation (98); auth, "Scholarship, Local Life, and the Necessity of Worldliness," in Herman van der Wusten, ed, The Urban University and Its Identity (98); auth, "Cities, Intellectuals, and Citizenship: The United States in the 1890s and 1990s," in James Holston, ed, Cities and Citizenship (99); auth, "New York City, 1910-1935: The Politics and Aesthetics of Two Modernities," in Steven Spier, ed, Urban Visions (2000). **CONTACT ADDRESS** Dept Hist, New York Univ, 53 Washington Sq S, New York, NY 10012. **EMAIL** thomas.bender@nyu.edu

BENDER, TODD K.
PERSONAL Born 01/08/1936, Stark County, OH, m, 1958, 2 children **DISCIPLINE** ENGLISH, CLASSICAL LANGUAGES **EDUCATION** Kenyon Col, BA, 58; Stanford Univ, PhD(class lang & English), 62. **CAREER** Instr English, Stanford Univ, 61-62; instr, Dartmouth Col, 62-63; asst prof, Univ Va, 63-65; assoc prof, 65-73, Prof English, Univ Wis, Madison, 73-, Am Coun Learned Soc grant-in-aid, Oxford Univ, 63 & fel, Bibliot Nat, Paris, 65-66; Am Philos Soc grant, Paris, 69; vis prof, World Campus Prog, 73; Fulbright lectr, Univ Athens, Greece, 78-79. **MEMBERSHIPS** MLA. **RESEARCH** Nineteenth century English and European literature; Homeric Greek; computational linguistics. **SELECTED PUBLICATIONS** **CONTACT ADDRESS** Dept of English, Univ of Wisconsin, Madison, Madison, WI 53706.

BENDERSKY, JOSEPH WILLIAM
PERSONAL Born 07/30/1946, Carbondale, PA **DISCIPLINE** MODERN EUROPEAN & MODERN GERMAN HISTORY **EDUCATION** City Col NYork, BA, 69; Mich State Univ, MA, 70, PhD(German hist), 75. **CAREER** Instr humanities, Mich State Univ, 74-75; asst prof German hist, Marquette Univ, 75-76; instr, 76-79, asst prof, 79-82, Assoc Prof German Hist, VA Commonwealth Univ, 82- **MEMBERSHIPS** Southern Hist Asn; Conf Group for Cent Europ Hist. **RESEARCH** Political and legal theory of Carl Schmitt; Weimar and Nazi Germany; history of German conservatism. **SELECTED PUBLICATIONS** Auth, Progenitors of National Socialism?, Intellect, 78; Ernst Bohle & Nazi Foreign Organization, Int Rev Hist & Polit Sci, 78; Carl Schmitt & English-speaking world, Can J Polit & Social Theory, 78; Carl Schmitt in 1932: A reexamination, Rev europeenne des sci sociales, 78; The expendable Kronjurist, J of Contemp Hist, 79; Carl Schmitt, Theorist for the Reich, Princeton Univ Press, 82. **CONTACT ADDRESS** Dept of Hist, Virginia Commonwealth Univ, Box 2001, Richmond, VA 23284-9004.

BENDINER, KENNETH PAUL
PERSONAL Born 06/06/1947, New York, NY, m, 1974, 3 children **DISCIPLINE** ART **EDUCATION** Univ Mich, BA, 69; Columbia Univ, PhD, 79. **CAREER** Instr, 77-78, Vassar Col; asst prof, 78-79, Wellesley Col; asst prof, 79-80, Columbia Col; assoc prof, prof, 85-99, Univ Wisc - Milwaukee. **RESEARCH** 19th & 20th century art, esp victorian painting, Matisse. **SELECTED PUBLICATIONS** An Introduction to Victorian Painting, Yale Univ Pr (New Haven), 85; Ford Madox Brown: Il Lavoro, Lindau (Turin), 91; The Art of Ford Madox Brown, Penn State Pr (Univ Park, Pa), 98. **CONTACT ADDRESS** Art History, Univ of Wisconsin, Milwaukee, PO Box 413, Milwaukee, WI 53201. **EMAIL** bendiner@uwm.edu

BENEDICT, MICHAEL LES
PERSONAL Born 03/18/1945, Chicago, IL, m, 1968 **DISCIPLINE** AMERICAN & LEGAL CONSTITUTIONAL HISTORY, CIVIL WAR RECONSTRUCTION **EDUCATION** Univ Ill, Urbana-Champaign, BA, 65, MA, 67; Rice Univ, PhD(hist), 71. **CAREER** Asst prof, 70-75, assoc prof, 75-81, prof Hist, Ohio State Univ, 81-, Nat Endowment for Humanities Younger Humanist fel, 73-74; vis mem, Inst Advan Study, Princeton Univ, 74; Guggenheim Mem Found fel, 77-78; fel, Woodrow Wilson Int Ctr Scholars, 79; Fulbright sr lectr, Japan, 82-83; vis prof, Yale Law Sch, 90-91; vis prof, Law Faculty, Doshisha Univ, Kyoto, Japan, 92; adunct prof, Ohio State Univ Sch of Law, 96-; **HONORS AND AWARDS** Samuel I. Golieb Res fel, New York Univ, School of Law, 86-87; ACLS/Ford Fel, Am Council of Learned Soc, 86-87; Vis fellow, The Huntington Library, 86, 87, 88; Fellow, Japan Society for the Promotion of Sci, 89; Fellow, Society of Am Historians, elected 88; Distinguished Lecturer, Fulbright Commission, United Kingdom, 96; Vis fellow, Cunliffe Centre for the Study of Constitutionalism and National Identity, Univ of Sussex, 96, 00 Fellow, Ohio State Univ Center for Law, Policy, and Social Science, 99-02 **MEMBERSHIPS** Southern Hist Asn; Orgn Am Historians; Am Soc Legal Hist; Soc Sci Hist Asn. **RESEARCH** American legal and constitutional history; American Civil War and Reconstruction. **SELECTED PUBLICATIONS** Auth, The Impeachment and Trial of Andrew Johnson, 73 & A Compromise of Principle: Congressional Republicans and Reconstruction, 1863-1869, 74, Norton; The Fruits of Victory: Alternatives in Restoring the Union, Lippincott, 75; rev ed 86; The Blessings of Liberty: A Concise History of the Constitution of the United States, Heath, 95; Preserving Federalism: Reconstruction and the Waite Court, Super Ct Rev, 78; Southern Democrats in the Crisis of 1876-1877: A Reconsideration of Reunion and Reaction, J Southern Hist, 11/80; "Laissez Faire and Liberty: A Re-Evaluation of the Meaning and Origins of Laissez-Faire Constitutionalism," Law and History Review, 3, Fall 85: 293-331 **CONTACT ADDRESS** Dept of History, Ohio State Univ, Columbus, 230 W 17th Ave, Columbus, OH 43210-1361. **EMAIL** benedict.3@osu.edu

BENEDICT, PHILIP
PERSONAL Born 08/20/1949, Washington, DC, m, 1970, 2 children **DISCIPLINE** HISTORY **EDUCATION** Cornell Univ, BA, 70; Princeton Univ, MA, 72; PhD, 75. **CAREER** Visiting asst prof, Cornell Univ, 75-76; asst prof, Univ MD, 76-78; asst to full prof, Brown Univ, 78-. **HONORS AND AWARDS** Fulbright Fel, NEH Fel for Univ teachers, Guggenheim Mem Fel. **MEMBERSHIPS** Am Soc for Reformation Res; Soc for French Hist Studies. **RESEARCH** Early modern Europe, especially religious and social. **SELECTED PUBLICATIONS** Auth, "The Saint Bartholomew's Massacres in the Provinces," the Historical Journal (78): 205-225; auth, Rouen during the Wars of Religion, Cambridge Univ Press, 81; auth, "Rouen's Foreign Trade in the Age of the Religious Wars (1560-1600)," Journal of European Economic History, (84): 29-74; ed, Reformation, Revolt and Civil War in France and the Netherlands, 1555-1585, Amsterdam, 99; auth, "Between Whig Traditions and New Histories: American Historical Writing about Reformation and Early Modern Europe," in Imagined Histories: American Historians Explore the Past, 98; auth, "Un roi, une loi, deux fois: Parameters for the History of Catholic-Reformed Coexistence in France, 1555-1685," in Tolerance and Intolerance in the European Reformation, Cambridge, 96; auth, "Faith, fortune and Social Structure in Seventeenth-Century Montpellier," Past & Present, (96): 46-78. **CONTACT ADDRESS** Dept Hist, Brown Univ, Providence, RI 02912-9100. **EMAIL** philip_benedict@brown.edu

BENKO, STEPHEN
PERSONAL Born 06/13/1924, Budapest, Hungary, m, 1952, 4 children **DISCIPLINE** RELIGION, ANCIENT HISTORY **EDUCATION** Reformed Theol Sem Budapest, BD, 47; Univ Basel, PhD(relig), 51. **CAREER** Res fel, Divinity Sch, Yale Univ, 53-54; instr, Sch Theol, Temple Univ, 57-59 & lectr, Grad Sch Philos & Relig, 59-61; prof Bibl studies & patristics, Conwell Sch Theol, 60-69; Prof Ancient Hist, Calif State Univ, Fresno, 69-. **MEMBERSHIPS** Am Hist Asn; Am Philol Asn; Am Soc Church Hist; Soc Bibl Lit. **RESEARCH** Ancient church history; ecumenical relations. **SELECTED PUBLICATIONS** Auth, Education, Culture and the Arts Transylvanian Cultural Hist, Hungarian Quart, Vol 0035, 94. **CONTACT ADDRESS** Dept of Hist, California State Univ, Fresno, Fresno, CA 93740.

BENN, CARL E.
PERSONAL Born 03/04/1953, Toronto, ON, Canada **DISCIPLINE** MILITARY HISTORY **EDUCATION** Univ Toronto, BA, 80, MDiv, 83; York Univ, PhD, 95. **CAREER** Hist interp, Toronto Hist Bd, 71-75; sr hist interp, Borough Etobicoke, 75-80; cur collections, Regional Municipality Waterloo, 83-85; Cur Military Hist, Toronto Hist Board, 85-; Tchr (part-time), Univ Toronto, 90-. **MEMBERSHIPS** Ont Mus Asn; Ont Hist Soc. **SELECTED PUBLICATIONS** Auth, The King's Mill on the Humber, 79; auth, The Battle of York, 84; auth, Historic Fort York 1793-1993, 93; auth, The Iroquois in the War of 1812, 98. **CONTACT ADDRESS** Dept Hist, Univ of Toronto, 100 St George St, 2074 Sidney Smith Hall, Toronto, ON, Canada M5S 3G3. **EMAIL** c.benn@utoronto.ca

BENNETT, DAVID HARRY
PERSONAL Born 01/22/1935, Syracuse, NY, m, 1961, 2 children **DISCIPLINE** AMERICAN HISTORY **EDUCATION** Syracuse Univ, AB, 56; Univ Chicago, AM, 58, PhD(hist), 63. **CAREER** Lectr hist, Univ Chicago, 58-60; instr Am studies, 61-63, asst prof hist & Am studies, 63-69, assoc prof, 69-75, Prof Hist & Chmn Dept, Hist, Syracuse Univ, 70-76; Prof, 75-- **HONORS AND AWARDS** Gustavius Meyers Prize, 88. **MEMBERSHIPS** AHA; Orgn Am Historians. **RESEARCH** Recent Amer history; Amer studies. **SELECTED PUBLICATIONS** Auth, Demagogues in the Depression: American Radicals and the Union Party, 1932-36, New Brunswick, NJ: Rutgers Univ Press, 69; auth, The Party of Fear: From Nativist Movements to the Far Right in American History, Chapel Hill: Univ of North Carolina Press, 88; auth, The Party of Fear: The American Far Right From Nativism to the Militia Movement, New York: Vintage Book, 95; auth, Religion and the Racist Right in the Origins of the Christian Identity Movement, Amer Hist Rev, Vol 0101, 96; Forging New Freedoms in Nativism, Education, and the Constitution, 1917-1927, J of Amer Hist, Vol 0083, 96; The Populist Persuasion in An American History, Amer Hist Rev, Vol 0101, 96. **CONTACT ADDRESS** Syracuse Univ, 320 Berkeley Dr, Syracuse, NY 13210.

BENNETT, EDWARD MOORE
PERSONAL Born 09/28/1927, Dixon, IL, m, 1950, 1 child **DISCIPLINE** AMERICAN HISTORY **EDUCATION** Butler Univ, BA, 52; Univ Ill, MA, 56, PhD(Am diplomatic hist), 61. **CAREER** Teaching asst, Univ Ill, 56-60; instr Am hist, Agr & Mech Col Tex, 60-61; from asst prof to assoc prof Am & Russ hist, 61-71, Prof Hist, Wash State Univ, 71-94, prof emer, 94-; Participant, Ford Found Community Sem, 65; pres, Pac-Eight Conf Coun, 72-73. Pac-iu, 73-91. **HONORS AND AWARDS** Outstanding Fac Awd, Wash State Univ, 79. **MEMBERSHIPS** Orgn Am Historians; AAUP; Soc Hist Am Foreign Rels. **RESEARCH** Russian-Amer diplomacy, especially the 1930's; Amer diplomatic history; Amer Far Eastern relations 1932-1941. **SELECTED PUBLICATIONS** Auth, Franklin D. Roosevelt and the Search for Security: American-Soviet Relations, 1933-1939, 85; auth, Franklin D. Roosevelt and the Search for Victory: American-Soviet Relations, 1939-45, 90; auth, Fdr and His Contemporaries in Foreign Perceptions of An Amer President, Amer Hist Rev, Vol 0098, 93; Davies, Joseph, E in Envoy to the Soviets, Amer Hist Rev, Vol 0100, 95; the Vulnerability of Empire, Amer Hist Rev, Vol 0100, 95. **CONTACT ADDRESS** Dept of Hist, Washington State Univ, 323 Wilson Hall, Pullman, WA 99164. **EMAIL** embennet@wsunix.wsu.edu

BENNETT, JAMES D.
PERSONAL Born 08/02/1926, Calhoun, KY, m, 1951 **DISCIPLINE** HISTORY **EDUCATION** Centre Col Ky, BA, 47; Tex Christian Univ, MA, 54; Vanderbilt Univ, PhD(hist), 68. **CAREER** Asst, Tex Christian Univ, 53-54; from instr to asst prof US Hist, San Antonio Col, 54-59; assoc prof, 59-69, Prof US Hist, Western KY Univ, 69- **MEMBERSHIPS** Southern Hist Asn; Orgn Am Historians; Western Hist Asn. **RESEARCH** Urban history; trans-Mississippi west; Tennessee Valley Authority. **SELECTED PUBLICATIONS** Coauth, A Guide to Historical Research and Writing, Western Ky Univ, 70 & rev ed, 74; auth, Frederick Jackson Turner: American Historian, Twayne, 73. **CONTACT ADDRESS** Dept of Hist, Western Kentucky Univ, Bowling Green, KY 42101.

BENNETT, JUDITH M.
PERSONAL Born 01/12/1951, Neptune, NJ **DISCIPLINE** HISTORY **CAREER** Asst prof to prof, Univ of NC, 81-; vis prof, Univ of London, 98-; Dir, Grad Studies, 98-. **HONORS AND AWARDS** Am coun of Learned Soc Fel, 84; Am Philos Soc Res Grant, 86; NEH Summer Stipend, 87; Guggenheim Fel, 89-90; Walter D. Love Prize for 92; Nat Humanities Fel, 93-4; Folger Shakespeare Libr Fel, 97; Otto Grundler Prize in Medieval Studies, 98. **RESEARCH** Women in medieval and early modern Europe, especially England. **SELECTED PUBLICATIONS** Auth, Women in the Medieval English Countryside: Gender and Household in Brigstock before the Plague, Oxford Univ Pr, 87; coed, Sisters and Workers in The Middle Ages, Oxford Univ Pr, 89; auth, Ale, Beer, and Brewsters in England: Women's Work in a Changing World, 1300 to 1600, Oxford Univ Pr, 96; auth, A Medieval Life: Cecilia Penifader of Brigstock, c. 1297-1344, McGraw-Hill, 98; coed, Singlewomen in the European Past, 1250-1800, Univ of Pa Pr, 99; auth, Medieval Women in Modern Perspective, AHA, 00. **CONTACT ADDRESS** Dept Hist, Univ of No Carolina, Chapel Hill, 440 W Franklin St, Chapel Hill, NC 27599-2319. **EMAIL** bennett@email.unc.edu

BENNETT, NORMAN ROBERT
PERSONAL Born 10/31/1932, Marlboro, MA, m, 1976, 2 children **DISCIPLINE** AFRICAN, WINE & PORTUGUESE HISTORY **EDUCATION** Tufts Univ, AB, 54; Fletcher Sch Law, MA, 56; Boston Univ, PhD, 61. **CAREER** From instr to asst prof African hist, 60-67, assoc prof, 67-70, Prof Hist, Boston Univ, 70-98, Prof Emer, 98-; Am Philos Soc fel, 66; ed, African Studies Asn Bull, 66-70 & Int J Hist African Studies, 68-99; vis scholar, Eduardo Mondlane Univ, Mozambique, 77. **HONORS AND AWARDS** Ford Found African Scholar, 58-60; Smith-Mundt lectr, Kivukoni Col, Tanganyika, 62-63; Gulbenkian Foundation Fellowship, 84-87. **MEMBERSHIPS** AHA; African Studies Asn (pres, 81); Tanzania Soc; Acad Royale des Sci d'Outre-Mer, Belgium. **RESEARCH** African history; Portuguese history; Wine history. **SELECTED PUBLICATIONS** ed, Leadership in Eastern Africa, 68, From Zanzibar to Ujiji: The Journal of Arthur W Dodgshun, 69, Stanley's Dispatches to the New York Herald, 1871-1872, 1874-1877, 70 & co-ed, The Central African Journal of L J Procter, 1860-1864, 71, Bos-

ton Univ; auth, Mirambo of Tanzania, Oxford Univ, 71; ed, The Zanzibar Letters of E D Ropes, Jr, 1882-1892, Boston Univ African Studies Ctr, 73; auth, Africa and Europe from Roman Times to the Present, Africana, 75; A History of the Arab State of Zanzibar, Methuen, Inc, 78; Arab Versus European Diplomacy & War in 19th Century East Central Africa, Africana, 86. **CONTACT ADDRESS** African Studies Ctr, Boston Univ, 270 Bay State Rd, Boston, MA 02215-1403. **EMAIL** bennet-l@idt.net

BENNETT, Y. ALEKSANDRA
DISCIPLINE HISTORY **EDUCATION** Univ Windsor, BA, MA; McMaster Univ, PhD. **CAREER** Assoc prof. **RESEARCH** Peace, religion, war and society in twentieth-century Britain. **SELECTED PUBLICATIONS** Auth, A Question of Responsibility and Tactics: Vera Brittain and Food Relief for Occupied Europe, 1941-1944, The Pacifist Impulse in Historical Perspective, Toronto UP, 96. **CONTACT ADDRESS** Dept of Hist, Carleton Univ, 1125 Colonel By Dr, 440 Patterson Hall, Ottawa, ON, Canada K1S 5B6. **EMAIL** bennett@ccs.carleton.ca

BENNETT PETERSON, BARBARA
DISCIPLINE HISTORY **EDUCATION** Ore State Univ, BA, 64; BS, 64; Stanford Univ, MA, 65; Univ Haw, PhD, 78; London Inst Applied Res, Honorary PhD,91; Australian Inst for Coordinated Res, Honorary PhD, 95. **CAREER** Asst Prof, Chapman Col, 74; Assoc Prof, Univ Colo, 78; Assoc Prof, Univ Haw, 81; Visiting Prof, Sichuan Univ, 89; Prof, Wuhan Univ, 88-89; Res Assoc, Intl Biography Center, 92; Adj Prof, Haw Pacific Univ, 96-; Fel, World Literary Acad, 97-; emeritus prof, Univ Haw, 95-. **HONORS AND AWARDS** Distinguished alumni Awd, Univ Haw Alumni Asn, 97; Excellence in Teaching Awd, Univ Haw, 93; Outstanding Teacher of the Year, Wuhan Univ, 88-89; Grand ambassador of Achievement, am Biographical Inst, 92; Woman of the Year, am Biographical Inst, 90-91; world Decoration of Excellence, Am Biographical Inst, 89-90; Leader for the 1980s, AAWCJC, 85; NEH-Woodrow Wilson Fel, 80; Outstanding Educator of Am, 73Fulbright Scholar, Sophia Univ, 67; Intl Relations Awd, Kiwanis club of W San Jose, 67; Phi Kappa Phi; Mortar Board, OSU, 64; Outstanding Sen Woman, OSU, 64; Kappa Delta Pi, 64; Pi Delta Phi, 64; Clara H Waldo Awd, OSU, 62. **MEMBERSHIPS** Intl Biographical Asn, Bishop Museum Coun, Nat Coun for History Educ, Am Biographical Inst Res Asn, Am Biographical Inst, Haw Foundation for Women's Hist. **SELECTED PUBLICATIONS** Co-ed, American National Biography, 24 volumes, 98; auth, Notable Women of china, M.E. Sharpe Pub, New York, 00; auth, John Bull's Eye on America, Fulbright Asn, 95; ed, America: 19th and 20th Centuries, American Heritage, 94; ed, American History, 17th, 18th and 19th Centuries, American Heritage, New York, 93; co-ed, The Pacific Region 1990, Fulbright Asn, 91; auth, America in British Eyes, Fulbright Asn, 88; ed, Notable Women of Hawaii, Univ of Haw Press, 84; co-auth, Woman's Place is in the History Books, Her Story, 1620-1980. A curriculum Guide for American History Teachers, Woodrow Wilson Inst, 80; auth, "Andre Gide," in Europe since 1945: An Encyclopedia, Garland Press, 99 **CONTACT ADDRESS** Dept History, Univ of Hawaii, Honolulu Comm Col, 1601 East-West Rd, Burns Hall, Honolulu, HI 96822.

BENSON, JACK LEONARD
PERSONAL Born 06/25/1920, Kansas City, MO, m, 1954 **DISCIPLINE** CLASSICAL ARCHAEOLOGY **EDUCATION** Univ Mo, BA, 41; Ind Univ, MA, 47; Univ Basel, Switz, PhD, 52. **CAREER** Instr, Yale Univ, 52-53; res assoc class archaeol, Univ Mus, Univ Pa, 53; assoc prof classics, Univ Miss, 58-61; vis assoc prof art, Princeton Univ, 60-61; assoc prof, Wellesley Col, 61-64; prof Ancient Art, 65-85, prof emeritus, 85-, Univ Mass, Amherst; Res assoc, Univ Mus, Univ Pa, 54-85; Fulbright res scholar & Guggenheim fel, 56-58; mem, Brit Sch Archaeol, Jerusalem, 57-75; Am Philos Soc Penrose Fund fel, 61; mem, Inst Advan Study, Princeton Univ, 55, 64-65 & 70; Am Coun Learned Soc fel, 65; guest prof, Univ Freiburg, 76. **MEMBERSHIPS** Archaeol Inst Am; Class Asn New England. **RESEARCH** Theory of period setting in Greek art; archaic Greek vases; Cypriote archaeology. **SELECTED PUBLICATIONS** Auth, Horse Bird & Man: The Origins of Greek Painting, Univ of Mass Press, 70; auth, Bamboula at Kourion, Univ of Pa Press, 72; auth, The Necropolis of Kaloriziki, Studies in Mediterranean Archaeology XXXVI, 73; Coauth, Corinth, vol XV pt 3, The Potters' Quarter: The Corinthian Pottery, Princeton, 84; auth, Earlier Corinthian Workshops, Amsterdam, 89; auth, The Inner Nature of Greek Art, 92; auth, CVA Fascicule 29, Univ Mus Fascicule II: Corinthian Pottery, Penn, 95; auth, Greek Color Theory and the Four Elements, 00; auth, Greek Sculpture and the Four Elements, 00. **CONTACT ADDRESS** Art History Dept, Univ of Massachusetts, Amherst, Amherst, MA 01003. **EMAIL** jlb@vgernet.net

BENSON, KEITH RODNEY
PERSONAL Born 07/22/1948, Portland, OR, d, 1980 **DISCIPLINE** HISTORY **EDUCATION** Whitworth Col, BA, 70; Ore State Univ, MA, 73, PhD(biol sci), 79. **CAREER** Instr biol, Whitworth Col, 77-78; asst prof, Pac Lutheran Univ, 79-81; Asst Prof Biomedical Hist, Univ Wash, 81-87; Assoc, 87-94; Prof, 94-. **MEMBERSHIPS** Sigma Xi; Hist Sci Soc. **RESEARCH** Hist of marine biology; development of Amer science; evolution theory. **SELECTED PUBLICATIONS** Auth, Dohrn,Anton in A Life For Science, Hist and Philos of the Life Sciences, Vol 0014, 92; Experimental Ecology on the Pacific Coast in Shelford, Victor and His Search For Appropriate Methods, Hist and Philos of the Life Sciences, Vol 0014, 92; Experimental Ecology on the Pacific Coast in Shelford, Victor and His Search For Appropriate Methods, Hist and Philos of the Life Sciences, Vol 0014, 92; Reading the Shape of Nature in Comparative Zoology At the Agassiz Museum, Hist and Philos of the Life Sciences, Vol 0014, 92; Dohrn, Anton in A Life For Science, Hist and Philos of the Life Sciences, Vol 0014, 92; Reading the Shape of Nature in Comparative Zoology At the Agassiz-Museum, Hist and Philos of the Life Sciences, Vol 0014, 92; Making Sex in Body and Gender From the Greeks to Freud, Hist and Philos of the Life Sciences, Vol 0015, 93; Making Sex in Body and Gender From the Greeks to Freud, Hist and Philos of the Life Sciences, Vol 0015, 93; Sovereign Oceanographers, Hist and Philos of the Life Sciences, Vol 0017, 95; Sovereign Oceanographers, Hist and Philos of the Life Sciences, Vol 0017, 95; Styles of Scientific Thought in the German Genetics Community, 1900-1933, Annals of Sci, Vol 0052, 95; Styles of Scientific Thought in the German Genetics Community, 1900-1933, Annals of Sci, Vol 0052, 95; To Make A Spotless Orange in Biological-Control in California, J of Amer Hist, Vol 0084, 97. **CONTACT ADDRESS** Dept of Hist, Univ of Washington, PO Box 353560, Seattle, WA 98195. **EMAIL** krbenson@u.washington.edu

BENSON, LEGRACE
PERSONAL Born 02/23/1930, Richmond, VA, w, 1952, 3 children **DISCIPLINE** ART; PHILOSOPHY; PERCEPTUAL PSYCHOLOGY **EDUCATION** Meredith Coll, AB, 51; Univ Georgia Athens, MFA, 56; Cornell Univ, PhD, 74. **CAREER** Asst prof, Cornell Univ, 68-71; assoc prof/assoc dean for special programs, Wells Coll, 71-77; assoc dean, SUNY-Empire State Coll, 77-80; coordinator of arts, humanities and communications study, center for distance learning, SUNY-Empire State Coll, 81-92. **HONORS AND AWARDS** Empire State Coll Excellence in Scholarship, 92. **MEMBERSHIPS** Natl Coalition of Independent Scholars; Haitian Studies Assn; Coll Art Assn; Latin Amer Studies Assn; Arts Council African Studies Assn; African Studies Assn; Canadian Assn Latin Amer and Caribbean Studies. **RESEARCH** Arts and Culture of Haiti; adult distance learning **SELECTED PUBLICATIONS** Auth, The Utopian Vision in Haitian Painting, Callaloo, Spring 92; Journal of Caribbean Studies, Observations on Islamic Motifs in Haitian Visual Arts, Winter 92/Spring 93; The Arts of Haiti Considered Ecologically, Paper for Culture Change and Technology in the Americas conference, Nov 95; Three Presentations of the Arts of Haiti, Journal of Haitian Studies, Autumn 96; Habits of Attention: Persistence of Lan Ginee in Haiti, in The African Diaspora African Origins and New-world Self-fashioning, 98; How Houngans Use the Light from Distant Stars; Muslim and Breton Survivals in Haitian Voudou Arts, 99; The Artists and the Arts of Haiti in Their Geographical and Conversational Domains, 99. **CONTACT ADDRESS** 314 E. Buffalo St., Ithaca, NY 14850-4227. **EMAIL** legracebenson@clarityconnect.com

BENSON, RENATE
PERSONAL Born, Germany **DISCIPLINE** GERMAN STUDIES **EDUCATION** Univ Cologne, 61-62; Univ Montreal, LL, 65; McGill Univ, PhD, 70. **CAREER** Lectr to Prof, German Studies, Univ Guelph, 67-. **HONORS AND AWARDS** Distinguished Prof Awd, Col Arts, 90. **MEMBERSHIPS** MLA; CAUTG; OATG; Hum Asn. **SELECTED PUBLICATIONS** Auth, Erich Kastner, Studien zu seinem Werk, 73; auth, Aspects of Love in Anne Hebert's Short Stories, in J Can Fiction, 79; auth, German Expressionist Drama: Ernst Toller and Georg Kaiser, 84. **CONTACT ADDRESS** Dept of German Studies, Univ of Guelph, Guelph, ON, Canada N1G 2W1. **EMAIL** rbenson@uoguelph.ca

BENSON, WARREN S.
PERSONAL Born 08/23/1929, Chicago, IL, m, 1953, 2 children **DISCIPLINE** HISTORY OF EDUCATION **EDUCATION** NW Col, BA, 52; Dallas Theol Sem, ThM, 56; SW Baptist Theol Sem, MRE, 57; Loyola Univ Chicago, PhD, 75. **CAREER** Min of Education, Winnetka Bible Church, 57-62; Min of Youth & Education, First Covenant Church, Minn, 62-65; Min of Education, Lake Ave Congregational Church, Pasedena, 65-69; Assoc prof, Christian Education, Dallas Theol Sem, 74-78; asst prof, Christian Education, Trinity Evangelical Divinity School, Deerfield, 70-74 & 78-. **HONORS AND AWARDS** Distinguished Prof of Christian Education (NAPCE) **MEMBERSHIPS** N Amer Prof Christian Education; Asn Prof & Res Relig Educ **SELECTED PUBLICATIONS** Coauth, A History and Philosophy of Christian Education, Moody Press; coed, Youth Education in the Church, Moody Press; The Complete Book of Youth Ministry, Moody Press; auth, Leading the Church in Education, Word Publishing. **CONTACT ADDRESS** Trinity Evangelical Divinity Sch, 2065 Half Day Rd., Deerfield, IL 60015.

BENTLEY, JERRY HARRELL
PERSONAL Born 12/09/1949, Birmingham, AL, s **DISCIPLINE** WORLD HISTORY **EDUCATION** Univ Tenn, BA, 71; Univ Minn, MA, 74, PhD (hist), 76. **CAREER** Asst prof, 76-82, Assoc Prof Hist, 82-87; Prof 87-, Univ Hawaii. **MEMBERSHIPS** Renaissance Soc Am; Am Soc Reformation Res; AHA. **RESEARCH** Renaissance Europe; Renaissance humanism; politics and culture. **SELECTED PUBLICATIONS** Auth, "Traditions and Encounters: A Global Perspective on the Past," New York, 00; auth, "Hemispheric Integration, 500-1500 C.E.," Journal of World History, 9, 98: 237-54; auth, "Shapes of World History in Twentieth-Century Scholarship," Washington, D.C., 96; auth, "Cross-Cultural Interaction and Periodization in World History," American Historical Review 101, 96: 749-70; auth, "Old World Encounters: Cross-Cultural Contacts and Exchanges in Pre-Modern Times," New York 93; auth, "Politics and Culture in Renaissance Naples," Pinceton, 87; auth, "Humanists and Holy Writ: New Testament Scholarship in the Renaissance," Princeton, 83. **CONTACT ADDRESS** Dept of Hist, Univ of Hawaii, Manoa, 2530 Dole St, Honolulu, HI 96822-2303. **EMAIL** jbentley@hawaii.edu

BENTON, CATHERINE
PERSONAL m, 1944 **DISCIPLINE** HISTORY OF RELIGION **EDUCATION** Columbia Univ, PhD, 91. **CAREER** LECTR, RELIG, LAKE FOREST COL, 87-. **MEMBERSHIPS** AAR; AAS; Asia Network. **CONTACT ADDRESS** Dept of Relig, Lake Forest Col, 555 N Sheridan Rd, Saint Louis, MO 60045. **EMAIL** benton@lfc.edu

BENTON, RUSSELL E.
PERSONAL Born, FL, s **DISCIPLINE** HISTORY **EDUCATION** Erskine Col, AB, 61; Stetson Univ, MA, 62; La State Univ, PhD, 75. **CAREER** Instr, Univ of SC, 62-64; asst prof, Gardner-Webb, 65-66; prof, Lenoir-Rhyne Col, 67-. **HONORS AND AWARDS** R.J. Reynolds Fel, UNC, 65; Vis Scholar, Cambridge Univ, 89; Vis Prof, Harlaxton Col, 94. **MEMBERSHIPS** SHA. **RESEARCH** Royal biography, King Alexander I of Greece. **SELECTED PUBLICATIONS** Auth, The Downfall of a King: Dom Manuel II of Portugal, Univ Pr of Am, 77; auth, Emma Naea Rooke - Beloved Queen of Hawaii, Mellon Pr, 88. **CONTACT ADDRESS** Dept Hist, Lenoir-Rhyne Col, PO Box 7224, Hickory, NC 28601-3904. **EMAIL** benton_r@lrc.edu

BERCUSON, DAVID JAY
PERSONAL Born 08/31/1945, Montreal, PQ, Canada, m, 1966, 1 child **DISCIPLINE** CANADIAN HISTORY **EDUCATION** Sir George Williams Univ, BA, 66; Univ Toronto, MA, 67, PhD (hist), 71. **CAREER** Asst prof, 71-80, Prof Hist, Univ Calgary, 80-. **MEMBERSHIPS** Can Hist Asn. **RESEARCH** Modern Canadian political, Military and diplomatic history, hist of Israel and Zionism, and modern Jewish hist. **SELECTED PUBLICATIONS** Auth, Canada and the Birth of Israel: A Study in Canadian Foeign Policy, by David J. Bercuson, 85; auth, Canada and the Burden of Unity, by David J. Bercuson, 86; auth, Relations, and the General Strike, by David J. Bercuson, 90; auth, True Patriot: The Life of Brooke Clcaxton, 1898-1960, by David J. Bercuson, 93; coauth, The Valour and the Horror Revisited, by David J. Bercuson, S.F. Wise, 94; coauth, The Valour and the Horror Revisited, by David J. Bercuson, S. F.Wise, 94; auth, Maple Leaf Against th eAxis: Canada's Second World War, by David J. Bercuson, 95; auth, Significant Incident: Canada's Army, the Airborne, and the Murder in Somalia, by David Bercuson, 97; auth, Maple Leaf Against the Axis: Canada's Second World War, by David J. Bercuson, 98; auth, Blood on the Hills: The Canadian Army in the Korean War, by David J. Bercuson, 99. **CONTACT ADDRESS** Dept of Hist, Univ of Calgary, 2500 Univ Dr NW, Social Sciences 656, Calgary, AB, Canada T2N 1N4. **EMAIL** dbercuson@stratnet.ucalgary.ca

BERG, GERALD MICHAEL
PERSONAL Born 06/29/1946, New York, NY, m **DISCIPLINE** HISTORY **EDUCATION** Univ Calif, Berkeley, BA, 69, PhD, 75. **CAREER** From asst prof to prof History, Sweet Briar Col, 75-; Nat Endowment Hum fel, 82; Fulbright fel 89-90. **MEMBERSHIPS** AHA; African Studies Asn. **RESEARCH** Madagascar; civic religion; ideology; Modern Isreal, gender. **SELECTED PUBLICATIONS** Auth, The myth of racial strife and Merina Kinglists, History in Africa, 77; Royal ritual in 19th century Imerina, Madagascar in History, Found Malagasy Studies, 80; Some Words about Merina Historical Literature, The African Past Speaks, Dawson, 80; Riziculture and the Founding of Monarchy in Imerina, J African Hist, Vol 22, 289-308; The Sacred Musket, Comp Studies in Soc and History, (27/2) 85; Sacred Acquisition, J African Hist, (29) 88; Writing Ideology, Hist in Africa, (22) 95; Virtue and Fortuna.., Hist in Africa (23) 96; Radama's Smile, Hist in Africa (25) 98. **CONTACT ADDRESS** Dept Hist, Sweet Briar Col, Sweet Briar, VA 24595. **EMAIL** gberg@sbc.edu

BERGEN, BARRY
PERSONAL Born 07/05/1955, Newark, NJ, s **DISCIPLINE** HISTORY **EDUCATION** Univ Rochester, BA, 78; Univ Pa, MA; PhD, 87. **CAREER** Lectr/Vis Asst Prof, Univ of NC at Wilmington, 86-88; Vis Asst Prof, Auburn Univ at Montogomery, 88-89; Vis Lectr/Asst Prof, Rice Univ, 90-92; Asst/Assoc Prof, Gallaudet Prof, 92-. **HONORS AND AWARDS** Henry Bernard Prize, Hist of Educ Soc, 80-81; Bourse Chateaubriand,

83-84; Post-Doctoral Fel, Harvard Univ Minda du Gunzberg Ctr for Europ Studies, 89-90; Nat Acad of Educ Spencer Post-Doctoral Fel, 89-90; Gaullaudet Univ Res Grants, 95, 99, 00. **MEMBERSHIPS** AHA, Soc for French Hist Studies, Western Soc for French Hist, Int Standing Conf on the Hist of Educ. **RESEARCH** Modern France, Primary Education, Modern Europe. **SELECTED PUBLICATIONS** Auth, "Only a schoolmaster: Gender, Class and the Effort to Professionalize Elementary Teaching in England, 1870-1910," Hist of Educ Quart 22-2 (Spring 82): 1-21, and in Schoolwork: Approaches to the Labor Process of Teaching, ed. Jenny Ozga (Philadelphia and Milton Keynes, England: The Open Univ Press, 88); auth, "Primary Education in Third Republic France: Recent French Works," Hist of Educ Quart 26-2 (Summer 86): 271-285; auth, "Secularizing the Schools in France, 1870-1900: Controversy, Continuity, and Consensus," Harvard Univ Center for Europ Studies Working Papers, Series 26 (July 90). **CONTACT ADDRESS** Dept Hist and Govt, Gallaudet Univ, 800 Florida Ave NE, Washington, DC 20002-3660. **EMAIL** barry.bergen@gallaudet.edu

BERGEN, DORIS L.

PERSONAL Born 10/19/1960, Saskatoon, Canada, m, 1998 **DISCIPLINE** HISTORY OF MODERN EUROPE **EDUCATION** Univ Saskatchewan, BA, 82; Univ Alberta, MA, 84; Univ N Carolina, Chapel Hill, PhD, 91. **CAREER** Asst prof, Univ Vermont, 91-96; asst prof, 96-98, assoc prof, 98- , Univ Notre Dame. **HONORS AND AWARDS** DAAD grant, 98; fel, German Marshall Fund, 98; Charles H Revson Fel, Ctr for Advanced Holocaust Stud, US Holocaust Mem Mus, 98. **MEMBERSHIPS** Am Hist Asn; German Stud Asn; Berkshire Conf of Women Hist. **RESEARCH** Religion; ethnicity and gender in National Socialist Germany; Holocaust; World War II; German military chaplains; ethnic Germans in Eastern Europe. **SELECTED PUBLICATIONS** Auth, The Nazi Concept of Volksdeutsche and The Exacerbation of Antisemitism in Eastern Europe, 1939-1945, J of Contemp Hist, 94; auth, Catholics, Protestants, and Anti-Jewish Christianity in Nazi Germany, Cent Europ Hist, 94; auth, Nazi Christians and Christian Nazis: The German Christian Movement in National Socialist Germany, in Rubenstein, ed, What Kind of God: Essays in Honor of Richard L. Rubenstein, Univ Press of Am, 95; auth, Twisted Cross: The German Christian Movement in the Third Reich, Univ No Carolina Press, 96; auth, Germany Is Our Mission--Christ Is Our Strength!: The Wehrmacht Chaplaincy and the German Christian Movement, Church Hist, 97; auth, What God Has Put Asunder, Let No Man Join Together: Overseas Missions and the German Christian View of Race, in Tobler, ed, Remembrance, Repentance, Reconciliation: The 25th Anniversary Volume of the Annual Scholars' Conference on the Holocaust and the Churches, Univ Press of America, 98; auth, The Volksdeutschen, World War II, and the Holocaust, in Bullivant, ed, Germany and Eastern Europe, 1870-1996: Cultural Identities and Cultural Differences, Walter De Gruyter, 98. **CONTACT ADDRESS** Dept of History, Univ of Notre Dame, 219 O'Shaughnessy Hall, Notre Dame, IN 46556-0368. **EMAIL** Bergen.4@nd.edu

BERGER, CARL

PERSONAL Born 01/28/1925, Chicago, IL **DISCIPLINE** AMERICAN HISTORY **EDUCATION** Univ Iowa, AB, 49; Drake Univ, MA, 51. **CAREER** Reporter and asst city ed, Des Moines Register, Iowa, 49-53; historian, US Army, Japan, 53-55, Tech Serv Corps, Washington, DC, 56-57, writer-analyst, spec opers res off, Am Univ, 57-59; historian, 1st Strategic Aerospace Div, Vandenberg AFB, Calif, 59-61, Cambridge Res Labs, Bedford, Mass, 61-62 and hq, Washington, DC, 62-69, Chief Hist Div, Off Air Force Hist, Hq, US Dept Air Force, Washington, DC, 69- **MEMBERSHIPS** AHA; Orgn Am Historians. **RESEARCH** Far Eastern history; the Jacksonian period. **SELECTED PUBLICATIONS** Auth, Source Studies on Ockeghem, Johannes Motets, Musiktheorie, Vol 0007, 92; Haydn Farewell Symphony and the Idea of Classical Style-Through Composition and Cyclic Integration in his Instrumental Music, Musiktheorie, Vol 0009, 94; Stevens, Wallace, The Plain Sense of Things, Mod Philol, Vol 0092, 94; Musical Form Theory in the Context of National Traditions of the 17th Century--The Lamento from Biber, Heinrich, Ignaz, Franz Rosenkranzsonate Nr. 6, Acta Musicologica, Vol 0064, 92; Poetry of Mourning--The Modern Elegy from Hardy to Heaney, Mod Philol, Vol 0095, 97; Wagner Das Rheingold, Musikforschung, Vol 0048, 95; Biber, Heinrich, Franz 1644-1704--Music and Culture in Salzburg During the High Baroque Period, Musikforschung, Vol 0048, 95; pour Doulz Regard--A Newly Discovered Manuscript Page with French Chansons from the Beginning of the 15th Century, Archiv Musikwissenschaft, Vol 0051, 94; Opera Incerta--Authenticity as a Problem of Complete Musicological Editions, Musikforschung, Vol 0046, 93; An Analysis of Rabanus Maurus Views on Atonality and Tradition--Webern, Anton Vier Stucke fur Geige und Klavier, Op.7, Archiv Musikwissenschaft, Vol 0053, 96; music, Musiktheorie, Vol 0008, 93; Sound and Structure of 13th Century English Polyphonic Compositions--Interchange of Parts in the Worcester Fragments, Musikforschung, Vol 0047, 94; Sicilian Contrafacta--The Unity of Music and Lyrics in 13th Century Sicilian and Siculo Tuscan Music and Poetry, Musikforschung, Vol 0046, 93; The Granddaughters Archive--Dove, Rita Thomas and Beulah, Western Hum Rev, Vol 0051, 97; Corpus Troporum, Vol 7, Tropes Du Sanctus, Musikforschung, Vol 0046, 93; Stevens, Wallace, The Plain Sense of Things, Mod Philol, Vol 0092, 94; Reading as Poets Read,, Philos Lit, Vol 0020, 96; The Monographic Songs in the Roman de Fauvel, Musikforschung, Vol 0046, 93; Macahut Mass--An Introduction, Musiktheorie, Vol 0007,92; The Rondeau Ay Las Quant Je Pans in the Lucca Codex, Musikforschung, Vol 0048, 95; Quadruplum and Trimplum Parisian Organum--A Collection of Plainchants, Musikforschung, Vol 0048, 95; The Man with Night Sweats, Raritan Quart Rev, Vol 0013, 93; Foundations of Medieval Music, Mus, Vol 0049, 95. **CONTACT ADDRESS** 927 Clintwood Dr, Silver Spring, MD 20902.

BERGER, DAVID

PERSONAL Born 06/24/1943, Brooklyn, NY, m, 1965, 3 children **DISCIPLINE** HISTORY **EDUCATION** Yeshiva Col, BA, 64; Yeshiva, Univ, Rabbinic Ordination, 67; Columbia Univ, MA, 65, PhD, 70. **CAREER** Instr, Yeshiva Col, 68-70; asst prof to prof, Brooklyn Col, City Univ of NY, 70-. **HONORS AND AWARDS** John Nicholas Brown Prize, Med Acad of Am, 83; Fel, Am Acad for Jewish Res. **MEMBERSHIPS** Assoc for Jewish Studies; Am Acad for Jewish Res; World Union of Jewish Studies; Med Acad of Am; AHA. **RESEARCH** Medieval Jewish History, Jewish-Christian Relations, Intellectual History of the Jews. **SELECTED PUBLICATIONS** Coauth, Jews and "Jewish Christianity", Ktav, 78; auth, The Jewish-Christian Debate in the High Middle Ages: A Critical Edition of the Nizzahon Vetus with an Introduction, Translation and Commentary, Jewish Pub Soc, 79; ed, The Legacy of Jewish Migration: 1881 and Its Impact, Brooklyn Col Pr, 83; ed, History and Hate: The Dimensions of Anti-Semitism, Jewish Pub Soc, 86; auth, From Crusades to Blood Libels to Expulsions: Some New Approaches to Medieval Antisemitism, Touro Col Grad School of Jewish Studies, 97. **CONTACT ADDRESS** Dept History, Brooklyn Col, CUNY, 2901 Bedford Ave, Brooklyn, NY 11210-2813. **EMAIL** dberger@gc.cuny.edu

BERGER, GORDON

DISCIPLINE HISTORY **EDUCATION** Yale Univ, PhD, 72. **CAREER** Prof, Univ Southern Calif. **RESEARCH** Modern Japanese history; history of Japanese politics in the 20th century. **SELECTED PUBLICATIONS** Auth, Politics and Militarism in the 1930s"; Parties Out of Power in Japan. **CONTACT ADDRESS** East Asian Studies Center, Univ of So California, University Park Campus, Los Angeles, CA 90089.

BERGER, HENRY WEINBERG

PERSONAL Born 07/12/1937, Frederick, MD, m, 1966, 2 children **DISCIPLINE** UNITED STATES HISTORY **EDUCATION** Ohio State Univ, BA, 59; Univ Wis, MS, 61, PhD(Hist) 66. **CAREER** From instr to asst prof Hist, Univ Vt, 65-70; asst prof, 70-72, assoc prof Hist, Wash Univ, 72-, vis prof Hist, Concordia Univ, 75-76; chemn Jewish Studies, Washington Univ, 81-84; chemn Jewish and Near Eastern Studies, 84-89, Washington Univ. **HONORS AND AWARDS** fac res grant, 68-69; Nat Endowment for Humanities jr fel, 72-73; consult, Mo Comt, Nat Endowment for Humanities, 77-78; Alfred P Sloan Found grant, 81, 83; Arts and Sciences Undergraduate Teaching and Service Awd, 84; William T. Kemper Awd Found grant for teaching, 97-98. **MEMBERSHIPS** Orgn Am Historians; Phi Beta Kappa, Soc for Historians of Am Foreign Relations. **RESEARCH** United States foreign relations, especially in the 20th century; United States labor history. **SELECTED PUBLICATIONS** Contribr, Senator Robert A Taft dissents from military escalation, In: Cold War Critics, Quadrangle, 71; Crisis diplomacy in the 1930's, In: From Colony to Empire, Wiley, 72; auth, Warren Austin in China, 1916-1917, Vt Hist, Fall 72; Bipartisanship, Senator Taft and the Truman Administration, Polit Sci Quart, Summer 75; Unions and empire: Organized labor and American corporations abroad, Peace & Change, Spring 76; Ed and Commentator, William Appleman Williams Reader: Selections from His Major Historical Writings, Ivan R Dee, 92. **CONTACT ADDRESS** Dept of History, Washington Univ, 1 Brookings Dr, Box 1062, Saint Louis, MO 63130-4899. **EMAIL** hwberger@artsci.wustl.edu

BERGER, IRIS B.

PERSONAL Born 10/12/1941, Chicago, IL, m, 1963, 2 children **DISCIPLINE** AFRICAN & WOMEN'S HISTORY **EDUCATION** Univ Mich, BA, 63; Univ Wis, MA, 67, PhD(African hist), 73; **CAREER** Kaaga Elementary School, Meru, Kenya, 63; Kenya-Israel Sch of Social Work, Machakos, Kenya, adult educ, 64-65; Machakos Girl's High Sch, head hist teacher, 64-65; Res Assoc, Makerere Univ, Uganda, 70; Res Assoc, Univ of Dar es Salaam, Tanzania, 70; Adj lectr hist, State Univ NY Oneonta, 72-75, 76-79; asst prof, Wellesley Col, 75-76; Dewar Chair Lectr in Non-Western Hist, Hartwick College, 77-78; Res Assoc African Hist, Boston Univ, 79-83; from Vis Asst Prof to Assoc Prof, 81-93, Prof of Hist, Africana and Women's Studies, State Univ of NY, Albany, 93-, Dir, Women's Studies Prog, 81-84, Dir, Grad Studies, Hist Dept, 96-97; Dir, Inst for Res on Women, 91-95; Pres, African Studies Asn, 95-96. **HONORS AND AWARDS** Nat Endowment for Humanities fel, 79-80, 86-87; Soc Sci Res Coun res fel, 80-81; Annual book award from the Academie Royale des Sciences d'Outre Mer, Brussels, to: Religion and Resistance: East African Kingdoms in the Precolonial Period, 82; The Rockefeller Found, Res Fel, 87; ACLS, Int Travel Awd, Summer 90, Summer 95; Soc Sci Res Coun, Joint Comt on African Studies, Res Fel, Fall 90; Ford Found, Individual Awd, 91; Distinguished Africanist Awd, NY African Studies Asn, 97; recipient of numerous grants, research awards, graduate and undergraduate awards. **MEMBERSHIPS** African Studies Asn; Am Historical Asn. **RESEARCH** Women, and gender in Africa; South Africa; work women and comparative perspectives; African American--South africa Connections. **SELECTED PUBLICATIONS** Contribr, East African Culture History, Syracuse Univ, 76; Women in Africa: Studies in Social and Economic Change, Stanford Univ Press, 76; The African Past Speaks, Dawson Publ Co, 80; auth, Religion and Resistance: East African Kingdoms in the Precolonial Period, Mus Royal Afrique Cent, 81; coed, Women and Class in Africa, Holmes and Meier/Africana Publ Co, 86; auth, Threads of Solidarity: Women in South African Industry, 1900-1980, Ind Univ Press/James Currey, 92; coauth, Women in Sub-Saharan Africa: Restoring Women to History, Ind Univ Press, 00. **CONTACT ADDRESS** History Dept, SUNY, Albany, 1400 Washington, Albany, NY 12222-1000. **EMAIL** iberger@albany.edu

BERGER, MARK LEWIS

PERSONAL Born 12/02/1942, Brooklyn, NY, m, 1969, 2 children **DISCIPLINE** MIDDLE PERIOD OF AMERICAN HISTORY **EDUCATION** Queens Col, NYork, BA, 64; City Univ NYork, PhD, 72. **CAREER** Asst prof, 69-80, prof hist, Columbus Col, 80-. **MEMBERSHIPS** AHA; Orgn Am Historians; Southern Hist Assn. **RESEARCH** Pre-Civil War era. **SELECTED PUBLICATIONS** Auth, The Revolution in the New York Party Systems, 1840-1860, Kennikat. **CONTACT ADDRESS** Dept of History, Columbus State Univ, 4225 University Ave, Columbus, GA 31907-5645. **EMAIL** berge_mark@colstate.edu

BERGER, MARTIN A.

DISCIPLINE ART HISTORY **EDUCATION** Yale Univ, PhD. **CAREER** Prof, Northwestern Univ **RESEARCH** Construction of gender and race; 19th century painting. **SELECTED PUBLICATIONS** Auth, Man Made: Thomas Eakins and the Construction of Victorian Manhood, Univ Calif Press; essays on, 19th-century Am painting. **CONTACT ADDRESS** Dept of Art Hist-Clemens, SUNY, Buffalo, PO Box 604640, Buffalo, NY 14260-0001.

BERGER, MARTIN EDGAR

PERSONAL Born 11/22/1942, Columbus, OH, m, 1965, 3 children **DISCIPLINE** MODERN EUROPEAN HISTORY **EDUCATION** Columbia Univ, BA, 64; Univ Pittsburgh, MA, 64, PhD(hist), 69. **CAREER** Asst prof, 69-77, from assoc prof to prof Hist, Youngstown State Univ, 77-. **HONORS AND AWARDS** Distinguished Prof, teaching, 99. **MEMBERSHIPS** AHA; Study Group Int Labor & Working Class Hist; Conf Group Cent Europ Hist. **RESEARCH** Socialist movement; fascism; modern Germany. **SELECTED PUBLICATIONS** Auth, Engels, Armies, and Revolution: The Revolutionary Tactics of classical Marxism, Archon, 77. **CONTACT ADDRESS** Dept of History, Youngstown State Univ, One University Plz, Youngstown, OH 44555-3452. **EMAIL** meberger@cc.ysu.edu

BERGER, PATRICE

DISCIPLINE HISTORY OF OLD REGIME EUROPE AND FRANCE **EDUCATION** Univ Chicago, PhD, 72. **CAREER** Assoc prof, dir, Honors prog, Univ Nebr, Lincoln. **HONORS AND AWARDS** Acad of Distinguished Tchr; Chancellor's Awd for Exemplary Serv to Stud, 92; Outstanding Tchg and Instruct Creativity Awd, 95. **RESEARCH** Biography of Louis de Pontchartrain. **SELECTED PUBLICATIONS** Published several articles on 17th century France. **CONTACT ADDRESS** Univ of Nebraska, Lincoln, 634 Oldfather, Lincoln, NE 68588-0417. **EMAIL** pberger@unlinfo.unl.edu

BERGERON, PAUL H.

PERSONAL Born 02/08/1938, Alexandria, LA, m, 1968, 3 children **DISCIPLINE** HISTORY **EDUCATION** La Col, BA, 60; Vanderbilt Univ, MA, 62, PhD(hist), 65. **CAREER** From instr to assoc prof hist, Vanderbilt Univ, 65-72; from assoc prof to prof hist, Univ Tenn, Knoxville, 72-; ed, The Papers of Andrew Johnson, 87-00. **MEMBERSHIPS** Orgn Am Historians; Southern Historical Asn; Soc for Historians of the Early Am Republic (SHEAR). **RESEARCH** United States middle period, 1787-1865; political history of the Jacksonian era, 1830-60; Southern history. **SELECTED PUBLICATIONS** Co-ed, Correspondence of James K Polk, Vanderbilt Univ, Vols I & II, 69-72; auth, Paths of the Past, Tennessee, 1770-1970, Univ Tenn Press, 79; Antebellum Politics in Tennessee, Univ Press Ky, 82; The Presidency of James K. Polk, Univ Press Kans, 87; ed, The Papers of Andrew Johnson, Vol 8-16, Univ Tenn Press, 89-00; coauth, Tennesseans and Their Hist, Univ Tenn Pr, 99. **CONTACT ADDRESS** Dept of History, Univ of Tennessee, Knoxville, Dunford Hall, Knoxville, TN 37996-4065. **EMAIL** bergeron@utk.edu

BERGQUIST, JAMES
PERSONAL Born 02/01/1934, Council Bluffa, IA, m, 1969, 2 children **DISCIPLINE** HISTORY **EDUCATION** Univ of Notre Dame, BA, 55; Northwestern Univ, MA, 56; PhD, 66. **CAREER** Instr, Coe Col, Iowa, 61-62; From Instr to Prof, Villanova Univ, 63-. **HONORS AND AWARDS** NEH Summer Fel, 67, 77, 80. **MEMBERSHIPS** AAUP, AHA, OAH, AM Studies Asn, Hist Soc of Pa, Immigration and Ethnic Hist Soc, Am Asn for State and Local Hist, Balch Inst for Ethnic Studies, 88-92, 94-. **RESEARCH** American social history, immigration and ethnicity. **SELECTED PUBLICATIONS** Auth, "German America in the 1980's: Illusion and Realities," in Germans in America: Aspects of German-American Relations in the Nineteenth Century, ed. E. Allen McCormick (NY: Brooklyn Col Press, 83), 1-14; auth, "German Communities and American Cities: A Review of the Nineteenth-Century Experience," J of Am Ethnic Hist 4 (84): 9-30; auth, "The Concept of Nativism in Historical Study since 'Strangers in the Land'," Am Jewish Hist 76 (86): 125-141; auth, "The Mid-Nineteenth Century Slavery Crisis and the German-Americans," in States of Progress: Germans and Blacks in America over 300 Years, ed. Randall Miller (Philadelphia: Ger Soc of Pa, 89), 55-71; auth, "The Forty-Eighters and the Republica Convention of 1860," in The German Forty-Eighters in the United States, ed. Charlotte L. Brancaforte (NY: Peter Lang, 89), 141-156; auth, "German-Americans," in Multiculturalism in the United States: A Comparative Guide to Acculturation and Ethnicity, ed. John D. Buenker and Lorman A. Ratner (Westport, CT: Greenwood, 92), 53-76; auth, "The Val J. Peter Newspapers: The Rise and Decline of a Twentieth-Century German-Language Newspaper Empire," Yearbk of Ger-Am Studies 29 (94): 117-128; auth, "German-American Organizational Life," Invisible Philadelphia: Community through Voluntary Organizations, ed. J.B. Toll and M. Gilliam (Philadelphia: Atwater Kent Mus, 95); auth, "Germans and German-Speaking Peoples," in Our Multicultural Heritage: A Guide to American Ethnic Groups, ed. Elliott Barkan (Westport, CT: Greenwood Press, 99). **CONTACT ADDRESS** Dept Hist, Villanova Univ, 800 E Lancaster Ave, Villanova, PA 19085-1603. **EMAIL** jbergqui@email.villanova.edu

BERINGER, RICHARD E.
PERSONAL Born 12/29/1933, Madison, WI, m, 1964, 2 children **DISCIPLINE** HISTORY **EDUCATION** Lawrence Col, BA, 56; Northwestern Univ Evanston Il, MA, 57, PhD, 66. **CAREER** Teaching asst, 60-62, Northwestern Univ; personnel off, 57-60, USAF; instr, 63-64, Wisc St Univ--Oshkosh; asst prof, 65-69, Calif United States Air Force, Kansas, Texas, Alaska, Personnel Officer, 57-60; Northwestern Teaching Asst, 60-62; St Univ Hayward; assoc prof, to prof, grad faculty, dept chair, prof emeritus, 70-99, Univ ND. **HONORS AND AWARDS** Phi Beta Kappa, Magna Cum Laude, Lawrence Col, 56; Nat Hist Publ & Records Comm Fel, 69-70; Jefferson Davis Awd, 73, 87; Charles Sackett Sydnor Awd, 73; Rev Elmer & Min West Outstanding Faculty Awd, 87; Chester Fritz Distinguished Professorship, 88; Fulbright Travel Awd, Germany, 94. **MEMBERSHIPS** S Hist Assoc; Hist Soc; Soc of Civil War Historians. **RESEARCH** U S Civil War era; nineteenth century U S mil hist. **SELECTED PUBLICATIONS** Coauth, The Anatomy of the Confederate Congress, Vanderbilt Univ Press, 72; vis coed, auth of intro, The Papers of Jefferson Davis, v. 4 La St Univ Press, 83; coauth, Historical Analysis: Contemporary Approaches to Clio's Craft, John Wiley, 78, reprint Robert E. Krieger, 86; coauth, Why the South Lost the Civil War, Univ Ga Press, 86, 88; rev, American Against Itself, rev of Battle Cry of Freedom: The Civil War Era, NY Rev of Books, 88; auth, Jefferson Davis's Pursuit of Ambition: The Attractive Features of Alternative Decisions, Civil War Hist, 92; essay, Confederate Identity and the Will to Fight, On the Road to Total War: The American Civil War and the German Wars of Unification, 1861-1871, Cambridge Univ Press, 96. **CONTACT ADDRESS** Dept of History, Univ of No Dakota, Univ Station, Box 8096, Grand Forks, ND 58202. **EMAIL** richard_beringer@und.nodak.edu

BERKELEY, EDMUND
PERSONAL Born 04/01/1937, Charlottesville, VA, m, 2 children **DISCIPLINE** HISTORY **EDUCATION** Univ of the South, BA, 58; Univ Va, MA, 61. **CAREER** Asst archv, Va State Lib, 63-65; from sr asst to acting cur, 65-69, asst prof & Cur of Manuscripts, 70-76, assoc prof & univ archv, 76-87, agency records adminr, 79- , dir special collections, 87-94, Univ Archv & Coordr, Special Collections Digital Ctr, 95- , Univ Va. **HONORS AND AWARDS** Phi Beta Kappa; fel, Soc of Am Archv, 76; fel, Va Ctr for Hum and Public Policy, 88. **MEMBERSHIPS** Albemarle Co Hist Soc; Asn for Documentary Editing; Bibliog Soc of Univ Va; Book Arts Press; Mid-Atlantic Regional Arch Conf; Mid-West Archv Conf; Soc of Am Archv; Soc of Ga Archv; Va Asn of Gov Arch and Records Adminr; Va Hist Soc. **SELECTED PUBLICATIONS** Ed, Robert Carter as Agricultural Administrator: His Letters to Robert Jones, 1727-1729, Va Mag of Hist and Biog, 93; auth, The Great War Exhibit at the University of Virginia Library, in Dictionary of Literary Biography Year Book 1993, Gale, 94; auth, Linton R. Massey, in Rosenblum, ed, American Book Collectors and Bibliographers, Second Series, Gale, 97. **CONTACT ADDRESS** Special Collections Dept, Univ of Virginia, Charlottesville, VA 22903-2498. **EMAIL** eb2c@virginia.edu

BERKEY, JONATHAN P.
PERSONAL Born 12/05/1959, Northampton, MA, m, 1988, 2 children **DISCIPLINE** HISTORY **EDUCATION** Williams, BA, 81; Princeton, MA, 86, PhD, 89. **CAREER** Asst Prof Relig, Mt Holyoke Col, 90-93; Asst Prof Hist, Davidson Col, 93-96; Assoc Prof, 96-. **HONORS AND AWARDS** Fulbright/IIE, 86-87; NEH Fellow, 92-93. **MEMBERSHIPS** Inst for Adv Stud, 94-95; Mid E Stud Asn. **RESEARCH** Medieval Islamic History. **SELECTED PUBLICATIONS** Auth, The Transmission of Knowledge in Medieval Cairo: A Social History of Islamic Education, Princeton Press, 92; auth, Tradition, Innovation and the Social Construction of Knowledge in the Medieval Islamic Near East, Past & Present, 146, 38-65, 95; auth, Women in Medieval Islamic Society, Women & Medieval Culture, Garland Pub, forthcoming; auth, Popular Preaching and Religious Authority in the Medieval Islamic Near East, Univ Wa Press, (in press). **CONTACT ADDRESS** Dept Hist, Davidson Col, Davidson, NC 28036. **EMAIL** joberkey@davidson.edu

BERKIN, CAROL RUTH
PERSONAL Born 10/01/1942, Mobile, AL, d, 2 children **DISCIPLINE** AMERICAN HISTORY **EDUCATION** Barnard Col, AB, 64; Columbia Univ, MA, 66, PhD(Am hist), 72. **CAREER** Mem ed staff, Papers of Alexander Hamilton, 64-65; lectr, Columbia Univ, 69 & Hunter Col, City Univ New York, 69-70; asst prof, 72-75, assoc prof, 75-79, Prof Hist, Baruch Col, City Univ New York, 79-, Prof, Grad Ctr, CUNY, 80-. **HONORS AND AWARDS** Bancroft Dissertation Awd, Columbia Univ, 72; Am Coun Learned Socs study fel, 78-79. **MEMBERSHIPS** AHA; Orgn Am Historians; Soc Am Historians; Am Studies Asn; Am Soc 18th Century Studies; Coord Comt Women in Hist Profession. **SELECTED PUBLICATIONS** Auth, Jonathan Sewall: Odyssey of an American Loyalist, Columbia Univ, 74; Within the Conjurer's Circle: Women in Colonial America, Gen Learning, 74; co-ed, Women of America: A History, Houghton-Mifflin, 79; auth, Private Woman, Public Woman: The contradictions of Charlotte Perkins Gilman, In: The Women of America, 79, Houghton-Mifflin; co-ed, Women, War and Revolution, Holmes-Meier, 79; auth, First Generations: Women in Colonial America, Hill & Wang, 96; co-ed, Women's Voices, Women's Lives: Documents in Early American History, Northeastern Univ Press, 98. **CONTACT ADDRESS** Dept of History, Graduate Sch and Univ Ctr, CUNY, 365 5th Ave, New York City, NY 10016. **EMAIL** cberkin@gc.cuny.edu

BERKMAN, JOYCE A.
PERSONAL Born 11/20/1937, San Jose, CA, m, 1962, 2 children **DISCIPLINE** HISTORY, WOMEN'S STUDIES **EDUCATION** Univ Calif, Los Angeles, BA, 58; Yale Univ, MA, 59, PhD, 67. **CAREER** Instr, Conn Col, 62-63; instr, 66-68, asst prof, 68-80,Danforth Found assoc, 75-; Assoc Prof Hist, Univ Mass, 80-; Prof of Hist., 00-; Adjunct Prof of Women's Studies, 00-. **HONORS AND AWARDS** Distinguished Teacher Awd, Univ Mass, 80. **MEMBERSHIPS** Am Hist Assoc; Berkshire Orgn Women Historians; Conf Brit Historians; Northeast Victorian Studies Asn; New Eng Hist Asn; Nat Women's Studies Asn. **RESEARCH** 19th and 20th century British and American women's history; African-American women's history; Victorian social and intellectual history; historical methodology; European Women's History. **SELECTED PUBLICATIONS** Auth, The Healing Imagination of Olive Schreiner: Beyond South African Colonialism, Univ Mass Press, 89; co-ed, African American Women and the Vote, Univ mass Press, 97; co-ed, Contenplating Edith Stein, Univ of Notre Dame Press, forthcoming. **CONTACT ADDRESS** Univ of Massachusetts, Amherst, Amherst, MA 01003-0002. **EMAIL** jberkman@history.umass.edu

BERKOWITZ, EDWARD D.
PERSONAL Born 01/11/1950, Passaic, NJ, m, 1981, 2 children **DISCIPLINE** HISTORY **EDUCATION** Princeton Univ, AB, 72; Northwestern Univ, MA, 73, PhD, 76. **CAREER** Asst prof, Univ Ma, Boston, 77-80; chair to prof, dir, George Washington Univ, Washington, DC, 82- . **HONORS AND AWARDS** Ed bd member, J of Policy Hist; assoc ed & book rev ed, J of Disability Policy Stud; ed bd member, J of Gerontology-Soc Sci; ed bd member, Soc Insurance Update; founding member, Nat Acad of Soc Insurance; Mary Switzer Scholar, 84; robert wood johnson found faculty fel, health care fin, johns hopkins med inst, 87-88. **MEMBERSHIPS** Amer Hist Assoc, Org of Amer Hist; Soc Sci Hist Assoc. **RESEARCH** History & public policy; soc welfare policy, hist of Soc Sec; disability policy; hist of med care; the presidency. **SELECTED PUBLICATIONS** Auth, Disabled Policy: America's Programs for the Handicapped--A Twentieth Century Fund Report, Cambridge Univ Press, 87, 89; America's Welfare State: From Roosevelt to Reagan, Johns Hopkins Press, 91; Mr. Social Security: The Life of Wilbur J. Cohen, Univ Press Ks, 95; To Heal A Nation: A History of the Institute of Medicine, Nat Acad Press, 98; coauth, Group Health Association: A Portrait of a Health Maintenance Organization, Temple Univ Press, 88. **CONTACT ADDRESS** Dept of History, The George Washington Univ, Washington, DC 20052. **EMAIL** ber@qwv.edu

BERLANSTEIN, LENARD RUSSELL
PERSONAL Born 11/29/1947, Brooklyn, NY **DISCIPLINE** EUROPEAN HISTORY **EDUCATION** Univ Mich, BA, 69; Johns Hopkins Univ, MA, 71, PhD, 73. **CAREER** Asst prof, 73-79, assoc prof, 79-86, Prof History, Univ VA, 86-. **MEMBERSHIPS** AHA; Soc Fr Hist Studies. **RESEARCH** French social and cultural history. **SELECTED PUBLICATIONS** Auth, The Advocates of Toulouse in the Eighteenth Century, 1750-1793, Johns Hopkins Univ, 75; The Working People of Paris, 1871-1914, Johns Hopkins Univ Press, 86; Big Business and Industrial Conflict in Nineteenth Century France, Univ Calif Press, 91. **CONTACT ADDRESS** Dept of Hist, Univ of Virginia, 1 Randall Hall, Charlottesville, VA 22903-3284. **EMAIL** lrb@virginia.edu

BERLIN, ADELE
PERSONAL Born 05/23/1943, Philadelphia, PA, m, 2 children **DISCIPLINE** BIBLICAL STUDIES, ANCIENT NEAR EASTERN STUDIES **EDUCATION** Univ PA, PhD, 76. **CAREER** Robert H Smith prof of Hebrew Bible, Univ MD. **HONORS AND AWARDS** Guggenheim fel; ACLS fel; NEH translation fel; fel, Am Academy of Jewish Res. **MEMBERSHIPS** Soc of Biblical Lit; Asn for Jewish Studies; Am Oriental Soc. **RESEARCH** Biblical literature. **SELECTED PUBLICATIONS** Auth, Zephaniah, Anchor Bible; The Dynamics of Biblical Parallelism; Poetics and Interpretation of Biblical Narrative. **CONTACT ADDRESS** Dept of English, Univ of Maryland, Col Park, College Park, MD 20742. **EMAIL** aberlin@deans.umd.edu

BERLIN, ANDREA MICHELLE
DISCIPLINE HELLENISTIC AND ROMAN CERAMICS, HELLENISTIC AND ROMAN NEAR EAST, ARCHAEOLOG **EDUCATION** Univ Mich, AB, 76; Univ Chicago, AM, 79; Univ Mich, PhD, 88. **CAREER** Instr, Univ Mich, 81-84; instr, Hebrew Univ, Jerusalem, 85; lectr, George Washington Univ, 88; lectr, Univ Va, 89; lectr, Univ Md, 90; adj asst prof, Georgetown Univ, 94-95; asst prof, Univ Minn, Twin Cities, 97-; asst prof, Univ Minn, Twin Cities, 97-99; assoc prof, Univ Minn, Twin Cities, 00-. **HONORS AND AWARDS** Samuel H Kress fel, Am Sch of Orient Res & Albright Inst of Archaeol, Jerusalem, 84-85; Fulbright-Hays jr res fel, Greece, 85-86; Homer A and Dorothy B Thompson fel, Am Sch of Class Stud, Athens, 86-87; Grad Col Scholar Awd, Univ Ill, Urbana-Champaign, 93-94; jr fel, Ctr for Hellenic Stud, Wash, 96-97; Shelby White-Leon Levy fel, 97-98. **MEMBERSHIPS** Archaeological Institute of Am, Am Schools of Oriental Res. **RESEARCH** Persian, Hellenistic, and Roman pottery. **SELECTED PUBLICATIONS** Auth, Excavations at Tel Anafa, vol II, i. The Persian, Hellenistic, and Roman Plain Wares, J of Roman Archaeol Suppl Ser vol 10.2, 97; From Monarchy to Markets: The Phoenicians in Hellenistic Palestine, Bull of Am Sch of Orient Res 306: 75-88, 97; Between Large Forces: Palestine in the Hellenistic Period, Bibl Archaeol 60.1: 2- 57, 97; auth, "Studies in Hellenistic Ilion: The Lower City, Stratified Assemblages and Chronology," Studia Troica 9, (99, 00): 73-157; auth, "Tel Kedesh, 97-99," Israel Exploration Journal 50, with Sharon C. Herbert, (00): 118-123. **CONTACT ADDRESS** Univ of Minnesota, Twin Cities, 9 Pleasant St. SE, 305 Folwell Hall, Minneapolis, MN 55455. **EMAIL** aberlin@tc.umn.edu

BERLIN, IRA
PERSONAL Born 05/27/1941, New York, NY, m, 1963, 2 children **DISCIPLINE** HISTORY **EDUCATION** Univ Wis Madison, BS, 63; MA, 66; PhD, 70. **CAREER** Instr to asst prof, Univ of Ill, 69-72; asst prof, Federal City Col, 72-74; vis asst prof to prof, Univ of Md, 74-99, Distinguished Univ Prof, 99-. **HONORS AND AWARDS** Thomas Jefferson Prize, 85; J. Franklin Jameson Prize, 85; Fel, Ctr for Advan Studies in the Behav Sci, 89-90; Distinguished Teacher, Univ of Md, 90-91; State's Outstanding Fac Mem, Md Asn for Higher Educ, 91; Abraham Lincoln Prize, 94; Percy Adams Prize, 98; Douglas Adair Mem Awd, 98; Bancroft Prize, 99; Frank and Harriet Owsley Awd, 99; Frederick Douglass Prize, 99; Presidential Medal, Univ of Md, 99; Cordozo Prof, Yale, Univ, 99. **MEMBERSHIPS** Nat Soc Sci Hist Assoc; Southern Hist Assoc; Org of Am Hist; AHA; Int Sociol Assoc; Europ Am Studies Assoc; Milan Group of Am Hist. **RESEARCH** History of Slaver, History of the United States. **SELECTED PUBLICATIONS** Coed, Culture and Cultivation: Labor and the Shaping of Slave Life in the Americas, Univ of Va Pr, 93; coauth, Slaves No More: Three Essays on Emancipation and the Civil War, Cambridge Univ Pr, 92; coauth, Free At Last: A Documentary History of Slavery, Freedom, and the Civil War, New Pr, 92; coauth, Families and Freedom: A Documentary History of African-American Kinship in the Civil War Era, New Pr, 97; coauth, Freedom's Soldiers: The Black Military Experience and the Civil War, Cambridge Univ Pr, 98; coauth, Remembering Slavery: African Americans Talk About Their Personal Experiences of Slavery and Emancipation, New Pr, 98; auth, Many Thousands Gone: The First Two Centuries of African-American Slavery in Mainland North America, Harvard Univ Pr, 98. **CONTACT ADDRESS** Dept Hist, Univ of Maryland, Col Park, 2115 Francis Scott Key Hall, College Park, MD 20742-0001. **EMAIL** ib3@umail.umd.edu

BERLIN, ROBERT HARRY
PERSONAL Born 10/24/1946, Pittsburgh, PA, m, 1971 **DISCIPLINE** AMERICAN AND MILITARY HISTORY **EDUCATION** Rockford Col, BA, 68; Univ Calif, Santa Barbara, PhD (hist), 76. **CAREER** Instr hist, Allan Hancock Community Col, 76-79; vis assoc prof mil hist, 79-81, Assoc Prof Mil Hist, US Army Command and Gen Staff Col, 81-, Vis asst prof hist Am Revolution, Mansfield State Col, 76; lectr, Continuing Educ Div, Santa Barbara City Col, 76. **MEMBERSHIPS** Orgn Am Historians; Am Mil Inst; fel Inter-Univ Sem on Armed Forces & Soc; Soc Hist Fed Govt. **RESEARCH** American military history; American Revolution. **SELECTED PUBLICATIONS** Auth, US Marines in the Persia -Gulf, 1990-1991--With he 1st Marine Division in Desert Shield and Desert Storm, Pub Hist, Vol 0017, 95; Infamous Day--Marines at Pearl Harbor, 7 December 1941, Pub Hist, Vol 0017, 95; 1st Offensive--The Marine Campaign for Guadalcanal, Pub Hist, Vol 0017, 95; United States Marines in Vietnam--The War that Would Not End, 1971-1973, Pub Hist, Vol 0017, 95. **CONTACT ADDRESS** 1716 Miami St, Leavenworth, KS 66048.

BERLO, JANET CATHERINE
DISCIPLINE ART HISTORY **EDUCATION** Yale Univ, PhD, 80. **CAREER** Prof & Susan B. Anthony ch Gender and Women's Stud. **HONORS AND AWARDS** Sr res grant, J. Paul Getty Found, 94-96; fel col tchr(s), Nat Endowment for the Humanities, 94; fac res grant, Can Govt, 94; presidential awd excellence tchg, Univ MO, 94 & Summer grant, Am Philos Soc, 89. **RESEARCH** North Am Indian art hist; mus studies; arts of the colonial encounter; Pre-Columbian art and archaeol. **SELECTED PUBLICATIONS** Auth, Plains Indian Drawings 1865-1935: Pages from a Visual History, NY, Abrams Press, 96; Ed, Art and Ideology at Teotihuacan, WA, Dumbarton Oaks Res Ctr, 93; The Early Years of Native American Art History: The Politics of Scholarship and Collecting, Univ WA Press, 92; co-ed, Arts of Africa, Oceania and the Americas: Selected Readings, Prentice Hall Co, 92. **CONTACT ADDRESS** Dept of Art and Art Hist, Univ of Rochester, 601 Elmwood Ave, Ste. 656, 421 Morey , Rochester, NY 14642. **EMAIL** brlo@uhura.cc.rochester.edu

BERMAN, HYMAN
PERSONAL Born 02/20/1925, New York, NY, m, 1950 **DISCIPLINE** HISTORY **EDUCATION** City Col NYork, BS, 48; Columbia Univ, PhD (hist), 56. **CAREER** Instr Hist, Brooklyn Col, 57-60; asst prof Am thought, Mich State Univ, 60-61; from asst prof to assoc prof hist, 61-61, dir soc sci prog, 68-71, Prof Hist and Dir Exp Courses Prog, Univ Minn, Minneapolis, 71-, Vis lectr, Osmania Univ, India, 64; mem screening comt, Woodrow Wilson Fel Found, 66-; vis prof, Univ Calif, Berkeley, 67-68. **MEMBERSHIPS** AHA; Immigration Hist Group (exec secy, 67); Orgn Am Historians; Labor Historians. **RESEARCH** US labor; immigration and social history. **SELECTED PUBLICATIONS** Auth, Cloakmakers strike of 1910, Essays in Jewish Life & Thought, 60; Labor in America, In: Dictionary of American History, Scribner, 62; Historiography of the American Jewish labor movement, Am Jewish Hist Quart, 62; coauth, American Worker in the Twentieth Century, Free Press, 63; auth, From Socialism to Pragmatism, Greenwood, 68. **CONTACT ADDRESS** Univ of Minnesota, Twin Cities, 267 19th Ave., 614 Soc Sci, Minneapolis, MN 55455.

BERNARD, PAUL PETER
PERSONAL Born 05/07/1929, Antwerp, Belgium, m, 1949, 3 children **DISCIPLINE** HISTORY **EDUCATION** Univ Denver, BA, 48; Univ Colo, MA, 52, PhD (hist), 55. **CAREER** Instr French, Univ Colo, 55; from instr to assoc prof hist, Colo Col, 55-68; prof hist, Univ Ill, Urbana-Champaign, 68-, Ford Found pub affairs fel, Austria, 60-61; assoc, Ctr Advan Study, Univ Ill, 71-72 and 79-80. **HONORS AND AWARDS** Graduate Fel, Univ of Colorado, 53-54; Fulbright Fel to Austria, 53-54; Ford Foundation Fel, 60-61; Am Philosophical Soc Fel, 71-72; NEH Sr Fel, 75-76; Center for European Studies Res Grant, 85; **MEMBERSHIPS** AHA. **RESEARCH** Hussite movement; Joseph II of Austria; Austrian enlightenment. **SELECTED PUBLICATIONS** Auth, Joseph II and Bavaria, The Hague, 65; auth, Joseph II, New York, 68; auth, Jesuits and Jacobins, Urbana, 71; auth, Rush to the Alps, Boulder, 78; auth, The Limits of Enlightenment, Urbana, 79; auth, From the Enlightenment to the Police State, Urbana, 91; auth, From the Enlightenment to the Police State, Urbana, 91; "The Invisibility of the Obvious: French Military Planning before 1914," Swords and Ploughshares, I, 4, (88); auth, "Austria's Last Turkish War Reconsidered," Austrian History Yearbook, (88): auth, "Von der Aufklarung zum Polizeistaat: Der Weg des grafen Johann Anton Pergen," Veroffentlichungen des Instituts fur Europaische Geschichte, Mainz, (89); auth, "Poverty and Poor Relief in 18th Century Austria - Proceeding for the 3rd Symposium on the Holy Roman Empire, (in press), 94. **CONTACT ADDRESS** Dept of Hist, Univ of Illinois, Urbana-Champaign, Urbana, IL 61801. **EMAIL** pbernard@staff.uiuc.edu

BERNBECK, REINHARD W.
DISCIPLINE ARCHAEOLOGY, NEAR EAST, CRITICAL THEORY **EDUCATION** Univ de Paris, DEUG, 80; Freie Univ, Berlin, MA, 87; PhD, 91. **CAREER** Wissenschaftlicher mitarbeiter, Freie Univ, Berlin, 92-96; fel, Alexander von Humboldt Found, SUNY, Binghamton, 95-96; vis lectr, Ithaca Col, 96; postdoc assoc, SUNY, Binghamton, 95-96; asst prof, Bryn Mawr Col, 96-98; asst prof, SUNY, Binghamton, 99-. **MEMBERSHIPS** AAA; SAA; AIA; Deutsche Gesellschaft fur Urund Fruhgeschichte. **RESEARCH** Near East; concepts of intentionality and agency in archaeology; critical theory and theories of ideology; social inequality in early complex societies; the political use of the past; New Mueology; mobility and sedentariness. **SELECTED PUBLICATIONS** Auth, Theorien in der Archaologie, Francke-Verlag (Tuibingen), 97; auth, Die Auflbsung der Hauslichen Produktionsweise: das Beispiel Mesopotamiens. Berliner Beitrage zum Vorderen Orient, Band 14, Dietrich Reimer (Berlin), 94; co-ed, Fluchtpunkt Uruk. Archaologische Einheit aus methodischer Vielfalt. Schriften fur Hans J. Nissen, Rahden (Germany), 99; co-ed, Prestige, Prestigeguter, Sozialstrukturen. Beispiele aus dem europaischen und vorderasiatischen Neolithikum. Deutsche Gesellschaft fur Ur und Fruhgeschicht, Archaiologische Berichte, (Bonn: Holos: Verlag), 96; co-ed, Zwischen Euphrat und Indus. Aktuelle Forschungsprobleme in der vorderasiatischen Archaologie, Georg Olms: Verlag (Hildesheim), 95; coauth, "And They Said, Let Us Make Gods in Our Image: Gendered Ideologies in Ancient Mesopotamia," in Reading the Body: Representations and Remains in the Archaeological Record, ed. Alison Rautman (Philadelphia: Univ Penn Press, 00), 150-164; coauth, "Fistikli Hoyuk 1998: Sistematik Yuzey Arastirmasi ve Kaziland Systematic Survey and Sounding," in Ilisu ve Karkamis Baraj Golleri Altinda Kalacak Arkeolojik Kultur Varliklarini Kurtarma Projesi 1998 Yili Calismalari, ed. Numan Tuna, Jean Ozturk (Ankara: ODTU Tarihsel Cevre Arastirma Merkezi, 99); auth, "An Empire and Its Sherds," in Iron Age Pottery in Northern Mesopotamia, Northern Syria and South Eastern Anatolia, ed. Arnulf Hausleiter, Andrzej Reiche (Munster: Ugarit: Verlag, 99); co-ed, "Land, Stadt, Wanderung und Ethnizitat im alten Mesopotamian, " in Fluchtpunkt Uruk. Archaologische Einheit aus methodischer Vielfalt. Schriften fur Hans J. Nissen, Rahden (Germany), 99; auth, "Structure Strikes Back: Implicit Meanings of Ceramics from Qale Rostam, Iran," in Material Symbols, Culture and Economy in Prehistory, ed. John Robb Cen Archaeol Investigations (Carbondale: Southern Ill Univ, 96). **CONTACT ADDRESS** Dept Anthropology, SUNY, Binghamton, Binghamton, NY 13902-6000.

BERNHARD, VIRGINIA P.
PERSONAL Born 11/15/1937, Austin, TX, m, 1961, 3 children **DISCIPLINE** HISTORY **EDUCATION** Rice Univ, BA, 59; PhD, 71; Univ Pa, MA, 61. **CAREER** Lectr, Rice Univ, 71-72; asst prof, 72-75; assoc prof, 75-78; prof, 78-. **HONORS AND AWARDS** Woodrow Wilson Fel; TSHC Awd. **MEMBERSHIPS** AHA; OAH; SHA; SAWH. **RESEARCH** Colonial America; slavery; Bermuda; women's history. **SELECTED PUBLICATIONS** Auth, Ima Hogg: The Governor's Daughter, 84, 86, 96; auth, A Durable Fire, 90, 91; co-ed, "Birth of American Feminism: The Seneca Falls," Women's Rights (95); auth, Slaves and Slave Holders in Bermuda, 1616-1782, 99. **CONTACT ADDRESS** Dept History, Univ of St. Thomas, Texas, 3800 Montrose Blvd, Houston, TX 77006-4626. **EMAIL** bernhard@basil.stthom.edu

BERNSTEIN, BARTON JANNEN
PERSONAL Born 09/08/1936, New York, NY, m, 1967 **DISCIPLINE** AMERICAN HISTORY **EDUCATION** Queens Col, AB, 57; Harvard Univ, PhD, 64. **CAREER** Mem fac soc sci, Bennington Col, 63-65; asst prof hist, 65-68, assoc prof, 68-82, Prof Hist, Stanford Univ, 82-, Am Coun Learned Soc grant-in-aid, 64-65; Charles Warren fel, Harvard Univ, 67-68; Harry S Truman Inst fel, 67-68; fel, Ctr Advan Studies, Univ Ill, Urbana, 70-71 and Comt Res Int Studies grant, 74; adv ed, Little, Brown and Co, 70-73; Hoover Inst peace fel, 74-75; Nat Endowment for Humanities fel, 77-78; Ford Found fel, 80. **HONORS AND AWARDS** Goldstein Prize in Civil War Hist, 58; Dean's Teaching Awd, Stanford Univ, 77; Koontz Prize, Pac Hist Rev, 78. **MEMBERSHIPS** AHA; Orgn Am Historians; Conf Peace Res Hist; Soc Hist & Am Foreign Rels. **RESEARCH** Twentieth century American history; history of the cold war; American social history and foreign policy. **SELECTED PUBLICATIONS** Co-ed, The Truman Administration: A Documentary History, Harper, 66; ed & contribr, Towards a New Past: Dissenting Essays in American History, Pantheon, 68; co-ed & contribr, Twentieth-century America: Recent Interpretations, 69, 72 & ed & contribr, Policy and Politcs of the Truman Administration, 70, Quadrangle; auth, The 1952 election, Vol IV, In: History of American Presidential Elections, McGraw, 71; co-ed & contribr, Understanding the American Experience, Quadrangle, 73; ed & contribr, The Atomic Bomb: The Critical Issues, Little, 76; auth, The week we went to war: American intervention in the Korean Civil War, Foreign Serv J, 77. **CONTACT ADDRESS** Dept of Hist, Stanford Univ, Stanford, CA 94305-1926.

BERNSTEIN, GAIL LEE
PERSONAL Born 02/22/1939, Brooklyn, NY **DISCIPLINE** JAPANESE HISTORY **EDUCATION** Barnard Col, Columbia Univ, BA, 59; Radcliffe Col, MA, 61; Harvard Univ, PhD(hist), 68. **CAREER** From asst prof to assoc prof, 67-84, Prof Orient Studies, Univ Ariz, 84-; Ed, J Asian Studies, 78-83. **HONORS AND AWARDS** John K Fairbank Awd East Asian Hist, Am Hist Asn, 77; Univ of Ariz Soc and Behav Sci Gen Educ Teaching Awd, 92; Univ of Ariz Soc and Behav Sci Res Inst Res Professorship, 94; Asn for Asian Studies Distinguished Lectr on Japan, 96; Mortar Bd Recognition Awd, Univ of Ariz, 97. **MEMBERSHIPS** Asn Asian Studies. **RESEARCH** Modern Japanese intellectual and social history. **SELECTED PUBLICATIONS** Auth, Japanese Marxist, A Portrait of Kawakami Hajime, Harvard Univ Press, 76; Women in Rural Japan, In: Women in Changing Japan, Westview Press, 76; The Early Japanese Socialists, the Russian Revolution and the Problem of Dogmatism, Studies in Comparative Communism, 76; coauth (with Yasve Aoki Kidd), Child bearing in Japan, In: An Anthropology of Childbearing, F A Davis Co, 81; auth, Haruko's World, A Japanese Farm Woman and Her Community, Stanford Univ Press, 83, rev ed, 96; Women in the Silk Reeling Industry in Nineteenth-Century Japan, In: Japan and the World, St Martin's Press, 88; co-ed, Japan and the World, St Martin's Press, 88; auth, Recreating Japanese Women, Univ Calif Press, 91. **CONTACT ADDRESS** Dept of Hist, Univ of Arizona, Social Sci 215, Tucson, AZ 85721-0001. **EMAIL** glbernst@u.arizona.edu

BERNSTEIN, IVER
DISCIPLINE HISTORY **EDUCATION** Brown Univ, BA, 77; Yale Univ, MA, 79, Mphil, 82, PhD, 85. **CAREER** Act instr, Yale Univ, 82; Adj asst prof, NY Univ, 84; Vis asst prof, Univ Chicago, 85-86; Asst prof to prof, Washington Univ, 86. **HONORS AND AWARDS** Nat Endowment Hum stipend, 87; Am Coun Learned Societies, 87-88; Hist Soc Pa & Library Comp fel Recent Recipients Ph.D. Phil fel, 90; Mayer Fund fel, Huntington Library, 93; Am Coun Learned Societies fel, 95-96. **SELECTED PUBLICATIONS** Co-Auth, Work, Family And Class Values In The Nineteenth Century, International Labor And Working Class History, 81; Expanding The Boundaries The Political: Workers And Political Change In The Nineteenth Century, International Labor And Working Class History, 87; What Did The New York City Draft Rioters Think They Were Doing?, The Rise Am Capitalism, NY Hist Soc, 89; The New York City Draft Riots: Their Significance For Am Society And Politics In The Age The Civil War, Oxford Univ Profess, 90; Moral Perspective And The Cycles Jacksonian History, Jour Policy Hist, 94. **CONTACT ADDRESS** Washington Univ, 1 Brookings Dr, Saint Louis, MO 63130.

BERNSTEIN, JOANNE G.
DISCIPLINE HISTORY OF ART **EDUCATION** Univ Pa, BA, 62; NYork Univ, MA, 64, PhD, 72. **CAREER** Prof; Mills Col, 89-. **RESEARCH** Italian Renaissance art; women in European art and society. **SELECTED PUBLICATIONS** Auth, Patronage, Autobiography, and Iconography: the Facade of the Colleoni Chapel, In Giovanni Antonio Amadeo: Scultura e Architettura del suo tempo, Milan: Cisalpino, 93; The Female Model and the Renaissance Nude: Durer, Giorgione, and Raphael, Artibus et Historiae, XIII, 92; Work in progress: problems in methodology, and The Portal of the Medici Bank in Milan, In Verrocchio and Late Quattrocento Italian Sculpture, Florence: Le Lettere, 92; Milanese and Antique Aspects of the Colleoni Chapel: Site and Symbolism, Arte Lombarda, 100, 92; rev, Janice Shell, Grazioso Sironi, Giovanni Antonio Amadeo, Documents / I documenti, in Arte Lombarda, 94-95, 90; Restauro della Cappella Colleoni: Primi Ritrovamenti, Arte Lombarda, 92-93, 90. **CONTACT ADDRESS** Dept of Art, Mills Col, 5000 MacArthur Blvd, Oakland, CA 94613-1301. **EMAIL** jobern@mills.edu

BERNSTEIN, JOHN ANDREW
PERSONAL Born 03/25/1944, Boston, MA **DISCIPLINE** MODERN EUROPEAN INTELLECTUAL HISTORY **EDUCATION** Harvard Univ, AB, 66; AM, 67; PhD(hist), 70. **CAREER** Asst prof, 70-79; assoc prof, 79-88; prof hist, Univ Del, 89-. **RESEARCH** Eighteenth through twentieth century ethical thought. **SELECTED PUBLICATIONS** Ed, Select Sermons of Benjamin Whichcote, Scholar's Facsimiles and Reprints, 77; auth, Shaftesbury's Identification of the Good with the Beautiful, Eighteenth-Century Studies, spring 77; auth, Adam Ferguson and the Idea of Progress, Studies in Burke and His Times, spring 78; auth, Shaftesbury, Rousseau and Kant, Fairleigh Dickinson, 80; auth, Ethics, Theology and the Original State of Man: An Historical Sketch, Anglican Theol Rev, spring 79; auth, Nietzsche's Moral Philosophy, Faircloth Dickinson, 87; auth, Progress and the Quest for Meaning, Faircloth Dickinson, 87. **CONTACT ADDRESS** Dept of Hist, Univ of Delaware, Newark, DE 19711. **EMAIL** John.Bernstein@mvs.udel.edu

BERROL, SELMA CANTOR
PERSONAL Born 06/07/1924, New York, NY, w, 1948, 2 children **DISCIPLINE** AMERICAN HISTORY **EDUCATION** Hunter Col, BA, 45; Columbia Univ, MA, 46; City Univ NYork, PhD (hist), 67. **CAREER** Instr hist, Hunter Col, 46-49; teacher social studies, NY City High Sch, 49-55; lectr hist, Queens Col, City Univ NY, 67-68; asst prof hist, 68-73, assoc prof, 73-77, asst dean lib arts, 72-78, prof Hist, Baruch Col, City Univ New York, 77-95. **HONORS AND AWARDS** Distinguished Teaching Awd, Baruch Col, 82. **MEMBERSHIPS** AHA; Orgn Am Historians; Immigration Hist Soc; Am Jewish Hist Soc; Yivo Inst Jewish Studies. **RESEARCH** American immigration hist; New York City history; public schools. **SELECTED PUBLICATIONS** Auth, Immigrants At School:

New York, 1898-1914, Arno Press, 78; auth, Getting Down to Business: Baruch College in the City of New York, Greenwood Press, 89; co-ed, Immigration to New York, Associated Universities Press, 91; auth, "Immigrant Working Class Families," A Guide to the History of the Family," Greenwood Press, (91); auth, "Immigrant Children At School: A Child's Eye View," Small Worlds, Children and Adolescents in America, Univ Press of Kansas, 92; auth, Julia Richman: A Notable Woman, Associated Universites Press, 93; auth, East Side/East End: Eastern European Jews in London and New York, Praeger Publishers, 94; auth, Growing Up American: Immigrant Children in the United States, Twayne Publishers, 95; auth, "The City University of New York," Encyclopedia of New York, Kenneth Jackson, (95); auth, The Empire City: New York and Its People, 1624-1996, Praeger Publishers, 97. **CONTACT ADDRESS** Dept Hist, 111 E 85th St, New York, NY 10028.

BERRY, BRIAN J. L.
PERSONAL Born 02/16/1934, Sedgley, United Kingdom, m, 1958, 3 children **DISCIPLINE** GEOGRAPHY **EDUCATION** Univ London, BA, 55; Univ Wash, MA, 56; PhD, 58. **CAREER** Asst prof to prof, Univ of Chicago, 58-76; Frank Backus Prof, Harvard Univ, 76-81; prof, Carnegie-Mellon Univ, 81-86; prof, Univ of Tex, 86-. **HONORS AND AWARDS** Award, Asn of Am Geogr, 68; Fel, Urban Land Inst, 75; Fel, Am Acad of Arts and Sci, 76; James R. Anderson Medal of Honor, Assoc of Am Geogr, 87; Victoria Medal, Royal Geog Soc, 88; Fel, Southern Reg Sci Assoc. **RESEARCH** Urban ecology, geographic information systems, growth center theory, the concept of counterurbanization, long-wave macroeconomic/historical processes. **SELECTED PUBLICATIONS** Auth, Long-Wave Rhythms in Economic Development and Political Behavior, Johns Hopkins Univ Pr, (Baltimore), 91; auth, America's Utopian Experiments. Communal Havens from Long-Wave Crises, Univ Pr of New England (Hanover, NH), 92; coauth, The Global Economy. Resource Use, Location Choice, and International Trace, Prentice-Hall, (Englewood Cliffs, NJ), 93; coauth, "Long Swings in American Inequality: The Kuznets Conjecture Revisited", Papers in Regional Sci 74, (95): 153-174; auth, "From Malthusian Frontier to Demographic Steady State: The Concordian Birth Rate, 1635-1993", Population and Develop Rev 22 (96): 207-229; coauth, The Rhythms of American Politics, Univ Pr of Am, (Lanham, MD), 98; coauth, "Measurement of Campaign Efficiency Using Data Envelopment Analysis", Electoral Studies 18, (99): 379-395. **CONTACT ADDRESS** Univ of Texas, Dallas, Box 830688, Richardson, TX 75083. **EMAIL** heja@utdallas.edu

BERRY, J. DUNCAN
PERSONAL Born 12/14/1959, OH, m, 1989, 1 child **DISCIPLINE** HISTORY OF ART AND ARCHITECTURE **EDUCATION** Col Wooster, BA, 82; Brown Univ, AM, 85; PhD, 89. **CAREER** Adj prof, Roger Williams Univ, 86-87; adj prof, RI Sch of Design, 86-90; adj prof, Brown Univ, 89-90. **HONORS AND AWARDS** NEA Curatorial Fel, 82; Fulbright scholar, Univ Vienna, 87-88; IREX scholar, Tech Univ Dresden, 88; dissertation fel, Inst for Int Studies, 88-89. **MEMBERSHIPS** Soc of Archit Hist. **RESEARCH** Architectural theory; German/Austrian/Swiss/French architecture 1500-1900; architectural drawings and fantasies; history of ideas; Freemasonry. **SELECTED PUBLICATIONS** Auth, Pamet Cottage: An Updated Truro Retreat, Cape Cod Home, 97; auth, Reaping what is Soane, The New Criterion, 97; auth, A Richardson Round-up, The New Criterion, 98; auth, A Vibrant Tetonic Strain, The New Criterion, 98; auth, "Heinrich Hubsch," in Encyclopedia of Aesthetics (Oxford Univ Press, 98). **CONTACT ADDRESS** 94 Main St, West Harwich, MA 02671-0517. **EMAIL** duncanb@capecod.net

BERRY, LEE ROY, JR.
PERSONAL Born 11/05/1943, Lake Placid, FL, m **DISCIPLINE** HISTORY **EDUCATION** Eastern Mennonite Col, BA, 1966; University of Notre Dame, PhD, 1976; Indiana University Bloomington, School of Law, JD, 1984. **CAREER** Cleveland Public Schools, teacher, 66-68; Goshen College, prof, 69-79, leader, study serv trimester, 79-80, Dept of History & Government, associate professor, 80-. **HONORS AND AWARDS** John Hay Whitney Fellow, 1970-71; Natl Fellowships Fund Felow, 1975-76. **MEMBERSHIPS** General Board, Mennonite Ch; chairman, High Aim Committee, member, Relief & Service Committee, Mennonite Board of Missions; Peace Sect, Mennonite Central Committee. **CONTACT ADDRESS** Dept of History & Government, Goshen Col, S Main St, Goshen, IN 46526-4795.

BERTELSEN, LANCE
PERSONAL Born 10/24/1947, Inglewood, CA, d, 2 children **DISCIPLINE** ENGLISH LITERATURE, EIGHTEENTH CENTURY ENGLISH CULTURE **EDUCATION** Dartmouth Col, AB, 69; Univ WA, PhD(English), 79. **CAREER** Asst prof, 79-85, assoc prof English, Univ Tex, Austin, 86-, assoc ch, 94-97. **HONORS AND AWARDS** Fel, Nat Humanities center, 83; fel, Yale Center for British Art, 84; TX Inst of Letters O. Henry Awd, 90; URI Fac Res assignment, 91; Frank C. Erwin Centennial Honors Prof, 94; Dean's Fel, 97; President's Associates Teaching Awd, 00. **MEMBERSHIPS** Am Soc 18th Century Studies; S Cent Am Soc 18th Century Studies. **RESEARCH** Fielding; WWII. **SELECTED PUBLICATIONS** Auth, Ireland, temple, and the Origins of the Drapier, Papers on Lang & Lit, 77; The Smollettian View of life, Novel, 78; David Garrick and English painting, 18th Century Studies, 78; Have at you all: Or, Bonnell Thornton's Journalism, Huntington Libr Quart, 81; New Information on a Brush for the Sign Painters, Eighteenth-Century Life, 7, 82; The Interior Structures of Hogarth's Marriage a la Mode, Art History, 6, 83; the Crab: An Unpublished Poem by Charles Churchill, Philol Quart, 63, 84; Jane Austen's Miniatures: Painting, Drawing, and the Novels, Modern lang Quart, 4, 84; The Nonsense Club: Literature and Popular Culture, 1749-1764, Oxford: Clarendon Press, 86; The Significance of the 1731 Revisions to The Fall of Mortimer, Restoration and Eighteenth-Century Theatre Res, 2nd ser, 2, winter 87; Icons on Two, J of Popular Culture, 22, spring 89; San Pietro and the Art of War, Southeast Rev, 74, 89; How Texas Won the Second World War, SE Rev, 76, 91; Journalism, Carnival, and Jubilate Agno, ELH, 59, 92; Committed by Justice Fielding, Eighteenth-Century Studies, 30, 97; auth, Henry Fielding at Work: Magistrate, Businessman, Writer, St. Martins Press, New York, 00. **CONTACT ADDRESS** Dept English, Univ of Texas, Austin, 0 Univ of TX, Austin, TX 78712-1026. **EMAIL** lberte@uts.cc.utexas.edu

BERTHOLD, RICHARD M.
PERSONAL Born 01/22/1946, San Francisco, CA, m **DISCIPLINE** CLASSICAL HISTORY **EDUCATION** Stanford Univ, BA, great distin, 67; Cornell Univ, MA, 69, PhD, 71. **CAREER** Cornell Univ, pt lectr, 71-72; Univ New Mexico, asst prof, 72-85, assoc prof, 85-; Faculty Advisor, Cam Librit, 96-, Am-Arab Anti-discrim comm, 96-, col repub, 96-, Iranian hum rts org, 92-93, Weregamers guild, 90-94, Regular Columnist for UNM LOBO, 82-91, 92-; numerous other Univ serv positions. **HONORS AND AWARDS** Republic of Rome, Avalon Hill Games, with Robert Haines, 90, Awd for Best Pre-20th Century Board Game, Res Publica Romana, french ver, 94; new mex humanities council, accepted and pub 3 essays in sev nm newspapers. **SELECTED PUBLICATIONS** Monograph on Marathon, Hear, O Israel, a Novel about Moses, Three Hour Video Documentary on the Greeks, in progress; Game Simulation of Weimar Republic politics, in progress; Rhodes in the Hellenistic Age, Ithaca, 84; Dare to Struggle: The History and Society of Greece, seeking pub; Day of the Long Night: A Palestinian Refugee Remembers the Nakba, Albuquerque Journal, 98; many numerous reviews and articles. **CONTACT ADDRESS** Dept History, Univ of New Mexico, Albuquerque, Albuquerque, NM 87131. **EMAIL** qqduckus@unm.edu

BERTHRONG, DONALD JOHN
PERSONAL Born 10/02/1922, La Crosse, WI, m, 1942, 2 children **DISCIPLINE** US HISTORY **EDUCATION** Univ Wis, BS, 46, MS, 47, PhD (hist), 52. **CAREER** Instr Am hist, Univ Kansas City, 51-52; from asst prof to prof, Univ Okla, 52-64, chmn dept hist, 66-70; prof to prof emer and head Dept Hist, Purdue Univ, Lafayette, 70-, Consult, US Dept Justice, 57-64. **HONORS AND AWARDS** Awd of Merit, Am Asn State and Local Hist, 64; Fulbright lectr, Univ Hong Kong, 65-66. **MEMBERSHIPS** AHA; Orgn Am Historians; AAUP; Western Hist Asn. **SELECTED PUBLICATIONS** Auth, Walter Stanley Campbell: Plainsman, Ariz & the West, summer 66; ed, A Confederate in the Colorado Goldfields, Univ Okla, 70; auth, Cattleman on the Cheyenne-Arapaho reservation, 1883-1885, Ariz & the West, spring 71; The American Indian: From pacifism to activism, In: Forums in History, Forum, 73; Indians in Northern Indiana and Southwestern Michigan, Garland, 74; The Cheyenne and Arapaho Ordeal, Okla Univ, 76; Changing Concepts: Indians Learn about Long Knives and Settlers, 1849-1800's, In: Red Men and Hat Weavers, Pruett, 76; Black Kettle, A Friend of Peace, In: Indian Leaders: Oklahoma's First Statesmen, Okla Hist Soc, 79. **CONTACT ADDRESS** Dept Hist, Purdue Univ, West Lafayette, West Lafayette, IN 47907.

BERTOLAS, RANDY
PERSONAL Born 09/19/1957, Virginia, MN, m, 1985 **DISCIPLINE** GEOGRAPHY **EDUCATION** Univ Minn, BA, 80; Univ Vt, MA, 82; SUNY Buffalo, PhD, 95. **CAREER** Lectr, SUNY Buffalo, 90-94; assoc prof, Wayne State Col, 95-. **HONORS AND AWARDS** Who's Who Among Am Teachers, 98. **MEMBERSHIPS** AAG; NCGE. **RESEARCH** Geography of Recreation, Tourism, Sports and Environmental Perception. **CONTACT ADDRESS** Dept Soc Sci, Wayne State Col, 1111 Main St, Wayne, NE 68787.

BERTRAND, CHARLES L.
DISCIPLINE MODERN EUROPEAN HISTORY **EDUCATION** Univ Wis, PhD. **CAREER** Assoc prof, 67-. **SELECTED PUBLICATIONS** Ed, Revolutionary Situations in Europe, 1917-1922: Germany, Italy, Austria-Hungary; auth, articles on Italian revolutionary syndicalism, the Italian trade union movement and Italian anarchism. **CONTACT ADDRESS** Dept of Hist, Concordia Univ, Montreal, McConnell Library Buliding, 1400 de Maisonneuve Blvd W, Montreal, QB, Canada H3G 1W8. **EMAIL** bertran@vax2.concordia.ca

BERWANGER, EUGENE H.
PERSONAL Born Calumet City, IL, m **DISCIPLINE** HISTORY **EDUCATION** Illinois State Univ, BA, 51; MA, 52; PhD, Univ of Illinois, Urbana, 64. **CAREER** Asst Prof of History, Illinois College Jacksonville, Illinois, 64-67; Prof of History, Colorado State Univ, 67-. **HONORS AND AWARDS** Fulbright Fellowship, 82; Pennock Teaching-Service Awd, 83; John N Stern Distinguished Professorship, 91. **MEMBERSHIPS** Organization of Amer Historians; Southern Historical Assoc. **RESEARCH** United States History 1800-1877; race relations; Civil War diplomacy. **SELECTED PUBLICATIONS** Auth, "My Diary North and South, by William H. Russell; "British Foreign Service and the American Civil War;" "West and Reconstruction: Frontier Against Slavery: Western Anti-Negro Prejudice and the Slavery Extension Controversy;" "As They Saw Slavery." **CONTACT ADDRESS** Dept History 1776, Colorado State Univ, Fort Collins, CO 80523-0001. **EMAIL** eberwanger@vines.colostate.edu

BEST, GARY DEAN
PERSONAL Born 09/18/1936, Estherville, IA, s **DISCIPLINE** HISTORY **EDUCATION** Univ Haw, Manoa, BA, 68, MA, 69, PhD(Hist), 73. **CAREER** Asst prof, Sophia Univ, Japan, 73-74; asst prof, 75-78, assoc prof, 79-82, prof Hist, Univ Hawaii, HILO, 82-, Am-E Asian rel fel Hist, AHA, 73-74; Fulbright scholar Hist, Japan, 74-75; Nat Endowment of Humanities fel, 82-83; vis scholar, Hoover Inst, 83; vis scholar, Social Philos and Policy Center, bowling Green State U, 00. **MEMBERSHIPS** Orgn Am Historians; Am Hist Asn. **RESEARCH** Twentieth century United States political history; United States diplomatic history. **SELECTED PUBLICATIONS** Auth, Pride, Prejudice and Politics, Praeger, 91; auth, Nickle and Dime Decade, Praeger, 92; Witch Hunt in Wise County: The Persecution of Edith Maxwell, Praeger, 93; The United States in the Pacific: Private Interests and Public Policies with Donald D Johnson, Praeger, 94; Herbert Hoover: The Elder Statesman, Norton, in prep. **CONTACT ADDRESS** Dept of History, Univ of Hawaii, Hilo, 200 W Kawili St, Hilo, HI 96720-4091. **EMAIL** gbest@hawaii.edu

BEST, HENRY
DISCIPLINE HISTORY **EDUCATION** Laval Univ, BA, MA, PhD. **CAREER** Prof. **HONORS AND AWARDS** Knight of the Order of Italy, 84; Commander of the Order of St. Lazarus of Jeruslem, 90. **RESEARCH** Biography of Charles Herbert Best and Margaret Mohan Best. **SELECTED PUBLICATIONS** Auth, "The Viceroy of Sable Island," a paper about the Marquis de la Roche Mesgouez," The Varsity Graduate, 59; auth, "George-Etienne Cartier and the North West," Canadian Historical Asn Annual Meeting, Winnipeg, 70; auth, "The Scot in New France," Scottish Colloquium Proceedings, Vol. 4, Univ of Guelph, 71; co-ed, "The Scot in Canada during the Old Regime,"' Chapter I of The Scot in Canada, Univ of Guelph, (76); ed, The Scot in New France, Scottish Colloquium Proceedings, Guelph, 71; art, L'Etat culturel du Canada a la cession, Revue de l'Universite Laval, 61; auth, "Charles and Margaret Best", Diabetes 1988, Excerpta Medica, (89): 821-830; auth, "The 75th Anniversary of the Discovery of Insulin," Academy of Medicine, Toronto, 96. **CONTACT ADDRESS** Dept of History, Laurentian Univ, 935 Ramsey Lake Rd, Sudbury, ON, Canada P3E 2C6.

BETANCOURT, PHILIP PAUL
PERSONAL Born 10/17/1936, Los Angeles, CA, m, 1959, 2 children **DISCIPLINE** ART HISTORY, CLASSICAL ARCHAEOLOGY **EDUCATION** Southwest Mo State Univ, BS, 59; Wash Univ, St Louis, MA, 67; Univ Pa, PhD (class archaeol), 70. **CAREER** Asst prof, 70-74, assoc prof, 75-78, Prof Art Hist, Temple Univ, 78-, Vis lectr class archaeol, Univ Pa, 76-; res assoc Bronze Age archaeol, Univ Mus, Univ Pa, 77-. **MEMBERSHIPS** Archaeol Inst Am; Col Art Asn. **RESEARCH** Aegean prehistory. **SELECTED PUBLICATIONS** Auth, An Unpublished Minoan Stone Quarry from Eastern Crete, Am J Archeol, Vol 0100, 96; Investigations at the Amnissos Cave, Am J Archeol, Vol 0098, 94; Excavations at Chrysokamino, Crete, 1996, Am J Archaeol, Vol 0101, 97. **CONTACT ADDRESS** Dept of Art Hist, Temple Univ, 1301 Cecil B Moore, Philadelphia, PA 19122-6029.

BETLYON, JOHN WILSON
PERSONAL Born 05/05/1949, York, PA, m, 9 children **DISCIPLINE** NEAR EASTERN LANGUAGES AND CIVILIZATIONS **EDUCATION** Bucknell Univ, AB (cum laude), 71; Harvard Univ, MTS, 73, PhD, 78. **CAREER** Asst prof, Relig, NC Wesleyan Col, 78-80; Campus minister, Lycoming Col, 80-81; Chaplain & assoc prof, Relig, Smith Col, 81-89; Chaplain, US Army, 89-92; Chaplain & assoc prof, Univ North FL & Jacksonville Univ, 92-95; lect, PA State Univ, 95-. **MEMBERSHIPS** SBL; ASOR. **RESEARCH** Persian Period history and religion. **SELECTED PUBLICATIONS** Auth, Coins, Commerce, and Politics: Coins from the Limes Arabicus Project, 1976-1985, in The Roman Frontier in Central Jordan: Interim Report of the Limes Arabicus Project, 1980-1985, S Thomas Parker, ed, British Archaeological Reports Int Series 340, part ii, Oxford British Archaeological Reports, 87; Archaeological Evidence of Military Operations in Southern Judah during the Early Hellenistic Period, The Biblical Archaeologist, 91; Canaanite Myth and the Early Coinage of the Phoenician City-States, in Ancient Economy in Mythology: East and West, Morris Silver, ed, Rowman & Littlefield, 91; Coinage, in Anchor

Bible Dictionary, vol 1, D N Freedman, ed, Doubleday, 92; Money, in HarperCollins Bible Dictionary, rev ed, P J Achtemeier, ed, Harper, 96; many other publications. **CONTACT ADDRESS** 1243 Haymaker Rd, State College, PA 16801. **EMAIL** jwb14@psu.edu

BETTS, RAYMOND FREDERICK
PERSONAL Born 12/23/1925, Bloomfield, NJ, m, 1956, 3 children **DISCIPLINE** HISTORY **EDUCATION** Rutgers Univ, AB, 49; Columbia Univ, MA, 50, PhD, 58; Univ Grenoble, France, D'Univ(hist), 55; Univ Paris, cert, 55. **CAREER** From Instr to asst prof hist, Bryn Mawr Col, 56-61; from asst prof to prof, Grinnell Col, 61-71; Prof Hist, Univ KY, 71-98, dir, Honors Prog, 78-90, founding dir Gains Ctr for Hum, 83-98. **HONORS AND AWARDS** Assoc Cols, Midwest-Ford Found res fel, 66-67; consult, Nat Endowment for Humanities, 72-75; co-ed Fr Colonial Hist Studies, 76-80; Camargo Found res fel, 80; chm, Ky Humanities Coun, 81- ; distinguished prof,Univ Ky, 85; Outstanding Ky Hum Awd, Ky Hum Coun, 89; Chancellor's Awd for Excellence in Tchg, 90; Acorn Awd for Outstanding Excellence in Service and Commitment to Tchg, Ky Advocates of Higher Educ, 92. **MEMBERSHIPS** Fr Colonial Hist Studies; Soc Fr Hist Studies; Ky Hum Coun, chm 81-82; Nat Hum and Liberal Arts Fac. **RESEARCH** Modern European, French Colonial and Modern African history. **SELECTED PUBLICATIONS** Auth, Assimilation and Association in French Colonial Theory, 1890-1914, Columbia Univ, 61; ed, The Scramble for Africa, Heath, 66, 2nd ed, 72; auth, Europe Overseas; Phases of Imperialism, Basic Bks, 68, contribr, From the Ancient Regime to the Popular Front, Columbia Univ, 69, ed, The Ideology of Blackness, Heath, 71; auth, The False Dawn: European Imperialism in the Nineteenth Century, Univ Minn, 75; Tricouleur: A Brief History of French Colonial Empire, Gordon & Cremonsei, 78; Europe in Retrospect: A Brief History of the Last Two Hundred Years, Heath, 79; auth, Uncertain Dimensions: Western Overseas Empire in the Twentieth Century, Minnesota, 85; auth, France and Decolonization, Macmillan, 91; auth, Decolonization, Routledge, 98. **CONTACT ADDRESS** Dept of History, Univ of Kentucky, Lexington, KY 40506.

BHANA, SURENDRA
PERSONAL Born 05/15/1939, India, m, 1966, 3 children **DISCIPLINE** HISTORY **EDUCATION** Univ Witwatersrand, South Africa, BA, 62; Univ South Africa, BA, 65; Univ Kansas, MA, 68; PhD, 71. **CAREER** Teach, Lenasia Indian HS, 63-66; teach asst, Univ of Kansas, 67-69; asst instr, Univ of Kansas, 69-71; lectr, Univ Durban-Westville, 72-75; sr lectr, 76-79; prof, 80-87; vis prof, Univ of Kansas, 88-91; assoc prof, 91-98; prof, 98-. **HONORS AND AWARDS** Res Aff, Jawaharlal Nehru Univ, 99; Vis Prof, Univ of Durban-Westville, SA, 96; Langston Hughes Prof, Univ of Kansas; SA Res Prog Fel, Yale Univ; Eleanor Roosevelt Inst Gnt; George L. Anderson Awd; Harry S. Truman Inst Gnt; Awd, Nat Coun Phi Alpha Theta for Conspicuous Attain Schol of Hist; Bursary Awd, UNIV Witwatersrand. **MEMBERSHIPS** AHA. **RESEARCH** South Africa with special reference to the Indian experience. **SELECTED PUBLICATIONS** Auth, Gandhi's Legacy: The Natal Indian Congress, 1894-94 (97; auth, Indentured Indian Emigrants to Natal, 1860-1902: A Study Based on Ships' Lists (91); ed, Essays on Indentured Indians in Natal (91); coauth, Setting Down Roots: Indian Migrants in South Africa, 1860-1911 (90); co-ed, A Documentary History of Indian South Africans, 1860-1982 (84); auth, The United States and the Development of the Puerto Rican Status Question, 1836-1968 (75). **CONTACT ADDRESS** Dept History, Univ of Kansas, Lawrence, Lawrence, KS 66045-0001. **EMAIL** bhana@falcon.cc.ukans.edu

BIANCHI, ROBERT S.
PERSONAL Born 11/30/1943, New York, NY, m, 1998, 1 child **DISCIPLINE** ART HISTORY **EDUCATION** New York Univ, Inst of Fine Arts, PhD, 96. **CAREER** Cur, Dept of Egyptian Class and Ancient Middle Eastern Art, Brooklyn Mus of Art, 76-91; dir acad and cur aff, Broughton Int, Inc, St. Petersburg, Fla, 96- . **HONORS AND AWARDS** Scholar, Am Sch of Class Stud, Athens, 69; Fulbright-Hayes scholar, 77; J. Clawson Mills fell, Metropolitan Mus of Mod Art, 92-93. **MEMBERSHIPS** Archaeol Inst Am; Am Res Ctr in Egypt. **RESEARCH** Ancient glass; women of antiquity. **SELECTED PUBLICATIONS** Auth, Nana Tokatah: En Apxn Hn Aeyko, Corfu, Antonia Havani Contemp Art, 96; auth, Alexander the Great: The Exhibition, Docent Manual, St. Petersburg, Fla, 96; auth, Raneferef's Carnelian, in van Dijk, ed, Essays on Ancient Egypt in Honour of Herman te Velde, Groningen, 97; auth, Egipcios-Soberanos de la tierra negra, Estrella 8, 98; auth, A Memphite Plaque of Athena, in Bible Lands Museum Jerusalem. Sixth Anniversary Dinner in Honor of Museum Founder Dr. Elie Borowski, Jerusalem, 98; auth, A Question of Political Identity: Nicholas II's Dilemma, Del Hum Forum, Newsl, 98; auth, Egito Milenario: Vida Cotidiana en la Epoca de Los Faraones, Fundacio, 98; auth, Egipte Mil lenair: Vida Quotidiana en l'Epoca Dels Faraons, Fundacio, 98; auth, Nicholas and Alexandra: The Last Imperial Family of Tsarist Russia, Curriculum Guide for Educators and Docents, Broughton Int, 98. **CONTACT ADDRESS** 263 Kenywood Court North, Baxter, MN 56425-7919. **EMAIL** drbob04@attglobal.net

BIDDLE, TAMI DAVIS
PERSONAL Born 06/29/1959, Chester, PA, m, 1988, 1 child **DISCIPLINE** HISTORY **EDUCATION** Lehigh Univ, BA, 81; Yale Univ, PhD, 95. **CAREER** Asst prof, Duke Univ. **HONORS AND AWARDS** Smithsonian Institution Fel; Harvard-McArthur Fel; SSRC-MacArthur Fel. **MEMBERSHIPS** AHA; Soc for Military Hist; Soc for Hist of Am Foreign Relations. **RESEARCH** History of air warfare, particularly strategic bombing; law of war; history of the Cold War. **SELECTED PUBLICATIONS** Auth, Rhetoric and Reality in Air Warfare: the Evolution of British and American Thinking about Strategic Bombing 1914-1945; auth, "British and American Approaches to Strategic Bombing: Their Origins and Implementation in the World War II Combined Bomber Offensive," Jour Strategic Studies (95); auth, "Bombing by the Square Yard: Sir Arthur Harris At War 1942-1945," International History Review (99). **CONTACT ADDRESS** Dept of Hist, Duke Univ, Bix 90719, Durham, NC 27708. **EMAIL** tbiddle@duke.edu

BIEBER, JUDY
DISCIPLINE BRAZIL & LATIN AMERICA HISTORY **EDUCATION** Johns Hopkins Univ, PhD, 95. **CAREER** Asst Prof, Univ NMex, ed bd, Colonial Lat Am Hist Rev. **RESEARCH** Brazilian hist, Comparative slavery, Social hist, Race, Gender, and Fam hist. **SELECTED PUBLICATIONS** Auth, Slavery and Social Life: Attempts to Reduce Free People to Slavery in the Sertao Mineiro, Brazil, 1850-1871, Journal of Latin American Studies, 26, 94; auth, Plantation Socities duting the Era of European Expansion 1450-1800, Varorium Press. **CONTACT ADDRESS** Univ of New Mexico, Albuquerque, Albuquerque, NM 87131. **EMAIL** jbieberr@unm.edu

BIETENHOLZ, PETER GERARD
PERSONAL Born 01/07/1933, Basel, Switzerland, m, 1958, 3 children **DISCIPLINE** RENAISSANCE AND REFORMATION HISTORY **EDUCATION** Univ Basel, PhD (hist, Ital lit), 58. **CAREER** Res fel hist, Warburg Inst, Univ London, 58-59; lectr, Univ Khartoum, 59-63; from asst prof to assoc prof, 63-70, head dept, 74-77, Prof Hist, Univ Sask, 70-, Ed, Can J Hist-Ann Can Hist, 67; Swiss Nat fund sci Res and Can Coun grants; mem exec comt, Collected Works of Erasmus, Univ Toronto Press, 68- 74; res fel, Harvard Inst Ital Renaissance Studies, Florence, 69-70. **MEMBERSHIPS** Can Hist Asn; Renaissance Soc Am; Soc Reformation Res. **RESEARCH** Renaissance humanism, radical reformation, place of myths and legends in European historical thought. **SELECTED PUBLICATIONS** Auth, Basle and France in the sixteenth century; the Basle humanists and printers in their contacts with Francophone culture, by Peter G. Bietenholz; ed, Contemporaries if Erasmus: A Biographical Register of the Renaissance and Reformation/ A-E (A-E), by Peter G. Bietenholz, 85; ed, Contemporaries of Erasmus: A Biographical Register of the Renaissance and Reforamtion: F-M, Peter G. Bietenholz, 86; ed, Contemporaries of Erasmus: A Biographical Register of Renaissance and Reformation: N-Z, by Peter G. Bietenholz, Thomas B. Deutscher, 87; coed, The Correspondence of Erasmus: Letters 1122-1251 (1520-1521), by Desiderius Erasmus, Peter Bietenholz, 88; auth, Historia and Fabula: Myths and Legends in Historial Thought from Antiquity to the Modern Age (Brill's Studies in Intellectual History, Vol 59, by Peter G. Bietenholz, 97. **CONTACT ADDRESS** Dept of Hist, Univ of Saskatchewan, 9 Campus Dr, Saskatoon, SK, Canada S7N 5A5. **EMAIL** bietenholz@sask.usask.ca

BIGGS, DOUGLAS L.
PERSONAL Born 06/01/1960, Ames, IA, m, 1993 **DISCIPLINE** HISTORY **EDUCATION** Iowa State Univ, BA, 82; MA, 86; Univ Minn PhD, 96. **CAREER** Adj Asst Prof, Des Moines Area Community Col, 94-97; Asst Prof to Chair, Waldorf Col, 97-. **HONORS AND AWARDS** Grant, Iowa Humanities Board, 97; Teaching Excellence Awd, Des Moines Area Community Col, 94; Excellence in Research Awd, Iowa State Univ, 86; Clarence H Matterson Awd, Iowa State Univ, 81; Phi Alpha Theta. **MEMBERSHIPS** Medieval Acad of Am, Am Hist Asn, White Hart Soc, NACBS, Richard III Soc. **SELECTED PUBLICATIONS** Auth, "The Appellant and the Clerk; The Officers of Central Government and the First Appeal of Treason, 1387-89," in The Reign of Richard II: Politics, Personalities and Perceptions, Univ Press, forthcoming; auth, "The reign of Henry IV: The Revolution of 1399 and the Establishment of the Lancastrian Regime," in Fourteenth Century Studies, forthcoming; auth, "Henry IV and his Justices of the Peace: The Lancastrianization of Justice, 1399-1413," in Fifteenth Century England, forthcoming; auth, "The Plantagenet Revolution in Government? The Officers of Central Government and the Lancastrian Usurpation of 1399," Medieval Prosopography, forthcoming; auth, "Henry Iv," "The Exchequer," "The Chancery," "Edmund of Langley," "The Unlearned Parliament," "The Earls' Rebellion," "The Free Companies" in Dictionary of Medieval England, forthcoming; auth, "The Trinity Guild of Coventry and the Royal Affinity, 1392-1413," Journal of the Rocky Mountain Medieval and Renaissance Association, (96): 91-113; auth, "Sheriffs and Justices of the Peace: The Patterns of Lancastrian Governance, 1399-1402," Nottingham Medieval Studies, (96): 149-166. **CONTACT ADDRESS** Dept Soc & Beh Sci, Waldorf Col, 106 S 6th St, Forest City, IA 50436-1713. **EMAIL** biggsd@waldorf.edu

BIGGS, ROBERT DALE
PERSONAL Born 06/13/1934, Pasco, WA **DISCIPLINE** ASSYRIOLOGY **EDUCATION** Eastern Wash State Col, BA, 56, Johns Hopkins Univ, PhD(Assyriol), 62. **CAREER** Res assoc Assyriol, Orient Inst, 63-64, from asst prof to assoc prof, 64-72, Prof Assyriol, Univ Chicago, 72-, Fel, Baghdad Sch, Am Schs Orient Res, 62-63; assoc ed, Assyrian Dictionary, 64-; ed, J Near Eastern Studies, 71- **MEMBERSHIPS** Am Orient Soc; Archaeol Inst Am. **RESEARCH** Babylonian and Assyrian languages; Sumerian language. **SELECTED PUBLICATIONS** Auth, The Abu Salabikh tablets: A preliminary survey, J Cuneiform Studies, 66; Semitic names in the Fara Period, Orientalia, 67; SA ZI GA: Ancient Mesopotamian Potency Incantations, J J Augustin, 67; An esoteric Babylonian commentary, Rev Assyriologie, 68; coauth, Cuneiform Texts from Nippur: The Eighth and Ninth Seasons, Univ Chicago, 69; auth, Inscriptions from al-Hiba-Lagash: The First and Second Seasons, 76 & co-ed, Seals and Sealing in the Ancient Near East, 77, Undena, Malibu; coauth, Nippur II: The North Temple and Sounding E, Univ Chicago, 78. **CONTACT ADDRESS** Orient Inst, Univ of Chicago, 1155 E 58th St, Chicago, IL 60637-1540. **EMAIL** r-biggs@uchicago.edu

BIGHAM, DARREL E.
PERSONAL Born 08/12/1942, Harrisburg, PA, m, 1965, 2 children **DISCIPLINE** UNITED STATES HISTORY **EDUCATION** Messiah Col, BA, 64; Univ Kans, PhD, 70. **CAREER** Asst instr US hist, Univ Kans, 68-70; co-dir regional arch proj, 72-75, from Asst Prof to Prof, 70-89, Distinguished Prof Hist, Univ Southern Ind, Evansville, 89-, Dir, Historic Southern Ind, 86-; Exec dir, Leadership Evansville, 76-79. **HONORS AND AWARDS** Paul Harris Fel, Evansville Rotary Club, 92; Rotarian of the Decade, 97. **MEMBERSHIPS** AHA; Orgn Am Historians; AASLH; NCSS. **RESEARCH** American cultural and intellectual history; religion in American history; state and local history. **SELECTED PUBLICATIONS** Auth, From the Green Mountains to the Tombigbee: Henry Hitchcock in territorial Alabama, 1817-1819, Ala Rev, 7/73; Charles Leich and company: A note on the dilemma of German Americans during World War I, Ind Mag Hist, 6/74; The Black family in Evansville and Vanderburgh County, Indiana, in 1880, 6/79 & Work, residence, and the origins of the Black ghetto in Evansville, 1865-1900, 12/80, Ind Mag Hist; Reflections on a heritage: The German Americans of southwest Indiana, ISUE, 80; War as obligation in the thought of American Christians, 1898-1900, Peace & Change, winter 81; The Black family in Evansville and Vanderburgh County: A 1900 post-script, Ind Mag Hist, 6/82; contribr, Their Infinite Variety: Essays on Indiana Politicians, Ind Hist Bur, 82; We Ask Only a Fair Trial: A History of the Black Community of Evansville, Indiana, Ind Univ Press, 87; An Evansville Album, Ind Univ Press, 88; contribr, Always a River, Ind Univ Press, 91; auth, Towns and Villages of the Lower Ohio, Univ Press Ky, 98; Images of America: Evansville, Arcadia, 98. **CONTACT ADDRESS** Dept of Hist, Univ of So Indiana, 8600 University Blvd, Evansville, IN 47712-3591. **EMAIL** dbigham@usi.edu

BIJLEFELD, WILLEM A.
PERSONAL Born 05/08/1925, Tobelo, Indonesia, m, 1950, 4 children **DISCIPLINE** ISLAMIC STUDIES, HISTORY OF RELIGIONS **EDUCATION** Univ Groningen, BD, 46, Drs Theol, 50; Univ Utrecht, Dr Theol, 59. **CAREER** Chaplain to overseas studies, Univ Leiden, 50-55; consult, Islam in Africa Proj, Northern Nigeria, 59-64; asst prof Arabic and Islamic studies, Univ Ibadan, 64-66; assoc prof, 66-68, acad dean, 69-74, Prof Islamics, Hartford Sem Found, 68-90, Dir, Duncan Black Macdonald Ctr, 74-88, Dir, Pierre Benignus Studies Ctr, Islam in Africa Proj, Ibadan, 64-66; ed, Muslim World, 67-90 **RESEARCH** Qur'anic studies; history of the discipline of history of religions; Muslim-Christian relations, past and present. **SELECTED PUBLICATIONS** Auth, A Century of Arabic and Islamic Studies at Hartford Seminary, Muslim World, Vol 0083, 93. **CONTACT ADDRESS** D B Macdonald Ctr, Hartford Sem, 110 Sherman St, Hartford, CT 06105. **EMAIL** wablfld@sover.net

BILHARTZ, TERRY D.
DISCIPLINE HISTORY **EDUCATION** Dallas Baptist Univ, BS; Emory Univ, MA; George Washington Univ, PhD. **CAREER** Prof, Sam Houston State Univ, 79-. **HONORS AND AWARDS** Vis fel, Australian Nat Univ, 91-. **RESEARCH** American religion, historiography and philosophy of history. **SELECTED PUBLICATIONS** Auth, Urban Religion and the Second Great Awakening: Church and Society in Early National Baltimore, Fairleigh Dickinson UP, 86; Francis Asbury's America: An Album of Early American Methodism, 84; co-ed, Constructing the American Past. **CONTACT ADDRESS** Dept of History, Sam Houston State Univ, 1903 University Ave, Suite 314, PO Box 2239, Huntsville, TX 77341-2239. **EMAIL** his_tdb@shsu.edu

BILLIAS, GEORGE ATHAN
PERSONAL Born 06/26/1919, Lynn, MA, m, 1948, 3 children **DISCIPLINE** AMERICAN HISTORY **EDUCATION** Bates Col, AB, 48; Columbia Univ, MA, 49, PhD, 58. **CAREER** From instr to assoc prof Am hist, Univ Maine, 54-62; assoc prof Am colonial hist, 62-66, Prof Am Hist, Clark Univ, 66-; mem

coun, Inst Early Am Hist and Cult, Col William and Mary, 68-71; mem heritage comt, Am Revolution Bicentennial Comn, 72-; Hiatt Prof Am Hist, 83-89 **HONORS AND AWARDS** Guggenheim Mem Found fel, 61-62; Am Philos Society Grant, 65; Am Coun Learned Soc fel, 68-69; NEH grant, 70-71, 79, 86; Exxon Foundation grant, 83; Who's Who in Am, 86-; Earhart Foundation grant, 88; Huntington Library Fel, 89-90; Symposium in Home of G.A.B. Am Antiq Soc, 89. **MEMBERSHIPS** AHA; Manuscript Soc; Am Antiq Soc. **RESEARCH** Am Colonial Hist, Maritime history of the US, American military history, Comparative Const Hist. **SELECTED PUBLICATIONS** Auth, Mass. Land Bankers of 1740, Univ of Maine, 59; auth, General John Glover and His Marblehead Mariners, holt, 60; ed, Am Constitutionalism Abroad, Greenwood, 90; auth, Knight, Russell, Wallace--Proceedings of the American Antiquarian Society, Vol 0104, 94; Privileged Person, William Mary Quart, Vol 0052, 95; A Culture of Rights, The Bill of Rights in Philosophy, Politics and Law, 1791-1991, William And Mary Quart, Vol 0050, 93; My Intellectual Odyssey, Proc Am Antiq Soc, Vol 0102, 92; ed, George Washington's Generals and Opponents, DaCapo 94. **CONTACT ADDRESS** Dept of Hist, Clark Univ, Worcester, MA 01610.

BILLINGS, WILLIAM M.
DISCIPLINE HISTORY **EDUCATION** William & Mary, AB, 62; Pitt, AM, 63; N Ill Univ, PhD, 68. **CAREER** Asst profprof, Univ New Orleans, 68-78; res prof, 88; prof, Univ New Orleans, 94-; Historian of the Supreme Ct of Louisiana. **HONORS AND AWARDS** Phi Beta Kappa; Am Bar Found Fel, 82; Weddell Lectr, Va Hist Soc, 88; LS Fac Found Fel, 87; VHS Mellon Found Fel, 89, 92. **MEMBERSHIPS** Va Hist Soc; La Hist Asoc; Southern Hist Asoc; Am Asoc of Law Libr; British-Irish Asoc of Law Librns. **RESEARCH** Early American law; 17th century Virginia; documentary editing, 19th century law. **SELECTED PUBLICATIONS** Auth, Vignettes of Jamestown, Va Cavalcade, 95; co-ed with Judith Kelleher Schafer, An Uncommon Experience: Law and Judicial Institutions in Louisiana, 1803-2003, 97; auth, The Return of Sir William Berkeley, Va Cavalcade, 98; auth, The Papers of Sir William Berkeley, 1605-1677, forthcoming; auth, Councils, Assemblies, and Courts of Judicature: The General Assembly of Virginia, 1619-1699, forthcoming. **CONTACT ADDRESS** History Dept, Univ of New Orleans, New Orleans, LA 70148. **EMAIL** wmbhi@uno.edu

BILLINGTON, JAMES H.
PERSONAL Born 06/01/1929, Bryn Mawr, PA, m, 1957, 3 children **DISCIPLINE** EUROPEAN HISTORY **EDUCATION** Princeton Univ, BA, 50; Oxford Univ, DPhil, 53. **CAREER** From instr to asst prof hist and gen educ, Harvard Univ, 57-62, res fel, Russian Res Ctr, 58-59; asst prof hist, 62-64, Hodder fel, Coun Humanities, 61-62, prof, 64-75, Dir, Woodrow Wilson Int Ctr Scholars, Princeton Univ, 73-, Fulbright res prof, Univ Helsinki, 60-61; Guggenheim fel, 60-61; guest prof, Univ Leningrad, 61; exchange prof, Univ Moscow, 64 and Inst Hist, Soviet Acad Sci, Moscow, 66-67, chmn bd foreign scholar, Fulbright Prog, 71-73; historian-host, Humanities Film Forum, Nat Pub TV, 73-74. **HONORS AND AWARDS** LittD, Lafayette Col, 81, LeMoyne Col, 82. **MEMBERSHIPS** AHA; Am Asn Advan Slavic Studies; Coun Foreign Rels; PEN Club. **RESEARCH** Russian history, especially cultural and intellectual history of 17th and 19th to 20th centuries; general European history. **SELECTED PUBLICATIONS** Auth, The Intellectual and Cultural Dimensions of International Relations--Present Ironies and Future Possibilities, J Arts Mgt Law Soc, Vol 0022, 92; The Church in the World, Conflict and Hope in the Russian Orthodox Christian Renewal, Theol Today, Vol 0052, 95; Libraries, The Library of Congress, and the Information Age, Daedalus, Vol 0125, 96. **CONTACT ADDRESS** Smithsonian Inst, Washington, DC 20560.

BILLINGTON, MONROE
PERSONAL Born 03/04/1928, m, 1951, 3 children **DISCIPLINE** HISTORY **EDUCATION** Okla Baptist Univ, BA, 50; Univ Okla, MA, 51; Univ Ky, PhD (hist), 55. **CAREER** From instr to prof hist, Univ SDak, 55-66; prof, Univ Toledo, 66-68; head dept, 68-75, Prof Hist, N Mex State Univ, 68-, News ed, Historian, 60-70; vis Fulbright prof, Univ Vienna, 62-63. **MEMBERSHIPS** Orgn Am Historians; Southern Hist Asn. **RESEARCH** Twentieth century US history; the American South; the Negro and civil rights. **SELECTED PUBLICATIONS** Auth, College courses in Southern history: a survey, J Southern Hist, 8/65; Thomas P Gore: the Blind Senator from Oklahoma, Univ Kans, 67; ed, The South: A Central Theme?, Holt, 68; co-ed, Forging of a Nation, 68 & American Democracy on Trial, 68, McCutchan; auth, The American South: A Brief History, Scribner, 71; The Political South in the 20th Century, Scribner's, 75; Lyndon B Johnson and Blacks: the early years, J Negro Hist, 77. **CONTACT ADDRESS** Dept of History, New Mexico State Univ, Las Cruces, NM 88001.

BILLOWS, RICHARD A.
DISCIPLINE ANCIENT GREEK AND ROMAN HISTORY **EDUCATION** Oxford Univ, BA, 78; Univ Calif-Berkeley, PhD, 85. **CAREER** Assoc **RESEARCH** Greek epigraphy **SELECTED PUBLICATIONS** Auth, Antigonos the One-Eyed and the Creation of the Hellenistic State, 90; Kings and Colonists: Aspects of Macedonian Imperialism, 95. **CONTACT ADDRESS** Dept of Hist, Columbia Col, New York, 2960 Broadway, New York, NY 10027-6902.

BILSKY, LESTER JAMES
PERSONAL Born 12/20/1935, St. Louis, MO, m, 1960, 3 children **DISCIPLINE** CHINESE HISTORY **EDUCATION** Wash Univ, BA, 56; Univ Wash, Seattle, PhD(hist), 71. **CAREER** Instr hist, Univ Akron, 62-71; asst prof, 72-76, assoc prof, 76-81, prof hist, Univ Ark, Little Rock, 81-, chm dept, 80-86, 98-. **MEMBERSHIPS** Asn Asian Studies; Soc Study Early China; Southwest Conf Asian Studies. **RESEARCH** Ancient China, especially religious history and environmental history. **SELECTED PUBLICATIONS** Auth, The State Religion of Ancient China, Orient Cult Serv, Taipei, 75; ed, Historical Ecology: Essays on Environment and Social Change, Kennikat Press, 80. **CONTACT ADDRESS** Dept of Hist, Univ of Arkansas, Little Rock, 2801 S University Ave., Little Rock, AR 72204-1000. **EMAIL** ljbilsky@ualr.edu

BILSTEIN, ROGER EUGENE
PERSONAL Born 01/19/1937, Hyannis, NE, m, 1964, 2 children **DISCIPLINE** HISTORY OF TECHNOLOGY **EDUCATION** Doane Col, BA, 59; Oh State Univ, MA, 60, PhD (recent US), 65. **CAREER** Asst prof recent US, Wis State Univ-Whitewater, 65-69, assoc prof hist technol, 69-72; asst prof technol and aero hist, Univ Ill, Urbana, 72-74; assoc prof, 74-79, Prof Technol, Aero Hist and Recent US, Univ Houston, Clear Lake City, 79-00, emeritus, 00-, Sr res assoc, Res Inst, Univ Ala, Huntsville, 70-72; vis scholar aerospace hist, Nat Air and Space Mus, Smithsonian Inst, 77-78; consult, Epic of Flight series, Time and Life, Inc, 80-82; vis prof hist, United States Air Force, Air War Col, 95-96. **HONORS AND AWARDS** Writing Awds, Aviation and Space Writers Asn, 75, 80 and 82; Goddard Essay Awd, Am Inst Astronaut, 77; Manuscript Awd, An Inst Aeronaut and Astronaut, 79; Am Hist Asn; Sr fel in Aerospace hist, 91; Charles Lindbergh Chair of Aerospace Hist, Smithsonian, 92-93; Stellar Awd, Nat Rotary Space Achievement Found, 93; Am Aerospace Industry, cited by Am Libr Asn as one of outstanding academic books of 97. **MEMBERSHIPS** Soc Hist Technol; Orgn Am Historians; Int Comm for the hist of technology. **RESEARCH** History of aviation and space flight; technology since 1900; social, political and diplomatic history of the US since 1900. **SELECTED PUBLICATIONS** Auth, Technology and Commerce: Aviation in the Conduct of American Business, 1918-1929, Technol & Culture, 69; contributor, "The Wrights, the Airplane, and the American Public," in The Wright Brothers (Smithsonian Inst, 78); auth, The Stages of Saturn: A Technological History of the Apollo/Saturn Launch Vehicles, NASA & Government Printing Office, 81; auth, Flight Patterns: Aviation in the US, 1918-1929, Univ Ga, 83; auth, Flight in America: From the Wrights to the Astronauts, Smithsonian Inst, 84, 94, 01; coauth, "Aviation in Texas," Texas Monthly Press (85); coauth, Orders of Magnitude: History of NACA and NASA, 1915-1990, NASA & Government Printing Office, 89; auth, The American Aerospace Industry: From Workshop to Global Enterprise, Twayne Publishers, 96; auth, Airlift and Airborne Operations in World War II, office of Air Force History & Government Printing Office, 98. **CONTACT ADDRESS** 18000 Montevista Cove, Dripping Springs, TX 78620. **EMAIL** bilstein@airmail.net

BINDER, FREDERICK MELVIN
PERSONAL Born 06/19/1931, Chelsea, MA, m, 1964, 1 child **DISCIPLINE** AMERICAN HISTORY **EDUCATION** Boston Univ, BS, 53; Columbia Univ, MA, 54, EdD(Am hist), 62. **CAREER** Asst prof US hist, Ball State Univ, 62-65; from asst prof to prof Am educ hist, City Col New York, 65-74, chmn dept social and psychol found, 68-72; assoc dean fac, 74-79, Prof Hist, Col Staten Island, City Univ New York, 74-, Dir NDEA US Hist Inst, Ball State Univ, 65 and City Col New York, 67. **MEMBERSHIPS** AHA; Orgn Am Historians; Hist Educ Soc; Am Studies Asn. **RESEARCH** American educational, social and intellectual history; the age of the common school, 1830-1865; race and ethnicity in American educational history. **SELECTED PUBLICATIONS** Auth, The Color Problem in Early National America as Viewed by John Adams, Jefferson and Jackson, Mouton, The Hague, 68; ed, Education in the History of Western Civilization: Selected Readings, Macmillan, 70; auth, The Age of the Common School: 1830-1865, Wiley, 74; The growth of the American Republic, 1783-1865, In: A Bibliography of American Educational History, AMS Press, 75. **CONTACT ADDRESS** Col of Staten Island, CUNY, Staten Island, NY 10301.

BINDON, K.
PERSONAL Born Toronto, ON, Canada **DISCIPLINE** HISTORY **EDUCATION** Sir George Williams Univ, BA, 71; Queen's Univ MA, 73, PhD, 79. **CAREER** Lectr, 78-80, asst prof, 80-83, prin, Sch Community & Pub Affairs, 81-84, Concordia Univ; assoc prof, 83, assoc prof, 87-91, Mt St Vincent Univ; Prin & Prof History, Sir Wilfred Grenfell Col, 91-. **HONORS AND AWARDS** Woodrow Wilson Fel, 71-72; R. Samuel McLaughlin Scholar, Queen's Univ, 71-72; Sir John A. Macdonald Grad Fel, 72-74. **MEMBERSHIPS** Can Hist Soc; Champlain Soc; Nova Scotia Coun Higher Learning; Gov Gen Can Stud Conf. **SELECTED PUBLICATIONS** Auth, Canada at War, 1914-1918, 79; coauth, Newfoundland: More Canadian Than British, But Longer Getting There in Higher Education in Canada: Different Systems, Different Perspectives. **CONTACT ADDRESS** Dept of Hist, Okanagan Univ Col, 1000 KLO Rd, Kelowna, BC, Canada V1Y 4X8. **EMAIL** kbindon@beothuk.swgc.mun.ca

BINFORD, HENRY C.
PERSONAL Born 05/02/1944, Berea, OH, m **DISCIPLINE** HISTORY **EDUCATION** Harvard Univ, AB 1966, PhD 1973; Univ of Sussex England, MA 1967. **CAREER** Northwestern Univ, asst prof 1973-79, assoc prof 1979-. **MEMBERSHIPS** Dir Business and Professional People for the Public Interest 1985-; mem Sigma Pi Phi 1985-; editorial board, Chicago Reporter, 1988-. **SELECTED PUBLICATIONS** Author, The First Suburbs, Univ of Chicago Press, 1985. **CONTACT ADDRESS** Northwestern Univ, Evanston, IL 60208.

BING, J. DANIEL
PERSONAL Born 02/11/1938, Jacksonville, FL, m, 1965, 3 children **DISCIPLINE** ANCIENT HISTORY **EDUCATION** Univ Ind, PhD. **CAREER** Assoc prof emer, Hist, Univ Tenn. **MEMBERSHIPS** Asn of Ancient Historians. **RESEARCH** Ancient Greece and near East. **SELECTED PUBLICATIONS** Auth, pubs on Sumerian and Babylonian literature, Assyrian, Persian and early Hellenistic imperial policy in southeast Anatolia, and Athenian political-military development. **CONTACT ADDRESS** Dept Hist, Univ of Tennessee, Knoxville, 915 Volunteer Blvd, 6th Fl, Dunford Hall, Knoxville, TN 37996-4065. **EMAIL** dbing@utk.edu

BINGHAM, EDWIN RALPH
PERSONAL Born 01/21/1920, Denver, CO, 4 children **DISCIPLINE** HISTORY **EDUCATION** Occidental Col, AB, 41, MA, 42; Univ Calif, Los Angeles, PhD, 51. **CAREER** From instr to assoc prof, 49-63, Prof Hist, Univ Ore, 64-, Ford Found advan educ grant, Yale Univ, 54-55; sr Fulbright lectr, Mysore Univ, India, 78-79; Pres., Pacific Coast Branch, Amer. Hist. Assoc. 1985. **MEMBERSHIPS** Oregon Hist Society; Am Historians; AHA; Western Hist Asn. **RESEARCH** Cultural and intellectual history; American biography; American biography; history of the American West; **SELECTED PUBLICATIONS** Auth, "Charles F. Lummis, Editor of the Southwest," Huntington Library, San Marino, 55, Oregon, Palo Alto, CA and Layton, Utah, Peregrine Smith, 79; 2nd ed., 85, Public School Text; ed. With Tim Barnes, "Wood Works: Life and Writings of Charles Erskine Scott Wood, Corvallis, Oregon State University Press, 97. **CONTACT ADDRESS** 697 Crest Dr., Eugene, OR 97405.

BINION, RUDOLPH
PERSONAL Born 01/18/1927, New York, NY, m, 2000 **DISCIPLINE** HISTORY **EDUCATION** Columbia Col, BA, 45, PhD, 58. **CAREER** Instr hist, Rutgers Univ, 55-56; instr hum, Mass Inst Technol, 56-59; from asst prof to assoc prof hist, Columbia Univ, 59-67; prof hist, Brandeis Univ, MA, 67, Coun Res Soc Sci res grant, Columbia Univ, 60; Am Coun Learned Soc fel, 61; Deutscher Akademischer Austauschdienst fel, 81. **HONORS AND AWARDS** Clarke F Ansley Awd, Columbia Univ, 58; George Louis Beer Prize, AHA, 60; medal, Col de France, 80. **MEMBERSHIPS** International Psychohistorical Asn. **RESEARCH** Mod Europ polit, thought and cult, psychohist. **SELECTED PUBLICATIONS** Defeated Leaders, the Political Fate of Caillaux, Jouvenel and Tardieu, Columbia Univ, 60; Frau Lou: Nietzsche's Wayward Disciple, Princeton Univ, 68; Hitler Among the Germans, Elsevier, 76; Soundings, Psychohistory Press, 81; Introduction a la psychohistoire, Pressses Univ France & Col Frane, 82; After Christianity, Logbrigde-Rhodes, 86; Love Beyond Death: The Anatomy of a Myth in the Arts, NYU, 93; Freud uber Aggression und Tod, Picus, 95; Sounding the Classics: From Sophocles to Thomas Mann, Greenwood, 97. **CONTACT ADDRESS** Dept of Hist, Brandeis Univ, 415 South St, Waltham, MA 02454-9110. **EMAIL** binion@brandeis.edu

BIRCH, BRUCE CHARLES
PERSONAL Born 12/03/1941, Wichita, KS, m, 1990, 4 children **DISCIPLINE** OLD TESTAMENT, ANCIENT NEAR EASTERN STUDIES **EDUCATION** Southwestern Col, BA, 62; Southern Methodist Univ, BD, 65; Yale Univ, MA, 67, MPhil, 68, PhD, 70. **CAREER** Asst prof relig, Iowa Wesleyan Col, 68-70; asst prof Bible & relig, 70-71, Erskine Col; assoc prof Old Testament, 71-77, prof Old Testament, 77-, dean, 98-, Wesley Theol Sem; Chmn Nat Intersem Coun, 64-67; mem bd dir, Washington Int Col, 71-74; dir & chmn bd, Int Prog Human Resources Develop, 75-; res fel, Asn Theol Schs, 77-78; vis prof, Sch Theol, summer 82, Claremont. **MEMBERSHIPS** Soc Bibl Lit. **RESEARCH** Deuteronomic history; Biblical theology; Biblical ethics. **SELECTED PUBLICATIONS** Auth, Let Justice Roll Down: Old Testament, Ethics, and Christian Life, Westminster, 91; auth, Hosea, Joel, Amos: Westminster Bible Companion, Westminster, 97; auth, 1 and 2 Samuel: The New Interpreter's Bible, v.2, Abingdon, 98. **CONTACT ADDRESS** Wesley Theol Sem, 4500 Mass Ave N W, Washington, DC 20016-5632. **EMAIL** bbirch@wesleysem.edu

BIRD, HAROLD WESLEY
PERSONAL Born 08/23/1937, Nottingham, England, m, 1962, 2 children **DISCIPLINE** ANCIENT HISTORY AND LITERATURE **EDUCATION** Cambridge Univ, BA, 60, dipl, 61, MA, 64; McMaster Univ, MA, 63; Univ Toronto, PhD (Greek and Roman hist), 72. **CAREER** Head Latin Dept, Salt Fleet High Sch, Ont, 63-64; from lectr to asst prof classics, Univ NB, 64-67; from asst prof to assoc prof, 69-75, Prof Classics, Univ Windsor, 75-, Head, Dept Class and Mod Lang, 82- **MEMBERSHIPS** Class Asn Can; Am Asn Ancient Historians. **RESEARCH** Roman imperial history; history of the late Roman Republic; Roman historiography. **SELECTED PUBLICATIONS** Auth, Julian and Aurelius Victor--Did Victor Receive the Governorship of Pannonia Secunda for Writing De Caesaribus, Latomus, Vol 0055, 96. **CONTACT ADDRESS** Dept of Class Studies, Univ of Windsor, Windsor, ON, Canada N9B 3P4. **EMAIL** hbird@uwindsor.ca

BIRELEY, ROBERT LEE
PERSONAL Born 07/26/1933, Evanston, IL **DISCIPLINE** EARLY MODERN EUROPEAN HISTORY **EDUCATION** Loyola Univ, Chicago, AB, 56, MA, 63; Hochschule Sankt Georgen, Frankfurt, STL, 65; Harvard Univ, PhD, 72. **CAREER** Instr hist, St Ignatius High Sch, Cleveland, 58-61; instr, 71-72, asst prof, 72-76, assoc prof, 76-82, prof hist, Loyola Univ, Chicago, 82, adv ed, Cath Hist Rev, 79-; mem, Inst for Advanced Study, Princeton, 86-86. **HONORS AND AWARDS** Nat Endowment for Hum fel, Rome, Vienna, Brno, Czech & Gyor, Hungary, 72-73; Am Coun Learned Soc res fel, 79; Guggenheim fel, 83; NEH Sr Res Fel, 86-87; Fel, Nat Hum Ctr, Research Triangle Parl, NC, 98-99. **MEMBERSHIPS** AHA; Am Cath Hist Asn; Ren Soc Am; Am Soc Reformation Res; 16th Century Studies Conf; Coun of the Renaissance Soc of Am. **RESEARCH** Early mod Catholicism; Thirty Years War; Hist of the Jesuits; early mod polit thought. **SELECTED PUBLICATIONS** Auth, Maximilian von Bayern, Adam Contzen, S J, und die Gegen reformation in Deutschland 1624-1635, Vandenhoeck & Ruprecht, G"ttingen, 75; The Peace of Prague (1635) and the Counterreformation in Germany, J Mod Hist, 76; Religion and Politics in the Age of Counterreformation, Univ NC Press, 81; The Counter-Reformation Prince. Antimachiavellianism or Catholic Statecraft in Early Modern Europe, Univ NC Press, 90; The Thirty Years' War as Germany's Religious War, In: Krieg und Politik, 1618-1648, Kolloquien 8, 88; Confessional Absolutism in the Habsburg Lands in the Seventeenth Century, In: State and Society in Early Modern Austria, Purdue Univ Press, 94; Scholasticism and Reason of State, In: Aristotelismo politico e ragion di stato, Centro di Studi sul pensiero politico, Studi e Testi 4, 95; Neue Orden, Katholische Reform, und Konfessionalisierung, In: Die katholische Konfessionalisierung, Aschendorff, 95; auth, The Refashioning of Catholicism: A Reassessment of the Counter-Reformation, Catholic Univ of Am Pr (Washington) & Macmillan (London), 99. **CONTACT ADDRESS** Dept of Hist, Loyola Univ, Chicago, 6525 N Sheridan Rd, Chicago, IL 60626-5385. **EMAIL** rbirele@orion.it.luc.edu

BIRKNER, MICHAEL J.
PERSONAL Born 03/26/1950, Teaneck, NJ, m, 1979, 3 children **DISCIPLINE** HISTORY **EDUCATION** Gettysburg Col, BA, 72; Univ Va, MA, 73, PhD, 81. **CAREER** Vis asst prof, Univ Ky, 79-81; assoc ed, Dartmouth Col, 81-83; ed, Concord Monitor, 83-85; asst prof, Millersville Univ, 85-89; from assoc to prof to chemn, Gettysburg Col, 89-. **HONORS AND AWARDS** John A. Booth Prize, New Jersey Hist Society; NEH Summer Fel, 89; Cert of Commendation, Am Asn of State and Local Hist, 95; phi beta kappa, 72; thomas jefferson fel, 72-74. **MEMBERSHIPS** AHA; OAH **RESEARCH** American political history **SELECTED PUBLICATIONS** Coed, The Governor's of New Jersey, 82; auth, Samuel L. Southard: Jeffersonian Whig, 84; coed, Correspondence of Daniel Webster, 1850-1852, 86; auth, A Country Place No More: The Transformation of Bergenfield, New Jersey 1894-1994, 94; ed, James Buchanan and the Political Crisis of the 1850s, 96. **CONTACT ADDRESS** Dept of History, Gettysburg Col, Gettysburg, PA 17325. **EMAIL** mbirkner@gettysburg.edu

BIRN, DONALD S.
PERSONAL Born 08/11/1937, New York, NY, m, 1964, 2 children **DISCIPLINE** MODERN HISTORY **EDUCATION** Union Col, NYork, AB, 59; Columbia Univ, MA, 60, PhD(hist), 64. **CAREER** Foreign serv officer, US Info Serv, Madras, India, 64-66; asst prof, 66-81, Assoc Prof Hist, State Univ NY Albany, 81-, Fel, Richardson Inst for Conflict and Peace Res, London, 73-74. **MEMBERSHIPS** Conf on Brit Studies; AHA; Conf Peace Res in Hist. **RESEARCH** Twentieth century Europe; modern Britain; British cultural propaganda. **SELECTED PUBLICATIONS** Auth, Open diplomacy at the Washington Conference, Comp Studies in Soc & Hist, 5/69; The history teacher as propagandist, Hist Teacher, 5/72; A peace movement divided: Pacifism and internationalism in Britain, J Peace & Change, 6/73; The League of Nations Union and collective security, J Contemporary Hist, 74; The League of Nations Union 1918-1945, Oxford Univ Press, 81. **CONTACT ADDRESS** Dept of Hist, SUNY, Albany, Albany, NY 12054.

BIRN, RAYMOND
PERSONAL Born 05/10/1935, New York, NY **DISCIPLINE** HISTORY **EDUCATION** NYork Univ, BA, 65; Univ IL, MA, 57; PhD, 61. **CAREER** Instructor to Full Prof and Dept Head, Univ Ore, 61-. **HONORS AND AWARDS** Fel, Center for the Hist of Freedom Washington Univ, 92; NEH, 87-88; Fulbright Fel, France, 68-69. **MEMBERSHIPS** Am Hist Asn, Soc for French Hist Studies, Am Soc for 18th Century Studies. **RESEARCH** Eighteenth-Century European History; History of the Book. **SELECTED PUBLICATIONS** Auth, Forging Rousseau: Print, commerce, and Cultural manipulation in the Late enlightenment, Oxford, forthcoming; auth, Crisis, Absolutism, Revolution: Europe, 1648-1789, London: Harcourt, 92; auth, Pierre Rousseau and the Philosophes of Bouillon, Geneva, 64; ed, "Transmitting Rousseau," in The Transmission of Culture in 18th and 19th Century Europe, Berne, 99; auth, "Fashioning an Icon: Jean-Jacques Rousseau and the Memoires Secrets," in The Memoires Secrets and the Culture of Publicity, Oxford, 98; auth, "A Certain Place for Memory: Rousseau, the Confessions, and the Publishing History of the Discours sur l'Inegalite," in Le Livre et l'Historien, Geneva, 97. **CONTACT ADDRESS** Dept Hist, Univ of Oregon, Eugene, OR 97403. **EMAIL** rbirn@oregon.uoregon.edu

BIRNBAUM, LUCIA CHIAVOLA
PERSONAL Born 01/03/1924, Kansas City, MO, m, 1946, 3 children **DISCIPLINE** HISTORY **EDUCATION** Univ Calif, Berkeley, PhD. **CAREER** Res assoc, 83-85, Women's Ctr; res assoc, 90-96, dept hist, Univ Calif; affil scholar, 87-94, Inst Res & Gender, Stanford Univ; vis scholar, 84, 95, Grad Theol Union Berkley; instr, 94-, Women's Spirituality, Calif Inst of Integral Stud; 98- Italian Res & Stud Prog, Ctr of Western Europe Stud. **RESEARCH** Cultural history **CONTACT ADDRESS** 349 Gravatt Dr., Berkeley, CA 94705-1503. **EMAIL** cowari@aol.com

BISCHOF, GUNTER J., JR.
PERSONAL Born 10/06/1953, Mellau, Austria, m, 1990, 3 children **DISCIPLINE** HISTORY **EDUCATION** Univ Innsbruck, Mag Phil, 82; Univ New Orleans, MA, 80; Harvard Univ, MA, 83; PhD, 89. **CAREER** Assoc prof to prof, Univ New Orleans, 89-; assoc dir, Eisenhower Center, 89-97; assoc dir to exec dir, Center for Austrian culture and Comm, 97-. **HONORS AND AWARDS** Guest Prof, Univ of Munich, 92-94; Guest Prof, Univ of Innsbruck, 93, 94; Guest Prof, Univ of Salzburg and Univ of Vienna, 98; Guest Scholar, Inst of Human Sci, Vienna, 98; Guest Lectr, Austrian Diplomatic Acad, 98. **MEMBERSHIPS** AHA; Ger Studies Assoc; Soc of Hist of Am Foreign Relations; Austrian Assoc for Am Studies; Europ Assoc for Am Studies. **RESEARCH** World War II, Cold War, 20th Century Austria, Prisoners of War. **SELECTED PUBLICATIONS** Coauth, Eisenhower: A Centenary Assessment, LSU Pr, 95; auth, Contemporary Austrian Studies, 8 Vol, 93-00; auth, Austria in the First Cold War, 1945-55, St Martin's, 99; ed, Cold War Respite: The Geneva Summit of 1955, LSU Pr, 00. **CONTACT ADDRESS** Dept Hist, Univ of New Orleans, 2000 Lakeshore Dr, New Orleans, LA 70148-0001. **EMAIL** camc@uno.edu

BISHOP, C. JAMES
PERSONAL Born 11/09/1935, Loretto, PA, m, 1959, 4 children **DISCIPLINE** HISTORY **EDUCATION** Clarion State Col, BS, 61; Ohio Univ, MA, 64; Univ Wis, Madison, MA, 66; Univ Va, PhD, 72. **CAREER** Asst prof, Winthrop Col, 64-67; lectr, Kans State Univ, 68-69; Prof Asian Hist, Manchester Col, 69-; Fulbright Scholar hist, US Educ Found in India, 67-68; NEH grant hist of socialism, Duke Univ, 67-67 & 77. **MEMBERSHIPS** AHA, Am Asn Asian Studies. **RESEARCH** Social and political structure and history of South and Southeast Asia, particularly Modern India, 1857-1947. **SELECTED PUBLICATIONS** Auth, The Chinese Laborer in Malaya 1900-1922, Univ Singapore, 72; coauth, The Indian World, Forum Press, 77. **CONTACT ADDRESS** Dept Hist, Manchester Col, 601 E College Ave, North Manchester, IN 46962-1226.

BISHOP, DONALD M.
PERSONAL Born 10/20/1945, Nashville, TN, m, 1973, 3 children **DISCIPLINE** AMERICAN STUDIES **EDUCATION** Trinity Col, BA, 67; Ohio State Univ, MA, 74. **CAREER** Res Hist, Aerospace Studies Inst, 70-71; Asst Prof, US Air Force Acad, 74-79; For Serv Off, 79-87; Info Off, Am Inst in Taiwan, 88-91; Congressional Fel, House of Rep, 91-92; Course Dir, US Info Agency, 92-94; County Pub Affairs Off, Am Embassy Dhaka, 94-97; Dep Pub Affairs Off, Am Embassy Beijing, 97-00; Country Pub Affairs Off, Am Embassy Nigeria, 00-. **HONORS AND AWARDS** Colt Firearms Prize, Trinity Col, 67; Bronze Star Medal, 70; Air Force commendation Medal, 72; Meritorious Serv Medal, 79; USIA Sustained Superior Honor Awds, 94, 98. **MEMBERSHIPS** Hist Soc. **RESEARCH** American-East Asian relations; Religion in American Society **SELECTED PUBLICATIONS** Ed, Gontantra O Pujibad Nirbachito Probondhaj (Essays on Democracy and Capitalism), US Information Service, Dhaka, 97; auth, "The Place of Religion in American Society," Meiguo Yanjiu (American Studies, 98; auth, "Closing the Understanding Gap: American Fulbright Professors in China," Vital Speeches of the Day, 98. **CONTACT ADDRESS** Dept of State, 8320 Abuja Pl, Washington, DC 20521-8320. **EMAIL** donald.bishop.67@trincoll.edu

BISMANIS, MAIJA
PERSONAL Born Riga, Latvia **DISCIPLINE** ART HISTORY **EDUCATION** Univ BC, BA, MA, 68; Univ Nottingham, PhD, 74; Oriel Col, Oxford, post-doc, 74-76. **CAREER** Educ & Res curator, Vancouver Art Gallery, 68-70; Prof Univ Regina 70-. **HONORS AND AWARDS** Heritage Awd, City Regina, 82. **MEMBERSHIPS** Univ Art Asn Can; Int Ctr Medieval Art; Medieval Soc Am; Soc Archit Hists. **SELECTED PUBLICATIONS** Auth, Canada Collects: the Middle Ages; auth, The English Medieval Timber Roof: A Handbook of Types; auth, Medieval Sculpture in Canadian Collections. **CONTACT ADDRESS** Dept of Art History, Univ of Regina, 3737 Wascana Pkwy Dr, Regina, SK, Canada S4S 0A2.

BISSON, DOUGLAS R.
PERSONAL Born 05/17/1954, Rockville Centre, NY, m **DISCIPLINE** HISTORY **EDUCATION** Fla Atlantic Univ, BA, 76; Ohio State Univ, MA, 81; PhD, 87. **CAREER** Asst prof to prof, Belmont Univ, 87-. **HONORS AND AWARDS** Univ Fel, Ohio State Univ, 79; Diss Year Fel, Ohio State Univ, 85-86; Fulbright, Great Britain, 83-84. **MEMBERSHIPS** N Am Conference on British Studies; Europ Hist Sec, S Hist Assoc. **RESEARCH** Tudor History, Economic History. **SELECTED PUBLICATIONS** Auth, The Merchant Adventurers of England: the Company and The Crown, 1474-1564. **CONTACT ADDRESS** Dept Hist, Belmont Univ, 1900 Belmont Blvd, Nashville, TN 37212-3758. **EMAIL** bissond@mail.belmont.edu

BISSON, THOMAS N.
PERSONAL Born 03/30/1931, New York, NY, m, 1962, 2 children **DISCIPLINE** HISTORY **EDUCATION** Haverford Col, BA, 53; Princeton Univ, MA, 55, PhD, 58. **CAREER** Instr, Amherst Col, 57-60; asst prof, Brown Univ, 60-65; assoc prof, Swarthmore Col, 65-67; from assoc prof to prof, Univ of Calif, Berkeley, 67-87; prof, Harvard Univ, 87-. **HONORS AND AWARDS** J.S. Guggenheim Mem Fel, 64-65; Univ of Calif Res Comt Fels for the Hums, 68-69, 76, 80; Am Philos Soc, Grants-in Aid, 69, 78; Inst for Advan Study, Princeton, vis mem, 71-72; Nat Endowment for the Hums, sen fel, 75-76; Am Coun of Learned Socs, sen fel, 79-80; All Souls Col, Oxford, vis fel, 83-84; Fulbright Fel for West European Studies, 83-84; W. Channing Cabot Fel in the Fac of Arts and Scis, Harvard Univ, 89-90. **MEMBERSHIPS** Medieval Acad of Am; Am Acad of Arts and Scis; Reial Academia de Bones Lletres; Brit Acad; Royal Hist Soc; Institut d'Estudis Catalans; Am Philos Soc; AHA. **RESEARCH** Medieval history: power and cultural change, tenth to thirteenth centuries. **SELECTED PUBLICATIONS** Auth, Assemblies and Representation in Languedoc in the Thirteenth Century, 64; Medieval Representative Institutions: Their Origins and Nature, 73; Conservation of Coinage: Monetary Exploitation and its Restraint in France, Catalonia and Aragon (c.A.D. 1000-c.1225), 79; Fiscal Accounts of Catalonia under the Early Count-Kings (1151-1213), 84; The Medieval Crown of Aragon: a Short History, 86; Medieval France and her Pyrenean neighbours: studies in early institutional history, 89; The war of the two Arnaus: a memorial of the broken peace in Cerdanya, in Miscellania en homenatge al P. Agusti Altisent, 91; Utilia perniciem operantur: forme et objet dans le Memorial del'eveque Aldebert III de Mende, in Histoire et societe. Melanges offerts a Georges Duby, 92; The 'Feudal revolution,' in Past and Present, 142, 94; Medieval lordship, in Speculum 1xx, 95; Cultures of Power: Lordship, Status, and Process in Twelfth-Century Europe, 95; The politicising of west European societies (c.1175-c.1225), in Georges Duby. L'ecriture de l'histoire, 96; The origins of the Corts of Catalonia, in Parliaments, Estates and Representation 16, 96; Els origens de l'impost sobre la moneda a Catalunya: una reconsideracio, in Acta historica et archaelogica mediavalia 16-17, 96; 'Statebuilding' in the medieval Crown of Aragon, in XV Congreso de Historia de la Corona de Aragon. Actas tomo1. El poder real en la Corona de Aragon (Siglos XIV-XVI), 96; In memoriam: Georges Duby, in French Politics & Society, 15:1, 97; The 'Feudal revolution': Debate: Reply, in Past & Present, 155, 97; L'Impuls de Catalunya: recerques sobre l'epoca dels primers comtes-reis (vers 1140-vers 1225), 97; Tormented Voices: Power, Crisis and Humanity in Rural Catalonia, 1140-1200, 98. **CONTACT ADDRESS** Dept of History, Harvard Univ, 213 Robinson Hall, Cambridge, MA 02138. **EMAIL** tnbisson@fas.harvard.edu

BITTLE, WILLIAM GEORGE
PERSONAL Born 03/01/1943, Warren, OH, m, 1963, 2 children **DISCIPLINE** ENGLISH HISTORY **EDUCATION** E Stroudsburg State Col, BA, 70, MA, 71; Kent State Univ, PhD(hist), 75. **CAREER** Asst Prof Hist, Kent State Univ, 75- **MEMBERSHIPS** AHA; Friend's Hist Asn; Conf Quaker Historians; Conf Brit Studies. **RESEARCH** Cromwellian England; English radical movements of the 17th century. **SELECTED PUBLICATIONS** Coauth, Inflation and Philanthropy in England: A reassessment of W K Jordan's data, 76 & A reassessment reiterated, 78, Econ Hist Rev; contribr, A Biographical History of Seventeenth Century English Radicals (in prep). **CONTACT ADDRESS** Dept of Hist, Kent State Univ, Canton, OH 44720.

BIZZARRO, TINA WALDEIER
PERSONAL Born Media, PA, m, 1977, 2 children **DISCIPLINE** HISTORY OF ART **EDUCATION** Hamilton Col and Univ Pittsburgh, BA, 71; Bryn Mawr Col, PhD(hist art), 85. **CAREER** Prof, 85-, chair, Arts Division, 85-, Rosemont Coll. **HONORS AND AWARDS** Phi Beta Kappa **MEMBERSHIPS** Int Center for Medieval Art; Col Art Asn; Am Asn Univ Women; Soc Architectural Historians; Del Valley Medieval Asn. **RESEARCH** History of criticism; medieval architecture, Mediterranean Studies Summer Program in Messina, Sicily. **SELECTED PUBLICATIONS** Auth, Romanesque Architectural Criticism: A Prehistory, Cambridge Univ Press, 93. **CONTACT ADDRESS** 511 N. Wynnewood Ave., Narberth, PA 19072. **EMAIL** tbizzarro@rosemont.edu

BLACK, BRIAN C.
PERSONAL Born 08/08/1966, Altoona, PA, m, 1988, 2 children **DISCIPLINE** AMERICAN STUDIES **EDUCATION** Gettysburg Col, BA, 88; NYork Univ, MA, 91; Univ Kansas, PhD, 96 **CAREER** Visiting asst prof, Gettysburg Col, 94-97; visiting asst prof, Skidmore Col, 97-99; Asst Prof, Penn St Altoona, 99-. **HONORS AND AWARDS** NEH Fel, 96; Beeke-Levy Res Fel, 97; Skidmore Col Faculty Development Grant, 98; Aldo Leopold Prize, 99. **RESEARCH** North America Environmental History; 19th & 20th Centuries; New Deal **SELECTED PUBLICATIONS** Auth, "PETROLIA: The Landscape of America's First Oil Boom," Johns Hopkins Univ, 00; auth, "Organic Planning: Ecology and Design in Landscape of the Tennessee Valley Authority, 1930-1945," Environmentalism in Landscape Architecture, 00. **CONTACT ADDRESS** Dept of History, Pennsylvania State Univ, Altoona, Ivyside Park, Altoona, PA 16601. **EMAIL** bcb4@psu.edu

BLACK, EUGENE CHARLTON
PERSONAL Born 12/15/1927, Boston, MA, m, 1983, 5 children **DISCIPLINE** MODERN EUROPEAN HISTORY **EDUCATION** Col William & Mary, AB, 48; Harvard Univ, AM, 54, PhD, 58. **CAREER** From instr to prof, 58-69, Springer Prof Hist, Brandeis Univ, 71-; Vis prof, Boston Univ, 69. **HONORS AND AWARDS** Mazer Fellow, 83, 86, 90; Tauber Fellowship, 83; APS grant, 85, 87; Sacher Fellowship, 86; NEH Grant, 87; Guest Fellow, Wolfson Col, Oxford, 88; Who's Who in America, 87-; Who's Who Among American Teachers, 98-. **MEMBERSHIPS** AHA; Hist Asn UK; Conf Brit Studies; fel Royal Hist Soc; Econ Hist Soc; Athenaeum. **RESEARCH** Transition from voluntarism to collectivism; feminism and liberalism; diplomacy of minority rights in Eastern Europe, 1914-1930; universal Judaism and the Republican tradition; modern British social history. **SELECTED PUBLICATIONS** Auth, The Association: British Extraparliamentary Political Organization, 1769-1793, Harvard Univ, 63; Posture of Europe, 1815-1940: Readings in European Intellectual History, Dorsey, 64; European Political History, 1815-70: Aspects of Liberalism, 67, British Politics in the Nineteenth Century, 69 & Victorian Culture and Society, 73, Harper; Feminists, Liberalism, and Morality: The Unresolvable Triangle, Fawcett Libr Papers, 81; Social Politics of Anglo-Jewry, 1880-1920, 88. **CONTACT ADDRESS** Dept of Hist, Brandeis Univ, Mailstop 036, Waltham, MA 02454. **EMAIL** blackec@brandeis.edu

BLACK, J. LAURENCE
DISCIPLINE HISTORY **EDUCATION** Mount Allison Univ, BA; Boston Univ, MA; McGill Univ, PhD. **CAREER** Prof, Carleton Univ; dir of the Centre for Res, Carleton Univ. **RESEARCH** Russian and Soviet Education; Inter-ethnic conflict, human rights and issues in the Russian Federation and the successor states to the USSR. **SELECTED PUBLICATIONS** Auth, Into the Dustbin of History: The USSR from August Coup to Commonwealth, 1991, Gulf Breeze, Fla: Acad Intl Press, 93; Skovoroda as Teacher: The Image as Model, Hyrhorij Savyc Skovoroda, An Anthology of Critical Articles, Can Inst Ukrainian Stud Press, Univ Toronto Press, 94; "Canada in the Soviet Mirror: English-Canadian Literature in Soviet Translation," Jour Can Stud/Rev d'etudes canadiennes 30:2, 95; Canada in the Russian Mirror: The 'Canada Card' in Russian politics and Foreign policy, 1802-1860, Occasional Paper No 4, Ctr for Res on Can-Russ Rel(s), 95; ed, "Kana-Votchina Amerikanskogo Imperializma: Canada and Canadian Communists in the Soviet Coming War Paradigm, 1946-1951," with Greg Donaghy, Canada and the Cold War, Ottawa: Canadian Committee for the History of the Second World War, 97; ed, Russia and Eurasia Documents Annual, 1987-1996, Gulf Breeze, Fla: Academic International Press, 99-98; ed, "G.-F. Muller and the Popularization of Siberian History, geography, and Ethnography in the 18th Centrury," in Boris Chichlo, ed., Siberie II, Questions Siberiennes, Paris: Institut d'Etudes Slaves, 99. **CONTACT ADDRESS** Dept of Hist, Carleton Univ, 1125 Colonel By Dr, Ottawa, ON, Canada K1S 5B6. **EMAIL** larry_black@carleton.ca

BLACK, NAOMI
PERSONAL Born 02/13/1935, Newcastle-upon-Tyne, England **DISCIPLINE** POLITICAL SCIENCE, HISTORY **EDUCATION** Cornell Univ, AB, 55; Yale Univ, MA, 57, PhD, 64. **CAREER** Instr, polit sci, Brown Univ, 63-64; instr, govt, Ind Univ, 64-65; asst prof, 65-71, assoc prof, 71-84, PROF POLITICAL SCIENCE, YORK UNIV, 85-. **SELECTED PUBLICATIONS** Auth, Social Feminism, 89; coauth, Canadian Women: A History, 88, 2nd ed, 96. **CONTACT ADDRESS** Dept of Polit Sci, York Univ, 4700 Keele St, North York, ON, Canada M3J 1P3.

BLACK, SHIRLEY JEAN
PERSONAL Born 04/20/1935, Tulsa, OK **DISCIPLINE** MODERN EUROPEAN HISTORY, FRENCH HISTORY **EDUCATION** Univ Okla, BA, 67, MA, 69, PhD(hist), 74. **CAREER** Asst Prof Hist, Tex AandM Univ, 73-, Ed adv hist, Military Affairs, 76-79. **MEMBERSHIPS** Soc Fr Hist Studies; Western Soc Fr Hist (secy, 78-81); AHA; Fr Colonial Hist Soc. **RESEARCH** Napoleon III and the French intervention in Mexico; nineteenth century French diplomatic history. **SELECTED PUBLICATIONS** Auth, Napoleon III's quest for silver in Mexico, Proc Western Soc Fr Hist, Vol I, 4/74; Napoleon III et le Mexique: Un triomphe monetaire, Rev Hist, 1-3/78; The silver problem of the second French Empire: Motivation for intervention in Mexico, Proc Fr Colonial Hist Soc, Vol 4, 4/78; Napoleon III and European colonization in Mexico: The substance of an imperial dream, In: Festschrift for Max L Moorhead, Perdido Bay Press, 79; Olivenza: An Iberian Alsace-Lorraine, Americas, Vol 35, 4/79. **CONTACT ADDRESS** Dept of Hist, Texas A&M Univ, Col Station, College Station, TX 77843.

BLACKBOURN, DAVID G.
PERSONAL Born 11/01/1949, Spilsby, United Kingdom, m, 1985, 2 children **DISCIPLINE** HISTORY **EDUCATION** Cambridge Univ, BA, 70; MA, 74; PhD, 76. **CAREER** Res Fel, Jesus Col, 73-76; lectr, Queen Mary Col, 76-79; vis Kratter prof, Stanford Univ, 89-90; lectr to prof, Birkbeck Col, 79-92; prof to Coolidge prof, Harvard Univ, 92-. **HONORS AND AWARDS** Fel, Royal Hist Soc; Best Book in Ger Hist Prize, Am Hist Asn. **MEMBERSHIPS** Ger Hist Soc, Ger Studies Asn, Confr Group on Central European Hist of Am Hist Asn. **RESEARCH** Social, cultural, and political history of modern Germany (18th-20th centuries). **SELECTED PUBLICATIONS** Auth, Class, Religion and Local Politics in Wilhelmine Germany. The Center Party in Wurttemberg before 1914, 80; coauth, The Peculiarities of German History. Bourgeois Society and Politics in Nineteenth-Century Germany, 84; auth, Populists and Patricians. Essays in Modern German History, 87; co-ed, Ther German Bourgeoisie: Essays in the Social History of the Early German Middle Classes from the Late Eighteenth to the Early Twentieth Century, 91; auth, Marpingen: Apparitions of the Virgin Mary in Bismarckian Germany, 93, 94, & 97; auth, The Long Nineteenth Century. A History of Germany 1780-1918, 97. **CONTACT ADDRESS** Dept Hist, Harvard Univ, Robinson Hall, Cambridge, MA 02138. **EMAIL** dgblackb@fas.harvard.edu

BLACKBURN, GEORGE MCCOY
PERSONAL Born 05/05/1926, Bloomington, IN, m, 1952, 5 children **DISCIPLINE** AMERICAN HISTORY **EDUCATION** State Univ NYork Albany, BA, 47; Ind Univ, MA, 50, PhD(hist), 56. **CAREER** Teacher social studies, Alpena Community Col, 55-58; asst prof hist, Ferris Inst, 58-59; from asst prof to assoc prof, 59-67, assoc dean arts and sci, 70-76, chmn dept, 76-82, Prof Hist, Cent Mich Univ, 67- **MEMBERSHIPS** AHA; Orgn Am Historians. **RESEARCH** Civil War; Reconstruction; demographic history. **SELECTED PUBLICATIONS** Auth, Unequal Opportunity on a Mining Frontier - the Role of Gender, Race, and Birthplace, Pac Hist Rev, Vol 0062, 93. **CONTACT ADDRESS** Dept of Hist, Central Michigan Univ, Mount Pleasant, MI 48859. **EMAIL** blacklg@cmich.edu

BLACKEY, ROBERT ALAN
PERSONAL Born 12/17/1941, New York, NY, m **DISCIPLINE** ENGLISH HISTORY, HISTORY OF REVOLUTIONS, HISTORY **EDUCATION** City Col New York, BA, 63; NYork Univ, MA, 64, PhD(hist), 68. **CAREER** Prof Hist, Calif State Univ, San Bernadino, 68-, Fel, William Andrews Clark Mem Libr, Univ Calif, Los Angeles, 69; chief reader, Col Bd Advan Placement Exam in Europ Hist, 77-80. **MEMBERSHIPS** AHA; Conf Brit Studies; Anglo-Am Asn. **RESEARCH** Eighteenth century English history. **SELECTED PUBLICATIONS** Auth, Fanon and Cabral: A Contrast in Theories of Revolution for Africa, J Mod African Studies, 6/74; coauth, Revolution and the Revolutionary Ideal, Schenkman, 76; auth, Modern Revolutions and Revolutionists: A Bibliography, ABC-Clio Bks, 76; A Politician in Ireland: The Lord Lieutenancy of the Earl of Halifax, 1761-63, Eire-Ireland, Winter, 79; Free at Last: Portuguese Colonies After Independence, African Studies Assoc Rev of Bks, 79; Beginning an Advanced Placement Course in European History, Col Entrance Exam Bd, 80; A Guide to the Skill of Essay Construction in History, Social Educ, 3/81; Revolution and Revolutionists: A Comprehensive Guide to the Literature, ABC-Clio Bks, 82. **CONTACT ADDRESS** Dept of History, California State Univ, San Bernardino, 5500 University Pky, San Bernardino, CA 92407-7500. **EMAIL** rblackey@wiley.csusb.edu

BLACKFORD, MANSEL GRIFFITHS
PERSONAL Born 05/12/1944, Seattle, WA, m, 1966, 2 children **DISCIPLINE** HISTORY **EDUCATION** Stanford Univ, BA, 66; Univ Wash, MA, 67; Univ Calif, Berkeley, PhD(hist), 72. **CAREER** Asst prof, 72-78, Assoc Prof Hist, Ohio State Univ, 79-83, Fulbright lectr, Japan, 80-81, 85-86; Prof, 84-01. **HONORS AND AWARDS** Pres, Bus Hist Conf, 97. **MEMBERSHIPS** Bus Hist Conf; AHA; OAH; ASEH. **RESEARCH** Business history; history of American West. **SELECTED PUBLICATIONS** Auth, Business Enterprise in American History, Houghton Mifflin, 86; auth, The Rise of Modern Business in Great Britain, the United States and Japan, Univ of North Carolina Press, 88; auth, Local Businesses: Exploring Thus Histor, AASLH, 90; auth, A History of Small Business in America, Twayne, 91; auth, The Lost Dream: Businessmen and City Planning on the Pacific Coast, 1890-1920, Ohio State Univ Press, 93; auth, BF Goodrich: Tradition and Transformation, 1870-1995. Ohio State Univ Press, 96; auth, Fragile Paradise: The Impact of Tourism on Maui, 1959-2000, Univ Press of Kansas, 01. **CONTACT ADDRESS** Dept of History, Ohio State Univ, Columbus, 230 W 17th Ave, Columbus, OH 43210-1361. **EMAIL** blackford@osu.edu

BLACKMAR, ELIZABETH
DISCIPLINE UNITED STATES HISTORY **EDUCATION** Smith Univ, BA, 72; Harvard Univ, PhD, 81. **CAREER** Prof. **RESEARCH** Social and urban history. **SELECTED PUBLICATIONS** Auth, Manhattan for Rent 1785-1850, 89; co-auth, The Park and the People: A History of Central Park, 92. **CONTACT ADDRESS** Dept of History, Columbia Col, New York, 2960 Broadway, New York, NY 10027-6902.

BLACKWELL, FREDERICK WARN
PERSONAL Born 09/09/1936, Spokane, WA, m, 1 child **DISCIPLINE** SOUTH ASIAN CULTURE, HISTORY **EDUCATION** WA State Univ, BA, 58, MA, 60; Univ Wis, MA, 65, PhD(SAsian lang & lit), 73. **CAREER** Asst prof hist, WA State Univ, 69-72, asst prof English, 70-72, asst prof foreign lang & lit, 72-76, univ ombudsman, 79-81, assoc prof Foreign Lang & Lit, 76-90, assoc prof hist, WA State Univ, 90-, dir East & South Asia Program, 80-93; Exec comt, Indian Studies Asn, 77-80 & Philol Asn Pac Coast, 78-81; educ consult, Educ Resources Ctr, New Delhi, 80; assoc ed, J SAsian Lit, 81-. **RESEARCH** Literature of and about India, in English; concepts of M. K. Gandhi; journals of Lewis Thompson; translation of contemporary Hindi writers. **SELECTED PUBLICATIONS** Auth, Comment on Mohan Rakesh and Socialist Realism, SAsia Ser Occas Paper, 74; Four Plays of Nissim Ezekiel, J SAsian Lit, 76; Experiences of Teaching South Asian Literature to Non-Asians, SAsia Perspectives, 77; ed, Feminine Sensibility and Characterization Issue, J SAsian Lit, Vol 13, No 3 & 4; auth, Perception of the Guru in the Fiction of Ruth Prawer Jhabvala, J Indian Writing English, 77; Krishna Motifs in the Poetry of Sarojini Naidu and Kamala Das, 78 & coauth, Mohan Rakesh's Lahrom Ke Rajhans and Ashvagosha's Saundarananda, 78, J SAsian Lit; auth, In Defense of Kaikeyi and Draupadi, Indian Lit, 78; co-ed, English Poetry by Indians, 88; co-ed, Letters from Chittagong, 92. **CONTACT ADDRESS** History, Washington State Univ, 301 Wilson Hall, PO Box 644030, Pullman, WA 99164-4030. **EMAIL** blackwel@wsu.edu

BLAINE, BRADFORD BENNETT
PERSONAL Born 05/29/1930, Cedar Rapids, IA, m, 1954, 2 children **DISCIPLINE** MEDIEVAL HISTORY **EDUCATION** Stanford Univ, BA, 52, MA, 54; Univ Calif, Los Angeles, PhD, 66. **CAREER** Asst dean men, Stanford Univ, 53-54; asst dean men, Univ Ore, 54-56; teaching asst hist, Univ Calif, Los Angeles, 59-62; instr, Fullerton Col, 62-64; prof hist, Scripps Col, 64-; prof emeritus, 98. **MEMBERSHIPS** AHA; Soc Hist Technol; Mediaeval Acad Am; Medieval Assn Pac; Int Molinological Soc; member of Scripps College Board of Trustees, 99-. **RESEARCH** Medieval technology; 7th century Europe. **SELECTED PUBLICATIONS** Auth, Enigmatic Water-Mill, Lynn White Festschrift, Univ Calif, 74; art, Technology and the Muses, Humanitas-Essays in Honor of Ralph Ross, Scripps Col, 77; art, Mills: Wind and Water, Dictionary of the Middle Ages, Am Coun Learned Socs, Charles Scribner's Sons, 82; art, Mills and Milling, Medieval France: An Encyclopedia, Garland Publishing, 95. **CONTACT ADDRESS** 586 W 11th St, Claremont, CA 91711. **EMAIL** Blaine1066@aol.com

BLAISDELL, CHARMARIE JENKINS
PERSONAL Born 01/23/1934, Philadelphia, PA, d, 2 children **DISCIPLINE** HISTORY **EDUCATION** Boston Univ, BA. (Cum laude), 55; Tufts Univ, MA, 64; PhD (History), 70. **CAREER** Asst Prof Hist, Boston Col, 70-71; Asst Prof Northeastern Univ, 71-77; Assoc Prof Hist, Northeastern Univ, 77-; Assoc Prof of History and Education, Northeastern Univ, 99-. **HONORS AND AWARDS** Am Assoc of Univ Women, Predoctoral fel, 69; Northeastern Univ Teaching Excellence Awd, 91; Senior Fel, Sixteenth Century Studies Conference; Garth Pitman Awd for Teaching Excellence, Northeastern Univ, 99. **MEMBERSHIPS** AHA; Sixteenth Century Studies; Church History; AASLH; Oral History Assoc. **RESEARCH** Women in Early Modern France and Italy; Women's diaries. **SELECTED PUBLICATIONS** Auth, Women Who Would Be Kings - Female Rulers in the 16th-Century, 16th Century J, Vol 0023, 92; Conversini-Da-Contributor of chapters to books, numerous articles and reviews in Sixteenth Century Studies Journal, Church History, Archive for Reformation History. **CONTACT ADDRESS** Northeastern Univ, Boston, MA 02115. **EMAIL** cblaisdell@historicalperspectives.com

BLAKE, STEPHEN
DISCIPLINE SOUTH ASIAN AND MIDDLE EASTERN HISTORY **EDUCATION** Dartmouth Col, BA; Univ Chicago, MA, PhD. **CAREER** History, St. Olaf Col. **SELECTED PUBLICATIONS** Auth, Shanjahanabad: The Soverign City in Mughal India, 1639-1739, Cambridge Univ Press, 91; Indian paperback ed, Found Books, 93. **CONTACT ADDRESS** St. Olaf Col, 1520 St Olaf Ave, Northfield, MN 55057. **EMAIL** blake@stolaf.edu

BLAKELY, ALLISON
PERSONAL Born 03/31/1940, Clinton, AL, m, 1968, 2 children **DISCIPLINE** HISTORY **EDUCATION** Univ Ore, BA, 62; Univ Calif, Berkeley, MA, 64, PhD, 71. **CAREER** Instr, Stanford Univ, 70-71; from Asst Prof to Assoc Prof, 71-87, prof hist, Howard Univ, 87-. **HONORS AND AWARDS** Andrew Mellon fel humanities, Aspen Inst Humanities Studies, 76-77; Fulbright-Hays Res Fel, 85-86; Am Book Awd, 88; Phi Beta Kappa Soc Senator, 94-2000. **MEMBERSHIPS** AHA; Am Asn Advan Slavic Studies; World Hist Asn; Am Asn Neth Studies. **RESEARCH** Modern Russia; comparative populism; African Diaspora. **SELECTED PUBLICATIONS** Auth, The Dynamics of Revolutionary Populism in Russian and American Society, Studia Africana, spring 78; The Making of Populist Revolution in Russia 1900-1907, in Latin American Populism in Comparative Perspective, Univ NMex Press, 82; Russia and the Negro: Blacks in Russian History and Thought, Howard Univ Press, 86; American Influences on Russian Reformist Thought in the Era of the French Revolution, The Russ Rev, 10/93; Blacks in the Dutch World: The Evolution of Racial Imagery in a Modern Society, Ind Univ Press, 94. **CONTACT ADDRESS** Dept of Hist, Howard Univ, 2400 6th St NW, Washington, DC 20059-0002. **EMAIL** ablakely@fac.howard.edu

BLAKEY, GEORGE THOMAS
PERSONAL Born 08/25/1939, Beattyville, KY, m, 1970 **DISCIPLINE** UNITED STATES HISTORY **EDUCATION** Berea Col, BA, 61; Vanderbilt Univ, MA, 62; IN Univ, Bloomington, PhD, 69. **CAREER** From instr to asst prof, 67-73, assoc prof, 73-81, prof hist, IN Univ East, 81, Eli Lilly fac res fel, 75-76. **MEMBERSHIPS** Orgn Am Historians. **RESEARCH** The New Deal and Progressivism in the US; IN hist. **SELECTED PUBLICATIONS** Auth, Ham that never was: 1933 Emergency Hog Slaughter, Historian, 11/67; Historians on the Home Front, Univ KY, 70; Calling a boss a boss, NY Hist, 4/79; Hard Times and New Deal in KY, Univ Press Ky, 86; Wendell Willkie as a Hoosier, In: Wendell Willkie: Essays, IN Univ Press, 92; Batling the Great Depression on Stage in IN, IN Mag Hist, 3/94; auth "Stalking the Elusive Hoosier's Nest," Traces Magazine (99). **CONTACT ADDRESS** Dept of Hist, Indiana Univ, East, 2325 Chester Blvd, Richmond, IN 47374-1220. **EMAIL** gblakey@indiana.edu

BLANCHARD, PETER
DISCIPLINE LATIN AMERICAN HISTORY **EDUCATION** Univ Toronto, BA, 67; Univ London, PhD(hist), 75. **CAREER** Asst prof, 75-82, Assoc Prof Hist, Univ Toronto, 82-. **MEMBERSHIPS** Can Asn Latin Am and Caribbean Studies. **RESEARCH** Social history of Spanish Am, especially Peru in the 19th Century, slavery, and the Wars of Independence. **SELECTED PUBLICATIONS** Auth, The Origins of the Peruvian Labor Movement, 1883-1919, 82; auth, Markham in Peru: The Travels of Clements R Markham, 1852-1853, 91; auth, Slavery and Abolition in Early Republican Peru, 92. **CONTACT ADDRESS** Dept Hist, Univ of Toronto, 100 St George St, Rm 2074, Toronto, ON, Canada M5S 3G3. **EMAIL** blanchar@chass.utoronto.ca

BLAND, SIDNEY RODERICK
PERSONAL Born 10/31/1936, Caroleen, NC, m, 1962, 2 children **DISCIPLINE** WOMEN'S HISTORY, AMERICAN HISTORY **EDUCATION** Furman Univ, BA, 59; Univ Md, College Park, MA, 61; George Washington Univ, PhD(Am civilization), 72. **CAREER** Asst prof, 65-72, assoc prof, 72-81, Prof Hist, James Madison Univ, 81-, Co-chmn, Am Studies Comt, 73-; grant, Am Philos Soc, 81. **RESEARCH** Militancy in the woman suffrage movement in the early twentieth century; women in Southern history; late 19th-early 20th century American history. **SELECTED PUBLICATIONS** Auth, Aspects of Woman Suffrage Militancy in England, 1905-1914, Studies & Res, 3/70; New life in an Old Movement: The Great Suffrage Parade of 1913, Records, Columbia Hist Soc, 71-72; Mad Women of the Cause: The National Women's Party and the South, Furman Univ Studies, 12/80; Lucy Burns, In: Notable American Women: The Modern Period, Harvard Univ Press, 80; Fighting the Odds: Militant Suffragists in South Carolina, SC Hist Mag, 1/81; Never Quite as Committed as We'd Like: The Suffrage Militancy of Lucy Burns, J Long Island Hist, XXII, No 2, spring 81. **CONTACT ADDRESS** Dept of Hist, James Madison Univ, Harrisonburg, VA 22801.

BLANKE, RICHARD
PERSONAL Born 07/08/1940, Pasadena, CA, m, 1977, 4 children **DISCIPLINE** MODERN EUROPEAN HISTORY **EDUCATION** CA State Univ Northridge, BA, 63; Univ Calif, Berkeley, MA, 64, PhD(hist), 70. **CAREER** Asst prof, 69-74, Assoc Prof Hist, Univ Maine, Orono, 74-; Prof, Univ of Maine, 83-; Adelaide and Alan Bird Prof, 95-. **MEMBERSHIPS** AHA; Am Asn Advan Slavic Studies. **RESEARCH** Modern German and Polish history, nationalism, German Studies Assoc, Am Asn Advan Slavic Studies, Assoc for the Study of Nationalities. **SELECTED PUBLICATIONS** Auth, Prussian Poland in the German Empire, 1871-1900, 81; auth, Orphans of Versailles: Germans in Western Poland, 1918-1939, 93; auth, Polish-Speaking Germans? Language and National Identity among the Masurians, 00. **CONTACT ADDRESS** Dept of Hist, Univ of Maine, Orono, ME 04473. **EMAIL** blanke@maine.maine.edu

BLANKEN, PETER D.
PERSONAL Born 11/08/1965, Burlington, ON, Canada **DISCIPLINE** GEOGRAPHY **EDUCATION** McMaster Univ, BS, 90; MS, 93; Univ BC, PhD, 97. **CAREER** Postdoc Fel, McMaster Univ, 97-98; Asst Prof, Univ Colo, 98-. **HONORS AND AWARDS** Fel, Nat Sci and Engineering Res Coun of Can, 92-96; Grad Scholar, Univ BC; Scholar, McMaster Univ; Develop Awd, Univ Colo. **MEMBERSHIPS** Am Meterol Soc; Am Geophysical Union. **RESEARCH** Climatology; Agricultural and Forest Meteorology; Arctic and Alpine Ecosystems; Air Pollution. **SELECTED PUBLICATIONS** Co-auth, "The role of willow-birch forest in the surface energy balance at arctic treeline," Arctic and Alpine Res, 94; co-auth, "Modeling evaporation from a high subarctic willow-birch forest," Intl J of Climatol, 95; co-auth, "Evidence of water conservation mechanisms in several subarctic wetland species," J of App Ecol, 96; co-auth, "Energy balance and canopy conductance of a boreal aspen forest: Partitioning overstory and understory components," J of Geophys Res, 97; co-auth, "Turbulent flux measurements above and below the overstory of a boreal aspen forest," Boundary-Layer Meteorol, 98; co-auth, "Eddy covariance measurements of evaporation from Great Slave Lake, Northwest Territories, Canada," Water Resources Res, 00; co-auth, "The impact of an air quality advisory program on voluntary mobile source air pollution reduction," Atmospheric Environ, 01; co-auth, "Seasonal energy and water exchange above and within a boreal aspen forest," J of Hydrology, 01. **CONTACT ADDRESS** Dept Geog, Univ of Colorado, Boulder, 260 UCB, Boulder, CO 8039-0260. **EMAIL** blanken@colorado.edu

BLANTZ, THOMAS E.
PERSONAL Born 06/18/1934, Massillon, OH, s **DISCIPLINE** AMERICAN HISTORY **EDUCATION** Univ Not Dam, AB, 57; MA, 63; Gregor Univ, Rome, STL, 61; Colum Univ, PhD, 68. **CAREER** VP stud aff, Univ Not Dam, 70-72; archiv, 69-78; asst prof, assoc prof, 68-; ch, 80-87. **HONORS AND AWARDS** Solon J Buck Awd; Thomas Madden Awd; James E Armstrong Awd. **MEMBERSHIPS** AHA; OAH; ACHA. **RESEARCH** 20th century American political history; 20th century American diplomatic history; history of American Catholicism. **SELECTED PUBLICATIONS** Auth, A Priest in Public Service: Francis J Haas and the New Deal, Univ Notre Dame Press (82); auth, George N Shuster: On the Side of Truth, Univ Notre Dame Press (93). **CONTACT ADDRESS** Dept History, Univ of Notre Dame, 219 O'Shaugnessy Hall, Notre Dame, IN 46556-5639. **EMAIL** thomas.e.blantz.1@nd.edu

BLASER, L. KENT
PERSONAL Born 02/18/1949, Manhattan, KS, m, 1971, 3 children **DISCIPLINE** HISTORY **EDUCATION** Kans State Univ, BA, 71; Univ NC, PhD, 77. **CAREER** Lecturer, Univ NC, 76-77; Vis Asst Prof, Univ Neb, 77-79; Asst Prof to Full Prof, Wayne State Col, 79-. **HONORS AND AWARDS** Outstanding Fac Awd, 85. **MEMBERSHIPS** Phi Alpha Theta, am Studies Asn, Neb Sate Hist Preservation Board, Exec Board of MidAm am Studies Asn. **RESEARCH** Historiography; Philosophy of history; American cultural/intellectual history (20th century); West/Midwest. **SELECTED PUBLICATIONS** Auth, "The History of Nature and the Nature of History: Stephen Jay Arnold on History, Science and Philosophy," History Teacher, 99; auth, "Where is Nebraska, Anyway/," Nebraska History, 99; auth, "What Happened to New Left History?," South Atlantic Quarterly, 86; auth, "Apocalypse Now? Social Change in Contemporary America," American Stuies, 96; auth, "Something Old, Something New: Understanding the American West," Nebraska History, 96. **CONTACT ADDRESS** Dept Soc Sci, Wayne State Col, 1111 Main St, Wayne, NE 68787-1119. **EMAIL** kblaser@wscgate.wsc.edu

BLASZAK, BARBARA J.
PERSONAL Born 02/23/1950, Buffalo, NY, m, 1975 **DISCIPLINE** HISTORY **EDUCATION** SUNY, Buffalo, PhD, 78. **CAREER** Assoc acad dean, Le Moyne Col, 82-90, asst prof to assoc prof, 90-2000. **MEMBERSHIPS** Am Hist Asn, Nat Asn of Conferences on British Studies. **RESEARCH** Women and labor in late-Victorian and Edwardian England. **SELECTED PUBLICATIONS** Auth, "The Women's Cooperative Guild, 1883-1921," Int Soc Sci Rev, vol 61, no 2 (Spring 86); auth, George Jacob Holyoake and the Development of the British Cooperative Movement, Lewiston, NY: Edwin Mellon Press (88); auth, "The Secularist Movement and Anti-Catholicism in Victorian Britain," The Proceedings, vol VI (91); auth, "Margaret Llewelyn Davies: At Study in Female Leadership," J of Cooperative Studies, vol 33-3, no 94 (Jan 99); auth, "The Gendered Geography of the English Co-operative Movement at the Turn of the Century," Women's Hist Rev (forthcoming June 2000); auth, The Matriarchs of England's Cooperative Movement: A Study in Gender Politics and Female Leadership, 1882-1921, Westport, CT: Greenwood Press (2000). **CONTACT ADDRESS** Dept Hist, Le Moyne Col, 1419 Salt Springs Rd, Syracuse, NY 13214-1302. **EMAIL** blaszabj@maple.lemoyne.edu

BLATZ, PERRY K.
DISCIPLINE HISTORY **EDUCATION** Princeton Univ, PhD, 87. **CAREER** Assoc prof to Chair, Duquesne Univ, 94-. **RESEARCH** U.S. labor and business history, 1815 - 1920. **SELECTED PUBLICATIONS** Auth, Democratic Miners: Work and Labor Relations in the Anthracite Coal Industry, 1875 - 1925, 94; coauth, Keystone of Democracy: A History of Pennsylvania's Workers, 99. **CONTACT ADDRESS** Dept Hist, Duquesne Univ, 600 Forbes Ave, Pittsburgh, PA 15282-0001. **EMAIL** blatz@duq.edu

BLEDSTEIN, ADRIEN
PERSONAL Born 03/04/1939, Los Angeles, CA, m, 1959, 2 children **DISCIPLINE** HISTORY; ENGLISH **EDUCATION** Univ California at Los Angeles, BA, 60; Teaching Certificate, 61. **CAREER** KAM Isiah Israel Congregation, Chicago, 30 years. **MEMBERSHIPS** SBL; Chicago Soc for Biblical Research **RESEARCH** Bible and ancient near Eastern lit. **SELECTED PUBLICATIONS** Auth, Was Eve Cursed (Or Did a Woman Write Genesis), Bible Review, 93; Are Women Cursed in Genesis 3.16, A Feminist Companion to Genesis, 93; Binder, Trickster, Heel and Hairy-man: Re-reading Genesis 27 as a Trickster Tale Told by a Woman, A Feminist Companion to Genesis, 93; Is Judges a Woman's Satire of Men Who Play God, A Feminist Companion to Judges, 93; Female Companionships: If the Book of Ruth Were Written by a Woman, A Feminist Companion to Ruth, 93; Dr. Tamar, Bible Review, 95; Tamar and the Coat of Many Colors, A Feminist Companion to Samuel and Kings II, forthcoming. **CONTACT ADDRESS** 5459 S. Hyde Pk. Blvd., Chicago, IL 60615-5801. **EMAIL** ajb@icanbreathe.com

BLEDSTEIN, BURTON J.
PERSONAL Born 07/05/1937, Los Angeles, CA, m, 1959, 2 children **DISCIPLINE** AMERICAN INTELLECTUAL AND SOCIAL THOUGHT **EDUCATION** Univ Calif, Los Angeles, BA, 59; Princeton Univ, MA, 63 PhD(hist), 67. **CAREER** Asst prof, 67-77, Assoc Prof Hist, Univ Ill, Chicago Circle, 77-, Nat Endowment for Humanities fel, 72-73; fel, Nat Humanities Inst, Univ Chicago, 77-78. **MEMBERSHIPS** Orgn Am Historians; Am Studies Asn; AHA. **RESEARCH** American social thought and culture in the 19th and 20th centuries. **SELECTED PUBLICATIONS** Auth, Architects of Charleston, Miss Quart, Vol 0045, 92; The Quest For Authority and Honor in the American Professions, 1750-00, Am Hist Rev, Vol 0098, 93; The Definition of a Profession - the Authority of Metaphor in the History of Intelligence-Testing, 1890-30, Rev in Am Hist, Vol 0022, 94; The True Professional Ideal in America - a History, J of Interdisciplinary Hist, Vol 0025, 95; Patricians, Professors, and Public-Schools - the Origins of Modern Educational-Thought in America, J of Am Hist, Vol 0082, 95; Hunting-ton,Henry,Edwards - a Biography, Am Hist Rev, Vol 0101, 96. **CONTACT ADDRESS** Dept of Hist, Univ of Illinois, Chicago, Box 4348, Chicago, IL 60680.

BLETHEN, H. TYLER
DISCIPLINE HISTORY **EDUCATION** Bowdoin Col, BA, 67; Univ N Carolina, Chapel Hill, MA, 69, Phd, 72. **CAREER** From asst prof to full prof, 72- , dir, Mountain Heritage Ctr, 85- , actg head, Dept of Hist, 81-82, Western Carolina Univ. **HONORS AND AWARDS** Hist Soc N Carolina; Phi Kappa Phi; Phi Alpha Theta. **MEMBERSHIPS** Appalachian Consortium; Appalachian Stud Asn; Carolinas Symp on Brit Stud; N Am Conf on Brit Stud; N Carolina Lit and Hist Soc; S Conf on Brit Stud; S Hist Asn. **RESEARCH** History of Southern Appalachia; early Stuart Britain. **SELECTED PUBLICATIONS** Auth, A Mountain Heritage: The Illustrated History of Western Carolina University, Western Carolina Univ, 89; ed, Diversity in Appalachia: Images and Realities, v 5 of J of the Appalachian Stud Asn, 93; co-ed, Ulster and North America: Transatlantic Perspectives on the Scotch-Irish, Alabama, 97; coauth, From Ulster to Carolina: The Migration of the Scotch-Irish to Southwestern North Carolina, North Carolina Archives and History, 98. **CONTACT ADDRESS** Dept of History, Western Carolina Univ, Cullowhee, NC 28723. **EMAIL** blethen@wcu.edu

BLEWETT, MARY H.
PERSONAL Born 12/17/1938, St. Louis, MO, m **DISCIPLINE** AMERICAN SOCIAL HISTORY **EDUCATION** A.B. University of Missouri, 60, Political Science major; M.A. University of Missouri, 62 History; Ph.D., University of Missouri, 65, History; Dissertation Dir: Dr. Richard S. Kirkendall: Roosevelt, Truman, and the Frustration of the New Deal Revival, 65. **CAREER** Full Prof, 67; Visiting Graduate Prof, Univ of Massachusetts Amherst, 92-96; Visiting Graduate Prof, Yale Univ, Spring Semester, 99. **HONORS AND AWARDS** Harvey A. Kantor Awd for Distinguished Contribution to the Field of Oral History, 90; Joan Kelly Memorial Prize of the American Historical Association, 89; Herbert G. Gutman Awd in Social History,

89; New England Historical Association Book Awd, 89; Berkshire Conference of Women Historians Article Awd, 83. **RESEARCH** Truman administration; municipal reform in textile cities of Massachusetts; sex and class in shoe industry. **SELECTED PUBLICATIONS** Auth, Religion and the Working-Class in Antebellum America, Jour Soc Hist, Vol 0030, 96; Women of the Commonwealth--Work, Family, and Social-Change in 19th-Century Massachusetts, Labor Hist, Vol 0037, 96; Dishing It Out--Waitresses and Their Unions in the 20th-Century, Int Rev Soc Hist, Vol 0037, 92; Transforming Womens Work--New-England Lives in the Industrial-Revolution, Jour Soc Hist, Vol 0029, 95; A Very Social Time--Crafting Community in Antebellum New-England, Jour Interdisciplinary Hist, Vol 0026, 96. **CONTACT ADDRESS** Dept of Hist, Univ of Massachusetts, Lowell, 28 wannalancit St., Lowell, MA 01854-3226. **EMAIL** mary_blewett@uml.edu

BLIER, SUZANNE PRESTON
PERSONAL Born 10/22/1948, Burlington, VT, m, 1969 **DISCIPLINE** ART HISTORY; AFRICAN STUDIES **EDUCATION** Univ Vt, BA, 73; Columbia Univ, MA, 76, MPhil, 76, PhD, 81. **CAREER** Res asst primitive art, Metropolitan Mus of Art, 79-81; Mellon asst prof Art Hist, Northwestern Univ, 81-, Cur, primitive slide collection, Columbia Univ, 73-75, adj lectr, 79; vis lectr, Vassar Col, 79-81; consult, Am Mus of Natural Hist, 80-81; vis asst prof, Univ Ill, Chicago Circle, 82. **HONORS AND AWARDS** Ailsa Mellon Bruce Sr Fel, Center for Advanced Study in the Visual Arts, 88; John Simon Guggenheim Memorial Fel, 88-89; Getty Scholar, Getty Center for the Hist of Art and Humanities, 90-91; Seaver Foundation, 93-98; Charles Rufus Morey Awd from Col Art Asn, 97; Arnold Rubin Awd for African Vodun, 98; Melville Herskovits Awd for African Vodun, 98; Choice Awd, Book Selection - for African Royal Art, 99. **MEMBERSHIPS** Col Art Asn; Soc Archit Historians; African Studies Asn; Am Soc Aesthetics. **RESEARCH** Art and architecture of Africa, art hist and sociocultural study. **SELECTED PUBLICATIONS** Auth, Beauty and the Beast, A Study in Contrasts, Tribal Arts, New York, 76; auth, African Art as Theatre: The Mount Collection, Vassar Col, 80; auth, Africa's Cross River: Art of the Nigerian-Cameroon Border Redefined, L.Kahan, New York, 80; auth, Gestures in African Art, L. Kahan, New York, 82; auth, The Anatomy of Architecture: Ontology and Metaphor inBatammaliba Architectural Expression, Cambridge Univ Press, New York, 87; auth, African Vodun: Art, Psychology, and Power, Univ of Chicago Press, 95; coauth, The Art of Identity: African Art in the Teel Collection, exhibition catalog with Aimee and Mark Bessire, Fogg Museum, Harvard Univ, 96; auth, L'Art Royal Africain, Paris: Flammarion, 98; auth, African Royal Art: The Majesty of Form, London: Calmann and King: New York: Abrams/Prentice Hall, 98; auth, "The Woman, the Snake and the Ocean: A Masterpiece of Vodun Sculpture from Southern Benin," Arts and Cultures, Geneva, No. 1, (00). **CONTACT ADDRESS** Dept of Art History, Harvard Univ, Sackler Museum - 485 Bdwy, Cambridge, MA 02138. **EMAIL** blier@fas

BLISS, JOHN W. M.
PERSONAL Born 01/18/1941, Leamington, ON, Canada **DISCIPLINE** HISTORY **EDUCATION** Univ Toronto, BA, 62; MA, 66, PhD, 72. **CAREER** Tchg asst, Harvard Univ, 67-68; mem Gov Coun Univ, 75-78; Prof History, Univ Toronto. **HONORS AND AWARDS** F-X Garneau Medal & Sir John A Macdonald Prize, Can Hist Asn; Univ BC Medal Can Biog; City Toronto Book Awd; Toronto Hist Bd Awd Merit; Jason Hannah Medal, Royal Soc Can; Wm H Welch Medal, Am Asn Hist Med. **MEMBERSHIPS** Royal Soc Can **RESEARCH** Modern Canadian political, business, and medical history. **SELECTED PUBLICATIONS** Auth, A Living Profit: Studies in the Social History of Canadian Business 1883-1911, 74; A Canadian Millionaire: The Life and Business Times of Sir Joseph Flavelle, Bart, 78; The Discovery of Insulin, 82; Banting: A Biography, 84; Northern Enterprise: Five Centuries of Canadian Business, 87; Plague: A Story of Smallpox in Montreal, 91; Right Honourable Men: The Descent of Canadian Politics from Macdonald to Mulroney, 94. **CONTACT ADDRESS** History of Medicine, Univ of Toronto, 88 College St, Toronto, ON, Canada M5G 1L4.

BLISS, KATHERINE
DISCIPLINE HISTORY **EDUCATION** Univ Chicago, PhD, 96. **CAREER** Asst prof, Univ MA Amherst. **RESEARCH** Latin Am hist, mod Mex, gender and sexuality, public health. **CONTACT ADDRESS** Dept of Hist, Univ of Massachusetts, Amherst, 161 President's Dr, Amherst, MA 01003-9312.

BLISS, ROBERT M.
PERSONAL Born 04/30/1943, Portland, OR, m, 1966, 2 children **DISCIPLINE** HISTORY **EDUCATION** Univ Pa, BA, 65; Univ Wis,Madison, MA, 67, PhD, 83. **CAREER** Wis Res Fel, Linacre Col, Oxford Univ, 69-70; lect to sen lect, hist, Lancaster Univ, 70-97; principal, Grizedale Col, Lancaster Univ, 78-93; dir Am Stud, 92-97; Dean Pierre Laclede Honors, Assoc Prof, Hist, Univ MO, 97-. **HONORS AND AWARDS** Dist Bk Awd, Soc Colonial Wars, NY, 93; res fel, Newberry Library, 81; Lancaster Univ Res Fund, 84-85; John Carter Brown Library, 91. **MEMBERSHIPS** Org Am Hist; Inst Early Am Hist & Cult; Hist Asn (UK); British Asn for Am Stud. **RESEARCH** Anglo-Am politics and culture 1550-1700. **SELECTED PUBLICATIONS** Auth, Revolution and Empire: English Politics and the American Colonies in the Seventeenth Century, 90,93; 'Paradigms Lost? British-Amican Colonial History and the Encyclopedia of the North Amican Colonies,' in Jour of Am Stud 29, 95. **CONTACT ADDRESS** Pierre Laclede Honors Col, Univ of Missouri, St. Louis, 8001 Natural Bridge Rd, Saint Louis, MO 63121. **EMAIL** rmbliss@umsl.edu

BLOCKER, H. GENE
PERSONAL Born 11/29/1937, Dallas, TX, m, 1962, 1 child **DISCIPLINE** AESTHETICS **EDUCATION** Univ Chicago, BA, 60; Univ Calif, Berkeley, PhD(philos), 66. **CAREER** Lectr moral philos, Univ Aberdeen, 65-68; lectr philos, Univ Sierra Leone, W Africa, 68-70; asst prof, Ill State Univ, Bloomington-Normal, 70-72; assoc prof, 72-77, Prof Philos, Ohio Univ, 77-; vis prof, Univ Ibadau, Nigeria, 80-81. **HONORS AND AWARDS** Am Coun Learned Soc fel, 75-76. **RESEARCH** Philosophy of primitive art. **SELECTED PUBLICATIONS CONTACT ADDRESS** Dept of Philos, Ohio Univ, Athens, OH 45701.

BLODGETT, RALPH EDWARD
PERSONAL Born 11/05/1941, Goodland, KS, m, 1966, 2 children **DISCIPLINE** AMERICAN HISTORY **EDUCATION** Univ Colo, Boulder, BA, 64, MA, 69, PhD, 71. **CAREER** Teacher hist, Mapleton Publ Schs, Denver, 64-67; teaching asst US hist, Univ CO, 69-71; asst prof hist, Lenior Rhyne Col, 71-72; asst prof, 72-75, assoc prof, 75-79, Prof Hist, Cameron Univ, 79-. **MEMBERSHIPS** Orgn Am Hist. **RESEARCH** American colonial and Revolutionary War era; US diplomatic history; Western US--history and development. **SELECTED PUBLICATIONS** Auth, The Colorado Territorial Board of Immigration, CO Mag, CO State Hist Soc, 69. **CONTACT ADDRESS** Dept of Hist, Cameron Univ, 2800 Gore Blvd, Lawton, OK 73505-6377.

BLOMQUIST, THOMAS W.
PERSONAL Born 03/03/1931, St. Paul, MN, m, 1963, 2 children **DISCIPLINE** MEDIEVAL EUROPEAN AND ITALIAN HISTORY **EDUCATION** Dartmouth Col, BA, 53; Univ Minn, MA, 59, PhD(hist), 66. **CAREER** From instr to asst prof, 65-71, Assoc Prof, N Ill Univ, 71-. **HONORS AND AWARDS** Am Coun Learned Socs fel, 70-71. **MEMBERSHIPS** Mediaeval Acad Am; Soc Ital Hist Studies; Econ Hist Soc. **RESEARCH** Medieval Italian social and economic history. **SELECTED PUBLICATIONS** Auth, The drapers of Lucca and the marketing of cloth in the mid-thirteenth century, Explor Econ Hist, 69; The Castracani family of thirteenth century Lucca, Speculum, 71; Commercial association in thirteenth century Lucca, Bus His Rev, 71; Administration of a thirteenth century mercantile-banking partnership: The Ricciardi of Lucca, Int Rev Banking, 73; De Roover on business, banking and economic thought, J Econ Hist, 75; The First Consuls at Lucca: 10 July 1119, Actum Luce, Vol VII, 78; The dawn of banking in a medieval commune: Thirteenth century Lucca, In: The Dawn of Modern Banking, Ctr Medieval & Renaissance Studies, Univ Calif, Los Angeles, 79; Land, lineage and business in the thirteenth century: The Guidiccioni family of Lucca, Part I, Actum Luce, Vol IX, 80. **CONTACT ADDRESS** Dept of Hist, No Illinois Univ, 1425 W Lincoln Hwy, De Kalb, IL 60115-2825.

BLOOM, ALEXANDER
PERSONAL Born 10/10/1947, Los Angeles, CA, d, 2 children **DISCIPLINE** AMERICAN HISTORY **EDUCATION** Univ Calif, Santa Cruz, BA, 68; Boston Col, MA, 73, PhD, 79. **CAREER** Asst prof, prof, 80-, Wheaton Col. **MEMBERSHIPS** AHA; Orgn Amer Hist; AAUP; Amer Stud Assn. **RESEARCH** American intellectual history; American radicalism; the 1960s: post 45 R.S. **SELECTED PUBLICATIONS** Auth, Prodigal Sons: The New York Intellectuals and Their World, Oxford Press, 84; auth, Takin' It To The Streets, Oxford Univ Press, 95; auth, For What It's Worth: Looking Back at Sixties America, Oxford Univ. Press, 01. **CONTACT ADDRESS** History Dept, Wheaton Col, Massachusetts, 26 E Main St, Norton, MA 02766-2322. **EMAIL** abloom@wheatonma.edu

BLOOMER, JENNIFER A.
PERSONAL Born 11/13/1951, Knoxville, TN, m, 1990, 3 children **DISCIPLINE** ARCHITECTURAL HISTORY, THEORY AND CRITICISM **EDUCATION** Georgia Inst Technol, PhD, 89; Georgia Inst Technol, MA, 81; Mount Holyoke Col, AB, 73 **CAREER** Prof, Iowa State Univ, 98-; assoc prof, Iowa State Univ, 91-98; asst prof, Univ Flor, 88-91; instr, Georgia Tech Univ, 82-88 **HONORS AND AWARDS** Distinguished Visting Critic, Yale Univ, 95; Ruth & Norman Moore Lectr, Washington Univ, 94; Eva Maddox Lectr, Univ Illinois Chicago, 92; Annual Discourse, Royal Inst British Architects, 92; Swanson Lectr, Cranbrook Acad Art, 90 **MEMBERSHIPS** Soc Archit Historians; Ed Boards: Archit New York, Assemblage, Space and Culture **RESEARCH** Architecture and Literature; Architecture and Hypertextuality; Critical Theory **SELECTED PUBLICATIONS** The Longing for Gravity, Academy Editions, 97; "Nature Morte," Architect: Reconstructing Her Practice, MIT, 96; "The Matter of the Cutting Edge," Desiring Practices, Black Dog, 96; Architecture and the Text: The (S)crypts of Joyce and Piranesi, Yale Univ, 93 **CONTACT ADDRESS** Dept Archit, Iowa State Univ of Science and Tech, Ames, IA 50011. **EMAIL** jbloomer@iastate.edu

BLOOMFIELD, MAXWELL H.
PERSONAL Born 08/17/1931, Galveston, TX, m, 1965 **DISCIPLINE** HISTORY **EDUCATION** Rice Univ, BA, 52; Harvard Univ, LLB, 57; Tulane Univ, PhD, 62. **CAREER** Instr, Ohio State Univ, 62-66; asst prof to Prof Emeritus, Cath Univ, 66-. **HONORS AND AWARDS** Phi Beta Kappa; Am Bar Found Fel, 68-69; Project '87 Fel, 81; Benemerenti Medal, Cath Univ, 94; Carl Bode Awd of Am Cult Asn, 961 **MEMBERSHIPS** Org of Am Hist; AHA; Am Cult Assoc; Am Soc for Legal Hist; State Bar of Tex. **RESEARCH** American legal and constitutional history, American cultural history. **SELECTED PUBLICATIONS** Auth, Alarms and Diversions: The American Mind Through American Magazines, 1900-1914, Mouton (The Hague), 67; auth, American Lawyers in a Changing Society, 1776-1876, Harvard Univ Pr (Cambridge), 76; auth, "The Supreme Court in American Popular Culture", Jour of Am Culture 4, 81; coauth, Law and American Literature: A Collection of Essays, Knopf (NY), 83; auth, "Constitutional Values and the Literature of the Early Republic", Jour of Am Culture 11 (88): 53; auth, "Creative Writers and Criminal Justice: Confronting the System (1890-1920), Criminal Justice Rev 15 (90):208; auth, "The Warren court in American Fiction", Jour of Supreme Court Hist (91):86; auth, "Constitutional Ideology and Progressive fiction", Jour of Am culture 18 (95):77; auth, "Peaceful Revolution: Constitutional Change and American Culture from Professivism to the New Deal (forthcoming). **CONTACT ADDRESS** Dept Hist/ Columbus School of Law, Catholic Univ of America, 620 Michigan Ave NE, Washington, DC 20064-0001.

BLOUET, OLWYN
PERSONAL Born 12/17/1948, Stockport, United Kingdom, m, 1970, 3 children **DISCIPLINE** HISTORY **EDUCATION** Univ Sheffield UK, BA, 70; Univ Nebr-Lincoln, MA, 72; PhD, 77. **CAREER** Vis asst prof, Univ of Nebr-Lincoln, 79-82; vis asst prof, Tex A & M Univ, 83-89; vis asst prof, Col of William & Mary, 91-92; from asst prof to assoc prof, Va State Univ, 92-. **MEMBERSHIPS** AHA, Asn of Caribbean Historians, Barbados Mus of Hist Soc. **RESEARCH** History of the Caribbean **SELECTED PUBLICATIONS** Auth, Latin America and the Caribbean: A Systematic and Regional Survey, Hohn Wiley (NY), 97. **CONTACT ADDRESS** Dept Hist & Philos, Virginia State Univ, PO BOX 9070, Petersburg, VA 23806.

BLUE, FREDERICK J.
PERSONAL Born 04/18/1937, Staten Island, NY, m, 1962, 2 children **DISCIPLINE** AMERICAN HISTORY **EDUCATION** Yale Univ, AB, 58; Univ Wis, MS, 62, PhD(hist), 66. **CAREER** From asst prof to assoc prof, 64-75, prof hist, Youngstown State Univ, 75-. **MEMBERSHIPS** Orgn Am Historians; Soc Historians Early Am Repub. **RESEARCH** Pre-Civil War political history; Ohio; 19th century American West. **SELECTED PUBLICATIONS** Auth, The Ohio Free Soilers and Problems of Factionalism, Ohio Hist, winter-spring 67; The Free Soilers: Third Party Politics, 1848-1854, Univ Ill, 73; Chase and the Governorship: A Stepping Stone to the Presidency, Ohio Hist, summer 81; A Reformer for all Seasons, in The Pursuit of Public Power: Political Culture in Ohio, 1787-1861, co-authored with Robert McCormick, Kent State Univ, Ohio, 94; Charles Sumner and the Conscience of the North, Harlan Davidson, 94; The Poet and the Reformer: Longfellow, Sumner and the Bonds of Male Friendship, 1837-1874, Journal of the Early Republic, summer, 95. **CONTACT ADDRESS** Dept of History, Youngstown State Univ, One University Plz, Youngstown, OH 44555-0002. **EMAIL** fjblue@cc.ysu.edu

BLUESTONE, DANIEL
DISCIPLINE ARCHITECTURAL HISTORY **EDUCATION** Harvard Univ, BA, 75; Univ Chicago, PhD, 84. **CAREER** Assoc prof, Univ Va. **HONORS AND AWARDS** Int Bk Awd, 91; Nat Hist Preservation Bk Prize, 91. **RESEARCH** Nineteenth century American architecture and urbanism. **SELECTED PUBLICATIONS** Auth, Constructing Chicago, 91. **CONTACT ADDRESS** School of Architecture, Univ of Virginia, PO Box 400122, Campbell Hall, Charlottesville, VA 22904-4122. **EMAIL** dblues@virginia.edu

BLUM, ALBERT A.
PERSONAL Born 04/05/1924, New York, NY, m, 1949, 2 children **DISCIPLINE** HISTORY **EDUCATION** City Col NYork, BS, 47; Columbia Univ, MA, 48, PhD, 53. **CAREER** Labor hist, Office of Chief of Mil Hist, Washington DC, 51-53; lect, Queens Col, Brooklyn Col, 54-56; labor rel, Natl Industrial Conf Bd, 56-58; asst prof, NYU, 57-58; asst prof, Cornell Univ, 58-59; assoc prof, Am Univ, 59-60; res assoc, Int Labour Off, Geneva, 66-67; Fulbright res prof, Danish Natl Inst for Soc Res, and lectr Univ Copenhagen, 68; Exec sec, Natl Acad Sci, 73-74; prof, chm, Sch of Labor and Ind Rel, Michigan St Univ, 60-74; dean, prof, Stuart School of Bus Adm, Ill Inst Tech, 78-82; George Wilson prof Int Mgt, Univ of the Pacific, 82-84; prof, chm, Int Bus Dept, Am Univ of Paris, 87-89; vis prof, Univ Witwatersrand, 91-92; vis prof, Helsinki Sch of Bus Admin and Econ, 93; guest prof, Aalborg Univ, 96; prof, New Mex State Univ, 85-; Prof of Emer of Management, New Mexico State Univ. **HONORS AND AWARDS** Phi Beta Kappa; Soc Sci Res Council National Security Program Grant, 58-59; Res Fulbright, Denmark, 67-68; Dept Labor Res Grant, 74-76; Lyndon B Johnson Found Grant, 75-76. **MEMBERSHIPS** Int Ind Rel

Asoc. **RESEARCH** Labor history; international labor; negotiation and conflict management. **SELECTED PUBLICATIONS** Auth, Drafted or Deferred: Practices Past and Present, Univ Michigan, 67; ed, Teacher Unions and Associations: A Comparative Study, Univ Ill, 69; co-auth, White Collar Workers, Random, 71; auth, A Brief History of the American Labor Movement, Am Hist Assoc, 72; auth of numerous articles. **CONTACT ADDRESS** Dept of Management, New Mexico State Univ, Dept 3DJ, PO Box 30001, Las Cruces, NM 88003. **EMAIL** ablum@nmsu.edu

BLUM, GEORGE PAUL
PERSONAL Born 02/05/1932, Kibartai, Lithuania, m, 1961, 2 children **DISCIPLINE** MODERN EUROPEAN HISTORY **EDUCATION** Hamline Univ, BA, 56; Univ Minn, MA, 58, PhD(mod Ger hist), 62. **CAREER** From asst prof soc sci to prof, Raymond Col, 62-77, prof hist, Raymond-Callison Col, 77-80; Prof Hist, Univ Pac, 80-, Chair Dept, 91-; Nat Endowment for Humanities young scholar, 67-68. **MEMBERSHIPS** AHA; AAUP; Conf Group Cent Europ Hist; Conf Group Ger Politics; Ger Studies Asn **RESEARCH** Modern German and European history; social democracy. **SELECTED PUBLICATIONS** Contrib, Research Guide to European Historical Biography, Beacham, 92-93; Statesmen Who Changed the World, Greenwood, 93; Events That Changed the World in the Twentieth Century, Greenwood, 95; Auth, The Rise of Fascism in Europe, Greenwood, 98. **CONTACT ADDRESS** Dept. of History, Univ of the Pacific, Stockton, 3601 Pacific Ave, Stockton, CA 95211-0197. **EMAIL** gblum@uop.edu

BLUMBERG, ARNOLD
PERSONAL Born 05/09/1925, Philadelphia, PA, m, 1954, 3 children **DISCIPLINE** MODERN EUROPEAN HISTORY **EDUCATION** Univ Pa, PhD, 52. **CAREER** Assoc prof, 58-64, prof, hist, 64-, prof emer, 96- Towson Univ; found sum res grant, 61; abstractor, Hist Abstr, 63-80; ed consult, Am Hist Rev, The Hist and the Pacific Coast Hist Rev. **HONORS AND AWARDS** Amer Philos Soc Johnson res fund grant, 66; res grants, Towson Univ. **MEMBERSHIPS** AHA; Soc Hist Studies; Southern Hist Assn; AAUP. **RESEARCH** French second empire; Italian unification; diplomatic history; mid-19th century British and Prussian consular correspondence at the Israel State Archives in Jerusalem. **SELECTED PUBLICATIONS** Auth, The Diplomacy of the Mexican Empire, 1963-1867, Amer Philos Soc, 71; auth, A View from Jerusalem, 1849-1858, Fairleigh Dickinson Univ/Assoc Univ Press, 80; auth, Zion Before Zionism, 1838-1880, Syracuse Univ Press, 86; auth, A Carefully Planned Accident; The Italian War of 1859, Susquehanna Univ Press/Assoc Univ Press, 90; auth, Great Leaders, Great Tyrants? Contemporary Views of the World Rulers Who Made History, Greenwood Press, 95; auth, A History of Israel, Greenwood Press, 98. **CONTACT ADDRESS** Dept of History, Towson State Univ, Linthicum Hall, 119c, Baltimore, MD 21204. **EMAIL** ablumberg@towson.edu

BLUMBERG, BARBARA
PERSONAL Born 10/27/1936, Bronx, NY, m, 1974, 2 children **DISCIPLINE** HISTORY **EDUCATION** Univ Calif Berkeley, AB, 58; MA, 62; Columbia Univ, PhD, 74. **CAREER** From Adj Instr to Prof and Chairperson of Hist Dept, Pace Univ NY, 71-. **HONORS AND AWARDS** Phi Beta Kappa, 58; Kenan Awd for Teaching Excellence, Pace Univ, 96. **MEMBERSHIPS** AHA, Orgn of Am Historians. **RESEARCH** 20th Century US History: Political, New Deal and 1930s, NYC, Immigration. **SELECTED PUBLICATIONS** Auth, The New Deal and the Unemployed: The View from New York City, Bucknell Univ Press (Lewisburg, PA), 79; auth, Celebrating the Immigrant: An Administrative History of the Statue of Liberty National Monument, 1952-1981, US Dept of Interior, Nat Park Serv, 85; auth, "A National Park Emerges: The Statue as Park and Museum," in Liberty: The French-American Statue in Art and History (Harper & Row, 86); auth, Student Guide to The Enduring Vision: A History of American People, DC Heath and Co (Lexington, MA), 90; auth, "Celler, Emanuel," in Encyclopedia of the Unites States Congress (Simon & Schuster, 95); auth, "Ellis Island," "Statue of Liberty," "Works Progress Administration(WPA)," in The Encyclopedia of the New York City (Yale Univ Press, 95); auth, "Work Projects Administration(WPA)," in Encyclopedia of African-American Culture and History (MacMillan and Simon & Schuster, 96); auth, "Cahill, Holger," "Henderson, Leon," "Guffey, Joseph," "Lubin, Isador," "Niles, David K.," "Smith, Harold Dewey," "Taber, John," "Williams, Aubrey Willis," in American National Biography (Oxford Univ Press, 99). **CONTACT ADDRESS** Dept Hist, Pace Univ, New York, 1 Pace Plz, New York, NY 10038-1502. **EMAIL** bblumberg@pace.edu

BLUMENFELD, DAVID
DISCIPLINE HISTORY OF MODERN PHILOSOPHY, METAPHYSICS, ETHICS, ANALYTIC PHILOSOPHY **EDUCATION** Univ Calif, Berkeley, PhD, 66. **CAREER** Prof, assoc dean, Hum and Fine Arts, Ga State Univ. **SELECTED PUBLICATIONS** Author of over twenty-five articles, including two recent ones in The Cambridge Companion to Leibniz, and an article on free will in Am Philos Quart; co-ed; Overcoming Racism and Sexism. **CONTACT ADDRESS** Georgia State Univ, Box 4038, Atlanta, GA 30303-4038. **EMAIL** dblumenfeld@gsu.edu

BLUMENFELD, RODICA
PERSONAL Born Bucharest, Romania **DISCIPLINE** ITALIAN STUDIES **EDUCATION** Columbia Univ, PhD, 93. **CAREER** Asst Prof, Vassar Col, 91-99; Assoc Prof, Vassar Col, 99-. **MEMBERSHIPS** MLA, SCS. **RESEARCH** Italian cinema, cultural studies, feminist film theory. **SELECTED PUBLICATIONS** Auth, "Born Illiterate: Gender and Representation in Gadda's Pasticciaccio," Hull Ital Texts, Market Harborough (UK: 99); ed, The Pleasure of Writing: Critical Essays on Dacia Maraini, Purdue Univ Pr (West Lafayette, IN), 00. **CONTACT ADDRESS** Dept Lang, Vassar Col, 124 Raymond Ave, Poughkeepsie, NY 12604-0002. **EMAIL** blumenfeld@vassar.edu

BLUMENSHINE, GARY BAKER
PERSONAL Born 11/23/1944, Rockford, IL, m, 1968, 1 child **DISCIPLINE** HISTORY **EDUCATION** Northwestern Univ, AB, 66; Univ Ill, AM, 68; PhD, 73. **CAREER** Res asst hist, Univ Ill, 69-70, teaching asst, 70-71; from lectr to assoc prof, Ind Univ-Purdue Univ, Fort Wayne, 71-; vis lectr, New Col, Durham, England, 78-79. **HONORS AND AWARDS** Grants-in-aid, Ind Univ, 74, 75, 81 & 82; summer grants, 74 & 82; travel grants, 75 & 82; Nat Endowment Humanities Summer Sem, 80. **MEMBERSHIPS** AHA, Am Cath Hist Asn; Am Soc Church Hist; Medieval Acad Am; Int Ctr Medieval Art. **RESEARCH** Medieval intellectual history; Medieval Latin; stained glass iconography. **SELECTED PUBLICATIONS** Ed, Liber Alcuini Contra Haeresim, 80. **CONTACT ADDRESS** Dept of Hist, Indiana Univ-Purdue Univ, Fort Wayne, 2101 Coliseum Blvd E, Fort Wayne, IN 46805-1445. **EMAIL** blumensh@ipfw.edu

BLUMHOFER, EDITH L.
PERSONAL Born 09/13/1975, Brooklyn, NY, m, 1975, 3 children **DISCIPLINE** AMERICAN RELIGIOUS HISTORY, AMERICAN HISTORY **EDUCATION** Hunt Col, BA, 71; MA; Harv Univ, PhD, 77. **CAREER** Adj prof, Hunt Col, 79-82; asst prof, SW Missou Univ, 82-84; assoc prof, Wheat Col, 87-95; assoc dir, Univ Chic, 96-99; prof, dir, Wheat Col, 99-. **HONORS AND AWARDS** Phi Beta Kappa; Danforth Fel. **MEMBERSHIPS** AHA; ASCH; AAR. **RESEARCH** American religious history; Protestant hymnody; Pentecostalism. **SELECTED PUBLICATIONS** Auth Restoring the Faith: The Assemblies of God, Pentecostalism, and American Culture, Univ Ill Press, 93; auth, Aimee Semple McPherson: Everybody's Sister, W B Erdmans, 93. **CONTACT ADDRESS** Dept History, Wheaton Col, Illinois, 501 College St, Wheaton, IL 60187-5501.

BLUMIN, STUART
PERSONAL Born 03/29/1940, Miami, FL, m, 1965, 2 children **DISCIPLINE** HISTORY **EDUCATION** Univ PA, BS, 62, MA, 63, PhD, 68. **CAREER** Asst prof Am studies, Skidmore Col, 67-69; asst prof hist, Mass Inst Technol, 69-73; asst prof, 74-77, assoc prof, 77-87, prof hist, Cornell Univ, 87-, Res fel, Charles Warren Ctr Studies in Am Hist, Harvard Univ, 71-72; vis lectr, Brandeis Univ, 72. **HONORS AND AWARDS** NEH Fel Univ Tchr(s), 87-88, 97-98; Kerr Prize (NYSHA), 75; Urban Hist Asn Best Book Prize, 89; Binkley-Stephenson Prize (OAH), 97. **MEMBERSHIPS** AHA; Orgn Am Historians; Urban Hist Asn. **RESEARCH** Am soc hist; the Am city. **SELECTED PUBLICATIONS** Auth, The Historical Study of Vertical Mobility, Hist Methods Newsletter, 68; Mobility and Change in Ante-Bellum Philadelphia, In: Nineteenth-Century Cities: Essays in the New Urban History, Yale Univ, 69; Residential Mobility in the Nineteenth-Century City, In: The Peoples of Philadelphia, Temple Univ, 73; Rip Van Winkle's Grandchildren: Family and Household in the Hudson Valley, 1800-1860, J Urban Hist, 75; Church and Community: A Case Study of Lay Leadership in Nineteenth-Century America, New York Hist, 75; The Urban Threshold: Growth and Change in A Nineteenth-Century American Community, Univ Chicago, 76; Black Coats to White Collars: Economic Change, Nonmanual Work, and the Social Structure of Industrializing America, In: Small Business in American Life, Columbia Univ, 80; The Short Season of Sharon Springs: Portrait of Another New York, Cornell Univ, 80; The Emergence of the Middle Class: Social Experience in the American City, Cambridge, 89; ed, New York by Gas-Light and Other Urban Sketches by George G Foster, Calif, 90; The Social Implications of American Economic Development, In: The Cambridge Economic History of the United States, Cambridge, 00; co-auth (with Glenn C Altschauler), Rude Republic: Americans and Their Politics in the Nineteenth Century, Princeton, 99. **CONTACT ADDRESS** Dept of Hist, Cornell Univ, Mcgraw Hall, Ithaca, NY 14853-0001. **EMAIL** smb5@cornell.edu

BLUSTEIN, BONNIE ELLEN
PERSONAL Born 04/17/1951, Middletown, CT **DISCIPLINE** HISTORY OF SCIENCE & MEDICINE **EDUCATION** Harvard Univ, AB, 73; Univ Pa, PhD(hist & sociol sci), 79. **CAREER** Asst prof hist, Univ Louisville, 79-81; Researcher, Mus Sci & Indust, 81- **MEMBERSHIPS** Hist Sci Soc; Am Asn Hist Med; Cheiron Soc. **RESEARCH** History of neurosciences; social relations of science and medicine; history of American science and technology. **SELECTED PUBLICATIONS** Auth, Neurology in New York: A case study in the specialization of medicine, Bull Hist Med, 79; The Philadelphia biological society, 1857-1861: A failed experiment?, J Hist Med & Allied Sci, 80; contribr, Madhouses, Mad-doctors, and Madmen, Univ Pa Press, 81. **CONTACT ADDRESS** Pasadena, CA. **EMAIL** blustein@worldnet.att.net

BOBER, PHYLLIS PRAY
PERSONAL Born 12/02/1920, Portland, ME, d, 2 children **DISCIPLINE** ARCHAEOLOGY, HISTORY OF ART **EDUCATION** Wellesley Col, BA, 41; NYork Univ, MA, 43, PhD(fine arts), 46. **CAREER** Instr art, Wellesley Col, 47-49; census coordinator, antique art known to Renaissance artists, Warburg Inst, Univ london, 49-84; lectr & cur mus, 51-54; res assoc, Inst Fine Arts, NY Univ, 54-73; from assoc prof to prof, Univ Col, 67-73; chemn, dept fine arts, Univ Col, 67-73; panelist, educ progrs, Nat Endowment for Humanities, 72-; dean, Grad Sch Arts & Sci, Bryn Mawr Col, 73-80; prof, classical & near Eastern archaeology, Bryn Mawr Col, 73-91; prof, hist of art, Bryn Mawr Col, 73-91; mem, Nat Bd Consult, 74-; bd mem, Grad Record Exam, 76-80; exec comt chemn, Serv Comt, 77-80; pres, Asn Pa Grad Deans, 77-78; adj prof fine arts, New York Univ, 81-82; Leslie Clark Prof in the Humanities, Bryn Mawr Col, 87-91. **HONORS AND AWARDS** Corresponding fel, German Archaeological Inst, 58-; planning grant, Archit Ecol, 71; Guggenheim fel, 79-80; sr fel, Soc for the Humanities, Cornell Univ, 84; DHL, honoris causa, Univ Rome, 93; hon fel, Warburg Inst, Univ London, 93-; elected to "Les Dames Escoffier," 95-; Charles Homer Haskins lectr, ACLS, " A Life of Learning," 95; fel, Accademia Nazionale dei Lincei, 96-; Appleton Eminent Scholar in the Arts, Florida State Univ, 98; vis prof, dept educ, Am Academy in Rome, 99; Kennedy Prof in the Renaissance, Smith Col, 00; DHL Bowdoin Col, 00. **MEMBERSHIPS** Am Inst Archaeol; Col Art Asn Am; Victorian Soc in Am; Am Mycol Asn; Northeast Asn Grad Schs; Renaissance Soc Am; bd of corporators, Medical Col of Pa, 79-96; bd of dirs, Coun of Grad Schs in US, 77-79. **RESEARCH** Relationships between Renaissance and antique art; late antique art and thought; history of city planning. **SELECTED PUBLICATIONS** Auth, Drawings After the Antique by Amico Aspertini: Sketchbooks in the British Museum, Studies of the Warburg Inst, London, 57; coauth, Renaissance Artists and Antique Sculpture, Harvery Miller and Oxford Pr, 86; auth, Art, Culture and Cuisine: Ancient and Medieval Gastronomy, Chicago Univ Pr, 99. **CONTACT ADDRESS** 29 Simpson Rd, Ardmore, PA 19003.

BOBINSKI, GEORGE SYLVAN
PERSONAL Born 10/24/1929, Cleveland, OH, m, 1953, 2 children **DISCIPLINE** LIBRARY AND INFORMATION SCIENCE, HISTORY **EDUCATION** Case Western Univ, BA, 51, MLS, 55; Univ of Mich, MA, 61, PhD, 66. **CAREER** Ref asst, Cleveland Pub Libr, 54-55; asst dir, Royal Oak Pub Libr, 55-59; dir of libraries, SUNY Col at Cortland, NY, 60-67; asst dean/assoc prof, Sch of Libr Sci, Univ of Ky, 67-70; Dean and Prof, Sch of Infor and Libr Studies, Univ at Buffalo, 70-99; Prof, 99-. **HONORS AND AWARDS** Beta Phi Mu Int Libr Sci Hon Soc; Fulbright Sch Lectr, Univ of Warsaw, 77; Vis Sch, Jagiellonian Univ-Krakow, 92, 97; Meritorious Medal, 97. **MEMBERSHIPS** Am Libr Asn; Asn for Libr and Infor Sci Educ. **RESEARCH** History of Libraries; Library Education; Comparative Librarianship-Poland. **SELECTED PUBLICATIONS** auth, Carnegie Libraries: Their History and Impact on American Public Library Developments, ALA, 69; auth, Dictionary of American Library Biography, Libraries Unlimited, 78; auth, "The Golden Age of American Librarianship 1945-1970," Wilson Libr Bull, 84; ed, "Current and Future Trends in Library and Information Science, " Libr Trends; auth, "Carnegie Libraries: Their Current and Future Status," Public Libraries, 92; "Libraries in the Democratic Process," Jagiellonian Press, 95. **CONTACT ADDRESS** Sch of Infor and Libr Studies, SUNY, Buffalo, Buffalo, NY 14260. **EMAIL** bobinski@acsu.buffalo.edu

BOCK-WEISS, CATHERINE C.
PERSONAL Born 08/05/1931, Chicago, IL, m, 1991 **DISCIPLINE** ART HISTORY **EDUCATION** Cath Univ Am, MFA, 57; Univ CA, PhD, 77. **CAREER** Instr, Univ WI; prof, 77-; Assoc prof, painting, Alverno College, Milwaukee, WI, 57-67; Instr., Univ WI-Milwaukee, 73-77; Prof, Sch. Of the Art Inst. Of Chicago, 77-96; Prof Emeritus, 96-; Prof Emerita, Dept of Art History, Theory and Criticism School of the Art Institute of Chicago. **HONORS AND AWARDS** Grant for res in Fr, Univ CA, LA Arts Coun. **SELECTED PUBLICATIONS** Auth, Henri Matisse and Neo-Impressionism, 1898-1908; Henri Matisse: A Guide to Research, 94. **CONTACT ADDRESS** Dept of Art Hist, Theory and Criticism, Sch of the Art Inst of Chicago, 37 S Wabash Ave, Chicago, IL 60603. **EMAIL** bockweissc@atsglobaldialog.com

BODDE, DERK
PERSONAL Born 03/09/1909, Brant Rock, MA **DISCIPLINE** EAST ASIAN STUDIES **EDUCATION** Harvard Univ, AB, 30; Univ Leyden, Neth, PhD, 38. **CAREER** Lectr Chinese, 38, from asst prof to prof, 38-75, Emer Prof Chinese, Univ PA, 75-, Specialist on China, Off Strategic Serv & Off War Info, 42-45; Fulbright res fel, Peking, China, 48-49; Guggenheim fel, 70-71; Nat Endowment for Humanities fel, Cam-

bridge, Eng, 74-75; Dr Sun Yat-sen distinguished vis prof China studies, Georgetown Univ, 81. **MEMBERSHIPS** Am Orient Soc (pres, 68-69); Asn Asian Studies; Am Acad Arts & Sci; Am Philos Soc. **RESEARCH** Chinese philosophy, history and law; Chinese popular religion. **SELECTED PUBLICATIONS** Auth, Peking Diary, Fawcett; Tolstoy and China, Johnson Reprint, 50; translr, History of Chinese Philosophy, Vol I, 52 & Vol II, 53, Princeton Univ; coauth, Law in Imperial China, Harvard Univ, 67; auth, Festivals in Classical China, Princeton Univ, 75; Essays on Chinese Civilization, Princeton Univ, 81. **CONTACT ADDRESS** Univ of Pennsylvania, 29 W Phil-Ellena St, Philadelphia, PA 19119.

BODE, FREDERICK AUGUST
PERSONAL Born 12/12/1940, Geneva, IL, m, 1971, 1 child **DISCIPLINE** HISTORY **EDUCATION** Univ Calif, Los Angeles, BA, 62; Yale Univ, MA, 63, PhD(hist), 69. **CAREER** Instr hist, Univ NC, Chapel Hill, 67-70; asst prof, 70-73, Assoc Prof Hist, Concordia Univ, 73- **MEMBERSHIPS** AHA; Orgn Am Historians; Southern Hist Asn; Econ Hist Asn. **RESEARCH** Pre-Civil War South, slavery, religion and culture, social class, gender. **SELECTED PUBLICATIONS** Auth, Protestantism and the New South, 75; Auth, Farm Tenancy and the Census in Antebellum Georgia, with, Donald Ginter, 86. **CONTACT ADDRESS** Dept of Hist, Concordia Univ, Montreal, 1400 de Maisonneuve Blvd W, LB-601, Montreal, QC, Canada H3G 1W8. **EMAIL** frbod@alcor.concordia.ca

BODIAN, MIRIAM
PERSONAL Born Baltimore, MD **DISCIPLINE** HISTORY, JUDAIC STUDIES **EDUCATION** Harvard Univ, BA, 69; Hebrew Univ, Jerusalem, PhD, 88. **CAREER** Asst prof, Yeshiva Univ, 88-90; asst prof, Univ Mich, 90-97; assoc prof, PaState Univ, 98-2000. **HONORS AND AWARDS** Nat Jewish Book Awd in Hist, 98; Koret Jewish Book Awd in Hist, 98. **SELECTED PUBLICATIONS** Auth, Hebrews of the Portuguese Nation: Conversos and Community in Early Modern Amsterdam, Indiana Univ Press (97). **CONTACT ADDRESS** Dept Hist, Pennsylvania State Univ, Univ Park, 108 Weaver Bldg, University Park, PA 16802-5500. **EMAIL** mxb59@psu.edu

BODLING, KURT A.
DISCIPLINE HISTORICAL THEOLOGY, LIBRARY SCIENCE **EDUCATION** Concordia Col, AA, 74; Concordia Sen Col, BA, 76; Concordia Sem, MDiv, 80, MST, 86; Univ Ill, MS; Fordham Univ, PhD cand. **CAREER** Ref, res asst, 81-86; asst dir, ref svcs, 86-87, Concordia Hist Inst; free-lance ed, Concordia Pub, 88-89; assoc lib, Winterthur Mus, 90-91; dean, spiritual life, 95-96, COL ARCH, 93- , asst prof, 91-98, ASSOC PROF, RELIG, 98-, DIR LIBR SVCS, 91-, CONCORDIA COL. **HONORS AND AWARDS** Beta Phi Mu. **MEMBERSHIPS** Soc of Am Archivists, Am Library Society, Asn of Col and Res Libraries. **RESEARCH** Am Lutheran History; Religious History of Am. **CONTACT ADDRESS** Concordia Col, New York, 171 White Plains Rd., Bronxville, NY 10708.

BODNAR, JOHN EDWARD
PERSONAL Born 05/19/1944, m, 1968, 2 children **DISCIPLINE** AMERICAN SOCIAL HISTORY, PUBLIC HISTORY **EDUCATION** John Carroll Univ, BA, 66 MA, 68; Univ Conn, PhD, 74. **CAREER** Chief historian, Pa Hist Mus Comn, 71-81; Assoc Prof, 81-85, prof hist, 85-97, Chancellor's prof and Chair, Dept Hist, Ind Univ, 97-; Adj Prof Am studies, Pa State Univ, Middletown, 74-80. **HONORS AND AWARDS** Res grant Rockefeller Found, 75 & Am Coun Learned Soc, 76; Beveridge grant, AHA, 81; Guggenheim Fel, 83-84; Fulbright Chair, Europ Univ Inst, Florence, Italy, 94; NEH grant; selected speaker, Int Hist Congr, Bucharest, 80. **MEMBERSHIPS** Orgn Am Historians; Immigration Hist Soc; AHA. **RESEARCH** American immigration and labor history, public history, impact of mass culture on traditional American political ideas, relationship between mass culture and the representation of the past. **SELECTED PUBLICATIONS** Ed, Ethnic Experience in Pennsylvania, Bucknell Univ, 73; auth, Materialism and Morality: Slavic Americans and Education, J Ethnic Studies, 76; Immigration and Modernization: Slavic Peasants in Industrial America, J Soc Hist, 76; Immigration and Industrialization: Ethnicity in an American Mill Town, Univ Pittsburgh, 77; Migration, Kinship and Urban Adjustment: Blacks & Poles in Pittsburgh, J Am Hist, 79; Immigration, Kinship, and the Rise of Working-Class Realism, J Social Hist, 80; coauth, Lives of Their Own: Blacks, Italians, and Poles in Pittsburgh, Univ Ill, 82; Workers' World: Kinship, Community and Protest in an Industrial Society, Johns Hopkins, 82; auth, The Transplanted: A History of Immigrants in Urban America, Ind, 85; Remaking America: Public Memory, Commemoration, and Patriotism, Princeton, 92; ed, Bonds of Affection: Americans Define Their Patriotism, Princeton, 96; auth, Generational Memory in an American Town, J Interdisciplinary Hist, 96. **CONTACT ADDRESS** Dept of Hist, Indiana Univ, Bloomington, 1020 E Kirkwood Ave, 702 Ballantine Hall, Bloomington, IN 47405. **EMAIL** bodnar@indiana.edu

BOEGER, PALMER HENRY
PERSONAL Born 03/27/1919, Plymouth, WI, m, 1957, 2 children **DISCIPLINE** UNITED STATES & MODERN EUROPEAN HISTORY **EDUCATION** Univ Wis, BS, 41, PhM, 42, PhD(hist), 53. **CAREER** Instr US & mod Europ hist, Exten Div, Univ Wis, 48-49, Exten Ctr, Milwaukee, 49-51; assoc prof US hist, 53-57, prof hist, E Cent State Col, 57-, chemn dept hist & govt, 62-; US Nat Park Service ranger/interpretor, summers, 69-94. **MEMBERSHIPS** Orgn Am Historians; Southern Hist Asn. **RESEARCH** United States Civil War army supply; the war and American industrial development; teaching history via television. **SELECTED PUBLICATIONS** Auth, Hardtack and burned beans, Civil War Hist, 3/58; The great Kentucky hog swindle, J Southern Hist, 2/62; General Burnside's Knoxville Packing Project, E Tenn Hist Soc Publ, 63; From Platt NP to Chickasaw NRA, Western Heritage Press, 87; auth, "Flowing with Blood and Whiskey: Stand Watie and the Battles of Cabin Creek," I.T. Jrnl of the Indian Wars (00). **CONTACT ADDRESS** Dept of History, East Central Univ, 1100 E 14th St, Ada, OK 74820-6999.

BOEHLING, REBECCA
PERSONAL Born 09/19/1955, Leesburg, VA, m, 1995 **DISCIPLINE** HISTORY **EDUCATION** Univ Wis Madison, PhD. **CAREER** Assoc prof, Univ MD Baltimore County. **HONORS AND AWARDS** Fulbright fel, 77-78; German Academic Exchange Service Dissertation fel, 81-83; Volkswagen Postwar German Hist Res fel, 93-94; res fel, Center for Advanced Holocaust Studies, 00. **MEMBERSHIPS** Am Hist Asn; Am Asn of Univ Professors; German Studies Asn; Peace Hist Soc; Berkshire Conference of Women Historians. **RESEARCH** Europ hist; Ger Am rel(s); Ger women in the postwar era; Denazification. **SELECTED PUBLICATIONS** Auth, A Question of Priorities: Democratic Reforms and Economic Recovery in Postwar Germany. **CONTACT ADDRESS** Dept of Hist, Univ of Maryland, Baltimore County, 1000 Hilltop Circle, Baltimore, MD 21250. **EMAIL** boehling@umbc.edu

BOERSMA, HANS
PERSONAL Born 05/03/1961, Urk, Netherlands, m, 1984, 5 children **DISCIPLINE** HISTORICAL SOCIETY **EDUCATION** State Univ of Utrecht, ThD, 93. **CAREER** Pastor, 94-98. **HONORS AND AWARDS** MTh, Univ of Utrecht with high honors. **MEMBERSHIPS** SBL; ETS; Calvin Theol Soc. **RESEARCH** History of Doctrine, Justification, Historical Jesus, Worldview Studies. **SELECTED PUBLICATIONS** Auth, The Life of Jeremiah, Eating God's Words, Study Guide, RevelationSeries, Grand Rapids, CRC Pub, 98; The Weak and the Strong, Koinwnja, 95; A Hot Pepper Corn: Richard Baxter's Doctrine of Justification in Its Seventeenth-Century Context of Controversy, Zoetermeer: Boekencentrum, 93; review, The Origins of the Federal Theology in Sixteenth-Century Reformation Thought, by David A. Weir, Evangelical Quarterly, 93, Jesus and the Victory of God, Christian Origins and the Question of God, by NT Wright, Calvin Theo J, 97; Clavinism, Authentic Calvinism, A Clarification, by Alan C. Clifford, Westminster Theo J, 96. **CONTACT ADDRESS** 20571 49A Ave, Langley, BC, Canada V3A 5T. **EMAIL** boersma@universe.com

BOGGER, TOMMY L.
PERSONAL Born 05/07/1944, Williamsburg, VA, 1 child **DISCIPLINE** SOUTHERN & AFRO-AMERICAN HISTORY **EDUCATION** Norfolk State Col, BA, 68; Carnegie-Mellon Univ, MA, 69; Univ Va, PhD(hist), 76. **CAREER** From instr to asst prof, 69-76, Assoc Prof Hist, Norfolk State Col, 76- **MEMBERSHIPS** Asn Study Afro-Am Life & Hist; Southern Hist Asn. **RESEARCH** The free Black community; Black families. **SELECTED PUBLICATIONS** Auth, Revolutionary sentiment and the growth of Norfolk's free Black population, Va Soc Sci J, 4/77; Slave resistance in Virginia during the Haitian Revolution, Hampton Inst J Ethnic Studies, 11/78; coauth, A historical study of Norfolk's Church Street Corridor, Norfolk Housing & Redevelop Admin, (in press). **CONTACT ADDRESS** Norfolk State Univ, 2401 Corprew Ave, Norfolk, VA 23504-3993.

BOGGESS, JENNIFER H.
DISCIPLINE FINE ART **EDUCATION** WV Univ, BA, 79; MA, 96; MFA, 00. **CAREER** Adj Instr, Fairmont State Col, 94-98; Asst Prof, Alderson-Broaddus Col, 99-. **HONORS AND AWARDS** Gov Awd, WV Watercolor Soc; Awd of Merit, WV Juried Exhibition. **RESEARCH** Solo Exhibitions of Paintings: Recent Paintings, 00; Mapping Appalachia. **CONTACT ADDRESS** Dept Art, Alderson-Broaddus Col, 722 Coleman, Fairmont, WV 26554. **EMAIL** Boggess@ab.edu

BOGIN, RUTH
PERSONAL Born New York, NY **DISCIPLINE** AMERICAN HISTORY **EDUCATION** Univ Wis, BA, 41; Sarah Lawrence Col, MA, 65; Union Grad Sch, PhD(Am hist), 78. **CAREER** Assoc hist, Sarah Lawrence Col, 65-70; Adj Prof Hist, Pace Univ, 65-, Vis asst prof, NY Univ, summer, 80; res fel, Nat Endowment for Humanities, 80-81. **MEMBERSHIPS** Inst Res Hist; Orgn Am Historians; AHA; Am Studies Asn; Soc Historians Early Am Repub. **RESEARCH** History of the American Revolutionary era; history of women, particularly black women; egalitarianism. **SELECTED PUBLICATIONS** Auth, Race and Revolution, William and Mary Quart, Vol 0051, 94. **CONTACT ADDRESS** 3 Brook Lane, Great Neck, NY 11023.

BOGUE, ALLAN G.
PERSONAL Born 05/12/1921, London, ON, Canada, m, 1950, 3 children **DISCIPLINE** AMERICAN HISTORY **EDUCATION** Univ Western Ont, BA, 43, MA, 46; Cornell Univ, PhD, 51. **CAREER** Lectr econ & hist & asst librn, Univ Western Ont, 49-52; from asst prof to prof hist, Univ Iowa, 52-64, chmn dept, 59-63; prof hist, 64-68, chmn dept, 72-73, Frederick Jackson Turner Prof Hist, Univ Wis-Madison, 68-91, prof emer, 91-; Soc Sci Res Coun fel, 55 & 66; mem hist adv comt, Math Soc Sci Bd, 65-71; Scand-Am Found Thord-Gray lectr, 68; Guggenheim fel, 70; mem, Coun Inter-Univ Consortium Polit Res, 71-73; vis prof hist, Harvard Univ, 72; dir, Soc Sci Res Coun, 73-76; Sherman Fairchild distinguished fel, Calif Inst Technol, 75; fellow, Cntr for Adv Study in the Behavioral Sciences 85-86; NEH Sr Fellow, 85-86; Huntington Library Fellow, 92, 94. **HONORS AND AWARDS** Elected Mem National Acad of Sciences, 85; honorary life mem, Western Hist Assoc, 93; fellow of the Agricultural Hist Soc, 94; Warren E. Miller awd for meritorious service to the soc sciences, **MEMBERSHIPS** Agr Hist Soc (pres, 63-64); Orgn Am Historians (pres, 82-83); NAS, 85; Econ Hist Asn (pres, 81-82); Soc Sci Hist Asn (pres, 77-78). **RESEARCH** Nineteenth century American economic and political history; the American West. **SELECTED PUBLICATIONS** Auth, Money at Interest, Cornell Univ, 55; auth, From Prairie to Corn Belt, Univ of Chicago, 63; ed, Emerging Theoretical Models in Social and Political History, Sage, 73; co-ed, The History of American Electoral Behavior, Princeton Univ, 78; auth, The Earnest Men: Republicans of the Civil War Senate, Cornell Univ, 81; Clio and the Bitch Goddess: Quantification in American Political History, Sage, 83; auth, The Congressman's Civil War, Cambridge Univ, 89; co-ed, The Jeffersonian Dream: Studies in the History of American Land Policy by Paul W. Gates, Univ of NM, 96; auth, Frederick Jackson Turner: Strange Roads Going Down, Univ OK, 98. **CONTACT ADDRESS** Univ of Wisconsin, Madison, 1914 Vilas Ave, Madison, WI 53711. **EMAIL** boguezg@mhub.history.wisc.edu

BOHNSTEDT, JOHN WOLFGANG
PERSONAL Born 02/22/1927, Berlin, Germany, m, 1948, 2 children **DISCIPLINE** HISTORY **EDUCATION** Mich State Col, BA, 50; Univ Minn, MA, 52, PhD(hist), 59. **CAREER** Instr Europ hist, Univ SDak, 55-56; from instr to assoc prof, 56-68, Prof Hist, Calif State Univ, Fresno, 68-, Am Philos Soc res grant, Harvard Univ, 65; res grants, Calif State Univ, Fresno, 65-67. **HONORS AND AWARDS** Distinguished Teaching Awd, Fresno State Col, 66. **MEMBERSHIPS** AHA. **RESEARCH** History of Germany in the nineteenth and twentieth centuries, intellectual history of modern Europe. **SELECTED PUBLICATIONS** Auth, The Infidel Scourge of God: The Turkish Menace as Seen by German Pamphleteers of the Reformation Era, Am Philos Soc, 68. **CONTACT ADDRESS** Dept of History, California State Univ, Fresno, 5340 N Campus Dr, Fresno, CA 93740-0021. **EMAIL** johnbo@csufresno.edu

BOHSTEDT, JOHN
PERSONAL Born 09/28/1943, Des Moines, IA, m, 1988, 2 children **DISCIPLINE** MODERN BRITISH SOCIAL HISTORY **EDUCATION** Cornell Col, BA, 64; Oxford Univ, BA, 66; MA, 70; Harvard Univ, PhD, 72. **CAREER** Asst prof, Harvard Univ, 73-79; assoc prof, Univ of Tenn, 79-. **HONORS AND AWARDS** Rhodes Scholar, 64-66; Danforth Fel, 66-71; NEH Summer Stipend, 74; ACLS Grant, 85; Guggenheim Res Grant, 88-89; NEH Grant, 93-96; LeRoy P Graf Awd, 93; Alexander von Humboldt Grant, 94-98. **RESEARCH** Riots in Britain 1550-1990. **SELECTED PUBLICATIONS** Auth, Riots and Community Politics in England and Wales, 1790-1810, Harvard Univ Pr, 83; coauth, "The Diffusion of Riots: The Patterns of 1766, 1795, and 1801 in Devonshire, J of Interdisciplinary Hist XIX.1 (88): 1-24; auth, "Gender, Household, and Community Politics: Women in English Riots, 1790-1810", Past and Present 120, (88): 88-122; auth, "The Myth of the Feminine Food Riot: women as Proto-Citizens in English Community Politics, 1790-1810", Women and Politics in the Age of Democratic Revolution, ed Darline Gay Levy and Harriet B. Applewhite, Univ of Mich Pr, (90): 21-60; auth, "More than One Working Class: Protestant-Catholic Riots in Edwardian Liverpool", Popular Politics, Riot and Labour: Essays in Liverpool History, 1790-1940, ed John C. Belchem, Liverpool Univ Pr, (92): 173-216; auth, "The Moral Economy and the Discipline of History Context", J of Soc Hist 26, (92): 265-284; auth, "Food Riots", Encyclop of Soc Hist, ed Peter N. Stearns, Garland (NY, 94): 286-287; auth, "The Dynamics of Riots: Escalation and Diffusion/Contagion", The Dynamics of Aggression: Biological and Social Processes in Dyads and Groups, ed Michael Potegal and John F. Knutson, Lawrence Erlbaum, (Hillsdale, 94): 257-306; auth, "The Pragmatic Economy, the Politics of Provisions, and the Invention of the Food Riot Tradition in 1740", Moral Economy and Popular Protest: Crowds, Conflict and Authority, eds Adrian Randall and Andrew Charlesworth, Macmillan (London, 00): 55-92. **CONTACT ADDRESS** Dept of Hist, Univ of Tennessee, Knoxville, 1345 Circle Pk, Knoxville, TN 37996-0001. **EMAIL** john-bohstedt@utk.edu

BOIME, ALBERT
PERSONAL Born 03/17/1933, St Louis, MO, m, 1965, 2 children **DISCIPLINE** HISTORY **EDUCATION** UCLA, BA, 61; Columbia Univ, MA, 63; PhD, 68. **CAREER** Instr, Columbia

Univ, 66-67; asst prof to assoc prof, SUNY Stony Brook, 68-72; prof to dept chmn, SUNY Binghamton, 72-78; prof, UCLA, 79-. **HONORS AND AWARDS** Guggenheim Fel, 74-75; 84-85; Rome Prize Fel, 79-80; Smithsonian Regents Fel, 88-89, 89-90; Myers Cen Awd, 99. **RESEARCH** Social history of modern art. **SELECTED PUBLICATIONS** Auth, The Academy and French Painting in the Nineteenth Century, 71; auth, Thomas Couture and the Eclectic Vision, 80; auth, Van Gogh's Starry Night, 89; auth, Art in the Age of Revolution, 87; auth, The Art of Exclusion: Representing Blacks in the Nineteenth Century, 90; auth, Art in the Age of Bonapartism, 91; Art and the French Commune, 95; ed, Violence and Utopia: The Work of Jerome P. Boime, 96; auth, The Unveiling of the National Icons, 98. **CONTACT ADDRESS** Dept Art Hist, Univ of California, Los Angeles, 100 Dodd Hall, PO Box 95147, Los Angeles, CA 90095-1417. **EMAIL** boime@humnet.ucla.edu

BOIRE, GARY
DISCIPLINE EARLY ROMAN IMPERIAL HISTORY **EDUCATION** Loyola, BA; McMaster, MA, PhD. **CAREER** Prof. **RESEARCH** Literary theory, postcolonial lit, Canadian fiction and drama, law, and lit, interdisciplinary approaches to lit. **SELECTED PUBLICATIONS** Auth, Morley Callaghan: Literary Anarchist, 94; Tribunalations: George Ryga's Postcolonial Trial Play; Inside Out: Prison Theatre from Australia, Canada, and New Zealand; Wide-Wasting Pest: Social History in The Vanity of Human Wishes; Canadian Twink: Surviving the Whiteouts. **CONTACT ADDRESS** Dept of English, Wilfrid Laurier Univ, 75 University Ave W, Waterloo, ON, Canada N2L 3C5. **EMAIL** gboire@wlu.cas

BOKER, HANS J.
PERSONAL Born 03/30/1953, Dalhausen, Germany, m, 1994 **DISCIPLINE** ART HISTORY **EDUCATION** Univ Saarbrucken, PhD, 79. **CAREER** Univ Hanover Germany, asst prof, 82-88; Ruhr-Universitat Bocham Germany, prof, 88-89; McGill Univ, prof, 89-. **MEMBERSHIPS** SAH, SFd'A **RESEARCH** Medieval Architecture. **SELECTED PUBLICATIONS** auth, "Englische Sakralarchitektur des Mittelalters," (Darmstadt: Wissenschaftliche Buchgesellschaft, 84), 371; auth, "Mittelalterliche Backsteinarchitektur Norddeutschlands," (Darmstadt: Wissenschaftliche Buchgesellschaft, 88), 309; author, "Die Marktpfarrkirche St. Lamberti in Munster: Die mittelalterliche Bau-und Resturierungsgeschichte einer spatgotischen Stadtkirche," Denkmalpflege und Forschung in Westfalen, Vol. XVIII, (Bonn: Rudolf Habelt, 89), 228; auth, Idensen: Architekur und Ausmalung einer romanischen Hofkapelle, (Berlin: Gebr Mann, 95); coauth, Respiciendo et prospiciendo: Allegories of Architecture and Sculpture on the Frontispieces of Leoni's Editions of Palladio and Alberti, in; Architecture and the Emblem, Montreal: McGill- Queens Univ Press, forthcoming; auth, Cologne Cathedral, Intl Dict Architects and Architecture, Bd 2: Architecture, ed. R. van Vynckt, Chicago: St James Press, 93; auth, The Bishops Chapel at Hereford and the Question of Architectural Copies in the Middle Ages, Gesta, 98; auth, Per Grecos Operarios: Die Bartholomauskapelle in Paderborn und ihr Byzantinisches Vorbild, Niederdeutsche Beitrage zur Kunstgeschichte, 97; auth, Ein heiliger Georg aus Soest? Zur Deutung der Patroklusstatue in Munster, Soester Zeitschrift, 96. **CONTACT ADDRESS** Dept of Art History, McGill Univ, 853 Sherbrooke St W, Montreal, QC, Canada H3A 2T6. **EMAIL** boker@leacock.ian.mcgill.ca

BOLES, JOHN B.
PERSONAL Born 10/20/1943, Houston, TX, m, 1967, 2 children **DISCIPLINE** HISTORY **EDUCATION** Rice Univ, BA, 65; Univ of Va, PhD, 69. **CAREER** Asst to Full Prof, Towson State Univ, 69-76; NEH Post-Doctoral Fel, Johns Hopkins Univ, 76-77; Vis Assoc Prof, Rice Univ, 77-78; Assoc to Full Prof, Tulane Univ, 78-81; Prof, Rice Univ, 81-; Managing Ed, J of Southern Hist, 83-. **HONORS AND AWARDS** Woodrow Wilson Dissertation Fel; NEH Fel for Col Teachers; Grad Student Asn Teaching Awd, Rice Univ. **MEMBERSHIPS** Southern Hist Asn. **RESEARCH** US South. **SELECTED PUBLICATIONS** Auth, The Great Revival, 1787-1805: The Origins of the Southern Evangelical Mind, (Kentucky), 72; auth, Black Southerners, 1619-1869, (Kentucky), 83; auth, The South Through Time: A History of an American Region, Prentice-Hall, 95, 99; co-ed, Interpreting Southern History, LSU. **CONTACT ADDRESS** Dept Hist, Rice Univ, 6100 Main St, Houston, TX 77005-1827. **EMAIL** boles@rice.edu

BOLES, LAWRENCE H., JR.
PERSONAL Born 12/09/1940, East Cleveland, OH, m, 1978, 1 child **DISCIPLINE** HISTORY **EDUCATION** Yale Univ, BA, 63; Case W Res, MA, 66; N Ariz Univ, PhD, 94. **CAREER** Asst teach, N Ariz Univ, 87-88; instr, 88-; assoc fac, Coconino CC, 95-. **MEMBERSHIPS** AHA; SFHS. **RESEARCH** Early modern Europe; modern Europe; United States. **SELECTED PUBLICATIONS** Auth, The Huguenots, the Protestant Interest, and the War of the Spanish Succession, 1702-1714, Peter Lang Pub (97). **CONTACT ADDRESS** Dept History, No Arizona Univ, PO Box 6023 NAU, Flagstaff, AZ 86011-0001.

BOLGER, FRANCIS W. P.
PERSONAL Born 07/08/1925, Stanley Bridge, PE, Canada **DISCIPLINE** HISTORY **EDUCATION** St Dunstan's Univ, BA, 47; Univ Montreal, STL, 51; Univ Toronto, MA, 56, PhD, 59. **CAREER** Diocese Charlottetown, 51-; assoc pastor, St. Dunstan's Basilica, Charlottetown, 51-53; prof, St. Dunstan's Univ, 59-69; prof, 69-94, PROF EMER HISTORY, UNIV PEI, 94-; chaplain, Air Force Reserve, 54-60; USSO Off, RCAF, 60-67. **HONORS AND AWARDS** Islander Year, 74; Awd excellence tchg, Univ PEI, 86-87; PEI Model Educ Prize, 90; mem, Order Can, 95; Int Rotary Paul Harris fel, 97; o. roman cath priest, 1951 **MEMBERSHIPS** Can Cath Hist Asn (pres, 64, pres-gen, 65); PEI rep, Hist Sites & Monuments Can, 66-78, 90-; chmn, Lucy Maud Montgomery Found Bd, 80. **RESEARCH** PEI history & literature; L.M. Montgomery. **SELECTED PUBLICATIONS** Auth, PEI and Confederation 1863-1873, 64; auth, The Years Before Anne, 74; coauth, Spirit of Place, 82; coauth, Memories of the Old Home Place, 84; ed, Canada's Smallest Province, 73; co-ed, My Dear Mr. M.: Letters of L.M. Montgomery to G.B. Macmillan, 80. **CONTACT ADDRESS** Dept of History, Univ of Prince Edward Island, 550 University Ave, Charlottetown, PE, Canada C1A 4P3.

BOLIN, JOHN SEELYE
PERSONAL Born 09/20/1943, Ft Bragg, NC, m, 1965, 1 child **DISCIPLINE** DRAMATIC LITERATURE, THEATRE HISTORY **EDUCATION** Kalamazoo Col, BA, 65; Univ MI, Ann Arbor, MA, 65, PhD, 70. **CAREER** Prof eng & theatre ,Berea Col, 70, dir repertory theatre festival, 81-83, Assoc dean Gen Educ, 89-94, Dean Fac, 98-; Mellon Found, Berea Col, Sabbatical fel, 77-78. **HONORS AND AWARDS** Kellog Nat Fel, 83-86; Canadian Embassy, Fac Res Grant, 94-95. **MEMBERSHIPS** AAUP; William Morris Soc; Asn Canadian Studies in U S; Midwestern Asn canadian Studies; KY Hum Coun, bd mem,, Asn Am Col and Univ, 94-98. **RESEARCH** Theatre aesthetics; theatre hist; criticism of drama. **SELECTED PUBLICATIONS** Auth, var rev & articles on Canadian Theatre and drama. **CONTACT ADDRESS** Dept of Eng, Berea Col, 101 Chestnut St, Berea, KY 40404-0003. **EMAIL** john_bolin@berea.edu

BOLL, MICHAEL MITCHEL
PERSONAL Born 03/03/1938, Antigo, WI, m, 1960, 2 children **DISCIPLINE** SOVIET & MODERN EUROPEAN HISTORY **EDUCATION** Univ Wis-Madison, BS, 61, MS, 65, PhD(soviet hist), 70. **CAREER** Instr Soviet hist, Ripon Col, 66-68; Soviet analyst, Radio Free Europe, Munich, 68-69; foreign serv officer soviet affairs, US Info Agency, Washington DC, 70; asst prof, 70-74, assoc prof, 75-80, Prof Soviet Hist, San Jose State Univ, 80- **MEMBERSHIPS** Am Asn Advan Slavic Studies; AHA. **RESEARCH** The militia and Red Guard in the Russian revolutions; the evolution of Soviet policy toward East Europe in the 70's; contemporary Soviet foreign affairs. **SELECTED PUBLICATIONS** Auth, Soviet policy toward East Europe & East Europea after the Czechoslovak Invasion, E Europe, 2/69; The dilemma of the Warsaw Pact, Mil Rev, 7/69; Problemy idealizma and Russian liberalism, Indian Polit Sci Rev, 1/74; Soviet strategy for the seventies, Mil Rev, 4/74; India looks to the Eastern Bloc, The New Leader, 4/74; Why do the Soviets want detente?, Mil Rev, 10/74. **CONTACT ADDRESS** Dept of Hist, San Jose State Univ, 1 Washington Sq, San Jose, CA 95192-0001.

BOLSTER, W. JEFFREY
DISCIPLINE EARLY AMERICAN SOCIAL AND CULTURAL HISTORY; AFRICAN-AMERICAN HISTORY; CARIBBEAN HISTORY; MARITIME HISTORY **EDUCATION** Johns Hopkins Univ, PhD. **CAREER** Asst prof, Univ NH. **HONORS AND AWARDS** NEH fel; Nat Mus of Am Hist fel, Smithsonian; Paul Cuffe fel, Mystic Seaport Mus; Binkley-Stephenson Awd, JAH; Louis Pelzer Mem Awd, JAH; New York Times Book Review "Notable Book" award, 97; John Lyman Book Awd for maritime hist, 97; Hortense Cavis Shepherd prof, UNH, 95-98; Co-winner of the A.H.A.'s Wesley-Logan book prize, 98; Asn of Am Publishers award for Hist, 98. **RESEARCH** African American and Caribbean identify-formation, accultruation, and social life; The Nature of a Place: A Social and Environmental History of the Piscataqua Watershed; Ships and Seafaring in the Atlantic World; Maritime of New England. **SELECTED PUBLICATIONS** Auth, 'To Feel Like a Man': Black Seamen in the Northern States, 1800-1860, J of Am Hist 76, 90; An Inner Diaspora: Black Sailors marking Selves, in Through a Glass Darkly: Reflections on Self in Early America, eds, Ronald Hoffman, et al, Omohundro Inst of Early Am Hist and Cult 97; Black Jacks: African American Seamen in the Age of Sail, 97; coauth, Soldiers, Sailors, Slaves, and Ships: The Civil War Photographs of Henry P. Moore, New Hampshire Hist Soc, Concord, 99. **CONTACT ADDRESS** History Dept., Univ of New Hampshire, Durham, 111 Green Hill Rd, Barrington, NH 03825. **EMAIL** jbolster@christa.unh.edu

BOLSTERLI, MARGARET JONES
PERSONAL Born 05/10/1931, Watson, AR, 2 children **DISCIPLINE** ENGLISH, CULTURAL HISTORY **EDUCATION** Univ Ark, BA, 53; Wash Univ, MA, 53; Univ Minn, PhD(English), 67. **CAREER** Asst prof English, Augsburg Col, 67-68; Prof English, Univ Ark, 68-, Nat Endowment Humanities Younger Humanist Award, 70-71; Ark Endowment Humanities grant, 80-81. **MEMBERSHIPS** MLA; SCent Mod Land Asn; Am Asn State & Local Hist. **RESEARCH** Nineteenth century Britain; the American south; women's studies. **SELECTED PUBLICATIONS** Auth, Porter,Katherine,Anne and Texas, Mod Fiction Stud, Vol 0038, 92; An Interview with Bolsterli,Margaret,Jones, Ark Hist Quart, Vol 0055, 96; Warren,Robert,Penn And The American Imagination--Mod Fiction Stud, Vol 0038, 92. **CONTACT ADDRESS** Dept of English, Univ of Arkansas, Fayetteville, Fayetteville, AR 72701.

BOLT, ERNEST C., JR.
DISCIPLINE HISTORY **EDUCATION** Furman Univ, BA, 58; Univ GA, MA, 63, PhD, 66. **CAREER** Samuel Chiles Mitchell-Jacob Billikopf prof, 82-88 & reapp, 88 and 94, Univ Richmond; Univ Richmond, 66-; Furman Univ, 65 & 68; grad tchg asst, Univ GA, 61-66; consul on Boatwright Mem Libr, Univ Richmond, 69-74; dir, 4 proj Dept Hist, 84-87; ch, Dept Hist, 83-89 & interim ch, 66; dir, Univ Richmond Self-Study, 96-98. **HONORS AND AWARDS** Grant & co-dir, Libr-Fac Partnership Prog, 73-78, Nat Endowment Hum and the Coun on Libr Rsrc(s); Frederick Jackson Turner awd, 74; mem, Phi Kappa Phi; Phi Alpha Theta; Omicron Delta Kappa & Phi Beta Delta; Who's Who in the South and Southwest and Contemp Authors. **MEMBERSHIPS** Act dir, Va Baptist Hist Soc, 75-79; AHA, Southern Hist Asn, 73-74; Orgn Am Historians; Soc for Historians Am For Rel; Conf on Peace Res in Hist; past VP and sec local chap, AAUP; exec comt and pres several terms, VA Baptist Hist Socy; pres, Richmond Oral Hist Asn 76-78 & exec coun, Friends of Boatwright Mem Libr. **RESEARCH** Am diplomatic hist, 1919 to 1941 and since 1945; Am peace movement hist; Am biog; Vietnam War. **SELECTED PUBLICATIONS** Auth, Isolation, Expansion, and Peace: American Foreign Policy Between the Wars, chap 8, American Foreign Relations: A Historiographical Review, Greenwood Press, 81; Reluctant Belligerent: The Career of Louis L. Ludlow, chap 11, Their Infinite Variety: Essays on Indiana Politicians, Indiana Hist Bureau, 82; William McClannahan: Early Virginia Bi-Vocational Minister and His Family, The Virginia Baptist Register, 97; Samuel Chiles Mitchell 1864-1948, in Biog Dictionary of Internationalists, Greenwood Press, 83; rev(s) in, J Amer Hist, 75; J Southern Hist, 77, 95; Amer Hist Rev, 79, 84, 87, 89, 90; Hist Tchr, 83, 84, 86 & Histy: Rev(s) New Bk(s), 97. **CONTACT ADDRESS** Dept of Hist, Univ of Richmond, 28 Westhampton Way, Richmond, VA 23173.

BOLT, ROBERT
PERSONAL Born 08/16/1930, Grand Rapids, MI, m, 1952, 5 children **DISCIPLINE** AMERICAN HISTORY **EDUCATION** Calvin Col, AB, 52; Univ Mich, AM, 53; Mich State Univ, PhD(hist), 63. **CAREER** Asst hist, Mich State Univ, 60-62; asst prof Am hist, Ill State Univ, 62-65; assoc prof, 65-73, Prof Hist, Calvin Col, 73- **MEMBERSHIPS** AHA; Orgn Am Historians. **RESEARCH** Biographical study of Donald M Dickson; twentieth century American history; local history. **SELECTED PUBLICATIONS** Auth, Apologia--The Screenplay for Lean 'Lawrence of Arabia, Cineaste, Vol 0021, 95. **CONTACT ADDRESS** Dept of Hist, Calvin Col, Grand Rapids, MI 49506.

BOLTON, CHARLES C.
DISCIPLINE HISTORY **EDUCATION** Univ Southern Mississippi, BS, 82; Duke Univ, MA, 86; Duke Univ, PhD, 89. **CAREER** Dir, Center for Oral History and Cultural Heritage; Asst Prof of History, Univ of Southern Miss, 90-94; Dir, Center for Oral History and Cultural Heritage; Assoc Prof of History, Univ of Southern Mississippi, 94- **HONORS AND AWARDS** Aubrey K. Lucas Fac Excellence Awd; Univ of Southern Mississippi, 95; Public Humanities Scholar Awd; Mississippi Humanities Council, 00. **MEMBERSHIPS** Mississippi Historical Society; Southern Historical Association; Organization of American Historians. **RESEARCH** US South; Oral History **SELECTED PUBLICATIONS** Auth, "Poor Whites of the Antebellum South: Tenants and Laborers in Central North Carolina and Northeast Mississippi, Duke Univ Press, 94; auth, "The Confessions of Edward Isham: A Poor White Life of the Old South," edited jointly with Scott P. Culclasure, Univ of Georgia Press, 98. **CONTACT ADDRESS** Dept History, Univ of So Mississippi, 2805 Hardy St, PO Box 5047, Hattiesburg, MS 39406-0001. **EMAIL** charles.bolton@usm.edu

BOLTON, SIDNEY CHARLES
PERSONAL Born 04/18/1943, Brooklyn, NY, m, 1999, 3 children **DISCIPLINE** AMERICAN HISTORY **EDUCATION** St Lawrence Univ, BA, 66; Univ Wis-Madison, MA, 68, PhD(hist), 73. **CAREER** Asst prof hist, Ill State Univ, 70-73; asst prof, 73-77, Assoc Prof Hist, Univ Ark, Little Rock, 77- **MEMBERSHIPS** Orgn Am Historians; Soc Historians of Early Republic. **RESEARCH** Early Republic, Arkansas. **SELECTED PUBLICATIONS** Auth, Southern Anglicanism: The Church of England in Colonial South Carolina, 82; auth, Territorial Ambition: Land and Society in Arkansas, 1800-1840, 93; auth, Arkansas 1800-1860: Remote and Restless, 98. **CONTACT ADDRESS** Dept of Hist, Univ of Arkansas, Little Rock, 33rd & University, Little Rock, AR 72204. **EMAIL** scbolton@ualr.edu

BOMBERGER, E. DOUGLAS
PERSONAL Born 11/15/1958, Lancaster, PA, m, 1982, 2 children **DISCIPLINE** HISTORICAL MUSICOLGY **EDUCATION** Univ of MD-Col Park, PhD, 91, Univ of NC-Chapel Hill, MM, 83, Goshen IN Col, BA, 81. **CAREER** Univ of HI-Manoa assoc prof, 98-, asst prof, 94-98 Ithaca Col asst prof, 92-94 Sweet Briar Col lectr, 89-90, Goshen Col asst prof, 83-87. **HONORS AND AWARDS** Deutscher Akademischer Austauschdienst fel, 90-91 Irving Lowens Student Research in Music Award, 88 Dean's Fel, Univ of MD, 87-89. **MEMBERSHIPS** Am Musicological Soc, ch, Capital Chapter, 93-94; Col Music Soc; Soc for Am Music; Am Liszt Soc. **RESEARCH** Am and Ger music of the late 19th century, hist and lit of the piano. **SELECTED PUBLICATIONS** Auth, "Opera in Context", ed. Mark A. Radice (Amadeus, 98), auth, Brainard's Biographies of American Music, (Greenwood 99); auth, Articles in "Piano Roles", ed. James Parakilas (Yale, 99); Musical Quarterly, Notes, American Music, etc. **CONTACT ADDRESS** Univ of Hawaii, Manoa, 2411 Dole Street, Honolulu, HI 96822. **EMAIL** edb@hawaii.edu

BOND, GERALD ALBERT
PERSONAL Born 03/15/1944, Rochester, NY, m, 1966, 2 children **DISCIPLINE** FRENCH AND GERMAN LANGUAGE, MEDIEVAL HISTORY **EDUCATION** William Col, BA, 65; Tufts Univ, MA, 66; Yale Univ, PhD(Medieval studies), 73. **CAREER** Instr Ger, 70-73, asst prof French & Ger, 73-78, Assoc Prof French & German, 78- **HONORS AND AWARDS** Younger humanist fel, Mellon Found, 76; Camargo Found fel, 77. **MEMBERSHIPS** Medieval Acad; MLA; Int Courtly Lit Soc. **RESEARCH** Medieval lyric poetry; courtly love; game and literature. **SELECTED PUBLICATIONS** Auth, The Game of Love, Troubadour Wordplay, Romance Philol, Vol 0048, 94; The Envy of Angels--Cathedral Schools and Social Ideas in Medieval Europe, Speculum- Jour Medieval Stud, Vol 0071, 96. **CONTACT ADDRESS** Dept of Foreign Lang Lit & Ling, Univ of Rochester, Rochester, NY 14627.

BOND, GORDON CREWS
PERSONAL Born 11/17/1939, Ft Myers, FL, m, 1974, 2 children **DISCIPLINE** MODERN EUROPEAN HISTORY **EDUCATION** Fla State Univ, BS, 62, MA, 63, PhD(hist), 66. **CAREER** Asst prof hist, Univ Southern Miss, 66-67; asst prof, 67-76, Assoc Prof Hist, Auburn Univ, 76- **MEMBERSHIPS** AHA; Soc Fr Hist Studies; Belg Soc Napoleonic Studies. **RESEARCH** The French Revolution and Napoleon. **SELECTED PUBLICATIONS** Auth, The Grand Expedition: The British Invasion of Holland in 1809, Univ Ga Press, 79. **CONTACT ADDRESS** Dept of Hist, Auburn Univ, Auburn, AL 36830.

BOND, JULIAN
PERSONAL Born 01/14/1940, Nashville, TN **DISCIPLINE** HISTORY **EDUCATION** Morehouse Col, BA, 71. **CAREER** Pappas Fel, Univ Pa, 89; Vis Prof, Harvard Univ, 89, 91; Vis Lecturer, Occidental Col, 91; Vis Prof, Williams Col, 92; Prof, American Univ, 91-.; Prof, Univ Va, 93-. **HONORS AND AWARDS** Honorary Degrees: Dalhousie Univ, Univ Bridgeport, Wesleyan Univ, Univ Ore, Syracuse Univ, Eastern Mich Univ, Lincoln Univ, Wilberforce Col, Patterson State Col, NH Col, Detroit Inst of Technol, Tuskegee Inst, Howard Univ, Morgan State Univ, Edward Waters Col, Gonzaga School of Law, Bates Col, Northeastern Univ; Time Magazine's 200 Leaders List; Bill of Rights Awd, Mass, 90; bill of Rights Awd, ACLU of Ga, 85; Outstanding Service Awd, Ga Municipal Asn, 84. **MEMBERSHIPS** NAACP, Am Inst for Public Service. **SELECTED PUBLICATIONS** Auth, "It Just Takes Organizing," Southern Exposure, 99; auth, "In Defense of affirmative Action," Gonzaga Law Review, 98; auth, "civil Rights, Then and Now," Poverty and Race, 98; auth, "Civil rights," Proteus, 98; auth, "Gonna Sit at the Welcome Table, am Heritage Pub, 95; auth, Forward, On Higher Ground: Education and the Case for affirmative Action, Teachers Col Press, 98; auth, "Excellence and Equity," in the Most Important Thing I Know, Cader Books, 97; auth, foreword, The Star Creek Papers: Washington Parish & The Lynching of Jerome Wilson, Univ Ga Press, 97; auth, "Democracy Demands Memory," Southern Changes, 97 **CONTACT ADDRESS** Dept Hist, Univ of Virginia, Charlottesville, VA 22903-3244. **EMAIL** hjb7g@virginia.edu

BONE, QUENTIN
PERSONAL Born 09/03/1918, Bond Co, IL **DISCIPLINE** MODERN EUROPEAN AND ENGLISH HISTORY **EDUCATION** Univ Ill, Urbana, AB, 40, MA, 41, PhD(hist), 54. **CAREER** Teacher social studies, Sorento High Sch, 41-42; master, DeVeaux Sch, 46-48; teacher, East Peoria Community High Sch, 48-52; asst prof hist, Fairmont State Col, 54-55; Prof Hist, Ind State Univ, Terre Haute, 55- **MEMBERSHIPS** AHA. **RESEARCH** Seventeenth and nineteenth century English history. **SELECTED PUBLICATIONS** Auth, An Old Radical and His Brood, Notes And Records Of The Royal Society Of London, Vol 0050, 96; Pittrivers, The Life And Archaeological Work Of Pittrivers,Augustus,Henry,Lane,Fox, Notes And Records Of The Royal Society Of London, Vol 0049, 95; Sir Bowring,John, 1792-1872--Aspects of His Life and Career, Notes and Records of the Royal Society of London, Vol 0050, 96. **CONTACT ADDRESS** 2524 N 10th St, Terre Haute, IN 47804.

BONEY, FRANCIS NASH
PERSONAL Born 11/10/1929, Richmond, VA, m, 1959, 2 children **DISCIPLINE** AMERICAN HISTORY **EDUCATION** Hampden-Sydney Col, BS, 52; Univ Va, MA, 60, PhD, 63. **CAREER** Asst prof hist, Murray State Col, 62-63 and Univ Ga, 63-65; from asst prof to assoc prof, Wash State Univ, 65-68; assoc prof, 68-72, Prof Hist, Univ GA, 72-. **HONORS AND AWARDS** Am Philos Soc grants, 72, 73 and 79. **MEMBERSHIPS** Southern Hist Asn. **RESEARCH** American Civil War; antebellum South; American Middle Period, 1800-1877. **SELECTED PUBLICATIONS** Auth, Andersonville the Last Depot, J Am Hist, Vol 0082, 95; For the Sake of my Country--The Diary of Ward, W.W., 9th Tennessee Cavalry, Morgans Brigade, CSA, Va Mag Hist Biog, Vol 0102, 94; The Georgia Gold Rush-Twenty Niners, Cherokees, and Gold Fever, Am Hist Rev, Vol 0099, 94. **CONTACT ADDRESS** Dept of Hist, Univ of Georgia, Athens, GA 30602-1602.

BONFANTE, LARISSA
PERSONAL Born Naples, d, 2 children **DISCIPLINE** ETRUSCAN STUDIES, ROMAN HISTORY **EDUCATION** Barnard Col, BA, 54; Univ Cincinnati, MA, 57; Columbia Univ, PhD (archaeol), 66. **CAREER** From instr to Prof of Classics, Univ of NY, 63-. **MEMBERSHIPS** Archaeol Inst Am; Instituto di Studi Etruschi, German Archaeological Institute. **RESEARCH** Etruscan studies; Roman history; Latin language and literature. **SELECTED PUBLICATIONS** Auth, "Roman Triumphes and Etruscan Kings: The Changing Face of The Triumph," Journal of Roman Studies, 60 (70): 49-66; auth, Etruscan Dress, 75; auth, Out of Etraria, 81; Estruscan Life and Afterlife, ed 86; auth, The Etruscan Language: An Introduction, with A. Bonfonte, 83; auth, "Nudity as a Costume in Classical Art," American Journal of rchaeology, 93 (89): 543-570; auth, Reading the Past: Etruscan, 90; auth, Etruscan Mirrors, The Metropolitan Museum of Art, 97. **CONTACT ADDRESS** Dept of Classics, New York Univ, 25 Waverly Pl, New York, NY 10003. **EMAIL** lb11@is2.nyu.edu

BONNER, ROBERT ELLIOTT
PERSONAL Born 06/06/1938, Covina, CA, m, 1962, 2 children **DISCIPLINE** AMERICAN HISTORY **EDUCATION** Univ Wyo, BA, 61; Univ Ore, MA, 63; Univ Minn, PhD(Hist), 68. **CAREER** From instr to prof hist, Carlton col, 67-00; Marjorie Crabb Garbisch Prof of the Liberal Arts, Carlton Col, 00-. **MEMBERSHIPS** Am Studies Assoc, Western Hist Assn. **RESEARCH** Am West **CONTACT ADDRESS** Dept of American Studies, Carleton Col, 1 N College St, Northfield, MN 55057-4044. **EMAIL** RBonner@Carleton.edu

BONNER, THOMAS NEVILLE
PERSONAL Born 05/28/1923, Rochester, NY, 2 children **DISCIPLINE** HISTORY **EDUCATION** Univ Rochester, AB, 47, MA, 49; Northwestern Univ, PhD, 52. **CAREER** Acad dean, William Woods Col, 51-54; Fulbright prof Am civilization, Univ Mainz, 54-55; from assoc prof to prof hist, Univ Omaha, 55-62; legis asst, Sen George McGovern, 62-63; prof hist and chmn dept, Univ Cincinnati, 63-68, vpres and provost, 67-71; prof hist and pres, Univ NH, 71-74; pres and chancellor, Union Col, 74-78; pres, 78-82, Distinguished Prof Hist, Wayne State Univ, 82-, vpres, Acad Affairs. **HONORS AND AWARDS** Guggenheim Mem fels, 58-59, 64-65. **MEMBERSHIPS** AHA; Orgn Am Historians. **RESEARCH** Recent American history; history of medicine; American intellectual history. **SELECTED PUBLICATIONS** Auth, Medicine in Chicago, 1850-1950, Am Hist Res Ctr, 57; Kansas Doctor, Univ Kans, 59; Our Recent Past, Prentice-Hall, 63; American Doctors and German Universities, 1870-1914, Univ Nebr, 63. **CONTACT ADDRESS** Division of Acad Affairs, Wayne State Univ, Detroit, MI 48202-3919. **EMAIL** aa1289@wayne.edu

BONOMI, PATRICIA UPDEGRAFF
PERSONAL Born 01/16/1928, Longview, WA, m, 1953, 2 children **DISCIPLINE** EARLY AMERICAN HISTORY **EDUCATION** Univ Calif, Los Angeles, BA, 48; NYork Univ, MA, 63; Columbia Univ, PhD (hist), 70. **CAREER** Lectr Am hist, Lehman Col, 67-70, vis asst prof, 70; from asst prof to assoc prof, 70-78, Prof Am Hist, NY Univ, 78-, Mem, Columbia Univ Sem Early Am Hist and Cult, 70-; Am Coun Learned Socs fel, 73-74; Guggenheim fel, 76-77; Rockefeller Found Humanities fel, 79-80; vis fel, Shelby Cullom Davis Ctr, Princeton Univ, 79-80. **MEMBERSHIPS** AHA; Inst Early Am Hist and Cult; Orgn Am Historians. **RESEARCH** Political, social and religious history. **SELECTED PUBLICATIONS** Auth, Political Patterns in Colonial New York City: The General Assembly Election of 1786, Polit Sci Quart, 9/66; A Factious People: Politics and Society in Colonial New York, Columbia Univ, 71; contribr, Perspectives on Early American History: Essays in Honor of Richard B Morris, Harper, 73; Aspects of Early New York Society and Politics, Sleepy Hollow Restorations, 74; ed, Party and Political Opposition in Revolutionary America, Sleepy Hollow Press, 80; co-ed, The American Constitution Under Strong and Weak Parties, Praeger, 81; coauth, Church Adherence in the Eighteenth Century British American Colonies, William & Mary Quart, 4/82. **CONTACT ADDRESS** Dept of Hist, New York Univ, 19 University Pl, New York, NY 10003.

BONTTY, MONICA
PERSONAL Born 02/13/1959, Santa Monica, CA, s **DISCIPLINE** ARCHAEOLOGY, EGYPTOLOGY **EDUCATION** Univ Calif at Los Angeles, BA, 83; MA, 83; PhD, 97. **CAREER** Conf coordr, TA/reader, res asst, libr asst & lectr, Univ Calif, Los Angeles, 89-; museum asst, Lancaster Museum, 92. **HONORS AND AWARDS** German Acad Exchange Scholar, 81; Dept Scholar, Dean's Honor List, 81-83; Grad Advancement Opportunity Fel, 89-92; Grad Advancement Fel, 92-93; Friends of Archaeol Travel Grant, Inst of Archaeol, 93-94; Gottinger Contact Fel, 93-94; Grad Div Fel, 94-96. **MEMBERSHIPS** ARCE **RESEARCH** Egyptology, coptology, ancient history, sociology of law, general sociology. **SELECTED PUBLICATIONS** Auth, "The Haunebu," GM 145 (95): 45-58; auth, "P. Deir El-Medinah VII," JARCE 33 (96): 65-68; rev, of "Die Admonitions," by W. Helck, LingAeg 6 (99). **CONTACT ADDRESS** Dept Near Eastern Lang & Lit, Univ of California, Los Angeles, PO Box 951584, Los Angeles, CA 90095-1584. **EMAIL** Uhura@humnet.ucla.edu

BOON, KEVIN A.
PERSONAL Born 10/13/1956, Tampa, FL, d **DISCIPLINE** ENGLISH, AMERICAN STUDIES **EDUCATION** Univ S Fla, BA, 83; MA, 91; PhD, 95. **CAREER** Instr, Univ S Fla, 95-96; instr, Univ Alabama, 96-97; asst prof, Maritime Col, SUNY, 97-00; asst prof, Pa State, 00-. **HONORS AND AWARDS** Hon Men, USF Fic Con; Eng Poetry Awd; Anspaugh Fic Awd; Flora Zbar Grad Teach Awd. **MEMBERSHIPS** NYCEA; MLA. **RESEARCH** 20th Century literature and culture; Kurt Vonnegut; Chaos Theory; Technology; Film; Science and Literature. **SELECTED PUBLICATIONS** Auth, Chaos Theory and the Interpretation of Literary Texts: The Case of Kurt Vonnegut, Edwin Mellon Press, 97; auth, An Interpretive Commentary on Virginia Woolf's The Waves, Edwin Mellon Press, 98; auth, Reading the Sea: New Essays on Sea Literature, Ft Schuyler Press, 99; auth, Absolute Zero, Ft Schuyler Press, 99; auth, At Millennium's End: New Essays on the Work of Kurt Vonnegut, SUNY Press, in press; auth, "Efrem Zimbalist, Sr," Scribner Encycl Am Lives v2 (98); auth, "In Defense of John Carpenter's Thing," Creat Screen Writ 44 (99): 66-74; auth, "Mrs Mallory's Mummified Dog," Lullwater Rev 6 (95): 35-43; auth, "Last Rites," Sandhill Rev (95): 14-17; auth, "Clean and Simple," Sandhill Rev (forthcoming); auth, "Railroad Men," Sandhill Rev (95); auth, "In the Corridors of the Cardiac Unit," Poetry Motel (98). **CONTACT ADDRESS** Dept Humanities, SUNY, Maritime Col, 6 Pennyfield Ave, Bronx, NY 10465-4127.

BOORSTIN, DANIEL JOSEPH
PERSONAL Born 10/01/1914, Atlanta, GA, m, 1941, 3 children **DISCIPLINE** HISTORY **EDUCATION** Harvard Univ, AB, 34: Oxford Univ, BA, 36; BCL, 37; Yale Univ, JSD, 40. **CAREER** Instr hist and lit, Harvard and Radcliffe Cols, 38-42; instr legal hist, Law Sch, Harvard Univ, 39-42; asst prof hist, Swarthmore Col, 42-44; from assoc prof to prof, Univ Chicago, 44-64, Preston and Sterling Morton distinguished prof Am hist, 64-69; Librn of Cong, Cong Libr, 75-, Barrister-at-law, Inner Temple, London, England, 37-; Fulbright vis prof, Univ Rome, 50-51; Walgreen lectr Am civilization, Univ Chicago, 52; ed, Am hist, Encycl Britannica, 52-55; consult, Soc Sci Res Ctr, Univ PR, 55; vis prof, Kyoto Univ, 57; State Dept lectr, Turkey, Iran, Nepal, India and Ceylon, 59-60, India, Pakistan and Iceland, 74, Philippines, Thailand, Malaysia, India and Egypt, 75; first holder, Chair of Am Hist Sorbonne, 61-62; Pitt prof, Cambridge Univ and fel, Trinity Col, 64-65; mem, Am Revolution Bicentennial Comm, 66-70 and Indust Govt Spec Task Force on Travel, 68; trustee, Colonial Williamsburg, 68-; lectr, William W Cook Lect Ser, Univ Mich, 72; trustee, Am Film Inst, 72-76, John F Kennedy Ctr Performing arts, 75-, Woodrow Wilson Int Ctr Scholars, 75- and Nat Humanities Ctr, 77-78; Shelby and Kathry Davis lectr, Grad Inst Int Studies, Geneve, 73-74; mem, Comn Critical Choices for Am, 73-75; mem adv bd, Morris and Gwendolyn Cafritz Found, 76-; mem, Japan-US Friendship Comn, 78-; mem, Carl Albert Cong Res and Studies Ctr, 79-; mem, pres task force, Arts and Humanities, 81. **HONORS AND AWARDS** Bancroft Prize, Columbia Univ, 59; Frances Parkman Prize, Soc Am Historians, 66; Nat Bk Award; Pulitzer Prize for Hist, 74; Dexter Prize, 74; 50 hon degrees from various Univs & Cols; 18 hon degrees from various cols and univs. **MEMBERSHIPS** AHA; Orgn Am Historians; Am Antiq Soc; Am Acad Arts and Sci; Am Studies Asn (pres, 69-71). **RESEARCH** American history; intellectual and social history; world history. **SELECTED PUBLICATIONS** Auth, Portraits from the Americans: The Democratic Experience, 76; auth, The Exploring Spirit, 77; auth, The Republic of Technology, 78; co-auth, A History of the United States, 80; auth, The Discoverers, 83; auth, Hidden History, 87; auth, The Creators, 92; auth, Cleopatra's Nose, 94; auth, The Modern Library Boorstin Reader, 96; auth, The Seekers, 98. **CONTACT ADDRESS** 3541 Ordway St NW, Washington, DC 20016.

BOOTH, ALAN R.
PERSONAL Born 03/20/1934, Manchester, NH, m, 1956, 3 children **DISCIPLINE** AFRICAN HISTORY **EDUCATION** Dartmouth Col, AB, 56; Boston Univ, MA, 62, PhD (hist), 64. **CAREER** Asst prof hist, 64-68, dir African studies, 66-73, chmn dept, 75-80, Assoc Prof Hist, Ohio Univ, 68-, Ohio Univ Fund grant, 64-65; lectr African hist, Foreign Serv Inst, 65; Am

Philos Soc grant, 65; Fulbright fel, 65-66; US Off Educ grant, Lesotho Field Proj, 67; consult, African Studies Ctr, Cent State Univ, 67-68; consult, Choice. **HONORS AND AWARDS** Outstanding Grad Fac Awd, Ohio Univ, 77. **MEMBERSHIPS** AHA; African Studies Asn. **RESEARCH** Role of Lord Selborne in South Africa and the protectorates; American role in South Africa, 19th and 20th centuries; labour migrations in southern Africa. **SELECTED PUBLICATIONS** Auth, American whalers in south African waters, S African J Econ, 12/64; Alabama at the Cape, 1863, Am Neptune, 4/66; ed, Journal of Rev George Champion, 1835-1839, C Struik, 67; auth, Lord Selborne and the British protectorates, J African Hist, 1/69; Polaroid's experiment in the disengagement from South Africa, In: Foreign Investment in South Africa: The Policy Debate, Africa Publ Trust, 75; The United States Experience in South Africa, 1784-1870, AA Balkema, Cape Town, 76; Development of the Swazi labour market, S African Labour Bull, 82. **CONTACT ADDRESS** Dept of Hist, Ohio Univ, Bentley Hall, Athens, OH 45701.

BORCHERT, JAMES A.
PERSONAL Born 01/13/1941, Cleveland, OH, m, 1982 **DISCIPLINE** HISTORY **EDUCATION** Miami Univ, BA, 63; Ind Univ, MSEd, 65; Univ Cincinnati, MA, 66; Univ Md, PhD, 76. **CAREER** Instr, Ala A & M Col, 66-67; Instr, Univ Md, 68; Vis Assoc Prof, Case Western Reserve Univ, 81; Vis asst Prof to Assoc Prof, Univ Calif, 73-84; Assoc Prof, Cleveland State Univ, 84-. **HONORS AND AWARDS** Fel, Smithsonian Inst, 74-75; Ralph Henry Gabriel Prize, Am Studies Asn, 77; Outstanding Achievement Awd, Lakewood Hist Soc, 90; Best Paper, Ohio Acad of Hist, 99. **MEMBERSHIPS** Am Asn for State and Local Hist, Am Asn of Univ Prof, Am Hist Asn, Am Urban Hist Asn, Asn for the study of Afro-Am Life and Hist, Intl Planning Hist Soc, Intl Visual Sociol Asn, Nat Coun on Pub Hist, Org of Am Hist, Slovak Stud Asn, Soc for Am city and Reg Planning Hist, Vernacular Archit Forum. **RESEARCH** US Social and cultural, Urban and suburban, African American History, Race, Class and Ethnicity in the US and Research Methods: Visual Analysis. **SELECTED PUBLICATIONS** Auth, Alley Life in Washington: Family, community, Religion and folklife in the City, 1850-1970, Univ Ill Press, 80; auth, Lakewood: The first Hundred Years, Donning Co Pub, 94; auth, "Residential City Suburbs: The emergence of a New Suburban Type, 1880-1930," Journal of Urban History, (96): 283-307; auth, "Cities in the Suburbs: Heterogeneous Communities on the US Urban Fringe, 1920-1950," Urban History, (96): 211-227; auth, "Visual Landscapes of a Streetcar Suburb," in Understanding Ordinary Landscapes, Yale Univ Press, 97; auth, "Viewing the Underclass and Ghetto from the top down," Journal of Urban History, (99): 583-593; auth, "From City to Suburb: the Strange Case of Cleveland's Disappearing elite and their Changing Residential Landscapes," Ohio Acad of History Proceedings, 00. **CONTACT ADDRESS** Dept Hist, Cleveland State Univ, 1983 E 24th St, Cleveland, OH 44115-2403. **EMAIL** j.borchert@popmail.csuohio.edu

BORELLI, JOHN
PERSONAL Born 07/19/1946, Oklahoma City, OK, m, 1971, 3 children **DISCIPLINE** HISTORY OF RELIGIONS, THEOLOGY **EDUCATION** Fordham Univ, PhD, 76. **CAREER** Instr, Dept Theology, Fordham Univ, Bronx, NY, 75-76; Prof Religious Studies, Col Mount St Vincent, Riverdale, NY, 76-87; dir, Interreligous Relations, US Conference of Catholic Bishops, 87-. **HONORS AND AWARDS** Phi Beta Kappa, St. Louis Univ, 68. **MEMBERSHIPS** Consultor, Pontifical Coun for Interreligous Dialogue, Vatican; Int Buddhist-Christian Theological Encounter Group; Exec Coun, World Conference on Religion and Peace, USA; adv bd, Monastic Interreligous Dialogue; advisory bd, Institute for Interreligious Study and Dialogue, Catholic Univ of Am; ; Soc for Buddhist-Christian Studies; Soc for Hindu-Christian Studies. **RESEARCH** Interreligous relations; theology of religions; the Hindu tradition; Yoga and meditation; ecumenical relations. **SELECTED PUBLICATIONS** Auth, Children of Abraham: Muslim-Christian-Jewish Relations, Mid-Stream 34, 2, April 95; The 1994 International Buddhist-Christian Theological Encounter, with Judith Simmer-Brown, Buddhist-Christian Studies, 15, 95; Interreligous Relations, Annual report, 1994, Pro Dialogo, Bul of the Pontifical Coun for Interreligous Dialogue, 89, 95; The Goal and Fruit of Catholic-Muslim Dialogue, The Living Light, Dept of Ed, US Cath Conference, 32, 2, winter 95; Talking With Muslims, Faith Alive, Cath News Service, Feb 96; Indispensable Resources on the Christian East and Other Important Books, Ecumenical Trends, 25, 6, June 96; Jesus Christ's Challenge to World Religions: A Response, The Continuing Challenge of Jesus Christ to the World, a Symposium on the Coming of the Third Millenium and the Jubilee Year 2000, sponsored by the NCCB Subcommittee on the Millenium, Sept 7-8, 96, Proceedings; The Virgin Mary in the Breadth and Scope of Interreligious Dialogue, Marian Spirituality and Interreligous Dialogue, Marian Studies, 47, 96; Introductory Address for Imam Warith Deen Mohammed, Living City, Oct, 97; The Catholic Church and Interreligious Dialogue, in Vatican II: The Continuing Agenda, ed by Anthony J Cernera, Sacred Heart Univ Press, 97; Religous Pluralism in India and the Mission of the Church, Periodic Paper #4, US Cath Mission Asn, in Mission Update 6, 4, Dec 97; Interreligous Relations, 1996, Annual Report, Pro Dialogo, Bul of the Pontifical Coun for Interreligious Dialogue, 96, 97; Islamic-Catholic Relations in the USA: Activities of the National Conference of Catholic Bishops (1996) and Recent Developments, Islamochristiana 23, 97; ed with John H Erickson, The Quest for Unity, Orthodox and Catholics in Dialogue, St Vladimir's Seminary Press/US Cath Conf, 96. **CONTACT ADDRESS** Interreligious Relations, 3211 Fourth St NE, Washington, DC 20017. **EMAIL** seiamail@nccbuscc.org

BOREN, HENRY C.
PERSONAL Born 02/10/1921, Pike Co, IL, m, 1942, 1 child **DISCIPLINE** ANCIENT HISTORY **EDUCATION** Southwest Mo State Col, AB, 49; Univ Ill, MA, 50, PhD, 52. **CAREER** Instr English and hist, Southwest Mo State Col, 52-54; instr hist, Univ Nebr, 55; asst prof, Southern Ill Univ, 55-60; assoc prof, 60-67; Prof Hist, Univ NC, Chapel Hill, 67-86; Secy Fac, 69-84; Nat Endowment for Humanities sr fel and scholar in residence, Am Acad Rome, 67-68; consult-panelist, Nat Endowment for Humanities, 76- **MEMBERSHIPS** AHA; Am Philol Asn; Am Numis Soc; Archaeol Inst Am; Soc Promotion Roman Studies. **RESEARCH** Roman Republic; economic and social history; numismatics. **SELECTED PUBLICATIONS** Auth, The Roman Republic, Anvil Books, 65; auth, The Graechi, Twayne, 68; auth, The Ancient World, Prentice Hall, 76, 2nd ed., 86; auth, Roman Society, D.C. Heath, 77, 2nd ed., 92; auth, Coins of the Roman-Empire, Class World, Vol 0086, 92; Cicero and the Roman-Republic, Hist, Vol 0056, 94. **CONTACT ADDRESS** Dept of Hist, Univ of No Carolina, Chapel Hill, Chapel Hill, NC 27514. **EMAIL** hboren@Attglobal.net

BORG, DANIEL RAYMOND
PERSONAL Born 08/01/1931, Tracy, MN, m, 1959, 4 children **DISCIPLINE** MODERN EUROPEAN HISTORY **EDUCATION** Gustavus Adolphus Col, BA, 53, Yale Univ, MA, 57, PhD (hist), 63. **CAREER** From instr to prof emer, Clark Univ, 61-; Chmn Dept Hist, 69-72, 77-83. **HONORS AND AWARDS** Nat Endowment for Humanities fel, 68. **MEMBERSHIPS** AHA. **RESEARCH** Modern German history, German Protestants in the Weimar Republic and Nazi period, ecumenical history. **SELECTED PUBLICATIONS** Auth, The Old Prussian Church and The Weimar Republic, Univ Press of New England (Hanover, NH), 84. **CONTACT ADDRESS** Dept of Hist, Clark Univ, Worcester, MA 01610.

BORG, DOROTHY
PERSONAL Born 09/04/1902, Elberon **DISCIPLINE** HISTORY, PUBLIC LAW **EDUCATION** Wellesley Col, AB, 23; Columbia Univ, MA, 31, PhD (pub law and govt), 46. **CAREER** Res assoc Am-Chinese rels, Inst Pac Rels, 38-59; res assoc, EAsian Res Ctr, Harvard Univ, 59-61; Sr Res Assoc, Am Far East Policy, East Asian Inst, Columbia Univ, 62-, Lectr, Peking Univ, 47-48. **HONORS AND AWARDS** Bancroft Prize Hist, 65. **MEMBERSHIPS** AHA; Asn Asian Studies, Acad Polit Sci. **SELECTED PUBLICATIONS** Auth, Social Protestantism in the 20th Century--History of the Inner Mission 1914-1945, J Mod Hist, Vol 0064, 92. **CONTACT ADDRESS** 22 Riverside Dr, New York, NY 10023.

BORN, JOHN D., JR.
PERSONAL Born 07/07/1934, Ellis Co., TX, m, 1971, 2 children **DISCIPLINE** COLONIAL AMERICAN HISTORY; AMERICAN REVOLUTION & THE EARLY REPUBLIC, OLD SOUTH, THE AMERICANS **EDUCATION** Univ Tex, BA, 52; Univ Houston, MA, 58; Univ Nmex, PhD, 63. **CAREER** Asst graduate dean; grad co-ord, hist dept, 78-; assoc prof-. **HONORS AND AWARDS** Summer and Academic yr grants, NEH, 76,80,83; Fel in Residence, UCSB, 79-80, 92. **MEMBERSHIPS** SHEAR, Nat Soc Sci Asn. **RESEARCH** Early Am. **SELECTED PUBLICATIONS** Co-auth, History of the United States With Topics and Readings in United States History With Topics, Vol I and Vol. II, 96; contribu, Soc Sci Perspectives Jour, Psychohist Rev, Jour Miss Hist, Jour Ala Hist, Wichita State Univ Stud, Nat Soc Sci Journal. **CONTACT ADDRESS** Dept of Hist, Wichita State Univ, 1845 Fairmont, Wichita, KS 67260-0045.

BORNE, LAWRENCE ROGER
PERSONAL Born 01/08/1939, Indianapolis, IN, s **DISCIPLINE** UNITED STATES HISTORY **EDUCATION** Xavier Univ, Ohio, BS, 59, MA, 66; Univ Colo, Boulder, PhD, 70. **CAREER** Instr hist, Univ Colo, 68-70; Instr hist, Xavier Univ, summers 69-70; from asst prof to prof hist, Northern Ky Univ, 70-; mem adv bd, League of Kentucky Property Owners. **HONORS AND AWARDS** NDEA fel, 66-69. **MEMBERSHIPS** Western Hist Asn. **RESEARCH** Western tourism; communism in the United States; conservation. **SELECTED PUBLICATIONS** Auth, The Wootton Land and Fuel Company, 1905-1910, Colo Mag, summer 69; auth, Triumph to Disaster: Colonel James A Ownbey, Colo Mag, fall 71; art, The Cowboy and Dude Ranching, Red River Valley Hist Rev, spring 75; contribr, The Cowboys: Six-Shooters, Songs and Sex, Univ Okla, 76; auth, Recreation, Government and Freedom, World Res INK, 8/77; auth, Dude Ranches and the Development of the West, J of the West, 7/78; contribr, Sports and Recreation in the West, Sunflower Univ Press, 78; auth, Welcome to My West, I.H. Larom: Dude Rancher, Conservationist, Collector, Buffalo Bill Hist Ctr, 82; auth, Dude Ranching : A Complete Hist, Univ NMex Pr (Albuquerque), 83; auth, Western Railroads and the Dude Ranching Industry, The pacific Hist, 86; auth, Dude Ranching in the Rockies, Montana: The Magazine of Western Hist, 88. **CONTACT ADDRESS** 2945 Wild Rose Dr, Edgewood, KY 41017. **EMAIL** bornel@nku.com

BORNSTEIN, DANIEL E.
PERSONAL Born 09/10/1950, New Haven, CT, m, 1998, 1 child **DISCIPLINE** MEDIEVAL AND RENAISSANCE HISTORY **EDUCATION** Oberlin Col, BA, 72; Univ Chicago, MA, 77; PhD, 85. **CAREER** Asst Prof, Univ Mich, 83-86; Lecturer, Univ Calif, 86-89; Asst Prof to Prof, Tex A & M Univ, 89-; visiting Prof, Central European Univ, 97; Visiting Prof, Universite degli studi di Milano, 97. **HONORS AND AWARDS** Fel, NEH, 89-902, 93, 95; Grant, Am Philos Soc, 90, 96, 98; Grant, Gladys Krieble Delmas Foundation, 96. **MEMBERSHIPS** AHA, Renaissance Soc of Am, Medieval Acad of Am, Am Soc for Church History. **RESEARCH** Medieval and Renaissance Italy; Women and religion in medieval Europe. **SELECTED PUBLICATIONS** Auth, Dino Compagni's Chronicle of Florence, Univ Penn Press, 86; auth, The Bianchi of 1399: Popular Devotion in Late Medieval Italy, Cornell Univ Press, 93; ed, "Bartolomea Riccoboni," Life and Death in a Venetian Convent: The Chronicle and Necrology of Corpus Domini, 1395-1436, Univ Chicago Press, 00; ed, Mistiche e Devote nell'Italia tardomedievale, Naples, 92; ed, Women and Religion in Medieval and Renaissance Italy, Univ of Chicago Press, 96; auth, "Giovanni Dominici, the Bianchi, and Venice: Symbolic Action and Interpretive Grids," Journal of Medieval and Renaissance Studies, (93): 143-171; auth, "The Uses of the Body: The Church and the Cult of Santa Margherita da Corona," Church History, (93): 163-177; auth, "Dominican Friar, Lay Saint: the Case of Marcolino of Forli," Church History, (97): 252-267; auth, "Parish Priests in late Medieval Cortona: The Urban and Rural Clergy," Quaderni di Storia Religiosa, (97): 165-193. **CONTACT ADDRESS** Dept Hist, Texas A&M Univ, Col Station, MSC 166, College Station, TX 77843-4236. **EMAIL** d.bornstein@tamu.edu

BOROWSKI, ODED
PERSONAL Born 08/26/1939, Petakh Tikva, Israel, m, 1964, 2 children **DISCIPLINE** BIBLICAL ARCHAEOLOGY **EDUCATION** Midrasha Col of Jewish Studies, BHL, 68; Wayne State Univ, BA, 70; Univ of Mich, AM, 72; PhD, 79. **CAREER** Instr, Schoolcraft Col, 73-77; lectr, Univ of Mich, 75-77; instr to assoc prof, Emory Univ, 77-. **HONORS AND AWARDS** Ford Found Grant, 72; Mem Found for Jewish Culture Grant, 79; Emory Univ Grant, 79, 82, 84; NEH Grant 82-84; Lilly Found Fel, 85-86; Annual Prof, Albright Inst, 88; Joe Alon Center Grant, 88; Cobb Inst Grant, 88, 90; Dorot Res Prof, AIAR, Jerusalem 91-92; Mem Found for Jewish Culture, 94-95; Annual Prof, AIAR, Jerusalem, 95-96; Assoc Fel, AIAR, Jerusalem, 99. **MEMBERSHIPS** Israel Exploration Soc; Am Schools of Oriental Res; Soc for Bibl Lit; Nat Assoc of Prof of Hebrew; AAUP. **RESEARCH** Ancient agriculture, daily use of animals in ancient Isreael, space utilization in daily life activities, use of ground penetrating radar and global positioning systems in archaeology. **SELECTED PUBLICATIONS** Auth, Agriculture in Iron Age Israel", Eisenbrauns, (Winona Lake), 87; "Agriculture", Anchor Bible Dictionary, Doubleday, (NY, 92): 95-98; auth, "Halif, Tel: The Iron Age Cemetery", New Encycl of Archaeol Excavations in the Holy Land, Israel Exploration Soc (Jerusalem, 93): 559-560; auth, "The Language of the Media and Daily use of Hebrew", Bulletin of Higher Hebrew Educ 6.7 (94-95): 73-77; auth, "The Pomegranate Bowl from Tell Halif", Israel Exploration J 45 (95): 150-154; coauth, "A Penetrating Look: An Experiment in Remote Sensing at Tell Halif", Retrieving the Past: Essays on Archaeological Research and Methodology in Honor of Gus W Van Beek, ed JD Seger, Eisenbrauns, (96): 25-34; auth, "Irrigation", "Granaries and Silos", and "Food Storage", Oxford Encycl of Near Eastern Archaeol, Oxford Univ Pr, (NY, 97); auth, Every Living Thing: the Daily use of Animals in Ancient Israel, AltaMira Pr, (Walnut Creek, CA), 97. **CONTACT ADDRESS** Dept Middle East Studies, Emory Univ, 1364 Clifton Rd NE, Atlanta, GA 30322-1061.

BORSTELMANN, THOMAS
PERSONAL Born 04/29/1958, Durham, NC, m, 1988, 2 children **DISCIPLINE** HISTORY **EDUCATION** Stanford Univ, BA, 80; Duke Univ, MA, 86, PhD, 90. **CAREER** Visiting asst prof, Duke Univ, 91; Asst Prof, 91-97, Assoc Prof, 97-, Cornell Univ. **HONORS AND AWARDS** Stuart Bernath Book Prize, Hist of Am Foreign Relations, 94; Robert & Helen Appel Fel, Cornell Univ, 98. **MEMBERSHIPS** Org of Am Historians; Am Hist Asn; Soc for Hist of Am Foreign Relations. **RESEARCH** Twentieth Century United States; U.S. foreign relations; the Cold War; race relations. **SELECTED PUBLICATIONS** Auth, Apartheid's Reluctant Uncle: The United States and Southern Africa in the Early Cold War, Oxford Univ Press, 93, reprint 01; auth, A World of Color: Race Relations and American Foreign Policy Since 1945, forthcoming. **CONTACT ADDRESS** Dept of Hist, Cornell Univ, 450 McGraw Hall, Ithaca, NY 14853-4601. **EMAIL** borstel@dreamscape.com

BORZA, EUGENE N.
PERSONAL Born 03/03/1935, Cleveland, OH **DISCIPLINE** ANCIENT HISTORY **EDUCATION** Baldwin-Wallace Col,

AB, 57; Univ Chicago, AM, 62, PhD (hist), 66. **CAREER** Asst prof, 64-71, assoc prof hist, 71-81, Prof to Prof Emer Ancient Hist, PA State Univ, University Park, 81-; mem managing comt, Am Sch Class Studies Athens, 75-; nat lectr, Archaeol Inst Am, 76-; hist consult, Nat Gallery Art. **HONORS AND AWARDS** Archaeol Inst Am Olivia James traveling fel, 70-71; Am Coun Learned Socs-Nat Endowment for Humanities travel grant, 73, 77; Am Philos Soc res grant, 79. **MEMBERSHIPS** AHA; Am Philol Asn; Archaeol Inst Am; Asn Ancient Historians. **RESEARCH** Alexander the Great; Macedonia; the classical tradition. **SELECTED PUBLICATIONS** Auth, The Tomb of Lyson and Kallikles--A Painted Macedonian Tomb, Am J Archaeol, Vol 0099, 95. **CONTACT ADDRESS** Dept of Hist, Pennsylvania State Univ, Univ Park, University Park, PA 16802. **EMAIL** enb1@psu.edu

BOSKIN, JOSEPH
PERSONAL Born 08/10/1929, Brooklyn, NY, s, 1955, 3 children **DISCIPLINE** AMERICAN HISTORY, SOCIAL CULTURAL HISTORY **EDUCATION** State Univ NYork, BS, 51; NYork Univ, MA, 52; Univ Minn, PhD, 59. **CAREER** Instr hist, State Univ Iowa, 59-60; assoc prof hist & Am studies, Univ Southern Calif, 60-69; co-dir, Urban Studies Prog, 77-81, prof hist, Boston Univ, 69-, Tozer Found res award, 59; Univ Southern Calif res grant, 61-63; consult, Gov Comn on Los Angeles riot, 65-66; US Comn Civil Rights, 71-72; vis prof, Univ Calif, San Diego, 67-68; NIMH study grant, 68-69; vis prof, Univ Calif, Los Angeles, 70-71; dir, Inst Law & Urban Studies, 70-71; Russell Sage Found fel, 76-77. **HONORS AND AWARDS** Outstanding Teacher Award, Univ Southern Calif, 62 & 67; Emmy Award for NBC TV ser, The Afro-American in American Culture, 68; Danforth Found Assocs Award, 81. **MEMBERSHIPS** AHA; Orgn Am Historians; Popular Cult Asn; Am Humor Asn. **RESEARCH** Recent social and cultural American history; Afro-American history; popular culture. **SELECTED PUBLICATIONS** Auth, Goodbye, Mr Bones, NY Times Mag, 5/1/66; ed & contribr, The Revolt of the Urban Ghettos, Annals Acad Polit & Soc Sci, 3/69; auth, Sambo: The National Jester in the Population Culture, In: The Great Fear, 70 & co-ed & contribr, Seasons of Rebellion, 71, Holt; auth, Aftermath of an Urban Crisis: Watts, In: Social Theory and Ethnic Conduct, Wiley, 72; ed & contribr, Urban Racial Violence in the Twentieth Century, Glencoe, 69 & 76; auth, Into Slavery: Racial Decisions in the Virginia Colony, Lippincott, 76; Humor and Society, Boston Pub Libr, 78; auth, Rebellious Laughter: People's Humor in American Culture, Syracuse Univ Press, 97; The Humor Prism in 20th Century America, Wayne State Univ Press, 97. **CONTACT ADDRESS** Dept of Hist, Boston Univ, 226 Bay State Rd, Boston, MA 02215-1403. **EMAIL** Jboskin@bu.edu

BOSWELL, JACKSON CAMPBELL
PERSONAL Born 10/02/1934, Whiteville, NC, m, 1969 **DISCIPLINE** ENGLISH LITERATURE, AMERICAN STUDIES **EDUCATION** Univ NC, Chapel Hill, AB, 60, MA, 62; George Wash Univ, MPhil, 73, PhD, 74. **CAREER** Instr English, Col William & Mary, 62-63; Randolph-Macon Woman's Col, 63-65; asst prof, DC Teachers Col, 68-77; Prof English, Univ DC, 77-. **HONORS AND AWARDS** NEH Fel, Folger Shakespeare Libr, 78-79; Fulbright Fel, Brit Libr, Univ London, 81-82. **MEMBERSHIPS** Milton Soc Am; Col Lang Asn; Southeastern Renaissance Conf. **RESEARCH** Renaissance reputations of Chaucer, Dante, Petrarch, Cervantes and others; Am thought and culture; North Atlantic civilization. **SELECTED PUBLICATIONS** Contr, MLA International Bibliography, PMLA, 69-77; auth, Milton's Library, Garland, 75; auth, Register of Paul's Cross Sermons, Dovehouse, 89; auth, Sir Thomas More in the English Renaissance, MRTS, 94; auth, Dante's Fame in England, Delaware/AUP, 99. **CONTACT ADDRESS** Dept of English, Univ of District of Columbia, 4200 Connecticut N W, Washington, DC 20008-1175. **EMAIL** jboswell@udc.edu

BOTHWELL, ROBERT S.
PERSONAL Born 08/17/1944, Ottawa, ON, Canada **DISCIPLINE** HISTORY **EDUCATION** Univ Toronto, BA, 66; Harvard Univ, AM, 67, PhD, 72. **CAREER** Tchg fel, Harvard Univ 68-70; lectr 70, asst prof 72, assoc prof 75, prof Hist, Univ Toronto, 81-; vis fel Woodrow Wilson Int Ctr Scholars 97-98. **HONORS AND AWARDS** Corey Prize, Can & Am Hist Asns 80 **RESEARCH** A specialist in post-1945 Canadian hist. **SELECTED PUBLICATIONS** Auth, The World of Lester Pearson 78; Eldorado: Canada's National Uranium Company 1984; A Short History of Ontario 86; Years of Victory 87; Nucleus 88; Loring Christie 88; Laying the Foundations 91; Canada & the United States 92; Canada & Quebec 95; coauth, CD Howe: A Biography 79; Canada Since 1945, 81, 2nd ed, 89; The Great Brain Robbery 84; Canada 1900-1945, 87; Pirouette, 90; The Petrified Campus, 97; co-ed Policy By Other Means, 72; The In-Between Time, 75. **CONTACT ADDRESS** Dept of History, Univ of Toronto, Toronto, ON, Canada M5S 3G3. **EMAIL** bothwell@chass.utoronto.ca

BOTJER, GEORGE
DISCIPLINE EUROPEAN HISTORY, ECONOMIC GEOGRAPHY AND THIRD WORLD HISTORY **EDUCATION** NYork Univ, BS, 59, MA, 61; FL State Univ, PhD, 73. **CAREER** Prof, Univ of Tampa . **SELECTED PUBLICATIONS** Auth, A Short History of Nationalist China 1919-1949, Putnam, 80; Sideshow War: A History of the Italian Campaign, 1943-45, Tex A&M UP, 96. **CONTACT ADDRESS** Dept of Hist, Univ of Tampa, 401 W. Kennedy Blvd, Tampa, FL 33606-1490.

BOTSTEIN, LEON
PERSONAL Born 12/14/1946, Zurich, Switzerland, m, 3 children **DISCIPLINE** HISTORY **EDUCATION** Univ Chicago, BA, 67; Harvard Univ, MA, 68, PhD, 85. **CAREER** Teaching Fel and Non-Resident Tutor, Harvard Univ, 68-69; Lectr, Boston Univ, 69; Special Asst to the Pres Bd Educ, City of New York, 69-70; Pres, Franconia Col, 70-75; Vis Fac, Manhattan Sch Music, 86; Vis Prof, Vienna, 88; Ed, The Musical Quart, 92-; Artistic Dir, Am Russ Young Artists Orchestra, 95-; Music Dir, Am Symphony Orchestra, 92-; Pres, Simon's Rock Col of Bard, 79-; Leon Levy Prof Arts & Humanities, Bard Col, 75-, Pres, 75-. **HONORS AND AWARDS** Howell Murray Alumni Awd, Univ Chicago, 67; Woodrow Wilson Fel, 67; Danforth Found Fel, 67; Sloan Found Urban Fel, 69; Annual Awd, Nat Conf Christians and Jews, 75; Rockefeller Fel, Aspen Inst Humanistic Studies, 78; Honorary Doctorate Humane Letters, Cedar Crest Col, 80; Professional Achievement Awd, Univ Chicago Alumni Asn, 84; Honorary Doctorate Humane Letters, Salisbury State Univ, 88; Fel, Am Acad Arts & Sci, 93-; Nat Arts Club Gold Medal, 95; Centennial Medal, Harvard Grad Sch Arts & Sci, 96; Honorary Doctorate Humane Letters, Western Conn State Univ, 97; Berlin Prize Fel, Am Acad in Berlin, 00. **MEMBERSHIPS** Mem brd, Ctr for Curatorial Stud, 00-; mem advis brd, Paul J. Tsang Fnd, 99-; mem advis brd, Music of Remembrance, 99-; mem brd of trustees, Sch for Strings, 99-; mem brd, Ball Fnd, 99-; mem brd, Natl Fnd for Jewish Culture, 96-; mem brd, Cntrl European Univ, 95-; mem brd of trustees, Interschool Orchs of NY, 94-; mem brd, Open Soc Inst, 93-; mem Natl Advis Comm, Yale-New Haven Teachers Inst, 84-; past chair, NY Coun for the Humanities, past chair, Harper's Mag Fnd; past chair, Assoc of Episco[al Colleges. **RESEARCH** Jewish Culture. **SELECTED PUBLICATIONS** Auth, Hearing is Seeing: Thoughts on the History of Music and the Imagination, The Musical Quart, 95; Music and Ideology: Thoughts on Bruckner, The Music Quart, 96; The Future of the Orchestra, The Music Quart, 96; Realism Transformed: Franz Schubert and Vienna, The Cambridge Companion to Schubert, Cambridge Univ Press, 97; The Demise of Philosophical Listening: Haydn in the 19th Century, Haydn and His World, Princeton Univ Press, 97; Brahms the performer, editor and collector, BBC Proms, BBC Radio 3 Publ, 97; Jefferson's Children: Education and the Promise of American Culture, Doubleday, 97; The Compleat Brahms, WW Norton & Co, 99; Music and Its Public: Habits of Listening and the Crisis of Musical Modernism in Vienna, 1870-1914, Univ Chicago Press (forthcoming); author of numerous other articles and chapters; conductor on many classical recordings. **CONTACT ADDRESS** Bard Col, Annandale, NY 12504. **EMAIL** president@bard.edu

BOTTIGHEIMER, KARL S.
PERSONAL Born 03/19/1937, Louisville, KY, m, 1960, 2 children **DISCIPLINE** HISTORY **EDUCATION** Harvard Coll, AB, 58; Univ Wisconsin, MA, 59; Univ Oxford, 59-60; Univ Cal, Berkeley, PhD, 65. **CAREER** Act instr, Univ Cal, Berkeley, 63-64; instr, SUNY, Stony Brook, 64-65; asst prof, 65-71; assoc prof, 71-94; prof, 94-. **HONORS AND AWARDS** Woodrow Wilson Fel, 62-63; SUNY Res Found Fel, 65, 66, 68; NEH Fel, 69; Guggenheim Fel, 73-74; Vis Fel, Princeton Univ, 82-83; NEH Fel, 84. **MEMBERSHIPS** RHS; Am Con Irish Stud. **RESEARCH** Early modern Ireland. **SELECTED PUBLICATIONS** Auth, "The Restoration Land Settlement in Ireland: A Structural View," J British Studies (72); auth, "The Reformation in Ireland Revisited," J British Studies (76); auth, "Kingdom and Colony: Ireland in the Westward Enterprise, 1536-1660" in The Westward Enterprise: English Activity in Ireland the Atlantic, and America, 1500-1650, ed. PEH Hair (Univ of Liverpool Press, 78); auth, "Why the Reformation Failed in Ireland," J of Ecclesiastical History (85); auth, "The New-New History of Ireland," J of British Studies (88); auth, "The Glorious Revolution and Ireland" in The Revolution of 1688-1689: Changing Perspectives, ed. Lois G Schwoerer (Cambridge Univ Press, 92); auth, "Nackte Wahrheit Kontra Brauchbare Vergangenheit: Die Irische 'Historikerdebatte," (Innsbrucker Historische Studien, 94); auth, "The Hagiography of William Bedell", in A Miracle of Learning: Irish Manuscripts, Their Owners and Their Uses, ed. TC Barnard, Scolar Press (Aldershot, England, 98); coauth, "The Irish Reformation in European Perspective," The Archive for Reformation History, 89 (98) 268-309; auth, "Revisionism and the Irish reformation," J of ecclesiastical History (00) vol 51, no 2. **CONTACT ADDRESS** Dept History, SUNY, Stony Brook, 100 Nicholls Rd, Stony Brook, NY 11794-0001.

BOTZENHART-VIEHE, VERENA
PERSONAL Born 11/08/1952, Germany, 2 children **DISCIPLINE** EUROPEAN HISTORY, AMERICAN DIPLOMATIC HISTORY **EDUCATION** Univ Tulsa, BA, 74; Univ Calif, Santa Barbara, MA, 75, PhD, 80. **CAREER** 1977-78 Pres, Hist Grad Stud Assn, Univ Calif, 77-78; tchg asst, Univ Calif, 75-78; adjunct prof, Youngstown State Univ, 86-90; assist prof, 90; fac consult, Princeton, 94-; assoc prof, 96-. **HONORS AND AWARDS** Sullins award, Univ Tulsa, 74; grant, Sem Fur Politische Bildung in Munich, 88-93; Silver memorial scholar, 89. **MEMBERSHIPS** Mem, President's Admissions Task Force. **RESEARCH** Cold War, German American Relations. **SELECTED PUBLICATIONS** Auth, George Bancroft, Notable U.S. Ambassadors 1775-1995: A Biographical Dictionary, Greenwood Press, 96. Andrew White, Notable U.S. Ambassadors 1775-1995: A Biographical Dictionary, Greenwood Press, 96; rev(s), Origins of a Spontaneous Revolution: East Germany, 1989, by Karl Dieter Opp, Peter Voss, and Christiane Gern, History, Rev of New Bk(s), 96; The End of an Era? Europe 1945-1990s, by Antonio Varsori, Hist Rev of New Bk(s), 96; The Cold War- A History, by Martin Walker, Hist Rev of New Bk(s), 95; James B. Conant: Harvard to Hiroshima and the Making of the Nuclear Age, by James G. Hershberg, The Historian, 94; Chester Bowles: New Dealer in the Cold War, by Howard B Schaffer, Hist Rev(s) of New Bk(s), 94. **CONTACT ADDRESS** Rel, Hist, Philos, Classics Dept, Westminster Col, Pennsylvania, New Wilmington, PA 16172-0001. **EMAIL** verenabv@westminster.edu

BOUCHARD, CONSTANCE BRITTAIN
PERSONAL Born 05/17/1948, Syracuse, NY, m, 1970 **DISCIPLINE** MEDIEVAL HISTORY **EDUCATION** Middlebury Col, AB, 70; Univ Chicago, AM, 73, PhD 76. **CAREER** Prof hist, Univ Akron, 90- . **HONORS AND AWARDS** NEH Fellow, 82; John Simon Guggenheim Mem Fellow, 95. **MEMBERSHIPS** Medieval Acad Am; Am Hist Assoc; Ohio Acad Hist; Soc French Hist; Catholic Hist Asn. **RESEARCH** Medieval history, especially relations between nobility and the church. **SELECTED PUBLICATIONS** Auth, The Cartulary of St-Marcel-les-Chalon Medieval Academy, 98; Strong of Body, Brave and Noble: Chivalry and Society in Medieval France, Cornell Univ Press, 98; The Cartulary of Flavigny, Medieval Acad, 91; Holy Entrepreneurs: Cistercians, Knights, and Economic Exchange in Twelfth-Century Burgundy, Cornell Univ Press, 91; Life and Society in the West: Antiquity and the Middle Ages, HBJ, 88; Sword, Miter, and Cloister: Nobility and the Church in Burgundy, 980-1198, Cornell Univ Press, 87; auth, Spirituality and Administration: The Role of the Bishop in Twelf-Century Auxerre Medieval Academy, 78. **CONTACT ADDRESS** Univ of Akron, Dept of History, Akron, OH 44325-1902. **EMAIL** CBouchard@UAkron.edu

BOUCHER, PHILIP P.
PERSONAL Born 07/22/1944, Hartford, CT, m, 1989, 3 children **DISCIPLINE** HISTORY **EDUCATION** Univ of Hartford, BA, 66; Univ of Connt, MA, 67; PhD, 73. **CAREER** Instructor, Univ of North Carolina, 73-74; Asst Prof, Univ of Alabama, 74-81; Assoc Prof, Univ of Alabama, 81-89; Prof, Univ of Alabama, 89-96; Distinguished Prof History, Univ of Alabama, 96-. **HONORS AND AWARDS** Univ of Alabama in Huntsville Research Awd, 92; Named Distinguished Prof of History, 96. **MEMBERSHIPS** Amer Historical Assoc; French Colonial Historical Society; Assoc of Caribbean Historians. **RESEARCH** French Colonial History; French Caribbean; The Atlantic World. **SELECTED PUBLICATIONS** Auth, "Les Nouvelles Frances: France and America," (Providence, RI), 89; auth, "Cannibal Encounters: Europeans and Island Caribs, 1492-1763," Johns Hopkins Univ Press, 92. **CONTACT ADDRESS** Dept History, Univ of Alabama, Huntsville, 301 Sparkman Dr Northwest, Huntsville, AL 35805-1911. **EMAIL** boucherp@email.uah.edu

BOUDREAU, JOSEPH A.
PERSONAL Born 12/23/1934, San Francisco, CA, m, 1961, 3 children **DISCIPLINE** CANADIAN HISTORY **EDUCATION** Univ Calif, Los Angeles, BA, 56, MA, 58, PhD(Hist), 65. **CAREER** Lectr hist, Univ BC, 61-62; asst prof, Univ Alta, Calgary, 62-66; from asst prof to assoc prof, 66-75, Prof Hist, San Jose State Univ, 75-, Faculty Early Retirement Prog, 98-03; Nat Endowment for Humanities fel, Yale, 81; Can govt enrichment grant, 82-83. **HONORS AND AWARDS** Mem & chair, Corey Prize Comt, Am Hist Asn, 95-00. **MEMBERSHIPS** Am Hist Asn; Can Hist Asn; Asn Can Studies in US **RESEARCH** Canadian history. **SELECTED PUBLICATIONS** Auth, Western Canada's enemy aliens in World War I, Alta Hist Rev, winter, 64; Alberta, In: Canadian Annual Review for 1963, 64, 65 & 66, Univ Toronto, 64-67; Interning Canada's enemy aliens, Canadian Hist Mag, 9/74; Alberta, Aberhart and Social Credit, Holt, 75; The medium and the message of Wm Aberhart, Am Rev Can Studies, spring 78; Social credit Reconsidered, in: The Man on the Spot, 95. **CONTACT ADDRESS** Dept of Hist, San Jose State Univ, 1 Washington Sq, San Jose, CA 95192-0001. **EMAIL** jboudrea@pacbell.net

BOURDON, ROGER J.
PERSONAL Born 05/08/1937, St. Paul, MN, m, 1967, 3 children **DISCIPLINE** UNITED STATES HISTORY **EDUCATION** Loyola Univ, Calif, BS, 59; Univ Calif, Los Angeles, MA, 61, PhD(US Hist), 65. **CAREER** Asst prof US Hist, Wichita State Univ, 56-67 & Marquette Univ, 67-68; from asst prof to assoc prof, 68-75, prof US Hist, Mary Washington Col, Univ VA, 75-, bicentennial lect ser Campus & Community, 75; chmn fac Welfare Comt, Mary Washington Col, 76-77; emeritus, 00. **HONORS AND AWARDS** Simpson Award for Excellence in Teaching, 89. **MEMBERSHIPS** Inst Early Am Hist & Cult AHA; Western Hist Asn; Orgn Am Hist. **RESEARCH** Westward expansion; colonial United States history. **CON-**

TACT ADDRESS Dept of History, Mary Washington Col, 1301 College Ave, Fredericksburg, VA 22401-5300. **EMAIL** rbourdon@mwc.edu

BOURGUIGNON, HENRY J.
PERSONAL Born 08/19/1931, Lakewood, OH, m, 1971, 2 children **DISCIPLINE** LEGAL HISTORY; LAW **EDUCATION** Loyola Univ Chicago, AB, 54, MA, 58; Univ Mich, PhD(legal hist), 68, JD, 71. **CAREER** Trial atty, Dept Justice, 71-74; from Assoc Prof to Distinguished Univ Prof Law, Col Law, Univ Toledo, 74-. **HONORS AND AWARDS** Am Coun Learned Soc fel, England, 80-81. **MEMBERSHIPS** Am Soc Legal Hist (secy, 78-83). **RESEARCH** History of international law; constitutional law. **SELECTED PUBLICATIONS** Auth, The First Federal Court: The Federal Appellate Prize Court of the American Revolution, 1775-1787, Am Philos Soc, 77; Incorporation of the law of Nations during the American Revolution -- the case of the San Antonio, Am J of Int Law 71, 77; The Second Justice Harlan - His Principles of Judicial Decision Making, Supreme Ct Rev, 79; A Revisionist Revises Himself - A Review Essay, Tex Law Rev 64, 85; The Articles of Confederation, In: Encyclopedia of the American Judicial System, Charles Scribner's Sons, 87; Sir William Scott, Lord Stowell, Judge of the High Court of Admiralty, 1798-1828, Cambridge Univ Press, 87; The Belilos Case - New Light on Reservations to Multilateral Treaties, Va J of Int Law 29, 89; coauth, Coming to Terms with Death -- The Cruzan Case, Hast L.J. 42, 91; auth, Human Rights Decisions by the United Supreme Court - October Term 1990, Human Rights L.J. 13, 92; Human Rights Decisions by the United Supreme Court - October Term 1991, Human Rights L.J. 13, 92; The United States Supreme Court and Freedom of Expression - October Term 92, Human Rights L.J. 15, 94; Persons with Mental Retardation - The Reality Behind the Label, Cambridge Quart of Healthcare Ethics 3, 94; The Federal Key to the Judiciary Act of 1789, SC Law Rev 46, 95. **CONTACT ADDRESS** Col of Law, Univ of Toledo, 2801 W Bancroft St, Toledo, OH 43606-3391.

BOUWSMA, WILLIAM JAMES
PERSONAL Born 11/22/1923, Ann Arbor, MI, m, 1944, 4 children **DISCIPLINE** HISTORY **EDUCATION** Harvard Univ, AB, 43, AM, 47, PhD, 50. **CAREER** From instr to assoc prof hist, Univ Ill, 50-57; from assoc prof to prof, Univ Calif, Berkeley, 57-69, chmn dept, 66-67, vchancellor acad affairs, 67-69; prof hist, Harvard Univ, 69-71; Sather Prof Hist, Univ Calif, Berkeley, 71-, Chmn Dept, 81-, Guggenheim fel and Fulbright res fel, Italy, 59-60; fel, Ctr advan Studies Behav Sci, 63-64; Nat Humanities Inst, New Haven, fel, 76-77. **MEMBERSHIPS** AHA (pres, 78); Am Soc Reformation Res (pres, 63); Renaissance Soc Am; fel Am Acad Arts and Sci; fel Am Philos Soc. **CONTACT ADDRESS** Dept of Hist, Univ of California, Berkeley, Berkeley, CA 94720.

BOWDEN, HENRY WARNER
PERSONAL Born 04/01/1939, Memphis, TN, m, 1997, 2 children **DISCIPLINE** HISTORY, RELIGION **EDUCATION** Baylor Univ, AB, 61; Princeton Univ, AM, 64, PhD (relig), 66. **CAREER** From instr to asst prof, 64-71, asst dean col, 69-71, assoc prof, 71-79, Prof Relig, Douglass Col, Rutgers Univ, 79-. **MEMBERSHIPS** Am Soc Church Hist; American Catholic Hist Assn. **RESEARCH** Historiographical studies, chiefly in the United States; religion of American Indians and missionary activities by Europeans. **SELECTED PUBLICATIONS** Ed, Religion in America, Harper, 70; auth, Church History in the Age of Science, Univ NC, 71; Dict of American Religious Biography, 77 & 93 & ed, John Eliot's Indian Dialogues, 80, Greenwood; auth, American Indians and Christian missions, Chicago, 81; auth, Church History in an Age of Uncertainty, Carbondale, 89; auth, Native and Christian--Indigenous Voices on Religious Identity in the United States and Canada, Am Indian Cult Res J, Vol 0021, 97; Historians of the Christian Tradition--Their Methodology and Influence on Western Thought, Church Hist, Vol 0066, 97; Missionary Conquest--The Gospel and Native American Cultural Genocide, Church Hist, Vol 0064, 95; Historians of the Christian Tradition--Their Methodology and Influence on Western Thought, Church Hist, Vol 0066, 97 Choctaws and Missionaries in Mississippi, 1818-1918, Am Hist Rev, Vol 0102, 97; Converting the West--A Biography of Whitman, Narcissa, Pac Hist Rev, Vol 0061, 92. **CONTACT ADDRESS** Dept of Relig Douglass Col, Rutgers, The State Univ of New Jersey, New Brunswick, P O Box 270, New Brunswick, NJ 08903-0270.

BOWDEN, JAMES HENRY
PERSONAL Born 10/28/1934, Louisville, KY, d, 3 children **DISCIPLINE** AMERICAN STUDIES, RELIGION **EDUCATION** Univ Louisville, MA, 59; Univ MN, Minneapolis, PhD, 70; Louisville Presbyterian Theol Sem, MA, 87. **CAREER** Instr Eng, Univ KY, 60-61, Univ MT, 62-64 & Colgate Univ, 65-66; from Instr to Assoc Prof, 66-80, Prof English, 80-98, Prof Emeritus, Ind Univ SE, 98-, Chmn Hum Div, 80-85; Assoc Dir, Am Studies Ctr, Warsaw, 85-86; Prof, Institut Teknologi Mari, Malaysia, 89-91. **HONORS AND AWARDS** Nat Endowment for the Humanities summer fel, Univ MI, 77; fel, Bread Loaf Writers Conf, 80. **RESEARCH** Relig in Am life; imaginative writing; theories of humor. **SELECTED PUBLICATIONS** Auth, The bland leading the bland, New Oxford Rev, 77; Go purple, West Branch, 77; The grief of Terry Magoo, Great River Rev, 77; The Bible and other Novels, Cresset, 78; Don't Lose This, It's My Only Copy, Col English, 79; ICU, Thornleigh Rev, 82; Conwell Lives, New Oxford Rev, 82; Peter DeVries, A Critical Study, G K Hall, 83. **CONTACT ADDRESS** Dept of Hum, Indiana Univ, Southeast, 4201 Grant Line Rd, New Albany, IN 47150-2158. **EMAIL** jhbowden@iusmail.ius.indiana.edu

BOWEN, LYNNE E.
PERSONAL Born 08/22/1940, Indian Head, SK, Canada **DISCIPLINE** HISTORY **EDUCATION** Univ Alta, BS, RN, 63; Univ Victoria, MA, 80. **CAREER** Victorian Order Nurses, 63-64; vis guest lectr, various univ, 80-; Maclean Hunter Lectr, Univ BC, 92-. **HONORS AND AWARDS** Eaton's BC Bk Awd, 83; Can Hist Asn Reg Cert Merit, 83, 92; BC Lt-Gov Awd Writing Hist, 87; Hubert Evans Non-fiction Prize, BC Bk Awds, 92. **MEMBERSHIPS** Writer's Union Can; BC Fedn Writers; Nanaimo Harbourfront Ctr Soc; Nanaimo Hist Soc; Int PEN. **SELECTED PUBLICATIONS** Auth, Boss Whistle: The Coal Miners of Vancouver Island Remember, 82; auth, Three Dollar Dreams, 87; auth, The Dunsmuirs of Nanaimo, 89; auth, Muddling Through: The Remarkable Story of the Barr Colonists, 92; auth, Those Lake People, 95. **CONTACT ADDRESS** 4982 Fillinger Cr., Nanaimo, BC, Canada V9V 1J1.

BOWERS, RICHARD HUGH
PERSONAL Born 07/30/1937, Onawa, IA, m, 1960, 2 children **DISCIPLINE** MEDIEVAL HISTORY **EDUCATION** Miss State Univ, BA, 59, MA, 60 PhD(hist), 65. **CAREER** Asst prof hist, Univ Southwestern La, 65-66; assoc prof, 66-76, Honors Prof Hist, Univ Southern Miss, 76-, Assoc Dir Hons Col, 57-. **MEMBERSHIPS** Mediaeval Acad Am; AHA; Selden Soc. **RESEARCH** Economic history of Medieval England; development of the royal household in England. **SELECTED PUBLICATIONS** Auth, Italian merchants in England, 1216-1272, 1/68, The baronial movement (1258-1267): Reform or reaction, 7/68 & The first English wool embargo, 1270-1274, 10/72, Southern Quart. **CONTACT ADDRESS** Southern Station, Box 135, Hattiesburg, MS 39401.

BOWERS, WILLIAM LAVALLE
PERSONAL Born 06/09/1930, Mason City, IA, m, 1954, 4 children **DISCIPLINE** HISTORY **EDUCATION** Univ Northern Iowa, BA, 55, MA, 58; Univ Iowa, PhD, 68. **CAREER** From instr to assoc prof, 62-76, Prof Hist, Bradley Univ, 76-00, Emeritus Prof Hist, 00-. **MEMBERSHIPS** AAUP; AHA; Orgn Am Hist. **RESEARCH** American social history; agricultural history. **CONTACT ADDRESS** Bradley Univ, 1314 Schneblin Ct, Peoria, IL 61604. **EMAIL** wlb@hilltop.bradley.edu

BOWLES, SUZANNE
PERSONAL Born 11/12/1950, Somerville, NJ, m, 1994 **DISCIPLINE** HISTORY **EDUCATION** Syracuse Univ, BA, 71; Rutgers Univ, MA, 72; Drew Univ, MTS, 79; Syracuse Univ, PhD, 76. **CAREER** Lect, Drew Univ, 77-79; Adjunct Prof, Upsala Col, 79-95; Adjunct Prof, William Paterson Univ, 95-99; Asst Prof, William Paterson Univ, 99-. **HONORS AND AWARDS** Who's Who in the East, 79; Who's Who in Am Relig, 92; Who's Who in Am, 00. **MEMBERSHIPS** Am Hist Assoc, Orgn of Am Hist, Am Soc of Church Hist, Hist Soc of the Episcopal Church, Soc for Military Hist. **RESEARCH** American religious history. **SELECTED PUBLICATIONS** Auth, "'A Piece of Epic Action': The Trial of Aaron Burr," Courier, 12 (75): 3-22; auth, "Aaron Burr, Jr -- 'Darling of the Presbyterians'," J of Presbyterian Hist, 56 (78): 134-147; auth, Jonathan Edwards to Aaron Burr, Jr: From the Great Awakening to Democratic Politics, Edwin Mellen Pr, 81; auth, "Reflections on a Royal Wedding," Hist Mag of the Protestant Episcopal Church, 50 (81): 171-175; auth, "A Step on the Swedish Lutheran Road to Anglicanism," Hist Mag of the Protestant Episcopal Church, 54 (85): 39-49; auth, History of Grace Church 1854-1984, Grace Episcopal Church (Madison, NJ), 87; auth, Lutheranism and Anglicanism in Colonial New Jersey: An Early Ecumenical Experiment in New Sweden, Edwin Mellen Pr, 88; auth, "'Mystery Years' 1780-1792 -- Explored in Academy History," Newark Acad Alumnus, 21 (89): 13-15; auth, "The Young Man Who Never Went to School: John Croes," Anglican and Episcopal Hist, 60 (91): 43-56; auth, "Church, State and Arbitration: Admiral Mahan Speaks Out," Naval Hist (forthcoming). **CONTACT ADDRESS** Dept Hist, William Paterson Col of New Jersey, 300 Pompton Rd, Wayne, NJ 07470-2103. **EMAIL** bowless@wpunj.edu

BOWLING, KENNETH R.
PERSONAL Born 09/12/1940, Baltimore, MD, 1 child **DISCIPLINE** EARLY AMERICAN HISTORY **EDUCATION** Dickinson Col, BA, 62; Univ Wis-Madison, MA, 64, PhD(hist), 68. **CAREER** Proj assoc hist, 67-70, Nat Endowment for Humanities bicentennial fel, 70-71, asst prof hist, Inst Environ Studies, Univ Wis-Madison, 71-74; Mem Staff, First Fed Cong Proj, George Washington Univ, 75-, Am Philos Soc res grant, 77. **HONORS AND AWARDS** Charles Thomson Prize, Nat Archives, 76. **RESEARCH** Late 18th century American politics; American reactions to the environment; cultural ecology. **CONTACT ADDRESS** The George Washington Univ, Washington, DC 53703. **EMAIL** kbowling@gwu.edu

BOWLUS, BRUCE
PERSONAL Born 12/20/1946, Sandusky, OH, m, 1989, 2 children **DISCIPLINE** HISTORY **EDUCATION** Bowling Green State Univ, PhD, 92. **CAREER** Asst Prof to Assoc Prof, Tiffin Univ, 93-. **MEMBERSHIPS** Hist Soc. **RESEARCH** 19th Century Am (Gilded Age/Great Lakes); Early 20th Century European-Military. **CONTACT ADDRESS** Dept Arts & Sci, Tiffin Univ, 155 Miami St, Tiffin, OH 44883-2109. **EMAIL** bbowlus@tiffin.edu

BOWMAN, JEFFREY A.
DISCIPLINE HISTORY **EDUCATION** Carleton Col, BA, 88; Yale Univ, MA, 92; Mphil, 94; PhD, 97. **CAREER** Asst prof, Kenyon Coll, 97-; Fel, Yale Univ, 90-94; tchg asst, Yale Univ, 93-94; instr, Yale Summer Lang Inst, 94-96; fel, John F. Enders, 95; instr, Yale Univ, 95; Whiting Found Diss fel, 95-96; Bourses Chateaubriand, 95-96; Yale Univ Diss Fel, 96-97; asst prof, Kenyon Col, 97-. **HONORS AND AWARDS** Sterling Prize for Outstanding Entering Grad Students, Yale Univ, 90-92; res grant, Prog for Cult Coop, 93; res grant, Am Hist Assoc Bernadotte E. Schmitt, 93. **RESEARCH** European history. **SELECTED PUBLICATIONS** Auth, Do Neo-Romans Curse? Land, Law, and Ritual in the Midi (900-1100), Viator 28, 97; Sicilian Identity and the Middle Ages (1000-1300), Sicilia Bella: The Other Side of Italy, proceedings of a symposium at the Museo ItaloAmericano, 96. **CONTACT ADDRESS** Dept of Hist, Kenyon Col, Gambier, OH 43022. **EMAIL** bowmanj@kenyon.edu

BOWMAN, JOYE L.
DISCIPLINE HISTORY **EDUCATION** UCLA, PhD, 80. **CAREER** Prof, Univ MA Amherst. **RESEARCH** Hist of Portuguese Africa. **SELECTED PUBLICATIONS** Auth, Ominous Transition: Commerce and Colonial Expansion in the Senegambia and Guinea 1857-1919, 97; publ(s) on Guinea-Bissau; African Affairs. **CONTACT ADDRESS** Dept of Hist, Univ of Massachusetts, Amherst, Mass Ave, Amherst, MA 01003.

BOWMAN, L. M.
DISCIPLINE GREEK STUDIES **EDUCATION** Univ Toronto, BA, 81; Univ Brit Col, MA, 86; UCLA, PhD, 94. **CAREER** Asst prof, Univ of Victoria, 92. **RESEARCH** Greek tragedy and religion, Women in antiquity, Hellenistic literature. **SELECTED PUBLICATIONS** Auth, Interview with David Halperin, Favonius 3, 91; Klytaimnestra's Dream: Prophecy in Sophokles' Elektra, Phoenix 51, 97. **CONTACT ADDRESS** Dept of Greek and Roman Studies, Univ of Victoria, PO Box 1700 STN CSC, Victoria, BC, Canada V8W 2Y2. **EMAIL** lbowman@uvic.ca

BOWMAN, SHEARER DAVIS
PERSONAL Born Richmond, VA, m, 1972, 2 children **DISCIPLINE** HISTORY **EDUCATION** Univ Virginia, BA, 71; MA, 76, PhD, 86, Univ California-Berkeley. **CAREER** Asst Prof, Hampden-Sydney Col, VA, 84-86; Asst Prof, 86-93, Assoc Prof, 93-, Univ Texas-Austin **MEMBERSHIPS** AHA, OAH. **RESEARCH** 19th Century. **CONTACT ADDRESS** Dept of History, Univ of Texas, Austin, Austin, TX 78712-1163. **EMAIL** s.bowman@mail.utexas.edu

BOWMAN, STEVEN
PERSONAL Born 08/30/1942, Boston, MA, 3 children **DISCIPLINE** HISTORY **EDUCATION** Univ Mass, BA, 64; Ohio State Univ, PhD, 74. **CAREER** Ind Univ, 74-76; Asst prof to prof, Univ of Cincinnati, 80-. **HONORS AND AWARDS** Koerner Fel; Mem Found for Jewish Culture Fel; Fulbright; NEH; Gennadeion, Taft. **MEMBERSHIPS** Assoc for Jewish Studies; US Nat Comm for Byzantine Studies. **RESEARCH** Bible, Greek and Jewish History - all periods, Middle East, Holocaust. **SELECTED PUBLICATIONS** Auth, Jews in Byzantium, 1204-1453, 85; ed, Birkenan, Camp of Death, ed, In lure veritas, 91; auth, "Yosippon and Jewish Nationalism", Proceedings of the am Acad for Jewish Res, 95. **CONTACT ADDRESS** Dept Judaic Studies, Univ of Cincinnati, PO Box 210169, Cincinnati, OH 45221-0169. **EMAIL** steven.bowman@uc.edu

BOWSKY, WILLIAM MARVIN
PERSONAL Born 04/16/1930, New York, NY, m, 1986, 2 children **DISCIPLINE** MEDIEVAL HISTORY **EDUCATION** NYork Univ, BA, 52; Princeton Univ, MA, 53, PhD, 57. **CAREER** Instr hist, Princeton Univ, 56-57 & Univ Ore, 57-58; from asst prof to prof, Univ Nebr, 58-67; Prof Hist, Univ Calif, Davis, 67-94, prof emer, 94-; Asst, Inst Advan Studies, 56-57. **HONORS AND AWARDS** Fulbright Fel, 54-55, 55-56; Guggenheim Fel, 63-64, 87-88; fel, Medieval Acad of Am; fel, Deputazione di Storia Patria per la Toscana; fel, Accademia Senese di Storia Patria; sr fel, Nat Endowment for the Humanities; pres, Soc for Ital Hist Studies, 78-79; distinguished sr scholar, Soc for Ital Hist Studies, 94. **MEMBERSHIPS** AHA; fel Mediaeval Acad Am; Renaissance Soc Am; Medieval Asn Pac; Soc Ital Hist Studies. **RESEARCH** Italian history; institutional history; urban history; Italian Church. **SELECTED PUBLICATIONS** Auth, Henry VII in Italy: The Conflict of Empire and City-State, 1310-1313, Univ of Nebr Press, 60; auth, The Black Death: A Turning Point in History?, Holt, 70;

auth, The Finance of the Commune of Siena, 1287-1355, Oxford Univ Press, 70; auth, A Medieval Italian Commune: Siena under the Nine, 1287-1355, Univ of Calif Press, 80; auth, Piety and Property in Medieval Florence: A House in San Lorenzo, Giuffre, 90; auth, La Chiesa di San Lorenzo a Firenze nel Medioevo, Florence, 99. **CONTACT ADDRESS** Dept of Hist, Univ of California, Davis, Davis, CA 95616. **EMAIL** wmbowsky@ucdavis.edu

BOYAJIAN, JAMES CHARLES

PERSONAL Born 10/26/1949, Fresno, CA **DISCIPLINE** MODERN EUROPEAN AND LATIN AMERICAN HISTORY **EDUCATION** Univ Calif, Santa Barbara, BA, 71; Univ Calif, Berkeley, MA, 72, PhD(hist), 78. **CAREER** Lecter urban hist, Univ Calif, Berkeley, 79; res fel hist, Fundacao Calouste Gulbenkian, Lisbon, 79-80; Res & Writing, 81- **MEMBERSHIPS** AHA; Soc Span & Portuguese Hist Studies; Conf Group Mod Portugal. **RESEARCH** Iberian social and economic history; Iberian overseas expansion and trade; Iberian Inquisitions. **SELECTED PUBLICATIONS** Auth, The new Christians reconsidered: Evidence from Lisbon's Portuguese bankers, Studia Rosenthaliana, 79; Portuguese Bankers at the Court of Spain, 1626-1650, Rutgers Univ Press, 82. **CONTACT ADDRESS** 7349 S Cherry Ave, Fresno, CA 93725.

BOYD, CARL

PERSONAL Born 03/27/1936, Philadelphia, PA **DISCIPLINE** MILITARY HISTORY **EDUCATION** Ind Univ, Bloomington, AB, 62, AM, 63; Univ Calif, Davis, PhD, 71. **CAREER** Instr hist, Henderson St Col, 63-64; instr, asst prof, 69-75, Ohio St Univ; asst prof, assoc prof, prof, 75-85, eminent scholar, 94-, Louis I Jaffe Prof, Col of Arts & Letters, 95-, Old Dominion Univ; vis scholar, 87-89, US Army Ctr Mil Hist; vis, 93, Inst Advan Stud, Princeton; vis prof, 95, 96, Kitakyushu Univ, Japan; Scholar in res, 96-97, Natl Sec Agency. **HONORS AND AWARDS** Amer Philos Soc res grant, 90; Huntington Fel, Mariners' Museum, 96; Charles O & Elisabeth C Burgess Fac Res & Creativity Awd, 98; Fulbright Awd to Poland, 99-00. **MEMBERSHIPS** AHA; Int Naval Res Orgn; Amer Comt Hist Second World War; US Naval Inst; Amer Mil Inst. **RESEARCH** War studies; naval history; code breaking; modern German and Japanese military strategy and policy. **SELECTED PUBLICATIONS** Auth, " American Naval Intelligence of Japanese Submarine Operations Early in the Pacific War," Journal of Military History 53, no 2, (89): 169-189; auth, "Anguish under Siege: High-Grade Japanese Signal Intelligence and the Fall of Berlin," Cryptologia: A Quarterly Journal of Cryptology 13. No 3, (89): 193-209; auth, " Significance of MAGIC and the Japanese Ambassador to Berlin: (V) News of Hitler's Defense Preparations for Allied Invasion of Western Europe," Intelligence and National Security 4, (89): 461-481; auth, " Introductory Essay" to Top Secret Studies on U S Communications Intelligence during World War II, 3pts, Bethesda, MD, Univ Publications of America, (99): v-ix; auth, " Japanese Diplomacy in Berlin during Hitler's Preparations for War, January-August 1939." World War II: A Fifty Year Perspective on 1939, Albany, NY, Siena, College Research Institute Press, (92): 59-79; auth, " Cryptologic Intelligence in the interwar Years, 1919-1939," Innovation in the Interwar Period, Washington, DC, The Pentagon, (94): 493-552; auth, "Arlington Hall and Tokyo's Links with Berlin and Moscow, 1944-1945," 1945: Consequences an Sequels of the Second World War, Paris: Institut d historie du Temps Present, (95): 81-91; auth, "Anglo-America-Japanese Cryptologic Preparations for the Second World War," The Enigma Bulletin, (97): 17-52; auth, " The Role of Cryptologic Intelligence in the Pacific War, 1941-1943," The Enigma Bulletin, (98): 5-33; auth, " U S Navy Intelligence and the Sinking of the Japanese Submarine I-52 in 1944," Journal of Military History 63, no 2, (99): 339-354. **CONTACT ADDRESS** Dept of History, Old Dominion Univ, Norfolk, VA 23529-0091. **EMAIL** CBOYD31480@aol.com

BOYD, CAROLYN PATRICIA

PERSONAL Born 06/01/1944, San Diego, CA, m, 1975, 1 child **DISCIPLINE** SPANISH HISTORY **EDUCATION** Stanford Univ, AB, 66; Univ Wash, MA, 69, PhD, 74. **CAREER** Instr, 73-74, asst prof, 74-79, assoc prof, 79-95, prof hist, Univ TX, Austin, 95, ch, 94-, Am Coun Learned Soc grant hist, 77-78, 85; Am Philos Soc grant hist, 78-79. **HONORS AND AWARDS** Phi Beta Kappa, Phi Alpha Theta. **MEMBERSHIPS** Soc Span & Port Hist Studies; AHA; Coun for Europ Studies. **RESEARCH** Mod Span hist, polit and cult; civil-mil rel; hist of educ; nationalism. **SELECTED PUBLICATIONS** Auth, The Anarchists and Education in Spain, 1868-1909, J Mod Hist, 76; Praetorian Politics in Liberal Spain, Univ NC, 79; Responsibilities and the Second Spanish Republic, European Hist Quart, 84; Las reformas militares, Historia general de Espana y America, vol 17, 86; La politica pretoriana en el reinado de Alfonso XIII, Alianza Editorial, 90; Historia Patria: Politics, History and National Identity in Spain, 1875-1975, Princeton, 97. **CONTACT ADDRESS** Dept of Hist, Univ of California, Irvine, Irvine, CA 92697. **EMAIL** cpboyd@uci.edu

BOYER, JOHN WILLIAM

PERSONAL Born 10/17/1946, Chicago, IL, m, 1968, 3 children **DISCIPLINE** EUROPEAN HISTORY **EDUCATION** Loyola Univ, Chicago, BA, 68; Univ Chicago, MA, 69, PhD, 75. **CAREER** Lectr western civilization, 73-74, from Instr Europ Hist to Prof Modern Hist, 74-95, Martin A. Ryerson Distinguished Service Professor of History, Univ Chicago, 95-, Dean of the Col, 92-; Assoc Ed, 78-80, Co-ed, J Mod Hist, 80-; Christensen Vis Fel, St Catherine's Col, Oxford Univ, 83. **HONORS AND AWARDS** Foreign Area Fel, Am Coun Learned Soc & Soc Res Coun, 70-72; Grant-in-Aid, Am Coun Learned Soc, 76, 82; Spencer Found Res Awds, 77, 80, 82; Theodor Korner Prize, 78; Alexander von Humboldt fel, 80-81; John Gilmary Shea Prize, Am Cath Hist Asn, for: Political Radicalism in Late Imperial Vienna, 82; NEH Sr Res Fel, 83-84; Res Grant, Lilly Found, 88; Ludwig Jedlicka Memorial Prize, for: "Culture and Political Crisis in Vienna", 96. **MEMBERSHIPS** Am Hist Asn. **RESEARCH** Austrian and Ger hist; relig and polit in mod Europ hist; comp Europ and Am polit hist. **SELECTED PUBLICATIONS** Auth, Catholic priests in lower Austria, Proc Am Philos Soc, 74; A J P Taylor and the art of modern history, 77 & Freud, marriage and late Viennese liberalism, 78, J Mod Hist; Karl Lueger and Viennese Jewry, Leo Baeck Inst Yearbk, 81; Political Radicalism in Late Imperial Vienna, Univ Chicago Press, 81; Veranderungen im politischen Leben Wiens, Jahrbuch des Vereins fuer Geschichte der Stadt Wien, 80-81; co-ed, Nineteenth Century Europe. Liberalism and its Critics, Univ Chicago Press, 87; Twentieth Century Europe, Univ Chicago Press, 87; auth, Some Reflections on the Problem of Austria, Germany, and Mitteleuropa, Central Europ Hist, 89; Culture and Political Crisis in Vienna: Christian Socialism in Power, 1879-1918, Univ Chicago Press, 95; ed, The Aims of Education, Col of the Univ Chicago, 97. **CONTACT ADDRESS** Dept of Hist, Univ of Chicago, 1126 E 59th St, Chicago, IL 60637-1476. **EMAIL** jwboyer@midway.uchicago.edu

BOYER, LEE R.

DISCIPLINE HISTORY **EDUCATION** Univ Notre Dame, PhD. **CAREER** Prof, Eastern Michigan Univ, 70-. **RESEARCH** US, native american. **SELECTED PUBLICATIONS** Auth, US Indians: A Brief History. **CONTACT ADDRESS** Dept of History and Philosophy, Eastern Michigan Univ, 701 Pray-Harrold, Ypsilanti, MI 48197.

BOYER, MARJORIE NICE

PERSONAL Born 11/16/1912, Pelham, MA, m, 1935, 4 children **DISCIPLINE** MEDIEVAL HISTORY **EDUCATION** Ohio State Univ, AB, 33; Columbia Univ, MA, 34, PhD, 58. **CAREER** Lectr hist, Brooklyn Col, 56-66 & Univ Kans, 66; asst prof, 67-71, assoc prof, 72-78, Prof Hist, York Col, 79- **MEMBERSHIPS** AHA; Mediaeval Acad Am; Renaissance Soc Am; Soc Hist Technol; Soc Hist Paris & l'Ile-de-France. **RESEARCH** History of travel, technology and bridges in medieval France. **SELECTED PUBLICATIONS** Auth, The Art of Medieval Technolog--Images of Noah the Shipbuilde, Amer Hist Rev, Vol 0098, 93. **CONTACT ADDRESS** Dept of Hist, York Col, CUNY, 150-14 Jamaica Ave, Jamaica, NY 11432.

BOYER, PAUL S.

PERSONAL Born 08/02/1935, Dayton, OH, m, 1962, 2 children **DISCIPLINE** AMERICAN HISTORY **EDUCATION** Harvard Univ, BA, 60, MA, 61, PhD, 66. **CAREER** Coordr, staff mem, Comt for Int Voluntary Work Camps, UNESCO, Paris, 55-57; asst ed, Notable American Women, 1607-1950, Radcliffe Col, 63-67; asst to prof, Univ Mass, Amherst, 67-80; prof, Univ Wisc, Madison, 80-, Merle Curti Prof of Hist, 92-, Dir, Inst for Res in the Humanities, 93-2001. **HONORS AND AWARDS** John Simon Guggenheim Fel; Rockefeller Found Fel; John H. Dunning Prize, Am Hist Asn, for Salem Possessed; elected mem: Soc of Hists, Am Acad of Arts and Scis, Am Antiquarian Soc. **MEMBERSHIPS** Org of Am Hists, Am Hist Asn. **RESEARCH** American intellectual and cultural history. **SELECTED PUBLICATIONS** Auth, Purity in Print: The Vice Society Movement and Book Censorship in America (68); asst ed, Notable American Women, 1600-1950, 3 vols (71); coauth, Salem Possessed: The Social Origins of Witchcraft (74); auth, Urban Masses and Moral Order in America, 1820-1920 (78); auth, By the Bomb's Early Light: American Thought and Culture at the Dawn of the Atomic Age (85); auth, When Time Shall Be No More: Prophecy Belief in Modern American Culture (92); auth, Fallout: A Historian Reflects on America's Half-Century Encounter With Nuclear Weapons (98); coauth, The Enduring Vision: A History of the American People, 4th ed (99); coauth, Promises to Keep: The United States Since 1945, 2nd ed (99); auth, Boyer's American Nation, 3rd ed (99); ed-in-chief, The Oxford Companion to United States History (forthcoming 2000). **CONTACT ADDRESS** Dept Hist, Univ of Wisconsin, Madison, 3211 Humanities Bldg, 455 N Park St, Madison, WI 53706-1405. **EMAIL** psboyer@facstaff.wisc.edu

BOYER, RICHARD

PERSONAL Born Los Angeles, CA **DISCIPLINE** LATIN AMERICAN HISTORY **EDUCATION** Westmont Col, BA, 59; Univ Wash, MA, 62; Univ Conn, PhD(hist), 73. **CAREER** Teacher hist, Lakeside Sch, 63-67 & 71-72; from instr to asst prof, 72-77, Assoc Prof Hist, Simon Fraser Univ, 77- **MEMBERSHIPS** AHA; Conf Latin Am Hist; Can Asn Latin Am Studies. **RESEARCH** Social history of New Spain in the 17th century; urban history of Latin America. **SELECTED PUBLICATIONS** Auth, Urbanization in Nineteenth Century Latin America; Statistcs and Sources, Keith A Davies, (Los Angeles: Univ of California Press, 73); ed, "Women, La Mala Vida, and th ePolitics of Marriage in Asuncion" Lavrin, ed, Sexuality and Marriage in Colonial Latin America, (Lincoln and London: Univ of Nebraska Press, 89), 252-286; ed, "People, Places and Gossip: The Flow of Information in Colonial Mexico," Ricardo Sanchez, Eric Van Young and Gisela von Wobeser, eds, (Mexico City: Universidad Nacional Antonoma de Mexico, 92), 143-150; auth, "The Inquisitor, the Witness and the Historian: The Document as Dialogue," Revista Canadiense de Estudios Hispanicos 18, 3, (Primavera, 94): 393-403; auth, Lives of the Bigamists: Marriage, Family and Community in Colonial Mexico, (Albuquerque: Univ of New Mexico Press, 95); auth, La gran inudacion: vida y sociedad en la ciudad de Mexico 1629-1635, (Mexico City: Secretaria de Educacion Publica, 95); auth, "Caste and Identity in Colonial Mexico: A Proposal and an Example," Latin American Studies Consortium of New England, No 7, 96; auth, "Clientelismo y trabajadores en el Mexico colonial, Algunos efectos en la vida privada," In Pilar Gonzalbo Aizpuru y Cecilia Rabell Romero, coordinadoras, Familia y vida privada en la historia de iberomamerica, (Mexico City: El Colegio de Mexico/Universidad Nacional Autonoma de Mexico, 96): 387-400; auth, "Negotiating Calidad: The Everyday Struggle for Status in Mexico," Historical Archaeology 31:1, (97): 64-73. **CONTACT ADDRESS** Dept of Hist, Simon Fraser Univ, 8888 Univ Dr, Burnaby, BC, Canada V5A 1S6. **EMAIL** richard_boyer@sfu.ca

BOYLAN, ANNE M.

PERSONAL Born 04/09/1947, Thurles, Ireland, m, 1975, 2 children **DISCIPLINE** HISTORY **EDUCATION** Mundelein Col, BA, 68; Univ Wis, MA, 70; PhD, 73. **CAREER** Vis Asst Prof, Univ Minn, 73-76; Vis Asst Prof, Univ Tex, 77-79; Asst Prof, Univ NMex, 79-85; Adjunct Prof, Univ Del, 86-88; Assoc Prof, Univ Del, 88-. **HONORS AND AWARDS** Phi Kappa Phi; NEH Summer Fel, 79; Awd for Best Article, Western Assoc of Women Historians, 85; Res Grants, Univ Del, 91, 00. **RESEARCH** United States social history, United States women's history. **SELECTED PUBLICATIONS** Auth, "Women in Groups: An Analysis of Women's Benevolent Organizations in New York and Boston 1797-1840," J of Am Hist, 71 (84): 497-523; auth, "Timid Girls, Venerable Widows and Dignified Matrons: Life-Cycle Patterns Among Organized Women in New York and Boston 1797-1840," Am Quart, 38 (86): 779-797; auth, "Women and politics in the Era Before Seneca Falls," J of the Early Republic, 10 (90): 363-382; auth, Sunday School: The Formation of an American Institution 1790-1880, Yale Univ Pr (New Haven, CT), 88, 90; auth, "Benevolence and Antislavery Activity Among African-American Women in New York and Boston 1820-1840," in The Abolitionist Sisterhood: Women's Polit Cult in Antebellum Am (Ithaca, NY: Cornell Univ Pr, 94), 119-137. **CONTACT ADDRESS** Dept Hist, Univ of Delaware, Newark, DE 19716-2555.

BOYLE, EDWARD A.

PERSONAL Born 05/01/1949 **DISCIPLINE** GEOLOGY **EDUCATION** Univ Calif, San Diego, BA, 71; Mass Inst Tech, Woods Hole Oceanographic Inst, PhD, 76. **CAREER** Postdoctoral fel, Univ Edinburgh, 76-77; asst prof to prof, Mass Inst Tech, 77-. **HONORS AND AWARDS** Nat Sci Foun Grad Fel, 71-75; NATO Postdoctoral Fel, 76-77; Guggenheim Fel, 91-92; Fel, Am Geophysical Union, 94; Huntsman Awd, Bedford Inst of Oceanography, 94; Geochemistry Fel, Geochemical Soc and European Asn for Geochemistry, 98; Fel, Am Asn for the Advan of Sci, 99. **MEMBERSHIPS** Am Geophysical Union, Geochemical Soc, Oceanography Soc, Am Asn for the Advan of Sci, Am Chemical Soc. **SELECTED PUBLICATIONS** Auth, "Cadmium: chemical tracer of deep-water paleoceanography," Paleoceanography, 3:471-490.48 (88); auth, "Quaternary deep water paleoceanography," Sci 249:863-870 (90); auth, "Cadmium and 13C paleochemical ocean distributions during the stage 2 glacial maximum," Ann Rev Earth Planet, Sci 20: 245-287 (92); coauth with R. A. Sherrell and M. P. Bacon, "Lead variability in the western North Atlantic and Central Greenland: implications for the search for decadal trends in anthropogenic emissions, " Geochim, Cosmochim, Acta 58:3227-3238 (94); coauth with L. Labeyie and J. C. Duplessy, "Calcitic foraminiferal data confirmed by cadmium in aragonitic Hoeglundina: application to the last glacial maximum northern Indian Ocean," Paleoceanogr, 10:881-900 (95); coauth with J. F. Wu, "Lead in the western North Atlantic Ocean: completed response to leaded gasoline phaseout," Geochim, Cosmochim, Acta 61:3279-3283 (97); coauth with J. F. Adkins, L. Keigwin, and E. Cortijo, "Variability of the North Atlantic thermohaline circulation during the last interglacial period," Nature, 390: 154-156 (97); coauth with J. Adkins, H. Cheng, E. R. M. Druffel and R. L. Eddwards, "Deep-Sea Coral Evidence for Rapid Change in Ventilation of the Deep North Atlantic at 15.4 ka," Sci 280:725-728 (98); coauth with L. D. Keigwin, "Surface and deep ocean variability in the Northern Sargasso Sea during marine isotope stage 3," Paleoceanography, 14:164-170 (99); auth, "Is Ocean Thermohaline Circulation Linked to Abrubt Stadial/ Interstadial Transitions?," Quat Sci Rev, 19:255-272 (2000). **CONTACT ADDRESS** Dept Earth Sci, Massachusetts Inst of Tech, 77 Massachusetts Ave, Cambridge, MA 02139. **EMAIL** eaboyle@mit.edu

BOYLE, JOHN HUNTER
PERSONAL Born 10/06/1930, Huron, SD, m, 1958, 2 children **DISCIPLINE** HISTORY OF EAST ASIA **EDUCATION** Georgetown Univ, BS, 53; Harvard Univ, MA, 58; Stanford Univ, PhD(hist), 68. **CAREER** Assoc prof, 68-74, Prof Hist, Calif State Univ, Chico, 74-, Fulbright grant for asst ed, Japan Interpreter, Tokyo, 69-70. **MEMBERSHIPS** Asn Asian Studies; AHA; Pac Area Intercol Coun Asian Studies. **RESEARCH** History of Sino-Japanese War, 1937-45. **SELECTED PUBLICATIONS** Auth, China and Japan at War, 1937-1945: The Politics of Collaboration, Stanford Univ, 72. **CONTACT ADDRESS** Dept Hist, California State Univ, Chico, Chico, CA 95929.

BOYLE, KEVIN
DISCIPLINE HISTORY **EDUCATION** Univ Detroit, BA, 82; Univ Michigan , MA, 84, PhD, 90. **CAREER** Asst Prof, 90-94, Univ Toledo; Asst Prof, 94-97, Assoc Prof, 97-, Univ Massachusetts. **CONTACT ADDRESS** Dept of History, Univ of Massachusetts, Amherst, Amherst, MA 01003. **EMAIL** kboyle@history.umass.edu

BOZEMAN, THEODORE D.
PERSONAL Born 01/27/1942, Gainesville, FL, m, 1973 **DISCIPLINE** AMERICAN RELIGIOUS HISTORY **EDUCATION** Eckerd Col, BA, 64; Union Theol Sem, NYC, BD, 68; Univ Theol Sem, Richmond, ThM, 70; Duke Univ, PhD, 74. **CAREER** Instr to prof, Univ Iowa, 73- . **HONORS AND AWARDS** NEH fel, 84, 92. **MEMBERSHIPS** Orgn Am Hist; Am Hist Asn; Am Soc Church Hist. **RESEARCH** Puritanism, American religious thought. **SELECTED PUBLICATIONS** Auth, Protestants in an Age of Science, Chapel Hill, (78); auth, To Live Ancient Lives, Chapel Hill, (88). **CONTACT ADDRESS** Dept Hist, Univ Iowa, 205 Schaeffer Hall, Iowa City, IA 52242-1409. **EMAIL** d-bozeman@uiowa.edu

BRACKENRIDGE, ROBERT DOUGLAS
PERSONAL Born 08/06/1932, Youngstown, OH, m, 1954, 5 children **DISCIPLINE** HISTORY, CHURCH HISTORY **EDUCATION** Muskingum Col, BA, 54; Pittsburgh Theol Sem, BD, 57, ThM, 59; Glasgow Univ, PhD(church hist), 62. **CAREER** Pastor, Cross Rd United Presby Church, 58-60; from asst prof to assoc prof, 62-72, Prof Relig, Trinity Univ, Tex, 72-, Assoc, Danforth Found, 72- **HONORS AND AWARDS** Thornwell Awd, 68; Piper Prof, Minnie Stevens Piper Found, 73; Distinguished Serv Awd, Presby Hist Soc, 81. **MEMBERSHIPS** Presby Hist Soc (pres, 76-); Am Soc Church Hist; Am Acad Relig; Scottish Church Hist Soc. **SELECTED PUBLICATIONS** Auth, The Sabbath War 1865-1866, Records Scottish Church Hist Soc, Part I, 66; The Growth and Development of Sabbatarianism in Scotland 1560-1650, 10 & 12/67 & Sumner Bacon, the Apostle of Texas, 10 & 12/67, J Presby Hist; Voice in the Wilderness, 68 & Beckoning Frontiers, 76, Trinity Univ; Eugene Carson Blake: Prophet With Portfolio, Seabury, 78. **CONTACT ADDRESS** Dept of Relig, Trinity Univ, San Antonio, TX 78287.

BRADBURY, MILES L.
PERSONAL Born 06/16/1938, Sioux City, IA **DISCIPLINE** AMERICAN HISTORY **EDUCATION** Harvard Univ, AB, 60, AM, 61, PhD(hist), 67. **CAREER** Asst Prof Hist, Univ MD, College Park, 67- **RESEARCH** Early American and American church history. **SELECTED PUBLICATIONS** Auth, Frontier Faiths--Church, Temple, and Synagogue in Los Angeles, 1846-1888--Engh, Am Jewish Hist, vol 0082, 94. **CONTACT ADDRESS** Dept of Hist, Univ of Maryland, Col Park, 2115 Francis Scott Key Hall, College Park, MD 20742-0001. **EMAIL** mb58@umail.umd.edu

BRADDOCK, ROBERT COOK
PERSONAL Born 05/31/1939, Mt Holly, NJ, m, 1962, 2 children **DISCIPLINE** ENGLISH & EARLY MODERN EUROPEAN HISTORY **EDUCATION** Middlebury Col, AB, 61; Northwestern Univ, MA, 63, PhD(hist), 71. **CAREER** From instr to asst prof, 70-75, chmn dept, 76-78, 96-98, assoc prof to prof Hist, Saginaw Valley State Univ, 75-. **HONORS AND AWARDS** Dist Fac Awd, State Univ Mich, 91; Fel of Early Mod Studies, Sixteenth Century Studies Conf, 98. **MEMBERSHIPS** AHA; Renaissance Soc Am; Conf Brit Studies. **RESEARCH** Administrative history especially early modern Europe; the court in Tudor-Stuart England; office holding. **SELECTED PUBLICATIONS** Auth, The Character and Composition of the Duke of Northumberland's Army, Albion VI, 74; The Rewards of Office-Holding in Tudor England, J Brit Studies XIV, 75; J. H. Plumb and the Whig Tradition, In: Recent Historians of Great Britain, Iowa State Univ Press, 90; contribr, Historical Dictionary of Tudor England, Greenwood Press, 91; Dict of National Biography, Oxford Univ Press, forthcoming; Reader's Guide to British History, Fitzroy-Dearborn Press, forthcoming. **CONTACT ADDRESS** Dept of Hist, Saginaw Valley State Univ, 7400 Bay Rd, University Center, MI 48710-0001. **EMAIL** rcbrad@svsu.edu

BRADFORD, JAMES CHAPIN
PERSONAL Born 04/07/1945, Detroit, MI, m, 1964, 2 children **DISCIPLINE** AMERICAN NAVAL & MILITARY HISTORY **EDUCATION** Mich State Univ, BA, 67, MA, 68; Univ Va, PhD(hist), 76. **CAREER** Res asst, Thomas Jefferson Mem Found, 72-73; asst prof hist, US Naval Acad, 73-81; assoc prof hist, Tex A&M Univ, 81-, Ed, The Papers of John Paul Jones, 78-; mem, Int Comn Maritime Hist, 80-; bk rev ed, J Early Repub, 80- **HONORS AND AWARDS** John Lyman Awd for "Best Book in U.S. Naval History," 85; K. Jack Bauer Awd for Scholarship and Service, North Am Soc for Oceanic Hist. **MEMBERSHIPS** AHA; Orgn Am Historians; NAm Soc Oceanic Hist; Soc Historians of Early Am Repub; Asn Documentary Editing. **RESEARCH** Naval history of the age of sail; local government in Virginia, 1750-1820; early American history. **SELECTED PUBLICATIONS** Auth, The Military and Conflict Between Cultures, 97; auth, Quarterdeck and Bridge, 96; auth, Admirals of the New Steel Navy, 90; auth, Captains of the Old Steam Navy, 86; auth, The Papers of John Paul Jones, 86; auth, Command Under Sail, 85. **CONTACT ADDRESS** Dept of Hist, Texas A&M Univ, Col Station, Campus MS 4236, College Station, TX 77843. **EMAIL** jcbradford@tamu.edu

BRADFORD, RICHARD HEADLEE
PERSONAL Born 04/14/1938, Waynesburg, PA, m, 1966 **DISCIPLINE** AMERICAN HISTORY **EDUCATION** Pa State Univ, BA, 62; Ind Univ, MA, 64, PhD(hist), 73. **CAREER** Instr hist, St Louis Jr Col Dist, 64-66; teaching assoc, Ind Univ, 66-68; from asst prof to prof Hist, WVa Univ Inst Technol, 68-. **HONORS AND AWARDS** Phi Alpha Theta Best First Book Awd, 81; Am Philos Soc research grant, 82; WVa Writers Asn 1st Prize Dramatic Writing for Knight, Death, and the Devil, 89; WVa Humanities Coun Fel, 97-00. **RESEARCH** American history. **SELECTED PUBLICATIONS** Auth, Religion and Politics: Alfred E Smith and the 1928 Presidential Primary in West Virginia, WVa Hist, 4/75; And Oregon Rushed Home, Am Neptune, 10/76; John F Kennedy and the 1960 Presidential Primary in West Virginia, S Atlantic Quart, spring 76; That prodigal son: Philo McGiffin and the Chinese Navy, 1885-1894, Am Neptune, 7/78; The Virginius Affair, Colo Assoc Univ Press, 80, 81; The Spanish Problem in American Politics, In: La Republique Imperialiste, Univ De Provence, 87; coauth, An American Family on the American Frontier, Rinehart, 94. **CONTACT ADDRESS** Dept of Hist, West Virginia Univ Inst of Tech, 405 Fayette Pike, Montgomery, WV 25136-2436. **EMAIL** rbradford@wvutech.edu

BRADLEY, JOSEPH C.
PERSONAL Born 12/15/1945, Madison, WI, m, 1992, 1 child **DISCIPLINE** HISTORY **EDUCATION** Univ Wis, BA, 68; Harvard Univ, AM, 71; PhD, 77. **CAREER** Asst prof, Univ Tulsa, 79-86, assoc prof, 86-91; prof, Univ Tulsa, 91-. **HONORS AND AWARDS** Phi Beta Kappa; Grad Prize Fel, Harvard, 68-74; Fulbright-Hays Fel, 72-73; Weatherhead Fel, Russian Res Ctr, Harvard,, 78-79; Int Res and Exchanges Bd; NEH grants, 81, 88,. 93; Nat Coun of Soviet and East European Res, 93-94. **MEMBERSHIPS** Am Hist Asn, Am Asn for the Advancement of Slavic Studies. **RESEARCH** Modern Russian history. **SELECTED PUBLICATIONS** Auth, Muzhik and Muscovite: Urbanization in Late Imperial Russia, Berkeley: Univ Calif Press (85); auth, Guns for the Tsar: American Technology and the Small Arms Industry in Nineteenth-century Russia, Dekalb, Ill: Northern Ill Univ Press (90); auth, "Dobrovol'nye obshchestva I grazhdanskoe obshchestvo v Moskve (Voluntary Societies and Civil Society in Moscow)," Obshchestvennye nauki I sovremennost' (The Natural Social Sciences and Modernity), no 5 (94): 77-89; auth, "Russia's Cities of Dreadful Delight," J of Urban Hist, 24, no 1 (Nov 97): 120-129; ed's intro, "Was the USSR Planning to Attack Germany in 1941?," Russian Studies in History, Vol 36, No 2 (fall 97): 3-7; ed's intro, "Russia -- A Divided Civilization?," Russian Studies in History, Vol 36, No 1 (summer 97): 3-7; ed's intro, "The Russian People: Destiny in the 20th Century," Russian Studies in History, Vol 37, No 2 (fall 98): 3-7; auth, Voluntary Associations and the Formation of Civil Society in Russia, 1750-1930 (in progress). **CONTACT ADDRESS** Dept Hist, Univ of Tulsa, 600 S Col Ave, Tulsa, OK 74104-3126. **EMAIL** joseph-bradley@utulsa.edu

BRADLEY, KEITH RICHARD
PERSONAL Born 04/30/1946, Oldswinford, England, m, 1976, 3 children **DISCIPLINE** ANCIENT HISTORY, CLASSICAL LANGUAGES **EDUCATION** Sheffield Univ, BA, 67, MA, 68; Oxford Univ, BLitt, 75; Sheffield, LittD, 97. **CAREER** Asst prof, Johns Hopkins Univ, 72-77; vis asst prof, Stanford Univ, 77-80; Asst Prof Classics & Ancient Hist, Univ Victoria, 80- **HONORS AND AWARDS** Fel, of the Soc of Antiquaries, 93; Canada Council Killam Res Fel, 96-98; Fel, of Royal Soc of Canada, 96. **MEMBERSHIPS** Soc Prom Roman Studies, Am Philol Asn, Class Asn Can, Soc for Libyan Studies. **RESEARCH** Greek and Roman social and cultural history; Roman historiography. **SELECTED PUBLICATIONS** Auth, Suetonius' Life of Nero: An Historical Commentary, Brussels, 78; auth, Slaves and Masters in the Roman Empire, New York & Oxford, 86; auth, Slavery and Rebellion in the Roman World, Bloomington & London, 89, 98; auth, Discovering the Roman Family, New York & Oxford, 91; auth, Slavery and Society at Rome, Cambridge, 94; auth, Slaves And Freedmen in Roman Society Under the Empire--A Selection of Texts With Translations--German, Greek And Latin, vol 0068, 96; Suetonius, 'Lives Of Galba, Otho And Vitellius', Latomus, vol 0055, 96; coed, A Historical Guide to World Slavery, eds, S. Engerman & S. Drescher, New York, 98. **CONTACT ADDRESS** Greek and Roman Studies, Univ of Victoria, PO Box 3045, Victoria, BC, Canada V8W 3P4. **EMAIL** kbradley@uvic.ca

BRADLEY, OWEN
DISCIPLINE HISTORY **EDUCATION** Cornell Univ, PhD, 93 **CAREER** Asst prof, Hist, Univ Tenn. **RESEARCH** Modern European cultural and intellectual history. **SELECTED PUBLICATIONS** Auth, A Modern Maistre: The Social and Political Thought of Joesph de Maistre, Univ Neb Pr (Lincoln), 99. **CONTACT ADDRESS** Dept Hist, Univ of Tennessee, Knoxville, 915 Volunteer Blvd, 6th Fl, Dunford Hall, Knoxville, TN 37996-4065. **EMAIL** obradley@utk.edu

BRADY, PATRICK S.
PERSONAL Born 10/27/1933, Broken Hill, Australia, D **DISCIPLINE** FRENCH LITERATURE & COMPARATIVE LITERATURE, ART, CULTURE **EDUCATION** Sorbonne Univ, DUP, 60. **CAREER** Prof, French, Univ Tenn. **HONORS AND AWARDS** Schumway Chair of Excellence. **MEMBERSHIPS** SCLA, ACLA, ICLA. **RESEARCH** Provost, Zola, The Moco-co; Interdiscplinary apparatus to art, literature, culture. **SELECTED PUBLICATIONS** "L'Oeurve d'Emile Zola, roman sur les arts: manifeste, autobiographie, roman a clef, (Geneva, Dorz), 67; Marcel Proust, G.K. Hall, (Boston), 77; Structuralist Perspectives in Criticism of Fiction: Essays on "Manon Lescaut' and "La Vie de Marianne," Bern, (Lang), 78; Le Bouc emissaire chez Emile Zola: Quarte essais sur "Germinal" et "L'Oeuvre" Carl Winter Verlag, (Heidelberg), 81; Rococo Style versus Enlightenment Novel, Slatkine, (Geneva), 84; "From Transactual Analysis to Chaos Theory: New Critical Perspectives," Australian Journal of French Studies, vol XXVI, no 2 (May-August 89): 176-193; Memory and History as Fiction: An Archetypal Approach to the Historical Novel, New Paradigm Press, (Knoxville), 93; Chaos in the Humanities, New Paradigm Pr, (Knoxville), 94; "Does God Play Dice? Deterministic and Stochastic Chance in Proust's Recherche," Michigan Romance Studies, vol XIV, (94): 133-149; Interdisciplinary Interpretation of Art and Literature: The Principle of Convergence, New Paradigm Pr, (Knoxville), 95. **CONTACT ADDRESS** Dept of ModFor Langs & Lits, Univ of Tennessee, Knoxville, 701 McClung Tower & Plaza, Knoxville, TN 37996. **EMAIL** pbrady@utk.edu

BRAEMAN, JOHN
DISCIPLINE 20TH CENTURY AMERICAN HISTORY **EDUCATION** Johns Hopkins Univ, PhD, 60. **CAREER** Prof, Univ Nebr, Lincoln; vis scholar, Bowling Green State Univ, 95; instr, Univ Hannover, Ger, 97. **RESEARCH** The Supreme Court and its civil liberties rulings. **SELECTED PUBLICATIONS** Auth, Albert J. Beveridge: American Nationalist, Univ Chicago Press, 71; Before The Civil Rights Revolution: The Old Court and Individual Rights, Greenwood Press, 88. **CONTACT ADDRESS** Univ of Nebraska, Lincoln, 643 Oldfather, Lincoln, NE 68588-0417. **EMAIL** jbraeman@unlinfo.unl.edu

BRAESTER, YOMI
PERSONAL Born 06/24/1964, Israel, m, 1998 **DISCIPLINE** COMPARATIVE LITERATURE, EAST ASIAN STUDIES **EDUCATION** Hebrew Univ, BA, 85, MA, 91; Yale Univ, MA, 92, PhD, 97. **CAREER** Post-doc fel, CCS, Univ Calif, Berkeley, 97-98; Asst Prof, Comp Lit, Univ GA, 98-; dir, Chinese Lang Prog, Univ Ga, 98-. **HONORS AND AWARDS** Pacific Cult Fnd Res Grant; China Times Cultural Fnd Awd. **MEMBERSHIPS** MLA, AAS. **RESEARCH** Comparative lit, E Asian stud **SELECTED PUBLICATIONS** Auth, "Shanghai's Economy of the Spectacle: The Shanghai Race Club in Liu Na'ou's and Mu Shiying's Stories," Modern Chinese Lit, 9:1, 95; "The Cruelty in Writing: Lu Xun's 'Diary of a Madman' and Authorial Complicity," Literature and Cruelty: Proceedings of the Sixth Annual Graduate Conference in French Francophone and Comparative Literature, 96; "Modern Identity and Karmic Retribution in Clara Law's Reincarnations of Golden Lotus," Asian Cinema 10, 98. **CONTACT ADDRESS** 133 Ashley Cir, Apt 3, Athens, GA 30605. **EMAIL** yomi@arches.uga.edu

BRAISTED, WILLIAM REYNOLDS
PERSONAL Born 03/14/1918, Washington, DC **DISCIPLINE** HISTORY **EDUCATION** A.A., George Wash Univ, 37; Stanford Univ, BA, 39; Univ Chicago, AM, 40, PhD, 50; Post-doctora, Special Student, Harvard Univ, 52-53. **CAREER** Instr, Univ of Tex, 42-50; Naval Japanese Lang Sch, 43; War Dept, Mil Intelligence Serv, Res Consult, 44-46; Asst prof, 50-58, Assoc prof, 58-66, Prof, 66-; Vis prof of Naval Hist, US Naval Acad, 76-77; Prof emer, 88; Secy of the Navy's Res Prof, Naval Hist Ctr, 88-89. **HONORS AND AWARDS** Ford Found, Fund for the Advancement of Educ, 52-53; Fulbright Res Fel, 55-56; Mershon Fel in Mil Hist, Ohio State Univ, 60-61; Univ Res Inst, 65-66; Am Coun of Learned Societies with U.R.I. Supplement, 67-68, Summer Grants from the Am Philos Soc, the Soc Sci res Coun and U.R.I.; Univ Res Inst, 80; Nat Endowment for the Humanities, 82; Univ Res Inst, 85; Order of Sacred Treasurer for the Emperor of Japan, 88. **RESEARCH** Far Eastern history; United States Navy in the Far East. **SELECTED PUBLICATIONS** Auth, The United State Navy in

the Pacific, 1897-1909, Austin: The Univ of Texas Press, 58; auth, The United States Navy in the Pacific, 1909-1922, Austin: The Univ of Texas Press, 71; auth, "The Navy in the Early Twentieth Century, 1890-1941;" in Robin Higham, A Guide to the Sources of United States Military Hist (Hamden, Conn.: Archon Books, 75), 344-378; auth, Meiroku Zasshi: Journal of Japanese Englightenment, Tokyo: Univ of Tokyo Press, 76 and Cambridge, Mass.: Harvard Univ Press, 77; auth, "On the American Red and Red-Orange Plans, 1919-1939," in Gerald Jordan, Naval Warfare in the Twentieth Century (London: Crown Helm, 77), 167-185; auth, "Amerika Kaigun to Orenji Sakusen Keikaku," The American Navy's Orange Plans, 1919-1931), in Hosoya Ohihiro and Saito Makoto, eds., Washington taisei to Nichi Bei Kankei (Tokyo: Tokyo Univ Press, 78), 415-440; auth, "Naval Diplomacy," in Alexander DeConde, Encyclopedia of American Foreign Policy (New York: Scribners, 78), 668-678; auth, "Charles Frederick Hughes, 14 November 1927-17 September 1930," in Robert Love, ed., The Chiefs of Naval Operations (US Naval Institute Press, 80); auth, "Mid-Pacific Bases," in Paolo Coletta and K. Jack Bauer, eds., United States Naval and Marine Coprs Bases, overseas: A Historical Encyclopedia (Westport, Conn., Greenwood Press, 85); auth, "Admiral Mark Lambert Bristol: Naval Diplomat Extraordinary in the Battleship Age," in Professor James C. Bradford, ed., Admirals of the Steel Navy (Annapolis, Naval Institute Press), 90. **CONTACT ADDRESS** Dept of Hist, Univ of Texas, Austin, Austin, TX 78712.

BRAND, CHARLES MACY
PERSONAL Born 04/07/1932, Stanford, CA, m, 1954, 2 children **DISCIPLINE** MEDIEVAL HISTORY **EDUCATION** Stanford Univ, AB, 53; Harvard Univ, AM, 54, PhD, 61. **CAREER** Teaching fel, Harvard Univ, 58-61, vis fel, Dumbarton Oaks Res Libr, 61-62, 88; asst prof hist, San Francisco State Col, 62-64; from asst prof to assoc prof, 64-76; pro hist, Bryn Mawr Col, 76-; Fulbright res fel, Greece, 68-69; gov bd, Byzantine Studies Conf, 81-84; Guggenheim Fel, 72-73. **MEMBERSHIPS** AHA; Mediaeval Acad Am. **RESEARCH** Byzantine history; relations between Byzantium and the West. **SELECTED PUBLICATIONS** Auth, Byzantines and Saladin, 1185-1192: opponents of the third crusade, Speculum, 4/62; Byzantium Confronts the West, 1180-1204, Harvard Univ, 68; translr, John Kinnamos, Deeds of John and Manuel Comnenus, Columbia Univ, 76. **CONTACT ADDRESS** Dept of History, Bryn Mawr Col, 101 N Merion Ave, Bryn Mawr, PA 19010-2899.

BRANDIMARTE, CYNTHIA A.
DISCIPLINE AMERICAN CIVILIZATION **EDUCATION** Univ Texas, BA, 72; MA, 75; PhD, 80 **CAREER** Asst Instr, Univ of Tex Austin, 75-79; Res Dir, Winedale Summer Inst for Historic Preservation, 77-79; Asst Instr, Univ of Tex Austin, 79-80; Lectr, Univ of Tex Austin, 81-82; Dir, Harrington House, 83-84; Cur and Registrar, Harris County Heritage Soc, 84-86; Planner, Tex Parks and Wildlife Dept, 87-89; Historian, 89-92, Dir Cult Resources, 92-; asst prof and dir Public Hist Prog, Southwest Tex State Univ, 97-. **HONORS AND AWARDS** Am Ceramic Circle Grant, 84-85; Cunningham Found Grant, 85-86; Tex Architectural Found Grant, 85-86; Nat Endowment for the Humanities/Am Asn for State and Local Hist Grant, 86; Victorian Soc of Am Scholarship, 87; Nat Endowment for the Humanities, Summer fel, 95; Coral H. Tullis Award, 92; Kate Broocks Bates Award, 92; T.R. Fehrenbach Bk Award, 92; Historic Preservation Award, 92; Outstanding Bk Award, 92. **SELECTED PUBLICATIONS** Auth, "Growing Number of Museums Offer Varied Service to the Public," Texas Libraries, (78): 183-88; auth, "Fannie Hurst: A Missouri Girl Makes Good," Missouri Historical Review, (87): 275-95; auth, "Somebody's Aunt and Nobody's Mother: The American China Painter and Her Work, 1870-1920," Winterthur Portfolio 23, (88): 203-24; auth, "Darling Dabblers," American Ceramic Circle Journal 6 (88): 6-27; auth, Inside Texas: Culture, Identity and House, 1878-1920, Texas Christian Univ Press (Fort Worth), 91; auth, "Japanese Novelty Stores," Winterthur Portfolio 26, (91): 1-25; auth, "Domesticating the World: Nature and Culture in the Victorian Home," In Dwelling: Social Life, Buildings, and the Spaces Between Them, Center: A Journal for Architecture in America 8 (93): 44-51; auth, "To Make the Whole World Homelike: Gender, Space, and America's Tea Room Movement," Winterthur Portfolio 30, (96): 1-19; auth, "Immaterial Girls: Prints of Pageantry and Dance in Texas, 1900-1936," In Proceedings of the 1988 North American Print Conference, Austin: Texas State Historical Asn, in press. **CONTACT ADDRESS** Southwest Texas State Univ, 808 Westlake Dr., Austin, TX 78746. **EMAIL** cb22@swt.edu

BRANDT, BEVERLY K.
PERSONAL Born 08/26/1951, Evanston, IL, s **DISCIPLINE** DESIGN **EDUCATION** Univ Mich, BFA, 73; Mich State Univ, MA, 77; Boston Univ, PhD, 85 **CAREER** Asst Prof, Iowa State Univ, 84-87; Asst Prof, 87-92, Arizona State, Assoc Prof with tenure, Ariz State Univ, 92-00, Dir, Herberger Ctr for Design Excellence, 92-95; Full Prof, Ariz State Univ, 00-. **HONORS AND AWARDS** Kappa Omicron Nu; Burlington Resources Found Fac Achievement Awd for excellence in teaching, 91; Fel, Ariz Wakonse Conf on Teaching, 93-94; Lincoln Fel, Joan & David Lincoln Ctr for Ethics, ASU's Col Bus, 96; Fac of the Year award, Student Asn Interior Designers, Ariz State Univ, 98; recipient of numerous grants. **MEMBERSHIPS** Soc Archit Hist; Int Interior Design Asn; Am Soc Interior Designers; Decorative Arts Soc; William Morris Soc. **RESEARCH** History of interior design, ancient to the present; history of decorative arts in interiors, ancient to the present; history of textiles in interiors, ancient to the present; design criticism. **SELECTED PUBLICATIONS** Auth, "Introduction", "Afterword", and chapters on "Interior Design" and "Architecture", The Encyclopedia of Arts & Crafts: The International Arts Movement 1850-1920, EP Dutton/Headline, 89; The Critic and the Evolution of Early-Twentieth-Century American Craft, The Ideal Home. The History of Twentieth-Century American Craft, 1900-1920, Harry N. Abrams, Inc, 93; Foreword, Innovation and Derivation: The Contribution of L & JG Stickley to the Arts and Crafts Movement, The Craftsman Farms Found, 95; One Who Has Seen More and Knows More: The Design Critic and the Arts and Crafts, The Substance of Style: Perspectives on the American Arts and Crafts Movement, The Henry Francis du Pont Winterthur Museum, 96; Overview: Gustave Stickley's Craftsman Magazine, The Craftsman on CD-ROM, Interactive Bureau, 98; author of numerous articles and other publications. **CONTACT ADDRESS** College of Architecture & Environmental Design, School of Design, Arizona State Univ, Tempe, AZ 85287-2105. **EMAIL** beverly_brandt@asu.edu

BRANHAM, JOAN R.
DISCIPLINE ART HISTORY **EDUCATION** Fla State Univ, BA, 83, MA, 85; Diplome d-etudes francaises, 86; Grad Inst, Lib Arts, Emory Univ, PhD, 93. **CAREER** Fel, Getty Ctr Hist Art, Hum, 93-94; fel, Ecole Pratique des Hautes Etudes, Sorbonne, 94-95; assoc prof, Art Hist, Providence Col, Presently. **HONORS AND AWARDS** Received the Awd for Excellence in Graduate Res in the Humanities, Emory Univ, 93. **RESEARCH** Sacred space and Gendered space in the early Middle Ages, the Temple Mount in Jerusalem, Byzantine art and architecture, Jewish art in Late Antiquity, and Islamic art; incorporating various technologies into teaching. **SELECTED PUBLICATIONS** Auth, "Sacred Space Under Erasure in Ancient Synagogues and Early Churces," The Art Bulletin, LXXIV, 3, (92): 375-394; auth, "Sacrality and Aura in the Museum: Mute Objects and Articulate Space," The Journal of the Walters Art Gallery, LII/LIII, (94/95): 33-47; auth, "Vicarious Sacrality: Temple Space in Ancient Synagogues," Ancient Synagogues: Historical Analysis and Archaeological Discoverey, II, eds. Dan Urman and Paul V. M. Flesher, (Leiden: E.J. Brill, 95): 319-345; auth, "Ot-Ha-Kalon--Badge of Shame: Traces of Medieval Markings," Exhibition by Marcia Cohen, Atlanta: Marcia Wood Gallery, 95; auth, "Blood in Flux, Sanctity at Issue," RES Anthropology and Aesthetics, XXXI, (97): 53-70; auth, "Negotiating Women's Space in Early Christian Architecture: The Jerusalem Temple as Burden of Authority," 98; auth," Ritual Elements in the Art of Barnaby Evans," Exhibition Notes, no. 7, (Providence: The Rhode Island School of Design Museum, 99); auth, "Bloody Women and Bloody Spaces: Menses and the Eucharist in Late Antiquity and the Early Middle Ages," (in German translation), Vortrage aus dem Warbug-Haus, Band 3, (99): 129-161; auth, "Mapping Tragedy in the U.S. Holocaust Memorial Museum," Architectural Design: The Tragic in Architecutre, (Chichester, England: John Wiley & Sons, Ltd., 00). **CONTACT ADDRESS** Dept of Art & Art Hist, Providence Col, Providence, RI 02918-0001. **EMAIL** jbranham@providence.edu

BRANSON, SUSAN
DISCIPLINE HISTORY **EDUCATION** Northern Ill Univ, PhD, 94. **CAREER** Asst prof. **RESEARCH** U.S. women's history; 18th and 19th century; U.S. early republic. **SELECTED PUBLICATIONS** Auth, Women and the Family Economy in the Early Republic: The Case of Elizabeth Meredith, Jour Early Repub, 96; Beyond Respectability: the Female World of Love and Crime in Nineteenth-Century Philadelphia, 96. **CONTACT ADDRESS** Dept of History, Univ of Texas, Dallas, Richardson, TX 75083-0688. **EMAIL** sbranson@utdallas.edu

BRASSEAUX, CARL A.
PERSONAL Born 08/19/1951, Opelousas, LA, m, 1973, 3 children **DISCIPLINE** HISTORY **EDUCATION** Univ Southwestern La, BA, 74; MA, 75; Univ de Paris, doctorat de 3e cycle, 82. **CAREER** Asst dir, Center for La Studies, 75-; adj asst prof to prof, Univ of Southwestern La, 87-. **HONORS AND AWARDS** Kemper Williams Prize, 79; Robert L Brown Prize, 80; Presidents's Mem Awd, La Hist Assoc; 86; Book Prize, Fr Colonial Hist Soc, 87; Chevalier Ordre de Palmes Academiques, 94; Univ Distinguished Prof, 95; Fel, La Hist Assoc, 99. **MEMBERSHIPS** La Hist Assoc. **RESEARCH** French Colonial America, Spanish Borderlands, Acadian Studies, Cajun Studies, Creole Studies, Steamboats, Ethnohistory, Historical Anthropology. **SELECTED PUBLICATIONS** Coauth, The Courthouses of Louisiana, USL Arch Series, (Lafayette), 77; ed, transl, A Comparative View of French Louisiana: The Journals of Pierre Le Moyne d'Iberville and Jean-Jacques-Blaise d'Abbadie, USL Hist Series, 79; ed, A Franco-American Overview: Louisiana, Vol V-VII, Nat Assessment and Dissemination Center for Bilingual/Bicultural Educ, 82; auth, "The Moral Climate of French Louisiana, 1699-1763", La Hist XXVII, (86); 27-41; auth, The Founding of New Acadia: Beginnings of Acadian Life in Louisiana, 1765-1803, LSU PR, 87; auth, "Creoles of Color in Louisiana's Bayou Country, 1766-1877", Creoles of Color of the Gulf South, ed James H Dormon, Univ of Tenn Pr, (96): 67-86; auth, "Hennepin, Louis", "Lamothe Cadillac, Antoine Laumet de", "Caffery, Donelson", and "Le Moyne, Pierre", American National Biography, Oxford Univ Pr, 99; coauth, "Observations on Fauna, Flora, and Geography of the Bayou Laforuche Region, 1772-1786, by Pioneer Amateur Naturalist Louis Judice", J of Southern Hist, (forthcoming). **CONTACT ADDRESS** Dept Hist and Geog, Univ of Southwestern Louisiana, PO Box 40831, Lafayette, LA 70504-0831. **EMAIL** cab6944@louisiana.edu

BRATTON, TIMOTHY L.
PERSONAL Born 04/21/1947, Cleveland, OH, m, 1975, 3 children **DISCIPLINE** HISTORY **EDUCATION** Bryn Mawr College, Phd, 79, Michigan State Univ, MA, 71; Baldwin-Wallace College, BA, 69. **CAREER** Chair, Dept of History/Political Science, Jamestown College, 97-; Prof, 94-; Assoc Prof, 87-93; Assist Prof, 82-86; Parttime Instructor in Western Civilization, Villanova Univ, Villanova, PA, 80-82; Asst Editor of the Transactions and Studies of the College of Physicians of Philadelphia, 80-82; Archival Asst, Historical Collections of the College of Physicians of Philadelphia, 79-80; Teachng Asst, Dept of History, Bryn Mawr College, 9-80; Library Asst, Library of the Pennsylvania State Univ Graduate Center at King of Prussia, Pa; 77-78; Asst Librarian, Historical Society of Pennsylvania, Philadelphia, Pa, 73-77; Teaching Asst, Dept of History, Michigan State Univ, East Lansing Michigan, 69-71; Teaching Asst, Baldwin-Wallace College, Berea, Ohio, 68-69. **HONORS AND AWARDS** National Science Foundation grant for summer workshop on the teaching of introduction to astronomy, 94; Burlington Northern Faculty Achievement Awd, 99; Professor of the Year, 85. **MEMBERSHIPS** Amer Assoc for the History of Medicine; Society for Ancient Medicine; Paleopatology Assoc; Amer Historical Assoc; Medieval Academy of America. **RESEARCH** Historical epidemiology; History of Medicine; Paleopathology; History of Astrology/Astronomy. **SELECTED PUBLICATIONS** Auth, "Spengler, Time, and the Autonomy of History," Dialogue 10, no. 2 Nov. 68: 19-23; auth, "The Identity of the Plague of Justinian," Transactions and Studies of the College of Physicians of Philadelphia ser", 5, 3, 81: 113-24, 174-80; rev, "Luke Demaire's Doctor Bernard de Gordon, in Journal of the History of Medicine and Allied Sciences 37, 82: 241-143; coauth, "A Catalogue of the Manuscripts and Archives of the Library of the College of Physicians of Philadelphia," Philadelphia: Univ of Pa Press, 83; auth, "The Identity of the New England Indian Epidemic of 1616-19," Bulletin of the History of Medicine 62, 88: 351-83. **CONTACT ADDRESS** Dept History & Political Science, Jamestown Col, 6006 College Lane, Jamestown, ND 58405-0001. **EMAIL** bratton@jc.edu

BRAUDE, BENJAMIN
DISCIPLINE HISTORY **EDUCATION** Harvard Univ, BA, 67; MA, 75; PhD, 78. **CAREER** Asst prof to assoc prof, Boston Col, 78-; Director Comm on Middle Eastern Studies, 86. **SELECTED PUBLICATIONS** Coed, Christians and Jews in the Ottoman Empire, the Functioning of a Plural Society, Vol I: the Central Lands, Vol II: The Arabic-Speaking Lands, (NY), 82; coed, "Open thou Mine Eyes..": Essays on Aggadah and Judaica Presented to Rabbi William G. Braude on His Eightieth Birthday and Dedicated to His Memory, (NY), 92; auth, ""Burckhardt, Jean Louis, I", "Burton, Richard, I", Canning, Stratford (Viscount Stratford de Redcliffe), I", Encyclopedia of the Modern Middle East, eds R.S. Simon, P. Mattar, R.W. Bulliet, (NY), 96; auth, "The Sons of Noah and the Construction of Ethnic and Geographical Identities in the Medieval and Early Modern Periods", William and Mary Quarterly 54, (97): 103-142; auth, "Les contours indecis d'une nouvelle geographic", Cahiers de Science et Vie 44, (96): 46-53; auth, "Jew and Jesuit at the Origins of Arabism: William Gifford Palgrave", The Jewish Discovery of Islam, ed Martin Kramer, Tel-Aviv Univ Pr, (99): 77-93; auth, "The Nexus of Diaspora, Enlightenment and Nation: Thoughts on Comparative History", Enlightenment and Diaspora, the Armenian and Jewish Cases, eds, David Myers and Richard Hovanissian, Scholars Pr, (Atlanta, 99): 5-44; auth, "Jews in Muslim Society", History of Humanity, Vol IV, From the Seventh to the Sixteenth Century, Routeledge, (London), (forthcoming); auth, "The Myth of the Sefardi Economic Superman", Trading Cultures: The Worlds of Western Merchants, eds J. Adelman and S. Aron, Brepols (Antwerp), (forthcoming); auth, Sex, Slavery, and Racism: the Secret History of the Sons of Noah, Alfred J. Knopf (NY), (forthcoming). **CONTACT ADDRESS** Dept Hist, Boston Col, Chestnut Hill, 140 Commonwealth Ave, Chestnut Hill, MA 02467-3800. **EMAIL** braude@bc.edu

BRAUER, CARL MALCOLM
PERSONAL Born 09/13/1946, Jersey City, NJ, m, 2 children **DISCIPLINE** HISTORY **EDUCATION** Rutgers Univ, New Brunswick, BA, 68, Harvard Univ, MA, 69, PhD(hist), 73. **CAREER** Vis asst prof hist, Univ Mo-Columbia, 73-74; vis asst prof, Brown Univ, 74-75; asst prof hist, Univ Va, 75-81; Fellow & Project Director; Kennedy Sch Govt, Harvard Univ, 82- ; Winthrop Group, 89-91; Freedance, 91- . **RESEARCH** Recent American history; business history; biography; public history. **SELECTED PUBLICATIONS** Auth, Calculating Visions--Kennedy, Johnson, And Civil-Rights--Stern, J Am Hist, vol 0079, 93. **CONTACT ADDRESS** 67 Leonard Street, Belmont, MA 02478. **EMAIL** cbrauer@erols.com

BRAUER, JERALD
PERSONAL Born 09/16/1921, Fond du Lac, WI, m, 1945, 3 children **DISCIPLINE** HISTORY OF CHRISTIANITY **EDUCATION** Carthage Col, AB, 43; Northwestern Lutheran Theol Sem, BD, 45; Univ Chicago, PhD, 48. **CAREER** Instr church hist & hist Christian thought, Union Theol Sem, NY, 48-50; from asst prof to prof church hist, 50-69, dean federated theol fac, 55-60, dean divinity sch, 60-70, Prof Hist Christianity, Univ Chicago, 69-, Naomi Shenstone Donnelley Prof, 69-, Kessler lectr, Hamma Divinity Sch & Wittenberg Col, 54; Merrick lectr, Ohio Wesleyan, 58; mem bd dirs, Rockefeller Theol Fel Prog & Inst Advan Pastoral Studies; trustee, Carthage Col; pres bd theol educ, Lutheran Church in Am, 62-68; deleg observer, Vatican Coun II, session 3, 64, session 4, 65; vis lectr, Univ Tokoyo & Kokagokuin Univ, 66; consult, NY State Dept Educ, 70-; vis fel, Ctr Studies Democratic Insts, 72 & 74; pres bd gov, Int House, 73-; Am Asn Theol Schs grant; fel, Ctr Policy Study, 74-79; Nat Endowment for Humanities fel, 77-78; chmn bd, Coun Relig & Int Affairs, 79- **HONORS AND AWARDS** DD, Miami Univ, 56; LLD, Carthage Col, 57; STD, Ripon Col, 61; LHD, Gettysburg Col, 63. **MEMBERSHIPS** Am Soc Church Hist (pres, 60). **RESEARCH** Puritanism influence in the United States and England; revivalism; religion in America. **SELECTED PUBLICATIONS** Auth, Protestantism in America, Westminster, 53; coauth, Luther and the Reformation, 53 & auth, Basic questions for the Christian scholar, 54, Nat Lutheran Coun; ed, Essays in Divinity (7 vols), Univ Chicago, 67-69; Reinterpretation in American Church History, Univ Chicago, 69; Paul Tillich, My Travel Diary, Harper, 70; Westminster Dictionary of Church History, Westminster, 71; Religion and the American Revolution, Fortress, 76. **CONTACT ADDRESS** Divinity Sch, Univ of Chicago, 207 Swift Hall, Chicago, IL 60637.

BRAUER, KINLEY
PERSONAL Born 04/16/1935, Jersey City, NJ, m, 1961, 2 children **DISCIPLINE** HISTORY **EDUCATION** Univ Rochester, BA, 57; Univ Calif, PhD, 63. **CAREER** Lectr, Oxford Univ, 76-77; vis prof, Univ Munich, 87; dir, Ctr for Austrian Studies, 88-89; dir, Intl Relations Prog, 93-94; Fulbright prof, Univ of Graz, 94-95; prof, Univ Minn Twin Cities; ch, Dept of Hist, 94-00; prof emer, 01. **HONORS AND AWARDS** McKnight Foundation Humanities Awd, 67. **MEMBERSHIPS** Soc for Hist of Am Foreign Relations, Soc for Hist of the Early Am Republic, Organization of Am Hist. **RESEARCH** Hist of American-foreign relations; Pre-Civil War period. **SELECTED PUBLICATIONS** Auth, pubs on history of American foreign relations; ed, Austria in the Age of the French Revolution, 90. **CONTACT ADDRESS** History Dept, Univ of Minnesota, Twin Cities, 614 Social Sciences Tower, 267 19th Ave. S, Minneapolis, MN 55455. **EMAIL** braue001@umn.edu

BRAY, R. MATTHEW
DISCIPLINE HISTORY **EDUCATION** Univ Manitoba, BA, MA; York Univ, PhD. **CAREER** Prof. **RESEARCH** Hist of Can Copper Co. **SELECTED PUBLICATIONS** Co-ed, A Vast and Magnificent Land, Laurentian Univ, Sudbury, (84): 205; co-ed, Un Vast et Merveilleux Pays, Sudbury, Laurentian Univ, (85): 205; co-ed, Temagami A Debate on Wilderness, Toronto, Dundurn Press, (90): 255; co-ed, At The End of the Shift Mines and Single-Industry Towns in Northern Ontario, Toronto, Dundurn Press, (92): 208; co-ed, Reappraisals in Caanadian History: Post-Confederation, Toronto: Prentice Hall, (92): 594; co-ed, Reappraisals in Canadian History: Pre-Confederation, Toronto: Prentice Hall, (93): 581; co-ed, "1910-1920", in C.M. Wallace and A. Thomson, eds., Sudbury: From Rail Town to Regional Capital, (Toronto: Dundurn Press, 93): 86-112; co-ed, Reappraisals in Canadian History: Post-Confederation, Toronto: Prentice Hall, 96; co-ed, Reappraisals in Canadian History: Pre-Confederation, Toronto: Prentisc Hall, 96. **CONTACT ADDRESS** Dept of History, Laurentian Univ, 935 Ramsey Lake Rd, Sudbury, ON, Canada P3E 2C6. **EMAIL** mbray@nickel.laurentian.ca

BRECKENRIDGE, JAMES
PERSONAL Born 06/30/1935, St. Louis, MO, m, 1969, 2 children **DISCIPLINE** HISTORY OF RELIGIONS, CHURCH HISTORY **EDUCATION** Biola Col, BA, 57; Calif Baptist theol Sem, BD, 60; Univ Southern Calif, MA, 65, PhD(relig), 68. **CAREER** Lectr church hist & world relig hist, Am Baptist Sem the West, 67-74; Assoc Prof Hist Relig, Baylor Univ, 74-, Lectr philos, Calif State Polytech Univ, 69-74. **MEMBERSHIPS** Am Acad Relig. **SELECTED PUBLICATIONS** Auth, Pelagius, Evangel Quart,70; Julian and Athanasius, theology, 73; Augustine and the Donatists, Foundations, 76; Religion and the problem of death, J Dharma, 79. **CONTACT ADDRESS** Dept of Relig, Baylor Univ, Waco, Waco, TX 76703.

BREECE, WILLIAM H.
PERSONAL Born 06/12/1942, m, 1988 **DISCIPLINE** ARCHAEOLOGY **EDUCATION** Calif State Univ, Long Beach, BA, 73; Univ Calif at Los Angeles, MA, 77, PhD, 92. **CAREER** Project archaeol, 78-81; instr and consultant, 81-91; prof, Anthropol and Archaeol, 91-. **HONORS AND AWARDS** Phi Kappa Phi Nat Honor Soc, 72-. **MEMBERSHIPS** Am Anthropol Asn, Register of Prof Archaeologists, Archaeol Inst Am; Soc Am Anthropol. **RESEARCH** Prehistoric Western Europe, particularly S W France. **CONTACT ADDRESS** Dept Soc Sci, Orange Coast Col, 2701 Fairview Rd, Costa Mesa, CA 92626.

BREEN, TIMOTHY HALL
PERSONAL Born 09/05/1942, Cincinnati, OH, m, 1963, 2 children **DISCIPLINE** HISTORY, AMERICAN CULTURE **EDUCATION** Yale Univ, BA, 64, MA, 66, PhD(hist), 68. **CAREER** Asst prof hist, Yale Univ, 68-70; assoc prof hist, 70-75, dir Am cult prog, 75-79, Prof Hist, Northwestern Univ, 75-, Am Coun Learned Socs res fel, 71 & Guggenheim res fel, 75; mem, inst Adv Study, 79; Bellagio-Rockefeller Ctr, scholar, 81. **MEMBERSHIPS** Inst Early Am Hist & Cult. **RESEARCH** Colonial America; American cultural history; social and cultural anthropology. **SELECTED PUBLICATIONS** Auth, Changing labor force and race relations in Virginia, 1660-1710, J Soc Hist, 73; Persistent localism in New England, William & Mary Quart, 75; ed, Shaping Southern Society, Oxford Univ, 76; auth, Horses and gentlemen: significance of gambling in seventeenth-century Virginia, William & Mary Quart, 77; Looking out for number one: conflicting cultural values in early Virginia, S Atlantic Quart, 78; Transfer of culture: chance and design in shaping Massachusetts, 1630-1660, New Eng Hist & Geneal Regist, 78; coauth, Myne Owne Ground: Race and Freedom, 81 & auth, Puritans and Adventurers: Change and Persistence in Early America, 81, Oxford Univ. **CONTACT ADDRESS** Dept of Hist, Northwestern Univ, Evanston, IL 60201.

BREIHAN, JOHN R.
PERSONAL Born 08/24/1947, St. Louis, MO, m, 1970, 3 children **DISCIPLINE** MODERN ENGLISH HISTORY; 20TH CENTURY AMERICAN HISTORY; AVIATION HISTORY. **EDUCATION** Princeton Univ, AB, 69; Univ Cambridge, PhD, 78. **CAREER** Asst instr hist, Mercer County Community Col, 69-70; prog dir, Regional Conf Hist Agencies, 77; Assoc Prof to Prof Hist, Loyola Col, 77-. Chair, Dept Hist, 83-87; Assoc dir, Fac Inst Writing Across the Curric, Md Writing Prof, 81-82; co-dir, Empirical Rhetoric II writing prog, Loyola Col, 82-87. **HONORS AND AWARDS** Loyola Col summer research grants, 80, 86, 91; sabbatical grant, 88-89, 96-97; Merit Awds for teaching and service, Loyola Col, 82, 83, 96; NEH Summer Inst in Writing Across the Curriculumn, 81; NEH, program implementation grant for Empirical Rhetoric II, cross-curricular writing program at Loyola Col, 82-87; Md Hist Trust, Md Humanities Coun, Nat Trust for Historic Preservation: grant funding for Past and Future of a Planned Suburb: Community Hist and Community Planning for Middle River (Md); Baltimore County Landmarks Preservation Comn, Awd for Excellence in Historic Preservation, 96; Verville Fel in Aviation Hist, Smithsonian Inst, 96-97. **MEMBERSHIPS** Nat Trust Hist Preserv; Soc Military Hist; Soc Hist Technol. **RESEARCH** The reform of British government administration during the fifty years between the American War and the Reform Act of 1832; writing in college history courses; historic preservation and local history; history of aircraft industry and effects on city planning. **SELECTED PUBLICATIONS** Auth, The Addington party and the Navy in British politics, 1801-1806, in New Aspects of Naval History, US Naval Inst Press, 81; The abolition of Sinecures, 1782-1834, Proc Consortium on Revolutionary Europe, 81; William Pitt and the Commission on Fees, 1785-1801, The Hist J 27, 84; coauth, Thinking and Writing in College: A Naturalistic Study in Four Disciplines, NCTE, 91; Martin Aircraft 1909-1960, Thompson/Narkiewicz, 95. **CONTACT ADDRESS** Dept of Hist, Loyola Col, 4501 N Charles St, Baltimore, MD 21210-2694. **EMAIL** breihan@loyola.edu

BREINES, PAUL
PERSONAL Born 04/16/1941, New York, NY, m, 1964, 2 children **DISCIPLINE** MODERN HISTORY **EDUCATION** Univ Wis-Madison, BA, 63, MA, 67, PhD(hist), 72. **CAREER** Asst prof soc sci, Boston Univ, 71-74; asst prof hist, 74-80, Assoc Prof Hist, Boston Col, 80-, Dir Grad Studies, 80-, Book rev ed, Telos, 69-; contrib ed, theory & Soc, 77-. **RESEARCH** Social theory; Marxism: intellectuals. **SELECTED PUBLICATIONS** Ed & contribr, Critical Interruptions: New Left Perspectives on Herbert Marcuse, Herder, 70; auth, Introduction to Lukacs, 71 & Praxis and Its Theorists, 72, Telos; Lukacs, revolution and Marxism: 1885-1918, Philos Forum, 73; Marxism and Romanticism, In: Studies in Romanticism, 16: 4, 77; coauth, Nietzsche, Marx and the German left, In: Marx und Nietzsche, 79; Young Lukacs & Origins of Western Marxism, Seabury, 80; Germans, Journals, & Jews, New German Critique, winter 81. **CONTACT ADDRESS** Dept of Hist, Boston Col, Chestnut Hill, 140 Commonwealth Ave, Chestnut Hill, MA 02167.

BREISACH, ERNST ADOLF
PERSONAL Born 10/08/1923, Schwanberg, Austria, m, 1945, 2 children **DISCIPLINE** HISTORY **EDUCATION** Univ Vienna, PhD(hist), 46; Dr rer oec, Vienna Sch Econ, 50. **CAREER** Prof hist & geog, Realsch, Vienna, 46-52; assoc prof hist, Olivet Col, 53-57; Prof Hist, Western Mich Univ, 57-96, Fulbright fel & UN off Educ grant, 51-52; fel, Am Philos Soc, 65. **HONORS AND AWARDS** Fulbright Fellow, 51-52; Conference dedication, 74; Distinguished Fac Scholar - WMU, 83; Academic Excellence Awd, 88; NEH Fellow, 89-90; Elected Founding mem of the Theta chpt of Phi Beta Kappa National Honor Soc, 98. **MEMBERSHIPS** AHA. **RESEARCH** History of Renaissance and Reformation; theory of history; historiography. **SELECTED PUBLICATIONS** Auth, Introduction to Modern Existentialism, Grove Press, New York, 62; auth, Caterina Sforza. A Renaissance Virago, The Univ of Chicago Press, Chicago, 68; auth, Renaissance Europe, The Macmillan Company, New York, 73; auth, Historiography: Ancient, Medieval Modern, The Univ of Chicago Press, Chicago, 83; ed, Classical Rhetoric and Medieval Historiography, Studies in Medieval Culture XIX, Medieval Institute Publications, Kalamazoo, Michigan, 85; auth, American Progressive History: An Experiment in Modernization, The Univ of Chicago Press, 1993. **CONTACT ADDRESS** Western Michigan Univ, 228 W Ridge Circle, Kalamazoo, MI 49008. **EMAIL** breisach@wmich.edu

BREIT, FREDERICK JOSEPH
PERSONAL Born 03/19/1936, Chicago, IL, m, 1957, 3 children **DISCIPLINE** RUSSIAN & MODERN EUROPEAN HISTORY **EDUCATION** Roosevelt Univ, BA, 63; Duke Univ, MA, 66, PhD, 72. **CAREER** Asst prof, 67-74, assoc prof hist, Whitman Col, 75-, Nat Endowment for Hum fel, 77-78. **MEMBERSHIPS** Am Comt Study World War II; AHA. **RESEARCH** International communism. **SELECTED PUBLICATIONS** Auth, Concerning the Origins of World War I, In: Problems in European History, Moore Pub Co. **CONTACT ADDRESS** Dept of Hist, Whitman Col, 345 Boyer Ave, Walla Walla, WA 99362-2083. **EMAIL** breitfj@whitman.edu

BREIT, PETER K.
DISCIPLINE HISTORY **EDUCATION** Univ CO, BA; Univ MA, MA, PhD. **CAREER** Prof, Univ Hartford. **HONORS AND AWARDS** Distinguished Serv Awd; Oscar and Shoshana Trachtenberg Awd; Roy E. Larsen Awd; **MEMBERSHIPS** Northeastern Polit Sci Asn. **RESEARCH** Europ polit and hist; Holocaust studies. **SELECTED PUBLICATIONS** Auth, Culture as Authority: US Cultural Influences in Germany 1945-1949; International Relations; Alliances; Postwar Alliances; The Encyclopedia Americana; The Christian Response to the Holocaust; Military Occupation as an Instrument of National Policy; War and Morality. **CONTACT ADDRESS** Hist Dept, Univ of Hartford, Bloomfield Ave, PO Box 200, West Hartford, CT 06117. **EMAIL** moore@uhavax.hartford.edu

BREITMAN, RICHARD D.
PERSONAL Born 03/27/1947, Hartford, CT, m, 2 children **DISCIPLINE** HISTORY **EDUCATION** Yale Univ, BA, 69; Harvard Univ, MA, 71, PhD, 75. **CAREER** From Asst Prof to Assoc Prof, 76-85, Prof Hist, Am Univ, 85-, Chair, Hist Dept, 95-97; co-ed, 94-95, ed-in-chief, Holocaust and Genocide Studies, 95-98; mem ed bd, J Contemp Hist, 94-98. **HONORS AND AWARDS** Phi Beta Kappa, Yale Univ; Graduation Honors, Summa cum Laude, Yale Univ; Fel, Woodrow Wilson Int Ctr for Schol, 87; Merit of Distinction Award, Ctr for Holocaust Studies, anti-Defamation League, for: Breaking the Silence; Fraenkel Prize for Contemp Hist, for: The Architect of Genocide. **MEMBERSHIPS** AHA. **RESEARCH** Europ Socialism: twentieth-century Germany; Am Refugee Policy and Europ Jews, 1933-1945. **SELECTED PUBLICATIONS** Auth, German Socialism and Weimar Democracy, Univ NC Press, 81; coauth, Breaking the Silence, Simon & Schuster, 86, multiple international editions, revised Am Paperback ed: Breaking the Silence: The German Who Exposed the Final Solution, Univ Press New England, 94; American Refugee Policy and European Jewry, 1933-1945, Ind Univ Press, 88; auth, The Architect of Genocide: Himmler and the Final Solution, Alfred A. Knopf, 91, & multiple international editons; Official Secrets: What the Nazis Planned, What the British and Americans Knew, Farrar, Straus, and Giroux (forthcoming Fall 98); author of numerous journal articles. **CONTACT ADDRESS** Dept of Hist, American Univ, 4400 Massachusetts Ave NW, Washington, DC 20016-8200. **EMAIL** rbreit@american.edu

BREMER, FRANCIS JOHN
PERSONAL Born 01/26/1947, New York, NY, m, 1968, 3 children **DISCIPLINE** AMERICAN HISTORY **EDUCATION** Fordham Univ, BA, 68; Columbia Univ, MA, 69, PhD, 72. **CAREER** Adj instr, 69-70, Fordham Col; lectr, 70-71, Richmond Col, CUNY; intr, 71-72, asst prof, 72-76, assoc prof, 76-77, tenured, 76, dir, Hum Enrich Prog, 73-76, dir, Hist Cooperative Ed, 76-77, Thomas More Col; assoc prof, 77-80, prof, 80-, reg dir, 79-81, 85-89, Natl History Day, grad coord, hist, 81-85, dir, Applied History Prog, 82-, chmn, 92, dept Econ, Millersvile Univ; co-dir, NEH sum sem, 94-95. **HONORS AND AWARDS** Herbert H Lehman Fel, 68; Woodrow Wilson Found Dis Fel, 70. **MEMBERSHIPS** Orgn Am Historians. **RESEARCH** 17th century trans-Atlantic Puritanism; anthropological approaches to Colonial America. **SELECTED PUBLICATIONS** Co-ed, Research Guide to Pennsylvania History, Greenwood, 93; ed, Puritanism: TransAtlantic Perspectives on a 17th Century Anglo-American Faith, Mass Hist Soc, 93; auth, The Growth of Puritanism, Christian Hist, 94; auth, Shaping New Englands: Puritan Clergymen in 17th Century England and New England, Twayne, 94; auth, Congregationalist Communion: Clerical Friendship in the Anglo-American Puritan Community, 1610-1690, Northeastern Univ Press, 94; auth, The Puritan Experiment: New England Society from Bradford to Edwards, Univ Press New England, 95; auth, Puritans in the

Pulpit: Center Stage in the Theater of God's Judgement, Hist Today, 95; auth, The Heritage of John Winthrop: Religion along the Stour Valley, 1548-1630, New England Quart, 97; coauth, The Boxford Lecture in 1620, Suffolk Rev, 98. **CONTACT ADDRESS** History Dept, The Winthrop Papers, Millersville Univ of Pennsylvania, Millersville, PA 17551. **EMAIL** francis.bremer@millersv.edu

BREMER, WILLIAM WALLING
PERSONAL Born 01/08/1942, Chicago, IL, d **DISCIPLINE** UNITED STATES HISTORY **EDUCATION** Stanford Univ, BA, 64; Univ Wis, MA, 66; Stanford Univ, PhD, 73. **CAREER** Instr, 69-72, chmn dept, 75-76, 79-82, 86-89, 96-97, from assoc prof to prof hist, 82-98, prof emeritus, Lawrence Univ. **HONORS AND AWARDS** New York State Historical Association Manuscript Awd, 82; Awd of Merit of State Historical Society of Wisconsin, 84; Excellent Teaching Awd, Lawrence University, 94. **MEMBERSHIPS** Orgn Am Historians; AHA; Am Hist Assn Social Welfare Hist Group; Am Studies Assn. **RESEARCH** Twentieth-century United States history; United States social welfare history. **SELECTED PUBLICATIONS** Art, Along the American Way: The New Deal's Work Relief Programs For The Unemployed, J Am Hist, 75; art, Into The Grain: Golf's Ascent In American Culture, J Am Cult, 81; auth, A Little Ways Ahead: The Centennial History of Thilmany Pulp & Paper Company, Kaukauna, Wisconsin, 83 auth, Depression Winters: New York Social Workers and the New Deal, 84. **CONTACT ADDRESS** 301 Kirkwood Dr, Chapel Hill, NC 27514. **EMAIL** bremerww@aol.com

BREMNER, ROBERT HAMLETT
PERSONAL Born 05/26/1917, Brunswick, OH, m, 1950, 2 children **DISCIPLINE** AMERICAN HISTORY **EDUCATION** Baldwin-Wallace Col, AB, 38; Ohio State Univ, AM, 39; PhD, 43. **CAREER** From instr to assoc prof Am hist, 46-60, prof hist, 60-80, Emer Prof Hist, Ohio State Univ, 80-, NATO res fel, 61; Soc Sci Res Coun fel, 63; Huntington Libr fel, 63; res assoc, Charles Warren Ctr, Harvard Univ, 66-69 & res ed, Child & State Proj, 67-73; sr fel, Nat Endowment for Humanities, 73-74. **SELECTED PUBLICATIONS** Auth, From the Depths, The Discovery of Poverty in the United States, NY Univ, 56, Transaction, 92; auth, American Philanthropy, Univ Chicago, 60, 88; ed, Children and Youth in America (3 vols), Harvard Univ, 70-74; auth, Public Good, Knopf, 80; auth, Giving, Charity and Philanthropy in History, Transaction, 94. **CONTACT ADDRESS** 33 Orchard Drive, Worthington, OH 43085.

BRENNAN, JOHN JAMES
PERSONAL Born 08/20/1933, Brooklyn, NY, m, 1959, 3 children **DISCIPLINE** MODERN EUROPEAN HISTORY **EDUCATION** St Vincent Col, BA, 55; Fordham Univ, MA, 59, Ph-D(hist), 69. **CAREER** From instr to asst prof, 59-75, dir honors prog, 69-76, chmn div soc sci, Notre Dame Col, 71-76, Assoc Prof Hist, St John's Univ, NY, 75-, Assoc Dean, Norte Dame Col, 79-, Danforth Found assoc, 74; mem Community Planning Bd 3, Staten Island, 76-; vchmn, Community Planning Bd #3, Staten Island, NY, 80- **RESEARCH** Sixteenth and 17th century French history; Anglo-French relations in the 16th century. **SELECTED PUBLICATIONS** Auth, Campeggio, Lorenzo, Cardinal, Ferdinand V, King of Aragon & Auto-da-Fe, In: Catholic Encylcopedia for Home and School, McGraw, 67. **CONTACT ADDRESS** Dept of Hist, St. John's Univ, 300 Howard Ave, Staten Island, NY 10301-4496.

BRENNAN, PAT
PERSONAL Born 02/05/1947, New York, NY, d, 2 children **DISCIPLINE** HISTORY **EDUCATION** St John's Univ, BA, 68; NYork Univ, MA, 70; Univ London, MA, 97. **CAREER** Prof and Chair, Piedmont Tech Col, 83-. **MEMBERSHIPS** AHA. **RESEARCH** British Empire and Commonwealth. **CONTACT ADDRESS** Dept Gen Educ, Piedmont Tech Col, PO Drawer 1467, Greenwood, SC 29648. **EMAIL** brennan_p@ped.tec.sc.us

BRENNEMAN, WALTER L., JR.
PERSONAL Born 12/05/1936, Harrisburg, PA, m, 1963, 6 children **DISCIPLINE** HISTORY OF RELIGION **EDUCATION** Gettysburg Col, BA; Univ Chicago, BA; Union Inst, PhD. **CAREER** Prof relig, Univ Vt, 69-99. **MEMBERSHIPS** Am Acad Relig; Am Comt Irish Stud. **RESEARCH** Irish Celtic religion; Irish Celtic Christianity; phenomenological method. **SELECTED PUBLICATIONS** Auth, Spirals: A study in Symbol, Myth and Ritual, Univ Press Am, 78; coauth, The Seeing Eye: Hermeneutical Phenomenology in the Study of Religion, Penn State, 82; coauth, Crossing the Circle at the Holy Walls of Ireland, Univ Press of Vir, 95. **CONTACT ADDRESS** 1853 County Rd, PO Box 760, Montpelier, VT 05602. **EMAIL** wbrennem@zoo.uvm.edu

BRENNER, LOUIS
PERSONAL Born 06/19/1937, Memphis, TN, m, 1959, 2 children **DISCIPLINE** AFRICAN HISTORY **EDUCATION** Univ Wis, BS, 59; Columbia Univ, MA, 64, PhD(hist), 68. **CAREER** Asst Prof Hist & Fac Mem, African Studies Ctr, Boston Univ, 67-80. **MEMBERSHIPS** AHA; African Studies Asn. **RESEARCH** West African history, especially the Lake Chad Basin; history of Sufism in West Africa. **SELECTED PUBLICATIONS** Auth, Separate realities: A review of literature of Sufism, Int J African Hist Studies, 72; The Shehus of Kukawa: A History of the Al-Kanemi Dynasty of Bornu, Clarendon, Oxford, 73. **CONTACT ADDRESS** 46 Craftsman Rd, Brookline, MA 02167.

BRENTANO, ROBERT
PERSONAL Born 05/19/1926, Evansville, IN, m, 1956, 3 children **DISCIPLINE** MEDIEVAL HISTORY **EDUCATION** Swarthmore Col, BA, 49; Oxford Univ, DPhil, 52. **CAREER** From instr to assoc prof, 52-65, chmn dept, 75-78, Prof Hist, Univ Calif, Berkeley, 65-, Fulbright fel, Italy, 56-57; Am Coun Learned Soc fel, 60-61; Guggenheim fel, 65-66 & 78-79; Nat Endowment for Humanities fel, 72-73. **HONORS AND AWARDS** Haskins Medal, Mediaeval Acad Am, 70; John Gilmary Shea Prize, Am Cath Hist Asn, 70; Howard R Marraro Prize, AHA, 75. **MEMBERSHIPS** Mediaeval Acad Am; Royal Hist Soc; Deputazione di storia patria per le Venezie; Soc Ital Hist Studies. **RESEARCH** English Medieval history; Italian ecclesiastical history; writing of history in the 19th century. **SELECTED PUBLICATIONS** Auth, York Metropolitan Jurisdiction and Papal Judges Delegate (1279-1296), U of Cal, 59; auth, Two Churches, England and Italy in the Thirteenth Century, Princeton, 68, U of Cal, 88; auth, Rome before Avignon , A Social of the Thirteenth-Century Rome, Basic, 74, U of Cal, 90; auth, A New World in a Small Place, Church and Religion in the Diocese of Rieti, 1188-1378, U of Cal, 94; auth, " Frederic William Maitland (1850-1906)," Medieval Scholarship, Garland, 95; auth, "Sulmona Society and the Miracles of Peter of Morrone," Monks and Nuns, Saints and Outcasts, Cornell, 00. **CONTACT ADDRESS** Dept of Hist, Univ of California, Berkeley, 3229 Dwinelle Hall, Berkeley, CA 94720.

BRESLAW, ELAINE
DISCIPLINE HISTORY **EDUCATION** Univ Md, PhD; Hunter Col, BA; Smith Col, MA; Pratt Institute, MLS. **CAREER** Lectr, Hist, Univ Tenn. **RESEARCH** Early American history. **SELECTED PUBLICATIONS** ed, Records of the Tuesday Club of Annapolis, Md., Univ of Illinois, 88; auth, Tituba, Reluctant Witch of Salem, Univ NY, 96; ed, Witches of the Atlantic World, NY Univ, 00. **CONTACT ADDRESS** Dept of Hist, Univ of Tennessee, Knoxville, 915 Volunteer Blvd, 6th Fl, Dunford Hall, Knoxville, TN 37996-4065. **EMAIL** ebreslaw@utk.edu

BRESLIN, THOMAS ALOYSIUS
PERSONAL Born 05/23/1944, Philadelphia, PA, m, 1977, 2 children **DISCIPLINE** HISTORY & INTERNATIONAL RELATIONS **EDUCATION** Fordham Univ, BA, 68; Univ Va, MA, 69, PhD, 72. **CAREER** Asst prof hist, 76-77, asst prof, Int Rels,77-81; assoc Prof, Int Rels 81-; assoc dean, Int Affairs, 77-82; Dir Div Sponsored Research and training, 82-93; asst vice pres, acad Affairs, 85-87; Assoc Vice Pres, Acad affairs, 87-88; vice provost, 87-96; vice pres, research and grad studies, 96-; Fac Fulbright adv, FL Int Univ, 77-82; mem adv bd, Univ Presses FL, 80-82; consult, Global Educ Prog, FL Dept Educ, 79-80; board mem, Center for Health Tech, Miami, 91-97. **MEMBERSHIPS** Soc Historians Am Foreign Rels; Assoc Asian Studies; Authors Guild. **RESEARCH** US diplomatic hist; mod China; Roman Cath Church. **SELECTED PUBLICATIONS** Coauth, State of Danger: Childhood Lead Paint Poisoning in Massachusetts, Mass Advocacy Ctr, 74; auth, Roman Catholic Mission to China: Victim of Religious Myopia, Holy Cross Quart, 6/75; Trouble Over Oil: America, Japan, and the Oil Cartel, 1934-35, Bull Concerned Asian Scholars, 7-9/75; coauth, Brainwashing and Managed Group Experiences: Converging New Techniques, Reason Papers, fall 75; auth, Mystifying the Past: Establishment Historians and the Origins of the Pacific War, Bull Concerned Asian Scholars, 10-12/76; China, American Catholicism, and the Missionary, Pa State Univ Press, 80; coauth, An Ordinary Relationship: American Opposition to Republican Revolution in China, FIU and U Presses of FL, 86; auth, The Administration of International Education at Florida International University in Backman, Approaches to International Education, Macmillan, 84. **CONTACT ADDRESS** Div Sponsored Res & Training, Florida Intl Univ, 1 FIU U Park, Miami, FL 33199-0001. **EMAIL** breslint@dsrt.fiu.edu

BRESLOW, BOYD
PERSONAL Born 09/08/1937, Lincoln, NE, s **DISCIPLINE** HISTORY **EDUCATION** Univ NE, BA, 59, MA 63; OH State Univ, PhD, 68. **CAREER** From instr to asst prof hist, Univ Ariz, 67-71; asst prof, 71-81, assoc prof hist, Fla Atlantic Univ, 81-. **HONORS AND AWARDS** Am Philos Soc grant, 70. **MEMBERSHIPS** Mediaeval Acad Am; Conf Brit Studies; Haskins Soc; AHA; London Rec Soc. **RESEARCH** Medieval Eng constitutional, admin and urban hist. **SELECTED PUBLICATIONS** Auth, The social status and economic interests of Richer de Refham, Lord Mayor of London, J Medieval Hist, 12/77; Ambiguities of political loyalties in Edwardian England, The case of Richer de Refham, Medieval Prosopography, 85; London merchants and the origins of the House of Commons, Medieval Prosopography, 89. **CONTACT ADDRESS** Dept of Hist, Florida Atlantic Univ, 777 Glades Rd., Boca Raton, FL 33431-0991. **EMAIL** breslow@fau.edu

BRESLOW, MARVIN A.
PERSONAL Born 01/09/1936, Lincoln, NE **DISCIPLINE** HISTORY **EDUCATION** Univ Nebr, BA, 57; Harvard Univ, MA, 58, PhD(hist), 63. **CAREER** From instr to asst prof, 62-68, assoc prof Hist, Univ MD, Col Park, 68-, Consult Elizabethan hist, Educ Serv, inc, 65-67; fel, Folger Shakespeare Libr, 66. **HONORS AND AWARDS** Folger Fel, 66; NEH Grant, 89. **MEMBERSHIPS** AHA; Conf Brit Studies. **RESEARCH** Puritanism; political thought. **SELECTED PUBLICATIONS** Auth, A Mirror of England: English Puritan Views of Foreign Nations, 1618-1640; ed, The Political Writing of John Knox; auth, George Calvert. **CONTACT ADDRESS** Dept of His, Univ of Maryland, Col Park, 2100 Washington Ave #6-B, Silver Spring, MD 20910. **EMAIL** mb62@umail.umd.edu

BRETON, RAYMOND J.
PERSONAL Born 08/19/1931, Montmartre, SK, Canada **DISCIPLINE** SOCIAL HISTORY, POPULATION HISTORY **EDUCATION** Univ Man, BA, 52; Univ Chicago, MA, 58; Johns Hopkins Univ, PhD, 61. **CAREER** Res dir, Soc Res Gp, Montreal, 57-64; prog dir, Inst Res Pub Policy, 76-81; dir, grad stud soc, 81-85, PROF SOCIOLOGY, UNIV TORONTO; William Lyon MacKenzie King Prof Can Stud, Harvard Univ, 96-97. **HONORS AND AWARDS** Samuel S. Fels fel, 60-61; Can Coun leave fel, 72-73, 81-82; sr res fel, Statistics Can, 87-88; sr Connaught fel soc sci, 88-89; Outstanding Contrib Awd, Can Soc & Anthrop Asn, 90; DL (honoris causa), Univ Guelph, 94. **MEMBERSHIPS** Royal Soc Can **SELECTED PUBLICATIONS** Auth, Academic and Social Factors in Career Decision-Making: A Study of Canadian Secondary School Students, 72; auth, The Governance of Ethnic Communities: Political Structures and Processes in Canada, 91; auth, Why Meech Lake Failed: Lessons in Canadian Constitutionmaking, 92; coauth, The Social Impact of Changes in Population Size and Composition: An Analysis of Reactions to Patterns of Immigration, 74; coauth, Cultural Boundaries and the Cohesion of Canada, 80; coauth, Why Disunity: An Analysis of Linguistic and Regional Cleavages in Canada, 80; coauth, The Illusion of Difference: Realities of Ethnicity in Canada and the United States, 94; ed, Aspects of Canadian Society, 74; ed, Ethnic Identity and Equality: Varieties of Experience in a Canadian City, 90; ed, Can Rev Soc Anthrop, 73-76. **CONTACT ADDRESS** Dept of Sociology, Univ of Toronto, 203 College St, 5th Fl, Toronto, ON, Canada M5T 1P9. **EMAIL** rbreton@chass.utoronto.ca

BRETT-SMITH, SARAH
DISCIPLINE ART HISTORY **EDUCATION** Yale Univ, PhD, 82. **CAREER** Assoc prof, Rutgers Univ. **HONORS AND AWARDS** Hon Men Victor Turner Prize, Soc Hum Anthro, 95; Arts Coun African Studies Asn, 93-95; Arnold J Rubin awd outstanding bk African Art. **RESEARCH** Bamana (Bambara) sculpture: gender and art making; the symbolism of Bamana, Dogon, Malinke, Minianka, Senufo and Bobo textiles; surrealism and primitive art. **SELECTED PUBLICATIONS** Auth, The Mouth of the Komo, Res: Anthropology and Aesthetics, 97; The Artfulness of M'Fa Jigi: An Interview with Nyamaton Diarra, Univ Wis, 96; The Making of Bamana Sculpture: Creativity and Gender, Cambridge UP, 94; Bamanakan ka Gelen or The Voice of the Bamana is Hard, Art Tribal, Musee Barbier-Mueller, 87; The Poisonous Child, Res: Anthropology and Aesthetics, 83; Symbolic Blood: Cloths for Excised Women, RES: Anthro Aesthetics), 82. **CONTACT ADDRESS** Dept of Art Hist, Rutgers, The State Univ of New Jersey, Rutgers Col, Hamilton St., New Brunswick, NJ 08903. **EMAIL** brettsmi@rci.rutgers.edu

BRICELAND, ALAN VANCE
PERSONAL Born 04/17/1939, Baltimore, MD, w, 1962, 2 children **DISCIPLINE** AMERICAN HISTORY **EDUCATION** Col William & Mary, AB, 61; Duke Univ, MA, 63, PhD, 65. **CAREER** Asst prof hist, N TX State Univ, 65-66; asst prof, 66-74, assoc prof hist, VA Commonwealth Univ, 74. **MEMBERSHIPS** AHA; Orgn Am Historians; Southern Hist Asn; AAUP; Soc Hist Early Am Repub. **RESEARCH** South side Virginia in mid 17th century; frontier Alabama: 1800-1805; Virginia ratifying conviction of 1788. **SELECTED PUBLICATIONS** Auth, Daniel McCalla, 1746-1809: New Side Revolutionary and Jeffersonian, J Presby Hist, fall 78; The Search for Edward Bland's New Britain, Va Mag Hist & Biog, 4/79; Land, Law, and Politics on the Tombigbee Frontier, 1804, Ala Rev, 4/80; The Group-Task Approach: Developing Analytical Skills in the United States History Survey, The Hist Teacher, 2/81; Westward from Virginia: The Exploration of the Virginia-Carolina Frontier, 1650-1710, Univ Press Va, 87; 1788: The Year of Decision: Virginia's Ratification of the U.S. Constitution, Va Dept Educ: Soc Studies Prog, 89; British Exploration of the United States Interior 1707-1804, In: The Exploration of North America, vol II, Univ Nebr Press, 97; North America: Inland from the East Coast, 1607-1769, In: The Times Atlas of World Exploration, HarperCollins Publ, 91; Batts and Fallam Explore the Backbone on the Continent, In: Appalachian Frontiers: Settlement, Society & Development in the Preindustrial Era, Univ Press KY, 91. **CONTACT ADDRESS** Dept of Hist, Virginia Commonwealth Univ, Box 2001, Richmond, VA 23284-2001. **EMAIL** abricela@atlas.vcu.edu

BRIDENTHAL, RENATE
PERSONAL Born 06/13/1935, Germany **DISCIPLINE** GERMAN HISTORY **EDUCATION** City Col New York, BA, 60; Columbia Univ, MA, 61, PhD(hist), 70. **CAREER** Lectr hist, Borough Manhattan Community Col, 66-67; lectr, 67-74, asst prof, 74-80, assoc prof 80-86, Prof Hist, Brooklyn Col, 86-, Ed, Sci & Soc, 72- **HONORS AND AWARDS** PSC-BHE res award, 80; Intl Res and Exchanges Bd, 83; NEH, 83-84; Fulbright, 83-84 (declined), PSC-BHE Res Awd, 99-00. **MEMBERSHIPS** AHA; Coord Coun for Women in Hist; Berkshire Conf Women Historians; Phi Beta Kappa **RESEARCH** Research Intrests: Russian-German Diaspora **SELECTED PUBLICATIONS** Auth, The Greening of Germany: 1848: Karl Grun's true socialism, Sci & Soc, 71; The dialectics of production and reproduction in history, Radical Am 3-4, 76; contrib/co-ed, Becoming Visible: Women in European History, Houghton, 77; auth, Critique of family history, Feminist Studies, spring 79; The family: The view from the room of her own, In: Rethinking the Family: Some Feminist Questions, Longmans, 82; Class struggle around the hearth: Women and domestic service in the Weimar Republic, In: Towards the Holocaust: Anti-Semitism and Fascism in the Weimar Republic, Greenwood, 83; co-ed & contrb, When biology became destiny: Women in Weimar and Nazi Germany, Monthly Rev, 84; Women and the Conservative Mobilization Of The Countryside in Weimar Republic, in: Between Reform, Reaction, and Resistance: Studies in the History of German Conservativism from 1789 to the Present, Berg, 93; contrib/co-ed, Becoming Visible: Women in European History, 3rd ed, Houghton, 98; auth, "Making and Writing History Together," Nupur Chaudhuri, Indiana UP, 99. **CONTACT ADDRESS** Dept of Hist, Brooklyn Col, CUNY, 2900 Bedford Ave, Brooklyn, NY 11210-2889. **EMAIL** RBriden1@juno.com

BRIDGES, ROGER DEAN
PERSONAL Born 02/10/1937, Marshalltown, IA, m, 1960, 3 children **DISCIPLINE** UNITED STATES HISTORY **EDUCATION** Univ Northern Iowa, BA, 59, MA, 63; Univ Ill, Urbana-Champaign, PhD(hist), 70. **CAREER** Teacher-librn, Jr High Sch, Keokuk, Iowa, 59-62; asst soc sci, Univ Northern Iowa, 62-63 & hist, Univ Ill, Urbana-Champaign, 63-68; asst prof, Univ SDak, 68-69; Nat Hist Publ Comn fel, Ulysses S Grant Asn & vis adj lectr hist, Southern Ill Univ, Carbondale, 69-70; dir res, Ill state hist libr, 70-85, head librn, 77-85, Lectr Hist, Ill State Univ, 74-88; head, Ill State hist libr/division, Ill historic Preservation Agency, 85-87; asst Ill state historian and ed, The Lincoln Legals Project, Ill Historic Preservation Agency, 87-88; exec dir, Rutherford B. Hayes Presidential Center, Fremont, Ohio, 88-; Adjunct prof pf hist, Bowling Green State Univ, 88-. **HONORS AND AWARDS** Hon doctorate in Humane Letter, Lincoln Univ, Lincoln, Ill, 87; Tiffin Univ, 95; Awd for Distinguished Service to Ill hist, Ill State Historical Soc, 88. **MEMBERSHIPS** AHA; Orgn Am Hist; Southern Hist Asn; Asn Doc Editing; Soc for Historians of the Gilded Age and Progressive Era. **RESEARCH** Nineteenth-century United States history; Illinois history; Afro-American history; Public history. **SELECTED PUBLICATIONS** Coed, Papers of Ulysses S. Grant, Jan 8-March 31, 1862, Vol 4, Southern Ill Univ, 72; auth, John Sherman and the Impeachment of Andrew Johnson, Ohio Hist, 73; auth, "Origins and Early Years of the Illinois State Historical Society," J Ill State Hist Soc (75); auth, "Bibliography of Dissertation Related to Illinois History, 1884-1976," J Ill State Hist Soc (77); auth, "Lincoln Reacts to the Civil War,: Lincoln Herald (79); auth, "Equality Deferred: Civil Rights for Illinois Blacks, 1865-1895," J Ill State Hist Soc (81); coed, Illinois: Its History and Legacy, 84; auth, "Dark Faces on the Antebellum West Central Illinois Landscape," Western Illinois Regional Studies (83); auth, "Founding the Illinois Baptist Convention, 1830-1834," American Baptish Quarterly (84); auth, "Lincoln's Impact on President Rutherford B. Hayes," in Abraham Lincoln: Comtemporary, ed. Frank J. Williams and William D. Pederson (Campbell, Calif, Savas Woodbury, 95); auth, "John Sherman, Republican Senator," in The Human Conidtion in the American Civil War and Reconstruction, ed. Steven E. Woodworth (Wilminton, Delaware, Scholarly Resources, 00). **CONTACT ADDRESS** Rutherford B. Hayes Presidential Center, Spiegel Grove, Fremont, OH 43420-2796. **EMAIL** rbridges@rbhayes.org

BRIEGER, GERT HENRY
PERSONAL Born 01/05/1932, Hamburg, Germany, m, 1955, 3 children **DISCIPLINE** HISTORY OF MEDICINE **EDUCATION** Univ Calif, Berkeley, AB, 53; Univ Calif, Los Angeles, MD, 57; Harvard Univ, MPh, 62; Johns Hopkins Univ, PhD, 68. **CAREER** Asst prof hist med, Sch Med, Johns Hopkins Univ, 66-70; assoc prof, Duke Univ, 70-75; Prof Hist Med, Univ Calif, San Fransisco, 75-. **MEMBERSHIPS** Hist Sci Soc; AHA; Orgn Am Historians; Am Asn Hist Med (vpres, 78-80, pres, 80-82). **RESEARCH** History of American medicine; 19th and 20th century history of medical education. **SELECTED PUBLICATIONS** Auth, Medical America in the 19th Century, Johns Hopkins, 72; Theory and practice in American medicine, Sci Hist, 76. **CONTACT ADDRESS** Sch Med, Johns Hopkins Univ, Baltimore, 3400 N Charles St, Baltimore, MD 21218.

BRIGGS, J. M.
DISCIPLINE HISTORY OF SCIENCE, EARLY MODERN EUROPE, AND HISTORY THROUGH SCIENCE FICTIO **EDUCATION** Columbia Univ, PhD, 62. **CAREER** Dept Hist, Univ of RI **RESEARCH** Sci, technol and cult. **SELECTED PUBLICATIONS** Publ on, effects of industrial pollution in 18th century Fr. **CONTACT ADDRESS** Dept of Hist, Univ of Rhode Island, 8 Ranger Rd, Ste. 1, Kingston, RI 02881-0807.

BRILLIANT, RICHARD
PERSONAL Born 11/20/1929, Boston, MA, m, 1951, 4 children **DISCIPLINE** HISTORY OF GREEK & ROMAN ART **EDUCATION** Yale Univ, BA, 51, MA, 56, PhD(art hist), 60; LLB, Harvard Univ, 54. **CAREER** From asst prof to prof hist of art, Univ Pa, 62-70; prof art hist, Columbia Univ, 70-; Anna S. Garbedian prof in the Humanities (Columbia), 90-; dir, Italian Academy for Advanced Studies in America at Columbia, 96-00; Fulbright grant, Italy, 57-59; Am Acad Rome fel, 60-62; Guggenheim fel, 67-68; vis Mellon prof fine arts, Univ Pittsburgh, 71; Nat Endowment Humanities sr fel, 72-73; vis Lincei prof, Scuola Normale Superiore, Pisa, 74, 80, & 88; ed in chief, The Art Bulletin, 91-94. **MEMBERSHIPS** Corresp mem, Ger Archaeol Inst; Col Art Asn; Am Numis Soc; Archaeol Inst Am; Soc Prom Hellenic Studies. **RESEARCH** Greek and Roman art and archaeology; theory in the historiography of art; the city of Rome, antiquity to the early Renaissance. **SELECTED PUBLICATIONS** Auth, Gesture and Rank in Roman Art, Conn Acad, 63; The Arch of Septimius Severus in the Roman Forum, Am Acad Rome, 67; Arts of the Ancient Greeks, McGraw, 73; Roman Art, Phaidon, 74; Pompeii: AD 79, The Treasure of Rediscovery, 79; Visual Narratives, Cornell, 84; Portraiture, Harvard, 91; Commentaries on Roman Art, London, 94; Facing the New World, NY, 97; auth, My Laocoon, UCAL Press, 00; auth, Un Americano a Roma, Direnzo (Rome), 00. **CONTACT ADDRESS** Dept of Art Hist & Archaeol, Columbia Univ, 2960 Broadway, New York, NY 10027-6900.

BRINGHURST, NEWELL G.
PERSONAL Born 04/03/1942, Salt Lake City, UT, m, 1969, 1 child **DISCIPLINE** HISTORY, POLITICAL SCIENCE **EDUCATION** Univ Ut, BS, 65; MS, 67; Univ Calif Davis, PhD, 75. **CAREER** Lectr, San Jose State Univ, 72-75; instr, Bosie State Univ, 75-76; asst prof, Ind univ at Kokomo, 77-81; instr, Col of the Sequoias, 81-. **HONORS AND AWARDS** Fac Recognition Awd, Col of the Sequoias, 86-87; Best Article Awd, Mormon Hist Asn, 79 & 90; Dale L. Morgan Awd, Ut Hist Asn, 90. **MEMBERSHIPS** Western Hist Asn, Am Hist Asn, Mormon Hist Asn. **RESEARCH** U.S. political, social, and cultural history, the American West, American religious history with a focus on Mormonism. **SELECTED PUBLICATIONS** Auth, Mormonism, 81; Saints, Slaves, and Blacks: The Changing Place of Black People within Brigham Young and the Expanding American Frontier, 86; auth, Fawn McKay Brodie: A Biographer's Life, 99. **CONTACT ADDRESS** Dept Soc Sci, Col of the Sequoias, 915 S Mooney Blvd, Visalia, CA 93277-2214. **EMAIL** newellb@giant.sequoias.cc.ca.us

BRINK, JAMES EASTGATE
PERSONAL Born 02/28/1945, Santa Fe, NM, m, 1968, 1 child **DISCIPLINE** HISTORY **EDUCATION** Univ Kans, BA, 67; Univ Wash, MA, 70, PhD(hist), 74. **CAREER** Asst prof to assoc prof hist, Tex Tech Univ, 76-; interim vice pres for Enrollment of Management, 97; vice provost, 98. **MEMBERSHIPS** AHA; Int Comn Hist Representative & Parliamentary Inst; Soc Reformation Res; Western Soc French Hist. **RESEARCH** Representative institutions of early modern Europe; the estates general of Languedoc: sixteenth century political and social history. **SELECTED PUBLICATIONS** Auth, A Tax Loop-Hole in the Sixteenth Century, Western French Hist, 76; Les Etats de Languedoc de 1515-1560, Annales du Midi, 7-9/76; The Case for Provincial Autonomy: The Estates of Languedoc, 1515-1560, Legis Studies Quart, Vol 3, 437-446. **CONTACT ADDRESS** Office of the Provost, Texas Tech Univ, Box 42019, Lubbock, TX 79409-0001. **EMAIL** jim.brink@ttu.edu

BRINKLEY, ALAN
PERSONAL Born 06/02/1944, Washington, DC, m, 1989, 1 child **DISCIPLINE** HISTORY **EDUCATION** Princeton Univ, AB, 71; Harvard Univ, PhD, 79. **CAREER** Asst Prof, MIT, 78-82; Assoc Prof, Harvard Univ, 82-88; Prof, CUNY, 88-91; Prof, Columbia Univ, 91-; Prof, Oxford Univ, 98-99. **HONORS AND AWARDS** Nat Book Awd, 83. **MEMBERSHIPS** Am Acad of Arts and Sci. **RESEARCH** 20th Century U.S. History **SELECTED PUBLICATIONS** Auth, The End of Reform: New Deal Liberalism in Recession and War, Alfred A. Knopf, 95; co-auth, New Federalist Papers, W.W. Norton, 97; co-auth, Eyes of the Nation: A Visual History of the United States, Alfred A. Knopf, 97; auth, The Unfinished Nation: A concise History of the American People, Alfred A. Knopf, 97; auth, Liberalism and Its discontents, Harvard Univ Press, 98; auth, American History: A Survey, McGraw-Hill, 98; co-auth, The Chicago Handbook for Teachers: A Practical Guide to the College Classroom, Chicago Univ Press, 99; co-ed, The Readers companion to the American Presidency, Houghton-Mifflin, 00. **CONTACT ADDRESS** Dept Hist, Columbia Univ, 2960 Broadway, New York, NY 10027-6944. **EMAIL** ab65@columbia.edu

BRINKLEY, GEORGE A.
PERSONAL Born 04/20/1931, Wilmington, NC, m, 1959, 1 child **DISCIPLINE** INTERNATIONAL RELATIONS, RUSSIAN AND EAST EUROPEAN STUDIES **EDUCATION** Davidson Col, BA, 53; Columbia Univ, MA, 55, PhD, 64. **CAREER** Instr, Columbia Univ, 57-58; Instr to prof emer, 58-91, dir, 69-87, Prog of Soviet and East European Stud, Univ of Notre Dame. **HONORS AND AWARDS** Phi Beta Kappa, 52; Ford Found Fel, 54-57; Beer Prize, Am Hist Asn, 67; Fel Coun on For Rel, 68. **MEMBERSHIPS** Am Asn for Advan of Slavic Stud. **RESEARCH** Soviet/Russian government and foreign relations. **SELECTED PUBLICATIONS** Auth, The Volunteer Army and Allied Intervention in South Russia, 1917-1921, Univ Notre Dame Pr, 66. **CONTACT ADDRESS** 19539 Cowles Ave, South Bend, IN 46637.

BRINKMAN, JOHN ANTHONY
PERSONAL Born 07/04/1934, Chicago, IL, m, 1970, 1 child **DISCIPLINE** ANCIENT NEAR EASTERN HISTORY **EDUCATION** Loyola Univ, AB, 56, AM, 58; Univ Chicago, PhD, 62. **CAREER** From asst prof to assoc prof, 64-70; chmn, Dept Near Eastern Lang & Civilizations, 69-72; dir, Orient Inst, 72-81; Prof, Mesopotamian History, Orient Inst, Univ Chicago, 70-, Charles H. Swift Distinguished Serv Prof, 84- , Chair of the Visiting Committee of the Dept Near Eastern Lang & Civs, Harvard, 95- ,Am Coun Learned Soc fel, 63-64; annual prof, Am Schs Orient Res, Baghdad, 68-69, chmn Baghdad sch comt, 71, chmn exec comt, 73-75; res fel, Am Res Inst Turkey, 71; mem vis comt, Dept Near Eastern Lang & Lit, Harvard Univ, 73-80; Nat Endowment for Humanities sr fel, 73-74; cur tablet collection, Orient Inst, 77; ed, Chicago Assyrian Dict, 77-. **MEMBERSHIPS** Am Orient Soc; Brit Inst Persian Studies; Brit Inst Archaeol Ankara; Brit Sch Archaeol Iraq; Deutsche Orient Ges. **RESEARCH** Political history of Babylonia; Assyrian historiography; ancient Oriental numismatics. **SELECTED PUBLICATIONS** Auth, A political history of post-Kassite Babylonia, Pontif Bibl Inst, 68; Foreign relations of Babylonia from 1600 to 625 BC, Am J Archaeol, 72; Comments on the Nassouhi Kinglist and the Assyrian Kinglist tradition, Orientalia, 73; Sennacherib's Babylonian problem: An interpretation, J Cuneiform Studies, 73; Materials and Studies for Kassite History, Vol I, Orient Inst, Univ Chicago, 76; Prelude to Empire, 84. **CONTACT ADDRESS** Oriental Inst, Univ of Chicago, 1155 E 58th St, Chicago, IL 60637-1540. **EMAIL** j-brinkman@uchicago.edu

BRINKMAN, JOHN T.
DISCIPLINE HISTORY OF RELIGION **EDUCATION** Fordham Univ, PhD, 88. **CAREER** Inst of Asian Stud, St John's Univ, 89-97. **MEMBERSHIPS** AAAS; AAR. **RESEARCH** Ecological dimension of world religion; East Asian thought; history of religions with refined focus in the sequence; Japan; Chiina; India; **SELECTED PUBLICATIONS** Auth, The Simplicity of Dogen, Eastern Buddhist, 94; auth, Harmony, Attribute of the Sacred and Phenomenal in Aquinas and Kukai, Buddhist-Christian Stud, 95; auth, The Simplicity of Nichiren, Eastern Buddhist, 95; auth, Simplicity: A Distinctive Quality of Japanese Spirituality, Peter Land, 96; auth, Cosmology and Consciousness, Buddhist-Christian Studies, 98; auth, The Kyoto Protocol and Exigent Ecological Vision, Int Shinto Found Symp Proc, 98-99. **CONTACT ADDRESS** 2 Darthouth Rd, Shoreham, NY 11786.

BRINKS, HERBERT JOHN
PERSONAL Born 05/25/1935, IL, m, 1957, 2 children **DISCIPLINE** HISTORY **EDUCATION** Calvin Col & Sem, AB, 57; Univ Mich, MA, 61, PhD, 65. **CAREER** Res asst, Mich Hist Collection, Univ Mich, 61-62; from instr to assoc prof, 62-71, Prof Hist, Calvin Col, 71- Cur Colonial Collection, 62-, Consult, Immigration Sources Proj, Univ Mich, 75-; Earhart Found fel, 76-77. **MEMBERSHIPS** Orgn Am Hist. **RESEARCH** Dutch-American immigration and Americanization. **SELECTED PUBLICATIONS** Auth, Michigan lumbering and mining, Mich Hist Mag, 60; Guide to Dutch-American Historical Collections of Western Michigan, Dutch-Am Hist Comn, 67; Peter White, 70 & A Michigan Reader, 73, Eerdmans; The Rationale for Denominational Colleges, Univ Col Quart, Mich State Univ, 76; Schrij of Spoedig Tervg, Boekencentrum, Den Haag, Neth, 78. **CONTACT ADDRESS** Dept of Hist, Calvin Col, Grand Rapids, MI 49506.

BRINNER, WILLIAM MICHAEL
PERSONAL Born 10/06/1924, Alameda, CA, m, 1951, 3 children **DISCIPLINE** PHILOLOGY, ISLAMIC HISTORY **EDUCATION** Univ Calif, Berkeley, AB, 48, MA, 50, PhD, 56. **CAREER** From instr to assoc prof, 56-64, chmn dept & dir Near Eastern Lang & Area Ctr, 65-70, dir Ctr Arabic Studies Abroad, 67-70, Prof Near Eastern Lang, Univ Calif, Berkeley, 64-, Lectr Arabic, Ctr Mid Eastern Studies, Harvard Univ, 61; Visiting Prof, Hebrew Univ of Jerusalem, 70-71; 73-75; Univ of San Francisco, 85; Univ of Washington, 91. Am Coun Learned Soc-Soc Sci Res Coun grant Near Eastern studies, 61-62; mem, Am Res Ctr Egypt, 68-70; consult, US off Educ, 65-68; 65-66; Guggenheim fel, 65-66; mem joint comt Near & Mid E, Am Coun Learned Soc-Soc Sci Res Coun, 66-70 & chmn, 69-70; mem exec comt, Am inst Iranian Studies, 68; Founder and U.S. Director, Center for Arabic Studies Abroad, Amer Univ in

Cairo, 66-70; Fulbright-Hays fac res award, 70-71 & sr consult, Comt int Exchange Persons, 72-73; Member, Evaluation Panels, Natl Endowmen for the Humanities, 78-81; 85-91; dir, Univ Calif Studies Ctr, Jerusalem, 73-75; Visiting Committee, Dept of Near Eastern Langs. And Lit, Harvard Univ, 84-90; Acting Dir, Annenberg Research Institute, Philadelphia, 92-93. **HONORS AND AWARDS** Berkeley Citation for Academic Achievement and Distinguished Service, 91; Hebrew Union College, Los Angeles, Doctor of Human Letters, 92; Honoree, International Interdisciplinary Conference, Bridging the Worlds of Judaism and Islam, Berkeley, 93. **MEMBERSHIPS** Am Orient Soc (pres, 76-77); Mediaeval Acad Am; Mid E Studies Asn (pres, 69-70); Am Asn Teachers Arabic (pres, 68-69); Soc for Judaco -Arabic Studies; Am Acad for Jewish Research; Association for Jewish Studies. **RESEARCH** Arabic and Hebrew language and literature; Islamic and Jewish history. **SELECTED PUBLICATIONS** Auth, "A Chronicle of Damascus, 1389-97 2 vols, Univ of Cal of Press, 63; auth, "Sutro Library Hebraica: A Handlist," Cal State Library, 67; auth, "Readings in Modern Arabic Literature," E.J. Brill, Leiden, 72; auth, "An Elegant Composition Concerning Relief After Adversity," Yak Univ Press, 78-, reprint by Jason Aronson Inc., 96; auth, "Studies in Islamic and Judaic Traditions," vol 1 86, vol 11 89, Atlanta Scholars Press; auth, "Prophets and Patriarchs," History of al-/ Tabari, vol 11, Suny Press, 87; auth, "The Children of Israel," History of al-Tabari, vol 111, Suny Press, 91. **CONTACT ADDRESS** Dept of Near Eastern Studies, Univ of California, Berkeley, 250 Barrows Hall, Berkeley, CA 94720-1940. **EMAIL** zebrin@socrates.berkeley.edu

BRISCO, THOMAS V.

PERSONAL m, 2 children **DISCIPLINE** BIBLICAL BACKGROUNDS AND ARCHAELOLOGY **EDUCATION** Ouachita Baptist Univ, BA, 69; Southwestern Baptist Theol Sem, MDiv, 73; Southwestern Baptist Theol Sem, PhD, 81; advan stud, Cambridge Univ, 86. **CAREER** Tchg fel, Southwestern Baptist Theol Sem, 75-76; instr, Ouachita Baptist Univ, 77-80; instr to prof, Southwestern Baptist Theol Sem, 80-; assoc dean, Spec Masters Degrees. **HONORS AND AWARDS** David Meier Intl Stud League Awd, Southwestern Baptist Theol Sem, 74; Outstanding Young Men of Am, 78, 79; Who's Who Among Students in Amer Univ(s) and Col(s), 76; Who's Who Among Biblical Archaeol; interim pastor, kingsland baptist church, 96-97; first baptist church, 95-96; first baptist church, humble, 94-95; intl baptist church, 93; first baptist church, arkadelphia, 92-93; vp, amer sch(s) oriental res, 82-83; president, 83-84; vp, nat assn bapti **SELECTED PUBLICATIONS** Auth, Biblical Illustrator, Baptist Sunday Sch Bd, 79; Intl Standard Bible Encycl, Eerdmans, 88; contribur, Holman Bible Dictionary, Broadman & Holman, 91; auth, Holman Bible Atlas; contribur, Eerdmans Dictionary of the Bible; contribur, New Int Dictionary of Old Testament Theol. **CONTACT ADDRESS** Sch Theol, Southwestern Baptist Theol Sem, PO Box 22000, Fort Worth, TX 76122-0418. **EMAIL** tvb@swbts.swbts.edu

BRISTOW, EDWARD

DISCIPLINE JEWISH HISTORY **EDUCATION** Yale Univ, PhD. **CAREER** Dean, prof, Fordham Univ. **HONORS AND AWARDS** Grants, NEH; Am Philos Soc. **RESEARCH** Mod Britain. **SELECTED PUBLICATIONS** Auth, Profit-Sharing, Socialism and Labor Unrest, Essays in Anti-Labor Hist, 75; Vice and Vigilance: Purity Movements in Britain Since 1700, Rowan and Littlefield, 78; Prostitution and Prejudice: The Jewish Fight Against White Slavery, 1875-1939, Clarendon Press, 82; Individualism Versus Socialism in Britain, 1880-1914, Garland Publ, 87. **CONTACT ADDRESS** Dept of Hist, Fordham Univ, 113 W 60th St, New York, NY 10023.

BRITSCH, R. LANIER

PERSONAL Born 11/16/1938, Provo, UT, m, 1961, 6 children **DISCIPLINE** HISTORY **EDUCATION** BYU, BA, 63, MA, 64; Claremont Grad Univ, PhD, 67. **CAREER** From instr to asst prof to assoc prof to prof, 66-, vp, academics, BYU, Hawaii Campus, 86-90; dir, David M. Kennedy Ctr, 91-97. **HONORS AND AWARDS** Nat Defense Foreign Lang Fel, 65-66; Fel, Blaisdell Inst, 66; Fulbright-Hays Summer Sem, 68; BYU Res Grant, 73; LDS Church Historians Grant, 74; Prof Development Leave, 78, 95, 97, 98. **MEMBERSHIPS** Mormon Hist Asn. **RESEARCH** History of the Church of Jesus Christ of Latter-day Saints in Asia and the Pacific; Christian mission history in Asia. **SELECTED PUBLICATIONS** Auth, Unto the Islands of the Sea: A History of the Latter-day Saints in the Pacific, 86; auth, Moramona: The Mormon in Hawaii, 89; auth, From the East: The History of the Latter-day Saints in Asia, 1851-1996, 98; auth, art, Faithful, Good, Virtuous, True: Pioneers in the Philippines, 98; auth, art, Mormon Intruders in Tonga: The Passport Act of 1922, 98; auth, Nothing More Heroic: The Compelling Story of the First Latter-day Saint Missionaries in India, 99. **CONTACT ADDRESS** Dept of History, Brigham Young Univ, Provo, UT 84602. **EMAIL** lanier_british@byu.edu

BRITTAIN, JAMES EDWARD

PERSONAL Born 05/20/1931, Mills River, NC, m, 1973 **DISCIPLINE** HISTORY OF SCIENCE & TECHNOLOGY **EDUCATION** Clemson Univ, BS, 57; Univ Tenn, MS, 58; Case Western Reserve Univ, MA, 68, PhD(hist), 70. **CAREER** Asst prof elec eng, Clemson Univ, 59-66; asst prof hist, Ga inst Technol, 69-72; res fel, Smithsonian inst, 72-73; Assoc Prof Hist, GA Inst Technol, 73-, Asst ed, Technol & Cult, 74-75, assoc ed, 76-77; chmn, inst Elec & Electronics Comn, 78-79. **HONORS AND AWARDS** Usher Awd, Soc Hist Technol, 71. **MEMBERSHIPS** Soc Hist Technol; Hist Sci Soc; inst Elect & Electronics Engrs; Soc indust Archaeol; Royal Soc Arts. **RESEARCH** History of electrical science and technology; history of technology in the American south. **SELECTED PUBLICATIONS** Auth, The Introduction of the Loading Coil, Technol & Cult, 1/70; The Internation Diffusion of Electric Power Technology, 1870-1920, J Econ Hist, 3/74; A Brief History of Engineering in Georgia, Ga Inst Technol, 76; C P Steinmetz and E F W Alexanderson, Proc Inst Elec & Electronic Engrs, 9/76; ed, Turning Points in American Electrical History, Inst Elec & Electronic Engrs, 77; auth, Power Electronics at General Electric, 1900-1941, Advances in Electronics & Electron Physics, 80. **CONTACT ADDRESS** Sch Soc Sci, Georgia Inst of Tech, Atlanta, GA 30332.

BROCK, KAREN L.

DISCIPLINE JAPANESE ART HISTORY **EDUCATION** Princeton Univ, PhD. **CAREER** Assoc prof Hist, Washington Univ, 85-. **HONORS AND AWARDS** Japan Found Prof Fel. **SELECTED PUBLICATIONS** Auth, "The Role of the Editor in Japanese Picture Scrolls: A Reexamination of Shigisan engi emaki," in Narrative Art, in International Symposium on Art Historical Studies 8, (90): 49-64; auth, "Chinese Maiden, Silla Monk: Zenmyo and her Thirteenth-century Japanese Audience," in Flowering in the Shadows: Women in the History of Chinese and Japanese Painting, ed. Marsha Weidner, (Honolulu: Univ of Hawaii Press, 90): 185-218; auth, "The Making and remaking of Miraculous Origins of Mt. Shigi," Archives of Asian Art 45, (92): 42-71; auth, "Pictorial Art Before 1600," in The Cambridge Encyclopedia of Japan, (Cambridge: Cambridge Univ Press, 93): 186-90; auth, "Seeing Myoe in Tale of Gangyo," in Tsuji Nobuo sensei kanreki kinen kai, ed. Nihon bijutshushi no suimyaku, (Tokyo: Perikan, 93): 355-91; auth, "The Shogun's Painting Match Monumenta Nipponica, Tokyo, (95): 433-84; coauth, The Dictionary of Art, London: MacMilan Publishers, 96. **CONTACT ADDRESS** Washington Univ, 1 Brookings Dr, Saint Louis, MO 63130. **EMAIL** YMatsusaka@wellesley.edu

BROCK, PETER DE BEAUVOIR

PERSONAL Born 01/30/1920, Guernsey Channel Is, United Kingdom **DISCIPLINE** HISTORY **EDUCATION** Univ Oxford, MA, 48, DPhil, 54; Univ Cracow, PhD, 50. **CAREER** Asst prof, Univ Alta, 58-60; assoc prof, Columbia Univ, 61-66; prof, 66-85, Prof Emer History, Univ Toronto, 85-. **HONORS AND AWARDS** Dlit(hon), Univ Toronto, 91. **MEMBERSHIPS** Can Asn Slavists; Czek Hist Conf; Peace Hist Soc; Polish Inst Arts Sci Am. **SELECTED PUBLICATIONS** Auth, Twentieth Century Pacifism, 70; auth, Pacifism in Europe to 1914, 72; auth, Nationalism and Populism in Partitioned Poland, 73; auth, The Slovak National Awakening, 76; auth, Polish Revolutionary Populism, 77; auth, The Roots of War Resistance, 81; auth, The Mahatma and Mother India, 83; auth, The Military Question in the Early Church, 88; auth, The Quaker Peace Testimony 1660 to 1914, 90; auth, Freedom from War, 91; auth, Freedom from Violence, 91; auth, Folk Cultures and Little Peoples, 92; auth, Breve historia del pacifismo, 97; ed, Records of Conscience, 93; ed, Testimonies of Conscience from the Soviet Union to the War Resisters' International 1923-1929, 97; co-ed, The Czech Renascence of the Nineteenth Century, 70. **CONTACT ADDRESS** Dept of History, Univ of Toronto, 100 St George St, 2074 Sidney Smith Hall, Toronto, ON, Canada M5S 3G3.

BRODHEAD, MICHAEL JOHN

PERSONAL Born 11/20/1935, Abilene, KS, m, 1969, 2 children **DISCIPLINE** HISTORY **EDUCATION** Univ Kans, BA, 59; MA, 62; Univ Minn, PhD, 67. **CAREER** Cur Kans Collection, Univ Kans Libr, 65-67; asst prof hist, 67-71, assoc prof, 71-79, Prof Hist, Univ Nev, Reno, 79-91, prof emer, 91-; archivist, Dept of Special Collections, Univ of Nev, Reno, Libr, 00. **HONORS AND AWARDS** Certificate of Appreciation, Army ROTC Mil Hist Expert, Univ of Nev, Reno, 91; Okla Hist Bk of the Year, Okla Hist Soc, 93; Outstanding Acad Bks of the Year, Choice, 93; Nat Archives and Records Admin Achievement Award, 96-97. **MEMBERSHIPS** Council on Am Military Past; Kans State Hist Soc; Nev Hist Soc; Nev Judicial Hist Soc; Western Hist Asn. **RESEARCH** Natural history; exploration and travel; populism. **SELECTED PUBLICATIONS** Auth, Persevering Populist: The Life of Frank Doster, Univ of Nev Press, 69; coauth, Elliott Coues: Naturalist and Frontier Historian, Univ of Ill Press, 81; coauth, Brushwork Diary: Watercolors of Early Nevada, Univ of Nev Press, 91; coed, A Naturalist in Indian Territory: The Journals of S.W. Woodhouse, Univ of Okla Press, 92; auth, David J. Brewer: The Life of a Supreme Court Justice, 1837-1910, Southern Ill Univ Press, 94; auth, "The Donner Party and Overland Emigration, 1840-1860," in The Archaeology of the Donner Party (NV: Univ of Nev Press, 97), 19-29; auth, "Fort Churchhill the Birthplace of Cavalry: Saddled with a Myth?," Sierra Sage (99). **CONTACT ADDRESS** 1790 W 12th St, Reno, NV 89503.

BRODMAN, JAMES W.

PERSONAL Born 12/09/1945, Rochester, NY, m, 1980, 2 children **DISCIPLINE** HISTORY **EDUCATION** Canisius Col, BA, 67; Univ Va, MA, 69, PhD, 74. **CAREER** Prof, Univ of Central Ark, 72-. **MEMBERSHIPS** Am Acad of Res Hists of Medieval Spain, Am Hist Asn, Am Cath Hist Asn, Medieval Acad of Am. **RESEARCH** Medieval Spain, medieval charity, medieval religious orders. **SELECTED PUBLICATIONS** Auth, A User's Guide to the Internet and LAN, Univ Central Ark (96); auth, "Boabdil," "Castile and Aragon," "Cid," and "Moors," in World Book Encyclopedia (96); auth, Charity and Welfare: Hospitals and the Poor in Medieval Catalonia, The Middle Age Series, Philadelphia: The Univ of Pa Press (98); auth, "Fable and Royal Power: The Origins of the Mercedarian Foundation Story," J of Medieval Hist, 25 (99): 229-241; review of Per Deu o per diners: Els mendicants I el clergat al Pais Valencia by Jill R. Webster, The Cath Hist Rev, 85 (99): 72-73; rev of La Orden de Santiago en el siglo XV: La Provincia de Castilla by Pedro Andres Porras Arbodedas, Speculum, 74 (99): 811-13; rev of The Kingdom of Leon-Castilla under King Alfonso VII by Bernard F. Reilly, The Cath Hist Rev, 85 (99): 608-9; auth, "E-publishing: Prospects, Promises, and Pitfalls," Perspectives: Am Hist Asn Newsletter, 38 (Feb 2000): 30-32; auth, "The Rhetoric of Ransoming: A Contribution to the Debate over Crusading in Medieval Iberia," Tolerance and Intolerance: Social Conflict in the Age of Crusades, ed Michael Gervers and James M. Powell, Syracuse: Syracuse Univ Press (forthcoming); auth, "Religious Orders," Encyclopedia of Medieval Iberia (forthcoming). **CONTACT ADDRESS** Dept Hist, Univ of Central Arkansas, 201 Donaghey Ave, Conway, AR 72035-5001. **EMAIL** JimB@mail.uca.edu

BRODY, AARON J.

PERSONAL Born 07/13/1966, Stanford, CA, m, 2001 **DISCIPLINE** ARCHAEOLOGY **EDUCATION** Univ Calif Berkeley, BA, 88; Harvard Univ, MA, 94; PhD, 96. **CAREER** Adj Asst Prof, Univ Ga, 97-98; Vis Asst Prof, 00-01; Lectr, MIT, 01-. **HONORS AND AWARDS** NEH, 00-01; Fel, Shelby White-Leon Levy Prog, 97-00; Fel, Albright Inst, 98; Fel, Haifa Univ, 97-98; Fel, U.S. Infor Agency, 95-96; Fel, Dorot Found, 93; G. Ernest Wright Fel, Harvard Univ, 88-90; Phi Beta Kappa. **MEMBERSHIPS** Am Sch of Oriental Res; Soc of Biblical Lit. **RESEARCH** Deep water archaeology; coastal archaeology; Sociology of seafaring; Archaeological approaches to the study of religion; Modeling of seafaring and trade in the ancient Near East & eastern Mediterranean; The maritime empire of the Phoenicians; The archaeology of death. **SELECTED PUBLICATIONS** Auth, 'Each Man Cried Out to His God': The Specialized Religion of Canaanite and Phoenician Seafarers, Scholars Press, 98. **CONTACT ADDRESS** Dept Archaeol, Massachusetts Inst of Tech, Bldg E51, 70 Memorial Dr, Cambridge, MA 02139. **EMAIL** ajbrody@postmark.net

BRODY, DAVID

PERSONAL Born 06/05/1930, Elizabeth, NJ, m, 1955, 3 children **DISCIPLINE** HISTORY **EDUCATION** Harvard Univ, AB, 52, MA, 53, PhD, 58. **CAREER** Instr hist, Northeastern Univ, 58-59; res assoc labor mgt hist, Harvard Univ, 59-61; asst prof hist, Columbia Univ, 61-65; assoc prof, Ohio State Univ, 65-67; Prof Hist, Univ Calif, Davis, 67-93, Emeritus, 93-; Soc Sci Res Coun fac fel, 66-67; vis prof US labor hist, Warwick Univ, 72-73; Fulbright sr lectr, Moscow State Univ, 75; sr fel, Nat Endowment for Humanities, 78-79; Dir, NEH Seminar for the Professions Labor leaders, 78,79; Senior Historical Consultant, Made in America Television Series, 78-90; USIA Lecturer, Korea, Taiwan, 88; U.S. Survey, 1865-; Emergence of Modern America, 1877-1914, 20th Century America 1914-1945, American Labor History upper division lecture courses; Historiography senior seminar; graduate seminars in American history; doctoral research. **HONORS AND AWARDS** Guggenheim Fellowship, 82-83. **MEMBERSHIPS** AHA; Orgn Am Hist; Labor Hist Asn. **RESEARCH** American labor, social and economic history. **SELECTED PUBLICATIONS** Auth, Steelworkers in America: The Nonunion Era, Harvard University Press, 60, Reprinted Harper & Row Torchboo 69, Univ of Illinois; auth, The Butcher Workmen: A Study of Unionization, Harvard University Press, 64; auth, Labor in Crisis: The Steel Strike of 1919, J. P. Lippincott Co., 65, Reprinted Greenwood Press, 82, University of Illinoi Press, 85; auth, Workers in Industrial America: Essays on the 20th Century Struggle, Oxford University Press, 80, Second edition, 93; auth, In Labor's Cause: Main Themes on the History of the American Worker, Oxford University Press, 93; ed., with James Henretta, Lynn Johnnson, Susan Ware, America's History, 2 vols, 4th ed., 00, Bedford/St. Marims. **CONTACT ADDRESS** Dept of Hist, Univ of California, Davis, Davis, CA 95616. **EMAIL** brodyiir@uclink4.berkeley.edu

BROESAMLE, JOHN JOSEPH

PERSONAL Born 02/10/1941, Long Beach, CA, m, 1963, 2 children **DISCIPLINE** UNITED STATES HISTORY **EDUCATION** Univ of the Pac, BA, 64; Columbia Univ, MA, 65, PhD (hist), 70. **CAREER** Assoc dean, Sch Social & Behav Sci, 73-76, from asst prof to assoc prof, 68-75, Prof Hist, CA State Univ, Northridge, 75-, Danforth Assoc, 81- **HONORS AND AWARDS** Woodrow Wilson fel, Woodrow Wilson Dissertation fel, 64-67; CA State Univ Northridge, Distinguished Teaching award, 73; CA State Univ, Northridge Scholarly Pub

Awd, 91. **MEMBERSHIPS** AHA; Orgn Am Hist; Academy of Political Science; Soc for Hist of the Gilded Age and Progressive Era; The Hist Soc; AAUP. **RESEARCH** Twentieth century United States political and cultural history. **SELECTED PUBLICATIONS** Auth, The Struggle for Control of the Federal Reserve System, 1914-1917, Mid-Am, 10/70; William Gibbs McAdoo: A Passion for Change, 1863-1917, Kennikat, 73; The Democrats from Bryan to Wilson, in: The Progressive Era, Syracuse Univ, 74; History: Cross-cultural Perspectives, in: Cross-cultural Prespectives in the Curriculum, Chandler & Sharpe, 86; Reform and Reaction in Twentieth Century American Politics, Greenwood, 90; Suddenly a Giant: A History of California State University, Northridge, Santa Susana, 93; William Gibbs McAdoo and the Hopeless Candidacy Syndrome, in Statesmen Who Were Never President, Univ Press Am, 97. **CONTACT ADDRESS** Dept Hist, California State Univ, Northridge, 18111 Nordhoff St, Northridge, CA 91330-8250.

BRONNER, EDWIN BLAINE
PERSONAL Born 09/02/1920, Yorba Linda, CA, m, 1946, 4 children **DISCIPLINE** HISTORY **EDUCATION** Whittier Col, BA, 41; Haverford Col, MA, 47; Univ Pa, PhD(hist), 52. **CAREER** From instr to assoc prof hist, Temple Univ, 47-62; Prof Hist & Cur Quaker Collection, Haverford Col, 62-, Librn, 69-, Am Philos Soc grant, 68; coun mem, Region 3 Arch Adv Coun, Nat Arch & Rec Serv, 72-74, Nat Endowment for Humanities grant, 81. **MEMBERSHIPS** Conf Early Am Hist; Orgn Am Historians; Friends Hist Asn (pres, 70-72); Friends Hist Soc (pres, 70); Conf Peace Res in Hist. **RESEARCH** Quaker history; early Pennsylvania history; William Penn. **SELECTED PUBLICATIONS** Coauth, Quaker Landmarks in Early Philadelphia, Am Philos Soc, 53; William Penn's Holy Experiment, Columbia, 62; ed, American Quakers Today, Friends World Comt, 66; auth, Quakerism and Christianity, Pendle Hill, 67; ed, An English View of American Quakerism, Journal of Walter Robson, 1877, Am Philos Soc, 70; auth, The Other Branch: London Yearly Meeting and the Hicksites, Friends Hist Soc, England, 74; ed, William Penn, 17th Century Founding Father, Pendle Hill, 75; auth, Sharing the Scriptures: The Bible Association of Friends in America, 1829-1979, Bible Assoc, 79; contribr, Friends in the Delaware Valley, 1681-1981, Friends Hist Asn, 81. **CONTACT ADDRESS** Libr, Haverford Col, Haverford, PA 19041.

BRONNER, SIMON J.
PERSONAL Born 04/07/1954, Haifa, Israel, m, 1998, 1 child **DISCIPLINE** AMERICAN STUDIES **EDUCATION** State Univ NYork, BA, 74, MA, 77; Ind Univ, PhD, 81. **CAREER** Asst prof, Pa St Univ, 81-84; assoc prof, 85-88; prof, 88-91; Distinguished Prof, Amer Studies, PA St Univ, 91-; vis prof, Univ Cal, 91; Fulbright prof, Osaka Univ, 96-97; vis prof, Harvard, 97; dir, Amer Studies Prog, 87-96, dir, Ctr Penn Culture Studies, 90-96, 98- . **HONORS AND AWARDS** Dickinson Col Memorial Awd, 74; Amer Folklore Soc Fels Awd, 80 & 81; James A. Jordan Memorial Awd for Teaching Excellence, 85; Chicago Folklore Prize, 86; John Ben Snow Found Prize, 87; Regional Coun of Hist Socs Awd of Merit, 88; Peter and Iona Opie Prize, 90; Wayland Hand Prize, 94; Penn-German Soc Awd of Merit, 96; Penn St Harrisburg Excellence in Res Awd, 98; NY St Scholar Incentive Awd, 71-74; NY St Regents Scholar, 71-74 NY St Coun on the Arts Fel, 74-75; Rockefeller Found Grad Fel, 78-81; NEH Res Fel, 84; opie prize comm, 88; chmn foodways sect, 79-80, chmn, history sect, 85-96, amer folklore soc; chmn, folklore fels prize comm, 95; ralph henry gabriel prize comm, 95 fel, amer folklore soc, 94- . **MEMBERSHIPS** Amer Studies Assn; Amer Folklore Soc; Org Amer Historians; Soc Folklife Studies; Penn Hist Assn. **RESEARCH** Folklore; material culture; ethnicity; industrial era. **SELECTED PUBLICATIONS** Ed, Folklore Forum 79; ed, Material Culture 83-86; ed, Folklore Historian, 83-89; ed, American Folk Art: A Guide to Sources, Garland, 84; ed, American Material Culture and Folklife series, UMI Res, 84-90; co-ed, Folk Art and Art Worlds, UMI Res, 86; ed, Folklife Studies from the Gilded Age: Object, Rite and Custom in Victorian America, UMI Res, 88; ed, Consuming Visions: Accumulation and Display of Goods in Amer, 1880-1920, WW Norton, 89; coed, Folk Art and Art Worlds, Utah St Univ, 92; ed, American Material Culture and Folklife, Utah St Univ, 92; ed, Creativity and Tradition in Folklore: New Directions, Utah St Univ, 92; ed, Pennsylvania Traditions, 94-96; ed, Material Worlds series, Univ Ky, 1996-; assoc ed, Jewish Folklore and Ethnology Review, 96-; auth, Chain Carvers: Old Men Crafting Meaning, Univ Ky, 85; auth, American Folklore Studies: An Intellectual History, Univ Kans, 86; auth, Grasping Things: Folk Material Culture and Mass Society in America, Univ Ky, 86; auth, Old-Time Music Makers of New York State, Syracuse Univ, 87; auth, American Children's Folklore, August House, 88; auth, Piled Higher and Deeper: The Folklore of Campus Life, August House, 90; auth, The Carver's Art: Crafting Meaning from Wood, Univ Ky, 96; auth, Popularizing Pennsylvania: Henry W Shoemaker and the Progressive Uses of Folklore and History, Penn St, 96; auth, Following Tradition: Folklore in the Discourse of American Culture, Utah St Univ, 98. **CONTACT ADDRESS** American Studies Prog, Pennsylvania State Univ, Harrisburg, The Capital Col, 777 W Harrisburg Pike, Middletown, PA 17057-4898. **EMAIL** sjb2@psu.edu

BRONSTEIN, HERBERT
PERSONAL Born 03/01/1930, Cincinnati, OH, m, 1954, 3 children **DISCIPLINE** RELIGIOUS HISTORY, JUDAISM **EDUCATION** Univ Cincinnati, BA, 52; MA, 54; Hebrew Union Col, MAHL, 56; DD, 82. **CAREER** Univ of Rochester; Univ of IL Chicago; Northwestern Univ; Lake Forest Col. **HONORS AND AWARDS** Taft Teaching Fel, 53, 54; Hirsch Fel, 55-56; Vis Scholar, Oxford Univ, 76, 93. **MEMBERSHIPS** Central Conf of Am Rabbis; Assoc of Jewish Studies; Midwest Assoc of Jewish Studies; Am Acad of Relig. **RESEARCH** Liturgy, Judaism and modernity, issues in comparative religion. **SELECTED PUBLICATIONS** Auth, Passover Haggadah, CCAR, (NY), 74; auth, The Five Scrolls, CCAR (NY), 84; Auth, "Time-Schemes, Order and Chaos: Periodization and History", Time Order Chaos, eds Fraser and Soulsby, Int Univ Pr, 98; auth, "Mitzvah and Autonomy", Duties of the Soul, UAHC, 99; auth, "Autonomy and Mitzvah: The Oxymoron of Reform Judaism", Tikkun, Summer 99; auth, "Social Action and Spirituality", Tikkun, May 00. **CONTACT ADDRESS** Dept Relig, Lake Forest Col, 555 N Sheridan Rd, Lake Forest, IL 60045-2338. **EMAIL** bronstein@lfc.edu

BROOKE, JOHN L.
PERSONAL Born 08/19/1953, Pittsfield, MA, m, 1979, 2 children **DISCIPLINE** AMERICAN HISTORY **EDUCATION** Cornell Univ, BA, 76; Univ Penn, MA, 77, PhD, 82. **CAREER** Vis asst prof, Amherst Col, 82-83; asst prof, 83-89, assoc prof, 89-97, prof, 97- Tufts Univ. **HONORS AND AWARDS** Charles Warren fel, Harvard Univ, 86-87; Am Coun of Learned Soc fel, 90-91; Orgn of Am Hist Merle Curtis Awd for Intellectual Hist, 91; Natl Hist Soc Book Prize, 91; New England Hist Asn Book Awd, 95; Soc of Hist of the Early Am Republic Book Prize, 95; Bancroft Prize, Columbia Univ, 95; NEH Fel for Ind Study and Res, 97-98; Guggenheim Fel, 97-98. **MEMBERSHIPS** Am Antiq Soc; Am Hist Assoc; Asn of Am Univ Prof; Orgn of Am Hist; Mass Hist Soc; New England Hist Asn; Soc for Hist of the Early Am Republic. **SELECTED PUBLICATIONS** Auth, The Heart of the Commonwealth: Society and Political Culture in Worcester County, Massachusetts, 1713-1861, Cambridge Univ Pr, 89; auth, The Refiner's Fire: The Making of Mormon Cosmology, 1644-1844, Cambridge, 94; auth, The True Spiritual Seed: Sectarian Religion and the Persistance of the Occult in Eighteenth-Century New England, in Benes, ed, Wonders of the Invisible World: 1600-1900, Boston Univ, 95; auth, Ancient Lodges and Self-Created Societies: Freemasonry and the Public Sphere in the Early Republic, in Hoffman, ed, The Beginnings of the Extended Republic: The Federalist Era, Univ Va, 96; auth, Reason and Passion in the Public Sphere: Habermas and the Cultural Historians, J of Interdisciplinary Hist, 98; auth, Press, Party, and Public Sphere in the United States, 1790-1840, in Kelly, ed, The History of the Book in America, v.2, forthcoming. **CONTACT ADDRESS** Dept of History, Tufts Univ, Medford, Medford, MA 02155. **EMAIL** jbrooke@tufts.edu

BROOKS, E. BRUCE
PERSONAL Born 06/23/1936, Akron, OH, m, 1964, 1 child **DISCIPLINE** CHINESE HISTORY **EDUCATION** Oberlin Conserv Music, MusB, 58; Univ Wash, PhD(Chinese lang & lit), 68. **CAREER** Lectr Chinese, Harvard Univ, 67-68, instr, 68-69, asst prof, 69-73, lectr, 73-74; Asst Prof Chinese Hist, Smith Col, 74-78; pres, Sinfac Minor, 68-80., Nat Endowment for Humanities res grant, 71-72; Am Coun Learned Socs, 76-77. **HONORS AND AWARDS** Waring Prize, Western Reserve Acad, 80. **RESEARCH** Prosody; stylistics; evolution of thought. **SELECTED PUBLICATIONS CONTACT ADDRESS** 39 Hillside Rd, Northampton, MA 01060.

BROOKS, E. WILLIS
PERSONAL Born Kingston, RI, m, 1960, 2 children **DISCIPLINE** HISTORY **EDUCATION** Dartmouth Col, AB, 58; Stanford Univ, MA, 62, PhD(hist), 70. **CAREER** Dep chmn, Comt Travel Grants, ind Univ, 66-68; lectr hist, 68-70, asst prof, 70-79, Assoc Prof Hist, Univ NC, Chapel Hill, 79-; Chief, Soviet and East European Research, US Information Agency, Washington, DC; 82-84. **HONORS AND AWARDS** Tanner Awd, Univ NC, 73; Tanner Teaching Awd, 82; Bowman and Gordon Gray term professorship for Excellence in Undergraduate Teaching, 94-97. **MEMBERSHIPS** Am Asn Advan Slavic Studies; Southern Conf Slavic Studies; Triangle Institute for Security Studies; UNC Academy of Distinguished Teaching Scholars. **RESEARCH** Modern Russian history. **SELECTED PUBLICATIONS** Twenty-three articles/entries in the Modern Encyclopedia of Russian and Soviet History, Gulf Breeze, FL, 76-82; auth, "Nicholas I as Reformer: Russian Attempts to Conquer the Caucasus," in Nation and Ideology, ed. Ivo Banac et al., Boulder CO, 81, 227-63; auth, "Reform in the Russian Army," 1856-1861," Slavic Review, 43:1, Spring 84, 63-82; auth, "The Improbable Connection: D.A. Miliutin and N.G. Chernyshevskii, 1848-1862," in Jahrbucher fur Geschicte Osteuropas, Band 37, Heft 1, January 89, 21-44; auth, "Russia's Conquest and Pacificatiion of the Caucasus: Relocation Becomes a Pogrom in the Post-Crimean War Period," Nationalities Papers 23:4, December 95, 675-86; auth, "The politics of the Conquest of the Caucasus, 1855-1864," Nationalities Papers 24:4, 96, 649-60. **CONTACT ADDRESS** Univ of No Carolina, Chapel Hill, 475 Hamilton Hall CB #3195, Chapel Hill, NC 27514. **EMAIL** ewbrooks@email.unc.edu

BROOKS, GEORGE E.
PERSONAL Born 04/20/1933, Lynn, MS, m, 1985, 4 children **DISCIPLINE** HISTORY **EDUCATION** Dartmouth Col, Ab 57; Boston Univ, MA 58, PhD 62. **CAREER** IN Univ, asst prof 62-68, assoc prof 68-75, prof 75-; Vis Prof, Shandong Univ, China 85; Univ Zimbabwe 84; Tufts Univ 69. **HONORS AND AWARDS** Bost Univ Fell; Phi Alpha Theta; Ford Found Fell; 8 Facul Res Gnts; Herman Frederic Lieber Awd; NEH; Fulbright Fell; ACLS Fell. **MEMBERSHIPS** ASA; AHA; LSA; MANSA; WHA. **SELECTED PUBLICATIONS** Climate and History in West Africa: in: Transformations in Africa, ed, Graham Connah, Leichester Univ Press, 98; Teaching a Non-Centric World History Course, in: The Aspen World History Handbook, ed George E Brooks, Dik A Daso, Marilynn Hitchens, Heidi Roupp, Denver, World Hist Assn, 94; Reports of Chimpanzee Natural History, Including Tool Use in 16th and 17th Century Sierra Leone, with Jeanne M Sept, Intl Journal of Primatology, 94; Getting Along Together: World History Perspectives for Living in the Twenty-First Century, auth,' Getting Along Together: World History Perspectives for the Twenty-First Century', (pg. 99, fall 99, brooks, Supp); **CONTACT ADDRESS** Dept of Hist, Indiana Univ, Bloomington, 1615 East University St, Bloomington, IN 47405. **EMAIL** BROOKSG@ucs.indiana.edu

BROOKS, JOHN
PERSONAL Born 09/06/1957, Chapel Hill, NC, m, 1994 **DISCIPLINE** HISTORY, GOVERNMENT **EDUCATION** Duke Univ, BA, 79; Univ Chicago, MA, 82; PhD, 90. **CAREER** Vis Asst Prof, Austin Col, 90-91; Asst Prof, Teikyo Loretto Heights Univ, 91-98; Asst Prof, Fayetteville State Univ, 98-. **HONORS AND AWARDS** Searle Fel, Univ Chicago, 71-84; George Lurcy Fel for Diss Res in France, 85-86; Tocqueville Awd and Soc Sci Res Coun Fel, 86-87; Phi Alpha Theta. **MEMBERSHIPS** AHA, Int Soc for the Hist of the Behav Sci, Forum for Hist of Human Sci, Hist of Sci Soc, Soc for Fr Hist Studies, World Hist Asn. **RESEARCH** History of human sciences, modern French history, modern European intellectual history. **SELECTED PUBLICATIONS** Auth, "Analogy and Argumentation in an Interdisciplinary Context: Durkheim's Individual and Collective Representations," Hist of the Human Sci 4 (91): 223-259; auth, "Philosophy and Psychology at the Sorbonne 1885-1913," J of the Hist of the Behav Sci 29 (93): 123-145; auth, "The Definition of Sociology and the Sociology of Definition: Durkheim's Rules of Sociological Method and High School Philosophy in France," J of the Hist of the Behav Sci 32 (96): 379-407; auth, The Eclectic Legacy: Academic Philosophy and the Human Sciences in Nineteenth-Century France, Univ Del Pr (Newark, NJ), 98. **CONTACT ADDRESS** Dept Hist, Fayetteville State Univ, 1200 Murchison Rd, Fayetteville, NC 28301-4252.

BROOKS, ROBIN
PERSONAL Born 05/28/1927, Moscow, USSR, m, 1950, 2 children **DISCIPLINE** AMERICAN HISTORY **EDUCATION** Brooklyn Col, BA, 57; Univ Rochester, PhD(hist), 64. **CAREER** From instr to asst prof hist, Rochester inst Technol, 61-64; asst prof, Calif State Col, Hayward, 64-65; from asst prof to assoc prof, 65-73, Prof Hist, San Jose State Univ, 73-, Fulbright-Hays lectr Am hist, Univ india, 75-76; mem, inst Early Am Hist & Cult, Williamsburg, Va. **MEMBERSHIPS** Am Studies Asn; Orgn Am Hist. **RESEARCH** American studies; environmental studies; United States social history. **SELECTED PUBLICATIONS** Auth, Alexander Hamilton, Melancton Smith and the ratification of the Constitution in New York, William & Mary Quart, 67; Domestic violence and America's wars, In: Violence in America, US Govt Printing Off, 69; Environmental education as general education, J Environ Educ, 73. **CONTACT ADDRESS** Dept of Hist, San Jose State Univ, San Jose, CA 95192.

BROOKSHIRE, JERRY
PERSONAL Born 10/17/1943, Athens, GA, m, 1968, 2 children **DISCIPLINE** HISTORY **EDUCATION** Univ Ga, BA, 65; Vanderbilt Univ, MA, 67; PhD, 70. **CAREER** Captain, US Army, 70-72; Prof, Middle Tenn State Univ, 72-. **MEMBERSHIPS** Am Hist Asn, The Hist Soc, Southern Hist Asn, N Am conf on British Studies, Soc for the Study of Labor Hist, Am Asn of Univ Prof, Phi Kappa Phi, Phi Beta Kappa. **RESEARCH** Twentieth-century British political history, Labor party history. **SELECTED PUBLICATIONS** Auth, clement Attlee, Manchester Univ Press, 95; auth, "Speak for England; Act for England: Labor's Leadership and British national Security under the Threat of War in the Late 1930s," European History Quarterly, (99): 251-287; auth, "The National Council of Labor, 1921-1946," Albion, (86): 43-69; auth, "Clement Attlee and Cabinet Reform, 1930-1945," Historical Journal, (81): 175-188. **CONTACT ADDRESS** Dept History, Middle Tennessee State Univ, 1301 E Main St, Murfreesboro, TN 37132-0001. **EMAIL** jbrookshire@mtsu.edu

BROSS, JAMES BEVERLEY
PERSONAL Born 11/21/1938, Knoxville, TN, m, 1959, 4 children **DISCIPLINE** RELIGION; HISTORY **EDUCATION** Cent Wesleyan Col, AB, 59; Univ Ill, MA, 65; Univ Iowa, PhD(relig), 72. **CAREER** Teacher math, Tenn Pub Schs, 59-60, 62-63 & All Tribes Indian Mission Sch, 60-62; instr, Southern

Wesleyan Univ, 63-64; asst prof, Iowa Wesleyan Col, 65-68; teacher, Iowa Publ Schs, 72-73; Prof Relig, Southern Wesleyan Univ, 73-. **MEMBERSHIPS** Wesleyan Theol Soc; Am Soc Church Hist; Conf Faith & Hist; Evangelical Theol Soc. **RESEARCH** Puritanism in England; American religion. **CONTACT ADDRESS** So Wesleyan Univ, P O Box 1020, Central, SC 29630-1020. **EMAIL** jbbross@hotmail.com

BROUGHTON, THOMAS ROBERT SHANNON
PERSONAL Born 02/17/1900, Corbetton, ON, Canada, m, 1931, 2 children **DISCIPLINE** CLASSICS, ANCIENT HISTORY **EDUCATION** Univ Toronto, AB, 21, MA, 22; Johns Hopkins Univ, PhD (Latin), 28. **CAREER** Instr Greek, Amherst Col, 26-27; assoc Latin, Bryn Mawr Col, 28-30, from assoc prof to prof, 30-65; Paddison prof class, 65-70, Emer Prof Classics, Univ NC, Chapel Hill, 70-, Vis prof, Johns Hopkins Univ, 38-40; Guggenheim fel, 45-46; Fulbright res grant, Italy, 51-52; prof in charge, Sch Classical Studies, Am Acad Rome, 59-61; vpres, int Fed Soc Classical Studies, 59-69; mem comt res libr, Am Coun Learned Soc, 67; ann mem, inst Advan Studies, 71-72. **HONORS AND AWARDS** Awd, Am Philol Asn, 53; lld, johns hopkins univ, 69, univ toronto, 71 & univ nc, chapel hill, 74. **MEMBERSHIPS** Am Acad Arts & Sci; AHA; Archaeol inst Am (hon vpres, 53-58); Am Philol Asn (pres, 54); Class Asn Can. **RESEARCH** Economic history of Rome; provinces of the Roman Empire; Roman constitutional history and politics. **SELECTED PUBLICATIONS** Auth, Dionysus and the History of Archaic Rome, Classical J, Vol 0088, 93. **CONTACT ADDRESS** Dept of Classics, Univ of No Carolina, Chapel Hill, Murphey Hall, Chapel Hill, NC 27514.

BROUSSARD, RAY F.
PERSONAL Born 04/22/1926, Lafayette, LA, m, 1951, 3 children **DISCIPLINE** LATIN AMERICAN HISTORY **EDUCATION** Southwestern La Inst, BA, 49; Univ Tex, MA, 52, PhD, 59. **CAREER** Head dept foreign lang, Southwest Tex Jr Col, 52-55; instr hist, Howard County Jr Col, 55-57; dir, Bi-Nat Ctr, Cartagena, Colombia, 59-61; asst prof hist, Miss State Univ, 62-66; Assoc Prof Hist to Assoc Prof Emer, Univ Ga, 66-, Consult on Colombia, Spec Oper Res Off, Am Univ, 62-63; univ fel, Portuguese Inst, Univ Tex, 63. **MEMBERSHIPS** AHA; Conf Latin Am Hist; Southeastern Conf Latin Am Studies; Nat Social Sci Asn. **RESEARCH** Caribbean defense, Armada de Barlovento; Mexican reform; American West, Mexican-Texas relations. **SELECTED PUBLICATIONS** Auth, "John Quitman and the Lopez Expedition," Journal of Mississippi History, 66; San Antonio During the Texas Republic, Monogr 18, Southwestern Studies, Tex Western Press, 67; Comonfort: Misunderstood Reformer, WGa Col Study Soc Sci, 67; "Juarez, Vidaurri and Comonfort's Return from Exile," Hispanic American History Review, 69; auth, "Bautista Antonelli: Architect of Caribbean Defense," The Historian, 88. **CONTACT ADDRESS** Dept of History, Univ of Georgia, 202 LeConte Hall, Athens, GA 30602-1602. **EMAIL** raybruce@arches.uga.edu

BROWDER, GEORGE C.
PERSONAL Born 03/14/1939, Baltimore, MD, m, 1959, 3 children **DISCIPLINE** MODERN EUROPEAN HISTORY **EDUCATION** Univ Wis-Madison, PhD, 68. **CAREER** From asst prof to prof emeritus, State Univ NYork - Fredonia, 68-00. **HONORS AND AWARDS** SUNY Chancellor's Awd for Excellence in Teaching, 74; Kasling Lectr, SUNY-Fredonia, 97; Revson Fel, Inst for Advan Holocaust Studies, US Mem Holocaust Mus, 98. **MEMBERSHIPS** Conf Group on Central Europ Hist; World War II Studies Asn; German Studies Assoc; German Hist Soc; Int Gesellschaft fur Geschichtsdidaktik; Arbeitskreis Geschichte der Nachrichtendienste e V. **RESEARCH** German detective police and national security agencies, 1920-45; the Holocaust perpetrators; teaching-learning methodology and assessment in higher education. **SELECTED PUBLICATIONS** Auth, The Foundations of the Nazi Police State: The Formation of SIPO and SD, 90, Univ Press Ky; auth, "Captured German and Other Nations' Documents in the Osoby Archive Moscow," Central Europ Hist, 91; auth, "Update on the Captured Docuements in the Former Osoby Archive, Moscow," Central Europ Hist, 93; auth, "Non-Context Specific Assessment," The History Teacher, Aug 94; auth, Index of RG 15. 007M, Files of the Reichssicherheitshauptant, held by the Main Commission for the Investigation of Crimes against the Polish Nation, 95, US Holocaust Mem Research Inst; auth, Hitler's Enforcers: The Gestapo and the SS Security Service in the Nazi Revolution, 96, Oxford Univ Press; auth, "The Gestapo," "Kripo," "The Security Police," and "Security Service of the SS," in Encyclopedic History of Modern Germany, 98, Garland Publishing Inc. **CONTACT ADDRESS** Dept of History, SUNY, Col at Fredonia, Fredonia, NY 14063. **EMAIL** browder@fredonia.edu

BROWER, DANIEL ROBERTS
PERSONAL Born 01/09/1936, m, 1959, 3 children **DISCIPLINE** HISTORY **EDUCATION** Carleton Col, BA, 57; Columbia Univ, MA, 59, PhD, 63. **CAREER** Instr, Bowdoin Col, 62-63; asst prof, Oberlin Col, 63-68; prof, Univ CA-Davis, 68-. **MEMBERSHIPS** Am Asn for Advancement of Slavic Studies; Am Hist Asn; World Hist Soc. **RESEARCH** Russian empire; comparative colonialism. **SELECTED PUBLICATIONS** Auth, The New Jacobins: The French Communist Party and the Popular Front, Cornell Univ Press, 68; Training the Nihilists: Education and Radicalism in Tsarist Russia, Cornell Univ Press, 75; The Russian City between Tradition and Modernity, 1850-1900, Univ CA Press, 90; The Penny Press and Its Readers, in S Frank and M Steinberg, eds, Cultures in Flux: Lower Class Values, Practices, and Resistance in Late Imperial Russia, Princeton Univ Press, 94; Imperial Russia and Its Orient: The Renown of Nikolai Przhevalsky, The Russian Rev, v 53, July 94; Kyrgyz Nomads and Russian Pioneers: Colonization and Ethnic Conflict in the Turkestan Revolt of 1916, Jahrbucher fur Geschichte Osteuropas, v 44, 96; Russian Roads to Mecca: Religious Tolerance and Muslim Pilgrimage in the Russian Empire, Slavic Rev, v 55, fall 96; Islam and Ethnicity: Russia Colonial Policy in Turkestan, in Russia's Orient: Imperial Borderlands and Peoples, ed Daniel Brower & Edward Lazzerini, IN Univ Press, 97; Russia'a Orient: Imperial Borderlands and Peoples, 1700-1914, co-ed with Edward Lazzerini, IN Univ Press, 97; The World in the Twentieth Century: From Empires to Nations, 4th ed, Prentice-Hall, 99. **CONTACT ADDRESS** Dept of History, Univ of California, Davis, Davis, CA 95616. **EMAIL** drbrower@ucdavis.edu

BROWING, REED S.
PERSONAL Born 08/26/1938, New York, NY, m, 1963, 1 child **DISCIPLINE** HISTORY **EDUCATION** Dartmouth, BA, 60; Yale, MA, 64, PhD, 65. **CAREER** Asst Prof, Amherst Col, 64-67; Kenyon Col, 67-; Provost, 86-94; Acting Pres, 89. **MEMBERSHIPS** Historical Society, Ohio Academy of History, Society for Amer Baseball Research. **RESEARCH** 18th Century Britain & Europe; Baseball History. **SELECTED PUBLICATIONS** Auth, "The Duke of Newcastle," 75; "Political and Constitutional Ideas of the Cover Whigs," 82; "The War of the Austrian Succession," 94; "Young: A Baseball Life," 00. **CONTACT ADDRESS** Dept History, Kenyon Col, Seitz House, Gambier, OH 43022. **EMAIL** browning@kenyon.edu

BROWN, A. PETER
PERSONAL Born 04/30/1943, Chicago, IL, m, 1968, 1 child **DISCIPLINE** HISTORICAL MUSICOLOGY **EDUCATION** Northwestern Univ, BME, 65, MM, 66, PhD(music), 70. **CAREER** Asst prof music, Univ Hawaii, 69-74; assoc prof, 74-81, Prof Musicol, Ind Univ, Sch Music, 81-, Am Coun Learned Soc fel Ordonez, 72-73; Guggenheim Found fel haydn, 78-79; NEH Col Teaching Sem Dir, 84. **HONORS AND AWARDS** Malin Awd for Excellence in the res and editing of choral music. **MEMBERSHIPS** Am Musicol Soc; int Musicol Soc; Music Libr Asn; Nat Acad Rec Arts & Sci. **RESEARCH** Viennese music 1730-1830; history of orchestral music; Joseph Haydn. **SELECTED PUBLICATIONS** Auth, Carlo d'Ordonemz: A Thematic Catalogue, Info Coordr, 78; contribr, Papers for Haydn Festival and Conference, 75, Norton, 81; The Symphonies of Carlo d'Ordonez, Haydn Yearbk, XII; Approaching Musicol Classicism, CMS Symposium, XX; Joseph Haydn and Leopoid Hofmannn's Street Songs, XXXIII & Notes on some Viennere copyists, XXXIV, Am Musicol Soc J; ed, Seven Symphonies of Carlo d'Ordonez, Garland, 79; String Quartest op 1 of Carlo d'Ordonez, A-R, 80; auth, Performing Haydn's the Creation, Indiana, 85; auth, Haydn's Keyboard Music, Indiana, 86; auth, Music Publisher Guera of Lyon, Information Coordinators, 87; ed, Haydn, The Creation, Oxford, 91 & 95; auth, The Symphonic Reputoire (5 Vols.) Vol. III, Indiana, 01. **CONTACT ADDRESS** Sch of Music, Indiana Univ, Bloomington, Bloomington, IN 47401. **EMAIL** brownap@indiana.edu

BROWN, ALAN S.
PERSONAL Born 04/23/1922, Detroit, MI, m, 1950, 3 children **DISCIPLINE** HISTORY **EDUCATION** Univ Mich, AB, 49, MA, 50, PhD, 53. **CAREER** instr, Univ Mich, 53-54 & Kent State Univ, 54-55; from asst prof to assoc prof, 55-63, Prof Hist, Western Mich Univ, 63- **MEMBERSHIPS** Orgn Am Hist; AHA. **RESEARCH** American Revolution; American Colonial and Revolutionary eras; Michigan. **SELECTED PUBLICATIONS** Auth, The British peace offer of 1778, Mich Acad Sci, Lit & Arts, 55; The role of the Army in Western settlement: Josiah Harmar's command 1785-1790, Pa Mag & Biog, 4/69; Caroline Bartlett Crane and urban reform, Mich Hist, winter 72; The impossible dream: The north ministry, the structure of politics and conciliation, In: The American Revolution and a Candid World, Kent State Univ, 77. **CONTACT ADDRESS** Western Michigan Univ, 1201 Oliver St, Kalamazoo, MI 49008-3805.

BROWN, BLANCHE RACHEL
PERSONAL Born 04/12/1915, Boston, MA, w, 1938 **DISCIPLINE** HISTORY OF ART **EDUCATION** NYork Univ, BFA, 36, MA, 38, PhD, 67; cert, Univ Paris, 37. **CAREER** Lectr hist of art, Metropolitan Mus Art, 42-66; assoc prof, 67-73, prof hist of art, NY Univ, 73-85, Zacks Professor, Hebrew Univ, Jerusalem, 80, Emerita, 85-. **HONORS AND AWARDS** Assoc, Univ Sem Class Civilization, Columbia Univ, 71; Nat Endowment for Humanities fel, 76-77; John Simon Guggenheim Mem Found fel, 78-79. **MEMBERSHIPS** Archaeol Inst Am; Col Art Asn Am; fel Am Numismatic Soc. **RESEARCH** Hellenistic art. **SELECTED PUBLICATIONS** Auth, Ptolemaic Paintings and Mosaics, Archaeol Inst Am, Col Art Asn Am, 57; Five Cities, Doubleday, 64 & Anchor, 66; Anticlassicism in Greek Sculpture of the 4th Century BC, Archaeol Inst Am Col Art Asn Am Monogr Ser, 73; Questions about the Late Hellenistic Period, In: Art Studies for an Editor, NY, 75; The Iliad to Me, In: De Ilias Van Homerus, Antwerp, Galerie de Zwarte Panter, 76; Out of the Ashes: Glowing Treasures of Pompeii, NY Times Mag, 4/78 & Reader's Digest, 2/79; Deinokrates and Alexandria, Bulletin Am Soc Papyrologists, Vol XV, 78; Novelty, Ingenuity, Self-Aggrandisement, Ostentation, Extravagance, Gigantism and Kitsch in the Art of Alexander the Great and His Successors, In: Art the Ape Of Nature: Studies in Honor of HW Janson, Abrams, 81; Styles in the Alexander Portraits on the Coins of Lysimachos, Coins Culture and History: Studies in Honor of Bluma Trell, Wayne State Univ Press, 81; auth, Royal Portraits in Sculpture and Coins: Pyrrhos and the Successors of Alexander the Great, Peter Lang, 95; "Alexander the Great as Patron of the Arts," in The Fire of Hephaistos, Harvard Univ Press, 96; auth, "How Deinokrates Invented Alexandria," in Light from Cosa: in honor of Cleo Fitch, Peter Lang, forthcoming. **CONTACT ADDRESS** 15 W 70 St, New York, NY 10023.

BROWN, CANDY
PERSONAL Born 10/31/1971, Sanger, CA, m, 1998 **DISCIPLINE** AMERICAN STUDIES **EDUCATION** Harvard Univ, AB, 92; AM, 95; PhD, 00. **CAREER** Asst prof, Vanderbilt Univ, 00-01; asst prof, Saint Louis Univ, 01-. **HONORS AND AWARDS** Fel, Louisville Inst, 99-00; Fel, Packard, 99-00; Fel, Inst for the Study of Am Evangelization, 99-00; Fel, Harvard, 95, 98; Fulbright Fel, 92; John Clive Teaching Prize, 98; Sidney Mead Prize, 95; Houston Public Serv, 92; Phi Beta Kappa. **MEMBERSHIPS** Am Acad of Relig; Am Hist Asn; Am Soc of Church Hist; Am Soc for Eighteenth Century Studies; Am Studies Asn; MLA. **RESEARCH** American Religious History; Print, Communications Media; Popular Culture. **SELECTED PUBLICATIONS** Auth, "The Spiritual Pilgrimage of Rachel Stearns, 1834-1837: Reinterpreting Women's Religious and Social Experiences in the Methodist Revivals of Nineteenth Century America," Church History, 96; auth, "Faith Working through Love: The Wesleyan Revivals and Social Transformation - Considerations for the Contemporary Filipino Church," Phronesis, 97. **CONTACT ADDRESS** Dept Am Studies, Saint Louis Univ, 3800 Lindell Blvd, Saint Louis, MO 63108. **EMAIL** cgbrown@post.harvard.edu

BROWN, CHRISTOPHER P.
DISCIPLINE GEOGRAPHY **EDUCATION** San Diego State Univ, BA, 86; Mich State Univ, MA, 91; San Diego State Univ, PhD, 98. **CAREER** Asst Prof, W Chester Univ, 97-. **HONORS AND AWARDS** Int Travel Awd, NFS, 94; Phi Beta Delta, San Diego St Univ, 94-95; Travel Scholar, Univ Calif, 96; Sigma Xi Grant-in-Aid Awd, San Diego St Univ, 96; Ford Found Fel, Univ Ariz, 99; Res Awd, W Chester Univ, 00. **MEMBERSHIPS** SCRA, AAG, ABSS, APCG, ASPRS. **RESEARCH** Geography and planning. **SELECTED PUBLICATIONS** Coauth, "Modeling the Impacts of Surface Water Hydrology and Land Use on Water Quality in the Tijuana River Watershed," Watershed Management: Moving from Theory to Implementation Spec Conf (98); coauth, "Geographic Information System (GIS) Characterization of Metal Loading in the Binational Tijuana River Watershed," J of Borderland Studies (99); coauth, "Quality of Urban Stormwater in the Tijuana River Watershed," San Diego St UP (99); auth, "Reform Options for Improved Water Resource Management on the U S-Mexico Border," SCAMASG (99); auth, "River Basin Commissions and Watershed Councils: Perspectives from the Large and the Small," SCRA (99); auth, "Consejos de Cuencas as Tools for Environmental Conflict Resolution: Preliminary Work in the upper Santa Cruz Basin," Udall Ctr Fels Colloquia Ser (99); **CONTACT ADDRESS** Dept Geog, West Chester Univ of Pennsylvania, 700 S High St, West Chester, PA 19383-0001. **EMAIL** cbrown@wcupa.edu

BROWN, D. CLAYTON
PERSONAL Born 04/12/1941, Houston, TX, m, 1963, 2 children **DISCIPLINE** HISTORY **EDUCATION** N Tex State Univ, BA, 65; MA, 66; Univ Calif at Los Angeles, PhD, 70. **CAREER** Asst Prof, E Tex State Univ, 70-71; Asst Prof to Full Prof, Tex Christian Univ, 71-. **HONORS AND AWARDS** NEH Young Humanist Awd, 75; Best Article of the Year, Southwestern Hist Quarterly, 75. **MEMBERSHIPS** Agricultural Hist Soc, Tex State Hist Asn, E Tex Hist Asn, S Hist Asn. **RESEARCH** US Agricultural History (Modern). **SELECTED PUBLICATIONS** Auth, Electricity for Rural America: The Fight for the REA; auth, Eisenhower: A Biography (children's reader). **CONTACT ADDRESS** Dept Hist, Texas Christian Univ, Fort Worth, TX 76129. **EMAIL** d.c.brown@tcu.edu

BROWN, DOROTHY M.
PERSONAL Born 12/23/1932, Baltimore, MD **DISCIPLINE** HISTORY **EDUCATION** Coll of Notre Dame Maryland, BA, 54; Georgetown Univ, MA, 59, PhD, 62. **CAREER** Asst Prof, 59-66, interim pres, 96-97, Coll of Notre Dame Maryland; Asst Prof, Assoc Prof, Prof, 66-, interim provost, 98-99, Georgetown Univ. **MEMBERSHIPS** AHA, OAH, ASA. **RESEARCH** 20th century American society & culture, history of American women. **SELECTED PUBLICATIONS** Co-auth, The Poor Belong to Us, Catholic Charities and American Welfare, Cambridge Harvard Univ Press, 97; auth, Setting a Course, Ameri-

can Women in the 1920s, Boston Twayne/G K Hall, 87; Mabel Walker Willebrandt, A Study in Power Loyalty and Law, Knoxville Univ of Tenn Press, 84. **CONTACT ADDRESS** Provost, Georgetown Univ, Washington, DC 20057. **EMAIL** browndo@gunet.georgetown.edu

BROWN, IRA VERNON
PERSONAL Born 08/14/1922, Albemarle Co, VA, m, 1955, 1 child **DISCIPLINE** HISTORY **EDUCATION** George Washington Univ, AB, 41; Univ Va, AM, 42; Harvard Univ, AM, 43; PhD, 46. **CAREER** From instr to assoc prof, 47-60, prof to prof emeritus, Am Hist, PA State Univ, 60-. **HONORS AND AWARDS** Brewer Prize, Am Soc Church Hist, 49; Fund for Advan of Educ fel, 52-53. **MEMBERSHIPS** AHA; Orgn Am Historians. **RESEARCH** American social and cultural history; the formative period, 1776-1828; abolition and feminism. **SELECTED PUBLICATIONS** Auth, Women of the Antislavery Movement in the Weston Sisters, Amer Hist Rev, 96; auth, The Abolitionists and the South, 1831-1861, Amer Hist Rev, 96. **CONTACT ADDRESS** Dept of Hist, Pennsylvania State Univ, Univ Park, 208 Weaver Bldg, University Park, PA 16802.

BROWN, JAMES SEAY, JR.
PERSONAL Born 11/12/1944, Boston, MA, m, 1966, 3 children **DISCIPLINE** EUROPEAN HISTORY **EDUCATION** TN Technological Univ, BA (Hist), 66; Vanderbilt Univ, MA (Hist), 68, PhD (European Hist), 71. **CAREER** Full-Time Teaching, Dept of Hist and Philos, Sanford Univ, 71-. **HONORS AND AWARDS** Buchanon Teaching Awd, Samford Univ; George Macon Memorial Teaching Awd, Samford Univ. **MEMBERSHIPS** Southern Hist Asn; AL Folklife Asn; Southern Conference on Slavic Studies. **RESEARCH** Nationalism. **SELECTED PUBLICATIONS** Ed, Up Before Daylight: Life Histories from the Alabama Writer's Project, 1938-1939, Univ AL Press, 82, 97. **CONTACT ADDRESS** Samford Univ, Box 292206, Birmingham, AL 35229. **EMAIL** jsbrown@samford.edu

BROWN, JENNIFER S. H.
PERSONAL Born 12/30/1940, Providence, RI **DISCIPLINE** HISTORY **EDUCATION** Brown Univ, AB, 62; Harvard Univ, AM, 63; Univ Chicago, PhD, 76. **CAREER** Asst prof, Collby Col, N Ill Univ, Univ Ind, 66-82; vis distinguished prof Can stud, Univ Alta, 82; assoc prof, 82-88, PROF HISTORY, UNIV WINNIPEG, 88-, dir, Ctr Rupert's Land Stud, 97-; Woodrow Wilson fel, 62-63; publs ed, Middle Am Res Inst, Tulane Univ, 75-82; res fel, Newberry Libr Chicago, 82; gen ed, Rupert's Land Record Soc, 86-. **HONORS AND AWARDS** Phi Beta Kappa Honor Soc; hon men, Sir John A. Macdonald Prize. **MEMBERSHIPS** Man Record Soc; Champlain Soc **RESEARCH** First Nations history **SELECTED PUBLICATIONS** Auth, Strangers in Blood: Fur Trade Company Families in Indian Country, 80; coauth, The Orders of the Dreamed: George Nelson on Cree and Northern Ojibwa Religion and Myth, 88; ed, The Ojibwa of Berens River, Manitoba: Ethnography into History, 92; co-ed, The New Peoples: Being and Becoming Metis in North America, 85; co-ed, Reading Beyond Words: Contexts for Native History, 96; contribur, Dictionary of Canadian Biography; contribur, Canadian Encyclopedia. **CONTACT ADDRESS** Dept of History, Univ of Winnipeg, 515 Portage Ave, Winnipeg, MB, Canada R3B 2E9. **EMAIL** jennifer.brown@uwinnipeg.ca

BROWN, JERRY WAYNE
PERSONAL Born 02/24/1936, Frederick, OK, m, 1958, 1 child **DISCIPLINE** RELIGION, HISTORY **EDUCATION** Harvard Univ, AB, 58; Eastern Baptist Theol Sem, BD, 61; Univ Pa, MA, 61; Princeton Univ, MA, 63, PhD(relig), 64. **CAREER** Teaching fel relig, Princeton Univ, 63-64; asst prof, Bowdoin Col, 64-69, actg chmn dept, 64-65, resident prof, Sr Ctr, 65-66, dean students, 66-69; Assoc Prof Hist, Rider Col 69-, VPres Acad Affairs, 70-;, Provost, 75-. **RESEARCH** Religion in America. **SELECTED PUBLICATIONS** The Rise of Biblical Criticism in American, 1800-1870, Wesleyan Univ, 69. **CONTACT ADDRESS** Dept of Hist, Rider Univ, Lawrenceville, NJ 08648.

BROWN, JOHN E.
PERSONAL Born 05/28/1939, Lawrence, KS, m, 1961, 1 child **DISCIPLINE** ENGLISH HISTORY **EDUCATION** Univ Kans, BA, 61; Stanford Univ, MA, 62, PhD(hist), 66. **CAREER** Instr hist, Stanford Univ, 65-67; asst prof, 67-72, assoc prof, 72-81, prof, 81-82, VPres Acad Affairs & Dean Fac, Lewis & Clark Col, 72-, Provost, Lewis & Clark Col, 79-82; Pres Elect, COE Col, 82-. **RESEARCH** British business and the education of a gentleman in late Victorian England. **SELECTED PUBLICATIONS** The Goddess as Excellent Cow: Selling the Education of a Gentleman as a Prescription for Success in Late Victorian England, Albion, 70; The Sacred Center + the Peace-Pipe/, Parabola-Myth Tradition and the Search for Meaning, Vol. 21, 1996. **CONTACT ADDRESS** Off of Vpres for Acad Affairs, Lewis and Clark Col, Portland, OR 97219.

BROWN, JONATHAN CHARLES
PERSONAL Born 10/02/1942, Fond du Lac, WI, m, 1965, 1 child **DISCIPLINE** ECONOMIC HISTORY **EDUCATION** Univ Wis, Madison, BA, 66; Univ Ariz, MA, 68; Univ Tex, Austin, PhD(hist), 76. **CAREER** Lectr hist, Univ Calif, Santa Barbara, 76-77; Lectr Hist, Univ Calif, Los Angeles, 77-. **MEMBERSHIPS** AHA; Conf Latin Am Hist; Econ Hist Asn; Can Econ Asn. **RESEARCH** Argentina; Latin American economic history; Venezuela. **SELECTED PUBLICATIONS** Auth, Dynamics and autonomy of a traditional marketing system: Buenos Aires, 1810-1860, Hisp Am Hist Rev, 76; A nineteenth century Argentine cattle empire, Agr Hist, 78; The genteel tradition of nineteenth century Colombian culture, Americas, 78; A Socioeconomic History of Argentina, Cambridge Univ, 79. **CONTACT ADDRESS** Dept of Hist, Univ of California, Los Angeles, Los Angeles, CA 90024.

BROWN, JONATHAN M.
PERSONAL Born 07/15/1939, Springfield, MA, m, 1966 **DISCIPLINE** ART HISTORY **EDUCATION** Dartmouth Col, AB, 60; Princeton Univ, MFA, 63, PhD(art hist), 64. **CAREER** From instr to assoc prof art hist, Princeton Univ, 65-73; assoc prof, 73-77, actg dir, 73-75, Dir, Inst Fine Arts, NY Univ, 75-, Prof Art Hist, 77-. **HONORS AND AWARDS** A K Porter Prize, Art Asn Am, 70; Nat Endowment for Humanities fel, 78-79. **MEMBERSHIPS** Art Asn Am. **RESEARCH** Spanish art of the 17th century. **SELECTED PUBLICATIONS** Auth, Hieroglyphs of death and salvation: The decoration of the Church of the Hermandad de la Caridad, Seville, Art Bull, 9/70; co-ed, Sources and Documents in the History of Art: Italy and Spain 2600-2750, Princeton-Hall, 70; auth, Jusepe de Ribera: Prints and Drawings, 73, Murillo and His Drawings, 76 & Images and Ideas in 17th Century Spanish Painting, 78, Princeton Univ. **CONTACT ADDRESS** Inst of Fine Arts, New York Univ, 1 E 78 St, New York, NY 10021.

BROWN, KENDALL H.
PERSONAL Born Los Angeles **DISCIPLINE** ASIAN ART **EDUCATION** Yale Univ, PhD, 94. **CAREER** Asst prof, CSULB. **RESEARCH** Japanese art in the 20th century; Asian art history. **SELECTED PUBLICATIONS** Auth, The Politics of Reclusion: Painting and Power in Momoyama Japan, Hawai'i, 97; Shin-hanga: New Prints in Modern Japan, Los Angeles Co Mus Art, 96 & Light In Darkness: Women in Japanese Prints of Early Showa 1926-1945, Fisher Gallery, 96; auth, Japanese-Style Gardens of the Pacifid West Coast, Rizolli, 99. **CONTACT ADDRESS** Dept of Art, California State Univ, Long Beach, Long Beach, CA 90840-3501. **EMAIL** kbrown@csulb.edu

BROWN, KENDALL WALKER
PERSONAL Born 01/14/1949, American Fork, UT, m, 1974, 2 children **DISCIPLINE** LATIN AMERICAN HISTORY **EDUCATION** Brigham Young Univ, BA, 73; Duke Univ, MA, 75, PhD, 79. **CAREER** Vis prof Span Am hist, Univ Fed de Santa Catarina, Brazil, 79-81; vis asst prof Latin Am hist, Univ NC, Charlotte, 81-82; asst prof Latin Am Hist, Hillsdale Col, 82-. **MEMBERSHIPS** AHA; Conf Latin Am Hist; Latin Am Studies Asn. **RESEARCH** Economic history of Colonial Spanish America; prices in Viceregal Peru; commerce and trade in Southern Brazil. **SELECTED PUBLICATIONS** Auth, A Evolucao da Vinicultura em Arequipa, 1550-1800, Estudos Ibero-Americanos, 80; A documentacao da real hacienda como fonte para a historia economica da America Espanhola, Memorias da II Semana de Hist, 81; co-ed, Peru, In: Royal Treasuries of the Spanish Empire in America, Vol 1, Duke Univ Press, 82. **CONTACT ADDRESS** Dept of History and Political Science, Hillsdale Col, Hillsdale, MI 49242.

BROWN, KENNETH
PERSONAL Born 03/05/1943, Chicago, IL, 2 children **DISCIPLINE** BIBLE, THEOLOGY, HISTORY **EDUCATION** Asbury Theol Sem, BA Theol, 66; Mdiv 76; Drew Univ, PhD, 88. **CAREER** Pastor/Minister, 66-; Prof, Vennard Coll, 76-79. **MEMBERSHIPS** Amer Acad Rel; ATLA; Wesleyan Theol Soc; Christian Holiness Partnership. **RESEARCH** Camp Meeting History; History of the Holiness Movement; Biographical Studies. **SELECTED PUBLICATIONS** Auth, Holy Ground, Too, The Camp Meeting Family Tree, Hazleton, Holiness Archives, 98; co-auth, "Wholly and Forever Thine," Leadership in the Early Natl Camp Meeting Assoc for the Promotion of Holiness, Holiness Archives (Hazleton), 99. **CONTACT ADDRESS** 243 S Pine St, Hazleton, PA 18201. **EMAIL** cmbooks@ptdprolog.net

BROWN, KRISTEN M.
DISCIPLINE 19TH CENTURY GERMAN PHILOSOPHY, ANCIENT PHILOSOPHY **EDUCATION** Stanford Univ, BA; Vanderbilt Univ, MA, PhD. **CAREER** Dept Philos, Millsaps Col **SELECTED PUBLICATIONS** Publ on, Embodiment and Feminine Other in Nietzsche & Form as Logos in Aristotle's Metaphysics Z and Politics. **CONTACT ADDRESS** Dept of Philosophy, Millsaps Col, 1701 N State St, Jackson, MS 39210. **EMAIL** brownkm@okra.millsaps.edu

BROWN, LESLIE
PERSONAL Born 12/02/1954, New York, NY, s **DISCIPLINE** HISTORY **EDUCATION** Duke Univ, PhD, 97. **CAREER** Asst Prof, Univ of MO at St. Louis; asst prof hist and African-Am stud, Wash Univ in St. Louis. **MEMBERSHIPS** AHA; OAH; CCWH; NWSA. **RESEARCH** African American women. **CONTACT ADDRESS** Dept of Hist, Washington Univ, 1 Brookings Dr., Saint Louis, MO 63130. **EMAIL** lbrownb@artsci.wustl.edu

BROWN, MARGARET T.
PERSONAL Born 11/18/1958, Austin, MN, s **DISCIPLINE** UNITED STATES HISTORY **EDUCATION** Univ Minn, BS, 81; Univ Kentucky, MA, 90; PhD, 95. **CAREER** Adj prof, Kennesaw state Univ, Univ Tenn, 94-96; asst prof, Brevard Col, 96-. **HONORS AND AWARDS** Outstand Teach Awd, United Meth, 99. **MEMBERSHIPS** ASEH; SHA; ASA. **RESEARCH** Environmental history; twentieth century US; Appalachian. **SELECTED PUBLICATIONS** Auth, The Wild East: A Biography of the Great Smoky Mountains (Univ Press FL, Gainesville, 00). **CONTACT ADDRESS** Dept Social Science, Brevard Col, PO Box 21, Brevard, NC 28712. **EMAIL** mbrown@brevard.edu

BROWN, MARILYN
DISCIPLINE ART HISTORY **EDUCATION** Birmingham-S Col, BA, 72; Yale Univ, MA, 74, Mphil, 75, PhD, 78. **CAREER** Lecturer, Yale Univ, 77; vis asst prof, ReedCol, 77-78; asst prof, Univ CA, 78-79; asst prof, Tulane Univ, 79-85; grad coord, 93-94; 95-96; 97-98; prof, 95-. **HONORS AND AWARDS** Summer stipend, NEH, 79; grant, ACLS, 82; grant-in-aid, ACLS, 87, 88, 89; vis arts comm,contemp arts ctr, 85-86; fel selection comm, acls, 91-92; bd trustees, new orleans mus art, 1996-; bd dir(s), col art assn am, 97-01. **SELECTED PUBLICATIONS** Auth, Two Generations of Abstract Painting, Alice Trumbull Mason, Emily Mason, NY Eaton House, 82; Gypsies and Other Bohemians, The Myth of the Artist in Nineteenth-Century France, UMI Res Press, Avant-Garde Series, 85; The Degas-Musson Family Papers, An Annotated Inventory, Tulane Univ Lib, 91; Degas and the Business of Art: A Cotton Office in New Orleans, Penn State Press/CAA Monogr, 94. **CONTACT ADDRESS** Dept of Art, Tulane Univ, 6823 St Charles Ave, New Orleans, LA 70118.

BROWN, MARK M.
DISCIPLINE ART; ARCHITECTURAL HISTORY **EDUCATION** Macalester Col, BA, 80; State Univ NYork, MA, 83; Univ Pittsburgh, PhD, 95. **CAREER** Historian, Hist Am Engineering Record, Nat Park Service, 89-92, 96-97; Asst Prof Art Hist & Curator, Earlham Col, 97-. **HONORS AND AWARDS** H.B. du Pont Fel, 94; Henry Luce Found/ACLS Doctoral Dissertation Fel in Am Art, 94-95. **MEMBERSHIPS** Col Art Asn; Soc Archit Hist; Vernacular Archit Forum; Soc Industrial Archeol; Soc Hist Technol. **RESEARCH** Interdisciplinary approaches to diverse themes of architecture, urbanism, structural systems, and cultural landscapes; especially: American steel industry, bridges. **SELECTED PUBLICATIONS** Coauth, The History of the Duquesne Club, Duquesne Club, 89; auth, Nineteenth-Century Cable-Stayed Bridges in Texas, [Proceedings], Fifth Annual Hist Bridges Conf, 97; Technology and the Homestead Steel Works: 1879-1945, Canal History and Technology Proceedings, Canal Hist and Technol Press, 92; The Cathedral of Learning: Concept, Design, Construction, Univ Art Gallery, Univ Pittsburgh, 87, 2nd printing, 95. **CONTACT ADDRESS** Art Dept, Earlham Col, Richmond, IN 47374. **EMAIL** brownma1@earlham.edu

BROWN, NORMAN D.
PERSONAL Born 06/28/1935, Pittsburgh, PA, m, 1966, 2 children **DISCIPLINE** AMERICAN, SOUTHERN & TEXAS HISTORY **EDUCATION** IN Univ, BA, 57; Univ NC, Chapel Hill, MA, 59, PhD, 63. **CAREER** From instr to asst prof, 62-69, assoc prof, 69-83, prof hist, Univ TX, Austin, 83-84, Barbara White Stuart Centennial prof TX hist, 84. **HONORS AND AWARDS** Fel, TX State Hist Asn; Hon life mem, TX State Hist Asn; Earl R Davis Awd for Contrib to TX Conf Hist; UDC's Jefferson Davis Medal; John Bell Hood Awd, Hill Col Conf Hist Symposium. **MEMBERSHIPS** Soc Historians Early Am Repub; Orgn Am Hist; Southern Hist Asn; TX State Hist Asn; Soc of Civil War Hist; Civil War Round Table Assoc. **RESEARCH** The Whig Party; Civil War and Reconstruction; TX polit, 1921-1938. **SELECTED PUBLICATIONS** Auth, A Union Election in Civil War North Carolina, NC Hist Rev, autumn 66; Edward Stanly: First Republican Candidate for Governor of California, Calif Hist Soc Quart, 9/68; Daniel Webster and the Politics of Availability, Univ Ga, 69; Edward Stanly: Whiggery's Tarheel Conqueror, Univ Ala, 74; Dan's the Man, Me for Ma, and Lynch is a Cinch: The Gubernatorial Election of 1926 in Texas, WTex Hist Asn Year Bk, 79; ed, One of Cleburne's Command: The Civil War Reminiscences and Diary of Capt Samuel T Foster, Granbury's Texas Brigade, CSA, Univ Tex Press, 80; ed, Journey to Pleasant Hill: The Civil War Letters of Captain Elijah P Petty, Walker's Texas Division, CSA, Inst Texan Cult, 82; Hood, Bonnet, and Little Brown Jug: Texas Politics, 1921-1928, Tex A&M Univ Press, 84; A Brief History of Walker's Texas Division, In: Joseph P Blessington's Campaigns of Walker's Texas Division, 1875, reprint, Austin, State House Press, 94. **CONTACT ADDRESS** Dept of Hist, Univ of Texas, Austin, Austin, TX 78712-1026.

BROWN, PETER B.
DISCIPLINE RUSSIAN, SOVIET, EASTERN EUROPEAN HISTORY **EDUCATION** Stanford Univ, BA; Univ Chicago, MA, PhD. **CAREER** Instr, RI Col. **RESEARCH** 14th-18th century Russian soc hist; comp Medieval and Early Mod hist; late Imperial-early Soviet economic hist. **SELECTED PUBLICATIONS** Auth, Anthropological Perspective and Early Muscovite Court Politics, Russian Hist; Muscovy, Poland, and the Seventeenth-Century Crisis, The Polish Rev; ed, Studies and Essays on the Soviet and Eastern European Economies. **CONTACT ADDRESS** Rhode Island Col, Providence, RI 02908.

BROWN, R. CRAIG
PERSONAL Born 10/14/1935, Rochester, NY, m, 1960, 3 children **DISCIPLINE** CANADIAN HISTORY **EDUCATION** Univ Rochester, BA, 57; Univ Toronto, MA, 58, PhD(hist), 62. **CAREER** Asst prof hist, Univ Calgary, 61-64; from asst prof to assoc prof, 64-70, dir, Grad Studies, Dept Hist, 72-73, assoc chmn, Dept Hist, 74-77, Prof Hist, Univ Toronto, 70-, Assoc Dean Sch Grad Studies, 81-, Can Coun grants, 62, 63, 65, 73; ed, Can Hist Rev, 68-73; sr res scholar, Izaak Walton Killam Scholar, 77-78. **MEMBERSHIPS** AHA; Can Hist Asn (pres, 80). **RESEARCH** Canadian-American relations; Canadian history. **SELECTED PUBLICATIONS** Auth, Canada's National Policy 1883-1900, 64; auth, Robert Laird Borden: A Biography, vol 1, 75, vol 2, 80; coauth, Canada Views the United States, 66; coauth, Confederation to 1949, 66; coauth, The Canadians 1867-1967, 67; coauth, Canada 1896-1921, 74; coauth, Twentieth Century Canada, 83; coauth, Nation: Canada Since Confederation, 90; ed, The Illustrated History of Canada, 87; ed, Histoire Generale du Canada, 88. **CONTACT ADDRESS** Dept of Hist, Univ of Toronto, 100 St George St, Room 2074, Sidney Smith Hall, Toronto, ON, Canada M5S 1A1. **EMAIL** craig.brown@utoronto.ca

BROWN, RICHARD CARL
PERSONAL Born 04/09/1919, Logan, OH, m, 1946 **DISCIPLINE** HISTORY **EDUCATION** Ohio State Univ, BSc 47; Colgate Univ, MA, 48; Univ Wis, PhD(Am hist), 51. **CAREER** Instr social studies, Colgate Univ, 47-48; from instr to prof, 52-77, Distinguished serv prof, 77-79, Emer Prof Hist, State Univ NY, Col Buffalo, 79-. **MEMBERSHIPS** AHA; Am Studies Asn; Orgn Am Hist. **RESEARCH** American social and intellectual history; immigration and ethnicity. **SELECTED PUBLICATIONS** Auth, Human Side of American History, Ginn, 62; coauth, United States of America: A History for Young Citizens, 63 & The American Achievement, 66, Silver Burdett; Man in America, Gen Learning Corp, 73; auth, Let Freedom Ring, 76; Social Attitudes of American Generals, Arno Press, 79; auth, The Presbyterians, 200 years in Danville Church, 83; auth, A History of Danville and Boyle County, Kentucky 1774-1992, Bicentennial Publications, 92. **CONTACT ADDRESS** Charleston Greene, Danville, KY 40422.

BROWN, RICHARD D.
PERSONAL Born 10/31/1939, New York, NY, m, 1962, 2 children **DISCIPLINE** HISTORY **EDUCATION** Oberlin Col, BA, 66; Harvard Univ, AM, 62; PhD, 66. **CAREER** Fulbright lectr, Univ Toulouse, France, 65-66; asst prof, Oberlin Coll, 66-71; assoc prof, Univ Conn, 71-75; dept hd, 74-80, 94-95; prof, 75-. **HONORS AND AWARDS** Univ Conn, Awd Excel, Res, 99; Guggenheim Fel, 98-99; Alumni Awd, Excel; NEH, 84-85. **MEMBERSHIPS** OAH; AAS; MHS; AHA. **RESEARCH** Social and cultural history of early America. **SELECTED PUBLICATIONS** Auth, The Strength of a People: The Idea of an Informed Citizenry in America 1650-1870 Univ NC Press (Chapel Hill: NC), 96; auth, Knowledge is Power: The Diffusion of Information in Early America 1700-1865, Oxford Univ Press (NY), 89; co-rev, Massachusetts: A Concise History, Univ Mass Press (Amherst), 00; auth, Modernization: The Transformation of American Life 1600-1865, Hill and Wang (NY), 76; auth, Revolutionary Politics in Massachusetts: The Boston Committee of Correspondence and the Towns, 1772-1774, Harvard Univ Press (Cambridge, Mass), 70; ed, Major Problems in the Era of The American Revolution 1760-1791, DC Heath (Lexington, Mass: 92), 2nd ed rev, (Boston, Houghton Mifflin, 00). **CONTACT ADDRESS** Dept History, Univ of Connecticut, Storrs, 241 Glenbrook Rd, Storrs, CT 06269-9005. **EMAIL** richard.d.brown@uconn.edu

BROWN, RICHARD HOLBROOK
PERSONAL Born 09/25/1927, Boston, MA **DISCIPLINE** HISTORY **EDUCATION** Yale Univ, BA, 49, MA, 52, PhD(hist), 55. **CAREER** From instr to asst prof hist, Univ Mass, 55-62; assoc prof, Northern Ill Univ, 62-64; dir, Amherst Proj, Amherst & Hampshire Cols & Newberry Libr, 64-73; dir res & educ & academic vpres, Newberry Libr, 73-94; mem bd dirs, Soc Sci Educ Consortium, 73-79; pres, 75-77; mem, Nat Endowment for Humanities Bd Consults, 77-; chmn, Teaching Resource Group, Nat Coord Comt for Prom Hist, 77-80; sr res fel, Newberry Libr, 94-. **HONORS AND AWARDS** Egleston Hist Prize, Yale Univ, 55; Andrew Mellon fel, Univ Pittsburgh, 60-61; **MEMBERSHIPS** AHA; Orgn Am Historians; Am Antiquarian Soc. **RESEARCH** Pre-Civil War American history and the South; Jackson-Van Buren era; history education. **SELECTED PUBLICATIONS** Auth, The Hero and the People: The Meaning of Jacksonian Democracy, Macmillan, 63; History and the new social studies, Saturday Rev, 10/66; The Missouri crisis, slavery, and the politics of Jacksonianism, South Atlantic Quart, winter 66. **CONTACT ADDRESS** 880 N Lake Shore Dr Apt 16E, Chicago, IL 60611. **EMAIL** brownr@newberry.dre

BROWN, RICHMOND F.
DISCIPLINE LATIN AMERICA AND THE CARIBBEAN, SOCIAL HISTORY **EDUCATION** Spring Hill Col, BA; Tulane Univ, MA, PhD. **CAREER** Asst prof, Univ Kans, 89-90; Asst Prof, Univ South Al, 90-. **SELECTED PUBLICATIONS** Auth, Juan Fermin de Aycinena: Central American Colonial Entrepreneur, 1729-1796, Norman, Univ Okla Press, 97; Profits, Prestige, and Persistence: Juan Fermin de Aycinena and the Spirit of Enterprise in the Kingdom of Guatemala, Hisp Amer Hist Rev 75, 95 & Charles Lennox Wyke and the Clayton-Bulwer Formula in Central America, 1852-1860, The Americas 47, 91. **CONTACT ADDRESS** Dept of History, Univ of So Alabama, 379 Humanities, Mobile, AL 36688-0002. **EMAIL** rbrown@jaguar1.usouthal.edu

BROWN, ROBERT W.
DISCIPLINE HISTORY **EDUCATION** Univ NC Chapel Hill, AB, 69; Marshall Univ, MA, 71; Duke Univ, MA, 73; PhD, 79. **CAREER** Nat Teacher Corps, 69-71; lectr, European Div of Univ Md, 75-76; Lehrbeauftragter, Univ Munster, 76-77; part-time instr, Duke Univ, 77-78; part-time instr, NC State Univ, 78-79; instr, NC Wesleyan Col, 79; from asst prof to prof & dept chemn, Univ NC Pembroke, 79-. **HONORS AND AWARDS** NEH summer sem, 81, 85, & 93; NEH summer inst, 86, 88, 90, & 94; Outstanding Teacher Awd, Univ NC Pembroke, 97. **MEMBERSHIPS** Am Hist Asn, Col Art Asn, Associations of Historians of Nineteenth-century Art, Soc for French Hist Studies, Western Soc for French Hist, Soc for Hist Educ, Consortium on Revolutionary Europe, NC Asn of Historians. **RESEARCH** Nineteenth-Century France, Germany During the Nazi Era, The History and Topography of Paris, Topogarphy and Townscapes in the Visual Arts, The Preservation of Historical Monuments during the Nineteenth-Century. **SELECTED PUBLICATIONS** Auth, "Ancien Paris/Vieux Paris: Images of Old Paris During the Restoration and the July Monarchy," proceedings, The Consortium on Revolutionary Europe, 1750-1850 18 (88): 339-356; auth, "Paris 1900: Exposition universelle," in Historical Dictionary of the World's Fairs and Expositions, 1851-1988, ed. John E. Findling (CT: Greenwood Press, 90), 155-164; auth, "Albert Robida's Vieux Paris Exhibit: Art and Historical Re-creation at the Paris World's Fair of 1900," in Year Book of Interdisciplinary Studies in the Fine Arts Vol 2, eds. William E. Grimm and Michael B. Harper (NY: The Edwin Mellen Press, 91), 421-455; auth, "[The London] Diorama," "Landscape Painting, 1780-1830," and "Topographical and Travel Prints, 1780-1830," in Encyclopedia of Romanticism: Culture in Britain, 1780s-1830s, ed. Laura Dabundo (NY: Garland Pub, Inc., 92), 164-166, 326-328, and 579-582; auth, "Topography," in The Dictionary of Art, ed. Jane Shoaf Turner (London: Macmillan Pub Co., & NY: Grove, 96), 154-157; auth, "Horst Wessel Song," The Encyclopedia of Propaganda, ed. Robert Cole (NY: M. E. Sharpe, 97). **CONTACT ADDRESS** Dept Hist, Univ of No Carolina, Pembroke, PO Box 1510, Pembroke, NC 29372-1510. **EMAIL** rwb@papa.uncp.edu

BROWN, RONALD CONKLIN
PERSONAL Born 04/25/1945, Brownwood, TX, m, 1969, 1 child **DISCIPLINE** UNITED STATES NATIONAL HISTORY **EDUCATION** Wabash Col, AB, 67; Univ Ill, Urbana, AM, 68, PhD(hist), 75. **CAREER** Instr, 75-78; Asst Prof, 78-81; Assoc Prof, 81-85, Prof US Hist, Southwest TX St Univ, 85-; Univ Archivist, 79-82; Dir Hon Prog, 80-95; Acting Dean, General Studies, 95-99, Dean Univ Col, 99-. **HONORS AND AWARDS** Phi Alpha Theta, Donald B. Hoffman Scholarship, SWT Presidential Seminar, SWT Student Body Educ of the Year, Alpha Lambda Delta, Golden Key National Honor Society. **MEMBERSHIPS** AHA; Mining Hist Asn; Texas St Hist Asn; AAHE, ACAD, NCHC, CAGLS; Nat Col Hon Coun. **RESEARCH** Trans-Mississippi West; labor; historiography; mining; oral history; business history. **SELECTED PUBLICATIONS** Auth, Dedication to Fred A Shannon, Ariz and the West, spring 78; Hard-Rock Miners: The Intermountain West, 1860-1920, Tex A&M Press, 79; Beacon on the Hill: Southwest Texas State University, 1903-1978, Southwest Tex, 79; auth, "Western Miners in the Twentieth Century," in Duane A. Smith, ed, Natural Resources in Colorado and Wyoming, Sunflower Univ Press, 82; auth, Up the HIll, Down the Years: A Century in the Life of the College in San Marcos, with David C. Nelson, Southwest Texas St Univ, 1899-1999, Downing Company, 99; auth, No One Ailing Except a Physician: Medicine in the Mining West, 1848-1919, ed Duane A. Smith, Associated Presses of Colorado, 00. **CONTACT ADDRESS** Dept of Hist, Southwest Texas State Univ, 601 University Dr, San Marcos, TX 78666. **EMAIL** rb04@swt.edu

BROWN, RONALD PAUL
PERSONAL Born 03/19/1938, Ravenna, OH, m, 1961, 3 children **DISCIPLINE** HISTORY **EDUCATION** Univ of Akron, BS, history & govt, 1967, MS, counseling & guidance, 1969, PhD, counselor educ, 1974. **CAREER** Univ of Akron, coord of dev serv & student adv 69-74; Cuyahoga Co Bd of Mental Retardation, dir of habilitation serv 74-80; Co of Summit, admin asst 81-84; Kent State Univ, asst to the dean for minority & women affairs 84-87; Kent State Univ Ashtabula Campus, asst dean and asst prof of counselor educ 87-92, assistant professor of Pan African Studies/dir of multicultural affairs, 92-98; Joparo, Owner currently. **HONORS AND AWARDS** Chmn of the Educ Comm Eta Tau Lambda 1982-84; Outstanding Serv Awd Eta Tau Lambda 1983; chairman Univ of Akron's Black Alumni 1984; Key to the City of Ashtabula Ohio, 1990; Developed African American Speaker Series, Ashtabula Campus, 1990; NAACP, Ashtabula Chapter, Man of the Year, 1991, 1995. **MEMBERSHIPS** Univ of Akron Alumni Council 1978-81; bd of trustees Cuyahoga Valley Mental Health 1982-84; Natl Cert Counselor Natl Bd for Certified Couns Inc 1984; bd of trustees St Paul AME Church 1978-; Alpha Phi Alpha, 1982-; board of directors Alpha Homes Inc 1982-; chap sec Natl Old Timers Inc 1984-87; treasurers Black Alumni Assoc 1987-; vice pres, Comm Action Council Ashtabula OH; adv board member Ashtabula Salvation Army; dir Community Resource Economic Comm Ashtabula, Home Safe Inc, bd of trustees 1990, adv bd, 1992; Private Industry Council Advisory Board, 1990, vice pres, Jobs for Ohio's Graduates, president, 1992; Goodwill Industries, bd of advisors. **SELECTED PUBLICATIONS** Auth, African-Americans In Dual Career Commuter Marriages: Personal, Family, Financial, Cultural, and career realities, co-authorship, Journal of Marriage and Family, Spring,00; auth, Slavery with Honor and Freedom, OATYC (Ohio Assoc for two year colleges, Spring, 97); "The Joys and Pain of Brotherhood: A Neophyte Expressed Himself" Alpha Newsletter 1983. **CONTACT ADDRESS** PO Box 9301, Akron, OH 44305-9301. **EMAIL** joparoco@aol.com

BROWN, SALLIE
DISCIPLINE HISTORY **EDUCATION** Ga State Univ, PhD. **CAREER** Asst prof. **HONORS AND AWARDS** E. Merton Coulter Awd; Leroy Collins Prize. **MEMBERSHIPS** Fla Hist Asn. **RESEARCH** United States history; modern South; civil rights. **SELECTED PUBLICATIONS** Auth, Standing Against Dragons: Three Southern Lawyers in the Era of Fear 1945-1965, 98; Federal Anti-Communism and the Segregationist South: From New Orleans to Atlanta 1954-1958, Ga Hist Quarterly, 96. **CONTACT ADDRESS** History Dept, Florida Atlantic Univ, 777 Glades Rd, Boca Raton, FL 33431.

BROWN, SCOTT KENT
PERSONAL Born 10/01/1940, Murray, UT, m, 1966, 5 children **DISCIPLINE** EARLY CHRISTIAN HISTORY & LITERATURE **EDUCATION** Univ Calif, Berkeley, BA, 67; Brown Univ, PhD (Bibl studies), 72. **CAREER** Asst prof, 71-76, Assoc Prof to prof, Ancient Scripture, Brigham Young Univ, 76-; Mem, Inst Ancient Studies, Brigham Young Univ, 73-; corresp mem, Inst Antiquity & Christianity, Calif, 73-. **MEMBERSHIPS** Soc Bibl Lit. **RESEARCH** New Testament; New Testament apocrypha. **SELECTED PUBLICATIONS** Auth, James the Just and the question of Peter's leadership in the light of new sources, In: Sperry Lectr Series, Brigham Young Univ, 73; The book of Lehi: A lost record?, spring 74 & The Apocalypse of Peter (CG VII, 3): A translation, spring 74, Brigham Young Univ Studies; Masada + Excavations and Discoveries from the World of the New-Testament - Herod Fortress and the Zealots Last Stand - a Brigham-Young-University forum address, Brigham Young Univ Studies, Vol 36, 1997. **CONTACT ADDRESS** Dept of Ancient Scripture, Brigham Young Univ, 5435 HBLL, Provo, UT 84602. **EMAIL** skb@byu.edu

BROWN, SIDNEY DEVERE
PERSONAL Born 01/29/1925, Douglass, KS, m, 1948, 4 children **DISCIPLINE** HISTORY **EDUCATION** Southwestern Col, BA, 47; Univ Wis, MA, 50, PhD(hist), 53. **CAREER** From instr to assoc prof hist, Okla State Univ, 52-66, prof 66-71; Prof East Asian Hist, Univ Okla, 71-95, Ford Found fel, Japan, 56-57; ed, Studies Asia, Univ Nebr, 62, 67; vis prof, Univ Ill, Urbana-Champaign, 68-69; Am Philos Soc Grant travel & res in Japan, 71; Japan Found fel, Tokyo Univ, 77-78, 84-85; Prof Emeritus of History, Univ of Okla: regents Prof of History, Univ of Sci and Arts of Okla. **MEMBERSHIPS** AHA; Asn Asian Studies; Japan Soc; Midwest Conf Asian Affiars (pres, 59-60); Southwest Conf Asian Studies (pres, 78). **RESEARCH** Meiji leaders in Japan's modernization. **SELECTED PUBLICATIONS** Auth, Okubo Toshimichi: Meiji economic policies, J Asian Studies, 2/62; Okubo and the first home ministry bureaucracy, In: Japan's Modern Leadership, Univ Ariz, 66; contribr, Political assassination in Early Meiji Japan: the plot against Okubo, In: Meiji Japan's Centennial, Univ Kans, 71; Shidehara Kijuro: The Diplomacy of the Yen, In: Diplomacy in Crisis, Clio Press, 74; auth, The Diary of Kido Takayoshi, 1868-1877, 3 vols, Univ of Toyko Press, 83-96, [biographical essay and annotated translation] with Akiko Hirota; The Self-Image of an Early Meiji Statesman: Through the Diary of Kido Takayoshi, Selected Papers on Asia, Vol I, 197-207; 'Seijoki No Kikoenai Heya' - Levy,IH/, World Lit Today, Vol 67, 1993; 'Youth' and Other Stories - Ogai,M, Rimer,JT, ed/, World Lit Today, Vol 69, 1995; Saigo,Takamori - The Man Behind the Myth - Yates,CL/, Monumenta Nipponica, Vol 51, 1996; On Familiar Terms - A Journey Across Cultures - Keene,D/, World Lit Today, Vol 70, 1996. **CONTACT AD-**

DRESS Dept of Hist, Univ of Oklahoma, 455 W Lindsey St, Norman, OK 73019. **EMAIL** sdbrown4@juno.com

BROWN, SPENCER HUNTER
PERSONAL Born 06/10/1928, Knoxville, TN, m, 1951, 1 child **DISCIPLINE** HISTORY **EDUCATION** Univ Ill, BA, 54, MA, 55; Northwestern Univ, PhD(African hist), 64. **CAREER** Teacher, Carl Sandburg High Sch, 55-56, chmn dept social studies, 56-59; from asst prof to assoc prof hist, 62-71, Prof Hist, Western Ill Univ, 71-98, Chmn Dept, 76-84, Gen ed, J Developing Areas, 65-76, bus mgr, 77-93; Asst ed, 76-84, Assoc Ed., 84-00. **HONORS AND AWARDS** Phi Beta Kappa, 54; Ford Foundation Foreign Areas Fellow, 61-62; ACT/NACADA Certificate of Merit for Advising, 91. **MEMBERSHIPS** African Studies Asn; AHA. **RESEARCH** Social history of Lagos, Nigeria, 1852-1900. **SELECTED PUBLICATIONS** Auth, Publ Health in Lages, 1850-1900: Perceptions, Patterns, and Perspectives, Int & African Hist Studies, Vol. 25; auth, British Army Surgeons Commissioned 1840-1909 with West-Indian/ West-African Service - A Prosopographical Evaluation/, Med Hist, Vol 37, 1993; auth, Public-Health in United-States and West-African Cities, 1870-1900/, Historian, Vol 56, 1994; Colonialism on the Cheap - A Tale of 2 English Army Surgeons in Lagos, Samuel Rowe, and Frank Simpson, 1862-1882/, Int J African Hist Studies, Vol 27, 1994. **CONTACT ADDRESS** Dept of Hist, Western Illinois Univ, 1 University Cir, Macomb, IL 61455-1390.

BROWN, STEWART JAY
PERSONAL Born 07/08/1951, Oak Park, IL, m, 1972, 2 children **DISCIPLINE** MODERN BRITISH & EUROPEAN HISTORY **EDUCATION** Univ Ill, Urbana, BA, 73; Univ Chicago, MA, 74, PhD(hist), 81. **CAREER** Head, Foreign Newspaper Microfilm Proj, Ctr Res Libr, 78-79; asst to dean, Col Arts & Sci, Northwestern Univ, 80-82, lectr hist, 81-82; Asst Prof Hist, Univ GA, 82- **MEMBERSHIPS** Am Hist Asn; Conf on Brit Studies; Am Soc Church Hist; Scottish Church Hist Soc. **RESEARCH** Modern Scottish and Irish & nineteenth century British social and religious history; history of the British Empire. **SELECTED PUBLICATIONS** Auth, The disruption and urban proverty: T Chalmers and the West Port in Edinburgh 1844-47, Records of the Scottish Church Hist Soc, 78; Thomas Chalmers and the Godly Commonwealth in Scotland, Oxford Univ Press, 82. **CONTACT ADDRESS** Dept of Hist, Univ of Georgia, Athens, GA 30602-0001.

BROWN, WALTER R.
PERSONAL Born 05/22/1940, Meridian, MS **DISCIPLINE** HISTORY **EDUCATION** Millsaps Col, BA, 62; Emory Univ, MA, 63, PhD, 72. **CAREER** From instr to asst prof, Memphis State Univ, 65-84; assoc prof, Univ of Memphis, 84-. **MEMBERSHIPS** Furniture Hist Soc, The Pewter Soc, Antique Metalware Soc, French Hist Soc, Regional Furniture Soc, Carolinas Symposium for British Studies, Western Soc for French Hist. **RESEARCH** History of furniture and material culture in England 1450-1700. **SELECTED PUBLICATIONS** Auth, The Stuart Legacy: English Art 1603-1715, Univ of Wash Press (Seattle, WA and London, Eng), 91. **CONTACT ADDRESS** Dept Hist, Univ of Memphis, 3706 Alumni St, Memphis, TN 38152-0001.

BROWNE, GARY LAWSON
PERSONAL Born 09/21/1939, Lansing, MI, m, 1984, 1 child **DISCIPLINE** AMERICAN HISTORY **EDUCATION** Univ Mich, BA, 62; Wayne State Univ, MA, 65, PhD(hist), 73. **CAREER** Instr hist, Wayne State Univ, 72-73, asst prof, 73-75; asst prof, 76-81, Assoc Prof Hist, Univ MD, Baltimire, 81-, Ed, Md Hist Mag, 77- & Md Mag Genealogy, 77- **MEMBERSHIPS** Orgn Am Historians; Southern Hist Asn; AHA. **RESEARCH** American early republic; business history; Maryland history. **SELECTED PUBLICATIONS** Auth, Business Innovation and Social Change: The career of Alexander Brown after the War of 1812, Md Hist Mag, fall 74; The Panic of 1819 in Baltimore, In: Law, Society, and Politics in Early Maryland, Johns Hopkins Univ, 77; Baltimore in the Nation, 1789-1861, Univ NC Press, 80; Cultural Conservatism and the Industrial Revolution: The case of Baltimore, 1776-1860, Continuity, 1/81. **CONTACT ADDRESS** Dept of Hist, Univ of Maryland, Baltimore, Baltimore, MD 21228. **EMAIL** browne@umbc.edu

BROWNING, C. R.
PERSONAL Born 05/22/1944, Durham, NC, m, 1970, 2 children **DISCIPLINE** MODERN EUROPEAN HISTORY **EDUCATION** Oberlin Col, BA 67; Univ Wisconsin Madison, MA 68, PhD 75. **CAREER** Allegheny Col PA, instr 69-71; Pacific Lutheran Univ, all ranks, 74-99; Univ N Carolina Chapel Hill, Frank Porter Graham Dist Prof, 99-. **HONORS AND AWARDS** Woodrow Wilson Fel; DAAD; Humboldt; Fulbright; Inst Adv Stud Princeton and Hebrew U; Schhapior Sr Sch in Res US Holocaust Mem Museum. **MEMBERSHIPS** AHA; GSA; Holocaust Edu Found. **RESEARCH** Holocaust; Nazi Germany; Second World War. **SELECTED PUBLICATIONS** Auth, Fateful Months: Essays on the Emergence of the Final Solution, NY 85; The Path to Genocide, NY 92; Ordinary Men: Reserve Police Battalion 101 and the Final Solution in Poland, NY 92; auth, Naji Policy; auth, Jewish Workers, auth, German Killers, Cambridge Univ Press; Auth, Der Weg zur Endlosung, Entscheidungen und Taeter, Bonn 98. **CONTACT ADDRESS** Univ of No Carolina, Chapel Hill, Chapel Hill, NC 27599. **EMAIL** crbrownn@email.unc.edu

BROWNING, DANIEL C.
PERSONAL Born 10/26/1956, Albany, GA, m, 1982, 2 children **DISCIPLINE** ARCHAEOLOGY; BIBLICAL BACKGROUNDS **EDUCATION** Univ Alabama Huntsville, BSE, 80; MDiv, 84, PhD, 88, Southwestern Baptist Theological Seminary. **CAREER** Instr, Texas Christian Univ, 87-89; Teaching Fel, 85-87, Adjunct Instr, 87-89, Southwestern Baptist Theological Seminary; Instr, 88-90, Tarrant County Jr. Col; Asst Prof, 90-93, Assoc Prof, 93-, William Carey Col. **HONORS AND AWARDS** Endowment for Biblical Research/American Schools of Oriental Research Travel Grant, 84; Research Fel, Albright Inst of Archaeological Research, Jerusalem, 88; Outstanding Faculty Member 95/96, William Carey Col (Student Govt Assoc Awd), 96; Teaching Excellence Grants William Carey Col, 93-97. **MEMBERSHIPS** Amer Schools of Oriental Research; Israel Exploration Soc; Soc of Biblical Lit. **RESEARCH** Biblical backgrounds; culture of New Testament times; archaeological field work **SELECTED PUBLICATIONS** Auth, Land of Goshen, Biblical Illustrator 19, 93; The Other Side of the Sea of Galilee, Biblical Illustrator, 20, 94; Standards of Greatness in the First Century, Biblical Illustrator 21, 95; Coauth, Of Seals and Scrolls, Biblical Illustrator 22, 96; Auth, The Strange Search for the Ashes of the Red Hefer, Biblical Archaeologist, 96; The Hill Country is not Enough for Us: Recent Arcaheology and the Book of Joshua, Southwestern Journal of Theology, 98; Jesus as Carpenter, Biblical Illustrator, 98; Iron Age Loom Weights from Timnah, Tell Batash (Timnah) II: The Finds from the Iron Age II, forthcoming. **CONTACT ADDRESS** William Carey Col, Hattiesburg, MS 39401. **EMAIL** browning@wmcarey.edu

BROWNING, REED ST. CLAIR
PERSONAL Born 08/26/1938, New York, NY, m, 1963, 1 child **DISCIPLINE** HISTORY **EDUCATION** Dartmouth Col, BA, 60; Yale Univ, PhD, 65. **CAREER** Amherst Col, 64-67; Kenyon Col, instr to asst prof, 67-86, asst prof to prof provost, 86-94, act pres, 89. **HONORS AND AWARDS** Fulbright Scholarship; NEH summer stipend; dir NEH summer sem for school teachers; Jacob Javits Fel Board. **MEMBERSHIPS** Ohio Acad Hist, Hist Soc, Soc for Am Baseball Res. **RESEARCH** 18th-century Britain; 18th-century Europe; baseball hist. **SELECTED PUBLICATIONS** The Duke of Newcastle, 75; Political and Constitutional Ideas of the Court Whigs, 82; The War of the Austrian Succession, 94; auth, Cy Young: A Baseball Life, 00. **CONTACT ADDRESS** Kenyon Col, Gambier, OH 43022. **EMAIL** browninr@kenyon.edu

BROXTON, RANDALL
DISCIPLINE HISTORY **EDUCATION** Univ S Ala, BS, 68; Troy State Univ, MA, 78; MS, 78. **CAREER** Prof, Pensacola Jr Col, 68-. **HONORS AND AWARDS** Kappa Delta Pi; Teaching Excellence Awd, 68; Spec Recognition Teaching Excellence Awd, NISOD Conf, 98; Who's Who Among Am Teachers, 94, 96, 00. **MEMBERSHIPS** Gulf S Hist and Humanities Conf, Pensacola Hist Soc, Fla Hist Soc, Fla Endowment for the Humanities, Nar Trust for Hist Preserv, Orgn of Am Historians, Southern Hist Asn, Santa Rosa Hist Soc. **RESEARCH** Muckraker period, the Waltons, Escambia County and Pensacola history. **SELECTED PUBLICATIONS** Auth, Pensacola Historical Society 1933-1990; auth, Docie Clubbs: Her Role in History and Education; co-ed, Emerald Coast Review; auth, The Historical Impact of Letters; auth, Ghosts, Letters and Legends of Pensacola History; auth, The Waltons. **CONTACT ADDRESS** Dept Hist, Pensacola Junior Col, 1000 College Blvd, Pensacola, FL 32504. **EMAIL** rbroxton@pjc.cc.fl.us

BROYLES, MICHAEL
DISCIPLINE MUSIC HISTORY, HISTORY **EDUCATION** Austin Coll, BA, 61; Univ Texas at Austin, MA, 64, PhD, 76. **CAREER** Prof, mus, Univ Maryland Baltimore; PROF, MUS & AM HIST, PENN STATE UNIV. **MEMBERSHIPS** Am Antiquarian Soc **SELECTED PUBLICATIONS** Auth, A Yankee Musician in Europe: The European Journals of Lowell Mason, UMI Research Press, 90; auth, "Music and Class Structure in Antebellum Boston," Jour of the Am Mus Soc, 91; auth, "Music of the Highest Class": Elitism and Populism in Antebellum Boston, Yale Univ Press. 92. **CONTACT ADDRESS** Sch of Mus, Pennsylvania State Univ, Univ Park, University Park, PA 16802. **EMAIL** broyles@psu.edu

BRUCE, D. D.
PERSONAL Born 04/11/1946, Dallas, TX, m, 1967, 1 child **DISCIPLINE** AMERICAN CIVILIZATION **EDUCATION** Univ Pa, PhD, 71. **CAREER** Asst prof, Univ Calif, Irvine; assoc prof, 76-81; prof, 81- . **HONORS AND AWARDS** James Mooney Awd, Southern Anthrop Soc, 73; Fulbright lectr in Am lit, Szeged, Hungary, 87-88. **RESEARCH** 19th century U.S. history; African-American intellectual/cultural history. **SELECTED PUBLICATIONS** Auth, And They All Sang Hallelujah: Plain-Folk Camp-Meeting Religion, 1800-1845, 74; auth, Violence and Culture in the Antebellum South, 79; auth, The Rhetoric of Conservatism: The Virginia Convention of 1829-30 and the Conservative Tradition in the South, 82; auth, Black American Writing from the Nadir: The Evolution of a Literary Tradition, 1877-1915, 89; auth, Archibald Grimke: Portrait of a Black Independent, 93. **CONTACT ADDRESS** History Dept, Univ of California, Irvine, Irvine, CA 92697-3275. **EMAIL** ddbruce@uci.edu

BRUCE, ROBERT VANCE
PERSONAL Born 12/19/1923, Malden, MA **DISCIPLINE** HISTORY **EDUCATION** Univ NH, BS, 45; Boston Univ, AM, 47, PhD(hist), 53. **CAREER** Instr hist & math, Univ Bridgeport, 47-48; master hist, Lawrence Acad, 48-51; from instr to assoc prof, 55-66, prof hist, 66-90, Prof Emer, 84- Boston Univ. **HONORS AND AWARDS** Guggenheim Mem fel, 57-58; vis assoc prof hist, Univ Wis, 62-63; Henry E Huntington Libr fel, 66; Pulitzer Prize History, 88. **MEMBERSHIPS** AAAS Fel; Orgn Am Hist; Soc Am Hist Fel. **RESEARCH** American Civil War; United States history, 1846-1897; history of American science and technology. **SELECTED PUBLICATIONS** Auth, Lincoln and the Tools of War, Bobbs,56; 1877: Year of Violence, Bobbs,59; Chap, In: Abraham Lincoln: A New Portrait, Putnam, 59; Chap, In: Lincoln for the Ages, Doubleday, 60; contribr, Nineteenth Century American Science: A Reappraisal, Northwestern Univ, 72; auth, Bell: Alexander Graham Bell and the Conquest of Solitude, Little, 73; Packaging the Past, J Interdisciplinary Hist, winter 76; auth, The Launching of Modern American Science, Knopf, 87; chap, in Lincoln the War President, Oxford, 92; chap, In Feeding Mars, Westview, 93; chap, in War Comes Again, Oxford, 95; auth, "The Riddle of Death," in The Lincoln Enigma, (Oxford, 01). **CONTACT ADDRESS** Dept of History, Boston Univ, 226 Bay State Rd, Boston, MA 02215. **EMAIL** vov1877@webtv.net

BRUCKER, GENE ADAM
PERSONAL Born 10/15/1924, Cropsey, IL, m, 1949, 3 children **DISCIPLINE** HISTORY **EDUCATION** Univ Ill, AB, 47, MA, 48; Oxford Univ, BLitt, 50; Princeton Univ, PhD(hist), 54. **CAREER** From instr to assoc prof, 54-64, prof, 64-80, Shepard Prof Hist, Univ Calif, Berkeley, 80-91; Emeritus, 91-; Guggenheim fel, 60-61; Am Coun Learned Soc fel, 64-65; fel, Inst Advan Studies, Princeton Univ, 68-69. **RESEARCH** Renaissance Italian history; history of Florence. **SELECTED PUBLICATIONS** Auth, Renaissance Florence, Wiley, 69; ed, The Society of Renaissance Florence, Harper, 72; auth, The Civic World of Early Renaissance Florence, Princeton Univ, 77; Ecclesiastical Courts in 15th-Century Florence and Fiesole/, Mediaeval Studies, Vol 53, 1991; The Criminal-Law System of Medieval and Renaissance Florence - Stern,LI/, Renaissance Quart, Vol 48, 1995; The 'Consulte e Pratiche' of the Florentine Republic 1498-1505 - Italian - Fachard,D, ed/, Renaissance Quart, Vol 48, 1995; Charity and State in Late Renaissance Italy - The Monte-de-Pieta of Florence - Menning,CB/, Renaissance Quart, Vol 48, 1995; Institutional Legislation and Documents from the Florentine Republic, 1494-1512, Vol 1 - 2-December,1494 to 14-February,1497 - Italian - Cadoni,G, Ed/, Speculum- a J Medieval Studies, Vol 71, 1996; Lucca 1439-1494 - The Reconstruction of an Italian City-Republic - Bratchel,ME/, J Interdisciplinary Hist, Vol 27, 1997. **CONTACT ADDRESS** Dept of Hist, Univ of California, Berkeley, Berkeley, CA 94720.

BRUEGMANN, ROBERT
PERSONAL Born 05/21/1948, Chicago, IL, s **DISCIPLINE** HISTORY OF ARCHITECTURE **EDUCATION** Principia Col, BA, 70; Univ Pa, PhD, 76. **CAREER** Phil Col Art, lectr, 76-77; Univ Ill Chicago, asst prof, 77-83; assoc prof, 83-93; dir Preservation Prog, 77-83; Dir Grad Study, 87-90; prof, 94- . **HONORS AND AWARDS** Teaching fel, Univ Pa, 72-74; Head Teaching fel, Univ Pa, 73-74; Penfield Scholar in Diplomacy, Int Affaris and Belles lettres, 73-74; Founder's Awd, Soc of Archit Hist, 78; Univ Ill Chicago, fac summer fel, 80; NEH fel, 83-84; Graham Found for Advan Studies in the Arts, 85; Sr fel, Temply Hoyne Bell Ctr for the Study of Am Archit, Columbia Univ, 89-90; fel, Inst for the Human, Univ Ill Chicago, 92-93; scholar, Great Cities Inst, Univ Ill Chicago, 98-99; Spro Kostof Awd, Soc of Archit Hist, 98. **MEMBERSHIPS** Int Planning Hist Soc; Nat Trust for Hist Preserv; Soc of Archit Hist; Metrop Planning Coun, Chicago; Chicago Archit Club; Vernacular Archit Forum. **RESEARCH** Modern and contemporary architecture, urbanism, planning and landscape; contemporary urban built evironment and urban sprawl. **SELECTED PUBLICATIONS** Auth, Benicia: Portrait of an Early California Town: An Architectural History, 1846 to the Present, 80; auth, Holabird & Roche/Holbird & Root, Catalog of Work 1910-1940, 91; ed, Modernism at Mid-Century: The Architecture of the United States Air Force Academy, 94; auth, The Architects and the City: Holabird and Roche of Chicago 1880-1918, 97. **CONTACT ADDRESS** Art History M/C 201, Univ of Illinois, Chicago, 935 W. Harrison St., Chicago, IL 60607. **EMAIL** bbrueg@uic.edu

BRUMBERG, JOAN JACOBS
PERSONAL Born 04/29/1944, Mt Vernon, NY, m, 1972, 1 child **DISCIPLINE** AMERICAN HISTORY **EDUCATION** Univ Rochester, BA, 65; Boston Col, MA, 71; Univ Va, PhD, 78. **CAREER** Vis asst prof, State Univ NY, Binghamton, 78-

79; from asst prof to prof, 79-96, Stephen H. Weiss Presidential Fel and prof hist, Cornell Univ, 96-. **HONORS AND AWARDS** Fel, Charles Warren Ctr, Harvard Univ, 82-83; fel, Rockefeller Found, 84-85; Berkshire Book Prize, 88; John Hope Franklin Prize, 89; Watson Davis Prize, 89; Basker Memorial Prize, 89; fel, NEH, 90-91; fel, John Simon Guggenheim Found, 91-92; fel, OAH Japanese Am Studies Asn, 97; fel, Am Col Obstetricians & Gynecologists, 91; fel, Soc Am Hist, 98-. **MEMBERSHIPS** Orgn Am Historians; Berkshire Womens Hist Conf; ASA; AAHM. **RESEARCH** Nineteenth century social and cultural history of the United States; history of women, childhood, and the family; history of medicine. **SELECTED PUBLICATIONS** Auth, Mission for Life: The Judson Family and American Evangelical Culture, The Free Press, 80, NY Univ Press pb, 84; coauth, Women in the professions: A research agenda for American historians, in Rev Am Hist, 6/82; auth, Zenanas and Girlless villages: The ethnology of American evangelical women, 1870-1910, in J Am Hist, 9/82; Chlorotic girls, 1870 to 1920: An historical perspective on female adolescence, in Child Develop, 12/82; Fasting Girls: The Emergence of Anorexia Nervosa as a Modern Disease, Harvard Univ Press, 88 (selected for numerous book prizes); The Body Project: An Intimate History of American Girls, Random House, 97; auth numerous articles and book reviews. **CONTACT ADDRESS** Dept of Human Development, Cornell Univ, Martha Van Rensselaer Hall, Ithaca, NY 14853-0001. **EMAIL** jjb10@cornell.edu

BRUMFIELD, WILLIAM CRAFT
PERSONAL Born 06/28/1944, Charlotte, NC, s **DISCIPLINE** RUSSIAN LITERATURE & ART HISTORY **EDUCATION** Tulane Univ, BA, 66; Univ Calif, Berkeley, MA, 68, PhD (Slavic lang), 73 **CAREER** Vis lectr Russ lit, Univ Wis-Madison, 73-74; asst prof Russ lit, Harvard Univ, 74-79; Asst Prof Russ Lit, Tulane Univ, 81-, Res dir, ACTR Moscow, 79-80. **HONORS AND AWARDS** Woodrow Wilson fel, 66; IREX sr exchange scholar, Moscow, 83-84; fel, Kennan Inst, Washington, 89; NEH fel, Nat Humanities Ctr, 92-93; "Notable Books of the Year 1993", for A History of Russian Architecture, New York Times Book Rev, 93; fac res award, Tulane Univ, 97; Guggenheim fel, 00-01. **MEMBERSHIPS** Am Asn Advan Slavic Studies; Am Coun Teachers of Russian; Soc Architectural Historians. **RESEARCH** Russian cultural hist; Russian architectural history. **SELECTED PUBLICATIONS** Auth, Gold in Azure: One Thousand Years of Russian Architecture, David Godine (Boston), 83; ed, Reshaping Russian Architecture: Western Technology, Utopian Dreams, Cambridge Univ Pr, Wilson Ctr, 90; ed, Christianity and the Arts in Russia, Cambridge Univ Pr, 91; auth, The Origins of Modernism in Russian Archietecture, Univ Calif, 91; auth, A History of Russian Architecture, Cambridge Univ Pr, 93; ed, Russian Housing in the Modern Age: Design and Social Hist, Cambridge Univ Pr, Wilson Ctr, 93; auth, An Architectural Survey of St. Petersburg, 1840-1916: Building Inventory, Kennan Inst, Woodrow Wilson Ctr, 94; auth, Lost Russia: Photograhping the Ruins of Russian Architecture, Duke Univ Pr, 95; auth, Landmarks of Russian Architecture: A Photographic Survey, Gordon and Breach, 97. **CONTACT ADDRESS** Dept of Ger & Slavic Lang, Tulane Univ, 305 Newcomb Hall, New Orleans, LA 70118. **EMAIL** brumfiel@mailhost.tcs.tulane.edu

BRUMMETT, PALMIRA
DISCIPLINE HISTORY **EDUCATION** Univ Ill, MPH, 81; Univ Chicago, PhD, 88. **CAREER** Assoc prof, Hist, Univ Tenn. **RESEARCH** Ottoman history. **SELECTED PUBLICATIONS** Auth, Ottoman Seapower and Levantine Diplomacy in the Age of Discovery,SUNY Pr, 94; auth, Image and Imperialism in the Ottoman Revolutionary Press, SUNY Pr, 00; auth, Civilizations Past and Present, Longman's, 00. **CONTACT ADDRESS** Dept of History, Univ of Tennessee, Knoxville, 915 Volunteer Blvd, 6th Fl, Dunford Hall, Knoxville, TN 37996-4065. **EMAIL** palmira@utk.edu

BRUNDAGE, JAMES A.
PERSONAL Born 02/05/1929, Lincoln, NE, d, 6 children **DISCIPLINE** HISTORY **EDUCATION** Univ Nebraska, BA, 50, MA, 51; Fordham Univ, PhD, 55. **CAREER** Lectr, Fordham Univ, 53-55; asst prof, Univ Wisconisn Milwaukee, 57-60; from assoc prof to Ahmanson-Murphy Distinguished Prof hist, Univ Kansas, 60-89; Courtesy Prof law, Univ Kansas, 90-. **HONORS AND AWARDS** Guggenheim Fel; Fulbright Fel Spain; NEH Fel. **MEMBERSHIPS** RHS; MAA; ASLH; CLSA; AHA; ACHA. **RESEARCH** History of Medieval Law; Canon Law; Roman Law; Ius Commune; History of Universities; History of the Crusades. **SELECTED PUBLICATIONS** Auth, Sex Law and Marriage in the Middle Ages, London, Variorum, 93; Medieval Canon Law, London, Longmans, 95; coed, Handbook of Medieval sexuality, NY, Garland, 96; The Calumny Oath and Ethical Ideals of Canonical Advocates, in: Proceedings of the Ninth Intl Congress of Medieval Canon Law, ed, Peter Landau, Joers Mueller, Vatican City, BAV, 97; auth, Obscene and Lascivious: Behavioral Obscenity in Canon Law, in: Obscenity: Social Control and Artistic Creation in the European Middle Ages, ed, Jan M Ziolkowski, Cultures Beliefs and Traditions: Medieval and Early Modern Peoples, Leiden Brill, 98; auth, Taxation of Costs in Medieval Cononical Courts, in: Forschungen zur Reichs-Papst und Landesgeschichte: Peter Herde zum 65, Geburtstag, ed, Karl Borchardt, Enno Bunz, Stuttgart, Anton Hiersemann, 98. **CONTACT ADDRESS** 1102 Sunset Dr, Lawrence, KS 66044-4548. **EMAIL** brundage@eagle.cc.ukans.edu

BRUNDAGE, WILLIAM F.
PERSONAL Born 11/05/1959, PA, m, 1985, 1 child **DISCIPLINE** HISTORY **EDUCATION** Univ Chicago, BA, 81; Harvard Univ, MA, 84; Harvard Univ, PhD, 88. **CAREER** Instr, Univ Ga, 88-89; From Asst Prof to Assoc Prof, Queen's Univ, 89-97; From Assoc Prof to Prof, Univ Fla, 97-. **HONORS AND AWARDS** E Merton Coulter Awd, Ga Hist Soc, 90; Grant, Soc Sci and Humanities Res Coun, 92-95; Elliot Rudwick Awd, Ind Univ, 92; Merle Curti Awd, Orgn of Am Historians, 94; Fel, Am Coun of Learned Soc, 95-96; Fel, Nat Humanities Ctr, 95-96; Choice Outstanding Acad Book of the Year, 98. **MEMBERSHIPS** Orgn of Am Hist, AHA, SHA, GHA, VHS, ASA. **RESEARCH** Southern history, American history, African-American history. **SELECTED PUBLICATIONS** Auth, Lynching in the New South: Georgia and Virginia 1880-1930, Univ Ill Pr (Urbana, IL), 93; auth, A Socialist Utopia in the New South: The Ruskin Colonies in Tennessee and Georgia 1894-1901, Univ Ill Pr (Urbana, IL), 96; ed, Under Sentence of Death: Essays on Lynching in the South, Univ NC Pr (Chapel Hill, NC), 97; auth, "Class, Gender and Mob Violence in the South," in Identity and Intolerance: Nationalism, Racism and Xenophobia in Ger and the U S (New York: Cambridge Univ Pr, 97); ed, Where These Memories Grow: History, Memory and Regional Identity in the American South, Univ NC Pr (Chapel Hill, NC), 00; auth, "Racial Violence, Lynchings and Modernization in the Mountain South," in Appalachians and Race: The Mountain South from Slavery to Segregation (Lexington, KY: UP of KY, forthcoming); auth, "White Women and the Politics of Historical Memory in the South 1880-1920," in Jumpin' Jim Crow: Southern Polit from Civil war to Civil Rights (Princeton: Princeton Univ Pr, forthcoming). **CONTACT ADDRESS** Dept Hist, Univ of Florida, PO Box 117320, Gainesville, FL 32611-7320. **EMAIL** brundage@history.ufl.edu

BRUNETTE, PETER
PERSONAL Born 09/18/1943, Richwood, WV, m, 1974 **DISCIPLINE** VISUAL ARTS **EDUCATION** Univ Wis, PhD. **CAREER** Prof. **MEMBERSHIPS** Modern Lang Asn, Soc for Cinema Studies. **RESEARCH** Literary theory; film theory and history; theories of visual representation. **SELECTED PUBLICATIONS** Roberto Rossellini, 87; co-auth, Screen/Play: Derrida and Film Theory, 90; ed, Shoot the Piano Player, 93; coed, Deconstruction and the Visual Arts: Art, Media, Architecture, 94; auth, The Films of Michelangelo Autonioni, 98; ed, Martin Scoraese: Interviews, 99. **CONTACT ADDRESS** Dept of English, George Mason Univ, Fairfax, 4400 University Dr, Fairfax, VA 22030. **EMAIL** pbrunette@gmu.edu

BRUNGARDT, MAURICE P.
PERSONAL Born 03/30/1941, Oklahoma City, OK, m, 1971, 1 child **DISCIPLINE** HISTORY **EDUCATION** Univ Notre Dame, BA, 63; Univ Tex at Austin, PhD, 74. **CAREER** Adj prof, Pontif Univ Javeriana, 70-71; from instr to assoc prof, Loyola Univ, 71-; Fulbright vis prof, La Univ Pedagogica Y Tecnologica de Colombia, 94; Fulbright vis prof, Univ Nac, 94. **HONORS AND AWARDS** Fulbright Grant, 94. **MEMBERSHIPS** Am Hist Asn, Latin Am Studies Asn, Soc for Span & Port Hist Studies, Confr on Latin Am Hist, Louisiana Hist Asn, S Eastern Confr of Latin Am Studies. **RESEARCH** Columbia, Northern South America, Spanish Empire. **SELECTED PUBLICATIONS** Auth, "Mitos Historicos y Literarios: La Casa Grande," De Ficciones y Realidades. Perspectivas sobre Literatura e Historia Colombianas (Bogota: Tercer Mundo, 89), 63-72; auth, "The Economy of Colombia in the Late Colonial and Early National Periods," Reform and Insurrection in Bourbon New Granada and Peru (LA: La State Univ Press, 90), 164-193; auth, A Reference Guide to Latin American History, Sharpe (Armonk, NY), 00. **CONTACT ADDRESS** Dept Hist, Loyola Univ, New Orleans, 6363 Saint Charles Ave, New Orleans, LA 70118-6143. **EMAIL** brungard@loyno.edu

BRUNK, SAMUEL
PERSONAL Born 08/27/1959, Charlottesville, VA, m, 1989, 1 child **DISCIPLINE** HISTORY, LATIN AMERICA **EDUCATION** Wash Univ, BA, 81; Univ MN, MA, 87; PhD, 92. **CAREER** Instr, Univ Minn, 90-93; asst prof, Univ Neb, 93-98; assoc prof, Univ Tex, 98-. **HONORS AND AWARDS** Dist Teach Awd; Fulbright Awd. **MEMBERSHIPS** CLAH. **RESEARCH** 20th Century Mexico; Mexican Revolution (Emiliano Zapata); political culture; environmental history. **SELECTED PUBLICATIONS** Auth, Emiliano Zapata: Revolution and Betrayal in Mexico, Univ New Mexico Press (Albuquerque), 95; auth, "Zapata and the City Boys: In Search of a Piece of the Revolution," Hisp Am Hist Rev 73 (93); auth, "'The Sad Situation of Civilians and Soldiers': The Banditry of Zapatismo in the Mexican Revolution," Am Hist Rev 101 (96); auth, "Remembering Emiliano Zapata: Three Moments in the Posthumous Career of the Martyr of Chinameca," Hisp Am Hist Rev 78 (98). **CONTACT ADDRESS** Dept History, Univ of Texas, El Paso, 500 West Univ Ave, El Paso, TX 79968-8900. **EMAIL** sbrunk@miners.utep.edu

BRUSH, STEPHEN GEORGE
PERSONAL Born Bangor, ME, m, 1960, 2 children **DISCIPLINE** HISTORY OF SCIENCE **EDUCATION** Harvard Univ, AB, 55; Oxford Univ, DPhil, 58. **CAREER** NSF fel physics, Imp Col, Univ London, 58-59; physicist, Lawrence Radiation Lab, Univ Calif, Livermore, 59-65; res assoc educ, Harvard Proj Physics, Harvard Univ, 65-68, lectr physics & hist sci, 66-68; assoc prof, 68-71, Prof, Dept Hist & Inst Phys Sci & Technol, Univ MD, College Park, 71-; Prin investr res grants, NSF, 65-; adv ed, Isis, 79-. **HONORS AND AWARDS** Pfizer Awd, Hist Sci Soc, 77; Distinguished Univ Prof of Hist of Sci, 95. **MEMBERSHIPS** Hist Sci Soc; Am Phys Soc; AAAS; Am Hist Asn. **RESEARCH** History of modern physical science, especially geophysics and astrophysics. **SELECTED PUBLICATIONS** Auth, Kinetic Theory (3 vols), Pergamon, New York, 65, 66 & 72; ed, Resources for the History of Physics, 72 & co-ed, History in the Teaching of Physics, 72, Univ New England; coauth, Introduction to Concepts and Theories in Physical Science, Addison-Wesley Publ Co, 73; auth, The Kind of Motion We Call Heat: A History of the Kinetic Theory of Gases in the 19th Century, North-Holland, 76; The Temperature of History; Phases of Science & Culture in the 19th Century, Burt Franklin, 78; Statistical Physics and the Atomic Theory of Matter from Boyle and Newton to Landau and Unsager, 83; A History of Modern Planetary Physics, 96. **CONTACT ADDRESS** Dept of Hist, Univ of Maryland, Col Park, College Park, MD 20742-0001. **EMAIL** brush@ipst.umd.edu

BRUZELIUS, CAROLINE
PERSONAL Born 04/18/1949, Stockholm, Sweden, s, 1 child **DISCIPLINE** ART HISTORY **EDUCATION** Yale Univ, PhD. **CAREER** Prof, art hist, Duke Univ. **HONORS AND AWARDS** Duke Alumni Distinguished Tchg Awd, 85; Fulbright Fel, 93; Guggenheim Fel, 98-99. **RESEARCH** Gothic archit and sculpture in France and Italy. **SELECTED PUBLICATIONS** Auth, The Thirteenth Century Church at Saint Denis; The Architecture of the Cistercians in the Early Thirteenth Century; auth The Brummer Collection of Medieval Art. **CONTACT ADDRESS** Dept of Art and Art Hist, Duke Univ, East Duke Building, Durham, NC 27706.

BRYSON, WILLIAM HAMILTON
PERSONAL Born 07/29/1941, Richmond, VA **DISCIPLINE** ENGLISH & AMERICAN LEGAL HISTORY **EDUCATION** Hampden-Sydney Col, BA, 63; Harvard Univ, LLB, 67; Univ Va, LLM, 68; Cambridge Univ, PhD, 72. **CAREER** Max Planck Inst grant, Frankfurt, 72-73; prof law, Univ Richmond, 73-. **HONORS AND AWARDS** Yorke Prize, Cambridge Univ, 73; Am Coun Learned Soc fel, 80. **MEMBERSHIPS** Fel Royal Hist Soc; Selden Soc; Am Soc Legal Hist; Medieval Acad Am. **RESEARCH** English legal history (particularly the history of equity); Virginia legal institutions; Virginia civil procedure. **SELECTED PUBLICATIONS** Auth, Dict of Sigla and Abbreviations to and in Law Books Before 1607, Hein, 96; ed, Legal Education in Virginia, 1779-1979, Univ Press Va, 82; ed, Sir John Randolph's King's Bench Reports, Hein, 96; auth, Legal Education in 19th Century Virginia, essay, Hein, 98; auth, Virgina Law Books, Am Philosophical Soc, 00, auth, samuel Dodd's reports, Carolina Acad Press, 00. **CONTACT ADDRESS** Law School, Univ of Richmond, 28 Westhampton Way, Richmond, VA 23173. **EMAIL** hbryson@richmond.edu

BUCCELLATI, GIORGIO
PERSONAL Born 02/08/1937, Milano, Italy, m, 1966 **DISCIPLINE** HISTORY OF MESOPOTAMIA & SYRIA **EDUCATION** Cath Univ Sacred Heart, Milan, Phil Dr, 58; Fordham Univ, MA, 60; Univ Chicago, PhD, 65. **CAREER** Instr hist, Loyola Univ, Ill, 63-65; from asst prof to prof, 65-76, Dir, Inst Archaeol, Univ Calif, Los Angeles, 76-, Epigrapher Cuneiform texts, Orient Inst, Chicago, 62-63 & 66-67; Am Sch Orient Res fel, Bagdad, 62-63; Univ Calif Humanities Inst fel, 66 & 68; codir archeol exped, Korucu Tepe, Turkey, 68-72; vis prof Assyriol, Pontif Bibl Inst, Rome, 72; dir, Old Babylon Ling Anal Proj, 72-; gen ed, Monographic Journals of the Near East, Undena Publ, 74; dir, Joint Exped to Terga, Syria, 76- **MEMBERSHIPS** Am Orient Soc; AHA; Soc Bibl Lit; Cath Bibl Asn Am; Soc Am Archaeol. **RESEARCH** Political institutions of Syria and Mesopotamia; archaeology of Mesopotamia; Akkadian linguistics. **SELECTED PUBLICATIONS** Auth, Cities and Nations of Ancient Syria, Univ Rome, 67; An interpretation of the Akkadian stative, J Near Eastern Studies, 68; coauth, Cuneiform Texts from Nippur, Orient Inst, Chicago, 69; auth, On the use of Akkadian infinitive after sha or construct state, J Semitic Studies, 72; Tre saggi sulla sapienza Mesopotamia, Oriens Antiquus, 72; ed, Approach to the Study of the Ancient Near East, Pontif Bibl Inst Rome, 73; auth, Terga preliminary report, Vol 10, 80; co-ed, The Shape of the Past, 81; Urkesh, the first Hurrian Capital/, Bibl Archaeol, Vol 60, 1997. **CONTACT ADDRESS** Cotsen Inst of Archeol, A210 Fowler, Los Angeles, CA 90095-1510. **EMAIL** buccella@ucla.edu

BUCHANAN, HARVEY
PERSONAL Born 09/18/1923, New Haven, CT **DISCIPLINE** HISTORY, ART HISTORY **EDUCATION** Yale Univ, BA, 44, MA, 48, PhD(hist), 53. **CAREER** From instr to assoc prof, 52-64, head dept humanities & soc sci, 63-68, assoc dean humanities & fine arts, 68-71, dean, 71-72, provost, 72-77, Prof

Hist, Case Western Reserve Univ, 64-, Prof Humanities, 77-, Relief worker, Am Friends Serv Comt, Normandy, Ger & Palestine, 45-49; Fulbright scholar, Crose Inst, Naples, Italy, 49-51; mem Nat Bd Consults, Nat Endowment for Humanities, 75-. **HONORS AND AWARDS** Ordre des Palmes Academiques, Fr Govt, 75. **MEMBERSHIPS** AHA; Am Soc Reformation Res; Renaissance Soc Am; Ancient Hist Soc, Naples. **RESEARCH** The enlightenment of Italy; Luther and the Turks; Renaissance political thought. **CONTACT ADDRESS** Mather Hall, Case Western Reserve Univ, Cleveland, OH 44106.

BUCHOLZ, ARDEN K.
PERSONAL Born 05/14/1936, Chicago, IL, m, 1962, 2 children **DISCIPLINE** HISTORY **EDUCATION** Dartmouth Col, AB, 58; Univ Vienna, Diploma, 70; Univ Chicago, AM, 65, PhD, 72. **CAREER** English teacher, Am Orta Okulu, Talas-Kaysenm Turkey, 58-60; US Army, 2nd Armored Cavalry Regiment, Nuernberg, Ger, 61-64; Hist teacher, The Latin School of Chicago, 65-70; Prof hist, SUNY Brockport, 70-; prof hist, Brunel Univ, Uxbridge England, 87-88. **HONORS AND AWARDS** SUNY Res Found Fel, 74-76, 77; SUNY Chancellor's Awd for Excellence in Teaching, 77; Queen Awd for Excellence in the Teaching of History, 85; Advanced Res Assoc, US Army Military Hist Inst, 85; Dennis Fel, Houghton Library, Harvard Univ, 99. **SELECTED PUBLICATIONS** Auth, Hans Delbruck and the German Military Establishment, Iowa City (85); auth, Moltke, Schlieffen and Prussian War Planning, Oxford (91); auth, Delbruck's Modern Military History, London (97); more than a hundred books, articles and reviews. **CONTACT ADDRESS** Dept Hist, SUNY, Col at Brockport, 350 New Campus Dr, Brockport, NY 14420-2997. **EMAIL** abucholz@acspr1.acs.brockport.edu

BUCK, DAVID
PERSONAL Born 12/31/1936, Denver, CO, m, 1964, 2 children **DISCIPLINE** HISTORY **EDUCATION** Stanford Univ, BA, 58; PhD, 72; Harvard Univ, MA, 60. **CAREER** Instr to prof, Univ of Wisc Milwaukee, 69-. **HONORS AND AWARDS** UWM Teaching Awd, 75; UWM Fel, 87; 96. **MEMBERSHIPS** Assoc for Asian Studies; AHA; Nat Comm on US China Rel. **RESEARCH** Urban History of Modern China, History of Boxer Uprising, History of the Tea Trade 1800-1950. **SELECTED PUBLICATIONS** Auth, "China and the Containment of Ethnonationalism", Global Convulsions: Race, Ethnicity, and Nationalism at the End of the Twentieth Century, ed Winston A. Van Horne, SUNY Pr, (Albany, 97): 281-297; auth, "Biography of Owen Lattimore", American National Biography, eds John A. Garraty and Mark C. Carnes, Oxford Univ Pr, (NY, 99): 248-250; auth, "Was It Pluck or Luck that Made the West Grow Rich", J of World Hist, 10.2 (Fall 99): 413-430; auth, "Railway City and National Capital: Two Faces of the Modern in Changchun", Remaking the Chinese City: Modernity and National Identity, 1900-1950, ed Joseph Esherick, Univ of Haw Pr, (Honolulu, 00): 68-89. **CONTACT ADDRESS** Dept Hist, Univ of Wisconsin, Milwaukee, PO Box 413, Milwaukee, WI 53201-0413. **EMAIL** davebuck@uwm.edu

BUCK, HARRY MERWYN
PERSONAL Born 11/18/1921, Enola, PA, m, 1943, 2 children **DISCIPLINE** HISTORY OF RELIGIONS **EDUCATION** Albright Col, AB, 42; Evangel Sch Theol, MDiv, 45; Univ Chicago, PhD, 54. **CAREER** Pastor, Evangel United Brethren Church, Md, 42-46, Pa, 46-49; from instr to asst prof Bibl hist, 51-59, assoc prof Bible & relig, 59-68, prof Relig Studies, Wilson Col, 68-; consult, New Testament Greek Text Proj, Am Bible Soc, 55; mem, East-West Philosophers Conf, Honolulu, Hawaii, 59; comt lectionary study, Int Greek New Testament Proj, 59-; seminar Indian Civilization, Hyderabad, India, 61; managing ed, J Am Acad Relig, 61-73; chmn, Am Textual Criticism Sem, 60-62; fac training fel, Am Inst Indian Studies & hist relig fel, Soc Relig Higher Educ, 65-66; partic fel, Int Conf-Sem on Tamil Studies, Univ Malaya, 66; ed, Anima, 74-. **MEMBERSHIPS** Am Acad Relig; Soc Bibl Lit; Soc Study New Testament; Asn Asian Studies; Int Soc Study Relig. **RESEARCH** Epic literature of South Asia; function of sacred tradition; methodology in the history of religions. **SELECTED PUBLICATIONS** Auth, People of the Lord, History, Scriptures and Faith of Ancient Israel, Macmillan, 66; co-ed, Religious Traditions and the Limits of Tolerance, Anima, 88; auth, Rama in Buddhist Cultures, 95; art, Beyond Walls, Fences, and Interreligious Dialogue, J of Ecumenical Stories, 97; auth, Beware the Self Evident, Dharma World, 98. **CONTACT ADDRESS** 1053 Wilson Ave, Chambersburg, PA 17201.

BUCKLAND, ROSCOE LAWRENCE
PERSONAL Born 07/28/1918, Blackfoot, ID, m, 1941, 2 children **DISCIPLINE** ENGLISH, AMERICAN CIVILIZATION **EDUCATION** Univ Idaho, BA & MA, 48; State Univ Iowa, PhD(Am civilization), 55. **CAREER** Instr English, Wash State Col, 48-51; from asst prof to prof, Long Beach State Col, 55-70, chmn dept, 60-68; chmn dept, 70-78, Prof Lib Studies, Western Wash Univ, 70-, Asst, Univ Iowa, 52-55; lectr, Workers Educ Asn & Nat Arts Coun, Sydney, Australia, 68-69, Exchange Prof, Tokyo, Spring 85. **MEMBERSHIPS** Am Studies Asn; Brit Asn Am Studies; Am Cult Asn; Western Lit Asn; Am Folklore Asn. **RESEARCH** Australian and American frontier literature; American folklore; 19th century popular culture. **SELECTED PUBLICATIONS** Reviews in Western American Literature, 1967-1996; reviews in Studies in Short Fiction, 1969-1994; reviews in Pacific Northwest Quarterly, 1994; "Jack Hamlin: Bret Harte's Romantic Rogue," Western American Literature, Fall 73, reprinted in Short Story Criticism, Gale 1991; "Contrasting Views, Lynching in Two Western Stories," Wyoming Annals, Winter 93; Frederic Remington: The Writer, Twayne's U.S. Authors Series, 2000; papers read at Western American Literature annual conferences 1972-1999. **CONTACT ADDRESS** 1719 E Maple St, Apt 131, Bellingham, WA 98226.

BUCKLER, JOHN
DISCIPLINE GREEK HISTORY **EDUCATION** Univ Louisville, AB, 67; Am School of Classical Studies, Athens, 70-71; Harvard Univ, MA, 68, PhD, 73. **CAREER** Vis lectr, 73-75, asst prof, 75-80, assoc prof, 80-89, prof hist, Univ IL, 90- . **HONORS AND AWARDS** Am Coun Learned Soc, 83; Am Philos Soc, 83; Deutscher Akademischer Austauschdienst, 84; Alexander von Humboldt Found, 84-; Alexander von Humboldt fel, Univ Munich, 84-86. **MEMBERSHIPS** Am Ancient Hist. **RESEARCH** Greek history; fourth century BC; Greek topopography, Greek diplomatic and military history. **SELECTED PUBLICATIONS** Auth, The Theban Hegemony, 371-362 BC, 80; Philip II and the Sacred War, 89; coauth, A History of Western Societies, 6 eds, A History of World Socities, 5 eds, Boiotika: Vortrage vom 5, Int Bootien-Kolloquium, 89; William Abbott Oldfather, Encyclopedia of Classical Scholars, 90; Plutarch and Autopsy, Aufstieg und Niedergang der romischen Welt, 91; Il Federalismo in Grecia e in America, Federazione e federalismo nell'Europa antica, 94; co-ed, Of the Athenian Government, George Grote Reconsidered, 96; Philip's Designs on Greece, Transitions to Empire, 96; Helikon and Klio, La Montagne des Muses, 96; 56 articles in American Historical Association's Guide to Historical Literature, 3rd ed, 95; 28 articles, The Oxford Classical Dictionary, 3rd ed, 96; 6 articles, Encyclopedia of Greece and the Hellenic Tradition, 99. **CONTACT ADDRESS** Dept of Hist, Univ of Illinois, Urbana-Champaign, 810 S Wright St, 309 Gregory Hall, Urbana, IL 61801-3611. **EMAIL** jbuckler@uiuc.edu

BUCKLEY, THOMAS HUGH
PERSONAL Born 09/11/1932, Elkhart, IN, m, 5 children **DISCIPLINE** HISTORY **EDUCATION** Ind Univ, AB, 55, MA, 56, PhD, 61. **CAREER** From instr to prof hist, Univ SDak, 60-71; chmn dept, 71-81, chmn fac humanistic studies, 74-81, Prof Hist, Univ Tulsa, 71-, Assoc Dean of the Graduate Sch, 95-00; vis prof hist, Ind Univ, 69-71; ed, Research and Roster Guide, Soc Historians Am Foreign Rels, 80-83. **HONORS AND AWARDS** Denver Sch Int Rels res fel, 64-65; Stanford Univ fel, 68-69; Best First Bk by Hist Awd, Phi Alpha Theta, 71; Fulbright, Univ Western Australia, 86. **MEMBERSHIPS** Orgn Am Hist; AHA; Soc Hist Am Foreign Rels. **RESEARCH** American Foreign policy; American East Asian policies; national defense and national security since 1939. **SELECTED PUBLICATIONS** Auth, The United States and the Washington Conference, 1921-1922, Univ Tenn, 70; ed, Challenge Was My Master, Univ Tulsa, 79; contribr, Guide to US Foreign Relation Since 1700, Clio, 82; auth, Walter Helmerich, Independent Oilman, Okla, 82; coauth, American Foreign and National Security Policies, 1914-1945, Univ Tenn, 87; contribr, Treaty Ratification, St. Martin's Press, 91; Encyclopedia of Arms Control and Disarmament, Scribner's, 92; The Washington Conference; The Politics of Arms control, Cross, 94. **CONTACT ADDRESS** Dept of History, Univ of Tulsa, 600 S College, Tulsa, OK 74104.

BUCKLIN, STEVE
PERSONAL Born 05/17/1955, Huron, SD, m, 1985, 2 children **DISCIPLINE** HISTORY **EDUCATION** Univ SDak, BA, 83; MA, 86; Univ Iowa, PhD, 93. **CAREER** Vis asst prof, Cornell Col, 92-94; vis asst prof, Univ of Iowa, 94-95; asst prof, Univ of SDak, 96-. **HONORS AND AWARDS** Christol, Sterling and Weaver Awds, Univ SDak, 83-85; Elizabeth Bennett Ink Diss Fel, 89; Grant, Karl Mundt Found, 96; Grant, Nat Parks Serv, 98; Grnat, Allene R Chiesman Fund, 98; Grant, SDak Humanities Coun Teachers Inst. **MEMBERSHIPS** OAH; SHAFR. **RESEARCH** U.S. Diplomatic, Frontier, History. **SELECTED PUBLICATIONS** Auth, Problems in Human History: Twentieth Century Crisis. A Course Guide, Univ of Iowa, 91; auth, "Quincy Wright's Blue Print for a Durable Peace", Mid-America 76.3 (94); auth, The United State in World Affairs: 1900-1995. A Course Guide, Unit of Iowa, 96; auth, The United States in World Affairs: 1760-1900. A Course Guide, Univ of Iowa, 97; rev, of "Keeping America Sane", by Ian Dowbiggin, Annals of Iowa 57.1 (98); auth, "A Pioneer Remembered: Frank Bloodgood's Memoir of Life in Beadle County, Dakota Territory", SDak Hist 29.2 (99): auth, Realism and American Foreign Policy; Wilsonians and the Kennan-Morgenthan Thesis, Greenwood, 00; auth, Wilsonian Realism: Quincy Wright, Denna Fleming, and Frederick Schuman, Greenwood, (New Haven), 00; auth, From Cold War to Gulf War: The South Dakota National Guard, 1945-2000, Pine Hills Pr, (Freeman, SD), 00; auth, "Those in Reserve Also Serve: The South Dakota National Guard and the Korean War", SDak Hist, (forthcoming). **CONTACT ADDRESS** Dept Hist, Univ of So Dakota, Vermillion, 414 E Clark St, Vermillion, SD 57069-2307. **EMAIL** sbucklin@usd.edu

BUCKNER, PHILLIP ALFRED
PERSONAL Born 06/04/1942, Toronto, ON, Canada, m, 1969 **DISCIPLINE** CANADIAN HISTORY, BRITISH IMPERIAL HISTORY **EDUCATION** Univ Toronto, BA, 65; Univ London, PhD(hist), 69. **CAREER** Lectr, 68-69, asst prof, 69-79, Prof Hist, Univ NB, Fredericton, 80-. **MEMBERSHIPS** Can Hist Asn; Can Asn Univ Teachers. **RESEARCH** Nineteenth century British imperial history. **SELECTED PUBLICATIONS** Auth, The Transition to Responsible Government: British Policy in North America 1825-1850, 85; ed, Eastern and Western Perspectives, 81; ed, The Acadiensis Reader: Volumes One and Two, 85; ed, Teaching Maritime studies, 86; ed, The Atlantic Region to Confederation: A History, 94. **CONTACT ADDRESS** Dept Hist, Univ of New Brunswick, Fredericton, PO Box 4400, Fredericton, NB, Canada E3B 5A3. **EMAIL** pbuckner@unb.ca

BUEL, RICHARD (VAN WYCK)
PERSONAL Born 07/22/1933, Morristown, NJ, m, 1992, 1 child **DISCIPLINE** HISTORY **EDUCATION** Amherst Coll, Amherst, MA, 55, BA: Harvard Univ, Cambridge, MA, 57, Phd 62. **CAREER** Asst Prof, Wesleyan Univ, 62-69; Asoc Prof, Wesleyan Univ, 69-75; Full Prof Wesleyan Univ, 75. **HONORS AND AWARDS** PBK; ACLS Fac Fellowships 67-68, 74-75, NEH fellowships, 71-72, 85, Guggenheim Fellowship, 86; Charles Warren Fellowship, 67-68; John Carter Brown Library Fellowship, 86. **MEMBERSHIPS** Amer Hist Assoc; Organization of Amer Hist; Amer Hist and Culture; Soc for Hist of the Early Amer Rep; CT Academy of Arts and Sci; Soc for the Study at CT Hist; New England Asn. **RESEARCH** Revolutionary Amer 1730-1830. **SELECTED PUBLICATIONS** Securing the Revolution, 72; Dear Liberty, 80; The Way of Duty, 84; In Irons, 98. **CONTACT ADDRESS** Dept of Hist, Wesleyan Univ, Middletown, CT 06457. **EMAIL** Rbucl@Wesleyan.edu

BUENKER, JOHN D.
PERSONAL Born 08/11/1937, Dubuque, IA, m, 1962, 5 children **DISCIPLINE** UNITED STATES HISTORY **EDUCATION** Loras Col, BA, 59; Georgetown Univ, MA, 62, PhD, 64. **CAREER** Instr hist, Prince George's Community Col, 62-65; asst prof, Eastern Ill Univ, 65-70; assoc prof, 70-73, dir ethnic studies, Ctr Multicult Studies, 77-81, 88-91, prof hist, Univ of Wis Parkside, 73-, Vis Prof, Holy Redeemer Col, 73-85; Vis Prof, Univ Wis-Madison, 86-87. **HONORS AND AWARDS** William Adee Whitehead Awd, NJ Hist Soc, 70; Harry E Pratt Awd, Ill State Hist Soc, 71; John Simon Guggenheim Found fel, 75-76; Newberry Libr fel, 79; Univ Wis-Parkside Awd for Excellence in Schol Activity, 89; Wis CASE Prof of the Year, 90-91; SEastern Wis Educ Hall of Fame, 91; Fel, Univ Wis System Ctr for Res in the Humanities, 91-92. **MEMBERSHIPS** Orgn Am Hist; Immigration Hist Soc; Urban Hist Asn; Soc Hist of the Gilded Age and Progressive Era; Nat Coun for Hist Educ; Kappa Delta Pi; Phi Kappa Delta; Am Hist Asn; Soc for Ger-Am Studies. **RESEARCH** Immigration, urban; the progressive era. **SELECTED PUBLICATIONS** Auth, The Urban Political Machine and the Seventeenth Amendment, J Am Hist, 69; The Progressive Era: Search for a Synthesis, Mid-Am, 69; The Politics of Resistance, New England Quart, 6/74; Urban Liberalism and Progressive Reform, Norton, 77; coauth, Progressivism, Schenkman, 77; co-ed, Immigration and Ethnicity: Guide to the Information Sources, 77, Progressive Reform: Guide to the Information Sources, 80 & Urban History: Guide to the Information Sources, 81, Gale Res Co; auth, The Income Tax and the Progressive Era, Garland, 85; co-ed, Historical Dictionary of the Progressive Era, Greenwood, 88; Multiculturism in the U.S., Greenwood, 92; Those United States, Harcourt Brace, 98; auth, Wisconsin The Progressive Era, Univ Wis Press, 98; Invention City, Racine Heritage Museum, 98. **CONTACT ADDRESS** Dept of Hist, Univ of Wisconsin, Parkside, Box 2000, Kenosha, WI 53141-2000. **EMAIL** buenker@execpc.com

BUETTINGER, CRAIG
PERSONAL Born 01/20/1951, Cincinnati, OH **DISCIPLINE** HISTORY **EDUCATION** John Hopkins Univ, BA, 73; Northwestern Univ, MA, 78; PhD, 82. **CAREER** Jacksonville Univ. **RESEARCH** 19th Century American social history. **SELECTED PUBLICATIONS** Auth, "Antivivisection and the Charge of Zoophil-Psychosis in the Early Twentieth Century," Hist 55 (93): 277-88; auth, "Sarah Cleghom, Antivivisection, and Victorian Sensitivity about Pain and Cruelty," Ver Hist 62 (94): 88-100; auth, "Women and Antivivisection in Late Nineteenth-Century America," J Soc Hist 30 (97): 857-872; auth, "Masters on Trial: The Enforcement of Laws against Self-Hire by Slaves in Jacksonville and Palatka, Florida," Civil War Hist 46 (00): 91-106. **CONTACT ADDRESS** Dept History, Jacksonville Univ, 2800 University Blvd N, Jacksonville, FL 32211. **EMAIL** cbuetti@ju.edu

BUETTNER, BRIGITTE
DISCIPLINE ART HISTORY **EDUCATION** Maitrise Paris-X Nanterre, PhD. **CAREER** Dir, JYA Prog, Hamburg, Ger, 97-98; assoc prof, Smith Col. **RESEARCH** Late medieval art, particularly secular art produced within the context of court cult. **SELECTED PUBLICATIONS** Auth, Boccaccio's, Des cleres et nobles femmes: Systems of Signification in an Illuminated Manuscript, Col Art Asn Monograph Ser, Univ WA Press, 96. **CONTACT ADDRESS** Dept of Art, Smith Col, 45 Round Hill Rd, Bell Hall, Northampton, MA 01063. **EMAIL** bbuettne@smith.edu

BUHLE, MARI JO
PERSONAL Born 12/07/1943, Waukegan, IL, m, 1963 **DISCIPLINE** HISTORY, AMERICAN STUDIES **EDUCATION** Univ Ill, BA, 66; Univ Conn, MA, 68; Univ Wisc-Madison, PhD, 74. **CAREER** Prof, Brown Univ, 72-. **HONORS AND AWARDS** John D. and Catherine T. MacArthur Fel. **MEMBERSHIPS** Org of Am Hist, Am Studies Asn, Cherion. **RESEARCH** US history, intellectual; gender and women. **SELECTED PUBLICATIONS** Coed with Paul Buhle, The Concise History of Women Suffrage, Urbana: Univ Ill Press (78); auth, Women and American Socialism, 1870-1920, Urbana: Univ Ill Press (81); auth, Women and the American Left; A Guide to Sources, Boston: G. K. Hall (83); coed with Paul Buhle and Dan Georgakas, Encyclopedia of the American Left, NY: Garland (90), 2nd ed, Oxford Univ Press (98); coauth with John Faragher, Daniel Czitrom, and Susan Armitage, Out of Many: A History of the American People, Upper Saddle River, NJ: Prentice Hall (94, 97, 2000, brief ed 95, 98, 2000); coed with Paul Buhle and Harvey Kaye, The American Radical, NY: Routledge (94); auth, Feminism and Its Discontents: A Struggle with Psychoanalysis, Cambridge: Harvard Univ Press (98).(**CONTACT ADDRESS** Dept Am Culture, Brown Univ, PO Box 1892, Providence, RI 02912-9100. **EMAIL** Mari_Buhle@Brown.edu

BUHNEMANN, GUDRUN
PERSONAL Born Goslar **DISCIPLINE** INDIAN AND BUDDHIST STUDIES, SANSKRIT STUDIES **EDUCATION** Vienna Univ, PhD, 80. **CAREER** Prof, Univ Wis Madison. **HONORS AND AWARDS** Nat Endow for the Humanities; Amer Coun of Learned Soc; Japan Soc for the Promotion of Sci. **MEMBERSHIPS** Amer Acad of Relig; Amer Orient Soc; Amer Coun of Southern Asian Art. **RESEARCH** Classical Indian studies; Religions of India. **SELECTED PUBLICATIONS** Auth, Sadhanasataka and Sadhanasatapancasika. Two Buddhist Sadhana Collections in Sanskrit Manuscript, Wien, Univ Wien, 94; auth, Nispannayogavali. Two Sanskrit Manuscripts from Nepal, Tokyo, The Ctr for East Asian Cultural Studies, 91; auth, The Hindu Deities Illustrated according to the Pratisthalaksanasarasamuccaya, Tokyo, The Ctr for East Asian Cultural Studies, 90; auth, Forms of Ganesa. A Study based on the Vidyarnavatantra, Wichtrach, Inst fur Indologie, 89; auth, The Worship of Mahaganapati according to the Nityotsava, Wichtrach, Inst fur Indologie, 88; auth, Puja. A Study in Smarta Ritual, Vienna, Inst fur Indologie, Univ Wien, 88; auth, The Iconography of Hindu Tantric Deities, 2 vols, Egbert Forsten, 00. **CONTACT ADDRESS** Dept of Lang and Cult of Asia, Univ of Wisconsin, Madison, 11220 Lindon Dr., Madison, WI 53706. **EMAIL** gbuhnema@facstaff.wisc.edu

BUISSERET, DAVID
PERSONAL Born 12/18/1934, Totland Bay, United Kingdom, m, 1961, 5 children **DISCIPLINE** HISTORY **EDUCATION** Cambridge Univ, BA, 58; PhD, 61. **CAREER** Fel, Corpus Christ Col at Cambridge, 61-64; prof, Southern Univ of the West Indies, 64-80; Newberry Libr, 80-95; prof, Univ Tex at Arlington, 95-. **HONORS AND AWARDS** NEH Fel; Fels at Newberry, Huntington, & Wolfenbuttel. **MEMBERSHIPS** Royal Hist Soc, Hist Asn. **RESEARCH** Sixteenth- and Seventeenth-Century France, Sixteenth- through Eighteenth-Century Caribbean, the History of Cartography. **SELECTED PUBLICATIONS** Auth, Historic Jamaica from the Air, 90; ed, Monarchs, Ministers, and Maps, 92; ed, Rural Images, 96; ed, Envisioning the City, 98. **CONTACT ADDRESS** Dept Hist, Univ of Texas, Arlington, PO Box 19529, Arlington, TX 76019.

BUKEY, EVAN B.
PERSONAL Born 04/24/1940, Cincinnati, OH, m, 1963, 2 children **DISCIPLINE** HISTORY **EDUCATION** Ohio Wesleyan, BA, 62; Ohio State Univ, MA, 64; PhD, 69. **CAREER** From asst prof to prof, Univ of Ark, 69-. **HONORS AND AWARDS** Vis Fel, Wolfsou Col, Univ of Cambridge, 93-94; Master Teacher Awd, Fulbright Col, 97. **MEMBERSHIPS** Ger Studies Asn, Confr Group for Central European Hist, The Hist Soc, Am Hist Asn. **RESEARCH** Modern Austria, National Socialism, World War II. **SELECTED PUBLICATIONS** Auth, Hitler's Hometown: Linz, Austria, 1908-1945, Ind Univ Press (Bloomington, IN), 86; auth, "Nazi Rule in Austria: A Review Essay," Austrian Hist Yearbook XXII (92): 202-234; auth, Patenstadt des Fuhrers. Eine Politik-und Sozialgeschichte von Linz 1908-1945, Campus Verlag, 93; auth, "Between Stalingrad and the Night of the Generals: Popular Opinion in the Danubian and Alpine Regions," in Austria 1938-1988: Anschluss and Fifty Years, ed. William Wright (Ariadne Press, 95), 167-196; auth, "Great Men and the Twentieth Century," The Hist J 39.1 (96): 277-283; auth, "The Austrians and the 'Ostmark' 1938-1945," in Ungleiche Partner? Osterreich and Deutschland in ihrer gegenseitigen Wahrnehmung. Historische Analysen and Vergleiche aus den 19. and 20. Jahrhundert, eds. Michael Gehler and Rainer Schmidt (Innsbruck, 96), 513-31; auth, "Die Heimatfront: Von der 'Ostmark' zu den Alpen-und Donaugauen 1939/40-1945," in Osterrich im 20. Jahrhundert: Fragen-Schwerpunkte-Antworten, ed Rolf Steiniger (Bohlau, 97), 465-498; auth, Hitler's Austria: Popular Sentiment in the Nazi Era 1938-1945, Univ of NC Press (Chapel Hill, NC), 00. **CONTACT ADDRESS** Dept Hist, Univ of Arkansas, Fayetteville, 416 Old Main, Fayetteville, AR 72701-1201. **EMAIL** ebukey@comp.uark.edu

BULL, ROBERT JEHU
PERSONAL Born 10/21/1920, Harrington, DE, m, 1959 **DISCIPLINE** CHURCH HISTORY, ARCHAEOLOGY **EDUCATION** Randolph-Macon Col, BA, 43; Duke Univ, BD, 46; Yale Univ, MA, 51, PhD, 56. **CAREER** Instr philos, Colgate Univ, 54-55; from instr to assoc prof, 55-70, field supvr, Drew Univ-McCormick Archaeol Exped, Jordan, 56-57, 60-62, 64, Prof Church Hist, Drew Univ, 70-, Dir, Inst Archaeol Res, 68-, Mem, Hazen Theol Discussion Group; Am Asn Theol Sch fel, Univ Utrecht, 59-60; Am Sch Orient Res, Jordan, 66-67; field supvr, Wooster Exped, Pella, 66; dir, Tell er Ras Exped, 66, 68; vpres, Comm Arch & Hist, United Methodist Church, 68; dir, Am Sch Orient Res, Jerusalem, 70-71, Joint Exped Khirbet Shemac, 70 & Joint Exped Caesarea, 71; res prof, William Foxwell Albright Inst Archaeol Res, 74. **MEMBERSHIPS** Am Soc Church Hist; Am Sch Orient Res; Albright Inst Archaeol Res; Nat Lectr Archaeol Inst Am. **RESEARCH** Patristics; Palestinian archaeology; early American Methodist history. **SELECTED PUBLICATIONS** Auth, The Making of Our Tradition, Westminster, 67; coauth, The sixth campaign at Balatah, Bull Am Sch Orient Res, 4/68; The excavation of Tell er Ras, Bull Am Sch Orient Res, 4/68; The excavation of Tell er Ras on Mt Gerigim, Bibl Archaeologist, 5/68; Towards a Corpus Inscriptonum Latinarum Britannecarum in Palestina, Blestine Exploration Quart, 70; Tell er Ras, The Pottery, 71 & Tell er Ras, The Coins, 71, Smithsonian; co-ed, Eaesarea, The Preliminary Reports, Vol I, Harvard Univ, 74; auth, The Gold Coin Hoard at Caesarea + Ancient Numismatic Studies/, Bibl Archaeol, Vol 56, 1993; Caesarea and King Herod Magnificent City Plan/, Am J Archaeol, Vol 100, 1996. **CONTACT ADDRESS** Dept of Hist, Drew Univ, Madison, NJ 07940.

BULLARD, ALICE
PERSONAL Born 03/05/1963, South Bend, IL, s **DISCIPLINE** HISTORY **EDUCATION** Johns Hopkins Univ, BA, 85; Univ Calif, MA, 89; PhD, 94. **CAREER** Instructor to Visiting Lecturer, Univ Calif, 88-94; Asst Prof, Ga Inst of Technol, 94-. **HONORS AND AWARDS** Camargo Foundation Residential Fel, 99; Am Philos Soc Res Grant, 99; NEH Summer Sem Fel, 98; Res Fel, Humanities Ctr Australian Nat Univ, 97. **MEMBERSHIPS** Am Hist Asn. **RESEARCH** 19th and 20th Century France; Colonial and Postcolonial; Feminism; Human rights; Cross cultural Psychiatry. **SELECTED PUBLICATIONS** Auth, Exile to Paradise: savagery and Civilization in Paris and the south Pacific, 1790-1900, Stanford Univ Press, forthcoming; auth, "Le theatre des plages en Nouvelle-Caledonie: La Presentation du corps et l'art kanak feminist," Journal de la societe des oceanistes, (99): 133-143; auth, "Becoming Savage? The first Step Toward Civilization and The Practices of Intransigence," History and anthropology, (98): 319-374; auth, "the French Idea of subjectivity and the Kanak of New Caledonia: recuperating the Category of Affect," History and anthropology, (98): 375-405; auth, "Self-Representation in the Arms of Defeat: Fatal Nostalgia and the Surviving comrades," Cultural anthropology, (97): 179-211; auth, "Kant in the third Republic: Charles Renouvier and the Constructed Self," in Selected Proceedings of the Western Society for French History, Univ N C Press, 97; auth, "Paris 1871/New Caledonia 1878: Human rights and the Managerial State," in Human rights and Revolutions, forthcoming. **CONTACT ADDRESS** Dept History, Georgia Inst of Tech, 225 N Ave Northwest, Atlanta, GA 30332-0001.

BULLARD, MELISSA MERIAM
PERSONAL Born 03/12/1946, Berkeley, CA, m, 1969, 1 child **DISCIPLINE** HISTORY **EDUCATION** Duke Univ, AB, 67; Cornell Univ, MA, 69, PhD(hist), 77. **CAREER** Asst Prof Hist, Univ NC, Chapel Hill, 77-81; assoc, 81-89; prof, 89-; Wm. Smith Wells, prof of hist, 94-96. **HONORS AND AWARDS** Best unpubl manuscript in Ital hist, Soc Ital Hist Studies, 77. **MEMBERSHIPS** AHA; Renaissance Soc Am; Soc Ital Hist Studies; Res Italian Renaissance and Mediterranean history of the early modern period. **SELECTED PUBLICATIONS** Auth, Filippo Strozzi and the Medici: Favor and Finance in Sixteenth-Century Florence and Rome, Cambridge Univ Press, 80; auth, Lorenzo de' Medici: Image and Anxiety, Politics and Finance, Istituto Nazionale di Studi sul Rinascimento and Leo S. Olschki, Florence, 94; auth, art, Il credito in un nome, Storia e Dossier, 95; auth, art, House of Medici, The Oxford Reformation Encyclopedi, New York: Oxford Univ Press, 96; auth, art, Lorenzo and Patterns of Diplomatic Discourse in the Late Fifteenth Century, Lorenzo the Magnificent. Culture and Politics, Warburg Inst, Univ of London: London, 96; auth, art, Adumbrations of Power and the Politics of Appearances in Medicean Florence, Renaissance Studies, 98; co-auth, art, Where and When did Lorenzo de' Medici acquire the 'sigillo neroniano?, Journal of the Warburg and Courtauld Institutes, 99; auth, art, Where Self and Culture Intersect: Narrating a Fitting End to a Condottiere's Life, Self and Culture in the Renaissance, UC Press, 00; auth, art, Renaissance Spirituality and the Ethical Dimensions of Church Reform in the Age of Savonarola: The Dilemma of Cardinal Marco Barbo, The World of Savonarola: Italian Elites in Crisis, 1494-1519, Ashcroft and Soc for Renaissance Studies: London, 00. **CONTACT ADDRESS** Dept of Hist, Univ of No Carolina, Chapel Hill, Hamilton Hall, CB # 3195, Chapel Hill, NC 27599. **EMAIL** mbullard@email.unc.edu

BULLARD, REUBEN
PERSONAL Born 03/08/1928, Wheeling, WV, m, 1956, 4 children **DISCIPLINE** ARCHAEOLOGICAL GEOLOGY **EDUCATION** Cincinnati Bible Col & Sem, ThB, 56; MA, 57; BD, 58; Univ Cincinnati, BA, 61; MS, 64; PhD, 69. **CAREER** Instru to prof, chair, Cincinnati Bible Col & Sem; asst prof, lectr, Univ of Cincinnati. **HONORS AND AWARDS** Fenneman Fel, Univ of Cincinnati, 66; Best Teacher, CC of CU, 91. **MEMBERSHIPS** Geol Soc of Am; Nat Assoc of Geol Teachers; Archeol Inst of Am; Near East Archeol Soc; Am Schools of Orient Res; Soc of Bibl Lit; Soc of Econ Palaeontologists & Mineralogists; Evangel theol Soc. **RESEARCH** Geology, Archaeology, Environment. **SELECTED PUBLICATIONS** Auth, "Archaeological Geology", Sedimentary Environments and Litholgic Materials at Two Archaeological Site, Yale Pr, 85; auth, Revised International Standard Bible Encyclopedia, Berdmans Pub, 88; auth, Precious Stones, Berdmans Pub, 88; auth, Encyclopedia of Near Eastern Archaeology, Oxford Pr, 96; auth, Magnetic Archaeolmetry, Oxford Pr, 96. **CONTACT ADDRESS** Dept Gen Educ, Cincinnati Bible Col and Sem, 2700 glenway Ave, Cincinnati, OH 45204-1738. **EMAIL** reuben.bullard@cincybible.edu

BULLIET, RICHARD
PERSONAL Born 10/30/1940, Rockford, IL, m, 1962, 1 child **DISCIPLINE** MIDDLE EASTERN HISTORY **EDUCATION** Harvard Univ, BA, 62, MA, 64, PhD, 67. **CAREER** Prof. **RESEARCH** The social and institutional history of Islamic countries; history of technology history of animals. **SELECTED PUBLICATIONS** Auth, The Patricians of Nishapur: a Study in Medieval Islamic Hist, 72; The Tomb of the Twelfth Imam, 72; The Camel and the Wheel, 75; auth, Conversion to Islam on the Medieval Period, 79; The Gulf Scenario, 84; The Sufi Fiddle, 91; Islam: the View from the Edge, 94; coauth, The Earth and Its Peoples, 97; ed, Columbia History of the Twentieth Century, 98. **CONTACT ADDRESS** Dept of Hist, Columbia Col, New York, 2960 Broadway, New York, NY 10027-6902. **EMAIL** rwb3@columbia.edu

BULLION, JOHN LEWIS
PERSONAL Born 10/23/1944, Washington, DC, m, 1976, 2 children **DISCIPLINE** HISTORY **EDUCATION** Stanford Univ, BA, 66; Univ of Tex at Austin, MA, 68, PhD, 77. **CAREER** Instr of Hist, Southwest Tex State Univ, 74-78; Chemn, 91-96, Asst Prof to Prof, Univ of MO-Columbia, 78-. **HONORS AND AWARDS** Phi Beta Kappa, 66; Colonial Dames Commemorative Awd for Best Masters Thesis or Doctoral Dissertation in The Southeastern United States, 68; Univ of Mo Curators' Publication Awd, 83; Am Military Inst Distinguished Article Awd, 88; Burlington Northern Foundation Faculty Achievement Awd for Significant and Meritorious Tchg in the Univ of Mo System, 90. **MEMBERSHIPS** Am Hist Asn; Am Soc of Eighteenth-Century Studies; North Am Coun of British Studies. **RESEARCH** British politics and the American Revolution; race relations in early Twentieth-Century Mo. **SELECTED PUBLICATIONS** Auth, A Great and Necessary Measure: George Grenville and the Genesis of the Stamp Act, 82; Securing the Peace: Lord Bute, the plan for the army, and the origins of the American Revolution, Lord Bute: Essays in Reinterpretation, 88; Security and Economy: The Bute Administration's Plans for the American Army and Revenue, William and Mary Quart, 88; British Ministers and American Resistance tot he Stamp Act, October-December, 1765, William and Mary Quart, 92; George III on Empire 1783, William and Mary Quart, 94; George, be a King! The Relationship between Princess Augusta and George III, Hanoverian Britain and Empire, 98. **CONTACT ADDRESS** Dept of Hist, Univ of Missouri, Columbia, Read Hall Rm 101, Columbia, MO 65211. **EMAIL** jlbullio@gte.net

BULLIVANT, KEITH
PERSONAL Born 02/11/1941, Derby, England, m, 1965, 2 children **DISCIPLINE** GERMAN STUDIES **EDUCATION** Birmingham Univ, BA, 63; PhD, 68. **CAREER** Asst prof, Birmingham Univ, 65-70; prof, Univ of Warwick, 70-89; prof, chair, Univ of Fla, 89-. **HONORS AND AWARDS** Brit Coun, 80; Dist Vis Prof, NMex State Univ, 89; Gastprofessor, Univ of Paderborn, 91; Ger-Am Acad Coun, 99-01 **MEMBERSHIPS** MLA, SAMLA, Ger Studies Assoc, Am Assoc of Teachers of Ger. **RESEARCH** Modern German Studies. **SELECTED PUBLICATIONS** Coauth, Literature in Upheaval, Manchester UP, 74; coauth, Industrie und deutsche Literature 1830-1914, Deutscher Taschenbuch Verlag, 76; ed, Culture and Society in the Weimar Republic, 77; auth, Between Chaos and Order: The work of Gerd Gaiser, Manchester UP, 80; auth, Realism Today, Heinz, 87; auth, The Future of German Literature, Berg Publ, 94; coed, Dieter Wellershoff, Werke 1-6, Kiepenheur & Witsch, 96-97; ed, Beyond 1989: Re-reading German Literature Since 1945, Bergham Books, 97; coed, Germany and Eastern Europe, Rodopi, 99; coed, Literarisches Krisenbewusstsein, Iudicium, 01. **CONTACT ADDRESS** Univ of Florida, 6237 NW 19th Pl, Gainesville, FL 32605. **EMAIL** kbulli@germslav.ufl.edu

BULLOCK, STEVEN C.
DISCIPLINE HISTORY **EDUCATION** Houghton Coll, BA, 78; State Univ NYork-Binghamton, MA, 80; Brown Univ, AM,

82, PhD, 86. **CAREER** ASSOC PROF, HIST, WORCESTER POLYTECH INST **MEMBERSHIPS** Am Antiquarian Soc **SELECTED PUBLICATIONS** Auth, "According to Their Rank: Masonry and the Revolution, 1775-1792", in Heredom: The Transaction of the Scottish Rite Society, IV, 95; auth, Revolutionary Brotherhood: Freemasonry and the Transformation of the American Social Order, 1730-1840, IEAHC and Univ NC Press, 96; auth, "Review Essay - Initiating the Enlightenment?: Recent Works on European Freemasonry," Eighteenth-Century Life, 20, 96. **CONTACT ADDRESS** 2 Eagle Terr, Worcester, MA 01602. **EMAIL** sbullock@wpi.edu

BULLOUGH, ROBERT V., JR.
PERSONAL Born 02/12/1949, Salt Lake City, UT, m, 1976, 4 children **DISCIPLINE** EDUCATIONAL STUDIES; HISTORY **EDUCATION** Univ of Utah, BS, 71, MEd, 73; Ohio State Univ, PhD, 76. **CAREER** Prof, Educ Stud, Univ of Utah, 76-99; prof emeritus, Educational Studies, Univ Utah, 99-; prof, teacher educ, Brigham Young Univ. **HONORS AND AWARDS** Phi Beta Kappa; Phi Kappa Phi, 71; AACTE Outstanding Writing Awd, 97. **MEMBERSHIPS** Am Educ Res Asn; Prof of Curriculum; Phi Delta Kappa. **RESEARCH** Teacher development; curriculum studies; lives of children. **SELECTED PUBLICATIONS** Auth, Trends in teacher education reform in America: A personal perspective, Teacher Educators' Annual Handbook, Queensland Univ of Tech, 87-97, 93; co-auth, Becoming a Student of Teaching: Methodologies for Exploring Self and School Context, Garland Publishing Inc, 95; auth, Professorial dreams and mentoring: A personal view, Teachers and mentors: Profiles of distinguished 20th century professors of education, Garland Publishing Inc, 257-267, 96; auth, Becoming a teacher: Self and the social location of teacher education, Int Handbook of Tchrs and Tchng, Kluwer Acad Publishers, 87-148; auth, Practicing theory and theorizing practice in teacher education, Purposes, passion, & pedagogy in teacher education, The Falmer Press, 13-21, 97; co-auth, First year teacher--after eight years: An inquiry into teacher development, Tchrs Col Press, 97; auth, Musing on life writing: Biography and case studies in teacher education, Writing educational biography: Adventures in qualitative research, Garland Publishing, 19-32, 98; auth, Children's Lives - On the Other Side of Teacher's Desk, Teachers Col Pr, 00. **CONTACT ADDRESS** 413 4th Ave, Salt Lake City, UT 84103. **EMAIL** bob_bullough@byu.edu

BULLOUGH, WILLIAM ALFRED
PERSONAL Born 01/03/1933, CA **DISCIPLINE** URBAN HISTORY **EDUCATION** Univ Calif, Santa Barbara, BA, 55, MA, 67, PhD(hist), 70. **CAREER** Teacher, Calif Pub Schs, 57-65; asst prof, 70-74, assoc prof, 74-79, Prof Hist, Calif State Univ, Hayward, 79-. **MEMBERSHIPS** Orgn Am Historians; AHA; Western Hist Asn. **RESEARCH** Urban institutional history; western municipal politics; California history. **SELECTED PUBLICATIONS** Auth, It is better to be a country boy: The lure of the country in urban education in the Gilded Age, Historian, 2/73; The steam beer handicap: Chris Buckley and the San Francisco municipal election of 1896, Calif Hist Quart, fall 75; Hannibal versus the blind boss: The Junta, Chris Buckley and democratic reform politics in San Francisco, Pac Hist Rev, 5/77; The Blind Boss and His City: Christopher Augustine Buckley and Nineteenth Century San Francisco, Univ Calif Press, 79. **CONTACT ADDRESS** Dept of Hist, California State Univ, Hayward, Hayward, CA 94542.

BUNCH, RICHARD ALAN
PERSONAL Born 06/01/1945, Honolulu, HI, m, 1990, 2 children **DISCIPLINE** HISTORY **EDUCATION** Napa Col, AA, 65; Stanford Univ, BA, 67; Univ Ariz, MA, 69; Vanderbilt Univ, MDiv, 70; DD, 71; postgrad, 75; Temple Univ, postgrad, 76; Univ Memphis, JD, 80; Sonoma State Univ, teaching cred, 88. **CAREER** Teaching asst, Vanderbilt Univ, 73-74; instr, Belmont Univ, 73-74; law clerk, Shelby County Tenn, 79-81; atty, Horne & Peppel Memphis, 81-83; law clerk, Tenn Ct appeals, 83; instr, Chapman Univ, 86-87; instr, Sonoma State Univ, 86-87, 89-90; lecturer, Univ Calif, 90-95; adj prof, Napa Valley Col, 85-. **HONORS AND AWARDS** Ina Coobrith Nat Poetry Day Contest, 89; Jessamyn West Creative writing prize, 90; Pushcart Prize nominations,88, 96, 97. **MEMBERSHIPS** Ina Coolbrith Circle, Acad of Am Poets. **RESEARCH** Relations between literature and the arts, Holocaust, Comparative religion. **SELECTED PUBLICATIONS** Auth, "Evolution and Contemporary Religious Sensibility," Dissertation Abstract, 71; auth, South By Southwest (poetry), Cedar Bay Press: Beaverton, Ore, 97; auth, Sacred Space (poetry), Dry Bones Press: San Francisco, 98; auth, Rivers of the Sea (poetry), Phoenix Press: Berkeley, 98. **CONTACT ADDRESS** Dept Soc Sci, Napa Valley Col, 2277 Napa Vallejo Hwy, Napa, CA 94558-6236. **EMAIL** rbgunch@ucdavis.edu

BUNI, ANDREW
PERSONAL Born 06/12/1931, Manchester, NH, m, 1960, 4 children **DISCIPLINE** AMERICAN NEGRO HISTORY **EDUCATION** Univ NH, BA, 58, MA, 59; Univ Va, PhD(hist), 65. **CAREER** From asst prof to assoc prof hist, Mary Washington Col, Univ Va, 64-68; Assoc Prof Hist, Boston Col, 68- **MEMBERSHIPS** AHA; Soc Am Hist; Southern Hist Asn; Asn Study Negro Life & Hist. **RESEARCH** Negro in American history; Negro press in the 20th century. **SELECTED PUBLICATIONS** Auth, The Negro in Virginia Politics, 1902-1965, Univ Va, 67; Robert L Vann and the Pittsburgh Courier, Univ Pittsburgh, 74. **CONTACT ADDRESS** Dept Hist, Boston Col, Chestnut Hill, Chestnut Hill, MA 02167.

BUNTROCK, DANA
DISCIPLINE ARCHITECTURE **EDUCATION** Tulane Univ, B Arch, 81; The Univ MI, M Arch, High Distinction, May, 88, MUP, Dec, 88. **CAREER** Visit Asst Prof, Carnegie Mellon Univ, 89-91; Visit Academic, Univ of Adelaide S. Australia, 94; Asst Prof, Univ Ill at Chicago, 94-00; Research Assoc, Univ of Tokyo, 98; Asst Prof, Univ of California, Berkeley, 00-. **HONORS AND AWARDS** Henry Adams Certificate, Marion Sarah Parker Mem Prize. **MEMBERSHIPS** Assn of Collegiate Schs of Architecture; Assn for Asian Studies, Patron; Ctr for the Study of the Practice of Architecture, sustaining member. **SELECTED PUBLICATIONS** coauth, The Use of Tradition in Japanese Architecture, Identity, Tradition, and Built Form: the Role of Culture in Planning and Development, Dec 96; Collaborative Production: Building Opportunities in Japan, Journal of Architectural Education, May 97; Japanese Building Production: Four Models of Design Development and Delivery, Oct 98. **CONTACT ADDRESS** 1242 North Lake Shore Dr. #17N, Chicago, IL 60610. **EMAIL** danab@uclink.berkeley.edu

BURCKEL, NICHOLAS C.
PERSONAL Born 08/15/1943, Evansville, IN, m, 1969 **DISCIPLINE** UNITED STATES HISTORY **EDUCATION** Georgetown Univ, BA, 65; Univ Wis-Madison, MA, 67, PhD(hist), 71. **CAREER** Asst archivist, Univ Wis-Madison, 71-72; Dir, Arch & Area Res Ctr, Univ Wis-Parkside, 72-, Exec Asst to Chancellor, 75-00; Dean of Libraries and Prof of hist, Marquette Univ, 00. **HONORS AND AWARDS** Cert Commendation, Am Asn State & Local Hist, 78. **MEMBERSHIPS** AHA; Orgn Am Historians; Soc Am Archivists; Midwest Arch Conf; Am Asn State & Local Hist. **RESEARCH** Progressivism, Wisconsin history; archival administration. **SELECTED PUBLICATIONS** Auth, From Beckham to McCreary: The progressive record of Kentucky governors, Regist Ky Hist Soc, 10/78; co-ed, Govenor Albert B White and the beginning of progressive reform, 1901-05, WVa Hist, fall 78; auth, Business archives in a university setting: Status and prospect, Col & Res Libr, 5/80; co-ed, Progressive Reform, Gale, 80; Kenosha Retrospective: A Biographical Approach, Kenosha County, 81; auth, A O Stanley and progressive reform, 1902-1919, Regist Ky Hist Soc, spring 81; Govenor Austin Lane Crothers and progressive reform in Maryland, 1908-1912, Md Hist Mag, summer 81; Publicizing progressivism: William M O Dawson, WVa Hist, spring-summer 81. **CONTACT ADDRESS** Marquette Univ, PO Box 1881, Milwaukee, WI 53201-1881.

BURDICK, DAKIN
PERSONAL Born 12/10/1962, New York, NY, m, 1990, 2 children **DISCIPLINE** US MILITARY HISTORY, SPORTS HISTORY **EDUCATION** Ind Univ, BA, 85; MA, 87; PhD, 99. **CAREER** Adj Prof and Instr, Ind Univ, 92-. **MEMBERSHIPS** OAH, NASSH **RESEARCH** Nineteenth Century US, Sports history, Canadian history, east Asian history. **SELECTED PUBLICATIONS** Auth, British Boxing and Japanese Judo: Transnational Influences on American Unarmed Combat, 1845-1945, forthcoming; auth, "People & Events in T'aekwondon's Formative Years," Journal of Asian Martial Arts, (97): 30-49. **CONTACT ADDRESS** Dept Kinesiology, Indiana Univ, Bloomington, HPER 032, Bloomington, IN 47405.

BURFORD, JIM
PERSONAL Born 07/25/1945, Vancouver, WA, m, 1972, 2 children **DISCIPLINE** STUDIO ARTS **EDUCATION** Univ Or, BS, 71; Carnegie Mellon Univ, MFA, 78. **CAREER** Instr, Duquesne Univ, 77-78; instr, Carnegie Mellon Univ, 77-78; adjunct lectr, Md Col, 99-; assoc prof, Mt Vernon Col, 78-99; dir, Gatehouse Gallery, Mount Vernon Col, 79-98; adjunct instr, Marymount Univ, 99-. **HONORS AND AWARDS** Who's Who, 92-93; guest lectr, Hirshhorn Museum, 89, 90, 92; Cert of Merit, Mount Vernon Col, 95-96; Faculty Develop Grant, 79, 97; Arts and Humanities Fund and Workshop grants, Mount Vernon Col, 81, 83, 89-90. **MEMBERSHIPS** Col Art Asn. **RESEARCH** Exhibitions of painting & drawings. **CONTACT ADDRESS** 3222 First Rd N, Arlington, VA 22201. **EMAIL** JEBURFORD@aol.com

BURG, B. R.
PERSONAL Born 08/02/1938, Denver, CO, m, 1982, 2 children **DISCIPLINE** HISTORY **EDUCATION** Univ Colo, BA, 60; Western State Col, MA, 63; Univ Colo, PhD, 67. **CAREER** Instr, Univ Colo, 65-66; from asst prof to prof, Ariz State Univ, 65-, dir, Am Studies Res Center, 95-97. **HONORS AND AWARDS** Fel, Ford Found, 69-70; Fulbright Fel, 81-82, 89-90, 95-97. **MEMBERSHIPS** Nat Asn of Seafaring Hist; W Soc Sci Asn. **RESEARCH** Seventeenth to nineteenth-century seafaring; Piracy; Male group behavior; History of human sexuality. **SELECTED PUBLICATIONS** Auth, An American Seafarer in the Age of Sail: The Erotic Diaries of Philip C. Van Buskirk, 1851-1870, Yale Univ Press, 94; ed, Gay Warriors: A Documentary History of Homosexuals in the Military from the Iliad to the Present, NY Univ Press, 01. **CONTACT ADDRESS** Dept of Hist, Arizona State Univ, Tempe, AZ 85287-2501. **EMAIL** burg@asu.edu

BURGGRAAFF, WINFIELD J.
PERSONAL Born 05/21/1940, Brooklyn, NY, m, 1966 **DISCIPLINE** HISTORY **EDUCATION** Hope Col, AB, 61; Univ NMex, PhD(Latin Am hist), 67. **CAREER** Asst prof, 66-72, Assoc Prof Hist, Univ MO-Columbia, 72-, Actg dir, Div Inter-Am Studies, Univ NMex, 70. **HONORS AND AWARDS** Cur Publ Awd, Cur of Univ Mo, 72. **MEMBERSHIPS** AHA; Conf Latin Am Hist; Latin Am Studies Asn. **RESEARCH** Modern Venezuelan history; the Latin American military; oil politics in Latin America. **SELECTED PUBLICATIONS** Auth, The military origin of Venezuela's 1945 revolution, Caribbean Studies, 10/71; The Venezuelan Armed Forces in Politics, Univ Mo, 72; El ocaso de una era, Bol Hist, 9/72; Andeanism and Anti-Andeanism in Twentieth-Century Venezuela, The Americas, 7/75; co-ed, El petroleo en Venezuela: Una bibliografia, Edicionex Centauro, 77. **CONTACT ADDRESS** Dept of Hist, Univ of Missouri, Columbia, Read Hall, Rm 101, Columbia, MO 65211. **EMAIL** histwb@atsshowme.missouri.edy

BURGUENO, MARIA C.
PERSONAL Born 07/02/1951, Montevideo, Uruguay, m, 1984, 2 children **DISCIPLINE** LATIN AMERICAN CULTURE **EDUCATION** Instituto de profesores, 77; Ohio State Univ, MA, 94; PhD, 96. **CAREER** Prof, Montevideo Uruguay, 77-92; teacher asst, Ohio State Univ, 92-95; asst prof, Marshall Univ, 96-. **MEMBERSHIPS** Latin Am Studies Asn, South Central Mod Lang Asn. **RESEARCH** National and cultural identites in Latin America. **SELECTED PUBLICATIONS** Auth, El imaginerio uruguayo: La patria, las tumbas, editorial linardi, (forthcoming). **CONTACT ADDRESS** Dept Modern Lang, Marshall Univ, 400 Hal Greer Blvd, Huntington, WV 25755-0001. **EMAIL** burgueno@marshall.edu

BURKE, ALBIE
PERSONAL Born 03/21/1932, Rugby, ND, d, 1960, 2 children **DISCIPLINE** AMERICAN CONSTITUTIONAL & LEGAL HISTORY **EDUCATION** Univ Chicago, BA, 58, MA, 65, PhD, 68. **CAREER** Assoc prof, 72-77, prof hist, Calif State Univ, Long Beach, 77-. **MEMBERSHIPS** Am Civil Liberties Union; Orgn Am Historians; Am Soc Legal Hist. **SELECTED PUBLICATIONS** Auth, Federal regulation of congressional elections in Northern cities 1871-94, Am J Legal Hist, 1/70; ed, The Hist Teacher, 79-85. **CONTACT ADDRESS** Dept Hist, California State Univ, Long Beach, 1250 N Bellflower, Long Beach, CA 90840-0001. **EMAIL** aburke@csucb.edu

BURKE, BERNARD V.
PERSONAL Born 08/13/1924, Springfield, MA, m, 1945, 5 children **DISCIPLINE** HISTORY **EDUCATION** Univ Washington, BA, 51, MA, 55, PhD, 66. **CAREER** Asst prof to Prof Emeritus, Portland State Univ. **HONORS AND AWARDS** Burlington Northern Awd for Fac Excellence. **MEMBERSHIPS** Am Hist Asn, Org of Am Hists, Soc for Hist of Am Foreign Relations. **RESEARCH** Fear as a factor in early American history. **SELECTED PUBLICATIONS** Auth, Ambassador Frederic Sackett and the collapse of the Weimar Republic, 1930-1933: The United States and Hitler's rise to power. **CONTACT ADDRESS** Dept Hist, Portland State Univ, PO Box 751, Portland, OR 97207-0751.

BURKE, COLIN B.
DISCIPLINE HISTORY **EDUCATION** WA Univ, PhD. **CAREER** Emeritus, Dept of History, UMBC. **HONORS AND AWARDS** Research Fellow, Yale Univ, Ponpo Eugene Garfield Fellow, CHF. **RESEARCH** 19th-century Am hist; hist of computing and computers; hist of information policy. **SELECTED PUBLICATIONS** Auth, American Collegiate Populations: A Test of the Traditional View; Information and Secrecy: Vannevar Bush; Ultra; Other Memex. **CONTACT ADDRESS** Dept of Hist, Univ of Maryland, Baltimore, Hilltop Circle, PO Box 1000, Baltimore, MD 21250. **EMAIL** burke@umbc.edu

BURKE, EDMUND
PERSONAL Born 07/30/1940, Washington, DC, m, 1974, 1 child **DISCIPLINE** HISTORY **EDUCATION** Univ Notre Dame, BA, 62; Princeton Univ, MA, 65, PhD, 70. **CAREER** Univ of Calif, Santa Cruz, 68-. **HONORS AND AWARDS** Woodrow Wilson Fel; Danforth Fel, Fulbright Hayes, NEH Grants; Carnegie Fel. **MEMBERSHIPS** AHA; World Hist Assoc; Middle East Studies Assoc. **RESEARCH** French colonialism, world history, modern Middle East history, North African history. **SELECTED PUBLICATIONS** Auth, Prelude to Protectorate in Morocco, 1860-1912: Patterns of Pre-Colonial Protest and Resistance, Univ of Chicago Pr, 76; ed, Global Crises and Social Movements: Artisans, Peasants, Populists and the World Economy, Westview Pr, (Boulder, CO), 88; coed, Islam, Politics and Social Movements, Univ of Calif Pr, (Berkeley), 88; ed, Rethinking World History: Essays on Europe, Islam and World History, Cambridge Univ Pr, (Cambridge), 93; ed, Struggle and Survival in the Modern Middle East, Univ of Calif Pr, I.B. Tauris, (Berkeley/London), 93; coed, Orientalism

and History: A Reader, 99; auth, Orientalism and Power: France and Morocco, 1890-1925, Princeton Univ Pr, (forthcoming), coed, The Environment and World History, 1500-2000 (forthcoming), auth, France and the Sociology of Islam, 1798-1962, (forthcoming). **CONTACT ADDRESS** Dept Hist, Univ of California, Santa Cruz, 1156 High St, Santa Cruz, CA 95064-1077.

BURKE, MARTIN J.
DISCIPLINE HISTORY **EDUCATION** City Col NYork, AB, 73; Univ Mich, AM, 77, PhD, 87. **CAREER** LECT, HIST, UNIV COLL, GALWAY, IRELAND **MEMBERSHIPS** Am Antiquarian Soc **SELECTED PUBLICATIONS** Auth, "Mathew Carey and the Vindicia Hibernicae," in The Literature of Politics and the Politics of Literature, RoDoPi, 94; auth, "A German Academic in the Wilderness: Francis Lieber and the Higher Learning in America," in The Fate of Liberal Education, Open Court, 95; auth, The Conundrum of Class: Public Discourse on the Social Order in America, Univ Chicago Press, 95. **CONTACT ADDRESS** Sch of Hist Stud, Inst for Advanced Studies, Olden Lane, Princeton, NJ 08540.

BURKE, MICHAEL E.
DISCIPLINE LATIN AMERICAN HISTORY **EDUCATION** Holy Cross Col, AB, 64; Duke Univ, MA, 67, PhD, 71. **CAREER** Assoc prof; dir, Villanova Hon(s) Prog, 82-93; founding pres, Villanova Phi Beta Kappa Chap. . **HONORS AND AWARDS** Sears-Roebuck Found Awd; Danforth Tchg Assoc; NEH, Brazil. **RESEARCH** Colonial Latin America; Mexico; Cultural & religious diversity; Reform and Revolution; Comparative Colonialism. **SELECTED PUBLICATIONS** Auth, The Royal College of San Carlos: Surgery and Spanish Medical Reform in the Eighteenth Century Enlightenment, Duke Univ Press, 77; Mexico's New Prisons, Corrections Today, 81; Mexico, Hippocrene Press, 92; Mexico como 'el otro', Vertebracion, 97; ed, dir, Signpost Biographies; articles on, colonial Latin American medicine, 20th century Mexico, teaching. **CONTACT ADDRESS** Dept of History, Villanova Univ, 800 Lancaster Ave., Villanova, PA 19085-1692. **EMAIL** mburke@email.vill.edu

BURKE, SARA Z.
DISCIPLINE HISTORY **EDUCATION** McMaster Univ, BA, MA; Carleton Univ, PhD. **CAREER** Asst prof. **RESEARCH** Coeducation in Canada **SELECTED PUBLICATIONS** Auth, Seeking the Highest Good: Social Service and Gender at the University of Toronto 1888-1937, Univ Toronto, 96; art, Science and Sentiment: Social Service and Gender at the University of Toronto, 1888-1910, Jour Can Hist Asn, 93. **CONTACT ADDRESS** Dept of History, Laurentian Univ, 935 Ramsey Lake Rd, Sudbury, ON, Canada P3E 2C6. **EMAIL** sburke@nickel.laurentian.ca

BURKETT, DELBERT ROYCE
PERSONAL Born 08/22/1949, Lamesa, TX, s **DISCIPLINE** NEW TESTAMENT; CHRISTIAN ORIGINS **EDUCATION** Abilene Christian Col, BA, 71; Harvard Divinity School, MA, 73; Duke Univ, Phd, 89. **CAREER** Vis asst prof, W Ky Univ, 89-90; vis asst prof, Appalachian St Univ, 90-93; asst prof, Lebanon Valley Col, 93-96; asst prof, La St Univ, 96-. **MEMBERSHIPS** Soc Bibl Lit. **RESEARCH** The canonical gospels and apocalyptic thought. **SELECTED PUBLICATIONS** Auth, "Four Sahidic Songs to St. John the Evangelist," Coptic Church Review 9, (88): 83-86; auth, The Son of the Man in the Gospel of John, Sheffield Academic Press, 91; auth, "The Nontitular Son of Man: A History and Critique," New Testament Studies 40, (94): 504-21; auth, "Two Accounts of Lazarus' Resurrection in John 11." Novum Testamentum 36, (94): 209-32; auth, The Son of Man Debate: A History and Evaluation, New Testament Studies Monograph Series, Cambridge Univ Press, 99. **CONTACT ADDRESS** Dept of Philosophy and Relig Stud, Louisiana State Univ, Baton Rouge, LA 70803-3901. **EMAIL** dburket@lsu.edu

BURKETT, RANDALL KEITH
PERSONAL Born 10/23/1943, Union City, IN, m, 1965 **DISCIPLINE** RELIGION, HISTORY **EDUCATION** Am Univ, AB, 65; Harvard Divinity Sch, MTS, 69; Univ Southern Calif, PhD(social ethics), 75. **CAREER** Admin asst curric develop, Univ Southern Calif, 72-73; assoc dir spec studies, 73-77, assoc coordr grants & res, 76-79, Dir Spec Studies, Col of Holy Cross, 77-, Coordr Grants & Res, 79-, Lectr, Ctr Exp Studies; ed, Afro-Am Relig Hist Group Newsletter, Am Acad of Relig, 76-; Nat Endowment for the Humanities fel, 79-80. **MEMBERSHIPS** Am Acad Relig; Am Soc Church Hist; Asn for Study Afro-Am Life & Hist. **RESEARCH** Afro-American religious history. **SELECTED PUBLICATIONS** Auth, Black Redemption: Churchmen Speak for the Garvey Movement, Temple Univ, 78; co-ed, Black Apostles: Afro-American Clergy Confront the Twentieth Century, G K Hall, 78; auth, Garveyism as a Religious Movement: The Institutionalization of a Black Civil Religion, Scarecrow, 78. **CONTACT ADDRESS** Off of Spec Studies, Col of the Holy Cross, Worcester, MA 01610.

BURKHARDT, RICHARD W.
DISCIPLINE HISTORY **EDUCATION** Harvard Col, AB, 66; Harvard Univ, AM, 67; PhD, 72. **CAREER** Asst prof, Univ Ill Champaign Urbana, 72-76; assoc prof, Univ of Ill, 76-84; prof, Univ of Ill, 84-; dir, Univ of Ill, 78-81; acting ch, Univ of Ill, 81; ch, Univ of Ill, 81-85. **HONORS AND AWARDS** Woodrow Wilson Honorary Fel, 66; NEH Summer Fel, 73; Nsf Res Fel, 78-79; John Simon Guggenheim Fel, 92-93; NSF Res Fel, 92-93; Fel, Am Asn for the Advancement of Science, 92; NSF Res Fel, 96-97. **RESEARCH** Scientific and social dimensions of animal behavior studies from 1800 and the present and the social and cultural history of zoos. **SELECTED PUBLICATIONS** Auth, "Struggling for identity: the study of animal behavior in America, 1930-1945," in Keith Benson, Ronald Raninger, and Jane Maienschein, eds., The Expansion of American Biology, New Brunswick, New Jersey: Rutgers Univ Press, (91): 164-194; auth, "Le comportement animal et l'deologie de domestication chez Buffon et les ethologistes modernes," in J.-C. Beaune et al, eds. Buffon 88, Actes du Colloque international pour le bicentenaire de la mort de Buffon, Paris: J. Vrin, (92): 569-582; auth, "Julian Huxley and the rise of ethology," in C. Kenneth Waters and Albert Van Helden, eds., Julian Huxley; Biologist and Statesman of Science, Houston: Rice Univ Press, (92): 127-149; auth, "Konrad Lorenz et le pas de l'oie," in Claude Blanckaert, ed., Des Sciences contrel'homme, vol II: Au nom du Bien, Paris: Editions Autrement, (93): 46-57; auth, " Le Comportement animal et la biologie francaise, Animal Behavior and French Biology, 1920-1950," in Claude Debru, Jean Gayon, and Jean-Franzois Picad, eds., Les Sciences Biologiques et Medicales en France 1920-1950, Paris: CNRS Editions, (94): 99-111; auth, "Ernst Mayr: Biologist-Historian," Biology and Philosophy, 9, (94): 359-371; auth, "Animal behavior and organic mutability in the age of Lamarck," in: Istituto Italiano per gli Studi Filosofici, Lamarck e il Lamarckismo, Napoli: La Citta del Sole, (96): 63-89; auth, "The founders of ethology and the problem of animal subjective experience," In: Marcel Dol et al., eds., Animal Consciousness and Animal Ethics: Perspectives form the Netherlands, Assen: Van Gorcum, (97): 1-13; auth, "Unpacking Baudien: models of scientific practice in the age of Lamarck," in Goulven Laurent, ed., Jean-Baptiste Lamarck, 1744-1829, Paris: Eeditions du CTHS, (97): 497-514; auth, The Spirit of System: Lamarck and Evolutionary Biology, Cambridge, Mass: Harvard Univ Press, 97. **CONTACT ADDRESS** History Dept, Univ of Illinois, Urbana-Champaign, 306 W Vermont St, Urbana, IL 61801. **EMAIL** burkhard@staff.uiuc.edu

BURKHOLDER, MARK A.
PERSONAL Born 09/03/1943, Chicago, IL, m, 2000, 2 children **DISCIPLINE** HISTORY **EDUCATION** Muskingum Col, BA, 65; Univ Or, MA, 67; Duke Univ, PhD, 70. **CAREER** Acad assoc to assoc v pres, Univ Mo, 83-84; asst dean to assoc dean to chair, asst prof to assoc prof to prof, Univ Mo St Louis, 70- . **HONORS AND AWARDS** Phi Beta Kappa; Phi Kappa Phi; Phi Alpha Theta; Chancellor's Awd for Excellence in Svc, 97; Edwin Lieuwin Awd; Hubert Herring Awd for Best Book. **MEMBERSHIPS** Amer Hist Assoc; Conf on Latin Amer Hist; Rocky Mountain Coun of Latin Amer Stud; Pac Coast Coun of Latin Amer Stud, Soc for Spanish & Portuguese Hist Stud. **RESEARCH** Bureaucracy in eighteenth-century Spain & Spanish Amer **SELECTED PUBLICATIONS** Auth, Latin American Colonial Era, in Latin American Military History: An Annotated Bibliography, Garland Press, 93; Honest Judges Leave Destitute Heirs: the Price of Integrity in Eighteenth-Century Spain, in Virtue, Corruption, and Self-Interest: Political Values in the Eighteenth Century, Lehigh Univ Press, 94; coauth, Colonial Latin America, Oxford Univ Press, 90, 94, 98; ed, Latin America to 1800, in The American Historical Association's Guide to Historical Literature, Oxford Univ Press, 95; Administrators of Empire Latin America to 1800, Ashgate Publ Ltd, 98. **CONTACT ADDRESS** Dept of History, Univ of Missouri, St. Louis, Saint Louis, MO 63121. **EMAIL** burkholder@umsl.edu

BURKINSHAW, ROBERT K.
DISCIPLINE CANADIAN HISTORY **EDUCATION** Vancouver Bible Col, BTh; UBC, BA; Univ Waterloo, MA; UBC, PhD, 88. **CAREER** Prof and Dean, Trinity Western Univ. **RESEARCH** Evangelicalism in Western Canada espec B.C; Bible school movement in Canada; religious, social and ethnic significance. **SELECTED PUBLICATIONS** Auth, Pilgrims in Lotus Land: Conservative Protestantism in British Columbia, 1917-1981, Montreal & Kingston: McGill-Queen's UP, 95. **CONTACT ADDRESS** Dept of History and Political Science, Trinity Western Univ, 7600 Glover Rd, Langley, BC, Canada V2Y 1Y1. **EMAIL** burkinsh@twu.ca

BURKMAN, THOMAS
PERSONAL Born 01/28/1944, Philadelphia, PA, m, 1982, 4 children **DISCIPLINE** HISTORY, MODERN JAPAN **EDUCATION** Univ MI, PhD, 75. **CAREER** Instr, Colby Col, 75-76; assoc prof of hist, Old Dominion Univ, 76-91; vis assoc prof, Hamilton Col, 92-93; dir of Asian Studies, SUNY at Buffalo, 94-. **HONORS AND AWARDS** Fulbright scholar, 78. **MEMBERSHIPS** Asn for Asian Studies; Soc of Peace Hist; Conf on Faith and Hist. **RESEARCH** 20th century Japan; East Asian int relations. **SELECTED PUBLICATIONS** Ed, The Occupation of Japan: Arts and Culture, The MacArthur Memorial, 88; auth, Reflections on the Occupation's Grassroots and the Eight Symposia, in W Nimmo, ed, The Occupation of Japan: The GrassRoots, 92; The Geneva Spirit, in John F Howes, ed, Nitobe Inazo: Japan's Bridge Across the Pacific, Westview Press, 95; Japanese trans, 97; Japan and the League of Nations: An Asian Power Confronts the European Club, in World Affairs, summer 95; The Immigration Act of 1924: The Limits of American Progressivisn, in Miwa Kimitada, ed, 1924-nen Amerika Shinminho no kokusai kankyo to Nihon no taio, Tokyo, 96. **CONTACT ADDRESS** Asian Studies, SUNY, Buffalo, 715 Clemens Hall, Buffalo, NY 14260-4610. **EMAIL** burkman@buffalo.edu

BURLINGAME, MICHAEL A.
PERSONAL Born 09/13/1941, Washington, DC, d, 1968, 2 children **DISCIPLINE** HISTORY **EDUCATION** Princeton Univ, BA; John Hopkins Univ, PhD. **CAREER** Prof; Conn Col, 68-; past Woodrow Wilson fel and Fulbright schol. **HONORS AND AWARDS** Abraham Lincoln Asn awd; Lincoln Diploma of Honor, Lincoln Memorial U; Sadowsik Prof of History. **MEMBERSHIPS** Am Hist Assoc, Organization of Am Historians, The Hist Soc, The Abraham Lincoln Assoc, The Abraham Lincoln Institute of the Mid- Atlantic, Conn Asn Scholars; National Asn Scholars. **RESEARCH** US History; Civil War; Abraham Lincoln; Psychohistory. **SELECTED PUBLICATIONS** Auth, The Inner World of Abraham Lincoln, Univ Ill Press, 94; An Oral History of Abraham Lincoln, Southern Ill UP, 96; auth, Inside Lincolns White House, Southern IL U Press, 97; auth, Lincoln Observed, John Hopkins U Press, 98; auth, A Reporters Lincoln, U of Nebrasks Press, 98; auth, Lincoln's Journalist, Southern IL U Press, 98; auth, Inside the White House in War Times, U of Nebraska Press, 00; auth, At Lincolns Side, Southern IL U Press, 00; auth, With Lincoln in the White House, Southern IL U Press, 00. **CONTACT ADDRESS** Dept of History, Connecticut Col, 270 Mohegan Ave, Box 5426, New London, CT 06320. **EMAIL** mabur@conncoll.edu

BURMAN, THOMAS
DISCIPLINE HISTORY **EDUCATION** Univ Toronto, MA, 86; PhD, 91. **CAREER** Assoc prof, Hist, Univ Tenn **HONORS AND AWARDS** Rockefeller Found Res Fel, 92-93; Am Philos Soc Res Grant, 95; Univ Tenn Fac Develop Grants, 95, 98, 99; Univ Tenn Col of Arts & Scis Fac Advis Awd, 97. **RESEARCH** Medieval Jewish-Christian-Muslim relations; medieval intellectual history. **SELECTED PUBLICATIONS** Auth, Religious Polemic and the Intellectual History of the Mozarabs 1050-1200, E.J. Brill (Leiden), 94; auth, "'Tafsir' and Translation: Traditional Qur'an Exegesis and the Latin Qur'ans of Robert of Ketton and Mark of Toledo," Speculum 73 (98): 703-32. **CONTACT ADDRESS** Dept Hist, Univ of Tennessee, Knoxville, 915 Volunteer Blvd, 6th Fl, Dunford Hall, Knoxville, TN 37996-4065. **EMAIL** tburman@utk.edu

BURNELL, DEVIN
DISCIPLINE ART HISTORY **EDUCATION** Smith Col, BA, 61; Boston Univ, MA, 66; Univ Chicago, PhD, 76. **CAREER** Instr, Univ Ill; vis assoc prof, 77. **HONORS AND AWARDS** Unendowed grants, Univ Chicago; res fel, Ford Foundation; res grant, Amer Assn Univ Women; grant-in-aid, Am Coun of Learned Soc(s). **SELECTED PUBLICATIONS** Pub(s), var prof papers and articles on 18th and 19th century Europ art. **CONTACT ADDRESS** Dept of Art Hist, Sch of the Art Inst of Chicago, 37 S Wabash Ave, Chicago, IL 60603.

BURNER, DAVID B.
PERSONAL Born 05/10/1937, Cornwall, NY, m, 1958, 2 children **DISCIPLINE** HISTORY, LITERATURE **EDUCATION** AB Hamilton Col, 58; PhD Columbia Univ, 65. **CAREER** Colby Col, 62-63; Oakland Univ, 63-67; SUNY, Stony Brook, 67-. **HONORS AND AWARDS** Guggenheim Fellowship; NYS Excellence Awd; Natl Hum Found. **MEMBERSHIPS** ASA; OAH; AHA. **RESEARCH** 20th century Am Poli. **SELECTED PUBLICATIONS** Making Peace with the 60s, Princeton Univ Press, 96; John F Kennedy and a New Generation, Little Brown, 89; Herbert Hoover: A Public Life, Alfred A Rucpt, 68; The Polotics of Provincialism: The Democratic Party in Transition, 1918-1932. **CONTACT ADDRESS** Dept Hist, SUNY, Stony Brook, Stony Brook, NY 11794. **EMAIL** DBBurner@AOL.com

BURNETT, AMY
PERSONAL Born 04/27/1957, Madison, WI **DISCIPLINE** EARLY MODERN EUROPE HISTORY **EDUCATION** Univ Wis, Madison, PhD, 89. **CAREER** Assoc prof, Univ Nebr, Lincoln, 95-. **RESEARCH** The Protestant Reformation in Basel. **SELECTED PUBLICATIONS** Auth, The Yoke of Christ: Martin Bucer and Christian Discipline, 16th Century J, 94. **CONTACT ADDRESS** Univ of Nebraska, Lincoln, 626 Oldfather, Lincoln, NE 68588-0327. **EMAIL** aburnett1@unl.edu

BURNETT, DAVID G.
PERSONAL Born 10/01/1940, Lincoln, England **DISCIPLINE** CURATOR **EDUCATION** Univ London, Birkbeck Col, BA 65; Courtauld Inst Art, MA, 67, PhD, 73. **CAREER** Lectr hist art, Univ Bristol, 67-70; assoc prof art hist, 70-80, dept chair, 74-77, 78-79, Carleton Univ; curator, Art Gallery Ont, 80-84; dir, Drabinsky Gallery, 90. **HONORS AND AWARDS** Can Coun grants, 74, 80 **MEMBERSHIPS** Univ Art Asn; Asn Univs & Cols Scholar Bd; Int Asn Art Critics.

RESEARCH Canadian art SELECTED PUBLICATIONS Auth, Alex Colville, 83; auth, Town, 86; auth, Anton Cetin, 86; auth, Jeremy Smith, 88; auth, Cineplex Odeon: The First Ten Years, A Celebration of Contemporary Canadian Art, 89; auth, Masterpieces of Canadian Art from the National Gallery of Canada, 90; coauth, Contemporary Canadian Art, 83. CONTACT ADDRESS 601-10 Tichester Rd, Toronto, ON, Canada M5P 3M4.

BURNETT, G. WESLEY
PERSONAL Born 07/20/1944, St Louis, MO, m, 1966, 2 children **DISCIPLINE** GEOGRAPHY **EDUCATION** Southern Methodist Univ, BA, 66; Univ Okla, MA, 74; PhD, 76. **CAREER** Chief, Planning and Project Admin Bur, Mont Dept of Fish and Game, Helena, Mont, 74-79; St Lectr and Dept Chair, Dept of Geog, Kenyatta Univ, Nairobi, Kenya, 84-86; Prof, Clemson Univ, 79-. **HONORS AND AWARDS** Fulbright Hays Scholar, Cameroon, 83; US Infor Agency Scholar, Am Ctrs for Oriental Res, Amman Jordan, 96; Sr Joseph E. and Caroline G. Dixon Fel, Clemson Univ Hon Col. **MEMBERSHIPS** George Wright Soc, SC Native Plant Soc, Southeast Regional Middle E and Islamic Studies Soc, Third World Studies Asn, Royal Geog Soc with the Inst of Brit Geogr. **RESEARCH** Historical geography of parks and equivalent reserves, Conservation in the Third World, Africa, Middle East, Ethnophilosophy of nature and wilderness, Portrayal of nature in literature, Portrayal of leisure in literature. **SELECTED PUBLICATIONS** Coauth, "Hgugi wa Thiong'o and the Search for a Populist Landscape Aesthetics," Environ Values 3 (94): 47-59; coauth, "Early National Park Adoption in Sub-Saharan Africa," Soc and Natural Resources 7 (94): 155-168; coauth, "Wilderness and the Bantu Mind," Environ Ethics 16 (95): 145-160; coauth, "A Willing Benefactor: An Essay on Wilderness in Nilotie and Bantu Thought," Soc and Natural Resources 9 (96): 201-212; auth, "Ecology Control in East Africa: A Review Essay," J of Third World Studies 14 (97): 223-230; coauth, "Kurt Vonnegut's 'Player Piano' and American Anti-leisure: Idle Time in Hell," Studies in Am Cult 20-2 (97): 17-27; coauth, "A Private Affair: Nature Reserves in the Hashemite Kingdom of Jordan," George Wright Soc Forum 16-2 (99): 75-83; coauth, "The Situation of the Bedouin of Jordan's Karak Plateau," Third World Studies 16-2 (99): 121-131. **CONTACT ADDRESS** Dept Parks Res and Tourism, Clemson Univ, Clemson, SC 29634-0001. **EMAIL** karlosk@clemson.edu

BURNETT, STEPHEN G.
PERSONAL Born 10/06/1956, Madison, WI, m, 1981, 3 children **DISCIPLINE** HISTORY, RELIGIOUS STUDIES **EDUCATION** Univ Wis-Madison, BA, 78; MA, 83; PhD, 90. **CAREER** Vis prof, hist & Judaic studies, 93-96, lectr, hist, classics and Judaic studies, Univ Neb Lincoln, 96-; Asst Prof of Classics/Religious Studies and History, 00-. **HONORS AND AWARDS** Friends of the Univ Wisc libr grant-in-aid, 98; res grant, Amer Philos Soc, 95, Frank S. Elizabeth D. Brewer prize, Amer Soc of Church Hist, 94; Fellow, Center for Advance Judaic Studies, Univ of Pennsylvania, 99; ACLS Research Fellowhip, 99-00. **MEMBERSHIPS** Asn of Jewish Studies; Asn of Jewish Libr; Sixteenth Century Studies Conf. **RESEARCH** Christian Hebrew scholarship; Christian-Jewish relations in early modern Europe. **SELECTED PUBLICATIONS** Auth, From Christian Hebraism to Jewish Studies: Johannes Buxtorf (1564-1629) and Hebrew Learning in the Seventeenth-Century, Studies in the History of Christian Thought, vol 68, Leiden, E. J. Brill, 96; article, From Israel to Germany: A Conference Report, Judaic Studies Newsletter, Univ Neb Lincoln, 97-98; article, The Regulation of Hebrew Printing in Germany, 1555-1630: Confessional Politics and the Limits of Jewish Toleration, 329-348, Infinite Boundaries: Order, Disorder, and Reorder in Early Modern German Culture, Sixteenth Century Jour Publ, 98; article, Jews and Anti-Semitism in Early Modern Germany: A Review Article, Sixteenth Century Jour, 27/4, 1057-1064, 96; article, Hebrew Censorship in Hanau: A Mirror of Jewish-Christian Coextistence in Seventeenth Century Germany, 199-222, The Expulsion of the Jews: 1492 and After, Garland Studies in the Renaissance, vol 2, 94; article, Buxtorf Family Papers, 71-88, Die Handschriften der Universitat Basel: Die hebraische Handschriften, Verlag der Universitatsbibliothek, 94; auth, Christian Hebrew Printing in the Sixteen Century: Printers, humanism and the impact of the Reformation, Helmantica, (00): 13-42. **CONTACT ADDRESS** Dept of Hist, Univ of Nebraska, Lincoln, 612 Old Father Hall, Lincoln, NE 68588-0327. **EMAIL** sburnett1@unl.edu

BURNETTE, RAND
PERSONAL Born 08/10/1936, Evansville, IN, m, 1958, 3 children **DISCIPLINE** HISTORY **EDUCATION** Wabash Col, AB, 58; Univ Wis, Madison, MS, 59; Ind Univ, PhD, 67. **CAREER** Instr, Carthage Col, 62-63; asst to prof hist, MacMurray Col, 63-; chair, MacMurray Col, 74-77, 80-83, 86-89, 92-00. **HONORS AND AWARDS** Phi Alpha Theta; Outstanding Educator Am, 75; fel, Hermon Dunlap Smith Ctr Hist Cartography, Newberry Libr, 90; fel, Early Mod Stud, 98; neh inst, 80, 88, 91, 93; neh summer seminar, 84. **MEMBERSHIPS** Am Hist Asn; Org Am Hist; Soc Hist Discoveries; Sixteenth Cent Stud Conf; Renaissance Soc Am; Soc Reformation Res; Indiana Hist Soc; Ill St Hist Soc; His Soc Pa; Communal Stud Asn; Am Soc 18th Century Stud; Am Asn Univ Prof. **RESEARCH** Early Am hist; hist cartography; hist of Am animation. **SELECTED PUBLICATIONS** Auth, "British Rule and American Settlement 1765-1818" in A Guide to the History of Illinois, 91; "So You Want to Teach a Mickey Mouse Course: An Undergraduate Course in the History of Animation," Teaching History: A Jour of Methods, 17, 92. **CONTACT ADDRESS** Dept of History, MacMurray Col, 447 E. Colege, Jacksonville, IL 62650. **EMAIL** rburnett@mac.edu

BURNHAM, JOHN CHYNOWETH
PERSONAL Born 07/14/1929, Boulder, CO, m, 1957, 4 children **DISCIPLINE** UNITED STATES HISTORY **EDUCATION** Stanford Univ, BA, 51, PhD, 58; Univ Wis, MA, 52. **CAREER** Actg instr hist, Stanford Univ, 56; lectr, Claremont Men's Col, 56-57; actg instr hist, Stanford Univ, 57-58, instr, 58; fel, Found Fund Res Psychiat, 58-61; asst prof hist, San Francisco State Col, 61-63; from asst prof to assoc prof, 63-69, Prof Hist, Ohio State Univ, 69-, Fulbright lectr, Univ Melbourne, 67 & Univs Tasmania & New England, Australia, 73; Tallman vis prof hist & psychol, Bowdoin Col, 82; vis prof, Univ of Sydney, Australia, 99. **MEMBERSHIPS** AHA; Orgn Am Historians; Am Asn Hist Med; Am Studies Asn; Hist Sci Soc. **RESEARCH** History of psychiatry; history of American medicine, science, and society. **SELECTED PUBLICATIONS** Auth, Psychoanalysis and American Medicine, 1894-1918: Medicine, Science, and Culture, Int Univ, 67; ed, Science in America: Historical Selections, Holt, 71; coauth, Progressivism, Schenkman, 77; auth, Jellife: American Psychoanalyst and Physician, Chicago, 83; How Superstition Won and Science Lost: Popularizing Science and Health in the United States, Rutgers, 87; Paths into American Culture: Psychology, Medicine, and Morals, Temple, 88; Bad Habits: Drinking, Smoking, Taking Drugs, Gambling, Sexual Misbehavior, and Swearing American History, NY Univ, 93; auth, How the Idea of Profession Changed the Writing of Medical History, Wellcome Inst for the Hist of Med (London), 98. **CONTACT ADDRESS** Dept Hist, Ohio State Univ, Columbus, 230 W 17th Ave, Columbus, OH 43210-1367. **EMAIL** burnham.2@osu.edu

BURNHAM, PATRICIA
PERSONAL Born 11/21/1935, Greenwich, CT, m, 1958, 2 children **DISCIPLINE** ART HISTORY **EDUCATION** Albertus Magnus Col, B.A., 57; Boston Univ, PhD, 84. **CAREER** Sr lectr & lectr, Univ TX, 88-. **HONORS AND AWARDS** Montana Hist Soc Sr Bradley Fel, 97; Nat Endowment for the Humantities Summer Stipend, 94; Nat Endowment for the Humanities Travel to Collections Grant, 92; Smithsonian Fel at the Nat Mus of Am Art, 91; Univ of Tex Col of Fine Arts Res Awd, 89; Rockefeller-Boston Univ Dissertation Fel in Am Art, 79-80. **MEMBERSHIPS** Col Art Asn; Am Studies Asn; Asn of Historians of Am Art; Women's Caucus for Art. **RESEARCH** American history painting; Public art; The art of John Trumbull, Charles Marion Russell and Theresa Bernstein. **SELECTED PUBLICATIONS** Co-ed, Redefining American History Painting, Cambridge UP, 95. **CONTACT ADDRESS** Dept of Art and Art Hist, Univ of Texas, Austin, ART 3.404, Austin, TX 78712. **EMAIL** tishmb@aol.com

BURNS, CAROL J.
PERSONAL Born 11/24/1954, Cedar Rapids, IA, m, 1989, 1 child **DISCIPLINE** ARCHITECTURE **EDUCATION** Bryn Mawr Co, BA, 75; Yale Col, BA, 80; Yale Sch of Architecture, MA, 83. **CAREER** Asst Prof, Univ Cincinnati, 84-86; Adj Prof, Rhode Island School of Design, 86-87; Asst Prof to Assoc Prof, 87-99. **HONORS AND AWARDS** Milton grant, Harvard Univ, 92; Joint Center for Housing Studies, 91; Fac Merit Awd, Univ of Cincinnati, 86; Eero Saarinen Fel, Yale Univ, 83; Am Inst of Architects scholarship, 83; Peter Rolland landscape Awd, Yale Univ, 82; Clareth Awd, Bryn Mawr Col, 74. **MEMBERSHIPS** Am Inst of Archit, Boston soc of archit, citizens Housing and Planning Asn, Soc of archit Hist, Yale club of Boston. **RESEARCH** Condition of the post-WWII era, relating architectural theory to professional and social practices and to evolving urban form; An academic entrepreneurial initiative for students to design fifty units of manufactured housing for a settlement in Rhode Island; : The physical residential environment as a vehicle for mobility in physical, spatial, economic, and social terms; Professional practice and education, site issues in design. **SELECTED PUBLICATIONS** auth, Housing and Mobility, forthcoming; auth, "Approaching alignment," in the Discipline Architecture, forthcoming; auth, "Review of Building community," Journal of Architectural and Planning Research, forthcoming; auth, "Land as a commodity of Limited supply, Thresholds 4," MIT Student Journal, 98; auth, "Housing/Site/Settlement," Architecture Reading Lists and Course Outlines, 98; auth, "A Review of Bauhaus in America," Journal of the Society of Architectural Historians, 96; auth, "Introduction to Global Economy and Architecture," Reflections on Architectural, 96; auth, "Globalization and architectural Practices: A double Project," ACSA Annual Proceedings, 96; auth, "The Gehry Phenomenon," Thinking the Present: Recent American Architecture, 90; auth, "Alternate Parking Lots," Landscape Architecture, 90. **CONTACT ADDRESS** Dept Archit, Harvard Univ, Gund Hall, Cambridge, MA 02138. **EMAIL** cb@taymacbur.com

BURNS, CHESTER RAY
PERSONAL Born 12/05/1937, Nashville, TN, m, 1962, 2 children **DISCIPLINE** HISTORY OF MEDICINE, AMERICAN HISTORY **EDUCATION** Vanderbilt Univ, BA, 59, MD, 63; Johns Hopkins Univ, PhD, 69. **CAREER** Asst prof hist of med, 69-71, James Wade Rockwell asst prof, 71-74, dir div, 69-74, assoc dir, Inst Med Humanities, 74-80, James Wade Rockwell assoc prof, 75-79, James Wade Rockwell prof hist of med & mem, inst med humanities, 79-, Asst prof, Dept Prev Med & Community Health, Univ Tex Med Br, 74-75; from assoc prof to prof, 75-79; assoc, Univ Tex Grad Sch Biomed Sci Galveston, 74-77, mem, 77-; consult, Nat Ctr Health Servs Res, 76-78; Nat Bd Consult, Nat Endowment for Humanities, 78-. **HONORS AND AWARDS** Philos Soc TX, 97 **MEMBERSHIPS** Am Assn Hist Med; Hist Sci Soc; AHA; Orgn Am Hist; Assn Am Med Col. **RESEARCH** History of medical ethics and philosophy; history of American medicine; history of medical education. **SELECTED PUBLICATIONS** Auth, The Development of Hospitals in Galveston During the Nineteenth Century, Southwestern Historical Quarterly, 93; auth, Thirty-three biographical essays for the New Handbook of Texas, Texas State Historical Association, 96; auth, Eight non-biographical essays for the New Handbook of Texas, Texas State Historical Association, 96; auth, Philosophy of Medicine and Bioethics: A Twenty-Year Retrospective and Critical Appraisal, Dordrecht: Kluwer Academic Publishers, 97. **CONTACT ADDRESS** Inst for the Med Humanities, Univ of Texas, Med Branch at Galveston, 301 University Blvd, Galveston, TX 77555-1311. **EMAIL** cburns@utmb.edu

BURNS, MICHAEL
PERSONAL Born 12/30/1947, New York, NY, m, 1986, 1 child **DISCIPLINE** HISTORY **EDUCATION** Univ Calif Los Angeles, BA, 76; Yale Univ, PhD, 81. **CAREER** Acting instr, Yale Univ, 79-80; Prof, Mount Holyoke Coll, 81-; Visiting Prof, Ecole des Hautes Etudes, 91. **HONORS AND AWARDS** Best Book Awd, Phi Alpha Theta; Prix Lecache; Woodrow Wilson Int Center for Scholars Fel; Fulbright; Rockefeller; Tocqueville Awd. **RESEARCH** Modern Europe; Modern France. **SELECTED PUBLICATIONS** Auth, Rural Society and French Politics, 84; Dreyfus: A Family Affair, 1789-1945, 92; Auth, Disturbed Spirits: minority rights and New World Orders 1919 and 1990, New European Orders, 96; France and the Dreyfus Affair, 98 . **CONTACT ADDRESS** Dept of History, Mount Holyoke Col, South Hadley, MA 01075. **EMAIL** mburns@mtholyoke.edu

BURNS, SARAH
DISCIPLINE AMERICAN ART **EDUCATION** Univ Ill, PhD. **CAREER** Prof. **RESEARCH** Social history of American art; popular prints; consumer culture; gender studies. **SELECTED PUBLICATIONS** Auth, Pastoral Inventions: Rural Life in Nineteenth-Century American Art and Culture, Temple, 89; Inventing the Modern Artist: Art and Culture in Gilded Age America, Yale, 96. **CONTACT ADDRESS** Dept of History and Art, Indiana Univ, Bloomington, 300 N Jordan Ave, Bloomington, IN 47405. **EMAIL** burnss@indiana.edu

BURNS, THOMAS S.
PERSONAL Born 06/07/1945, Michigan City, IN, m, 1968, 1 child **DISCIPLINE** HISTORY **EDUCATION** Wabash Col, BA, 67; Univ Mich, MA, 68; PhD, 74. **CAREER** Samuel Candler Dobbs Prof Hist, Emory Univ, 85-. **HONORS AND AWARDS** NEH Fel, 85, 88; Fulbright Fel, 86; Emory Williams Awd for Distinguished Teaching. **MEMBERSHIPS** Medieval Acad of Am; Am Inst of Archaeol; Soc for Late Antiquity. **RESEARCH** Late Roman History and Archaeology. **SELECTED PUBLICATIONS** Auth, The Ostrogoths: Kingship and Society, Historia Einzelschriffen, Wiesbaden, 80; auth, A History and the Ostrogoths, IN Univ Press, 84; auth, Barbarians Within the Gates of Rome: Roman Military Policy and the Barbarians ca 395-425AD, IN Univ Press, 94. **CONTACT ADDRESS** Dept of Hist, Emory Univ, 223 Bowden Hall, Atlanta, GA 30322. **EMAIL** histsb@emory.edu

BURNSTEIN, DANIEL
DISCIPLINE AMERICAN HISTORY, WESTERN CIVILIZATION **EDUCATION** Univ TX, Austin, BA, 73; Tulane Univ, MSW, 80; Rutgers Univ, Doctorate, 92. **CAREER** Instr, Seattle Univ. **MEMBERSHIPS** Am Asn for the Hist of Med; AHA; Orgn of Am Hist; Nat Asn of Soc Workers; Urban Hist Asn. **SELECTED PUBLICATIONS** Auth, Progressivism and Urban Crisis: The New York City Garbage Workers' Strike of 1907, J of Urban Hist 16, 90; Rev of The Sanitarians: A History of American Public Health, by John Duffy, ISIS 82, 91; The Vegetable Man Cometh: Political and Moral Choices in Pushcart Policy in Progressive Era New York City, NY Hist 77, 96. **CONTACT ADDRESS** Seattle Univ, Seattle, WA 98122-4460. **EMAIL** danielbu@seattleu.edu

BURRELL, BARBARA
DISCIPLINE CLASSICAL ARCHAEOLOGY **EDUCATION** NYork Univ, AB, 73; Harvard Univ, MA, 75, PhD, 80. **CAREER** Tutor, NY Univ, 75; Tchg Fel, Harvard Univ, 78-80; Asst prof, Univ Pa, 81-83; Vis Lecturer, Johns Hopkins Univ, 87; Asst prof, Swarthmore Col, 84-90; Lecturer, Hebrew Union Col, 92-; Assoc Res Prof, Univ Cincinnati, 91-. **HONORS**

AND AWARDS Magna cum laude, 73; Phi beta Kappa, 73; Fel Am Numismatic Soc, 74; Norton Fel, 75-76; Fel Royal Numismatic Soc, 77; May Isabel Sibley Fel, 77-78; Eugene Lang Fel, 88-89. **SELECTED PUBLICATIONS** Coauth, Notes on some Archaeological Contexts, Greek, Roman and Islamic Coins from Sardis, Archaeological Exploration of Sardis, 81; auth, Neokoroi, Harvard Studies in Classical Philol, 85; coauth, Uncovering Herod's Seaside Palace, Biblical Archaeol Rev, 93; auth, Two Inscribed Columns from Caesarea Maritima, Zeitschrift fur Papyrologie und Epigraphik, 93; auth, Palace to Praetorium: The Romanization of Caesarea, Caesarea Maritima: a Retrospective After Two Milennia, 96. **CONTACT ADDRESS** Dept of Classics, Univ of Cincinnati, PO Box 210226, Cincinnati, OH 45210-0226. **EMAIL** barbara.burrell@classics.uc.edu

BURROUGHS, CHARLES

PERSONAL m, 1 child **DISCIPLINE** URBAN HISTORY **EDUCATION** Oxford, BA; M.Phil; London, PhD, 75. **CAREER** Assoc prof/dir Ctr Medieval/Renaissance Studies. **HONORS AND AWARDS** Vis member, Institute for Advanced Study, 89; assoc ed, mediaevalia. **RESEARCH** Italian Renaissance art: archit and urban design, landscape. **SELECTED PUBLICATIONS** Auth, From signs to design: environmental process and reform in early Renaissance Rome, MIT Press, Cambridge, Mass, 90; auth, The Italian Renaissance palace facade: structures of authority, surfaces of sense, Cambridge Univ Press, (in press); auth, "Michelangelo at the Campidoglio: artistic identity, patronage, and manufacture," Artibus et Historiae 28, (93): 85-111; auth, "The Last Judgement of Michelangelo: pictorial space, sacred toography, and the social world, " Artibus et Historiae 32, (96): 55-89; auth, "The altar and the city: Botticelli's mannerism and the reform of sacred art," Artibus et Historiae 33, (97): 9-40; auth, "Grammar and expression in early Renaissance architecture: Brunelleschi and Alberti," Res: Anthropology and Aesthetics 34, (98): 39-63; auth, "Spaces of arbitration and the organization of space in late-medieval Italian cities," in Hanawalt and Kobialka, ed. Medieval practices of space, (Minneapolis and London: Univ of Minn Press, 00): 64-199. **CONTACT ADDRESS** SUNY, Binghamton, PO Box 6000, Binghamton, NY 13902-6000. **EMAIL** cburrou@binghamton.edu

BURROWS, EDWIN G.

PERSONAL Born 05/15/1943, Detroit, MI, m, 1978, 2 children **DISCIPLINE** HISTORY **EDUCATION** Univ Mich, BA, 64; Columbia Univ, PhD, 74. **CAREER** Prof, CUNY Brooklyn, 86-. **HONORS AND AWARDS** Claire and Leonard Tow Prof of Hist, 99; Pulitzer Prize in Hist, 99. **RESEARCH** Early America, New York City. **SELECTED PUBLICATIONS** Auth, Gotham: A History of NYC to 1898, Oxford, 98. **CONTACT ADDRESS** Dept Hist, Brooklyn Col, CUNY, 2901 Bedford Ave, Brooklyn, NY 11210-2813. **EMAIL** eburrows@brooklyn.cuny.edu

BURSTEIN, ANDREW

DISCIPLINE HISTORY **EDUCATION** Columbia Univ, ABA, 74; Univ Mich, MA, 75; Univ VA, PhD, 94. **CAREER** Asst prof, hist, Univ N Iowa, 96-. **MEMBERSHIPS** Am Antiquarian Soc **SELECTED PUBLICATIONS** Auth, The Inner Jefferson: Portrait of a Grieving Optimist, Univ Va Press, 95; auth, Sentimental Democracy: The Evolution of Americais Romantic Self-Image, 99; auth, Americais Jubliee, (forthcoming). **CONTACT ADDRESS** Dept of Hist, Univ of No Iowa, Seerley 319, Cedar Falls, IA 50614-0701.

BURSTEIN, STANLEY M.

PERSONAL Born 09/16/1941, Methuen, MA, m, 1966, 2 children **DISCIPLINE** HISTORY **EDUCATION** Univ Calif at Los Angeles, BA, 63; MA, 65; MPhil, 67; PhD, 72. **CAREER** Prof, Calif State Univ at Los Angeles, 68-00. **HONORS AND AWARDS** Independent Study & Res Fel, NEH, 76; Transl Grant, NEH, 85; Fel for Col Professors & Independent Scholars, NEH, 94; Outstanding Prof, Calif State Univ at Los Angeles, 93; President's Distinguished Prof, Calif State Univ at Los Angeles, 96. **MEMBERSHIPS** Asn of Ancient Historians, Am philol Asn, Am Res Ctr in Egypt, World Hist Asn, Calif Coun for the Soc Studies, Calif Classical Asn, Hakluyt Soc. **RESEARCH** Greek History, History of Ancient Egypt and Africa, Classical Tradition. **SELECTED PUBLICATIONS** Co-ed, Ancient History: Reading Lists and Course Outlines from American Colleges and Universities Vol 1, Markus Wiener Pub, Inc., 94 & 86; auth, The Hellenistic Age from the Battle of Ipsos to the Death of Kleopatra VII: Translated Documents of Greece and Rome Vol 3, Cambridge Univ Press, 85; ed & transl, Agatharchides of Cnidus On the Erythraean Sea, The Hakluyt Soc, 90; auth, Graeco-Africana: Studies in the History of History of Greek Relations with Egypt and Nubia, Aristide D. Caratzas, 95; coauth, The Ancient World: Readings in Social and Cultural History, Prentice Hall, 95; auth, Ancient African Civilizations: Kush and Axum, Markus Wiener Pub, Inc., 98; coauth, Ancient Greece: A Political, Social, and Cultural History, Oxford Univ Press, 99. **CONTACT ADDRESS** Dept Hist, California State Univ, Los Angeles, 5151 State University Dr, Los Angeles, CA 90032-4226. **EMAIL** sburste@calstatela.edu

BURT, LARRY

PERSONAL Born 09/14/1950, Sioux City, IA, m, 1972, 2 children **DISCIPLINE** HISTORY **EDUCATION** Morningside Col, BS, 72; Univ SDak, MA, 74; Univ Toledo, PhD, 79. **CAREER** Asst dir of the Am W Ctr, Univ of Ut, 86-87; from instr to asst prof, Northern Mont Col, 79-86 & 87-88; assoc prof & chemn of div of business and soc sci, Univ of Sci and Arts of Okla, 88-90; from asst prof to assoc prof, Southwest Mo State Univ, 90-. **RESEARCH** Native American Studies, Environmental History. **SELECTED PUBLICATIONS** Auth, "Factories on Reservations: The Industrial Development Programs of Commissioner Glenn Emmons, 1953-1961," Ariz and the W 19.4 (77): 317-332; auth, Tribalism in Crisis: Federal Indian Policy 1953-1961, Univ of NMex Press (Albuquerque, NM), 82; auth, "Roots of the Native American Urban Experience: Relocation Policy in the 1950s," Am Indian Quart 10.2 (86): 85-99; auth, "In a Crooked Piece of Time: The Dilemma of the Montana Cree and Metis," J of Am Culture 9.1 (86): 45-51; auth, "Nowhere Left to go: Montana's Cree, Metis, and Chippewa and the Creation of Rocky boy's Reservation," Great Plains Quart 7.3 (87): 195-209; auth, "Western Tribes and Balance Sheets: Business Development Programs in the 1960s and 1970s," Western Hist Quart 23.4 (92): 475-495; coauth, The National Forest of the Northern Region: Living Legacy, Intaglio Press (College Station, TX), 93; auth, "Unlikely Activism: O.K. Armstrong and Federal Indian Policy in the Mid-Twentieth Century," Mo Hist Rev (forthcoming). **CONTACT ADDRESS** Dept Hist, Southwest Missouri State Univ, Springfield, 901 S National Ave, Springfield, MO 65804-0027. **EMAIL** lwb644f@mail.smsu.edu

BURTON, DAVID HENRY

PERSONAL Born 08/04/1925, Oil City, PA, m, 1960, 3 children **DISCIPLINE** HISTORY **EDUCATION** Univ Scranton, BSS, 49; Georgetown Univ, MA, 51, PhD, 53. **CAREER** Instr soc sci, St Joseph's Col, Pa, 53-55; asst prof hist, Duquesne Univ, 55-56; from asst prof to assoc prof, 56-62, prof hist, St Joseph's Col, PA, 62-, Vis lectr Am hist, Georgetown Univ, 54; English-Speaking Union Winston Churchill traveling fel, 72. **HONORS AND AWARDS** Themis Awd for Contributions to the Study of Law, 80; Tengelmann Awd for Distinguished Research and Teaching, 96; Earhart Fel, 85, 95. **MEMBERSHIPS** AHA; Am Cath Hist Asn; Orgn Am Historians; English-Speaking Union. **RESEARCH** American intellectual history, 19th and 20th centuries; British interpretations of American history; Oliver Wendell Holmes, Jr. **SELECTED PUBLICATIONS** Auth, Theodore Roosevelt: Confident Imperialist, Univ Pa, 69; Theodore Roosevelt: A Biography, Twayne, 72; Theodore Roosevelt and his English Correspondents, Am Philos Soc, 73; ed, American History--British Historians, Nelson-Hall, 76; Holmes-Sheehan Correspondence, Kennikat, 76; The Friendship of Justice Holmes and Canon Sheehan, Harvard Libr Bull, 4/77; Oliver Wendell Holmes, Jr, Twayne, 80; Progressive Masks, Univ of Del Press, 82; Clara Barton In The Service of Humanity, Greenwood, 95; Theodore Roosevelt American Politician, Fairleigh Dickinson Univ Press, 97; auth, The Learned Presidency, Fairleigh Dickinson Univ Press, 88; auth, Cecil Spring Rice A Diplomat's Life, Fairleigh Dickinson Univ Press, 90; auth, Political Ideas of Justice Holmes, Fairleigh Dickinson Univ Press, 92; Taft, Holmes and the 1920s Court, Fairleigh Dickinson Univ Press, 98. **CONTACT ADDRESS** Dept of History, Saint Joseph's Univ, 5600 City Ave, Philadelphia, PA 19131-1376.

BURTON, J. D.

PERSONAL Born 05/28/1959, Mankato, MN **DISCIPLINE** HISTORY OF EDUCATION **EDUCATION** St Olaf Coll, BA, 81; Univ Chicago, MA, 85; Coll of William & Mary, MA, 89; PhD, 96. **CAREER** Res Assoc, De Paul Univ, 85-88; Sr Res Asoc, Asoc Dir Inst Plan Res, De Paul Univ91-92; Dir Inst Plan Res, De Paul Univ, 92-94; Dir, Mgt Support De Paul Univ, 94-96; dir acad support De Paul Univ, 96-. **MEMBERSHIPS** Orgn of Am Historians; Hist of Educ Soc; Soc Sci Hist Asn; Asn for the Stduy of Hist Educ. **RESEARCH** History of Education; History of Higher Education; Colonial New England. **SELECTED PUBLICATIONS** Auth, Crimson Missionaries: Harvard College and the Robert Boyle trust, The New England Quart, 94; Harvard Tutors: The Beginning of an Academic Profession, Hist of Higher Educ Annual, 96; Philanthropy and the Origins of Educational Cooperation: Harvard College, the Hopkins Trust and the Cambridge Grammar School, The Hist of Educ Quart, 97; coauth, Data Linking: A Model of Student Outcomes Assessment, A Collection of Papers on Self-Study and Institutional Improvement, 94; Faculty Vitality in the Comprehensive University: Changing Context and Concerns, Res and Higher Educ, 96; From Retention to Satisfaction: New Outcomes for Assessing the Freshmen Experience, Res in Higher Educ, 96. **CONTACT ADDRESS** DePaul Univ, 2320 N Kennore Ave, Chicago, IL 60614. **EMAIL** jburton@wppost.depaul.edu

BURTON, ORVILLE VERNON

PERSONAL Born 04/15/1947, Royston, GA, m, 1980, 5 children **DISCIPLINE** AMERICAN HISTORY **EDUCATION** Furman Univ, BA, 69; Princeton Univ, MA, 71, PhD(hist), 76. **CAREER** Instr hist, Mercer County Community Col, 71-72; asst master admin, dean Woodrow Wilson Residential Col, Princeton Univ, 72-74; instr, 74-75, asst prof, 75-82, assoc prof, 82-89, Prof Hist and Sociol, 89- Univ Il; senior res sci and head, Initiative for Soc Sci and Hum, Nat Ctr for Supercomputing Applications, Univ Ill, 94- . **HONORS AND AWARDS** The Pew Nat Fel Prog for Carnegie Scholars, 00-01; US Prof of the Year, Outstanding Res and Doctoral Univ Prof, 99-00; Univ Distinguished Teacher/Scholar, 99; Univ Scholar, 88; Mark Clark Distinguished Vis Chair Hist at the Citadel, 00-01; Pres Agr Hist Soc, 01-02. **MEMBERSHIPS** AHA; Orgn Am Historians; Southern Hist Asn; Social Sci Hist Asn; Conf Faith & Hist; Assoc for the Study of AFro American Hist and Life; So Asn for Women Hist; Soc Sci Computing Asn; H-Net; Nat Adv Bd, Alan Lomax's Global Jukebox: Giving Voice to the Human Species; Abraham Lincoln Hist Digitization Project; Univ Ill Press Bd, 96-00, chr, 99-00; Agr Hist Asn. **RESEARCH** United States southern history; race relations; family; community; religion; agrarian society; voting rights. **SELECTED PUBLICATIONS** Auth, In My Father's House Are Many Mansions: Family and Community in Edgefield, South Carolina, Chapel Hill: Univ of NC Pr, 85; co-auth, A Gentleman and an Officer: A Military and Social History of James B Griffin's Civil War, NY: Oxford Univ Pr, 96; co-ed, Class, Conflict, and Consensus: Antebellum Southern Community Studies, Westport, Conn: Greenwood Pr, 82; co-ed, Toward a New South? Studies in Post-Civil War Southern Communities, Westport, Conn: Greenwood Pr, 82; ed, Computing in the Humanities and Social Sciences, Urbana: Univ of IL Pr, 01; co-ed, Wayfarer: Charting Advances in Social Science Computing, Urbana: Univ of IL Pr, 01; auth, The Modern New South in a Postmodern Academy, Journ of Southern Hist, LXII, no 4, 96: 767-786; auth, Race Relations in the Rural South Since 1945, 28-58, in The Rural South Since World War II, Baton Rouge: Louisana State Univ Pr, 98; auth, Legislative and Congressional Redistricting in South Carolina, 290-314, in Race and Redistricting in the 1990s, NY: Agathon Pr, 98. **CONTACT ADDRESS** Dept of History, Univ of Illinois, Urbana-Champaign, 810 S Wright S, Urbana, IL 61801. **EMAIL** o-burton@uiuc.edu

BURTON, WILLIAM LESTER

PERSONAL Born 09/20/1928, Moundsville, WV, m, 1958, 2 children **DISCIPLINE** UNITED STATES HISTORY **EDUCATION** Bethany Col, WVa, AB, 49; Univ Wis, MS, 52, PhD, 58. **CAREER** Instr hist, high sch, Va, 49-50; from asst prof to assoc prof, 57-68, chmn dept, 69-76, Prof Hist, Western Ill Univ, 68-, Acad coordr, Independent Travel Study Prog. **MEMBERSHIPS** AHA; Orgn Am Hist. **RESEARCH** Social and intellectual history; recent United States history; teaching of history. **SELECTED PUBLICATIONS** Auth, First Wisconsin railroad commission, Wis Mag Hist, 62; Revolution and American mythology, Midwest Quart, 63; Illinois in the age of exploration, Study Ill Hist, 66; A Descriptive Bibliography of Civil War Manuscripts in Illinois, Northwestern Univ, 66; ed, A Manual for History Teachers, Ill Off Pub Instr, 67; auth, Illinois: A Student's History of the Prairie State, Panoramic, 68; coauth, Exploring Regions Near and Far, 77 & Exploring Regions of the Western Hemisphere, 77, Follett. **CONTACT ADDRESS** Dept of Hist, Western Illinois Univ, Macomb, IL 61455.

BUSCH, BRITON COOPER

PERSONAL Born 09/05/1936, Los Angeles, CA, m, 1958, 2 children **DISCIPLINE** MODERN EUROPEAN & MIDDLE EASTERN HISTORY **EDUCATION** Stanford Univ, AB, 58; Univ Calif, Berkeley, MA, 60, PhD(mod Europ hist), 65. **CAREER** From instr to assoc prof, 63-73, prof hist, 73-78, William R Kenan Jr Prof, Colgate Univ, 78-, Chmn Dept, 80-, Nat Endowment for Humanities fel, 68; Soc Sci Res Coun fel, 69. **MEMBERSHIPS** AHA; Mideast Inst; fel Am Asn Mideast Studies; Royal Soc Asian Affairs; NAm Soc Oceanic Hist. **RESEARCH** Maritime history; nineteenth and twentieth century Middle East and India. **SELECTED PUBLICATIONS** Auth, Britain and the Persian Gulf, 1894-1914, 67; Britain, India and the Arabs 1914-1921, 71; auth, Mudros to Lausanne: Britains Frontier in West Asia 1918-1923, 76; auth, Master of Desolation: The Reminiscences of Capt. Joseph J. Fuller, 80; auth, Hardinge of Penshurst: A Study in The Old Diplomacy, 80; auth, Alta California 1840-1842: The Journal and Observations of William Dane Phelps, Master of the Ship Alert, 83; auth, The War Against the Seals: A History of the North American Seal Fishery, 85; auth, Fremont's Private Navy: the 1846 Journal of Capt. W.D. Phelps, 1987, Whaling Will Never Do For Me: The American Whaleman in the 19th Century, 94; coauth, Fur Traders From New England: The Boston Men, 1787-1800, 96. **CONTACT ADDRESS** Dept Hist, Colgate Univ, 13 Oak Dr, Hamilton, NY 13346. **EMAIL** bbusch@mail.colgate.edu

BUSH, JOHN M.

DISCIPLINE HISTORY **EDUCATION** Ark Tchr Col, BSE, 60; MS State Univ, MA, 62, PhD, 64. **CAREER** Tchr, Benton Jr High Sch, 60-61; tchg asst, MS State Univ, 62-62; instr Am hist, Ark Polytech inst, 64-65; assoc prof hist, 65-69, prof hist, La Tech Univ, 69-. **MEMBERSHIPS** Am Hist Asoc; La Hist Asoc; N La Hist Asoc. **RESEARCH** Hist of the late 19th century; recent Am hist; diplomatic hist. **SELECTED PUBLICATIONS** Auth, The Tensas Gazette: A Brief Sketch, N La Hist Asoc Jour, 74; Hale Boggs in Dic La Biog, La Hist Asoc, 88. **CONTACT ADDRESS** Dept of Hist, Louisiana Tech Univ, PO Box 3178, Ruston, LA 71272.

BUSH, PERRY
DISCIPLINE HISTORY **EDUCATION** Univ Calif Berkeley, BA, 81; Carnegie Mellon Univ, MA, 87; PhD, 90. **CAREER** TA, Carnegie Mellon Univ, 86-87; instr, Community Col of Baltimore, 88-89; asst prof, Phillips Univ, 90-94; assoc prof, Bluffton Col, 94-. **HONORS AND AWARDS** Res Grant, Billy Graham Ctr, 91; Grant, Okla Found for the Humanities, 91; Dean Shirley Outstanding Fac Teaching Awd, Phillips Univ, 92-93; Grants, Bluffton Col, 95, 97; C Henry Smith Pace Lectr, 97-98. **MEMBERSHIPS** Org of Am Hist; Conf on Faith and Hist; Mennonite Hist Soc; Peace Hist Soc. **SELECTED PUBLICATIONS** Auth, "Military Service, Religious Faith, and Acculturation: Mennonite GI's and their Church, 1941-1945", Mennonite Quarterly Rev LXVII, (93): 261-282; auth, "Prophetic Anger: The Lingering Power of Evangelical Populism", Sojourners, (97): 34-37; auth, "Can Martin Luther King be Rescued from the Taming of Pop Culture?", Gospel Herald 90, (98): 1-3; auth, "The Flexibility of the Center: Mennonite Church Conflict in the 1960's", Mennonite Quarterly Rev LXXII, (98): 189-206; auth, Two Kingdoms, Two Loyalties: Mennonite Pacifism in Modern America, Johns Hopkins Univ Pr, (Baltimore), 98; auth, "Christian Propriety and the Fourth of July", Mennonite 2, (99): 6-7; auth, "Vietnam and the Burden of Mennonite History", Conrad Grebel Rev, (99); auth, "The Solidification of Nonresistance: Bluffton and World War, 1917-1945", Mennonite Life 55.1 (00): 1-10; auth, Dancing with the Kobzar: Bluffton College and Mennonite Higher Education, Pandora Pr, (Telford, PA), 00; auth, "United Progressive Mennonites: Bluffton College and Mennonite Higher Education, 1913-1945", Mennonite Quarterly Rev LXXIIV (forthcoming). **CONTACT ADDRESS** Dept Hist and Philos, Bluffton Col, 280 W College Ave, Bluffton, OH 45817-1196. **EMAIL** bush@bluffton.edu

BUSHMAN, CLAUDIA
PERSONAL Born 06/11/1934, Oakland, CA, m, 1955, 6 children **DISCIPLINE** HISTORY **EDUCATION** Wellesley Coll, AB, 56; Brigham Young Univ, MA, 63, Boston Univ PhD, 78. **CAREER** ADJ PROF, HIST, COLUMBIA UNIV **HONORS AND AWARDS** Virginia Foundation for the Humanities, 94; Virginia Historical Society, 92; Rockefeler foundation, Bellagio, Italy, 92; Huntington Library, 91; American Antiquarian Society, 91; Winterthue Museum, 82; Order of the First State, Conferred by Gov. Michael Castle of Delaware, Acad for Dist. Service to the Humanities, Del. Humanities Forum, My Mother of the Year, 00. **MEMBERSHIPS** Am Antiquarian Soc **RESEARCH** American Social and local history; American women and Literature; Mormon Studies; John Walker of Virginia. **SELECTED PUBLICATIONS** Auth, America Discovers Columbus: How an Italian Explorer Became and American Hero, Univ Press of New England, 92; auth, Mormon Sisters: Women in Early Utah, Emmeline Press, 76, and Olympus Publ, 80; auth, "A Good Poor Man's Wits," Univ Press of New England, 81, 99; auth, "Mormons in America" with Richard Lyman Bushman, Oxford Univ Press, 98. **CONTACT ADDRESS** 456 Riverside Dr, 10A, New York, NY 10027. **EMAIL** cmb35@columbia.edu

BUSHMAN, RICHARD
PERSONAL Born 06/20/1931, Salt Lake City, UT, m, 1955, 6 children **DISCIPLINE** UNITED STATES HISTORY **EDUCATION** Harvard Univ, BA, 55, PhD, 61. **CAREER** Prof. **HONORS AND AWARDS** Bancroft Prize, 68 **SELECTED PUBLICATIONS** Auth, Joseph Smith and the Beginnings of Mormonism, 84; King and People in Provincial Massachusetts, 85; The Refinement of America: Persons, Houses, Cities, 92. **CONTACT ADDRESS** Dept of History, Columbia Univ, 2960 Broadway, New York, NY 10027-6902. **EMAIL** rlb7@columbia.edu

BUSHNELL, DAVID
PERSONAL Born 05/14/1923, Philadelphia, PA, m, 1945, 3 children **DISCIPLINE** HISTORY **EDUCATION** Harvard Univ, BA, 43, PhD(hist), 51. **CAREER** Res analyst, Off Strategic Serv & US Dept State, 44-46; from instr to asst prof hist, Univ Del, 49-56; historian, US Air Force Missile Develop Ctr, 56-61, chief hist div, Off Aerospace Res, 61-63; assoc prof, 63-68, Prof Hist, Univ Fla, 68-91, Contrib ed, Handbook Latin Am Studies, 56-91. **MEMBERSHIPS** Conf Latin Am Hist; Latin Am Studies Assn; corresp mem Agentine Colombian Acads Hist. **RESEARCH** Nineteenth century Colombia and Argentina. **CONTACT ADDRESS** Dept of Hist, Univ of Florida, Gainesville, FL 32611. **EMAIL** dav@ufl.edu

BUSS, DIETRICH
PERSONAL Born 09/20/1939, Tokyo, Japan, m, 1966, 3 children **DISCIPLINE** HISTORY **EDUCATION** Biola Univ, BA, 63; Calif State Univ-Los Angeles, MA, 65; Claremont Univ, PhD, 76. **CAREER** Prof, dept chemn hist, Biola Univ, 66- . **HONORS AND AWARDS** Who's Who Among Am Educ; Charles J. Kennedy Awd, Econ & Bus Hist Soc; Nat Endowment for Hum. **MEMBERSHIPS** Orgn Am Hist; Hist Soc; Confr on Faith & Hist; Asn Public Justice. **RESEARCH** Henry Villard and his many business interests, Mission aviation fellowship worldwide. **SELECTED PUBLICATIONS** Auth, Henry Villard: Transatlantic Investment and Interests; auth, Giving Wings to the Gospel: The Remarkable Story of mission aviation fellowship. **CONTACT ADDRESS** Dept Hist & Geog, Biola Univ, 13800 Biola Ave, La Mirada, CA 80639-0002. **EMAIL** dietrich_buss@peter.biola.edu

BUTLER, JEFFREY ERNEST
PERSONAL Born 09/27/1922, Cape Province, South Africa, m, 1947, 3 children **DISCIPLINE** MODERN HISTORY **EDUCATION** Rhodes Univ, S Africa, BA, 47; Oxford Univ, MA, 56, DPhil, 63. **CAREER** Staff tutor delegacy extramural studies, Oxford Univ, 53-57; vis asst prof govt, Boston Univ, 57-58, res assoc hist govt, 58-64; Prof Hist, Wesleyan Univ, 64-, Lectr hist, Wellesley Col, 60-64; prof of hist emer, Wesleyan, 91. **MEMBERSHIPS** Mem African Studies Asn; South African Inst of Race Relations. **RESEARCH** British liberal colonial policy, particularly South Africa; African political organizations; South African history and politics. **SELECTED PUBLICATIONS** Auth, The Liberal Party and the Jameson Raid, Clarendon, Oxford, 68; ed and auth, Democratic Liberalism in South Africa, Wesleyan, 87. **CONTACT ADDRESS** Dept of Hist, Wesleyan Univ, Middletown, CT 06457. **EMAIL** jbutler@wesleyan.edu

BUTLER, JON
PERSONAL Born 06/04/1940, Fort Smith, AK, m, 1970, 2 children **DISCIPLINE** HISTORY **EDUCATION** Univ Minnesota BA 64, PhD 72. **CAREER** Yale Univ prof of Amer studies, history and religious studies, 85 to 98-; Univ Illinois, Chicago, asst prof to prof, hist, 75-85; California State Col, asst prof, hist, 71-75. **HONORS AND AWARDS** Beveridge Prize of AHA for Best Book in Amer Hist: Awash in a Sea of Faith; Outler Prize; Theodore Saloutos Prize; Gilbert Chinard Prize. **MEMBERSHIPS** AHA; ASA; OAH; ASCH **RESEARCH** Am Religious History; Early Am History; Religion in Urban Am. **SELECTED PUBLICATIONS** Auth, Religion in American History: A Reader, co-ed Harry S Stout, NY 97; Awash in a Sea of Faith: Christianizing the American People, Cambridge MA, Harvard Univ Press, 90; The Christianization of Modern America, Kirchliche Zeitgeschichte, 98; Protestant Success in the New American City, 1870-1920, The Anxious Secrets of Rev Walter Laidlaw PhD, IN: Harry S. Stout and Darryl G. Hart, eds, New Directions in American Religious History, NY Oxford Press 97; Coercion, Miracle, Reason: Rethinking Religion in the Revolutionary Age, in: Religion in the Revolutionary Age, ed Ronald Hoffman, Char VA, Univ Press Of VA 94; Becoming America: The Revolution Before 1776, Cambridge, MA, Harvard Univ Press, 00; Relioion in Colonial Am, NY, Oxford Univ Press, 00. **CONTACT ADDRESS** Dept of History, Yale Univ, 208324, New Haven, CT 06520-8324. **EMAIL** jon.butler@yale.edu

BUTLER, KIM D.
PERSONAL Born Brooklyn, NY **DISCIPLINE** HISTORY, AFRICAN STUDIES **EDUCATION** Sarah Lawrence Col, BA, 82; Harvard Univ, MA, 89; Johns Hopkins Univ, MA, 92, PhD, 95. **CAREER** Asst prof, Dept of Africana Studies, Rutgers Univ. **HONORS AND AWARDS** George Owens Fel, 90-93; Fulbright Scholar, 91-92; Book Awds: Leticia Woods Brown Prize, Asn of Black Women's Hist, 98, Wesley Logan Prize, Am Hist Soc, 99. **MEMBERSHIPS** Am Hist Asn, Asn of Black Women Hist. **RESEARCH** African Diaspora history, Afro-Brazilian history. **SELECTED PUBLICATIONS** Auth, "Up From Slavery: Afro-Brazilian Activism in Sao Paulo, Brazil, 1888-1938," The Americas, 49:2, 179-206 (Oct 92); auth, Freedoms Given, Freedoms Won: Afro-Brazilians in Post-Abolition Sao Paulo and Salvador, New Brunswick, NJ: Rutgers Univ Press (98); auth, "Jinga Baiana: The Politics of Race, Class, and Power in Salvador, Bahia," in Hendrik Kraay, ed, Afro-Brazilian Culture and Politics: Bahia, 1790s-1990s, Armonk, NY: M. E. Sharpe Press (98); auth, "Abolition and the Politics of Identity in the Afro-Atlantic Diaspora: Towards a Comparative Approach," in Darlene Clark Hine, ed, Comparative History of Black People in Diaspora, Bloomington: Ind Univ Press, 121-133 (99); auth, "Africa in the Reinvention of Nineteenth Century Afro-Brahian identity," Slavery and Abolition (forthcoming 2000); auth, "From Black History to Diasporan History: Brazilian Abolition inAfro-Atlantic Perspective," African Studies Rev (forthcoming 2000). **CONTACT ADDRESS** DEPT Afro-Am Studies, Rutgers, The State Univ of New Jersey, New Brunswick, PO Box 5062, New Brunswick, NJ 08903-5062.

BUTLER, LESLIE
DISCIPLINE HISTORY **EDUCATION** Univ of Rochester, BA, 91; Yale Univ, Phil, 94; PhD, 97. **CAREER** VIS ASST PROF, HIST, REED COLL **MEMBERSHIPS** Am Antiquarian Soc **RESEARCH** James Russell Lowell **CONTACT ADDRESS** History Dept, Reed Col, 3203 SE Woodstock Blvd, Portland, OR 97202. **EMAIL** leslie.butler@reed.edu

BUTOW, ROBERT J. C.
PERSONAL Born 03/19/1924, San Mateo, CA, d, 1 child **DISCIPLINE** HISTORY **EDUCATION** Stanford Univ, PhD(hist), 53. **CAREER** Res fel, Ctr Int Studies, Princeton Univ, 53-54, res assoc, 57-60, from instr to asst prof, 54-60; assoc prof, 60-66, Prof Hist, Univ Wash, 66-, Mem Fac, Sch Int Studies, 60-90, Rockefeller Found & Soc Sci Res Coun res fel, Japan, 56-57; mem, Inst Advan Study & Rockefeller Found grant int rels res, 62-63; Guggenheim Mem Found fel, 65-66 & 78-79. **MEMBERSHIPS** Asn Mem Inst Advan Study; Soc Hist Am Foreign Rel. **RESEARCH** Japanese-American relations. **SELECTED PUBLICATIONS** Auth, Japan's Decision to Surrender, Stanford Univ, 54 & 67; The Hull-Nomura Conversations: A Fundamental Misconception, Am Hist Rev, 7/60; Tojo and the Coming of the War, Princeton Univ, 61 & Stanford Univ, 69; Backdoor Diplomacy in the Pacific: The Proposal for a Konoye-Roosevelt Meeting, 1941, J Am Hist, 6/72; The John Doe Associates: Backdoor Diplomacy for Peace, 1941, Stanford Univ, 74; The FDR Tapes: Secret Recordings Made in the Oval Office of the President in the Autumn of 1940, Am Heritage, 2-3/82; auth, "Pearl Harbor Jitters: Defending the WhitHouse against Attack," Quarterly of the National Archives 23 (91); Marching Off to War on the Wrong Foot, The Final Note Tokyo Did Not Send to Washington/, Pac Hist Rev, Vol 63, 1994; How Roosevelt Attacked Japan at Pearl-Harbor - Myth Masquerading as History/, Prologue-Quarterly of the National Archives, Vol 28, 1996; auth, "A Notable Passage to China: Myth and Memory in FDR's Family History," Quarterly of the National Archives 31 (99). **CONTACT ADDRESS** Univ of Washington, Box 353650, Seattle, WA 98195-3650. **EMAIL** rbutow@u.washington.edu

BUTTENFIELD, BARBARA P.
PERSONAL Born 08/14/1952, Pittsburgh, PA **DISCIPLINE** GEOGRAPHY **EDUCATION** Clark Univ, BA, 74; Univ Kans, MA, 79; Univ Wash, PhD, 84. **CAREER** Acting asst prof, Univ Calif, 82-84; asst prof, Univ Wis, 84-87; asst prof to assoc prof, 87-95; res scientist, Nat Center for Geog Infor and Analysis, 88-96; res scientist, U.S. Geol Survey, 93-94; assoc prof to prof, Univ Colo, 96-; guest prof, Univ Wien, 97. **HONORS AND AWARDS** Fel, Am Congress on Surveying and Mapping, 97; Best Res Paper, Geosci Infor Soc, 99. **MEMBERSHIPS** AAUW; ACA; ACSM; AAG; CaGIS; ICA; NOW; NACIS; Nat Geog Soc; Smithsonian Inst Assoc. **RESEARCH** Digital libraries: data delivery via Internet, interface design and usability, evaluation; Scientific visualization: information design, representations of uncertainty, map animation; Scale dependent geometry: map generalization, multi-scale geospatial databases, data fusion. **SELECTED PUBLICATIONS** Co-ed, Map Generalization: Making Rules for Knowledge Representation, Longman, 94; auth, "GIS and Digital Libraries: Issues of Size and Scalability," GIS and Libraries; Patrons, Maps and Spatial Data, (Univ Ill Press, 96), 69-80; co-auth, "The Alexandria Digital Library Project: Distributed Library Services for Spatially Referenced Data," Proceedings, (96): 76-84; auth, "Looking Forward: Geographic Information Services and Libraries in the Future," Cartography and GIS, (98): 161-171; auth, "Usability Evaluation of Digital Libraries," Sci and Technol Libr, (99): 39-59; co-auth, "Scaling Models of Digital Library Use," Intl J of Human-Computer Systems, 00; co-auth, Digital Library Use and Social Practice, MIT Press, 00. **CONTACT ADDRESS** Dept Geog, Univ of Colorado, Boulder, 260 UCB, Boulder, CO 80309-0260. **EMAIL** babs@colorado.edu

BUTTS, MICHELE T.
PERSONAL Born 12/23/1952, Clarksville, TN **DISCIPLINE** HISTORY **EDUCATION** Austin Peay State Univ, BA, 73; MA, 74; Univ NMex, PhD, 92. **CAREER** Assoc prof, Prestonburg Community Col, 75-82; adj instr Santa Fe Community Col, 83-84; teacher, Albuquerque Public School, 82-89; adj instr Albuquerque Tech Voc Inst, 87-88; adj instr, Hopkinsville Community Col, 91-92; adj instr to assoc prof, Austin Peay State Univ, 89-. **HONORS AND AWARDS** NEH Summer Sem, 93; Grant, Austin Pea State Univ. **MEMBERSHIPS** Conf on Faith and Hist; Org of Am Hist; Soc for Milit Hist; Southern Assoc for Women Hist; Western Hist Assoc. **RESEARCH** US Religious history, Native America, Social history, American West, Civil War Era, Comparative Frontiers. **SELECTED PUBLICATIONS** Auth, "John Sevier" and "Zebulon Montgomery Pike", Encycl of the War of 1812, eds Davis S Heidler and Jeanne T Heidler, ABC-CLIO, (Santa Barbara, 97); auth, "Native American Resistance and Presbyterian Missions in Post-Civil War New Mexico, 1867-1912", Am Presby: J of Presby Hist 74, (96): 241-52; auth, "Galvanized Yankees on the Upper Missouri", Mont: Mag of Western Hist (99); auth, "Galvanized Yankees", Encycl of the Great Plains, Univ of Nebr Pr, 98; auth, Galvanized Yankees on the Upper Missouri: A History of the First United States Infantry Regiment, Univ Pr of Colo, (forthcoming). **CONTACT ADDRESS** Dept Hist and Philos, Austin Peay State Univ, 601 College St, Clarksville, TN 37044-0001. **EMAIL** Buttsmt@apsu.edu

BYMAN, SEYMOUR DAVID
PERSONAL Born 10/26/1934, Chicago, IL, m, 1956, 3 children **DISCIPLINE** RELIGIOUS HISTORY **EDUCATION** Univ Ill, Urbana, BA, 56; Roosevelt Univ, MA, 67; Northwestern Univ, PhD(hist), 71. **CAREER** Asst prof, 70-75, assoc prof, 75-78, Prof Hist, Winona State Univ, 78-, Assoc, Inst Psychohistory, 77-78. **MEMBERSHIPS** AHA. **RESEARCH** Martyrology. **SELECTED PUBLICATIONS** Auth, Tudor death stands, Moreana, 73; Suicide and alienation: Martyrdom in Tudor England, Psychoanal Rev, 74; Guilt and martyrdom: The case of John Bradford, Harvard Theol Rev, 75; A defense of psychohistory, 78 & Child raising and melancholia in Tudor England, 78, J Psychohistory; Ritualistic acts and compulsive behavior: The pattern of sixteenth century martyrdom, Am Hist

Rev, 78; Humanities and the Law School Experience, J of Legal Educ, 85; The Perils of Psychohistory, J of Psychohistory, 88. **CONTACT ADDRESS** Dept of History, Winona State Univ, P O Box 5838, Winona, MN 55987-0838. **EMAIL** sbyman@vax2.winona.msus.edu

BYNUM, CAROLINE WALKER
PERSONAL Born 05/10/1941, Atlanta, GA, m, 1983, 1 child **DISCIPLINE** HISTORY, MEDIEVAL EUROPE **EDUCATION** Univ Mich, BA, 62; Harvard Univ, PhD, 69. **CAREER** Asst prof, Harvard Univ, 69-74, assoc prof, 74-76; assoc prof and prof, Univ WA, Seattle, 76-88; prof, Columbia Univ, NYC, 88-, Morris and Alma Schapiro chair in History, 90-; Univ Prof, 99-. **HONORS AND AWARDS** Berkshire Prize, for Best Historical Article Written by a Woman, 85; MacArthur Fel, July 86-July 91; Nelson Prize for best article, Renaissance Soc of Am, 87; fel, Medieval Academy of Am, 89; Philip Schaff prize of the ASCH/AHA for the best book in any field of Church History, for Holy Feast, Holy Fast; Trilling Prize for the Best Book by a Columbia Faculty Member, 92, for Fragmentation and Redemption, given by the Am Academy of Religion, 92; Ralph Waldo Emerson Prize of Phi Beta Kappa given for the best book of the year on "the intellectual and cultural condition of man," 95, for Resurrection of the Body; Jacques Barzun Prize for the best work in cultural history, given by the Am Philos Soc for Resurrection of the Body, 96; Presidential Awd for Outstanding teaching, Columbia Univ, May, 97; seven honorary degrees; Jefferson Lecturer in The Humanities for NEH, 99. **MEMBERSHIPS** Am Hist Asn; Medieval Academy of Am; Am Soc of Church History; Am Cath Hist Asn; Am Academy of Relig; Am Soc for the Study of Relig (86); Am Academy of Arts and Sciences (93); Am Philos Soc (95). **RESEARCH** The religious and intellectual history of medieval Europe, ca 500-ca 1500; escatology; hagiography; women's religious movements; mysticism; the history of science; scholasticism. **SELECTED PUBLICATIONS** Auth, Jesus as Mother: Studies in the Spirituality of the High Middle Ages, Univ CA Press, 82; Gender and Religion: On the Complexity of Symbols, ed Caroline Bynum, Stevan Harrell, and Paula Richman, Beacon Press, 86; Holy Feast and Holy Fast: The Religious Significance of Food to Medieval Women, Univ CA Press, 87; Fragmentation and Redemption: Essays on Gender and the Human Body in Medieval Religion, Urzone Pubs, 91; The Resurrection of the Body in Western Christianity, 200-1336, Columbia Univ Press, 95; Why All the Fuss About the Body? A Medievalist's Perspective, Critical Inquiry 22, autumn 95; auth, The Resurrection of the body in Western Christianity, 200-1336, Columbia Univ Pr, 95; Wonder, The Am Hist Rev 102 1, Feb 97; Metamorphosis, or Gerald and the Werewolf, Speculum 73, Oct 98; coed, Last Things; Death and the Apocalypse in the Middle Ages, Univ of Pa Pr, 00; auth Metamorphosis and Identity, Urzone Publs, 01. **CONTACT ADDRESS** History Dept, Columbia Univ, Fayerweather Hall, MC 2546, New York, NY 10027.

BYRNE, FRANK LOYOLA
PERSONAL Born 05/12/1928, Hackensack, NJ, m, 1962, 2 children **DISCIPLINE** UNITED STATES HISTORY **EDUCATION** NJ State Col, Trenton, BS, 50; Univ Wis, MS, 51, PhD(hist), 57. **CAREER** Instr hist, La State Univ, 57-58; from asst prof to assoc prof, Creighton Univ, 58-66; assoc prof, 66-68, chmn, Grad Prog Hist, 69-72, Prof Hist, Kent State Univ, 68-, Mem, Nebr Civil War Centennial Comn, 60-65; Wis Civil War Centennial Comn res grant, 62-63; Am Philos Soc res grant, 65; Kent State Univ fac res grant, 67, 69, 72. **MEMBERSHIPS** AHA; Orgn Am Hist; Southern Hist Asn. **RESEARCH** Civil War; temperance movement; Reconstruction. **SELECTED PUBLICATIONS** Auth, Libby Prison: A Study in Emotions, J Southern Hist, 11/58; Prophet of Prohibition: Neal Dow and His Crusade, 61 & ed, The View From Headquarters: Civil War Letters of Harvey Reid, 65, Wis State Hist Soc; auth, A Terrible Machine: General Neal Dow's Military Government on the Gulf Coast, Civil War Hist, 3/66; compiler, Prisons and Prisoners of War, In: Civil War Books: A Critical Bibliography, La State Univ, Vol I, 67; co-ed, Haskell of Gettysburg: His Life and Civil War Papers, Wis State Hist Soc, 70; ed, Bound to See the President: A Michigan Private Calls on Lincoln, Mich Hist, 7-8/79; auth, Libby Prison, Salisbury Prison, In: Encyclopedia of Southern History, La State Univ, 79; The Sultana Tragedy - America Greatest Maritime Disaster - Potter,JO/, Civil War History, Vol 38, 1992; Civil-War Prisons and Escapes - A Day-to-Day Chronicle - Denney,RE/, Civil War Hist, Vol 40, 1994; Andersonville - The Last Depot - Marvel,W/, Civil War Hist, Vol 41, 1995; Recollected Words of Lincoln,Abraham - Fehrenbacher,DE, Fehrenbacher,V/, Civil War History, Vol 43, 1997. **CONTACT ADDRESS** Dept of Hist, Kent State Univ, Kent, OH 44242.

BYRNE, JOHN M.
PERSONAL Born 11/02/1949, Chicago, IL, 2 children **DISCIPLINE** URBAN AFFAIRS **EDUCATION** Univ Del, BA, 71; MA, 73; PhD, 80. **CAREER** Vis asst prof to prof, Univ of Del, 81-; Dir, Center for Energy and Environ Policy, Univ of Del, 84-. **HONORS AND AWARDS** Postdoctoral Fel, Univ of Del, 80-81; Excellence in Teaching Awd, Univ of Del, 88; Fulbright Sr Lectr, Korea, 95; Evaluator, USEPA, 99; Environ Expert, China Nat Foreign Expert Agency Register, 97-; Policy Advisor, Environ Forum, Korea Nat Assembly, 98-. **MEMBERSHIPS** Nat Assoc of Sci, Tech and Soc. **RESEARCH** Energy and Environmental Policy, Environmental Justice, Sustainable Development, Political Ecology. **SELECTED PUBLICATIONS** Coed, The Solar Energy Transition: Implementation and Policy Implications, Westview Pr, Boulder, (CO), 83; coed, "Energy and Cities", "The Politics of Energy R&D", "Planning for Changing Energy Conditions", "Energy and Environment: The Policy Challenge", and "Governing the Atom: The Policies of Risk", Energy and Environ Policy Series, Transaction Books, (New Brunswick, NJ), 86-96; coauth, "Commercializing Photovoltaics: The Importance of Capturing Distributed Benefits", Proc of the Am Solar Energy Soc Solar 98 Conf, (Albuquerque, NM), (98): 231-237; coauth, "An Equity- and Sustainability-Based Policy Response to Global Climate Change", Energy Policy 26.4 (98): 335-343; coauth, "Environmental Impacts of Building Integrated PV Applications in the State Public Buildings Sector", Proc of the Am Solar Energy Soc Solar 99 Conf, (99): 425-429; coauth, "Evaluating the Persistence of Residential Water Conservation: A 1992-97 Panel Study of a Water Utility Program in Delaware, J of Am Water Resources Assoc 35.5, (99): 1269-1276; coauth, "Efficient Global Warming: Contradictions in Liberal Democratic Responses to Global Environmental Problems", Bull of Sci Tech and Soc 19.6, (99): 493-500. **CONTACT ADDRESS** Center for Energy and Environ Policy, Univ of Delaware, Newark, DE 19716. **EMAIL** jbbyrne@udel.edu

BYRNES, JOSEPH FRANCIS
PERSONAL Born 10/25/1939, Waterbury, CT, m, 2 children **DISCIPLINE** HISTORY OF CHRISTIANITY; MODERN EUROPEAN HISTORY **EDUCATION** De Montfort Col BA, 66; Univ Notre Dame, MA, 67; Univ Chicago, MA, 74, PhD(relig & psychol), 76. **CAREER** From Asst Prof to Prof Relig Studies, 77-88, Prof History, Okla State Univ, 88-. **HONORS AND AWARDS** Fel, Inst for the Med Humanities, Univ Tex Med Branch, 80-81; Fel, Inst for the Advanced Study of Relig, Univ Chicago, 81-82; Southwestern Bell Res Fel, OSU, 89; NEH Travel Grant, 84, 91; Okla Found for the Humanities Res Grant, 90, 92, 94, 96. **MEMBERSHIPS** Am Acad Relig; Soc for Fr Hist Studies; Western Soc for Fr Hist; Am Soc of Church Hist; Cath Hist Soc. **RESEARCH** Religion and nationalism in modern France; Priests of the French Revolution. **SELECTED PUBLICATIONS** Auth, The Virgin of Chartres, Fairleigh Dickinson Univ Press, 81; The Psychology of Religion, Free Press, 84; Chateaubriand and Destutt de Tracy, Church Hist, 91; Christianity, in Rel World, Macmillan, 93; Revolutionary Festivals under the Directory, Church Hist, 94; Emile MÓle (1862-1954), Cath Hist Rev, 97. **CONTACT ADDRESS** Dept of History, Oklahoma State Univ, Stillwater, 501 Life Sciences W, Stillwater, OK 74078. **EMAIL** byr6620@okstate.edu

BYRON, KRISTINE ANN
DISCIPLINE HISPANIC STUDIES **EDUCATION** Wash Univ St Louis, BA, 90; Univ Conn, MA, 97; PhD, 01. **CAREER** Instr, Univ Conn, 92-00; asst prof, Mich State Univ, 01-. **HONORS AND AWARDS** Phi Beta Kappa; Edward Victor Grant Fel. **MEMBERSHIPS** MLA; ACIS; LASA. **RESEARCH** Women's studies; Latin American studies; Irish studies. **SELECTED PUBLICATIONS** Auth, "El Extasis de la Comunicacion: La Imagen en Tres Tristes Tigres," Torre de Papel 4 (94): 43-52; auth, "Entre la Luz y el Abismo: Voces al Atardecer de Francisco Rivera," Cinc Romance Rev (97): 127-134; auth, "(De)Constructing Historiography: 'Organic Intellectuals' and the 1933 Revolution in Cuba," Entrecaminos: J Lat Am Aff 4 (99): 43-64; rev, "Brigid," by Jill Blee, Irish Study Rev (01); auth, "Edith Dimo and Amarilis Hidalgo de Jesus," in Narradoras Venezolanas del Siglo, eds. Escritura, Desafio (INTI, 01) auth, "In the Name of the Mother': The Epilogue of Edna O' Brien's Country Girls Trilogy," Women's Study J (02). **CONTACT ADDRESS** Dept Romance Class Lang, Michigan State Univ, 258 Old Horticulture Bldg, East Lansing, MI 48824-1112. **EMAIL** kristine.byron@uconn.edu

C

CABAN, PEDRO
DISCIPLINE POLITICS AND COMPARATIVE LITERATURE, PUERTO RICAN STUDIES **EDUCATION** City Col NYork, BA; Columbia Univ, PhD. **CAREER** Assoc prof, dir, Puerto Rican and Lat Am Stud Prog, Fordham Univ; assoc prof, Rutgers, State Univ NJ, Livingston Col, 90-; ed bd, Latin Am Res Rev; bd dir, 85-91, chemn, 87-89, Inst for Puerto Rican Policy. **HONORS AND AWARDS** Fel, Ford Found; fel, Rockefeller Found. **MEMBERSHIPS** Lat Am Stud Asn; Puerto Rican Studies Asn. **RESEARCH** The nature of economic change and the role of the state in Puerto Rico during the post World War II era. **SELECTED PUBLICATIONS** Auth, Constructing a Colonial People: Puerto Rico and the United States, 1898-1932, Westview Prerss, 99. **CONTACT ADDRESS** Dept of Puerto Rican & Hisp Carib Stud, Rutgers, The State Univ of New Jersey, Livingston Col, Tillett Hall 237, Livingston, NJ 50011. **EMAIL** caban@rci.rutgers.edu

CAFFERTY, PASTORA SAN JUAN
PERSONAL Born 07/29/1940, Cienfuegos, Cuba, w **DISCIPLINE** HISTORY **EDUCATION** St. Bernard Col, BA, 62; George Washington Univ, MA 66, PhD, 71. **CAREER** Inst, Sacred Heart Acad, 62-64; inst, George Washington Univ, 67-69; spec asst to the Sec Transp, 69-70; spec asst to General Asst Sec, HUD, 70-71; sr study dir, Nat Opinion Res Ctr, 75-70, res assoc 80-88, Nat Opinion Res Ctr; asst prof, 71-76, assoc prof, 76-85, Prof, Sch of Social Serv Admin, Univ Chicago, 76- . **HONORS AND AWARDS** Wall St. J fel, 62; Smithsonian Res fel, 66-67; White House fel 69-70; Operation PUSH Woman of the Year, 75; Founder's Day Awd, 76; Outstanding Achievement Awd YWCA, 79; Dr of Humane Letters, honoris causa, Columbia Col, 87; Outstanding Achievement Awd, Girl Scouts of Amer, 89; Comm of 100, Hull House Assn, 89. **RESEARCH** Language and culture; race and ethnicity; politics and governance. **SELECTED PUBLICATIONS** Coauth, Youth and the Environment: Report to the White House, GPO, 70; auth, Chicago's Spanish-Speaking Population: Selected Statistics, Chicago Dept Develop & Planning, 73; auth, LaPolacion Hispana de Chicago, Chicago Dept Develop & Planning, 73; coauth, Diverse Society: Implication for Social Policy, Nat Assn of Social Workers, 76; coauth, Selected Bibliography on Ethnicity and Social Policy: Health Care Delivery to Meet the Changing Needs of the American Family, DHEW, 78; coauth, Politics of Language: The Dilemma of Bilingual Education for Puerto Ricans, Westview, 81; coauth, Backs Against the Wall: Urban-Oriented Colleges and Universities with the Urban Poor and Disadvantaged, Ford Found, 83; coauth, The Dilemma of Immigration in America: Beyond the Golden Door, Transaction-Rutger Univ, 83; auth, Chicago Project: A Report on Civic Life in Chicago, Crain's Business, 87; coauth, Hispanics in the USA: A New Social Agenda, Transaction-Rutger Univ, 4th ed., 94; coauth, Hispanics in the United States: A Agenda for the Twenty-First Century, Rutger Univ, 00. **CONTACT ADDRESS** Sch of Social Serv Admin, Univ of Chicago, 969 E 60th St, Chicago, IL 60637. **EMAIL** p-cafferty@uchicago.edu

CAFFREY, MARGARET M.
DISCIPLINE AMERICAN STUDIES **EDUCATION** Univ Texas, PhD 86. **CAREER** Memphis State Univ, asst prof, 88-93; Univ Memphis, assoc prof, 93-. **HONORS AND AWARDS** Facu Res Gnt; Outstnd Young Res Awd; Critics Choice Awd. **MEMBERSHIPS** SHA; ASA; OAH; Southern Asn Womens Historians. **RESEARCH** Am Women; cultural hist. **SELECTED PUBLICATIONS** Ruth Benedict: Stranger in this Land. **CONTACT ADDRESS** Dept History, Univ of Memphis, Memphis, TN 38152. **EMAIL** MCAFFREY@mocha.memphis.edu

CAGNIANT, PIERRE
PERSONAL Born 07/04/1951, Rethel, France, m, 1979, 3 children **DISCIPLINE** ROMAN HISTORY, ART, ARCHAEOLOGY **EDUCATION** Univ Paris, JD, 76; MA, 77; Univ Tex, PhD, 86; Univ Tex Law Sch, MCJ, 92. **CAREER** Assoc prof, SW Tex State Univ. **MEMBERSHIPS** AHA. **RESEARCH** Roman public and private life; Roman history and Latin literature; Roman Military; philosophy of history. **SELECTED PUBLICATIONS** Auth, "L Cornelius Sulla's Quarrel with C Marius at the Time of the Germanic Invasions (104-101 BC), Athenaeum 67 (89):139-149; auth, "L. Cornelius Sulla in the Nineties: A Reassessment," Latomus 50 (91): 285-303; auth, "Victori receptaculum, victo perfugium: Note a propos des camps de marche de l'armee romaine," Les Etudes Classiques 60 (92): 217-234; auth, "Studies on Caesar's use of Cavalry during the Gallic War, 58-50 BC," Ancient World 23 (92):71-85; auth, "Strategy and Politics in Caesar's Spanish Campaign, 49 BC: Variation on a Theme by Clausewitz," Ancient World (95): 29-44; auth, "The Persian and the Greek World," and "The Hellenistic World and the Rise of Rome," and "The Roman World," in World History: Continuity and Change, ed. W T Hanes (Holt, Rinehart and Winston, 97); auth, "Le soldat et l'armee dans le th¤¤tre de Plaute: L'antimilitarisme de Plaute, Latomus 58 (99): 753-779; auth, "The Philosopher and the Gladiator," Classical World (forthcoming); auth, "Seneca's Attitude towards Sport and Athletics," Ancient History Bulletin (forthcoming). **CONTACT ADDRESS** Dept History, Southwest Texas State Univ, 601 University Dr, San Marcos, TX 78666-4685.

CAHAN, DAVID
DISCIPLINE HISTORY OF SCIENCE **EDUCATION** Johns Hopkins Univ, PhD, 80. **CAREER** Prof, Univ Nebr, Lincoln. **HONORS AND AWARDS** Nat Sci Found Award, 85; NEH fel, 94-96; vis fel, Ctr de la Recherche en Hist des Sci et des Techniques, Paris, Fr, 97; Fulbright Res Fel Reicpient to the Federal Republic of Germany, 75-76. **MEMBERSHIPS** Hist of Sci Soc. **RESEARCH** 19th century German scientist Hermann von Helmholtz; 19th century sci; Sci and soc, 1600-. **SELECTED PUBLICATIONS** Auth, An Institute for an Empire: The Physikalisch-Technische Reichsanstalt, 1871-1918, Cambridge UP, 89; ed, Letters of Hermann von Helmholtz to His Parents: the Medical Education of a German Scientist, 1837-1846, Stuttgart: Franz Steiner Verlag, 93; ed and contrib, Hermann von Helmholtz and the Fuondations of Nineteenth-Centruy Science, Berkeley, Los Angeles, and Oxford: Univ of calif Press, 94; ed and transl, Science and Culture: Popular and Philosophical Essays, Chicago and London: Univ of Chicago Press, 95; coauth, Sciene at the American Frontier: A Biography of DeWitt Bristol Brace, Lincoln and London: Univ of Nebraska Press, 00. **CONTACT ADDRESS** Univ of Nebraska, Lincoln, 629 Oldfather, Lincoln, NE 68588-0417. **EMAIL** dcahan@unlnotes.unl.edu

CAINE, STANLEY PAUL
PERSONAL Born 02/11/1940, Huron, SD, m, 1964, 3 children **DISCIPLINE** AMERICAN HISTORY **EDUCATION** Macalester Col, BA, 62; Univ Wis-Madison, MS, 64, PhD(hist), 67. **CAREER** Asst prof hist, Lindenwood Cols, 67-71 & DePauw Univ, 71-77; Prof Hist & V Pres Acad Affairs, Hanover Col, 77- **MEMBERSHIPS** Orgn Am Historians; Nat Humanities Fac. **RESEARCH** Late 19th century American history; early 20th century America. **SELECTED PUBLICATIONS** Auth, The Myth of a Progressive Reform, State Hist Soc Wis, 70; Why railroads supported regulation: The case of Wisconsin, 1905-1910, Bus Hist Rev, summer 70; co-ed, Political reform in Wisconsin. **CONTACT ADDRESS** Hanover Col, Hanover, IN 47243.

CAIRNS, HUGH A. C.
PERSONAL Born 03/02/1930, Galt, ON, Canada **DISCIPLINE** LAW, POLITICAL SCIENCE, HISTORY **EDUCATION** Univ Toronto, BA, 53, MA, 57; St. Antony's Col, Oxford Univ, Dphil, 63. **CAREER** Instr to prof, polit sci, 60-95, chmn, 73-80, PROF EMER, UNIV BC, 95-; vis prof, Memorial Univ Nfld, 70-71; vis prof, Can stud, Univ Edinburgh, 77-78; vis prof, Can stud, Harvard Univ 82-83; Brenda and David McLean ch Can stud, 93-95; John Willis vis prof law, Univ Toronto, 95-96; PROF AND LAW FOUNDATION OF SASK CHAIR, COLLEGE OF LAW, UNIV OF SASKATCHEWAN, 97-. **HONORS AND AWARDS** Gold Medal Polit Sci & Econ, 53; Queen's Silver Jubilee Medal, 77; Pres Medal Univ Western Ont, 77; Molson Prize Can Coun, 82; Killam res fel, 89-91; Gov Gen Int Awd Can Stud, 94; DLaws(hon), Carleton Univ, 94; DLaws(hon), Univ Toronto, 96; DLaws(hon), Univ BC, 98. **MEMBERSHIPS** Can Polit Sci Asn (pres, 76-77); Int Polit Sci Asn (mem coun, 76-79). **SELECTED PUBLICATIONS** Auth, Prelude to Imperialism: British Reactions to Central African Society 1840-1890, 65; coauth, A Survey of the Contemporary Indians of Canada: Economic, Political and Educational Needs and Policies, vol 1, 66; coauth, Constitution, Government and Society in Canada: Selected Essays by Alan C. Cairns, 88; coauth, Disruptions: Constitutional Struggles from the Charter to Meech Lake, 91; coauth, Charter versus Federalism: The Dilemmas of Constitutional Reform, 92; coauth, Reconfigurations: Canadian Citizenship and Constitutional Change, 95. **CONTACT ADDRESS** 1866 Main Mall, Vancouver, BC, Canada V6T 1Z1.

CALDER, LENDOL
PERSONAL Born 11/19/1958, Beaumont, TX, m, 1990, 2 children **DISCIPLINE** HISTORY **EDUCATION** Univ Tex, BA, 80; Univ Chicago, MA, 86, PhD, 93. **CAREER** Asst prof, Univ Wash, 92-93; asst prof, Colby-Sawyer Col, 93-96; asst prof, Augustana Col, 96-. **HONORS AND AWARDS** Phi Beta Kappa, 79; Charles Kennedy Awd, 96, Econ Bus Hist Soc. **MEMBERSHIPS** Org Am Hist. **RESEARCH** Consumer culture; the sixties; US social and cultural hist. **SELECTED PUBLICATIONS** Auth, Financing the American Dream: A Cultural History of Consumer Credit, 99. **CONTACT ADDRESS** Dept of History, Augustana Col, Illinois, 639 38th St, Rock Island, IL 61201. **EMAIL** hicalder@augustana.edu

CALDWELL, L. K.
PERSONAL Born 11/21/1913, Montezuma, IA, m, 1940, 2 children **DISCIPLINE** HISTORY, GOVERNMENT **EDUCATION** Univ Chicago, PhB, 34 PhD, 43; Harvard Univ, MA, 38; Western Mich Univ, LLD, 77. **CAREER** Dir Res, Council of State Governments, 44-47; prof polit sci, Syracuse Univ, 47-53; co-dir, Public Admin Inst for Turkey and Middle East, United Nations, 53-54; vis prof, Univ Calif, Berkeley, 54-55; prof Polit Sci & Public and Environ Affairs to Arthur F. Bentley prof emer , Indiana Univ, 55- . **HONORS AND AWARDS** UN Global 500, 91; John Gaus Awd, Am Polit Sci Asn, 96; Natural Rsrc Coun Awd, 97; Hon Life Member, Int Asn of Impact Assessment; fel, Am Asn for Advanc of Sci; fel, Nat Acad of Public Admin; fel, Royal Soc of the Arts. **MEMBERSHIPS** Am Polit Sci Asn; Am Soc for Public Admin; Asn for Polit and Life Sci. **RESEARCH** Public policy, law, and administration; policy for science, technology, and the environment. **SELECTED PUBLICATIONS** Coauth, Policy for Land: Law and Ethics, Rowman and Littlefield, 93; auth, Environment as a Focus for Public Policy, Texas A & M, 95; co-ed, Environmental Policy: Transnational Issues and National Trends, Quorum, 96; auth, International Environmental Policy, 3d ed, Duke, 96; auth, Scientific Assumptions and Misplaced Certainty in Natural Resources and Environmental problem-Solving, in Lemons, ed, Scientific Uncertainty and Environmental Problem-Solving, Blackwell, 96; auth, Implications for a World Economy for Environmental Policy and Law, in Dasgupta, ed, The Economics of Transnational Commons, Oxford, 97; auth, The national Environmental Policy Act: Agenda for the Future, Indiana, 98; auth, The Concept of Sustainability: A Critical Approach, in Lemons, Ecological Sustainability and Integrity; Concepts and Approaches, Kluwer Academic, 98. **CONTACT ADDRESS** School of Public and Environmental Affairs, Indiana Univ, Bloomington, 1315 E Tenth St, Bloomington, IN 47405. **EMAIL** lkcaldwe@indiana.edu

CALDWELL, RONALD JAMES
PERSONAL Born 07/02/1943, Pensacola, FL, m, 1966, 2 children **DISCIPLINE** MODERN EUROPEAN HISTORY **EDUCATION** Fla State Univ, BS, 65; MA, 66; PhD, 71; M.L.I.S., Univ Al, 88. **CAREER** Instr hist, Orlando Jr Col, 66-68; assoc prof hist, 71-83, prof of hist, 83-99; prof emeritus, 99-, Jacksonville State Univ. **MEMBERSHIPS** AHA; Southern Hist Asn; Soc Fr Hist Studies. **RESEARCH** Political history of the French Revolution. **SELECTED PUBLICATIONS** The Era of the French Revolution: A Bibliography of the History of Western Civilization, 1789-1799, 85; The Era of Napolean: A Bibliography of the History of Western Civilization, 1799-1815, 91. **CONTACT ADDRESS** Dept of Hist, Jacksonville State Univ, 700 Pelham Rd N, Jacksonville, AL 36265-1602. **EMAIL** rcaldwel@jsucc.jsu.edu

CALHOON, ROBERT M.
PERSONAL Born 10/03/1935, Pittsburgh, PA, m, 1966 **DISCIPLINE** AMERICAN HISTORY **EDUCATION** Wooster Col, BA, 58; Western Reserve Univ, MA, 49, PhD, 64. **CAREER** Jr high sch teacher, Ohio, 59-60; from instr to assoc prof, 64-74, prof hist, Univ Nc, Greensboro, 74-; vis asst prof hist, Univ Conn, 66-67. **HONORS AND AWARDS** Fel, Duke-Univ NC Prog Humanities, 69-70; Nat Endowment Humanities res grant, 75; fel, ACLS Ford; fel, Dew Christian Scholars, 98-99. **MEMBERSHIPS** AHA; Orgn Am Historians; Southern Hist Assn. **RESEARCH** Early American political and intellectual history; the American Revolution; religion and cultural change in the south, 1750-1840. **SELECTED PUBLICATIONS** Auth, The Loyalists in Revolutionary America, 1760-1781, 73; auth, Revolutionary America: An Interpretive Overview, Harcourt, 76; ed, Religion and the American Revolution in North Carolina, NC Div Archives & Hist, 76; auth, A Troubled Culture: North Carolina in the New Nation, Writing North Carolina History, 79; Evangelicals and Conservations in The Early South 1740-1861, 88; The Logalist Perception and Other Essays, 89; Doinion and Liberty, 94. **CONTACT ADDRESS** Dept of History, Univ of No Carolina, Greensboro, 1000 Spring Garden, PO Box 6170, Greensboro, NC 27402-6170. **EMAIL** vmcalhoo@uncg.edu

CALHOUN, CHARLES W.
PERSONAL Born 02/24/1948, South Bend, IN, m, 1972, 1 child **DISCIPLINE** HISTORY **EDUCATION** Yale Univ, BA, 70; Columbia Univ, MA, 72, MPhil, 74; PhD, 77. **CAREER** Prof, Austin Peay State Univ, 78-89; hist dept chemn, Austin Peay State Univ, 87-89; prof, E Carolina Univ, 89-; hist dept chemn, E Carolina Univ, 89-92; general ed, The Human Tradition in American History series, Scholarly Resources, 96-. **HONORS AND AWARDS** NEH Fel, 88-89. **MEMBERSHIPS** Am Hist Asn, Orgn of Am Historians, Southern Hist Asn, Soc for Historians of Am For Relations, Soc for Historians of the Gilded Age and Progressive Era. **RESEARCH** The Gilded Age, Nineteenth-century U. S. Politics. **SELECTED PUBLICATIONS** Co-ed, Biographical Directory of the Ind General Assembly, 1816-1899, Ind Hist Bureau, 80; auth, Gilded Age Cato: The Life of Walter Q. Gresham, Univ Pr of Ky, 88; auth, The Gilded Age: Essays on the Origins of Modern America, Scholarly Resources, 96. **CONTACT ADDRESS** Dept Hist, East Carolina Univ, 1000 E 5th St, Greenville, NC 27858-2502. **EMAIL** calhounc@mail.ecu.edu

CALHOUN, DANIEL FAIRCHILD
PERSONAL Born 06/21/1929, Bridgeport, CT, m, 1952, 3 children **DISCIPLINE** MODERN HISTORY **EDUCATION** Williams Col, AB, 50; Univ Chicago, MA, 51, PhD(hist), 59. **CAREER** From instr to assoc prof, 56-66, Prof Hist, Col Wooster, 66-94, prof emer, 94-. **MEMBERSHIPS** AHA. **RESEARCH** Russian history; Anglo-Soviet relations. **SELECTED PUBLICATIONS** Auth, Hungary and Suez, 56; auth, The United Front: The TUC and the Russians, 1923-1928, Cambridge Univ, 76; auth, An Exploration of Who Makes History, Univ Press of America, 91. **CONTACT ADDRESS** Dept of Hist, The Col of Wooster, Wooster, OH 44691. **EMAIL** dcalhour@acs.wooster.edu

CALHOUN, ROBERT M.
PERSONAL Born 10/03/1935, Pittsburgh, PA, m, 1966, 1 child **DISCIPLINE** HISTORY **EDUCATION** Col Wooster, BA, 58; Western Reserve Univ, 59, PhD; 64. **CAREER** Instr, 64-65; Asst Prof, 65-69; Assoc Prof, 69-74; Prof, 74-, Univ of North Carolina at Greensboro. **HONORS AND AWARDS** Univ of North Carolina/Duke Univ Co-operative Program in the Humanities, Fellow, 69-70; National Endowment in the Humanities, Research Grant, 75; Ford Fel, 83. **MEMBERSHIPS** Amer Council of Learned Societies; Endowment Evangelical Scholars Fellowship, 98-99; Southern Historical Assoc; Historical Society of North Carolina; North Carolina Literary and Historical Assoc; Center on Religion in the South; The Historical Society; Organization of Amer Historians. **RESEARCH** Amer Revolution; Loyalists; Southern Religious History; Political Moderation. **SELECTED PUBLICATIONS** Auth, "The Loyalists in Revolutionary America, 1760-1781; auth, "Revolutionary America: An Interpretive Overview;" "Evangelicals and Conservatives in the Early South, 1740-1861;" "The Loyalist Perception and Other Essays;" "Dominion and Liberty: Ideology in the Anglo-American World, 1660-1801." **CONTACT ADDRESS** Dept History, Univ of No Carolina, Greensboro, PO Box 26170, Greensboro, NC 27402-6170. **EMAIL** rmcalhoo@uncg.edu

CALKINS, KENNETH ROY
PERSONAL Born 02/19/1935, Detroit, MI, m, 1966, 3 children **DISCIPLINE** MODERN EUROPEAN HISTORY **EDUCATION** Haverford Col, BA, 57; Univ Chicago, MA, 58, PhD(hist), 66. **CAREER** From instr to asst prof hist, Lake Forest Col, 63-67; asst prof, 67-75, assoc prof, 75-81, Prof Hist, Kent State Univ, 81-, Nat coun, AAUP, 81-84. **MEMBERSHIPS** AHA. **RESEARCH** Late 19th and 20th century German and Austrian history; the development of European Socialism. **SELECTED PUBLICATIONS** Auth, Hugo Haase: Demokrat and Revolutionar, Colloquium, Berlin, 76. **CONTACT ADDRESS** Dept of Hist, Kent State Univ, Kent, OH 44240.

CALKINS, ROBERT GILMER
PERSONAL Born 12/29/1932, Oakland, CA, m, 1962, 3 children **DISCIPLINE** HISTORY OF ART **EDUCATION** Princeton Univ, AB, 55; Harvard Univ, MA, 62, PhD, 67. **CAREER** Assoc prof, 66-80, chmn dept, 76-81, Prof Hist of Art, Cornell Univ, 80-, Am Coun Learned Soc grant-in-aid, 73; Am Philos Soc grant-in-aid, 80. **MEMBERSHIPS** Col Art Asn Am; Mediaeval Acad Am; Int Ctr Medieval Art. **RESEARCH** Fifteenth century manuscript illumination; Medieval architecture; Flemish painting. **SELECTED PUBLICATIONS** Auth, A Medieval Treasury, Medieval Art Exhib Catalogue, Cornell Univ, 10/68; Medieval and Renaissance Illuminated Manuscripts in the Cornell University Library, Cornell Libr J, 5/72; Stages of Execution: Procedures of Illumination as Revealed in an Unfinished Book of Hours, Gesta, 78; Parallels Between Inculabula and Manuscripts from the Circle of the Master of Catherine of Cleves, Oud Holland, 78; Distribution of Labor: The Illuminators of the Hours of Catherine of Cleves and Their Workshop, Trans of Am Philos Soc, 79; Monuments of Medieval Art, E P Dutton, 79; An Italian in Paris: The Master of the Brussels Initials and His Participation in the French Book Industry, Gesta, 81; auth The Question of the Origins of the Master of Catherine of Cleves, Masters and Miniatures: Proceedings of the Congress on Medieval Manuscript Illumination in the Northern Netherlands, 92; Pictorial Emphases in Early Biblical Manuscripts, The Bible in the Middle Ages: Its Influence on Literature and Art, Medieval and Renaissance Texts and Studies, 92; Narrative in Image and Text in Medieval Illuminated Manuscripts, Medieval Perspectives, 92; Secular Objects and Their Implications in Early Netherlandish Painting, Art into Life: Collected Papers from the Kresge Art Museum Symposia, Mich State Univ Press, 95; The Cathedral as Text, Hum, 95; Medieval Architecture in Western Europe from AD 300 to 1500, Oxford Univ Press, 98; auth, Gerard Horenbout and his Associates: Illuminating Activities in Ghent, 1480-1521, In Detail: New Studies of Northern Renaissance Art in Honor of Walter Gibson, Brepols, 98. **CONTACT ADDRESS** Dept Hist of Art, Cornell Univ, Goldwin Smith Hall, Ithaca, NY 14850. **EMAIL** rgc1@cornell.edu

CALLAHAN, DANIEL FRANCIS
PERSONAL Born 11/28/1939, Boston, MA, m, 1974, 3 children **DISCIPLINE** MEDIEVAL & CHURCH HISTORY **EDUCATION** St John's Sem, Mass, BA, 62; Boston Col, MA, 66; Univ Wis-Madison, PhD(hist), 68. **CAREER** Asst prof to prof hist, Univ Delaware, 68-. **HONORS AND AWARDS** Am Coun Learned Soc grant, 82. **MEMBERSHIPS** Medieval Acad Am; AHA; Am Cath Hist Asn. **RESEARCH** The church in France, 750-1050; Medieval pilgrimages. **SELECTED PUBLICATIONS** Auth, "Ademar of Chabannes, Millennial Fears and the Development of Western Anti-Judaism," The J of Ecclesiastical Hist, 46 (95): 19-35; auth, "When Heaven Came Down to Earth: The Family of St. Martial of Limoges and the 'Terrors of the Year 1000,'" in Portraits of Medieval and Renaissance Living: Essays in Memory of David Herlihy, ed. S. Cohn and S. Epstein (Ann Arbor, 95), 245-258; auth, "Ecclesia Semper Reformanda: Clerical Celibacy and Reform in the Church," in Medieval Piety and Purity, ed. M. Frassetto (New York, 98), 377-388. **CONTACT ADDRESS** Dept of Hist, Univ of Delaware, Newark, DE 19711. **EMAIL** dfcao@udel.edu

CALLAHAN, RAYMOND ALOYSIUS
PERSONAL Born 11/30/1938, Trenton, NJ, m, 1964, 2 children **DISCIPLINE** MODERN BRITISH HISTORY **EDUCATION** Georgetown Univ, AB, 61; Harvard Univ, MA, 62, PhD(hist), 67. **CAREER** From asst prof to assoc prof, 67-76, Prof Hist, Univ Del, 76- **MEMBERSHIPS** AHA; Conf Brit Studies; Am Comt Hist Second World War; Am Comt Irish Studies. **RESEARCH** Modern Britain; British empire; Second World War. **SELECTED PUBLICATIONS** Auth, Cornwallis and the Indian Army, Mil Affairs, 70; The East India Company and Army Reform, Harvard Univ, 72; What about the Dardanelles?, Am Hist Rev, 73; The Illusion of Security: Singapore 1919-1942, J Contemp Hist, 74; The Worst Disaster: The Fall of Singapore, Univ Del, 77; Burma 1942-45, Davis-Poynter Ltd, 78; Servants of the Raj: The Jacob Family in India, J Soc Army Hist Res, 78. **CONTACT ADDRESS** Dept of Hist, Univ of Delaware, 401 KOF, Newark, DE 19711.

CALLAHAN, WILLIAM JAMES
PERSONAL Born 01/22/1937, Winchester, MA **DISCIPLINE** EARLY MODERN EUROPEAN HISTORY **EDUCATION** Boston Col, AB, 58; Harvard Univ, AM, 59, PhD,hist, 64. **CAREER** From asst prof to assoc prof, 65-75, Prof Hist, Univ Toronto, 75-00; prof emer, Univ of Toronto, 00. **MEMBERSHIPS** Soc Span-Port Hist Studies, Can Hist Asn. **RESEARCH** Early modern and 18th century Spain. **SELECTED PUBLICATIONS** Auth, La Santa y Real Hermandad del Refugio y Piedad de Madrid 1618-1832; auth, Church, Politics, and Society in Spain 1750-1874, 84; auth, The Catholic Church in Spain 1875-1998, 00. **CONTACT ADDRESS** Dept of Hist, Univ of Toronto, 100 St George St, Room 2074, Sidney Smith Hall, Toronto, ON, Canada M5S 3G3. **EMAIL** wj.callahan@utoronto.ca

CAMERON, ALAN
PERSONAL Born 03/13/1938, Windsor, England, m, 1961, 2 children **DISCIPLINE** CLASSICAL PHILOLOGY, BYZANTINE STUDIES **EDUCATION** Oxford Univ, BA, 61, MA, 64. **CAREER** Lectr Latin, Univ Glasgow, 61-64, Bedord Col, Univ London, 64-71 & Kings Col, 72-76; Anthon Prof Latin, Columbia Univ, 77- **HONORS AND AWARDS** N H Baynes Prize, London Univ, 67; J Conington Prize, Oxford Univ, 68; fel, British Acad, 75. **MEMBERSHIPS** Soc Roman Studies; Am Philol Asn; fel Am Acad Arts & Sci. **RESEARCH** Latin literature; Roman history; Byzantine history and literature. **SELECTED PUBLICATIONS CONTACT ADDRESS** Columbia Univ, 2960 Broadway, New York, NY 10027-6900.

CAMERON, JAMES D.
DISCIPLINE HISTORY **EDUCATION** Univ Prince Edward Island, BA, 81; BEd, 81; Acadia Univ, MA, 85; Queen's Univ, PhD, 90. **CAREER** Hist Prof, St francis Xavier Univ. **SELECTED PUBLICATIONS** Auth, pubs about Canadian higher education; Canadian congregations of women religious; and Celtic fiddle music; auth, For the People: A History of St Francis Xavier Univ. **CONTACT ADDRESS** History Dept, St. Francis Xavier Univ, Antigonish, NS, Canada B2G 2W5. **EMAIL** jdcamero@stfx.ca

CAMERON, JAMES REESE
PERSONAL Born 08/27/1929, Columbus, OH, m, 1950, 2 children **DISCIPLINE** HISTORY **EDUCATION** Eastern Nazarene Col, AB, 51; Boston Univ, MA, 52, PhD, 59. **CAREER** Instr hist, 51-55; asst prof to assoc prof, 55-64, prof, 64-, Eastern Nazarene Col. **MEMBERSHIPS** AHA; Mediaeval Acad Am; Conf Brit Studies; fel Pilgrim Soc. **RESEARCH** English constitutional history; history of the Middle Ages; Massachusetts local history. **SELECTED PUBLICATIONS** Auth, Frederick William Maitland and the History of English Law, Greenwood, 77; auth, The Public Career of Josiah Quincy, 1802-1882, Quincy Coop Bank, 62; art, The Christian Perspective and The Teaching of Political Science, J Am Sci Affil, 66; auth, New Beginnings: Quincy and Norfolk County, Massachusetts, Quincy Hist Soc, 66; auth, Eastern Nazarene College: The First Fifty Years, 1900-1950, Nazarene Publ House, 68; auth, Church on the Campus, Wollaston Church of the Nazarene, 72; auth, Economic Life, Quincy, 350 Years, City of Quincy, Mass, 74; ed, Calendar of the papers of General Joseph Palmer, 1716-1788, Quincy Hist Soc, 78; auth, Semper Fidelis: The Life of James R. McIntyre, ENC Press, 90; auth, The Spirit Makes the Difference: Eastern Nazarene College, 1948-98, ENC Press, 00. **CONTACT ADDRESS** Dept of History, Eastern Nazarene Col, 23 E Elm Ave, Quincy, MA 02170. **EMAIL** cameronj@enc.edu

CAMFIELD, THOMAS M.
DISCIPLINE HISTORY **EDUCATION** Univ Tex at Austin, BA, PhD; Univ Calif Berkeley, MA. **CAREER** Sr tenured prof, Sam Houston State Univ, 69-; **RESEARCH** American social and intellectual history, late 19th and early 20th-century america. **SELECTED PUBLICATIONS** Auth, The American Psychological Association and World War I, in The American Psychological Association: A Historical Perspective, 93; rev, A Can or Two of Worms: Virginia Bernhard and the Historiography of Early Virginia, 1607-1610, J Southern Hist, 94; co-ed, Exploring United States History. **CONTACT ADDRESS** Dept of History, Sam Houston State Univ, Huntsville, TX 77341.

CAMP, HELEN C.
PERSONAL Born 02/19/1939, Mobile, AL, m, 1959, 1 child **DISCIPLINE** HISTORY **EDUCATION** Univ Missouri, AB, 68; Columbia Univ, MA, 70; PhD, 80. **CAREER** Adj prof, Manhattan Col, 73-78; adj prof, Brooklyn Col, 81; adj prof, Baruch Col, 81; adj prof, Lehman Col, 82-85; adj prof, Empire State Col, 84-85; adj prof, NYU, 87; adj prof, Pace Univ, 85-96; assoc prof, 98-00. **MEMBERSHIPS** Coord Comm Women Hist Profession, IRH; OAH; AHA. **SELECTED PUBLICATIONS** Rev, Regulating Danger: The Struggle for Mine Safety in the Rocky Mountain Coal Industry, West Hist Quart, 91; contrib auth, World Leaders, ed. Carol Nagy (Detroit, 94); contrib auth, American National Biography, ed. John Garraty (Oxford Univ Press, NY, forthcoming); contrib auth, Encyclopedia of Protest Movements, ed. Irwin Unger (Gale Group, Farmington Hill, forthcoming); co-ed, From World War to Cold War and Beyond: Readings in Foreign and Domestic Policy (NY, 95); assoc ed, Women and History, Inst Res Hist and Hawthorn Press, 80-82; auth, Iron in Her Soul: Elizabeth Gurley Flynn and the American Left, Wash St Univ Press (Pullman, WA), 95. **CONTACT ADDRESS** 8818 Dolphin Lane, Gulf Shores, AL 36547.

CAMP, RICHARD
PERSONAL Born 03/31/1936, Yankton, SD, m, 1963 **DISCIPLINE** MODERN EUROPEAN HISTORY **EDUCATION** Goshen Col, BA, 58; Columbia Univ, MA, 60, PhD(hist), 65. **CAREER** Asst prof Europ hist, Goshen Col, 62-65; Prof Hist & Coordr Interdisciplinary Humanities Prog, Calif State Univ, Northridge, 65- **MEMBERSHIPS** AHA; Soc Italian Hist Studies; AAUP; Conf Group Women's Hist. **RESEARCH** Italy in the 19th and 20th centuries; social and intellectual history of modern Europe; women in Italy and Europe since 1815. **SELECTED PUBLICATIONS** Auth, The Papal Ideology of Social Reform: A Study in Historical Development, 1878-1967, Brill, 69; Corporate reform or comanagement, Am Ecclesiastical Rev, 5/71. **CONTACT ADDRESS** Dept of Hist, California State Univ, Northridge, Northridge, CA 91324.

CAMPBELL, BALLARD C.
PERSONAL Born 11/30/1940, Orange, NJ, m, 1988, 3 children **DISCIPLINE** AMERICAN HISTORY **EDUCATION** Northwestern Univ, BA, 62; Northeastern Univ, MA, 64; Univ Wisc, Madison, PhD, 70. **CAREER** Inst, 69-70, Asst Prof, 70-76, Assoc Prof, 76-82, Prof, 82-, Dept Hist, NorthEastern Univ; Pres, (SHGAPE), 02-04. **HONORS AND AWARDS** Fellow, Charles Warren Ctr, 76-77; Fellow, Am Coun of Learned Soc, 82. **MEMBERSHIPS** AHA; OAH; Soc Sci Hist Asn; Econ Hist Asn, SHGAPE. **RESEARCH** American governmental history; economic & business history, Comparative history. **SELECTED PUBLICATIONS** Auth, Representative Democracy, Harvard Univ Press, 80; auth, Federalism and American Legislatures, Encyclopedia of the American Legislative System, Charles Scribner Sons, I, 71-88, 94; auth, The Growth of American Government: Governance from the Cleveland Era to the Present, Ind Univ Press, 95; auth, Public Policy and State Government, The Gilded Age: Essays on the Origins of Modern America, Schol Res Inc, 309-329, 96; auth, Tax Revolts and Political Change, J of Policy Hist, 10, 153-178, 98; ed, contributor, The Human Tradition in the Gilded Age and Progressive Era, Scholarly Resources, 00. **CONTACT ADDRESS** Dept Hist, Northeastern Univ, 360 Huntington Ave, Boston, MA 02115. **EMAIL** campbell@neu.edu

CAMPBELL, JOAN
PERSONAL Born 06/22/1929, Berlin, Germany, m, 1954, 4 children **DISCIPLINE** MODERN EUROPEAN HISTORY, GERMAN HISTORY **EDUCATION** Radcliffe Col, BA, 50; Oxford Univ, MA, 52; Queen's Univ, Ont, PhD(hist), 75. **CAREER** Asst Prof Hist, Univ Toronto, 77- **MEMBERSHIPS** AHA; Can Hist Asn. **RESEARCH** German Werkbund; the idea of Arbeitsfreude (joy in work). **SELECTED PUBLICATIONS** Auth, At the Turn of a Civilization--Jones, David and Modern Poetics, Rel & Lit, Vol 0027, 95; At the Turn of a Civilization--Jones, David and Modern Poetics, Rel & Lit, Vol 0027, 95; The Language of Gender and Class--Transformation in the Victorian Novel, Intl Fiction Rev, Vol 0024, 97; New Women, New Novels--Feminism and Early Modernism, Intl Fiction Rev, Vol 0019, 92; Country Parsons, Country Poets--Hebert,George and Hopkins, Gerard, Manley as Spiritual Autobiographers, Rel and Lit, Vol 0026, 94; The Concept of Work--Ancient, Medieval, and Modern, Amer Hist Rev, Vol 0099, 94; Visions of Modernity--American Business and the Modernization of Germany, Amer Hist Rev, Vol 0101, 96; Labor and Power in the Iron-And-Steel-Industry--Industrial and Labor-Relations in the German and American Iron-and-Steel-Industry from the 1860s to the 1930s-Ger, Amer Hist Rev, Vol 0100, 95; Protecting Motherhood--Women and the Family in the Politics of Postwar West-Germany, Labor Hist, Vol 0035, 94. **CONTACT ADDRESS** 43 Cross St, Dundas, ON, Canada L9H 2R5.

CAMPBELL, JOHN COERT
PERSONAL Born 10/08/1911, New York, NY **DISCIPLINE** EASTERN EUROPEAN HISTORY **EDUCATION** Harvard Univ, AB, 33, AM, 36, PhD, 40. **CAREER** Instr polit sci, Univ Louisville, 40-41; Rockefeller fel, 41-42; div asst, US Dept State, 42-46; ed, Coun Foreign Rels, 46-49; officer-in-chg Balkan Affairs, US Dept State, 49-52 & Nat War Col, 52-53; mem policy planning staff, US Dept State, 53-55; dir polit studies & sr res fel, Coun Foreign Rels, 55-78; Consult & Adv, US Dept State, 63-, Consult, US Dept State, 63-67 & 68-, mem policy planning coun, 67-68; mem joint comt Slavic studies, Am Coun Learned Soc--Soc Sci Res Coun, 65-67; vis lectr, Columbia Univ, 68; consult, Brookings Inst, 72-73. **MEMBERSHIPS** Int Studies Asn; Am Asn Advan Slavic Studies; Mideast Inst (vpres, 67-77); Mideast Studies Asn; AHA. **RESEARCH** United States foreign relations; Balkan history; Middle East studies. **SELECTED PUBLICATIONS** Auth, Moscow and the Middle-East--Soviet-Policy Since the Invasion of Afghanistan, Russian Rev, Vol 0052, 93; Beacons in the Night--With the Oss and Tito Partisans in Wartime Yugoslavia, Jour Amer Hist, Vol 0081, 94; Yugoslavias Bloody Collapse--Causes, Course and Consequences, Amer Hist Rev, Vol 0101, 96; Nationalism and Federalism in Yugoslavia, 1962-1991, 2nd Edition, Amer Hist Rev, Vol 0098, 93. **CONTACT ADDRESS** 220 S Main St, Cohasset, MA 02025.

CAMPBELL, JOHN POLLOCK
PERSONAL Born 06/03/1933, New Milns, Scotland **DISCIPLINE** MODERN HISTORY **EDUCATION** Glasgow Univ, MA, 55; Yale Univ, MA, 59 PhD,hist, 61. **CAREER** Asst prof, 62-68, Assoc Prof Hist, McMaster Univ, 68- **MEMBERSHIPS** AHA; Orgn Am Historians. **RESEARCH** United States Foreign Policy in 20th Century, Military History since 1914. **CONTACT ADDRESS** 479 Dundurn St S, Hamilton, ON, Canada L8P 4M2. **EMAIL** jcampbel@mcmaster.ca

CAMPBELL, MARY SCHMIDT
PERSONAL Born 10/21/1947, Philadelphia, PA, m, 1968 **DISCIPLINE** ART HISTORY **EDUCATION** Swarthmore Coll, BA English Lit 1969; Syracuse Univ, MA art history 1973, PhD, 1982. **CAREER** Syracuse University, Syracuse, NY, lecturer; Nkumbi Intl Coll, Kabwe, Zambia, instr, 69-71; Syracuse New Times, writer, art editor, 73-77; Everson Museum, curator, guest curator, 74-76; The Studio Museum in Harlem, exec dir, 77-87; New York City Department of Cultural Affairs, New York, commissioner, 87-91; Tisch School, Dean, 91-. **HONORS AND AWARDS** Ford Fellow, 1973-77; Rockefeller Fellowship in the Humanities, 1985; Municipal Art Society Certificate, 1985; Candace Awd, 100 Black Women, 1986; consultant to the Ford Foundation as part of their mid-decade review; lectures on American & African-American Art, The Studio Museum in Harlem and the issues involved in the Institutionalization of Diverse Cultures and Public Policy and the Arts; City College, NY, Honorary Doctorate, 1992. **MEMBERSHIPS** Chair, Student Life Committee, Swarthmore College Board of Managers, 1991-; member, Visiting Committee on Fine Arts, Harvard College Board of Overseers, 1991-93; chair, Advisory Committee for African American Institutional Study, Smithsonian Institute, 1989-91; advisory board member , Barnes Foundation, 1991-; fellow, Institute for Humanities, New York University, 1989-. **SELECTED PUBLICATIONS** Author, Black American Art & Harlem Renaissance, 1987; author of numerous articles on Black American art. **CONTACT ADDRESS** Tisch Sch of the Arts, New York Univ, 721 Broadway, New York, NY 10003.

CAMPBELL, RANDOLPH B.
PERSONAL Born 11/16/1940, Charlottesville, VA, m, 1962, 2 children **DISCIPLINE** HISTORY **EDUCATION** Univ Va, BS, 61; MA, 63; PhD, 66. **CAREER** Asst prof, N Tex St Univ, 66-69; assoc prof, 69-77; prof, 77-. **HONORS AND AWARDS** Phi Beta Kappa. **MEMBERSHIPS** OAH; SHA; TSHA; SHEAR; The Hist Soc. **RESEARCH** Nineteenth-century Texas. **SELECTED PUBLICATIONS** Auth, A Southern Community in Crisis: Harrison County, Texas, 1850-1880, Texas State Hist Asn (Austin), 83; auth, An Empire for Slavery: The Peculiar Institution in Texas, 1821-1865, Louisiana State Univ Press (Baton Rouge), 89, pb ed, 91; auth, Sam Houston and the American Southwest, HarperCollins Publishers (NY), 93; auth, Grass-Roots Reconstruction in Texas, 1865-1880 Louisiana State Univ Press (Baton Rouge), 98; auth, "The Slave-Hire System in Texas: A Research Note," Am Hist Rev 93 (88): 107-14; auth, "Grass Roots Reconstruction: The Personnel of County Government in Texas, 1865-1876," J Southern Hist (92): 99-116; auth, "Carpetbagger Rule in Reconstruction Texas: An Enduring Myth," Southwestern Hist Quart (94): 587-596; auth, "Reconstruction in McLennan County, Texas, 1865-1876," Prologue: Quart Nat Arch (95): 17-35. **CONTACT ADDRESS** Dept History, Univ of No Texas, PO Box 310650, Denton, TX 76203-0650. **EMAIL** rbc0003@unt.edu

CAMPBELL, STUART LORIN
PERSONAL Born 04/15/1938, Whittier, CA, m, 1960, 1 child **DISCIPLINE** MODERN & FRENCH HISTORY **EDUCATION** Univ Ore, BA, 59, MA, 61; Univ Rochester, PhD, 69. **CAREER** Instr hist, Ore State Univ, 65-66; asst prof, 66-71, assoc prof, 71-79, prof, 79-80, Hagar Prof Hum, Alfred Univ, 81-86; Chief Ed, Hist Reflections/Reflexions Historiques, 91-; Kruson Distinguished Prof of History, 99-. **HONORS AND AWARDS** Col Ctr Finger Lakers res grant, 72-73; NEH fel, 82-83. **MEMBERSHIPS** AHA; Soc Fr Hist Studies; Soc Mod Hist. **RESEARCH** Historiography of the French Second Empire; political and social history of the French Second Republic; 20th century French political-intellectual. **SELECTED PUBLICATIONS** Auth, The Second Empire Reconsidered: A Study in French Historiography, Rutgers Univ, 78. **CONTACT ADDRESS** Div of Human Studies, Alfred Univ, 26 N Main St, Alfred, NY 14802-1222. **EMAIL** fcampbell@bigvax.alfred.edu

CAMPBELL, TED A.
PERSONAL Born 09/03/1953, Beaumont, TX, m, 1975, 2 children **DISCIPLINE** CHURCH HISTORY **EDUCATION** Univ N Tex, BA, 76; Oxford Univ, BA/MA, 79; SMU, PhD, 84 **CAREER** Visiting lctr, Methodist Thelog School, 84-85; asst prof, Duke Divinity, 85-93; prof, Wesley Theolog Seminary, 93 **MEMBERSHIPS** AAR; ASCH; World Methodist Hist Soc **RESEARCH** Wesleyan Studies; History of Christian Doctrine **SELECTED PUBLICATIONS** Auth, Christian Con-

fessions, Westminister John Knox Press, 96; auth, John Wesley and Christian Antiquity, Kingsword Bks, 91; **CONTACT ADDRESS** Wesley Theol Sem, 4500 Massachussettes, Washington, DC 20016. **EMAIL** tcamp@clark.net

CANNADINE, DAVID
DISCIPLINE MODERN BRITISH HISTORY **EDUCATION** Cambridge Univ, PhD, 72; Oxford Univ, PhD, 75. **CAREER** Moore Collegiate prof. **RESEARCH** Biography of Andrew Mellon. **SELECTED PUBLICATIONS** Auth, Lords and Landlords: the Aristocracy and the Towns, 1774-1967, 80; The Pleasures of the Past, 89; The Decline and Fall of the British Aristocracy, 90; G M Trevelyan: a Life in History, 92; Aspects of Aristocracy: Grandeur and Decline, Mod Britain, 94. **CONTACT ADDRESS** Dept of Hist, Columbia Col, New York, 2960 Broadway, New York, NY 10027-6902.

CANNING, PAUL
PERSONAL Born 01/10/1947, m, 1987, 3 children **DISCIPLINE** HISTORY **EDUCATION** Univ Washington, BA 69; Univ Connecticut, MA 71; Univ Washington, 79. **CAREER** Gunzaga Univ, instr, 76-77, vis prof 82; Marymont Col, vis prof, 83-84; Univ Connecticut, asst prof, assoc prof, 85 to 89-. **MEMBERSHIPS** AHA; NACBS; ACIS. **RESEARCH** Modern Britain, Modern Ireland and Modern Africa. **SELECTED PUBLICATIONS** Auth, British Policy Towards Ireland, Oxford, Clarendon Press of OUP, 85. **CONTACT ADDRESS** Dept of History, 85 Lawler Rd, West Hartford, CT 06117.

CANNISTRARO, PHILIP VINCENT
PERSONAL Born 11/13/1942, New York, NY **DISCIPLINE** MODERN ITALIAN HISTORY **EDUCATION** NYork Univ, BA, 65, MA, 66, PhD(hist), 70. **CAREER** Instr hist, NY Univ, 69-70; from asst prof to assoc prof, 70-78, Prof Hist, Fla State Univ, 78-, Am ed, Storia Contemporanea, 72-; mem, Columbia Univ Sem Mod italy, 73-; Fulbright sr fel, Rome 77-78; Distinguished prof, Queens Col, CUNY. **MEMBERSHIPS** Soc Ital Hist Studies; AHA; Am Ital Hist Asn. **RESEARCH** Italian history; history of fascism; Italian-Americans and fascism. **SELECTED PUBLICATIONS** Coauth, Il Duce's Other Woman: The Untold Story of Margherita Sarfatti, New York: William Morrow, 93; coauth, Civilizations of the World, New York: HarperCollins/Longman, 96. **CONTACT ADDRESS** Queens Col, CUNY, 65-30 Kissena Blvd., Flushing, NY 11367.

CANNON, DONALD QUAYLE
PERSONAL Born 12/24/1936, Washington, DC, m, 1960, 5 children **DISCIPLINE** AMERICAN COLONIAL HISTORY **EDUCATION** Univ Utah, BA, 61, MA, 62; Clark Univ, PhD(hist), 67. **CAREER** Asst prof Am hist, Univ Maine, Portland, 67-73; assoc prof, 73-80, Prof Church Hist & Doctrine, Brigham Young Univ, 80-, Mem, Inst Early Am Hist & Cult, Va. **MEMBERSHIPS** AHA. **RESEARCH** History of geography; early history of the Mormon Church. **SELECTED PUBLICATIONS** Auth, Wilford Woodruff's mission to Maine, Improv Era, 9/70; Topsfield, Massachusetts: Ancestral home of the prophet Joseph Smith, fall 73 & Thomas L Kane meets the Mormons, fall 77, Brigham Young Univ Studies; Who is Jesus Christ?, New Era, 3/78. **CONTACT ADDRESS** Dept of Church Hist, Brigham Young Univ, Joseph Smith Bldg, Provo, UT 84602-0002.

CANTOR, LOUIS
DISCIPLINE HISTORY **EDUCATION** Duke Univ, PhD, 63. **CAREER** Prof. **SELECTED PUBLICATIONS** Auth, A Prologue to the Protest Movementand Wheelin' on Beale: How WDIA Memphis became the Nation's First All-Black Radio Station and Created the Sound that Changed America. **CONTACT ADDRESS** Dept of History, Indiana Univ-Purdue Univ, Fort Wayne, 2101 Coliseum Blvd, Fort Wayne, IN 46805.

CANTOR, MILTON
DISCIPLINE HISTORY **EDUCATION** Columbia Univ, PhD, 54. **CAREER** Prof, Univ MA Amherst. **SELECTED PUBLICATIONS** Auth, Max Eastman, 70; The Divided Left: American Radicalism in the Twentieth Century, 78; ed, American Working Class Culture,79; co-ed, Sex, Class and the Women Worker, 77; Documents of American History, 89. **CONTACT ADDRESS** Dept of Hist, Univ of Massachusetts, Amherst, Mass Ave, Amherst, MA 01003.

CANTOR, NORMAN FRANK
PERSONAL Born 11/19/1929, Winnipeg, MB, Canada, m, 1957, 2 children **DISCIPLINE** MEDIEVAL & ENGLISH LEGAL HISTORY, HISTORICAL SOCIOLOGY **EDUCATION** Univ Man, BA, 51; Princeton Univ, MA, 53, PhD, 57. **CAREER** From instr to asst prof hist, Princeton Univ, 55-60; vis prof, Johns Hopkins Univ, 60; from assoc prof to prof, Columbia Univ, 60-66; prof, Brandeis Univ, 66-68, Leff prof, 68-70; chmn dept, State Univ NY, Binghamton, 70-74, distinguished prof hist, 70-76, provost for grad studies, 75-76, vpres acad affairs, 75-76; vchancellor acad affairs & prof hist, Ill-Chicago Circle, 76-78; dean fac arts & sci, 78-81, prof hist, 78-81, Prof Hist & Sociol, New York Univ, 81-; Can Coun fel, 60; Am Coun Learned Soc fel, 60; consult, Bar Asn NYC, 63-67; consult, Encycl Britannica, 64-65; consult, Life mag, 66-68; vis prof, Brooklyn Col, 72-73, Adelphi Univ, 87; Fulbright prof, Tel Aviv, 87-88; consult, NEH 73, 89-91. **HONORS AND AWARDS** Nat Book Critics Circle Nomination, 91; NY Public Libr Awd, 97; Fel Royal Hist Soc, 74; lld, univ winnipeg, 73. **MEMBERSHIPS** AHA; AAUP. **RESEARCH** Medieval cultural history; legal history; comparative European history. **SELECTED PUBLICATIONS** Inventing the Middle Ages, Morrow, 91; Civilization of the Middle Ages, HarperCollins, 93; The Sacred Chain, HarperCollins, 94; Medieval Lives, HarperCollins, 94; The Medieval Reader, 95; The Jewish Experience, HarperCollins, 95; The American Century, HarperCollins, 97; Imagining the Law, HarperCollins, 97. **CONTACT ADDRESS** Dept Hist, New York Univ, 53 Washington Sq S, New York, NY 10012-4556.

CANTRELL, GREGG
PERSONAL Born 06/20/1958, Sweetwater, TX, m, 1997, 2 children **DISCIPLINE** HISTORY **EDUCATION** Tx A&M Univ, BBA, 79, MBA, 80, PhD, 88 **CAREER** Asst prof to assoc prof, Sam Houston St Univ, 88-98; Rupert N. Richardson Prof, Hardin-Simmons Univ, 98-00; Assoc Prof, Univ of North Texas, 00- . **HONORS AND AWARDS** Tullis Mem Awd, Tx St Hist Assoc, 94; Phi Alpha Theta Book Awd, 94; Fel, Nat Endow for the Humanities, 94-95; Carroll Awd, Tx St Hist Assoc, 96; Res Fel, Clements Center for SW Stud, S Methodist Univ, 96-97; Presidio La Bahia Awd and Summerfield G. Roberts Awd, Sons of The Republic of Texas, 99; Miss Ima Hogg Awd, Center for American History, Univ of Texas, 00; T.R. Fehrenbach Awd, Texas Historical Commission, 00; Citation of Merit, Texas Historical Foundations, 00. **MEMBERSHIPS** Tx St Hist Assoc; S Hist Assoc; E Tx Hist Assoc; W Hist Assoc. **RESEARCH** Hist of the Amer south; the southwest; Tx. **SELECTED PUBLICATIONS** Auth, Southerner and Nativist: Kenneth Rayner and the Ideology of Americanism, NC Hist Rev, 92; Sam Houston and the Know-Nothings: A Reappraisal, SW Hist Quart, 93; The Partnership of Stephen F. Austin and Joseph H. Hawkins, SW Hist Quart, 95; Kenneth and John B. Rayner and the Limits of Southern Dissent, Univ of Il Press, 93; Stephen F. Austin: Empresario of Texas, Yale Univ Press, 99. **CONTACT ADDRESS** Dept of History, Univ of No Texas, Box 310650, Denton, TX 76203-0650. **EMAIL** cantrell@unt.edu

CANTRILL, DANTE
DISCIPLINE AMERICAN STUDIES **EDUCATION** Univ Wash, PhD, 76. **CAREER** Prof. **RESEARCH** History of ideas. **SELECTED PUBLICATIONS** Auth, Adam's Apple. **CONTACT ADDRESS** Dept of English and Philosophy, Idaho State Univ, Pocatello, ID 83209. **EMAIL** cantdant@isu.edu

CANUP, JOHN
DISCIPLINE HISTORY **EDUCATION** Univ Georgia, AB, 73; Univ Hawaii-Manoa, MA, 75; Univ N Carol at Chapel Hill, PhD, 86. **CAREER** ASST PROF, HIST, TEXAS A&M UNIV **MEMBERSHIPS** Am Antiquarian Soc **SELECTED PUBLICATIONS** Auth, Out of the Wilderness, Wesleyan Univ Press, 90; Drem Castles, Viking, 99; Andrew Deutsch, London, 66; El Escorial, Newsbreak Books, 71; The Cry of Sodom Enquired Into, Procs of AAS 98, 88; Cotton Mather and Criolian Degeneracy, Early Am Lt 24, 89. **CONTACT ADDRESS** Dept of Hist, Texas A&M Univ, Col Station, College Station, TX 77843-4236.

CAPRON, ALEXANDER M.
PERSONAL Born 08/16/1944, Hartford, CT, m, 1989, 4 children **DISCIPLINE** ECONOMICS & HISTORY, LAW **EDUCATION** Swarthmore Col, BA, 66; Yale Law Sch, LLB, 69. **CAREER** USC Law School **HONORS AND AWARDS** Fellow, Am Asn for Advan of Sci; Hon Fellow, Am Col of Legal Med. **MEMBERSHIPS** Inst Med; Nat Acad Sci; Int Asn of Bioethics; Am Soc of Law, Med, & Ethics (past pres). **RESEARCH** Ethical & social issues in medical & the life sciences. **CONTACT ADDRESS** USC Law School, Univ of So California, Los Angeles, CA 90089-0071. **EMAIL** acapron@law.usc.edu

CAPSHEW, JAMES H.
PERSONAL Born 10/14/1954, Indianapolis, IN **DISCIPLINE** HISTORY OF SCIENCE **EDUCATION** Ind Univ, BA, 79; Univ Pa, AM, 82; PhD, 86. **CAREER** Res assoc, Univ of Md, 86-89; asst prof to assoc prof, Ind Univ, 90-, dir, Grad Studies, 98-. **HONORS AND AWARDS** Phi Beta Kappa, 79; Nat Sci Found Grad Fel, 80-84; Mellon Grad Fel, Univ of Pa, 85-86; Joan Cahalin Robinson Prize, Soc for the Hist of Tech, 86. **MEMBERSHIPS** Hist of Sci Soc; Hist of Educ Soc; AAUP. **RESEARCH** History of American psychology, history of higher education, historiography, biography. **SELECTED PUBLICATIONS** Coauth, "The Power of Service: World War II and Professional Reform in the American Psychological Association", The American Psychological Association: A Historical Perspective, eds Rand B. Evans, Virginia S. Sexton and Thomas C. Cadwallader, Am Psychol Assoc, (Washington), (92): 149-175; auth, "Psychologist on Site: A Reconnaissance of the Historiography of the Laboratory", Am Psychol, 47 (92): 132-142; coauth, "Big Science: Price to the Present", Osiris 7; (92): 3-25; auth, "Engineering Behavior: Project Pigeon, World War II, and the Conditioning of B.F. Skinner", Tech and Culture 34, (93): 835-357; auth, "The Yale Connection in American Psychology: Philanthropy, War, and the Emergence of an Academic Elite", The Development of the Social Sciences in the United States and Canada: The Role of Philanthropy, eds Theresa R. Richardson and Donald Fisher, Ablex Pub Corp, (Greenwich, Conn, 99): 143-154; auth, Psychologist on the March: Science, Practice, and Professional Identity in America, 1929-1969, Cambridge Univ Pr, (NY/Cambridge), 99. **CONTACT ADDRESS** Dept Hist and Philos of Sci, Indiana Univ, Bloomington, Goodbody Hall 130, Bloomington, IN 47405. **EMAIL** jcapshew@indiana.edu

CAPUTI, JANE
PERSONAL Born 10/27/1953, Brooklyn, NY **DISCIPLINE** AMERICAN STUDIES, WOMENS STUDIES **EDUCATION** Boston Col, BA, 74; Simmons Col, MA, 77; Bowling Green State Univ, PhD, 82. **CAREER** Prof, Amer Studies, Univ Nmex, 95-97; prof, women's studies, Fla Atlantic Univ, 97-. **HONORS AND AWARDS** Emily Toth Awd, for The Age of Sex Crime, 88; Honorable Mention, Carl Bode Awd, Amer Culture Asn, for The New Founding Fathers: The Lore and Lure of the Serial Killer, 91; Kathleen Gregory Klein Awd, Popular Culture Asn, for American Psychos: The Serial Killer in Contemporary Fiction, 92. **RESEARCH** New spiritualities; Violence against women; Popular culture. **SELECTED PUBLICATIONS** Auth, Unthinkable Fathering: Connecting Incest and Nuclearism, Hypatia: A Journal of Feminist Philosophy, vol 9, no 2, 102-122, 94; auth, American Psychos: The Serial Killer in Contemporary Fiction, Jour of Amer Culture, 16, no 4, 101-112, 93; auth, The Heart of Knowledge: Nuclear Themes in Native American Thought and Literature, Amer Indian Culture and Res Jour, 14, no 4, 1-27, 92; auth, Gossips, Gorgons & Crones: The Fates of the Earth, Bear and Co, 93; co-auth, Websters' First New Intergalactic Wickedary of the English Language, Beacon Press, Boston, 87; auth, The Age of Sex Crime, Bowling Green State Univ Popular Press, Bowling Green, Oh, 87; auth, The Seocnd Coming of Diana," National Womens Studies Asn Journal 11:2, (99): 103-123. **CONTACT ADDRESS** Women's Studies, Florida Atlantic Univ, Boca Raton, FL 33431. **EMAIL** jcaputi@fau.edu

CARANFA, ANGELO
PERSONAL Born 05/24/1942, Rotello, Italy, s **DISCIPLINE** AESTHETICS, PHILOSOPHY **EDUCATION** Stonehill Col, BS, 66; Boston Col, MA, 71; Univ Florence, PhD, 72. **CAREER** Adj instr, Newbury Jr Col, 75-76, Boston State Col, 76-78, Bridgewater State Col, 85-87, Stonehill Col, 78-85, 90-. **MEMBERSHIPS** Am Philos Asn **RESEARCH** 20th Century French aesthetics. **SELECTED PUBLICATIONS** Auth, Obedience, Love and Marriage in the Philosophy of St John, Licacre Quarterly, 83; coed, Western Heritage: Man's Encounter with Himsef and the World, Lanham, Md: Univ Press of Am, 84; auth, Proust and Augustine on Time, Hist of Eurpean Ideas, 86; auth, Claudel: Beauty and Grace, Lewisburg, Penn: Bucknell Unvi Press, 89; auth, Proust: The Creative Silence, Lewisburg, Penn: Bucknell Univ Press, 90; auth, The Interior Life in claudel's Art Criticism of renaissance Dutch Painting, Art Critcism, 97; auth, Toward an Aesthetric Model of Teaching and Writing in the Humanitie, J of Aesthetic Ed, 99; auth, Camille Claudel: A Sculptuer of Interior Solitued, Bucknell Univ Press, 99. **CONTACT ADDRESS** 27 Sprague Ave., Brockton, MA 02302. **EMAIL** acaranfa@stonehill.edu

CARBY, HAZEL V.
PERSONAL Born 01/15/1948, Oakhampton, England, m, 1982 **DISCIPLINE** AFRICAN-AMERICAN STUDIES **EDUCATION** Birmingham University, Center for Contemporary Cultural Studies, PhD, 1984. **CAREER** Wesleyan University, associate professor, 82-89; Yale Univ, Prof, 89-. **CONTACT ADDRESS** African-American Studies, Yale Univ, PO Box 3388, Yale Station, New Haven, CT 06520.

CARDENAS, MARIA DE LA LUZ RODRIGUEZ
PERSONAL Born 09/03/1945, Laredo, TX, m, 1971, 3 children **DISCIPLINE** HISTORY, WOMEN'S STUDIES **EDUCATION** Tex Woman's Univ, BA, 69; MA, 74; Colegio de Mex, Cert Women's Study, 94. **CAREER** Instr, Laredo Community Col, 70-; Staff Develop Office, Laredo Community Col, 74-76; Asst to Acad Dean, Laredo Community Col, 76-81; St. Augustine High Sch Life Vocations/Hist/Rel, 81-88; Laredo Community Col Dir of Familias Pueden, Ford Found, 96-. **HONORS AND AWARDS** Fel for Master' Degree, Summer Inst in Mex City, Grant; Ford Found Rural Community Col Initiative, 96-99; Pathfinder Awd, Tex A&M Int Univ 99-00; S Tex Writing Proj, 00-02. **MEMBERSHIPS** Tex Community Col Teachers, AAUW, Delta Kappa Gamma, Tex State Hist Asn, Int Good Neighbor Coun, Las Mujeras, Laredo Comn for Women, Domestic Violence Coalition, Tex State Cath Hist Conf. **RESEARCH** Women's history, Hispanic educational models, Women vowed religions, Church history, Women in politics. **SELECTED PUBLICATIONS** Auth, "Anglo-American Relations, 1844-46,"; auth, "Laredo Vietnam Causalities & their Families,", 93, 97; auth, "Jovita Perez, First Woman Licensed Custom House Broker in U.S.;" auth, "Fearless Voices in a Common Struggle, Laredo Women in Politics;" auth, "The Role of the Laity-Diocese of Corpus Christi Synod

Doc;" auth, "Familias Pueden," LCC's Rural Community Col Initiative; auth, "Hispanic Women in Communication, Texas Tamaulipas Border." **CONTACT ADDRESS** Dept Soc and Behav Sci, Laredo Comm Col, 1 W End Wash, Laredo, TX 78040. **EMAIL** lrcardenas@laredo.cc.tx.us

CARDOSO, JOAQUIN JOSE
PERSONAL Born 08/20/1932, Mahoning Township, PA, m, 1968, 3 children **DISCIPLINE** UNITED STATES HISTORY **EDUCATION** Pa State Teachers Col, BS, 58; Lehigh Univ, MA, 59; Univ Wis-Madison, PhD(hist), 67. **CAREER** Instr English, Parkland High Sch, Orefield, Pa, 58-60; instr econ, social & hist, Madison West High Sch, Wis, 60-62; instr Am Hist, San Bernardino High Sch, Calif, 62-65; asst prof Am Hist, Chico State Col, 65-68; assoc prof, 68-72, Prof Am Hist, State Univ NY Col Buffalo, 73-, State Univ NY Res Found fels, 71 & 73; ed consult, World Mag, 73-75. **HONORS AND AWARDS** Voelkers Fel, Claremont Grad Sch, 62; William Robertson Coe Fel, Stanford Univ, 63; Hist Fel Univ Wyo, 64. **MEMBERSHIPS** Orgn Am Historians; AHA; Southern Hist Asn; Can Am Studies Asn. **RESEARCH** Canadian-United States relations; political and economic history of mid-19th century United States. **SELECTED PUBLICATIONS** Auth, "Canada in the Korean War," "Matthew bunker Ridgway," "S.L.A. Marshall," "Lin Piao," in The Korean War: An Encyclopedia (NYork: Garland Publ), 95; rev, Portrait of an Abolitionist--A Biography of Stearns, George, Luther, 1809-1867, Jour Amer Hist, Vol 0083, 97; auth, "Michael Shaara," in Am Lives, 2 (97); auth, "Harvey Penick," and "Christopher Lasch," in Am Lives, 3 (forthcoming). **CONTACT ADDRESS** Dept of Hist, SUNY, Buffalo, 1300 Elmwood Ave, Buffalo, NY 14222-1095. **EMAIL** cardosjj@buffalostatecollege.edu

CARDOZA, ANTHONY L.
PERSONAL Born 01/31/1947, Berkeley, CA, m, 1989, 1 child **DISCIPLINE** HISTORY **EDUCATION** Princeton Univ, PhD. **CAREER** Hist, Loyola Univ. **HONORS AND AWARDS** Howard R. Marraro prize; Am Historical Asn, 98. **RESEARCH** Modern Italian soc and Polit history. **SELECTED PUBLICATIONS** Auth, Agrarian Elites and Italian Fascism, Princeton UP, 82; The Long Goodbye: The Landed Aristocracy in Northwestern Italy, 1880-1930, Europ Hist Quart 23, 93; auth, Aristocrats in Bourgeois Italy, (Cambridge U.P., 97); auth, Patrizi in un Mondo Plebeio, (Donzelli Editor: Rome, 99). **CONTACT ADDRESS** History Dept, Loyola Univ, Chicago, 6525 N. Sheridan Rd., Chicago, IL 60626. **EMAIL** acardoz@atswpo.it.luc.edu

CARELESS, JAMES M. S.
PERSONAL Born 02/17/1919, Toronto, ON, Canada **DISCIPLINE** HISTORY **EDUCATION** Univ Toronto, BA, 40; Harvard Univ, AM, 41, PhD, 50. **CAREER** Sheldon Trav fel, Harvard Univ, 42-43; lectr to assoc prof, 45-59, chmn, 59-67, prof 59-84, PROF EMER HISTORY, UNIV TORONTO, 84-; dir, Ont Heritage Found, 75-81; chmn, Ont Hist Stud Ser, 82-93. **HONORS AND AWARDS** Tyrrell Medal Can Hist, 62; Gov Gen Awd non-fiction, 64; Cruickshank Medal Ont Hist Soc, 68; sr res fel, Australian Nat Univ, 78; Order Ont, 87. **MEMBERSHIPS** Multicultural Hist Soc, 76-88; Hist Sites & Monuments Bd Can, 80-85; Can Hist Asn (pres, 67-68); Ont Hist Soc (pres, 59). **RESEARCH** Canadian history **SELECTED PUBLICATIONS** Auth, Canada: A Story of Challenge, 53; auth, Brown of the Globe, vol 1 59, vol 2 63; auth, The Union of the Canadas, 67; auth, Rise of Cities in Canada, 78; auth, Toronto to 1918, 84; auth, Frontier and Metropolis, 89; auth, Ontario: A Celebration of Heritage, vol 1 91, vol 2 92; auth, Canada: A Celebration of Heritage, vol 1 94, vol 2 95; coauth, The Pioneers, 69; coauth, Colonist and Canadiens, 71; coauth, Aspects of 19th Century Ontario, 74; coauth, Pre-Confederation Premiers, 80. **CONTACT ADDRESS** 121 Ranleigh St, Toronto, ON, Canada M4N 1X2.

CAREY, JAMES CHARLES
PERSONAL Born 04/01/1915, Bancroft, NE **DISCIPLINE** HISTORY **EDUCATION** Nebr State Teachers Col, AB, 37; Univ Colo, AM, 40, PhD, 48; Univ San Marcos, Peru, cert, 42. **CAREER** Dir, Col Am Deleg Callao, Peru, 41-45; instr, Univ Colo, 46-48; assoc prof, 48-54, Prof Hist Kans State Univ, 54-, Dir, Pub Libr, Callao, Peru; chief party, USAID/Southwest Alliance Latin Am, Univ Santa Maria Antigua, CZ, 68-69. **RESEARCH** Latin American history; United States colonial history; Yucatan in the 20th century. **SELECTED PUBLICATIONS** Auth, Setting the Virgin on Fire--Cardenas, Lazaro, Michoacan Peasants, and the Redemption of the Mexican-Revolution, Hisp Amer Hist Rev, Vol 0077, 97; Indigenous Rulers--An Ethnohistory of Town Government in Colonial Cuernavaca, Jour West, Vol 0032, 93; How the West Was Also Won--An Account of the Family Of Omaha Chief Laflesche, Joseph Iron-Eye, Jour W, Vol 0035, 96. **CONTACT ADDRESS** Dept of Hist, Kansas State Univ, Manhattan, KS 66502.

CAREY, PATRICK W.
PERSONAL Born 07/02/1940, m, 2 children **DISCIPLINE** RELIGIOUS STUDIES; HISTORY OF AMERICAN RELIGION **EDUCATION** St John's Univ, BA, 62; St John's Sem, M Div, 66; Union Theol Sem, STM, 71; Fordham Univ, PhD, 75. **CAREER** Asst prof, St Peter's Col, 75-76; Elisabeth Seton Col, 76; Carleton Col, 76-77; Gustavus Adolphus, 77-78; from asst prof to assoc prof, Marquette Univ, 78-. **MEMBERSHIPS** Am Acad of Rel; Am Soc of Church Hist; U.S. Cath. Hist Soc; Am Cath. Hist Asn; Am Cath. Hist Soc of Philadelphia; Col Theol Soc; Cath. Theol Soc of Am. **RESEARCH** Hist of Am Rel. **SELECTED PUBLICATIONS** Auth, Orestes A. Brownson: Selected Writings, 91; The Roman Catholics, 93; The Roman Catholics in America, 96; Orestes A. Brownson: A Bibliography, 1826-1876, 96; Ontologism in American Catholic Thought, 1840-1900, Revue d'Histoire Ecclesiastique 91/3-4, 96; Catholicism, Encycl of the United States in the Twentieth Century, ed S. I. Kutler et al, 96; After Testem Benevolentiae and Pascendi, Catholic Southwest: A Jour of History and Culture 7, 96; ed, The Pastoral Letters of the United States Catholic Bishops, vol 6, 1989-1997, 98; coed, Theological Education in the Catholic Tradition: Contemporary Challenges, 97. **CONTACT ADDRESS** Dept of Theology, Marquette Univ, 100 Coughlin Hall, PO Box 1881, Milwaukee, WI 53233-2295. **EMAIL** careyp@csd.mu.edu

CARGILL, JACK
PERSONAL Born 05/19/1941, TX, d, 1 child **DISCIPLINE** ANCIENT HISTORY **EDUCATION** Univ Tex, Austin, BA, 63, MA, 66; Univ Calif, Berkeley, PhD, 77. **CAREER** Lect, vis, asst prof, 65-66, 75-80; asst prof to prof history, Rutgers Univ, 81-. **MEMBERSHIPS** Am Philological Asn; Asn Ancient Historians. **RESEARCH** Ancient Greece, Rome, Near East; Greek Epigraphy. **SELECTED PUBLICATIONS** Auth, Handbook for Ancient History Classes, Regina Books, 97; auth, Athenian Settlements of the Fourth Century B.C., Leiden, 95; auth, The Second Athenian League: Empire or Free Alliance? Univ Calif Press, 81; auth, The Decree of Aristoteles: Some Epigraphical Details, Ancient World 27, 96; auth, David in History: A Secular Approach, Judaism 35, 86; auth, Demosthenes, Aischines, and the Crop of Traitors, Ancient World 11 (85). **CONTACT ADDRESS** Dept Hist, Rutgers, The State Univ of New Jersey, New Brunswick, 16 Seminary Place, New Brunswick, NJ 08901-1108. **EMAIL** jcargill@rci.rutgers.edu

CARILLI, THERESA M.
PERSONAL Born 12/29/1956, Hartford, CT **DISCIPLINE** CREATIVE ARTS **EDUCATION** Univ Conn, BA, 78; MA, 81; Southern IL Univ, PhD, 89. **CAREER** Prof, Purdue Univ Calumet, 89- **MEMBERSHIPS** Nat Commun Assoc; Nat Women's Studies Assoc; Am Ital Studies Assoc. **SELECTED PUBLICATIONS** Auth, Women As Lovers, 96; coauth, Cultural Diversity and the U.S. Media, 98. **CONTACT ADDRESS** Dept Speech and Creative Arts, Purdue Univ, Calumet, 2233 - 171 St, Hammond, IN 46323. **EMAIL** carilli@calumet.purdue.edu

CARLEBACH, MICHAEL L.
PERSONAL Born New York, NY, m, 1981, 2 children **DISCIPLINE** HISTORY **EDUCATION** Colgate Univ, AB, 67; Fla State Univ, MA, 80; Brown Univ, PhD, 88. **CAREER** Asst prof, hist, PROF COMM & AM STUD, UNIV MIAMI **MEMBERSHIPS** Am Antiquarian Soc **SELECTED PUBLICATIONS** Auth, The Origins of Photojournalism in America, Smith Inst Press, 92; auth, Art and Propaganda: The Photograhy Project of the Farm Security Administration, Jour of Decorative and Propaganda Arts 8, 88; coauth, Farm Security Administration Photographs of Florida, Univ Fla Press, 93; American Photojournalism Comes of Age, Smith Inst Press, 98; auth, This Way to the Crypt, Southeast Museum of Photography, 99. **CONTACT ADDRESS** Sch of Comm, Univ of Miami, PO Box 248127, Coral Gables, FL 33124. **EMAIL** mcarleba@umiami.ir.miami.edu

CARLETON, DON E.
PERSONAL Born 01/22/1947, Dallas, TX, m, 1974, 2 children **DISCIPLINE** HISTORY **EDUCATION** Univ Houston, BS, 69, MA, 74; PhD, 78. **CAREER** Founding dir, Houston Metrop Res Ctr, 75-79; dir, Barker Texas Hist Ctr, 79-91; dir, Ctr Am Hist, 91- ; sr lectr, dept hist, 86-; sr lectr, dept jour, Univ Texas-Austin, 98-. **HONORS AND AWARDS** J.R. Parten Chr Arch Am Hist, Univ Texas, 88; fel Texas State Hist Asn. **MEMBERSHIPS** Texas State Hist Asn. **RESEARCH** 20th Century US Political History, Texas history, Historical research methods, Broadcast journalism history. **SELECTED PUBLICATIONS** Auth, Red Scare, Austin 85; auth, A Breed so Rare: The Life of J.R. Parten, Liberal Texas Oil Man, 1896-1992, Austin, 98. **CONTACT ADDRESS** Dept Hist, Univ of Texas, Austin, Ctr Am Hist, Austin, TX 78712. **EMAIL** d.carleton@mail.utexas.edu

CARLETON, MARK THOMAS
PERSONAL Born 02/07/1935, Baton Rouge, LA, m, 1963, 3 children **DISCIPLINE** HISTORY OF LOUISIANA AND THE SOUTH **EDUCATION** Yale Univ, AB, 57; Stanford, Univ, MA, 64, PhD(US hist), 70. **CAREER** From instr to asst prof, 65-73, Assoc Prof US Hist, LA State Univ, Baton Rouge, 73-, Mem, Gov Coun of Econ Adv, State of La, 73-; mem exec comt, La Comt for Humanities, 78-81. **HONORS AND AWARDS** Cert Commendation, Am Asn State & Local Hist, 73. **MEMBERSHIPS** Southern Hist Asn. **RESEARCH** Late 19th century United States. **SELECTED PUBLICATIONS** Auth, Acadian to Cajun--Transformation of a People, 1803-1877, Jour Amer Hist, Vol 0081, 94; Prisons and the American Conscience--History of United-States Federal Corrections, Amer Jour Legal Hist, Vol 0037, 93. **CONTACT ADDRESS** Dept of Hist, Louisiana State Univ and A&M Col, Baton Rouge, LA 70803.

CARLISLE, RODNEY
PERSONAL Born 10/10/1936, Hempstead, NY, m, 1988, 2 children **DISCIPLINE** UNITED STATES HISTORY **EDUCATION** Harvard Univ, Ab, 58; Univ Calif, Berkeley, MA, 62, PhD(hist), 65. **CAREER** Instr hist, Merritt Col, 64-66; asst prof, 66-73 dir dept urban univ, 69-71, chmn dept, 73-80, 92 & 97, Prpf Hist, Rutgers Univ, Camden, 80-, Pres fac senate, Rutgers Univ, Camden, 77-78; vis scholar, Dept Energy, 79-80; sr assoc, Hist Assoc Inc, 81-. **RESEARCH** Maritime history; Political biography of W R Hearst; Afro-American history **SELECTED PUBLICATIONS** Auth, Prologue to Liberation, A History of Black People in America, Appleton, 72, 2nd ed, Univ Press Am, 79; Black Nationalism, an Integral Tradition, Black World, 2/73; auth, The Roots of Black Nationalism, Kennikat, 75; auth, Production Reactors: An Outline Overview 1944-1988, U S Dept of Energy, 10/92; Probabilistic Risk Assessment in New Production Reactors: Background and Issues to 1991, U S Dept of Energy, 10/92; Management of the U S Navy Research and Development Centers, Naval Hist Center, 96; Supplying the Nuclear Arsenal: American Production Reactors, 1942-1992, Johns Hopkins Univ Press, 96; A Guide to Writing the Longer Piece, Serenus Press, 97; The Relationship of Science and Technology, A Bibliographic Guide, Naval Hist Center, 97; coauth, Our Man in Acapulco--The Life and Times of Col. Frank M Brandstetter, Univ of N Texas Press, 99; coauth, Jack Tar-A Sailor's Life 1750-1910, antique Collectorys Club, 99. **CONTACT ADDRESS** Dept of Hist, Rutgers, The State Univ of New Jersey, Camden, 311 N 5th St, Camden, NJ 08102-1461. **EMAIL** carlisle@crab.rutgers.edu

CARLS, ALICE-CATHERINE
PERSONAL Born 06/14/1950, Mulhouse, France, m, 1977, 3 children **DISCIPLINE** HISTORY **EDUCATION** Univ de Paris IV-Sorbonne, BA, 70; MA, 72; VA, 73; Univ de Paris I-Sorbonne,Doctorat de Troisieme Cycle, 76. **CAREER** Adj prof, Sterling Col, 78-83; Union Univ, 83-85; asst prof, Lambuth Col, 85-92; asst prof to assoc prof, chair, Univ of Tenn Martin, 92-. **HONORS AND AWARDS** Herbert Hoover Grants, 79, 84; Who's Who in the World, 92; Who's Who in Polish Am, 96; Int Authors and Writers Who's Who, 97; Int Scholar Awd, Univ of Tenn, 99; Who's Who in Am, 94-01; 20th Century Awd for Achievement, Outstanding Scholars of 20th Century, Int Woman of the Year, Int Biographical Centre, England, 00. **MEMBERSHIPS** S Assoc for Slavic Studies; S Hist Assoc; Phi Kappa Phi; United Nat Assoc of the U.S.; Phi Alpha Theta; Pi Delta Phi, Polish-Am Hist Assoc; AHA; Assoc for Public Justice; Am Assoc for the Advan of Slavic Studies. **RESEARCH** Poland - 20th Century - Cultural history - Literature - diplomacy, 20th Century Europe including Russia and East-Central Europe. **SELECTED PUBLICATIONS** Auth, La Ville Libre de Dantzig en crise ouverte, 24.10.1938-1.9. 1939--Politique et diplomatie, Ossolineu, (Warsaw), 82; auth, "46 Years of Libella", Polish Rev XXXVI.3, (91): 339-344; auth, "European Welfare Systems in Transition", Pub Justice Rep 15.8 (92): 4; auth, "Of Two Minds", Pub Justice Rep, 16.5 (93): 5; auth, "Ksiegarnia Polska - Librairie Polonaise. 160 years of Polish Presence in Paris", Polish Rev XXXIX.3 (94): 301-305; trans, Louis Loucheur and the Shaping of Modern France, 1916-1931, by Stephen D. Carls, Les Editions du Septentrion, (Lille, France), 99; auth, "Soviet Union", "Russification", "Stalin", Encycl of Mod East Europe 1815-1989, Garland, (forthcoming); auth, "Hostage to a Pipeline: Russia, the Caucasus, and the Silk Road of the 21st Century", Pub Justice Rep, (forthcoming). **CONTACT ADDRESS** Dept Hist and Philos, Univ of Tennessee, Martin, 554 University St, Martin, TN 38238-0001. **EMAIL** accarls@utm.edu

CARLS, STEPHEN
PERSONAL Born 02/15/1944, Minneapolis, MN, m, 1977, 3 children **DISCIPLINE** HISTORY **EDUCATION** Wheaton Col, BA, 66; Univ Minn MA, 68; PhD, 82 **CAREER** Asst Prof to Assoc Prof, Sterling Col, 71-81-90; Assoc Prof to Prof, Union Univ, 90-. **HONORS AND AWARDS** Publication recommended by Am Hist Asn First Books Program, 83; Grant, Southern Regional Educ Board, 85; Fac Recognition Awd, Union Univ, 87. **MEMBERSHIPS** Am Hist Asn, Coun for European Studies, Economic Hist, W Tenn Hist Soc, Phi Alpha Theta, Delta Psi chapter Faculty Sponsor, 83-. **RESEARCH** French Industrial Mobilization during World War I; France between the two world wars; Twentieth century Europe. **SELECTED PUBLICATIONS** auth, Louis Loucheur and the Shaping of Modern France, 1916-1931, Louisiana State Univ Press, 93; auth, Louis Loucheur, 1872-1931: Ingenieur, homme d'etat, modernisateur de la France, Presses Universitaires du septentrion, 00. **CONTACT ADDRESS** Dept Hist & Govt, Union Univ, 1050 Union Univ Dr, Jackson, TN 38305-3656. **EMAIL** scarls@uu.edu

CARLSON, ANDREW
PERSONAL Born 08/19/1934, Ludington, MI, m, 1959, 2 children **DISCIPLINE** HISTORY **EDUCATION** West Mich Univ, BA, 60; MA, 61; Mich State Univ, PhD, 70. **CAREER** Asst prof, Eastern Kent Univ, 67-70; asst prof, Ferris State Univ, 70-73; Kalamazoo Cty Govt, 76-00; adj prof, Western Mich Univ, 74-75, 89-. **HONORS AND AWARDS** Pi Gamma Mu; Phi Alpha Theta. **MEMBERSHIPS** AHA; GSA; Wissenschaftliche Korrespondenz; CCEH; SHA; CES; AAA; MAA. **RESEARCH** Germany 1871-1945; Wilhelm II; film in Nazi Germany; postal system in Nazi Germany; 1936 Berlin Olympics; anarchism in Germany; German foreign and colonial policy; World War I; World War II. **SELECTED PUBLICATIONS** Auth, Anarchism in Germany, The Early Years (Metuchen, 72); auth, "Anarchism and Individual Terror in the German Empire 1870-1890," in Social Protest, Violence & Terror in Nineteenth & Twentieth Century Europe, ed. Wolfgang J Morninsen (Macmillan; London, 82); auth, Sozialprotest, Gewalt, Terror, Gewaltanwendung durch politische und gesellschaftliche Randgruppen im und 20. Jahrundert, ed. Wolfgang J Mommsen (Klett-Cotta: Stuttgart, 82); auth, "Wilhelm II and the Hale Interview," University Microfilms, 89; auth, Modern Germany: An Encyclopedia of History, People, and Culture, 1871-90 (Garland: New York & London, 98); auth, "National Malaise, National Unity: Wilhelm II's Attempt to Consolidate the Reich," Michigan Academician 30 (98): 131-146, auth, of articles on Wilhelm II and Karl von Clausewitz in the 2000 ed of the Encyclopedia of Military History. **CONTACT ADDRESS** Dept History, Western Michigan Univ, 1201 Oliver St, Kalamazoo, MI 49008-3804. **EMAIL** andrew.carlson@wmich.edu

CARLSON, ARVID JOHN
PERSONAL Born 09/12/1928, East Tawas, MI, m, 1950, 2 children **DISCIPLINE** EARLY MODERN EUROPEAN HISTORY **EDUCATION** Univ Mich, AB, 50, AM, 51; Princeton Univ, AM, 58, PhD, 62. **CAREER** Instr social studies, Emory-at-Oxford, 51-55; Danforth teacher grant, 55-56; assoc prof hist, Wofford Col, 58-61; assoc prof, 62-65, Prof Hist & Basic Studies, Austin Col, 65-, Chmn Humanities, 67-, Assoc Dean Col, 71-, retired, 94. **MEMBERSHIPS** World Hist Asn; Conf Brit Studies. **RESEARCH** Elizabethan history; influence of Puritanism on early Elizabethan bishops, Reformation studies, effect of Martin Butzer and reformed theology in general; higher education, impact of change on liberal arts education. **SELECTED PUBLICATIONS** Rev, The Sign of the Golden Grasshopper--A Biography of Sir Gresham, Thomas, Sixteenth Century Jour, Vol 0027, 96; Auth, Mundus-Muliebris--The World of Women Reviled and Defiled C.195-Bc and 1551-Ad and Other Things, Sixteenth Century Jour, Vol 0024, 93; Rev, The English-Civil-War--A Contemporary Account, Vol 1, 1625-1639, Sixteenth Century Jour, Vol 0028, 97. **CONTACT ADDRESS** Dept of Hist, Austin Col, Sherman, TX 95090. **EMAIL** ajcarl@texoma.net

CARLSON, LEWIS H.
PERSONAL Born 08/01/1934, Muskegon, MI, m, 1960, 2 children **DISCIPLINE** RECENT AMERICAN HISTORY **EDUCATION** Univ Mich, BA, 57, MA, 62; Mich State Univ, PhD(hist), 67. **CAREER** Asst prof hist, Ferris State Col, 65-68; asst prof hist, 68-80, prof hist and dir of Am studies, Western Mich Univ, 80-99; Emeritus. **HONORS AND AWARDS** Western Mich Univ Alumni Awd, 72. **MEMBERSHIPS** Asn Popular Cult. **RESEARCH** Oral history and popular culture. **SELECTED PUBLICATIONS** Co-auth, with George Colburn, In Their Place: White America Defines Her Minorities, John Wiley & Sons, 71;auth, Energy and the Way We Live, The Humanist's Guide to Energy, 79; co-auth, with John J. Fogarty, Tales of Gold: Olympic Stories as Told by Those Who Lived Them, Chicago: Contemporary Books, 87; writer and producer, Images in Black and White: a Documentary Film on Racial Images in Popular Culture, 88; co-auth, with Frank Unger, Amerika - der gespaltene Traum (America the Fragmented Dream), Berlin: Aufbau Verlag, Berlin, 92; with James Ferreira, Beyond the Red, White, and Blue: A Student's Introduction to American Studies, Dubuque, Iowa: Kendall/Hunt, 93; with Frank Unger, Highland Park oder Stadt der Zukunft (Highland Park: City of the Future?), Berlin: Aufbau Verlag, 94; with Kevin Vichcales, American Popular Culture at Home and Abroad, Kalamazoo, Mi: New Issues Press, 96; with Norbert Haase, Warten auf Freiheit: Deutsche und Amerikanische Kriegsgefangene des Zweiten Weltkrieges Erzahlen (Waiting for Freedom: An Oral History of World War II German and American Prisoners of War, Berlin: Aufbau Verlag, 96; auth, Remember Prisoners of a Forgotten War: An Oral Hiatory of Korean War POWs, NY: St. Martins Press, 02. **CONTACT ADDRESS** Dept of Hist, Western Michigan Univ, 3760 Ravine Vista, SE, Grand Rapids, MI 49508. **EMAIL** lewis.carlson@wmich.edu

CARLSON, PAUL
PERSONAL Born Minneapolis, MN, m **DISCIPLINE** AMERICAN HISTORY **EDUCATION** Dakota Wesleyan Univ, BA, 62; Minn State Univ, MS, 67; Texas Tech Univ, PhD, 73. **CAREER** Prof, Texas Lutheran Univ, 73-85; prof, Tex Tech Univ, 85-. **HONORS AND AWARDS** Mrs. Percy Jones Awd, 78, 82, 91; Fel, Tex State Hist Assoc, 92; Outstanding Grad Fac Instr, Tex Tech Univ, 93; President's Excellence in Teaching Awd, Texas Tech Univ, 93; Rupert N. Richardson Awd, WTHA, 98; Barnie E. Rushing Jr. Fac Distinguished Res Awd, 99. **MEMBERSHIPS** AHA; Org of Am Hist; W Hist Assoc; Tex State Hist Assoc; Western Writers Assoc; Am Assoc of State and Local Hist. **RESEARCH** American West. **SELECTED PUBLICATIONS** Auth, The Plains Indians, Texx A&M Univ Pr, (College Station), 98. **CONTACT ADDRESS** Dept Hist, Texas Tech Univ, 1 Tex Tech Univ, Lubbock, TX 79409-0999. **EMAIL** k6phc@ttacs.ttu.edu

CARLSON, ROBERT E.
PERSONAL Born 01/22/1922, Johnstown, PA, m, 1946, 2 children **DISCIPLINE** HISTORY **EDUCATION** Univ Pittsburgh, AB, 43, MA, 50, PhD(hist), 55. **CAREER** Lectr & instr hist, Univ Pittsburgh at Johnstown, 47-49, from lectr to asst prof, Univ Pittsburgh, 49-61; Prof Hist, West Chester Univ, 61-84; Prof Emer, 84-. Am Coun Learned Soc & Am Philos Soc grants, 60-61; Am Philos Soc grant, 69. **HONORS AND AWARDS** Distinguished prof hist, West Chester Univ, 79. **MEMBERSHIPS** AAUP; AHA. **RESEARCH** Hist of Am and Brit railways; Chester County hist. **SELECTED PUBLICATIONS** Auth, British railroads and engineers and the beginnings of American railroad development, Bus Hist Rev, 60; The Pennsylvania Improvement Society and its promotion of canals and railroads, 1824-1826, Pa Hist, 7/64; The Liverpool and Manchester Railway Project 1821-1831, David & Charles, Newton Abbot, Devon & Kelley, NY, 69; Chester County Pennsylvania Bibliography, KNA Press, 81; Dictionary of Chester County Biography, 82. **CONTACT ADDRESS** 1343 W Baltimore Pike, Media, PA 19063.

CARLSON, ROY L.
PERSONAL Born 06/25/1930, Bremerton, WA **DISCIPLINE** ARCHAEOLOGY, ART **EDUCATION** Univ Wash, BA, 52, MA, 55; Univ Ariz, PhD, 61. **CAREER** Asst prof, Univ Colo, 61, field dir, 4th Nubian Exped, 65; asst prof to prof, 66-95, dept ch, 71-79, 84-89, prof emer Archaeology, Simon Fraser, Univ, 95-. **HONORS AND AWARDS** Smith-Wintemberg Awd, Can Archaeol Asn, 95. **MEMBERSHIPS** Can Archaeol Asn; Soc Am Archaeol; Am Indian Art Stud Asn; Am Asn Advan Sci. **RESEARCH** North American archaeology and prehistory with particular interests in the Northwest Coast, the Southwest, and PaleoIndian cultures. **SELECTED PUBLICATIONS** Auth, Indian Art Traditions of the Northwest Coast, Archaeology Press, Simon Fraser Univ, Burnaby, 83; auth, "Cultural Antecedents," in Handbook of North American Indians 7 Northwest Coast, ed. W. Suttles, Smithsonian Institution, (Washinigton D.C., 90): 60-69; auth, "Clovis from the Perspective of the Ice Free Corridor," in Clovis Origins and Adaptions, eds. R. Bonnichsen and K.L. Turnmire, (Oregon State Univ, Corvallis, 91); auth, "Before Malaspina: the Archeology of Northwest Coast Indian Cultures," in Malaspina'92, eds. M. Palau Baquero and N. Orozco Acuaaviva, (Real Academia Hispano-Americana, Cadiz, 94); auth, Early Human Occupation in British Columbia, Univ of British Columbia Press, Vancouver, 96. **CONTACT ADDRESS** Dept of Archaeol, Simon Fraser Univ, Burnaby, BC, Canada V5A 1S6. **EMAIL** royc@sfu.ca

CARLTON, DAVID L.
PERSONAL Born 01/06/1948, Spartanburg, SC, s **DISCIPLINE** HISTORY **EDUCATION** Amherst Col, BA, 70; Yale Univ, MA, MPhil, 74, PhD, 77. **CAREER** Vis asst prof, Tex Tech Univ, 79-80; lectr in Hist, Coastal Carolina Col, 81-82; Asst Prof of Hist, 83-89; Assoc Prof, Vanderbilt Univ, 89-. **HONORS AND AWARDS** NEH Fel, 80-81; Fel, Nat Humanities Center, 94-95. **RESEARCH** History of the American South; Industrialization. **SELECTED PUBLICATIONS** Auth, Mill and Town in South Carolina, 1880-1920, La State Univ Press, 82; The Revolution From Above: The National Economy and the Beginnings of Industrialization in North Carolina, J of Am Hist, 90; Paternalism and Southern Textile Labor: A Historiographical View, Race, Class, and Community in Southern Labor Hist, Univ of Ala Press, 94; coauth, Capital Mobilization and Southern Industry, 1880-1920: The Case of the Southern Piedmont, J of Economic Hist, 89; co-ed, Confronting Southern Poverty in the Great Depression: The Report on Economic Conditions of the South and Supplementary Documents, Bedford Books of St. Martin's Press, 96. **CONTACT ADDRESS** Dept of History, Vanderbilt Univ, PO Box 1802, Sta B, Nashville, TN 37235. **EMAIL** david.l.carlton@vanderbilt.edu

CARMACK, NOEL A.
PERSONAL Born 11/21/1967, Paso Robles, CA, m, 1990, 1 child **DISCIPLINE** ART, ILLUSTRATION **EDUCATION** Utah State Univ, BFA, 93, MFA, magna cum laude, 97. **CAREER** Pres lib, 94-, Utah State Univ; Conservator, 91-94, archive Asst, 89-91, Spec Collections. **HONORS AND AWARDS** Mountain W Cen Reg Stud Fel; Liquitex Excel Art Prod Gnt; W Mont Timmons Awd; Liquitex Excel Art Univ Awd; George B and Marie Eccles Caine Art Schsp; CVHS Hist Preser Awd; SMA, Awd of Merit; 3rd PL Eccles Comm Art Cent Blk/Wht Competition. **MEMBERSHIPS** MHA; CIA; USHS; ULA; UASAL. **RESEARCH** Art, preservation, conservation, collections mgmt; American culture and religious history with emphasis in Mormon experience. **SELECTED PUBLICATIONS** Auth, Before the Flapper: The Utah Beginnings of John Held Jr., UT Historical Qtly, 98; A Memorable Creation: The Life and Art of Effie Marquess Carmack, BYU Studies, 97-98; One of the Most Interesting Seeneries that can be Found in Zion: Philo Dibble's Panorama, and Museum, Nauvoo J, 98; Conservation Note: Selection for Preservation: A Few Considerations, Con Inter-Mountain Archv NewsLetter, 98; Portrait of a Lady Rediscovered?, Marginalia, 97; Saving the Serials: Preserving Mass Culture at the Utah State Univ Libraries, Archv Prod News, 97; The Yellow Ochre Club: B.F. Larson and the Pioneer Trail Art Tour 1936, UT Hist Qtly, 97; Of Prophets and Pale Horses: Joseph Smith Benjamin West and the American Millenarian Tradition, Dialogue, J Mormon Thought, 96; Labor in the Construction of the Logan Temple, 1877-18884, J Mormon History, 96; A Note on Nauvoo Theater, BYU Studies, 94; The Seven Ages of Thomas Lyne: A Tragedian Among the Mormons, John Whitmer Hist Assoc, 94; Images of christ in Latter-day Saint Visual Culture, 1900-1999, BYU Studies, forthcoming; auth, Out of the Black Patch: The Autobiography of Effie Marques Carmack, Folk Musician, Artist, and Writer edited by Noel Carmack and Karen Lynn Davidson Logan, UT; Utah State University Press, 99; Other articles: auth, "Conservation Note: UP to Standards", Con Inter-Mountain Archv Newsletter, 99; auth, "Conservation Note: Reserving and Inspecting Microfilm: Things to Look for, Con Inter-Mountain Archv Newsletter, 98. **CONTACT ADDRESS** Special Collections and Archives, Utah State Univ, 3000 Old Main Hill, Logan, UT 84322-3000. **EMAIL** noecar@ngw.lib.usu.edu

CARMAN, CHARLES
PERSONAL Born 09/08/1943, Pryor, OKLA, m, 4 children **DISCIPLINE** ART HISTORY **EDUCATION** Johns Hopkins Univ, PhD. **CAREER** Fac, SUNY Buffalo. **HONORS AND AWARDS** Summer Research in Italy Awd, UUP. **RESEARCH** Italian Renaissance and Baroque Art; 18th Century Europ Art. **SELECTED PUBLICATIONS** Auth, Images of Humanist Ideas in Italian Renaissance Art. **CONTACT ADDRESS** Dept Art, SUNY, Buffalo, 202 Center for the Arts, Buffalo, NY 14260-6010. **EMAIL** ccarman@acsu.buffalo.edu

CARMICAL, OLINE, JR.
PERSONAL Born 12/08/1944, Evarts, KY, m, 1968, 1 child **DISCIPLINE** HISTORY **EDUCATION** Cumberland Col, BA, 66; Univ Ky, MA, 70; PhD, 75. **CAREER** Asst Prof, Warren Wilson Col, 70-74; Asst Prof to Prof, Cumberland Col, 75-. **HONORS AND AWARDS** James Still Fel, Univ KY, 84. **MEMBERSHIPS** Am Hist Asn; Org of Am Hist; Phi Alpha Theta. **RESEARCH** American Constitutional History; British Colonial American History to 1783; British Constitutional and Legal History. **CONTACT ADDRESS** Dept Hist & Polit Sci, Cumberland Col, Williamsburg, KY 40769-1387. **EMAIL** ocarmica@cc.cumber.edu

CARMICHAEL, ANN GRAYTON
PERSONAL Born 08/28/1947, Roanoke, VA, d, 1 child **DISCIPLINE** HISTORY OF MEDICINE **EDUCATION** DePauw Univ, BA, 69; Duke Univ, MD, 78, PhD, 78. **CAREER** Indiana Univ, asst prof, assoc prof, 79-. **MEMBERSHIPS** AAHM, AHA, HSS, RSA. **RESEARCH** Hist of infectious diseases; hist medicine; renaissance Italy. **CONTACT ADDRESS** Dept of History, Indiana Univ, Bloomington, 742 Ballantine Hall, Bloomington, IN 47405. **EMAIL** carmicha@indiana.edu

CARMICHAEL, PETER S.
PERSONAL Born 02/23/1966, Indianapolis, IN **DISCIPLINE** CIVIL WAR AND RECONSTRUCTION **EDUCATION** PA State Univ, PhD. **CAREER** Hist Dept, Western Carolina Univ; UNC Greensboro. **SELECTED PUBLICATIONS** Auth, Lee's Young Artillerist: William R. J. Pegram, 95. **CONTACT ADDRESS** Univ of No Carolina, Greensboro, Greensboro, NC 28723. **EMAIL** pcarmich@aol.com

CARNEAL, THOMAS WILLIAM
PERSONAL Born 04/08/1934, Plattsmouth, NE, 1 child **DISCIPLINE** UNITED STATES URBAN & ECONOMIC HISTORY **EDUCATION** Univ Mo-Kansas City, BA, 63, MA, 66. **CAREER** Instr hist, Kemper Mil Acad, 65-68; asst prof, 68-80, assoc prof hist, 80-, chemn, hist humanities & philos dept, Northwest Mo State Univ, 93-, dir Missouriana Collection, 69-, Dir, Patee House Mus, 70-73; grant humanities, 77-80 & Dept Interior-Mo Off Hist Preserv grant, 78-79, 79-80 & 80-81. **MEMBERSHIPS** Orgn Am Historians; Econ Hist Asn; AAUP. **RESEARCH** Urban problems; Missouri urban and economic problems. **SELECTED PUBLICATIONS** Auth, Issac Miller House, St Joseph, 79; Caleb Burns House, Maryville, 79; Walnut Inn, Tarkio, 80; Fenton House, Buchanan County, 80; Slatten Thousand Acres, Bethany, 80; Delaney House, 80 & Mathias House, 80, DeKalb County; Jessie James House, 80 & American Electric Company, 80, St Joseph. **CONTACT ADDRESS** Dept of History, Humanities and Philos, Northwest Missouri State Univ, 800 University Dr, Maryville, MO 64468-6001. **EMAIL** tcarnea@mail.nwmissouri.edu

CARNES, MARK C.
PERSONAL Born 11/17/1950, Pocatello, ID, m, 1976, 1 child **DISCIPLINE** HISTORY **EDUCATION** Harvard Univ, BA, 74; Columbia Univ, PhD, 82. **CAREER** Gen ed, Am National

Biography; asst prof, 82-89, assoc prof, 89-92, Prof Hist, Barnard Col, Columbia Univ, 92-. **MEMBERSHIPS** OAH, AHA, Soc Am Historians **RESEARCH** Am social hist **SELECTED PUBLICATIONS** various **CONTACT ADDRESS** Dept Hist, Barnard Col, 3009 Broadway, New York, NY 10027. **EMAIL** mc422@columbia.edu

CARNEY, JUDITH A.
PERSONAL Born Detroit, MI **DISCIPLINE** GEOGRAPHY **EDUCATION** Mich State Univ, BA, 69; Univ Calif Berkeley, MA, 79; PhD, 86. **CAREER** Assoc scientist, CIMMYT, 88-89; asst prof to assoc prof, UCLA, 88-. **HONORS AND AWARDS** Univ Calif President's Res Fel, 98; Wenner-Gren Found for Anthropol Res, 97; UCLA Luckman Distinguished Teaching Awd, 96; Eby Awd, 96. **MEMBERSHIPS** Asn of Am Geogr. **RESEARCH** Environment and development: Latin America and West Africa; Cultural and ecological knowledge transfers with the African Diaspora; African indigenous knowledge systems. **SELECTED PUBLICATIONS** Co-auth, "Manufacturing Dissent: Work, Gender, and the Politics of Meaning in a Peasant Society," Africa, (92): 207-241; co-auth, "Disciplining Women? Rice, Mechanization and the Evolution of Mandinka Gender Relations in Senegambia," Signs, (92): 651-681; auth, "From Hands to Tutors: African Expertise in the South Carolina Rice Economy," Agricultural Hist, (93): 1-30; auth, "Converting the Wetlands, Engendering the Environment: The Intersection of Gender with Agrarian Change in the Gambia," Econ Geog, (93): 329-349; auth, "Landscapes of Technology Transfer: Rice Cultivation and African Continuities," Technol and Culture, (96): 5-35; auth, "Gender and Slave Labour in Colonial South Carolina," Pas and Present, (96): 108-134; auth, "The Role of African Rice and Slaves in the History of Rice Cultivation in the Americas," Human Ecology, (98): 525-545; auth, "The African Origins of Carolina Rice culture," Ecumene, (00): 125-149. **CONTACT ADDRESS** Dept Geog, Univ of California, Los Angeles, 1255 Bunche, Box 951524, Los Angeles, CA 90095-1524. **EMAIL** carney@geog.ucla.edu

CAROLI, BETTY BOYD
PERSONAL Born 01/09/1938, Mt Vernon, OH, m, 1966 **DISCIPLINE** AMERICAN HISTORY **EDUCATION** Oberlin Col, BA, 60; Univ Pa, MA, 61; NYork Univ, PhD(Am civilization), 72. **CAREER** Instr speech, State Univ NY Brockport, 61-63; teacher English as second lang, British Col, Sicily & English Sch, Rome, Italy, 64-65; lectr debate, Queens Col, 65-66; instr, 66-78, Prof Hist, Kingsborough Community Col, 78-95. **MEMBERSHIPS** Am Ital Hist Asn (secy, 78-82); Immigration Hist Soc. **RESEARCH** American women's history; immigration history. **SELECTED PUBLICATIONS** Auth, Italian Repatriation From the United States, 1900-1914, Ctr Migration Studies, 73; co-ed, The Italian Immigrant Woman in North America, Multicult Hist Soc, 78; coauth, Today's Immigrants: Their Stories, Oxford Univ Press, 81; contrib, Images: A Photographic History of Italian Americans, Ctr Migration Studies, 81; Rhetoric of Protest and Reform, Ohio Univ Press, 80; auth, First Ladies, Oxford, 87, expanded ed, 95; auth, Immigrants Who Returned Home, Chelsea, 90; auth, Inside the White House, Doubleday, 92, expanded ed, 99; auth, America's First Ladies, Doubleday, 96; auth, The Roosevelt Women, Basic, 98. **CONTACT ADDRESS** 30 Fifth Ave, New York, NY 10011. **EMAIL** bbckb@aol.com

CARP, E. WAYNE
PERSONAL Born 08/02/1946, New York, NY, s **DISCIPLINE** HISTORY **EDUCATION** Univ of CA, Berkeley, PhD, 81; MA, 73; AB, 72 **CAREER** Prof, 98-, Chair, 95-99, Assoc Prof, 92-98, Asst Prof, 86-92, Pac Luth Univ; Visit Asst Prof, 84-85, Univ of WA; vis asst prof, Stanford Univ, 88; vis lecturer, Univ of Calif, Berkeley, 83, 81. **HONORS AND AWARDS** Univ Faculty Excel Awd, 98; assoc ed, The Nathanael Greene papers, Rhode Island Hist Soc, Jan 84-Sept 85; ed, fel, The Papers of Thomas Jefferson, Nat Hist Publications and Record Commission, Dept of Hist, Princeton Univ, 82-83; Nat Endowment fo the Humanities, Fel for Col Teachers and Independent Scholars, 94-95; Nat Endowment for the Humanities, Summer stipend, 92; F. leroy Hill Summer fac fel, Inst for Humane Studies, summer, 89; John M. Olin Found fel, 87-88; Vis fel, The Henry E. Huntington Libr, June 87; Nat Hist Soc Bk Prize, 85; Phi Beta Kappa Soc, 72; grad cum laude, 72 **MEMBERSHIPS** Am Hist Asn; Orgn of Am Historians; assoc, Inst of Early Am Hist and Culture; H-Net; Social Welfare Hist Group; Southern Hist Asn. **RESEARCH** History of adoption. **SELECTED PUBLICATIONS** Auth, To Starve the Army at Pleasure: Continental Army Administration and American Political Culture, 1775-1783, Univ of NC Press (Chapel Hill), 84; auth, "Two Cheers for Orphanages," Reviews in Am Hist 24 (96): 277-284; auth, "The Rise and Fall of the U.S. Children's Bureau," Reviews in Am Hist 25 (97): 606-611; auth, "Orphanages vs. Adoption: The Triumph of Biological Kinship, 1800-1930," in Always With Us: A History of Charity and Welfare, ed. Donald C. Critchlow and Hal Parker (Boston, Rowman and Littlefield, 98), 124-144; auth, "Orphanages: The Strength and Weakness of a Macroscopic View," Reviews in Am Hist (99): 105-111; auth, "Thomas Fitzsimons," in American National Biography (99); auth, "Spock on the Examining Table," Reviews in Am Hist 28 (00); ed, Adoption in History: New Interpretive Essays, forthcoming; auth, Jean Paton and the Adoption Right Movement: The Search for Identity, forthcoming. **CONTACT ADDRESS** Dept of History, Pacific Lutheran Univ, Tacoma, WA 98447-0003. **EMAIL** carpw@plu.edu

CARPENTER, GERALD
PERSONAL Born 11/04/1945, Elkin, NC, m, 1968, 2 children **DISCIPLINE** HISTORY **EDUCATION** NC State Univ, BA, 68; Tulane Univ, MA, 70; PhD, 73. **CAREER** Vis Asst Prof of History and Research Assoc Center for Business History Studies, 74-78; Asst Prof Niagara Univ, 78-; Assoc Prof Niagara Univ, 81-82; Prof of History, Niagara Univ, 82. **HONORS AND AWARDS** Phi Kappa Phi, Outstanding Teacher Awd, Niagara Univ, 96. **MEMBERSHIPS** Organization of American Historians, Southern Historical Assoc. **SELECTED PUBLICATIONS** Auth, With Bennett H. Hall, Growth in a Changing Environment: History of Exxon Corporation, 50-75; auth, co-ed. With D.F. Peters, Echoes of the Future: American Voices Since 1945. **CONTACT ADDRESS** Dept History, Niagara Univ, Timon Hall, Niagara, NY 14109. **EMAIL** cgc@niagara.edu

CARPENTER, JOEL A.
PERSONAL Born 02/02/1952, South Haven, MI, m, 1978, 2 children **DISCIPLINE** HISTORY **EDUCATION** Calvin Col, BA, 74; Johns Hopkins, MA, 77, PhD, 84. **CAREER** Vis instr, 76-77, Calvin Col; res asst, 77-78, Johns Hopkins; asst prof, 78-83, Trinity Col, IL; asst to assoc prof, 83-89, Wheaton Col; admin to dir, 83-89, Inst for Study of Am Evangelicals; dir, 89-96, Relig Prog, Pew Charitable Trusts; provost, 96-, Calvin Col. **HONORS AND AWARDS** Honors scholar, Calvin Col; Lilly Fel, Johns Hopkins Univ; Earthen Vessels: yrs best, 91, Int Bul of Missionary Res; Revive Us Again: 98 Christianity Today bk award. **MEMBERSHIPS** Am Hist Asn; Am Soc of Church Hist; Conf on Faith and Hist. **RESEARCH** Am relig and cult hist; evangel & fundamentalist Christianity; foreign missions. **SELECTED PUBLICATIONS** Co-ed, Twentieth-Century Evangelicalism: A Guide to the Sources, Garland, 80; co-ed, Making Higher Education Christian: The History and Mission of Evangelical Colleges in America, Eerdmans, 87; ed, Fundamentalism in American Religion, a 45-volume repr ser, Garland, 88; co-ed, Earthen Vessels: American Evangelicals and Foreign Missions, 1880-1980, Eerdmans, 90; auth, Revive Us Again: The Reawakening of American Fundamentalism, Oxford Univ Press, 97. **CONTACT ADDRESS** Provost's Office, Calvin Col, 3201 Burton St SE, Grand Rapids, MI 49546. **EMAIL** jcarpent@calvin.edu

CARPENTER, JOSEPH, II
PERSONAL Born 07/21/1937, Aliceville, AL, m **DISCIPLINE** AFRICAN-AMERICAN STUDIES **EDUCATION** MATC, AA 1965; Marquette U, BA 1967; Fisk U, 1968-69; Marquette U, PhD 1970; Univ of IA, Post Doctorate 1972. **CAREER** Univ of WI, prof Afro-Educ, soc research, 72-. **HONORS AND AWARDS** Distinguished Christian Fellowship Awd for Comm Serv 1973; distinguished political serv Awd 1974. **MEMBERSHIPS** Dir Carthage Coll 1970-72; asst prof Lehman Coll Bronx Summer 1971; NEA Fellow Marquette Univ 1968-70; chmn City of Milwaukee Bd of Election Commr; chmn bd dir Northcott Youth Serv Bur for Prevention of Juvenile Delinq; chmn Univ of WI Afro-am Stud Comm Rel Comm; exec bd mem Social Studies Council of WI; consult State of NJ Dept of Ed; mem Phi Delta Kappa; alpha Psi Alpha; Milwaukee Frontiers Internat; bd dir Nat Council for Black Child Develop Inc. **SELECTED PUBLICATIONS** numerous articles **CONTACT ADDRESS** Dept of Afro Am Studies, Univ of Wisconsin, Milwaukee, Milwaukee, WI 53201.

CARPENTER, T. H.
PERSONAL Born 07/07/1944, Eugene, OR, m **DISCIPLINE** CLASSICAL ARCHAEOLOGY **EDUCATION** Johns Hopkins Univ, BA, 66; Harvard Univ, MTS, 71; Oxford Univ, DPhil, 83. **CAREER** Teacher, Groton Sch, Groton, MA, 71-76; teacher and admr, St. Stephen's Sch, Rome, Italy, 76-80; chief res, Beazley Archive Ashmolean Mus, Oxford, England, 82-86; prof, Va Polytechnic Inst and State Univ, 86-97; prof, Oh Univ, Athens, Oh, 97-. **HONORS AND AWARDS** Charles J. Ping Prof of Humanities. **MEMBERSHIPS** Amer Philol Asn; Archaeol Asn of Amer; Col Art Asn. **RESEARCH** Ancient Greek vase painting; Greek iconography (archaic and classical); Ancient Greek religion. **SELECTED PUBLICATIONS** Auth, Dionysian Imagery in Fifth Century Athens, Oxford Univ Press, Clarendon, 97; auth, Masks of Dionysus, Cornell Univ Press, 93; auth, Art and Myth in Ancient Greece, Thames and Hudson, World of Art Series, 91; auth, Beazley Addenda, Additional References to ABV, ARV and Paralipomena, 2nd ed, Oxford Univ Press for the Brit Acad, 89; auth, Dionysian Imagery in Archaic Greek Art, Oxford Univ Press, Clarendon, 86; auth, Summary Guide to the Corpus Vasorum Antiquorum, Oxford Univ Press for the Brit Acad, 84; co-auth, Mythology, Greek and Roman, Independent Sch Press, 77; article, Nymphs, not Maenads, Amer Jour of Archaeol, 99, 314, 95; article, A Symposium of Gods, In Vino Veritas, Oxford, 145-63, 95; article, The Terrible Twins in Sixth Century Attic Art, Apollo, Origins and Influences, Univ Ariz Press, 61-79, 94; article, Harmodios and Apollo in Fifth Century Athens. What's in a Pose?, in J. Oakley ed. Athenian Potters and Painters, American School of Classical Studies, Athens, 97. **CONTACT ADDRESS** Classics Dept., Ohio Univ, Ellis Hall, Athens, OH 45701. **EMAIL** carpentt@ohio.edu

CARR, AMELIA J.
PERSONAL Born 04/22/1955, Columbus, OH **DISCIPLINE** ART HISTORY **EDUCATION** Ohio State Univ, BA, 76; Northwestern Univ, PhD, 84. **CAREER** Lectr, Northwestern Univ, 82; asst prof, 82-87, dir, prog in Greece and Turkey, Lake Forest Col, 85; asst prof, 87-94, dir, summer prog in Fr, 90, assoc prof, 94-, dir, Women's Stud prog, Allegheny Col, 96-. **RESEARCH** Klosterneuburg, Austria. **SELECTED PUBLICATIONS** Auth, Narrative Pictorial Cycles of the Renaissance and Baroque; trans, The Seal of Blessed Mary, by Honorius Augustodunensis (Peregrina Publ, 1991); auth, "Women's Manuscripts at Klosterneuburg," Early Drama Art and Music Rev (00). **CONTACT ADDRESS** Allegheny Col, Meadville, PA 16335.

CARR, DAVID RANDOLPH
PERSONAL Born 08/03/1942, San Francisco, CA, m, 1965 **DISCIPLINE** MEDIEVAL HISTORY **EDUCATION** Colo State Univ, BA, 64; Univ Nebr, Lincoln, MA, 68, PhD, 71. **CAREER** Asst prof Hist, Univ South Fla, 71-80; assoc prof Hist, 80-; coord, Col of Arts and Sciences, 99-. **MEMBERSHIPS** AHA; Medieval Acad Am; Soc Ital Hist Studies; Wiltshire Record Society, Haskins Soc, Am Soc for Legal Hist. **RESEARCH** Medieval urban history, especially Italy and England; philosophy of history, social history (medieval, Renaissance, Reformation). **SELECTED PUBLICATIONS** Coauth, The process of criticism in interpretive sociology and history, Human Studies, 78; auth, The prince and the city: Ideology and reality in the thought of Marsilius of Padua, Medioevo rivista di storia della filos medievale, 81; Marsilius of Padua: The use and image of history in Defensor Pacis, Altro Polo, 82; auth, "Marsilius of Padua and the Role of Law," Italian Quarterly, 87; auth, "The Problem of Urban Patriciates: Office Holders in Fifteenth-Century Salisbury," Wiltshire Archaeology and Natural Magazine, 89; auth, "Frederick Barbarossa and the Lombard League: The Role of Law in the Emergence of the Cities of Northern Italy," Journal of the Rocky Mountain Medieval and Renaissance Association, 89; From Pollution to Prostitution: Supervising the Citizens of Fifteenth-Century Salisbury, Southern History: A Review of the History of Southern England, 97; Judaism in Christendom, in Blackwell Companion to Judaism, ed Jacob Nuesner & Alan Avery-Peck, London, Blackwell, 00; Judaism in Christendom, in Blackwell Reader in Judaism, ed. J. Neusner & A. Avery-Peck, London, Blackwell, 01; auth, Salisbury City First General Entry Book, Wiltshire Record Society, Devizes, 00. **CONTACT ADDRESS** Dept of History, Univ of So Florida, 140 7th Ave S, Saint Petersburg, FL 33701-5016. **EMAIL** carr@stpt.usf.edu

CARR, GRAHAM
DISCIPLINE MODERN NORTH AMERICAN CULTURAL HISTORY **EDUCATION** Queen's Univ, BA, MA; Univ Maine, PhD. **CAREER** Assoc prof. **RESEARCH** Post WWII cultural and public history. **SELECTED PUBLICATIONS** Pub(s), on culture and free trade, literary history, and historiography. **CONTACT ADDRESS** Dept of Hist, Concordia Univ, Montreal, McConnell Library Bldg, 1455 de Maisonneuve W, Montreal, QC, Canada H3G 1W8. **EMAIL** gcarr@vax2.concordia.ca

CARR, LOIS GREEN
PERSONAL Born 03/07/1922, Holyoke, MA, m, 1963, 1 child **DISCIPLINE** AMERICAN COLONIAL & LEGAL HISTORY **EDUCATION** Swarthmore Col, AB, 43; Radcliffe Col, AM, 44; Harvard Univ, PhD(hist), 68. **CAREER** Asst ed, Alfred A Knopf, Inc Col Dept, 51-52; jr archivist, Hall of Rec Comn, Annapolis, 56-64; adj prof hist, Historian, Historic St Mary's City Comn, MD, 67-, vis prof hist, St Mary's Col Md, 70; coun mem, omohundro, Inst Early Am Hist & Cult, 80-82; mem, Res Div, AHA, 80-82; adv bd, McNeil Ctr for Early Am Stud, 81- ; adj prof hist, Univ Md, 82- ; sr adj scholar, Md State Archv, 88- ; sr hist, Md Hist Trust, 89- ; pres, Econ Hist Asn, 90-91; publ comt, Md Hist Soc, 90- ; Bd of Trustees, Charles Carroll House of Annapolis, 94- ; Md Hum Coun, 98- . **HONORS AND AWARDS** Phi Beta Kappa; Vis prof hist, St Mary's Col; co-prin investr, Nat Sci Found grant, 72-73 & Nat Endowment for Humanities grant, 76-79; fel, Regional Econ Hist Res Ctr, Eleutherian Mills-Hagley Found, 79-80; sr res assoc, Nat Endowment for Humanities grant, 81-83; proj dir, Am Asn for State and Local Hist grant, 88-89; co-winner, Md Hist Soc Book Prize, 93; co-winner, Econ Hist Asn Alice Hanson Jones Prize, 94; co-winner, Eisenberg Prize for Excellence in the Hum, Md Hum Coun, 96; Woman of the Year, 00; Md Commission on Women, 00. **MEMBERSHIPS** AHA; Orgn Am Historians; Econ Hist Asn; Soc Sci Hist Asn.; So Hist Asn; Am Soc for Legal Hist. **RESEARCH** Colonial Chesapeake society and economy; local government and the courts of colonial Maryland; social analysis of communities. **SELECTED PUBLICATIONS** Auth, The Metropolis of Maryland: A Comment on Town Development Along the Tobacco Coast, Md Hist Mag, summer 74; coauth, Maryland's Revolution of Government, 1689-1692, Cornell Univ, 74; The Planter's Wife: The Experience of White Women in Seventeenth Century Maryland, William & Mary Quart, 10/77; auth, The Development of the Maryland Orphan's Court, 1654-1715, In: Law, Society and Politics in Early Maryland, Johns Hopkins Univ Press, 77; The Foundations of Social Order: Local Government in Colonial Maryland, In: Town and County: Essays on the Structure of Local Govern-

ment in the American Colonies, Wesleyan Univ Press, 78; coauth, Immigration and Opportunity: The Freedman in early Colonial Maryland, In: The Chesapeake in the Seventeenth Century: Essays on Anglo-American Society and Politics, Univ NC Press, 79; Inventories and the Analysis of Wealth and Consumption Patterns in St Mary's County, Maryland, 1658-1777, Hist Methods, spring 80; The Lords Baltimore and the Colonization of Maryland, In: Maryland in a Wider World, Wayne State Univ Press, 82; Robert Cole's World: Agriculture and Society in Early Maryland, North Carolina, 91; auth, Emigration and the Standard of the Living: The Seventeenth Century Chesapeake, in J of Econ Hist, 92; co-auth, Changing Life Styles and Consumer Behavior in the Colonial Chesapeake, In: Of Consuming Interests: Styles of Life in the Eighteenth Century, Univ Pr of Va, 94; auth, Wealth and Welfare in the Colonial Chesapeake, William and Mary Q, 99. **CONTACT ADDRESS** Maryland State Archives, 350 Rowe Blvd, Annapolis, MD 21401. **EMAIL** loisc@mdmarchives.state.md.us

CARR, MICHAEL HAROLD
PERSONAL Born 05/26/1935, Leeds, England, m, 1961, 1 child **DISCIPLINE** GEOLOGY **EDUCATION** London, BSc, 56; Yale, PhD, 60. **CAREER** Res assoc, Univ W Ontario, 60-62; Geologist, US Geol Surv, 62-. **HONORS AND AWARDS** NASA Medal Except Sci Achievement, 77; Dept Interior Distinguished Serv Awd, 88; Geol Soc Am Gilbert Awd, 93; Natl Air & Space Mus Lifetime Achievement Awd, 94. **MEMBERSHIPS** Am Asn Advanced Sci; Geol Soc Am; Am Geophys Soc **RESEARCH** Planetary Science **SELECTED PUBLICATIONS** The Surface of Mars, Yale; Water on Mars, Oxford. **CONTACT ADDRESS** US Geol Survey, Menlo Park, CA 94025. **EMAIL** carr@usgs.gov

CARRENO, ANTONIO
PERSONAL Born 07/01/1938, Orense, Spain, m, 1962, 2 children **DISCIPLINE** HISPANIC STUDIES **EDUCATION** Escuela Normal Magisterio, BA, 63; Trinity Col, MA, 70; Yale Univ, MPhil, 74; PhD, 75. **CAREER** Acting instr, Yale Univ, 74-75; asst prof, Columbia Univ, 75-78; assoc prof to prof, Univ of IL, 79-85; prof, Brown Univ, 85-. **HONORS AND AWARDS** Ramon Menendez Pidal Prize, 78; W Duncan MacMillan Family Prof in the Humanities, 93. **MEMBERSHIPS** MLA; Int Assoc of Hispanist; Assoc of Teachers of Span and Port. **SELECTED PUBLICATIONS** Auth, "A un rio lo llamban Carlos", La moderna critica literaria hispanica. Antologia, ed Miguel Angel garrido Gallardo, Editorial Mapfre, (Madrid, 96): 31-37; auth, "The Poetics of Closure in Calderon's Plays", The Calderonian Stage: Body and Soul, ed Manuel Delgado Morales, Bucknell Univ Pr, (97): 25-44; auth, "De mi vida, Amarilis, os he escrito / lo que nunca pense. Las biografias liricas de Lope de Vega", Anuario de Lope de Vega, Univ Autonoma de barcelona, (97): 25-44; auth, "Las dulces / amargas prendas en don Ouijote: Eldiscurso de la locura", Cervantes, Gongora y Ouevedo, Univ Nacional de Cuyo (Argentina, 97): 50-71; auth, "Los concertados disparates de don Quijote: sobre el discurso de la locura", En un lugar de la Mancha: estudios cervantinos en honor de Manuel Duran, Salmanda, Ediciones almar (99): 57-75; auth, "Los silencios criticos de una recepcion: Lope de Vega: Del 98 al 98: literatura e historia literaria en el siglo XX hispano, eds Victor Garcia Ruiz, rosa Fernandez Urtasun, David K Herzberger, RILCE 15.1 , (99): 141-155; auth, "Un canto en disfrazado velo: las Angelicas de Lope de Vega", Dule et decorum est philogican colere: Festchrift fur Dietrich Briesemesiter zu seinment 65 Geburtstag, Domus Editoria europeae (Berlin, 99); 145-165; ed, Lope de Vega, Rimas humanas y otros versos, Editorial Critica, (Barcelona), 98; ed, Lope De Vega, Rimas humanas y divinas de tome de burguillos, Editorial almar (Salmanca), (forthcoming); ed, Lope de Vega, Poesia completa, Ediciones de Castro, (Madrid), (forthcoming). **CONTACT ADDRESS** Dept Hispanic Studies, Brown Univ, 1 Prospect St, Providence, RI 02912-9100. **EMAIL** antonio_carreno@brown.edu

CARRIGAN, DAVID O.
PERSONAL Born 11/30/1933, New Glasgow, NS, Canada **DISCIPLINE** HISTORY **EDUCATION** St Francis Xavier Univ, BA, 54; Boston Univ, MA, 55; Univ Maine, PhD, 66. **CAREER** Asst prof, 57-61, assoc prof & dept ch, Xavier Col, St Francis Xavier Univ, 61-67; assoc prof, Wilfrid Laurier Univ, 67-68; prin & dean arts, King's Col, Univ Western Ont, 68-71; pres, 71-79, Prof Hist to Prof Emer, St Mary's Univ, 79-. **MEMBERSHIPS** Am Hist Asn. **SELECTED PUBLICATIONS** Auth, Canadian Party Platforms 1867-1968, 68; auth, Crime and Punishment in Canada, A History, 91; auth, Juvenile Delinquency in Canada, 97. **CONTACT ADDRESS** Dept of History, Saint Mary's Univ, 923 Robie St, Halifax, NS, Canada B3H 3C3.

CARRIKER, ROBERT C.
PERSONAL Born 08/18/1940, St. Louis, MO, m, 1963, 3 children **DISCIPLINE** AMERICAN HISTORY **EDUCATION** St Louis Univ, BS, 62, AM, 63; Univ OK, PhD, 67. **CAREER** From asst prof to prof hist, Gonzaga Univ, 67, Henry E Huntington Libr fels, 69 & 71; Am Philos Soc grant, 70; vis lectr Am Indian hist, AZ State Univ, 71-72. **HONORS AND AWARDS** Burlington Northern Scholar of the Year, 85, 96. **MEMBERSHIPS** Western Hist Asn; Orgn Am Historians. **RESEARCH** Frontier and Western American history; Southwestern military frontier; American Indians. **SELECTED PUBLICATIONS** Fort Supply: Indian Territory, Univ OK, 70, 2nd ed, 90; Kalispel people, Indian Tribal Series, 73; ed, An Army Wife on The Frontier, Univ UT, 75; ed, Microfilm Edition IN Lang Collection, 76; Microfilm Edition Alaska Missions Collection, 80; Microfilm Edition Pacific Northwest Tribes Missions Collection, 86; Father Peter John De Smet: Jesuit in the West, 95; Bk rev ed, Columbia, Mag of Northwest Hist, 87; ed, Great River of The West, Univ WA, 99. **CONTACT ADDRESS** Dept of Hist, Gonzaga Univ, 502 E Boone Ave, Spokane, WA 99258-0001. **EMAIL** carriker@gonzaga.edu

CARRINGER, ROBERT L.
PERSONAL Born 05/12/1941, Knoxville, TN, m, 1968 **DISCIPLINE** FILM STUDIES, CULTURAL STUDIES, AMERICAN STUDIES **EDUCATION** Univ Tenn, AB, 62; Johns Hopkins Univ, MA, 64; Ind Univ, PhD, 70. **CAREER** Prof English & Film Studies, Univ Ill, Urbana, 70-, fel, Fac Study Second Discipline (Cognitive psychol), 90-91; assoc, Center for Advan Studies, 83-84; NEH res ed grant, 86-87; Getty Scholar, 96-97. **HONORS AND AWARDS** Undergrad Instr Awd, 79; Amoco Curric Develop Awd, 80; Distinguished Prof Awd, 85; Apple Computer Curric Innovation Awd, 88. **MEMBERSHIPS** Soc Cinema Studies; Univ Film Asn; Film Div, Mod Lang Asn; Film Studies Sect, Midwest Mod Lang Asn. **RESEARCH** American film; American Literature. **SELECTED PUBLICATIONS** Auth, Circumscription of space and the form of Poe's Arthur Gordon Pym, PMLA, 5/74; Citizen Kane, The Great Gatsby, and some conventions of American narrative, Critical Inquiry, winter 75; Rosebud, dead or alive, PMLA, 3/76; coauth, Ernst Lubitsch, G K Hall, 78; auth, The Scripts of Citizen Kane, Critical Inquiry, fall 78, ed, The Jazz Singer, Univ Wis, 79; auth, Orson Wells and Gregg Toland, Critical Inquiry, summer 82; ed, Citizen Kane, Criterion Laserdisc 84, rev ed, 92; auth, The Making of Citizen Kane, Univ Calif, 85, rev ed, 96; ed, The Magnificent Ambersons, Criterion Laserdisc, 84, rev ed, 92; auth, The Magnificent Ambersons: A Reconstruction, Univ Calif, 93; Designing Los Angeles: Richard Sylbert, Wide Angle, 98; Hollywood's LA, in Looking at Los Angeles, Getty, 00. **CONTACT ADDRESS** Dept of English, Univ of Illinois, Urbana-Champaign, 608 S Wright St, Urbana, IL 61801-3613. **EMAIL** fergus@uiuc.edu

CARRINGTON, LAUREL
DISCIPLINE MEDIEVAL AND EARLY MODERN EUROPE **EDUCATION** Wellesley Col, AB, 76; Cornell Univ, MA, 81; PhD, 86. **CAREER** Instr, Cornell Univ, 85; Tchg & Res Fel, Stanford Univ, 86-88; asst prof, 88-93, assoc prof, St Olaf Col, 93- . **MEMBERSHIPS** Amer Hist Asn; Renaissance Soc of Amer; Erasmus of Rotterdam Soc; Sixteenth Cent Studies. **SELECTED PUBLICATIONS** Auth, "Erasmus' 'Lingua': The Double-Edged Tongue," The Erasmus of Rotterdam Soc Yrbk Nine (89): 106-118; auth, "The Writer and his Style: The Correspondence of Erasmus and Guallaume Bude," The Erasmus of Rotterdam Soc Yrbk Ten (90); auth, "Erasmus on the Use and Abuse of Metaphor," in Neo-Latin Acta: Toronto, (Binghamton, NY: Medieval & Renaissance Texts & Studies, 90); auth, "Rhetoric and Letter Writing: THe Correspondence between Marguerite d'Alencon and Bichop Briconnet of Meaux," in Essays on the Rhetorical Activities of Historical Women, ed Molly Meier Wertheimer (Univ of SCarolina Pr, 96), auth, "The Boundaries Between Text and Reader: Erasmus's Approach to Reading Scripture," in Archiv fur Reformationsgechichte (97). **CONTACT ADDRESS** St. Olaf Col, 1520 St Olaf Ave, Northfield, MN 55057. **EMAIL** carrington@stolaf.edu

CARROLL, BRET E.
DISCIPLINE HISTORY **EDUCATION** Emory, BA, 83; Cornell Univ, MA, 88, PhD, 91. **CAREER** VIS ASST PROF, HIST, UNIV TEXAS ARLINGTON **MEMBERSHIPS** Am Antiquarian Soc **RESEARCH** Religion **SELECTED PUBLICATIONS** Religion and Masuclinity in Antebellum America **CONTACT ADDRESS** Dept of Hist, Univ of Texas, Arlington, PO Box 19529, Arlington, TX 76019-0529.

CARROLL, CHARLES FRANCIS
PERSONAL Born 10/05/1936, Cambridge, MA, m, 1970, 1 child **DISCIPLINE** AMERICAN HISTORY **EDUCATION** Boston Col, AB, 59, MA, 61; Brown Univ, PhD(hist), 70. **CAREER** Instr hist,62-63, 66-68 & Univ RI, 65-66; asst prof, assoc prof, 68-74, prof, 74-, chmn, Dept Hist, Univ Mass, Lowell **MEMBERSHIPS** Colonial Soc of Mass; Orgn Am Hist; Am Hist Assn; Soc for Hist of Tech. **RESEARCH** Colonial history of New England; American Colonial history; American economic history. **SELECTED PUBLICATIONS** Auth, Timber Economy of Puritan New England, Brown Univ, 73; The Forest Society of New England, America's Wooden Age, Sleepy Hollow Restorations, 74; contrib, 3 chap on Chelmsford, Mass, Cotton Was King, NH Publ Co. 76; contrib, 4 art, Encycl of Am Forest & Conservation Hist, Free Press, Macmillan Pub, 83; auth, Empirical Technology and the Early Industrial Development of Lowell, Continuing Revolution: A History of Lowell, Mass, Lowell Hist Soc, 91; auth, The Human Impact on the New England Landscape, Thoreau's World and Ours: A Natural Legacy, No Am Press, 93. **CONTACT ADDRESS** Box 172, Harvard, MA 01451. **EMAIL** Charles_Carroll@uml.edu

CARROLL, FRANCIS MARTIN
PERSONAL Born 01/31/1938, Cloquet, MN, m, 1963, 1 child **DISCIPLINE** AMERICAN & IRISH HISTORY **EDUCATION** Carleton Col, BA, 60; Univ Minn, MA, 62; Dublin Univ, PhD(hist), 70. **CAREER** Instr English, SDak State Univ, 62-64; vis instr hist, Kalamazoo Col, 67-68; asst prof, 69-74, Assoc Prof Hist, St John's Col, Univ Man, 74-, Assoc Head Dept, 82-, Dean studies, St John's Col, Univ Man, 76-78; vis scholar, Columbia Univ Law Sch, 80. **MEMBERSHIPS** Am Comt Irish Studies; Am Hist Asn; Forest Hist Soc; Orgn Am Historians; Soc Historians Am Foreign Rels. **RESEARCH** Diplomacy of the Wilson Era, Anglo-Irish-Am Relations 1910-37, Anglo-Canadian-Am Relations 1814-48, Irish Nationalism, Northern Minnesota. **SELECTED PUBLICATIONS** Auth, Crossroads in Time: A History of Carlton County Minnesota, by Francis M. Carroll, 87; auth, The Wpa Guide to the Minnesota Arrowhead Country, by Workers on the Wpa Writers Program, Francis M. Carrol, 88; coauth, Fires of Autumn: The Cloquet-Moose Lake Disaster of 1928, by Franklin R. Raiter, Francis M. Carroll, 90; coauth, Reflections of Our Past: A Pictorial History of Carlton County, Minnesota, by Francis M. Carroll, 97. **CONTACT ADDRESS** Dept of Hist, Univ of Manitoba, 403 Fletcher Bldg, Winnipeg, MB, Canada R3T 5V5. **EMAIL** fcarrol@cc.umanitoba.ca

CARROLL, JAMES T.
PERSONAL Born 12/11/1961, Queens, NY, s **DISCIPLINE** HISTORY **EDUCATION** Iona Col, BA, 84; Univ Notre Dame, MA, 87; Providence Col, MEd, 92; Univ Notre Dame, Phd, 97. **CAREER** Asst Prof, Iona Col, 97-. **MEMBERSHIPS** Am Hist Asn, Am Catholic Hist Asn, Western Hist Asn. **RESEARCH** Native Americans, Maerican Catholicism, Gilded age. **SELECTED PUBLICATIONS** Auth, Seeds of Faith: Catholic Indian Boarding School, Garland Pub, New York, forthcoming; auth, "Catholic Sisterhoods," in Encyclopedia of the Great Plains, forthcoming; auth, "Self-Direction, Activity, and Syncretism: Catholic Indian Boarding Schools on the Northern Great Plains at Contact," US Catholic Historian, (98): 78-89; rev, of "Education for Extinction: American Indians and the Boarding School Experience," by David Wallace Adams, North Dakota History, (Winter 97): 36-37; rev. of ""The Massacre at Sand Creek: Narrative Voices," by Bruce Cutler, South Dakota History, (Winter 96): 260-262; rev, of "From Fort Laramie to Wounded Knee: In the West That Was," by Charles Allen, South Dakota History, (Winter 97): 264-265; rev, of "On the Padres' Trail," by Christopher Vecsey, Journal of the West, (April 99): 102; rev, of "Of Bison and Man," by Harold P. Danz, south Dakota History, (Fall 98): 191-192; rev, of "Rethinking American Indian History," by ed Donald Fixico, North Dakota History, (Fall 98): 35; rev, of "Sunset to Sunset: A Lifetime With My Brothers, The Dakota," by Thomas Lawrence Riggs, South Dakota History, (Spring 99): 52-53. **CONTACT ADDRESS** Dept Hist & Govt, Iona Col, 715 North Ave, New Rochelle, NY 10801-1830. **EMAIL** jcarroll@iona.edu

CARROLL, JOHN M.
PERSONAL Born 03/29/1943, Providence, RI, m, 1985, 2 children **DISCIPLINE** US HISTORY **EDUCATION** Brown Univ, BA, 65; Prov Col, MA, 67; Univ Ky, PhD, 73. **CAREER** Lamar Univ, 72-. **HONORS AND AWARDS** Herbert Hoover Lib Fel; Dist Lectr; Regents Prof. **MEMBERSHIPS** AHA; OAH; NASSH. **RESEARCH** Sport, popular culture; diplomatic; military. **SELECTED PUBLICATIONS** Auth, Red Grange and the Rise of Modern Football, Univ Ill Press, 99; auth, Fritz Pollard: Pioneer in Racial Advancement, Univ Ill Press, 92; auth, "Modern American Diplomacy," Schl Res (95). **CONTACT ADDRESS** Dept History, Lamar Univ, Beaumont, PO Box 10048, Beaumont, TX 77710-0048. **EMAIL** carrolljm@hal.lamar.edu

CARROLL, ROSEMARY F.
PERSONAL Born 10/15/1935, Providence, RI, s **DISCIPLINE** HISTORY, LAW **EDUCATION** Brown Univ, BA, 57; Wesleyan Univ, MA, 62; Rutgers Univ, PhD, 68; Univ Iowa, JD, 83. **CAREER** Asst prof, Notre Dame Col, 68-70; vis asst prof, Denison Univ, 70-71; asst prof, Coe Col, 71-75, 75-84; prof, 84-. **HONORS AND AWARDS** Radcliffe-Hicks Prize, Brown Univ, 56; teaching assistantship, Rutgers NDEA Summer Inst, 65, 67; res assistantship, Rutgers, 65-66; Squire Fel, Wesleyan Univ, 61-62; Coe Found Fel, Yale Univ, summer 63; General Electric Found Fel, Union Col, summer 64; Fel, Sem for Hist Adminrs, Williamsburg, Va, summer 66; Univ Fel, Rutgers, 66-67; Hoover grant, Hoover Pres Library Asn, 87-88; Olmsted Fel, Hoover Pres Library Asn, 87-92; Edward S. Murray Memorial Res Awd, Coe Col, 87-88; Fac Develop grant, Coe Col, 92-93; NEH travel grant, 92-93; listed in: Phi Kappa Phi, Who's Who in the Midwest, Who's Who of Contemporary Women, Who's Who in Am Law, Who's Who in Am Educ, The Dir of Distinguished Ams, The Int Biography of Women, The World's Who's Who of Women, Community Leaders of the World, The Int Dir of Distinguished Leadership, Two Thousand Notable Am Women, Lexington's Who's Who. **MEMBERSHIPS** Am Bar Asn, Iowa State Bar Asn, Linn Co Bar Asn, Linn Co Women Attorneys, Am Hist Asn, Org of Am Hists, Am Asn of Univ Profs, Southern Hist Asn, Southern Asn of Women Hists. **RESEARCH** U.S. Women's History, U.S. Law. **SELECTED PUBLICATIONS** Auth, "Margaret Clark Griffis: Plantation Teacher," Tenn Hist Quart, fall 67; rev of N. D. Mar-

kowitz, The Rise and Fall of the People's Century, The Historian (fall 75); auth, "A Plantation Teacher's Perception of the Impending Crisis," Southern Studies (fall 79); rev of Kent Folmar, This State of Wonders, The Annals of Iowa (fall 88); rev of Tim Purdy, The Journals of Sylvester Daniels, The Annals of Iowa (winter 89); rev of Ruth Dennis, The Homes of the Hoovers, The Annals of Iowa (spring 89); auth, "Lou Henry Hoover: The Emergence of a Leader, 1874-1916," an essay in Dale Mayer, ed, Lou Henry Hoover: Essays on a Busy Life (fall 93); auth, "Lou Henry Hoover: The Early Years," Hoover VII Symposium (forthcoming); auth, "Lou Henry Hoover: The London Years," Hoover VIII Symposium (forthcoming). **CONTACT ADDRESS** Dept Hist, Coe Col, 1220 1st Ave Northeast, Cedar Rapids, IA 52402-5008. **EMAIL** rcarroll@coe.edu

CARROLL, WARREN HASTY
PERSONAL Born 03/24/1932, Minneapolis, MN, m, 1967 **DISCIPLINE** CATHOLIC HISTORY **EDUCATION** Bates Col, BA, 53; Columbia Univ, MA, 54, PhD(hist), 59. **CAREER** Instr hist, Ind Univ, 57-58; asst command historian, Sec Air Force, US Strategic Air Command, 60-61; admin asst, Calif State Senator John G Schmitz, 67-70, legis asst, 70-72; dir, Christian Commonwealth Inst, 73-75; Pres, Christendom Col, 77-85, Contrib ed, Triumph Mag, 73-75; trustee, Seton Sch, Manassas, 76-. **MEMBERSHIPS** Fel Catholic Scholars. **RESEARCH** Church history in the broadest sense; history of the Spanish-speaking peoples; history of modern revolutionary movements, since 1789. **SELECTED PUBLICATIONS** Auth, Law: The Quest for Certainty, Am Bar Asn J, 1/63; The West come to Judgment, Triumph, 5/72; Philip II versus William Cecil: The Cleaving of Christendom, Faith & Reason, winter 75-76; coauth, Reasons for Hope, Christendom Col Press, 78; auth, The dispersion of the Apostles: Overview, Peter, spring 81, The Dispersion of the Apostles: Thomas, summer 81 & The Dispersion of the Apostles: St Jude and the Shroud, fall 81, Faith & Reason; 1917: Red Banners, White Mantle, Christendom Publ, 81; Our Lady of Guadalupe and the Conquest of Darkness, 83; The Founding of Christendom , 85; The Guillotine and the Cross, 86; The Building of Christendom, 87; Isabel of Spain, the Catholic Queen, 91; The Glory of Christendom, 93; The Rise and Fall of the Communist Revolution, 95; The Last Crusade, 96. **CONTACT ADDRESS** Christendom Col, 134 Christendom Dr, Box 87, Front Royal, VA 22630-6534. **EMAIL** Warren.h.carroll@trincomm.org

CARSON, BARBARA
PERSONAL Born 07/07/1941, m, 1965, 1 child **DISCIPLINE** URBAN STUDIES **EDUCATION** Brown Univ, AB, 63; Univ Delaware, MA, 65. **CAREER** Assoc prof, adj, George Wash Univ, Col Will Mary, New School Univ. **HONORS AND AWARDS** HF du Pont Winthrop Fel; CC Fel. **RESEARCH** Material culture; native arts. **CONTACT ADDRESS** Dept Am Studies, Col of William and Mary, PO Box 8795, Williamsburg, VA 23187-8795.

CARSON, CLAYBORNE
DISCIPLINE HISTORY **EDUCATION** Univ Calif at Los Angeles, BA, 67; MA, 71; PhD, 75. **CAREER** Prof, Stanford Univ. **HONORS AND AWARDS** Rosa Parks Distinguished Citizen Awd, MLK Jr Asn of Santa Clara Valley, 91; Fel, Ctr for Advanced Study in the Behav Scis, 93-94; Jessie and John Lectureship, Univ of Washington, 98 **SELECTED PUBLICATIONS** Auth, In Struggle: SNCC and the Black Awakening of the 1960s, Harvard Univ Press (Cambridge), 81; auth, Malcolm X: The FBI File, Carroll & Graf (New York, NY), 91; co-ed, The Eyes on the Civil Rights Leader, Penguin Books ((New York, NY), 91; coauth, American Voices: A History of the United States, Scott Forseman (Glenview, IL), 92; co-ed, The Papers of Martin Luther King, Jr., Volume 1: Called to Serve, January 1929-June 1951, Univ of Calif Press (Berkeley, CA), 92; co-ed, The Papers of Martin Luther King, Jr., Volume 2: Rediscovering Precious Values, July 1951-November 1955, Univ of Calif Press (Berkeley, CA), 94; co-ed, The Papers of Martin Luther King, Jr., Volume 3: Birth of a New Age, December 1955-December 1956, Univ of Calif Press (Berkeley, CA), 97; co-ed, A Knock at Midnight: Inspiration from the Great Sermons of Reverend Martin Luther King, Jr, IPM/Warner Books (New York, NY), 98; ed, The Autobiography of Martin Luther King, Jr, IPM/Warner Books (New York, NY), 98. **CONTACT ADDRESS** Dept Hist, Stanford Univ, Cypress Hall D, Stanford, CA 94305-4146. **EMAIL** ccarson@stanford.edu

CARSON, DAVID
PERSONAL Born 06/10/1956, Newport, TN, m, 1991, 1 child **DISCIPLINE** HISTORY **EDUCATION** E Tenn State Univ, BS, 77; MA, 80; Tex Christian Univ, PhD, 83. **CAREER** Prof, Buffalo State Col, 83-. **HONORS AND AWARDS** Chancellor's Awd for Excellence in Teaching, 99; Phi Alpha Theta. **MEMBERSHIPS** Soc for Hist of the Early Republic. **RESEARCH** The new nation. **SELECTED PUBLICATIONS** Auth, "That Ground Called Quiddism: John Randolph's War with the Jefferson Administration," in The Cong of the US 1789-1989, 20 vols, vol 2; auth, "Jefferson, Congress and the Question of Leadership in the Tripolitan War," in The Cong of the US 1789-1989, 20 vols, vol 1; auth, "The Role of Congress in the Acquisition of the Louisiana Territory," La Purchase Bicentennial Ser in La Hist, vol 3. La Purchase: The Purchase and its Aftermath 1800-1830; auth, "The Role of Congress in the Acquisition of the Louisiana Territory," La Hist, 85; auth, "That Ground Called Quiddism: John Randolph and the Origins of the Tertium Quid Revolt," J of Am Studies (Cambridge), 86; auth, "Jefferson, Congress and the Question of Leadership in the Tripolitan War," Va Mag of Hist and Biog (86); auth, Quiddism and the Candidacy of James Monroe in the Election of 1808," Mid-Am (88); auth, "Blank Paper of the Constitution: The Louisiana Purchase Debates," in Taking Sides: Clashing Views on Controversial Issues in Am Hist, 99; auth, "Blank Paper of the Constitution: The Louisiana Purchase Debates," The Historian (95). **CONTACT ADDRESS** Dept Hist & Soc Sci, Buffalo State Col, 1300 Elmwood Ave, Buffalo, NY 14222-1004. **EMAIL** samwise2@msn.com

CARTER, DAN T.
DISCIPLINE HISTORY **EDUCATION** Univ SC, BA, 62; Univ Wis, MA, 64; Univ NC, PhD, 67. **CAREER** Prof **HONORS AND AWARDS** Anisfield Wolfe Awd; 2 times Jules Landry Prize; Lillian Smith Awd; Bancroft Prize; Avery Craven Prize, Organ Am Hist; Robert F. Kennedy Bk Awd; Seltzer Prize. **RESEARCH** Southern history. **SELECTED PUBLICATIONS** Auth, Scottsboro: A Tragedy of the American South; When the War Was Over: the Failure of Self-Reconstruction in the South, 1865-1867; Politics of Rage: George Wallace, the Rise of the New Conservatism and the Transformation of American Politics; From George Wallace to Newt Gingrich: Race in the Conservative Counterrevolution, 1963-1994. **CONTACT ADDRESS** Dept History, Emory Univ, Bowden 222, Atlanta, GA 30322. **EMAIL** dcarter@emory.edu

CARTER, DORIS
PERSONAL Born 12/10/1945, Homer, LA **DISCIPLINE** HISTORY, GEOGRAPHY **EDUCATION** Grambling State Univ, BA, 69; La Tech Univ, MA, 71; La State Univ, PhD, 89. **CAREER** Prof, Grambling State Univ, 71-. **HONORS AND AWARDS** Max Bradbury Awd, 99. **MEMBERSHIPS** N La Hist Asn, La Hist Asn, SHA. **RESEARCH** Louisiana history, African-American history, African-American women in history. **SELECTED PUBLICATIONS** Auth, "Governor Robert Floyd Kennon: The Early Years 1902-1925," N La Hist J XXV (94); auth, Robert Floyd Kennon: Reform Governor, Ctr for La Studies (Lafayette, LA), 98; auth, "Fidelia Adams Johnson and Grambling state University," N La Hist Asn J XXIX (98); auth, "Martha Adams," in A Dict of La Biog: Ten-Year Supplement 1988-1998, 99; auth, "Wilbur L Hayes," in A Dict of La Biog: Ten-Year Supplement 1988-1998, 99; auth, "Fidelia Adams Johnson," in A Dict of La Biog: Ten-Year Supplement 1988-1998, 99; auth, "Minnie Ridley Merritt," in A Dict of La Biog: Ten-Year Supplement 1988-1998, 99; auth, Fascinating Tidbits and More: The African-American Experience in Louisiana History, Self-Publ (Minden, LA), 00. **CONTACT ADDRESS** Dept Hist & Geog, Grambling State Univ, 99 S Main St, Grambling, LA 71245.

CARTER, EDWARD C., II
PERSONAL Born 01/10/1928, Rochester, NY, m, 1975, 4 children **DISCIPLINE** AMERICAN HISTORY, AMERICAN LANDSCAPE, CALIFORNIA **EDUCATION** Univ Penn, AB, 54, MA, 56; Bryn Mawr Col, PhD, 62. **CAREER** Vis lect, hist, Univ of PA, 62-64; chemn, dept of hist, St. Stephen's Sch, Rome, 65-69; prof, hist, Catholic Univ Am, 69-80; ed-in-chief, Papers of Benjamin Henry Latrobe, Baltimore, 70-95; adj prof, hist, Univ of Penn, 80- ; librn, Am Philos Soc, 80- . **HONORS AND AWARDS** Elected Am Philos Soc, 83 and Am Antiq Soc, 87; 7 NEH grants; 12 NHPRC grants, 2 NSF grants; Huntington Lib Fel, 89; English-Speaking Union Ambassador Book Awd; 2 APS res grants; ACLS grant-in-aid. **RESEARCH** Creation of American landscape; California history; Philadelphia. **SELECTED PUBLICATIONS** Co-ed, Enterprise and Entrepreneurs in Nineteenth and Twentieth Century France, Johns Hopkins, 76; co-ed, Beyond Confederation: Origins of the Constitution and American National Identity, Univ of North Carolina Pr, 87; auth, One Grand Pursuit: A Brief History of the American Philosophical Society's First 250 Years, 1743-1993, Am Philos Soc, 93; ed-in-chief, The Papers of Benjamin Henry Latrobe, 10 vols, Yale, 95; ed, Surveying the Record: North American Scientific Exploration to 1930, Am Philos Soc, 98; ed, Three Journals of the Louis and Clark Expedition 1804-1806, from the American Philosophical Society Collection: A Facsimile Edition, Am Philos Soc, 00. **CONTACT ADDRESS** 105 South Fifth St, Philadelphia, PA 19106. **EMAIL** ecarter@sas.upenn.edu

CARTER, GUY C.
PERSONAL Born 02/21/1951, Austin, TX, m, 1994, 2 children **DISCIPLINE** HISTORICAL THEOLOGY **EDUCATION** Univ St. Thomas, BA, 73; Marquette Univ, MA, 80; Lutheran Sch Theol, MDiv, 86; Marquette Univ, PhD, 87. **CAREER** Pastor, Evangel Lutheran Abbey of St. Boniface, hameln, Ger, 89-91; pastor, Grace Evangel Lutheran Church, NJ, 92-94; pastor, Trinity Evangel Lutheran Church, NJ, 94-89; adj lectr, St. Peter's Col, 92-98, asst prof, 98- . **HONORS AND AWARDS** Magna cum Laude, 73; Arthur J. Schmitt Doctoral Fel, 81-82, 82-83. **MEMBERSHIPS** Am Acad Relig; Soc of Bibl Lit; Int Bonhoeffer Soc for Arch & Res. **RESEARCH** Historical theology of the German Church struggle, 1933-45; Holocaust studies. **SELECTED PUBLICATIONS** Auth, "Walter A. Maier," Twentieth Century Shapers of American Ppular Religion, Greenwood, 89; co-ed, "Bonhoeffer's Ethics," Kok Pharos, 91; auth, "Evangelische Theologie und ihre Didaktik," Damit wir einander nahe sind, Haensel-Hohenhausen, 98. **CONTACT ADDRESS** Theology Dept, Saint Peter's Col, 2641 Kennedy Blvd, Jersey City, NJ 07306. **EMAIL** gcemc@earthlink.net

CARTER, JANE B.
DISCIPLINE CLASSICAL ARCHAEOLOGY **EDUCATION** Mount Holyoke Col, AB, 70; Univ VA, MA, 71; Harvard Univ, PhD, 84. **CAREER** Assoc prof, Tulane Univ. **SELECTED PUBLICATIONS** Auth, Greek Ivory-Carving in the Orientalizing and Archaic Periods, Garland Publ Inc, 85; Ancestor Cult and the Occasion of Homeric Performance, The Ages of Homer, Univ Tex Press, 95; Thiasos and Marzeah: Ancestor Cult in the Age of Homer, From Pasture to Polis: Art in the Age of Homer, Univ Mo Press, 97; co-ed, The Ages of Homer, Univ Tex Press, 95; Egyptian Bronze Jugs from Crete and Lefkandi, Jour Hellenic Stud, 98. **CONTACT ADDRESS** Dept of Class Stud, Tulane Univ, 6823 St Charles Ave, New Orleans, LA 70118. **EMAIL** jcarter@mailhost.tcs.tulane.edu

CARTER, JEFFREY D. R.
PERSONAL Born 04/18/1963, Boston, MA, m, 1996 **DISCIPLINE** THE HISTORY OF RELIGIONS; THE RELIGIONS OF AFRICA **EDUCATION** Univ of Chicago, PhD, 97 **CAREER** Vis asst prof, Davidson Col, 97-98; vis asst prof, Univ S Carolina, 98-99. **HONORS AND AWARDS** Fulbright Dissertation Fel Nigeria; Pre-dissertation Fel Soc Sci Res Coun Nigeria; Inst Advan Study Relig Chicago. **MEMBERSHIPS** Amer Acad Relig **RESEARCH** Comparative religions; Indigenous religious traditions; Religions of Africa; Methods & theories in the study of religion. **SELECTED PUBLICATIONS** rev, Prey into Hunter: The Politics of Religious Experience, Jour Relig, 93; rev, The Social Control of Religious Zeal: A Study of Organizational Contradictions, Jour Relig, 95; rev, A History of Christianity in Africa: From Antiquity to the Present, Jour Relig, 97; Religion and Politics in Nigeria: A Study of Middle Belt Christianity, Jour Relig, 97; auth, Description is not Explanation: A Methodology of Comparison, Method & Theory in the Study of Religion, 98. **CONTACT ADDRESS** Dept of Religious Studies, Univ of So Carolina, Columbia, Columbia, SC 29208. **EMAIL** carterj@garnet.cla.sc.edu

CARTER, JOHN ROSS
PERSONAL Born 06/22/1938, Baytown, TX, m, 1960, 2 children **DISCIPLINE** HISTORY OF RELIGIONS, BUDDHIST STUDIES **EDUCATION** Baylor Univ, BA, 60; Southern Baptist Theol Sem, BD, 63; Univ London, MTh, 65; Harvard Univ, PhD(hist relig), 72; D Litt Kelaniya Univ, 98. **CAREER** Asst prof, 72-80, assoc prof, Colgate Univ, 80-, Dir, Fund Study Great Relig & Chapel House, Colgate Univ, 74-; Asst prof of phil and rel, 72-79; assoc prof, 79-83; prof, Colgate Univ, 83-; dir, Chapel House & Fund for the study of the Great rel, 74-; Robert Ho prof, Asian Studies, 96-. **MEMBERSHIPS** Am Acad Relig; Asn Asian Studes. **RESEARCH** History of religion; Buddhist studies. **SELECTED PUBLICATIONS** Auth, Dhamma: Western Academic and Sinhalese Buddhist Interpretations, Hokuseido Press, Tokyo, 78; ed, Religiousness in Sri Lanka, Marga Inst, Colombo, 79; co-ed, Religiousness in Yoga by T K V Desikachar, Univ Press Am, 80; cotranslator, The Dhammapada, Oxford Univ Press, 87; auth, On Outstanding Buddhits, State Univ, NY, 93; ed, Religious Heritage of Japan, Book East, 99. **CONTACT ADDRESS** Colgate Univ, 13 Oak Dr, Hamilton, NY 13346-1379.

CARTER, JOSEPH COLEMAN
PERSONAL Born 12/23/1941, New York, NY, 3 children **DISCIPLINE** CLASSICAL ARCHAEOLOGY, CLASSICS **EDUCATION** Amherst Col, BA, 63; Princeton Univ, MA, 67, PhD, 71. **CAREER** Asst prof, 71-76, prof class & class Archaeol, Univ TX Austin; Class Archaeol, Univ TX, Nat Endowment for Humanities younger humanist fel, 73-74; Am Coun Learned Soc fel, 79; NEH Fellowships, 88-89; Guggenheim Fellowships, 94-95. **HONORS AND AWARDS** James R. Wiseman Book, Awd Archaeological Institute of Am. **MEMBERSHIPS** Soc Promot Hellenic Studies; Archaeol Inst Am; Soc Promotion Roman Studies; Inst per la Storia della Magna Precia; Fellow Soc of An of London, 84. **RESEARCH** Excavation & research of Greek colonies on the Black Sea; Archaeological excavation, survey and research in Greek colonial S Haly. **SELECTED PUBLICATIONS** Auth, Relief sculpture from the Necropolis of Taranto, 74 & The Tomb of the Sire, 78, Am J Archaeol; The Sculpture of Taras, Philadelphia, 75; auth, The Chora of Metaponto: The Necropoleis, 97. **CONTACT ADDRESS** Dept of Class, Univ of Texas, Austin, Austin, TX 78712-1026. **EMAIL** j.carter@mail.utexas.edu

CARTER, NANCY CORSON
PERSONAL Born 03/28/1943, Williamsport, PA, m, 1967, 1 child **DISCIPLINE** AMERICAN & WOMEN'S STUDIES **EDUCATION** Susquehanna Univ, BA, 65; Univ Iowa, MA, 68, PhD(Am Civics), 72. **CAREER** Dir, Learning Resources Ctr, 74-76, asst prof Am Studies, 76-78, asst prof Lit & Human-

ities, 78-79, asst prof Lit & Creative Writing, Eckerd Col, 79-; prof Humanities, 91; fel, Cross-Disciplinary Inst, Summer, 75 & Inst Ecumenical & Cult Res, St John's Univ, Fall, 77; Fla Corresp, Art Voices/South, 78-82; poet-in-schs, Pinellas County Arts Coun, 81. **HONORS AND AWARDS** Dana Fellow, Southeastern Consortium Humanities Program, Emory Univ, 89-90; Visiting Prof, Duke Univ School of the Environment, 95-96. **MEMBERSHIPS** Soc Values Higher Educ; Am Studies Asn; Southeast Women's Studies Asn; MLA. **RESEARCH** Writings of Doris Lessing, especially mythical and evolutionary aspects; interdisciplinary approaches to theme and process of the spiritual journey; psycho-historical, mythical and spiritual ramifications of Jean Houston's work. **SELECTED PUBLICATIONS** Contribr poems, Survivor's Box, Possum Press, 77; 1970's images of the machine and the garden: Kosinski, Crews & Pirsig, Soundings: An Interdisciplinary J, 78; Artist profiles for Florida artists issue: Beckett, Crane, Hodgell, Rigg, Art Voices/South, 79; Demeter & Persephone in Margaret Atwood's novels: Mother-daughter transformations, J Anal Psychol, 10/79; coauth, Spirit of Eve: The Art of Marion Beckeet (videotape), produced on WEDU, 81; Journey toward wholeness: A meditation on Doris Lessing's The Memoirs of a Survivor, J Evolutionary Psychol, 8/81; Dragon Poems, Lewiston/Queenston/Lampeter: Mellen Poetry Press, 93. **CONTACT ADDRESS** Lett Collegium Eckerd Col, 4200 54th Ave S, Saint Petersburg, FL 33711-4744. **EMAIL** carternc@eckerd.edu

CARTER, PAUL ALLEN
PERSONAL Born 09/03/1926, New Bedford, MA, m, 1962, 4 children **DISCIPLINE** AMERICAN HISTORY **EDUCATION** Wesleyan Univ, BA, 50; Columbia Univ, MA, 51, PhD(hist), 54. **CAREER** Lectr hist, Columbia Univ, 54-55; actg asst prof, Cornell Univ, 55; asst prof, Univ Md, 55-56; from asst prof to assoc prof, Univ Mont, 56-62; vis assoc prof hist, Smith Col, 62-63; vis lectr, Univ Calif, Berkeley, 63-64; vis assoc prof, Univ Mass, 64-65; vis assoc prof relig, Amherst Col, 65-66; from assoc prof to prof, Northern Ill Univ, 66-73; PROF HIST, UNIV ARIZ, 73-, Hist consult, Nat Pub Radio, DC, 77-79. **RESEARCH** American intellectual and religious history; 20th century American history; history of American science fiction. **SELECTED PUBLICATIONS** Auth, The Social-Gospel in Black-and-White--American Radical Reform, 1885-1912, Church Hist, Vol 0062, 93; Protestantism and Social Christianity, Church Hist, Vol 0063, 94; Soul in Society--The Making and Renewal of Social Christianity, Church Hist, Vol 0065, 96; Oxnam, G.Bromley--Paladin of Liberal Protestantism, Jour Amer Hist, Vol 0080, 94; Soul in Society--The Making and Renewal of Social Christianity, Church History, Vol 0065, 96. **CONTACT ADDRESS** Dept of Hist, Univ of Arizona, Tucson, AZ 85721.

CARTWRIGHT, JOSEPH HOWARD
PERSONAL Born 05/16/1939, Nashville, TN, m, 1959, 2 children **DISCIPLINE** AMERICAN HISTORY **EDUCATION** Murray State Univ, BS & MA, 62; Vanderbilt Univ, MA, 68, PhD, 73. **CAREER** From asst prof to assoc prof, 70-81, prof hist and dept chmn, 81-91, dean, Col Humanities, Murray State Univ, 91-. **MEMBERSHIPS** Orgn Am Historians; Southern Hist Asn. **RESEARCH** Southern United States history: reconstruction, race relations, politics. **SELECTED PUBLICATIONS** Auth, Black legislators in Tennessee in the 1880s: a case study in Black political leadership, in Tenn Hist Quart, fall 73; The Triumph of Jim Crow: Race Relations in Transition in Tennessee, Univ Tenn, 76. **CONTACT ADDRESS** Dept of Hist, Murray State Univ, 1 Murray St, Murray, KY 42071-3310. **EMAIL** Joseph.Cartwright@MurrayState.edu

CARY, NOEL D.
PERSONAL Born 06/22/1950, San Francisco, CA **DISCIPLINE** HISTORY **EDUCATION** Univ Calif at Davis, BS, 71; Univ Va, MA, 73; Univ Calif at Berkeley, PhD, 88. **CAREER** Adj Asst Prof, Montana State Univ, 86-87; Vis Instr, Swarthmore Col, 87-88; Vis Asst Prof, Oakland Univ, 88-89; Asst to Assoc Prof, Col of the Holy Cross, Worcester, 89-. **HONORS AND AWARDS** Ger Acad Exchange Serv Doctoral Fel, 81-82; Soc Sci Res Coun Doctoral Fel, 82-83; Charlotte Newcombe Fel, 83-84. **MEMBERSHIPS** AHA, Ger Studies Asn. **RESEARCH** Modern German History, Cold War and Postwar History. **SELECTED PUBLICATIONS** Auth, The Path to Christian Democracy: German Catholics and the Party System from Windthorst to Adenauer, Harvard Univ Press (Cambridge, MA), 96. **CONTACT ADDRESS** Dept Hist, Col of the Holy Cross, 1 College St, Worcester, MA 01610-2322. **EMAIL** ncary@holycross.edu

CASDORPH, PAUL DOUGLAS
PERSONAL Born 09/05/1932, Charleston, WV, m, 1972 **DISCIPLINE** AMERICAN HISTORY **EDUCATION** Univ Tex, Austin, BA, 60, MA, 61; Univ Ky, EdD, 70. **CAREER** Social worker, Tex Dept of Pub Welfare, 62-66; instr sociol & hist, 66-71, from asst prof to assoc prof hist, 71-77, Prof Hist, WVA State Col, 77-, Lectr, WVa Univ, 71-72; instr, Morris Harvey Col, 71-73; lectr, WVa Col Grad Studies, 72-73. **MEMBERSHIPS** Southern Hist Asn. **RESEARCH** Southern Republicanism; the Bull Moose or progressive politics; American politics and education. **SELECTED PUBLICATIONS** Auth, Army Surveillance in America, 1775-1980, Historian, Vol 0056, 93; The Draft, 1940-1973, Historian, Vol 0056, 94; Lees Terrible Swift Sword--From Antietam to Chancellorsville, An Eyewitness History, Jour Amer Hist, Vol 0080, 93. **CONTACT ADDRESS** West Virginia Univ, Charleston, 1413 Alexander Pl, Charleston, WV 25314.

CASEBIER, ALLAN
PERSONAL Born 10/01/1934, Los Angeles, CA, m, 1994 **DISCIPLINE** PHILOSOPHY; HISTORY **EDUCATION** UCLA, MA, 64; Michigan, PhD, 69. **CAREER** Philos Prof, USC, IL; Cinema/Television, Usc, Miami, FL. **HONORS AND AWARDS** Fulbright, India, 82. **MEMBERSHIPS** Amer Philos Assoc; Amer Soc for Aesthetics; Soc for Cinema Studies. **RESEARCH** Aesthetics; ethics; ontology; film hist. **SELECTED PUBLICATIONS** Auth, Film Appreciation, NY: Harcourt Brace Jovanovich, 76; Social Responsibilities of the Mass Media, Washington, DC: Univ Press Amer, 78; The Phenomenology of Japanese Cinema, Quart Rev Film & Video, 90; Film and Phenomenology, NY: Cambridge Univ Press, 91; Phenomenology and Aesthetics, Encyclopedia of Aesthetics, Oxford Univ Press, 97; A Phenomenology of Motion Picture Experience, Film and Philosophy, vol 4, 98; The Japanese Aesthetic, Journal of Comparative Lit and Art, fall 98; Theorizing the Moving Image, Film and Philos, vol 5, 99; Representation: Cultural Representations and Signifying Practices, World Communication, winter 99; Critical Communication, manuscript in progress. **CONTACT ADDRESS** Philosophy Dept, Univ of Miami, Coral Gables, FL 33124-4670. **EMAIL** acasebie@miami.edu

CASEY, JOHN DUDLEY
PERSONAL Born 01/18/1939, Worcester, MA, m, 1982, 4 children **DISCIPLINE** HISTORY, LAW, AND LITERATURE **EDUCATION** Harvard Col, BA; Harvard Law School, LLB; Univ of Iowa, MFA. **CAREER** Prof of English, Univ of Va, 72-92. **HONORS AND AWARDS** Nat Board Awd for Fiction, 89. **MEMBERSHIPS** P.E.N. **SELECTED PUBLICATIONS** Auth, The Half-life of Happiness, 98; auth, Supper at the Black Pearl, 95; auth, Spartina, 89; auth, Testimony & Demeanor, 79; auth, An American Romance, 77. **CONTACT ADDRESS** Dept of English, Univ of Virginia, Bryant Hall, Charlottesville, VA 22904.

CASEY, MICHAEL S.
PERSONAL Born 11/10/1955, New Haven, CT, m, 1978, 2 children **DISCIPLINE** HISTORY **EDUCATION** S Conn State Col, BA, 78; Providence Col, MEd, 85; U.S. Army Command & General Staff Col, MMAS, 90; Salve Regina Univ, PhD, 98. **CAREER** Dep Dir, Naval Staff Col, 94-98; Assoc Dean, Graceland Univ, 98-. **HONORS AND AWARDS** Hon Mention, Arter-Darby Military Hist Prize, 90. **MEMBERSHIPS** Am Hist Asn; Am Soc for Eighteenth-Century Studies; RI Marine Archaeol Project; Soc of Ancient Military Hist; W Front Asn. **RESEARCH** Great White Fleet; American Frontier; Military Technology. **SELECTED PUBLICATIONS** Auth, Rebel Privateers - The Winners of American Independence, U.S. Army Command and Staff Col, 98; auth, America's Technological Sailor: A Retrospective on a Century of 'Progress' in the United States Navy, UMI Co, 98; auth, Abbas the Great, Magill's Guide to Military History, 00; auth, The Parthian Empire, Magill's Guide to Military History, 00; auth, The Siege of Famagusta, Magill's Guide to Military History, 00. **CONTACT ADDRESS** Dept Hist, Graceland Col, 1 University Pl, Lamoni, IA 50140. **EMAIL** caseym@graceland.edu

CASH, PHILIP
PERSONAL Born 01/28/1931, South Portland, ME, m, 1962 **DISCIPLINE** AMERICAN COLONIAL AND MEDICAL HISTORY **EDUCATION** Gorham State Teachers Col, BS, 53; Boston Col, MA, 55, PhD(hist), 68. **CAREER** Chmn dept, 63-72, Prof Hist, Emmanuel Col, Mass, 60-, Chmn Dept, 82-. **MEMBERSHIPS** AAUP; AHA; Am Asn Hist Med; Am Inst Hist Pharm; Int Soc Hist Med. **RESEARCH** Anglo-American colonial medical and military history; American medical history. **SELECTED PUBLICATIONS** Auth, Medical men at the siege of Boston, Am Philos Soc, 73; sr ed, Medicine in Masachusetts, 1620-1820, Colonial Soc Mass Publ, Vol 57, 80. **CONTACT ADDRESS** Dept Hist, Emmanuel Col, Massachusetts, Boston, MA 02115.

CASHDOLLAR, CHARLES D.
PERSONAL Born 10/24/1943, Pittsburgh, PA, m, 1968 **DISCIPLINE** HISTORY **EDUCATION** Ind Univ of Pa, BS, 65; Univ of Pa, MA, 66; PhD, 69. **CAREER** Fel to Inst, Univ of Pa, 65-69; Asst Prof to Univ Prof, Ind Univ of Pa, 69-. **HONORS AND AWARDS** Fel, Am Coun of Learned Soc, 95-96. **MEMBERSHIPS** AHA, Orgn of Am Hist, Am Acad of Relig, Am Soc of Church Hist, Pa Hist Asm, Presby Hist Soc. **RESEARCH** 19th Century American and British Religious History. **SELECTED PUBLICATIONS** Auth, The Transformation of Theology, 1830-1890: Positivism and Protestant Thought in Britain and America, Princeton Univ Press (Princeton, NJ), 89; auth, A Spiritual Home: Life in British and American Reformed Congregations, 1830-1915, Pa State Univ Press (Univ Park), 00. **CONTACT ADDRESS** Dept Hist, Indiana Univ of Pennsylvania, Indiana, PA 15705-0001. **EMAIL** cashdolr@grove.iup.edu

CASPER, SCOTT E.
DISCIPLINE HISTORY **EDUCATION** Princeton Univ, AB, 86; Yale Univ, MA, MPhil, 90, PhD, 92. **CAREER** ASSOC PROF, HIST, UNIV NEVADA RENO **HONORS AND AWARDS** Theron Rockwell Field prize, Yale Univ; NEH Fel, Winterthur Museum and Library, 98-99; Peterson Fel, Am Antiqurian Soc, 98-99; Soc for the Hist of Authorship, Reading and Publishing Book Prize, 00. **MEMBERSHIPS** Am Antiquarian Soc **SELECTED PUBLICATIONS** Auth, Constructing American Lives: The Cultural History of Biography in Nineteenth-Century America, Yale, 92; auth, "The Two Lives of Franklin Pierce: Hawthorne, Political Culture, and the Literary Market," Am Lit Hist 5, 93; auth, "An Uneasy Marriage of Sentiment and Scholarship: Elizabeth F. Ellet and the Domestic Origins of American Women's History," Jour Women's Hist 4, 92; auth, "Defining the National Pantheon: The Making of Houghton Mifflin's Biographical Series, 1880-1900," in Reading Books: Essays on the Material Text and Literature in America, Amherst, 97. **CONTACT ADDRESS** Dept of Hist/308, Univ of Nevada, Reno, Reno, NV 89557. **EMAIL** casper@unr.nevada.edu

CASS, MICHAEL MCCONNELL
PERSONAL Born 07/01/1941, Macon, GA, m, 1965, 2 children **DISCIPLINE** AMERICAN LITERATURE & HISTORY **EDUCATION** University of the South, BA, 63; Emory Univ, PhD(Am Studies), 71. **CAREER** From instr to asst prof, 69-76, from assoc prof to prof Interdisciplinary Studies, Mercer Univ, 76-84; chmn, Lamar Mem Lec Comm, 92. **MEMBERSHIPS** SAtlantic Mod Lang Assn; Soc for the Study of Southern Lit. **RESEARCH** Southern literature; southern culture. **SELECTED PUBLICATIONS** Auth, Charles C Jones Jr and the lost cause, Ga Hist Quart, Summer 71; The South Will Rise Again, Anniversary & October Poem (poems), Southern Rev, Autumn 74; foreword to Lewis P Simpson's The Dispossessed Garden: Pastoral and History in Southern Literature, 74 & to Walter L Sullivan's A Requiem for the Renaissance: The State of Fiction in the Modern South, 75, Univ Ga Press; Joshua & Coming Back to Poetry (poems), World Order, Summer 75; At Home in the Dark, The Fairest Lass in All Christendom & The Lonesome End (poems), Southern Rev, Spring 77; Georgia Preacher (poem), Christian Century, 10/4/78; Survivors (poem), Christianity & Lit, Winter 79; foreword to Fred C. Hobson, Jr, The Writer in the Postmodern South, Athens, 91; to Jack Temple Kirby, The Counter-Cultural South, Athens, 96; auth, "Walker Percy," in Contemporary Southern Authors, ed Roger Matuz, St James Press, 98. **CONTACT ADDRESS** Interdisciplinary Studies, Mercer Univ, Macon, 1400 Coleman Ave, Macon, GA 31207-0003. **EMAIL** cass_mm@mercer.edu

CASSAR, GEORGE H.
PERSONAL Born 10/31/1938, Shebrooke, PQ, Canada, m, 1984, 3 children **DISCIPLINE** HISTORY **EDUCATION** McGill Univ, PhD. **CAREER** Prof, Eastern Michigan Univ. **HONORS AND AWARDS** Fac awd for res and pub. **RESEARCH** Modern Europe, military. **SELECTED PUBLICATIONS** Auth, Kitchener: Architect of Victory; Asquith as War Leader; Beyond Courage; auth, The Tragedy of Sir John French; The French and the Dadanelles; The Forgotten Front. **CONTACT ADDRESS** Dept of History and Philosophy, Eastern Michigan Univ, 701 Pray-Harrold, Ypsilanti, MI 48197. **EMAIL** nancy.snyder@emich.edu

CASSEDY, JAMES HIGGINS
PERSONAL Born Gloversville, NY, m, 1949, 2 children **DISCIPLINE** AMERICAN HISTORY **EDUCATION** Middlebury Col, AB, 41; Brown Univ, AM, 50, PhD, 59. **CAREER** Personnel officer, US Vet Admin, 46-48; instr employ pract & placement officer, Northeastern Univ, 48-49; dir, Haitian-Am Inst, Port-au-Prince, 51-53, Burma Am Inst, Rangoon, 53-55 & Pakistan-Am Cult Ctr, Karachi, 60-62; exec secy, Hist Life Sci Study Sect, Nat Inst Health, 62-66, dep chief Europ off, NIH, Paris, 66-68; Historian, Nat Libr Med, 68-, Instr Am hist, Williams Col, 59-60; Garrison lectr, Am Asn Hist Med, 78; Sigerist lectr, Yale Univ, 82; **HONORS AND AWARDS** Welch Medal, Am Asn Hist Med, 87; Lifetime Achievement Awd, 00. **MEMBERSHIPS** AHA; Am Asn Hist Med; Hist Sci Soc; Orgn Am Historians. **RESEARCH** History of statistics and demography; history of American medicine and science; American social and intellectual history. **SELECTED PUBLICATIONS** Auth, Charles V. Chapin and the Public Health Movement, 62; auth, Demography in Early America: Beginnings of the Statistical Mind 1600-1800, 69; auth, American Medicine and Statistical Thinking 1800-1860, Harvard Univ, 84; auth, Medicine and American Growth 1800-1860, Univ of WI, 86; auth, Medicine in America: A Short History, Johns Hopkins Univ, 91. **CONTACT ADDRESS** Hist of Med Div, National Libr of Med, 8600 Rockville Pike, Bethesda, MD 20894. **EMAIL** james_cassedy@nlm.mih.gov

CASSELS, ALAN
PERSONAL Born 02/20/1929, Liverpool, England, m, 1961, 2 children **DISCIPLINE** MODERN EUROPEAN HISTORY **EDUCATION** Oxford Univ, BA, 52, MA, 56; Univ Mich, PhD(europ diplomatic hist), 61. **CAREER** Teaching fel, Univ Mich, 52-54 & 57-58; vis lectr hist, Sweet Briar Col, 56-57; instr, Trinity Col, Conn, 59-62; asst prof, Univ Pa, 62-67; assoc

prof, 67-71, Prof Hist, McMaster Univ, 71-, Vis asst prof, Haverford Col, 63-64; Can Coun fel, 73-74 & 80-81; adv bd, Can J Italian Studies, 81- **HONORS AND AWARDS** Soc Ital Hist Studies Essay Prize, 62. **MEMBERSHIPS** Soc Ital Hist Studies (vpres, 78-79); Interuniv Ctr Europ Studies; Am Comt Hist of Second World War; AHA. **RESEARCH** Twentieth century European diplomatic history; fascism. **SELECTED PUBLICATIONS** Auth, A Disobedient Faithful Follower--Grandi, Dino from the Palazzo-Chigi to the 25th-of-July, Intl Hist Rev, Vol 0016, 94; Genoa, Rapallo, and European Reconstruction in 1922, Intl Hist Rev, Vol 0014, 92; A Nation Banished--Italian Armistice of September 1943-Ital, Amer Hist Rev, Vol 0100, 95; Italian Fascists on Trial, 1943-1948, Amer Hist Rev, Vol 0098, 93; The Crisis of Liberal Italy-- Monetary and Financial Policy, 1914-1922, Amer Hist Rev, Vol 0100, 95; Britain and Italy, 1943-1949--The Decline of British Influence, Intl Hist Rev, Vol 0019, 97; The Faces of Fraternalism--Nazi Germany, Fascist Italy, and Imperial Japan, Intl Hist Rev Vol 0014, 92. **CONTACT ADDRESS** Dept of Hist, McMaster Univ, 1280 Main St W, Hamilton, ON, Canada L8S 4M4.

CASSIDY, DAVID C.
PERSONAL Born 08/10/1945, Richmond, VA, m **DISCIPLINE** HISTORY OF SCIENCE **EDUCATION** Rutgers Univ, BA, 67, MS, 70; Purdue Univ, PhD, 76. **CAREER** Res fel, Univ Calif. Berkeley, 76-77; Humboldt fel, Univ. Stuttgart, Germany, 77-80; asst prof, Univ Regensburg, Germany, 80-83; assoc ed, Einstein Papers, Princeton and Boston, 83-90; from assoc prof to prof, Hofstra Univ, 90-. **HONORS AND AWARDS** Sci Writing Awd, Am Inst Physics, 93; Fel, Am Physical Soc, 94; Pfizer Awd, Hist of Sci Soc, 95; Hon Dr Sci, Purdue Univ, 97. **MEMBERSHIPS** Hist of Sci Soc; Am Phys Soc; NY Acad of Scis, Ed Board, Phys in Perspective. **RESEARCH** Hist of German Physics, espec 18th and 20th centuries, biographies of Albert Einstein and Werner Heisenberg, science education. **SELECTED PUBLICATIONS** Auth, Meteorology in Mannheim, The Palatine Meteorological Society 1781-1795, Sudhoffs Archiv, 69, 85; Uncertainty: The Life and Science of Werner Heisenberg, 92; Werner Heisenberg--Die deutsche Wissenschaft und das Dritte Reich, Naturwissenschaft und Technik in der Geschichte, Helmuth Albrecht, ed, 93; Controlling German Science I: U.S. and Allied Forces in Germany, 1945-1947, Historical Studies in the Physical and Biological Sciences, 24, 94; Einstein and Our World, 95; Introduction to reprint of Samuel Goudsmit, Alsos: The Failure of German Science, 95; German Scientists and the Nazi Atomic Bomb, Dimensions: A Jour of Holocaust Studies, 10/2, 96; Controlling German Science II: U.S. and Allied Forces in Germany, 1945-1947, Historical Studies in the Physical and Biological Sciences, 26, 96; Reading Gothic German Print and Manuscript, 98. **CONTACT ADDRESS** Dept of Natural Science, Hofstra Univ, Hempstead, NY 11549. **EMAIL** chmdcc@hofstra.edu

CASSIDY, JAMES G.
DISCIPLINE HISTORY OF SCIENCE **EDUCATION** St Anselm Col, BA, 79; St John's Sem, MATheol, 84; Univ Toronto, MA, 87; Univ PA, MA, 89; Univ PA, PhD, 91. **CAREER** Fac, 85-87; to asst prof, 91-, St Anselm Col. **RESEARCH** Develop of sci and sci educ in Am hist, with particular interest in the role of the federal government as a patron of sci in the Gilded Age and Progressive Era; develop of the US Geological and Geographical Survey in the immediate post-Civil War decades; develop of the Marine Hospital Service. **SELECTED PUBLICATIONS** Auth, Monastic Silence and Solitude as Supports of Prayer in the Teaching of Pope Paul VI, Am Benedictine Rev, 87; George Frederic Matthew--Invertebrate Paleontologist, Geoscience Canada, 88. **CONTACT ADDRESS** Saint Anselm Col, 100 Saint Anselm Dr, Manchester, NH 03102-1310. **EMAIL** jcassidy@anselm.edu

CASSON, LIONEL
PERSONAL Born 07/22/1914, New York, NY, 2 children **DISCIPLINE** ANCIENT HISTORY **EDUCATION** NYork Univ, AB, 34, AM, 35, PhD, 39. **CAREER** From instr to assoc prof, 36-59, Prof Classics, Washington Square Col, NY UNIV, 59-79, Guggenheim fels, 52-53 & 59-60; dir summer session, Am Acad Rome, 63-66; Nat Endowment for Hum sr fel, 67-68 dir, Nat Endowment for Hum, summer seminar in Classics, 78; Prof Emeritus 79-; Andrew W Mellon prof class studies, Am Acad Rome, 81-82. **MEMBERSHIPS** Am Philo Asn; Archaeol Inst Am; Am Soc Papyrologists. **RESEARCH** Greek and Roman maritime hist; papyrology; hist of naval technol. **SELECTED PUBLICATIONS** Auth, Selected Satires of Lucian, Anchor, 62; auth, Six Plays of Plautus, Anchor, 63; Illustrated History of Ships and Boats, Doubleday, 64; Ancient Egypt, Time-Life, 65; The Plays of Menander, NY Univ, 71; Daily Life in Ancient Rome, Horizon Bks, 75; Periplus Maris Erythraei, Princeton Univ, 89; The Ancient Mariners, 2nd ed, Princeton Univ, 91; Ships and Seamanship in the Ancient World, 3rd ed, Johns Hopkins Univ, 95; Travel in the Ancient World, 2nd ed, John Hopkins Univ, 94; auth, Ships and Seafaring in Ancient Times, British Museum Press, 94; auth, Everyday Life in Ancient Rome, Johns Hopkins Univ, 98. **CONTACT ADDRESS** 100 Bleecker, New York, NY 10012.

CAST, DAVID JESSE DALE
PERSONAL Born 01/08/1942, London, England, m, 1981 **DISCIPLINE** ART HISTORY **EDUCATION** Oxford Univ, BA, 65; Columbia Univ, MA, 67, PhD, 70. **CAREER** Asst/assoc prof, Yale Univ, 70-80; Assoc/Full prof, Bryn Mawr Coll, 81-. **MEMBERSHIPS** Coll Art Asn; Royal Soc Arts; Renaissance Soc Am **RESEARCH** Renaissance art; British painting. **CONTACT ADDRESS** Bryn Mawr Col, 244 Thomas, Bryn Mawr, PA 19010. **EMAIL** dcast@brynmawr.edu

CASTAGNA, JOANN E.
PERSONAL Born 04/21/1951, New London, CT **DISCIPLINE** AMERICAN STUDIES **EDUCATION** East Conn, BA, 75; Univ Iowa, MA, 83, PhD, 89. **CAREER** Administration, UNIV IOWA. **SELECTED PUBLICATIONS** Coauth, "Making Rape Romantic: A Study of Rosemary Rogers' 'Steve and Ginny' Novels" in Violence Against Women in Literature, Garland, 89; auth, bio entries on 19th and early 20th-century Am women writers in The Feminist Companion to Literature in English, Batsford/Yale, 90; auth, "Mary Daly," in The Oxford Companion to Women's Writing in the United States, Oxford Univ Press, 94; contr, Chronlogy of Women Worldwide, Gale Research, 97; auth, bio entries in the American National Biography series; auth, "Caption" for Mary Jane Holmes, 'Lena Rivers, Gale Group's American Literature Archive, forthcoming; auth, "Elinor Glyn," for the New Dictionary of National Biography, London, Oxford University Press, forthcoming; Three entries for the ABC-CLIO Encyclopedia of the Civil War, forthcoming; auth, "Solon Robinson," for the ABC-CLIO CD-ROM History of Indiana, forthcoming; auth, "Booknote," on Women of Principle, by Janet Bennion in Religious Studies Review. **CONTACT ADDRESS** Ofc of Acad Prog, Univ of Iowa, 120 Schaeffer Hall, Iowa City, IA 52242. **EMAIL** joann-castagna@uiowa.edu

CASTEEN, JOHN
PERSONAL Born 12/11/1943, Portsmouth, VA, 1 child **DISCIPLINE** OLD ENGLISH LITERATURE, HISTORY OF THE ENGLISH LANGUAGE **EDUCATION** Univ Va, BA, 65, MA, 66, PhD(English), 70. **CAREER** Asst to dean, Co of Arts & Sci, Univ Va, 69-70; asst prof English, Univ Calif, Berkeley, 70-75; asst prof, 75-77, Assoc Prof English, Univ VA, 77-, Dean of Admis, 75- **RESEARCH** Patristics; early American literature. **SELECTED PUBLICATIONS** Auth, Poem for Mary Magdalene, Shenandoah, Vol 0046, 96. **CONTACT ADDRESS** Dept of English, Univ of Virginia, Charlottesville, VA 22901.

CASTIGLIONE, CAROLINE F.
PERSONAL Born 12/22/1962, San Antonio, TX, m, 1987, 1 child **DISCIPLINE** HISTORY **EDUCATION** Trinity Univ, BA, 85; Harvard Univ, MA; PhD, 95. **CAREER** Asst Prof, Univ Tex, 95-. **HONORS AND AWARDS** Fel, am Coun of Learned Soc, 99; Gladys Krieble Delmas Fel, 99; Jr Fel, Univ Tex, 98-. **RESEARCH** Early Modern Italy; Politics and Government; Popular Culture. **SELECTED PUBLICATIONS** Auth, "Accounting for Affection: Battles Between Aristocratic Mothers and Sons in Eighteenth-Century Rome," J of Family Hist, (00): 405-431; auth, "Political Culture in Seventeenth-Century Italian Villages," J of Interdisciplinary Hist, (01): 523-552; auth, Patrons and Adversaries: Nobles and Villagers in Italian Politics, 1640-1780, forthcoming. **CONTACT ADDRESS** Dept Hist, Univ of Texas, Austin, Garrison Hall, Austin, TX 78712. **EMAIL** castiglione@mail.utexas.edu

CASTILLO, ED
PERSONAL Born 08/25/1947, San Jacinto, CA, d, 2 children **DISCIPLINE** AMERICAN ANTHROPOLOGY, U.S. HISTORY **EDUCATION** Univ Calif, Riverside, BA, 69; Univ Calif, Berkeley, MA, 74, PhD, 77. **CAREER** Prof & dept chmn, Native Am Stud, 72- , Univ Calif, Berkeley, Univ Calif, Santa Cruz, Sonoma State Univ. **HONORS AND AWARDS** Outstanding Fac of the Year, 74; Fac Meritorious Performance Awd, 89-90; Awd for Academic Excellence, 98; listed in Who's Who, 99. **MEMBERSHIPS** Am Indian Hist Soc; Am Hist Soc, Pacific Branch; Am Indian and Alaskan Native Prof Asn. **RESEARCH** California Indian history; North American Indian history. **SELECTED PUBLICATIONS** Auth, History of the Impact of Euro-American Exploration and Settlement on the Indians of California, and, Recent Secular Movements Among California Indians, 1900-1973, in Handbook of North American Indians, v.8, California, Smithsonian Inst, 78; coauth, A Bibliography of California Indian History, Ballena, 78; contribur, The Missions of California: A Legacy of Genocide, American Indian Historical Society, 87; auth, The Ethnography and History of the California Indians, in Champagne, ed, The Native North American Indian Almanac, Gale, 94; auth, The Language of Race Hatred, in Bean, ed, The Ohlone Past and Present: Native Americans of the San Francisco Bay Region, Ballen, 94; coauth, Indians, Franciscans and Spanish Colonization: The Impact of Franciscan Missionaries on the Indians of California, Univ New Mexico, 95; auth, Mission Indian Federation: Protecting Tribal Soverignty, 1919-1967, in Davis, ed, The Encyclopedia of Native Americans in the 20th Century, Garland, 95; auth, California Overview, in Encyclopedia of Native American Tribes, Gale, 98; auth, The Indians of Southern California, Bellerophon, 98. **CONTACT ADDRESS** Sonoma State Univ, 1501 E Colati Blvd, Rohnert Park, CA 94928.

CAUGHEY, JOHN L.
DISCIPLINE ETHNOGRAPHY AND AMERICAN STUDIES **EDUCATION** Harvard Col, BA, 63; Univ PA, MA, 67, PhD, 70. **CAREER** Am Stud Dept, Univ Md **RESEARCH** Ethnographic, comp investigation of contemp cult as syst of meaning. **SELECTED PUBLICATIONS** Auth, Imaginary Social Worlds: A Cultural Approach, Univ Nebr Press, 84; On the Anthropology of America, Epilogue to Symbolizing America, Univ Nebr Press, 86; Gina as Steven: The Social and Cultural Dimensions of a Media Relationship, Visual Anthrop Rev, Special issue on Culture/Media, 94; Imaginary Social Relationships, Media Jour: Reading and Writing About Popular Culture, Allyn and Bacon, 95; Personal Identity on Faanakkar, Pieces of The Personality Puzzle: Readings in Theory and Research, W W Norton and Co, 97. **CONTACT ADDRESS** Am Stud Dept, Univ of Maryland, Col Park, Taliferro Hall, College Park, MD 20742-8821. **EMAIL** jc29@umail.umd.edu

CAULFIELD, NORMAN
PERSONAL Born 10/17/1951, Dayton, OH, m, 1984, 1 child **DISCIPLINE** HISTORY **EDUCATION** Univ Houston, BA, 83; MA, 87; PhD, 90. **CAREER** Assoc Prof, Ft Hays State Univ, 88-. **HONORS AND AWARDS** Fulbright Lectr, Univ Panama, 83. **MEMBERSHIPS** Southwest Coun of Latin Am Studies, AAUP. **RESEARCH** Latin America, Mexico, labor. **SELECTED PUBLICATIONS** Auth, "Wobblies and Mexican Workers in Mining and Petroleum 1905-1924," Int Rev of Soc Hist 40 (95): 51-75; auth, Mexican Workers and the State: From the Porfiriato to NAFTA, Tex Christian UP, 98. **CONTACT ADDRESS** Dept Hist, Fort Hays State Univ, 600 Park St, Hays, KS 67601-4009. **EMAIL** ncaulfie@fhsu.edu

CAVAGLIERI, GIORGIO
PERSONAL Born 08/01/1911, Venice, Italy, w, 1942 **DISCIPLINE** ARCHITECTURAL ENGINEERING **EDUCATION** Superior School of Engineering, Doctor Arch Engineering, Milan, ITA, 32; Superior School, of Architecture, Specialized City Planning, Rome ITA, 35. **CAREER** Own office, Milan, Italy, & instr City Planning at Superior Schools of Engineering & Architecture, Milan, Italy, 34-39; to US, 39; draftsman NY and Baltimore, MD, 39-43; US Army, ETO, 43-45; own office, NY City, 46-; adjunct prof, Pratt School of Architecture, 56-71; vis prof and lect, Lawrence Inst of Architecture, Detroit, MI, & Columbia Univ School of Architecture. **HONORS AND AWARDS** Gold Medal, NY Architectural League, 56; fel, AIA, 65; Medal of Honor, NY Chapter AIA, 90; Presidential Citation, AIA, 90; Nat Academician, Nat Academy of Design. **MEMBERSHIPS** Nat Inst of Architectural Ed (pres, 56-58); NY Municipal Art Soc (pres, 62-64); Fine Art Federation (pres, 70-72, 74-76); NY Chapter AIA (pres, 70-71); NY Victorian Soc (pres, 74-76). **RESEARCH** Historic preservation; urban design. **SELECTED PUBLICATIONS** Auth, Landmark Buildings for Uses of Today, Empire State Architect, Sept/Oct, 67; Design in Adaptive Reuse, Hist Preservation, Jan/March 74; Review of La Citta american dalla guerra civile al New Deal, by Ciucci, Dal Co, et al, J of the Soc of Architectural Hist, Oct 74; Large Scale Preservation Projects, Preservation and Building Codes, Nat Trust for Hist Preservation, 74; Plus Factors of Old Buildings, Economic Benefits of Preserving Old Buildings, Nat Trust for Historic Preservation, 76; On Restoring Historic Residential Properties for Institutional Use, Saving Large Estates, Soc for the Preservation of Long Island Antiquities, 77; The Harmony That Can't Be Dictated, Old and New Architecture: Design Relationship, Nat Trust for Historic Preservation, 80; The Past is Present--the Adaptive Reuse of 19th Century Buildings, Around the Square, 1830-1890: Essays on Life, Letters and Architecture, NY Univ, 82; Review of New York 1930: Architecture and Urbanism Between the Two World Wars, by Robert A M Stern, Gregory Gilmartin, Thomas Mellins, Citizens Housing and Planning Council of New York Book News, June 89; Review of The Meissenhofsiedlung: Experimental Housing Built for the Deutscher Werkbund: Stuutgart, 1927, by Karin Kirsch, Citizens Housing and Planning Council of New York Book News, Sept 90; An Architect's View of 'Appropriateness,' District Lines, News and Views of the Historic Districts Council, vol 7, no 2, 3, 4, 92. **CONTACT ADDRESS** 250 West 57th St, Ste 2016, New York, NY 10107.

CAVALLARI, HECTOR MARIO
DISCIPLINE HISPANIC STUDIES **EDUCATION** San Francisco State Univ, BA, 69; Univ Calif at Irvine, MA, 72, PhD, 72. **CAREER** Prof; Mills Col, 86-. **RESEARCH** Contemporary Latin American literature; Hispanic cultures; literary criticism; critical theory, Hispanic cinema. **SELECTED PUBLICATIONS** Auth, La practica de la escritura. Concepcion, Chile: Ediciones LAR, 90; Leopoldo Marechal: El espacio de los signos. Xalapa, Mexico: Univ Vercruzana, 82; Antigona Velez: Justicialismo y obra dramatica, Gestos 10 20, 95; coauth, Escritura y desfetichizacion: En torno a El perseguidor, de Julio Cortazar, Revista de Critica Literaria Latinoamericana XXII, 96; bk contrib, Textualidadm modelacion, descentramiento: Notas sobre el proceso critico, In El puente de las palabras, Wash, EUA: Interamer/OEA, 94; Leopoldo marechal: ideologia, escritura, compromiso, In Ensaos de literatura europea e hispanoamericana, San Sebastian: Editorial de la Univ del Pais Vasco, 90; Liliana Heker: (d)enunciar el orden, In Commemorative Ser, Essays in Honor of Seymour Menton, Riverside: Univ Calif, 91; nJulio Cortazar: Todos los juegos el

juego, In Lôs ochenta mundos de Julio Cortazar, Madrid: Edi-6, 87; El agape de la escritura, In Homenaje a Leopoldo marechal, Buenos Aires: Corregidor, Articles: La tramoya de la escritura en La invencion de Morel, de Adolfo Bioy Casares, Bull Hisp Stud, Liverpool, UK 74, 97; La literatura latinoamericana: Busqueda problematica de una voz propia, Alba de Am 14, 96. **CONTACT ADDRESS** Dept of Hispanic Studies, Mills Col, 5000 MacArthur Blvd, Oakland, CA 94613-1301.

CAVE, ALFRED A.
PERSONAL Born 02/08/1935, Albuquerque, NM, m, 1950, 2 children **DISCIPLINE** AMERICAN HISTORY **EDUCATION** Linfield Col, BA, 57; Univ Fla, MA, 59, PhD, 61. **CAREER** Instr soc sci, Univ Fla, 59-61; instr hist, City Col New York, 61-62; from asst prof to assoc prof, Univ Utah, 62-73, dir honors prog, 65-67, assoc dean col lett & sci, 67-68, dean col humanities, 68-73; Dean Col Arts & Sci, Univ Toledo, 73-90, prof of Hist, 90-. **MEMBERSHIPS** Orgn Am Historians; Am Soc for Ethnohistory. **RESEARCH** The Jackson era; Native American History. **SELECTED PUBLICATIONS** Auth, Jacksonian Democracy and the Historians, Univ Fla, 64; coauth, American Civilization: A Documentary History, W C Browm, 66; auth, An American Consrbative of the Age of Jackson: The Political and Social Thought of Calvin Colton, Tex Christian Univ, 69; auth, The Pequot War, Mass, 96. **CONTACT ADDRESS** Dept Hist, Univ of Toledo, 2801 W Bancroft St, Toledo, OH 43606-3390.

CAVER, CHRISTINE
DISCIPLINE AMERICAN FICTION **EDUCATION** Univ TX at San Antonio, BA; Univ TX at Austin, MA, PhD. **CAREER** Asst prof; taught at, Univ TX at Austin. **RESEARCH** Contemp Am fiction. **SELECTED PUBLICATIONS** Publ on res interest. **CONTACT ADDRESS** Col of Fine Arts and Hum, Univ of Texas, San Antonio, 6900 N Loop 1604 W, San Antonio, TX 78249.

CAVINESS, MADELINE H.
PERSONAL Born 03/27/1938, London, England, m, 1962, 2 children **DISCIPLINE** ART HISTORY **EDUCATION** Newnham Col, Cambridge Univ, BA, 59; Harvard Univ, PhD, 70. **CAREER** Prog organizer, British Council, 59-60; asst to librarian, Harry Elkins Widener Rare Book Collection, Harvard Univ, 62-63; res asst, Paintings Dept, Boston Museum of Fine Arts, 63; instr, Art Dept, Wellesley Col, 70-71; Radcliff Inst Fel, Harvard Univ, 70-72; asst prof, Tufts Univ, 72-75; assoc prof, Tufts Univ, 76-81; chair, Fine Arts Dept, 75-82, 88-90; Mary Richardson prof, Dept of Art and the Hist of Art, Tufts Univ, 87-; Benjamin Sonnenberg vis prof, Inst of Fine Arts, NY Univ, 91; Robert Sterling Clark vis prof, Williams Col/Clark Art Inst, 96. **HONORS AND AWARDS** Haskins Medal of the Medieval Academy; Fel of Art Medieval Academy; Fel of the Soc of Antiquaries of London; Honorary Phi Beta Kappa; Fel Am Council of Learned Societies; Pres, Union Acad¤mique Internationale, 98-01; Pres, Conseil Int de la Philos et des Scis Humaines (CIPSH), 01- **MEMBERSHIPS** Corpus Vitrearum Committee for the USA; Am Council of Learned Societies; Col Art Asn of Am; Census of Am Stained Glass, Governing Board; Int Ctr for Medieval Art; British Soc of Master Glass-Painters; Soc for Medieval Feminist Schlrshp. **RESEARCH** Feminist critique of medieval art history. **SELECTED PUBLICATIONS** Auth, Sumptuous Arts at the Royal Abbeys in Reims and Braine, Ornatus elegantiae, varietate stupendes, Princeton Univ Pr, 90; auth, "Obscenity and Alterity: Images that Shock and Offend Us/Them, Now/Then?" Obscenity: Social Control and Artistic Creation in the European Middle Ages, (Cultures, Beliefs and Traditions 4), ed Jan M. Ziolkowski (Leiden: Brill, 98); auth, "Hildegard as Designer of the Illustrations to her Works," in Hildegard of Bingen: The Context of her Thought and Art, ed Charles Burnett and Peter Dronke (London: Warburg Inst, 98); auth, "Artist: To see, Hear, and Know, All at Once," in Voice of the Living Light: Hildegard of Bingen and her World, ed Barbara Newman (Berkeley: Univ Calif Pr, 98); auth, "Louis Grodecki (1910-1982)" in Medieval Scholarship: Biographical Studies on the Formation of a Discipline, 3: Philos & the Arts, ed Helen Damico (New York: Garland Publishing, 00); auth, Visualizing Women in the Middle Ages: Sight, Spectacle and Scopic Economy, Univ Pa Pr, 01; auth, Medieval Art in the West and its Audience: Viewers, Patrons, Interpreters, Aldershot, Variorum, 01. **CONTACT ADDRESS** Department of Art & Art History, Tufts Univ, Medford, 11 Talbot Ave., Medford, MA 02155. **EMAIL** Madeline.Caviness@tufts.edu

CAWELTI, JOHN GEORGE
PERSONAL Born 12/31/1929, Evanston, IL, m, 1955, 5 children **DISCIPLINE** AMERICAN CIVILIZATION, MODERN & CONTEMPORARY LITERATURE **EDUCATION** Oberlin Col, BA, 51; State Univ Iowa, MA, 56, PhD(Am civilization), 60. **CAREER** From instr to asst prof humanities, Univ Chicago, 57-64, assoc prof English & humanities, 64-68, prof, 68-80, chmn comt gen studies in humanities, 70-75; Prof English, Univ KY, 80- **MEMBERSHIPS** Am Studies Asn; Popular Cult Asn. **RESEARCH** History of popular culture; literature and culture; American literature. **SELECTED PUBLICATIONS** Coauth, Sources of The American Republic, Scott, 61; auth, Form as cultural criticism in the work of Henry James, In: Literature and Society, Univ Nebr, 64; Apostles of the Self-Made Man, Univ Chicago, 65; American on display: The World's Fairs of 1876, 1893 and 1933, In: America and the Age of Industrialism, Free, 68; The Six-Gun Mistique, Bowling Green Popular, 70; A Focus on Bonnie and Clyde, Prentice-Hall, 73; Adventure, Mystery and Romance, Univ Chicago, 76. **CONTACT ADDRESS** Dept of English, Univ of Kentucky, 500 S Limestone St, Lexington, KY 40506-0003.

CEBULA, JAMES E.
PERSONAL Born 07/28/1942, Dupont, PA, d, 1965, 2 children **DISCIPLINE** AMERICAN LABOR, POLITICAL, & URBAN HISTORY **EDUCATION** Univ Cincinnati, PhD(hist), 72. **CAREER** Teacher hist, Delaware Valley High Sch, Pa, 63-64; from instr to asst prof, 68-77, assoc prof hist, Raymond Walters Col, Univ, Cinncinnati, 77-; Prof of History, U of Cincinnati, 85. **MEMBERSHIPS** AHA; Orgn Am Historians, Ohio Academy of History. **RESEARCH** National and state politics; labor history. **SELECTED PUBLICATIONS** Auth, Kennedy Heights: A Fragmented Hilltop Suburb, Cincinnati Hist Soc Bull, 7/76; Glory and Despair, Challenge and Change, a History of the Molders Union, Cincinnati Int Molders Union, 8/76; James M. Cox: Journalist and Politician, NY: Garland Publishing, 85; James Cebula and James Wolfe, eds, Rhyme and Reason: Molders Portey from Sylvies to the Great Depression, Cincinnati: Sylvis Soc, 85. **CONTACT ADDRESS** Dept of Hist, Univ of Cincinnati, 9555 Plainfield Rd, Cincinnati, OH 45236-1007. **EMAIL** james.cebula@atsuc.edu

CECIRE, ROBERT C.
DISCIPLINE CHURCH HISTORY **EDUCATION** Wheaton Col, BA; Gordon Divinity Sch, BD; Univ Kans, MA, PhD. **CAREER** Adj prof, Bethel Col; Anoka-Ramsey Community Col; vis lectr, Univ Kans; lectr, Gordon Col; asst prof, Wiinebrenner Theol Sem, 97-; dir, Theol Stud. **MEMBERSHIPS** Mem, Soc Biblical Lit; Conf on Faith and History; Nat Hist Honor Soc. **SELECTED PUBLICATIONS** Rev(s), Jour Evangel Theol Soc; Res Publica Litterarum; pub, article on Encratism, Res Publica Litterarum. **CONTACT ADDRESS** Winebrenner Theol Sem, 701 E Melrose Ave, PO Box 478, Findlay, OH 45839.

CEDERBERG, HERBERT RENANDO
PERSONAL Born 08/11/1933, Spokane, WA, m, 1989, 2 children **DISCIPLINE** UNITED STATES ECONOMIC HISTORY, ART HISTORY, HISTORY OF PHILOSOPHY **EDUCATION** Univ Calif, Berkeley, AB, 59, MA, 63, PhD(hist), 68. **CAREER** From asst prof to prof US colonial hist, 66-78, admin dir minority serv off, 72-73, Prof Hist, Univ Wis-River Falls, 78-; guest prof, Univ Minn, 75-76; Chair, Bd of Dir of Jobs Now Coalition, 98-. **HONORS AND AWARDS** Wis State Legis res fels, 68-69, 75-76; Nat Endowment for Humanities fel in residence, 77; Outstanding Fac Mem of the Yr, Univ Wis-River Falls, Col of Arts & Scis, 99. **MEMBERSHIPS** AHA; Inst Early Am Hist & Cult; Hakluyt Soc. **RESEARCH** Economic analysis of early settlement in colonial America; colonial art history; probate and inventory records in 17th and 18th century Massachusetts. **SELECTED PUBLICATIONS** Auth, An Economic Analysis of English Settlement in North America 1583-1635, Arno, 77; co-auth, The Cost of Living in Minnesota, 2000: A Family Self-Sufficiency Wage Analysis (Part Three of the Job Gap Economic Literacy Project), 01. **CONTACT ADDRESS** Dept of History, Univ of Wisconsin, River Falls, 410 S 3rd St, River Falls, WI 54022-5013. **EMAIL** herbert.cederberg@uwrf.edu

CEH, BRIAN
PERSONAL Born 08/08/1964, ON, Canada **DISCIPLINE** GEOGRAPHY **EDUCATION** Univ Waterloo, BES, 87; Sir Wilfrid Laurier Univ, MA, 89; Univ Western Ont, PhD, 94. **CAREER** Asst Prof, Ind State Univ. **MEMBERSHIPS** Can Asn of Geog, Am Asn of Geog. **RESEARCH** Economic Geography; Business Geographics; Quantitative Analysis; Industrial Geography. **CONTACT ADDRESS** Dept Geog, Indiana State Univ, 210 N 7th St, Terre Haute, IN 47809-0002. **EMAIL** geceh@scifac.indstate.edu

CELL, JOHN W.
PERSONAL 3 children **DISCIPLINE** HISTORY **EDUCATION** Duke Univ, BA, 57, PhD, 65. **CAREER** Prof, Duke Univ. **RESEARCH** Brit Empire Commonwealth. **SELECTED PUBLICATIONS** Auth, British Colonial Administration in the Mid-Nineteenth Century: The Policy-Making Process, 70; By Kenya Possessed: The Correspondence of Norman Leys and J.H. Oldham, 76; The Highest Stage of White Supremacy: The Origins of Segregation in South Africa and the American South, 82; Hailey: A Study in British Imperialism 1872-1969, 92. **CONTACT ADDRESS** Dept of Hist, Duke Univ, Carr Bldg, Durham, NC 27706. **EMAIL** jcell@acpub.duke.edu

CELMS, PETER
DISCIPLINE HISTORY **EDUCATION** Duke Univ, AB, MA; Union Grad Sch, PhD. **CAREER** Prof, 62-; **HONORS AND AWARDS** Woodrow Wilson fel; Danforth fel, Fulbright Scholar; NEH Fel. **RESEARCH** German historiography since late 18th century, Friedrich Mienecke. **SELECTED PUBLICATIONS** Area: Wilhelmian Germany. **CONTACT ADDRESS** Wittenberg Univ, Springfield, OH 45501-0720.

CENKNER, WILLIAM
PERSONAL Born 10/25/1930, Cleveland, OH **DISCIPLINE** HISTORY OF RELIGIONS **EDUCATION** Providence Col, AB, 54; Pontif Fac Theol, STL, 59; Fordham Univ, PhD(hist relig), 69. **CAREER** Assoc prof hist, 69-80, Assoc Prof HistRelig & Relig Educ, CaTh Univ Am, 80-, Chauncey Stillman Found res grant, 69; mem, Nat Coun Relig & Pub Educ, 72-; assoc ed, Col Theol Soc, 73- **MEMBERSHIPS** Col Theol Soc (pres, 78-80); Am Acad Relig; Asn Asian Studies. **RESEARCH** Encounter of world religions; religion and education; Sankaracarya's. **SELECTED PUBLICATIONS** Auth, Rabindranath Tagore and aesthetic man, Int Philos Quart, 73; The emergence of an Indian-Christian theology, Z Missionswissenschaft & Religionswissenchaft, 73; The covergence of religions, Cross Currents, 73; Relgion & education: Models from contemporary Hinduism, Relig Educ, 75; The Hindu Personality in Education, South Asia Bks, 76; Tagore's vision of relationality, Humanitas, 76; Understanding the religious personality, Horizons, 78. **CONTACT ADDRESS** Sch of Relig Studies, Catholic Univ of America, 620 Michigan Ave NE, Washington, DC 20064-0002.

CENSER, JACK R.
PERSONAL Born 12/08/1946, Memphis, TN, m, 1976, 2 children **DISCIPLINE** HISTORY **EDUCATION** Duke Univ, BA, 68; Johns Hopkins Univ, MA, 71; PhD, 73. **CAREER** Asst prof, Col of Charleston, 74-77; asst prof to prof, George Mason Univ, 77-; Chair, George Mason Univ, 95-. **HONORS AND AWARDS** NEH Grant; ACLS Grant; Am Philos Soc Grant; Grant, Max Plunck Inst fur Geschichte. **MEMBERSHIPS** AHA; Soc for French Hist Studies. **RESEARCH** History of the Press, Old Regime France, the French Revolution. **SELECTED PUBLICATIONS** Auth, Prelude to Power: The Parisian Radical Press, 1789 - 91, Johns Hopkins Univ Pr, 76; coed, Press and Politics in Pre-Revolutionary France, Univ of Calif Pr, 87; ed, The French Revolution and Intellectual History, Wadsworth Pr, 89; auth, The French Press in the Age of Enlightenment, Routledge, 94; coed, Visions and Revisions in Eighteenth-Century France, Univ Pr, 97; coed, Liberty, Fraternity, Equality: Exploring the French Revolution, Pa State Pr, (forthcoming). **CONTACT ADDRESS** Dept Hist, George Mason Univ, Fairfax, 4400 University Dr, Fairfax, VA 22030-4422. **EMAIL** jcenser@smu.edu

CENSER, JANE TURNER
PERSONAL Born 07/13/1951, Glasgow, KY, m, 1976, 2 children **DISCIPLINE** HISTORY **EDUCATION** Transylvania Univ, AB, 73; Johns Hopkins Univ, MA, 75; PhD, 80. **CAREER** Asst to assoc editor, Frederick Law Olmstead Papers, Am Univ, 80-89; asst prof to assoc prof, George Mason Univ, 89-. **HONORS AND AWARDS** Fellow, Nat Humanities Ctr, 83-84; R.D.W. Connor Awd, 96, A. Elizabeth Taylor Prize, 97; NEH Fel, 98-99. **MEMBERSHIPS** AHA; S Hist Assoc; Org of Am Hist; S Assoc of Women Hist; Va Soc of Hist Teachers. **RESEARCH** Women and family in 19th Century American South. **SELECTED PUBLICATIONS** Auth, North Carolina Planters and Their Children, 1800-1860, La State Univ Pr, (Baton Rouge) 84; ed, Defending the Union: The Civil War and the U.S. Sanitary Commission, 1861-1863, Vol 4, Papers of Frederick Law Olmstead, John Hopkins Univ Pr, (Baltimore), 86; auth; "What Ever Happened to Family History? A Review Essay", Comp Studies in Soc and Hist, 33.3 (91):528-38; auth, "Southwestern Migration among North Carolina Planter Families: The Disposition to Migrate", Jour of S Hist 57 (91):407-26; auth, "Videobites: Ken Burns's The Civil War in the Classroom", am Quarterly 44, (92):244-54; auth, "The Nineteenth Century Bookshelf", Va Mag of Hist and Biog 104 (96):121-28; auth, "A Changing World of Work: North Carolina Elite Women, 1865-1895" NC Hist Rev 73 (96):28-55; auth, "Reimagining the North-South Reunion: Southern Women Writers and the Intersectional romance, 1876-1900", S Cult 5, (99):64-91. **CONTACT ADDRESS** Dept Hist, George Mason Univ, Fairfax, 4400 University Dr, Fairfax, VA 22030-4422. **EMAIL** jcensel@gmu.edu

CERILLO, AUGUSTUS
DISCIPLINE HISTORY AND POLITICAL SCIENCE **EDUCATION** Northwestern Univ, PhD. **CAREER** Adj prof; full-time fac, CA State Univ at Long Beach. **HONORS AND AWARDS** Outstanding prof, CA State Univ at Long Beach. **RESEARCH** Hist since the Civil War; urban hist; hist of the involvement of Evangelicals in Am politics. **SELECTED PUBLICATIONS** Auth, Reform in New York City: A Study of Urban Progressivism; co-ed, Salt and Light: Evangelical Political Thought in Modern America. **CONTACT ADDRESS** Dept of Hist and Polit Sci, So California Col, 55 Fair Dr., Costa Mesa, CA 92626.

CHALFANT, WILLIAM Y.
PERSONAL Born 10/03/1928, Hutchinson, KS, m, 1956, 2 children **DISCIPLINE** HISTORY; LAW **EDUCATION** Univ Kans, AB, 50; Univ Mich, Juris Dr, 56. **CAREER** Atty at Law, Branwe, Chalfant, & Hill, 56-. **HONORS AND AWARDS** Various. **MEMBERSHIPS** Kans Bar Asn; Am Bar Asn; SW Bar Asn; W Hist Asn; Santa Fe Trail Asn. **RESEARCH** Spanish Entrada on Western Plains; military history of Southern Plains; Plains Indians. **SELECTED PUBLICATIONS** Auth,

Cheyennes and Horse Soldiers, Univ Okla Press, 89; auth, Without Quarter, Univ Okla Press, 91; Dangerous Passage, Univ Okla Press, 94; Cheyennes at Darkwater Creek, Univ Okla Press, 97. **CONTACT ADDRESS** Branine, Chalfant & Hill, 418 First Nat Ctr, PO Box 2027, Hutchinson, KS 67504-2027.

CHALK, FRANK
DISCIPLINE HISTORY **EDUCATION** Univ Wis, BS, MS, PhD. **CAREER** Instr, Tex A & M Univ; Fulbright prof, Univ Ibadan, Nigeria; assoc prof. **RESEARCH** History of genocide and humanitarian intervention, modern American foreign policy. **SELECTED PUBLICATIONS** Coauth, The History and Sociology of Genocide: Analyses and Case Studies; pub(s), chapters in various bk(s) and articles, Can Jour of African Stud; Holocaust and Genocide Stud. **CONTACT ADDRESS** Dept of Hist, Concordia Univ, Montreal, 1455 de Maisonneuve W, Montreal, QC, Canada H3G 1M8. **EMAIL** drfrank@alcor.concordia.ca

CHALLENER, RICHARD DELO
PERSONAL Born 01/15/1923, Pittsburgh, PA, m, 1947, 3 children **DISCIPLINE** HISTORY **EDUCATION** Princeton Univ, AB, 47; Columbia Univ, AM, 48, PhD(hist), 52. **CAREER** From instr to assoc prof, 49-64, asst dean, 57-61, assoc dean, 61-66, chmn dept hist, 70-71 & 73-77, Prof Hist, Princeton Univ, 64-, Mem, Col Entrance Exam Bd Advan Placement Comt, 58-61; vis prof, Johns Hopkins Univ, 67-68. **MEMBERSHIPS** AHA; Am Mil Inst. **RESEARCH** American diplomatic and military history since 1861; modern French history. **SELECTED PUBLICATIONS** Auth, French Theory of the Nation in Arms, 1866-1939, Columbia Univ, 55; co-ed, National Security in the Nuclear Age, Praeger, 60; contribr, An Uncertain Tradition, McGraw, 61; ed, From Isolation to Containment, 1921-1952 (doc of mod hist ser), St Martins, US & Arnold, London, 70; auth, Admirals, Generals, and American Foreign Policy, 1898-1914, Princeton Univ, 73. **CONTACT ADDRESS** Dept of Hist, Princeton Univ, Princeton, NJ 08544.

CHAMBERLAIN, GORDON BLANDING
PERSONAL Born 06/10/1939, New York, NY, m, 1964, 2 children **DISCIPLINE** MODERN JAPANESE HISTORY **EDUCATION** Yale Univ, BA, 60; Univ Calif, Berkeley, MA, 5 65, PhD(hist), 72. **CAREER** Lectr hist, Leland Stanford Jr Univ, 71; asst prof, Macalester Col, 73-76; Asst Prof, Ore State Univ, 76-80. **MEMBERSHIPS** Asn Asian Studies; AHA. **RESEARCH** Pre-1914 Japanese foreign policy. **CONTACT ADDRESS** 1915 NW Arthur, Corvallis, OR 97330.

CHAMBERLAIN, KATHLEEN P.
PERSONAL Born 01/13/1947, Lakewood, OH, 1 child **DISCIPLINE** HISTORY **EDUCATION** Oh State Univ, BS, 69; Univ Colo, MA, 92; Univ NM, PhD, 98. **CAREER** Asst Prof, Castleton State Col, 98-. **HONORS AND AWARDS** Tom L. Popejoy Dissertation Awd, Univ NM, 99; John Topham and Susan Redd Butler Fac Res Grant, 99-00; Grant, Am Philos Soc, 97; Dudley L. Philips Dissertation Grant, 97. **MEMBERSHIPS** Ofg of Am Hist; W Hist Asn; Coalition for W Women's Hist; Nat Coun for Hist Educ; VT Hist Soc. **RESEARCH** Native American History; Western and Southwestern History; Popular Culture. **SELECTED PUBLICATIONS** Auth, "Competitions for the Native American Soul," in Religion in Modern New Mexico, (Univ NM Press, 97); auth, "Patrick Floyd Garrett: The Man Who Shot Billy the Kid," in With Badges and Bullets: Lawmen and Outlaws in the Old West, Fulcrm Pub, 99; co-ed, Negotiation and Conflict: Essays in American and Mexican Hitory, Albuquerque, 97; comp, Billy the Kid and the Lincoln County War: A Bibliography, Albuquerque, 97; comp, Wild Westerners: A Bibliography, Albuquerque, 98; auth, Under Sacred Ground: The Navajo Fight to Control Oil Development, 1922-1982, Univ NM Press, 00. **CONTACT ADDRESS** Dept Hist, Geog, Economics, & Polit Sci, Castleton State Col, Castleton, VT 05735.

CHAMBERLAIN, MICHAEL
DISCIPLINE HISTORY **EDUCATION** Univ of California, Berkeley, PhD, 92. **CAREER** Acting Asst Prof, Stanford Univ, 89-91; Asst Prof, 92-97, Assoc Prof, 97-, Univ Of Wisconsin, Madison, ch, Middle East Studies Program, Univ of Wis, 97-. **RESEARCH** Medieval Islamic social & cultural history, comparative history. **SELECTED PUBLICATIONS** Auth, Knowledge and Social Practice in Medieval Damascus, Cambridge, UK, 94; auth, "The Ayyubids and the Crusader Era," in The Cambridge History of Egypt, vol. 1, ed. C. Petry (Cambridge, 99). **CONTACT ADDRESS** 455 N Park St, #4118, Madison, WI 53706. **EMAIL** mchamber@facstaff.wisc.edu

CHAMBERLIN, EUGENE KEITH
PERSONAL Born 02/15/1916, Gustine, CA, m, 1940, 5 children **DISCIPLINE** HISTORY **EDUCATION** Univ Calif, BA, 39, MA, 40, PhD(hist), 49. **CAREER** Teacher, Lassen Union H.S. and Jr. Col, 41-43; teacher, Joint Union H.S., 43-45; teaching asst hist, Univ Calif, 46-48; instr, Mont State Univ, 48-51, asst prof, 51-54; from asst prof to prof San Diego City Col, 54-78; prof history, San Diego, Miramar Col, 78-83, San Diego Mesa Col, 83-86, ret. Part time cab driver San Diego Yellow Cab Co, 55-74, 79, 86; vis prof history, Mont State Col, 53, Univ Calif, Ext, 64-68, San Diego State Col, 65-68, instr, coord hist lectr, San Diego CC-TV, 69-77; prof, MiraCosta Col, 98; mem adv com, Quechan Crossing Master Plan Proj, 89-90; historian San Diego First Ch of the Brethren, 54-98. **HONORS AND AWARDS** Rockerfeller Found Grant, Huntington Libr, 52; Merit award Congress of Hist San Diego County, 78, Fulbright-Hays grant in Peru, 82; award for dedicated svc. To local hist San Diego Hist. Soc, 91; Ben Dixon award Congress Hist, San Diego and Imperial Counties, 97; Who's Who in America, 00; **MEMBERSHIPS** AAUP, San Diego County Congree of Hist; AHA; Pacific Coast Coun on Latin Am Studies; Cultural Asn of the Californias; The Westerners (Calafia, S.D. chpt), E Clampus Vitus Squibob Chpt; San Diego Hist Soc (hon life); Phi Alpha Theta (sec U Calif Berkeley chpt; Democrat, Mem Church of the Brethren. **RESEARCH** Auth, Mission Dam and Flume, 92; auth, San Diego Presidio, 92; auth, Cabrillo Landing, 92; auth, Fort Rosecrans, 93; auth, Yuha Well, 93; auth, Mesquite Mine and its Neighbors, 93; auth, Getting into and Out of Death Valley, 93; auth, Casa de Carrillo, 94; auth, El Campo Santo, 94; auth, El Desembarcadero, 95-96. **SELECTED PUBLICATIONS** Auth, Mexican colonization versus American interests in lower California, Pac Hist Rev, 2/51; Baja California after Walker: The Zerman Enterprise, Hisp Am Hist Rev, 5/54; The Japanese scare at Magdalena Bay, 11/55 & Nicholas Trist and Baja California, 2/63, Pac Hist Rev; The 1894 wheelbarrow odometer survey of Porter Perrin Wheaton, Brand Book Number Three, 73 & Joseph P Hale and the Orchilla Era in Baja California, Brand Book Number Four, 76, San Diego Corral of the Westerners; The Magdalena Plain: From the time of the Jesuits to the development of the Santo Domingo Valley, Proceedings, Symp XVI, Asoc Cult las Califs, 78; auth, El Campo Santo, Old Foun, San Diego, 96. **CONTACT ADDRESS** 3033 Dale St, San Diego, CA 92104-4929.

CHAMBERS, HENRY EDMUND
PERSONAL Born 08/27/1941, Detroit, MI, m, 1967, 2 children **DISCIPLINE** HISTORY **EDUCATION** Xavier Univ, Ohio, AB, 63, MA, 64; Ind Univ, Bloomington, PhD(ancient hist), 68. **CAREER** From Asst Prof to Assoc Prof, 67-80, prof ancient hist, Calif State Univ, Sacramento, 80-. **MEMBERSHIPS** -Asn Ancient Historians. **RESEARCH** Ancient Near East, Greece and Rome, modern Middle East. **CONTACT ADDRESS** Dept of History, California State Univ, Sacramento, 6000 J St, Sacramento, CA 95819-2694. **EMAIL** hchamber@csus.edu

CHAMBERS, JOHN W., II
PERSONAL Born 08/06/1936, West Chester, PA, m, 1982, 4 children **DISCIPLINE** HISTORY **EDUCATION** Temple Univ, BS, 58; Calif State Univ, MA, 65; Columbia Univ, PhD, 73. **CAREER** Asst Prof, Columbia Univ, 72-82; Asst Prof to Prof and Dept Chair, Rutgers Univ, 82-. **HONORS AND AWARDS** Scholar in Residence, Univ Tokyo, 97; Ernest McMahon Awd, Rutgers Univ, 95; distinguished Book Awd, Soc for Military Hist, 88; Fulbright Fel, Univ Rome, 82; Rockefeller Humanities Fel, 81-82; Albert J Beveridge Grant, am Hist Asn, 81; Andrew W Mellon Foundation Grant, Barnard Col, 79; ford Foundation Grant, 97-99; NEH, 93-95. **MEMBERSHIPS** Intl Asn for Media and Hist, Historial de la Grande Guerre, Coun on Peace Res in Hist, Org of Am Hist, Rutgers Oral Hist Archives of World War II, Soc for Military Hist. **RESEARCH** 20th Century US History, especially war, peace, and society; also political/cultural history; film and history. **SELECTED PUBLICATIONS** Auth, To Raise an Army: The Draft comes to Modern America, Macmillan, 87; auth, The Tyranny of Change: America in the Progressive Era, 1890-1920, St Martin's Press, 80; ed, The Oxford Companion to American Military History, Oxford Univ Press, 99; co-ed, Major Problems in American Military History, Houghton Mifflin, 98; co-ed, World War II, Film, and History, Oxford Univ Press, 96; co-ed, The New Conscientious Objection: From Sacred to Secular Resistance, Oxford Univ Press, 93; auth, "Jimmy Carter's Public Policy Ex-Presidency," Political Science Quarterly, (98): 405-425; auth, "All Quiet on the Western Front (1930): The Antiwar film and the Image of the First World War," Historical Journal of Film, Radio, and Television, (94): 377-411 **CONTACT ADDRESS** Dept Hist, Rutgers, The State Univ of New Jersey, New Brunswick, 16 Seminary Pl, New Brunswick, NJ 08901-1108. **EMAIL** chamber@rci.rutgers.edu

CHAMBERS, MARJORIE BELL
DISCIPLINE HISTORY **EDUCATION** Mt. Holyoke Col, BA; Cornell Univ, MA; Univ NMex, PhD. **CAREER** Prof. **RESEARCH** Contemporary American history; Soviet and Chinese studies; European history; social, intellectual, and women's History; history of art. **SELECTED PUBLICATIONS** Auth, pubs about women's striving for equal opportunity and citizenship. **CONTACT ADDRESS** History Dept, Union Inst, 440 E McMillan St, Cincinnati, OH 45206-1925.

CHAMBERS, SARAH
DISCIPLINE HISTORY **EDUCATION** Univ Wis Madison, PhD, 92. **CAREER** Assoc prof, 00-. **RESEARCH** Eighteenth- and nineteenth-century social, cultural, and legal history. **SELECTED PUBLICATIONS** Auth, From Subjects to Citizens: Honor, Gender and Politics in Arequipa, Peru, 1780-1854, Penn State Univ; 'To the company of a man like my husband; no law can compel me': Women's Strategies against Domestic Violence in Arequipa, Peru, 1780-1850, J Women's Hist. **CONTACT ADDRESS** History Dept, Univ of Minnesota, Twin Cities, 614 Social Sciences Tower, 267 19th Ave. S, Minneapolis, MN 55455. **EMAIL** chambers@tc.unm.edu

CHAMPLIN, EDWARD JAMES
PERSONAL Born 06/03/1948, New York, NY, m, 1972, 2 children **DISCIPLINE** ANCIENT HISTORY **EDUCATION** Univ Toronto, BA, 70, MA, 72; Oxford Univ, DPhil(Literae Humaniores), 76. **CAREER** Instr, 75-76, asst prof, 76-81, assoc prof, 81-86, Prof Classics, 86-, Cotsen Prof Humanities Princeton Univ, 87-; Master of Butler Col Princeton Univ, 95-. **HONORS AND AWARDS** Alexander von Humboldt fel, Heidelberg Univ, 84-85; Fowler Hamilton fel, Christ Church, Oxford Univ, 89-91; Resident in Classics, Am Academy in Rome, 94; corresponding member, German Archaelogical Inst, 91-. **MEMBERSHIPS** Am Philol Asn; Class Asn Can; Asn Ancient Historians; Soc Prom Roman Studies. **RESEARCH** Roman history; Roman law; Latin literature. **SELECTED PUBLICATIONS** Auth, Fronto and Antonine Rome, Harvard Univ, 80; Final Judgments, CA Univ, 91; ed, Cambridge Ancient History vol X, 96. **CONTACT ADDRESS** Dept Classics, Princeton Univ, 104 East Pyne, Princeton, NJ 08544. **EMAIL** champlin@princeton.edu

CHAN, LOREN BRIGGS
PERSONAL Born 09/10/1943, Palo Alto, CA **DISCIPLINE** AMERICAN HISTORY **EDUCATION** Stanford Univ, AB, 65, AM, 66; Univ Calif, Los Angeles, MA, 67, CPhil, 69, PhD(hist), 71. **CAREER** Lectr hist, San Fernando Valley State Col, 70-71; lectr, 71-72, asst prof, 72-76, Assoc Prof Hist, San Jose State Univ, 76-, Partic, Workshop in hist, Danforth Found, 75; adj lectr mod Chinese hist, Univ Santa Clara, 77-78. **MEMBERSHIPS** AHA; Orgn Am Historians; Am Studies Asn; Western Hist Asn; Chinese Hist Soc Am. **RESEARCH** United States, 1900-1940; Nevada, 1864-1940; Chinese-Americans, 1920-1950. **SELECTED PUBLICATIONS** Auth, Foot health in the school curriculum, J Am Podiatry Asn, 4/70; Sagebrush Statesman: Tasker L Oddie of Nevada, Univ Nev, 73; Example for the Nation: Nevada's execution of Gee Jon, Nev Hist Soc Quart, summer 75; ed, Chinese-American History Reader and Workbook, Spartan Bookstore, 76; contribr, Proceedings of the National Conference on the Life, Influence, and Role of the Chinese in the United States, 1776-1960, Chinese Hist Soc Am, 76; ed, New Light on a New Land: Recent Research in Western History, Spartan Bookstore, 76; The Silver State in 1878, Nev Hist Soc Quart, summer 77; contribr, Biographical Directory of the Governors of the United States, 1789-1978, (4 vols), Meckler Bks, 78. **CONTACT ADDRESS** Dept of Hist, San Jose State Univ, San Jose, CA 95192.

CHANCELLOR, JAMES D.
PERSONAL Born 11/23/1944, St. Louis, MO, m, 1969, 2 children **DISCIPLINE** HISTORY OF RELIGION, ISLAM **EDUCATION** Duke Univ, PhD, 88. **CAREER** Assoc prof Relig, 85-89, Col Baptist Univ; dean, prof Rel, Col Christian Univ, 89-92; prof Rel, S Bapt Theol Sem, 92- . **MEMBERSHIPS** AAR; SSR; CESNUR. **RESEARCH** New Religious Movements; The Family **SELECTED PUBLICATIONS** Auth, The Night of the Cross, The Dividing Edge, Fall, 91; Christ and Religious Pluralism, Rev and Expositor, vol 91, no 4, Fall, 94; Religion in the Middle East, in Introduction to Missions, Broadman and Holman Publ, 98; auth, Life in the Family: An Oral History of the Children of God, Syracuse Univ Press, 00. **CONTACT ADDRESS** Dept of Religion, So Baptist Theol Sem, 2825 Lexington Rd, Louisville, KY 40280. **EMAIL** jchancellor@sbts.edu

CHANDLER, JOAN
DISCIPLINE HISTORY **EDUCATION** Univ Tex, PhD, 72. **CAREER** Prof. **RESEARCH** Sport in culture; U.S. popular culture; southwestern U.S. history and literature. **SELECTED PUBLICATIONS** Auth, Television and National Sport: The United States and Britain, Univ Ill, 88; Camping for Life: Transmission of Values at a Girls' Summer Camp, Hall, 81; American Televised Sport: Business as Usual, Bucknell, 85; Sport as TV Product: A Case Study of Monday Night Football, Univ Ill, 91. **CONTACT ADDRESS** Dept of History, Univ of Texas, Dallas, Richardson, TX 75083-0688. **EMAIL** jchandlr@utdallas.edu

CHANDLER, ROBERT JOSEPH
PERSONAL Born 07/31/1942, Salt Lake City, UT, m, 1975, 2 children **DISCIPLINE** AMERICAN HISTORY **EDUCATION** Earlham Col, BA, 64; Univ Calif, Riverside, MA, 66, PhD(hist), 78. **CAREER** Pub Relations Officer & Sr Res Specialist, Hist Dept, Wells Fargo Bank, 78- **MEMBERSHIPS** Orgn Am Historians. **RESEARCH** Civil war; California and the west; journalism. **SELECTED PUBLICATIONS** Auth, Spreading the News--The American Postal System from Franklin to Morse, New Eng Quart-Hist Rev of New Eng Life and Letters, Vol 0070, 97; In the Van--Spiritualists As Catalysts for the California Womens Suffrage Movement, Calif Hist, Vol 0073, 94; A San-Francisco Scandal--The California of Gordon, George, Calif Hist, Vol 0074, 95; Spreading the News--The American Postal System From Franklin To Morse, New Eng Quart-Hist Rev of New Eng Life and Letters, Vol 0070, 97; In-

tegrity Amid Tumult, Wells-Fargo-And-Cos Gold-Rush Banking, Calif Hist, Vol 0070, 91; The Other California--The Great-Central-Valley in Life and Letters, Jour W, Vol 0032, 93; Newhall, Henry, Mayo and His Times--A California Legacy, Pacific Northwest Quart, Vol 0084, 93; Patterson,Tom--Colorado Crusader For Change, Jour W, Vol 0036, 97. **CONTACT ADDRESS** 4625 Stillwater Ct, Concord, CA 94521.

CHANDRA, VIPAN

PERSONAL Born 01/20/1940, Rawalpindi, India, m, 1969, 1 child **DISCIPLINE** ASIAN HISTORY & POLITICS **EDUCATION** Agra Univ, India, BA, 59, MA, 61; Harvard Univ, MA, 71, PhD, 77. **CAREER** Lectr pol sci, Meerut Col, India, 61-65; lectr Hindi, Hanguk Univ Foreign Studies, Seoul, 66-68; prof Asian hist, Wheaton Col, 77-, Coordr Asian studies, Wheaton Col, 78-; consult, Harvard Law Sch, 80; Book Review Ed, J Korean Studies, Univ Calif Los Angeles; Chair, Dept of Hist, Wheaton Col, 88-91, 99-01. **MEMBERSHIPS** Asn Asian Studies. **RESEARCH** Modern Korean and Japanese history. **SELECTED PUBLICATIONS** Auth, An Outline Study of Korea's Advancement Society, 74 & Korea's First Proposal for a National Assembly, 75, in Occasional Papers on Korea, Soc Sci Res Coun & Am Coun Learned Soc; The Concept of Popular Sovereignty: The Case of So Chael-p'il and Yun Ch'i-ho, Korea J, Seoul, 4/81; The Korean Enlightenment: A Reexamination, Korea J, 5/82; Imperialism, Resistance and Reform in Late 19th-Century Korea: Enlightenment and the Independence Club, Inst E Asian Studies, Univ Calif, 88. **CONTACT ADDRESS** Dept of Hist, Wheaton Col, Massachusetts, 26 E Main St, Norton, MA 02766-2322. **EMAIL** vchandra@wheaton.ma.edu

CHANEY, WILLIAM ALBERT

PERSONAL Born 12/23/1922, Arcadia, CA, s **DISCIPLINE** MEDIEVAL HISTORY **EDUCATION** Univ CA, Berkeley, AB, 43, PhD, 61. **CAREER** From asst prof to George McKendree Steel prof hist emeritus, Lawrence Univ, 52-; lectr, MI State Univ, 58; chemn dept hist, Lawrence Univ, 67-71, 95-96. **HONORS AND AWARDS** Am Coun Learned Soc grant-in-aid, 66-67; Royal Soc of Arts fel, 77. **MEMBERSHIPS** AHA; MLA; Am Soc Church Hist; Mediaeval Acad Am; Archaeol Inst Am. **RESEARCH** Anglo-Saxon Engl; medieval rulership, sacred space. **SELECTED PUBLICATIONS** Auth, Grendel and the Gifstol: A legal view of monsters, PMLA, 62, Aethelberht's code and the king's number, Am J Legal Hist, 62; A Louisiana planter in the Gold Rush, La Hist, 62; Anglo-Saxon Church dues, Church Hist, 63; The economics of ruler-cult in Anglo-Saxon law, J Brit Studies, 65; Paganism to Christianity in Anglo-Saxon England: In: Early Medieval Society, Appleton, 67; The Cult of Kingship in Anglo-Saxon England: The Transition from Paganism to Christianity, Univ Calif & Manchester Univ, 70, 99; Eleven articles in New Catholic Encycl, Schafer Williams: A Memoir in In Iure Veritas: Studies in Canon Law in Memory of Schafer Williams, univ on cin col law, 91. **CONTACT ADDRESS** Dept of Hist, Lawrence Univ, 115 S Drew St, Appleton, WI 54911-5798.

CHANG, CHUN-SHU

PERSONAL Born 04/25/1934, Shantung, China, m, 1959, 3 children **DISCIPLINE** ANCIENT CHINESE HISTORY, CHINESE LANGUAGE **EDUCATION** Taiwan Univ, BA, 56; Harvard Univ, PhD(hist), 64. **CAREER** Res asst hist, Inst Hist & Philol, Acad Sinica, China, 56-57; lectr Chinese hist, Univ Iowa, 64; dir Far Eastern studies, Wis State Univ, 64-66; assoc prof, 66-73, prof, Hist, Univ Mich, 73- . **HONORS AND AWARDS** Am Coun Learned Soc res grant, 65-66; Soc Sci Res Coun res grant, 66-67; fel Acad Sinica, China; Rackham fac res grants, 67, 70-71, 72-73, 76; Warner G Rice Humanities Awd, Univ Mich, 77. **MEMBERSHIPS** AHA; Asn Asian Studies; Soc Ch'ing Studies; Social Studies Pre-Han China; Soc Sung Studies. **RESEARCH** Hist and civil of China, 1600 BC-1800 AD: sociocultural, intellectual-literary, military-diplomatic, historiography, science & technology **SELECTED PUBLICATIONS** Auth, Premodern China: A Bibliographical Introduction, Ann Arbor Publ, 71; coauth, The world of P'u Sung-ling's Liao-chai Chih-i: Literature and the intelligentsia during the Ming-Ch'ing dynastic transition, J Inst Chinese Studies, 73; auth, Han-tai pien-chiang shih lun-chi, Taipei, 74; The Making of China: Main Themes in Premodern Chinese History, Appleton, 74; coauth, K'ung Shang-jen and his T'ao-hua Shan: A dramatist's reflections on the Ming-Ch'ing Dynastic transition, J Inst Chinese Studies, 77; auth, Understanding China's international behavior: Old traditions and new perspectives, Mich Quart Rev, 77; Social Change and Military Expansion in Early Han China, Ann Arbor Publ, 78; South China in the Twelfth Century, Hong Kong & Ann Arbor, 78. **CONTACT ADDRESS** Dept of Hist, Univ of Michigan, Ann Arbor, 1029 Tisch Hall, 555 S State St, Ann Arbor, MI 48109-1003. **EMAIL** cschang@umich.edu

CHANG, SEN DOU

PERSONAL Born 08/16/1928, China, m, 1981, 2 children **DISCIPLINE** GEOGRAPHY **EDUCATION** Univ Wisc, MA, 55; Univ WA, PhD, 61. **CAREER** Assoc Prof to Prof, Univ Haw, 67-. **HONORS AND AWARDS** Fulbright Scholar, 77-78. **MEMBERSHIPS** An for Asian Studies; Asn of Am Geog. **RESEARCH** Urbanization; Water Resouces Management of China. **SELECTED PUBLICATIONS** Co-auth, "The Economic Performance and Regional Systems of Chinese Cities," Review of Urban and Regional Development Studies (94): 58-77; co-ed, "A Preliminary Study of Chinese Urban System," in Geographical Research and Development, (Hong Kong Univ Press, 95), 113-122; auth, "Agriculture, Rural Development and Labor Transfer," in Regional Development in Northeast China, (East-West Center, 94), 105-132; auth, "The Floating Population: An Informal Process of Urbanization in China," Intl Journal of Population Geography (96): 197-214; auth, "Beijing: Perspectives on Preservation, Environment, and Development," Cities (98): 1-13. **CONTACT ADDRESS** Dept Geog, Univ of Hawaii, Manoa, 2424 Maile Way, Honolulu, HI 96822. **EMAIL** sdchag@hawaii.edu

CHANG, SIDNEY H.

PERSONAL Born 01/01/1934, China, m, 1962, 2 children **DISCIPLINE** HISTORY **EDUCATION** Nat Taiwan Univ, BA, 56; Univ Miss, MA, 59; Fla State Univ, MS, 61; Univ Wisc, PhD, 66; Harvard Univ, Postdoctoral, 69-70. **CAREER** Asst prof to prof, Cal State Univ, Fresno, 66-. **HONORS AND AWARDS** Teaching and Mentoring Awd, 93; Res Grant, The Pac Cul Found, 92, 95; Chinese Aviation Dev Found, 96; Cal State Univ Fac Pub Awd, 99. **MEMBERSHIPS** AHA; Assoc for Asian Studies; Am Ass for Chinese Studies; Reg Fac Res Sem, Center for Chinese Studies. **RESEARCH** USA-China-Soviet Relations. **SELECTED PUBLICATIONS** Coauth, Bibliography of Sun-Yat-sen in China's Republican Revolution, 1885-1925, 90, 98; coauth, All Under Heaven: Sun Yat-sen and His Revolutionary Thought, 91; coauth, Storm Clouds Clear Over China: Memoir of Ch'en Li'fu, 1900-1993, 94. **CONTACT ADDRESS** Dept Hist, California State Univ, Fresno, 5340 N Campus Dr, Fresno, CA 93740-8019. **EMAIL** schang@csufresno.edu

CHANNELL, DAVID

DISCIPLINE HISTORY **EDUCATION** Case Western Reserve Univ, PhD, 75. **CAREER** Prof. **HONORS AND AWARDS** Fel, Nat Humanities Inst at the Univ of Chicago, 78-79; Nat Sci Found Res Grant, 87-83; Nat Endowment for the Humanities, Summer Stipend, 92; Nat Sci Found Int Prog Grant, 95-97; John Templeton Fond Sci & Relig Course Prize, 97; Ctr for Theol and the Natural Sci(s) Dev Awd,99; Nat Sci Found Sci-Technology Studio Scholars Awd, 99-01. **MEMBERSHIPS** Soc for the Hist of Technology, Hist of Sci Soc, Int Comt for the Hist of Technology, Am Assoc for the Advancement of Sci, Sigma Xi. **RESEARCH** History of science, technology and medicine; philosophy of science and technology; 18th to 20th century European intellectual history; 19th century British history; Science, Technology and Religion. **SELECTED PUBLICATIONS** Auth, The Vital Machine: A Study of Technology and Organic Life, Oxford, 91; The History of Engineering Science, Garland, 89; Scottish Men of Science-W.J.M. Rankine, F.R.S.E., F.R.S., Scotland's Cult Heritage, 86. **CONTACT ADDRESS** Dept of History, Univ of Texas, Dallas, Richardson, TX 75083-0688. **EMAIL** channell@utdallas.edu

CHANZIT, GWEN

DISCIPLINE EUROPEAN MODERN ART **EDUCATION** Univ Iowa, PhD, 84. **CAREER** Experience-cur, Mod and Contemporary Art and Herbert Bayer Collection and Archive, Denver Art Mus; sr lectr, Univ of Denver. **SELECTED PUBLICATIONS** Auth, Herbert Bayer and Modernist Design in America, UMI Res Press, 87; The Herbert Bayer Collection and Archive at the Denver Art Museum, Denver Art Mus, 88. **CONTACT ADDRESS** Dept of Art and Art Hist, Univ of Denver, 2199 S Univ Blvd, Denver, CO 80208. **EMAIL** gchanzit@du.edu

CHAPELLE, SUZANNE E. G.

PERSONAL Born 09/21/1942, Philadelphia, PA, w, 1984, 1 child **DISCIPLINE** HISTORY **EDUCATION** Harvard Univ, BA, 64; John Hopkins Univ, MA, 66; PhD, 70. **CAREER** Asst prof, Towson Univ, 69-71; adj prof, John Hopkins Univ, 70-85; asst prof, 71-73; assoc prof, 73-75; prof, Morgan State Univ, 75-. **HONORS AND AWARDS** Pub Comm, MHS; Advisory Panel, Archives of MD. **MEMBERSHIPS** AHA; MHS; ASA; Am Stud Environ Hist. **SELECTED PUBLICATIONS** Auth, Books for Pleasure: Best Selling Books in America 1914-1945, Bowling Green Univ Popular Press, 76; auth, Baltimore: An Illustrated History, Windsor Pub, 80; auth, Maryland: A History of Its People, John Hopkins Univ Press, 86; rev auth, A Child's History of the World, Calvert School, 94; coauth, African American Leaders in Maryland, MHS, 00; auth, The Maryland Adventure, Gibbs Smith Pub, 00. **CONTACT ADDRESS** Dept History, Morgan State Univ, 1700 East Cold Spring Lane, Baltimore, MD 21251-0001. **EMAIL** suechapelle@hotmail.com

CHAPMAN, H. PERRY

DISCIPLINE ART HISTORY **EDUCATION** Swarthmore Col, BA, 75; Princeton Univ, MFA, 78; PhD, 83. **CAREER** Instr, Swarthmore Col, 81; lectr, Amer Univ, 82; instr, 82-83; asst prof, 83-89;assoc prof, 89-96; dept assoc ch, 91-93;prof, 96. **HONORS AND AWARDS** Kress fel, Princeton Univ, 79; gen res grant, Univ Del, 89, 84, 92; res grant, Am Philos Soc, 84; stipend, NEH, 85; supplemental funds grant, Univ Del, 86, 88; publ grant, Getty Grant Prog, 90; fel, Woodrow Wilson Intl Ctr for Scholars, 90-91; fel, NEH, Univ tchr(s), 93-94; gst cur, nat gallery of art, wash, dc, 96. **MEMBERSHIPS** Mem, Amer Assn Netherlandic Stud; Col Art Assn; Historians of Netherlandish Art. **SELECTED PUBLICATIONS** Auth, Rembrandt's Self-Portraits: A Study in Seventeenth-Century Identity, Princeton Univ Press, 90; Rembrandt's burgerlijk Self-Portraits, Leids Kunsthistorisch Jaarboek 89, The Hague, 90; Jan Steen's Household Revisited, Simiolus, 91; Persona and Myth in Houbraken's Life of Jan Steen, The Art Bulletin, 93. **CONTACT ADDRESS** Dept of Art Hist, Univ of Delaware, 162 Ctr Mall, Newark, DE 19716. **EMAIL** pchapman@udel.edu

CHAPPELL, DAVID L.

PERSONAL Born 03/28/1959, Chicago, IL, s **DISCIPLINE** HISTORY **EDUCATION** Yale Univ, BA, 82; Univ of Rochester, PhD, 92. **CAREER** Lectr, SUNY, 90; asst prof, Hartwick Col, 91-92; asst prof to assoc prof, Univ of Ark. **HONORS AND AWARDS** Fulbright Lectr, 93; NEH Res Stipend, 99; Guggenheim Grant, 99-00. **MEMBERSHIPS** AHA, Org of Am Hist, S Hist Assoc, Hist Soc. **RESEARCH** Civil rights, racist, cultural and intellectual history. **CONTACT ADDRESS** Dept Hist, Univ of Arkansas, Fayetteville, 416 Old Main, Fayetteville, AR 72701-1201. **EMAIL** dchappel@comp.uark.edu

CHAPPELL, DAVID WELLINGTON

PERSONAL Born 02/03/1940, St. John, NB, Canada, 2 children **DISCIPLINE** HISTORY OF RELIGIONS **EDUCATION** Mt Allison Univ, BA, 61; McGill Univ, BD, 65; Yale Univ, PhD(Chinese Buddhism), 76. **CAREER** Teaching asst world relig, Yale Univ, 70-71; actg asst prof Chinese relig, Univ Hawaii, 71-77; asst prof, Univ Toronto, 77-78; asst prof, 78-80, Prof Chinese Relig, Univ Hawaii, Manoa, 85- **MEMBERSHIPS** Asn for Asian Studies; Am Acad Relig; Soc Study Chinese Relig; NAm Soc Buddhist Studies; Soc for Buddhist-Christian Stu. **RESEARCH** Formation of Chinese Buddhism; Buddhist-Christian comparisons. **SELECTED PUBLICATIONS** Auth, Introduction to the T'ien-t'ai ssu-chiao-i, Eastern Buddhist, 5/76; A perspective on the Pure Land Doctrine of T'ien-t'ai Chih-i (538-597), (in Japanese), Taisho Daigaku Bukkyo gaku, 76; coed & contribr article, In: Buddhist and Taoist Studies (Vol I), Univ Hawaii, 77; contribr, Early Ch'an in China and Tibet, 82; ed, T'ien-t'ai Buddhism, Dai-ichi-Shobo, 83; auth, Pure Land Buddhism: History, Culture and Doctrine, Univ Calif, 97; ed, Buddhist Peacework, Wisdom, 99. **CONTACT ADDRESS** Dept of Relig, Soka Univ of America, 2530 Dole St, Aliso Viejo, CA 92656. **EMAIL** alohachap@aol.com

CHAPPLE, C. K.

PERSONAL Born 09/04/1954, Medina, NY, m, 1974, 2 children **DISCIPLINE** HISTORY OF RELIGION **EDUCATION** SUNY Stony Brook, BA, 76; Fordham Univ, MA, 78, PhD, 80. **CAREER** Prof, 85-, Loyola Marymont Univ; Lectr, 80-85, SUNY Stony Brook; Asst Dir, 80-85, Inst Adv Stud Wld Rel. **HONORS AND AWARDS** 2 NEH Fels; Lily Gnt; College Fel; Chilton Ch Awd; Gannett Schlshp; IAAPEA Res Awd; CWHE Appre Certif; Grant Devel Gnt. **MEMBERSHIPS** AAR; AAS; AIIS. **RESEARCH** Yoga Traditions; Jainism; Hinduism; Buddhism. **SELECTED PUBLICATIONS** Ed, Ecological Prospects: Scientific Religious and Aesthetic Perspectives, Albany, SUNY Press, 94, Intl edition, Delhi, Indian Books Cen, 95; auth, Nonviolence to Animals Earth and Self in Asian Traditions, Albany, NY, SUNY Press, 93, Intl edition, Delhi, Indian Books Cen, 95; ed, Jesuit Tradition in Education and Missions, Scranton, U of Scranton Press, 93; Haribhadra's Analysis of Patanjala and Kula Yoga in the Yogadrstisamuccaya, in: Open Boundaries: Jain Communities and Cultures in Indian History, ed, John E Cort, Albany, SUNY Press, 98; India: The Land of Plentitude, Satya, 98; Animals in the Buddhist Birth Stories, in: Buddhism and Ecology: The Interconnection of Dharma, and Deeds, ed, Mary Evelyn Tucker, Duncan Ryuken Williams, Cambridge MA, Harv Univ Cen Stud Of World Rel, 97; Renouncer Traditions Of India: Jainism and Buddhism, in: Ananya: A Portrait of India, ed, S Sn Sridhar, Nirmal K Mattoo, NY, Assoc of Indians in Amer, 97; co-ed, Hinduism and Ecology, Cambridge, CSWR, Harvard Press, 00. **CONTACT ADDRESS** Dept Theol Studies, Loyola Marymount Univ, 7900 Loyola Blvd, Los Angeles, CA 90045. **EMAIL** cchapple@lmu.edu

CHAPUT, DONALD

PERSONAL Born 12/19/1933, Houghton County, MI, m, 1960, 2 children **DISCIPLINE** UNITED STATES HISTORY **EDUCATION** Northland Col, BA, 57; Mich State Univ, MA, 58. **CAREER** Instr hist, Elgin Community Col, 64-66; ed & chief, Mich Hist Comn, 66-71; Sr Cur Hist to Cur Emer, Natural Hist Mus, Los Angeles, 72-, US consult, Dict Can Biog, 66-**MEMBERSHIPS** Orgn Am Historians. **RESEARCH** Exploration; military; mining. **SELECTED PUBLICATIONS** Auth, In Search of Silver and Gold--Cashman, Nellie, Miner and Philanthropist in the Late 1800s, Amer Hist, Vol 0030, 96; Brothers on the Santa-Fe and Chihuahua Trails-- Glasgow, Edward, James and Glasgow , William, Henry 1846-1848, Pacific Hist Rev, Vol 0064, 95. **CONTACT ADDRESS** Hist Div Natural Hist, Mus Exposition Park, Los Angeles, CA 90001.

CHARBRAN, H. RAFAEL
PERSONAL Born 02/02/1947, Monterey, CA **DISCIPLINE** HISTORY OF SCIENCE, HISTORY OF MEDICINE, LATINO STUDIES, SPANISH LITERATURE **CAREER** Asst prof, La State Univ, 83-85; asst prof to prof, Whittier Col, 85-. **HONORS AND AWARDS** Harry Nerhood Teach Excell Awd; Fulbright Fel; NEH; Albert and Elaine Borchard Found. **MEMBERSHIPS** MLA; ATSP; SLS; AHF. **RESEARCH** History of medicine; history of science; life and works of Miguel Unamuno, 1864-1936; life and works of Francisco Hernandez, 1515-1587. **SELECTED PUBLICATIONS** Co-ed, Latino Encyclopedia, 6 vols, Marshall Cavendish (NY), 96; contrib, The World of Dr Francisco Hernandez, Stanford Univ Press, 00. **CONTACT ADDRESS** Dept Modern Lang, Whittier Col, 13406 Philadelphia St, Whittier, CA 90601-4446. **EMAIL** rchabran@whittier.edu

CHARLESWORTH, MICHAEL
DISCIPLINE 19TH-CENTURY EUROPEAN PAINTING AND PHOTOGRAPHY **EDUCATION** Univ Manchester, MA; Univ Kent at Canterbury, Engl, PhD. **CAREER** Assoc prof; Univ TX, 93-; taught at, Kent & Univ SC. **RESEARCH** Panoramic representation of landscape. **SELECTED PUBLICATIONS** Ed, 3-vol bk, The English Garden: Literary Sources and Documents, 93; contrib chap, gothic architecture and the picturesque movement to The Politics of the Picturesque, 94; auth, series of essays on 19th century photography. **CONTACT ADDRESS** Dept of Art and Art Hist, Univ of Texas, Austin, 2613 Wichita St, FAB 1.112, Austin, TX 78705.

CHARLTON, THOMAS L.
PERSONAL Born 12/18/1936, Helena, AR, m, 1988, 2 children **DISCIPLINE** HISTORY **EDUCATION** Baylor Univ, BA, 59; Univ TX Austin, MA, 61; PhD, 69. **CAREER** San Antonio Coll, 62-70; asst prof, Baylor Univ, 70-; dir, 70-93; vice prov, 93-. **HONORS AND AWARDS** Phi Alpha Theta; Alpha Kappa Delta; OHA, p-pres. **MEMBERSHIPS** OAH; NCPH; SHA; WHA; OHA; TSHA; NCURA; SRA. **RESEARCH** Texas and Southwest; oral history; public history. **SELECTED PUBLICATIONS** Auth, Oral History for Texans, Texas Hist Comm, Austin, 77, 86. **CONTACT ADDRESS** Dept History, Baylor Univ, Waco, PO Box 97286, Waco, TX 76798-7286. **EMAIL** thomas_charlton@baylor.edu

CHARNON-DEUTSCH, LOU
PERSONAL Born 07/02/1946, Freeport, IL, m, 1972 **DISCIPLINE** SPANISH STUDIES **EDUCATION** Mount Mary Col, BA, 68; Purdue Univ, MA, 71; Univ Chicago, PhD, 78. **CAREER** Asst prof to prof, SUNY Stony Brook, 80-; Chair 89-91; 99-00. **HONORS AND AWARDS** SUNY Fac Grant, 85; Presidents Awd for Excellence in Teaching, 90; Fac Travel Grant, SUNY, 87, 91, 92, 93; NEH Grant, 91; PDQWL Continuing Fac Awd, 93, 98; Ministry of Culture Res Grant, Spain, 95; Grant, Ministry of Culture, Spain, 99. **MEMBERSHIPS** Am Assoc of Teachers of Span and Port; MLA, Midwest MLA; Feministas Unidas; Teachers for a Democratic Cult; Asociacion Int de Hispanista. **RESEARCH** Spanish culture and literature, feminist theory. **SELECTED PUBLICATIONS** Auth, The Nineteenth-Century Spanish Short Story: Textual Strategies of a Genre in Evolution, Tamesis (Madrid), 85; auth, Gender and Representation: Women in Nineteenth-Century Spanish Realist Fiction, John Benjamins (Amsterdam), 90; ed, Estudios sobre escritoras hispanicas en honor de Georgina Sabat-Rivers, Castalia (Madric), 92; auth, Narratives of Desire: Nineteenth-Century Spanish Fiction by Women, Penn State Univ Pr, 94; coed, Culture and Gender in Nineteenth-Century Spain, Oxford Univ Pr, (London), 95; auth, Fictions of the Feminine in Nineteenth-Century Spanish Press, Penn State Pr, (University Park, 99. **CONTACT ADDRESS** Dept Hispanic Lang and Lit, SUNY, Stony Brook, 100 Nicolls Rd, Stony Brook, NY 11794-0002. **EMAIL** ldeutsch@notes.cc.sunsb.edu

CHARTIER, YVES
DISCIPLINE HISTORY OF MUSIC **EDUCATION** Univ Ottawa, BA, MA; Univ Paris, DU. **CAREER** Assoc prof, Univ Ottawa. **RESEARCH** Musicology (Middle Ages, Renaissance), aesthetics. **SELECTED PUBLICATIONS** Auth, L'Oeuvre musicale d'Hucbald de Saint-Amand, Mont real-Paris, Editions Bellarmin-Vrin, 94; Clavis opervm Hvcbaldi Elnonensis, Jour of Medieval Latin 4, 95; Les outils du musicologue, Dubuque, 91; coauth, Glossaire de Musique, Toronto, 90; ed, Georges MIGOT, Douze hymnes liturgiques, Paris, 87. **CONTACT ADDRESS** Dept of Music, Univ of Ottawa, PO Box 450 Stn A, Ottawa, ON, Canada K1N 6N5.

CHASE, JAMES S.
DISCIPLINE HISTORY **EDUCATION** Univ Chicago, PhD. **CAREER** Prof. **RESEARCH** United States political parties; early national period. **SELECTED PUBLICATIONS** Auth, Democratizing the Old Dominion: Virginia and the Second Party System, 1824-1861 (rev), 98; DeWitt Clinton and the Rise of the People's Men (rev), Am Hist Rev, 97; Character Above All: Ten Presidents from FDR to George Bush (rev), Ark Hist Rev, 97; The Presidency of Andrew Jackson (rev), Hist Rev New Brooks, 94; The 1992 Presidential Election in the South (rev), Ark Hist Quarterly, 94. **CONTACT ADDRESS** History Dept, Univ of Arkansas, Fayetteville, 406 Old Main, Fayetteville, AR 72701. **EMAIL** jchase@comp.uark.edu

CHASE, PHILANDER DEAN
PERSONAL Born 03/10/1943, Eikin, NC, m, 1971 **DISCIPLINE** AMERICAN HISTORY **EDUCATION** NC State Univ, BA, 65; Duke Univ, MA, 68, PhD(hist), 73. **CAREER** Nat Hist Publ & Rec Comn fel, Papers George Washington, 73-74; asst ed, 74-89, assoc ed, 89-98, Editor, Papers of George Washington, Alderman Libr, Univ VA, Charlottesville, 98-. **HONORS AND AWARDS** Philip M Hamer Awd, Soc Am Archivists, 78; Distinguished Alumnus Awd, Col of Humanities and Social Sciences, NC State Univ, 94. **MEMBERSHIPS** AHA; Southern Hist Asn; Asn Doc Ed; Inst Early Am Hist & Cult. **RESEARCH** American Revolution; 18th century military history. **SELECTED PUBLICATIONS** Auth, A la recherche de l'esprit et de l'ame de la Revolution Americaine, Annales Hist Revolution Fr, Vol 48, 76; co-ed, The Diaries of George Washington, Univ Press VA (6 vols), 76-79; co-ed, The Papers of George Washington: Colonial Series (10 vols), Univ Press VA, 83-95; ed, The Papers of George Washington: Revolutionary War Series (11 vols to date), Univ Press VA, 85-; auth, Years of Hardships and Revelations: The Convention Army at the Albemarle Barracks, 1779-1781, Mag of Albemarle County Hist, 41, 83; A Stake in the West: George Washington as Back Country Surveyor and Landowner, in Warren R. Hofstra, ed, George Washington and the Virginia Back Country, Madison, WI: Madison House, 97. **CONTACT ADDRESS** Alderman Libr, Univ of Virginia, P O Box 400117, Charlottesville, VA 22904-4117. **EMAIL** pdc7m@virginia.edu

CHASE, WILLIAM JOHN
PERSONAL Born 09/04/1947, Glen Cove, NY, m, 1972, 2 children **DISCIPLINE** RUSIAN AND SOVIET HISTORY **EDUCATION** Lafayette Col, BA, 69; Boston Col, MA, 73, PhD, 79. **CAREER** Instr, Boston Col, 76-79; asst prof hist, Univ Pittsburgh, 79-85; assoc prof, 85-; co-dir, Russ Archive Series, 91-; dir, Russ Pub Proj, 90; ed, Carl Beck Papers Russ & East Europ studies, 82-; dir, Cen for Russ and Eur Studies, Univ of Pittsburgh, 89-91. **HONORS AND AWARDS** Nat Coun for Soviet & East European Res grants, 83, 84, 85, 92, 95; NEH-84; SSRC, 91; IREX, 90; ACLS, 81; Sr Fel, Harriman Inst for Adv Stud of Sov Union, Columbia Univ, 82; Distinguished Teaching Awd, 84; **RESEARCH** International communist and revolutionary movements, urbanization **SELECTED PUBLICATIONS** Coauth, "Worktime and Industrialization in the USSR, 1917-1941," in Worktime and Industrialization, ed. Gary Cross An Int Hist, (89), 183-216; auth, "Voluntarism, Mobilazation and Coercion: Subbotniki, 1919-1921," Soviet Studies, 31, (89), 111-128; coauth, The Soviet Bureaucracy in 1935: A Socio-Political Profile, John W Strong, essays on Revolutionary Culture and Stalinism, (90), 192-223; auth, L'Irrealisable Smycka," revue des Etudes Slaves, 64, (92), 53-74; auth, Patterns of Repression among the Soviet Elite in the Late 1930's: A Biographical Approach," J. Arch Getty and Roberta Manning, Stalinist Terror: New Perspectives, (93), 225-246; auth, Case of Diego Rivera and the U.S. State Department, Zona Abierta, 93; co-ed, Rossiiskii Gosudarstvennyi Arkhiv Ekonomiki, Putevodital, Vol 1, Moscow, 94; auth, Trotskii v Mekcike: K istorii ero Neglasnykh Kontaktov s Pravitel Stvom SSha 1937-1940," Othechestvennaia istoriia, (95), 76-02; auth, Enemies Within the Gates? The Comintern and the Stalinist Repression, 1934-1939, Yale Univ Press, 01. **CONTACT ADDRESS** Univ of Pittsburgh, 3s25 W. Posvar Hall, Pittsburgh, PA 15260-0001. **EMAIL** wchase@pitt.edu

CHASSEN-LOPEZ, FRANCIE R.
PERSONAL Born 07/04/1947, New York, NY, 1 child **DISCIPLINE** HISTORY **EDUCATION** Vassar Col, BA, 69; Univ Nac Autonoma Mexico, MA, 75, PhD, 86. **CAREER** Prof, Univ Autonoma, Estado Mexico, 77-78, 80-81; assoc prof, Univ Nac Autonoma Mexico, Mexico City, 76-81; assoc prof, Univ Autonoma Metropolitana, Ixtapalapa, 81-86; vis instr, Fla Int Univ, 86-87; vis instr, Fla Atlantic Univ, 86-88; asst prof, 88-91, ASSOC PROF, 91-; act dir Lat Am Stud Prog, Univ Ky, 97; ed bd, Guchachi Reza, 96-. **HONORS AND AWARDS** Gabino Berreda Meda acad exc, Univ Nac Autonoma Mexico, 88; PRONAES grant res reg Hist, 84-86; Univ Ky res fund grant, 89; NEH summer inst, 92; Univ Ky grant, 94, 96. **MEMBERSHIPS** Conf Lat Am Hist; Lat Am Stud Asn; Rocky Mountain Counc Lat Am Stud; Midwest Asn Lat Am Stud; Phi Alpha Theta; Vassar Alumni Asn. **SELECTED PUBLICATIONS** Co-auth, Diccionario Historico de la Revolucion en Oaxaca, Univ Autonoma Benito Juarez Oaxaca and Inst Estatal Educ Pub Oaxaca, 97; co-auth, La Revolucion en Oaxaca 1900-1930, Mins Adm Pub Oaxaca, 85, Consejo Nac Cult, Artes, 93; auth, Capitalismo o comunalismo: Cambio y Continuidad en la Tenencia de la Tierra en la Oaxaca Profirista, in El Porfiriato: Sintesis y Perspectivas, Univ Iberoamericana, 98; auth, Dona Juana Cata Romero, in Forjando Matrias. Las mujeres y la Historia Mexicana, Univ Calif Press and Col Mex, forthcoming; auth, Maderismo or Mixtec Empire? Class and Ethnicity in the Mexican Revolution (Costa Chica of Oaxaca, 1911) The Americas, 55:1, Jul 98; auth, El Ferrocarril Nacional de Tehuantepec, Acervos 10, Oct/Dec 98; auth, Cheaper than Machines: Women in Agriculture in Porfirian Oaxaca, in Creating Spaces, Shaping Transitions: Women of the Mexican Countryside, 1850-1990, Univ Az, 94, Sp trans, 96. **CONTACT ADDRESS** Dept of History, Univ of Kentucky, 1715 Patterson Off, Lexington, KY 40506-0027. **EMAIL** frclopz@pop.uky.edu

CHASTAIN, CATHERINE
DISCIPLINE ART HISTORY **EDUCATION** Rhodes Col, BA, 90; Emory Univ, MA, 93, PhD, 98. **HONORS AND AWARDS** Res fel(s), 93, 96. **SELECTED PUBLICATIONS** Publ, articles, essays in the field of American Modernism, Oxford Univ Press22,Woman's Art Jour. **CONTACT ADDRESS** Art Dept, Piedmont Col, 165 Central Ave., PO Box 10, Demorest, GA 30535. **EMAIL** cgoldsle@piedmont.edu

CHASTAIN, JAMES G.
PERSONAL Born 03/15/1939, Chickasha, OK, m, 1965, 2 children **DISCIPLINE** MODERN EUROPEAN HISTORY **EDUCATION** Harvard Univ, BA, 61; Univ Okla, MA, 66, PhD, 67. **CAREER** Asst prof, 67-72, Assoc Prof Hist, Ohio Univ, 72-; Prof emer, Ohio Univ. **MEMBERSHIPS** AHA; Soc Fr Hist Studies; Conf Group Cent Europ Hist; Western Soc Fr Hist. **RESEARCH** Modern French history; modern German history; 19th century revolutions. **SELECTED PUBLICATIONS** Contribr, Annual Proceedings of the Consortium on Revolutionary Europe, 1750-1850, Vol II, Univ Fla, 74; auth, Jules Bastide et l'unite allemande, 1848, Rev Hist, 74; translr, Rudolf Stadelmann Social and Political History of the German 1848 Revolution, Ohio Univ, 75; auth, Franciaorszag Magyarorszagi Politikaja 1848-ban, Leveltari Kozlemenyek A Magyar Orszagos Leveltar Folyoirata, 76; France in 1848: the diplomatic revolution Manque, Rev Europ Hist, 9/76; contribr, France's proposed Danubian Confederation in 1848, In: Proceedings of the 8th Consortium on Revolutionary Europe, Fla Univs. **CONTACT ADDRESS** Villa des Lucioles, 21 Bd Princess Grace, Villefranche, France 06230. **EMAIL** Lucioles@aol.com

CHATFIELD, E. CHARLES
PERSONAL Born 03/11/1934, Philadelphia, PA, m, 1957, 2 children **DISCIPLINE** HISTORY **EDUCATION** Monmouth Col, BA, 56; Vanderbilt Univ, MA, 58, Phd, 65; Univ of Chicago, postdoctoral work, 66. **CAREER** Vis prof, hist, Gustavus Adlphus Col, 74; vis prof, hist, Univ of Toledo, 87-88; Prof, Hist, Wittenberg Univ, 61- . **HONORS AND AWARDS** Named to endowed chair: H. Orth Hirt Prof of Hist, 98; Hon PhD, Monmouth Col, 95; Danforth Fel, 56-65; Warren Kuehl Prize of the Soc for Hists of Am For Policy for an Am Ordeal; Publ Prize of the Ohio Acad of Hist For Peace and Justice: Pacifism in Am, 72. **MEMBERSHIPS** Am Hist Asn; Ohio Acad of Hist; Peace Hist Soc; Int Peace Res Asn. **RESEARCH** History of peace and antiwar movements, in U.S. and twentieth century; history of internationalism. **SELECTED PUBLICATIONS** Coauth, An American Ordeal: The Antiwar Movement of the Vietnam Era, Syracuse Univ Pr, 90; auth, The American Peace Movement: Ideals and Activism, Syracuse Univ Pr, 92; co-ed, Peace/Mir: An Anthology of Historic Alternatives to War, Syracuse Univ Pr, 94; co-ed, Transnational Movements and Global Politics: Solidarity Beyond the State, Syracuse Univ Pr, 1997; co-ed, Peace Movements and Political Cultures, Tenn Univ Pr, 88. **CONTACT ADDRESS** Wittenberg Univ, PO Box 720, Springfield, OH 45501-0720. **EMAIL** echatfield@wittenberg.edu

CHATTERJEE, LATA
PERSONAL Born 02/11/1938, Calcutta, India, m, 1979, 2 children **DISCIPLINE** GEOGRAPHY **EDUCATION** Calcutta Univ, PhD, 70; Johns Hopkins Univ, PhD, 73. **CAREER** Asst prof, Rutgers Univ, 73-75; asst prof, Johns Hopkins Univ, 75-78; assoc prof to prof, Boston Univ, 78-. **HONORS AND AWARDS** Sen Fulbright Fel, Amsterdam, 84; Vis Scholar, Royal Inst of Technol; Vis Scholar, Nat Urban Inst, India. **MEMBERSHIPS** Regional Sci Asn; Asn of Am Geogr/ **RESEARCH** Geography of Development; Trade and Development; Transportation and Trade; Environmental Studies; Disability Studies. **CONTACT ADDRESS** Dept Geog, Boston Univ, 675 Commonwealth Ave, Stone Science Bldg, Boston, MA 02215. **EMAIL** lata@bu.edu

CHAUSSE, GILLES
PERSONAL Born 06/06/1931, Montreal, PQ, Canada **DISCIPLINE** THEOLOGY, CHURCH HISTORY **EDUCATION** Univ Montreal, MA, 58, PhD, 73. **CAREER** Prof hist, Col Jean-de-Brebeuf Montreal, 69-85; PROF D'HISTOIRE DE L'EGLISE, FACULTE DE THEOLOGIE, UNIV MONTREAL, 86-. **HONORS AND AWARDS** Collaborateur a l'Institut historique de la Compagnie de Jesus a Rome; recipiendaire du Merite Diocesain 'Monseigneur Ignace Bourger', 86. **MEMBERSHIPS** Societe Canadienne d'Histoire de l'Eglise catholique **SELECTED PUBLICATIONS** Auth, Jean-Jacques Lartigue, premier eveque de Montreal, 80; coauth, Les Ultramontains canadiens-francais, 85; coauth, Le Christianisme d'ici a-t-il un avenir?, 88; coauth, L'Image de la Revolution francaise au Quebec 1789-1989, 89; coauth, Quebec, terre d'Evangile: les defis de l'evangelisation dans la culture contemporaine, 91; coauth, Montreal 1642-1992, 92; coauth, Dictionnaire Biographique du Canada, tomes 4-8; coauth, A Concise History of Christianity in Canada, 96. **CONTACT ADDRESS** Fac de Theologie, Univ of Montreal, CP 6128, Succ Centre Ville, Montreal, QC, Canada H3C 3J7. **EMAIL** chausseg@magellan.umontreal.ca

CHAVALAS, MARK W.
DISCIPLINE HISTORY **EDUCATION** Univ Calif Los Angeles, PhD, 88. **CAREER** Instr, Univ Wis, 89-; Prof, Univ Wis, 98-. **HONORS AND AWARDS** NEH Summer Sem, Cornell, 98; NEH Summer Inst, Univ Ariz, 96; NEH Summer Inst, Brown, 95. **MEMBERSHIPS** Am Oriental Soc; Am Schs of Oriental Res; Archeol Inst of Am; Soc of Bibl Lit. **RESEARCH** Ancient Near East history; archaeology; Biblical studies; classical studies. **SELECTED PUBLICATIONS** Co-ed, New Horizons in the Study of Ancient Syria, 92; Ed, Emar: The History, Religion, and Culture of a Syrian Town in the Late Bronze Age, 96; Co-ed, Crossing Boundaries and Linking Horizons: Studies in Honor of Michael C. Astour on his 80th Birthday, 97; Co-ed, Syro-Mesopotamia and the Bible, 99. **CONTACT ADDRESS** Dept of History, Univ of Wisconsin, La Crosse, 1725 State St, La Crosse, WI 54601. **EMAIL** chavalas.mark@uwlax.edu

CHAVEZ, JOHN R.
PERSONAL Born 01/12/1949, Pasadena, CA, m, 1984, 2 children **DISCIPLINE** HISTORY **EDUCATION** Calif State, BA, 71; MA, 72; BA, 75; Univ Mich, MA, 78; PhD, 80. **CAREER** Asst Prof, Texas A & M Univ, 86-89; Assoc Prof to Prof, Southern Methodist Univ, 89-. **HONORS AND AWARDS** Pulitzer Prize nomination; Hispanic Educator of the Year nomination. **MEMBERSHIPS** Nat Asn for Chicano Studies, Western Hist Asn. **RESEARCH** Ethnic, regional and US history, especially as related to Mexican Americans and the Southwest. **SELECTED PUBLICATIONS** Auth, Eastside Landmark; A History of the East Los Angeles Community Union, Stanford Univ Press, 98; auth, The Lost Land: The Chicano Image of the Southwest, Univ of New Mexico Press, 84. **CONTACT ADDRESS** Dept Hist, So Methodist Univ, PO Box 750176, Dallas, TX 75275-0176. **EMAIL** jchavez@mail.smu.edu

CHEAL, CATHERYN LEDA
PERSONAL Born 04/11/1951, Mich **DISCIPLINE** CLASSICAL ARCHEOLOGY, NUMISMATICS **EDUCATION** Univ Mich, BS, 73; Brown Univ, PhD(class archaeol), 78. **CAREER** Teaching asst to assoc Latin & archaeol, Brown Univ, 76-78; instr hist archit, Roger Williams Col, 77-79; Lectr Classics & Art Hist, Calif State Univ, Northridge 81-. **MEMBERSHIPS** Am Inst Archaeol. **RESEARCH** Greek sculpture. **SELECTED PUBLICATIONS** Auth, The early Hellenistic clay sculptures from Salamis, Cyprus, Quaderni Ticinesi, 80; The Coins of Selinus, Edizioni Arte e Moneta, Bellizona, Switzerland (in prep). **CONTACT ADDRESS** 1343 Erringer Rd, Simi Valley, CA 93065.

CHEATHAM, CARL W.
PERSONAL Born 08/04/1940, Lincoln, AR, m, 1961, 4 children **DISCIPLINE** MODERN CHURCH HISTORY **EDUCATION** Harding Univ, BA, 62; Harding Graduate Sch, MTh, 65; Vanderbilt, MA, 79, PhD, 82. **CAREER** Prof, Faulkner Univ, 81-. **MEMBERSHIPS** Am Soc Church Hist; AAR; SBL; ETS. **RESEARCH** Restoration History **CONTACT ADDRESS** Faulkner Univ, 5345 Atlanta Hwy, Box 44, Montgomery, AL 36109. **EMAIL** ccheatha@faulkner.edu

CHECK, ED
DISCIPLINE ART HISTORY **EDUCATION** Univ Wis, Milwaukee, BFA, 80, MS, 87, PhD, 96. **CAREER** Lectr, McPherson Col-Milwaukee Ctr, 89; tchg asst, 89-95, lectr, Univ WI, Madison, 95; asst prof, TX Tech Univ, 96-; rev bd mem, J of Gender Issues in Art and Educ. **HONORS AND AWARDS** Frederick M Logan scholar, Univ WI, 93; Univ Res Enhancement Fund Grant, Tex Tech Univ, 99. **MEMBERSHIPS** Nat Art Educ Asn; TX Art Educ Asn; Col Arts Asn; Southern Poverty Law Ctr; Lubbock Arts Alliance; Nat Orgn of Men Against Sexism; S Plains Art Educ Asn. **RESEARCH** Gender (masculinity) and sexuality; cult criticism. **SELECTED PUBLICATIONS** Auth, Queers, art and education, in M. Zurmuehlen, ed, Working Papers In Art Education, Univ Iowa, 92; coauth, Living the discourses, J of Soc Theory in Art Educ, 17, 38-68, 97; coauth, "Teaching more of the story: Sexual and cultural diversity in art and the classroom," Advisory (99); auth, "Caught between control and creativity: Boredom and the classroom," in Realworld readings in art education: Things your professors never told you, ed. D. Fehr and K. Fehr and K. Keifer-Boyd (NY: Falmer Press, 00): 137-145; coauth, "Notes toward a theory of dialogue," J of Soc Theory in Art Educ 19 (00): 7-23. **CONTACT ADDRESS** School of Art, Texas Tech Univ, Lubbock, TX 79409. **EMAIL** echeck@ttacs.ttu.edu

CHEETHAM, MARK A.
DISCIPLINE ART **EDUCATION** Univ Toronto, BA; MA; Univ London, PhD. **RESEARCH** Art theory. **SELECTED PUBLICATIONS** Auth, Alex Colville: The Observer Observed, ECW, 94; The Rhetoric of Purity: Essentialist Theory & the Advent of Abstract Painting, Cambridge, 91; Remembering Postmodernism: Trends in Recent Canadian Art, Oxford, 91; coauth, Disturbing Abstraction: Christian Eckart, 96; co-ed, Theory Between the Disciplines: Authority/Vision/Politics, Michigan, 90. **CONTACT ADDRESS** Dept of Visual Arts, Univ of Western Ontario, London, ON, Canada N6A 5B8. **EMAIL** cheetham@julian.uwo.ca

CHEHABI, HOUCHANG E.
PERSONAL Born 02/22/1954, Teheran, Iran **DISCIPLINE** INTERNATIONAL RELATIONS, HISTORY **EDUCATION** Univ Caen, Licence, 75; Sciences Po, Paris, Diploma, 77; Yale Univ, MA, 79; PhD, 86. **CAREER** Asst to assoc prof, Harvard Univ, 86-94; vis fel, Oxford Univ, 94-95; vis assoc prof, UCLA, 95-97; prof, Boston Univ, 98-. **HONORS AND AWARDS** Centre for Lebanese Studies Fel, 94-95; Woodrow Wilson Fel, 97-98; Gregory Luebbert Prize, Am Polit Sci Assoc, 99. **MEMBERSHIPS** Middle Eastern Studies Assoc, Soc for Iranian Studies, Center for Iranian Res and Analysis, Assoc for the Study of Persianate Soc. **RESEARCH** Iranian politics and culture, Cultural history of Iran, Turkey, and Afghanistan, the politics of small island states. **SELECTED PUBLICATIONS** Auth, "Self-Determination, Territorial Integrity, and the Falkland Islands," Polit Sci Quart, (85); auth, Iranian Politics and Religious Modernism: The Liberation Movement of Iran under the Shah and Khomeini, Cornell Univ Pr, 90; auth, "Ardabil Becomes a Province: Center-Periphery Relations in the Islamic Republic of Iran," Int Jour of Middle East Studies, (97); coed, Sultanistic Regimes, Johns Hopkins Univ Pr, 98; auth, "The Political Regime of the Islamic Republic of Iran in Comparative Perspective," Govt and Opposition, (01); auth, "US-Iranian Sports Diplomacy," Diplomacy and Statecraft, (01). **CONTACT ADDRESS** Boston Univ, 152 Bay State Rd, Boston, MA 02215. **EMAIL** chehabi@bu.edu

CHEN, CHING-CHIH
PERSONAL Born 05/24/1937, Taoyuan, Taiwan, m, 1965, 2 children **DISCIPLINE** EAST ASIAN HISTORY **EDUCATION** Tunghai Univ, Taiwan, BA, 60; Harvard Univ, MA, 65, PhD(hist & EAsian lang), 73. **CAREER** Teaching asst polit sci, Tunghai Univ, Taiwan, 61-63; asst prof, 69-77, Assoc Prof Hist, Southern Ill Univ, Edwardsville, 77- **MEMBERSHIPS** AHA; Asn Asian Studies. **RESEARCH** History of Japanese colonial expansion; history of Sino-Japanese relations; history of Taiwan. **SELECTED PUBLICATIONS** Auth, The police and hoko systems in Taiwan under Japanese administration, 1895-1945, In: Papers on Japan, (Vol 4), Harvard Univ, 67; The Japanese adaptation of the Pao-chin system in Taiwan, 1895-1945, J Asian Studies, 2/75. **CONTACT ADDRESS** Dept of Hist Studies, So Illinois Univ, Edwardsville, 6 Hairpin Dr, Edwardsville, IL 62026-0001.

CHEN, XIANG
DISCIPLINE PHILOSOPHY OF SCIENCE, HISTORY OF SCIENCE **EDUCATION** Zhongshand Univ, BA, 82; MA, 85; Va Polytechnic Inst and State Univ, MS, 88; PhD, 92. **CAREER** Asst prof, Calif Lutheran Univ, 92-98; Sr Residential Fel, Dibner Inst for the Hist of Sci and Tech at MIT, 98-99; assoc prof, Calif Lutheran Univ, 98-. **HONORS AND AWARDS** Fel for Sr Resident Fel, Dibner Inst for the Hist of Sci and Tech at MIT, 98-99; NEH res stipend, Johns Hopkins Univ, 92. **MEMBERSHIPS** Philos of Sci Asn, Hist of Sci Soc, Am Philos Asn. **RESEARCH** Theories of scientific revolutions, cognitive psychology and philosophy of science, history of optics in 19th century. **SELECTED PUBLICATIONS** Auth, "Recent Progress in the Studies of Incommensurability," Sci, Philos, and Culture, Zhongshan Univ Press (96): 169-190; coauth, "Kuhn's Mature Philosophy of Science and Cognitive Psychology," Philos Psychol 9 (96): 347-363; auth, "Thomas Kuhn's Latest Notion of Incommensurability," J for General Philos of Sci 28 (97): 257-273; auth, "The Debate on the Polarity of Light during the Optical Revolution," Archive for Hist of Exact Sci 50 (97): 359-393; coauth, "Kuhn's Theory of Scientific Revolutions and Cognitive Psychology," Philos Psychol 11 (98): 5-28; auth, "Dispersion, Experimental Apparatus, and the Acceptance of the Wave Theory of Light," Annals of Sci 55 (98): 401-420; auth, "Instrumental Unification: Optical Apparatus in the Unification of Dispersion and Selective Absorption," Studies in Hist and Philos of Modern Physics 30 (99): 519-542; coauth, "Continuity through Revolution: A Frame-based Account of Conceptual Change during Scientific Revolutions," Philos of Sci 67 (00): A1-A9; Auth, Instrumental Traditions and Theories of Light: The Uses of Instruments in the Optical Revolution, Kluwer Acad, 00. **CONTACT ADDRESS** Dept Philos, California Lutheran Univ, 60 W Olsen Rd, Thousand Oaks, CA 91360-2700. **EMAIL** Chenxi@clunet.edu

CHENG, WEIKUN
DISCIPLINE HISTORY **EDUCATION** Johns Hopkins Univ, PhD. **CAREER** Vis asst prof, SUNY Oswego. **RESEARCH** Mod China; mod Japan; Chinese soc and cult hist. **SELECTED PUBLICATIONS** Auth, The Challenge of the Actresses: Female Performers and the Cultural Alternatives in the Early Twentieth-Century Beijing and Tianjin, in Modern China, 96; The Politics of Headdress: Agitations Regarding the Queue in the Beginning and the End of Qing China in Hair in Asian Cultures: Context and Change, SUNY Albany P, 96. **CONTACT ADDRESS** Dept Hist, SUNY, Oswego, 423 Mahar Hall, Oswego, NY 13126.

CHERNOW, BARBARA A.
PERSONAL Born 04/18/1948, New York, NY, s **DISCIPLINE** AMERICAN HISTORY **EDUCATION** Hunter Coll, CUNY, BA, 68; Columbia Univ, MA, 69, PhD, 74. **CAREER** Assoc edr, 69-76; ref edr, MacMillan Publ Co, 77-82; PRES, CHERNOW EDIT SERVS, 82-. **MEMBERSHIPS** Soc Women Geog; Womens City Club of NY **RESEARCH** Early national period of American history **SELECTED PUBLICATIONS** Ed, The Paper of Alexander Hamilton, vols. 17-25, Columbia Univ Press, 71-79; Co-ed, The Columbia Encyclopedia 5th ed, Columbia Univ Press/Houghton Mifflin, 93. **CONTACT ADDRESS** Chernow Editorial Services, 1133 Broadway, New York, NY 10010. **EMAIL** bchernow@chernow.com

CHERNY, ROBERT WALLACE
PERSONAL Born 04/04/1943, Marysville, KS, m, 1967, 1 child **DISCIPLINE** AMERICAN HISTORY **EDUCATION** Univ NE, BA, 65; Columbia Univ, MA, 67, PhD(hist), 72. **CAREER** Instr Am hist, 71-72, asst prof, 72-77, assoc prof, 77-81, PROF AM HIST, SAN FRANCISCO STATE UNIV, 81-, Chair, 87-92, 95; Vis assoc prof, Univ NE-Lincoln, 80, vis prof, 82. **HONORS AND AWARDS** Vis Res Scholar, Univ Melbourne, 97; Distinguished Fulbright Lect, Moscow State Univ, 96; fel, Nat Endowment for the Humanities, 92-93. **MEMBERSHIPS** AHA; Orgn Am Historians; Southwest Labor Studies Asn (pres, 82-86); Am Hist Asn, Pacific Coast Branch: Council, 91-94; Soc Hist of the Gilded Age and the Progressive Era, pres, 95-96. **RESEARCH** United States political, labor, and urban history, 1877-1945; US West, especially CA. **SELECTED PUBLICATIONS** Auth, Isolationist voting in 1940: A statistical analysis, Nebr Hist, 71; Anti-imperialism on the middle border, 1898-1900, Midwest Rev, 79; Populism, Progressivism and the Transformation of Nebraska Politics, 1885-1915, Univ NE Press, 81; Lawrence Goodwyn and Nebraska Populism: A review essay, Gt Plains Quart, summer 81; Willa Cather and the Populists, Gt Plains Quart, 83; A Righteous Cause: The Life of William Jennings Bryan, Little, Brown, 85, reprint, Univ OK Press, 94; coauth, San Francisco, 1865-1932: Politics, Power, and Urban Development, Univ CA Press, 86; auth, Democratic Party in the Era of William Jennings Bryan, Democrats and the Am Idea, Center for Nat Policy Press, 92; City Commercial, City Beautiful, City Practical: The San Francisco Visions of Willliam Ralston, James Phelan, and Michael O'Shaughnessy, CA Hist, 95; coauth, Making America: A History of the United States, Houghton Mifflin, 95, 2nd ed, 99;auth, The Making of a Labor Radical: Harry Bridges, 1901-1934, Pacific Hist Rev, 95; William Jennnings Bryan and the Historians, NE Hist, 96; American Politics in the Gilded Age, 1868-1900, Harlan Davidson, 97. **CONTACT ADDRESS** Dept of Hist, San Francisco State Univ, 1600 Holloway Ave, San Francisco, CA 94132-1740. **EMAIL** cherny@sfsu.edu

CHERU, FANTU
DISCIPLINE AFRICAN AND DEVELOPMENT STUDIES **EDUCATION** Colo Col, BA; Portland State Univ, MS, PhD. **CAREER** Prof, Am Univ. **HONORS AND AWARDS** Consult, UN. **SELECTED PUBLICATIONS** Auth, The Financial Implications of Divesting from South Africa: A Review of the Evidence; Underdevelopment and Unemployment in Kenya, Int Jour African Hist Studies, 88; The Silent Revolution in Africa: Debt, Development and Democracy, Zed Press, 89: Ethiopia: Options for Rural Development, Zed Press, 90, The Not So Brave New World: Rethinking Regional Integration in Post-Apartheid Southern Africa, Bradlow Occasional Paper Series 92. **CONTACT ADDRESS** American Univ, 4400 Massachusetts Ave, Washington, DC 20016.

CHESSON, MICHAEL
PERSONAL Born 09/05/1947, Richmond, VA, m, 1988, 2 children **DISCIPLINE** HISTORY **EDUCATION** Col William and Mary, AB, 69; Harvard Univ, PhD, 78. **CAREER** Teaching Fel, Harvard Univ, 75-78; asst prof to prof, 78-, chmn, Dept of Hist, 96-98, Univ Mass. **HONORS AND AWARDS** Pulitzer Prize board nominee, 81; Jefferson Davis Awd, 81; Mellon Fel, VA Hist Soc, 89; LA Endowment for the Humanities Grant, 97. **MEMBERSHIPS** Org of Am Hist; S Hist Asn; Am Hist Asn; VA Hist Soc. **RESEARCH** Civil War and Reconstruction; American slavery; The Old South. **SELECTED PUBLICATIONS** Auth, Richmond After the War, 1865-1890, Richmond, 81; auth, "Prison Camps and Prisoners of War," in The American Civil War: A Handbook of Literature and Research, (Greenwood Press, 96), 466-478; auth, "Judah P. Benjamin," "Clement C. Clay, Jr.," "Linton Stephens," "Robert A. Toombs," and "Henry A. Wise," in American National Biography, Oxford Univ Press, 99; co-ed, In Exile: The Civil War Journal of Henri Garidel, Citizen of New Orleans, in Richmond, 1863-1865, Univ Press of VA, 00. **CONTACT ADDRESS** Dept of Hist, Univ of Massachusetts, Boston, 100 Morrissey Blvd, Boston, MA 02125-3393. **EMAIL** michael.chesson@umb.edu

CHESTNUT, PAUL IVAR
PERSONAL Born 06/07/1939, Charleston, SC **DISCIPLINE** AMERICAN HISTORY **EDUCATION** Duke Univ, AB, 61, PhD(Am hist), 74; Yale Univ, BD, 64. **CAREER** Asst cur of manuscripts for reader serv, Perkins Libr, Duke Univ, 72-78; Asst State Archivist, VA State Library, 78-, Adj fac, Va Commonweatlh Univ, 80-81. **MEMBERSHIPS** Soc Am Archivists; Nat Asn State Archives & Records Adminr; Am Asn State & Local Hist. **RESEARCH** American religious and social history; archives administration. **SELECTED PUBLICATIONS** Auth, A tribute to Montrose Jonas Moses, Libr Notes, 12/73; The Moravians, In: Encycl of Southern History, La State Univ Press, 79. **CONTACT ADDRESS** 221 N 25th St, Richmond, VA 23223.

CHEYETTE, FREDRIC LAWRENCE
PERSONAL Born 01/13/1932, New York, NY, w, 1957, 3 children **DISCIPLINE** MEDIEVAL HISTORY **EDUCATION** Princeton Univ, AB, 53; Harvard Univ, MA, 55, PhD, 59. **CAREER** From instr to asst prof Hist, Stanford Univ, 59-61; asst prof, Oberlin Col, 62-63; from asst prof to assoc prof, 63-74, prof Hist, Amherst Col, 74-, book rev ed, Speculum, 78-00. **HONORS AND AWARDS** Webb-Smith Essay Prize, Univ Tex-Arlington, 77; A H Cole Prize, Econ Hist Asn, 77; Nat Endowment Humanities grant, 77-78; Guggenheim fel, 83-84. **MEMBERSHIPS** Medieval Acad. **SELECTED PUBLICATIONS** Auth, Lordship and Community in Medieval Europe, Holt, 68; Origins of European villages, J Econ Hist, 77; The invention of the state, Walter P Webb Mem Lect (12), 78. **CONTACT ADDRESS** Dept of History, Amherst Col, Amherst, MA 01002-5003. **EMAIL** flcheyette@amherst.edu

CHIARENZA, CARL
PERSONAL Born 09/06/1935, Rochester, NY, m, 1978, 3 children **DISCIPLINE** ART, HISTORY **EDUCATION** Roch Inst Tech, BFA, 57, MS, 59; Boston Univ, AM, 64; Harvard Univ, PhD, 73. **CAREER** Vis prof, Cornell Univ, 91; **HONORS AND AWARDS** Recipient of two Danforth Teacher Grants, 66-68; Kress Found res Grant, 70-71; Harnish Visiting Artist, Smith Col, 83-84; selected by the Mass Coun of the Arts to work with the Polaroid 20 x 24 Camera as a Vis Artist, School of the Museum of Fine Arts in Boston, 83, 86; received the Artist Award of the Arts and Cultural Council for Greater Rochester, 96; Special Opportunity Stipend Award from the New York Found fro the Arts, 97; Lillian Fiarchild Artist Award, 99. **CONTACT ADDRESS** Dept Art & Art Hist, Univ of Rochester, Morey Hall 424, Rochester, NY 14627. **EMAIL** ccrz@db1.cc.rochester.edu

CHIKEKA, CHARLES
PERSONAL Born 12/25/1931, Oinerri, Nigeria, m, 1978, 7 children **DISCIPLINE** AFRICAN AMERICAN STUDIES **EDUCATION** Univ Minn, BA, 63; MPA, 64; Columbia Univ, MA, 66; MPhil, 78; PhD, 82. **CAREER** Asst prof, Jackson State Col, 67-68; asst prof, Fla A & M Univ, 68-69; assoc prof, Morgan State Univ, 70-00. **MEMBERSHIPS** African Studies Asn, Nat Asn of African-American Studies, Am Hist Asn, Am Political Sci Asn. **SELECTED PUBLICATIONS** Auth, Britain, France and the New African States: A Study of Post-Independence Relationships, 1960-1985, The Edwin Mellen Press (Lewiston, NY), 90; auth, Africa and the European Economic Community 1957-1992, The Edwin Mellen Press (Lewiston, NY), 93; auth, Decolonization Process in Africa During the Post-War Era, 1960-1990, The Edwin Mellen Press (Lewiston, NY), 98. **CONTACT ADDRESS** Dept Hist, Morgan State Univ, 1700 E Cold Spring Ln, Baltimore, MD 21251-0001.

CHILCOTE, WAYNE L.
PERSONAL Born 09/12/1945, Ft Oglethorpe, GA, m, 1980, 3 children **DISCIPLINE** ENGLISH, GEOGRAPHY **EDUCATION** Univ Tenn, BS, 71; E Tenn State. Univ, MA, 73. **CAREER** Res Asst, Univ of SC, 81-84; instr, Tusculun Col, 84-85; instr, Univ of Tenn, 85-86; instr, Piedmont Va Community Col, 86-89. Assoc Prof, Univ of SC Salkehatchie, 89-. **MEMBERSHIPS** SC Acad of Sci, Gamma Theta Upsilon, Tenn Alumni Relations Coun, Va Community Col Asn, SC Geog Alliance, SA Hist Asn. **RESEARCH** Southern Appalachian Culture, particulary music and religion, Geography/history of SC, interdisciplinary studies. **SELECTED PUBLICATIONS** Auth, "The Search for National Idendity: The U.S. in the Modern World. An Interdisciplinary Approach", The Proceedings of the South Carolina Historical Association (00): 43-50; auth, "The Evolution of Bluegrass Music from Appalachian Mountain Music", Highland Heritage, (74): 3-6. **CONTACT ADDRESS** Dept Humanities & Soc Sci, Univ of So Carolina, Salkehatchie Regional, PO Box 617, Allendale, SC 29810. **EMAIL** waynelc@yahoo.com

CHILDS, ELIZABETH C.
PERSONAL Born 07/05/1954, Denver, CO, m, 1987, 1 child **DISCIPLINE** ART HISTORY **EDUCATION** Wake Forest Univ, BA, Art Hist & Anthrop, 76; Columbia Univ, MA, 80, PhD, 89. **CAREER** Intern/ consult/ lectr, Metro Museum Art, 76-82; curat consult, Peggy Guggenheim Coll, Venice, 84-85; res assoc, Contemp Am Art, Solomon R Guggenheim Museum, 87-91; asst prof, Art Hist, SUNY-Purchase Coll, 87-92; asst prof, Wash Univ, 93-98; ASSOC PROF, ART HIST & ARCHAEOL, WASH UNIV, 98-. **HONORS AND AWARDS** National Endowment for the Humanities; National for the Humanities; National Galley of Art; Metropolitan Museum of Art. **RESEARCH** Art & censorship; Nineteenth century French painting; Photography; Printmaking; Exoticism in modern art. **SELECTED PUBLICATIONS** Coed, Femmes d'Espirit: Women in Daumieis Caucahue, Middlebury, 90; In Search of Paradise: Painting and Photography in Tahiti, 1880-1910, Univ Calif Press, forthcoming; edr, Suspended License: Censorship and the Visual Arts, Univ Wash Press, 97; contrib, Making the News: Modernity and the Mass Press in Nineteenth-Century France, Univ Mass Press, 98. **CONTACT ADDRESS** Dept Art Hist & Archaeol, Washington Univ, One Brookings Dr, Campus Box 1189, Saint Louis, MO 63130. **EMAIL** ecchilds@artsci.wustl.edu

CHING, ERIK K.
PERSONAL Born 10/06/1967, Duluth, MN, s **DISCIPLINE** HISTORY **EDUCATION** Pacific Lutheran Univ, BA, 90; Univ Calif at Santa Barbara, MA, 92; PhD, 97. **CAREER** Instr, Highline Community Col, 97-98; asst prof, Furman Univ, 98-. **HONORS AND AWARDS** Fulbright Res Grant, 94; Area Studies Fel, Acad for Educ Development, 95; Hubert Herring Prize, Pacific Coast Coun of Latin Am Studies, 98; Confr on Latin Am Hist Prize, 99. **MEMBERSHIPS** Latin Am Studies Asn, Am Hist Asn, Confr on Latin Am Hist. **RESEARCH** El Salvador, Central America, Patronage, Communist Parties. **SELECTED PUBLICATIONS** Auth, "In Search of the Party: Communism, the Comintern and the Rebellion of 1932 in El Salvador," The Americas 55.2 (98): 204-239; coauth, "Indians, the Military and the Rebellion of 1932 in El Salvador," J of Latin Am Studies 30.1 (98): 121-156. **CONTACT ADDRESS** Dept Hist, Furman Univ, 3300 Poinsett Hwy, Greenville, SC 29613-0002. **EMAIL** erik.ching@furman.edu

CHINNICI, JOSEPH PATRICK
PERSONAL Born 03/16/1945, Altadena, CA **DISCIPLINE** HISTORY THEOLOGY **EDUCATION** San Luis Rey Col, BA, 68; Grad Theol Union, MA, 71; Franciscan Sch Theol, MDiv, 72; Oxford Univ, DPhil(hist, theol), 76. **CAREER** Asst prof church hist, Franciscan Sch Theol, 75-; asst prof, Grad Theol Union, 75-. **HONORS AND AWARDS** Univ Notre Dame travel grant, 78. **MEMBERSHIPS** AHA; Am Cath Hist Asn; US Cath Hist Soc. **RESEARCH** Church and the Enlightenment; American Catholicism; American religious history. **SELECTED PUBLICATIONS** Auth, Living Stones, The History and Sturcture of Catholic Spiritual Life in the United States, Orbis Books, 96; coauth, Prayer and Practice in the Am Catholic Community, 1785-1979, Orbis Books, 00. **CONTACT ADDRESS** Franciscan Sch of Theol, 1712 Euclid Ave, Berkeley, CA 94709-1294. **EMAIL** jpchinnici@aol.com

CHIPMAN, DONALD EUGENE
PERSONAL Born 11/19/1928, Hill City, KS, d, 1955, 2 children **DISCIPLINE** LATIN AMERICAN HISTORY **EDUCATION** Ft Hays Kans State Col, AB, 55, MS, 58; Univ NMex, PhD(hist), 62. **CAREER** Teacher pub sch, Kans, 55-57; asst prof, Ft Hays Kans State Col, 62-64; assoc prof, 64-67, Prof Hist, University of North Texas, 67-, Am Coun Learned Soc grant-in-aid, 63-64; ed hist gen, Handbk Latin Am Studies, 73-; Am Philos Soc grant-in-aid, 76. **HONORS AND AWARDS** Presidio la Bahio Award, 92, 00; Texas Inst of Letters, 92; Kate Broocks Bates Award, 93; Choice Outstanding Academic Book Award, 92; Catholic Historical Society Book Award, 01. **MEMBERSHIPS** Latin Am Studies Asn; Conf Latin Am Hist. **RESEARCH** Mexican history. **SELECTED PUBLICATIONS** Auth, In Search of Cabeza de Vaca's Route across Texas, Southwestern Historical Quarterly, 87; auth, Spanish Texas, 1519-1821, Univ of Texas Press, 92; auth, The Desoto Chronicles--The Expedition of Desoto,Hernando to North-America, 1539-1543, Volume 1, Southwestern Hist Quart, Vol 0097, 94; San-Antonio De Bexar--A Community on New-Spain Northern Frontier, Amer Hist Rev, Vol 0101, 96; The Desoto Chronicles--The Expedition of Desoto, Hernando to North-America, 1539-1543, Volume 2, Southwestern Hist Quart, Vol 0097, 94; Flags Along the Coast--Charting the Gulf-Of-Mexico, 1519-1759, Southwestern Hist Quart, Vol 0099, 95; Depineda, Alonso, Alvarez and The Rio-De-Las-Palmas--Scholars and the Mislocation of a River, Southwestern Hist Quart, Vol 0098, 95; Tejano Origins in 18th-Century San-Antonio, Hisp Amer Hist Rev, Vol 0072, 92; Tejanos and Texas Under the Mexican Flag, 1821-1836, Amer Hist Rev, Vol 0101, 96; The Dominguez-Escalante Journal, Southwestern Hist Quart, Vol 0099, 95; Spanish Observers and the American-Revolution, 1775-1778, Southwestern Hist Quart, Vol 0097, 93; auth, Alonso Alvarex de pineda and the Rio de las Palmas, Southwestern Historical Quarterly, 95; To the Royal Crown Restored--The Journals of Don Vargas, Diego, De, New-Mexico, 1692-1694, Hisp Amer Hist Rev, Vol 0077, 97; Along Ancient Trails--The Mallet Expedition of 1739, Jour Amer Hist, Vol 0083, 96; coauth, Notable Men and Women of Spanish Texas, Univ of Texas Press, 99; coauth, Explorers and Settlers of Spanish Texas, Univ of Texas Press, 01; auth,. **CONTACT ADDRESS** Dept of Hist, Univ of No Texas, PO Box 310650, Denton, TX 76203-0650. **EMAIL** dchipman@unt.edu

CHMIELEWSKI, WENDY E.
PERSONAL Born 11/06/1955, United Kingdom, s **DISCIPLINE** US HISTORY **EDUCATION** State Univ NYork, BING, PhD 89, MA 81; Goucher Col, BA 77. **CAREER** Swathmore Col, Curator, Peace Collection, 88, lectr, peace studies 94. **MEMBERSHIPS** Peace Hist Soc; Communal Stud Asn. **RESEARCH** Women in intentional communities; women in 19th and 20th century peace movement. **SELECTED PUBLICATIONS** Binding Themselves the Closer to Their Own Peculiar Duties: Gender and Women's Work for Peace, 1818-1860, Peace and Change, 95; Mid the Din a Dove Appeared: Women's Work in the Nineteenth-Century Peace Movement, in: Over Here, 97. **CONTACT ADDRESS** Swathmore Col Peace Collection, Swarthmore Col, 500 College Av, Swarthmore, PA 19081. **EMAIL** wchmiel1@swathmore.edu

CHO, JOANNE M.
DISCIPLINE MODERN EUROPEAN AND GERMAN HISTORY **EDUCATION** Univ Chicago, MA, 84; Univ Calif, Los Angeles, BA, 83; Univ Chicago, PhD, 93. **CAREER** Asst prof, William Paterson Univ, 95-; asst prof, Hope Col, 92-95; tchg intern, Univ Chicago, 88-89; res asst, Univ Chicago, 84-90; acad serv, World Hist Comt, William Paterson Col, 95-96; fac adv to freshmen, Hope Col, 93-; AP Reader in Europ His, 94; Hope Col Rep, Midwest Fac Sem, Univ Chicago; Professionalization in the Mod World, 92; Pierre Bourdieu, 92. **HONORS AND AWARDS** DAAD post-doctoral res fel, Univ Tubingen, 95; Summer res grant, Hope Col, Mich, 94; Knight Found Grant, Hope Col, Mich, 93; Dissertation fel, Inst fur europaische Geschichte, Mainz, Ger, 91-92; Progetto Federico II, Int Workshop, Trani, Italy, 91; Awd, Ger Hist Inst & the Stiftung Volkswagenwerk, Herzog August Bibliothek in Wolfenbuttel, Ger, 90; Awd, Atlantic Coun of the US for a study-tour of NATO, 89; DAAD fel(s), Univat Regensburg, Ger, 87, Univat Mannheim, Ger, 86 & Univ Calif, Berkeley, 84; grad fel(s), Univ Chicago, 85-88. **MEMBERSHIPS** AHA, Ger Stud Asn; Ernst Troeltsch Gesellschaft. **RESEARCH** Mod European and German History; The Idea of Europeanism; German Liberalism; Ernst Troeltsch; Weimar Culture; The image of Asia in Mod Germany and Europe. **SELECTED PUBLICATIONS** Auth, "The Crisis of Historicism and Troeltsch's Europeanism," Hist of European Ideas 21 (95): 195-207; auth, "The Idea of Compromise in Ernst Troeltsch (1865-1923): Modernism and Ambivalence," The European Legacy 3 (98): 65-85; auth, "A New Frontier in German Universal History: Continuity and Mutuality in Karl Jaspers," Yearbk of the Austrian Karl-Jaspers Soc 12 (99): 59-81; auth, "Historicism and Civilizational Discontinuity in Spengler and Troeltsch," J of Relig and Intellectual Hist 51 (99): 238-262; auth, "A Cosmopolitan Faith in Karl Jaspers: From Exclusion to Inclusion," J of Ecumenical Studies (00); auth, "The German Debate over Civilization: Troeltsch's Europeanism and Jaspers' Cosmopolitanism," J of European Ideas (00). **CONTACT ADDRESS** Dept of History, William Paterson Col of New Jersey, 300 Pompton Rd., Atrium 210, Wayne, NJ 07470. **EMAIL** choj@wpunj.edu

CHOE, YONG-HO
PERSONAL Born 06/13/1931, Kyongsan, Korea, m, 1966, 2 children **DISCIPLINE** ASIAN HISTORY **EDUCATION** Univ Ariz, BA, 61; Univ Chicago, AM, 63, PhD(hist), 71. **CAREER** Res assoc Korean hist, EAsia Res Ctr, Harvard Univ, 68-70; asst prof, 70-77, Assoc Prof Hist, Univ Hawaii, Manoa, 77-. **HONORS AND AWARDS** Phi Beta Kappa **MEMBERSHIPS** Asn Asian Studies; Korean Hist Asn; Acad Asn Koreanology Japan. **RESEARCH** Civil service examinations in traditional Korea; social structure in traditional Korea. **SELECTED PUBLICATIONS** Auth, Sino-Korean relations, 1866-1876: A study of Korea's tributary relationship to China, Asea Yon'gu, 3/66; Commoners in early Yi Dynasty civil examinations, J Asian Studies, 74; History in North Korea, J East & West Studies, 5/76; The Civil Examinations & the Social Structure in Early Yi Korea, 87; co-ed, Sourcebook of Korean Civilisation, 2 vols, 93, 96; auth, Sources of Korean Tradition, 97. **CONTACT ADDRESS** Dept of History, Univ of Hawaii, Manoa, 2530 Dole St, Honolulu, HI 96822-2303. **EMAIL** choeyh@hawaii.edu

CHOKSY, JAMSHEED
PERSONAL Born 01/08/1962, Bombay, India, m, 1993, 1 child **DISCIPLINE** MIDDLE EASTERN STUDIES, MEDIEVAL HISTORY **EDUCATION** Columbia Univ, AB, 85; Harvard Univ, PhD, 91. **CAREER** Tech Fel, 88, Jr Fel, 88-91, Harvard Univ; Vis Asst Prof, Stanford Univ, 91-93; Mem School of Hist Stud, Inst for Adv Stud , Princeton, 93-94; Asst Prof, 93-97, Dir, UderGrad Stud, 95-99; Chairman, dept of Near East Lang, 99-2000. **HONORS AND AWARDS** Guggenheim Memorial Foundation Fel, 96-97; Res Grant, Am Acad of Relig, 95-96; Outstanding Junior Fac Awd, Ind Univ, 95-96; NEH Fel, Princeton, 93-94; Mellon Foundation Fel, Stanford Univ, 91-93; Fel, Am Numismatic Soc, 87. **RESEARCH** Anthropology, Archaeology, History, Languages, Numismatics and Religions of the Near East, Central Asia, and South Asia. **SELECTED PUBLICATIONS** Auth, Etched in Stone: Inscriptions by Early Muslims in Pakistan, forthcoming; auth, "Evil, Good, and Gender Images: Representations of the Feminine in Zoroastrian Belief and Epic," Tafazzoli Memorial Volume, Mazda Pub, forthcoming; auth, "Ancient Iranian Ideas in a Modern Context," Jamshid Soroush Soroushian Memorial vol, forthcoming; auth, "Zoroastrian Notions of Sacred Space," Proceedings of the First International Avest Conference, forthcoming; auth, "Dualism of the Feminine in Manichaeism: The Mother of Life and the Demoness of Concupiscence," Proceedings of the third International Congress of the K. R. Cama Oriental Institute, forthcoming; auth, "Women during the Transition from Sasanian to Early Islamic Times," Women in Iran from Medieval Times to the Islamic Republic, forthcoming; auth, Conflict and Cooperation: Zoroastrian Subalterns and Muslim Elites in Medieval Iranain Society, Columbia Univ Press, 97; auth, Earliest Zoroastrianism: Archaeological and Textual Evidence, Cama Oriental Inst, 98; **CONTACT ADDRESS** Dept Near Eastern Lang Cultures, Indiana Univ, Bloomington, 1011 E 3rd St, Bloomington, IN 47405-7005. **EMAIL** jchoksy@indiana.edu

CHOLDIN, MARIANNA TAX
PERSONAL Born 02/26/1942, Chicago, IL, m, 1962, 2 children **DISCIPLINE** RUSSIAN AND SOVIET STUDIES **ED-**

UCATION Univ Chicago, BA, 62, MA, 67, PhD(librarianship), 79. **CAREER** Slavic bibliogr, Mich State Univ, 67-79; Slavic Bibliogr, Univ Ill Urbana-Champaign, 69-, RES Dir, Russ & East Europ Ctr, Univ Ill Urbana-Champaign, 80-, dept affil, Grad Sch Libr & Info Sci, 80-; mem, exec comt, Midwest Slavic Conf, 81-84. **MEMBERSHIPS** Am Asn Advan Slavic Studies; Am Libr Asn; Midwest Slavic Conf. **RESEARCH** Russian and Soviet censorship; Russian bibliography; Russian history, culture and literature. **SELECTED PUBLICATIONS** Auth, Censorship in Soviet Literature, 1917-1991, Slavic Rev, Vol 0056, 97; Russian Libraries in Transition--An Anthology of Glasnost Literature, Slavic Rev, Vol 0051, 92. **CONTACT ADDRESS** Univ of Illinois, Urbana-Champaign, 1111 S Pine St, Champaign, IL 61820. **EMAIL** mcholdin@uiuc.edu

CHOMSKY, AVIVA
DISCIPLINE HISTORY **EDUCATION** Univ Calif, Berkeley, BA, 82; Univ Calif, Berkeley, MA, 85; Univ Calif, Berkeley, PhD, 90. **CAREER** Teaching asst, Spanish Dept, Univ Calif, Berkeley, 85-87; teaching asst, Hist Dept, Univ Calif, Berkeley, 97-90; asst prof, Bates Col, 90-97; assoc prof, Salem State Col, 97-present. **HONORS AND AWARDS** Best Book Prize, New England Coun of Latin Am Studies; Fac Res Assoc, Inst for Health and Social Justice; Cuban Studies Travel Grant, Johns Hopkins Univ; vis scholar, Harvard Univ; Univ Fla Ctr for Latin Am Studies Library Travel Grant; Bates Col Mellon Professional Leave Grant; Bates Col McGinty Fac Res Grant; Bates Col Mellon Summer Res Grant; Bates Col Lincoln and Gloria Ladd Fac Res Grant; Mabelle McLeod Lewis Memorial Fund Dissertation Grant; Soc of Women Geographers Fel; Ctr for Latin Am Studies/Tinker Found Grant; Univ Calif Berkeley Hist Dept Outstanding Teaching Award; Comite Conjunto Hispano-Norteamericano para la Cooperacion Cultural y Educativa Cooperative Res Grant; Departmental Citation, Dept of Spanish and Portuguese, Univ Calif, Berkeley. **MEMBERSHIPS** Asn of Caribbean Historians; AHA; Latin Am Labor Hist Group; Latin Am Studies Asn; New England Council on Latin Am Studies; New England Historical Asn. **SELECTED PUBLICATIONS** Auth, West Indian Workers in Costa Rican Radical and Nationalist Ideology, 1900-1950, in The Americas: A Quarterly Review of Inter-American Cultural History 51:1, 94; auth, Labor in Coasta Rica's Gold Mines, 1900-1940, in Journal of Third World Studies XI:2, 94; auth, Recent Historiography of Cuba, in Latin American Research Review 29:3, 94; auth,Afro-Jamaican Traditions and Labor Organizing on United Fruit Company Plantations in Costa Rica, 1910, in Journal of Social History 28:4, 95; auth, West Indian Workers and the United Fruit Company in Costa Rica, 1870-1940, Louisiana State Univ Press, 96; coed, with Aldo Laura-Santiago, Indentity and Struggle at the Margins of the Nation-State: Central America and the Hispanic Caribbean, Duke UP, 98; auth, "The Aftermath of Repression: Race and Nation in Cuba After 1912," Journal of Ibrian and Latin American Studies, 4:2 (98); auth, "'Barbados or Canada?' Race, Immigration and Nation in Early Twentieth-Century Cuba," Hispanic American Historical Review 80:30 (00). **CONTACT ADDRESS** Dept of History, Salem State Col, Salem, MA 01970. **EMAIL** achomsky@salem.mass.edu

CHRISLOCK, C. WINSTON
PERSONAL Born 11/08/1940, Owatonna, MN, m, 1965, 2 children **DISCIPLINE** MODERN HISTORY **EDUCATION** Univ Minn, Minneapolis, BA, 62; Ind Univ, Bloomington, MA, 64 PhD(hist), 71. **CAREER** Instr hist, Augsburg Col, 64-65; assoc, Ind Univ, Bloomington, 65-67; asst prof, Calif State Univ, Northridge, 68-73; asst prof, 72-80, from assoc prof to prof hist, Univ St Thomas, 80-91, prof hist, 91-; travelling prof, Nat Humanities Ser, Woodrow Wilson Found, 70, consult, 71; Nat Endowment for Humanities grant, 75-76. **MEMBERSHIPS** AHA; Am Asn Advan Slavic Studies. **RESEARCH** Modern Czechoslovak political, cultural and social history. **SELECTED PUBLICATIONS** Coauth, A more perfect union, an annotated bibliography, Nat Humanities Ser, 72; Charles Jonas: Czech National Liberal, Wisconsin Bourbon Democrat, Balch Press-Associated University Presses, 93, Cranbury, NJ. **CONTACT ADDRESS** Dept of History, Univ of St. Thomas, Minnesota, 2115 Summit Ave, Saint Paul, MN 55105-1096. **EMAIL** cwchrislock@stthomas.edu

CHRISMAN, MIRIAM USHER
PERSONAL Born 05/20/1920, Ithaca, NY, m, 1943, 2 children **DISCIPLINE** EARLY MODERN SOCIAL HISTORY **EDUCATION** Smith Col, AB, 41, MA, 55; Am Univ, MA, 48; Yale Univ, PhD(hist), 62. **CAREER** Res asst, Nat Planning Asn, 43-46; teacher, Tenacre Sch, Mass, 46-47, Bryn Mawr Sch, Md, 47-49 & Northampton Sch Girls, Mass, 49-59; instr hist, Smith Col, 55-57; from instr to assoc prof, 62-71, Prof Hist, Univ Mass, Amherst, 71-. **MEMBERSHIPS** AHA; Am Soc Reformation Res (pres, 76-77); Sixteenth Century Studies Conf. **RESEARCH** Renaissance and Reformation; early modern social and intellectual history; early modern urban history. **SELECTED PUBLICATIONS** Auth, Women and the Reformation in Strasbourg, Arch Reformations Geschichte, 63; Strasbourg and the Reform, Yale Univ, 67; coauth, People and Issues in the Western World, Scott, 72; auth, L'Imprimere a Strasbourg, 1480-1599, Strasbourg Coeur Relig XVIC Siecle, Libr Istra, Strasbourg, 76. **CONTACT ADDRESS** Hist Dept, Univ of Massachusetts, Amherst, Amherst, MA 01003.

CHRISTENSEN, CARL C.
PERSONAL Born 02/15/1935, Chicago, IL, m, 1960, 3 children **DISCIPLINE** RENAISSANCE & REFORMATION HISTORY **EDUCATION** Univ Iowa, BA, 60; Ohio State Univ, MA, 61, PhD(hist), 65. **CAREER** From instr to asst prof, 65-70, assoc prof, 70-78, Prof Hist, Univ Colo, Boulder, 78-, Fac fel, Univ Colo, Boulder, 71; vis lectr hist, Univ Kent at Canterbury, 75-76. **MEMBERSHIPS** Soc Reformation Res; Sixteenth Century Studies Conf. **RESEARCH** Reformation and art in Germany. **SELECTED PUBLICATIONS** Auth, Municipal patronage and the crisis of the arts in Reformation Nuernberg, Church Hist, 6/67; Durer's Four Apostles and the dedication as a form of Renaissance art patronage, Renaissance Quart, 67; Luther's theology and the uses of religious art, Lutheran Quart, 70; Iconoclasm and the preservation of ecclesiastical art in Reformation Nuernberg, Arch Reformations-Ges, 70; The Reformation and the decline of German art, Cent Europ Hist, 9/73; Patterns of iconoclasm in the early Reformation: Strasbourg and Basel, In: The Image and the Word: Confrontations in Judaism, Christianity and Islam, Scholars Press, 77; Art and the Reformation in Germany, Wayne State Univ, 79; Five biographical essays, In: The Holy Roman Empire: A Dictionary Handbook, Greenwood Press, 80; Reformation and Art, In: Reformation Europe: A Guide to Research, Ctr for Reformation Res, 82; John of Saxony's Diplomacy, 1529-1530: Reformation or Realpolitik?, The Sixteenth Century J 15, 84; Princes and Propaganda: Electoral Saxon Art of the Reformation, Sixteenth Century Journal Publ, Inc, 92; Art, In: The Oxford Encyclopedia of the Reformation, Oxford Univ Press, 96; auth, The Reformation of Bible Illustration: Genesisi Woodcuts in Wittenberg, 1523-1534, Archive Fro Reformation Hist, 99. **CONTACT ADDRESS** Dept of Hist, Univ of Colorado, Boulder, Box 234, Boulder, CO 80309-0234. **EMAIL** cchrist@stripe.colorado.edu

CHRISTENSEN, LAWRENCE
PERSONAL Born 08/08/1937, Glasgow, MT, m, 1961 **DISCIPLINE** AMERICAN HISTORY **EDUCATION** NE Mo State Univ, BS, 60, MA, 62; Univ Mo-Columbia, PhD, 72. **CAREER** Instr, Univ Mo-Whitewater, 68; instr to distinguished teaching prof, Univ Mo-Rolla, 69-00. **HONORS AND AWARDS** Distinguished Teaching Prof Univ Mo, 93; Thomas Jefferson Awd, 99. **MEMBERSHIPS** Hist Soc Mo; State Hist Soc Mo; Orgn Am Hist; S Hist Asn. **RESEARCH** Black America, Missouri history. **SELECTED PUBLICATIONS** Co-auth, A History of Missouri, 1875-1919, (97); co-auth, Dictionary of Missouri Biography, (99). **CONTACT ADDRESS** Dept Hist, Univ of Missouri, Rolla, 118 H-SS, Rolla, MO 65409. **EMAIL** christen@UMR.edu

CHRISTENSEN, MICHAEL
PERSONAL 2 children **DISCIPLINE** THEOLOGY; RELIGIOUS STUDIES; HISTORICAL THEOLOGY **EDUCATION** Point Loma Col, BA, 77; Yale Univ Divinity School, MA, 81; M.Phil, 95, PhD, 97, Drew Univ. **CAREER** Asst Prof, 97-, Dir of Doctor of Ministry Program, 95-, Drew Univ. **HONORS AND AWARDS** John Wesley Fel, 93-97; Will Herberg Merit Scholarship, Drew Univ, 93-96; Crossroads Scholar Program (research stipend for writing public policy monograph on nuclear issues in former Soviet Union), 94-96; Research Fel, Newark Project, 94-95; Recipient of the Helen Le Page and William Hale Chamberlain Prize awarded for the PhD Dissertation that is singularly distinguished by creative thought and excellent prose style, 97; Recipient of the Martin Luther King Jr. and Abraham Joshua Heschel Humanitarian Awd for Spirituality and Social Justice, 98; Research Fel, Senior Research Scholar for Russia, The Princeton Project on Youth, Globalization and the Church, 98-01. **MEMBERSHIPS** Amer Acad of Religion; Phi Delta Lamba Honor Soc; The Patristic Soc, Center for Millenial Studies, Boston Univ. **RESEARCH** Theology and Culture; Russian Eschatology; Spirituality **SELECTED PUBLICATIONS** Auto, The Samaritan's Imperative: Compassionate Ministry to People Living With Aids, Abingdon, 91; auth, Aids Ministry and the Article of Death: A Westleyan Pastoral Theological Perspective, Catalyst, 95; " Evangelical-Orthodox Dialogue in Russia" The Journal of Ecumenical Studies, 96; auth, " The Russian Idea of Apocalypse: Nikolai Berdyaev's Theory of Russian Cultural Apocalyptic" , The Journal of Millennial Studies, 98; auth, " Believers Without Borders: Bringing Hope to Kosovo Refugees, The Covenant Companion, 99; auth, " The Chernobyl Prophecy in Russian Apocalyptic Eschatology" The Living Pulpit, vol 8, no 1, 99; auth, " The psychosocial Impact of Chernobyl: Thirteen Years After" The Journal of Intergroup Relations, Vol XXVI, no 1, 99; auth, " Millennial Moments" in forthcoming Encyclopedia of Millenialism and Millennial Movements, Routledge/Berkshire Reference Works, 00; assoc ed, Routledge Encyclopedia of Millennialism and Millennial Movements, Routledge, 00; gen ed, TheNextChurch Series, Three volume series in practical theology, forthcoming , Abingdon: vol 1: Equipping the Saints: Mobilizing Laity for Ministry, 00. **CONTACT ADDRESS** Drew Univ, 12 Campus Dr., Madison, NJ 07940. **EMAIL** mchriste@drew.edu

CHRISTENSON, ALLEN J.
PERSONAL Born 08/21/1957, Sherman Oaks, CA, m, 1980, 3 children **DISCIPLINE** ART HISTORY **EDUCATION** Brigham Young Univ, BS, 80; UCLA, DDS, 84; Univ Tx Austin, MA, 96, PhD, 98. **CAREER** Instr, Merced Col, 85-90; instr to asst prof, Brigham Young Univ, 90- . **MEMBERSHIPS** CAA; AAA. **RESEARCH** Maya ethnology, art history **SELECTED PUBLICATIONS** Auth, Bare Bones and the Divine Right of Kings: The Carved Femurs of Chiapa de Corzo, Mexico, Univ of Tx Austin, 96; Prehistory of the K'iche'an People of Highland Guatemala, Univ of Tx, 96; The World Tree of the Ancient Maya, BYU Stud, 97; Scaling the Mountain of the Ancients: The Altarpiece of Santiago Atitlan, Univ Tx Austin, 98; Popol Vuh, BYU Press, 99. **CONTACT ADDRESS** 2975 N Iroquois Dr, Provo, UT 84604. **EMAIL** allen_christenson@byu.edu

CHRISTIAN, GARNA
PERSONAL Born 01/06/1935, Houston, TX, m, 1958, 2 children **DISCIPLINE** HISTORY **EDUCATION** Mex City Col, BA, 59; Texas W Col, MA, 61; Texas Tech Univ, PhD, 77. **CAREER** S Texas Jr Col, 62-73; prof of History, Univ Houston-Downtown, 74-; E Texas Hist Asn Ottis Lock Award Excellence Tchg, 85. **HONORS AND AWARDS** T R Fehrenback Awd Texas Hist Comn; State & local Hist Asn; Hum Rights Found. **MEMBERSHIPS** Texas State Hist Asn; E Texas Hist Asn; S Conf Afro-Am Cult. **RESEARCH** Texas history; Black history; Music history. **SELECTED PUBLICATIONS** Black Soldiers in Jim Crow Texas 1899-1917, Texas A&M Univ Press, 95; articles on black military in Texas, country music, and jazz. **CONTACT ADDRESS** Univ of Houston, One Main St, Houston, TX 77002. **EMAIL** Christian@DT3.DT.UH.EDU

CHRISTIANSON, ERIC HOWARD
PERSONAL Born 11/24/1946, Peoria, IL, 1 child **DISCIPLINE** HISTORY **EDUCATION** Univ Southern Calif, AB, 68, AM, 70, PhD(hist), 76. **CAREER** Instr, 75-76, Asst Prof Hist, Univ KY, 76- **MEMBERSHIPS** Am Assoc Hist Med; Soc Social Studies Sci; Am Soc Eighteenth Century Studies. **RESEARCH** History of science and medicine post-1700; quantitative methods; United States social history. **SELECTED PUBLICATIONS** The confederacy of physicians: An historical oversight?, J Hist of Med Allergol Sci, 77. **CONTACT ADDRESS** Dept of Hist, Univ of Kentucky, 500 S Limestone St, Lexington, KY 40506-0003.

CHRISTIANSON, GALE EDWARD
PERSONAL Born 06/29/1942, Charles City, IA **DISCIPLINE** MODERN HISTORY, HISTORY OF SCIENCE **EDUCATION** Univ IA, BA, 64; Univ Northern IA, MA, 66; Carnegie-Mellon Univ, DA, 71. **CAREER** Instr hist, Northern IA Area Community Col, 66-69 & Carnegie-Mellon Univ, 69-71; asst prof, 71-75, assoc prof, 75-80, prof hist, IN State Univ, 80, IN State Univ Fac Res Comt res grants, 72 & 73; Am Philos Soc res grant, 72-73, Am Coun of Learned Soc grant, 84, Am Inst of Physics grant, 91, Nat Endowment for the Hum summer stipend, 91, Fletcher Jones Foun fel: The Huntington Lib, 91, John Simon Guggenheim Mem Fel, 92. **HONORS AND AWARDS** Distinguished Prof, Col Arts & Sci, IN State Univ, 87, First Place Awd: Prof Papers, Nineteenth Annual Dakota Hist Conf, 88, Loren Eiseley Medal, 95, Science Writing Awd, Rockwell Int, 97. **MEMBERSHIPS** AHA; AAUP; Hist of Sci Soc. **SELECTED PUBLICATIONS** Auth, This Wild Abyss: The Story of the Men who Made Modern Astronomy, The Free Press/Macmillan, 78; In the Presence of the Creator: Isaac Newton and His Times, The Free Press/Macmillan, 84; Fox at the Wood's Edge: A Biography of Loren Eiseley, Henry Holt, 90; Writing Lives is the Devil! Essays of a Biographer at Work, Archon Books, 93; Edwin Hubble: Mariner of the Nebulae, Farrar, Straus and Giroux, 95; Isaac Newton and the Scientific Revolution, Oxford Univ Press, 96; Greenhouse: The 200-Year Story of Global Warming, Walker, 99. **CONTACT ADDRESS** Dept of Hist, Indiana State Univ, 210 N 7th St, Terre Haute, IN 47809-0002. **EMAIL** Higalee@ruby.indstate.edu

CHRISTIANSON, JOHN ROBERT
PERSONAL Born 01/21/1934, Mankato, MN, m, 1964, 2 children **DISCIPLINE** SCANDINAVIAN HISTORY **EDUCATION** Minn State Univ, BA, 56; Univ Minn, Minneapolis, MA, 59 PhD(hist), 64. **CAREER** Asst prof hist, Univ SDak, 64-66; vis asst prof, Univ Minn, Minneapolis, 66-67; assoc prof, 67-72, Prof Hist, Luther Col, Iowa, 72-96, Chmn Dept, 67-83, Emeritus, Asst dir, Norweg-Am Mus, 69-90; exec bd mem, Norweg-Am Hist Asn, 71-; Am Coun Learned Socs fel & George C Marshall Mem Fund in Denmark grant, 73-74; mem, 16th Century Studies Coun, 76-80; Board of Dir mem, Danish-Am Heritage Soc, 98-. **HONORS AND AWARDS** Knight, Royal Norwegian Order of Merit, 95. **MEMBERSHIPS** AHA; Soc Advan Scand Studies; Am-Scand Found; Norweg-Am Hist Asn. **RESEARCH** Tycho Brahe; 16th century Denmark; Scandinavian population movements. **SELECTED PUBLICATIONS** Coed and Transl with Birgitte Christianson, The Dream of America, 7 vols. (Mankato MN: Creative Education, 82); Ed, Scandinavians in America: Literary Life (Decorah: Symra, 85); auth, Victor E. Thosen, The Lord of Urauiborg: A Biography of Tycko Brahe, with contributions by JRC, Cambridge UP, 90; auth, on Tycho's Island: Tycho Brahe and His Assistants 1570-160, Cambridge UP, 00. **CONTACT ADDRESS** Dept of Hist, Luther Col, Decorah, IA 52101. **EMAIL** christjr@luther.edu

CHRISTIE, JEAN
PERSONAL Born Manila, Philippines, m, 2 children **DISCIPLINE** UNITED STATES HISTORY **EDUCATION** Columbia Univ, PhD(Am hist), 63. **CAREER** Lectr hist, Brooklyn Col, 55-58 & 59-60; instr, Vassar Col, 59; lectr, Hunter Col, 60-62 & Bronx Community Col, 62-63; lectr, 63-64, from asst prof to assoc prof, 64-75, prof, 75-77, Emer Prof Hist, Fairleigh Dickinson Univ, Teaneck Campus, 77-, Fairleigh Dickinson Univ fac res grant, 77-78. **MEMBERSHIPS** Berkshire Conf Women Historians; Conf Group on Women's Hist; AHA; Orgn Am Historians; Conf Peace Res in Hist. **RESEARCH** Conservation movement; women in the 1920's. **SELECTED PUBLICATIONS** Auth, Machine-Age Ideology--Social Engineering and American Liberalism, 1911-1939, Tech and Cult, Vol 0036, 95; Steinmetz-- Engineer and Socialist, Tech and Cult, Vol 0034, 93; auth, Christie Stevens: Schoolwoman which, originally published in MINNESOTA HISTORY, 48/6, summer 83 has now been included in AMERICAN PORTRAITS: BIOGRAPHIES IN UNITED STATES HISTORY, Stephen G. Weisner and William F. Hartford, eds. McGraw-Hill, 98, pp. 38-55. **CONTACT ADDRESS** 34 Bellingham Ln, Great Neck, NY 11023.

CHRISTMAN, CALVIN
PERSONAL Born 07/12/1942, Lakewood, OH, m, 1968, 2 children **DISCIPLINE** HISTORY **EDUCATION** Dartmouth Col, AB, 64; Vanderbilt Univ, MA & MAT, 66; Ohio State Univ, PhD, 71. **CAREER** Ohio State Univ, 71-72; William Penn Col, 72-76; Adj Prof, Univ Tex , 96-; Prof, Cedar Valley Col, 77-. **HONORS AND AWARDS** Who's Who among Am Teachers, 94, 95, 96, 97, 99; Excellence in Teaching Awd, Cedar Valley Col, 80-81. **MEMBERSHIPS** Soc of Military Hist, Inter-Univ Seminar on Armed Forces and Soc, Nat Security Fel, Inst for Advanced Technol. **RESEARCH** United States military history; History of World War II. **SELECTED PUBLICATIONS** Ed, Lost in the Victory: Reflections of American War Orphans of World War II, Univ North Texas Press, 98; ed, America at War, Naval Institute Press, 95; co-ed, Was and the Southwest, Univ of North Texas Press. **CONTACT ADDRESS** Dept Liberal Arts, Cedar Valley Col, 3030 N Dallas Ave, Lancaster, TX 75134. **EMAIL** cchristman@dcccd.edu

CHU, JONATHAN M.
PERSONAL Born 11/04/1945, Honolulu, HI, m, 1985, 1 child **DISCIPLINE** HISTORY **EDUCATION** Univ Penn, AB, 67; Univ Hawaii, MA, 69; Univ Washington, PhD, 78; Yale Law Sch, MSL, 83. **CAREER** Asst prof, Univ Mass, 78-85; vis assoc prof, Univ Hawaii, 86; assoc prof, Univ Mass, 85-. **HONORS AND AWARDS** NEH, AAS, 88; Fulbright Lectureship to Peoples Republic of China, 01. **MEMBERSHIPS** OAH; SHEAR; IEAH; MHS; CSM; FHS; ASLH; Soc de Jean Bodin. **RESEARCH** Legal and economic impact of the American revolution; 19th Naturalization law. **SELECTED PUBLICATIONS** Auth, "Debt Litigation and Shays's Rebellion," in Debt to Shays, Colonial Society of Massachusetts ed. R Gross (Univ Press of Virginia, 92); auth, "Does Real History Begin at Jamestown and Plymouth?" Org Am Hist Mag (96); auth, "Debt and Taxes: Public Finance and Private Economic Behavior in Post-Revolutionary Massachusetts," in Entrepreneurs: The Boston Business Community, 1700-1850, eds. Conrad Wright, Kathryn Viens (Boston: Northeastern Univ. Press, 97); auth, "Richard Coote, Earl of Bellomont," "Elisha Cooke Sr," "Jeremiah Dummer," "William Dummer," "John Endecott," "William Phips," "Joseph Russell," "Samuel Sewall," American National Biography (Oxford: Oxford Univ Press, 98); auth, "An Independent Means: Capitalism, the American Revolution and the Rise of a National Economy, " J Interdisciplinary Hist (forthcoming). **CONTACT ADDRESS** Dept History, Univ of Massachusetts, Boston, 100 Morrissey Blvd, Dorchester, MA 02125-3300. **EMAIL** jonathan_chu@umb.edu

CHU, PAO-CHIN
PERSONAL Born 08/05/1928, Ho-pei, China, m, 1961, 2 children **DISCIPLINE** CHINESE HISTORY **EDUCATION** Nat Taiwan Univ, BA, 54; Univ PA, MA, 62, PhD, 70. **CAREER** Interpreter Eng-Chinese, Combat Air Command, Chinese Air Force, 55-57; asst prof, 67-70, assoc prof, 71-81, prof Chinese hist, San Diego State Univ, 82-, dir, Center for Asian Studies, 81-84, dir, China Studies Inst, 88-90, 95-96. **MEMBERSHIPS** AHA; Asn Asian Studies. **RESEARCH** Diplomatic hist of Republican China, 1912-1949; hist of the Chinese Communist Party, 1919-1949. **SELECTED PUBLICATIONS** The Impact of External War: The Demise of Chiang's China, In: Civil Wars in the Twentieth Century (Robin Higham, ed), Univ KY, 72; V K Wellington Koo: Diplomacy of Nationalism, In: Diplomats in Crisis: The Coming of the Pacific War (E Bennett and R D Burns, ed), Clio Press, 74; From Paris Peace Conference to Manchurian Incident: The Diplomacy of Resistance Against Japan (Hilary Conroy and Alvin Coox, ed), Clio Press, 78; V K Wellington Koo: A Case Study of China's Diplomat and Diplomacy of Nationalism, 1912-1966, Chinse Univ Hong Kong Press, 81; Yen Hui-ch'ing, In: Biographical Dictionary of Modern Peace Leaders (Harold Josephson, ed), Greenwood Press, 85; The American View of China, 1957-1982: the Personal Experience of a China-born Sinologist, In: America Views China: American Images of China Then and Now (Jonathan Goldstein, Jerry Israel, Hilary Conroy, ed), Assoc Univ Presses, 91; Sheng Hsuan-huai and the Self-Protection of the Southeastern Provinces during the Boxer Movement, In: Yi-he-tuan yun-dong yu jin-dai Zhongguo she-hui guo-je xue-so tao-lung hui lung-wen-je (Collected Papers of the Int Conf on Boxer Movement and the Modern Chinese Society), Jinan, Qi-lu Press, 92. **CONTACT ADDRESS** Dept of Hist, San Diego State Univ, 5500 Campanile Dr, San Diego, CA 92182-0002.

CHU, PETRA
PERSONAL Born 10/15/1942, Zeist, Netherlands, m, 1971, 4 children **DISCIPLINE** ART HISTORY **EDUCATION** Diplome superieur du Cours de civilisation Francaise, 60-61; Utrecht Univ, doctoraal, 61-67; Columbia Univ, PhD, 67-72. **CAREER** Res, Institut Neerlandais, 65-72; vis prof, Princeton Univ, 90-92; prof, Seton Hall Univ, 72-. **HONORS AND AWARDS** Institute for Advanced Study, Princeton, 90; Wheatland Found, 90; John Simon Guggenheim Memorial Found, 91; Nat Endowment, 94; Jane and Morgan Whitney Art Hist Fel, 94-95. **SELECTED PUBLICATIONS** Auth, French Realism and the Dutch Masters, 74; auth, Courbet in Perspective, 77; auth, Dominique Vivant Denon, 85; auth, The Letters of Gustave Courbet, 92; auth, The Popularization of Images, 94; Gustave Courbet: Artiste et promoteur de son oeuvre, Paris, Flammarion, 1999 (with Jorg Zutter). **CONTACT ADDRESS** Dept of Art and Music, Seton Hall Univ, So Orange, 400 S Orange Ave, South Orange, NJ 07079-2697. **EMAIL** chupetra@shu.edu

CHUDACOFF, HOWARD PETER
PERSONAL Born 01/21/1943, Omaha, NE, m, 1967 **DISCIPLINE** UNITED STATES HISTORY **EDUCATION** Univ Chicago, BA 65, MA 67, PhD 69. **CAREER** Vis asst prof, Univ Cincinnati, 69-70; from asst to prof, hist, 70-92, Brown Univ, now Univ Prof & Prof of History, 92- . **MEMBERSHIPS** Am Hist Asn; Orgn of Am Hist; Urban Hist Asn. **RESEARCH** United States urban and social history. **SELECTED PUBLICATIONS** Auth, How Old Are You? Age Consciousness in American Culture, Princeton, 89; coauth, A People and a Nation, 3d through 6th ed, 90, 94, 97, 20000; Houghton Mifflin; auth, Major Problems in American Urban History, Heath, 93; coauth, The Evolution of American Urban Society, 4th ed, 93, 5th ed, 99, Prentice-Hall; auth, The Age of the Bachelor: Creating an American Subculture, Princeton, 99. **CONTACT ADDRESS** 84 Cole Ave, Providence, RI 02906. **EMAIL** Howard_Chudacoff@Brown.edu

CHUNG, SUE FAWN
PERSONAL Born Los Angeles, CA, m, 1980, 2 children **DISCIPLINE** HISTORY **EDUCATION** Univ of Calif, Los Angeles, BA, 65; Harvard Univ, AM, 67; Univ of Calif, Berkeley, PhD, 75. **CAREER** From asst prof to assoc prof, Univ Nev Las Vegas, 75-. **HONORS AND AWARDS** Nev Human Awd, 96; Rita Abbey Tchr of the Yr Awd, UNLV, 98; Las Vegas Chamber of Commerce Commun Achievement Awd for Excel in Educ, 99. **MEMBERSHIPS** Am Hist Asn; Asn for Asian Studes; Asn for Asian Am Studies; Nev Hist Soc; Nat Trust for Hist Preserv; Harvard Alum Club of Nev. **RESEARCH** China; Chinese-Americans; Asian-Americans. **CONTACT ADDRESS** Hist Dept, Univ of Nevada, Las Vegas, 4505 Md Pkwy, Box 455020, Las Vegas, NV 89154-5020. **EMAIL** chung@nevada.edu

CHURCHILL, CHARLES B.
PERSONAL Born 09/09/1944, MI, m, 1984, 3 children **DISCIPLINE** HISTORY **EDUCATION** UC Santa Barbara, PhD, 89; Univ Hawaii, MA, 72; UC Irvine, BA, 68. **CAREER** Lecturer, CSU Chico, 96-; Writing Prof, Oregon State Univ, 94-96. **HONORS AND AWARDS** NEH Summer Scholar, 84; NEH Grant, 85. **MEMBERSHIPS** Amer Historical Assn; Western Historical Assn. **RESEARCH** Mexican California & South West. **SELECTED PUBLICATIONS** Auth, "Adventurers and Prophets American Autobiography in Mexican California," Arthur H. Clark, Spokane, 95. **CONTACT ADDRESS** California State Univ, Chico, 400 West 1st St, Chico, CA 95929-0001. **EMAIL** cchurchill@csuchico.edu

CHURCHILL, FREDERICK BARTON
PERSONAL Born 12/14/1932, Boston, MA, m, 1981, 2 children **DISCIPLINE** HISTORY OF SCIENCE **EDUCATION** Harvard Univ, AB, 55, PhD(hist of sci), 67; Columbia Univ, MA, 61. **CAREER** Lectr, 66-67, asst prof, 67-70, assoc prof, 70-80, Prof Hist & Philos of Sci, Ind Univ, Bloomington, 80-, Ed, Mendel Newsletter, 76-91. **MEMBERSHIPS** Hist Sci Soc; Int Soc Hist Phil and Soc Studies of Biology. **RESEARCH** History of biology. **SELECTED PUBLICATIONS** Auth, Frederick B Churchill and Helmet Risler, eds. August Weismann Ausgewahlfe Briefe und Dotumenta 2 vols, Freiburg, 99. **CONTACT ADDRESS** Dept of Hist & Philos of Sci, Indiana Univ, Bloomington, Bloomington, IN 47401.

CHYET, STANLEY F.
PERSONAL Born Boston, MA, m, 1956, 2 children **DISCIPLINE** AMERICAN JEWISH HISTORY **EDUCATION** Brandeis, BA, 52 Univ; Hebrew Union Col, PhD, 60. **CAREER** Prof; ordained, Rabbi, HUC-JIR, Cincinnati, 57; fac, HUC-JIR, Cincinnati, 60-; fac, HUC-JIR, Los Angeles, 76-. **RESEARCH** Contemp. Hist./Lit. **SELECTED PUBLICATIONS** Pub(s), Amer Jewish biographies, history and literature/translations of 20th Century Israeli Poetry. **CONTACT ADDRESS** Hebrew Union College-Jewish Institute Of Religion, Univ of So California, 3077 University Ave., Los Angeles, CA 90007. **EMAIL** gernbear@aol.com

CIENCIALA, ANNA M.
PERSONAL Born 11/08/1929, Gdansk, Poland, s **DISCIPLINE** EUROPEAN DIPLOMATIC HISTORY WITH EMPHASIS ON POLAND **EDUCATION** Univ Liverpool, BA, 52; McGill Univ, MA, 55; Ind Univ, PhD(mod Europ hist), 62. **CAREER** Lectr Europ & Russ hist, Univ Ottawa, 61-62; Instr, Univ Toronto, 62-65; from asst prof to assoc prof, 65-71, Prof Europ & Russ Hist, Univ Kans, 71-; res dir, Kans Studies Poznan, 71; mem, Kosciuszko Found, Polish Inst Arts & Sci. **HONORS AND AWARDS** Res grants, Univ Kans, 65-68, 70 & 72, Fulbright-Hays NDEA fac fel, 68-69; other grants and fellowships from NEH, IREX, ACLS, Lawrence, Ks, Kosciuszko Found, Univ Kans; award, Jozef Pilsudski Inst, New York , book prize,68; award, Jerzy Lojek Foundation, book prize, 90; medal, 1000 anniv of he city Gdansk, 97; book honor awardee, gdansk, 00; Polish Cross of Merit, Polish Inst of Arts and Sciences of America, Krakow, 00. **MEMBERSHIPS** Am Asn Advan Slavic Studies; Polish Am Hist Asn; AAUP; Polish Inst Arts & Sci Am; Joseph Pilsudski Inst Am. **RESEARCH** European diplomatic and political history, 1914-45; modern East European history. **SELECTED PUBLICATIONS** Auth, Poland and the Western powers, 1938-1938, Univ Toronto, 68: and Routledge, London; co-ed, Sir James Headlam-Morley, a memoir of the Paris Peace Conference 191 9, London, 72; coauth, From Versailles to Locarno. Keys to Polish Foreign Policy, 1919-1925, Lawrence, Ks, 84; ed, annotated version of: Jozef Beck, Polska Polityka Zagraniczna, 1926-1939, (Polish Foreign Policy, 1926-1939), Paris, 90; author of numerous of articles in U.S., German, and Polish professional journals. **CONTACT ADDRESS** Dept of Hist, Univ of Kansas, Lawrence, Lawrence, KS 66045-0001. **EMAIL** annacien@eagle.cc.ukans.edu

CIFELLI, EDWARD M.
PERSONAL Born 04/28/1942, Newark, NJ, m, 1966, 2 children **DISCIPLINE** AMERICAN STUDIES **EDUCATION** Rutgers Univ, BA, 64; Tex Tech Univ, MA, 67; NYork Univ, MA, 70 PhD, 77. **CAREER** Lectr, Rutgers Univ, 67-69; prof, County Col Morris, 69-. **HONORS AND AWARDS** Tchg Excellece Awd, 98, NISOD; Outstanding Acad Book Awd, 99, Choice Magazine. **RESEARCH** Colonial American studies and twentieth century American poetry. **SELECTED PUBLICATIONS** Auth, David Humphreys, 82; auth, art, Ciardi, John (Anthony), 94; auth, art, John Ciardi, Birth of a Poet, 96; auth, art, John Ciardi and the Italian American Question, 97; auth, John Ciardi: A Biography, 97. **CONTACT ADDRESS** 147 Merriam Ave, Newton, NJ 07860. **EMAIL** ecifelli@garden.net

CIMBALA, PAUL A.
DISCIPLINE AFRICAN-AMERICAN HISTORY **EDUCATION** Emory Univ, PhD. **CAREER** Assoc prof, Fordham Univ. **HONORS AND AWARDS** Ed, Fordham UP. **MEMBERSHIPS** Mem, Adv Coun Lincoln Prize, Gettysburg Col. **SELECTED PUBLICATIONS** Auth, The Black Abolitionist Papers, vol 2: Canada, 1830-1865, Univ NC 86; Against the Tide: Women Reformers in American Society, 96; Historians and Race: Autobiography and the Writing of History, 96; American Reform and Reformers: A Biog Dictionary, 96; Under the Guardianship of the Nation: The Freedmen's Bureau and the Reconstruction of Georgia, 1865-1870, 97; co-ed,The Freedmen's Bureau and Reconstruction: Interpretive Essays on an Organization and its Failure, 98. **CONTACT ADDRESS** Dept of Hist, Fordham Univ, 113 W 60th St, New York, NY 10023.

CIMPRICH, JOHN
PERSONAL Born 06/26/1949, Middleton, OH, m, 1985 **DISCIPLINE** HISTORY **EDUCATION** Thomas More Col, AB, 71; Ohio St Univ, MA, 73; PhD, 77. **CAREER** Lecturer, Ohio State Univ, 77-79; Instructor to visiting Asst Prof, Southeast Missouri State Univ, 80-85; Lecturer to Prof, Thomas More College, 85-; Chairman, History Dept, 91-97; 98-. **HONORS AND AWARDS** Phi Alpha Theta Faculty Advisor Research Grant, 97; Mellon Fellowship in Historical Editing, 79-80. **MEMBERSHIPS** Organization of Amer Historians; Phi Alpha Theta Honor Society in History; World History Assoc. **RESEARCH** American Civil War Period. **SELECTED PUBLICATIONS** Auth, Slavery's End in Tennessee, 1861-1865, 85; auth, "A Critical Moment and Its Aftermath for George H. Thomas," in Randall M. Miller & John R. McKivigan, eds., The Moment of Decision, 94; auth, "The Fort Pillow Massacre: A Statistical Note," Journal of American History, Dec 89; auth, "Fort Pillow Revisited: New Evidence about an Old Controversy," Civil War History, Dec, 82. **CONTACT ADDRESS** Dept History & Government, Thomas More Col, 333 Thomas More Pkwy, Crestview Hills, KY 41017-3428. **EMAIL** cimpricj@thomasmore.edu

CITINO, ROBERT M.
DISCIPLINE HISTORY **EDUCATION** Univ Ind, PhD. **CAREER** Prof, Eastern Michigan Univ. **RESEARCH** Europe, Germany Europe, military. **SELECTED PUBLICATIONS** Auth, Armored Forces: A History and Sourcebook; The Evolu-

tion of Blitzkrieg Tactics. **CONTACT ADDRESS** Dept of History and Philosophy, Eastern Michigan Univ, 701 Pray-Harrold, Ypsilanti, MI 48197.

CITRON, HENRY
PERSONAL Born 01/15/1937, Philadelphia, PA, m, 1963, 2 children **DISCIPLINE** HISTORY, POLITICAL SCIENCE **EDUCATION** Temple Univ, BA, 60, MA, 61, NYork Univ, PhD, 76. **CAREER** Substitute teacher, Philadelphia Pub Sch, 60-61; instr hist, Moravian Col, Bethlehem, Pa, 61-63; teacher social studies, Glen Cove High Sch, Glen Cove, NY, 63-65; dean students & group leader hist dept, Pa State Univ, Monaca, 65-68; prof hist & chemn dept Hist & Polit Sci, County Col Morris, 68-; asst presiding partner, Oglethorpe Group Holdings. **MEMBERSHIPS** AHA, Community Col Social Sci Asn: Eastern Community Col Social Sci Asn. **RESEARCH** Study of the arguments of interest groups which opposed federal aid to education from 1949-1965. **SELECTED PUBLICATIONS** Auth: Some recent discoveries at the Ohioview Archaeological Site, Ohio Archaeologist, 2/66; The Discovery of the Bakery at Old Economy, Pa Hist Comn, 68; Technology and New Teaching Techniques, Community Col Social Sci Conf, Dallas, 11/74; The End of History, Eastern Community Col Social Sci Conf, Princeton, 75; Search for the Czar: Russian Oral History, Kentucky Hist Comn, Frankfort, 3/76; "The American Reaction to the Boxer Rebellion," Community College Social Science Review, winter 76. **CONTACT ADDRESS** County Col of Morris, 214 Center Grove Rd, Randolph, NJ 07869-2086. **EMAIL** hcitron@ccm.edu

CIVIL, MIGUEL
PERSONAL Born 05/07/1926, Sabadell, Spain, d, 2 children **DISCIPLINE** ASSYRIOLOGY, LINGUISTICS **EDUCATION** Univ Paris, PhD, 58. **CAREER** Res assoc Assyriol, Univ Pa, 58-63; from asst prof to assoc prof Near Eastern Lang & civilizations & ling, 63-70, Prof Near Eastern Lang & Civilizations & Ling, Univ Chicago, 70-, Mem ed bd, Chicago Assyrian Dict, 67-; dir d'etudes associe etranger, Sorbonne, 68-70; ed, Materials for the Sumerian Lexicon, 68- **HONORS AND AWARDS** Hon PhD, Univ Barcelona, 00. **MEMBERSHIPS** Am Orient Soc; Am Sch Orient Res. **RESEARCH** Sumerian grammar and literature; anthropology of Mesopotamia; lexicography. **SELECTED PUBLICATIONS** Auth, Prescriptions medicales Sumeriennes, Rev D'Assyriol, 60; The message of Lu-dingirra, J Near Eastern Studies, 64; Notes on Sumerian lexicography, J Cuneiform Studies, 66; coauth, Vol IX, Materials for the Sumerian Lexicon, 67 & auth, Vol XIII-XIV, 71, Pontificio Inst Biblico, Rome. **CONTACT ADDRESS** Oriental Institute Univ, Univ of Chicago, 1155 E 58th St, Chicago, IL 60637-1540. **EMAIL** mcivil@uchicago.edu

CLAGETT, MARSHALL
PERSONAL Born 01/23/1916, Washington, DC, m, 1946, 3 children **DISCIPLINE** MEDIEVAL HISTORY **EDUCATION** George Washington Univ, AB, 37, AM, 38; Columbia Univ, PhD, 41. **CAREER** Instr hist & hist sci, Columbia Univ, 46-47; from asst prof to prof hist sci, Univ Wis, 47-64, dir inst res humanities, 59-64; Prof Hist Sci, Inst Advan Study, 64-, Guggenheim fels, 46, 50-51; Nat Sci Found grant, Rome & London, 55-56. **HONORS AND AWARDS** LLD, George Washington Univ, 69; LHD, Univ Wis, 74. **MEMBERSHIPS** Hist Sci Soc (pres, 62-64); fel Mediaeval Acad Am; fel Am Acad Arts & Sci; Am Philos Soc; Int Acad Hist Sci. **RESEARCH** Ancient and medieval science and mathematics. **SELECTED PUBLICATIONS** Auth, Sarton Medal Citation, Isis, Vol 0084, 93. **CONTACT ADDRESS** Inst for Advan Study, Princeton, NJ 08540.

CLANTON, ORVAL GENE
PERSONAL Born 09/14/1934, Pittsburg, KS, m, 1959, 2 children **DISCIPLINE** UNITED STATES HISTORY **EDUCATION** Kans State Col, Pittsburg, BS, 59, MS, 61; Univ Kans, PhD(US hist), 67. **CAREER** Teacher, high sch, Colo, 60-62; from instr to asst prof US hist, Tex A&M Univ, 66-68; asst prof, 68-71, assoc prof, 71-78, prof Emeritus, US Hist, Wash State Univ, 78-. **MEMBERSHIPS** AHA; Orgn Am Historians. **RESEARCH** Populism and progressivism; Gilded Age; the Congressional Populist delegations. **SELECTED PUBLICATIONS** Auth, Mary Elizabeth Lease: Intolerant Populist?, Kans Hist Quart, summer 68; Kansas Populism: Ideas and Men, Univ Press of Kans, 69; A Rose by Any Other Name: Kansas Populism and Progressivism, fall 69 & coauth, G C Clemens: The Sociable Socialist, winter 74, Kans Hist Quart; Populism, Progressivism and Equality: The Kansas Paradigm, Agr Hist, 7/77; Multiple entries, The Readers Encyclopedia of the American West, T Y Crowell, 77; Populism: The Humane Preference in America, 1890-1900, Twayne Pub, 91; Congressional Populism and the Crisis of the 1890's, Univ Press of Kansas, 98. **CONTACT ADDRESS** Dept of Hist, Washington State Univ, P O Box 644030, Pullman, WA 99164-4030. **EMAIL** geno@iea.com

CLAPPER, MICHAEL
DISCIPLINE ART HISTORY **EDUCATION** Swarthmore Col, BA, 87; Washington Univ, MFA, 89; Northwestern, PhD, 97. **CAREER** ASST PROF, ART HIST, SKIDMORE COLL **SELECTED PUBLICATIONS** Auth, "Art, Industry and Education in Prang's Chromolithograph Company, " Procs of the AAS, 105:1, April, 95; auth, "The Chromo and the Art Museum: Popular and Elite Art Institutions in Late Nineteenth-Century America," in Not at Home: The Suppression of Domesticity in Modern Art and Architecture, 33-47. **CONTACT ADDRESS** Dept of Art & Art Hist, Skidmore Col, 815 North Broadway, Saratoga Springs, NY 12866-1632.

CLARDY, JESSE V.
PERSONAL Born 02/15/1931, Olney, TX, m, 1964 **DISCIPLINE** RUSSIAN AND MODERN CHINESE HISTORY **EDUCATION** Tex A&I Univ, BS & MS, 60; Univ Mich, PhD(hist), 61. **CAREER** Prof Hist, Univ MO-Kansas City, 64-. **MEMBERSHIPS** Am Asn Advan Slavic Studies; Asn Slavic & East Europ Studies. **SELECTED PUBLICATIONS** Auth, Philosophical Ideas of Alexander Radishchev, Vision, 64; The Dropout Problem in Russia, Clearing House, 64; Communist Publications in the US Mail, Western Humanities Rev, 66; G R Derzhavin, A Political Biography, Mouton, The Hague, 67; Alexander Solzhenitsyn and His Concept of the Role of the Artist in Society, Slavonic Rev, 74; Tsar and the Vatican, Church & State, winter 77; Solzhenitsyn and World War I, Red River Hist J, summer 77. **CONTACT ADDRESS** Dept Hist, Univ of Missouri, Kansas City, 5100 Rockhill Rd, Kansas City, MO 64110-2499.

CLARK, ANDREW
DISCIPLINE WEST AFRICAN HISTORY **EDUCATION** Mich State Univ, PhD, 90. **CAREER** Prof, Univ NC, Wilmington. **RESEARCH** West African economic and social history; Slavery and its demise in West Africa. **SELECTED PUBLICATIONS** Published articles in the J of African Hist, Slavery and Abolition, Oral Hist Rev, J of 3rd World Stud, Can J of African Stud Africa Today; and the Int J of African Hist Stud. He is author of Historical Dictionary of Senegal; New 3rd Edition, From Frontier to Backuater: Economy and Society in the Upper Senegal Valley, 1850-1920. **CONTACT ADDRESS** Univ of No Carolina, Wilmington, 227 Morton Hall, Wilmington, NC 28403-3297. **EMAIL** clarka@uncwil.edu

CLARK, ANNA
DISCIPLINE MODERN BRITAIN HISTORY, EUROPEAN WOMEN'S HISTORY, HISTORY OF SEXUALITY **EDUCATION** Rutgers Univ, PhD, 87; Harvard, BA; Univ of Essex, MA. **CAREER** Assoc prof, Univ NC, Charlotte; assoc prof, Univ of Minn. **HONORS AND AWARDS** N Am Conf on Brit Stud Prize in the Hum. **RESEARCH** Gender and Politics in late 18th and Early 19th Century Britain; domesticity and the Poor Laws in the 19th Century. **SELECTED PUBLICATIONS** Auth, Women's Silence, Men's Violence: Sexual Assault in England, 1770-1845, Pandora, 87; auth, The Struggle for the Breeches: Gender and the Making of the British Working Class, Univ Calif Press 95; auth, "Anne Lister's Construction of Lesbian Identity," Journal of the History of Sexuality, 96; auth, "Wilkes and d'Eon: the Politics of Masculinity, 1763-1778," Eighteenth-Century Studies, 98. **CONTACT ADDRESS** Dept of Hist, Univ of Minnesota, Twin Cities, 774 Social Science Bldg, 267 19th Ave S, Minneapolis, MN 55455. **EMAIL** clark106@umn.edu

CLARK, CHARLES EDWIN
PERSONAL Born 04/28/1929, Brunswick, ME, m, 1952, 4 children **DISCIPLINE** AMERICAN HISTORY **EDUCATION** Bates Col, AB, 51; Columbia Univ, MS, 52; Brown Univ, PhD(Am civilization), 66. **CAREER** Reporter, Providence Jour & Evening Bull, RI, 56-61; asst prof hist, Southeastern Mass Technol Inst, 65-67; from asst prof to prof, 67-97, chmn dept, 77-80, James H. Hayes and Claire Short Hayes Chair in the Humanities, 93-97 Emeritus Prof Hist, Univ NH, 98-; researcher, Prog Loyalist Studies & Publ, 71. **HONORS AND AWARDS** Nat Endowment Arts & Humanities fel, 68; Henry E Huntington fel, 72; Am Coun Learned Soc fel, 73-74; Daniels fel, Am Antiquarian Soc, 80; Commonwealth Fel, Col of William and Mary, 90. **MEMBERSHIPS** AHA; Asn Inst Early Am Hist & Culture; OAH, SHARP. **RESEARCH** Intellectual and cultural history of early America; regional history of northern New England; eighteenth-century English and American journalism. **SELECTED PUBLICATIONS** Coauth, New England's Tom Paine: John Allen and the Spirit of Liberty, William & Mary Quart, 10/64; auth, Science, Reason and an Angry God: The Literature of an Earthquake, New Eng quart, 9/65; A Test of Religious Liberty: The Ministry Land Case in Narragansett, 1668-1752, J Church & State, 69; The Eastern Frontier: The Settlement of Northern New England, 1610, 1763, Knopf, 70; Maine during the Colonial Period: A Bibliographical Guide, Maine Hist Soc, 74; Maine: A Bicentennial History, Norton, 77; History, literature, and Belknap's social happiness, Hist NH, Vol XXXV, 1-22; coauth, The Measure of Maturity: The Pennsylvania Gazette, 1728-1765, William and Mary Quart, 3rd ser, XLVI, 89; auth, Metropolis and Province in Eighteenth-Century Press Relations: The Case of Boston, J Newspaper and Periodical Hist, Autumn 89; The Newspapers of Provincial America, Am Antiquarian Soc Proceedings, 100, 90; Boston and the Nurturing of Newspapers, New Eng Quart LXIV, 91; The Public Prints: The Newspaper in Anglo-American Culture, 1665-1740, Oxford, 94; The Meetinghouse Tragedy: An Episode in the Life of a New England Town, Univ Press of New Eng, 98; auth, "Early American Journalism: News and Opinion in the Popular Press" in Amory & Hall, eds, The Colonial Book in the Atlantic World, Cambridge, 00. **CONTACT ADDRESS** 2 Thompson Ln, Durham, NH 03824. **EMAIL** ceclark@christa.unh.edu

CLARK, CLIFFORD E., JR.
PERSONAL Born New York, NY, m, 1966, 3 children **DISCIPLINE** HISTORY, AMERICAN STUDIES **EDUCATION** Yale Univ, BA, 63; Harvard Univ, MA, 64; PhD, 68. **CAREER** Instr to asst prof, Amherst, Col, 67-70; asst prof to prof, Carleton Col, 70-, chair, 86-90. **HONORS AND AWARDS** Woodrow Wilson Fel, 64, 67; NEH Summer Fel, 73, 80; Hunt Found Grant, 74; **MEMBERSHIPS** AHA; Org of Am Hist; Am Studies Assoc. **RESEARCH** Architecture, material culture, intellectual history. **SELECTED PUBLICATIONS** Auth, Henry Ward Beecher: Spokesman for a Middle-Class America, Univ of IL Pr, (Urbana), 78; auth, "Henry Ward Beecher", Dict of Literary Biography, Vol III, Detroit Res, 79; auth, "The Piano and American Victorian Thought", The Piano - Mirror of American Life, ed Bruce Carson, Schubert Club (St Paul, 81); auth, The American Family Home, 1800-1960; Univ of NC Pr, (Chapel Hill), 86; auth, "American and Canadian Intellectual History: 1789-1960", General History of the Americas, Org of Am States, (Caracas, 93); coauth, The Enduring Vision: A History of the American People, DC Heath, (Lexington, MA), 90; coauth, Northfield: the History and Architecture of a Community, city of Northfield, 98. **CONTACT ADDRESS** Dept Hist, Carleton Col, 1 N College St, Northfield, MN 55057-4001. **EMAIL** cclark@carleton.edu

CLARK, GEOFFREY W.
DISCIPLINE HISTORY **EDUCATION** Wesleyan Univ, BA, 81; Princeton Univ, MA, 87, PhD, 93. **CAREER** Asst prof **RESEARCH** Early modern British history; social and economic history of Augustan England; cultural history of financial speculation. **SELECTED PUBLICATIONS** Auth, Betting on Lives: Providence, chance, and the culture of life insurance in England 1695-1775. **CONTACT ADDRESS** Dept History, Stevens Inst of Tech, Pierce Complex, Hoboken, NJ 07030. **EMAIL** gclark@stevens-tech.edu

CLARK, HUGH R.
DISCIPLINE HISTORY AND EAST ASIAN STUDIES **EDUCATION** Univ Pa, PhD. **CAREER** Prof Hist and E Asian Stud, ch, dept Hist, Ursinus Col. **HONORS AND AWARDS** Laughlin Prof Achievement Awd, Ursinus Col; grant, Chiang Ching-kuo Found, NEH, Comt for Scholarly Res in China. **RESEARCH** Middle period Chinese history. **SELECTED PUBLICATIONS** Auth, Community, Trade, and Networks: Southern Fujian Province from the 3rd to the 13th Centuries. **CONTACT ADDRESS** Ursinus Col, Collegeville, PA 19426-1000.

CLARK, LINDA L.
PERSONAL Born 09/18/1942, Syracuse, NY, m, 1989 **DISCIPLINE** HISTORY **EDUCATION** Duke Univ, BA, 64; Univ of NC Chapel Hill, PhD, 68. **CAREER** Asst prof, hist, Shepherd Col, 69-70; asst prof, 70-72, assoc prof hist, Millersville State Col, 72-, prof, 79, Nat Endowment for Humanities fel in residence for col teachers, 75-76; res fel, Bunting Inst, Radcliffe Col, 79-80. **HONORS AND AWARDS** Phi Beta Kappa; NEH Fel, 75-76 & 86-87; Fel, Radcliffe Col, 79-80. **MEMBERSHIPS** Am Hist Asn, Soc for French Hist Studies, Hist of Ed in Soc. **RESEARCH** Women's education and careers in France primary education in France. **SELECTED PUBLICATIONS** Auth, "Bringing Feminine Qualities into the Public Sphere: The Third Republic's Appointment of Women Inspectors," Gender and the Politics of Social Reform in France 1870-1914, Johns Hopkins Univ Press, 95; auth, "Les Carrieres des inspectrices du travail 1892-1939," Inspecteurs et Insection du travail Actes du colloque, 98; auth, "Higher-Ranking Women Civil Servants and the Vichy Regime: Firings and Hirings, Collaboration and Resistance," French Hist 13 (99); auth, "Feminist Maternalists and the French State: Two Inspectresses General in the Pre-World War I Third Republic," J of Women's Hist 12 (00); auth, The Rise of Professional Women in France: Gender and Public Administration since 1830, Cambridge Univ Press, 00. **CONTACT ADDRESS** Dept Hist, Millersville Univ of Pennsylvania, PO Box 1002, Millersville, PA 17551-0302.

CLARK, MALCOLM CAMERON
PERSONAL Born 01/24/1930, Washington, DC, m, 1972 **DISCIPLINE** AMERICAN & EUROPEAN HISTORY **EDUCATION** George Washington Univ, BA, 53, MA, 59; Georgetown Univ, PhD(hist), 70. **CAREER** From asst prof to assoc prof, 66-75, chmn dept, 72-75, prof Hist, 75-95, DISTINGUISHED PROF EMERITUS COL CHARLESTON, 95-. **HONORS AND AWARDS** SC Hist Soc: pres, 82-85, ed bd, 68-98, chmn, 76-98, Mary Elizabeth Prior Awd, 96. **MEMBERSHIPS** AHA; Orgn Am Historians; Southern Hist Asn. **RESEARCH** American colonial history; American economic history. **SELECTED PUBLICATIONS** Auth, Federalism at high tide: the election of 1796 in Maryland, Md Hist Mag, 9/66; The birth of an enterprise: Baldwin locomotive, 1831-1842, Pa Mag Hist & Biog, 10/66. **CONTACT ADDRESS** Dept of Hist, Col of Charleston, 66 George St, Charleston, SC 29424-0001.

CLARK, MARK
PERSONAL Born 04/20/1961, San Antonio, TX, m, 1992 **DISCIPLINE** HISTORY OF TECHNOLOGY **EDUCATION** Rice Univ, BS, 94; Univ Houston, MA, 87; Univ Del, PhD, 92. **CAREER** Hist res contractor, 92-95; temp asst prof, Iowa State Univ, 95-96; asst prof hist, Oregon Inst Technol, 96-. **HONORS AND AWARDS** Fulbright fel, Univ Aarhus Denmark, 97. **MEMBERSHIPS** Soc Hist Technol; His Sci Soc. **RESEARCH** History of magnetic recording, History of the engineering profession, History of water & reclamation. **SELECTED PUBLICATIONS** Auth, Magnetic Recording: The First 100 Years, IEEE Press, 98. **CONTACT ADDRESS** Dept Hum & Soc Sci, Oregon Inst of Tech, 3201 Campus Dr, Klamath Falls, OR 97601-8801.

CLARK, MICHAEL D.
PERSONAL Born 11/05/1937, Baltimore, MD, m, 1965, 2 children **DISCIPLINE** HISTORY **EDUCATION** Yale Univ, BA, 59; Univ of NC Chapel Hill, MA, 62; PhD, 65. **CAREER** From Asst Prof to Prof, Univ of New Orleans, 64-. **HONORS AND AWARDS** Excellence in Teaching Awd, Univ of New Orleans Alumni Asn; Hellman Found Scholar; Waddell Fel. **MEMBERSHIPS** Am Studies Asn, Southern Am Studies Asn, Southern Hist Asn. **RESEARCH** American intellectual and cultural history, American religious history. **SELECTED PUBLICATIONS** Auth, Worldly Theologians: The Persistence of Religion in Nineteenth Century American Thought, Univ Press of Am (Wash, DC), 81; auth, Coherent Variety: The Idea of Diversity in British and American Conservative Thought, Greenwood Press (Wesport, CT), 83. **CONTACT ADDRESS** Dept Hist, Univ of New Orleans, 2000 Lakeshore Dr, New Orleans, LA 70148-0001. **EMAIL** mdclark943@prodegy.net

CLARKE, DUNCAN
DISCIPLINE U.S. FOREIGN AND NATIONAL SECURITY POLICY **EDUCATION** Clark Univ; AB; Cornell Univ, JD; Univ Va, PhD. **CAREER** Prof, Am Univ. **HONORS AND AWARDS** Ten Best Professors, Am Univ; Tchg/schol yr, Scool of Int Serv. **SELECTED PUBLICATIONS** Auth, American Defense and Foreign Policy Institutions Harper and Row, 89; Send Guns and Money: Security Assistance and United States Foreign Policy, Praeger, 97. **CONTACT ADDRESS** American Univ, 4400 Massachusetts Ave, Washington, DC 20016.

CLARKE, ERNEST GEORGE
PERSONAL Born 06/16/1927, Varna, ON, Canada, m, 1951, 4 children **DISCIPLINE** NEAR EASTERN STUDIES **EDUCATION** Univ Toronto, BA, 49, BD, 52, MA, 53; Univ Leiden, DLitt(Aramaic), 62. **CAREER** Lectr Old Testament, Queen's Theol Col, Kingston, 56-58, prof, 58-61; assoc prof, 61-64, chmn dept, 70-75, Prof Near Eastern Studies, Victoria Col, Univ Toronto, 64-, Mem, Br Sch Archaeol; Can Conn leave fel, 69-70; vis fel, Univ Col, Cambridge, 69-70; gov, gov counc, Univ Toronto, 79-97. **MEMBERSHIPS** Am Orient Soc, Soc Bibl Lit, Can Soc Bibl Studies; International Organization for the Study of Targums and the International Soc of Old Testament. **RESEARCH** Preparation of a computer generated keyword in context concordance to Targum Pseudo-Jonathan to the Pentateuch. **SELECTED PUBLICATIONS** Auth, The Selected Questions of Isho 'Bar Nun, 62, auth, Wisdom of Solomon, 72; auth, Targum Pseudo-Jonathan of the Pentateuch: Text and Concordance, 84; transl, Targum Pseudo-Jonathan: Numbers: Translated with Notes, 95. **CONTACT ADDRESS** Dept of Near Eastern Studies, Univ of Toronto, Toronto, ON, Canada M5S 1A1.

CLARKE, JOHN R.
PERSONAL Born 01/25/1945, Pittsburgh, PA, S **DISCIPLINE** ART HISTORY **EDUCATION** Yale Univ, PhD, 73. **CAREER** Prof; Univ TX at Austin, 80-; critic, contemp art. **MEMBERSHIPS** Pres, Board of Dir, Col Art Asn Am, 91-01. **RESEARCH** Ancient Roman art. **SELECTED PUBLICATIONS** Auth, Roman Black-and-White Figural Mosaics, 79; Houses of Roman Italy 100 BC-AD 250: Ritual, Space, and Decoration, 91; publ in, Arts Mag and Art in Am; auth, Looking at Lovemaking: Constructions of Sexuality in Roman Art, 100 B.C.-AD 250, 98. **CONTACT ADDRESS** Dept of Art and Art Hist, Univ of Texas, Austin, Austin, TX 78712-1104. **EMAIL** j.clarke@mail.utexas.edu

CLASSEN, ALBRECHT
PERSONAL Born 04/23/1956, Germany, m, 1984, 1 child **DISCIPLINE** GERMAN LITERATURE, GERMAN HISTORY **EDUCATION** Univ Marburg, MA, 82; Univ Va, PhD, 86. **CAREER** From asst prof to assoc prof to prof, 87-, Univ Ariz. **HONORS AND AWARDS** Edgar-Shannon-Awd, 86, Univ Va; El Paso Natural Gas Found Fac Achievement Awd, 95; Univ Tchr Grant, 99, Rotary Int; pres, aatg, 97-98; pres, aatg, 92-98. **MEMBERSHIPS** MLA; SEMA; Oswald von Wolkenstein Gesellschaft; Rocky Mountain MLA; ICLS. **RESEARCH** Medieval and early modern German literature and history. **SELECTED PUBLICATIONS** Auth, The German Volksbuch. A Critical History of a Late-Medieval Genre, 95; auth, Tristania, Vol. XVI, 95; auth, Tristania, Vol. XVII, 96; auth, Diu Klage, Mittelhochdeutsch-neuhochdeutsch. Einleitung Ubersetzung, Kommentar und Anmerkungen, 97; auth, Trisania, Vol. XVII, 98. **CONTACT ADDRESS** 2413 E 4th St, Tucson, AZ 85719. **EMAIL** aclassen@u.arizona.edu

CLASTER, JILL NADELL
PERSONAL Born 05/14/1932, New York, NY, m, 1979 **DISCIPLINE** ANCIENT & MEDIEVAL HISTORY **EDUCATION** NYork Univ, AB, 52, MA, 54; Univ PA, PhD, 59. **CAREER** Teaching asst, Univ PA, 55-57; from instr to asst prof hist, Univ KY, 59-62; asst prof classics, 63-64, asst prof medieval hist, 64-67, dir, Master Arts Liberal Studies Prog, 76-78, actg dean, Col Arts & Sci, 78, assoc prof, 67-83, Prof Hist, NY Univ, 84-; Dean, Washington Sq & Univ Col, 79-86; dir, Center for Near Eastern Studies, NYU, 91-96. **HONORS AND AWARDS** Fulbright Awd (to Italy) 1958-59; Danforth Found Awdee 1966-68. **MEMBERSHIPS** AHA; Mediaeval Acad Am; Classical Asn Atlantic States. **RESEARCH** Social and intellectual late Roman and medieval history; the classical tradition in the Middle Ages. **SELECTED PUBLICATIONS** Auth, Anthenian Democracy: Triumph or Travesty?, Holt, 67; The Medieval Experience 300-1400, NY Univ Press & Columbia Univ Press, 81. **CONTACT ADDRESS** Dept of Hist, New York Univ, 53 Washington Sq. S, New York, NY 10012. **EMAIL** jill.claster@nyu.edu

CLAUSEN, MEREDITH L.
PERSONAL Born 06/10/1942, Hollywood, CA, w, 1967 **DISCIPLINE** ARCHITECTURAL HISTORY **EDUCATION** Univ Cal Berk, PhD 75, MA 72; Scripps College, BA. **CAREER** Univ Washington prof 79-. **HONORS AND AWARDS** Graham Foun Ad Stud; Mellon Fell; Res Professorshp Awd; NEH; Fulbright-Hays Fel; J Paul Getty Gnt; available on the web,http://www.washington.edu/ark2/cities/building archive, digitized images for academic use throughout the univ and prof comm. **MEMBERSHIPS** SAH; FA; AIA. **RESEARCH** 20TH Cent Architecture; Amer architecture. **SELECTED PUBLICATIONS** Auth, Craig Ellwood, the Art Center College of Design: Shattering the Image, Casabella, 98; Pietro Belluschi, Modern American Architect, MIT Press, 94; Spiritual Space, The Religious Architecture of Pietro Belluschi, U of W Press, 92; The Michael Graves Portland Building and Its Problems, coauth, Architronic, 97; Essays on Art Dans La Rue, Department Store, Pietro Belluschi, Frantz Jourdain, Shopping Malls, in: Dictionary of Art, Macmillam Pub, London, 96; in progress, The Pan Am Building and the Demise of Modernism. **CONTACT ADDRESS** Dept of Aritectural History, Univ of Washington, 4332 Thackeray Place NE, Seattle, WA 98105. **EMAIL** mlc@washington.edu

CLAYSON, S. HOLLIS
PERSONAL 1 child **DISCIPLINE** ART HISTORY **EDUCATION** Wellesley Col, BA, 68; Univ Calif Los Angeles, MA 75, PhD, 84. **CAREER** Instr, Calif Inst Arts, 74-76; instr, Schiller Col, 77-78; asst prof, Wichita State Univ, 78-82; asst prof, Univ Ill Chicago, 84-85; vis assoc prof, Univ Chicago, 96; from vis asst prof to asst prof to assoc prof, Northwestern Univ, 82-. **HONORS AND AWARDS** Edward A. Dickson Support Fel in Hist Art, 75-77; US Dept Educ FIPSE Grant, 82; Lilly Endowment Post-Dr Awd, 85-86; ACLS Res Fel, 87-88, 90-91; Univ Res Grants Comm Northwestern Univ Res Awd, 88, 90, 93, 99; CIRA Northwestern Univ Fel, 90-91, 91-92; AAUW Educ Found Am Fel, 94-95; Sr Fel Ctr Hum Northwestern Univ, 94-95; UCLA Distinguished Tchg Asst Awd Honor Mention, 74-75; Fac Honor Roll, Assoc Student Govt List Outstanding Instructors, Northwestern Univ, 83-84, 86-87, 87-88, 92-93, 94, 96-97; Awd Outstanding Tchg, Col Arts Sci, Northwestern Univ, 87; Col Art Asn, Distinguished Tchg Art Hist Awd Jr Prof, 90; Charles Deering McCormick Prof Tchg Excellence, Northwestern Univ, 93-94, 95-97; Carnegie Found Advan Tchg US Prof Year Prg, Northwestern Univ nominee, 94, 95; Lake Park High Sch Educ Found Distinguished Alumna Awd, 94. **RESEARCH** Nineteenth century European art concentrating on painting and printmaking in France; women and visual representation; sexual identity and cultural representation; feminist and gender theory; artistic identity and practice in the Franco-Prussian War; Orientalism; post-ethnographic physiognomy in Edgar Degas' later work. **SELECTED PUBLICATIONS** Auth, Painted Love: Prostitution in French Art of the Impressionist Era, 91; coauth, Quaecumque sunt vera? Revising the Intro Course at Northwestern University, Art Jour, Fall, 95; auth, Materialist Art History and its Points of Difficulty, Range Critical Perspectives: Art Hist, The Art Bull, Sept, 95; auth, A Wintry Masculinity: Art, Soldiering and Gendered Space in Paris Under Siege, Nineteenth-Century Contexts, 98. **CONTACT ADDRESS** Dept of Art History, Northwestern Univ, 244 Kresge Hall, Evanston, IL 60208. **EMAIL** shc@northwestern.edu

CLAYSON, W.
PERSONAL Born 02/13/1970, Glean, NY, m, 1994, 1 child **DISCIPLINE** HISTORY **EDUCATION** Tex Technol Univ, ABD, 98; MA, 96; Univ Nev. **CAREER** Teacher's asst, Tex Technol Univ, 96-98; partime instr, Tex Technol Univ, 97-98; adj fac, San Antonio Col, 98-. **HONORS AND AWARDS** Phi Alpha Tueta, International Hist Honors Soc; Phi Kappa Phi. **MEMBERSHIPS** AHA, Southwest Soc Sci Asn. **RESEARCH** Recent United States history, the war on poverty. **SELECTED PUBLICATIONS** Auth, "Cubans in Las Vegas," Nev Hist Soc Quart (95): 1; auth, "The Lubbock Chamber of Commerce, The New Deal, and the Roseville Resettlement Project," Great Plains Quart (98): 3. **CONTACT ADDRESS** Dept Hist, San Antonio Col, 1300 San Pedro Ave, San Antonio, TX 78212-4201. **EMAIL** bdclayson@email.msn.com

CLAYTON, JAMES L.
PERSONAL Born 07/28/1931, Salt Lake City, UT, m, 1957, 3 children **DISCIPLINE** ECONOMIC & LEGAL HISTORY **EDUCATION** Univ Utah, BA, 58; Cornell Univ, PhD(Econ Hist), 64. **CAREER** Case officer, Cent Intel Agency, 57-58; instr Hist, Hamilton Col, 62-63; from instr to assoc prof, 63-71, dir honors prog, 67-70, prof Hist, Univ Utah, 71-, dean, grad school, 78-86; provost, 86-90; vis asst prof, Dartmouth Col, 66-67; mem, Coun Grad Schs, US, 78-84. **HONORS AND AWARDS** Distinguished Teaching Awd, Univ Utah, 66; Minn Hist Soc Solon J Buck Prize, 67; Distinguished Hon Prof, Univ Utah, 77; Univ Prof, 77-78; Phi Kappa Phi; Phi Beta Kappa; Vis Fel, Cambridge Univ, 02. **MEMBERSHIPS** Western Asn Grad Schs (pres, 82); GRE Board, 82-87. **RESEARCH** Economic and social impact of war since 1945; Economic Consequence of Debt; Bear Markets in G7 Natcous; American economic history; legal history. **SELECTED PUBLICATIONS** Coauth, American Civilization: A Documentary History, W C Brown, 66; auth, The growth and economic significance of the American fur trade, Minn Hist, Winter 66; ed, The Economic Impact of the Cold War, In: Forces in Am Growth series, Harcourt, 70; auth, The fiscal cost of the Cold War to the United States: the first 25 years, 1947-1971, Western Polit Quart, 9/72; The fiscal limits of the warfare-welfare state, Western Polit Quart, 76; A comparison of defense and welfare spending in the US and the UK, J Biol & Social Welfare, 77; A Farewell to the Welfare State, Univ Utah Press, 76; Does Defense Beggar Welfare?, Nat Strategy Info Ctr, 79; auth, The Global Debt Boub, M.E. Sharpe, 00. **CONTACT ADDRESS** Univ of Utah, 217 Carlson Hall, Salt Lake City, UT 84112-0311. **EMAIL** Jclayton@lec.hum.utah.edu

CLAYTON, LAWRENCE A.
DISCIPLINE COLONIAL LATIN AMERICA **EDUCATION** Tulane Univ, PhD. **CAREER** Univ Ala **HONORS AND AWARDS** Two Fulbright Awds; dir grad studies hist; dir, latin am studies prog. **SELECTED PUBLICATIONS** Auth, Los astilleros de Guayaquil colonial 78; The Bolivarian Nations, 84; Alabama and the Borderlands: From Prehistory to Statehood, 85; Grace, W. R. Grace & Co., The Formative Years, 1850-1930, 85; The Hispanic Experience in North America: Sources for Study in the United States, 92; The DeSoto Chronicles, 93. **CONTACT ADDRESS** Dept of History, Univ of Alabama, Tuscaloosa, Box 870212, Tuscaloosa, AL 35487-0212. **EMAIL** lclayton@simplecom

CLAYTON, PHILIP
PERSONAL Born 04/03/1956, Berkeley, CA, m, 1981, 2 children **DISCIPLINE** PHILOSOPHICAL THEOLOGY; RELIGION & SCIENCE; MODERN RELIGIOUS THOUGHT **EDUCATION** Westmont Col, BA, 78; Fuller Theolog Sem, MA, 80; Ludwig-Maximilians-Universitat, Munich, MA, 81-83; Yale Univ, MA, 84; Yale Univ, M.Phil, 85; Yale Univ, PhD, 86. **CAREER** Sonoma St Univ, 91-; Williams Col, 86-91; vis asst prof, Haverford Col, 86 **HONORS AND AWARDS** CSU Grant, 97; Templeton Grant, 97; Univ Merit Awd, 96; Univ Best Prof, 95; Alexander von Humboldt Prof, Ludwig-Maximilians-Universitat, 94-95; Fulbright Senior Res Fel, Univ Munich, 90-91. **MEMBERSHIPS** Amer Acad Relig; Amer Philos Assoc; Center for Theolog & Natural Sci; Pacific Coast Theolog Soc; Leibniz Soc N Amer; Metaphysical Soc Amer; Soc Study of Process Philos. **SELECTED PUBLICATIONS** Beyond Apologetics: Integrating Scientific Results and Religious Explanations, Fortress Pr, forthcoming; Das Gottesproblem. Moderne Losungsversuche, forthcoming; auth, God and Contemporary Science, Edinburgh Univ Press, 97; auth, Infinite and Perfect? The Problem of God in Modern Thought, Eerdmans Publ, 00. **CONTACT ADDRESS** Dept of Philosophy, Sonoma State Univ, Rohnert Park, CA 94928. **EMAIL** claytonp@sonoma.edu

CLAYTON, TOM
PERSONAL Born 12/15/1932, New Ulm, MN, w, 1955, 4 children **DISCIPLINE** ENGLISH, CLASS & NEAR EASTERN STUDIES **EDUCATION** Univ Minn, BA, 54; Oxford Univ, DPhil, 60. **CAREER** Instr English, Yale Univ, 60-62; asst prof, Univ Calif, Los Angeles, 62-67, assoc prof, 67-68; assoc prof, 68-70, Prof English, Univ Minn, Minneapolis, 70-99, Prof Class & Near Eastern Studies, 80-, Chmn, Class Civilization Prog, 82-, Morse-Alumni Distinguished Teaching Prof Engl & Classical Studies, 93-; Am Coun Learned Soc grant, 62-63; fel, Inst for Humanities, Univ Calif, 66-67; assoc, Danforth Assoc Prog, 72-77; Guggenheim fel, 78-79; Bush fel, Univ Minn, 85-86; NEH award, Div Res Tools, 88; Regents Prof English, 99-. **HONORS AND AWARDS** Rhodes Scholar, Minn and Wadham College, Oxford, 54; Distinguished Teaching Awd, Col Lib Arts, Univ Minn, 71; Morse-Alumni Awd, Outstanding contrib undergrad educ, Univ Minn 82. **MEMBERSHIPS** Asn of Am Rhodes Scholars; Asn Literary Scholars and Critics; Renaissance English Text Soc; Int Shakespeare Asn;

Shakespeare Asn Am. **RESEARCH** Shakespeare; literary criticism; earlier 17th Century English literature. **SELECTED PUBLICATIONS** Ed & auth, The Shakespearean Addition in the Books of Sir Thomas Moore, Ctr Shakespeare Studies, 69; ed & auth, The Non-Dramatic Works of Sir John Suckling, Clarendon, 71; ed & auth, Cavalier Poets, Oxford Univ, 78; auth, Is this the promis'd end?, Revision in the role of the King [himself], in The Division of the Kingdoms, Clarendon, 83; The texts and publishing vicissitudes of Peter Nichols's Passion Play, in The Library, 87; ed & auth, The Hamlet First Published (Q1, 1603), Univ Del, 92; That's she that was myself: Not-so-famous last words and some ends of Othello, Shakespeare Survey, 94; So our virtues lie in the interpretation of the time: Shakespeare's Coriolanus and Coriolanus, and Some Questions of Value, Ben Jonson J, 94; Who has no children in Macbeth?, in Festschrift for Marvin Rosenbert, Univ Del, 98 (forthcoming); So quick bright things come to confusion, or what else was A Midsummer's Night Dream about?, in Festschrift for Jay L Halio, 99. **CONTACT ADDRESS** Dept of English, Univ of Minnesota, Twin Cities, 207 Church St SE, Minneapolis, MN 55455-0134. **EMAIL** tsc@unm.edu

CLEGERN, WAYNE M.
PERSONAL Born 11/25/1929, Edmond, OK, m, 1954, 2 children **DISCIPLINE** HISTORY **EDUCATION** Univ of Okla, BA, 51; MA, 54; Univ of Calif Berkeley, Phd, 59. **CAREER** La State Univ, New Orleans, 59-69, chair 62-65; Colo State Univ, 69-00, Emeritus, 00-. **HONORS AND AWARDS** Doherty Fel in Latin Am. **MEMBERSHIPS** Conf on Latin Am Hist; Caribbean Studies Assoc. **RESEARCH** Belize, Late 19th Century Latin America, Third World **SELECTED PUBLICATIONS** Auth, Brit Honduras: Colonial Dead End, 1859-1900, LSU Pr, (Baton Rouge), 67; auth, Origins of Liberal Dictatorship in Central America: Guatemala, 1865-1871, Univ Press of Colo (Niwot), 94; historical ed, A Pocket Eden: Guatemalan Journals of Caroline Salvin, 1873-1874, Plumsock Inst, 00. **CONTACT ADDRESS** Dept Hist, Colorado State Univ, Fort Collins, CO 80523-0001. **EMAIL** hch88@juno.com

CLEMENS, DIANE SHAVER
PERSONAL Born 09/05/1936, Cincinnati, OH, m, 1960, 1 child **DISCIPLINE** DIPLOMATIC HISTORY **EDUCATION** Univ Cincinnati, BA & BS, 58, MA, 60; Univ Calif, PhD(hist), 66. **CAREER** Instr hist, Santa Barbara City Col, 60-62; lectr, Boston Univ, 64-66; asst prof, Mass Inst Technol, 66-72; Assoc Prof Hist, Univ Calif, Berkeley, 72-, Lectr Ger, Univ Hawaii & asst to dean, East-West Ctr, 60-61; travel grants, Moscow, 67-68 & Budapest, 68; Old Dominion fel, 69. **MEMBERSHIPS** Peace Res Soc; AHA; Am Asn Advan Slavic Studies; Soc Historians of Am Foreign Rels; Orgn Am Historians. **RESEARCH** Soviet-American diplomacy; the Cold War; 19th and 20th century European and American diplomacy. **SELECTED PUBLICATIONS** Auth, The structure of negotiation, Int Papers, Peace Res Soc, 68; Yalta, Oxford Univ, 69. **CONTACT ADDRESS** Dept of Hist, Univ of California, Berkeley, 3229 Dwinelle Hall, Berkeley, CA 94720-2551.

CLEMENTS, BARBARA EVANS
PERSONAL Born 05/26/1945, Richmond, VA **DISCIPLINE** RUSSIAN HISTORY **EDUCATION** Univ Richmond, BA, 67; Duke Univ, MA, 69, PhD, 71. **CAREER** Asst prof, 71-78, assoc prof, 78-86, Prof Hist, Univ Akron, 86-; Am Coun Learned Soc-Soc Sci Res Coun grant Soviet studies, 72-73. **HONORS AND AWARDS** NEH grants, 88, 93. **MEMBERSHIPS** AHA; Am Asn Advan Slavic Studies. **RESEARCH** Russian Revolution; Russian woman's movement; early Soviet history. **SELECTED PUBLICATIONS** Auth, Emancipation through Communism: The ideology of A M Kollontai, Slavic Rev, 6/73; Kollontai's contribution to the workers' opposition, Russ Hist, 75; Aleksandra Kollontai: Libertine or feminist?, Reconsideration Russ Revolution, 76; Bolshevik Feminist: The Life of Aleksandra Kollontai, Ind Univ Press, 79; Bolshevik women: The first generation, in Women in Eastern Europe and The Soviet Union, Praeger, 80; Working-class and peasant women in the Russian Revolution, 1917-1923; Signs, winter 82; The enduring kinship of the Baba and the Bolshevik women, Soviet Union, 85; The birth of the new Soviet woman, in Bolshevik Culture: Experiment and Order in the Russian Revolution, Ind Univ Press, 85; The impact of the Civil War on women and family relations, in Party, State, and Society in the Russian Civil War, Ind Univ Press, 89; Images of women: Views from the discipline of history, in Foundations for a Feminist Restructuring of Academic Disciplines, Harrington Park Press, 90; co-ed, Russia's Women: Accommodation, Resistance, Transformation, Univ Calif Press, 91; The Utopianism of the Zhenotdel, Slavic Rev, fall 92; Daughters of Revolution: A History of Soviet Women, Harlan Davidson, 94; Women in Russia: Images and realities, in Reemerging Russia: Search for Identity, Simon and Schuster, 95; Bolshevik Women, Cambridge Univ Press, 97; Women and the gender question, in Critical Companion to the Russian Revolution, Arnold, 97. **CONTACT ADDRESS** Dept of Hist, Univ of Akron, Akron, OH 44325-1902. **EMAIL** bclements@uakron.edu

CLEMENTS, KENDRICK A.
PERSONAL Born 02/07/1939, Rochester, NY, m, 1964, 2 children **DISCIPLINE** HISTORY **EDUCATION** Williams Col, BA, 60; Univ Calif at Berkeley, MA, 61; PhD, 70. **CAREER** From instr to prof, Univ SC, 67-. **HONORS AND AWARDS** Fulbright Lectureship, 77-78 & 91-92. **MEMBERSHIPS** Am Hist Asn, Orgn of Am Historians, Soc for the Historians of Am For Relations, Soc for the Historians of the Gilded Age and Progressive Era, Southern Historical Asn, Forest Hist Soc, Asn for Canadian Studies in the United States. **RESEARCH** Twentieth-Century U.S. History (diplomatic and environmental), Biography (especially William Jennings Bryan, Herbert Hoover, Woodrow Wilson). **SELECTED PUBLICATIONS** Auth, Woodrow Wilson: World Statesman, Twayne Publ (Boston, MA), 87 & 99; auth, The Presidency of Woodrow Wilson, Univ Press of Kans (Lawrence, KS), 92 & 94; auth, "Secretary of State William Jennings Bryan," Nebr Hist 77 (96): 167-76; auth, "Woodrow Wilson and Administrative Reform," Presidential Studies Quart 28 (98): 320-336; auth, Hoover, Conservation, and Consumerism: Engineering the Good Life, Univ Press of Kans (Lawrence, KS), 00. **CONTACT ADDRESS** Dept Hist, Univ of So Carolina, Columbia, Columbia, SC 29225. **EMAIL** kclements@sc.edu

CLIFFORD, DALE LOTHROP
PERSONAL Born 09/18/1945, Knoxville, TN **DISCIPLINE** HISTORY **EDUCATION** Vanderbilt Univ, BA, 66; Univ Tenn, MA, 68, PhD(hist), 75. **CAREER** Asst prof, 72-81, Assoc Prof Hist, Univ North Fla, 81-; Dept chair, 99-. **MEMBERSHIPS** AHA; Soc Fr Hist Studies; Western Soc Fr Hist; Coord Comt Women Hist Profession. **RESEARCH** French National Guard; direct democracy in the French Revolutionary tradition. **SELECTED PUBLICATIONS** Auth, Elihu Benjamin Washburne: An American diplomat in Paris, 1870-71, Prologue: J Nat Arch, winter 70; The quest for direct democracy: The National Guard and the siege of Paris, 1870-71, Hist Reflections, summer 77; L'Affaire Guillotte: A case study in parisian municipal politics, 1789-90, Proc Consortium Revolutionary Europe, 80; auth, Developing a Municipal Administration: Parisian Politics and the Management of the Paid National Guard, Proceedings of the Consortium on Revolutionary Europe, 89; auth, "The National Guard and the Parisian Community, 1789-90," Fr Historical Studies 4 (90): 849-78; auth, "Command Over Equals: The Officer Corps of the Parisian National Guard," Proceedings of the Annual Meeting of the Western Society for Fr Hist 18 (91): 152-165; auth, Can the Uniform Make the Citizen? Paris, 1789-1791, Eighteenth-Century Studies, 01. **CONTACT ADDRESS** Dept of Hist, Univ of No Florida, Jacksonville, FL 32216. **EMAIL** clifford@unf.edu

CLIFFORD, GERALDINE JONCICH
PERSONAL Born 04/17/1931, San Pedro, CA, w, 1969 **DISCIPLINE** HISTORY OF AMERICAN EDUCATION **EDUCATION** Univ Calif, Los Angeles, AB, 54, MEd, 57; Columbia Univ, EdD(hist educ), 61. **CAREER** Lectr hist & soc found educ, Univ Calif, Santa Barbara, 61-62; from asst prof to assoc prof educ, 62-72, res & travel grant, 63, assoc dean, Sch Educ, 76-80, chmn, Dept Educ, 78-81, Prof Hist Educ, Univ Calif, Berkeley, 72-, Guggenheim fel, 65-66; humanities res fel, 73-74 & 81-82; Rockefeller Humanities fel, Rockefeller Found, 77-78. **HONORS AND AWARDS** Phi Beta Kappa, Willystine Goodsell Awd (for service to women in education). **MEMBERSHIPS** AHA; Am Studies Asn; Hist Educ Soc (pres, 76-77); Am Educ Studies Asn; Am Educ Res Asn (vpres, 73-75). **RESEARCH** Autobiographical sources in the history of American education; women in educational history; nineteenth century American schools and colleges; history of the American Women teacher. **SELECTED PUBLICATIONS** Ed, Psychology and the Science of Education, Columbia Univ, 62; auth, The Sane Positivist: A Biography of E L Thorndike, Wesleyan Univ, 68; Edward Lee Thorndike: A biography, In: New International Encyclopedia of the Social Sciences, Crowell Collier & Macmillan, 68; A history of the effects of research on teaching, In: Second Handbook, Rand McNally, 73; The Shape of American Education, Prentice-Hall, 76; Home and school in nineteenth century America, Hist Educ Quart, 78; ed, School: A Brief for Professional Education, Chicago 99; auth, Lone Voyagers, Feminist Press, 89. **CONTACT ADDRESS** Sch of Educ, Univ of California, Berkeley, 1501 Tolman Hall, Berkeley, CA 94720-1671.

CLIFFORD, JOHN GARRY
PERSONAL Born 03/22/1942, Haverhill, MA **DISCIPLINE** AMERICAN DIPLOMATIC HISTORY **EDUCATION** Williams Col, BA, 64; Ind Univ, MA, 65, PhD(hist), 69. **CAREER** Teaching asst hist, Ind Univ, 65-67; instr, Univ Tenn, 68-69; asst prof polit sci, Univ Conn, 69-72; vis assoc prof hist, Dartmouth Col, 72-73; Assoc Prof Polit Sci, Univ Conn, 73-, Nat Endowment for Humanities younger humanist fel, 72. **HONORS AND AWARDS** Frederick Jackson Turner Awd, Orgn Am Historians, 71. **MEMBERSHIPS** AHA; Soc Historians Am Foreign Rels. **RESEARCH** FDR and the American entry into World War II. **SELECTED PUBLICATIONS** Auth, The Citizen Soldiers: The Plattsburg Training Camp Movement, 1913-1920, 72; ed, Memoirs of a Man: Brenville Clark, 75; auth, The First Peacetime Draft, 86; auth, Am Foreign Relations: A History, 4th edition, 95; auth, America Ascendant: U.S. Foreign Relations Since, 1939, 95. **CONTACT ADDRESS** Dept of Political Sci, Univ of Connecticut, Storrs, Monteith Bldg, Unit 1024, Storrs, CT 06269. **EMAIL** clifford@uconnvm.uconn.edu

CLIFFORD, NICHOLAS R.
PERSONAL Born 10/12/1930, Radnor, PA, m, 1957, 4 children **DISCIPLINE** MODERN HISTORY **EDUCATION** Princeton Univ, AB, 52; Harvard Univ, AM, 57, PhD (hist), 61. **CAREER** Instr humanities, Mass Inst Technol, 61-62; instr hist, Princeton Univ, 62-66; asst prof, 66-68, assoc prof, 68-76, chmn dept, 71-76, prof hist, 76-85, col prof, 85-93, vpres acad affairs and provost, 79-85, dean, E Asian Summer Lang Sch, 73-81, emeritus prof, 93- Middlebury Col. **MEMBERSHIPS** Am Hist Asn; Asn Asian Studies. **RESEARCH** China and the West; early 20th century. **SELECTED PUBLICATIONS** Auth, Retreat from China: British policy in the Far East, 1937-1941, Longmans, Green & Univ Wash, 67; auth, Urban Nationalism and the Defense of Foreign Privilege, Univ Mich, 79; auth, Spoilt Children of Empire: Westerners in Shanghai and the Chinese Revolution of the 1920s, Univ Press of New England, 91; auth, House of memory, Ballantine, 94; auth, "A Truthful Impression of the Country": British and American Travel Writing in China, 180-1949, Univ of Mich Press, 01. **CONTACT ADDRESS** 125 Sherman Ln, New Haven, VT 05472. **EMAIL** clifford@middlebury.edu

CLINE, CATHERINE ANN
PERSONAL Born 07/27/1927, West Springfield, MA **DISCIPLINE** HISTORY **EDUCATION** Smith Col, AB, 48; Columbia Univ, MA, 50; Bryn Mawr Col, PhD, 57. **CAREER** Instr hist, St Mary's Col, Ind, 53-54; from asst prof to prof, Notre Dame Col Staten Island, 54-68; assoc prof, 68-73, Prof Hist, Cath Univ AM, 73-. **MEMBERSHIPS** AHA; Conf Brit Studies; Am Cath Hist Asn. **RESEARCH** Twentieth century England; 20th Century European Foreign Policy. **SELECTED PUBLICATIONS** Auth, E.D. Morel: The Strategies of Protest, (Belfast), 81; auth, "British Historians and the Treaty of Versailles," Alion (88); auth, "Ecumenism and Appeasement," J Mod Hist (89); auth, Labor at War--France and Britain, 1914-1918, Jour Mod Hist, Vol 0066, 94; Defending the Empire--The Conservative Party and British Defense Policy, 1899-1915, Jour Mod Hist, Vol 0066, 94; Contemporary British History 1931-1961-- Politics and the Limits of Policy, Albion, Vol 0025, 93; Labors War--The Labor-Party During the World-War-2, Amer Hist Rev, Vol 0099, 94; Political-Change and the Labor-Party, 1900-1918, Jour Mod Hist, Vol 0066, 94; The Politics of Continuity--British Foreign-Policy and the Labor Government, 1945-46, Amer Hist Rev, Vol 0100, 95. **CONTACT ADDRESS** Dept of Hist, Catholic Univ of America, Washington, DC 20064.

CLINE, ERIC
PERSONAL Born 09/01/1960, Washington, DC, m, 1990, 2 children **DISCIPLINE** ANCIENT HISTORY **EDUCATION** Dartmouth Col, AB, 82; Yale Univ, MA, 84; Univ Pa, PhD, 91. **CAREER** Adj Asst prof, Col Sequoias, 92-94; Instr, Fresno City Col, 92-94; Adj Asst prof, Calif State Univ, 92-94; Adj Asst Prof, Miami Univ Ohio, 94-97; Adj Res Ast Prof, Univ Cincinnati, 94-97; Lecturer & Vis Ast Prof , Xavier Univ, 94-97; Lecturer & Postdoctoral Tchg Fel, Stanford Univ, 97-98; Asst Prof, George Washington Univ, 00-. **HONORS AND AWARDS** Kress Found INSTAP, AIA, & Semple Fund Conf Grants; Fulbright Sch; ASOR/EBR Summer Res Grant; AIA Olivia James Traveling Fel; INSTAP Publ Subvention. **RESEARCH** Trade and Interconnections in Bronze Aegean, Middle East Military History. **SELECTED PUBLICATIONS** Auth, Sailing the Wine-Dark Sea: International Trade and the Late Bronze Age Aegean, Tempus Reparatum, 94; auth, Amenhotep III: Perspectives on his Reign, Univ Mich Press, 97. **CONTACT ADDRESS** 10209 Drumm Ave, Kensington, MD 20895. **EMAIL** clinee@email.uc.edu

CLINE, PETER KNOX
PERSONAL Born 03/04/1942, La Crosse, WI, d **DISCIPLINE** MODERN BRITISH HISTORY **EDUCATION** Univ Wis-Madison, BA, 64; Stanford Univ, MA, 65, PhD(Brit hist), 69. **CAREER** Actg asst prof hist, Univ Wash, 67; asst prof, Univ Calif, Davis, 68-76; asst prof, 76-80, assoc prof, 80-83, Prof Hist, Earlham Col, 83-, assoc acad dean, 88-90; Chair of Social Sciences, 97-; Regional coordr of Hist Day, Nat Endowment for Humanities, 77-; Humanities Develop grant, Earlham Col, 88-90. **MEMBERSHIPS** Conf Brit Studies; Soc Study of Labour Hist **RESEARCH** Nineteenth and 20th century British commercial policy; European politics and gender since 1789; gay and lesbian studies. **SELECTED PUBLICATIONS** Auth, Reopening the case of Lloyd George and the postwar transition 1918-19, J Brit Studies, 11/70; Eric Geddes: Experiment with businessmen in Lloyd George's coalition governments 1915-1922, in: Essays in Anti-Labour History, Macmillan, London, 74; The Problem Of Economic Recovery, 1915-1919, in: War and the State, The Transformation of British Government, 1914-1919, Geo Allen & Unwin, London, 82. **CONTACT ADDRESS** Earlham Col, 801 National Rd W, Richmond, IN 47374-4095. **EMAIL** peterc@earlham.edu

CLINGAN, EDMUND
PERSONAL Born 10/12/1962, New York, NY, s **DISCIPLINE** HISTORY **EDUCATION** Queens Col, BA, 85; Univ Wisc, MA, 87; PhD, 91. **CAREER** Adj to asst prof, City Univ of NY, 92-95; asst to assoc prof, Univ ND, 95-. **HONORS AND AWARDS** Fulbright Scholarship, Germany, 88-89.

MEMBERSHIPS Am Hist Asn, Ger Studies Asn, Austrian Studies Centre **RESEARCH** Modern Germany **SELECTED PUBLICATIONS** Auth, Finance from Kaise to Fuhrer: Budget Politics in Germany 1912-34, Greenwood, 00; auth, "The Budget Debate of 1926: A Case Study in Weimar Democracy," European History Quarterly, 00. **CONTACT ADDRESS** Dept History, Univ of No Dakota, PO Box 8096, Grand Forks, ND 58202-8096. **EMAIL** clingan@plains.nodak.edu

CLOTHEY, FREDERICK WILSON

PERSONAL Born 02/29/1936, Madras, India, m, 1962, 4 children **DISCIPLINE** HISTORY OF RELIGIONS **EDUCATION** Aurora Col, BA & BTh, 57; Evangel Theol Sem, BD, 59; Univ Chicago, MA, 65, PhD(hist relig), 68. **CAREER** Dir youth work, Advent Christian Gen Conf, 59-62; from instr to asst prof relig Boston Univ, 67-77; Assoc Prof, Prof Hist Relig, Univ Pittsburgh, 77-, Chmn Dept Relig Studies, 78-88; 95-98, Resident coordr, Great Lakes Cols Asn Year in India Prog, 71-72; producer & dir films, Yakam: A Fire Ritual in South India, spring 73, Skanda-Sasti: A Festival of Conquest, fall 73 & Pankuni Uttiram: A Festival of Marriage, spring 74. **HONORS AND AWARDS** Fulbright fel, 78, 82, 91, 98; AIIS Fellow 66-67, 81, 85, 91, 94. **MEMBERSHIPS** Am Acad Relig; Soc Indian Studies; Conf So Indian Relig; Soc Sci Study Relig; Asn Asian Studies. **RESEARCH** Religion in South India; nature of myth, symbol, ritual; ethnic religion in America; South Indians Abroad. **SELECTED PUBLICATIONS** Auth, The many faces of Murukan: The history and meaning of a South Indian God, Mouton, The Hague, 78; contribr, Chronometry, cosmology and the festival calendar of the Murukan Cultus, In: Interludes: Festivals of South India and Sri Lanka, Manohar Bks, 82; "Sasta-Aiyanar-Aiyappan: The God as prism of social History," Images of Man: Relgion and Historical Process in South Asia, 82; The construction of a temple in an American city & The acculturation process, In: Rythm & Intent: Ritual Studies from South India, Blackie & Son, 82; auth, Quiscence and passion: The vision of Arunakiri, Tamil Mystic Austin and Winfield, 1996; Rhythm & intent: Ritual studies from South India, Blackie & Son, 82; ed, Experiencing Siva: Encounters with a Hindu Deity, Manohar Bks, 82; Images of man: Religion and historical process, New Era Publ, 82; auth, Tale of Four Cities: Religin, Indentity and Tamil Expatriates, forthcoming, Co-Founder, co-ed, Journal of Ritual Studies, 86-98; auth, Tamil Religion in Encyclopedia of Religion, 87; auth, . **CONTACT ADDRESS** Dept of Relig Studies, Univ of Pittsburgh, 2604 Cathedral/Learn, Pittsburgh, PA 15260-0001. **EMAIL** clothey+@pitt.edu

CLOUSE, ROBERT G.

PERSONAL Born 08/26/1931, Mansfield, OH, m, 1955, 2 children **DISCIPLINE** EARLY MODERN EUROPEAN HISTORY **EDUCATION** Bryan Col, BA, 54; Grace Theol Sem, BD, 57; Univ Iowa, MA, 60, PhD(hist), 63. **CAREER** Assoc prof, 63-72, Prof Hist, Ind State Univ, Terre Haute, 72-, Fel, Folger Shakespeare-Libr, Washington, DC, 64; grant, Penrose Rund, Am Philos Soc, 68; grants, Newberry Libr, 72, Lilly Libr, 76 & Nat Endowment for Humanities, 80. **HONORS AND AWARDS** Ind St Univ Res Creativity Awd, 87; Ind St Univ Distinguished Service Awd, 00. **MEMBERSHIPS** AHA; Am Soc Church Hist; Renaissance Soc Am. **RESEARCH** Millennial thought in early modern Europe; Calvinism before the Age of reason; the rise of Pietism. **SELECTED PUBLICATIONS** Auth, The Protestant Evangelical Revival, Amer Hist Rev, Vol 0099, 94; The Formation of Hell--Death and Retribution in the Ancient and Early-Christian Worlds, Amer Hist Rev, Vol 0100, 95; Atheism from the Reformation to the Enlightenment, Church Hist, Vol 0064, 95; auth, The New Millennium Manual, A Once and Future Guide, Baker (Grand Rapids, MI), 99. **CONTACT ADDRESS** Dept of Hist, Indiana State Univ, 210 N 7th St, Terre Haute, IN 47809-0002. **EMAIL** hiclouse@ruby.indstate.edu

CLOVER, FRANK M.

PERSONAL Born 05/05/1940, Denver, CO, w, 1965, 2 children **DISCIPLINE** ANCIENT HISTORY **EDUCATION** Univ of Chicago, PhD, 66. **CAREER** Prof of Hist and Classics, Univ Wis, Madison, 78-. **HONORS AND AWARDS** Netherlands Inst for Advanced Study, 91 & 94. **MEMBERSHIPS** Soc for Promotion of Roman Studies; Asn pour l'Antiquite Tardive. **RESEARCH** Roman empire; hellenistic age. **SELECTED PUBLICATIONS** Auth, The Late Roman West and the Vandals, Variorum, 93. **CONTACT ADDRESS** History Dept, Univ of Wisconsin, Madison, 455 N Park St., Madison, WI 53706. **EMAIL** fmclover@facstaff.wisc.edu

CLOWSE, CONVERSE DILWORTH

PERSONAL Born 04/15/1929, Burlington, VT, m, 1964, 2 children **DISCIPLINE** AMERICAN HISTORY **EDUCATION** Univ Vt, BA, 51, MA, 53; Northwestern Univ, PhD(hist), 63. **CAREER** Admin asst sales, Procter & Gamble Co, Boston & Cincinnati, 55-57; from instr to asst prof, 62-69, Assoc Prof Hist, Univ NC, Greensboro, 69-. **MEMBERSHIPS** AHA; Orgn Am Historians. **RESEARCH** American Colonial history; American economic history. **SELECTED PUBLICATIONS** Auth, Economic Beginnings in Colonial South Caroline, 1670-1730, Univ. SC, 71. **CONTACT ADDRESS** Dept of Hist, Univ of No Carolina, Greensboro, Greensboro, NC 27412.

CLULEE, NICHOLAS H.

PERSONAL Born 02/13/1945, Oak Park, IL, m, 1973, 2 children **DISCIPLINE** HISTORY **EDUCATION** Hobart Col, BA, 66; Univ of Chicago, MA, 68; PhD, 73. **CAREER** Prof, Frostburg State Univ, 71-; Chair, 97-. **HONORS AND AWARDS** NEH Fel, 84-85; Fac Achievement Awd, Frostburg State Univ, 90. **MEMBERSHIPS** AHA; Renaissance Soc of am; Hist of Science Soc. **RESEARCH** Sixteenth-century Natural Philosophy and Science. **SELECTED PUBLICATIONS** Auth, "John Dee's Mathematics and the Grading of Compound Qualities", Ambix 18 (73):178-211; auth, "Astrology, Magic and Optics: Facets of John Dee's Early Natural Philosophy", Renaissance Quarterly 30, (77):632-680; auth, "At the Crossroads of Magic and Science: John Dee's Archemastrie", in Occult and Scientific Mentalities in the Renaissance, ed Brian Vickers, (Cambridge: Univ Pr, 84) 57-71; auth, John Dee's Natural Philosophy. Between Science and Religion, Routledge, (London and NY), 88; auth, "John Dee and the Paracelsians" in Reading the book of Nature: The Other Side of the Scientific Revolution, Sixteenth Century Essays and Studies 41, ed Allen g. Debus and Michael t. Walton, (98):111-32. **CONTACT ADDRESS** Dept Hist, Frostburg State Univ, 101 Braddock Rd, Frostburg, MD 21532-2303. **EMAIL** nclulee@frostburg.edu

CLYMER, KENTON JAMES

PERSONAL Born 11/17/1943, Brooklyn, NY, m, 1967, 2 children **DISCIPLINE** UNITED STATE DIPLOMATIC HISTORY **EDUCATION** Grinnell Col, AB, 65; Univ MI, MA, 66, PhD, 70. **CAREER** Asst prof, 70-75, assoc prof, 75-82, Prof US Hist, Univ TX, El Paso, 82-; Fulbright prof, Silliman Univ, Phillipines, 77-78, Univ Indonesia, 90-91; George Bancroft Prof, Univ Gottingen, Germany, 92-93; Ch, Dept. Hist, Univ TX, El Paso, 84-85, 93-96; Assoc provost, TX Int Educ Consortium Prog, Malaysia, 86. **HONORS AND AWARDS** NEH summer stipends, 83, 98; Am Philos Soc, 72, 76, 81; Indo-US Subcomn on Educ and Cult, 87; Distinguished Res Awd, UTEP, 94; NEH Fel for Col Teachers, 00; Rockefeller Bellegn Center Awd, 00. **MEMBERSHIPS** Orgn Am Historians; AHA; Soc Historians Am For Rel(s); AAS. **RESEARCH** The US and Cambodia. **SELECTED PUBLICATIONS** Auth, John Hay: The Gentleman as Diplomat, Univ MI, 75; Protestant Missionaries in the Phillippines, 1893-1916: An Inquiry into the American Colonial Mentality, Univ Ill, 86; Quest for Freedom: The United States and India's Independence, Columbia Univ Press, 95; ed, The Vietnam War: It's History, Literature, and Music, TX Western Press, 98. **CONTACT ADDRESS** Dept Of US Hist, Univ of Texas, El Paso, 500 W University Ave, El Paso, TX 79968-0532. **EMAIL** kclymer@utep.edu

COAKLEY, JOHN

PERSONAL Born 04/05/1949, Washington, DC **DISCIPLINE** CHURCH HISTORY **EDUCATION** Wesleyan Univ, AB, 71; Harvard Divinity Sch, Mdiv, 74; ThD, 80. **CAREER** Fac, New Brunswick Theol Sem, 84-. **HONORS AND AWARDS** NEH Fel, 97-98. **MEMBERSHIPS** Am Soc of church Hist, Am Hist Asn, Medieval Acad of Am, Am Acad of Relig. **RESEARCH** History of Christianity (especially Medieval). **SELECTED PUBLICATIONS** Auth, "Gender, Friars and Sanctity: Mendicant Encounters with Saints, 1250-1325," in Medieval Masculinities, ed. Clare Lees (MN: Univ Minn Pr, 94), 91-110; auth, "Devotion, literature de," and "Direction spirituelle," in Dictionnaire encyclopedique du moyen age chretienne, ed. Andre Vauchez (Paris: Editions du Cerf, 97), 458-459, 468; auth, "A Marriage and Its Observer: Christine of Stommeln, the Heavenly Bridegroom, and Friar Peter of Dacia," in Gendered Voices: Medieval Saints and Their Interpreters, ed. Catherine Mooney (PA: Univ Penn Pr, 99), 99-117; co-ed, Patterns and Portraits: Women in the History of the Reformed Church in America, Eerdmans, 99. **CONTACT ADDRESS** Dept Church Hist, New Brunswick Theol Sem, 17 Seminary Place, New Brunswick, NJ 08901-1107. **EMAIL** jwc@nbts.edu

COAKLEY, THOMAS M.

PERSONAL Born 05/25/1929, Hamilton, OH, m, 1973, 5 children **DISCIPLINE** BRITISH HISTORY **EDUCATION** Miami Univ, AB, 51; Univ Minn, Minneapolis, MA, 53, PhD, 59. **CAREER** Asst prof hist, St John's Col, Man, 58-63; from asst prof to assoc prof, 63-93, prof emer, Miami Univ, 93-. **HONORS AND AWARDS** Phi Beta Kappa **MEMBERSHIPS** Conf Brit Studies; Midwest Conf Brit Studies. **RESEARCH** Tudor-Stuart. **SELECTED PUBLICATIONS** Auth, "Robert Cecil in Power: Elizabethan Politics in Two Regions," in Early Stuart Studies: Essays in Honor of David Harris Willson (MN: Univ Minn Press, 71); auth, "George Calvert and Newfoundland: 'The Sad Face of Winter,'" Md Hist Mag 0071 (76); auth, "George Calvert, First Lord Baltimore: Family, Status, and Arms," Md Hist Mag 0079 (84); auth, Sir John Bramston, the Younger (1611-1700), Oxford Univ Press, forthcoming. **CONTACT ADDRESS** Dept of Hist, Miami Univ, Oxford, OH 45056-1879. **EMAIL** coakletm@muohio.edu

COALE, SAMUEL CHASE

PERSONAL Born 07/26/1943, Hartford, CT, m, 1972, 1 child **DISCIPLINE** ENGLISH, AMERICAN CIVILIZATION **EDUCATION** Trinity Col, Conn, AB, 65; Brown Univ, Am & PhD, 70. **CAREER** Instr Eng, 68-71, asst prof, 71-76, assoc prof, 76-81, asst dean, 78-80, prof eng & Am lit, Wheaton Col, 81, Co-Ch, Am hist & lit, 70, Wheaton res & travel grant, Wordsworth-Coleridge Conf, Engl, 72; Fulbright sr lectureship, Aristotelian Univ, Greece, 76-77, Universidade Federal de Minas Gerais, Brazil, 94; lectr, Engl, 72 & 96, Ann Poznan Am Cult Sem, Poland, 77, 78 & 79, India and Pakistan, 81, Sweden, 81, Czechoslovakia, 83-89, Israel and Egypt, 87, Pakistan, 90 & 93, Brazil, 90, Ygoslavia, 91, India, 94; Nat Endowment for Hum fel, 81-82; Teaching, Brazil at UFMG, 98; Prof, A. Howard Meneely, 00; Book reviewer for the Providence Journal; theatre and film reviewer for the East Side Monthly. **HONORS AND AWARDS** A Howard Meneely Prof Hum, Wheaton, 98; Awded the Faculty Appreciation Awd from the graduating class, 99. **MEMBERSHIPS** MLA; Northeast Mod Lang Asn; Hawthorne Soc; Poe Soc; Knight of Mark Twain. **RESEARCH** Mod Am lit; 19th century Am lit; Engromantic poets. **SELECTED PUBLICATIONS** Auth, Faulkner and the Southern Imagination, Grammata, Greece, 77; John Cheever, Ungar, 77; Hawthorne's American Notebooks: Contours of a haunted mind, Nathaniel Hawthorne J, 78; The Marble Faun: A frail structure of our own rearing, Essays in Lit, 80; Anthony Burgess, Ungar, 81; A Quality of Light: The fiction of Paul Theroux, Critique, 81; An interview with Anthony Burgess, In: The Ludic loves of Anthony Burgess, Mod Fiction Studies, 81; Into the Farther Darkness: The Manichean pastoralism of John Gardner, In: Critical Essys on John Gardner, Southern Ill Univ Press, 82; Didion's Disorder: An American Romancer's Art, Critique, 84; Paul Theroux, Twayne, 87; William Styron Revisited, Twayne, 91; The Scarlet Letter as Icon, ATQ, 92; Hawthorne's Black Veil: From Image to Icon, CEA Critic, 93; Red Noses, The Black Death, and AIDS: Cycles of Despair and Disease, Ill, 93; Spiritualism and Hawthorne's Romance: The Blithedale Theater as False Consciousness, Literature and Belief, 94; The Resurrection of Bullet Park: John Cheever's Curative Spell, Greenwood, 94; The Romance of Mesmerism: Hawthorne's Medium of Romance, Studies in the Am Renaissance, 94; Hillerman and Cross: The Re-Invention and Mythic (Re)-Modeling of the Poplar Mystery, Clues, 95; The Dark Domain of James Lee Burke: Mysteries within Mystery, Clues, 97; Mesmerism and Hawthorne: Mediums of American Romance, Alabama, 98; Blood Rites (a novel), Commonwealth, 98. **CONTACT ADDRESS** Dept of Eng & Am Lit, Wheaton Col, Massachusetts, 26 E Main St, Norton, MA 02766-2322. **EMAIL** samcoale@aol.com

COBB, WILLIAM HENRY

PERSONAL Born 04/19/1938, Little Rock, AR, m, 1961, 2 children **DISCIPLINE** FRENCH HISTORY **EDUCATION** Univ Ark, Fayetteville, AB, 60, MA, 62; Tulane Univ, PhD(hist), 70. **CAREER** Instr hist, Memphis State Univ, 62-65; asst prof, Zavier Univ, La, 67-69; Asst Prof Hist, E Caroline Univ, 69-. **MEMBERSHIPS** Soc Fr Hist Studies. **RESEARCH** Reign of Louis XIII: French political institutions and diplomatic history; Arkansas history. **CONTACT ADDRESS** Dept of Hist, East Carolina Univ, Greenville, NC 27834.

COBBLE, DOROTHY SUE

PERSONAL Born 06/28/1949, Atlanta, GA, m, 1997, 3 children **DISCIPLINE** WOMEN'S STUDIES, LABOR STUDIES **EDUCATION** Univ Calif, Berkeley, BA, 72; Stanford Univ, PhD, 86. **CAREER** Dept chair and Dir, Labor Studies Dept, City Col of San Francisco, 80-86; assoc prof, Rutgers Univ, 86-. **HONORS AND AWARDS** H. Gutman Book Awd, 92; Rutgers Univ Bd of Trustees Res Awd, 92; ALCS and NEH Res Awds; Funding Dir, Centre for Women and Work, 930-96; Woodrow Wilson Fel, 99-2000. **MEMBERSHIPS** Org of Am Hists, Industrial Relations Res Asn. **RESEARCH** American labor and women's history; women and work; service work. **SELECTED PUBLICATIONS** Auth, Dishing It Out: Waitresses and Their Unions in the Twentieth Century, Urbana: Univ Ill Press (91); ed, Women and Unions: Forging A Partnership, Ithaca: Cornell Univ ILR Press (93); auth, "Lost Ways of Organizing: Reviving the AFL's Direct Affiliate Strategy," Industrial Relations, 36, no 3 (July 97): 278-301; auth, "The Next Unionism: Structural Innovations for a Revitalized Labor Movement," Labor Law J, 48, no 8 (Aug 97): 439-443; auth, "Knowledge Workers and the New Unionism," Thought and Action: The National Education Association Higher Education Journal, 15, no 2 (fall 99): 19-24; auth, "A Spontaneous Loss of Enthusiasm': Workplace Feminism and the Transformation of Women's Service Jobs in the 1970's," Int Labor and Working-Class Hist, 56 (fall 99): 23-44; coauth, "Historical Perspectives on Representing NonStandard Workers," in Non-Traditional Work Arrangements and the Changing Labor Market, ed by Francoise Carre, et al, Wisc: Industrial Relations Res Asn (2000). **CONTACT ADDRESS** Dept Labor and Industrial Relations, Rutgers, The State Univ of New Jersey, New Brunswick, PO Box 5062, New Brunswick, NJ 08903-5062.

COBEN, STANLEY

PERSONAL Born 08/06/1929, Flushing, NY, m, 1984, 2 children **DISCIPLINE** UNITED STATES HISTORY **EDUCATION** Univ Southern Calif, BA, 54; Columbia Univ, MA, 59, PhD(hist), 61. **CAREER** Lectr hist, Hunter Col, 60-62, asst prof, 62-64; asst prof, Princeton Univ, 64-67; assoc prof, 67-68, Prof Hist, Univ Calif, Los Angeles, 68-, Mem Am hist adv comt, NY State Bd Higher Educ, 64-66; Soc Sci Res Coun fac res fel, 67-68; vis prof hist, Univ Calif, Berkeley, 71; Am Philos

Soc fel, 72, Guggenheim Mem Found fel, 72-73; Woodrow Wilson Int Ctr for Scholars fel, 74-75; mem, Univ Calif Liason Comt, Educ Progs, 77- **MEMBERSHIPS** AHA; Orgn Am Historians; Am Studies Asn; Econ Hist Asn. **RESEARCH** Twentieth century United States history: American nativism and race relations; American culture. **SELECTED PUBLICATIONS** The scientific establishment and the transmission of quantum mechanics to the United States, 1919-1932, Am Hist Rev, 71; co-ed, The Development of an American Culture, Prentice-hall, 71-79; coauth, The Democratic Heritage, Xerox, 72; ed, Reform War and Reaction, 1922-1932, 73; auth, The first years of modern America, 1918-1933, In: The Unfinished Century, 73, Harper; The assault on Victorianism in the twentieth century, Am Quart, 12/75; Innovation in the Patronage of Science, Minerva, summer 76; auth, Rebellion Against Victorianism, Oxford, 91. **CONTACT ADDRESS** Dept of Hist, Univ of California, Los Angeles, Los Angeles, CA 90024.

COBLE, PARKS
DISCIPLINE HISTORY OF EAST ASIA **EDUCATION** Univ Ill, Urbana, PhD, 75. **CAREER** Prof, Univ Nebr, Lincoln; ed bd, 20th Century China; assoc-in-res, Fairbank Ctr for E Asian Res, Harvard Univ. **HONORS AND AWARDS** Distinguished Tchg Awd, Univ Nebr, Lincoln, 90. **RESEARCH** The Japanese occupation of China during the World War II. **SELECTED PUBLICATIONS** Auth, The Shanghai Capitalists and the Nationalist Government, 1927-1937, Harvard E Asian Monogr Ser, 80; Facing Japan: Chinese Politics and Japanese Imperialism, 1931-1937, Harvard E Asian Monogr Ser, 91. **CONTACT ADDRESS** Univ of Nebraska, Lincoln, 622 Oldfather, Lincoln, NE 68588-0417. **EMAIL** pcoble@unlinfo.unl.edu

COBURN, THOMAS BOWEN
PERSONAL Born 02/08/1944, New York, NY, m, 1998, 2 children **DISCIPLINE** HISTORY OF RELIGION **EDUCATION** Princeton Univ, AB, 65; Harvard Univ, MTS, 69, PhD(-comp relig), 77. **CAREER** Teaching fel relig, Phillips Acad, 65-66; instr math & physics, Am Community Sch, Lebanon, 66-67; from Instr to Prof, 74-90, Charles A. Dana Prof Rel Studies, St Lawrence Univ, 90-, Vice Pres St Lawrence Univ and Dean of Acad Affairs, 96-. **HONORS AND AWARDS** Sr res fel, Am Inst Indian Studies, 81-82; Nat Endowment for Humanities fel, 82. **MEMBERSHIPS** Am Acad Relig; Asn Asian Studies; Network liberal arts education. **RESEARCH** South Asian religion, especially the literature and mythology of popular religion in India; goddesses; methods in comparative study. **SELECTED PUBLICATIONS** Auth, The Conceptualization of Religious Change and the Worship of the Great Goddess, St Lawrence Univ, 80; auth, Consort of none, Sakti of all: The vision of the Devi-Mahatmya, In: The Divine Consort: Radha and the Goddesses of India, Berkeley Res Publ, 1982, rev ed, 95; Devi-Mahatmya: The Crystallization of the Goddess Tradition: Motilal Banarsidass, New Delhi, 84; Scripture in India, IN, Rethinking Scripture, SUNY Press, repr 89; Encountering the Goddess: A Trans. of the Devi-Mahatmya and a Study of Its Interpretation, State Univ of NY Press, 91; guest ed, Education About Asia, 2/97; author of numerous other journal articles; auth, Climbing The Mountain of God, Inl. Am Acad. Of Rel., Spring 95; auth, Three-Fold Vision of The Devi-Mahatmya, In Devi: The Great Goddess, Smithsonian Institution, 99; auth, Asia and The Undergraduate Curriculum, In Asia in The Undergraduate Curriculum, M.E. Sharpe, 00. **CONTACT ADDRESS** Vice Pres and Dean of Acad Affairs, St. Lawrence Univ, Canton, NY 13617-1499. **EMAIL** tcoburn@stlawu.edu

COCHRAN, SHERMAN
DISCIPLINE HISTORY **EDUCATION** Yale Univ, BA, 62, MA, 67, PhD, 75. **CAREER** Asst prof, 73-79; assoc prof, 79-86; prof, 86-. **SELECTED PUBLICATIONS** Auth, Big Business in China: Sino-Foreign Rivalry in the Cigarette Industry 1890-1930, Cambridge, 80; coauth, One Day in China: May 21 1936, Yale, 83. **CONTACT ADDRESS** Dept of History, Cornell Univ, Ithaca, NY 14853-2801. **EMAIL** sgc11@cornell.edu

COCHRAN, THOMAS CHILDS
PERSONAL Born 04/29/1902, Brooklyn, NY **DISCIPLINE** HISTORY **EDUCATION** NYork Univ, BS, 23, AM, 25; Univ Pa, PhD, 30; Cambridge Univ, MA, 65. **CAREER** From instr to prof hist, NY Univ, 27-50; prof, 50-68, Benjamin Franklin prof, 68-72, Emer Benjamin Franklin Prof Hist, Univ PA, 72-, Mem historiography comt, Soc Sci Res Coun, 43-64, exec comt, 62-65; co-ed jour, Econ Hist Asn, 45-50, ed, 50-55; chmn & pres, Nat Records Mgt Coun, 48-50; vis lectr, Harvard Univ, 48-49; sem assoc, Columbia Univ, 49-; dir, Nat Bur Econ Res, 49-52; mem adv comt, Eleutherian-Milla-Hagley Found, 62-69; Pitt prof, Cambridge Univ, 65-66; fel, St Anthony's Col, Oxford Univ, 70; sr fel, Eleutherian Mills Libr, 73-74, 77-; Robert Lee Bailey prof, Univ NC, Charlotte, 73-74; guest ed, Am Hist Rev, 73-74. **HONORS AND AWARDS** LLD, Univ Pa, 72; LittD, Rider Col, 76. **MEMBERSHIPS** AHA (Pres, 72-); Am Acad Arts & Sci; Am Philos Soc: Orgn Am Historians (vpres, 64-65, pres, 65-66); Econ Hist Asn (secy-treas, 42-46, pres, 58-60). **RESEARCH** American social and economic history; the cultural approach to history. **SELECTED PUBLICATIONS** Auth, The Culture of Technology--An Alternative View of the Industrial-Revolution in the United-States, Science in Context, Vol 0008, 95. **CONTACT ADDRESS** Dept Hist, Univ of Pennsylvania, Philadelphia, PA 19104.

COCKFIELD, JAMIE H.
PERSONAL Born 06/20/1945, Charleston, SC, s **DISCIPLINE** HISTORY **EDUCATION** Univ SCar, BA, 67; MA, 68; Univ Va, PhD, 72. **CAREER** Extension Div, Univ Va, 72; Asst Prof to Prof, Mercer Univ, 72-. **MEMBERSHIPS** Am Asn for the Advancement of Slavic Studies; Southern Conf on Slavic Studies; Western Soc of French Hist. **RESEARCH** Reign of Tsar Nicholas II of Russia. **SELECTED PUBLICATIONS** Auth, dollars and diplomacy, Duke Univ Press, 81; auth, with Snow on their Boots, St Martin's Press, 98. **CONTACT ADDRESS** Dept History, Mercer Univ, Macon, 1400 Coleman Ave, Macon, GA 31207-0001. **EMAIL** cockfield_jh@mercer.edu

COCKS, GEOFFREY C.
PERSONAL Born 11/13/1948, New Bedford, MA, m, 1971, 1 child **DISCIPLINE** HISTORY **EDUCATION** Occidental Col, BA 70; UCLA, MA 71, PhD 75. **CAREER** Occidental Col, inst 74-75; Albion Col, asst prof, assoc prof, prof, 75-; UCLA, vis asst prof, 80; Albion Col, Royal G. Hall Prof, 94-. **HONORS AND AWARDS** Scholar of Year; Outstanding Jr Fac Mem; Honor Prog Sch Tchg Awd; 3 NEH; 2 DAAD; NIH; Fulbright Fel. **MEMBERSHIPS** AHA **RESEARCH** Modern Germany; Hist of Psychotherapy; Medicine; Health Nazi Germany. **SELECTED PUBLICATIONS** Auth, Treating Mind and Body: Essays in the History of Science, Professions and Society Under Extreme Conditions, New Bruns NJ, Transaction, 98; Psychotherapy in the Third Reich: The Goring Institute, New Bruns NJ, Transaction, 97; Medicine and Modernity: Public Health and Medical Care in Nineteenth and Twentieth Century Germany, coed, Cambridge, CUP, 96; The Goring Institute: Context and Contents of the History of Psychiatry, in: Power and Knowledge: Perspectives in the History of Psychiatry, ed Matthias Weber, Munich, 98; Teaching Undergraduates Psychohistory, Clio's Psych, 97; The Old as New: the Nuremberg Doctor's Trial and Medicine in Modern Germany, in: Medicine and Modernity, co-ed, 96. **CONTACT ADDRESS** Dept of History, Albion Col, 611 East Porter St, Albion, MI 49224. **EMAIL** gcocks@albion.edu

CODELL, JULIE
PERSONAL Born 09/19/1945, Chicago, IL, 1 child **DISCIPLINE** ART **EDUCATION** Vassar Col, BA, 67; Univ Mich, MA, 68; Ind Univ Bloomington, MA, 75, PhD, 78. **CAREER** Prof, 79-90, Univ Mt; dir, 91-, Az St Univ. **HONORS AND AWARDS** NEH Summer Stipend, 88; NEH Fel, 93; Yale British Art Center Fel, 94. **MEMBERSHIPS** Res Soc for Victorian Per; CAA; HBA; MLA; INCS. **RESEARCH** 19th cent British art; lit; early modernism; critical theory; film. **SELECTED PUBLICATIONS** Art, The Public Image of Victorian Artists: Family Biographies, J Pre-Raphaelite St, 96; auth, The Artist Colonized: Holman Hunt's 'Bio-History', Masculinity, Nationalism & The English School, Re-framing the Pre-Raphaelites, Scolar, 96; art, Charles Fairfax Murray and the Pre-Raphaelite Academy: Writing and Forging the Artistic Field, Collecting the Pre-Raphaelites, Scolar, 97; art, Ford Madox Brown, Carlyle, Macaulay, Bakhtin: The Pratfalls and Penultimates of History, Art Hist, 98; coed, Orientalism Transposed: The Impact of the Colonies on British Culture, 98; auth, "Victorian Artists Family Biographies: Domestic Authority, the Marketplace, and the Artist's Body," Biographical Passages: Essays on Victorian and Modernist Biography, ed. L. Hughes and J. Law, (Univ of MO Press, 00): 65-108; auth, "Righting the Victorian Artist: The Redgraves A Century of Painters of the English School and the Serialization of Art History," Oxford Art Journal, 23, (00): 93-118; auth, "Serialized Artists Biographies: A Culture Industry in Late Victorian Britain," Book History, 3, (00): 94-124; auth, "Constructing the Victorian Artist: National Identity, the Political Economy of Art, and Biographical Mania in the Periodical Press," Victorian Periodicals Review, 33, (00): 283-316; auth, "Empiricism, Naturalism, and Science in Millais's Paintings," John Everett Millais: New Context, Studies in British Art, ed. D. Mancoff, (Yale Univ Press, 01). **CONTACT ADDRESS** Sch of Art, Arizona State Univ, Tempe, AZ 85287-1505. **EMAIL** Julie.Codell@asu.edu

CODLING, JIM
PERSONAL Born 11/28/1949, Lloydminster, SK, Canada, m, 1982, 2 children **DISCIPLINE** HISTORY, PHILOSOPHY, EDUCATION **EDUCATION** Univ Saskatchewan, B Ed, 72; Knox Col, M Div, 76; Convent Sem, Th M, 81; Mississippi State Univ, M Ed, 89; Concordia, St Louis, Th D, 90. **CAREER** Prof, Mary Holmes Col, 91-. **HONORS AND AWARDS** Concordia Res Fel; Fisher Prize, Knox Coll; Fac Mem of the Year, 94; Res, 94; Teach, 95. **MEMBERSHIPS** Convent Presbytery. **RESEARCH** Ethics; Reformation History; Local Histories. **SELECTED PUBLICATIONS** Auth, 'The New Deal in Public Policy," 97; auth, Cross Cultural Missions, Coast to Coast (92); auth, Why So Many Churches, Coast to Coast (94). **CONTACT ADDRESS** Dept Soc Science, Education, Mary Holmes Col, PO Box 1257, West Point, MS 39773-1257.

COFFEY, JOAN L.
DISCIPLINE HISTORY **EDUCATION** Barat Col, BA, 65; Univ Colo, MA, 86, PhD, 90. **CAREER** High sch teachr, 65-84; asst prof, Sam Houston State Univ, 90-97; assoc prof, 97-. **HONORS AND AWARDS** Gilbert Chinard Scholarship, Inst Francais de Washington, 87; Dissertation Fel, Univ of Colorado, 88; Phi Alpha Theta National History Honor Soc, 88; Pi Delta Phi Nat French Honor Soc, 93: **MEMBERSHIPS** Am Hist Asn, Soc for French Hist Studies, Western Soc for French Hist, World Hist Asn, World His Asn of Tex, Nat Coun for Hist Educ, Tex Coun for Hist Educ, Tex, Catholic Histol Educ, Southern Histol Asn. **RESEARCH** France and southern Europe, world history. **SELECTED PUBLICATIONS** Auth, "The First Indochina War: Perceptions and Realities of French and American Policy," Handbook of Vietnam Literature and Research, Greenwood Publishing Group, 93; auth, "The Worker Pilgrimage; Religious Experience or Media Event?," Proceedings of the Western Society for French History, 93; auth, "Labor Law and the Christian Corporation at Val des Bois, 1840-1914," Historical Reflections Reflexions Historique, 84; auth, "Church-State Conflict: Bilingualism and Religious Education, 1891-1906," Proceedings of the Western Society for French History," 95; auth, "Tradition in French Fin de Siecle films," Proceedings of the Western Society for French History, 96; auth, "O Catechisms and Sermons: Church-State Relations in France, 1890-1905," Church History, 97; auth, "The Aix Affair of 1891: A Turning Point in Church-State Relations before the Separation?," French Historical Studies, 98; auth, "For God and France: The Military Law of 1889 and the Soldiers of Saint-Sulpice," The Catholic Historical Review, (forthcoming). **CONTACT ADDRESS** Dept of History, Sam Houston State Univ, 306 Estill Bldg, Huntsville, TX 77341.

COFFIN, DAVID ROBBINS
PERSONAL Born 03/20/1918, New York, NY, m, 1947, 4 children **DISCIPLINE** HISTORY OF ART **EDUCATION** Princeton Univ, AB, 40, MFA, 47, PhD(hist of art), 54. **CAREER** Instr fine arts, Univ Mich, 47-49; lectr art & archaeol, 49-54, from asst prof to assoc prof, 54-60, Marquand prof, 66-70, chmn dept, 64-70, Prof Art & Archaeol, Princeton Univ, 60-, H C Butler Prof Hist of Archit, 70-, Ed-in-chief, Art Bull, 59-62; Am Coun Learned Socs fel, 63-64; Guggenheim Found fel, 72-73. **HONORS AND AWARDS** Kress Prof, CASVA **MEMBERSHIPS** Col Art Asn; Soc Archit Hist (treas, 69-70); Renaissance Soc Am. **RESEARCH** History of Renaissance and Baroque architecture; history of Italian Renaissance art. **SELECTED PUBLICATIONS** Auth, Villa d'Este at Tivoli, Princeton Univ, 60; ed, the Italian garden, Dumbarton Oaks, 73; auth, Villa in The Life of Renais, Rome, Princeton, 79; auth, Gardens and Gardening in Papal Rome, Princeton, 91; auth, The English Garden: Meditation and Memorial, Princeton, 94; auth, Princeton University Graduate College, Princeton, 00. **CONTACT ADDRESS** Dept of Arts & Archaeol, Princeton Univ, Princeton, NJ 08540.

COFFMAN, EDWARD M.
PERSONAL Born 01/27/1929, Hopkinsville, KY, m, 1955, 3 children **DISCIPLINE** AMERICAN HISTORY **EDUCATION** Univ Ky, ABJ, 51, MA, 55, PhD, 59. **CAREER** From instr to asst prof hist, Memphis State Univ, 57-61; from asst prof to assoc prof hist, 61-68, Prof Hist, Univ Wis-Madison, 68-, Am Philos Soc grant, 60; res assoc, G C Marshall Found, 60-61; Nat Security Study Group grant-in-aid, 63; vis Dwight D Eisenhower prof, Kans State Univ, 69-70; mem adv comt, Off Chief Mil Hist, Dept Army, 72-76; mem, Nat Hist Publ Comn, 72-76; Guggenheim fel, 73-74; dir, US Comn on Mil Hist; vis prof US Mil Acad, 77-78; Harmon lectr, US Air Force Acad, 76. **MEMBERSHIPS** AHA; Am Mil Inst; Orgn Am Historians; Southern Hist Asn. **RESEARCH** American history, especially military and social history; the life of Gen Peyton C March; the United States in World War I. **SELECTED PUBLICATIONS** Auth, Army life on the frontier, 1865-1898, Mil Affairs, 56; The Hilt of the Sword: The Career of Peyton C March, Univ Wis, 66; The War to End All Wars: The American Military Experience in World War I, Oxford Univ, 68; American command and commanders in World War I, In: New Dimensions in Military History, Presidio, 75; The second battle of the Marne, In: Transformation of a Continent: Europe in the Twentieth Century, Burgess, 75; Batson of the Philippine Scouts, Parameters, VII, No 3, 77; coauth, The American regular Army Officer Corps between the World Wars, Armed Forces & Soc, 11/77; auth, The American military and strategic policy in World War I, In: War Aims and Strategic Policy in The Great War: 1914-1918, Croom-Helm, 77. **CONTACT ADDRESS** Dept of Hist, Univ of Wisconsin, Madison, Madison, WI 53706.

COHASSEY, JOHN F.
PERSONAL Born 11/02/1961, Pontiac, MI, m, 1993 **DISCIPLINE** HISTORY **EDUCATION** Oakland Univ, BA, 90; Wayne State Univ, MA, 93. **CAREER** Freelance Writer, 88-; Author, 98-; Guest Lectr, Wayne State Univ, Oaklnad Univ, Detroit Pub Sch, 99-. **HONORS AND AWARDS** Award of Merit, for book Toast of the Town: The Life and Times on Sunnie Wilson, Hist Soc of Mich, 98. **MEMBERSHIPS** Pontiac Hist Dist Comn, 99-. **RESEARCH** American cultural history. **SELECTED PUBLICATIONS** Coauth,Toast of the Town: The Life and Times on Sunnie Wilson, Wayne State Press, 98; articles in Contemporary Black Biography, Contemporary Musicians, African American Almanac, Encyclopedia of Latin American History, The Detroit News, Har magazine, Big City Blues. **CONTACT ADDRESS** 398 W Irgvois, Pontiac, MI 48341. **EMAIL** jfcohass@oakland.edu

COHEN, ADA
DISCIPLINE ART HISTORY **EDUCATION** Brandeis Univ, BA; Harvard Univ, MA, PhD. **CAREER** Assoc prof, Dartmouth Col. **RESEARCH** Greek large-scale painting and mosaic in the late Classical/early Hellenistic periods; ancient art and gender. **SELECTED PUBLICATIONS** Auth, The Alexander Mosaic: Stories of Victory and Defeat, Cambridge UP, 97; Portrayals of Abduction in Greek Art: Rape or Metaphor? in Sexuality in Ancient Art, Cambridge UP, 96; Alexander and Achilles: Macedonians and 'Mycenaeans,' in The Ages of Homer, Univ Tex P, 95. **CONTACT ADDRESS** Dartmouth Col, 3529 N Main St, Ste. 207, Hanover, NH 03755. **EMAIL** ada.cohen@dartmouth.edu

COHEN, ALVIN PHILIP
PERSONAL Born 12/12/1937, Los Angeles, CA, m, 1984, 2 children **DISCIPLINE** CHINESE PHILOLOGY & CULTURAL HISTORY **EDUCATION** Univ Calif, Berkeley, BS, 60, MA, 66, PhD(Orient Lang), 71. **CAREER** Lectr Orient Lang, Univ Calif, Davis, 70-71; asst prof, 71-77, assoc prof Chinese, Univ Mass, Amherst 77-83; actg bibliogr Orient Collection, Univ Mass, Amherst, 71-; prof, Chinese Univ Mass, Amherst, 83-; Dept Chair, 91-97. **HONORS AND AWARDS** Fulbright-Hays Fel, 68-69; China and Inner Asia Council of the Assoc for Asian Studies grant, 95-97. **MEMBERSHIPS** Am Orient Soc; Soc Study Chinese Relig; Assn for Asian Studies; Early Medieval China Group; Tang Studies Soc. **RESEARCH** Chinese historiography; Chinese folk religion; Classical Chinese Language. **SELECTED PUBLICATIONS** Auth, Grammar Notes for Introductory Classical Chinese, Chinese Materials Ctr, 75, 2nd ed, 80; Notes on a Chinese workingclass bookshelf, J Am Orient Soc, 76; Coercing the rain deities in ancient China, Hist Relig, 78; ed, Selected Works of Peter A Boodberg, Univ Calif, Berkeley, 79; Legend, Lore and Religion in China, Chinese Materials Ctr, 79; auth, Introduction to Research in Chinese Source Materials, Far Eastern Publications, Yale Univ, 00. **CONTACT ADDRESS** Asian Lang and Lit Dept, Univ of Massachusetts, Amherst, Amherst, MA 01003-9277. **EMAIL** cohen@asianlan.umass.edu

COHEN, GARY BENNETT
PERSONAL Born 10/26/1948, Los Angeles, CA **DISCIPLINE** HISTORY **EDUCATION** Univ Southern Calif, BA, 70; Princeton Univ, MA, 72, PhD(hist), 75. **CAREER** Instr, Princeton Univ, 74-76; asst prof, 76-82, assoc prof, Univ Okla, 82-95; res fel, dept hist, Princeton Univ, 78, Fulbright Hays & Int Res & Exchange Bd, 82, 97. **MEMBERSHIPS** AHA; Conf Group Cent Europ Hist; Social Sci Hist Asn. **RESEARCH** Social history of modern Central and East Central Europe; Bohemian lands and Austria; European ethnic minorities. **SELECTED PUBLICATIONS** Auth, Jews in German Society: Prague 1860-1914, Cent Europ Hist, 3/77; Recent research on Czech nation-building, J Mod Hist, 12/79; The Politics of Ethnic Survival: Germans in Prague, 1861-1914, Princeton Univ Press, 81; Education and Middle-class Society in Imperial Austria 1848-1918, Purdue Univ Press, 96. **CONTACT ADDRESS** Dept of History, Univ of Oklahoma, 455 W Lindsey St, Norman, OK 73019-2000. **EMAIL** gcohen@ou.edu

COHEN, GEORGE MICHAEL
PERSONAL Born 09/24/1931, Brookline, MA, m, 1964, 2 children **DISCIPLINE** ART HISTORY **EDUCATION** Harvard Univ, AB, 55, AM, 58; Boston Univ, PhD, 62. **CAREER** Asst prof art hist, Mass Col Art, 63-68; assoc prof, C W Post Col, Long Island Univ, 68-69 & Newark State Col, 69-70; prof art hist, Hofstra Univ, 70. **MEMBERSHIPS** Col Art Asn Am; AAUP; Appraisers Asn Am; Authors Guild. **RESEARCH** Am art. **SELECTED PUBLICATIONS** Auth, The paintings of Charles Sheeler, 59 & The lithographs of Thomas Hart Benton, 62, Am Artist; A History of American Art, Dell, 71; American impressionism, Ford Motor Co, 72; An art historical discovery and its importance to personal property appraisal, 6/75 & Interest and rise in market valuation of 19th century American genre painting, 12/77, Valuation; Outlines of art history, Univ Col Tutors, 77; Essentials of Art History & Essentials, J Am Art. **CONTACT ADDRESS** Fine Arts Dept, Hofstra Univ, 113 Calkins Hall, Hempstead, NY 11549-0000.

COHEN, JEFFREY A.
PERSONAL Born 04/17/1952, Boston, MA **DISCIPLINE** HISTORY OF ARCHITECTURE **EDUCATION** Univ Pa, PhD, 91. **CAREER** Tchg fel, dept art hist, Univ Pa, 75-77; archit draftsman and surveyor, Univ Mus Exped, Cyrene, Libya, summers, 78-79; instr, art dept, Muhlenberg Col, Allentown, Pa, fall 79; res, surveyor, and photographer, Philadelphia Hist Sites Surv, Clio Grp Inc, Phildelphia, 77-80; lectr, archit dept, Drexel Univ, Philadelphia, sept 77-dec 80; asst ed for archit hist, The Papers of Benjamin Henry Latrobe, Md Hist Soc, feb 81-jan 86; assoc ed for archit hist, The Papers of Benjamin Henry Latrobe, Md Hist Soc, feb 86-sep 94; consult, Marianna Thomas Archit, Philadelphia, jul 93-dec 94; lectr, hist of art dept, Univ Pa, sep-dec 93; adjunct prof, archit dept, Drexel Univ, sept-dec 95; adjunct instr, MA prog in hist preserv, Goucher Col, Baltimore, Md, jun-dec 96; lectr, Growth and Structure of Cities dept, Bryn Mawr Col, jan 95-; dir, Digital Media and Visual Resource Ctr, Bryn Mawr Col, jan 97-. **HONORS AND AWARDS** Robert Smith Fel, Carpenters' Co of the City and County of Philadelphia, 92; Andrew W. Mellon Fel, Amer Philos Soc, 89; Charles E. Peterson Fel, Athenaeum of Philadelphia, 89-91; Dept Kress Found Fel, Univ Pa, 88-89; Dean's Scholar, Univ Pa, 88; Mellon Grad Fel, Univ Pa, 82-83; Dept Kress Found Fel, Univ Pa, 81-82; Victorian Soc Summer Sch Scholarship, 77; Rockefeller Found Travel Grant, 77; Nat Merit Scholarship, 70-74. **MEMBERSHIPS** Soc of Archit Hist, Philadelphia Chap, vpres, 96-98, pres, 98-00; Soc of Archit Hist, nat, Educ Comt, 96-; Soc of Archit Hist, nat, Elec Media Comt, 95-; chair, 98-. **SELECTED PUBLICATIONS** Auth, with Charles B. Brownell, The Architectural Drawings of Benjamin Henry Latrobe, 2 vol, New Haven, Yale Univ Press, 95; auth," Accommodation and Redefinition in the Twentieth Century," in Norman Johnston, Eastern State Penitentiary: Crucible and Good Intentions, Philadelphia, Philadelphia Mus of Art, 80-99, 94; "Building a Discipline: Early Institutional Settings for Architectural Education in Philadelphia, 1804-1890," Jour of the Soc of Archit Hist, 53, 139-83, jun 94; "Rowhouse Heaven," ed Kenneth Finkel, Philadelphia Almanac and Citizens' Manual, Philadelphia, 100, 94; coauth, with George E. Thomas and Michael J. Lewis, Frank Furness: The Complete Works, NY, Princeton Archit Press, 91, expanded and corrected in rev ed, 96; assoc ed, The Correspondence and Miscellaneous Papers of Benjamin Henry Latrobe, vol 2, 1805-10, New Haven, Yale Univ Press, 86; vol 3, 1811-20, New Haven, Yale Univ Press, 88; coauth, with James F. O'Gorman, George E. Thomas and G. Holmes Perkins, Drawing Toward Building: Philadelphia Architectural Graphics 1732-1986, Philadelphia, Univ Pa Press, 15-116, 151-53, 86; asst ed, The Correspondence and Miscellaneous Papers of Benjamin Henry Latrobe, vol 1, 1784-1804, ed John C. Van Horne and Lee W. Formwalt, New Haven, Yale Univ Press, 84. **CONTACT ADDRESS** Rhys Carpenter Library A5, Bryn Mawr Col, 101 N. Merion Av., Bryn Mawr, PA 19010-2899. **EMAIL** jcohen@brynmawr.edu

COHEN, JEREMY
PERSONAL Born New York, NY, m, 1977, 1 child **DISCIPLINE** JEWISH AND MEDIEVAL HISTORY **EDUCATION** Columbia Univ, AB, 74; Jewish Theol Sem Am, BHL, 74; Cornell Univ, MA, 76, PhD(hist), 78. **CAREER** Instr Jewish hist, Cornell Univ, 77-78, asst prof, 78-81 & coordr prog Jewish studies, 78-81; Melton Chair Jewish Hist, Ohio State Univ, 82-, Fac fel, Soc for Humanities, Cornell Univ, 80-81. **HONORS AND AWARDS** Nat Jewish Bk Awd, 82, 89, 99. **MEMBERSHIPS** AHA; Medieval Acad Am; Asn Jewish Studies. **RESEARCH** Judaism and Christianity: comparative cultural history; anti-semitism; history of western religious traditions. **SELECTED PUBLICATIONS** Auth, Refertile and Increase, Fill the Earth and Master It, Cornell Univ Press, 89; auth, Kentucky, Amer Jewish Arch, Vol 0046, 94; Political Liberalism, Mich Law Rev, Vol 0092, 94; Alfonsi,Petrus and His Medieval Readers, Amer Hist Rev, Vol 0100, 95; auth, Living Letters of the Law, Univ of Calif Press, 99. **CONTACT ADDRESS** Dept Jewish Hist, Tel Aviv Univ, 69978 Tel Aviv, Israel. **EMAIL** jecohen@pgt.tau.ac.il

COHEN, JOEL ALDEN
PERSONAL Born 09/06/1938, Providence, RI, m, 1986, 2 children **DISCIPLINE** AMERICAN HISTORY **EDUCATION** Univ RI, BA, 60; Univ Conn, MA, 62, PhD, 67. **CAREER** From instr to asst prof, 65-73, assoc prof, 73-79, prof hist, Univ RI, 79-; Ed, RI Hist, 70-75. **HONORS AND AWARDS** Univ of RI Teaching in Excellence Awd, 78 **RESEARCH** Colonial America; social and political history of the American Revolution; Rhode Island history. **SELECTED PUBLICATIONS** Auth, Rhode Island Loyalism and the American Revolution, 10/68; art, Democracy in Revolutionary Rhode Island: A Statistical Analysis, 2 & 5/70; art, Molasses to Muskets-Rhode Island 1763-1775, 11/75, RI Hist; coauth, Rule, Rhode Island (play), 76. **CONTACT ADDRESS** Dept of History, Univ of Rhode Island, Kingston, RI 02881.

COHEN, JUDITH
PERSONAL Born 12/09/1949, Montreal, PQ, Canada **DISCIPLINE** MUSIC, HISTORY **EDUCATION** McGill Univ, BA, 71; Concordia Univ, BFA, 75; Univ Montreal, MA, 80, PhD, 89; Univ Toronto BEd, 96. **CAREER** Pres, Can Soc Traditional Mus, 93-97; Adj Grad Fac Mus, York Univ. **HONORS AND AWARDS** Can Coun grants; SSHRCC grants. **MEMBERSHIPS** Iberian Ethnomusicol Soc; Europ Sem Ethnomusicol; Folklore Stud Asn Can; Int Coun Traditional Mus. **SELECTED PUBLICATIONS** Auth, Sonography of Judeo-Spanish Song in Jewish Folklore & Ethnol Rev, 93; auth, Women's Role in Judeo-Spanish Song in Active Voices, 95; auth, Pero la voz es muy educada in Hommage H.V. Sophia, 96. **CONTACT ADDRESS** 751 Euclid Ave, Toronto, ON, Canada M6G 2V3.

COHEN, MARTIN AARON
PERSONAL Born 02/10/1928, Philadelphia, PA, m, 1953 **DISCIPLINE** JEWISH HISTORY AND THEOLOGY **EDUCATION** Univ Pa, BA, 46, MA, 49; Hebrew Union Col, Ohio, BHL, 55, MAHL, 57, PhD(Jewish hist), 60. **CAREER** Asst instr Roman lang, Univ Pa, 46-48, instr, 48-50; instr, Rutgers Univ, New Brunswick, 50-51; instr Jewish hist, Jewish Inst Relig, Hebrew Union Col, Ohio, 60-62; from asst prof to assoc prof, 62-69, prof Jewish Hist, Jewish Inst Relig, Hebrew Union Col, NY, 69-, Nat chaplain, Am Vets World War II & Korea, 61-62; vis lectr, Antioch Col, 61-62; vis prof, Temple Univ, 63-65 & Hunter Col, 73-74; chmn, Nat Comt Jewish-Cath Rels Anti-Defamation League, B'rith, 76- **HONORS AND AWARDS** Chadabee Awd for Outstanding Achievement, Nat Fedn Temple Brotherhoods, 76. **MEMBERSHIPS** Am Jewish Hist Soc; Cent Conf Am Rabbis; Soc Bibl Lit; Am Acad Relig; Am Soc Sephardic Studies (pres, 76-66). **RESEARCH** General Jewish history; Sephardic history; Jewish theology. **CONTACT ADDRESS** Jewish Inst of Relig, Hebrew Union Col-Jewish Inst of Religion, New York, 40 W 68th St, New York, NY 10023. **EMAIL** mcohen@huc.edu

COHEN, MIRIAM J.
PERSONAL Born 11/16/1950, Chicago, IL, m, 1974, 2 children **DISCIPLINE** HISTORY **EDUCATION** Univ of Rochester, AB, 71; Univ of Mich, MA, 73, PhD, 78. **CAREER** Instr, 77-78, Asst Prof, 78-85, Assoc Prof, 86-92, Prof, 92-, Chemn, Dept of Hist, Vassar Col, 96-99. **HONORS AND AWARDS** Phi Beta Kappa, 71; Ford Fel, ACLS, 87-88; Woodrow Wilson Nat Fel in Women's Studies, 75-76. **MEMBERSHIPS** Am Hist Asn; Org of Am Historians; Soc Sci Hist Asn; Coord Comt on Women in the Hist Profession; Berkshire Confr of Women Historians; Am soc his, women's hist, hist of the welfare st. **SELECTED PUBLICATIONS** Coauth, Politics, Unemployment and Citizenship: Unemployment Policy in England, France and the United States 1890-1950, Citizenship, Identity and Soc Hist, Cambridge Univ Press, 96; coauth, Work, School and Reform: A Comparison of Birmingham, England and Pittsburgh USA: 1900-1950, Int Labor and Working Class Hist, 91; coauth, The Politics of Gender and the Making of the Welfare State: A Comparative Perspective, J of Soc Hist, 91; auth, Workshop to Office: Two Generations of Italian Women in New York 1900-1950, Cornell Univ Press, 93; auth, Progressivism," In The Eleanor Roosevelt Encylopedia, Greenwook Press, 01. **CONTACT ADDRESS** Dept of Hist, Vassar Col, 124 Raymond Ave, Box 369, Poughkeepsie, NY 12604-0369. **EMAIL** Cohen@vassar.edu

COHEN, NAOMI WIENER
PERSONAL Born 11/13/1927, New York, NY, m, 1948, 2 children **DISCIPLINE** AMERICAN HISTORY **EDUCATION** Hunter Col, BA, 47; Sem Col Jewish Studies, BHL, 48; Columbia Univ, MA, 49, PhD(hist), 55. **CAREER** Asst prof, 62-67, assoc prof, 68-72, Prof Hist, Hunter Col, 73-. **MEMBERSHIPS** AHA; Orgn Am Historians; Am Jewish Hist Soc; Asn Jewish Studies; Conf Jewish Social Studies. **RESEARCH** History of the United States in the twentieth century; American Jewish history. **SELECTED PUBLICATIONS** Auth, Ambassador Straus in Turkey, Miss Valley Hist Rev, 3/59; An American Jew at the Paris Peace Conference of 1919, In: Essays on Jewish Life and Thought, Columbia Univ; Abrogation of Russo-American treaty of 1832, Jewish Social Studies, 1/63; A Dual Heritage, 69 & Not Free to Desist, 72, Jewish Publ Soc Am; American Jews and the Zionist Idea, 75 & contrib, An uneasy alliance, In: Bicentennial Festschrift for J R Marcus, 76, Ktav, auth, Pioneers of American Jewish defense, Am Jewish Arch, 11/77. **CONTACT ADDRESS** Dept of Hist, Hunter Col, CUNY, 695 Park Ave, New York, NY 10021.

COHEN, NORMAN SONNY
PERSONAL Born 06/30/1933, Washington, DC, m, 1957, 2 children **DISCIPLINE** UNITED STATES HISTORY **EDUCATION** George Washington Univ, AB, 58; Pa State Univ, MA, 60; Univ Calif, Berkeley, PhD(Hist), 66. **CAREER** Instr US & English Hist, Purdue Univ, 64-65; instr, Ind Univ, 65-66; asst prof, 66-70, from assoc prof to prof Hist, Occidental Col, 70-82; ret Emeritus status. **HONORS AND AWARDS** The Robert Glass Prof Am Hist. **MEMBERSHIPS** AHA; Orgn Am Historians. **RESEARCH** American Revolution; class conflict and crowd action in early America; the Confederation period. **SELECTED PUBLICATIONS** Auth, The Philadelphia election riot 1742, Pa Mag Hist & Biog, 7/68; ed, Civil Strife in America, Dryden, 72. **CONTACT ADDRESS** Dept of History, Occidental Col, 1600 Campus Rd, Los Angeles, CA 90041-3314.

COHEN, PATRICIA CLINE
PERSONAL Born 03/22/1946, Ann Arbor, MI **DISCIPLINE** HISTORY **EDUCATION** Univ Chicago, BA, 68; Univ Calif, Berkeley, PhD, 77. **CAREER** Asst prof, 77-83; assoc prof, 83-93; PROF HIST, 93-; ACTG DEAN HUM, UNIV CALIF SANTA BARBARA, 96-98. **HONORS AND AWARDS** Woodrow Wilson Fel, 68; ACLS, 80; NEH, 87; NEH, 94; UC President's Humanities Fel, 00; Mellon Sr Scholar in Residence; Am Antiquarian Soc, 01. **MEMBERSHIPS** Am Antiquarian Soc; OAH; SHEAR; Advisory Council, 01-03; Omohundro Institute of Early Am Hist and Culture, (OIEAHC), 00-02. **SELECTED PUBLICATIONS** Auth, "Statistics and the State: Changing Social Thought and the Emergence of a Quantitative Mentality in America, 1790-1820," Will & Mary Quar 3d ser, 38, 81; A Calculating People: The Spread of Numeracy in Early America, 82; "The Helen Jewett Murder: Gender, Licentiousness and Violence in Antebellum America," NWSA Jour, 90; "The Early (and soon broken) Marriage and Statistics: Boston, 1839," Hist Methods, 90; "Safety and Danger: Women on American Public Transport, 1750-1850," in Gendered Domains: Beyond the Public-Private Dichotomy in Women's His-

tory, 92; "Unregulated Youth: Masculinity and Murder in the 1830s City," Radical Hist Rev 52, 92; "Reckoning with Commerce: Numeracy in 17th and 18th Century America," in Consumption and the World of Goods, 93; "Doing Women's History at the American Antiquarian Society," Procs of the AAS 103, 93; "The Mystery of Helen Jewett: Romantic Fiction and the Eroticization of Violence," Legal Stud Forum, 93; "Ministerial Misdeeds: Bishop Onderdonk's Trial for Sexual Harassment in the 1840's," The Jour of Women's Hist 7, 95; The American Promise, 97; The Murder of Helen Jewett, 98; coauth, The American Promis, 98, 00, 02; auth, The Murder of Helen Jewett, 98; auth, A Calculating People: The spread of Numeracy in Early America, 82, 99. **CONTACT ADDRESS** Dept of Hist, Univ of California, Santa Barbara, Santa Barbara, CA 93106. **EMAIL** cohen@humanitas.ucsb.edu.

COHEN, PAUL ANDREW

PERSONAL Born 06/02/1934, New York, NY, 4 children **DISCIPLINE** CHINESE HISTORY **EDUCATION** Univ Chicago, BA, 55; Harvard Univ, MA, 57, PhD(E Asian hist), 61. **CAREER** Vis lectr hist, Univ Mich, 62-63; asst prof, Amherst Col, 63-65; assoc prof, 65-71, Edith Stix Wasserman Prof Asian Studies, Wellesley Col, 71-, Assoc, E Asian Res Ctr, Harvard Univ, 65- **MEMBERSHIPS** Asn Asian Studies; Soc Ch'ing Studies; AHA; AAUP. **RESEARCH** Nineteenth century Chinese history. **SELECTED PUBLICATIONS** Auth, China and Christianity: The Missionary Movement and the Growth of Chinese Anti-foreignism, 1860-1870, Harvard Univ, 63; Wang T'ao and incipient Chinese nationalism, J Asian Studies, 8/67; Wang T'ao's perspective on a changing world, In: Approaches to Modern Chinese History, Univ Calif, 67; contribr, Ch'ing China: Confrontation with the West, 1850-1900, In: Modern East Asia: Essays in Interpretation, Harcourt, 70; Between Tradition and Modernity: Wang T'ao and Reform in Late Ch'ing China, Harvard Univ, 74. **CONTACT ADDRESS** Dept of Hist, Wellesley Col, 106 Central St, Wellesley, MA 02181-8204.

COHEN, PAUL M.

PERSONAL Born 07/05/1955, Washington, DC, m, 1993, 2 children **DISCIPLINE** HISTORY **EDUCATION** Clark Univ, BA, 77; Univ Chicago, MA, 79; PhD, 84. **CAREER** Lecturer, Univ Chicago, 82-84; Asst Prof to Full Prof, Lawrence Univ, 85-. **HONORS AND AWARDS** Freshman Studies Teaching Awd, Lawrence Univ, 99. **MEMBERSHIPS** Am Hist Asn, Soc for French Hist Studies. **RESEARCH** Modern France: intellectual history, 1789 to present. **SELECTED PUBLICATIONS** Auth, Piety and Politics: Catholic Revival and the Generation of 1905-1914 in France, Garland Press, 87; auth, Freedom's Moment: An Essay on the French Idea of Freedom from Rousseau to Foucault, Chicago, 77. **CONTACT ADDRESS** Dept Hist, Lawrence Univ, PO Box 599, Appleton, WI 54912-0599. **EMAIL** paul.m.cohen@lawrence.edu

COHEN, RONALD DENNIS

PERSONAL Born 08/03/1940, Los Angeles, CA, d, 1965, 2 children **DISCIPLINE** HISTORY OF AMERICAN POPULAR MUSIC **EDUCATION** Univ Calif, Berkeley, BA, 62; Univ Minn, Minneapolis, MA, 64, PhD(Am colonial hist), 67. **CAREER** Asst prof Am hist, Hartwick Col, 67-69; fel, Macalester Col, 69-70; asst prof to prof hist, Ind Univ NW, 70-00. **MEMBERSHIPS** Orgn Am Historians; Hist Educ Soc (past pres and mem board of dir, 96-98); Sonneck Soc; Hist of Am Communism (pres, 00). **RESEARCH** History of education in the United States; History of popular music in the United States. **SELECTED PUBLICATIONS** Coauth, The Paradox of Progressive Education: The Gary Plan and Urban Schooling, Kennikat, 79; Gary: A Pictorial History, Donning Co, 83; auth, Children of the Mill: Schooling and Society in Gary, Indiana, 1906-1960, Ind Univ Press, 90; ed, Wasn't That a Time!: First-hand Accounts of the Folk Music Revival, Scarecrow Press, 95; co-prod, Songs for Political Action: Folk Music, Topical Songs and the American Left, 1926-1954, Bear Family Records, 96; co-ed, Moonlight in Duneland: The Illustrated Story of the Chicago South Shore and South Bend Railroad, Ind Univ Press, 98; ed, Red Dust and Broadsides: The Autobiography of Sis Cunningham and Gordon Friesen, Univ Mass Press, 99; co-ed, Folk Music and Musicians, book series, Scarecrow Press; auth and coauth of numerous articles and other publications. **CONTACT ADDRESS** Indiana Univ, Northwest, 3400 Broadway, Gary, IN 46408-1101. **EMAIL** rcohen@iunhaw1.iun.indiana.edu

COHEN, SHELDON S.

PERSONAL Born 09/29/1931, Akron, OH, m, 1965, 2 children **DISCIPLINE** HISTORY **EDUCATION** NYork Univ, PhD. **CAREER** Hist, Loyola Univ. **HONORS AND AWARDS** Scholarship prize for book on Am naval prisoners in Britain, Sons of the Am Revolution, 97. **RESEARCH** American history. **SELECTED PUBLICATIONS** Auth, Thomas Wren: Portsmouth's Patron of American Liberty, Portsmouth Papers, 91; Yankee Sailors in British Gaols; Prisoners of War at Forton and Mill, 1777-1783, Univ Delaware Press, 95. **CONTACT ADDRESS** Fine Arts Dept, Loyola Univ, Chicago, 6525 N. Sheridan Rd., Chicago, IL 60626. **EMAIL** scohen@wpo.it.luc.edu

COHEN, WARREN I.

PERSONAL Born 06/20/1934, Brooklyn, NY, m, 1988, 2 children **DISCIPLINE** HISTORY **EDUCATION** Columbia Col, AB, 55; Fletcher Schl Law & Diplomacy, AM, 56; Univ Wash, PhD, 62. **CAREER** Lectr, 62-63, Univ Calif, Riverside; asst prof to prof, 63-93, Mich St Univ; dist univ prof, 93-, Univ Maryland. **RESEARCH** Intl rels, esp Amer-E Asian. **CONTACT ADDRESS** Dept of History, Univ of Maryland, Baltimore County, Baltimore, MD 21250. **EMAIL** wcohen@umbc2.umbc.edu

COHEN, WILLIAM

PERSONAL Born 06/27/1936, Los Angeles, CA, s, 3 children **DISCIPLINE** UNITED STATES HISTORY **EDUCATION** Brooklyn Col, BA, 57; Columbia Univ, MA, 60; NYork Univ, PhD, 68. **CAREER** Lectr US hist, Hunter Col, 65-68; res assoc Negro in the cities, Ctr Urban Studies, Univ Chicago, 68-71; from Asst Prof to Assoc Prof, 71-88, prof hist, Hope Col, 88; Vis asst prof, Univ Ill, Chicago, 68-69. **HONORS AND AWARDS** Nat Endowment for Hum fel, 80-81; Francis Butler Simkins Awd for best first bk in southern hist in the past two years, Southern Hist Asn, for: At Freedom's Edge, 93. **MEMBERSHIPS** AHA; Orgn Am Historians; Southern Hist Asn. **RESEARCH** Reconstruction; agricult labor in the South; Black hist. **SELECTED PUBLICATIONS** Auth, Thomas Jefferson and the Problem of Slavery, J Am His, 12/69; Riots, Racism and Hysteria: The Response of Federal Investigative Officials to the Race Riots of 1919, Mass Rev, summer 72; Negro Involuntary Servitude in the South, 1865-1940, J Southern Hist, 2/76; Black Immobility and Free Labor: The Freedmen's Bureau and the Relocation of Black Labor, 1865-1868, Civil War Hist, 9/84; The Great Migration as a Lever for Social Change, In: Black Exodus: The Great Migration from the American South, Univ Miss Press, 91; At Freedom's Edge: Black Mobility and the Southern White Quest for Racial Control, 1861-1915, La State Univ Press, 91. **CONTACT ADDRESS** Dept Hist, Hope Col, 126 E 10th St., Holland, MI 49424-9000. **EMAIL** cohen@hope.edu

COHEN, WILLIAM B.

PERSONAL Born 05/02/1941, Jakobstad, Finland, m, 1988, 3 children **DISCIPLINE** MODERN EUROPEAN HISTORY **EDUCATION** Pomona Col, BA, 62; Stanford Univ, MA, 63; PhD, 68. **CAREER** Vis instr, Northwestern Univ, 66-67; from lectr to full prof, Ind Univ, 67-; chemn, Dept Hist, Ind Univ, 80-87. **HONORS AND AWARDS** Fulbright Fac Res Fel, 83-84; Ind Univ Teaching Dev Fel; Nat Endowment for the Humanities; Hoover Inst Res Grant; NDEA Fel. **MEMBERSHIPS** AHA; Soc Fr Hist Studies; The Fr Colonial Hist Soc; Coun for Europ Studies; Soc francaise d'histoire d'outre-mer; Soc de l'histoire de l'administration fran¤aise. **RESEARCH** French racial thought; colonial history; modern Europe; French social history. **SELECTED PUBLICATIONS** Auth, "Symbols of Power: Statues in Nineteenth Century Provincial France," Comp Studies in Soc and Hist 31 (89): 491-513; auth, "De Gaulle and Europe prior to 1958," Fr Polit and Soc 8.4 (90): 1-12; ed, De Gaulle et son siecle, Plon (Paris), 92; coauth, Western Civilization: The Continuing Experiment, Houghton Mifflin (Boston, MA), 94, 2nd ed, 98; auth, "European Nationalism," in Bonds of Affection: Americans Define their Patriotism, ed. John Bodnar (NJ: Princeton Univ Press, 95), 323-339; ed, The Transformation of Modern France--Essays in Honor of Gordon Wright, Houghton Mifflin (Boston, MA), 97; auth, "The Development of an Urban Society," in The Transformation of Modern France (Boston: Houghton Mifflin, 97), 47-65; auth, Urban Government and the Rise of the French City: Five Municipalities in the Nineteenth Century, St Martin's Press (New York), 98; auth, "The European Background," in American Philanthropy, ed. Larry Friedman, in press; auth, "France's Algerian War: a Review Essay," Contemp Europ Hist (forthcoming). **CONTACT ADDRESS** Dept of Hist, Indiana Univ, Bloomington, Bloomington, IN 47401. **EMAIL** cohenw@indiana.edu

COHN, BERNARD SAMUEL

PERSONAL Born 05/13/1928, Brooklyn, NY, m, 1950, 4 children **DISCIPLINE** ANTHROPOLOGY, HISTORY **EDUCATION** Univ Wis, BA, 49; Cornell Univ, PhD(anthrop), 54. **CAREER** Res assoc anthrop, Univ Chicago, 56-57; fel hist, Rockefeller Found, 57-59; asst prof, Univ Chicago, 59-60; assoc prof anthrop, Univ Rochester, 60-64; assoc prof, 64-67, chmn dept anthrop, 69-71, Prof Anthrop & Hist, Univ Chicago, 67-, Guggenheim fel, 64-65; vis prof, Univ Mich, 66-67; fel, Ctr Advan Study Behav Sci, 67-68; Richards lectr, Univ Va, 65; Am Coun Learned Soc-Soc Sci Res Coun fel, Comt Southern Asia, 73-74; Am Inst Indian Studies fel, 74-75; NSF grant, 75-77. **MEMBERSHIPS** Am Anthrop Asn; Asn Asian Studies; Royal Anthrop Inst; Am Soc Ethnohist; AHA. **RESEARCH** History of South Asia; comparative colonial systems; representations of authority in colonial India. **SELECTED PUBLICATIONS** Auth, The Sepoy and the Raj--The Indian Army, 1860-1940, Intl Hist Rev, Vol 0017, 95. **CONTACT ADDRESS** Dept of Anthrop, Univ of Chicago, Chicago, IL 60637.

COKER, WILLIAM SIDNEY

PERSONAL Born 07/18/1924, Des Moines, IA, m, 1944, 4 children **DISCIPLINE** LATIN AMERICAN AND UNITED STATES HISTORY **EDUCATION** Univ Okla, BA, 59, PhD(Mex hist), 65; Univ Southern Miss, MA, 62. **CAREER** From asst prof to assoc prof Latin Am hist, Univ Southern Miss, 66-69; assoc prof, 69-74, Prof Latin Am Hist, Univ W Fla, 74-. **MEMBERSHIPS** Latin Am Studies Asn; Southeastern Conf Latin Am Studies; Southern Hist Asn; Soc Hist Discoveries. **RESEARCH** Spain in the Old Southwest and the Floridas; Mexico; United States-Latin American relations. **SELECTED PUBLICATIONS** Auth introd, A Description of the English Province of Carolana, By the Spaniards called Florida . . ., Univ Presses Fla, 76; Historical Sketches of Panton, Leslie and Company, Univ WFla, 76; ed, The Military Presence on the Gulf Coast, Gulf Coast & Humanities Conf, 78; transl & ed, John Forbes' Description of the Spanish Floridas, 1804, ed, Hispanic-American Essays in Honor of Max Leon Moorhead, coauth (with G Douglas Inglish, The Spanish Censuses of Pensacola, 1784-1820 & (with Hazel P Coker), The Siege of Pensacola, 1781, in Maps with Data on Troop Strength, Military Units, Ships, Casualties, and Related Statistics, 81, Perdido Bay Press; Historical Sketches of Panton, Leslie and Company, Univ WFla, 76; ed, The Military Presence on the Gulf Coast, Gulf Coast Hist & Humanities Conf, 78. **CONTACT ADDRESS** Fac Hist, Univ of West Florida, Pensacola, FL 32504.

COLANTUONO, ANTHONY

PERSONAL Born 05/05/1958, Somerville, NJ, m, 1993, 1 child **DISCIPLINE** ART HISTORY **EDUCATION** Rutgers Univ, BA, 80; Johns Hopkins Univ, MA, 82, PhD, 87. **CAREER** Vis asst prof, 86-88, Kenyon Col; vis asst prof, 88-89, Wake Forest Univ; asst prof, 89-90, Vanderbilt Univ; assoc prof, 90-, Univ Maryland Col. **HONORS AND AWARDS** Recipient of the 2-year Kress "Rome Prize" fel at the Am Academy in Rome; grant from the NEH. **RESEARCH** 16th & 17th century Italian, French & Spanish art. **SELECTED PUBLICATIONS** Auth, The Tender Infant 'Invenzione' and 'Figura' in the Art of Poussin, PhD. Dissertation: The Johns Hopkins Univ, 86; auth, "Titian's Tender Infants: On the Imitation of Venetian Paianting in Baroque Rome," I Tatti Studies 3, (89): 207-234; auth, "Dies Alcyoniae: The Invention of Bellini's Feast of the Gods," The Art Bulletin 73, (91): 237-256; auth, "Invention and Caprice in an Iconographical Programme by G. B. Passeri," Storia dell'arte 87, (96): 188-203; auth, "Jennifer Montague, The Expression of the Passions: the Origin and Influence of Charles Le Brun's Conference sur l'expression generale et particuliere, Yale Univ Press, The Art Bulletin 78, (96): 355-358; auth, "Interpreter Poussin: metaphore, similarite et maniera Magnifica," in Acts of the International Colloquium, Musee du Louvre, Paris 1994, ed. A. Merot, (Paris, Reunion des Musees Nationaux, 96): 649-665; auth, Guido Reni's 'The Abduction of Helen': The Politis and Rhetoric of Painting in Seveenth-Century Europe, New York, Cambridge Univ Press, 97; auth, "The Mute Diplomat: Theorizing the Role of Images in Seventeenth-Century Political Negotiations," in The Diplomacy of Art-Artistic Creation and Politics in Seicento Italy, ed. Elizabeth Cropper, (Villa Spelman Colloquia, 7), (Milan, Nuova Alfa Editoriale, 00): 51-76; auth, "Poussin's Osservazioni sophra la pittura: Notes or Aphorism?" Studi Secenteschi, Biblioteca dell'Archivum Romanicum 41, (00): 285-311; auth, "Commemorating Poussin: reception and interpretation of the artist, Cambridge Univ Press, 1999," Burlington Magazine 142, (00): 572. **CONTACT ADDRESS** Dept of Art History & Archaeology, Univ of Maryland, Col Park, Art-Sociology Bldg, College Park, MD 20742-1335. **EMAIL** ac65@umail.umd.edu

COLBERT, THOMAS BURNELL

PERSONAL Born 09/23/1947, Carroll, IA, m, 1978, 1 child **DISCIPLINE** HISTORY **EDUCATION** Univ Iowa, BA, 69, MA, 75; Oklahoma St Univ, PhD, 82. **CAREER** Vis instr, 79-80, Huron Col, SD; tchng asst, 75-79, 80-81, Oklahoma St Univ; instr, 81-87, chmn, social sci dept, 88-92, chmn social sci & physical ed, 92-96, prof, 92-, Marshalltown Comm Col. **RESEARCH** Amer Indian hist; political hist; 19th century rural western & midwestern hist. **CONTACT ADDRESS** 3700 S Center, Marshalltown, IA 50158. **EMAIL** tcolbert@iavalley.cc.ia.us

COLBURN, DAVID RICHARD

PERSONAL Born 09/29/1942, Providence, RI, m, 1966, 3 children **DISCIPLINE** US HISTORY **EDUCATION** Providence Col, AB, 64, MA, 65; Univ NC, PhD(hist), 71. **CAREER** Asst prof hist, East Carolina Univ, 71-72; Assoc Prof Hist, Univ Fla, 72-, Consult, Pa Ethnic Heritage Proj, 76-77; ed consult, Fla Hist Quart, 76- **HONORS AND AWARDS** Teacher of the Year, Univ Col, Univ Fla, 77; Social Sciences Publication Awd, Dept Social Sci, Univ Fla, 77. **MEMBERSHIPS** Southern Hist Asn; Orgn Am Historians; Am Acad Polit Sci. **RESEARCH** Twentieth century American history; the Civil Rights Movement; American politics in the twentieth century. **SELECTED PUBLICATIONS** Auth, Crusaders in the Courts--How a Dedicated Band of Lawyers Fought for the Civil-Rights Revolution, Rev(s) Amer Hist, Vol 0023, 95; Inside Agitators--White Southerners in the Civil-Rights-Movement, Rev(s) Amer Hist, Vol 0023, 95; Race in America--The Struggle for Equality, Rev(s) Amer Hist, Vol 0023, 95; The Civil-Rights Era--Origins and Development of National Policy, 1960-1972, Jour Amer Ethnic Hist, Vol 0012, 93; New Directions in Civil-Rights Studies, Jour So Hist, Vol 0059, 93; The Color of Their Skin--Education and Race in Richmond, Virginia, 1954-89, Jour Amer Hist, Vol 0080, 93. **CONTACT ADDRESS** Office of the

Provost, Univ of Florida, PO Box 113175, Gainesville, FL 32611-3175.

COLBY-HALL, ALICE MARY

PERSONAL Born 02/25/1932, Portland, ME, w, 1976, 3 children **DISCIPLINE** MEDIEVAL FRENCH LITERATURE **EDUCATION** Colby Col, BA, 53; Middlebury Col, MA, 54; Columbia Univ, PhD, 62. **CAREER** Teacher high sch, Maine, 54-55; teacher French, Gould Acad, Bethel, Maine, 55-57; lectr, Columbia Univ, 59-60; from instr to assoc prof Romance Studies, 62-75, Prof Romance Studies, Cornell Univ, 75-97; prof emer, 97-. **HONORS AND AWARDS** Fulbright grant, 53-54; NEH Fel, 84-85; recipient, Medaille des Amis d'Orange, 85; Chevalier des Arts et Lettres, French Govt, 97. **MEMBERSHIPS** Mediaeval Acad Am; MLA; Soc Rencesvals; Int Arthurian Soc; Acad de Vaucluse; Les Amis d'Orange; Soc Guilhem IX; Asn Internationale d'Etudes Occitanes. **RESEARCH** Chretien de Troyes; the style of medieval French literary texts; William cycle epics. **SELECTED PUBLICATIONS** Auth, The Portrait in 12th Century French Literature: An Example of the Stylistic Originality of Chretien de Troyes, Droz, 65; In Search of the Lost Epics of the Lower Rhone Valley, Olifant, 80/81; Frustration and Fulfillment: The Double Ending of the Bel Inconnu, Yale Fr Studies, 84; William of Orange in the Canso de la Crosada, Magister Regis: Studies in Honor of Robert Earl Kaske, 86; L'Heraldique au service de la linguistique: le cas du cor nier de Guillaume, Au carrefour des routes d'Europe: la chanson de geste, 87; Guillaume d' Orange sur un nouveau sceau medieval de l'abbaye de Saint-Guilhem-le-Desert, Olifant, 90; Guillaume d' Orange, l'abbaye de Gellone et la vache pie de Chateauneuf-de-Gadagne, Etudes sur l' Herault, 93. **CONTACT ADDRESS** Dept of Romance Studies, Cornell Univ, Morrill Hall, Ithaca, NY 14853-4701. **EMAIL** amc12@cornell.edu

COLE, BRUCE

PERSONAL Born 08/02/1938, Cleveland, OH, m, 1962, 2 children **DISCIPLINE** ART HISTORY **EDUCATION** Western Reserve Univ, BA, 62; Oberlin Col, MA, 64; Bryn Mawr Col, PhD(art hist), 69. **CAREER** Asst prof art hist, Univ Rochester, 69-73; assoc prof, 73-77, prof art hist, Ind Univ, 77-, distinguished prof, 88; Nat Endowment for Humanities fel art hist, 72; Guggenheim Foundation fel, 76; Am Coun Learned Soc fel, 81. **RESEARCH** Italian Renaissance. **SELECTED PUBLICATIONS** Auth, Old and new in the early Trecento, Klara Steinweg-In Memoriam, 73; Some Sinopie by Taddeo Gaddi Reconsidered, Pantheon, 76; Giotto and Florentine Painting 1280-1375, Harper & Row, 76; Agnolo Gaddi, Oxford Univ, 77; Italian Maiolica from Midwestern Collections, Ind Univ Art Mus, 77; Musaccio and the Art of Early Renaissance Florence, Ind Univ Press, 80; Sienese Painting From Its Origins to the Fifteenth Century, 80 & The Renaissance Artist at Work, 82, Harper & Row; Pieio deua Francesca, Harper Colllins, 92; Siotto, The Scrovegni Chapel, Brazilier, 93; Studies in de Histoy of Italian Art, Pindar Press, 96; Titian and Venetian Painting, Westview Press, 98. **CONTACT ADDRESS** Hist of Art Dept, Indiana Univ, Bloomington, 1201 E 7th St, Fine Arts 132, Bloomington, IN 47405. **EMAIL** coleb@indiana.edu

COLE, DONALD BARNARD

PERSONAL Born 03/31/1922, Lawrence, MA, m, 1949, 4 children **DISCIPLINE** HISTORY **EDUCATION** Harvard Univ, AB, 43, AM, 47, PhD, 57. **CAREER** Instr hist, 47-71, chmn dept, 61-66, dean, 75-80, Prof Hist, Phillips Exeter Acad, 71-, Consult, US Off Educ, 65-66; vis prof, Univ Calif, Los Angeles, 67-78; mem vis comt hist, Harvard Univ, 68-71; Am Coun Learned Soc grant-in-aid, 70-71; mem adv comt, Papers of Martin Van Buren, 71-; mem admin bd, Papers of Andrew Jackson, 72- **HONORS AND AWARDS** Yale Sec Sch Teaching Awd, 65; Kidger Awd, New Eng Hist Teachers Asn, 68. **MEMBERSHIPS** AHA; Orgn Am Historians. **RESEARCH** American immigration history; Jackson period in American history; biography of Martin Van Buren. **SELECTED PUBLICATIONS** Auth, The Jacksonian Promise--America, 1815-1840, Jour Amer Hist, Vol 0083, 96; Clinton,Dewitt and the Rise of the Peoples Men, Jour Early Republic, Vol 0017, 97. **CONTACT ADDRESS** Phillips Exeter Acad, Tan Lane, Exeter, NH 03833.

COLE, JOHN R.

PERSONAL Born 10/09/1941, Worcester, MA, m, 1978, 4 children **DISCIPLINE** HISTORY **EDUCATION** Haverford Univ, BA, 63; Harvard Univ, PhD, 70. **CAREER** Prof, Bates Col, 63-. **MEMBERSHIPS** Asn of Ancient Hist; Soc for French Hist Studies; Montsigne Studies Asn; Pascal Studies Asn. **SELECTED PUBLICATIONS** Auth, The Youthful Rebellion and Olympian Dreams of Rene Descartes, 92; auth, Pascal, The Man and His Two Loves, 95. **CONTACT ADDRESS** Dept Hist, Bates Col, 146 Wood St, Lewiston, ME 04240-6017.

COLE, JUAN R.

PERSONAL Born 10/23/1952, Albuquerque, NM, m, 1982, 1 child **DISCIPLINE** HISTORY **EDUCATION** Northwestern Univ, BA, 75; Am Univ in Cairo, MA, 78; Univ Calif, PhD, 84. **CAREER** From Asst Prof to Prof, Univ of Mich, 84-. **HONORS AND AWARDS** Fulbright Fel, Islamic Civilization Egypt, 85-86; NEH Fel, 91; Res Excellence Awd, Col of LSA, 97. **MEMBERSHIPS** Am Hist Asn, Asn for Asian Studies, Middle East Studies Asn, Am Inst for Pakistan Studies, Soc for Iranian Studies, Soc for the Sci Study of Relig. **RESEARCH** Modern Egypt, modern Iran, modern South Asia, Islam, Shi'ism, Bahai. **SELECTED PUBLICATIONS** Auth, Colonialism and Revolution in the Middle East, Princeton Pr, 83; auth, Roots of North Indian Shi'ism in Iran and Iraq, Univ Calif Pr, 89; auth, Modernity and the Millennium, Columbia UP, 98. **CONTACT ADDRESS** Dept Hist, Univ of Michigan, Ann Arbor, 435 S State St, 1029 Angell Hall, Ann Arbor, MI 48109-1003. **EMAIL** jrcole@umich.edu

COLE, MARY HILL

PERSONAL Born 07/24/1957, Richmond, VA **DISCIPLINE** HISTORY **EDUCATION** James Madison Univ, BA, 79; Univ Va, MA, 82, PhD, 85. **CAREER** Asst prof hist, Wilson Col, 85-87; asst to prof, Mary Baldwin Col, 87-. **HONORS AND AWARDS** Outstanding Teach Awd, Mary Baldwin Col, 89; Alpha Lambda Delta, Freshman Teach Awd, 92, 93; NEH Summer Inst, 91; Omicron Delta Kappa, 94; phi kappa phi, 79; governor's fel, univ va, 80,79. **MEMBERSHIPS** Am Hist Asn, Folger Shakespeare Libr. **RESEARCH** 16th century English political hist. **SELECTED PUBLICATIONS** Auth, "James II and the Royal Bounty," in Essays in History XXVII, 83; "The Ceremonial Dialogue of Elizabeth and her Civic Hosts," in Ceremony and Text in the Renaissance, 96; auth, The Portable Queen: Elizabeth I and the Politics of Ceremony. **CONTACT ADDRESS** History Dept, Mary Baldwin Col, Staunton, VA 24401. **EMAIL** mhcole@mbc.edu

COLE, RICHARD G.

PERSONAL Born 11/24/1934, Sioux Falls, SD, m, 1962, 4 children **DISCIPLINE** EUROPEAN HISTORY **EDUCATION** Eastern NMex Univ, BA, 56; Univ of Iowa, MA, 58; Ohio State Univ, PhD, 63. **CAREER** Instr hist, Ohio State Univ, 63-64; from asst prof to assoc prof, 64-74, actg chmn dept, 73-74, prof hist, Luther Col, Iowa, 74-, Dept Head, 86-98. **HONORS AND AWARDS** Fel inst res, Univ Wis, 66-67; Deutsche Forschungsgemeinschaft award to participate in reformation pamphlet conference, Tuebingen, Ger, 80; Fulbright Summer Seminar Awd, Bonn and Berlin, Germany, 88; named Fel of Early Mod Studies, Sixteenth-Century Studies Coun, 98. **MEMBERSHIPS** AHA; Am Soc Reformation Res. **RESEARCH** Renaissance and reformation; modern Europe; sixteenth century Germany. **SELECTED PUBLICATIONS** Auth, European attitudes toward non-western peoples in sixteenth century French and German pamphlets, in Yearbook Am Philos Soc, 70; Sixteenth century travel books as a source of European attitudes toward non-white and non-western culture, Proc Am Philos Soc, 2/72; Dynamics of printing in the sixteenth century, in The Social History of the Reformation, Ohio State Univ, 73; The reformation in print, Arch Reformation Hist, 75; The Reformation Pamphlet and Communication Processes, In: Flugschriften als Massenmedium der Reformationzeit, Stuttgart: Klett-Cota, 81; Pamphlet Woodcuts in the Communication Processes of Reformation Germany, in Pietas et Societas: New Trends in Reformation Social History, Forum Press, 85; Humanists and Professors Encounter the New World in the Age of Discovery, in Platte Valley Rev, 92; The Interface of Academic and Popular Medicine in the Sixteenth Century, in J Popular Culture, Spring 93. **CONTACT ADDRESS** Dept of Hist, Luther Col, 700 College Dr, Decorah, IA 52101-1045. **EMAIL** coler@martin.luther.edu

COLE, ROBERT

PERSONAL Born 08/24/1939, Harper, KS, m, 1990, 1 child **DISCIPLINE** HISTORY **EDUCATION** Ottawa Univ, BA; Kans State Univ, MA; Claremont Grad Univ, PhD. **CAREER** Prof of Hist, Utah State Univ, 70-. **HONORS AND AWARDS** Hon Lecturer Awd, USU, 92, 94; HAST Col Res of the Yr, 93; elected Fellow of Royal Hist Soc, 94. **MEMBERSHIPS** N Am Conf on Brit Stud; West Conf on Brit Stud (co-founder & 1st pres). **RESEARCH** Modern Brit propaganda in war; film hist. **SELECTED PUBLICATIONS** Auth, A.J.P. Taylor: The Traitor Within the Gates, Macmillan, 93; auth, Traveller's History of Paris, Windrush, 2nd ed, 94; auth, Good Relations: Irish Neutrality and the Propaganda of John Betjeman, 1941-1943, Eire-Ireland, vol 30, no 4, 96. **CONTACT ADDRESS** Dept of Hist, Utah State Univ, Logan, UT 84322-0710. **EMAIL** rcole@hass.usu.edu

COLE, TERRENCE M.

DISCIPLINE TWENTIETH CENTURY AMERICA **EDUCATION** Univ WA, PhD, 83. **CAREER** Univ Alaska **HONORS AND AWARDS** Usibelli Awd. **SELECTED PUBLICATIONS** Auth,The Cornerstone on College Hill, Univ Alaska Press, 94; Crooked Past: The History of A Frontier Mining Camp, Univ Alaska Press 91; Nome: City of the Golden Beaches, Alaska Geog Soc, 84. **CONTACT ADDRESS** Univ of Alaska, Fairbanks, PO Box 757480, Fairbanks, AK 99775-7480. **EMAIL** fftmc@aurora.alaska.edu

COLE, THOMAS RICHARD

PERSONAL Born 03/15/1949, New Haven, CT, m, 1972, 2 children **DISCIPLINE** AMERICAN HISTORY **EDUCATION** Yale Univ, BA, 71; Wesleyan Univ, MA, 75; Univ Rochester, PhD(hist), 81. **CAREER** prof and grad prog dir, 92-. **HONORS AND AWARDS** Honors in Philos, Yale Univ, 71; Rush Rhees Fel, Univ Rochester, 75-78; Newberry Libr Fel Summer Workshop in Family and Community Hist, 76; Nat Sci Found Grant for Supporting Doctoral Dissertation Res, 78; NIMH Predoctoral Fel; The Gerontological Soc of Am; Journey of Life, nominated for Pulitizer Prize, 92; McGovern Awd for Humanities in Med, Yale Univ Sch of Med, 97; nominee, Nat Humanities Medal, Tex Coun for the Humanities, 98; Bronze Apple Awd Nat Educ Media Assn, 98; CINE Golden Eagle Awd for "The Strange Demise of Jim Crow," 98. **MEMBERSHIPS** Gerontological Soc of Am; Orgn of Am Historians; Am Soc for Bioethics and Humanities; Int Soc for the Hist of Medicine; Int Documentary Assn. **RESEARCH** Aging and culture. **SELECTED PUBLICATIONS** Coauth, "The Meaning of Aging and the Future of Social Security," Generations, 23:4 (99-00), 72-76; co-ed, The Oxford Book of Aging, Oxford Univ Press, 94; auth, No Color is My Kind: The Life of Eldrewey Stearns and the Integration of Houston, Tex, Univ Tex Press, 97; creator and exec producer, "The Strange Demise of Jim Crow: How Houston Desegregated Its Public Accommodations, 1959-1963," distributed by California Newsreel, 97; co-edu, Handbook of the Humanities and Aging, Springer Publ Co, 99; coauth, "Visible Lives: Life Stories and Ritual in American Nursing Homes," in Caring for the Elderly in Japan and the US: Practices and Policies, Routledge, 00. **CONTACT ADDRESS** Inst for Med Humanities, Univ of Texas, Med Branch at Galveston, 301 University Blvd, 2.210 Ashbel Smith Bldg., Galveston, TX 77555-1311. **EMAIL** tcole@utmb.edu

COLE, WAYNE S.

PERSONAL Born 11/11/1922, Manning, IA, m, 1950, 1 child **DISCIPLINE** AMERICAN DIPLOMATIC HISTORY **EDUCATION** Iowa State Teachers Col, BA, 46; Univ Wisc, MS, 48; PhD(hist), 51. **CAREER** Instr social studies, Bedford High Sch, Iowa, 46-47; from instr to asst prof hist, Univ Ark, 50-54; asst prof, Iowa State Col, 54-56; from assoc prof to prof, Iowa State Univ, 56-65; vis asst prof, Iowas State Col, 52-53; Prof, 65-92, prof emer, Hist, Univ Md, College Park, 92- . **HONORS AND AWARDS** Fulbright Sect Lectr, Univ Kelle, 62-63; Woodrow Wilson Fel, 73; NEH Fel, 78-79; dist schlr tchr, Univ Md, 89-90; SHAFR Graebner Awd, 94. **MEMBERSHIPS** Soc Historians Am; Foreign Rels (pres, 73). **RESEARCH** History of American foreign relations; American isolationism; Roosevelt and the isolationists; Norway and U.S. **SELECTED PUBLICATIONS** Auth, America First: Battle Against Intervention, 1940-1941, Univ Wisc, 52; auth, American Entry into World Warr II: A historiographical appraisal, Miss Val Hist Rev, 57; auth, Senator Gerald P. Nye and American Foreign Relations, Univ Minn, 62; An Interpretive History of American Foreign Relations, Dorsey, 68, rev ed, 74; auth, Charles A. Lindbergh and the Battle Against American Intervention in World War II, Harcourt Brace Jovanovich, 74; auth, Roosevelt and the Isolationists, Univ Neb Pr, 83; auth, Norway and the United States, ISU Pr, 89; auth, Determinism and the American Foreign Relations During the Franklin D. Roosevelt Era, Univ Pr of Amer, 95. **CONTACT ADDRESS** Dept of Hist, Univ of Maryland, Col Park, College Park, MD 20742. **EMAIL** wc14@umail.umd.edu

COLEMAN, JOHN E.

PERSONAL Born 04/23/1940, Vancouver, BC, Canada **DISCIPLINE** CLASSICAL ARCHEOLOGY, GREEK **EDUCATION** Univ BC, BA, 61; Univ Cincinnati, PhD(classics), 67. **CAREER** Asst prof classics, Univ Colo, 67-69; lectr classical archaeol, Bryn Mawr Col, 69-70; asst prof, 70-74, Assoc Prof Classics, Cornell Univ, 74-, prof 81-, Dir, Excavations at Elean Pylos, Greece, 68 & Cornell Excavations at Alambra, Cyprus, 76-84; Haki and East Lokris Proj, Greece, 98-. **MEMBERSHIPS** Archaeol Inst Am; Am Sch Class Studies Athens. **RESEARCH** Classical archaeology; Aegean archaeology; Cypriot archaeology. **SELECTED PUBLICATIONS** Auth, Alambra, 96; auth, "Haki: the 1992-1994 Field Seasons," Hesperia 68 (99). **CONTACT ADDRESS** Dept of Classics, Cornell Univ, 120-A Goldwin Smith, Ithaca, NY 14853-0001. **EMAIL** jec13@cornell.edu

COLEMAN, RONALD GERALD

PERSONAL Born 04/03/1944, San Francisco, CA, s **DISCIPLINE** HISTORY **EDUCATION** Univ of UT, BS Sociology 1966, PhD History 1980; CA State Univ Sacramento, CA teaching certificate secondary 1968, MA Social Science 1973. **CAREER** General Mills Inc, grocery sales rep 1966-67; San Francisco Unified Sch Dist, faculty teacher social studies phys ed 1968-70; Sacramento City Coll, faculty instructor social science 1970-73; Univ of UT, dir of Afro-Amer studies 1981-, coord of ethnic studies 1984-; CA State Univ Haywood, visiting prof Afro-Amer studies 1981; Univ of UT, prof of history, Diversity and Faculty Development, associate vice president 1989-. **HONORS AND AWARDS** Phi Kappa Phi 1979; Merit Society for Distinguished Alumni George Washington High School; University of Utah, Hatch Price Awd for Distinguished Teaching, 1990. **MEMBERSHIPS** Consultant UT State Cultural Awareness Training Prog 1974-76; consultant UT State Bd of Educ 1981; consultant UT State Historical Soc 1981; mem UT Endowment for the Humanities 1982-88; commissioner Salt Lake City Civil Service Comm 1983-; chairperson Salt Lake City Branch NAACP Educ Comm 1984-85; mem UT Chapter American Civil Liberties Union 1989-; mem Salt Lake Sports

Advisory Board 1990-. **SELECTED PUBLICATIONS** "Blacks in Pioneer Utah 1847-1869" UOMOJA Scholar/Journal of Black Studies 1979; "Blacks in Utah History: An Unknown Legacy" The Peoples of Utah 1976; "The Buffalo Soldiers, Guardians of the Uintah Frontier 1886-1901" Utah Historical Quarterly 1979; Martin Luther King Jr: Apostle of Social Justice, Peace and Love pamphlet printed for Univ of Utah Martin Luther King Jr Comm 1985 **CONTACT ADDRESS** Professor of History, Univ of Utah, Salt Lake City, UT 84112.

COLETTA, PAOLO E.
PERSONAL Born 02/03/1916, Plainfield, NJ, m, 1940, 3 children **DISCIPLINE** UNITED STATES HISTORY **EDUCATION** Univ Mo, BS, 38, MA, 39, PhD(Brit hist), 42. **CAREER** Instr Am hist, Univ Mo, 40-42 & SDak State Col, 46; instr soc sci, Stephens Col, 42-43 & Univ Louisville, 46; from instr to asst prof hist, 46-55, assoc prof, 58-63, Prof Hist, US Naval Acad, 63-, Fulbright sr lectr Am hist, Univ Genoa, 71. **MEMBERSHIPS** AHA; Orgn Am Historians: Am Mil Inst; Nav Inst; Southern Hist Asn. **RESEARCH** Recent United States history; naval history. **SELECTED PUBLICATIONS** Auth, Launching the Doolittle Raid on Japan, April 18, 1942, Pacific Hist Rev, Vol 0062, 93; A Selectively Annotated-Bibliography of Naval Power in the American-Civil-War, Civil War Hist, Vol 0042, 96; Moffet, William,A. and His Disastrous Dirigibles--The Rear Admiral and His Promotion of Nonrigid Airships, Amer Neptune, Vol 0056, 96; Macarthur Ultra Codebreaking and the War Against Japan, 1942-1945, Pacific Hist Rev, Vol 0063, 94. **CONTACT ADDRESS** Dept of Hist, United States Naval Acad, Annapolis, MD 21402.

COLISH, MARCIA L.
PERSONAL Born 07/27/1937, Brooklyn, NY **DISCIPLINE** HISTORY **EDUCATION** Smith Col, BA, 58; Yale Univ, MA, 59; PhD, 65. **CAREER** Instr, Skidmore Col, 62-63; instr to prof, Oberlin Col, 63-; Frederick B Artz Prof, 85-. **HONORS AND AWARDS** Phi Beta Kappa; Hazel Edgerly Prize, 58; Samuel S Fel Fel, 61-62; ACLS Grants, 74, 87; Guggenheim Fel, 89-90; Wilbury Cross Medal, Yale Grad School Alumni Assoc; 93; NEH Sem, 93; Fel, Woodrow Wilson Center, 94-95; Rockefeller Found Writing Residency, 95; Haskins Medal, 98; Marianist Awd, Univ of Dayton, 00; Etienne Gilson Lectr, Pontifical Inst of Medieval Studies, 00. **MEMBERSHIPS** AHA; Medieval Acad of Am; Renaissance Soc of Am; AAUP; Ohio Humanities Coun; Medieval Assoc of the Midwest. **SELECTED PUBLICATIONS** Auth, The Mirror of Language: A Study in the Medieval Theory of Knowledge, Yale Univ Pr, (New Haven), 68; auth, "Peter of Bruys, Henry of Lausanne, and the Facade of St Gilles", Traditio 28, (72): 451-460; auth, "The Roman Law of Persons and Roman History: A Case for an Interdisciplinary Approach", Am J of Jurisprudence 19, 974): 112-27; auth, "Medieval Allegory: A Historiographical Consideration", Clio 4 (75): 341-3561; auth, "Sir Thomas Aquinas in Historical Perspective: The Modern Period, Church Hist 44 (75): 433-49; auth, "The Stoic Tradition from Antiquity to the Early Middle Ages, I: Stoicism in Classical Latin Literature", Studies in the History of Christian Thought 34, ed Heiko A Oberman, Brill (Leiden), 85; auth, "The Stoic Tradition from Antiquity to the Early Middle Ages, II: Stoicism in Classical Latin Literature", Studies in the History of Christian Thought 34, ed Heiko A Oberman, Brill (Leiden), 85; auth, "Peter Lombard", Brill's Studies in Intellectual History, ed A.J. Vanderjagt, E.J. Brill (Leiden), 94; auth, Medieval Foundations of the Western Intellectual Tradition, 400-1400, Yale Intellectual History of the West, Yale Univ Pr, (New Haven/London), 97; auth, "Remapping Scholasticism", Etienne Gilson Series 21, Pontifical Inst of Mediaeval Studies, (Toronto), 00. **CONTACT ADDRESS** Dept Hist, Oberlin Col, Oberlin, OH 44074. **EMAIL** marcia.colish@oberlin.edu

COLL, BLANCHE D.
PERSONAL Born 12/26/1916, Baltimore, MD **DISCIPLINE** AMERICAN AND SOCIAL HISTORY **EDUCATION** Johns Hopkins Univ, BS, 43, MA, 48. **CAREER** Historian Labor hist, Hist Div, US Maritime Comn, 46-48 & Am mil hist, Engr Hist Div, US Dept Army, 48-60; historian social welfare hist, Social & Rehab Serv, 64-77, chief, planning & eval br, Off Child Support Enforcement, Hew, 77-79; Res & Writing, 79- **HONORS AND AWARDS** Sustained Superior Performance Awd, US Army Corps Engrs, 59. **MEMBERSHIPS** Orgn Am Historians; Soc Hist Fed Govt. **RESEARCH** Social Welfare; labor and military history. **SELECTED PUBLICATIONS** Auth, Improving Poor People--The Welfare-State, the Underclass, and Urban-Schools as History, Jour Econ Hist, Vol 0056, 96. **CONTACT ADDRESS** Dept of Health & Human Services, 314 Massachusetts Ave NE, Washington, DC 20002.

COLL-TELLECHA, REYES
PERSONAL Born 11/17/1960, Spain, s **DISCIPLINE** HISPANIC STUDIES **EDUCATION** Univ Mass, PhD. **CAREER** Vis Prof, Wellesley Col; vis prof Wash Univ; assoc prof, Univ of Mass. **MEMBERSHIPS** Amnesty Intl. **RESEARCH** Literature and Society. **SELECTED PUBLICATIONS** Ed, La Vida de Lazarillo de Tormes, Akal (Madrid, Spain), 97. **CONTACT ADDRESS** Dept Hisp Studies, Univ of Massachusetts, Boston, 100 Morrissey Blvd, Dorcherster, MA 02125-3300.

COLLIE, MICHAEL J.
PERSONAL Born 08/08/1929, Eastbourne, England **DISCIPLINE** ENGLISH, HISTORY OF SCIENCE **EDUCATION** St Catharine's Col, Cambridge Univ, MA, 56. **CAREER** Asst prof, Univ Man, 57; lectr, Univ Exeter, 61; assoc prof, Mt Allison Univ, 62; prof Eng, 65-90, dept ch, 67-69, dean grad stud, 69-73, Prof Emer, York Univ, 90-. **MEMBERSHIPS** Int Asn Univ Profs Eng; Mod Hum Res Asn; Bibliog Soc; Bibliog Soc Am; Asn Can Univ Tchrs Eng (pres, 68-69); Can Bibliog Soc; Soc Hist Sci; Geol Soc Am; Geol Soc London; Edinburgh Bibliog Soc. **SELECTED PUBLICATIONS** Auth, George Borrow Eccentric, 82; auth, George Borrow: A Bibliographical Study, 84; auth, George Gissing: A Bibliographical Study, 85; auth, Henry Maudsley: Victorian Psychiatrist, 88; auth, Huxley at Work, 91; auth, Murchison in Moray: the Geologist on Home Ground, 95; auth, George Gordon: A Catalogue of His Scientific Correspondence, 96. **CONTACT ADDRESS** Winters Col, York Univ, 4700 Keele St, Toronto, ON, Canada M3J 1P3.

COLLIER, CHRISTOPHER
PERSONAL Born 01/29/1930, New York, NY, m, 1969, 3 children **DISCIPLINE** HISTORY **EDUCATION** Clark Univ, BA, 51; Columbia Univ, MA, 55; PhD, 64. **CAREER** From instr to prof, Univ of Bridgport, 61-84; prof, Univ of Conn, 84-; Conn State Historian, 85-. **HONORS AND AWARDS** Christopher Awd, Jane Addams Peace Prize, Newbery Honor. **MEMBERSHIPS** AHA, OAH, AAS, Author's Guild. **RESEARCH** Early American History, U.S. Constitutional History, the History of Connecticut. **SELECTED PUBLICATIONS** Auth, Roger Sherman's Connecticut: Yankee Politics and the American Revolution, Wesleyan Univ Press (Middletown, CT), 71; auth, My Brother Sam is Dead, Four Winds, 74; auth, The Literature of Connecticut History, Conn Humanities Coun (Middletown, CT), 82; auth, Decision in Philadelphia: The Constitutional Convention of 1787, Random House (New York, NY), 85 and Ballantine, 86; auth, The Drama of American History (22 Vols), Marshall Cavandish (Tarry town, NY), 98-00. **CONTACT ADDRESS** Dept Hist, Univ of Connecticut, Storrs, 241 Glenbrook Rd, Storrs, CT 06269-9005.

COLLIER-THOMAS, BETTYE
PERSONAL Born 02/18/1941, Macon, GA, m, 1963 **DISCIPLINE** HISTORY **EDUCATION** Allen Univ, BA, 63; Atlanta Univ, MA, 66; George Wash Univ, 74. **CAREER** Instr, 66-69, Dir of Hon, 69-71, Howard Univ; lectr, 71-74, asst prof, 74-76, Univ Maryland; spec consul, 77-81, Natl Endowment for Hum; founding exec dir, 77-89, Bethune Mus & Archives; assoc prof, 89-97, prof, 98-, dir, Ctr for African Am Hist & Cult, 89-97, Temple Univ. **HONORS AND AWARDS** Ford Found Fel; Southern Fel Fund Grant; Atlanta Univ Pres Scholar; Mark Schaeffer Awd Hist; Am Asn of Univ Women's Awd Scholar; Delta Sigma Theta Awd Scholar; Alpha Kappa Mu Natl Honor Soc; Howard Univ Res Grant; Who's Who in Am Col and Univ; Who's Who in Black Am; Lilly Endow multi-yr grant; Septima Poinsett Clark Awd, Alpha Kappa Alpha Sorority, 98; Mary McLeod Bethune Awd, Phil Coun of Natl Council of Negro Women, 94; Conservation Svc Awd, U S Dept of Interior, 94; Carlton Qualey Awd, best article, J of Am Ethnic Hist, Immigration Hist Soc, 95; Black Women in Sisterhood for Action, 95 Dist Black Women. **MEMBERSHIPS** AHA; Asn for Stud of Afro-AM Hist & Cult; Org of Am Hist; Asn of Black Women Hist; Southern Hist Asn. **RESEARCH** Amer soc & intel hist; African Am hist; women; relig & popular cult. **SELECTED PUBLICATIONS** Coauth, "Race, Class and Color: The African American Discourse on Identity," Journal of American Ethnic Hist, vol. 14, no. 1, (94): 5-31; co-ed, African American Women and the Vote, 1837-1965, Univ of Mass, 97; ed, A Treasury of African American Christmas Stories, vols. I and II, Henry Holt, 97, 99; auth, Daughters of Thunder: Black Women Preachers and Their Sermons, 1850-1979, Jossey Bass Publishers, 97; coauth, My Soul Is A Witness: A Chronology of the Civil Rights Era, 1954-1965, Henry Holt, 00. **CONTACT ADDRESS** Ctr for Afro-Am Hist & Cult, Temple Univ, 13th St and Cecil B Moore Ave, Philadelphia, PA 19122. **EMAIL** bcollier@astro.temple.edu

COLLIN, RICHARD H.
PERSONAL Born 03/04/1932, Philadelphia, PA, m, 1969 **DISCIPLINE** CULTURAL AND RECENT AMERICAN HISTORY **EDUCATION** Kenyon Col, AB, 54; NYork Univ, PhD(Am civilization), 66. **CAREER** Asst prof, 66-71, Assoc Prof Hist, Univ New Orleans, 71-, Am Philos Soc res grant, 67; columnist, New Orleans States-Item, 70- **MEMBERSHIPS** AHA; Orgn Am Historians; Am Studies Asn. **RESEARCH** Theodore Roosevelt and the Progressive Era; American cultural and social history. **SELECTED PUBLICATIONS** Auth, New Orleans Underground Gourmet, Simon & Schuster, 70; Theodore Roosevelt's New Orleans progressive campaign, 1914, La Hist, 71; Henry Pringle's Theodore Roosevelt: A study in historical revisionism, NY Hist, 71; ed, Theodore Roosevelt and Reform Politics, Heath, 72; coauth, New Orleans Cookbook, Knopf, 74; New Orleans Restaurant Guide, Strether & Swann, 76; Pleasures of Seafood, Holt, 77. **CONTACT ADDRESS** Dept of Hist, Univ of New Orleans, Lakefront St, New Orleans, LA 70122.

COLLINS, DONALD E.
PERSONAL Born 12/06/1934, Miami, FL, m, 1969, 3 children **DISCIPLINE** HISTORY **EDUCATION** Fla State Univ, BA, 62; MS, 63; Univ Ga, MA, 70; PhD, 75. **CAREER** Ref Librn, Univ of Ga, 63-70; Assoc Prof, E Carolina Univ, 72-. **MEMBERSHIPS** Southern Hist Asn, NC Lit and Hist Asn, Asn of Historians in NC. **RESEARCH** Japenese American History, U.S. Civil War, North Carolina. **SELECTED PUBLICATIONS** Auth, Native American Aliens: Disloyalty and Renunciation of Citizenship during World War II, Greenwood Press (Westport, CT), 85; auth, Libraries and Research, Kendall/Hunt Publ Co (Dubuque), 94. **CONTACT ADDRESS** Dept Hist, East Carolina Univ, 1000 E 5th St, Greenville, NC 27858-2502. **EMAIL** collins@mail.ecu.edu

COLLINS, ELLIOTT
PERSONAL Born 03/18/1943, Eastman, GA, m, 1967, 1 child **DISCIPLINE** HISTORY **EDUCATION** Univ of DE, BA 1966; New York Univ, MPA 1971; Drew Univ, Madison, NJ, MA, political science, 1983; New York Univ, American Studies, PhD, 00. **CAREER** Passaic (NJ) County Community Col, Paterson, NJ, Professor, Hist and Political Sci, 96-, Passaic Cty Community Col, pres, 91-96, interim pres, 90-91, dean of academic services, 86-89, dean of students, 79-86; Upsala Col, East Orange, NJ, coordinator of science enrichment prog, 76-77; Upsala Col, Drew Univ, lecturer political science, 74-; Upsala Col, asst dean for acad counseling, 76-77; Upsala Col, affirmative action officer, 74-77; Educ Opportunity Fund Prog Upsala Coll, dir and coordinator, 70-76; City of E Orange NJ, asst city planner, 69. **HONORS AND AWARDS** Alpha Phi Alpha Scholarship 1962-64; Young Man of the Year Unity Club Wilmington DE 1965; Martin Luther King Scholarship 1968-70, New York Univ. **MEMBERSHIPS** Vp United Way & Community Serv Council 1971-75; vice pres bd of dir Rotary Club of E Orange NJ 1971-72; bd of trustees Family Servs & Child Guidance Center 1975-76; board of directors, Opportunities Industrialization Center, 1987-95; board of directors, Paterson YMCA, 1983-87; board of trustees, Passaic-Clifton YMCA, 1989-93; United Way of Passaic Valley, board of directors, 1992-95; Inner City Christian Action for Housing Inc, board of trustees, 1992-96; North Jersey Regional Chamber of Commerce, 1991-95; Greater Paterson Chamber of Commerce, 1991-95; Passaic Valley Council Boy Scouts of America, executive board member, 1992-95. **CONTACT ADDRESS** Passaic County Comm Col, One College Blvd, Paterson, NJ 07509.

COLLINS, JACQUELIN
PERSONAL Born 12/27/1933, Kenaston, SK, Canada, m, 1961, 2 children **DISCIPLINE** BRITISH HISTORY **EDUCATION** Rice Univ, BA, 56, MA, 59; Univ Ill, PhD(hist), 64. **CAREER** Asst prof, 62-66, Assoc Prof Hist, Tex Tech Univ, 66-. **MEMBERSHIPS** AHA; AAUP; Conf Brit Studies. **RESEARCH** Seventeenth century England; 16th and 17th century Scotland. **SELECTED PUBLICATIONS** Auth, The English Civil-War, Albion, Vol 0024, 92; Historical Dictionary of Tudor England, 1485-1603, Albion, Vol 0024, 92; Powle,Stephen of Court and Country, Memorabilia of a Government Agent for Elizabeth-I, Chancery Official, and English Country Gentleman, Albion, Vol 0026, 94. **CONTACT ADDRESS** Dept of Hist, Texas Tech Univ, Lubbock, TX 79409-0001.

COLLINS, PATRICIA HILL
PERSONAL Born 05/01/1948, Philadelphia, PA, m **DISCIPLINE** AFRICAN-AMERICAN STUDIES **EDUCATION** Brandeis Univ, AB 1969, PhD 1984; Harvard Univ, MAT 1970. **CAREER** Harvard UTTT Program, teacher/curriculum spec 70-73; St Joseph Community School, curriculum specialist 73-76; Tufts Univ, dir African Amer Ctr 76-80; Univ of Cincinnati, assoc prof of African-American Studies, 87-94, Prof, 94-, assoc prof of Sociology, 88-. **HONORS AND AWARDS** Career Woman of Achievement Awd, YWCA of Cincinnati, 1993. **MEMBERSHIPS** Chair Minority Fellowship Program Comm 1986-1989; mem Amer Sociological Assn; vp Great Rivers Girl Scouts Council 1992-94. **SELECTED PUBLICATIONS** C Wright Mills Award for "Black Feminist Thought," 1990. **CONTACT ADDRESS** African-American Studies, Univ of Cincinnati, ML 370, Cincinnati, OH 45221.

COLLINS, ROBERT MAURICE
PERSONAL Born 12/29/1943, Kearny, NJ **DISCIPLINE** AMERICAN HISTORY **EDUCATION** Jersey City State Col, AB, 67; Columbia Univ, MA, 68; Johns Hopkins Univ, PhD, 71. **CAREER** Asst prof, NC State Univ, 75-80; Assoc Prof Am Hist, Univ MO-Columbia, 80-, Vis prof, Univ Manchester, 82-83. **MEMBERSHIPS** Orgn Am Historians; AHA. **RESEARCH** Public policy; business-government relations; political history. **SELECTED PUBLICATIONS** Auth, Positive business responses to the New Deal: The roots of the committee for economic development, 1933-1942, Bus Hist Rev, fall 78; The Business Response to Keynes, 1929-1964, Columbia Univ Press, 81; American corporatism: The committee for economic development, 1942-1964, The Historian, 2/82; auth, The Originality Trap: Richard Hofstadter on Populism, Journal of American History, 89; auth, The Economic Crisis of 1968 and the Waning of the American Century, American Historical review, 96; auth, More: The Politics of Growth in Postwar America, 00.

CONTACT ADDRESS Dept Hist, Univ of Missouri, Columbia, 316 Read Hall, Columbia, MO 65211-0001. **EMAIL** CollinsR@missouri.edu

COLLINS, ROBERT O.
PERSONAL Born 04/01/1933, Waukegan, IL, m, 1974, 3 children **DISCIPLINE** AFRICAN HISTORY **EDUCATION** Dartmouth Col, BA, 54; Balliol College, Oxford Univ, AB, 56, MA, 60; Yale Univ, MA, 58, PhD, 59. **CAREER** From instr to asst prof Hist, Williams Col, 59-65; dir UC Santa Barbara Washington Cen; assoc prof, 65-69, prof Hist, Univ Calif, Santa Barbara, 69-94; prof Emeritus, 94; dean Grad Div, 70-80, lectr, Univ Mass, Pittsfield, 60-61 & Shiloah Ctr, Tel-Aviv Univ, 73; vis asst prof, Columbia Univ, 62; Soc Sci Res Coun fel, 62 & 68; chmn, Herskovits Prize Comt, 71-73; consult, Sudan Govt & High Exec Coun Southern Sudan Regional Govt, 75-; mem comt, Coun Grad Schs, 76-. **HONORS AND AWARDS** Order of Sciences, Arts and Art-Gold Class, Democratic Republic of the Sudan, 80; Senior Associate Member, St Antony's College, 81, 87, 89; Who's Who in American, the West, American Authors, American Scholars, Contemporary Authors, International Dictionary of Scholars in the Third World, International Authors and Writers. **MEMBERSHIPS** AHA; African Studies Asn; Conf Brit Studies. **RESEARCH** African history; history of Sudan and East Africa. **SELECTED PUBLICATIONS** Auth, King Leopold, England, and the Upper Nile, 1898-1909, Yale Univ, 68; ed, Problems in African history, Prentice-Hall, 68; An Arabian diary, Univ Calif, 69; The partition of Africa, Wiley, 69; Problems in the History of Colonial Africa, Prentice-Hall, 70; auth, Europeans in Africa, Knopf, 71; African History: Test and Readings, Random, 71; Land beyond the rivers: The Southern Sudan, 1898-1918, Yale Univ, 71.; Historical Problems of Imperial Africa, Markus Wiener, 94; Problems in Modern Africa, Markus Wiener, 96; auth, Africa's Thirty Years' War: Chad, Libya, and the Sdn, 63-93, 99. **CONTACT ADDRESS** Dept of History, Univ of California, Santa Barbara, Santa Barbara, CA 93106-0001. **EMAIL** rcollins@humanitas.ucsb.edu

COLMAN, GOULD P.
PERSONAL Born 04/30/1926, Medina, NY, m, 1957, 2 children **DISCIPLINE** AGRICULTURAL ORAL HISTORY **EDUCATION** Cornell Univ, BA, 51, MA, 53, PhD(Am hist), 62. **CAREER** Asst archivist, Cornell Univ, 53-55; instr Am hist, Storm King Sch, 56-59; col historian, NY State Col Agr, 61-63, dir, Oral Hist Proj, 63-65, prog in oral hist, 67-71, chmn dept manuscripts & univ arch, 71-79, Univ Archivist, Cornell Univ, 71-, Res specialist, Dept Rural Sociol. **MEMBERSHIPS** Agr Hist Soc; Oral Hist Asn (vpres, 68, pres, 69-70); Orgn Am Historians; Soc Am Arch; Rural Sociol Soc. **RESEARCH** Institutional studies; oral history techniques; archives administration. **SELECTED PUBLICATIONS** Auth, The Agrarian Origins of American Capitalism, NY Hist, Vol 0075, 94. **CONTACT ADDRESS** John M Olin Libr, Cornell Univ, Ithaca, NY 14853.

COLTON, JOEL
PERSONAL Born 08/23/1918, New York, NY, m, 1942, 2 children **DISCIPLINE** MODERN HISTORY **EDUCATION** City Col New York, AB, 37, MS, 38; Columbia Univ, AM, 40, PhD, 50. **CAREER** Lectr, Columbia Univ, 46-47; from instr to prof, hist, Duke Univ, 47-74, chmn dept, 67-74, chmn acad coun, 71-72; dir for humanities, Rockefeller Found, 74-81; Prof Hist, Duke Univ, 82-, Guggenheim fel, 57-58; Rockefeller Found fel, 61-62; chmn, Europ Hist Advan Placement Comt, Col Entrance Exam Bd, 67-70; Nat Endowment for Humanities sr fel, 70-71. **HONORS AND AWARDS** Bk Awd, Mayflower Soc, 67. **MEMBERSHIPS** AHA; fel Am Acad Arts & Sci; Southern Hist Assoc; Soc Fr Hist Studies (vpres 72-73). **RESEARCH** Modern and contemporary history; modern France; history of social thought. **SELECTED PUBLICATIONS** Auth, Lost Comrades--Socialists of the Front Generation 1918-1945, Amer Hist Rev, Vol 0099, 94; Choice and Democratic Order--The French Socialist-Party, 1937-1950, Amer Hist Rev, Vol 0101, 96; Loucheur, Louis and the Shaping of Modern France, 1916-1931, Amer Histl Rev, Vol 0100, 95; Stanzione, Massimo-- Complete Works-Italian, Renaissance Quart, Vol 0050, 97. **CONTACT ADDRESS** 215 East 68th, New York, NY 10021. **EMAIL** jcolton@duke.edu

COLVIN, WILLIAM E.
PERSONAL Born 05/27/1930, Birmingham, AL, m, 1956 **DISCIPLINE** AFRICAN-AMERICAN STUDIES **EDUCATION** AL State Univ, BS 1951; IN Univ, MS 1960; Academic Affairs Conf of Midwestern Univs, Cert of Administration; IL State, EdD 1971. **CAREER** Stillman Coll, Department of Art, chair 1958-69; Illinois State Univ, dir of ethnic studies 1974-78, prof of art 1971-91; Eastern Illinois Univ, Professor of Art, 87-, Chair Afro-American Studies, 91-. **HONORS AND AWARDS** Rockefeller Fellow 1973-74; Phelps-Stokes Fund Grant 1973; publs exhibitions in field; Martin Luther King BLM Normal Human Relations 1983; Outstanding Artist in the Field AL State Univ 1985; Outstanding Service Awd IL Committee on Black Concerns in Higher Educ 1985; Fulbright Lecture/Rsch Fulbright Brazil 1981-85; univ grant to Belize for research, 1989. **MEMBERSHIPS** Elected rep to US/Brazilian Mod Art Soc 1981-; dir career program IL Comm on Black Concerns in Higher Educ 1983-; mem Natl Conf of Artists; mem Natl Art Educ Assn; mem Phi Delta Kappa Hon Soc in Educ. **CONTACT ADDRESS** Eastern Illinois Univ, Charleston, IL 61920.

COMACCHIO, CYNTHIA
DISCIPLINE CANADIAN SOCIAL HISTORY **EDUCATION** Glendon, BA; York, MA; Univ Guelph, PhD. **CAREER** Prof. **RESEARCH** Canadian social hist, specifically the interrelations of class, gender, family and state in post-Confederation Canada; child and maternal welfare in the twentieth century; fatherhood; adolescence; the politics of health and health care; and the not-entirely-unrelated topics of industrial hygiene and the technological subline. **SELECTED PUBLICATIONS** Auth, "The Mothers of the Land Must Suffer: Maternal and Child Welfare in Rural and Outpost Ontario, 1900-1940," Ontario Hist 80, (88): 183-206; auth, The Infant Soldier: Canadian Child Welfare and the Great War," in V. Fildes, L. Marks, H. Marland, eds., Women and Children First: Child and Maternal Welfare in International Perspective, (London: Routledge, 92); auth, Nations are Built of Babies, McGill-Queen's Univ Press, 93; coauth, "Regulating Nuptiality: restricting Access to Marriage in Early 20th-Century English Canada," in T. Loo, ed., Essays in Canadian Law, (Toronto: Copp Clark, 94); auth, "Motherhood in Crisis: Women, Medicine and the State in Canada, 1900-1940," in R. Hennessey, C. Ingraham, eds., Materialist Feminisms: A Reader, (New York: Routledge, 96). **CONTACT ADDRESS** Dept of History, Wilfrid Laurier Univ, 75 University Ave W, Waterloo, ON, Canada N2L 3C5. **EMAIL** ccomacch@mach1.wlu.ca

COMBS, JERALD A.
PERSONAL Born 04/19/1937, Long Beach, CA, m, 1958, 2 children **DISCIPLINE** UNITED STATES HISTORY **EDUCATION** Univ Calif, Santa Barbara, BA, 58, Los Angeles, Ph-d(hist), 64. **CAREER** Assoc prof, 64-73, Prof Hist, Calif State Univ, San Francisco, 73-. **MEMBERSHIPS** AHA; Conf Early Am Hist; Soc Hist Am Foreign Rel. **RESEARCH** United States diplomacy and Revolutionary and Federalist Eras. **SELECTED PUBLICATIONS** Auth, The Jay Treaty, Univ Calif, 70; ed, Nationalist, Realist and Radical: Three Views of American Foreign Policy, Harper, 71. **CONTACT ADDRESS** Dept of History, San Francisco State Univ, 1600 Holloway Ave, San Francisco, CA 94132-1740.

COMBS, WILLIAM L.
PERSONAL Born 10/06/1937, Worth County, MO, m, 1977, 2 children **DISCIPLINE** HISTORY **EDUCATION** Northwest Mo State Univ, BS, 59; MA, 60; Purdue Univ, PhD, 82. **CAREER** Prof, Western Ill Univ, 66-. **MEMBERSHIPS** Ger Studies Asn, Confr Group for Central European Hist. **RESEARCH** German National Socialism. **SELECTED PUBLICATIONS** Auth, Voice of the SS: A History of the SS Journal 'Das Schwarze Korps,' Peter Lang, 86; auth, "Fatal Attraction: Dueling and the SS," Hist Today (97). **CONTACT ADDRESS** Dept Hist, Western Illinois Univ, 1 University Cir, Macomb, IL 61455-1367. **EMAIL** william_combs@ccmail.wiu.edu

CONARD, REBECCA
PERSONAL Born 08/10/1946, Ida Grove, IA **DISCIPLINE** HISTORY **EDUCATION** Calif State Polytech Univ, BS, 73; Univ Calif at Los Angeles, MA, 76; Univ Calif Santa Barbara, PhD, 84. **CAREER** Prin, PHR Assocs Santa Barbara, 82-92; asst prof, Wichita State Univ, 92-98; assoc prof, Middle Tenn State Univ, 98-; partner, Tallgrass Historians, 93-. **MEMBERSHIPS** Nat Council on Pub Hist, Orgn of Am Historians, Am Soc for Environ Hist, W Hist Asn, Am Asn of State and Local Hist. **RESEARCH** Public and environmental history. **SELECTED PUBLICATIONS** Auth, Places of Quiet Beauty: Parks, Preserves, and Environmentalism, Univ of Iowa Press, 97; auth, Benjamin Shambaugh and the Intellectual Foundations of Public History, Univ of Iowa Press (forthcoming). **CONTACT ADDRESS** Dept Hist, Middle Tennessee State Univ, 1301 E Main St, Murfreesboro, TN 37132-0001. **EMAIL** rconard@mtsu.edu

CONDON, RICHARD HERRICK
PERSONAL Born 05/29/1935, Lewiston, ME, m, 1957, 3 children **DISCIPLINE** BRITISH HISTORY **EDUCATION** Bates Col, AB, 56; Brown Univ, AM, 57, PhD(hist), 62. **CAREER** Instr hist, Kent State Univ, 60-64; asst prof, State Univ NY Col Oneonta, 64-65; from asst prof to assoc prof, 65-68, Prof Hist, Univ Maine, Farmington, 68-, Chmn Dept, 69- **MEMBERSHIPS** AHA; Hist Asn, England. **RESEARCH** British 18th and 19th century social reform. **SELECTED PUBLICATIONS** Auth, James Neild, forgotten reformer, Studies Romanticism, 64; The Fleet prison, Hist Today, 64. **CONTACT ADDRESS** Dept of Hist, Univ of Maine, 86 Main St, Farmington, ME 04938-1990.

CONGDON, KRISTIN G.
PERSONAL Born 10/09/1948, Boston, MA, m, 1970 **DISCIPLINE** ART-ART EDUCATION, FOLKLORE, ART HISTORY **EDUCATION** PhD Univ of Oregon, 83; MS IN Univ, 72; BA Valparaiso Univ, 70. **CAREER** Prof of Art, Univ of Central FL, Orlando, Coordinator AA Hist Prog 88-present; Asst Prof, AA Edu Bowling Green State Univ,OH, 84-87. **HONORS AND AWARDS** Natl Art Edu Assoc, Zeigfeld Awd, Res of the Year Awd, Southeastern Region's Natl Art Edu Assoc Higher Edu Div Natl Art Educator of the Year Awd, NAEA Barkan Awd. **MEMBERSHIPS** Am Folklore Assoc, Col Art Assoc, Intl Soc for Edu through AA, Natl Art Edu Assoc, Woman's Caucus for AA. **RESEARCH** Commun AAS Soc Eco, Feminist& AA Criticism, Folklore At/Traditional AA, Art and Eco multi-cultural Edu. **SELECTED PUBLICATIONS** Review ed,: Indigenous Teaching(Webb-based Pub) 98-present; Member, Review Bd, The Journal of Gender Issues in Art and Education, 96-present; Outside Review Ed, Aouthern Folklore, 93-95; Member Ed Advisory Bd, Studies in Art Education, 91-95; Journal of Multi-cultural and Cross-cultural Research in Art Education, 87-present; Asst Ed: Journal of Social Theory and Art Education, 90-91; Browne, R Browne P, Congdon, KG et al, The Encyclopedia of Popular Culture in the United States, NY ABC-CLIO Publishing Co, in press. **CONTACT ADDRESS** Col of Arts and Sci, Univ of Central Florida, Orlando, FL 32816. **EMAIL** kcongdon@pegasus.cc.ucf.edu

CONGDON, LEE W.
PERSONAL Born 08/11/1939, Chicago, IL, m, 1967, 2 children **DISCIPLINE** HISTORY **EDUCATION** Wheaton Col, BA, 61; Northern Ill Univ, MA, 67; PhD, 73. **CAREER** Editorial asst & writer, Encyclopedia Britannica, 65 & 67-68; from asst prof to prof, James Madison Univ, 72-. **HONORS AND AWARDS** Fulbright-Hays Fac Res Abroad, Hungary, 77-78; Order of Merit, Small Cross of Republic of Hungary, 99. **MEMBERSHIPS** Am Asn for the Study of Hungarian Hist. **RESEARCH** Modern European intellectual history, history of Hungary. **SELECTED PUBLICATIONS** Auth, The Young Lukacs, Univ NC Press, 83; auth, Exile and Soc Thought: Hungarian Intellectuals in Germany and Austria, 1919-1933, Princeton Univ Press, 91. **CONTACT ADDRESS** Dept of Hist, James Madison Univ, 800 S Main St, Harrisonburg, VA 22807. **EMAIL** congdolw@jmu.edu

CONKIN, PAUL K.
PERSONAL Born 10/25/1929, Chuckey, TN, m, 1954, 3 children **DISCIPLINE** HISTORY **EDUCATION** Milligan Col, BA, 51; Vanderbilt Univ, MA, 53; PhD, 57. **CAREER** Asst prof, Univ of Southwestern La, 57-59; from asst prof to prof, Univ of Md, 59-67; vis prof, Univ of Mont, 67; prof, Univ of Wis, 67-75; Merle Curti Prof of Hist, Univ of Wis, 75-79; Distinguished Prof of Hist, Vanderbilt Univ, 79-; Chair of Dept of Hist, Vanderbilt Univ, 84-87. **HONORS AND AWARDS** Albert J. Beveridge Awd, 58; John Simon Guggenheim Memorial Fel, 66-67; Sr Fel, NEH, 72-73; Univ Fel, NEH, 90. **MEMBERSHIPS** Am Hist Asn, Orgnn of Am Historians, Southern Hist Asn, Am Soc of Church Hist. **RESEARCH** American Intellectual History, Recent American History, Philosophy of History, History of Religion. **SELECTED PUBLICATIONS** Auth, Big Daddy from the Pedernales: Lyndon Baines Johnson, G.K. Hall (Boston, MA), 86; auth, The southern Agrarians, Univ of Tenn Press (Knoxville, TN), 88; auth, Cane Ridge: America's Pentecost, Univ of Wis Press (Madison, WI), 91; auth, The Four Foundations of American Government: Consent, Limits, Balance, and Participation, Harlan Davidson (Arlington Heights, IL), 94; auth, The Uneasy Center: Reformed Christianity in Antebellum America, Univ of NC Press (Chapel Hill, NC), 95; auth, American Originals: Homemade Varieties of Christianity, Univ of NC Press (Chapel Hill, NC), 97; auth, When All the Gods Trembled: Darwinism, Scopes, and American Intellectuals, Roman & Littlefield (New York, NY), 98; auth, Requiem for the American Village, Roman & Littlefield (New York, NY), 00. **CONTACT ADDRESS** Dept of History, Vanderbilt Univ, PO Box 1802, Sta B, Nashville, TN 37235. **EMAIL** conkinpk@vanderbilt.edu

CONLEY, CAROLYN
DISCIPLINE HISTORY **EDUCATION** Duke Univ, BA, 75, PhD, 84; Univ Chicago, MA, 76. **CAREER** Asst prof to prof grad student, Univ Ala Birmingham, 85- . **HONORS AND AWARDS** LA Prade Prize; NEH fel; Schyugill fel. **MEMBERSHIPS** AHA, ACIS, NACBS, **RESEARCH** Social history of crime and violence in the British Isles. **SELECTED PUBLICATIONS** Auth, The Unwritten Law: Criminal Justice in Victoria Kent, Oxford, (91); auth, "No Pedestals" Women & Violence in Late 19th Century Ireland, J Soc Hist, (95); auth, "The Agreeable Recreator of Fighting, J Soc Hist, (99); auth, Melancholy Accidents: The Meaning of Violence in Post-Famine Ireland, Lexington Books, (99). **CONTACT ADDRESS** Dept Hist, Univ of Alabama, Birmingham, 1530 3 Ave S, Birmingham, AL 35294-0001. **EMAIL** cconley@uab.edu

CONLEY, PATRICK THOMAS
PERSONAL Born 06/22/1938, New Haven, CT, m, 1962, 6 children **DISCIPLINE** AMERICAN HISTORY, CONSTITUTIONAL LAW **EDUCATION** Providence Col, AB, 59; Univ Notre Dame, MA, 61, PhD(hist), 70; Suffolk Univ, JD, 73. **CAREER** Prof Hist, Providence Col, 63-93, Spec asst to Congressman Robert O Tiernan, RI, 67-74; secy, RI Constitutional Convention, 73; chmn, RI Bicentennial Comn/Found, 74-; chairman U.S. Constitution Council, 88-91. **HONORS AND AWARDS** Elected to Rhode Island Heritage Hall of Fame, 95. **MEMBERSHIPS** AHA; Orgn Am Historians; RI Historical Soc (life member of each). **RESEARCH** Rhode Island history; American ethnic history; constitutional history. **SELECTED PUBLICATIONS** Auth, Proceedings of the Rhode Island Constitutional Convention of 1973, Providence: Oxford Press, 73; auth, Democracy in Decline: Rhode Island's Constitutional Development, 1776-1841, Providence: Rhode Island Historical Society,

77; coauth, Providence: A Pictorial History, with Paul R. Campbell, Norfolk: The Donning Company, 82; auth, Rhode Island Profile, Providence: Rhode Island Publications Society, 82; auth, The Irish in Rhode Island: A Historical Appreciation, Providence: Rhode Island Heritage Commission, 86; auth, An Album of Rhode Island History, 1636-1986, Norfolk: Donning Company, 86; auth, First in War, Last in Peace: Rhode Island and the Constitution, 1786-1790, Providence: Rhode Island Bicentennial Foundation, 87; coauth, The Bill of Rights and the States: The Colonial and Revolutionary Origins of American Liberties, with John P. Kaminski, Madison, Wis: Madison House Publishers, 92; auth, Liberty and Justice: A History of Law and Lawyers in Rhode Island, 1636-1998, Providence: Rhode Island Publications Society, 98; auth, Neither Separate Nor Equal: Legislature and Executive in Rhode Island Constitutional History, Providence: Rhode Island Publications Society, 99. **CONTACT ADDRESS** 1 Bristol Point Rd, Bristol, RI 02809.

CONLEY, TOM C.
PERSONAL Born 12/07/1943, New Haven, CT, m, 1967, 2 children **DISCIPLINE** FRENCH STUDIES **EDUCATION** Lawrence Univ, BA, 65; Columbia Univ, MA, 66; Univ Wis, PhD, 71. **CAREER** Asst prof to prof, Univ Minn, 71-95; vis prof, Univ Mich, 78; vis assoc prof, Univ Calif Berkeley, 78-79; vis prof, CUNY, Grad Center, 85-87; vis prof, Miami Univ Ohio, 89-93; vis prof, Univ Calif Los Angeles, 95; prof, Bryn Mawr Col, 01. **HONORS AND AWARDS** Fulbright Fel, 68; Ford Diss Fel, 71; ACLS Fel, 76; MEH Fel, 75, 89; Inst for Res in Humanities Fel, 90; Hermon Dunlap Smith Fel, 91; Cornell Soc fof the Humanities Fel, 98. **MEMBERSHIPS** MLA, Renaissance Soc of Am, Asn for the Study of Dada, Surrealism, Soc for Cinema Studies, Soc for the Hist of Discoveries. **RESEARCH** Early modern French literature and culture, film and visual studies, contemporary criticism and writing. **SELECTED PUBLICATIONS** Auth, Film Hieroglyphics: Ruptures of Classical Cinema, Univ Minn Pr, 91; auth, The Graphic Unconscious in Early Modern French Writing, Cambridge Univ Pr, 92; transl, ed, The Fold: Leibniz and the Baroque, by Gilles Deleuze, Univ Minn Pr, 93; coed, Identity Papers: Contested Nationhood in 20th Century France, Univ Minn Pr, 96; transl and ed, The Capture of Speech and Cultural in the Plural by Michel de Certeau, Univ Minn Pr, 97; auth, The Self-Made Map: Cartographic Writing in Early Modern France, 97; coed, The World and its Rival: Essays in Honor of Per Kykrog, Rodopi Editions, 99; auth, L'inconscient graphique: essai sur la lettre a la Renaissance, 00. **CONTACT ADDRESS** Dept Romance Lang, Harvard Univ, Boylston Hall, Cambridge, MA 02138. **EMAIL** tconley@fas.harvard.edu

CONLON, FRANK FOWLER
PERSONAL Born 11/06/1938, Omaha, NE, m, 1972 **DISCIPLINE** HISTORY OF INDIA **EDUCATION** Northwestern Univ, Evanston, AB, 60; Univ Minn, Minneapolis, MA, 63, PhD(hist), 69. **CAREER** Asst prof, 68-75; assoc prof hist, Univ Wash, 75-83, Asia rev ed, Journal Asian Studies, 78-80; chmn bd, 82-83; prof, 83-01; co-founder and editor H-ASIA, 94-; prof emer, Univ Wash, 01- **HONORS AND AWARDS** Sr fel Am Inst, Indian Studies, 71, 77-78, 90-91; **MEMBERSHIPS** Asn Asian Studies; AHA. **RESEARCH** Modern India; social history of India; Maharashtra and west coast. **SELECTED PUBLICATIONS** Auth, Marathas, Marauders, and State Formation in 18th-Century India, Jour Amer Oriental Soc, Vol 0116, 96; The New Cambridge History of India, Vol 2, Pt 4, The Marathas 1600-1818, Amer Hist Rev, Vol 0100, 95; In the Absence of God - the Early Years of an Indian Sect--A Translation of Smrtisthal with an Introduction, Jour Amer Oriental Soc, Vol 0115, 95; The Unification and Division of India, Historian, Vol 0055, 93. **CONTACT ADDRESS** Dept of Hist, Univ of Washington, Seattle, WA 98195-3560. **EMAIL** conlon@u.washington.edu

CONNELL-SZASZ, MARGARET
PERSONAL Born Pasco, WA, 3 children **DISCIPLINE** WESTERN AMERICA, INDIAN AND SCOTTISH HISTORY **EDUCATION** Univ NMex, PhD, 72. **CAREER** Instr, Univ Exeter, Eng; instr, Univ Aberdeen, Scottland; prof, Univ NMex. **HONORS AND AWARDS** D'Arcy McNickle Ctr fel; Spencer Found grant. **RESEARCH** History of Am Indian education; Scottland. **SELECTED PUBLICATIONS** Auth, Education and the American Indian, The Road to Self-Determination, 74, 77, 99; Between Indian and White Worlds: The Cultural Broker, 94. **CONTACT ADDRESS** Univ of New Mexico, Albuquerque, Albuquerque, NM 87131. **EMAIL** conszasz@unm.edu

CONNELLY, OWEN S.
PERSONAL Born 01/24/1929, Morganton, NC, m, 1965, 3 children **DISCIPLINE** HISTORY, MODERN EUROPEAN **EDUCATION** Wake Forest, BS, 48; Univ NCar, Chapel Hill, PhD, 60. **CAREER** From assoc prof to McKissick Dial Prof, Univ of SCar, 67-; chmn, Europ Sect, SHA, 82; Bd Dir Consortium Revolutionary Europ, 71-; instr, assoc prof, Duke. **HONORS AND AWARDS** Pres, Soc for French Hist Studies, 88. **MEMBERSHIPS** Soc d'Hist Mod; Inst Napoleon; Soc Mil Hist; Asn Mem Inst for Advan Study. **RESEARCH** French Revolution; Napoleonic era; Military history. **SELECTED PUBLICATIONS** Auth, The Gentle Bonaparte..Joseph, Napoleon's Elder Brother, 68; The Epoch of Napoleon, 72 & 78; ed, Historical Dictionary of Napoleonic France, 85; auth, Napoleon's Satellite Kingdoms, 65 & 69 & 90; Blundering to Glory: Napoleon's Military Campaigns, 87 & 90 & 99; The French Revolution and Napoleonic Era, 79 & 91 & 99. **CONTACT ADDRESS** History Dept, Univ of So Carolina, Columbia, 221 Gambrell, Columbia, SC 29208. **EMAIL** Connelly@gwm.sc.edu

CONNER, VALERIE JEAN
PERSONAL Born 10/23/1945, Jennings, LA, m **DISCIPLINE** HISTORY **EDUCATION** Loyola Univ, BA, 67; Univ VA, MA, 69, PhD, 74. **CAREER** Res staff local govt, style & drafting, La Const Conv, 73-74; asst prof, 74-81, assoc prof Am hist, FL State Univ, 82. **MEMBERSHIPS** Orgn Am Historians. **RESEARCH** US polit, economic, and soc hist: 1890-1940. **SELECTED PUBLICATIONS** Auth, The Mothers of the Race in World War I: The National War Labor Board and Women in Industry, Labor Hist, Vol 21, winter 80; The National War Labor Board in 1918-1919: Stability and Social Justice in the Voluntary State, Univ NC Press, 83. **CONTACT ADDRESS** Florida State Univ, 600 W College Ave, Tallahassee, FL 32306-1096. **EMAIL** vconner@mailer.fsu.edu

CONNOLLY, THOMAS J.
PERSONAL Born 03/01/1954, Fargo, ND, m, 1982, 1 child **DISCIPLINE** ANTHROPOLOGY, ARCHAEOLOGY **EDUCATION** Univ Oregon, PhD, 86 **CAREER** Research div dir, State Mus Anthrop, Univ Oregon, 86- **MEMBERSHIPS** Soc Amer Archaeol; Soc Calif Archaeol; Assoc Ore Archaeologist; Plains Archaeol Soc **RESEARCH** Archaelogy of Western North America **SELECTED PUBLICATIONS** "Radiocarbon Evidence Relating to Northern Great Basin Basketry Chronology." Jour Calif & Great Basin Anthrop, 98; "Newberry Crater: A Ten-Thousand-Year Record of Human Occupation and Environmental Change in the Basin-Plateau Borderlands." Univ Utah Anthro Papers; "Oregon Wet Site Basketry: A Review of Structural Type." Contribution to the Archaeology of Oregon, 95-97; coauth, "Population Dynamics on the Northwestern Great Basin Periphery: Clues from Obsidian Geochemistry," Jrnl of Calif and Great Basin Antrho 19 (2) (97): 241-250; coauth, "Mapping the Mosier Mounds: The Significance of Rock Feature Complexes on the Southern Columbia Plateau," Jrnl of Archaeological Sce, 24 (97): 289-300; coauth, "Comments on 'America's Oldest Basketry,'" Radiocarbon 41 (3) (99): 309-313. **CONTACT ADDRESS** Dept Anthro, Univ of Oregon, Eugene, OR 97403. **EMAIL** connolly@darkwing.uoregon.edu

CONOLLY-SMITH, PETER
PERSONAL Born 09/03/1964, Munich, Germany, s **DISCIPLINE** AMERICAN STUDIES **EDUCATION** Freie Univ, Berlin, BA, 87; Yale Univ, MA, 92; MPhil, 93; PhD, 96. **CAREER** Instr, High Sch Summers Prog, Columbia Univ, 96; Post-doctoral Fel, Longfellow Inst, Harvard Univ, spring 97; adjunct asst prof, Master of Liberal Arts Prog, Columbia Univ, spring 97; assoc prof, General Educ, DeVry Inst, 96-, coordr, Social Scis and Humanities, 96-. **HONORS AND AWARDS** DAAD Fel, 88-89; Prize Teaching Fel, Yale Univ, 93-94; Diss Fel, Yale Univ, 94-95; AAA-Compendium, Nat Asn Visual Anthropol, 95; Grand Jury Prize, Bettina Russell Festival, 96; John D. Sawyer Fel, Harvard, 97; selected for Young Am Conf, Harvard Univ, 98; Best Student Ctred Technique, DeVry Fac Symposium, 98; selected for NY Coun for Humanities Lect Series, 2000; Who's Who Among America's Teachers, 2000. **MEMBERSHIPS** MLA, AHA, ASA. **RESEARCH** 20th century social/political/cultural/diplomatic American and world history; immigration; pop culture; literature; film. **SELECTED PUBLICATIONS** Auth, "New Yorker Deutschtum des 19. Und 20. Jahrhunderts," in Stephan Loose, ed, New York: Kultur und Geschitchte, Loose Travel Pubs, Berlin (98); auth, "Ersatz-Drama and Ethnic (Self-)Parody: Adolf Philipp and the Decline of New York's German-Language Stage: 1890-1920," in Werner Sollors, ed, Multilingual America, New York Univ Press (98); auth, "On Agents, Archives, and Historians: Censorship, Language and the Early History of the (F)BI," in Werner Sollors, ed, Young Americanists, New York Univ Press (2000); auth, The Translated Community: New York's German-Language Press as an Agent of Cultural Resistance and Integration, 1910-1920, Smithsonian Inst Series on Am Studies, Mark Hirsch, series ed (forthcoming 2000). **CONTACT ADDRESS** Dept General Educ, DeVry Inst, 630 US Highway 1, North Brunswick, NJ 08902-3311.

CONRAD, DAVID C.
PERSONAL Born 03/25/1939, USA, m, 1998 **DISCIPLINE** HISTORY **EDUCATION** Idaho State Univ, BA, 61, Univ of Nev, MA, 64; San Francisco State Univ, MA, 71; Univ of London, PhD, 81. **CAREER** Lect, San Francisco State Univ, 71-72; asst prof to prof, SUNY, 85-; res asst prof, State Univ of NY, Inst Teknologi Mara, Malaysia, 88-90; vis prof, Ecole des hautes Etudes en Sciences Sociales, Paris, 99. **HONORS AND AWARDS** Fel, Royal Georg Soc, 92-94; Fulbright Res Grant, 94; Pres Awd for Achievement in Scholarly Res, SUNY-Oswego, 98. **MEMBERSHIPS** African Studies Assoc; MANSA; WARA. **RESEARCH** West African Epic Tradition, Indigenous Systems of Belief, Early West African States. **SELECTED PUBLICATIONS** Auth, "Islam in the Oral Traditions of Mali: Bilai and Surakata", Jour of African Hist 26, (85): 33-49; auth, State of Intrigue: The Epic of Bamana Segu According to Tayiru Banbera, Oxford Univ Pr for the British Acad, 90; auth, "Searching for History in the Sunjata Epic: the Case of Fakoli", Hist in Africa 19 (92):147-200; auth, "A Town Called Dakajalan: The Sunjata Tradition and the Question of Ancient Mali's Capital", Jour of African Hist 35 (94):355-377; auth, "Blind Man Meets Prophet: Oral Tradition, Islam, and fune Identity" in Status and Identity in West Africa: Nyamakalaw of Mande, eds David C. Conrad and Barbara E. Frank, (IN: Ind Univ Pr, 95), 86-132; coauth, Status and Identity in West Africa: Nyamakalaw of Mande, Ind Univ Pr (Bloomington), 95; auth, Segu Maana Bamanankan Na: Bamana Language Edition of the Epic of Segu, Univ of Wis African Studies Prog (Madison), 98; auth, Epic Ancestors of the Sunjata Era: Oral Tradition from the Maninka of Guinea, Univ of Wis African Studies Prog (Madison), 99; auth, Almani Samori: A Nineteenth-Century Conqueror in Mande Epic Tradition, Univ of Wis African Studies Prog (Madison) 00. **CONTACT ADDRESS** Dept Hist, SUNY, Oswego, 7060 State Route 104, Oswego, NY 13126-3560. **EMAIL** dconrad@oswego.edu

CONRAD, GLENN RUSSELL
PERSONAL Born 09/03/1932, New Iberia, LA, m, 1955, 4 children **DISCIPLINE** MODERN FRANCE FRENCH NORTH AMERICAN COLONIAL LOUISIANA **EDUCATION** Georgetown Univ, BS, 53, MA, 59. **CAREER** Instr hist, Univ Southwestern La, 58-62; asst prof, Southern State Col, 63-64; instr, 65-70, asst prof, 70-76, Assoc Prof Hist, Univ Southwestern La, 76-91, Dir Ctr La Studies, 73-93, Sec/Treas, La Hist Asn, 93-, Ed, La Hist, La Hist Asn, 73. **HONORS AND AWARDS** Univ Dist Prof, Fel, La Hist Asn **MEMBERSHIPS** Southern Hist Asn; Fr Hist Soc; Fr Soc Overseas Hist. **RESEARCH** Modern France, Louisiana, local. **SELECTED PUBLICATIONS** Ed, French Louisiana: A Commemoration of the French Revolution Bicentellial, ed. With Robert B. Holtman, Univ of Southwestern Louisiana, (Lafayette, La), 89; auth, Land Records of the Attakapas District, vol. I, The Attakapas Domesday Book: Land Grants, Claims, and Confirmations in the Attakapas District, 1764-1826, Univ of Southwestern Louisiana (Lafayette, La), 90; auth, Land Records of the Attakapas District, vol II part I, Conveyance Records of Attakapas County, 1804-1818, Univ of Southwestern Louisiana (Lafayette, La), 92; ed, The Road to Louisiana: The Saint-Domingue Refugees, 1792-1809, (Lafayette, La), 92; co-auth, A Bibliography of Scholarly Literature on Colonia Louisiana and New France, Lafayette, La, 92; auth, Land Records of the Attakapas District, vol. II, part 3, Attakapas-St Martin Estates, 1804-1818, Univ of Southwestern Lousiana (Lafayette, La), 93; gen ed and contrib, Cross, Crozier, & Crucible: A Volume Celebrating the Bicentennial of a Catholic Diocese in Louisiana, 1793-1993, Univ of Southwestern Lousiana (Lafayette, La), 93; co-auth, Crevasse! The 1927 Flood in Acadiana, Univ of Southwestern Louisiana, (Lafayette, La), 94; co-auth, White Gold: A Brief History of the Louisiana Sugar Industry, Univ of Southwestern Louisiana (Lafayette, La), 95; auth, Louisiana Purchase Bicentennial Series in Louisiana History, vol I, The French Experience in Louisiana, Univ of Southwestern Louisiana (Lafayette, La), 95. **CONTACT ADDRESS** Ctr for La Studies, Univ of Louisiana, Lafayette, PO Box 40831, Lafayette, LA 70504. **EMAIL** conrad@louisiana.edu

CONRAD, MARGARET R.
PERSONAL Born 12/14/1946, Bridgewater, NS, Canada **DISCIPLINE** HISTORY, WOMEN'S STUDIES **EDUCATION** Acadia Univ, BA, 67; Univ Toronto, MA, 68, PhD, 79. **CAREER** Ed, Clark, Irwin Publ, 68-69; lectr to assoc prof, 69-87, Prof History, Acadia Univ, 87-; adj prof, Dalhousie Univ, 91-; Nancy Rowell Jackman Chair Women's Stud, Mt St Vincent Univ, 96-98. **HONORS AND AWARDS** Fel, Royal Soc Canada, 95. **MEMBERSHIPS** Asn Can Stud; Can Hist Asn; Can Res Inst Advan Women; Can Women's Stud Asn; Planter Stud Ctr. **RESEARCH** History of Atlantic Canada. **SELECTED PUBLICATIONS** Auth, Recording Angels, 83; auth, George Nowlan: Maritime Conservative in National Politics, 86; coauth, Twentieth Century Canada, 74; coauth, Women at Acadia University: The First Fifty Years 1884-1934, 83; coauth, No Place Like Home: The Diaries and Letters of Nova Scotia Women 1771-1938, 88; coauth, History of the Canadian Peoples, 2 vols, 93, 2nd ed 97; supv ed, New England Planters in Maritime Canada, 93; ed, They Planted Well, 88; ed, Making Adjustments: Change and Continuity in Planter Nova Scotia, 91; ed, Intimate Relations, 95; co-ed, Atlantis: A Women's Stud J, 75-85; co-ed, Can Hist Rev, 97-. **CONTACT ADDRESS** History Dept, Acadia Univ, Wolfville, NS, Canada B0P 1X0. **EMAIL** margaret.conrad@acadiau.ca

CONSENSTEIN, PETER
DISCIPLINE FRENCH STUDIES **EDUCATION** SUNY at Plattsburgh, BA, 81; Univ Laval, MA, 86; Columbia Univ, PhD, 93. **CAREER** Preceptor, Columbia Univ, 87-92; Coord, Columbia Univ, 92-93; Assoc Prof, Bor Manhattan Community Col, 93-. **HONORS AND AWARDS** Presidents Fel, Columbia Univ, 90, 91-92; New York Jr Fac Awd, CUNY, 94, 96; NISOD Excellence Awd, Nat Inst for Staff and Orgn Develop, 97; Who's Who Among America's Teachers, 01; Who's Who in the World, 18th ed, 01. **RESEARCH** French poetry after World

War II, 20th-century French literature, the group Oulipo, literary criticism and theory, Francophone literature. **SELECTED PUBLICATIONS** Auth, "The Asian Influences in the Poetry of Jacque Roubaud and Raymond Queneau," W Va Univ Philol Papers 40 (94): 56-63; auth, "Memory and 'Oulipian' Constraints," Postmodern Culture 6:1 e-J, Oxford Univ Pr (95); auth, "The Rhythm of Irony," Cincinnati Romance Rev XV (96): 8-19; auth, "Dominique Fourcade-Confluences," Sites 3:1 (99): 203-216. **CONTACT ADDRESS** Dept Lang, Borough of Manhattan Comm Col, CUNY, 205 W 88th St, #12C, New York, NY 10024-2350. **EMAIL** pconsenstein@bmcc.cuny.edu

CONSER, WALTER H., JR.
PERSONAL Born 04/04/1949, Riverside, CA, m, 1986, 3 children **DISCIPLINE** AMERICAN RELIGIOUS HISTORY **EDUCATION** Univ Calif Irvine, BA, 71; Brown Univ, MA, 74, PhD, hist, 81. **CAREER** James A. Gray fel in relig, Univ NC Chapel Hill, 82-84; adjunct facul, Univ San Francisco, 85; vis asst prof to asst prof, 85-89, assoc prof, 89-94, chmn, 92-98, prof relig, 94-, Univ NC Wilmington; fel, Albert Einstein Inst for Nonviolent Alternatives, 84-87; vis prof, JF Kennedy Inst for North Amer Studies, Free Univ Berlin, 90; prof, hist, Univ NC Wilmington, 95-. **HONORS AND AWARDS** German Academic Exchange Service Fellowship 77; North Carolina Humanities Grant 87, 98. **MEMBERSHIPS** Amer Acad of Relig; Amer Hist Asn. **SELECTED PUBLICATIONS** Auth, Religious Diversity and American Religious History, Univ Ga Press, 97; auth, God and the Natural World: Religion and Science in Antebellum America, Univ SC Press, 93; co-ed, Experience of the Sacred: Readings in the Phenomenology of Religion, Brown Univ Press, 92; auth, James Marsh and the Germans, New Eng Quart, 86; auth, Church and Confession: Conservative Theologians in Germany, England and America, 1815-1866, Mercer Univ Press; auth, Conservative Critique of Church and State, Jour of Church and State, 83; auth, John Ross and the Cherokee Resistance Campaign, Jour of Southern Hist, 78; co-auth, Cherokee Reponses to the Debate Over Indian Origins, Amer Quart, 89; co-auth, Cherokees in Transition, Jour of Amer Hist, 77. **CONTACT ADDRESS** Dept. of Philosophy and Religion, Univ of No Carolina, Wilmington, 601 S. College Rd., Wilmington, NC 28403.

CONSTANCE, JOSEPH
PERSONAL Born 04/16/1952, Montaul, MA, m, 1982, 2 children **DISCIPLINE** HISTORY, LIBRARY SCIENCE **EDUCATION** St. Michael's Col, BA (magna cum laude), 76; Univ VT, MA (Hist), 79; SUNY, Albany, MLS, 83; Boston Univ, PhD Candidate, 95-. **CAREER** Archivist and curator of Manuscripts, Soc of St. Edmund, Burlington, VT, 78-80; archivist and curator of Special Collections, Middle GA Hist Soc, Macon, 80-81; Univ archivist and curator of Rare Books, GA State Univ, Atlanta, 83-87; Head, Archives and Manuscripts Dept, John J. Burns Library of Special Collections, Chestnut Hill, MA, 87-90; College Librarian, Saint Anselm Col, Manchester, NH, 90-. **SELECTED PUBLICATIONS** Auth, Time Management for Archivists, with Robert C. Dinwiddie in Provenance, fall 85; book reviewer for Library Journal, 83-. **CONTACT ADDRESS** Geisel Library, Saint Anselm Col, 87 St. Anselm Dr., Manchester, NH 03102-1323.

CONSTANTELOS, DEMETRIOS J.
PERSONAL Born 07/27/1927, Spilia, Messenia, m, 1954, 4 children **DISCIPLINE** BYZANTINE HISTORY **EDUCATION** Holy Cross Orthodox Theol Sch, BA, 58; Princeton Theol Sem, ThM, 59; Rutgers Univ, MA, 63, PhD(hist), 65. **CAREER** Tchng asst hist, Rutgers Univ, 61-62; from asst prof to assoc prof, Hellenic Col, 65-71; prof, 71-86, Charches Cooper Townsend Dist Prof, hist & relig stud, 86-, Richard Stockton Col, , Ed, Greek Orthodox Theol Rev, 66-71; vis lectr, Boston Col, 67-68; mem, Anglican-Orthodox Theol Consult, 68-& Orthodox-Cath Theol Consult, 69-; pres, Orthodox Theol Soc Am, 69-71; mem, Natl Comm Byzantine Studies, 73-. **MEMBERSHIPS** Mediaeval Acad Am; Am Soc Church Hist; Mod Greek Studies Assn. **RESEARCH** Byzantine civilization; Greek orthodox theology; ecclesiastical history. **SELECTED PUBLICATIONS** Auth, Byzantine Philanthropy and Social Welfare, Rutgers Univ, 68, 2nd ed, Aristide D Caratzas Publ, 91; contribr, Southeastern Europe: A Guide to Basic Publications, Univ Chicago, 69; auth, Kyros Panopolites, Rebuilder of Constantinople, Greek-Roman and Byzantine Studies, 71; The Moslem conquests of the Near East as revealed in the Greek sources, Byzantion, 72; ed, Encyclicals and Documents of the Greek Archdiocese (1922-1972), Patriarchal Inst, 76; contribr, The Oxford Annotated Apocrypha, Oxford Univ, 77; ed, Orthodox Theology and Diakonia: Trends and Prospects, Hellenic Col Press, 81; auth, Understanding the Greek Orthodox Church, Seabury, 82, 3rd ed,Hellenic Col Press, 98; auth, Poverty, Society and Philanthropy in the Late Mediaeval Greek World, Aristide D Caratzas, Publ, 92; auth, The Greeks: Their Heritage and its Value Today, Hellenic Col Press, 96; contr, The Parallel Apocrypha, Oxford Univ, 97; auth, Christian Hellenism: Essays and Studies in Continuity and Change, Caratzas: Melissa Media Assn, 98. **CONTACT ADDRESS** Dept of Arts & Humanities, Richard Stockton Col, Pomona, NJ 08240.

CONTOSTA, DAVID RICHARD
PERSONAL Born 02/03/1945, Lancaster, OH, m, 1984, 5 children **DISCIPLINE** UNITED STATES CULTURAL AND INTELLECTUAL HISTORY; URBAN HISTORY **EDUCATION** Miami Univ, OH, AB, 67, MA, 70, PhD, 73. **CAREER** Prof Hist, Chestnut Hill Col, 74-, Fulbright fel, 72. **HONORS AND AWARDS** Phi Beta Kappa, 67; Fulbright fel, 72. **MEMBERSHIPS** AHA; Am Studies Asn. **RESEARCH** Henry Adams. **SELECTED PUBLICATIONS** Auth, Henry Adams and the American Experiment, Little, Brown & Co, 80; Rise to World Power: Selected Letters of Whitelaw Reid, 1895-1912, Am Philos Soc, 86; America in the Twentieth Century: Coming of Age: HarperCollins, 88; A Philadelphia Family: The Houstons and the Woodwards of Chestnut Hill, Univ Penn Press, 88; Suburb in the City: Chestnut Hill, Philadelphia, 1850-1990, Ohio State Univ Press, 92; Henry Adams and His World, Am Philos Soc, 93; The Private Life of James Bond, Sutter House, 93; Villanova University, 1842-1992: American-Catholic-Augustinian, Penn State Press, 95; Philadelphia's Progressive Orphanage: The Carson Valley School, Penn State Press, 95; auth, "Lancaster, Ohio: Frontier Town to Edge City, 1800-2000," Ohio State Univ Press, 99; auth, "Saint Joseph's: Philadelphia's Jesuit University," St. Joseph's Univ Press, 00. **CONTACT ADDRESS** Dept of Hist, Chestnut Hill Col, 9601 Germantown Ave, Philadelphia, PA 19118-2693. **EMAIL** contosta@msn.com

CONTRENI, JOHN JOSEPH
PERSONAL Born 08/31/1944, Savannah, GA, m, 1986, 6 children **DISCIPLINE** MEDIEVAL HISTORY **EDUCATION** St Vincent Col, BA, 66; Mich State Univ, MA, 68, PhD, 71. **CAREER** From asst prof to assoc prof, 71-82, prof hist, Purdue Univ, West Lafayette, 82-, asst dean, Sch Humanities, Soc Sci, & Educ, 81-85, interim head, Dept For Lang & Lit, 83-85, head, Dept Hist, 85-97; co-ed, French Hist Studies, 92-00. **HONORS AND AWARDS** Excellence in Graduate Teaching Citation, Mich State Univ, 71; Grant, Summer Sem Paleography, Univ Chicago, 73; Am Philos Soc grant, 73 & 76; Nat Endowment for Humanities summer grant, 75; Am Coun Learned Soc study fel, 77-78; Liberal Arts Excellence in Teaching Awd, Purdue Univ, West Lafayette, 81; John Nicholas Brown Prize for "The Cathedral School of Laon..", Medieval Acad Am, 82; Liberal Arts Educational Excellence Awd, Purdue Univ, West Lafayette, 90; recipient of numerous research grants. **MEMBERSHIPS** AHA; Mediaeval Acad Am; Soc Prom Eriugenian Studies (Dublin). **RESEARCH** Carolingian renaissance; early medieval intellectual and cultural history; the liberal arts; education in the Middle Ages; Latin manuscripts and Palaeography. **SELECTED PUBLICATIONS** Transl, Pierre Riche, Education and culture in the Barbarian West, Sixth Through Eighth Centuries, Univ SC, 76; auth, The Cathedral School of Laon from 850 to 930: Its Manuscripts and Masters, Arbeo Gesellschaft, Munich, 78; co-ed, Religion, Culture and Society in the Early Middle Ages: Studies in Honor of Richard E. Sullivan, Western Mich Univ Press, 87; auth, Carolingian Learning, Masters and Manuscripts, Collected Studies Series, CS 363, Variorum, 92; coauth, Glossae Divinae Historiae: The Biblical Glosses of John Scottus Eriugena, Millennio Medievale 1, Testi 1, SISMEL: Edizioni del Galluzzo, 97; author of numerous journal articles, review essays, and book chapters. **CONTACT ADDRESS** Dept of Hist, Purdue Univ, West Lafayette, West Lafayette, IN 47907-1358. **EMAIL** contreni@purdue.edu

CONTRERAS, RAOUL
DISCIPLINE LATINO STUDIES **EDUCATION** Univ Calif, PhD, 92. **CAREER** From Asst prof to Assoc prof, Ind Univ, Northwest. **RESEARCH** Chicano studies; Latino studies; race ethnic studies; political science. **SELECTED PUBLICATIONS** Auth, Principles and Foundations of Chicano Studies: Chicano Organization on University Campuses in California, Univ Houston, 92; Chicano Movement Chicano Studies: Social Science and Self-conscious Ideology: Perspectives in Mexican American Studies-Mexican Americans in the 1990's, 97; auth, "Chicano Studies: A Political Strategy of the Chicano Movement," in Mapping Strategies: NACCS and the Challenge of Multiple Oppressions (99); auth, " What is Latino Studies? The Idealogical Dimension of Program Construction and porgram Location," Lation Studies J 11 (00). **CONTACT ADDRESS** Dept of Minority Studies, Indiana Univ, Northwest, 3400 Broadway, Gary, IN 46408. **EMAIL** Rcontrer@iunhaw1.iun.indiana.edu

CONVERSE, HYLA STUNTZ
PERSONAL Born 10/31/1920, Lahore, Pakistan, m, 1951, 2 children **DISCIPLINE** HISTORY OF RELIGIONS, SOUTH ASIAN LITERATURE **EDUCATION** Smith Col, BA, 43; Union Theol Sem, BD, 49; Columbia Univ, PhD(hist of relig), 71. **CAREER** Relief & rehab worker, Eglise Reforme France, 45-48; dir student work, Judson Mem Church, New York, 52-55; dir lit & study, Nat Student Christian Fed, 57-63; asst prof Asian relig & humanities, 68-78, chmn humanities fac, 73-78, assoc prof, 78-80, Prof Asian Relig & Humanities, Okla State Univ, 80-, Fulbright res fel, India, 74-75; Am Inst Pakistan Studies fel, 78-79. **MEMBERSHIPS** Am Orient Soc; Bhandarkar Oriental Res Inst. **RESEARCH** Religions of South Asia; literature of South Asia; arts of South Asia. **SELECTED PUBLICATIONS** Auth, An Ancient Sudra Account of the Origins of Castes, Jour Amer Oriental Soc, Vol 0114, 94. **CONTACT ADDRESS** Dept Relig Studies, Oklahoma State Univ, Stillwater, Stillwater, OK 74074.

CONWAY, JOHN S.
PERSONAL Born 12/31/1929, London, England **DISCIPLINE** HISTORY **EDUCATION** Cambridge Univ, BA, 52; MA, 55, PhD, 56. **CAREER** Asst prof, Univ Man, 55-57; asst prof, 57-64, assoc prof, 64-69, prof, 69-95, PROF EMER HISTORY, UNIV BC, 95-; moderator, Asn Contemp Church Hist, 95-. **HONORS AND AWARDS** Queen's Jubilee Medal, 77 **RESEARCH** Church history **SELECTED PUBLICATIONS** Auth, The Nazi Persecution of the Churches 1933-45, 68, reissued 97. **CONTACT ADDRESS** Dept of History, Univ of British Columbia, Vancouver, BC, Canada V6T 1Z1. **EMAIL** jconway@interchange.ubc.ca

CONWAY, MELISSA
PERSONAL m **DISCIPLINE** MEDIEVAL STUDIES **EDUCATION** Yale Univ, PhD, 94. **CAREER** Cur, Wash D.C., 91-; codir, UMCC, De Ricci Census Update Project, 96-. **MEMBERSHIPS** Medieval Acad Am; Am Libry Asn; Am Inst Conservation. **RESEARCH** Manuscripts and early printing **CONTACT ADDRESS** 25705 Horado Ln, Moreno Valley, CA 92551-1985. **EMAIL** drmconway@aol.com

CONYERS, JIM
PERSONAL Born 06/17/1961, Jersey City, NJ, m, 1985, 3 children **DISCIPLINE** AFRICAN STUDIES **EDUCATION** Rannapo Col, BA; State Univ NY (SUNY), MA; Temple Univ, PhD. **CAREER** Assoc Prof, Univ Nebr, -. **HONORS AND AWARDS** Alpha Phi Alpha. **MEMBERSHIPS** Nat Coun of Black Studies, African Heritage Asn. **RESEARCH** African-American history and sociology. **SELECTED PUBLICATIONS** Ed, Carter G Woodson: A Historical Reader; ed, Africana Studies: A Disciplinary Quest for Theory and Method. **CONTACT ADDRESS** Dept African Studies, Univ of Nebraska, Omaha, 6001 Dodge St, Omaha, NE 68182-0001. **EMAIL** James_conyers@unomaha.edu

COOK, BERNARD ANTHONY
PERSONAL Born 07/11/1941, Meridian, MS, m, 1966, 2 children **DISCIPLINE** MODERN EUROPEAN HISTORY **EDUCATION** Notre Dame Sem, BA, 63; St Louis Univ, MA, 66, PhD(hist), 70. **CAREER** Instr hist, Northern Mich Univ, 68; from instr to asst prof, 68-74, Assoc Prof Hist, Loyola Univ, LA, 74-; Chair Hist, 83-89; Prof Hist, Loyola Univ, LA, 85-; Co-director, Loyola Univ, 93; Assoc for Study/Ethnicity and Nationalism. **MEMBERSHIPS** AHA, LASEN. **RESEARCH** Ethnic Conflict, Belguim. **SELECTED PUBLICATIONS** Auth, Louisiana Labor, UPA, 1985; auth, Europe Since 1945: An Encyclopedia, Garland, 00. **CONTACT ADDRESS** Dept of Hist, Loyola Univ, New Orleans, 6363 St Charles Ave, New Orleans, LA 70118-6195. **EMAIL** cook@loyno.edu

COOK, BLANCHE WIESEN
PERSONAL Born 04/20/1941, New York, NY **DISCIPLINE** UNITED STATES HISTORY **EDUCATION** Hunter Col, BA, 62; Johns Hopkins Univ, MA, 64, PhD(hist), 70. **CAREER** Hampton Inst, 63; instr hist, Stern Col, Yeshiva Univ, 64-67; assoc prof, 69-80, Dist Prof Hist, John Jay Col Criminal Justice, & Grad Ctr 80-, Mem, Fac Sem Am Civilization, Columbia Univ, 70-; consult, World Law Fund-Inst Int Order, 71-76; co-chairwoman, Coord Comt of Women in Hist Prof, New York, 72-73; co-chairwoman, Freedom Info Off, Orgn Am Hist, 80-82. **MEMBERSHIPS** AHA; Orgn Am Hist; Am Studies Asn; Conf Peace Res in Hist (exec secy, 70-73, vpres, 76-78). **RESEARCH** Violence; war and peace; women. **SELECTED PUBLICATIONS** Sr ed, Garland Lib on War and Peace (360 vol reprint ser), Garland, 70-73; co-ed & contribr, Past--Imperfect, Knopf, 73; The Woman's Peace Party: Collaboration and Non-Cooperation in World War I, J Peace & Change, 72; Democracy in Wartime, Am Studies J, 72; contribr, American Peace Movements, Schocken, 73; auth, Female Support Networks and Political Activism, Chrysalis, Autumn 77; contribr, The D D Eisenhower Library: The Manuscript Fiefdom at Abilene, AHA-PAH-SAA, 77; ed, Crystal Eastman on Women & Revolution, Oxford Univ, 10/78; The Declassified Eisenhower: A Divided Legacy of Peace & Political Warfare, Doubleday, 81; Eleanor Roosevelt, Vol I, Viking-Penguin, 92; Eleanor Roosevelt, Vol II, Spring 99. **CONTACT ADDRESS** John Jay Col of Criminal Justice, CUNY, 445 W 59th St, New York, NY 10019.

COOK, HAROLD J.
PERSONAL Born 05/07/1952, Evanston, IL, m, 1985 **DISCIPLINE** HISTORY **EDUCATION** Cornell Col, BA, 74; Univ Mich, MA, 75; PhD, 81. **CAREER** Vis asst prof, Univ Okla, 81-82; asst professor/head tutor, Harvard Univ Dept of the Hist of Sci, 82-85; asst prof, Harvard Univ, 85-88; from assoc prof to prof, Univ Wis at Madison, 88-; chemn, Univ Wis at Madison Dept of the Hist of Medicine, 93-. **HONORS AND AWARDS** Welch Medal of AAHM; NEH; NLM; Fulbright; Inst of Advanced Study. **MEMBERSHIPS** AHA, AAHM, HHS. **RESEARCH** Early Modern Europe, History of Medicine, History of Science. **SELECTED PUBLICATIONS** Auth, "Medical Ethics, History of: IV. Europe: B. Renaissance and Enlighten-

ment," in Encyclopedia of Bioethics, editor-in-chief Warren T. Reich (NY: Macmillan Libr Ref, 95), 1537-1543; auth, "The Moral Economy of Natural History and Medicine in the Dutch Golden Age," in Publications of the American Association of Netherlandic Studies Volume 9, eds. William Z. Shetter and Inge Van der Cruysse (96), 39-47; auth, "Physicians and Natural History," in Cultures of Natural History, eds. Nicholas Jardine, James Secord, and Emma Spary (MA: Cambridge Univ Press, 96), 91-105; auth, "Institutional Structures and Personal Belief in the London College of Physicians," in Religion Medici: Medicine and Religion in 17th-Century England, eds. Ole Peter Grell and Andrew Cunningham (Scholar Press, 96), 91-114; auth, "From the Scientific Revolution to the Germ Theory," in Western Medicine: An Illustrated History, ed. Irvine Loudon (Oxford Univ Press, 97), 80-101; coauth, "Closed Circles or Open Networks?: Communicating at a Distance During the Scientific Revolution," Hist of Sci 36 (98): 179-211. **CONTACT ADDRESS** Dept Hist of Medicine, Univ of Wisconsin, Madison, 1300 University Ave, Madison, WI 53706-1320. **EMAIL** hjcook@facstaff.wisc.edu

COOK, NOBLE DAVID
PERSONAL Born 04/18/1941, Gary, IN, m, 1975, 3 children **DISCIPLINE** HISTORY **EDUCATION** Univ Florida, BA, 62, MA, 64; Univ Texas, PhD, 73. **CAREER** Fulbright Prof, 74, 84, Catholic Univ Peru; vis prof, 89-90, Yale Univ; instr, prof, 69-92, Univ Bridgeport; prof, 92-, chmn, 95-98, Florida Intl Univ. **HONORS AND AWARDS** Fel, Doherty Foundation, 68; fel, Wenner-Gren Foundation, 77; fel, John Simon Guggenheim Memorial Foundation, 91-92; fel, American Council of Learned Studies, 98-99. **RESEARCH** Colonial Hispanic Amer, early modern Spain. Disease and Population **SELECTED PUBLICATIONS** Auth, Demographic Collapse: Indian Peru,1520-1620, Cambridge U P, 81; auth, People of the Colca Valley: A Population Study, Westview Press, 82; coed, " Secret Judgments of God: Old World Disease in Colonial Spanish America, Oklahoma U P , 92; coauth, " Good Faith and Truthful Ingnorance," A Case of Transatlantic Bigamy, Duke U P , 92; cotransl, coed, The Discovery and Conquest of Peru by Pedro de Cieza de Leon, Duke U P , 98; auth, " Born to Die," Disease and New World Conquest, 1492-1650, Cambridge, 97. **CONTACT ADDRESS** Dept of History, Florida Intl Univ, Miami, FL 33199-0001. **EMAIL** cookn@fiu.edu

COOK, PHILIP C.
PERSONAL Born 10/31/1933, Ringgold, LA, m, 1971, 1 child **DISCIPLINE** HISTORY **EDUCATION** La State Univ, BA, 56; La Tech Univ, MA, 66; Univ GA, PhD, 68. **CAREER** Instr hist, La Tech Univ, 63-64; tchg asst, Univ Ga, 64-67; asst prof hist, NE La Univ, 67 69; assoc prof hist, 69-87, prof-hist, La Tech Univ, 87-. **HONORS AND AWARDS** Louisiana Tech Found Teaching Awd; Garnie W. McGinty Prof of Hist, 92. **MEMBERSHIPS** La Hist Rec Adv Comn; Southern Hist Asn; La Hist Asn; N La Hist Asn; Southwestern Hist Asn; Louisiana Review Comt of the Nat Register of Hist Phces. **RESEARCH** Louisiana hist; mod Europ hist. **SELECTED PUBLICATIONS** Auth, Louisiana: A Political History in Cartoon and Narrative, Dean. La Hist,96; End of the Land: A South Carolina Family on the Louisiana Frontier, Shreveport Times, 94; The Foreign French: Immigration into Ninteenth Century Louisiana, Vol I, 1820-1837, Brasseaux. La Hist, 92; The Roads and Trails of Early North Louisiana, N La Geneal Soc Jour, 88; The Pioneer Preachers of the North Louisiana Hill Country, N La Hist Asoc Jour, 83; A Case Study of Functional Preservation The Kidd-Davis House of Ruston, N La Hist Asoc Jour, 78; auth, The North Louisiana Upland Frontier, North Louisiana, vol. One, 84. **CONTACT ADDRESS** Dept of Hist, Louisiana Tech Univ, PO Box 3178, Ruston, LA 71272.

COOK, THEODORE F., JR.
DISCIPLINE JAPANESE HISTORY **EDUCATION** Trinity Col, BA, 69; Univ London, MA, 70; Princeton Univ, PhD, 87. **CAREER** Asst intr, Princeton Univ, 73-74; sponsored lectr, Far E Div, Univ Md, 77-81; mil and polit anal, Off E Asian Anal, Cent Intel Agency, Washington, DC, 81-85; lectr, Merrill Col, Univ Calif Santa Cruz, 87; lectr, Univ Calif San Diego, 87-88; assoc prof, William Paterson Col, 88-; dir, Japanese Hist and Cult Curric, , Univ Calif San Diego & Japan Performing Arts Ctr Prog, Higashi-Tonami Gun, Toyama Prefecture, Japan, 88-93; vis prof, US Naval War Col, 94-95; vis prof, Australian Defense Force Univ, Univ New South Wales, Australia, 00. ' **HONORS AND AWARDS** res fel, Inst Soc Sci Res, Tokyo Univ, 75-76, 77-78; sr res fel, Inst Soc Sci Res, Tokyo Univ, 88-89; Prof fel for Res in Japan, Japan Foundation, 88-89; NEH Travel to Collections Grant for Japan, Nat Endowment for the Humanities, 90; Japan Found, Int Conf Awd, William Paterson Col, 91; tes travel grant Northeast Asia Coun, Asn Asian Stud, 91; Nat Endowment for the Humanities, Summer Stipend, NEH Small Col Div, 93; Nobel Res fel, Norwegian Nobel Inst, 94; Nat Endowment for the Humanities Res fel, Col Tchr(s) Div, 94-95; sr res fel, Japan, 94-95; NJ State Fac fel, Rutgers Ctr for Hist Anal, Rutgers Univ, 94-95; sr res fel, Inst for Soc Sci Res, Tokyo Univ, 94-95; res fel, Defense Res Inst, Japan Defense Agency, Tokyo, 95; Harry Frank Guggenheim Found, 98-00. **MEMBERSHIPS** Ch, Columbia Univ Sem on Mod Japan, 91-93 & exec comt, 91-; Int-Univ Sem on Armed Forces & Soc; Gunjishi Gakkai, Mil Hist Asn Japan; Mil Hist Asn US; World War Two Stud Asn & the Comte Int d'Hist de la Deuxieme Guerre Mondiale; NY Mil Aff Symp; AHA; Asn Asian Stud; Int House of Japan; Japan Soc NY; Asia Soc NY. **RESEARCH** War and society in Japan, a study of modern Japanese history from the prospective of war and society. **SELECTED PUBLICATIONS** Auth, Cataclysm and Career Rebirth: The Imperial Military Elite, Work and Lifecourse in Japan, Albany: SUNY Press, 83; Tokyo: December 8, 1941; Dawn of a New War, MHQ: The Quart J of Mil Hist, 91; coauth, Japan at War, An Oral History, NY: The New Press, 92; auth, The Merchant Seaman's Tale, MHQ: The Quart J of Mil Hist, 93; auth, Heishi to kokka, heishi to shakai: Yo"bei sekai e Nihon no Sannyu- The Soldier and the State, Soldiers and Society: Japan Joins the Western World, Nihon Kin-Gendaishi, A Hist of Mod and Contemporary Japan, vol 2: Shihonshugi to Jiyu-shugi Capitalism and Liberalism, Tokyo: Iwanami Sho"ten, 93; rev(s) J Japanese Stud & J Asian Stud; in, Rev in Hist. **CONTACT ADDRESS** Dept of History, William Paterson Col of New Jersey, 300 Pompton Rd., Wayne, NJ 07470. **EMAIL** cookt@upunj.edu

COOK, WARREN LAWRENCE
PERSONAL Born 07/29/1925, Spokane, WA, m, 1963 **DISCIPLINE** LATIN AMERICAN HISTORY **EDUCATION** Univ San Marcos, Peru, BA, 50; Yale Univ, MA, 57, PhD, 60. **CAREER** From asst prof to assoc prof hist, 60-70, chmn dept soc sci, 67-68, Prof Hist & Anthrop, Castleton State Col, 70-. **HONORS AND AWARDS** Bolton Prize, Conf Latin Am Hist, 74; dlitt, univ san marcos, peru, 55. **MEMBERSHIPS** AHA; Conf Latin Am Hist; Soc Hist Discoveries; Epigraphic Soc. **RESEARCH** Andean history and anthropology; Spanish explorations in North America, especially in the Pacific Northwest; ancient lithic culture of New England. **SELECTED PUBLICATIONS** Auth, The Roots of Country-Music, Amer Heritage, Vol 0046, 95. **CONTACT ADDRESS** Dept of Hist, Castleton State Col, Castleton, VT 05735.

COOK, WILLIAM ROBERT
PERSONAL Born 12/27/1943, Indianapolis, IN, s, 3 children **DISCIPLINE** MEDIEVAL HISTORY, HISTORY OF CHRISTIANITY **EDUCATION** Wabash Col, AB, 66; Cornell Univ, MA, 70, PhD(medieval hist), 71. **CAREER** Asst prof hist, 70-77, Assoc Prof Hist, State Univ NY Col Geneseo, 77-82; Prof, 82-84; Distinguished Teaching Prof, 84-; Nat Endowment for Humanities fel in residence, Harvard Univ, 76-77; adj prof lit, Attica Correctional Facil, 80 & 81; adj prof relig studies, Siena Col, NY, 81. **HONORS AND AWARDS** Phi Beta Kappa; CASE Prof of the Year for NY, 92. **MEMBERSHIPS** AHA; Mediaeval Acad Am; Am Soc Church Hist; Am Friends Bodley; Dante Soc Am. **RESEARCH** Medieval Franciscanism; Monasticism; Siena, Italy. **SELECTED PUBLICATIONS** Coauth, The Medieval World View, Oxford, UP, 83; auth, Frances: The Way of Poverty and Humility, Liturgical Press, 89; auth, St. Francis in America, Franciscan Press, 98; auth, Images of St. Francis in Painting, Stone and from the Earlect Image to ca. 1320 in: A Catalogue. **CONTACT ADDRESS** Dept of Hist, SUNY, Col at Geneseo, 1 College Cir, Geneseo, NY 14454-1401. **EMAIL** cookb@geneseo.edu

COOKE, JACOB ERNEST
PERSONAL Born 09/23/1924, Aulander, NC, m, 1956 **DISCIPLINE** HISTORY **EDUCATION** Columbia Univ, PhD, 55. **CAREER** Instr hist, Columbia Univ, 52-55, asst prof, 60-61; prof & head dept, Carnegie Inst technol, 61-62; MacCracken Prof Hist, Lafayette Col, 62-, Assoc ed, Papers of Alexander Hamilton, 55-72; assoc, sem, Columbia Univ, 67-72, vis prof, univ, 68-69; Guggenheim fel, 68-69; Nat Endowment for Humanities fel, 72-73; Nat Humanities Ctr fel, 81; resident scholar, Bellagio Study and Conf Ctr, spring 82. **MEMBERSHIPS** AHA; Orgn Am Historians. **RESEARCH** American history, 1763-1815; United States constitutional history; American history, post World War II. **SELECTED PUBLICATIONS** Auth, Encyclopedia of the North American; auth, Colonies, 4 vols, Scribner's, 93; auth, When Illness Strikes the Leader--The Dilemma of the Captive King from George-III to Reagan,Ronald, Jour Interdisciplinary Hist, Vol 0025, 95; Historian by Happenstance--One Scholars Odyssey, William and Mary Quart, Vol 0052, 95. **CONTACT ADDRESS** 212 W Wayne Ave., Easton, PA 18042-1561. **EMAIL** cookj82@cs.com

COOKE, JAMES JEROME
PERSONAL Born 08/02/1939, Baltimore, MD, m, 1961, 4 children **DISCIPLINE** NORTH AFRICAN, MILITARY, & FRENCH HISTORY **EDUCATION** MS Col, BA, 65, MA, 66; Univ GA, PhD(hist), 69. **CAREER** Asst prof, 69-73, assoc prof, 73-79, PROF HIST, UNIV MS, 79-99-. **HONORS AND AWARDS** Order of the Academic Palms, Knight, Min of Educ, Fr Govt, 75. **MEMBERSHIPS** Western Front Asn; fel, Royal Hist Soc; League of WWI Aviation Historians. **SELECTED PUBLICATIONS** Auth, New French Imperialism: The Third Republic Colonial Expansion, 1880-1910, 73 & A Dict of Modern French History, 1789-1962, 75, Newton Abbot, England & David & Charles; coauth, Through Foreign Eyes: Western Attitudes Toward North Africa, Univ Press Am, 81; auth, The Old South in the Crucibles of War, Univ Press MS, 83; 100 Miles From Bagdad, 93; The Rainbow Division in the Great War, 1917-1919, 94; The US Air Service in the Great War, 1917-1919, 96; Pershing and His Generals: Command and Staff in the AEF, Praeger Pub, 97; auth, The All-Americans at War: The 82nd Division in The Great War, Praeger Pub, 99. **CONTACT ADDRESS** Dept of Hist, Univ of Mississippi, General Delivery, University, MS 38677-9999. **EMAIL** jjcooke@olemiss.edu

COOLEY, ROBERT E.
PERSONAL Born Kalamazoo, MI, m, 1952, 2 children **DISCIPLINE** HEBREW STUDIES; NEAR EASTERN ARCHAEOLOGY **EDUCATION** Wheaton Col, BA; Wheaton Col Grad Sch, MA; NYork Univ, PhD. **CAREER** Asst to the pres, Dropsie Univ; acad dean, Evangel Col; prof, Southwest Mo State Univ; dir, Ctr Archaeol Res, Southwest Mo State Univ; pres, 81-97; chancellor, Gordon-Conwell Theol Sem, 97-00; Exec. Dir., CTI Found, 00-. **HONORS AND AWARDS** Ch bd dir(s), World Relief Corp; pres, Assn Theol Sch(s), US, Can; bd dir(s), InTrust mag; pres, In Trust, Inc. **MEMBERSHIPS** SBL **SELECTED PUBLICATIONS** Sr ed, Christianity Today. **CONTACT ADDRESS** Gordon-Conwell Theol Sem, 130 Essex St, South Hamilton, MA 01982. **EMAIL** recgcts@aol.com

COOLEY, THOMAS WINFIELD
PERSONAL Born 06/24/1942, Gaffney, SC, m, 1989, 1 child **DISCIPLINE** AMERICAN LITERATURE, AMERICAN STUDIES **EDUCATION** Duke Univ, BA, 64; Ind Univ, Bloomington, MA, 68, PhD(English), 70. **CAREER** Asst prof, 70-79, Assoc Prof English, Ohio State Univ, 80-99; Prof of English, 00. **HONORS AND AWARDS** NEH Research grants; U.S. State Dept "Participant", Australia, New Zealand, and Taiwan; Exec Comnr of Am Lit Section of MLA. **MEMBERSHIPS** MLA. **RESEARCH** American literature; autobiography; psychology of narrative; composition. **SELECTED PUBLICATIONS** Auth, Educated Lives: The Rise of Modern Autobiography in America, Columbus: OSU Press, 76; auth, The Norton Sampler, New York: Norton 97; auth, The Norton Critical Edition of Huckleberry Finn, New York: Norton, 99; auth, The Ivory Leg in the Ebony Cabinet: Madness, Race, and Gender in Victorian America, Univ of MA Press, 01; auth, The Selected Letters of Sophia Hawthorne, Ohio State Univ Press; auth, American Literature, Twentieth-Century Literature, College Composition and Communication, Ohio History. **CONTACT ADDRESS** Dept of English, Ohio State Univ, Columbus, 164 W 17th Ave, Columbus, OH 43210-1326. **EMAIL** Cooley.1@osu.edu

COOMBS, FRANK ALAN
PERSONAL Born 09/26/1938, Belleville, KS, m, 1961, 2 children **DISCIPLINE** RECENT UNITED STATES HISTORY **EDUCATION** Univ Kans, BA, 60; Univ Ill, MA, 64, PhD(Hist), 68. **CAREER** Asst prof, 68-73, assoc prof Hist, Univ Utah, 73-, vis prof, Univ Hawaii, Hilo, 77-78. **MEMBERSHIPS** AHA; Orgn Am Historians. **RESEARCH** The New Deal; American politics; Truman and Eisenhower eras; 20th Century Am West. **SELECTED PUBLICATIONS** Auth, The impact of the new deal on Wyoming politics, In: The New Deal, Vol 2, The State and Local Levels, Ohio State Univ Press, 75; Twentieth-century western politics, In: Historians and the American West, Univ of Nebraska Press, 83; Congressional opinion and war relocation, 43, In: Japanese Americans from Relocation to Redress, Univ of Utah Press, 86. **CONTACT ADDRESS** Dept of History, Univ of Utah, 380 S 1400 E Rm 211, Salt Lake City, UT 84112-0311. **EMAIL** ACoombs@mail.hum.utah.edu

COON, DAVID L.
DISCIPLINE EARLY AMERICA HISTORY **EDUCATION** Univ Ill Urbana, PhD, 72. **CAREER** Assoc prof, Washington State Univ. **HONORS AND AWARDS** Burlington Northern Fac Achievement Awd, 88. **RESEARCH** George Washington's Mount Vernon slave community and a general survey of American agricultural history. **SELECTED PUBLICATIONS** Auth, The Development of Market Agriculture in South Carolina, 89. **CONTACT ADDRESS** Dept of History, Washington State Univ, 301 Wilson Hall, PO Box 644030, Pullman, WA 99164-4030. **EMAIL** coond@wsu.edu

COON, LYNDA L.
DISCIPLINE HISTORY **EDUCATION** Univ Va, PhD. **CAREER** Assoc prof. **RESEARCH** Medieval European history. **SELECTED PUBLICATIONS** Auth, Sacred Fictions: Holy Women and Hagiography in late Antiquity, Univ Pa, 97; co-ed, That Gentle Strength: Historical Perspectives on Women and Christianity, Univ Va, 90. **CONTACT ADDRESS** History Dept, Univ of Arkansas, Fayetteville, 509 Old Main, Fayetteville, AR 72701. **EMAIL** llcoon@comp.uark.edu

COONEY, TERRY ARNOLD
PERSONAL Born 06/20/1948, Presque Isle, ME, s, 2 children **DISCIPLINE** UNITED STATES HISTORY **EDUCATION** Harvard Univ, BA, 70; State Univ NYork, Stony Brook, MA, 71, PhD(hist), 76. **CAREER** Asst Prof Hist, Univ Puget Sound, 76-82, Assoc Prof 83-88, Prof 89, Assoc Dean 89-95, Academic VP, 97-, Nat Endowment Humanities fel, 80-81, 88-99. **HONORS AND AWARDS** Phi Beta Kappa, Phi Kappa Phi, Gaves Awd in the Humanities, 84, John D. Regaster Lectureship, 87, Burlington Northern Faculty Achievement Awd, 85,88, Ap-

pointed Robert G. Albertson Prof, 96. **MEMBERSHIPS** AHA; Orgn Am Historians, ASA. **RESEARCH** Literary radicalism in the twentieth century; American cultural values; Intellectual Tolerance. **SELECTED PUBLICATIONS** Auth, New Readings on the Old Left, Am Literacy History, vol 0011, 99; auth, Renewing The Left--Politics, Imagination, and the New-York Intellectuals, Amer Hist Rev, Vol 0102, 97; auth, Balancing Act: American Thought and Culture in the 1930's, Twayne, 95; Remaking America--Public Memory, Commemoration, and Patriotism in the 20th-Century, Pacific Northwest Quart, Vol 0084, 93; auth, The Rise of NY Intellectuals, Univ of Wiscousin Press, 86. **CONTACT ADDRESS** Dept of Hist, Univ of Puget Sound, 1500 N Warner St, Tacoma, WA 98416-0005. **EMAIL** cooney@ups.edu

COONS, RONALD E.
PERSONAL Born 07/24/1936, Elmhurst, IL, s **DISCIPLINE** HISTORY **EDUCATION** DePauw Univ, BA, 58; Harvard Univ, AM, 59; PhD, 66. **CAREER** Asst prof to prof, Univ of Conn Storrs, 66-. **HONORS AND AWARDS** Teaching Fel, Harvard Univ, 61-62, 63-66; Res Fel, Inst fur Europaische Geschichte, Germany, 62-63. **MEMBERSHIPS** AHA; Phi Beta Kappa; Phi Alpha Theta; AAUP; Ger Studies Assoc; Conf Group for Central European Hist; Soc for Austrian and Habsburg Hist; New England Hist Assoc; Hist Soc. **RESEARCH** Austrian History 1815 - 1848. **SELECTED PUBLICATIONS** Auth, Steamships, Statesmen, and Bureaucrats. Austrian Policy towards the Steam Navigation Company of the Austrian Lloyd 1836-1848, Veroffentlichungen des Instituts fur Europaische Geschichte Mainz, Band 74, Franz Steiner Verlag, 75; auth, I primi anni del Lloyd Austriaco. Politica di governo a Vienna ed iniziative imprenditoriali a Trieste, 1836-1848, Civilta del Risorgimento, 15 (Undine: Del Bianco Editore), 82; auth, "Kubeck and the Pre-Revolutionary Origins of Austrian Neoabsolutism" in Gesellschaft, Politik und Verwaltung in der Habsburgermonarchie 1830-1918, eds Ferenc Glatz and Ralph Melville, (Stuttgart/Budapest: Franz Steiner Verlag), 55-86; auth, "Steamships and Quarantines at Trieste, 1837-1848", J of the Hist of Medicine and Allied Sci, 44.1 (89): 28-55; auth "Austrian Maritime Quarantine Reform During the Vormarz", Etudes Danubiennes 5.1 (89): 23-38; coauth, "An Audacious Proposal: A Memorandum Attributed to Finance Minister Karl Ludwig Freiherr von Bruck" Mitteilungen des Osterreichischen Staatsarchivs, Sonderband 3 (97): 151-174; auth, "Over Land and Sea, 1857 - 1909. Memoir of an Austrian Rear Admiral's Life in Europe and Africa, 1857-1909", eds Ronald E. Coons and Pascal James Imperato, Homes and Meier, (NY), 00. **CONTACT ADDRESS** Dept Hist, Univ of Connecticut, Storrs, 241 Glenbrook Rd, Storrs, CT 06269-2103. **EMAIL** recoons@hotmail.com

COOPE, JESSICA
DISCIPLINE MEDIEVAL EUROPEAN HISTORY **EDUCATION** Univ Calif, Berkeley, PhD, 88. **CAREER** Assoc prof, Undergrad Ch, Univ Nebr, Lincoln. **HONORS AND AWARDS** Distinguished Tchg Awd, Univ Nebr, Lincoln, 98. **RESEARCH** Medieval Spain. **SELECTED PUBLICATIONS** Auth, The Martyrs of Cordoba: Community and Family Conflict in an Age of Mass Conversion, Univ Nebr Press, 95. **CONTACT ADDRESS** Univ of Nebraska, Lincoln, 625 Oldfather, Lincoln, NE 68588-0417. **EMAIL** jcoope@unlinfo.unl.edu

COOPER, DANIELLE CHAVY
PERSONAL Born 12/11/1921, Paris, France, m, 1947, 1 child **DISCIPLINE** FRENCH STUDIES **EDUCATION** Univ Paris, BA, 39, MA, 41, PhD(Am lit), 42; Univ Southern Calif, PhD, 63. **CAREER** Teacher English & Span, Sec Schs, France, 42-44; asst French, Whalley Range High Sch & Univ Manchester, 45-46; Marcelle Parde teaching fel, Bryn Mawr Col, 46-47; lang coordr, Isabelle Buckley Schs, Los Angeles, Calif, 55-56; instr French & Ger, Immaculate Heart Col, 57-60, asst prof French, 60-63; lectr, Univ Colo, 63-65; from assoc prof to prof, Keuka Col, 65-70, chmn dept mod lang, 65-70; chmn div lang & civilizations, 71-73, chmn dept lang & humanities, 75-77, Prof French, Monterey Inst Int Studies, Instr French, Fr Found Calif, Los Angeles, 56-58; bd reviewer, Bks Abroad/World Lit Today, 58-; instr, Univ Southern Calif, 58; mem, Alliance Francaise. **HONORS AND AWARDS** Chevalier, Ordre des Palmes Academiques, 72. **MEMBERSHIPS** Am Asn Teachers Fr; MLA; African Studies Asn; Am Name Soc; Philol Asn Pac Coast. **RESEARCH** French phonetics; African and Caribbean literature of French expression; translation theory and practice. **SELECTED PUBLICATIONS CONTACT ADDRESS** Monterey Inst of Intl Studies, PO Box 1978, Monterey, CA 93940.

COOPER, DONALD B.
PERSONAL Born 08/20/1931, Columbus, OH, m, 1957, 3 children **DISCIPLINE** LATIN AMERICAN HISTORY **EDUCATION** Ohio State Univ, BA, 57; Univ Tex, MA, 58, PhD, 63. **CAREER** Asst prof Latin Am hist, Okla State Univ, 61-63; from asst prof to assoc prof, Tulane Univ, 63-69; Prof Latin Am Hist, Ohio State Univ, 69-, Nat Libr Med & Commonwealth Fund spec res fels, Brazil, 67-68. **MEMBERSHIPS** AHA; Latin Am Studies Asn; Conf Latin Am Hist. **RESEARCH** Medical and social history of Latin America, especially 19th and 20th century Brazil and 18th century Mexico. **SELECTED PUBLICATIONS** Auth, Selective list of the colonial manuscripts, 1564-1800, in the archives of the Department of Health and Wefare, Mexico City: A newly-discovered source for religious and architectural history, Hisp Am Hist Rev, 8/62; Withdrawal of the United States from Haiti, 1928-1934, J Inter-Am Studies, 1/63; Epidemic Disease in Mexico City, 1761-1813, an administrative, social, and medical study, Univ Tex, 65; The establishment of the Anglican Church in the Leeward Islands, Okla State Univ Monogr Humanities, 66; Brazil's long fight against epidemic disease, 1849-1917, with special emphasis on yellow fever, Bull NY Acad Med, 5/75. **CONTACT ADDRESS** Dept of Hist, Ohio State Univ, Columbus, Columbus, OH 43210.

COOPER, FREDERICK A.
PERSONAL Born 12/12/1936, Sewickley, PA, m, 1991, 5 children **DISCIPLINE** GREEK AND ROMAN ART, GREEK ARCHITECTURE, ARCHAEOLOGY **EDUCATION** Yale Univ, AB, 59; Univ Pittsburg, MA, 62; Univ Pa, PhD, 70. **CAREER** Prof, Univ Minn, Twin Cities. **HONORS AND AWARDS** CLA Distinguished Tchr Awds, Univ Minn, 72-73, 89-90; Guggenheim fel, 79-80; Morse-Minn Alumni Awd, 91; Excellence in Undergrad Tchg Awd, Archaeol Inst of Am, 96. **RESEARCH** Medieval architecture. **SELECTED PUBLICATIONS** Auth, The Temple of Zeus at Nemea: The Reconstruction Project, 83; coauth, Dining in Round Buildings, in Sympotika, ed, O Murray, 90; Satellite Spectral Data and Archaeological Reconnaissance in Western Greece, in Applications of Space-Age Technology in Anthropology, eds, C Behrens and L Sever, 91; The Quarries of Mt. Taygetos in the Peloponessos, Greece, in Marble in Ancient Greece and Rome: Geology, Quarries, Commerce, Artifacts, ed, N Herz and M Waelkens, 92; The Temple of Apollo Bassitas, 92-97. **CONTACT ADDRESS** Univ of Minnesota, Twin Cities, 9 Pleasant St SE, 305D Folwell Hall, Minneapolis, MN 55455. **EMAIL** coope002@tc.umn.edu

COOPER, GAIL
PERSONAL Born 03/20/1954, Visalia, CA, m, 1988 **DISCIPLINE** HISTORY **EDUCATION** Univ Calif, Santa Barbara, PhD, 87. **CAREER** Asst prof, 87-96, assoc prof, 96-, Lehigh Univ. **MEMBERSHIPS** Soc History Tech; Amer Hist Assn. **RESEARCH** History of technology; Japanese industrialization; technology and gender. **SELECTED PUBLICATIONS** Auth, Air-conditioning America: Engineers and the Controlled Environment, 1900-1960, 98; auth, "Love, War, and Chocolate: Gender and the American Candy Industry, 1890-1930," in His and Hers: Gender, Consumption, and technology, 98. **CONTACT ADDRESS** Dept of History, Lehigh Univ, 9 W Packer Ave, Bethlehem, PA 18015. **EMAIL** gc05@lehigh.edu

COOPER, JERROLD STEPHEN
PERSONAL Born 11/24/1942, Chicago, IL, 3 children **DISCIPLINE** ASSYRIOLOGY **EDUCATION** Univ Calif, Berkeley, AB, 63, AM, 64; Univ Chicago, PhD(Assyriol), 69. **CAREER** Asst prof, 68-74, assoc prof, 74-79, prof Near Eastern Studies, Johns Hopkins Univ, 79-, dept chair, 84-91, Co-ed, J Cuneiform Studies, 72-89. **MEMBERSHIPS** Am Orient Soc; Am Schools of Oriental Res. **RESEARCH** Sumerian literature, Mesopotamian history, gender and sexuality in antiquity, early writing systems. **SELECTED PUBLICATIONS** Auth, The Return of Ninurta to Nippur, Pontif Bibl Inst, 78; Symmetry and repetion in Akkadian narrative, J Am Orient Soc, 78; Apodotic death and the historicity of historical omens, Mesopotamia, Vol 8, 80; Studies in Mesopotamian Lapidary Inscription, Vol I & II, J Cuneiform Studies & Rev'd Assyriologie, 80; The Curse of the Agade, Johns Hopkins Press, 82; ed, Mesopotamian Civilizations, 87-; auth, Reconstructing History from Ancient Sources: The Lagash-Umma Border Conflict, Malibu, Udena Publ, 87; auth, Sumerian and Akkadian royal Inscriptions Vol.1: Presargonic Inscriptions, New Haven, Am Oriental Soc, 86; co-ed, The Study of the Ancient Near East in the 21st Century: The WF Albright Centenary Conference, Eisenbrauns, 96; auth, Paradigm and Propaganda: The Dynasty of Akkade in the 21st Century BC, Akkad, the First World Empire: Structure, Ideology, Traditions, ed. M. Liverani, 11-23, 93; Magic and M(is)use: Poetic Promiscuity in Mesopotamian Ritual, Mesopotamian Poetic Language: Sumerian and Akkadian, Styx Publ, 47-57, 96. **CONTACT ADDRESS** Dept of Near Eastern Studies, Johns Hopkins Univ, Baltimore, 3400 N Charles St, Baltimore, MD 21218-2680. **EMAIL** anzu@jhu.edu

COOPER, JERRY MARVIN
PERSONAL Born 11/25/1939, Three Rivers, MI, 1 child **DISCIPLINE** AMERICAN HISTORY **EDUCATION** Western Mich Univ, BA, 65; Univ Wis-Madison, MA, 68, PhD(Am hist), 71. **CAREER** Asst prof, 71-77, assoc prof Am Hist, Univ Mo-St Louis, 77-. **MEMBERSHIPS** Orgn Am Historians; Soc of Military History; Society for Historians of American Foreign Relations. **RESEARCH** American military history; 20th century American history. **SELECTED PUBLICATIONS** Auth, The Wisconsin National Guard in the Milwaukee riots of 2886, Wis Mag Hist, fall 71; National Guard reform, the Army, and the Spanish-American war: the view from Wisconsin, Mil Affairs, 2/78; The Army and Civil Disorder: Federal Military Intervention in American Labor Disputes, Greenwood Press, 80; Citizens As Soldiers: A History of the North Dakota National Gueard, North Dakota State U. Press, 86; The Militia and National Guard In America Since Colonial Times: A Research Guide, Greenwood Press, 93; The Rise of the National Guard: Evolution of the American Militia, 1865-1920, University of Nebraska Press, 97. **CONTACT ADDRESS** Dept of History, Univ of Missouri, St. Louis, 8001 Natural Bridge, Saint Louis, MO 63121-4499. **EMAIL** cooperj@msx.umsl.edu

COOPER, SANDI E.
PERSONAL Born 05/11/1936, New York, NY, m, 1967, 2 children **DISCIPLINE** MODERN HISTORY **CAREER** Grad asst hist,59-60, NY Univ; instr,61-65, lectr, 66-67, Douglass Col, Rutgers Univ; asst prof, 67-71, assoc prof, 71-79, prof hist, div soc sci, chmn, 94-98, Univ Fac Senate, Col Staten Island, Grad Schl - CUNY; Natl co-pres, Coord Comt Women in Hist Profes, 71-73; pres, Berkshire Conf Women Historians, 79-81. **HONORS AND AWARDS** NEH; USIP Fels. **MEMBERSHIPS** AHA; Soc Hist Studies, France; Peace Hist Soc; Inst Res Hist. **SELECTED PUBLICATIONS** Auth, Patriotic Pacifism: Waging War on War in Europe 1815-1914, Oxford, 91; auth, of 30 introd & ed, Garland Library of War and Peace, Garland, 71-76; ed, Biographical Dictionary of Modern Peace Leaders, Greenwood (in prep). **CONTACT ADDRESS** Dept of History, Col of Staten Island, CUNY, Staten Island, NY 10301. **EMAIL** sansi@cunyvm.cuny.edu

COOPER, WILLIAM
PERSONAL Born 10/22/1940, Kingstree, SC, m, 1962, 2 children **DISCIPLINE** HISTORY **EDUCATION** Princeton Univ, AB, 62; Johns Hopkins Univ, PhD, 66. **CAREER** Asst prof, 68-70, Assoc prof, 70-78, prof 78-89, dean, graduate sch, 82-89, Boyd prof, 89-, Louisiana State Univ. **MEMBERSHIPS** Amer Hist Assn; Organization of Amer Historian; Southern Historical Assn. **RESEARCH** Amer Hist; Hist of the South (19th century) **SELECTED PUBLICATIONS** auth, The Conservative Regime: South Carolina 1877-1890, LSU Press, 91; coauth, The American South: A History, McGraw Hill, NY, 96; coauth, Writing the Civil War: The Quest to Understand, Univ S. Carolina Press, 98. **CONTACT ADDRESS** Dept of History, Louisiana State Univ and A&M Col, Baton Rouge, LA 70803. **EMAIL** wcooper@lsu.edu

COOPERSMITH, JONATHAN C.
DISCIPLINE HISTORY **EDUCATION** Princeton Univ, AB, 78; Oxford Univ, PhD, 85. **CAREER** Asst prof to assoc prof, Tex A&M Univ, 88-. **HONORS AND AWARDS** Fel, IREX, 85-86; Fe. IEEE, 86-87; Grant, Texas A&M Univ, 93, 94, 95-96; Grant, Nat Sci Found, 94-95. **RESEARCH** History of the facsimile machine, 1843 - present. **SELECTED PUBLICATIONS** Auth, The Electrification of Russian, 1880-1926, Cornell Univ Pr, 92; auth, "Soviet Electrification: The Roads Not Taken," IEEE Tech and Soc Mag 12.2 (93): 13-20; auth, "The Failure of Fax: When a Vision is Not Enough," Bus and Econ Hist 23.1, (94): 272-282; auth, "Technological Innovation and Failure: The Case of the Fax Machine," Proc of the Conf on Bus Hist, Erasmus Univ, (95): 61-77; auth, "Disposal of Nuclear Waste in Space," Space News, (Feb 13, 95):15; auth, "Texas Politics and the Fax Revolution," Infor Syst Res 7.1 (96): 37-51; auth, "Pornography, Technology, and Progress," ICON 4, (98): 94-125; auth, "Creating the Commons: Establishing a Civic Space for a New Form of Communications," Bus and Econ Hist 28.1 (99): 115-24; auth, "Pornography, Videotape, and the Internet," IEEE Tech and Soc 19.1, (00):27-34. **CONTACT ADDRESS** Dept Hist, Texas A&M Univ, Col Station, College Station, TX 77843. **EMAIL** j-coopersmith@tamu.edu

COPE, ESTHER SIDNEY
PERSONAL Born 09/09/1942, West Chester, PA **DISCIPLINE** ENGLISH AND EUROPEAN HISTORY **EDUCATION** Wilson Col, BA, 64; Univ Wis, MA, 65; Bryn Mawr Col, PhD(hist), 69. **CAREER** Instr hist, Ursinus Col, 68-70, asst prof, 70-75; asst prof, 75-77, assoc prof, 77-81, Prof Hist, Univ Nebr-Lincoln, 81-. **MEMBERSHIPS** Conf Brit Studies (rec secy, 77-81); AHA; Int Comn Study Rep & Parliamentary Inst; fel Royal Hist Soc. **RESEARCH** Political history of early Stuart England. **SELECTED PUBLICATIONS** Auth, The short Parliament and convocation, J Ecclesiastical Hist, 74; co-ed, Proceedings of the Short Parliament, Royal Hist Soc Camden Ser, 77; ed, The Earl of Bedford's Journal of the Short Parliament, Bull Inst Hist Res, 80; auth, The inconveniences of a long absence of Parliament and a remedy for them, Albion, 80; The Life of a Public Man: Edward, Lord Montagu of Boughton, 1562-1644, Am Philos Soc, 81; Public images of Parliament during its absence, Legis Studies Quart, 82. **CONTACT ADDRESS** Dept of Hist, Univ of Nebraska, Lincoln, Lincoln, NE 68588.

COPELAND, HENRY JEFFERSON
PERSONAL Born 06/13/1936, Griffin, GA, m, 1958, 2 children **DISCIPLINE** MODERN EUROPEAN HISTORY **EDUCATION** Baylor Univ, AB, 58; Cornell Univ, PhD, 66. **CAREER** Instr hist, Cornell Univ, 65-66; from asst prof to assoc prof, 66-74, assoc dean, 69-74, dean fac, 74-77, Pres, Col Wooster, 77-95, prof hist, 74-99. **HONORS AND AWARDS** Woodrow Wilson Fellow. **MEMBERSHIPS** AHA; Soc Fr Hist Studies. **RESEARCH** French Revolution. **SELECTED PUBLICATIONS** Auth, An Improbable College. **CONTACT ADDRESS** P.O. Box 1347, Montreal, NC 28757.

COPP, JOHN T.
PERSONAL Born 10/28/1938, Ottawa, ON, Canada **DISCIPLINE** HISTORY **EDUCATION** Sir George Williams Col, BA, 59; McGill Univ, MA, 62. **CAREER** Lectr, Loyola Col & McGill Univ, 63-70; lectr, Sir George Williams Col & Concordia Univ, 70-75; fac mem, 75-81, Prof History, Wilfrid Laurier Univ, 81-, ch hist, 82-95, co-dir, Laurier Ctr Mil Strategic & Disarmament Stud; vis prof, Univ Victoria, 71-72; vis prof, Univ Ottawa, 71-73. **HONORS AND AWARDS** C.P. Stacey Bk Awd, 90, 92. **RESEARCH** Canadian social, labor and military history. **SELECTED PUBLICATIONS** Auth, The Anatomy of Poverty: The Condition of the Working Class in Montreal 1897-1929, 74; auth, The Brigade: The Fifth Canadian Infantry Brigade 1939-1945, 92; auth, A Canadian's Guide to the Battlefields of Normandy, 94; auth, No Price Too High, 95; coauth, Maple Leaf Route, 5 vols, 82-88; coauth, Battle Exhaustion: Soldiers and Psychiatrists in the Canadian Army 1939-1945, 90. **CONTACT ADDRESS** Dept of History, Wilfrid Laurier Univ, Dr Alvin Wood Bldg 4-210B, Waterloo, ON, Canada N2L 3C5. **EMAIL** tcopp@wlu.ca

COPPA, FRANK JOHN
PERSONAL Born 07/18/1937, New York, NY, m, 1965, 2 children **DISCIPLINE** MODERN EUROPEAN HISTORY **EDUCATION** Brooklyn Col, BA, 60; Cath Univ, MA, 62, PhD, 66. **CAREER** Lectr hist, Brooklyn Col, 64; from instr to prof hist, St. John's Univ; chemn dept, St. John's Univ, 79-; assoc, Sem on Studies in Mod Italy, Columbia Univ, 71-80; chmn,80-82; mem, Nat Comt of USA Bicentennial--The Italian Contrib, 75-76 & Inst Storia Risorgimento Ital. **HONORS AND AWARDS** Generoso Pope Scholarship, 56; Knights of Columbus Fel, 60-64; Fulbright Grant to Italy, 64-65; Grant by the US Ed Found in BEL, 65; Univ Grants, summers of 67 and 69; res grants on Italy, St. John's Univ, 67 & 69; Faculty Research Awd, 74; NEH, Sr div grant, summer 77; grants from the Italian Ministry of Foreign Affairs and the Banca Commerciate Italiana, Int Conference on Post-War Italy at Columbia Univ, 89. **MEMBERSHIPS** AHA; Am Cath Hist Asn, exec coun, 91-; Soc Ital Hist Studies; NY State Asn European Hist; Instituto per la storia del Risorgimento; Columbia Sem on Modern Italy, sec, 76-77, chair, 80-81; Interuniversity Center for European Studies. **RESEARCH** Modern European history 1800 to present; modern Italian history; relations between church and state in Italy; examination of counter-Risorgimento with emphasis on Pope Pius IX and his Secretary of State Cardinal Giacomo Antonelli; Giovanni Giolitti, Italian Prime Minister dominating Italian political life from 1901-1914. **SELECTED PUBLICATIONS** Co-ed, Modern From Vienna to Vietnam: War and Peace in the Modern World, W. C. Brown (Dubuque), 69; auth, Economics and Politics in the Giolittian Age, Cath Univ Am, DC, 71; Camillo di Cavour, Twayne Pubs, 73; co-ed, Cities in Transition: From the Ancient World to Urban America, Nelson-Hall, 74; ed, Religion in the Making of Western Man, NY: St John's Univ Press, 74; ed, The Immigrant Experience in America, Twayne Pubs (Boston and New York), 76; ed, Screen and Society: The Impact of Television upon Aspects of Contemporary Civilization, Nelson-Hall, 79; auth, Papal Rome in 1848: From Reform to Revolution, Proc Consortium Revolutionary Europ, 79; co-ed, Technology in the Twentieth Century, Kendall-Hunt Pub Co, 83; ed, Dictionary of Modern Italian History, Greenwood Press (Westport, Conn), 85; ed, Studies in Modern Italian History: From the Risorgimento to the Republic, NY and Berne: Peter Lang, 86; ed, Italian History: An Annotated Bibliography, Greenwood Press (NYork), 90; auth, "Christopher Columbus and Italy," in Review of Nat Literatures (NYork, 92), 83-94; auth, "From Liberalism to Fascism: The Church-State Conflict over Italy's Schools," The History Teacher 28 (95): 135-148; auth, The Modern Papacy since 1789, Longman (London/NYork), 98; auth, "The Vatican between Anti-Judaism and Anti-Semitism in its Response to Nazi Racialism," Proceedings of the Fifth Biennial Conference on Christianity and the Holocaust, Princeton, 5 (99): 31-52; ed, Controversial Concordats: The Vatican's Relations with Napoleon, Mussolini, and Hitler, The Catholic Univ Pr (Washington, D.C.), 99; ed, Encyclopedia of the Vatican and Papacy, Greenwood Pr (Wesport, Conn), 99. **CONTACT ADDRESS** Dept of Hist, St. John's Univ, 8150 Utopia Pky, Jamaica, NY 11439-0002. **EMAIL** coppaf@stjohns.edu

CORAZZO, NINA
DISCIPLINE ART HISTORY **EDUCATION** IN Univ, BA, 69; MA, 71; Phd, 77. **CAREER** Assoc prof, Valparaiso Univ. **HONORS AND AWARDS** Hellenic Laurel Outstanding Tchg, 96 and 97. **SELECTED PUBLICATIONS** Auth, The Enclosed Garden (hortus conclusus) as Sign of the Virgin Mary in Paradise by the Upper Rhine Master, c. 1410, Semiotics, 97; Women and Monocles, Semiotics, 97; Two studies of Art History: The Virgin Mary as Enclosed Garden and The Construction of Masculine Evil: Francois-Eduard Cibot's 'The Fallen Angels,' 1833; Remembering and Dis-membering: Agatha's Breast, Semiotics, 94; The Construction of Sexual Difference: The Representation of Woman as the Deadly Sin Gluttony, Semiotics, 93; The Collapse of Time: Baubo's Obscene Display and Magritte's painting 'Le Viol', Semiotics, 94; The Unnatural Woman in 18th Century France: Charlotte Corday and the femme homme in Literate Women and French Revolution of 1789. **CONTACT ADDRESS** Valparaiso Univ, 1500 E Lincoln Way, Valparaiso, IN 46383-6493. **EMAIL** ncorazzo@exodus.valpo.edu

CORBETT, WILLIAM P.
PERSONAL Born 11/19/1948, Clarion, PA, m, 1983, 2 children **DISCIPLINE** HISTORY **EDUCATION** Clarion State Col, BS, 70; Univ SD, MA, 76; OK State Univ, PhD, 82. **CAREER** US Navy, 70-74; Tchr, Clarion-Limestone Sch, 75; Grad Tchg Fel, OK State Univ, 76-80; instr, 80-88, N OK Col; from asst prof to prof, 88-, Northeastern State Univ; Dept Chair, Northeastern State Univ, 91-00. **HONORS AND AWARDS** Pi Gamma Mu; Phi Alpha Theta; Gilbert Fite Awd; Homer L. Knight Awd; Albert Pike Awd; Jefferson Davis Awd; Muriel H Wright Awd. **MEMBERSHIPS** Western Hist Asn; OK Hist Soc, Board of Dir, 94-, chair, Historic Sites Committee, member, Indian Heritage Committee. **RESEARCH** State and local history. **SELECTED PUBLICATIONS** Auth, Oklahoma Passage: The Telecourse Study Guide; "Men, Mud, and Mules: The Good Roads Movement in Oklahoma"; "Peerless Princess of the Best Country: Early Years of Tonkawa"; "They Hired Every Farmer in the Country: Establishing the Prisoner of War Camp at Tonkawa," in The Chronicles of OK. **CONTACT ADDRESS** Dept of History, Northeastern State Univ, 600 N Grand Ave, Tahlequah, OK 74464. **EMAIL** corbett@nsuok.edu

CORDASCO, FRANCESCO
PERSONAL Born 11/02/1920, New York, NY, m, 1942, 2 children **DISCIPLINE** AMERICAN EDUCATIONAL HISTORY **EDUCATION** Columbia Univ, BA, 44; NYork Univ, MA, 45, PhD(sociol), 59. **CAREER** Assoc prof English, Long Island Univ, 46-53; prof educ, Fairleigh Dickinson Univ, 53-58; prof, Seton Hall Univ, 58-63; prof educ, 63-89, Prof Emer Educ, 89- ,Montclair State Col, 63- ; Educ consult, Migration Div, Commonwealth of PR, 61-71; vis prof educ, NY Univ, summer, 62; consult, US Off of Educ, 67-70; vis prof educ, Univ of PR, summer, 69 & City Univ New York, 72-73. **HONORS AND AWARDS** Order of Merit, Repub of Italy, 76; Brotherhood Awd, Nat Conf Christians & Jews, 67. **MEMBERSHIPS** Am Sociol Asn; Am Asn Hist Professors; Hist Educ Soc; British Sociol Asn; Immigration Hist Soc. **RESEARCH** American ethnic communities; immigrant children in American schools. **SELECTED PUBLICATIONS** Auth, Brief History of Education, Littlefield, Adams, 63, rev ed, 70 & 76; Jacob Riis Revisited: Poverty & the Slum, Doubleday, 68; Education in the Urban Community, Am Book Co, 69; Minorities & American City, David McKay, 70; Shaping of American Graduate Education, Rowman & Littlefield, 72; School in the Social Order, Intext, 73; Italian Community & Its Language in United States, Rowman & Littlefield, 75; Bilingual Schooling in the United States, McGraw-Hill, 76; Italian Mass Emigration, Rowman & Littlefield, 80; American Medical Imprints, 1820-1910, Rowman & Littlefield, 85; Immigrant Woman in North American, Scarecrow/Grolier, 85; The Puerto Rican Community, Scarecrow/Grolier, 82; The New American Immigration, Garland Publ, 87; Dictionary of American Immigration History, Scarecrow/Grolier, 90; Theodore Besterman: Bibliographer & Editor, Scarecrow/Grolier, 92. **CONTACT ADDRESS** 6606 Jackson St, West New York, NJ 07093.

CORDELL, DENNIS DALE
PERSONAL Born 01/01/1947, St. Louis, MO **DISCIPLINE** HISTORY **EDUCATION** Yale Univ, BA, 68; Univ Wis, MA, (History) 72, PhD, 77; Maitrise es-Science, (Demography), 87. **CAREER** Assoc prof, Dept Demog, Univ Montreal, 89-; chmn, Dept History, prof History, 95, South Methodist Univ, Dallas; assoc dean Gen Ed, 97. **HONORS AND AWARDS** Univ Research Coun, Southern Methodist Univ, Travel Grant, 95; Int Migration Proj, Social Science Research Coun, Planning Grant, 96; American Philosophical Soc Awd, 96; National Science Foundation, 01. **MEMBERSHIPS** African Studies Asn; AHA; Western Asn Africanists; Southern Africanists Asn; Comt Concerned Africanist Scholars; IUSSP; PAA; UAPS. **RESEARCH** History of Equatorial Africa; Islamic Africa; Trans-Saharan slave trade; Migration in Africa; Immigration to USA. **SELECTED PUBLICATIONS** Coauth, Sara Madjingaye: Guide pour L-Etude Orale de la Langue, US Peace Corps, 69; auth, Throwing knives in Equatorial Africa: A distribution study, BaShiru, 73; A History of the Central African Republic, US Peace Corps, 75; Research resources in Chad and the Central African Republic, Hist Africa, 75; coauth, Southern Africa films: A selected listing of 16mm socio-political films, African Studies Newslett, 76; auth, Eastern Libya, Wadai and the Sanusiya: A Tariqa and a trade route, J African Hist, 77; Population, reproduction, societes, Perspecitives et enjeux de demographie sociale, Melanges en l'honneur de Joel Gregory, Montreal: Les presses de lUniversite de Montreal, 93; Hoe and Wage: A Social History of a Circular Migration System in West Africa, 1900-1975, Doulder, San Francisco and London: HarperCollins/Westview Press, 96, with Joel W Gregory and Victor Piche. **CONTACT ADDRESS** Dept of History, So Methodist Univ, PO Box 750176, Dallas, TX 75275-0176. **EMAIL** dcordell@mail.smu.edu

CORDERY, SIMON
PERSONAL Born 07/08/1960, London, England, m, 1992, 1 child **DISCIPLINE** LEGAL AND SOCIAL HISTORY **EDUCATION** Northern Ill Univ, Ba, 82; Univ of York, MA, 84; Univ of Tex at Austin, PhD, 95. **CAREER** Res asst, Am Hist Asn, 85-88; instr, Louisburg Col, 92-94; instr, Monmouth Col, 94-; instr, Knox Col, 00. **HONORS AND AWARDS** NEH summer stipend, 98. **MEMBERSHIPS** AHA; NACBS; RLHS; LHS. **RESEARCH** Modern British labor and social history; the history of mutualism. **SELECTED PUBLICATIONS** Auth, Joshua Hobson 1810-1876, Dictionary of Labour Bio, Macmillan, 87; Joshua Hobson and the Business of Radicalism, Bio: An Interdisciplinary Quart, 88; Friendly Societies and the Discourse of Respectability in Britain 1825-1875, J of British Studies, 95; Friendly Societies and the British Labour Movement Before 1914, J of the Asn of Historians in NC, 95; Mutual Benefit Societies in the United States: A Quest for Protection and Identity, Social Security Mutualism: The Comparative Hist of Mutual Benefit Societies, Peter Lang, 96. **CONTACT ADDRESS** Hist Dept, Monmouth Col, 700 E Broadway, Monmouth, IL 61462. **EMAIL** simon@monm.edu

CORDERY, STACY A. ROZEK
PERSONAL Born 05/22/1961, Saqinaw, MI, m, 1992, 1 child **DISCIPLINE** HISTORY **EDUCATION** Univ of Tex, BA, 83, MA, 86, PhD, 92. **CAREER** Vis asst prof, East Carolina Univ, 92-94; Asst Prof of Hist & Coord of Women's Studies, 94-98, Assoc Prof of Hist & Coord of Women's Studies, Monmouth Col, 95-00; Assoc Prof of Hist, 95-. **HONORS AND AWARDS** Prof of the Year, 97 & 98. **MEMBERSHIPS** AHA; SHQAPE; WHOM; Theodore Roosevelt Asn. **RESEARCH** Gilded age; progressive era; women; the Roosevelt family. **SELECTED PUBLICATIONS** Auth, Gertrude Vanderbilt Whitney, Women in World Hist, Yorkin Pub, 98; Juliette Gordon Low, Women in World Hist, Yorking Pub, 98; Alice Roosevelt Longworth, The Biographical and Genealogical Directory of the Roosevelt Family, 97; Alice Roosevelt Longworth, Am Nat Bio, Oxford Univ Press, 98; Helen H. Taft, Am Nat Bio, Oxford Univ Press, 98. **CONTACT ADDRESS** Dept of Hist, Monmouth Col, 700 E Broadway, Monmouth, IL 61462. **EMAIL** stacy@monm.edu

CORDOVA, CARLOS E.
PERSONAL Born 03/30/1965, San Miguel, El Salvador, m, 1997 **DISCIPLINE** GEOGRAPHY **EDUCATION** Natl Autonomous Univ MEX, BA, 88, MA, 91; Univ TX, PhD, 97. **CAREER** Asst prof, OK Univ, 97. **HONORS AND AWARDS** ED Farmer Fel, 93-94; Univ TX Dissertation Grant Fel, 94-95. **MEMBERSHIPS** Amer Schs of Oriental Research **RESEARCH** Geomorphology; Soils; Geoarchaeology **CONTACT ADDRESS** Dept of Geography, Oklahoma State Univ, Stillwater, 225 Scott Hall, Stillwater, OK 74078. **EMAIL** cordova@okway.okstate.edu

CORNELIUS, JANET DUITSMAN
PERSONAL Born 01/20/1938, Danville, IL, m, 1956, 4 children **DISCIPLINE** HISTORY **EDUCATION** Univ Ill, Urbana-Champaign, BA, 68, MA, 69, PhD(hist), 77. **CAREER** Instr soc sci, Danville Jr Col, 69-77; asst prof Am hist, Univ Ill, Urbana-Champaign, 77-78; Chmn Soc Sci Dept, Danville Jr Col, 82-, Fel col teachers, Nat Endowment Humanities, 80-81. **MEMBERSHIPS** Orgn Am Historians; Southern Hist Asn; AHA; Community Col Social Sci Asn; Community Col Humanities Asn. **RESEARCH** Southern religion and slavery; comparative slave systems; family in antebellum United States. **SELECTED PUBLICATIONS** Auth, Sapelos People--A Long Walk Into Freedom, Jour So Hist, Vol 0061, 95; The Abolitionist Sisterhood--Womens Political-Culture in Antebellum America, Jour Amer History, Vol 0082, 1995 **CONTACT ADDRESS** Dept of Soc Sci, Danville Area Comm Col, 1900 E Main St, Danville, IL 61832.

CORNELL, PAUL G.
PERSONAL Born 09/13/1918, Toronto, ON, Canada **DISCIPLINE** HISTORY **EDUCATION** Univ Toronto, BA, MA, PhD. **CAREER** Lectr to prof hist, Acadia Univ, 49-60; dept ch, 60-68, prof hist, 60-85, dean arts, 70-73, acting vice pres, 72, hon archivist, 77-85, PROF EMER, UNIV WATERLOO, 94-; **HONORS AND AWARDS** Fel, Royal Soc Can; Cruickshank medal, 78. **MEMBERSHIPS** Can Hist Asn (ed, Report, 53-56); Ont Hist Soc (pres, 73-74) **RESEARCH** Canadian history **SELECTED PUBLICATIONS** Auth, The Alignment of Political Groups in the Province of Canada, 62; auth, The Great Coalition, 67, repr 71; coauth, Canada: Unity in Diversity, 67, Fr transl 71; co-ed, Ontario Hist, 63-78. **CONTACT ADDRESS** 202 Laurier Pl, Waterloo, ON, Canada N2L 1K8.

CORNWALL, PETER G.
DISCIPLINE MODERN JAPAN **EDUCATION** Univ Mich, PhD, 70. **CAREER** Univ Alaska **SELECTED PUBLICATIONS** Ed, Alaska's Rural Development. **CONTACT ADDRESS** Univ of Alaska, Fairbanks, PO Box 757480, Fairbanks, AK 99775-7480.

CORNWALL, ROBERT D.
PERSONAL Born 03/03/1958, Los Angeles, CA, m, 1983, 1 child **DISCIPLINE** HISTORICAL THEOLOGY **EDUCATION** Northwest Christian Col, BS, 80; Fuller Theol Sem, M Div, 85, PhD, 91. **CAREER** Dir of the Lib, 92-94, William Carey Int Univ; vis asst prof of Church Hist, 94-95, Fuller Theol Sem; assoc prof Theol, 95-97, Manhattan Christian Col; pastor, First Christian Church, Santa Barbara, CA, 98-. **HONORS AND AWARDS** Winner, Land O' Lakes Essay Competition, Shaw Hist Library, 91. **MEMBERSHIPS** North Am Conf of

Brit Stud; Am Acad of Relig; Am Soc of Church Hist. **RESEARCH** Anglicanism 17th & 18th century; church-state issues; Nonjurors; Jacobites; Sacramental Theol. **SELECTED PUBLICATIONS** Auth, Visible and Apostolic: The Constitution of the Church in High Church Anglican and Non-Juror Thought 1688-1745, Univ DE Press, 93; auth, The Later Non-Jurors and the Theological Basis of the Usages Controversy, Anglican Theol Rev, 75, 93; auth, The Church and Salvation: An Early Eighteenth-Century High Church Anglican Perspective, Anglican and Episcopal History, 62, 93; auth, Advocacy of the Independence of the Church from the State in Eighteenth Century England: A Comparison of a Nonjuror and a Nonconformist View, Enlightenment and Dissent, 12, 93; auth, The Crisis in Disciples of Christ Ecclesiology: The Search for Identity, Encounter 55, 94; auth, Unity, Restoration, and Ecclesiology: Why the Stone-Campbell Movement Divided, J of Relig Stud, 19, 95; auth, The Ministry of Reconciliation: Toward a Balanced Understanding of the Global Mission of the Christian Church (Disciples of Christ), Lexington Theol Sem Quart, 30, 95; auth, Education for Ministry in the Augustan Age: A Comparison of the Views of Gilbert Burnet and George Bull and Their Implications for the Modern Church, Anglican Theol Rev, 78, 96; auth, The Scandal of the Cross: Self-Sacrifice, Obedience, and Modern Culture, Encounter 58, 97; ed, Gilbert Burnet, Discourse of the Pastoral Care, Edwin Mellon Press, 97; auth, The Agricultural Revolution: An Interpretive Essay, in Events that Changed the World in the Eighteenth Century, Greenwood Press, 98. **CONTACT ADDRESS** First Christian Church, 1905 Chapala St, Santa Barbara, CA 93101. **EMAIL** bobcornwall@juno.com

CORRALES, EDWIN
PERSONAL Born 02/22/1956, Costa Rica, d, 1 child **DISCIPLINE** HISTORY, LITERATURE **EDUCATION** Univ Costa Rica, BA Hist, 80; BA Soc Studies, 82; EdD, 81. **CAREER** Adj Prof, Ulster Co Community Col, 90-. **HONORS AND AWARDS** Essay Awd, Govt of Venezuela. **RESEARCH** Latin American Literature. **CONTACT ADDRESS** Dept Commun, Ulster Co Comm Col, Cottekill Rd, Stone Ridge, NY 12484. **EMAIL** corraleE@sunyulster.edu

CORRIGAN, JOHN
DISCIPLINE RELIGION; AMERICAN STUDIES **EDUCATION** Univ of Chicago, PhD; 82 **CAREER** Asst prof, rel stud, Univ Va; current, PROF, AM STUD, ARIZ STATE UNIV **MEMBERSHIPS** Am Antiquarian Soc **RESEARCH** 18th century religion **SELECTED PUBLICATIONS** Auth, The Hidden Balance: Religion and the Social Theories of Charles Chauncy and Jonathan Mayhew, 87; auth, The Prism of Piety: Catholic Congregational Clergy at the Beginning of the Enlightenment, 91; auth, "Habits from the Heart: The American Enlightenment and Religious Ideas about Emotion and Habit," Jour of Rel 73, 93; Jews, Christians, Muslims, 97; coauth, Religion in America, 98. **CONTACT ADDRESS** 15236 N 6th Cir, Phoenix, AZ 85023. **EMAIL** john.corrigan@asu.edu

CORRIGAN, KATHLEEN
DISCIPLINE ART HISTORY **EDUCATION** UCLA, BA, MA, PhD. **CAREER** Assoc prof, Dartmouth Col. **RESEARCH** Medieval manuscript illumination; Byzantine monasticism; Byzantine icons. **SELECTED PUBLICATIONS** Auth, Visual Polemics in the Ninth-Century Byzantine Psalters, Cambridge UP, 92; var articles on Byzantine icons and ivories. **CONTACT ADDRESS** Dartmouth Col, 3529 N Main St, Ste. 207, Hanover, NH 03755. **EMAIL** kathleen.corrigan@dartmouth.edu

CORRIN, JAY PATRICK
PERSONAL Born 12/18/1943, Duluth, MN, m, 1967 **DISCIPLINE** MODERN EUROPEAN HISTORY **EDUCATION** Mich State Univ, BA, 66; Univ Hawaii, MA, 68; Boston Univ, PhD(hist mod Europe), 76. **CAREER** Teacher English, Misurata Prep School, Libya N Africa, 68-69; asst prof hist, Col Lib Arts, 76-77, Asst Prof Social Sci, Col Basic Studies, Boston Univ, 77-. **MEMBERSHIPS** AHA; New Eng Hist Asn; Chesterton Soc. **RESEARCH** British intellectual and social history. **SELECTED PUBLICATIONS** Auth, Reinhold,Hans,Anscar--Liturgical Pioneer and Antifascist, Cath Hist Rev, Vol 0082, 96. **CONTACT ADDRESS** Col of Basic Studies, Boston Univ, 755 Commonwealth Ave, Boston, MA 02215-1401.

CORTES, CARLOS ELISEO
PERSONAL Born 04/06/1934, Oakland, CA, m, 1978, 1 child **DISCIPLINE** ETHNIC HISTORY, MEDIA HISTORY **EDUCATION** Univ Calif, Berkeley, BA, 56; Columbia Univ, MS, 57; Am Inst Foreign Trade, BFT, 62; Univ N Mex, MA, 65, PhD(hist), 69. **CAREER** Actg asst prof hist, 68-69, asst prof, chmn Latin Am studies & asst to VChancellor Acad Affairs, 69-72, assoc prof hist, 72-76, Prof Hist, Univ Calif, Riverside, 78-94, Chmn Chicano Studies, 72-79., Faculty, Harvard Institutes for Higher Education, 90-; Prof Emeritus, 94-; Faculty, Summer Institute fr Intercultural Communication, 94-. **HONORS AND AWARDS** Hubert Herring Mem Awd, Pac Coast Counc Latin Am Studies, 74; Distinguished Teaching Awd, Univ Calif, Riverside, 76; Eleanor Fishburn Awd, Wash Ed Press Asn, 77; Distinguished Calif Humanist Awd, Calif Coun Humanities, 80; National Multicultural Trainer of the Year, Am Society for Training and Development, 89. **MEMBERSHIPS** Nat Counc Social Studies; Nat Asn Chicano Studies. **RESEARCH** Comparative ethnic history; multicultural education; history of mass media. **SELECTED PUBLICATIONS** Auth, The Children Are Watching: How the Media Teach about Diversity, Teachers College Press, 00. **CONTACT ADDRESS** Dept of Hist, Univ of California, Riverside, Riverside, CA 92521. **EMAIL** carlos.cortes@ucr.edu

COSGROVE, DENIS E.
PERSONAL Born 05/03/1948, Liverpool, England, m, 1989, 2 children **DISCIPLINE** GEOGRAPHY **EDUCATION** Oxford Univ, BA, 66; Univ Toronto, MA, 70; Oxford Univ, DPhil, 75. **CAREER** Lectr, Oxford Polytech, 72-80; Lectr, Loughborough Univ, 80-93; Prof, Royal Holloway Univ, 94-99; Prof, UCLA, 00-. **HONORS AND AWARDS** Nuffield Fel, 88-89; Leverhulme Fel, 91; Back Medal, Royal Geog Soc, 88. **MEMBERSHIPS** Asn of Am Geog; Royal Geog Soc **RESEARCH** Landscape meanings and images; Venetian landscapes of the 16th century; Cartography and geographic representation; Extra-terrestrial geographies. **SELECTED PUBLICATIONS** Co-ed, Water, Engineering and Landscape, Belhaven Press, 90; co-ed, The Palladian Landscape, Pa State Univ Press, 93; ed, Mappings, Reaktion Books, 99; auth, Apollo's Eye: A Cartographic genealogy of the earth in the Western Imagination, Johns Hopkins Univ Press, 01. **CONTACT ADDRESS** Dept Geog, Univ of California, Los Angeles, 1170 Bunche Hall, 405 Hilgard Ave, Los Angeles, CA 90095. **EMAIL** cosgrove@geog.ucla.edu

COSGROVE, RICHARD A.
PERSONAL Born 02/26/1941, Jersey City, NJ, m, 1963, 4 children **DISCIPLINE** MODERN BRITISH HISTORY **EDUCATION** Holy Cross Col, BS, 62; Univ Calif, Riverside, MA, 63, PhD(Hist), 67. **CAREER** Asst prof, 67-72, from assoc prof to prof Hist, Univ Ariz, 72-. **MEMBERSHIPS** Conf Brit Studies. **RESEARCH** Nineteenth and 20th century British hist; British legal hist. **SELECTED PUBLICATIONS** Auth, The Rule of Law: A V Dicey, Victorian Jurist, Univ NC Press, 80; Our Lady the Common Law: An Anglo-American Legal Community, 1870-1930, NYU Press, 87; Scholars of the Law: English Jurisprudence from Blackstone to Hart, NYU Press, 96. **CONTACT ADDRESS** Dept of History, Univ of Arizona, Tucson, AZ 85721-0001. **EMAIL** rcosgrov@u.arizona.edu

COSTA, GUSTAVO
PERSONAL Born 03/21/1930, Rome, Italy, m, 1963, 1 child **DISCIPLINE** ITALIAN, HISTORY **EDUCATION** Univ Rome, DPhilos, 54. **CAREER** Asst hist of mod & contemporary philos, Univ Rome, 57-60; lectr Ital, Univ Lyon, 60-61; from instr to assoc prof, 61-72, chmn dept, 73-76, 88-91, Prof Ital, Univ Calif, Berkeley, 72-91, prof emer, 91-; vis prof, Naples, 84; vis prof, Inst of Philos, Univ of Rome, 92; ed staff, Cuadernos sobre Vico, New Vico Studies, Forum Italicum & Nouvelles de la Republique des lettres. **HONORS AND AWARDS** Ist Ital Studi Storici, Naples fel, 54-57; French & Belg govt grants, 56; Am Philos Soc grant, 67; Nat Endowment for Humanities fel, 70-71; Guggenheim Mem Found fel, 76-77. **MEMBERSHIPS** AATI; Renaissance Soc Am; Am Soc Aesthet. **RESEARCH** Literary criticism; history; philosophy. **SELECTED PUBLICATIONS** Auth, La leggenda dei secoli d'oro nella letteratura italiana, Laterza, 72; auth, Le antichita germaniche nella cultura italiana da Machiavelli a Vico, Bibliopolis, 77; auth,Il sublime e la magia da Dante a Tosso, Edizioni Scientifiche Italiane, 94; auth, Vico e l'Europa: Contro la "boria delle nazioni", Guerini e Associati, 96. **CONTACT ADDRESS** Dept of Ital, Univ of California, Berkeley, Berkeley, CA 94720.

COSTELLO, DONALD PAUL
PERSONAL Born 08/04/1931, Chicago, IL, m, 1952, 6 children **DISCIPLINE** AMERICAN STUDIES, DRAMA & FILM **EDUCATION** DePaul Univ, AB, 55; Univ Chicago, MA, 56, PhD, 62. **CAREER** Instr, Roosevelt Univ, 57-60 & Chicago City Jr Col, 58-59; from instr to assoc prof, 60-71, prof English, Univ Notre Dame, 71-, chmn Am studies & commun arts, 79-, soc relig higher educ fel, 64-65; consult, Educ Assoc, Inc for Proj Upward Bound, Wash, DC, 66-; consult/panelist, Nat Endowment for Humanities Lit & Fine Arts Panel, 77-. **MEMBERSHIPS** Soc Values Higher Educ; MLA. **RESEARCH** American literature; modern drama; cinema. **SELECTED PUBLICATIONS** Auth, The Language of The Catcher in the Rye, Am Speech, 10/59; art, Graham Greene and the Catholic Press, Renaissance, autumn 59; art, The Structure of the Turn of the Screw, Mod Lang Notes, 4/60; art, The Serpent's Eye: Shaw and the Cinema, Univ Notre Dame, 65; contribr, Black Man as Victim: The Drama of LeRoi Jones, Five Black Writers, New York Univ, 70; art, Counter-culture to Anti-culture: Woodstock, Easy Rider, and A Clockwork Orange, The Rev Polit, 10/72; art, Tennessee Williams' Fugitive Kind, Mod Drama, 5/72; art, Fellini's Road, Univ Notre Dame, 82. **CONTACT ADDRESS** Dept of English, Univ of Notre Dame, 356 Oshaugnessy Hall, Notre Dame, IN 46556.

COSTIGLIOLA, FRANK CHARLES
PERSONAL Born 11/01/1946, Spring Valley, NY, 3 children **DISCIPLINE** HISTORY **EDUCATION** Hamilton Col, BA, 68; Cornell Univ, PhD(hist), 73. **CAREER** Asst prof, 72-80, assoc prof Hist, Univ RI, 80-84, prof 85-, prof Univ Conn, 98-, Nat endowment for Humanities fel, 77. **MEMBERSHIPS** AHA, Orgn Am Historians. **RESEARCH** The formation of meaning in the Cold War and the Western Alliance, the role of emotion and cultural difference in shaping foreign policy. **SELECTED PUBLICATIONS** Auth, Awkward Dominion: American Political, Economic, and Cultural Relations with Europe, 1919-1933, Ithaca: Cornell Univ Press, 84, 87; auth, France and the United States: The Cold Alliance Since World War II, New York: Twayne/Macmillan, 92; auth, "An 'Arm Around the Shoulder': The United States, NATO and German Reunification, 1989-90," Contemporary European History, (94): 87-110; auth, "Kennedy, the European Allies, and the Failure to Consult," Political Science Quarterly, (95): 105-23; auth, "The Nuclear Family: Tropes of Gender and Pathology in the Western Alliance," Diplomatic History, (97): 163-83; auth, "Unceasing Pressure for Penetration': Gender, Pathology, and Emotion in George Kennan's Formation of the Cold War," The Journal of American History, (97): 1309-39; auth, "Mixed Up' and 'Contact': Culture and Emotion among the Allies in the Second World War," International History Review, (98): 791-805; auth, "I Had Come as a Friend': Emotion, Culture, and Ambiguity in the Formation of the Cold War," Cold War History, (00): 103-28. **CONTACT ADDRESS** Dept of Hist, Univ of Connecticut, Storrs, Wood Hall, Unit 2103, Storrs, CT 06269. **EMAIL** frank.costigliola@uconn.edu

COTE, JOANNE
PERSONAL Born Montreal, PQ, Canada **DISCIPLINE** MUSEUM STUDIES **EDUCATION** Univ Quebec Montreal, BA, 79; John F. Kennedy Univ, San Francisco, MA, 87. **CAREER** Asst Registr, Collections Mgmt Svs, Montreal Mus Fine Arts, 79-84; mgr Mus Move & Proj Coordr, Bldg Expansion & Reno Proj, McCord Mus Can Hist, 88-92, head, special proj, 92, head, Educ Svs & Cultural Prog, 94-96. **HONORS AND AWARDS** Joy Feinberg Scholar, 87. **MEMBERSHIPS** Can Mus Asn; Int Coun Mus. **SELECTED PUBLICATIONS** Auth, Moving A Museum: Nightmare or Opportunity, in MUSE, 90. **CONTACT ADDRESS** Museum Studies, Univ of Montreal, Montreal, QC, Canada H3C 3J7. **EMAIL** joanne.cote@umontreal.ca

COTERA, MARIA E.
PERSONAL Born 07/17/1964, Austin, TX, m, 1999 **DISCIPLINE** AMERICAN STUDIES, WOMEN'S STUDIES, LATINO STUDIES **EDUCATION** Univ Tex, BA, 86; MA, 94; Stanford Univ, PhD, 00. **CAREER** Asst prof, Univ Mich, 00-. **HONORS AND AWARDS** Postdoc Fel Univ Mich, 00-01; Dis Fel Ford Found, 99-00; Am Dis Fel, AAUW Edu Found, 00; Grad Res Opp Awd, 99; Dis Res Fel, Sch Hum Sci, Stan Univ, 99; Escobedo Sum Res Fel, Cen Chicana Res, Stan Univ, 97; Prog Dev Fel, Grad Opp Prog, Univ Tex, 93-94; Tex Achiev Awd, 82-86; Frederick Cervantes Stud Premio, Nat Asn Chicano/Chicana Stud, 99; James W. Lyons Awd Ser to the Stan Comm, 98-99; Dean of Stud, Stan Univ, 99; Galarza Prize for Excel, Stan Cen Chicana/o Res, 96. **MEMBERSHIPS** MLA; ASA; NACCS. **RESEARCH** Writing by women of color; ethnic and racial consciousness in the inter-war years, 1920-1940; Latina/o studies; American Indian studies; women's studies; comparative approaches to ethnic studies. **SELECTED PUBLICATIONS** Co-ed, Caballero, Tex AM Press, 95; auth, contrb, "Refiguring the 'American Congo:' Jovita Gonzdlez, John Gregory Bourke and the Battle Over Ethnohistorical Representations of the Borderlands," in Recovering a Mexican American, West Lit Ser (00); auth, contrb, "Engendering a 'Dialectics of Our America:' Jovita Gonzalez' Pluralist Dialogue as Feminist Testimonio," Las Obreras: The Politics of Work and Family, UCLA Chi Stud Res Cent (00); auth, contrb, "Jovita Gonzalez Mirelés" in Latinas in the United States, Hist Encycl (forthcoming); auth, "Deconstructing the Corrido Hero, Caballero and its Gendered Critique of Nationalist Discourse," Mex Am Persp (95). **CONTACT ADDRESS** Am Cultures Prog, Univ of Michigan, Ann Arbor, 419 S State St, 2402 Mason Hall, Ann Arbor, MI 48109. **EMAIL** mcotera@umich.edu

COTHREN, MICHAEL W.
PERSONAL Born 04/09/1951, Nashville, AR, m, 2 children **DISCIPLINE** ART HISTORY **EDUCATION** Vanderbilt Univ, BA, 73; Colombia Univ, MA, 74; PhD, 80. **CAREER** Prof, Swarthmore Col. **HONORS AND AWARDS** Consult curator, Glencairn Mus (Bryn Athyn, PA); pres, Am Corpus Vitrearum; bd dir, Int Ctr Medieval Art. **RESEARCH** Medieval art. **SELECTED PUBLICATIONS** Auth, Restaurateurs et createurs de vitraux a la cathedrale de Beauvais dans les annees 1340, Revue de l'art, 96; Replacing the Survey at Swarthmore, Art Jour, 95; A propos de trois panneaux du musee de Picardie provenant de l'ancienne vitrerie de la cathedrale de Beauvais in Groupe d'Etude des Monuments et Oeuvres d'art de l'Oise et du Beauvaisis, Bulletin, 95; Who is the Bishop in the Virgin Chapel of Beauvais Cathedral?, Gazette des Beaux Arts, 95; Is the 'Tete Gerente' from Saint-Denis?, Jour Glass Studies, 93. **CONTACT ADDRESS** Swarthmore Col, Swarthmore, PA 19081-1397. **EMAIL** mcothre1@swarthmore.edu

COTRONEO, ROSS RALPH
PERSONAL Born 07/24/1930, Lewiston, ID, m, 1962, 1 child **DISCIPLINE** AMERICAN HISTORY **EDUCATION** Univ Idaho, BS, 59, MA, 62, PhD(hist), 66. **CAREER** Asst prof hist, Valley City State Col, 63-66; from asst prof to assoc prof, 66-76, Prof Hist, Western Ore State Col, 76-, Chmn, Dept Soc Sci, 79-. **MEMBERSHIPS** Orgn Am Historians; Western Hist Asn. **RESEARCH** Land grant history of the Northern Pacific Railway. **SELECTED PUBLICATIONS** Auth, The Northern Pacific: Years of difficulty, Kans Quart, 70; Colonization of the Northern Pacific land grant, 1900-1920, NDak Quart, 70; Northern Pacific officials and the disposition of the railroad's land grant in North Dakota, NDak Hist, 70; Reserving the subsurface: The mineral lands policy of the Northern Pacific Railway, 1900-1954, NDak Hist, summer 73; A time of disintegration: The Coeur d'Alene and the Dawes Act, Western Hist Quart, 10/74; Timber marketing by the Northern Pacific Railway, 1920-1952, J Forest Hist, 7/76; United States v Northern Pacific Railway company: The final settlement of the land grant case, 1924-1941, Pac Northwest Quart, 7/80. **CONTACT ADDRESS** Dept of Hist, Western Oregon State Col, Monmouth, OR 97361.

COTT, NANCY FALIK
PERSONAL Born 11/08/1945, Philadelphia, PA, d, 1969, 2 children **DISCIPLINE** HISTORY **EDUCATION** Cornell Univ, BA, 67; Brandeis Univ, PhD, 74. **CAREER** Instr hist, Wheaton Col, 71, Clark Univ, 72 & Wellesley Col, 73-74; asst prof, 75-79, assoc prof hist Am studies, Yale Univ, 79-81, prof, 81-91; Fel, law & hist, Harvard Law School, 78-79; Stanley Woodward Prof, 91-; Rockefeller Found Hum fel, 78-79; Guggenheim, 85; NEH, 93-94; Radcliffe res scholar, 82, 97; Ctr for Adv Study in Behav Sci 98-99. **MEMBERSHIPS** OHA; Am Studies Asn; Coord Comt Women Hist Profession; AHA. **RESEARCH** Women and gender hist in USA. **SELECTED PUBLICATIONS** Ed, Root of Bitterness: Documents of the History of American Women, E P Dutton, 72; auth, Young Women in the 2d Great Awakening in New England, Feminist Studies, 75; Divorce and the Changing Status of Women in 18th-Century Massachusetts, William & Mary Quart, 76; 18th-Century Family and Social Life Revealed in Massachusetts Divorce Records, J Social Hist, 76; The Bonds of Womanhood: Woman's Sphere in New England, 1780-1835, Yale Press, 77; Passionlessness: An Interpretation of Victorian Sexual Ideology, Signs, 78; co-ed, A Heritage of Her Own, Simon & Schuster, 79; The Grounding of Modern Feminism, Yale, 1987; A Woman Making History: Mary Ritter Beard Through Her Letters, Yale Press, 91; auth, Public Vows: A History of Marriage and The Nation, Harvard Univ Press, 00. **CONTACT ADDRESS** American Studies Prog, Yale Univ, PO Box 208236, New Haven, CT 06520-8236.

COTTER, JOHN LAMBERT
PERSONAL Born 12/06/1911, Denver, CO, m, 1941, 2 children **DISCIPLINE** HISTORICAL ARCHEOLOGY, ANTHROPOLOGY **EDUCATION** Univ Denver, BA, 34, MA, 35; Univ Pa, PhD(anthrop), 59. **CAREER** Supvr, Archaeol Surv Ky, 38-40; archaeologist, US Nat Park Serv, 40-77; res & writing, 77-, Adj assoc prof Am Civilization, Univ Pa, 60-79, Assoc Cur, Am Hist Archaeol, Univ Mus, 70-79, Emer Assoc Cur, 79-; ed, Bibliog Hist Archaeol. **HONORS AND AWARDS** J A Mason Awd, Archaeol Soc Pa, 74; D E Finley Awd, Nat Trust for Hist Preserv, 78. **MEMBERSHIPS** Fel Am Anthrop Asn; fel AAAS; Soc Prof Archaeologists; Archaeol Inst Am; Soc Hist Archaeol (pres, 66-67). **RESEARCH** Archaeology of historical American sites and their conservation; archaeology of prehistoric American sites, and conservation. **SELECTED PUBLICATIONS** Coauth, Archaeology of Bynum Mounds, 52 & auth, Archaeological Excavations at Jamestown, Virginia, 58, Govt Printing Off; ed, Bibliography of Historical Sites Archaeology, Univ Microfilms, 66; Handbook for Historical Archaeology, J L Cotter, 68; auth, Above Ground Archaeology, Govt Printing Off, 74; contribr, chap 5, In: The Study of American Culture, Everett-Edwards, 78; contribr, chap 5, In: Historical Archaeology: A Guide, Baywood, 78; auth, Premier etablissement Francais en Acadie: St Croix, Dossiers de l'Archeologie, 78. **CONTACT ADDRESS** Univ Museum, 34th & Spruce Sts, Philadelphia, PA 19174.

COTTRELL, JACK WARREN
PERSONAL Born 04/30/1938, Scott County, KY, m, 1958, 3 children **DISCIPLINE** HISTORY OF DOCTRINE **EDUCATION** Cincinnati Bible Coll, AB, 59, ThB, 60; Univ Cincinnati, AB, Philos, 62; Westminster Theol Sem, MDiv, 65; Princeton Theol Sem, PhD, 71. **CAREER** Stud instr, Cincinnati Bible Coll, 59-62; Prof, Theol, Cincinnati Bible Sem, 67-. **MEMBERSHIPS** Evan Theol Sem **SELECTED PUBLICATIONS** Auth, Feminism and the Bible: An Introduction to Feminism for Christians, Coll Press, 92; auth, Gender Roles and the Bible: Creation, the Fall, and Redemption. A Critique of Feminist Biblical Interpretation, Coll Press, 94; Faith's Fundamentals: Seven Essentials of Christian Belief, Standard Publ, 95; TheCollege Press NIV Commentary: Romans, Volume 1, Coll Press, 96; auth, The College Press NIV Commentary: Romans, Volume 2, Coll Press, 98. **CONTACT ADDRESS** Cincinnati Bible Col and Sem, 2700 Glenway Ave, Cincinnati, OH 45204. **EMAIL** Jack.Cottrell@cincybible.edu

COUDERT, ALLISON P.
PERSONAL Born 12/02/1941, New York, NY, m, 2 children **DISCIPLINE** HISTORY **EDUCATION** Vassar Col, BA, 63; Univ London, Warburg Inst, PhD. **CAREER** Prof, Ariz St Univ. **MEMBERSHIPS** AHA; AAR; AJS; Renaissance Soc of Am; Int Soc for Intellectual Hist; Authors Guild; PEN. **RESEARCH** The relation between religion and science in early modern history; women's hist. **SELECTED PUBLICATIONS** Auth, Alchemy: The Philosopher's Stone, Wildwood House, 80, Shambhala, 80; co-ed, The Politics of Gender in Early Modern Europe vol xii Sixteenth Century Essays & Studies, Sixteenth Century J Pubs, 89; co-ed, Playing With Gender: A Renaissance Pursuit, Univ Ill Press, 91; co-ed, transl, & intro, The Principles of the Most Ancient and Modern Philosophy, of Anne Conway's Principia Philosophiae Antiquissimae & Recentissimae, Amsterdam, 1690, Cambridge Texts in the History of Philosophy, Cambridge Univ Press, 96; auth, Leibniz and the Kabbalah, Kluwer Acad Pubs, 95; auth, The Impact of the Kabbalah in the Seventeenth Century: The Life and Thought of Francis Mercury van Helmont, E. J. Brill, 99; co-ed, Leibniz, Mysticism and Religion, Kluwer, 98. **CONTACT ADDRESS** Dept of Relig Studies, Arizona State Univ, Tempe, AZ 85287-3104. **EMAIL** acoudert@aol.com

COUGHTRY, JAY
DISCIPLINE HISTORY **EDUCATION** Univ Wis Madison, PhD, 78. **CAREER** Assoc prof, Univ Nev Las Vegas. **RESEARCH** Colonial and early national US history; social history; Afro-American history. **SELECTED PUBLICATIONS** Auth, The Notorious Triangle: Rhode Island and the African Slave Trade, 1700-1807, 81. **CONTACT ADDRESS** History Dept, Univ of Nevada, Las Vegas, 4505 Md Pky, Las Vegas, NV 89154.

COULTER, HARRIS L.
PERSONAL Born 10/08/1932, Baltimore, MD, 4 children **DISCIPLINE** MEDICAL HISTORY **EDUCATION** Yale Univ, Columbia Univ, PhD, 69. **CAREER** Medical historian, lectr, and analyst of medical practice, 72-94. **HONORS AND AWARDS** Centenary Gold Medal, Academica Medico-Homeopatica de Barcelona; Hahnemann Prize, Belgian Fac of Homeopathy; honors at the 39th Congress of the Int Homeopathic Medical League. **MEMBERSHIPS** NIH Workshop on Alternative Medicine; Ad Hoc Advisory Panel of the Office of Alternative Medicine, 93. **SELECTED PUBLICATIONS** Auth, Divided Legacy Vol IV: Twentieth Century Medicine: The Bacteriological Era; The Controlled Clinical Trial: an Analysis; Vaccination, Social Violence, and Criminality; AIDS and Syphilis: the Hidden Link; Homeopathic Science and Modern Medicine; Divided Legacy Vol II: The Origins of Modern Western Medicine: J.B. Van Helmont to Claude Bernard; Divided Legacy Vol I: The Patterns Emerge: Hippocrates to Paracelus; Divided Legacy Vol III The Conflict Between Homeopathy and the American Medical Association and Homeopathic Influences in Nineteenth-Century Allopathic Therapeutics; Homeopathic Medicine; coauth, DPT: A Shot in the Dark. **CONTACT ADDRESS** 237 W 11th St, New York, NY 10014.

COULTER, MATTHEW
PERSONAL Born 05/18/1956, Moline, IL, s, 1 child **DISCIPLINE** HISTORY **EDUCATION** Southern Ill Univ, BS, 77; MA, 81; Univ N Tex, PhD, 96. **CAREER** Instr of hist, Hibbing Community Col, 83-88; prof, Collin County Community Col, 88-. **HONORS AND AWARDS** NEH summer sem fel, 84. **MEMBERSHIPS** Soc for Hist of Am For Relations, Tex Community Col Teacher's Asn. **RESEARCH** Franklin D. Roosevelt presidency, Texas petroleum industry. **SELECTED PUBLICATIONS** Auth, "The Franklin D. Roosevelt Administration and the Special Committee on Investigation of the Munitions Industry," Mid-America 67 (85): 23-36; auth, "FDR and Palestine: The Role of Special Agents," Franklin D. Roosevelt: The Man, the Myth, the Era 1882-1945, Greenwood Press (Westport, CT), 87; auth, "The Joint Anglo-American Statement on Palestine, 1943," The Historian 54 (92): 465-476; auth, "Modern Teachers and Postmodern Students," Community Col J 17 (93): 51-58; auth, The Senate Munitions Inquiry of the 1930s: Beyond the Merchants of Death, Greenwood Press (Westport, CT), 97. **CONTACT ADDRESS** Dept Soc Sci, Collin County Comm Col, 2800 E Spring Creek Pkwy, Plano, TX 75074-3300. **EMAIL** mcoulter@ccccd.edu

COUNTRYMAN, EDWARD
DISCIPLINE AMERICAN HISTORY **EDUCATION** Manhattan, BA, 66: Cornell Univ, MA, 67, PhD, 71. **CAREER** Sr Lect, Warwick; PROF, AM HIST, S METH UNIV **MEMBERSHIPS** Am Antiquarian Soc **SELECTED PUBLICATIONS** Auth, A People in Revolution: The American Revolution and Political Society in New York, 81; auth, The People's American Revolution, 84; auth, The American Revolution, 85; contribur, The British Film Institute Companion to the Western,88; coauth, vol 1, Who Built America, 89; auth, "The Uses of Capital in Revolutionary America: The Case of the New York Loyalist Merchants," Will & Mary Quar, 92; auth, "To Secure the Blessings of Liberty: Language, Capitalism and the Revolution," in Beyond the American Revolution, 93; auth, "Indians, the Colonial Order, and the Social Significance of the American Declaration," Will & Mary Quar, 96; America: A Cousin of Histories, 96; coauth, A New History of New York State, forthcoming. **CONTACT ADDRESS** Dept of Hist, So Methodist Univ, Dallas, TX 75275-0176. **EMAIL** ecountry@mail.smu.edu

COURTEMANCHE, REGIS ARMAND
PERSONAL Born 05/05/1933, Scranton, PA, m, 1967, 7 children **DISCIPLINE** BRITISH & NAVAL HISTORY **EDUCATION** St John's Univ, BA, 59, MA, 62; London Sch Econ, PhD, 67. **CAREER** Instr hist, Delehanty High Sch, 61-64; assoc prof, 67-77, Prof Hist, CW Post Col, Long Island Univ, 77-, Mem bd, Educ Reviewer, Inc, 72. **RESEARCH** Nineteenth century Brit hist. **SELECTED PUBLICATIONS** Auth, The Royal Navy and the end of William Walker, Historian, 5/68; Home and history, Designer, 10/71; An American at the London School of Economics, Univ Bookman, summer 73; No Need of Glory, the British Navy in American Waters, 1860-64, Naval Inst, 77. **CONTACT ADDRESS** Dept of Hist, Long Island Univ, C.W. Post, 720 Northern Blvd, Greenvale, NY 11548-1300.

COURTENAY, WILLIAM JAMES
PERSONAL Born 11/05/1935, Neenah, WI **DISCIPLINE** MEDIEVAL HISTORY **EDUCATION** Vanderbilt Univ, AB, 57; Harvard Univ, STB, 60; PhD, 67. **CAREER** Instr hist, Stanford Univ, 65-66; from asst prof to assoc prof, 66-71, prof hist, Univ Wis-Madison, 71-; chairman, Hist Dept, Univ Wis-Madison, 85-88; pres, Am Soc of Church Hist, 88; chairman, Classics Dept, Univ Wis-Madison, 99-02; C.H. Haskins prof, Univ Wis-Madison, 88-; Hilldale prof, Univ Wis-Madison, 98-. **HONORS AND AWARDS** Nat Endowment for Humanities younger scholar award, 68-69; A von Humboldt fel, Tubingen, Ger, 75-76, 79-80; Guggenheim fel, 80; NEH fel, Newberry Libr, 83; Inst for Adv Study, Princeton, mem, 88-89; A von Humboldt Preistrager, 90; Am Council of Learned Societies fel, 95-96; Am Acad in Rome, vis sch, 95, 97; Herzog August Bibl Wolfenbuttel, Ger, fel, 98; Fel Medieval Acad of Am, 79-; Fel Am Acad of Arts and Sciences, 96-. **MEMBERSHIPS** Medieval Acad Am; Am Soc Church Hist; Int Soc Study Medieval Philos. **RESEARCH** Intellectual history of the high and late Middle Ages; History of medieval universities. **SELECTED PUBLICATIONS** Auth, Adam Wodeham, Brill (Leiden), 78; auth, Covenant and Causality in Medieval Thought, Variorum (London), 84; auth, Schools and Scholars in Fourteenth-century England, Princeton, 87; auth, Capacity and Volition. A History of the Distinction of Absolute and Ordained Power, Pierluigi Lubrina (Bergamo), 90; auth, Parisian Scholars in the Early Fourteenth-century, Cambridge, 99; ed, Universities and Schooling in Medieval Society, Brill (Leiden), 00. **CONTACT ADDRESS** Dept of Hist, Univ of Wisconsin, Madison, Madison, WI 53706. **EMAIL** wjcourte@facstaff.wisc.edu

COURTWRIGHT, DAVID T.
PERSONAL Born 04/10/1952, Kansas City, MO, m, 1976, 2 children **DISCIPLINE** HISTORY **EDUCATION** Univ of Kans, BA, 74; Rice Univ, PhD, 79. **CAREER** Assoc Prof, Univ of Hartford, 79-88; Prof, Univ of N Fla, 88-. **HONORS AND AWARDS** NEH Fel, 81 & 98-99; ACLS Fel, 93-94; Outstanding Undergraduate Teaching Awd, 98; Univ N Fla, Dist Prof, 98. **MEMBERSHIPS** OAH, AHA, AAHM, SHA, Phi Beta Kappa. **RESEARCH** History of Drug use and Drug Policy; Male Violence; and other aspects of social; legal; and medical history. **SELECTED PUBLICATIONS** Auth, "Dark Paradise: Opiate Addiction in America before 1940, Harvard Univ Pr, 82; auth, Addicts Who Survived: An Oral History of Narcotic Addiction in America, 1923-1965, Univ Tenn Pr, 89; auth, Violent Land: Single Men and Social Disorder from the Frontier to the Inner City, Harvard Univ Pr, 96; auth, Drug World: Five Centuries fo Pleasure, Profit, and Power, Harvard Univ Press, 01. **CONTACT ADDRESS** Dept History, Univ of No Florida, 4567 Saint Johns Bluff Rd S, Jacksonville, FL 32224-2645. **EMAIL** dcourtwr@unf.edu

COUTENAY, LYNN
PERSONAL Born 07/08/1943, Nashville, TN, d, 2 children **DISCIPLINE** ENGLISH; HISTORY; ART HISTORY **EDUCATION** Vassar Col, BA, 65; MA, PhD, 79, Univ of Wis-Madison. **CAREER** Visiting lectr, University of WI-Madison; lectr, sr lectr, 84-96, asst prof, 96-, University of WI-Whitewata. **HONORS AND AWARDS** Fel in humanities, Newberry Library, 90-91; NEH Cooperative Project Grant, 91; Honorary Fel in Art hist, 94-97; elected Fel of the Soc of Antiquaries (members by invitation only), 95; Who's Who Among America's Teachers, Natl Honor Students' nomination, 96; University of WI System Fel: Inst for research in the humanities, 98-99 **MEMBERSHIPS** Soc of Antiquairies; ICMA; AVISTA; CAA; Vernacular Architecture Group; RAI; AIA (USA). **RESEARCH** Medieval Architecture; historic carpentry; Roman architecture; late medieval social and cultural hist; hist of technology. **SELECTED PUBLICATIONS** Auth, The Westminster Hall Roof: A New Archaeological Source, British Archaeological Association Journal, 90; Architectural Technology up to the Scientific Revolution: The Art and Structure of Large-scale Buildings, 93; Scale and Scantling: Technological Issues in large-scale Timberwork of the High Middle Ages, in Technology and Resource Use in Medieval Europe, Cathedrals, the Mills, and Mines, Dec 97; The Engineering of Gothic Cathe-

drals, Studies in the History of Civil Engineering, Dec 11, 1997. **CONTACT ADDRESS** 3100 Lake Mendota Dr., #504, Madison, WI 53705. **EMAIL** hcourte@facstoff.wise.edu

COUTTS, BRIAN E.
PERSONAL Born 01/29/1948, Lethbridge, Canada, m, 1978, 1 child **DISCIPLINE** HISTORY, LIBRARY AND INFORMATION SCIENCE **EDUCATION** La State Univ, MLS, 83, Phd, 81. **CAREER** Hist bibliog, Fondren Libr, Rice Univ, 84-86; Coord, Collection Dev. Western Ky Univ, 87-90; PROF, HEAD, DEPT LIBRARY PUB SVCS, WESTERN KY UNIV, 91-. **HONORS AND AWARDS** Distinguished Research, Western Ky Univ, 91, 94; Outstanding Public Serv, 99; Louis Shores-Oryx Press Awd, ALA, 99. **MEMBERSHIPS** ALA, ACRL, La Hist. **RESEARCH** Colonial La hist, reference books publishing, hsitory of Belize. **SELECTED PUBLICATIONS** Auth, Belize, Clio Press, 93; auth, Reference Sources in History, 90, 2nd ed. 00; auth, Best Reference Sources of 1999, Libr J, Apr 15, 00; auth, Best Reference Websites of 1999, Libr J, apr 15, 00; auth, The Reference Revolution:Wired for the 90s, Libr J, Nov 15, 97; auth, Central America: From Civil Wars to Tourist Mecca, Libr J, Mar 1, 97. **CONTACT ADDRESS** Dept Libr Pub Svcs, Western Kentucky Univ, 1 Big Red Way, Bowling Green, KY 42101-3576. **EMAIL** brian.coutts@wku.edu

COUVARES, FRANCIS G.
PERSONAL Born 03/26/1948, Brooklyn, NY, m, 1969, 1 child **DISCIPLINE** HISTORY **EDUCATION** Univ Pittsburgh, BA, 69; Univ Mich, MA, 74; PhD, 80. **CAREER** Asst Prof, Clark Univ, 80-83; from asst prof to prof, 83-, dean of new students, 96-, Amherst Col. **HONORS AND AWARDS** J. Paul Getty Trust, 92-94; NEH, 90, 86; Amherst Col Res Awd, 98-99, 89-90. **MEMBERSHIPS** Am Hist Asn; Org of Am Hist; Am Studies Asn; Am Asn of Univ Prof. **RESEARCH** Nineteenth and Twentieth Century U.S. Social History; History of Free Speech and Censorship. **SELECTED PUBLICATIONS** Auth, "Hollywood, Main Street, and the Church: Trying to Censor the Movies before the Production Code," Am Quart, 92; auth, "The Good Censor: Race, Sex, and Censorship in the Early Cinema," Yale J of Criticism, 94; ed, Movie Censorship and American Culture, Smithsonian Press, 96; co-ed, Interpretations of American History, 7th ed, Free Press, 00. **CONTACT ADDRESS** Dept Hist, Amherst Col, Amherst, MA 01002. **EMAIL** fgcouvares@amherst.edu

COVERT, JAMES THAYNE
PERSONAL Born 04/20/1932, Cimarron, KS, m, 1952, 6 children **DISCIPLINE** ENGLISH AND MODERN EUROPEAN HISTORY **EDUCATION** Univ Portland, BA, 59; Univ Ore, MA, 61, PhD(hist), 67. **CAREER** From instr to assoc prof hist, 61-71, chmn dept, 67-72, Prof Hist, Univ Portland, 71-97, Danforth assoc, 70- **HONORS AND AWARDS** Standard Oil Calif Leadership Awd, 57; Nat Asn Manufacturers' Presidential Awd, 58; Am Red Cross Recognition Awd for Vol Serv, 64; Culligan Fac Awd, 68 & Distinguished Prof Awd, 96, Univ Portland. **RESEARCH** Victorian and Edwardian England and England in the twentieth century; social, intellectual, political history. **SELECTED PUBLICATIONS** Auth, "Student Freedom in American Higher Education," edited with Louis Vacaro, New York: Teachers College Press, Columbia University, 69; auth, "A Point of Pride: The University of Portland Story," Portland: University of Portland Press, 76; auth, "Memory Makers: More than 100 Just-For-Fun Ways to Give Children Memories to Last a Lifetime," with Jan Smith, Portland: Frank Amato Publication, 88; auth, "Memoir of a Victorian Woman: Reflections of Louise Creighton, 1850-1936," Bloomington: Indiana University Press, 94; auth, "A Victorian Family as Seen through the Letters of Louise Creighton to her Mother, 1872-1880," Lewiston, NY: Edwin Mellen Press, 98; auth, "A Victorian Marriage: Mandell and Louise Creighton," London: The Hambledon Press, 01. **CONTACT ADDRESS** Dept of Hist, Univ of Portland, Portland, OR 97203. **EMAIL** covert@up.edu

COWAN, RICHARD O.
PERSONAL Born 01/24/1934, Los Angeles, CA, m, 1958, 6 children **DISCIPLINE** CHURCH HISTORY **EDUCATION** Occidental Col, BA, 58; Stanford Univ, MA, 59, PhD, 61. **CAREER** Asst prof relig instr, 61-65, assoc prof hist relig, 65-71, prof of church hist, Brigham Young Univ, 71-; Danforth Fel, 58. **HONORS AND AWARDS** Phi Beta Kappa, 57. **MEMBERSHIPS** Mormon Hist Asn; Utah Hist Soc. **RESEARCH** Latter-day Saint history and theology. **SELECTED PUBLICATIONS** Coauth, Mormonism in the Twentieth Century 64, auth, The Doctrine and Covenants: Our Modern Scripture, 67, Temple Building Ancient and Modern, 71 & coauth, The Living Church, 74, Brigham Young Univ, Doctrine and Covenants: Our Modern Scripture, 84; Church in the Twentieth Century, 85; Temples to Dot the Earth, 89; Joseph Smith and the Doctrine and Covenants, 92; California Saints, 96; auth, Answers to Your Questions About the Doctrine and Covenants, 96; auth, The Latter-day Saint Century, 99; coauth, Encyclopedia of Latter-day Saint History, 00. **CONTACT ADDRESS** Brigham Young Univ, 270L Joseph Smith Bldg, Provo, UT 84602. **EMAIL** richard_cowan@byu.edu

COWAN, RUTH SCHWARTZ
PERSONAL Born 04/09/1941, Brooklyn, NY, m, 1968, 3 children **DISCIPLINE** HISTORY OF SCIENCE AND TECHNOLOGY **EDUCATION** Barnard Col, AB, 61; Univ Calif, Berkeley, MA, 64; Johns Hopkins Univ, PhD(hist sci), 69. **CAREER** From instr to full prof, SUNY, Stony Brook, 67-; NIH grad res asst, Johns Hopkins Univ, 65-66; vis asst prof hist, Princeton Univ, 72-73. **HONORS AND AWARDS** Phi Beta Kappa Lectr, 81-82; Dexter Prize, Soc for the Hist of Technol, 84; John Simon Guggenheim Mem Fel, 88-89; Sherman Fairchild Dist Scholar, Calif Inst of Technol, 89-90; Leonardo daVinci Medal, Soc for the Hist of Technol, 97. **MEMBERSHIPS** Hist Sci Soc; Soc Hist Technol; AAAS. **RESEARCH** History of biology; history of technology; women's history. **SELECTED PUBLICATIONS** Auth, More Work for Mother: The Ironies of Household Technology from the Open Hearth to the Microwave, 83; auth, Sir Francis Galton and the Study of Heredity in the Nineteenth Century, 85; coauth, Our Parent's Lives: The Americanization of Eastern European Jews, 89; auth, A Social History of American Technology, 97. **CONTACT ADDRESS** Dept of Hist, SUNY, Stony Brook, 100 Nicolls Rd, Stony Brook, NY 11794-4348. **EMAIL** rcowan@sunysb.edu

COWARD, HAROLD G.
PERSONAL Born 12/13/1936, Calgary, AB, Canada **DISCIPLINE** RELIGION, HISTORY **EDUCATION** Univ Alta, BA, 58, BD, 67, MA, 69; McMaster Univ, PhD, 73. **CAREER** Prof, Univ Calgary, 73-92, head relig stud, 76, 79-83, assoc dean hum, 77, dir, univ press, 81-83; dir, Calgary Inst Hum, 80-92; Dir, Centre for studies in Relig and Soc & prof Hist, Univ Victoria, 92-. **HONORS AND AWARDS** Fel, Royal Soc Can **MEMBERSHIPS** Pres, Can Soc Stud Relig, 84-86; pres, Shastri Indo-Can Inst, 86-88; pres, Can Corp Stud Relig, 87-90; pres, Can Fedn Hum, 90-91. **RESEARCH** Eastern religions; Hindu thought & religion; religious pluralism. **SELECTED PUBLICATIONS** Auth, Hindu Ethics: Purity, Euthanasia and Abortion, 88; auth, Derrida and Indian Philosophy, 90; auth, Philosophy of the Grammarians, 90; ed, Mantra: Hearing the Divine in India, 91; auth, Aging and Dying: Legal, Scientific and Religious Challenges, 93; auth, Anger in Our City: Youth Seeking Meaning, 94; auth, Population, Consumption and the Environment, 95; auth, Life After Death in World Religions, 97; auth, Traditional and Modern Approaches to the Environment on the Pacific Rim: Tensions and Values, 98; auth, Religious Conscience, the State and the Law, 98. **CONTACT ADDRESS** Ctr for Stud in Relig & Society, Univ of Victoria, Victoria, BC, Canada V8W 3P4. **EMAIL** csrs@uvic.ca

COWDEN, JOANNA DUNLAP
PERSONAL Born 02/09/1933, Woburn, MA, m, 1998, 4 children **DISCIPLINE** NINETEENTH CENTURY AMERICAN HISTORY **EDUCATION** Radcliffe Col, AB, 55; Trinity Col, Conn, MA, 65; Univ Conn, PhD(hist), 75. **CAREER** Prof 19th Century Am Hist, Calif State Univ, Chico, 76-. **MEMBERSHIPS** Orgn Am Historians; AHA; Western Assn of Women Historians. **RESEARCH** Study of Civil War and Reconstruction politics. **SELECTED PUBLICATIONS** Co-ed, Slavery in America: Theodore Weld's American Slavery as It Is, F E Peacock, 72. **CONTACT ADDRESS** Dept of History, California State Univ, Chico, 101 Orange St, Chico, CA 95929-0001. **EMAIL** jcowden@csuchico.edu

COWIE, JEFFERSON R.
DISCIPLINE HISTORY **EDUCATION** Univ Calif, BA, 87; Univ Washington, MA, 90; Univ NC, PhD, 96. **CAREER** Vis Asst Prof, Cornell Univ. **HONORS AND AWARDS** MacIntyre Awd, Cornell Univ, 99; Spec Res Grant Awd, Cornell Univ, 99; Fel, Ctr for US-Mexican Studies, 95-96; NJ Hist commission Res Grant, 96; FLAS Fel, Universidad Nacional Autonoma de Mexico, 95; Albert j Beveridge Grant, Am Hist Asn, 94. **SELECTED PUBLICATIONS** Auth, Capital Moves: RCA's Seventy-Year Quest for Cheap Labor, Cornell Univ Press, 99; auth, Labor and NAFTA: A Briefing Book, Durham, 94; auth, "The New Industrial Frontier: Mexican and US Workers in the Creation of the Border Industrialization Program, 1964-1974," in The Workers' West, Univ of Okla Press, forthcoming; auth, "Working Xlass," Encyclopedia of American Culture and Intellectual History, forthcoming; auth, "Anything but an Industrial Town," BookPress: The Newspaper of the Literary Arts, 98; auth, "National Struggles in a Transnational Economy: A Critical Analysis of Labor's Response to NAFTA," Labor Studies Journal, (97): 3-32; auth, "NAFTA's Labor Side Accord: A Textual Analysis," Latin Americna Labor News, 94; auth, "US Labor and Free Trade: The Future and History," Latin American Labor News, 94. **CONTACT ADDRESS** Sch Indust & Labor Relations, Cornell Univ, Ives Hall, Ithaca, NY 14853. **EMAIL** jrc32@cornell.edu

COWING, CEDRIC BRESLYN
PERSONAL Born 07/29/1926, Pasadena, CA, m, 1963, 1 child **DISCIPLINE** AMERICAN HISTORY **EDUCATION** Stanford Univ, AB, 48, AM, 51; Univ Wis, PhD(hist), 55. **CAREER** Actg instr hist, Univ Calif, Santa Barbara, 55-57; from asst prof to assoc prof, 57-68, Prof Hist, Univ Hawaii, Manoa, 68-. **HONORS AND AWARDS** Annual Awd, Am Studies Asn, 68. **MEMBERSHIPS** Orgn Am Historians; Am Studies Asn; Am Soc Church Hist. **RESEARCH** Social and religious history. **SELECTED PUBLICATIONS** Auth, Populists, Plungers, and Progressives, Princeton Univ, 65; Sex and preaching in the great awakening, Am Quart, fall 68; The Great Awakening and the American Revolution, Rand, 71; The American Revolution: Its Meaning to Asians & Americans, East-West Ctr, 77. **CONTACT ADDRESS** Dept of Hist, Univ of Hawaii, Manoa, Honolulu, HI 96822.

COX, CAROLINE
PERSONAL Born 11/23/1954, Scotland, m **DISCIPLINE** HISTORY **EDUCATION** Univ Calif, Berkeley, AB, 90, MA, 93, PhD, 97. **CAREER** Asst prof, 98-, Univ Pacific. **RESEARCH** Early Amer, Native Amer, Africa Amer. **CONTACT ADDRESS** Dept of History, Univ of the Pacific, Stockton, Stockton, CA 95211. **EMAIL** ccox@uop.edu

COX, GARY D.
PERSONAL Born, MI, m, 1993, 3 children **DISCIPLINE** SLAVIC STUDIES **EDUCATION** Earlham Col, BA, 69; Ind Univ, MA, 73; Columbia Univ, PhD, 78. **CAREER** Asst prof, Univ Mo/Columbia Inst, 76-81; asst/assoc prof, Southern Methodist Univ, 81- . **HONORS AND AWARDS** Phi Beta Kappa; SMU Authors' Awd, 92. **MEMBERSHIPS** Am Asoc of Teachers of Slavic/Eastern Europ Lang; Am Asoc for Advan of Slavic Studies; Human Behavior and Evolution Soc. **RESEARCH** Russian literature and culture; Dostoevsky; evolution of cultural systems. **SELECTED PUBLICATIONS** Tyrant and Victim in Dostoevsky, 84; auth, Crime and Punishment: A Mind to Murder, 90. **CONTACT ADDRESS** Foreign Langs & Lits, Russian Area, So Methodist Univ, Dallas, TX 75275. **EMAIL** gcox@post.smu.edu

COX, HAROLD E.
PERSONAL Born 06/27/1931, Lynchburg, VA, m, 1956 **DISCIPLINE** HISTORY **EDUCATION** William and Mary, AB, 51; Univ of Va, MA, 54; PhD, 56. **CAREER** Asst Prof, Temple Univ, 56-63; Hist Dept Chair, Wilkes Univ, 66-67, 91-99; Dean Col of Lib Arts, Wilkes Univ, 97; From Assoc Prof to Prof, Wilkes Univ, 63-. **HONORS AND AWARDS** Phi Beta Kappa, Alpha of Va, 51. **RESEARCH** History of Technology, Gilded Age. **SELECTED PUBLICATIONS** Coauth, A Concise Historical Atlas of Eastern Europe, St Martin's Press, 96. **CONTACT ADDRESS** Dept Hist, Wilkes Univ, PO Box 111, Wilkes-Barre, PA 18766-0999. **EMAIL** hcox@wilkes.edu

COX, JOSEPH W.
PERSONAL Born 05/26/1937, Hagerstown, MD, m, 1963, 3 children **DISCIPLINE** EARLY AMERICAN HISTORY, HIGHER EDUCATION **EDUCATION** Univ Md, BA, 59, PhD(hist), 67. **CAREER** Asst hist, Univ Md, 60-64; assoc dean English, hist & soc sci, Towson State Univ, 69-72, dean eve col & summer session, 72-75, dir fac develop, 75-77, prof hist, 64-81, vpres acad affairs & dean univ, 77-81; VPres Acad Affairs, Northern Ariz Univ, 81-, Consult on col governance, Bd Trustees, Md State Cols, 68; consul on fac teaching awards, Pa State Dept Educ, 76-78. **MEMBERSHIPS** Am Asn Higher Educ; AAUP. **RESEARCH** Early American history; Maryland history; history of higher education; cultural philanthropy in 19th century America; the Historical Society movement. **SELECTED PUBLICATIONS** Contribr, Racial sensitivity: A model program, Am Personnel & Guide Asn, 70; auth, Champion of Southern Federalism: Robert Goodloe Harper, Kennikat, 72; coauth, Programs that don't lock you in: The flexible degree structure, Col Mgt, 73; auth, The second bachelor's program, Md Higher Educ, 73; The Army Corps of Engineers in the Early National Era 1781-1812, Govt Printing Off, 78; The Origins of the Md Historical Society, Md Hist Mag, 79; Surviving the 1980's, Nacubo, 81. **CONTACT ADDRESS** Dept of History, No Arizona Univ, Flagstaff, AZ 86001.

COX, KEVIN R.
PERSONAL Born 03/22/1939, Warwick, England, m, 1966, 2 children **DISCIPLINE** GEOGRAPHY **EDUCATION** Cambridge Univ, BA, 61; Univ Ill, MA, 63; PhD, 66. **CAREER** Asst Prof, Ohio State Univ, 65-68; Assoc Prof, Ohio State Univ, 68-71; Vis Prof, Univ Reading, 95-99; Prof, Ohio State Univ, 71-. **HONORS AND AWARDS** Hon Awd, Asn of Am Geogrs, 85; Distinguished Scholar Awd, Ohio State Univ, 97. **MEMBERSHIPS** Assoc of Am Geogrs. **RESEARCH** The politics of local economic development, neighborhood politics, migrant labor and its politics in South Africa. **SELECTED PUBLICATIONS** Co-ed, Behavioral Problems in Geography, Northwestern Univ Pr, 69; auth, Man, Location and Behavior: An Introduction to Human Geography, John Wiley (New York, NY), 72; auth, Conflict, Power and Politics in the City: A Geographic Approach, McGraw-Hill (New York, NY), 73; co-ed, Locational Approaches to Power and Conflict, Sage Publ (Beverly Hills, CA), 74; ed, Urbanization and Conflict in Market Societies, Maarouga Pr (Chicago, IL), 78; auth, Location and Public Problems: An Introduction to Political Geography, Maaroufa Pr (Chicago, IL), 79; co-ed, Behavioral Geography Revisited, Methuen (London, UK), 81; co-ed, Conflict, Politics and the Urban Scene: Case Studies in Urban Political Geography, Longman (London, UK), 82; ed, Spaces of Globalization: Reasserting the Power of the Local, Guilford Pr (New York, NY), 97. **CONTACT ADDRESS** Dept Geog, Ohio State Univ, Columbus, 154 N Oval Mall, 1035 Derby Hall, Columbus, OH 43210-1361. **EMAIL** kcox@geography.ohio-state.edu

COX, SHARON G.
PERSONAL 3 children **DISCIPLINE** ART **EDUCATION** Mercer Univ, BA, 82; Univ Georgia, MFA, 83. **CAREER** Lectr, art, Mercer Univ, 83-85; asst prof, journalism, Jackson State Univ, 87-89; asst prof journalism, Lynchburg Col, 89-91; head, Art Dept, Jamestown Col, 92- . **HONORS AND AWARDS** Outstanding Citizen, Warner Robins, GA, 69; Outstanding Student, hum div, Macon Jr Col, 80; press awards for newspaper work. **MEMBERSHIPS** CAA; AAUW; SPJ; Ga Press Assoc; Asia Soc. **RESEARCH** Native American pigment sites in the Dakotas. **CONTACT ADDRESS** Jamestown Col, 6003 College Ln, Box 1559, Jamestown, ND 58402. **EMAIL** cox@jc.edu

COX, THOMAS C.
DISCIPLINE HISTORY **EDUCATION** Princeton Univ, PhD, 80. **CAREER** Assoc prof, Univ Southern Calif. **RESEARCH** Grasshopper Plague in the Trans-Mississippi West, 1874-1878. **SELECTED PUBLICATIONS** Auth, Blacks in Topeka, Kansas, 1865-1915: A Social History, La State, 82. **CONTACT ADDRESS** Dept of History, Univ of So California, University Park Campus, Los Angeles, CA 90089. **EMAIL** tcox@bcf.usc.edu

COX, THOMAS RICHARD
PERSONAL Born 01/16/1933, Portland, OR, m, 1954, 4 children **DISCIPLINE** AMERICAN HISTORY **EDUCATION** Ore State Univ, BS, 55; Univ Ore, MS, 59, PhD(hist), 69. **CAREER** Teacher, Pub High Schs, 56-63; from asst prof to assoc prof hist, 67-74, Prof US Hist, San Diego State Univ, 74-, Fulbright prof, Kyushu Univ & Seinan Gakuin Univ, Japan, 75-76; Forest Hist Soc vis fel, Univ Calif, Santa Cruz, 79-80. **HONORS AND AWARDS** Max Savelle Prize, 65; Emil & Kathleen Sick Lect-Bk Awd, 74; Theodore Blegen Awd, Forest Hist Soc, 74. **MEMBERSHIPS** Orgn Am Historians; Agr Hist Soc (pres, 78-80); Forest Hist Soc; Western Hist Asn; Asn Asian Studies. **RESEARCH** Forest and conservation history; late 19th and early 20th century United States history; Asian-American relations. **SELECTED PUBLICATIONS** Contribr, Reflections of Western historians, Univ Ariz, 69; auth, Lumber and ships: The business empire of Asa Mead Simpson, Forest Hist, 70; Harbingers of change: American merchants and the Formosa annexation scheme, Pac Hist Rev, 73; Conservation by subterfuge, Pac Northwest Quart, 73; Mills and Markets, Univ Wash, 74; Treaty Port Press & 100 days reforms, Historian, 74; The 1880's as an intellectual watershed in the US, Seinan Law Rev, 76; Transition in the woods: Log drivers, raftsmen, and the emergence of modern lumbering in Pennsylvania, Pa Mag Hist Biog, 80. **CONTACT ADDRESS** Dept of Hist, San Diego State Univ, 5500 Campanile Dr, San Diego, CA 92182-0002.

COYLE, J. KEVIN
PERSONAL Born 04/25/1943, Iroquois Falls, ON, Canada, s **DISCIPLINE** EARLY CHRISTIAN HISTORY **EDUCATION** Univ of Ottawa, BA, BPh, 63; Catholic Univ of Amer, BTh, LTh, 65 and 67; Univ de Fribourg en Suisse, DTh, 79. **CAREER** Lectr, 76-79, Asst Prof, 79-84, Assoc Prof, 84-87, Full Prof, 87-, Universite Saint-Paul, Ottawa. **MEMBERSHIPS** Canadian Soc of Patristic Studies; North Amer Patristic Soc; Intl Assoc for Patristic Studies; Intl Assoc of Manichaean Studies; Societe quebecoise pour l etude de las religion; Soc of Biblical Lit. **RESEARCH** History of early Christianity; Latin Palaeography; Development of Christian Thought; Manichaeism **SELECTED PUBLICATIONS** Auth, De moribus ecclesiae catholicae: Augustin chretien a Rome, De moribus ecclesiae catholicae et de moribus Manichaeorum: De quantitate animae, 91; Mary Magdalene in Manichaeism, Le Museon, 91; Augustine's Millenialism Reconsidered, Charisteria Augustiniana Iosepho Oroz Reta dicata, 93; Recent Reviews on the Origins of Clerical Celibacy, Logos, 93; Hands and the Impositions of Hands in Manichaesim, Pegrina Curiositas: Eine Reise durch den orbis antiquus. Zu Ehren von Dirk van Damme, 94; Early Monks, Prayer and the Devil, Prayer and Spirituality in the Early Church, 98. **CONTACT ADDRESS** Saint Paul Univ, 223 Main St., Ottawa, ON, Canada K1S 1C4. **EMAIL** jkcoyle@ustpaul.uottawa.ca

CRABTREE, LOREN WILLIAM
PERSONAL Born 09/02/1940, Aberdeen, SD, m, 1987, 3 children **DISCIPLINE** HISTORY; ASIAN STUDIES **EDUCATION** Univ Minn, BA, 61, MA, 65, PhD(hist), 69. **CAREER** Instr hist, Bethel Col, St Paul, Minn, 65-67; from instr to assoc prof, 67-85, Prof Hist, Colo State Univ, 85-, Dean, Col Liberal Arts, 91-97, Provost, 97-. **HONORS AND AWARDS** Nat Endowment for Humanities Younger Humanist fel, 73-74. **MEMBERSHIPS** Asn Asian Studies; AHA; Asia Soc; Conf Faith & Hist; Western Soc Sci Asn. **RESEARCH** Chinese history, 1900-1937; rural development in Asia; Christian missions in China and India. **SELECTED PUBLICATIONS** Auth, The papers of the National Federation of Settlements, Soc Serv Rev, 66; Communism and the Chinese cultural tradition, Int Quart, 68; coauth, Descriptive Inventories of Collections in the Social Welfare Archives Center, Greenwood, 70; From Mohensodaro to Mao: Perspectives on reaching Asian civilization, Hist Teacher, 73; auth, New perspectives on Sino-American relations, 73 & coauth, Interpreting Asia to Americans, 74, Rocky Mountain Soc Sci J; auth, Seeing red in China: Missouri Synod missionaries and the Chinese Revolution, 1913-30, Selected Papers on Asia, 76; coauth, The Lion and the Dragon: An Introduction to the Civilizations of India and China, J Weston Walch, 79. **CONTACT ADDRESS** Off of the Provost, Colorado State Univ, Fort Collins, CO 80523-0001. **EMAIL** 1crabtree@lamar.colostate.edu

CRAFT, GEORGE S., JR.
PERSONAL Born 12/13/1942, Atlanta, GA, w, 5 children **DISCIPLINE** HISTORY **EDUCATION** Univ Notre Dame, AB, 64; Oxford Univ, BA, 66; Stanford Univ, PhD, 71. **CAREER** Prof, CA State Univ, Sacramento, 70-. **RESEARCH** Modern France, culture, history, and film. **SELECTED PUBLICATIONS** Auth, The Emergence of National Sentiment in French Lorraine, 1871-1889, Third Republic/Troisieme republique, no 2, 76; California State University, Sacramento: The First Forty Years, 1947-1987, 87. **CONTACT ADDRESS** Dept of Hist, California State Univ, Sacramento, Sacramento, CA 95819. **EMAIL** gcraft@csus.edu

CRAIG, ALBERT MORTON
PERSONAL Born 12/09/1927, Chicago, IL, m, 1953, 3 children **DISCIPLINE** JAPANESE HISTORY **EDUCATION** Northwestern Univ, BS, 49; Harvard Univ, PhD, 59. **CAREER** Instr hist, Univ MA, 57-59; from instr to asst prof Japanese hist, 59-63, assoc prof hist, 63-67, assoc dir, E Asian Res Ctr, 70-76, prof Hist, Harvard Univ, 67-, dir, Yenching Inst, 76-87, Harvard-Yenching Prof Hist, 89-99; Fulbright res prof & Am Coun Learned Soc grant, Kyoto Univ, 62-63; Guggenheim fel, 67-68; fellow, Pembroke Col, Oxford Univ, 95; vis prof, Inst of Social Science, Tokyo Univ, 96; Burns vis prof, Univ HI, 97; Harvard-Yenching Res Prof of History, 99-. **MEMBERSHIPS** Asn Asian Studies; Hist Soc Japan. **RESEARCH** Modern Japanese thought; comparative studies of Asian development, society and religion, Meiji restoration. **SELECTED PUBLICATIONS** Auth, Choshu in the Meiji Restoration, Harvard Univ, 61; coauth, East Asia the Modern Transformation, Houghton, 65; co-ed, Personality in Japanese History, Univ CA, 70; coauth, East Asia: Tradition and Transformation, 73 & Japan: Tradition and Transformation, 78, Houghton; Japan, A Comparative View, Princeton Univ Press, 80; Heritage of World Civilization (with others), Prentice Hall, 86, 90, 94, 97. **CONTACT ADDRESS** Dept of Hist, Harvard Univ, Robinson Hall, Cambridge, MA 02138-3800. **EMAIL** acraig@fas.harvard.edu

CRAIG, GORDON ALEXANDER
PERSONAL Born 11/26/1913, Glasgow, Scotland **DISCIPLINE** HISTORY **EDUCATION** Princeton Univ, AB, 36, AM, 39 PhD, 41. **CAREER** Instr hist, Yale Univ, 39-41; from instr to prof, Princeton Univ, 41-61; prof, 61-69, J E Wallace Sterling Prof Humanities, Stanford Univ, 69-, Vis prof, Columbia Univ, 47-48, 49-50; fel, Ctr Advan Study Behav Sci, 56-57; prof mod hist, Free Univ, Berlin, 62-; mem soc sci adv bd, US Arms Control & Disarmament Agency, 64-70; mem, US Air Force Acad Adv Coun, 68-71. **HONORS AND AWARDS** Historians Prize, City of MInster, Westphalia, 81; littd, princeton univ, 70; blitt, oxford univ, 38. **MEMBERSHIPS** AHA (pres, 82); AAAS; Am Philos Soc. **RESEARCH** German history; modern diplomacy; military history. **SELECTED PUBLICATIONS** Auth, Politics of the Prussian Army, 1640-1945, Oxford Univ, 55; From Bismarck to Adenauer: Aspects of German Statecraft, Johns Hopkins Univ, 58; Europe since 1815, Holt, 61, 66; The Diplomats, 1919-39, 2 Vols, Atheneum, 63; The Battle of Koniggratz, Lippincott, 64; War, Politics and Diplomacy, Praeger, 66; Germany 1866-1945, Oxford Univ, 78; The Germans, Putmam's, 82; coauth (with Alexander L George), Force and Statecraft, Oxford Univ, 82. **CONTACT ADDRESS** Dept of Hist, Stanford Univ, Stanford, CA 94305.

CRAIG, JOHN ELDON
PERSONAL Born 07/23/1941, Sherbrooke, PQ, Canada, m, 1975 **DISCIPLINE** MODERN EUROPEAN HISTORY, COMPARATIVE EDUCATION **EDUCATION** Bowdoin Col, AB, 62; Stanford Univ, AM, 63, PhD, 73. **CAREER** Actg instr hist, Stanford Univ, 67; actg asst prof, Univ Va, 67-73; asst prof, 75-81, assoc prof, Educ, Univ Chicago, 81-. **MEMBERSHIPS** AHA; Conf Group Cent Europ Hist; Soc Fr Hist Studies; Soc Sci Hist Asn; Int Sociol Asn. **RESEARCH** Modern European social history; educational expansion in developed and developing countries. **SELECTED PUBLICATIONS** Auth, Maurice Halbwachs a Strasbourg, Rev Fr Sociol, Vol 20, 273-292; "On the Development of Educational Systems," American Journal of Education, 89; The Expansion of Education, Rev Res in Educ, 9: 151-213; Die Durkheim-Schule und die Annales, Gerschichte der Soziologie, Suhrkamp (4 vols), 3: 298-322; Higher Education and Social Mobility in Germany, 1850-1930, The Transformation of Higher Learning, 1850-1930, Klett-Cotta, 82; coauth (with N. Spear), Explaining Educational Expansion: An Agenda for Historical and Comparative Research, & Rational Actors, Group Processes, and the Development of Educational Systems, The Sociology of Educational Expansion, Sage, 82; auth, Scholarship and Nation Building: The Universities of Strasbourg and Alsatian Society, 1870-1939, Univ Chicago Press, 84. **CONTACT ADDRESS** Dept of Educ, Univ of Chicago, 5835 Kimbark Ave, Chicago, IL 60637-1684. **EMAIL** j-craig@uchicago.edu

CRAIG, ROBERT
PERSONAL Born 02/07/1942, San Jose, CA, m, 1963, 2 children **DISCIPLINE** HISTORY, INTERNATIONAL STUDIES **EDUCATION** Univ Calif at Santa Barbara, BA, 65; Union Theol Sem, MDiv, 68; Columbia Univ, PhD, 75. **CAREER** Assoc prof, Mount Union Col, 90-96; dir of general educ, Col of St Scholastica, 96-99; prof, Col of St Scholastica, 99-. **HONORS AND AWARDS** Burma-Bucknell Awd for Promoting Int Understanding, 86; Wye Fel, 92; NEH summer sem, Univ of Okla, 95; listed in Who'sWho Among America's Teachers, 00. **MEMBERSHIPS** Am Historical Asn, Acad of Polit Sci, Soc of Christian Ethics. **RESEARCH** Challenges posed by indigenous communities with respect to environmental ethics and the nature of American jurisprudence. **SELECTED PUBLICATIONS** Auth, "Christianity and Empire: A Case-Study of American Protestant Colonialism and Native Americans," Am Indian Culture and Res J 21,2 (97); auth, "Making a Living, Making a Life: Education with a Purpose," Volume 5: The Management of Values: Organizational and Educational issues, Univ Press of Am, Inc and Oxford Univ Center for the Study of Values in Educ and Business, 98; auth, "The Search for Justice in an Unjust World: John Macmurray and Criminal Justice," J for Peace and Justice Studies 9,1 (98); auth, "Institutionalized Relationality: A native American Perspective on Law, Justice, and Community," Annual of the Soc of Christian Ethics 1999 Vol 19, The Soc of Christian Ethics (Chicago), 99; auth, "The Commodification of Education: Education as Business," Volume 6: Business, Education and Training Series: On the Threshold of a New Millenium, Univ Press of Am, Inc. (Lanham, MD) and Oxford Univ Center for the Study of Values in Education and Business, 00. **CONTACT ADDRESS** Dept Hist and Dept Lang & Int Studies, Col of St. Scholastica, 1200 Kenwood Ave, Duluth, MN 55811-4199. **EMAIL** rcraig@css.edu

CRAIG, ROBERT M.
PERSONAL Born 05/29/1944, St. Louis, MO, m, 1975, 1 child **DISCIPLINE** ARCHITECTURURAL HISTORY **EDUCATION** Principia Col, BA, 66; Univ Ill, MA, 67; Cornell Univ, PhD (hist archit), 73. **CAREER** Instr, Meremac Jr Col, 67-68; instr, Principia Col, 72-73; asst prof, Ga Inst Tech, 73-78, assoc prof, 78-99; prof, 99-. **HONORS AND AWARDS** Donaghey Dist Lectr, 93; Who's Who in Sci and Engg. 92, 95; Who's Who in the World, 94; Men of Achievement, 93, 94; Who's Who in Am Educ, 90, 92; Dictionary of International Biography, 22nd ed, 92, 29th ed., 01; Who's Who in the South and Southwest, 22nd & 23rd & 24th eds., 89, 92, 95; 2000 Outstanding Scholars of the 20th Century, 00; Outstanding People of the 20th Century 2nd ed., 00; Outstanding Scholars of the 21st Century, 1st ed., 01. **MEMBERSHIPS** SAH; SESAH; SECAC; NCSA; SCA; SEASECS; PCAS/ACAS; VAF. **RESEARCH** Nineteenth and twentieth century American and English architecture; Bernard Maybeck; art deco; arts and crafts movement; garden history. **SELECTED PUBLICATIONS** Auth, "Passages to a Different Universe: The Three Gardenes of Zhuo Zheng Yuan, Suzhou," in SECAC Rev, 88; auth, Is Atlanta Losing Its Early Modern Heritage?, in Atlanta Hist, 95; auth, Atlanta Architecture:Art Deco to Modern Classic, Gretna, 95; auth, Functional Sculpture: The early work of Julian H. Harris, SECAC Rev, 96; auth, Atlanta's Moderne Diner Revival: History, Nostalgia, Youth and Car Culture, in On the Culture of the American South, Stud in Am/Popular Culture, 96; auth, Edwin Lutyens, Frank Lloyd Wright, Gustav Stickley, essays in Encyclopedia of Interior Design, 97; coauth, John Portman: An Island on an Island, L'Arca'Edizioni, 97; auth, "The Archaeology of Atlanta's First Automobile Age," in Atlanta Hist., 00. **CONTACT ADDRESS** College of Architecture, Georgia Inst of Tech, Atlanta, GA 30332-0155. **EMAIL** rob.craig@arch.gatech.edu

CRAIS, CLIFTON C.
PERSONAL Born 04/04/1960 **DISCIPLINE** AFRICAN HISTORY **EDUCATION** Univ of Md, BA, 82; Johns Hopkins Univ, MA, 84; PhD, 88; Mellon Fac Sem on Post-Modernism, Kenyon Col, 88. **CAREER** Visiting Sch, Rhodes Univ, 85; visiting instr, Kenyon Col, 87-88; visiting asst professor, Univ of Cape Town, 88-89; res asst, Univ of Cape Town, 88-89; Post-Doc Res Fel, Univ of Cape Town, 88, 89; ch, African and African-Am Studies Comm, 90-91; ch, Kenyon Sem, 90-96; ch, African-Am Hist Search Comm, 90-91; visiting assoc, Univ of Cape Town, 89, 91; Univ res scholar, Rhodes Univ, 92; Univ res scholar, Rhodes Univ, 92; asst prof, 88-93; assoc prof, Kenyon Col, 93-; visiting assoc prof, Stanford Univ 95; ch, Fac Aff Comm, 96-97. **HONORS AND AWARDS** Full Tuition Scholar, Johns Hopkins Univ, 82-88; tchg fel, 83-84; grad fel, 85,Kenan spec tchg fel, 87; Fulbright full fel, 84-85; fac devel grants, Kenyon Col, 88, 91, 92; Univ Res Fel, Rhodes Univ, 92; ACLS Fel,-In-Aid, 93; fac devel grant, Stanford Univ, 94-5; fel, Stanford Hum Center, 95; fel, Stanford Univ, 94-95; Spring Quarter, 1995; panels ch, African Studies Assoc, 97; ch, Fac Aff Comm, Kenyon Col, 96-98; ch, Kenyon Col, 95-98. **MEMBERSHIPS** World Hist Assoc, 93-4; Inst of Histl Res, Univ of London, 85-86; Inst of Commonwealth Studies, Sch of Oriental and African Studies, 85-94; Ctr for African Studies, 84-95; Ctr for African Studies, 84-95; Am Hist Assoc, 88-. **RESEARCH** Pre-colonial, colonial and contemporary Africa, slavery and emancipation. **SELECTED PUBLICATIONS** Auth, White Supremacy and Black Resistance in Pre-Industrial South Africa: The Making of the Colonial Order in the Eastern Cape, 1770-1865, Cambridge Univ Press, 92, Witwatersrand Univ

Press, 92; Breaking the Chains: Slavery and its Legacy in Nineteenth-Century South Africa, Witwatersrand Univ Press, 94; Representation and the Politics of Identity in South Africa: An Eastern Cape Example, Intl Jour of African Hist Studies, 92; Rev of Carolyn Hamilton, The Mfecane Aftermath, Intl Jour of African Hist Studies, 97; Rev of E. Eldredge and F. Morton, Slavery in South Africa: Captive Labor on the Dutch Frontier, Jour of Soc Hist, 97. **CONTACT ADDRESS** Dept of Hist, Kenyon Col, Gambier, OH 43022. **EMAIL** Crais@kenyon.edu

CRAMER, RICHARD S.
PERSONAL Born 10/08/1928, Bandon, OR, m, 1950, 3 children **DISCIPLINE** UNITED STATES HISTORY **EDUCATION** Univ OR, BS, 50, MS, 52; Stanford Univ, PhD, 60. **CAREER** Instr western civilization, Stanford Univ, 60-61; from asst prof to assoc prof US hist, 61-70, prof hist, CA State Univ, San Jose, 70-96, Col Found res grant, 62. **MEMBERSHIPS** AHA; Orgn Am Historians; Pac Coast Br AHA; Southern Hist Asn; Soc for Historians for the Early Republic. **RESEARCH** The ante-bellum South; 19th century Am polit hist; 19th century, Anglo-Am soc and intellectual rel(s). **SELECTED PUBLICATIONS** Auth, British magazines and the Oregon question, Pac Hist Rev, 11/63; Ole P Balling: Painter of Civil War heroes, Am Scand Rev, summer 66; coauth, Portraits of Nobel Peace Prize Laureates, Abelard, 69 & American Humor and Humorists (2 vols), Spartan Bk Store, 70-71. **CONTACT ADDRESS** Dept of Hist, San Jose State Univ, 1 Washington Sq, San Jose, CA 95192-0001.

CRANE, CONRAD CHARLES
PERSONAL Born 01/22/1952, Wilkes-Barre, PA, m, 1979, 2 children **DISCIPLINE** MILITARY HISTORY **EDUCATION** U.S. Military Acad, BS, 74; Stanford Univ, MA, 83, PhD, 90. **CAREER** From asst prof to prof, hist, 83-99, U.S. Mil Acad.; U.S. Army officer, 74- ; Strategic Studies Inst. 00-. **HONORS AND AWARDS** John A. Hotell III Awd for modern history, 74; Phi Kappa Phi Awd for Scholarship, 86; graduate of u.s. army war col & u.s. army command and general staff col. **MEMBERSHIPS** Soc for Mil Hist; Hist Soc; World War II Studies Asn; Phi Kappa Phi; Phi Alpha Theta. **RESEARCH** Airpower; Twentieth Century warfare and wars; experience of combat; American Civil War. **SELECTED PUBLICATIONS** Co-ed, rev WWI vol of The West Point Atlas of American Wars, Holt, 97; auth, Twilight of the Superfortresses: Strategic Airpower in the Korean War, Inst for Security Stud, 97; auth, A Clarion of Thunderclaps and Hurricanes; The Search for Victory Through Airpower in Europe, in Brower, ed, World War II in Europe: The Final Year, St Martin's, 98; auth, Eagle Over the Sun: The Air War Against Japan and the End of the War in the Pacific, in Lee, ed, World War II in Asia and the Pacific and the War's Aftermath, with General Themes: A Handbook of Literature and Research, Greenwood, 98; auth, Raiding the Beggar's Pantry: The Search for Airpower Strategy in the Korean War, J of Mil Hist, 99; auth, American Airpower Strategy in Korea, 1950-1953, Kansas, 99. **CONTACT ADDRESS** US Army War College, Strategic Studies Institute, Carlisle Barracks, Carlisle, PA. 17013-5050. **EMAIL** conrad.crane@carlisle.army.mil

CRANE, ELAINE F.
PERSONAL Born 07/23/1939, New York, NY, m, 1960, 2 children **DISCIPLINE** AMERICAN HISTORY **EDUCATION** Cornell Univ, BA, 61; NYork Univ, MA, 73, PhD(Am hist), 77. **CAREER** Asst ed, Papers Robert Morris, 76-77, Papers William Livingston, 77-78; asst prof Hist, 78-83, assoc prof, 84-91, Prof Hist, Fordham Univ, 91-. **HONORS AND AWARDS** Soc of Am Archivists, 92. **MEMBERSHIPS** Orgn Am Historians. **RESEARCH** Colonial and revolutionary history; women's history. **SELECTED PUBLICATIONS** Auth, A Dependent People: Newport, Rhode Island in the Revolutionary Era, NY: Fordhan Univ Press, 85; ed, The Diary of Elizabeth Drinker, 3 vols, Boston: Northeastern Univ Press, 91; auth, Ebb Tide in New England: Women, Seaports, and Social Change 1630-1800, Boston: Northeastern Univ Press, 98. **CONTACT ADDRESS** Dept of Hist, Fordham Univ, 501 E Fordham Rd, Bronx, NY 10458-5191. **EMAIL** ecrane@fordham.edu

CRAPOL, EDWARD P.
PERSONAL Born 09/29/1936, Buffalo, NY, m, 1973, 4 children **DISCIPLINE** HISTORY **EDUCATION** SUNY Col at Buffalo, BS, 60; Univ Wisc, Madison, MS, 64, PhD, 86. **CAREER** Instr, Wisc State Univ, Eau Claire, 66-67; asst prof, Col of William & Mary, 67-71, assoc prof, 71-77, prof, 78-94, Chancellor prof, 94-99, William E. Pullen Prof, 99-. **HONORS AND AWARDS** Exchange prof, Exeter Univ, 76-77; NEH grants, Summer Inst for Secondary Teachers, 84, 86; William & Mary's Thomas A. Graves Awd for Sustained Excellence in Teaching, 91; Jefferson Awd, 92. **MEMBERSHIPS** Am Hist Asn, OAH, SHAFR, SHEAR, SHGAPE. **RESEARCH** 19th century American foreign relations, American Imperialism. **SELECTED PUBLICATIONS** Auth, America for Americans: Economic Nationalism and Anglophobia in the Late Nineteenth Century, Greenwood Press (73); ed, Women and American Foreign Policy: Lobbyists, Critics, and Insiders, Greenwood Press (87), 2nd ed, Scholarly Resources (92); auth, "From Anglophobia to Fragile Rapprochement: Anglo-American Relations in the Early Twentieth Century," in Confrontation and Cooperation: Germany and the United States in the Era of World War I, 1900-1924, ed Hans-Juergen Schroder, Berg Pubs (93); auth, "John Tyler and the Pursuit of National Destiny," J of the Early Republic (fall 97); auth, James G. Blaine: Architect of Empire, Scholarly Resources (2000); auth, "Coming to Terms with Empire: The Historiography of Late Nineteenth-Century American Foreign Relations," in Paths to Power: The Historiography of American Foreign Relations to 1941, ed Michael Hogan, Cambridge Univ Press (2000). **CONTACT ADDRESS** Dept Hist, Col of William and Mary, PO Box 8795, Williamsburg, VA 23187-8795. **EMAIL** edpcal@wm.edu

CRAUSAZ, WINSTON
PERSONAL Born 04/15/1943, McKeesport, PA, d, 2 children **DISCIPLINE** SCIENCE, GEOLOGY, GEOGRAPHY **EDUCATION** Kent State Univ, BS, 75; Bowling Green State Univ, MA, 76. **CAREER** Instr, SW Missouri State Univ, 76-88; engin lab super, PSI, 98-99; Blue River Comm Col, 99-. **HONORS AND AWARDS** GSA Fel. **MEMBERSHIPS** GSA; AEG. **RESEARCH** Physical geography; high Mexican volcanoes. **SELECTED PUBLICATIONS** Auth, "Dr Atl: Pioneer Mexican Volcanologist," Geo Soc Am 1 (85): 251-256; auth, "Dr Atl at Paricutin," in Paricutin: The Volcano Born in a Mexican Cornfield, eds. Jane F Luhr, Tom Simkin (Phoenix, Ariz: Geoscience Press, 93); auth, Pico de Orizaba or Citlaltepetl: Geology, Archaeology, History, Natural History, and Mountaineering Routes: With Additional Material on the High Mexican Volcanoes, Geo Press Intl (Amherst, OH), 93. **CONTACT ADDRESS** Dept Science, Blue River Community Col, 1501 W Jefferson St, Blue Springs, MO 64015. **EMAIL** crausazw@blueriver.cc.mo.us

CRAVEN, WAYNE
PERSONAL Born 12/07/1930, Pontiac, IL, m, 1953 **DISCIPLINE** AMERICAN PAINTING AND SCULPTURE **EDUCATION** Columbia Univ, PhD. **CAREER** Prof. **MEMBERSHIPS** College Art Assn; Philadelphia Athenaeum; Am Antiquarian Soc; Nat Sculpture Soc; ed boards of Smithsonian Stud in Am Art, Am Art Jrnl, Peale Family Papers, Univ of Del Press; brd of trustees, Brookgreen Sculpture Gardens, SC. **RESEARCH** The Gilded Age. **SELECTED PUBLICATIONS** Publ, Cat of Amer Portraits, NY Hist Soc, Yale, 74; Sculpture in America from the Colonial Period to the Present, Del Univ Press, 84; Colonial American Portraiture, Cambridge, 86; American Art: History and Culture, McGraw Hill, 93. **CONTACT ADDRESS** Dept of Art Hist, Univ of Delaware, Newark, DE 19716. **EMAIL** 46830@udel.edu

CRAVENS, HAMILTON
PERSONAL Born 08/12/1938, Evanston, IL, m, 2000, 2 children **DISCIPLINE** AMERICAN HISTORY, HISTORY OF SCIENCE, MEDICINE, AND TECHNOLOGY **EDUCATION** Univ WA, BA, 60, MA, 62; Univ IA, PhD, 69. **CAREER** Teaching asst hist, Univ WA, 60-62; teaching asst, Univ IA, 62-64, instr, 64-65; instr, OH State Univ, 65-68; from instr to asst prof, 68-69, asst prof, 69-73, assoc prof, 73-80, Prof, IA State Univ, 80-; Vis asst prof hist, Univ MD, College Park, 71-72; consult, Soc for Research in Child Development, 80-83, Rand Corp, 81, Distinguished Senior Lecturer, German Fulbright Prog, Goettingen Univ, 88-89, Distinguished Senior Lecturer, German Fulbright Prog, Bonn Univ and Cologne Univ, summer sem, 97. **HONORS AND AWARDS** Ford Foundation Fellow, 60-61, Univ WA, Univ IA Fellow, 64-65; Charles M Gates Mem Awd, WA St Hist Soc, 66; NEH Summer Stipend, 73; Bicentennial Awd, Nat Sci Teachers Asn, 76; NSF Grants, 78, 79, 80-83; Vis Fellow, Hoover Institution, 86; Fellow, Stanford Humanities Center, 86; George Bancroft Prof of Am Hist, Goettingen Univ, GER, 88-89; Fellow, Davis Humanities Center, Univ CA, Davis, 90-92; Vis Scholar, Hist, Univ CA, Berkeley, 90-92; J. William Fulbright Distinguished Prof Am Studies, Bonn and Cologne Univs, 97; Vis Scholar, Max Planck Institut fuer Geschichte, Goettingen, GER, 97. **MEMBERSHIPS** AHA; ASA; Hist Sci Soc; OAH; MAASA. **RESEARCH** Am intellectual hist; American cultural hist; the hist of Am science, medicine, and technology. **SELECTED PUBLICATIONS** Auth, The Triumph of Evolution: American Scientists and the Heredity-Environment Controversy, 1900-1941, Univ PA, 78; ed, Ideas in America's Cultures: From Republic to Mass Society, IA State Univ Press, 82; auth, Child-Saving in the Age of Professionalism, 1915-1930, in J. Hawes and N. R. Hiner, eds, American Childhood, Greenwood, 85; History of the Social Sciences, in S. G. Kohlstedt and M. G. Rossiter, eds, Historical Writing on American Science, Johns Hopkins Univ Press, 86; The Triumph of Evolution. The Heredity-Environment Controversy, 1900-1941, paper ed, Johns Hopkins Univ Press, 88; Before Head Start. The Iowa Station and America's Children, Univ NC Press, 93; co-auth and co-ed, Technical Knowledge in America, Science, Medicine, and Technology in America since 1800, Univ AL Press, 96; auth, Scientific racism in Modern America, 1870's-1990's, Prospects, 21, 96; co-auth and co-ed, Health Care Policy in Contemporary America, PA State Univ Press, 97; co-auth, History in an Ahistorical World, Teachers College Record, 98. **CONTACT ADDRESS** Dept of Hist, Iowa State Univ of Science and Tech, Ames, IA 50011-1202. **EMAIL** hcravens@iastate.edu

CRAWFORD, JOHN S.
DISCIPLINE ANCIENT ART AND ARCHAEOLOGY **EDUCATION** Harvard Univ, PhD. **CAREER** Prof. **SELECTED PUBLICATIONS** Auth, The Byzantine Shops at Sardis, Harvard, 89. **CONTACT ADDRESS** Dept of Art Hist, Univ of Delaware, 318 Old College, Newark, DE 19716-2516. **EMAIL** jstephens@udel.edu

CRAWFORD, KATHERINE B.
PERSONAL Born 05/13/1966, Boston, MA, p **DISCIPLINE** HISTORY **EDUCATION** Columbia Univ, AB, 88; Univ Chicago, MA, 91; PhD, 97. **CAREER** Fel, Univ Chicago, 97-99; asst prof, Vanderbilt Univ, 99-. **HONORS AND AWARDS** Honorable Mention, Soc Sci Dissertation Prize, Univ Chicago, 97; Von Holst Teaching Prize, 95; Am Can Dissertation Res Fel, 94; Mellon Dissertation Writing Fel, 96. **MEMBERSHIPS** French Hist Studies; Sixteenth Century Studies; W Soc for French Hist; NE Am 18th Century Studies; Am Hist Asn. **RESEARCH** Early Modern France; Gender and Sexuality; Visual Culture. **SELECTED PUBLICATIONS** Auth, "Catherine de Medicis and the Performance of Political Motherhood," Sixteenth Century J, (00): 643-673; auth, "Gender and History," in Intl Encyclopedia of the Social and Beh Sci, (forthcoming); auth, Perilous Performances: Gender and Regency I Early Modern France, (forthcoming). **CONTACT ADDRESS** Dept Hist, Vanderbilt Univ, PO Box 1802, Sta B., Nashville, TN 37235. **EMAIL** katherine.b.crawford@vanderbilt.edu

CRAWFORD, MICHAEL JOHN
PERSONAL Born 06/03/1950, St. Louis, MO, m, 1982, 1 child **DISCIPLINE** AMERICAN AND BRITISH HISTORY **EDUCATION** Washington Univ, AB, 71, AM, 72; Boston Univ, PhD(hist), 78. **CAREER** Vis asst prof Am hist, Tex Tech Univ, 78-80; Nat Hist Publ & Rec Comn fel, Adams Papers, 80-81; Historian, Naval Hist Ctr, 82- **HONORS AND AWARDS** John Lyman Book Awd of the North American Society for Oceanic History, for best reference work of 1996, Naval Documents of the American Revolution, Volume 10. **MEMBERSHIPS** AHA; Asn Doc Ed; Soc Hist Fed Govt; North American Society for Oceanic History. **RESEARCH** Religion in early modern America and Britain; political culture in early modern America and Britain; early United States Naval history. **SELECTED PUBLICATIONS** Auth, "Seasons of Grace: Colonial New England's Revival Tradition in its Britis Context," Oxford University Press, 91; auth, "The Spanish-American War: Historical Overview and Select Bibliography," Mark L. Hayes and Michael D. Sessions, co-authors, Washington, D.C.: Naval Historical Center 98; auth, "The Reestablishment of the Navy, 1787-1801: Historical Overview and Select Bibliography," Christine Hughes, co-author, Washington, D.C.: Naval Historical Center, 95; auth, "History of Natick, Massachusetts, 1650-1976," Historical Commission of Natick, Revolution, Volume 10, Washington, D.C.: Naval Historical Center, 96; Assoc. Editor "The Naval War of 1812: A Documentary History, Volume I, 1812," William S. Dudley, ed., Washington: "Government Printing Office," 85. **CONTACT ADDRESS** Naval Historical Ctr, 805 Kidder Breese, SE, Washington, DC 20374. **EMAIL** crawford.michael@nhc.navy.mil

CRAWFORD, SIDNIE WHITE
PERSONAL Born 01/08/1960, Greenwich, CT, m, 1994 **DISCIPLINE** NEAR EASTERN LANGUAGES AND CIVILIZATIONS **EDUCATION** Trinity Col, BA, 81; Harvard Divinity Sch, MTS, 84; Harvard Univ, PhD, 88. **CAREER** Instr, Harvard Div Sch, 87-88; asst prof, St Olaf Col, 88-89; asst prof, 89-96, ch of fac, 95-96, assoc prof, Relisios Studies, Albright Col, 96 -; assoc prof & ch, Classics, Unic Neb-Lincoln, 96- . **HONORS AND AWARDS** Abraham Joshua Heschel Prize, 81; Cert of Distinct in Tchg, Harvard Univ, 87; Jacob Albright Awd, Fac Mem of the Yr, 91; United Methdist Church Awd, Albright Col, 95. **MEMBERSHIPS** Am Acad Rel; Am Schs of Oriental Res; Int Org for the Study of Qumran; Soc of Bib Lit. **RESEARCH** Second Temple Judaism, Dead Sea Scrolls, Hebrew Bible Textual Criticism. **SELECTED PUBLICATIONS** Co-auth, 4Qdeuteronomy a, c, d, f, g, I, n, o, p, Discoveries in the Judaean Desert XIV, Oxford Univ, 95; coauth, 4Qreworked Pentateuch: 4Q364-367, Discoveries in the Judaean Desert XIII, Oxford Univ, 94; auth, A Response to Elizabeth Owen's "4Qdeut": A Pre-Samaritan Manuscript, Dead Sea Discoveries 5, 98; Has Esther been Found at Quamran?, 4Qproto-Esther and the Esther Corpus, Revue ke Qumran 17, 96; Amram, Testament of, "Angelic Liturgy" and eighteen other entries in Dictionary of Biblical Judaism, NY, Macmillan, 95. **CONTACT ADDRESS** Dept of Classics, Univ of Nebraska, Lincoln, 236 Andrews Hall, Lincoln, NE 68588-0337. **EMAIL** scrawfor@unl.edu

CRAY, ROBERT
PERSONAL Born 04/29/1956, Mamareneck, NY, m, 1993, 1 child **DISCIPLINE** HISTORY **EDUCATION** Stony Brook Univ, BA, 78; PhD, 84. **CAREER** Vis Asst Prof, Univ of Puget Sound, 84-85; Asst Prof, Tenn Technol Univ, 85-88; Asst/Assoc Prof, Montclair State Univ, 88-. **HONORS AND AWARDS** Ralph D. Gray Awd for Best Essay, J of the Early Repub, 98. **MEMBERSHIPS** Orgn of Am Historians, Soc for Historians of the Early Am Repub, Inst Assoc Onohundro. **RESEARCH** Early American History, Early American Republic. **SELECTED PUBLICATIONS** Auth, "White Welfare and

Black Strategies: The Dynamics of Race and Poor Relief in Early New York, 1700-1825," Slavery and Abolition 7 (Dec 86): 273-284; auth, Paupers and Poor Relief in New York City and Its Rural Environs, 1700-1830, Temple Univ Press (Philadelphia), 88; auth, "Memorialization and Enshrinement: George Whitefield and Popular Religious Culture, 1770-1850," J of the Early Repub 10 (Fall 90): 339-361; auth, "The John Andre Memorial: The Politics of Memory in Gilded Age," NY Hist 77 (Jan 96): 5-32; auth, "The Post Bonfire Ministry of James Davenport, 1743-1757," The Historian 59 (Fall 96): 59-73; auth, "Major John Andre and the Three Captors: Class Dynamics and Revolutionary Memory Wars in the Early Republic," J of the Early Repub 17 (Fall 97): 371-397; auth, "Commemorating the Prison Ship Dead: Revolutionary Memory and the Politics of Sepulture in the Early Republic, 1776-1808," William and Mary Quart 66 (July 99): 565-590. **CONTACT ADDRESS** Dept Hist, Montclair State Univ, 1 Normal Ave, Montclair, NJ 07043-1624. **EMAIL** crayr@mail.montclair.edu

CRECELIUS, DANIEL
PERSONAL Born 01/15/1937, St. Louis, MO, m, 1963, 1 child **DISCIPLINE** MODERN MIDDLE EASTERN HISTORY **EDUCATION** CO Col, BA, 59; Princeton Univ, MA, 62, PhD, 67. **CAREER** From asst prof to assoc prof, 64-73, prof mid east hist, CA State Univ, Los Angeles, 73-, Ch, Dept Hist, 80-83, actg chair, summer 86; Ch, 98-; Vis lectr, UCLA, 66-67; Vis prof, CO Col, 10/90; Vis prof, Cairo Univ, 1/92-2/92; Trustees Scholarship, CO Col, 55-59; Esden Award, Outstanding Student in Soc Sci, CO Col, 59; Dunniway Prize, Outstanding Student in Hist, CO Col, 59; Woodrow Wilson Nat Fel, Princeton Univ, 59-60; Ford Found Foreign Area Traineeship, Princeton Univ, 60-61; Princeton Univ Near East Fel, 61-62; Five Universities' summer grant for intensive study of Arabic, Univ MI, 60; Princeton Univ summer grant for intensive study of Arabic at Princeton Univ, 61; Fulbright award, Al-Azhar Univ, Cairo, 62-63; Nat Defense For Lang Award, Am Univ of Beirut, 63-64; Am Res Center grant, Egypt, WAQF archives, 68-69, summer 72, summer 79; Soc Sci Res Counc grant, joint res London and Paris, ulama in Cairo and Damascus in 18th Century, 73; Am Phil Soc summer res grant, Cairo, Shari'ah court archives, 75 and 80; Fulbright award, joint res on Acehnese royal decrees, Australia, Indonesia, and Malayasia; CA State Univ, Los Angeles Found, 18th century Egyptian hist, 79 and 81; Nat Endowment for Hum, transl al-Jabarti's Aja'ib al-Athar fi al-Tarajim wa al-Akhbar, 80-82; Nat Endowment for Hum grant, archival res on late 18th Century Egyptian hist, London, Paris, Vienna, and Cairo, 83-84; Am Res Center summer grant, archival res, late 18th Centry Egyptian hist, Egypt, 84; Am Res Center summer grant, annotated transl of manuscript of Ahmad Katkhuda Azaban al-Damurdashi, Egypt, 87; Nat Endowment for the Hum Travel to Collections summer grant, Cairo's Nat Libr, 87; CA State Univ, Los Angeles Found, mini-grant, manuscript of Ahmad Katkhuda Azaban al-Damurdashi, 87; Am Philo Soc summer grant, al-Damurdashi's manuscript, Cairo, 89; CA State Univ, Los Angeles, mini-grant, annotated transl of al-Damurdashi's al-Durrah al-Musanah, 90; Sch of Natural and Soc Sci, CA State Univ, Los Angeles, and Fulbright/Cairo, int conf on Arabic Manuscript Sources for 18th Century Egyptian Hist, 90; Fulbright sr scholar area award, Istanbul and Cairo, 91-92; Nat Endowment for Hum, Travel to Collections summer grant, Cairo, 92; Fulbright Found, Cairo, grant to publ selected papers of the Int Conf on Soc and Econ Hist of Ottoman Egypt, 92; Fulbright Inst award, 95-96; Fulbright collaborative res award, edit and annotate Shaykh al-Rajabi's Ta'rikh al-Wazir Muhammad Ali Basha, 95-96; CA State Univ, Los Angeles, Sch of Natural and Soc Sci summer mini-grant, Cairo, 95; Am Res Center, Eqypt, res Egyptian archives, 96; Fulbright award, Int Conf on Econ and Soc Hist of Ottoman Egypt, Cairo, 96. **HONORS AND AWARDS** CA State Univ, Los Angeles, Outstanding Prof Awd, 74; Meritorius Service Awd, 84, 85, 86, 87, 88 & 89. **MEMBERSHIPS** MidE Inst; Am Asn MidE Studies; Turkish Studies Assoc; Nat Geog Soc. **RESEARCH** Eighteenth to twentieth century Egyptian hist; mod Arab polit; Acehnese sarakatas. **SELECTED PUBLICATIONS** Auth, Al-Azhar in the Revolution, Middle East Jour, winter 66, reprint, Schools in Transition: Essays in Comparative Education (Erwin H Epstein and Andreas Kazamais), 68; Al-Azhar, In: Encyclopedia Americana, 67; Die religion im Dienste des islamischen Staatssozialismus in Aegypten, Bustan, 67; Waqf Archives in the U A R, Newsletter of the Am Res Center in Egypt, 10/69; Report on Research in Cairo's Archives, Bull of the Am Res Center in Eqypt, 5/15/70; Al-Azhar: A Millenium of Faithfulness to Tradition, Mid East, 4/70; The organization of Waqf documents in Cairo, IJMES, 71; Emergence of the Shaykh al-Azhar as the pre-eminent religious leader in Egypt, Colloque Int sur l-Hist du Caire, 72; Nonideological Responses of the Egyptian Ulama to Modernization, In: Scholars, Saints and Sufis (Nikki Keddie, ed), Berkeley and Los Angeles, 72; The Course of Secularization in Modern Egypt, In: Religion and Political Modernization (Donald E Smith, ed), New Haven, 74; Sa'udi-Egyptian Relations, Int Studies, 75; Co-auth (with Anahid Crecelius), An Egyptian Battalion in Mexico: 1863-1867, Der Islam, 2/76; The waqfiyah of Muhammad Bey Abu al-Dhabab, JARCE, 78 & 79; A Reputed Acehense Sarakata of the Jamal al-Layl Dynasty, JMBRAS, 79; The Course of Secularism in Modern Egypt, In: Islam and Development (John Esposito, ed), Syracuse, 80; Co-auth (with Edward A Beardow), Another Acehnese Sarakata, Proceedings of the Third Int Symposium on Asian Studies, Hong Kong, 81; Archival Sources for Demographic Studies of the Middle East, In: The Islamic Middle East, 700-1900: Studies in Economic and Social History (A L Udovitch, ed), Princeton, 81; The Roots of Modern Egypt: A Study of the Regimes of Ali Bey al-Kabir and Muhammad Bey Abu al-Dhahab, 1760-1775, Minneapolis and Chicago, 81, Juthur Misr al-Haditha, Arabic transl, Cairo, 85; Des Incidences de cas du waqf dans trois cours du Caire (1640-1802), Jour Econ and Soc Hist of the Orient, 86; Unratified Commercial Treaties between Egypt and England and France, 1773-1794, Revue d'Histoire Maghrebine, 6/85; Egypt's Reawakening Interest in Palestine during the Regimes of Ali Bey al-Kabir and Muhammad Bey Abu al-Dhahab, 1760-1775, In: Palestine in the Late Ottoman Period: Political, Social and Economic Transformation (David Kushner, ed), Jerusalem, 86; The Attempt by Greek Catholics to Control Egypt's Trade with Europe in the Second Half of the Eighteenth Centruy, In: La vie sociale dans les provinces arabes a l'epoque ottomane (Abdeljelil Temimi, ed), Zaghouan, 88; Russia's Relations with the Mamluk Beys of Egypt, 1770-1798, In: A Way Prepared, Essays on Islamic Culture in Honor of Richard Bayly Winder (Farhad Kazemi and R D McChesney, ed), New York, 88; A Source for al-Jabarti's History, Newsletter of the Am Res Center in Egypt, spring 89; Ahmad Shalabi ibn Abd al-Ghani and Ahmad Katkhuda Azaban al-Damurdashi: Two Sources for al-Jabarti's Aja'ib al-Athar fi 'l-Tarajim wa 'l-Akhbar, In: Eighteenth Century Egypt: The Arabic Manuscript Sources (Daniel Crecelius, ed), Claremont, 90; The Importance of Qusayr in the Late Eighteenth Century, JARCE, 90; Masadir Ta'rikh al-Jabarti fi Awakhir al-Qarn al-Sabi Ashar wa Awa'il al-Qarn al-Thamin Ashar (Sources for al-Jabarti's History of the Latter Part of the 17th Century and the Early 18th century), al-Majallah al-Ta'rikhiyah al-Maghribiyah, 7/90; Al-Hudud al-Siyasiyyah li al-Bayt al-Mamluki (The Political Parameters of the Mamluk Faction), Majallat Kulliyyat al-Adab, Jami'at Zagazig, 90; Co-auth (with Butrus Abd al-Malik), A Late Eighteenth Century Egyptian Waqf Endowed by a Sister of the Mamluk Shaykh al-Balad Muhammad Bey Abu al-Dhahab, Arab Hist Rev for Ottoman Studies, 1/90; Ed, Al-Damurdashi's Chronicle of Egypt, 1688-1755, Leiden, 91; The Waqf of Muhammad Bey Abu al-Dhahab in Historical Perspective, Int Jour of Middle East Studies, 2/91; Makhtutat al-Durrah al-Musanah fi Akhbar al-Kinanah li al-Amir Ahmad al-Damurdashi Katkhuda Azaban, Cairo, 92; Ed, Fihris Waqfiyyat al-Asr al-Uthmani al-Mahfudhah bi Wizarat al-Awqaf wa Dar al-Watha'iq al-Ta'rikhiyya al-Qawmiyyah bi al-Qahirah (Index of Waqfiyyat from the Ottoman Period Preserved in the Ministry of Awqaf and the Dar al-Watha'iq in Cairo), Dar al-Nahdah al-Arabiyyah, Cairo, 92; Co-ed (with Hamza Abd al-Aziz Badr and Daniel Crecelius), A Short Manuscript History of the Career of Murad Bey, al-Maktabah al-Arabiyyah, Cairo, 92; Co-auth (with Hamza Abd al-Aziz Badr), The Waqfs of Shahin Ahmad Agha, Annales Islamologiques, 92; Co-ed (with Ra'uf Abbas and Daniel Crecelius), Abhath Nadwah Ta'rikh Misr al-Iqtisadi wa al-Ijtima'i fi al-Asr al-Uthmani: 1517-1798, Majallat Kulliyyat al-Adab, Jami'at al-Qahirah, 2/93; Co-auth (with Hamza Abd al-Aziz Badr), An Egyptian Grain Shipment of 1763 to the Imperial Pantry in Istanbul, JARCE, 93, Arabic transl, Shuhnat Ghilal Misriyyah illa al-Kilar al-Sultani bi Istanbul: 1763, Al-Mu'arrikh al-Misri, 1/93; Hawliyat Awqaf Dumyat fi Awakhir al-Qarn al-Thamin Ashar, Majallat Kulliyyat al-Adab, Jami'at al-Qahirah, 2/93; Co-auth (with Hamza Abd al-Aziz Badr), The Awqaf of al-Hajj Bashir Agha in Cairo, Annales Islamologiques, 93; Co-auth, (with Hamza Abd al-Aziz Badr), The Awqaf of Hasan Bey al-Jiddawi, Arab Hist Rev for Ottoman Studies, 8/94; Co-auth (with Hamza Abd al-Aziz Badr), French Ships and Their Cargoes Sailing between Damiette and Ottoman Ports, 1777-1781, Jour Econ and Soc Hist of the Orient, 94; An Austrian Attempt to Develop the Red Sea Trade Route in the Late Eighteenth Century, Middle Eastern Studies, 4/94; Shaykh Abd al-Rahman ibn Hasan al-Jabarti's Aja'ib al-Athar fi al-Tarajim wa al-Akhbar, annotated transl (with Butrus Abd al-Malik), Franz Steiner Verlag, Stuttgart, 94; Guest ed & contr, Introduction, Jour Econ and Soc Hist of the Orient, 8/95; Co-auth (with Hamza Abd al-Aziz Badr), The Waqfiyya of the Two Hammams in Cairo Known as al-Sukkariyya, In: Le waqf dans l'espace islamique (Randi Deguilhem, ed), Damascus, 95; Co-auth (with Hamza Abd al-Aziz Badr), The Usurpation of Waqf Revenues in Sixteenth Century Damiette, JARCE, 95; Co-auth (with Hamza Abd al-Aziz Badr), An Agreement between the Ulama and the Mamluk Amirs in 1795: A Test of the Accuracy of Two Contemporary Chronicles, In: Dirasat fi Ta'rikh Misr al-Iqtisadi wa al-Ijtima'i fi al-Asr al-Uthmani (Daniel Crecelius, Hamza Badr, and Husam al-Din Isma'il, ed), Dar al-Afaq al-Arabi, Cairo, 97; Co-ed (with Hamza Badr and Husam al-Din Ismail), Dirasat fi Ta'rikh al-Iqtisadi wa al-Ijtima i fi al-Asr al-Uthmani, dar al-Afaq al-Arabi, Cairo, 97; Co-ed (with Hamza Badr and Husam al-Din Ismail), Ta-rikh al-Wazir Muhammad Ali Basha li al-Shaykh Khalil ibn Ahmad al-Rajabi, Dar al-Afaq al-Arabi, Cairo, 97. **CONTACT ADDRESS** Dept of Hist, California State Univ, Los Angeles, 5151 State Univ Dr, Los Angeles, CA 90032-4202. **EMAIL** dcrecel@calstatela.edu

CREGIER, DON MESICK
PERSONAL Born 03/28/1930, Schenectady, NY, m, 1965 **DISCIPLINE** BRITISH AND AMERICAN HISTORY **EDUCATION** Union Col, NY, AB, 51; Univ Mich, MA, 52. **CAREER** Asst instr govt, Clark Univ, 52-54; instr hist & polit sci, Univ Tenn, 56-57; from instr to asst prof, Baker Univ, 58-61; asst prof, Keuka Col, 62-64; vis asst prof hist, St John's Univ, 64-65; sr fel hist & polit sci, Mary Hopkins Col, 65-66; asst prof hist, St Dunstan's Univ, 66-68, assoc prof, 68-69; Assoc Prof Hist, Univ Prince Edward Island, 69-, Can Coun fel, 72-73; abstractor, Am Bibliog Ctr, Santa Barbara, Calif, 78- **MEMBERSHIPS** AHA; Conf Brit Studies; Hist Asn, Eng; Am Polit Sci Asn; Asn Contemporary Hist; hon mem, Mark Twain Soc. **RESEARCH** Nineteenth and 20th century British, Irish and American history. **SELECTED PUBLICATIONS** Auth, The Age of Upheaval--Edwardian Politics, 1899-1914, Albion, Vol 0028, 96; Lloydgeorge, David--A Political Life--Organizer of Victory 1912-1916, Amer Hist Rev, Vol 0099, 94. **CONTACT ADDRESS** Dept of Hist, Univ of Prince Edward Island, Charlottetown, PE, Canada C1A 4P3.

CRESSON, BRUCE COLLINS
PERSONAL Born 10/27/1930, Lenoir, NC, m, 1955, 2 children **DISCIPLINE** RELIGION, ARCHEOLOGY **EDUCATION** Wake Forest Col, BA, 52; Southeastern Baptist Theol Sem, BD, 55, ThM, 56; Duke Univ, PhD(relig), 64. **CAREER** Instr Hebrew, Southeastern Baptist Theol Sem, 62-63; instr relig, Duke Univ, 63-66; assoc prof, 66-77, Prof Relig, Baylor Univ, 77-00, prof emer, 00-; Mem, excavation staff, Aphek-Antipatris, 74-76, Wardeh, 77; dir, excavation to Tel Dalit, 78-80; Tel Ira, 80-81; Horvat Uza, 82-88; Horvat Radarn 89; Tel Malhata, 90-00. **MEMBERSHIPS** Am Sch Org Res; Soc Bibl Lit. **RESEARCH** Edom; history of Old Testament and intertestamental period in its world setting; Biblical archaeology. **SELECTED PUBLICATIONS** Auth, Isaiah and the restoration community, Rev & Exposito, fall 68; auth, Obadiah, In: Broadman Commentary, Broadman, 72; The condemnation of Edom in post-exilic Judaism, In: Use of the Old Testament in the New and or Other Essays, Duke Univ, 72; coauth, Introduction to the Bible, Ronald, 73; auth, Ammon, Moab and Edom--Early States-Nations of Jordan in the Biblical Period, Biblical Archaeol, Vol 0059, 96; contrib, Excovation at Tel Dalit, 96; contrib, Tel Ira, 99. **CONTACT ADDRESS** 212 Harrington, Waco, TX 76706. **EMAIL** bruce_cresson@baylor.edu

CRESSY, DAVID
PERSONAL Born 04/04/1946, Isleworth, England, m, 1966, 2 children **DISCIPLINE** HISTORY **EDUCATION** Univ Cambridge, BA, 67; MA, 71; PhD, 73. **CAREER** Tutorial supervisor, Cambridge Univ, 68-70; instructor, Pitzer Col, 70-80; visiting assoc prof, Claremont Col, 80-84; assoc to full prof, Calif State Univ, 84-98; prof, Ohio State Univ, 98-. **HONORS AND AWARDS** Guggenheim Fel, 77; NEH Fel, 81,90,96. **MEMBERSHIPS** AHA, NACRS, Royal Hist Soc. **RESEARCH** Society, Culture and religion in post-reformation on Revolutionary England. **SELECTED PUBLICATIONS** Auth, Travesties and Transgressions in Tudor and Stuart England: Tales of Discord and Dissension, Oxford, 00; auth, Birth, Marriage and Death: Ritual, Religion and the Life Cycle in Tudor and Stuart England, Oxford, 97; auth, Religion and Society in Early Modern England, London, 96; auth, Bonfires and Bells: National Memory and the Protestant Calendar in Elizabethan and Stuart England, London, 89; auth, Coming Over: Migration and communication between England and New England in the Seventeenth Century, Cambridge, 87; auth, Literacy and the Social Order: Reading and Writing in Tudor and Stuart England, Cambridge, 80. **CONTACT ADDRESS** Dept Hist, Ohio State Univ, Columbus, 230 W 17th Ave, Columbus, OH 43210-1361. **EMAIL** cressy.3@osu.edu

CREW, DAVID F.
PERSONAL Born 02/14/1946, London, England **DISCIPLINE** HISTORY **EDUCATION** McMaster Univ, BA, 67; Cornell Univ, PhD, 75. **CAREER** Asst Prof, Columbia Univ, 74-80; Lectr, Cambridge Univ, 80-84; Asst Prof to Prof, Univ Tex, 84-. **HONORS AND AWARDS** Fel, German Acad Exchange Service, 70-71; Grant, Am Coun of Learned Soc Res, 78; Grant, Brit Acad, 83; NEH Summer Stipend, 87; German Marshall Fund of the U.S., 87-88. **MEMBERSHIPS** AHA; GSA; German Hist Soc. **RESEARCH** Twentieth Century German Social and Cultural History. **SELECTED PUBLICATIONS** Ed, Nazism and German Society, 1933-1945, Routledge Press, 95; auth, Germans on Welfare: From Weimar to Hitler, Oxford Univ Press, 98. **CONTACT ADDRESS** Dept Hist, Univ of Texas, Austin, 3121 Hemphill Pk, Austin, TX 78705. **EMAIL** dfcrew@mail.utexas.edu

CREW, SPENCER R.
PERSONAL Born 01/07/1949, Poughkeepsie, NY, m, 1971 **DISCIPLINE** CURATOR **EDUCATION** Brown Univ, Providence RI, AB, 1967-71; Rutgers Univ, New Brunswick NJ, MA, 1971-73; Rutgers Univ, New Brunswick NJ, PhD, 1973-79. **CAREER** Univ of MD Baltimore County, Catonsville MD, asst profr, 78-81; Smithsonian Institution, Natl Museum of Amer History, Washington DC, historian, 81-87; Natl Museum of Amer History, curato, 87-89; Natl Museum of Amer History, chair, Dept of Social and Cultural History, 89-91, deputy director, 91-92, acting director, 92-94; director, 94. **HONORS AND AWARDS** Curator for exhibition "Field to Factory: Afro-American Migration 1915-1940"; Osceola Awd, Delta Sigma Theta Sorority, Inc 1988; co-curator: "Go Forth and Serve: Black Land Grant Colleges Enter a Second Century," 1990, "African American Images in Postal Service Stamps," 1992; **MEMBERSHIPS** Program chairperson, 1985-86, executive bd

member, 1986-90, Oral History in the Mid-Atlantic Region; mem Oral History Assn 1988-; 2nd vice pres African Amer Museums Assn, 1988-91; program co-chairperson, Oral History Assn 1988; commissioner (bd mem), Banneker-Douglass Museum, 1989-93; editorial board mem, Journal of Amer History, 1989-93; program chairperson, African Amer Museums Assn, 1989; senior youth group coordinator, St John Baptist Church, 1989, co-editor, Newsletter for the American Historical Assn, 1990-; trustee, Brown Univ, 1995-; mem of bd Amer Assn of Museums, 1995-98. **SELECTED PUBLICATIONS** Author of booklet Field to Factory: Afro-American Migration 1915-1940, 1987; author, Black Life in Secondary Cities: A Comparative Analysis of the Black Communities of Camden and Elizabeth, NJ, 1860-1920, 1993. **CONTACT ADDRESS** Natl Museum of American History, Smithsonian Inst, Rm 5112, Washington, DC 20560.

CREWS, DANIEL A.
PERSONAL Born 10/17/1956, Lawrenceburg, TN, m, 1975, 1 child **DISCIPLINE** HISTORY **EDUCATION** Univ N Ala, BA, 77; Memphis State Univ, MA, 79; Auburn Univ, PhD, 84. **CAREER** Asst prof, Okla Baptist Univ, 84-87; asst to Prof, Hist, Central Missouri State Univ, 87-; edit bd, Med Studies, 90-; gen ed, Bull, Soc Span & Port Hist Stud, 89-99. **HONORS AND AWARDS** Invited lectr, Spanish fac, Oxford Univ, 99; phi kappa phi **MEMBERSHIPS** Soc Span, Port Hist Stud; Soc for Sixteenth Century Studies. **RESEARCH** Span humanism, diplomacy of Charles V, imperial ideology. **SELECTED PUBLICATIONS** Auth, "Vives: Edicions Princeps," bk rev in The 16th Cent J, 95; auth, "Uprising of the Comuneros," and "The Defeat of the Spanish Armada," in Chron Eur Hist, 97; "De Armas y Letras: el cursus honorum de Juan de Valdes," in Actas del XIII Congreso de la Asociacion Internacional de Hispanistas, Madrid: Editorial Castalia, 00; "Juan de Valdes y la crisis de Camerino, 1534-1535," in Aspectos historicos y culturales bajo Carlos V, Frankfut am Maini Velvuert, 01. **CONTACT ADDRESS** History Dept, Central Missouri State Univ, Wood 136E, Warrensburg, MO 64093. **EMAIL** crews@cmsul.cmsu.edu

CRIMANDO, THOMAS
PERSONAL s **DISCIPLINE** HISTORY **EDUCATION** St John Fisher Col; BA; Univ Rochester, MA, PhD. **CAREER** Adj lectr. **RESEARCH** Renaissance and Reformation Europe; Modern Europe. **SELECTED PUBLICATIONS** Auth, Two French Views of the Council of Trent, 88; auth, "Biographical Sketch of Bruce Catton," American National Biography, Oxford: Oxford University Press, 99; auth, "French Wars of Religion," "Normandy Invasion," and "Pavia," Magill's Guide to Military History, Salem Press, forthcoming; auth, "Battle of Adrianople," "Marcus Aurelius," "Theodosius the Great," and "Valentinian I," Encyclopedia of the Ancient World, Salem Press, forthcoming. **CONTACT ADDRESS** Dept of History, SUNY, Col at Brockport, Brockport, NY 14420. **EMAIL** tcrimando@acspr1.acs.brockport.edu

CRIMM, CAROLINA CASTILLO
DISCIPLINE HISTORY **EDUCATION** Univ Miami, Florida, BA, 69; Tex Tech Univ, MA, 86; Univ Tex-Austin, PhD, 94. **CAREER** Asst prof, Sam Houston State Univ, 92-. **HONORS AND AWARDS** Excellence in Teaching Awd, 98-99; Trull Foundation Awd, 97; auth, Sammie Awds, Advisor, 95 **MEMBERSHIPS** Conference on Latin Am History; Latin Am Scholars Assoc; Hispanic Am Historical Assoc; Texas State Historical Assoc; Western History Assoc; Southern History Assoc **RESEARCH** Latin America, Texas and the Southwest. **SELECTED PUBLICATIONS** Auth, Founding Families: The Mexican-Americans of Victoria, South Tex Stud, 92; auth, Chapter "Colonizacion de Victoria, Texas, 1825-1836" in collected papers of Saltillo Conference PRIMER ENCUENTRO DE HISTORIADORES FRONTERIZOS, MEXICO-TEXAS, December, 93; auth, Chapter "Mexican-Texans after the the Texas Revolution, 1836-1870," in Tejano Journey, edited collection by Gerald E. Poyo and Jesus F. de la Teja, San Antonio: Institute of Texan Cultures, August 96; auth, Introduction, Vaqueros of the Wild Horse Desert, Authors Jane Monday and Betty Coley, Austin: University of Texas Press, 98; auth, "Mathew Hooks," Black Cowboys of Texas, Austin: University of Texas Press, Fall, 99; auth, "J. Frank Dobie," Dictionary of Literary Biography, Vol: 20th Century American Western Writiers, Columbia, S.C.: Bruccoli, Clark, Layman, Inc., Fall 99; auth, "Aqui todos somos primos," Journal of South Texas, Fall 99, Victoria Community College, Victoria, Texas, 99 **CONTACT ADDRESS** Dept of History, Sam Houston State Univ, Huntsville, TX 77341. **EMAIL** his_ccc@shsu.edu

CRIMP, DOUGLAS
DISCIPLINE ART HISTORY AND VISUAL AND CULTURAL STUDIES **EDUCATION** CUNY, PhD, 94. **CAREER** Prof, Univ of Rochester. **HONORS AND AWARDS** Rockefeller Foundation Humanities Fellowship, 00; Publication Grant, J. Paul Getty Foundation, 92; Frank Jewett Mather Awd for Distinction in Art Criticism, College Art Association, 88; Art Critics Fellowship, National Endowment for the Arts, 73, 84. **RESEARCH** Contemporary art, queer theory, AIDS. **SELECTED PUBLICATIONS** Auth, On the Museum's Ruins, Cambridge: MIT Press, 93 & AIDS Demo Graphics, Seattle: Bay Press, 90; co-ed, How Do I Look Queer Film and Video, Seattle: Bay Press, 91; ed, AIDS: Cultural Analysis/ Cultural Activism, Cambridge: MIT Press, 88. **CONTACT ADDRESS** Dept of Art and Art Hist, Univ of Rochester, 424 Morey Hall, Rochester, NY 14642. **EMAIL** crmp@mail.rochester.edu

CRIPPS, THOMAS
PERSONAL Born 09/17/1932, m, 1954, 3 children **DISCIPLINE** AMERICAN HISTORY **EDUCATION** Towson State Col, BS, 54; Univ Md, MA, 57, PhD(hist), 67. **CAREER** Asst prof hist, Pembroke State Col, 57-58; asst prof hist & soc sci & chmn soc sci div, Harford Jr Col, 58-61; asst prof 61-67, assoc prof hist, 67-68, Prof Hist Morgan State Univ, 68-, Coordr Grad Prog Popular Cult, 73-, Lectr, Univ Md, 63 & Johns Hopkins Univ, 67-68; consult Negro hist, Westinghouse Learning Corp & Md Educ TV Comn, 67-68; Am Philos Soc study grant cinema in Europ arch, 67 & 72; co-producer, writer & host, 30 show ser & talk shows, Westinghouse Broadcasting Co, 68-69; vis prof Afro-Am hist, Stanford Univ, 69-70, Am Coun Learned Soc fel, 71-72; Rockefeller Found fel humanities & Woodrow Wilson Int Ctr for Scholars fel, 75-76; Am Coun Learned Soc & Nat Humanities Ctr fel, 80-81, Nat Endowment for Humanities grant, 82. **HONORS AND AWARDS** Charles Thomson Prize Essay, 82. **MEMBERSHIPS** AHA; Am Film Inst; Brit Film Inst; Popular Cult Asn; Int Asn AV Media Hist Res. **RESEARCH** Black history; cinema history; popular culture. **SELECTED PUBLICATIONS** Auth, Negro reaction to the motion picture, Birth of a Nation, Historian, 5/63; Death of Rastus: Negro in American Film Since 1945, Phylon, 67; Paul Robeson and Black identity in American movies, Mass Rev, spring 70; contrib, Myth of Southern box office, In: The Black Experience in America, Univ Tex, 70; auth, Native Son in the movies, New Letters, spring 72; Black Shadows on a Silver Screen (film), Post-News-Week TV, 75; Slow fade to black: Negro in American film, 1900-42, Oxford Univ, 77; Black film as genre, Ind Univ, 78; ed & contribr, The Green Pastures, Wis Univ Press, 79. **CONTACT ADDRESS** 1714 Bolton St, Baltimore, MD 21217.

CRISCENTI, JOSEPH THOMAS
PERSONAL Born 08/07/1920, Detroit, MI **DISCIPLINE** HISTORY **EDUCATION** Univ Detroit, PhB, 42; Harvard Univ, MA, 47, PhD(hist), 56. **CAREER** From instr to asst prof, 55-62, Assoc Prof Latin Am Hist, Boston Col, 62-, Chmn comt, James Alexander Robertson Mem Prize, 62 & 72; Am Philos Soc grant, 63; mem, Exec Comt, Conf Latin Am Hist, 63-64; consult, Cooperative Res Inst Collection, Asn Col & Res Libr, 71-72; mem, Regional Liaison Comt, Latin Am Studies Asn, 73-; judge Domingo Faustino Sarmiento Prize Comt, Argentine Embassy, 75; chmn, Comt on Chile Rio de la Plata Studies, Conf Latin Am Hist, 75-76. **HONORS AND AWARDS** James Alexander Robertson Mem Prize, 61. **MEMBERSHIPS** Latin Am Studies Asn; AHA; Conf Latin Am Hist; New England Coun Latin Am Studies (secy-treas, 72-). **RESEARCH** National period of Argentina and Uruguay; economic aspects of foreign policy of Brazil in the 19th century; bibliographical guide to the travel literature of Argentina, Urguay and Paraguay, 1810-1910. **SELECTED PUBLICATIONS** Auth, Argentine Constitutional History, 1810-1852: A Re-examiantion, Hisp Am Hist Rev, 61; contribr, Latin America: A Guide to the Historical Literature, Univ Tex, 71; Latin American Scholarship Since World War II, Univ Nebr, 71; Encyclopedia of Latin America, McGraw-Hill, 74; coauth, The New England Council of Latin American Studies, Latin Am Res Rev, 79. **CONTACT ADDRESS** Dept of Hist, Boston Col, Chestnut Hill, Chestnut Hill, MA 02167.

CRISP, JAMES E.
PERSONAL Born 05/28/1946, Wichita Falls, TX, m, 1968, 1 child **DISCIPLINE** HISTORY **EDUCATION** Rice Univ, BA, 68; Yale Univ, MPhil, 71; PhD, 76. **CAREER** TA, Yale Univ, 71-72; instr to assoc prof, NC State Univ, 72-. **HONORS AND AWARDS** Beinecke Diss Prize, Yale, 76; Acad of Outstanding Teachers, NC State Univ, 81; Rockefeller Fel, 92-93; H.B. Carroll Awd, Tex State Hist Assoc, 94. **MEMBERSHIPS** Southern Hist Assoc; Western Hist Assoc; Tex State Hist Assoc. **RESEARCH** Texas Revolution and Texas Republic, Race Relations in the U.S. Southwest. **SELECTED PUBLICATIONS** Auth, "Sam Houston's Speechwriters: The Grad Student, the Teenager, the Editors, and the Historians" Southwestern Hist Quarterly 97.2 (93): 202-237; auth, "The Little Book That Wasn't There: The Myth and Mystery of the de la Pena Diary", Southwestern Hist Quarterly 98.2 (94): 261-296; auth, "When Revision Becomes Obsession: Bill Groneman and the de la Pena Diary", Military Hist of the West 25.2 (94): 143-154; auth, "Race, Revolution, and the Texas Republic: Toward a Reinterpretation" The Texas Military Experience, ed Joseph G. Dawson III, Tex A&M Univ Pr, 95; auth, "Introduction" and "La Semana Perdida", With Santa Anna in Texas: A Personal Narrative of the Revolution, ed Carmen Perry, Tex A&M Univ Pr, 97; auth, "In Pursuit of Herman Ehrenberg: A Research Adventure", Southwestern Hist Quarterly 102.4 (99): 422-439; auth, "A Fresh Look at the Texas Revolution", J of S Tex 13.1 (00): 52-77. **CONTACT ADDRESS** Dept Hist, No Carolina State Univ, Box 8108, Raleigh, NC 27695-0001. **EMAIL** james_crisp@ncsu.edu

CRIST, LYNDA LASSWELL
PERSONAL Born 11/03/1945, Bay City, TX, m, 1977 **DISCIPLINE** SOUTHERN AMERICAN HISTORY **EDUCATION** Rice Univ, BA, 67, MA, 69; Univ Tenn, Knoxville, PhD(hist), 80. **CAREER** Asst ed, 73-76, assoc ed, 76-79, Ed, Papers of Jefferson Davis, 79-. **MEMBERSHIPS** Southern Hist Asn; Asn Doc Ed; Southern Asn of Women Historians; Am Libr Asn. **RESEARCH** Jefferson Davis; Mississippi history; American art and architecture. **SELECTED PUBLICATIONS** Ed, Jefferson Davis ponders his future, J Southern Hist, 75; auth, Rugby: A Brave Failure, A Brave Success, Rugby Inc, 75; Walter Prescott Webb's expansive frontier, W Tex Hist Asn Yearbk, 77; contribr, Lives of Mississippi Authors, 1817-1967, Univ Press Miss, 81; co-ed, The Papers of Jefferson Davis, Vol III, 81 & ED, Vol 4-10 83-00, La State Univ Press, 82; contribr, Encyclopedia of the Confederacy and Encyclopedia of the American Civil War. **CONTACT ADDRESS** Rice Univ, Houston, TX 77251. **EMAIL** llc@rice.edu

CRISTI, RENATO
DISCIPLINE INTELLECTUAL IMPACT OF SCIENCE IN CANADA **EDUCATION** St. Louis Univ, Purdue Univ, Univ of Toronto, Mphil, 72; PhD, 80. **CAREER** Prof. **RESEARCH** Political and social philosophy, legal philosophy, and the hist of Ancient Greek and nineteenth century philosophy. **SELECTED PUBLICATIONS** Coauth, El pensamiento conservador en Chile: Seis ensayos, Santiago: Editorial Universitaria, 92; Auth, Le liberalisme conservateur: Trois essais sur Schmitt, Hayek et Hegel, 93; auth, "Carl Schmitt ono Sovereignty and Constituent Power," Canadian Journal of Law and Jurisprudence, 97; rev, of David Dyzenhaus, Legality and Legitimacy: Carl Schmitt, Hans Kelsen and Hermann Heller in Weimar, in The Univ of Toronto Quarterly, 97; rev, of Heinrich Meier, Carl Schmitt and Leo Strauss: The Hidden Dialogue, in The European Legacy, 97; auth, "La Critica Comunitaria a la Moral Liberal," Estudios Publicos, 98; Carl Schmitt and Authoritarian Liberalism: Strong State, Free Economy, U of Wales P, 98; auth, "La nocion de sociedad civil en la Filosofia del Derecho de Hegel," in Sociedad civil, La democracia y su destino, ed. By R. Alvira, N. Grimaldi & M. Herrero, (Pamplona: Ediciones Universidad de Navarra, 99); auth, "Hayek on Liberalism and Democracy," in Democracy in Central Europe, ed. by J. Miklaszewska, (Krakow: Meritum, 99); auth, "The Metaphysics of Constituent Power: Carl Schmitt and the Genesis of Chile's 1980 Constitution," Crdozo Law Review, 00. **CONTACT ADDRESS** Dept of Philosophy, Wilfrid Laurier Univ, 75 University Ave W, Waterloo, ON, Canada N2L 3C5. **EMAIL** rcristi@wlu.ca

CRITCHLOW, DONALD T.
PERSONAL Born 05/18/1948 **DISCIPLINE** AMERICAN PUBLIC POLICY AND BUSINESS **EDUCATION** San Francisco State Univ, BA, 70; Univ of Calif, Berkeley, MA, 72; Ph.D, 78. **CAREER** Asst to assoc prof, Notre Dame Univ, 83-91; prof, St Lous Univ, 91-. **HONORS AND AWARDS** Guest Scholar, Brookings Inst, 76-77; NEH Fel, 80; Rockefeller Fel, 83, 94; USIA Lectr, 88-89, grant, 95; Woodrow Wilson Fel, 96-97; Fulbright Fel, 97-98; ed, jour policy hist. **RESEARCH** History of US Public Policy. **SELECTED PUBLICATIONS** Auth, The Brookings Institution, 1916-1952: Expertise and the Public Interest in a Democratic Society, 85; coauth, America!: A Concise History, 93; auth, Historia Stanow Zjednoczonych Ameryki (A History of the United States), Polish Acad Pr (Warsaw), 95; auth, The Politics of Abortion and Birth Control in Historical Perspective, Pennsylania State Pr (University Park, PA), 96; auth, Studebaker: The Life and Death of an American Corporation, 96; ed, Journal Policy Hist; auth, With Us Always: Private Charity and Public Welfare in Historical Perspective, Rowman and Littlefield (Lanham, MD), 98; auth, Intended Consequences: Birth Control, Abortion, and the Federal Government in Modern America, Oxford Univ Pr, 99. **CONTACT ADDRESS** Dept of Hist, Saint Louis Univ, 3800 Lindell Blvd, PO Box 56907, Saint Louis, MO 63156-0907. **EMAIL** critchdt@slu.edu

CROCE, LEWIS HENRY
PERSONAL Born 12/21/1933, Washington, DC **DISCIPLINE** AMERICAN HISTORY **EDUCATION** Univ Md, BA, 64, MA, 65, PhD(hist), 68. **CAREER** From asst prof Am hist to assoc prof, 68-77, Prof Hist, Mankato State Univ, 77-, Sr lectr hist, Univ London, 72-73; res grants, Henry E Huntington Libr & Harry S Truman Libr Inst, 77; adj fac, Princeton Univ, summer 81; prof, US Military Acad, summer 82. **MEMBERSHIPS** AHA; Orgn Am Historians; Southern Hist Asn. **RESEARCH** United States, 1815-1877; Abraham Lincoln; American Civil War. **SELECTED PUBLICATIONS** Auth, Sykes Regular Infantry Division, 1861-1864--A History of Regular United-States Infantry Operations in the Civil-Wars Eastern Theater, Civil War Hist, Vol 0039, 93. **CONTACT ADDRESS** Mankato State Univ, 734 Marsh St, Mankato, MN 56001-4490.

CROCE, PAUL JEROME
PERSONAL Born 06/24/1957, Washington, DC, m, 1985, 2 children **DISCIPLINE** AMERICAN HISTORY **EDUCATION** Georgetown Univ, BA, 79; Brown Univ, PhD, 87. **CAREER** Vis Asst Prof, Rollins Col, 87-89; From Asst Prof to Assoc Prof, Stetson Univ, 89-. **HONORS AND AWARDS**

Summer Stipend, Nat Endowment Humanities, 89; Fel, 95; Hand Awd for Creative Excellence, 99. **MEMBERSHIPS** Am Studies Asn, AHA, Orgn of Am Historians, Hist of Sci Soc, Am Acad of Relig. **RESEARCH** Science and religion, William James. **SELECTED PUBLICATIONS** Auth, "The Scientific Education of William James," Hist of the Human Sci, vol 8, no 1 (95): 9-27; auth, "Science and the Moral Religion of William James," Bull of the Honors Prog, vol 2, no 1(96); auth, "Accommodation Vs Struggle," The W E B DuBois Encycl, Greenwood Pr (97). Auth, "Probabilistic Darwinism: Louis Agassiz vs Asa Gray on Science, Religion and Certainty," J of Relig Hist, vol 22, no 1 (98); auth, "Science and Religion," in The Encycl of Am Cult and Intellectual Hist (99); auth, "Charles Sanders Peirce," Am Nat Biog, Oxford UP (99); auth, "William James," The Hist of Sci in the U S: An Encycl, Garland Publ (forthcoming). **CONTACT ADDRESS** Dept Am Hist, Stetson Univ, De Land, 421 N Woodland Blvd, Deland, FL 32720-3760. **EMAIL** pcroce@stetson.edu

CROCKER, RICHARD LINCOLN
PERSONAL Born 02/17/1927, Roxbury, MA, m, 1948, 3 children **DISCIPLINE** HISTORY OF MUSIC **EDUCATION** Yale Univ, BA, 50, PhD(music), 57. **CAREER** From inst to asst prog, Yale Univ, 55-63; prof, Univ of CA at Berkeley, 63-94; chmn of dept, 75-78; prof emer, 94-; prof in grad studies, 95. **HONORS AND AWARDS** Alfred Einstein Mem Prize, Am Musicol Soc, 67; Guggenheim Fellowship, 69-70; Kinkeldey Award of the Am Musicological Soc, 78. **MEMBERSHIPS** Am Musicol Soc. **RESEARCH** Early Medieval music, sequences. **SELECTED PUBLICATIONS** Auth, History of Musical Style, McGraw-Hill, 66, reprint, Dover, 86; co-auth, Listening to Music, McGraw-Hill, 70; The Early Medieval Sequence, Univ of Calif Press, 77; co-ed & contrib, The Early Middle Ages to 1300, New Oxford History of Music, vol. II, 90; auth, Studies in Medieval Music Theory and the Early Sequence, 97; auth, Introduction to Gregorian Chant, Yale Univ Press, 00. **CONTACT ADDRESS** Dept of Music, Univ of California, Berkeley, Berkeley, CA 94720.

CROFTS, DANIEL WALLACE
PERSONAL Born 06/25/1941, m, 1966, 2 children **DISCIPLINE** AMERICAN HISTORY **EDUCATION** Wabash Col, BA, 63; Yale Univ, MA, 64, PhD(hist), 68. **CAREER** Asst prof hist, Dickinson Col, 68-69 & NY Univ, 69-72; lectr hist & Afro-Am studies, Yale Univ, 72-74; Asst Prof Hist, Trenton State Col, 75-, Nat Endownment for Humanities res fel, 74-75. **RESEARCH** Nineteenth century American political and social history. **SELECTED PUBLICATIONS** Auth, The Black response to the Blair Education Bill, 2/71 & The Warner-Foraker Amendment to the Hepburn Bill: Friend or foe of Jim Crow?, 8/73, J Southern Hist; The Union Party of 1861 and the secession crisis, Perspectives in Am Hist, 78; John A Gilmer's secession crisis dilemma: Southern Unionism and the struggle to shape Lincoln's Cabinet, Civil War Hist, 9/78. **CONTACT ADDRESS** 1373 Butternut Dr, Southampton, PA 18966.

CROMLEY, ELIZABETH COLLINS
PERSONAL Born, NJ, w, 2 children **DISCIPLINE** ARCHTECTURAL HISTORY **EDUCATION** Univ Penn, BA, 63; New York Univ, MA, 66; City Univ of New York, PhD, 82 **CAREER** Lectr Art Dept, Bronx Comm Col, 74-75; lectr, Archit & Art Hist, City College, City Univ New York, 72-80; visit assoc prof, Univ Calif Berkeley, 87; asst prof Archit Hist, SUNY, 80-86, assoc prof Archit Hist, SUNY, 86-92; prof Archit Hist, SUNY, 92-96; chair & prof Art & Archit, Northeastern Univ, 97- **HONORS AND AWARDS** Mary Wahington Col Hist Presev Prize, 96; Nat Endowment Humanities Fel, 94; Abbot Lowell Cummings Awd, 92; Nat Endowment Humanities Fel, 90-91; Benno Forman Fel, 88; NEH Schlr, 01-02. **MEMBERSHIPS** Vernacular Archit Forum; Soc Archit Historians; Amer Studies Assoc **RESEARCH** American Architecture. **SELECTED PUBLICATIONS** Auth, "Public History and Preservation in Brooklyn," in Past Meets Present, ed Jo Blatti (Washington & NYork: Smithsonian Pr & the NYork Coun for the Human, 87): 30-37; auth, "Apartments and Collective Life in Turn-of-the-Century New York," in Housing for Non-Traditional Households, eds Franck & Ahrentsen (NY: van Nostrand, 89); auth, Alone Together: a History of New York's Early Apartment Houses, Cornell Univ Pr, 90, paperback, 99; ed, "Elements of Style," in American Editor (London: Mitchell-Beazley, 91; 2nd ed, 96); auth, "History of the Bedroom," Perspectives in Vernacular Architecture 4 (91); co-ed, Gender, Class, and Shelter: Perspectives in Vernacular Architecture 5, Univ Tenn Pr, 95; co-ed, Shaping Communities: Perspectives in Vernacular Architecture 6, Univ Tenn Pr, 97; auth, "The First House," Intersight (Spring 97); auth, "Transforming the Food Axis," Material Hist Rev 44 (Fall 96): 8-22; auth, "Masculine/Indian," Winterthur Portfolio (Spring 97). **CONTACT ADDRESS** Dept Art & Architecture, Northeastern Univ, 239 Ryder Hall, Boston, MA 02115. **EMAIL** ecromley@lynx.neu.edu

CROMPTON, LOUIS
PERSONAL Born 04/05/1925, Port Colborne, ON, Canada **DISCIPLINE** ENGLISH HISTORY **EDUCATION** Univ Toronto, BA, 47, MA, 48; Univ Chicago, AM, 50, PhD(English), 54. **CAREER** Lectr math, Univ BC, 48-49; lectr English, Univ Toronto, 53-55; from asst prof to assoc prof, 55-64, Prof English, Univ Nebr, 64-; Eme, 89-. **HONORS AND AWARDS** Christian Gauss Bk Awd, Nat Phi Beta Kappa, 69; Christian Gauss Awd for Literary Criticism. **RESEARCH** Bernard Shaw; 19th century literature; homosexual history and literature. **SELECTED PUBLICATIONS** ed., Bernard Shaw, Arms and the Man, Bobbs- Mevill, 68; Show the Dramalist, U. of Nebraska Press, 69; ed., Bernard Shaw, The Road to Equality, Beacon Press, 71; ed., Bernard Shaw, The Great Composers, U. of California Press, 78; auth, Byron and Greek Love: Homophobia in 19th-Century England, U. of California Press, 85; auth, An Army of Lovers--Male Love and Military Prowess in Classical Greece --The Sacred Band of Thebes, Hist Today, Vol 0044, 94. **CONTACT ADDRESS** Dept of English, Univ of Nebraska, Lincoln, Lincoln, NE 68588. **EMAIL** lcrompton@unl.edu

CRONIN, JAMES E.
PERSONAL Born 09/14/1947, Boston, MA, d, 2 children **DISCIPLINE** HISTORY **EDUCATION** Boston Coll, BA, 69; Northeastern Univ, 73; Brandeis Univ, PhD, 77. **HONORS AND AWARDS** NEH Fel; German Marshall Found Fel; Dist Res Awd. **MEMBERSHIPS** AHA; NCBS. **RESEARCH** Social history; State-Society relations; contemporary history. **SELECTED PUBLICATIONS** Auth, Industrial Conflict in Modern Britain, 79; auth, Labour and Society in Britain, 84; auth The Politics of State Expansion, 92; auth, The World the Cold War Made, 96. **CONTACT ADDRESS** Dept History, Boston Col, Chestnut Hill, 140 Commonwealth Ave, Chestnut Hill, MA 02467-3800. **EMAIL** croninj@bc.edu

CROOKS, JAMES BENEDICT
PERSONAL Born 09/27/1933, Paterson, NJ, m, 1958, 2 children **DISCIPLINE** AMERICAN HISTORY **EDUCATION** Yale Univ, BA, 57; Johns Hopkins Univ, MA, 62, PhD(hist), 64. **CAREER** Contract worker, Conn Gen Life Ins Co, 57-59; vis lectr hist, Univ Col, Dublin, 64-66; asst prof & chmn dept, Hollins Col, 66-72; Prof Hist, Chmn Dept & Asst Dean Col Interim Dean, Arts & Sci, Univ N Fla, 72-. **HONORS AND AWARDS** Univ Distnguished Prof; Outstanding Teacher Awd. **MEMBERSHIPS** AHA; Orgn Am Historians; Fla Hist Soc; Urban Hist Soc. **RESEARCH** Progressive era in American history; urban history; Contemporary US. **SELECTED PUBLICATIONS** Auth, Jacksonville After the Fire: 1901-1909 A New South City, Univ Press of Fla, 91; auth, The Promise of Paradise--Recreational and Retirement Communities in the United-States since 1950, Jour Amer Hist, Vol 0082, 95; Florida--A Short History, Jour Amer Hist, Vol 0081, 94; Language Death, Language Genesis, and World-History, Jour World Hist, Vol 0006, 95. **CONTACT ADDRESS** Dept of Hist, Univ of No Florida, Jacksonville, FL 32224. **EMAIL** jcrooks@unf.edu

CROSBY, ALFRED W.
PERSONAL Born 01/15/1931, Boston, MA, m, 1983, 2 children **DISCIPLINE** HISTORY **EDUCATION** Harvard, AB, 52; AMT, 56; Boston Univ, PhD, 61. **CAREER** Asst prof, Albion Col, 60-61; asst prof, Ohio State Univ, 61=65; asst prof, San Fernando Valley State Col, 65-66; prof, Wash State Univ, 66-77; prof, Univ of Texas, 77-99. **HONORS AND AWARDS** Med Writers Book Awd, 76; Ralph Waldo Emerson Book Prize, 88; Dr of Humane Letters, Grinnel Col, 92; Fel, Acad of Finalnd, 95; Fel, Am Acad of Arts and Sciences, 95; Fel, Am Philos Soc, 00; Dist Scholar Awd, Am Soc for Environ Hist, 01. **MEMBERSHIPS** AHA, World Hist Assoc, Am Soc for Environ Hist. **RESEARCH** Environmental History, Science and Technology History, Disease History. **SELECTED PUBLICATIONS** Auth, Ecological Imperialism: The Biological Expansion of Europe, 900-1900; auth, The Columbian Exchange: Biological and Cultural Consequences of 1492; auth, America's Forgotten Pandemic, The Influenza of 1918; auth, The Measure of Reality: Quantification and Western Society, 1250-1600; auth, Germs, Seeds, and Animals: Studies in Ecological History; auth, America, Russia, Help and Napoleon: American Trade with Russia and the Baltic, 1783-1812; auth, "Epidemic Disease as a Factor in the Aboriginal Depopulation In America," William and Mary Quarterly, Vol 33, (76); auth, "The Columbian Voyages, the Columbian Exchange, and their Historians," Essays on Global and Comparative Hist, AHA, (87); coauth, "Language Death, Language Genesis, and World History," Jour of World Hist VI, (95). **CONTACT ADDRESS** 67 North Centre St, Nantucket, MA 02554. **EMAIL** acrosby@nantucket.net

CROSBY, EDWARD WARREN
PERSONAL Born 11/04/1932, Cleveland, OH, m, 1956 **DISCIPLINE** AFRICAN-AMERICAN STUDIES **EDUCATION** Kent State Univ, BA 1957, MA 1959; Univ of KA, PhD 1965. **CAREER** Educ Resources Inst Inc E St Louis, vice pres program devel 1968; Experiment in Higher Educ SIU, dir of educ 1966-69; Inst for African Amer Affairs Kent State Univ, dir 1969-76; Univ of WA, dir Black Studies Program 1976-78; Kent State Univ, assoc prof 1969-94, chm, dept of Pan-African Studies, 76-94; Network for Educ Devel & Enrichment, Kent OH, vp, 88-. **HONORS AND AWARDS** Hon Leadership Awd Omicron Delta Kappa 1976; Hon mem Alpha Kappa Mu; **MEMBERSHIPS** Resident consult Regional Council on Intl Educ; Faculty Inst on the Black World 1970-72; consult Peat Marwick Mitchell & Co 1971-72; pres NE OH Black Studies Consortium 1974; pres OH Consortium for Black Studies 1980-; former board member, Harriet Tubman, African American Museum 1985-. **SELECTED PUBLICATIONS** Publ The Black Experience, "An Anthology" 1976; published "Chronology of Notable Dates in the History of Africans in the Am & Elsewhere" 1976; publ "The Educ of Black Folk, An Historical Perspective" The Western Journal of Black Studies 1977; publ "The African Experience in Community Devel" Two Vols 1980; Your History, A Chronology of Notable Events 1988. **CONTACT ADDRESS** Kent State Univ, Rm 117, Center of Pan-African Culture, Kent, OH 44242.

CROSBY, TRAVIS L.
DISCIPLINE BRITISH HISTORY; MODERN EUROPEAN HISTORY **EDUCATION** Univ Tex, BA; Johns Hopkins Univ; PhD. **CAREER** Hist, Wheaton Col. **RESEARCH** Psychological studies of British politicians. **SELECTED PUBLICATIONS** Auth, Two Mr. Gladstones: A Study in Psychology and History, Yale UP, 97. **CONTACT ADDRESS** Dept of Hist, Wheaton Col, Massachusetts, 26 East Main St, Norton, MA 02766. **EMAIL** tcrosby@wheatonma.edu

CROSS, GARY
PERSONAL Born 09/25/1946, Spokane, WA, m, 1984, 3 children **DISCIPLINE** HISTORY **EDUCATION** Wash State Univ, BA, 68; Harvard, MDiv, 73; Univ Wis, PhD, 77. **CAREER** Prof, Pa State, 90. **HONORS AND AWARDS** Fulbright, Melbourne, Australia, 92; Marshall Fel, 93; Leverhulme Prof, 01-. **RESEARCH** Twentieth century American and Western European consumer society, family, and technology. **SELECTED PUBLICATIONS** Auth, Immigrant Workers in Industrial France, 83; ed, Worktime and Industrialization: An International History, 88; auth, A Quest for Time: The Reduction of Work in Britain and France, 1840-1940, 89; auth, A Social History of Leisure Since 1600, 90; ed, Worktowners at Blackpool: Mass-Observation and Popular Leisure in the 1930s, 90; auth, Time and Money: The Making of Consuemr Culture, 93; coauth, Technology and American Society, 95; auth, Kids' Stuff: Toys and the Changing World of American Childhood, 97; auth, An All-Consuming Century: Why Commercialism Won in Modern America, 00. **CONTACT ADDRESS** Dept of History, Pennsylvania State Univ, Univ Park, University Park, PA 16802. **EMAIL** gsc2@psu.edu

CROSS, ROBERT DOUGHERTY
PERSONAL Born 01/21/1924, Grinnel, IA, m, 1951, 2 children **DISCIPLINE** HISTORY **EDUCATION** Harvard Univ, AB, 47, AM, 51, PhD(hist), 55. **CAREER** From instr to asst prof hist, Swarthmore Col, 52-59; assoc prof, Columbia Univ, 59-64, prof & chmn dept, 64-67; prof hist & pres, Hunter Col, 67-69; pres, Swarthmore Col, 69-72; dean fac arts & sci, 72-74, Prof Hist, 72-, Asst Dean Arts & Sci, 81-. **HONORS AND AWARDS** DHL, Villanova Univ, 68 & St Mary's Univ, Md, 71; LLD, Univ, Pa, 70. **MEMBERSHIPS** AHA; Am Studies Asn. **RESEARCH** American church history; social history of the 20th century; immigration history. **SELECTED PUBLICATIONS** Auth, Emergence of Liberal Catholicism in America, Harvard Univ, 58; ed, The Churches and the City, Bobbs, 66. **CONTACT ADDRESS** Univ of Virginia, 218 Randall Hall, Charlottesville, VA 22903.

CROSTHWAITE, JANE FREEMAN
PERSONAL Born 11/07/1936, Salisbury, NC, m, 1964 **DISCIPLINE** AMERICAN RELIGIOUS HISTORY **EDUCATION** Wake Forest Univ, BA, 59; Duke Univ, MA, 62, PhD(relig), 72. **CAREER** Asst dean women & instr philos, Wake Forest Univ, 62-64; head corp rec, Harvard Bus Sch Libr, 64-65q instr English, Queens Col, NC, 69-72, registr, 72-74, assoc prof relig, 74-76; lectr philos & relig, Univ NC, Charlotte, 76-79; Asst Prof Relig, Mount Holyoke Col, 79- **MEMBERSHIPS** Am Acad Relig; MLA; Church Hist Soc. **RESEARCH** American religious history; Emily Dickinson; women in American religion. **SELECTED PUBLICATIONS** Auth, Spiritual Spectacles--Vision and Image in Mid-19th-Century Shakerism, Jour Interdisciplinary Hist, Vol 0026, 95; The Carmelite Adventure--Dickinson, Clare,Joseph Journal of the Trip To America and Other Documents, Church Hist, Vol 0063, 94. **CONTACT ADDRESS** Dept of Relig, Mount Holyoke Col, 50 College St, South Hadley, MA 01075-1461.

CROTHERS, A. GLENN
PERSONAL Born 03/04/1963, Toronto, ON, Canada, m, 1999 **DISCIPLINE** HISTORY **EDUCATION** Univ Florida, Phd, 97; Univ Toronto, MA, 90; BA, 88. **CAREER** Asst Prof of History, 97- ; Dir, Floyd County Oral History Project; Indiana Univ Southeast. **HONORS AND AWARDS** Kentuckiana Metroversity Awd of Special Merit for Instructional Development, 99; Kentuckiana Metroversity Awd for Instructional Development, 99; Finalist, Conomic History Association's, Allan Nevins Dissertation Prize, 98; St. George Tucker Society's Dissertation Prize, 98; Indiana Heritage Research Grant, 99; Social Sciences & Humanities Research Council of Canada (SSHRC) Doctoral Fel, 91-94. **MEMBERSHIPS** Amer Historical Assoc; Economic History Assoc; Omohundro Institute of Early Amer History and Culture; Organization of Amer Historians; Society for Historians of the Early Amer Republic; Southern Historical Assoc; St. George Tucker Society; Virginia Historical Society.

RESEARCH Early Amer History; Revolutionary America; Early Republic; Social and Economic History; Oral History. **SELECTED PUBLICATIONS** Auth, "Public Culture and Economic Liberalism in Post Revolutionary Northern Virginia," Canadian Review of Amer Studies, 29, No. 3, 99: 1-30; auth, "The Projecting Spirit's Social Economic and cultural change in Post-Revolutionary Northern Virginia," Journal of Economic History, 59, June 99: 473-476; auth, "Banks and Economic Development in Post-Revolutionary Northern Virginia," Business History Review, 73, Spring 99, 1-39. **CONTACT ADDRESS** Division of Social Sciences, Indiana Univ, Southeast, 4201 Grant Line Rd, New Albany, IN 47150-2158. **EMAIL** acrother@ius.edu

CROUCH, DORA POLK
PERSONAL Born 02/15/1931, Ann Arbor, MI, 7 children **DISCIPLINE** ARCHITECTURAL AND URBAN HISTORY **EDUCATION** Univ Calif, Los Angeles, BA & MA, 65, PhD(art hist), 67. **CAREER** Asst prof art hist, San Francisco State Univ, 69-70; vis asst prof archit hist, Univ Calif, Berkeley, 70-71; lectr art hist, Univ Calif, Los Angeles, 71-72; asst prof, Calif State Univ, Dominguez Hills, 72-75; Assoc Prof Archit Hist, Rensselaer Polytech Inst, 75-, Ed newslett, Soc Archit Historians, 77-80; fel, Ctr Advan Study, Nat Gallery Art, 80-81. **MEMBERSHIPS** Soc Archit Historians; Col Art Asn; Am Inst Archeol. **RESEARCH** Urban history especially Spanish colonial; ancient Greek water systems; Palmyra. **SELECTED PUBLICATIONS** Auth, Geological Differences in Ancient Water-Supply--Syracuse and Agrigento, Amer Jour Archaeol, Vol 0101, 97. **CONTACT ADDRESS** Sch of Archit, Rensselaer Polytech Inst, Troy, NY 12181.

CROUCH, TOM DAY
PERSONAL Born 02/28/1944, Dayton, OH, m, 1963, 3 children **DISCIPLINE** AMERICAN HISTORY, HISTORY OF TECHNOLOGY **EDUCATION** Ohio Univ, BA, 66; Miami Univ, MA, 68; Ohio State Univ, PhD(hist), 76. **CAREER** Dir educ, Ohio Hist Soc, 69-70; dir, Ohio Am Revolution Bicentennial Comn, Ohio Hist Soc, 72-74; Cur Aeronaut, Nat Air & Space Mus, Smithsonian Inst, 74-, Adj prof, Dept Hist, Univ Md, 76-; mem, Am Inst Aeronaut & Astronaut Hist Comt, 76-; Distinguished Lectr, Am Inst Aeronaut & Astronaut, 78-79. **HONORS AND AWARDS** Hist Awd, Am Inst Aeronaut & Astronaut, 76. **RESEARCH** History of technology; history of aeronautics; United States social and cultural history. **SELECTED PUBLICATIONS** Auth, The Dream Machines--An Illustrated History of the Spaceship in Art, Science and Literature, Tech and Cult, Vol 0035, 94; Local Hero--Montgomery, John, Joseph and the First Winged Flight in America, Jour W, Vol 0036, 97; The Dream Machines--An Illustrated History of the Spaceship in Art, Science and Literature, Tech and Cult, Vol 0035, 94; Triumph at Kitty-Hawk--The Wright Brothers and Powered Flight, Pub Historian, Vol 0017, 95; auth, The Bishop's Boys: A Life of Wilbur and Orville Wright (New York: W.W. Norton, 89); auth, Aiming for the Stars: Dreamers and Doers of the Space Age (Washington, DC, 99). **CONTACT ADDRESS** Aeronautics Dept Natl Air and Sp, Smithsonian Inst, Washington, DC 20560. **EMAIL** tom.crouch@nasm.si.edu

CROUSE, MAURICE A.
PERSONAL Born 02/15/1934, Lincolnton, NC, m, 1958, 3 children **DISCIPLINE** HISTORY **EDUCATION** Davidson Col, BS, 56; Northwestern Univ, MA, 57; PhD, 64; Univ Memphis, MS, 86. **CAREER** Asst, NWU, 60-61; asst prof, Univ Memphis, 62-66; assoc prof, 66-72; prof, 72-. **HONORS AND AWARDS** Phi Beta Kappa; Omicron Delta Kappa. **MEMBERSHIPS** AHA; OAH; SCHS; AAUP. **RESEARCH** Provincial South Carolina; early American civilization; methods of historical research. **SELECTED PUBLICATIONS** Auth, The Public Treasury of Colonial South Carolina, Univ SC, 77. **CONTACT ADDRESS** Dept Hist, Univ of Memphis, Box 52610, Memphis, TN 38152-6120. **EMAIL** mcrouse@memphis.edu

CROUTER, RICHARD E.
PERSONAL Born 11/02/1937, Washington, DC, m, 1960, 2 children **DISCIPLINE** HISTORY OF THEOLOGY **EDUCATION** Occidental Col, AB, 60; Union Theol Sem, BD, 63, ThD, 68. **CAREER** From instr to asst prof 67-73, assoc prof, 73-79, prof relig, Carleton Col, 79-, John M. and Elizabeth Musser Prof of Religious Studies, 97-, Univ Toronto, 72-73; Am Coun Learned Soc fel, 76-77; sr Fulbright scholar, Univ Marburg, 76-77, 91-92; David and Marian Adams Bryn-Jones Distinguished Teaching Prof of Humanities, 93-96, DAAD (German Academic Exchange Service) Fellowship, Univ Munich, 01. **MEMBERSHIPS** Am Soc Church Hist; Am Acad Relig; Hegel Soc Am. **RESEARCH** History of Christian thought; Schleiermacher, Hegel, Kierkegaard. **SELECTED PUBLICATIONS** Auth, Schleiermacher and the Theology of Bourgeois Society: A Critique of the Critics, 86; coauth,Traveling with Luther and Marx: On and Off the Luther Trail in the GDR, 84; auth, Ambrose, Bishop of Milan, 87; transl, Friedrich Schleiermacher, on Religion: Spelcher to its Cultural Despisers, 88, 96; auth, A Historical Demurral,88; auth, Revolution and the Religious Imagination in Kierkegaard's Two Ages, 91; auth, Friedrich Schleiermacher Between Enlightenment and Romantiscism, 03. **CONTACT ADDRESS** Dept of Relig, Carleton Col, 1 N College St, Northfield, MN 55057-4044. **EMAIL** rcrouter@carleton.edu

CROUTHAMEL, JAMES L.
PERSONAL Born 01/29/1931, Lansdale, PA, 3 children **DISCIPLINE** AMERICAN HISTORY **EDUCATION** Franklin & Marshall Col, BA, 52; Univ Rochester, PhD, 58. **CAREER** Instr hist, Ill Col, 56-58 & Pa State Univ, 58-60; from asst prof to assoc prof, 60-69, Prof Hist, Hobart & William Smith Cols, 69-. **MEMBERSHIPS** Orgn Am Historians; Southern Hist Asn; Soc Hist Early Am Repub. **RESEARCH** History of newspapers; American politics, 1828-1860; history of New York. **SELECTED PUBLICATIONS** Auth, James Watson Webb, A Biography, Wesleyan Univ, 69. **CONTACT ADDRESS** Dept of Hist, Hobart & William Smith Cols, Geneva, NY 14456.

CROUTHER, BETTY JEAN
PERSONAL Born 03/02/1950, Carthage, MS, d **DISCIPLINE** ART **EDUCATION** Jackson State Univ, BS (Summa Cum Laude) 1972; Univ of MS, MFA 1975; Univ of MO Columbia, PhD 1985. **CAREER** Lincoln Univ, asst prof of art 1978-80; Jackson State Univ, asst prof of art 1980-83; Univ of MS, assoc prof of art history 1983-. **HONORS AND AWARDS** University of Missouri, Superior Graduate Achievement Awd, 1985; Stanford University, J Paul Getty Postdoctoral Fellowship, 1986; participant in Fulbright Group Studies program, India, 1989; Southeastern Coll Art Conference, Awd for Excellence in Teaching, 1994. **MEMBERSHIPS** College Art Assn; Southeastern College Art Conference; Natl Art Ed Assn; MS Art Ed Assn; Phi Kappa Phi Honor Society; Kappa Pi International Honorary Art Fraternity; Pi Delta Phi Honorary Fraternity; University of Mississippi, University Museum, friends of the museum. **SELECTED PUBLICATIONS** Juried exhibition, "Images '84," The Mississippi Pavilion, Louisiana World Exposition, 1984; contributor, exhibition catalogue "Dean Cornwell, Painter As Illustrator," Museum of Art and Archaeology Univ of MO-Columbia 1978; co-moderator with Dr Joanne V Hawks in enrichment program "Uniting Generations Together/The Search for Meaning," 1984; author, "Deciphering the Mississippi River Iconography of Frederick Oakes Sylvester," MUSE, vol 20, pp 81-9, 1986; reader for Jacob K Javit's Fellowship Fund, U S Department of Education 1989-90; invited papers: "Diversity in Afro-American Art," University of Missouri, Columbia, 1990; "Iconography of a Henry Gudgell Walking Stick," Southeastern College Art Conference, Memphis, 1991; "Iconography in the Art of Contemporary African-Americans: Lawrence A Jones and Roger Rice," James A Porter Colloquium, Howard University, 1992; "Marriage and Social Aspiration in the Art of Rembrandt," Mississippi Museum of Art, 1992; "Images of Peace and African Heritage in the Art of Lawrence A Jones," Southeastern College Art Conference, Birmingham, AL, 1992; Betty J Crouther, "Iconography of a Henry Gudgell Walking Stick," SECAC REVIEW, p 187-91, 1993; Southeastern College Art Conference, New Orleans, LA, "The Hand as a Symbol for African American Artists," 1994. **CONTACT ADDRESS** Univ of Mississippi, University, MS 38677.

CROW, JEFFREY JAY
PERSONAL Born 05/29/1947, Akron, OH, m, 1979, 1 child **DISCIPLINE** AMERICAN HISTORY **EDUCATION** Ohio State Univ, BA, 69; Univ Akron, MA, 72; Duke Univ, PhD, 74. **CAREER** Historian, NC Bicentennial Comt, NC Div Archives & Hist, 74-76; hist publ ed, 76-82, Adminr, Div Archives & Hist, Hist Publ Sect, NC, 82-. **HONORS AND AWARDS** Best article in 1980 award, William & Mary Quart, 81. **MEMBERSHIPS** Orgn Am Historians; Southern Hist Asn. **RESEARCH** Colonial and revolutionary South; Afro-American history; New South. **SELECTED PUBLICATIONS** Auth, Settle,Thomas Jr, Reconstruction, and the Memory of the Civil-War, Jour So Hist, Vol 0062, 96; Tyron,Willian and the Course of Empire--A Life in British Imperial Service, William and Mary Quart, Vol 0050, 93. **CONTACT ADDRESS** Division of Archives and History, 4610 Mail Service Center, Raleigh, NC 27699-4610.

CROWE, DAVID
PERSONAL Born 09/20/1943, Norfold, VA, m, 1989, 2 children **DISCIPLINE** HISTORY **EDUCATION** SE La Col, BA, 66; Univ Ga, PhD, 74. **CAREER** Arch, Nat Arch US, 74-77; prof hist, Elon Col, 77- ; pres, Asn Student Nat, Columbia Univ, 98- ; chr, NC Coun Holocaust, 95- . **HONORS AND AWARDS** V. Stanley Vardys Pres Prize Books Baltic Studententententent; vis schol, Harriman Inst, Columbia Univ; fel Ctr Slavic, Eurasian, & E Europ Studententententent. **MEMBERSHIPS** Asn Studenty Nat; Ger Student Asn; Am Asn Advan Slavic Student; SE Con Slavic Student; Gypsy Lore Soc. **RESEARCH** Roma (gypsies), Oskar chindler, Holocaust, Baltic states, Ethnic studies, Central Asia. **SELECTED PUBLICATIONS** Co-ed, The Gypsies of Eastern Europe, M.E. Sharpe, (91); auth, The Baltic States and the Great Powers: Foreign Relations, 1938-1940, Westview Press, (93); auth, A History of the Gypsies of Eastern Eurpoe and Russia, St Martins Press, (94-95); co-ed, Roma and Forced Migration: An Annotated Bibliography, Open Soc Inst, (98); c0-ed, Kazakstan: History, Ethnicity, and Society, Nat Papers, (98); auth, Oskar Schindler: A Life, Westview Press, (01). **CONTACT ADDRESS** Dept Hist, Elon Col, 3505 Henderson Rd, Greensboro, NC 27410. **EMAIL** crowed@numen.elon.edu

CROWE, MICHAEL J.
PERSONAL Born 03/18/1936, Minneapolis, MN, m, 1994, 4 children **DISCIPLINE** HISTORY OF SCIENCE **EDUCATION** Univ Notre Dame, BA, 58, BS, 58; Univ Wisc, PhD, 65. **CAREER** Instr, 61-65, asst prof, Univ Notre Dame, 65-68, Dir, Col Honors Prog, 66-67, assoc prof, 68-73, chemn, 67-73, prof, 73-2000, Rev. John J. Cavanaugh Prof in History and Philos of Sci, 2000-. **HONORS AND AWARDS** Phi Beta Kappa, 87; Woodrow Wilson Fel, 58; Jean Scott Prize from La Maison des Sciences de l'Homme in Paris; Nat Sci Found Grants, 77, 80, 86, 90; grants from the Indiana Comt for the Humanities and the Wilbur Found. **MEMBERSHIPS** Hist of Sci Soc, Midwest Hist of Sci Soc, Hist of Astronomy Div of the Am Astronomical Soc, William Herschel Soc, Asn for Core Texts and Courses. **RESEARCH** History of astronomy, physics, and mathematics 1750-1900; science and religion; history of ideas of extraterrestrial life; Sir John Herschel. **SELECTED PUBLICATIONS** Auth, A History of Vector Analysis: The Evolution of the Idea of a Vectorial System, Notre Dame, Ind: Univ Notre Dame Press (67), paperback, New York: Dover Pubs (85, 94); auth, The Extraterrestrial Life Debate 1750-1900: The Idea of a Plurality of Worlds from Kant to Lowell, Cambridge: Cambridge Univ Press (86), paperback ed, Cambridge: Cambridge Univ Press (88), revised ed, New York: Dover Pubs (99); auth, Theories of the World from Ptolemy to the Copernican Revolution, New York: Dover Pubs (90); ed, The Letters and Papers of Sir John Herschel: A Guide to the Manuscripts and Microfilm, in the series: Collections from the Royal Society, Bethesda, Md: Univ Pubs of Am (91); auth, Modern Theories of the Universe from Herschel to Hubble, New York: Dover (94); ed, David R. Dyck and James J. Kevin, assoc eds, Calendar of the Correspondence of Sir John Herschel, Cambridge, England: Cambridge Univ Press (98). **CONTACT ADDRESS** Prog of Liberal Studies, Univ of Notre Dame, 215 O'Shaughnessy Hall, Notre Dame, IN 46556-5639. **EMAIL** crowe.1@nd.edu

CROWLEY, JOHN G.
PERSONAL Born 07/16/1955, Hahina, GA, s **DISCIPLINE** HISTORY **EDUCATION** Valdosta State Univ, BA, 77; MA, 81; Fla State Univ, PhD, 96. **CAREER** From asst prof to assoc prof, Valdosta State Univ, 94-. **MEMBERSHIPS** AAUP, Ga Asn of Hist, Southern Hist Asn, Ga Baptist Hist Soc, Phi Alpha Theta, Ga Hist Soc. **RESEARCH** Southern Religion, especially Baptist. **SELECTED PUBLICATIONS** Auth, The Primitive Baptists of the Wiregrass South, Univ Pr of Fla, 99. **CONTACT ADDRESS** Dept Hist, Valdosta State Univ, 1500 N Patterson St, Valdosta, GA 31698-0100. **EMAIL** jcrowley@valdosta.edu

CRUIKSHANK, KENNETH
DISCIPLINE HISTORY **EDUCATION** Carleton Univ, BA; York Univ, MA, PhD. **RESEARCH** Hist of business; development of the administrative state in Canada and the United States. **SELECTED PUBLICATIONS** Auth, Close Ties: Railways, Government and the Board of Railway Commissioners, 1851-1933. Auth of scholarly articles in Acadiensis, Canadian Historical Review, and Canadian Papers in Business History. **CONTACT ADDRESS** History Dept, McMaster Univ, 1280 Main St W, Hamilton, ON, Canada L8S 4L9. **EMAIL** cruiksha@mcmaster.ca

CRUMMEY, DONALD E.
PERSONAL Born 01/26/1941, New Glasgow, Canada, m, 3 children **DISCIPLINE** HISTORY **EDUCATION** Honours History, Univ of Toronto, BA, 62, 58; Univ London, PhD, 67 **CAREER** Vis Assoc, Prof of African History, and Assoc Dir of the African Studies Program, Univ of Ill Urbana-Champaign, 77-79; Assoc Prof of African History, Univ of Ill Urbana-Champaign, 79-83; Prof of African History, Univ of Ill Urbana-Champaign, 83; Dir, Center for African Studies, Univ of Ill Urbana-Champaign, 84-94; Prof, Univ Ill Urbana Champaign **HONORS AND AWARDS** Nat Endow for the Humanities fell, 79-80; Nat Endow for the Humanities grant, 87; renewed April 90, for two years; Burlington Northern Foundation Faculty Achievement Awd, 88 **RESEARCH** History of east and southern Africa since the eighteenth century. **SELECTED PUBLICATIONS** Auth, Priests and Politicians, Protestant and Catholic Missions in Orthodox Ethiopia 1830-1868, Oxford: Clarendon Press, 72; coed, with C.C. Stewart, Modes of Production in Africa: The Pre-colonial Era, Beverly Hills, 81; auth, Banditry, Rebellion, and Social Protest in Africa, edited collection, James Currey: London, 86; auth, "Society, State and Nationality in the Recent Historiography of Ethiopia," J. Afr. Hist., XXXI, 1, 90, 103-119; eds, With Shumet Sishagne and Daniel Ayana, "Oral Tradition in a Literate Culture: The Case of Christian Ethiopia," pp. 137-149 inS. Pilaszewicz and E. Rzewuski, Unwritten Testimonies of the African Past, Proceedings of the International Symposium held in Wjrzanow n. Warsaw on 07-08 November 89, Orientalia Varsoviensia, Warsaw, 91; auth, with Shumet Sishagne, "Land Tenure and the Social Accumulation of Wealth in Eighteenth Century Ethiopia: Evidence from the Qwesqwam Land Register," Int. J. Afr. Hist. St. XXIV, 2, 91, 241-58; auth, with Shumet Sishagne, "The Lands of the Church of Dabra Sa'hay Qwesqwam, Gondar," J. Eth. St. XXVI, 2, 93, 53-62; coed, with T. Bassett, Land in African Agrarian Systems, Madison: University of Wisconsin Press, 93; auth, "Church and State in Ethiopia: The Sixteenth through Eighteenth Centuries," pp. 43-6 in African Zion: The Sacred Art

of Ethiopia, New Haven: Yale University Press, 93; ed, with Daniel Ayana and Shumet Sishagne, "A Gondarine Land Grant in Gojjam: The Case of Qaranyo Madhane Alam," pp. 103-116 in volume I of Bahru Zewde, Richard Pankhurst and Taddese Beyene, Proceedings of the Xith International Conference of Ethiopian Studies, Addis Ababa, April 91, Addis Ababa: 2 vols., 94. **CONTACT ADDRESS** History Dept, Univ of Illinois, Urbana-Champaign, 52 E Gregory Dr, Champaign, IL 61820. **EMAIL** dcrummey@uiuc.edu

CRUMMEY, ROBERT OWEN
PERSONAL Born 04/12/1936, New Glasgow, NS, Canada, m, 1980, 1 child **DISCIPLINE** RUSSIAN HISTORY **EDUCATION** Univ Toronto, BA, 58; Univ Chicago, PhD(hist), 64. **CAREER** Asst prof hist, Univ Ill, 64-65; from asst prof to assoc prof hist, Yale Univ, 65-74; assoc prof, 74-79, prof Hist, Univ Calif, Davis, 79-. **MEMBERSHIPS** Am Asn Advan Slavic Studies. **RESEARCH** Russian hist of the 16th and 17th centuries, especially social and religious hist. **SELECTED PUBLICATIONS** Auth, The Old Believers and the World of Antichrist: The Vyg Community and the Russian State, 1694-1856, Univ of Wis Press, 70; auth, Aristocrates & Servitors: The Boyar Elite in Russia, 1613-1689, Princeton Univ Press, 83; auth, Old-Belief as Popular Religion--New Approaches, Slavic Rev, Vol 0052, 93. **CONTACT ADDRESS** Dept of Hist, Univ of California, Davis, Davis, CA 95616. **EMAIL** rocrummey@ucdavis.edu

CRUZ, JO ANN HOEPPNER MORAN
PERSONAL Born 05/12/1944, Eau Claire, WI, m, 3 children **DISCIPLINE** MEDIEVAL HISTORY **EDUCATION** Harvard Univ, BA, 66; Brandeis Univ, MA, 69, PhD(hist ideas), 75. **CAREER** Lectr hist, Boston Col, 71-72; assoc prof lectr, George Washington Univ, 75-78; Asst Prof Hist, 78-84, assoc prof, 84-, chair, Georgetown Univ, 97-. **HONORS AND AWARDS** Alpha Sigma Nu Hon fel; Brown Bk Prize, Med Acad of Am; Exec Cmt, N Am Conf on British Stu; Councillor, Med Acad Am. **MEMBERSHIPS** Mediaeval Acad Am; Am Hist Asn. **RESEARCH** Education and literacy in late medieval Britain; ecclesiastical history in late medieval Britain; use of wills as a historical source. **SELECTED PUBLICATIONS** Auth, Education and Learning in the City of York, 1300- 1548, Univ York, 79; Literacy and education in Northern England, 1350-1550: A methodological inquiry, Northern Hist, 81; Clerical recruitment in the Diocese of York, 1340-1530: Data and commentary, J Ecclesiastical Hist, 82; The 73rd Annual-Meeting Of The American-Catholic-Historical-Association, Catholic Historical Review, Vol 0079, 1993;. **CONTACT ADDRESS** Dept of Hist, Georgetown Univ, 1421 37th St N W, Washington, DC 20057-0001. **EMAIL** moranj@gunet.georgetown.edu

CUDJOE, SELWYN REGINALD
PERSONAL Born 12/01/1943, s, 2 children **DISCIPLINE** AFRICAN STUDIES **EDUCATION** Fordham Univ, BA 69, MA 72; Cornell Univ, PhD 76. **CAREER** Fordham Univ, instructor, 70-72; Ithaca Coll, adjunct asst prof, 73-75; Ohio Univ, assoc prof, 75-76; Harvard Univ, asst prof, 76-81; Wellesley Coll, Marion Butler McLean, Professor in the History of Ideas, prof, African studies. **HONORS AND AWARDS** NEH Fellowship, 91-92, 97-98; American Council of Learned Societies Fellowship 91-92; Senior Fellow, Society for the Humanities, Cornell University 92; Visiting Fellow, WEB DuBois Institute for African-American Research, Harvard University 91; Visiting Scholar, African-American Studies Department, Harvard University 92-97. **SELECTED PUBLICATIONS** Resistance and Caribbean Literature, Ohio Univ Press 80; Movement of the People Calaloux, 83; A Just and Moral Society Calaloux, 84; VS Naipaul: A Materialist Reading, Univ of Mass Press, 88; Caribbean Women Writers: Essays from the First International Conference, Calaloux & University of Mass Press, 90; ed, Eric E Willliams Speaks, 93; co-ed, CLR James: His Intellectual Legacies, 95; ed, Maxwell Philip, EmmanueL Appadocca, Univ of Massachusetts, 97. **CONTACT ADDRESS** Africana Studies, Wellesley Col, Wellesley, MA 02181. **EMAIL** scudjoe@wellesley.edu

CULBERT, DAVID H.
PERSONAL Born 07/07/1943, San Antonio, TX, m, 1979 **DISCIPLINE** HISTORY **EDUCATION** Oberlin Col, BA, 66; Oberlin Conserv of Music, BMus, 66; Mozarteum, Austria, Bmus, 63-64; NW Univ Evanston, PhD, 70. **CAREER** Asst prof, Yale Univ, 70-71; asst prof to prof, La State Univ, 70-; Assoc prod and Dir of Hist Res, Ken Burn's Huey Long, 85; ed, Hist Jour of Film, Radio and Television, Oxford, 92- **HONORS AND AWARDS** Phi Beta Kappa, Pi Kappa Lamba, NDEA Title IV Fel, 66-70; Wilson Center for Scholars, Smithsonian, 76-77; Nat Humanities Inst, Yale, 77-78; Kellogg Found Nat Fel, 81-84; Thyssen Stiftung Grant, 92; ACLS-DAAD Coll Res Grant, 93; Vis Fel, Princeton, 95. **MEMBERSHIPS** AHA; OAH; IAMHIST; SHAFR; Hanns Eisler Gesellschaft. **RESEARCH** Mass media and propaganda. **SELECTED PUBLICATIONS** Coed, History of Mass Communications, Cambridge Univ Pr; coed, Series in Propaganda, Althone Pr, Univ of London; auth, News for Everyman: Radio and Foreign Affairs in Thirties America, 76; auth, Mission to Moscow, 80; ed, Film and Propaganda in America, 5 vols, 90-93; coauth, Competing Nazi Cimena Propaganda and the Riefenstahl Myth, Cambridge Univ Pr (forthcoming). **CONTACT ADDRESS** Dept Hist, La State Univ Baton Rouge, La State Univ, Baton Rouge, LA 70803-3601. **EMAIL** dculbert@lsu.edu

CULHAM, PHYLLIS
PERSONAL Born 06/22/1948, Junction City, KS, m, 1969, 1 child **DISCIPLINE** ANCIENT HISTORY, CLASSICAL LITERATURE **EDUCATION** Univ Kans, BA, 70; State Univ NYork Buffalo, MA, 72, PhD, 76. **CAREER** Lectr classics, Univ Calif, Irvine, 75-77; asst prof hist, Univ Ill, Chicago, 77-79; from Asst Prof to Assoc Prof, 79-91, prof hist, US Naval Acad, 91-. **HONORS AND AWARDS** NEH Curriculum Grant, 94. **MEMBERSHIPS** Asn Ancient Historians; Am Philol Asn. **RESEARCH** Roman bureaucratic history; Latin epigraphy. **SELECTED PUBLICATIONS** Auth, Classics: A Discipline and Profession in Crisis, 89; Seneca's on Favors, 95. **CONTACT ADDRESS** Dept of Hist, United States Naval Acad, Annapolis, MD 21402. **EMAIL** culham@nadn.navy.mil

CULLEY, JOHN JOEL
PERSONAL Born 11/13/1938, Clovis, NM **DISCIPLINE** AMERICAN HISTORY **EDUCATION** Univ NMex, BA, 61, MA, 62; Univ Va, PhD(hist), 67. **CAREER** Teaching asst, Univ Va, 63-65 & 66-67; asst prof, 67-72, Assoc Prof US Hist, West Tex State Univ, 72-. **MEMBERSHIPS** Southern Hist Asn; Orgn Am Historians; Western Hist Asn. **RESEARCH** Recent United States history; United States cultural & social; southern history. **SELECTED PUBLICATIONS** Coauth, Hard times on the high plains: FSA photography during the 1930's, Panhandle-Plains Hist Rev, 79; auth, World War II and a western town: The internment of the Japanese railroad workers of Clovis, New Mexico, Western Hist Quart, 1/82. **CONTACT ADDRESS** Dept of Hist, West Texas A&M Univ, 2501 4th Ave, Canyon, TX 79016-0001.

CULTER, SUZANNE
DISCIPLINE EAST ASIAN STUDIES **EDUCATION** Univ Hawaii, PhD. **CAREER** Asst prof. **RESEARCH** Sociology of Japan **SELECTED PUBLICATIONS** Auth, Industry Restructuring and Family Migration Decisions: A Community Study in Japan, 94; auth, Coal Industry Decline in Japan: Community and Household Response, JAI, 92. **CONTACT ADDRESS** East Asian Studies Dept, McGill Univ, 845 Sherbrooke St, Montreal, QC, Canada H3A 2T5.

CUMMINGS, RAYMOND L.
PERSONAL Born 11/06/1922, Baltimore, MD, m, 1950, 3 children **DISCIPLINE** MODERN EUROPEAN HISTORY **EDUCATION** Villanova Univ, BA, 48; Georgetown Univ, MA, 52; Univ Pa, PhD(hist), 64. **CAREER** Assoc prof, 49-69, Prof to Prof Emer Hist, Villanova Univ, 69-. **MEMBERSHIPS** AHA; Soc Fr Hist Studies; Soc Ital Hist Studies; Cath Hist Asn. **RESEARCH** European diplomatic history, 19th century: the Risorgimento; French history, 19th century. **SELECTED PUBLICATIONS** Auth, The French Effort to Block Garbaldi at the Straits, Historian, 2/69; Francis II of Naples: Shield for Pio Novo?, Cath Hist Rev, 4/74; auth, Vatican City, In: The New Guide to the Diplomatic Archives of Western Europe, Univ Pa, 75; contribr, The Nunciature at Naples, its Archives and the National Revolution, August-September 1860, Archivum Hist Pontificiae, 79; auth, Come La Nunciatura Di Napoli Informava Roma Nel 1859-1860, Rassegna Storica Del Risorgimento, 4/80. **CONTACT ADDRESS** Dept of Hist, Villanova Univ, 800 Lancaster Ave, St. Augustine Liberal Arts Center, Room 403, Villanova, PA 19085.

CUMMINS, LIGHT TOWNSEND
PERSONAL Born 04/23/1946, Derby, CT, m, 1977, 2 children **DISCIPLINE** HISTORY **EDUCATION** Southwest Texas State Univ, BS, 68, MA, 72; Tulane Univ, PhD, 77. **CAREER** Abraham Baldwin Agricultural Col, 76-78; vis asst prof, Tulane Univ, 82; Austin Col, 78- , Guy M. Bryan, Jr. Prof of History, 86- . **HONORS AND AWARDS** Fulbright scholar, 74-76; NEH Summer Seminar, 79; Danforth Assoc, 81- ; Rice Univ Sem Fel, 84; Sid Richardson Grants, 80, 82, 84-85; Columbus Quincentennial Prize, 86; NEH Sum Sem, 89; Sid Richardson Sabbatical Grant, 91-92; Francisco Bouligny Prize, Louisiana Hist Asn, 93. **MEMBERSHIPS** Texas State Hist Asn; AHA; So His Asn; SW Hist Asn; Publ Comm, Social Sci Q; LA Hist Asn; Conf on Latin Am Hist. **RESEARCH** Southeastern Spanish Borderlands; The Old Southwest; Anglo-Spanish rivalry in the eighteenth century Gulf Coast and lower Mississippi Valley; colonial Texas. **SELECTED PUBLICATIONS** Co-ed, A Guide to the History of Louisiana, Greenwood, 82; co-ed, A Guide to the History of Texas, Greenwood, 88; auth, Spanish Observers and the American Revolution, 1775-1783, Louisiana State Univ, 92; auth, "An Enduring Community: British Settlers at Colonial Natchez and in the Spanish Felicianas," Journal of Mississippi History 55 (93): 133-154; auth, "Church Courts, Marriage Breakdown, and Separation in Spanish Louisiana, West Florida, and Texas, 1763-1836," Journal of Texas Catholic History and Culture 4 (93): 97-114; auth, "The Governors of Spanish Colonial Louisiana and Espionage in the Southeastern Borderlands, 1766-1795," Locus: An Historical Journal of Regional Perspectives 6 (93): 23-37; auth, "Keeping Score: Winners and Losers in the Atlantic Sea Trade," Reviews in American History 21 (93): 379-384; coauth, Louisiana: A History, 3d ed, Harlan Davidson, 96; auth, Austin College: A Sesquicentennial History, 1849-1999, Eakin Press, 99; co-ed, Spanish Borderlands History: A Sourcebook and Interviews with Scholars, Texas A&M, forthcoming. **CONTACT ADDRESS** Dept of History, Austin Col, 900 N Grand Ave, Ste 61606, Sherman, TX 75090-4440. **EMAIL** lcummins@austinc.edu

CUMMINS, VICTORIA HENNESSEY
PERSONAL Born 03/10/1951, Yonkers, NY, m, 1975 **DISCIPLINE** LATIN AMERICAN AND EUROPEAN HISTORY **EDUCATION** Univ Md, BA, 72; Tulane Univ, MA, 74, PhD(hist), 79. **CAREER** Instr hist, Abraham Baldwin Agr Col, 77-78; Asst Prof Hist, Austin Col, 78- **MEMBERSHIPS** Conf Latin Am Hist; Southern Hist Asn; Am Hist Asn; Latin Am Studies Asn; Southwestern Conf Latin Am Studies. **RESEARCH** Catholic church in colonial Mexico and Peru; bureaucracies in colonial Mexico and Peru; imperial policy in the Spanish Empire. **CONTACT ADDRESS** Austin Col, 900 N Grand Ave, Sherman, TX 75090-4400.

CUNNIFF, ROGER LEE
PERSONAL Born 10/29/1932, Stonewall, CO, m, 1959, 4 children **DISCIPLINE** LATIN AMERICAN AND BRAZILIAN HISTORY **EDUCATION** Univ Northern Colo, BA, 54, MA, 58, Univ Tex, Austin, PhD(hist), 70. **CAREER** Teacher social studies, Riverton High Sch, Wyo, 58-59 & Hana Sch, Maui, Hawaii, 59-61; teaching asst hist, Univ Tex, Austin, 62-65; asst prof, 67-72, assoc prof, 72-80, Prof Hist of Brazil, San Diego State Univ, 80-. **MEMBERSHIPS** AHA: Conf Latin Am Hist; Latin Am Studies Asn; Pac Cost Coun Latin Am Studies (pres, 73). **RESEARCH** Social history of northeast Brazil; history of natural disasters; history of education in Latin America. **SELECTED PUBLICATIONS** Auth, the Spanish Cortes and Mexican municipal electoral reform, In: Mexico and the Spanish Cortes, Univ Tex, 67; Regional image and social change in northeast Brazil, J Inter-Am Studies & World Affairs, 8/73; Vol ed, Proceedings of the Pacific Coast Coun on Latin American Studies, San Diego State Univ, Vol III, (in prep). **CONTACT ADDRESS** Dept of Hist, San Diego State Univ, 5500 Campanile Dr, San Diego, CA 92182-0002.

CUNNINGHAM, NOBLE E., JR.
PERSONAL Born 07/25/1926, Evans Landing, IN, m, 1954 **DISCIPLINE** HISTORY **EDUCATION** Duke Univ, PhD 52, MA 49; Univ Louisville, BA 48. **CAREER** Univ Missouri CO, assoc prof , prof, chemn, 64-74, Byler Dist Prof, 80-81, Frederick A Middlebush Prof 86-88; curators prof hist 88-97, Curators' Prof Emer 97-. **HONORS AND AWARDS** Phi Beta Kappa; Guggenheim Fel; Outstanding Prof; NHPC Gnt; 2 NEH Fel; APS Penrose Gnt; Thomas Jefferson Awd; Chancellors Awd; Fac Alum; Thomas Jefferson Mem Foun Medal; MO Conf on Hist Awd; Awd for Schly Excellence. **MEMBERSHIPS** AHS' OAH; SHA; SHER. **SELECTED PUBLICATIONS** Auth, The Presidency of James Monroe, Lawrence, Univ Press of Kansas, 96; Popular Images of the Presidency: From Washington to Lincoln, Columbia, Univ of MO Press, 91; In Pursuit of Reason: The Life of Thomas Jefferson, Baton Rouge, LA State Univ Press, 87. **CONTACT ADDRESS** Dept of History, Univ of Missouri, Columbia, Columbia, MO 65211.

CUNNINGHAM, SARAH GARDNER
PERSONAL Born 12/30/1956, Rochester, MN, 2 children **DISCIPLINE** HISTORY AND RELIGION **EDUCATION** Princeton Univ, BA, 79; Union Theol Sem, MDiv, 89, PhD, 84. **CAREER** Macmillan Lib Ref, Simon and Schuster Acad Ref, 94-98; Marymont Sch, Upper Sch History, 98-. **MEMBERSHIPS** AAR; AHA; ASCH. **RESEARCH** US Religious History; Hist of Christianity; Gender Studies. **CONTACT ADDRESS** 1735 York Ave, #6C, New York, NY 10128. **EMAIL** sgcunningham@atsearthlink.net

CUNO, KENNETH M.
PERSONAL Born 01/04/1950, Syracuse, NY, m, 1986, 2 children **DISCIPLINE** HISTORY **EDUCATION** Lewis & Clark Col, BA, hist, 72; Univ Calif Los Angeles, MA, hist, 77, PhD, hist, 85. **CAREER** Vis asst prof, Amer Univ in Cairo, 85-90; asst prof, 90-96, assoc prof, 96-, Univ Ill Urbana-Champaign. **HONORS AND AWARDS** SSRC res fel, 99; Fulbright Sr Res fel, 98-99; US Info Agency, US speaker and specialist grant, 98; vis res scholar, Amer Univ Cairo, 94, 96; fel, Ctr for Advan Study, UIUC, 94-95; fel, Amer Res Ctr in Egypt, 94; honorable mention, Albert Hourani Book Prize, Middle East Studies Asn, 93; humanities released time award, 93; teachers rated excellent by students, UIUC, 90, 94; outstanding teacher, AUC Student Union, 87, 89; soc sci res coun intl doctoral res fel, 81-82; Fulbright-Hays dissertation res abroad fel, 80-81; fel, Ctr for Arabic Studies, 79-80; fel, Amer Res Ctr in Egypt, 79-80. **MEMBERSHIPS** Amer Hist Asn; Middle East Studies Asn of North Amer; Amer Res Ctr in Egypt; Ctr for Middle Eastern Studies at Univ of Chicago; Soc Sci Hist Asn; Turkish Studies Asn. **RESEARCH** Pre-modern and modern family history. **SELECTED PUBLICATIONS** Auth, A Tale of Two Villages: Family, Property, and Economic Activity in Rural Egypt in the 1840s, land, Settlement and Agriculture in Egypt from Pharaonic to

Modern Times, Oxford Univ Press, 98; auth, Ideology and Juridical Discourse in Ottoman Egypt: the Uses of the Concept of Irsad, Islamic Law and Soc, 98; co-auth, The Census Registers of Nineteenth-Century Egypt: A New Source for Social Historians, Brit Jour of Middle Eastern Studies, 97; auth, Migrants, Islam, Refugees and Behind the Veil, Imagining the Twentieth Century, Univ Ill Press, 97; auth, In Memoriam (Ronald C. Jennings), Turkish Studies Asn Bull, 96; auth, Joint Family Households and Rural Notables in Nineteenth-Century Egypt, Intl Jour of Middle East Studies, 95; auth, Was the Land of Ottoman Syria Miri or Milk? An Examination of Juridical Differences within the Hanafi School, Studia Islamica, 95; auth, The Origins of Private Ownership of Land in Egypt: a Reappraisal, The Modern Middle East: a Reader, Univ Calif Press, 94. **CONTACT ADDRESS** Dept. of History, Univ of Illinois, Urbana-Champaign, 309 Gregory Hall, 810 S. Wri, Urbana, IL 61801. **EMAIL** k-cuno@uiuc.edu

CUNSOLO, RONALD S.
PERSONAL Born 05/03/1923, New York, NY, m, 1951, 2 children **DISCIPLINE** MODERN EUROPEAN HISTORY **EDUCATION** NYork Univ, BA, 49, PhD(hist), 62; Univ Chicago, MA, 56. **CAREER** Permanent substitute hist, Brooklyn Col, 62-63; from instr to assoc prof, 63-71, chmn dept hist & polit sci, 66-73, Prof Hist, Nassau Community Col, 71-, Assoc, Sem Mod Ital Hist, Columbia Univ, 70-, chmn, 73-74; chmn Sem Studies Mod Italy, 74-75; exec secy, Matteotti Int Symp, Columbia Univ, 75-78. **HONORS AND AWARDS** Great Teacher Awd, State Univ NY, 81-82. **MEMBERSHIPS** AHA; Acad Polit Sci; Soc Ital Hist Studies. **RESEARCH** Modern Italian history; nationalism; imperialism. **SELECTED PUBLICATIONS** Auth, "Libya, Italian Nationalism, and the Revolt Against Giolitti," Journal of Modern History, XXXVII (65): 186-207; auth, "The Great Debate on Prime Minister Giolitti and Giolittian Italy," Canadian Review of Studies in Nationalism, XVIII (91): 95-115; auth, Nationalists and Catholics in Giolittian Italy--An Uneasy Collaboration, Cath Hist Rev, Vol 0079, 93; auth, Italian Nationalism from its Origins to World War II, Krieger (Malabar, FL), 90; **CONTACT ADDRESS** Nassau Comm Col, Garden City, NY 11530.

CURET, LUIS ANTONIO
PERSONAL Born 10/20/1960, San Juan, PR, m, 1990, 2 children **DISCIPLINE** ANTHROPOLOGY, ARCHAEOLOGY **EDUCATION** Arizona State Univ, PhD, 92. **CAREER** Asst prof, Gettysburg Col, 93-96; asst prof, Univ of Colorado, Denver, 96- . **HONORS AND AWARDS** Res awd, Univ Colorado, 98. **MEMBERSHIPS** Soc for Am Archaeol; Sigma Xi Sci Soc; Int Asoc Caribbean Archaeol; Asociacion Puertorriquencia de Antropologos y Arqueologos. **RESEARCH** Caribbean and Mesoamerica; complex societies. **SELECTED PUBLICATIONS** Auth, Ceramic Production Areas and Regional Studies: An Example From La Mixtequilla, Veracruz, Mexico, in J of Field Archaeol, 93; auth, Prehistoric Demographic Changes in the Valley of Maunabo, Puerto Rico: A Preliminary Report, in Proc of the 14th Int Cong for Caribbean Archaeol, 93; coauth, Post classic Changes in Veracruz, Mexico, Ancient Mesoamerica, 94; auth, Ideology, Chiefly Power, and Material Culture: An Example from the Greater Antilles, Latin Am Antiq, 96; auth, Technological Changes in Prehistoric Ceramics from Eastern Puerto Rico: An Exploratory Study, in J of Archaeol Sci, 97; auth, New Formulae for Estimating prehistoric Populations for Lowland South America and the Caribbean, in Antiquity, 98; coauth, Poder e ideologia: el control del simbolismo en los cacicazgos tempranos de Puerto Rico, Historia y Sociedad, 98; coauth, Mortuary Practices, Social Development and Ideology in Precolumbian Puerto Rico, Latin Am Antiq, in press; coauth, Informe Preliminar del Proyecto Arqueologico del Centro Indigena de Tibes, Ponce, Puerto Rico, in Proc of the 16th Int Cong for Caribbean Archaeol, in press. **CONTACT ADDRESS** Dept of Anthropology, Univ of Colorado, Denver, Campus Box 103, PO Box 173364, Denver, CO 80217-3364. **EMAIL** lcuret@carbon.cudenver.edu

CURL, DONALD WALTER
PERSONAL Born 10/07/1935, East Liberty, OH **DISCIPLINE** UNITED STATES HISTORY **EDUCATION** Ohio State Univ, BScEd, 57, MA, 58, PhD (Hist), 64. **CAREER** Instr Hist, Kent State Univ, 62-64; from asst prof to assoc prof, 64-71, chmn dept, 69-75, 90-92, 94-98; prof Hist, Fla Atlantic Univ, 71-. **HONORS AND AWARDS** Cert of Commendation, Am Asn State & Local Hist, 71; Awd for Best Book, FL Hist, 84; Awd for best article in Florida Hist Quarterly, 93; Awd of Merit, Am Assn State & Local Hist, 96. **MEMBERSHIPS** AHA. **RESEARCH** United States social and intellectual history; Florida history; political party history. **SELECTED PUBLICATIONS** Auth, The Senate Rejects, Ohio Hist, summer 67; Murat Halstead, In: For the Union, Ohio State Univ, 68; ed, Pioneer Life in Southeast Florida, Univ Miami, 70; auth, An American reporter and the Franco-Prussian War, Jour Quart, Fall 72; The pioneer cook in SE Florida, Boca Raton Hist Soc, 75; Murat Halstead and the Cincinnati Commercial, Univ Fla, 80; auth, Mizner's Florida: American Resort Architecture, MIT Press, 84; Joseph Urban's Palm Beach Architecture, FL Hist Quarterly, April 93; Palm Beach County: In a Class by Itself, ed, Copperfield, 98; The Florida Architecture of F Burrall Hoffman, Jr, 1882-1980, FL Hist Quarterly, Spring 98. **CONTACT ADDRESS** Dept of History, Florida Atlantic Univ, PO Box 3091, Boca Raton, FL 33431-0991. **EMAIL** curld@fau.edu

CURNOW, KATHY
DISCIPLINE AFRICAN AND AFRICAN-AMERICAN ART HISTORY **EDUCATION** PA State Univ, BA, 76; IN State Univ, MA, 80, PhD, 83. **CAREER** Instr, Univ PA; Lincoln Univ; Univ Arts, NTA TV Col, Nigeria; assoc prof, 80-. **HONORS AND AWARDS** NEH grant; Fulbright; Soc Sci Res Coun grant. **RESEARCH** Fiction writing. **SELECTED PUBLICATIONS** Publ, art Benin Kingdom; Itsekiri; Nupe of Nigeria; articles, Benin's ideal man, Art Jour; Benin's Ague Festival, African Arts; dwarf figures from Benin, exhib cat, Linz, Austria. **CONTACT ADDRESS** Dept of Art, Cleveland State Univ, 83 E 24th St, Cleveland, OH 44115.

CURRAN, BRIAN A.
PERSONAL Born 06/25/1953, Boston, MA, m, 1987 **DISCIPLINE** ITALIAN RENAISSANCE ART **EDUCATION** Mass Coll Art, BFA; Univ Mass, MA; Princeton Univ, MA, PhD. **CAREER** 84-90, Museum of Fine Arts, Boston; Tchg fel, Columbia Univ, 96-97; asst prof, Pa State Univ, 97-;. **HONORS AND AWARDS** Fel, Am Acad, Rome; fel, Bibliotheca Hertziana, Rome. **MEMBERSHIPS** Renaissance Soc of Am, Col Art Asn; Natl Trust for Historic Pres. **RESEARCH** History of archaeology, humanism, renaissance "egyptology," portraiture; patronage of private families in early modern Rome. **SELECTED PUBLICATIONS** Articles, Art Bull; Jour Warburg & Courtauld Insts; Words & Image. **CONTACT ADDRESS** Pennsylvania State Univ, Univ Park, 229 Arts Bldg, University Park, PA 16802. **EMAIL** bac18@psu.edu

CURRAN, DANIEL JOHN
PERSONAL Born 10/27/1932, Brooklyn, NY **DISCIPLINE** HISTORY **EDUCATION** Manhattan Col, BA, 52; Fordham Univ, MA, 53, PhD (hist), 62. **CAREER** Assoc prof, 58-72, Prof Hist, King's Col, PA, 72-. **MEMBERSHIPS** AHA; Am Cath Hist Asn; Orgn Am Historians; Am Asn Slavic Studies. **RESEARCH** American contemporary political history; modern Russian history. **SELECTED PUBLICATIONS** Auth, Polk, Politics and Patronage--The Rejection of Woodward, George,W. Nomination to the Supreme-Court, Pa Mag Hist and Biog, Vol 0121, 97. **CONTACT ADDRESS** Dept of Hist, King's Col, 133 N River St, Wilkes-Barre, PA 18711-0801.

CURRAN, ROBERT EMMOTT
PERSONAL Born 05/23/1936, Baltimore, MD, m, 1998 **DISCIPLINE** HISTORY **EDUCATION** Col of Holy Cross, AB, 58; Fordham Univ, MA, 65; Yale Univ, PhD, 74. **CAREER** Instr to asst prof to assoc prof to prof, 72-, Georgetown Univ. **MEMBERSHIPS** Amer Hist Assoc; Org of Amer Hist; Amer Stud Assoc; Amer Catholic Hist Assoc; S Hist Assoc; Immigration Hist Assoc; Amer Soc of Church Hist. **RESEARCH** US religions; education; US South. **SELECTED PUBLICATIONS** Auth, The Bicentennial History of Georgetown University, 93; auth, The Jesuits as Educators in Anglo-America in Jesuit Encounters in the New World: Jesuit Chroniclers, Geographers, Educators and Missionaries in the Americas, 1549-1767, Jesuit Hist Inst, 97; art, Christianity: Roman Catholicism, Encyclopedia of Slaver, 99. **CONTACT ADDRESS** History Dept, Georgetown Univ, Washington, DC 20057. **EMAIL** currane@GUNET.GEORGETOWN.EDU

CURRAN, THOMAS F.
DISCIPLINE US CIVIL WAR **EDUCATION** Univ Mass Amherst, 83, MA, 86; Univ Notre Dame, PhD. **CAREER** Asst prof, St Louis Univ. **HONORS AND AWARDS** Managing ed, Jour Policy Hist. **SELECTED PUBLICATIONS** Auth, '"Resist Not Evil': The Ifeological Roots of Civil War Pacifism," Civil War History 36 (90): 197-208; auth, "Colonel Moses Little," in The War of the American Revolution, 1775-1783: An Encyclopedia, Garland Publishing, 93; auth, "Pacifists, Peace Democrats, and Politics of Perfection in the Civil War Era," Journal of Church and State 38 (96): 487-505. **CONTACT ADDRESS** Dept of Hist, Saint Louis Univ, 3800 Lindell Blvd, PO Box 56907, Saint Louis, MO 63159-0907. **EMAIL** currantf@slu.edu

CURRAN, THOMAS J.
PERSONAL Born 10/03/1929, Brooklyn, NY, 2 children **DISCIPLINE** AMERICAN HISTORY **EDUCATION** Manhattan Col, AB, 48; Columbia Univ, MA, 51, PhD, 63. **CAREER** Instr hist, Manhattanville Col Sacred Heart, 55-56; from instr to asst prof, 56-65, assoc prof Hist, St John's Univ, NY, 65-, Acad coordr, Nat Broadcasting Co-TV & consult, Columbia Broadcasting Syst-TV, 71-. **MEMBERSHIPS** AHA; Am Cath Hist Asn; Orgn Am Historians. **RESEARCH** Nineteenth century American history--know nothing movement. **SELECTED PUBLICATIONS** Auth, Assimilation and nativism, Int Migration Rev, spring 66; Seward and the know-nothings, 4/67 & ed, The diary of Henry Van Der Lyn, spring 71, NY Hist Soc Quart; auth, Xenophobia and Immigration, 76 & co-ed, Immigrant in American History, 77, Twayne. **CONTACT ADDRESS** Dept of History, St. John's Univ, 8150 Utopia Pky, Jamaica, NY 11439-0002.

CURRENT, RICHARD NELSON
PERSONAL Born 10/05/1912, Colorado City, CO, m, 1937, 2 children **DISCIPLINE** AMERICAN HISTORY **EDUCATION** Oberlin Col, AB, 34; Fletcher Sch Law, AM, 35; Univ Wis, PhD, 39. **CAREER** Instr soc sci, Md State Teachers Col, Salisbury, 38-42; asst prof hist & polit sci, Rutgers Univ, 42-43; asst prof hist, Hamilton Col, 43-44; prof, Northern Mich Col Educ, 44-45; assoc prof, Lawrence Col, 45-47; Morrison prof Am hist, Mills Col, 47-50; from assoc prof to prof hist, Univ Ill, 50-55; prof hist & polit sci & head dept Woman's Col, Univ NC, 55-60; prof hist, Univ Wis, Madison, 60-66; Distinguished Prof Hist, Univ NC, Greensboro, 66-, Lectr, Doshisha Univ, 58; lectr, Am specialist prog, India & Fulbright Lectr, Univ Munich, 59; Harmsworth prof, Oxford Univ, 62-63; lectr, India, 65, 67-68, Chile & Arg, 65, Australia & Europe, 66, Japan, Taiwan & Philippines, 67, Chile & Ecuador, 68. **HONORS AND AWARDS** Bancroft Prize, Columbia Univ, 56; Banta Awd, Wis Libr Asn, 77; ma, oxford univ, 62. **MEMBERSHIPS** AHA; Orgn Am Historians; Soc Am Historians; Southern Hist Asn (pres, 74-75). **RESEARCH** American diplomatic history; American political biography; the Civil War and Reconstruction. **SELECTED PUBLICATIONS** Auth, Foote,Shelby--Novelist and Historian, Jour So Hist, Vol 0059, 93. **CONTACT ADDRESS** 1805 Brookcliff Dr, Greensboro, NC 27408.

CURREY, CECIL B.
PERSONAL Born 11/29/1932, Clarks, NE, m, 1952, 3 children **DISCIPLINE** AMERICAN MILITARY HISTORY **EDUCATION** Ft Hays State Univ, M.Sc, 59; Univ Kans, PhD(hist), 65. **CAREER** Asst prof Am hist, Nebr Wesleyan Univ, 65-67, assoc prof, 67; assoc prof, 67-69, Prof Colonial, US Military & Revolution Am Hist, Univ S Fla, Tampa, 69-, S & H Lectureship Found grants, 67, 68. **HONORS AND AWARDS** Outstanding Alum Awd (FHSU), 75; Tchr of the Yr, 78; Outstanding Prof Awd, 91; St of FL Tchng Awd, 95. **MEMBERSHIPS** AHA; Orgn Am Historians. **RESEARCH** The career of Benjamin Franklin; Viet Nam; WW II; Am Rev. **SELECTED PUBLICATIONS** Auth, Road to Revolution, 68; auth, Code Number 72, 73; auth, Reason & Revelation, 77; auth, Self-Destruction, 81; auth, With Wings as Eagles, 84; auth, Follow me & Die, 84; auth, Edward Lausdale, 89; auth, Victory at any Cost, 97; auth, Long Binh Jail, 00. **CONTACT ADDRESS** Dept of Hist, Univ of So Florida, 4202 Fowler Ave, Tampa, FL 33620-9951. **EMAIL** cbcthor@aol.com

CURRY, LAWRENCE H., JR.
PERSONAL Born 02/04/1935, Anderson, SC, m, 1994, 3 children **DISCIPLINE** HISTORY **EDUCATION** Univ SC, BS, 57, MA, 59; Duke Univ, PhD, 71. **CAREER** From instr to asst prof to assoc dean, 68-, Univ Houston. **HONORS AND AWARDS** Univ Houston Tchg Excellence, 77, 97, 00. **MEMBERSHIPS** Am Hist Asn; Southern Hist Asn. **RESEARCH** Recent US history **CONTACT ADDRESS** Dept of History, Univ of Houston, Houston, TX 77204-3785. **EMAIL** lcurry@uh.edu

CURRY, LEONARD PRESTON
PERSONAL Born 03/23/1929, Cave City, KY, m, 1959, 2 children **DISCIPLINE** UNITED STATES HISTORY **EDUCATION** Western Ky State Col, AB, 51; Univ Ky, MA, 56, PhD, 61. **CAREER** From instr to asst prof hist, Memphis State Univ, 58-62; from asst prof to assoc prof, 62-69, Prof Hist, Univ Louisville, 69-, Prof hist, 66-99, Emer Prof, Univ Louisville, 99-; Am Philos Soc res grants, 62, 72 & 76; vis asst prof, Univ Maine, 64-65; vis assoc prof, Univ Md, 68-69; vis res assoc, Smithsonian Inst, 70-71; mem, Adv Comt Ky Arch & Rec Comn, 72-; fac res grants, 63, 66, 67 & 73-81; fac res grants, 63,66,67,73-83 & 90-98; Am Coun Learned Socs res grant, 76; mem, Ky Comn Pub Doc, 76-; consult, Nat Endowment for Humanities, 76, 77, 78 & 81; Southern Regional Educ Bd res grant, 81; Southern Regional Educ Bd res grant, 81, 86; Nat Endowment for Humanities summer stipend, 85 & senior scolars fellowship, 88-89. **MEMBERSHIPS** AHA; Orgn Am Historians; Southern Hist Asn. **RESEARCH** United States history, 1820-1877; urban development in the United States, 1800-1850; United States congressional history. **SELECTED PUBLICATIONS** Auth, "Election Year--Kentucky, 1828; Register of the Ky Hist Soc, 6/57; auth, "Congressional Democrats: 1861-1863, Civil War Hist," 9/66; auth, "Blueprint for Modern America: Nonmilitary Legislation of the First Civil War Congress," Vanderbilt Univ, 68; auth, "Rail Routres South: Louisville's Fight for the Southern Market, 1865-1872," Univ Ky, 69; auth, "Urbanization and Urbanism in the Old South: A Comparative View," J Southern Hist, 2/74; auth, "Urban Life in the Old South," Forum 76; auth, "The Free Black in Urban America, 1800-1850: The Shadow of the Dream," Univ Chicago, 81, 86; auth, "Urban Slavery, in Dictionary of Afro-American Slavery," Greenwood, 88; auth, "The Corporate City: The American City as a Political Entity, 1800-1850, vol 1 of The Emergence of American Urbanism, 1800-1850," Greenwood, 97. **CONTACT ADDRESS** Dept of Hist, Univ of Louisville, 2350 Valletta Lane, Louisville, KY 40205.

CURRY, RICHARD ORR
PERSONAL Born 01/26/1931, White Sulphur Springs, WV, m, 1953, 4 children **DISCIPLINE** UNITED STATES HISTORY **EDUCATION** Marshall Univ, BA, 52, MA, 56; Univ Pa, PhD(hist), 61. **CAREER** Instr Europ hist, Morris Harvey Col, 59-60; instr US hist, Pa State Univ, 60-62; vis asst prof, Univ Pittsburgh, 62-63; from asst prof to assoc prof, 63-71, Prof US

Hist, Univ Conn, 71-, Am Asn State & Local Hist grant, 64; Soc Relig Higher Educ & Harvard Divinity Sch fel, 65-66; Am Philos Soc grant, 67 & 70. **HONORS AND AWARDS** Haynes Lectr, 74; US Int Commun Agency Lectr, Philippines, 78 & Australia, 81; Fulbright Lectr, 81; Charles Hill Moffat Lectr, 82. **MEMBERSHIPS** Orgn Am Historians; Southern Hist Asn; Am Studies Asn. **RESEARCH** Nineteenth century United States social political and intellectual history. **SELECTED PUBLICATIONS** Auth, The New Individualists--The Generation After the Organization-Man, Jour Amer Hist, Vol 0080, 93; Untitled, Jour Amer Hist, Vol 0082, 95. **CONTACT ADDRESS** Dept of Hist, Univ of Connecticut, Storrs, Storrs, CT 06268.

CURTIN, N. J.
PERSONAL Born 07/01/1952, Reedsburg, WI **DISCIPLINE** HISTORY **EDUCATION** Univ of Wisconsin-Madison, BA 76, MA 80, PhD 88. **CAREER** Fordham Univ, asst prof to prof, 88 to 98-. **MEMBERSHIPS** AHA; Amer Conf for Irish Studies; North Amer Conf for British Studies **RESEARCH** Modern Ireland, nationalism, republicanism and gender. **SELECTED PUBLICATIONS** Auth, Eire-Ireland: An Interdisciplinary Jour of Irish Studies, co-ed, 96-; The United Irishmen: Popular Politics in Ulster and Dublin, 1791-1798, Oxford Clarendon Press 94, ppbk 98; Matilda Tone and Virtuous Republican Femininity, Women in '98 ed Daire Keogh, 98; Radicals and Rebels: The United Irishmen in County Down, in Down Hist and Soc, ed Lindsay Proudfoot, 97; forthcoming, A Perfect Liberty: The Irish Whigs, 1789-1797, in Political Discourse in Early Modern Ireland, eds W. G. Boyce, R. R. Eccleshall, V. Geoghegan, London Macmillan; Reclaiming Gender: Transgressive Identities in Modern Ireland, co-ed Marilyn Cohen, NY St Martins press, 99. **CONTACT ADDRESS** Dept of History, Fordham Univ, Bronx, NY 10458. **EMAIL** nancycurtin@telocity.com

CURTIN, PHILIP DE ARMOND
PERSONAL Born 05/22/1922, Philadelphia, PA, m, 1957, 3 children **DISCIPLINE** HISTORY **EDUCATION** Swarthmore Col, AB, 48; Harvard Univ, MA, 49, PhD, 53. **CAREER** From instr to asst prof hist, Swarthmore Col, 53-56; from asst prof to prof, Univ WI Madison, 56-70, chmn, Prog Comp World Hist, 59-75,chmn, Dept African Languages and Lit, 63-64, 65-66; mem, African Studies Prog, 61-66, Melville J Herskovits prof, 70-75, co-dir res prog in African econ hist, 71-75; Prof Hist, Johns Hopkins Univ, 75-82, Herbert Baxter Adams Prof of Hist, 82-; Ford Found African area training fel, 58-59; US-African Leader Exchange Prog fac exchange travel grant, 62-63; mem joint comt African studies Soc Sci Res Coun-Am Coun Learned Socs, 63-73, chmn, 71-73; Guggenheim fel, 66 & 80; mem coun, Soc Sci Res Coun, 67-71; Nat Endowment for Humanities sr fel, 68-69;chmn, Prog Atlantic Studies in Hist and Culture, 76-79; Univ of Hawaii, John A. Burns Distinguished Vis Prof of Hist, spring semester, 88; Univ MN, Union Pacific Vis Prof, spring semester, 90. **HONORS AND AWARDS** Phi Beta Kappa, 48; Ford Fellowship, 58-59; United States-South Africa Leader Exchange Program Fellowship, 62-63; Guggenheim Fellowship, 66, 80; Robert Livingston Schuyler Prize, 66; Sr Fellowship, NEH, 68-69; MacArthur Prize Fellowship, 83-88; Phi Beta Kappa Assoc, 83; Presented with Africans in Bondage, ed Paul Lovejoy, essays in honor of Philip D. Curtin, by African Studies Program, Univ WI, Oct 86; Doctor of Humane Letters, Swarthmore Col, 87; Welch Medal from the Am Assoc for the Hist of Medicine, 92; Distinguished Africanist Awd, 92. **MEMBERSHIPS** AHA, pres 83; African Studies Asn (pres, 70-71); Int Cong Africanists (vpres, 69-73); Am Anthrop Asn; Econ Hist Asn; Am Philos Soc, 96. **RESEARCH** African history; Caribbean history; world history. **SELECTED PUBLICATIONS** Auth, Two Jamaicas, Harvard Univ, 55; The Image of Africa, 64, Africa Remembered, 67, The Atlantic Slave Trade: A Census, 69 & ed & Contrib, Africa and the West, 69, Univ WI; coauth, Africa and Africans, Natural Hist, 71; auth, Economic Change in Pre-Colonial Africa, Univ WI, 75; coauth, African History, Little, 78; Cross-Cultural Trade in World History, NY, Cambridge Univ Press, 84; Death by Migration: Europe's Encounter with the Tropical World in the Nineteenth Century, NY, Cambridge Univ Press, 89; The Rise and Fall of the Plantation Comples: Essays in Atlantic History, NY, Cambridge Univ Press, 90; Why People Move: Migration in African History, Waco, Tx: Baylor Univ Press, 95.; auth, Disease and Empire, Cambridge Univ Press, 98; The World and the West, Cambridge Univ Press, 00; contrib ed to: Current History, 55-59, Jnal of African Hist, 60-76, Jnal of African Studies, 74-, African Economic Hist, 75-, Social Science Hist, 76-, Am Hist Rev, 77-80, Hist in Africa, 74-, J of Economic Hist, 75-78, Plantation Soc, 78-. **CONTACT ADDRESS** Dept of Hist, Johns Hopkins Univ, Baltimore, 3400 N Charles St, Baltimore, MD 21218-2680. **EMAIL** curtinpd@aol.com

CURTIS, JAMES C.
PERSONAL Born 07/12/1938, Evanston, IL, m, 1961, 2 children **DISCIPLINE** AMERICAN HISTORY **EDUCATION** Carleton Col, BA, 59; Northwestern Univ, MA, 66, PhD (Am hist), 67. **CAREER** Asst prof, Univ Tex, Austin, 67-70; assoc prof, 70-76, Prof Hist & Am Studies, Univ Del, 76-, Nat Endowment for Humanities fel, 73-74. **HONORS AND AWARDS** Excellence in Teaching Awd, Univ Del, 76. **MEMBERSHIPS** AHA; Orgn Am Historians. **RESEARCH** Jacksonian politics; the history of the 19th century Presidency; history and media. **SELECTED PUBLICATIONS** Auth, The Fox at Bay: Martin Van Buren and the Presidency, 1837-1841, Univ Ky, 70; co-ed, The Black Experience in America, Univ Tex, 70; Andrew Jackson and the Search for Vindication, Little Brown, 76. **CONTACT ADDRESS** Dept of Hist, Univ of Delaware, Newark, DE 19711.

CURTIS, ROBERT I.
PERSONAL Born 10/17/1943, Waycross, GA, m, 1976, 1 child **DISCIPLINE** ANCIENT HISTORY **EDUCATION** Univ Maryland, PhD 78. **CAREER** From asst prof to prof, Univ Georgia, 78-; vis prof, Univ Leeds, 97. **HONORS AND AWARDS** Outstanding Honors Prof, 91 **MEMBERSHIPS** AIA; ISCT; AAH **RESEARCH** Roman social and econ history; Roman food and drink; Pompeii and Herculaneum. **SELECTED PUBLICATIONS** Auth, Garum and Salsamenta: The Production and Commerce of Materia Medica, Leiden, E. J. Brill, 91; Confederate Classical Textbooks: A Lost Cause? In: The Intl Jour for the Classical Tradition, 97; The Bingham School and Classical Education in North Carolina, 1793-1873, The North Carol Hist Rev, 96. **CONTACT ADDRESS** Dept of Classics, Univ of Georgia, Park Hall, Athens, GA 30602-6203. **EMAIL** ricurtis@arches.uga.edu

CURTIS, SUSAN
PERSONAL Born 07/09/1956, Red Oak, IA, m, 1992 **DISCIPLINE** HISTORY **EDUCATION** Graceland Col, BA, 77; Univ Mo-Columbia, MA, 81, PhD, 86. **CAREER** Asst prof, Fla Int Univ, 86-89; asst prof, Purdue Univ, 89-94; Assoc Prof, Purdue Univ, 94-99; Prof, Purdue Univ, 99-; Chair of American Studies, Purdue Univ, 99-. **MEMBERSHIPS** Org Am Historians; Am Stud Asn; Am Hist Asn; Am Soc Church Hist; John Whitmer Hist Asn **RESEARCH** American Cultural History; American Religious History. **SELECTED PUBLICATIONS** A Consuming Faith: The Social Gospel and Modern American Culture, JHUP, (Baltimore), 91; "Scott Joplin and Sedalia: The King of Ragtime in the Queen City of Missouri," Gateway Heritage, 94; Dancing to a Black Man's Tune: A Life of Scott Joplin, Columbia: Univ Mo Press, 94; The First Black Actors on the Great White Way, Columbia: Univ Mo Press, 98. **CONTACT ADDRESS** Dept Hist, Purdue Univ, West Lafayette, West Lafayette, IN 47907-1358. **EMAIL** curtis@purdue.edu

CUSHING, JAMES T.
DISCIPLINE HISTORY **EDUCATION** Loyola Univ, BS, 59; Northwestern Univ, MS, 60; Univ Iowa, PhD, 63. **CAREER** Prof. **RESEARCH** History and philosophy of quantum physics. **SELECTED PUBLICATIONS** Auth, Underdetermination, Conventionalism, and Realism, 93; Why Local Realism?, 93; A Bohmian Response to Bohr's Complementarity, 94; Hermeneutics, Underdetermination and Quantum Mechanics, 94; Bohmian Mechanics and Quantum Theory: An Appraisal, 96; co-ed, Quantum Mechanics: Historical Contingency and the Copenhagen Hegemony, 94. **CONTACT ADDRESS** History and Philosophy of Science Dept, Univ of Notre Dame, Notre Dame, IN 46556. **EMAIL** Cushing.1@nd.edu

CUTCLIFFE, STEPHEN HOSMER
PERSONAL Born 01/17/1947, Melrose, MA, s **DISCIPLINE** SCIENCE, TECHNOLOGY & SOCIETY; HISTORY OF TECHNOLOGY **EDUCATION** Bates Col, AB, 68; Lehigh Univ, MA, 73, PhD(hist), 76. **CAREER** Admin asst, Sci, Technol & Soc Prog, 76-81, dir, Sci, Technol & Soc Prog, 88-, ed, Science, Technology and Society Newsletter, 77-. **MEMBERSHIPS** Orgn Am Historians; Soc Hist Technol; Nat Assn for Sci, Technol, and Soc. **RESEARCH** Technology and society; history of technology. **SELECTED PUBLICATIONS** Coauth, Technology and Values in American Civilization Detroit, Gale Res, 80; Responsibility and the technological process, Technol in Society, spring 80; auth, Colonial Indian policy as a measure of rising imperialism: New York and Pennsylvania, 1700-1755, Western Pa Hist Mag, 7/81; coauth, Technology and Values in American Civilization, Gale Research, 80; co-ed, In Context: History and the History of Technology-Essays in Honor of Melvin Kranzberg, Research in Technol Studies, vol 1, Lehigh Univ Press, 89; co-ed, New Worlds, New Technologies, New Issues, Research in Technol Studies, vol 6, Lehigh Univ Press, 92; co-ed, Technology and the West and Technology and American History, Univ Chicago Press, 97; The Emergence of STS as an Academic Field, Research in Philosophy and Technology 9, 287-301, 89; The Warp and Woof of Science and Technology Studies in the United States, Education, 352, 391-91, Spring 93; auth, Ideas, Machines, and Values: An Introduction to Science, Technology and Society Studies, Ronman and Littlefield, 00. **CONTACT ADDRESS** Lehigh Univ, 9 W Packer Ave, Bethlehem, PA 18015-3081. **EMAIL** shc0@lehigh.edu

CUTLER, ANTHONY
PERSONAL Born 02/18/1934, London, England, m, 1961, 2 children **DISCIPLINE** ART HISTORY **EDUCATION** Cambridge Univ, BA, 55, MA, 60; Emory Univ, PhD, 63. **CAREER** Instr humanities, Morehouse Col, 60-63; asst prof fine arts, 63-67, Emory Univ; assoc prof, 67-74, prof art hist, 74-, PA State Univ, Univ Park; Rockefeller res scholar, Inst Hist Studies, Naples, Italy, 56; Brit Coun Scholar, Univ Belgrade, 62; Am Numis Soc grant-in-aid, 63; vis assoc prof archit hist, 69, Univ Calif, Berkeley; Gennadeion fel, Am Sch Classical Studies, Athens, 70-71; fel, Dumbarton Oaks Ctr for Byzantine Studies, 75-76; consult, NEH, 76-; Am Coun Learned Soc, grant-in-aid, 81; sr res scholar, Corpus Christi Col, 82-83; Visiting Scholar, Univ of Chicago, 01. **HONORS AND AWARDS** Choice's list of Outstanding Academic Books of 1994; American Society of Eighteenth-Century Studies Fellow, Houghton Library, Harvard University, 94-95; Visiting Fellow, Princeton Univ, 95; Francois Ier medal, Coll de France, Paris, 95; Paul Mellon Sen Fel, Cen; vis fel, Princeton Univ, Spring, 95; Humboldt Prize, 00-01. **MEMBERSHIPS** Soc Am Archaeol; Mediaeval Acad Am; Col Art Assn; Byzantine Studies Conf. **RESEARCH** Byzantine art history, especially late antique and early Christian ivories. manuscript illumination, mosaic and fresco painting. **SELECTED PUBLICATIONS** Auth, The Hand of the Master, Craftsmanship, Ivory and Society in Byzantium, Princeton University Press, 94. **CONTACT ADDRESS** Dept of Art Hist, Pennsylvania State Univ, Univ Park, 229 Arts Bldg, University Park, PA 16802-2901. **EMAIL** axcb@psu.edu

CUTLER, WILLIAM W., III
DISCIPLINE HISTORY OF AMERICAN EDUCATION, AMERICAN URBAN HISTORY **EDUCATION** Cornell Univ, PhD. **CAREER** Assoc prof Hist and Educ Policy Stud, Temple Univ; guest lectr, Univ Algiers, 89. **HONORS AND AWARDS** The best article, Am Quart, 72. **RESEARCH** The hist of the home-school relationship in Am since the middle of the 19th century; the material cult of Am educ. **SELECTED PUBLICATIONS** Auth, Status, Values and the Education of the Poor: The Trustees of the New York Public School Society, 1805-1853, Am Quart, 72; Continuity and Discontinuity in the History of Childhood and the Family: A Reappraisal, Hist of Educ Quart, 86; Cathedral of Culture: The Schoolhouse in American Educational Thought and Practice since 1820, Hist of Educ Quart, 89; Symbol of Paradox in the New Republic: Classicism in the Design of Schoolhouses and Other Public Buildings in the United States, 1800-1860, in Aspects of Antiquity in the History of Education, F-P. Hager, et al, eds, 92; In Search of Influence and Authority: Parents and the Politics of the Home-School Relationship in Philadelphia and Two of its Suburbs, 1905-1035, Pa Hist, 96; auth, "The History Course Portfolio," Perspectives 35, (97): 17-20; auth, Parents and Schools: The 150-Year Struggle for Control in American Education, Chicago: Univ of Chicago Press, 00. **CONTACT ADDRESS** Temple Univ, Philadelphia, PA 19122. **EMAIL** wcutler@astro.ocis.temple.edu

CUTRER, THOMAS W.
PERSONAL Born 05/01/1947, Spring Creek, LA, m, 1978, 2 children **DISCIPLINE** AMERICAN STUDIES **EDUCATION** La State Univ, BA, 69; MA, 74; Univ of Tex, PhD, 80. **CAREER** Res assoc, Univ of Tex, 80-90; vis asst prof to prof, Ariz State Univ, 90-. **HONORS AND AWARDS** Gen L. Kamper Williams Prize, La Hist Soc, 84; La Lit Awd, La Libr Assoc, 84; Summerfield g. robers Awd, Sons of Rep of Tex, 93. **RESEARCH** Cultural history of the American South, Civil War and Reconstruction, Nineteenth century United States military history. **SELECTED PUBLICATIONS** Auth, Parnassus on the Mississippi: The Southern Review and the Baton Rouge Literary Community, 1935-1942, La State Univ Pr (Baton Rouge), 84; auth, Ben McCulloch and the Frontier Military Tradition, Univ of NC Pr (Chapel Hill), 93; auth, Longstreet's Aide: The Civil War Letters of Major Thomas J. Goree, Univ Pr of Va (Charlottesville), 95; coed, Brothers in Gray: The Civil War Letters of the Pierson Family, La State Univ Pr (Baton Rouge), 97. **CONTACT ADDRESS** Dept American Studies, Arizona State Univ, West, PO Box 37100, Glendale, AZ 85306. **EMAIL** cutrer@asu.edu

CUTTER, DONALD C.
PERSONAL Born 01/09/1922, Chico, CA, m, 1945, 9 children **DISCIPLINE** HISTORY **EDUCATION** Univ Calif, Berkeley, AB, 43, MA, 47, PhD, 50. **CAREER** Inst of Hist, San Diego St Col, 50-51; asst prof, 51-56, assoc prof, 56-61, prof, 61-62, Univ of So Calif; prof, 62-82, prof emeritus, 82-, Univ N Mex; O'Connor Prof, Spanish Colonial Hist of Texas & S W, 82-88, prof emer, 88-, St Mary's Univ. **RESEARCH** Spanish SW; Spanish naval explor; Amer Indian legal status. **SELECTED PUBLICATIONS** Auth, Changing Tides--Twilight and Dawn In the Spanish Sea, 1763-1803, Pacific Hist Rev, Vol 0066, 97; Malaspina,Alejandro--Impossible America-Spanish, Pacific Hist Rev, Vol 0064, 95; The Red Captain--The Life of Oconor, Hugo, Commandant-Inspector of New-Spain, NMex Hist Rev, Vol 0071, 96; The Discovery of San-Francisco-Bay--Spanish and English, Calif Hist, Vol 0072, 93; The Pueblo Revolt of 1680--Conquest and Resistance in 17th-Century New-Mexico, Jour W, Vol 0036, 97; Hail, Columbia--Gray, Robert, Kendrick, John and the Pacific Fur Trade, Pacific Hist Rev, Vol 0064, 95; They Are Coming--The Conquest of Mexico, Jour W, Vol 0034, 95. **CONTACT ADDRESS** 2508 Harold Place NE, Albuquerque, NM 87106. **EMAIL** dcutter@unm.edu

CUTTLER, CHARLES DAVID
PERSONAL Born 04/08/1913, Cleveland, OH, 1 child **DISCIPLINE** HISTORY OF ART **EDUCATION** NYork Univ, PhD(art hist), 52. **CAREER** Asst art hist, Ohio State Univ, 35-37;

asst prof, Mich State Univ, 47-57; assoc prof hist of art, 57-65, res prof, 65-66, 75-76 & 82, Prof Hist of Art, Univ Iowa, 65-, Sr Fulbright fel, Belgium, 65-66; consult, Nat Endowment for Humanities, 73-; guest lectr Europe, 66 & 76 & Japan, 79. **MEMBERSHIPS** Col Art Asn Am; Renaissance Soc Am; Mediaeval Acad Am; Midwest Art Hist Soc (pres, 73-77). **RESEARCH** Medieval art; late medieval art. **SELECTED PUBLICATIONS** Auth, Holbein Inscriptions, Sixteenth Century Jour, Vol 0024, 93. **CONTACT ADDRESS** Sch of Art & Art Hist, Univ of Iowa, Iowa City, IA 52242.

CUVALO, ANTE
PERSONAL Born, Bosnia/Herzegovina, m, 2 children **DISCIPLINE** HISTORY **EDUCATION** St Francis Col, BA, 68; John Carroll Univ, MA, 83; Ohio State Univ, PhD, 87. **CAREER** Lectr, Ohio State Univ, 87-91; prof, Joliet Jr Coll. **MEMBERSHIPS** AAASS; ACS; CAA. **RESEARCH** Croatia; Bosnia and Herzegovina; Balkans; US Emigration. **SELECTED PUBLICATIONS** Auth, The Croatian National Movement, 1966-1972, Hist Dictionary of Bosnia and Herzegovina; coauth, ed, Croatia and the Croatians, Removing the Mask, in press; contr, assoc ed, American Croatian Rev. **CONTACT ADDRESS** Dept Sociology, Behavioral Sci, Joliet Junior Col, 1215 Houbolt Rd, Joliet, IL 60431-8938. **EMAIL** cuv@netzero.com

CVORNYEK, BOB
DISCIPLINE AFRICAN-AMERICAN, LABOR HISTORY **EDUCATION** Univ Del, BA; Columbia Univ, MPhil, PhD. **CAREER** Instr, RI Col. **RESEARCH** 19th-20th century African-Am and labor. **SELECTED PUBLICATIONS** Coed, A Documentary History of the Black Worker: From the AFL-CIO Merger to the Present. **CONTACT ADDRESS** Rhode Island Col, Providence, RI 02908.

CYR, MARY
PERSONAL Born Fargo, ND **DISCIPLINE** MUSIC, HISTORY **EDUCATION** Univ Calif, BA, 68, MA, 70, PhD, 75. **CAREER** Prof, McGill Univ, 76-92, dir grad studs, 91-92; prof & ch, Music, Univ Guelph, 92-. **HONORS AND AWARDS** Noah Greenberg Awd Excellence, Am Musicological Soc. **MEMBERSHIPS** Can Univ Music Soc; Early Music Soc; Am Musicological Soc. **SELECTED PUBLICATIONS** Auth, Performing Baroque Music, 92; auth, Violin Playing in Late Seventeenth-Century England: Baltzar, Matteis and Purcell in Performance Practice Review 8:1, 95. **CONTACT ADDRESS** Dept of Fine Art & Music, Univ of Guelph, Guelph, ON, Canada N1G 2W1. **EMAIL** mcyr@arts.uoguelph.ca

CZUMA, STANISLAW
PERSONAL Born 10/26/1935, Warsaw, m, 1962, 1 child **DISCIPLINE** ART OF INDIA AND SOUTHEAST ASIA **EDUCATION** Jagiellon Univ, BA; MA; Univ Mich, PhD, 69. **CAREER** Art, Cleveland Mus of Art; Case Western Univ. **HONORS AND AWARDS** Paderewski Found; National Defense; Ford Found; Am Inst Indian Studies; Am Philos Soc; George P. Bickford grant; Andrew W. Mellon grant. **RESEARCH** Indian Sculpture. **SELECTED PUBLICATIONS** Auth, Bull Cleveland Mus Art; auth, Indian Art from the George P. Bickford Collection, CMA, 75; auth, Kushan Sculpture, CMA, 85; auth, Masterworks of Asian Art, CMA, 98. **CONTACT ADDRESS** Cleveland Mus of Art, 11150 East Blvd, Cleveland, OH 44106. **EMAIL** czuma@cma-oh.org

D

D'AGOSTINO, ANTHONY W.
DISCIPLINE HISTORY **EDUCATION** Univ Calif, BA, 59, MA, 61; Univ Calif at Los Angeles, PhD, 71. **CAREER** Prof hist, San Fran State Univ. **HONORS AND AWARDS** Res fel NEH & State Dept & Hoover Inst. **MEMBERSHIPS** Hist Soc; Am Hist Soc; World Asn Int Student. **RESEARCH** Nineteenth & Twentieth century international history, The Russian revolution. **SELECTED PUBLICATIONS** Auth, Sovet Succession Struggles, (88); auth, Gorbachev's Revolution, 1985-1991, (98); auth, The Russian Revolution, 1917-1945, (00). **CONTACT ADDRESS** Dept Hist, San Francisco State Univ, 1600 Holloway Ave, San Francisco, CA 94132-1722. **EMAIL** dagostin@sfsu.edu

D'AGOSTINO, PETER R.
PERSONAL Born 12/22/1962, New York, NY, s **DISCIPLINE** RELIGIOUS STUDIES; HISTORY **EDUCATION** Brown Univ, BA, 80-84; Univ Chicago, MA, 86-87; Univ Chicago, PhD, 87-93 **CAREER** Visiting asst prof, Univ Ill, 94-95; asst prof Relig Studies & History, Stonehill Col, 95 **HONORS AND AWARDS** PEW Grant for Relig in Amer History, 98-99; Fulbright Jr Fac Res Fel, 96; Jr Fel, Univ Chic, 91-92; Giovanni Agnelli Found Italian Amer Studies Fel, 90-91; John T. McNeil Fel, 88-89 **MEMBERSHIPS** Orgn Amer Historians; Immigration History Soc; Amer Italian Historical Assoc; Amer Cath Historical Assoc; Amer Soc Church History; Amer Acad Relig **RESEARCH** U.S. Immigration History; U.S. Religious History; U.S. Society, 1877-1945; Modern Italy **SELECTED PUBLICATIONS** "The Sacraments of Whiteness: Racial Ambiguity and Religious Discipline Among Italians in Urban America," Religion and the City, forthcoming; "Urban Restructuring and the Religious Adaptation: Cardinal Joseph Bernardin of Chicago (1982-1995)," Public Religion and Urban Transformation, NY Univ Pr, forthcoming; "The Crisis of Authority in American Catholicism: Urban Schools and Cultural Conflict," Records of the American Catholic Historical Association of Philadelphia, forthcoming **CONTACT ADDRESS** 22 Bradbury St, Allston, MA 02134. **EMAIL** pdagostino@stonehill.edu

D'ALLAIRE, MICHELINE
PERSONAL Born 04/23/1938, Montreal, PQ, Canada **DISCIPLINE** HISTORY **EDUCATION** Univ Montreal, BA, MA; Univ Ottawa, PhD. **CAREER** Prof, 65-86, prof Titulaire D'histoire, Univ Ottawa, 86-. **RESEARCH** Canadian history; Quebec history; socio-religious history. **SELECTED PUBLICATIONS** Auth, Talon, 70; auth, L'Hopital-General de Quebec, 1692-1764, 71; auth, Montee et declin d'une famille noble: Les Ruette d'Auteuil, 1617-1737, 80; auth, La Crise des communautes religieuses, 83; auth, Les Dots des religieuses au Canada francais, 1639-1800, 86; auth, Les communautes religieuses a Montreal, Tome I: L'assistance sociale a Montreal, 1659-1900, 97. **CONTACT ADDRESS** History Dept, Univ of Ottawa, 155 Seraphim Marion, Ottawa, ON, Canada K1N 6N5.

D'ELIA, DONALD JOHN
PERSONAL Born 06/16/1933, Jersey City, NJ, m, 1957, 4 children **DISCIPLINE** AMERICAN HISTORY **EDUCATION** Rutgers Univ, BA, 56, MA, 57; Pa State Univ, PhD, 65. **CAREER** Teaching asst hist, Pa State Univ, 59-61; from asst prof to assoc prof social studies, Bloomsburg State Col, 61-65; assoc prof, 65-71, prof hist, SUNY New Paltz, 71-; Boyd Lee Spahr lect Americana, Dickinson Col, 66; fac res fel, State Univ NY, 68, 74. **MEMBERSHIPS** Am Catholic Hist Asn; Fellowship Catholic Scholars. **RESEARCH** Early American scientific and religious thought; American intellectual history; the American Revolution. **SELECTED PUBLICATIONS** Auth, Dr Benjamin Rush and the Negro, J Hist Ideas, 7/69; auth, Dr Benjamin Rush, David Hartley, and the Revolutionary Uses of Psychology, Proc Am Philos Soc, 4/70; auth, Jefferson, Rush and the Limits of Philosophical Friendship, Proc Am Philos Soc, 10/73; auth, Benjamin Rush: Philosopher of the American Revolution, Trans Am Philos Soc, 74. **CONTACT ADDRESS** Dept of History, SUNY, New Paltz, New Paltz, NY 12561.

D'EVELYN, MARGARET M.
PERSONAL Born 08/23/1948, Brookline, MA, m, 1970, 1 child **DISCIPLINE** HISTORY OF ART **EDUCATION** Princeton Univ, PhD 94. **CAREER** Author **RESEARCH** 15th, 16th century illustrated architectural books; art and architecture of renaissance. Venice **SELECTED PUBLICATIONS** Auth, Venice as Vitruvius's City in Daniele Barbaro's Commentaries, Studi Venezian, 96. **CONTACT ADDRESS** 48 Pratt St, Providence, RI 02906. **EMAIL** mdevelyn@cs.com

DAHLSTRAND, FREDERICK CHARLES
PERSONAL Born 07/22/1945, Corry, PA, m, 1989, 1 child **DISCIPLINE** AMERICAN HISTORY **EDUCATION** Thiel Col, Ba, 67; Univ KS, MPhil, 76, PhD, 77. **CAREER** From asst prof to assoc prof hist and assoc dean, OH State Univ, Mansfield. **HONORS AND AWARDS** Univ Distinguished Tchg Awd, 83. **RESEARCH** Am transcendentalism; impact of sci and technol on Am thought. **SELECTED PUBLICATIONS** Auth, Amos Bronson Alcott: An Intellectual Biography, Fairleigh-Dickinson Univ Press, 82. **CONTACT ADDRESS** Dept of Hist, Ohio State Univ, Mansfield, 1680 University Dr, Mansfield, OH 44906-1547. **EMAIL** dahlstrand.1@osu.edu

DAILY, JONATHAN
PERSONAL Born 05/07/1958, Port Chester, NY, m, 1989, 2 children **DISCIPLINE** HISTORY **EDUCATION** Universite de Montreal, BA, 83; Georgetown Univ, MA, 86; Harvard Univ, AM, 87, PhD, 92. **CAREER** Tutor, 88-92, Senior Thesis Adv, 91-92, Harvard Univ; lectr to asst prof to assoc chemn, Univ Ill, 92-. **HONORS AND AWARDS** HF Guggenheim Res Grant, 95-96. **MEMBERSHIPS** Am Assoc Adv Slavic Stud. **RESEARCH** Political, institutional, and legal history of late Imperial Russia and early Soviet history. **SELECTED PUBLICATIONS** Auth, art, On the Significance of Emergency Legislation in Late Imperial Russia, 95; auth, Autocracy under Siege: Security Police and Opposition in Russia, 1866-1905, 98. **CONTACT ADDRESS** Dept of History, Univ of Illinois, Chicago, UH 913, Chicago, IL 60607-7109. **EMAIL** daly@uic.edu

DAIN, NORMAN
PERSONAL Born 10/05/1925, Brooklyn, NY, m, 1950, 1 child **DISCIPLINE** AMERICAN HISTORY **EDUCATION** Brooklyn Col, BA, 53; Columbia Univ, MA, 57, PhD, 61. **CAREER** Res asst psychiat, Med Col, Cornell Univ, 58-61; from instr to assoc prof, 61-68, Prof Am Hist, Rutgers Univ, Newark, 68-, Mem ed staff, Hist Behav Sci Newslett, 60-65; Rutgers Univ Res Coun fac fels, 66-67 & 71-72; Soc Sci Res Coun grant-in-aid, 63-65; mem ed bd, J Hist Behav Sci, 65-81; NIH res grant, 66-69; sem assoc, Columbia Univ, 66-; res assoc, Med Col, Cornell Univ, 68-76, adj prof, 76- **MEMBERSHIPS** AHA; Am Asn Hist Med; Orgn Am Historians; Int Soc Hist Behav & Soc Sci; AAUP. **RESEARCH** American intellectual history; history of psychiatric thought; social history of the United States. **SELECTED PUBLICATIONS** Coauth, Social Class and Psychological Medicine in the United States, 1789-1824, Bull Hist Med, 9-10/59; Moral Insanity in the United States, 1835-1866, Am J Psychiat, 3/62; auth, Concepts of Insanity in the United States, 1789-1865, Rutgers Univ, 64; Disordered Minds: The First Century of Eastern State Hospital in Williamsburg, Virginia, 1766-1866, Colonial Williamsburg Found & Univ Va, 71; American Psychiatry in the Eighteenth Century, In: American Psychiatry: Past, Present and Future, Univ Press Va, 75; From Colonial America to Bicentennial America: Two Centuries of Vicissitudes in the Institutional Care of Mental Patients, Bull NY Acad Med, 12/76; The Chronic Patient in Nineteenth-Century Mental Institutions, Psychiat Annals, 9/80; Clifford W Beers, Advocate for the Insane, Univ Pittsburgh Press, 80. **CONTACT ADDRESS** Dept of History, Rutgers, The State Univ of New Jersey, Newark, Newark, NJ 07102.

DALE, WILLIAM S. A.
PERSONAL Born 09/18/1921, Toronto, ON, Canada **DISCIPLINE** ART HISTORY **EDUCATION** Univ Toronto, BA, 44, MA, 46; Harvard Univ, PhD, 55; Courtauld Inst, London Univ, 48-50. **CAREER** Staff, 50-57, asst dir, 61-66, dep dir, Nat Gallery Can, 66-67; curator, Art Gallery Toronto, 57-59; dir, Vancouver Art Gallery, 59-61; prof 67-87, dept ch, 67-75, 85-87, Prof Emer Visual Arts, Univ Western Ont, 87-; res fel, Dumbarton Oaks Res Libr, Washington, 56-57. **MEMBERSHIPS** Arts & Letters Club Toronto; Col Art Asn Am; Medieval Acad Am; Royal Soc Arts; Int Ctr Medieval Art; Univ Art Asn Can. **SELECTED PUBLICATIONS** Contribur, Apollo; contribur, Art Bull; contribur, Brit Mus Yearbk; contribur, Burlington Mag; contribur, Can Art; contribur, RACAR; contribur, Speculum. **CONTACT ADDRESS** Dept Visual Arts, Univ Western Ontario, 1151 Richmond St, Ste 2, London, ON, Canada N6A 5B8. **EMAIL** wdale@uwo.ca

DALES, RICHARD C.
PERSONAL Born 04/17/1926, Akron, OH, m, 1950, 2 children **DISCIPLINE** HISTORY **EDUCATION** Univ Rochester, BA, 49; Univ Colo, MA, 52, PhD, 55. **CAREER** Instr hist, NDak Agr Col, 54-55; from instr to assoc prof, Lewis & Clark Col, 55-64; assoc prof, 64-66, Prof Hist, Univ Southern Calif, 66-, Am Coun Learned Soc fel, 60-61; vis assoc prof, Univ Southern Calif, 62-63; mem, Inst Advan Studies, 66-67; Am Philos Soc fel, 68. **MEMBERSHIPS** Medieval Acad Am. **RESEARCH** Medieval intellectual history; history of science. **SELECTED PUBLICATIONS** Auth, Roberti Grosseteste commentarius in octo libros physicorum Aristotelis, Univ Colo, 63; Robert Grosseteste's scientific works, 61 & Anonymi de elementis, 65, Isis: Grosseteste's views on astrology, Mediaeval Studies, 67; The achievement of medieval science, Univ Pa, 73; ed, Marius on the Elements, Univ Calif, 76; auth, A medieval view of human dignity, J Hist of Ideas, 77. **CONTACT ADDRESS** Dept of Hist, Univ of So California, Los Angeles, CA 90007.

DALEY, BRIAN EDWARD
PERSONAL Born 01/18/1940, Orange, NJ **DISCIPLINE** HISTORICAL THEOLOGY, CHURCH HISTORY **EDUCATION** Fordham Univ, BA, 61; Oxford Univ, BA, 64, MA, 67, DPhil(theol), 79; Loyola Sem, PhL, 66; Hochschule Sankt Georgen, Frankfurt, Lic theol, 72. **CAREER** Instr classics, Fordham Univ, 66-67; Asst Prof Hist Theol, Weston Sch Theol, 78-, Ed, Traditio, 78-; trustee, Le Moyne Col, 79- **MEMBERSHIPS** Asn Int Etudes Patristiques; Am Soc Church Hist; Soc Values Higher Educ; Am Asn Rhodes Scholars. **RESEARCH** Greek patristic theology; history of spirituality; Neoplatonism. **SELECTED PUBLICATIONS** Auth, Position and Patronage in the Early-Church--Distinguishing Between Personal or Moral Authority and Canonical or Structural Jurisdiction in the Early-Christian Community and Civil-Society--The Original Meaning of Primacy-Of-Honor, Jour Theol; Regnum-Caelorum--Patterns of Future Hope in Early Christianity, Jour Theol Stud, Vol 0045, 94; Apollo as a Chalcedonian--Tracing the Trajectory of a Christian Oracle and Christological Apologia--A New Fragment of a Controversial Work From Early 6th-Century Constantinople, Traditio-Stud Ancient and Medieval Hist Thought and Rel. **CONTACT ADDRESS** Dept of Hist Theol, Weston Jesuit Sch of Theol, Cambridge, MA 02138.

DALLEK, ROBERT
PERSONAL Born 05/16/1934, Brooklyn, NY, m, 1965 **DISCIPLINE** AMERICAN DIPLOMATIC HISTORY **EDUCATION** Univ Ill, BA, 55; Columbia Univ, MA, 57, PhD, 64; Oxford Univ, Honorary MA, 95. **CAREER** Lectr hist, City Col New York, 58-60; instr, Columbia Univ, 60-64; from asst prof to assoc prof, 64-73, Grad Advisor, Dept of Hist, UCLA, 66-68, Vice Chairman, Dept of Hist, 72-74; Prof Hist, Univ Calif, Los Angeles, 73-94; Vis prof, Calif Inst of Technology, Spring, 93; Harmsworth Vis Prof, Univ of Oxford, 94-95; Vis Prof, LBJ Sch of Public Affairs, Univ of Tex, 96; Prof, Boston Univ, 96-. **HONORS AND AWARDS** John Simon Guggenheim Fel, 73-74; Sr Fel, Nat Endowment for the Humanities, 76-77; Bancroft Prize, Franklin D. Roosevelt and Am Foreign Policy 1932-

1945, 80; Humanities Fel, Rockefeller Found, 81-82; Henry L. Eby Awd for the Art of Teaching, UCLA, 84; Fel, Am Coun of Learned Societies, 84-85; Elected Fel, Am Acad of Arts and Sciences, 94; Herbert Marcuse Lecture in Modern Hist, Brandeis Univ, 99; The University's Endowed Annual Lect, Boston Univ, 99. **MEMBERSHIPS** AHA; Orgn Am Historians; Soc Hist Am Foreign Relat. **RESEARCH** Franklin D Roosevelt's diplomacy. **SELECTED PUBLICATIONS** Auth, Democrat and Diploma: The Life of William E. Dodd, Oxford University Press, 68; ed., Western Europe, Vol. 1 of The Dynamics of World Power: A Documentary History of United States, Foreign Policy, 1945-1973, Chelsea House/McGraw Hill, 73; auth, Franklin D. Roosevelt and American Foreign Policy, 1932-1945, Oxford Univ Press, 79, 2nd ed. 95; auth, The American Style of Foreign Policy: Cultural Politics and Foreign Affairs, Alfred A. Knopf, 83, New American Library, 85, Oxford Univ press, 91; auth, Ronald Reagan: The Politics of Symbolism, Harvard Univ Press, 84; auth, Part Six of The Great Republic: A History of the American People, 85, 4th 91; auth, Lone Star Rising: Lyndon Johnson and His Times, 1908-1960, Oxford Univ Press, 91; assoc ed, The Encyclopedia of 20th-Century American History, Simon & Schuster, 95; auth, Hail to the Chief: The Making and Unmaking of American Presidents, Hyperion, 96; auth, Flawed Giant: Lyndon Johnson and His Times, 1961-73, Oxford Univ Press, 98; auth, Ronald Reagan: The Politics of Symbolism, Harvard Univ Press, 99. **CONTACT ADDRESS** Los Angeles, CA 90024.

DALSTROM, HARL A.
PERSONAL Born 04/11/1936, Omaha, NE **DISCIPLINE** UNITED STATES HISTORY **EDUCATION** Munic Univ Omaha, BA, 58, MA, 59; Univ Nebr, PhD(hist), 65. **CAREER** Instr hist, 63-65, from asst prof to assoc prof, 65-74, chmn dept, 71-75, Prof Hist, Univ Nebr, Omaha, 74-. **MEMBERSHIPS** Orgn Am Historians; Southern Hist Asn; Western Hist Asn; Agr Hist Soc. **RESEARCH** Regional, state, and local history. **SELECTED PUBLICATIONS** Auth, Eugene C. Eppley: His Life and Legacy, 69; auth, A.V. Sorensen and the New Omaha, 88. **CONTACT ADDRESS** Dept of Hist, Univ of Nebraska, Omaha, 6001 Dodge St, Omaha, NE 68182-0002. **EMAIL** kdalstrom@msn.com

DALTON, KATHLEEN MARY
PERSONAL Born 11/18/1948, Martinez, CA, m, 1981 **DISCIPLINE** AMERICAN HISTORY & STUDIES **EDUCATION** Mills Col, AB, 70; Johns Hopkins Univ, MA, 75, PhD(Am hist), 79. **CAREER** Instr hist, Hartford Col for Women, 76, Nat Cathedral Sch, 73-74 & 78-79; adj prof hist & Am studies, Am Univ, 79-80; Instr Hist & Soc Sci, Phillips Acad, 80-, Consult, Nat Geog Soc, 79-80; assoc ed, Psychohist Rev, 81- **MEMBERSHIPS** Orgn Am Historians; AHA; Coord Comt Women in Hist Profession; Am Studies Asn; Group for Use of Psychol in Hist. **RESEARCH** American social, intellectual and cultural history; Theodore Roosevelt and his America; sex roles in recent United States history. **SELECTED PUBLICATIONS** Auth, Ives,Charles--My Fathers Song--A Psychoanalytic Biography, Amer Hist Rev, Vol 0098, 93; The Inner World of Lincoln,Abraham, Amer Hist Rev, Vol 0101, 96; Icons of Democracy--American Leaders as Heroes, Aristocrats, Dissenters, and Democrats, Jour Interdisciplinary Hist, Vol 0025, 95. **CONTACT ADDRESS** Phillips Acad, 137 Main St, Andover, MA 01810.

DALY, JOHN P.
DISCIPLINE HISTORY **EDUCATION** Univ VA, BA, 86; Rice Univ, MA, PhD 93. **CAREER** Am hist instr, Univ St Thomas, 90-94; col instr, Univ Houston, 91-92; Am hist instr, Tex Southern Univ, 93-94; relig and hist instr, Rice Univ, 92-95; hist adj, Univ Houston, 94-95; vis asst prof, Austin Col, 95-96; asst prof, La Tech Univ, 96-. **HONORS AND AWARDS** Barbara Field Kennedy Awd in Am Hist, 93. **RESEARCH** Am hist; Am intellectual and cult hist; southern hist. **SELECTED PUBLICATIONS** Auth, Redeeming America, Jour of Southern Hist, 95; Henry Hughes and Proslavery, Jour of Southern Hist, 95; Virtue is Power: Sectionalism, Slavery, and the Moral Culture of Antebellum America, 1830-1865, Univ Ky. **CONTACT ADDRESS** Dept of Hist, Louisiana Tech Univ, PO Box 3178, Ruston, LA 71272.

DALY, LAWRENCE JOHN
PERSONAL Born 02/07/1938, Middletown, OH, m, 1960, 4 children **DISCIPLINE** HISTORY **EDUCATION** Xavier Univ, Ohio, AB, 60, MA, 61; Loyola Univ, Ill, PhD(hist), 70. **CAREER** From instr to asst prof, 65-72, asoc prof hist, Bowling Green State Univ, 72- **MEMBERSHIPS** Soc Prom Roman Studies; Asn Ancient Historians. **RESEARCH** Late Roman Empire; the pagan opposition; imperial ideology. **SELECTED PUBLICATIONS** Auth, Themistius' Plea for Religious Tolerance, Greek Roman & Byzantine Studies, 71; The Mandarin and the Barbarian: Themistius' Response to the Gothic Challenge, 72 & Verginius at Vesontio: The Incongruity of the Bellum Neronis, 75, Historia; Themistius' Concept of Philanthropia, Byzantion, 75; Varro Murena, cos 23 BC: (magistratu motus) est, Historia, 78. **CONTACT ADDRESS** Dept of Hist, Bowling Green State Univ, 1001 E Wooster St, Bowling Green, OH 43403-0001. **EMAIL** ldaly@bgnet.bgsu.edu

DALY, WILLIAM M.
PERSONAL Born 12/27/1920, Great Barrington, MA, m, 1947, 3 children **DISCIPLINE** HISTORY **EDUCATION** Boston Col, BA, 42, MA, 47; Brown Univ, PhD, 55. **CAREER** From instr to assoc prof, 47-71, Prof Hist, Boston Col, 71-, Vis assoc prof hist, Brown Univ, 60; fac res fel, Boston Col, 61-62; Am Coun Learned Soc fel, 68-69. **MEMBERSHIPS** Mediaeval Acad Am; AHA. **RESEARCH** Early Medieval France, especially political and social thought; Medieval English constitutional history. **SELECTED PUBLICATIONS** Auth, Clovis--A Portrayal of the First Frankish King of Gaul Through Primary and Secondary Source Material--How Barbaric, How Pagan, Speculum-A Jour Medieval Stud, Vol 0069, 94. **CONTACT ADDRESS** Dept of Hist, Boston Col, Chestnut Hill, Chestnut Hill, MA 02167.

DAMERON, GEORGE WILLIAMSON
PERSONAL Born Durham, NC, m, 1984, 1 child **DISCIPLINE** HISTORY **EDUCATION** Duke Univ, BA, 75; Harvard Univ,AM, 79, PhD, 83. **CAREER** Asst prof, 83-87, 87-; Assoc prof, 91-, Prof, 97-,St. Michael's Col. **HONORS AND AWARDS** Sch.& Artistic Achievement Awd, Numerous Saint Michael's Col Fac Develop Grants; Am Philos Soc; Nat Endowment Hum, Fel, Harvard Ctr Italian Renaissance Studies; Harvard Lehman Fund Grad Sch Fel. **SELECTED PUBLICATIONS** Auth, Episcopal Power and Florentine Society, 1000-1320, Harvard Univ Press, 91. **CONTACT ADDRESS** Dept of History, Saint Michael's Col, Winooski Park, Colchester, VT 05439. **EMAIL** gdameron@smcvt.edu

DANBOM, DAVID BYERS
PERSONAL Born 03/29/1947, Denver, CO, m, 1971, 2 children **DISCIPLINE** AMERICAN HISTORY **EDUCATION** CO State Univ, BA, 69; Stanford Univ, MA, 70, PhD, 74. **CAREER** Prof Am hist, ND, State Univ, 74, Assoc ed, NDak Inst Regional Studies, 81-92. **HONORS AND AWARDS** Fargo Chamber of Commerce Distinguished Prof, 90; CASE ND Prof of the Year, 1990; NDSU Fac Lectr, 98. **MEMBERSHIPS** Orgn Am Historians; Agr Hist Soc. **RESEARCH** Progressivism; rural and agricultural hist; ND hist. **SELECTED PUBLICATIONS** Auth, The Resisted Revolution: Urban America and the Industrialization of Agriculture, 1900-1930, Iowa State Univ Press, 79; The World of Hope: Progressives and the Struggle for an Ethical Public Life, Temple Univ Press, 87; Our Purpose Is to Serve: The First Century of the North Dakota Agricultural Experiment Station, NDIRS, 90; Born in the Country: A History of Rural America, Johns Hopkins Univ press, 95. **CONTACT ADDRESS** Dept of Hist, No Dakota State Univ, PO Box 5075, Fargo, ND 58105-5075. **EMAIL** danbom@plains.nodak.edu

DANDO, WILLIAM
PERSONAL Born 06/13/1934, Newell, PA, m, 1958, 3 children **DISCIPLINE** GEOGRAPHY, GEOLOGY **EDUCATION** Calif State Univ, BS, 59; Univ Minn, MA, 62; Univ Miss, PhD, 69. **CAREER** Prof, Ind State Univ, 89-. **HONORS AND AWARDS** Distinguished Teaching Achievement Awd, NCGE, 84; Burlington Northern Found Fac Achievement Awd, Univ NDak, 88; Outstanding Teacher Awd, AAG, 95; Phi Sigma Psi; Gamma Theta Upsilon. **MEMBERSHIPS** AAG, NCGE, HAST, IASS, GENI. **RESEARCH** Hunger and famine in Russia, CIS and developing nations, multiple sclerosis. **SELECTED PUBLICATIONS** Coauth, Russia and the Independent Nations of the Former U S S R: Geofact and Maps, William C Brown, Inc (Dubuque, IA), 95; auth, "Population, Hunger and Famine: Critical Issues for the 21st Century," Tension Areas of the World, 2nd ed, Park Pr (97): 15-33; auth, "Changing Geographic Personality of Indiana," Renaissance in the Heartland: The Ind Experience, NCGE Pr (98): 1-8; coauth, "Biblical Geography: An Application of Geographic Concepts and Methods to Enhance Understanding of Biblical Lands and Peoples," Geog in Am at the Dawn of the 21st Century, Oxford UP (99). **CONTACT ADDRESS** Dept Geog & Geol, Indiana State Univ, 210 N 7th St, Terre Haute, IN 47809-0002.

DANIEL, CLETUS EDWARD
PERSONAL Born 12/26/1943, Salinas, CA, m, 1976, 2 children **DISCIPLINE** HISTORY **EDUCATION** San Jose State Univ, BA, 67, MA, 69; Univ Washington, PhD, 72. **CAREER** Vis asst prof, hist, Univ Wash, 73; asst prof, 73-79, assos prof, 79-88, prof, 88 -, Sch Indus and Labor Rel, Cornell Univ. **HONORS AND AWARDS** Magna cum laude; Woodrow Wilson Diss Fel, 71-72; NEH Fel, 74-75; ACLS Fellowship, 76; ILR Excellence in Teaching Awd, 79-80, 82-83; Univ Paramount Prof for Tchg Excellence, 92-93. **MEMBERSHIPS** Ed Bd, Labor History; ed consult NY State Labor Legacy Project. **SELECTED PUBLICATIONS** Auth, The ACLU and the Wagner Act: An Inquiry into the Depression-Era Crisis of American Liberalism, ILR Press, 81; auth, Bitter Harvest: A History of California Farmworkers, 1870-1941, Cornell, 81; auth, Cesar Chavez, in Dubofsky, ed, Labor Leaders in Industrial America, Univ Ill, 87; auth, Cesar Chavez and the Unionization of California Farm Workers, in Nash, ed, Retracing the Past: Readings in the History of the American People, v.2, 2d ed, Harper & Row, 90; auth, Chicano Workers and the Politics of Fairness: The FEPC in the Southwest, 1941-1945, Univ Texas, 91; auth, Cesar Chavez and California Farm Workers, in Cornford, ed, Working People of California, Univ Calif, 95; auth, Communist Involvement in Agricultural Labor Struggles, in Chan, ed, Major Problems in California History: Documents and Essays, Houghton Mifflin, 97; auth, "Culture of Misfortune: An Interpretive History of Textile Unionism in the United States," Cornell University Press, forthcoming. **CONTACT ADDRESS** School of Industrial and Labor Relations, Cornell Univ, Ithaca, NY 14853.

DANIEL, MARCUS L.
DISCIPLINE HISTORY **EDUCATION** Cambridge Univ, BA, 84; Princeton Univ, MA, 89, PhD, 97. **CAREER** ASST PROF, HIST, UNIV HAWAII MANOA **MEMBERSHIPS** Am Antiquarian Soc **SELECTED PUBLICATIONS** Auth, "Ribaldry and Billingsgate: Popular Journalism and Political Culture in the Early Republic, 97. **CONTACT ADDRESS** Dept of Hist, Coll of Arts & Human, Univ of Hawaii, Manoa, 2530 Dole St, Honolulu, HI 96822. **EMAIL** mdaniel@hawaii.edu

DANIEL, PETE
PERSONAL Born 11/24/1938, Rocky Mount, NC **DISCIPLINE** SOUTHERN UNITED STATES AND AGRICULTURAL HISTORY **EDUCATION** Wake Forest Univ, BA, 61, MA, 62; Univ Md, College Park, PhD(hist), 70. **CAREER** Instr hist, Univ NC, Wilmington, 63-66; asst ed, Booker T Washington Papers, Univ Md, 69-70; Nat Endowment for Humanities fel Afro-Am hist, Johns Hopkins Univ, 70-71; asst prof, Univ Tenn, Knoxville, 71-73, assoc prof, 73-78, prof, 78; FEL, Woodrow Wilson Int Ctr Scholars, 79-, Vis prof hist, Univ Mass, Boston, 74-75; Nat Endowment for Humanities Independent Study res fel, 78-79; consult, US Dept Educ, 81 & Smithsonian Inst, 81. **HONORS AND AWARDS** Louis Pelzer Prize, Orgn Am Historians, 70. **MEMBERSHIPS** Orgn Am Historians; AHA; Southern History Asn. **RESEARCH** United States Southern history; agricultural history. **SELECTED PUBLICATIONS** Auth, Black Power in the 1920's: The Case of Tuskegee Veterans Hospital, J Southern Hist, 8/70; Up From Slavery and Down to Peonage: The Alonzo Bailey Case, J Am Hist, 12/70; co-ed, The Booker T Washington Papers, Univ Ill, Vol II, 72; auth, The Shadow of Slavery: Peonage in the South, 1901-1969, Univ Ill, 72 & Oxford, 73; coauth, A Talent for Detail: The Photographs of Miss Frances B Johnston, 1889-1910, Harmony, 74; auth, Deep'n as it Come: The 1927 Mississippi Flood, Oxford Univ, 77; The Metamorphosis of Slavery, 1865-1900, J Am Hist, 6/79; The Transformation of the Rural South, 1930 to the Present, Agr Hist, 7/81. **CONTACT ADDRESS** Natl Museum Amer Hist, Smithsonian Inst, Div Agr and Nat Resour, Washington, DC 20560.

DANIEL, WILBON HARRISON
PERSONAL Born 09/25/1922, Lynchburg, VA, m, 1950, 1 child **DISCIPLINE** AMERICAN HISTORY **EDUCATION** Lynchburg Col, BA, 44; Vanderbilt Univ, BD, 46, MA, 47; Duke Univ, PhD(Am hist, Am Christianity), 57. **CAREER** Teacher hist, Va Intermont Col, 47-54; from instr to assoc prof, 56-69, chmn dept, 69-74, prof, 69-80, William Binford Vest Prof Hist, Univ Richmond, 80-93; William Bonford West, hist, emer, 93. **MEMBERSHIPS** AHA; Southern Hist Asn; Orgn Am Historians. **RESEARCH** Civil War period; American church history; 19th century United States. **SELECTED PUBLICATIONS** Auth, Bible Publication and Procurement in the Confederacy, J Southern Hist, 5/58; Southern Presbyterians in the Confederacy, NC Hist Rev, summer 67; Protestantism and Patriotism in the Confederacy, Miss Quart, spring 71; the Methodist Episcopal Church and the Negro in the Early National Period, Methodist Hist, 7/73; Southern Presbyterians and the Negro in the Early National Period, J Negro Hist, 7/73; Virginia Baptists and the Myth of the Southern Mind, 1865-1900, Satlantic Quart, winter 74; The Response of the Church of England to the Civil War and Reconstruction in America, Hist Mag of Protestant Episcopal Church, 3/78; Old Lynchburg College, 1855-1869, Va Mag Hist & biog, 10/80; auth, Jimmie Foxx, The Life and Times of a Baseball Hall of Famer, 1907-1967, Jefferson, McFarland and Company, Inc., Publishers (North Carolina), 96. **CONTACT ADDRESS** Dept of Hist, Univ of Richmond, Richmond, VA 23173.

DANIELL, JERE
PERSONAL Born 11/28/1932, Millinocket, ME, m, 1969, 5 children **DISCIPLINE** HISTORY **EDUCATION** Dartmouth Col, AB, 55; Harvard Univ, PhD, 64. **CAREER** From asst prof to Class of 1925 Prof, Dartmouth Col, 64-. **HONORS AND AWARDS** Who's Who in Am; NH Notables. **RESEARCH** Early American History; History of New England. **SELECTED PUBLICATIONS** Auth, "How Did They Begin and Who Owns Them Anyway," Yankee Homes, 87; auth, "Charitable Giving in New Hampshire: A Brief History," Annual Report of the New Hampshire Charitable Funds, 87; auth, "Counting Noses: Delagate Sentiment in New Hampshire's Ratifying Convention," Historical New Hampshire, (88): 136-155; auth, "Frontier and Constitution: Why Grafton County Delegates Voted 10-1 for Ratification," Historical New Hampshire, (90): 207-229; auth, "A Sense of Place: Lobstermen, Milltowns and Witchcraft Shape New England Still," Dartmouth Alumni Magazine, (90): 14-15; auth, "New Hampshire," in Encyclopedia Britannica, 91; auth, "Introduction," in Indian Stream Republic:

Selling a New England Frontier, 1785-1842, 97; auth, "New Hampshire" and "Town Meeting," in Encyclopedia of New England Culture, forthcoming. **CONTACT ADDRESS** Dept Hist, Dartmouth Col, 6107 Reed Hall, Hanover, NH 03755-3506. **EMAIL** jere.r.daniell@dartmouth.edu

DANIELS, BRUCE C.
PERSONAL Born 08/27/1943, Baldwin, NY **DISCIPLINE** HISTORY **EDUCATION** Syracuse Univ, AB, 64; Univ Conn, MA, 67, PhD, 70. **CAREER** PROF HISTORY, UNIV WINNIPEG, 70-. **HONORS AND AWARDS** Awd merit, Am Asn State Local Hist, 90; Homer Babbidge Awd, 90. **SELECTED PUBLICATIONS** Auth, Connecticut's First Family, 75; auth, Town and Country, 78; auth, The Connecticut Town, 79; auth, Dissent and Conformity on Narragansett Bay, 83; auth, Power and Status in the American Colonies, 86; auth, The Fragmentation of New England, 89; auth, Puritans at Play, 95; ed, Can Rev Am Stud, 77-86; assoc ed, Am Nat Biogr, 91-. **CONTACT ADDRESS** Dept of History, Univ of Winnipeg, Winnipeg, MB, Canada R3B 2E9. **EMAIL** bruce.daniels@uwinnipeg.ca

DANIELS, DOUGLAS HENRY
PERSONAL Born 10/12/1943, Chicago, IL, m, 1987, 3 children **DISCIPLINE** HISTORY **EDUCATION** Univ Chicago, BA 64; Univ Cal Berk, Ma and PhD, 69 and 75. **CAREER** Univ Texas, asst prof 75-78; Univ Cal Santa Barb, prof 79-. **HONORS AND AWARDS** Fulbright fel; Mellon fel; Ford fel; NEH **MEMBERSHIPS** OAH; ASAALA **RESEARCH** Hist of Jazz; urban hist; photography; E African pop music. **SELECTED PUBLICATIONS** Auth, Pioneer Urbanites: A Social and Cultural History of Black San Francisco, ed et al; Peoples of Color in the American West; transl, Charlemagne Peralte and the First American Occupation of Haiti, by George Michael. **CONTACT ADDRESS** Dept of Black Studies, Univ of California, Santa Barbara, Santa Barbara, CA 93106-3150. **EMAIL** daniels@sscf.ucs.edu

DANIELS, ROBERT V.
PERSONAL Born 01/04/1926, Boston, MA, m, 1945, 4 children **DISCIPLINE** HISTORY **EDUCATION** Harvard Univ, AB 45, MA 47, PhD 51. **CAREER** Univ Vermont, chmn 64-69, prof 58-88, prof emer 88-. **HONORS AND AWARDS** Guggenheim fel; Kennan Inst fel; LLD Honors **MEMBERSHIPS** AAASS; CAS; VAAS **RESEARCH** Russian hist politics since 1917. **SELECTED PUBLICATIONS** Auth, The Conscience of the Revolution, Harvard, 60; auth, The Nature of Communism, Random House, 62; auth, Red October, Scribners, 67; auth, Year of the Heroic Guerrilla, Basic Books, 89; auth, The End of the Communist Revolution, Routledge, 93; A Documentary History of Communism, ed, Univ Press New Eng, 94; Russia's Transformation, Rowman Littlefield, 97. **CONTACT ADDRESS** Dept of History, Univ of Vermont, 195 South Prospect St, Burlington, VT 05401. **EMAIL** rdaniels@zoo.uvm.edu

DANKER, DONALD FLOYD
PERSONAL Born 10/07/1922, Riverton, NE, m, 1946, 2 children **DISCIPLINE** AMERICAN HISTORY **EDUCATION** Univ Nebr, BS, 48, MA, 49, PhD, 55. **CAREER** Prof Am hist & polit sci, York Col, 49-51; instr Am hist, Univ Nebr, 55-63; asst prof US hist, Washburn Univ Topeka, 63-64; historian, Nebr State Hist Soc, 64-67; assoc prof, 67-71, Prof Hist, Washburn Univ Topeka, 71-, Archivist, Nebr State Hist Soc, 52-63; mem, Kans Hist Sites Bd Rev, 71-77. **MEMBERSHIPS** Orgn Am Historians; Western Hist Asn. **RESEARCH** Western history. **SELECTED PUBLICATIONS** Ed, Mollie, The Journal of Mollie Dorsey Sanford, 1857-1866, 59 & Man of the Plains: Recollections of Luther North, 61, Univ Nebr; Transportation influence in Nebraska Territory, Nebr Hist, 6/66; Populist cartoons, Kans Quart, fall 69; The Eli Ricker Papers, Prairie Scout, 73. **CONTACT ADDRESS** Dept of Hist, Washburn Univ of Topeka, Topeka, KS 66621.

DANNER, DAN GORDON
PERSONAL Born 07/05/1939, Salt Lake City, UT, m, 1961, 2 children **DISCIPLINE** RELIGION, HISTORY OF CHRISTIAN THOUGHT **EDUCATION** Abilene Christian Col, 61, MA, 63; Univ Iowa, PhD(relig), 69. **CAREER** Dir, Church Christ Bible Chair Bibl Lit, Tyler Jr Col, 62-66; asst prof, 69-73, assoc prof, 73-81, Prof theol, Univ Portland 81- **MEMBERSHIPS** Am Acad Refig; Am Soc Reformation Res; Am Soc Church Hist. **RESEARCH** Reformation; Reformation in England; Puritanism and the Geneva exiles, 1555-1560. **SELECTED PUBLICATIONS** Auth, Revelation 20: 1-10 in a history of interpretation of the Restoration movement, Restoration Quart, 63; Anthony Gilby: Puritan in exile--a bibliographical approach, Church Hist, 71; Women's lib or Adam's rib--the problem of women and the church, 72 & Not peace but a sword--an essay on war and peace, fall 76, Univ Portland Rev; Christopher Goodman and the English Protestant tradition of civil disobedience, Sixteenth Century J, 77; The contributions of the Geneva Bible of 1560 to the English Protestant tradition, Sixteenth Century J, 81; Resistance and the ungodly magistrate in the sixteenth century: The Marian Exiles, J Am Acad Relig, 81; auth, Pilgrimage to Puritanism: History and Theology of the Manan Exiles at Geneva, 1555 to 1560, Peter Lang, 98. **CONTACT ADDRESS** Dept of Theol, Univ of Portland, 5000 N Willamette, Portland, OR 97203-5798.

DANYSK, CECILIA
PERSONAL 2 children **DISCIPLINE** HISTORY **EDUCATION** Concordia Univ, Montreal, BA, 78; McGill Univ, Montreal, MA, 81, PhD, McGill Univ, Montreal, 91. **CAREER** Lectr, Dept Hist, Univ Alberta, Can, 86-88; Lectr, Dept Hist & Can Stud Prog, Trent Univ, Can, 88-91; Asst prof, Dept Hist & Can Stud, Dalhousie Univ, Can, 91-96; Asst Prof, Dept Hist & CAN-AM Prog, W Wash Univ, 96-00; Assoc Prof, Dept of hist & Can-am prog, Westen Washington Univ, 00-. **HONORS AND AWARDS** Res fel Can Plains Res Ctr, Univ Regina, Can, 94; Soc Sci & Hum Res Coun Can grant, 93-97. **MEMBERSHIPS** Can Hist Asn; Asn Can Stud; Can Comm Labour Hist; Can Comm Women's Hist; Asn Atlantic Hist; Women in AB & SK Hist; Soc Soc Stud; Asn Can Stud in US, Am Hist Asn. **RESEARCH** Western Canadian rural, labour and social history; Current research project on Bonanza Farming in Prairie Canada, 1880-1930. **SELECTED PUBLICATIONS** Auth, No Help for the Farm Help: The Farm Placement Plans of the 1930's in Prairie Canada, Prairie Forum, 94; Recreating the Pluralism of the Past, Teaching Women's History: Challenges and Solutions, Athabasca Univ, 95; When Agribusiness Failed: The Qu'Appelle Valley Farming Company, 1882-1889, Rural Res in Hum & Soc Sci II: Proceedings of the Second Annual Colloquium of Rural Res Ctr, Nova Scotia Agr Col, 95; Hired Hands: Labour and the Development of Prairie Agriculture, 1880 to 1930, Oxford Univ Press, 95; A Bachelor's Paradise: Homesteaders, Hired Hands and the Construction of Masculinity, Making Western Canada: Essays on European Colonization and Settlement, Garamond Press, 96; 'James Speakman' and 'Edwin Carswell' Dictionary of Can Biog, Volume XIV, 1911-1920, Univ Toronto Press, 98. **CONTACT ADDRESS** Hist Dept, Western Washington Univ, Bellingham, WA 98225-9056. **EMAIL** danysk@cc.wwu.edu

DANZER, GERALD
PERSONAL Born 11/09/1938, Chicago, IL, m, 1960, 3 children **DISCIPLINE** HISTORY, EDUCATION **EDUCATION** Concord Col, BS, 59; Nwest Univ, MA, 61; PhD, 67. **CAREER** Prof, Univ Ill, 67-. **HONORS AND AWARDS** James Harvey Robinson Prize; 87, 90. **MEMBERSHIPS** AHA; OAH; AAG; NCSS. **RESEARCH** History of Cartography; historical geography; cities and the built environment; state and local history. **SELECTED PUBLICATIONS** Auth, People Space and Time, 86; auth, World History: An Atlas, 98; auth, Public Places: Exploring Their History, 87; auth, Discovering World History Through Maps and Views, 96. **CONTACT ADDRESS** Dept History, Univ of Illinois, Chicago, 851 South Morgan St, Box 723, Chicago, IL 60607-7042. **EMAIL** gdanzer@uic.edu

DANZIGER, EDMUND J.
PERSONAL Born 02/10/1938, Newark, NJ, m, 1961, 2 children **DISCIPLINE** HISTORY **EDUCATION** Col of Wooster, BA, 60; Univ Ill, MA, 62, PhD, 66. **CAREER** Dist Teach Prof, Bowling Green State Univ, 66-. **MEMBERSHIPS** Western Hist Asn; Org of Am Hist. **RESEARCH** American & Canadian Indian History. **SELECTED PUBLICATIONS** Auth, United States Indian Policy during the Late Nineteenth Century: Change and Continuity, Hayes Hist J, vol 12, 27-39, Fall 92; auth, Conflict, Cooperation, and Accomodation Along the Great Lakes Frontier, NW Ohio Quart, vol 65, 129-33, summer 93; auth, Self-Determination, Native Am in the 20th cent, an Encycl, Garland Publishing, Inc, 223-25, 94; auth, Native American Resistance and Accomodations in the Late Nineteenth Century, The Gilded Age: Essays on the Origins of Modern America, Schol Resources, Inc., 163-84, 95; co-auth, Taking Hold of the Tools: Post-Secondary Education for Canada's Walpole Island First Nation, 1965-1994, Can J of Native Stud, 16(no 2), 229-46, 96; Auth, A People Living Apart: Indians of the Great Lakes, 1855-1900, Univ Mich Press, (in press). **CONTACT ADDRESS** Dept Hist, Bowling Green State Univ, Bowling Green, OH 43403. **EMAIL** edanzig@bgnet.bgsu.edu

DARDEN, LINDLEY
PERSONAL Born 12/17/1945, New Albany, MS **DISCIPLINE** PHILOSOPHY AND HISTORY OF SCIENCE **EDUCATION** Rhodes College, BA, 68; Univ Chicago, AM, 69, SM, 72, PhD, 74. **CAREER** Asst prof, 74-78, Assoc Prof Philos and Hist, Univ MD, College Park, 78-92, prof of phil, 92-; NSF grant, 78-80, 99-01; Am Coun Learned Soc fel, 82. **HONORS AND AWARDS** Fel, AAAS, 95. **MEMBERSHIPS** ISHPSSB, Philos Sci Asn; Hist Sci Soc; AAAS. **RESEARCH** Theory construction in science; discovering mechanisms. **SELECTED PUBLICATIONS** Auth, Theory Change in Science, Oxford Univ Press, 91; coauth, " Thinking About Mechanisms," Phil Sci 67, 1-25, 00. **CONTACT ADDRESS** Dept of Philos, Univ of Maryland, Col Park, College Park, MD 20742. **EMAIL** darden@carnap.umd.edu

DARDESS, JOHN W.
PERSONAL Born 01/17/1937, Albany, NY, d, 1 child **DISCIPLINE** HISTORY **EDUCATION** Geotwn Univ, BS, 58; Columbia Univ, PhD, 68. **CAREER** Prof, Univ Kan, 79-. **MEMBERSHIPS** AAS. **RESEARCH** Yuan; Ming; Qing history. **SELECTED PUBLICATIONS** Auth, A Ming Society, Univ Cal Press (Berkeley), 96. **CONTACT ADDRESS** Dept History, Univ of Kansas, Lawrence, Lawrence, KS 66045-0001. **EMAIL** jdardess@falcon.cc.ukans.edu

DARLING, LINDA T.
PERSONAL Born 02/16/1945, s **DISCIPLINE** HISTORY **EDUCATION** Univ of Conn, BA, 67; Univ of Chicago, MAT, 73, MA, 80, PhD, 90. **CAREER** Asst prof, 89-96, Assoc Prof of Hist, Univ of Ariz, 96-. **HONORS AND AWARDS** Am Coun of Learned Soc Fel; Outstanding Fac member, Mortar Board and Golden Key Honor Societies. **MEMBERSHIPS** Am Hist Asn; Middle East Studies Asn; Turkish Studies Asn. **RESEARCH** Ottoman Empire; admin and govt; taxation and political relations; Lyria and Lebanon in the Ottoman period; world hist. **SELECTED PUBLICATIONS** Auth, Rethinking Europe and the Islamic World in the Age of Exploration, The J of Early Modern Hist, 98; Ottoman Provincial Treasuries: The Case of Syria, Arab Hist Rev for Ottoman Studies, 97; Ottoman Fiscal Administration: Decline or Adaptation, The J of European Economic Hist, 97; Revenue Raising and Legitimacy: Tax Collection and the Central Finance Department in Capitulations, Oxford Encycl of the Modern Islamic World, Oxford Univ Press, 95; Ottoman Politics through British Eyes: Paul Rycaut's The Present State of the Ottoman Empire, The J of World Hist, 94; The Finance Scribes and Ottoman Politics, Decision Making in the Ottoman Empire, Thomas Jefferson Univ Press and Univ Press of Am, 93. **CONTACT ADDRESS** Dept of Hist, Univ of Arizona, Tucson, AZ 85721. **EMAIL** ldarling@u.arizona.edu

DAUBEN, JOSEPH WARREN
PERSONAL Born 12/29/1944, Santa Monica, CA **DISCIPLINE** HISTORY OF SCIENCE & MATHEMATICS **EDUCATION** Claremont Men's Col, AB, 66; Harvard Univ, AM, 68, PhD(hist of sci), 72. **CAREER** Tutor & teaching fel hist of sci, Harvard Univ, 67-72; vis prof hist ancient sci, Clark Univ, 72; asst prof hist & hist of sci, 72-78, assoc prof, 78-81, Prof Hist of Sci, Lehman Col & Grad Prog Hist, Grad Ctr, City Univ New York, 81-; mem, Inst Advan Study, Princeton, 77-78; vis prof, Columbia Univ, 79-84 & Oberlin Col, 80-81, NY Botanical Garden, 89-, NYU, 89-93, Nat Tsing-Hua Univ, Taiwan, 91, Nat Normal Univ, Taiwan 95; Guggenheim fel, 80-81; vis scholar, Harvard Univ, 81; Nat Endowment for Humanities younger humanist fel, 73-74, fel, 91-94; ACLS sr fel, 98-; ed, Historia Mathematica, 76-86. **HONORS AND AWARDS** Mead-Swing lectr, Oberlin Col, 77 & 80; Bolzano Medal, Czech Acad Sci, 78; Lenin Medal, Univ Tashkent, USSR, 86. **MEMBERSHIPS** Fel, AAAS, NY Acad Sci; Hist Sci Soc; Int Comn Hist of Math (chmn 85-94); Sigma Xi, Phi Beta Kappa **RESEARCH** History of mathematics in the 19th century; history of science in the 16th and 17th centuries; history of philosophy from Descartes to Kant. **SELECTED PUBLICATIONS** Auth, Marat: His science and the French Revolution, Arch Int Hist Sci, 69; The Trigonometric Background to Georg Cantor's Theory of Sets, Arch Hist Exact Sci, 71; C S Peirce and American mathematics in the 19th century, Math Mag, 77; Georg Cantor and Pope Leo XIII: Philosophical and Theological Dimensions of Transfinite Set Theory, J Hist of Ideas, 77; Georg Cantor: The Personal Matrix of His Mathematics, Isis, No 69, 534-550; Georg Cantor, His Mathematics and Philosophy of the Infinite, Harvard Univ, 79; The Development of Cantorian Set Theory, in: From the Calculus to Set Theory, 1630-1910, Duckworths, London, 81; ed, Mathematical Perspectives: Essays on the History of Mathematics in Honor of Kurt R Biermann, NY Acad Press, 81. **CONTACT ADDRESS** Dept of Hist, Lehman Col, CUNY, Bedford Park Blvd W, Bronx, NY 10468. **EMAIL** jdauben@email.gc.cuny.edu

DAVENPORT, ROBERT WILSON
PERSONAL Born 08/19/1929, Elizabeth, NJ, m, 1960, 1 child **DISCIPLINE** AMERICAN HISTORY **EDUCATION** Pomona Col, BA, 51; Univ CA, Berkeley, MA, 53; UCLA, MS, 56, PhD, 69. **CAREER** Asst jour, Univ CA, Los Angeles, 59-60; from instr to asst prof hist, 64-70, actg dean, Col Arts & Lett, 71-73, chmn dept hist, 76-78, assoc prof hist, Univ NV, Las Vegas, 70; emer assoc prof hist, 98-. **MEMBERSHIPS** Orgn Am Historians; Western Hist Asn. **RESEARCH** Am west; progressives; Am journalism hist. **SELECTED PUBLICATIONS** Auth, Weird note for the Vox Populi: The Los Angeles Municipal News, Calif Hist Soc Quart, 3/65; ed, Desert Heritage: Readings in Nevada History, Ginn Press, 89; Early Years, Early Workers: The Genesis of the University of Nevada, Nevada Hist Soc Quart, spring 92. **CONTACT ADDRESS** Dept of Hist, Univ of Nevada, Las Vegas, PO Box 455020, Las Vegas, NV 89154-5020. **EMAIL** davenpr1@nevada.edu

DAVID, ARTHUR LACURTISS
PERSONAL Born 04/13/1938, Chicago, IL, m **DISCIPLINE** HISTORY **EDUCATION** Lane Coll, BA 1960; Phillips Sch of Theol, BD 1963; NE U, MA 1970; ITC, MDiv 1971; Middle TN State U, Arts D 1973. **CAREER** Soc Sci Div Lane Coll, chmn; Lane Coll, prof of hist, 63-67 69-77; NE Wesleyan Univ, 67-69; Motlow State Commn Coll, 72-73; Lane Coll, dean, 79-93; Prof of History, 93-. **MEMBERSHIPS** Mem So Hist Assn; Am Hist Assn; Orgn of Am Historians; mem Pi Gamma Mu Social Sci, Hon Soc; Phi Alpha Theta Hist Hon Soc; Sigma Theta Epsilon Hon Soc for Clergymen; Kappa Kappa Psi Hon Band Frat; Alpha Phi Alpha Frat Inc. **SELECTED PUBLICATIONS** You Can Fool Me But You Can't Fool God, 76; An Anthology of a Minister's Thoughts, 77; He Touched Me, 92. **CONTACT ADDRESS** History, Lane Col, 545 Lane Ave, Jackson, TN 38301.

DAVIDOV, JUDITH FRYER
PERSONAL Born 08/05/1939, Minneapolis, MN, d, 2 children **DISCIPLINE** AMERICAN STUDIES **EDUCATION** Univ Minn, BA, 61, MA, 67, PhD, 73. **CAREER** Miami Univ, Ohio, , 74-84; DEPT ENG, DIR, AM STUD; UNIV MASS, AMHERST, PROF, ENG, 84-; dir, grad prog Am Stud, 88-98, UNIV MASS, AMHERST. **HONORS AND AWARDS** ACLS; NEH (4); Rockefeller, Getty, Fulbright (2); Mellon, CASUA. **MEMBERSHIPS** Am Studies Asn. **RESEARCH** Visual culture (esp. phogography), interdisciplinary method, nature and the environment. **SELECTED PUBLICATIONS** Auth, The Faces of Eve: Women in the 19th Century American Novel; Felicitous Space: The Imaginative Structures of Edith Wharton and Willa Cather; Women's Camera Work: Self/ Body/Other in American Visual Culture. **CONTACT ADDRESS** Dept of English, Univ of Massachusetts, Amherst, Bartlett Hall, Amherst, MA 01003.

DAVIDSON, ABRAHAM A.
PERSONAL Born 06/27/1935, Dorchester, MA **DISCIPLINE** HISTORY OF AMERICAN ART **EDUCATION** Harvard Univ, AB, 57; Hebrew Teachers Col, BSEd, 60; Boston Univ, AM, 60; Columbia Univ, PhD(art hist), 65. **CAREER** Vis lectr art hist, Univ Iowa, 63-64; instr, Wayne State Univ, 64-65; asst prof, Oakland Univ, 65-68; from asst prof to assoc prof, 68-75, Prof Art Hist, Tyler Sch Art, Temple Univ, 75-. **RESEARCH** Early American modernism in painting; painting of William Sydney Mount; painting of Charles Willson Peale. **SELECTED PUBLICATIONS** Auth, Utopia and Dissent--Art, Poetry, and Politics in California, Amer Hist Rev, Vol 0101, 96. **CONTACT ADDRESS** Dept Art Hist, Temple Univ, 7725 Penrose Ave, Elkins Park, PA 19027-1098.

DAVIES, CAROLE BOYCE
PERSONAL Born 12/13/1948, Tobago, Trinidad, d, 2 children **DISCIPLINE** AFRICAN STUDIES **EDUCATION** Univ Md, BA, 71; Howard Univ, MA, 74; Univ Ibadan, PhD. **CAREER** Prof. **HONORS AND AWARDS** Herskovits Professof of African Studies, Northwestern Univ, 00-. **MEMBERSHIPS** African Lit Asn; African Studies Asn; CAFRA; MLA; Nat Women's Studies Asn; Women's Caucus African Lit Asn. **RESEARCH** Black women's writing; African American literature; comparative black literature; African literature; Caribbean oral and written literature; cross cultural feminist theory; oral tradition and written literature; Afican Diaspora Culture. **SELECTED PUBLICATIONS** Ed, Ngambika, Studies of Women in African Literature, 86; ed, Out of Kumbla, Caribbean Women and Literature, 90; auth, Migrations of the Subject, Black Women, Writing Identity, London, Routledge, 94; auth, Black Women, Writing, and Identity, Routledge, 94; Moving Beyond Boundaries, Univ NY, 95; Moving Beyond Boundaries, Pluto, 95; ed, Moving Beyond Boundaries, v 1, International Dimensions of Black Womens Writing, V V 2 Black Women's Diasporas 95; Under African Skies (rev), 97; coed, The African Diaspora, African Origins and New World Identities, Indiana Univ Press, 99. **CONTACT ADDRESS** Northwestern Univ, Kresge 314, Kresge 314, Evanston, IL 60208. **EMAIL** cboyced@northwestern.edu

DAVIES, MORGAN
DISCIPLINE MEDIEVAL ENGLISH, WELSH, IRISH LANGUAGE, LITERATURE AND CULTURE **EDUCATION** Stanford, BA; Univ CA, MA, Cphil, PhD. **CAREER** Asst prof, Colgate Univ. **HONORS AND AWARDS** NEH Fel, Col Tchr(s), 95. **RESEARCH** Old Eng lit, old and middle Irish lit, middle Welsh lit. **SELECTED PUBLICATIONS** Auth, Dafydd Ap Gwilym and the Friars: The Poetics of Antimendicancy, Studia Celtica; Aed I'r Coed I Dorri Cof: Dafydd Ap Gwilym and the Metaphorics of Carpentry, Cambrian Medieval Celtic Studies. **CONTACT ADDRESS** Dept of Eng, Colgate Univ, 13 Oak Drive, Hamilton, NY 13346.

DAVIS, ALLEN FREEMAN
PERSONAL Born 01/09/1931, Hardwick, VT, d, 2 children **DISCIPLINE** AMERICAN HISTORY **EDUCATION** Dartmouth Col, AB, 53; Univ Rochester, MA, 54; Univ Wis, PhD(Am Hist), 59. **CAREER** Instr Hist, Wayne Univ, 59-60; from asst prof to assoc prof, Univ Mo-Columbia, 60-68; prof Hist, Temple Univ, 68-; vis prof Univ Texas Austin, 83; prof, Univ of Amsterdam, 86-87. **HONORS AND AWARDS** John Adams chmn, Bode-Pearson Awd; Sr fel, Am Coun Learned Soc; NEH fel, Fulbright sen fel. **MEMBERSHIPS** AHA; Orgn Am Historians; Soc Am Historians; Am Studies Asn (treas, 79-72, exec secry, 72-77, pres, 89-90). **RESEARCH** American cultural history. **SELECTED PUBLICATIONS** Co-ed, Conflict and Concensus in American History, Heath, Houghton and Mifflin, 66, 68, 72, 76, 80, 84, 86, 92, 97; ed, For Better of Worse, Greenwood, 81; auth, Spearheads for Reform, Oxford Univ, 67, Rutgers, 84; co-ed, Eighty Years at Hull House, Quadrangle, 69; auth, Introduction to Jane Addams, Spirit of youth and the city streets, Univ Ill, 72; co-ed, The Peoples of Philadelphia, Temple Univ, 73, Univ of PA, 98; auth, American Heroine: The Life and Legend of Jane Addams, Oxford Univ, 73, Ivan Dee Inc, 00; coauth, Generations: Your Family in Modern American History, Knopf, 74, 78 & 83; coauth, 100 Years at Hull House, Ind Univ Press, 90; coauth, The American People!, Harper Collins, 86, 90, 94, Addison Wesley, Longmans, 98. **CONTACT ADDRESS** 2032 Waverly St., Philadelphia, PA 19146. **EMAIL** davisafd@aol.com

DAVIS, AUDREY BLYMAN
PERSONAL Born 11/09/1934, Hicksville, NY, m, 1960, 2 children **DISCIPLINE** HISTORY OF SCIENCE AND MEDICINE **EDUCATION** Adelphi Univ, BS, 56; Johns Hopkins Univ, PhD(hist of sci), 69. **CAREER** Teacher biol, physics & chem, Sewanhaka High Sch, NY, 56-59; teacher biol & physics, Windsor Sch & Saugus High Sch, Mass, 61-62; consult sci educ, Sci Serv, Washington, DC, 64-66; Cur, Mus Am Hist, Smithsonian Inst, 67-, Curator, Smithsonian Res Found Grant, 71-72, Commonwealth Found grant, 72-73; prof, Univ Md, College Park, 73-74; prof, Univ Md, Baltimore, 82. **MEMBERSHIPS** Hist Sci Soc (secy, 82-); Am Asn Hist Med. **RESEARCH** History of biology, medicine and the technology of medicine from the 17th century to the present; history of women. **SELECTED PUBLICATIONS** Auth, Circulation Physiology and Medical Chemistry in England, 1650-1680, Coronado, 73; History of Medical Technology, In: Vol 6, A History of Technology, 78; Historical Studies of Medical instruments, Hist Sci, 78; Bloodletting instruments, In: The National Museum of History and Technology, Smithsonian, 78; Medicine and Its Technology: An Introduction to the History of Medical Instrumentation, Greenwood Press, 81. **CONTACT ADDRESS** Div of Med Sci Mus Am Hist, Smithsonian Inst, Washington, DC 20560.

DAVIS, BARBARA BECKERMAN
DISCIPLINE EUROPEAN HISTORY, 16TH CENTURY URBAN FRANCE HISTORY **EDUCATION** CUNY, Uptown, BA; Univ CA, Berkeley, MA, PhD. **CAREER** Assoc prof, Antioch Col. **HONORS AND AWARDS** NEH inst, 91 NEH sem, 95. **RESEARCH** Poor relief institutions and the poor in Toulouse and spirituality. **SELECTED PUBLICATIONS** Articles appeared in Hist Reflections/Reflexions historiques (91) and Fr Hist (93); she reviews for the 16th Century J, Cath Hist J, and J of Mod Hist. **CONTACT ADDRESS** Antioch Col, Yellow Springs, OH 45387. **EMAIL** bdavis@antioch-college.edu

DAVIS, CALVIN D.
PERSONAL Born 12/03/1927, Westport, IN **DISCIPLINE** HISTORY **EDUCATION** Franklin Col, AB, 49; Ind Univ MA, 56, PhD, 61. **CAREER** Teacher pub schs, Ind, 49-54 & Univ Sch, Ind Univ, Bloomington, 54-55; asst prof hist, Ind Cent Col, 56-57; assoc Ind Univ, 58-59; asst prof, Univ Denver, 59-62; from asst prof to assoc prof, 62-76, Prof Hist, Duke Univ, 76-95, Consult, Nat Endowment for Humanities, 74-75; Prof Emeritus of History, Duke University, 95-. **HONORS AND AWARDS** Beveridge Awd, AHA, 61. **MEMBERSHIPS** AHA; Orgn Am Historians; Soc Historians Am Foreign Rels. **RESEARCH** American foreign relations; American diplomacy and the Hague system; the Paris Peace Conference of 1919. **SELECTED PUBLICATIONS** Auth, The United States and the First Hague Peace Conference, Cornell University Press, 62; auth, The United States and the Second Hague Peace Conference, Duke University Press, 76. **CONTACT ADDRESS** Dept of Hist, Duke Univ, Durham, IN 27708.

DAVIS, CARL L.
PERSONAL Born 08/27/1934, Bartlesville, OK, m, 1967, 2 children **DISCIPLINE** HISTORY, POLITICAL SCIENCE **EDUCATION** Okla State Univ, AB, 58, MA, 59, PhD(hist), 71. **CAREER** Instr hist & polit sci, 61-64, from asst prof to assoc prof hist, 74-77, Prof Hist, Stephen F Austin State Univ, 77-. **MEMBERSHIPS** AHA; Orgn Am Historians; Southern Hist Asn; Southwestern Soc Sci Asn. **RESEARCH** United States military-industrial; modern United States (since 1945) social attitudes. **SELECTED PUBLICATIONS** Auth, Study Guide to American History to 1865, 71 & Study Guide to American History, 1865-Present, 71, Okla State Univ; contribr, The Mexican War, In: Fighting Men, Kendall, 71; coauth, Dragoons in Indian territory, Chronicles Okla, spring 72; auth, Arming the Union, Kennikat, 74; coauth (with A P McDonald), The War with Mexico, Forum Press, 79; auth, James W Ripley, George D Ramsay & Alexander B Dyer, In: Dict Union Biog, 82. **CONTACT ADDRESS** Dept of Hist, Stephen F. Austin State Univ, Box 3013, Nacogdoches, TX 75962.

DAVIS, DANIEL CLAIR
DISCIPLINE CHURCH HISTORY **EDUCATION** Wheaton Col, AB, 53, MA, 57; Westminster Theol Sem, BD, 56; Georg-August Univ, Guttingen, ThD, 60. **CAREER** Asst prof, Olivet Col, 60-63; vis prof, asst prof, Wheaton Col, Grad Sch Theol, 63-66; prof, Westminster Theol Sem, 66-. **SELECTED PUBLICATIONS** Contrib, John Calvin: His Influence in the Western World; Challenges to Inerrancy; Inerrancy and the Church; Pressing Toward the Mark; Theonomy: A Reformed Critique. **CONTACT ADDRESS** Westminster Theol Sem, Pennsylvania, PO Box 27009, Philadelphia, PA 19118. **EMAIL** cdavis@wts.edu

DAVIS, DAVID BRION
PERSONAL Born 02/16/1927, Denver, CO, m, 1971, 5 children **DISCIPLINE** HISTORY **EDUCATION** Dartmouth Col, AB, 50; Harvard Univ, AM, 53, PhD, 56. **CAREER** Instr hist & Ford Fund Advan Educ intern, Dartmouth Col, 53-54; from asst prof to Ernest I White prof hist, Cornell Univ, 55-69; Harmsworth prof Am hist, Oxford Univ, 69-70; prof, 69-72, Farnam prof, 72-78, Sterling Prof Hist, Yale Univ, 78-, Guggenheim Mem fel, 58-59; Fulbright lectr, Hyderabad, India, 67; fel, Ctr Advan Studies Behav Sci, 72-73; Henry E Huntington Libr fel, 76; Nat Endowment for Humanities res grants, 79-80 & 80-81; Fulbright traveling fel, 80-81; French-Am Found Chair Am Civilization, Ecole des Hautes Etudes en Sciences Sociales, Paris, 80-81. **HONORS AND AWARDS** Anisfield-Wolf Awd, 67; Nat Mass Media Awd, Nat Conf Christians & Jews, 67; Pulitzer Prize, 67; Albert J Beveridge Awd, AHA, 75; Bancroft Prize, Columbia Univ, 76; Nat Bk Awd, Nat Inst Arts & Lett, 76; Benjamin Rush lectr, Am Psychiat Asn, 76; O Meredith Wilson lectr, Univ Utah, 78; Walter Lynwood Fleming lectr, Southern Hist, La State Univ, 79; Pierce lectr, Oberlin Col, 79; ma, oxford univ, 69; ma, yale univ, 70; littd, dartmouth col, 77, littd columbia, 99. **MEMBERSHIPS** AHA; Orgn Am Historians; Am Acad Arts & Sci; Soc Am Historians; Am Antiqn Soc. **RESEARCH** Intellectual history of the United States; slavery and antislavery; Anglo-American nineteenth century culture. **SELECTED PUBLICATIONS** Auth, Life in Black-And-White--Family and Community in the Slave South, NY Rev Bk(s), Vol 0044, 97; Witness for Freedom--African-American Voices on Race, Slavery and Emancipation, NY Rev Bk(s), Vol 0040, 93; Constructing Race--European-History and the Definition of Race--A Reflection, William and Mary Quart, Vol 0054, 97; Tumult and Silence at Second-Creek--An Inquiry Into a Civil-War Conspiracy, NY Rev Bk(s), Vol 0040, 93; The Age of Federalism, NY Rev Bk(s), Vol 0041, 94; Slavery and the Jews--Clarification on a Statement Made in a Recently Published Essay, NY Rev Bk(s), Vol 0042, 95; At the Heart of Slavery--Essay, NY Rev Bk(s), Vol 0043, 96; Free at Last--A Documentary History of Slavery, Freedom and the Civil-War, NY Rev Bk(s), Vol 0040, 93; The Southern Tradition--The Achievement and Limitations of an American Conservatism, NY Rev Bk(s), Vol 0042, 95; The Southern Front--History and Politics in the Cultural War, NY Rev Bk(s), Vol 0042, 95; The Slave-Trade and the Jews, NY Rev Bk(s), Vol 0041, 94; The Slaveholders Dilemma--Freedom and Progress in Southern Conservative Thought, 1820-1860, NY Rev Bk(s), Vol 0042, 95. **CONTACT ADDRESS** Dept of Hist, Yale Univ, P O Box 208301, New Haven, CT 06520-8301. **EMAIL** david.b.davis@yale.edu

DAVIS, DAVID D.
PERSONAL Born 08/08/1956, Boston, MA, m, 1978, 2 children **DISCIPLINE** LIBRARY SCIENCE; HISTORY **EDUCATION** Catholic Univ Am, MSLIS, MS. **CAREER** Publ Libr, 82-88; Corp Libr, 88-94; Copyright Clearance Ctr, 94-. **MEMBERSHIPS** SLA **RESEARCH** Service quality; copyright; digital rights management (DRM) systems. **SELECTED PUBLICATIONS** Auth, "Copyright Dilemma," Computers in Libraries, 99; auth, "What DRM Means Today," Computers in Libraries, 01. **CONTACT ADDRESS** Copyright Clearance Ctr, 222 Rosewood Dr, Danvers, MA 01923. **EMAIL** ddavis@copyright.com

DAVIS, DONALD G., JR.
PERSONAL Born 12/06/1939, San Marcos, TX, m, 1969, 3 children **DISCIPLINE** LIBRARY SCIENCE, HISTORY **EDUCATION** UCLA, BA, 61; UC Berkeley, MA, 63, MLS, 64; Univ Ill, Champaign-Urbana, PhD, 72; Austin Presbyterian Theol Sem, MA, 96. **CAREER** Libry asst, UC Berkeley, 61-64; sen ref librn, Fresno State Col, 64-68; prof, Univ Tx Austin, 71-. **HONORS AND AWARDS** Beta Phi Mu; Phi Kappa Phi; HEA Title-B Fel; Newberry Libry Fel; Am Inst Indian Stud Fel; Berner-Nash Awd, Univ Ill; GLSIS; John P. Commons Tchg Fel, Univ Tex Austin; Beta Phi Mu, Golden Anniversary Awd, 99. **MEMBERSHIPS** Am Hist Asn; Am Libry Asn; Asn Bibliography Hist; Am Printing Hist Asn; Conference on Faith and Hist; Nat Asn Scholars; Org Am Hist; Tex Libry Asn; Tex State Hist Asn; American: History and Life; Annual Bibliography of the History of the Printed Book and Libraries. **RESEARCH** Hist of books and libraries; American library history; history of printing; Christian missions. **SELECTED PUBLICATIONS** Auth, Libraries & Culture, University of Texas Press, Quarterly Journal; auth, art, Problems in the Life of a University Librarian: Thomas James, 1600-1620, 70; auth, The Association of American Library Schools, 1915-1968: An Analytical History, 74; auth, art, Education for Librarianship, 76; auth, Reference Books in the Social Sciences and Humanities, 77; auth, art, The Status of Library History in India: A Report of an Informal Survey and a Selective Auth, Bibliographic Essay, 89; auth, American Library History: A Comprehensive Guide to the Literature, 89; auth, Encyclopedia of Library History, 94; auth, art, Destruction of Chinese Books in the Peking Siege of 1900, 97; auth, art, Arthur E. Bostwick and Chinese Library Development: A Chapter in International Cooperation, 98; auth, Library History Research in America,00. **CONTACT ADDRESS** Graduate School of Library and Information Science, Univ of Texas, Austin, Austin, TX 78712-1276. **EMAIL** dgdavis@gslis.utexas.edu

DAVIS, EDWARD B.
PERSONAL Born 08/05/1953, Philadelphia, PA, m, 2 children **DISCIPLINE** HISTORY OF SCIENCE **EDUCATION** Drexel Univ, BS, 75; Indiana Univ Bloomington, PhD, 84. **CAREER** Vis asst prof, Dept of Hist & Philos, Vanderbilt Univ, 84-85; asst prof, 85-90, assoc prof, 90-96, Sci & Hist, prof, the history of science, 96-, Messiah Col, 85-. **HONORS AND**

AWARDS Diss Year fel Charlotte W. Newcombe Found, 83-84; Nat Sci Found Res Grant, 89; Mellon fel Hum Univ Penn, 91-92; Lilly Fellows Prog Hum & Arts Summer Inst grant, 98; Scholar chr Messiah Col, 98-00; Net Sci Found Res Grants, 99-01; Exemplary Papers Awd Program, John M Templeton Found, 96-97; Esther L Kinsley PhD Diss Prize Ind Univ, 85. **MEMBERSHIPS** Amer Sci Affil; Hist Sci Soc **RESEARCH** Robert Boyle; Religion and science since 1650; Antievolutionism. **SELECTED PUBLICATIONS** Auth, Parcere nominibus: Boyle, Hooke, and the Rhetorical Interpretation of Descartes, Robert Boyle Reconsidered, Cambridge, 94; The Anonymous Works of Robert Boyle and the Reasons Why a Protestant Should not Turn Papist (1687), Jour Hist Ideas, 94; ed, The Antievolution Pamphlets of Harry Rimmer, Creationism in Twentieth Century America, Garland Publ, 95; auth, Fundamentalism and Folk Science Between the Wars, Relig and Amer Cult, 95; coauth, The Making of Robert Boyles Free Enquiry into the Vulgarly Receiv d Notion of Nature (1686); Early Sci Med, 96; co-ed, Robert Boyle A Free Enquiry into the Vulgarly Received Notion of Nature, Cambridge Texts, Cambridge Univ Press, 96; auth, Newtons Rejection of the Newtonian World View: The Role of Divine Will in Newtons Natural Philosophy, Facets of Faith and Science Vol 3: The Role of Beliefs in the Natural Sciences, Univ Press Amer, 96; Rationalism, Voluntarism, and Seventeenth-Century Science, Facets of Faith and Science Vol 3: The Role of Beliefs in the Natural Sciences, Univ Press Amer, 96; co-ed, The Works of Robert Boyle, 14 vols. Pickering and Chatto, 99-00. **CONTACT ADDRESS** Messiah Col, Grantham, PA 17027. **EMAIL** tdavis@messiah.edu

DAVIS, ELLEN NANCY

PERSONAL Born 07/20/1937, Hackensack, NJ **DISCIPLINE** ART HISTORY, ARCHAEOLOGY **EDUCATION** St John's Col, BA, 60; Inst Fine Arts, NYork Univ, PhD, 73. **CAREER** Res asst ancient art, Inst Fine Arts, NY Univ, 60-66; from lectr to asst prof, 66-78, Assoc Prof Ancient Art, Queens Col, 78-, Nat Endowment for Humanities res grant, prin investr ancient metallurgy, 77-79. **MEMBERSHIPS** Archaeol Inst Am; New York Aegean Bronze Age Col; Anc Civilizat Sem; Am Res Ctr in Egypt; Am Sch of Class Stu, Athens; Columbia Univ Sem, Archaeology of the Mediteranean; New York Egyptological Sem. **RESEARCH** Aegean Bronze Age; ancient metallurgy. **SELECTED PUBLICATIONS** Coauth, Catalogue of Anatolian Metal Vessels, Ancient Art: The Norbert Schimmel Collection, 74; auth, The Vapheio cups: One Minoan and One Mycenean?, Art Bull, Vol 56, 74; coauth, The Classic Ideal, In: Sculpture, Newsweek: The History of Culture, NY, 75; auth, Metal Inlaying in Minoan and Mycenean Art, Temple Univ Aegean Symp, Vol I, 76; ed, Symposium on the Dark Ages, Archaeol Inst Am, NY, 77; Auth, The Vapheio Cups and Aegian Gold and Silver Ware, Garland Publ Inc, NY & London, 77; auth, Youth and the Age in the Thera Frescoes, Am Jou of Archaeology, 399-40, 86; The Cyclasic Style of the Thera Frescoes, Thera and the Aegean World III, Vol 3, Third Int Thera Congress, 214-227, 90; Art and Politics in the Aegean: The Missing Ruler, The Role of the Ruler in the Prehistoric Aegean, Aegaeum, Vol 11, 11-20, 5; The Iconography of the Thera Ship Fresco, Greek Art and Iconography, Madison, 40-54, 83. **CONTACT ADDRESS** Dept of Art, Queens Col, CUNY, 6530 Kissena Blvd, Flushing, NY 11367-1597.

DAVIS, ELLIOT BOSTWICK

PERSONAL Born 02/28/1962, New York, NY, m, 1988, 2 children **DISCIPLINE** ART HISTORY **EDUCATION** Princeton Univ, AB, 84; Univ NYork, MA, 85; Columbia Univ, MA, 86, MPhil, 88, PhD, 92. **CAREER** Teach asst, Harvard Univ; current, ASST CUR, DEPT American Paintings and Sculpture, METROPOLITAN MUSEUM ART **MEMBERSHIPS** Am Antiquarian Soc; Am Historical Print Collectors; Print Council of Am; Art Table, Inc; Am Assoc of Museums; CAA. **RESEARCH** Am drawing books, 1820-1880 **SELECTED PUBLICATIONS** Auth, Training the Eye and the Hand; Fitz Hugh Lane and Nineteenth-Century Drawing Books, Cape Ann Historical Soc, 93; auth, "Fitz Hugh Lane and John B. Chapman's American Drawing Book," The Mag Antiques, 93; auth, "American Drawing Books and Their Impact on Winslow Homer," Winterthur Portfolio 31, 96; auth, "WPA Color Prints: Images from the Federal Art Project, Am Art Rev VIII, 96; auther, "American Drawing Books and Their Impact on Fitz Hugh Lane," in The Cultivation of Artists in Nineteenth-Century America, ASS, 97. **CONTACT ADDRESS** Dept of American Paintings and Sculpture, Metropolitan Mus of Art, 1000 Fifth Ave, New York, NY 10028.

DAVIS, GEORGE H.

PERSONAL Born 05/18/1938, Pittsburgh, PA, m, 1961, 2 children **DISCIPLINE** AMERICAN HISTORY **EDUCATION** Bowdoin Col, AB, 60; Univ Chicago, MAT, 62, PhD, 66. **CAREER** Lectr hist, Ind Univ, Gary, 64-65; instr, Lake Forest Col, 65-66; from Asst Prof to Assoc Prof, 66-79, prof hist, Wabash Col, 79-. **MEMBERSHIPS** AHA; Orgn Am Historians. **RESEARCH** Truman administration; urban and social history. **SELECTED PUBLICATIONS** Co-compiler, Who Was Who 1604-1896, Marquis, 64; auth, The puritan idea of success, in Present in the Past, Macmillan, 72. **CONTACT ADDRESS** Dept of Hist, Wabash Col, PO Box 352, Crawfordsville, IN 47933-0352. **EMAIL** davisg@wabash.edu

DAVIS, HENRY VANCE

PERSONAL Born 08/14/1946, Detroit, MI, s, 5 children **DISCIPLINE** AFRICAN-AMERICAN HISTORY **EDUCATION** Western Mich Univ, BS, 70; Univ Mich, MA, 72, PhD, 90. **CAREER** Lectr, Univ Mich, 72-73; asst prof, Univ Detroit, 72-73; asst prof, Saw Col at Detroit, 73-75; adjunct asst prof, Univ Mich, Flint, 90-91; asst to assoc prof, Dept Hist, Western Mich Univ, 90-97, assoc prof, Dept of Extended Learning, 94-98; assoc prof, Ramapo Col of NJ, 98-. **MEMBERSHIPS** Am Asn of Univ Profs, Alliance of Black Sch Educators, Nat Asn African Am Studies. **RESEARCH** Harold Cruse, The Black Press 1827-1927. **SELECTED PUBLICATIONS** Auth, "The High-tech Lynching and the High-tech Overseer: Thoughts from the Anita Hill/Clarence Thomas Affair," in The Court of Appeal, ed by Robert Chrisman, Ballantine Books: NY (92); auth, "Environmental Voting Record of the Congressional Black Caucus," in Race and the Incidence of Environmental Hazards: A Time for Discourse, ed by Bunyan Bryant and Paul Mohai, Boulder: Westview Press (92); auth, "An African-American Perspective on the Reagan-Bush Years and Beyond," Beyond the Red, White, and Blue," Lewis H. Carlson and James M. Ferreira, Dubuque, Iowa: Dendal/Hunt Pub Co (93, 98); auth, "NAAPID, A Defining Day in African American History," Washtenaw Enquirer (Feb 5, 96); auth, "Comments on the First Anniversary of the Million Man March," Washtenaw Enquirer (Oct 15, 96); coauth, "The Carter G. Woodson Commission Report on the Campus Climate at Eastern Mich Univ," Million Man March Asn of Washtenaw Co (Nov 97); auth, Social Changes in Western Michigan 1930-1990, Kalamazoo: Western Mich Univ (97); auth, "Other Voices," Ann Arbor News (April 4, 98); auth, "Arthur P. Davis, Gardner: On the Landscape of African-American Intellectual History," Callalou (in press). **CONTACT ADDRESS** Sch of Soc Sci and Human Services, Ramapo Col of New Jersey, 505 Ramapo Valley Rd, Mahwah, NJ 07430-1623.

DAVIS, JACK E.

PERSONAL Born 07/13/1956, s **DISCIPLINE** HISTORY **EDUCATION** Brandeis Univ, PhD, 94. **CAREER** Asst prof, Univ Ala, Birmingham; asst prof hist, Eckerd Col; dir, Environmental Studies, Eckerd Col. **HONORS AND AWARDS** N Am Soc Sport Historians, essay prize, 91; NEH Summer Inst, Harvard Univ, 98; Frederick W. Conner Prize in the Hist of Ideas, 98. **RESEARCH** U.S. race relations, civil rights, environmental history. **SELECTED PUBLICATIONS** Contr, Encyclopedia of African-American Civil Rights: From Whitewash in Florida: The Lynching of Jesse James Payne and its Aftermath, Florida Historical Quarterly 63 (Jan 90); contr, Encyclopedia of African-American Civil Rights: From Emancipation to the Present, Greenwood Press, 92; Baseball's Reluctant Challenge: Desegregating Major League Spring Training Sites, 1960-1963; Journal of Sport History 20 (fall 92); Making the Cut: Racial Discrimination in Major League Spring Training, Journeys for the Junior Historian, spring/summer 93; Changing Places: Slave Movement in the South, The Historian 55 (summer 93); Making the Cut: Racial Discrimination in Major League Spring Training, Journeys for the Junior Historian, spring/summer 93; coauth, Only in Mississippi: A Guide for the Adventurous Traveler, Quail Ridge Press, 97; New Left, Revisionist, In Your Face History: Oliver Stone's Born on the Fourth of July Experience, Film and History, Oct 98; ed, The Civil Rights Movement, Blackwell Publ, 00; auth, Race Against Time: Culture and Separation in Natchez Since 1930, Louisiana State Univ Pr, forthcoming. **CONTACT ADDRESS** 633 Idlewild Cr, A8, Birmingham, AL 35205. **EMAIL** davisje@uab.edu

DAVIS, JAMES EDWARD

PERSONAL Born 09/27/1940, Detroit, MI, m, 1966, 2 children **DISCIPLINE** HISTORY, GEOGRAPHY **EDUCATION** Wayne State Univ, AB, 62, MA, 66 Univ MI, PhD(hist), 71. **CAREER** Teacher, Dearborn Pub Schs, 62-71; assoc prof to prof hist, IL Col, 71-. **HONORS AND AWARDS** Distinguished Service Awd, Ill State Historical Soc, 77. **MEMBERSHIPS** Orgn Am Historians; Soc for Hist for the Early Am Republic. **RESEARCH** The social and political history of the early National era of America; the settlement process of early America and other frontier societies; the civil war era. **SELECTED PUBLICATIONS** Auth, New Aspects of Men and New Forms of Society, the Old Northwest, 1790-1920, J Ill State Historical Soc, 8/76; Frontier America, 1800-1840: A Comparative Demographic Analysis of the Settlement Process, Arthur Clark, 77; ed, Dreams to Dust, Univ NE, 89; auth, Frontier Illinois, IN Univ Press, 99. **CONTACT ADDRESS** Dept Hist, Illinois Col, 1101 W College Ave, Jacksonville, IL 62650-2299. **EMAIL** davis@hilltop.ic.edu

DAVIS, JOHN

PERSONAL Born 09/24/1961, OH **DISCIPLINE** ART HISTORY **EDUCATION** Cornell Univ, AB; Columbia Univ, MA, MPhil, PhD. **CAREER** Priscilla Paine Van der Poel prof, Smith Col. **RESEARCH** Artists' studios; the painting of Johnson Eastman; urban cult in 19th-century NY City; Cath imagery in the Antebellum Era; Am concepts of gender and space. **SELECTED PUBLICATIONS** Auth, The Landscape of Belief: Encountering the Holy Land in the Nineteenth Century, Amer Art and Cult; coauth, Nineteenth-Century American Paintings: Collections of the National Gallery of Art, Syst Catalogue; coauth, Smith College Museum of Art: European and American Paintings and Sculpture, 1760-1960. New York: Hudson Hills Press, 00. **CONTACT ADDRESS** Dept of Art, Smith Col, Hilyer Hall 311, Northampton, MA 01063. **EMAIL** JDAVIS@smith.edu

DAVIS, LEROY

DISCIPLINE HISTORY **EDUCATION** Howard Univ, BA, 76; Kent State Univ, MA, 78, PhD, 90. **CAREER** Assoc prof **RESEARCH** African-American history; American history; comparative education in the African Diaspora. **SELECTED PUBLICATIONS** Coauth, African Experience in Community Development: The Continuing Struggle in Africa and the Americas (v I/II); A Clashing of the Soul: John Hope and the Dilemma of African American Leadership and Black Education in the Early 20th Century. **CONTACT ADDRESS** Dept History, Emory Univ, 221 Bowden Hall, 561 Kilgo Cir, Atlanta, GA 30322-1950. **EMAIL** ldavi04@emory.edu

DAVIS, MIRIAM

PERSONAL Born 03/18/1963, Ft Rucker, AL, m, 1993 **DISCIPLINE** HISTORY **EDUCATION** Emory Univ, BA, 86; Univ Calif at Santa Barbara, MA, 89; PhD, 95; Univ York, MA, 90. **CAREER** Asst prof, Delta State Univ, 95-. **HONORS AND AWARDS** Fulbright, 89-90. **RESEARCH** Dame Kathleen Kenyon. **SELECTED PUBLICATIONS** Auth, "The English Medieval Urban Environment Before the Black Death: Learned Views and Popular Practice," Medieval Perspectives Vol 8 (98): 69-83. **CONTACT ADDRESS** Dept Hist, Delta State Univ, 1003 W Sunflower Rd, Cleveland, MS 38733-0001. **EMAIL** mdavis@dsu.deltast.edu

DAVIS, NATALIE ZEMON

PERSONAL Born 11/08/1928, Detroit, MI, m, 1948, 3 children **DISCIPLINE** EARLY MODERN AND SOCIAL HISTORY **EDUCATION** Smith Col, BA, 49; Radcliffe Col, MA, 50; Univ Mich, PhD(hist), 59. **CAREER** Brown Univ, 59-63; York Univ, 63-64; Univ of Toronto, 63-71; Univ of Calif, Berkeley, 71-77; Ecole des Hautes Etudes en Sciences Sociales, Paris, 77; Yale Univ, Henry Luce Vis prof, 87; Prof, Princeton Univ, 81-, Henry Charles Lea Prof emer, 96-, Dir, Shelby Cullom Davis Ctr of Historical Studies, 90-94; George Eastman Prof, Balliol Col Oxford, 94-95; Northrop Frye Vis Prof of Literary Theory, Univ of Toronto, 96-97, Adj Prof of Hist, Anthropology, Medieval Studies, 97-, Sr Fel, Centre for Comparative Lit, 97-. **HONORS AND AWARDS** Chevalier, L'Ordre des Palmes Academiques, 76; Fel Am Acad of Arts and Sciences, 79; Radcliffe Grad Soc Medal for Distinguished Achievement, 83; Howard T. Berhman Awd for Distinguished Achievement in the Humanities at Princeton, 83; Eugene Asher Distinguished Teaching Awd, Am Historical Asn, 94; Corresponding Fel, The British Acad, 95; Smith Col Medal, 96; Fel of Early Mod Studies, Sixteenth Century Studies Conf, 98; Toynbee Prize, 00. **MEMBERSHIPS** Am Soc Reformation Res; AHA; Soc Fr Hist Studies; Renaissance Soc Am. **RESEARCH** Sex roles in early modern Europe; religion and society in 16th century France; popular culture. **SELECTED PUBLICATIONS** Auth, Society and Culture in Early Modern France, Stanford Univ Press, 75; auth, The Return of Martin Guerre, Harvard Univ Press, 83; auth, Frauen und Gesellschaft am Beginn der Neuzeit, trans. Wolfgang Kaiser, Berlin: Wagenbach, 86; auth, Fiction in the Archives, Pardon Tales and their Tellers in Sixteenth Century France, Stanford Univ Press, 87; co-ed, A History of Women, 3: Renaissance and Enlightenment Paradoxes, Harvard Univ Press, 93; auth, Women on the Margins, Three Seventeenth-Century Lives, Harvard Univ Press, 95; auth, Lebensgange, trans. Wolfgang Kaiser, Berlin: Wagenbach, 98; auth, Slaves on Screen: Film and Historical Vision, The Barbara Frum Lectures, Toronto: Random House of Canada, 00; auth, The Gift in Sixteenth-Century France, Madison: Univ of Wisconsin Press, September 00. **CONTACT ADDRESS** Dept of History, Princeton Univ, 768 Euclid Ave., Toronto, ON, Canada M6G 2V2.

DAVIS, RICHARD W.

PERSONAL Born 12/08/1935, Somers, CT, m, 1965, 2 children **DISCIPLINE** HISTORY **EDUCATION** Amherst Col, BA, 57; Cambridge Univ, M Lit, 62; Columbia Univ, MA, 58; PhD, 63. **CAREER** Instr, Univ RI, 62-64; asst prof, Univ Cal, Riverside, 64-69; assoc prof to prof, Washington Univ, 69-; chair, 74-77; Cen dir, 89-. **HONORS AND AWARDS** Fel, RHS; NEH, 67, 81; Guggenheim Fel; Dist Vis Prof, Christ's Coll, Cambridge. **MEMBERSHIPS** AHA; MVSA; NACBS. **RESEARCH** Modern Britain, political, social, religious, history, 1780-1914. **SELECTED PUBLICATIONS** Auth, Politics, 1780-1830 (71); auth, Political Change & Continuity, 1760-1830: A Buckinghamshire Study (72); auth, Disraeli (76); auth, The English Rothschilds (82); co-ed, Religion and Irreligion in Victorian Society (92); ed, Lords of Parliament, 1714-1914 (95); ed, The Origins of Modern Freedom in the West (95). **CONTACT ADDRESS** Cen Hist Freedom, Washington Univ, PO Box 1223, Saint Louis, MO 63130. **EMAIL** rwdavis@artsci.wustl.edu

DAVIS, RODNEY

PERSONAL Born 07/14/1932, Newton, KS, m, 1954, 3 children **DISCIPLINE** HISTORY **EDUCATION** Univ Kans, BS, 54; MA, 59; Univ Iowa, PhD, 66. **CAREER** From Instr to Prof,

Knox Col, 63-97; Co-Dir, Lincoln Studios Ctr, Knox Col, 97-. **HONORS AND AWARDS** Philip Greon Wright Prize for Excellence in Teaching, 67, 89; Emma Lou & Gayle Thornbrough Awd, 93; Huntington Libr Fels, 91-92, 99. **MEMBERSHIPS** OAH, ISHS **RESEARCH** Abraham Lincoln, Illinois history. **SELECTED PUBLICATIONS** Co-ed, Hernoon's Informants: Letters, Interviews and Statements About Abraham Lincoln, Univ Ill Pr, 98; ed, Thomas Ford: A History of Illinois, Univ Ill Pr, 99; ed, Ward Hill Lamon: Abraham Lincoln, Univ Nebr Pr, 99. **CONTACT ADDRESS** Lincoln Studies Center, Knox Col, Illinois, Galesburg, IL 61401-4938. **EMAIL** rodavis@knox.edu

DAVIS, RONALD LEROY
PERSONAL Born 09/22/1933, Cambridge, OH **DISCIPLINE** AMERICAN CULTURAL HISTORY **EDUCATION** Univ Tex, BA, 55, MA, 57, PhD(hist), 61. **CAREER** Asst prof hist, Kans State Teachers Col (Emporia State Univ), 61-62; asst prof humanities, Mich State Univ, 62-65; from asst prof to assoc prof, 65-72, PROF HIST, SOUTHERN METHODIST UNIV, 72-; Mich State Univ All-Univ res grant, 63-64, Univ Grad Coun grant, 67-68; dir oral hist prog on performing arts, Southern Methodist Univ, 72-; dir, DeGolyer Inst Am Studies, 74- **HONORS AND AWARDS** Phi Beta Kappa. **MEMBERSHIPS** Orgn Am Historians; Western Hist Asn. **RESEARCH** American cultural history, particularly history of American music, theater, and film. **SELECTED PUBLICATIONS** Auth, A History of Opera in the American West, Prentice-Hall, 64; Opera in Chicago, Appleton, 66; Culture on the Frontier, SW Rev, fall 68; Sopranos and Six-Guns: The Frontier Opera House as a Cultural Symbol, Am West, 11/70; ed, The Social and Cultural Life of the 1920's, Holt, 72; auth, A History of Music in American Life, Krieger Publ Co, 80-82; Hollywood Beauty: Linda Darnell and the American Dream, Univ OK Press, 91; The Glamour Factory, SMU Press, 93; John Ford: Hollywood's Old Master, Univ Ok Press, 95; Celluloid Mirrors: Hollywood and American Society Since 1945, Harcourt Brace, 97; Duke: The Life and Image of John Wayne, Unvi OK Press, 98; auth, La Scala West: The Dallas Opera Under Kelly and Rescigno, SMU Press, 00. **CONTACT ADDRESS** Dept of Hist, So Methodist Univ, P O Box 750001, Dallas, TX 75275-0001. **EMAIL** rldavis@mail.smu.edu

DAVIS, THOMAS JOSEPH
PERSONAL Born 01/06/1946, New York, NY **DISCIPLINE** HISTORY **EDUCATION** SUNY at Buffalo, JD 1993; Ball State Univ, MA 1976; Columbia Univ, PhD 1974, MA 1968; Fordham Univ, AB 1967. **CAREER** Columbia Univ, instr, 68; Southern Univ, instr 68-69; Manhattanville Coll, dir Afro-Amer stud 70-71; Earlham Coll, assoc/asst prof 72-76; Howard Univ, prof/assoc prof 77-87; State Univ of NY at Buffalo, prof, 86-96; Arizona State Univ, prof, 96-. **HONORS AND AWARDS** Fellow Ford Found 1971, Herbert H Lehman 1969-71; Fulbright 1972, 1994; Francis Cardinal Spellman Youth Awd 1962; Newberry Library Fellow 1982; Smithsonian Inst Faculty Fellow 1983; Alpha Kappa Alpha, Gamma Iota Chapter, Educator of the Year, 1982; NY African American Inst, 1986, 1987; Amer Bar Found, Visiting Fellow, 1994-95. **MEMBERSHIPS** Bd mem New York City Council Against Poverty 1965-67; consultant Natl Endowment for Humanities 1980, Educational Testing Serv 1979-88, US Dept of Labor 1978-79; **SELECTED PUBLICATIONS** Auth, A Rumor of Revolt, Macmillian/Free Press, 1985, Univ Mass, 1990; Africans in the Americas, St Martin's Press, 1994. **CONTACT ADDRESS** Dept of History, Arizona State Univ, Box 872501, Tempe, AZ 85287-2501.

DAVIS, THOMAS WEBSTER
PERSONAL Born 10/03/1942, Richmond, VA, m, 1967, 1 child **DISCIPLINE** BRITISH & WORLD HISTORY **EDUCATION** Va Mil Inst, BA, 64; Univ NC, Chapel Hill, MA, 66, PhD(Brit hist), 72. **CAREER** Asst prof, 72-78, assoc prof, 78-82, Prof Hist, Va Mil Inst, 82-, Am Philos Soc res grant, 74; Danforth assoc, 76-. **HONORS AND AWARDS** Who's Who Among Teachers in America **MEMBERSHIPS** World Hist Asn; AHA; Southern Conf Brit Studies **RESEARCH** Eighteenth-nineteenth century ecclesiastical history; social history. **SELECTED PUBLICATIONS** Ed, Committees for repeal of the Test and Corporation Acts, minutes 1786-90 and 1827-28, London Rec Soc, 78 **CONTACT ADDRESS** Dept of Hist, Virginia Military Inst, Lexington, VA 24450. **EMAIL** davistw@vmi.edu

DAVIS, WHITNEY
DISCIPLINE ART HISTORY **EDUCATION** Harvard Univ, PhD. **CAREER** Porf, Northwestern Univ; Lectr, Thomas Harris Lectures in History of Art, Univ Col London, 93; prof Humanities, Northwestern Univ, 93-94; tchg and res prof, Arthur Andersen Univ 94-95; dir, Alice Berline Kaplan Center for the Humanities, Northwestern Univ; Getty fel; Guggenheim fel. **SELECTED PUBLICATIONS** Auth, The Canonical Tradition in Ancient Egyptian Art, 89; Masking the Blow: The Scene of Representation in Late Prehistoric Egyptian Art, 92; Drawing the Dream of the Wolves: Homosexuality, Interpretation, and Freud's Wolf Man, 96; replications: Archaeology, Art History and Psychoanalysis, 96; Pacing the World: Construction in the Sculpture of David Rabinowitch, 96; ed, Gay and Lesbian Studies in Art History, 94. **CONTACT ADDRESS** Dept of Art History, Northwestern Univ, 1801 Hinman, Evanston, IL 60208.

DAVIS, WINSTON
PERSONAL Born 11/05/1939, Jamestown, NY, m, 1974, 2 children **DISCIPLINE** HISTORY OF RELIGION **EDUCATION** Univ Chicago, PhD, 73. **CAREER** Wash and Lee Univ, 92-; Southwestern Univ, 83-92; Kwansei Gakuin Japan, 79-83; Stanford Univ, 73-79. **HONORS AND AWARDS** Phi Beta Kappa; NEH Fel; Dist Lectr, Univ Lectr, U of AZ. **MEMBERSHIPS** AAAR; ASSR. **RESEARCH** Max Weiber; The Ethics of Responsibility. **SELECTED PUBLICATIONS** Auth, DoJo: Magil and Exorcism in Modern Japan; Japanese Religion and Society; The Moral and Political Naturalism of Baron Kate Hiroyuki. **CONTACT ADDRESS** Dept of Religion, Washington and Lee Univ, Lexington, VA 24450. **EMAIL** davis.w@wlu.edu

DAVISON, JEAN MARGARET
PERSONAL Born 04/19/1922, Glens Falls, NY **DISCIPLINE** CLASSICAL LANGUAGES, ANCIENT HISTORY **EDUCATION** Univ Vt, AB, 44; Yale Univ, AM, 50, PhD(class archaeol), 57; Univ Ital Stranieri, Perugia, dipl, 60. **CAREER** Cryptanalyst, US Dept War, 44-45; foreign serv clerk, US Dept State, Athens, 45-46 & Vienna, 47-49; instr ancient hist, Latin, Greek & Greek art, 55-59, from asst prof to prof, 59-72, Roberts Prof Class Lang & Lit, Univ VT, 72-, Am Philos Asn res grant, 67-68; mem managing comt, Am Sch Class Studies, Athens, 65, mem exec comt, 73, vis prof, 74-75. **MEMBERSHIPS** Archaeol Inst Am; Vergilian Soc Am; Class Asn New England; Am Sch Orient Res; Asn Field Archaeol. **RESEARCH** Greek Archaeology; Homeric studies; pre-Roman Italy. **SELECTED PUBLICATIONS** Auth, Vitruvius on Acoustical Vases in Greek and Roman Theaters, Amer Jour Archaeol, Vol 0100, 96. **CONTACT ADDRESS** Dept of Classics, Univ of Vermont, Burlington, VT 05401.

DAVISON, NANCY R.
DISCIPLINE AMERICAN CULTURE **EDUCATION** Smith, BA, 66; Univ Mich, MA, 73, PhD, 80. **CAREER** ARTIST, PRINTMAKER & GALLERY OWNER **MEMBERSHIPS** Am Antiquarian Soc **SELECTED PUBLICATIONS** Author, American Sheet Music Illustration: Reflections of the Nineteenth-Century, Clements Library Exhibition, 73; auth, "Andrew Jackson in Cartoon and Caricature," American Printmaking Before 1876: Fact, Fiction, and Fantasy, Lib Congress, 75; auth, "Bickham's Musical Entertainer and Other Curiosities," in Eighteenth-Century Prints in Colonial America: To Educate and Decorate, Colonial Williamsburg Found, 79; auth, E. W. Clay and the American Caricature Business, in Prints and Printmakers of New York State, 1825-1940, Syracuse Univ Press, 86; York Beach Activity Book, Blue Stocking, 96. **CONTACT ADDRESS** PO Box 1257, York Beach, ME 03910.

DAVISON, RODERIC HOLLETT
PERSONAL Born Buffalo, NY, m, 2 children **DISCIPLINE** HISTORY **EDUCATION** Princeton Univ, AB, 37; Harvard Univ, AM, 38, PhD(hist), 42. **CAREER** Inst hist, Princeton Univ, 40-42, 46-47; from asst prof to assoc prof, 47-54, chmn dept, 60-64, 69-70, Prof Hist, George Washington Univ, 54-, Lectr hist, Sch Advan Int Studies, Johns Hopkins Univ, 51-52 & 55-58 & Harvard Univ, 59-60; Ford fel, Fund for Advan Educ, 53-54; Soc Sci Res Coun grant, Mid East, 64-65 & 77-78; fel, Am Res Inst, Turkey, 64-65; Guggenheim fel, 70-71. **MEMBERSHIPS** AHA (treas, 74); Mid East Inst (vpres, 76-82); Mid East Studies Asn NAm (pres, 74-75); Turkish Studies Asn NAm (pres, 80-81). **RESEARCH** European diplomatic history since 1815; Ottoman and Turkish modern history; diplomacy of the Eastern question. **SELECTED PUBLICATIONS** Coauth, The Diplomats, 1919-1939, Princeton Univ, 53; auth, Turkish attitudes concerning Christian-Muslim equality, Am Hist Rev, 7/54; The Near and Middle East: An Introduction to History and Bibliography, Am Hist Asn, 59; Where is the Middle East?, Foreign Affairs, 7/60; Reform in the Ottoman Empire, 1856-1876, Princeton Univ, 63; Turkey, Prentice-Hall, 68; The treaty of Kuchuk Kainardji reconsidered, Slavic Rev, 9/76; The First Ottoman Experiment with Paper Money, In: Social and Economic History of Turkey, 80. **CONTACT ADDRESS** Dept of Hist, The George Washington Univ, Washington, DC 20052.

DAWSON, ANNE
DISCIPLINE ART HISTORY **EDUCATION** Brown Univ, PhD. **CAREER** Eng Dept, Eastern Conn State Univ **MEMBERSHIPS** Asn Study Conn Hist; Conn Rev; Jour Am Hist. **SELECTED PUBLICATIONS** Auth, exhib catalogues. **CONTACT ADDRESS** Eastern Connecticut State Univ, 83 Windham Street, Willimantic, CT 06226.

DAWSON, JOHN PHILIP
PERSONAL Born 11/28/1928, Ann Arbor, MI, m, 1997, 2 children **DISCIPLINE** HISTORY **EDUCATION** Harvard Univ, PhD, 61. **CAREER** Instr, Harvard Univ, 61-64; asst prof, 64-70, assoc prof, 70-73, Stanford Univ; prof, Brooklyn Col, CUNY, 73-98. **HONORS AND AWARDS** NEH fel, 87-88. **MEMBERSHIPS** Soc des Etudes Robespierristes; Soc Hist de Paris et de l'Ile-de-France; Asn Hist Soc Rurales; Soc for French Hist Stud. **RESEARCH** French Revolution. **SELECTED PUBLICATIONS** Auth, Provincial Magistrates and Revolutionary Politics in France, 1789-1795, Harvard, 72; contribur, Aydelotte, ed, The Dimensions of Quantitative Research in History, Princeton, 72; contribur, Waldinger, ed, The French Revolution and the Meaning of Citizenship, Greenwood, 93. **CONTACT ADDRESS** 56 Seventh Ave, New York, NY 10011. **EMAIL** ph.dawson@worldnet.att.net

DAWSON, JOSEPH G., III
PERSONAL Born 09/22/1945, Beford, OH, m, 1969, 2 children **DISCIPLINE** HISTORY **EDUCATION** La State Univ, BA, 67; MA, 70; PhD, 78. **CAREER** Instr, La State Univ at Eunice, 78-79; from asst prof to prof, Tex A & M Univ, 79-. **HONORS AND AWARDS** General L. Kemper Williams Prize, La Hist Asn, 83; Certificate of Commendation, Am Asn for State and Local Hist, 91; Colonel Robert D. Heinl Awd, Marine Corps Heritage Found, 99. **MEMBERSHIPS** Soc for Military Hist, Southern Hist Asn, Western Hist Asn, La Hist Asn. **RESEARCH** American Military History, Louisiana History. **SELECTED PUBLICATIONS** Auth, Army Generals and Reconstruction: Louisiana 1862-1877, La State Univ Press, 82; ed, The Louisiana Governors, La State Univ Press, 90; auth, "William T. Sampson: Progressive Technologist as Naval Commander," in Admirals of the New Stell Navy, ed. J. C. Bradford (Naval Inst Press, 90)); auth, The Late 19th Century U.S. Army 1865-1898, Greenwood Press, 90; ed, Commanders in Chief: Presidential Leadership in Modern Wars, Univ Press of Kans, 93; ed, The Texas Military Experience, Tex A & M Univ Press, 95; auth, "With Fidelity and Effectiveness: General Archibald Henderson's Lasting Legacy to the U.S. Marine Corps," J of Military Hist vol 62 (98); auth, Doniphan's Epic March, Univ Press of Kans, 99. **CONTACT ADDRESS** Dept Hist, Texas A&M Univ, Col Station, College Station, TX 77843-4236. **EMAIL** jgdawson@tamu.edu

DAY, LYNDA
PERSONAL Born, NC, m, 1 child **DISCIPLINE** AFRICAN STUDIES **EDUCATION** Harvard Univ, BA, 75; Univ Wisc, PhD, 88. **CAREER** Asst prof, William Paterson Col, 88-92; Asst Prof to Assoc Prof, CUNY, 92-. **HONORS AND AWARDS** Fulbright Lecture/Res Awd, 99-00. **MEMBERSHIPS** African Studies Asn, Caribbean Studies Asn. **RESEARCH** African women in politics. **SELECTED PUBLICATIONS** Auth, Making a Way to Freedom: A History of African Americans on Long Island, Heart of the Lakes Press, 97. **CONTACT ADDRESS** Dept African Studies, Brooklyn Col, CUNY, 2901 Bedford Ave, Brooklyn, NY 11210-2813. **EMAIL** lday@brooklyn.cuny.edu

DAY, RICHARD B.
PERSONAL Born 07/22/1942, Toronto, ON, Canada **DISCIPLINE** POLITICAL SCIENCE, HISTORY **EDUCATION** Univ Toronto, BA, 65, MA, 67, Dip REES, 67; Univ London, PhD, 70. **CAREER** Asst to assoc prof, 70-79, PROF POLITICAL SCIENCE, ERINDALE COL, UNIV TORONTO, 79-. **HONORS AND AWARDS** Killam sr res fel, 78, 79. **MEMBERSHIPS** Int Soc Study Europ Ideas; Asn Can Slavists; Can Polit Sci Asn. **SELECTED PUBLICATIONS** Auth, Leon Trotsky and the Economics of Political Isolation, 73; auth, The 'Crisis' and the 'Crash' - Soviet Studies of the West (1917-1939), 81; auth, Cold War Capitalism: The View from Moscow (1945-1975), 95; ed/transl, Selected Writings on the State and the Transition to Socialism (N.I. Bukharin); ed/transl, The Decline of Capitalism (E.A. Preobrazhensky), 85; co-ed, Democratic Theory and Technological Society, 88. **CONTACT ADDRESS** Dept o Political Sci, Univ of Toronto, 100 St George St, Rm 3018, Mississauga, ON, Canada M5S 3G3. **EMAIL** rbday@credit.erin.utoronto.ca

DAY, RONNIE
PERSONAL Born 09/20/1939, London, KY, m, 1985, 2 children **DISCIPLINE** HISTORY **EDUCATION** Cumberland Col, BA, 63; Tex Christian Univ, MA, 65, PhD, 71. **CAREER** Prof, East Tenn State Univ, 68-. **MEMBERSHIPS** Society for Military Hist. **RESEARCH** World War II, South Pacific. **SELECTED PUBLICATIONS** Ed, South Pacific Diary: 1942-1943, 96. **CONTACT ADDRESS** East Tennessee State Univ, PO Box 70672, Johnson City, TN 37614. **EMAIL** dayr@etsu.edu

DAY, TERENCE PATRICK
PERSONAL Born 02/02/1930, London, England, m, 1969, 3 children **DISCIPLINE** HISTORY OF RELIGIONS, BUDDHISM **EDUCATION** London Col Divinity, ALCD, 59; Univ London, BD Hons, 60; King's Col, MTh, 63, PhD(hist of relig), 66. **CAREER** Lectr philos, St John's Col, Univ Agra, India, 66-71; lectr hist of relig, Univ Nairobi, Kenya, 71-73; Asst Prof Hist/Relig, Univ Manitoba, 74-. **MEMBERSHIPS** Can Soc Study Relig, Am Acad Relig, Int Asn of Buddhist Studies, Am Oriental Soc, Can Asian Studies Assoc. **RESEARCH** Iconography of Religion, Folk Religion, Modern Movements in Religion. **SELECTED PUBLICATIONS** Auth, Great Tradition and Little Tradition in Theravada Buddhsit Studies (Studies in Asian Thought and Religion, Vol 7), 88. **CONTACT ADDRESS** Dept of Relig, Univ of Manitoba, 327 Fletcher Argue Bldg, Winnipeg, MB, Canada R3T 5V5. **EMAIL** day@ms.umanitoba.ca

DAYTON, CORNELIA H.
DISCIPLINE HISTORY **EDUCATION** Harvard-Radcliffe, AB, 79; Princeton Univ, PhD, 86 **CAREER** Assoc prof, hist, Univ Calif Irvine; current, ASSOC PROF, HIST, UNIV CONN STORRS; Instr, Col of William and Mary. **HONORS AND AWARDS** 1996 Homer D Babbidge Jr Awd; Douglass Adair Memorial Awd, 96; NEH Fel. 99-00; Post Doctoral Fel. **MEMBERSHIPS** Am Antiquarian Soc. **SELECTED PUBLICATIONS** Auth, Taking the Trade: Abortion and Gender Relations in an Eighteenth-Century New England Village, Will & Mary Q, 3rd Ser, 91; auth, Women Before the Bar: Gender, Law and Society in Connecticut, 1639- 1789, Inst of Early Am Hist & Cult with Univ of NC Press, 95; auth, "Excommunicating the Governor's Wife: Religious Dissent in the Puritan Colonies Before the Era of Rights Consciousness," in Religious Conscience, the State, and the Law in Anglo-American History," SUNY Press, 99; auth, "Was there a Calvinist Type of Patriarchy? New Haven Colony Reconsidered in the Early Modern Contest," in The Many Legalities of Early America (Univ of NCar Press, forthcoming). **CONTACT ADDRESS** Dept of Hist, V-2103, Univ of Connecticut, Storrs, 241 Glenbrook Rd, Storrs, CT 06269-3722. **EMAIL** dayton@sp.uconn.edu

DAYTON, DONALD WILBER
PERSONAL Born 07/25/1942, Chicago, IL, m, 1969 **DISCIPLINE** THEOLOGY, AMERICAN RELIGIOUS HISTORY **EDUCATION** Houghton Col, BA, 63; Yale Univ, BD, 69; Univ Ky, MS, 69; Univ Chicago, PhD, 83. **CAREER** From asst to asst prof theol, Asbury Theol Sem, 69-72, acquisitions librn, B L Fisher Libr, 69-72; asst prof theol, North Park Theol Sem, 72-77, assoc prof, 77-80, dir, Mellander Libr, 72-80; Prof Theol, Northern Baptist Theol Sem, 80-97; prof, Drew Univ, 97-. **MEMBERSHIPS** Karl Barth Soc NAm; Wesleyan Theol Soc; Am Theol Libr Asn; Am Soc Church Hist; Am Acad Relig. **RESEARCH** Theology and ethics of Karl Barth; 19th century American religious thought; holiness and Pentecostal churches. **SELECTED PUBLICATIONS** Auth, Creationism in 20th-Century America--A 10-Volume Anthology of Documents, 1903-1961, Zygon, Vol 0032, 97. **CONTACT ADDRESS** Drew Univ, 36 Madison Ave, Madison, NJ 07940.

DE BACA, VINCENT C.
PERSONAL Born 05/29/1950, San Diego, CA, m, 1977, 5 children **DISCIPLINE** HISTORY **EDUCATION** Univ Calif, BA, 81; MA, 85; PhD, 91. **CAREER** Instr, Miracosta Col, 86-87; Instr, San Diego Community Col, 90-92; Lectr, Univ San Diego, 92; Lectr, Univ Calif, 92; From Asst Prof to Assoc Prof, Metropolitan State Col, 93-. **HONORS AND AWARDS** President's Fel, Univ Calif, 86-87; Pew Found Fel, 90; Outstanding Scholar Awd, Metro St Col, 97; Leroy Haten Awd, Colo Hist Soc, 99. **MEMBERSHIPS** CHSRB, CHS, NACS, HLRC, LRPC, NSHG. **RESEARCH** Mexican history, United States and Mexico border, Chicano history, United States and Mexico War, New Mexico history, Hispanos in Colorado, Hispano genealogy. **SELECTED PUBLICATIONS** Auth, "Emilio Zamora," NMex Hist Rev, 70:1 (95); auth, "Chicano Studies at Metro State College," Resources in Educ, Appalachia Educ Lab (96); auth, "Pastimes in the Life of Pablo C de Baca," La Gente: Hispano His and Life in Colo, Colo Hist Soc (98); ed, La Gente: Hispano History and Life in Colorado, Colo Hist Soc (Denver, CO), 98; auth, Susan Calafate Boyle, Color Heritage Pr, 99; auth, "The 'Shame Suicides' and Tijuana," J of the Southwest (forthcoming). **CONTACT ADDRESS** Dept Hist, Metropolitan State Col of Denver, PO Box 173362, Denver, CO 80217-3362.

DE BARY, WM. THEODORE
PERSONAL Born 08/09/1919, NY, m, 1942, 4 children **DISCIPLINE** EAST ASIAN STUDIES **EDUCATION** Columbia Col, BA 41; Columbia Univ, MA 48, PhD 53. **CAREER** Columbia Univ, Special Serv Prof 90-; Heyman Cen Humanities, dir 81-; John Mitchell Mason Prof 79-90; exe vp 71-78; pres assoc Asian Stud 69-70; chemn univ sen 69-70; Carpenter Prof Oriental stud 66-78; chmn dept E Asian lang and cult 60-66; dir E Asian lang 60-72; chemn comm Oriental stud 53-61. **HONORS AND AWARDS** Hon Doc of Letters and Humane Letters, Col Univ, St Lawrence Univ, Loyola Univ; Order of the Rising Sun; Pres Townsend Harris Medal; John Jay Awd; Alexander Hamilton Medal; Lionel Trilling Book Awd; Mark Van Doren Prize; Great Teacher Awd; Awd for Excell Grad Fac Alum; Frank Tannenbaum Mem Awd; Guggenheim Fel; Watumull Prize; Fishburn Prize. **MEMBERSHIPS** Founder or co-founder of, Heyman Cen for Humanities; The Society of Fellows in the Humanities; The Society of Senior Scholars; The Univ Lectures; Trilling Seminars; The Univ Seminars in Asian Thought and Religion and Neo-Confucian Studies; Alumni Colloquia in the Humanities. **RESEARCH** Confucianism; Civil society; Human rights. **SELECTED PUBLICATIONS** Auth, Asian Values and Human Rights, Harvard Univ Press, 98; Confucianism and Human Rights, Columbia Univ Press, 97; Sources of Korean Tradition, CUP, 97; Waiting for the Dawn: A Plan for the Prince, CUP, 93; auth or coauth. **CONTACT ADDRESS** Committee on Asia and the Middle East, Columbia Univ, 502 Kent Hall, New York, NY 10027. **EMAIL** wtd1@columbia.edu

DE BRETTEVILLE, SHEILA LEVRANT
PERSONAL Born 11/04/1940, New York, NY, m, 1965, 1 child **DISCIPLINE** ART **EDUCATION** Barnard Col, Columbia Univ, BA 62; Yale Univ, MFA 64. **CAREER** Cal Inst of Arts, fac 70-73, pres woman's bldg 73-80, ch Otis A&D 80-90; Yale Univ Art Sch, prof 90-. **HONORS AND AWARDS** Moore College Art Des and Cal College Art & Craft-Hon Doct. **RESEARCH** Public Art; Immigrant neighborhoods. **SELECTED PUBLICATIONS** coauth, The Architecture of the Everyday, Princeton Univ Press, 97. **CONTACT ADDRESS** Dept of Art, Yale Univ, PO Box 208339, New Haven, CT 06520-8339. **EMAIL** sheila.debretteville@yale.edu

DE GIROLAMI CHENEY, LIANA
DISCIPLINE ART HISTORY **EDUCATION** Univ Miami, BA, 68, MA, 70; Boston Univ, PhD, 78. **CAREER** Asst prof, Framingham Col, 74-76; asst prof, Univ Lowell, 76-82; vis prof, York Univ, 79-86; vis prof, Emmanuel Col, 86-95; prof, Univ Lowell, 85-. **HONORS AND AWARDS** Governor's Awd, 85; Outstanding Young Woman Am Awd, 76; pres, asn textual scholar, 97-98; pres, s cent renaissance asn, 98-. **MEMBERSHIPS** Asn Textual Scholar; S Cent Renaissance Asn; Div Humanities Soc Sci; Art Text Asn; Am Asn Italian Studies; British Art Hist Soc; Col Art Asn Am; Emblematic Soc; Hagiographic Soc; Master Drawings Soc; Pre Raphaelite Soc; Renaissance Soc Am. **RESEARCH** Renaissance hist and art. **SELECTED PUBLICATIONS** Auth, Readings in Italian Mannerism, Peter Lang, 97; Botticelli's Neoplatonic Images, Scripta Humanistica, 93; Symbolism of 'Vanitas' in the Arts, Literature, and Music, Edwin Mellen, 93; Medievalism and Pre-Raphaelitism, Edwin Mellen, 93. **CONTACT ADDRESS** Univ of Massachusetts, Lowell, One Univ Ave, Lowell, MA 01854. **EMAIL** lianacheney@earthlink.net

DE GRAZIA, VICTORIA
DISCIPLINE CONTEMPORARY HISTORY OF WESTERN EUROPE **EDUCATION** Smith Col, BA, 68; Columbia Univ, PhD, 76. **CAREER** Prof. **SELECTED PUBLICATIONS** Auth, The Culture of Consent: Mass Organization of Leisure in Fascist Italy, 81; How Fascism Ruled Women: Italy, 1922-1945, 92; ed, The Sex of Things: Gender and Consumption, Hist Perspective, 96. **CONTACT ADDRESS** Dept of Hist, Columbia Col, New York, 2960 Broadway, New York, NY 10027-6902.

DE HART, JANE S.
PERSONAL Born Asheville, NC, m, 1986 **DISCIPLINE** HISTORY **EDUCATION** Duke Univ, BA, 58; MA, 63; PhD, 66. **CAREER** Prof of Hist, Univ NC, Greensboro, 76-81; Bicentennial Prof of Am Studies, Univ Helsinki, Finland, 81-82; prof, Univ NC, Chapel Hill, 82091, Dir, Women's Studies Prog, 82-87; prof, Univ of Calif, Santa Barbara, 92-. **HONORS AND AWARDS** NEH Fel, 75, 98-99; Am Coun of Learned Socs Grant-in-Aid, 76; Fulbright Fel, 81-82; Am Political Sci Asn, Ida Cornelia Beam Distinguished Vis Prof, Univ Iowa, 96. **MEMBERSHIPS** Am Hist Asn, Am Studies Asn, Am Political Sci Asn, Org of Am Hists, Coord Comt of Women in the Hist Prof, West Coast Asn of Women Hists, UCLA Teaching Workshop on Women's Hist. **RESEARCH** U.S. History (primarily 20th century), Political, Legal, and Cultural Conflicts involving Public Policy, and Issues of Gender, Sexuality, Race, and National Identity. **SELECTED PUBLICATIONS** Auth, The Federal Theatre, 1935-39: Plays, Relief, and Politics, Princeton: Princeton Univ Press (67, paperback, 71); ed with Linda K. Kerber, Women's America: Refocusing the Past, NY: oxford Univ Press (82, 87, 91, 95, 99); coauth with Donald G. Mathews, Sex, Gender, and the Politics of ERA: A State and the Nation, NY: Oxford Univ Press (90); auth, Litigating Equality: Ruth Bader Ginsburg, Feminist Lawyers, and the Court, Univ of Chicago Press (forthcoming 2001); auth, Defining America: Personal Politics and the Politics of National Identity, Univ Chicago Press (forthcoming 2003). **CONTACT ADDRESS** Dept Hist, Univ of California, Santa Barbara, 552 Univ Rd, Santa Barbara, CA 93106-0002.

DE JESUS, MELINDA L.
PERSONAL Born Bethlehem, PA, m, 1991 **DISCIPLINE** ASIAN AMERICAN STUDIES **EDUCATION** Lehigh Univ, BA, 87; Univ York, UK, MA, 89; Univ Calif Santa Cruz, PhD, 95. **CAREER** Asst prof, San Francisco State Univ, 96-99; asst prof, Ariz State Univ, 99-. **HONORS AND AWARDS** Citibank Fel, 95-96; Rockefeller Fel, 97; Ariz Wakonse Teaching Fel, 01. **MEMBERSHIPS** MLA, MELUS, AAAS. **RESEARCH** Asian American literature and culture, US Third World feminist theory, Filipino American Studies, popular culture. **SELECTED PUBLICATIONS** Auth, "Fictions of Assimilation: Nancy Drew, Cultural Imperialism, and the Filipina/American Experience," Delinquents and Debutantes, ed Sherrie Iness, (98); auth, "Transforming Pedagogy: Integrating New Media Technologies and Asian American Studies," Works and Days, (99); auth, "A walkin' of de (Rice) Kake: A Filipina American Feminist's Adventures in Academia or, A Pinay's Progress," SOCI Online Jour, (00); auth, "Two's Company, Three's a Crowd? Reading Interracial (Heterosexual) Romance in Contemporary Asian American," LIT: Literature, Interpretation, Theory, (01); auth, "Refiguring History/Transgressing Desire: Tracing the Homoerotic in Carlos Bulosan's America Is in the Heart," Jour of Asian Am Studies, (02). **CONTACT ADDRESS** Asian Pacific Am Studies, Arizona State Univ, Tempe, AZ 85287-0803. **EMAIL** dejesus@asu.edu

DE LA PEDRAJA, RENE
PERSONAL Born 11/26/1951, Havana, Cuba, m, 1976, 1 child **DISCIPLINE** HISTORY **EDUCATION** Univ of Houston, BA, 73; Univ of Chicago, MA, 74, PhD, 77. **CAREER** Res prof, School of Economics, Universidad de los Andes, 76-85; asst prof, Dept of Hist, Kans State Univ, 86-89; ASST PROF, 89-92, ASSOC PROF, 92-97, PROF, 97-, DEPT OF HIST, CANISIUS COL, pres faculty senate, 00-. **HONORS AND AWARDS** Choice Outstanding Academic Boox Awd, Am Libr Asn, 94. **MEMBERSHIPS** Am Hist Asn; Latin Am Studies Asn; Confr of Latin Am Hist. **RESEARCH** Business history; military history. **SELECTED PUBLICATIONS** Auth, Latin American Merchant Shipping in the Age of Global Competition, Greenwood Press, 99; auth, Oil and Coffee: The Merchant Shipping of Latin America from the Imperial Era to the 1950s, Greenwood Press, 98; auth, A Historical Dictionary of the U.S. Merchant Marine and Shipping Industry: Since the Introduction of Steam, Greenwood Press, 94; auth, The Rise and Decline of U.S. Merchant Shipping in the Twentieth Century, Twayne Pub, 92; auth, Energy Politics in Colombia, Westview Press, 89; auth, Fedemetal y la industrializacion de Colombia, Op Graficas, 86; auth, Historia de la energia en Colombia 1538-1930, El Ancora Editores, 85. **CONTACT ADDRESS** Dept of Hist, Canisius Col, 2001 Main St, Buffalo, NY 14208-1098. **EMAIL** delapedr@canisius.edu

DE LA TEJA, J. F.
PERSONAL Born 07/17/1956, Cuba, m, 1983, 2 children **DISCIPLINE** HISTORY **EDUCATION** Seton Hall Univ, BA, 79, MA, 81; Univ of Tx at Austin, PhD, 88. **CAREER** Asst archivist, 85-89, archivist, 89-91, dir of archives and records, Tex General Land Office, 90-91; Asst Prof, 91-95, Assoc Prof, Southwest Tex State Univ, 96-. **HONORS AND AWARDS** Carlos Edvardo Castaneda Service Awd, Tex Catholic Hist Soc, 97; San Antonio Conservation Soc Book Citation and Sons of the Republic of Tex Presidio La Bahia Awd; Southwest Tex State Univ Presidential Awd for Scholarly/Creative Activities, 96; Elected to membership Texas Institute of Letters, 00; Elect Fel of the Tex State Hist Assoc, 01. **MEMBERSHIPS** Tex State Hist Assoc; Western Hist Assoc; Conf on Latin Am Hist. **RESEARCH** Spanish borderlands, Colonial Mexico, 19th Century Texas. **SELECTED PUBLICATIONS** Auth, Spanish Colonial Texas, New Views of Borderland Hist, Univ of Nmex Press, 98; Discovering the Tejano Community in Early Texas, J of the Early Republic, 98; The Colonization and Independence of Texas: A Tejano Perspective, Myths, Misdeeds, and Misunderstandings: The Roots of Conflict in United States-Mexico Relations, Scholarly Resources, 97; Rebellion on the Frontier, Tejano Journey 1770-1860, Univ of Tex Press, 96; San Antonio de Bexar: A Community on New Spain's Northern Frontier, Univ of NMex Press, 95; coed, "The Human Tradition in Texas," Wilmington," DE: Scholarly Resources, 01; auth, "St. James at the Fair: Religious Ceremony and Civic Boosterism on the Colonial Mexican Frontier," The Americas, 01. **CONTACT ADDRESS** Dept of Hist, Southwest Texas State Univ, San Marcos, TX 78666. **EMAIL** jd10@swt.edu

DE LEON, DAVID
PERSONAL Born 03/16/1947, Fargo, ND, s **DISCIPLINE** HISTORY **EDUCATION** Univ Iowa, PhD, 72. **CAREER** Asst prof, Univ of Md, 72-79; asst prof, Calif Inst of Tech, 79-80; assoc prof to prof, Howard Univ, 80-. **HONORS AND AWARDS** Grant, Am Philos Soc, 75; Grant, Am Coun of Learned Soc, 75; NEH Fel, 76-77; ACLS, 79, 88, 92; NEH, 79, 84, 96. **MEMBERSHIPS** Am Studies Assoc; AHA, Org of Am Hist; Popular culture Assoc. **RESEARCH** U.S. social and intellectual, comparative radical and reform movements. **SELECTED PUBLICATIONS** Auth, The American as Anarchist: Reflections on Indigenous Radicalism, Johns Hopkins Univ Pr, (Baltimore), 78; coed, Reinventing Anarchy: What Are Anarchists Thinking These Days?, Routledge and Kegal Paul, (London), 79; auth, Everything is changing: Contemporary U.S. Movements in Historical Perspective, Praeger (NY), 88; auth, Leaders from the 1960s: A Biographical Sourcebook of American Activism, Greenwood Pr, (Westport, CT), 94. **CONTACT ADDRESS** Dept Hist, Howard Univ, 2400 6th St Northwest, Washington, DC 20059-0001. **EMAIL** dde@howard.edu

DE PAUW, LINDA GRANT
PERSONAL Born 01/19/1940, New York, NY, d, 2 children **DISCIPLINE** AMERICAN HISTORY **EDUCATION** Swarthmore Col, BA, 61; Johns Hopkins Univ, PhD, 64. **CAREER** Asst prof hist, George Mason Col, Univ Va, 64-65; from asst prof to assoc prof, 66-75, Prof Hist, George Washington Univ, 75-89; Ed in Chief Doc Hist, First Fed Cong, Nat Hist Publ Comn, 66-84; prof emer, Washington Univ, 98-. **HONORS AND AWARDS** Beveridge Awd, AHA, 64 **RESEARCH** Early American history; women and war. **SELECTED PUBLICATIONS** Auth, The Eleventh Pillar: New York State and the Federal Constitution, Cornell Univ, 66; ed, Documentary History of the First Federal Congress, Johns Hopkins Univ, 72; auth, Land of the unfree: Legal limitations on liberty in pre-revolutionary America, Md Hist Mag, 73; Four traditions:

Women of New York During the American Revolution, Albany, 74; Founding Mothers: Women of America in the Revolutionary era, Houghton, 75; coauth, Remember the Ladies: Women in America, 1750-1815, Viking, 76; Women in Combat: The Revolutionary War Experience, Armed Forces & Soc, winter 81; Seafaring Women, Houghton, 82; Battle Cries and Lullabies, Univ Okla, 98. **CONTACT ADDRESS** Minerva Center, Inc., 20 Granada Rd, Pasadena, MD 21122. **EMAIL** minervacen@aol.com

DE PUMA, RICHARD DANIEL
PERSONAL Born 05/15/1942, DuBois, PA, d, 1 child **DISCIPLINE** CLASSICAL ARCHAEOLOGY, ETRUSCOLOGY **EDUCATION** Swarthmore Col, BA, 64; Bryn Mawr Col, MA, 67, PhD(Class Archaeol), 69. **CAREER** From instr to assoc prof, 68-86, prof Art Hist & Archael, Univ Iowa, 86-, Am Philos Soc fel, 70; Univ Iowa Grad Col grants, 70, 73, 77, 82, 87, 94, 99, 00. **HONORS AND AWARDS** NEH, 84, 91, 93, 99; German Arch Inst, 95. **MEMBERSHIPS** Archaeol Inst Am; Col Art Asn Am; Natl Inst Etruscan Studies; Etruscan Found. **RESEARCH** Etruscan pottery and minor arts; Roman and Hellenistic mosaics; Greek vase painting. **SELECTED PUBLICATIONS** Auth, Corpus Speculorum Etruscorum USA 1, 97 and USA 2, 93; Murlo and the Etruscans, with J Small, 94; Corpus Vasorum Antiquorum: J Paul Getty Museum, fasc 6, 95; fasc 9, 00. **CONTACT ADDRESS** Sch of Art & Art History, Univ of Iowa, E 100, Art Building, Iowa City, IA 52242-1706. **EMAIL** richard-depuma@uiowa.edu

DE SCHAEPDRIJVER, SOPHIE
PERSONAL Born 09/11/1961, Kortrijk, Belgium, m, 1995, 1 child **DISCIPLINE** HISTORY **EDUCATION** Free Univ Brussels, MA, 83; Univ Amsterdam, PhD, 90. **CAREER** Assoc Prof, Univ of Groningen, 90; Assoc Prof, Univ Leiden, 91-95; Vis Assoc Prof, New York Univ., 96-. **HONORS AND AWARDS** Maurits Naessens Awd, 90; Free Speech Awd, 99; Fel, Nat Humanities Ctr, 95-96. **MEMBERSHIPS** Soc for Netherlandic Hist. **RESEARCH** World War One; Urban history; Europe - 19th and 20th centuries; History of the European middle classes. **SELECTED PUBLICATIONS** Auth, Elites for the Capital? Foreign Migration to 19th Century Brussels, Amsterdam, 90; auth, De Groote Oorlog: Het Konikrijk Belgie Tjdens de Eerste Wereldorlog, Atlas Pub, 97; auth, "Occupation, Progaganda, and the Idea of Belgium," in European Culture in the Great War: The Arts, Entertainment, and Propaganda, Cambridge Univ Press, 99. **CONTACT ADDRESS** Dept Hist, New York Univ, 19 University Pl, New York, NY 10003-4556.

DE SYON, GUILLAUME
PERSONAL Born 03/02/1966, Paris, France, m, 1994 **DISCIPLINE** HISTORY **EDUCATION** Tufts Univ, BA, 87; George Wash Univ, MA, 89; Boston Univ, PhD, 94. **CAREER** Contributing Ed, Einstein Papers project, 92-94; Asst prof, Albright Col, 95-. **HONORS AND AWARDS** George M and Paige Laughlin Distinguished Fac Awd, Albright Col, 99; A Shirk Class of 49 Res Awd; Albright Col, 98; Max-Plank Inst fuer Geschichte, Summer Fel, 98. **MEMBERSHIPS** Am Hist Asn, Soc for the Hist of Technol, German Studies Asn, Hist of Sci Soc, Nat Coun for Hist Educ. **RESEARCH** Modern Germany; History of Technology; History of travel. **SELECTED PUBLICATIONS** Auth, Zeppelin! Germany and the Airship Experience, 1900-1939, Johns Hopkins Univ Press, forthcoming; auth, "The Zeppelin Museum in Friedrichshafen," Technology and Culture, (99): 116-121; auth, "Switzerland," in The Encyclopedia of Historians and Historical Writing, Fitzroy Dearborn, 99; auth, "Searching for the German Hero: Biographies of Count Zeppelin, 1908-1938," in Memory, History and Critique, European Identity at the Millennium. Proceedings of the Fifth ISSEI Conference at the Unvisited for Humanist Studies, Utrecht, The Netherlands, August 1996, MIT Press, 98; co-ed, The Collected Papers of Albert Einstein, volumes 8A & 8B, The Berlin Years: Correspondence 1914-1918, Princeton Univ Press, 98; auth, "PostCARds: Spreading the Good Word about the Automobile During the Belle Epoque," Image file, (97): 1-7; auth, "Aviation," American Decades: 1980-1989, Gale Research, 96; auth, "Science and Technology," American Decades: 1930-1939, Gale Research, 95. **CONTACT ADDRESS** Dept Hist, Albright Col, PO Box 15234, Reading, PA 19612-5234.

DE VRIES, BERT
PERSONAL Born 03/04/1939, Netherlands, m, 1962, 4 children **DISCIPLINE** NEAR EAST HISTORY **EDUCATION** Calvin Col, BSc, 60; Calvin Theol Sem, BD, 64; Brandeis Univ, PhD(Hittite), 67. **CAREER** From asst prof to assoc prof, 67-77, Prof Hist, Calvin Col, 77-, Chmn Dept, 80-, Architect-survr, Heshbon Archeol Exped, 68-76; Albright fel, Am Schs Orient Res, 72; dir, Umm El-Jimal archeol exped, 72- **MEMBERSHIPS** Am Orient Soc. **RESEARCH** Middle East archaeology. **CONTACT ADDRESS** Dept of History, Calvin Col, Grand Rapids, MI 49506.

DE VRIES, JAN
PERSONAL Born 11/14/1943, Netherlands, m, 1968, 2 children **DISCIPLINE** HISTORY, ECONOMICS **EDUCATION** Yale, PhD, 70; Columbia Univ, BA, 65. **CAREER** Univ Calif, Berkeley, Prof, 77-, Assoc Prof 73-77; MI State Univ, asst Prof, 70-73. **HONORS AND AWARDS** Gugganheim fel, vis fel, All Souls Col, Oxford; fel, British Academy; fel, Am Academy of Arts & Sciences; fel, Royal Netherlands Academy of Sciences; Heineken Prize in History, 00. **MEMBERSHIPS** Ec Hist Asn; Am Ec Asn; Soc Sci Hist Asn. **RESEARCH** European Economic Hist; Demographic Hist. **SELECTED PUBLICATIONS** The Dutch Economy in the Golden Age, 1500-1700, New Haven, Yale Univ Press, 74; The Economy of Europe in an Age of Crisis, 1600-1750, Cambridge, Cambridge Univ press, 76, Span trans, 79, Port trans, 83, Catalan trans, 93; Barges and Capitalism: Passenger Transportation in the Dutch Economy, 1632-1839, A A G Bijdragen no 21, Wageningen, The Neth, 78, reissued, Utrecht, Hes Pub 81; European Urbanization, 1500-1800, London, Methuen and Co, Cambridge MA, Harvard Univ Press 84, Span trans 87; with A M van der Woude, The First Modern Economy: Success, Failure and Perseverance of the Dutch Economy, 1500-1815, Cambridge, Cambridge Univ Press, 97, Dutch ed, Nederland, 1500-1815: De eerste ronde van modern economisch groei, Amsterdam, Uitgeverij Balans, 95; ed, with Ad van der Woude and Akira Hyami, Urbanization in History, Oxford, Oxford Univ Press, 90; with David Freedberg, Art in History, History in Art: Studies in 17th Century Dutch Culture, Chicago, Univ Chicago Press, 91. **CONTACT ADDRESS** Univ of California, Berkeley, Dept History, Berkeley, CA 94720-2550. **EMAIL** devries@socrates.berkeley.edu

DEAK, ISTVAN
PERSONAL Born 05/11/1926, Szekesfehervar, Hungary, m, 1959, 1 child **DISCIPLINE** MODERN EUROPEAN HISTORY **EDUCATION** Columbia Univ, MA, 58, PhD, 64. **CAREER** Instr Hist, Smith Col, 62-63; from Instr to Prof Hist, 63-93, Seth Low Prof Hist, Columbia Univ, 93-97, actg dir, Inst E Cent Europe, 67-68, dir, Inst E Cent Europe, 68-78; Vis lectr, Yale Univ, 66; vis prof, Univ Calif, Los Angeles, 75 & Univ Siegen, Fed Repub of Ger, 81; emer, 97-. **HONORS AND AWARDS** Guggenheim fel, 70-71; Fulbright-Hays travel fel, 73; Lionel Trilling Book Awd, 79; Am Coun Learned Soc fel, 81; mem, Inst for Advan Study, 81; mem, Hungarian Acad Sci, 90; Wayne S. Vuchinich Book Prize, 91. **MEMBERSHIPS** Am Asn Advan Slavic Studies; Conf Group Slavic & East Europ Hist (vpres, 75-77); Mid-Atlantic Slavic Asn (pres, 77). **RESEARCH** Hist of the Habsburg Monarchy; the Central European Revolutions of 1848-1849; the army in society and polit in Central and Eastern Europe; collaboration, resistance, and retribution in World War II Europe. **SELECTED PUBLICATIONS** Auth, Hungary, In: The European Right, a Historical Profile, 65-66 & Weimer Germany's Left-Wing Intellectuals, 68, Univ CA; The Decline and Fall of Habsburg Hungary, In: Hungary in Revolution, 1918-1919, Univ Nebr, 71; co-ed, Eastern Europe in the 1970's, Praeger, 72; Everyman in Europe: Essays in Social History, Prentice-Hall, 74 & 81; auth, An Army Divided: The Loyalty Crisis of the Habsburg Officer Corps, 1848-49, In: Jahrbuch, Univ Tel-Aviv, 79; The Lawful Revolution, Louis Kossuth and the Hungarians, 1848-49, Univ Columbia, 79; Reform Triumphant, In: The American and European Revolutions, 1776-1848, Univ Iowa, 80; Beyond Nationalism: A Social and Political History of the Habsburg Officer Corps, 1848-1918, Oxford Univ Press, 90, 91, Ger ed, 91, 93, Hungarian ed, 93, Ital ed, 94; coed, The Politics of Retribution in Europe: World War II and its Aftermath, Princeton Univ Press, 00. **CONTACT ADDRESS** Inst of E Cent Europe, Columbia Univ, 420 W 118th St, New York, NY 10027. **EMAIL** id1@columbia.edu

DEAL, J. DOUGLAS
DISCIPLINE HISTORY **EDUCATION** Harvard, AB, 71; Univ Rochester, MA, 74; PhD, 82. **CAREER** Prof, SUNY Oswego. **RESEARCH** Colonial and Revolutionary Am; slavery, the South, and the Civil War era; Am labor hist. **SELECTED PUBLICATIONS** Auth, Race and Class in Colonial Virginia: Indians, Englishmen, and Africans on the Eastern Shore During the Seventeenth Century, Garland, 93; A Constricted World: Free Blacks on Virginia's Eastern Shore, 1680-1750 in Colonial Chesapeake Society, Univ NC P. **CONTACT ADDRESS** Dept Hist, SUNY, Oswego, 110 Mahar Hall, Oswego, NY 13126. **EMAIL** deal@oswego.edu

DEAN, DAVID M.
DISCIPLINE EARLY MODERN BRITISH AND EUROPEAN HISTORY **EDUCATION** Univ Auckland, BA, MA; Univ Cambridge, PhD. **CAREER** Assoc prof, Carleton Univ. **RESEARCH** Political and cultural history, comparative constitutional history; early modern British and European hist; law and soc. **SELECTED PUBLICATIONS** Ed, Interest Groups and Legislative Activity in Elizabeth's Parliaments, a Special Issue of Parliamentary History 8, 2, with N.L. Jones, ed., 89; ed, The Parliaments of Elizabethan England, Oxford: Basil Blackwell, with N.L. Jones, 90; ed, 'Locality and Parliament: The Legislative Activities of Devon's MP's during the Reign of Elizabeth' in T. Grey, M. Rowe and A. Erskine, eds., Tudor and Stuart Devon: The Common Estate and Government, Essays Presented to Joyce Youings, (Exeter, 92): 75-95; ed, 'Image and Ritual in the Tudor Parliament' in Dale Hoak, ed., Tudor Political Culture, (Cambridge Univ Press, 95): 243-71; auth, Law, Law-Making and Society: The Parliament of England 1584-1601, (Cambridge Univ Press, 96). **CONTACT ADDRESS** Dept of Hist, Carleton Univ, 1125 Colonel By Dr, Ottawa, ON, Canada K1S 5B6. **EMAIL** davdean@ccs.carleton.ca

DEAN, KENNETH
DISCIPLINE EAST ASIAN STUDIES **EDUCATION** Stanford Univ, PhD. **CAREER** Assoc prof. **RESEARCH** Taoist studies; popular culture; Chinese lit. **SELECTED PUBLICATIONS** Auth, Taoist Ritual and Popular Cults of Southeast China, Princeton, 93; .Auth, Comic Inversion and Cosmic Renewal in the Ritual Theater of Putian: The God of Theater in Southeast China, 94; auth, Irrigation and Individuation: Cults of Water Deities along the Putian Plains, 94; auth, Lord of the Three in One: the Spread of the Cult in southeast China, Princeton Univ Press, 98; ed, Epigraphical Materials on the History of Religion in Fujian. **CONTACT ADDRESS** East Asian Studies Dept, McGill Univ, 845 Sherbrooke St, Montreal, QC, Canada H3A 2T5. **EMAIL** kdean@leacock.lan.mcgill.ca

DEAN, WARREN
PERSONAL Born 10/17/1932, Passaic, NJ **DISCIPLINE** HISTORY **EDUCATION** Univ Miami, BA, 53; Univ Fla, MA, 61, PhD(hist), 64. **CAREER** Asst prof hist, Univ Tex, Austin, 65-70; assoc prof, 70-77, Prof Hist, NY Univ, 77-, Univ Tex fel hist, 64-65; Social Sci Res Coun fel, 68-69; Guggenheim fel, 80-81. **HONORS AND AWARDS** Robertson Prize, 69. **MEMBERSHIPS** Conf Latin Am Hist; Am Soc Environ Hist. **RESEARCH** Latin America; environmental history; Brazil. **SELECTED PUBLICATIONS** Auth, Industrialization of Sao Paulo, Univ Tex, 69; Latifundia and Land Policy, Hispanic Am Rev, 71; Rio Claro: A Brazilian Plantation System, Stanford Univ, 76; A Pequena Propriedade Dentro do Complexo Cafeeiro: Sitiantes no Municipio de Rio Claro, 1870-1920, Revista de Historia, 76; coauth, Brazil, In: Latin America: A Guide to Economic History, Princeton Univ, 76; co-ed, Essays in the Socioeconomic History of Brazil and Portuguese India, 77; ed, Reflections on the Brazilian Counter-Revolution, 81. **CONTACT ADDRESS** Dept of Hist, New York Univ, 19 University Pl, New York, NY 10003.

DEANE, SEAMUS
PERSONAL Born 02/09/1940, Ireland **DISCIPLINE** IRISH STUDIES **EDUCATION** Cambridge Univ, PhD. **CAREER** Donald and Marilyn Keough Prof Irish Stud, Univ Notre Dame; dir, Field Day Theatre and Publ Co. **HONORS AND AWARDS** Guardian Fiction Prize, 97; Irish Times Intl and Irish Fiction Awds, 97. **MEMBERSHIPS** Royal Irish Academy. **RESEARCH** Irish Literature, History, Enlightenment Studies, Critical Theory. **SELECTED PUBLICATIONS** Auth, Celtic Revivals: Essays in Modern Irish Literature 1880-1980; A Short History of Irish Literature; The French Revolution and Enlightenment in England 1789-1832; ed, The Field Day Anthology of Irish Writing; Reading in the Dark; co-ed, Future Crossings. **CONTACT ADDRESS** Univ of Notre Dame, Notre Dame, IN 46556. **EMAIL** seamus.f.deane.4@nd.edu

DEBLAUWE, FRANCIS
PERSONAL Born 08/01/1961, Kuurne, Belgium, m, 1989, 3 children **DISCIPLINE** ARCHAEOLOGY AND ART HISTORY **EDUCATION** Univ Calif Los Angeles, PhD, 94; Univ Leuven Belgium, Licentiaat Katholieke, 84. **CAREER** Adj doc fac, lectr, 95-, Univ Missouri; lectr, 95-97, Kansas City Art Inst. **HONORS AND AWARDS** Spec instr KCAI; Lectr St Mary's College and Univ MD. **MEMBERSHIPS** AIA; AHA; FAGDM. **RESEARCH** Mesopotamia; Ancient Near East; Archaeology; History; Spatial Analysis of Architecture. **SELECTED PUBLICATIONS** Auth, Discriminant Analysis of Selected Spatial Variables Derived from Mesopotamian Buildings of the Late Bronze Age till the Parthian Period, in: Mesopotamia Rivista di Archeologia Epigrafia e Storia Orientale Antica, 97; A Test Study of Circulation and Access Patterns in Assyrian Architecture, in: Hartmut Waetzzold, Harald Hauptmann, eds, Assyrien im Wandel der Zeiten, Recontre Assyriologique Intl, Heidelberg, 97; Spacings and Stats or a Different Method to Analyze Buildings, A Test with Mesopotamian Houses from the Late Bronze and Iron Ages, in, Akkadia, 94. **CONTACT ADDRESS** 101 E 113th Terrace, Kansas City, MO 64114. **EMAIL** fdeblauwe@compuserve.com

DEBUYS, WILLIAM ENO
PERSONAL Born 10/30/1949, Baltimore, MD, m, 1977 **DISCIPLINE** HISTORY **EDUCATION** Univ Texas, PhD, 82; Univ Texas, MA, 80; Univ North Carolina, BA, 72; Unversite de Lyon, France, Certificat des Etudes Francaises, 70 **CAREER** Writer and conservation consultant, 86-; editor, Common Ground, bimonthly newsletter by Conservation Fund, 89-97; exec dir, North Carolina Nature Conservancy, 82-86; asst instr, Univ Texas, 80-81; writer and instr, Northern New Mexico Community Col, 75-79 **HONORS AND AWARDS** Calvin Horn Lectr, Univ New Mexico, 97; Evans Biography Awd, 91; Pulitzer Prize Finalist, 91; New York Times Notable Book of the Year, 90; Distinguished Visiting Prof, New Mexico State Univ, 87; Chairman's Awd, North Carolina Nature Conservancy, 87 **MEMBERSHIPS** Chairman, New Mexico Recreational Trails Advisory Board, 96-; United Way Santa Fe County Allocations Committee, 96-; Dir EarthWorks, 94-; Founding Dir, Santa Fe Conservation Trust, 93-; Chairman, Rio Grande Bosque Conservation Initiative, 91-93 **RESEARCH** Environmental History of North American West; Social//Cultural His-

tory of North American West **SELECTED PUBLICATIONS** Enchantment and Exploitation: the Life and Hard Times of a New Mexico Mountain Range, Univ New Mexico, 85; River of Traps: a Village Life, Univ New Mexico, 90; coauth, Toward a Scientific and Social Framework for Ecological-based Stewardship of Federal Lands and Waters, Elsevier, forthcoming **CONTACT ADDRESS** 1511 Don Gaspar, Santa Fe, NM 87505. **EMAIL** wdebuys@aol.com

DECARIE, GRAEME
DISCIPLINE HISTORY **EDUCATION** Sir George Univ, BA; Acadia Univ, MA; Queen's Univ, PhD. **CAREER** Instr, Univ Prince Edward Island; Shue Yan Col, Hong Kong; Univ Groeningen; assoc prof. **RESEARCH** Prohibition in Canada. **SELECTED PUBLICATIONS** Auth, book on the history of Montreal. **CONTACT ADDRESS** Dept of Hist, Concordia Univ, Montreal, 1455 de Maisonneuve W, Montreal, QC, Canada H3G 1M8. **EMAIL** decarie@vax2.concordia.ca

DECKER, HANNAH S.
PERSONAL Born 03/19/1937, New York, NY, m, 1957, 2 children **DISCIPLINE** HISTORY **EDUCATION** Barnard Col, AB, 57; MA, 58, PhD, 71, Columbia Univ. **CAREER** Asst Prof/Assoc Prof/Prof, Univ Houston, 74-; Adj Asst/Assoc/Prof, Baylor Col of Medicine, 80-; Adj Mem, Houston-Galveston Pschoanalytic Inst, 94-. **HONORS AND AWARDS** NEH fel, 87-88; NSF Scholars Awd, 88-89; Univ of Houston Res Excellence Awd, 91; Univ of Houston Teacing Excellence Awd, 83; Federal Republic of Germany-Foreign Office, Historical Studies Tour in Germany,84. **MEMBERSHIPS** Am Assoc for the Hist of Medicine; Am Historical Assoc; CHEIRON- Int Soc for the Hist of the Behavorial and Soc Sci(s); Forum for the Hist of Human Sci; Group fot the Use of Psychology in Hist; Hist of Sci Soc; Sigmund Freud-Gesellschaft, Wien; Southern Historical Assoc-European Intellectual Hist. **SELECTED PUBLICATIONS** auth, "The Choice of a Name: Dora and Freud's Relationship to Breuer," Journal of the American Psychoanalytic Association, 82, Vol 30 (1); auth,"Comparative Reception in Germany," Comparative Studies in Society and History, 82, Vol 24 (4); auth, The Lure of Non-Materialism in Materialist Europe: Investigations of Dissociative Phenomena, 1880-1915," Split Minds/Split Brains: Historical and Current Perspectives, New York Univ Press, 86; auth, Freud in Germany: Revolution and Reaction in Science, International Universities Press, 77, Freud, Dora, and Vienna 1900, Free Press, 91; auth," Freud's 'Dora" Case in Perspective: The Medical Treatment of Hysteria at the Turn of the Century," Freud and the History of Psychoanalysis, The Analytic Press, 1992; auth, What Will Happen if My Zurichers Desert me?: The Favorable Reception of Psychoanalysis in Switzerland, " The Psychiatric Clinics of North America, 94, Vol 17 (3); auth, essay review of Beyond Psychology : Wilhelm Reich's Letters and Journals, 1934-1939, In Psychoanalytic Books, 96 Vol 7 (1) , auth, Freud's 'Dora' Case: The Crucible of the Psychoanalytic Concept of Transference," Freud: Culture and Conflict, Alfred A Knopf, 98; auth, Freud's 'Dora' Case: The Classical Freudian Explanations and the Overlooked Cultural Determinants," Psychoanalysis and Psychotherapy, 99, Vol 16 (2). **CONTACT ADDRESS** Dept of History, Univ of Houston, Houston, TX 77204-3785. **EMAIL** hsdecker@jetson.uh.edu

DECKER, LESLIE EDWARD
PERSONAL Born 06/14/1930, Wellington, ME, m, 1948, 2 children **DISCIPLINE** AMERICAN HISTORY **EDUCATION** Univ Maine, BA, 51; Okla State Univ, MA, 52; Cornell Univ, PhD, 61. **CAREER** Teaching fel, Okla State Univ, 51-52; teaching fel, Cornell Univ, 52-55; Cornell Univ Soc Sci Res Council Fel, 55-56; ed, Wis Mag Hist, 56-57; asst prof hist, State Univ NY Col Potsdam, 58-61; from asst prof to assoc prof, Univ Maine, 61-69; prof, 69-75, Emer Prof Hist, Univ Ore, 75-, Ed consult, Am hist publs, 57-. **HONORS AND AWARDS** Fel, Relm Found, 64-65. **MEMBERSHIPS** Orgn Am Historians; AHA; United Methodist Econ Ministry; Me chap Nat Multiple Sclerosis Soc. **RESEARCH** Peopling and politics of the trans-Mississippi country; agricultural abandonment in northern New England; economic history of the Northwest. **SELECTED PUBLICATIONS** Coauth, The anniversary publication: objectives and research, Wis Mag Hist, 57; auth, The railroads and the land office: administrative policy and the land patent controversy, 1864-1896, Miss Valley Hist Rev, 60; Railroads, Lands, and Politics: The Taxation of the Railroad Land Grants, 1864-1897, Brown Univ, 64, 66; collabr, The Torch is Passed: The United States in the Twentieth Century, Addison-Wesley, 68; auth, The great speculation, In: The Frontier in American Development: Essays in Honor of Paul Wallace Gates, Cornell Univ, 69; coauth, The Last Best Hope: A History of the United States (3 vols), 72 & co-ed, America's Major Wars: Crusaders, Critics, and Scholars (2 vols), 73, Addison-Wesley; co-auth, Place of Peace: Salem, Maine 1815-1995, forthcoming. **CONTACT ADDRESS** RFD Salem, RRI Box 884, Strong, ME 04983. **EMAIL** lesdme@tustelme.net

DECONDE, ALEXANDER
PERSONAL Born 11/13/1920, Utica, NY, m, 1973, 4 children **DISCIPLINE** HISTORY **EDUCATION** San Francisco State Col, AB, 43; Stanford Univ, AM, 47, PhD, 49. **CAREER** Actg instr hist, Stanford Univ, 47-48; from asst prof to assoc prof, Whittier Col, 48-52; res assoc, Duke Univ, 52-53, asst prof, 53-57; assoc prof, Univ Mich, 57-61; chmn dept, 63-67, Prof Hist, Univ Calif, Santa Barbara, 61-, Pac Coast Br AHA Am hist award, 49; Soc Sci Res Coun grants, 51 & 56; Guggenheim fel, 59-60 & 67-68; Am Philos Soc grant, 63 & res grant Am diplomatic hist, 72-73; Fulbright grant, Ctr Am Studies, Rome, 64 & Fulbright-State Dept inter-country lectr Am hist & Am foreign rels, India and SE Asia, 71; fac res lectr, 67; resident scholar, Rockefeller Ctr, Bellagio, Italy, 75; State Dept lectr, Ger & Austria, 75; Italian comt Am hist lectr, Italy, 75. **HONORS AND AWARDS** Co-winner, annual book prize; Pacific Coast Branch of Am Hist Assoc and Pres, 84; Guggenheim Fels, 59-60, 67-8; Fulbright Scholar, 64-5; Lifetime achievement award, 71; Norman and Laura Greeber Awd, Soc fir Hist of Am Foreign Relations, 88. **MEMBERSHIPS** AHA; Orgn Am Historians; Soc Hist Am Foreign Rels (vpres, 68, pres, 69). **RESEARCH** American diplomatic and political history; intercultural history. **SELECTED PUBLICATIONS** Auth, Herbert Hoovers Latin American Policy, Stanford Univ Press, 51; auth, Entangling Alliance, Duke Univ Press (Durham, NC), 58; auth, The American Secretary of State, Praeger (NY), 62; auth, The Quasi-War, Scribners', 66; auth, Decisions for Peace, (Putnam, NY), 70; auth, A History of American Foreign Policy, Scribners, NY, 3rd, edition, 78; auth, Ethnicity, Race, and American Foreign Policy, Northeastern Univ Press (Boston), 92; auth, Presidential Machismo, Northeastern Univ Press (Boston), 00; auth, Gun Violence in America, Northeastern, 01. **CONTACT ADDRESS** Dept of Hist, Univ of California, Santa Barbara, Santa Barbara, CA 93106.

DECREDICO, MARY A.
PERSONAL Born 03/28/1959, Cleveland, OH, s **DISCIPLINE** US HISTORY WITH EMPHASIS ON SOUTHERN HISTORY **EDUCATION** Bucknell Univ, BA; Vanderbilt Univ, MA, PhD. **CAREER** Asst prof to assoc prof to Prof History, US Naval Acad, 86-. **HONORS AND AWARDS** Jefferson Davis Awd Outstanding Monogr; Meritorious Civilian Serv Medal. **MEMBERSHIPS** Am Hist Asn; S Hist Asn; Soc Civil War Hist; GA Hist Soc; VA Hist Soc; St George Tucker. **RESEARCH** Urban Confederacy **SELECTED PUBLICATIONS** Patriotism for Profit: Georgia's Urban Entrepreneurs and the Confederate War Effort, Univ NC Press, 90; Mary Boykin Chesnut: A Confederate Women's Life, Madison House, 96. **CONTACT ADDRESS** Dept of History, United States Naval Acad, Annapolis, MD 21402. **EMAIL** decredic@novell.nadn.navy.mil

DEERING, RONALD F.
PERSONAL Born 10/06/1929, Ford County, IL, m, 1966, 2 children **DISCIPLINE** HISTORY; NEW TESTAMENT; LIBRARY SCIENCE **EDUCATION** Georgetown Col, BA, 51; MDiv, 55, PhD, 61, Southern Baptist Theological Seminary; Columbia Univ, MSLS, 67. **CAREER** Instr, 58-61, Research Librarian, 61-67; Assoc Librarian, 67-71, Seminary Librarian, 71-95, Assoc VP for Academic Resources, Southern Baptist Theological Seminary. **HONORS AND AWARDS** Lilly Endowment Scholarship in Theological Librarianship **MEMBERSHIPS** Amer Theological Library Assoc; Amer Library Assoc; Kentucky Library Assoc; Soc of Biblical Lit; Southeastern Library Assoc; Church and Synagogue Library Assoc. **RESEARCH** Theological librarianship **CONTACT ADDRESS** So Baptist Theol Sem, 2825 Lexington Rd., Louisville, KY 40280. **EMAIL** rdeering@compuserve.com

DEETER, ALLEN C.
PERSONAL Born 03/08/1931, Dayton, OH, m, 1952, 3 children **DISCIPLINE** RELIGION, HISTORY **EDUCATION** Manchester Col, BA, 53; Bethany Theol Sem, BD, 56; Princeton Univ, MA, 58, PhD(hist Christianity), 63. **CAREER** Instr relig, 59-60, from asst prof to assoc prof, 60-72, dir, Peace Studies Inst & Prog Conflict Resolution, 67-80, assoc acad dean, 69-80, Prof Relig & Philos, Manchester Col, 72-; Adminr, Brethren Cols Abroad, 75-, Vchmn bd gov, John F Kennedy Am Haus, Marburg, 65-66; dir Brethren Cols Abroad, Univ Marburg & Univ Strasburg, 65-66; Soc Relig Higher Educ grant, 68-69; lectr, Punjabi Univ & Dibrugarh Univ, India, spring 69; exec secy, Consortium Peace Res, Educ & Develop, 71-72; consult on world order studies, various cols, univs & consortia, 71-; ed, Bull, Peace Studies Inst, Manchester Col, 71-80; spring inaugural lectr, Christian Theol Sem, Indianapolis, 72. **HONORS AND AWARDS** Hon Doctorate, Bridgewater Col. **MEMBERSHIPS** Int Studies Asn; Am Soc Church Hist; Am Acad Relig. **RESEARCH** The origins of modern radical religious and political thought; mysticism and pietism East and West, especially as related to social ethics; Tolstoyan and Gandhian political, social and religious tactics of transformation. **SELECTED PUBLICATIONS** Coauth, In His Hand, Brethren Press, 64; auth, Pietist views of the Church, Brethren Life & Thought, winter 64; Western mysticism and social concern, J Inst Traditional Cult, spring 69; Religion as a social and political force in America, Bull Ramakrishna Inst, fall 69; Toyohiko Kagawa: Mystic and Social Activist, Punjabi Univ, 70; Heirs of a Promise, Brethern Press, 72; auth, The Paradoxical Necessity of Realism and Idealism, Bull of Peace Stu Inst, 98. **CONTACT ADDRESS** Dept of Relig, Manchester Col, 601 E College Ave, North Manchester, IN 46962-1226.

DEGLER, CARL NEUMANN
PERSONAL Born 02/06/1921, Orange, NJ, w, 2 children **DISCIPLINE** HISTORY **EDUCATION** Upsala Col, AB, 42; Columbia Univ, MA, 47, PhD, 52. **CAREER** Instr hist, Wash Sq Col, NY Univ, 47-50 & Adelphi Col, 50-51; lectr, City Col New York, 52; lectr, Vassar Col, 52-54, from asst prof to prof, 54-68; Prof Hist, Stanford Univ, 68-90; emeritus, Tutor, Hunter Col, 47-48; mem exam comt Am hist, Col Entrance Exam Bd, 61-66; vis prof, Grad Sch, Columbia Univ, 63-64; Am Coun Learned Soc fel, 64-65; mem exam comt, Hist Grad Rec Exam Bd, 70-72; Guggenheim fel, 72-73; Harmsworth prof, Oxford Univ, 73-74; Nat Endowment Humanities fel, 76-77; Ctr Advan Study in Behavioral Scis fel, 79-80. **HONORS AND AWARDS** Beveridge Prize, 71; Pulitzer Prize in Hist, 72; Bancroft Prize, 72; Dean's Awd for Teaching, Stanford Univ, 79; lhd, upsala col, 69; ma, oxford univ, 74; lld, ripon col, 76; littd, colgate univ, 78. **MEMBERSHIPS** Econ Hist Asn; AHA; Orgn Am Historians (pres, 79-80); Am Studies Asn; fel Am Acad Arts & Sci; Pres of AHA, 85-86; Pres of Southern Historical Assoc, 85-86. **RESEARCH** American social history; history of the American South; history of women and the family in the United States. **SELECTED PUBLICATIONS** Auth, Out of Our Past 1959-1984; auth, The Other South, 74; auth, Neither Black Nor White, 71; auth, Place Over Time, 77; auth, At Odds, Women and the Family, 80; auth, In Search of Human Nature, 91. **CONTACT ADDRESS** Dept of Hist, Stanford Univ, Stanford, CA 94305. **EMAIL** dealer@leland.stanford.edu

DEGRAFF, AMY
DISCIPLINE FRENCH CIVILIZATION, FRENCH CONVERSATION, FRENCH LITERATURE **EDUCATION** Sorbonne, Univ Paris, Diplome d'Etudes Superieures; Univ Va, PhD. **CAREER** Assoc prof Fr, ch, dept Romance Lang, Randolph-Macon Col. **RESEARCH** Psychological criticism in film and literature; the 17th century French fairy tale **SELECTED PUBLICATIONS** Auth, The Tower and the Well: A Psychological Interpretation of the Fairy Tales of Mme d'Aulnoy; From Glass Slipper to Glass Ceiling, or 'Cinderella', the Endurance of a Fairy Tale, Merveilles et Contes. **CONTACT ADDRESS** Dept of Romance Lang, Randolph-Macon Col, Ashland, VA 23005-5505. **EMAIL** adegraff@rmc.edu

DEGROAT, JUDITH A.
PERSONAL Born 07/12/1955, Milwaukee, WI, m **DISCIPLINE** HISTORY **EDUCATION** Univ Wisc, Milwaukee, BA, 81, MA, 83; Univ Rochester, PhD, 91. **CAREER** Instr, Univ Georgia, 88-89; instr, Univ Alabama, Birmingham, 89-91; asst and assoc prof, hist, St Lawrence Univ, 91- . **HONORS AND AWARDS** Susan B. Anthony Dissertation Fel, 87-88; ACLS grant-in-aid, 92; Dean's Res Fund Grant, 94, 97. **MEMBERSHIPS** Soc for French Hist Stud; Am Hist Asn; Soc Sci Hist Asn; European Women's Stud Asn; Radical Hist Rev, ed colective. **RESEARCH** Modern France; gender; women; labor; cultural/national identities; transnational studies. **SELECTED PUBLICATIONS** Coauth, Cultural Encounters: Interdisciplinary Faculty Development for an Intercultural Core Curriculum, in 1993 Conference Proceedings of the Institute for the Study of Postsecondary Pedagogy at the State University of New York, Inst for the Stud of Postsecondary Pedagogy, 94; auth, Cultural Encounters in European History, Radical Hist Rev, 97; auth, The Public Nature of Women's Work: Definitions and Debates During the Revolution of 1848, Fr Hist Stud, 97; auth, Challenging Impoverished Curricula, Radical Hist Rev, 97. **CONTACT ADDRESS** Dept of History, St. Lawrence Univ, Canton, NY 13617. **EMAIL** jdeg@ccmaillink.stlawu.edu

DELANCEY, JULIA
DISCIPLINE ART HISTORY **EDUCATION** Univ MI, BA; Univ St Andrews, Scotland, PhD. **CAREER** Asst prof, Truman State Univ. **RESEARCH** Archival research on the pigment trade in Renaissance Italy. **SELECTED PUBLICATIONS** Auth, Quiet, Silence and Solitude: the Carthusian Order, the Certosa of Florence and Jacopo Pontormo's Passion Cycle, Inferno: St Andrews Jour Art Hist, 95; Before Michelangelo: Colour Usage in Domenico Ghirlandaio and Filippino Lippi, Apollo, 97. **CONTACT ADDRESS** Dept of Art, Truman State Univ, 100 E Normal St, Kirksville, MO 63501-4221.

DELANEY, JEANE
DISCIPLINE LATIN AMERICA **EDUCATION** Stanford Univ, PhD, 89. **CAREER** History, St. Olaf Col. **SELECTED PUBLICATIONS** Auth, Rediscovering Spain: The Hispanismo of Manuel Galvez; Making Sense of Modernity: Changing Attitudes toward the Immigrant and the Gaucho in Turn-of-the-Century Argentina; Nation, National Identity and Immigration in Argentina, 1810-1930. **CONTACT ADDRESS** St. Olaf Col, 1520 St Olaf Ave, Northfield, MN 55057. **EMAIL** delaney@stolaf.edu

DELANEY, JOHN J.
PERSONAL Born 11/04/1956, Charleston, SC, m, 1984, 2 children **DISCIPLINE** HISTORY **EDUCATION** Boston Col, BA, 79; MA, 85; SUNY Buffalo, PhD, 95. **CAREER** Adj prof, SUNY Fredonia, 92-94; instr to asst prof, Kutztown Univ, 94-. **HONORS AND AWARDS** Holocaust Educ Found Fel; Fulbright Fel, 90-91. **MEMBERSHIPS** AHA; Conf Group for Central European Hist; Ger Studies Assoc; Ger Hist Soc. **RE-**

SEARCH Forced Labor, Racial Policy, Gestapo Authority and Everyday Life in Nazi Germany. **SELECTED PUBLICATIONS** Auth, Rural Catholics, Polish workers, and Nazi Racial Policy in Bavaria, 1939-1945, Univ Microfilms (Ann Arbor), 95. **CONTACT ADDRESS** Dept Hist, Kutztown Univ of Pennsylvania, Kutztown, PA 19530. **EMAIL** delaney@kutztown.edu

DELANEY, NORMAN
PERSONAL Born 04/13/1932, Rockport, MA, m, 1966, 2 children **DISCIPLINE** HISTORY **EDUCATION** State Col at Salem, Mass, BS, 55; Boston univ, AM, 56; Duke Univ, PhD, 67. **CAREER** Instr, State Col at Bridgewater, Mass, 59-62; Peace Corps Teacher, Osmania Univ, 62-64; prof, Del Mar Col, 67-. **HONORS AND AWARDS** Mrs. Simon Baruch Univ Awd, United Daughters of the Confederacy; Piper Prof, Minnie Stevens Piper Found. **RESEARCH** American Civil War (military & naval). **SELECTED PUBLICATIONS** Auth, John McIntosh Kell of the Raider Alabama, 73; auth, Ghost Ship: The Confederate Raider Alabama, 89; auth, Raiders and Blockaders: The American Civil War Afloat, 98. **CONTACT ADDRESS** Dept Soc Sci, Del Mar Col, 101 Baldwin Blvd, Corpus Christi, TX 78404-3897. **EMAIL** ndelaney@delmar.edu

DELEEUW, PATRICIA ALLWIN
PERSONAL Born 04/29/1950, Frankfurt, Germany, m, 1971 **DISCIPLINE** CHURCH AND MEDIEVAL HISTORY **EDUCATION** Univ Detroit, BA, 71, PhD(medieval studies), 79; Univ Toronto, MA, 72; Pontifical Inst Medieval Studies, MSL, 75. **CAREER** Asst Prof Theol, Boston Col, 79-. **MEMBERSHIPS** Mediaeval Acad Am; Am Soc Church Hist. **RESEARCH** Religious social history; early medieval Germany; history of pastoral care. **SELECTED PUBLICATIONS** Auth, The changing face of the village parish I: The parish in the early middle ages, In: Pathways to Medieval Peasants, Pontifical Inst Medieval Studies, Toronto, 81. **CONTACT ADDRESS** Dept of Theol, Boston Col, Chestnut Hill, Chestnut Hill, MA 02167.

DELIO, ILIA
PERSONAL Born 08/20/1955, Newark, NJ, s **DISCIPLINE** CHURCH HISTORY **EDUCATION** Univ Mon, PhD, 83; Fordham Univ, MA, 92; PhD, 96. **CAREER** Vis asst prof, Trinity Coll, 96; asst prof, Washington Theo Univ, 97-. **HONORS AND AWARDS** Pres Schlp, 92. **MEMBERSHIPS** AAR; SSCS; MAA. **RESEARCH** Franciscan theology; religion and science. **SELECTED PUBLICATIONS** Auth, Crucified Love: Bonaventure's Mysticism of the Crucified Christ Quincy, Franciscan Press (IL), 98; auth, "The Humility of God in a Scientific World." New Theo Rev 11 (98): 36-49; auth, "The Dangerous Memory of Francis." The Cord 48 (98): 218-23; auth, "Mirrors and Footprints: Metaphors of Relationships in Clare of AssisiÛs Writings," in Resource Study for the Study of Franciscan Christology (Wash, D.C.: Franc Fed, 98); auth, "Bonaventure and Bernard: On Human Image and Mystical Union." Cister Stud 34 (99): 251-63; auth, "The Renaissance of Franciscan Theology: Retrieving the Tradition of the Good." Spirit and Life: A J Contem Franc 8 (99): 21-41; auth, "Bonaventure's Metaphysics of the Good," Theol Stud 60 (1999): 228-46; auth, "Francis of Assisi and Global Consciousness." The Cord 49.6 (99): 273 - 88. **CONTACT ADDRESS** Dept Church History, Washington Theol Union, 6896 Laurel St, Washington, DC 20012. **EMAIL** delio@wtu.edu

DELISLE, JEAN
PERSONAL Born 04/13/1947, Hull, PQ, Canada **DISCIPLINE** TRANSLATION STUDIES, HISTORY **EDUCATION** Laval Univ, BA, 68; Univ Montreal, LTrad, 71, MTrad, 75; Sorbonne Nouvelle (Paris), DTrad, 78. **CAREER** Prof, School Transl & Interpretation, Univ Ottawa, 74-. **HONORS AND AWARDS** Can Coun schol, 76. **MEMBERSHIPS** Soc traducteurs Que, 72-92; Union ecrivains que, 87-94; Can Asn Transl Stud, 87- (pres 91-93); pres, Comt Hist Transl, 90-. **SELECTED PUBLICATIONS** Auth, L'Analyse du discours comme methode de traduction, 80; auth, Les Obsedes textuels, 83; auth, Au coeur du trialogue canadien/Bridging the Language Solitudes, 84; auth, La Traduction au Canada/Translation in Canada 1534-1984, 87; auth, The Language Alchemists, 90; auth, La Traduction raisonee, 93; coauth, Bibliographic Guide for Translators, Writers and Terminologists, 79; coauth, International Directory of Historians of Translation, 3rd ed 96; ed, L'enseignement de l'interpretation et de la traduction: de la theorie a la pedagogie, 81; ed, Les Traducteurs dans l'histoire, 95; ed, Translators Through History, 95. **CONTACT ADDRESS** School of Transl & Interpretation, Univ of Ottawa, 70 Laurier Ave E, Room 401, PO Box 450, Station A, Ottawa, ON, Canada K1N 6N5. **EMAIL** jdelisle@uottawa.ca

DELONG, DAVID G.
PERSONAL Born 02/10/1939, Topeka, KS **DISCIPLINE** ARCHITECTURE **EDUCATION** Univ Kans, BArch, 62; Univ Pa, MArch, 63; Columbia Univ, PhD, 76. **CAREER** Vis Critic Archit Design, Middle East Tech Univ, 67-68; Asst Prof to Assoc Prof, Columbia Univ, 76-84, Chair, Prog Hist Preservation, 81-84; Assoc Prof, 84-87, Prof Archit, Univ Pa, 87-, Prof City & Regional Planning, 95-, Chair, Grad Group Hist Preservation, 84-96; Vis Prof, Univ Sydney, 92. **HONORS AND AWARDS** Kellogg Schol, 57-58; Summerfield Schol, Univ Kans, 59-62; Am Inst Archit Schol, 62-63; Preceptor in Archit, Columbia Univ, 71-75; Charles F. Montgomery Prize, for: Design in America, 83; Distinguished Alumnus Awd, Univ Kans, 84; Vis Schol, Getty Ctr Hist Art & Humanities, 89; Am Inst Archit Int Archit Bk Awd, 92; Soc Archit Hist Bk Awd, 93; Service Awd, Univ Pa, 94; Am Inst Archit Int Bk Awd, 96; recipient of numerous grants and fellowships. **MEMBERSHIPS** Libr Co Philadelphia; Athenaeum Philadelphia; Nat Coun Preservation Educ (Dir 81-92, VChair 89-92, Treasr 86-89); Soc Archit Hist (Dir 95-, VPres NY Chap 75-78); Asn Preservation Technol; Preservation Action; Nat Trust Hist Preservation. **SELECTED PUBLICATIONS** Auth, Eliel Saarinen and the Cranbook Tradition in Architecture and Urban Design, Design in America: the Cranbook Vision, 1925-1950, Abrams, 83; coauth, Louis I. Kahn: In the Realm of Architecture, Universe Publ, 91; ed, Wright in Hollywood: Visions of a New Architecture, Archit Hist Found & MIT Press, 94; James Gamble Rogers and the Architecture of Pragmatism, Archit Hist Found & MIT Press, 94; Working with Mr. Wright: What it was Like, Cambridge Univ Press, 95; ed & principal auth, Frank Lloyd Wright: Designs for an American Landscape, 1922-1933, Abrams, 96; Frank Lloyd Wright and the Living City, Skira, 98; author of numerous articles and other publications. **CONTACT ADDRESS** Univ of Pennsylvania, Philadelphia, PA 19104-6311.

DELORIA, VINE, JR.
PERSONAL Born 03/26/1933, Martin, SD, m, 1958, 3 children **DISCIPLINE** HISTORY **EDUCATION** Iowa State Univ, BS, 58; Lutheran Sch Theol, MST, 63; Univ Colo Sch Law, JD, 70. **CAREER** Exec dir, Nat Cong of Am Indians, 65-67; lectr, Western Wash Univ, 70-72; Lectr, Am Indian Cult & Res Ctr, Univ Calif - Los Angeles, 72-73; Exec Dir, Southwest Intergroup Coun, 72; Special Coun, Native Am Rights Fund, 72; Script Writer, Indian Series, KRMA-TV, Denver, Colo, 72-74; Researcher, Am Indian Resource Assoc, 73-74; Researcher, Am Indian Resource Consult, 74-75; Vis Lectr, Pac Sch Relig, 75; Vis Lectr, New Sch Relig, 76; Vis Lectr, Colo Col, 77-78; Vis Prof, 78, Prof Law & Polit Sci, Univ Ariz, 78-90; Prof Am Indian Studies, Prof Hist, Adj Prof Law, Relis Studies, & Polit Sci, 90-00. **HONORS AND AWARDS** Anisfield-Wolf Awd, 70; Special Citation for We Talk, You Listen, Nat Conf Christians & Jews, 71; Hon Doctor Humane Letts, Augustana Col, 72; Indian Achievement Awd, Indian Coun Fire, 72; Named one of eleven Theological Superstars of the Future, Interchurch Features, 74; Hon Doctor Letters, Scholastica Col, 76; Distinguished Alumni Awd, Iowa State Univ, 77; Hon Prof, Athabasca Univ, 77; Hon Doctor Humane Letts, Hamline Univ, 79; Distinguished Alumni in Field Legal Educ, Univ Colo Sch Law, 85; Hon Doctor Humane Letts, Northern Mich Univ, 91; Senate Resolution No. 118, State of Mich, "A Resolution Honoring Vine Deloria, Jr.", 91; Lifetime Achievement Awd, Mountains and Plains Booksellers Asn, 96; Non-Fiction Book of the Year Awd, Colo Ctr for the Bk, 96; Lifetime Achievement Awd, Native Writers Am, 96; "Spirit of Excellence" award, Am Bar Asn, 01. **SELECTED PUBLICATIONS** Auth, Custer Died For Your Sins: An Indian Manifesto, Macmillan, 69 (and numerous editions outside the U.S.); coauth, The Nations Within: The Past and Future of American Indian Sovereignty, Pantheon Bks, 84; auth, American Indian Policy in the Twentieth Century, Univ Okla Press, 85, 92; auth, Indian Education in America: Eight Essays, Am Indian Sci & Engineering Soc, 91; auth, Frank Waters: Man and Mystic, Swallow Press, 93; auth, Red Earth, White Lies, Scribner, 95; auth, Singing for a Spirit, 99; auth, Spirit and Reason, 99; auth, Documents of American Indian Diplomacy, 99; auth, For This Land, 99; auth, Tribes, Treaties and Constitutional Tribulations, 00. **CONTACT ADDRESS** Univ of Colorado, Boulder, Boulder, CO 80309-0234. **EMAIL** vine@spot.colorado.edu

DELORME, ROLAND L.
PERSONAL Born 06/12/1937, Aberdeen, WA, 5 children **DISCIPLINE** AMERICAN HISTORY **EDUCATION** Univ Puget Sound, BA, 59; Univ PA, MA, 60; Univ CO, PhD, 65. **CAREER** Instr US hist, Skagit Valley Col, 64-66; asst prof hist & dir gen studies, 66-68, assoc prof hist, Western WA Univ, 68-, chmn hist, 71-80 and 84-89, Provost & vpres Acad Affairs, 90; Mem, Fed Regional Arch Adv Coun, 69. **RESEARCH** Twentieth century US soc and intellectual hist; 20th century Am western hist; Pacific Northwest hist. **SELECTED PUBLICATIONS** Auth, Turn-of-the-century Denver: An invitation to reform, Colo Mag, winter, 68; Colorado's mugwump interlude: The state voters' league, 1905-1906, J West, 10/68; coauth, Anti-Democratic Trends in Twentieth Century America, Addison-Wesley, 69; auth, The United States Bureau of Customs and smuggling on Puget Sound, 1851-1913, Prologue, summer 73. **CONTACT ADDRESS** Pres/Provost Office, Western Washington Univ, M/S 9033, Bellingham, WA 98225-5996. **EMAIL** ldelorme@cms.wwu.edu

DELPH, RONALD
PERSONAL Born 10/04/1951, Pontiac, MI, m, 1987, 2 children **DISCIPLINE** HISTORY **EDUCATION** Univ Mich, PhD. **CAREER** Asst prof to assoc prof, Eastern Mich Univ; Honors adv; Students Hist Assoc Adv. **HONORS AND AWARDS** Phi Alpha Theta Adv;Teaching Awd, Stanford Univ, 91; Listed In Who's Who Among America's Teachers, 99, 00. **MEMBERSHIPS** Exec Committee for Sixteenth Century Studies Conference; Sixteenth Century Studies Soc; Renaissance Soc of Am; Italian Hist Studies Asn. **RESEARCH** Europe, renaissance, Europe, reformation. **SELECTED PUBLICATIONS** Publ in, J Hist Idea; Renaissance Quart; 16th-Century J. **CONTACT ADDRESS** Dept of History and Philosophy, Eastern Michigan Univ, 701 Pray-Harrold, Ypsilanti, MI 48197. **EMAIL** ron.delph@emich.edu

DEMOLEN, RICHARD LEE
PERSONAL Born 08/19/1938, Hartford, WI **DISCIPLINE** EARLY MODERN EUROPE **EDUCATION** Univ Mich, AB, 62, AM, 63, PhD(hist), 70. **CAREER** Instr hist, Crowder Col, 64-66; asst prof, Drury Col, 66-67 & Ithaca Col, 67-70; Res & Writing, Folger Shakespeare Libr, 70-, Folger Shakespeare Libr fel, 69, 70 & 73; Am Philos Soc grants-in-aid, 69 & 70; Nat Endowment for Humanities younger humanist fel, 71-72; Huntington Libr fel, 73; Newberry Libr fel, 70, 73, & 76; sr Fulbright, Univ London, 74-75; ed, Erasmus Rotterdam Soc Yearbook, 80- **MEMBERSHIPS** AHA; Renaissance Soc Am; Erasmus Rotterdam Soc (secy & treas, 80-). **RESEARCH** Renaissance intellectual and cultural history; Tudor and Stuart biography. **SELECTED PUBLICATIONS** Auth, Man On His Own--Interpretations of Erasmus, C.1750-1920, Cath Hist Rev, Vol 0079, 93. **CONTACT ADDRESS** Erasmus Rotterdam Society, Fort Washington, MD 20744.

DEMOSS, DOROTHY DELL
PERSONAL Born 02/17/1942, Houston, TX, s **DISCIPLINE** AMERICAN AND LATIN AMERICAN HISTORY **EDUCATION** Rice Univ, BA, 63; Univ Tex Austin, MA, 66; Tex Christian Univ, PhD(hist), 81. **CAREER** Teacher social studies, Blair High Sch, Silver Spring, Md, 63-65; instr hist, Tex Woman's Univ, 66-79; teaching asst, Tex Christian Univ, 79-81; Asst Prof Hist, Tex Woman's Univ, 82-; assoc prof and prof, 84-98. **MEMBERSHIPS** Southern Hist Asn; Southern Asn Women Historians. **RESEARCH** Recent (20th century) United States history; Texas history; urban and economic history. **SELECTED PUBLICATIONS** Rev, Women and Texas History--Selected Essays, Jour So Hist, Vol 0060, 94; Pioneer Woman Educator--The Progressive Spirit Blanton, Annie,Webb, Jour So Hist, Vol 0061, 95; auth, "George Bush," Profiles in Power, ed Hendrickson and Collins; Harlan Davidson, 93. **CONTACT ADDRESS** Dept of Hist & Govt, Texas Woman's Univ, P O Box 425889, Denton, TX 76204-5889.

DEMY, TIMOTHY J.
PERSONAL Born 12/06/1954, Brownsville, TX, m, 1978 **DISCIPLINE** THEOLOGY & HISTORY **EDUCATION** Tex Christian Univ, BA, 77; Dallas Theol Sem, Th M, 81, ThD, 90; Salve Regina Univ, MA, 90; Univ Tex at Arlington, MA, 94; Noval War Col, MA, 99; Ph.D, 99. **CAREER** Military chaplain, 81-; adj instr, Naval War Col, 96-. **HONORS AND AWARDS** Phi Alpha Theta; Outstanding Young Men in Amer; Who's Who in the South and Southwest; Who's Who in America; numerous military awards. **MEMBERSHIPS** Evang Theol Soc; Soc of Bibl Lit; Orgn of Amer Hist; Ctr for Bioethics and Human Dignity. **RESEARCH** Bioethics; The crusades; Evangelical theology; Church history. **SELECTED PUBLICATIONS** Coed, Genetic Engineering: A Christian Response, Kregel Pub. 99; coed, Politics and Public Policy: A Christian Response, Kregel Pub, 00; co-auth, Basic Questions on Suicide and Euthanasia, Basic Questions on End of Life Decisions, Basic Questions on Sexuality and Reproductive Technology, Basic Questions on Alternative Medicine, Kregel Publ, 98; co-ed, Suicide: A Christian Response, Kregel Publ, 98; co-auth, Winning the Marriage Marathon, Kregel Publ, 98; co-auth, Prophecy Watch, Harvest House, 98; auth, Onward Christian Soldiers? Christian Perspectives on War, The Voice, 98; auth, Suicide and the Christian Worldview, Conservative Theol Jour, 97; auth, Chaplain Walter Colton and the California Gold Rush, Navy Chaplain, 97; co-auth, The Coming Cashless Society, Harvest House, 96; auth, A Dictionary of Premillennial Theology, Kregel Books, 96; co-ed, When the Trumpet Sounds!, Harvest House, 95; auth, Blackwell's Dictionary of Evangelical Biography, Blackwells, 95; co-auth, The Rapture and an Early Medieval Citation, Bibliotheca Sacra, 95. **CONTACT ADDRESS** 7 Ellen Rd., Middletown, RI 02842. **EMAIL** tdemy@efortress.com

DENHAM, JAMES M.
PERSONAL Born 07/17/1957, m, 2 children **DISCIPLINE** HISTORY **EDUCATION** Fla State Univ, PhD, 88. **CAREER** Instr, Fla State Univ, 85-86; instr, Ga Southern Univ, 87; asst prof, Limestone Col, 87-91; asst to assoc prof, Fla Southern Col, 91-. **HONORS AND AWARDS** Governor's Distinguished Prof Awd, 90; Fullerton Merit Awd, 91; Athur Thompson Prize, Fla Hist Soc, 92; Fac Develop Grant, 90, 94, 95-99; Fel, Grady McWhiney Res Found, 97; NEH, 99. **RESEARCH** U.S. 19th-Century, concentration in the Antebellum South. **SELECTED PUBLICATIONS** Auth, "Dropping State History?", Lakeland Ledger, Mar 95; auth, "Florida's Sesquicentennial", Polk County Hist Quarterly 22, (June 95): 1-3; auth, "From a Territorial to a Statehood Judiciary: Florida's Antebellum Courts and Judges", Fla Hist Quarterly 73, (April 95): 443-55; auth, "Bringing Justice to the Frontier: Crime and Punishment in Antebellum Hillsborough County", Tamp Bay Hist 19, (97): 77-91; auth, "Cracker Women and Their Families in Nineteenth Century Florida", Florida's Heritage of Diversity: Essays in the

Honor of Samuel Proctor, eds William Rogers, Canter Brown and Mark E. Greenberg, Sentry Pr, (Tallahassee, 97): 15-28; auth, A Rogue's Paradise: Crime and Punishment in Antebellum Florida, 1821-1961, Univ of Ala Pr, (Tuscaloosa), 97; coauth, "With Scott in Mexico: Letters of Captain James W. Anderson in the Mexican War, 1846-1847", Military Hist of the West 28 (Spring 98): 19-48; auth, "Charles E. Hawkins", "Thomas S. Jesup", "Jose Antonio Mexia", Edward Ward Moore", "Texan Navy", and "John Tyler", the United States and Mexico at War: Nineteenth-Century Expansionism and Conflict, ed Donald S. Frazier, Simon and Schuster, (NY), 98; coauth, Cracker Times and Pioneer Lives: The Florida Reminiscences of George Gillett Keen and Sarah Pamela Williams, Univ of SC Pr, (Columbia), (forthcoming). **CONTACT ADDRESS** Dept Soc Sci and Educ, Florida So Col, 111 Lake Hollingsworth Dr, Lakeland, FL 33801-5607. **EMAIL** jdenham@flsouthern.edu

DENNEY, COLLEEN J.
DISCIPLINE ART HISTORY **EDUCATION** La State Univ, BA, 78, MA, 83; Univ IA, PhD, 84-87; Univ MN, PhD, 90. **CAREER** Assoc prof; adj assoc prof, Women's Stud; mem, Women's Stud Resource Fac & Prof Staff; Comt on Instnl Coop Traveling Scholar, Univ MN, 86-87. **HONORS AND AWARDS** Funded projects as PI, Fac Mentor, Nat Endowment for the Hum Younger Scholars Prog, $500; funded projects as Co-PI, Nat Endowment for the Hum Implementation Grant, $250,000 given outright, $50,00 given in match. **RESEARCH** 19th century Engl and France; hist of exhibition syst. **SELECTED PUBLICATIONS** Auth, The Grosvenor Gallery: A Palace of Art in Victorian England, Yale UP, 96; Exhibitions in Artists' Studios: Francois Bonvin's 1859 Salon des Refuses, Gazette des Beaux Arts, Vol CXXII, 93; The Role of Sir Coutts Lindsay and the Grosvenor Gallery in the Reception of Pre-Raphaelitism on the Continent, IN: Pre-Raphaelitism in its European Context, Assoc UP, 95. **CONTACT ADDRESS** Dept of Art, Univ of Wyoming, PO Box 3964, Laramie, WY 82071-3964. **EMAIL** CDENNEY@UWYO.EDU

DENNIS, DAVID B.
DISCIPLINE HISTORY **EDUCATION** UCLA, PhD, 91. **CAREER** Hist, Loyola Univ. **RESEARCH** Modern European intellectual & cultural history. **SELECTED PUBLICATIONS** Auth, Beethoven in German Politics, 1870-1989, New Hvn: Yale UP, 96; rev(s)NY Times, La Stampa Milano, Financial Times. **CONTACT ADDRESS** Fine Arts Dept, Loyola Univ, Chicago, 6525 N. Sheridan Rd., Chicago, IL 60626. **EMAIL** dennis@orion.it.luc.edu

DENNIS, GEORGE THOMAS
PERSONAL Born 11/17/1923, Somerville, MA **DISCIPLINE** BYZANTINE HISTORY **EDUCATION** Gonzaga Univ, AB, 48; Alma Col, STL, 54; Pontif Inst Orient Studies, Rome, PhD, 60. **CAREER** Asst prof hist & theol, Loyola Univ, Los Angeles, 61-67; from adj assoc prof to assoc prof, 67-72, Prof Hist, Cath Univ Am, 72-, Am Coun Learned Soc grant-in-aid, 62; Guggenheim Mem fel, 64-65. **MEMBERSHIPS** Mediaeval Acad Am; AHA; Am Cath Hist Asn; Am Soc Church Hist. **RESEARCH** Fourteenth century Byzantine history. **CONTACT ADDRESS** Catholic Univ of America, Washington, DC 20064. **EMAIL** nauarchos@aol.com

DENNY, DON WILLIAM
PERSONAL Born 08/19/1926, Cedar Rapids, IA, m, 1953, 2 children **DISCIPLINE** HISTORY OF ART **EDUCATION** Univ Fla, BA, 59; NYork Univ, MA, 61, PhD, 65. **CAREER** Instr design, Univ Fla, 54-59; instr hist of art, NY Univ, 61-62 & Princeton Univ, 62-65; from asst prof to assoc prof, 65-72, prof hist of art, Univ of Md, College Park, 72-, Nat Found for Humanities fel, 68. **RESEARCH** Medieval art and iconography. **SELECTED PUBLICATIONS** Auth, The trinity in Enguerrand Quarton's coronation of the Virgin, in Art Bull, 3/63; Simone Martini's Holy family, J Warburg & Courtauld Inst, 67; Notes on the Avignon Pieta, in Speculum, 69; Some symbols in the Arena Chapel Frescoes, in Art Bull, 73; Portal sculpture of Auxerre Cathedral, in Speculum, 76; Annunciation from the Right, Garland, 77; Historiated initials of the Lobbes Bible, in Revue Belge d'Archeologie, 77. **CONTACT ADDRESS** Dept of Art, Univ of Maryland, Col Park, College Park, MD 20742-0001. **EMAIL** dd18@umail.umd.edu

DEPAUW, LINDA GRANT
PERSONAL Born 01/19/1940, New York, NY **DISCIPLINE** AMERICAN HISTORY **EDUCATION** Swarthmore Col, BA, 61; Johns Hopkins Univ, PhD, 64. **CAREER** Asst prof hist, George Mason Col, Univ Va, 64-65; from asst prof to assoc prof, 66-75, Prof Hist, George Washington Univ, 75-98; Ed in Chief Doc Hist, First Fed Cong, Nat Hist Publ Comn, 66-84, emeritus 99-; Pres, The Minerva Center, 83-. **HONORS AND AWARDS** Beveridge Awd, AHA, 64. **RESEARCH** Early American history; women in America, Women and War. **SELECTED PUBLICATIONS** Auth, Disorderly Women--Sexual Polities and Evangelicalism in Revolutionary New-England, Jour Church and State, Vol 0038, 96; Encyclopedia of the North-American Colonies, Jour Amer Hist, Vol 0081, 95; Battle Cries and Lullabies: Women in War from Prehistory to the Present, Oklahoma, 98. **CONTACT ADDRESS** The Minerva Center, 20 Granada Rd., Pasadena, MD 21122.

DEPILLIS, MARIO STEPHEN
PERSONAL Born 01/22/1926, Philadelphia, PA, m, 1952, 3 children **DISCIPLINE** AMERICAN HISTORY **EDUCATION** Univ Chicago, BA, 52, MA, 54; Yale Univ, PhD, 61. **CAREER** From instr to asst prof Am hist, Univ Mass, 58-61; vis asst prof, Univ Calif, Berkeley, 61-62; from asst prof to assoc prof, 62-75, prof, Am Hist, Univ Mass, Amherst, 76-91, Teacher's res grants, Univ Mass, 63; Fulbright exchange prof, Univ Munich, 66-67; US State Dept lectr, Europe, 77; sr fel in res, Smith Institute, BYU, 00-01; prof emer, Univ Mass, Amherst, 91-. **HONORS AND AWARDS** Eggleston Prize, 61. **MEMBERSHIPS** AHA; Pac Coast Br AHA; Orgn Am Historians; Western Hist Asn; Mormon Hist Asn. **RESEARCH** The west in American history; Mormonism; United States social history. **SELECTED PUBLICATIONS** Auth, The Quest for Religious Authority and the Rise of Mormonism, Dialogue: J Mormon Thought, spring 66; Trends in American Social History and the Possibilities of Behavioral Approaches, J Social Hist, fall 67; The Social Sources of Mormonism, Church Hist, 3/68. **CONTACT ADDRESS** Smith Institute, Brigham Young Univ, 132 KMB, Provo, UT 84602-4485. **EMAIL** depillis@history.umass.edu

DERBY, WILLIAM EDWARD
PERSONAL Born 10/26/1925, Canton, NY, m, 1956, 7 children **DISCIPLINE** AMERICAN HISTORY **EDUCATION** Harvard Univ, AB, 47; St Lawrence Univ, MEd, 49; Univ Wis, PhD, 63. **CAREER** Teacher high schs, NY 49-51 & 5354; from asst prof to assoc prof, 57-70, Prof Am Hist, State Univ NY Col Gebeseo, 70-. **MEMBERSHIPS** Orgn Am Hist; AHA; Southern Hist Asn; Econ Hist Asn. **RESEARCH** American economic and urban history; Civil War and Reconstruction period; history of the Great Lakes region. **CONTACT ADDRESS** Dept of History, SUNY, Col at Geneseo, Geneseo, NY 11454.

DERDEN, JOHN K.
PERSONAL Born 12/17/1947, Ft. Benning, GA, m, 2 children **DISCIPLINE** HISTORY **EDUCATION** Reinhardt Col, AA, 67; Univ Ga, BSEd, 69, MA, 73, PhD, 81. **CAREER** High sch teacher, 69-70; inst, 73-76, asst prof, 76-85, assoc prof, 85-90, CHAIR, SOC SCI, 90-, PROF HIST, 98-, Acting Vice Pres of Academic Affairs, 99-, E GA COL. **HONORS AND AWARDS** Kappi Phi Kappa; Phi Theta Kappa; Phi Alpha Theta. **CONTACT ADDRESS** Chair, Soc Sci Div, East Georgia Col, 131 College Cr, Swainsboro, GA 30401. **EMAIL** jderden@mail.peachnet.edu

DERFLER, LESLIE A.
PERSONAL Born 01/11/1933, New York, NY, m, 1962, 4 children **DISCIPLINE** HISTORY **EDUCATION** City Col NYork, BA, 54; Columbia Univ, MA, 57; PhD, 62. **CAREER** Instr, City Col NY, 59-62; asst prof, Carnegie-Mellon Univ, 62-68; assoc prof, Univ of Mass, 68-69; prof, Florida Atlantic Univ, 69- . **HONORS AND AWARDS** Florida Atlantic Univ Tchg Incentive and Professorial Excellence Awds; Nat Endowment for Humanities Fellowship; Koren Prize for outstanding article on French hist. **MEMBERSHIPS** Soc for French Hist Studies; Southern Hist Asn; Western Soc for French Hist. **RESEARCH** History of Socialism; Political Biography. **SELECTED PUBLICATIONS** Auth, The Dreyfus Affair: Tragedy of Errors, 63; The Third French Republic, 1870-1940, 66; Socialism Since Marx, 73; Alexandre Millerand: The Socialist Years, 77; President and Parliament. A Short History of the French Presidency, 84; An Age of Conflict: Readings in 20th Century European History, 90; Paul Lafargue and the Founding of French Marxism, 1842-1882, 91; Paul Lafargue and the Flowering of French Socialism, 1882-1911, 98. **CONTACT ADDRESS** Dept of History, Florida Atlantic Univ, Boca Raton, FL 33432. **EMAIL** derflerl@fau.edu

DERFLER, STEVEN
PERSONAL Born 12/22/1951, Columbus, OH, m, 1981, 1 child **DISCIPLINE** ARCHAEOLOGY **EDUCATION** Ind Univ, BA, 73; Univ Minn, MA, 75, PhD, 83. **CAREER** Instr, Ind Univ, 72; from teaching asst to assoc, Univ Minn, 73-78; adj fac, Tel Aviv Univ, 75-84; Metropolitan State Univ, 97-95; adj assoc prof, Univ Wis, 90-97; dir Jewish Studies, Hamline Univ, 79-93; **MEMBERSHIPS** Am Jewish Com. **RESEARCH** Archaeology; Biblical history; Comparative religions; Jewish-Christian Relations. **SELECTED PUBLICATIONS** Auth, "Its Unfair to Compare Palestinians and American Indians," 98; "Religious Freedom Amendment is Dangerous," 98; "A Night to Remember," 97; "Which will it be? Peace or Jihad?," 97; "Pluralism and the Role of Constructive Interference," 97; "Survival of Israel Depends on Celebrating Diversity," 97; "No Light at the End of This Tunnel," 96; "Collective Soul-Searching in Israel," 96; "A Democratic Experiment that Became Chaotic," 96; "Israel Comes of Age in the Democratic World," 95; "A Painful Comong of Age for Israel," 95; "A Threat to Freedom," 95; "A Cellular Phone on His Bike, Nobody's Laughing Anymore," 95; "The Pitfalls of School Vouchers," 95. **CONTACT ADDRESS** 1885 University Ave, Ste 85, Saint Paul, MN 55104. **EMAIL** 70264.1320@compuserve.com

DEROCHE, ANDREW
PERSONAL Born 10/25/1966, Caribou, ME, s, 1997 **DISCIPLINE** HISTORY **EDUCATION** Princeton Univ, History BA, 89; Univ Maine, History MA, 93; Univ Colorado, History PhD, 97. **CAREER** History Instr, Front Range Comm. Col, 98-. **MEMBERSHIPS** Society of Historians of Amer foreign Relations. **RESEARCH** US relations with Africa; Career of Andy Young. **SELECTED PUBLICATIONS** Auth, "Standing Firm for Principles: Jimmy Carter and Zimbabwe," Diplomatic History, Fall 99; auth, "Black, White, and Chrome: US Relations with Zimbabwe, 53-98, Africa-World Press, 00. **CONTACT ADDRESS** Dept Communications, Front Range Comm Col, 2255 North Main St, No S118, Longmount, CO 80501-1488. **EMAIL** fr_andrewd@cccs.cccdes.edu

DES GAGNIERS, JEAN
PERSONAL Born 02/07/1929, St. Joseph-de-la-Rive, PQ, Canada **DISCIPLINE** ARCHAEOLOGY, MUSEUM STUDIES **EDUCATION** Col Jean de Brebeuf (Montreal), BA, 49; Diplome de l'Ecole de Marine (Rimouski), 51; Univ Laval, LPh, 53; Diplome de l'Ecole du Louvre (Paris), 56. **CAREER** Laodikaia Excavations (Turkey), 61-64; Soli Excavations (Cyprus), 64-74; Trustee, Nat Mus Can, 72-79; Asst to Vice-Rector, Laval Univ, 76-94, Centre Museographique, 79-94 (RETIRED). **HONORS AND AWARDS** Mem, Royal Soc Can **SELECTED PUBLICATIONS** Auth, Fouilles de Laodicee du Lycos; auth, L'Acropole d' Athenes; auth, La ceramique chypriote a decor figure; auth, Vases et figurines de l'Age du Bronze; auth, Objets d'art grec du Louvre; auth, Soloi: dix campagnes de fouilles; auth, La conservation du patrimoine museologique du Quebec; auth, L'Ile-aux-Coudres; auth, Charlevoix, pays enchante; auth, Monseigneur de Charlevoix. **CONTACT ADDRESS** St-Joseph-de-la-rive, QC, Canada G0A 3Y0.

DESAI, GAURAV GAJANAN
DISCIPLINE AFRICAN AND DIASPORA STUDIES, POSTCOLONIAL LITERATURE **EDUCATION** Northwestern Univ, BA, 88; Duke Univ, PhD, 97. **CAREER** Engl, Tulane Univ. **SELECTED PUBLICATIONS** Auth, Theater as Praxis: Discursive Strategies in African Popular Theater, African Stud Rev 33, 90; The Invention of Invention, Cult Critique 24, 93; English as an African Language, Eng Today 9, 93; Out in Africa, Genders 25, 97. **CONTACT ADDRESS** Dept of Eng, Tulane Univ, 6823 St Charles Ave, New Orleans, LA 70118. **EMAIL** gaurav@mailhost.tcs.tulane.edu

DESHMUKH, MARION FISHEL
PERSONAL Born Los Angeles, CA, m, 1969, 1 child **DISCIPLINE** MODERN GERMAN CULTURAL HISTORY **EDUCATION** Univ Calif, Los Angeles, BA, 66; Columbia Univ, MA, 67, PhD(hist), 75. **CAREER** Lectr hist, Nassau Community Col, 68 & Brooklyn Col, 69; lectr, 69-75, asst prof, 75-80, ASSOC PROF HIST, GEORGE MASON UNIV, 80-, Dept Chair 84-95; Proposal reviewer, Nat Endowment for Humanities, 78-; lectr, US Dept State, Foreign Serv Off Inst, 79- & Smithsonian Inst, 82-. **HONORS AND AWARDS** Phi Beta Kappa, DAAD; J P Getty Stipend, Fulbright Scholars Awd. **MEMBERSHIPS** AHA; Conf Group Cent Europ Hist; College Art Asn; Western Asn German Studies; Southern Hist Asn, Europ Sect. **RESEARCH** German art history: 1800-1914; sociology of German cultural institutions; 19th and 20th century cultural history of Europe. **SELECTED PUBLICATIONS** Auth, Max Liebermann: Observations on painting & politics in Germany, Ger Studies Rev, 5/80; German impressionist painters & World War I, Art Hist; contribr, Arts & politics in turn of the century Berlin, In: The Turn of the Century: German Literature & Art, 1890-1915, Herbert Grundmann, Bonn, 81; ed, Cultures in Conflict East German Visual Arts, 90; Berlin National Gallery after 1945, Central Euro Hist, 94. **CONTACT ADDRESS** Dept Hist, George Mason Univ, Fairfax, 4400 University Dr, Fairfax, VA 22030-4444. **EMAIL** mdeshmuk@gmu.edu

DESPALATOVIC, ELINOR MURRAY
PERSONAL Born 08/10/1933, Cleveland, OH, m, 1962, 2 children **DISCIPLINE** MODERN EUROPEAN AND EAST EUROPEAN HISTORY **EDUCATION** Columbia Univ, BA, 55, MA and cert area studies, 59, PhD (hist), 69. **CAREER** Lectr hist, Univ Mich, 62-63; res asst Southern Slavic hist, Yale Univ, 63-65; from instr to asst prof, 65-74, assoc prof, 74-79, actg chemn dept, 74, prof hist, Conn Col, 79-86; Chemn, Hist Dept, Conn Col, 80-84, 90-91; Brigida Pacchiani Ardenghi Prof, Conn Col, 86-. **HONORS AND AWARDS** Am Coun Learned Soc fel, 71; Fulbright area studies fel, 72; Int Res and Exchanges Bd fel, 72, 78-79; mem, E Europ selection comt, 73-74; Distinguished Alumnae Awd, The George Sch, Bucks County, Pa, 77. **MEMBERSHIPS** AHA; Am Asn Advan Slavic Studies; Am Asn Southeast Europ Studies. **RESEARCH** Croatian nationalism; the Illyrian Movement; the Croatian Peasant Party. **SELECTED PUBLICATIONS** Auth, The Balkan Express--Fragments from the Other Side of the War, Slavic Rev, Vol 53, 94. **CONTACT ADDRESS** Dept of Hist, Connecticut Col, 270 Mohegan Ave, New London, CT 06320-4125. **EMAIL** emdes@conn.coll.edu

DETHLOFF, HENRY CLAY
PERSONAL Born 08/10/1934, New Orleans, LA, m, 1961, 2 children **DISCIPLINE** AMERICAN ECONOMIC AND SOUTHERN HISTORY **EDUCATION** Univ Tex, BA, 56; Northwestern State Col, La, MA, 60; Univ Mo, PhD (hist), 64. **CAREER** From instr to assoc prof Am hist, Univ Southwestern La, 62-69; assoc prof, 69-75, Prof Hist, Tex AM Univ, 75-, Dept Head, 80-. **MEMBERSHIPS** Southern Hist Asn; Agr Hist Asn; Econ Hist Asn. **RESEARCH** Economic history; agricultural history; Southern history. **SELECTED PUBLICATIONS** Auth,Davis, Edgar, B. and Sequences in Business Capitalism--From Shoes to Rubber to Oil - Froh, J Southern Hist, Vol 60, 94; Cinderella of the New South--A History of the Cottonseed Industry, 1855-1955, Am Hist Rev, Vol 102, 97. **CONTACT ADDRESS** Dept of Hist, Texas A&M Univ, Col Station, 1 Texas A and M Univ, College Station, TX 77843. **EMAIL** h-dethloff@tamu.edu

DETWILER, DONALD SCAIFE
PERSONAL Born 08/19/1933, Jacksonville, FL, m, 1956, 1 child **DISCIPLINE** EUROPEAN HISTORY **EDUCATION** George Washington Univ, BA, 54; Univ Goettingen, Dr phil(hist), 61. **CAREER** Lectr hist, Montgomery Col, Md, 62, from instr to asst prof hist, 62-65; asst prof, WVa Univ, 65-57; from asst prof to assoc prof, 67-77, prof, 77-98; Prof Emer Hist, Southern Ill Univ, 98-; concomitantly, secr. & newsletter ed, Amer Committee on the Hist of the Second World War, 76-90; co-chair, Committee on Hist in the Classroom, 76-00; dir, SIUC-USICA Ger-Amer Hist Textbook Proj, 79-82; pres, Asso for the Bibl of Hist, 84; vis res prof hist, National Taiwan Univ, 87; chairman, World War Two Studies Asso, 91-. **MEMBERSHIPS** PBK; AHA; Assoc Bibl Hist, Committee on Hist in the Classroom; Ger Studies Asso; Soc Mil Hist; Soc Span and Port Hist Studies. **RESEARCH** Germany; modern Spain; political and military history of the twentieth century. **SELECTED PUBLICATIONS** Auth, Germany, Hitler Franco und Gibraltar, Steiner, Wiesbaden ,62; auth, Germany: A Short History, SIU Press, 76, 3rd ed 99; coauth, West Germany: The Federal Republic of Germany, vol 72, World Bibl Ser, Clio Oxford 87; ed, transl, P.E. Schramm's Hitler: The Man and the Military, Quadrangle, Chicago 71, Allan Lane/Penguin, London, 72, repr, Academy Chicago 99; ed, World War II German Military Studies, 24 vols, Garland, N Y 79; ed, War in Asia and the Pacific: Japanese and Chinese Studies and Documents, 15 vols, Garland, N Y 80. **CONTACT ADDRESS** Dept of Hist, So Illinois Univ, Carbondale, 201 S. Travelstead Lane, Carbondale, IL 62901-4519. **EMAIL** detwiler@midwest.net

DEUTSCH, HAROLD CHARLES
PERSONAL Born 06/07/1904, Milwaukee, WI, m, 1923, 3 children **DISCIPLINE** HISTORY **EDUCATION** Univ Wis, AB, 24, AM, 25; Harvard Univ, AM, 27, PhD (French hist), 29. **CAREER** From asst prof to prof, 29-72, chmn dept, 60-66, Emer Prof Hist, Univ Minn, Minneapolis, 72-; Mem Fac, US Army War Col, Carlisle, PA, 74-, Soc Sci res fel, 35-36; mem, Bd Econ Warfare, 42-43; consult, Off Strategic Serv, 43-45 and Bur Europ Affairs, US Dept State, 45 and 67-72; mem civilian staff, Nat War Col, 48-50, dir Europ Studies and prof int rels, 72-74; Fulbright fel, Ger, 57-59 and 69-70; vis prof, Free Univ Berlin, 63. **MEMBERSHIPS** AHA; Am Mil Inst; Int Inst Strategic Studies; US Comn Mil Hist; Oral Hist Asn. **RESEARCH** Military opposition to Hitler; current European affairs; history of World War II. **SELECTED PUBLICATIONS** Auth, Hitler Greatest Defeat--The Collapse of Army-Group Center, June 1944, J Mil Hist, Vol 59, 95. **CONTACT ADDRESS** US Army War Col Fac, Barracks Carlisle, PA 17013.

DEUTSCH, SANDRA MCGEE
PERSONAL Born 10/18/1950, Chicago Heights, IL, s **DISCIPLINE** HISTORY **EDUCATION** Beloit Col, BA, 72; Univ Fla, MA, 73; PhD, 79. **CAREER** Vis prof, Indiana Univ, 79; asst prof, Manchester Col, 79-81; asst prof, DePaul Univ, 81-84; asst prof, 84-88, assoc prf, 88-95, prof, 95- , Univ Texas-El Paso. **HONORS AND AWARDS** Fulbright, 77, 89-90, 00; NEH, 81, 88, 93; ACLS, 89-90; Am Philos Soc, 87; Beveridge grant, 87; Phi Beta Kappa. **MEMBERSHIPS** AHA, CLAH, LASA, LAJSA. **RESEARCH** Extreme right, Women, Argentina, Brazil, Chile, Jews. **SELECTED PUBLICATIONS** Auth, Counterrevolution in Argentina, 1900-1932: The Argentine Patriotic League, Lincoln Univ Neb Press, (86); co-ed, The Argentine Right, Schol Res, (93); auth, Las Derechas: The Extreme Right in Argentina, Brazil, and Chile, 1890-1939, Stanford Univ Press, (99). **CONTACT ADDRESS** Dept Hist, Univ of Texas, El Paso, 500 W Univ Ave, El Paso, TX 79968-8900. **EMAIL** sdeutsch@miners.utep.edu

DEVER, WILLIAM GWINN
PERSONAL Born 11/27/1933, Louisville, KY, m, 1953, 1 child **DISCIPLINE** SYRO PALESTINIAN ARCHEOLOGY **EDUCATION** Milligan Col, AB, 55; Christian Theol Sem, Ind, BD, 59; Butler Univ, MA, 59; Harvard Univ, PhD, 66. **CAREER** Sr archaeol fel, Biblical and Archaeol Sch, Hebrew Union Col, Jerusalem, 66-67, from asst prof archaeol to prof ancient Near Eastern hist and archaeol, 67-75, resident dir, 68-71; head dept, 78-81, Prof Near Eastern Archaeol, Dept Orient Studies, Univ Ariz, 75-, Dir, Hebrew Union Col-Harvard Semitic Mus Excavations, Gezer, Israel, 66-71; dir, Hebrew Union Col Excavations, Khalit el-Ful, Hebron, 67-68 and 71; dir, W F Albright Inst Archaeol Res, Jerusalem, 71-75, trustee, 77-; Winslow lectr, Seabury Western Theol Sem, 72; dir, W F Albright Inst Excavations at Shechem, 72-73; Steloff lectr, Hebrew Univ Jerusalem, 73. **HONORS AND AWARDS** Univ Ariz Found travel grants, 76 and 78; ed, Bull Am Schs Orient Res, 78-; Nat Endowment for Humanities grant, 79 and 80; Percia Schimmel Prize, Israel Mus, 82; **MEMBERSHIPS** Am Sch Orient Res; Soc Bibl Lit; Archaeol Inst Am; Am Orient Soc. **RESEARCH** Ancient Near Eastern history in the third and second millennia BC; development of Syro-Palestinian archaeology as a modern independent discipline; relationship of archaeology to Biblical studies. **SELECTED PUBLICATIONS** Auth, People of the Sea--The Search for the Philistines, J Am Orient Soc, Vol 114, 94; Houses and Their Furnishings in Bronze Age Palestine--Domestic Activity Areas and Artifact Distribution in the Middle Bronze Age and the Late Bronze- age, J Am Orient Soc, Vol 114, 94; An Introduction to Biblical Archaeology, J Am Orient Soc, Vol 116, 96; Lower Galilee During the Iron Age, Israel Exploration J, Vol 45, 95; Ceramics, Ethnicity, and the Question of Israels Origins, Biblical Archaeol, Vol 58, 95; Burial Practices and Cultural Diversity in Late Bronze Age, Israel Exploration J, Vol 45, 95; The Archaeology of Ancient Israel - J Biblical Lit, Vol 114, 95. **CONTACT ADDRESS** Dept Near East Studies, Univ of Arizona, 1 University of Az, Tucson, AZ 85721-0001. **EMAIL** wdever@u.arizona.edu

DEVEREUX, DAVID R.
PERSONAL Born 02/06/1961, London, ON, Canada, m, 1989, 1 child **DISCIPLINE** HISTORY **EDUCATION** Univ Western Ontario, BA, 84; Dalhousie Univ, MA, 85; Univ London, PhD, 88. **CAREER** Mount Allison Univ, vis asst prof, 88-89; postdoctoral fel, social sciences/humanities, 89-91; asst prof, St John Fisher Coll, 91-96; asst prof, Canisius Coll, 96-. **MEMBERSHIPS** Amer Historical Assn; North Amer Conf British Studies. **RESEARCH** British decolonization; aviation. **SELECTED PUBLICATIONS** Auth, The Formulation of British Defense Policy Towards the Middle East 1948-56, 91. **CONTACT ADDRESS** Dept of History, Canisius Col, 2001 Main St, Buffalo, NY 14208. **EMAIL** Devereud@canisius.edu

DEVINATZ, VICTOR G.
PERSONAL Born 10/19/1957, St Louis, MO, s **DISCIPLINE** LABOR HISTORY **EDUCATION** Northwestern Univ, BSE, 79; MA, 80; Univ Mass, MS, 86; Univ Minn, PhD, 90. **CAREER** From Asst Prof to Prof, Ill State Univ, 91-. **HONORS AND AWARDS** Outstanding MBAA Paper McGraw-Irwin Awd; Col of Bus Outstanding Researcher, 97; Caterpillar Fac Scholar, 99. **MEMBERSHIPS** Indust Rels Res Asn, United Asn for Labor Educ. **RESEARCH** Twentieth-Century U S labor history, U S labor relations, union organizing. **SELECTED PUBLICATIONS** Auth, "'Instead of Leaders They Have Become Bankers of Men': Gramsci's Alternative to the U S Neoinstitutionalists Theory of Trade-Union Bureaucratization," in Nature, Soc and Thought, vol 8, no 4 (96), 381-403; coauth, "Third Party Dispute Resolution - Interest Disputes," in The Human Resource Mangement Handbk, (Greenwich, CT: JAI Pr, 97), 95-135; auth, "What Do We Know About Mutual Gains Bargaining Among Educators?" J of Collective Negotiations in the Public Sector, vol 27, no 2 (98): 79-91; auth, "The Real Difference Between the Old Unionism and the New Unionism: A Strategy for U S Public Sector Unions," J of Collective Negotiations in the Public Sector, vol 28, no 1 (99): 29-39; auth, "The Ideology of Wildcat Strikes and Shop Floor Governance Regimes: The Institutionalization of Collective Bargaining, Shop Floor Contractualism and Fractional Bargaining," Advances in Indust and Labor Rels, vol 9 (99): 211-237; auth, High-Tech Betrayal: Working and Organizing on the Shop Floor, Mich St UP, 99; auth, "'Uncle Sam Does Not Want You to Organize': The 1977 Senate Armed Services Committee Hearings on Outlawing Military Unionization," J of Collective Negotiations in the Public Sector (forthcoming). **CONTACT ADDRESS** Dept Indust Rels, Illinois State Univ, 1 Campus, Box 5580, Normal, IL 61790-0001. **EMAIL** vgdevin@ilstu.edu

DEVINE, JOSEPH A., JR.
PERSONAL Born 06/10/1940, Philadelphia, PA, m, 1967, 3 children **DISCIPLINE** HISTORY **EDUCATION** Georgetown Univ, AB, 62; MA, 64, PhD, 68, Univ Virginia **CAREER** Prof, Stephen F. Austin State Univ **MEMBERSHIPS** AHA; OAH; SHA; TACT; ETHA; TSHA. **RESEARCH** Colonial America; 20th century Texas **CONTACT ADDRESS** Dept of History, Stephen F. Austin State Univ, Nacogdoches, TX 75962. **EMAIL** jdevine@sfasu.edu

DEVINE, MICHAEL JOHN
PERSONAL Born 01/05/1945, Aurora, IL, m, 1970, 3 children **DISCIPLINE** AMERICAN HISTORY **EDUCATION** Loras Col, BA, 67, Ohio State Univ, MA, 68, PhD (hist), 74. **CAREER** Instr hist, Loras Col, 68-69; Peace Corps vol English, US Dept State, Korea, 69-70; asst prof hist, Ohio Univ, 72-74; adminr, Ohio Am Revolution Bicentennial Comn, 74-76; Asst Dir, Ohio Hist Soc, 77-, Am Philos Soc grant, 78. **MEMBERSHIPS** AHA; Am Asn Mus; Am Asn State and Local Hist; Soc Historians Am Foreign Rels. **RESEARCH** Late 19th century American political and diplomatic; Ohio history; United States-East Asian relations. **SELECTED PUBLICATIONS** Ed, Ohio American Revolution Bicentennial Conference Series, Numbers 1-6, Ohio Hist Soc, 75-77; auth, John W Foster and the Annexation of Hawaii, Pac Hist Rev, 2/77. **CONTACT ADDRESS** Ohio Historical Ctr, 1982 Velma Ave, Columbus, OH 43211.

DEW, CHARLES BURGESS
PERSONAL Born 01/05/1937, St. Petersburg, FL, m, 1968, 2 children **DISCIPLINE** AMERICAN HISTORY **EDUCATION** Williams Col, AB, 58; Johns Hopkins Univ, PhD, 64. **CAREER** Instr hist, 63-64, asst prof, 64-65, Wayne St Univ, ; asst prof, 65-68, La State Univ,; Vis assoc prof hist, 70-71, Univ Va;from assoc prof to prof, 68-78, Univ Mo-Columbia; prof hist, 78-85, Class 1956 prof Am stud, 85-96; chmn dept hist, 86-92, dir, Oakley Ctr for Hum & Soc Sci, 94-97, W. Van Alan Clark Third Century Prof in Soc Sci, Williams Col; Am Coun Learned Soc fel, 75-76. **HONORS AND AWARDS** Fletcher Pratt Awd, 66; Awd of Merit, Am Assn State & Local Hist, 67. **MEMBERSHIPS** AHA; Orgn Am Historians; Southern Hist Assn. **RESEARCH** Antebellum South; slavery: Civil War and Reconstruction. **SELECTED PUBLICATIONS** Auth, The Slavery Experience, Interpreting So History: Historiographical Essays in Hon of Sanford W. Higginbotham, La St Univ Press, 87; auth, Slavery and Technology in the Antebellum Southern Iron Industry: The Case of Buffalo Forge, Sci & Med in the Old South, La St Univ Press, 89; auth, Bond of Iron: Master and Slave at Buffalo Forge, Norton & Co, 94; auth, Industrial Slavery, Encycl of Slavery, Garland Pub, 97. **CONTACT ADDRESS** Dept of History, Williams Col, 880 Main St, Williamstown, MA 01267-2600.

DEWAR, MARY
PERSONAL Born 02/13/1921, Mossley, England, m, 1944, 2 children **DISCIPLINE** MEDIEVAL AND MODERN HISTORY **EDUCATION** Oxford Univ, BA, 43, MA, 52; Univ London, PhD (medieval and mod hist), 56. **CAREER** Lectr econ and Social hist, Workers Educ Asn, Oxford Univ, 45-47; English, Maidenhead Tech Inst, 46-49; Res Assoc Hist, Univ Tex, Austin, 63-. **RESEARCH** Tudor history. **SELECTED PUBLICATIONS** Auth, Sir Thomas Smith, A Tudor Intellectual in Office, Univ London, 64; A Discourse of the Commonweal, Univ Va, 68. **CONTACT ADDRESS** Dept of Hist, Univ of Texas, Austin, Austin, TX 78712.

DEWEY, DONALD ODELL
PERSONAL Born 07/09/1930, Portland, OR, m, 1952, 3 children **DISCIPLINE** AMERICAN HISTORY **EDUCATION** Univ OR, BA, 52; Univ UT, MS, 56; Univ Chicago, PhD, 60. **CAREER** Instr hist, Univ Chicago, 60-62; from asst prof to assoc prof, 62-70, prof hist, CA State Univ, Los Angeles, 70, Dean, Sch Lett & Sci, 70-84, Dean, Sch Nat & Soc Sci, 84-96, Asst ed, Papers of James Madison, Univ Chicago, 60-61, assoc ed, 61-62; Am Philos Soc res grant, 65. **HONORS AND AWARDS** Outstanding Prof, Calif State Univ, Los Angeles, 75-76; CSLA nom for State Outstanding Prof, 89. **MEMBERSHIPS** Orgn Am Historians; AHA. **RESEARCH** US constitutional hist; James Madison; impeachment of federal judges. **SELECTED PUBLICATIONS** Coauth, The Papers of James Madison, Univ Chicago, Vols I-III, 62-63; The Continuing Dialogue, Pac Bks, Vols I & II, 63 & 64; auth, Hoosier Justice: The Journal of David McDonald, 1864-1868, Ind Mag Hist & Biog, 66; Union and Liberty, McGraw, 69; Marshall Versus Jefferson: The Political Background of Marbury v Madison, Knopf, 70; coauth, Becoming Informed Citizens: Lessons on the constitution for Junior High School Students, Regina, 88; Invitation to the Dance, RSVP, 91; The Congressional Salary Amendment: 200 Years Later, Glendale Law Rev, 91; auth, Samuel Chase, William Cushing, William Paterson in Melvin Urofsky, The Supreme Court Justices, Garland, 94; 19 Essays in Robert Rutland, James Madison and the American Nation, Simon & Schuster, 94; coauth, Becoming Informed Citizens: Lessons on the Bill of Rights for Secondary School Students, Regina, 95; Becoming Informed Citizens: Lessons on the Constitution for Secondary School Students, Regina, 95; auth, Truly the Weakest Branch: The United States Supreme Court, 1789-1803 in Roberto Martucci, Constitution & Revolution, Univ Macerata, 95; That's a Good One: Cal State LA at 50, CSULA, 97; The Federalist and Antifederalist Papers, Regina, 98. **CONTACT ADDRESS** Dept of Hist, California State Univ, Los Angeles, 5151 State University Dr, Los Angeles, CA 90032-4202. **EMAIL** ddewey@calstatela.edu

DEWEY, TOM
DISCIPLINE 19TH AND 20TH CENTURY ART, SOUTHERN ART AND ARCHITECTURE, HISTORY OF PRINTS **EDUCATION** Univ Southern IL, BA, MA; Univ Wis, Madison, PhD. **CAREER** Assoc prof, Univ MS, 76-; archv, Southern Graphics Coun, 77. **SELECTED PUBLICATIONS** Publ(s) on contemp Southern printmaking; 19th century Southern archit; the themes of horse racing, ballet, prostitution in the work of Edgar Degas and his contemp(s); the International Exhibition of Decorative and Industrial Arts, Paris 1925; critical essays on major 19th and 20th century Europ painters and archit(s), plus major Mod Movement buildings. **CONTACT ADDRESS** Univ of Mississippi, Oxford, MS 38677.

DEWINDT, ANNE R.
PERSONAL Born 08/08/1943, m, 1969 **DISCIPLINE** MEDIEVAL STUDIES **EDUCATION** Univ Toronto, PhD, 72. **CAREER** Instr, Hist and Philos Depts, Wayne County Community Col, 72-. **MEMBERSHIPS** Am Hist Asn; Royal Hist Soc. **RESEARCH** Medieval England; social history. **SELECTED PUBLICATIONS** Auth, Redefining the Peasant Community in Medieval England: The Regional Perspective, J British Studies, 4/87; auth, Local Government in a Small Town: A Medieval Leet Jury and its Constituents, Albion, Winter 91; auth, Monks and the Town Court of Ramsey: Overlapping Communities, In: La societe rurale et les institutions gouvernementales au moyen Age, Actes du Colloque de Montreal, 5/93; auth, Witchcraft and Conflicting Visions of the Ideal Village Community, J British Studies, 10/95; auth, The Town of Ramsey: The Question of Economic Development, 1290-1523, in The Salt of Common Life: Individuality and Choice in the Medieval Town, Countryside, and Church, Essays Presented to J. Ambrose Raftis, Kalamazoo, 96. **CONTACT ADDRESS** 3446 Cambridge Rd., Detroit, MI 48221. **EMAIL** AandE@compuserve.com

DEWINDT, EDWIN B.
DISCIPLINE HISTORY **EDUCATION** Univ Detroit, PhB; Pontifical Inst Mediaeval Stud, LMS; Univ Toronto, PhD. **CAREER** Prof, 68-. **HONORS AND AWARDS** Guggenheim fel; fel, Royal Hist Soc. **SELECTED PUBLICATIONS** Auth, ed, several bk(s) on society and law in the English Middle Ages; Royal Justice; Medieval English Countryside. **CONTACT ADDRESS** Dept of Hist, Univ of Detroit Mercy, 4001 W McNichols Rd, PO BOX 19900, Detroit, MI 48219-0900. **EMAIL** DEWINDTE@udmercy.edu

DI MAIO, IRENE S.
PERSONAL Born New York, NY, 1 child **DISCIPLINE** GERMAN STUDIES **EDUCATION** Vassar Col, BA; Univ Chicago, MA, La State Univ, PhD, 76. **CAREER** From instr to assoc prof, La State Univ, 65-. **HONORS AND AWARDS** DAAD; SCMLA Travel Grant; NEH Summer Sem; IREX; Southern Region Educ Travel Board; Fulbright Summer Sem. **MEMBERSHIPS** AATG, MLA, SCMLA, INCS, Women in German, Forum Vormurz Forschung. **RESEARCH** German-Jewish Relations, Cultural Diversity, Eighteenth- through Twentieth-Century German Literature--especially Realism, Raabe, Lewald, Auerbach, Gerstucker. **SELECTED PUBLICATIONS** Auth, The Multiple Perspective: Wilhelm Raabe's Third-Person Narratives of the Braunschweig Period, John Benjamins, 81; auth, "The Frauenfrage and the Reception of Wilhelm Raabe's Female Characters," in Wilhelm Raabe: Studien zu seinem Leben und Werk, eds. Leo Lensing and Hans-Werner Peter (Braunschweig: pp-Verlag, 81), 406-413; auth, "Nochmals zu den Akten: Sphinx, Indianerprinzessin, Nilschlange," Jarbuch der Raabe-Gesellschaft (87): 228-242; auth, "Heimat, Ortlichkeiten, and Mother-Tongue: The Cases of Jean Amery and Elias Canetti," in The Concept of "Heimat" in Contemporary German Literature, ed. H. W. Seliger (Munich: Iudicium Verlag, 87), 211-224; auth, "Berthold Auerbach's Dichter und Kaufmann: Enlightenment Thought and Jewish Identity," Lessing Yearbook (88): 265-283; auth, "Fanny Lewald," in Dictionary of Literary Biography. Nineteenth-Century German Writers, 1841-1900, eds. James Hardin and Siegfried Mews (MI: Gale Research, Inc., 93), 202-213; auth, "Borders of Culture: The Native American in Friedrich Gerstacker's North American Narratives," Yearbook of German-American Studies Vol 28 (93): 53-75; auth, "Fanny Lewald and Bismarck: Forty-Eighter Turned Monarchist?," Forum Vormarz Forschung, Jahrbuch (98): 233-250. **CONTACT ADDRESS** Dept For Lang & Lit, La State Univ, Baton Rouge, LA 70803-5306. **EMAIL** idmaio@lsu.edu

DIACON, TODD
DISCIPLINE HISTORY **EDUCATION** Univ Wisc, MA, 83; PhD, 87. **CAREER** Assoc prof, Hist, Univ Tenn. **RESEARCH** Latin American history. **SELECTED PUBLICATIONS** Auth, Millenarian Vision, Capitalist Reality: Brazil's Contestado Rebellion 1912-1916, Duke Univ Pr, 95. **CONTACT ADDRESS** Dept of Hist, Univ of Tennessee, Knoxville, Knoxville, TN 37996. **EMAIL** tdiacon@utk.edu

DIAMOND, SANDER A.
PERSONAL Born 11/25/1942, New York, NY, m, 1966, 2 children **DISCIPLINE** MODERN EUROPEAN HISTORY **EDUCATION** State Univ NYork Col New Paltz, AB, 64; State Univ NYork Binghamton, MA, 66, PhD, 71. **CAREER** From instr to asst prof, 68-72, assoc prof, 74-78, prof hist, Keuka Col, 74-, chmn dept, 78-, Nat Endowment Humanities course develop grant, 74; vis prof hist, Hobart & William Smith Col, 76-77; vis prof hist, State Univ NY, Binghamton, 77; NEH fel, 79; Danforth teaching fel, 81-86. **MEMBERSHIPS** AHA. **RESEARCH** German history, the Nazi years; German-American diplomatic relations; study of extremist movements; historical fiction. **SELECTED PUBLICATIONS** Auth, The Nazi Movement in the United States, 1924-1941, Cornell Univ, 74; Zur Typologie de Amerikadeutschen NS-Bewegung, 75 & Aus den Papieren des Amerikanischen Botschafters in Berlin, 1922-1925, 79, Vierteljahrshefte fur Zeitgeschichte; The Bund Movement in the United States, in Germany and America: Essays on Problems of International Relations and Immigration, Brooklyn Col Press, 80; The Soul of a Nation, in Newsday, 79; Herr Hitler: Amerikas Diplomaten, Washington, und der Untergang Weimars, Droste Verlag, 85; Starik, E.P. Dutton, 89; Starik, Pinnacle Paperbacks, 90; The Red Arrow, E.P. Dutton, 92; The German Table: The Education of a Nation, DISC-US Books, Inc, 98. **CONTACT ADDRESS** Dept Hist, Keuka Col, Keuka Park, NY 14478. **EMAIL** Sdiamond@mail.keuka.edu

DIAMOND, SIGMUND
PERSONAL Born 06/14/1920, Baltimore, MD, m, 1945, 2 children **DISCIPLINE** HISTORY, SOCIOLOGY **EDUCATION** Johns Hopkins Univ, AB, 40; Harvard Univ, PhD (US hist), 53. **CAREER** Reader-coder, Off Facts and Figures, Washington, DC, 42; head radio intel unit, Bd Econ Warfare, 42-43; int rep, United Auto Workers-Cong Indust Orgn, Mich, 43-49; from asst prof to assoc prof, 55-63, Prof Sociol and Hist, Columbia Univ, 63-, Fel, Ctr Advan Studies Behav Sci, 59-60; ed, Polit Sci Quart, 63-73; sr res fel, Newberry libr, Ill, 67; vis prof, Hebrew Univ, Jerusalem, 69-70; mem panel III, comt brain sci, Nat Res Coun, 72-; Fulbright prof, Tel-Aviv Univ, 75-76; deleg, Am Coun Learned Soc, 78-80. **MEMBERSHIPS** Conf Jewish Social Studies; Inst Early Am Hist and Cult; AHA; Econ Hist Asn; Am Sociol Asn. **RESEARCH** Sixteenth and 17th century theories of human nature and social organization; comparative studies of colonization in the New World; sociology of the arts. **SELECTED PUBLICATIONS** Auth, Whos Afraid of George and Marthas Parlor, Lit Film Quart, Vol 24, 96; Mothers in the Margins--Hardy, Thomas, Lawrence,D. H., And Suffragisms Discontents, Colby Quart, Vol 32, 96; Menand Review of Hershberg Book on Conand, James,B.--A Comment, NY Rev Books, Vol 41, 94; Diamond, Sara, Womens Stud Interdisciplinary J, Vol 25, 96. **CONTACT ADDRESS** Dept of Sociol, Columbia Univ, New York, NY 10027.

DICK, ERIC L.
PERSONAL Born 11/19/1951, Brandon, MB, Canada **DISCIPLINE** HISTORY **EDUCATION** Brandon Univ, BA, 72; Univ Man, MA, 78. **CAREER** Hist, Hist Sites Planner, Cultur Rsrc Mgt Specialist, Prairie & NWT Reg, 77-92, Nat Hist Sites Directorate, 92-95, HISTORIAN, PARKS CANADA, DEPT CAN HERITAGE, WESTERN CAN SERV CTR, 96-; partner, Ronald Thomas Frohwerk, 87-; adj prof, landscape archit, Univ Man, 91-92. **HONORS AND AWARDS** Can Hist Asn Reg Hist Cert Merit, 90; Merit Awd, City Winnipeg, 90; Parks Can Merit Awd, 96. **RESEARCH** Canadian agricultural history & architectural history. **SELECTED PUBLICATIONS** Auth, A History of Prairie Settlement Patterns, 87; auth, Farmers "Making Good": The Development of Abernethy District, Saskatchewan 1880-1920, in Stud Archaeol, Archit Hist, 89; auth, "Pibloktoq" (Arctic Hysteria): A Construction of European-Inuit Relations? in Arctic Anthrop, 95; contribur, The Canadian Encyclopedia, 85, 88; contribur, Making Western Canada: Essays on European Colonization and Settlement, 96 **CONTACT ADDRESS** 1102-888 Hamilton St., Vancouver, BC, Canada V6B 5W4.

DICKASON, OLIVE P.
PERSONAL Born 03/06/1920, Winnipeg, MB, Canada **DISCIPLINE** HISTORY **EDUCATION** Notre Dame Col, BA, 43; Univ Ottawa, MA, 72, PhD, 77. **CAREER** Reporter, The Leader-Post, 44-56; Globe & Mail, 56-67; chief info serv, Nat Gallery Can, 67-70; asst prof, 76-79, assoc prof, 79-85, prof, 85-92, prof emer Hist, Univ Alta, 92-; Adj prof, Univ Ottawa, 97-. **HONORS AND AWARDS** SSHRCC res grant, 85; Sr Rockefeller fel, 89; Sir John A. Macdonald Prize, 92; Metis Woman Year, 92; DLitt(hon), Univ NB, 93; DLitt(hon), Univ Alta, 95; Order of Can, 96; DLitt(hon), Univ Windsor, 96; LLD(hon), Univ Calgary, 96; DLitt(hon), Lakehead Univ, 97; DLitt(hon), Univ Guelph, 97; Nat Aboriginal Achievement Awd, 97. **MEMBERSHIPS** Mem, Metis Nation Alta; bd mem, Nat Aboriginal Achievement Found; mem coun, Champlain Soc; Can Hist Asn; Am Soc Ethnohist; Fr Colonial Hist Soc; Soc francaise d'histoire d'outre-mer; Soc d'histoire de l'Amerique francaise. **RESEARCH** First Nations history; colonisation of the Americas. **SELECTED PUBLICATIONS** Auth, The Myth of the Savage and the Beginnings of French Colonialism in the Americas, 84; auth, The Law of Nations and the New World, 89; auth, Indian Arts in Canada, 92; auth, The Native Imprint, 2 vols., 95-96; auth, Canada's First Nations, 97; auth, Visions of the Heart, 00. **CONTACT ADDRESS** Univ of Ottawa, 147 Seraphin-Marion, Ottawa, ON, Canada K1N 6N5. **EMAIL** dickason@uottawa.ca

DICKE, THOMAS SCOTT
PERSONAL Born 11/09/1955, St. Mary's, OH, m, 2 children **DISCIPLINE** HISTORY **EDUCATION** The Ohio State Univ, PhD, 88. **CAREER** Asst Prof, Univ GA, 89-90; Asst Prof, Southwest Missouri State Univ, 90-93; Assoc Prof Southwest Missouri State Univ, 93-. **MEMBERSHIPS** Business Hist Conf. **RESEARCH** Small Bussiness; Industrialization in global context; Hist of Edu. **SELECTED PUBLICATIONS** Franchising in America, Univ of NC Press, 92. **CONTACT ADDRESS** Dept Hist, Southwest Missouri State Univ, Springfield, 901 South National Ave, Springfield, MO 65802-0089. **EMAIL** tomdicke@mail.smsu.edu

DICKERMAN, EDMUND H.
PERSONAL Born 09/02/1935, Haverhill, MA, m, 1962, 1 child **DISCIPLINE** HISTORY **EDUCATION** Univ NH, BS, 57; Brown Univ, PhD (hist), 65. **CAREER** Instr hist, Conn Col, 64-65; from asst prof to assoc prof, 65-78, Prof Hist, Univ Conn, 78-. **MEMBERSHIPS** AHA; Renaissance Soc Am; Soc Fr Hist Studies. **RESEARCH** Renaissance and reformation history of Europe; early modern history of France. **SELECTED PUBLICATIONS** Auth THE CHOICE OF HERCULES - HENRY-IV AS HERO/, HISTORICAL JOURNAL, Vol 39, 1996 **CONTACT ADDRESS** Dept of Hist, Univ of Connecticut, Storrs, Storrs, CT 06268.

DICKINSON, GLORIA HARPER
PERSONAL Born 08/05/1947, New York, NY, m **DISCIPLINE** AFRICAN-AMERICAN STUDIES **EDUCATION** City Coll of NYork, BA European Hist 1968; Howard Univ, MA African Studies 1970, PhD African Stud 1978. **CAREER** Camden High School Camden NJ, geography/Social studies teacher 70-71; English Dept Trenton State Coll, instructor 71-73; Dept of African-Am Studies Trenton State Coll, Chmn Assoc Prof 1973-. **HONORS AND AWARDS** NEH summer fellowship for coll fac Univ of IA 1977, NY Univ School of Bus 1979, Univ of PA 1981, Princeton Univ 1984; Fac Mem of the Year Trenton State Coll 1984; Proj Dir NEH Summer Inst in African-Amer Culture Trenton State Coll 1987;Mentor of the Year, Trenton State College Minority Scholars, 1990 Blue Key Honor Society, Trenton State College, 1989. **MEMBERSHIPS** Editorial bd mem Journal of Negro History 1983-93; mem NJ Committee on The Humanities 1984-90; mem ASALH; mem ASA; mem AHSA; mem NCBS; mem NCNW; faculty advisor Zeta Sigma Chptr Alpha Kappa Alpha 1972-; contrib scholar NJ Women's Project 1984; proj dir TSC Summer Study Tours to Africa 1984-; mem NJ Historic Trust 1986-89; Alpha Kappa Alpha Sorority, chair, International Nominating Committee, 1988-92, archives comm, 1994-98; Supreme Grammateus, 1998-2000. **CONTACT ADDRESS** African-American Studies, Trenton State Col, PO Box 7718, Ewing, NJ 08628. **EMAIL** dickinsg@tcnj.edu

DICKISON, SHEILA KATHRYN
PERSONAL Born 11/14/1942, Walkerton, ON, Canada **DISCIPLINE** CLASSICS, ANCIENT HISTORY **EDUCATION** Univ Toronto, BA, 64; Bryn Mawr Col, MA, 66, PhD (Latin and Greek), 72. **CAREER** From instr to asst prof Greek, Latin and ancient hist, Wellesley Col, 69-76; actg chmn classics, 77-78, Assoc Prof Classics, Univ Fla, 76-. **MEMBERSHIPS** Archaeol Inst Am; Am Class League. **RESEARCH** Roman historiography; ancient social history **SELECTED PUBLICATIONS** Auth, The Reasonable Approach to Beginning Greek and Latin, Class J, Vol 87, 92. **CONTACT ADDRESS** ASB-3C, Univ of Florida, 3c Arts and Sciences, Gainesville, FL 32611-9500.

DICKS, SAMUEL EUGENE
PERSONAL Born 06/15/1935, St. Louis, MO, m, 1959, 4 children **DISCIPLINE** MEDIEVAL HISTORY, WOMEN'S HISTORY **EDUCATION** Dakota Wesleyan Univ, AB, 57; Univ SDak, AM, 58; Univ Okla, PhD (hist), 66. **CAREER** From asst prof to assoc prof, 65-67, Prof Hist, Emporia State Univ, 75-. **MEMBERSHIPS** AHA; Renaissance Soc Am; Medieval Acad Am. **RESEARCH** Late medieval diplomacy. **SELECTED PUBLICATIONS** Auth, Henry VI and the daughters of Armagnac: A problem in medieval diplomacy, 67 & Antoine Saugrain, 1763-1820: A French scientist on the American frontier, 75, Emporia State Res Studies. **CONTACT ADDRESS** Dept of Hist, Emporia State Univ, 1200 Commercial St, Emporia, KS 66801-5087.

DICKSON, CHARLES ELLIS
PERSONAL Born 06/13/1935, Bellevue, PA, m, 1964, 2 children **DISCIPLINE** HISTORY **EDUCATION** Ind Univ, BS, 57; Univ Pittsburgh, MA, 61; Ohio State Univ, PhD, 71. **CAREER** Assoc Prof and Fac Develop Coordr, Clark State, 89-; Asst Prof, Wright State Univ, 85-89; Fac Mem, Cottey College, 78-81; Instr, King Col, 76-77; Asst Prof, Geneva Col, 70-77. **HONORS AND AWARDS** Fulbright grant. **MEMBERSHIPS** Am Hist Asn; Ohio Acad Hist; Nat Coun for Staff, Prog and Orgn Develop. **RESEARCH** Early national political and religious history; James Monroe. **SELECTED PUBLICATIONS** John Sherman Hoyt, Dict Am Bio, NY, Charles Scribner's Sons, 77; The Election of 1816, The Election of 1820, and Thomas Pinckney (1750-1828), in Encycl Southern Hist, La State Univ Press, 79; Prosperity Rides on Rubber Tires: The Impact of the Automobile on Minot during the 1920's, N Dak Hist: Jour Northern Plains, 53, Summer 86, 14-23; Jeremiads in the New American Republic: The Case of National Fasts in the John Adams Administration, The New Eng Quart, 60, 87, 187-207; And Ladies of the Church: The Origins of the Episcopal Congregation in Minot, North Dakota, Hist: Jour Northern Plains, 55, 88, 8-19. **CONTACT ADDRESS** Clark State Comm Col, 570 E Leffel Ln, Springfield, OH 45501. **EMAIL** DicksonC@clark.cc.oh.us

DIEFENDORF, BARBARA BOONSTOPPEL
PERSONAL Born 12/19/1946, Oakland, CA, m, 1972 **DISCIPLINE** EUROPEAN HISTORY **EDUCATION** Univ Calif,

Berkeley, AB, 68, MA, 70, PhD, 78. **CAREER** Asst prof humanities, Univ NH, 79-80; from asst to assoc prof 80-93, prof history, 93-, Boston Univ; Visiting Prof, Harvard Univ Divinity School, 99-. **HONORS AND AWARDS** Nat Endowment for the Humanities Fell, 83-84, 01; Am Coun of Learned Soc Res Fell, 87-88; Outstanding Teaching, Boston Univ, 00; Nancy Lyman Roelker Pr, Sixteenth Century Stud Conf, 83, 96; Nat Huguenot Soc, Biennial Book Pr, 91-92; New England Hist Assoc, Book Pr, 92. **MEMBERSHIPS** AHA; Soc Fr Hist Studies; Sixteenth Century Studies. **RESEARCH** Sixteenth century France; wars of religion in Paris. **SELECTED PUBLICATIONS** Auth, "An Age of Gold? Parisian Women, the Holy League, and the Roots of Catholic Renewal," in Dissent, Identity and the Law in Early Modern France: Essays in Honor of Nancy Lyman Roelker, ed Michael Wolfe (Durham and London: Duke Univ Pr, 77) 169-90; auth, Paris' City Councillors in the Sixteenth Century: The Politics of Patrimony, Princeton, 83; auth, "Houses Divided: Religious Schism in Parisian Families in the Sixteenth Century," in Urban Life in the Renaissance, ed Ronald Weissman and Susan Zimmerman, (Univ of Del Pr, 89), 80-99; auth, "Prologue to a Massacre: Popular Unrest in Paris, 1557-1572," American Historical Review, (90), (December 85), 1067-91; auth, Beneath the Cross: Catholics and Huguenots in Sixteenth-Century Paris, Oxford, 91; co-ed, Culture and Identity in Early Modern Europe (1500-1800), Michigan, 93; co-ed, "The Huguenot Psalter and the Faith of French Protestants in the Sixteenth Century," in Culture and Identity in Early Modern Europe (1500-1800), (Univ of Mich Pr, 93), 41-63; auth, "Women and Property in Ancien Regime France: Theory and Practice in Dauphine and Paris," Early Modern Conceptions of Property, ed. John Brewer and Susan Staves (London and New York: Routledge, 94), 170-93; "Give Us Back Our Children: Patriarchal Authority and Parental Consent to Religious Vocations in Early Counter-Reformation France," Journal of Modern History 68, (96), 1-43; "La Saint-Barthelemy et la bourgeoisie parisienne," Histoire, economie et societe, 17, (98), 341-53. **CONTACT ADDRESS** Dept of History, Boston Univ, 226 Bay State Rd, Boston, MA 02215-1403. **EMAIL** bdiefend@bu.edu

DIEFENDORF, JEFFRY MINDLIN
PERSONAL Born 10/19/1945, Pasadena, CA, m, 1972 **DISCIPLINE** MODERN EUROPEAN HISTORY **EDUCATION** Stanford Univ, BA, 67; Univ Calif, Berkeley, MA, 68, PhD, 75. **CAREER** Teacher hist, Stanford Univ, 73-76, lectr, 75; from Asst Prof to Assoc Prof, 76-91, prof hist, Univ NH, 91-, Dept Chair, 91-97, Sr Fac Fel, 97-. **HONORS AND AWARDS** Am Coun Learned Soc grant-in-aid, 77-78; fel, NEH, 81-82; Nat Sci Found Res Initiation Grant, 81-83; Fel, Woodrow Wilson Int Ctr for Schol, 87; Fel, Alexander von Humboldt Found, 89-90, 94; NEH Summer Fel, 94. **MEMBERSHIPS** AHA; Conf Group Cent Europ Hist; German Studies Asn; New England Hist Asn; Int Planning Hist Soc; Urban Hist Soc. **RESEARCH** Comparative urban change in Germany, Switzerland, Boston. **SELECTED PUBLICATIONS** Auth, Businessman and Politics in the Rhineland, 1789-1834, Princeton Univ Press, 80; ed, The Rebuilding of Europe's Bombed Cities, MacMillan Press/ St. Martin's Press, 90; auth, In the Wake of War: The Reconstruction of German Cities after World War II, Oxford Univ Press, 93; co-ed, America's Policy and the Reconstruction of Germany, 1945-1955, Cambridge Univ Press, 94; author of 24 journal articles and chapters. **CONTACT ADDRESS** Dept of Hist, Univ of New Hampshire, Durham, Horton Soc Sci Ctr, Durham, NH 03824-4724. **EMAIL** jeffryd@christa.unh.edu

DIERENFIELD, BRUCE
PERSONAL Born 07/26/1951, Waterloo, IA, m, 1984, 1 child **DISCIPLINE** HISTORY **EDUCATION** St Olaf Col, BA, 73; Univ of Va, MA, 77; PhD, 81. **CAREER** Vis asst prof, Univ of Ala, 81-82; vis asst prof, Purdue Univ, 82-83; lectr, Tex Women's Univ, 83-86; asst prof to prof, Canisius Col, 86-. **HONORS AND AWARDS** Phi Beta Kappa; Phi Alpha Theta; DuPont Fel, 77; Fac Fel, Canisius Col, 88, 92, 96, 99; NEH Grants, 87, 93, Gerald R Ford Found Grant, 93; Ball Bros Found Fel, 93; Fulbright Prof, 57, 88, 93; Vis Prof, Univ of Helsinki, 93; Vis Prof, China, 94-95. **MEMBERSHIPS** AHA; Am United for Separation of Church and State; Christian Coalition; J of Church and State; Nat Counc on Relig and Public Educ; Org of Am Hist; Pa Hist Assoc; People for the Am Way; Southern Hist Assoc; Theodore Roosevelt Inaugural Nat Site Found. **RESEARCH** 20th century, especially politics and public policy, social movements, Constitution, African American, Religion, South. **SELECTED PUBLICATIONS** Auth, Keeper of the Rules: Congressman Howard W Smith of Virginia, Univ Pr of Va, 87; auth, "The Speaker and the Rules Keeper: Sam Rayburn, Howard Smith, and the Liberal Democratic Temper", Developing Dixie: Modernization in a Traditional Society, ed JF Tripp, Greenwood Pr, (88): 199-213; auth, "A Year in Cologne", Fulbright Funnel, (92): 14-25; auth, "Rolando Blackman", "Chuck Daly", and "Hakeem Olajuwon", Biographical Dict of American Sports: 1992-1995 Supplement for Baseball, football, Basketball and Other Sports, Greenwood Pr, 95; auth, "China Through My Eyes: One Child Gets Caught in the Cultural Gap", China Daily, Jan 96; auth, "A Nation Under God: Ronald Reagan and the Crusade for School Prayer", Ronald's Reagan's America, eds Eric J Schmertz et al, Greenwood Pr, (97): 215-241; auth, The Civil Rights Movement, Addison Wesley Longman, (forthcoming); auth, Defending the Wall: The Minnesota Civil Liberties Union and the War Against Religious Establishment, Friends of the Bill of Rights Found, (forthcoming); auth, A Godless Nation? The School Prayer Case of Engel vs Vitale, Univ Pr of Kans, (forthcoming); auth, God in the Classroom: A History of Religious Expression in American Public Schools, Ivan R Dee Pub, (forthcoming). **CONTACT ADDRESS** Dept Hist, Canisius Col, 2001 Main St, Buffalo, NY 14208-1035. **EMAIL** dierenfb@canisius.edu

DIETRICH, CRAIG
PERSONAL Born 08/15/1937, Butte, MT **DISCIPLINE** CHINESE SOCIAL AND ECONOMIC HISTORY **EDUCATION** Univ Chicago, AB, 61, PhD (Chinese hist), 70. **CAREER** Asst prof Chinese hist, Univ Minn, 66-67; from instr to asst prof, 68-73; Assoc Prof Chinese Hist, Univ Maine, Portland-Gorham, 73-, Instr Chinese hist, Bowdoin Col, 68-70, asst prof, 71-73; Am Coun Learned Soc res grant Chinese civilization, 73-74. **MEMBERSHIPS** Asn Asian Studies. **RESEARCH** Late traditional Chinese economic organization; 17th century Chinese-European intellectual contacts. **SELECTED PUBLICATIONS** Auth, Les Opera Parfumes, Aspects of Orientalism in 19th Century French Opera, Theatre Research International, Vol 22, 97. **CONTACT ADDRESS** Dept of Hist, Univ of Maine, Portland, ME 04103.

DIETRICH, WILFRED O.
PERSONAL Born 05/22/1924, Burton, TX, m, 1969 **DISCIPLINE** ENGLISH, HISTORY **EDUCATION** Blinn Col, AA, 43; Sam Houston State Univ, BA, 46, MA, 48; East Tex State Univ (now Tex A & M Commerce), Doctor Education and English, 78. **CAREER** Public school teacher, Burton Independent Sch District, 43-58; instr and chemn of the Div of Humanities, Blinn Col, 58-. **HONORS AND AWARDS** Several fels during the summers; distinguished teacher Awd several times from public schools; many teaching Awds from Blinn Col. **MEMBERSHIPS** Tex Jr Col Asn, Tex Coun of English, Nat Coun of English, Am Folk Soc, Tex Hist Soc, many others. **RESEARCH** History--country, regional, families, special groups that have made an impact on the heritage of Washington County and the State of Texas, for example, several Indian tribes, Old Three Hundred, family history and the like. **SELECTED PUBLICATIONS** Auth, The Blazing Story of Washington County; auth, revision of The Blazing Story of Washington County; auth, History of the Brenham Manifest; auth, Work of Junior College Registrars. **CONTACT ADDRESS** Dept Humanities, Blinn Col, 902 College Ave, Brenham, TX 77833-4049.

DIETZ, HANNS-BERTOLD
PERSONAL Born, Germany, 3 children **DISCIPLINE** MUSIC, HISTORICAL MUSICOLOLOGY **EDUCATION** Univ Insbruck, PhD, 56. **CAREER** Prof, Univ of Tx at Austin; Prof Emeritus, 99. **HONORS AND AWARDS** 3 Tchg Excellence awd(s); **RESEARCH** Neapolitan opera and church music. **SELECTED PUBLICATIONS** Auth, Die Chorfuge be Georg Friedrich Handel; publ, Analecta Musicologica, Int J Musicol, J Amer Musicol Soc, Musikforschung, Notes, Pergolesi Stud; contrib to, Die Musik in Geschichte und Gegenwart, New Grove Dictionary of Music and Musicians & New Grove Dictionary of Opera. **CONTACT ADDRESS** School of Music, Univ of Texas, Austin, 2613 Wichita St, Austin, TX 78705. **EMAIL** hbd@mail.utexas.edu

DIGBY, JOAN
DISCIPLINE EIGHTEENTH CENTURY BRITISH LITERATURE, ART AND LITERATURE **EDUCATION** NYork Univ, PhD. **CAREER** Prof, dir, honors prog, Long Island Univ, C.W. Post Campus. **SELECTED PUBLICATIONS** Auth, Philosophy in the Kitchen; or, Problems in Eighteenth-Century Culinary Aesthetics; Reading Goya's Dispartes; A Sound of Feathers; coauth, The Collage Handbook; coed, Permutations, Food for Thought; Inspired by Drink. **CONTACT ADDRESS** Long Island Univ, C.W. Post, Brookville, NY 11548-1300.

DILLON, CLARISSA F.
PERSONAL Born 07/24/1933, Chicago, IL, d, 1 child **DISCIPLINE** POLITICAL SCIENCE; AMERICAN HISTORY; HISTORY **EDUCATION** Bryn Mawr Col, AB, 55; Univ Chicago, MA, 60; Bryn Mawr Col, PhD, 86. **CAREER** Classrom teacher, The Latin School of Chicago, grades 1, 2, 5, 6, 7, 8, 11-12; Ithan Elementary, Radnor, PA, grades 1, 4, 5, 6 (public school certification through Immaculata Col); consultant and free-lance Living History demonstrator at Historic Sites and Museums, 73-. **MEMBERSHIPS** Radnor Twp Ed Asn; PA State Ed Asn; NEA; Nat Coalition of Independent Scholars; Asn for Living History, Farms, and Agricultural Museums (ALHFAM). **RESEARCH** 18th century women's work/lives among the English in southeastern PA (demonstration/ interpretation of processes based on research findings). **SELECTED PUBLICATIONS** Auth, A Most Comfortable Dinner-18th Century Foods "to subsist a great Number of Persons at a small Expense," printed for the author, 94; "To Make the Face Faire and Smooth," ALHFAM Proceedings for Annual Conference, 95; Beef--It's What's for Dinner, ALHFAM Bul, spring, 96; Barbecues, with Sandra Oliver, Food History News, spring 96; Lewd, Enormous, and Disorderly Practices: Prostitution in 18th-Century Philadelphia and Its English Background, ALHFAM Proceedings for Annual Conference, 96; Margaret Morris Burlington-NJ 1804 Gardening Memorandum, with Nancy V Webster, No 6 in Am Horticultural Series, The AM Botanist, Booksellers, Chillicothe, IL, 96; This is the Way We Wash Our Clothes, Past Masters, Newsletter, winter 98; "Under the Shadow of My Wing", ALHFAM Proceedings for Annual Conference, 98; 18th-Century Dyeng in Pennsylvania, Past Masters Newsletter, summer 98; auth, "So Serve It Up: Eighteenth-Century English Foodstuffs in Eastern Pennsylvania," printed for the author, 99. **CONTACT ADDRESS** 768 Buck Ln, Haverford, PA 19041-1202.

DILLON, DIANE
DISCIPLINE ART HISTORY **EDUCATION** Yale Univ, PhD. **CAREER** Prof, Northwestern Univ. **RESEARCH** Gender studies, critical theory, and post-colonial studies. **SELECTED PUBLICATIONS** Writing a book about the visual culture of the World Colombian Exposition of 1893. **CONTACT ADDRESS** Dept of Art History, Northwestern Univ, 1801 Hinman, Evanston, IL 60208.

DILLON, MERTON LYNN
PERSONAL Born 04/04/1924, Addison, MI **DISCIPLINE** AMERICAN HISTORY **EDUCATION** Mich State Norm Col, AB, 45; Univ Mich, AM, 48, PhD (hist), 51. **CAREER** Instr hist, Mich State Norm Col, 51; asst prof, NMex Mil Inst, 51-56; from asst prof to prof, Tex Tech Col, 56-65; assoc prof, Northern Ill Univ, 65-67; Prof Hist, Ohio State Univ, 67-, Nat Endowment for Humanities sr fel, 73-74. **MEMBERSHIPS** AHA; Orgn Am Historians; Southern Hist Asn. **RESEARCH** Nineteenth Century United States; antislavery movement; slavery and antislavery. **SELECTED PUBLICATIONS** Auth, In Retrospect--Barnes, Gilbert, H. and Dumond, Dwight, L., Revs Am Hist, Vol 21, 93; Antiracism in United States History--The 1st 200 Years, J Southern Hist, Vol 59, 93; Witness for Freedom--African American Voices on Race, Slavery and Emancipation, African Am Rev, Vol 29, 95. **CONTACT ADDRESS** Dept of Hist, Ohio State Univ, Columbus, Columbus, OH 43210.

DIN, GILBERT C.
PERSONAL Born 11/11/1932, Holtville, CA, m, 1989, 1 child **DISCIPLINE** COLONIAL AND MODERN LATIN AMERICAN HISTORY **EDUCATION** Univ Calif, Berkeley, AB, 57, MA, 58; Univ Madrid, PhD (hist), 60. **CAREER** Instr hist and anthrop, Imperial Valley Col, 61-65; from asst prof to assoc prof, 64-75, chmn dept, 73-80, Prof Hist, Ft Lewis Col, 75-90. **HONORS AND AWARDS** kemper Williams Awd for best bk published in La Hist, 98, 99; best article in La Hist for 78, 96; McGinty Lifetime Meritorious Awd, 94; Certificate of Commendation from Am Asn for Stae and local hist in 94 for Francisco Bouligny: A Bourbon Soldier in Spanish Louisiana; Fel of the La Hist Asn, 98; prof emeritus, 90. **MEMBERSHIPS** AHA; Conf Latin Am Hist. **RESEARCH** Eighteenth century French and Spanish Louisiana. **SELECTED PUBLICATIONS** Auth, "Louisiana in 1776: A Memoria of Francisco Bouligny," La Collection Series, 77; auth, Getting to Know Latin, J Weston Walsh, 78; auth, "Canary Islander Settlements of Louisiana: An Overview," La Hist, 86; auth, Louisiana, LSU press, 88; auth, Francisco Bouligny: A Bourbon Soldier in Spanish Louisiana, LSU Press, 93; auth, Europeans in Arkansas, Compiler: J. Whayne, Univ of Ark Press, 95; auth, Spanish Prescence in Louisiana, 1763-1803, Center for La studies, Univ of Southwestern La, 96; auth, Spainards, Planters, and Slaves: The Spanish Regulation of Slavery in Louisiana, 1763-1803, Tex A and M Univ Press, 99; numerous other articles and essays. **CONTACT ADDRESS** 2533 Little Vista Terr., Olney, MD 20832-1568.

DINAN, SUSAN A.
PERSONAL Born 05/15/1965, Buffalo, NY, m, 1996 **DISCIPLINE** HISTORY **EDUCATION** Cornell Univ, BS, 87; Univ Wash, BA, 89; Univ IL, MA, 90; Univ Wisconsin, PhD, 96. **CAREER** Lect, Univ Wis-Madison, 94-96; asst prof, Long Island Univ, CW Post Campus, 97-. **HONORS AND AWARDS** George Mosse Teach Fel, 95; TLII Devel Grant, 98-99. **MEMBERSHIPS** ACHA; AHA; FHA; SEMS; SEMW. **RESEARCH** Reformation; Catholic reformation; Early modern France; Gender. **SELECTED PUBLICATIONS** Auth "An Ambiguous Sphere: the Daughters of Charity between a Confraternity and a Religious Order," in Confraternities and Catholic Reform in Italy France and Spain, eds. John Patrick Donnelly, Michael Maher (Kirksville, MO: Thomas Jefferson University Press, 99), 191-214; auth, "Public Charity and Public Piety: The Missionary Vocation of the Daughters of Charity of Charity," under review with Proceedings of the Western Society for French History; auth, "Spheres of Female Religious Expression in Catholic Reformation France," in Gender and Religion in the Old and New Worlds, under review with Routledge; rev, Budding Codes: The Aesthetics of Calvinism in Early Modern Europe. Catharine Randall. Univ of Penn Press (Philadelphia, PA, 99); co-ed, Gender and Religion in the Old and New Worlds, under review with Routledge; rev, Renaissance and Reformation, forthcoming. **CONTACT ADDRESS** Dept Hist, Long Island Univ, C.W. Post, 720 Northern Blvd, Greenvale, NY 11548-1319. **EMAIL** sdinan@liu.edu

DINCAUZE, DENA F.
PERSONAL Born 03/26/1934, Boston, MA, d, 2 children **DISCIPLINE** ARCHAEOLOGY **EDUCATION** Barnard Col, BA, 56; Cambridge Univ, Dip, 57; Harvard Univ, PhD, 67. **CAREER** Lecturer, Harvard Univ, 68-69; Asst Prof, SUNY Buffalo, 72-73; Asst Prof to Prof, Univ Mass, 73-. **HONORS AND AWARDS** Phi Beta Kappa, 56; Sigma Xi, 67; Fulbright Sch, Cambridge Univ, 56-57; Fel, Am Asn Adv of Sci, 88; Distinguished Service Awd, Soc for Am Archaeol, 97; Chancellor's Medal, Univ MA, 89. **MEMBERSHIPS** Soc for Am Archaeol; Soc of Prof Archeol; Am Asn Adv of Sci; Am Arth Asn. **RESEARCH** Prehistory and ethnohistory of northwestern North America; Human Paleo-ecology; Geoarchaeology; Archaeology Resource Management; Field Methods. **SELECTED PUBLICATIONS** Auth, "Centering," Northeast Anthropology, (93): 33-37; auth, "Federal Archaeological Preservation Programs in the Northeast: An Assessment for 1997," Northeast anthropology, (97): 15-21; co-auth, "On the Pleistocene antiquity of Monte Verde, Southern Chile," American Antiquity, (97): 659-663; auth, Environmental Archaeology: Principles and Practice, Cambridge Univ Press, 00. **CONTACT ADDRESS** Dept Anthropol, Univ of Massachusetts, Amherst, PO Box 34805, Amherst, MA 01003. **EMAIL** doncauze@authro.umass.edu

DINER, STEVEN J.
PERSONAL Born 12/14/1944, Bronx, NY, m, 1970, 3 children **DISCIPLINE** HISTORY **EDUCATION** Binghamton Univ, BA, 66; Univ Chicago, MA, 68, PhD, 72. **CAREER** Asst prof to assoc prof to prof Urban Stud, Univ DC, 72-85; prof Hist, George Mason Univ, 85-98; Dean, Fac Arts, Scis, Prof History, 98-, Rutgers, Newark. **MEMBERSHIPS** Am Hist Asn; Org Am Hist; Soc Hist Gilded Age & Progressive Era; Urban Hist Asn. **RESEARCH** US urban history; US immigration and ethnic history; Progressive Era; history of US higher education. **SELECTED PUBLICATIONS** Auth, A Very Different Age: Americans of the Progressive Era, Hill & Wang, 98; auth, A City and Its Universites: Public Policy In Chicago, 1892-1919 , Univ of North Carolina Press, 80.; auth, Housing Washington's People: Public Policy in Retrospect, Washington, DC, 83. **CONTACT ADDRESS** Office of Dean, Arts & Scis, Rutgers, The State Univ of New Jersey, Newark, 360 Martin Luther King Jr. Blvd., Newark, NJ 07102-1801. **EMAIL** sdiner@andromeda.rutgers.edu

DINGMAN, ROGER V.
PERSONAL Born 10/19/1938, Los Angeles, CA, m, 1965, 4 children **DISCIPLINE** HISTORY **EDUCATION** Stanford Univ, BA, 60; Harvard Univ, MA, 63; PhD, 69. **CAREER** Vis Prof, Calif State Univ, 63-64; Teaching Asst to Lecturer, Harvard Univ, 64-71; Asst Prof to Assoc Prof, Univ Southern Calif, 71-75; Prof, US Naval War Col, 77-78; Assoc Prof, Univ Southern Calif, 78-97; Visiting Prof, Griffith Univ, 85; Distinguished Visiting Prof, US Air Force Acad, 88-89; Visiting Prof, Mesa State Col, 91; Visiting Prof, Yokohama Nat Univ, 99; Prof, Univ Southern Calif, 98-. **HONORS AND AWARDS** Vice Admiral E.B. Hooper Fel, Naval Hist Foundation, 98; Iriye Intl Hist Book Prize, 98; Japan Defense Agency Distinguished Visiting Lectureship Award, Nat Inst of Defense, 97; Univ Distinguished visiting Lectureship Award, Northern Ariz Univ, 96; Korea Res Foundation Award, 91; Res/Travel Awards, Am Coun of Learned Soc, 86, 83; Distinguished Lecturer, United States-Japan Friendship Commission for Asian Studies, 83; Sen Fel, Australian Nat Univ, 82; Sen Fel, United States NEH, 82; Bernath Award, soc of Hist of Am foreign Relations, 77; Res Award, Am Philos soc, 76; Haynes foundation Award, 75; Nat Fel, Stanford Univ, 73-74; Harvard Canaday Award, 70; Honors Prize, Stanford Univ, 59; Phi Beta Kappa, 59. **MEMBERSHIPS** Society for Historians of Am Foreign Relations, Society for Military History, International Hose of Japan, United States Navel Institute. **RESEARCH** American diplomatic, military, and naval history; American-East Asian relations; International history of the Pacific in the Twentieth Century. **SELECTED PUBLICATIONS** Auth, Ghost of War: the sinking of the Awa maru and Japanese-American Relations, 1945-1995, naval Inst Press, 97; auth, Power in the Pacific: The Origins of Naval Arms Limitation, 1914-1922, Univ Chicago Press, 76; ed, Kindai Nihon no taigai taido, Tokyo Univ Press, 74; auth, Anchor of Peace: The United States Navy in Japan, forthcoming; auth, "Protested Presence: The Nuclear Navy Comes to Japan, 1961-1968," in Proceedings of the XVth Naval History Symposium, forthcoming; auth, "Not without the Other: The Non-American in Ernest R. May's History," in Rethinking International Relations, 99; auth, "Paths to Officership: Military Education in Japan Before and After 1945," in Forging the Sword: Selecting, Educating, and Training Cadets and Junior Officers in the Twentieth Century, 99; auth, "Reflections on Pearl Harbor Anniversaries Past," Journal of American-East Asian Relations, (94): 279-293; auth, "Jih-pen yu Mahan," in Li-shih tui Ma-han chih, ying-hsiang, Taipei, 94; auth, "Destinies Intertwined: An Historical overview of United States-Japan-Korea Relations, 1890-1990," in JS-Japan Cooperation in Conflict Management: The Case of Korea, 93; auth, "The Dagger and the Gift: The Impact of the Korean War on Japan," Journal of American-East Asian Relations, (93): 29-55 **CONTACT ADDRESS** Dept History, Univ of So California, 3502 Trousdale Pkwy, Los Angeles, CA 90089-0034. **EMAIL** dingman@mizar.usc.edu

DINKIN, ROBERT J.
PERSONAL Born 05/26/1940, Brooklyn, NY, m, 1988, 2 children **DISCIPLINE** AMERICAN HISTORY **EDUCATION** Brooklyn Col, BA, 63; Columbia Univ, MA, 64, PhD(hist), 68. **CAREER** From Asst Prof to Assoc Prof, 68-78, Prof Hist, Calif State Univ Fresno, 78-. **MEMBERSHIPS** AHA; Orgn Am Historians; Inst Early Am Hist & Culture. **RESEARCH** Early American history; women's history. **SELECTED PUBLICATIONS** Ed, Selected Readings in Early American History, McCutchan, 69; auth, Seating the meetinghouse in early Massachusetts, New Eng Quart, 70; Elections in Colonial Connecticut, Conn Hist Soc Bull, 72; Nominations in Provincial America, Historian, 73; Voting in Provincial America, Greenwood, 77; Voting in Revolutionary America, Greenwood, 82; Campaigning in America, Greenwood, 89; Before Equal Suffrage, Greenwood, 95. **CONTACT ADDRESS** Dept of Hist, California State Univ, Fresno, 5340 N Campus Dr, Fresno, CA 93740-8019.

DINNERSTEIN, LEONARD
PERSONAL Born 05/05/1934, New York, NY, m, 1961, 2 children **DISCIPLINE** AMERICAN HISTORY **EDUCATION** City Col New York, BSS, 55; Columbia Univ, MA, 60, PhD(Am hist), 66. **CAREER** Lectr Am hist & Am govt, NY Inst Technol, 60-65; lectr hist, City Col New York, 66-67; asst prof, Fairleigh Dickinson Univ, 67-70; from assoc prof to prof Am Hist, Univ Ariz, 70-, dir Judaic Studies, 93-00; dir, NEH Summer Seminars for Col Teachers: Minorities in the Southwest, Univ Ariz, 80, 83. **HONORS AND AWARDS** Anisfield-Wolf Awd, 69; NEH fel, 70, 77, 78, 85, 87, 89, 91-92; National Jewish Book Awd, 94; Myers Ctr Awd for the Study of Hum Rights in Am, 94. **MEMBERSHIPS** AHA; Orgn Am Historians; Am Jewish Hist Soc; Immigration Hist Soc. **RESEARCH** American immigration; American Jewish history; 20th century America. **SELECTED PUBLICATIONS** Auth, The Leo Frank Case, Columbia Univ, 68; co-ed, The Aliens, Appleton, 70; American Vistas, Oxford Univ, 71, 75, 79, 83, 87, 91, 95; ed, Antisemitism in the United States, Holt, 72; co-ed, Jews in the South, La State Univ, 73; Decisions and Revisions, Praeger, 75; coauth, Ethnic Americans, 77 & Natives and Strangers, 79, 89, 96, Oxford Univ; auth, America and the Survivors of the Holocaust, Columbia Univ, 82; Antisemitism in America, Oxford, 94. **CONTACT ADDRESS** Hist Dept, Univ of Arizona, 1 University of Az, PO Box 210027, Tucson, AZ 85721-0027. **EMAIL** dinnerst@u.arizona.edu

DIRKS, NICHOLAS
DISCIPLINE SOUTH ASIAN HISTORY **EDUCATION** Wesleyan Univ, BA, 72; Univ Chicago, PhD, 78. **CAREER** Prof. **SELECTED PUBLICATIONS** Auth, The Home and the Nation: Consuming Culture and Politics in Roja, 98. **CONTACT ADDRESS** Dept of History, Columbia Col, New York, 2960 Broadway, New York, NY 10027-6902.

DIRKS, PATRICIA
PERSONAL Born, ON, Canada **DISCIPLINE** HISTORY **EDUCATION** Queen's Univ, BA, 63, MA, 66; Univ Toronto, PhD, 72. **CAREER** Lectr, SUNY Buffalo, 70-71; lectr to asst prof, 71-90, assoc prof, Brock Univ, 90-. **MEMBERSHIPS** Can Hist Asn; Soc Can Studs; Can Inst Int Affairs; Ont Hist Soc. **RESEARCH** Early twentieth-century voluntary associations for English-Canadian Protestant youngsters. **SELECTED PUBLICATIONS** Auth, Finding the Canadian Way: Origins of the Religious Education Council of Canada, in Studs Rel/Sci Rel, 87; auth, L'Action liberale nationale: A Failed Attempt to Reconcile Modernization with Tradition, 91. **CONTACT ADDRESS** History Dept, Brock Univ, 500 Glenridge Ave, Saint Catherines, ON, Canada L2S 3A1. **EMAIL** pdirks@spartan.ac.BrockU.CA

DIRLIK, ARIF
PERSONAL Born 11/23/1940, Mersin, Turkey, s, 2 children **DISCIPLINE** MODERN CHINESE HISTORY **EDUCATION** Robert Col, Istanbul, BS, 64; Univ Rochester, PhD (hist), 73. **CAREER** From instr to asst prof, 71-77, Assoc Prof Hist, Duke Univ, 77-; prof hist, Duke Univ, 89; prof hist and cultural anthrolpology, Dunk Univ, 00; vis prof, Univ Victoria, BC, summer, 80, 85, 92; and Univ BC, 80-81; UCLA, 85; Homg Kong Univ of Sci and Technology, 98. **HONORS AND AWARDS** Fel, netherlands Inst for Advanced Studies, Nordic inst for Asian Studies; Fulbright NEH. **MEMBERSHIPS** Editorial Boards of China Quarterly, Ameraisa, Boundary 2, Interventions, Asian Studies Review, Zhongguo xueshu. **RESEARCH** Marxism in China; modern Chinese historiography; Socialist thought in China; modern Chinese political thought; Pacific studies; Asian-American Studies; Postcolonial and cultural studies. **SELECTED PUBLICATIONS** Auth, Revolution and History, California, 78; auth, Origins of Chinese Communism, Oxford, 89; auth, Anarchism in the Chinese Revolution, California, 91; coauth, Schools in the Fields and Factories: Anarchists, the Guomindang, and the Labor University in Shanghai, 1927-1932, Duke 92; auth, After the Revolution: Waking to Globacl Capitalism, Wesleyan, 94; auth, "The Postcolonial Aura, 3rd World Criticism in the Age of Global Capitalism," Critical Inquiry, Vol 20 (94); ed, What is in a Rim, Rowman and Littlefield, 98; coed, Postmodernism and China, Duke, 00; auth, Postmodernity's Histories, Rowman and Littlefield, 00; ed, Chinese on the American Frontier, Rowman and Littlefield, 01; coed, Places and Politics in an Age of Global Capital, Rowman and Littlefield, 01. **CONTACT ADDRESS** Dept of Hist, Duke Univ, Durham, NC 27706. **EMAIL** adirlik@duke.edu

DITTMER, JOHN
PERSONAL Born 10/30/1939, Seymour, IN, m, 1961, 2 children **DISCIPLINE** HISTORY **EDUCATION** Ind Univ, BS, 61; MA, 63; PhD, 71. **CAREER** From asst prof to assoc prof, Tougaloo Col, 67-79; acad dean, Tougaloo Col, 68-70; vis assoc prof, Brown Univ, 79-84; vis assoc prof, Mass Inst of Technol, 82-84; from assoc prof to prof, DePauw Univ, 85-. **HONORS AND AWARDS** NEH Younger Humanist Fel, 73-74; NEH Fel, Vanderbilt Univ, 76-77; Rockefeller Found Fel, 80-81; ACLS Fel, 83-84; Ctr for the Study of Civil Rights Fel, 88-89; Lillian Smith Book Awd, 94; McLemore Prize, 95; Bancroft Prize, 95; NEH Fel for Col Teachers, 99. **MEMBERSHIPS** Am Hist Asn, Orgn of Am Historians, Southern Historical Asn, Southern Asn for Women Historians. **RESEARCH** African-American History, History of the South, The United States in the Twentieth Century. **SELECTED PUBLICATIONS** Auth, Black Georgia in the Progressive Era, 1900-1920, Univ Ill Press, 77 & 81; auth, Local People: The Struggle for Civil Rights in Mississippi, Univ Ill Press, 94 & 95. **CONTACT ADDRESS** Dept Hist, DePauw Univ, 313 S Locust St, Greencastle, IN 46135-1736. **EMAIL** rip@depauw.edu

DIUBALDO, RICHARD J.
DISCIPLINE HISTORY OF THE CANADIAN NORTH **EDUCATION** McMaster Univ, BA, MA; Univ W Ontario, PhD. **RESEARCH** The history of the Canadian North. **SELECTED PUBLICATIONS** Pub(s), extensively on Arctic sovereignty, Can-US relations, and Can government policy toward the Inuit; auth, Stefansson and the Canadian Arctic. **CONTACT ADDRESS** Dept of Hist, Concordia Univ, Montreal, 1400 de Maisonneuve Blvd W, Montreal, QB, Canada H3G 1W8. **EMAIL** history@alcor.concordia.ca

DIVINE, ROBERT ALEXANDER
PERSONAL Born 05/10/1929, Brooklyn, NY, m, 1955, 4 children **DISCIPLINE** AMERICAN HISTORY **EDUCATION** Yale Univ, BA, 51, MA, 52, PhD (hist), 54. **CAREER** From instr to assoc rpof, 54-63, chmn dept, 63-68, prof hist, 63-81, George W Littlefield Prof Am Hist, Univ Tex, Austin, 81-96, Fel, Ctr Advan Studies Behav Sci, 62-63; Albert Shaw lectr diplomatic hist, Johns Hopkins Univ, 68; Rockefeller Found humanities fel, 76-77; prof emer,96-. **HONORS AND AWARDS** Eugene Emme Astronautical Literature Awd, 93; Norman and Laura Graebner Awd, Soc Hist Am Foreign Rels, 00. **MEMBERSHIPS** AHA; Orgn Am Historians; Soc Hist Am Foreign Rels (pres, 76); Am Comt Hist 2nd World War. **RESEARCH** American diplomatic history; United States since 1945; 20th century American history. **SELECTED PUBLICATIONS** Auth, Illusion of Neutrality, 62; auth, Second Chance, 67; auth, Roosevelt and World War Ii, 69; auth, Blowing on the Wind , 78; auth, The Reluctant Belligerent, 2nd ed, 79; auth, Eisenhower and the Cold War, 81; auth, The Sputnik Challenge, 93; auth " Historians and the Gulf War," Dipl Hist, Vol 19, 95; auth, ' The Persian Gulf War Revisited , " Dipl Hist, vol 24, 00; auth, Perpetual War for Perepetual Peace, 00; coauth, America Past and Present, 5th ed, 99. **CONTACT ADDRESS** Dept of Hist, Univ of Texas, Austin, 0 Univ of Texas, Austin, TX 78712-1026.

DIVITA, JAMES JOHN
PERSONAL Born 01/20/1938, Chicago, IL, m, 1964, 4 children **DISCIPLINE** MODERN EUROPEAN HISTORY **EDUCATION** DePaul Univ, BA, 59; Univ Chicago, AM, 60; Univ Chicago, PhD(hist), 72. **CAREER** From instr to assoc prof, 61-76, prof, 76- Marian Col, Ind, dept ch, 83-. **HONORS AND AWARDS** Pi Gamma Mu, 59; Teaching Excellence and Campus Leadership Awd, Marian Col, 98; **MEMBERSHIPS** AHA; Am Cath Hist Asn; Soc Ital Hist Studies; IN Relig Hist Assn; Ital Heritage Soc of Ind; Indiana Historical Soc. **RESEARCH** Western European integration; contemporary Italy; Italian-American history; Indiana ethnic and religios hist **SELECTED PUBLICATIONS** Auth, Ethnic Settlement Patterns in Indianapolis, 88; Contr Auth, Indiana Churches and the Italian Immigrant 1890-1935, Liptak, ed, A Church of Many Cultures, 88; Auth, Rejoice and Remember: A Centennial History of the Catholic Community of St. Anthony of Padua Indianapolis, 92; Auth, Workers Church, Centennial History of the Catholic Parish of the Assumption of the Blessed Virgin Mary in West Indianapolis, 94; Contr Auth, Italians and Slovenes, Mcbirney, ed, Peopling Indiana: the Ethnic Experience, 96; auth, Splendor of the South Side: a History of Sacred Heart of Jesus Catholic Parish in Indpls, 00. **CONTACT ADDRESS** Dept of Hist, Marian Col, 3200 Cold Springs Rd, Indianapolis, IN 46222-1997. **EMAIL** jdivita@marian.edu

DIXON, LAURINDA S.
PERSONAL Born 09/04/1948, Toledo, OH, m, 1986 **DISCIPLINE** ART HISTORY **EDUCATION** Univ Cincinnati, Coll Conserv Music, BA, 70, MA, 72; Boston Univ,PhD, 80. **CAREER** Dir, Adult Educ, Ind Museum Art, 79; asst prof, John Carroll Univ, 80-81; PROF, SYRACUSE UNIV, 82-. **MEM-**

BERSHIPS Coll Art Asn; Am Asn Netherlandish Stud; Hist Netherlandish Art; Hermetic Text Soc; Womens Caucus for Art **RESEARCH** Northern European painting; Pre-Enlighten Medicine; Art; Music. **SELECTED PUBLICATIONS** Perilous Chastity: Women and Illness in Pre-Enlightenmnet Art and Medicine, Cornell Univ Press, 95; Nicolas Flamel, His Exposition of the Hieroglyphicall Figures 1624, English Renaissance Hermeticism Vol 2, Garland Press, 94; co-edr, The Documented Image: Visions in Art History, Syracuse Univ Press, 87; "Beware the Wandering Womb: Painterly Reflections of Early Gynecological Theory," Cancer Investigation, 94; "Some Penetrating Insights: The Imagery of Enemas in Art," Art Journal, 93; auth, In Detail: New Studies of Northern Renaissance Art, Brepols, 98. **CONTACT ADDRESS** Dept Fine Arts, Syracuse Univ, 308 Bowne Hall, Syracuse, NY 13244-1200. **EMAIL** ldixon@mailbox.syr.edu

DJEBAR, ASSIA
DISCIPLINE FRENCH STUDIES **EDUCATION** Univ Paris-Sorbonne, DES, 59. **CAREER** LSU Found Distinguished Prof, La State Univ, Dir, Ctr for Fr and Francophone Stud. **HONORS AND AWARDS** Doctor Honoris Causa, Univ of Vienna, 95; elected mem of the Belgian Royal Acad of French Lang and Lit, 99; Medal of Francophony, Academie Francaise de Paris, 99; Prize from the Review: Etudes Francaises, Montreal for Ces voix qui m'assiegent, 99; Int Prize of Palmi (Italy) for all creative work, 98; Marguerite Yourcenar Prize for Literature, Boston, for Oran Langue Morte, 97; Fonlon-Nichols Prize, African Lit Asn, USA, for all creative work, 97; Int Literary Neustadt Prize, World Lit Today, Oklahoma, for all creative work, 96; Maurice Maeterlinck Int Prize, Societe des gens de Lettres, Brussels, for all creative work, 95. **SELECTED PUBLICATIONS** Auth, Chronique d'un ete Algerien Paris: Plume, 93; auth, Vaste est la prison Paris, Albin Michel, 94; auth, Le blanc de l'Algerie Paris: Albin Michel, 96; auth, Oran, langue morte Paris: Actes Sud, 97; auth, Les nuits de Strasbourg Paris: Actes Sud, 97; auth, Ces voix qui m'assiegent: En marge de ma francophonie Paris: Albin Michel and Montreal: Les presses de l'universite de Montreal, 99. **CONTACT ADDRESS** Dept of Fr Grad Stud, Louisiana State Univ and A&M Col, Baton Rouge, LA 70803.

DJORDJEVIC, DIMITRIJE
PERSONAL Born 02/27/1922, Belgrade, Yugoslavia, m, 1944, 1 child **DISCIPLINE** MODERN EUROPEAN HISTORY **EDUCATION** Univ Belgrade, BA, 54, PhD (hist), 62. **CAREER** Asst hist, Hist Inst, Serbian Acad Sci, Yugoslavia, 58-63, sr staff mem, 63-69, Inst Balkan Studies, 69-70; chmn Russian area studies, 76-82, Prof Hist, Univ Calif, Santa Barbara, 70-, Mem, Yugoslav Nat Comt Hist Sci, 64-70; mem, Yugoslav Nat Comt Balkan Studies, 65-70. **MEMBERSHIPS** AHA; Am Asn Advan Slavic Studies. **RESEARCH** History of Southeast Europe in the 19th and 20th century. **SELECTED PUBLICATIONS** Auth, Yugoslavia --The Process of Disintegration, Slavic Rev, Vol 53, 94; The Development of Education in Serbia and Emergence of Its Intelligentsia 1838-1858, Slavic Rev, Vol 56, 97. **CONTACT ADDRESS** Dept of Hist, Univ of California, Santa Barbara, Santa Barbara, CA 93106.

DMYTRYSHYN, BASIL
PERSONAL Born 01/14/1925, Poland, m, 1949, 2 children **DISCIPLINE** RUSSIAN HISTORY **EDUCATION** Univ Ark, BA, 50, MA, 51; Univ Calif, Berkeley, PhD, 55. **CAREER** Asst res historian, Univ Calif, Berkeley, 55-56; from asst prof to assoc prof, 56-64, Prof Hist, Portland State Univ, 64-, Res assoc, Columbia Univ, 56; curric consult, pub high sch, Portland, Ore, 60-62; vis prof, Univ Ill, Champaign, 64-65; Fulbright-Hays res fel, WGer, 67-68; vis prof, Harvard Univ, 71, Univ Hawaii, 76 and Hokkaido Univ, Japan, 78-79; fel, Kennan Inst, 78. **HONORS AND AWARDS** John Mosser Awd, 66 and 67. **MEMBERSHIPS** AHA; Am Asn Advan Slavic Studies; Western Slavic Asn; Conf Slavic and E Europ Hist (secy, 72-75); Can Asn Slavists. **RESEARCH** Russian and modern European history; history of Eastern Europe; Russian expansion to the Pacific and America. **SELECTED PUBLICATIONS** Coauth, USSR: A Concise History, Scribner's, 65, 71 & 78; German occupation policy in the Ukraine, 1918: Some new evidence, Can Slavic & East Europ Studies, fall-winter 66; Medieval Russia: A Source Book, 900-1700, 67 & 73 & Imperial Russia: A Source Book, 1700-1917, 67 & 74, Holt; Modernization of Russia Under Peter I and Catherine II, Wiley, 74; co-ed, Colonial Russian America, Ore Hist Soc, 76; auth, A History of Russia, Prentice-Hall, 77; co-ed, The end of Russian America, Ore Hist Soc, 79. **CONTACT ADDRESS** Dept of Hist, Portland State Univ, Portland, OR 97207.

DOAK, KEVIN M.
DISCIPLINE EAST ASIAN STUDIES **EDUCATION** Quincy Col, BA, 82; The Univ of Chicago, MA, 83; St. Paul's Univ, 85-87; Univ of Tokyo, 85-87; Univ of Chicago, PhD, 89. **CAREER** Dana fac fel and asst prof, Wake Forest Univ, 89-94; dir, Tokai Univ, 92-93; asst prof, Univ of Illinois, 94-97; assoc prof, Univ Ill Urbana Champaign, 97-. **HONORS AND AWARDS** Nat Resource Fel, 84-85; Fulbright, 85-87; Social Science Res Council/Am Council of Learned Societies, 87-88; Mrs. Giles Whiting Fel, 88-89; Pew Memorial Trust, 90; Z. Smith Reynolds Junior Fac Semester Leave, Wake Forest, 93; William and Flora Hewitt Summer International Res Grant, 95; Incomplete List of Teachers Rated as Excellent by Their Students, 96; Conference Grant, (w/Kai Wing Chow and Poshek Fu) "Narratives, Arts, and Ritual: Imaging and Constructing Nationalhood in Modern East Asia," 96; Cneter for Avdanced Studies Fel, 97; Advanced Res Grant, 98. **MEMBERSHIPS** Am Hist Asn, Asn for Asian Studies, Midwest Regional Conference, Conference on Asian Hist, The Asn for the Study of Ethnicity and Nationalism, Japanese Anthropology Workshop, Modern Japan Res Asn. **RESEARCH** Modern Japanese cultural and intellectual hist, nationalism, and romanticism as social ideology, the idiom of race and ethnic-nationalsim in prewar Japan, prewar Japanese political culture, and romanticism and modernism in twentieth-century Japan. **SELECTED PUBLICATIONS** Auth, Dreams of Difference: The Japan Romantic School and the Crisis of Modernity, Univ of California Press, 94; auth, "Ethnic Nationalism, Romanticism and the Problem of Japan: Some Dilemmas in the Construction of Asian Unity," Center for International Studies Occasional Papers, No 94-03, Univ of Wisconsin--Milwaukee, (94); auth, "Nationalism as Dialectics: Ethnicity; Ethnicity, Moralism, and the State in Early Twentieth Century Japan," in James Heisig and John Maraldo, eds, Rude Awakenings: Zen, the Kyoto School & the Question of Nationalism, Univ of Hawaii Press, (94); auth, "Hiroshima as History: Some Preliminary Thoughts," Swards and Ploughshares Vol, IX nos. 3 & 4, (95); auth, "Bungei no basho: Nihon romanha ni tsuite" The Place of Culture: An Essay on the Japan Romantic School, Shincho, in Japanese, (95); auth, "What is a Nation and Who Belongs? National Narratives and the Ethnic Imagination in Twentieth-Century Japan," The American Historical Rev, Vol, 20, (97): 283-309; auth, "Colonialism and Ethnic Nationalism in the Political Thought of Yanaihara Tadao (1893-1961)," East Asian History, No 10, (97): 283-309; auth, "Ethnicity," "Anachronism," "Olympics," "Tokyo," in Charles C. Stewart and Peter Fritzsche, eds, Imagining the Twentieth Century, Urbana: Univ of Illinois Press, (97); auth, "Culture, Ethnicity and the State in Twentieth-Century Japan," In Germaine Hoston and Sharon Minichiello, eds, Competing Modernities in Twentieth Century Japan: Taisho Democracy, Honolulu: Univ of Hawaii Press, 98; auth, "Under the Banner of the New Science: History, Science and the Problem of Particluarity in Early 20th Century Japan," Philosophy East and West, Vol 48, No 2, (98); **CONTACT ADDRESS** Dept East Asian Languages and Cultures, Univ of Illinois, Urbana-Champaign, 309 Gregory Hall, mc 466, 810 S Wright, Champaign, IL 61801. **EMAIL** k-doak@uiuc.edu

DOAN, JAMES E.
PERSONAL Born 04/11/1953, Palo Alto, CA **DISCIPLINE** FOLKLORE, CELTIC STUDIES, MEDIEVAL LITERATURE **EDUCATION** Univ Calif, BA, 75; MA, 77; Harvard Univ, MA, 78; PhD, 81. **CAREER** Assoc prof, dean, Chamberlayne Jr. Col, 81-88; prof, Nova Southeastern Univ, 88-. **HONORS AND AWARDS** NEH, 84; British Coun, 93, 96; Nova Southeastern Univ Fac Awd, 01. **MEMBERSHIPS** MLA, Am Conf for Irish Studies, Int Assoc for the Study of Irish Lit. **RESEARCH** Folklore, Celtic Studies, Medieval Literature, Irish-American Studies. **SELECTED PUBLICATIONS** Auth, The Romance of Cearbhall and Fearbhlaidh, Dolmen Pr, 85; auth, Women and Goddesses in Early Celtic History, Myth and Legend, Northeastern Univ, 87; auth, Cearbhall O Dalaigh: An Irish Poet in Romance and Oral Tradition, Garland Pr, 90; auth, Early Celtic, Irish and Mediterranean Connections, Tema, Cagliari, Italy, 96; auth, The Otherworld Journey: A Celtic and Universal Theme, Princess Grace Libr, Monaco, 98; auth, "How the Irish and Scots Became Indians: Colonial Traders and Agents and the Southeastern Tribes," New Hibernia Rev, (99); auth, "The Voyage of St Brendan: Otherworld Tale, Christian Apologia or Medieval Travelog?" ABEI Jour, (00); auth, "Revisiting the Blasket Island Memoirs," Irish Studies Rev, (00); coauth, "Reverine Crossings: Gender, Identity and the Reconstruction of National Mythic Narrative in the Crying Game," Cult Studies, (01). **CONTACT ADDRESS** Dept Lib Arts, Nova Southeastern Univ, Fort Lauderdale, 3301 College Ave, Ft Lauderdale, FL 33314. **EMAIL** doan@nova.edu

DOBSON, JOHN MCCULLOUGH
PERSONAL Born 07/20/1940, Las Cruces, NM, m, 1963 **DISCIPLINE** AMERICAN HISTORY **EDUCATION** Mass Inst Technol, BS, 62; Univ Wis, MS, 64, PhD, 66. **CAREER** Asst prof hist, Chico State Col, 66-67; foreign serv off, Dept State, Washington, DC, 67-68; from asst prof to assoc prof, 68-78, Prof to prof emer Hist, Iowa State Univ, 78-, Historian, US Int Trade Comn, 76. **HONORS AND AWARDS** Fulbright lectr, Univ Col, Dublin, 79-80. **MEMBERSHIPS** AHA; Orgn Am Historians. **RESEARCH** Nineteenth century United States history; political and diplomatic history. **SELECTED PUBLICATIONS** Auth, The Tariff Question in The Gilded Age--The Great Debate of 1888, Am Hist Rev, Vol 101, 96. **CONTACT ADDRESS** Dept of Hist, Iowa State Univ of Science and Tech, Ames, IA 50011-0002.

DOCKERY, DAVID S.
PERSONAL Born 10/28/1952, Tuscaloosa, AL, m, 1975, 3 children **DISCIPLINE** HISTORY; RELIGION **EDUCATION** Texas Christian Univ, MA, 86; Univ TX, PhD, 88. **CAREER** Dean & Acad VP, S Baptist Theol Sem, 88-96; pres, Union Univ, 96-. **HONORS AND AWARDS** Who's Who Relig; Who's Who Bibl Studies **MEMBERSHIPS** Soc Bibl Lit; Inst Bibl Res; Amer Acad Relig; Evangelical Theol Soc **RESEARCH** New Testament Studies; Hermeneutics; Baptist Theology. **SELECTED PUBLICATIONS** Auth, New Dimensions in Evangelical Thought, Intervarsity; Our Blessed Hope, LifeWay; Christian Scripture, Broadman & Holman; Biblical Interpretation Then and Now, Baker; auth, Ephesians, Convention; Holman Bible Handbook, Holman. **CONTACT ADDRESS** 1050 Union Univ Dr., Jackson, TN 38305. **EMAIL** ddockery@uu.edu

DODDS, DENNIS R.
PERSONAL Born 03/04/1940, OK, m, 1991, 1 child **DISCIPLINE** ARCHITECTURE; CITY PLANNING; URBAN DESIGN; ARCH. HISTORY (ISLAMIC) **EDUCATION** Ariz State Univ, B Arch, 69; Univ Pa, M Arch, 72.; MCP, 73; **CAREER** Pres, Dennis R. Dodds & Assoc; Secretary-General. **HONORS AND AWARDS** Medal, Azerbaijan Acad of Sci and Archit; Medal, Alpha Rho Chi; AIA fel; McMullen Awd for Scholar in Islamic Textiles. **MEMBERSHIPS** Soc of Archit Historians **RESEARCH** Islamic art & architecture; Early Turkish carpet weaving. **SELECTED PUBLICATIONS** auth, Oriental Rugs in the Virginia Museum of Fine Art; auth with Murray Eiland, Jr., Oriental Rugs in Atlantic Collections. **CONTACT ADDRESS** PO Box 4312, Philadelphia, PA 19118. **EMAIL** dennisdobbs@juno.com

DODDS, GORDON B.
PERSONAL Born 03/12/1932, Milwaukee, WI, m, 5 children **DISCIPLINE** HISTORY **EDUCATION** Harvard, AB, 54; Univ of IL, AM, 55; Univ of Wis, PhD, 58 **CAREER** Inst, Asst Prof, 58-66, Knox Col; Assoc Prof, Prof, 66-, Portland St Univ **MEMBERSHIPS** West Hist Asn **RESEARCH** Pacific NW Hist **SELECTED PUBLICATIONS** Auth, Varieties of Hope: An Anthology of Oregon Prose, OR St Univ Press, 93 **CONTACT ADDRESS** Dept of History, Portland State Univ, PO Box 751, Portland, OR 97207-0751. **EMAIL** doddsg@px.edu

DODGE, TIMOTHY
PERSONAL Born 04/15/1957, Boston, MA **DISCIPLINE** LIBRARY SCIENCE & HISTORY **EDUCATION** Swarthmore Col, BA, 79; Columbia Univ, MLS, 80; Univ NH, MA, 82 PhD, 92. **CAREER** Librn, Univ NH, 82-84, 87-92; librn, Barry Univ, 84-87; librn, Auburn Univ, 92-. **HONORS AND AWARDS** Prof Achievement Awd, 86-87, Barry Univ. **MEMBERSHIPS** Am Libr Asn; Ala Libr Asn; Asn Col & Res Librs; Ala Asn Col & Res Librs; Psi Gamma Mu; Phi Alpha Theta; Org Am Hist; NH Hist Society. **RESEARCH** Modern American history; library science. **SELECTED PUBLICATIONS** Auth, art, From Spirituals to Gospel Rap: Gospel Music Periodicals, 94; auth, art, Crime and Punishment in New Hampshire, 1812-1914, 95; auth, Poor Relief in Durham, Lee, and Madbury, New Hampshire, 1732-1891, 95; auth, art, US Department of Commerce CD-ROM Serial Databases, 96; auth art, Criminal Justice Web Sites, 98. **CONTACT ADDRESS** 1772 Lee Rd 88, Waverly, AL 36879. **EMAIL** dodgeti@auburn.edu

DOENECKE, JUSTUS D.
PERSONAL Born 03/05/1938, Brooklyn, NY, m, 1970 **DISCIPLINE** HISTORY **EDUCATION** Colgate Univ, BA, 60; Princeton Univ, MA, 62, PhD, 66. **CAREER** Instr, Colgate Univ, 63-64; Instr to Asst Prof, Ohio Wesleyan Univ, 65-69; Asst Prof to Assoc Prof, New Col, 69-75; Assoc Prof, 75-77, Prof Hist, New Col, Univ S Fla, 77-. **HONORS AND AWARDS** Phi Beta Kappa; Woodrow Wilson Nat Fel, 60; Danforth Fel, 60; Arthur S. Link Prize for Documentary Editing, Soc Hist Am For Relations, 91. **MEMBERSHIPS** Am Hist Asn; Peace Hist Soc (coun 75-79, 98-); Soc Hist Am For Relations (program co-chair 86, Link Award Comt, 92-); Am Soc Church Hist; Hist Soc Episcopal Church. **RESEARCH** American isolationism and pacifism; the gilded age. **SELECTED PUBLICATIONS** Auth, When the Wicked Rise: American Opinion-makers and the Manchurian Crisis, 1931-1933, Bucknell Univ Press, 84; Anti-Intervention: A Bibliographical Introduction to Isolationism and Pacifism from World War I to the Early Cold War, Garland, 87; In Danger Undaunted: The Anti-Interventionist Movement of 1940-1941 as Revealed in the Papers of the America First Committee, Hoover Inst Press, 90; coauth, From Isolation to War, 1931-1941, Harlan Davidson, 2nd ed, 91; auth, The Battle Against Intervention, 1939-1941, Krieger, 97; Storm on the Horizon: The Challenge to American Intervention, 1939-1941, Rowmond, Littlefield, 00. **CONTACT ADDRESS** Social Science Division, New Col of the Univ of So Florida, Sarasota, FL 34243-2197. **EMAIL** doenecke@virtu.sar.usf.edu

DOENGES, NORMAN ARTHUR
PERSONAL Born 08/23/1926, Ft Wayne, IN, m, 1952, 3 children **DISCIPLINE** ANCIENT HISTORY, CLASSICS **EDUCATION** Yale Univ, BA, 47; Oxford Univ, BA, 49; Princeton Univ, MA, 51, PhD (classics), 54; American School Classical Studies, 51-52. **CAREER** Instr classics, Princeton Univ, 49-50 and 52-53; from instr to assoc prof, 55-65, chmn dept classics, 59-63, 67-71 and 78-79, chmn div humanities, 63-67, assoc dean fac, 64-66, prof-in-chg, Intercol Ctr Class Studies, Rome, Italy, 66-67, Prof Classics, Dartmouth Col, 65-, Mem managing comt, Am Sch Class Studies; mem adv coun, Am Acad in

Rome; Field Dir Excavation of the Roman colony of Pollentia, Mallorca, Spain, 84-97. **HONORS AND AWARDS** Woodrow Wilson Fellow, 50-51; Fulbright Fellow, 51-52. **MEMBERSHIPS** Soc Prom Hellenic Studies; Am Philol Asn; Class Asn Can; Class Asn New Eng(secy-treas, 63-68); Asn of Ancient Historians. **RESEARCH** Greek and Roman history; Greek pseudonymic letters. **SELECTED PUBLICATIONS** Auth, The Letters of Themistokles, New York: Arno Press, 81; auth, A. Arribas y N. Doenges, Piezas Singulares de una Estancia del Area Commercial del Foro de Pollentia, Travalhos de Antropologia e Etnologia 35, 95, 397-412; auth, Ostracism and the Boulai of Kleisthenes, Hist Zeitschrift Alte Geschichte, Vol 45, 96; The Campaign and Battle of Marathon, Historia 47 (1998)1-17. **CONTACT ADDRESS** Dept of Classics, Dartmouth Col, Hanover, NH 03755. **EMAIL** doenges@dartmouth.edu

DOHANIAN, DIRAN KAVORK
DISCIPLINE ART HISTORY **EDUCATION** Harvard Univ, PhD. **CAREER** Prof, Univ of Rochester. **RESEARCH** Hist of the art and cult of ancient Lanka; Buddhism: art and cult; comp studies of the art of east and west; art as relig expression; elite cult: arts of China, arts of Japan; popular art: east/west; connoisseurship and collecting. **SELECTED PUBLICATIONS** Auth, Sinhalese Sculptures in the Pallava Style, Archives of Asian Art, XXXVI, 83; The Mahayana Buddhist Sculpture of Ceylon, NY and London: Garland Pub, 77; The Wata-Da-Ge in Ceylon: the Circular Relic House of Polonnaruva and its Antecedents, Arch Asian Art, XXIII & The Colossal Buddha at Aukana, Arch of the Chinese Art Soc in Am, XIX. **CONTACT ADDRESS** Dept of Art and Art Hist, Univ of Rochester, 601 Elmwood Ave, Ste. 656, 424 Morey , Rochester, NY 14642. **EMAIL** urhomepage@cc.rochester.edu

DOHERTY, BARBARA
PERSONAL Born 12/02/1931, Chicago, IL **DISCIPLINE** THEOLOGY, HISTORY OF RELIGIONS **EDUCATION** St Mary-of-the-Woods Col, BA, 53; St Mary's Col, MA, 63; Fordham Univ, PhD (theol), 79. **CAREER** Assoc prof theol, St Mary-of-the-Woods Col, 63-75; Prov Super, Sisters of Providence, 75-, Chairperson, Leadership Conf Women Relig, Region 8, 79-82. **RESEARCH** Eastern and western spirituality. **SELECTED PUBLICATIONS** Auth, Contemplation, New Cath Encycl, Vol 17, 78; I Am What I Do, Thomas More Asn, 81. **CONTACT ADDRESS** 215 Ridge Terrace Park, Ridge, IL 60068.

DOLAN, JAY P.
DISCIPLINE AMERICAN RELIGIOUS HISTORY **EDUCATION** Gregorian Univ, Italy, STL, 62; Univ Chicago, PhD, 70. **CAREER** Asst prof, Univ San Francisco, 70-71; asst prof, 71-77, dir, Ctr for Stud of Am Cath, 77-93, assoc prof, 77-86, prof, Univ Notre Dame, 86-; Fulbright prof, Univ Col, Ireland, 86; vis instr, Boston Col, 91; chemn, publ ser, Notre Dame Stud in Am Cath, Univ Notre Dame Press, 77-93; publ comt, Immigration Hist Soc, 77-80; ed bd, J of Am Ethnic Hist, 80-; ed bd, Church Hist, 82-86; ed bd, Hebrew Un Co-Jewish Inst of Relig, 84-89; ed bd, Sources of Am Spirituality, publ ser, Paulist Press, 86-90; ed bd, Statue of Liberty-Ellis Island Centennial publ ser, Univ Ill Press, 86-; assoc ed, Am Nat Biogr Mid-America, 88-; assoc ed, Am Nat Biogr, 89-; ed bd, Rel and Am Cult: J of Interp, 89-; ed bd, Church Hist, 94-. **HONORS AND AWARDS** Rockefeller fel, Univ Chicago, 69-70; O'Brien Fund grant, Univ Notre Dame, 72; fac res grant, Univ Notre Dame, 73; fel, Princeton Univ, 73-74; John Gilmary Shea Awd, Am Cath Hist Asn, 75; res grant, Word of God Inst, 76; Frank O'Malley Awd, Univ Notre Dame, 77; fel, Am Coun of Learned Soc, 78-79; fac develop grant, Univ Notre Dame, 80; Alumnus of the Yr, Univ Chicago, 87; Emily Schossberger Awd, Univ Notre Dame Press, 88; res grant Lilly Endowment, 81, 81-87, 83-84, 86-88, 90-93, 91-92. **MEMBERSHIPS** Pres, Am Soc of Church Hist, 87; pres, Am Cath Hist Asn, 95; Immigration Hist Soc; Am Acad of Relig. **RESEARCH** Am Religious History, Immigratin History. **SELECTED PUBLICATIONS** Auth, Patterns of Leadership in the Congregation, in James P Wind and James W Lewis, eds, American Congregations, vol 2: New Perspectives in the Study of Congregations, Univ Chicago Press, 94; Conclusion, in Jay P Dolan and Allan Figueroa Deck, SJ, eds, Hispanic Catholic Culture in the U.S., Univ Notre Dame Press, 94; The People As Well As The Prelates: A Social History of a Denomination, in R Mullin and R Richey, eds, Reimagining Denominationalism: Interpretive Essays, Oxford UP, 94; coed, Mexican Americans and the Catholic Church. 1900-1965, Univ Notre Dame Press, 94; Puerto Rican and Cuban Catholics in the U.S. 1900-1965, Univ Notre Dame Press, 94; Hispanic Catholic Culture in the U.S.: Issues and Concerns, Univ Notre Dame Press, 94. **CONTACT ADDRESS** Dept of Hist, Univ of Notre Dame, Notre Dame, IN 46556.

DOLCE, PHILIP CHARLES
PERSONAL Born 11/23/1941, New York, NY, m, 1966, 2 children **DISCIPLINE** AMERICAN HISTORY **EDUCATION** St John's Univ, NYork, BA, 63; Fordham Univ, MA, 66, PhD(Am Hist), 71; Management Development Program Certificate, Harvard Univ, 91. **CAREER** Teacher hist, St Helena's High Sch, 63-66; lectr Am hist, St John's Univ, 66-68, instr, 68-71; asst prof, 71-75, assoc prof Am hist, Bergen Commun Col, 75-79, prof, 79-; coordr Pub Media progr, 73-80, Bus mgr, J Social Hist, 70-72; Harry S Truman Libr Inst grant, 72; creator, producer & moderator of many TV & radio progs; vchairperson, Am Asn Commun Jr Cols; instr, Telecommun Consortium; exec dir, Eastern Educ Consortium; assoc, Columbia Univ Seminar on the City. **HONORS AND AWARDS** Finalist Awd, Int Film and Television Festival, 87; ACE nomination, Distinguished Programming Achievement, 87; Admin Innovation and Team Leadership Awd, AAU Admin, 90; First Place Awd Personality Profile and Public Service Radio Reporting, N Jersey Press Club, 93; First Place Awds for Radio Feature Reporting and Sports Feature Reporting, 94; Finalist Awd for Social commitment, Global Int Healthcare Commun Competition, 95; First Place Awd for Sports Reporting, 96 and First Place Awd Public Service Awd, 97, North Jersey Press Club; Four TV Series created and produced now part of the permanent collection of Museum of Radio and Television, 97, one part of permanent collection of National Archives, 99. **RESEARCH** American urban and suburban history; American presidential history. **SELECTED PUBLICATIONS** Co-ed, Cities in transition: From the Ancient World to Urban America, Nelson-Hall, 73; ed, Surburbia: The American Dream and Dilemma, Doubleday, 11/76; co-ed, Power and the Presidency, Scribner, 76; creator & producer of CBS TV ser, Paradox of power: US foreign policy, 78; Suburbia: The promised land, 79; Asia: Half the human race, 79; Metropolitan America, 80; Post industrial America: Economic strategies for the 1980's, 81; produce TV documentary The Cubans of New Jersey, 87; producer and host of Weekly WPAT radio program Suburbia: The American Dream and Dilemma, 89-96. **CONTACT ADDRESS** Dept of Soc Sci, Bergen Comm Col, 400 Paramus Rd, Paramus, NJ 07652-1595.

DOLNIKOWSKI, EDITH W.
PERSONAL Born 07/21/1959, Pittsburgh, PA, m, 1980 **DISCIPLINE** HISTORY **EDUCATION** Coll of Wooster, BA, 81; Michigan State Univ, PhD, 84, PhD, 89; Episcopal Divinity Sch, M. Div., 94. **CAREER** Graduate Tchg Asst, Dept of Hist, 81-84, Res Asst, Dept of Hist, 84-85, Undergraduate Adviser, Dept of Hist, 85-86, Michigan State Univ; instr, Univ of Warwick, United Kingdom, 88-89; instr, Univ of Nebraska, 89-90; Field Edu Minister, The Harvard-Radcliffe Episcopal Chaplaincy, 90-92; minisry intern, 94-95, deacon, 95-96, priest-in-charge, 96, asst to the rector, 97, The Church of Our Saviour, Brookline, Massachusetts; parish administrator, St. Andrew's Church, Wellesley, Mass, 98. **HONORS AND AWARDS** Fulbright Res Grant; Michigan State Univ Arts and Letters Graduate Fellowship; Phi Kappa Phi; Phi Beta Kappa; Dept Honors; Kellogg Fellow for Ministry in Higher Edu, 93-94 **MEMBERSHIPS** AMA, ASCH, Medieval Acad of Amer, AAR, Intl Medieval Sermon Studies Soc; Soc for Medieval Feminist Scholarship. **RESEARCH** Late Medieval Theology, English and Latin Sermons. **SELECTED PUBLICATIONS** Auth, Time and Memory in the Thought of Thomas Bradwardine, in: Disputatio, Vol II, Constructions of Time in the Late Middle Ages, eds, C Poster & R Utz, Northwestern Univ Press, 97; Feminine Exemplars of Reform: Women's Voices in John Foxe's Acts and Monuments, Women Preachers and Prophets through Two Millenia fo Christianit, eds, B Mayne & PJ Walker, Univ of California Press, 98; Thomas Bradwardine's Sermo epinicius: Some Reflections on it's Political, Theological and Pastoral Significance, Medieval Sermons and Society, Cloister, City, UnivTextes et etudes du moyen, 9, eds, Federation Internationale des Instituts d'Etudes Medievales, 98. **CONTACT ADDRESS** 59 Lincoln St, Natick, MA 01760. **EMAIL** ewd@standrewswellesley.org

DOMARADZKI, THEODORE F.
PERSONAL Born 10/27/1910, Warsaw, Poland **DISCIPLINE** SLAVIC & EUROPEAN STUDIES **EDUCATION** Acad Polit Sci (Warsaw), Polit Sci Dipl, 36; Univ Warsaw, MA (Hist), 39; Univ Rome, LittD (Slavic Philol), 41. **CAREER** Lectr, Univ Rome, 41-47; dir, prof & founder, dept Slavic stud, Ctr Polish & Slavic Res, Univ Montreal, 48-76; PROF & DIR, INST COMPARATIVE CIVILIZATIONS OF MONTREAL, 76-. **HONORS AND AWARDS** Order Can; Order Polonia Restituta; Papal Order St Gregory Great; Order St Sava; Ordo Constantini Magni; Sovereign Order St John Jerusalem; Polish Golden Cross Merit; Medal Polish Educ Merit. **MEMBERSHIPS** Can Asn Slavists; Can Soc Comp Stud Civilizations; Can Int Acad Hum Soc Sci; Que Ethnic Press Asn; PEN; Soc ecrivains Can; Inst Ital Cultur. **SELECTED PUBLICATIONS** Auth, Norwid poet of Christianity, 84; auth, Entre le romantisme et le symbolisme: C. Baudelaire et C. Norwid, in Les Cahiers de Varsovie, 86; auth, C.K. Norwid in Canada, 89; auth, Personalite ethniques au Quebec, 91; ed, Slavic & East Europ Stud, 56-76; ed, Slavic Publ/Publ Slaves, 73-. **CONTACT ADDRESS** Inst Comp Civilizations of Montreal, PO Box 759, Succ Outremont, Montreal, QC, Canada H2V 4N9.

DOMBROWSKI, NICOLE
PERSONAL Born 12/30/1964, NC, m, 1999 **DISCIPLINE** HISTORY **EDUCATION** Univ Wis Madison, BA, 87; NY Univ, MA, 90, PhD, 95. **CAREER** Lectr, Princeton Univ, 95-98. **HONORS AND AWARDS** Franco-Am Found, Bicentennial Scholarship, 92; Mellon Fel, 94. **MEMBERSHIPS** AHA. **RESEARCH** Modern Europe, France, Women and War. **SELECTED PUBLICATIONS** Auth, Women and War in the 20th Century: Enlisted With or Without Consent, Garland, 99. **CONTACT ADDRESS** Dept Hist, Towson State Univ, 8000 York Rd, Baltimore, MD 21252-0001.

DOMENICO, ROY P.
PERSONAL Born 02/09/1954, New Orleans, LA, m, 1988, 4 children **DISCIPLINE** HISTORY **EDUCATION** Univ Wis, BA, 77; Univ Conn, MA, 79; Rutgers Univ, PhD, 87. **CAREER** Vis Asst Prof, Moore Col, 86-87; Asst Prof, Upsala Col, 87-92; Asst Prof, Truman State Univ, 92-97; Asst Prof, Univ Scranton, 97-99; Assoc Prof, Univ Scranton, 99-. **HONORS AND AWARDS** Howard R and Helen Marar Prize, Soc for Ital Hist Studies, 92. **MEMBERSHIPS** Soc for Ital Hist Studies. **RESEARCH** 20th-Century Ital, political, cultural. **SELECTED PUBLICATIONS** Auth, "Anglo-American Impressions of the Partisans Along the Gothic Line: The Case of the Patriots Branch," in Al di qua e al di la della Linea Gotica, (Bologna-Florence: Regioni Emilia-Romagna e Toscana, 93); auth, "America, The Holy See and the War in Vietnam," in Papal Diplomacy in the Mod Age (Westport: Praeger, 94); auth, "The Many Meanings of Italian Anti-Fascism," J of Mod Ital Studies, vol 4, no 1(99); auth, Italian Fascists on Trial 1943-1948, Univ NC (Chapel Hill, NC), 96. **CONTACT ADDRESS** Dept Hist, Univ of Scranton, 800 Linden St, Scranton, PA 18510-2429. **EMAIL** domenicor2@uofs.edu

DOMINICK, RAYMOND
PERSONAL Born 10/18/1945, Atlanta, GA, m, 1979, 1 child **DISCIPLINE** EUROPEAN HISTORY **EDUCATION** Univ NC, PhD, 73 **CAREER** From instr to assoc prof, Univ NC, 73-92; prof hist, Ohio St Univ-Mansfield, 92-. **HONORS AND AWARDS** Sr Fulbright Fel, Jena, 95; Outstanding Publ Awd, Ohio Hist Acad, 92; Outstanding Tchr, Mansfield, 84. **MEMBERSHIPS** Ger Stud Asn; Am Soc Environ Hist. **RESEARCH** History of the Environmental Movement. **SELECTED PUBLICATIONS** Auth, Wilhelm Liebknecht and the Founding of the German Social Democratic Party, Univ NC,82; Nascent Environmental Protection in the Second German Empire, Ger Studies Rev, 86; The Nazis and the Nature Conservationists, The Hist, 87; The Roots of the Green Movement in West Germany and the USA, Environ Rev, 88); The Environmental Movement in Germany: Prophets and Pioneers, 1871-1971, Ind Univ, 92;. **CONTACT ADDRESS** Ohio State Univ, Mansfield, 1680 University Dr., Mansfield, OH 44906. **EMAIL** dominick.1@osu.edu

DONAGHAY, MARIE
PERSONAL Born 01/10/1943, Wilmington, DE **DISCIPLINE** HISTORY **EDUCATION** Univ DE, BA, 65; Univ VA, MA, 67, PhD, 70. **CAREER** Assoc prof, Hist, Radford Col, 70-74; adjunct prof, 83-89, asst prof, 90-92, Hist, Villanova Univ; assoc prof, Hist, East Stroudsburg Univ, 92-. **MEMBERSHIPS** World Hist Asn, 92-00; Am Hist Asn; Soc for French Hist Studies; Southern Hist Asn. **RESEARCH** France on the eve of the French Revolution, French foreign policy; Anglo-French relations (commercial and diplomatic). **SELECTED PUBLICATIONS** Auth, Comment on a Bit of Total History: the Transfer of Technology between France and Britain during the Eighteenth Century, The Consortium on Revolutionary Europe Proceedings, 1984, Athens, GA, 86; A propos du traite commercial franco-anglais de 1786, Revue d'Histoire Diplomatique, 87; The Vicious Circle: The Anglo-French Commercial Treaty of 1786 and the Dutch Crisis of 1787, Consortium on Revolutionary Europe 1750-1850, Proceedings 1989, Tallahasse, FL, 90; The Exchange of Products of the Soil and Industrial Goods in the Anglo-French Commercial Treaty of 1786, J of European Economic Hist, 90; The French Debate on the Free Trade Treaty of 1786, in Ilaria Zilli, ed, Fra Spazio E Tempo Studi in Onori di Luigi de Rosa, Settecento E Ottocento, Naples, Italy, 95; Britain and France at the Close of the Old Regime, A Commentary, The Consortium on Revolutionary Europe, 1750-1850, selected papers, 1995, Tallahassee, FL, 95; several other publications. **CONTACT ADDRESS** History Dept, East Stroudsburg Univ of Pennsylvania, 200 Prospect St, East Stroudsburg, PA 18301-2999.

DONAGHY, THOMAS J.
PERSONAL Born 10/20/1928, Sharon Hill, PA **DISCIPLINE** AMERICAN HISTORY **EDUCATION** Cath Univ Am, AB, 51; Univ Pittsburgh, MA, 54, PhD (hist), 60; St Charles Sem, MA, 78. **CAREER** Teacher, Cent Cath High Sch, Pa, 51-55, La Salle High Sch, 55-56 and Cent Cath High Sch, 56-61, assoc prof, 61-72, prof hist, La Salle Col, 72-79, dir summer sessions, 62-72; Acad Dean, St Mary's Sem and Univ, 79-. **HONORS AND AWARDS** MA, St Charles Sem, Philadelphia, 78. **MEMBERSHIPS** AHA; Am Cath Hist Asn; Lexington Group. **RESEARCH** Railway transportation, Great Britain; Colonial Philadelphia; history of educational institutions. **SELECTED PUBLICATIONS** Auth, Villanova University, 1842-1992-American Catholic Augustinian, Cath Histl Rev, Vol 83, 97. **CONTACT ADDRESS** 5450 Roland Ave, Baltimore, MD 21210.

DONAHOE, BERNARD FRANCIS
PERSONAL Born 03/16/1932, Madison, WI **DISCIPLINE** AMERICAN POLITICAL & INTELLECTUAL HISTORY **EDUCATION** Univ Notre Dame, BA, 55, MA, 59, PhD, 65. **CAREER** Tchr hist, parochial high sch, OH, 56-57 & Ind, 57-61; master novices, St Joseph Novitiate, 64-68; asst prof, Holy Cross Jr Col, 67-74; asst prof, 68-74, assoc prof hist, St Mary's Col, IN, 74; assoc prof hist Holy Cross Jr Col, 74. **MEMBER-**

SHIPS AHA; Orgn Am Historians. **RESEARCH** Polit of the New Deal; Am intellectual hist. **SELECTED PUBLICATIONS** Auth, Private Plans and Public Dangers: The Story of FDR's Third Nomination, Univ Notre Dame, 66; coauth, The congressional power to raise armies: The constitutional ratifying conventions, 1787-1788, Rev Polit, 4/71; Politics and Federal-State Programs for the Unemployed: The Case of the Indiana WPA, Humboldt J Social Relations, Vol 6, No 2; The Dictator and the Priest, Prologue, Vol 22, No 6. **CONTACT ADDRESS** Holy Cross Col, Notre Dame, IN 46556. **EMAIL** bdonahoe@saintmarys.edu

DONAKOWSKI, CONRAD L.
PERSONAL Born 03/13/1936, Detroit, MI, m, 1961, 2 children **DISCIPLINE** RELIGION, HISTORY, MUSIC **EDUCATION** Xavier Univ, BA, 58, MA, 59; Columbia Univ, PhD, 69. **CAREER** Instr humanities, Mich State Univ, 66-69; coordr, James Madison Col, Mich State Univ, 67-72; from asst to assoc prof humanities, 69-78, prof, 78-81, prof music hist, Mich State Univ, 81-, asst dean arts & lett, 79-, Am Coun Learned Soc grant, 73. **HONORS AND AWARDS** American Revolutionary Bicentennial Article Prize, Ohio Hist Comt, 76; Rockefeller Found grants, 76 & 77; DAAD, 88, 95. **MEMBERSHIPS** AHA; Am Soc Eighteenth Century Studies; Am Soc Church Hist; Soc Fr Hist Studies. **RESEARCH** Romanticism; enlightenment; popular culture; ritual and liturgy; music. **SELECTED PUBLICATIONS** Auth, A Muse for the Masses: Ritual and Music in an Age of Democratic Revolution, Univ Chicago, 77. **CONTACT ADDRESS** School of Music, Michigan State Univ, East Lansing, MI 48824-1043. **EMAIL** donakows@msu.edu

DONALD, DAVID HERBERT
PERSONAL Born 10/01/1920, Goodman, MS, m, 1955, 1 child **DISCIPLINE** AMERICAN HISTORY **EDUCATION** Millsaps Col, AB, 41; Univ Ill, AM, 42, PhD, 46. **CAREER** Res assoc hist, Univ Ill, 46-47; instr, Columbia Univ, 47-49; assoc prof, Smith Col, 49-51; from asst prof to prof, Columbia Univ, 51-59; prof, Princeton Univ, 59-62; prof, Johns Hopkins Univ, 62-63, Harry C Black Prof Am hist, 63-73; Charles Warren prof Am Hist, Prof Emer, 91- , Harvard Univ, 73-91, Prof Am Civilization, 74-91, Chr Grad Prog Am Civilization, 79-85, Vis assoc prof, Amherst Col, 50; Fulbright prof, Univ Col, NWales, Bangor, 54-55; mem, Inst Advan Studies, 57-58; George A & Eliza Gardner Howard fel, 57-58; Harmsworth prof, Oxford Univ, 59-60; Guggenheim fel, 64-65; Am Coun Learned Soc fel, 69-70; fel, Ctr Advan Studies Behav Sci, 69-70; Nat Endowment for Humanities sr fel, 71-72; gen ed, Making of Am Series & Doc Hist Am Life Series; commonwealth lectr, Univ Col London, 76. **HONORS AND AWARDS** Pulitzer Prize Biog, 61 & 88; Lincoln Prize Gettysburg Col, 96; Jefferson Davis Awd, Mus Confederacy, 96; ma, oxford univ, 59, harvard univ, 73; lhd, millsaps col, 76; col charleston, 85; univ of calgary, 00. **MEMBERSHIPS** Orgn Am Historians; Southern Hist Asn; Soc Am Hist; AHA. **RESEARCH** The United States during the Civil War-Reconstruction Period; The Jacksonian Era; Southern history and literature. **SELECTED PUBLICATIONS** Auth, Lincoln's Herndon, 48, Lincoln Reconsidered, 56, rev ed, 61 & Charles Sumner and the Coming of the Civil War, 60, Knopf; coauth, The Civil War and Reconstruction, Heath, 61, rev ed, Little, 69, rev ed, Norton, 00; auth, The Politics of Reconstruction, 1863-1867, La State Univ, 65; Charles Sumner and the Rights of Man, Knopf, 70; coauth, The Great Republic: A History of the American People, 77 & auth, Liberty and Union, 78, DC Heath/Little-Brown; Look Homeward: A Life of Thomas Wolfe, Little-Brown, 87; Lincoln, Simon & Schuster, 95; auth, Lincoln at Home, Thornwillow, 99. **CONTACT ADDRESS** PO Box 6158, Lincoln, MA 01773. **EMAIL** donald@fas.harvard.edu

DONALDSON, SCOTT
PERSONAL Born 11/11/1928, Minneapolis, MN **DISCIPLINE** AMERICAN LITERATURE, AMERICAN STUDIES **EDUCATION** Yale Univ, Ba, 51; Univ Minn, MA, 52, PhD (Am studies), 66. **CAREER** Reporter, Minneapolis Star, 55-57; ed and publ, Bloomington Sun, 58-63; from asst prof to assoc prof English, 66-74, Prof English, Col William and Mary, 74-, Fulbright lectr, Turku Univ, 70-71; vis prof, Univ Leeds, 72-73; Fulbright lectr, Univ Milan, 79. **MEMBERSHIPS** MLA; Am Studies Asn; Fulbright Alumni Asn; Int PEN; Auths Guild. **RESEARCH** Fitzgerald and Hemingway; American poetry; modern American fiction. **CONTACT ADDRESS** Dept of English, Col of William and Mary, Williamsburg, VA 23185. **EMAIL** scottd@amug.org

DONALDSON, THOMAS
DISCIPLINE ASIAN ART HISTORY **EDUCATION** Wayne State Univ, BFA, 59, MA, 63; Case Western Reserve Univ, PhD, 73. **CAREER** Prof, Cleveland State Univ, 69-. **RESEARCH** Indian painting, Buddhist sculpt, erotic art. **SELECTED PUBLICATIONS** Auth, Hindu Temple Art of Orissa, Leiden, 85-87; Kamadeva's Pleasure Garden-Orissa, Delhi, 87; sch articles, maj intl jour(s). **CONTACT ADDRESS** Dept of Art, Cleveland State Univ, 83 E 24th St, Cleveland, OH 44115.

DONEGAN, JANE BAUER
PERSONAL Born 09/24/1933, Brooklyn, NY, m, 1981, 2 children **DISCIPLINE** AMERICAN SOCIAL AND CULTURAL HISTORY **EDUCATION** Syracuse Univ, AB, 54, MA, 59, PhD (hist), 72. **CAREER** Teacher Am hist, Fabius Cent Sch, 55-59 and 60-62; teacher Europ hist, Deposit Cent Sch, 59-60; Prof Am Hist, Onondaga Community Col, 62-, Nat Endowment for Humanities summer grant, 77; State Univ NY fac res fel, 78; Nat Endowment for Humanities fel, 80-81. **MEMBERSHIPS** Orgn Am Historians; Am Asn Hist Med; Soc Social Hist Med; Soc Historians Early Am Repub; AHA. **RESEARCH** American medical history; history of American women; American social and cultural history. **SELECTED PUBLICATIONS** Auth, Man midwifery and the delicacy of the sexes, In: Remember the Ladies, Syracuse Univ, 75; Early medical co-education in Central New York, Onondaga Med Soc Bull, 7/76; Women and Men Midwives: Medicine Morality and Misogyny in Early America, Greenwood, 78. **CONTACT ADDRESS** Dept of Soc Sci, Onondaga Comm Col, Syracuse, NY 13215.

DONHAUSER, PETER L.
DISCIPLINE ART, ARCHITECTURAL HISTORY **EDUCATION** Vassar Col, BA, 81; Columbia Univ, MA, 89; New York Univ, PhD candidate. **CAREER** History teacher, Trinity School, New York City. **SELECTED PUBLICATIONS** Auth, A Key to Uemeer?, Artibus et Historiae, vol XIV, no 27, 93; The Encyclopedia of New York City, Yale Univ Press, 96, entries on the Metropolitan Museum of Art, Brooklyn Museum, Guggenheim Museum, and Cooper-Hewitt Museum. **CONTACT ADDRESS** 1680 York Ave, Apt 6-H, New York, NY 10028. **EMAIL** pdonhauser@trinity.nyc.ny.us

DONNELLY, J. PATRICK
PERSONAL Born 09/23/1934, Milwaukee, WI, s **DISCIPLINE** HISTORY **EDUCATION** St Louis Univ, BA, 58; PhL, 59; MA, 63; St Mary's Col, STL, 67; Univ Wis Madison, PhD, 72. **CAREER** Instr to prof, Marquette Univ, 71-. **HONORS AND AWARDS** Phi Alpha Theta; Lawrence G. Haggerty Awd for Teaching Excellence, Marquette Univ, 88; Vis Jesuit Prof, Fordham Univ, 95. **MEMBERSHIPS** Am Soc for reformation Res; AHA; Sixteenth Century Studies Conf; Am Cath Hist Assoc; Soc for Ital Hist Studies; Soc for Reformation Res. **RESEARCH** Peter Martyr Vermigli, Ignatius of Loyola, Antonio Possevino, Early Jesuits. **SELECTED PUBLICATIONS** Ed, transl, "Dialogue on the Two Nature's of Christ" by Peter Martyr Vermigli, Sixteenth Century Essay and Studies Vol XXXI, 95; ed, transl, "Annotations on First Corinthians", by Philipp Melachthon, Reformation Texts with Translation (1350-1650), Marquette Univ Pr, 95; ed, transl, "Sacred Prayers Drawn from the Psalms of David", by Peter Martyr Vermigli, Sixteenth Century Essay and Studies XXXIV, 96; coed, "Cofraternities and Catholic Reform in Italy, France and Spain", Sixteenth Century Essay and Studies XXXXIV, Truman State Univ Pr, 99; ed, transl, "Life, Letters, and Sermons", by Peter Martyr Vermigli, Sixteenth Century Essay and Studies XXXXII, Truman State Univ Pr, 99; coed, The Peter Martyr Reader, Truman State Univ Pr, (Kirksville, MO), 99. **CONTACT ADDRESS** Dept Hist, Marquette Univ, PO Box 1881, Milwaukee, WI 53201-1881. **EMAIL** john.p.donnelly@marquette.edu

DONNER, FRED M.
PERSONAL Born 09/30/1945, Washington, DC, m, 1982, 2 children **DISCIPLINE** HISTORY **EDUCATION** Princeton Univ, BA, Oriental Studies, 68; MA, Near Eastern Studies, 73; PhD, Near Eastern Studies, 75. **CAREER** Instr/Asst Prof/Assoc Prof, History Dept, Yale Univ, 75-82; Assoc Prof/Prof, Dept of Near Eastern Languages & Civilization, Univ of Chicago, 82-. **HONORS AND AWARDS** NEH Fellowship for Univ Teachers, 87-88; Quantrell Awd for Excellence in Undergraduate Teaching, Univ of Chicago, 92. **MEMBERSHIPS** Middle East Medievalists; Middle East Studies Assoc; Amer Oriental Society. **RESEARCH** Early Islamic History. **SELECTED PUBLICATIONS** Auth, "The Early Islamic Conquests, Princeton Univ Press, 82; auth, "Narratives of Islamic Historical Writing, Darwin Press, 88. **CONTACT ADDRESS** Dept Near Eastern Languages, Univ of Chicago, 1155 East 58th St, Chicago, IL 60637-1540. **EMAIL** f-donner@uchicago.edu

DONOHUE, JOHN WALDRON
PERSONAL Born 09/17/1917, New York, NY **DISCIPLINE** HISTORY & PHILOSOPHY OF EDUCATION **EDUCATION** Fordham Univ, AB, 39; St Louis Univ, MA, 44; Woodstock Col, STL, 51; Yale Univ, PhD, 55. **CAREER** Teacher high sch, NY, 44-47; from assoc prof to prof hist & philos of educ, Sch Educ, Fordham Univ, 55-70, adj prof, 77-80; Assoc Ed, America, 72- . **HONORS AND AWARDS** Mem, Society of Jesus, 39- ; ordained Roman Catholic priest, 50; Trustee, Fordham Univ, 69-77, 78-87, St Peter's Col, 80- ; St Louis Univ, 67-81. **MEMBERSHIPS** Philos Educ Soc; Nat Cath Ed Asn. **RESEARCH** Theory of Christian education; contemporary problems concerning religion and education. **SELECTED PUBLICATIONS** Auth, Work and Education, Loyola Univ, 59; Jesuit Education: An Essay on the Foundations of Its Idea, Fordham Univ, 63; St Thomas Aquinas and Education, Random, 68; Catholicism and Education, Harper, 73. **CONTACT ADDRESS** America 106 W 56th St, New York, NY 10019.

DONOVAN, MARY ANN
PERSONAL Born Cincinnati, OH **DISCIPLINE** HISTORICAL THEOLOGY **EDUCATION** St Michaels, Toronto, 77 **CAREER** Prof, 94-pres, Jesuit Sch of Theol, Assoc Prof, 81-94, Assist Prof, 77-81 **HONORS AND AWARDS** Col Theology Bk Awd, 98; Elizabeth Seton Medal, Distinguished Woman Theologian **MEMBERSHIPS** Cath Theol Soc of Am; Col Theology Soc; N Amer Patristics Soc; Soc for Study of Christian Spirituality **RESEARCH** History, Spirituality; Early Christianity; Women's Issues **SELECTED PUBLICATIONS** Auth, One Right Reading? A Guide to Irenaeus, Liturgical Press, 97; Auth, Sisterhood as Power, The Past and Passion of Ecclesial Women, Crossroad, 89 **CONTACT ADDRESS** Jesuit Sch of Theol, Berkeley, 1735 LeRoy Ave, Berkeley, CA 94709. **EMAIL** mdonovan@jstb.edu

DOOLEY, HOWARD JOHN
PERSONAL Born 09/12/1944, Pittsburgh, PA, m, 1972, 2 children **DISCIPLINE** HISTORY **EDUCATION** Univ Notre Dame, BA, 66, MA, 70, PhD (hist), 76. **CAREER** Instr, 70-72; asst prof, 72-78; dir of forensics (Intercollegiate Debate Coach), 75-81; assoc prof, 78-85; asst to the dean of international education, 81-88; prof, 85-89; prof, 90-; asst dean, 88-91; senior adviser to the pres for international affairs (Acting), Western Mich Univ, 91-93; exec dir of international affairs, 93-. **HONORS AND AWARDS** NDEA, 66-70; Fac Res Fel, Western Mich Univ, 77; Nat Endowment for the Humanities, Summer Inst Fel, 82; Nat Endowment, for the Humanitiesm Travel to Collections Grant, 87; Mich Coun for the Humanities Publications Grant, 87; WMU Fac Res Travel Grant, 87; Mich Coun for the Humanities Conf Grants, 89 & 91; Nat Endowment for the Humanities Conf Matching Grants, 89 & 90; Canadian Embassy Conf Grant, 89; Travel Grant 91; Kalamazoo Consortium for Higher Educ Conf Grant, 90; Atlantic Coun Grant, NATO Discussion Series, Brussels, Belgium, 93; Danforth Assoc, 81-86; Acad Assoc, Atlantic Counc of the US, 92-. **MEMBERSHIPS** NAFSA: Asn of Int Educrs; Asn of Int Educ Adminrs (AIEA); Middle East Studies Asn (MESA); Rotary Club of Kalamazoo. **RESEARCH** Modern Middle East; America since World War I; 20th century Europe; international education. **SELECTED PUBLICATIONS** Auth, Hesburgh's Notre Dame: Triumph in Transition, Hawthorn, (New York), 72; co-ed, Changing Asia, Asian Forum Publications (Kalamazoo and Seoul), 87; auth, "The Suez Crisis of 1956: Select Bibliography," eds. Wm. Roger Louis and Roger Owen, Suez 1956: The Crisis and Its Consequences (Oxford: Oxford Univ Press, 89); auth, "Eisenhower affronta la questione orientale, Gli Stati Uniti e la crisi di Suez," in Ombre di guerra fredda, Gli Stati Uniti nel Medio Oriente durante gli anni di Eisenhower Cold War Shadows: The United States in the Middle East during the Eisenhower Years, 1953-2961, (Naples: Edizioni Scientifiche Italiana, 98); auth, The Rights Struggle: Making of a Rebel, Chicago Sunday Sun-Times: Viewpoint, 73; auth, Room for the Poets: New Directions in State Humanities Programs, Michigan Council for the Humanities: A Report to the State, 79; auth, Chautauqua: Then and Now, The Michigan Connection, 84; auth, Great Britain's Last Battle in the Middle East: Notes on Cabinet Planning during the Suez Crisis of 1956, The Internation History Review, 89; auth, With NAFTA We Hafta: International Education for our Common North American Home, Translation News, November 94, and December 94. **CONTACT ADDRESS** Office of Int Affairs, Western Michigan Univ, B-200 Ellsworth Hall, Kalamazoo, MI 49008. **EMAIL** howard.dooley@wmich.edu

DOOLITTLE, JAMES
PERSONAL Born 10/08/1917, Morristown, NJ, m, 1944, 6 children **DISCIPLINE** FRENCH LANGUAGE & LITERATURE, FRENCH HISTORY **EDUCATION** Princeton Univ, AB, 39, MA, 42, PhD, 48. **CAREER** Teacher French and English, Thacher Sch, Calif, 39-40; instr French, Princeton Univ, 46-49; from asst prof to prof, Ohio State Univ, 49-61; prof Romance lang and head dept, Univ Cincinnati, 61-65; Prof French Lit, Univ Rochester, 65-, Ohio State Univ fel, 59-60; Guggenheim fel, 62-63 and 65; Am Coun Learned Soc grant, 69-70. **RESEARCH** History of ideas in France, 1600-1900; French literature of the 17th, 18th and 19th centuries; 17th century French memoirs. **SELECTED PUBLICATIONS** Auth, The Hungry Spirit, Selected Plays and Prose of Gowan, Elsie, Park, Theatre Rsrc Can Recherches Theatrales Can, Vol 13, 1992 The Nowlan, Alden Papers--An Inventory of the Archive at the University Of Calgary Libraries, Theatre Rsrc Int, Vol 19, 94. **CONTACT ADDRESS** Dept of Foreign Lang, Lit and Ling, Univ of Rochester, Rochester, NY 14627.

DORAN, KATHERYN
PERSONAL Born 05/30/1954, PA, m, 1989, 1 child **DISCIPLINE** HISTORY **EDUCATION** Univ Pittsburgh, BA, 76; UNC Chapel Hill, MA, 80, PhD, 83. **CAREER** Asst prof, Wellesley Col, 82-90; asst to assoc prof, Hamilton Col, 91-. **MEMBERSHIPS** Am Philos Assoc. **RESEARCH** Epistemology, early analytic. **CONTACT ADDRESS** Dept Philos, Hamilton Col, New York, Clinton, NY 13323. **EMAIL** kdoran@hamilton.edu

DORINSON, JOSEPH
PERSONAL Born 11/15/1936, Jersey City, NJ, m, 1968, 3 children **DISCIPLINE** HISTORY **EDUCATION** Columbia

Col, BA, 58; Columbia Univ, MPhil, 76. **CAREER** Instr to prof, chair, 66-, Long Island Univ. **HONORS AND AWARDS** NY St Scholar; NY St Regents Col Teaching Fel, Scholar for study at Oslo Univ, 61; Danforth Associateship, 80-86; NEH Summer Grants, 80, 87, 89, 91; highest rank in student-faculty eval; David Newton Awd for Excellence in Teaching, 88. **MEMBERSHIPS** Amer Popular Culture Assoc; DANY; Intl Soc for Humor Stud. **RESEARCH** Brooklyn hist; sports hist; ethnic hist; Jackie Robinson; Paul Robeson; Frank Sinatra, Jewish humor. **SELECTED PUBLICATIONS** Auth, Anyone Here A Sailor?: Popular Entertainment and the Navy with Dennis Carpenter, Brightlights Publ, 94; auth, The Enigma of Babe Ruth, Nine, 96; art, Marianne Moore & The Brooklyn Dodgers, Long Island Women: Activists and Innovators, Greenwood Press, 98; art, From Jack Johnson to Muhamad Ali: Black Heroes in American Sports, J Popular Culture, 97; art, Jackie Robinson: Man of the Times: Mentsch for All Seasons, NY Times: Newspaper in Educ Curric Guide, 97; auth, Paul Robeson: A Symposium with William Pencak, Pa Hist, 99; coauth, Jackie Robinson: Race, Sports and the American Dream, M E Sharpe, 99. **CONTACT ADDRESS** History Dept, Long Island Univ, Brooklyn, 1 University Plaza, Brooklyn, NY 11201. **EMAIL** jdorinso@liu.edu

DORN, JACOB HENRY
PERSONAL Born 09/21/1939, Chicago, IL, m, 1964, 2 children **DISCIPLINE** RECENT AMERICAN HISTORY **EDUCATION** Wheaton Col, Ill, BA, 60; Univ Ore, MA, 62, PhD(hist), 65. **CAREER** From asst prof to assoc prof, 65-74, vpres fac, 77-78, Prof Am Hist, Wright State Univ, 74-, Dir Univ Honors Prog, 72-87. **HONORS AND AWARDS** Danforth Found assoc, 69; Outstanding Educator Am, 74; Wright State Univ Lib Arts Outstanding Teacher, 77; Ohio Acad Hist, Outstanding Teacher Awd, 86; Mid-East Honors Asn Leadership Awd, 88; Ohio Acad Hist, Distinguished Service Awd, 97. **MEMBERSHIPS** AHA; Orgn Am Historians; Am Soc Church Hist; Conf Faith & Hist **RESEARCH** American religious history, late 19th and 20th centuries; 20th century American history, especially social and intellectual history. **SELECTED PUBLICATIONS** Auth, Washington Gladden: Prophet of the Social Gospel, Ohio State Univ, 67; Subsistence Homesteading in Dayton, Ohio, 1933-35, Ohio Hist, spring 69; co-ed, A Bibliography of Sources for Dayton, Ohio, 1850-1950, Wright State Univ, 71; auth, Sunday Afternoon: The Early Social Gospel in Journalism, New England Quart, 6/71; Religion and the City, in: The Urban Experience: Themes in American History, Wadsworth, 73; The Rural Idea and Agrarian Realities: Arthur E. Holt and the Vision of a Decentralized America in the Interwar Years, Church Hist, 3/83; Religion and Reform in the City: the Re-thinking Chicago Movement in the 1930's, Church Hist, 9/86; Episcopal Priest and Socialist Activitist: The Case of Irwin St. John Tucker, Anglican and Episcopal Hist, 6/92; The Social Gospel and Socialism: A Comparison of the Thought of Francis Greenwood Peabody, Washington Gladden, and Walter Rauschenbusch, Church Hist, 3/93; Washington Gladden and the Social Gospel, in: American Reforms and Reformers, 95; ed, Socialismm and Christianity in Early 20th Century America, Greenwood Press, 98; auth, "Univ Bookman" and "Intercollegiate Review," in The Conservative Press in Twentieth-Century America, Greenwood Press, 99. **CONTACT ADDRESS** Dept of Hist, Wright State Univ, Dayton, 3640 Colonel Glenn, Dayton, OH 45435-0002. **EMAIL** jdorn@desire.wright.edu

DORNISH, MARGARET HAMMOND
PERSONAL Born 07/25/1934, St. Marys, PA **DISCIPLINE** HISTORY OF RELIGIONS **EDUCATION** Smith Col, AB, 56; Claremont Grad Sch, MA, 67, PhD(relig), 69. **CAREER** Teacher English, Orme Sch, 60-65; asst prof relig, 69-74, assoc prof, 74-92, prof relig & chair, relig studies, Pomona Col, 93-. **MEMBERSHIPS** Am Acad Relig; Pac Coast Theol Soc; Asn Asian Studies; Int Asn Buddhist Studies. **RESEARCH** Buddhist studies. **SELECTED PUBLICATIONS** Auth, D T Suzuki's early interpretation of Buddhism and Zen, Eastern Buddhist, 70. **CONTACT ADDRESS** Dept of Religious Studies, Pomona Col, 551 N College Ave., Claremont, CA 91711-6319. **EMAIL** mdornish@pomona.edu

DORONDO, DAVID R.
DISCIPLINE MODERN GERMANY **EDUCATION** Oxford Univ, PhD. **CAREER** Hist Dept, Western Carolina Univ **SELECTED PUBLICATIONS** Auth, Bavaria and German Federalism: Reich to Republic, 1918-1933, 92. **CONTACT ADDRESS** Western Carolina Univ, Cullowhee, NC 28723.

DORSETT, LYLE WESLEY
PERSONAL Born 04/17/1938, Kansas City, MO, m, 1970, 2 children **DISCIPLINE** US HISTORY **EDUCATION** Univ Mo, Kansas City, BA, 60, MA, 62; Univ Mo, Columbia, PhD (hist), 65. **CAREER** Asst prof hist, Univ Mo, St Louis, 65-66 and Univ Southern Calif, 66-68; assoc prof, Univ Mo, St Louis, 68-71 and Univ Colo, 71-72; Prof Hist, Univ Denver, 72-, Nat Endowment for Humanities fel, 68; Henry Haskell Distinguished Lectr, Univ Mo, Kansas City, 77-78. **HONORS AND AWARDS** W A Whitehead Awd, NJ Hist, 77. **MEMBERSHIPS** AHA; Orgn Am Historians; Southern Hist Asn; Western Hist Asn; Conf Faith and Hist. **RESEARCH** Urban history; alcoholism in the 19th century; biography. **SELECTED PUBLICATIONS** Auth, Town Promotion in the 19th Century Vermont, New England Quart, 6/67; The Pendergast Machine, Oxford Univ, 68, Nebr, 80; The Challenge of the City, Heath, 68; coauth, Was the Antebellum South Antiurban?, J Southern Hist, 2/72; auth, The city boss and reformer: A reappraisal, Pac Northwestern Quart, 10/72; The Queen City: A History of Denver, Pruett, 77; Franklin D Roosevelt and the City Bosses, Kennikat, 77; coauth, K C: A History of Kansas City, Mo, Pruett, 78. **CONTACT ADDRESS** Dept of Hist, Univ of Denver, Denver, CO 80210.

DORSEY, CAROLYN ANN
PERSONAL Born, OH, s **DISCIPLINE** AFRICAN-AMERICAN STUDIES **EDUCATION** Kent State Univ, BS 1956, MEd 1961; Yale Univ, Danforth Fellow in Black Studies 1969-70; New York Univ, PhD 1976. **CAREER** Cleveland Public Schools, teacher 1956-62; Tabora Girls Sch, Tanzania, E Africa, teacher 1962-64; Cleveland Job Corps Ctr, social studies dept chair & teacher 1965-67; Southern IL Univ Exper in Higher Educ Prog, curriculum spec & instructor 1967-69; Yale Univ Transitional Year Program, assoc dir & teacher, 69-70; NY Univ Inst of Afro-Amer Affairs, jr fellow 1970-74; IN State Univ, asst prof of afro-amer studies 1976-77; Univ of MO, coord of Black studies & asst prof of higher educ 1977-81, coord of Black studies & assoc prof of higher educ 1981-85, assoc prof of higher educ 1985-, dir of graduate studies, 86-91. **HONORS AND AWARDS** Danforth Found Black Studies Fellowship yr spent at Yale Univ 1969-70; Southern Fellowship used for Dissertation Study at New York Univ 1973-74; Danforth Found Assoc 1980-86; resident participant in Summer Inst for Women in Higher Educ Admin, Bryn Mawr Coll, 1989; University of Missouri Faculty Awd, 1990; University of Missouri Alumnae Anniversary Awd for Contributions to the Education of Women, 1990. **MEMBERSHIPS** Stephens Coll Bd of Curators, 1981-91; Amer Assn of Higher Educ, Natl Council for Black Studies; Phi Delta Kappa; Phi Lambda Theta; Assn for the Study of Afro-American Life & History; Alpha Kappa Alpha Sorority; mem of bias panel Amer Coll Testing Program Tests 1982- & The Psychological Corp Stanford Achievement Test, 7th & 8th editions. **CONTACT ADDRESS** Univ of Missouri, Columbia, 301 Hill Hall, Columbia, MO 65211.

DORSEY, KURK
DISCIPLINE U.S. FOREIGN RELATIONS, ENVIRONMENTAL HISTORY, CANADA **EDUCATION** Yale Univ, PhD. **CAREER** Asst prof, Univ NH, 95-. **HONORS AND AWARDS** Co-Winner Stuart L. Bernath Prize for the Soc for Hist of Am Foreign Relations; Univ Excellence in Teaching Awd; UNH Outstanding Fac Awd, 99. **RESEARCH** Diplomacy of whaling since 1930. **SELECTED PUBLICATIONS** Auth, Putting a Ceiling on Sealing: Conservation and Cooperation in the International Arena, Environ Hist Rev, 91; Scientists, Citizens, Statesmen: U.S.-Canadian Wildlife Protection Treaties in the Progressive Era, Diplomatic Hist, 95; auth, The Dawn of Conservation Diplomacy: Canadian-American Wildlife Protection Treaties in the Progressive Era, 98. **CONTACT ADDRESS** Univ of New Hampshire, Durham, 9 River St, Apt C14, Newmarket, NH 03857. **EMAIL** kd@hopper.unh.edu

DORSEY, LEARTHEN
DISCIPLINE HISTORY OF AFRICA **EDUCATION** Mich State Univ, PhD. **CAREER** Assoc prof Hist & Ethnic Stud, Univ Nebr, Lincoln. **RESEARCH** The colonial economic history of Rwanda. **SELECTED PUBLICATIONS** Auth, Historical Dictionary of Rwanda, Scarecrow Press, 94. **CONTACT ADDRESS** Univ of Nebraska, Lincoln, 615 Oldfather Hall, Lincoln, NE 68588-0417. **EMAIL** ldorsey7@unl.edu

DORWART, JEFFREY M.
PERSONAL Born 02/10/1944, Willimantic, CT, m, 1969, 3 children **DISCIPLINE** HISTORY **EDUCATION** Univ Conn, BA, 65; Univ Mass Amherst, MA, 68; PhD, 71. **CAREER** From asst prof to prof, Rutgers Univ, 71-. **HONORS AND AWARDS** Phi Beta Kappa; Phi Sigma Alpha. **MEMBERSHIPS** US Naval Inst. **RESEARCH** Naval, Military, New Jersey, US History. **SELECTED PUBLICATIONS** Auth, Office of Naval Intelligence, 80; auth, Eberstadt and Forvestal, 91; auth, Fort Mifflin of Philadelphia, 98; auth, The Philadelphia Navy Yard, 00. **CONTACT ADDRESS** Dept Hist, Rutgers, The State Univ of New Jersey, Camden, 311 N 5th St, Camden, NJ 08102-1405. **EMAIL** dorwart@crab.rutgers.edu

DOSTER, JAMES FLETCHER
PERSONAL Born 12/08/1912, Tuscaloosa, AL, m, 1936, 2 children **DISCIPLINE** HISTORY **EDUCATION** Univ Ala, AB, 32; Univ Chicago, AM, 36, PhD, 48. **CAREER** From instr to assoc prof, 36-62, Prof Hist, Univ Ala, 62-, Instr, Howard Col, 44-45; Danforth Found assoc, 50-53; fel, Harvard Univ, 53-54; mem conf nature and writing of hist, Univ Kans, 55; consult Creek Nation on claims pending before Indian Claims Comn, 57-73; mem transp prize comt, Ford Motor Co, 61-64; mem fac sem, Standard Oil Co, Calif, 62; distinguished sr fel, Ctr Study Southern Hist and Cult, Univ Ala, 76-. **MEMBERSHIPS** AHA; Southern Hist Asn; Am Econ Asn; Econ Hist Orgn Am Historians. **RESEARCH** American railway history; United States history; Creek Indian Confederacy, 1740-1825. **SELECTED PUBLICATIONS** Auth, Alabama's First Railroad Commission, privately publ, 49; Alabama political revolution of 1904, Ala Rev, 4/54; Vicissitudes of the South Carolina railroad, Bus Hist Rev, 6/56; Railroads in Alabama Politics, Univ Ala, 57; The Georgia Railroad & Banking Company in the Reconstruction Era, Ga Hist Quart, 3/64; The Creek Indians and Their Florida Lands, (2 vols), Garland, 74. **CONTACT ADDRESS** Dept of Hist, Univ of Alabama, Tuscaloosa, Box 1955, University, AL 35486.

DOTSON, JOHN EDWARD
PERSONAL Born 06/12/1939, Frederick, OK **DISCIPLINE** RENAISSANCE HISTORY **EDUCATION** Univ Okla, BA, 61; Univ Nebr, MA, 63; Johns Hopkins Univ, PhD (hist), 69. **CAREER** Asst prof, Concordia Univ, 67-70; Asst Prof Hist, Southern Ill Univ Carbondale, 70-. **SELECTED PUBLICATIONS** Auth, Jal's Nef X and Genoese naval architecture in the 13th century, Mariner's Mirror, 5/73; Merchant and naval influences on galley design at Venice and Genoa in the fourteenth century, In: New Aspects of Naval History, Naval Inst Press, 81; A problem of cotton and lead in medieval Italian shipping, Speculum, 1/82. **CONTACT ADDRESS** Dept of Hist, So Illinois Univ, Carbondale, Carbondale, IL 62901-4300.

DOTY, CHARLES STEWART
PERSONAL Born 09/08/1928, Fredonia, KS, m, 1954, 3 children **DISCIPLINE** MODERN EUROPEAN AND FRENCH HISTORY **EDUCATION** Washburn Univ, AB, 50; Univ Kans, MA, 55; Ohio State Univ, PhD (hist), 64. **CAREER** Instr hist, Kent State Univ, 61-64; asst prof, 64-67, assoc prof, 67-76, from Prof to prof emer, Univ Maine, Orono, 76-. **MEMBERSHIPS** AHA; Soc Fr Hist Studies. **RESEARCH** Comparison of French nationalism with French North American nationalism. **SELECTED PUBLICATIONS** Auth, Alsatian Emigration to the United States, 1815-1870, J Am Hist, Vol 80, 93; American Immigration--Example or Counterexample for France, J Am Hist, Vol 82, 95; The American Identity of Dantin, Louis, More Francophone American Than Franco American, Can Rev Am Stud, Vol 24, 94; Monsieur Maurras Est Ici--French Fascism in Franco American New England, J Contemporary Hist, Vol 32, 97. **CONTACT ADDRESS** 18 Sunrise Terr, Orono, ME 04473. **EMAIL** doty@maine.maine.edu

DOUDNA, MARTIN KIRK
PERSONAL Born 06/04/1930, Louisville, KY, m, 1962, 3 children **DISCIPLINE** ENGLISH LITERATURE, AMERICAN CULTURE **EDUCATION** Oberlin Col, AB, 52; Univ Louisville, MA, 59; Univ Mich, PhD (Am cult), 71. **CAREER** Asst prof English, Mackinac Col, 66-69; assoc prof, 71-78, Prof English, Univ Hawaii, Hilo, 78-. **MEMBERSHIPS** MLA; Thoreau Soc; Thoreau Lyceum. **RESEARCH** Nineteenth century American literature; American liberalism and radicalism; American magazine journalism. **SELECTED PUBLICATIONS** Auth, Nay Lady Sit, The Dramatic and Human Dimensions of Comus, Anq A Quart J Short Articles Notes Revs, Vol 8, 95. **CONTACT ADDRESS** Humanities Div, Univ of Hawaii, Hilo, Hilo, HI 96720.

DOUGAN, MICHAEL BRUCE
PERSONAL Born 02/26/1944, Burbank, CA, m, 1970 **DISCIPLINE** AMERICAN HISTORY **EDUCATION** Southwest Mo State Col, AB, 66; Emory Univ, MA, 67, PhD (hist), 70. **CAREER** Instr, 70-71, asst prof, 71-77, Assoc Prof Hist, Ark State Univ, 77-. **MEMBERSHIPS** Southern Hist Asn; Am Asn Legal Hist; Am Asn State and Local Hist. **RESEARCH** Southern history; legal history; local history. **SELECTED PUBLICATIONS** Auth, Confederate Arkansas: The People and Policies of a Frontier State in Wartime, Univ Ala Press, 76; contribr, Thomas C Hindman, In: Rank and File: Civil War Essays in Honor of Bell I Wiley, Presidio, 76; auth, Mary Lewis: An Arkansas girl in Grand Opera, Record Collector, 12/76; co-ed, By the Cypress Swamp: The Arkansas Stories of Octave Thanet, Rose Publ Co, 80; auth, The doctrine of creative destruction, Ark Hist Quart, summer 80. **CONTACT ADDRESS** P O Box 1690, Box 2607, State University, AR 72467-1690.

DOUGHERTY, PATRICIA M.
PERSONAL Born 12/07/1944, CA **DISCIPLINE** MODERN EUROPEAN HISTORY **EDUCATION** Georgetown Univ, MA 79, PhD 84. **CAREER** Dominican Col SR, prof 84-. **HONORS AND AWARDS** Tchr of the Yr; NEH Fel; Fulbright Fel. **MEMBERSHIPS** ACHA; AHA; SFHS; WSFH; WAWH. **RESEARCH** France 19th century, esp July Monarchy Press; Women and religion. **SELECTED PUBLICATIONS** Auth, The French Catholic Press and the July Revolution, French History, forthcoming; Voyage sans carte: Mary Goemaere et la fondation des Soeurs dominicaines en Californie, Memoire dominicaine, 98; auth, L'Ami de la Religion, et les eveques francais sous le Concordat, 1815-1850, Rev d'hist ecclesiastique, 94; auth, The Rise and Fall of L'Ami de la Religion: History Purpose and Readership of a French Catholic Newspaper, Cath Hist Rev, 91; auth, Baudrillart Blum Freundlich Gerlier, Jeunesse ouvriere chretienne, Historical Dictionary of World War II France: The Occupation Vichy and the Resisitance, 1938-1946, ed, Bertram M. Gordon, Westport CT, Greenwood Press, 98; auth, Goemaere, Mary of the Cross, European Immigrant Women in the United State: A Biographical Dictionary, eds, Judy B. Litoff, Judith McDonnell, NY, Garland Press, 94.

CONTACT ADDRESS Dept of History, Dominican Col of San Rafael, 50 Aracia Ave, San Rafael, CA 94901-2298. **EMAIL** dougherty@dominican.edu

DOUGHTY, ROBERT
PERSONAL Born 11/04/1943, Tullos, LA, m, 1967, 2 children **DISCIPLINE** HISTORY **EDUCATION** Us Mil Acad, BS, 65; UCLA, MA, 72; Univ Kansas, PhD, 79. **CAREER** Instr, 72-75, assoc prof, 81-84, prof, 84-, US Mil Acad; instr, 76-79, Dept of Strategy, Command & Gen Staff Col; **HONORS AND AWARDS** Am Historical Assoc's Paul Birdsall Prize in European Militiary and Strategic History, 86. **MEMBERSHIPS** Soc for Militiary History, Soc for French Historical Studies. **RESEARCH** French military in 19th & 20th centuries **SELECTED PUBLICATIONS** Auth, Seeds of Disaster: The Development of French Army Doctrine, 1919-1939, Archon, 85; auth, The Breaking Point: Sedan and the Fall of France, 1940, Archon, 90; co-ed; Warefare in the Western World, D.C. Health, 95. **CONTACT ADDRESS** Dept of History, United States Military Acad, West Point, NY 10996. **EMAIL** kr0724@usma.edu

DOUGLAS, DONALD MORSE
PERSONAL Born 09/07/1924, Los Angeles, CA, m, 1943, 2 children **DISCIPLINE** EUROPEAN HISTORY **EDUCATION** Kans State Univ, BA, 61, MA, 63; Univ Kans, PhD (hist), 68. **CAREER** Asst prof, 65-75, Assoc Prof Hist, Wichita State Univ, 75-. **MEMBERSHIPS** Western Asn German Studies. **RESEARCH** The Holocaust; Nazi Germany. **SELECTED PUBLICATIONS** Auth, The Anatomy of the Nuremberg Trials--A Personal Memoir, Hist, Vol 56, 93; The Rhetoric of Moderation--Desegregating the South During the Decade After Brown, Northwestern Univ Law Rev, Vol 89, 94; The Limits of Law in Accomplishing Racial Change--School Segregation in the Pre Brown North, Ucla Law Rev, Vol 44, 97; Race, Law and American History 1700-1990--The African American Experience, Am J Legal Hist, Vol 37, 93; Dismantling Desegregation --The Quiet Reversal of Brown V., Michigan Law Rev, Vol 95, 97. **CONTACT ADDRESS** Dept of Hist, Wichita State Univ, Wichita, KS 67208.

DOUGLAS, GEORGE HALSEY
PERSONAL Born 01/09/1934, East Orange, NJ, m, 1961, 1 child **DISCIPLINE** AMERICAN LITERATURE & STUDIES **EDUCATION** Lafayette Col, AB, 56; Columbia Univ, MA, 66; Univ Ill, PhD(philos), 68. **CAREER** From instr to prof, 66-88, prof English, Univ Ill, Urbana, 88-. **MEMBERSHIPS** MLA; Am Soc Aesthet; Am Studies Asn; Popular Cult Asn. **RESEARCH** American culture and social history. **SELECTED PUBLICATIONS** Auth, H L Mencken: Critic of American Life, Archon, 78; Rail city: Chicago and the Railroad, Howell-North Bks, 82; auth, Edmund Urban's America, Ky, 83; auth, Women of the Twenties, Saybrook, 86; auth, The Early Days of Radio Broadcasting, McFarland, 87; All Aboard: The Railroad in American Life, Paragon House, 92; Education Without Impact, Birch Lane Press, 92; Skyscraper Odyssey, McFarland, 96; Postwar America, Krieger Publishing, 98; auth, The Golden Age of the Newspaper, Greenwood, 99. **CONTACT ADDRESS** Dept of English, Univ of Illinois, Urbana-Champaign, 608 S Wright St, Urbana, IL 61801-3613. **EMAIL** ghdougla@vivc.edu

DOWNEY, DENNIS B.
DISCIPLINE UNITED STATES HISTORY **EDUCATION** Fla State Univ, BA, 74, MA, 76; Marquette Univ, PhD, 81. **CAREER** Prof & actg dir, Univ Grad Stud. **HONORS AND AWARDS** Outstanding bk awd,Gustavus Myers Ctr Human Rights, 92. **MEMBERSHIPS** Org Amer Historians; AHA; Southern Hist Asn; Soc Historians of the Gilded Age and Progressive Era. **RESEARCH** US social and cultural history; society and culture, 1865-1930; race relations, esp 1865-1930; racialvViolence, esp lynching. **SELECTED PUBLICATIONS** Auth, Historical, Architectural and Archeological Survey of Duval County, Florida, State Fla, Misc Proj No 37, 81; Pennsylvania, in Microsoft Encarta, Microsoft Corp, 97; An Interview with Thomas Flanagan, Contemp Lit 35, 94; Revisionism and the Holocaust, OAH Newsl 21, 93; The Second Industrial Revolution 1865-1900, Lessons From Hist, 92, in OAH Chairs' Newsl, 92; Accidents and Incidents, Friends' Folio, 91; coauth, Industrial Pennsylvania, 1876-1919, A Guide to the History of Pennsylvania, Westport: Greenwood Press, 93; co-ed, A Guide to the History of Pennsylvania, Westport: Greenwood Press, 93; coauth, Crooked Death: Coatesville, Pennsylvania and the Lynching of Zachariah Walker, Champaign: Univ Ill Press, 91. **CONTACT ADDRESS** Dept of History, Millersville Univ of Pennsylvania, PO Box 1002, Millersville, PA 17551-0302. **EMAIL** ddowney@mu3.millersv.edu

DOWNING, MARVIN LEE
PERSONAL Born 03/21/1937, Brownwood, TX, m, 1967, 2 children **DISCIPLINE** UNITED STATES HISTORY **EDUCATION** Wayland Baptist Col, BA, 59; Tex Christian Univ, MA, 63; Univ Okla, PhD(hist), 70. **CAREER** Instr hist, Wayland Baptist Col, 63-66; asst prof, 69-73, Prof Hist, Univ Tenn, Martin, 73-, Nat Endowment for Humanities, grant W Tenn Frontier, 73-74. **MEMBERSHIPS** Orgn Am Historians; Asn Asian Studies. **RESEARCH** American frontier; American agricultural history; Northwest Tennesse frontier. **SELECTED PUBLICATIONS** Auth, The PWA and the acquisition of the Fort Worth Public Library building 1933-1939, Tex Libr, fall 65; Davy Crockett in Northwest Tennessee, 75 & Christmasville and its origins, 75, River Region Monographs, Univ Tenn, Martin; coauth, Brief History of the First Baptist Church, Martin, Tennessee, First Baptist Church, 76. **CONTACT ADDRESS** Univ of Tennessee, Martin, 554 University St, Martin, TN 38238-0002. **EMAIL** mdowning@utm.edu

DOYLE, DON H.
PERSONAL Born Long Beach, CA, s, 2 children **DISCIPLINE** HISTORY **EDUCATION** Univ Calif, Davis, BA, 67; Northwestern Univ, PhD, 73. **CAREER** Asst, 74-79, assoc, 79-86, Prof, 86-, VANDERBILT UNIV; vis prof, Univ Leeds, England, 97-98; Fulbright sen lectr, Univ Genoa, 95; Fulbright sen lect, Univ Rome, 91; lectr, 71-73, asst prof, 73-74, Univ Mich, Dearborn; Nelson Tyrone, prof of Hist, 00-. **SELECTED PUBLICATIONS** Auth, The Social Order of a Frontier Community, 78; auth, Nashville in The New South, 85; author Nashville Since the Twenties, 85; auth, New Men, New Cities, New South, 90; coed, The South as an American Problem, 95; auth, Fulkner's County: The Historical Roots of Yoknapa Tawpha, 01. **CONTACT ADDRESS** Dept of History, Vanderbilt Univ, PO Box 1802, Sta B, Nashville, TN 37235. **EMAIL** don.h.doyle@vanderbilt.edu

DOYLE, MICHAEL W.
PERSONAL Born 07/17/1953, Oak Park, IL, m, 1980, 1 child **DISCIPLINE** HISTORY **EDUCATION** Univ Wis Madison, BA, 85; Cornell Univ, MA, 92; PhD, 97. **CAREER** Asst prof, Ball State Univ, 96-. **HONORS AND AWARDS** Mellon Fel in the Humanities, 89; Jacob K. Javits Fel (declined), 89; Phi Beta Kappa, 89. **MEMBERSHIPS** Am Asn for State and Local Hist, Am Hist Asn, Am Studies Asn, Asn of Ind Museums, Communal Studies Asn, Ind Asn of Historians, Nat Coun on Public Hist, Orgn of Am Historians. **RESEARCH** Twentieth-century U.S. Cultural History, Utopianism, Political Radicalism and the Arts, Public History. **SELECTED PUBLICATIONS** Rev, of "Frontier Indiana," by Andrew R.L. Cayton, Mich Hist Rev 23.2 (97): 205-206; rev, of "Rock and Roll: A Social History," Mich Hist Rev 24.1 (98): 171; auth, "Be-ins," "Flower Children," and "Death of Hippie," in The Sixties in America, ed. Carl Singleton (CA: Salem Press, 99); auth, "Debating the Counterculture: Ecstasy and Anxiety over the Hip Alternative," in Columbia Guide to America in the Sixties, eds. David Farber and Beth Bailey (NY: Columbia Univ Pr, forthcoming); co-ed & contribur, Imagine Nation: American Cultural Radicalism in the 1960s and 70s, Univ Calif Press (Berkeley, CA), forthcoming. **CONTACT ADDRESS** Dept Hist, Ball State Univ, 213 Burkhardt Bldg, Muncie, IN 47306-0480.

DOZIER, ROBERT R.
PERSONAL Born 04/07/1932, New Orleans, LA, m, 1954, 4 children **DISCIPLINE** HISTORY, POLITICAL SCIENCE **EDUCATION** Univ Calif, PhD, 69. **CAREER** Prof, Univ Mont, 82-89; Prof Emer, Univ Mont, 89-. **HONORS AND AWARDS** Teacher of the Year, 77; Outstanding Educr, 82. **RESEARCH** Military history. **SELECTED PUBLICATIONS** Auth, For King, Constitution and Country, Univ KY Pr, 83. **CONTACT ADDRESS** Dept Hist, Univ of Montana, Missoula, MT 59812. **EMAIL** rrdozier@aol.com

DRACHMAN, VIRGINIA GOLDSMITH
PERSONAL Born 01/12/1948, New York, NY, 2 children **DISCIPLINE** AMERICAN MEDICAL & WOMEN'S HISTORY **EDUCATION** Univ Rochester, BA, 70; State Univ NYork, Buffalo, MA, 74, PhD, 76. **CAREER** Assoc prof hist med & hist women, Tufts Univ, 77, Rockefeller Found fel hist & women med movement, 77-78. **HONORS AND AWARDS** ACLS Ford, 88; NSF Law & Soc Sci, 88; NEH Summer Fel, 94. **MEMBERSHIPS** AHA; Orgn Am Historians; Am Studies Asn. **RESEARCH** Women in med. **SELECTED PUBLICATIONS** Auth, Women Lawyers & the Origins of Professional Identity in America: The Letters of the Equity Club, 1887-1890, Univ Mich Press, 94; Sisters in Law: Women Lawyers in Modern American History, Harvard Univ Press, 98; Hospital with a Heart: Women Doctors and the Paradox of Separation at the New England Hospital, 1862-1969, Cornell Univ Press, 98. **CONTACT ADDRESS** Dept of Hist, Tufts Univ, Medford, 520 Boston Ave, Medford, MA 02155-5555. **EMAIL** drachman@tiac.net

DRAKE, FRED
PERSONAL Born 05/25/1937, Barrow in, England, m, 1963, 2 children **DISCIPLINE** NORTH AMERICAN DIPLOMATIC, NAVAL, AND MILITARY HISTORY **EDUCATION** Univ Manchester, BA, MA; Cornell Univ, PhD. **CAREER** Prof. **HONORS AND AWARDS** Great Lakes Hist prize, Cleveland State Univ, Fr-Amer Endowed Library Fund. **RESEARCH** Naval history. **SELECTED PUBLICATIONS** Auth, "The Niagara Peninsula and Naval Aspects of the War of 1812," Proc of Eighth Niagara Peninsula Hist Conf, Vanwell Press, 90; The Empire of the Seas: A Biography of Rear Admiral Shufeldt, Univ Hawaii Press. **CONTACT ADDRESS** Dept of Hist, Brock Univ, MacKenzie Chown Complex, room C422, Saint Catharines, ON, Canada L2S 3A1. **EMAIL** fcdrake@spartan.ac.brocku.ca

DRAKE, FRED
DISCIPLINE HISTORY **EDUCATION** Harvard Univ, PhD, 71. **CAREER** Prof, Univ MA Amherst. **SELECTED PUBLICATIONS** Auth, publ(s) on aspects of Sino-Western cult interaction; role of Western missionaries in China; pioneer photography in China; early Manchu acceptance of Chinese cult. **CONTACT ADDRESS** Dept of Hist, Univ of Massachusetts, Amherst, Mass Ave, Amherst, MA 01003.

DRAKE, HAROLD A.
PERSONAL Born 07/24/1942, Cincinnati, IL, m, 1969, 1 child **DISCIPLINE** HISTORY, CLASSICS **EDUCATION** Univ S Calif, AM, 63; Univ Wis, MA, 66; MA, 69; PhD, 70. **CAREER** Teach asst, Univ Wis, 62-65; lectr, asst prof, assoc prof, prof, UCSB, 70-. **HONORS AND AWARDS** NEH Fel, Inst Adv Stud, 73-74; Sr Fel, Annenburg Res Inst, 91-92; Asn Stud Out Teach Awd, 73-74; Plous Memo Awd, Out Asst Prof, 76; Mortar Bd Prof of Yr, 86-87; Alumni Dist Teach Awd, 95-96. **MEMBERSHIPS** Phi Beta Kappa; APA; AIA; SPRS; AAH; NAPS; BSA; ASCH; SBL. **RESEARCH** Late Roman empire; early Christianity; late antiquity; ancient histiography. **SELECTED PUBLICATIONS** Auth, In Praise of Constantine, Univ Calif Press, 76; co-auth, Eudoxia and the Holy Sepulchre, Cisalpino Golliardica (Milan), 81; auth, "Eusebius on the True Cross," Eccle Hist (85); auth, "Lambs Into Lions," Past and Pres (96); auth, Constantine and the Bishops, John Hopkins Press, 00. **CONTACT ADDRESS** Hist Dept, Univ of California, Santa Barbara, Santa Barbara, CA 93106-9410. **EMAIL** drake@humanities.ucsb.edu

DRAPER, JOAN E.
DISCIPLINE ARCHITECTURE, ARCITECTURAL HISTORY **EDUCATION** Univ of Calif, Berkeley, BA, 69, MA, 72, PhD, 79. **CAREER** Asst prof, Mont State Univ, 76-70; asst prof, Univ of Ill at Chicago, 79-85; ASSOC PROF, UNIV OF COLO AT BOULDER & DENVER, 85-. **MEMBERSHIPS** Soc of Archit Historians; Soc of Am City & Regional Planning Hist. **RESEARCH** History of American architecture & planning, 19th and 20th centuries. **SELECTED PUBLICATIONS** Auth, John Galen Howard, Toward the Simple Life: Arts and Crafts Architects of Calif, Univ of Calif Press, 97; auth, Architectural Education and Multiculturalism, Doing Diversity, Asn of Collegiate Schools of Archit, 96; auth, Chicago: Small Parks of 1902-1903 and Park Planning in the United States, Planning the Am City: Hist, Practice and Prospects, Johns Hopkins Univ Press, 96; auth, Chicago: Planning Wacker Drive, Streets: Critical Perspectives on Public Space, Univ of Calif Press, 94; auth, Landscape Design, Oxford Companion to Am Hist, Oxford Univ Press, forthcoming; auth, Edward H. Bennett, Am Nat Bio, Oxford Univ Press and the Am Coun of Learned Socs, 98; auth, John Galen Howard, Dizionario de Architettura Contemporaneo, UTET, 97. **CONTACT ADDRESS** Archit and Planning, Univ of Colorado, Boulder, EnvD Bldg, Boulder, CO 80309.

DRAZNIN, YAFFA CLAIRE
PERSONAL Born 05/19/1922, WI, m, 1942, 2 children **DISCIPLINE** MODERN BRITISH HISTORY (VICTORIAN STUDIES) **EDUCATION** Univ Chicago, BA, 43; Univ Southern Calif, MA, 82, PhD, 85. **CAREER** Professional editor and staff writer (community activity, law enforcement, aerospace and computer hardware), 54-70; freelance magazine writer, author, 70-81; affiliated scholar, USC faculty status, SWMS program, 85-87; visiting scholars (faculty status), Dept History, Univ Chicago, 95-98. **HONORS AND AWARDS** Dr. George P. Hammond Awd, Phi Alpha Theta Historical Soc, for best paper, cash award; Barbara Kanner Prize, Western Assn of Women Historians, best book, cash award, 94. **MEMBERSHIPS** Amer Hist Soc; Assn Documentary Editing; Natl Coalition Independent Scholars; Coordinating Group, Women Historians, MESNA. **RESEARCH** Victorian England, women in late 19th-century. **SELECTED PUBLICATIONS** Auth, "Victorian London's Middle-class Housewife: What Did She Do All Day"; auth, "My Other Self": The Letters of Olive Schreiner and Havelock Ellis, 1884-1920, 92/93; auth, book review of The Rise of Respectable Society: A Social History of Victorian Britain, 1830-1900, in The Historian, v 52, 90; auth, book review, A Mid-Victorian Feminist: Barbara Leigh Smith Bodichon, in The Historian, v 50, 88. **CONTACT ADDRESS** 5532 S Shore Dr, #14F, Chicago, IL 60637-1990. **EMAIL** ydraznin@aol.com

DREIFORT, JOHN E.
DISCIPLINE HISTORY **EDUCATION** Bowling Green State Univ, BA, 65; MA, 66; Kent State Univ, PhD, 70. **CAREER** Exec secy, Wichita Comm For Rel, 73-; affil, Coun For Rel; Amer Comm For Rel; interim VP, acad aff, 93-94; dept ch, 86-; prof-. **HONORS AND AWARDS** Pres award for achievement; fac senate pres, 77-78. **SELECTED PUBLICATIONS** Auth, Yvon Delbos at the Quai d'orsay: French Foreign Policy During the Popular Front, 36-38, Univ Press Kans, 73; Myopic Grandeur: The Ambivalence of French Foreign Policy toward the Far East, 1919-1945, Kent State Univ Press, 91; Reappraising the Munich Pact, Woodrow Wilson Ctr, Smithsonian Institute. **CONTACT ADDRESS** Dept of Hist, Wichita State Univ, 1845 Fairmont, Wichita, KS 67260-0062. **EMAIL** dreifort@wsuhub.uc.twsu.edu

DREISBACH, DONALD FRED
PERSONAL Born 06/25/1941, Allentown, PA, d **DISCIPLINE** PHILOSOPHY & HISTORY OF RELIGION **EDUCATION** MA Inst Technol, BS, 63; Northwestern Univ, MA, 69, PhD, 70. **CAREER** Assoc prof, 69- 80, Prof Philos, Northern MI Univ, 80. **MEMBERSHIPS** AAUP; Am Acad Relig; Am Philos Asn; NAm Paul Tillich Soc. **RESEARCH** Philosophical theology; Paul Tillich. **SELECTED PUBLICATIONS** Auth, Paul Tillich's Herrmeneutic, J Am Acad Relig, Vol XLIII, No 1; Paul Tillich's Doctrine of Religious Symbols, Encounter, Vol 37, No 4; On the love of God, Anglican Theol Rev, Vol LIX, No 1; Circularity and consistency in Descartes, Can J Philos, Vol VIII, No 1; Agreement and obligation in the Crito, New Scholasticism, Vol LII, No 2; The unity of Paul Tillich's existential analysis, Encounter, Vol 41, No 4; On the hermeneutic of symbols: The Buri-Hardwick debate, Theologische Zeitschrift, 9-10/79; Essence, existence and the fall: Paul Tillich's analysis of existence, Harvard Theol Rev, Vol 73, No 1-2; Symbols and Salvation, Univ Press Am, 93. **CONTACT ADDRESS** Dept of Philos, No Michigan Univ, 1401 Presque Isle Av, Marquette, MI 49855-5301. **EMAIL** ddreisba@nmu.edu

DRESCHER, SEYMOUR
PERSONAL Born 02/20/1934, New York, NY, m, 1955, 3 children **DISCIPLINE** HISTORY **EDUCATION** CUNY, BA, 55; Univ Wisc, MS, 56; PhD, 60. **CAREER** Instructor, Harvard Univ, 60-62; Asst Prof to Prof, Univ Pittsburgh, 62-. **HONORS AND AWARDS** Fulbright Scholar, 57-58; NEH Sen Fel, 73-74; Guggenheim Fel, 77-78; Woodrow Wilson Fel, 83-84. **MEMBERSHIPS** Am Hist Soc; Hist Soc; Soc for French Hist Studies. **RESEARCH** Modern Europe; Tocqueville; Slavery and Abolition. **SELECTED PUBLICATIONS** Auth, "Servile Insurrection and John Brown's Body in Europe," in His Soul Goes Marching On: Responses to the John Brown Raid, (Charlottesville, 95(, 253-295; co-auth, "Statement on the Jews and the Atlantic Slave Trade," Perspectives (95): 27; auth, "Abolitionism," in The Encyclopedia of Democracy, (congressional Quarterly Books, 96); auth, "The Atlantic Slave Trade and the Holocaust: A comparative Analysis," in Is the Holocaust Unique?: Perspectives on comparative Genocide, (Westview Press, 96), 65-85; auth, "Capitalism and Slavery after Fifty Years," Slavery and Abolitions, (97): 212-227; co-ed, A Historical Guide to World Slavery, Oxford Univ Press, 98; auth, From Slavery to Freedom: comparative Studies in the Rise and Fall of Atlantic Slavery, NYU Press, 99. **CONTACT ADDRESS** Dept Hist, Univ of Pittsburgh, 3P38 Forbes Quad, Pittsburgh, PA 15260. **EMAIL** syd@pitt.edu

DRESSLER, RACHEL
DISCIPLINE ART HISTORY **EDUCATION** Emory Univ, BA, 74; MA, 81; Columbia Univ, PhD, 93. **CAREER** Univ Albany - SUNY **HONORS AND AWARDS** Georges Lurcy Charitable & Educational Trust; Howard Hibbard Fund, 88; Fac Develop Awd, 94; Fac Res Awds Prog, 96. **SELECTED PUBLICATIONS** Auth, Gary Keown at The Atlanta Art Workers' Coalition, Art Papers, 81; Duane Michals at The Atlanta Gallery of Photography, Art Papers, 81; Entries in French Romanesque Sculpture: An Annotated Bibliography, 87; Deus Hoc Vult: Visual Rhetoric at the Time of the Crusades, Medieval Encounters, 95. **CONTACT ADDRESS** SUNY, Albany, 1400 Washington Ave, Albany, NY 12222.

DREW, KATHERINE FISCHER
PERSONAL Born 09/24/1923, Houston, TX, m, 1951 **DISCIPLINE** MEDIEVAL HISTORY **EDUCATION** Rice Inst, AB, 44, AM, 45; Cornell Univ, PhD (hist), 50. **CAREER** Instr Hist, Rice Univ, 46-48; asst, Cornell Univ, 48-50; from asst prof to assoc prof, 50-63, chmn dept, 70-80, Prof Hist, Rice Univ, 63., Guggenheim fel, 59; Fulbright seminarist, 65; ed, Rice Univ Studies, 67-81; Nat Endowment for Humanities fel, 74-75. **MEMBERSHIPS** AHA; Mediaeval Acad Am; Int Comn Hist Rep and Parliamentary Insts; Am Soc Legal Hist. **RESEARCH** Medieval legal history; medieval social and economic history. **SELECTED PUBLICATIONS** Auth, Burgundian Code, Univ Pa, 49, rev ed, 72; Notes on Lombard Institutions, Rice Inst, 56; ed, Immunity in Carolingium Italy, Speculum, 4/62; The Carolingium military frontier in Italy, Traditio, 64; The Italian monasteries of Nonantola, San Salvatore and Santa Maria Teodota in the eighth and ninth centuries, Manuscripta, 65; The Barbarian Invasions, Holt, 70; auth, The Lombard Laws, Univ Pa, 73.; Law of the family in Germanic barbarian kingdoms: A synthesis, Studies in Medieval Cult, Vol XI, 77. **CONTACT ADDRESS** Dept of Hist, Rice Univ, Houston, TX 77001.

DREYER, EDWARD L.
PERSONAL Born 07/26/1940, San Diego, CA, m, 1964, 2 children **DISCIPLINE** HISTORY **EDUCATION** Harvard Univ, BA, 61; MA, 62; PhD, 71. **CAREER** From Asst Prof to Prof, Miami Univ, 70-. **HONORS AND AWARDS** Fulbright Fel, 68-69. **RESEARCH** Chinese history, military history. **SELECTED PUBLICATIONS** Auth, Early Ming China: A Political History, Stanford UP, 82; auth, China at War 1901-1949, Longman Pr, 95. **CONTACT ADDRESS** Dept Hist, Univ of Miami, PO Box 248107, Miami, FL 33124-8107. **EMAIL** edreyer@umiami.ir.miami.edu

DRIEVER, STEVEN L.
PERSONAL Born 04/27/1947, Nyack, NY, d, 1 child **DISCIPLINE** GEOGRAPHY **EDUCATION** Univ Va, BA, 69; Northwestern Univ, MS, 70; Univ Ga, PhD, 77. **CAREER** From Asst Prof to Prof, Univ Mo, 77-. **HONORS AND AWARDS** Phi Kappa Phi; Fulbright Sen Res Fel, 96. **MEMBERSHIPS** Soc for Span & Port Hist Studies, AGA, AAG. **RESEARCH** Historical geography of Spain, literary geography of Spain and Latin America. **SELECTED PUBLICATIONS** Rev, "An Early Encounter with Tomorrow: Europeans, Chicago's Loop and the World's Columbian Exposition," J of Hist Geog, vol 25 (99): 431-432; auth, "Juan Carlos I," in Biog Encycl of 20th-Century World Leaders, vol 1 (Tarrytown, NY: Marshall Cavendish Corp, 00), 792-794; auth, "Allende Salvador," in Biog Encycl, of 20th-Century world Leaders, vol 2 (Tarrytown, NY: Marshall Cavendish Corp, 00), 30-33; auth, "Mallada and Spain's Regenerationist Movement," Iberian Studies (forthcoming); auth, "Lucas Mallada and the Modern View of Spain's Environment, Paper in Proceedings of 1898: Entre la Crisi d'Identitat I la Modernitzacio, Int Cong at Barcelona, 1998 (forthcoming); rev, "Urbanismo europeo de Caracas (1870-1940), by Arturo Almandoz Marte, J of Hist Geog (forthcoming). **CONTACT ADDRESS** Dept Geosciences, Univ of Missouri, Kansas City, 5100 Rockhill Rd, Kansas City, MO 64110. **EMAIL** drievers@umkc.edu

DRINKARD-HAWKSHAWE, DOROTHY
PERSONAL Born 06/22/1938, Greensboro, GA, w, 1963, 1 child **DISCIPLINE** HISTORY **EDUCATION** Howard Univ, BA, 60; MA, 63; Catholic Univ of Am, PhD, 74. **CAREER** Instructor, Va Union Univ, 63-66; Asst prof, Coppin State Col, 66-74; Assoc prof, Bowie State Col, 74-83; Visiting Prof, Howard Univ, 85-88; Assoc Prof to Full Prof and Chair, East Tenn State Univ, 89-. **HONORS AND AWARDS** NEH Summer Faculty Fel, 76, 80; Phelps-Stokes Faculty grant, 79; Woman of the Year Ward, Johnson city, 99. **MEMBERSHIPS** Am Hist Asn, Asn of Univ Prof. **RESEARCH** Civil War and reconstruction; Civil rights; Legal History. **SELECTED PUBLICATIONS** Auth, Illinois Freedom Fighters: A civil War Saga of the 29th Infantry US colored Troops, Simon & Schuster, 98; auth, The Legacy of Reconstruction, 1865-1877, Harcourt Brace pub, 98; auth, Indomitable: A Biography of James Farmer and the civil Rights Movement, forthcoming. **CONTACT ADDRESS** Dept Hist, East Tennessee State Univ, PO Box 10001, Johnson City, TN 37614-0001. **EMAIL** drinkard@access.etsu.edu

DUBE, JEAN-CLAUDE
PERSONAL Born 01/12/1925, Riviere-du-Loup, PQ, Canada **DISCIPLINE** HISTORY **EDUCATION** Univ Ottawa, LPhil, 46, LTheol, 50, MA, 61; Univ Paris, PhD, 66. **CAREER** Fac mem to prof, 61-90, Prof Emer History, Univ Ottawa, 90-; founder & first dir, Ctr de rech en hist relig du Can, St Paul Univ. **HONORS AND AWARDS** Prix litt Que (Hist), 70; fel, Royal Soc Can, 89. **MEMBERSHIPS** Soc d'Hist de France (Paris); Soc archeol de Tours; pres, Soc can d'hist de l'Eglise cath, 95-97. **SELECTED PUBLICATIONS** Auth, Claude-Thomas Dupuy, intendant de la Nouvelle-France, 69; co-ed, Rencontres de l'historiographie francaise avec l'histoire sociale, 78; auth, Les intendants de la Nouvelle-France, 84; auth, Les Bigot du XVIe siecle a la Revolution, 87. **CONTACT ADDRESS** Dept of History, Univ of Ottawa, Ottawa, ON, Canada K1N 6N5.

DUBERMAN, MARTIN
PERSONAL Born 08/06/1930, New York, NY **DISCIPLINE** UNITED STATES HISTORY **EDUCATION** Yale Univ, BA, 52; Harvard Univ, MA, 53, PhD, 57. **CAREER** Teaching fel, Harvard Univ, 55-57; from instr to asst prof Am hist, Yale Univ, 57-62; from asst prof to prof hist, Princeton Univ, 62-72; Distinguished Prof Hist, Lehman/The Graduate Center, CUNY, 72-, founder and dir, The Center for Lesbian and Gay Studies (CLAGS), the CUNY Graduate School; Morse fel, Yale Univ, 61-62; bicentennial preceptor, Princeton Univ, 62-65; Am Coun Learned Soc grant-in-aid, 62; Rockefeller Found grant studies, Black Mountain Col, 67-68; Princeton McCosh fac fel, 68-69; var productions of plays, The Memory Bank, 70-71, Payments, New Dramatists, 71, Inner Limits, Easthampton, 71, Visions of Kerouac, Lion, 76, Back Alley, 76, Odyssey, Los Angeles, 77 & Vancouver, 78: Rockefeller fel in humanities, 76; vis Randolf Distinguished Prof, Vassar, fall 92. **HONORS AND AWARDS** Bancroft Prize, 62; Vernon Rice-Drama Desk Awd, 63; Nat Acad Arts & Lett Special Awd, 71; Finalist for: Nat Book Awd, L.A. Times Book Awd, Robert Kennedy Book Awd, James Ramsey Prize, 93-94 and 97-98 Lambda Book Awds, Am Library Asn Gay and Lesbian Book Awd; Runner-up in Non-fiction for the Am Library Asn Best Gay Book of the Year; Best Twenty-Five Books of the Year, The Village Voice; Best Seven Books of the Year, The Boston Globe; Winner: Manhattan Borough President's Gold Medal in Literature (88), The George Freedley Memorial Awd from the New York Public Library for best book of the year, two Lambda Book Awds, Gustavus Myer Awd for best books of the year, Gustavus Myers Center Awd for an outstanding work on intolerance in North America (94); Public Service Awd from LeGal (Asn Gay and Lesbian Lawyers), 95; Distinguished Service Awd from the Asn of Gay and Lesbian Psychiatrists, 96; Public Service Awd from GAYLA (Gay and Lesbian Analyists), 98; Guest of Honor, Harvard Gay and Lesbian Rev annual banguet, 98; Annual Awd from the Asn of Men's Studies, 98. **MEMBERSHIPS** AHA; Orgn Am Historians; ACLU. **RESEARCH** American intellectual history; United States history, 1820-1877; history of sex roles and sexual behavior in America. **SELECTED PUBLICATIONS** Auth, Charles Francis Adams, 1807-1886, Houghton Mifflin, 60; In White America, Houghton, 64; ed, The Anti-slavery Vanguard, Princeton Univ, 65; auth, James Russell Lowell, Houghton Mifflin, 66; The Uncompleted Past, Random House, 69; The Memory Bank, Dial, 70; Black Mountain: An Exploration in Community, Dutton, 72; Male Armor: Selected Plays, 1968-1974, Dutton, 75; Visions of Kerouac, Little, Brown, 77; About Time: Exploring the Gay Past, Gay Presses of NY, 86, rev and enlarged 2nd ed, NAL, 91; co-ed, Hidden from History: Reclaiming the Gay and Lesbian Past, New Am Lib, 89; auth, Paul Robeson, Knopf, 89; Cures: A Gay Man's Odyssey, Dutton/NAL, 91; Mother Earth: An Epic Play on the Life of Emma Goldman, St Martins, 91; Stonewall, Dutton, 93; co-ed and intro, The CLAGS Directory of Scholars in Gay and Lesbian Studies, 94-95; gen ed, Lives of Notable Gay Men and Lesbians and Issues in Gay and Lesbian Life, Chelsea House (14 books to date); Midlife Queer, Scribner, 96, Univ WI Press (paper), 98; ed, A Queer World: The Center for Lesbian and Gay Studies Reader, NYU Press, 97; ed, Queer Representations: Reading Lives, Reading Cultures, NYU Press, 97; assoc ed, J of the Hist of Sexuality, 93-; assoc ed, Masculinities: Interdisciplinary Studies on Gender, 93-; auth, Left Out: The Politics of Exclusion, Basic Books, 99; many articles and reviews. **CONTACT ADDRESS** Dept of Hist, Lehman Col, CUNY, 250 Bedford Park W, Bronx, NY 10468-1527.

DUBLIN, THOMAS
PERSONAL Born 12/01/1946, Norwalk, CT, m, 1988, 2 children **DISCIPLINE** HISTORY **EDUCATION** Harvard, BA, 68; Columbia, MA, 71, PhD, 75. **CAREER** Vis asst prof, Wellesley Col, 75-76; asst to assoc prof, Univ Calif, San Diego, 76-88; prof, State Univ of New York, Binghamton, 88-. **HONORS AND AWARDS** Summa cum laude in Chemistry, Harvard; Phi Beta Kappa; Bancroft Diss Awd, Columbia Univ, 75; Bancroft Prize for Women at Work, 80; Merle Curti Awd, Women at Work, 80. **MEMBERSHIPS** Soc Am Hists. **RESEARCH** U. S. women's history, labor history, ethnic history. **SELECTED PUBLICATIONS** Auth, Women at Work: The Transformation of Work and Community in Lowell, Massachusetts, 1826-1860, Columbia Univ Press (79, 2nd ed, 94): auth, Farm to Factory: Women's Letters, 1830-1860, Columbia Univ Press (81, 2nd ed, 93); coed with Kathryn Kish Sklar, Women and Power in American History: A Reader, 2 vols, Prentice-Hall (91); auth, Immigrant Voices: New Lives in America, 1773-1986, Univ Ill Press (93); auth, Transforming Women's Work: New England Lives in the Industrial Revolution, Cornell Univ Press (94, paperback 95); auth, Becoming American, Becoming Ethnic: College Students Explore Their Roots, Temple Univ Press (96); auth, When the Mines Closed: Stories of Struggles in Hard Times, Cornell Univ Press (98). **CONTACT ADDRESS** Dept Hist, SUNY, Binghamton, PO Box 6000, Binghamton, NY 13902-6000. **EMAIL** tdublin@binghamton.edu

DUBOFSKY, MELVYN
PERSONAL Born 10/25/1934, Brooklyn, NY, w, 1959, 2 children **DISCIPLINE** HISTORY **EDUCATION** Brooklyn College, BA, 55; Univ of Rochester, PhD, 60. **CAREER** Asst to Assoc Prof, Northern Illinois Univ, 59-67; Assoc Prof, Univ of Massachusetts-Amherst, 67-69; Assoc Prof, Univ of Wisconsin-Milwaukee, 69-71; Distinguished Prof of History and Sociology, Binghamton Univ-SUNY, 71. **HONORS AND AWARDS** NEH Senior and Summer Fellowships; ACLS and APS Awds; John Adams Prof of American History; Univ of Amsterdam, 00; Fulbright Distinguished Prof, Univ of Salzburg, Austria, 88-89 BA, Magna Cum Laude; Phi Beta Kappa. **MEMBERSHIPS** AHA, OAH, LAWCHA, NYSTATE, Labor. **RESEARCH** Labor and social history, 20th century. **SELECTED PUBLICATIONS** Auth, When Workers Organize: New York City in the Progressive Era, 67; auth, We Shall Be All: A History of the IWW; 69; Industrialism and the American Worker, 75, 85, 96; auth, John L. Lewis: A Biography, (with Warren Van Tine), 77; auth, ed, Labor Leaders in America, (with Warren Van Tine), 85; auth, The State and Labor in Modern America, 94; auth, Hard Work: The Making of Labor History, 00. **CONTACT ADDRESS** Dept History, SUNY, Binghamton, PO Box 6000, Binghamton, NY 13902-6000. **EMAIL** dubof@binghamton.edu

DUBOIS, ELLEN CAROL
PERSONAL Born 03/11/1947, Baltimore, MD, s **DISCIPLINE** HISTORY **EDUCATION** Wellesley Col, BA, 68; Northwestern Univ, PhD, 75. **CAREER** Asst prof to prof, SUNY Buffalo, 72-88; prof, UCLA, 88-. **HONORS AND AWARDS** Guggenheim Found Fel, 99-00; Joan Kelly Prize, Am Hist Asn, 98; Migunyah distinguished Fel, Univ Melbourne, 98. **MEMBERSHIPS** Org of Am Hist; Am Hist Asn. **RESEARCH** History of women in the United States; History of feminism; History of woman suffrage movements in the United States and around the world. **SELECTED PUBLICATIONS** Ed, Elizabeth Cady Stanton, Susan B. Anthony: A Reader, Northeastern Univ Press, 92; auth, Harriot Stanton Blatch and the Winning of Woman Suffrage, Yale Univ Press, 97; auth, Woman Suffrage and Women's Rights, NY Univ

Press, 98; co-ed, Unequal Sisters: A Multicultural Reader in U.S. Women's History, Routledge, 00; auth, Feminism and Suffrage: The Emergence of an Independent Women's Movement in America, Cornell Univ Press. **CONTACT ADDRESS** Dept Hist, Univ of California, Los Angeles, 6265 Bunche, Box 951473, Los Angeles, CA 90095-1473. **EMAIL** edubois@ucla.edu

DUCKER, JAMES H.
PERSONAL Born 07/24/1950, Rochester, NY **DISCIPLINE** AMERICAN HISTORY **EDUCATION** Villanova Univ, BA, 72; Univ Ill, AM, 74, PhD (hist), 80. **CAREER** Historian, Bureau of Land Management, 81-. **MEMBERSHIPS** Orgn Am Historians. **RESEARCH** American social and Western history; Alaska History. **SELECTED PUBLICATIONS** Auth, Kusiq--An Eskimo Life from the Arctic Coast of Alaska, J West, Vol 32, 93; Inuit--Glimpses of an Arctic Past, A Indian Cult Rsrc J, Vol 21, 97; Gold Rushers North--A Census Study of the Yukon and Alaskan Gold Rushes, 1896-1900, Pac Northwest Quart, Vol 85, 94; Arctic School Teacher--Kulukak, Alaska, 1931-1933, J West, Vol 34, 95; A Hogheads Random Railroad Reminiscences, Pac Northwest Quart, Vol 88, 97; Pioneering on the Yukon 1892-1917, J West, Vol 34, 95; Out of Harms Way--Relocating Northwest Alaska Eskimos, 1907-1917, Am Indian Cult Rsrc J, Vol 20, 96; Tourism in Katmai Country--A History of Concessions Activity in Katmai National Park and Preserve, Public Historian, Vol 17, 95; Gold at Fortymile Creek--Early Days in the Yukon, J West, Vol 35, 96; Chilkoot Trail--Heritage Route to the Klondike, Public Historian, Vol 19, 97; Aleutian Echoes, J West, Vol 36, 97. **CONTACT ADDRESS** 1611 Early View Dr, Anchorage, AK 99504.

DUCLOW, DONALD F.
PERSONAL Born 01/11/1946, Chicago, IL, m, 1970 **DISCIPLINE** ENGLISH, PHILSOSOPHY, MEDIEVAL STUDIES **EDUCATION** DePaul Univ, BA, English, philosophy, 68, MA, philosophy, 69; Bryn Mawr Coll, MA, medieval studies, 72, PhD, philosophy, 74, Divinity School, Unv. Of Chicago, 98. **CAREER** Visiting prof, philosophy, Fordham Univ, 78; asst prof of philosophy, 74-79, assoc prof of philosophy, 79-89, prof of philosophy, 89-, Gwynedd-Mercy Coll. **HONORS AND AWARDS** Mellon Fellow in the Humanities, Univ Pa, 80-81; NEH summer seminars, 87, 93; Senior Fellow, Institute for the Advanced Study of Religion, Divinity School, University of Chicago, Spring, 98; Inst for the Advan Study of Relig Sen Fel. **MEMBERSHIPS** Amer Acad Religion; Medieval Acad Am; sec, Amer Cusanus Soc; Amer Assn Univ Profs; pres, Gwynedd-Mercy Coll Chap, 96-97; Exec Committee, Pennsylvania AAUP, 00. **RESEARCH** Medieval philosophy and religion. **SELECTED PUBLICATIONS** Auth, "Divine Nothingness and Self-Creation in John Scotus Eriugena," The Journ of Religion, vol 57, 77; "'My Suffering Is God': Meister Eckhart's Book of Divine Consolation," Theological Studies, vol 44, 83, reprinted in Classical and Medieval Literature Criticism, 93; "Into the Whirlwind of Suffering: Resistance and Transformation," Second Opinion, Nov 88; "Nicholas of Cusa," in Medieval Philosophers, vol 15, Dictionary of Literary Biography, 92; "Isaiah Meets the Seraph: Breaking Ranks in Dionysius and Eriugena?" in Eriugena: East and West, 94. **CONTACT ADDRESS** Gwynedd-Mercy Col, Gwynedd Valley, PA 19437-0901. **EMAIL** duclow.d@gmc.edu

DUDDEN, ARTHUR POWER
PERSONAL Born 10/26/1921, Cleveland, OH, m, 1965, 3 children **DISCIPLINE** HISTORY **EDUCATION** Wayne Univ, AB, 42; Univ Mich, AM, 47, PhD(hist), 50. **CAREER** From asst prof to prof emer hist, Bryn Mawr Col, 50-; chm dept, Bryn Mawr Col, 68-78, 81-86. **HONORS AND AWARDS** Sr Fulbright res scholar, Denmark, 59-60 lectr, 92; mem screening comt, Inst Int Educ, Scandinavia, 61, 62; dist lectr, US Dept State, 63; pres, Fulbright Alumni Asn, 77-80, executive dir, 80-84; Penn Commonwealth Speaker, 91, 95; Bode-Pearson Prize, Am Studies Asn, 91; Bd Dir, Hist Soc Penn, 93-99 ; consult, Nat Archives, 93-. **MEMBERSHIPS** AHA; Orgn Am Historians; Am Studies Asn (treas, 68-69 & 72, exec secy, 69-72). **RESEARCH** American history, biography and humor; international relations. **SELECTED PUBLICATIONS** Ed, Woodrow Wilson and World of Today, Univ Pa, 57; The Assault of Laughter: A Treasury of American Political Humor, Barnes, 62; The United States of America: A Syllabus of American Studies (2 vols), Univ Pa, 63; Joseph Fels and the Singletax Movement, Temple Univ, 71; Pardon Us, Mr President!, a Treasury of American Political Humor, Barnes, 75; co-ed, The Fulbright Experience, 1946-1986, Rutgers, 87; ed, American Humor, Oxford, 87; auth, The American Pacific from the Old China Trade to the Present, Oxford, 92; ed, The Logbook of the Captain's Clerk: Adventures in the China Seas, Donnelley, 95. **CONTACT ADDRESS** Dept of History, Bryn Mawr Col, Bryn Mawr, PA 19010. **EMAIL** 76511.3300@compuserve.com

DUDDEN, FAYE E.
PERSONAL Born 06/03/1948, m, 1976 **DISCIPLINE** HISTORY **EDUCATION** Cornell Univ, AB, 70; Rochester, PhD, 81. **CAREER** Asst prof, hist, Union Coll; current, PROF, HIST, COLGATE UNIV **HONORS AND AWARDS** George Freedley Mem Awd **MEMBERSHIPS** Am Antiquarian Soc, Berkshire Conference of Women Historians, Org of Am Historian, Am Historical Asn. **RESEARCH** Women in theater, 1790-1870. **SELECTED PUBLICATIONS** Auth, Serving Women: Household Service in Nineteenth-Century America, 83; auth, "Experts and Servants, " Jour of Soc Hist, 86; "Small Town Knights," Labor Hist, 87; Women in the American Theater: Actresses and Audiences, 1790-1870, Yale Univ PRess, 94. **CONTACT ADDRESS** Dept of Hist, Colgate Univ, Hamilton, NY 13346. **EMAIL** fdudden@mail.colgate.edu

DUDLEY, WILLIAM SHELDON
PERSONAL Born 07/14/1936, Brooklyn, NY, m, 1965, 2 children **DISCIPLINE** AMERICAN & LATIN-AMERICAN HISTORY **EDUCATION** Williams Col, BA, 58; Columbia Univ, MA, 66, PhD (hist), 72. **CAREER** Asst prof Latin Am hist, Southern Methodist Univ, 70-77; asst head res br, 77-81, Head Res Br, Naval Hist Ctr, Washington Navy Yard, 82-90; Sr Hist, 90-95; Dir of Novel History, 95-. **HONORS AND AWARDS** Thomas Jefferson Prize by Soc for Histin the Federal Government, 93; Sr Executive Service, 95. **MEMBERSHIPS** Orgn Am Historians, Conf Latin Am Hist, North Am Soc Oceanic Hist, Soc Hist Federal Govt (treas), Am Military Inst, NASOH. **RESEARCH** Latin Am Hist-Brazil, Civil Military Relations. **SELECTED PUBLICATIONS** Ed, The Naval War of 1812: A Documentary History, Naval Historical Center, Washington, DC, Vol I, 85, Vol II 92; auth, To Shining Sea--A History of the United States Navy, 1775-1991, Intl Hist Rev, Vol 15, 1993; auth, "The War of 1812" in Encyclopedia of the American Military, Vol I, McGraw-Hill, 94. **CONTACT ADDRESS** Naval Historical Ctr, 805 Kidder Breese St SE, Washington, DC 20374. **EMAIL** wsdudley@earthlink.net

DUDZIAK, MARY L.
PERSONAL Born 06/15/1956, Oakland, CA, d, 1 child **DISCIPLINE** LAW, LEGAL HISTORY **EDUCATION** Univ Calif, Berkeley, AB, 78; Yale, JD, 84, MA, 86, MPhil, 86, PhD, 92. **CAREER** Assoc prof, Univ Iowa, 86-90, prof, 90-98; vis prof, Univ Southern Calif, 97-98, prof, 98-. **HONORS AND AWARDS** Charlotte W. Newcombe Fel/Woodrow Wilson Fel, 86-89; Scholars Development Awd, Nancy S. Truman Library Inst, 92; travel grant, Eisenhower World Affairs Inst, 93; Theodore C. Sorenson Fel, Kennedy Library Found, 97; Moody grant, Johnson Library, 98; OAH-JAAS Fel for Short-term travel to Japan, 2000. **MEMBERSHIPS** Org of Am Hists, Am Studies Asn, Am Hist Asn, Am Soc for Legal Hist, Law & Soc Asn, Soc for Hists of Am Foreign Relations, Soc Sci Hist Asn. **RESEARCH** Impact of foreign affairs on U.S. civil rights policy during the cold war; role of U.S. Constitutionalism overseas during the 20th century. **SELECTED PUBLICATIONS** Auth, Cold War Civil Rights: Race and the Image of American Democracy, Princeton Univ Press (forthcoming 2000); articles in J of Am Hist, Stanford Law Rev, Southern Calif Law Rev, etc. **CONTACT ADDRESS** Sch of Law, Univ of So California, 699 Exposition Blvd, Los Angeles, CA 90089-0040.

DUFFIN, JACALYN
PERSONAL Born London, ON, Canada **DISCIPLINE** HISTORY OF MEDICINE **EDUCATION** Univ Toronto, MD, 74; Univ Sorbonne, DEA, 83; PhD, 85. **CAREER** Gen practice locum tenens, Come-by-Chance, NF, 77; haematology/oncology, Ont Cancer Treatment & Res Found, Thunder Bay, 80-82; Hannah Postdoc Fel Hist Med, Univ Ottawa, 85-88; consult haematologist, Kingston Gen Hospital, 88-94; Hannah Prof Hist Medicine, Queen's Univ, 88-. **HONORS AND AWARDS** W.F.Connell Awd Tchg Exellence, Queen's Univ, Fac Med, 92. **MEMBERSHIPS** Am Asn Hist Med; Can Fedn Hum; Can Soc Hist Med; Hist Sci Soc. **RESEARCH** Medical epistemology, nineteenth-century French and Canadian medicine, medical illustrations, and medical saints. **SELECTED PUBLICATIONS** Auth, In View of the Body of Job Broom: A Glimpse of the Medical Knowledge and Practice of John Rolph, in Can Bull of Med Hist, 90; auth, The Death of Sara Lovell and the Constrained Feminism of Emily Stowe, in Can Med Asn J, 92; auth, Langstaff: A Nineteenth-Century Medical Life, 93; auth, To See With a Better Eye: A Life of R.T.H. Laennec, Princeton U Press, 98. **CONTACT ADDRESS** Dept of Hist, Queen's Univ at Kingston, 99 University Ave, Kingston, ON, Canada K7L 3N6. **EMAIL** duffinj@post.queensu.ca

DUFFY, JOHN JOSEPH
PERSONAL Born 04/25/1931, Charleston, SC, m, 1959, 3 children **DISCIPLINE** UNITED STATES HISTORY **EDUCATION** Col Charleston, BS, 52; Univ SC, MA, 55, PhD (hist), 63. **CAREER** Resident dir, Beaufort Regional Campus, 59-66, acad coordr Col Gen Studies, 66-67, assoc provost, Regional Campuses, 67-72, assoc prof hist and assoc vprovost, 72-77, VPres Two Year Campuses and Continuing Educ, Univ SC, 77-. **MEMBERSHIPS** Southern Hist Asn. **RESEARCH** Oral history; South Carolina politics; contemporary United States. **SELECTED PUBLICATIONS** Auth, Charleston at the turn of the century, St Andrews Quart, fall 72; A Short History of Beaufort County, 75; Charleston, Dict Southern Hist, 79. **CONTACT ADDRESS** Univ of So Carolina, Columbia, 1626 College St, Columbia, SC 29208.

DUFOUR, RON
PERSONAL Born 10/22/1947, Lawrence, MA, m, 1973, 1 child **DISCIPLINE** COLONIAL AND REVOLUTIONARY AMERICA **EDUCATION** Merrimack Col, BA; Col William and Mary, MA, PhD. **CAREER** Prof, ch dept Hist, RI Col. **RESEARCH** Early Am, esp. soc, intellectual, cult; 20th century Am music and cult, esp. jazz, blues, rock. **SELECTED PUBLICATIONS** Auth, Modernization in Colonial Massachussetts; Colonial America **CONTACT ADDRESS** Rhode Island Col, Providence, RI 02908. **EMAIL** rdufour@ric.edu

DUGGAN, LAWRENCE GERALD
PERSONAL Born 02/18/1944, Hartford, CT, m, 1977, 2 children **DISCIPLINE** RENAISSANCE AND REFORMATION HISTORY **EDUCATION** Col of the Holy Cross, AB, 65; Harvard Univ, AM, 66, Harvard Univ, PhD (hist), 71. **CAREER** Asst prof, 70-77, Lecture on Sixteenth-Century Paleography, Inst of the Ctr for Reformation Research, 76, Assoc Prof Hist, Univ Del, 77-90, Alexander von Humboldt Found fel, 76-77; Visiting Member, School of Hist Studies, Inst for Advanced Study, Princeton, 87-88; Visiting Prof of Hist, Columbia Univ, 90. **MEMBERSHIPS** Cath Hist Asn; Int Comn Study Rep and Parliamentary Inst; Past and Present Soc; Woodrow Wilson, Danforth, German Academic Exchange Service, and Harvard Sheldon Travelling fellowships, 65-70; Univ of Delaware General Univ Research Fund grants, 80, 87; German Academic Exchange Service grants, 71, 74; Alexander von Humboldt Stiftung Fellow, 76-77, 80, 83, 87, 92, 97; Am Philosophical Society grant, 83; Stipendiary Member, School of Historical Studies, Inst for Advanced Study, Princeton, 87-88; Harry Frank Guggenheim Foundation grant, 88; Member, Center for Advanced Study, Univ of Delaware, 91-92; Excellence in Undergraduate Advising Award, Univ of Delaware, 99. **RESEARCH** Ecclesiastical and Germany history; representative institutions. **SELECTED PUBLICATIONS** Auth, "The Church as an Institution of th Reich," in James A. Vann and Steven W. Rowan, eds, The Old Reich. Essays on German Political Institutions 1495-1806, Brussels (74): 149-64; auth, "The Unresponsiveness of the Late Medieval Church: A Reconsideration," The Sixteenth Century Journal 9/1 (78): 3-26; auth, Bishop and Chapter. The Governance of th Bishopric of Speyer to 1552. Studies Presented to the International Commission for the History of Representative and Parliamentary Institutions, 62, New Brunswick: Rutgers Univ Press, 78; auth, "Melchoir von Meckau: A Missing Link in the Eck ZinsDisputes of 1514-1516? Archiv Fur Reformationsgeschichte 74 (83): 25-37; auth, "Fear and Confession on the Eve of the Reformation," Archiv fur Reformatinsgeschichte 75 (84): 153-75; auth, "Representative Assemblies, German, " in The Dictionary of the Middle Ages, 10 New York (88): 328-34; auth, "Zur Bedeutung des spatmittelalterlichen Kreditsystmes fur die fruhneuzeitliche deutsche Geschicht," in Georg Schmidt, ed., Stande ud Gesellschaft im alten Reich, Veroffentlichungen des Instituts fur europaische Geschichte Mainz, Abteilung Universalgeschichte 29 Stuttgart (89): 201-209; auth, Contributions to the History and Structure of the Medieval Germania Sacra - German - Crusius,I, Editor/, Speculum-A J Medieval Studies, Vol 68, 93; The German Episcopacy and the Implementation of the Decrees of the 4th Lateran Council, 1216-1245--Watchmen on the Tower, Am Hist Rev, Vol 101, 96; Noble Bondsmen--Ministerial Marriages in the Archdiocese of Salzburg,, Cath Hist Rev, Vol 82, 96; Pflug, Julius 1499-1564 and the Religious Crisis in Germany During the 16th Century--An Attempt at Biographical and Theological Synthesis, Cath Hist Rev, Vol 80, 94; The Way to the Reichstag--Studies on Changes in the Nature of Centralized Power in Germany, 1314-1410, Am Hist Rev, Vol 99, 94; Contributions to the History and Structure of the Medieval Germania Sacra, Speculum J Medieval Stud, Vol 68, 93; auth, Arma Clerumque Cano. The Clergy and Armsbearing in the History of Western Civilization (to be published by Princeton Univ Press in 00 or 01). **CONTACT ADDRESS** Dept of Hist, Univ of Delaware, 213 Sypherd Dr, Newark, DE 19711-3626. **EMAIL** lgjd@udel.edu

DUKES, JACK RICHARD
PERSONAL Born 01/21/1941, Indianapolis, IN, m, 1963, 1 child **DISCIPLINE** MODERN EUROPEAN HISTORY **EDUCATION** Beloit Col, AB, 63; Northern Ill Univ, MA, 65; Univ Ill, Urbana, PhD, 70. **CAREER** Asst prof, Macalester Col, 69-70; asst prof, 70-75, dir, Russ & E Europ Studies Prog, 72-74, Assoc Prof, 75-83, prof mod europ hist, Carroll Col, 83-, Chmn Dept, 72-96; Fel, Univ Ill, 68-69; Nat Endowment for Humanities fel in residence Ger hist, Univ Calif, Santa Barbara, 77-78; vis assoc prof Russ hist, Univ Calif, Santa Barbara, 80-81; Pres, Exec Dir-Waukesha Sister City Asn, 88; Exec Dir, 89-99. **HONORS AND AWARDS** NEH Fellow Ger Hist, SUNY Albany, 74; NEH Fellow Russian Hist, Univ IL, 77-; US Dept State Fellow, 77; Reader's Digest Humanitarian Awd, 90; Benjamin F. Richardson Awd for Excellence in Teaching, Res and Educ Innovation, Carroll Col; NEH Fel Russ Hist, St. Petersburg, USSR, 91; Distinguished Alumni Awd, Beloit Col, 93; Honorary Citizenship, Kokshetan, Kazakstan, 95; Eurasia Found grants for promoting international education, 95-96, 96-97; Carroll Col Community Service Awd, 98. **MEMBERSHIPS** AHA; Conf Group Cent Europ Hist; Coun Europ Studies; Western Asn Ger Studies; Waukesha Area Sister Asn; Am Asn Advan Slavic Studies. **RESEARCH** Armaments policy; German history; Russian history. **SELECTED PUBLICATIONS** Coauth, Another Germany, Westview Press, 88; author of numerous articles. **CONTACT ADDRESS** Dept of Hist, Carroll Col, Wisconsin, 100 N East Ave, Waukesha, WI 53186-5593. **EMAIL** jdukes@cc.edu

DULAI, SURJIT SINGH
PERSONAL Born 11/06/1930, Danubyu, Burma, m, 1965, 2 children **DISCIPLINE** COMPARATIVE LITERATURE, SOUTH ASIAN STUDIES **EDUCATION** Panjab Univ, BA, 50, MA, 54; Mich State Univ, PhD, 65. **CAREER** Lectr English, Urdu, Panjab Univ, 54-59; headmaster, G N High Sch, Partab, Pura, 59-60; asst English & comp lit, Mich State Univ, 62-67, fel, 64-65; asst prof English, Long Island Univ, 65-66; asst prof humanities, 66-70, assoc prof humanities & Asian studies, 70-74, prof English, 74-, Mich State Univ; co-ed, J SAsian Lit, 69-. **HONORS AND AWARDS** Fulbright-Hays fel, Off Health, Educ, Welfare, 70-71; Rockefeller Found award, 76; Mich State Univ Excellence in Diversity Award, 95. **MEMBERSHIPS** Asn Asian Studies; Can Asn SAsian Studies; MLA; Popular Cult Asn; Asn Gen & Lib Studies. **RESEARCH** Interdisciplinary humanities; Indian & comparative literature; Anglo-Indian literature. **SELECTED PUBLICATIONS** Co-ed, Punjab in Perspective, 91; coauth, Contemporary Poets, St James Press, 95; co-ed, World Literature and Thought, 4 v, 00. **CONTACT ADDRESS** Dept of English, Michigan State Univ, 201 Morrill Hall, East Lansing, MI 48824-1036. **EMAIL** dulai@pilot.msu.edu

DULEY, MARGOT I.
DISCIPLINE HISTORY **EDUCATION** Memorial Univ of Newfoundland, B.A.; Duke Univ, M.A.; Univ London, PhD. **CAREER** Assoc dir, Honors Prog, Univ of Mich; Assoc prof of hist and dir, Women's studies, Denison Univ; Assoc prof of hist and dir univ honors prog, Univ of Toledo; prof and former head, hist and philos dept, Eastern Mich Univ. **HONORS AND AWARDS** Rothermere Fel, Univ of London; Canada Coun Doctoral Fel. **RESEARCH** South Asia; International feminist movements; Newfoundland history. **SELECTED PUBLICATIONS** Auth, Where Once Our Mothers Stood We Stand; co-ed, The Cross-Cultural Study of Women. **CONTACT ADDRESS** Dept of Hist and Philos, Eastern Michigan Univ, 701 Pray-Harrold, Ypsilanti, MI 48197. **EMAIL** his_duley@online.emich.edu

DULLES, JOHN W. F.
PERSONAL Born 05/20/1913, Auburn, NY, m, 1940, 4 children **DISCIPLINE** AMERICAN STUDIES **EDUCATION** Princeton Univ, AB, 35; Harvard Univ, MBA, 37; Univ Ariz, BS, 43; MS, 51; Harvard Bus Sch, PhD, 52. **CAREER** Adj prof, Univ Ariz, 66-91; prof, Univ Tex, 62-. **HONORS AND AWARDS** 75th Anniversary Medallion of Merit, Univ Ariz, 60; Brazilian Govt Alliance for Progress Medal, 66; Theta Tau Alumni Hall of Fame, Phi Kappa Phi; Tau Beta Pi; Pi Mu Epsilon; Phi Lambda Epsilon; Fel, Calif Inst of Int Studies; Who's Who in Am; Who's Who in the World; Mellon Found Grant, Denver Grad Sch. **MEMBERSHIPS** Am Soc of the Most Venerable Order of St John of Jerusalem, Tex Inst of Letters, AHA, Calif Inst of Int Studies. **RESEARCH** Twentieth-Century Brazilian politics. **SELECTED PUBLICATIONS** Auth, Yesterday in Mexico; auth, Vargas in Mexico; auth, Unrest in Brazil; auth, Anarchists and Communists in Brazil; auth, Castello Branco: The Making of a Brazilian President; auth, President Castello Branco; auth, Brazilian Communism; auth, The Sao Paulo Law School; auth, Carlos Lacerda, Brazilian Crusader: vol 1, 1914-1960; auth, Carlos Lacerda, Brazilian Crusader: vol 2, 1960-1977. **CONTACT ADDRESS** Dept Am Studies, Univ of Texas, Austin, Box 7934, Univ Station, Austin, TX 78712-1013. **EMAIL** dulles@mail.utexas.edu

DUMOND, D. E.
PERSONAL Born 03/23/1929, Childress, TX, m, 1950 **DISCIPLINE** ANTHROPOLOGY, ARCHAEOLOGY **EDUCATION** Univ New Mexico, BA, 49; Mexico City College, MA, 57; Univ Oregon, PhD, 62. **CAREER** Asst Prof, Assoc Prof, Prof, 62-94, Univ Oregon; Dir 77-96, OR State Museum of Anthropology; Dir 82-96, U of OR Museum Nat Hist; Prof Emeritus of Anthropology. **HONORS AND AWARDS** SSRC Fel; NEH Fel; Japan Soc Promo Sci Fel; SI Fel; Arctic Inst NA Elec Fel; AAAS Elec Fel; AAA Career Achv Awd. **MEMBERSHIPS** AAA; SAA; AAA. **RESEARCH** Archaeology and Ethnohistory of the American Arctic; Archaeology and Ethnohistory of Mexico. **SELECTED PUBLICATIONS** Auth, The Machete and the Cross: Campesino Rebellion in Yucatan, Lincoln, Univ of NE Press, 97; Poison in the Cup: The South Alaskan Smallpox Epidemic of 1835, in: Chin Hills to Chiloquin: Papers Honoring the Versatile Career of Theodore Stern, edited, Univ of Oregon Anthro Papers, 96; Holocene Prehistory of the Northernmost North Pacific, J World Prehistory, 95; co auth, Paugvik: A Nineteenth Century Native Village on Bristol Bay Southwestern Alaska, Fieldiana Anthro, Field Museum of Natural History, Chicago, 95; auth, Western Arctic Culture, a section in the article, The Arctic, Encyc Britannica, Macropaedia, 93; co auth, Holocene Prehistory of the Northernmost North Pacific. **CONTACT ADDRESS** Dept of Anthropology, Univ of Oregon, Eugene, OR 97403-1218. **EMAIL** ddumond@oregon.uoregon.edu

DUMONT, MICHELINE
PERSONAL Born 07/02/1935, Verdun, PQ, Canada **DISCIPLINE** HISTORY **EDUCATION** Univ Montreal, BA, 57, LL, 59; Univ Laval, DES, 64. **CAREER** Tchr, Inst Cardinal-Leger (Montreal), 59-68; Prof History, Univ Sherbrooke, 70-. **HONORS AND AWARDS** L'Academie I de la Soc Royale Can, 93. **MEMBERSHIPS** Institut d'histoire d'Amerique Francaise (pres, 95-97); Can Hist Asn (Coun 89-92); Soc des professeurs d'histoire du Quebec (vice-pres, 75-77). **SELECTED PUBLICATIONS** Auth, L'histoire apprivoisee, 79; coauth, Histoire des femmes au Quebec depuis quatre siecles, 82, 2nd ed 92 (Eng transl, Quebec Women: A History, 87); coauth, Les couventines, 86; coauth, Les Religieuses sont-elles feministes?, 95. **CONTACT ADDRESS** Dep d'histoire, Univ of Sherbrooke, Ste. Foy, QC, Canada J1K 2R1.

DUNAR, ANDREW J.
PERSONAL Born 01/25/1946, Milwaukee, WI, m, 1968, 3 children **DISCIPLINE** HISTORY **EDUCATION** Northwestern Univ, BA, 68; Univ Calif, Los Angeles, MA, 74; Univ S Calif, PhD, 81. **CAREER** Asst prof, Manchester Col, 81-83; vis asst prof, Union Col, 83-84; from asst prof to prof, Univ Ala, Huntsville, 84-94. **MEMBERSHIPS** OAH, AHA, Oral Hist Asn. **RESEARCH** Harry S. Truman, aerospace hist, 20th cent US society. **SELECTED PUBLICATIONS** Auth, The Truman Scnadals and the Politics of Morality, Univ Mo Press, 84, paperback, 97; co-auth, Building Hoover Dam: An Oral History of the Great Depression, Twayne Pubs, 93; co-auth, Power to Explore: The History of Marshall Space Flight Center, 1960-1990, NASA, 99; ed, Oral Hist Review, 99. **CONTACT ADDRESS** Dept of History, Univ of Alabama, Huntsville, Huntsville, AL 35899. **EMAIL** dunara@email.uah.edu

DUNCAN, CAROL G.
PERSONAL Born 11/10/1936, Chicago, IL, m, 1998 **DISCIPLINE** ART HISTORY **EDUCATION** Univ Chicago, BA, 58, AM, 60; Columbia Univ, PhD, 68. **CAREER** Vis appointments, Univ Calif, Los Angeles, 74, Univ Calif, San Diego, 76, Univ Queensland, 85; vis Eminent Appelton Scholar, Fla State Univ, 99; vis Mellon Prof, Univ Pittsburg; 72-, Ramapo Col, NJ. **HONORS AND AWARDS** ACLS; NJers Coun of the Arts Book Awd. **MEMBERSHIPS** CAA; AHA. **RESEARCH** 19th & 20th century art; art museums. **SELECTED PUBLICATIONS** Auth, The Aesthetics of Power, Cambridge Univ Pr, 93; auth, Civilizing Rituals, Routledge, 95. **CONTACT ADDRESS** 400 Central Park W, New York, NY 10025.

DUNCAN, RICHARD R.
PERSONAL Born 08/30/1931, Cincinnati, OH, s **DISCIPLINE** HISTORY **EDUCATION** Ohio Univ, AB, 54, MA, 55; Ohio State Univ, PhD, 63. **CAREER** Instr, Kent State Univ, 61-64; asst prof, Univ Richmond, 64- 67; asst prof, 67-70, ed, Maryland Historical Magazine, 67-74; assoc prof, 70-98, PROF, prof emer, GEORGETOWN UNIV, 00-. **RESEARCH** Civil War History. **SELECTED PUBLICATIONS** Auth, Theses and Dissertations on Virginia History: A Bibliography, 86; auth, Alexander Neil and the Last Valley Campaign, 96; auth, Lee's Extended Left Flank: The War in Western Virginia, Spring of 1864, 98; auth, "Maryland: A History, "Catholics in the Old South," "Battles Lost and Won: Essays from Civil War History. **CONTACT ADDRESS** 6101Edsall Rd., Apt. 1802, Alexandria, VA 22304.

DUNCAN, RUSSELL
DISCIPLINE HISTORY **EDUCATION** Geor South Univ, BS, 73; Valdosta State Univ, MS, 75; Univ of Geor, MA, 84, PhD, 88. **CAREER** ASST PROF, HIST, JOHN CARROLL UNIV **MEMBERSHIPS** Am Antiquarian Soc **CONTACT ADDRESS** Dept of Hist, John Carroll Univ, 20700 N Park Blvd, University Heights, OH 44118.

DUNKAK, HARRY MATTHEW
PERSONAL Born 04/14/1929, New York, NY **DISCIPLINE** AMERICAN HISTORY **EDUCATION** Iona Col, BA, 51; Fordham Univ, MA, 59; St John's Univ, PhD, 68. **CAREER** Teacher, Rice High Sch, NY, 52-54, Cardinal Hayes High Sch, 54-65 & Power Mem Acad, 65-66; instr, 67-69, assoc prof 69-85, asst dean, Sch Arts & Sci, 78-85, Prof Hist, Iona Col, 85-. **MEMBERSHIPS** Am Cath Hist Asn; Orgn Am Historians; AHA; Huguenot-Thomas Paine Hist Asn. **RESEARCH** The 1767-1770 non-importation agreements and the newspapers of Boston; American colonial history, especially New York in the 18th century; New York Whig politics, 1752-1769 and the role of J M Scott. **SELECTED PUBLICATIONS** Auth, Samuel Pintard, a New Rochelle loyalist, Westchester Hist Quart; The Papers of an Unheralded Irish-American Historian, Michael J O'Brien (1870-1960), in Eire - Ireland, A Journal of Irish Studies, Irish Am Cultural Inst, Morristown, NJ; The 1733 Eastchester Election, the Zenger Trial & Freedom of the Press, Westchester His, spring 88; A Colonial & Revolutionary Parish in New York: St Paul's Church in Eastchester, in Anglican & Episcopal History, 12/88; St Columbo of the Isle of Iona, Iona Mag, spring 88; The Lorillard Family of Westchester County: Tobacco, Property & Nature, Westchester Hist, summer 95; The Irish of Early Westchester County, monogr, Iona College, 94. **CONTACT ADDRESS** Dept of Hist, Iona Col, 715 North Ave, New Rochelle, NY 10801-1890. **EMAIL** mdunkak@atgnet.com

DUNLOP, ANNE
DISCIPLINE ART HISTORY **EDUCATION** Univ Warwick, PhD, 97. **CAREER** Dept Art Hist, Concordia Univ **HONORS AND AWARDS** Rome award, Brit Sch at Rome. **RESEARCH** Methodological and gender issues in late-medieval and early-modern art and society; rise of tourism and the promotion of new miracle and pilgrimage cults in the Quattrocento Papal States. **SELECTED PUBLICATIONS** Rev, articles in Art Hist and Renaissance Stud; auth, El vostro poeta, The First Florentine Printing of Dante's Commedia, RACAR XX, 93. **CONTACT ADDRESS** Dept Art Hist, VA-432, Concordia Univ, Montreal, 1455 de Maisonneuve W, Montreal, QC, Canada H3G 1M8. **EMAIL** adunlop@alcor.concordia.ca

DUNN, DENNIS JOHN
PERSONAL Born 10/23/1942, Cleveland, OH, m, 1966, 2 children **DISCIPLINE** RUSSIAN HISTORY **EDUCATION** John Carroll Univ, BA, 66, MA, 67; Kent State Univ, PhD(Hist), 70. **CAREER** Asst Hist, John Carroll Univ, 66-67; instr, Borremeo Sem-Col, 68; instr, Cleveland State Univ, 68-69; asst prof, 73-79, prof Hist, Southwest Tex State Univ, 70-, dir Inst Studies Relig & Communism, 80-, Vis fel, London Sch Econ & Polit Sci, 75-76. **MEMBERSHIPS** Am Asn Advan Slavic Studies; Am Cath Hist Asn; AHA. **RESEARCH** Russian history; Eastern European history; church-state relations. **SELECTED PUBLICATIONS** Auth, The Disappearance of the Ukranian Uniate Church, Ukrainskii Istorik, 72; coauth, Folktales and Footprints: Stories From the Old World, Benson, 73; auth, Pre-World War II Relations Between Stalin and the Catholic Church, J Church & State, Spring 73; Stalinism and the Catholic Church during the Era of World War II, Cath Hist, Rev, 10/73; Papal-Communist Detene: Motivation, Surv, 76; Religious Renaissance in USSR, J Church & State, 77; ed, Religion and Modernization in Soviet Union, Westview, 77; auth, The Catholic Church & Soviet Government, 1939-49, Columbia Univ, 77; Caught Between Roosevelt and Stalin: American Ambassadors in Russia; Lexington's University Press of Kenturcky, 98. **CONTACT ADDRESS** Dept of History, Southwest Texas State Univ, 601 University Dr, San Marcos, TX 78666-4685. **EMAIL** DD05@Academia.swt.edu

DUNN, DURWOOD
PERSONAL Born 11/30/1943, Chickamauga, GA **DISCIPLINE** HISTORY **EDUCATION** Univ TN, Knoxville, BA, 65, MA, 68, PhD, 76. **CAREER** Instr, Hiwassee Col, 70-74; from instr to prof to chair, 75-, TN Wesleyan Col. **HONORS AND AWARDS** Phi Beta Kappa; Phi Kappa Phi; Woodrow Wilson Nat Fel, 65; Danforth assoc, 77; Fel Independent Study and Res, 78-79, 94-95, Nat Endowment Hum; Thomas Wolfe Memorial Lit Awd, 88. **MEMBERSHIPS** Am Hist Asn; Org Am Hist; Southern Hist Asn; Appalachian Studies Asn; AAUP. **RESEARCH** Tennessee state and local history; Appalachian regional history and folklore. **SELECTED PUBLICATIONS** Auth, "Mary Noailles Murfree: A Reappraisal," Appalachian Jour, 79; "Apprenticeship and Indentured Servitude in Tennessee Before the Civil War," W TN Hist Soc Publications, 82; Cades Cove: The Life and Death of A Southern Appalachian Community, 1818-1937, Univ TN Press, 88; "A Meditation on Pittman Center: An Interview with Jessie Mechem Ledford," TN Hist Quart, 91; An Abolitionist in the Appalachian South: Ezekiel Birdseye on Slavery, Capitalism, and Separate Statehood in East Tennessee, 1841-1846, Univ TN Press, 97; ed, Appalachian Echoes, Univ Tenn. **CONTACT ADDRESS** PO Box 1041, Athens, TN 37371-1041. **EMAIL** dunnd@tnwc.edu

DUNN, JOE PENDER
PERSONAL Born 09/21/1945, Cape Girardeau, MO, m, 1972, 1 child **DISCIPLINE** AMERICAN HISTORY, INTERNATIONAL RELATIONS **EDUCATION** Southeast Mo State Col, BS, 67; Univ Mo-Columbia, MA, 68, PhD (hist), 73. **CAREER** Asst prof hist and polit sci, Univ Md, Europe Div, 73-77; asst prof, 77-81, Assoc Prof Hist 81-88, Prof & Department Chair, 88-; Converse Col. **RESEARCH** Recent American political and social history; national security; the Vietnam war. **SELECTED PUBLICATIONS** Auth, "Teaching The Vietnam War," Center for the Study of Armament and Disarmament, 90; auth, "The Future South," University of Illinois Press, 91; auth, "Desk Warrior: Memoirs of a Combat REMF," Pearson Publishing, 99. **CONTACT ADDRESS** Dept of History, Converse Col, Spartanburg, SC 29301. **EMAIL** joe.dunn@converse.edu

DUNN, LAURA
PERSONAL Born 08/16/1960, Cincinnati, OH **DISCIPLINE** ANCIENT HISTORY **EDUCATION** Trinity Evangelical Divinity School, MA, 91; Miami Univ, PhD, 98. **CAREER** Adjunct instr, Palm Beach Community Col, 98-; Indian River Community Col, 98-. **MEMBERSHIPS** Soc of Bibl Lit. **RESEARCH** Early Christianity; Sexual relationships in the Ancient World. **SELECTED PUBLICATIONS** Auth, "A New Look at Same-Sex Relationships in 1 Cor 6:9 and 1 Tim 1:10" in J for the Critical Study of Relig, 98. **CONTACT ADDRESS** 574 Frink Ave., Sebastian, FL 32958-4330. **EMAIL** laurad@gate.net

DUNN, PATRICK PETER
PERSONAL Born 05/05/1942, Cudahy, WI, m, 1965, 2 children **DISCIPLINE** RUSSIAN HISTORY, PSYCHOHI-

STORY **EDUCATION** Marquette Univ, BA, 64; Duke Univ, PhD(hist), 69. **CAREER** Asst prof hist, Duke Univ, 69-70 & Univ Wis, La Crosse, 70-74; asst prof, 74-80, assoc prof hist, Worcester Polytech Inst, 80-, Nat Endowment for Humanities younger humanist fel, 73. **MEMBERSHIPS** AHA; Am Asn Advan Slavic Studies. **RESEARCH** Russian social and intellectual history; history of childhood. **SELECTED PUBLICATIONS** Auth, Childhood of Vissarion Belinskii, Hist Childhood Quart, 12/73; contrib, History of Childhood, At com, 74; What Happened to the Hyphen in Psychohistory?, fall 74 & Intuitive and Over Forty: Barzun's Attack on the New Historians, spring 75, Book Forum; Modernization and the Family, J Psychohist, fall 76; Belinskii and Bakunin: Adolescence in Nineteenth Century Russia, spring 79 & Lithuanian Psychology and History, summer 82, Psychohist Rev. **CONTACT ADDRESS** Dept of Humanities, Worcester Polytech Inst, 100 Institute Rd, Worcester, MA 01609-2247.

DUNN, RICHARD SLATOR

PERSONAL Born 08/09/1928, Minneapolis, MN, m, 1960, 2 children **DISCIPLINE** HISTORY **EDUCATION** Harvard Univ, AB, 50; Princeton Univ, MA, 52, PhD (hist), 55. **CAREER** Instr hist, Univ Mich, 55-57; from asst prof to assoc prof, 57-68, chmn dept, 72-77, dir Philadephia Ctr Early Am Studies, 77-80, Prof Hist, Univ PA, 68-, Guggenheim fel, 66-67; mem coun Inst Early Am Hist and Cult, 67-69; vis prof hist, Univ Mich, 69-70; Nat Endowment Humanities fel, 74-75; mem coun Hist Soc Pa, 76-; mem Inst Adv Study, 74-75; Am Coun Learned Soc fel, 77-78; co-ed, Papers William Penn, 78-; chmn coun, Philadelphia Ctr Early Am Studies, 80-; mem, Ctr Adv Study Behav Sci, 82-83. **HONORS AND AWARDS** Jamestown Found Awd, 72; Love Prize, Conf Brit Studies, 73. **MEMBERSHIPS** AHA; Royal Hist Soc Fel; Orgn Am Hist; Am Antique Soc. **RESEARCH** American colonial history; Caribbean history; Anglo-american social history, 1607-1775. **SELECTED PUBLICATIONS** Auth, Puritans and Yankees: The Winthrop Dynasty of New England, 1630-1717, Princeton Univ, 62; Sugar and Slaves: The Rise of the Planter Class in the English West Indies, 1624-1713, Univ NC, 72; Social History of Early New England, Am Quart, 12/73; Tale of Two Plantations, William & Mary Quart, 1/77; Experiments holy and unholy, In: Westward Enterprise: English Activity in Ireland, the Atlantic and America, 1500-1650, Liverpool Univ, 78; Age of Religious Wars, 1559-1715, Norton 79; Papers of William Penn, 1644-1679, Univ Pa, 81. **CONTACT ADDRESS** Dept Hist, Univ of Pennsylvania, Philadelphia, PA 19104.

DUNNELL, RUTH W.

DISCIPLINE HISTORY **EDUCATION** Middlebury Col, BA, 72; Univ of Wash, MA, 75; Princeton Univ, PhD, 83. **CAREER** Postdoc res assoc, University of Wash, 83-84; instr, Roosevelt Univ, 85; visiting asst prof, Univ of Ore, 85-87; visiting for scholar, Chinese Acad of Soc Sci, 87-88; res assoc, Univ of Calif-Berkeley, 88-89; asst prof, 89-95; assoc prof, Kenyon Col, 95-. **HONORS AND AWARDS** FLAS/NDSL grants, 74-75, 76-78; Full Princeton Univ fel, 76-78, 79-80, 81-83; Andrew Mellon lang trng fel (ACLS), 83-84; IREX Emergency Support grant, 84-85; Nat Prog for Advanceded Study and Res in China Grantee, Nat Acad Sci, 87-88; Am Coun of Learned Soc Proj grant, 92; fac res grant-in-Residence, Univ of Mich, 93; Short-Term Travel grant, IREX, 93; IREX Individual Advanced Res Opportunity in Eurasia grant, 96; NEH fel for Col tchr(s) and Independent Scholars, 96-97; **MEMBERSHIPS** Assn Asian Studies; Mongolia Soc; Tibet Soc; T'ang Studies Soc. **RESEARCH** Chinese-Inner Asian political, institutional, & cultural history. **SELECTED PUBLICATIONS** Auth, The Great State of White and High: Buddhism and State Formation in Eleventh-Century Xia, Univ. of Hawaii Press, 96; The Recovery of Tangut History, Orientations 27:4, 96; Weiming (Li) Renxiao,1124-1193, Xia Biog Ser, Jour of Sung-Yuan Studies 95; Significant Peripheries: Inner Asian Perspectives on Song Studies, Jour of Sung-Yuan Studies, 94; Hsi-Hsia, The Cambridge Hist of China, Vol 6, Cambridge Univ. Press, 94; rev, Juha Janhunen, Manchuria, An Ethnic History, Jour of Sung-Yuan Studies 98; S.A.M. Adshead, Central Asia in World History, Jour of Asian Studies 94. **CONTACT ADDRESS** Dept of Hist, Kenyon Col, Gambier, OH 43022. **EMAIL** dunnell@kenyon.edu

DUPLESSIS, ROBERT S.

PERSONAL Born 06/01/1945, New York, NY, m, 1965, 1 child **DISCIPLINE** HISTORY **EDUCATION** Williams Col, BA, 66; Columbia Univ, MA, 68, PhD, 74. **CAREER** Asst prof to Isaac H. Clothier prof, Swarthmore Col, 73-. **HONORS AND AWARDS** Foreign Area Fel, 70-72; Mellon Fel, 80-81; Fulbright Fel, 66-67, 85-86; Nat Endow for the Humanities Fel for Col Teachers, 96-97; Guggenheim Fel, 00-01; Camargo Fel, 01; chair, div of soc sci, dept of hist, co-chair, women's stud prog, pres, amer assoc of univ prof, swarthmore col **MEMBERSHIPS** Amer Hist Assoc; Econ Hist Assoc; Renaissance Soc of Amer; French Colonial Hist Soc. **RESEARCH** Early modern Atlantic economic and cultural hist. **SELECTED PUBLICATIONS** Auth, Lille and the Dutch Revolt, Cambridge Univ Press, 91; auth, "Weber Thesis," in Encyclopedia of the Reformation, Oxford Univ Press, 96; auth, Transitions to Capitalism in Early Modern Europe, Cambridge Univ Press, 97; auth, Mercantilism, in Encyclopedia of the Renaissance, Scribner's, 99; auth, Transatlantic Textiles: European Linen in the Cloth Cultures of Colonial North American, in Linen in Europe, Oxford Univ Press, forthcoming; auth, Circulation et appropriation des mouchoirs chez les colons et aborigenes de la Nouvelle-France aux XVIIe et XVIIIe siecles, in Le Mouchoir Dans Tous Ses Etats, Musee du Textile, Cholet, France, 00; auth, Was There A Consumer Revolution in Eighteenth Century New France?, in Proceedings of the Annual Conference of the French Colonial Historical Society, 1997, Mich St Univ Press, forthcoming; auth "Capitalism and Commercialization," in Encyclopedia of European Social History, Scribner's, forthcoming. **CONTACT ADDRESS** Dept of History, Swarthmore Col, 500 College Ave, Swarthmore, PA 19081. **EMAIL** rduples1@swarthmore.edu

DUPRE, DAN

DISCIPLINE AMERICAN HISTORY **EDUCATION** Brandeis Univ, PhD, 90. **CAREER** Assoc prof, Univ NC, Charlotte. **RESEARCH** The Old South; soc and polit hist of the early republic. **SELECTED PUBLICATIONS** Auth, Transforming the Cotton Frontier: Madison County, Alabama, 1800-1840, La State UP, 97. **CONTACT ADDRESS** Univ of No Carolina, Charlotte, Charlotte, NC 28223-0001.

DUPREE, ANDERSON HUNTER

PERSONAL Born 01/29/1921, Hillsboro, TX, m, 1946, 2 children **DISCIPLINE** HISTORY **EDUCATION** Oberlin Col, AB, 42; Harvard Univ, AM, 47, PhD (hist), 52. **CAREER** Asst prof hist, Tex Technol Col, 50-53; res fel, Gray Herbarium, Harvard Univ, 52-54, 55-56; vis asst prof hist, Univ Calif, Berkeley, 56-58, from assoc prof to prof hist, Univ Calif, Berkeley, 58-68, asst to chancellor, 60-62; George L Littlefield prof, 68-81, Emer Prof Hist, Brown Univ, 81-, Fel, Ctr Advan Studies Behav Sci, 67-68; mem, hist adv comt, NASA, 64-73, hist adv comt, Atomic Energy Comn, 67-73, adv comt govt prog in behav sci, Nat Res Coun, 66-68; Smithsonian coun, 75-. **MEMBERSHIPS** AHA; Orgn Am Historians; Soc Hist Technol; Am Acad Arts and Sci (secy, 73-76); Hist Sci Soc. **RESEARCH** American social and intellectual history; history of science in America; history of science and technology. **SELECTED PUBLICATIONS** Auth, Science in the Federal Government, 57 & Asa Gray, 59, Harvard Univ; Science and the Emergence of Modern America, Rand McNally, 63. **CONTACT ADDRESS** 975 Memorial Dr. Unit 201, Cambridge, MA 02138.

DURAM, JAMES C.

PERSONAL d, 2 children **DISCIPLINE** US CONSTITUTIONAL, LEGAL, POLITICAL, FAMILY HISTORY AND HISTORIOGRAPHY **EDUCATION** W Michigan Univ, Ba, MA; Wayne State Univ, PhD. **CAREER** Dept prelaw adv; prof-. **HONORS AND AWARDS** Fulbright fel, Intl Inst Soc Hist, Amsterdam. **RESEARCH** Uses and dynamics of constitutional argumentation. **SELECTED PUBLICATIONS** Auth, books on Norman Thomas, US Supreme Court Justice; William O. Douglas, President Dwight D Eisenhower's role in the School Segregation Cases; Biography of a Civil War Chaplain. **CONTACT ADDRESS** Dept of Hist, Wichita State Univ, 1845 Fairmont, Wichita, KS 67260-0062. **EMAIL** duram@twsuvm.uc.twsu.edu

DURAM, LESLIE

PERSONAL Born Detroit, MI, m, 1993, 1 child **DISCIPLINE** GEOGRAPHY **EDUCATION** Wichita State Univ, BA, 88; Kansas State Univ, MA, 91; Univ Col, PhD, 94. **CAREER** Asst prof, S IL Univ Carbondale, 95-. **MEMBERSHIPS** Assoc of Am Geog. **RESEARCH** Rural land use, sustainable agriculture, watershed management. **SELECTED PUBLICATIONS** Coauth, "Central Great Plains Land Use/Cover Modeling Project: A Pilot Study in Northeastern Colorado", High Plains Appl Anthrop 16.1 (96):19-28; auth, "Characteristics of US Organic Farming: An Illinois Case Study", Bull of the IL Geog Soc 39.2 (97):26-34; auth, "A Pragmatic Study of Conventional and Alternative Farmers in Colorado", The Prof Geog 49.2 (97):202-213; auth, "The Continuum From Conventional to Alternative Farmers in Colorado" in Agr Restructuring and Sustainability, eds B. Ilbery, T. Richard, Q. Chiotti (UK: CAB Int, 97) 153-166; auth, "Taking a Pragmatic Behavioral Approach to Alternative Agriculture Research", Am Jour of Alternative Agr 13, (98):92-97; auth, "Organic Agriculture in the United States: Current Status and Future Regulation", Choice: Food, Farm and Res Issues (98):34-38; coauth, "An Assessment of Public Participation in Federally funded Watershed Planning Initiatives", Society and Nat Res 12 (99):455-467; auth, "Factors in Organic Farmers' Decisionmaking: Diversity, Challenge and Obstacles", Am Jour of Alternative Agr 14.1 (99):2-10; auth, "Agents Perceptions of Structure: How Illinois Organic Farmers View Political, Economic, and Social Factors", Agr and Human Values 17.1 (00):35-47; coauth, "Contemporary Agriculture and Rural Land Use" in Geog in Am, eds G. Gaile and C. Willmott (Oxford: Oxford Univ Pr) (forthcoming). **CONTACT ADDRESS** Dept Geography, So Illinois Univ, Carbondale, S IL Union, Mc4514, Carbondale, IL 62901. **EMAIL** duram@siu.edu

DURDEN, ROBERT FRANKLIN

PERSONAL Born 05/10/1925, Graymont, GA, m, 1952, 2 children **DISCIPLINE** HISTORY **EDUCATION** Emory Univ, AB, 47, MA, 48; Princeton Univ, MA, 50, PhD, 52. **CAREER** Asst instr hist, Princeton Univ, 50-52; from instr to assoc prof, 52-64, chmn dept, 74-80, Prof Hist, Duke Univ, 65-96, Emer prof, 96-, Fulbright prof, Am hist, Johns Hopkins Sch Int Rels, Bologna, Italy, 65-68; Fulbright prof Am hist, Monash Univ, Melbourne, Australia, 80. **HONORS AND AWARDS** LLD, Emory Univ, 81. **MEMBERSHIPS** Southern Hist Asn **RESEARCH** American history. **SELECTED PUBLICATIONS** Auth, James S Pike: Republicanism and the American Negro, 1850-1882, 56 & Reconstruction Bonds and Twentieth Century Politics: South Dakota Versus North Carolina, 62, Duke Univ; Climax of Populism, Univ Ky, 65; ed, The Prostrate State, Harper, 68; auth, The Gray and the Black: the Confederate Debate on Emancipation, La State Univ, 72; The Dukes of Durham, 1865-1929, Duke Univ, 75; coauth, Maverick Republican in the Old North State: a Political Biography of Daniel L Russell, La State Univ, 77; auth, The Self-Inflicted Wound: Southern Politics in the Nineteenth Century, Univ KY, 85; auth, The Launching of Duke University, 1924-1949, Duke Univ, 93; auth, Charter G. Woodson: Father of African-American History, Enslow, 98; auth, Lasting Legacy to the Carolinas, The Duke Endowment, 1924-1994, Duke Univ, 98. **CONTACT ADDRESS** Dept of Hist, Duke Univ, PO Box 90719, Durham, NC 27708.

DURNBAUGH, DONALD F.

PERSONAL Born 11/16/1927, Detroit, MI, m, 1952, 3 children **DISCIPLINE** CHURCH HISTORY, MODERN EUROPEAN HISTORY **EDUCATION** Manchester Col, BA, 49; Univ Mich, MA, 53; Univ Pa, PhD (hist), 60. **CAREER** Dir, Brethren Serv Comn, Austria, 53-56; lectr Brethren hist, Bethany Theol Sem, 58; from instr to asst prof hist, Juniata Col, 58-62; assoc prof, 62-70, Prof Church Hist, Bethany Theol Sem, 70-, Alternate serv, Brethren Serv Comn, Austria and Ger, 49-51 and 53-56; dir in Europe, Brethren Cols Abroad, 64-65; adj prof church hist, Northern Baptist Theol Sem, 68-71; assoc, Ctr Reformation and Free Church Studies, Chicago Theol Sem, 68-; Nat Endowment for Humanities res fel, 76-77. **MEMBERSHIPS** Am Soc Church Hist; Orgn Am Historians; NAm Acad Ecumenists; AHA; Am Soc Reformation Res. **RESEARCH** Modern European church history; German sectarian movements in America; Communitarian societies. **SELECTED PUBLICATIONS** Auth, Spiritual Life in Anabaptism, Church Hist, Vol 66, 97; The German Peasant War and Anabaptist Community of Goods, Church Hist, Vol 63, 94; Mennonite Entrepreneurs, Church Hist, Vol 66, 97; The German Peasant War and Anabaptist Community of Goods, Church Hist, Vol 63, 94; Spiritual Life in Anabaptism, Church Hist, Vol 66, 97; Mennonite Entrepreneurs, Church Hist, Vol 66, 97; The Writings of Philips, Dirk, J Church State, Vol 35, 93. **CONTACT ADDRESS** Bethany Theol Sem, Oak Brook, IL 60521.

DUROCHER, RENE

PERSONAL Born 06/28/1938, Montreal, PQ, Canada **DISCIPLINE** HISTORY **EDUCATION** Univ Montreal, BA, 60, BPed, 60, LL, 65, DES Histoire, 68. **CAREER** Asst to assoc prof, York Univ, 71-74; vis prof, Univ Calgary, 72; Prof History, Univ Montreal, 74-, dept ch, 84-87, dir res office, 94-; vis prof, Israel, 80. **MEMBERSHIPS** Conseil de la Sci et de la Technologie du Que, 81-86; pres, Can Hist Asn, 86-87. **SELECTED PUBLICATIONS** Coauth, Le retard du Quebec et l'inferiorite economique des Canadiens francais, 71; coauth, Histoire du Quebec contemporain 1867-1929, 79; coauth, Nouvelle histoire du Canada et du Quebec; coauth, Le Quebec depuis 1930. **CONTACT ADDRESS** Dep d'histoire, Univ of Montreal, CP 6128, Succ Centre-ville, Montreal, QC, Canada H3C 3J7. **EMAIL** durochr@hst.umontreal.ca

DURRILL, WAYNE K.

PERSONAL Born 08/01/1953, Sedalia, MO, d **DISCIPLINE** HISTORY **EDUCATION** Northwestern Univ, BA, 75, MA, 76; Univ NC at Chapel Hill, PhD, 87. **CAREER** Asst ed, Freedman and Southern Soc Proj, Univ Md, 1987-90; asst prof, Hist Dept, Univ Cincinnati, 90-94; Fulbright lectr and researcher, Hist Dept, Univ Cape Town, South Africa, Jan-Dec 96; assoc prof, Univ Cincinnati, 94-, Asst Dept Head and dir of Undergrad Studies, 98-; co-ed, Ohio Valley History: The Bulletin of the Cincinnati Hist Soc, 200-. **HONORS AND AWARDS** Louis Pelzer Memorial Awd, Org of Am Hists, 84; Predoctoral Fel, Nat Museum of Am Hist, Smithsonian Inst, 86; Postdoctoral Fel, Am Coun of Learned Socs, 90; Res grant, Spenser Found, 92; Spenser Found Post-doctoral Fel, Nat Acad of Educ, 93; Taft Competitive Fel, Taft Memorial Fund, Univ of Cincinnati, 95; Fel, Fulbright Foreign Scholarship Bd, 95; Res grant, Spenser Found, 97; Univ Fac Achievement Awd, Univ Cincinnati, 97. **MEMBERSHIPS** Am Hist Asn, Org of Am Hists, Southern Hist Asn. **SELECTED PUBLICATIONS** Auth, War of Another Kind: A Southern Community in the Great Rebellion, New York: Oxford Univ Press (90, paperback, 94); auth, "An Uncivil War," Southern Exposure: A J of Politics & Culture, 18 (90): 18-21; auth, "The South Carolina Black Code," in True Stories from the American Past, ed by William Graebner, New York: McGraw-Hill (92): 1-15; auth, "Slavery, Kinship, and Dominance: The Black Community at Somerset Place Plantation, 1786-1860," Slavery and Abolition, 16 (95): 161-87; auth, "The Struggle for Black Freedom before Emancipation," OAH Mag of Hist, 8 (93): 7-10; auth, "Farming," and "Hinton Rowan Helper," in Encyclopedia of the Confederacy, ed by

Richard N. Current, NY: Simon & Schuster (95); auth, "New Schooling for a New South: A Community Study of Education and Social Change, 1875-1885," J of Soc Hist, 31 (97): 156-81; auth, "The Power of Ancient Words: Classical Teaching and Social Change at South Carolina College, 1801-1860," J of Southern Hist, 65 (99): 469-98; auth, "Shaping a Colonial Elite: Students, Competition, and Leadership at South African College, 1829-1895," J of African Hist (forthcoming 2000). **CONTACT ADDRESS** Dept Hist, Univ of Cincinnati, Cincinnati, OH 45221-0373. **EMAIL** durrilwk@email.uc.edu

DUTT, ASHOK K.
PERSONAL Born 11/01/1931, Hazaribagh, India, m, 1956, 2 children **DISCIPLINE** GEOGRAPHY **EDUCATION** Patna Univ, BA, 53; MA, 55; MA, 56; PhD, 61. **CAREER** Lecturer, D.K. College, 56-58; Asst Prof, Patna Univ, 58-62; Chief Geog Team and Reg Planning, Govt of West Bengal, 62-66; Asst Prof, St Anselm's Col, 66-68; Prof, E Carolina Univ, 67; Asst Prof to Prof, Univ Akron, 68-. **HONORS AND AWARDS** Fel, OH Acad of Sci, 81; Fel, Ford Foundation, 64; Fulbright Prof, Delhi Univ, 88-89; Distinguished Service Awd, Asn of Am Geog, 91; Distinguished Scholar Awd, Asn of Am Geog, 92; **MEMBERSHIPS** OH Acad of Sci; Asian Urban Res Org; Asn of Am Geog; Bengali Cult Soc; Am Geog Soc; APA; Reg Sci Asn; Nat Asn of Geog in India. **RESEARCH** Urban geography; Cultural and medical geography; Planning. **SELECTED PUBLICATIONS** Auth, The Asian City: Processes of Development, Characteristics and Planning, Kluwer Acad Pub, 94; ed, Southeast Asia: A Ten Nation Region, Kluwer Acad Pub, 96; auth, "Place of Geography in Ancient India," National Geographical Journal of India, (96): 1-8; co-auth, Atlas of South Asia: A Geographic Analysis by Countries, IBH Pub Co, 98. **CONTACT ADDRESS** Dept Geog, Univ of Akron, 302 Buchtel Mall, Akron, OH 44325-0002. **EMAIL** dutt@uakron.edu

DUTTON, PAUL V.
PERSONAL Born Palo Alto, CA **DISCIPLINE** HISTORY **EDUCATION** Univ Calif, BA; Johns Hopkins Univ, MA; Univ Calif, PhD. **CAREER** Asst prof hist, N Az Univ, 97- . **HONORS AND AWARDS** Fulbright fel, 88. **MEMBERSHIPS** Soc Fr Hist Student; Am Hist Asn. **RESEARCH** Modern France, Social reform. **SELECTED PUBLICATIONS** Auth, "French Versus German Approaches to Family Welfare in Lorraine," Fr Hist, (Dec 99); auth, "An Overlooked Source of Social Reform: Family Policy in French Agriculture," J Mod Hist, (June 00). **CONTACT ADDRESS** Dept Hist, No Arizona Univ, Liberal Arts, Box 6023, Flagstaff, AZ 86011-0001. **EMAIL** Paul.Dutton@nau.edu

DVORSKY-ROHNER, DOROTHY
DISCIPLINE ART HISTORY **EDUCATION** Univ CO, BFA, MA, PhD. **CAREER** Asst prof Art, Univ NC, Asheville, 96-. **RESEARCH** The art and archit of the Ancient World. **SELECTED PUBLICATIONS** Her articles on Greek and Etruscan archit have appeared in Archaeology News and other professional jour(s). **CONTACT ADDRESS** Univ of No Carolina, Asheville, Asheville, NC 28804-8510. **EMAIL** rtynes@unca.edu

DWYER, EUGENE JOSEPH
PERSONAL Born 09/14/1943, Buffalo, NY, m, 1969, 1 child **DISCIPLINE** CLASSICAL ARCHEOLOGY, ART HISTORY **EDUCATION** Harvard Univ, BA, 65; NYork Univ, MA, 67, PhD(art hist), 74. **CAREER** Prof Art Hist, Kenyon Col, 73-. **HONORS AND AWARDS** Tatiana Warsher Awd, Am Acad, Rome, 72-73. **MEMBERSHIPS** Am Numis Soc; Archaeol Inst Am; Col Art Asn. **RESEARCH** Hellenistic and Roman art; Pompeii. **SELECTED PUBLICATIONS** Auth, The Subject of Durer's Four Witches, Art Quart, 71; Augustus and the Capricorn 73 & Pompeian Oscilla Collections, 81, Romische Mitteilungen; Temporal Allegory of Tazza Farnese, Am J of Archaeol, 92; articles: Macmillan Dictionary of Art, 96; articles: Encyclopedia of Comparative Iconography, 98. **CONTACT ADDRESS** Kenyon Col, Gambier, OH 43022-9623. **EMAIL** dwyere@kenyon.edu

DYCK, CORNELIUS JOHN
PERSONAL Born 08/20/1921, Russia, m, 1952, 3 children **DISCIPLINE** HISTORY, HISTORICAL THEOLOGY **EDUCATION** BA, Bethel Col, N Newton KS, 53; MA Wichita State Univ, 55; BD Divinity School Univ Chicago, 59, PhD, 62. **CAREER** Prof Assoc Mennonite Seminaries, 59-89; Dir Inst of Mennonite Studies, 58-79; Exec Sec, Mennonite World Conf, 61-73. **MEMBERSHIPS** Mennonite Hist Soc, Goshen IN; Mennonitischer Geschichtsverein, Weierhof Germany; Doopsgezind Historische Kring, Amsterdam; Doc for Reformation Res; NA Soc Of Church Hist. **RESEARCH** 16th century Dutch Anabaptism. **SELECTED PUBLICATIONS** Mennonite Encyclopedia vol V ed, 90; Introduction to Mennonite History, 3rd ed, 93; Spiritual Life in Anabaptism, 95. **CONTACT ADDRESS** Associated Mennonite Biblical Sem, 3003 Benham Ave, Elkhart, IN 46514. **EMAIL** ejwdyck@juno.com

DYE, JAMES WAYNE
PERSONAL Born 12/22/1934, Appalachia, VA, m, 1985, 1 child **DISCIPLINE** PHILOSOPHY, HISTORY OF PHILOSOPHY **EDUCATION** Carson-Newman Col, AB, 55; New Orleans Baptist Theol Sem, BD, 58; Tulane Univ, PhD, 60. **CAREER** Teaching asst philos, Tulane Univ, 58-59; from instr to asst prof, Washington Univ, 60-66; assoc prof, 66-76, dir, Philos Inst, 67-70, prof philos, Northern Ill Univ, 76-, assoc ed, The Philos Forum, 67-70. **MEMBERSHIPS** Am Philos Asn; Soc Ancient Greek Philos; Hume Soc; S Soc Philos Psy Psychol, Pres, 94-95. **RESEARCH** Ancient Greek philosophy; philosophy of religion and culture; German idealism; Hume. **SELECTED PUBLICATIONS** Coauth, Religions of the World, Appleton, 67, Irvington, 75; auth, Denton J Snider's interpretation of Hegel, Mod Schoolman, 1/70; Unspoken philosophy: The presuppositions and applications of thought, Studium Gererale, 71; Kant as ethical naturalist, J Value Inquiry, 78; Plato's concept of causal explanation, Tulane Stud Philos, 78; Aristotle's matter as a sensible principle, Int Studies Philos, 78; Nikolai Bendyaev and his ideas on ultimate reality, J Ultimate Reality & Meaning, 79; The sensibility of intelligible matter, Int Studies Philos, 82; In Search of the Philosopher-King, Archeol News, 82; The Poetization of Science, Studies in Sci and Cult II, 86; Hume on Curing Superstition, Hume Stud, 86; Superhuman Voices and Biological Books, Hist Philos Quart, 88; A Word on Behalf of Demea, Hume Stud, 89; Demea's Departure, Hume Stud, 93. **CONTACT ADDRESS** Dept of Philosophy, No Illinois Univ, 1425 W Lincoln Hwy, De Kalb, IL 60115-2825. **EMAIL** jdye@niu.edu

DYKES, DEWITT S., JR.
PERSONAL Born 01/02/1938, Chattanooga, TN, m **DISCIPLINE** HISTORY **EDUCATION** Fisk Univ, BA (Summa Cum Laude) 1960; Univ of MI, MA 1961, PhD 65. **CAREER** MI State Univ, instructor Amer Thought & Language 1965-69; Oakland Univ, asst prof of history 1969-73; Oakland Univ, dean's asst for affirmative action 1975-78, coordinator Afro-Amer studies 1975-83; Univ of SC School of Public Health, consultant 1977; Oakland Univ, assoc prof of History 1973-. **MEMBERSHIPS** African Heritage Studies Assn 1970; life mem Assn for the Study of Afro-Amer Life & History; charter mem Afro-Amer Historical & Genealogical Soc 1978; Alpha Phi Alpha Fraternity; bd of editors Detroit in Perspective, A Journal of Regional History 1978-84; vice chmn Historic Designation Advisory Bd City of Detroit 1980-82, chmn 1982-84; book review editor Journal of the Afro-Amer Historical & Genealogical Soc 1981-85; pres The Fred Hart Williams Genealogical Soc 1980-86; bd of trustees Historical Soc of MI 1983-; summer fellowship Natl Endowment for the Humanities 1985; pres Michigan Black History Network 1986-; bd of trustees, Historical Soc of MI, 1983-89; pres, MI Black History Network, 1986-88. **SELECTED PUBLICATIONS** Published "Mary McLeod Bethune"; "Ida Gray Nelson Rollins DDS" Profiles of the Negro in Amer Dentistry 1979; "Augusta Savage;" "Jerome Cavanagh & Roman Gribbs;" "Amer Blacks as Perpetual Victims, An Historical Overview" Victimization of the Weak 1982; "The Black Population in MI, Growth, Distribution & Public Office, 1800-1983" Ethnic Groups in MI Vol 2 1983; Phi Beta Kappa, Honorary Fraternity, 1969; "The Search for Community: MI Soc and Educ, 1945-80" in MI: Visions of our Past, 1989. **CONTACT ADDRESS** Dept of History, Oakland Univ, 378 O'Dowd Hall, Rochester, MI 48309-4401.

DYKSTRA, ROBERT R.
PERSONAL Born 08/29/1930, Ames, IA, m, 1980, 3 children **DISCIPLINE** HISTORY **EDUCATION** Univ of IA, ba, 53; MA 59; Ph.D. 64. **CAREER** Ed, Civil War History, 62-65; U. of New Mexico 65-67; U. of Nebraska Lincoln, 67-68; U. of Iowa, 68-80; SUNY Albany, 80-;Ed consul; 78-, Annals of Iowa; mem ed bd, 79-82, J Am Hist; mem ed bd, 80-81, Am Stud; mem ed bd, 81-, Upper Midwest Hist; dir, 84, 7th Am Stud Sem, Am Antiquarian Soc; consult, 85, Natl Endowment Hum; res assoc 85-86, Am Antiquarian Soc; res fel, 85-86, 88-90, Natl Endowment Hum, prof, 81-, SUNY. **HONORS AND AWARDS** Binkley-Stephenson Awd, Org Am Historians, 86; Myers Ctr Awd, Gustavus Myers Ctr for Stud of Human Rights, N Am, 94; Shambaugh Awd, St Hist Soc of Iowa, 94. **MEMBERSHIPS** Fel Soc Am Hist; Am Antiquarian Soc; Kansas St Hist Soc; St Hist Soc of Iowa. **SELECTED PUBLICATIONS** Auth, Dr Emerson's Sam: Black Iowans Before the Civil War, Palimsest, 82; auth, White Men, Black Laws: Territorial Iowans and Civil Rights, 1838-1843, Annals of Iowa, 82; auth, The Issue Squarely Met: Toward an Explanation of Iowans' Racial Attitudes, 1865-1868, Annals of Iowa, 84; coauth, Serial Marriage and the origins of the Black Stepfamily: The Rowanty Evidence, J Am Hist, 85; coauth, Doing Local History: Monographic Approaches to the Smaller Community, Am Quart, 85; auth, Ecological Regression Estimates: Alchemist's Gold? Soc Sci Hist, 86; auth, Bright Radical Star: Black Freedom and White Supremacy on the Hawkeye Frontier, Harvard Univ, 93; auth, The Know Nothings Nobody Knows: Political nativists in Antebellum Iowa, Annals of Iowa, 94; auth, Iowans and the Politics of Race in America, 1857-1880, In: Iowa History Reader, St Hist Soc of Iowa, 96; auth, Overdosing on Dodge City; Western Hist Quart, 96; auth, To Live and Die in Dodge City: Body Counts, Law and Order,a nd the Case of Kansas v. Gill, In: Lethal Imagination: Violence and Brutality in American History, NY Univ, 99; auth, Violence, Gender, and Methodology in the New Western History, Rev in Am Hist, 99. **CONTACT ADDRESS** 39 Waterford Dr, Worcester, MA 01602. **EMAIL** dykstra@cse.albany.edu

DYSART, JANE ELLEN
PERSONAL Born 06/25/1938, Ft Worth, TX **DISCIPLINE** LATIN AMERICAN HISTORY **EDUCATION** Tex Wesleyan Col, BA, 59; Tex Christian Univ, MA, 67, PhD (hist), 72. **CAREER** Pub sch teacher English and hist, 59-68; Asst Prof Latin Am Hist, Univ W Fla, 71-. **MEMBERSHIPS** AHA; Western Hist Asn. **RESEARCH** Borderlands; 19th century; sociology. **SELECTED PUBLICATIONS** Auth, Mexican women in San Antonio 1830-1860: The assimilation process, Western Hist Quart, 10/76. **CONTACT ADDRESS** Dept of Hist, Univ of West Florida, Pensacola, FL 32504.

DYSON, ROBERT HARRIS, JR.
PERSONAL Born 08/02/1927, York, PA **DISCIPLINE** ANTHROPOLOGY, ARCHAEOLOGY **EDUCATION** Harvard College, BA magna cum laude 50; Harvard Univ, PhD 66; Univ Penn, MA hon 71. **CAREER** Univ Penn, asst prof, assoc prof, 54-94; prof emer, Univ Penn Museum, asst, assoc, curator, curator emer, 54-95, dir, dir emer, 82-94; Univ Penn Arts Sci, dean, 79-82. **HONORS AND AWARDS** R H Dyson Ch Endow, NEA; Elect Cors Mem; Elect APA; Elect Cors Mem Deutchees Arch. **MEMBERSHIPS** AIAP; AIIS; AIA; Brit Sch Arch Iraq; Brit Sch Arch Iran; Brit Sch Arch Turkey; SAA. **RESEARCH** Archaeol and prehistory; Near East and Iran; paleoecoogy; technology; archit; cultural change; hist of Near Eastern archaeol; chronology; and urbanization. **SELECTED PUBLICATIONS** Auth, Triangle-Festoon Ware Reconsidered, Iranica Ant, in press 99; The Achaemenid Triangle Ware of Hasanlu IIIA, Anatolian Iron Ages, BIAT, 98; Hasanlu, ditto vol 2, 97; History of the Field: Archaeology in Persia, The Oxford Encycl of the Near East, OUP, 97. **CONTACT ADDRESS** Near East Laboratory, Univ of Pennsylvania, Philadelphia, PA 19104. **EMAIL** robertd@sas.upenn.edu

DZAMBA, ANNE
PERSONAL m, 1987 **DISCIPLINE** HISTORY, WOMEN'S STUDIES **EDUCATION** Swarthmore Col, BA, 60; Univ Del, PhD, 73. **CAREER** Prof of hist and women's studies, chairperson, hist dept, West Chester Univ, Pa, 95-99. **SELECTED PUBLICATIONS** Auth (as Anne Dzamba Sessa), Richard Wagner and the English, and various articles. **CONTACT ADDRESS** Dept Hist, West Chester Univ of Pennsylvania, 700 S High St, West Chester, PA 19383-0003.

DZIEWANOWSKI, MARIAN KAMIL
PERSONAL Born 06/01/1913, Zhitomir, Ukraine, m, 1946, 2 children **DISCIPLINE** HISTORY **EDUCATION** Univ Warsaw, LLM, 37; French Inst, Warsaw, cert, 37; Harvard Univ, MA, 48, PhD(hist), 51. **CAREER** Res fel, Russ Res Ctr, Harvard Univ, 49-51; res assoc, Ctr Int Studies, Mass Inst Technol, 52-53; from asst prof to prof hist, Boston Col, 54-65; prof hist, Boston Univ, 65-78; Prof Hist, Univ Wis, Milwaukee, 79-, Ford exchange prof, Poland, 58; Am Philos Soc res fels, 59-60; assoc Russ Res Ctr, Harvard Univ, 60-78; vis prof, Brown Univ, 61-62 & 66-67; prof int rels, Boston Univ Br Brussels & West Berlin, 72-73; vis prof, NAtlantic Treaty Orgn & Supreme Hq Allied Powers Europe, 72-73; vis prof, Grad Univ Europ Community, 79. **MEMBERSHIPS** AHA; Inst Am; Polish Inst Arts & Sci Am; Am Asn Advan Slavic Studies. **RESEARCH** Modern eastern Europe; contemporary Russia; Poland. **SELECTED PUBLICATIONS** Auth, Dualism or Trialism, Slavonic Rev, 6/60; coauth, Communist States at the Crossroads, Praeger, 65; Bibliography of Soviet Foreign Relations, Princeton Univ, 65; auth, The C.P. of Poland, Harvard, 69; auth, A European Federalist, Stanford Univ, 68; Poland in the 20th Century, Columbia Univ, 77 & 79; A History of Soviet Russia, Prentice-Hall, 79-96; coauth, Communist Parties of Eastern Europe, Columbia, 80; European Federalism, Europ Univ, 82; auth, War at Any Price, Prentice-Hall, 79; Russia in the 20th Century, (Prentice Hall) 00. **CONTACT ADDRESS** 3352 N Hackett Ave, Milwaukee, WI 53211.

DZUBACK, MARY ANN
PERSONAL Born 03/17/1950, Chattanooga, TN, m, 1983 **DISCIPLINE** HISTORY; EDUCATION **EDUCATION** Franconia Col, BA, 74; Columbia Univ, PhD, 87. **CAREER** From asst prof to assoc prof, Wash Univ, 87-. **HONORS AND AWARDS** Rockefeller Arch Ctr grant; Spencer Found grant, Wash Univ fac res grant, Oberlin Col Arch grant. **MEMBERSHIPS** Hist of Educ Soc; Am Educ Res Asn, Am Hist Asn; Org of Am Hists; Hist of the Behavioral Scis Asn. **RESEARCH** Soc and intellectual hist of educ and higher educ; Women's hist, gender and cult. **SELECTED PUBLICATIONS** Auth, Robert M. Hutchins: Portrait of an Educator, 91; various articles. **CONTACT ADDRESS** Dept of Education, Washington Univ, 1 Brookings Dr, Campus Box 1183, Saint Louis, MO 63130. **EMAIL** madzubac@artsci.wash.edu

E

EADIE, JOHN W.
PERSONAL Born 12/18/1935, Ft Smith, AR, m, 1957, 2 children **DISCIPLINE** ANCIENT HISTORY **EDUCATION** Univ Ark, BA, 57; Univ Chicago, MA, 59; Univ London, PhD

(hist), 62. **CAREER** Asst prof hist, Ripon Col, 62-63; from asst prof to assoc prof, 63-73, Prof Hist, Univ Mich, Ann Arbor, 73-, Rackham res fel, 67-68; vis fel, Clare Hall, Cambridge Univ, 68-69; sr res, Joint Am-Yugoslavian Excavation, Sirmium, Yugoslavia, 68-72; Am Coun Learned Soc grant-in-aid, 74; humanities and arts adv to vpres for res, Univ Mich, 74-; dir, Summer Inst in Ancient Hist, Asn Ancient Historians, 77; chmn, Mich Coun for Humanities, Nat Endowment for Humanities State Coun, 77-80; dir, archaeol explor of Humayma region in southern Jordan, 82-. **MEMBERSHIPS** Asn of Ancient Historians; Soc Prom Roman Studies; AHA; Archaeol Inst Am. **RESEARCH** Roman Empire; Roman frontiers and provinces; historiography. **SELECTED PUBLICATIONS** Auth, The development of Roman mailed cavalry, J Roman Studies, 67; The Breviarium of Festus, Athlone, London, 67; ed, The Conversion of Constantine, Holt, 71; auth, The reliability and origin of the vita Didii Iuliani, Annali Scuola Norm Super Pisa, 74; co-ed, Ancient and Modern: Essays in Honor of Gerald F Else, Ctr Coord Ancient & Mod Studies, 77; auth, Civitates and clients: Roman frontier policies in Pannonia and Mauretania Tingitana, In: The Frontier, Univ Okla, 77; The Barbarian invasions and frontier politics in the reign of Gallienus, Roman Frontier Studies, 79 & In: BAR Int Ser, 71, 80; City and countryside in late Roman Pannonia: The regio Sirmiensis, In: City, Town and Countryside in the Early Byzantine Era, Columbia Univ, 82. **CONTACT ADDRESS** Dept of Hist, Univ of Michigan, Ann Arbor, Ann Arbor, MI 48109.

EAGLES, CHARLES W.
PERSONAL Born 09/22/1946, Spartanburg, SC, m, 1978, 2 children **DISCIPLINE** HISTORY **EDUCATION** BA, Presbyterian College, 68; MA, North Carolina, 73; PhD, North Carolina, 78. **CAREER** NC State Univ, 77-80; Southeast Missouri State Univ, 80-82; Vanderbilt Univ, Univ of Mississippi, Asst Prof 83-86; Assoc Prof 86-91, Prof 91-. **HONORS AND AWARDS** Lillian Smith Awd 93. **MEMBERSHIPS** Southern Historical Association; Amer Historical Association; Organization of Amer Historians; Mississippi Historical Society. **RESEARCH** Recent US, modern South, civil rights and race relations **SELECTED PUBLICATIONS** Jonathan Daniels and Race Relations; The Evolution of a Southern Liberal 82, The Civil Rights Movement in America (ed) 86; Urban-Rural Conflict in the 1920s: A Historiographical Assessment, The Historian 49 p26-48, 86; Congressional Voting in the 1920s: A Test of Urban-Rural Conflict, Journal of American History 76, p528-34, 89; Democracy Delayed: Congressional Reapportionment and Urban-Rural Conflict in the 1920s, 90; The Mind of the South After Fifty Years, 92; Outside Agitator: Jon Daniels and the Civil Rights Movement in Alabama, 93; Is There a Southern Political Tradition?, 96; auth, "Toward New Histories of the Civil Rights Era," Jrnl of Southern History 66 (00). **CONTACT ADDRESS** Dept of History, Univ of Mississippi, University, MS 38677. **EMAIL** eagles@olemiss.edu

EAKIN, MARSHALL C.
PERSONAL Born 12/26/1952, Madisonville, TX, m, 1977, 2 children **DISCIPLINE** HISTORY **EDUCATION** Univ Kans, BA, 75; MA, 77; Univ Calif, Los Angeles, PhD, 81. **CAREER** Vis asst prof, Loyola Marymount Univ, 81-83; asst prof, 83- 89, Assoc prof, Vanderbit Univ, 89-; Dept Chair, 00-. **HONORS AND AWARDS** Ful Hays Doctoral Fel, 79-80; Tinker Found Postdoctoral Fel, 87-88; Case/Carnegie Found for the Advancement of Teaching, Tenn Prof of the Year, 00. **MEMBERSHIPS** AHA; LASA; HSS; SHOT. **RESEARCH** 19th and 20th Century Latin America, especially Brazil. **SELECTED PUBLICATIONS** Auth, British Enterprise in Brazil, Duke, 89; auth, Brazil: The Once and Future Country, St. Martin's, 96; auth, Tropical Capitalism, St. Martin's, 01. **CONTACT ADDRESS** Dept of History, Vanderbilt Univ, PO Box 1802, Sta B, Nashville, TN 37235. **EMAIL** marshall.c.eakin@vanderbilt.edu

EAMON, WILLIAM
PERSONAL Born 06/05/1946, Williston, ND, m, 1975, 1 child **DISCIPLINE** HISTORY OF SCIENCE AND MEDICINE; ITALIAN RENAISSANCE **EDUCATION** Univ Mont, BA, 68, Ma, 70; Univ Kans, PhD(hist sci), 77 **CAREER** Instr hist, Univ Miami, Coral Cables, 73-74; instr, 76-77, asst prof, 77-80, assoc prof, 80-93, Prof Hist, Nmex State Univ, 94-. **MEMBERSHIPS** Hist Sci Soc; Renaissance Soc Am; Soc Hist Medicine. **RESEARCH** Renaissance science and medicine: the scientific revolution; science and popular culture. **SELECTED PUBLICATIONS** Science and the Secrets of Nature, Princeton Univ Press, 94; Cannibalism and contagion: Framing syphilis in Counter-Reformation Italy, in: Early Science and Medicine, 98; auth, Alchemy in Popular Culture: Leonardo Fioravanti and the Search for the Philosopher's Stone, Early Science and Medicine, 00. **CONTACT ADDRESS** Dept of Hist, New Mexico State Univ, PO Box 30001, Las Cruces, NM 88003-8001. **EMAIL** weamon@nmsu.edu

EARHART, HARRY BYRON
PERSONAL Born 01/07/1935, Aledo, IL, m, 1956, 3 children **DISCIPLINE** HISTORY OF RELIGIOUS, ASIAN STUDIES **EDUCATION** Univ Chicago, BD and MA, 60, PhD, 65. **CAREER** Asst prof relig, Vanderbilt Univ, 65-66; from asst prof to assoc prof, 66-69, prof Relig, Western Mich Univ, 75-, Fac res fels, 68 and 73; Fulbright res grant and prof relig, Int Summer Sch Asian Studies, Ewha Womans Univ, Korea, 73; adv Far Eastern relig, Encycl Britannica; ed, Relig Studies Rev, 75-80. **HONORS AND AWARDS** Distinguished Fac Scholar Award, 81; Distniguished Fac Award (from the Michigan asn of Governing Bd), 82; Philo T. Farnsworth Award for his videotape "Fuji: Sacred Mountain of Japan." **MEMBERSHIPS** Am Acad Relig; Asn Asian Studies; Am Soc Study Relig. **RESEARCH** Hist of Japanese relig; Japanese new religions; new religious movements. **SELECTED PUBLICATIONS** Auth, A Religious Study of the Mount Haguro Sect of Shugendo, 70; auth, The New Religions of Japan: A Bibliography of Western-language Material, 2nd ed, 83; auth, Gedatsu-kai and Reilgion in Contemporary Japan, 89; auth, Japanese Religion: Unity an ddiversity, 82; auth, Religious Traditions of the World, 92. **CONTACT ADDRESS** Dept of Relig, Western Michigan Univ, Kalamazoo, MI 49008. **EMAIL** earhart@wmich.edu

EARLY, GERALD
PERSONAL Born 04/21/1952, Philadelphia, PA, m, 1982 **DISCIPLINE** ENGLISH, AFRICAN-AMERICAN STUDIES **EDUCATION** University of Pennsylvania, Philadelphia, PA, BA, 1974; Cornell University, Ithaca, NYork, MA, 1982, PhD, 1982. **CAREER** Washington University, St Louis, MO, professor of English & African & Afro-American studies, 82; Randolph Macon College for Women, Lynchburg, VA, writer in residence, 90. **HONORS AND AWARDS** Whiting Foundation Writer's Awd, Whiting Foundation, 1988; CCLM/General Electric Foundation Awd for Younger Writers, 1988; The Passing of Jazz's Old Guard, published in Best American Essays, 1986; University of Kansas Minority Postdoctoral Fellowship, 1985-87. **SELECTED PUBLICATIONS** Daughters: On Family and Fatherhood, Addison-Wesley, 1994. **CONTACT ADDRESS** Professor, African and Afro-American Studies, Washington Univ, One Brookings Dr, Box 1109, Saint Louis, MO 63130-4899.

EARLY, JAMES
PERSONAL Born 04/19/1923, Worcester, MA, m, 1949, 3 children **DISCIPLINE** HISTORY AMERICAN CIVILIZATION **EDUCATION** Bowdin Col, BA, 47; Harvard Univ, MA, 49; PhD, 53. **CAREER** Teach fel, Harvard Univ, 52-53; instr, Yale Univ, 53-57; instr, asst prof, Vassar, 57-64; assoc prof, prof, Southern Methodist Univ, 64-. **MEMBERSHIPS** MLA. **RESEARCH** American literature; American and Mexican architecture; urbanism. **SELECTED PUBLICATIONS** Auth, Romanticism and Architecture, 65; auth, The Making of Go Down Moses, 72; auth, The Colonial Architecture of Mexico, 94. **CONTACT ADDRESS** Dept English, So Methodist Univ, PO Box 750001, Dallas, TX 75275-0001.

EASTMAN, JOHN ROBERT
PERSONAL Born 06/30/1945, San Diego, CA **DISCIPLINE** HISTORY, MEDIEVAL EUROPEAN HISTORY **EDUCATION** VA Polytechnical Inst & State Univ, BA, 68; Julius-Maximilians-Universitat zu Wurzburg, PhD, 85. **CAREER** Teacher, math, Southern High School, Harwood, MD, 68-69; instr, English, Dolmetscher Inst, Wurzburg, Germany, 76-83; tourist guide, Arbeitsamt, Wurzburg, Germany, 76-85; graduate/postgraduate asst, Dept of Hist, Univ of Wurzburg, 78-82, 85; substitute teacher, Anne Arundel Co, MD, 87-97; teacher, Latin & German, Peninsula Catholic High School, Newport News, VA, 97-; contrib to Int Medieval Bibliography, Univ of Leeds United Kingdom, 95-. **HONORS AND AWARDS** William John Bennett Memorial Scholarship, Annapolis High School, 63. **MEMBERSHIPS** Am Hist Asn; Southeastern Medieval Asn; Nat Coalition of Independent Scholars; Int Platform Asn; Am Philol Asn. **RESEARCH** Medieval scholasticism; religion; history of Germany. **SELECTED PUBLICATIONS** Auth, Editing Medieval Texts: A Modern Critical Edition of De renunciatione pape by Aegidius Romanus, Medieval Perspectives 3, 88; Giles of Rome and His Use of St Augustine in Defense of Papal Abdication, Augustiniana 38, 88; Das Leben des Augustiner-Eremiten Aegidius Romanus (c 1243-1316), Zeitschrift fuer Kirchengeschichte 100, 89; Giles of Rome and Celestine V: The Franciscan Revolution and the Theology of Abdication, Cath Hist Rev 76, 90; Papal Abdication in Later Medieval Thought, Edwin Mellen Press, 90; ed/Herausgeber, Aegidius Romanus, De Renunciatione Pape, Edwin Mellen Press, 92; auth, Giles of Rome and His Fidelity to Sources in the Context of Ecclesiological Political Thought as Exemplified in De renunciatione papae, Documentui e studi sulla tradizione filosofica medievale 3:1, 92; Relating Martin Luther to Giles of Rome: How to Proceed!, Medieval Perspectives 8, 93; Die Werke des Aegidius Romanus, Augustiniana 44, 94; Peter of Auvergne: Life, Master Regent, and the First Quodlibet of 1296, Forschungen zur Reichs-, Papst-und Landesgeschichte, Peter Herde zum 65, Geburtstag, eds, Karl Borchardt & Enno Buenz, Anton Hiersemann, 98. **CONTACT ADDRESS** 11311 Winston Place, Apt 8, Newport News, VA 23601.

EASTWOOD, BRUCE STANSFIELD
PERSONAL Born 02/08/1938, Worcester, MA, m, 1958, 3 children **DISCIPLINE** HISTORY OF SCIENCE **EDUCATION** Emory Univ, AB, 59, MA, 60; Univ Wis, PhD (Grosseteste's optics), 64. **CAREER** Instr hist, Russell Sage Col, 63-64; asst prof, Ithaca Col, 64-67; asst prof hist sci, Clarkson Col Technol, 67-70; assoc prof medieval hist sci, Kans State Univ, 70-73; Assoc Prof to Prof Intellectual Hist Sci, Univ KY, 73-. **HONORS AND AWARDS** Am Philos Soc res grant, 66-67; Nat Sci Found res grant, 66-67. **MEMBERSHIPS** Hist Sci Soc; AHA. **RESEARCH** History of optics before Newton; medieval Franciscans; 17th century physics and culture. **SELECTED PUBLICATIONS** Auth, Mediaeval empiricism, Speculum, 4/68; The revolution in science, In: Harper Encycl Modern World, 70; Metaphysical derivations of a law of refraction, Arch Hist Exact Sci, 70. **CONTACT ADDRESS** Dept of Hist, Univ of Kentucky, 1757 Patterson Office Tower, Lexington, KY 40506. **EMAIL** bseast01@pop.uky.edu

EATON, RICHARD MAXWELL
PERSONAL Born 12/08/1940, Grand Rapids, MI **DISCIPLINE** ISLAMIC STUDIES, INDIAN HISTORY **EDUCATION** Col Wooster, BA, 62; Univ Va, Charlottesville, MA, 67; Univ Wis-Madison, PhD(hist), 72. **CAREER** Teacher Hist, Walton High Sch, WVa, 64-65; teaching asst, Univ Wis-Madison, 67-69; asst prof, 72-78, from assoc prof to prof Hist, Univ Ariz, Tuscon, 78-. **HONORS AND AWARDS** Fulbright-Hays Sr Awd, fel field res Pakistan, 75-76. **MEMBERSHIPS** Asn Asian Studies; Soc Iranian Studies. **RESEARCH** History of medieval India; Islamic studies; comparative religion. **SELECTED PUBLICATIONS** Auth, The court and the dargah in the seventeenth century Deccan, Indian Econ & Social Hist Rev, Vol 10, No 1, 3/73; Sufi folk literature and the expansion of Indian Islam, Hist Religions, Vol 14, No 2, 11/74; Sufis of Bijapur, 1300-1700: Social roles of Sufis in Medieval India, Princeton Univ, 78; The Rise of Islam and the Bengal Frontier, 1204-1760, Univ of California, 93; Nonbelief and Evil, Prometheus Books, Amherst, NY, 98. **CONTACT ADDRESS** Dept of Hist, Univ of Arizona, 215 Social Sciences, Tucson, AZ 85721. **EMAIL** reaton@u.arizona.edu

EBERWEIN, JANE DONAHUE
PERSONAL Born 09/13/1943, Boston, MA, m, 1971 **DISCIPLINE** AMERICAN LITERATURE AND STUDIES **EDUCATION** Emmanuel Col, AB, 65; Brown Univ, PhD (Am civilization), 69. **CAREER** Asst prof, 69-75, assoc prof, 75-84, prof, English, Oakland Univ, 84-. **MEMBERSHIPS** MLA; Col English Asn; Am Studies Asn; Emily Dickinson Int Soc; Soc for the Study of Am Women Writers; Soc of Early Americanists. **RESEARCH** Colonial American literature; American poetry; Emily Dickinson. **SELECTED PUBLICATIONS** Auth, Early American Poetry: Bradstreet, Taylor, Dwight, Freneau, and Bryant, Madison, Univ Wisc Pr, 78; auth, Dickinson: Strategies of Limitation, Univ Mass Pr (Amherst), 85; auth, "Graphicer for Grace: Emily Dickinson's Calvinist Language," Studies in Puritan American Sprituality 1 (90): 170-201; auth, "Introducing a Religious Poet: The 1890 Poems of Emily Dickinson," Christianity and Literature 39 (90): 241-260; auth, "Civil War and Bradstreet's Monarchies," Early American Literature 26 (91): 119-44; auth, "Harvardine quil: Benjamin Tompson's Poems on King Philip's War," Early American Literature 28 (93): 1-20; auth, An Emily Dickinson Encyclopedia, Greenwood Press (Westport, CT), 98; "Emily Dickinson" entry American National Biography New York: Oxford Univ Press (99): 563-66; auth, "Dickinson's Local, Global, and Cosmic Perspectives," Emily Dickinson Handbook, ed. Gudrun Grabher, Roland Hagenbuchle, and Cristanne Miller, University of Massachusetts Press, (98): 27-43; auth, "Art, natures Ape: The Challenge to the Puritan Poet," Poetics in the Poem: Critical Essays on American Self-Reflexive Poetry, ed. Dorothy Z. Baker, New York: Peter Lang (97): 24-25; **CONTACT ADDRESS** Dept of English, Oakland Univ, Rochester, MI 48309-4401. **EMAIL** jeberwei@oakland.edu

EBNER, MICHAEL HOWARD
PERSONAL Born 04/22/1942, Paterson, NJ, m, 1966, 2 children **DISCIPLINE** HISTORY **EDUCATION** Univ Toledo, BA, 64; Univ Va, MA, 66, PhD, 74. **CAREER** Lectr hist, Herbert H Lehman Col, 69-72 & City Col, City Univ NY, 72-74; asst prof, 74-80, assoc prof hist, Lake Forest Col, 80-88; prof hist, A.B. Dick, 1994-; vis prof hist, Univ of Chicago, 90. **HONORS AND AWARDS** Outstanding Teaching Contrib Awd, City Col New York, 73; Chicago Tribune All-Star Team of Col Prof, 94; Nancy Roelker Mentorship Awd, Am Hist Assn, 94; Trustee Awd for Com Serv, Lake Forest Col, 98; Great Tchr Awd from class of 00, Lake Forest Col, 00. **MEMBERSHIPS** AHA; Orgn Am Historians; Soc Hist Educ; AAUP; Urban Hist Assn; Chicago Hist Soc. **RESEARCH** American urban history; American social history. **SELECTED PUBLICATIONS** Co-ed, The Age of Urban Reform, Kennikat, 77; auth, Creating Chicago's North Shore, Univ of Chicago Press, 88; art, Experiencing Megapolis in Princeton, Journal of Urban History, 19:2, Feb 93; art, Technoburb, Inland Architect 37:1, Jan-Feb 93; co-art, Harold Moser's Naperville, Ill Hist Tchr 7:1, 99. **CONTACT ADDRESS** Lake Forest Col, 555 N Sheridan Rd, Lake Forest, IL 60045-2399. **EMAIL** ebner@lfc.edu.

EBY, CECIL DEGROTTE
PERSONAL Born 08/01/1927, Charles Town, WV, m, 1956, 2 children **DISCIPLINE** AMERICAN LITERATURE AND STUDIES **EDUCATION** Shepherd Col, BA, 50; Northwestern Univ, MA, 51; Univ Pa, PhD, 58. **CAREER** From instr to asst

prof English, High Point Col, 55-57; from asst prof to assoc prof, Madison Col, Va, 57-60; from asst prof to assoc prof, Washington and Lee Univ, 60-65; assoc prof, 65-68, Prof English, Univ Mich, Ann Arbor, 68-, chmn, Dept English, Univ Miss, 75-76. **HONORS AND AWARDS** Fulbright lectr Am lit, Lit Univ Salamanca, 62-63; Fulbright lectr Am studies, Univ Valencia, 67-68; Rackham res grants, 67, 71 and 77. **RESEARCH** Literature of the First World War; Spanish Civil War in literature; midwestern literature. **SELECTED PUBLICATIONS** Auth, Popular Fiction in England, 1914-1918, Eng Lit Transition 1880-1920, Vol 36, 93; Hemingway the Short Happy Life of Francis Macomber, Explicator, Vol 51, 92; Fitzgerald Babylon Revisited, Explicator, Vol 53, 95. **CONTACT ADDRESS** Dept of English, Univ of Michigan, Ann Arbor, Ann Arbor, MI 48104. **EMAIL** cdeby@umich.edu

ECHOLS, JAMES KENNETH
PERSONAL m, 2 children **DISCIPLINE** AMERICAN CHURCH HISTORY **EDUCATION** Temple Univ, BA, 73; Lutheran Theol Sem at Phil, MDiv, 77 Yale Univ, MA, 79, MPhil, 84, PhD, 89. **CAREER** Dean, Lutheran Theol Sem at Phil; pres-. **HONORS AND AWARDS** Daniel Alexander Payne awd for Ecumenical srv, African Methodist Episcopal Church, 96; bd mem, elca div for ministry; black lutheran commn develop corporation. **MEMBERSHIPS** Mem, ELCA Delegation to Natl Coun of Churches of Christ. **SELECTED PUBLICATIONS** Pub(s), in the areas of church history, theology and Black American Lutheranism. **CONTACT ADDRESS** Dept of American Church History, Lutheran Sch of Theol at Chicago, 1100 E 55th St, Chicago, IL 60615.

ECKARDT, ALICE LYONS
PERSONAL Born 04/27/1923, Brooklyn, NY, m, 1944, 2 children **DISCIPLINE** HISTORY OF RELIGIONS, CHRISTIAN-JEWISH RELATIONS **EDUCATION** Oberlin Col, BA, 44; Lehigh Univ, MA, 66; DHL, Leigh Univ, 92. **CAREER** Asst Prof, Lehigh Univ, 76-85; Assoc Prof, 85-87; Adjunct Prof, Cedar Crest Col, 81, 82; Spec Advisor, Educ Comm, U S Holocaust Meml Coun, 81-86; Co-Founder and Co-Dir Leigh Univ, 76-85; Prof Emer, 87; **HONORS AND AWARDS** DHL, Lehigh Univ, 92 **MEMBERSHIPS** Am Acad Relig; Nat Inst Holocaust; Am Professors Peace Mid East.; Christian Scholars Group on Judiasm and the Jewish People, 73; Institute for Jewis-Christian Understanding, Steering Comm, 95-00; Exec Comm 87-88; Journal of Ecumenical Studies, Executive Editorial Review Bd, Advisory Bd, 87-; Berman Center for Jewish Studies, 85-89; United Church of Christ Jewish-Christain Dialogue Project, 88-95. **RESEARCH** History and theology of Jewish-Christian relations; the Holocaust, and post-Holocaust theology; sexism and world religions. **SELECTED PUBLICATIONS** Coauth, Encounter with Israel, 70; coauth, Long Night's Journey Into Day, 82, revised 88; auth, Jerusalem: City of the Ages, 87; auth, " The Refromation and the Jews , " Interwoven Destinies: Jews and Christians Through the Ages, 93; auth, ed, Burinig Memory: Times of Testing and Reckoning, 93; ed, Collecting Myself: A Writer's Perspective, 93; auth, " Suffering, Theology, and the Shoah," The Holocaust Now, , 96; auth, "Creating Christian Yom HaShoah Gutman, 96; auth, " The Shoah Road to a Revised-Revived Christianity," From the Unthinkable to the Unavoidable, 97; auth, " Leiden: Herausforderung des Glaubens - Herausforderung Gottes," Kultur allein inst nicht genug, 98. **CONTACT ADDRESS** Beverly Hill Rd, Box 619A, Coopersburg, PA 18036. **EMAIL** AliceEck@aol.com

ECKERT, EDWARD K.
DISCIPLINE HISTORY **EDUCATION** Univ FL, PhD. **CAREER** Prof Hist and vpres Acad Affairs. **RESEARCH** US hist; the Am Civil War; mil hist; the Vietnam War. **SELECTED PUBLICATIONS** Auth, In War and Peace: An American Military History Anthology, Wadsworth , 89; "Fiction Distorting Fact:" The Prison Life, Annotated by Jefferson Davis, Mercer UP, 87; coauth, Ten Years in the Saddle: The Military Memoir of William W. Averell, Presidio, 79; The McClellans and the Grants: Generalship and Strategy in the Civil War. **CONTACT ADDRESS** St. Bonaventure Univ, Saint Bonaventure, NY 14778. **EMAIL** eeckert@sbu.edu

ECKHARDT, PATRICIA
PERSONAL Born 06/27/1939, Toledo, OH, m, 1961, 3 children **DISCIPLINE** ART HISTORY **EDUCATION** Lindenwood Col, BA, 61; Univ Iowa, MA, 73, MFA, 78, PhD, 90. **CAREER** Field Svc, grant manag, 77-82, St Hist Soc of Iowa; principal, 90-, Eckhardt Research. **MEMBERSHIPS** Society of Architectural Historians, Dowd Society of the Archaeological Institute of America. **RESEARCH** Amer Archit, 1880-1920 **CONTACT ADDRESS** 514 North Linn St, Iowa City, IA 52245. **EMAIL** peckhardt@juno.com

ECKSTEIN, ARTHUR M.
PERSONAL Born 09/13/1946, Hempstead, NY **DISCIPLINE** ANCIENT HISTORY **EDUCATION** UCLA, BA 68, MA 70; Univ Calif Berkeley, PhD 78. **CAREER** Univ N Carolina, asst prof 78-80; Univ Maryland, asst prof, assoc prof, prof 80-94-. **HONORS AND AWARDS** Woodrow Wilson Fel; svral tchrs and serv Awds UM. **MEMBERSHIPS** AHA; APA; AAAH. **RESEARCH** Roman Imperial Expansion; Hellenistic Politics; Ancient Histiography. **SELECTED PUBLICATIONS** Auth, Senate and General: Individual Decision-Making and Roman Foreign Relations, 264-194 BC, Univ Calif Press, 87; auth, Moral Vision in the Histories of Polybius, Univ Calif Press, 95; auth, Polybius Demetrius of Pharus and the Origins of the Second Illyrian War, Classical Philology, 94; auth, Glabrio and the Aetolians: A Note on deditio, Trans of the Amer Philos Assoc, 96; Physis and Nomos: Polybius the Romans and Cato the Elder, in: Peter Cartledge, Peter Garnsey, Erich Gruen, eds, Hellenistic Constructs, Univ Calif Press, 97. **CONTACT ADDRESS** Dept Hist, Univ of Maryland, Col Park, 2115 Francis Scott Key Hall, College Park, MD 20742. **EMAIL** ae1@umail.umd.edu

EDELMAN, DIANA V.
DISCIPLINE BIBLICAL STUDIES; ANCIENT SYNO-PALESTINIAN HISTORY & ARCHAEOLOGY **EDUCATION** Smith Col, AB, 75; Univ Chicago, MA, 78, PhD, 86. **CAREER** Lectr, St Xavier Univ, 90-91; assoc prof, James Madison Univ, 93-00; lectr, Univ Sheffield, 00-; staff mem, Tel Rehov Excavations, Israel. **HONORS AND AWARDS** Grant-in-aid Am Coun Learned Studies, 88; vis prof Ecole biblique et archeol Jerusalem, 96. **MEMBERSHIPS** Soc Bibl Lit; Am Schools of Orient Res; Cath Bibl Asn. **RESEARCH** Ancient Syno-Palestinian history & archaelology; Deuteronomistic history; Ancient Israelite religion; 2nd temple Judaism. **SELECTED PUBLICATIONS** Auth, King Saul in the Historiography of Judah, Journal for the Study of the Old Testament Supplement Series, 91; ed, The Fabric of History: Text, Artifact, & Israels Past, Journal for the Study of the Old Testament Supplement Series, 91; auth, You Shall Not Abhor an Edomite for He is Your Brother: Edom and Seir in History and Tradition, Archaeology and Biblical Studies, 95; The Triumph of Elohim: From Yahuisims to Judaisms, Biblical Exegesis and Theology, 95. **CONTACT ADDRESS** Western Bank, Univ of Sheffield, Sheffield S10 2TN. **EMAIL** d.edelman@sheffield.ac.uk

EDELSTEIN, ARTHUR
PERSONAL Born New York, NY **DISCIPLINE** AMERICAN LITERATURE, AMERICAN STUDIES **EDUCATION** Brooklyn Col, BA, 56; Stanford Univ, MA, 63, PhD (Englisb), 77. **CAREER** Lectr English, Hunter Col, City Univ NY, 63-66; asst prof English and Am studies, Brandeis Univ, 66-76; assoc prof English, Col William and Mary, 77-78; Adj Prof English, Brandeis Univ, 79-, Dir writing prog, Brandeis Univ, 71-74; Nat Endowment for Humanities fel Am social hist, 73-74; mem adv comt to bd trustees humanities, Suffolk Univ, Boston, 78-79; vis prof English, Wellesley Col, fall, 81; Consult, Mass Found Humanities and Public Policy, 80-. **MEMBERSHIPS** MLA. **RESEARCH** American realist fiction; American working class history; contemporary world literature. **SELECTED PUBLICATIONS** Auth, Weber, Max and the Jewish Question--A Study of the Social Outlook of His Sociology, Am Hist Rev, Vol 99, 94. **CONTACT ADDRESS** 2 Dale St, Wellesley, MA 02181.

EDELSTEIN, MELVIN A.
PERSONAL Born 05/23/1939, New York, NY, m, 1969, 1 child **DISCIPLINE** HISTORY **EDUCATION** Univ of Chicago, BA, 60; Princeton Univ, MA, 62, PhD, 65. **CAREER** Instr in History of Western Civilization, Stanford Univ, 64-67; asst prof of hist, Herbert H. Lehman Col of CUNY, 67-73; Assoc Prof, 73-79, Prof, 79-, Chemn, William Paterson Univ of New Jersey, 81-87. **HONORS AND AWARDS** Grant, Am Philos Soc, 69, 75, 90, 94, 99; summer stipend, 89, travel-to-collections grant, NEH, 90; Fulbright fel for res, 96. **MEMBERSHIPS** Am Hist Asn; Soc of French Hist Studies; Societe des Etudes Robespierristes. **RESEARCH** French revolutionary elections; French revolutionary press. **SELECTED PUBLICATIONS** Auth, La Feuille Villageoise: Communication Et Modernisation Dans Les Regions Rurales Pendant La Revolution: Comission D'Histoire Economique Et Sociale De La Revolution Francaise. Memoires Et Documents, Bibliotheque Nationale, 77; Le Comportement Electoral sous la Monarchie Constitutionnelle (1790-91): Une Interpretation Communautaire, Annales Historiques de la Revolution Francaise, 95; Participation ed Sociologie Electorales des Landes en 1790, Annales Historiques de la Revolution Francaise, 99; Participation et Sociologie Electorales de l'Aisne en mai 1790 et juin 1791, AnnalesHistoriques Compiegnoises, 98; Le Militaire-Citoyen, ou le droit de vote des militaires pendant la Revolution francaise, Annales Historiques de la Revolution Francaise, 97. **CONTACT ADDRESS** Dept of Hist, William Paterson Col of New Jersey, 300 Pompton Rd, Wayne, NJ 07470. **EMAIL** edelsteinm@wpunj.edu

EDGAR, WALTER B.
PERSONAL Born 12/10/1943, Mobile, AL, m, 1966, 2 children **DISCIPLINE** HISTORY **EDUCATION** Davidson Col, AB, 65; Univ SC, MA, 67; PhD, 69. **CAREER** Asst prof hist to prof, dir Inst S Student, 80- , Univ S Carolina, 72- ; vis prof hist, Middlebury Col, 86. **HONORS AND AWARDS** Neuffer Prof S Studententententent, 95; Mortar Bd "Exc in Teaching" Awd, 95, 00; George Wash Distinguished Prof Hist, 99. **MEMBERSHIPS** Orgn Am Hist; S Hist Asn; S Student Forum. **RESEARCH** American South, South Carolina. **SELECTED PUBLICATIONS** Auth, The Letterbook of Robert Pringle, (72); auth The Biographical Directory of the SC House of Representatives, (74); auth, A Southern Renaascence Man: Views of Robert Penn Warren, (84); auth, Southern Landscapes, (96); auth, South Carolina in the Modern Age, (92); auth, South Carolina: A History, (98). **CONTACT ADDRESS** Dept Hist, Univ of So Carolina, Columbia, Columbia, SC 29225. **EMAIL** edgar@gwm.sc.edu

EDIE, CAROLYN A.
PERSONAL Born 08/09/1930, Boston, MA, m, 1960 **DISCIPLINE** HISTORY **EDUCATION** Wellesley Col, AB, 51; Univ Wis, MA, 54, PhD, 57. **CAREER** Instr hist, Hobart and William Smith Cols, 57-59, asst prof 59-61; from asst prof to assoc prof, 61-74, Prof Hist, Univ Ill, Chicago Circle, 74-, Am Philos Soc res grant 67; fels, Huntington Libr and Grad Col, Univ Ill, 71; Am Philos Soc grant, 74. **MEMBERSHIPS** AHA; Conf Brit Studies (rec secy, 71-73); Am Soc Legal Hist; Conf Study Soc and Polit Thought. **RESEARCH** British history, 17th century; early modern Europe. **CONTACT ADDRESS** Dept of Hist, Univ of Illinois, Chicago, Chicago, IL 60680. **EMAIL** cedie@uic.edu

EDLUND-BERRY, INGRID E. M.
PERSONAL Born 09/18/1942, Lund, Sweden, m, 1987, 2 children **DISCIPLINE** CLASSICAL ARCHAEOLOGY; ANCIENT HISTORY **EDUCATION** Univ of Lund, SWE, FK, FM, 65, FL, 69; Bryn Mawr Col, MA, 69, PhD, 71. **CAREER** Instr, The Intercollegiate Center for Classical Studies, 71-72, asst prof, 77-78; Univ GA, vis asst prof, 73-78; vis prof, Univ MN, 82; asst prof, 78-87, assoc prof, 87-98, Prof, Univ TX at Austin, 98-. **HONORS AND AWARDS** ACLS; Fondazione Familglia Rausing; Andrew W. Mellon Found; Alexander von Humboldt-Siftung; Univ Res Inst , Univ TX at Austin. **MEMBERSHIPS** Amer Philological Assoc; Archaeological Inst Amer; Associazone internationale di archaeologia classica; Classical Assoc of the Middle West and South; Etruscan Found; Svenska klassikerforbundet. **RESEARCH** Archaeology of ancient Italy, ancient relig. **SELECTED PUBLICATIONS** Auth, The Iron Age and Etruscan Vases in the Olcott Collection at Columbia Univ, NY, Amer Philos Soc, Transaction 70, 80; The Gods and the Place: Location and Function of Sanctuaries in the Countryside of Etruria and Magna Graecia (700-400 B. C.), Acta Instituti Romani Regni Sueciae, Stockholm, 87; Poggio Civitate (Murlo) 1966-1987: an annotated bibliography of primary and secondary publications, with the late Kyle M. Phillips, Jr, in In the Hills of Tuscany, ed, Karen B. Velluci, The Univ Museum, Univ PA, 93; The Seated and Standing Statue Akroteria from Poggio Civitate (Murlo), Giorgio Bretschneider, Rome, 92, Archaeologica, 96; numerous articles in Archaeological News, Eranos, Classical Bull, Rivista di Studi Classici, Talanta, CA Studies in Classical Antiquity, Medusa, Mededelingen van het Nederl, Historisch Instituut te Rome, Rivista di Archaeologia, Amer J of Archaeology, Vergilius, Parola del Passato, Opuscula Romana, Acta Instituti Romani Regni Sueciae: Deliciae Fictiles, Opus mixtum, Acta Universitatis Upsaliensis: Boreas, Bollettino d'Arte, Praktika, Etruscan Studies, Kotinos. **CONTACT ADDRESS** Dept of Classics, Univ of Texas, Austin, Waggener 123, Austin, TX 78712. **EMAIL** IEMEB@mail.utexas.edu

EDMONDS, ANTHONY OWENS
PERSONAL Born 06/11/1940, Biloxi, MS, m, 1964, 3 children **DISCIPLINE** RECENT UNITED STATES & BLACK HISTORY **EDUCATION** Yale Univ, BA, 62; Vanderbilt Univ, MA, 66, PhD, 70. **CAREER** Instr hist, Univ TN, Nashville, 68-69; from Asst Prof to Assoc Prof, 69-78, prof hist, Ball State Univ, 78; Outstanding Honors Col Prof, 99. **HONORS AND AWARDS** Outstanding Tchr, Ball State Univ, 81, 91, 96; Outstanding Fac Advisor ,96. **MEMBERSHIPS** Southern Historical Asn; Orgn Am Historians; Pop Cult Asn; Soc Study For Rels; Am Stud Asn; Nat Collegiate Honors Coun. **RESEARCH** Am cult in the 1950's; sports hist; Vietnam War; higher educ. **SELECTED PUBLICATIONS** Auth, Joe Louis, Eerdmans, 73; Resources for Teaching the Vietnam War, Ctr for Soc Studies Educ, 92; The War in Vietnam, Greenwood, 98. **CONTACT ADDRESS** Dept of Hist, Ball State Univ, 2000 W University, Muncie, IN 47306-0002. **EMAIL** 00aoedmonds@bsuvc.bsu.edu

EDMONDSON, CLIFTON EARL
PERSONAL Born 05/14/1937, Shreveport, LA, m, 1964, 2 children **DISCIPLINE** MODERN EUROPEAN HISTORY **EDUCATION** Miss Col, BA, 59; Duke Univ, MA, 62, PhD (hist), 66. **CAREER** From instr to asst prof hist, Univ NC, Chapel Hill, 62-70, Univ Res Coun fac grant, 67-69; asst prof 70-77, Assoc Prof Hist, Davidson Col, 77-85; prof hist, 85-; chair, 97-. **MEMBERSHIPS** AHA; AAUP; SHA. **RESEARCH** Central Europe; Fascism; Cold War. **SELECTED PUBLICATIONS** auth, article, Early Heimwehr Aims and Activities, Austrian History Yearbook, vol. VII, 72; auth The Heimwehr and Austrian Politics, 1918-1936, Ahtens, Univ of Georgia Press, 78; auth, article, The Heimwehr and February 1934: Reflections and Questions, The Austrian Socialist Experiment: Social Democracy and Austromarxism, 1918-1934, Boulder, London: Westview Press, 85; auth, article, Heimwehren und andere Wehrverbande, Handbuch des politischen Systems Osterreichs: Erst Repulik 1918-1933, 95; auth, articles

about Ruth Fischer, Hans Gatzke, Georg Grosz, Carlton J.H. Hayes, Hajo Holborn, and Kurt von Schuschnigg, American National Biography, Oxford Univ Press, 99. **CONTACT ADDRESS** Dept of Hist, Davidson Col, PO Box 1719, Davidson, NC 28036-1719. **EMAIL** eaedmondson@davidson.edu

EDMONDSON, JONATHAN C.
PERSONAL Born 01/14/1959, Liverpool, United Kingdom, m, 1983, 3 children **DISCIPLINE** HISTORY **EDUCATION** Cambridge Univ, BA, 79; MA; PhD, 84. **CAREER** Vis Asst Prof to Assoc Prof, York Univ, 87-. **MEMBERSHIPS** Class Asn of Can; Soc for Promotion of Roman Studies; Am Philol Asn; Cambridge Philol Soc. **RESEARCH** Roman Spain, especially Lusitania; Roman imperialism; Roman spectacle, especially gladiators. **SELECTED PUBLICATIONS** Auth, Dio: The Julio-Claudians, London, 92; auth, "Dynamic arenas: gladiatorial presentations in the city of Rome and the construction of Roman society," in Roman Theater and Society, Univ Mich Press, 96; auth, "Two dedications to Divus Augustus and Diva Augusta from Augusta Emerita and the early development of the imperial cult in Lusitania re-examined," Madrider Mitteilungen, 97; auth, "The cultural politics of public spectacle in Rome and the Greek East, 167-166 BCE," in The Art of Ancient spectacle, 99; auth, "Epigraphy and History of Roman Hispania," J of Roman Archaeol, 99; auth, "Conmemoracion funeraria y relaciones familiares en Augusta Emerita," Sociedad y cultura en Lusitania romana, 00; co-ed, Law and Social Status in Classical Athens, Oxford Univ Press, 00; co-auth, Imagen y Memoria: Monumentos funerarios con retrato de Augusta Emerita, Madrid, 01. **CONTACT ADDRESS** Dept Hist, York Univ, 4700 Keele St, Toronto, ON, Canada M3J 1P3. **EMAIL** jedmond@yorku.ca

EDMONSON, JAMES MILTON
PERSONAL Born 02/12/1951, Muncie, IN, m, 2 children **DISCIPLINE** HISTORY OF TECHNOLOGY **EDUCATION** Col of Wooster, BA, 73; Univ of Del, MA, 76; Univ of Del, PhD, 81. **CAREER** Curator, Dittrick Museum of Med Hist, Case Western Reserve Univ and Cleveland Med Lib Assoc, 81-; teach asst, Col Wooster, 71-72; teach asst, Univ Del, 77; Adj asst prof, Case Western Reserve University, 81-. **HONORS AND AWARDS** Hagley Fellow, 74-78; Fulbright-Hays Fellow, Paris, 78-79; Willbur Owen Sypherd Prize, Univ Del, 81; Smithsonian Inst Res Fellow, 88; FC Clark Wood Fellow, 90; Wellcome Museum Fellow, London, 92. **MEMBERSHIPS** Handerson Med Hist Soc; Ohio Acad of Med Hist; Soc Hist of Technol; Euro Asn Museums of Hist of Med Sciences; Med Museums Assoc; Am Asn Hist Med. **RESEARCH** History of American surgical instrument trade; medical patents; medical furniture; endoscopy. **SELECTED PUBLICATIONS** United States patents for medical devices: patterns of inventive activity in the nineteenth century, Proceedings of the Seventh Symposium of the European Association of Museums of History of Medical Sciences,Zurich, 94; Endoscope, in Instruments of Science: An Historical Encyclopedia, London, 97; American Surgical Instruments: An Illustrated History of Their Manufacture and a Directory of Instrument Makers to 1900, San Francisco, Norman Pub, 97. **CONTACT ADDRESS** Case Western Reserve Univ, 11000 Euclid Ave., Cleveland, OH 44106-1714. **EMAIL** jme3@po.cwru.edu

EDSALL, NICHOLAS CRANFORD
PERSONAL Born 07/14/1936, Boston, MA **DISCIPLINE** MODERN ENGLISH HISTORY **EDUCATION** Harvard Univ, BA, 58, PhD, 66; London Sch Econ, MA, 60. **CAREER** From asst lectr to lectr hist, Univ Nottingham, 64-66; asst prof, 66-72, assoc prof Hist, 72-88, prof Hist, 88-98, Prof Emeritus, Univ VA, Charlottesville, 98-. **MEMBERSHIPS** AHA; Conf Brit Studies; AAUP. **RESEARCH** Victorian political and social history; history of homosexuality. **SELECTED PUBLICATIONS** Auth, The Antipoor Law Movement, Manchester Univ, 71; Varieties of radicalism: Attwood, Cobden and the local politics of municipal incorporation, Hist J, 73; A failed national movement: The Parliamentary and Financial Reform Association, 1848-54, Bull Inst Hist Res, 5/76; Richard Cobden, Independent Radical, Harvard Univ Press, 86. **CONTACT ADDRESS** 1924 Thomson Rd, Charlottesville, VA 22903.

EDWARDS, LEE M.
PERSONAL Born 10/20/1937, Sydney, Australia, 1 child **DISCIPLINE** ART HISTORY **EDUCATION** Columbia Univ, PhD, 84 **CAREER** Writer, consultant, Fac, Sarah Lawrence Coll. **MEMBERSHIPS** Natl Coalition of Independent Scholars; Historians of Nineteenth Century Art; The Victorian Soc **RESEARCH** Victorian Painting; The Idyllists and their followers; Hubert von Herkomer **SELECTED PUBLICATIONS** Auth, numerous book and exhibition reviews since 92 for The Art Book; Herkomer: A Vicotiran Artist, Scolar Press, Ashgate Publishing, Fall 99. **CONTACT ADDRESS** P O Box 489, Locust Valley, NY 11560. **EMAIL** ledwal1234@aol.com

EDWARDS, MARY
DISCIPLINE ART HISTORY **EDUCATION** Columbia Univ, MLS, BS, MA, PhD. **CAREER** Adjunct prof. **HONORS AND AWARDS** Samuel H. Kress diss fel, 82; NEH Travel to Coll(s) grant, 87. **SELECTED PUBLICATIONS** Co-auth, Wind Chant and Night Chant Sandpaintings: Studies Iconography; Source, Jour of Arch Hist, Il Santo, Bollettino del Museo Civico di Padova. **CONTACT ADDRESS** Dept of Art Hist, Pratt Inst, 200 Willoughby Ave, Brooklyn, NY 11205.

EDWARDS, REBECCA
DISCIPLINE HISTORY **EDUCATION** Col of William and Mary, BA, 88; MA, 90, PhD, 95, Univ Virginia. **CAREER** Asst Prof, Vassar Col, 95-. **CONTACT ADDRESS** Vassar Col, 124 Raymond Ave, Box 493, Poughkeepsie, NY 12604. **EMAIL** reedwards@vassar.edu

EDWARDS, WENDY J. DEICHMANN
PERSONAL Born 12/07/1957, Waterbury, CT, m, 1992, 1 child **DISCIPLINE** HISTORY, RELIGIOUS **EDUCATION** Drew Univ, PhD, 91. **CAREER** Adj Prof Church History, 94-, Ashland Theo Sem; United Theo Sem. **MEMBERSHIPS** ASCH, AAR, HSUMC. **RESEARCH** American Religious History, Social gospel history, history of Christian missions, women in history of Christianity, Methodism. **SELECTED PUBLICATIONS** Ed, "Mission Becomes Institution: The Example of U.s. Methodism" in The World is My Parish (Lewiston NY: Edwin Mellen Press, 1992); Manifest Destiny, the Social Gospel and the Coming Kingdom, Josiah Strong's Program of Global Reform, 1885-1916, in: Perspectives on the Social Gospel, Papers from the Inaugural Social Gospel Conference at Colgate Rochester Divinity School, Lewiston NY, Edwin Mellen Press, 98; Forging an Ideology for American Missions, Josiah Strong and Manifest Destiny in North American Foreign Missions, 1810-1914; Theology, Theory and Policy, Curzon Press, London, and Eerdmans, Grand Rapids, 00; Domesticity with a Difference, Woman's Sphere Woman's Leadership and the Founding of the Baptist Missionary Training School in Chicago, 1881, in: Amer Baptist Qtly, 90. **CONTACT ADDRESS** 12645 Coal Bank Rd, Doylestown, OH 33230.

EGAN, MARY JOAN
PERSONAL Born 06/23/1932, Tuscaloosa, AL, m, 1974 **DISCIPLINE** ENGLISH LITERATURE, IRISH STUDIES **EDUCATION** Univ Ala, BA, 52; Cath Univ Am, MA, 58, PhD (English and philos), 69. **CAREER** Instr English, Univ Md, 66-69; asst prof, Centenary Col La, 69-72; asst prof, 72-80, Assoc Prof English, Slippery Rock State Col, 80-, Instr English, Wiley Col, 69-70. **MEMBERSHIPS** Wallace Stevens Soc; Irish Am Cult Inst. **RESEARCH** Modern poetry; myth and archetype. **SELECTED PUBLICATIONS** Auth, Stevens, Wallace Homunculus et la Belle Etoile--An Echo of Goethe Faust, Eng Lang Notes, Vol 31, 93. **CONTACT ADDRESS** Dept of English, Slippery Rock Univ of Pennsylvania, Slippery Rock, PA 16057.

EGENHOFER, MAX J.
DISCIPLINE GEOGRAPHY **EDUCATION** Stuttgart Univ, Dipl-Ing, 85; Univ Maine, PhD, 89. **CAREER** Grad res asst, Inst for Geodesy and Photogrammetry, Swiss Federal Inst of Technol, 82-83; grad res asst to res asst, Stuttgart Univ, 83-85; from grad res asst to prof, Univ Maine, 85-. **MEMBERSHIPS** Res Projects Comt of the Univ Consortium for Geog Infor Sci, Am Inst of Urban and Regional Affairs, NCGIA. **SELECTED PUBLICATIONS** Auth, "Consistency Revisited," GeoInformatica 1.4 (97): 323-325; coauth, "Comparing the Complexity of Wayfinding Tasks in Built Environments," Environment and Planning B 25.6 (98): 895-913; coauth, "Metric Details for Natural-Language Spatial Relations," ACM Transactions on Infor Systems 16.4 (98): 295-321; coauth, "Using Digital Spatial Archives Effectively," Int J of Geog Infor Sci 13.1 (99): 1-8; coauth, "Robust Inference of the Flow Direction in River Networks," Algorithmica (in press); coauth, "Visualization in an Early Stage of the Problem Solving Process in GIS," Computers and Geosciences (in press); coauth, "Spatial Relations in SQL/Multimedia," Transactions in GIS 3.3 (in press). **CONTACT ADDRESS** Dept Spatial Infor Sci & Engineering, Univ of Maine, 348B Boardman Hall, Orono, ME 04469-5711. **EMAIL** max@spatial.maine.edu

EGERTON, FRANK N.
PERSONAL Born 02/06/1936, Louisburg, NC, m, 1966, 2 children **DISCIPLINE** WORLD HISTORY, HISTORY OF SCIENCE, ENV HISTORY **EDUCATION** Duke Univ, BS, 58; Univ Wis-Madison, PhD, 67. **CAREER** Dept History, Univ Wisc-Parkside **HONORS AND AWARDS** Hunt Inst Bot Doc, 67, 68, 69 & 70; Nat Sci Found, 81; Univ WI Sea Grant Inst. **MEMBERSHIPS** Am Soc Environmental Hist **RESEARCH** History of science; environmental history. **SELECTED PUBLICATIONS** Ed, Landmarks of Botanical History, Stanford Univ Press; Overfishing or Pollution Case History of a Controversy on the Great Lakes, Ann Arbor: Great Lakes Fishery Comn, 85. **CONTACT ADDRESS** Dept of Hist, Univ of Wisconsin, Parkside, PO Box 2000, Kenosha, WI 53141-2000. **EMAIL** frank.egerton@uwp.edu

EGGENER, KEITH L.
PERSONAL Born Portland, OR **DISCIPLINE** ART, ARCHITECTURAL HISTORY **EDUCATION** Portland State Univ, BA, 85; Univ WA, MA, 89; Stanford Univ, PhD, 95. **CAREER** Asst prof, Art Hist, Carleton Col, Northfield, MN, 95-97; asst prof of Architecural Hist, Univ NV, Las Vegas, 97-99; historic preservation consultant, Portland, OR, Charleston, SC, Las Vegas, NV, 84-; advisor, Barragan Found, Basel, Switzerland, 95-; asst prof, Univ Missouri, Columbia, 99-. **HONORS AND AWARDS** Samuel H Kress Found fel, 93; Sally Kress Tompkins fel, 93; Jacob K Javits fel, 93-95; Best Article of 1997, South Carolina Hist Magazine. **MEMBERSHIPS** Soc of Architectural Hist; Col Art Asn; Am Collegiate Schools of Architecture. **RESEARCH** Modern architecture in Mexico and the US; architectural photography; nationalism; melancholia. **SELECTED PUBLICATIONS** Auth, Diego Rivera's Proposal for El Pedregal, Source: Notes in the History of Art, spring 95; Expressionism and Emotional Architecture in Mexico: Luis Barragan's Collaborations with Max Cetto and Mathias Goeritz, Architectura--J of the Hist of Architecture, no 1, 95; Old Folks, New South: Charleston's William Enston Home, SC Hist Mag, July 97; Reflecting Psyche: Mirrors and Meaning at the Salon de la Princesse, hotel de Soubise, Constructing Identity: Proceedings of the 86th ACSA Annual Meeting, ACSA Press, 98; Towards an Organic Architecture in Mexico, Frank Lloyd Wright: Europe and Beyond, Anthony Alofsin, ed, Univ CA Press, 99; Past Knowing: Photography, Preservation, and Decay at the Gardens of El Pedregal, Memory and Architecture: Proceedings of the 1998 ACSA West Central Regional Conference; Image and Identity in Post-War Mexican Architecture, forthcoming; The Integration of Architecture and Landscape at the Gardens of El Pedregal, forthcoming. **CONTACT ADDRESS** Dept of Art Hist & Archaeology, Univ of Missouri, Columbia, 109 Pickard Hall, Columbia, MO 65211. **EMAIL** eggenerk@missouri.edu

EGGERT, GERALD G.
PERSONAL Born 04/12/1926, Berrien Co, MI, m, 1953, 3 children **DISCIPLINE** U.S. HISTORY **EDUCATION** Western Mich Univ, AB, 49; Univ Mich, AM, 51, PhD (US hist), 60. **CAREER** Teacher pub sch, Mich, 49-54; instr US hist, Univ Md, 57-60; from instr to asst prof, Bowling Green State Univ, 60-65; from asst prof to assoc prof, 65-72, Prof to Prof Emer US Hist, PA State Univ, 72-, Head Dept Hist, 80-, Vis lectr, Univ Mich, 63. **MEMBERSHIPS** AHA; Orgn Am Historians. **SELECTED PUBLICATIONS** Auth, Richard Olney and the income tax cases, Miss Valley Hist Rev, 61; A missed alternative, federal courts as arbiters of railway labor disputes 1877-95, Labor Hist, 66; Our man in Havana: Fitzhugh Lee, Hisp Am Hist Rev, 67; Railroad Labor Disputes-Beginnings of Federal strike policy, Univ Mich, 67; Richard Olney, Evolution of a Statesman, Pa State Univ, 74; Steelmasters and Labor Reform, 1886-1923, Univ Pittsburg, 81. **CONTACT ADDRESS** Dept of Hist, Pennsylvania State Univ, Univ Park, University Park, PA 16802. **EMAIL** gge1@psu.edu

EGLER, DAVID G.
PERSONAL Born 06/04/1937, Chicago, IL, m, 1965, 2 children **DISCIPLINE** HISTORY **EDUCATION** Univ Chicago, AB, 59; Vanderbilt Univ, MAt, 60; Univ Mich, MA 63; Univ Ariz, PhD, 78. **CAREER** Instr, Univ Ariz, 68-69; instr, Univ Colo, 71-72; prof, Western Ill Univ, 72-. **HONORS AND AWARDS** Fulbright, NEH, Ford Foundation, Univ Chicago Scholarship. **MEMBERSHIPS** Asn for Asian Studies. **RESEARCH** Japanese imperialism/colonialsim. **SELECTED PUBLICATIONS** Auth, Civilization Past and Present Study Guide; auth, **CONTACT ADDRESS** Dept Hist, Western Illinois Univ, 1 University Circle, Macomb, IL 61455-1367. **EMAIL** david_egler@ccmail.wiu.edu

EGLIN, JOHN
PERSONAL Born 04/26/1962, Santa Montana, CA, s **DISCIPLINE** HISTORY **EDUCATION** Davidson Col, BA, 84; MA, 89; Univ Ga, MA, 90; Yale Univ, M Phil, 92; PhD, 96. **CAREER** Asst Prof, Univ of Montana, 96-. **MEMBERSHIPS** AHA, Am Soc for Eighteenth Century Studies, N Am Coun on British Studies. **RESEARCH** Eighteenth Century British Culture and Politics. **SELECTED PUBLICATIONS** Auth, "Venice and the Thames: Venetian Vedutisti and the London View in the Eighteenth Century," in Italian Culture in Northern Europe in the Eighteenth Century, ed. Shearer West (Cambridge: Cambridge Univ Press, 99); auth, Venice Transfigured: The Myth of Venice in British Culture, 1660-1797, St. Martin's Press (NY), forthcoming. **CONTACT ADDRESS** Dept Hist, Univ of Montana, 1310 Gerald Ave 3, Missoula, MT 59812. **EMAIL** eglin@selway.umt.edu

EHRET, CHRISTOPHER
PERSONAL Born 07/27/1941, San Francisco, CA **DISCIPLINE** AFRICAN HISTORY, HISTORICAL LINGUISTICS **EDUCATION** Univ Redlands, BA, 63; Northwestern Univ, Evanston, MA and cert African studies, 66, PhD (African hist), 68. **CAREER** Asst prof, 68-72, assoc prof, 72-78, Prof African Hist, Univ Calif, Los Angeles, 78-, Ford Found grant African relig hist, 71-74; Fulbright grant, 82. **MEMBERSHIPS** Kenya Hist Soc; Hist Soc Tanzania; African Studies Association life member. **RESEARCH** Development and use of linguistic evidence in historical reconstruction; eastern and southern African history; African historical linquistics. **SELECTED PUBLICATIONS** Auth, "Southern Nilotic History," 71; auth, "Ethiopians and East Africans," 74; auth, "The Archaeological and Linguistic Reconstruction of African History," 82; auth, "Reconstructing Proto-Afroasiatic, 95; auth, An African Classical Age," 98 **CONTACT ADDRESS** Dept of Hist, Univ of California, Los Angeles, Los Angeles, CA 90024. **EMAIL** ehret@history.ucla.edu

EICK, GRETCHEN
PERSONAL Born 12/17/1942, Fairview Park, OH, m, 1991, 6 children **DISCIPLINE** HISTORY **EDUCATION** Kalamazoo Col, BA, 64; NW Univ, MA, 65; Univ Kans, PhD, 97. **CAREER** Exec Dir, National Impact, 87-91; Res Project Admin, 92-93; Instructor to Assoc Prof, Friends Univ, 93-. **HONORS AND AWARDS** Woodrow Wilson Fel, 64-65; Fulbright Fel, 00. **MEMBERSHIPS** Org of Am Hist; Asn for the Study of African Am Life and Hist; Am Studies Asn. **RESEARCH** Civil rights movement; US foreign policy since 1945; Womens history - 19th and 20th Century; Literature and history; African American Studies. **SELECTED PUBLICATIONS** Auth, Women: Economic Exile in the Promised Land, 92; auth, Lifted Voices: The Civil Rights Movement, The NAACP, and America's Heartland, Univ IL Press, forthcoming. **CONTACT ADDRESS** Dept Relig & Humanities, Friends Univ, 2100 W Univ St, Wichita, KS 67213-3379. **EMAIL** eick@friends.edu

EID, LEROY VICTOR
PERSONAL Born 12/22/1932, Cincinnati, OH, m, 1970 **DISCIPLINE** AMERICAN HISTORY **EDUCATION** Univ Dayton, BS, 53; St John's Univ, MA, 58, PhD, 61; Univ Toronto, MA, 68. **CAREER** From instr to asst prof, 61-73, assoc prof, 73-79, prof hist, Univ Dayton, 79-, chmn dept, 69-83. **RESEARCH** American Irish; Indian military history. **SELECTED PUBLICATIONS** Auth, The Colonial Scotch-Irish, Eire-Ireland, Winter, 86; auth, Irish, Scotch and Scotch-Irish, A Reconsideration, American Presbyterians: Journal of Presbyterian History, vol 64, winter, 86; auth, Their Rules of War: The Validity of James Smith's Analysis of Indian War, The Register of the Kentucky Historical Society, Winter, 86; auth A Kind of Running Fight: Indian Battlefield Tactics in the Late Eighteenth Century, The Western Pennsylvania Historical Mazagine, 88; auth, No Freight Paid So Well, in Eire-Ireland, Summer, 92; auth, American Indian Leadership, Journal of Military History 57, 93; auth, The Slaughter Was Reciprocal: Josiah Harmer's Two Defeats, 1790, Northwest Ohio Quarterly 65, Spring, 93. **CONTACT ADDRESS** Dept of History, Univ of Dayton, 300 College Park, Dayton, OH 45469-1540.

EIDELBERG, MARTIN
PERSONAL Born 01/30/1941, New York, NY **DISCIPLINE** BAROQUE AND ROCOCO, MODERN DECORATIVE ARTS **EDUCATION** Princeton Univ, PhD. **CAREER** Prof, Rutgers, The State Univ NJ, New Brunswick, NJ. **RESEARCH** French 18th-century painting; history of modern crafts and design. **SELECTED PUBLICATIONS** Auth, Watteau in the Atelier of Gillot, in Antoine Watteau (1684 - 1721), le peintre, son temps et sa le gende, eds Francois Moreau and Margaret Morgan Grasselli, Paris and Geneva 87; Tiffany and the Cult of Nature, in Masterworks of Louis Comfort Tiffany, Alastair Duncan, Martin Eidelberg, and Neil Harris, London and NY, 89; Myths of Style and Nationalism: American Art Pottery at the Turn of the Century, The J of Decorative and Propaganda Arts 20, 94; Watteau's Italian Reveries, in Gazette des Beaux-Arts ser 6, 126, 95; 'Dieu invenit, Watteau pinxit.' Un nouvel eclairage sur une ancienne relation, La revue de l'art 115, 97; coauth, The Dispersal of the Last Duke of Mantua's Paintings, in Gazette des Beaux-Arts ser 6, 123, 94; Watteau's Chinoiseries at La Muette, in Gazette des Beaux-Arts ser 6, 130, 97; ed, Design 1935-1965, What Modern Was; Selections from the Liliane and David M. Stewart Collection, New York, 91. **CONTACT ADDRESS** Dept of Art Hist, Rutgers, The State Univ of New Jersey, New Brunswick, Voorhees Hall, 71 Hamilton St, New Brunswick, NJ 08903. **EMAIL** eidelber@rci.rutgers.edu

EINHORN, ROBIN
PERSONAL Born 07/19/1960, NJ **DISCIPLINE** HISTORY **EDUCATION** Univ Chicago, AB, 82; MA, 83; PhD, 88. **CAREER** Asst prof to assoc prof, 88-. **HONORS AND AWARDS** John Simon Guggenheim Mem Found Fel, 96-97. **MEMBERSHIPS** Am Hist Asn; Org of Am Hist; Econ Hist Asn. **RESEARCH** U.S. politics and government from the Revolution to the Civil War; U.S. urban history. **SELECTED PUBLICATIONS** Auth, "Slavery and the Politics of Taxation in the Early United States," Studies in am Polit Develop, (00): 156-183; auth, Property Rules: Political Economy in Chicago, 1833-1872, Univ Chicago Press, 91; 2nd ed, 01. **CONTACT ADDRESS** Dept Hist, Univ of California, Berkeley, 3229 Dwinelle Hall, Berkeley, CA 94720-2550. **EMAIL** reinhorn@socrates.berkeley.edu

EISENSTADT, ABRAHAM S.
PERSONAL Born 02/18/1920, Brooklyn, NY, w, 1949, 3 children **DISCIPLINE** HISTORY **EDUCATION** Brooklyn Col, AB, 40; Columbia Univ, PhD, 55. **CAREER** Instructor to adj emeritus prof, 56-. **HONORS AND AWARDS** Fulbright, Johns Hopkins Univ, 62-63; Nat Endowment of Humanities Fel, 82-83; Am Philos Soc Grant, 65; City Univ of NY rants, 66, 67. **MEMBERSHIPS** Phi Beta Kappa Soc, Org of Am Hist, Am Hist Asn, Fulbright Asn, British Studies Asn, Am Studies Asn. **RESEARCH** American Historical writing, British-American relationships 1776-1920. **SELECTED PUBLICATIONS** Auth, "History and Historians," in The Reader's Companion to American History, Houghton Mifflin Co, 92; auth, Reconsidering Tocqueville's Democracy in America, Rutgers Univ Press, 89; auth, Before Watergate: Problems of Corruption in American History, Columbia Univ Press, 78; auth, American History: Recent Interpretations, 2 volumes, Thomas Y Crowell, 69; auth, The Craft of American History, Harper and Row, 66; ed, Major Issues in American History Series, Pitman Publ Co, 67-73; auth, Charles McLean Andrews: A Study in American Historical Writing, Columbia Univ Pr, 56. **CONTACT ADDRESS** Dept Hist, Brooklyn Col, CUNY, 2901 Bedford Ave, Brooklyn, NY 11210-2813. **EMAIL** ASE567@aol.com

EISENSTADT, PETER
DISCIPLINE HISTORY **EDUCATION** NYork Univ; PhD,90. **CAREER** MNG ED, ENCYCLOPEDIA OF NEW YORK CITY **MEMBERSHIPS** Am Antiquarian Soc **SELECTED PUBLICATIONS** Auth, "Weather Prediction in Seventeenth-Century Massachusetts Almanacs," in Travail et Loisir dans les Societes Pre-Industrielles, 91. **CONTACT ADDRESS** Dept of Hist, New York Univ, 576 5th St, New York, NY 11215. **EMAIL** peisenst@mail.nysed.gov

EISENSTEIN, ELIZABETH LEWISOHN
PERSONAL Born 10/11/1923, New York, NY, m, 1948, 3 children **DISCIPLINE** EUROPEAN HISTORY **EDUCATION** Vassar Col, BA, 44; Radcliffe (Harvard) Univ, MA, 47, PhD, 53; Mt Holyoke Col, D.Litt, hon degree, 79. **CAREER** Lectr/adj prof, Am Univ, 59-75; Alice Freeman Palmer prof, Hist, Univ Mich, 75-88; vis prof, Wolfson Coll, 90; Lyell lectr, Bodleian Libr, oxford Univ, 90; fel, Center Advanced Stud, Palo Alto Univ, 92-93; fel, Nat Human Center, Australian Nat Univ Canberra, 88, Emer Prof, Univ Mich, 88-. **HONORS AND AWARDS** NEH Fel, 77; Guggenheim Fel, 82; Phi Beta Kappa, Junior Year Vassar, and the Ralph Waldo Emerson Phi Beta Kappa Prize received for my 79 bk. **MEMBERSHIPS** Fr Hist Studies; Am Soc 18th Cent Stud; Renaissance Soc Am; Am Acad Arts & Sci; Royal Hist Soc London **RESEARCH** History of communication; Early Modern Europe intellectual history; Enlightenment & French Revolution **SELECTED PUBLICATIONS** Auth, The First Professional Revolutionist: F. M. Buonarroti, Harvard Univ Press, 59; auth, The Printing Press as an Agent of Change, 2 vols., Cambridge Univ press, 79, Paperback 2 vols in 1, 81; auth, The Printing Revolution in Early Modern Europe, abridged illustrated version of 2 vol. Book, Cambridge Univ Press, 83, auth, "Revolution and the Printed Word," Revolution in History, ed. Roy Porter and M. Teich, Cambridge Univ Press, (86): 186-206; Reissued in Canto series, 93 and 00; auth, Grub Street Abroad: Aspects of the Eighteenth Century French Cosmopolitan Press, Lyell Lectures, 90, Oxford Univ Press, 92; auth, "The End of the Book?" Am Scholar, (95); auth, "The End of the Book? The American Scholar, Autumn (95): 541-549, Reprinted in A Passion for Books, ed. Dale Salwack London: Macmillan (99): 181-199; "From the Printed Word to the Moving Image," Soc Res, (97); "The Libraire-Philosophe," Le Livre et L'Historien, (97); auth, "From the Printed Word to the Moving Image," Social Research vol. 64, no. 3, fall (97): 1049-1065; auth, "The Libraire-Philosophe: Four Sketches for a group portrait," Le Livre et L'Historien, Festschrift for Henri-Jean Marting, ed. F. Barbier et. Al, Geneva: Droz, (97): 539-550; auth, "Gods, Devils, and Gutenberg: The Eighteenth Century Confronts the Printing Press," in Studies in Eighteenth Century Culture, vol 27, Baltimore: Johns Hopkins, (98): 1-24; auth, "Bypassing the Enlightenment: Taking the underground route to Revolution," The Darnton Debate: Books and Revolution in eighteenth century, ed. H.T. Mason, Oxford (98): 157-179. **CONTACT ADDRESS** 82 Kalorama Circle, NW, Washington, DC 20008-1616. **EMAIL** eisenst@mindspring.com

EISLER, COLIN
PERSONAL Born 03/17/1931, Hamburg, Germany, m, 1961, 1 child **DISCIPLINE** HISTORY OF ART **EDUCATION** Yale Univ, BA, 52; Harvard Univ, PhD, 57. **CAREER** Cur dept prints and drawings, art gallery, and instr art hist, Yale Univ, 55-57; from asst prof to prof art hist, inst fine arts, 58-77, Robert Lehman Prof Fine Arts, NY Univ, 77-, Yale Univ lectr grant, Int Cong, Paris, 57; Ford lect grant, Int Cong, Bonn; fel, Inst Advan Studies, 57-58; consult, paintings dept, Metropolitan Mus Art, 58-60; Guggenheim fel, 66-67; mem vis comt, Smith Col Art Mus; Cooper-Hewitt Print and Drawing Dept; secy, Nat Comt Hist Art; visual arts consult, Renaissance Soc; Nat Endowment for Humanities sr fel, 72-73; mem bd, The Drawing Ctr and The Archit Hist Found, Am Friends Israel Mus. **MEMBERSHIPS** Drawing Soc. **RESEARCH** Western European art, 1350-1650; graphic arts, photography and decorative arts. **SELECTED PUBLICATIONS** Auth, "A Study of Lorenzo Monaco," Speculum J Medieval Stud 67 (92); "Giotto to Durer--Early Renaissance Painting in the National Gallery," Renaissance Quart 47 (94); "The Renaissance Print, 1470-1550," Speculum J Medieval Stud 70 (95). **CONTACT ADDRESS** Inst of Fine Arts, New York Univ, 1 E 78th St, New York, NY 10021. **EMAIL** cte1@nyu.edu

EITELJORG, HARRISON, II
PERSONAL Born 03/04/1943, Indianapolis, IN, m, 1964, 3 children **DISCIPLINE** ARCHAEOLOGY **EDUCATION** Amherst Col, BA, 63; Butler Univ, MA, 68; Univ of Pa, PhD, 73. **CAREER** Vis Lectr, 77-78, Bryn Mawr Col, Dir, 91-, Archaeol Data Archive Project, Dir, 86-, Center for the Study of Architecture. **MEMBERSHIPS** AIA, SAA, SAH, CAA, ASOR. **RESEARCH** Architecture of Classical Greece, computers in archaeology. **SELECTED PUBLICATIONS** Auth, "Reconstructing with Computers," Bibl Archaeol Rev (91); auth, "Computer-Assisted Drafting and Design Programs for Presenting Architectural History and Archaeology," in Hypermedia and Interactivity in Museums: Proceedings of an International Conference, ed. David Bearman (Pittsburgh Archives and Museums Informatics, 91); auth, The Entrance to the Athenian Acropolis Before Mnesicles, Archaeol Inst of Am, 94; contribr, Historical Dictionary of Classical Archaeology, Greenwood Press, 96; auth, "Where Do We Put Our Files?," Bulletin of the Soc for Am Archaeol (97). **CONTACT ADDRESS** 142 Grays Lane, Haverford, PA 19041. **EMAIL** nicke@csanet.org

EKECHI, FELIX KAMALU
PERSONAL Born 10/30/1934, Owerri, Nigeria, m, 1966, 4 children **DISCIPLINE** AFRICAN HISTORY **EDUCATION** Univ MN, Minneapolis, BA, 63; KS State Univ, MA, 65; Univ Wis-Madison, PhD, 69. **CAREER** Headmaster, St Dominic's Sch, Afara-Mbieri, Owerri, 55-56 & 57-58; asst headmaster, Cent Sch Oboro-Ogwa, 56-57; tutor hist & Igbo, Mt St Mary's Col, Azaraegbelu, 59-60; tchg asst hist, KS State Univ, 63-64; instr hist & polit sci, Alcorn Agr & Mech Col, 64-65; asst prof, 69-71, assoc prof, 71-77, prof African hist, Kent State Univ, 78-, Res Coun res fel, 73, 75 & 79; Am Philos Soc grant, 79, 82. **HONORS AND AWARDS** NEH grants, 89, 92, 96; Creative Contrib Awd, KSU, 97. **MEMBERSHIPS** AHA; African Studies Asn; Hist Soc Ghana; Hist Soc Nigeria. **RESEARCH** Soc and polit hist; pre-colonial Igbo hist. **SELECTED PUBLICATIONS** Auth, Christianity and colonialism in West Africa, J African Hist, 71; Missionary Enterprise and Rivalry in Igboland, 1857-1914, Frank Cass, London, 72; The Holy Ghost Fathers in Eastern Nigeria: Observation on Missionary Strategy, African Studies Rev, 72; Traders, Missionaries and the Bombardment of Onitsha, 1879-1880, Conch Mag, 73; 1960 Response to British imperialism: The episode of Dr Stewart and the Ahiara Expedition, 1905-1916, 74 & African polygamy and Western Christian ethnocentrism, 76, J African Studies; The Missionary Career of T J Dennis in West Africa, 1893-1917, J African Relig, 78; The Igbo and Their History: The Problem of Cultural Origins, Alvana Jour Soc Sci, 82; Owerri in Transition, Owerri, 84; Tradition and Transformation in Eastern Nigeria, Kent, 89; Studies on MIssions, African Histography, 93; co-ed, African Market Women and Economic Power, Westport, 95; Gender and Economic Power: The Case of Igbo Market Women of Eastern Nigeria, African Market Women, 95; An African Initiative in Education, Educ and Develop in Africa, 98. **CONTACT ADDRESS** Dept of Hist, Kent State Univ, PO Box 5190, Kent, OH 44242-0001. **EMAIL** fekechi@kent.edu

EKIRCH, A. ROGER
PERSONAL Born 02/06/1950, Washington, DC, m, 1988, 3 children **DISCIPLINE** HISTORY **EDUCATION** Dartmouth Col, AB, 72; Johns Hopkins Univ, MA, 74, PhD, 78. **CAREER** Inst, 77-78, asst prof, 78-82, assoc prof, 82-88, Prof, VA Tech, 88-; vis ed, Inst Early Am History & Culture, 87-88. **HONORS AND AWARDS** NEH fel, 82, 86, 92; Guggenheim fel, 98; Paul Mellon fel, Cambridge Univ, 81; fel Commoner, Peterhouse, 81. **MEMBERSHIPS** AHA; Assocs Omohundo Inst Early Am Hist and Culture. **RESEARCH** Early Am hist; British hist. **SELECTED PUBLICATIONS** Auth, Poor Carolina Politics and Society in Colonial North Carolina, 1729-1776, Univ NC Press, 81; auth, Bound for America: The Transportation of British Convicts to the Colonies, 1718- 1775, Clarendon/Oxford Univ Press, 87; auth, The North Carolina Regulators on Liberty and Corruption, 1766-1771, in Perspectives in American History, Harvard Univ, Charles Warren Ctr for Studies in Am Hist, XI, 77-78; auth, Great Britain's Secret Convict Trade to America, 1783-1784, Am Hist Rev, LXXXIX, no 5, Dec 84; auth, Bound for America: A Profile of British Convicts Transported to the Colonies, 1718-1775, Wm and Mary Q, 3d Ser, XLII, no 2, Apr 85. **CONTACT ADDRESS** Dept Hist, Virginia Polytech Inst and State Univ, Blacksburg, VA 24061. **EMAIL** arekirch@vt.edu

EL-BAZ, FAROUK
PERSONAL Born 01/01/1938, Zagazig, Egypt, m, 1962, 4 children **DISCIPLINE** GEOLOGY, REMOTE SENSING **EDUCATION** Ain Shams Univ, Cairo, Egypt, B Sc, 58; MO School of Mines and Metallurgy, MS, 61; Univ MO, PhD, 64; New England Col, Henneker, NH, D Sc Honoris, 84. **CAREER** Supervisor, Lunar Science Operations, Bellcomm, Inc (NASA contractor), Washington, DC, 67-72; Res Dir, Center for Earth and Planetary Studies, Smithsonian Inst, Washington, DC, 73-82; Vice-pres for Science and Technology, Itek Optical Systems, Lexington, MA, 82-86; dir, Center for Remote Sensing, Boston Univ, Boston, MA, 86-. **HONORS AND AWARDS** NASA Exceptional Achievement Medal; Univ MO Alumni Achievement Awd for Extraordinary Scientific Accomplishments; Certificate of Merit of the World Aerospace Ed Org; Arab Republic of Egypt Order of Merit-First Class; AAPG Human Needs Awd. **MEMBERSHIPS** Geological Soc of Am; Am Asn for the Advancement of Science; Royal Astronomical Soc; Am Asn of Petroleum Geologists, Explorers Club; World Aerospace Ed Org; Am Soc of Photogrammetry and Remote Sensing. **RESEARCH** Interpretation of satellite images of desert regions, particularly for groundwater exploration. **SE-**

LECTED PUBLICATIONS Auth, Origin and Evolusion of the Desert, Interdisciplinary Science Reviews, Dec 88; Finding a Pharoah's Funeral Bank, Nat Geographic, April 88; The Gulf War and the Environment, co-ed with R M Makharita, Gordon and Breach, Lausanne, Switzerland, 94; Space Age Archaeology, Scientific American, Aug 97; coed, Atlas of the State of Kuwait from Satellite Images, with M 41-Sarawi, Kuwait Foundation for the Advancement of Sciences, 00. **CONTACT ADDRESS** Center for Remote Sensing, Boston Univ, 725 Commonwealth Ave, Boston, MA 02215. **EMAIL** farouk@bu.edu

ELAM, EARL HENRY
PERSONAL Born 12/07/1934, Wichita Falls, TX, m, 1964, 3 children **DISCIPLINE** AMERICAN HISTORY **EDUCATION** Midwest Univ, BA, 61; Tex Tech Univ, MA, 67; PhD, 71. **CAREER** Instr US hist, Lubbock High Sch, Tex, 61-67; Part-time instr, Tex Tech Univ, 67-71; from asst prof to prof US hist, 71-74, dir div soc sci, 73-74, VPres Acad Affairs to prof emeritus hist, Sul Ross State Univ, 74-, Consult, Indian Claims Sect, US Dept Justice, 71-. **MEMBERSHIPS** Western Hist Asn. **RESEARCH** Indians of the southern plains and of the southwest; frontier history of the southwest; twentieth century western history. **SELECTED PUBLICATIONS** Auth,War Pony, J West, Vol 35, 96;, Noble Brutes--Camels on the American Frontier, Southwestern Hist Quart, Vol 99, 95; Portraits of the Pecos Frontier, Southwestern Hist Quart, Vol 97, 94;Lone Hunter and the Cheyennes, J West, Vol 35, 96; Lone Hunters Gray Pony, J West, Vol 35, 96. **CONTACT ADDRESS** 407 N Cockrell, Alpine, TX 79830.

ELBERT, SARAH
PERSONAL Born 01/05/1937, New York, NY, d, 2 children **DISCIPLINE** HISTORY **EDUCATION** Cornell Univ, AB, 65, MAT, 66, MA, 68; PhD, 74. **CAREER** Res Assoc, 68-72, Vis Asst Prof, 77, Vis Assoc Prof, Cornell Univ, 81-84; Vis Asst Prof, 73-74, Asst Prof, 74-81, Assoc Prof Hist, Binghamton Univ, 81-; Vis Prof, Calif Polytechnic State Univ, 86-87; Fulbright Prof, Univ Tromso, Norway, 92-93. **HONORS AND AWARDS** NY Chancellors Awd for Excellence in Teaching, 98. **MEMBERSHIPS** Am Studies Asn; Org Am Hist; Berkshire Conf Women Hist; Louisa May Alcott Soc. **RESEARCH** 19th & 20th century cultural and intellectual history in the US; Louise May Alcott; nature/culture studies. **SELECTED PUBLICATIONS** Ed, Two Little Confederates, Garland Publ, 76; The Little Colonel, Garland Publ, 76; auth, A Hunger for Home: Louisa May Alcott and Little Women, Temple Univ Press, 86; A Hunger for Home: Louise Alcott's Place in American Culture, Rutgers Univ Press, 87; Diana and Persis, In: Alternative Alcott, Rutgers Univ Press, 89; Louisa May Alcott on Race, Sex, and Slavery, Northeastern Univ Press, 98; auth, Louisa May Alcott's Work: A Story Experience, The Alcott Encyclopedia, Glenwood Press, (99); auth, Taming the Call of the Wild From Jack London to Lassie Come Home, Rutgers Univ Press (forthcoming). **CONTACT ADDRESS** History Dept, SUNY, Binghamton, PO Box 600, Binghamton, NY 13902-6000. **EMAIL** se30@cornell.edu

ELBOW, GARY S.
PERSONAL Born 11/15/1938, San Francisco, CA, m, 1967 **DISCIPLINE** GEOGRAPHY, ECONOMICS **EDUCATION** Ore State Col, BS, 60; Univ Ore, MA, 64; Univ Pittsburgh, PhD, 72. **CAREER** Asst to prof, Tex Tech Univ, Lubbock, 70-; vis prof, Pontifical Cath Univ of Ecuador, 90, 92, 93; vis prof, Pan Am Inst for Res and Ed, Quito, Ecuador, 88, 90, 92, 93; contributing ed, Handbook of Latin Am Studies, Library of Congress, 76-2001. **HONORS AND AWARDS** Fulbright Scholar, 83, 90, 92; academic specialist, US Information Agency, Quito, Ecudor, 90, 92; Who's Who Among Am Teachers, 96, 97; President's Academic Acheivement Awd, Tex Tech Univ, 98. **MEMBERSHIPS** Asn Am Geog, Latin Am Studies Asn, Nat Coun for Geog Ed. **RESEARCH** Settlements, urban geography, geography education, Latin America. **SELECTED PUBLICATIONS** Auth, "Creating an Atmosphere: Depiction of Climate in the Works of Gabriel Garcia Marquez," in J. Perez and W. Aycock, eds, Climate and Literature: Reflections of Environment, Lubbock, TX: Tex Tech Univ Press (95); auth, "Marketing in Latin America: A Photo Essay," J of Cultural Geog, vol 15, no 2, 55-77 (summer/fall 95); auth, "Territorial Loss and National Image: The Case of Ecuador," Yearbk, Conf of Latin Am Geog, vol 22, 93-107 (96); coauth with Tom L. Martinson, "Geography, Middle America," in Dolores M. Martin, ed, Handbook of Latin Am Studies, Austin,TX: Univ Tex Press (97); auth, "Economic Integration in the Caribbean: The Association of Caribbean States," J of Geograohy, vol 96, no 1, 29-38 (Jan-Feb 97); auth, "Coming Out of the Country: Population Growth, Migration, and Urbanization," in Alfonzo Gonzalez and Jim Norwine, The New Third World, Boulder, Colo: Westview (98); auth, "Scale and Regional Identity in the Caribbean," in David Kaplan and Guntram Herb, eds, Nested Identities: Nationalism, Territory, and Scale,Totowa, NJ: Rowman & Littlefield (99). **CONTACT ADDRESS** Dept Econ & Geog, Texas Tech Univ, Lubbock, TX 79409-1014. **EMAIL** adgse@ttacs.ttu.edu

ELDER, ELLEN ROZANNE
PERSONAL Born 05/21/1940, Harrisburg, PA **DISCIPLINE** MEDIEVAL STUDIES **EDUCATION** Western MI Univ, AB, 62, AM, 64; Univ Toronto, PhD, 72. **CAREER** Instr hist, 68-72, prof hist & dir inst Cistercian Studies, Western MI Univ, 73; Ed Dir, Cistercian Publ, Inc, 73, Co-ed, Studies in Medieval Cult, Vols IV, V, VI & VII. **HONORS AND AWARDS** H. L.D. honoris causa, Nashotah House Theol Sem, Nashotah, WI, 95. **RESEARCH** Twelfth century Christological controversy; early Cistercian Christology. **SELECTED PUBLICATIONS** Auth, Cistercian Order, Trappistine Sisters, and Trappists, In: The Harper Encyclopedia of Catholicism, HarperSan, 95; coauth, Receiving the Vision: The Reality of Anglican-Roman Catholic Relations Today, Liturgical Press, 95; ed, The Joy of Learning and the Love of God: Essays in Honor of Jean Leclercq, Cistercian Studies Series, No 160, Cistercian Publ, 95; auth, Bernard of Clairvaux, In: The International Encyclopedia of the Church, Eerdmans, 97; Trappisten, In: Theologische Realenzyklodie. Verlag Walter de Gruyter, 99; auth and editor of numerous other publs. **CONTACT ADDRESS** Cistercian Publ, Western Michigan Univ, 1201 Oliver St, Kalamazoo, MI 49008-3805.

ELEY, GEOFF
PERSONAL Born 05/04/1949, Burton-on-Treat, England, 2 children **DISCIPLINE** MODERN GERMAN & EUROPEAN HISTORY **EDUCATION** Oxford Univ, BA, 70, MA, 81; Sussex Univ, DPhil(Hist), 74; Cambridge Univ, MA, 75. **CAREER** Lectr Hist, Univ Keele, 74-75; col lectr & dir Hist Studies, Emmanuel Col, Univ Cambridge, 75-79; asst prof Europ Hist, 79-81, assoc prof Europ Hist, Univ Mich, Ann Arbor, 81-, rev ed, Comp Studies Soc & Hist, 80-87; rev assoc, New Ger Critique, 81-86. **MEMBERSHIPS** Conf Group Cent Europ Hist; Coun Europ Studies; Soc Ger Historians Brit; Past & Present Soc, UK. **RESEARCH** Liberalism in German and Britain in 19th and 20th century; nationalism and popular politics; European Left from mid-19th century to the present; history & film. **SELECTED PUBLICATIONS** Auth, Defining social imperialism: Use and abuse of an idea, Social Hist, 76; Reshaping the German Right: Radical Nationalism and Political Change after Bismark, Yale Univ Press, 80; coauth, Mythen deutscher Geschichteschreibung: Die gescheiterte Grgerliche Revolution von 1848, Ullstein Materialien, 80; Why does social history ignore politics?, 80 & auth, Nationalism and social history, 81; co-ed Culture/Power/History, Princeton UP, 94; coed, Becoming National, Oxford UP, 96; ed, Society, Culture, & the State in Germany 1870-1930, U-Michigan Press, 96. **CONTACT ADDRESS** Dept of History, Univ of Michigan, Ann Arbor, Ann Arbor, MI 48109. **EMAIL** ghe@umich.edu

ELFENBEIN, JESSICA
DISCIPLINE HISTORY **EDUCATION** Barnard Col, AB, George Washington Univ, MA; Univ Delaware, MA, PhD. **CAREER** Asst Prof, Univ Baltimore, 95-. **SELECTED PUBLICATIONS** Auth, Civics, Commerce, and Community: the History of the Greater Washington Board of Trade, 1889-1989, Kendall-Hunt Publ Co, 89; auth, Philadelphia Board of Trade, 1833-1899, Atwater Kent Museum, 95; auth, 'An Agressive Christian Enterprise': The Baltimore YMCA and the Making of Institutional Legitimacy, NY Univ Press, 96. **CONTACT ADDRESS** Univ of Baltimore, 1420 N. Charles Street, Baltimore, MD 21201.

ELKINS, JAMES
PERSONAL Born 10/13/1955, Ithaca, NY, m **DISCIPLINE** ART HISTORY **EDUCATION** Cornell Univ, BA, 77; Univ Chicago, MFA, 83, MA, 84, PhD, 84-89. **CAREER** Vis assoc prof, Northwestern Univ, 96; vis assoc prof, Univ Chicago, 96; vis assoc prof, Univ CA-Berkeley, 96; assoc prof, 89-. **HONORS AND AWARDS** PhD with hon(s), Univ Chicago, 89. **SELECTED PUBLICATIONS** Auth, The Poetics of Perspective, Cornell UP, 94; The Object Stares Back: On the Nature of Seeing, Simon and Schuster, 96; Our Beautiful, Dry, and Distant Texts: Art History as Writing, Penn State Press, 97; The Question of the Body in Mesoamerican Art, Res 26, 94; Parallel Art History / Studio Program, The Art Jour, 95; There are No Philosophic Problems Raised by Virtual Reality, Computer Graphics 28, 94; Art Criticism, The Dictionary of Art, Macmillan Publishers, 96; Visual Schemata, The Encycl of Aesthet, Garland Press, 96; Marks, Traces, Traits, Contours, Orli, and Splendores: Nonsemiotic Elements in Pictures, Critical Inquiry 21, 95; Between Picture and Proposition: Torturing Paintings in Wittgenstein's Tractatus, Visible Lang 30, 96; On the Impossibility of Close Reading: The Case of Alexander Marshack, Current Anthrop 37, 96; Art History and Images that are Not Art, The Art Bulletin 77, 95; Histoire de l'art et pratiques d'atelier, transl Why Art Historians should Draw: The Case for Studio Experience, Hist de l'art 29-30, 95; Why Are Our Pictures Puzzles? Some Thoughts on Writing Excessively, New Lit Hist 27, 96. **CONTACT ADDRESS** Dept of Art Hist, Sch of the Art Inst of Chicago, 37 S Wabash Ave, Chicago, IL 60603. **EMAIL** j.elkins@artic.edu

ELLER, DAVID B.
PERSONAL Born 04/30/1945, Roanoke, VA, m, 1979, 3 children **DISCIPLINE** HISTORY, RELIGION **EDUCATION** La Verne Col, Calif, BA, 67; Bethany Theol Sem, MA, 71; Miami Univ, Oxford, Oh, PhD, 76. **CAREER** Lectr, Dir of Pub Studies, Rosemont Col, Pa, 96-97; Dir of the Young Center and prof of Hist and Relig, Elizabethtown Col, Pa, 97-. **HONORS AND AWARDS** Phi Alpha Theta, 74; Summer Res Fe3l, Miami Univ, 73, 74; NEH Summer Sem for Col Teachers, Indiana Univ, 83; Smithsonian Inst, Short-Term Vis Awd, 84; Newberry Library, Short-Term Vis Fel, 84. **MEMBERSHIPS** Am Acad of Relig, Communal Studies Asn, Conf on Faith and Hist, Soc for Scholarly Pub. **RESEARCH** Anabaptism, Pietism, communal societies. **SELECTED PUBLICATIONS** Auth, "George Wolfe III and the 'Church of California'," Messenger, 146 (May 97): 12-16; auth, "The Dissent of the Congregational Brethren," Brethren Life and Thought, 42 (summer and fall 97): 158-179; auth, "Tending the Garden: Memories of My Father," in Going For It: Perspectives on Living, ed, Carol S. Lawson, West Chester, Pa: Chrysalis Books (97); ed, From Age to Age: Historians and the Modern Church. A Festschrift for Donald F. Durnbaugh, vol 42, (summer and fall 97) in Brethren Life and Thought (fall 98); auth, Illuminating the World of Spirit. A Sesquicentennial Record of the Swedenborg Foundation, 1850-2000, West Chester, Pa: Swedenborg Found (99). **CONTACT ADDRESS** Dir of the Young Center, Elizabethtown Col, 1 Alpha Dr, Elizabethtown, PA 17022-2298.

ELLER, RONALD
PERSONAL Born 04/23/1948, m, 1992, 3 children **DISCIPLINE** HISTORY **EDUCATION** Col of Wooster, BA, 70; Univ NC, MA, 73; PhD, 79. **CAREER** Asst to Assoc Prof, Mars Hill Col, 76-85; Assoc Prof, Univ Ky, 85-. **HONORS AND AWARDS** Willis D Weatherford Awd, 83; Thomas Wolfe Literary Awd, 82; Rockefeller Foundation Scholar, 73-76; Ky Appalachian Commission, 95-00; Jim Wayne Miller Awd, 97; William E Lyons Awd, Univ Ky, 98; John D Whisman School, Appalachian Reg Commission, 98-00; E Ky Leadership Foundation Awd, 99; President's Service Awd, Southeast Community Col, 99. **RESEARCH** History of Appalachia; Economic development and social change; Development policy. **SELECTED PUBLICATIONS** Auth, Miners, Millhands, and Mountaineers: The Industrialization of the Appalachian South, 1880-1930, Univ Tenn Press, 82; co-auth, Capacity for Leading Institutional and Community Change: The Rural Community College Initiative, Am Asn of Community Colleges, 99; co-auth, Building Teams for Institutional and Community Change: The Rural Community College Initiative, Am Asn of Community Col, 99; co-auth, "The Rural Community College Initiative," in Creating and Benefiting From Institutional Collaborations, Jossey-Bass Pub, 99; auth, "Give Rural Areas Comprehensive Community-based Development," Herald-Leader, 99; auth, "Forward" in Recycling Appalachia: Backtalk from an American Region, Univ Press of Ky, 99; co-auth, Economic Development and Rural Community Colleges, Am Asn of Community Colleges, 98; co-auth, Access to Rural Community Colleges: Removing Barriers to Participation, Am Asn of Community Colleges, 98; auth, "Lost and Found in the Promised Land: the Education of a Hillbilly," in One Hundred Years of Appalachian Visions, Berea, 97; co-auth, Kentucky Highways: Some History and Prospects for Planning, Univ Ky, 97; co-auth, "Exploring and Documenting the Challenge and Opportunities Faced by Institutions Participating in the Rural Community College Initiative: A Preliminary Report of Key Findings, Am Coun on Educ, 96. **CONTACT ADDRESS** Dept Hist, Univ of Kentucky, 500 S Limestone St, Lexington, KY 40506-0001. **EMAIL** eller@pop.uky.edu

ELLINGTON, DONNA S.
PERSONAL Born 01/09/1955, Charlotte, NC, m, 1974 **DISCIPLINE** MEDIEVAL, RENAISSANCE HISTORY **EDUCATION** Appal State Univ, BA, 77; MA, 84; Duke Univ, PhD, 91. **CAREER** Instr, Appal Univ, 81-84; instr, Univ Caroli, 88; instr, Gard Webb Univ, 88-91; asst prof, 91-95; assoc prof, 95-00, prof, 00-. **HONORS AND AWARDS** Fulbright Schlp Decl; Medieval Ren Fel; Cratis D Williams Thes Awd. **MEMBERSHIPS** RSA. **RESEARCH** Medieval renaissance religious history; medieval popular devotion and popular sermons; the relationship between literacy and religious practice; use of the body and body symbolism in medieval religion. **SELECTED PUBLICATIONS** Auth, "Impassioned Mother or Passive Icon: The Virgin's Role in Late Medieval and Early Modern Passion Sermons," Renai Quart 48 (95): 227-261; rev of, "The Boubaries of Faith: The Development and Transmission of Medieval Spirituality," by John C Hirsh, Renai Quart 5 (98): 1002-1004; auth, From Sacred Body to Angelic Soul: Understanding Mary in Late Medieval and Early Modern Europe, Cath Univ Press, forthcoming. **CONTACT ADDRESS** Dept Religion, Philosophy, Gardner-Webb Univ, Boiling Springs, NC 28017-9999. **EMAIL** dellington@gardner-webb.edu

ELLIOTT, B. S.
DISCIPLINE CANADIAN HISTORY **EDUCATION** Carleton Univ, BA, PhD; Univ Leicester, MA. **CAREER** Prof, Carleton Univ. **RESEARCH** English immigration, Irish Protestant immigration; gravestones and gravestone carvers of Prince Edward Island. **SELECTED PUBLICATIONS** Auth, Irish Migrants in the Canadas: A New Approach, McGill Queen's UP, Inst Irish Stud, 88; The City Beyond: A History of Nepean, Birthplace of Canada's Capital, 1792-1990, Corporation of the City of Nepean, 91; co-ed, The McCabe List: Early Irish in The Ottawa Valley, Ontario Genealogical Soc, 95; ed,

Settling the Land: Records of the Upper Canadian District Land Boards, 1819-1825, with Fawne Stratford-Devai, (forthcoming 97). **CONTACT ADDRESS** Dept of Hist, Carleton Univ, 1125 Colonel By Dr, Ottawa, ON, Canada K1S 5B6. **EMAIL** belliott@ccs.carleton.ca

ELLIOTT, BRIDGET
DISCIPLINE ART **EDUCATION** Univ Toronto, BA; Univ British Columbia, MA; Univ London, PhD. **RESEARCH** Theories of sexual difference and feminist art practices; analysis of arts institutions, critical reception and hierarchies of cultural value; theories of cultural studies and art history's relationship to film, literature, music, theatre and social history. **SELECTED PUBLICATIONS** Coauth, Women Artists and Writers: Modernist (im)positionings, Routledge, 94; Peter Greenaway: Architecture and Allegory, Academy, 97. **CONTACT ADDRESS** Dept of Visual Arts, Univ of Western Ontario, London, ON, Canada N6A 5B8. **EMAIL** belliott@julain.uwo.ca

ELLIOTT, CAROLYN S.
PERSONAL Born 02/20/1947, Glen Ridge, NJ, m, 1970, 2 children **DISCIPLINE** RELIGION AND CULTURE; HISTORY **EDUCATION** Syracuse Univ, BA, 70, MA, 73; SUNY, MLIS, 94. **CAREER** From dir to adj fac to full-time fac, 72-, Keystone Col. **HONORS AND AWARDS** Theta Chi Beta; Beta Phi Mu. **MEMBERSHIPS** Am Libr Asn; Asn Col & Res Librs; Pa Libr Asn. **RESEARCH** Religion and culture of Asia; library computing options. **SELECTED PUBLICATIONS** Auth, art, NREN Update, 1993: Washington Policy, 94. **CONTACT ADDRESS** Miller Library, Keystone Col, One College Green, La Plume, PA 18440-0200. **EMAIL** celliott@kstone.edu

ELLIOTT, CLARK ALBERT
PERSONAL Born 01/22/1941, Ware, MA, m, 1965, 2 children **DISCIPLINE** ARCHIVES, BIBLIOGRAPHY, HISTORY OF SCIENCE **EDUCATION** Marietta Col, AB, 63; Western Reserve Univ, MSLS, 65; Case Western Reserve Univ, MA, 68, PhD(libr & info sci), 70. **CAREER** Archivist, Case Inst Technol, 64-66; asst prof libr sci, Sch of Libr Sci, Simmons Col, 69-71; assoc cur, Harvard Univ archives, 71-97; Librn, Burndy Libr, Dibner Inst for the Hist of Sci and Technol, 97-00. **MEMBERSHIPS** Soc Am Archivists; New England Archivists; Hist Sci Soc; Forum for the Hist of Sci in Am, chm, 97-99. **RESEARCH** History of science in America, especially scientific careers, and institutions; documentation and historiography in history of science. **SELECTED PUBLICATIONS** Auth, The Royal Society Catalogue as an Index to Nineteenth Century American Science, J of Am Soc for Info Sci, 11-12/70; Sources for the History of Science in the Harvard University Archives, Havard Libr Bull, 1/74; Experimental Data as a Source for the History of Science, Am Archivist, 1/74; A Descriptive Guide to the Harvard University Archives, Harvard Univ Libr, 74; The American scientist in Antebellum Society: A Quantitative View, Social Studies of Sci, 1/75; Biographical Dict of American Science: The Seventeenth Through the Nineteenth Centuries, Greenwood Press, 79; Citation patterns and Documentation for the History of Science: Some Methodological Considerations, Am Archivist, Spring 81; Models of the American scientist: A look at Collective Biography, Isis, 3/82; auth, Biographical Index to American Science: The Seventeenth Century to 1920, Greenwood, 90; co-ed, Science at Harvard University: Historical Perspectives, Lehigh, 92; auth, History of Science in the United States: A Chronology and Research Guide, Garland, 96; coed, Commemorative Practices in Science: Historical Perspectives on the Politics of Collective Memory, Univ of Chicago Press, 99. **CONTACT ADDRESS** 105 Beech St No. 2, Belmont, MA 02478. **EMAIL** claelliott@earthlink.net

ELLIOTT, DEREK W.
PERSONAL Born 10/03/1958, Nashville, TN, s **DISCIPLINE** HISTORY **EDUCATION** Harvard Univ, AB, 80; Univ Calif at Berkeley, MA, 85; George Washington Univ, PhD, 92. **CAREER** Curator, Smithsonian Inst Nat Air & Space Museum Dept of Space Hist, 82-92; from asst prof of Hist, 92-98; assoc prof, Tenn State Univ, 98-. **HONORS AND AWARDS** Listed in Who's Who Among Black Americans, 92-; Phi Kappa Phi, 97-. **MEMBERSHIPS** Am Hist Asn, Orgn of Am Historians, Soc for the Hist of Technol, Ctr for the Study of the Presidency, Tenn Hist Soc, Phi Alpha Theta Honor Soc in Hist. **RESEARCH** Recent U.S. Political and Social Theory. **SELECTED PUBLICATIONS** Auth, "Joann Gibson Robinson," in Notable Black American Women, Book II, ed. Jessie Carney Smith (MI: Gale Research, 96), 562-564; auth, "George R. Carruthers," in The Biographical Encyclopedia of Scientists (NY: Marshall Cavendish Corp., 98), 241-244; auth, "Space: The Final Frontier of the New Frontier," in Kennedy: New Frontiers Revisited, ed. Mark J. White (NY: NY Univ Pr, 98), 193-221; auth, "Project Apollo Crew: Virgil Grissom, Edward White, Roger Chaffee," in American National Biography (NY: Oxford Univ Pr, 99), 902-903. **CONTACT ADDRESS** Hist, Geog, Polit Sci, Tennessee State Univ, 3500 John A. Merritt Blvd, Nashville, TN 37209-1500. **EMAIL** delliott@tnstate.edu

ELLIOTT, HAROLD M.
PERSONAL Born, FL, m, 1975, 3 children **DISCIPLINE** GEOGRAPHY **EDUCATION** San Francisco State Univ, BA, 64; Infantry Off Candidate St, Dipl, 65; Univ Okla, PhD, 78. **CAREER** Instr, Cameron State Col, 70-72; Instr, Fla Int Univ, 77-78; From Asst Prof to Prof, Weber State Univ, 79-. **HONORS AND AWARDS** Geog Proof of the Year, Weber State Univ, 81-82; Examr Teaching Awd, Ogden Standard, 92; ROTC Fac Mentor Awd, Weber State Univ, 99. **MEMBERSHIPS** Assoc. of Am Geogrs, Ut Geog Soc, Reserve Offs assoc. **RESEARCH** Urban systems, historical geography. **SELECTED PUBLICATIONS** Auth, "Cardinal Place Geometry in the American South," Southeastern Geogr, vol 24, no 2 (84): 65-77; auth, "Cardinal Places and the Urban Gradient," Urban Geog, col 5, no 3 (84): 223-239; auth, "Cardinal Place Geometry," Geog Analysis, vol 17, no 1 (85): 16-35; auth, "Changing Spatial Structure in the Rocky Mountain Regional System," Yearbk of the Assoc of Pac Coast Geogrs, vol 48 (86): 149-167; auth, "Cardinal Directions, Southpaws and Geographic Place Names," Sport Place: Int J of Sports Geog, vol 2, no 2 (88): 39-41; auth, "Maps of Holmes County and Its Surrounding Neighbors: Some Observations," The Ohio Geneal Soc Report, vol 35, no 1 (95): 4-7; auth, Scots in the United States," The Scottish-Am Patriot, vol 19, no 3 (99): 10-13. **CONTACT ADDRESS** Dept Geog, Weber State Univ, 3750 Harrison Blvd, Ogden, UT 84408-0001. **EMAIL** helliott@weber.edu

ELLIOTT, SHIRLEY B.
PERSONAL Born 06/04/1916, Wolfville, NS, Canada **DISCIPLINE** HISTORY **EDUCATION** Acadia Univ, BA, 37, MA, 39; Simmons Col (Boston), SB(LibrSci), 40; DCL(hon), Acadia Univ, 84; LLD(hon), Dalhousie Univ, 85. **CAREER** Ref asst, Brookline (Mass) Pub Libr, 40-46; asst librn, Univ RI Libr, 46-49; asst ed, Canadian Index, Can Libr Asn, 49-50; chief librn, Reg Libr, Truro(NS), 50-54; legis librn, Legis Libr NS, 54-82. **HONORS AND AWARDS** Canada 125 Medal; Atlantic Provinces Libr Asn Merit Awd, 81; CASLIS Merit Awd, 88. **MEMBERSHIPS** Can Fedn Univ Women; Heritage Trust NS; Royal NS Hist Soc; Bibliog Soc Can; Atlantic Provinces Libr Asn. **SELECTED PUBLICATIONS** Auth, Nova Scotia in Books 1752-1967, 67; auth, Province House, 66; auth, Nova Scotia Book of Days, 80; auth, The Legislative Assembly of Nova Scotia 1758-1983: a biographical directory, 84; auth, Nova Scotia in Books: A Quarter Century's Gleanings, 87; auth, Nova Scotia in London: a History of its Agents General 1762-1988, 88; ed & comp, Atlantic Provinces Checklist 1957-65; contribur, Dictionary of Canadian Biography. **CONTACT ADDRESS** 15 Queen St, Box 342, Wolfville, NS, Canada B0P 1X0.

ELLIS, EDWARD EARLE
PERSONAL Born 03/18/1926, Ft Lauderdale, FL **DISCIPLINE** THEOLOGY, HISTORY **EDUCATION** Univ Va, BS, 50; Wheaton Col, Ill, MA and BD, 53; Univ Edinburgh, PhD (Bibl studies), 55. **CAREER** Asst prof Bible and philos, Aurora Col, 56-58; asst prof New Testament interpretation, Southern Baptist Theol Sem, 58-60; from vis prof to prof Bibl Studies, 62-77, Res Prof New Testament, New Brunswick Theol Sem, 77-, Am Asn Theol Schs fel, 68-69; von Humbolt scholar, 68-69 and 75-76; lectr, Princeton Theol Sem, 74, 76, 78; Guggenheim fel, 75-76; lectr, Drew Univ, 67-68 and Univ Tubingen, 75-76; vis distinguished prof Evangel Christianity, Juniata Col, 78-79; Bye fel, Robinson Col, Cambridge Univ, 82-83; exec Comt, Soc Studies New Testament, 67-69. **HONORS AND AWARDS** DD, Wheaton Col, Ill, 82. **MEMBERSHIPS** Soc Bibl Lit (treas, 67-68); Soc Studies New Testament; Inst Biblical Res. **RESEARCH** Early Christian history and thought; Biblical studies. **SELECTED PUBLICATIONS** Auth, Paul's Use of the Old Testament, Oliver & Boyd, London & Eerdmans, 57 & Baker, 81; Paul and His Recent Interpreters, Eerdmans, 61; The World of St John Lutterworth, London & Abingdon, Nashville, 65; The Gospel of Luke, Olifants, London, 66, 2nd ed, 74 & Eerdmans, 81; Eschatology in Luke, Fortress, 73; Prophecy and Hermeneutic in Early Christianity, Mohr, Tubingen & Eerdmans, 78; Dating the New Testament, New Testament Studies, Vol 26: 487-502. **CONTACT ADDRESS** Dept of Bibl Studies, New Brunswick Theol Sem, New Brunswick, NJ 08901.

ELLIS, JACK D.
PERSONAL Born 10/16/1941, Sulphur, OK, m, 1966, 2 children **DISCIPLINE** HISTORY **EDUCATION** Baylor Univ, BA, 63; Tulane Univ, MS, 65, PhD, 67. **CAREER** Asst prof, 67-70, assoc prof, 70-80, prof, 80-92, chair, dept hist, Univ Del; dean, Col Lib Arts, 92-96, PROF, UNIV ALA, HUNTSVILLE, 92-. **HONORS AND AWARDS** Wm P. Lyons Master's Essay Awd, 65; ACLS fel, 80; Univ Del Ctr Adv Study fels, 83-84. **MEMBERSHIPS** AHA; Soc Fr Historical Stud; So Hist Asn; Oral Hist Asn; Am Asn Hist Med. **RESEARCH** France, Third Republic; soc hist med; African-Am physicians in the South. **SELECTED PUBLICATIONS** Auth, The French Socialists and the Problem of The Peace, 1904-1914, Loyola Univ Chicago Press, 67; auth, The Early Life of Georges Clemenceau, 1841-1893, Regents Press Kans, 80; auth, The Physician-legislators of France, 1870-1914, Cambridge Univ Press, 92. **CONTACT ADDRESS** Dept of History, Univ of Alabama, Huntsville, 415 Roberts Hall, Huntsville, AL 35899. **EMAIL** ellisj@email.uah.edu

ELLIS, R. CLYDE
PERSONAL Born 03/29/1958, Greenville, NC, m, 1990 **DISCIPLINE** HISTORY **EDUCATION** Lenoir Rhyne Col, BA 80; Univ N Carolina, MA 86; Okla State Univ, PhD 93. **CAREER** Elon Col, asst prof 94-99; East Cen Univ, asst prof 93-94; Assoc Prof, 99-. **HONORS AND AWARDS** Gustavus Myers AWD; winner of the gustavus myers book award for outstanding work on intolerance in n america. **MEMBERSHIPS** OHS; WHA. **RESEARCH** Amer Indians; Indian Edu; Cultural adaptation; ethnography **SELECTED PUBLICATIONS** Auth, "'A Remedy For Barbarism': Indian Schools, The Civilizing Program, and the Kiowa-Comanche-Apache Reservation, 1871-1915," American Indian Cultrue and Research Journal, 94; auth, To Change Them Forever: Indian Education at the Rainy Mountain Boarding School, 1893-1920, Norman, Univ Oklahoma Press, 96; She Gave us the Jesus Way: Isabel Crawford, The Kiowas and the Saddle Mountain Indian Baptist Church, intro to Kiowa: A Woman Missionary in Indian Territory, Lincoln, Univ Nebraska Press, 98; E E Dale and Tales of the Tepee, intro to Tales of the Tepee, Lincoln, Univ Nebraska Press, 98; auth, "Applying Communitas to Kiowa Powwows," American Indian Quarterly, 98; The Kiowa Gourd Dance, in: Native Amer Values: Survival and Renewal, eds, Thomas E. Schirer, Susan Branstner, Sault Ste Marie MI, Lake Superior State Univ Press, 93; Harrah's Casino and the Eastern Cherokees, Our State, 98; Boarding School Life at the Kiowa-Comanche Agency, 1893-1920, The Historian, 96; auth, "'We Don't Want Your Rations, We Want This Dance': The Changing Use of Song and Dance on the Southern Plains," Western Historical Quarterly, 98. **CONTACT ADDRESS** Dept of History, Elon Col, PO Box 2143, Elon College, NC 27244. **EMAIL** ellisrc@elon.edu

ELLIS, RICHARD E.
PERSONAL Born 09/07/1937, New York, NY, m, 1959, 4 children **DISCIPLINE** AMERICAN HISTORY **EDUCATION** Univ Wis-Madison, BA, 60; Univ Calif, Berkeley, MA, 61, PhD, 69. **CAREER** Teaching asst Am hist, Univ Calif, Berkeley, 61-63 & 64-65; instr hist & soc sci, Dept Hist & the Col, Univ Chicago, 65-68; from asst prof to assoc prof hist, Univ Va, 68-74; prof hist, 74-, chemn hist dept, 97-, SUNY Buffalo; John Simon Guggenheim Mem Found fel, 72-73; fel law & hist, Law Sch & fel, Charles Warren Ctr, Harvard Univ, 72-73; Nat Endowment for Humanities fel, Am Enterprise Inst, 78-79. **MEMBERSHIPS** AHA; Orgn Am Historians; Am Soc Legal Hist; Econ Hist Asn; Southern Hist Asn. **RESEARCH** Early American Constitutional and legal history; United States politics, 1776-1845; historiography. **SELECTED PUBLICATIONS** Auth, The Jeffersonian Crisis: Courts and Politics in the Young Republic, Oxford, 71; contribr, The Political Economy of Thomas Jefferson, Thomas Jefferson..The Man..His World.. His Influence, Putnam, 73; art, John Quincy Adams, Andrew Jackson and Martin Van Buren, Response of the President to Charge of Misconduct, 74; art, United States vs Nixon: A Historical Perspective, Loyola Los Angeles Law Rev, 12/75; art, The Impeachment of Samuel Chase, American Publical Trials, Greenwood Press, 81; auth, The Union at Risk: Jacksonian Democracy, States' Rights and the Nullification Crisis, Oxford, 81; auth, The Persistence of Antifederation after 1789, Before Confederation, Chapel Hill, 87; auth, The Path Not Taken: Virginia and the Supreme Court, 1789-1821, Virginia and the Constitution, Univ Virginia, 92; auth, The Market Revolution as the Transformation of American Politics, 1801-1837, The Market Revolution in America, Univ Press of Virginia, 96. **CONTACT ADDRESS** Dept of History, SUNY, Buffalo, 546 Park Hall, Buffalo, NY 14260. **EMAIL** reellis@acsu.buffalo.edu

ELLIS, RICHARD N.
PERSONAL Born 06/06/1939, Brooklyn, NY, m, 1967 **DISCIPLINE** AMERICAN FRONTIER HISTORY **EDUCATION** Univ Colo, BA, 61, MA, 63, PhD (hist), 67. **CAREER** Asst prof, Murray State Univ, 67-68; asst prof, 68-71, assoc prof, 71-80, Prof Hist, Univ NMex, 80-, Asst dir and dir, Doris Duke Am Indian Oral Hist Proj, Univ NMex, 68-71; consult, Nat Park Serv, 71-72; Am Coun Learned Soc res grant, 71-72; assoc ed, Red River Valley Hist Rev, 73-; vis prof, Univ Md, 74; sr lectr, Fulbright Prog, Aarhus Univ, Aarhus, Denmark, 79; co-coordr Am Indian exhibition, Moesgaard Forhistorisk Mus, Aarhus, Denmark. **MEMBERSHIPS** AHA; Orgn Am Historians; Western Hist Asn; Am Indian Hist Soc; Am Soc Ethnohist. **RESEARCH** American Indian history; trans-Mississippi West; the Southwest. **SELECTED PUBLICATIONS** Auth, Miles, Nelson, A. and the Twilight of the Frontier Army, Southwestern Hist Quart, Vol 98, 94; The Most Promising Young Officer--A Life of Mackenzie, Ranald, Slidell, J Am Hist, Vol 81, 94; Yellowstone Command Miles, Nelson, A. and the Great Sioux War, 1876-1877, J Am Hist, Vol 80, 93; Texas, New Mexico, and the Compromise of 1850--Boundary Dispute and Sectional Crisis, J Am Hist, Vol 84, 97; Dangerous Passage--The Santa Fe Trail and the Mexican War, J Am Hist, Vol 82, 95; On Rims and Ridges--The Los Alamos Area Since 1880, Am Hist Rev, Vol 99, 94; Cochise--Chiricahua Apache Chief, Montana Mag W Hist, Vol 43, 93; By Force of Arms--The Journals of Don Diego De Vargas, New-Mexico, 1691-93, NMex Hist Rev, Vol 70, 95; Matthews, Watt of Lambshead, NMex Hist Rev, Vol 69, 94; Glory Hunter--A Biography of Connor, Patrick, Edward, Pac Hist Rev, Vol 63, 94. **CONTACT ADDRESS** Dept of Hist, Fort Lewis Col, 1000 Rim Dr, Durango, CO 81301-3999.

ELLIS, WILLIAM ELLIOTT
PERSONAL Born 01/01/1940, Danville, KY, m, 1960, 2 children **DISCIPLINE** HISTORY **EDUCATION** Georgetown Col, AB, 62; Eastern Ky Univ, MA, 67; Univ Ky, PhD, 74. **CAREER** Instr hist, Lees Jr Col, 67-70; prof hist, Eastern Ky Univ, 70-. **MEMBERSHIPS** Southern Hist Asn. **RESEARCH** American intellectual history; southern Protestantism; evolution, education, and religion. **SELECTED PUBLICATIONS** Auth, Children, youth, and the social gospel: The reaction of Washington Gladden, Foundations, 9/80; Tenement house reform: Another episode in Kentucky progressivism, Filson Club Hist Quart, 10/81; Robert Worth Bingham and the crisis of cooperative marketing in the Twenties, Agr Hist, 1/82; Evolution, fundamentalism, and the historians: An historiographical Rev, The Historian, spring 82; A Man of Books and a Man of the People: E.Y. Mullins and the Crisis of Moderate Southern Baptist Leadership, Mercer Univ Press, 85; Patrick Henry Callahan: Progressive Catholic Layman in the American South, The Edwin Mellen Press, 89; Robert Worth Bingham and the Southern Mystique, Kent State Univ Press, 97. **CONTACT ADDRESS** Dept of Hist, Eastern Kentucky Univ, 521 Lancaster Ave, Richmond, KY 40475-3102. **EMAIL** hisellis@acs.eku.edu

ELLISON, CURTIS WILLIAM
PERSONAL Born 10/03/1943, Jasper, AL, m, 1966, 2 children **DISCIPLINE** AMERICAN STUDIES **EDUCATION** Univ Ala, BA, 65; Univ Minn, Minneapolis, MA, 67, PhD (Am studies), 70. **CAREER** Asst prof English, 70-74, assoc prof, 74-76, dir prog Am Studies, 70-74, Prof Interdisciplinary Studies, Miami Univ, 76-, Dean, 80-96, interim dean, education and allied professions, 98-01. **MEMBERSHIPS** Am Studies Asn; Southern Hist Asn; Integrative Studies Asn. **RESEARCH** Am culture studies; Popular Music and Culture; History of Education. **SELECTED PUBLICATIONS** Auth, Country Music Culture, UNW Press of Mississippi, 95; ed, The Big Ballad Jamborce, by D. Davidson, UNW Press Mississippi, 96. **CONTACT ADDRESS** Miami Univ, 20 McGuffey Hall, Oxford, OH 45056. **EMAIL** ellisocw@muoluo.edu

ELLISON, HERBERT J.
PERSONAL Born 10/03/1929, Portland, OR, m, 1952, 2 children **DISCIPLINE** RUSSIAN HISTORY **EDUCATION** Univ Wash, BA, 51; MA, 52; Univ London, PhD, 55. **CAREER** Instr hist, Univ Wash, 55-56; asst prof, hist, Univ Okla, 56-62; assoc prof hist, chmn Slavic and Soviet studies, Univ Kans, 62-65, prof hist, 65-68, assoc dean fac int progs, 67-68; prof, hist, Russian and East European studies, Univ Wash, 68-; dir div int progs, 68-72, vice provost for educational development, 69-72; dir, inst Comparative and Fgn. Area Studies, ?-77; chmn, Russian and East European studies, 73-83; sec. Kennan inst Advanced Russian Studies, Washington, 83-85; trustee, Nat Coun for Russia and East European Res, 83-87; dir, Erasian res, Nat Bureau of Asian res, 90-00, board of directors, 93-; chmn board of directors Int res and exchange baord; dir, The New Russia in Asia res and conf proj, 93-96; chmn, Acad coun, Kennan Inst for Advanced Russian studies, 97. **MEMBERSHIPS** AHA; Am Asn Advan Slavic Studies (vpres, 72-75); Conf Slavic and E Europ Hist (secy, 67-69). **RESEARCH** Russia and the Soviet Union; Histoyr of Communism; Russian Foreign Policy. **SELECTED PUBLICATIONS** Auth, History of Russia, 64; auth, Sino-Soviet Conflict, 82; coauth, The Soviet-Cuba Role in Grenada and US Intervention, 83; ed, contributor, Soviet Policy Toward Western Europe, 83; auth, Japan and the Pacific Quadrille, 87; exec dir, Messengers from Moscow, PBS/BBS TV series, 95; auth, Twentieth Century Russia, 00; exec dir, Yeltsin, PBS Special, 00. **CONTACT ADDRESS** Jackson Sch Int Studies, Univ of Washington, DR-05, Seattle, WA 98195. **EMAIL** hellison@u.washington.edu

ELLSWORTH, SAMUEL GEORGE
PERSONAL Born 06/19/1916, Safford, AZ, m, 1942, 2 children **DISCIPLINE** HISTORY **EDUCATION** Ut State Agr Col, BS, 41; Univ Calif, AM, 47, PhD, 51. **CAREER** From asst prof to assoc prof, 51-63, chmn dept, 66-69, Prof Hist, Ut State Univ, 63-, Ed, Western Hist Quart, 70-79. **HONORS AND AWARDS** Awd of Merit, Am Asn for State and Local Hist, 74. **MEMBERSHIPS** AHA; Orgn Am Historians; Western Hist Asn. **RESEARCH** The American West; Utah; the Mormons. **SELECTED PUBLICATIONS** Auth, Men With a Mission--The Quorum of the 12 Apostles in the British Isles, 1837-1841 W Hist Quart, Vol 24, 93. **CONTACT ADDRESS** Dept Hist, Utah State Univ, Logan, UT 84322.

ELMAN, B. A.
DISCIPLINE CHINESE HISTORY **EDUCATION** Univ Hawaii, jr yr, 66-67; Hamilton Col, BA honors, 68; Inter Univ Stanford in Taiwan, lang stud, chin 73-74, in Japan, 76-77; Univ Penn, PhD 80. **CAREER** Chinese Science, editor, 92-98-; UCLA Cen of Chinese Studies, prof, dir. **HONORS AND AWARDS** NEH; Fulbright Fel; NAS Res Fell; Res/Teach Fel Japan Foun; NSC Taiwan vis prof; Ecoles des Hautes Etudes Soc Sci dir; Soc Hist Stud Princeton vis prof. **SELECTED PUBLICATIONS** Auth, The Impact of Qing Dynasty Classicism in Tokugawa Japan, in progress; A Cultural History of Modern Science in China 1850-1920; in progress; A Cultural History of Civil Examinations in Late Imperial China, UCP, 99; Classical Historiography for Chinese History: Bibliography and Exercises, published and periodically updated on the WWW since 1996; Education and Society in Late Imperial China 1600-1900, co ed, Berkeley, UCP, 94; Classicism Politics and Kinship: the Ch'ang Chou New Text School of Confucianism in Late Imperial China, Berkeley, UCP, 90, Berkeley Prize 91, Jiangsu People's Press, Chin ed, 98; From Philosophy to Philology: Social and Intellectual Aspects of Change in Late Imperial China, Cambridge, Harv Univ, Coun on E Asian Stud, 84, pbk 90, Chin Ed 95. **CONTACT ADDRESS** Dept of Chinese Studies, Univ of California, Los Angeles, Los Angeles, CA 90024.

ELMAN, BENJAMIN
PERSONAL Born 09/06/1946, Germany, m, 1984 **DISCIPLINE** HISTORY **EDUCATION** Hamilton Col, AB, 68; Univ Pa, PhD, 80. **CAREER** Lectr, Colby Col, 80-82; res fel, Univ Mich, 84-85; asst prof, Rice Univ, 85-86; assoc prof to prof, Univ Calif, 86-; vis prof, Inst for Adv Study, 99-01. **HONORS AND AWARDS** Fulbright Prog Res Fel, Taiwan, 83-84, 90-91; NEH Fel, 82-83; Nat Acad of Sci, China, 83-84, 94-95; Japan Found Fel, 91; Berkeley Prize, Univ Calif, 90; Squire's Prize, Phi Beta Kappa, Hamilton Col. **MEMBERSHIPS** Asn for Asian Studies; Am Hist Asn; Soc for the Study of E Asian Sci, Technol and Med. **RESEARCH** Chinese cultural and intellectual history, 1400-1900; History of science in China; History of education in China. **SELECTED PUBLICATIONS** Auth, From Philosophy to Philology: Social and Intellectual Aspects of Change in Late Imperial China, Harvard Univ Press, 90; auth, Classicism, Politics, & Kinship: The ch'ang-chou New Text School of Confucianism in Late Imperial China, Univ Calif Press, 90; co-ed, Education & Society in Late Imperial China, 1600-1900, Univ Calif Press, 94; auth, A Cultural History of Civil Examinations in Late Imperial China, Univ Calif, 00; co-ed, Rethinking Confucianism: Past and Present in China, Japan, Korea, and Vietnam, Univ Calif, 02. **CONTACT ADDRESS** Dept Hist, Univ of California, Los Angeles, 6265 Bunche, Box 951473, Los Angeles, CA 90095-1473. **EMAIL** elman@history.ucla.edu

ELPHICK, RICHARD
DISCIPLINE SOUTH AFRICA **EDUCATION** Univ Toronto, BA; Univ Calif, MA; Yale Univ, PhD. **CAREER** Wesleyan Univ. **HONORS AND AWARDS** Assoc Ed, History & Theory. **SELECTED PUBLICATIONS** Area: South Africa. **CONTACT ADDRESS** Wesleyan Univ, Middletown, CT 06459. **EMAIL** relphick@wesleyan.edu

ELWOOD, R. CARTER
PERSONAL Born 07/23/1935, Chicago, IL **DISCIPLINE** HISTORY **EDUCATION** Dartmouth Col, BA, 58; Columbia Univ, MA, 62, PhD, 69; Russian, Univ of Edinburgh; Certificate of Russian Institute, Columbia Univ. **CAREER** Asst prof, Univ Alta, 68-70; asst prof to assoc prof, 68-76, prof history, carleton univ, 76-, ch dept, 82-85; vis scholar, St Antony's Col, Oxford, 70-71, 74; vis scholar, Univ Fribourg, 77-78; vis scholar, London Sch Econ, 84-85; vis scholar, Russian Res Ctr, Harvard Univ, 91-92. **HONORS AND AWARDS** Excellence Tchg Awd, 85; Marston LaFrance Fel, 87-88; Heldt Prize, Best Bk, Slavic Women's Stud, 92; Tchg Achievement Awd, 95. **MEMBERSHIPS** Can Asn Slavists (pres 81-82). **RESEARCH** Lenin and the dev of the Bolshevik Party, 1907-1914, a biography of Reed, Am poet, journalist and revolutionary, 1887-1920. **SELECTED PUBLICATIONS** Auth, Vserossiiskaya konferensiya Ros. Sots. - Dem. Rab. Partii, 1912 goda and Izveshenie o konferentsii organizatsii RSDRP, London and New York: Kraus International Publications, (82): 155; auth, Inessa Armand: Revolutionary and Feminist, Cambridge: Cambridge Univ Press, (92): 304; auth, Russian and Eastern European History: Selected Papers from the Second Congress for Soviet and East European Studies, Berkeley: Berkeley Slavic Specialities, (84): 306; auth, "Inessa Armand," "Aleksandra Kollontai," "Angelika Balabanoff," "Ekaterina Furtseva," "Elizaveta Koval'skaia," and "Praskovia Ivanovskaia," in Woman in World History, ed. by Anne Commire, (in press); auth, "The Malinovskii Affair: 'A Very Fishy business,'' Revolutionary Russia, No. 1, (98): 1-16. **CONTACT ADDRESS** Dept of History, Carleton Univ, 1125 Colonel By Dr, 400 Patterso Hall, Ottawa, ON, Canada K1S 5B6. **EMAIL** r_c_elwood@carleton.ca

ELY, MELVIN PATRICK
PERSONAL Born 06/11/1952, Richmond, VA, m, 1983, 2 children **DISCIPLINE** HISTORY **EDUCATION** Princeton Univ, AB, 73; Univ Tex Austin, MA, 78; Princeton Univ, MA, 82; PhD, 85. **CAREER** Asst prof to assoc prof, Yale Univ, 86-95; prof, Col of William & Mary, 95-. **HONORS AND AWARDS** Teaching Excellence Prize, Yale Col, 89; Notable Book of 1991, NY Times Book Rev; Theatre Libr Asn Awd, 92; Heyman Prize, Yale, Col, 92; Fulbright Prof, Israel, 98-99. **MEMBERSHIPS** AHA; Va Hist Soc; Southern Hist Assoc. **RESEARCH** African American history, history of the American South. **SELECTED PUBLICATIONS** Auth, The Adventures of Amos 'n' Andy: A Social History of an American Phenomenon, Free Pr, (NY), 91. **CONTACT ADDRESS** Dept Hist, Col of William and Mary, PO Box 8795, Williamsburg, VA 23187-8795.

EMBREE, AINSLIE THOMAS
PERSONAL Born 01/01/1921, NS, Canada, m, 1947, 2 children **DISCIPLINE** MODERN INDIAN HISTORY **EDUCATION** Dalhousie Univ, BA, 41; Pine Hill Divinity Sch, BD, 47; Union Theol Sem, NYork, MA, 47; Columbia Univ, MA, 55, PhD (Brit imperial hist), 60. **CAREER** Lectr hist, Indore Christian Col, India, 48-58; from instr to assoc prof Indian hist, Columbia Univ, 58-69; prof hist, Duke Univ, 69-72; assoc dean fac int affairs, 72-78, Prof Hist to Prof Emer, Columbia Univ, 72-, Vpres to pres, Am Inst Indian Studies, 67-73, fel, 68-69; coun cult affairs, Am Embassy, India, 78-80. **HONORS AND AWARDS** Am Coun Learned Soc fel, 68; Nat Endowment for Humanities fel, 77. **MEMBERSHIPS** AHA; Asn Asian Studies; Am Orient Soc; Coun Foreign Rel. **RESEARCH** Nineteenth century Indian history; modern SAsia. **SELECTED PUBLICATIONS** Contribr, Land Control and Soil Structure in Indian History, Univ Wis, 69; coauth, The Non-European World, Scott, 70; auth, India's Search for National Identity, Knopf, 71; ed, Alberuni's India, Norton, 71; contribr, Columbia History of the World, Harper, 71; The Last Empire, Aperture, 76; Realm and Region in Traditional India, Duke Univ, 77; ed, Pakistan's Western Borderlands, Carolina Academic, 77. **CONTACT ADDRESS** 54 Morningside Dr, New York, NY 10025. **EMAIL** ate1@columbia.edu

EMERICK, JUDSON
PERSONAL Born 07/03/1941, Kingston, NY, m, 1963 **DISCIPLINE** ART HISTORY **EDUCATION** Hope Col, BA, 63; Univ Mich, MA, 65; Univ Pa, PhD, 75. **CAREER** Instr, Pomona Col, 73-75; asst prof, 75-81; assoc prof, 81-97; prof, 97- . **HONORS AND AWARDS** Pennfield Scholoar, 70-71; Samuel H. Kress Found Fel, 71-73; NEH Fel, 81. **MEMBERSHIPS** Col Art Asoc; Soc of Archit Hist; Int Ctr of Medieval Art; Byzantine Studes Conf; Art Hist of Souther Cal. **RESEARCH** Late antique and early medieval art in Italy; the Corinthian order in ancient and medieval architecture; archaeology of standing walls. **SELECTED PUBLICATIONS** Co-auth with C. Davis-Weyer, The Early Sixth-Century Frescoes at S. Martino at Monti in Rome, Romisches Jahrbuch fur Kuustgeschichte, 84; auth, The Tempiettodel Clitunno near Spoleto, 98. **CONTACT ADDRESS** Dept. of Art and Art History, Pomona Col, 145 E. Bonita Ave., Claremont, CA 91711. **EMAIL** jje04747@pomona.edu

EMERY, TED
DISCIPLINE ITALIAN EIGHTEENTH CENTURY **EDUCATION** Trinity Col, BA; Brown Univ, MA, PhD. **CAREER** Asst prof-. **HONORS AND AWARDS** Commentator on Giacomo Casanova, Arts and Entertainment Network's biog prog. **RESEARCH** Singing and acting, scenery, costumes and dance. **SELECTED PUBLICATIONS** Auth, monograph on the opera libretti of Carlo Goldoni, Peter Lang, 91; ed, co-transl, Five Tales for the Theatre by Carlo Gozzi, Univ Chicago Press, 89. **CONTACT ADDRESS** Dept of Fr and Ital, Dickinson Col, PO Box 1773, Carlisle, PA 17013-2896.

EMGE, STEVEN W.
PERSONAL Born 05/15/1958, Council Bluffs, IA, m, 2 children **DISCIPLINE** VOICE; MUSIC **EDUCATION** Drake Univ, BME, 80; Drake Univ, MME, 92; Univ Iowa, MA, 95; Univ Iowa, PhD, 96. **CAREER** Elementary/junior high music specialist, 86-91; instr, Univ Iowa, 92-95; instr, Coe Col, 93-95; instr, Augustana Col, 95; asst prof, Southeastern Oklahoma State Univ, 96-. **HONORS AND AWARDS** Undergraduate vocal scholarship, Drake University; graduate music educ scholarship, Drake Univ; Univ Iowa graduate teaching assistantship. **MEMBERSHIPS** National Asn of Teachers of Singing; Music Educators National Conference. **RESEARCH** Voice development; vocal pedagogy. **SELECTED PUBLICATIONS** Coauth, "Vocal Registration as it Affects Vocal Range for Seventh- and Eighth-Grade Boys", in The Journal of Research in Singing and Applied Vocal Pedagogy 18(1), 94. **CONTACT ADDRESS** Southeastern Oklahoma State Univ, 5th & University, Durant, OK 74701-0609. **EMAIL** semge@sosu.edu

EMISON, PATRICIA A.
DISCIPLINE ART, ART HISTORY **EDUCATION** Bryn Mawr Col, BA, 78; Columbia Univ, PhD, 85. **CAREER** Lectr, Smith Col, 87; asst pro, Univ of New Hampshire, 87-92, assoc prof, 93-. **HONORS AND AWARDS** UNH Ctr for the Humanities Discretionary Grant, 94; UNH Class of 1954 Grant, 96; Samuel H. Fress Found Fel in Renaissance Art Hist, Awded by the Renaissance Soc of Am, 99; Inst fir Advanced Study, Princeton, membership in Sch of Hist Studies, Awd for Spring Semester, 200-2001. **SELECTED PUBLICATIONS** Auth, "The Paysage Moralise," Artibus et Historiae, XXXI (95): 125-37; auth, "Prolegomenon to the Study of Italian Renaissance Prints," Word and Image, XI (95): 1-15; auth, Low and High Style in Italian Renaissance Art, New York (97); auth, "The Igundo as Proto-Capriccio," Word and Image, XIV (98): 281-95. **CONTACT ADDRESS** Dept of Art and Art Hist, Univ of New Hampshire, Durham, Paul Creative Arts Center, 30 Col Rd, Durham, NH 03824. **EMAIL** patricia.emison@unh.edu

EMMERSON, RICHARD K.
PERSONAL Born 05/11/1948, Mexico, m, 1976, 2 children **DISCIPLINE** ENGLISH AND MEDIEVAL STUDIES **EDUCATION** Columbia Union Col, BA, 70; Andrews Univ, MA, 71; Stanford Univ, PhD, 77. **CAREER** From Asst to Full Prof, Walla Walla Col, 75-86; Prog Officer, Summer Sem for Col Teachers, Nat Endowment for the Humanities, 83-85; Deputy Dir, Div of Fel and Sem, Nat Endowment for the Humanities, 87-90; Prof Lectr, Georgetown Univ, 87-90; Prof, Chair Dept of English, Western Wash Univ, 90-99; Exec Dit, Medieval Acad of Am, 99-. **HONORS AND AWARDS** Woodrow Wilson Fel, 70; Nat Endowment for the Humanities Fel, 78-79, 96-97. **MEMBERSHIPS** Medieval Acad of Am, Medieval and Renaissance Drama Soc, MLA, New Chaucer Soc. **RESEARCH** Medieval Apocalypticism, Medieval Drama and Visionary Poetry, Illustrated Manuscripts, 13th-15th centuries. **SELECTED PUBLICATIONS** Auth, Antichrist in the Middle Ages: A Study of Medieval Apocalypticism, Art, and Literature, (Seattle), 81; auth, Approaches to Teaching Medieval English Drama, (NY), 90; coauth, The Apocalyptic Imagination in Medieval Literature, (Philadelphia), 92; co-ed, The Apocalypse in the Middle Ages, (Ihaca, NY), 92; co-transl, co-ed, Antichrist and Doomsday: The Middle French 'Jour du Judgement', (Asheville, NC), 98. **CONTACT ADDRESS** Medieval Acad Of Am, 1430 Massachusetts Ave, Cambridge, MA 02138. **EMAIL** rke@medievalacademy.org

ENDELMAN, TODD MICHAEL
PERSONAL Born 11/10/1946, Fresno, CA, m, 1968, 2 children **DISCIPLINE** JEWISH HISTORY, EUROPEAN HISTORY **EDUCATION** Univ Calif, Berkeley, BA, 68; Hebrew Union Col-Jewish Inst Relig, Calif, BHL, 72; Harvard Univ, Am, 72, PhD (hist), 76. **CAREER** Asst prof Jewish hist, Yeshiva Univ, 76-79; asst prof hist, 79-81, Assoc Prof Hist, Ind Univ, 81-85, Lectr hist, Hebrew Union Col-Jewish Inst Relig, NY, 79; William Haber Prof of Mod Jewish Hist, Univ of Mich, 85-. **HONORS AND AWARDS** Frank and Ethel S Cohen Awd, Jewish Bd Coun, Nat Jewish Welfare Bd, 80; A S Diamond Mem Prize, Jewish Hist Soc England, 80. **MEMBERSHIPS** AHA; Jewish Hist Soc England; Leo Baeck Inst; Asn Jewish Studies. **RESEARCH** Anglo-Jewish history; social history of Western European Jewry; the entry of the Jews into European society, 1700-1880. **SELECTED PUBLICATIONS** Auth, The Jews of Georgian England, 1714-1830: Tradition and Change in a Liberal Society, 79; ed, Jewish Apostasy in the Modern World, 87; auth, Radical Assimilation in Anglo-Jewish History, 1656-1945, 90; ed, Comparing Jewish Societies, 97; auth, The Jews of Modern Britain, forthcoming. **CONTACT ADDRESS** Dept of Hist, Univ of Michigan, Ann Arbor, 555 S State St, 1029 Tisch Hall, Ann Arbor, MI 48109-1003. **EMAIL** endelman@umich.edu

ENDICOTT, ELIZABETH
DISCIPLINE CHINESE HISTORY, MONGOLIAN HISTORY, EAST ASIAN HISTORY **EDUCATION** Trinity Col, AB; Yale Univ, MA; Princeton Univ, MA, PhD. **CAREER** Assoc prof, Middlebury Col, 95-. **RESEARCH** China under Mongolian rule, 13th-14th centuries; Chinese-Mongolian-Russian relations, 19th-20th centuries. **SELECTED PUBLICATIONS** Auth, Mongolian Rule in China: Local Administration in the Yuan Dynasty, Harvard UP; coauth, The Modernization of Inner Asia, M.E. Sharpe. **CONTACT ADDRESS** Dept of History, Middlebury Col, Middlebury, VT 05753. **EMAIL** endicott@middlebury.edu

ENDICOTT, STEPHEN L.
PERSONAL Born 01/05/1928, Shanghai, China **DISCIPLINE** HISTORY **EDUCATION** Univ Toronto, BA, 49, MA, 66; Sch Orient African Stud Univ London, Univ Toronto, PhD, 73. **CAREER** Journalist, Jeunesse du Monde, Hungary, 52-54; mem, Labour Progressive Party Exec, Toronto, 54-57; high sch tchr, Peel Co, Ont, 60-68; lectr to assoc prof, 72-90, Sr Scholar, Dept Hist, Atkinson Col, York Univ, 90-; vis prof, Sichuan Univ (Chengdu), 80-81. **HONORS AND AWARDS** Can Coun scholar, 75-76; Killam fel, 76-78; SSHRCC fel, 83-84; Atkinson fel, 86. **RESEARCH** Chinese history. **SELECTED PUBLICATIONS** Auth, Diplomacy and Enterprise: British China Policy 1933-37, 75; auth, James G. Endicott: Rebel Out of China, 80; auth, Wen Yiuzhang Zhuan, 83; auth, Red Earth: Revolution in a Sichuan Village, 88; auth, The Red Dragon: China 1949-1990, 91. **CONTACT ADDRESS** School of Arts and Letters, York Univ, 4700 Keele St, 638 Atkinson College, Toronto, ON, Canada M3J 1P3.

ENG, ROBERT Y.
DISCIPLINE HISTORY **EDUCATION** Pomona Col, BA; Univ Calif Berkeley, MA; PhD. **CAREER** Prof,Redlands Univ. **RESEARCH** Social;economic and demographic history of modern China and Japan **SELECTED PUBLICATIONS** Auth, Land Reclamation, Merchant Wealth and Political Power in Qing and Republican China: Minglun Tang of Dongguan County, Beijing, 92; Luddism and Labor Protest Among Silk Artisans and Workers in Jiangnan and Guangdong, 1860-1930, Late Imperial China, 90; Institutional and Secondary Landlordism in the Pearl River Delta, 1600-1949, Modern China, 86; Chinese Entrepreneurs, the Government, and the Foreign Sector: The Canton and Shanghai Silk-reeling Enterprises, 1861-1932, Modern Asian Studies, 84. **CONTACT ADDRESS** History Dept, Univ of Redlands, 1200 E Colton Ave, Box 3090, Redlands, CA 92373-0999. **EMAIL** eng@uor.edu

ENGEBRETSEN, TERRY
DISCIPLINE AMERICAN STUDIES **EDUCATION** Wash State Univ, PhD, 82. **CAREER** Assoc prof. **RESEARCH** Seventeenth century American literature and culture; postmodernism. **SELECTED PUBLICATIONS** Auth, pubs in Studies in the Literary Imagination; Studies in Puritan American Spirituality. **CONTACT ADDRESS** Dept of English and Philosophy, Idaho State Univ, Pocatello, ID 83209.

ENGEL, ARTHUR JASON
PERSONAL Born 08/27/1944, Weehawken, NJ **DISCIPLINE** ENGLISH HISTORY **EDUCATION** Clark Univ, AB, 66; Princeton Univ, MA, 71, PhD, 75. **CAREER** Instr, 76-79, asst prof hist, 79-, Va Commonwealth Univ; assoc prof of history, Va Commonwealth Univ, 85-. **RESEARCH** English social history; history of education. **SELECTED PUBLICATIONS** Contribr, Emerging Concepts of the Academic Profession at Oxford 1800-54, The University in Society, Princeton Univ Press, Vol I, 305-52; auth, Oxford College finances 1871-1913: A Comment, Econ Hist Rev, 78; art, Immoral intentions: The University of Oxford and the Problem of Prostitution 1827-1914, Victorian Studies, 79; art, The University System in Modern England: Historography of the 1970's and Opportunities for the 1980's, Rev Higher Educ, Vol III, No 3, 80; art, Political Education in Oxford 1823-1914, Hist Educ Quart, 80; contribr, The English Universities and Professional Education, The Transformation of Higher Learning 1860-1930, Elsivir, 82; auth, From Clergyman to Don: The Rise of the Academic Profession in 19th century Oxford, Clarendon Press, 82. **CONTACT ADDRESS** Dept of History, Virginia Commonwealth Univ, Box 2001, Richmond, VA 23284-9004. **EMAIL** aengel@atlas.vcu.edu

ENGELS, DONALD W.
PERSONAL Born 05/15/1946, Rockville Centre, NY, s **DISCIPLINE** HISTORY, CLASSICS **EDUCATION** Univ of Fla, Ba, 69; Univ of Tex, MA, 72; Univ of Pa, PhD, 76. **CAREER** Instr for Greek & Roman Hist, Univ of Pa, 77; vis asst prof in Hist & Classics, Brandeis Univ, 77-78; asst prof of Hist & Greek & Latin, Wellesley Col, 78-85; from asst prof to prof, Univ Ark, 83-; vis asst prof o fhist & classics, Univ of Chicago, 83; vis asst prof, Boston Col, 85-86. **HONORS AND AWARDS** Tchg fel for Greek and Roman Hist, Univ of Pa, 75-76; Ford Found Archaeol Traineeship, 70; res & tchg fels, Univ of Pa, 73-76; Am Philos Soc Grant, 79; travel grant, Wellesley Col, 79; NEH summer stipend, Brown Univ, 81; res fel, Wolfson Col, Cambridge Univ, 00-01. **MEMBERSHIPS** Am Philol Asn; Asn of Ancient Historians; Friends of Ancient Hist; Soc for Ancient Medicine; Historical Soc. **RESEARCH** Greek and Roman history. **SELECTED PUBLICATIONS** Auth, Alexander the Greant the Logistics of the Macedonian Army, Univ Calif Pr, 78; auth, Roman Corinth: An Alternative Model for the Classical City, Univ of Chicago Press, 90; Classical Cats: The Rise and Fall of the Sacred Cat, Routledge, 99; Ptolemy I, World Book Encycl, 81; The Use of Historical Demography in Ancient History, Classical Quart, 84; The Length of Eratosthenes' Stade, Am J of Philol, 85; The Classical City Reconsidered, The Eye Expanded, Berkeley, 98. **CONTACT ADDRESS** Dept of Hist, Univ of Arkansas, Fayetteville, Fayetteville, AR 72701. **EMAIL** dengles@comp.uark.edu

ENGERMAN, STANLEY LEWIS
PERSONAL Born 03/14/1936, New York, NY, m, 1963, 3 children **DISCIPLINE** ECONOMICS, HISTORY **EDUCATION** NYork Univ, BS, 56, MBA, 58; Johns Hopkins Univ, PhD(econ), 62. **CAREER** Asst prof econ, Yale Univ, 62-63; from asst prof to assoc prof, 63-71, prof hist & econ, Univ Rochester, 71-, Nat Sci Found sci fac fel, 69-70; Nat Endowment for Humanities sr fel, 74-75; John Simon Guggenheim mem fel, 80-81. **MEMBERSHIPS** Am Econ Asn; Econ Hist Asn; AHA. **RESEARCH** Slavery; American social and economic history. **SELECTED PUBLICATIONS** Co-ed, The Reinterpretation of American Economic History, Harper, 71; coauth, Time on the Cross: The Economics of American Negro Slavery, Little, Brown, 74; co-ed, Race and Slavery in the Western Hemisphere: Quantitative Studies, Princeton Univ, 75. **CONTACT ADDRESS** Dept of Econ, Univ of Rochester, 500 Joseph C Wilson, Rochester, NY 14627-9000. **EMAIL** enge@troi.cc.rochester.edu

ENGLAND, JAMES MERTON
PERSONAL Born 11/30/1915, Deepwater, MO, m, 1944, 4 children **DISCIPLINE** AMERICAN HISTORY **EDUCATION** Cent Col, Mo, AB, 36; Vanderbilt Univ, AM, 37; PhD, 41. **CAREER** Ed asst, La State Univ, 41-42; from instr to asst prof, Univ Ky, 46-48, from assoc prof hist to prof, 48-61; prog dir inst grants for sci, 61-70, exec asst to dep asst dir instnl progs, 70-71, exec asst to asst dir, 71, spec asst to dir, 71-77, Historian, Nat Sci Found, 77-, Ed assoc, J Southern Hist, 49-52, managing ed, 53-58; Fulbright prof, Univ Birmingham, 56-57; lectr, Salzburg Sem Am Studies, 57; vis prof Am Civilization, sch int serv, Am Univ, 60-61. **HONORS AND AWARDS** LHD, WVa Inst Technol, 65. **MEMBERSHIPS** Southern Hist Asn; Orgn Am Historians; Am Hist Asn; AAAS. **RESEARCH** History of American education; science and federal government. **SELECTED PUBLICATIONS** Auth, To Foster the Spirit of Professionalism--Southern Scientists and State Academies of Science, J Southern Hist, Vol 59, 93. **CONTACT ADDRESS** National Sci Foundation, Washington, DC 20550.

ENGLAND, ROBERT
PERSONAL Born 01/29/1947, Birmingham, AL, d **DISCIPLINE** HISTORY, AMERICAN STUDIES **EDUCATION** Samford Univ, BS, 70; Univ Montevallo, MA, 76; Univ Ala, PhD, 79. **CAREER** Grad Teaching Asst, Univ of Ala, 89-92; Prof Adventurers, Morrison, England, & Lill, 85-; Prof, Dir of Outdoor Leadership, Northwest-Shoals Community Col, 92-. **HONORS AND AWARDS** Fel, Univ of Ala, 76-79, 89-92; Cited for lifesaving, State of Ala, 77; Fel, The Medici Found of Princeton Univ. **MEMBERSHIPS** Southern Hist Asn, Soc for Mil Hist, Ala Asn of Historians, Orgn of Am Historians, Am Hist Asn, Coun on Am's Mil past, Soc for Early Am Hist, Coast Defense Study Group. **RESEARCH** American national defense after the War of 1812, military planning, management of 19th century armies, ideological foundations of American strategy. **SELECTED PUBLICATIONS** Auth, "Whoa Boys! We've Got the Wrong Flag!," 93; auth, "The Bosnian Crisis Reduced to One," 93; auth, "Confederate Civilian Leadership," in Civil War Field Manual, ed. Stephen Woodworth (97); contrib, Fort Morgan, Arcadia Press, 00. **CONTACT ADDRESS** Dept Soc Sci, Northwest-Shoals Comm Col, PO Box 2545, Muscle Shoals, AL 35662-2545.

ENGLE, STEPHEN D.
PERSONAL Born 02/26/1962, Charlestown, WV, m, 1985, 2 children **DISCIPLINE** HISTORY **EDUCATION** Fla State Univ, PhD. **CAREER** Professor. **HONORS AND AWARDS** Fulbright Scholar, Martin Luther Univ, Germany, 95-96. **MEMBERSHIPS** Am Hist Asn; Southern Hist Asn; Asn German-Am. **RESEARCH** 19th century America; Civil War and reconstruction South. **SELECTED PUBLICATIONS** Auth, Yankee Dutchman: The Life of Franz Sigel, 93; Mountaineer Reconstruction: Blacks in the Political Reconstruction of West Virginia, Jour Negro Hist, 94; Don Carlos Buell, Military Philosophy, and Command Problems in the West, 95; auth, Don Carlos Buell: Most Promising of All, 99. **CONTACT ADDRESS** History Dept, Florida Atlantic Univ, 777 Glades Rd, Boca Raton, FL 33431. **EMAIL** engle@fau.edu

ENGLISH, ALLAN D.
DISCIPLINE HISTORY **EDUCATION** Royal Military Col Can, BA, 71; MA, 87; Queen's Univ, PhD, 94. **CAREER** Adj Asst Prof, Queen's Univ, 94-; Adj Assoc Prof, Royal Military Col of Can, 95-99. **RESEARCH** Military History; Air Warfare; Human Behaviour and War; Combat Stress; Military Culture. **SELECTED PUBLICATIONS** Auth, "The RAF Staff College and the Evolution of British Strategic Bombing Policy 1922-29," J of Strategic Studies, (93): 408-431; auth, "A Predisposition to Cowardice?: Aviation Psychology and the Genesis of 'Lack of Moral Fibre.'," War and Society, (95): 15-34; auth, The Cream of the Crop: Canadian Aircrew 1939-1945, Queen's Univ Press, 96; ed, The Changing Face of War, Queen's Univ Press, 98; auth, "Historical and Contemporary Interpretations of Combat Stress Reaction," in Proceedings in the Conference on Ethics in Canadian Defence, 99; auth, "Leadership and Operational Stress in the Canadian Forces," Can Military J, (00): 33-38; auth, "The Americanization of the Canadian Officer Corps: Myth and Reality?" in Contemporary Issues in Officership: A Canadian Perspective, (Toronto, 00), 181-204. **CONTACT ADDRESS** Dept Hist, Queen's Univ at Kingston, Dept Hist, Kingston, ON, Canada K7L 3N6. **EMAIL** english-a@rmc.ca

ENGLISH, JOHN CAMMEL
PERSONAL Born 12/04/1934, Kansas City, MO, m, 1966 **DISCIPLINE** HISTORY **EDUCATION** Wash Univ, BA, 55; Yale Univ, MDiv, 58; Vanderbilt Univ, PhD (church hist), 65. **CAREER** Asst prof hist, Stephen F Austin State Univ, 62-65; from asst prof to assoc prof, 65-68, chmn, Dept Hist and Polit Sci, 65-73, 83-93, chmn, Soc Sci Div, 70-72, chmn, Humanities Div, 78-81; Prof Hist, Baker Univ, 68-97; US Dept of Educ Fac Dev Award, Fl, Summer Fac Inst South and Southeast Asia,; US Educ fac develop award S Asian studies, Univs Minn and Chicago, 69-70; dir, Shaping of Western Thought Prog, 77-80. **HONORS AND AWARDS** US Dept. of Education Faculty Development Awd, South Asian Studies, Univs of MN, Chicago, 69-70; Distinguished Faculty Awd, Baker Univ, 85; Emeritus, 97- **MEMBERSHIPS** Am Soc Church Hist; Conf Brit Studies; Am Soc 18th Century Studies. **RESEARCH** European intellectual and religious history, particularly 17th and 18th century Britain; South Asian history and politics; methodology of historical research; Religious and intellectual history of England, 1558-1800; 18th century methodism; John Weslev. **SELECTED PUBLICATIONS** Auth, The Mind of Locke, John--A Study of Political-Theory in its Intellectual Setting, Church Hist, Vol 64, 95; auth, John Wesley and the Rights of Conscience, Journal of Church and State 37 (95):349-63; Wesley, John Conception and Use of Scripture, Church Hist, Vol 66, 97; The Mind of Locke, John--A Study of Political Theory in its Intellectual Setting, Church Hist, Vol 64, 95; Wesley, John and the Rights of Conscience Church and State, Vol 37, 95; Wesley,

John Conception and Use of Scripture, Church Hist, Vol 66, 97; auth, The Path to Perfection in Pseudo-Macarius and John Wesley, Pacifica 11 (98): 54-62; auth, John Wesley and His 'Jewish Parishioners: 'Jewish-Christian Relationships in Savannah, Georgia, 1736-1737, Methodist History 36 (98); 220-27; auth, The Scope of London Methodism: Walter Wilson's Evidence, Proceedings of the Wesley Historical Society 52 (99): 102-23; auth, John Hutchinson's Critique of Newtonian Heterodoxy, Church History 66 (99): 581-97. **CONTACT ADDRESS** PO Box 537, Baldwin City, KS 66006.

ENGS, ROBERT FRANCIS
PERSONAL Born 11/10/1943, Colorado Springs, CO, m, 1969, 1 child **DISCIPLINE** HISTORY **EDUCATION** Princeton U, AB (cum laude) 1965; Yale U, PhD History 1972. **CAREER** U Univ of PA, prof of history, 99-, assoc prof history 79-99; Univ of PA, asst prof history 72-79; Princeton U, instr history 70-72; NJ Black History Inst NJ Dept of Educ, dir 69-72; Coll of William & Mary, commonwealth visiting prof 84-85; Univ of PA, Philadelphia, PA, undergraduate chair History, 86-92, 00-02. **HONORS AND AWARDS** Short Term Am Grantee, US Dept of State 1971; William Penn Fellow, Moton Cntr for Ind Studies 1976-77; Freedom's First Generation, Univ of PA Press 1979; N&H Summer Fellowship, Natl Endowment of the Humanities 1980; Guggenheim Fellow 1982-83; Lindback Award for Excellence in Teaching, Univ of Pennsylvania 1988. **MEMBERSHIPS** Faculty mem/cons Nat Humanities Faculty 1972-80; adv Nat Humanities Center 1978-80; mem Orgn of Am Historians 1975-; mem Am Hist Assn 1975; mem Assn for Study of Afro-Am Life History 1975; chmn Presidents Forum Univ of PA 1985-87. **RESEARCH** African American history 1860-1920. **SELECTED PUBLICATIONS** Auth, Freedom's First Generation, Phila, 79; auth, Educating the Disfranchised Disinherited: Samuel Chapman Armstrong and Hampton Institute, Knoxville, 00. **CONTACT ADDRESS** Univ of Pennsylvania, 3401 Walnut St, Philadelphia, PA 19104. **EMAIL** rengs@sas.upenn.edu

ENGSTRAND, IRIS H. WILSON
PERSONAL Born 01/09/1935, Los Angeles, CA, m, 1970, 1 child **DISCIPLINE** HISTORY **EDUCATION** Univ Southern CA, BA, 56, MA, 57, PhD, 62. **CAREER** Res translr hist, Los Angeles County Mus, 59-60; instr hist, Long Beach City Col, 62-68; assoc prof, 68-74, prof hist, Univ San Diego, 74, Lectr & asst prof hist, Univ Southern CA, 62-68; Am Philos Soc fel res in Spain, 64-65; assoc prof hist, Univ CA, San Diego, 68-69; chmn, Bd Ed Consults, J San Diego Hist, 76-; Nat Endowment for Hum fel, 76; mem bd trustees, CA Hist Soc, 80; Huntington Lib fel, 89; Fulbright res scholar, Spain, 96. **HONORS AND AWARDS** Awd of Merit, San Diego Hist Soc, 75-76 & Calif Hist Soc, 78; Davies Awd for Fac Achievement, USD, 84; Distinguished Univ Prof, USD, 95; Am Hist Asn, pres, Pacific Coast Branch, 98-99. **MEMBERSHIPS** AHA; Latin Am Studies Asn; Western Hist Asn. **RESEARCH** Span Colonial empire; hist of sci; hist of CA. **SELECTED PUBLICATIONS** Auth, Investigacion sobre la planta maguey en Nueva Espana, Rev Indias, 63; Antonio Pineda y su Viaje Mundial, Rev Hist Militar, 64; William Wolfskill: Frontier Trapper to California Ranchero, 1798-1866, Arthur H Clark, 65; coauth, Southern California and its University: A History of USC, 1880-1964, Ward Ritchie, 69; ed & transl, Noticias de Nutka: An Account of Nootka Sound in 1792, Univ Wash, 70, rev 91; auth, Royal Officer in Baja California 1768-1770: Joaquin Velazquez de Leon, Dawson's 76; San Diego: California's Cornerstone, Continental Heritage Press, 80; Spanish Scientists in the New World: The Eighteenth Century Expeditions, Univ Wash, 81; San Diego: Gateway to the Pacific, Pioneer Publ, 92; Arizona Hispanica, Editorial Mapfre, 92; Documents for the History of California and the West, D C Heath, 92; co-auth (with Donald Cutter), Quest for Empire: Spanish Settlement in the Southwest, Fulcrum Publ, 96; coauth, Inspired by Nature: The San Diego Natural History Museum After 125 Years, Natural History Museum, 99. **CONTACT ADDRESS** Dept of Hist, Univ of San Diego, 5998 Alcala Park, San Diego, CA 92110-2492. **EMAIL** iris@acusd.edu

ENO, ROBERT BRYAN
PERSONAL Born 11/12/1936, Hartford, CT **DISCIPLINE** PATRISTICS, CHURCH HISTORY **EDUCATION** Cath Univ Am, BA, 58, MA, 59; Inst Cath de Paris, STD, 69. **CAREER** Asst prof, St Mary's Sem, Baltimore, 68-70; ASST PROF, 70-79, ASSOC PROF PATRISTICS, CATH UNIV AM, 79-, CHMN, DEPT CHURCH HIST, AND ASSOC CHMN, DEPT THEOL, 80-, Ed, Corpus Instrumentorum, 66-70; mem, NAT LUTHERAN-ROMAN CATH DIALOGUE, 76-; vis lectr, Princeton Theol Sem, spring, 77 and 80. **MEMBERSHIPS** NAm Patristic Soc; Asn Int des Etudes Patristiques; Am Soc Church Hist; Cath Hist Asn. **RESEARCH** Latin fathers, especially Augustine; ecclesiology; eschatology. **SELECTED PUBLICATIONS** Auth, Church, Book and Bishop--Conflict and Authority in Early Latin Christianity, Cath Hist Rev, Vol 83, 97; Historical Awareness in Augustine--Ontological, Anthropological and Historical Elements of an Augustinian Theory of History, Cath Hist Rev, Vol 80, 94; A Translation of Jerome Chronicon with Historical Commentary, Cath Hist Rev, Vol 83, 97; Desire and Delight--A New Reading of Augustine Confessions, Cath Hist Rev, Vol 79, 93; After the Apostles--Christianity in the 2nd Century, Church History, Vol 64, 95; Augustine, Arianism and Other Heresies, Cath Hist Rev, Vol 83, 97; Novitas Christiana - the Idea of Progress in the Old Church Before Eusebius, Cath Hist Rev, Vol 81, 95; Sacred and Secular--Studies on Augustine and Latin Christianity, Cath Hist Rev, Vol 83, 97; Augustine, Cath Hist Rev, Vol 83, 97; Augustine and the Catechumenate, Cath Hist Rev, Vol 83, 97; The Collection Sources Chretiennes--Editing the Fathers of the Church in the Xxth Century, Cath Hist Rev, Vol 83, 97; Chiliasm and the Myth of the Antichrist--Early Christian Controversy Regarding the Holy Land, Cath Hist Rev, Vol 80, 94; The Early Church--An Annotated Bibliography in English, Cath Hist Rev, Vol 80, 94; The Significance of the Lists of Roman Bishops in the Anti Donatist Polemic, Vigiliae Christianae, Vol 47, 93; Divine Grace and Human Agency--A Study of the Semi Pelagian Controversy, Theol Stud, Vol 57, 96; Reading the Apostolic Fathers--An Introduction, Cath Hist Rev, Vol 83, 97; After the Apostles--Christianity in the 2nd Century, Church Hist, Vol 64, 95. **CONTACT ADDRESS** Catholic Univ of America, 401 Michigan Ave NE, Washington, DC 20017.

ENS, GERHARD J.
DISCIPLINE HISTORY **EDUCATION** Univ Manitoba, BA, MA; Univ Alberta, PhD. **CAREER** Hist, Brandon Univ. **RESEARCH** Nineteenth and twentieth century metis society and politics. **SELECTED PUBLICATIONS** Auth, Homeland to Hinterland: The Changing Worlds of the Red River Metis in the nineteenth century, Univ Toronto, 96; Prologue to the Red River Resistance: Pre-liminal Metis Politics and the Triumph of Riel, Jour Can Hist Asn, 94; Metis Agriculture in Red River during the Transition from Peasant Society to Industrial Capitalism: The Example of St. Francois Xavier 1835-1870, Univ Alberta, 93; co-auth, Metis Land Grants in Manitoba: A Statistical Study, 94. **CONTACT ADDRESS** Dept of Hist and Class, Brandon Univ, Edmonton, AB, Canada T6G 2M7. **EMAIL** ens@BrandonU.ca

ENSSLE, MANFRED JOACHIM
PERSONAL Born 03/25/1939, Stuttgart, Germany, m, 1966, 2 children **DISCIPLINE** EUROPEAN & GERMAN HISTORY **EDUCATION** Univ Colo, BA, 61, MA, 63, PhD(hist), 71. **CAREER** Instr, 65-70, asst prof, 71-77, assoc prof Hist, Colo State Univ, 77-87, prof Hist, 87-, vis asst prof, Univ Del, summers 71 & 77; Danforth assoc, 80-. **HONORS AND AWARDS** Fellow, Institut fur Europaishe Geschichte (Institute for European History), Mainz, Germany, 67-68, 72; Research grant, Am Philosophical Soc, 72; Nat Endowment for the Humanities Summer Seminar for College Teachers, 80; 5 Teaching awards, Colorado State Univ, 87-93. **MEMBERSHIPS** General Studies Asn. **RESEARCH** German history; 20th century Europe. **SELECTED PUBLICATIONS** Auth, Stresemann's Diplomacy Fifty Years After Locarno: Some Recent Perspectives, Hist J, 77; Stresemann's Territorial Revisionism, Germany, Belgium, and the Eupen-Malmedy Question 1919-1929, Franz Steiner Verlag, 80; The Harsh Discipline of Food Scarcity in Postwar Stuttgart, 1945-1948, German Studies Review, X, 3 (Oct 87), pp481-502; Five Theses on German Everyday Life After World War II, Central European History 26, 1 (93), pp 1-19; Der Versorgungsalltag Stuttgarts 1945-1949, Aus den vertraulichen Stimmungsberichten der Polizeireviere, (chapter in) E. Lersch, H. Poker, and P. Saer, eds, Stuttgart in den ersten Nachkriegsjahren (Stuttgart: Klett-Cotta, 95), pp 353-397; (with Bradley J. MacDonald), The Wrapped Reichstag, 1995: Art, Dialogic Communities and Everyday Life, Theory & Event 1, 4 (97), pp 1-19. **CONTACT ADDRESS** Dept of Hist, Colorado State Univ, Fort Collins, CO 80523-0001. **EMAIL** menssle@colostate.edu

ENTENMANN, ROBERT
PERSONAL Born 05/11/1949, Seattle, WA, m, 1980, 2 children **DISCIPLINE** HISTORY **EDUCATION** Univ Wash, BA, 71; Stanford Univ, MA, 73; Harvard Univ, PhD, 82. **CAREER** Instructor, Harvard Univ, 80-81; Asst Prof to Prof, St Olaf Col, 82-; Visiting Prof, Carleton Col, 98. **MEMBERSHIPS** Am Hist Asn, Asn for Asian Studies. **RESEARCH** Chinese Catholics in 18th Century China. **CONTACT ADDRESS** Dept Hist, St. Olaf Col, 1520 Saint Olaf Ave, Northfield, MN 55057-1574. **EMAIL** entenman@stolaf.edu

ENTRIKIN, J. NICHOLAS
PERSONAL Born 11/22/1947, Toledo, OH, m, 1970, 2 children **DISCIPLINE** GEOGRAPHY **EDUCATION** Syracuse Univ, BA, 69; Univ Wisc, MA, 72; PhD, 75. **CAREER** Asst prof to prof, UCLA, 75-. **HONORS AND AWARDS** Guggenheim Fel, 83-84. **MEMBERSHIPS** Asn of Am Geogr. **RESEARCH** Cultural Geography and Contemporary Geographic Thought. **SELECTED PUBLICATIONS** Auth, The Betweenness of place: Towards a Geography of Modernity, Johns Hopkins Univ Press, 91; co-auth, "Lieu et sujet: Perspectives theoriques," L'Espace geographique, (98): 111-121; auth, "Political Community, Identity and Cosmopolitan Place," Intl Sociol, (99): 269-282; auth, "Le langage geographique dans la theorie democratique," in Logique de l'espace, esprit des lieux: Geographies a Cerisy, (Paris, 00), 189-199; auth, "Geographer as Humanist," in Textures of Place, (Minneapolis, 01), 426-440; auth, "Perfectibility and Democratic Place-making," in Progress: Essays in Geography, Johns Hopkins Univ Press, (forthcoming). **CONTACT ADDRESS** Dept Geog, Univ of California, Los Angeles, 1255 Bunche, PO Box 951524, Los Angeles, CA 90095-1524. **EMAIL** Entrikin@geog.ucla.edu

EPP, ELDON JAY
PERSONAL Born 11/01/1930, Mountain Lake, MN, m, 1951 **DISCIPLINE** CHRISTIAN ORIGINS, MANUSCRIPT STUDIES **EDUCATION** Wheaton Col, Ill, AB, 52; Fuller Theol Sem, BD, 55; Harvard Univ, STM, 56, PhD (hist, philos relig), 61. **CAREER** Spec res asst, Princeton Theol Sem, 61-62; from asst prof to assoc prof relig, Grad Sch Relig, Univ Southern Calif, 62-67, assoc prof classics, 66-68; from assoc prof to profrelig, 68-71, Fel Claremont Grad Sch, 66-68; AM EXEC COMT, INT GREEK NEW TESTAMENT PROJ, 68-; ASSOC ED, J BIBL LIT, 71-; Guggenheim fel, 74-75. **MEMBERSHIPS** Soc Bibl Lit; Am Acad Relig; Soc Study New Testament; Cath Bibl Asn; Soc Mithraic Studies. **RESEARCH** New Testament textual criticism; Greek and Latin manuscript studies; Greco-Roman religions. **SELECTED PUBLICATIONS** Auth, The International Greek New Testament--Project Motivation Hist, Novum Testamentum, Vol 39, 97. **CONTACT ADDRESS** Off of the Dean Case, Case Western Reserve Univ, 10900 Euclid Ave, Cleveland, OH 44106-4901.

EPSTEIN, CATHERINE A.
PERSONAL Born 01/27/1962, Providence, RI, m, 1995, 2 children **DISCIPLINE** HISTORY **EDUCATION** Brown Univ, AB, 85; London Sch of Econ, MS, 87; Harvard Univ, PhD, 98. **CAREER** Vis lectr, Stanford Univ, 98-99; vis asst prof, Mt Holyoke Col, 99-00; asst prof, Amherst Col, 00-. **HONORS AND AWARDS** Whiting Fel, 96-97; Dissertation Fel, Am Coun of Learned Societies, 95-96; Chancellor's Scholar, Alexander von Humboldt found, 94-95; Fulbright Scholar, 85-86. **MEMBERSHIPS** am Hist Asn; German Studies Asn. **RESEARCH** Twentieth Century Germany; German Democratic Republic. **SELECTED PUBLICATIONS** Auth, A Past Renewed: A Catalog of German Speaking Refugee Historians in the United States after 1933, Cambridge Univ Press, 93; auth, "The Politics of Biography: The Case of East German Old Communists," Daedalus, (99): 1-30. **CONTACT ADDRESS** Dept Hist, Amherst Col, PO Box 2254, Amherst, MA 01002-5000. **EMAIL** caepstein@amherst.edu

EPSTEIN, DAVID M.
PERSONAL Born 07/31/1930, Kansas City, MO, m, 1959 **DISCIPLINE** MODERN EUROPEAN HISTORY **EDUCATION** Univ Kansas City, BA, 55, MA, 59; Univ Nebr, PhD (hist), 67. **CAREER** Asst mod Europ hist, Univ Kansas City, 59-60; asst Western civilization, Univ Nebr, 60-62; asst prof mod Europ hist, Eastern Ky State Col, 63-67; asst prof, 67-70, Assoc Prof Hist, Univ Tulsa, 70-, Res grants, Univ Tulsa, 68; Am Philos Soc res grant, Univ Tulsa, 74-75. **MEMBERSHIPS** AHA; Soc Fr Hist Studies; Western Soc Fr Historians. **RESEARCH** Ancient regime; the French Revolution; French naval history. **SELECTED PUBLICATIONS** Auth, Bobolink, Hudson Review, Vol 49, 97; American Dryad, Am Scholar, Vol 63, 94; After Reading Le Demon de Lanalogy, Mic Quart Rev Vol 33, 94; Collection, Hudson Rev, Vol 49, 97; The Belled Buzzard of Roxbury Mills, Am Scholar, Vol 66, 97; Phidias in Exile, Am Scholar, Vol 64, 95; The Glories, Hudson Rev, Vol 49, 97; The Inheritance, Am Scholar, Vol 64, 95. **CONTACT ADDRESS** Dept of Hist, Univ of Tulsa, Tulsa, OK 74104.

EPSTEIN, JAMES A.
PERSONAL Born 04/13/1948, St. Louis, MO, d, 3 children **DISCIPLINE** HISTORY, BRITISH HISTORY & CULTURE **EDUCATION** Univ of Sussex, BA, 70; Univ of Birmingham, PhD, 77. **CAREER** Asst Prof, 86-90, Assoc Prof, 90-95, Prof, Vanderbilt Univ, 95-. **HONORS AND AWARDS** Center Fel, 85-86; Walter D Love Prize, 89; NEH Fel, 94-95; British Coun Prize in the Humanities, 95. **MEMBERSHIPS** Am Hist Asn; North Am Confr on British Studies; Soc for the Study of Labour Hist (UK). **RESEARCH** Mod Brit hist. **SELECTED PUBLICATIONS** Auth, Radical Expression: Political Language, Ritual, and Symbol in England, 1790-1850, Oxford Univ Press, 94; Our Real Constitution: Trial Defence and Radical Memory in the Age of Revolution, Re-reading the Constitution, Cambridge Univ Press, 96; Turn, turn, turn: Victorian Britain's Postmodern Season, J of Victorian Culture, 96; Signs of the Social, J of British Studies, 97; coauth, The Nineteenth-Century Gentleman Leader Revisited, Soc Hist, 97; auth, Spatial Practices/Democratic Vistas, Social History, 99; auth, America in Victorian Cultural Imagination, in Anglo-American Perspectives, Ashgate, 00; co-ed, Journal of British Studies, 01. **CONTACT ADDRESS** Dept of History, Vanderbilt Univ, PO Box 1802, Sta B, Nashville, TN 37235. **EMAIL** james.a.epstein@vanderbilt.edu

ERDEL, TIMOTHY PAUL
PERSONAL Born 08/07/1951, Decatur, IN, m, 1977, 3 children **DISCIPLINE** PHILOSOPHY; HISTORY; THEOLOGICAL LIBRARIANSHIP **EDUCATION** Fort Wayne Bible Col, BA, 73; Trinity Evangel Divinity School, M Div, 76; ThM, 81; Univ Chicago, AM, 78; Univ Ill, MA, 86; PhD, 00. **CAREER** Pastoral ministry, Chicago, 73-77; asst dir, Jesuit-Krauss-McCormick Libr, 77-78; ref librn, Trinity Evangel Divinity School, 78-82; vis lectr, Trinity Col, 82; lectr Hist & Philos Theol, Jamaica Theol Seminary & Carribean Grad School of Theol, 87-93; lectr, Jamaica Theol Sem, 87-93; librn, Zenas Gerig Libr, 87-93; teaching asst Philos & Relig Studies, Univ Ill, 82-87; vis lectr, Instituto Biblico-Teologico, I.E.M., 99; vis

lectr, Seminario Bautista Bereana, 99; asst prof Relig & Philos and Archivist & Theol Librn, Bethel Col, 94-. **HONORS AND AWARDS** Jamaica Theol Sem Teacher of Year, 92-93. **MEMBERSHIPS** Am Acad Relig; Am Philos Asn; Am Soc Church Hist; Am Theol Libr Asn; Anabaptist/Mennonite Theol Librn; Conference on Faith & History; Evangel Missiological Soc; Evangel Missiological Soc; Evangelical Theolog Soc; Ill Mennonite Historical & Genealogical Soc; Mennonite Historical Soc; Methodist Librn Fel; Soc Bibl Lit; Soc Am Archivists; Soc Christian Philos; Soc Ind Archivists; Wesleyan Theol Soc. **RESEARCH** History of Missionary Church; History of Ecuador; Faith and Reason; Theological Librarianship. **SELECTED PUBLICATIONS** From the Colonial Christ and Babylonian Captivity to Dread Jesus, 00; From Egly Amish to Global Mission: The Missionary Church Association, 98; The Missionary Church: From Radical Outcast to the Wild Child of Anabaptism, 97; compiler, Guide to the Preparation of Theses, Carribean Grad School of Theol, 89; coauth, Religions of the World, St Martin's Pr, 88. **CONTACT ADDRESS** Dept of Relig and Philos, Bethel Col, Indiana, 1001 W McKinley Ave, Mishawaka, IN 46545-5509. **EMAIL** erdelt@bethel-in.edu

ERENBERG, LEWIS
DISCIPLINE HISTORY **EDUCATION** Mich Univ, PhD. **CAREER** Fulbright lectr, Univ Munich, 90-91. **RESEARCH** American History. **SELECTED PUBLICATIONS** Auth, The War in American Culture, Univ Chicago Press, 96; Things to Come: Swing Bands, Bepop and the Rise of a PostwarJazz Scene, Recasting America: Culture and Politics in the Age of the Cold War, Univ Chicago Press, 89; Steppin' Out: New York City Nightlife and the Transformation of American Culture, 1890-1930, Univ Chicago Press, 84; ed, Swingin' The Dream: Big Band Jazz and The Rebirth of American Culture, Univ Chicago, 98 **CONTACT ADDRESS** Fine Arts Dept, Loyola Univ, Chicago, 6525 N. Sheridan Rd., Chicago, IL 60626. **EMAIL** lerenbe@wpo.it.luc.edu

ERICKSON, ERLING A.
DISCIPLINE HISTORY **EDUCATION** Luther Univ, BA, 58; ND Univ, MA, 59; IA Univ, PhD, 67. **CAREER** Prof emer, 69-, Univ Pacific. **RESEARCH** Business hist. **SELECTED PUBLICATIONS** Auth, Banking in Frontier Iowa, IA State Univ. **CONTACT ADDRESS** Hist Dept, Univ of the Pacific, Stockton, Pacific Ave, PO Box 3601, Stockton, CA 95211.

ERICKSON, NANCY LOU
PERSONAL Born 07/14/1941, Berea, OH, m, 1964, 2 children **DISCIPLINE** HISTORY, ENGLISH **EDUCATION** Kent State Univ, BS, 61; Univ IL, Urbana, AM, 64; Univ NC, Chapel Hill, PhD(hist), 70. **CAREER** Teacher hist, Champaign Sr High Sch, IL, 63-64; teacher, Maine Twp High Sch West, Des Plaines, IL, 64-66; assoc prof to prof hist, Erskine Col, 74-, dir of institutional res, 88-; Lilly Scholar Hist, Duke Univ, 76-77; pres acad affairs & prof hist, Iowa Wesleyan Col, 99- . **HONORS AND AWARDS** Excellence in Teaching Awd, 78; Renaissance Person of the Year, 92. **MEMBERSHIPS** Am Hist Asn; Orgn Am Historians; Coun Faith & Hist. **RESEARCH** Comparative cultures; United States-Soviet Union; national character; 17th century America. **CONTACT ADDRESS** Iowa Wesleyan Col, 601 N Main, Mount Pleasant, IA 52641. **EMAIL** nericksn@iwc.edu

ERICSON, ROBERT EDWARD
PERSONAL Born 07/19/1926, Poplar, MT, m, 1952, 3 children **DISCIPLINE** THEATRE HISTORY AND THEORY **EDUCATION** Pac Univ, BS, 51; Ind Univ, MA, 54; Univ Ore, PhD, 70. **CAREER** Grad asst theatre, Ind Univ, 53-54; asst prof, Radford Col, 54-55; instr, Columbia Basin Jr Col, 55-56; asst prof, Pac Univ, 56-60; grad asst, Univ Ore, 60-63; asst prof, Ore Col Educ, 63-64; dir univ theatre, Univ Nev, 64-70; Assoc Prof Theatre Arts, Boise State Col, 70-, Chmn Dept, 71-. **MEMBERSHIPS** Am Theatre Asn; Rocky Mountain Theatre Conf. **RESEARCH** American theatre history; cinema theory and history; classical theatre. **SELECTED PUBLICATIONS** Auth, Russia and The Nis in the World Economy--East West Investment, Financing and Trade, Slavic Rev, Vol 54, 95. **CONTACT ADDRESS** 2505 Sunrise Rim, Boise, ID 83705.

ERISMAN, FRED RAYMOND
PERSONAL Born 08/30/1937, Longview, TX, m, 1961, 1 child **DISCIPLINE** AMERICAN STUDIES & LITERATURE **EDUCATION** Rice Inst, BA, 58; Duke Univ, MA, 60; Univ Minn, Minneapolis, PhD(Am studies), 66. **CAREER** From instr to assoc prof, 65-77, actg dean, Col Arts & Sci, 70-71 & 72-73, dir honors prog, 72-74, prof English, Tex Christian Univ, 77-, Co-ed, The French-American Rev J, 76-; book rev ed, Soc Sci J, 78-82; publ ed & mem exec bd, Int Res Soc Children's Lit, 81-83; Hess fel, Univ Minn, 81; Kinnucan Arms Chair fel, Buffalo Bill Hist Ctr, 82; chrmn, dept English; Chm, Dept English, 83-89, 95-98; Lorraine Sherley Prof of Literature, Emeritus, 00. **HONORS AND AWARDS** Lorraine Sherley Prof of Literature, 86; Phi Beta Kappa, 88. **MEMBERSHIPS** Am Studies Asn; MLA; Orgn Am Historians; Western Lit Asn; Popular Cult Asn. **RESEARCH** American popular literature; detective and suspense fiction; Science Fiction. **SELECTED PUBLICATIONS** Auth, The environmental crisis and present-day romanticism, Rocky Mountain Soc Sci J, 73; The romantic regionalism of Harper Lee, Ala Rev, 73; Frederic Remington, Western Writers Ser, Boise State Univ, 75; Prolegomena to a theory of American life, Southern Quart, 76; Romantic reality in the spy stories of Len Deighton, Armchair Detective, 77; Jack Schaefer: The writer as ecologist, Western Am Lit, 78; Western regional writers and the uses of place, J of the West, 80; co-ed (with Richard W Etulain), Fifty Western Writers, Greenwood Press, 82; Barnboken i USA, 86; contribur, A Literary History of the American West, 87; Laura Ingalls Wilder, Western Writers Ser, 94; auth, The Technological Utopias of Thorstein Veblen and Nevil Shute, Weber Studeis, 94; auth, Robert A. Heinlein's Primers of Politics, Extrapolation, 97; Updating the Literary West; 97; auth, McCrumb's Comic Critiques of SF Fandom, Extrapolation, 99; auth, Thoreau, Alcott, and the Mythic West, Western Am Lit, 99; Reading A.B. Guthrie's THE BIG SKY, Western Writers Ser, 00. **CONTACT ADDRESS** Dept of English, Texas Christian Univ, Box 297270, Fort Worth, TX 76129-0002. **EMAIL** ferisman@swbell.net

ERLEBACHER, ALBERT
PERSONAL Born 09/28/1932, Ulm Wurttemberg, Germany, m, 1961, 3 children **DISCIPLINE** AMERICAN HISTORY **EDUCATION** Marquette Univ, BA, 54, MA, 56; Univ Wis, PhD, 65. **CAREER** Asst prof hist, Wis State Univ, Oshkosh, 62-65; from asst prof to assoc prof, 65-77, head div humanities, 75-79, Prof Hist, Depaul Univ, 77-, Head Div Common Studies, 80-82, chair, hist dept, 82-88. **MEMBERSHIPS** Wisc Historical Soc, AHA. **RESEARCH** History of insurance regulation; progressive period, political and economic aspects; American foreign relations since 1900. **SELECTED PUBLICATIONS** Auth, "The Wisconsin Life Insurance Reform of 1907," Wisc Magazine of Hist, vol 55.3 (72): 213-230. **CONTACT ADDRESS** Dept of Hist, DePaul Univ, 2323 N Kenmore, Chicago, IL 60614. **EMAIL** aerlebac@wppost.depaul.edu

ERLEN, JONATHON
PERSONAL Born 10/04/1946, Louisville, KY, m, 1978 **DISCIPLINE** HISTORY **EDUCATION** Indiana Univ, BA, 68; Univ KY, MA, 71; PhD, 73. **CAREER** Asst pof, Graduate School of Public Health, Univ Pittsburgh; faculty, Univ Honors Col, Univ Pittsburgh; adjunct asst prof, Univ Pittsburgh. **HONORS AND AWARDS** Golden Key Soc, Phi Alpha Theta History Honorary. **MEMBERSHIPS** Am Asn for the Hist of Med; APHA. **RESEARCH** History of medicine and public health, health care humanities. **SELECTED PUBLICATIONS** Auth, Bibliography of the History of Medicine and Health Care: 1700-1980, Garland Press (84); auth, The Skilful Physician, Gordon and Breach Pubs (97); auth, The Ladies Dispensatory, Gordon and Breach Pubs (2000). **CONTACT ADDRESS** Dept Hist, Univ of Pittsburgh, 200 Scaife Hall, Pittsburgh, PA 15261. **EMAIL** erlen+@pitt.edu

ERMARTH, ELIZABETH DEEDS
PERSONAL Born 11/30/1939, Denver, CO, m, 1977, 1 child **DISCIPLINE** HISTORY **EDUCATION** Carleton Col, BA, 61; Univ Calif Berkeley, MA, 63; Univ Chicago, PhD, 71. **CAREER** Instr, Northwestern Univ, 69-71; adj asst prof, Dartmouth Col, 72-74; asst prof, Reed Col, 74-78; asst prof to prof, Univ Md, 79-95; prof, Univ Edinburgh, 94-00. **HONORS AND AWARDS** Spec Res Initiative Grant, Univ Md, 87-88, 92-93; Pres Res, Univ Md, 91-95; Overseas Fel, Churchill Col, 92-93; Sr Fulbright Fel, 92-93. **MEMBERSHIPS** MLA; NCUP. **RESEARCH** Postmodernity; Cultural history of democratic institutions; Time, especially the history of modern historical conventions. **SELECTED PUBLICATIONS** Auth, Sequel to History: Postmodernism and the Crisis of Representational Time, Princeton, 92; auth, "Ph(r)ase Time: Chaos Theory and Postmodern Reports on Knowledge," Time and Society, 95; auth, Realism and Consensus, 2nd ed, Edinburgh, 98; auth, George Eliot, Macmillan, 98; auth, "Beyond the Subject: Individuality in the Discursive Condition," NLH, 00; auth, "Beyond History," Rethinking History, 01; auth, "Democracy and Postmodernity: The Problem of Agency Beyond the Founding Subject of History," History and Theory, 01. **CONTACT ADDRESS** 5289 S Joliet Way, Englewood, CO 80111-3827. **EMAIL** edermarth@aol.com

ERMARTH, HANS MICHAEL
PERSONAL Born 03/02/1944, Chicago, IL, m, 2 children **DISCIPLINE** HISTORY **EDUCATION** Wittenberg Univ, BA, 65; Univ Chicago, MA, 67, PhD(hist), 73. **CAREER** Asst prof, 71-78, assoc prof, 79-84, prof hist, 85- , Dartmouth Col. **HONORS AND AWARDS** Berman-Marshall, 84-85. **MEMBERSHIPS** AHA, GSA. **RESEARCH** Modern European intellectual history; modern Germany; theory of history. **SELECTED PUBLICATIONS** Auth, Wilhelm Dilthey: The Critique of Historical Reason, Univ Chicago, 6/78; Hermeneutics Old and New, The Monist, 4/81; ed, America and the Shaping of Germany, 1945-1955, Berg, 93. **CONTACT ADDRESS** Dept of History, Dartmouth Col, 6107 Reed Hall, Hanover, NH 03755-3506. **EMAIL** michael.ermarth@dartmouth.edu

ERNST, ELDON G.
PERSONAL Born 01/27/1939, Seattle, WA, m, 1959, 5 children **DISCIPLINE** HISTORY **EDUCATION** Yale, PhD, 68, MA, 65; Colgate Roch, MDiv, 64; Linfield Col, BA, 61 **CAREER** Prof, 67-82 Am Bapt Sem; Prof, 82-90, Grad Theol Un; Prof, 90-pres, Am Bapt Sem **MEMBERSHIPS** Am Soc of Church Hist; Am Hist Asoc; Am Acad of Relig; Calif Historical Soc **RESEARCH** American Social Christianity; California Religious History; History of Religion in North American Pacific Region **SELECTED PUBLICATIONS** Auth, Moment of Truth for Protestant Am, Scholars Pr, 74; auth, Without Help or Hindrance Religious Identity in American Culture, University Press of America, Inc, 87; coauth, Pilgrim Progression The Protestant Experience in California, Fithian Press, 93. **CONTACT ADDRESS** 1855 San Antonio Ave, Berkeley, CA 94707. **EMAIL** rjeernst@aol.com

ERNST, JOHN
PERSONAL Born 07/27/1952, Fort Dodge, IA, m, 1974 **DISCIPLINE** HISTORY **EDUCATION** Concordia Col, BA, 75; Wheaton Grad School, MA, 79; Univ MN, MA, 87; PhD, 91. **CAREER** Instructor, Northeast IA Cmty Col, 93-. **MEMBERSHIPS** AHA, Conf on Faith and Hist. **RESEARCH** Teaching history. **CONTACT ADDRESS** Dept Bus & Gen Studies, Northeast Iowa Comm Col, Calmar, PO Box 400, Calmar, IA 52132-0400. **EMAIL** ernstj@nicc.cc.ia.us

ERNST, JOSEPH ALBERT
PERSONAL Born 08/19/1931, Brooklyn, NY, m, 1956, 5 children **DISCIPLINE** UNITED STATES HISTORY **EDUCATION** Brooklyn Col, BA, 56; Univ Wis-Madison, MA, 58, PhD (hist), 62. **CAREER** Instr hist, Univ Wis, 61-62, vis lectr, 67; asst prof, San Fernando Valley State Col, 62-67 and Univ Calif, Los Angeles, 67-68; assoc prof, 68-71, Prof Hist, York Univ, 71-. **RESEARCH** American Revolution; economic history of colonial America. **SELECTED PUBLICATIONS** Auth, Money and Poitics in Americaa 1755-1775: A Study in the Currency Act of 1764 and the Political Economy of Revolution. **CONTACT ADDRESS** Dept of Hist, York Univ, 4700 Keele St, 2140 Vari Hall, Toronto, ON, Canada M3J 1P3. **EMAIL** jernst@yorku.edu

ERNST, ROBERT
PERSONAL Born 03/01/1915, New York, NY, m, 1950, 2 children **DISCIPLINE** MODERN HISTORY **EDUCATION** Columbia Univ, AB, 36, PhD, 47; Brown Univ, AM, 37. **CAREER** From instr to assoc prof, 46-58, Prof Hist, Adelphi Univ, 58-, Huntington Libr grant-in-aid, 60. **MEMBERSHIPS** AHA; Orgn Am Historians; AAUP; Immigration Hist Soc. **RESEARCH** Immigration to the United States in the nineteenth century and ethnic groups in the United States; Revolutionary and early national period of the United States; biography: Bernarr Macfadden. **SELECTED PUBLICATIONS** Immigrant Life in New York City, 1825-1863, King's Crown Press, 47, Ira J Friedman, 65 & Octagon Bks, 79; Rufus King, American Federalist, Univ NC, 68; Andrew Elliot, forgotten loyalist of occupied New York, New York Hist, 7/76. **CONTACT ADDRESS** Dept of Hist, Adelphi Univ, Garden City, NY 11530.

ERRINGTON, JANE
DISCIPLINE HISTORY **EDUCATION** Trent Univ, BA; Toronto, Bed; Queen's Univ, MA, PhD. **CAREER** High School tchr; prof, dept hd, history, Royal Milit Col. **RESEARCH** Life in early Upper Canada, the role of women in colonial soc - as workers, as emigrants, and in relation to the law, life of apprentices and indentured servants in the colony in the first half of the nineteenth century. **SELECTED PUBLICATIONS** Auth, Wives and Mothers, Schhol Mistresses and Scullery Maids. **CONTACT ADDRESS** Hist Dept, Royal Military Col, PO Box 17000, Kingston, ON, Canada K7K 7B4.

ERSHKOWITZ, HERBERT J.
DISCIPLINE AMERICAN HISTORY **EDUCATION** NYork Univ, PhD. **CAREER** Prof, Temple Univ. **RESEARCH** Jacksonian Politics and Soc; Am Business Hist; Nineteenth-Century Philadelphia; Antimasonic movement during the Jacksonian era. **SELECTED PUBLICATIONS** Auth, Business Attitudes toward American Foreign Policy, 1900-1914, 67; Political Behavior in the Jacksonian State Legislatures, J of Am Hist, 72; Origin of the Whig and Democratic Parties: New Jersey Politics, 1820-1837, 82; The Second Party System in New Jersey, NJ Hist, 90; History of the Philadelphia Gas Works, 92; auth, John Wanamaker: Philadelphia Merchant, 99. **CONTACT ADDRESS** Temple Univ, Philadelphia, PA 19122. **EMAIL** ersh@astro.temple.edu

ESCOTT, PAUL DAVID
PERSONAL Born 07/33/1947, St. Louis, MO, m, 1968, 1 child **DISCIPLINE** HISTORY **EDUCATION** Harvard Univ, BA, 69; Duke Univ, MA, 72, PhD (hist), 74. **CAREER** Asst prof, 74-79, Assoc Prof Hist, Univ NC, Charlotte, 79-, Whitney M Young, Jr Mem Found acad fel hist, 75-76. **HONORS AND AWARDS** Mayflower Cup, 79. **MEMBERSHIPS** Southern Hist Asn. **RESEARCH** The Old South; slavery; the South in the 20th century. **SELECTED PUBLICATIONS** Auth, The context of freedom: Georgia's slaves during the Civil War, spring 74 & Joseph E Brown, Jefferson Davis, and the problem of poverty in the Confederacy, spring 77, Ga Hist Quart; Jefferson Davis and slavery in the Territories, J Miss Hist, 5/77; The cry of the sufferer: the problem of poverty in the Confederacy, Civil War Hist, 9/77; Southern Yeomen and the Confederacy,

S Atlantic Quart, spring 78; After Secession: Jefferson Davis and the Failure of the Confederate Nationalism, La State Univ, Fall 78; Slavery Remembered: An Analysis of Twentieth-Century Slave Narratives, Univ NC, 79. **CONTACT ADDRESS** Dept of Hist, Univ of No Carolina, Charlotte, Charlotte, NC 28223.

ESHERICK, JOSEPH WHARTON
PERSONAL Born 08/14/1942, Ross, CA, m, 1984, 3 children **DISCIPLINE** CHINESE HISTORY **EDUCATION** Harvard Col, BA, 64; Univ Calif, Berkeley, MA, 66, PhD (hist), 71. **CAREER** Asst prof, 71-76, Assoc Prof, 76-85, full prof, 85-90, Chinese Hist, Univ Ore; prof hist and Hwei-Chih and Julia Hsiu, chair in chinese studies, U Calif, San Diego, 90-. **HONORS AND AWARDS** John K. Fairbank prize (Am Hist Assoc) and Joseph R. Levenson Prize (Assoc Asian Studies) for book origins of The Boxer Uprising. **MEMBERSHIPS** Am Historical Asn; Asn for Asian Studies. **RESEARCH** Modern Chinese history; Chinese society and political change. **SELECTED PUBLICATIONS** Coauth, Modern China: Story of a Revolution, Knopf, 72; ed, Lost Chance in China: The World War II Despatches of John S Service, Random House, 74; auth, Reform and Revolution in China: The 1911 Revolution in Hunan and Hubei, Univ Calif Press, 76; auth, The Origins of the The Boxer Uprising CA Calif, 87; coed, Chinese Local Elites and Patterns of Dominance, Univ Calif, 90; coauth, Chinese Archives: An Introductory Guide, UC Berkeley Inst of East Asian Studies, 96; ed, Remaking the Chinese City, 1900-1950, Univ Hawaii Press, 00. **CONTACT ADDRESS** Hist Dept, Univ of Oregon, Eugene, OR 97402. **EMAIL** jesheric@ucsd.edu

ESKEW, HARRY LEE
PERSONAL Born 07/02/1936, Spartanburg, SC, m, 1965, 2 children **DISCIPLINE** HYMNOLOGY, AMERICAN MUSIC HISTORY **EDUCATION** Furman Univ, BA, 58; New Orleans Baptist Theol Sem, MSM, 60; Tulane Univ, PhD(musicol), 66; La State Univ, MLIS, 95. **CAREER** Assoc prof, 65-75, Prof Music Hist & Hymnol, New Orleans Baptist Theol Sem, 75-, Music Librarian, 89-; Am Asn Theol Schs fel, Univ Erlangen, 70-71; mem Baptist hymnal rev comt, Southern Baptist Sunday Sch Bd, 73-75, 89-91; ed, The Hymn Quart, Hymn Soc Am, 76-83. **MEMBERSHIPS** The Hymn Soc in the U.S. and Canada; Southern Baptist Hist Soc; Southern Baptist Church Music Conf; Music Libr Asn. **RESEARCH** Church music; American folk and popular hymnody. **SELECTED PUBLICATIONS** Auth, American Folk Hymnody, Bull Hymn Soc Gt Brit & Ireland, 71; Music in the Baptist Tradition, Rev & Expositor, 72; A Cultural Understanding of Hymnody, Hymn, 72; Hymnody Kit, Part II, Convention Press, 75; coauth (with Hugh T McElrath), Sing With Understanding: An Introduction to Christian Hymnology, rev ed, Church Street Press, 95; Gospel Hymnody, Shape-note Hymnody In: The New Grove Dictionary of Music and Musicians, Macmillan, 80; coauth, Singing Baptists, Church Street Press, 94. **CONTACT ADDRESS** New Orleans Baptist Theol Sem, 3939 Gentilly Blvd., New Orleans, LA 70126-4858. **EMAIL** Heskew@nobts.edu

ESLER, ANTHONY J.
PERSONAL Born 02/20/1934, New London, CT, m, 1992, 2 children **DISCIPLINE** HISTORY **EDUCATION** Univ Ariz, BA, 56; Duke Univ, MA, 58; PhD, 61. **CAREER** Asst prof to prof, Col of William & Mary, 62-. **HONORS AND AWARDS** Fulbright Fel, 61-62; Vis Assoc Prof, Northwestern Univ, 68-69; ACSL Res Fel, 69-70; Fulbright Travel Grant, 83. **MEMBERSHIPS** AHA; World Hist Assoc; Authors Guild **RESEARCH** Conflict of generations in history, Global history, Globalization. **SELECTED PUBLICATIONS** Auth, The Aspiring Mind of the Elizabethan Younger Generation, Duke Univ Pr, (Durham, NC), 66; auth, Bombs Beards and Barricades: 150 Years of Youth in Revolt, Stein and Day, (NY), 71; ed, The Youth Revolution: The Conflict of Generations in Modern History, D.C. Heath, (Lexington, MA), 74; auth, Generations in History: An Introduction to the Concept, (Williamsburg, VA), 82; auth, The Human Venture: A World History, Prentice Hall, (Englewood Cliffs, NY), 86; auth, The Western World: Prehistory to the Present, Prentice Hall, (Englewood Cliffs, NJ), 94. **CONTACT ADDRESS** Dept Hist, Col of William and Mary, PO Box 8795, Williamsburg, VA 23187-8795. **EMAIL** anthonyesler@aol.com

ESLINGER, ELLEN T.
PERSONAL Born Chicago, IL **DISCIPLINE** HISTORY **EDUCATION** N Ill Univ, BS, 77; Univ Chicago, MA, 82; PhD, 88. **CAREER** Asst Prof, Assoc Prof, 92 to 97-, DePaul Univ; Asst Prof, 88-92, James Madison Univ. **HONORS AND AWARDS** Richard H Collins Awd; KHS Best Article. **MEMBERSHIPS** AHA; OAH; SHA; SHEAR. **RESEARCH** Early American and the frontier, African American history. **SELECTED PUBLICATIONS** Auth, Citizens of Zion: The Social Origins of Camp Meeting Revivalism, Univ Tenn Press, forthcoming; The Beginnings of Afro-American Christianity Among Kentucky Baptists, in: The Buzzel about Kentucky: Interpretations of the Promised Land 1750-1830, ed, Craig Friend, Lexington, Univ Press of KY, forthcoming; The Shape of Slavery on Virginia's Kentucky Frontier 1775-1800, in: Diversity and Accommodation: Essays on the Cultural Composition of the Virginia Frontier, ed, Michael Puglisi, Knoxville, Univ Tenn Press, 97; The Shape of Slavery on the Kentucky Frontier 11775-1800, Register KY Hist Soc, 94. **CONTACT ADDRESS** Dept of History, DePaul Univ, 2320 N Kenmore Ave, Chicago, IL 60614. **EMAIL** eeslinge@wppost.depaul.edu

ESPOSITO, JOHN L.
PERSONAL Born 05/19/1940, Brooklyn, NY, m, 1965 **DISCIPLINE** MIDDLE EAST STUDIES **EDUCATION** St. Anthony Col, BA, 63; St. John's Univ, MA, 66; Temple Univ, PhD, 74. **CAREER** Assoc Prof and Dept Chair, 75-84, Prof Relig Studies, Col Holy Cross, 84-, Loyola Prof Middle East Studies, 91-95, Univ Prof, 00; Prof Islamic Studies, 87-99, Prof and Dir Ctr Int Studies, 86-93; Adj Prof Diplomacy, The Fletcher Sch Law & Diplomacy, Tufts Univ, 91-95; Prof Relig & Int Affairs, and Prof Islamic Studies, Georgetown Univ, 93-, Dir, Ctr Muslim-Christian Understanding, 93-; Vis Prof, Oberlin Col, 86; ed, The Oxford History of Islam, Oxford Univ Press, 95-. **HONORS AND AWARDS** Fac Fel, Col Holy Cross, 77, 82-83, 90-91; Vis Schol, Ctr Study World Relig, Harvard Univ, 79-80; Elected Sr. Assoc, St. Antony's Col, Oxford Univ, 82-83; NEH Interpretive Res Grant, 90-93; U.S. Inst for Peace, 92-93. **MEMBERSHIPS** Middle East Studies Asn (Pres 88-89, Bd Dir, 83-86); Am Coun Study Islamic Soc (Bd Dir 84-, VPres 86-89, Pres 89-91); Am Soc Study Relig; Middle East Inst; Int Studies Asn; Asn Asian Studies; Maghreb Studies Asn; Am Acad Relig; Coun Study Relig; Col Theol Soc. **SELECTED PUBLICATIONS** Auth, The Islamic Threat: Myth or Reality?, Oxford Univ Press, 2nd rev ed, 95; ed-in-chief, The Oxford Encyclopedia of the Modern Islamic World, 4 vols, Oxford Univ Press, 95; coauth, Islam and Democracy, Oxford Univ Press, 96; Contemporary Islamic Revival Since 1988: A Critical Survey and Bibliography, Greenwood Press, 97; auth, Political Islam: Revolution, Radicalism or Reform?, Lynne Rienner Publ, 97; coauth, Islam, Gender and Social Change, Oxford Univ Press, 97; Muslims on the Americanization Path, Schol Press (forthcoming); Religion and Global Order, Univ Wales Press (forthcoming 98); auth, Oxford History of Islam; auth, Islam and Secularism in the Middle East; auth, Red and Senal Order; author of numerous other publications and articles. **CONTACT ADDRESS** School of Foreign Services, Georgetown Univ, Washington, DC 20057-1052. **EMAIL** jle2@georgetown.edu

ESSICK, ROBERT N.
DISCIPLINE BRITISH ROMANTIC LITERATURE AND ART **EDUCATION** UCLA, BA; Univ Calif-San Diego, PhD. **CAREER** Fac res lectr, 90-91; prof, English, Univ Calif, Riverside. **HONORS AND AWARDS** Outstanding Acad bk, Choice, 80-81; outstanding bk, Chioce, 91-92; fel(s), NEH; Amer Coun of Learned Soc; Guggenheim; on-line fel, inst adv tech in the hum, univ va. **MEMBERSHIPS** Mem, Bd of Overseers Huntington Lib; ed bd, Stud Eng Lit. **RESEARCH** William Blake, Blake electronic archive. **SELECTED PUBLICATIONS** Auth, William Blake, Printmaker, Princeton Univ Press, 80; William Blake and the Language of Adam, Oxford Univ Press, 89; William Blake's Commercial Book Illustrations, Oxford Univ Press, 91; William Blake at the Huntington, 94; **CONTACT ADDRESS** Dept of Eng, Univ of California, Riverside, Riverside, CA 92521-0209. **EMAIL** robert.essick@ucr.edu

ESSIN, EMMETT M.
DISCIPLINE HISTORY **EDUCATION** Austin Col, BA, 64; Univ Tex, MA, 65, PhD, 68. **CAREER** Prof. **SELECTED PUBLICATIONS** Auth, Shave Tails and Bell Sharpes: The History of the Army Mule, Univ Nebr, 97. **CONTACT ADDRESS** Dept of History, East Tennessee State Univ, PO Box 70717, Johnson City, TN 37614-0717. **EMAIL** EssinE@etsu.edu

ESSLINGER, DEAN ROBERT
PERSONAL Born 06/08/1942, Clifton, KS, m, 1963, 3 children **DISCIPLINE** AMERICAN URBAN & SOCIAL HISTORY **EDUCATION** Univ KS, BA, 64; Univ Notre Dame, MA, 66, PhD(hist), 72. **CAREER** Assoc prof, 68-75, prof Hist, Towson State Univ, 75-, dir Fac Develop, 77-88, assoc Dean for Faculty Develoment & Research, 88-94, assoc vice-pres for Int Education, 94-97, Assoc Vice-Pres for Academic Programs, 97-; Coordr, Baltimore Hist Res Group, 76-78. **HONORS AND AWARDS** Univ Merit Awd, 84-85, 87-88; President's Awd for Distinguished Service to the University, 88. **MEMBERSHIPS** Orgn Am Historians; Am Studies Asn; Immigration Hist Soc; Am Asn of Higher Ed; Am Asn State Colleges and Universities;Asn Am Colleges and Universities; Int Ed Asn; NAFSA; Nat Asn State Universities and Land Grant Colleges; Board of dirs, Am Cancer Soc-Baltimore; Asn Int Education Administrators; European Int Ed Asn; Maryland Sister State Comm; Oxford Capitol Foundation Board of Trustees. **RESEARCH** Social mobility of urban populations; social history of Baltimore; social history of Friends School in Baltimore, 1784-; Baltimore immigration history. **SELECTED PUBLICATIONS** Auth, American German and Irish Attitudes Toward Neutrality, 1914-1917: A Study of Catholic Minorities, Cath Hist Rev, 7/67; Immigrants and the City: Ethnicity and Mobility in a Nineteenth-Century Midwestern Community, Kennikat, 75; Catholics and Neutrality in the Great War, 1914-1917, In: Catholics in America, 76; Friends for 200 Years:A History of Baltimore: Oldest School, MD Hist Soc and Friends School, 83; co-auth, Maryland: A History of Its People, Johns Hopkins Univ, 86; chapter in Freedom's Doors, Balch Inst, 88; chapter in Unity and Diversity: Essays on Maryland Life and Culture, Kendall/Hunt, 89. **CONTACT ADDRESS** Academic Programs, Towson State Univ, Towson, MD 21252. **EMAIL** desslinger@towson.edu

ESTES, JAMES MARTIN
PERSONAL Born 10/04/1934, Hartford, MI **DISCIPLINE** MODERN HISTORY **EDUCATION** Mich State Univ, BA, 56, MA, 58; Ohio State Univ, PhD (hist), 64. **CAREER** Lectr, 62-65, asst prof, 65-69, Assoc Prof Hist, Univ Toronto, 69-, Dir, Centre Reformation and Renaissance Studies, Victoria Univ, 79-. **MEMBERSHIPS** Am Soc Reformation Res. **RESEARCH** German Reformation. **CONTACT ADDRESS** Dept of Hist, Univ of Toronto, 100 St George St, Sidney Smith Hall, Room 2074, Toronto, ON, Canada M5S 3G3. **EMAIL** jestes@chass.utoronto.ca

ESTHUS, RAYMOND ARTHUR
PERSONAL Born 03/17/1925, Chicago, IL, m, 1955, 2 children **DISCIPLINE** UNITED STATES DIPLOMATIC HISTORY **EDUCATION** Fla Southern Col, AB, 48; Duke Univ, MA, 51, PhD (hist), 56. **CAREER** Instr hist, Brevard Col, 54-55; from instr to asst prof, Univ Houston, 55-57; from asst prof to assoc prof, 57-66, Prof Hist, Tulane Univ, 66-, E Asia Lang and Area Ctr fel, Yale Univ, 66-67. **MEMBERSHIPS** Asn Asian Studies; Soc Historians of Am Foreign Rels (pres, 77). **RESEARCH** History of United States Far Eastern policy. **SELECTED PUBLICATIONS** Auth, The Taft-Katsura agreement--reality or myth, J Mod Hist, 3/59; The changing concept of the Open Door, 12/59 & President Roosevelt's commitment to Britain to intervene in a Pacific war, 6/63, Miss Valley Hist Rev; From Enmity to Alliance: US-Australian Relations, 1931-1941, 64 & Theodore Roosevelt and Japan, 66, Univ Wash; Theodore Roosevelt and the International Rivalries, Zerox, 70; Roosevelt, Russia, and peacemaking 1905, In: Perspectives in American Diplomacy, 76; Isolationism and world power, In: Diplomatic History, spring 78. **CONTACT ADDRESS** Dept of Hist, Tulane Univ, New Orleans, LA 70118.

ETHINGTON, PHILIP J.
DISCIPLINE US HISTORY **EDUCATION** Univ Mich, BA, 81; Stanford Univ, PhD, 89. **CAREER** Dir, ISLA: Inf Syst for Los Angeles proj; taught at, Brandeis Univ, 89-91 and Boston Univ, 92-93; Charles Warren Center for Studies in American History fel, 91-92; Schlesinger Libr for Res on the Hist of Women in Amer fel, 92-93; taught, Harvard-Radcliffe Univ; prof, Univ Southern Calif, 93-. **RESEARCH** Social, political, & cultural history of the US. **SELECTED PUBLICATIONS** Auth, The Public City; The Political Construction of Urban Life in San Francisco, 1850-1900, NY: Cambridge UP, 94; Toward a 'Borderlands School' for American Urban Ethnic Studies, rev of Becoming Mexican American: Ethnicity, Cluture & Identity in Chicano Los Angeles, 1900-1945, in Amer Quart, 96; Urban Constituencies, Regimes, & Policy Innovation In the Progressive Era: An Analysis of Boston, Chicago, New York City, & San Francisco, Stud in Amer Political Develop 7:2, Cambridge UP, 93; coauth, The Intellectual Legacy of the Johns Hopkins University Seminary of History & Politics: Reconsidering the Genealogy of the Social Sciences, Studies in American Political Development 8:2, Cambridge UP, 94; co-ed, Polity Forum: Institutions and Instutionalism, Polity 28: 1, 95. **CONTACT ADDRESS** Dept of History, Univ of So California, University Park Campus, Los Angeles, CA 90089. **EMAIL** philipje@mizar.usc.edu

ETULAIN, RICHARD W.
PERSONAL Born 08/28/1938, Wapato, WA, m, 1961, 1 child **DISCIPLINE** HISTORY **EDUCATION** NW Nazarene Col, Nampa, Id, BA, 60; Univ Or Eugene, MA, 62, PhD, 66. **CAREER** Grad asst, 63-66, Univ Or; asst prof, 66-68, NW Nazarene Col; assoc pro, 68-69f, E Nazarene Col; NHPRC Fel, 69-70, Dartmouth Col; assoc prof to prof, dept chair, 70-74, Id St Univ; prof, 79-, Univ NM; editor, 79-85, NM Hist Rev, 91; dir, 89-, Center Amer W; vis prof, 73, 78, Univ Or; vis prof, 78, UCLA; vis prof, 97, Pepperdine Univ. **HONORS AND AWARDS** HNPRC Fel, 69-70; NEH Awd, 73-74; Huntington Libr Fel, 74,84; USIA lectr, 10 countries; Alumnus of the Year, NW Nazarene Col, 75; Alumni Achievement Awd, Univ Or, 91; Ann Res Lectr, Univ NM, 91; W Heritage Awd, 96; John Caughey Awd, 96; NM End for the Humanities, Excellence in Humanities, 98; hilliard distinguished prof, univ nv, 85; petty-john distinguished lectr, washington st univ, 92. **MEMBERSHIPS** W Lit Assoc **RESEARCH** Hist & lit of Amer West; historiography; recent Amer. **SELECTED PUBLICATIONS** auth, Owen Wister, 73; auth, Conversations with Wallace Stegner on Western History and Literature, 83; coauth, The American West: A Twentieth-Century History, 89; ed, Contemporary New Mexico 1940-1990, 94; auth, Re-imagining the Modern American West: Century of Fiction, History, and Art, 96; coed, Researching Western History: The Twentieth Century, 97; coed, By Grit and Grace: Women Who Shaped the American West, 97; coed, Religion in Modern New Mexico, 97; auth, With Badges and Bullets: Lawmen and Outlaws in the Old West, 99; ed, Does the Frontier Experience Make American Exceptional, 99; auth, Telling Western Stories: From Buffalo Bill

to Larry McMurtry, 99. **CONTACT ADDRESS** Dept of History, Univ of New Mexico, Albuquerque, Albuquerque, NM 87131. **EMAIL** baldbasq@unm.edu

EUBANK, KEITH
PERSONAL Born 12/08/1920, Princeton, NJ, m, 1951, 2 children **DISCIPLINE** MODERN AMERICAN & EUROPEAN HISTORY **EDUCATION** Hampden-Sydney Col, BA, 42; Harvard Univ, MA, 47; Univ Pa, PhD (Europ hist), 51. **CAREER** Instr hist, Bloomfield Col, 50-53; from asst prof to prof, NTex State Univ, 54-64; Prof Hist, Queens Col, NY, 64-, Chmn Dept, 67-. **MEMBERSHIPS** AHA; Southern Hist Asn. **RESEARCH** Modern European history; United States and European diplomatic history. **SELECTED PUBLICATIONS** Auth, Paul Cambon: Master Diplomatist, Univ Okla, 60; ed, Fashoda crisis reexamined, Historian, 60; auth, Munich, Univ Okla, 63; ed, The Road to World War II, a Documentary History, Crowell, 63; The British pledge to Poland, Southwestern Soc Sci Quart, 65; auth, The Summit Conferences, 1919-1960, Univ Okla, 66; The Origins of World War II, Crowell, 69; ed, World War II: Roots and Causes, Heath, 75. **CONTACT ADDRESS** Dept of Hist, Queens Col, CUNY, Flushing, NY 11367.

EULA, MICHAEL JAMES
PERSONAL Born 05/18/1957, Passaic, NJ, m, 1993, 2 children **DISCIPLINE** HISTORY, LAW **EDUCATION** Rutgers Univ, BA (cum laude), 80; Calif State Univ, MA, 83; Univ of Calif at Irvine, MA, 84, PhD, 87; Newport Univ School of Law, JD, 98. **CAREER** Admin Law Judge, Riverside County, CA, 99-; Vis Lecturer in History and Criminal Justice, Champman Univ, 93-; Teaching asst/assoc, visiting asst prof of hist, Univ of Calif at Irvine, 91; lectr in hist, Calf State Univ, 89; PROF OF HIS, EL CAMINO COL, 89-. **HONORS AND AWARDS** Nat Endowment for the Humanities Fel, 90 & 95; New Jersey Hist Comn Fel, 92; Fac Res Fel, UCLA, 93; Phi Alpha Theta Iota Kappa, Rutgers Univ, 79. **MEMBERSHIPS** Am Hist Asn; Am Italian Hist Asn. **RESEARCH** Italian Americans; social history of ideas; legal history. **SELECTED PUBLICATIONS** Auth, Cultural Identity, Foodways, and the Failure of American Food Reformers Among Ital Immigrants in New York City 1891-1897, Ital Americana, 00; auth, The Politics of Ethnicity and Newark's Italian Tribune, 1934-1980, Ital Americana, forthcoming; Langage, Time, and the Formation of Self Among Italian-American Workers in New Jersey and New York 1880-1940, Ital Americana, 97; auth, Between Peasant and Urban Villager: Italian Americans of New Jersey and New York 1880-1980. The Structures of Counter Discourse, Peter Lang, 93; auth, Cultural Continuity and Cultural Hegemony: Italian Catholics in New Jersey and New York 1880-1940, Relig, 92; auth, Thinking Historically: Using Theory in the Introductory History Classroom, The Hist Teacher, 93. **CONTACT ADDRESS** Dept of History, El Camino Col, Torrance, CA 90506.

EVANS, DORINDA
PERSONAL Born 03/05/1944, Wakefield, MA **DISCIPLINE** ART HISTORY **EDUCATION** BA, Wheaton College, Massachusetts, 65, Univ Pa, MA, 67; Courtald Inst of Art, Univ London, PhD, 72; History of Art, Winterhur Summer Institute, Winterthur Museum, Winterthur, Del, 79 **CAREER** Mus curator, Nat Gallery of Art, Wash, 67-69; Asst Prof, Univ Ill, 72-74; Guest Curator, Philadelphia Mus of Art, 74-75; Guest Curator, Nat Portrait Gallery, Wash, 75-78; Asst Prof, Emory Univ, 78-84; Asn Prof, 84-. **HONORS AND AWARDS** Kress Foundation Fellow, 71-72; ACLS Grant-in-aid, 85; Smithsonian Sr Post-Doctoral Fellow, 86-87; Joshua C Taylor Res Fellow, 91. **MEMBERSHIPS** Col Art Asn; Hist of Am Art; Am Soc for 18th Cent Stud; Hist of Brit Art. **RESEARCH** Late 18th & 19th century Am painting, cultural ideology of the neoclassical and Romantic periods, concepts of the sublime **SELECTED PUBLICATIONS** Auth, Benjamin West and His American Students, Smithsonian Institution Press, Washington, D.C., 80, (203 pages, served as catalogue for traveling exh. At the National Portrait Gallery and the Pennsylvania Academy of the Fine Arts); auth, Mather Brown, Early American Artist in England, Wesleyan University Press, Middletown, Conn., 82, (309 pages), Subsidized by the Samuel H. Kress Foundation and the Barra Foundation; auth, "Art and Deception: Ralph Blakelock and His Guardian," The American Art Journal, 19:1, (Spr., 87), 39-50; auth, "Survival and Transformation: The Colonial Portrait in the Federal Era," in The Portrait in Eighteenth Century America, ed. E.G. Miles, University of Delaware Press, 93, 123-137; auth, The Genius of Gilbert Stuart, Princeton University Press, Princeton, N.J., 99 (216 pages). **CONTACT ADDRESS** Art Hist Dept, Emory Univ, Atlanta, GA 30322. **EMAIL** devon03@emory.edu

EVANS, ELLEN LOVELL
PERSONAL Born 11/17/1930, Paris, France, w, 3 children **DISCIPLINE** MODERN EUROPEAN HISTORY **EDUCATION** Swarthmore Col, BA, 51; Univ Wis, MA, 52; Columbia Univ, PhD (mod Europ hist), 56. **CAREER** From instr to asst prof, 54-68, Assoc Prof Hist, GA State Univ, 68-97. **MEMBERSHIPS** AHA; Southern Hist Asn; Conf Group Cent Europ Hist. **RESEARCH** Weimar Republic in Germany, Center Party; 19th and 20th century France and Germany. **SELECTED PUBLICATIONS** Auth, German Nationalism and Religious Conflict--Ideology, Politics, 1870-1914, Am Hist Rev, Vol 101, 96; Rural Protest in the Weimar Republic--The Free Peasantry in the Rhineland and Bavaria, Am Hist Rev, Vol 99, 94; Between Class and Confession--Catholic Burgertum in Rheinland 1794-1914, Cath Hist Rev, Vol 82, 96; Christian Labor Movement in Bavaria from the World War 1 to 1933, Am Hist Rev, Vol 97, 92; auth, The Cross and the Ballot: Catholic Political Parties in Germany, Switzerland, Austria, Belgium and the Netherlands 1785-1985, Humanities/Brill Press, 99. **CONTACT ADDRESS** Dept of Hist, Georgia State Univ, Atlanta, GA 30303. **EMAIL** ele1730@mindspring.com

EVANS, EMORY GIBBONS
PERSONAL Born 01/21/1928, Richmond, VA, m, 1953, 3 children **DISCIPLINE** AMERICAN HISTORY **EDUCATION** Randolph-Macon Col, BA, 50; Univ Va, MA, 54, PhD (Am hist), 57. **CAREER** Instr hist, Darlington Sch, 50-52; instr, Univ Md, 56-58; from instr to asst prof, Univ Pittsburgh, 58-64; from assoc prof to prof hist, Northern Ill Univ, 64-76, chmn dept, 64-76, acting vpres and provost, 75-76; Prof Hist and Chmn Dept, Univ MD, College Park, 76-, Vis prof hist, Univ Va, 70. **MEMBERSHIPS** AHA; Southern Hist Asn; Orgn Am Historians. **RESEARCH** Early American history; 18th century southern and Virginia history. **SELECTED PUBLICATIONS** Auth, A Planters Republic--The Search for Economic Independence in Revolutionary Virginia, J Southern Hist, Vol 63, 97. **CONTACT ADDRESS** Dept of Hist, Univ of Maryland, Col Park, College Park, MD 20742. **EMAIL** eel2@umail.umd.edu

EVANS, JOHN KARL
PERSONAL Born 02/27/1946, Los Angeles, CA, m, 1971, 2 children **DISCIPLINE** HISTORY **EDUCATION** Univ Calif Los Angeles, BA, MA; McMaster Univ, PhD, 74. **CAREER** Prof **HONORS AND AWARDS** Outstanding Academic Bk Awd, 93. **RESEARCH** Roman history. **SELECTED PUBLICATIONS** Auth, Resistance Movements in the Ancient World, Univ Tokyo; War, Women and Children in Ancient Rome, Routledge, 91. **CONTACT ADDRESS** History Dept, Univ of Minnesota, Twin Cities, 614 Social Sciences Tower, 267 19th Ave. S, Minneapolis, MN 55455. **EMAIL** evans002@tc.umn.edu

EVANS, JOHN WHITNEY
PERSONAL Born 08/06/1931, Kansas City, MO **DISCIPLINE** UNITED STATES CHURCH HISTORY **EDUCATION** St Paul Sem, Minn, MA, 57; Cath Univ Am, MA, 58; Univ Minn, PhD (hist, philos educl, 70. **CAREER** Instr social probs, Cathedral High Sch, Minn, 58-62; chaplain and lectr psychol and educ, Univ Minn, Duluth, 66-69; coord res campus ministry, Ctr Applied Res in Apostolate, Washington, DC, 69-71; dir, Nat Ctr Campus Ministry, Mass, 71-73; CHAPLAIN AND ASST PROF HIST AND RELIG STUDIES, COL ST SCHOLASTICA, 73-, Mem comn campus ministry, Nat Cath Educ Asn, 69-73; Underwood fel, 72-73. **HONORS AND AWARDS** Cath Campus Ministry Asn Serv Awd, 73. **MEMBERSHIPS** Nat Cath Educ Asn; Soc Sci Study Relig; AHA; Am Cath Hist Asn; Relig Educ Asn. **RESEARCH** History and religion in American higher education; philosophy of education; student movements. **SELECTED PUBLICATIONS** Coauth & co-ed, Perspectives for campus ministers, US Cath Conf, 72; coauth, Worship in the university environment, Living Worship, 4/72; auth, Exemplary presence as campus ministry, Counseling & Values, spring 73; The Newman Movement: Roman Catholicism in American Higher Education, 1883-1971, 80. **CONTACT ADDRESS** Off of Chaplain, Col of St. Scholastica, 1200 Kenwood Ave, Duluth, MN 55811-4199.

EVANS, MICHAEL J.
DISCIPLINE HISTORY **EDUCATION** Univ of Wash, BA, MA; Univ of Mich, PhD. **CAREER** Tchg asst, Univ of Wash, 60; tchg fel, Univ of Mich, 61-65; lectr in hist, Univ of Mich, Flint, 63; instr, asst prof, assoc prof, prof, Kenyon Col, 65-; interdisciplinary affil and prof of hist, 93-. **HONORS AND AWARDS** Campus rep, ACM/GLCA Czech Prog, 1996-; ACM/GLCA exec comm, Central Europ Studies Prog 1996-; acad policy comm, 1988-90; campus sen, 1983-4, 1968-70; ch, Judicial Comm, 1982; ch, dept hist, 1973-80. **MEMBERSHIPS** Ren Soc Am; OPH Roster Hum Scholars; Am Hist Assn; Ohio Hist Soc. **RESEARCH** Machiavelli, medieval and renaissance studies. **SELECTED PUBLICATIONS** Auth, Machiavelli and Castruccio: Reflections on the Vita. Machiavelli Studies, 91; rev, Hodges, Richard: Dark Age Economics, The Origins of Towns and Trade AD 600-1000; Tagliacozzo, Giorgio, ed: Vico and Marx; Pompa, Leon, ed: Vico, Selected Writings; Merriman, John, ed: French Cities in the Nineteenth Century; Dickinson, W Calvin: James Harrington's Republic. **CONTACT ADDRESS** Dept of Hist, Kenyon Col, Gambier, OH 43022.

EVANS, ROGER S.
PERSONAL Born 01/25/1949, Columbus, OH, m, 1974, 2 children **DISCIPLINE** CLASSICAL & HELLENISTIC GREEK; ROMAN EMPIRE REPUBLIC **EDUCATION** Columbia Union Col, BA, 76; Aandrews Theol Sem, MDiv, 79; Ohio State Univ, MA, 91, PhD, 96. **CAREER** Adj prof, History, Ohio Wesleyan Univ, 91 & 97; vis prof, Chruch History, Ecumenical Theol Sem, 98; asst prof, church history, payne theol sem, 90-. **MEMBERSHIPS** N Amer Patristic Soc; Asn Seventh-Day Adventist Hist; Andrews Univ Sem Stud; Amer Soc Church Hist; Am Soc Ancient Hist; Amer Hist Soc; Amer Acad Relig. **SELECTED PUBLICATIONS** Rev, Reading the Apostolic Fathers, Jour Early Christian Stud, Hendrickson Publ, 96; Apocalypse of Paul: a Critical Edition of Three Long Latin Versions, Jour Early Christian Stud, 97; auth, A Biblical Theology of Drinking, Min: An Int Jour for Clergy, 93; Soteriologies of Early Christianity Within the Intellectual Context of the Early Roman Empire: Barnabas and Clement of Rome as Case Studies, Dumbarton Oaks, 98. **CONTACT ADDRESS** 2945 Princeville Dr., Pickerington, OH 43147. **EMAIL** RSE121@aol.com

EVANS, SARA M.
PERSONAL Born 12/01/1943, McCormick, SC, d, 1966, 2 children **DISCIPLINE** HISTORY **EDUCATION** Univ NC, PhD, 76. **CAREER** Prof **RESEARCH** Women's studies; twentieth-century American social history. **SELECTED PUBLICATIONS** Auth, Personal Politics: The Roots of Women's Liberation in the Civil Rights Movement and the New Left, Knopf, 79; Born For Liberty: A History of Women in America, Free, 89, 2nd ed, 97; coauth, Free Spaces: The Sources of Democratic Change in America, Harper & Row, 86, Univ Chicago Pr, 92; Wage Justice: Comparable Worth and the Paradox of Technocratic Reform, Univ Chicago, 89. **CONTACT ADDRESS** History Dept, Univ of Minnesota, Twin Cities, 614 Social Sciences Tower, 267 19th Ave S, Minneapolis, MN 55455. **EMAIL** s-evan@tc.umn.edu

EVANS, WILLIAM MCKEE
PERSONAL Born 09/17/1923, St. Pauls, NC, 4 children **DISCIPLINE** AMERICAN HISTORY **EDUCATION** Univ NC, AB, 48, MA, 50, PhD (US hist), 65. **CAREER** Lectr hist, Westminster Col, Utah, 62-64; asst prof, Calif Lutheran Col, 64-68; from asst prof to assoc prof, 68-77, Prof Hist, Calif State Poly-Tech Univ, 77-. **HONORS AND AWARDS** Am Asn State and Local Hist Manuscript Prize, 66. **MEMBERSHIPS** AHA; Orgn Am Historians; Southern Hist Asn. **RESEARCH** The American South; comparative race relations; comparative slavery. **SELECTED PUBLICATIONS** Auth, Ballots and Fence Rails: Reconstruction on the Lower Cape Fear, Univ NC, 67; To Die Game: The Story of the Lowry Band, Indian Guerrillas of Reconstruction, La State Univ, 71; contribr, Indians of the Southeast Since the Removal Era, Univ Ga, 79; Dictionary of North Carolina Biography, Univ NC, 79; auth, From the Land of Canaan to the Land of Guinea: The Strange Odyssey of the Sons of Ham, Am Hist Rev, 2/80. **CONTACT ADDRESS** Dept of Hist, California State Polytech Univ, Pomona, Pomona, CA 91768.

EVERGATES, THEODORE
PERSONAL Born 09/16/1940 **DISCIPLINE** MEDIEVAL HISTORY **EDUCATION** Brown Univ, AB, 62; Johns Hopkins Univ, PhD, 71. **CAREER** Asst prof, 73-79, Assoc Prof Hist, Western MD Col, 79-, Johns Hopkins Univ fel, 71-73; Nat Endowment for Humanities fel, 75-76; Am Council Learned Soc grant, 79. **MEMBERSHIPS** AHA; Medieval Acad Am. **RESEARCH** Medieval social and economic history; history of France. **SELECTED PUBLICATIONS** Auth, The aristocracy of Champagne in the mid-thirteenth century, J Interdisciplinary Hist, 74; Historiography and sociology in early feudal society, Viator, 75; Feudal Society in the Bailliage of Troyes Under the Counts of Champagne 1152-1284, Johns Hopkins Univ, 75; ed, The Cartulary and Charters of Notre-Dame of Homblieres, Medieval Acad Am (in prep). **CONTACT ADDRESS** Dept of Hist, Western Maryland Col, 2 College Hill, Westminster, MD 21157-4390.

EWELL, JUDITH
PERSONAL Born Parksley, VA **DISCIPLINE** LATIN AMERICAN HISTORY **EDUCATION** Duke Univ, AB, 65; Univ NMex, PhD(Latin Am hist), 72. **CAREER** Asst prof, 71-77, Assoc prof hist, Col William & Mary, 77-, Orgn Am States fel Venezuelan hist, 74-75; Fulbright vis lectr, Univ Catolica Andres Bello, Caracas, Venezuela, 79-80. Prof hist 84-; Newton Family Prof hist 88-, Fullbright vis lectr, Univ Andina Simon Bolivar, Ecuador, 94-95. Ch, hist dept, Col of William & Mary, 91-98. **HONORS AND AWARDS** Orgn Am States Essay prize, 82; Sturgis Leavitt Awd, 83; Commonwealth of VA Outstanding Fac Awd, 89; pres, conf on Latin Am hist, 92; A.B. Thomas Awd, 97. **MEMBERSHIPS** AHA; Latin Am Studies Asn; Mid Atlantic Coun Latin Am Studies; Conf Latin Am Hist; Rocky Mountain Coun Latin Am Studies. **RESEARCH** Twentieth Century Venezuela; Nineteenth Century Ecuador. **SELECTED PUBLICATIONS** Auth, Venezuela's crucial decade: The dictatorship of Marcos Perez Jimenez, Rev Interam, fall 77; The extradition of Marcos Perez Jimenez, J Latin American Studies, England, 11/77; The Caribbean and the law of the sea, In: The Restless Carribean, Praeger, 79; Indictment of a Dictator: The Extradition of Marcos Perez Jimenez, Tex A&M Univ Press, 81; The development of Venezuelan geopolitical analysis since World War II, J Interam Studies & World Affairs, 8/82; Venezuela: A Century of Change, C. Hurst and Stanford Univ, 84; Venezuela and the United States: From Monroe's Hemisphere to Petroleum's Empire, Univ GA, 96; co-ed, The Human Tradition in Twentieth Century Latin America, Scholar-

ly Resources, 87; The Human Tradition in Nineteenth Century Latin America, Scholarly Resources, 89; The Human Tradition in Modern Latin America, Scholarly Resources, 97. **CONTACT ADDRESS** Dept of History, Col of William and Mary, PO Box 8795, Williamsburg, VA 23187-8795. **EMAIL** jxewel@mail.wm.edu

EYCK, F. GUNTHER
PERSONAL Born 07/10/1912, Magdeburg, Germany, m, 1948, 2 children **DISCIPLINE** WORLD WAR II DIPLOMACY AND COMPARATIVE FOREIGN POLICY **EDUCATION** NYork Univ, PhD. **CAREER** Prof, Am Univ. **HONORS AND AWARDS** Outstanding Teacher Award, American Univ, 96. **RESEARCH** Western European politics **SELECTED PUBLICATIONS** Auth, The Voice of Nations: European National Anthems and Their Authors, Greenwood Press, 95. **CONTACT ADDRESS** School of International Service, American Univ, 4400 Mass Ave., Washington, DC 20016.

EYCK, FRANK
PERSONAL Born 07/13/1921, Berlin, Germany, m, 1955, 2 children **DISCIPLINE** MODERN HISTORY **EDUCATION** Oxford Univ, BA, 49, MA, 54, BLitt, 58. **CAREER** News subed, Brit Broadcasting Corp, 49-56; temp asst lectr mod hist, Univ Liverpool, 58-59; lectr mod Europ hist, Univ Exeter, 59-68; Prof Hist, Univ Calgary, 68-, Vchmn coun, Inter-Univ Ctr Post-Grad Studies, Dubrovnik, Yugoslavia, 74-. **MEMBERSHIPS** AHA; Can Hist Asn; fel Royal Hist Soc; Royal Commonwealth Soc. **RESEARCH** German history; biography; church and state diplomatic history. **SELECTED PUBLICATIONS** Auth, Word and Power--Gentz, Friedrich as a Political Writer, Cent Europ Hist, Vol 28, 95; Bismarck and Mitteleuropa, Cent Europ Hist, Vol 28,95; Rhineland Radicals--The Democratic Movement and the Revolution of 1848-1849, Am Hist Rev, Vol 97, 92; Bucher, Lothar 1817-1892--A Political Life Between Revolution and Civil Service, Cent Europ Hist, Vol 26, 93; Bureaucratic Conservatism and Modernization--Studies on the Early History of the Conservative Party in Prussia 1810-1848, Cent Europ Hist, Vol 25, 92. **CONTACT ADDRESS** Dept of Hist, Univ of Calgary, Calgary, AB, Canada T2N 1N4.

EZERGAILIS, ANDREW
PERSONAL Born 12/10/1930, Latvia, m, 1957, 1 child **DISCIPLINE** RUSSIAN HISTORY, HISTORIOGRAPHY **EDUCATION** Mich State Univ, BA, 56; NYork Univ, MA, 60, PhD, 68. **CAREER** Asst prof, 63-73, prof hist, Ithaca Col, 73-, Res grant, Am Coun Learned Soc, 80. **MEMBERSHIPS** AHA; Am Asn Advan Slavic Studies; Am Asn Baltic Studies. **RESEARCH** The 1917 revolution in Russia; the socialist movement; Latvian history. **SELECTED PUBLICATIONS** Auth, The bolshevization of Latvian social democracy, Can Slavic Studies, 67; Anglo-Saxonism and fascism, Yale Rev, 6/69; October insurrection in Latvia: A chronology, J Baltic Studies, winter 73; The 1917 Revolution in Latvia, Columbia Univ, 74; The 1917 Revolution in Latvia; The Latvian Impact on the Bolshevik Revolution; The Holocaust in Latvia. **CONTACT ADDRESS** Ithaca Col, 953 Danby Rd, Ithaca, NY 14850-7002. **EMAIL** ezergail@ithaca.edu

F

FABEND, FIRTH HARING
PERSONAL Born 08/12/1957, Tappan, NY, m, 2 children **DISCIPLINE** AMERICAN STUDIES **EDUCATION** Barnard Col, BA; New York Univ, PhD, 88. **CAREER** Independent historian. **HONORS AND AWARDS** Res grant, New Jersey Hist Comn, 85; Hendricks Manuscript Awd, New Netherland Project, 89; NY State Hist Asn Annual Book Prize, 89; fel, Holland Soc, NY, 93; res grant, NJ Hist Comn, 94, 95; fel, New Netherland Project, 96. **MEMBERSHIPS** Am Hist Asn; Am Soc of Church Hist; Authors Guild; Natl Coalition of Independent Scholars; Omohundro Inst of Early Am Hist and Cult. **SELECTED PUBLICATIONS** Auth, The Dutch American Farmer: A Mad Rabble or Gentlemen Standing Up for Their Rights? de Halve Maen, 90; auth, A Dutch Family in the Middle Colonies, 1660-1800, Rutgers, 91; auth, According to Holland Custome: Jacob Leisler and the Loockermans Estate Feud, de Halve Maen, 94; auth, Suffer the Little Children: Evangelical Childrearing in Reformed Dutch Households, New York and New Jersey, de Halve Maen, 95; auth, The Synod of Dort and the Persistence of Dutchness in 19th-Century New York and New Jersey, NY Hist, 96; auth, Zion on the Hudson: Dutch New York nd New Jersey in the Age of Revivals, Rutgers, 00. **CONTACT ADDRESS** 54 Elston Rd, Upper Montclair, NJ 07043. **EMAIL** fhfabend@msn.com

FABIAN, ANN
DISCIPLINE AMERICAN STUDIES, HISTORY **EDUCATION** Univ Calif at Santa Cruz, BA, 71; Yale Univ, PhD, 82. **CAREER** Assoc prof, Am stud, Yale Univ; current, VIS SCHOLAR HIST, YALE UNIV. **MEMBERSHIPS** Am Antiquarian Soc **SELECTED PUBLICATIONS** Card Sharks, Dream Books & Bucket Shops: Gambling in 19th-Century America, Cornell Univ Press, 90. **CONTACT ADDRESS** 1165 5th Ave, #128, New York, NY 10029-6931.

FABOS, JULIUS GYULA
PERSONAL Born 04/15/1932, Marcali, Hungary, m, 1959, 3 children **DISCIPLINE** LANDSCAPE ARCHITECTURE **EDUCATION** Rutgers, Univ, BS, 61; Harvard Univ, MLA, 64; Univ Mich, PhD, 73. **CAREER** From asst prof to prof, Univ Mass, 64-97; prof emer, 98- . **HONORS AND AWARDS** Fel, ASLA, 85; hon doctorate, Univ Horticulture, Budapest, 92; Am Planning Asn Awd, 94; Am Soc Landscape Arch Medalist, 97. **MEMBERSHIPS** Am Soc Landscape Arch; Coun of Educ in Landsacpe Arch. **RESEARCH** Landscape planning and greenway planning. **SELECTED PUBLICATIONS** Auth, Land Use Planning, Chapman and Hall, 85; coed, Special Issue on Greenways, Landscape and Urban Planning J, 95; auth, How Can Land Use Planning Research Influence Land Use Policy Decisions? Proc ASLA, 95; co-ed, Greenways: The Beginning of an International Movement, Elsevier, 96. **CONTACT ADDRESS** Dept of Landscape, Archit, and Regional Planning, Univ of Massachusetts, Amherst, 109 Hills N, Amherst, MA 01003. **EMAIL** jfabos@larp.umass.edu

FACOS, MICHELLE
DISCIPLINE NINETEENTH CENTURY EUROPEAN PAINTING AND SCULPTURE **EDUCATION** Univ NYork, PhD. **CAREER** Asst prof. **RESEARCH** Romanticism; symbolism; nationalism. **SELECTED PUBLICATIONS** Auth, Nationalism and the Nordic Imagination: Swedish Painting in the 1890's, Univ Ca, 98; pubs on Scandinavian art. **CONTACT ADDRESS** Hist of Art Dept, Indiana Univ, Bloomington, 1201 E 7th St, Fine Arts 132, Bloomington, IN 47405. **EMAIL** mfacos@indiana.edu

FAHERTY, WILLIAM BARNABY
PERSONAL Born 12/17/1914, St. Louis, MO, s **DISCIPLINE** HISTORY **EDUCATION** St Louis Univ, AB, 36, AM, 38; St Mary's Col, STL, 45, PhD, 49. **CAREER** From instr to asst prof hist, Regis Col, Colo, 48-56; gen ed, Queen's Work Publ House, 56-63; Assoc Prof, 63-68, Prof Hist, St Louis Univ, 68-85, Chmn, Midwestern Jesuit Comt Hist Preserv, 71-; vis assoc prof hist and NASA grant, Univ Fla, 72-74; dir, St Stanislaus Jesuit Hist Mus, Inc, Florissant, Mo, 75. **HONORS AND AWARDS** Cath Pres Asn Nat Writing Awds, 43 and 44; Literary Awd, Mo Writers Guild, 77, 88, 92. **MEMBERSHIPS** Am Cath Hist Asn. **RESEARCH** Saint Louis regional history; Midwestern Church history; history of America's space program. **SELECTED PUBLICATIONS** Henry Shaw: His Life and Legacies (Univ. of Mo. Press); Moonport: A History of Apollo Launch Facilities and Operations (NASA) and 23 other books, reviews and articles in various historical journals. **CONTACT ADDRESS** Midwest Jesuit Archives, 4515 West Pine Blvd, Saint Louis, MO 63108. **EMAIL** archives@jesuits-mis.org.

FAHEY, DAVID MICHAEL
PERSONAL Born 05/18/1937, Ossining, NY, m, 1988, 1 child **DISCIPLINE** BRITISH AND WORLD HISTORY **EDUCATION** Siena Col, NYork, BA, 59; Univ Notre Dame, MA, 61, PhD(hist), 64. **CAREER** From instr to asst prof hist, Assumption Col, Mass, 63-66; asst prof, Ind Univ Northwest, 66-69; assoc prof, 69-80, prof Hist, Miami Univ, 80-, Dir Grad Studies, 82-85; dir undergrad Studies, 87, 95-98 Ed, Alcohol and Temperance History Group Newslett, 82-83; Alcohol in Hist, 83-86; moderator, ATHG listserv group, 95-; pres, Alcohol and Temperance Hist Group, 86-88; Pres, Ohio Academy of History, 00-01. **MEMBERSHIPS** American Historical Assoc; North American Conf British Studies; Social Hist Soc UK; Ohio Acad of Hist; World Hist Assn. **RESEARCH** British social history; Anglo-Am temperance and fraternal societies **SELECTED PUBLICATIONS** Auth, Henry Hallam: a conservative as Whig historian, Historian, 66; R H Tawney and the sense of community, Centennial Rev, 68; Temperance and the liberal party: Lord Peel's report, 1899, J Brit Studies, 71; ed, Samuel Rawson Gardiner looks at history, home rule and empire: some Bodleian letters, 1886-1899, Proc Am Philos Soc, 71; Rosebery, the Times and the Newcastle programme, Bull Inst Hist Res, 72; coauth, The English Heritage, Forum, 78; auth, The Politics of Drink: Pressure Groups and the British Liberal Party, 1883-1908, Soc Sci, 79; Brewers, Publicans, and Working-Class Drinkers: Pressure Group Politics in Late Victorian and Edwardian England, Hist Soc, 80; ed, The Collected Writings of Jessie Forsyth, 1847-1937: The Good Templars and Temperence Reform on Three Coutments, Edwin Mellen, 88; auth, "Slavery is a Sin against God and a Crime against Man": Alfred J. Anderson and Oxford's Black Convention of January 7, 1853, Old Northwest, 90; ed, The Black Lodge in White America: True Reformer Browne and His Economic Strategy, Wright State UP, 94; Temperance and Racism: John Bull, Johnny Reb and the Good Templars, Univ Press of Kentucky, 96; Blacks, Good Templars and Universal Membership in Jack S Blocker, Jr and Cheryl Krasnick Warsh, eds, The Changing Face of Drink, Histoire Sociale, 97; How the Good Templars Began: Fraternal Temperance in New York State, Social History of Alcohol Review, 99; auth, Blackboard Course Info: Supplementing In-Class Teaching with the Internet, History Computer Revew, 00. **CONTACT ADDRESS** Dept of History, Miami Univ, Oxford, OH 45056-1602. **EMAIL** faheydm@muohio.edu

FAHL, RONALD JENKS
PERSONAL Born 08/04/1942, Portland, OR, m, 1967, 2 children **DISCIPLINE** AMERICAN HISTORY **EDUCATION** Willamette Univ, BA, 64; Univ Ore, MA, 66. **CAREER** Instr hist, Eastern Ore State Col, 66-69; teaching assoc, Wash State Univ, 72-73; Bibliographer, 73-75, Ed, J Forest Hist, Forest Hist Soc, 75-, Dir Prog Develop, 80-. **MEMBERSHIPS** AHA; Orgn Am Historians; Western Hist Asn; Forest Hist Soc. **RESEARCH** Forest and conservation history; populism; American West. **SELECTED PUBLICATIONS** Auth, The National Forests of the Northern Region--Living Legacy, W Hist Quart, Vol 25, 94. **CONTACT ADDRESS** Forest Historical Society, 109 Coral St, Santa Cruz, CA 95060.

FAHMY-EID, NADIA
PERSONAL Born 09/09/1936, Egypt **DISCIPLINE** HISTORY **EDUCATION** Univ Laval, LL, 65; McGill Univ, MA, 67; Univ Montreal, PhD, 75. **CAREER** Prof hist, Col Edouard-Montpetit, 66-69; Prof Histoire, Univ Quebec Montreal, 69-, dir du prog d'etudes avancees, 74-76. **HONORS AND AWARDS** Membre de la Societe Royale du Can, 96-; Prix Guy Fregault, Inst d'hist de l'Amerique francais; Prix des Fondateurs, Asn can d'hist de l'educ; Marion Porter Prize, Can Res Inst Advan Women; Hilda Neatby Prize, Soc d'hist Can. **MEMBERSHIPS** Ch, Can Hist Asn, 95-96. **SELECTED PUBLICATIONS** Auth, Le clerge et le pouvoir politique au Quebec, 78; coauth, Si le travail m'etait conte autrement, 87; coauth, Femmes, sante et professions. Dietetistes et physiotherapentes au Quebec et en Ontario 1930-1980, 97; co-dir, Maitresses de maison, maitresses d'ecole, 83; co-dir, Les couventines, 86. **CONTACT ADDRESS** Dep d'histoire, Univ of Quebec, Montreal, CP 8888, Succ Centre-ville, Montreal, QC, Canada H3C 3P8.

FAHS, ALICE E.
DISCIPLINE HISTORY **EDUCATION** NYork Univ, PhD, 93. **CAREER** ASST PROF, HIST, UNIV CALIF IRVINE **MEMBERSHIPS** Am Antiquarian Soc **RESEARCH** Civil War **CONTACT ADDRESS** Dept of Hist, Univ of California, Irvine, Irvine, CA 92717-3275.

FAIR, JOHN
PERSONAL Born 09/06/1943, Waynesboro, PA, m, 1977, 2 children **DISCIPLINE** HISTORY **EDUCATION** Juniata Col, BA, 65; Wake Forest Univ, MA, 66; Duke Univ, PhD, 70. **CAREER** Instr, York Col, 67; instr, Mullersville Univ, 68; asst prof, Va Polytechnic Inst, 69-71; asst prof to prof, Auburn Univ Montgomery, 71-97; prof, chair, Ga Col and State Univ, 97-. **HONORS AND AWARDS** Alumni Prof Hist, Auburn Univ, 95-98; Fel, Royal Hist Soc, 96-. **MEMBERSHIPS** AHA; Hist Soc; Conf on British Studies; British Polit Group; Am Conf for Irish Studies; N Am Soc for Sport Hist; Ala Hist Assoc; Ga Assoc of Hist; Carolinas Symp on British Studies. **RESEARCH** British Political and Constitutional History, Modern Irish History, Sport History (Weightlifting and Bodybuilding). **SELECTED PUBLICATIONS** Auth, British Interparty Conferences: A Study of the Procedure of Conciliation in British Politics, 1867-1921, Clarendon Pr, (Oxford), 80; auth, Harold Temperley, A Scholar and Romantic in the Public Realm, 1879-1939, Univ of Del Pr, (Newark), 92; auth, Muscletown USA: Bob Hoffman and the Manly Culture of York Barbell, 1898-1985, Pa State Univ Pr, (University Park), 99. **CONTACT ADDRESS** Dept Hist and Geog, George Col and State Univ, PO Box 047, Milledgeville, GA 31061-0490. **EMAIL** jfair@mail.gcsu.edu

FAIR, THEOPOLIS
PERSONAL Born 02/03/1941, Pine Bluff, AR **DISCIPLINE** LATIN AMERICAN & BLACK HISTORY **EDUCATION** Fisk Univ, BA, 63; Columbia Univ, MA, 65; Univ Madrid, dipl hist, 65; Temple Univ, PhD(Latin Am hist), 72. **CAREER** Assoc Prof Hist, La Salle Univ, 67-. **HONORS AND AWARDS** Phi Beta Kappa; Woodrow Wilson; Fulbright. **MEMBERSHIPS** AHA; Latin Am Studies Asn **RESEARCH** Passage to and from Spain in the 16th century; Blacks in Latin America; Geraldine Farrar. **SELECTED PUBLICATIONS** Auth, The Impact of the New World on Spain, 1550-1650: Some Social Aspects, J of the Great Lake Hist Conf, Vol 2, 15-28; Asia in Latin American History, in: Asia in National & World History, 97. **CONTACT ADDRESS** Dept of Hist, La Salle Univ, 1900 W Olney Ave, Philadelphia, PA 19141-1199. **EMAIL** fair@lasalle.edu

FAIRBAIRN, BRETT T.
PERSONAL Born 04/24/1959, Winnipeg, MB, Canada **DISCIPLINE** HISTORY **EDUCATION** Univ Sask, BA, 81; Univ Oxford, BA, 84, DPhil, 88. **CAREER** Asst to assoc prof, 86-96, PROF, UNIV SASKATCHEWAN, 96-; ed, Can J Hist, 88-95; ch, Sask Archv Bd, 97-. **HONORS AND AWARDS** Rhodes schol, 81; SSHRC doctoral fel, 84-86; SSHRC res grant, 92-95; Alexander von Humboldt fel, 97-98. **RESEARCH** German soc and politics (1890-1914), particularly electoral hist, and the hist of cooperative movements in all countries but expecially in western Canada. **SELECTED PUBLICATIONS** Auth, Building a Dream: The Co-operative Retailing System in Western Canada, 89; auth, "Authority versus Democracy: Prussian Officials in the German Elections of 1898 and 1903," Hist Journal, 90; auth, Democracy in the Undemocratic State: The German

Reichstag Elections of 1898 and 1903, 97; coauth, Cooperatives and Community Development, 91; co-ed, Dignity and Growth, Citizen Participation in Social Change, 91; auth, "History from the Ecological Perspective: Gaia Theory and the Problem of Cooperatives in Turn-of-the-Century Germany," Am Hist Review, 94. **CONTACT ADDRESS** Univ of Saskatchewan, 101 Diefenbaker Pl, Saskatoon, SK, Canada S7N 5B8. **EMAIL** brett.fairbairn@usask.ca

FALER, PAUL G.
PERSONAL Born 09/10/1940, Worcester, MA, m, 1965, 3 children **DISCIPLINE** HISTORY **EDUCATION** Southern Meth Univ, BA,62; Univ Wis, MA, 65; PhD, 71. **CAREER** From asst prof to assoc prof, Univ of Mass, 70 - ; ch, Dept Hist, 92-96, 98- . **HONORS AND AWARDS** Eugene Asher Awd, Dist Teach, AHA, 89. **RESEARCH** American social history; Mass and local history. **SELECTED PUBLICATIONS** Auth, Mechanics and Manufacturing in the Early Industrial Revolution, 81. **CONTACT ADDRESS** Dept of Hist, Univ of Massachusetts, Boston, 100 Morrissey Blvd, Dorchester, MA 02125-3300. **EMAIL** paul.faler@umb.edu

FALK, CANDACE
PERSONAL Born New York, NY **DISCIPLINE** HISTORY; POLITICAL THEORY **EDUCATION** Univ Chicago, BA, 69; MA, 71; Univ Calif Santa Cruz, PhD, 84. **CAREER** Intermittent fac positions, Univ Calif Berkeley, Univ Calif Santa Cruz, Stockton State Col; dir/ed, The Emma Goldman Papers, 80- . **HONORS AND AWARDS** Guggenheim fel, 98-99. **MEMBERSHIPS** Asoc Documentary Eds; Orgn of Am Historians; Am Hist Asoc. **RESEARCH** History; women's studies; labor and left social movements; intellectual and cultural history; biography. **SELECTED PUBLICATIONS** auth, Love, Anarchy, and Emma Goldman, 84, 90, 99; auth, Emma Goldman Papers: A Comprehensive Microfilm Edition, 91; auth with S. Cole and S. Thomas, Emma Goldman: A Guide to her Life and Documentary Sources, 95; Selected Papers of Emma Goldman, forthcoming. **CONTACT ADDRESS** Emma Goldman Papers, Univ of California, Berkeley, 2372 Ellsworth St., Berkeley, CA 94720-6030. **EMAIL** cfalk@socrates.berkeley.edu

FALK, MARVIN W.
PERSONAL Born 01/29/1943, Wichita, KS, m, 1969, 3 children **DISCIPLINE** EUROPEAN, GERMANY, ARTIC, ALASKA, HISTORY OF CARTOGRAPHY **EDUCATION** Univ Iowa, PhD, 76. **CAREER** Univ Alaska **SELECTED PUBLICATIONS** Auth, Cartobibliography of AK, Garland, 83; ed, AK, CLIO Press, 95; auth, Rasmuson Library Historical Translation Series, Univ of AK Press, 85-. **CONTACT ADDRESS** Univ of Alaska, Fairbanks, PO Box 757480, Fairbanks, AK 99775-7480. **EMAIL** ffmwf@uaf.edu

FALK, NANCY ELLEN
PERSONAL Born 09/03/1938, Bethlehem, PA, m, 1967, 2 children **DISCIPLINE** HISTORY OF RELIGIONS **EDUCATION** Cedar Crest Col, AB, 60; Univ Chicago, AM, 63, PhD(hist of relig), 72. **CAREER** Asst prof, 66-71, assoc prof, 71-79, chmn dept, 72-75, Prof Relig, Western Mich Univ, 79-. **HONORS AND AWARDS** Fulbright, India, 84-85; AIIS sr fel, 91-92. **MEMBERSHIPS** Am Acad Relig. **RESEARCH** South Asian religion; women in religion. **SELECTED PUBLICATIONS** Co-ed (with Rita M Gross), Unspoken worlds: Women's Religious Lives, 80,89,00; auth, Women in Religion: An Annotated Bibliography of Sources in English, 1975-1992, 94. **CONTACT ADDRESS** Dept of Comp Relig, Western Michigan Univ, 1903 W Michigan, Kalamazoo, MI 49008-3805. **EMAIL** nancy.falk@wmich.edu

FALK, STANLEY LAWRENCE
PERSONAL Born 03/11/1927, New York, NY, m, 1956, 2 children **DISCIPLINE** MILITARY HISTORY **EDUCATION** Bard Col, BA, 45; Georgetown Univ, MA, 52, PhD(hist), 59. **CAREER** Historian, Off Chief Mil Hist, US Dept Army, 49-54, 59-62, bur soc sci res, Am Univ, DC, 54-56 & hist sect, Joint Chiefs of Staff, US Dept Defense, 56-59; assoc prof nat security affairs, Indust Col Armed Forces, 62-70, prof int rels, 70-74; chief historian, US Air Force, 74-80; Dep Chief Historian, Southeast Asia, US Army Ctr Military Hist, 80-82; independent historical consult, 83- . **HONORS AND AWARDS** Phi Alpha Theta. **MEMBERSHIPS** Soc Military Hist; World War Ii Stud Asn; Soc Hist Am Foreign Rels; AHA; Orgn Am Historians; Am Jewish Hist Soc. **RESEARCH** American history; American military history; national security affairs. **SELECTED PUBLICATIONS** Auth, Bataan: The March of Death, Norton, 62; auth, Decision at Leyte, Norton, 66; auth, Human Resources for National Strength, 66, The National Security Structure, 67 & 72, The Environment of National Security, 68 & 73, Defense Military Manpower, 70 & The World in Ferment: Problem Areas for the United States, 70 & 74, Indust Col Armed Forces; Liberation of the Philippines, 71 & The Palaus Campaign, 74, Ballantine; Seventy Days to Singapore, Putnam & Hale, 75. **CONTACT ADDRESS** 2310 Kimbro St, Alexandria, VA 22307.

FALOLA, TOYIN
PERSONAL Born 01/01/1953, Ibadan, Nigeria, m, 1981, 3 children **DISCIPLINE** HISTORY **EDUCATION** Univ Nigeria, BA, 76; Univ Ife, PhD, 81. **CAREER** Teacher, Nigeria, 70-77; admin off, Public Serv Commission Nigeria, 77; lectr to prof, Univ Ife, 77-90; prof, York Univ, 90-91; prof, Univ Tex Austin, 91-. **HONORS AND AWARDS** Holloway Awd, Smith Col, 00; Fel, Humanities Res Coun of Australian Nat Univ, 95; Smuts Fel, Univ Cambridge, 88-89. **SELECTED PUBLICATIONS** Ed, African Historiography, Longman, 93; co-ed, Pawnship in Africa. Debt Bondage in Historical Perspective, 94; auth, Development Planning and Decolonization in Nigeria, Univ Press of Fla, 96; auth, Violence in Nigeria: The Crisis of Religious Politics and Secular Ideologies, Univ Rochester Press, 98; auth, The History of Nigeria, Greenwood Press, 99; auth, Yoruba Gurus: Indigenous Production of Knowledge in Africa, Africa World Press, 00; ed, Africa, Vol. 2: Cultures and Societies, Carolina Acad Press, 00; ed, Africa, Vol. 1: Peoples and States, Carolina Acad Press, 00; auth, Nationalism and African Intellectuals, Univ Rochester Press, 01; auth, The Culture and Customs of Nigeria, Greenwood Press, 01; co-auth, Yoruba Warlords of the Nineteenth Century, Africa World Press, 01. **CONTACT ADDRESS** Dept Hist, Univ of Texas, Austin, Campus MC B7000, Austin, TX 78712. **EMAIL** toyin.falola@mail.utexas.edu

FANN, WILLERD REESE
PERSONAL Born 09/03/1932, Sacramento, CA, m, 1965 **DISCIPLINE** MODERN EUROPEAN HISTORY **EDUCATION** Univ Calif, Berkeley, AB, 57, MA, 59, PhD (hist), 65. **CAREER** Asst prof hist, La State Univ, New Orleans, 64-75; Assoc Prof Hist, Univ New Orleans, 74-. **MEMBERSHIPS** AHA; Col Mil Hist; Am Mil Inst; Conf Group on Cent Europ Hist. **RESEARCH** German history; military history. **SELECTED PUBLICATIONS** Auth, Military Conservatism--Veterans Associations and the Military Party in Prussia Between 1815 and 1848, Ger Stud Rev, Vol 15, 92. **CONTACT ADDRESS** Dept of Hist, Univ of New Orleans, New Orleans, LA 70122.

FANNING, STEVE
PERSONAL Born 02/17/1947, Weatherford, OK, m, 1992, 2 children **DISCIPLINE** MEDIEVAL HISTORY **EDUCATION** Tex Tech Univ, BA, 68; MA, 70; Univ Minn, PhD, 77. **CAREER** Vis Asst prof, 80-81, asst prof, 81-87, assoc prof, 87-, Univ Ill Chicago. **MEMBERSHIPS** AHA; MAA; NAPS; Haskins Soc; Majesta. **RESEARCH** Rulership in late antiquity and the early Middle Ages; France in the ten and eleventh centuries; mysticism. **SELECTED PUBLICATIONS** Auth, A Bishop and His World Before the Gregorian Reform, Hubert of Angers, 1006-1047, Transactions of the Am Philo Soc, 78 (88); auth, 'Lombard Arianism Reconsidered," Speculum 56 (81): 241-52; auth, "Bede, ImDerium, and the Bretwaldas," Speculum 66 (91): 1-26; auth, "Emperors and Empires in Fifth-Century Gaul," in a Crisis of Identity?, ed. John Drinkwater, Hugh Elton (Cambridge: Cambridge Univ Press, 92): 288-97. **CONTACT ADDRESS** Dept History, Univ of Illinois, Chicago, 601 South Morgan St, 913 University Hall, Chicago, IL 60607-7109. **EMAIL** sfanning@uic.edu

FARAGHER, JOHN MACK
PERSONAL Born 08/26/1945, Phoenix, AZ, 1 child **DISCIPLINE** AMERICAN HISTORY **EDUCATION** Univ Calif, Riverside, BA, 67, MA, 70; Yale Univ, PhD, 77. **CAREER** Soc worker, Dept Pub Soc Ser, Los Angeles County, 68-69; instr Am studies, Yale Univ, 75-77; asst prof hist, Univ Hartford, 77-78; Asst Prof Hist, Mt Holyoke Col, 78-; Arthur Unobskey prof hist, dir, Howard Lamar Ctr, Yale Univ. **HONORS AND AWARDS** John Addison Porter and Fredric Beinecke Prize, Yale Univ, 77; Fredrick Jackson Turner Awd, Orgn Am Historians, 80; Spec Citation, Soc Am Historians, 80. **MEMBERSHIPS** Western Hist Asn; AHA; New Eng Hist Asn; Mid Atlantic Radical Historians Asn. **RESEARCH** Sex and gender in history; Midwestern American society and culture; Antebellum America. **SELECTED PUBLICATIONS** Auth, Frontier Indiana, J Am Hist, Vol 84, 97; Past Imperfect--Fact and Truth, Am Heritage, Vol 46, 95; A Commentary on Hijiya, James, A. Article Why the West is Lost, William Mary Quart, Vol 51, 94; 3 Frontiers--Family, Land, and Society in the American West, 1850-1900, Pac Northwest Quart, Vol 87, 96; Belleville, Ottawa, and Galesburg--Community and Democracy On The Illinois Frontier, J Am Hist, Vol 84, 97; The Ohio Frontier--Crucible of the Old Northwest, 1720-1830, J Am Hist, Vol 84, 97; An Unsettled Country--Changing Landscapes of the American West, Environmental Hist, Vol 2, 97; All Over the Map--Rethinking American Regions, W Hist Quart, Vol 27, 96; Settling the Canadian American West, 1890-1915--Pioneer Adaptation and Community Building--An Anthropological History, J Soc Hist, Vol 30, 97. **CONTACT ADDRESS** Dept Hist, Yale Univ, TC 1137, New Haven, CT 06520. **EMAIL** john.faragher@yale.edu

FARAH, CAESAR E.
PERSONAL Born 03/13/1929, Portland, OR, m, 1987, 7 children **DISCIPLINE** HISTORY, RELIGION **EDUCATION** Stanford Univ, BA, 52; Princeton Univ, MA, 55; PhD, 57. **CAREER** Pub aff asst & educ exchange attache, US Info Serv, Delhi & Karachi, 57-59; asst prof hist & Near E lang, Portland State Univ, 59-63; consult US Army 62-63; asst prof hist, Los Angeles State Univ, 63-64; vis prof Harvard Univ 64-65; assoc prof Near Eastern lang & lit, Ind Univ, Bloomington, 64-69; prof Middle Eastern Studies, Univ Minn, Minneapolis, 69-, Consult, spec oper res off, Am Univ, 60; cult attache's comt, Arab Embassies in Washington, DC, 61; consult, col bks div, Am Libr Asn, 64-; Ford Found grant, 66-67; guest lectr Arabic Ottoman rels, Lebanese Univ, 66 & Univ Baghdad, 67; Fulbright award, Turkey, 67-68; Am Philos Soc res grant, 70-71; guest lectr For Min Spain, Iraq, Lebanon, Iran; Min Higher Educ Saudi Arabia, Yemen, Kuwait, Qatar, Tunisia, Morocco; Syrian Acad Sci, Acad Scis Beijing; vis scholar Cambridge Univ 74; rsrc person on Middle East svc gp MN, 77; bd dir chemn Upper Midwest Consortium for Middle East Outreach, 80-; vis prof Sanaa Univ, Yemen, 84, Karl-Franzens Univ, Austria, 90, Ludwig_Maximilian Univ, Munich, 92-93; exec secy ed Am Inst Yemeni Stud 82-86; secy-gen exec bd dir Int Comt for Pre-Ottoman & Ottoman Studies, 88-; fel Res Ctr Islamic Hist, Istanbul, 93; Ctr Lebanese Stydues & St Anthony Col, Oxford, Eng, 94; vis Fulbright-Hays scholar Univ Damascus, 94; Vice pres, CIEPO Gov Bd, 00-; Exec Dir and Gov Bd Mem, Upper Midwest Consortium. **HONORS AND AWARDS** Cert of Merit Syrian Min Higher Educ, 66-67; Stanford Univ Alumni Asn Ldr Recognition Awd; Fel, Am Res Cntr Egypt, 66-67. **MEMBERSHIPS** Am Orient Soc; Am Asn Arabic Studies; AHA; Royal Asiatic Soc; MidE Studies Asn NAm; Asn Tchr Arabic; Turkish Studies Asn; Pi Sigma Alpha; Phi Alpha Theta; Upper Midwest Consortium, exec dir and govern brd mem. **RESEARCH** Modern Arab world, sociopolitical changes; Islamic religion and mysticism; the West and the Arab world in the 19th century. **SELECTED PUBLICATIONS** Auth, ISLAM Beliefs and Observances, 1st ed, 67, 6th ed, 00; auth, Necib Pasa and the British in Syria, Archivum Ottomanicum, Budapest & Leiden, 72; Islam and revitalization, Quartet, London, 80; The quadruple alliance and proposed Ottoman reforms in Syria, 1839-41, Int J Turkish Studies II, 81; Tarikh Baghdad Ii-Ibn-al-Najjar, 80-83, 3 vols 2 edit 86; Al-Ghazali on Abstinence in Islam, 92; Decision Making in the Ottoman Empire, 92; The Road to Intervention: Fiscal Policies in Ottoman Mount Lebanon, 92; The Politics of Interventionism in Ottoman Lebanon, 2 vols, 97; ISLAM Beliefs and Observances, 1st ed. 67, 6th ed 00; auth, The Politics of Interventionism in Ottoman Lebanon 1831-1861, 00. **CONTACT ADDRESS** Univ of Minnesota, Twin Cities, 267 19th Ave S., 839 Soc Sci, Minneapolis, MN 55455. **EMAIL** farah001@maroon.tc.umn.edu

FARBER, PAUL L.
PERSONAL Born 03/07/1944, New York, NY, m, 1966, 2 children **DISCIPLINE** HISTORY OF SCIENCE **EDUCATION** Univ Pittsburgh, BS, 65; Ind Univ, Bloomington, MA, 68, PhD, 70. **CAREER** Asst prof, 70-76, prof hist of sci, Ore State Univ, 76-82; OSU Distinguished Prof. 93-. **MEMBERSHIPS** Am Assn Advan Sci; Hist Sci Soc; Am Hist Assn. **RESEARCH** History of life sciences **SELECTED PUBLICATIONS** Auth, The Emergence of Ornithology as as Scientific Discipline: 1760-1850, Reidel, 82; auth, The Temptations of Evolutionary Ethics, University of California, 92; auth, Finding Order in Nature: The Naturalist Tradition from Linnaeus to E.O. Wilson, Johns Hopkins, 00. **CONTACT ADDRESS** Dept of Hist, Oregon State Univ, Corvallis, OR 97331. **EMAIL** pfarber@orst.edu

FARGE, JAMES KNOX
PERSONAL Born 08/22/1938, Houston, TX **DISCIPLINE** EUROPEAN HISTORY **EDUCATION** Univ St Thomas, BA, 61; Univ Toronto, MA, 69, PhD (hist), 76. **CAREER** Instr hist, Univ St Thomas, 69-70; tutor church hist, Univ St Michael's Col, 73-75; asst prof hist, 76-80, Assoc Prof Hist, Univ St Thomas, 80-, Priest, Congregation of St Basil. **MEMBERSHIPS** Am Soc Reformation Res; Amici Thomae Morae; Cath Hist Asn; Renaissance Soc Am. **RESEARCH** University of Paris; Reformation in France; Erasmus. **SELECTED PUBLICATIONS** Auth, The Genesis of the French Reformation, 1520-1562, 16th Century J, Vol 28, 97; Soldiers of Christ--Preaching in Late Medieval and Reformation France, Cath Hist Rev, Vol 79, 93; The 5th Lateran Council 1512-17--Studies on its Membership, Diplomacy and Proposals for Reform,16th Century J, Vol 25, 94; Bouchet, Jean--La Deploration de Leglise Militante, Moreana, Vol 30, 93; Scholastic Humanism and the Unification of Europe, Vol 1, Theol Stud, Vol 57, 96. **CONTACT ADDRESS** Hist Dept, Univ of St. Thomas, Texas, Houston, TX 77006.

FARIES, MOLLY
DISCIPLINE NORTHERN EUROPEAN ART **EDUCATION** Bryn Mawr Col, PhD. **CAREER** Prof. **RESEARCH** Netherlandish and German painting. **SELECTED PUBLICATIONS** Auth, Art Before Iconoclasm, 86; Northern Renaissance Paintings; The Discovery of Invention, 86. **CONTACT ADDRESS** Dept of History and Art, Indiana Univ, Bloomington, 300 N Jordan Ave, Bloomington, IN 47405. **EMAIL** faries@indiana.edu

FARLEY, BENJAMIN WIRT
PERSONAL Born 08/06/1935, Manila, Philippines, m, 1962, 2 children **DISCIPLINE** HISTORICAL THEOLOGY, PHI-

LOSOPHY **EDUCATION** Davidson Col, AB, 58; Union Theol Sem, Va, BD, 63, ThM, 64, ThD, 76. **CAREER** Pastor, Franklin Presby Church, 64-68 & Cove & Rockfish Presby Churches, 68-71; instr relig, Lees-McRae Col, 73-74; assoc prof to Younts Prof Bible, Religion, and Philos, Erskine Col, 74-. **HONORS AND AWARDS** Excellence in Teaching Awd, Erskine Col, 77, 89, 00. **MEMBERSHIPS** Am Acad Refig; pres 97-99, Calvin Studies Soc. **RESEARCH** Reformation studies; philosophy of religion; literature and religion. **SELECTED PUBLICATIONS** Auth, Erskine Caldwell: Preacher's son and Southern prophet, fall 78 & George W Cable: Presbyterian Romancer, Reformer Bible Teacher, summer 80, J Presby Hist; John Calvin's Sermons on the Ten Commandments, 81 & Calvin's Treatises Against the Anabaptists and the Libertines, 82, Baker Book House; The Hero of St Lo and Other Stories, Attic Press, 82; The Providence of God, Baker Book House, 88; Calvin's Ecclesiastical Advice, Westminster/John Knox Press, 91; In Praise of Virtue, Eerdmans, 95; Mercy Road, Cherokee Publishing Co, 86; Corbin's Rubi-Yacht, Sandlapper Press, 92; auth, Son of the Morning Sky, Univ Press of Am, 99. **CONTACT ADDRESS** 1000 Woodleaf Ct., PO Box 595, Columbia, SC 29212. **EMAIL** aag@infoave.net

FARMER, CRAIG S.
PERSONAL Born 10/02/1961, Urbana, IL, m, 1982, 2 children **DISCIPLINE** HISTORY OF CHRISTIANITY **EDUCATION** Haverford Col, BA, 83; Univ Chicago, MA, 84; Duke Univ, PhD, 92. **CAREER** Asst prof of history and humanities, 93-98; assoc prof of hist and humanities, 98-present, Milligan Col. **MEMBERSHIPS** Amer Soc of Church Hist; Amer Acad of Relig; Medieval Acad of Amer; Sixteenth Century Studies Conf. **RESEARCH** Reformation theology; hist of biblical interpretation. **SELECTED PUBLICATIONS** Auth, Changing Images of the Samaritan Woman in Early Reformed Commentaries on John, Church History, 96; Eucharistic Exhibition and Sacramental Presence in the New Testament Commentaries of Wolfgang Musculus, Wolfgang Musculus, 97; The Gospel of John in the Sixteenth Century: The Johannine Exegesis of Wolfgang Musculus, The Oxford Studies in Historical Theology, Oxford University Press, 97; auth, "Revelation in the History of Exegesis, Leaven 8/1, (00). **CONTACT ADDRESS** Milligan Col, PO Box 500, Milligan College, TN 37682-0500. **EMAIL** csfarmer@milligan.edu

FARMER, EDWARD
PERSONAL Born 05/25/1935, Palo Alto, CA, m, 1958, 2 children **DISCIPLINE** HISTORY **EDUCATION** Stanford Univ, BA, 57; Harvard Univ, MA, 62; PhD, 68. **CAREER** Act instr, Yale Univ, 67-68; prof, Univ Minnesota, 68-. **HONORS AND AWARDS** NDEA Fels; ACLS Fel; Fulbright Fel; Morse Alumni Awd. **MEMBERSHIPS** AAS; AHA; SMS. **RESEARCH** Early modern Chinese history. **SELECTED PUBLICATIONS** Auth, Early Ming Government: The Evolution of Dual Capitals, 76; coauth, Ming History: An Introductory Guide to Research, 94; auth, Zhu Yuanzhang and Early Ming Legislation: The Reordering of Chinese Society Following the Era of Mongol Rule, 95. **CONTACT ADDRESS** Dept History, Univ of Minnesota, Twin Cities, 267 19th Ave, Minneapolis, MN 55455-0499. **EMAIL** efarmer@umn.edu

FARNSWORTH, BEATRICE
PERSONAL Born 02/03/1935, New York, NY, m, 1953, 3 children **DISCIPLINE** RUSSIAN HISTORY **EDUCATION** Ind Univ, AB, 55; Yale Univ, MA, 56, PhD, 59. **CAREER** Instr Russian Hist, Hobart and William Smith Cols, 61-64; from asst prof to assoc prof, 65-68, Assoc Prof to Prof Hist, Wells Col, 68-. **HONORS AND AWARDS** Fel, Radcliffe Inst Independent Studies, 64-65 and 66-67; assoc, Russ Res Ctr, Harvard Univ, 64-65. **MEMBERSHIPS** AHA; Am Asn Advan Slavic Studies **RESEARCH** Russian history. **SELECTED PUBLICATIONS** Auth, Armand, Inessa--Revolutionary and Feminist, Am Hist Rev, Vol 98, 93; Peasant Icons--Representations of Rural People in Late 19th Century Russia, Russ Rev, Vol 53, 94; Between the Fields and the City--Women, Work and Family in Russia, 1861-1914, Russ Hist Histoire Russe, Vol 23, 96; Perestroika and Soviet Women, Russ Rev, Vol 53, 94. **CONTACT ADDRESS** Dept of Hist, Wells Col, Aurora, NY 13026. **EMAIL** bfarnsworth@wells.edu

FARR, DAVID M. L.
PERSONAL Born Vancouver, BC, Canada **DISCIPLINE** HISTORY **EDUCATION** Univ BC, BA, 44; Univ Toronto, MA, 46; Oxford Univ, Dphil, 52. **CAREER** Lectr hist, Dalhousie Univ 46-47; asst prof 47, prof 61, dean of arts 63-69, prof emer hist, Carleton Univ, 87-; dir, Paterson Ctr Int Prog, Carleton Univ 79-85; vis lectr, assoc prof, Univ BC, 53, 57-58; vis assoc prof, Duke Univ, 60. **MEMBERSHIPS** Can Hist Asn; Soc Sci Fedn Can; Can Inst Int Affairs **SELECTED PUBLICATIONS** Auth, The Colonial Office and Canada, 1867-1887, 55; A Church in the Glebe: St. Matthew's, Ottawa, 1898-1988, 88; coauth, Two Democracies, 63; The Canadian Experience, 69; ed Documents on Canadian External Relations, vol 1, 1909-1918, 67. **CONTACT ADDRESS** Dept Hist, Carleton Univ, 1125 Colonel By Dr, 400 Paterson Hall, Ottawa, ON, Canada K1S 5B6.

FARRELL, FRANK
DISCIPLINE CHURCH HISTORY **EDUCATION** Edinburgh Univ, PhD. **CAREER** Instr, Alliance Theol Sem; vis prof, Reformed Theol Sem. **HONORS AND AWARDS** Founding ed, Christianity Today. **RESEARCH** Puritans. **SELECTED PUBLICATIONS** Ed-in-Chief, World Vision mag. **CONTACT ADDRESS** Dept of Church History, Reformed Theol Sem, Florida, 1231 Reformation Dr, Oviedo, FL 32765. **EMAIL** ffarrell@rts.edu

FARRIS, W. WAYNE
DISCIPLINE HISTORY **EDUCATION** Harvard Univ, PhD. **CAREER** Prof, Hist, Univ Tenn. **RESEARCH** Early Japanese history. **SELECTED PUBLICATIONS** Auth, Population, Disease, and Land in Early Japan 645-900, Harvard; Heavenly Warriors: The Evolution of Japan's Military 500-1300, Harvard; Sacred, Texts and Buried Treasures: Issues in Historical Archaeology of Ancient Japan, Univ Hawaii, 98. **CONTACT ADDRESS** Dept of History, Univ of Tennessee, Knoxville, 915 Volunteer Blvd, 6th Fl, Dunford Hall, Knoxville, TN 37996. **EMAIL** wfarris@utk.edu

FASOLT, CONSTANTIN
PERSONAL Born 03/18/1951, Bonn, Germany, m, 1998, 2 children **DISCIPLINE** HISTORY **EDUCATION** Beethoven-Gymnasium, Abitur, 69; Columbia Univ, MA, 76, MPhil, 78, PhD, 81. **CAREER** Preceptor in hist, 79-81, lectr in hist, 81-83, Columbia Univ; Asst Prof of Hist, 83-90, Assoc Prof of Hist, 90-98, visting prof of hist, Univ of Chicago; General Ed of New Perspectives on the past, 93-; visiting prof of hist, Univ of Va, 99-00. **HONORS AND AWARDS** Fel, Inst for European Hist, 85-86; Soc Scis Res Grants, Univ of Chicago, 87-88, 92-93, & 98-99; summer res fel, Max-Planck-Inst for European Legal Hist, 95; fel, Nat Humanities Center, 96-97; fel, John Simon Guggenheim Memorial Found, 96-97; Gerfog August Bilbiothek Wolfenbuttel, Res fel, 00. **MEMBERSHIPS** Am Cusanus Soc; Am Hist Asn; Medieval Acad of Am; Renaissance Soc of Am; Soc for Reformation Res; Conf for the Study of Political Thought . **RESEARCH** History of European political thought; history of historical thought. **SELECTED PUBLICATIONS** Auth, Council and Hierarchy: The Political Thought of William Durant the Younger, Cambridge Stud in Medieval Life and Thought 4th series, Cambridge Univ Press, 91; auth, Visions of Order in the Canonists and Civilians, Handbook of European Hist 1400-1600: Late Middle Ages, Renaissance and Reformation vol 2, Brill, 95; auth, William Durant the Younger and Conciliar Theory, J of the Hist of Ideas, 97; auth, A Question of Right: Hermann Conring's New Discourse on the Roman-German Emperor, Sixteenth Century J, 97; auth, Sovereignty and Heresy, Infinite Boundaries: Order, Disorder, and Reorder in Early Modern German Culture, 98. **CONTACT ADDRESS** Dept of Hist, Univ of Chicago, 1126 E 59th St., Chicago, IL 60637. **EMAIL** icon@midway.uchicago.edu

FASS, PAULA S.
PERSONAL Born 05/22/1947, m, 2 children **DISCIPLINE** AMERICAN HISTORY **EDUCATION** Barnard Col, AB, 67; Columbia Univ, MA, 68, PhD, 74. **CAREER** Asst prof, Rutgers Univ, New Brunswick, 72-74; asst prof, 74-78, assoc prof hist, Univ CA, Berkerley , 78, Rockefeller Hum fel hist, Rockefeller Found, 76-77; Nat Endowment for Hum, 78; fel, Center for Adv Study in Behavioral Sci, Stanford, 91-92; Nat Endowment for Hum Fel, 94-95; prof hist, Univ CA, 87. **HONORS AND AWARDS** Phi Beta Kappa; Chancellor's Prof, Univ CA, Berkeley. **RESEARCH** Am soc hist; family, youth and educ in the US; Am immigration. **SELECTED PUBLICATIONS** Contribr, The writings of Richard Hofstadter, a bibliography, In: The Hofstadter Aegis, Knopf, 74; Television as cultural document: Promises and problems, In: Television as a Cultural Force, Praeger, 76; auth, The Damned and the Beautiful: American Youth in the 1920's, Oxford Univ, 77; The IQ: A Cultural and Historical Framework, Am J Educ, 8/80; Outside In: Minorities and the Transformation of American Education, Oxford Press, 89; The Leopold and the Loeb Case in American Culture, J of American Hiatory, 93; Kidnapped: Child Abduction in America, Oxford Press, 97; Parental Kidnapping: A Sign of Family Disorder; contrib to All Our Families, Oxford Press, 98. **CONTACT ADDRESS** Dept of Hist, Univ of California, Berkeley, 3229 Dwinelle Hall, Berkeley, CA 94720-2551. **EMAIL** psfass@socrates.berkeley.edu

FAUE, ELIZABETH V.
PERSONAL Born 06/26/1956, Minneapolis, MN **DISCIPLINE** HISTORY **EDUCATION** Univ Minn, AB, 79, MA, 85, PhD, 87. **CAREER** Susan B. Anthony fel women's stud and hist, Univ Rochester, 88-90; asst prof, 90-93, Assoc Prof, Wayne State Univ, 93-. **HONORS AND AWARDS** Career Dev Dahir, Wayne State Univ, 95-96; Col Lib Arts teaching award, 98; Bd Gov fac rec, 92; Phi Beta Kappa, 79. **MEMBERSHIPS** AHA; Org Am Historians; Soc Sci Hist Asn. **RESEARCH** Labor, working class hist; U.S., comparative women's history, gender; political hist; 19th, 20th centuries. **SELECTED PUBLICATIONS** Auth, Community of Suffering and Struggle: Women, Men, and the Labor Movement in Minneapolis, 1915-1945, Univ NC Press, 91; ed, Gender and Labor History special issue, Labor Hist 34:2-3, Spring/Summer 93; auth, Outfoxing the Frost: Gender, Community- Based Organization, and the Contemporary American Labor Movement, Working Papers in Labor Studies No. 4, Jan 94; auth, Anti-Heroes of the Working Class, Int Rev Soc Hist 41, Dec 96; auth, Paths of Unionization: Community, Bureaucracy, and Gender in the Minneapolis Labor Movement, 1935-1945, in Work Engendered: Toward a New Labor History, Cornell Univ Press, 91; auth, Writing the Wrongs: Eva McDonald Valesh and the Political Culture of American Labor Reform, 1886-1920, Cornell Univ Press, forthcoming. **CONTACT ADDRESS** Dept Hist, Wayne State Univ, 3094 Faculty/Admn Bldg, Detroit, MI 48202. **EMAIL** efaue@aol.com

FAUL, KARENE TARQUIN
PERSONAL Born 10/16/1934, Pittsburgh, PA, m, 1971, 2 children **DISCIPLINE** ART **EDUCATION** Notre Dame, BA, 66, MA, 68, MFA, 70. **CAREER** prof, 70-, chmn, art dept, 83-, Col of St Rose, NY. **RESEARCH** Screen printing; history of printmaking, art careers, art portfolio for col acceptance. **CONTACT ADDRESS** 432 Western Ave, Albany, NY 12203. **EMAIL** faulk@rosnet.strose.edu

FAULK, ODIE B.
PERSONAL Born 08/26/1933, Winnsboro, TX, m, 1959, 2 children **DISCIPLINE** AMERICAN HISTORY **EDUCATION** Tex Technol Col, BS, 58, MA, 60, PhD, 62. **CAREER** Instr southwest hist, Tex Agr and Mech Col, 62-63; asst ed, Ariz and the West, 63-67; chmn div soc sci, Ariz West Col, 67-68; from assoc prof to prof hist, 68-77 and head dept, 72-77, Okla State Univ; Historian, Nat Cowboy Hall of Fame, Oklahoma City, 77-. **MEMBERSHIPS** AHA; Orgn Am Historians; Western Hist Asn. **RESEARCH** Southwest; Latin America. **SELECTED PUBLICATIONS** Auth, Land of Many Frontiers, 68, The Geronimo Campaign, 69, coauth, North America Divided, 71, auth, Tombstone: Myth and Reality, 72, Destiny Road: The Gila Trail, 73, Crimson Desert: The Indian Wars, 74, The Camel Corps: An Army Experiment, 76, Dodge City, 77, Oxford Univ. **CONTACT ADDRESS** 418 Ramblewood Terr, Edmond, OK 73034.

FAULKNER, RONNIE
PERSONAL Born 09/15/1952, Erwin, NC, s **DISCIPLINE** HISTORY, GOVERNMENT **EDUCATION** Campbell Col, BS, 74; Univ NC, MS, 78; East Carolina Univ, MA, 76; Univ SC, PhD, 83. **CAREER** Instr, TTU, 79-81; Asst Prof, TTU, 81-84; Asst Prof, Glenville State Col, 84-89; Asst Prof to Prof, Campbell Univ, 89-. **HONORS AND AWARDS** Gardner Soc Sci Awd, Campbell Col, 74; Weinefeld Hist Ward, Univ SC, 76; Southeast Libr Asn Wilson Awd, 84; Phi Alpha Theta; Phi Kappa Phi. **MEMBERSHIPS** NC Lit & Hist Asn, Southern Hist Asn, Southeast Libr Asn, NC Libr Asn. **RESEARCH** Southern history and politics, library science, North Carolina history. **SELECTED PUBLICATIONS** Auth, "North Carolina Democrats and Silver Fusion Politics 1892-1896," NC Hist Rev (82); auth, "Taking J C Calhoun to the UN," Polity (83); auth, "UN Ambassador Daniel Patrick Moynihan and the Calhounian Connection," Teaching Polit Sci (85-86); auth, "American Reaction to Hindenburg of the Weimar Republic," The Historian (89); auth, "Jesse Helms and the Legacy of Nathaniel Macon (98). **CONTACT ADDRESS** Dept Hist & Govt, Campbell Univ, Library, PO Box 98, Buies Creek, NC 27506-0098. **EMAIL** faulkner@camel.campbell.edu

FAUSOLD, MARTIN L.
PERSONAL Born 11/11/1921, Irwin, PA, m, 1996, 4 children **DISCIPLINE** POLITICAL HISTORY **EDUCATION** Gettysburg Col, AB, 45; Syracuse Univ, PhD (polit hist Am), 53. **CAREER** From asst prof to prof, State Univ NY Col Cortland, 52-58; prof and chmn dept, 58-65, Prof Hist, State Univ NY Col Geneseo, 65-92, Chmn div soc sci, State Univ NY Col Geneseo, 66-69, Res Found fel and grants-in-aid, 54-79, mem joint awards coun, Res Found, 69, chmn univ awards comt, 70-77, Pres, Suny Facans, 69-72. **MEMBERSHIPS** AHA; Orgn Am Historians. **RESEARCH** American political biography; presidency of Herbert Hoover; 20th century political history. **SELECTED PUBLICATIONS** Auth, Gifford Ponchat, Bull Moose Progressive, 61; ed, The Hoover Presidency, A Reappraisal, 74; auth, James W. Wadsworth Jr, The Geuthemoro from New York, 75; auth, The Presidency of Herbert Clark Hoover, 85; auth, co-ed, The Constitution and the American Presidency, 91. **CONTACT ADDRESS** Dept of Hist, SUNY, Col at Geneseo, Geneseo, NY 14454. **EMAIL** mlfausold@aol.com

FAUST, DREW GILPIN
PERSONAL Born 09/18/1947, New York, NY, 1 child **DISCIPLINE** AMERICAN STUDIES, AMERICAN HISTORY **EDUCATION** Bryn Mawr Col, BA, 68; Univ Pa, MA, 71, PhD, 75. **CAREER** Sr fel, 75-76, asst prof, 76-80, assoc prof am civilization, 80-84, prof, 84-88, chmn dept, 80-83, 84-86, Stanley I Sheerr Prof hist, 88-90, dir, Women's Stud, 96-, Annenberg Prof hist, 89-, Univ PA; Soc Sci Res Coun training fel, 75; Am Coun Learned Soc grant-in-aid, 78; Nat Endowment Humanities fel, 79-80. **HONORS AND AWARDS** Spencer Found Awd, 76; AACLS grant in Aid, 78; NEH Fel, indep res, 79-80; Lindback Awd for Dist tchng, 82; Jules F. Landry Awd, 82; assoc fel, Stanford Hum Ctr, Stanford Univ, 83-84; Prize of Soc of Hist of the Early Amer Rep, 83; Charles S Sydnor Prize of

the Southern Hist Assn, 84; Amer Coun of Learned Soc Fel, 86; Guggenheim Fel, 86; Walter Lynwood Fleming Lecturer La St Univ, 87; /Soc of Amer Hist, 93; Amer Acad of Arts & Sci, 96; Ira Abrams Awd for Dist tchng, Univ Pa, 96; Mothers of Invention - NY Times Notable Bk of Year, 96; Avery Craven Prize of the Org of Amer Hist, 96; Francis Parkman Prize, Soc of Amer Hist, 96. **MEMBERSHIPS** Orgn Am Historians; Southern Hist Assn. **RESEARCH** American South, American belief systems. **SELECTED PUBLICATIONS** Auth, A Sacred Circle, Johns Hopkins Univ Press, 77; auth, James Henry Hammon and the Old South, LSU Press, 82; auth, The Creation of Confederate Nationalism, LSU, 88; auth, Southern Stories, Univ of MO Press, 92; auth, Mothers of Invention: Women of the Salveholding South in the American Civil War, UNC Press, 96. **CONTACT ADDRESS** Dept of Hist, Harvard Univ, 10 Garden St, Cambridge, MA 02138. **EMAIL** dfaust@sas.upenn.edu

FAUSZ, JOHN FREDERICK
PERSONAL Born 11/28/1947, Covington, KY, m, 1981, 1 child **DISCIPLINE** HISTORY **EDUCATION** Thomas More Col, AB, 70; Col William and Mary Va, MA, 71; PhD, 77. **CAREER** Asst Ed, Complete Work of Capt. John Smith, Inst of Early Am Hist and Cult, Williamsburgh, Va, 74-76; NEH Predoctoral Fel, D'Arcy McNickle Center for Hist of the Am Indian, The Newberry Libr Chicago, 76-77; Mellon/NHPRC Ed Fel in Documentary Editing, The Papers of Benjamin Henry Latrobe, Md Hist Soc Baltimore, 77-78; Asst Prof to Prof, St. Mary's Col of Md, St. Mary's City, 78-91; Honors Prog Dir, St. Mary's Col of Md, 85-91; First Dean, The Pierre Laclede Honors Col, Univ of Missouri - St. Louis, 91-96; Tenured Assoc Prof, Univ of Missouri - St. Louis, 91-. **HONORS AND AWARDS** Phi Alpha Theta, 68; Woodrow Wilson Designated Fel, William and Mary, 70-71; Nat Defense Educ Act Fel, William and Mary, 71-74; First Prize, Grad Student Essay Contest, Southern Conf on Brit Studies, 72; Phi Beta Kappa, 76; Nat Endowment for the Humanities Summer Sem Grant, 80; Nat Endowment for the Humanities Res Fel for Col teachers, Inst of Early Am Hist and Cult, Williamsburgh Va, 82-93; Willaim M.E. Rachal Prize, Va Hist Soc, 91; funded "Am Mirror" Speaker, Missouri Humanities Coun, 93-99. **MEMBERSHIPS** Va Hist Soc, Missouri Hist Soc, , Inst of Early Am Hist and Cult. **RESEARCH** 17th Chesapeake Ethnohistory, English Colonization, American Fur Trades, 17th and 18th centuries, Tobacco and Smoking. **SELECTED PUBLICATIONS** Coauth, "A Letter of Advice to the Governor of Virginia, 1624," William and Mary Quart 34-1 (Jan 77): 104-129; auth, "Fighting 'Fire' with Firearms: The Anglo-Powhatan Arms Race in Early Virginia," Am Indian Cult and Res J (UCLA) 3-1(80): 33-50, and in The American Indian: Past and Present, ed. Roger Nichols (NY: Alfred Knopf), 61-72; auth, "Opechancanough: Indian Resistance Leader," in Struggle and Survival in Colonial America, ed. David Sweet and Gary Nash (Berkeley: Univ of Calif, 81), 21-37, and in American Indian: Past and Present, ed. Roger Nichols (McGraw Hill, 99); auth, "Patterns of Anglo-Indian Aggression and Accommodation Along the Mid-Atlantic Coast, 1584-1634," in Cultures in Contact: The Impact of European Contacts on Native American Cultural Institutions, AD 1000-1800, ed. William Fitzhugh (Smithsonian Inst Press, 85), 225-268; asst ed, The Complete Works of Captain John Smith, ed. Philip L. Barbour (Univ of NC Press for the Inst of Early Am Hist and Cult, 86); auth, "Merging and Emerging Worlds: Amglo-Indian Interest Groups and the Development of the 17-century Chesapeake," in Colonial Chesapeake Society, ed. Lois Green Carr, et al (Univ of NC Press for the Inst of Early Am Hist and Cult, 89), 47-98; auth, "'An Abundance of Blood Shed on Both Sides': England's First Indian War, 1609-1614," Va Magazine of Hist and Biog 98-1 (Jan 90): 3-56; auth, "Pocahontas," in Encyclopedia of North American Indians, ed. Frederick E. Hoxie (Boston and NY: Houghton Mifflin Comp, 96), 490-492; auth, "'Engaged in Enterprises Pregnant with Terror': George Washington's Formative Years among the Indians," in George Washington and the Virginia Backcountry, ed. Warren R. Hofstra (Madison House Press, 98), 115-155; auth, "Sir Samuel Argall," "Richard Bennett," "John Berkeley," in Dictionary of Virginia Biography Vol I (Richmong: Libr of Va, 99). **CONTACT ADDRESS** Univ of Missouri, St. Louis, 8001 Natural Bridge Rd, Saint Louis, MO 63121. **EMAIL** sjffaus@umslvma.umsl.edu

FAVIS, ROBERTA SMITH
DISCIPLINE ART HISTORY **EDUCATION** Bryn Mawr Col, BA; Univ Pa, PhD. **CAREER** Assoc prof, 85-. **RESEARCH** 19th and 20th century American painting. **SELECTED PUBLICATIONS** Auth, pubs on historical and contemporary art. **CONTACT ADDRESS** Dept of Art, Stetson Univ, De Land, Unit 8378, DeLand, FL 32720-3771.

FAXON, ALICIA CRAIG
PERSONAL Born 07/21/1931, New York, NY, m, 1953, 2 children **DISCIPLINE** ART HISTORY **EDUCATION** Vassar Col, BA, 52; Radcliffe Col, MA, 53; Boston Univ, BA, art hist, 75; PhD, 79. **CAREER** Lectr, 74-77, New England Schl Art & Design; asst prof, prof, 78-93, Simmons Col; ed, Rhode Island, Art New England, 93-98. **HONORS AND AWARDS** Hon degree, Simmons Col, 98; Honoree W CA, 96; Phi Beta Kappa, Vassar Col, award for art criticism, Art New England. **MEMBERSHIPS** Col Art Assn; Victorian Soc; Hist of British Art; SE Col Art Assn. **RESEARCH** Women artists; 19th century Eng & French art; Pre-Raphaelite art. **SELECTED PUBLICATIONS** Co-ed, Pre-Raphaelite Art in its European context, Assoc Univ Press, 95; auth, Dante Gabriel Rossetti, NY Abbeville, 94; auth, introduction, The Letters of Dane Gabriel and William Michael Rossetti, Ellen Clarke Bertrand Lib ed ser, Bucknell Univ, 95; ed & contr, Pilgrims & Pioneers: New England Women in the Arts, NY Midmarch, 87; auth, Jean-Louis Forain: Artist, Humanist, Realist, Wash DC: Intl Exhib Found, 82; auth, Jean-Louis Forain: A Catalogue Raisonne of the Prints, NY Garland, 82; art, Annette Messager, Art New Eng, 98; art, The Sculpture of B. Amore, Sculpture mag, 97; art, Art Collecting in Newport, Art New Eng, 97. **CONTACT ADDRESS** 2 Pond Cir, Jamaica Plain, MA 02130.

FAY, MARY ANN
DISCIPLINE HISTORY **EDUCATION** Georgetown Univ, PhD, 93. **CAREER** Prof, Va Mil Inst, 94-; adv, Model Arab League Club; Fulbright grant, 95; NEH-Amer Res Center grant, Egypt, 96. **SELECTED PUBLICATIONS** Publ on, women in Ottoman and Islamic society. **CONTACT ADDRESS** Dept of History, Virginia Military Inst, Lexington, VA 24450.

FAY, PETER WARD
PERSONAL Born 12/03/1924, Paris, France, m, 1957, 5 children **DISCIPLINE** EUROPEAN & ASIAN HISTORY **EDUCATION** Harvard Univ, BA, 47; Oxford Univ, BA, 49; Harvard Univ, PhD, 54. **CAREER** Instr hist, Williams Col, 51-55; Vis prof, Indian Inst Technol, Kanpur, 64-66; from asst prof to assoc prof, 55-70, Prof Hist, Calif Inst Technol, 70-97; prof emer, 97- . **HONORS AND AWARDS** Rhodes Scholar; 47-49; Silver medal, Commonwealth Club of Calif, 76; Am Coun Learned Soc res grant, 77; Am Inst Indian Studies res grant, 88. **MEMBERSHIPS** AHA; Asn Asian Studies. **RESEARCH** Britain in China, British India. **SELECTED PUBLICATIONS** Auth, The Opium War, 1840-42, Univ NC, 75, 97; auth, The Forgotten Army: India's Armed Struggle for Independence 1942-45, Univ Mich, 93. **CONTACT ADDRESS** Div of Humanities and Soc Sci, California Inst of Tech, Humanities, 228-77, Pasadena, CA 91125. **EMAIL** pfay@hss.caltech.edu

FEARS, J. RUFUS
PERSONAL Born 03/07/1945, Atlanta, GA, m, 1966, 2 children **DISCIPLINE** CLASSICS; HISTORY **EDUCATION** Emory Univ, BA, 66; Harvard Univ, MA, 67, PhD, 71. **CAREER** Asst Prof Classical Lang, Tulane Univ, 71-72; from Asst Prof to Prof Hist, Ind Univ, 72-86; Prof Classics and Dept Chair, Boston Univ, 86-90; Prof Classics, 90-92, G.T. and Libby Blankenship Prof Classics, Univ Okla, 92-, Dean Col Arts & Sci, 90-92. **HONORS AND AWARDS** Woodrow Wilson Fel, 66-67; Danforth Fel, 66-71; Harvard Prize Fel, 66-71; Sheldon Traveling Fel, 69-71; Fel of the Am Acad in Rome, 69-71; Howard Found Fel, 77-78; Guggenheim Fel, 76-77; Alexander von Humboldt Fel, 77-78, 80-81; Distinguished Fac Res Lectr, Ind Univ, 80; NEH Fel, 86; Woodrow Wilson Ctr Fel, 86; ACLS Fel, 86; Nat Humanities Ctr Fel, 86; Wash Univ Ctr Hist Freedom Fel, 89-90; Judah P. Benjamin Nat Merit Awd, 96; 15 awards for outstanding teaching, 76-00; Univ of Okla Prof of Year, 96, 99. **MEMBERSHIPS** Phi Beta Kappa; Golden Key Nat Honor Soc; Am Philol Asn; Archaeol Inst Am; Classical Asn Middle West and South; Vergilian Soc; Soc for Classical Tradition. **RESEARCH** Ancient history; history of freedom. **SELECTED PUBLICATIONS** Auth, Atlantis and the Myth of the Minoan Thalassocracy, Atlantis: Fact of Fiction, 78; Princeps A Diis Electus, 77; The Cult of Jupiter and Roman Imperial Ideology, 81; The Theology of Victory at Rome, 81; The Cult of Virtues and Roman Imperial Ideology, 81; Roman Liberty, 80; Gottesgnadentum, Reallexikon fur Antike und Christentum XI, 81; Herrscherkult, Reallexikon fur Antike und Christentum XIV, 88; Selected Writings of Lord Acton (3 vols), 85-88; Michael Rostovtzeff, Classical Scholarship: A Biographical Encyclopedia, 90; Antiquity: The Model of Rome, An Uncertain Legacy: Essays in Pursuit of Liberty, 97; Natural Law: The Legacy of Greece and Rome, Common Truths, 00; The Lessons of Rome for Our Own Day, Preparing America's Foreign Policy for the 21st Century, 99. **CONTACT ADDRESS** Dept of Classics, Univ of Oklahoma, Norman, OK 73019. **EMAIL** jrfears@ou.edu

FECHNER, ROGER J.
PERSONAL Born 01/20/1937, Springfield, MN, m, 1960, 2 children **DISCIPLINE** HISTORY **EDUCATION** Hamline Univ, BA, 59; Boston Univ, MA, 60; Univ Iowa, PhD, 74. **CAREER** Asst prof, Albion Col, 63-70; from asst prof to prof, Adrian Col, 70-00. **HONORS AND AWARDS** Woodrow Wilson Fel, 59-60 & 62-63; NEH Fel, Univ Mich, 75-76; NEH Fel, Univ Wis, 78; NEH Fel, Stanford, 84; Lilly Found Fel, 91-94. **MEMBERSHIPS** Am Hist Asn, Am Soc for Eighteenth-Century Studies, Eighteenth-Century Scottish Studies Soc, Int Soc for Eighteenth-Century Studies, Orgn of Am Historians. **RESEARCH** The American Enlightenment, The Scottish Enlightenment, The American Revolution, Eighteenth-Century Scottish-American Cultural and Intellectual History, Historiography and Philosophy of History. **SELECTED PUBLICATIONS** Auth, The Godly and Virtuous Republic of John Witherspoon; auth, Adam Smith and American Academic Moral Philosophers and Philosophy in the Age of Enlightenment and Revolution; auth, Burns and American Liberty; auth, John Witherspoon. **CONTACT ADDRESS** Dept of History, Adrian Col, 110 S Madison, Adrian, MI 49221.

FEE, ELIZABETH
PERSONAL Born 12/11/1946, Belfast, Northern Ireland **DISCIPLINE** HISTORY AND PHILOSOPHY OF SCIENCE **EDUCATION** Cambridge Univ, BA, 68, MA, 75; Princeton Univ, MA, 71, PhD (hist and philos sci), 78. **CAREER** Teaching asst hist med, Princeton Univ, 71-72; instr hist sci, State Univ NY Binghamton, 72-74; archivist, 74-78, asst prof, Sch Health Serv, 74-78, Asst Prof Hist Publ Health, Sch Hyg Publ Health, Johns Hopkins Univ, 78-, Ed consult, Int J Health Serv, 79-; consult, Col Allied Health Sci, Thomas Jefferson Univ, 79-80. **MEMBERSHIPS** Am Asn Hist Med; Hist Sci Soc; AHA; Berkshire Conf Women's Hist; Am Publ Health Asn. **RESEARCH** History of public health research and practice; history of Johns Hopkins School of Hygiene and Public Health; women and science and women and health. **SELECTED PUBLICATIONS** Auth, The sexual politics of Victorian social anthropology, Feminist Studies, 1: 23-29 & In: Clio's Consciousness Raised: New Perspectives on the History of Women, Harper & Row, 74; Science and the woman problem: Historical perspectives, In: Sex Differences: Social and Biological Perspectives, Doubleday-Anchor, 76; Women and health care: A comparison of theories, Int J Health Serv, 5: 397-415, Nursing Digest, 4: 74-78 & In: Health and Medical Care in the United States: A Critical Analysis, Baywood, 77; Psychology, sexuality and social control in Victorian England, Soc Sci Quart, 58: 632-646; Nineteenth century craniology: The study of the female skull, Bull Hist Med, 53: 415-433; coauth (with Michael Wallace), The history and politics of birth control: A review essay, Feminist Studies, 5: 201-215; auth, Is feminismm a threat to scientific objectivity?, J Col Sci Teaching, Vol 9, No 2; ed, Women and Health, Baywood Publ Co, 82. **CONTACT ADDRESS** Sch of Hygiene and Publ Health, Johns Hopkins Univ, Baltimore, 3400 N Charles St, Baltimore, MD 21205.

FEHL, PHILIPP P.
PERSONAL Born 05/09/1920, Vienna, Austria, m, 1945 **DISCIPLINE** HISTORY OF ART **EDUCATION** Stanford Univ, BA, 47, MA, 48; Univ Chicago, PhD (class sculpture), 63. **CAREER** Lectr humanities, Univ Col, Chicago, 50-52; instr, Univ Kansas City, 52-54; from asst prof to assoc prof art, Univ Nebr, 54-63; from assoc prof to prof hist of art, Univ NC, Chapel Hill, 63-69; Prof Hist of Art, Univ Ill, Urbana Champaign, 69-, Res fel, Warburg Inst, Univ London, 57-58; bk rev ed, Art Bull, 65-69; art Hist in residence, Am Acad Rome, 67; assoc, Ctr Advan Studies, Univ Ill, 70-71 and 81-82; fel, Nat Endowment for Humanities, 77-78; vis prof, Univ Tel Aviv, 82. **MEMBERSHIPS** Col Art Asn Am; Renaissance Soc Am; Am Soc Aesthet; Am Inst Archaeol; Int Survey Jewish Monuments (pres, 77). **RESEARCH** Renaissance painting and sculpture; history of the classical tradition in art; American art. **SELECTED PUBLICATIONS** Auth, Touchstones of Art and Art Criticism, Rubens and the Work of Junius, Franciscus, J Aesthet Educ, Vol 30, 96. **CONTACT ADDRESS** Dept of Art, Univ of Illinois, Urbana-Champaign, Champaign, IL 61820.

FEHRENBACH, HEIDE
DISCIPLINE HISTORY **EDUCATION** Rutgers Univ, AB, 79, PhD, 90. **CAREER** Assoc prof. **HONORS AND AWARDS** Co-winner, Biennial Bk Prize, AHA Conf Group Cent Europ Hist. **RESEARCH** Modern German history; Modern European cultural history; film; gender. **SELECTED PUBLICATIONS** Auth, Cinema in Democratizing Germany: Reconstructing National Identity after Hitler; coeditor of Transactions, Transgressions, Transformations: American Culture in Western Europe and Japan, (00). **CONTACT ADDRESS** Dept History, Emory Univ, 221 Bowden Hall, 561 Kilgo Cir, Atlanta, GA 30322-1950. **EMAIL** hfehren@emory.edu

FEHRENBACHER, DON EDWARD
PERSONAL Born 08/21/1920, Sterling, IL, m, 1944, 3 children **DISCIPLINE** AMERICAN HISTORY **EDUCATION** Cornell Col, AB, 46, Univ Chicago, AM, 48, PhD, 51. **CAREER** Asst prof hist, Coe Col, 49-53; from asst prof to prof, 53-66, Coe Prof Hist, Stanford Univ, 66-, Guggenheim fel, 59-60; Harmsworth prof Am hist, Oxford Univ, 67-68; Harrison prof hist, Col William and Mary, 73-74; Nat Endowment for Humanities fel, 75-76; Commonwealth Fund lectr, Univ Col London and Walter Lynwood Fleming lectr, La State Univ, 78. **HONORS AND AWARDS** Pulitzer Prize, 79; Seagram lectr, Univ Toronto, 81; dhl, cornell col, 70 and lincoln col, 81. **MEMBERSHIPS** AHA; Orgn Am Hists; Southern Hist Asn; Am Acad Arts and Sci; Soc Hists Early Am Repub. **RESEARCH** Nineteenth century United States; Civil War era; political and constitutional history. **SELECTED PUBLICATIONS** Auth, The Making of a Myth--Lincoln and the Vicr Presidential Nomination in 1864, Civil War Hist, Vol 41, 95. **CONTACT ADDRESS** PO Box 4024, Stanford, CA 94305.

FEINBERG, HARVEY MICHAEL
PERSONAL Born 04/17/1938, Hartford, CT, m, 1962, 2 children **DISCIPLINE** WEST AFRICAN & SOUTH AFRICAN HISTORY **EDUCATION** Yale Univ, BA, 60; Am Univ, MA, 63; Boston Univ, PhD(hist), 69. **CAREER** Arch asst, Libr Cong, 61-62; asst prof, 69-74, assoc prof, 74-79, Prof African Hist, Southern Conn State Univ, 79-. **HONORS AND AWARDS** Am Philos Soc, res fel Netherlands, summer 72 &

4-7/77, res fel South Africa, 2-6/85 & 8-11/92; postdoctoral fel, Dept Hist, Yale Univ, 76-77; vis fel, Yale Univ, 90-91; Fulbright-Hays Seminars Abroad fel, summer 91; assoc fel, South African Res Prog, Yale Univ, 93-94; National Endowment for the Humanities Fellowship, 99-00. **MEMBERSHIPS** African Studies Asn; Conn Acad Arts & Sci (vpres, 89-); Ghana Studies Coun; South African Hist Soc; Conn Coord Comt Promotion Hist **RESEARCH** Race and the Land: African challenges to land policy in South Africa, 1905-1936. **SELECTED PUBLICATIONS** Auth, Africans and Europeans in West Africa: Elminans and Dutchmen on the Gold Coast during the Eighteenth Century, Am Philos Soc, 89; art, The Natives Land Act of 1913 in South Africa: Politics, Race and Segregation in the Early 20th Century, Int J African Hist Studies, XXVI, 1, 93; art, South Africa and Land Ownership: What's in a deed?, in: History in Africa, 95; art, Pre-apartheid African Land Ownership and the Implication for the Current Restitution Debate in South Africa, Historia, 11/95. **CONTACT ADDRESS** Dept of Hist, So Connecticut State Univ, 501 Crescent St, New Haven, CT 06515-1330. **EMAIL** feinberg@scsu.ctstateu.edu

FEINGOLD, HENRY L.
PERSONAL Born 02/06/1931, Germany, m, 1954, 2 children **DISCIPLINE** UNITED STATES DIPLOMACY & AMERICAN JEWISH HISTORY **EDUCATION** Brooklyn Col, BA, 53, MA, 54; NYork Univ, PhD, 66. **CAREER** Tchr hist, Sec Schs, NY, 53-65; lectr, City Univ NY, 67-68; from instr to assoc prof hist, 68-76, grad ctr, 75, prof hist, Baruch Col, City Univ NY, 76-, Prof Emeritus, 98-, Dir, Jewish Resource Center, Baruch Col, CUNY; Lectr exten prog in Ger, Univ MD, 55-56; adj prof, Stern Col, Yeshiva Univ, 71-73; adj lectr, Inst Advan Study Hum Jewish Theol Inst Am, 73-76. **HONORS AND AWARDS** Leon Jolson Awd for best bk on Holocaust, 77; Presidential Awd for Excellence in Scholarship, Baruch Col, May 86; Lee Friedman Awd in Am Jewish Hist, 94; Morim Awd, Jewish Tchr(s) Asn, 95. **MEMBERSHIPS** Labor Zionist Alliance (pres, 89-92); Jewish Community Relations Coun (board of dir); World Zionist Org (gen coun); Jewish Agency for Israel (gen assembly); Am Zionist Movement (cabinet); dir, Jewish Resource Ctr, Baruch Col. **RESEARCH** Holocaust. **SELECTED PUBLICATIONS** Auth, The Politics of Rescue: The Roosevelt Administration and the Holocaust, 1938-1945, Rutgers Univ Press, 70; Zion in America: The Jewish Experience from Colonial Times to the Present, Twayne, 74; A Midrash on the History of American Jewry, NY State Univ Press, 82; A Time for Searching: Entering the Mainstream, 1920-1945, Johns Hopkins Univ Press, 92; Bearing Witness: How American and its Jews Responded to the Holocaust, Univ Syracuse Press, 95; Lest Memory Cease, Finding Meaning in the American Jewish Past, Univ Syracuse Press, 96. **CONTACT ADDRESS** Baruch Col, CUNY, 17 Lexington Ave, New York, NY 10010-5518. **EMAIL** jrc@baruch.cuny.edu

FELDHERR, ANDREW
DISCIPLINE ROMAN CULTURAL STUDIES **EDUCATION** Princeton Univ, AB, 85; U C Berkeley, PhD, 91. **CAREER** Asst prof, Princeton Univ. **RESEARCH** Livy, Ovid, Vergil, Roman cultural studies. **SELECTED PUBLICATIONS** Auth, Spectacle and Society in Livy's History. **CONTACT ADDRESS** Dept of Class, Princeton Univ, 109 E Pyne, Princeton, NJ 08544. **EMAIL** feldherr@princeton.edu

FELDMAN, GERALD DONALD
PERSONAL Born 04/24/1937, New York, NY, m, 1958 **DISCIPLINE** MODERN EUROPEAN HISTORY **EDUCATION** Columbia Col, BA, 58; Harvard Univ, MA, 59, PhD (hist), 64. **CAREER** From asst prof to assoc prof, 63-70, Prof Hist, Univ Calif, Berkeley, 70-. **HONORS AND AWARDS** Newcomen Prize, Newcomen Soc, 76; Soc Sci Res Coun fac res grant, 66-67; Am Coun Learned Soc fel, 66-67 and 70-71; Guggenheim fel, 73-74; Nat Endowment for Humanities fel, 77-78; comt mem Western Europe, Soc Sci Res Coun, 74-; mem, Historische Kommission for Berlin, 80-; Lehrman fel, 81-82; German Marshal fel, 81-82; res prof, Historisches Kolleg Munchen, 82-83; Univ of Calif Humanities Res Fel, 92; Woodrow Wilson Ctr Fel, 91-92; Bk Prize, Am Historical Asn, 95; DAAD Bk Prize of the Ger Studies Asn, 95; Co-winner, Financial Times/Booz-Allen & Hamilton Bus-Bk Awd, 95; Chancellor's Professorship, 97-00; Karl W. Deutsch Guest Prof, Wissenschaftszentrum Berlin, 97; Berlin Prize Fel, Am Acad in Berlin, 98-99; Commander's Cross of the Order of Merit of the Fed Republic of Ger, 00. **MEMBERSHIPS** AHA. **RESEARCH** Modern German social and economic history, European history, international relations. **SELECTED PUBLICATIONS** Co-ed, The Evolution of Modern Financial Institutions in the Twentieth Century, Proceedings, Eleventh International Economic History Congress, Milan, 94; co-ed, The Evolution of Financial Institutions and Markets in Twentieth-Century Europe, 95; co-ed, How to Write the History of a Bank, Aldershot, 95; co-ed, The Treaty of Versailles, A Reassessment after 75 Year, 98; auth, "War Aims, State Intervention, and Business Leadership in Germany: The Case of Hugo Stinnes," Great War, Total War, Combat and Mobilization on the Western Front, 1914-1918 (00): 349-368; auth, "The French Policies of Hugo Stinnes," in Deutschland und Frankreich, Vom Konflikt zur Aussohnung, Die Gestaltung der westeuropaischen Sicherheit 1914-1963 (00): 43-64; auth, "Mobilizing Economies for War," The Great War and the Twentieth Century (01): 21-29. **CONTACT ADDRESS** Dept of Hist, Univ of California, Berkeley, 3229 Dwinelle Hall, Berkeley, CA 94720-2551. **EMAIL** gfeld@socrates.berkeley.edu

FELIX, DAVID
PERSONAL Born 12/26/1921, New Britain, CT, m, 1966 **DISCIPLINE** MODERN HISTORY **EDUCATION** Trinity Col, Conn, BA, 42; Univ Chicago, MA, 47; Univ Paris, cert econ, Faculte de droit, 55; Columbia Univ, PhD (intel, soc & polit hist), 70. **CAREER** Reporter, Pittsburgh Sun-Tel, 47-50; info officer, US Econ Mission, Austria, 50-54; corresp, Int News Serv, Paris, 55-56; managing ed, Challenge, Mag Econ Affairs, NY Univ, 57-60; financial writer, 60-64; from instr to assoc prof, 65-74, Prof Hist, Bronx Community Col, 74-91, Grad Ctr, City Univ of NY, 81-91, Prof Emer Hist, 91- . **HONORS AND AWARDS** Am Coun Learned Socs res grant, 70; fac res award, City Univ NY, 70 & 71; Nat Endowment Humanities sr fel, 72-73; guest lectr, London Sch Econ, 73-74; consult on grants, Nat Endowment Humanities, 75-80; dir, Global Hist Curric Proj, City Univ New York, 81-82. **MEMBERSHIPS** AHA; AEA; Royal Econ Soc. **RESEARCH** Intellectual and political history; Marxism; Keynesianism. **SELECTED PUBLICATIONS** Auth, The sense of Coexistence, Am Scholar, winter 62-63; Protest: Sacco-Vanzetti and the Intellectuals, Ind Univ, 65; Walther Rathenau and the Weimar Republic: The Politics of Reparations, John Hopkins, 71; Reparations Reconsidered with a Vengeance, Cent Europ Hist, 6/71; Walther Rathenau: The Bad Thinker and His Uses, 1/75 & Access to Germany, 4/78, Europ Studies Rev; Marx as Politician, Southern Ill Univ, 83; auth, Biography of an Idea: John Maynard Keynes and The General Theory, Transaction, 95; auth, Marx and Keymes: The Primacy of Politics, Biography, 95; auth, Keynes: A Critical Life, Greenwood, 99. **CONTACT ADDRESS** 49 E 86th St, New York, NY 10028. **EMAIL** dflixx@aol.com

FELLER, DANIEL
PERSONAL Born 10/19/1950, Washington, DC, m, 1992, 1 child **DISCIPLINE** HISTORY **EDUCATION** Reed Col, BA, 72; Univ Wi., MA, 74, PhD, 81. **CAREER** Asst prof, Northland Col, 80-83; asst ed, The Papers of Andrew Jackson, 83-86; asst to full prof, Univ Nmex, 86-. **MEMBERSHIPS** Soc for Hist of the Early Amer Repub; Orgn of Amer Hist; Asn for Doc Ed; Southern Hist Asn. **RESEARCH** American political history; Jacksonian-antebellum and Civil War eras; Old northwest. **SELECTED PUBLICATIONS** Auth, "The Public Lands in Jacksonian Politics, University of Wisconsin Press, 84; coed, "The Paper of Andrew Jackson, 96; auth, "Politics and Society: Toward a Jascksonian Synthesis," Journal of the Early Republic, 90; auth, "The Jacsonian Promise: American, 1815-1840, Johns Hopkins University Press, 95. **CONTACT ADDRESS** Dept. of History, Univ of New Mexico, Albuquerque, Albuquerque, NM 87131-1181. **EMAIL** dfeller@unm.edu

FELLMAN, MICHAEL
PERSONAL Born 02/28/1943, Madison, WI **DISCIPLINE** HISTORY **EDUCATION** Univ Mich, 65; Northwestern Univ, PhD, 69. **CAREER** Asst prof to assoc prof, 68-83, prof Hist, Simon Fraaser Univ, 83-; Fulbright prof, Univ Haifa (Israel), 80-81; vis fel, Shelby Cullom Davis Ctr Hist Stud, Princeton Univ, 82-84; Marta Sutton Weeks sr res fel, 92-93, vis prof, Stanford Univ, 93. **MEMBERSHIPS** Can Asn Am Stud (pres, 81-83); Am Hist Asn; Orgn Am Hist; Southern Hist Asn. **SELECTED PUBLICATIONS** Auth, Inside War: The Guerilla Conflict in Missouri during the American Civil War, New York: Oxford Univ Press, 89; auth, R. Love, The Rise and Fall of Jesse James, (1926), Linton: Univ of Nebraska Press, 90; auth, "Bloody Sunday and News from Nowhere," Journal of the William Morris Society, 8, (90): 9-18; auth, "Inside Wars: The Cultural Crisis of Warfare and the Values of Ordinary People," Australian Journal of Am Studies 10, (91): 1-10; auth, "Women and Guerilla Warfare," in Divided Houses: Gender and the Civil War, eds. Catherine Clinton and Nina Silber, (Oxford Univ Press, 92): 147-65; auth, Citizen Sherman: A Life of William Tecumseh Sherman, New York, Random House, 95; auth, "At the Nihilist Edge: Reflections on Guerrilla Warfare during the American Civil War," in On the road to Total War: The American Civil War nad the German Wars of Unification, 1861-1871, eds. Stig Forster and Jeorg Nagler, (Cambridge: Cambridge Univ Press-German Historical Institute, 96). **CONTACT ADDRESS** Dept of History, Simon Fraser Univ, Burnaby, BC, Canada V5A 1S6. **EMAIL** michael_fellman@sfu.ca

FELSTINER, MARY LOWENTHAL
PERSONAL Born 02/19/1941, PA, 2 children **DISCIPLINE** COMPARATIVE HISTORY **EDUCATION** Harvard Univ, BA, 63; Columbia Univ, MA, 66; Stanford Univ, PhD, 71. **CAREER** Asst prof, 73-76, assoc prof, 76-81, prof, 81- , hist, San Francisco State Univ; vis prof Stanford Univ, 97; vis prof UC Santa Cruz, 98. **HONORS AND AWARDS** Junion Phi Beta Kappa, 62; For Area Fel, 64-66; Hubert Herring Awd, 74; Am Coun Learned Soc Fel, 90; Am Hist Asn Prize in Women's Hist, 95. **MEMBERSHIPS** Am Hist Asn; Western Asn of Women Hist. **RESEARCH** Colonial Latin Am; women's history; Nazi period; history of medicine. **SELECTED PUBLICATIONS** Coed & contribr, Chanzeaux: A Village in Anjou, Harvard Univ, 66; auth, Kinship politics in the Chilean independence movement, Hispanic Am Hist Rev, 2/76; auth, Family Metaphors: The Language of an Independent Revolution, Comp Stud in Soc and Hist, 83; auth, Seeing the Second Sex Through the Second Wave, Feminist Stud, 80; auth, Alois Brunner: Eichmann's Best Tool, Simon Wiesenthal Annual, 86; auth, Taking Her Life/History, Life/Lines, 88; auth, Charlotte Salomon's Inward-Turning Testimony, in, Shapes of memory, 93; auth, To Paint Her Life: Charlotte Salomon in the Nazi Era, Harper Collins, 94, Univ of Cal Press, 97. **CONTACT ADDRESS** Dept of History, San Francisco State Univ, 1600 Holloway Ave, San Francisco, CA 94132.

FELTON, CRAIG
DISCIPLINE ART HISTORY **EDUCATION** St Vincent Col, BA; Univ Pittsburgh, MA, PhD. **CAREER** Dept ch; taught at, Southern Methodist Univ & TX Christian Univ; res, Kimbell Art Mus. **HONORS AND AWARDS** Res on, Hispano-Italian painter, Jusepe de Ribera, led to the 1st exhibition of a selection of, Spagnoletto's works, and the exhibition catalogue: Jusepe Ribera, 1591-1652. **RESEARCH** Italian and Span painting of the first half of the 17th century, with an emphasis on Naples. **SELECTED PUBLICATIONS** Publ on, res interest. **CONTACT ADDRESS** Dept of Art, Smith Col, Hillyer Hall 314, Northampton, MA 01063. **EMAIL** cfelton@sophia.smith.edu

FERGUSON, ARTHUS BOWLES
PERSONAL Born 10/15/1913, Canada, m, 1942 **DISCIPLINE** HISTORY **EDUCATION** Univ Western Ont, BA, 35; Cornell Univ, PhD (hist), 39. **CAREER** From instr to assoc prof, 39-60, Prof Hist, Duke Univ, 60-, Fund Advan Educ fel, 54-55; Guggenheim Found fel, 71-72; assoc ed, J Medieval and Renaissance Studies, 71-. **MEMBERSHIPS** AHA; Renaissance Soc Am; Conf Brit Studies; fel Royal Hist Soc. **RESEARCH** English Renaissance; late medieval English culture; historiography. **SELECTED PUBLICATIONS** Auth, Indian Summer of English Chivalry, 60 & The Articulate Citizen and the English Renaissance, 65, Duke Univ; Reginald Pecock and the Renaissance Sense of History, Studies Renaissance, 66; The Historical Thought of Samuel Daniel: A Study in Renaissance Ambivalence, J Hist Ideas, 71; The Historical Perspective of Richard Hooker: A Renaissance Paradox, J Medieval & Renaissance Studies, 73; The Non-Political Past in Bacon's Theory of History, J Brit Studies, 74; Clio Unbound Perception of the Social and Cultural Past in Renaissance England, Duke Univ, 79. **CONTACT ADDRESS** Dept of Hist, Duke Univ, Durham, NC 27708.

FERGUSON, CLYDE RANDOLPH
PERSONAL Born 06/03/1930, Oklahoma City, OK, m, 1954, 3 children **DISCIPLINE** AMERICAN COLONIAL AND REVOLUTIONARY HISTORY **EDUCATION** Univ Okla, BA, 55; Duke Univ, MA, 57, PhD (hist), 60. **CAREER** Instr specialist hist and govt, 60-62, coordr home studies continuing educ, 62-66, asst prof, 66-80, Assoc Prof Hist, Kans State Univ, 80-. **MEMBERSHIPS** AHA; Southern Hist Asn. **RESEARCH** Colonial America; American revolution; guerrilla warfare. **SELECTED PUBLICATIONS** Auth, On Coon Mountain--Scenes from a Childhood in the Oklahoma Hills, J West, Vol 33, 94; The Papers of Bouquet, Henry, Vol 6, J Milit Hist, Vol 60, 96; National Rifle Association Money, Firepower and Fear, J West, Vol 35, 96. **CONTACT ADDRESS** Dept of Hist, Kansas State Univ, Manhattan, KS 66506.

FERGUSON, EUGENE S.
PERSONAL Born 01/24/1916, Wilmington, DE, m, 1948, 3 children **DISCIPLINE** HISTORY OF TECHNOLOGY **EDUCATION** Carnegie Inst Technol, BS, 37, Iowa State Col, MS, 55. **CAREER** Engr, E I du Pont de Nemours and Co, 38-42; instr mech eng, Iowa State Univ, 46-48, from asst prof to assoc prof, 49-58; engr, Foote Mineral Co, 48-49; cur civil and mech eng, Smithsonian Inst, US Nat Mus, 58-61; prof mech eng, Iowa State Univ, 61-69; prof hist, Univ Del, 69-79; cur of technol, Hagley Mus, Greenville, 69-79; Retired, Vchmn hist Am eng rec adv comt, Nat Park Serv, 72-77, chmn, 77-78. **HONORS AND AWARDS** Leonardo Da Vinci Medal, Soc Hist Technol, 77; lhd, univ del, 80. **MEMBERSHIPS** Soc Hist Technol (pres, 77-78); fel AAAS; Am Soc Mech Engrs; Newcomen Soc; AHA. **RESEARCH** Modern technological history. **SELECTED PUBLICATIONS** Auth, Engineering and the Mind's Eye, MIT Press (Cambridge, MA), 92. **CONTACT ADDRESS** 54 Winslow Rd, Newark, DE 19711.

FERGUSON, EVERETT
PERSONAL Born 02/18/1933, Montgomery, TX, m, 1956, 3 children **DISCIPLINE** HISTORY, PHILOSOPHY OF RELIGION **EDUCATION** Abilene Christ Univ, BA, 53, MA, 54; Harvard Univ, STB, 56, PhD, 60. **CAREER** Dean, Northeast Christ Jr Coll, 59-62; Prof, Abilene Christ Univ, 62-98. **HONORS AND AWARDS** Leiden, Brill, 98. **MEMBERSHIPS** North Am Patristics Soc; Am Soc Church Hist; Soc Biblical Lit; Ecclesiastical Hist Soc; Asn Int d'Etudes Patristiques; Inst Biblical Res **RESEARCH** Backgrounds Early Christianity; Early church history **SELECTED PUBLICATIONS** Auth, "Backgrounds of Early Christianity," 2nd ed., Grand Rapids, Eerdmans, 93; ed., "Encyclopedia of Early Christianity, 2nd ed., New York, Garland, 97; Auth, "Early Christians Speak," 3rd ed., Abilene, ACU Press, 99 . **CONTACT ADDRESS** Abilene Christian Univ, 609 E N 16th St, Abilene, TX 79601. **EMAIL** Ferguson@bible.acu.edu

FERGUSON, JAMES WILSON
PERSONAL Born 10/03/1933, Muncy, PA, m, 1 child **DISCIPLINE** EARLY MODERN EUROPEAN HISTORY **EDUCATION** Kenyon Col, AB, 55; Bryn Mawr Col, MA, 56; Princeton Univ, PhD, 61. **CAREER** Instr gen studies, Philadelphia Mus Col Art, 60-63; asst prof hist and humanities, Parsons Col, 63-66; Assoc Prof Hist, Russell Sage Col, 68-94. **HONORS AND AWARDS** Phi Beta Kappa. **MEMBERSHIPS** Sullivan County Hist Soc. **RESEARCH** Sullivan Count (PA) History. **SELECTED PUBLICATIONS** Auth, Churches of Sullivan County; auth, Cemeteries and Gravesites of Sullivan County, Pennsylvania. **CONTACT ADDRESS** Box 171, Laporte, PA 18626.

FERGUSSON, FRANCES D.
PERSONAL Born 10/03/1944, Boston, MA, m, 1988 **DISCIPLINE** ARCHITECTURAL HISTORY **EDUCATION** Wellesley Col, BA, 65; Harvard Univ, MA, 66, PhD, 74. **CAREER** Teaching Fel, Harvard Univ, 66-68; Asst Prof Art, Newton Col, 69-75, Dir Div Humanities & Fine Arts & Chair Dept Art, 72-75; Assoc Prof Art, Univ Mass - Boston, 75-82, Dir Urban Studies Prog, 78-79, Dir Am Civilization Prog, 79-80, Fac Representative to Bd Trustees, 79-80, Asst Chancellor, 80-82; Prof Art, Bucknell Univ, 82-86, Provost & VPres Acad Affairs, 82-86; Prof Art and Pres, Vassar Col, 86-. **HONORS AND AWARDS** Phi Beta Kappa; Founder's Awd, Soc of Archit Historians, 70; Danforth Assoc for Excellence in Teaching, 79; one of Am 200 most influential women, Vanity Fair, 98; Eleanor Roosevelt at Val-Kill Awd, 98; hon fel of the foreign policy, 99; Centennial Medal, Harvard Univ, 99; Alumnae Achievement Awd, Wellesley Col, 01. **MEMBERSHIPS** Bd of Trustees, Ford Found; Bd of Trustees, Mayo Found; Bd of Dir, HSBC Bank USA; Bd of Dir, CH Energy Group Inc. **RESEARCH** Late 18th - early 19th century French & English architecture; historians in architecture. **SELECTED PUBLICATIONS** Auth, Liberal Arts for the 80s, Vassar Quart, 88; Educating for a Vital Society, Vassar Quart, 89; A Commitment to Medicine and Society, Mayo Clinic Proceedings, Vol 65, 8/90; The Dilemma of Free Speech in a Diverse Society, Vassar Quart, 90; author of numerous other articles in Vassar Quarterly, and other publications. **CONTACT ADDRESS** Vassar Col, Box 43, Poughkeepsie, NY 12604-0043. **EMAIL** fergusson@vassar.edu

FERLEGER, LOUIS A.
PERSONAL Born 07/30/1947, Philadelphia, PA, m, 1980, 2 children **DISCIPLINE** HISTORY **EDUCATION** Temple Univ, BA, 71; MA, 73; PhD, 78. **CAREER** Assoc dean, Univ Mass Col Arts Sci, 89-91; prof to assoc dir to dept chmn, Univ Mass, 91-99; prof, Boston Univ, 99-. **HONORS AND AWARDS** Twentieth Century Res Grant, 92; Charles Warren Fel, 92; Arthur H. Cole Grant, 88; NEH Fel, 88; AASLH Res Grant, 85. **MEMBERSHIPS** Hist Soc; AHS; GHS. **RESEARCH** US economic history; 19th-20th-century; agricultural history; statistics. **SELECTED PUBLICATIONS** Co-auth, Statistics for Social Change, South End Pr (Boston), 80, 3rd printing, 90; auth, "Capital Goods and Southern Economic Development," J Econ Hist 65 (85): 411-417; auth, "Uplifting American Agriculture: Experiment Station Scientists and the OES in the Early Years After the Hatch Act," Agr Hist 64 (90): 5-23; ed, "Agriculture and National Development: Views on the Nineteenth Century," in Agricultural History and Rural Studies: Henry A. Wallace Series (Ames: Iowa State Univ Pr, 90); co-auth, "Americans' Hostility to Taxes," Challenge (91): 53-55; auth, "Response," Challenge (91): 54, reprinted, Duskin Pub (92, 93, 94, 95, 96); co-auth, "No Gain, No Pain: Taxes, Productivity and Economic Growth," Twentieth Century Fund (92), excerpted, Challenge 36 (93): 11-19; co-auth, "The Managerial Revolution and the Developmental State: The Case of U.S. Agriculture," Bus Econ Hist 22 (93): 67-98, reprinted, Organizational Capabilities and Competitive Advantage: Debates, Dynamics and Policy, eds. William Lazonick, William Mass (Vt: E Elgar Pub, 95); co-auth, A New Mandate: Democratic Choices for a Prosperous Economy, Univ Mo Pr, 94. **CONTACT ADDRESS** Dept Hist, Boston Univ, 226 Bay State Rd, Boston, MA 02215. **EMAIL** ferleger@bu.edu

FERLING, JOHN ERNIE
PERSONAL Born 01/10/1940, Charleston, WV, m, 1965 **DISCIPLINE** AMERICAN HISTORY **EDUCATION** Sam Houston State Univ, BA, 61; Baylor Univ, MA, 62; WVa Univ, PhD, 71. **CAREER** Asst prof, 65-68, Morehead State Univ; instr, 69-70, WVa Univ; assoc prof, 70-71, W Chester State Col; prof, 71-, St Univ W Ga. **HONORS AND AWARDS** George Washington Prof of Hist in Ga. **RESEARCH** Colonial-revolutionary America; United States military history. **SELECTED PUBLICATIONS** Auth, John Adams: A Life, Univ Tenn Press, 92; auth, Struggle for a Continent: The Wars of Early America, Harlan Davidson Pub, 93; art, John Adams, Diplomat, Wm & Mary Quart, 51, 94; art, John Adam's Health Reconsidered, Wm & Mary Quart, 55, 98; auth, Setting the World Ablaze: Washington, Adams, Jefferson, and the Am Revolution, Oxford Univ Pr, 00. **CONTACT ADDRESS** Dept of History, State Univ of West Georgia, Carrollton, GA 30118. **EMAIL** jferling@westga.edu

FERN, ALAN M.
PERSONAL Born 10/19/1930, Detroit, MI, m, 1957 **DISCIPLINE** ART HISTORY **EDUCATION** Univ of Chicago, BA, 50, MA, 50, PhD, 60. **CAREER** Asst to instr to asst prof, The Col, Univ of Chicago, 52-61; curator to asst chief to chief of prints & photographs to dir of res dept to dir of special collections, Library of Congress, 61-82; Dir, Nat Portrait Gallery, Smithsonian Inst, 82-00. **HONORS AND AWARDS** Fulbright scholar, 54-55; Ordre de la Couronne (Chevalier); Ordre des Arts des Letters (Chevalier); Order of the Polar Star (commander). **MEMBERSHIPS** Col Art Asn; Print Coun of Am; Grolies Club, Cosmos Club. **RESEARCH** History of graphic arts & photography; American art; art nouveau. **SELECTED PUBLICATIONS** Auth, The Project in Jack Delano, Puerto Rico Mio, Smithsonian Institution Press, 90; auth, Introduction ot Helma E. Wright, Prints at the Natl Mass Forward to N. & R.W.B. Lewis, American Characters, Yale Univ Press, 99; Entries on Holger Cahill and Joseph Pennell, Dictionary of Art, 96; Leadership in Arts-Oxymoron or Opportunity, Cosmos, 97. **CONTACT ADDRESS** National Portrait Gallery, Smithsonian Inst, Washington, DC 20560-0213. **EMAIL** afern@npg.si.edu

FERNANDEZ, JOSE A.
PERSONAL Born 11/06/1936, Mahon, Spain, s **DISCIPLINE** HISTORY **EDUCATION** Columbia Univ, BSc, 60; Indiana Univ, MA, 66; PhD, 70. **CAREER** From asst prof to prof, Calif State Univ, Hayward, 70-. **RESEARCH** History of ideas in early modern Spain. **SELECTED PUBLICATIONS** Auth, The State, War and Peace. Spanish Political Thought in the Renaissance 1516-1559, Cambridge, 77; auth, Reason of State and Statecraft in Spanish Political Thought 1595-1640, Lanham, Md, 83; auth, Baltasar Alamos de Barrientos, Aforismos al "Tacito espanol", 2 vols, Madrid, 87; auth, Juan Luis vives, Escepticismo y prudencia en el Renacimiento, Salamanca, 90; auth, La formacion de la sociedad y el origen del Estado, Ensayos sobre el pensamiento politico del siglo de Oro, Madrid, 97; auth, The Theater of Man, J.L. Vives on Society, Philadelphia, 98. **CONTACT ADDRESS** Dept Hist, California State Univ, Hayward, 25800 Carlos Bee Blvd, Hayward, CA 94542-3001.

FERNGREN, GARY BURT
PERSONAL Born 04/14/1942, Bellingham, WA, m, 1970, 3 children **DISCIPLINE** ANCIENT HISTORY & MEDICINE **EDUCATION** Western Wash State Col, BA, 64; Univ BC, MA, 67, PhD(classics), 73. **CAREER** Instr, 70-72, asst prof, 72-78, assoc prof Ancient Hist, Ore State Univ, 78-84, prof, 84-. **HONORS AND AWARDS** National Endowment for the Humanities fellow twice, Canada Council fellow three times, Joseph J. Malone fellow (Egypt), Vice President, Int Soc of the History of Medicine, 96-97, Councillor, 97-. **MEMBERSHIPS** Int Soc of the History of Medicine, Am Asn for the History of Medicine, Am Osler Soc, History of Science Soc. **RESEARCH** Social history of ancient medicine; history of medical ethics, historical relationship of religion to medicine and science. **SELECTED PUBLICATIONS** General ed, The History of Science and Religion in the Western Tradition: An Encyclopedia (New York: Garland 00), numerous articles and chapters. **CONTACT ADDRESS** Dept of Hist, Oregon State Univ, 306 Milam Hall, Corvallis, OR 97331-5104. **EMAIL** GFerngren@orst.edu

FERNIE, J. DONALD
PERSONAL Born 11/13/1933, Pretoria, South Africa **DISCIPLINE** ASTRONOMY, HISTORY OF SCIENCE **EDUCATION** Univ Cape Town, BS, 53, MS, 55; Ind Univ, PhD, 58. **CAREER** Lectr, Univ Cape Town, 58-61; asst prof to prof, 61-96, PROF EMER, UNIV TORONTO, 96-; Affil, Inst Hist Philos Sci Technol, 73-; dir, David Dunlap Observatory, 78-88. **MEMBERSHIPS** Royal Astron Soc Can; Int Astron Union. **SELECTED PUBLICATIONS** Auth, The Whisper and the Vision: The Voyages of the Astronomers, Clarke, Irwin & Co, 76. **CONTACT ADDRESS** Dept of Astronomy, Univ of Toronto, 60 St George St, Rm 1403, Toronto, ON, Canada M5S 3H8. **EMAIL** fernie@astor.utoronto.ca

FERNSTEIN, MARGARETE MYERS
PERSONAL Born 06/05/1962, CA, m, 1999 **DISCIPLINE** HISTORY **EDUCATION** Reed Col, BA, 83; Columbia Univ, MA, 84; Univ Calif Davis, PhD, 93. **CAREER** Asst prof, Susquehanna Univ, 93-97; asst prof, Ind Univ South Bend, 97-. **HONORS AND AWARDS** Fulbright Grad Res Fel, 89-90; AAUW Dissertation Awd, 90-91; Weber Chair in the Humanities, Susquehanna Univ, 93-95; IUSB Fac Res Grant, 99. **MEMBERSHIPS** AHA **RESEARCH** Post-WWII Germany, Jewish displaced persons. **SELECTED PUBLICATIONS** Auth, "Jewish Displaced Persons," Leo Baeck Year Book (97); auth, Recreating Germany, Humanities Press (forthcoming); auth, "Propaganda at the Post Office," Images of Germany (in press); auth, "Deutchland uber alles?" Cent Eurpean Hist (forthcoming). **CONTACT ADDRESS** Dept Hist, Indiana Univ, South Bend, PO Box 7111, South Bend, IN 46634-7111. **EMAIL** mfeinste@iusb.edu

FERRARI, ROBERTO
DISCIPLINE ART, ART HISTORY **EDUCATION** Univ S Fla, BA, 92, MLA, 94, MLS, 97. **CAREER** Student asst 88-89; Montclair State Univ Sprague Library; Teaching asst, Univ of South Florida, 92-94; adj prof, Hillsborough Community Col, 94-97; graduate asst, Univ of South Florida, 96-97;Library Intern, John & Mable Ringling Museum of Art Library, Sarasota, Florida, 97; assoc dean, Art Institute of Ft. Lauderdale, 97-99; librarian, Florida Atlantic Univ, 99; acting head, Florida Atlantic Univ, 00. **MEMBERSHIPS** ACRL: Asn of Col and Res Libraries; ACRL Arts Section; ALA: Am Library Asn; ARLIS/NA: Art Libraries Soc of North Am; ARLIS/SE: Southeast Chapter of ARLIS/NA; Art Institute of Fort Lauderdale General Education Advisory Committee; SEFLIN Circulation Committee; SEFLIN Collection Dev Committee; SLA: Special Libraries Asn; SLA Florida and Caribbean Chapter; SUS (State Univ System) Circulation Committee; SUS Electronic Collections (Sub)Committee for the Humanities. **RESEARCH** Visual Art and Art History Resources; Simeon Solomon (1840-1905), gay Jewish Victorian artist; Victorian Studies (Pre-Raphaelites, Aesthetes/Symbolists, Decadents, ca. 1850-1915); Gay and Gender Studies, particulary of the late 19th/early 20th centuries; Asian Culture (China, India, Japan), Ancient Greece, Rome, and Egypt, and Italian Renaissance Arts. **SELECTED PUBLICATIONS** Ed, "Art on the 'Net: Enhanced Research for Art and Architecture," article, Journal of Library Administration, Vol 30, No 1/2, Academic Research on the Internet, ed, Drs. William Miller and Helen Laurence, Binghamton, NY: Haworth, (00); auth, "The Art of Classification: Alternate Classification Systems in Art Libraries," Cataloging & Classification Quarterly, Vol 28, No 2, (00); rev, "The Architect's Portable Handbook," American Reference Books Annual, Vol 31, (00): rev, "Our Sunday Visitor's Encyclopedia of Saints,"CD-ROM review, American Reference Books Annual, Vol 31, 00; review, "A History of Photography," web site review, Electronic Resources Reviews, Vol 4, No 1/2, 00; auth, "Simeon Solomon: A Bibliographic Study," The Journal of Pre-Raphaelite Studies, 8, (99): 69-90; rev, "Victoria Res Wev," web site rev, Electronic Resources Review, Vol 3, No 9, 99; rev, "ArtSource," web site review, Electronic Resources Reviews, Vol 3, No 7, 99; rev, Inter-Play," web site review, Electronic Resources Rev, Vol 3, No 6, 99; rev, "Queer Forster?" book review, English Literature in Transition 1880-1920, vol 42, no 2, 99. **CONTACT ADDRESS** Florida Atlantic Univ, 777 Glades Rd, Boca Raton, FL 33431. **EMAIL** rferrari@fau.edu

FERRELL, ROBERT HUGH
PERSONAL Born 05/08/1921, Cleveland, OH, m, 1956, 1 child **DISCIPLINE** AMERICAN HISTORY **EDUCATION** Bowling Green State Univ, BS, 46, BA, 47; Yale Univ, MA, 48, PhD, 51, LLD, 71; Franklin Col, LLD, 84. **CAREER** Vis prof, Naval War Col, 74-75; vis prof, Eastern Illinois Univ, 85, 89; lectr, Doshisha Univ, 86; vis prof, United States Military Academy, 87-88; prof, Tex Christian Univ, 88. **HONORS AND AWARDS** John Addison Porter Prize, Yale Univ, 51; George Louis Beer Prize, Am Historical Asn, 52; Carnegie Corporation grant, 55-56; Social Science Res Coun grant, 56; Smith-Mundt grant to Egypt, 58-59; Social Science Res Coun grant, 61-62; Fulbright award to Belgium, 69-70; Distinguished teaching award, Indiana Univ, 69, 80; Distinguished teaching award, Col of Arts and Sciences and Graduate School alumni asn, Indiana Univ, 83; Honorary member, Gamma chapter of Phi Beta Kappa, Indiana Univ, 70; Fulbright award to Japan, 86; lld, bowling green state univ, 71. **RESEARCH** America diplomatic history; american preindustrial history. **SELECTED PUBLICATIONS** Auth, Harry S. Truman: A Life, Univ of Mo Press, 94; auth, Harry S. Truman an dthe Bomb, High Plains, 96; auth, Dictionary of American History, Supplement to the revised edition, 2 vols., Scribner's, 96; auth, The Strange Deaths of President Harding, Univ of Mo Press, 96; auth, FDR's Quiet Confidant: The Autobiography of Frank C. Walker, Univ Press of Colorado, 97; auth, The Dying President: Franklin D. Roosevelt, 1944-45, Univ of Mo Press, 98; auth, The Presidency of Calvin Coolidge, Univ Press of Kans, 98; auth, Truman and Pendergast, Univ of Mo Press, 99; auth, The Kansas City Investigation: Pendergast's Downfall, 193-1939, Univ of Mo Press, 99; auth, A Youth in the Meuse-Argonne: A Memoir of World War I, 1917-1918, Univ of Mo Press, 00. **CONTACT ADDRESS** Dept of Hist, Indiana Univ, Bloomington, Bloomington, IN 47401.

FERRILL, ARTHER L.
PERSONAL Born 11/26/1938, Enid, OK, m **DISCIPLINE** HISTORY **EDUCATION** Univ Wichita, BA, 60; Univ Delinors, MA, 61; PhD, 64. **CAREER** From asst prof to prof, Univ Wash, 64-. **HONORS AND AWARDS** Woodrow Wilson Fel, 60-61. **RESEARCH** Ancient History, Military History. **SELECTED PUBLICATIONS** Auth, Origins of War, 85; auth, Fall of the Roman Empire: The Military Explanation, 86; auth, Roman Imperial Grand Strategy, 91; auth, Caligula: Emperor of Rome, 91. **CONTACT ADDRESS** Dept Hist, Univ of Washington, PO Box 353560, Seattle, WA 98195-3560. **EMAIL** ferrill@u.washington.edu

FERRIS, NORMAN B.
PERSONAL Born 11/29/1931, Richmond, VA, m, 1962, 5 children **DISCIPLINE** AMERICAN HISTORY **EDUCATION** George Wash Univ, BA 53; Emory Univ, MA, 57; PhD, 62. **CAREER** Instr hist, Emory Univ, 59-60; asst prof, Univ Southwestern La, 60-61; from asst prof to assoc prof, 62-69, Prof Hist, Mid Tenn State Univ, 69-97, prof emer, 97-; Pres, Tenn Comt Humanities, 79-85. **HONORS AND AWARDS**

Grant, Nat Endowment for the Humanities; grant, NJers Hist Commission; Claxton Award, 91; Sumberg Award, Nat AAUP. **MEMBERSHIPS** AHA; AAUP; Orgn Am Hists; Southern Hist Asn; Soc Hist Am Foreign Rel. **RESEARCH** United States diplomatic history during Civil War period. **SELECTED PUBLICATIONS** Auth, "Diplomacy," in Civil War History (La State Univ Press, 67); auth, "Transatlantic Misunderstanding," in Rank and File (Presidio, 76); auth, Desperate Diplomacy, Univ of Tenn Press, 76; auth, The Trent Affair, Univ of Tenn Press, 77; auth, "William H. Seward and the Faith of a Nation," in Traditions and Values (Univ Press of Am, 85); auth, "Lincoln and Seward in Civil War Diplomacy: Their Relationship at the Outset Re-examined," in For a Vast Future Also: Essays from the Journal of the Abraham Lincoln Association, ed. Thomas F. Schwartz (NY: Fordham Univ Press, 99), 170-191. **CONTACT ADDRESS** 3210 E Compton Rd, Murfreesboro, TN 37130.

FETTER, BRUCE SIGMOND
PERSONAL Born 06/08/1938, Ashland, KY, m, 1966, 1 child **DISCIPLINE** AFRICAN HISTORY **EDUCATION** Harvard Univ, BA, 60; Oxford Univ, BPhil, 62; Univ Wis, PhD(hist), 68. **CAREER** From instr to asst prof, 67-74, from assoc prof to prof hist, Univ Wis-Milwaukee, 74-87, Dept Chair, 95-98; Fulbright sr lectr hist, Nat Univ Zaire, 72-73; Universite de Burundi, 86; res affil, Inst African Studies, Univ Zambia, 73; ed, Urbanism Past and Present, 75-84. **HONORS AND AWARDS** Kiekhofer Teaching Awd, 72; NSF Conference Awd, 86-87; USIAco-PI, 94-96. **MEMBERSHIPS** African Studies Asn; AHA; Soc Sci Hist Asn; Int Union for the Sci Stu of Population, 91. **RESEARCH** Central and Southern Africa; historical demography. **SELECTED PUBLICATIONS** Coauth, Backward sloping labor supply functions and African economic development, Econ Develop & Cult Change, 68; Auth, The Luluabourg Revolt at Elisabethville, Int J African Studies, 69; L'Union Miniere du Haut-Katanga, 1920-40, la mise en place d'une sousculture totalitaire, Les Cahiers du CEDAF, Brussels, 73; African associations at Elisabethville, 1910-1935, Etudes d'Hist Africaine, 74; The Creation of Elisabethville, Hoover Inst, 76; Colonial Rule and Regional Imbalance in Central Africa, Westview, 83; Colonial Rule in Africa: Readings from Primary Sources, Univ Wis Press, 79; Demography from Scanty Evidence: Central Africa in the Colonial Era, Lynne Rienner, 90; Coauth, Scars from a childhood disease: Measles in the concentration camps during the War, Social Science History 96; Trois siecles de politiques govvernementales enfaveuv de la sante publique, amales de demographic historique, 97. **CONTACT ADDRESS** Dept of History, Univ of Wisconsin, Milwaukee, PO Box 413, Milwaukee, WI 53201-0413. **EMAIL** bruf@uwm.edu

FETZER, JAMES HENRY
PERSONAL Born 12/06/1940, Pasadena, CA, m, 1977, 4 children **DISCIPLINE** HISTORY AND PHILOSOPHY OF SCIENCE **EDUCATION** Princeton Univ, AB, 62; Ind Univ, MA, 68; Ind Univ, PhD, 70. **CAREER** Asst prof, Univ Ky, 70-77; vis assoc prof, Univ Va, 77-78; vis assoc prof, Univ Cincinnati, 78-79; vis NSF res prof, Univ Cincinnati, 79-80; vis lectr, Univ NC at Chapel Hill, 80-81; vis assoc prof, New Col, Univ South Fla, 81-83; MacArthur vis distinguished prof, New Col, Univ South Fla, 83-84; adjunct prof, Univ South Fla, Fall, 84-85; vis prof, Univ Va, Spring, 84-85; prof, Univ Minn, Duluth, 87-96; dept chair, Univ Minn, Duluth, 88-92; dir, Master of Liberal Studies Program, Univ Minn, Duluth, 96-; distinguished McKnight univ prof, Univ Minn, 96-. **HONORS AND AWARDS** McKnight Endowment Fel, Univ Minn; Summer Faculty Res Fel, Univ Minn; Outstanding Res Awd, Univ Minn; Lansdowne Lectr, Univ Victoria; Pres, Minn Philosophical Society; Vice-pres, Minn Philosophical Society; Medal of the Univ of Helsinki; Summer Fac Res Fel, Univ Minn; Postdoctoral Fel in Computer Sci, Wright State Univ; Postdoctoral Res Fel, Nat Sci Found; Distinguished Teaching Awd, Univ Ky; Summer Fac Res Fellow, 72; Graduate Res Asst, Ind Univ; Fel of the Fac, Colombia Univ; NDEA Title IV Fel, Ind Univ; The Dickinson Prize, Princeton Univ; Magna Cum Laude, Princeton; res scholar, New Col, Univ South Fla, 85-86. **MEMBERSHIPS** Philos of Sci Asn; Am Philosophical Asn; Asn for Computing Machinery; Human Behavior and Evolution Society; Int Society for Human Ethnology; Am Asn of Univ Profs; Society for Machines and Mentality; Am Asn for the Advanc of Sci. **RESEARCH** Philosophy of science; computer science; artificial intelligence; cognitive science. **SELECTED PUBLICATIONS** Auth, Philosophy of Science, Paragon House Publ, 93; coauth, Glossary of Epistemology/Philosophy of Science, Paragon House Publ, 93; coauth, Glossary of Cognitive Science, Paragon House Publ, 93; ed, Foundations of Philosophy of Science, Paragon House Publ, 93; co-ed, Program Verification Fundamental Issues in Computer Science, Kluwer Academic Publ, 93; auth, Philosophy and Cognitive Science, Paragon House Publ, 96; coauth, Assassination Science: Experts Speak Out on the Death of JFK, Catfeet Press, 98, co-ed, The New Theory of Reference: Kripke, Marcusk, and Its Origins, Kluwer Academic Publ, 98. **CONTACT ADDRESS** Dept of Philosophy, Univ of Minnesota, Duluth, Duluth, MN 55812. **EMAIL** jfetzer@d.umn.edu

FEUERHAHN, RONALD R.
PERSONAL Born 12/01/1937, Cape Girardeau, MO, m, 1963, 3 children **DISCIPLINE** HISTORICAL THEOLOGY **EDUCATION** Concordia Sr Col, BA, 59; Concordia Sem, MDiv, 63; Univ Cambridge, England, MPhil, 80; PhD, 92. **CAREER** Pastor, St. David's, Cardiff, Wales, 64-70; pastor, Resurrection, Cambridge, Eng, 70-77; preceptor, Westfield House, Cambridge, England, 77-86; asst prof, 86-95, assoc prof hist theol, 95-, asst chaplain and coord musical and cultural activities, 90-92, acting dean of chapel, 98, Concordia Sem; contributing ed, Logia, 92-; assoc ed, Concordia Hist Inst Quarterly, 96-; vis prof, Urals State Univ, Dept of Arts and Culture, Yekaterinbury, Russia, 98-99; vis prof, Russian Acad of the State Service for the Pres of the Russian Federation, The Urals Acad of the State Service, Dept of Sociology and Psychology of the State Service, Yekaterinburg, Russia, 99; ELCA, LCMS Discussion Panel, 99-00; archivist, Concordia Seminary, St. Louis, MO, 99-. **MEMBERSHIPS** Cambridge Theol Soc; Soc for Liturgial Stud (Gr Britain); Societas Liturgica; Luther Acad; Lutheran Missiology Soc; Am Soc of Church Hist; Luthern Hist Conf; Governing Board, Lutheran Quarterly, 96-; Commission on Worship, LCMS; Liturgy Comm of the Lutheran Hymnal Project, Commission on Music, LCMS (chairman, 98-); Seminary Relations Standing Committee of the Int Lutheran Council (chairman, 00-). **RESEARCH** Liturgy and worship; ecumenical movement; law and Gospel; Hermann Sasse; movements of thought (Pietism, Rationalism. **SELECTED PUBLICATIONS** Co-ed, Scripture and the Church: Selected Essays of Hermann Sasse, Concordia Seminary, 95; auth, A Bibliography of Dr. Hermann Sasse, Scarecrow, 95; auth, "Ne Desperamus," in Logia, Reformation, 95; auth, Hermann Sasse and North American Lutheranism," in Logia, (Reformation, 95); auth, Hermann Sasse: Confessional Ecumenist, Lutherische Theologie und Kirche, 95; auth, Hermann Sasse-Gesetz und Evangelium in der Geshcichte, in Diestelemann, ed, Eintrachtig Lehren: Festrschrift fuer Bischof Dr. Jobst Schone, Heinrich Harms, 97; contrib, Hymnal Supplement, 98, St. Louis: Concordia, 98; contrib, Hymnal Supplement 98, Handbook, St. Louis: Concorida, 98. **CONTACT ADDRESS** Concordia Sem, 801 DeMun Ave, Saint Louis, MO 63105. **EMAIL** feuerhahnr@csl.edu

FEYERICK, ADA
PERSONAL Born 04/01/1928, m, 1962, 3 children **DISCIPLINE** HISTORY **EDUCATION** Douglass Col, BA, 48. **CAREER** Res, for affairs, , 50-55 Look Mag; res, pub affairs, 56-58, NBC-TV; asst ed, hist-archaeol, 58-62, Horizon Mag. **MEMBERSHIPS** Overseas Press Club; Am Oriental Soc; Am Schools of Oriental Res; Am Res Center in Egypt; Bibl Archaeol Soc of NY. **RESEARCH** Ancient Near East history/archaeology. **SELECTED PUBLICATIONS** Auth, Genesis: World of Myths and Patriarchs, NY Univ Press, 97. **CONTACT ADDRESS** 15 E Hartshorn Dr, Short Hills, NJ 07078.

FIALA, ROBERT D.
PERSONAL Born 09/27/1938, St. Louis, MO, m, 1962, 2 children **DISCIPLINE** BRITISH, RUSSIAN & EAST ASIAN HISTORY **EDUCATION** Concordia Teachers Col, Nebr, BSEd, 60; Univ Omaha, MA, 63; Wayne State Univ, PhD (Am colonial & Brit Imperial hist), 67; Nat Endowment for the Humanities, Summer Fellwo, 89; UCLA: World of Christopher Columbus, Univ Mich, 94; Imperial China: The Qianlong Era. **CAREER** Instr, High Sch, Tex, 60-61; from asst prof to assoc prof, 65-76, prof hist, Concordia Univ, Nebr, 76-, chmn dept soc sci, 73-, vis prof hist, Tunghai Univ, Taichung, Taiwan, 75-76; summer fel, Inst Mid East, 79, Inst East Asia, Hamline Univ, 81; vis prof hist, Normal Coll of Foreign Lang, Beijing, Peoples Repub of China, 87-88; vis prof hist, Oak Hill Col, London, England, 97. **MEMBERSHIPS** AHA; Conf Brit Studies; Soc Hist Educ. **RESEARCH** George III and English politics; British Empire; British Radicalism, 17th and 18th centuries; Asian Culture and Politics. **SELECTED PUBLICATIONS** Auth, Quakers and the British monarchy: A study in Anglo-American attitudes and practices in the early 1760's, Pa Hist, 4/70; contribr, Joseph Priestley, Thomas Fyshe Palmer, William Godwin, & Beatrice Webb, In: Biographical Dict of Modern British Radicals Since 1770, 78, 88, & Mrs Anne Hutchinson & Sir Nathaniel Rich, In: Biographical Dict of British Radicals in the Seventeenth Century, 81, Harvester; London Naval Treaty & Washington Naval Conference, Mod Japan: An Encycl of Hist, Cult, and Nationalism, Garland, 98; Numerous photographic essays on Europe and Asia. **CONTACT ADDRESS** Soc Sci Dept, Concordia Col, Nebraska, 800 N Columbia Ave, Seward, NE 68434-1556. **EMAIL** rfiala@seward.cune.edu

FICHTNER, PAULA SUTTER
PERSONAL Born 08/13/1935, Passaic, NJ, m, 1958 **DISCIPLINE** CENTRAL EUROPEAN HISTORY, RENAISSANCE AND REFORMATION **EDUCATION** Bryn Mawr Col, BA, 57; Ind Univ, MA, 60; Univ Pa, PhD (hist), 64. **CAREER** Lectr hist, 64-66, from asst prof to assoc prof, 66-77, Prof Hist, Brooklyn Col, 78-00, Univ grants, City Univ New York, 70 and 73. **HONORS AND AWARDS** National Endowment for Humanities University Fellowship, 87-88; American Academy of Religion Awd for Excellence in the Study of Religion in the Historical Category, 91; Broeklundian Prof, 94-96. **MEMBERSHIPS** Conf Group Cent Europ Hist; AHA. **RESEARCH** Habsburg monarchy; European intellectual history. **SELECTED PUBLICATIONS** Auth, Ferdinaud I. Of Austria: the Politics of Dynasticism in the Age of the Reformation, 82; auth, Primogeniture and Protestantism in Early Modern Germany, 89; auth, The Habsburg Empire: From Dynasticism in Multinationalism, 97; auth, An Historical Dictionary of Austria, 99. **CONTACT ADDRESS** Dept of Hist, 45 Grace Ct, Brooklyn, NY 11201. **EMAIL** psfichtner@aol.com

FICK, CAROLYN E.
DISCIPLINE HISTORY **EDUCATION** Wayne State Univ, BA; Univ of Mich, MA; Concordia Univ, PhD. **CAREER** Assoc prof, Concordia Univ. **RESEARCH** Colonial Caribbean slavery, the Haitian and French revolutions. **SELECTED PUBLICATIONS** Auth, The Making of Haiti: The Saint Domingue Revolution From Below, 90. **CONTACT ADDRESS** Dept of Hist, Concordia Univ, Montreal, 1400 de Maisonneuve Blvd W, Montreal, QC, Canada H3G 1W8. **EMAIL** cfick@vax2.concordia.ca

FICKLE, JAMES EDWARD
PERSONAL Born 05/21/1939, Royal Centre, IN, m, 1958, 3 children **DISCIPLINE** AMERICAN HISTORY **EDUCATION** Purdue Univ, BS, 61; La State Univ, MA, 63, PhD(hist), 70. **CAREER** Spec lectr hist, La State Univ, New Orleans, 65-67, instr, 67-68; from instr to asst prof, 68-75, assoc prof, 75-81, Prof Hist, Memphis State Univ, 81- **HONORS AND AWARDS** Theodore C Blegen Awd, Forest Hist Soc, 74. **MEMBERSHIPS** Orgn Am Historians; Southern Hist Asn. **RESEARCH** American economic and labor history. **SELECTED PUBLICATIONS** Contribr, Great Events in American History, Salem, 74; auth, Management Looks at the Labor Problem: The Southern Pine Association During the First World War and the Postwar Era, J Southern Hist, 2/74; The SPA and the NRA: A Case Study of the Blue Eagle in the South, Southwestern Hist Quart, 1/76; Defense Mobilization in the Southern Pine Industry: The Experience of World War I, J Forest Hist, 10/78; The New South and the New Competition, Univ Ill, 80; contribr, At the Point of Production: The Local History of the IWW, Greenwood, 81; Boxes, Baskets, and Boards: A History of the Anderson-Tully Company, Memphis State Univ, 82. **CONTACT ADDRESS** Dept of Hist, Univ of Memphis, 3706 Alumni St, Memphis, TN 38152-0001.

FIDELER, PAUL ARTHUR
PERSONAL Born 05/16/1936, Passaic, NJ, m, 1963, 2 children **DISCIPLINE** BRITISH AND EUROPEAN HISTORY, WESTERN POLITICAL THOUGHT, WORLD PHILOSOPHIES **EDUCATION** St Lawrence Univ, BA, 58; Brandeis Univ, MA, 62, PhD(hist), 71. **CAREER** Instr, Framingham State Col, 64-68; asst prof to prof hist, 69-91, prof hist and humanities, Lesley Col, 73-; adv ed, Brit Studies Monitor. **HONORS AND AWARDS** Fel in NEH Summer Seminars and Inst, 74, 76, 77, 84, 89; Res Fel, The Folger Shakespeare Library, spring 90; Am Coun of Learned Soc Fel in Humanities Curriculum Development and Vis Schol, Harvard Univ, 92-93. **MEMBERSHIPS** AAUP; AHA; New Eng Hist Asn (pres 87-88); Am Philos Asn; Conf for the Study of Political Thought; N Am Conf on Brit Studies; NE Conf on Brit Studies (pres 91-93). **RESEARCH** Poor relief policy and political theory in early modern England; historiography and humanities methodologies; character, values, ethics, and justice in the curriculum, K-16. **SELECTED PUBLICATIONS** Auth, Christian Humanism and Poor Law Reform in Early Tudor England, Societas, fall 74; Have Historians Lost Their Perspective on the Past?, Change, Jan/Feb 84; coed, Political Thought and the Tudor Commonwealth London and New York: Routledge, 92; Toward a Curriculum of Hope: The Essential Role of Humanities Scholarship in Public School Teaching, Am Coun of Learned Soc, Occasional Paper, No. 23, 94; Rescuing Youth Culture: Cultivating Children's Natural Abilities as Philosophers, Lesley Mag, winter 94; coauth, Autobiography in the Classroom: A Triptych, Teaching the Humanities, spring 95; auth, Societas, Civitas and Early Elizabethan Poverty Relief, In: State, Sovereigns and Society: Essays in Early Modern English History, St. Martins, 98. **CONTACT ADDRESS** Humanities Faculty, Lesley Col, 29 Everett St, Cambridge, MA 02138-2790. **EMAIL** pfideler@lesley.edu

FIDLER, ANN
DISCIPLINE HISTORY **EDUCATION** Univ of Kansas, BA, 84; Univ of Calif at Berkeley, JD, 90, PhD, 96. **CAREER** ASST PROF, HIST, OHIO UNIV **MEMBERSHIPS** Am Antiquarian Soc **SELECTED PUBLICATIONS** A Cultural History of the American Law Book, 1700-1900. **CONTACT ADDRESS** Dept of Hist, Ohio Univ, Bentley Hall, Athens, OH 45701-2979.

FIEGE, MARK T.
DISCIPLINE HISTORY **EDUCATION** W Wash Univ, BA, 81; Wash State Univ, MA, 85; Univ Utah, PhD, 94. **CAREER** Asst prof, Colo State Univ, 94-. **MEMBERSHIPS** Am Soc for Environmental Hist, W Hist Asn, Agr Hist Soc, Org of Am Hist, Am Hist Asn. **RESEARCH** Environmental history, Landscape history, Western American history. **SELECTED PUBLICATIONS** Auth, Irrigated Eden: the Making of an Agricultural Landscape in the American West, Univ of Wash Press: Seattle, 99. **CONTACT ADDRESS** Dept History, Colorado State Univ, Fort Collins, CO 80523-0001. **EMAIL** mfiege@vines.colostate.edu

FIELD, ARTHUR
PERSONAL Born 08/03/1948, Charleston, SC, s **DISCIPLINE** HISTORY **EDUCATION** Duke Univ, BA, 70; Univ Chicago, MA, 71; Univ Mich, PhD, 80. **CAREER** Adjunct asst prof, Hunter Col, 85-87; asst to Prof Paul Oskar Kristeller, Columbia Univ, 85-87; lectr, Princeton Univ, 87-89; assoc prof, Indian Univ, 89-, adjunct assoc prof, 99-. **HONORS AND AWARDS** Rome Prize Fel, Am Acad in Rome, 79-80; Fel, Harvard Univ Ctr for Italian Renaissance Studies, 83-84; Fulbright Fel, 83-84; Fel, Am Coun of Learned Socs, 84-85; Res Fel, Am Coun of Learned Socs, 92-93; Vis Scholar, Harvard Univ Ctr for Italian Renaissance Studies, 93-94; Fel, John Simon Guggenheim Memorial Found, 93-94; Resident, Am Acad in Rome, 96-97; Fel, Gladys Krieble Delmas Found, 97-98; William Nelson Prize, Renaissance Soc of Am, 99. **MEMBERSHIPS** Am Hist Asn, Renaissance Soc of Am. **SELECTED PUBLICATIONS** Auth, "Christoforo Landino's First Lectures on Dante," Renaissance Quart, 39 (86): 16-48; auth, The Origins of the Platonic Academy of Florence, Princeton: Princeton Univ Press (88); auth, "Lorenzo Buonincontri and the First Public Lectures on Manilius (Florence, 1475-76)," Rinascimento, 36 (96): 207-225; auth, "Leonardo Bruni, Florentine Traitor? Bruni, the Medici, and an Aretine Conspiracy of 1437," Renaissance Quart, 51 (98): 1109-1150; auth, "Francesco Filelfo and Carlo Marsuppini, 1429, in ms. Landi 31," Bollettino Storica Piacentino Dalla Biblioteca Comunale "Passerini Landi," (in press). **CONTACT ADDRESS** Dept Hist, Indiana Univ, Bloomington, Ballantine Hall 742, Bloomington, IN 47405. **EMAIL** AFIELD@INDIANA.EDU

FIELD, DANIEL
PERSONAL Born 07/26/1938, Boston, MA, m, 1959, 2 children **DISCIPLINE** HISTORY **EDUCATION** Harvard Univ, BA, 59; MA, 62; PhD, 69. **CAREER** Instr and Lectr, Harvard Univ, 68-70; Asst Prof, Columbia Univ, 70-76; From Assoc Prof to Prof, Syracuse Univ, 76-. **HONORS AND AWARDS** Res Fel, USSR, 78, 81; Fulbright-Hays Fel, 64-65, 78, 81; Res Fel, Russ Res Ctr, 72-73, 77-78, 81-82; Sr Fel, Harriman Inst for Advanced Study of the Soviet Union, 90-91. **MEMBERSHIPS** AHA, AAASS. **RESEARCH** Modern Russian political and social history, historiography. **SELECTED PUBLICATIONS** Auth, Quantitative Studies in Agrarian History, Iowa St UP, 93; auth, "Istoriia mentaliteta v zarubezhnoi istoricheskoi literature," in Mentalitet I agrarnoe razvitie Rossii (XIX-XX vv) (94), 14-15; auth, "Reforms and Political Culture in Prerevolutionary Russia," in Reform in Mod Russ Hist: Progress or Cycle? (Cambridge UP, 95), 125-136; auth, "Vospominaniia E K Breshko-Breshkovskoi o khozhdenii v narod 1870-kh gg: Opyt istochnikovedencheskogo analiza," in P A Zaionchkovskii (1904-1983): stat'l, publikatsii I vospominaniia o nem (Moscow: Rosspen, 98), 320-335. **CONTACT ADDRESS** Dept Hist, Syracuse Univ, 0 Eggers, Syracuse, NY 13244-1020. **EMAIL** dxfield@syr.edu

FIELD, EARLE
PERSONAL Born 01/14/1922, Syracuse, NY, m, 1946, 2 children **DISCIPLINE** EUROPEAN HISTORY **EDUCATION** Syracuse Univ, AB, 49, MA, 50, PhD, 54. **CAREER** Lectr hist, univ col, Syracuse Univ, 53-54; instr soc sci, State Univ NY, 54-59; from asst prof to assoc prof, 59-65, Prof Hist, Calif State Univ, Northridge, 65-. **MEMBERSHIPS** AHA. **RESEARCH** Ancient Near East; classical civilization; Jewish history. **SELECTED PUBLICATIONS** Auth, A Toast to Vera Soloviova, Mich Quart Rev, Vol 32, 93; Variety Photoplays, Parnassus Poetry Rev, Vol 22, 97; Tea at Paul Bowles, Raritan Quart Rev, Vol 12, 93; Old Aquaintance, Mich Quart Rev, Vol 33, 94; To My Country, Mich Quart Rev, Vol 35, 96; Paris 48, Kenyon Rev, Vol 16, 94; Doing it With Mirrors, Mich Quart Rev, Vol 33, 94. **CONTACT ADDRESS** 18132 Sunburst St, Northridge, CA 91325.

FIELD, LESTER L., JR
PERSONAL Born 10/31/1954, Red Bank, NJ, m, 1985, 2 children **DISCIPLINE** HISTORY **EDUCATION** Gonzega, BA, 77; Univ Calif at Los Angeles, MA, 79; PhD, 85. **CAREER** Lectr, Yale, 89; from asst prof to prof, Univ of Miss, 89-. **HONORS AND AWARDS** Henry R. Luce Postdoctoral Fel, Yale; Postdoctoral Scholar, Univ Calif, Los Angeles; Dissertation Grant, Univ Calif, Los Angeles. **MEMBERSHIPS** AHA, Medieval Acad of Am, Am Cath Hist Soc. **RESEARCH** Ancient & Medieval Christianity, late antiquity & early middle ages. **SELECTED PUBLICATIONS** Auth, "Liberty, Dominion, and the Two Swords: On the Origins of Western Political Theology," Publ in Medieval Studies 28 (Notre Dame: Notre Dame Press, 98): 180-298. **CONTACT ADDRESS** Dept Hist, Univ of Mississippi, University, MS 38677-9999. **EMAIL** hsfield@olemiss.edu

FIELD, PHYLLIS F.
PERSONAL Born 12/27/1946, Louisville, KY, m, 1977, 1 child **DISCIPLINE** HISTORY **EDUCATION** Univ of Louisville, BA, 67; Cornell Univ, PhD, 74. **CAREER** Vis asst prof, SUNY Stony Brook, 74-75; from asst prof to assoc prof, Ohio Univ, 75-. **MEMBERSHIPS** Orgn of Am Historians, Soc for Historians of the Early Am Republic, Southern Hist Asn, Ohio Acad of Hist. **RESEARCH** Nineteenth-Century U.S. Political History, Race Relations. **SELECTED PUBLICATIONS** Auth, The Politics of Race in New York: The struggle for Black Suffrage in the Civil War Era, Cornell Univ Press (Ithaca, NY), 82. **CONTACT ADDRESS** Dept Hist, Ohio Univ, Athens, OH 45701-2942. **EMAIL** fieldp@ohio.edu

FIELDS, BARBARA J.
DISCIPLINE UNITED STATES HISTORY **EDUCATION** Harvard Univ, BA, 68; Yale Univ, PhD, 78. **CAREER** Prof. **SELECTED PUBLICATIONS** Auth, Slavery and Freedom on the Middle Ground: Maryland during the Nineteenth Century, 85; Slaves No More: Three Essays on Emancipation and the Civil War, 92; Free at Last: A Documentary History of Slavery, Freedom, and the Civil War, 92; co-auth, The Destruction of Slavery, 85. **CONTACT ADDRESS** Dept of History, Columbia Col, New York, 2960 Broadway, New York, NY 10027-6902.

FIELDS, LANNY BRUCE
PERSONAL Born 05/10/1941, Indianapolis, IN, 2 children **DISCIPLINE** ASIAN HISTORY **EDUCATION** DePauw Univ, BA, 63; Univ Hawaii, Manoa, MA, 66; Ind Univ, PhD (hist), 72. **CAREER** Prof, Calif State Univ. **RESEARCH** World hist, Our Global Past. **SELECTED PUBLICATIONS** Auth, "The Legalists and the Fall if Ch'in" Journal of Asian History; Tso Tsung-t'and and the Muslims ni the Northwest China, 1868-1880; auth, "The Ch'in Dynasty: Confucianism and Legalism," Journal of Asian History; auth, "His Wu-chu: Physician to the first Ch'in Emperor," Journal of Asian History. **CONTACT ADDRESS** Col of Social & Behavioral Sci, California State Univ, San Bernardino, 5500 Univ Pkwy, San Bernardino, CA 92407. **EMAIL** lfields@csusb.edu

FIEMA, ZBIGNIEW
PERSONAL Born 03/07/1957, Poland, s **DISCIPLINE** ARCHAEOLOGY; ANTHROPOLOGY **EDUCATION** Univ Utah, PhD, 91 **CAREER** Assoc Instr, 86-92, Univ Utah; Visiting Prof, Univ Helsinki, Finland, 96-97; Chief Archaelogist, American Center of Oriental Research, Jordan, 92-97. **HONORS AND AWARDS** Phi Kappa Phi Honors Soc, Univ Utah **MEMBERSHIPS** Amer Schools of Oriental Research; Archaelogical Inst of Amer. **RESEARCH** Culture History of the Roman & Byzantine East; complex societies; archaelogical methodology **SELECTED PUBLICATIONS** Coauth, Report on the Petra Scrolls Project, Journal of Archaelogy, 95; Auth, Military Architecture and Defense System in Roman-Byzantine Southern Jordan. A Critical Appraisal of Recent Interpretations, Studies in the Archaeology and History of Jordan V, 95; Sr Coauth, The Petra Church Project 92-94, The Roman and Byzantine Near East: Some Recent Archaeological Research, 95; Auth, Nabataean and Palmyrene Commerce - The Mechanisms of Intensification, The Proceedings of the International Conference on Palmyra and the Silk Road, 96; Les papyri de Petra, Le Monde de la Bible, 97; Report on the Petra Church Project, American Journal of Archaeology, 97; Petra Romana et Byzantina, Petra - Antike Felsstadt zwischen Arabischer Tradition und Griechischer Norm, 97; At-Tuwan - The Development and Decline of a Classical Town in Southern Jordan, Studies in the History and Archaeology of Jordan VI, 97; Report on the Roman Street in Petra Project, American Journal of Archaeology, 98. **CONTACT ADDRESS** Dept. of Philosophy Stewart Building, Univ of Utah, University of Utah, Salt Lake City, UT 84112.

FIERCE, MILFRED C.
PERSONAL Born 07/06/1937, Brooklyn, NY **DISCIPLINE** HISTORY **EDUCATION** Wagner Coll, BA, MS; Columbia U, MA, MPhil, PhD. **CAREER** Vassar Coll, dir Black Studies 69-71; Hunter Coll, prof, 73-81; Brooklyn Col (CUNY), professor, 82-. **HONORS AND AWARDS** So Hist Assn recipient, NDEA 1965; EPDA 1969; delegate Intl Congress of Africanists 1973; recipient Natl Endowment for the Humanities Fellowship, City Univ of NY, 1976. **MEMBERSHIPS** Apptd exec dir Assn of Black Found Exec Inc 1976; apptd NY St Coll Proficiency Exam Com in African & Afro-Am History, fall 1976; apptd research dir Study Commn on US Policy toward South Africa 1979; mem African-Am Tchrs Assn; African Heritage Studies Assn; Assn for Study of Afro- Amer Life & History; mem Am Historical Assn; Orgn of Am Historians. **CONTACT ADDRESS** 2900 Bedford Ave, Brooklyn, NY 11210.

FIGUEIRA, THOMAS J.
PERSONAL Born 12/30/1948, New York, NY, m, 1976, 3 children **DISCIPLINE** ANCIENT HISTORY **EDUCATION** Fordham Univ, 66-70; Bensalem Col, BA (Huamanities), 70; Univ Chicago, 70-73 (Classics dept); Univ PA, PhD (Ancient History), 77. **CAREER** Teaching fel, Univ Pa, 74-75; acting asst prof of Classics, Stanford Univ, 77-78; asst prof of Classics, Dickinson Col, Carlisle, Pa, 78-79; asst prof of Classics and Archaeology, Rutgers Univ, 79-85, assoc prof of Classics and Ancient Hist, Rutgers Univ, 85-90; vis assoc prof of Classics, Princeton Univ, 85-86; prof of Classics and Ancient Hist, 91-99; prof II (full-time, with tenure), Rutgers Univ, 99-. **HONORS AND AWARDS** Fulbright res fel to Greece, 76-77; Nat Endowment for the Humanities, summer seminar fel, 81; res fel, Center for Hellenic Studies (Harvard Univ), Washington, DC, 92-93; Exxon Ed Found, travel grant, summer 85; Am Coun of Learned Soc, travel grant, summer 85; vis scholar, School of Hist Studies, Inst for Advanced Study, Princeton, NJ, 84-85; res fel, John Simon Guggenheim Memorial Found, 84-85. **MEMBERSHIPS** Am Philol Asn; Asn of Ancient Historians; Archaeological Inst of Am; Am Hist Asn. **RESEARCH** Ancient Greek history and literature; social and economic history of the ancient world; classical historiography. **SELECTED PUBLICATIONS** Auth, Aegina, Arno Press, 81-82, reprint 86, 98; auth, "Mess Contributions and Subsistence at Sparta," Transactions of the Am Philological Asn (84); coauth, Theognis and Megara: Poetry and the Polis, Johns Hopkins Univ Press, 85; auth, "Population Patterns in Late Archaic and Classical Sparta," Transactions of the Am Philological Asn (86); auth, Aigina in the Age of Imperial Colonization, Johns Hopkins Univ Press, 91; auth, Excursions in Epichoric History, Rowman and Littlefield, 93; auth, The Power of Money: Coinage and Politics in the Athenian Empire, Univ PA, 98; auth, "The Evolution of the Messenian Identity," in Sparta: New Perspectives, ed. S. Hodkinson and A. Powell (Classical Press of Wales, 99); coauth, Wisdom from the Ancients: Enduring Business Lessons from Alexander the Great, Julius Caesar, and the Illustrious Leaders of Ancient Greece and Rome, Perseus Press, 01. **CONTACT ADDRESS** Dept of Classics, Rutgers, The State Univ of New Jersey, New Brunswick, 131 George St., New Brunswick, NJ 08901-1414. **EMAIL** figueira@rci.rutgers.edu

FILENE, PETER GABRIEL
PERSONAL Born 01/28/1940, New York, NY, m, 1960, 2 children **DISCIPLINE** MODERN AMERICAN HISTORY **EDUCATION** Swarthmore Col, BA, 60; Harvard Univ, MA, 61, PhD (hist), 65. **CAREER** Asst prof hist, Lincoln Univ, Mo, 65-67; from asst prof to assoc prof, 65-75, Prof Hist, Univ NC Chapel Hill, 75-, Fel, Charles Warren Ctr Studies Am Hist, 73. **MEMBERSHIPS** Orgn Am Hists. **RESEARCH** American social history; sex roles; multimedia techniques. **SELECTED PUBLICATIONS** Auth, Him/Her/Self: Gender Identies in Modern America, 3rd edition, 98; auth, In the Arms of Others: A Cultural History of the Right-to-Die in America, 98. **CONTACT ADDRESS** Dept of Hist, Univ of No Carolina, Chapel Hill, Hamilton Hall, Chapel Hill, NC 27599. **EMAIL** filene@email.unc.edu

FILONOWICZ, JOSEPH
DISCIPLINE HISTORY OF ETHICS, SOCIAL AND POLITICAL PHILOSOPHY **EDUCATION** Hope Col, BA; Columbia Univ, MA, MPhil, PhD. **CAREER** Assoc prof, Long Island Univ. **MEMBERSHIPS** Ch, Long Island Philos Soc. **RESEARCH** History of the ideas of the British sentimental moralists, moral philosophy, psychology of ethics, American philosophy. **SELECTED PUBLICATIONS** Wrote on ethical sentimentalism for the History of Philos Quart; auth, "Black American Philosophy as American Philosophy," Am Phil Assoc newsletter on Philos and the Black Experience. **CONTACT ADDRESS** Long Island Univ, Brooklyn, Brooklyn, NY 11201-8423. **EMAIL** joseph.filonowicz@liu.edu

FINAN, JOHN J.
PERSONAL Born 09/01/1925, St. Louis, MO, m, 1964, 2 children **DISCIPLINE** LATIN AMERICAN HISTORY **EDUCATION** Wash Univ, AB, 45, AM, 47; Harvard Univ, PhD(Latin Am hist), 56. **CAREER** Latin Am specialist, manuscripts div, Libr Cong, 53-55; Brown Univ President's fel, Argentina, 56-58; polit off, US Embassy, Colombia, 58-61; assoc prof, 61-69, prof & dir Latin Am Studies, 69-95, Prof Emeritus, Latin Am Studies, 95-, Sch Int Serv, Am Univ; Vis prof, Nat War Col, 67-69 **MEMBERSHIPS** Conf Latin Am Hist (secy-treas, 63-72). **RESEARCH** Nineteenth century Argentina; Latin American foreign relations; Argentine foreign policy; moral economy of colonial Mexico. **SELECTED PUBLICATIONS** Auth, Maize in the great herbals, Chronica Botanica, 51; coauth, Diplomatic History of Latin America, La State Univ, 77. **CONTACT ADDRESS** Sch of Int Svc, American Univ, Washington, DC 20016.

FINDLAY, JAMES F.
PERSONAL Born 12/03/1930, Oklahoma City, OK, m, 1955, 3 children **DISCIPLINE** HISTORY **EDUCATION** Drury Col, BA, 52; Wash Univ, MA, 54; Northwestern Univ, PhD, 61. **CAREER** Vis Assoc Prof, Univ Wis, 69-70; Prof, Univ RI, 71-99; Emeritus Status in 99. **HONORS AND AWARDS** Danforth Fel, 53-58; Two Books Nominated for Pulitzer Prize, 71, 93; NEH Grant, 84; Eli Lilly Found Res Awd, 90-91; Fulbright Fel, 97-98 **MEMBERSHIPS** Soc for Values in Higher Educ, Am Soc of Church Historians, Orgn of Am Historians. **RESEARCH** American religious history, history of the civil rights era (1950-1970), evangelicalism in Nineteenth-Century America. **SELECTED PUBLICATIONS** Auth, Dwight L. Moody: American Evangelist 1837-1899, Univ Chicago Pr (Chicago, IL), 70; auth, "The Churches and the Civil Rights Act of 1964," J of Am Hist (90); auth, Church People in the Struggle: The National Council of Churches and the Black Freedom Movement 1950-1970, Oxford Univ Pr (New Your, NY), 93; auth, "The Maintive Churches and Head Start in Mississippi," Church Hist (94). **CONTACT ADDRESS** Dept Hist, Univ of Rhode Island, Kingston, RI 02881. **EMAIL** jfi7196u@postoffice.uri.edu

FINDLEN, PAULA
PERSONAL Born 05/19/1964, Washington, DC **DISCIPLINE** HISTORY **EDUCATION** Wellesley Col, BA, 84;

Univ Calif, MA, 85; PhD, 89. **CAREER** Asst Prof to Full Prof, Univ Calif, 89-96; Vis Assoc Prof, Harvard Univ, 95; Assoc Prof to Full Prof, Stanford Univ, 95-. **HONORS AND AWARDS** Guggenheim, 98; Getty Scholar, 95; ACLS, 92; Fulbright, Italy 87; Pfizer prize, 96; Howard Marraro Prize, 95; Derek price Awd, 95; Nelson Prize, 90. **MEMBERSHIPS** Am Hist Asn, Renaissance Soc of Am, Hist of Sci Soc. **RESEARCH** Renaissance Italy; Early Mod Europe; Sci Revolution; Gender and knowledge. **SELECTED PUBLICATIONS** Auth, A Fragmentary Past: The Renaissance Origins of the Museum, Stanford Univ Press, forthcoming; auth, Possessing Nature: Museums, Collecting and Scientific Culture in Early Modern Italy, Berkeley, 94; auth, "Possessing the Past: the Material World of the Italian Renaissance,". American Historical Review, (98): 83-124; auth, "The Janus Faces of Science in the Seventeenth Century: Athanasias Kircher and Isaac Newton," in Rethinking the Scientific Revolution, 00; auth, "Science as a Career in Enlightenment Italy: The Strategies of Laura Bassi," Isis, (93): 441-469; auth, "Masculine Prerogatives: Gender, Space and Knowledge in the early Modern Museum," in the Architecture of Science, Cambridge, 99; auth, "Controlling the Experiment: Rhetoric, Court Patronage and the Experimental Method of Francesco Redi," History of Science (93): 35-64; auth, "Jokes of Nature and Jokes of Knowledge: The Playfulness of Scientific Discourse in Early Modern Europe," Renaissance Quarterly, (90); 292-331; auth, "The Museum: Its Classical Etymology and Renaissance Genealogy," Journal of the History of Collection, (89): 59-78. **CONTACT ADDRESS** Dept Hist, Stanford Univ, Stanford, CA 94305. **EMAIL** pfindlen@leland.stanford.edu

FINDLEY, CARTER VAUGHN
PERSONAL Born 05/12/1941, Atlanta, GA, m, 1968, 2 children **DISCIPLINE** HISTORY; MIDDLE EASTERN STUDIES **EDUCATION** Yale Col, BA, 63; Harvard Univ, PhD, 69. **CAREER** Asst prof, 72-79, assoc prof hist, Ohio State Univ, 79-86, prof hist, 86-; Soc Sci Res Coun fel, 76-77, 79, 86-87, Inst Adv Study, 81-82; Fulbright-Hays Sr Res Fel, 94 & 98; vis prof, Ecole des Hautes en Sci Soc, Paris, 94; vis lect Dept Hist, Bilkent Univ, Ankara, 97. **HONORS AND AWARDS** OH Acad Publ Awd and M Fuat Koprulu Book Prize Turkish Stud Assoc. **MEMBERSHIPS** Fel MidE Inst; fel MidE Studies Asn NAm; AHA; Am Oriental Soc; Comite Int pour les Etudes Pre-Ottomanes et Ottomanes; Oh Acad Hist; Turkish Stud Assoc (pres 90-92), Economic Soc Hist Found Turkey; World Hist Assoc vpres, 98-00, pres elect, 00-02. **RESEARCH** Ottoman history; Turkish studies; world history. **SELECTED PUBLICATIONS** Auth, Bureaucratic Reform in the Ottoman Empire: The Sublime Porte, 1789-1922, Princeton Univ, 80; Ottoman Civil Officialdom: A Social History, Princeton Univ, 89; Economic Bases of Revolution and Repression in the Late Ottoman Empire, Comparative Studies in Society and History, 86; La soumise, la subversive: Fatma Aliye, romanciere et feministe, Turcica, 95; Ebu Bekir Ratib's Vienna Embassy Narrative: Discovering Austria or Propagandizing for Reform in Istanbul, Wiener Zeitschrift fur die Kunde des Morgenlandes, 95; An Ottoman Occidentalist in Europe, Ahmed Midhat Meets Madame Gulnar, 1889, Am Hist Rev, 98; coauth Twentieth-Century World, Houghton Mifflin, 98. **CONTACT ADDRESS** Dept Hist, Ohio State Univ, Columbus, 230 W 17th Ave, Columbus, OH 43210-1361. **EMAIL** findley.1@osu.edu

FINDLING, JOHN ELLIS
PERSONAL Born 03/16/1941, South Bend, IN, m, 1968, 1 child **DISCIPLINE** HISTORY OF WORLD'S FAIRS AND EXPOSITIONS, OLYMPIC MOVEMENT, U.S. DIPLOMATIC **EDUCATION** Rice Univ, BA, 63; Univ Tex, Austin, MA, 65, PhD, 71. **CAREER** Teacher English, Am Nicaraguan Sch, Managua, 65-67; from Asst Prof to Assoc Prof, 71-81, Prof Hist, Ind Univ Southeast, 81-, Chmn, Div Soc Sci, 81-87, Dir MLS Prog, 93-97. **HONORS AND AWARDS** Outstanding Res Award, Ind Univ SE, 88, 98. **MEMBERSHIPS** AHA; Soc Historians Am For Rels; NAm Soc Sport Hist; Int Soc Hist Phys Educ and Sport; Int Soc Olympic Hist. **RESEARCH** Worlds fairs and expositions; sports history. **SELECTED PUBLICATIONS** Auth, Dictionary of American Diplomatic History, 80, rev ed, 89; Close Neighbors, Distant Friends: United States-Central American Relations, 87; Historical Dictionary of World's Fairs and Expositions, 90; Chicago's Great World's Fairs, 94; Historical Dictionary of the Modern Olympic Movement, 96; Fair America, 00; author of various other edited works and articles. **CONTACT ADDRESS** Div of Soc Sci, Indiana Univ, Southeast, 4201 Grant Line Rd, New Albany, IN 47150-2158. **EMAIL** jfindlin@ius.edu

FINE, SIDNEY
PERSONAL Born 10/11/1920, Cleveland, OH, m, 1942, 2 children **DISCIPLINE** UNITED STATES HISTORY **EDUCATION** Western Reserve Univ, AB, 42; Univ Mich, AM, 44 PhD, 48. **CAREER** From instr to prof, 48-59, Andrew Dickson White distinguished prof hist, Univ Mich, Ann Arbor, 74-, Guggenheim fel, 57-58; fac mem Salzburg Sem Am Studies, 59; Richard Hudson res prof, Univ Mich, 63-64 & 76-77, chmn dept hist, 69-71; Nat Arch Adv Coun, 68-71. **HONORS AND AWARDS** Univ Mich Press Awd, 65, 71, 85, 91; Distinguished Fac Achievement Awd, Univ Mich, 69; Henry Russel Lectr, Univ Mich, 84-85; Doctor of Letters, Wittenberg Univ, 84; Gustavus Myers Ctr for Human Rights Awd, 90; Doctor of Humane Letters, DePaw Univ, 97; Doctor of Laws, Univ Mass, 97. **MEMBERSHIPS** AHA; Labor Historians (pres, 69-71); Orgn Am Historians. **RESEARCH** United States history since 1876; American labor history. **SELECTED PUBLICATIONS** Auth, Anarchism and the Assassination of McKinley, Am Hist Rev, 7, 55; Laissez Faire and the General-Welfare State: A Study of Conflict in American Thought 1865-1901, 56; auth, The Automobile Under the Blue Eagle, Univ Mich, 63; Mr Justice Murphy in World War II, J Am Hist, 6, 66; Sit-Down: The General Motors Strike of 1936-1937, 69 Frank Murphy: The Detroit Years, 75, Univ Mich; Frank Murphy: The New Deal Years, Chicago, 79; Frank Murphy: The Washington Years, 84; Violence in the Model City: The Cavanagh Administration, Race Relations and the Detroit Riot of 1967, 89; auth, "Without Blare of Trumpets: Walter," the National Erectors Assoc and the Open Shop Movement, (95), 1903-1957; auth, "Expanding the Fronters of Civil Rights: Michigan 1948-1968, 00. **CONTACT ADDRESS** Dept of Hist, Univ of Michigan, Ann Arbor, 435 S State St, Ann Arbor, MI 48109-1003. **EMAIL** sidneyf@umich.edu

FINGER, JOHN R.
DISCIPLINE HISTORY **EDUCATION** Univ Wash, PhD. **CAREER** Prof emer, Hist, Univ Tenn. **RESEARCH** Indian-White relations. **SELECTED PUBLICATIONS** Auth, The Eastern Band of Cherokees 1819-1900, Univ Tennessee; Cherokee Americans: The Eastern Band of the Cherokees in the Twentieth Century, Univ Nebr. **CONTACT ADDRESS** Dept Hist, Univ of Tennessee, Knoxville, 915 Volunteer Blvd, 6th Fl, Dunford Hall, Knoxville, TN 37996-4065. **EMAIL** jfinger@utk.edu

FINK, CAROLE K.
DISCIPLINE HISTORY **EDUCATION** Bard Col, BA, 60; Yale Univ, MA, 61; PhD, 68. **CAREER** Instr, Conn Col, 64-65' Lecturer, Albertus Magnus Col, 66-67; Asst Prof, Canisius Col, 68-71; Asst Prof, SUNY, 71-78; Asst Prof to Prof and Dir of Grad Studies, Univ NC, 78-91; Chair, Loyola Col, 87-88; Vis Prof, Vanderbilt Univ, 91; Prof, Ohio State Univ, 91-. **HONORS AND AWARDS** Sen Fel, Rutgers Inst, 94; NEH Res Fel, 91-92; NEH Summer Fel, 90; Fulbright Res Fel, 91-92; Woodrow Wilson Ctr, Guest Scholar, 90; Fel, Woodrow Wilson Ctr, 86-87; Res Fel, Am Coun of Learned Soc, 82-83; Res Awd, Am Philos Soc, 90, 82, 74; George Louis Beer Prize, Am Hist Asn, 85. **MEMBERSHIPS** am Hist Asn, Conf Group on Central European, German Studies Asn, Peace Hist Asn, Asn Internationale d'Histoire Contemporaine de l'Europe. **RESEARCH** 20th Century European International History; 20th Century Historiography; Minority rights and Human rights. **SELECTED PUBLICATIONS** Auth, 1968: The World transformed, Cambridge Univ Press, 98; co-ed, L'etablissement des frontieres en Europe apres les deux guerres mondiales, Peter Lang Pub, 96; auth, The Genoa conference: European Diplomacy, 1921-1922, Syracuse Univ Press, 94; auth, Genoa, Rapallo, and the reconstruction of Europe in 1922, Cambridge Univ Press, 91; auth, Marc Bloch: A Life in History, Cambridge Univ Press, 89; auth, "The Minorities Question at the Paris Peace conference," in The Treaty of Versailles: A Reassessment after 75 Years, Cambridge Univ Press, 98; auth, "Between the Second and Third Reichs: the Weimar Republic as Imperial Interregnum," in The end of Empire? The Transformation of the USSR in comparative Perspective, M.E. Sharpe, 96; auth, "The Murder of Walther Rathenau," Judaism, (95): 259-270. **CONTACT ADDRESS** Dept Hist, Ohio State Univ, Columbus, 230 W 17th Ave, Columbus, OH 43210-1361. **EMAIL** fink.24@osu.edu

FINK, GARY M.
PERSONAL Born 02/04/1936, Forsyth, MT, m, 1959, 4 children **DISCIPLINE** UNITED STATES HISTORY **EDUCATION** Univ MT, BS, 60; Univ MO, MA, 64, PhD, 68. **CAREER** Asst prof hist, Mankato State Col, 68-70; assoc prof, 70-80, prof hist, GA State Univ, 80- , dept ch, 84-92. **MEMBERSHIPS** AHA; Orgn Am Historians; Southern Hist Asn; Soc Sci Hist Asn. **RESEARCH** US polit hist; quantitative analysis; labor hist. **SELECTED PUBLICATIONS** Auth, The Fulton Bag and Cotton Mill Strike, 1914-1915, Univ Cornell, 93; co-ed, Essays in Southern Labor History, Greenwood, 78; co-ed, Race, Class, and Community in Southern Labor History, Univ Ala, 94; co-ed, The Carter Presidency: Policy Choices in the Post-New Deal Era, Univ Kans, 98, 01. **CONTACT ADDRESS** Dept of Hist, Georgia State Univ, Univ Plza, Atlanta, GA 30303-3080. **EMAIL** hisgmf@panther.gsu.edu

FINK, ROBERT J.
PERSONAL Born 02/17/1931, Rochester, NY, m, 1974, 1 child **DISCIPLINE** FRENCH RENAISSANCE, CINEMA **EDUCATION** Univ Toronto, BA, 54, MA, 58; Univ Chicago, PhD (Romance lang), 71. **CAREER** From instr to asst prof French, St Michael's Col, Univ Toronto, 65-73; arts officer, Can Coun, 73-77; assoc prof, St Francis Xavier Univ, 78-80; assoc prof, Mt Allison Univ, 80-81; Prof French, Acadia Univ, 81-. **MEMBERSHIPS** MLA; Renaissance Soc Am; Can Soc Renaissance Studies. **RESEARCH** French Renaissance humanism; French-Canadian novel and cinema. **SELECTED PUBLICATIONS** Auth, The National Wildlife Refuges--Theory, Practice, and Prospect, Harvard Environmental Law Rev, Vol 18, 94. **CONTACT ADDRESS** Dept of Mod Lang, Acadia Univ, Wolfville, NS, Canada B0P 1Z1.

FINK, WILLIAM BERTRAND
PERSONAL Born 05/11/1916, Yonkers, NY, m, 1941, 2 children **DISCIPLINE** HISTORY **EDUCATION** Wesleyan Univ, AB, 37; Columbia Univ, AM, 39, PhD (Am hist), 50. **CAREER** Teacher, Pub Schs, Md, 39-42; critic teacher, State Univ NY Col Teachers, Albany, 46-49; instr soc sci, Teachers Col, Columbia Univ, 49-51; supvr social studies, Pub Schs, NJ, 51-53; prof hist, State Univ NY Col Oneonta, 53-82, chmn, Dept Soc Sci Educ, 70-81; Retired, Fulbright lectr, Philippines, 61-62; surv consult, NY State Hist Trust, 67-68; vis prof, Trent Polytech, England, 78; fel, Hughes Hall, Cambridge, 78. **MEMBERSHIPS** AHA; Nat Coun Social Studies; Orgn Am Hists. **RESEARCH** New York state history; 20th century United States; social studies curriculum in secondary schools. **SELECTED PUBLICATIONS** Co-auth, New York, the Empire State, 1961-1980; auth, Getting to Know New York State, 70; Getting to Know the Hudson River, 70. **CONTACT ADDRESS** Laurens, NY 13796.

FINKEL, ALVIN
PERSONAL Born 05/17/1949, Winnipeg, MB, Canada **DISCIPLINE** HISTORY **EDUCATION** Univ Man, BA, 70, MA, 72; Univ Toronto, PhD, 76. **CAREER** Lectr, Univ Manitoba, Univ Brandon, 74; vis lectr, Queen's Univ, 75-76; lectr, Univ Alta, 76-78; asst to assoc prof, 78-86, PROF HISTORY, ATHABASCA UNIV, 86-. **MEMBERSHIPS** Can Hist Asn **SELECTED PUBLICATIONS** Auth, Social Reform in the Thirties, 79; auth, The Social Credit Phenomenon in Alberta, 89; auth, Our Lives: Canada 1945-1996, 97; coauth, History of the Canadian Peoples, vols 1 & 2, 93, 2nd ed 97; coauth, The Chamberlain-Hitler Collusion, 97; ed, Prairie Forum, 86-95. **CONTACT ADDRESS** History Dept, Athabasca Univ, Box 10,000, Athabasca, AB, Canada T0G 2R0. **EMAIL** alvinf@athabascau.ca

FINKELSTEIN, BARBARA
PERSONAL Born 03/22/1937, Brooklyn, NY, m, 1959, 2 children **DISCIPLINE** AMERICAN HISTORY, HISTORY OF EDUCATION **EDUCATION** Columbia Univ, BA, 59; MA, 60; EdD, 70. **CAREER** Lectr hist educ, Brooklyn Col, 61-62; asst prof, 70-74, assoc prof, 74-83, prof, 83- , hist educ, dir, Ctr Stud Educ Policy & Human Values, 79- , Univ Md, College Park; Nat Endowment for Humanities fel, 75-76; contrib ed, J Psychohist, 77- ; Japan Soc for Promotion of Sci fel, 91-92; ser ed, Reflective Hist, Teachers Col Press, Columbia Univ, 94- ; adv bd, US Ed, Pedagogica Hist, 89- ; Int Adv Bd, Hist of Educ, 96- . **HONORS AND AWARDS** Critic's Choice Awd, Am Educ Studies Asn, 81; recipient Key to the City of Osaka, 87; Am Educ Press Asn Awd, 89; Distinguished Int Service Awd, Univ Md, 94-95; Outstanding Woman of the Year, Univ Md, 97-98. **MEMBERSHIPS** Am Educ Studies Asn (pres, 81-82); Hist Educ Soc (pres, 98-99); Am Educ Res Asn (vpres, 89-91); Soc Res Child Develop. **RESEARCH** Family and education in historical perspective; childhood history in nineteenth century United States; learners and learning in American History; comparative cultural studies. **SELECTED PUBLICATIONS** Auth, Governing the Young: Teacher Behavior in Popular Primary Schools in Nineteenth Century United States, Taylor & Francis, 89; auth, Dollars and Dreams: Classrooms as Fictitious Message Systems, 1790-1930, Hist of Educ Q, 91; auth, Perfecting Childhood: Horace Mann and the Origins of Public Education in the United States, Biography, 91; auth, Education Historians as Mythmakers, Rev of Res in Educ, 92; auth, The Evolving Terrain of Teaching: Classroom Management in the United States, 1790-1990, in, Classroom Practices and Politics in Cross Cultural Perspective, Garland, 97; coauth, Discovering Culture in Education: An Approach to Cultural Education Program Evaluation and Design, 98; ed and contribur, Hidden Messages: Instructional Materials for Cultural Teaching and Learning, Intercultural, 98. **CONTACT ADDRESS** Dept of Educ Policy, Univ of Maryland, Col Park, College Park, MD 20742-0001. **EMAIL** bf6@umail.umd.edu

FINKELSTEIN, GABRIEL
PERSONAL Born 04/12/1963, Philadelphia, PA, m, 1995 **DISCIPLINE** HISTORY **EDUCATION** Amherst Col, BA, 85; Princeton Univ, MA, 89; PhD, 96. **CAREER** Sales trainer, The Southwestern Company, 84-87; teaching asst, Amherst Col, 83-84; instr, Landesbank Berlin, 92-94; teaching asst, Princeton Univ, 90-96; adj prof, Univ of Pa, 96; vis asst prof, Univ of Calif, 97-98; lectr, Princeton Univ, 98-99; asst prof, Univ of Colo at Denver, 99-. **HONORS AND AWARDS** Volkswagon Post-Doctoral Fel, Inst for the Hist of Sci at Gottingen Univ, 97; SSRC Fel, Free Univ of Berlin, 90-91; DAAD Fel, 90-91; Fel, Princeton Univ, 87. **MEMBERSHIPS** Am Hist Asn, Hist of Sci Soc, Int Soc for the Hist and Philos of the Biol Sci. **RESEARCH** Nineteenth-Century German science, history of exploration. **SELECTED PUBLICATIONS** Rev, of "Gustav Magnus und sein Haus: Im Auftrag der Deutschen Physikalischen Gesellschaft," Technol and Culture 39.3 (98): 568-569; auth, "New Perspectives on Alexander von Humboldt," NTM 6 (98): 60; auth, "Headless in Kashgar," Endeavour 23.1 (99): 5-9; auth, "Kultur-Evolution bei Emil du Bois-Reymond," Evolutionsbiologie von Darwin bis heute, 00; auth, "'Conquerors of the Kunlun'? The Schlagintweit Mission to High Asia, 1854-1857," Hist of Sci (forthcoming). **CONTACT ADDRESS** Dept Hist, Univ of Colorado, Denver, Campus Box 182, PO Box 173364, Denver, CO 80217-3364. **EMAIL** gabriel.finkelstein@cudenver.edu

FINKELSTEIN, JOSEPH
PERSONAL Born 05/13/1926, Troy, NY, m, 1955 **DISCIPLINE** HISTORY **EDUCATION** Union Col, NYork, BA, 46; Harvard Univ, MA, 49, PhD (hist), 52. **CAREER** Instr hist and econ, Union Col, NY, 46-48; teaching fel, Harvard Univ, 50-52; from asst prof to assoc prof, 53-63, Prof Hist and Econ and Admin Hist, Union Col, NY, 63-, Fulbright grant, London, 52-53. **MEMBERSHIPS** AHA; Econ Hist Asn; Hist Asn England; Acad Int Bus, Am Arbitration Asn. **RESEARCH** American economic history; American business history; multinational companies. **SELECTED PUBLICATIONS** Auth, Relevance and Renewal at the 92nd Street Y, Dance Mag, Vol 68, 94; Humphrey, Doris and the 92nd Street Y--A Dance Center for the People, Dance Rsch J, Vol 28, 96. **CONTACT ADDRESS** Dept of Hist, Union Col, New York, Schenectady, NY 12308.

FINKELSTEIN, RONA G.
PERSONAL Born 11/07/1927, Rochester, NY, w, 1950, 2 children **DISCIPLINE** ART; PHILOSOPHY **EDUCATION** Connecticut Col, BA, 49; MA, 61, PhD, 64, Univ Rochester. **CAREER** Delaware State Col, 64-70, chairperson, 66-70; Univ Delaware, Col Parallel Program, 70-72; Exec Dir, Delaware Humanities Forum, 72-81. **MEMBERSHIPS** APA **RESEARCH** Mind-Body **CONTACT ADDRESS** 115 Sorrel Dr., Surrey Pk., Wilmington, DE 19803. **EMAIL** rfinkel850@aol.com

FINKENBINE, ROY E.
PERSONAL Born 09/09/1953, Sidney, OH, m, 1982, 4 children **DISCIPLINE** HISTORY **EDUCATION** Taylor Univ, BS, 75; N Ariz Univ, MA, 76; Bowling Green State Univ, PhD, 82. **CAREER** Assoc ed, Black Abolitionist Papers Proj, Fla State Univ, 82-91; asst prof, Murray State Univ, 91-92; asst prof, Hampton Univ, 92-96; assoc prof, Univ Detroit Mercy, 98-. **HONORS AND AWARDS** Editing Fel, Nat Hist Publ and Records Comm, 81-82; Fel, NEH Summer Inst, 86. **MEMBERSHIPS** Am Hist Assoc; Org of Am Hist. **RESEARCH** African-American History, especially black abolitionists. **SELECTED PUBLICATIONS** Coed, The Black Abolitionist Papers, 1830-1865, Univ of NC Pr, 85-92; auth, "Our Little Circle: Benevolent Reformers, the Slater Fund and the Argument for Black Industrial Education, 1882-1908, Hayes Historical Journal, 86; coed, Witness for Freedom: African American Voices on Race, Slavery and Emancipation, Univ NC Pr, 93; auth, "Boston's Black Churches: Institutional Centers of the Antislavery Movement", Courage and Conscience: Black and White Abolitionists in Boston, Indiana Univ Pr, 93; auth, "The Symbolism of Slave Mutiny: Black Abolitionist Responses to the Amistad and Creole Incidents", Rebellion, Repression and Reinvention: Mutiny in Comparative Contexts, Praeger, 00. **CONTACT ADDRESS** Dept Hist, Univ of Detroit Mercy, PO Box 19900, Detroit, MI 48219-0900. **EMAIL** finkenre@udmercy.edu

FINLAY, ROBERT
DISCIPLINE HISTORY **EDUCATION** Univ Chicago, PhD. **CAREER** Assoc prof. **RESEARCH** Medieval and early modern European history. **SELECTED PUBLICATIONS** Auth, The Treasure-ships of Zheng He, J Hist Discoveries, 91; Portuguese and Chinese Maritime Imperialism: Camoes's Lusiads and Luo Maodeng's Voyage of the San Bao Eunuch, Comp Studies Soc Hist, 92. **CONTACT ADDRESS** History Dept, Univ of Arkansas, Fayetteville, 532 Old Main, Fayetteville, AR 72701. **EMAIL** rfinlay@comp.uark.edu

FINLAYSON, MICHAEL G.
PERSONAL Born 10/20/1938, Melbourne, Australia **DISCIPLINE** HISTORY **EDUCATION** Univ Melbourne, BA, 59, MA, 64; Univ Toronto, PhD, 68. **CAREER** Asst to assoc prof, 68-85, Prof Hist, 85-, ch hist, 87-91, Vice Pres (Admin & Human Resourdes), Univ Toronto, 94-; vis fel, La Trobe Univ Melbourne, 81; vis fel, Corpus Christi Col, Cambridge, 82; vis fel, Clare Hall, Cambridge, 89. **MEMBERSHIPS** Can Hist Asn; Conf Brit Stud. **RESEARCH** Seventeeth century English political and religious history and historiography. **SELECTED PUBLICATIONS** Auth, Historians, Puritanism and the English Revolution, 83; co-ed, The Struggle for Power, 87. **CONTACT ADDRESS** Univ of Toronto, 27 Kings College Cir, #112, Toronto, ON, Canada M5S 1A1. **EMAIL** michael,finlayson@utoronto.ca

FINLAYSON, WILLIAM D.
PERSONAL Born 03/01/1946, Toronto, ON, Canada **DISCIPLINE** ARCHAEOLOGY, HISTORY **EDUCATION** Univ Toronto, BA, 69, MA, 70, PhD, 76. **CAREER** Lectr, 73-76, vis asst prof, 76-79, adj prof, 79-82, adj assoc prof, Univ Western Ont, 95-; exec dir, 76-91, DIR GEN, LONDON MUS ARCHAEOLOGY, 91-; special lectr, 79-84, vis assoc prof, Univ Toronto, 78-79, 84-87; LAWSON PROF CAN ARCHAEOL, UNIV WESTERN ONT, 85-; dir gen, London and Middlesex Heritage Mus, 91-. **HONORS AND AWARDS** Milton Heritage Awd, 92; Ralph Sherwood Conserv Awd, Halton Reg Conserv Authority, 96. **MEMBERSHIPS** Ont Heritage Found; Ont Coun Archaeol. **SELECTED PUBLICATIONS** Auth, The Saugeen Culture, 76; auth, The 1975 and 1978 Rescue Excavations at the Draper Site: Introduction and Settlement Patterns, 85; coauth, What Columbus Missed!, 87; ed, Can Archaeol Asn Bull, 74-76. **CONTACT ADDRESS** London Mus of Archaeology, 1600 Attawandaron Rd, London, ON, Canada N6G 3M6. **EMAIL** wfinlays@julian.uwo.ca

FINLEY, GERALD E.
PERSONAL Born 07/17/1931, Munich, Germany **DISCIPLINE** ART HISTORY **EDUCATION** Univ Toronto, BA, 55, MA, 57; Johns Hopkins Univ, PhD, 65. **CAREER** Lectr, Univ Toronto, 59-60; lectr, Univ Sask, 62-63; fac mem 63, acting/head dept, 63-72, PROF EMER HISTORY OF ART, QUEEN'S UNIV; fel, Inst Advan Stud Hum, Univ Edinburgh, 79-80. **HONORS AND AWARDS** Fel, Royal Soc Can; Brit Coun; Can Coun; SSHRCC; Can Fedn Hum. **SELECTED PUBLICATIONS** Auth, In Praise of Older Buildings, 76; auth, George Heriot 1759-1839, 79; auth, Landscapes of Memory: Turner as Illustrator to Scott, 80; auth, Turner and George IV in Edinburgh 1822, 81; auth, George Heriot: Postmaster-Painter of the Canadas, 83. **CONTACT ADDRESS** Dept of Art, Queen's Univ at Kingston, Kingston, ON, Canada K7L 3N6.

FINN, MARGOT C.
DISCIPLINE HISTORY **EDUCATION** Syracuse Univ, BS, 80; Columbia Univ, MA 83, MPhil, 84, PhD 87. **CAREER** Assoc prof, Emory Univ. **HONORS AND AWARDS** NACBS John Ben Snow Found Prize, 94; NEH fel, 98; ed, jour brit studies. **RESEARCH** Modern British history. **SELECTED PUBLICATIONS** Auth, After Chartism: Class and Nation in English Radical Politics, 1848-1874. **CONTACT ADDRESS** Dept History, Emory Univ, 222 Bowden Hall, Atlanta, GA 30322. **EMAIL** mfinn01@emory.edu

FINN, THOMAS M.
PERSONAL Born 03/18/1927, New York, NY, m, 1968, 1 child **DISCIPLINE** PATRISTICS **EDUCATION** St. Paul's Col, AB, 56, MA, 58; Cath Univ Am, STL, 61, STD, 65. **CAREER** Chancellor Prof Relig. Col William and Mary, 73-. **HONORS AND AWARDS** Melone Fel, Coun on U.S. Arab Relations, 90; Res Fel, Inst Ecumenical and Cultural Res, 95. **MEMBERSHIPS** Am Acad Relig; Cath Bibl Asn; NAm Patristic Soc; Int Patristic Soc. **RESEARCH** Ritual in Greco-Roman antiquity, paganism, Judaism, and Christianity. **SELECTED PUBLICATIONS** Auth, Early Christian Baptism and the Catechumenate: Italy, North Africa and Egypt, Litturgical Press, 92; Early Christian Baptism and the Catechumenate: West and East Syria, Litturgical Press, 92; From Death to Rebirth: Conversion in Antiquity, Paulist Press, 97; Quodvultdeus: The Preacher and the Audience: The Homilies on the Creed, Studia Patristica 31, 97; Ritual and Conversion: The Case of Augustine, Nova & Vetera: Patristic Studies in Honor of Thomas Patrick Halton, Cath Univ Am Press, 98. **CONTACT ADDRESS** Religion Dept, Col of William and Mary, 310 Wren Building, Williamsburg, VA 23187-8795. **EMAIL** tmfinn@wm.edu

FINNEGAN, TERENCE ROBERT
PERSONAL Born 08/06/1961, Oak Park, IL, m, 4 children **DISCIPLINE** HISTORY **EDUCATION** Marquette Univ, BA, 83; MA, 86; Univ Ill, PhD, 93. **CAREER** Asst prof, William Paterson Col, 93-; vis prof, Nat Ctr for Supercomput Appln, Univ Ill, 94-95; postdr res assoc, Nat Ctr for Supercomput Appln(s), Univ Ill, 92-93; proj coordr, Univ Ill, Hist Census Database Proj, 91-92; asst to prin invesr, Univ Ill Hist Supercomputer Proj, 88-90; asst res, Univ Ill Lang Learning Lab, 88; coed, H-South, an H-Net electronic jour of US Southern Hist, 93-96; ed, Soc Sci Comput Asn Newsletter, 94-96; ed bd mem, H-MMedia, 94-96; fac affil, Univ Ill Hist Dept & Univ Ill Afro-Amer Stud Prog, 92-93 & 94-95; conf coordr, Conf on Comput for the Soc Sci, 93; VP, Hist Grad Stud Asn, 88; Hist Dept Comput Rsrc(s) Comt, 88-91; Archv, St John's Catholic Chapel & the Newman Found, Univ Ill, 88-92; grad res asst, Univ Ill, 87-89; asst prof, William Paterson Col, 93-94 & 95-96; instr, Hist Hon(s) Colloquium, Violence in America, 92; co-instr, Quantitative Methods in His, 90 & 92; asst, Family and Comm Hon(s) course, 90; tchg asst, Univ Ill, 86-87 & Marquette Univ, 84-86. **HONORS AND AWARDS** Postdoctoral fel, Nat Sci Found, CISE Inst Infrastructure Div, 92-93 & 94-95; co-investr, Nat Sci Found CISE/IRIS Div grant, 91-92; invited participant, Ctr for Documentary Stud, Duke Univ with NC Cent Univ, 91; conf fel, Wake Frst Univ, 91; Harry Frank Guggenheim Dissertation fel, 90-91; dissertation travel grant, Univ Ill, 90; Univ Ill Hist Dept fel, 89-90; Joseph L Swain Awd, Univ Ill Hist Dept, 88; Phi Kappa Phi, Univ Ill, 88; , Summer fel, Univ Ill Lang Learning Lab, 88; Summer fel, Univ Ill Soc Sci Quantitative Lab, 87; Incomplete List of Excellent Tchr(s), Univ Ill, 86; Phi Alpha Theta, Marquette Univ, 83. **RESEARCH** African-American history, Civil rights movement, comparative labor history. **SELECTED PUBLICATIONS** Auth, The Equal of Some White Men and the Superior of Others: Racial Hegemony and the 1916 Lynching of Anthony Crawford in Abbeville County, SC, The Proceedings of the SC Hist Asn, 94; coauth, Developing a Distributed Computing U.S. Census Database Linkage System, NCSA Tech Report no 027, 94; South Carolina, in Quiet Revolution in the South: The Impact of the Voting Rights Act 1965-1990, Princeton Univ Press, 94; It Ain't Broke, So Don't Fix It: The Legal and Factual Importance of Recent Attacks on Methods Used in Vote Dilution Litigation, San Francisco Law Rev, 93; The Civil War, chapter 15 of the Documents Collection that accompanies James Henretta, et al, America's Hist, vol 1, NY: Worth Publishers, 93; rev, Emancipation: The Making of the Black Lawyer, 1844-1944 in The Annals, 95; War of Another Kind: A Southern Community in the Great Rebellion, Agr Hist 65, 91. **CONTACT ADDRESS** Dept of History, William Paterson Col of New Jersey, 300 Pompton Rd., Wayne, NJ 07470. **EMAIL** finnegan@frontier.wilpaterson.edu

FINNEY, PAUL CORBY
DISCIPLINE HISTORY, ART & ARCHAEOLOGY, RELIGION **EDUCATION** Yale Univ, AB, 62; Maximilians Univ, Germany, 62-63; Harvard Univ, MA, PhD, 73. **CAREER** ASST PROF, ASSOC PROF, PROF, UNIV MO, ST LOUIS, 73-; area supervisor, Am Schs Oriental Res excavation Cathage, Tunisia, 75- 77; sen lectr, Hebrew Univ, Jerusalem, 79; vis lectr, Princeton Theol Sem, 83; sen assoc, Am Sch Class Stud, Athens, 87; assoc archaeologist, Gr Ministry Antiquities, 87; vis fel, Princeton Univ, 92, 95, 98, 99. **CONTACT ADDRESS** Dept of History, Univ of Missouri, St. Louis, 8001 Natural Bridge Rd, Saint Louis, MO 63121. **EMAIL** spcfinn@umslvma.umsl.edu

FIREMAN, JANET RUTH
PERSONAL Born 05/09/1945, Phoenix, AZ, m, 1980 **DISCIPLINE** AMERICAN AND MEXICAN HISTORY **EDUCATION** Univ Ariz, BA, 67; Univ NMex, MA, 68, PhD (hist), 72. **CAREER** From asst prof to assoc prof hist, Calif State Univ Fresno, 71-78; Assoc Cur Social and Cult Hist, Los Angeles County Mus Nat Hist, 76-, Ed consult hist, J San Diego Hist, 77- and Calif Hist, 80-. **MEMBERSHIPS** Western Hist Asn; Pac Coast Coun Latin Am Studies; AHA; Western Asn Women Hists. **RESEARCH** Spanish Southwest; Western American cultural history. **SELECTED PUBLICATIONS** Coauth, Miguel Costanso: California's forgotten founder, Calif Hist Soc Quart, 3/70; contribr, Spanish Military Weapons in Colonial America, 1700-1821, Stackpole, 72; auth, Reflections on teaching Women's history: first down and goal to go, J West, 4/73; Spain's Royal Corps of Engineers in the Western Borderlands; Instrument of Bourbon Reform, 1764 to 1815, Arthur H Clark, 77. **CONTACT ADDRESS** Los Angeles County Mus of Natural Hist, 900 Exposition Blvd, Los Angeles, CA 90007.

FISCHER, BERND
DISCIPLINE HISTORY **EDUCATION** Univ Ca, PhD, 82. **CAREER** Prof. **HONORS AND AWARDS** Res grantee, Am Coun Learned Socs, 89; NEH, 92; travel grantee, Mellon Found, 95. **MEMBERSHIPS** Soc for Albanian Studies; Int Asn for Southeast European Studies. **RESEARCH** Balkans history; Ottoman Empire history. **SELECTED PUBLICATIONS** Auth, King Zog and the Struggle for Stability in Albania, 84; ed, CLIO Jour Lit, Hist, and Philos of Hist, 95; contributor, Eastern European Nationalism in the 20th Century, 95; ed, Albanian Studies: International Registry of Scholars and Research, 98; auth, Albania at War, 1939-1945, 00. **CONTACT ADDRESS** Dept of History, Indiana Univ-Purdue Univ, Fort Wayne, 2101 Coliseum Blvd, Fort Wayne, IN 46805.

FISCHER, KLAUS P.
PERSONAL Born 12/12/1942, Munich, Germany, m, 1981, 3 children **DISCIPLINE** HISTORY **EDUCATION** Ariz State Univ, BA, 64; MA, 66; Univ Calif, PhD, 72. **CAREER** Instr, Ft Lewis Col, 68-69; Dir and Adj Prof, Chapman Col, 73-90; Prof, Allan Hancock Col, 90-. **HONORS AND AWARDS** Phi Alpha Theta; Fel, Univ Calif, 66-67; Instr of the Year, Hancock Col, 80. **MEMBERSHIPS** Am Hist Asn, Mencken Soc. **RESEARCH** Nazi Germany, the Holocaust, philosophy of history, political philosophy, youth movements. **SELECTED PUBLICATIONS** Auth, John Locke in the German Enlightenment, 72; auth, History and Prophecy: Oswald Spangler and the Decline of the West, Peter Lang Publ (New York, NY), 80; auth, Nazi Germany: A New History, Continuum (New York, NY), 95; auth, The History of an Obsession: German Judeophobia and the Holocaust, Continuum (New York, NY), 98. **CONTACT ADDRESS** Dept Soc Sci, Allan Hancock Col, 800 S College Dr, Santa Maria, CA 93454-6399. **EMAIL** kpfischer@hotmail.com

FISCHER, ROBERT HARLEY
PERSONAL Born 04/26/1918, Williamsport, PA, m, 1942, 1 child **DISCIPLINE** CHURCH HISTORY **EDUCATION** Gettysburg Col, AB, 39; Lutheran Theol Sem, Gettysburg, BD, 42; Yale Univ, PhD, 47. **CAREER** Minister, Hartland Community Parish, VT, 44-45; asst pastor, Zion Lutheran Church, Sunbury, Pa, 47-49; PROF HIST THEOL, LUTHERAN SCH THEOL, CHICAGO, 49-86, Kirchliche Hochschule, Berlin, 73 and Lutheran Sem, Tokyo, 80; tutor, Mansfield Col, Oxford Univ, 57-58; Am Asn Theol Schs fel, Tubingen, 64-65; assoc ed, Lutheran Quart, 66-72. **HONORS AND AWARDS** Phi Beta Kappa, Sterling Research Fellowship, Yale. **MEMBERSHIPS** Am Theol Soc Midwest Div; Am Soc Reformation Res (pres, 54); NAm Acad Ecumenists; Am Soc Church Hist; Lutheran Hist Conf (vpres, 72-76). **RESEARCH** Reformation history, especially theology of Luther; 19th century American Lutheranism; ecumenics. **SELECTED PUBLICATIONS** Ed, Luther's Large Catechism in Tappert, ed Book of Concord, 59; ed, Luther's Works V. 37 (Lord'sSupper Writings), 61; ed, Franklin Clark Fry, 72; ed, A Tribute to Arthur Voobus, 77; auth, Luther,

1966: A Servant of All People (W.A. Passerant), 97. **CONTACT ADDRESS** 5324 Central Ave, Western Springs, IL 60558.

FISCHER, ROGER ADRIAN
PERSONAL Born 05/08/1939, Minneapolis, MN, m, 1962, 3 children **DISCIPLINE** UNITED STATES HISTORY **EDUCATION** Univ MN, BA, 60, MA, 63; Tulane Univ, PhD, 67. **CAREER** Instr hist, Univ Southwestern La, 63-64; asst prof, Southern Univ, New Orleans Ctr, 65-67; asst prof, Sam Houston State Col, 67-69; assoc prof, Southwest MO State Col, 69-72; assoc prof, 72-80, prof hist, Univ MN, Duluth 80. **HONORS AND AWARDS** L. Kemper Williams Prize, 75; Carl Bode Awd, 87. **MEMBERSHIPS** Southern Hist Asn; AHA. **RESEARCH** Hist of the Negro, the South, the Civil War and Reconstruction, Am Polit Cult. **SELECTED PUBLICATIONS** Auth, Pioneer protest: The New Orleans street-car controversy of 1867, J Negro Hist, 7/68; Racial segregation in antebellum New Orleans, Am Hist Rev, 2/69; Ghetto and gown: The birth of Black studies, Current Hist, 11/69; The Segregation Struggle in Louisiana, 1862-1877, Univ Ill, Urbana, 74; American Political Ribbons & Ribbon Badges, 1825-1981 (with Edmund B. Sullivan), Quarterman Pub, 85; Tippecanoe and Trinkets Too: Material Culture in American Presidential Campaigns, 1828-1984, Univ of Ill, 88; Them Damned Pictures: Explorations in American Political Cartoon Art, Archon, 96. **CONTACT ADDRESS** Dept of Hist, Univ of Minnesota, Duluth, 10 University Dr, Duluth, MN 55812-2496.

FISHBURN, JANET FORSYTHE
PERSONAL Born 01/18/1937, Wilkinsburg, PA, m, 1958, 3 children **DISCIPLINE** AMERICAN CHURCH AND CULTURAL HISTORY **EDUCATION** Monmouth Col, BA, 58; Pa State Univ, PhD, 78. **CAREER** Dir Christian educ, 1st United Presby Church, Cleveland Heights, Ohio, 58-60; Instr humanities and Am studies, Pa State Univ, 77-78; Prof, Teaching Ministry and Church Hist, Theol Sch, Drew Univ, 78-95; Prof and Researchers Relig Educ, 95-. **MEMBERSHIPS** Am Acad Relig; Am Soc of Church Hist; ASC. **RESEARCH** American church history and contemporary Christian ministry; family studies and intergenerational education; theological; Reformed Tradition and Matrerial Culture in US; Social Gospel in the US. **SELECTED PUBLICATIONS** Auth, The Fatherhood of God and the Victorian Family: A Study of the Soicial Gospel in America, Fortress, 82; auth, Confronting the Idolatry of Family: A New Vision For the Household of God, Abingdon, 91; auth, Cultural Diversity and Seminary Teaching, Rel Educ, Vol 90, 95; Tennent, Gilbert, Established Dissenter, Church Hist, Vol 63.95; Preacher, Sunday, Billy and Big Time American Evangelism, Am Presbyterians J Presbyterian Hist, Vol 74, 96. **CONTACT ADDRESS** 74 Barnsdale Rd, Madison, NJ 07940. **EMAIL** jfishbur@drew.edu

FISHER, ALAN WASHBURN
PERSONAL Born 11/23/1939, Columbus, OH, m, 1963, 3 children **DISCIPLINE** RUSSIAN & EUROPEAN HISTORY **EDUCATION** DePauw Univ, BA, 61; Columbia Univ, MA, 64, PhD (hist), 67. **CAREER** From instr to asst prof, 66-70, assoc prof, 70-78, Prof Hist, Mich State Univ, 78-, Res fel, Am Res Inst, Turkey, 69, mem, bd gov, 70-74; fel, Am Coun Learned Socs, 76-77. **MEMBERSHIPS** Mid E Studies Asn; Turkish Studies Asn. **RESEARCH** Russian-Ottoman relations; biography of Suleyman the Magnificent. **SELECTED PUBLICATIONS** Auth, Russian Annexation of the Crimea, 1774-1783, Cambridge Univ Press, 70; auth, The Crimean Tatars, Hoover Institution Press, 78, 87; auth, Between Russians, Ottomans and Turks: Crimea and Crimean Tatars, Isis Press, 98; auth, A Precarious Balance: Conflict, Trade, and Diplomacy on the Russo-Ottoman Frontier, Isis Press, 99, auth, many articles. **CONTACT ADDRESS** Dept of Hist, Michigan State Univ, 301 Morrill Hall, East Lansing, MI 48824-1036. **EMAIL** fishera@msu.edu

FISHER, CRAIG B.
PERSONAL Born 05/10/1931, Alameda, CA **DISCIPLINE** MEDIEVAL HISTORY **EDUCATION** Univ Calif, Berkeley, BA, 52; Harvard Univ, MA, 56; Cornell Univ, PhD, 61. **CAREER** Asst prof hist, Univ Calif, Davis, 60-67, assoc prof, Conolly Col, 67-76, Prof Hist, Brooklyn Ctr, Long Island Univ, 76-. **RESEARCH** Italy and Germany in the High Middle Ages. **SELECTED PUBLICATIONS** Auth, American sychological ssociation 1992 Ethics Code and the Validation of exual Abuse in Day Care Settings, Psych Public Policy Law, Vol 1, 95. **CONTACT ADDRESS** Dept of Hist, Long Island Univ, Brooklyn, Brooklyn, NY 11201.

FISHER, JAMES T.
DISCIPLINE US RELIGIOUS HISTORY **EDUCATION** Rutgers Univ, PhD. **CAREER** Hist Dept, St Edward's Euniv **HONORS AND AWARDS** Managing ed, Jour Policy Hist. **SELECTED PUBLICATIONS** Auth, The Catholic Counterculture in America, 1933-1962; Dr. America: The Lives of Thomas A. Dooley. **CONTACT ADDRESS** St. Edward's Univ, 3001 S Congress Ave, Austin, TX 78704-6489.

FISHER, MARVIN
PERSONAL Born 11/19/1927, Detroit, MI, m, 1956, 3 children **DISCIPLINE** AMERICAN STUDIES **EDUCATION** Wayne Univ, AB, 50, AM, 52; Univ Minn, PhD, 58. **CAREER** Instr English, Gen Motors Inst, 52-53; instr, Univ Minn, 53-58; from asst prof to assoc prof, 58-66, prof to prof emer, Ariz State Univ, 66-; vis prof, Univ Calif, Davis, 69-70; chmn, Ariz State Univ, 77-. **HONORS AND AWARDS** Huntington Libr res fel, 60; Fulbright lectr, Greece, 61-63, Norway, 66-67. **MEMBERSHIPS** MLA; Am Studies Asn; NCTE; Melville Soc Am; AAUP. **RESEARCH** American Renaissance; 19th century technology and its impact on the American imagination; Herman Melville. **SELECTED PUBLICATIONS** Auth, Pattern of conservatism, In: Johnson's Rasselas and Hawthorne's Tales, J Hist Ideas, 58; The garden and the workshop, New England Quart, 61; Workshops in the wilderness, Oxford Univ, 67; Melville's Tartarus: The deflowering of New England, Am Quart, 71; coauth, Pudd'nhead Wilson: Half a dog is worse than none, Southern Rev, 72; auth, Benito Cereno: Old world experience, new world expectations and third world realities, Forum, 76; Going under: Melville's Short Fiction and the American 1850's, La State Univ, 77; coauth, Whitman and Dickinson, In: American Literary Scholarship, 75, 76, Duke Univ, 77 & 78. **CONTACT ADDRESS** Dept of English, Arizona State Univ, Tempe, AZ 85281.

FISHER, ROBERT BRUCE
PERSONAL Born 04/23/1947, Newark, NJ **DISCIPLINE** HISTORY, URBAN STUDIES **EDUCATION** Rutgers Univ, BA, 68; NYork Univ, MA, 70, PhD (US hist), 74. **CAREER** Instr hist and polit sci, Grahm Jr Col, 73-76; vis asst prof hist, Union Col, 77-78; Asst Prof Hist, Univ Houston, Downtown Col, 78-. **MEMBERSHIPS** AHA; Orgn Am Hists. **RESEARCH** History of urban social change; community organization; United States in the 20th century. **SELECTED PUBLICATIONS** Auth, Ad Hoc Justice Documented--The Paper Daguerreotypes of Fardon, George, Robinson, J West, Vol 33, 94. **CONTACT ADDRESS** Univ of Houston, One Main St, Houston, TX 77002.

FISHER, ROBIN
PERSONAL Born 02/24/1946, Palmerston N., New Zealand **DISCIPLINE** HISTORY **EDUCATION** Massey Univ, BA, 67; Univ Auckland, MA, 69; Univ BC, PhD, 74. **CAREER** Jr lectr hist, Massey Univ, 70; asst prof to prof hist, Simon Fraser Univ, 74-93; co-ed, Can Hist Rev, 84-87; founding ch hist, 93-96, acting dean arts sci, 94-96, dean arts, 96-97, dean of arts, social and health sciences, Univ Northern British Columbia, 97-. **HONORS AND AWARDS** John A. Macdonald Prize, Can Hist Asn, 77; Dafoe Book Prize, 92. **RESEARCH** Canadian history; First Nations-European relations; twentieth century politis and the history of higher education; aspects of comparative frontiers; New Zealand history particularly race relations. **SELECTED PUBLICATIONS** Auth, Duff Pattullo of British Columbia, Toronto: Univ of Toronto Press, (91): 445; auth, Vancouver's Voyage: Charting the Northwest Coast, 1791-1795, Vancouver and Seattle: douglas & McIntyre and Univ of Washington Press, (92): 145; auth, "Judging History: Reflections on The Reasons for Judgement in Delgamuukw v British Columbia," BC Studies, no. 95, (92): 43-54; auth, From Maps to Metaphors: The Pacific Worlld of George Vancouver, Vancouver, UBC Press, (93): 363; auth, "Matter for Reflection: BC Studies and British Columbia History," BC Studies no. 100, (Winter 93-94): 59-77; auth, "Native Land in the Okanagan Valley, British Columbia," Wellington: New Zealand Geographical Soc, (93): 176-81; auth, "Contact and Trade, 1774-1849," in The Pacific Province: A History of British Columbia, ed. Hugh Johnson, (Vancouver: Douglas & McIntyre, 96): 48-67; coauth, "Patterns of British Columbia Poitics Since 1916," in The Pacific Province: A History of British Columbia, ed. Hugh Johnson, (Vancouver: Douglas & McIntyre, 96): 254-272; auth, "The Northwest from the Beginning of Trade with Europeans to the 10s," in The Cambridge History of the Nativev Peoples of the Americas, vol. 1, eds. Bruce G. Trigger and Wilcomb E. Wsshburn, (New York: Cambridge Univ Press, 96): 117-182; auth, Out of the Background: Readings on Canadian Native History, Toronto: Copp Clark Pitman, (96). **CONTACT ADDRESS** Univ of British Columbia, 3333 University Way, Prince George, BC, Canada V2N 4Z9. **EMAIL** fisher@unbc.ca

FISHMAN, DAVID E.
PERSONAL Born, NY **DISCIPLINE** JEWISH HISTORY **EDUCATION** Yeshiva Univ, BA; Harvard Univ, MA, PhD. **CAREER** Instr, Brandeis Univ; instr, Russ State Univ, Moscow; fel, Hebrew Univ Inst Adv Studies; assoc prof and chr, Dept Jewish Hist, Jewish Theol Sem Am; sr resh assoc, YIVO Inst Jewish Res. **HONORS AND AWARDS** Dir Project Judaica, JTS and YIVO with the Russ State Univ for the Hum; ed, Yivo-Bletter. **SELECTED PUBLICATIONS** Auth, Russia's First Modern Jews, NY Univ Press; Embers Plucked from the Fire: The Rescue of Jewish Cultural Treasures in Vilna,YIVO; numerous articles on the history and culture of East European Jewry. **CONTACT ADDRESS** Jewish Theol Sem of America, 3080 Broadway, New York, NY 10027. **EMAIL** dafishman@jtsa.edu

FISHMAN-BOYD, SARAH
PERSONAL Born 03/31/1957, Syracuse, NY, m, 1983, 2 children **DISCIPLINE** HISTORY **EDUCATION** Oberlin Col, AB, 79; Univ S Calif, AM, 81; Harvard Univ, AM, 81; Harvard Univ, PhD, 87. **CAREER** From Asst Prof to Assoc Prof, Univ Houston, 93-. **HONORS AND AWARDS** Res Excellence Awd, Univ Houston, 93. **MEMBERSHIPS** Western Soc for Fr Hist, AHA, Soc for Fr Hist Studies. **RESEARCH** Modern French, World War II, social history, women's history. **SELECTED PUBLICATIONS** Auth, Femmes de Prisonniers 1940-1945, L'Harmattan, 96; auth, "Juvenile Delinquency as a 'Condition': Social Science Constructions of the Child Criminal 1936-1946," Proceedings of the Western Soc for Fr Hist, vol 24 (97); auth, "General Charles-Leon Huntziger," in Hist Dict of World War II France: The Occupation, Vichy and the Resistance 1938-1946 (Greenwood Pr), 98; auth, "Prisoners of War," in Hist Dict of World War II France: The Occupation, Vichy and the Resistance 1938-1946 (Greenwood Pr), 98; auth, "Prisoners of war, Wives of," in Hist Dict of World War II France: The Occupation, Vichy and the Resistance 1938-1946 (Greenwood Pr), 98; auth, "La Releve," in Hist Dict of World War II France: The Occupation, Vichy and the Resistance 1938-1946 (Greenwood Pr), 98; auth, "Les Swings," in Hist Dict of World War II France: The Occupation, Vichy and the Resistance 1938-1946 (Greenwood Pr), 98; auth, "Das Lange Warten - Die Ehefrauen Franzosischer Kreigsgefangenen 1940-1945," in Kreigsgefangenschaft im Zweitne Weltkrieg, Eine vergleichende Perspektive (98); auth, "Youth in Vichy France: The Juvenile Crime Wave and its Implications," in France at War: Vichy and the Historians (Berg Publ, 00); co-ed, France at War: Vichy and the Historians, Berg Publ, 00. **CONTACT ADDRESS** Dept Hist, Univ of Houston, Houston, TX 77204-0001. **EMAIL** sfishman@uh.edu

FISHWICK, MARSHALL W.
PERSONAL Born 05/07/1923, Roanoke, VA, m **DISCIPLINE** AMERICAN STUDIES **EDUCATION** Univ of Va, BA, 44; Univ of Wis, MA, 46; Yale Univ, PhD. **CAREER** Inst, Yale Univ, 49; prof, Wash and Lee Univ, 50-62; vis prof, Univ of Minn, 57; Dir, Wemyss Found, 62-64; Distinguished vis prof, Univ of Wyo, 63; prof, Lincoln Univ, 64-70; prof, Temple Univ, 70-76; vis prof, Yale Univ, 84; prof, Va Tech, 76-. **HONORS AND AWARDS** D. Phil, Krakow Univ, Poland, 67; D. Litt, Dhaka Univ, Bangladesh, 83. **MEMBERSHIPS** NEA; Am Studies Assoc; AHA; Org of Am Hist; MLA; AAUP; Va Hist Soc; S Hist Assoc; British Am Studies Assoc; Europ Am Studies Assoc; Am Studies Res Centre; Guild of Scholars; Centro Italiano di Studi Am; Conseils aux Etudiants d'Anglais, Institut fur Jugendkunde, Fulbright Alumni Assoc; Japanese Am Studies Assoc, Soc of Archit Hist; Popular Culture Assoc; Salzburg Advisory Faculty. **CONTACT ADDRESS** Popular Culture and Am Studies, Virginia Polytech Inst and State Univ, 100 Virginia Tech, Blacksburg, VA 24061-0227. **EMAIL** mfishwic@vt.edu

FISK, DEBORAH PAYNE
PERSONAL Born 07/17/1952, Los Angeles, CA, m, 1999, 1 child **DISCIPLINE** SEVENTEENTH- AND EIGHTEENTH-CENTURY STUDIES, THEATER HISTORY **EDUCATION** PhD, UCLA. **CAREER** Assoc prof, Depts of Literature and Performing Arts. **HONORS AND AWARDS** Distinguished Tchg Awd, Am Univ, 92; Huntington Lib Fel, 98; William Andrew Clark Mem Lib Fel, 99; Folger Shakespeare Lib/NEH Fel, 00-01. **MEMBERSHIPS** Am Soc for Eighteenth-Cent Stud; British Soc for Eighteenth-Cent Stud; Aphra Behn Soc; Am Soc for Theatre Res. **RESEARCH** Seventeenth- and eighteenth-century studies **SELECTED PUBLICATIONS** Co-ed, Cult Readings Restoration & Eighteenth-Century Eng Theatre, 95; ed, The Cambridge Companion to Restoration Theater, 00; ed, Four Libertine Plays, 01. **CONTACT ADDRESS** Dept of Literature, American Univ, 4400 Massachusetts Ave, Washington, DC 20016-8047. **EMAIL** paynefisk@earthlink.net

FISK, WILLIAM LYONS
PERSONAL Born 02/24/1921, Newark, OH, m, 1962, 2 children **DISCIPLINE** ENGLISH HISTORY **EDUCATION** Muskingum Col, AB, 41; Ohio State Univ, AM, 44, PhD (hist), 46. **CAREER** From asst prof to assoc prof hist, 46-55, dean and vpres, 68-76, Prof English Hist, Muskingum Col, 55-. **HONORS AND AWARDS** Distinguish Serv Awd, Muskingum Col, 77. **MEMBERSHIPS** AHA; Conf Brit Studies. **RESEARCH** Twenty years of English labor legislation, 1795-1815; 17th and 18th century English history. **SELECTED PUBLICATIONS** Auth, Walker, John--Renaissance Man, Amn Presbyterians-J Presbyterian Hist, Vol 71, 93. **CONTACT ADDRESS** Dept of Hist, Muskingum Col, New Concord, OH 43762.

FISS, KAREN A.
DISCIPLINE EUROPEAN CULTURE AND POLITICS BETWEEN THE WORLD WARS **EDUCATION** Yale Univ, PhD, 95. **CAREER** Hist, Washington Univ. **SELECTED PUBLICATIONS** Univ, Discourses: Conversations in Postmodern Art and Cult, M.I.T. Prof and the New Mus, 90; The German Pavilion at the 1937 Paris Exposition Internationale, in Art and Power: Europe under the Dictators, 1930-45, The South Bank Center London, 95. **CONTACT ADDRESS** Washington Univ, 1 Brookings Dr, Saint Louis, MO 63130. **EMAIL** kafiss@artsci.wustl.edu

FITE, GILBERT COURTLAND
PERSONAL Born 05/14/1918, Santa Fe, OH, m, 1941, 2 children **DISCIPLINE** HISTORY **EDUCATION** Univ SDak, AB and Am, 41; Univ Mo, PhD, 45. **CAREER** Prof, Wessington Springs Col, 41-42; from asst to prof to prof hist, Univ Okla, 45-58, chmn dept, 55-58, res prof, 58-71; pres, Eastern Ill Univ, 71-76; acting head hist dept, 77-78, Richard B Russell Prof Hist, Univ GA, Atens, 76-, Ford fel, 54-55; vis prof, Jadavpur Univ, India, 62-63; Guggenheim fel, 64-65; consult, US Off Educ, 65-68; dir, Am Studies Res Ctr, Hyderabad, India, 69-70; Int coun, Phi Alpha Theta, 78-80 (pres, 81-). **HONORS AND AWARDS** DLitt, Seattle Pac Col, 62; DLitt, Univ SDak, 75. **MEMBERSHIPS** AHA; Orgn Am Hists; Agr Hist Soc (pres, 60); Southern Hist Asn (vpres, 73, pres, 74); Econ Hist Asn. **RESEARCH** Farm movements; farm leaders; general recent agricultural history. **SELECTED PUBLICATIONS** Auth, Colleagues Russell, Richard, B. and his Apprentice, Johnnson, J Am Hist, Vol 81, 95 Bale O Cotton--The Mechanical Art of Cotton Ginning, Ark Hist Quart, Vol 52, 93; Interview with Fite, Gilbert, C., Hist, Vol 56, 93; American Agriculture--A Brief History, J Southern Hist, Vol 61, 95. **CONTACT ADDRESS** Dept of Hist, Univ of Georgia, Athens, GA 30602.

FITZ, EARL EUGENE
PERSONAL Born 03/07/1946, Marshalltown, IA, m, 1973, 1 child **DISCIPLINE** LUSO-BRAZILIAN STUDIES **EDUCATION** Univ Iowa, BA, 68, MA, 70; City Univ New York, MA, 73, PhD (comp lit), 77. **CAREER** Vis lectr Span and Port, Univ Mich, Ann Arbor, 76-77; asst prof, Dickinson Col, 77-78; Asst Prof Luso-Brazilian Studies and Span Am Lit, PA State Univ, 78-. **MEMBERSHIPS** MLA; Am Asn Teachers Span and Port; Am Translr Asn; Midwest Mod Lang Asn. **RESEARCH** Spanish Am Lit and culture; comparative literature. **SELECTED PUBLICATIONS CONTACT ADDRESS** Dept of Span Ital and Port, Pennsylvania State Univ, Univ Park, 352 Burrowes Bldg, University Park, PA 16802-6203.

FITZGERALD, E. P.
DISCIPLINE HISTORY **EDUCATION** Seton Hall Univ, BA; Univ de Geneve; Yale Univ, MA, PhD. **CAREER** Ch; assoc prof, Carleton Univ. **HONORS AND AWARDS** Adv, Mention francaise. **RESEARCH** International economic relations and their links to international politics. **SELECTED PUBLICATIONS** Auth, "Economic Constraints on the Continuation of Colonial Rule in French Colonial Africa: The Problem of Recurrent Costs," Proc Fr Colonial Hist Soc, 89; "The Iraq Oil Company, Standard Oil of California and the contest for eastern Arabia, 1930-32," Intl Hist Rev, 91; "Compagnie Francaise des Petroles and the Defense of the Red Line Regime in middle Eastern Oil, 1933-36," Bus and Econ Hist, 91; "Business diplomacy: Walter Teagle, jersey Standard, and the Anglo-French Pipeline Conflict in the Middle East," Bus Hist Rev, 93; "France's Middle Eastern Ambitions, the Sykes-Picot Negotiations, and the Oil Fields of Mosul, 1915-18," Jour Mod Hist, 94; "The Power of the Weak and the Weakness of the Strong: Explaining Corporate Behavior in Middle Eastern Oil, 1946-48," Bus and Econ Hist, 95. **CONTACT ADDRESS** Dept of Hist, Carleton Univ, 1125 Colonel By Dr, Ottawa, ON, Canada K1S 5B6. **EMAIL** fitz@ccs.carleton.ca

FITZGERALD, J. PATRICK
PERSONAL Born 04/05/1950, Evansville, IN, m, 1970, 2 children **DISCIPLINE** PHILOSOPHY, AESTHETICS **EDUCATION** Univ Southern Ind, BA, 74; Southern Ill Univ at Carbondale, MA, 76; PhD, 86. **CAREER** Instr, Southern Ill Univ at Carbondale, 77-79; chemn of Humanities, John A. Logan Col, 79-87; prof, Seminole Community Col, 88-. **HONORS AND AWARDS** Listed in Who's Who Among Am Teachers, 96. **MEMBERSHIPS** Am Philos Asn. **RESEARCH** Philosophy in the media. **SELECTED PUBLICATIONS** Auth, A Parliament of Minds, State Univ NY Pr, 99; auth, A Parliament of Minds (national PBS television series--18 episodes), 00. **CONTACT ADDRESS** Dept Humanities & Fine Arts, Seminole Comm Col, 100 Weldon Blvd, Sanford, FL 32773-6132. **EMAIL** patfitz@webtv.net

FITZGERALD, MICHAEL
PERSONAL Born 11/24/1953, Pueblo, CO, m, 1982, 2 children **DISCIPLINE** HISTORY **EDUCATION** Univ Southern Colo, BS, 76; Univ Chicago, MA, 79; Purdue Univ, PhD, 90. **CAREER** Asst/Assoc Prof, Pikeville Col, 90-00. **HONORS AND AWARDS** James Still Fel, Univ of Ky, 93, 95; Mellon Fac/Student Res Grant, Appalachian Col Asn, 94-96; John B. Stephenson Fel, Appalachian Col Asn, 96-97. **MEMBERSHIPS** The Hist Soc, Soc for Historians of the Early Am Republic, World Hist Asn. **RESEARCH** 19th century American diplomatic and military history. **SELECTED PUBLICATIONS** Auth, "Nature Unsubdued: Diplomacy, Expansion and the American Military Buildup of 1815-16," Mid-Am: An Hist Rev 77 (Winter 95): 5-32; auth, "Rejecting Calhoun's Expansible Army Plan: The Army Reduction Act of 1821," War in Hist 3 (Apr 96): 161-185. **CONTACT ADDRESS** Dept Soc Sci, Pikeville Col, 214 Sycamore St, Pikeville, KY 41501-1342. **EMAIL** mfitzger@pc.edu

FITZPATRICK, ELLEN
DISCIPLINE MODERN AMERICA, WOMEN'S HISTORY, INTELLECTUAL HISTORY **EDUCATION** Brandeis Univ, PhD. **CAREER** Assoc prof, Univ NH, 97-. **HONORS AND AWARDS** Charles Warren Ctr fel, Harvard Univ; Andrew Mellon fac fel in the Hum, Harvard Univ; Spencer Found grant; NEH grant. **RESEARCH** Reinventing history: American historians and the memory of modern history. **SELECTED PUBLICATIONS** Auth, Endless Crusade: Women Social Scientists and Progressive Reform; auth, Muckraking: Three Landmark Articles; ed, Century of Struggle by Eleanor Flexner; coauth, America in Modern Times. **CONTACT ADDRESS** Univ of New Hampshire, Durham, Durham, NH 03824. **EMAIL** effitz@mediaone.net

FITZSIMMONS, MICHAEL P.
DISCIPLINE HISTORY **EDUCATION** Belmont Abbey Col, BA, 71; Univ NC, Chapel Hill, MA, 76, PhD, 81. **CAREER** Mellon instr, Rice Univ, 82-85; asst prof to PROF, AUBURN UNIV, MONTGOMERY, 85-. **CONTACT ADDRESS** Dept of History, Auburn Univ, Montgomery, PO Box 244023, Montgomery, AL 36124-4023. **EMAIL** mpfitzsimmons@edla.aum.edu

FIX, ANDREW C.
PERSONAL Born 02/14/1955, Winston-Salem, NC, m, 1977, 1 child **DISCIPLINE** HISTORY **EDUCATION** Wake Forest Univ, BA, 77; Ind Univ, MA, 79; PhD, 84. **CAREER** Assoc instr, Ind Univ, 80-82; asst prof, Spring Hill Col, 84-85; vis prof, Vrije Univ Brussel, 89-90 & 93; from asst prof to prof, Lafayette Col, 85-. **HONORS AND AWARDS** Delta Phi Alpha; Phi Alpha Theta; Forrest Clonts Awd in Hist, Wake Forest Univ, 77; Phi Beta Kappa, Wake Forest Univ, 77; Dissertation Res Grant, Ind Univ Hist Dept, 82; Doctoral Dissertation Res Grant, Ctr Interuniversitaire d'etudes Europeenes, 82; Fulbright Fel, 82-83; Charlotte W. Newcombe Fel, Woodrow Wilson Nat Fel Found, 83-84; NEH Summer Res Stipend, 86; Thomas Roy and Laura Forrest Jones Fac Lectureship, Lafayette Col, 90; Res Grant, Am Philos Soc, 93; Res Grant, Lafayette Col, 94; Thomas Roy and Laura Forrest Jones Awd for Superior Teaching and Excellence of Scholar, Lafayette Col, 95. **MEMBERSHIPS** Renaissance Soc of Am, Sixteenth-Century Studies Soc, Am Asn for Netherlandic Studies, Werkgroep Sassen-Erasmus Univ, Werkgroep Zeventiende Eeuw, Maatschappij der Nederlandse Letterkunde, Am Asn of Univ Professors, Kerkhistorische Gesellschap. **RESEARCH** Early Modern European Intellectual History, History of Ideas. **SELECTED PUBLICATIONS** Auth, "Hendrik Niclaes," in Encyclopedia of the Reformation III (Oxford Univ Press, 96), 143-144; auth, "The Family of Love," in Encyclopedia of the Reformation II (Oxford Univ Press, 96), 98-99; auth, "Bekker and Bayle on Comets," Geschiedenis van de Wijsbegeerte in Nederland 10.2 (99); auth, Fallen Angels: Balthasar Bekker and the Spirit of Controversy in Seventeenth-Century Holland, Kluwer Acad Publ, 99; rev, of "Mutual Christianorum Tolerantia: Irenicism and Toleration in the Netherlands: The Stinstra Affair 1740-1745," by Joris van Eijnatten, The Catholic Hist Rev (forthcoming); auth, "Balthasar Bekker: Enlightened Foe of the Occult," J of Occult History (forthcoming). **CONTACT ADDRESS** Dept Hist, Lafayette Col, Easton, PA 18042. **EMAIL** fixa@lafayette.edu

FLACK, JAMES
PERSONAL Born 02/11/1937, Brooklyn, NY, m, 1960, 3 children **DISCIPLINE** HISTORY **EDUCATION** Albion Col, BA, 59; Wayne State Univ, MA, 63; PhD, 68. **CAREER** Instr, Wayne State Univ, 65-66; assoc prof, Univ MD, 67-. **HONORS AND AWARDS** Award of Merit, Washington, 89. **MEMBERSHIPS** Am Hist Asn. Org of Am Hist. **RESEARCH** Social History of Washington, DC; Historic preservation. **SELECTED PUBLICATIONS** Auth, Desideratum in Washington: The Intellectual Community in the Capital City, 75; ed, Records of the Columbia Historical Society of Washington, DC 89. **CONTACT ADDRESS** Dept History, Univ of Maryland, Col Park, 2115 F S Key Hall, College Park, MD 20742-0001. **EMAIL** jf14@umail.umd.edu

FLADER, SUSAN L.
PERSONAL Born 04/29/1941, Sheboygan, WI **DISCIPLINE** HISTORY **EDUCATION** Univ Wisc, BA, 63; Stanford Univ, MA, 65, PhD, 71. **CAREER** Instr, asst prof, 70-73, Univ Wisc; vis lectr, 86, 91, 96, Lanzhou, Qingdao, Nankai, Inner Mongolia, Wuhan, Sichuan, et al Univ, People's Rep of China; Fulbright Sr Lectr, 87-8, Univ Turku, Finland; vis scholar, 95, Univ W Cape S Africa;, asst prof, 73-75, assoc prof, 75-81, prof, 81- Univ Missouri-Columbia. **HONORS AND AWARDS** Forest Hist Soc, fel, 98. **MEMBERSHIPS** Am Soc for Environmental Hist, 97-99. **SELECTED PUBLICATIONS** Auth, Exploring Missouri's Lagacy: State Parks and Historic Sites, U MO Pr, 92; auth, The River of the Mother of God and Other Essays by Aldo Leapold, U Wis Pr, 93; auth, Thinking like a Mountain: Aldo Leopold and the Evolution of an Ecological Attitude Toward Deer, Wolves, and Forests, U Wis Pr, 94. **CONTACT ADDRESS** Dept of History, Univ of Missouri, Columbia, Columbia, MO 65211. **EMAIL** fladers@missouri.edu

FLANAGAN, MAUREEN ANNE
PERSONAL Born 02/20/1948, Chicago, IL **DISCIPLINE** AMERICAN HISTORY **EDUCATION** Loyola Univ, Chicago, PhD, 81. **CAREER** Lectr Hist, Loyola Univ; assoc prof, Michigan Stat Univ. **MEMBERSHIPS** Orgn Am Hists; AHA. **RESEARCH** Urban history; political culture of Chicago. **SELECTED PUBLICATIONS** Auth, Daley, Richard, J--Politics, Race, and the Governing of Chicago, Am Hist Rev, Vol 102, 97; Property Rules--Political Economy in Chicago, 1833-1872, Rev Am Hist, Vol 21, 93; The City Profitable, The City Livable--Environmental Policy, Gender, and Power in Chicago in the 1910s, J Urban Hist, Vol 22, 96; Women in the City, Women of the City--Where Do Women Fit in Urban History, J Urban Hist, Vol 23, 97. **CONTACT ADDRESS** Dept of History, Michigan State Univ, 407 Morrill Hall, East Lansing, MI 48824. **EMAIL** flanaga6@msu.edu

FLAYHART, WILLIAM H., III
PERSONAL Born 07/12/1944, Williamsport, PA, m, 1977, 3 children **DISCIPLINE** HISTORY **EDUCATION** Lycoming Col, BA, 66; Univ Va, MA, 68, PhD, 71. **CAREER** Asst Prof, 70-72, Assoc Prof, 72-74, Prof Hist, 74-, Del State Univ; Ch, Dept of Hist, Polit Sci, & Philos, Del State Univ, 93-00. **HONORS AND AWARDS** Vis Prof of Maritime Hist, Univ Lieden, 94-95; Fellow, Int Napoleonic Soc, 97; Legion of Merit, Int Napoleonic Soc, 00. **MEMBERSHIPS** AHA; SHA; US Naval Inst; NAOHS; CNRO; IMHA. **RESEARCH** Maritime & Naval history; Napoleonic history; British history. **SELECTED PUBLICATIONS** Coauth, Majesty at Sea: The Four Funnel Liners, WW Norton & Co, Inc, 81; coauth, QE2, WW Norton & Co, Inc, 85; auth, Counterpoint to Trafalgar: The Anglo-Russian Invasion of Naples, 1805-1806, Univ SC Press, 92; auth, British Rivalries in Sicily and Naples, 1803-1806, Consortium on Revolutionary Europe 1750-1850, Proceedings 1994, Fla State Univ, 95; auth, Oceanic Historiography: The American Dimension (1974-1994), Maritime History at the Crossroads, 249-276, Int Maritime Hist Asn, 95; auth, The Rise of the Compagnie Generale Transatlantique (French Line), Consortium on Revolutionary Europe, La State Univ, 97; auth, The American Line (1871-1902), WWNorton & Co, Inc, 00. **CONTACT ADDRESS** Dept of Hist & Polit Sci, Delaware State Univ, Dover, DE 19901. **EMAIL** wflayhar@dsc.edu

FLEENER, CHARLES JOSEPH
PERSONAL Born 11/22/1938, New Orleans, LA, m, 1967, 2 children **DISCIPLINE** LATIN AMERICAN HISTORY **EDUCATION** Georgetown Univ, BSFS, 60; Univ Fla, MA, 63, PhD, 69. **CAREER** From instr to asst prof, 66-76, Assoc Prof Latin Am Hist, St Louis Univ, 76-, Chmn Dept, 76-84, Dean, St Louis Univ/Spain, 92; Vis prof, Columbus Int Col, Spain, 73. **MEMBERSHIPS** Midwest Coun Latin Am Studies (pres, 69-70); AHA. **RESEARCH** Colonial Latin American history, 18th century; expulsions of the Jesuits from Spain and Spanish America. **SELECTED PUBLICATIONS** Coauth, The Guide to Latin American Paperback Literature, Univ Fla, 66; co-ed, Religious and Cultural Factors in Latin America, St Louis Univ, 71. **CONTACT ADDRESS** Dept of Hist, Saint Louis Univ, 221 N Grand Blvd, Saint Louis, MO 63103-2097. **EMAIL** fleener@slu.edu

FLEISCHER, MANFRED PAUL
PERSONAL Born 06/26/1928, Nieder Peilau-Schloessel, Germany, m, 1962, 3 children **DISCIPLINE** EUROPEAN HISTORY, HISTORY OF RELIGION **EDUCATION** Wagner Col, BA, 55; Philadelphia Lutheran Theol Sem, MDiv, 59; Univ Pa, MA, 61; Univ Erlangen, PhD (hist ideas and relig), 65. **CAREER** Lectr philos, Wagner Col, 55-56; pastor, Lutheran Church, NY, 59-61; lectr philos and relig, Wagner Col, 61; assoc, 63, from acting instr to assoc prof, 64-77, prof Hist, Univ Calif, Davis, 77-91, Fulbright res scholar, Univ Strabourg, 67-68; prof emer, 91-. **MEMBERSHIPS** Am Soc Church Hist. **RESEARCH** Interrelationships between humanism, Reformation, and counter-Reformation in central Europe. **SELECTED PUBLICATIONS** Ed, The Harvest of Humanism in Central Europe, St. Louis, Concordia, 92; auth, Der schlesische Spaethumanismus, in Quellenbuch zur Geschichte der Evangelischen Kirche in Schlesien, Munich, Oldenbourg, 92; Screech, M. A--Some Renaissance Studies, Church Hist, Vol 64, 95; auth, The Oxford Encyclopedia of Reformation, 96. **CONTACT ADDRESS** Dept of Hist, Univ of California, Davis, Davis, CA 95616. **EMAIL** mpfleischer@vcdavis.edu

FLEMING, JAMES RODGER
PERSONAL Born 05/28/1949, Windber, PA, m, 1982, 2 children **DISCIPLINE** HISTORY OF SCIENCE **EDUCATION** Penn State Univ, BS, 71; Colo State Univ, MS, 73; Princeton Univ, MA, 84; PhD, 88. **CAREER** Prof, Colby Col, 88-. **HONORS AND AWARDS** Bausch-Lomb Sci Awd, 67; Grant, Colby Col Res, 88-00; Fel, Smithsonian Inst, 85-87; Fel, Mellon Res, 91; Frederick W Beinecke Fel, Yale Univ, 92, NEH Fel, 92-93. **MEMBERSHIPS** AAAS, Intl Union Hist and Philos Sci; Am Geophys Union; Am Meteorol Soc; Brit Soc Hist of Sci; Hist of Sci Soc; Soc Hist Tech; Hist of the Earth Sci Soc. **RESEARCH** History of Geophysics, especially Meteorology. **SELECTED PUBLICATIONS** Auth, Meteorology in America, 1800-1870, 90; auth, Science, Technology and the Environment: Multidisciplinary Perspectives, 94; International Bibliog-

raphy of Meteorology: From the Beginning of Printing to 1889, 94; auth, Historical Essays on Meteorology, 1919-1995, 96; auth, Historical Perspectives on Climate Change, 98. **CONTACT ADDRESS** STS Prog, Colby Col, 5881 Mayflower Hill, Waterville, ME 04901. **EMAIL** jrflemin@colby.edu

FLEMING, JOHN EMORY
PERSONAL Born 08/03/1944, Morganton, NC, m, 1970, 2 children **DISCIPLINE** AFRICAN-AMERICAN HISTORY **EDUCATION** Berea Coll, BA 1966; Univ of KY, 1966-67; Howard U, MA, PhD 1970-74. **CAREER** KY Civil Rights Commn, educ specialist 1966-67; Peace Corps, visual aids special 1967-69; USCR Commn, program officer 1970-71; Inst for the Study of Educ Policy, sr fellow 1974-80; Natl Afro-American Museum, dir 1980-98; Natl Underground Railroad Freedom Ctr, dir, 98-. **HONORS AND AWARDS** Carter G Woodson Awd, Berea College; Martin Luther King Awd; OH Library Association Humanities Awd. **MEMBERSHIPS** Mem NAACP 1974-87; bd Assoc Study of Afro-Amer Life and History 1978-93; bd Journal of Negro History 1982-96; vice pres bd Art for Comm Expression 1984-87; panel Columbus Foundation 1986-87; v pres Ohio Museums Assoc 1989-90; board member, American Assn of Museums, 1990-95; board member, Museum Trustee Assn, 1989-95; president & board member, African-American Museums Assn, 1991-96; White House Conference on Travel and Tourism, 1995; Ohio Becentennial Commission, 1996-2003. **SELECTED PUBLICATIONS** "The Lenghtening Shadow of Slavery," Howard Univ Press 1976; "The Case for Affirmative Action for Blacks in Higher Education," Howard Univ Press 1978. **CONTACT ADDRESS** National Underground Railroad, 312 Elm St, 20th Floor, Cincinnati, OH 45202. **EMAIL** jfleming@nurfc.org

FLEMING, PATRICIA L.
PERSONAL Born 12/27/1939, Hamilton, ON, Canada **DISCIPLINE** HISTORY **EDUCATION** McMaster Univ, BA, 60; Univ Toronto, BLS, 64, MLS, 70; Univ London, MA, 77, PhD, 80. **CAREER** Staff, Metro Toronto Libr, 64-69; tchg asst to assoc prof, 70-90, Prof, Fac Information Stud, Univ Toronto, 90-; adv bd, Nat Libr Can, 83-86. **HONORS AND AWARDS** Tremaine Medal, 92. **MEMBERSHIPS** Bibliog Soc Can; Am Antiquarian Soc; Can Inst Hist Microrepro (bd mem, vice pres 89-92, pres 92-94), Bibliog Soc Can (coun 82-85, pres 86-89); Am Printing Hist Asn (trustee, 94-). **SELECTED PUBLICATIONS** Auth, Upper Canadian Imprints 1801-1841: A Bibliography, 88; auth, Atlantic Canadian Imprints 1801-1820: A Bibliography, 91. **CONTACT ADDRESS** Fac Info Stud, Univ of Toronto, Toronto, ON, Canada M5S 3G6. **EMAIL** fleming@fis.utoronto.ca

FLEMING, RAE B.
PERSONAL Born 05/17/1944, Lindsay, ON, Canada **DISCIPLINE** HISTORY **EDUCATION** Univ Toronto, BA, 66; Univ Sask, MA, 82, PhD, 88. **CAREER** Tchr, lectr, prof, 67-; vis fel, Ctr Can Stud, Univ Edinburgh, 91; lectr, Univ Winipeg; lectr, Univ Guelph; lectr, Ryerson Polytechnic Univ; res assoc, Leslie Frist Ctr, Trent Univ. **HONORS AND AWARDS** Thomas B. Symons Awd, Trent Univ; Fred Landon Awd, Ont Hist Soc. **MEMBERSHIPS** Can Hist Soc. **SELECTED PUBLICATIONS** Auth, Eldon Connections, 75; auth, The Railway King of Canada, 91; ed, Boswell's Children, 92; ed, The Lochaber Immigrants, 94; contribur, Canadian Encyclopedia, 85, 88; contribur, Dictionary of Canadian Biography, 94. **CONTACT ADDRESS** RR 6, Woodville, ON, Canada K0M 2T0.

FLETCHER, MARVIN EDWARD
PERSONAL Born 12/21/1941, San Francisco, CA, m, 1965, 2 children **DISCIPLINE** UNITED STATES HISTORY **EDUCATION** Univ Calif, Berkeley, BA, 63; Univ Wis-Madison, MA, 65, PhD, 68. **CAREER** Asst prof, 68-73, assoc prof hist, Ohio Univ, 73-89; prof hist, Ohio Univ, 89. **MEMBERSHIPS** Orgn Am Historians; Am Jewish Hist Soc; Soc of Military Hist. **RESEARCH** Black American history; American military history. **SELECTED PUBLICATIONS** Auth, The Black Volunteer in Reconstruction, 1865-66, 68; auth, The Black Volunteer in the Spanish American War, 73, Mil Affairs; art, The Black Soldier Athlete, Can J Hist Sport & Phys Educ, 73; auth, The Black Soldier and Officer in the United States Army, 1891-1917, Univ Mo, 74; auth, The United States Army in Peacetime, Mil Affairs/Aerospace Historian, 75; auth, The Black Bicycle Corps, Ariz & the West, summer 75; America's First Black General, U Press of Kansas, 89. **CONTACT ADDRESS** Athens, OH 45701-2979. **EMAIL** fletcher@ohio.edu

FLINT, ALLEN DENIS
PERSONAL Born 11/15/1929, Park River, ND, m, 1953, 5 children **DISCIPLINE** ENGLISH, AMERICAN STUDIES **EDUCATION** Univ Minn, BA, 55, MA, 56, PhD(Am studies), 65. **CAREER** Col Counsel & freshman adv, Col Lib Arts, Univ Minn, 56-58, scholastic comt rep, 58-59, sr scholastic comt rep, 59-62, instr & counsel, 62-64, asst dir, corres studies dept, 64-65, actg dir, 65-66; from asst prof to assoc prof English, Western Ill Univ, 66-70; chmn dept, 71-75, PROF ENGLISH, UNIV MAINE, FARMINGTON, 70-, Fulbright lectr, Romania, CIES, 75-76. **MEMBERSHIPS** MLA; Am Studies Asn. **RESEARCH** American renaissance; Black literature; contemporary literature. **SELECTED PUBLICATIONS** Auth, Hawthorne and the slavery crisis, New Eng Quart, 68; Essentially a daydream: Hawthorne's Blithedale, Hawthorne J, 72; The saving grace of marriage in Hawthorne's fiction, Emerson Soc Quart, 73. **CONTACT ADDRESS** Dept of English, Univ of Maine, Farmington, ME 04938.

FLINT, JOHN E.
PERSONAL Born 05/17/1930, Montreal, PQ, Canada **DISCIPLINE** HISTORY **EDUCATION** St John's Col, Cambridge, BA, 52, MA, 54; Royal Holloway Col & Sch Orient African Stud Univ London, PhD, 57. **CAREER** Asst lectr to reader, Univ London, King's Col, 54-67; prof, 67-92, ch hist, 68-71, 74-75, dir ctr African stud, 78-83, prof emer, Dalhousie Univ, 92-; vis prof, Univ Calif Santa Barbara, 60-61; vis prof, head hist, Univ Nigeria Nsukka, 63-64. **HONORS AND AWARDS** Fulbright fel, 60-61. **MEMBERSHIPS** Can Hist Asn (coun 68-69); Can Asn African Stud (vice pres 69-70, coun mem 77-79, 82-83); Nigerian Hist Soc (coun mem 64-65); African Stud Asn UK. **RESEARCH** History of Africa, Nigeria. **SELECTED PUBLICATIONS** Auth, Sir George Goldie and the Making of Nigeria, 60; auth, Nigeria and Ghana, 66; auth, Cecil Rhodes, 74; ed, West Africa Studies (Mary Kingsley), 64; ed, Travels in West Africa (Mary Kingsley), 65; ed, Cambridge History of Africa, vol V, 77; co-ed, Perspectives of Empire: Essays in Honour of Gerald Sandford Graham, 73; contribur, Oxford History of East Africa, vols I-II, 63, 65. **CONTACT ADDRESS** Dept of History, Dalhousie Univ, 6135 University Ave, Halifax, NS, Canada B3H 4P9.

FLORES, CAROL A.
PERSONAL Born Lockport, NY, m, 1968 **DISCIPLINE** ARCHITECTURE, HISTORY, THEORY & CRITICISM **EDUCATION** Univ NYork Albany, BA, 66; Ga Inst of Tech, MS, 90; Ga Inst of Tech, PhD, archit, 96. **CAREER** Teacher, LaSalle Sch for Boys, 66-71; asst to pres, Environment/One Corp, 71; svc adv, N Eng Telephone, 72-76; chief svc adv, Southern Bell, 76-77; mgr, Southern Bell, 78-79; district mgr, Southern Bell, 80-82; operations mgr, Bell South Svc, 83-85; owner and commercial and residential designer, Design Options, 86-90; grad teaching asst, Col of Archit, Ga Inst of Tech, 89; doctoral fel, Col of Archit, Ga Inst of Tech, 90-94; asst prof, Col of Archit and Planning, Ball State Univ, 96-; Assoc prof, College of Archit & Planning, Ball State Univ, 00. **HONORS AND AWARDS** Outstanding rating, Mgt Assessment Prog, Southern Bell, 78; Outstanding Mgt Candidate, Southern Bell, 80; Individual Incentive award, BellSouth Svc, 84; Fel, Colonial Williamsburg Found, Antiques forum, 93; Ga Tech Alumni Asn Student Leadership travel award for Rome study, 93; Scholar, Nineteenth Century Studies Prog in London, Victorian Soc, 94; GTA teaching excellence award, col of archit, Ga Inst of Tech, 94; CETL/AMOCO Found GTA teaching excellence award, 94; pres fel, col of archit, Ga Inst of Tech, 90-94; doctoral fel, col of archit, Ga Inst of Tech, 91-94; Best Article Awd, Southeast Chap, Soc of Archit Hist, 95; Outstanding Student in Archit, Ga Inst of Tech, dec, 96; Doctoral prog achievement award, Ga Inst of Tech, may, 97; Dept of Archit res award, 99; new faculty grant, 99. **MEMBERSHIPS** Soc of Archit Hist; Southeast Chap, Soc of Archit Hist; Vernacular Archit Forum; Soc for Am City and Regional Planning Hist; Asn of Coll Sch of Archit; Nineteenth-Century Studies Asn; Victorian Soc; Soc for Emblem Studies; Decorative Arts Soc; Intl Soc for Amer City and Regional Planning Hist; Wallpaper Hist Soc. **RESEARCH** 19th-Century British architecture, theory, and decorative arts; Architecture, theory and decorative arts of Owen Jones 1809-1874; Public housing; Inscriptions and Symbolism in architecture. **SELECTED PUBLICATIONS** Auth, Owen Jones, Architect, Ga Inst of Tech, 96; contr, The Grammar of Ornament, Professional Artists' Edition, Pasadena, Direct Imagination Inc, 96; auth, US public housing in the 1930s: the first projects in Atlanta, Georgia, Planning Perspectives, 9, 405-430, 94; coauth, " Sixty and Out: Termwood Houes Transformed by Enemies and Friends," Journal of Urban History, Vol 26, no 3, 00. **CONTACT ADDRESS** Col of Architecture and Planning, Ball State Univ, Muncie, IN 47306-0305. **EMAIL** cflores@gw.bsu.edu

FLORES, DAN
PERSONAL Born 10/19/1948, Vivian, LA, s **DISCIPLINE** HISTORY **EDUCATION** Texas A&M Univ, PhD, 78. **CAREER** Prof, 78-92, Texas Tech Univ; AB Hammond Prof, 92-, Univ Montana. **HONORS AND AWARDS** Best Contemporary Non-Fiction Book, 1st Runner -Up, Western Writers, 00; Nonfiction Book Prize Finalist, Oklahoma Book Awds, 00; Best short nonfiction finalist, Western writers, 98; Wrangler Awd, Nat'l Cowboy Hall of Fame, 97; Ray Allen Billington article prize, Western History Assoc, 1984; Westerners International best book on the West, 84; tullis Prize, Best Book on Texas, Texas state Hist. Assoc, 84; Carroll Prize, Best article, Texas state hist. Assoc. 84. **MEMBERSHIPS** Texas Institute of Letters; Amer Society for Environ. History; Western History Assoc; Organ of Am Historians. **RESEARCH** Environ hist of the Amer West. **SELECTED PUBLICATIONS** Auth, "Jefferson & Southwestern Exploration," 84; auth, "Journal of an Indian Trader," 85; auth, "Canyon Visions," with Amy Winton, 89; auth, "Caprock Canyon Lands," 90; auth, "Bison Ecology and Bison Diplomacy," Journal of American History, 91; auth, "The Missippi Kite," with Eric Bolen, 93; auth, Horizontal Yellow," 99; auth, "The Natural West," 01. **CONTACT ADDRESS** Dept of History, Univ of Montana, Missoula, MT 59812. **EMAIL** dflores@selway.umt.edu

FLORESCU, RADU R.
PERSONAL Born 10/23/1925, Bucharest, Romania, m, 1951, 4 children **DISCIPLINE** MODERN HISTORY **EDUCATION** Oxford Univ, BA, 47, MA, 50, BLitt, 51; Ind Univ, PhD(Rumanian hist), 59. **CAREER** From instr to asst prof, 53-63, assoc prof hist, Boston Col, 63-; dir East Europ Res Ctr, 80-, Am Philos Soc grant, 61-62; fel, St Antony Col, Oxford Univ, 61-62. **HONORS AND AWARDS** Doctor Honoris Causa Romanian Acad, 00. **MEMBERSHIPS** AHA; Am Romanian Acad, Soc Romanian Studies; Am Asn for Advancement of Seanic Studies; Southeastern Europe. **RESEARCH** Rumanian and East European history. **SELECTED PUBLICATIONS** Auth, The origin and development of science in Rumania, Ann Sci, 3/60; Stratford canning and the Wallachian revolution of 1848, J Mod Hist, 9/63; Struggle Against Russia in the Rumanian Principalities, 1821-54, Castaldi, Rome, 63; coauth, In Search of Dracula, NY Graphic Soc, 72; Dracula: A Biography of Vlad the Impaler 1431-1476, Hawthorn, 73; The Dracula debate, E Europ Quart, 74; In Search of Frankenstein, NY Graphic & Warner Books, 75; Dracula Prince of Many Faces, 87, Little Brown, 89, all Dracula books co-auth with Raymond T, McNally, The Essential Dracula, Mayflower Books, 80; 100 Years of American-Romanian Relations, Nagard, 81; co-ed, Romanian between East and West: Profesor C C Giurescu, Columbia Univ East European Monographs; Essay on Romanian History, auth, Center of Romanian Studies, 1451, 99; co-auth, Insearch of Dr Jekyll & Mr Hyde Renaissance Books, 01. **CONTACT ADDRESS** Boston Col, Chestnut Hill, 140 Commonwealth Ave, Chestnut Hill, MA 02167-3800. **EMAIL** florescu@BC.edu

FLORIAN, ROBERT BRUCE
PERSONAL Born 01/17/1930, Hartford, CT, m, 1951, 3 children **DISCIPLINE** MODERN BRITISH & EUROPEAN HISTORY **EDUCATION** Adrian Col, BA, 51: Garrett Theol Sem, MDiv, 56; WVa Univ, MA, 63, PhD(hist), 73. **CAREER** Fac chmn 80-84, prof Hist, Salem-Teikyo Univ, 75-00; Chmn dept Lib Studies, 74-90, Chmn Dept Humanities and Soc Sci(s), 90-93; retired 00; pastor, Wva United Methodist Churches, Haywood, 61-62, Jarvisvile, 71-73, Greenwood, 76-79, Wallace, 79-84, Riverside-Granville 86-90, Bristol, 99-. **HONORS AND AWARDS** Citation as Outstanding Instructor by Wva State Legis, 89. **MEMBERSHIPS** AAUP; AHA, mem, Wva State Antiquities Comm, treas comm on Archives and History, Wva Conf United Methodist Church, 84-88, 96-; treas comm on Archives and History, Northeastern Jurisdiction of United Methodist Church, 00-. **RESEARCH** Tudor England; history of United Methodist Church in West Virginia; Sen Jennings Randolph, 02-98. **SELECTED PUBLICATIONS** Auth, Condensation in Bootstraps, Salem Col Mag, Fall 73; ed, Bicentennial Historical Directory of West Virginia United Methodist Churches, WVa United Methodist, 5/76 & Suppl Article, 10/76; Sir Joh Cheke, Tudor Tutor, 73; Melting Times: A History of West Virginia United Methodism, 84-89; auth, Biography of Sen Randolph forthcoming. **CONTACT ADDRESS** Dept of Humantities and Soc Sciences, Salem-Teikyo Univ, PO Box 500, Salem, WV 26426-0500. **EMAIL** Florian@Salem.wvnet.edu

FLYNN, GEORGE QUITMAN
PERSONAL Born 02/12/1937, New Orleans, LA, m, 1960, 3 children **DISCIPLINE** RECENT AMERICAN HISTORY **EDUCATION** Loyola Univ, La, BS, 60; La State Univ, MA, 62, PhD(Hist), 66. **CAREER** Asst prof Hist, Seattle Univ, 66-69; vis assoc prof, Ind Univ, Bloomington, 69-71; assoc prof, Univ Miami, 71-73; assoc prof, 73-75, prof Hist, Tex Tech Univ, 75-. **MEMBERSHIPS** Orgn Am Historians. **RESEARCH** The New Deal and Franklin Delanor Roosevelt; home front World War II; General Lewis B Hershey of selective service system. **SELECTED PUBLICATIONS** Auth, American Catholics and the Roosevelt Presidency, 1932-1936, Univ Ky, 68; Franklin Roosevelt and the Vatican, Cath Hist Rev, 7/72; History and the social sciences, Hist Teacher, 5/74; Roosevelt and Romanism: Catholics and American Diplomacy, 1937-1945, Greenwood, 76; The Mess in Washington: Manpower Mobilization in World War II, Greenwood, 79; Lewis B Hershey, Mr Selective Service, North Carolina, 85; The Draft, 1940-1973, UP of Kansas, 93; Conscription and Equity in Western Democracies, 1940-1975, Journal of Contemporary History, Jan, 98. **CONTACT ADDRESS** Dept of History, Texas Tech Univ, Lubbock, TX 79409-0001. **EMAIL** g.flynn@ttu.edu

FLYNN, JAMES THOMAS
PERSONAL Born 04/11/1932, Norwood, MA, m, 1956, 3 children **DISCIPLINE** MODERN EUROPEAN HISTORY **EDUCATION** Boston Col, AB, 54, AM, 55; Clark Univ, PhD (hist), 64. **CAREER** From instr to assoc prof, 60-72, chmn dept, 68-70, Prof Hist, Col of the Holy Cross, 72-, Assoc, Russ Res Ctr, Harvard Univ, 70-. **MEMBERSHIPS** AHA; Am Cath Hist Asn; Am Asn Advan Slavic Studies. **RESEARCH** Russian higher education; Russian bureaucracy. **SELECTED PUBLICATIONS** Auth, Karazin, gentry, and Kharkov University, Slavic Rev, 6/69; Magnitskii's purge of Kazan University, J Mod Hist, 12/71; Uvarov's liveral years, Jahrbucher fur Gesch-

ichte Osteuopas, 12/72; Affair of Kostomarov's dissertation, Slavonic & E Europ Rev, 4/74; Uvarov and reaction in Russia, Slavic Rev, 6/76. **CONTACT ADDRESS** Dept of Hist, Col of the Holy Cross, 1 College St, Worcester, MA 01610-2322.

FLYNT, J. WAYNE
PERSONAL Born 10/04/1940, Pontotoc, MS, m, 1961, 2 children **DISCIPLINE** HISTORY **EDUCATION** Howard Col, AB, 61; Fla State Univ, MS, 62, PhD, 65. **CAREER** Asst to assoc prof, Samford Univ, 65-77; Head, Dept of Hist, Auburn Univ, 77-85; Hollifield Prof of Southern Hist, Auburn Univ, 82-90; Distinguished Univ Prof, Auburn Univ, 90-. **HONORS AND AWARDS** Woodrow Wilson Fel, 61; Woodrow Wilson Diss Fel, 64-65; NDEA Fel, 61-65; Ford Found Post Doc, 65; twelve teaching Awds including Prof of the Year for Ala from Coun for Advancement & Support of Ed; 18 writing Awds including Lillian Smith Awd for nonfiction, 90; Alabamian of the Year, Mobile Register, 92; public television documentary, "The Gospel According to Flynt.'' **MEMBERSHIPS** Ala Hist Soc, Ala Asn of Hists, Fla Hist Soc, Southern Hist Asn, Org of Am Hists, Church Hist Soc, Southern Baptist Hist Soc, Am Asn of Univ Profs. **RESEARCH** Southern U.S. political, social, religious history, history of poverty. **SELECTED PUBLICATIONS** Auth, Duncan Upshaw Fletcher: Dixie's Reluctant Progressive, Tallahassee: Fla State Univ Press (71); auth, Cracker Messiah: Governor Sidney J. Catts of Florida, Baton Rouge: La State Univ Press, Southern Biography Series (spring 77); auth, Dixie's Forgotten People: The South's Poor Whites, Bloomington: Ind Univ Press (79); auth, Montgomery: An Illustrated History, Woodland Hills, Calif: Windsor Pubs (80); coauth with Dorothy S. Flynt, Southern Poor Whites: An Annotated Bibliography, New York: Garland Pubs (81); auth, Mine, Mill and Microchip: A Chronicle of Alabama Enterprise, Woodland Hills, Calif: Windsor Pubs (87); auth, Poor But Proud: Alabama's Poor Whites, Tuscaloosa: Univ Ala Press (89); coauth with Leah Rawls Atkins, William W. Rogers, Davis Ward, Alabama: The History of a Deep South State, Tuscaloosa: Univ Ala Press (94); coauth with Gerald W. Berkley, Taking Christianity to China: Alabama Missionaries in the Middle Kingdom, 1850-1950, Tuscaloosa: Univ Ala Press (97); auth, Alabama Baptists: Southern Baptists in the Heart of Dixie, Tuscaloosa: Univ Ala Press (98). **CONTACT ADDRESS** Dept Hist, Auburn Univ, 310 Thach Hall, Auburn, AL 36849-5207. **EMAIL** henkewi@auburn.edu

FOGARTY, ROBERT STEPHEN
PERSONAL Born 08/30/1938, Brooklyn, NY, 2 children **DISCIPLINE** HISTORY **EDUCATION** Fordham Univ, BS, 60; Univ Denver, MA, 62, PhD, 68. **CAREER** Instr Am studies, Mich State Univ, 63-67; assoc prof, 68-80, chair humanities, 79-80, Prof Hist, Antioch Col, 80-; Mich Hist Comn grant, 71-72; consult, Nat Endowment Humanities, 73, Utopian films in Am, 77-; Am Philos Asn grant, 76; ed, Antioch Rev, 77-; Coord Coun Lit Mag Ed fel, 81. **HONORS AND AWARDS** Vis fel, All Souls, Oxford, 87; NYU Humanities Inst, 89; Lloyd Lews Fel Newberry Libr, 94; Distinguished Roving Lecturer, Korea, 00. **MEMBERSHIPS** Orgn Am Historians; Am Studies Asn. **RESEARCH** Reform movements; literary history; communal history. **SELECTED PUBLICATIONS** Auth, A nice piece of change, Antioch Rev, 69; ed, American Utopianism, AHM Publ, 72; ed, American Utopian Adventure (10 vols), Porcupine, 74; contribr, Wirtschaft und gesselschaft im industriezeitalter, Union Verlag Stuttgart, 74; auth, American communes: 1865-1914, Am Studies, 75; Dictionary of Communal History, Greenwood; The Righteous Remnant: The House of David, Kent State Press, 81; All Things New, Univ Chicago Press, 90; Special Love/Special Sex, Syracuse Univ Press, 94; auth, Desire and Duty at Oneida, Indiana Univ Press, 00. **CONTACT ADDRESS** Dept of Hist, Antioch Col, 795 Livermore St, Yellow Springs, OH 45387-1607.

FOGELSON, ROBERT M.
PERSONAL Born 05/19/1937, New York, NY **DISCIPLINE** URBAN STUDIES, HISTORY **EDUCATION** Columbia Univ, AB, 58; Harvard Univ, AM, 59, PhD, 64. **CAREER** Asst prof hist, Columbia Univ, 64-68; assoc prof, 68-76, prof urban studies & hist, MA Inst Technol, 76, Consult, Pres Comn Law Endorcement & Admin Justice 66; Soc Sci Res Coun fac res grant, 66-67 & legal & govt processes fel, 70-71; consult, Rand Corp, 67-68; consult, Nat Adv Comn Civil Disorders, 68-69 & Urban Inst, 70; Guggenheim fel, 73-74; consult, O'Melveny at Myers, 86-87; Macfarland Ferguson, 90-92; consult, Peabody Essex Museum, 00. **RESEARCH** Am urban hist. **SELECTED PUBLICATIONS** Auth, The Fragmented Metropolis: Los Angeles, 1850-1930, Harvard Univ, 67; Violence as Protest: A Study of Riots and Ghettos, Doubleday, 71; Big City Police, Harvard Univ, 77; auth, Pensions: The Hidden Costs of Public Safety, Columbia Univ, 84; America's Armories: Architecture, Society, and Public Order, Harvard Univ press, 89; auth, Downtown: Its Rise and Fall, 1880-1950, Yale Univ, 01. **CONTACT ADDRESS** Dept of Urban Studies, 77 Massachusetts Ave, Cambridge, MA 02139-4307.

FOGLEMAN, AARON S.
DISCIPLINE HISTORY **EDUCATION** Okla State Univ, BA; Albert-Ludwigs-Univ, Freiburg, Ger, MA; Univ Mich, PhD. **CAREER** Assoc prof & grad coordr Hist dept, Univ South Al. **RESEARCH** Early america, immigration, religion. **SELECTED PUBLICATIONS** Auth, Hopeful Journeys: German Immigration, Settlement, and Political Culture in Colonial America, 1717-1775, Philadelphia: Univ Pa Press, 96; The Transformation of Immigration into the US during the Era of the American Revolution, J Amer Hist, 98; Moravian Immigration and Settlement in British North America, 1734-1775, Transactions of the Moravian Hist Soc, 29, 96; Immigration, German Immigration, and Eighteenth Century America, in Emigration and Settlement Patterns of German Communities in North America, Indianapolis: Max Kade Ger Amer Ctr, 95 & Women on the Trail in Colonial America: A Travel Journal of German Moravians Migrating from Pennsylvania to North Carolina in 1766, Pa Hist 61, 94; auth, "Shadow Boxing Georgia: The Beginnings of the Moravian-Lutheran Conflict in British North America," Georgia Historical Quarterly, 83 (99). **CONTACT ADDRESS** Dept of History, Univ of So Alabama, Mobile, AL 36688-0002. **EMAIL** afoglema@jaguar1.usouthal.edu

FOLDA, JAROSLAV, III
PERSONAL Born 07/25/1940, Baltimore, MD, m, 1964, 2 children **DISCIPLINE** ART HISTORY **EDUCATION** Princeton Univ, AB, 62; Johns Hopkins Univ, PhD, 68. **CAREER** Instr, Dept of Art, 68, Asst Prof, 68-72, Assoc Prof, 72-78, Prof, 78-96, Ch Dept of Art, 83-87, N. Ferebee Taylor Prof of Hist of Art, 96-, Univ NC. **HONORS AND AWARDS** Tanner Awd for Undergrad Tchng, UNC, 94; Post-baccalaureate Tchng Awd, UNC, 98; Younger Humanist Fellow, NEH, 74-75; Fellow for Ind Study & Res, NEH, 81-82; Guggenheim Memorial Fellow, 88-89; Fellow, Ins for the Arts & Hum, UNC, 95; Vis Schol, J Paul Getty Mus, 95; Fellow for Univ Tchrs, NEH, 98-99. **MEMBERSHIPS** Am Soc of Oriental Res; Brit Sch of Archaeol in Jerusalem; Byzantine Stud Conf; Col Art Asn of Am; Medieval Acad of Am; Societe francaise d'archeologie; Soc for the Stud of the Crusades and the Latin E; US Nat Cmte for Byzantine Stud. **RESEARCH** History of Medieval art. **SELECTED PUBLICATIONS** Auth, The Art of the Crusaders in the Holy Land, 1098-1187, Cambridge Univ Press, 95; auth, The Kahn and Mellon Madonnas: Icon or Altarpiece?, Byzantine East, Latin West: Art-Historical Studies in Honor of Kurt Weitzman, Princeton Univ Press, 501-510, 95; auth, The Crusader Period and the Church of St Anne at Sepphoris, Sepphoris & Galilee, NC Mus of Art, 100-107, 96; auth, Paris, Bibl. Nat, MS lat 5334 and the Origins of the Hospitaller Master, Montjoie: Studies in Crusade History in Honor of Hans Eberhard Mayer, Variorium, 177-187, 97; auth, The South Transept Facade of the Church of the Holy Sepulchre in Jerusalem: As Aspect of rebuilding Zion, The Crusades and Their Sources: Studies Presented to Bernard Hamilton, Ashgate, 197-218, 98. **CONTACT ADDRESS** Dept of Art, Univ of No Carolina, Chapel Hill, 111 Hanes Art Ctr, Chapel Hill, NC 27599-3405. **EMAIL** jfolda@email.unc.edu

FOLEY, MARY BRIANT
PERSONAL Born 09/07/1921, Kansasville, WI **DISCIPLINE** AMERICAN HISTORY **EDUCATION** Mt Mary Col, BA, 50; DePaul Univ, MA, 62; Loyola Univ, Ill, PhD, 68. **CAREER** From instr to assoc prof, 66-77, prof hist, Mt Mary Col, 77-, chmn dept Hist & Polit Sci, 77-95; pres, Sch Sisters of Notre Dame, Mequon Prov, 71-75. **MEMBERSHIPS** AHA; Orgn Am Historians. **RESEARCH** United States history, Revolutionary period. **CONTACT ADDRESS** Dept of Hist, Mount Mary Col, 2900 N Menomonee Riv, Milwaukee, WI 53222-4597. **EMAIL** foleym@mtmary.edu

FOLEY, MARY KATHLEEN
DISCIPLINE ASIAN THEATER **EDUCATION** Rosemont Col, BA, 69; Univ Bochum, W Germany, Fulbright cert, 70; Univ Mass, Amherst, MA, 75; Univ Hawaii, PhD, 79. **CAREER** Asst to assoc PROF, UNIV CALIF, 80-, PROVOST PORTER COL, 89-, UNIV CALIF, SANTA CRUZ. **HONORS AND AWARDS** Fulbright Schlarship, NEH, NEA, Asian Cultural Council Grants, Chandra Bhandar, Endow Chair. **MEMBERSHIPS** Asn fro Asian Performance, Asn of Asian Studies, Assoc for Theatre in Higher Education, Puppeteers of America, UNIMA. **RESEARCH** Performance of South and Southeast Asia, Puppetry and Perfoming Objects. **SELECTED PUBLICATIONS** Auth, Local Manifestations and Corss-Cultural Implications: Essays on Southeast Asian Performing Arts, Berkeley, 92. **CONTACT ADDRESS** Porter Col, Univ of California, Santa Cruz, 301 Heller Dr, Santa Cruz, CA 95064. **EMAIL** kfoley@cats.ucsc.edu

FOLEY, NEIL
DISCIPLINE HISTORY, AMERICAN STUDIES **EDUCATION** Univ Va, BA; Georgetown Univ, MA, Univ Mich, MA, PhD, 90. **CAREER** Martin Luther King, Jr/Cesar Chavez/Rosa Parks fel, Univ Mich, 90-91; asst prof, 91-96, assoc dir, Ctr Mexican Am Stud, 96-97, ASSOC PROF, HIST, 97-, UNIV TEXAS, AUSTIN; consult dir, Ctr Mexican Am Studies, 97-98, Univ Tex, Arlington. **HONORS AND AWARDS** Winner of seven book awards for The White Scourge, (Berkeley, 1997). **CONTACT ADDRESS** History Dept, Univ of Texas, Austin, Campus Mail Code B7000, Austin, TX 78712. **EMAIL** nfoley@mail.utexas.edu

FOLEY, WILLIAM EDWARD
PERSONAL Born 09/20/1938, Kansas City, MO, m, 1967, 2 children **DISCIPLINE** UNITED STATES HISTORY **EDUCATION** Cent Mo State Univ, BS, 60, MA, 63; Univ Mo, PhD (hist), 67. **CAREER** Asst instr hist, Univ Mo, 63-66; from asst prof to assoc prof, 66-73, Prof Hist, Cent MO State Univ, 73-. **HONORS AND AWARDS** Awd of Merit, Am Asn State and Local Hist, 74; Author's Awd, State Hist Soc of Missouri, 78; Vivian Paladin Writing Awd, Montana Hist Soc, 79; James Neal Primm Awd, Missouri Hist Soc, 89. **MEMBERSHIPS** Organization of Am Historians; Western Hist Asn; Southern Hist Asn. **RESEARCH** Missouri territorial history; early national period in United States history; history of the American West. **SELECTED PUBLICATIONS** Coauth, The First Chouteaus: River Barons of Early St. Louis, Univ Illinois Pr (Urbana), 83; auth, "Different Notions of Justice: The Case of the 1808 St. Louis Murder Trials," Gateway Heritage 9 (88-89): 2-13; co-ed, An Account of Upper Louisiana by Nicolas de Finiels, Univ Missouri Pr (Columbia), 89; coauth, Missouri: Then and Now, Univ Missouri Pr (Columbia), 92; auth, Fremont, John Charles--Character as Destiny, Pac Northwest Quart, Vol 84, 93; co-ed, Dictionary of Missouri Biography, Univ Missouri Pr (Columbia), 99; auth, Biography of William Clark, forthcoming. **CONTACT ADDRESS** Dept of Hist, Central Missouri State Univ, Warrensburg, MO 64093-8888. **EMAIL** foleyw@iland.net

FOLMAR, JOHN KENT
PERSONAL Born Foley, AL **DISCIPLINE** UNITED STATES HISTORY **EDUCATION** Stanford Univ, AB, 55; Birmingham-Southern Col, MA, 61; Univ Ala, PhD (hist), 68. **CAREER** Teacher pub sch, Ala, 59-61; instr US hist, Univ Mil Sch, Ala, 61-63; instr, Univ Ala, 65-66; asst prof, Morehead State Univ, 66-69; chmn hist sect, Dept Soc Sci, 71-76, chmn, Dept Hist, 76-78, chmn, Dept Hist and Urban Affairs, 78-79, Prof Hist, California State Col, PA, 69-, Dir, Proj Adult Col Educ, 80-. **HONORS AND AWARDS** Commonwealth distinguished fac award, Asn Pa State Col and Univ Fac, 78. **MEMBERSHIPS** Southern Hist Asn; Orgn Am Hists. **RESEARCH** Civil War and Reconstruction, quantification; local and family history; Southern history. **SELECTED PUBLICATIONS** Auth, Lt Col James M Williams and the Ft Powell incident, Ala Rev, 4/64; The war comes to central Alabama: Ebenezer Church, April, 1865, Ala Hist Quart, 65; ed, Augusta, Georgia, 1860-1861: As seen in three letters, Ga Hist Quart, 69; Pre-Civil War sentiment from Belmont County: Correspondence of Hugh Anderson, Ohio Hist, 69; auth, United States History to 1877: An Outline and Workbook, Allegheny Press, 75; Reaction to Reconstruction: John Forsyth and the Mobile Advertiser-Register, 1865-1867, Ala Hist Quart, 75; Reaction to Reconstruction: The legislative behavior of Pennsylvania Republicans in the Forty-second Congress, 1871-1873, Western Pa Hist Mag, 78; From That Terrible Field: The Civil War Letters of James M Williams, Twenty-First Alabama Infantry Volunteers, Univ Ala Press, 81. **CONTACT ADDRESS** Dept of Hist and Urban Affairs, California Univ of Pennsylvania, 250 University Ave, California, PA 15419-1394.

FOLSOM, LOWELL EDWIN
PERSONAL Born 09/30/1947, Pittsburgh, PA, m, 1969, 1 child **DISCIPLINE** ENGLISH, AMERICAN STUDIES **EDUCATION** Ohio Wesleyan Univ, BA, 69; Univ Rochester, MA, 72, PhD(English), 76. **CAREER** Instr humanities, Eastman Sch Music, 74-75; vis asst prof English, State Univ NY, Geneseo, 75-76; asst prof, 76-81, assoc prof , 81-87, prof English & Am Studies, Univ Iowa, 87-; ed, Walt Whitman Qtly Rev, 83-, co-dir, Walt Whitman Hypertext Archive, 97-. **HONORS AND AWARDS** Director, NEH Summer Seminar, 84; Collaborative Research Awd, NEH, 91-94; Univ Rochester Distinguished Scholar Medal, 95; Iowa Regents Awd for Faculty Excellence, 96; Fullbright Senior Professorship, Germany, 96; F. Wendell Miller Distinguished Professorship, 97-. **MEMBERSHIPS** MLA; Midwest MLA; Am Lit Asn, Whitman Studies Asn. **RESEARCH** American poetry and culture; Walt Whitman; contemporary American literature. **SELECTED PUBLICATIONS** Ed, Walt Whitman: The Measure of His Song, Holy Cow! Press, 81, second ed, 98, Choice Best Academic Book, 82; Regions of Memory: Uncollected Prose of W.S. Merwin, Univ of Il Press, 87; W.S. Merwin: Essays on the Poetry, Univ of Il Press, 87; Walt Whitman: The Centennial Essays, Univ of Iowa Press, 94, Walt Whitman and the World, Univ of Iowa Press, 95; Major Authors: Walt Whitman, CD-ROM, Primary Source Media, 97, Choice Best Academic Book, 98; Auth, Walt Whitman's Native Representations, Cambridge UP, 94, Choice Best Academic Book, 95. **CONTACT ADDRESS** Dept of English, Univ of Iowa, 308 English Phil Bld, Iowa City, IA 52242-1492. **EMAIL** ed-folsom@uiowa.edu

FOLTZ, RICHARD
PERSONAL Born 04/19/1961, Columbus, OH, m, 1994, 1 child **DISCIPLINE** HISTORY AND MIDDLE EASTERN STUDIES **EDUCATION** Univ Utah, BA, 87, MA, 88; Harvard Univ, PhD, 96. **CAREER** Visiting Asst Prof, Brown Univ, 96-97; asst prof, Gettysburg Coll, 97-98; visiting asst prof, Columbia Univ, 98-00; asst prof, Univ of Florida, 00-. **MEMBERSHIPS** Amer Hist. Assoc; Amer Acad Religion; Iranian Sudies Assoc; Assoc Asian Studies **RESEARCH** Cultural history of central and south Asia; history of religion; religion and ecology

SELECTED PUBLICATIONS Conversations with Emperor Jahangir, Mazda Publishers, Costa Mesa, 98; Mughal India and Central Asia, Oxford Univ Press, Karachi, 98; Religions of the Silk Road, St. Martins Press, NY, 99. **CONTACT ADDRESS** Dept of Religion, Univ of Florida, PO Box 117410, Gainesville, FL 32611-7410. **EMAIL** rfoltz@religion.ufl.edu

FONER, ERIC
PERSONAL Born 02/07/1943, New York, NY, m, 1980, 1 child **DISCIPLINE** AMERICAN HISTORY **EDUCATION** Columbia Univ, BA, 63, PhD, 69; Oxford Univ, BA, 65. **CAREER** From instr to assoc prof hist, Columbia Univ, 69-73; prof hist, City Col New York, 73-82; prof hist, Columbia Univ, 82-, Vis prof, Princeton Univ, 76-77; vis prof, Univ SC, 78; vis prof, Univ Calif, Berkeley, 79; Pitt prof Am hist and insts, Cambridge Univ, 80-81; dir, Nat Endowment for the Humanities Summer Sem, 80 & 82; Harmsworth Prof Am Hist, Oxford Univ, 93-94. **HONORS AND AWARDS** Los Angeles Times Book Award, 89; Bancroft Prize, 89; Owsley Prize, 89; Parkman Prize, 89; Great Teacher Award, Columbia Univ, 91; Schol of the Year, NY Coun for the Humanities, 95. **MEMBERSHIPS** Am Hist Asn, 00; Southern Hist Asn; Orgn Am Historians, 93-94. **RESEARCH** Civil War period; history of American radicalism; Black history. **SELECTED PUBLICATIONS** Auth, Free Soil, Free Labor, Free Men: The Ideology of the Republican Party Before the Civil War, Oxford Univ, 70; ed, America's Black Past, Harper, 70; Nat Turner, Prentice-Hall, 71; auth, Tom Paine and Revolutionary America, 76 & Politics and Ideology in the Age of the Civil War, 81, Oxford Univ; Nothing But Freedom, 83; Reconstruction: America's Unfinished Revolution, 88; Freedom's Lawmakers, 93; The Story of American Freedom, 98. **CONTACT ADDRESS** Dept of Hist, Columbia Univ, Box 16, Fayerweather, New York, NY 10027-6900. **EMAIL** ef17@columbia.edu

FONG, GRACE
DISCIPLINE EAST ASIAN STUDIES **EDUCATION** Univ British Columbia, PhD. **CAREER** Assoc prof. **RESEARCH** Classical Chinese poetry; literary theory and criticism; gender and representation; Chinese film. **SELECTED PUBLICATIONS** Art, Inscribing Desire: Zhu Yizun's Love Lyrics in Jingzhi ju qinqu, Harvard Jour Asiatic Studies, 94; auth, The Early Literary Traditions, 94; auth, Wu Wenying and the Art of Southern Song Ci Poetry, Princeton, 87. **CONTACT ADDRESS** East Asian Studies Dept, McGill Univ, 845 Sherbrooke St, Montreal, QC, Canada H3A 2T5. **EMAIL** gfong@leacock.lan.mcgill.ca

FONGE, FUABEH P.
PERSONAL Born, Cameroon, 5 children **DISCIPLINE** HISTORY **EDUCATION** Univ Yaounde, BA, 75; Georgetown Univ, MA, 82; Howard Univ, PhD, 89. **CAREER** Vis asst prof, Guilford Col, 89-90; from asst prof to assoc prof, NC A & T State Univ, 90-. **HONORS AND AWARDS** Listed in Who's Who Among America's Teachers. **MEMBERSHIPS** African Studies Asn, Asn of Third World Studies, NC Hist Asn, Nat Geog, Am Asn of Univ Professors. **RESEARCH** African History, Politics, and Government; Africana Studies; Black Diaspora. **SELECTED PUBLICATIONS** Auth, Modernization Without Development in Africa, Africa World Press (Trenton, NJ), 97; auth, A Concise History of Africa Since 1800, Simon & Schuster Custom Publ (Needham Heights, MA), 97. **CONTACT ADDRESS** Dept Hist, No Carolina Agr and Tech State Univ, 1601 E Market St, Greensboro, NC 27401-3209.

FONROBERT, CHARLOTTE
PERSONAL Born 09/01/1965, Germany, s **DISCIPLINE** HISTORY **CAREER** Post-Doc, Syracuse Univ, 95-96; Asst Prof, Univ Judaism, 96-00; Asst prof, Stanford Univ, 00-. **HONORS AND AWARDS** Lady Davies Fel, 92-93; Hazel Cole Fel, 94-95; Interuniv Fel, 92-93; Memorial Fel, 93-94. **MEMBERSHIPS** AAR/SBL, AJS, NAPS. **RESEARCH** Talmud, Rabbinic Literature, Gender in Judaism, Jewish Christianity, Jewish-Christian Relationships in Late antiquity, Purity/Impurity in Judaism. **SELECTED PUBLICATIONS** Auth, Menstrual Purity: Rabbinic and Christian Reconstructions of Biblical Gender, Stanford Univ press, 00. **CONTACT ADDRESS** Dept Relig Studies, Stanford Univ, Building 70, Stanford, CA 94305-2165. **EMAIL** cfonrobert@uj.edu

FONTANA, BERNARD LEE
PERSONAL Born 01/07/1931, Oakland, CA, m, 1954, 3 children **DISCIPLINE** AMERICAN INDIAN AND SPANISH COLONIAL HISTORY **EDUCATION** Univ Calif, Berkeley, AB, 53; Univ Ariz, PhD, 60. **CAREER** Field Hist, Univ Ariz Libr, 59-61, Ethnologist, Ariz State Mus and Lectr Anthrop, Univ Ariz, 62-, Field Hist Libr, 78-, Consult, Papago Indian Tribe, 62-64; mem, Western Regional Adv Comt, Nat Park Serv, 74-78; bd mem, Southwest Parks and Monuments Asn, 79-. **HONORS AND AWARDS** Border Regional Libr Asn Book Awd, 79 and 81. **MEMBERSHIPS** Am Soc Ethnohist; Soc Hist Archaeol; Am Ethnol Soc; Soc Post-Medieval Archaeol; Southwestern Mission Res Ctr. **RESEARCH** Southwestern American Indian ethnology; southwestern colonial history and historical archaeology; contemporary American Indian studies. **SELECTED PUBLICATIONS** Auth, Kelemen, Pal 1894-1993, Hisp Am Hist Rev, Vol 73, 93; Reminiscences, J Southwest, Vol 38, 96; Sharing the Desert--The Tohono Oodham in History, Ethnohistory, Vol 43, 96; Archaeology of the Ak Chin Indian Community West Side Farms Project, Public Hist, Vol 15, 93; Arizona--A History, Ethnohistory, Vol 43, 96; Plants Without Water Ezell, Paul 1974 Manuscript Relating to Arizona and the Sonoran Desert, J Southwest, Vol 36, 94. **CONTACT ADDRESS** Libr, Univ of Arizona, Univ Library, Tucson, AZ 85721.

FONTANELLA, LEE
PERSONAL Born 07/23/1941, Stafford Springs, CT, m, 1974, 1 child **DISCIPLINE** HISPANIC STUDIES, COMPARATIVE LITERATURE. **EDUCATION** Williams Col, BA, 63; New York Univ, MA, 66; Princeton Univ, MA, 68, PhD (Romance lang and lit), 71. **CAREER** Instr Span, Williams Col, 63-64; asst prof, 70-76, Assoc Prof Span, Univ Tex, Austin, 76-, Coun Int Exchange Scholars fel, 77-78. **MEMBERSHIPS** SCent Mod Lang Asn; SCent Soc 18th Century Studies; Am Asn Teachers Span and Port; MLA; Am Soc 18th Century Studies. **RESEARCH** Spanish romantic literature and essay; comparative literature; 19th century popular science and photohistory. **SELECTED PUBLICATIONS CONTACT ADDRESS** Dept of Span and Port, Univ of Texas, Austin, Batts Hall, Austin, TX 78712.

FONTIJN-HARRIS, CLAIRE
PERSONAL Born 03/23/1960, Montreal, PQ, Canada, m, 2000 **DISCIPLINE** MUSIC, FRENCH, BAROQUE FLUTE, MUSICOLOGY **EDUCATION** Oberlin Col, BA, 82; Royal Conserv of the Hague, cert, 85; Duke Univ, MA, 89, PhD 94. **CAREER** Asst Prof Music, Dir Collegium Musicum, 94-, Wellesley Col. **HONORS AND AWARDS** Prize winner, Case Western Res Univ Baroque Mus Comp, 89; Gladys Krieble Delmas Grant, Venice, 94 and 00; Woodrow Wilson Nat Fellow Found Women's Stud Awd, 92, Am Musicol Soc Publ Subvertion, 00. **MEMBERSHIPS** Am Musicol Soc; Soc 17th Cent Mus; Int Assoc of Women in Mus; Heinrich Schuetz Soc. **RESEARCH** Baroque Music; Baroque Flute; Women in Music; Women in Baroque Music. **SELECTED PUBLICATIONS** Bembo, Antonia, entry in The Norton/Grove Dict of Women Composers, London, Macmillan, 94; Quantz's 'unegal': implications for the performance of 18th-century music, Early Mus, Feb 95, 55-62; In Honour of the Duchess of Burgundy: Antonia Bembo's Compositions for Marie-Adelaide of Savoy, Cahiers de l'IRHMES, 3, 95, 45-89; Antonia Bembo, in Women Composers: Music Through the Ages, New York, G.K. Hall, 96, 201-16. **CONTACT ADDRESS** Wellesley Col, 106 Central St., Dept. of M, Wellesley, MA 02481. **EMAIL** cfontijn@wellesley.edu

FOOS, PAUL W.
DISCIPLINE HISTORY **EDUCATION** Univ Mass, BA, 91; Yale Univ, PhD, 97. **CAREER** Author **MEMBERSHIPS** Am Antiquarian Soc **RESEARCH** Mexican Wars, 1835-1853 **CONTACT ADDRESS** 107 Foster St, New Haven, CT 06511. **EMAIL** paul.foos@yale.edu

FORAGE, PAUL C.
DISCIPLINE HISTORY **EDUCATION** Univ Toronto, PhD. **CAREER** Asst prof. **RESEARCH** Imperial China; Asian frontier history; history of science and technology; military history. **SELECTED PUBLICATIONS** Auth, pubs in Asian history journals. **CONTACT ADDRESS** History Dept, Florida Atlantic Univ, 777 Glades Rd, Boca Raton, FL 33431. **EMAIL** pforage@fau.edu

FORBES, GERALDINE MAY
PERSONAL Born 01/07/1943, Edmonton, AB, Canada **DISCIPLINE** ASIAN HISTORY **EDUCATION** Univ Alta, BEd, 65; Univ Ill, AM, 68, PhD(hist), 72. **CAREER** Teacher hist, Kings County High Sch, 64-66; asst prof, 71-76, assoc prof Hist, SUNY Oswego, 76-81; prof hist, 81-98; Distinguished Teaching Prof, 98; Dir Women's Studies, SUNY Oswego, 85-. **HONORS AND AWARDS** Rabindra Puraskar (Rabindranath Prize), 79. **MEMBERSHIPS** Asian Studies Asn; National Women's Studies Asn. **RESEARCH** Colonial and Postcolonial Indian History, Gender and Women's Roles. **SELECTED PUBLICATIONS** Auth, Positivism in Bengal: A Case Study in the Transmission and Assimilation of an Ideology (Book selected for the Rabindra Puraskar, awarded by the gov of West Bengal in 1979), Calcutta, Minerva, 75; ed, A Pattern of Life: the Memoirs of an Indian Woman, by Shudha Mazumdar, New Delhi, Manohar, 77; ed and intro, Shudha Mazumdar, Memoirs of an Indian Woman (revised ed of A Pattern of Life), NY, M.E. Sharpe, 89; ed and intro, Manmohini Zutshi Sahgal, An Indian Freedom Fighter Recalls Her Life, NY, M.E. Sharpe, 94; auth, Women in Modern India, New Cambridge History of India series, Cambridge Univ Press, 96; An Historian's Perspective: Indian Women and the Freedom Movement, RCWS Gender Series, S.N.D.T. Women's Univ, Bombay, 97. **CONTACT ADDRESS** Dept of Hist, SUNY, Oswego, 431 Mahar, Oswego, NY 13126-3599. **EMAIL** forbes@oswego.edu

FORBES, JOHN DOUGLAS
PERSONAL Born 04/09/1910, San Francisco, CA, m, 1980, 3 children **DISCIPLINE** ECONOMIC AND ARCHITECTURAL HISTORY **EDUCATION** Univ CA, AB, 31; Stanford Univ, AM, 32; Harvard Univ, AM & PhD(hist), 37. **CAREER** Curator paintings, San Francisco World's Fair, 38-40; chmn dept fine arts, Univ Kansas City, 40-42; mem fac hist, Bennington Col, 43-46; from assoc prof to prof hist & fine arts, Wabash Col, 46-54; prof, 54-80, EMER PROF BUS HIST, GRAD SCH BUS ADMIN, UNIV VA, 80-, Assoc ed, Am Enterprise Asn, 45-46; adv ed, Encycl Britannica, 56-58; mem adv bd, Hist Am Bldg Survey, US Dept Interior, 73-79. **HONORS AND AWARDS** Officier, Ordre des Palmes Academiques (France); Cavaliere, Ordine al Merito (Italy); Phi Beta Kappa. **MEMBERSHIPS** AHA; Soc Archit Hist (secy, 52, vpres, 60-61, pres, 62-63); hon mem Am Inst Archit; AAUP; Col Art Asn Am. **RESEARCH** Economic, political and architectural history. **SELECTED PUBLICATIONS** Auth, Victorian Architect, Ind Univ, 53; Israel Thorndike, Beverly, Mass Hist Soc, 53; Murder in Full View, Caravelle Bks, 68; Death Warmed Over, Pageant, 71; Stettinius, Sr, Portrait of a Morgan Partner, Univ Va, 74; J P Morgon, Jr, 1864-1944, Univ Va, 81; Death Among the Artists, Book Guild, 93. **CONTACT ADDRESS** Box 3607, Charlottesville, VA 22903.

FORD, BONNIE L.
PERSONAL Born 09/25/1938, Salt Lake City, UT, m, 1961, 2 children **DISCIPLINE** HISTORY **EDUCATION** Colo Col, BA, 60; Stanford Univ, MA, 62; Univ Calif, Davis, PhD, 85. **CAREER** Prof, Sacramento City Col, 71-. **HONORS AND AWARDS** Phi Beta Kappa; Fac Achievement Awd, Sacramento City Col; Awd for Excellence, Sacramento City Col. **MEMBERSHIPS** Am Fedn of Teachers. **RESEARCH** Women's history, early American history. **SELECTED PUBLICATIONS** Auth, bibliographic essays on slavery, the history of divorce, and the Seneca Falls Convention in The Reader's Guide to Women's Studies, Eleanor B. Amico, ed, Chicago: Fitzroy Dearborn, pubs 998); auth, "Jamestown" and "The Declaration of Independence" in The Encyclopedia of North American History, Tarrytown, New York: Marshall Cavendish Corp (99); auth, "Eleanor Roosevelt National Historic Site," Historical Places in the United States, Salem Press (2000). **CONTACT ADDRESS** Dept Social & Behav Sci, Sacramento City Col, 3835 Freeport Blvd, Sacramento, CA 95822-1318. **EMAIL** bonjimford@earthlink.net

FORD, FRANKLIN LEWIS
PERSONAL Born 12/26/1920, Waukegan, IL, m, 1944, 2 children **DISCIPLINE** HISTORY **EDUCATION** Univ Minn, AB, 42; Harvard Univ, AM, 48, PhD, 50; Suffolk Univ, LHD, 72. **CAREER** Mem fac, Bennington Col, 49-52; from asst prof to prof, 53-68, dean fac arts and sci, 62-70, McLean Prof Ancient and Mod Hist, Harvard Univ, 68-, Fulbright fel, France, 52-53; Guggenheim fel, Ger, 55-56; fel, Ctr Advan Studies Behav Sci, 61-62; trustee, Bennington Col, 62-72; fel, Inst Advan Studies, 74. **MEMBERSHIPS** Am Philos Soc. **RESEARCH** Modern Germany; early modern Europe; history of political assassination. **SELECTED PUBLICATIONS** Auth, Political Murder: Form Tyrannicide to Terrorism, Harvard Univ Pr, 85; auth, Communities and Conflict in Modern Colmar 1575-1730, Central Europ Hist, Vol 29, 96. **CONTACT ADDRESS** Harvard Univ, Cambridge, MA 02138.

FORD, PETER ANTHONY
PERSONAL Born 07/11/1934, Providence, RI, m, 1991, 3 children **DISCIPLINE** MEDIEVAL HISTORY **EDUCATION** Providence Col, BA, 56; Univ Notre Dame, MA, 58, MMedieval Stud, 59, DMedieval Stud, 64. **CAREER** From instr to asst prof hist, Tex A&M Univ, 60-65; assoc prof, 65-72, chmn dept, 71-73, actg dean humanities, 78-79, prof history, Merrimack Col 72-, Fulbright scholar, Paris, 59-60. **HONORS AND AWARDS** Tex A&M Univ Arts Sci Coun Awd Outstanding Tchr, 63; Edward G Roddy Awd Outstanding Teaching, Merrimack Col, 86. **RESEARCH** History of medieval universities; medieval intellectual history; American industrial history. **SELECTED PUBLICATIONS** Auth, The Medieval Account Books of the Parisian College of Dainville, Manuscripta, 11/65; John de Martigny, Principal and Benefactor of the College of Burgundy, In: Studium Generale: Studies Offered to A L Gabriel, Medieval Inst, Univ Notre Dame, 67; An American in Paris: Charles S Storrow and the 1830 Revolution, Proc Mass Hist Soc, 92; Charles S Storrow, Civil Engineer: A Case Study of European Training and Technological Transfer in the Antebellum Period, Technol and Cult, 93. **CONTACT ADDRESS** Dept of History, Merrimack Col, 315 Turnpike St, North Andover, MA 01845-5800.

FORDE, GERHARD OLAF
PERSONAL Born 09/10/1927, Starbuck, MN, 3 children **DISCIPLINE** CHURCH HISTORY, SYSTEMATIC THEOLOGY **EDUCATION** Luther Col, BA, 50; Luther Theol Sem, BTh, 55; Harvard Divinity Sch, ThD, 67; Oxford Univ, MA, 68. **CAREER** Instr relig, St Olaf Col, 55-56; lectr church hist, Luther Theol Sem, 59-61; asst prof relig, Luther Col, 61-63; assoc prof church hist, 64-71, Prof Syst Theol, Luther Theol Sem, 74-, Lutheran World Fed lectr, Mansfield Col, Oxford Univ, 68-70; Frederick A Schiotz fel, 72-73. **MEMBERSHIPS** Am Acad Relig. **RESEARCH** Theology of Martin Luther; 19th century theology. **SELECTED PUBLICATIONS** Auth, The Law-Gospel Debate, 69, Where God Meets Man, 72 & coauth, Free

To Be, 75, Augsburg; Justification By Faith: A Matter of Death & Life, 82; Theology is for Proclamation, 90; On Being a Theologian of the Cross, 97. **CONTACT ADDRESS** Luther Sem, 2481 Como Ave, Saint Paul, MN 55108-1445. **EMAIL** gforde@luthersem.edu

FORDERHASE, RUDOLPH EUGENE
PERSONAL Born 01/13/1934, Boonville, MO, m, 1963, 3 children **DISCIPLINE** MIDDLE PERIOD AMERICAN HISTORY **EDUCATION** Univ Mo, AB, 55, MA, 59, PhD, 68. **CAREER** Instr hist, Trenton Jr Col, 59-61 & Univ Mo, St Louis, 64-66; from asst prof to assoc prof, 66-73, prof hist, Eastern Ky Univ, 73-. **MEMBERSHIPS** Orgn Am Historians; Am Studies Asn; Southern Hist Asn. **RESEARCH** Jacksonian democracy; Civil War and Reconstruction. **CONTACT ADDRESS** Dept of History, Eastern Kentucky Univ, 521 Lancaster Ave, Richmond, KY 40475-3102.

FORDHAM, MONROE
PERSONAL Born 10/11/1939, Parrott, GA, m, 1961, 3 children **DISCIPLINE** HISTORY **EDUCATION** Emporia Kans State Univ, BS, 62, MA, 66; State Univ NYork, Buffalo, PhD (hist), 73. **CAREER** Soc studies teacher hist and current issues, Wichita Kans Pub Schs, 62-69; coord Afro-Am studies, Wichita State Univ, 69-70; asst prof, 70-78, Assoc Prof Hist, State Univ NY Col, Buffalo, 78-, State Univ NY res fel, 75; ed, Afro-Am in NY Life and Hist: Interdisciplinary J, 76-. **MEMBERSHIPS** Asn Study Afro-Am Life and Hist; African Heritage Studies Asn. **RESEARCH** Afro-American history; Afro-Americans in New York State. **SELECTED PUBLICATIONS** Auth, Lincoln's proposal to colonize Blacks, Afri-Am Studies, 4/71; Black Buffalonians in Antebellum reform movement, Courier Express Mag, 10/75; Major Themes in Northern Black Religious Thought (1800-1860), Exposition, 75; Some influences of the Santo Domingo Revolution on 19th century Black thought in US, J Black Studies, 12/75; The Black cooperative economic society of Buffalo NY, 1928-1961, Niagara Frontier, Summer 76. **CONTACT ADDRESS** Dept of Hist, SUNY, Buffalo, 1300 Elmwood Ave, Buffalo, NY 14222-1095.

FORGIE, GEORGE BARNARD
PERSONAL Born 05/31/1941, Philadelphia, PA **DISCIPLINE** AMERICAN HISTORY **EDUCATION** Amherst Col, BA, 63; Stanford Univ, LLB & MA, 67, PhD(Hist), 72. **CAREER** Lectr Am Hist, Princeton Univ, 69-72, asst prof, 72-74; asst prof, 74-80, assoc prof Am Hist, Univ Tex, Austin, 80-. **HONORS AND AWARDS** Allan Nevins Prize, Soc Am Historians, 73. **RESEARCH** American history, 1820-1880. **SELECTED PUBLICATIONS** Auth, Patricide in the House Divided: A Psychological Interpretation of Lincoln and His Age, Norton, 79. **CONTACT ADDRESS** Dept of History, Univ of Texas, Austin, Austin, TX 78712-1163. **EMAIL** forgie@mail.utexas.edu

FORMAN, MARY
PERSONAL Born 09/07/1947, Boise, ID **DISCIPLINE** MEDIEVAL STUDIES **EDUCATION** Idaho St Univ, BS, 70; St. John's Univ, Minn, MA, 82, MA, 88; Univ Toronto, Ctr for Medieval Stud, PhD, 95. **CAREER** Adj fac, Grad Sch of Theol, 90, Saint John's Univ; scholar in res, 96-, Benedictine Spirituality Ctr, Sacred Heart Monastery; adj fac, 97-, theol dept, Univ of Mary. **MEMBERSHIPS** Am Benedictine Acad; Fed of St Gertrude; St Benedict Ctr, Madison, Wis; AAR; ABA; NAPS; Am Pharmaceutical Asn. **RESEARCH** Early monasticism; medieval monastic women; hist of healing and med; early church hist; hist of Christian spirituality; Christian mysticism. **SELECTED PUBLICATIONS** Auth, Scripture and the Rule of Benedict as Sources of Benedictine Spirituality, Am Benedictine Rev, 39, 88; auth, Three Songs About St. Scholastica by Aldhelm and Paul the Deacon, transl, Vox Benedictina, 7, 90; auth, Syncletica: A Spirituality of Experience, Vox Benedictina, 10, 93; auth, Sapere--Tasting the Wisdom of the Monastic Tradition: The Biblical and Patristic Roots of Discerning, Benedictines, 49:1, 96; Ed & Transl, co-auth, Latin Cenobitic Rules of the West: 400-700, Am Benedictine Rev, 48:1, 97; auth, Gertrud of Helfta's Herald of Divine Love: Revelations Through Lectio Divina, Magistra 3.2, 97; auth, Desert Ammas: Midwives of Wisdom, Vetus Doctrina: Stud in Early Christianity in Honor of Fredric W. Schlatter, SJ, Peter Lang Pub, forthcoming; auth, Purity of Heart in the Life and Words of Amma Syncletica, Purity of Heart in Early Ascetical Literature: Essays in Honor of Juana Raasch OSB, Lit Press, 98. **CONTACT ADDRESS** School of Theology Seminary, Saint John's Univ, PO Box 7288, Collegeville, MN 56321-7288. **EMAIL** mforman@csbsju.edu

FORMAN, P.
PERSONAL Born 03/22/1937, Philadelphia, PA, d **DISCIPLINE** HISTORY OF SCIENCE **EDUCATION** Reed Col, BA 55-59; Northwestern Univ, grad stud, 59-60; Univ Caifl Berkeley, MA 62, PhD 67. **CAREER** Univ Rochester, asst prof, 67-72; Univ Calif Berk, vis fel, 72-73; Smithsonian Inst NMAH, mod phys curator, 72-; Princeton Univ, vis prof, 87; NY Univ, vis schl, 88-90; Hist Stud Physical Bio Sci, assoc editor, 80-. **HONORS AND AWARDS** APS Fel; AAAS Fel. **MEMBERSHIPS** AHA; HSS; SHT; SSSS; AAAS; APS. **RESEARCH** History of Physics and its social relations in the 20th century; historiography of science. **SELECTED PUBLICATIONS** Auth, Molecular Beam Measurements of nuclear moments before magnetic resonance: II Rabi and deflecting magnets to 1938, Annals of Science, 98; Recent Science: Late modern and Post modern, in: Thomas Soderqvist, ed, The historiography of contemporary science and technology, London and Chur, Harwood Acad Pub, 97; Into quantum electronics: the maser as gadget of Cold War America, P. Forman, JM Sanchez-Ron, eds, National Military establishments and the advancement of science and technology: studies in 20th century history, Dordrecht, Kluwer Acad Pub, 96; Swords into Ploughshares: breaking new ground with radar hardware and technique in physical research after World War II, Rev of Modern Physics, 95. **CONTACT ADDRESS** MRC-631, Smithsonian Inst, Washington, DC 20560. **EMAIL** formanp@nmah.si.edu

FORMISANO, RONALD P.
DISCIPLINE HISTORY **EDUCATION** Brown Univ, BA, 60; Univ Wis, MA, 62; Wayne State Univ, PhD, 66. **CAREER** Assoc prof, hist, Clark; current, PROF, HIST, UNIV FLA. **HONORS AND AWARDS** Fulbright, Pol Sci, Univ Bologna, 94. **MEMBERSHIPS** Am Antiquarian Soc **RESEARCH** US politics; political culture; social movements. **SELECTED PUBLICATIONS** Auth, The Transformation of Political Culture: Massachusetts Parties, 1790s-1840s, Oxford Univ Press, 83; co-ed, Boston 1700-1980: The Evolution of Urban Politics, Greenwood Press, 84; auth, The Birth of Mass Political Parties, Michigan, 1827-1861, Princeton Univ Press; auth, Toward a Reorientation of 'Jacksonian Politics,': A Review of the Literature, 1959-1974, Jour Am Hist 63, 76; auth, Boston Against Busing: Race, Class, and Ethnicity in the 1960s and 1970s, Univ NC PRess, 91; auth, The Great Lobster War, Univ Mass Press, 97. **CONTACT ADDRESS** Dept of Hist, Univ of Florida, Gainesville, FL 32601.

FORMWALT, LEE W.
PERSONAL Born 12/19/1949, Springfield, MA, m, 1972, 3 children **DISCIPLINE** HISTORY **EDUCATION** Catholic Univ Am, BA, 71; Univ Mass, MA, 72; Catholic Univ Am, PhD, 77. **CAREER** Albany State Col, asst prof hist, 77-82, assoc prof 82-88, prof hist 88-, dean grad school, 97-. **HONORS AND AWARDS** NEH; Res of the year; Hist teacher of the year. **MEMBERSHIPS** AHA; SHA; Org Am Histns; Georgia Asn Histns. **RESEARCH** Southern hist; Georgia Hist; African Am Hist. **SELECTED PUBLICATIONS** African American Persistence and Mobility in Postemancipation Southwest Georgia, Georgia Hist Quartly, forthcoming 98; Documenting the Origins of African American Politics in Southwest Georgia, J SW GA Hist, 93; several publications. **CONTACT ADDRESS** The Graduate School, Albany State Univ, 504 Col Dr, Albany, GA 31705. **EMAIL** lformwal@asurams.edu

FORREST, LARRY W.
PERSONAL Born 05/10/1957, Washington, DC, s **DISCIPLINE** ART HISTORY **EDUCATION** Univ of Louisville, BA, 80, MA, 83; Ind Univ, PhD, 91. **CAREER** Prof of Art Hist, Savannah Col of Art and Design, 90-. **HONORS AND AWARDS** Gennadeion Fel, Am School of Classical Studies of Athens, 86-87. **MEMBERSHIPS** CAA; AIA; Dunbarton Oaks. **RESEARCH** Byzantine architecture; Greek archaeology. **SELECTED PUBLICATIONS** Contrib, to Student and Instructor's Resource Manuel to Marilyn Stokstad's "Art Hist," 01. **CONTACT ADDRESS** Savannah Col of Art and Design, 212 W Taylor St, PO Box 3146, Savannah, GA 31402-3146. **EMAIL** lforrest@scad.edu

FORSE, JAMES HARRY
PERSONAL Born 01/26/1940, Binghamton, NY, m, 1961, 3 children **DISCIPLINE** MEDIEVAL HISTORY **EDUCATION** State Univ NYork, Albany, BA, 62; Univ Ill, MA, 63, PhD (hist), 67. **CAREER** Asst prof, 66-76, Assoc Prof Hist, Bowling Green State Univ, 76-. **MEMBERSHIPS** Cath Hist Asn; Mediaeval Acad Am. **SELECTED PUBLICATIONS** Auth, 25 articles, In: Westminster Dictionary of Church History, Westminster, 71; 6 articles, In: Great Events in History, Salem, 73. **CONTACT ADDRESS** Dept of Hist, Bowling Green State Univ, 1001 E Wooster St, Bowling Green, OH 43403-0001.

FORSLUND, CATHERINE
PERSONAL Born 10/17/1955, Evanston, IL, m, 1984 **DISCIPLINE** HISTORY **EDUCATION** WA Univ in St. Louis, MA, 93, PhD, 97; Univ of IL, BA, 77 **CAREER** Asst Prof, Rockford Col, 00-; Asst Prof, 97-00, Col Misericordia; Adj Faculty, 93-96; Wash Univ in St. Louis. **HONORS AND AWARDS** Mellon Travel/Diss Fel, 94-95; Moody Res Grant, 94; LBJ and Ford Presidential Libs Res Grants, 94-95. **MEMBERSHIPS** Am Hist Asn; Orgn of Am Hist; So Hist Am for Rel. **RESEARCH** Am diplom and cultural hist **SELECTED PUBLICATIONS** Auth, Anna Chennault: Woman of Two Worlds, Biographies in American Foreign Policy Series, Scholarly Resources, Inc (forthcoming, 00). **CONTACT ADDRESS** Dept of History, Rockford Col, 5050 East State St., Rockford, IL 61108-2393.

FORSTER, MARC R.
PERSONAL Born 10/18/1959, Lincoln, NE, m, 2 children **DISCIPLINE** HISTORY **EDUCATION** Swarthmore Col, BA; Harvard Univ, MA, PhD. **CAREER** Assoc prof; Conn Col, 90-; past vis prof, Ecole des Hautes Etudes en Sci Sociales, Paris; taught, For Lang Across Curric. **HONORS AND AWARDS** Conn Col Meredith prize, 93; Alexander von Humboldt Stiftung grant; Fulbright-Hays grant; Nat Endowment for the Humanities fel, 94; bk prize, Cent Europ Conf Gp of the AHA, 94; Guggenheim Fel, 00. **RESEARCH** Early modern European history; German history; religion and society in early modern Germany. **SELECTED PUBLICATIONS** Auth, The Counter Reformation in the Villages. **CONTACT ADDRESS** Dept of History, Connecticut Col, 270 Mohegan Ave, Box 5497, New London, CT 06320. **EMAIL** mrfor@conncoll.edu

FORSTER, ROBERT
PERSONAL Born 06/07/1926, New York, NY, m, 1955, 2 children **DISCIPLINE** HISTORY **EDUCATION** Swarthmore Col, BA, 49; Harvard Univ, MA, 51; Johns Hopkins Univ, PhD (hist), 56. **CAREER** From asst prof to assoc prof hist, Univ Nebr, 58-62; assoc prof mod Europ hist, Dartmouth Col, 62-65; assoc prof, 65-66, Prof Mod Europ Hist, Johns Hopkins Univ, 66-96, Gustav Bissing res fel, France, 57-58; Soc Sci Res Coun res grant, France, 62 and 64; John Simon Guggenheim res fel, France, 69-70; fel, Inst Advan Study, Princeton, 75-76; US deleg, Int Cong Hist Sci, 75-80; fel, Ctr Advan Study Behav Sci, Stanford, 79-80. **HONORS AND AWARDS** Citoyen d'Honneur, Commune of Vieillevigne, France, 78; Doctorat Honoris Causa, Univ of Toulouse, France, 1985; Palmes Academiques, Ambassade de France, 1992. **MEMBERSHIPS** AHA; Fr Hist Soc; Fr Col Hist. **RESEARCH** European social history; analyses of social groups in France and in the 18th and 19th century, revolutions in 18th and 19th century in France and the French Caribbean; slave societies in French Caribbean. **SELECTED PUBLICATIONS** Auth, The Nobility of Toulouse in the 18th Century, 1960; The House of Saulx-Tavanes: Versailles and Burgundy 1700-1830, 1971; Merchants, Landlords, Magistrates: The Depont Family in 18th-Century France, 1980; ed., with Elborg Foster, European Society in the 18th Century, 1969; ed., with Jack P. Greene, Preconditions of the Revolution in Early Modern Europe, 1970; ed., with Elborg Foster, European Diet from Pre-Industrial to Modern Times, 1975; ed., with Edwart Carter and Joseph Moody, Enterprise and Entrepreneurs in 19th- and 20th-Century France, 1976; ed., with Elborg Foster, Orest Ranum, and Patricia M. Ranum, Selections from the Annales, 7 Vol, 1975-1981; ed., with Elborg Foster, Sugar and Slaves, Family and Race: Letters and Diary of Pierre Dessalles, 1806-1856, 1996. **CONTACT ADDRESS** Dept of Hist, Johns Hopkins Univ, Baltimore, Baltimore, MD 21218.

FORSTER-HAHN, FRANCOISE
DISCIPLINE NINETEENTH AND TWENTIETH-CENTURY ART HISTORY **EDUCATION** Univ Bonn, PhD. **HONORS AND AWARDS** Fel, Alexander von Humboldt Found. **SELECTED PUBLICATIONS** Ed, Imagining Modern German Culture 1889-1910, Nat Gallery of Art, Wash DC, 96. **CONTACT ADDRESS** Dept of Art Hist, Univ of California, Riverside, 1156 Hinderaker Hall, Riverside, CA 92521-0209.

FORSYTH, PHYLLIS
PERSONAL Born Boston, MA, m, 1969 **DISCIPLINE** CLASSICAL STUDIES, HISTORY, FINE ART **EDUCATION** Mount Holyoke Col, BA, 66; Univ Toronto, MA, 67, PhD, 72. **CAREER** Tchr Fel, Univ Toronto, 67-69; prof, Univ Waterloo, 69-, founding ch, dept class studs, 79-88, acting ch 94-. **HONORS AND AWARDS** Distinguished Tchr Awd. **MEMBERSHIPS** Ont Class Asn; Can Fedn Hum; Archeol Inst Am; Can Mediter Inst. **RESEARCH** The Aegean Bronze Age; Thera in the Bronze Age; Minoan Civilization; Cycladic Civilization; Volcanic Eruptions in Antiquity; Natural Caatastrophes in the Ancient World; The Myth of Atlantis; Catullus. **SELECTED PUBLICATIONS** Auth, Atlantis: The Making of Myth, 80; ed, Labyrinth: A Classical Magazine for Secondary Schs, 73-84, 88-94; auth, Thera in the Bronze Age, Peter Lang Publ, 97. **CONTACT ADDRESS** Dept of Classical Studies, Univ of Waterloo, 200 University Ave W, Waterloo, ON, Canada N2L 3G1. **EMAIL** forsyth@watarts.uwaterloo.ca

FORTIN, MICHEL
PERSONAL Born 03/23/1950, Baie-Comeau, PQ, Canada, 3 children **DISCIPLINE** ARCHAEOLOGY **EDUCATION** Univ of London (England), PhD, 81. **CAREER** Prof adjoint, 81-86; Prof Agrege, 86-91; Prof litulaire, 91-, Univ Laval. **MEMBERSHIPS** Amer Inst of Archaelogy; Amer Schools of Oriental Research **RESEARCH** Near Eastern Archaeology **SELECTED PUBLICATIONS** Auth, Geomorphology Tell'Atij, Northern Syria', Geoarchaelogy, 94; Canadian Excavations at Tell Gudeda (Syria) 92-93, Bulletin of the Canadian Society for Mesopotamian Studies, 94; Canadian Excavations at Tell Atij (Syria) 92-93, Bulletin for the Canadian Society for Meopotamian Studies, 94; On the Fringe of Urbanization in Northern Mesopotamia (3000-2500 B.C.), Debating Complexity, Proceedings of the 26th Annual Chacmool Conference, 96; New Horizons in Ancient Syria, A view from Atij, New Eastern Archaelogy, 98. **CONTACT ADDRESS** Dept of History, Univ of Laval, Ste. Foy, QC, Canada G1K 7P4. **EMAIL** michel.fortin@mat.ulaval.ca

FOSS, BRIAN
DISCIPLINE CANADIAN ART HISTORY **EDUCATION** Concordia Univ, MA; Univ London, PhD. **CAREER** Dept Art Hist, Concordia Univ **HONORS AND AWARDS** Curator, co-curator, The imagery of urban site, 98; Young Montreal artists, 93; Military views and maps of Lower Canada, 92; The socio-political implications of the work of portraitist Robert Harris (1849-1919), 92; The visual representation of rural Quebec in the 19th and 20th centuries, 91. **RESEARCH** 19th and 20th-century Canadian art, 20th-century British art and patronage. **SELECTED PUBLICATIONS** Pub(s), articles and essays, especially on the intersections between war art, individual identity and national identity in Can and in Britain. **CONTACT ADDRESS** Dept Art Hist, Concordia Univ, Montreal, 1455 de Maisonneuve W, Montreal, QC, Canada H3G 1M8. **EMAIL** bffoss@alcor.concordia.ca

FOSS, CLIVE
PERSONAL Born 08/30/1939, London, England **DISCIPLINE** BYZANTINE HISTORY, ARCHEOLOGY; NUMISMATICS; HISTORY OF DICTATORSHIP **EDUCATION** Harvard Univ, AB, 61, AM, 65, PhD (hist and class archaeol), 73. **CAREER** Lectr, 67-78, Prof Ancient Hist and Classics, Univ Mass, Boston, 79-, Mem, Am Sch Class Studies, Athens, 61-62; asst prof hist, Boston Col, 68-69; mem, Sardis Excavation, 69-75 and 79-82; vis fel, Dumbarton Oaks Res Ctr, 73-74; assoc, Ephesus Excavations, 73-74; maitre de conf, Univ Lyon II, 77-79; vis prof, Univ SAfrica, 81; Vis fel, All Souls College, Oxford 83-84; Vis Prof University of California, Berkeley, 85; Vis Prof, Harvard University, 90-91; Fellow, Institute for Advanced Studies, Hebrew University, Jerusalem 93; Vis fel, Trinity College, Oxford 97; Fellow, Dumbarton Oaks, 99-00. **HONORS AND AWARDS** NEH Fellowship 75-76; Guggenheim Fellowhship, 83-84. **MEMBERSHIPS** Soc Antiquaries London; Am Philogical Assn; British Inst Archaeol Ankara; Royal Numis Soc; Am Numis Soc. **RESEARCH** Late antique and Byzantine history and archaeology; historical geography; ancient numismatics; dictators and dictatorship. **SELECTED PUBLICATIONS** Auth, "Byzantine and Turkish Sardis" 76; Rome and Byzantium, with Paul Magdalino77; auth, "Ephesus after Antiquity," 79; auth, "Survey of Medieval Castles of Anatolia I:" Kutahya, 85; II: "Nicomedia," 96; auth, "Byzantine Fortifications, an Introduction," with David Winfield 86; auth, "Roman Historical Coins," 90; auth, "History and Archaeology of Byzantine Asia Minor," 90; auth, "Cities, Villages and Fortresses of Byzantine Asia Minor," 96; auth, "Nicaea, A Byzantine Capital and its Praises," 96; auth, "Juan and Evan Peron," 99; auth, "Fidel Castro," 00; ed, "Studies in Honor of Wendell Clausen, 98. **CONTACT ADDRESS** Dept Hist, Univ of Massachusetts, Boston, 100 Morrissey Blvd, Boston, MA 02125-3300.

FOSS, D. PEDAR W.
DISCIPLINE CLASSICAL ART AND ARCHAEOLOGY **EDUCATION** Gustavus Adolphus Col, BA, 88; Univ Mich, MA, 91, PhD, 94. **CAREER** Tutor, Gustavus Adolphus Col, 87-88; Tchg Asst, Univ Mich, 92; Vis Asst Prof, Univ Mich, 95; Lecturer, Univ Mich, 95-96; Vis Asst Prof, Univ Cincinnati, 96-97; Adj Asst Prof, Uniiv Cincinnati, 97- . **HONORS AND AWARDS** Rackham One-Term Dissertation Grant; Rackham Dissertation/Thesis Grant; Mellon Dissertation Grant; Jacob K. Javits Fel; Alworth & Tozer Foundation Sch. **MEMBERSHIPS** Electronic Publ Comt; Archaeol Inst Am; Eta Sigma Phi. **SELECTED PUBLICATIONS** Coauth, A newly-discovered cryptoporticus and bath at Carthage, J of Roman Archaelogy, 93; coauth, The Rieti Surbey 1988-1001, Part II: Land-use patterns and gazetteer, Papers of the British School at Rome, 95; auth, Watchful Lares: Roman household organization and the rituals of cooking and dining, Domestic Space in the Ancient Mediterranean, 97; auth, Digitizing the ancient world: demograhics, resources, and future opportunities, Archaeological News, 97; auth, Cooking and cuisine, DIning rooms, The social ritual of dining, Oplontis, Boscoreale, and Boscotrecase, all in The Cambridge Guide to Classical Civilization, 98. **CONTACT ADDRESS** Dept of Classics, Univ of Cincinnati, PO Box 0226, Cincinnati, OH 45210-0226. **EMAIL** pfoss@depauw.edu

FOSTER, ANNE L.
DISCIPLINE HISTORY **EDUCATION** Am Univ, BA, 87; Cornell Univ, MA, 91; Cornell Univ, PhD, 95. **CAREER** Asst prof, 97-, St Anselm Col. **RESEARCH** Multiple layers of rel--strategic, economic, polit, and cult--between the US and Asia, particularly Southeast Asia; polit, economic, and cult rel(s) among Am(s), Europ(s), and Southeast Asians in 20th century colonial Southeast Asia; comp look at attempts by the Europ colonial governments and the US to control the use of opium in Southeast Asia from the middle of the th to the middle of the 20th century. **SELECTED PUBLICATIONS** Auth, Secret Police Cooperation and the Coming of the Cold War, Jour American-East Asian Relations, 95; French, Dutch, British and U.S. Reactions to the Nghe-Tinh Rebellions of 30-31 in Imperial Policy and Colonial Revolt, Nordic Inst Asian Studies, 95. **CONTACT ADDRESS** Saint Anselm Col, 100 Saint Anselm Dr, Manchester, NH 03102-1310. **EMAIL** afoster@anselm.edu

FOSTER, BENJAMIN READ
PERSONAL Born 09/15/1945, Bryn Mawr, PA, m, 1975, 2 children **DISCIPLINE** ASSYRIOLOGY **EDUCATION** Princeton Univ, BA, 68; Yale Univ, MA, MPhil, 74, PhD, 75. **CAREER** Instr Arabic, 73-75, asst prof Assyriol, 75-81, Assoc Prof Assyriol, Yale Univ, 81-86, prof, 86-; chmn dept Near East lang, 89-98. **HONORS AND AWARDS** Amer Res Inst in Turkey fel, 77, 79; Mellon Fel; NEH Translation Grant, 83-84. **MEMBERSHIPS** Am Orient Soc. **RESEARCH** Soc and economic hist of early Mesopotamia; Akkadian lit. **SELECTED PUBLICATIONS** Umma in the Sargonic Period, Memoirs of Conn Acad of Arts & Sci, No 20, 82; Administration and Use of Institutional Land in Sargonic Sumer, Copenhagen Studies in Assyriology, No 9, 82; coauth, Sargonic Tablets from Telloh in the Istanbul Archeological Museum, Babylonian Sect, Univ Mus, Philadelphia, 82; auth, Before the Muses An Anthology of Akkadian Literature, 93; auth, From Distant Days Myths Tales and Poetry of Ancient Mesopotamia, 95; auth, Un Arabo en el Neuvo Mundo 1668-1683, 89, (Argentina). **CONTACT ADDRESS** Sterling Mem Libr, Rm 318, Yale Univ, PO Box 208236, New Haven, CT 06520-8236. **EMAIL** benjamin.foster@yale.edu

FOSTER, DOUGLAS A.
PERSONAL Born 08/30/1952, Sheffield, AL, m, 1979, 2 children **DISCIPLINE** CHURCH HISTORY **EDUCATION** David Lipscomb Univ, BA, 74; Harding Grad Sch of Religion, 76; Scarritt Col, MA, 80; Vanderbilt Univ, PhD, 86. **CAREER** Assoc Min, Jackson Park Church of Christ, 74-83; Arch, Gospel Adv Co, 88-91; Retention, Inst, Asst Prof, David Lipscomb Univ, 85-91; Asst Prof, Assoc Prof, Abilene Christian Univ, 91-. **HONORS AND AWARDS** Outstanding Tchr Awd, College of Bibl Stud, ACU 94, 99; Outstanding Tchr Awd, DLU, 89; Mayhew Fel Vanderbilt Univ, 83-83. **MEMBERSHIPS** Amer Soc of Church History, Amer Acad of Religion, Conf on Faith and History, disciples of Christ Hist Soc, Rel Res Assn, Southern Baptist Hist Soc, Southwest Archivists, TN Archivists. **RESEARCH** Stone-Campbell History: American Church History; Ecumenism. **SELECTED PUBLICATIONS** Holding Back the Tide: T.B. Larimore and the Disciples of Christ and Churches of Christ, Discipliana, 93; Will the Cycle Be Unbroken: Churches of Christ Face the Twenty-First Century, ACU Press, 94; The Many Faces of Christian Unity: Disciples Ecumenism and Schism, 1875-1900, Nashville Disciples for Christ Hist Soc, 95; Millennial Harbinger, Pop Rel Mag of the USA, 95; Rethinking the History of Churches of Christ: Responses to Richard Hughes, Rest Quart, 96; Reflections on the Writing of Will the Cycle Be Unbroken: Churches of Christ Face the Twenty-First Century, Discipliana, 97. **CONTACT ADDRESS** Abilene Christian Univ, PO Box ACU 29429, Abilene, TX 79699-9429. **EMAIL** foster@bible.acu.edu

FOSTER, E. C.
PERSONAL Born 01/04/1939, Canton, MS, m **DISCIPLINE** HISTORY **EDUCATION** Jackson State Univ, BS 1964; Carnegie-Mellon Univ, MA 1967, DA 1970. **CAREER** Natchez Public School, teacher 1964-65; Brushton Inner City Project, community organizer 1965-66; Pittsburgh Public Schools, teacher 1967-68; Jackson MS City Council, pres 1985-94; Jackson State Univ, prof of history 1969-. **HONORS AND AWARDS** Jackson State Univ Alumni Service Awd 1985; Man of the Year Awd Omega Psi Phi 1985; NAEFO Presidential Citation Awd 1986; Dr Martin Luther King Service Awd JSU/SGA 1986. **MEMBERSHIPS** Pres Faculty Senate (JSU) 1974-79; bd mem Farish St YMCA 1976-79; assoc editor Journal of Negro History 1978-; pres Assn of Soc & Behav Scientists 1982; legislative comm chmn Local PTA 1984; city councilman Jackson MS 1985-; member, Chamber of Commerce, 1986-; member, Vicksburg/Jackson Trade Zone Commission, 1987-; MS Municipal Assn, bd of dirs, 1994-; Natl League of Cities Leadership Training Council, vice chair, 1994. **CONTACT ADDRESS** Jackson State Univ, Jackson, MS 39217.

FOSTER, KAREN POLINGER
PERSONAL Born 10/07/1950, New York, NY, m, 1975, 2 children **DISCIPLINE** ARCHAEOLOGY **EDUCATION** Mt Holyoke Col, AB, 71; Yale Univ, MA, MPhil, 74, PhD, 76. **CAREER** Vis Scholar, Yale, Wesleyan, Am Philos Soc fel, 77 & 81; Ludwig Vogelstein Found grant, 77; Am Coun Learned Soc fel, 78. **MEMBERSHIPS** Archaeol Inst Am; Am Res Ctr Egypt; Col Art Asn. **RESEARCH** Art and archaeology of the Bronze Age Aegean and ancient Near East. **SELECTED PUBLICATIONS** Auth, Aegean Faience of the Bronze Age, Yale Univ, 79; Minoan Ceramic Relief, Studies in Medit Archeol, 82; auth, The City of Rainbows: A Tale from Ancient Sumer, Univ Penn Museum, 99. **CONTACT ADDRESS** PO Box 208236, New Haven, CT 06520-8236. **EMAIL** karen.foster@yale.edu

FOSTER, MARK S.
PERSONAL Born 05/02/1939, Evanston, IL, m, 1998 **DISCIPLINE** AMERICAN HISTORY **EDUCATION** Brown Univ, AB, 61; Univ of Southern Calif, MA, 68, PhD, 71. **CAREER** Assist prof, Univ of Colo at Denver, 72-77; assoc prof, Univ of Colo at Denver, 77-81; prof, Univ of Colo at Denver, 81-00. **HONORS AND AWARDS** UCD Teaching Excellence Awd; UCD Faculty Fellowship. **MEMBERSHIPS** OAH, AHR. **RESEARCH** United States Urban History; American Biography. **SELECTED PUBLICATIONS** Auth, "From Streetcar to Superhighway: American City Planners and Urban Transportation, 1900-1940," (Philadelphia: Temple Univ Press, 81); auth, "Henry J. Kaiser: Builder in the Modern American West," (Auston,: Univ of Texas Press, 89); auth, "Henry Miller Porter: Rocky Mountain Empire Builder," (Niwot,: Univ of Press of Colo, 91); auth, "The Automobile and the Suburbanization of Los Angeles in the 1920s," in Howard P. Chudacoff, ed., Major Problems in American Urban History, (Toronto and Lexingeon, MA: D.C. Heath, 94): 318-325; auth, "Home Run in the Rockies: The History of Baseball in Colorado" (Denver: Hirschfeld Press, 97) with Irvin Moss; auth, "Little Lies: The Colorado 1976 Winter Olympics," (Colorado Heritage), Winter, 98: 22-23; auth, "In the Face of 'Jim Crow:' Prosperous Blacks and Vacations, Travel and Outdoor Leisure, 1890-1945," (Journal of Negro History 84:2) Spring, 99: 130-149; auth, "Castles in the Sand: The Life and Times of Carl G. Fisher, (Gainesville, Univ Press of Florida, 00). **CONTACT ADDRESS** Dept History, Univ of Colorado, Denver, PO Box 173364, Denver, CO 80217-3364. **EMAIL** msfoster@carbon.cudenver.edu

FOSTER, STEPHEN
PERSONAL Born 03/08/1942, New York, NY, m, 1971, 1 child **DISCIPLINE** EARLY AMERICAN HISTORY **EDUCATION** Univ Pa, BA, 61; Yale Univ, MA, 64, PhD (hist), 66. **CAREER** Asst prof to assoc prof, Northern Ill Univ, 66-93, pres res prof, 93-97, distinguished res prof, 97-; NEH, 68-69 & 79-80; Guggenheim Mem Found fel, 71-72; vis ed, William & Mary Quart, 77-78; Newberry Library - NEH Fel, 86-87. **HONORS AND AWARDS** Theron R Field Prize, Yale Univ, 66; Annual Awd Best Article, William & Mary Quart, 74. **MEMBERSHIPS** AHA; Conf Brit Studies. **RESEARCH** American colonial History; Jacobean-Caroline England. **SELECTED PUBLICATIONS** Auth, The Presbyterian Independents Exorcised: A Ghost Story for Historians, Past & Present, 69; Their Solitary Way, The Puritan Social Ethic in the First Century of Settlement in New England, Yale Univ, 71; coauth, The Puritans' Greatest Success: A Study of Social Cohesion in Massachusetts, J Am Hist, 73; coauth, Moving to the New World: The Pattern of Early Massachusetts Immigration, 73; Notes From the Caroline Under-Ground, Alexander Leighton, The Puritan Triumvirate and the Laudian Reaction to Nonconformity, Conf Brit Studies & Archon Bks, 78; auth, The Long Argument: English Puritanism and the Shaping of New England Culture, 1570-1700, Inst of Early am Hist and Cult, and Univ of N Ca Press, 91; The Historiography of British North America in the Seventeenth and Eighteenth Centuries, Oxford History of the British Empire, 5:4, 99. **CONTACT ADDRESS** Dept of Hist, No Illinois Univ, 1425 W Lincoln Hwy, De Kalb, IL 60115-2825. **EMAIL** sfoster@niu.edu

FOUCHE, RAYVON
DISCIPLINE HISTORY **EDUCATION** Univ Illinois, Urgana-Champaign, BA, 91; Cornell Univ, MA, 94, PhD, 97. **CAREER** Post-doctoral fel, African-Am Stud, Washington Univ, 96-98; asst prof hist and Af-Am Stud, Purdue Univ, 98- . **RESEARCH** African-American studies; science and technology studies; popular culture. **CONTACT ADDRESS** Dept of History, Purdue Univ, West Lafayette, 1358 University Hall, West Lafayette, IN 47904-1358. **EMAIL** fouche@purdue.edu

FOUQUET, PATRICIA ROOT
PERSONAL Born 06/16/1930, Brooklyn, NY, m, 1978, 2 children **DISCIPLINE** MODERN EUROPEAN HISTORY **EDUCATION** Barnard Col, BA, 53; Univ Calif, San Diego, PhD(hist), 72. **CAREER** Lectr hist, San Diego State Univ, 70; instr, Univ Calif, San Diego Extension, 72-73; lectr, Calif State Univ, Long Beach, 73-76; asst prof, Univ Nebr, Lincoln, 77-78; Asst Prof, 78-84, Assoc Prof Hist, Fayetteville State Univ, 84-98, retired, 98-; Assoc hist, Univ Calif, San Diego, 72-73; tour dir, Am Student Travel Asn, 76-78. **HONORS AND AWARDS** Fulbright Summer Seminar, 84, 86, 89, 94; John C. Moore Prize for Excellence in Teaching Humanities, 90; Col Arts & Sci Teacher of the Year, 92; Dept Geog, Hist, and Pol Sci Teacher of the Year, 97. **MEMBERSHIPS** AHA; Western Soc French Hist; West Coast Asn Women Historians (vpres, 73-75, pres, 75-76). **RESEARCH** The nature of prejudice in fascist movements; discrimination against women in the elite sciences. **SELECTED PUBLICATIONS** Coauth (with Joanna V Scott), The 1934 riots and the emergence of French fascism: The case of Jacques Doriot, 76 & auth, Fascism of the left or renegade Marxism?, The Case of Jacques Doriot, 78, Proc of the Western Soc for French Hist. **CONTACT ADDRESS** 1062, Bonsall, CA 92003. **EMAIL** prootfouq@aol.com

FOURNIER, ERIC J.
PERSONAL Born 10/17/1962, Biddeford, ME, m, 1991, 1 child **DISCIPLINE** GEOGRAPHY **EDUCATION** Syracuse Univ, BA, 86; Univ Ga, MA, 90; PhD, 95. **CAREER** Lab Instr, Univ of Ga, 87-90; Instr, Univ of Ga, 91-92; Adj Prof, Emmanuel Col, Frankling Springs, Ga, 92; Instr, Kennesaw State Col, 92-95; Asst Prof, Univ of Ga, 95-96; Asst Prof, Samford Univ, 97-; Acting Chair, Dept of Geog, Samford Univ, 98. **MEMBERSHIPS** Asn of Am Geogr, Nat Coun for Geog Educ. **RESEARCH** Urban revitalization, Waterfront revitalization, Geography education, Problem-based learning, Teaching

portfolios. **SELECTED PUBLICATIONS** Auth, Waterfront Revitalization: an Annotated Bibliography, Conc of Planning Librn Bibliog Ser, 84; coauth, "Cotton returns to the South: Evidence from Georgia," Southeastern Geogr 36-2 (96); coauth, "Finding the Southern Part of Cyberspace: Using the Internet to Teach the South," J of Geog 97-4/5 (98): 213-227; coauth, "Geography Teaching in Higher Education: Quality, Assessment and Accountability," J of Geog in Higher Educ (forthcoming). **CONTACT ADDRESS** Dept Geog, Samford Univ, 800 Lakeshore Dr, Birmingham, AL 35229-0002. **EMAIL** ejfourni@samford.edu

FOWLER, SHELLI
DISCIPLINE COMPARATIVE AMERICAN CULTURES. **EDUCATION** Univ Tex at Austin, PhD. **CAREER** Asst prof, Washington State Univ. **RESEARCH** African American literature, critical pedagogy; ethnic and cultural studies. **SELECTED PUBLICATIONS** Coauth, Site Visits: Itineraries for Writers, Houghton Mifflin. **CONTACT ADDRESS** Dept of English, Washington State Univ, 1 SE Stadium Way, PO Box 645020, Pullman, WA 99164-5020. **EMAIL** fowlers@wsu.edu

FOWLER, WILLIAM M.
PERSONAL Born 07/25/1944, Clearwater, FL, m, 1968, 2 children **DISCIPLINE** HISTORY **EDUCATION** Northeastern Univ, BA, 67; Univ Notre Dame, MA, 69; PhD, 71. **CAREER** From Asst Prof to Prof, Northeastern Univ, 71-. **MEMBERSHIPS** OAH, Marine Soc, Fellow Pilgrim Soc. **RESEARCH** Early New England, Naval maritime. **SELECTED PUBLICATIONS** Auth, Silas Talbot: Captain of Old Ironsides, Mystic Seaport, 98; auth, Samuel Adams: Radical Puritan, Longmans (New York, NY), 97; auth, "Marine Insurance in Boston," in Entrepreneurs: The Boston Bus Community 1750-1850 (Boston, MA: Massachusetts Hist Soc, 97), 150-179; coauth, America and The Sea: A Maritime History, Mystic Seaport, 98. **CONTACT ADDRESS** Dept Hist, Northeastern Univ, 360 Huntington Ave, Boston, MA 02115-5005. **EMAIL** wfowler@masshist.org

FOX, DOUGLAS A.
PERSONAL Born 03/20/1927, Mullumbimby, Australia, m, 1958, 2 children **DISCIPLINE** THEOLOGY, HISTORY OF RELIGIONS **EDUCATION** Univ Sydney, BA, 54; Univ Chicago, MA, 57; Pac Sch Relig, STM, 58, ThD, 63. **CAREER** From asst prof to assoc prof, 63-74, Prof Relig, Colo Col, 74-. **HONORS AND AWARDS** Carnegie found "Colorado prof of the year," 95. **MEMBERSHIPS** Am Acad Relig. **RESEARCH** Mahayana Buddhism; philosophy of religion; philosophical theology. **SELECTED PUBLICATIONS** Auth, Buddhism, Christianity, and the Future of Man, Westminster Press, 72; auth, The Heart of Buddhist Wisdom, Edwin Mellen Press, 85; auth, Meditation and Reality: A Critical View, John Knox Press, 86; auth, Dispelling Illusion: Gaudapada's Alatasanti, SUNY, 93; auth, Direct Awareness of the Self: A Translation of the Aparoksanubhuti by Sankara, Edwin Mellin, 95. **CONTACT ADDRESS** Dept of Relig, Colorado Col, Colorado Springs, CO 80903. **EMAIL** dfox@coloradocollege.edu

FOX, FRANK
PERSONAL Born 12/20/1923, Lodz, Poland, m, 1946, 2 children **DISCIPLINE** MODERN HISTORY **EDUCATION** Temple Univ, BS, 51; Univ Pa, MA, 52; Univ Del, PhD (hist), 66. **CAREER** Asst, Univ Del, 61-62; asst prof hist, Temple Univ, 63-67; assoc prof, 67-70, Prof Hist, West Chester Univ, 70-89. **HONORS AND AWARDS** Recipient of research grants from the Am Philosophical Society and the Eleutherian Mills (Dupont) Foundation. **MEMBERSHIPS** AHA; Am Asn Advan Slavic Studies; Soc Hist Studies, France. **SELECTED PUBLICATIONS** Auth, Am I a Murderer?: Testament of a Jewish Ghetto Policeman, edited and translated from Polish, Harper/Collins, 96; auth, "Poland and the American West," Washington State Univ Press in Western Anerykanski, 99; auth, God's, Eye: Aerial Photography and the Katyne Forest Massacre, West Chester Univ Press, 99. **CONTACT ADDRESS** 51 Merbrook Lane, Merion Station, PA 19066. **EMAIL** fischece@aol.com

FOX, FRANK WAYNE
PERSONAL Born 10/07/1940, Salt Lake City, UT, m, 1969, 2 children **DISCIPLINE** AMERICAN SOCIAL HISTORY **EDUCATION** Stanford Univ, PhD, 1973. **CAREER** Prof, Brigham Young Univ, 71-. **HONORS AND AWARDS** Disting. Tchg, 84, 85; Prof of the Year, 83, 97, 98; Alcuin Awd; Karl B. Maeser Awd. **MEMBERSHIPS** OAH; Am Studies Asn. **RESEARCH** Popular Culture; California; U.S. Constitution. **SELECTED PUBLICATIONS** Auth, Madison Avenue Goes To War: The Strange Wartime Career of American Advertising, 73; J. Reulark: The Public Years, 80; America: A Study in Heritage, 86; California and the Lost Continents: An Inquiry Into the California Garden, 99. **CONTACT ADDRESS** Dept of History, Brigham Young Univ, Provo, UT 84602. **EMAIL** frank_fox@byu.edu

FOX, MICHAEL
PERSONAL Born 12/12/1940, Detroit, MI, m, 1961, 2 children **DISCIPLINE** BIBLE STUDIES; ANCIENT NEAR EASTERN STUDIES **EDUCATION** Univ Mich, BA, 62; MA, 63; Hebrew Union Col, Rabbinical ordination, 68; Hebrew Univ Jerusalem, PhD, 72. **CAREER** Lectr, Haifa Univ, 71-74; lectr, Hebrew Univ Jerusalem, 75-77; asst prof to prof, Univ Wis-Madison, 77- . **HONORS AND AWARDS** Nat Endowment for the Humanities, Fel, 92-93; Honorary Doctorate of Hebrew Letters, Hebrew Union Col, 93; Rabbi Joseph L. Baron Faculty Achievement Award, 96; Jay C. and Ruth Halls-Bascom Prof in hebrew Studies, 99; Nat Center for the Humanities, Fel, 99; Nat Center for the Humanities, Fel, 99; Soc for Biblical Lit, Pres, 99-00; Nat Assoc of Prof of Hebrew, Vice-Pres, 99-; Kellett Mid-career Award, 00; Am Acad of Jewish Res, Fel, 00-. **MEMBERSHIPS** Soc for Bibl Lit; Nat Asoc of Profs of Hebrew. **RESEARCH** Biblical literature; ancient Egyptian literature. **SELECTED PUBLICATIONS** Auth, Ideas of Wisdom in Proverbs 1-9, JBL, 97; auth, Words for Folly, ZAH, 97; auth, What the Book of Proverbs is About, VTSup, 97; auth, Qohelet's Catalogue of Times, JNSL, 98; auth, Tearing Down and Building Up: A Rereading of Ecclesiastes, forthcoming. **CONTACT ADDRESS** Univ of Wisconsin, Madison, 1220 Linden Dr., Rm. 1346, Madison, WI 53706. **EMAIL** mfox@lss.wisc.edu

FOX, STEPHEN C.
PERSONAL Born 11/28/1938 **DISCIPLINE** MODERN HISTORY **EDUCATION** DePauw Univ, BA, 60; Univ Cincinnati, MA, 66, PhD, 73. **CAREER** Lectr hist, Univ Cincinnati, 68-69; asst prof, 69-73, assoc prof, 73-77, Prof Hist, Humboldt State Univ, 77-; Am-Italian Hist Asn, advisory board; Oral Hist Asn, editorial board; Una Storia Segreta: When Italian Americans were Enemy Aliens-Traveling Display; Bella Vista: An Unseen View of World War II (video) Internment of Italian seamen at Ft. Missoula, Mt; POW: Italian Prisoners in America (video in progress). **HONORS AND AWARDS** For General John DeWitt and the Proposed Internment of German and Italian Aliens during World War II, Louis Knott Koontz memorial award for most deserving article, 89, presented by the Board of Editors, Pacific Historical Rev; for The Unknown Internment, Gustavus Myers Center for the Study of Human Rights in the United States, Outstanding Book on the subject of human rights in the United States, 91; before Columbus Foundation, Am Book Award, 92. **MEMBERSHIPS** Oral Hist Asn. **RESEARCH** Jacksonian period; World War II. **SELECTED PUBLICATIONS** Auth, Politicians, Issues, and Voter Preference in Jacksonian Ohio: a Critique of an Interpretation, OH Hist, summer 77; The Bank Wars, the Idea of Party, and the Division of the Electorate in Jacksonian Ohio, OH Hist, summer 79; General John DeWitt and the Proposed Internment of German and Italian Aliens during World War II, Pacific Hist Rev 57, Nov 88; The Group Bases of Ohio Political Behavior, 1803-1848, NY: Garland Pub, Inc, 89; The Unknown Internment: An Oral History of the Relocation of Italian Americans during World War II, Boston: Twayne Pubs, 90; The Relocation of Italian Americans during World War II, in Struggle and Success: An Anthology of the Italian Immigrant Experience in California, ed by Paola A. Sensi-Isolani and Phyllis Cancilla Martinelli, NY: Center for Migration Studies, 92; The Deportation of Latin American Germans, 1941-1947: Fresh Legs for Mr. Monroe's Doctrine, Yearbook of German-American Studies 32, 97; Blunderbuss or Rifle? The Impact of World Wat II on Postwar Internal Security Policy (in preparation); Many are the Crimes: A Biography of German American Internment in World War II: History and Memory (completed manuscript); and numerous book reviews. **CONTACT ADDRESS** Dept of Hist, Humboldt State Univ, 1 Harpst St., Arcata, CA 95519-8299. **EMAIL** stfox@humboldt1.com

FOX-GENOVESE, ELIZABETH
DISCIPLINE HISTORY **EDUCATION** Bryn Mawr Col, AB, 63; Harvard Univ, MA, 66, PhD, 74. **CAREER** Eleonore Raoul Prof Hum. **RESEARCH** Comparative women's history; the antebellum South; cultural, literary, and intellectual history. **SELECTED PUBLICATIONS** Auth, The Origins of Physiocracy; Feminism without Illusions: A Critique of Individualism; Within the Plantation Household; Black and White Women of Old South; The Autobiography of P.S. Du Pont de Nemours; coauth, Fruits of Merchant Capital; "Feminism is Not the Story of My Life:" How Today's Feminist Elite Has Lost Touch with the Real Concerns of Women. **CONTACT ADDRESS** Dept History, Emory Univ, 221 Bowden Hall, 561 Kilgo Cir, Atlanta, GA 30322-1950. **EMAIL** efoxgen@emory.edu

FRAGER, RUTH
DISCIPLINE HISTORY **EDUCATION** Rochester Univ, BA; York Univ, MA, PhD. **MEMBERSHIPS** Ontario Hist Soc. **RESEARCH** Canadian women's history and women's studies; Canadian hist of immigrants. **SELECTED PUBLICATIONS** Auth, Sweatshop Strife: Class, Ethnicity and Gender in the Jewish Labour Movement of Toronto, 1900-1939. **CONTACT ADDRESS** History Dept, McMaster Univ, 1280 Main St W, Hamilton, ON, Canada L8S 4L9. **EMAIL** frager@mcmaster.ca

FRAKES, GEORGE EDWARD
PERSONAL Born 05/12/1932, Los Angeles, CA, m, 1954, 3 children **DISCIPLINE** AMERICAN HISTORY **EDUCATION** Stanford Univ, AB, 54, MA, 58; Univ Calif, Santa Barbara, PhD (Am hist), 66. **CAREER** Teacher, High Sch, Calif, 58-62; from instr to assoc prof, 62-71, chmn soc sci div, 73-77, Prof Hist, Santa Barbrar City Col, 71-, Lectr, Air Force Reserve Off Training Corps, Univ Southern Calif, 58-59; lectr, exten, Univ Calif, 65-66; supvr studies teachers, Univ Calif, Santa Barbara, 65-66. **MEMBERSHIPS** AHA. **RESEARCH** American colonial history; environmental history; California history. **SELECTED PUBLICATIONS** Auth, Laboratory for Liberty, Univ Ky, 70; coed, Pollution Papers, Appleton, 71; Minorities in California, Random, 71; co-auth, Columbus to Aquarius: An Interpretative History, Dryden/Holt, Rinehart & Winston, 76. **CONTACT ADDRESS** Dept of Hist, Santa Barbara City Col, Santa Barbara, CA 93109.

FRAKES, ROBERT
PERSONAL Born 12/30/1962, Santa Barbara, CA, m, 1991, 2 children **DISCIPLINE** GREEK AND ROMAN HISTORY **EDUCATION** Stanford Univ, BA, 84; MA, 85; Univ Calif Santa Barbara, MA, 87; PhD, 91. **CAREER** Asst prof to assoc prof, Clarion Univ, 91-. **HONORS AND AWARDS** Humboldt Fel, Univ of Munich, 95-96, 98, 00. **MEMBERSHIPS** AHA, Am Philog Assoc. **RESEARCH** Later Roman empire, Roman law, Church-State Relations, historiography. **SELECTED PUBLICATIONS** Auth, "Ammianus Marcellinus and his intended audience," Studies in Latin Lit and Roman Hist 10, (00): 392-442; coed, The Dance of Hippocleides: A Festschrift for Frank J. Frost, Ancient World 31 (00); auth, Contra Potentium Iniurias: The Defensor Civitatis and Late Roman Justice, forthcoming. **CONTACT ADDRESS** Clarion Univ of Pennsylvania, Clarion, PA 16214. **EMAIL** rfrakes@mail.clarion.edu

FRALEY, DAVID
PERSONAL Born 04/07/1941, Badin, NC, m, 1967, 1 child **DISCIPLINE** GERMAN HISTORY **EDUCATION** UNC, Chapel Hill, AB, 63; Duke Univ, MA, 65; PhD, 71. **CAREER** Asst Prof, Birmingham Southern Col, 67-72; Assoc Prof, 72-80; Prof of History, 80-; Chair, 72-76, 86-91. **HONORS AND AWARDS** Woodrow Wilson Fellow, 63-64; Exchange Fellow, Free Univ of Berlin, 65-66; Fulbright Summer Fellow, 88. **MEMBERSHIPS** Amer Historical Assoc; German Studies Assoc; Phi Beta Kappa. **RESEARCH** German History, 1890-1914. **SELECTED PUBLICATIONS** Auth, "Government by Procrastination: Chancellon Hoheaulohe and Kaisen Wilhelm II," Central European History, VII, 159-183; auth, "Reform or Reaction: The Dilemma of Prince Hoheulohe," European Studies Review IV, 317-343. **CONTACT ADDRESS** Dept Humanities, Birmingham-So Col, 900 Arkadelphia Rd, Birmingham, AL 35254-0001. **EMAIL** dfraley@bsc.edu

FRANCE, JEAN R.
PERSONAL Born 08/21/1923, Cleveland, OH, w, 1948, 3 children **DISCIPLINE** ART HISTORY **EDUCATION** Oberlin Col, BA, 46, MA, 48. **CAREER** Archit historian, adj assoc prof, 74-, Univ Rochester. **MEMBERSHIPS** Soc of Architectural Historians; Landmark Soc, Western NY; NY St Preservation League; Natl Trust for Historic Preservation. **RESEARCH** Architects Claude Bragdon, Harvey Ellis, Louis Kahn, Frank Lloyd Wright; Amer arts & crafts movement; local architecture, Rochester region. **SELECTED PUBLICATIONS** Auth, Of Town and the River, A Rochester Guide; auth, Harvey Ellis, Artist, Architect; auth, Made in Rochester (exhib catalogue). **CONTACT ADDRESS** 25 Hardwood Hill Rd,, Pittsford, NY 14534. **EMAIL** frnc@mail.rochester.edu

FRANCIS, ROBERT D.
PERSONAL Born 09/02/1944, Fenwick, ON, Canada **DISCIPLINE** HISTORY **EDUCATION** York Univ, BA, 67, PhD, 76; Univ Toronto, MA, 68. **CAREER** Instr, York Univ, 74-75; vis lectr, Univ BC, 75-76; asst to assoc prof, 76-88, prof, Univ Calgary, 88-; vis prof, Univ Tsukuba (Japan), 91-93. **HONORS AND AWARDS** Master Tchr Awd, Univ Calgary, 82; J.W. Dafoe Book Prize, 86; Awd Merit, Asn Can Stud, 89. **MEMBERSHIPS** Can Hist Asn; Alta Hist Asn; Asn Can Stud; Japanese Asn Can Stud. **RESEARCH** Canadian intellectual and social hist, particularly 20th century, and Western Canadian intellectual and social hist. **SELECTED PUBLICATIONS** Auth, Frank H. Underhill, 86; auth, Images of the West, 89; coauth, Origins: Canadian History Before Confederation, 88, 3rd ed 96; coauth, Destinies: Canadian History Since Confederation, 88, 3rd ed 96; co-ed, The Dirty Thirties in Prairie Canada, 80; co-ed, Readings in Canadian History, 2 vols, 82, 5th ed 98; co-ed, The Prairie West, 85, 2nd ed 92; co-ed, The Regions and Peoples of Canada: A Historical Approach (in Japanese), 93. **CONTACT ADDRESS** Dept of Hist, Univ of Calgary, 2500 University Dr, Calgary, AB, Canada T2N 1N4. **EMAIL** francis@ualgary.ca

FRANCIS, SAMUEL TODD
PERSONAL Born 04/29/1947, Chattanooga, TN **DISCIPLINE** BRITISH AND WORLD HISTORY **EDUCATION** Johns Hopkins Univ, BA, 69; Univ NC, MA, 71, PhD (hist), 79. **CAREER** Policy analyst--Foreign Affairs, Heritage Found 77-81; Legis Asst Nat Security, US Senate Staff, 81-, Washington ed, The Southern Partisan, 80-. **RESEARCH** Contemporary political and social conflicts; role of elites and counterelites in world history; sociobiology and political theory. **SELECTED PUBLICATIONS** Authy, Exploring Dance as Concept--Contributions from Cognitive Science, Dance Rsch J, Vol 28, 96. **CONTACT ADDRESS** Apt A1202 2801 Park Ctr, Alexandria, VA 22302.

FRANK, DAVID
PERSONAL Born 07/30/1949 **DISCIPLINE** CANADIAN HISTORY **EDUCATION** Univ Toronto, BA, 72; Dalhousie Univ, PhD (hist), 79. **CAREER** Mem fac, Col Cape Breton, 78-80, Mem Fac, Univ NB, 80-, Ed, Acadiensis: J Hist Atlantic Region, 81-. **MEMBERSHIPS** Can Hist Asn. **RESEARCH** History of Atlantic Canada; Canadian social and labour history; international working class history. **SELECTED PUBLICATIONS** Ed, Acadiensis: Journal of the History of the Atlantic Region; ed, Echoes from Labor's War, 76; ed, The Acadiensis Readers, 85, 88, 90; ed, The New Brunswick Worker: A Reader's Guide, 86; ed, George MacEachern: An Autobiography, 87; ed, Labour and Working-Class History in Atlantic Canada, 95. **CONTACT ADDRESS** Dept of Hist, Univ of New Brunswick, Fredericton, Fredericton, NB, Canada E3B 5A3. **EMAIL** dfrank@unb.ca

FRANK, SAM HAGER
PERSONAL Born 07/23/1932, King City, MO, m, 1955, 1 child **DISCIPLINE** MODERN HISTORY **EDUCATION** Fla State Univ, BA, 53, MA, 57; Univ Fla, PhD, 61. **CAREER** Hist consult, Res Studies Inst, Air Univ, 57-58; prof hist and head dept soc sci, Tift Col, 61-65; assoc prof hist, Augusta Col, 66-67; from assoc prof hist and asst dean faculties to prof hist and assoc dean faculties, Jacksonville Univ, 67-72, dean, Col Arts and Sci, 72-78; chancellor, La State Univ, Alexandria, 79-81; PRES, WAGNER COL, 81-, Vis Fulbright prof, Bhagalpur Univ, India, 65-66 and Osmania Univ, India, 66. **MEMBERSHIPS** Am Conf Acad Deans; AHA; Orgn Am Hists; Southern Hist Asn; Am Acad Polit and Soc Sci. **RESEARCH** Military, Far Eastern and United States history. **SELECTED PUBLICATIONS** Coauth, Air Force Combat Units of World War II, US Govt Printing Off, 60, Watts, 63; auth, A Kentucky missionary in Japan, Ky Hist Soc Regist, 7/60; coauth, American Air Service Observation in World War I, Univ Fla, 61; auth, Organizing the United States Air Service in war: The developments in Europe, J Soc World War One Aero Hist, 9/65; A history of the McMahon Line and its controversy, Proc Indian Hist Cong, 5/66. **CONTACT ADDRESS** Off of Pres, Wagner Col, Staten Island, NY 10301.

FRANKFORTER, ALBERTUS DANIEL
PERSONAL Born 05/17/1939, Waynesboro, PA, m, 1972 **DISCIPLINE** MEDIEVAL HISTORY, HISTORY OF RELIGION **EDUCATION** Franklin and Marshall Col, Artium Baccalaeurie, 61; Drew Univ, MDiv, 65; Pa State Univ, MA, 69, PhD (medieval hist), 71. **CAREER** Actg chaplain, Williams Col, 63-64; asst prof, 70-80, Assoc Prof Ancient and Medieval Hist, Behrend Col, PA State Univ, 80-88; prof, Penn State Erie, 80-. **MEMBERSHIPS** Mediaeval Acad Am; Am Soc Church Hist; AHA. **RESEARCH** Medieval English Episcopal registers; medieval female authors. **SELECTED PUBLICATIONS** Auth, A History of the Christian Movement: An Essay on the Development of Christian Institutions (Chicago), Nelson-Hall, 78; auth, Civilization and Survival, vol I (Landham, MD), University Press of Am, 88; co-auth, The Equality of the Two Sexes by Poullain de la Barre: Introduction and Translation (Lewiston, NY), The Edwin Mellen Press, 89; auth, Conversations in Clio's Classroom, Perspectives, 94; co-auth, The Shakespeare Name Dictionary (NY) Garland, 95; auth, Amalsuntha, Procopius, and a Woman's Place, The Journal of Women's History, 96; auth, The Shakespeare Name and Place Dictionary (London), Fitzroy-Dearborn, 99; co-auth, The Western Heritage (NY), Prentice, 96, 2nd edition, 99, 3rd edition, in press; auth, The Medieval Millenium: An Introduction (Upper Saddle River, NJ), Prentice Hall, 99; auth, Stones for Bread: A Critique of Contemporary Worship (Lexington, KY), Westminster/John Knox, in press. **CONTACT ADDRESS** Dept of Hist, Pennsylvania State Univ, Erie, The Behrend Col, Station Rd, Erie, PA 16510. **EMAIL** ADP1@psu.edu

FRANKLIN, ALLAN DAVID
PERSONAL Born 08/01/1938, Brooklyn, NY, m, 1994 **DISCIPLINE** HISTORY & PHILOSOPHY OF SCIENCE **EDUCATION** Columbia Col, AB, 59; Cornell Univ, PhD(physics), 65. **CAREER** Res assoc physics, Princeton Univ, 65-66, instr, 66-67; asst prof, 67-73, asoc prof physics, Univ Co, 73-82, prof, 82-. **HONORS AND AWARDS** Ch elect, Forum on History of Physics, Am Phys Soc; Exec Bd, Phil of Sci Asn.; Centennial speaker, Am Physical Soc. **MEMBERSHIPS** Fellow of Am Physical Soc; Hist Sci Soc; Phil of Sci Asn. **RESEARCH** The role of experiment in physics. **SELECTED PUBLICATIONS** Auth, The Principle of Inertia in the Middle Ages, CO Assoc Univ, 76; The Discovery and Nondiscovery of Partly Nonconservation, Studies in Hist & Philos of Sci, 10/79; The Neglect of Experiment, Cambridge Univ Press, 1986; Experiment, Right or Wrong, Cambridge Univ Press, 1990; The Rise and Fall of the Fifth Force, Am Institute of Physics, 1993; The Appearance and Disappearance of the 17-keV Neutrino, Rev. Modern Physics, 1995. **CONTACT ADDRESS** Dept of Physics & Astrophysics, Univ of Colorado, Boulder, Box 390, Boulder, CO 80309-0390. **EMAIL** Allau.Franklin@Colorado.edu

FRANKLIN, H. BRUCE
PERSONAL Born 02/28/1934, Brooklyn, NY, m, 1956, 3 children **DISCIPLINE** ENGLISH & AMERICAN STUDIES **EDUCATION** Amherst Col, BA, 55; Stanford Univ, PhD, 61. **CAREER** Asst prof English & Am lit, Stanford Univ, 61-64; asst prof English, Johns Hopkins Univ, 64-65; assoc prof, Stanford Univ, 65-72; vis fel, Ctr for Humanities, Wesleyan Univ, 74; prof English & Am stud, Rutgers Univ, Newark, 75-. **HONORS AND AWARDS** Alexander Cappon Prize, 78; Eaton Awd, 81; bd adv eds, ser wkg papers hist sys, nat, and peoples, 98- ; adv bd, viet nam gen, 94-; script consult, sugarloaf films, 93; pres, melville soc, 93. **MEMBERSHIPS** MLA; ASA. **RESEARCH** Literature and society; American literature; science fiction; Vietnam War. **SELECTED PUBLICATIONS** Auth, The Wake of the Gods: Melvilles Mythology, Stanford Univ, 63; Back Where You Came From: A Life in the Death of the Empire, Harper, 75; The Victim as Criminal and Artist: Literature from the American Prison, 78 & Robert A Heinlein: America as Science Fiction, Oxford Univ, 80; Prison Literature in America, Lawrence Hill, 82; ed, Countdown to Midnight, New Am Libr, 84; co-ed, Vietnam and America, Grove/Atlantic, 85,95; auth, War Stars: The Superweapon and the American Imagination, Oxford Univ, 90; ed, The Vietnam War in American Stories, Songs, and Poems, Bedford Books, 96; ed, Prison Writing in 20th Century America, Penguin, 98; auth, Vietnam and Other American Fantasies, Vair Mass, 00. **CONTACT ADDRESS** Dept of English, Rutgers, The State Univ of New Jersey, Newark, 180 University Ave, Newark, NJ 07102-1897. **EMAIL** hbf@andromeda.rutgers.edu

FRANKS, KENNY ARTHUR
PERSONAL Born 07/19/1945, Okemah, OK, m, 1996, 3 children **DISCIPLINE** HISTORY **EDUCATION** OK State Univ, PhD, hist 73, MA hist 71; Univ Cen OK, BA hist 69. **CAREER** OK State Univ, Grad tch asst, instr, adjunt asst prof; Univ Cen OK, lectr; Redlands Comm Col, adj instr; OK State Univ, adj facul, res asst, Res and Ed asst to the dir of Will Rogers Project; OK Historical Society and Heritage Society, Editor of the Chronicles of OK, The OK Series, The OK Trackmaker Series, The OK Heritage Magazine, The OK Horizon Series, The OK Heritage County Hist series, The OK Statesman Series, Dir of Publ for OK Historical Society and Dir of Educ and Publ of the OK Heritage Assn; Bk Rev Ed, Rural OK News, 91; Consultant and Legal Consultant; Auth; Ed; Coordr; Writer; etc. **HONORS AND AWARDS** Dean's Honor Roll; Phi Alpha Theta; Pres Hon Roll, Phi Alpha Theta; Awd of Merit from Amer Assn ST Local Hist; Mrs Simon Baruch Univ Awd for Best Book; Jefferson Davis Medal; Distinguished Service Awd, OK Petro Coun; Petro Herit Awd; Mem Okemah Hall Of Fame; consultant for numerous projects, to list a few, oil boom blues: tv documentary, cherokee culture series of oral roberts univ, big war little war: cen for the amer indian, kirkpatrick cen, usa postal ser commemorative stamp series. **MEMBERSHIPS** OHA; OHS. **RESEARCH** Energy, industry, Native Am, Am west. **SELECTED PUBLICATIONS** Oklahoma: Its Land and People, with Paul Lambert, Helena MT, Amer and World Geog Pub, 94; A History of Washington County Oklahoma, with Paul F Lambert, OK City, Oklahoma Herit Assn, 98; Pawnee Pride: A History of Pawnee Country, OK CTY, OK Herit Assn, 94; Glen D Johnston Sr" The Road to Washington, OK Cty, OK Herit Assn, 96; Where the Black Gold Rolls and Flows, OK Today, 97; many, many, more bks, chapters and articles. **CONTACT ADDRESS** Oklahoma Heritage Association, 201 Northwest 14th St, Oklahoma City, OK 73103. **EMAIL** oha@telepath.com

FRANTZ, JOHN B.
PERSONAL Born 01/10/1932, New Haven, CT, m, 1963, 1 child **DISCIPLINE** AMERICAN HISTORY **EDUCATION** Franklin & Marshall Col, AB, 54; Univ Pa, AM, 56, PhD, 61. **CAREER** From instr to asst prof, 61-66, assoc prof Am hist, PA State Univ, 66-98; emeritus 98-, Adj instr hist, Franklin & Marshall Col, 59-61; Am Philos Soc res grant, 65; Yale Univ Divinity Sch res fel, 67; bus secy, Pa Hist Asn, 65-68, exec coun, 69-77, 98-, pres, 84-86; hist coun, United Church Christ, 75-80. **MEMBERSHIPS** Orgn Am Historians; Am Soc Church Hist, Pa Hist Asn. **RESEARCH** Early Am relig hist; Colonial and Revolutionary Am; PA Ger(s). **SELECTED PUBLICATIONS** Auth, John C Guldin: Pennsylvania German revivalist, Pa Mag Hist & Biog, 4/63; The return to tradition: an analysis of the new measures movement in the German Reformed Church, Pa Hist, 6/64; Revivalism: a thesis concerning its effect on Protestant denominations, Theol & Life, summer 65; ed, Bacon's Rebellion: Prologue to the Revolution?, Heath, 69; auth, The awakening of religion among the German settlers in the middle colonies, William & Mary Quart, 4/76; Religion in Pennsylvania during the Revolution, Pa Heritage, 6/76; Pennsylvania, In: Encyclopedia Americana, Grolier, 76; Religious Freedom: Key to Diversity, Pennsylvania Heritage, 81; Co-ed, Pennsylvania Religions Leaders, 86; Early German Methodist in America, Yearbook of German-American Studies, 91; Franklin and the Pennsylvania Germans, Pa Hist, 98; Co-ed, Beyond Philadelphia: The American Revolution in the Pennsylvania Hinterland, 98. **CONTACT ADDRESS** Dept of Hist, Pennsylvania State Univ, 108 Weaver Bldg, University Park, PA 16802-5500. **EMAIL** jbf2@psu.edu

FRANTZ, MARY ALISON
PERSONAL Born 09/27/1903, Duluth, MN **DISCIPLINE** ARCHAEOLOGY **EDUCATION** Smith Col, AB, 24; Columbia Univ, PhD, 37. **CAREER** Teacher, Arden Sch, NJ, 25-27; reader Index Christian Art, Princeton Univ, 27-29; Mem Staff, Agora Excavations, Athens, 33-40, 49-, Analyst, Off Strategic Serv, Washington, DC, 42-45; cult attache, Am Embassy, Athens, 46-49; assoc ed, Allied mission to observ Greek elections, 46; vis mem, Inst Advan Study, Princeton, NJ, 76-77. **MEMBERSHIPS** Archaeol Inst Am; Mediaeval Acad Am; Am Philos Soc. **RESEARCH** Byzantine archaeology and literature; early Christian history and architecture; Athens in late antiquity. **SELECTED PUBLICATIONS** Auth, From Paganism to Christianity in the Temples of Athens, Dumbarton Oaks Papers, 65; The Church of the Holy Apostles, the Athenian Agora, Am Sch Class Studies Athens, Vol XX, 71; coauth, The Parthenon Frieze, Phaidon, 75; Did Julian the Apostate Rebuild the Panthenon?, Am J Archaeol, Vol 83, 79. **CONTACT ADDRESS** 27 Haslet Ave, Princeton, NJ 08540.

FRANZ, GEORGE W.
PERSONAL Born 03/31/1942, m, 2 children **DISCIPLINE** AMERICAN HISTORY **EDUCATION** Muhlenberg Col, AB, 64; Rutgers Univ, MA, 65, PhD(Am hist), 74. **CAREER** Instr, 68-73, asst prof hist, Pa State Univ, 74-, assoc ed, Papers Martin Van Buren, 75-76, proj dir & ed, 76-, dir of Academic Affairs, Penn State Delaware County, 97-. **HONORS AND AWARDS** Outstanding Teacher, Penn State Delaware County, 89; George W. Atherton Awd for Excellence in Undergraduate Teaching, Penn State Univ, 90; Outstanding Faculty Advisor, Col of the Liberal Arts, Penn State Univ, 93; McKay-Donkin Awd, Penn State Univ, 94. **MEMBERSHIPS** Orgn Am Historians. **RESEARCH** Colonial and revolutionary Pennsylvania history. **SELECTED PUBLICATIONS** Project dir and ed, The Papers of Martin Van Buren (55 reels of microfilm), Chadwyck-Healy, 88; Martin Van Buren, Research Guide to American Historical Biography, Beachem, 88; Paxton: A Study of community Structure and Mobility in the Colonial Pennsylvania Backcountry, Garland, 89. **CONTACT ADDRESS** Director of Academic Affairs, Pennsylvania State Univ, Delaware County, 25 Yearsley Mill Rd, Media, PA 19063-5522. **EMAIL** gwf1@psu.edu

FRASER, J(ULIUS) T(HOMAS)
PERSONAL Born 05/07/1923, Budapest, Hungary, m, 1973, 3 children **DISCIPLINE** STUDY OF TIME, HISTORY OF IDEAS **EDUCATION** Cooper Union, Bee, 51; Univ Hanover, PhD(philos), 70. **CAREER** Jr engineer, MacKay Radio & Telegraph, 51-53; design engineer, Westinghouse Electric Corp, 53-55; sr res scientist, Gen Precision Lab, Inc, 55-71; FOUNDER , INT SOC STUDY TIME, 66-; Adj Assoc Prof Hist Sci, Fordham Univ, 71-, Res asst physics, Mich State Univ, 62-66; vis lectr humanities & sci, Mass Inst Technol, 66-67, guest, 67-69; vis lectr study time, My Holyoke Col, 67-69; vis prof time & intellectual hist, Univ MD. **SELECTED PUBLICATIONS** Auth, Of Time, Passion, and Knowledge: Reflections on the Strategy of Existence, first ed, NY: Braziller, 75, 2nd ed, Princeton Univ Press, 90; Time as Conflict: a Scientific and Humanistic Study, Basel and Boston: Birkhauser, 78; The Genesis and Evolution of Time: a Critique of Interpretation in Physics, Amherst: Univ MA Press, Brighton, Sussex: The Harvester Press, 82, Tokyo: Kodansha Scientific Ltd, 84; Time, the Familiar Stranger, Amherst: Univ MA Press, 87, Redmond, WA: Tempest Books (paperback), 88, Stuart, FL: Triformation Braille Service, 89; Die Zeit: Vetraut und Fremd, trans of Time, the Familiar Stranger, Basel: Birkhauser Verlag, 88, 2nd ed (paperback), Munchen: Deutscher Taschenbuch Verlag, 91; Il Tempo: una Presenza Sconosciuta, trans of Time, the Familiar Stranger, Milano: Feltrinelli, 91; Genesis y Evolucion del Tiempo, trans of The Genesis and Evolution of Time, Irunea/ Pamplona: Pamiela, 95; Time, Conflict, and Human Values, Urbana and Chicago: Univ IL Press, 99; ed, The Voices of Time, 66, 81, 11 vols; ed, The Study of Time series, 72-00, 10 vols; numerous articles, book reviews, and other publications primarily concerning the study of time. **CONTACT ADDRESS** PO Box 815, Westport, CT 06881. **EMAIL** JT@Jfraser@cs.com

FRASER, SARAH
DISCIPLINE ASIAN ART **EDUCATION** Univ Calf, Berkeley, PhD. **CAREER** Prof, Northwestern Univ **MEMBERSHIPS** Turfan-Silk Road archeological team. **RESEARCH** Early Chinese painting, art of central Asia. **SELECTED PUBLICATIONS** Auth, Regimes of Production: The Use of Pounces in Temple Construction, Orientations, 96. **CONTACT ADDRESS** Dept of Art History, Northwestern Univ, 1801 Hinman, Evanston, IL 60208.

FRASSETTO, MICHAEL
DISCIPLINE HISTORY **EDUCATION** LaSalle Univ, BA, 83; MI State Univ, MA, 85; DE Univ, PhD, 93. **CAREER** Asst prof, 90-95; assoc prof, 95-, Jewish Theol Sem Am. **HONORS AND AWARDS** NEH summer sem, Bryn Mawr Col, 93; LaGrange Col summer res grant, 92; Fulbright-Hayes Res Fel, GDR, 1989-1990; Univ Del Grad Res Fel, 88. **RESEARCH** World civilization to 1648 and 1648 to present; ancient Rome; Middle Ages and Renaissance and Reformation. **SELECTED PUBLICATIONS** Auth, The Art of Forgery: The Sermons of Ademar of Chabannes and the Cult of St. Martial of Limoges, Comitatus, 95; Violence, Knightly Piety and the Peace of God in Aquitaine. **CONTACT ADDRESS** Dept of Hist, LaGrange Col, Broad St, PO Box 601, La Grange, GA 30240.

FRAZEE, CHARLES AARON
PERSONAL Born 07/04/1929, Rushville, IN, m, 1971, 2 children **DISCIPLINE** BYZANTINE AND CHURCH HISTORY **EDUCATION** St Meinrad Col, AB, 51; Cath Univ Am, MA, 54; Ind Univ, PhD (hist), 65, cert, Russ and Europ Inst, 65. **CAREER** Assoc prof hist, Marian Col, Ind, 56-70; assoc prof, 70-80, Prof Hist, Calif State Univ, Fullerton, 80-. **MEMBERSHIPS** Cath Hist Soc; Am Asn Slavic Studies; Mod Greek Studies Asn; Am Soc Church Hist. **RESEARCH** Christian communities in Eastern Europe and the Middle East. **SELECTED PUBLICATIONS** Auth, " The Orthodox and Eastern Chruches," The Religious Heritage of Southern Calfornia, Los Angeles CA, (76): 43-61; auth, " Church and State in Greece: Greece in Transition, London, (77): 128-152; auth, " The Orthodox Church of Greece: The Last Fifteen Years," Hellenic Perspectives, Lantham, MD, (80): 145-180; auth, Catholics and Sultans: The Church and the Ottoman Empire, 1453-1923, Cambridge Univ Press, 83; auth, " The Religious of Cyprus" Greece and Cyprus in History, Amsterdam, (85): 13-28; coauth, Princess of the Greek Islands: The Dukes of the Archipelago, 1207-1566, 88; auth, " Between East and West: The Balkan Churches in the First Christian Centuries" Following the Star from the East: essays in honour of Archimandrite Boniface Luykx, Ottawa, (92): 254-268; auth, " Using Vatican Archives in the Study of Eastern Christianity" Seeking God: The Recovery of Religious Identity in Orthodox Russia, Ukraine, and Georgian De Kalb, IL, (93): 164-282; auth, World History- the Easy Way 2 vols Barron's Educaitonal Series, 97; auth, World History: Original an Secondary Source Readings, 2 vols, Greenhaven Press, 99. **CONTACT ADDRESS** Episcopal Theological School at Claremont, 1325 No College Ave, Claremont, CA 91711-3199. **EMAIL** kfrazee@fullerton.edu

FRAZER, HEATHER
PERSONAL Born 11/25/1940, Honolulu, HI, m, 1976, 3 children **DISCIPLINE** HISTORY **EDUCATION** Duke Univ, PhD. **CAREER** Prof. **HONORS AND AWARDS** Tchg Incentive Prog Awd; Univ Distinguished Tchg Awd. **MEMBERSHIPS** AHA; OAH; AAS. **RESEARCH** India and British Empire; women's history. **SELECTED PUBLICATIONS** Auth, All Quiet on the Hollywood Front: Actor Lew Ayres as Conscientious Objector, 97; Curzon and His Indian Legacy: Consumate Imperialist and Preserver of Ancient Monuments, 95; coauth, We Have Just Begun Not to Fight, 96. **CONTACT ADDRESS** History Dept, Florida Atlantic Univ, 777 Glades Rd, Boca Raton, FL 33431. **EMAIL** frazer@fau.edu

FRAZIER, ALISON
DISCIPLINE HISTORY **EDUCATION** Columbia Univ, PhD, 97. **CAREER** Vis asst prof, Dartmouth, 95-96; Asst Prof Dept Hist, Univ TX, Austin, 96-. **HONORS AND AWARDS** Am Academy Rome, Mellon Awd, 97-98; Newcombe fel, 94-95; Delmas fel, 91; Phi Beta Kappa, 85. **MEMBERSHIPS** AHA, AAR; Am Philol Asn. **RESEARCH** Religious history, Italian Renaissance, biography. **CONTACT ADDRESS** Dept of History, Univ of Texas, Austin, Austin, TX 78712-1163. **EMAIL** akfrazier@mail.utexas.edu

FREDERICK, RICHARD G.
PERSONAL Born 07/16/1947, Ft. Wayne, IN, m, 1970 **DISCIPLINE** HISTORY **EDUCATION** Ind Univ, Bloomington, AB, 69; St Mary's Univ, San Antonio, MA, 71; Pa State Univ, PhD(hist), 79. **CAREER** Asst Prof to Prof Hist, Univ Pittsburgh, Bradford, 79-. **HONORS AND AWARDS** NEH Res grant; Chancellor's Distinguished Teaching Awd, Univ Pittsburgh. **MEMBERSHIPS** Orgn Am Historians. **RESEARCH** United States from 1900-1930: political, social and cultural. **SELECTED PUBLICATIONS** Auth, Warner G. Harding: A Bibliography, Greenwood Press, 92; Coauth, Dictionary of Theoretical Concepts in Biology, Scarecrow Press, 81 **CONTACT ADDRESS** Univ of Pittsburgh, Bradford, 300 Campus Dr, Bradford, PA 16701. **EMAIL** rgf1@pitt.edu

FREDERICK, WILLIAM HAYWARD
PERSONAL Born 09/02/1941, Boston, MA, m, 1964, 2 children **DISCIPLINE** HISTORY OF SOUTHEAST ASIA **EDUCATION** Yale Univ BA, 63; Univ Hawaii, PhD (hist), 78. **CAREER** Instr, 73-78, asst prof 78-88, assoc prof, Ohio Univ, 88-, Dir, Int Student Serv, Ohio Univ, 73-78; ed, Southeast Asia Series, Ctr Int Studies Publ, 78-; founder and ed, Antara Kita Bull, Indonesian Studies Comt, 73-76; ed, Southeast Asia Transl Publ Group, Asn Asian Studies, 79-; exec dir, Indonesian Studies Summer Inst, 81-83; vis sr res, Australian Nat Univ, Nordic Inst of Asian Stu and Int Inst for Asian Stu. **MEMBERSHIPS** Asn Asian Studies; Koninklijk Inst voor Taal-, Land- en Volkenkunde. **RESEARCH** Modern Indonesian history; Southeast Asian social change since 1750; literature, the popular arts, and society in contemporary Southeast Asia. **SELECTED PUBLICATIONS** Auth, The Putera Reports, SEA Prog, Cornell Univ, 71; Alexandre Varenne and Politics in Indochina, 1925-26, Univ Hawaii Press, 73; coauth, Sejarah Indonesia Masa Lampau dan Masa Kini, LP3ES, Jakarta, 82; auth, Rhoma Irama and the Dangdut style, Indonesia, Cornell Univ, 82; Kesatuan dan Keaneka-ragaman dalam Dua Kebudayaan: Bangsa dan Bahasa di Amerika dan Indonesia, PRISMA, Jakarta, 82. **CONTACT ADDRESS** Dept Hist, Ohio Univ, Athens, OH 45701-2979. **EMAIL** frederic@ohiou.edu

FREDRICK, DAVID
DISCIPLINE ROMAN SOCIAL HISTORY **EDUCATION** Univ Kans, BA, 82, MA, 84; Univ Southern Calif, PhD, 92. **CAREER** English and Lit, Univ Ark. **SELECTED PUBLICATIONS** Auth, Coming of Age in the Milky Way, Morrow, (88): 103, 131; auth, "Beyond the Atrium to Adriadne: Erotic Painting and Visual Pleasure in the Roman House," Classical Antiquity 14.2, (95): 266-287; auth, "Reading Broken Skin: Violence in Roman Elegy," in Roman Sexualities, eds. J. Hallett and M. Skinner, (Princeton, 97): 172-193; auth, Classics and Feminism: Gendering the Classics, in Vergilius 44, ed. Barbara F. McManus, (98): 164-168; auth, "Haptic Poetics," Arethusa 32, (99): 49-83. **CONTACT ADDRESS** Flan Dept, KIMP 425, Univ of Arkansas, Fayetteville, 1524 Stephens Ave, Fayetteville, AR 72703. **EMAIL** dfredric@comp.uark.edu

FREDRICKSON, GEORGE M.
PERSONAL Born 07/16/1934, Bristol, CT, m, 1956, 4 children **DISCIPLINE** AMERICAN HISTORY **EDUCATION** Harvard Univ, AB, 56, PhD, 64. **CAREER** Prof, Harvard Univ, Northwestern Univ; prof, Stanford Univ, 84-. **HONORS AND AWARDS** Fulbright Scholar, Univ of Oslo, 56-57; Guggenheim Fel; NEH Sen Fels; Ctr for Advan Study in the Behavioral Scis and the Hums Fel, Stanford Univ; Ford Found Fel, Harvard Univ; Harmsworth vis prof, Oxford; Fulbright lectr, Moscow Univ; Anisfield Wolf Awd in Race Relations Co-winner; Pulitzer Prize Finalist; Ralph Waldo Emerson Prize, Phi Beta Kappa; Merle Curti Awd, Org of Am Hists. **MEMBERSHIPS** Org of Am Hists; AHA; Southern Hist Asn; Am Antiquarian Soc; Am Acad of Arts and Scis. **RESEARCH** History of race relations in the U.S.; comperative history of race relationss in the U.S. and South Africa; nineteenth century American history; American intellectual history. **SELECTED PUBLICATIONS** Auth, The Inner Civil War: Northern Intellectuals and the Crisis of the Union, 65; The Black Image in the White Mind: The Debate on Afro-American Character and Destiny, 71; White Supremacy: A Comparative Study in American and South African History, 81; The Arrogance of Race: Historical Perspectives on Slavery, Racism, and Social Inequality, 87; Black Liberation: A Comparative History of Black Ideologies in the United States and South Africa, 95; The Comparative Imagination: On the History of Racism, Nationalism, and Social Movement, 97. **CONTACT ADDRESS** Dept of History, Stanford Univ, Stanford, CA 94305.

FREDRIKSEN, P.
PERSONAL Born 01/06/1951, RI, m, 2000, 3 children **DISCIPLINE** RELIGION & HISTORY **EDUCATION** Wellesley, BA, 73; Oxford, Dipl Theol, 74; Princeton, PhD, 79. **CAREER** Asst prof, History Dept, Univ Calif Berkeley, 81-86; assoc prof, Religious Studies, Univ Pitts, 86-89; aurelio prof, scripture, Boston Univ, 90-. **HONORS AND AWARDS** Lady Davis vis prof Jerusalem, 94; NEH Univ res grant, 92-93; Naitonal Jewish Book Awd, 99. **MEMBERSHIPS** Amer Acad Relig; Soc Bibl Lit; Nat Asn Patristic Studies **RESEARCH** Historical Jesus; Jews & Gentiles in antiquity; Augustine. **SELECTED PUBLICATIONS** Auth, Augustine on Romans, Sholars Press, 82; auth, From Jesus to Christ, Yale 88, 2nd ed 00; auth, "What You See is What You Get: Context and Content in Current Research on the Historical Jesus,' Theology Today 52.1(95), 75-97; auth, " Did Jesus Oppose Purity Laws?" Bible Review XI.3 (95), 18-25, 42-47; auth, " Excaecati Occulta Iustitia Dei: Augustine on Jews and Judaism," Journal of Early Christian Studies 3 (95), 299-324; auth, " Secundum Carnem: History nd Israel in the Theology of St Augustine," the Limits of Ancient Christianity, Essays on Late Antique Thought and Culture in Honor of R A Markus, Ann Arbor, Univ of Michigan, (99), 26-41; auth, Jesus of Nazareth, King of the Jews, Knopf, 99; auth, "The Human Condition in Formative Christianity: The Redemption of the Body," The Human Condtion: A Study of the Comparison of Religious Ideas, SUNY Press, (00); 133-156; auth, " Ultimate Reality in Ancient Christianity: Christ, Blood Sacrifice and Redemption," Ultimate Realities: A Study of the Comparison of Religious Ideas, SUNY Press, (00): 61-73. **CONTACT ADDRESS** Dept of Relig, Boston Univ, Boston, MA 02215. **EMAIL** augfred@bu.edu

FREE, KATHERINE B.
DISCIPLINE THEATRE HISTORY **EDUCATION** Marymount Col, BA; Univ Calif, Los Angeles, MA, PhD. **CAREER** Prof; consult & actress, theatre LA. **MEMBERSHIPS** Amer Soc Theatre Res, ASTR; Int Fedn for the Theatre Res, IFTR; Amer Edu Theatre Assoc, ATHE. **RESEARCH** Ancient Greek theatre & the folk theatre of India. **SELECTED PUBLICATIONS** Articles in, Theatre Res Int, Theatre J, & UCLA J of Dance Ethnol. **CONTACT ADDRESS** Dept of Theatre, Loyola Marymount Univ, 7900 Loyola Blvd, Los Angeles, CA 90045.

FREEBERG, E.
PERSONAL Born 06/11/1958, New York, NY, m, 2 children **DISCIPLINE** HISTORY **EDUCATION** Middlebury Col, BA; Emory Univ, MA; PhD. **CAREER** Asst Prof, Colby-Sawyer Col. **RESEARCH** Intellectual/Religious History; History of Education. **CONTACT ADDRESS** Dept of Humanities, Colby-Sawyer College, 100 Main St, New London, NH 03257-4651. **EMAIL** efreeber@colby-sawyer.edu

FREED, JOANN
DISCIPLINE HISTORY OF ARCHAEOLOGY AT CARTHAGE **EDUCATION** Alberta, PhD. **CAREER** Pottery analyst, San Giovanni di Ruoti in Southern Italy, 77-83; part of team working on the Second Canadian Theodosian Wall Site, Carthage, 84-86; Cataloguing the collection of amphorae, Musee National de Carthage, 90-. **RESEARCH** Roman pottery; amphoras and trade in the Mediterranean; hist of archaeology at Carthage. **SELECTED PUBLICATIONS** Auth, Deep Water Archaeology: A Late-Roman Ship from Carthage and an Ancient Trade Route near Skerki Bank off Northwest Sicily, 94; The Late Series of tunisian Cylindrical Amphoras at Carthage, 95; Early Roman Amphorae in the Collection of the Museum of Carthage, 96. **CONTACT ADDRESS** Dept of Classics, Wilfrid Laurier Univ, 75 University Ave W, Waterloo, ON, Canada N2L 3C5. **EMAIL** jfreed@mach1.wlu.ca

FREED, JOHN BECKMANN
PERSONAL Born 02/06/1944, New York, NY **DISCIPLINE** MEDIEVAL HISTORY **EDUCATION** Cornell Univ, AB, 65; Princeton Univ, PhD, 69. **CAREER** Asst prof, 69-75, Assoc Prof Hist, Ill State Univ, 75-, Shelby Cullom Davis fel, Princeton Univ, 72. **MEMBERSHIPS** AHA; Mediaeval Acad Am; Am Cath Hist Asn. **RESEARCH** Medieval religious history; medieval German social history. **SELECTED PUBLICATIONS** Auth, The Early Germans, Hist, Vol 55,93; Records of the Collegiate Foundation of St Castulus in Moosburg, Cath Hist Rev, Vol 81, 95; Beguines in the Lake Constance Area, Cath Hist Rev, Vol 81, 95; Communications and Power in Medieval Europe, Vol 2--The Gregorian Revolution and Beyond, Speculum J Medieval Stud, Vol 71, 96; The German Episcopacy and the Implementation of the Decrees of the 4th Lateran Council, Ad 1216-1245--Watchmen on the Tower, Cath Hist Rev, Vol 82, 96; Land and Lordship--Structures of Governance in Medieval Austria, Speculum J Medieval Stud, Vol 69, 94; Peasants in the Middle Ages, Cent Europ Hist, Vol 26, 93; Land and Lordship--Structures of Governance in Medieval Austria--Brunner, O, Speculum J Medieval Stud, Vol 69, 94; The Franciscans in Medieval Luneburg, Cath Hist Rev, Vol 83, 97; Germany in the Early Middle Ages C.800-1056, Cent Europ Hist, Vol 25, 92; Elenchus Fontium Historiae Urbanae, Vol 3, Pt 1--Source Documents on the Early History of the Austrian State up to Ad-1277, Speculum J Medieval Stud, Vol 69, 94; Medieval German Social History--Generalizations and Particularism, Cent Europ Hist, Vol 25, 92; The Cistercian Nunnery in Wald, Cath Hist Rev, Vol 79, 93; Chronicle of the Bishops of Wurzburg 742-1495, Vol 1, From the Beginning until Rugger 1125, Cent Europ Hist, Vol 26, 93; Elenchus Fontium Historiae Urbanae, Vol 3, Pt 1--Source Documents on the Early History of the Austrian State up to Ad 1277, Speculum J Medieval Stud, Vol 69, 94; Mendicant Orders in Mecklenburg--Contribution to the History of the Franciscans, The Nuns of the Order of Saint Clare, the Dominicans and the Augustinian Hermits in the Middle Ages - German - Ulpts,I/, Cath Hist Rev, Vol 83, 97; Itinerant Kingship and Royal Monasteries in Early Medieval Germany, C.936-1075, Cent Europ Hist, Vol 27, 94; The Letters of Hildegard of Bingen, Vol 1, Cent Europ Hist, Vol 28, 95; The Great Moravian Empire--Reality or Fiction--A New Interpretation of Sources on ihe History of 9th Century Middle Danube Region, Cent Europ Hist, Vol 30, 97; The Tradition of the Polling Foundation, Cath Hist Rev, Vol 80, 94; Fundatio and Memoria--Founders and Cloister Organizers in Images 1100-1350, Cath Hist Rev, Vol 80, 94; Registers of Documents of the Bishops of Passau, Vol 1, Cath Hist Rev, Vol 80, 94; Communications and Power in Medieval Europe, Vol 1--The Carolingian and Ottonian Centuries, Speculum J Medieval Stud, Vol 71, 96; The Making of Europe--Conquest, Colonization and Cultural Change, 950-1350, Cent Europ Hist, Vol 28, 95; Communications and Power in Medieval Europe, Vol 2--The Gregorian Revolution and Beyond, Speculum J Medieval Stud, Vol 71, 96; Schottenkloster--Irish Benedictines in Germany During the High iddle Ages, Cath Hist Rev, Vol 82, 96. **CONTACT ADDRESS** Dept of Hist, Illinois State Univ, Normal, IL 61761. **EMAIL** jbfreed@ilstu.edu

FREEDMAN, ESTELLE
DISCIPLINE HISTORY **EDUCATION** Barnard Col, BA; Columbia Univ, PhD. **CAREER** Stanford Univ, 76-. **HONORS AND AWARDS** Dinkelspiel Awd, 81; NEH Fel, 82-83, 92-93; Mellon Grant, 84-85; Fel, Stanford, 85-86; Fel, ACLS, 93; Thomas and Lillian Rhodes Prize, 96; Sierra Prize for Best Book, 96; Nancy Lyman Roelker Mentorship Awd, 98. **MEMBERSHIPS** AHA, Nat Women's Studies Assoc, Org of Am Hist, Jewish Women's Archiv. W Assoc of Women Hist, N Calif Lesbian and Gay Hist Soc. **RESEARCH** U.S. women's history, comparative women's history. **SELECTED PUBLICATIONS** Auth, Their Sisters' Keepers: Women's Prison Reform in America, 1830-1930, Univ of Mich Pr, (Ann Arbor) 81; coed, The Lesbian Issue: Essays From Signs, Univ of Chicago Pr, (Chicago), 85; coauth, Intimate Matters: A History of Sexuality in America, Harper and Row, (NY), 88; Univ of Chicago Pr, auth, Maternal Justice: Miriam Van Waters and the Female Reform Tradition, Univ of Chicago Pr, (Chicago), 96; auth, "The Social Construction of Homosexuality," Socialist Rev, (96); auth, "The Prison Lesbian: Race, Class, and the Construction of the Aggressive Female Homosexual, 1915-1965," Feminist Studies, (96); auth, "The History of the Family and the History of Sexuality," New Am Hist, ed Eric Foner, Temple Univ

Pr, (97); auth, "The Burning of Letters Continues: Elusive Identities and the Historical Construction of Sexuality," Jour of Women's Hist, (98); auth, "The Trials of Miriam Van Waters," Forgotten Heroes of America's Past, ed Susan Ware, Free Pr, (98). **CONTACT ADDRESS** Dept Hist, Stanford Univ, Bldg 200, Stanford, CA 94305. **EMAIL** ebf@stanford,.edu

FREEDMAN, ROBERT OWEN
PERSONAL Born 04/18/1941, Philadelphia, PA, m, 1965, 2 children **DISCIPLINE** DIPLOMATIC HISTORY; INTERNAL RELATIONS **EDUCATION** Univ Penn, BA 62; Columbia Univ, MA 65; Russian Inst Cert, 65, PhD, 69. **CAREER** Baltimore Hebrew Univ, , pres 97-00, acting pres, 95-97; dean grad sch, 75-97; Marquette Univ, assoc prof, asst prof, 67-75; US Military Acad, 67-70; Univ MD Baltimore, adj prof, 80-92; Geo Washington Univ, adj prof, 84-86; Natnl Sec Agncy, 88-90; Dept State Ser Inst, lectr, 80-90. **HONORS AND AWARDS** U of Penn full schshp, honors grad, Soc Sci honor, Political Sci honor, 2 German Prizes. **MEMBERSHIPS** AIS; APSA; AAASS; MEI; MESA; ISA; JSA. **SELECTED PUBLICATIONS** Auth, The Middle East and the Peace Process, con't ed, Gainesville, Univ Press Florida, 98; Israel Under Rabin, con't ed, Boulder CO, Westview Press, 95; The Middle East After the Iraqi Invasion of Kuwait, co-ed, Gainesville, Univ Press of FL, 93; Moscow and the Middle East: Soviet Policy Since the Invasion of Afghanistan, Cambridge Eng, CUP, 91. **CONTACT ADDRESS** Baltimore Hebrew Univ, 5800 Park Heights Ave, Baltimore, MD 21215. **EMAIL** Freedman@bhu.edu

FREEHLING, WILLIAM W.
PERSONAL Born 12/26/1935, Chicago, IL, m, 1971, 4 children **DISCIPLINE** AMERICAN CULTURAL HISTORY **EDUCATION** Harvard Univ, AB, 58; Univ Calif-Berkeley, MA, 59; Berkeley, PhD, 63. **CAREER** Tchg fel, Berkeley, 59-60 & 62-63; instr Univ S Carolina, 61-62; instr, Harvard Univ, 63-64; asst prof to prof, Univ Mich, 64-72; prof, Johns Hopkins Univ, 72-91; Thomas B. Lockwood Prof Am Hist, SUNY, Buffalo, 91-94; Otis A. Singletary Chr in Hum, Univ Kentucky, 94- . **HONORS AND AWARDS** Woodrow Wilson fel, Guggenheim fel, 69-70, nHF fel, 68; Horace Rockham fel, 70-71; Owsley Prize; Bancroft Prize, Nevins Prize; Univ Mich Russel Prize. **MEMBERSHIPS** Am Hist Soc; S Hist Asn; Orgn Am Hist; Am Antiq Soc; Soc Am Hist; Soc Hist of Early Repub; The Hist Soc. **RESEARCH** History of American furniture; History of the Civil War era. **SELECTED PUBLICATIONS** Auth, The Reintegration of American History: Slavery and the Civil War, NY, 94; The Road to Disunion, Disunionists at Bay, 1776-1854, NY, 90; ed, Secession Debated: Georgia's Showdown in 1860, NY, 93; rev, David Gollaher, Ddorothea Dix, Lexington Herald-Leader, 96; auth, "The South versus Te South: How AntiConfederate Southerners Shaped the Course of the Civil War," NY 01. **CONTACT ADDRESS** Singletary Chair in the Humanities, Univ of Kentucky, 1715 Patterson Office Tower, Lexington, KY 40506-0027. **EMAIL** wwfree0@pop.uky.edu

FREEMAN, JOANNE B.
PERSONAL Born 04/27/1962, Queens, NY **DISCIPLINE** HISTORY **EDUCATION** Pomona Col, BA, 84; Univ Va, MA, 93; PhD, 98. **CAREER** Asst prof of Hist, Yale Univ, 97-. **HONORS AND AWARDS** Phi Beta Kappa, 84; Andrew W. Mellon Fel, Mass Hist Soc, 95; Kate B. and Hall. J. Peterson Fel, Am Antiquarian Soc, 96; Salvatori Fel, Intercollegiate Studies Inst, 96; Shannon Awd for Scholarship and Leadership, Univ Va, 98; Morse Fel, Yale Univ, 2000. **MEMBERSHIPS** SHEAR, OAH, AHA, OIEAHC, AAUW. **RESEARCH** Revolutionary and early national political history and culture; honor culture. **SELECTED PUBLICATIONS** Auth, "Slander, Poison, Whispers, and Fame: Jefferson's 'Anas' and Political Gossip in the Early Republic," J of the Early Republic, 15 (spring 95): 25-57; auth, "Dueling as Politics: Reinterpreting the Burr-Hamilton Duel," William & Mary Quart, 53 (April 96): 289-318; auth, "The Election of 1800: A Study in the Process of Political Change," Yale Law J,.108 (June 99): 1959-1994; auth, Preface, Alexander Hamilton: A Concise Biography, by Broadus Mitchell, Oxford Univ Press (76), reprint, Barnes & Noble (99); auth, "Dueling," in Encyclopedia of American Studies, ed George Kurian and Miles Orvell, Bethel, Ct: Grolier Pub Co (forthcoming); auth, "The Presidential Election of 1796," in John Adams and the Founding of the Republic, Richard A. Ryerson, ed, Mass Hist Soc (forthcoming 2000); auth, " 'The Art and Address of Ministerial Management:' Secretary of the Treasury Alexander Hamilton and Congress," in Neither Separate Nor Equal: Congress and the Executive Branch in the 1790s, Ohio Univ Press (forthcoming 2000). **CONTACT ADDRESS** Dept of Hist, Yale Univ, PO Box 208324, New Haven, CT 06520-8324. **EMAIL** joanne.freeman@yale.edu

FREEZE, GREGORY L.
PERSONAL Born 05/09/1945, Dayton, OH, m, 1994, 3 children **DISCIPLINE** HISTORY **EDUCATION** DePauw Univ, BA, 67; Columbia Univ, MA, 68; PhD, 72. **CAREER** From asst to full prof, Brandeis Univ, 72- ; res assoc, Davis Ctr for Russian Stud, Harvard Univ, 72-; vis prof, Univ Calif, Berkeley, 89; vis prof, Univ Tuebingen, 84-85; vis prof, Heidelburg Univ, 91-92; vis prof, Goettingen Univ, 98. **HONORS AND AWARDS** Fulbright Fac Res Fel; IREX Fel; Guggenheim Fel; ACLS grant; Alexander von Humboldt Fel; NEH dir, Summer Sem for Col Tchrs, 88-89; NEH Res Fel, 89-90; NEH Dir of Summer Sem for Col Prof, 92-93, 93-94; principal investigator, Nat Coun for Soviet and E Europ Stud, 92-94, 95-97; Mazer grant, 98. **MEMBERSHIPS** Am Asn for the Advanc of Slavic Stud. **RESEARCH** Modern Russian history. **SELECTED PUBLICATIONS** Ed, Research Guide to the Central Party Archives, Moscow: Izd-vo Transakta, 93; ed, Special Files for I.V. Stalin from the NKVD, Blagovest, 94; ed, Russian Archive Series, v.4, Blagovest, 94; ed, Russian Archive Series, v,2, Iadatel'stvo Blagovest, 94; co-ed, Russian Archive Series, v.3, pt. 1, Izd-vo Blagovest, 94; ed, The Special Files for N.S. Khrushchev from the NKVD, Blagovest, 95; ed, The Special Files for V. Molotov from the NKVD, Blagovest, 95; ed, The Special Files for L.P. Beria from the NKVD, Blagovest, 96; ed, Russia, A History, Oxford, 97; ed, Pariahs, Partners, Predators: German-Soviet Relations, 1922-1941, Columbia Univ, 97. **CONTACT ADDRESS** Dept of History, Brandeis Univ, Waltham, MA 02254. **EMAIL** freeze@brandeis.edu

FREEZE, KAREN J.
PERSONAL Born Vancouver, WA **DISCIPLINE** HISTORY, MANAGEMENT **EDUCATION** Univ Wash, BA, 67; Columbia Univ, MA, 70; PhD, 74. **CAREER** Fulbright Lectr, Technical Univ of Liberec, Czech Republic, 95-96, vis lectr, 96-97; assoc prof, Eastern Nazarene Col, Quincy, Mass, 97-98; lectr and res fel, Univ of Washington, 98-. **HONORS AND AWARDS** German Marshall Fund Fel, 83-84; Am Coun of Learned Socs Fel and Int Res and Exchanges Bd Fel, 71-72, 74-75, 83-84, 88, 89; Fulbright Lectr, 95-96; Nat Res Coun Travel Grant, 2000-. **MEMBERSHIPS** Soc for the Hist of Technol, Int Comt on the Hist of Technol, Czechoslavak Hist Conf, Am Asn for the Advancement of Slavic Studies. **RESEARCH** Technological innovation in Central and Eastern Europe; history of technology and industry, especially the interaction of technology and human values; management of technology and product development; history and management of design in Europe and America. **SELECTED PUBLICATIONS** Auth, "Innovative Designing for Diabetics: Novo Nordisk A/S and Patient-Centered Systems," in M. Bruce and B. Jevaker, eds, Management of Design Alliances: Sustaining a Design-Based Competitive Advantage," NY (97): auth, "Design Management Lessons from Henry Dreyfuss," Innovation (spring 91): 17-20, reprinted in Bruce and Jevnaker, eds, Management of Design Alliances, NY (97); auth, "The New Eastern Europe: Reflections on Design in Czechoslovakia," Design Management J, vol 1, no 2 (summer 90): 42-48; auth, "Braun AG: Designing and Developing for a New Oral Care Category," (A), "Braun AG and the D5 Plaque Remover: Design and Technology Strategy,"(B) Design Management Inst Case Studies (2000). **CONTACT ADDRESS** History, Univ of Washington, PO Box 353560, Seattle, WA 98195-3560. **EMAIL** freezek@u.washington.edu

FRENCH, GOLDWIN S.
PERSONAL Born 01/24/1923, Dresden, ON, Canada **DISCIPLINE** HISTORY **EDUCATION** Univ Toronto, BA, 44, MA, 47, PhD, 58. **CAREER** Lectr to prof hist, McMaster Univ, 47-72, dept ch, 64-70; pres & vice chancellor, 73-87, PROF EMER, VICTORIA UNIV. **HONORS AND AWARDS** Can Coun jr res fel. **MEMBERSHIPS** Can Hist Asn; Am Hist Asn; CIIA; Soc Fr Hist Stud; Can Methodist Hist Soc. **SELECTED PUBLICATIONS** Auth, Parsons and Politics, 62; ed & contrib, Encyclopedia of World Methodism, 74; ed, The Churches and the Canadian Experience, 63; ed, The Shield of Achilles, 68; ed, Can Stud Hist Govt; ed-in-chief, Ont Hist Ser, 71-93. **CONTACT ADDRESS** Univ of Toronto, 73 Queen's Park Cr, Toronto, ON, Canada M5S 1K7.

FRENCH, HENRY P., JR
PERSONAL Born 11/21/1934, Rochester, NY, m, 1959, 4 children **DISCIPLINE** HISTORY, POLITICAL SCIENCE **EDUCATION** Univ Del, AB, 60; Univ Rochester, AM, 61; AMed, 62; EdD, 68. **CAREER** Chemn, Hist and Polit Sci Dept, SUNY Monroe Community Col, 79-85; Pres, Friends of the Rochester Public Libr, 88-91; Trustee Reynolds Libr Found, 91-; from Vice Pres to Pres, Rochester Public Libr, 96-00; Rochester Regional Libr Coun, 98-; Trustee, Rundel Libr Found, 99-; From Asst Prof to Prof, SUNY Monroe Community Col, 67-; **HONORS AND AWARDS** SUNY Bd of Trustees, Chancellor's Medal for Philanthropy Awd, 99. **MEMBERSHIPS** Asn for Asian Studies, Int Rochester Chapter, Int Asn of Historians of Asian. **RESEARCH** Chinese and Japanese Cultural History since 1800s. **SELECTED PUBLICATIONS** Coauth, China and Rochester, Easter 1990 and Beyond, Episcopal Diocese of Rochester (Rochester, NY), 91. **CONTACT ADDRESS** Dept Hist and Govt, Monroe Comm Col, 1000 E Henrietta Rd, Rochester, NY 14623-5701. **EMAIL** hfrench@monroe.edu

FRENCH, VALERIE
PERSONAL Born 01/16/1941, Toledo, OH, m, 1941, 4 children **DISCIPLINE** HISTORY **EDUCATION** Cornell Univ, BA, 64; UCLA, MA, 67; PhD, 71. **CAREER** Lectr to assoc prof and dept chair, Am Univ, 69-. **HONORS AND AWARDS** Woodrow Wilson Dissertation Fel, 69; NEH Fel, 79-80; Outstanding Teaching Awards, 72, 73, 75, 78, 86, 88; Outstanding Fac Admin Award, 81, 82. **MEMBERSHIPS** Am Hist Asn; Am Philol Asn; Archaeol Inst of Am; Asn of Ancient Hist; Class Asn of the Atlantic States; Class Asn of the Middle W and S; Wash Class Soc; Women's Class Caucus. **RESEARCH** Women in classical antiquity; Childrearing and parenting in the ancient world; Alexander the Great; Ancient Greek historians. **SELECTED PUBLICATIONS** Auth, "Children in Antiquity," in Children in Comparative and Historical Perspective, (Greenwood Pub, 90), 13-30; auth, "History of Parenting: The Ancient Mediterranean World," in Handbook of Parenting, Vol 2, (Lawrence Erlbaum, 95), 263-284; auth, "The Spartan Family and the Spartan Decline: Changes in Child-Rearing Practices and the Failure to Reform," in Polis and Polemos: Studies in Honor of Donald Kagan, (Regina Press, 97), 241-274; auth, "Aristophanes' Doting Dads: Adult Male Knowledge of Children," in Text and Tradition: Studies in Honor of Mortimer H. Chambers, (Regina Press, 99), 163-181. **CONTACT ADDRESS** Dept Hist, American Univ, Am Hist, Washington, DC 20016-8038. **EMAIL** vfrench@american.edu

FREY, LINDA
DISCIPLINE HISTORY **EDUCATION** Ohio State Univ, BS, 67; BA, 67; MA, 68; PhD, 71. **CAREER** Vis Lecturer, Denison Univ, 71; Asst Prof to Prof, Univ Mont, 71-; vis Prof, US Military Acad, 96-97. **HONORS AND AWARDS** Outstanding Civilian Service Medal, Dept of the Army, 97; Phi Kappa Phi, 94; Fel, Royal Hist Soc, 92; NEH travel grant, 91; Burlington Northern Awd, Univ Mont, 85; Outstanding Acad Book; Grant, Am Coun of Learned soc, USOE Fac Fel, Uralic and Inner Asian Lang and area Ctr, 80; NEH grant, 78-79; Univ Mont Res Grant, 74, 84, 87, 90; Delta Tau Kappa, 75; Outstanding Young Woman of the Year, 72; Nat Defense Educ Act Fel, 67-70; Stradley Scholarship, 64-67; Phi Beta Kappa, 67; Great Books Scholars Key Awd, 65; Alpha Lambda Delta, 65. **SELECTED PUBLICATIONS** Auth, The History of diplomatic Immunity, Ohio state Univ Press, 99; auth, The Treaties of the War of the Spanish succession, Greenwood Press, 95; auth, Women in Western European History: A Select Chronological, Geographical and Topical Bibliography - From Antiquity to the Present. Recent Research, Greenwood Press, 86; auth, women in Western European History: A Select Chronological, Geographical and Topical Bibliography - The Nineteenth and Twentieth Centuries, Greenwood Press, 84; auth, Friedrich I, the Man and His Times, Columbia Univ Press, 84; auth, "International Officials and the Standard of Diplomatic Privilege," Diplomacy and Statecraft, (98): 1-17; auth, "an Honest Messenger from the Past? An Examination of the National Standards for World History, (95): 25-31; auth, "A Matter of Asylum: European and south American Perspectives," History of European Ideas, (95): 81-88; auth, "Et Tu: Language and the French Revolution," History of European Ideas, (95): 505-510 **CONTACT ADDRESS** Dept Hist, Univ of Montana, Missoula, MT 59812.

FREY, MARSHA
DISCIPLINE HISTORY **EDUCATION** Ohio State Univ, BS, 67; BA, 67; MA, 68; PhD, 71. **CAREER** Lectr, Ore State Univ, 71-72; vis asst prof, Univ of Ore, 72-73; asst prof to prof, Kans State Univ, 73-. **HONORS AND AWARDS** Phi Kappa Phi; Phi Beta Kappa; NEH Grant, 77-78; ACLS Grant, 81; Choice Outstanding Acad Book, 82; MASUA Honors Lectr, 88-89; Am Philos Soc Grant, 90-91; Fulbright Grant, 94; 95-96; Fel, Royal Hist Soc, 92; Presidential Awd for Teaching Excellence, 97; Phi Alpha Theta Outstanding Book Awd, 00. **RESEARCH** War of the Spanish Succession, European diplomatic history. **SELECTED PUBLICATIONS** Coauth, A Question of Empire: Leopold I and the War of the Spanish Succession, 1701-1705, Columbia Univ Pr, 83; auth, Frederick I, The Man and His Times, Columbia Univ Pr, (NY), 84; coauth, Women in Western European History: A Select Chronological, Geographical, and Topical Bibliography from Antiquity to the Present: Recent Research, Greenwood Pr, (Westport), 86; coauth, Societies in Upheaval: Insurrections in France, Hungary, and Spain in the Early Eighteenth Century, Greenwood Pr, (Westport), 87; coauth, The Treaties of the War of the Spanish Succession: An Historical and Critical Dictionary, Greenwood Pr, (Westport), 95; auth, "A Diplomatic Analogy: International Functionaries and their Privileges", Diplomacy and Statecraft 93. (98): 1-17; coauth, "The History of Diplomatic Immunity, Part I and II", Ohio State Univ Pr, (Columbus, OH), 99; auth, "Maximillian I", Encycl of the Renaissance, (forthcoming); coed, Greenwood Guides to Historic Events, 1500-1900, (forthcoming). **CONTACT ADDRESS** Dept Hist, Kansas State Univ, Manhattan, KS 66506. **EMAIL** mfrey@ksu.edu

FREY, SLYVIA RAE
PERSONAL Born 05/03/1935, Eunice, LA **DISCIPLINE** AMERICAN AND BRITISH HISTORY **EDUCATION** Col Sacred Heart, BA, 56; La State Univ, MA, 65; Tulane Univ PhD (hist), 69. **CAREER** Teacher social studies, St Landry Parish Sch, 56-63 and Orleans Parish Sch, 63-66; instr, 69-72, asst prof, 72-81, Assoc Prof US Hist, Tulane Univ, 81-. **HONORS AND AWARDS** Moncado Prize, Am Mil Inst, 79. **RESEARCH** Colonial and revolutionary American history. **SELECTED PUBLICATIONS** Auth, The common British soldier in the late eighteenth century: A profile, Societas, spring 75; The British and the Black: A new perspective, Historian, 2/76; Courts and cats: British military justice in the eighteenth

century, Mil Affairs, 2/79; The British soldier in America, Univ Tex Press, 81; Between slavery and freedom, Virginia Blacks in the American Revolution, J Southern Hist (in press). **CONTACT ADDRESS** Dept Hist, Tulane Univ, 6823 St Charles Ave, New Orleans, LA 70118-5698.

FREYER, TONY ALLAN
PERSONAL Born 12/28/1947, Indianapolis, IN, m, 1976, 1 child **DISCIPLINE** HISTORY; LAW **EDUCATION** San Diego State Univ, AB, 70; Ind Univ, MA, 72, PhD, 75. **CAREER** Univ of Arkansas at Little Rock, 76-81; Univ Res Prof of History and Law, Univ of Ala, 81-. **HONORS AND AWARDS** University of Alabama's Burnum Distinguished fac awd, 92; sr Fulbright awd, Australia, 93; Abe Fellowship, Soc Sci Res Coun to Japan, 95-06; Harvard-Newcomer Postdoctoral Business History Fellow, Harvard Business School, 75-76; Research fellow, Charles Warren Center, Harvard Univ, 81-82; Sr. Fulbright Awd, United Kingdom, 1986; Fulbright Distinguished Chair, American Studies, Poland **RESEARCH** Legal history; Business History; History of Globalization. **SELECTED PUBLICATIONS** Auth, Forums of Order, 79; Harmony and Dissonance: The Swift and Erie Cases in American Federalism, 81; The Little Rock Crisis, 84; Justice Hugo L. Black and the Dilemma of American Liberalism, 90; Hugo L. Black and Modern America, 90; Regulating Big Business: Antitrust in Great Britain and America, 1880-1990, 92; Producers versus Capitalists: Constitutional Conflict in Antebellum America, 94; coauth, for Democracy and Judicial Independence, 95; auth, Defending Constitutional Rights: Frank M. Johnson, 01; auth, Rights Defied: Copper v. Aaron, the Little Rock Crisis, and America's Civil Rights Struggle, 04. **CONTACT ADDRESS** Law Dept, Univ of Alabama, Tuscaloosa, Box 870000, Tuscaloosa, AL 35487-0383. **EMAIL** tfreyer@law.ua.edu

FRIED, RICHARD M.
PERSONAL Born 04/14/1941, Milwaukee, WI, m, 1964, 2 children **DISCIPLINE** RECENT UNITED STATES HISTORY **EDUCATION** Amherst Col, BA, 63; Columbia Univ, MA, 65, PhD (hist), 72. **CAREER** Instr hist, Bowling Green State Univ, 67-70; vis assoc prof, Indiana Univ Pa, 70-71; asst prof, Fairmont State Col, 71-72; asst dept chmn, Univ Ill, Chicago Circle, 75-77; dir grad studies, Univ Ill, Chicago Circle, 79-81; from asst prof hist to prof, Univ Ill, Chicago Circle, 72-. **HONORS AND AWARDS** Phi Beta Kappa, 63. **MEMBERSHIPS** AHA; Orgn Am Hists. **RESEARCH** Recent American political history; McCarthy era. **SELECTED PUBLICATIONS** Auth, Men Against McCarthy, Columbia Univ Pr, 76; auth, Nightmare in Red, Oxford, 90; auth, The Russians Are Coming! The Russians Are Coming! Pageantry and Patriotism in Cold-War Am, Oxford, 98. **CONTACT ADDRESS** Dept of Hist, Univ of Illinois, Chicago, Chicago, IL 60680. **EMAIL** rmfried@uic.edu

FRIEDEL, ROBERT D.
PERSONAL Born 05/24/1950, Birmingham, AL **DISCIPLINE** HISTORY **EDUCATION** Brown Univ, AB, 71; Univ of London, MSc, 72; Johns Hopkins Univ, PhD, 77. **CAREER** Historian, Smithsonian Inst, 76-79; Dir, IEEE Center for Hist of Electrical Engineering, 80-84; prof, Dept of Hist, Univ Md, 84-. **MEMBERSHIPS** Soc for Hist of Technol. **RESEARCH** Technology, invention, environment-history. **SELECTED PUBLICATIONS** Auth, Edison's Electirc Light: A Biogaphy of an Invention, Rutgers Univ Press, 86; auth, "Crazy About Rubber," Am Heritage of invention & Tech 5, Winter 90; auth, Zipper: An Exploration in Novelty, WW Norton & Co, 94. **CONTACT ADDRESS** Dept Hist, Univ of Maryland, Col Park, 2115 F S Key Hall, College Park, MD 20742. **EMAIL** rf27@umail.edu

FRIEDLANDER, WALTER J.
PERSONAL Born 06/06/1919, Los Angeles, CA, m, 1976, 3 children **DISCIPLINE** MEDICAL ETHICS AND HISTORY **EDUCATION** Univ Calif, Berkeley, AB, 41; Univ Calif, San Francisco, MD, 45. **CAREER** Asst prof med, Sch Med, Stanford Univ, 54-56; asst prof neurol, Col Med, Boston Univ, 56-61; from assoc to prof neurol, Albany Med Col, 61-66; dir, Ctr Humanities and Med, 75-80, PROF NEUROL, COL MED, UNIV NEBR, 66-, Prof and Chmn Dept Med Humanities, 80-, Regional humanist, Nebr Comt for Humanities, 76-; consult, Nat Libr Med, 79-. **MEMBERSHIPS** Fel Am Col Physicians; Acad Aphasia. **RESEARCH** Medical history; applied medical ethics; medical sociology. **SELECTED PUBLICATIONS** Auth, The Evolution of Informed Consent in American Medicine, Perspectives Biol Med, Vol 38, 95. **CONTACT ADDRESS** Col of Med, Univ of Nebraska, Omaha, Omaha, NE 68105.

FRIEDMAN, EDWARD
PERSONAL Born 12/12/1937, New York, NY, m, 1969, 2 children **DISCIPLINE** POLITICAL SCIENCE, EAST ASIA **EDUCATION** Brandeis Univ, BA (Political Sci), 59; Harvard Univ, MA (East Asia), 61; PhD (Political Sci), 68. **CAREER** To prof, Dept of Political Science, Univ Wis, 67-; res fel, Univ Mich, spring 68; teaching, Harvard Univ, summers 68, 69, 71; res fel, MUCIA, Hong Kong, 70; res fel, Center for Advanced Study, Univ Ill, 71; fac, NYU, SUNY-Purchase, CUNY-Brooklyn, 71-72; SSRC, res grant, 73; consult, China Trade Services, fall 80; staff, US House of Representatives, Committee on Foreign Affairs, Jan 81-July 83; advisor, United Nations Develoment prog, Aug 83; lect, USAI: Australia, South Korea, Hong Kong, Burma, France, summer 84; Wang Found Res fel, 85; Guggenheim fel, 86-87; seminar, China and the Pacific Rim, Univ CA, La Jolla, summer 87; NEH fac seminar leader, summer 90; US AID, Albania, summer 92; US Dept of the Defense, consult, 93-94; US Naval Postgraduate School, Monterey, summer week, 93; US Naval Postgraduate School, summer sem, 94. **HONORS AND AWARDS** Phi Beta Kappa; Fels from Woodrow Wilson, Ford, Fulbright-Hays, Guggenheim; Book titled Chinese Village, Socialist State named best book on modern China for 1991 by AAS. **MEMBERSHIPS** AAS; APSA; AI. **RESEARCH** Democratization; International political economy; Leninist transitions; Revolution; US-Asian relations; Chinese politics. **SELECTED PUBLICATIONS** Auth, America's Asia, Pantheon; auth, Backward Toward Revolution, California; auth, Chinese Village, Socialist State China, Yale Univ Press, 91; auth, National Identity and Democratic Prospects in Socialist China, Sharpe; auth, The Politics of Democratization, ed, Westview; auth, What if China Doesn't Democratize? Implications for War and Peace, Routledge; auth, Revolution, Resistance, and Reform in Village China, fothcoming. **CONTACT ADDRESS** Dept of Political Science, Univ of Wisconsin, Madison, North Hall, Madison, WI 53706-1389. **EMAIL** friedman@polisci.wisc.edu

FRIEDMAN, ELLEN G.
PERSONAL Born 03/08/1939, New York, NY, 1 child **DISCIPLINE** SPANISH & EUROPEAN HISTORY **EDUCATION** NYork Univ, BA, 67; City Univ New York, PhD (hist), 75. **CAREER** Asst prof hist, Univ Ky, 75-78; Asst Prof Hist, Boston Col, 78-, Res grant, Joint Span-US Comt Educ and Cult Affairs, 78-79. **MEMBERSHIPS** Soc Span and Port Hist Studies (secy, 80-82); AHA; N Am Catalan Soc. **RESEARCH** Early modern Spanish social history; history of public health. **SELECTED PUBLICATIONS** Auth, The exercise of religion by Spanish captives in North Africa, Sixteenth Century J, 75; North African piracy on the coasts of Spain in the seventeenth century: A new perspective on the expulsion of the Moriscos, Int Hist Rev, 79; Christian captives at hard labor in North Africa, 16th-18th centuries, Int J African Hist Studies, 80; Trinitarian hospitals in Algiers: An early example of health care for prisoners of war, Cath Hist Rev, 80; Spanish Captives in North Africa in the Early Modern Age, Univ Wis Press, 83. **CONTACT ADDRESS** Dept of Hist, Boston Col, Chestnut Hill, 140 Commonwealth Ave, Chestnut Hill, MA 02167-3800.

FRIEDMAN, HAL M.
PERSONAL Born 12/24/1965, Trenton, MI, m, 1989, 1 child **DISCIPLINE** HISTORY **EDUCATION** E Mich Univ, BS, 87; Mich State Univ, MA, 91; PhD, 95. **CAREER** Instructor, Henry Ford Cmty Col, 96-. **HONORS AND AWARDS** Pi Sigma Alpha, 87-88; Phi Kappa Phi, 87-88; Fel, MI State Univ, 89, 90, 92, 95; Travel Grant, MI State Univ, 93, 94; Res Grant, Harry S. Truman Library Inst, 94, 95; Visiting Fel, Univ Windsor, 95; who's Who in the Midwest; Who's Who in Am; 2000 Outstanding Scholars of the 20th Century; Dictionary of Intl Biography. **MEMBERSHIPS** Omohundro Inst for Early Am Hist and Culture; World Hist Asn; Am Hist Asn; Org of Am Hist; Soc for Military Hist; Soc for Hist of Am For Relations. **RESEARCH** Red, White, and Black in the Motor City: Teaching the Early American Survey at a Comprehensive Metro Detroit Community College. **SELECTED PUBLICATIONS** Auth, "Arguing over Empire: American Interservice and Interdepartmental Rivalry over Micronesia, 1945-1947," The Journal of Pacific History, (94): 36-48; auth, "The Limitations of Collective Security: The United States and the Micronesian Trusteeship, 1945-1947," ISLA: A Journal of Micronesian Studies, (95): 339-370; auth, "Collective Bargaining, Shared Governance, and Professional Life at Henry Ford community College," Organization of American Historians Newsletter, (96): 9; auth, "Modified Mahanism: Pearl Harbor, the Pacific War, and Changes to U.S. National Security Strategy in the Pacific Basin, 1945-1947," The Hawaiian Journal of History, (97): 179-204; auth, "An Open Door in Paradise?: United States Strategic Security and Economic Policy in the Pacific Islands, 1945-1947," Pacific Studies, (97): 63-87; auth, "Races Undesirable from a Military Point of View: United States Cultural Security in the Pacific Islands, 1945-1947," The Journal of Pacific History, (97): 49-70; auth, "Painting Societal Portraits: One Approach to Teaching Critical Reading and Writing," Teaching History: A Journal of Methods, (97): 64-72; auth, "The Bear in the Pacific?: U.S. Intelligence Perceptions of Soviet Strategic Power Projection in the Pacific Basin and East Asia, 1945-1947," Intelligence and National Security, (97): 75-101; auth, "Americanism and Strategic Security: The Pacific Basin, 1943-1947," in American Diplomacy, Chapel Hill, 97; auth, "Truk," "Lieutenant Colonel Earl H. Pete Ellis, United States Marine Corps," "Admiral Jesse B. Oldendorf, United States Navy," The Kurile Islands," "Admiral Thomas c. Hart, United States Navy," and "American Airborne Operation in the Pacific War," in Garland's Encyclopedia of the Wars of the United States: World War II in the Pacific, Garland Pub, forthcoming. **CONTACT ADDRESS** Dept Soc Sci, Henry Ford Comm Col, 5101 Evergreen Rd, Dearborn, MI 48128-2407. **EMAIL** friedman@hanryford.cc.mi.us

FRIEDMAN, JEAN E.
DISCIPLINE HISTORY **EDUCATION** Moravian, BA, 63; Lehigh, MA, 67, PhD, 76. **CAREER** Assoc Prof, Hist, Univ Geor. **MEMBERSHIPS** Am Antiquarian Soc **CONTACT ADDRESS** 1141 hickory Hill Dr., Watkinsville, GA 30677-2122.

FRIEDMAN, JEROME
PERSONAL Born 02/05/1943, New York, NY **DISCIPLINE** MODERN EUROPEAN HISTORY, RENAISSANCE HISTORY **EDUCATION** Hebrew Univ Jerusalem, BA, 67; Univ Wis-Madison, MA, 68, PhD (hist), 71. **CAREER** Asst prof, 70-76, Assoc Prof Hist, Kent State Univ, 76-, Dir Jewish Studies, 77-, Lectr, Hillel Found Free Univ Kent State Univ, 73; mem, Ohio Renaissance-Reformation Forum; Nat Endowment for Humanities fel, 78. **MEMBERSHIPS** Am Soc Reformation Res; Sixteenth Century Studies Conf. **RESEARCH** Antitrinitarianism; Jewish-Christian dialogue; Reformation studies, Reformation radicalism. **SELECTED PUBLICATIONS** Coauth, The Crisis of Reformation: Confrontation and Conciliation, Kendall/Hunt Publishing Co. (Dubuque, Iowa), 75; auth, Michael Servetus: A Case Study in Total Heresy, Droz Press (Geneva, Switzerland), 78; auth, The Most Ancient Testimony: Sixteenth-century Christian-Hebraica in the Age of Renaissance Nostalgia, Ohio Univ Press (Athens), 83; auth, Blasphemy, Immortality, and Anarchy: The Ranters and the English Revolution, Ohio Univ press (Athens), 87; ed, Regnum, Religion et Ratio. Essays Presented to Robert M. Kingdon, Sixteenth Century Jour Press (Mo), 87; auth, The Battle of the Frogs and Fairford's Flies: Miracles and the Pulp Press During the English Revolution, St. Martin's Press (New York), 93; auth, The New Subminature Camera Darkroom Guide, 96; auth, the Complete Half Frame Guide: A History and Guide to 18x12 mm and 24x24mm Half Frame Cameras, 98. **CONTACT ADDRESS** Dept of Hist, Kent State Univ, PO Box 5190, Kent, OH 44242-0001. **EMAIL** smallcameraco@yahoo.com

FRIEDMAN, LAWRENCE JACOB
PERSONAL Born 10/08/1940, Cleveland, OH, m, 1966, 1 child **DISCIPLINE** AMERICAN HISTORY **EDUCATION** Univ Calif, Riverside, BA, 62; Los Angeles, MA, 65; PhD (hist), 67. **CAREER** Acting instr hist, Univ Calif, Los Angeles, 67; asst prof, Ind Univ, Ft Wayne, 67-68; asst prof, Ariz State Univ, 68-71; assoc prof, 71-77, Prof Hist and Am Studies, Bowling Green State Univ, 77-, Ind Univ fac res grant, 68; Nat Endowment for Humanities Younger Humanist fel, 71-72; res grant, Am Coun Learned Soc, 76; Nat Endowment for Humanities fel, 79-80; Ed Advisor, Black Abolitionist Papers Project, 83-90; Coordinator of Graduate Studies in Hist, Bowling Green State Univ, 89-93; Vis Scholar, Hist Sci Dept, Harvard Univ, 91; Prof of Hist, Indiana Univ, 93-; Consulting Ed, Hist Psychology, 96-. **HONORS AND AWARDS** Runner-up, Bancroft Book Prize, 91; Distinguished Univ Prof, Bowling Green State Univ, 91-93; Res Fel, Nat Endowment for the Humanities, 86-87, 94-95; Lilly Endowment Major Projects Res Grant, 98; John Adams Fel, Inst of United States, Univ of London, 99; Fel, Wellcome Inst for the Hist of Medicine, 99. **MEMBERSHIPS** Orgn Am Hists; Am Studies Asn; Group Use Psychol in Hist. **RESEARCH** American intellectual and Cultural History; History of American Philanthropy. **SELECTED PUBLICATIONS** Auth, The White Savage: Racial Fantasies in the Postbellum South, Prentice-Hall (Englewood Cliffs), 70; auth, Inventors of the Promised Land, 75; auth, Gregarious Saints: Self and Community in American Abolitionism, 1830-1870, Cambridge Univ Pr (Cambridge, New York), 82; auth, Menninger: The Family and the Clinic, Alfred A. Knopf (New York), 90; auth, "Erik Erikson's Critical Themes and Voices: The Task of Synthesis," in American Culture Critics, ed. David Murray, (Exeter, Univ of Exeter Pr, 95), 173-92; auth, "Psychological Advice in the Public Realm in America, 1940-1970: A Study in Mutability," Contemporary Psychology, 41 (96): 219-222; auth, "A Department's Advocacy Becomes Business as Usual," OAH Newsletter (96): 23-25; auth, 'Erik Erikson and Robert Lifton: The Pattern of a Relationship," in Trauma and Self, ed. Charles Strozier and Michael Flynn (Savage, Md, Rowman & Littlefield, 96), 131-150; auth, "Erik Erikson on Revolutionary Leadership: Thematic Trajectories," Contemporary Psychology 42 (97): 1063-1067; auth, Identity's Architect: A Biography of Erik Erikson, Scribner, 99. **CONTACT ADDRESS** Dept of Hist, Indiana Univ, Bloomington, 1020 E Kirkwood, 742 Ballantine Hall, Bloomington, IN 47405-7103. **EMAIL** ljfriedm@indiana.edu

FRIEDMAN, MURRAY
DISCIPLINE AMERICAN JEWISH HISTORY, AMERICAN SOCIAL AND POLITICAL HISTORY **EDUCATION** Georgetown Univ, PhD. **CAREER** Prof, dir, Myer and Rosaline Feinstein Ctr Am Jewish Hist, Temple Univ; lectr, US Infor Agency, African and India, 74; vice-ch, US Civil Rights Comn, DC, 86-89. **MEMBERSHIPS** Mid Atlantic States dir, Am Jewish Comt. **RESEARCH** Am Jewish Hist; Am Social and Political Hist. **SELECTED PUBLICATIONS** Auth, Overcoming Middle Class Rage, The Westminster Press, 71; Jewish Life in Philadelphia, 1830-1940, ISHI Publ, 83; The Utopian Dilemma: American Judaism in Public Policy, Ethics and Pub Policy Ctr, 85; Philadelphia Jewish Life: 1940 to 1985, Seth Press, 86; When Philadelphia Was the Capital of Jewish America, Assoc UP, 93; What Went Wrong: The Creation and Collapse of the

Black-Jewish Alliance, the Free Press, 95. **CONTACT ADDRESS** Temple Univ, Philadelphia, PA 19122.

FRIEDMAN, SAUL S.
PERSONAL Born 03/08/1937, Uniontown, PA, m, 1964, 3 children **DISCIPLINE** HOLOCAUST & MIDDLE EAST EDUCATION **EDUCATION** Kent State Univ, BA, 59; Ohio State Univ, MA, 62, PhD (hist), 69. **CAREER** Asst prof, 69-74, assoc prof, 74-80, Prof Hist, Youngstown State Univ, 80-; Univ Res Prof, Youngstown State, 76; dir, Holocaust and Judaic Studies prog, 98-. **HONORS AND AWARDS** Ohio Humanties Council Lifetime Achievement Awd, 98; Cleveland Regional Emmy Awds, 86, 88, 89, 91, 97; Brandeis Awd, Youngstown Zionist Dist, 89; Triumphant Spirit Awd for Edu, 99; Distinguished Univ Prof, YSU, 76, 82, 86, 90, 92. **MEMBERSHIPS** NEA. **RESEARCH** Holocaust; Zionism and Arab nationalism; Jews in Arab lands. **SELECTED PUBLICATIONS** auth, No Haven for the Oppressed: Official U.S. Policy toward European Jewish Refugees, 1933-1945, Wayne State, 72; auth, Pogromchik: The Assassination of Simon Petlura, Hart, 76; auth, The Incident at Massena: The Blood Livel in American, Stein & Day, 78; auth, Amcha: An Oral Testament of the Holocaust, Univ Press of Am, 79; auth, Land of Dust: Palestine at the turn of the Century, Univ Press, 82; auth, The Oberammergau Passion Play: A Lance against Civilization, Southern IL, 84; auth, Without Future: The Plight of Syrian Jewry, Praeger, 89; auth, The Terezin Diary of Gonda Redlich, Kentucky, 92; auth, Holocaust Literature, Greenwood, 94; auth, Jews and the American Slave Trade, Transaction, 97. **CONTACT ADDRESS** Dept of Hist, Youngstown State Univ, One University Plz, Youngstown, OH 44555-0002.

FRIEND, DONALD A.
PERSONAL Born 06/26/1960, San Francisco, CA, m, 1 child **DISCIPLINE** GEOGRAPHY **EDUCATION** Univ Cal, Berkeley, BA; 84; Univ Colorado, Boulder, MA, 88; Arizona State Univ, PhD, 97. **CAREER** Asst prof, prog dir, Minnesota State Univ, 97-. **HONORS AND AWARDS** J Warren Nystrom Awd, 99. **MEMBERSHIPS** AAG. **RESEARCH** Geomorphology; mountain environments; geographic and earth systems science education. **SELECTED PUBLICATIONS** Refereed, "Announcing tile Formation of a Mountain Geography Specialty Group," AAG Newsletter 34 (99):7-lO; ref, "Mountain Chronicle." Mountain Res Dev 19 (99): 167-168; ref, "Memoriam, Kirk H. Stone, I9l4-1997," Annals of the Asn Am Geographers 89 (99): 535-548; ref, "On Geography, Town and Global Awareness, " Alumni Magazine and Annual Report of Town School for Boys (97); ref, "Ice on the Equator: From the Beach to Glaciers in East Africa," in Locations, Patterns, and Regions: Introduction to Geography, eds. Miriam Lo, Carol Gersmehl, Martin Mitchell (WCB/McGraw Hill Custom Pub, 98); ref, "Revisiting William Morris Davis and Walther Penck to Purpose a General Model of Slope "Evolution" in Deserts" The Professional Geo 52 (00): 164-178. **CONTACT ADDRESS** Dept Geography, Minnesota State Univ, Mankato, 7 Armstrong Hall, Mankato, MN 56001. **EMAIL** friend@mankato.msus.edu

FRIEND, THEODORE W.
PERSONAL Born 08/27/1931, Wilkinsburg, PA, m, 1960, 3 children **DISCIPLINE** MODERN HISTORY **EDUCATION** Williams Col, BA, 53; Yale Univ, MA, 54, PhD, 58. **CAREER** Asst Instr Hist, Yale Univ, 55-57; from asst prof to prof, State Univ NY, Buffalo, 59-73, fac adv to pres, 68-69, exec asst to pres, 69-70; Pres, Swarthmore Col, 73-90, Am Philos Soc grant-in-aid, Philippines & Japan, 58; Rockefeller Found fel int rels, 61-62; Nat Defense Foreign Lang Act fel, Indonesia, 66-67; Guggenheim Found fel, Indonesia, Philippines & Japan, 67-68; nat consult, Nat Endowment for Humanities, 74-. **HONORS AND AWARDS** Bancroft Awd Am Hist, Diplomacy & Foreign Rels, 66; lld, williams col, 78. **MEMBERSHIPS** AHA; Asn Asian Studies; Soc Historians of Am Foreign Rels. **RESEARCH** History of American foreign relations; Southeast Asian history; Japanese imperialism. **SELECTED PUBLICATIONS** Auth, Between Two Empires: The Ordeal of the Philippines, 1929-1946, Yale Univ, 65; ed, The Philippine Polity: A Japanese View, Yale Southeast Asia Publ, 68. **CONTACT ADDRESS** Swarthmore Col, Swarthmore, PA 19081.

FRIER, BRUCE W.
PERSONAL Born 08/31/1943, Chicago, IL, s **DISCIPLINE** HISTORY OF LAW, CLASSICAL STUDIES **EDUCATION** Trinity Col, BA, 64; Fel, Am Acad in Rome, 68; Princeton Univ, PhD, 70. **CAREER** Asst prof to prof, Univ Mich, 69-. **HONORS AND AWARDS** Fel, Am Coun of Learned Soc; Fel, NEH, 76-77; Goodwin Awd, Am Philol Asn, 83; Guggenheim Fel, 84-85; Fel, Clare Hall, 84-85; Fel, NEH, 92-93; Fel, Am Acad of Arts and Sci, 93-; LS and A Excellence in Res Awd, 96. **MEMBERSHIPS** Am Philol Asn; Am Soc for Legal Hist. **RESEARCH** Roman law and legal history; Roman social, economic, and demographic history; Hellenistic and Roman historiography, especially Polybius, Sallust, and Livy; Legal theory and the sociology of law; Classical and modern rhetoric. **SELECTED PUBLICATIONS** Co-auth, The Demography of Roman Egypt, Cambridge Univ Press, 94; co-auth, The Census Register P.Oxy 984: The Reverse of Pindar's Paeans, Univ Brussels, 97; auth, Libri Annales Pontificum Maximorum: The Origins of the Annalistic Tradition, rev ed, Univ Mich Press, 99; co-auth, A Casebook on Roman Family Law, Scholars Press, (forthcoming); auth, Roman Law and the Social Sciences, Verlag, (forthcoming). **CONTACT ADDRESS** Sch of Law, Univ of Michigan, Ann Arbor, Univ Mich, Ann Arbor, MI 48109-1215. **EMAIL** bwfrier@umich.edu

FRIERSON, CATHY A.
DISCIPLINE RUSSIA AND THE SOVIET UNION, INTELLECTUAL HISTORY, WESTERN CIVILIZATION **EDUCATION** Harvard Univ, PhD. **CAREER** Assoc prof, Univ NH, 91-. **HONORS AND AWARDS** NEH summer stipend, 92; Hist Stud fel, Inst for Adv Stud, 93-95. **RESEARCH** Rural Russia; law and society in Russia. **SELECTED PUBLICATIONS** Auth, Peasant Icons: Representations of Rural People in Late Nineteenth Century Russia, 93; ed and transl, Aleksandr Nikolaevich Engelgardt: Letters from the Country, 1872-1887, 93. **CONTACT ADDRESS** Univ of New Hampshire, Durham, Durham, NH 03824. **EMAIL** cathyf@christa.unh.edu

FRIES, RUSSELL INSLEE
PERSONAL Born 05/15/1941, Glen Ridge, NJ, m, 1970 **DISCIPLINE** HISTORY OF SCIENCE & ECONOMIC HISTORY **EDUCATION** Yale Univ, BA, 63; Johns Hopkins Univ, MA, 67, PhD (econ hist), 72. **CAREER** Asst prof hist, Southern Methodist Univ, 70-73; asst prof, 73-78, Assoc Prof Hist, Univ Maine, Orono, 78-, Proj hist, Hist Am Eng Rec, Nat Parks Serv, Dept Interior, 73; dir, Great Falls Hist Dist, 75-76. **HONORS AND AWARDS** Abbott Payson Usher Prize, Soc Hist Technol, 76. **MEMBERSHIPS** AHA; Soc Hist Technol; Soc Indust Archaeol; Hist Sci Soc; Econ Hist Asn. **RESEARCH** Nineteenth Century industrial development and technology; maritime navigation and technology; hydroelectric development. **SELECTED PUBLICATIONS** Auth, The Jours of Gorgas, Josiah, 1857-1878, Technology and Culture, Vol 37, 96; The Jours of Gorgas, Josiah, 1857-1878, Tech Cult, Vol 37, 96. **CONTACT ADDRESS** Dept of Hist, Univ of Maine, Orono, ME 04473.

FRIGUGLIETTI, JAMES
PERSONAL Born 07/23/1936, Cleveland, OH **DISCIPLINE** FRENCH HISTORY **EDUCATION** Western Reserve Univ, BA, 58; Harvard Univ, PhD (hist), 66. **CAREER** Teaching Fel, Harvard Univ, 64-66; Asst prof hist, Univ Rochester, 66-69 and Case Western Reserve Univ, 69-76; asst prof, Eastern Montana Col, 76-78, Assoc prof, 78-82, prof, 82-94; Prof, Montana State Univ-Billings, 94. **HONORS AND AWARDS** Fulbright Grant, 58-59; Soc Sci Res Coun Res Training Fel, 63-64; Res Merit Awd, Eastern Mont Col, 77; Nat Endowment for Humanities fel, 77-82; Distinguished Teacher Awd, Mont State Col, 79, 00, Distinguished Scholar Awd, 83; Nat Endowment for the Humanities Summer Stipend, 87; Nat Endowment for the Humanities Summer Institute, 99. **MEMBERSHIPS** AHA; Soc Fr Hist Studies; West Soc Fr Hist. **RESEARCH** Historiography of French Revolution. **SELECTED PUBLICATIONS** Auth, "To the End of the Line: Why Richard Cobb Abandoned the Study of the French Revolution," Consortium on Revolutinary Europe, 1750-1850, Selected Papers, (98): 29-37; auth, "Jean Poperen," French Historical Studies, 3 (98): 499; auth, "Alphonse Aulard, Emmanuel Le Roy Ladurie, Georges Lefebvre, Albert Mathiez, and Albert Soboul," in D.R. Woolf, A Global Encyclopedia of Historicl Writing 2, New York and London (98); auth, "Fawn McKay Brodie," in Kenneth T. Jackson, The Scribner Encyclopedia of American Lives, 1981-1985, New York: Charles Scribner's Sons (98): 104-106; auth, "Jean Galtier-Boissiere, Henri Jeanson, Francois de La Rocque, and Lucien Romier," in Bertram M. Gordon, Historical Dictionary of World War II: The Occupation, Vichy, and the Resistance, 1938-1946 Westport, Conn.: Greenwood Press, (98); auth, "How George Frederick Elliot Rude Became the Historian George Rude," The Sphinx in the Tuileries and Other Essays in Modern French History, Sydney, Australia: Univ of Sydney (99): 49-55; "Rehabilitationg Robespierre: Albert Mathiez and Georges Lefebvre as Defenders of the Incorruptible," Robespierre, Cambridge, Eng.: Cambridge Univ Press (99): 212-23; auth, "Jacques Godechot" and "George Rude," in Kelly Boyd, Encyclopedia of Historians and Historical Writing, London and Chicago: Fitzroy Dearborn (99); "George Lincoln Burr, Bernard B. Fall, Garrett Mattingly, and James Harvey," in John A Garraty and Mark C. Carnes, American National Biography 24, New York and Oxford: Oxford Univ Press (99). **CONTACT ADDRESS** Dept of Hist, Montana State Univ, Billings, Billings, MT 59101.

FRINTA, MOJMIR SVATOPLUK
PERSONAL Born 07/28/1922, Prague, Czechoslovakia, m, 1948, 3 children **DISCIPLINE** ART HISTORY **EDUCATION** Karlova Univ, Prague, AB, 47; Univ Mich, MA, 53, PhD(art hist), 60. **CAREER** From asst prof to assoc prof, 63-69, prof Hist of Art, 69-93, emeritus, 93- , SUNY Albany; Am Philos Soc grants, 64 & 65; Am Coun Learned Soc grant, 68; S H Kress grant, 70; Nat Endowment for Humanities grant, 77; consult, Soc Sci & Humanities Res Coun Can. **HONORS AND AWARDS** Sr fel, Ctr for Advan Study, Washington, 84-85; Fulbright Fel to Yugoslavia, 87. **MEMBERSHIPS** Col Art Asn Am; Soc Am Archaeol; Int Inst Conserv Hist & Artistic Works; Int Ctr Medieval Art; Medieval Acad of Am. **RESEARCH** Fourteenth century painting and sculpture; 15th century Netherlandish painting; medieval art technology. **SELECTED PUBLICATIONS** Auth, The master of the Gerona Martyrology and Bohemian Illumination, 64 & An investigation of the punched decoration of medieval .. panel paintings, 65, Art Bull; The Genius of Robert Campin, Mouton, The Hague, 66; The authorship of the Merode Altarpiece, Art Quart, 68; A Seemingly Florentine yet not really Florentine altar-piece, Burlington Mag, 75; The puzzling raised decorations in the paintings of Magister Theodoric, Simiolus, 76; Deletions from the Oeuvre of Pietro Lorenzetti and related works, Mitteilungen des Kunsthistorischen Insts in Florenz, 76; The quest for a restorer's shop of beguiling invention: Restorations and forgeries in Italian panel painting, Art Bull, 3/78; auth, Punched Decoration on Late Medieval Panel and Miniature Painting, part I: Catalogue, Maxdorf, 98. **CONTACT ADDRESS** 12222. **EMAIL** frinta@juno.com

FRITZ, HARRY WILLIAM
PERSONAL Born 09/28/1937, Salisbury, MD, m, 1966, 2 children **DISCIPLINE** EARLY AMERICAN HISTORY **EDUCATION** Dartmouth Col, AB, 60; Mont State Univ, MA, 62; Wash Univ, PhD (hist), 71. **CAREER** Instr hist, Univ Col, Wash Univ, 63-66; from instr to assoc prof, 67-80, Prof Hist, Univ Mont, 80-. **MEMBERSHIPS** AHA; Orgn Am Hists; Western Soc Sci Asn; Soc Hists Early Am Republic; Southern Hist Asn. **RESEARCH** United States, 1789-1840; political parties; Montana. **SELECTED PUBLICATIONS** Auth, Racism and Democracy in Tocqueville's America, Soc Sci J, 10/76; War Hawks of 1812, Capitol Studies, spring 77; The Historical Literature of Montana, Mont Mag Western Hist, winter 82. **CONTACT ADDRESS** Dept of Hist, Univ of Montana, Missoula, MT 59812-0001.

FRITZ, HENRY EUGENE
PERSONAL Born 06/20/1927, Garrison, KS, m, 1950, 3 children **DISCIPLINE** AMERICAN HISTORY **EDUCATION** Bradley Univ, BS, 50, MA, 52; Univ Minn, PhD, 57. **CAREER** Instr Am hist, Univ Wis, Milwaukee, 56-58; from asst prof to assoc prof, 58-68, Prof Hist, St Olaf Col, 68-, Chmn Dept, 69-84. **HONORS AND AWARDS** Fac fel, Newberry Libr Sem in Humanities, Assoc Cols, Midwest, 68-69; Hon Life Membership, Western Hist Asn, 97. **MEMBERSHIPS** AHA; Orgn Am Hists; Western Hist Asn. **RESEARCH** American Indian policies and administration; development of American nationalism, 1800-1850; frontier and territorial expansion of the United States. **SELECTED PUBLICATIONS** Auth, "Last Hurrah of Humanitarian Ind Reform: Bd of Ind Com, 1909-18", Western Hist, Quarterly, 85; auth, The Fox Wars--The Mesquakie Challenge to New, Hist, Vol 57, 95; They Called it Prairie Light--The Story of Chilocco Indian School, J Am Hist, Vol 82, 95; American Indian Treaties--The History of a Political Anomaly, Pac Northwest Quart, Vol 87, 96; An American Dilemma--Administration of the Indian Estate Under the Dawesm Act and Amendments, J Southwest, Vol 37, 95; auth, "Humanitarian Rhetoric and Andrew Jackson's Indian Removal Policy", Chronicles of Oklahoma, 01 **CONTACT ADDRESS** Dept of Hist, St. Olaf Col, Northfield, MN 55057. **EMAIL** fritzh@redwing.net

FRITZ, ROBERT B.
PERSONAL Born 07/13/1929, Bridgeport, CT **DISCIPLINE** ART EDUCATION **EDUCATION** Syracuse Univ, BA, 51; Columbia Univ, MA, 52, Doctorate in Ed, 63. **CAREER** Prof Fine Arts, 61-92, Fitchburg State College; prof emer. **HONORS AND AWARDS** Emeritus Prof. **RESEARCH** American Architecture. **CONTACT ADDRESS** 30 Clover Lea Place, Stratford, CT 06615.

FRITZ, STEPHEN G.
PERSONAL Born 02/21/1949 **DISCIPLINE** HISTORY **EDUCATION** Univ Ill, BA, 71, MA, 73, PhD, 80; Goethe Inst, Zertifikat II, 77-78; Univ Heidelberg, Immatirkulation, 77-78. **CAREER** Tchg asst, 74-77, res asst, 78-79, vis instr, 80, Univ Ill; instr, Richland Col, 78; mgmt staff, Ill Res Ctr, 79-80; vis asst prof, Southern Ill Univ, 80-83; from asst prof to assoc prof to prof, 84-, East Tenn State Univ. **HONORS AND AWARDS** List of Excellent Teachers, Univ Ill, 76-77; Res Fel, German Acad Exchange Service, 77-78; List of Excellent Teachers, 80-83, Queen Awd, 83, Southern Ill Univ; Summer Res Grant, 85, 91, ETSU Res and Development Committee; Col of Arts and Sciences Res Awd, 96; Distinguished Univ Fac Res Awd, 96; distinction on phd exam. **MEMBERSHIPS** German Stud Asn; Conference Group Central European Hist; Soc German-Am Stud; European Hist Section, Southern Hist Asn; Fulbright Alumni Asn; Phi Alpha Theta; Delta Phi Alpha; Omicron Delta Kappa. **RESEARCH** Germany in World War II; Post-war Germany; Nazi Germany **SELECTED PUBLICATIONS** Auth, art, Benito Mussolini and Kaiser Wilhelm II, 91; auth, art, Frankfurt, 92; auth, Frontsoldaten: The German Soldier in World War II, 95; auth, Hitler's Frontsoldaten: Der erzahlte Krieg, 98; auth, art, We are trying to change the face of the world. Ideology and Motivation in the Wehrmacht on the Eastern Front: The View Fom Below, 98; auth, This is the Way Wars End With a Bang not a Whimper: Middle Franconia in April 45, 00. **CONTACT ADDRESS** Dept of History, East Tennessee State Univ, Box 70672, Johnson City, TN 37614-0672. **EMAIL** fritzs@etsu.edu

FRITZE, RONALD H.
DISCIPLINE HISTORY **EDUCATION** Concordia Univ, BA, 74; La State Univ, MA, 76; Cambridge Univ, PhD, 81; La State Univ, MLS, 82. **CAREER** Libr, Rice Univ, 82-84; from asst prof to prof, Lamar Univ, 84-. **HONORS AND AWARDS** Distinguished Fac Lectr, Lamar Univ; Phi Kappa Phi, **MEMBERSHIPS** AHA, Sixteenth Century Studies Conf, Past & Present Soc, Soc for Hist of Discoveries. **RESEARCH** English reformation, Age of Exploitation. **SELECTED PUBLICATIONS** Auth, Reference Sources in History, ABC-Clio, 90; auth, Historical Dictionary of Tudor England, Greenwood, 91; auth, Legend and Lore of the Americas Before 1492, ABC-Clio, 93; auth, Historical Dictionary of Stuart England, Greenwood, 96; auth, Travel Legend and Lore, ABC-Clio, 98. **CONTACT ADDRESS** Dept Hist, Lamar Univ, Beaumont, PO Box 10048, Beaumont, TX 77710-0048. **EMAIL** fritzerh@hal.lamar.edu

FRITZSCHE, PETER
PERSONAL Born 07/03/1959, Chicago, IL, m, 1988, 2 children **DISCIPLINE** HISTORY **EDUCATION** Univ Cal Berk, PhD 86. **CAREER** Univ IL, asst prof, assoc prof, prof, 87 to 94-; asst prof, 87-91; assoc prof, 91-94; prof, 94-; ch, Dept of Hist, 00-. **HONORS AND AWARDS** Humboldt Res Fel; Guggenheim, 99. **RESEARCH** Modernity; memory; German history. **SELECTED PUBLICATIONS** Auth, Rehearsals for fascism: Populism and Political Mobilization in Weimar Germany, Oxford, 90; auth, Germans into Nazis, Harvard Univ Press, 98; Reading Berlin 1900, Harvard Univ Press, 96; Imagining the Twentieth Century, coed, Univ of IL Press, 97; a Nation of Flyers: German aviation and Popular Imagination, Harvard Univ Press, 92. **CONTACT ADDRESS** Dept of History, Univ of Illinois, Urbana-Champaign, 810 S Wright St, Urbana, IL 61801. **EMAIL** pfritzsc@uiuc.edu

FRIZZELL, ROBERT
PERSONAL Born 06/26/1947, Marshall, MO, m, 1974, 1 child **DISCIPLINE** HISTORY **EDUCATION** Univ Mo, AB, 69; Univ Ill, MA, 73, MSLS, 75. **CAREER** Librn, Wesleyan Univ, 75-89; dir, Hendrix Col, 89-. **HONORS AND AWARDS** Auth Awd, 77, State Hist Society Mo. **MEMBERSHIPS** Society for German-Am Studies; Immigration Hist Society; State Hist Society Mo; Ill State Hist Society. **RESEARCH** Immigration history; German immigration to U.S.; Midwestern history. **SELECTED PUBLICATIONS** Auth, German Freethinkers in Bloomington: Sampling a Forgotten Culture, 88; auth, Reticent Germans: The East Frisians of Illinois, 92; auth, The New Bailey Library, 94; auth, Managing Through a Major Building Project: Three Academic Library Leaders Comment, 94; auth, The Low German Settlements of Western Missouri: Examples of Ethnic Cocoons, 98. **CONTACT ADDRESS** Bailey Library, Director, Hendrix Col, 1600 Washington Ave, Conway, AR 72032. **EMAIL** frizzellb@mercury.hendrix.edu

FROIDE, AMY
PERSONAL Born 06/22/1967, San Diego, CA **DISCIPLINE** EARLY MOD BRIT HIST, EUROPEAN WOMEN'S HIST **EDUCATION** Univ San Diego, MAT 90, BA 88; Duke Univ, PhD, 96, MA 93; **CAREER** Vis asst prof, Miami Univ Ohio, 96-98; asst prof, Univ Tenn Chattanooga, 98-. **HONORS AND AWARDS** 98-99 Rockefeller Found Fel Women's Hist; 98 Folger Shakespeare Libr Fel. **MEMBERSHIPS** AHA; NACBS; CCWH; WAWH. **RESEARCH** Women in Pre-Mod Europe; Singlewomen; Soc Hist of pre-mod Brit. **SELECTED PUBLICATIONS** Singlewomen in the European Past, ed, Judith M Bennett & Amy M Froide, Univ Penn, 98; Old Maids: The Lifecycle of Single Women in Early Modern England, ed, Lynn Botelho & Pat Thane; Old Women in Britain, 1500 to the Present, Longman, 01. **CONTACT ADDRESS** Dept of History, Univ of Tennessee, Chattanooga, 615 McCallie Ave, Chattanooga, TN 37403-2598. **EMAIL** Amy-Froide@utc.edu

FROST, FRANK J.
PERSONAL Born 12/03/1929, Washington, DC, 2 children **DISCIPLINE** ANCIENT HISTORY **EDUCATION** Univ Calif, Santa Barbara, AB, 55, Los Angeles, MA, 59, PhD, 61. **CAREER** Lectr hist and classics, Univ Calif, Riverside, 59-62; asst prof ancient hist, Hunter Col, 62-64; asst prof classics, Univ Calif, Riverside, 64-65; asst prof, 65-67, assoc prof, 68-80, Prof Hist, Univ Calif, Santa Barbara, 80-, County supvr, 73-77; assoc ed, Am J Ancient Hist, 76-. **MEMBERSHIPS** Soc Promotion Hellenic Studies; Brit Class Asn; Am Philol Asn; Archaeol Inst Am. **RESEARCH** Marine archaeology; Greek historiography, especially Plutarch; Athenian politics in the fifth century, BC. **SELECTED PUBLICATIONS** Auth, Voyages of the Imagination, Archaeol, Vol 46, 93. **CONTACT ADDRESS** 2687 Puesta del Sol, Santa Barbara, CA 93105.

FROST, GINGER S.
PERSONAL Born 08/19/1962, Sherman, TX **DISCIPLINE** HISTORY **EDUCATION** TX Woman's Univ, BA (Magna Cum Laude), 83; LA State Univ, MA, 86; Rice Univ, PhD, 91. **CAREER** Asst prof, Hist, Wesleyan Col, 91-93; Dept assoc, Northwestern Univ, 93-94; asst prof, Hist, Judson Col, 94-96; Asst Prof, Hist, Samford Univ, 96-99, Dir, Honors Prog, 98-; Assoc Prof, Hist, 99-. **HONORS AND AWARDS** North Am Conf on British Studies Dissertation Year fel, 89-90; Clifford Lefton Lawrence Awd in British Hist, Rice Univ, 91; John W. Gardner Awd for the Best Dissertation in Humanities and Social Sciences, Rice Univ, 91; Faculty Development grant, Samford Univ, 98; National Endowment for the Humanities Summer Research Stipend, 00; alumni federation graduate fel, la state univ, 84-87; rice presidential recognition award, rice univ, 87-88; lodieska stockbridge vaughan fel, rice univ, 89-90; history dept fel, rice univ, 87-91; member: pi gamma mu, mortar board, phi kappa phi, alpha ch **MEMBERSHIPS** Am Hist Asn; Southern Hist Asn (European Hist section); Southern Conference of British Studies (exec comm, 97-2000); Southern Asn of Women's Historians; North Am Conference on British Studies; Victorians Inst; Nineteenth Century Studies Asn. **RESEARCH** Modern Britain; family hist; women's hist. **SELECTED PUBLICATIONS** Auth, Through the Medium of the Passions: Cohabitation Contracts in England, 1750-1850, Proceedings of the 23rd Annual Consortium on Revolutionary Europe, 94; I Shall Not Sit Down and Crie: Feminism, Class and Breach of Promise Plaintiffs in England, 1850-1900, Gender and History 6, Aug 94; Promises Broken: Courtship, Class, and Gender in Victorian England, Univ Press VA, Nov 95; Bigamy and Cohabitation in Victorian England, J of Family Hist, 22, July 97; A Shock to Marriage? The Clitheroe Case and the Victorians, in Disorder in the Court, George Robb and Nancy Erber, eds, NY Univ Press, 99. **CONTACT ADDRESS** Dept of Hist, Samford Univ, Birmingham, AL 35229. **EMAIL** gsfrost@samford.edu

FROST, JAMES ARTHUR
PERSONAL Born 05/15/1918, Manchester, England, m, 1942, 2 children **DISCIPLINE** AMERICAN HISTORY **EDUCATION** Columbia Col, AB, 40; Columbia Univ, AM, 41, PhD, 49. **CAREER** Instr hist, Nutley High Sch, NJ, 46-47; instr, State Univ NY Col Oneonta, 47-50, asst to pres, 50-52, dean, 52-64; assoc provost acad planning, State Univ NY, 64-65, vchancellor univ cols, 65-72; Exec Secy Bd Trustees, Conn State Col, 72-, Exec Dir, 76-, Pres Connecticut State Univ, 83-85, Pres Emer, 85- , Conn State Univ, Smith-Mundt prof Am hist, Univ Ceylon, 59-60; mem comn higher educ, Mid States Asn Cols & Sec Schs, 67-73; mem, Comt Res & Develop, Col Entrance Eval Bd, 73-76; member advisory bord, Connecticut Review, 72-76; member editorial board State Univ of New York Press, 64-72; member National Council Heads of Systems of Public Higher Education, 76-85, Pres 79-80, now honrary member. **HONORS AND AWARDS** Fellow, New York State Historical assoc, Rockerfeller grants. **RESEARCH** American frontier; history of New York state; administration of higher education. **SELECTED PUBLICATIONS** Auth, Life on the Upper Susquehanna, 1783-1860, Columbia Univ, 51; coauth, A History of New York State, Cornell Univ Press, 2nd ed, 67; New York: The Empire State, Prentice-Hall, 5th ed, 80; A History of the United States: The Evolution of a Free People, Follett, 2nd ed, 69; The Establishment of the Connecticut State University, 1965-85, 91; The Country Club of Farmington, Conn, 1892-1995, 96. **CONTACT ADDRESS** 17 Neal Dr, Simsbury, CT 06070.

FROST, JERRY WILLIAM
PERSONAL Born 03/17/1940, Muncie, IN, m, 1963, 1 child **DISCIPLINE** AMERICAN & CHURCH HISTORY **EDUCATION** DePauw Univ, BA, 62; Univ Wis, MA, 65, PhD, 68. **CAREER** Asst prof Am hist, Vassar Col, 67-73; assoc prof & dir relig, Friends Hist Libr, 73-79, prof, 79, Jenkins prof Quaker hist & res, Swarthmore Col, 80-, Fel, John Carter Brown Libr, 70; USIP Fel, 85, Philadelphia Inst for Early Am Studies Fel, 80, Lang Fel, 81, 97; ed, Pa Mag Hist & Biog, 81-86. **HONORS AND AWARDS** Brit Friends Hist Asn, pres, 98. **MEMBERSHIPS** Friends Hist Soc; Am Soc Church Hist. **RESEARCH** Quakers; Am family; peace research. **SELECTED PUBLICATIONS** Auth, Quaker Family in Colonial America, St Martins, 73; Connecticut Education in the Revolutionary Era, Pequot, 74; Origins of the Quaker crusade against slavery: A review of recent literature, spring 78, Quaker Hist; ed, The Keithian Controversy in Early Pennsylvania, 80 & Quaker Origins of Antislavery, 81, Norwood; Years of crisis and separation: Philadelphia yearly meeting, 1790-1860, In: Friends in the Delaware Valley, 81; Seeking the Light, Essays in Quaker History, Pendle Hill, 87; co-auth, The Quakers, Greenwood, 88; auth, A Perfect Freedom: Religious Liberty in Pennsylvania, Cambridge, 90; Our deeds carry our message: The early history of the American Friends Service Committee, Quaker Hist, 92; co-auth, Christianity: a Social and Cultural History, Prentice Hall, 98. **CONTACT ADDRESS** Friends Hist Libr, Swarthmore Col, 500 College Ave, Swarthmore, PA 19081-1306.

FROST, PETER K.
PERSONAL Born 08/26/1936, Boston, MA, m, 1965, 3 children **DISCIPLINE** HISTORY **EDUCATION** Harvard Univ, BA, 58, MA, 62, PhD, 66. **CAREER** Asst to dean admis & scholar, Harvard Univ, 58-60; from instr to asst prof, 64-72, assoc dean admin, 69-72, dir assoc Kyoto prog, 72-73, assoc prof, 72-80, prof hist, Williams Col, 80-. **MEMBERSHIPS** Assn Asian Studies. **CONTACT ADDRESS** Dept of History, Williams Col, Stetson Hall, Williamstown, MA 01267-2600. **EMAIL** pfrost@williams.edu

FROST, RICHARD HINDMAN
PERSONAL Born 06/15/1930, Brooklyn, NY, m, 1963, 2 children **DISCIPLINE** UNITED STATES HISTORY **EDUCATION** Swarthmore Col, AB, 51; Univ Calif, Berkeley, MA, 54, PhD (hist), 60. **CAREER** Asst prof hist, Univ Winnipeg, 60-64; lectr, San Francisco State Col, 64-65; vis asst prof, Univ NMex, 65-66; assoc prof, 66-72, Prof Hist, Colgate Univ, 72-, Chmn Dept, 73-, Fel Ctr Hist Am Indian, Newberry Libr, 79-80. **MEMBERSHIPS** Orgn Am Hists; Am Soc Ethnohist. **RESEARCH** Twentieth century United States history; American civil liberties history; American Indian history. **SELECTED PUBLICATIONS** Auth, The Mooney Case, Stanford Univ, 68; Romantic inflation of the Pueblo Indians, Am West, 1/80. **CONTACT ADDRESS** Dept of Hist, Colgate Univ, Hamilton, NY 13346.

FRY, JOSEPH A.
DISCIPLINE HISTORY **EDUCATION** Univ Va, PhD, 74. **CAREER** Prof, Univ Nev Las Vegas. **SELECTED PUBLICATIONS** Auth, John Tyler Morgan and the Search for Southern Autonomy, Knoxville, 92; Henry S. Sanford: Diplomacy and Business in Nineteenth-Century America, Reno, 82. **CONTACT ADDRESS** History Dept, Univ of Nevada, Las Vegas, 4505 Md Pky, Las Vegas, NV 89154.

FRY, MICHAEL G.
PERSONAL Born 11/05/1932, Brierley, England, m, 1957, 3 children **DISCIPLINE** ECONOMICS, HISTORY **EDUCATION** London Sch of Econ, B Sc, 56, PhD, 63. **CAREER** Prof Hist, 66-77, Carleton Univ, Ottawa, Can; dean & prof, 77-80, Grad Sch of Int Stud, Univ Denver; dir & prof, 80-98, Univ So Calif, School of Int Affairs. **HONORS AND AWARDS** NATO fel; vpres Int Stud Asn; fel of the Royal Hist Soc, UK. **MEMBERSHIPS** Royal Hist Asn; SHAFR. **RESEARCH** North Atlantic relations; north Pacific relations; British foreign policy; Middle East. **SELECTED PUBLICATIONS** Auth, Eisenhower, Dulles and the Suez Crisis of 1956, Reexamining the Eisenhower Presidency, Greenwood Press, 93; auth, The Forgotten Crisis of 1957: Gaza and Sharm-el-Sheikh, Int Hist Rev 15, 1, 93, Revue d'Histoire Diplomatique, 93; auth, Epistemic Communities: Intelligence Studies & International Relations, Intel & Nat Security, 8, 3, 93; auth, Epistemic Communities: Intelligence Studies and International Relations, Espionage: Past, Present and Future, Cass, 94; auth, The Pacific Dominion and the Washington Conference, 1921-22, The Wash Conf, 1921-22 and The Road to Pearl Harbor, Cass, 94; auth, The United States, the United Nations and the Lebanon Crisis, 1958: Intelligence and Statecraft, in Intelligence and National Security 10,1, 95; auth, British Revisionism, Ctr for Ger & European Stud, Univ Calif, 95; auth, British Revisionism, in The 1919 Peace Settlement and Germany, Cambridge Univ Press, 96; auth, The North Pacific Triangle at Century's End: Canada, Japan and the United States, 98; ed, The Guide to Modern Politics and Diplomacy, Cassells, London. **CONTACT ADDRESS** School of Int Relations, Univ of So California, VKC 330, Univ Park, Los Angeles, CA 90089-0043.

FRYD, VIVIEN G.
PERSONAL Born 05/14/1952, Brooklyn, NY, m, 1983, 1 child **DISCIPLINE** ART HISTORY **EDUCATION** Ohio St Univ, BA, 70, MA 74; Univ Wisc, PhD, 84. **CAREER** Asst to Assoc Dean, Univ Wisc, Col Arts & Scui, 81-84; Vis Asst Prof, Ariz St, 84-85; Asst Prof, 85-92, Assoc Prof, 92-, Vanderbilt Univ. **HONORS AND AWARDS** Am Coun of Learned Soc Grant-in-Aid, 89; Smithsonian Short-term Vis Grant, 87; Capital Hist Soc Fellow, 87. **MEMBERSHIPS** Col Art Asn; Am Stud Asn. **RESEARCH** American art, public art, sculpture, Georgia O'Keefe, Edward Hopper, art in the US Capital. **SELECTED PUBLICATIONS** Auth, Art and Empire: The Politics of Ethnicity in the US Capitol, 1815-1860, Yale Univ Press, 92, reprint Ohio University Press, 01; auth, The Politics of Public Art: Art in the United States Capitol, The J of Art Mgt, Law & Soc, 23, 327-340, 94; auth, Rereading the Indian in Benjamin West's Death of General Wolfe, Am Art, 9, 73-85, 95; auth, Two US Capitol Statues: Horatio Greenough's Rescue and Luigi Persico's Discovery of America, Critical Issues in Am Art, Harper Collins, 93-108, 97; auth, Shifting Power Relations: Edward Hopper's Girlie Show American Art 14 (Summer 00): 52-75; auth, Georgia O'Keefe's Radiator Building: Gender, Sexaulity, and Urban Images Winterthur Portfolio, 35 (Wint. 01): 269-289; auth, Art and the Crisis of Marriage: Edward Hopps and Georgia O'Keeffe Chicago: University of Chicago Press, 02 **CONTACT ADDRESS** Dept of Fine Arts, Vanderbilt Univ, Nashville, TN 37235. **EMAIL** vivien.g.fryd@vanderbilt.edu

FRYE, RICHARD NELSON
PERSONAL Born 01/10/1920, Birmingham, AL, m, 1975, 4 children **DISCIPLINE** IRANIAN **EDUCATION** Univ Ill, AB, 39; Harvard Univ, Am, 40, PhD, 46. **CAREER** Exec secy Near East comt, 48-50, Am Coun Learned Soc; from asst prof to assoc prof Mid Eastern studies, 51-57, assoc dir, 55-57, Mid East Ctr, Aga Khan Prof Iranian, 57, Harvard Univ; asst ed, 50-58, Speculum; vis lectr Iranian archaeol, 66-67, Hermitage Mus; corresp fel, 66-, Ger Archaeol Inst; dir, 69-74, Asia Inst, Pahlavi Univ, Iran; ed bull & monogr ser, 69-74; consult, 76-, Pahlavi Libr, Tehran. **HONORS AND AWARDS** Hon PhD, 92, Univ Tajikistan. **MEMBERSHIPS** Hon mem Zorostrian Assn of NAm; Am Orient Soc (vice pres, 66); Nat Assn Armenian Studies & Res,founder. **RESEARCH** Iranian studies; middle Persian and central Asian history; archaeology. **SELECT-**

ED PUBLICATIONS Auth, The Heritage of Iran, London, 62; auth, The History of Ancient Iran, Beck Munich, 83; auth, The Heritage of Central Asia, Wiener, Princeton, 96; auth, The Histories of Nishapur, Harvard Univ, 65; auth, Bukhara the Medieval Achievement, Univ Okla, 65; auth, Persia, London, 68; ed, Middle Iranian inscriptions from Dura Europas, Corpus Inscriptionium Iranicarum, Lund Humphries, London, 68; auth, Sasanian Seals in the Collection of Mohsen Foroughi, Lund Humphries, London, 72; auth, Excavations of Qasr-i Abu Nasr, Harvard Univ, 73; auth, Neue Methodologie in der Iranistik, Harrasowitz, Wiesbaden, 74; auth, Opera Minora, Asia Inst, Shiraz, 76-77. **CONTACT ADDRESS** Harvard Univ, 6 Divinity Ave, Cambridge, MA 02138. **EMAIL** frye@fas.harvard.edu

FRYER, JUDITH
PERSONAL Born 08/05/1939, Minneapolis, MN, 2 children **DISCIPLINE** AMERICAN LITERATURE, HISTORY **EDUCATION** Univ Minn, PhD (Am studies), 73. **CAREER** Instr women's studies, Am studies and Am lit, Univ Minn, 68-73; asst prof, 74-78, ASSOC PROF AM STUDIES, MIAMI UNIV, OXFORD, OHIO, 78-, DIR AM STUDIES PROG, 74-, Instr Am lit, Macalester Col, St Paul, 72; guest prof Am studies, Univ Tİbingen, West Ger, 76-77; res grants, Miami Univ, summers, 75, 79 and 82, Nat Endowment for the Humanities, summers 76 and 78, 79-80; Fulbright grant, 76; fel, Bunting Inst, Harvard Univ, 79-80. **MEMBERSHIPS** Am Studies Asn; Nat Trust for Hist Preservation; Hist Keyboard Soc. **RESEARCH** Women's studies; early music. **SELECTED PUBLICATIONS** Auth, Review of Developments in State Securities Regulation, Business Lawyer, Vol 49, 93. **CONTACT ADDRESS** American Studies Prog, Miami Univ, Oxford, OH 45056.

FRYKENBERG, ROBERT E.
PERSONAL Born 06/08/1930, Ootacamund, India, m, 1952, 3 children **DISCIPLINE** SOUTH ASIAN HISTORY **EDUCATION** Bethel Col & Sem, BA, 51, BD, 55; Univ MN, MA, 53; Univ London, PhD, 61. **CAREER** Instr polit sci & hist, Oakland City Col, 57-58; Ford Found res & Carnegie teaching fels & vis asst prof Indian hist, Univ Chicago, 61-62; asst prof SAsian hist, 62-67, assoc prof hist & Indian studies, 67-71, chmn, Dept SAsian Studies, 70-73, dir, Ctr SAsian Studies, 70-74, Prof hist & S Asian studies, Univ WI-Madison, 71-97, Emeritus prof, 97. **HONORS AND AWARDS** Am Coun Learned Soc res grant, SIndia, 62-63; partic, SAsian Microform Proj, 62-; tchr, Peace Corps, 64; Fulbright-Hays fel Indian hist, 65-66; Am Coun Learned Soc-Soc Sci Res Coun grant-in-aid, Asia, 67; Guggenheim fel, 68-69; dir, Summer Prog SAsian Studies, 70-71; hon fel, Am Inst Indian Studies, 65-, trustee, 70-, chmn nominating comt, 73-74; consult, NDEA Title VI Ctr & Fel Progs, US Dept Health, Educ & Welfare, 71 & 73; Nat Endowment for Humanities sr fel & fel, Inst Res in Humanities, Univ WI-Madison, 75; ACLS-SSRC grant for res on SAsia, 77-78; travel fel, Am Inst Indian Studies, 78, 81, 84, 87, 90; Univ WI-Madison research grants, 68, 73-74, 75, 77-78, 79, 81, 82, 86, 88-90 (Vilas assoc), 97; NEH/UW-Madison summer semin dir, 86; IFACS Board, 79-87, 91; AM Phl Soc grant, 83; Woodrow Wilson Center Vis Sch, 86, Fell, 91-92; Rockfell Scholar in Res (Bellagio), 88; Pew (dir, Res Adv Grant: India), 94-97, 98-00; Pew Ev Sch Prog, senior fel, 97-98; Radhakrishnan Memorial Lecturer, vis fel, 98. **MEMBERSHIPS** Asn Asian Studies; fel Royal Asiatic Soc; AHA; fel Royal Hist Soc; India Inst Asian Studies; life member, India Intl Center. **RESEARCH** Hist; politics; relig India ad south Asia; cult and soc conflict in India; land and peasant in S Asia; fund movements ; hist of Christianity within Muslim-Hindu Env. **SELECTED PUBLICATIONS** Auth, India: Today's World in Focus, Ginn, 68 & 73; Elite formation in nineteenth century South India, First Conf Tamil Cult & Hist, Univ Malaysia, 68; auth, Land Control and Social Structure in Indian History, Univ Wis, 69; ed & auth, The partition of India a quarter century after, Am Hist Rev, 3/72; seven chap Asia Sect, In: European History in World Perspective, Heath 74; ed & auth, India's Imperial Tradition: Essays on the Logic of Political Systems, Indo-British Rev, Madras, 75; auth, The last emergency of the Raj, In: India Gandhi's India, West View, 76; ed & auth two chaps in: Land Tenure and Peasant in South Asia, Univ Wis Land Tenure Ctr & Orient Longman, Delhi, 77; co ed, Studies of South India: An Anthology, New Era, Madras, 86; auth ed, Delhi Through the Ages: Essays in History, Culture, and Society, Oxford univ press, 86, revised, 93; Accounting for Fundamentalisims, univ Chicago, 94; auth, History and Belief: The Foundations of Historical Understanding, Eerdmans, 96; auth, Oxford History of Christianity in Indian World, in progress. **CONTACT ADDRESS** Dept of Hist, Univ of Wisconsin, Madison, 455 North Park St, Madison, WI 53706-1483. **EMAIL** frykenberg@mhab.history.wisc.edu

FRYKMAN, GEORGE AXEL
PERSONAL Born 04/30/1917, South San Francisco, CA, m, 1942, 3 children **DISCIPLINE** HISTORY **EDUCATION** San Jose State Col, AB, 40; Stanford Univ, AM, 47, PhD (hist), 55. **CAREER** Teacher high sch, Calif, 41-42; actg instr hist, Stanford Univ, 49-50; instr, 50-51, asst librn and lectr, 51-53, from instr to asst prof, 53-61, asst to dean, Grad Sch, 61-64, assoc prof, 61-66, Prof Hist, Wash State Univ, 66-, State educ adv, Washington Encycl Americana, 59-64. **MEMBERSHIPS** AHA; Orgn Am Hists. **RESEARCH** Pacific Northwest; historiography; American intellectual history. **SELECTED PUBLICATIONS** Auth, Edmond S Meany, historian, 10/60 & Alaska-Yukon-Pacific exposition, 1909, 7/62, Pac Northwest Quart; Philosophy of Northwest history, Idaho Yesterdays, fall 64; Development of the Washington Historical Quarterly, 1906-1935, Pac Northwest Quart, 7/79. **CONTACT ADDRESS** Dept of Hist, Washington State Univ, Pullman, WA 99164.

FU, POSHEK
DISCIPLINE HISTORY **EDUCATION** Stanford Univ, PhD, 89. **CAREER** Assoc prof, Univ Ill Urbana Champaign. **RESEARCH** Modern Chinese cultural and intellectual history; popular culture and cultural criticism; cinema studies; comparative literature. **SELECTED PUBLICATIONS** Auth, Passivity, Resistance, and Collaboration: Intellectual Choices in Occupied Shanghai, 1957-1945, Stanford, 93; Patriotism or Profit: Hong Kong Cinema during the Second World War, Urban Council, 95; The Ambiguity of Entertainment: Chinese Cinema in Occupied Shanghai, 1941-1945, Cinema J, 97; co-auth, Struggle to Entertain: The Political Ambivalence of Shanghai Film Industry under Japanese Occupation, Urban Council, 94. **CONTACT ADDRESS** History Dept, Univ of Illinois, Urbana-Champaign, 52 E Gregory Dr, Champaign, IL 61820. **EMAIL** p-fu1@staff.uiuc.edu

FUCHS, CYNTHIA
DISCIPLINE VISUAL ARTS **EDUCATION** Univ Pa, PhD. **CAREER** Assoc prof. **RESEARCH** African American studies; queer theory; postmodern theory; popular mass culture studies. **SELECTED PUBLICATIONS** Auth, Between the Sheets, In the Streets: Queer, Lesbian, Gay Documentary, 97; Death is Irrelevant: Cyborgs, Reproduction, and the Future of Male Hysteria, Genders, 93; The Buddy Politic, 93. **CONTACT ADDRESS** Dept of Film and Media Studies, George Mason Univ, Fairfax, 4400 University Dr, Fairfax, VA 22030.

FUCHS, RACHEL G.
PERSONAL Born 06/25/1939, New York, NY, m, 1959, 2 children **DISCIPLINE** HISTORY **EDUCATION** Univ Mich,59; Boston Univ, BA, 60; MA, 62; Ind Univ, PhD, 80. **CAREER** Instr, Purdue Univ, 68-72; Vis Asst Prof, Ind Univ, 80; Dir, Purdue Univ, 80-83; Asst Prof to Prof, Ariz State Univ, 83-. **HONORS AND AWARDS** NEH Summer Stipend, 86; Fel, NEH, 88-89; Grant, Camargo Found 97; Alumni Teaching Awd, Ariz State Univ, 89, 94. **MEMBERSHIPS** Am Hist Asn; Soc for French Hist Studies; W Soc for French Hist; Soc Sci Hist Asn. **RESEARCH** Modern France: Women, children and the family; The social construction of the family; Paternity and property; Abortion; Adoption; Gender; The family and poverty in nineteenth-century Europe; Women in nineteenth-century Europe. **SELECTED PUBLICATIONS** Co-auth, "Pregnant, Single and Far from Home: Migrant Women in the Nineteenth-Century Metropolis," Am Hist Rev, 90; auth, Poor and Pregnant in Paris: Strategies for Survival in the Nineteenth Century, Rutgers Univ Press, 92; auth, Gender and the Politics of Social Reform in France, 1870-1914, Johns Hopkins Univ Press, 95; auth, "French Social Reform in a Comparative Perspective," in Gender and the Politics of Social Reform in France, 95; auth, "The Right to Life: Paul Strauss and the Politics of Motherhood," in Gender and the Politics of Social Reform in France, 95; co-auth, "Invisible Cultures: Poor Women's Networks and Reproductive Strategies in Nineteenth-Century Paris," in Situating Fertility: Anthropology and Demographic Inquiry, Cambridge Univ Press, 95; auth, "Seduction, Paternity, and the Law in Fin-de-Siecle France," J of Mod Hist, 00; auth, "Charity and Welfare," in History of the European Family, Vol 2, forthcoming. **CONTACT ADDRESS** Dept Hist, Arizona State Univ, 4525 E La Mirada Way, Phoenix, AZ 85044. **EMAIL** rfuchs@asu.edu

FULLER, JUSTIN
PERSONAL Born 07/26/1926, Birmingham, AL, m, 1960, 1 child **DISCIPLINE** AMERICAN HISTORY **EDUCATION** Ga Sch Technol, BS, 48; Emory Univ, MA, 58; Univ NC, PhD (hist), 66. **CAREER** Asst prof hist, Ala Col, 62-63; instr econ hist, Univ Ga, 63-65; from asst prof to assoc prof, 65-76, Prof Hist, Univ Montevallo, 76-. **MEMBERSHIPS** Southern Hist Asn. **RESEARCH** American business history; history of southern iron and steel industry. **SELECTED PUBLICATIONS** Auth, Les Vieilles Dames Indignes De Havergo Hill, Europe Revue Litteraire Mensuelle, Vol 71, 93; On Formal Verse and Free Verse, Poetry Wales, Vol 28, 93; First Day, Poetry Rev, Vol 85, 95. **CONTACT ADDRESS** 133 Tecumseh Rd, Montevallo, AL 35115.

FULLER, LAWRENCE BENEDICT
PERSONAL Born 07/27/1936, Orange, NJ, m, 1971, 2 children **DISCIPLINE** ENGLISH, HISTORY **EDUCATION** Dartmouth Col, AB, 58; Columbia Univ, MA, 63; Pennsylvania State Univ, MA, 83; Johns Hopkins Univ, PhD(Educ), 74. **CAREER** Prof English, Bloomsburg Univ, 71-00; Prof Emeritus, 00-. **HONORS AND AWARDS** Phi Betta Kappa; Phi Kappa Phi; Fulbright Scholar, Norway, 93-94; Czech Republic, 00-01. **MEMBERSHIPS** Hist Educ Soc; NCTE. **RESEARCH** History of education, media studies, literature for adolescents, methods of teaching secondary English. **SELECTED PUBLICATIONS** Auth, A sense of our own history, Independent Sch Bull, 12/71; Private secondary education: the search for a new model, 1880-1915, Foundational Studies, Spring 75; Research papers in English methods classes: introduction to varieties of opinion, English Educ, Summer 76; William M Sloane: A biographical study of turn of the century attitudes toward American education, Foundational Studies, Fall 78; Literature for adolescents: The early days, The ALAN Rev, Spring 79; Students' rights of expression: The decade since Tinker, English J, 12/79; Literature for adolescents: A historical perspective, English Educ, 2/80; Media Education: Where Have We Been? Where Are We Going?, English Education, February, 96. **CONTACT ADDRESS** Dept of English, Bloomsburg Univ of Pennsylvania, 400 E 2nd St, Bloomsburg, PA 17815-1399. **EMAIL** lfuller@planetx.bloomu.edu

FULLINWIDER, S. PENDLETON
PERSONAL Born 10/17/1933, Washington, DC, m, 1964, 1 child **DISCIPLINE** AMERICAN HISTORY **EDUCATION** US Naval Acad, BS, 55; Univ Wis, Madison, MS, 61, PhD (hist), 66. **CAREER** Instr Am hist, Stephens Col, 64-67; asst prof, 68-71, Assoc Prof Hist, Ariz State Univ, 71-, Rockefeller Found fel, 75-76. **RESEARCH** American psychiatry. **SELECTED PUBLICATIONS** Auth, The Natural and the Normative--Theories of Spatial PerceptionfFrom Kant to Helmholtz, Stud Hist Philos Science, Vol 24, 93. **CONTACT ADDRESS** Dept of Hist, Arizona State Univ, Tempe, AZ 85281.

FULLMER, JUNE ZIMMERMAN
PERSONAL Born 12/16/1920, IL, m, 1953 **DISCIPLINE** HISTORY OF SCIENCE **EDUCATION** Ill Inst Technol, BSAS, 43, MSChem, 45; Bryn Mawr Col, PhD (phys biochem), 48. **CAREER** Instr chem, Hood Col, 45-46; asst prof, Chatham Col, 50-53; assoc prof and head dept, Newcomb Col, Tulane Univ, 55-64; assoc prof hist, 66-70, Prof Hist, Ohio State Univ, 70-, Am Asn Univ Women fel, 48-49; Am Coun Learned Soc fel, 60-61; Guggenheim Found fel, 63-64. **MEMBERSHIPS** Hist of Sci Soc; Midwest Junto for Hist of Sci (pres, 75-76); Sigma Xi; AAAS; Am Asn Univ Women. **RESEARCH** History of science, especially 19th and 20th century physical sciences; women in science; chemical kinetics. **SELECTED PUBLICATIONS** Auth, On spontaneous combustion, 61 & Humphry Davy and the gun powder manufacture, 64, Annals of Sci; Humphry Davy's critical abstracts, Chymia, 64; Davy's biographers, Science, 67; Davy's MS sketches of his contemporaries, Chymia, 67; Sir Humphry Davy's Published Works, Harvard Univ, 69; Medical lives and medical letter, In: Modern Methods in the History of Medicine, Athlone, 71; Humphry Davy and the iodine priority dispute, Ambix, 75. **CONTACT ADDRESS** 781 Latham Ct, Columbus, OH 43214.

FUNCHION, MICHAEL FRANCIS
PERSONAL Born 10/04/1943, New York, NY, m, 1976, 2 children **DISCIPLINE** HISTORY **EDUCATION** Iona Col, BA, 66; Loyola Univ Chicago, MA, 68, PhD (hist), 73. **CAREER** Teaching asst, Loyola Univ Chicago, 67-70, lectr, 72; asst prof, 73-77, Assoc Prof Hist, SDak State Univ, 77-. **MEMBERSHIPS** AHA; Am Comt for Irish Studies; Orgn Am Hists; Immigration Hist Soc. **RESEARCH** Irish in America; United States immigration; Irish History. **SELECTED PUBLICATIONS** Auth, Irish Nationalists and Chicago politics in the 1880's Eire-Ireland: J Irish Studies, summer 75; Chicago's Irish Nationalists, 1881-1890, Arno, 76; Irish Chicago: Church, Homeland, Politics and Class-The Shaping of an Ethnic Group, 1870-1900, In: Ethnic Chicago, Eerdmans, 81. **CONTACT ADDRESS** Dept of Hist, So Dakota State Univ, Brookings, SD 57007-0001.

FUNIGIELLO, PHILIP J.
PERSONAL Born 06/28/1939, New York, NY, 1 child **DISCIPLINE** AMERICAN HISTORY **EDUCATION** Hunter Col, AB, 61; Univ Calif, Berkeley, MA, 62; NYork Univ, PhD, 66. **CAREER** From asst prof to assoc prof, 66-78, prof hist 78-, Col William & Mary; Fulbright lectr US hist, Univ Genoa, Italy, 77, Fulbright Comn, 77. **MEMBERSHIPS** AHA; Orgn Am Historians. **RESEARCH** History of natl health insurance; politics and public policy 1890-present. **SELECTED PUBLICATIONS** Art, Kilowatts for Defense: the New Deal and The Coming of The Second World War, J Am Hist, 69; auth, City Planning in World War II: the Experience of the National Resources Planning Board, Soc Sci Quart, 72; auth, The Bonneville Power Administration and the New Deal, Prologue: J Nat Arch, 73; auth, The Challenge to Urban Liberalism: Federal City Relations During World War II, Univ Tenn, 78; auth, American-Soviet Trade in the Cold War, Univ NC Press, 88; auth, Florence Lathrop Page: A Biography, Univ Va Press, 93. **CONTACT ADDRESS** Dept of History, Col of William and Mary, Williamsburg, VA 23185.

FUNK, ARTHUR LAYTON
PERSONAL Born 05/10/1914, Brooklyn, NY, m, 1944, 2 children **DISCIPLINE** HISTORY **EDUCATION** Dartmouth Col, AB, 36; Univ Chicago, PhD, 40. **CAREER** Instr hist, St Petersburg Jr Col, 40-42; asst prof, Drake Univ, 46; assoc prof humanities, Univ Fla, 46-56; cult affairs officer, US Info Agency, 56-62; chmn dept hist, 73-78, Prof Hist, Univ Fla, 62-, Grad Fac Hist, 68-, Guggenheim fel, 54-55; mem, Joint Comt Hists and Archivists, 76-79, chmn, 77-79; mem, Dept Army Historical Adv Comt, 81-. **MEMBERSHIPS** AHA, Soc Hist Studies,

France; Am Comt Hist 2nd World War (secy, 71-75); Soc Hist Am Foreign Rels; Int Comt Hist 2nd World War (vpres, 75-). **RESEARCH** Political history of World War II; history of France; Europe in the 20th century. **SELECTED PUBLICATIONS** Auth, In Search of the Maquis--Rural Resistance in Southern France, 1942-1944, J Mil Hist, Vol 57, 93; Secret Flotillas--Clandestine Sea Lines to France and French North Africa, 1940-1944, J Mil Hist, Vol 61, 97. **CONTACT ADDRESS** Dept of Hist, Univ of Florida, Gainesville, FL 32611.

FUNKENSTEIN, AMOS
PERSONAL Born 03/09/1937, Tel Aviv, Israel, m, 1958, 2 children **DISCIPLINE** HISTORY **EDUCATION** Free Univ, Berlin, DPhil(hist, philos), 65. **CAREER** Asst prof medieval hist, Free Univ, Berlin, 65-67; assoc prof, 67-72, Prof Jewish Hist and Medieval Intellectual Hist, Univ Calif, Los Angeles, 72-. **MEMBERSHIPS** Am Hist Asn; Hist Soc Israel; Mediaeval Acad Am. **RESEARCH** Medieval and early modern Jewish history; medieval and early modern European intellectual history; history of science. **SELECTED PUBLICATIONS** Auth, Heilslan und Naturliche Entwicklung, Nymphenburg, Munich, 65; Changes in the Patterns of Christian-Jewish Polemics in the 12th Century (Hebrew), Zion: Quart Res Jewish Hist, 68; Gesetz und Geschichte: zur historisierenden Hermeneutik bei Moses Maimonides und Thomas v Aquin, 70 & Some Remarks on the Concept of Impetus and the Determination of Simple Motion, 71, Viator. **CONTACT ADDRESS** Dept Hist, Univ of California, Los Angeles, Los Angeles, CA 90024.

FURDELL, ELLZABETH LANE
PERSONAL Born 04/13/1944, Harrisburg, PA, m, 1968 **DISCIPLINE** ENGLISH HISTORY, POLITICAL SCIENCE **EDUCATION** Univ Wash, BA, 66; Kent State Univ, MA, 68, PhD (hist), 73. **CAREER** Asst prof, 71-74, Assoc Prof Hist, Col Great Falls, 74-, Contribr, Hist Abstr, 73-78. **MEMBERSHIPS** AHA; Am Polit Sci Asn; Sixteenth Century Study Conf; Rocky Mountain Soc Sci Asn. **RESEARCH** London history; 16th century historiography; urban politics. **CONTACT ADDRESS** Dept of Soc Sci, Univ of Great Falls, Great Falls, MT 59405.

FURLONG, PATRICK JOSEPH
PERSONAL Born 02/07/1940, Lexington, KY, m, 1965, 2 children **DISCIPLINE** AMERICAN & NATIVE AMERICAN HISTORY **EDUCATION** Univ Ky, AB, 61; Northwestern Univ, MA, 62; PhD (hist), 66. **CAREER** Asst prof hist, Ariz State Univ, 65-67; asst prof, 67-71, assoc prof, 71-81, honors coordr, 75-78, Prof Hist, Ind Univ, South Bend, 81-. **HONORS AND AWARDS** LHD, Manchester Col, 80. **MEMBERSHIPS** Orgn Am Hists; AHA. **RESEARCH** Congress; Indiana; American Revolution. **SELECTED PUBLICATIONS** Auth, "Origins of the House Committee of Ways and Means," William and Mary Quarterly, vol 25 (68): 587-604; auth, Indiana: An Illustrated History, 85; auth, "The South Board Fugitive Slave Case," in We the People: Indiana and the U.S. Constitution, 87. **CONTACT ADDRESS** Dept of Hist, Indiana Univ, South Bend, PO Box 7111, South Bend, IN 46634. **EMAIL** pfurlong@iusb.edu

FURLOUGH, ELLEN
DISCIPLINE HISTORY **EDUCATION** Lander Col, BA, 75; Univ SC, MA, 78; Brown Univ, PhD, 87. **CAREER** Asst prof, 86-92; assoc prof, 92-96; prof, Kenyon Coll; assoc prof, Univ KY. **RESEARCH** Consumerism, contemporary social history. **SELECTED PUBLICATIONS** Coauth, bibliogr, The Sex of Things: Essays on Gender and Consumption, Univ Calif Press, 96; Packaging Pleasures: Club Mediterran and Consumer Culture in France, 1950-1968, Fr Hist Studies, 93, repro, Soc Hist W Civilization, 3rd ed, St Martin's, 95; co-auth, Composing a Landscape: Coastal Mass Tourism and Regional Development in the Languedoc, 1960s-1980s, Intl Jour Maritime Hist, 97. **CONTACT ADDRESS** Women's Studies, Univ of Kentucky, 112 Breckinridge Hall, Lexington, KY 40506-0056. **EMAIL** furloug@pop.uky.edu

FURMAN, NECAH STEWART
PERSONAL Born 01/29/1940, Del Rio, TX, m, 1962, 3 children **DISCIPLINE** HISTORY, AMERICAN STUDIES **EDUCATION** Univ Tex, El Paso, BA, 63; Univ Tex, Arlington, MA, 72; Univ NMex, PhD (Am studies), 75. **CAREER** Lectr US hist, Univ NMex, 76-77; chmn dept hist, Sandia Prep Sch, 76-77; Vis Asst Prof US Hist, Univ Tex, El Paso, 77-, Proj dir, New Mexico Humanities Coun grant on Cult Conflict in Borderlands, 76-77; Huntington fel, Southwestern Writers, Huntington Libr and Art Gallery, 77; Nat Endowment Humanities fel Mex and Borderlands Hist, 78. **MEMBERSHIPS** Western Hist Asn; AHA. **RESEARCH** Indian and borderlands history. **SELECTED PUBLICATIONS** Auth, Industrialization among the southern Pueblos, Ethnohistory, winter 75; Seedtime for Indian reform: An analysis of Commissioner Francis E Leupp, Red River Valley Hist Rev, winter 75; Walter Prescott Webb as environmentalist, NMex Hist Rev, 1/76; Walter Prescott Webb: His Life and Impact, Univ NMex, 76; La Vida Nueva: A reflection of Villista diplomacy 1914-1915, 4/78, Cultural conflict in the Spanish borderlands, 10/78 & Women's campaign for equality: A state and national perspective, NMex Hist Rev, 10/78. **CONTACT ADDRESS** 7421 El Morro Rd N E, Albuquerque, NM 87109.

FURTH, CHARLOTTE
DISCIPLINE HISTORY **EDUCATION** Stanford Univ, PhD, 65. **CAREER** Prof, Univ Southern Calif. **MEMBERSHIPS** Asn for Asian Studies, Am Hist Asn, International Soc for the Hist of East Asian Science, Technology and Medicine, editorial bd member. **RESEARCH** Late imperial and modern hist of culture, science and gender, hist of medicine. **SELECTED PUBLICATIONS** Auth, A Flourishing Yin: Gender in China's Medical History, 960-1665, U C Press, 99; Ting Wen-Chiang: Science and China's New Culture, Harvard, 70; ed and contribur, The Limits of Change: Essays on Conservative Alternatives in Republican China, Harvard, 76. **CONTACT ADDRESS** Dept of History, Univ of So California, University Park Campus, Los Angeles, CA 90089. **EMAIL** furth@usc.edu

FUSSNER, FRANK SMITH
PERSONAL Born 09/21/1920, Cincinnati, OH, w, 1943, 2 children **DISCIPLINE** HISTORY **EDUCATION** Harvard Univ, BS, 42, PhD (hist), 51. **CAREER** Instr hist and humanities, 50-52, from asst prof to prof, 53-74, Emer Prof Hist, Reed Col, 74-, Am Philos Soc grant, 54; Fulbright vis prof, Univ Col Swansea, Wales, 64-65; vis prof, Haverford Col, 68-69. **MEMBERSHIPS** AHA. **SELECTED PUBLICATIONS** Auth, The Historical Revolution, 62, reprint, 76; auth, Tudor History and The Historians, 70, ed, "William Camdens Discourse Concerning the Prerogative of the Crown," ed, Glimpses of Wheeler County's Past. **CONTACT ADDRESS** 4534 Hwy 207 S, Spray, OR 97874.

FUTRELL, ROBERT FRANK
PERSONAL Born 12/15/1917, Waterford, MS, m, 1944 **DISCIPLINE** MODERN HISTORY **EDUCATION** Univ Miss, BA, 38, MA, 39; Vanderbilt Univ, PhD, 50. **CAREER** Asst hist, Univ Miss, 38-39; spec consult, US War Dept, 46; Hist, Army Air Force and US Air Force Hist Off, 46-49; assoc prof mil hist, Res Studies Inst, Air Univ, 50-51, prof, Aerospace Studies Inst, 51-71, prof mil hist and sr Hist, Hist Res Ctr, 71-74, Emer Prof Mil Hist, Air Univ, 74-, Prof lectr int affairs, George Washington Univ Ctr, 63-68; consult, US Air Force Proj Corona Harvest eval air opers SE Asia, 66-73. **MEMBERSHIPS** Southern Hist Asn; Am Mil Inst; Air Force Hist Found. **RESEARCH** United States military history; airpower history; East Asian history. **SELECTED PUBLICATIONS** Coauth, Army Air Forces in World War II, Univ Chicago, 48-58; auth, United States Air Force in Korea, 1950-1953, Duell, 61; Ideas, Concepts, Doctrine: A History of Basic Thinking in the United States Air Force, 1907-1964, Air Univ, 74; The United States Air Force, The Advisory Years to 1965, Off Air Force Hist, 81. **CONTACT ADDRESS** 1871 Hill Hedge Dr, Montgomery, AL 36106.

G

GAAB, JEFFREY S.
PERSONAL Born 03/22/1963, Bethpage, NY, s **DISCIPLINE** HISTORY **EDUCATION** Hofstra Univ, BA, 85; State Univ NY at Stony Brook, MA, 87; PhD, 92. **CAREER** Adj, Nassau Community Col, 90-91; from adj to asst prof, SUNY at Farmingdale, 91-. **HONORS AND AWARDS** DAAD Fel, 89-90; NEH Scholar, 97. **MEMBERSHIPS** Am Hist Asn, NY State Asn of European Historians. **RESEARCH** Modern European & German History. **SELECTED PUBLICATIONS** auth, Justice Delayed: The Restoration of Justice in Bavaria Under American Occupation, 1945-1949, Peter Lang Pub, 99. **CONTACT ADDRESS** Dept Hist, SUNY, Col of Tech at Farmingdale, 1250 Melville Rd, Farmingdale, NY 11735-1313. **EMAIL** jsgaab@aol.com

GABACCIA, DONNA
DISCIPLINE MODERN U.S. SOCIAL HISTORY, WOMEN'S HISTORY, URBAN HISTORY **EDUCATION** Univ MI, PhD, 79. **CAREER** Charles H Stone Prof Hist, Univ NC, Charlotte. **RESEARCH** Migration to the US; the Italian diaspora. **SELECTED PUBLICATIONS** Auth, We Are What We Eat: Ethnic Food and the Making of Americans, Harvard UP, 96. **CONTACT ADDRESS** Univ of No Carolina, Charlotte, Charlotte, NC 28223-0001.

GABEL, CREIGHTON
PERSONAL Born 04/05/1931, Muskegon, MI, m, 1952, 3 children **DISCIPLINE** ARCHAEOLOGY, ANTHROPOLOGY **EDUCATION** Univ Mich, AB, 53, AM, 54; Univ Edinburgh, PhD(prehist archaeol), 57. **CAREER** From instr to asst prof anthrop, Northwestern Univ, 56-63; assoc prof, 63-69, Prof Anthrop, Boston Univ, 69-, NSF grants, Northern Rhodisia, 60-61 and Kenya, 66-67; res assoc, African Studies Ctr, 63-; chmn anthrop, Boston Univ, 70-72 and 76-; Sr Fulbright Hays award, Liberia, 73. **MEMBERSHIPS** Soc Am Archaeol; S African Archaeol Soc; Soc Africanist Archaeologists Am. **RESEARCH** Prehistoric archaeology Old World, expecially Africa; hunter-gatherers and early agricultural societies. **SELECTED PUBLICATIONS** Ed/contribr, Man Before History, Prentice-Hall Inc, 64; auth, Stone Age Hunters of the Kafue, Boston Univ, 65; analysis of Prehistoric Economic Patterns, Holt,. Rinehart & Winston, 67; co-ed/contribr, Reconstructing African Culture History, Boston Univ, 67. **CONTACT ADDRESS** African Studies Ctr, Boston Univ, 10 Lenox St, Brookline, MA 02146.

GABEL, JACK
PERSONAL Born 04/19/1930, New York, NY, m, 1974, 1 child **DISCIPLINE** AMERICAN HISTORY **EDUCATION** City Col New York, BA, 53, MA, 56; NYork Univ, PhD, 67. **CAREER** From asst prof to assoc prof, 61-74, Prof Hist, Long Island Univ, 74-, Asst dean, Col Arts & Sci, Long Island Univ, 80-81; Assoc Dean, Col of Arts, 81-86. **HONORS AND AWARDS** David Newton Awd for Excel in Teaching, 92. **MEMBERSHIPS** AHA; Orgn Am Historians. **RESEARCH** Twentieth century United States history; United States diplomatic and Hist of New York City. **CONTACT ADDRESS** 406 Pine Bark Ln, Hendersonville, NC 28739.

GADDIS, JOHN LEWIS
PERSONAL Born 04/02/1941, Cotulla, TX, m, 1965, 2 children **DISCIPLINE** UNITED STATES HISTORY **EDUCATION** Univ Tex, Austin, BA, 63, MA, 65, PhD(hist), 68. **CAREER** Asst prof, Ind Univ Southeast, 68-69; from asst prof to assoc prof, 69-76, Prof Hist, Ohio Univ, 76-99, Vis prof strategy, US Naval War Col, 75-77; Bicentennial prof Am hist, Univ Helsinki, 80-81; Harmeworth Prof, Oxford, 92-93; Eastman Prof, Oxford, 01; Robert A. Lovett Prof Hist, Yale Univ 1997-. **HONORS AND AWARDS** Bancroft Prize, 72; Nat Hist Soc Prize Best 1st Bk of Hist, 72; Bernath Prize, Soc Hist Am Foreign Rels, 72. **MEMBERSHIPS** AHA; Orgn Am Historians; Soc Hist Am Foreign Rels. **RESEARCH** Origins of the Cold War; Soviet-American relations; US national security policy. **SELECTED PUBLICATIONS** Auth, The Tragedy of Cold-War History, Diplomatic Hist, Vol 0017, 93; The Devil We Knew--Americans and the Cold-War, Am Hist Rev, Vol 0100, 95. **CONTACT ADDRESS** Dept. of History, Yale Univ, Yale University, New Haven, CT 06520. **EMAIL** john.gaddis@yale.edu

GAGLIANO, JOSEPH ANTHONY
PERSONAL Born 04/15/1930, Milwaukee, WI, w, 1961, 2 children **DISCIPLINE** LATIN AMERICAN HISTORY **EDUCATION** Marquette Univ, BS, 54, MA, 56; Georgetown Univ, PhD(Latin Am hist), 60. **CAREER** Instr hist, Aquinas Col, 59-62; from asst prof to assoc prof, 62-74, asst dean, 76-78, Prof Hist, Loyola Univ Chicago, 74-98, Assoc Dean Grad Sch, 78-86, Am Coun Learned Soc travel grant to 37th Int Cong Americanists, Buenos Aires and Mar del Plata, 66; Mellon grant, Mex, 79; Chair, 86-95, Emer Prof Hist, Loyola Univ, 98-. **MEMBERSHIPS** AHA; Am Cath Hist Asn; Conf Latin Am Hist; Latin Am Studies Asn. **RESEARCH** The Andean republics. **SELECTED PUBLICATIONS** Auth, "The Coca Debate in Colonial Peru," The Americas, 63; auth, Religion in the Andes--Vision and Imagination in Early Colonial Peru, Cath Hist Rev, Vol 0079, 93; The Coca Boom and Rural Social-Change in Bolivia, Americas, Vol 0051, 94; auth, "Coca Prohibition in Peru, Univ Ariz Pr, 94; Bolivia and Coca--A Study in Dependency, Americas, Vol 0051, 95; History of the Archdiocese of Bogota--Its Evangelist Itinerary, 1564-1993, Cath Hist Rev, Vol 0082, 96; Drug Lessons and Education-Programs in Developing-Countries, Hisp Am Hist Rev, Vol 0076, 96; The Cross and the Serpent--Religious Repression and Resurgence in Colonial Peru, Cath Hist Rev, Vol 0083, 97; The Andean Cocaine Industry, Americas, Vol 0053, 97; auth, "Jesuit Encounters in the New World, 97. **CONTACT ADDRESS** Dept Hist, Loyola Univ, Chicago, 6525 N Sheridan Rd, Chicago, IL 60626-5385. **EMAIL** jgaglia@luc.edu

GAGLIARDO, JOHN G.
PERSONAL Born 08/13/1933, Chicago, IL **DISCIPLINE** GERMAN & EARLY MODERN EUROPEAN HISTORY **EDUCATION** Univ Kans, AB, 54, MA, 57; Yale Univ, MA, 58, PhD(hist), 62. **CAREER** Asst instr Western civilization, Univ Kans, 55-57 & 59-60; from instr to asst prof hist, Amherst Col, 60-65; from asst prof to assoc prof, Univ Ill, Chicago, 65-68; assoc prof, 68-70, prof hist, Boston Univ, 70- **HONORS AND AWARDS** Metcalf Cup & Prize for Excellence in Teaching, Boston Univ, 84. **MEMBERSHIPS** AHA; Conf Group Cent Europ Hist; New Eng Hist Asn (pres, 74-75); German Studies Asn. **RESEARCH** European absolutism; German constitutional history; German agrarian history. **SELECTED PUBLICATIONS** Auth, Archives in East Germany, Am Archivist, 7/57; Germans and Agriculture in Colonial Pennsylvania, Pa Mag Hist & Biog, 4/59; Enlightened Despotism, Crowell, 67; Moralism, Rural Ideology and the German Peasant in the Late 18th Century, Agr Hist, 4/68; From Pariah to Patriot: The Changing Image of the German Peasant, 1770-1840, Univ Ky, 69; Reich and Nation: The Holy Roman Empire as Idea and Reality, 1763-1806, Ind Univ, 80; Germany Under the Old Regime 1600-1790, Longman, 91; translator, Otto Busch, Military System and Social Life in Old Regime Prussia, 1713-1807, Humanities Press, 97. **CONTACT ADDRESS** Dept of History, Boston Univ, 226 Bay State Rd, Boston, MA 02215-1403. **EMAIL** jgags@bu.edu

GAIDE, TANURE
PERSONAL Born 04/24/1948, Nigeria, m, 1976, 5 children **DISCIPLINE** LITERATURE, AFRICAN STUDIES **EDUCATION** Univ Ibadan, BA, 71; Syracuse Univ, MA, 79; PhD, 81. **CAREER** Lecturer, Univ Maiduguri Nigeria, 77-89; Visiting Prof, Whitman Col, 89-90; Asst Prof to Prof, Univ NCar, 90-. **HONORS AND AWARDS** Res Grant, UNC, 92-94, 95-96, 97, 99; Nigerian Authors' Poetry Awd, 94; All-Africa Okigbo Prize, 97; Fel, NEH, 00 **MEMBERSHIPS** African Studies Asn; African Lit Asn. **RESEARCH** African/Pan-African/Black Literatures; Non-western, World & Postcolonial literatures; Creative Writing/Poetry. **SELECTED PUBLICATIONS** Auth, The Blood of Peace, Oxford, 91; auth, "Orality in Recent West African Poetry," CLA Journal, (96): 302-319; auth, "African Literature and Its Context: Teaching Teachers of Chinua Achebe's Things Fall Apart," Women's Studies Quarterly, (97): 169-177; auth, Daydream of Ants, Malthouse, 97; auth, Delta Blues and Home Songs, Kraft books, 98; auth, Invoking the Warrior Spirit, Heinemann, 98; auth, Cannons for the Brave, Malthouse, 99; auth, Invoking the Warrior Spirit: New and Selected Poems, Africa World Press, 00. **CONTACT ADDRESS** Dept African Am Studies, Univ of No Carolina, Charlotte, 9201 University City Blvd, Charlotte, NC 28223-0001. **EMAIL** tojaide@email.unc.edu

GAILE, GARY L.
PERSONAL Born 08/03/1945, Cleveland, OH, m, 1983, 1 child **DISCIPLINE** GEOGRAPHY **EDUCATION** Univ Calif at Los Angeles, BA, 71; MA, 72; C Phil, 73; PhD, 76. **CAREER** Asst Prof, Northwestern Univ, 75-82; Assoc Prof, Univ of Conn, 82-84; From Assoc Prof to Prof and Dept Chair, Univ of Colo, 84-. **HONORS AND AWARDS** Distinguished Teaching Awd; Fulbright Hays Sr Scholar, 92-93; Vis Scholar, Cambridge Univ, 92-92. **MEMBERSHIPS** Asn of Am Geogr. **RESEARCH** Food security, Microenterprise Impacts, Africa, Development, Spatial Statistics. **SELECTED PUBLICATIONS** Coauth, The Work of Cities, Univ of Minn Press, 98; co-ed, Geography in America at the Dawn of the 21st century, Oxford Univ Press, forthcoming. **CONTACT ADDRESS** Dept Geog, Univ of Colorado, Boulder, Box 260, Boulder, CO 80309-0260. **EMAIL** gaile@spot.colorado.edu

GALAMBOS, LOUIS PAUL
PERSONAL Born 04/04/1931, Fostoria, OH, m, 1991, 4 children **DISCIPLINE** ECONOMIC HISTORY **EDUCATION** Ind Univ, BA, 55; Yale Univ, MA, 57, PhD, 60. **CAREER** Asst prof Hist, Rice Univ, 60-66 assoc prof Hist, 66-70; prof Hist, Livingston Col Rutgers Univ, 70-71; prof Hist, Johns Hopkins Univ, 71-, vis asst prof, Johns Hopkins Univ, 65-66; ed, Papers of Dwight D Eisenhower, 71-; coed, J Econ Hist, 76-78; Nat Endowment for Humanities sr fel, 78-79; Woodrow Wilson Center fel, 85-86. **HONORS AND AWARDS** Pres, Economic Hist Assn; pres, business hist conf, 91-92. **MEMBERSHIPS** AHA; Econ Hist Asn; Bus Hist Asn; Am Econ Asn; Orgn Am Historians. **RESEARCH** American economic history; business history. **SELECTED PUBLICATIONS** Auth, The Emerging Organizational Synthesis in Modern American History, Bus Hist Rev, Autumn 70; The Public Image of Big Business In America, 1880-1940, John Hopkins Univ, 75; ed, The Papers of Dwight David Eisenhower, Johns Hopkins Univ, Vol VI-IX, 78; co-ed, Studies in Economic History and Policy: The United States in the Twentieth Century, Cambridge Univ Press, 81; The Triumph of Oligopoly, in American Economic Development, Stanford Univ, 93; coauth, "Organizing and Reorganizing the World Bank, 1946-1972," Business History Review, 95; auth, "The Authority and Responsibility of the Chief Executive Officer," Industrial and Corporate change, 95; co-auth, "The McNamara Bank and Its Legacy, 1968-1987, Business and Economic History, 95; coauth, Networks of Innovation, Cambridge Univ Press, 95; co-auth, The Transformation of the Pharmaceutical Industry in the Twentieth Century, Science in the Twentieth Century, Harwood, 97; auth, "State Owned Enterprise in a Hostile Environment," and "Schumpeter Revisited," in The Rise and Fall of State Owned Enterprise, 00. **CONTACT ADDRESS** Dept of History, Johns Hopkins Univ, Baltimore, 3400 N Charles St, Baltimore, MD 21218-2680. **EMAIL** galambos@jhunix.hcf.jhu.edu

GALAVARIS, GEORGE
PERSONAL Born 00/00/1926, Greece, Greece **DISCIPLINE** HISTORY OF ART **EDUCATION** Univ Athens, MA, 51; Princeton Univ, MFA, 57, PhD(art, archaeol), 58. **CAREER** Vis fel Byzantine art, Dumbarton Oaks, Harvard Univ, 52-59; from asst prof to assoc prof, 59-65, Prof Hist of Art, McGill Univ, 65-, Vis prof hist of art, Univ Wis-Madison, 67-68; Can Coun leave award, 70-71, leave fel, 77-78; vis fel, Dept Art and Archaeol, Princeton Univ, 77. **MEMBERSHIPS** Int Asn Byzantine Studies; Mediaeval Acad Am; Am Numis Asn; Ger Soc Thomas von Kempen. **RESEARCH** History of early Christian and Byzantine art; liturgy; East Christian civilization. **SELECTED PUBLICATIONS** Auth, The Icon in the Life of the Church: Doctrine-Liturgy-Devotion (Iconography of Religions Section 24, Christianity), 81; auth, Bread and the liturgy; the symbolism of early Christian and Byzantine bread stamps; auth, Icons from the Elehjem Art Center; auth, The illustrations of the liturgical homilies of Gragory Nazianzenus; auth, The illustrations of the Prefaces in Byzantine gospels; coauth, The Monastery of Saint Catherine at Mount Sinai: The Illuminated Greek Manuscripts: From the Ninth to the Twelfth Century. **CONTACT ADDRESS** Dept of Art Hist, McGill Univ, 853 Sherbrooke St W, Montreal, QC, Canada H3A 2T6.

GALGANO, MICHAEL J.
PERSONAL Born 10/17/1942, Glen Ridge, NJ, m, 1965, 3 children **DISCIPLINE** HISTORY **CAREER** Instr, Middle Tenn State Univ, 69; Instr, Ohio State Univ, 69-71; Asst Prof to Prof, 71-84; Prof, James Madison Univ, 84-. **HONORS AND AWARDS** John Marshall Awd, Marshall Univ 84; Phi Alpha Theta, Omicron Delta Kappa, Golden Key Nat Honor Soc, James Madison Univ Grant, Folger Inst, 91; NEH Fel, Univ NC, 78-79 **MEMBERSHIPS** Am Hist Asn, N Am Conf on British Studies, world Hist Asn, S conf on British Studies, Carolinas Symposium on British Studies, Nat Coun for Hist Educ, Va Coun for Hist Educ. **RESEARCH** British social, family, and religious history, 1500-1700; Historical methods; The teaching of history. **SELECTED PUBLICATIONS** Auth, "The Best of Times: Teaching Undergraduate Research Methods Using the Great American History Machine and The Valley of the Shadow," History Computer Review, (99): 13-28; auth, "Infancy and Childhood: The Female Experience in the Restoration Northwest," in The Portrayal of Life Stages in English Literature, 1500-1800: Essays in Honor of Warren Wooden, Edwin Mellen Press, 89; auth, "Out of the Mainstream: Catholic and Quaker Women in the Restoration Northwest," The World of William Penn, Univ Penn Press, 117-137; auth, "Iron-Mining in Restoration Furness: The Case of Sir Thomas Preston," Recusant History, (76): 212-218; auth, "Negotiations for a Nun's dowry: Restoration Letters of Mary Caryll, O.S.B. and Ann Clifton, O.S.B.," American Benedictine Review, (73): 278-298; ed, Selected Papers of the West Virginia Shakespeare and Renaissance Association, 1977-1985. **CONTACT ADDRESS** Dept Hist, James Madison Univ, 800 S Main St, Harrisonburg, VA 22807-0001. **EMAIL** galganmj@jmu.edu

GALISHOFF, STUART
PERSONAL Born 04/18/1940, New York, NY **DISCIPLINE** URBAN HISTORY **EDUCATION** NYork Univ, BA, 60, MA, 66, PhD(hist), 69. **CAREER** Asst prof, 68-76, Assoc Prof Hist, GA State Univ, 76-. **HONORS AND AWARDS** William Adee Whitehead Awd, 70. **MEMBERSHIPS** Am Asn Med Hist; AHA; Orgn Am Historians. **RESEARCH** History of public health. **SELECTED PUBLICATIONS** Auth, Newark and the great influenza pandemic of 1918, Bull Hist Med, 5-6/69; Cholera in Newark, J Hist Med & Allied Sci, 10/70; The Passaic Valley trunk sewer, NJ Hist, winter 70; Safeguarding the Public Health, Newark, 1895-1918, Greenwood, 75; coauth, Atlanta's water supply, 1865-1918, Md Historian, Vol VIII, No 1, spring 77. **CONTACT ADDRESS** Dept of Hist, Georgia State Univ, 33 Gilmer St SE, Atlanta, GA 30303-3080.

GALLACHER, PATRICK
DISCIPLINE MEDIEVAL STUDIES **EDUCATION** Univ Ill, PhD, 66. **CAREER** Instr, Univ NMex, 66-. **SELECTED PUBLICATIONS** Coed, Hermeneutics and Medieval Culture, 89. **CONTACT ADDRESS** Dept of English, Univ of New Mexico, Albuquerque, Albuquerque, NM 87131. **EMAIL** gallache@umn.edu

GALLAGHER, GARY W.
PERSONAL Born 10/08/1950, Los Angeles, CA, m, 1986, 1 child **DISCIPLINE** HISTORY **EDUCATION** Adams State Col, BA, 72; Univ TX Austin, MA, PhD, 77, 82. **CAREER** Archivist, LBJ lib Austin TX, 77-86; vis lectr, Univ TX, Austin, 86; Asst, prof, assoc prof, Penn State, 86-91, hd dept, 91-95, prof, 91-98; Univ VA, prof hist, 98-. **HONORS AND AWARDS** Lincoln Prize, 98; George W Littlefield Lectr, 95-96; Citation, Soc Am Hist, 96; Frank L Klement Lectr, 95; Distg in Hum Awd, Penn State, 95; Richard Barksdale Harwell Awd, 91; Nevins Freeman Awd, 91; Douglas Southall Freman Awd, 90; Founders Awd, 89-90; Mellon Fellow, VA hist soc, 88, 89; Univ fel, Univ TX, Austin, 74, 75, 76, 77. **MEMBERSHIPS** Organ Am Historians; Southern Hist Asn. **RESEARCH** Am civil war; southern hist; military hist. **SELECTED PUBLICATIONS** Lee and His Generals in War and Memory, LA State Univ Press, 98; The Confederate War, Harvard Univ Press, 97; Lee The Soldier, Univ NE Press 96; Jubal A Early, the Lost Cause, and Civil War History: A Persistent Legacy, Marquette Univ Press, 95; many articles and essays. **CONTACT ADDRESS** Corcoran Dept Hist, Univ of Virginia, 227 Randall Hall, Charlottesville, VA 22903-3284. **EMAIL** gallagher@virgina.edu

GALLAGHER, MARY A. Y.
PERSONAL Born 12/09/1939, Hartford, CT, m, 1968, 1 child **DISCIPLINE** HISTORY **EDUCATION** Univ Notre Dame, MA, 67; Queen's Coll, CUNY, PhD, 78. **CAREER** From asst ed to co-ed, Papers of Robert Morris, 71-; adjunct prof, Brooklyn Coll, CUNY, 92-95; adjunct prof, Queens Coll, CUNY, 97. **MEMBERSHIPS** Assn Documentary Editors; Omobundo Inst Early Amer History and Culture. **SELECTED PUBLICATIONS** Co-ed, The Papers of Robert Morris, 1781-1784, vol. VIII, 95; auth, "Charting a New Course for the China Trade: The Late 18th-Century Model," The American Neptune, summer 97; auth, "Reinterpreting the 'very trifiling mutiny' at Philadelphia in 1783," Pennsylvania Magazine of History and Biography, Jan/Apr 95. **CONTACT ADDRESS** 763 E 39th St, Brooklyn, NY 11210. **EMAIL** magallagher@wans.net

GALLATIN, HARLIE KAY
PERSONAL Born 12/15/1933, Meadville, MO, m, 1954, 3 children **DISCIPLINE** ANCIENT & MEDIEVAL HISTORY **EDUCATION** William Jewell Col, BA, 55; Central Baptist Theol Sem, BD, 59; Central Mo State Univ, MA, 61; Univ Ill, Urbana, PhD(hist), 72. **CAREER** Instr hist & polit sci, 61-65, assoc prof, 67-73, chmn, Interdisciplinary Fac Mid Eastern Studies, 71-80, prof hist, Southwest Baptist Univ, 73-, chmn dept hist & polit sci, 70-, dir spec studies, 76-93. **HONORS AND AWARDS** Parkway Distinguished Prof, 97. **MEMBERSHIPS** AHA; Am Soc Church Hist; Conf Faith & Hist; Assoc of Ancient Hist. **RESEARCH** Relations and interactions between governments and popular religious movements in Hellenistic and Roman times; incidents and results of the use of religious ideology as political propaganda in ancient, medieval, and early modern settings in eastern and western Europe; the development of ancient and medieval Christianity in relation to its cultural context. **SELECTED PUBLICATIONS** Contribr, Eerdmans' Handbook to the History of Christianity, Eerdmans, 77; contribr, A Lion Handbook, The History of Christianity, Lion Publishing, 77, 90; contribr, Evangelical Dictionary of Theology, Baker Book House, 84,94. **CONTACT ADDRESS** Dept of Hist & Political Science, Southwestern Baptist Univ, 1600 Univ Ave, Bolivar, MO 65613-2597. **EMAIL** hgallati@sbuniv.edu

GALLICCHIO, MARC S.
DISCIPLINE HISTORY **EDUCATION** Temple Univ, BA, 75; Pa State Univ, MA, 77; Temple Univ, PhD, 86. **CAREER** Assoc prof. **HONORS AND AWARDS** Bernath Article Prize, Soc of Hist(s) of Amer For Rel(s) Stuart. **RESEARCH** US foreign relations; US military history; US and East Asia. **SELECTED PUBLICATIONS** Auth, The Cold War Begins in Asia: American East Asian Policy and the Fall of the Japanese Empire, 88; The Other China Hands: US Army Officers and America's Failure in China, 1941-1950, J of Amer E Asian Relations, 95; The Kuriles Controversy: US Diplomacy and Strategy in the Soviet-Japan Border Dispute, 1941-1956, Pac Hist Rev, 91; After Nagasaki: George Marshall's Plan for Tactical Nuclear Weapons in Japan, Prologue, 91; auth, The African American Encounter with Japan and China: Black Internationalism in Asia, 1895-1945, UNC Press, 00. **CONTACT ADDRESS** Dept of History, Villanova Univ, 800 Lancaster Ave., Villanova, PA 19085-1692. **EMAIL** marc.gallicchio@villanova.edu

GALLICK, ROSEMARY
PERSONAL Born 12/19/1949, Pittsburgh, PA, m, 1981, 2 children **DISCIPLINE** ART HISTORY **EDUCATION** SUNY, Stony Brook, BA, 71; Pratt Inst, MFA, 74; Cornell Univ, MPS, 76; SUNY, Buffalo, JD, 81. **CAREER** asst prof, N Va Comm Col. **HONORS AND AWARDS** Who's Who Among America's Teachers, 2000; Ser Learning Grant, 99-00; Achiev Awd, TAC/ELI, 98; NEH, 98. **MEMBERSHIPS** Am and Pop Culture Assocs. **SELECTED PUBLICATIONS** Auth, "Featuring the Funnies: 100 Years of the Comic Strip," INKS Mag ((Ohio State UP), 96; Auth, "The Tattoo: An American Pop Art Form," The Mid-Atlantic Almanack (96): vol.5:1-13; auth, "Bill Griffith's Zippy: A Renaissance Man," Pop Cult Rev (98): vol.9, no.1; auth, "Tribute to Woody Gelman, An Collector," The Genius of Winsor McKay, Ohio State UP (98); auth, Tattoo Parlors, Encycl of Am Studies, Grolier Encyclopedia (99). **CONTACT ADDRESS** Dept Humanities, No Virginia Comm Col, 15200 Neabsco Mills Rd, Woodbridge, VA 22191-4006.

GALUSH, WILLIAM J.
DISCIPLINE HISTORY **EDUCATION** Minn Univ, PhD. **CAREER** Ed, Mid-Am. **RESEARCH** Ethnic and religious history. **SELECTED PUBLICATIONS** Auth, Purity and Power: Chicago Polonia Feminists, 1880-1914, Polish Am Stud 47, 90. **CONTACT ADDRESS** Fine Arts Dept, Loyola Univ, Chicago, 6525 N. Sheridan Rd., Chicago, IL 60626. **EMAIL** wgalush@orion.it.luc.edu

GALVAN, DELIA V.
PERSONAL Born Mexico City, Mexico **DISCIPLINE** LITERATURE AND CIVILIZATION OF SPANISH AMERICA **EDUCATION** Univ Cincinnati, BA, MA, PhD. **CAREER** Instr, Bucknell Univ; John Carroll Univ; assoc prof, 91-. **SELECTED PUBLICATIONS** Publ, Spanish American Women Writers of Fiction. **CONTACT ADDRESS** Dept of For Lang, Cleveland State Univ, 83 E 24th St, Cleveland, OH 44115.

GALVARIS, GEORGE
PERSONAL Born 10/17/1926, Greece **DISCIPLINE** ART HISTORY **EDUCATION** Athens, MA, 51; Princeton Univ, MFA, 57, PhD, 58. **CAREER** Vis fel, Dumbarton Oaks, Harvard Univ, 57-59; asst prof, 59, prof art hist, 65, UNIV PROF EMER, McGILL UNIV; vis fel, Princeton Univ, 77; Inst Stud Icon Art, Holland, 78-81; vis prof, Univ Crete, 87, 94-96. **HONORS AND AWARDS** Fel, Royal Soc Can; Acad Athens Awd. **MEMBERSHIPS** Founder & first pres, Can Nat Comt Byzantine Stud; corresp mem, Acad Athens; fel, Greek Christian Archaeol Soc; Medieval Acad Am; Am Numismatic Soc; Soc Nubian Stud. **SELECTED PUBLICATIONS** Auth, The Illustrations of the Liturgical Homilies of Gregory Nazianzenus, 69; auth, Bread and the Liturgy, 70; auth, Icons from the

Elvehjem Centre, 73; auth, The Illustrations of the Prefaces in Byzantine Gospels, 79; auth, The Icon in the Life of the Church, 81; auth, Zografiki Vizantinon Cheirographon, 95; coauth, The Monastery of St. Catherine at Sinai, The Illuminated Manuscripts, vol 1, 90; coauth, Treasures at Sinai, 90. **CONTACT ADDRESS** 853 Sherbrooke St W, Montreal, QC, Canada H3A 2T6.

GAMBER, WENDY
DISCIPLINE HISTORY **EDUCATION** Univ Calif, AB, 80; Univ Calif, MA, 84; Brandeis Univ, PhD, 91. **CAREER** From Asst Prof to Assoc Prof, Ind Univ, 92-. **HONORS AND AWARDS** Mass Hist Soc Res Fel, 90-91; Ind Univ Summer Fac Fel, 93, 97; Dir Grant, Ind Hist Soc, 95-96; Judith Lee Ridge Article Prize, 96; Teaching Excellence Recognition Awd, Ind Univ, 96-97; Newberry Libr Short-Term Fel, 97; Fel, Ind Univ, 00-01. **MEMBERSHIPS** AHA, Berkshire Conf of Women Historians, Bus Hist Conf, Orgn of Am Historians, Soc Sci Hist Asn, Soc of Historians of the Early Am Republic, Am Studies Asn. **RESEARCH** Nineteenth-Century United States, women and gender, boarding houses in Nineteenth-Century America. **SELECTED PUBLICATIONS** Auth, "A Precarious Independence: Milliners and Dressmakers in Boston 1860-1890," J of Women's Hist 4 (92): 60-88; auth, "Gendered Concerns: Thoughts on the History of Business and the History of Women," Bus and Economic Hist 23 (94): 129-140; auth, "'Reduced to Science': Gender, Technology and Power in the American Dressmaking Trade 1860-1910," Technol and Cult 36 (95): 455-482; auth, The Female Economy: The Millinery and Dressmaking Trades 1860-1930, Univ Ill Pr (Urbana, IL), 97; auth, "A Gendered Enterprise: Placing Nineteenth-Century Businesswomen in History," Bus Hist Rev 72 (98): 188-218. **CONTACT ADDRESS** Dept Hist, Indiana Univ, Bloomington, 1020 E Kirkwood Ave, Bloomington, IN 47405-7103. **EMAIL** wgamber@indiana.edu

GAMBONI, DARIO
DISCIPLINE EUROPEAN ART OF THE 19TH CENTURY **EDUCATION** Univ Lausanne, BA, MA, PhD, 89. **CAREER** Curator, Museums of Fine Arts: Lausanne, Lucerne, Berne and Lugano. **HONORS AND AWARDS** Ailsa Mellon Bruce Sen fel Ctr Adv Study Visual Arts. **MEMBERSHIPS** Institut Universitaire de France; Nat Gallery Art; Revue de l'Art. **SELECTED PUBLICATIONS** Auth, La geographie artistique, Disentis: Desertina, 87, German and Italian translations; La plume et le pinceau. Odilon Redon et la litterature, Paris: Editions de Minuit, 89; The Destruction of Art: Iconoclasm and Vandalism since the French Revolution, New Haven and London: Yale U P, 97, German translation; and Odilon Redon: Das Fass Amontillado, Frankfurt-am-Main: Fischer, 98. **CONTACT ADDRESS** Inst of Art Hist, Univ of Amsterdam, Herengracht 286, NL-1016 BX, Amsterdam. **EMAIL** gamboni@hum.uva.nl

GANSON, BARBARA
PERSONAL Born 09/08/1953, CA, s **DISCIPLINE** HISTORY **EDUCATION** Univ Tex, PhD. **CAREER** Assoc prof. **HONORS AND AWARDS** Award for Excellence in Undergraduate Teaching, Florida Atlantic Univ, 96-97. **MEMBERSHIPS** American Historical Asn, Centro De Estudios Antropologicos, Catholic Univ, Paraguay. **RESEARCH** Latin America history; Rio De La Plata history; ethnohistory. **SELECTED PUBLICATIONS** Auth, Becoming Christian, Remaining Native: Guapani and Jesuit in the Rio De La Plata, forthcoming with Standard Univ Press; auth, The Evuevi of Paraguay: Adaptive Strategies and Responses to Colonialism 1528-1811, 89; Contacto intercultural: Un estudio de los payaguas del Paraguay 1528-1870, 89. **CONTACT ADDRESS** History Dept, Florida Atlantic Univ, 777 Glades Rd, Boca Raton, FL 33431. **EMAIL** bganson@fau.edu

GANZ, ALBERT HARDING
PERSONAL Born 12/12/1938, New York, NY, m, 1970, 2 children **DISCIPLINE** GERMAN & MILITARY HISTORY **EDUCATION** Wittenberg Univ, AB, 61; Columbia Univ, MA, 63; Lt 4th Armored Div, Germany, 64-66; Ohio State Univ, PhD(Ger hist), 72. **CAREER** Instr, Ohio State Univ at Newark, 71-72, asst prof 72-77, assoc prof Europ Hist, 77-. **MEMBERSHIPS** OAH, Ohio Acad of Hist; Soc Mil Hist; Ohio Arms Control Seminar (Mershon). **RESEARCH** Modern German history; Imperial German Navy; armored warfare; military history, national security. **SELECTED PUBLICATIONS** Auth, Abu Ageila-Two Battles, Armor, Part I, 5-6/74, Part II, 7-8/74; co-auth, The German Navy in the Far East and Pacific, In: Kennedy and Moses, Germany in the Pacific and Far East, 1870-1914, Univ Queensland, 77; auth, Colonial Policy and the Imperial German Navy, Militaergeschichtliche Mitteilungen, 1/77; Albion-The Baltic Islands Operation, 4/78, The German Expedition to Finland, 1918, 4/80, Military Affairs; auth, The Holy Roman Empire, ed Zophy, Greenwood Press, 80; auth, Breakthrough to Bastogne, Armor, 11-12/81; Return to Singling, Armor XCIV No 5: 32-39, Sept-Oct 85; Patton's Relief of General Wood, Journal of mil hist 53,3: 257-273, July 89; The 11th Panzers in the Defense, 1944, Armor CIII No 2: 26-27, Mar-Apr 94 (trans into German as Die 11. Panzer-Division an der Westfront 1944; Questionable Objective: The Brittany Ports, 1944, Journal of mil Hist, 59, 1: 77-95, Jan 95; Articles (7) in Spencer C. Tucker, ed, The European Powers in thr First World War, NY & London: Garland Pub, 96. **CONTACT ADDRESS** Dept of Hist, Ohio State Univ, Newark, 1179 University Dr, Newark, OH 43055-1797.

GANZ, MARGERY ANN
PERSONAL Born 07/04/1947, Trenton, NJ **DISCIPLINE** MEDIEVAL & RENAISSANCE HISTORY **EDUCATION** Univ Rochester, BA, 69; Syracuse Univ, MA, 71, PhD(Renaissance Hist), 79. **CAREER** Adj instr hist, Onondaga Community Col, 74-79; asst prof, Univ Tenn, Chattanooga, 79-80; asst prof hist, Spelman Col, 81-, Instr hist, Col Cortland, State Univ NY, 71-72 & Le Moyne Col, 76-79; chmn, dept of History, 97; prof History, 98, dir of study abroad, 88; Spelman College. **HONORS AND AWARDS** Harvard Univ Villa I Tatti, fel, 85; NAFSA Lily Von KempererAwd, 95; AMOCO Awd Outstanding Fac Feaching, 91; UNCF Mellon fel, 88-89. **MEMBERSHIPS** Renaissance Soc Am; Soc Ital Hist Studies; Am Hist Asn. **RESEARCH** Conspiracies against the Medici, 1450-1494; family history in Renaissance Florence; Buon Vivere Civile in the Renaissance. **SELECTED PUBLICATIONS** Auth, Donato Acciaiudi and the Medici: A strategy for survival in Quattrocento Florence, Rinascimento, 82; A Florentine Friendship: Donato Acciaindli & Vespasiano da Bisticci, Renaissance Quarterly 43, 90; Paying the Price for Political Failure: Florentine Women in the Aftermath of 1466, Rinascimento, 34, 94. **CONTACT ADDRESS** Dept of History, Spelman Col, 350 Spelman Lane, Box 1447, Atlanta, GA 30314-4398. **EMAIL** mganz@spelman.edu

GARA, LARRY
PERSONAL Born 05/16/1922, San Antonio, TX, m, 1946, 2 children **DISCIPLINE** AMERICAN HISTORY **EDUCATION** William Penn Col, BA, 47; Pa State Univ, MA, 48; Univ Wis, PhD, 53. **CAREER** Instr hist & govt, Bluffton Col, 48-49; lectr hist, Mexico City Col, 53-54; from instr to asst prof, Eureka Col, 54-57; prof, Grove City Col, 57-62, chmn, Dept Hist & Polit Sci, 58-62; Assoc Prof, 62-66, Prof Hist & Govt, 71-92, Prof Emeritus, Wilmington Col, Ohio, 92-, Chmn Dept Hist, 71-92. **HONORS AND AWARDS** T. Wistar Brown fel, Haverford Col, 68-69; War Resisters League Annual Peace Awd, 84; Distinguished Fac Awd, Wilmington Col, 96; Distinguished Service Awd, Ohio Acad Hist, 97. **MEMBERSHIPS** Orgn Am Hist; Southern Hist Asn; Ohio Acad Hist; Peace Hist Soc. **RESEARCH** Antislavery and other 19th century reform movements; the American peace movement; the Franklin Pierce Administration. **SELECTED PUBLICATIONS** Auth, Westernized Yankee: The Story of Cyrus Woodman, State Hist Soc Wis, 56; The Baby Dodd Story, Contemporary Press, 59, repr, LSU Press, 92; Liberty Line: The Legend of the Underground Railroad, Univ Ky, 61, repr, 96; A Short History of Wisconsin, State Hist Soc Wis, 62; Who was an Abolitionist?, In: The Antislavery Vanguard, Princeton Univ, 65; The Narrative of William Wells Brown, Addison-Wesley, 68; William Still and the Underground Railroad, In: The Making of Black America, Atheneum, 68; Horace Mann: Antislavery Congressman, Historian, 11/69; War Resistance in Historical Perspective Pendle Hill, 70; Propaganda Uses of the Underground Railroad, In: American Vistas 1607-1877, Oxford Univ, 71; Slavery and the Slave Power: a Crucial Distinction, In: The Abolitionists, 73; The Myth of the Underground Railroad, In: Annual Editions: Readings in American History, Dushkin, 81, Vol 1; The Presidency of Franklin Pierce, Univ Press Kans, 91; coauth, A Few Small Candles: War Resisters of World War II Tell Their Stories, Kent State Univ Press, 99. **CONTACT ADDRESS** 251 Ludovic St, Wilmington, OH 45177-2499. **EMAIL** larry_gara@wilmington.edu

GARBER, MARILYN
PERSONAL Born Brooklyn, NY, 2 children **DISCIPLINE** HISTORY, LAW **EDUCATION** Univ Calif, Los Angeles, BA, 57, MA, 60, PhD, 67; Calif State Univ, 67-80; Southwestern Univ, JD, 77; **CAREER** Prof hist, Calif State Univ, Dominguez Hills, 80-. **MEMBERSHIPS** Calif State Bar. **RESEARCH** Utopia; legal history; labor law; negotiation; conflict resolution **SELECTED PUBLICATIONS** Natural Law Liberalism, 67. **CONTACT ADDRESS** Dept Hist, California State Univ, Dominguez Hills, 1000 E Victoria, Carson, CA 90747-0005. **EMAIL** dhvx20@csudh.edu

GARCEAU, DEE
PERSONAL Born 10/08/1955, Boston, MA **DISCIPLINE** HISTORY **EDUCATION** Nasson Col, BA, 77; Wash St Univ, MA, 82; Brown Univ, PhD, 95. **CAREER** Vis Asst Prof, Univ Mont, 90-95; Asst Prof, Rhodes Col, 95-. **HONORS AND AWARDS** Ut Endowment for the Humanities Merit Awd, 87; Ut Arts Coun Develop Grant, 88, 89; Fel, Brown Univ; Grant, Mont Comt for the Humanities, 90; Grant, Western Studies Prog, 94; Fac Develop Grant, Rhodes Col, 97. **MEMBERSHIPS** OAW, WHA, CWWH. **RESEARCH** Gender in the American West, Native American women in the Northwest, cultures of manhood in the U S West. **SELECTED PUBLICATIONS** Auth, "Single Women Homesteaders and the Meanings of Independence: Places on the Map, Places in the Mind," Frontiers: A J of Women's Studies 15:3 (95): 1-26; auth, "'I Got a Girl Here, Would You Like to Meet Her?': Courtship, Ethnicity and Community in Sweetwater County, Wyoming 1900-1925," Writing the Range: Race, Class and Cult in the Women's West, Univ Okla Pr (97): 274-297; auth, The Important Things in Life: Women, Work and Family in Sweetwater County, Wyoming 1880-1929, Univ Neb Pr (Lincoln, NE); 97; rev, The Frontiers of Women's Writing: Women's Narratives and the Rhetoric of Westward Expansion, by Brigitte Georgi-Findlay, Mont: The Mag of Western Hist (99): 83-84; rev, Intimate Frontiers: Sex, Gender and Culture in Old California, by Albert L Hurtado, J of the Early Republic (forthcoming); co-ed, Crossing the Great Divide: Cultures of Manhood in the American West, Routledge Pr (New York), forthcoming; auth, "Sweetwater County: Desert Highway, Company Town, Cowboy West," The Worker's West, Univ Okla Pr (forthcoming); auth, "Bunkie, Prostitute's Friend, Cross-Dresser or Family Man: Cowboy Identity and the Gendering of Ranch Work," Crossing the Great Divide: Cult of Manhood in the Am West, Routledge Pr (forthcoming); auth, "Gender and Cultural Mediation in the Life and Work of Mourning Dove," Native Women's Lives, Oxford UP (forthcoming). **CONTACT ADDRESS** Dept Hist, Rhodes Col, 2000 N Parkway, Memphis, TN 38112-1624. **EMAIL** garceau@rhodes.edu

GARCIA, JUAN RAMON
PERSONAL Born 07/27/1947, Sebastian, TX, m, 3 children **DISCIPLINE** MEXICAN AMERICAN & AMERICAN HISTORY **EDUCATION** DePaul Univ, BA, 71, MA, 79; Univ Notre Dame, MA, 74, PhD, 77. **CAREER** Asst prof hist, Univ Mich-Flint, 75-78; prog dev bilingual educ, E Mich Univ, 78-79; assoc prof hist, Univ Mich-Flint, 79-81; Assoc prof hist, 81-, Dir Univ Teaching Ctr, 90-94, Assoc Dean, Col Social & Behavorial Sci, 94-98, Prof Hist, 97, Univ AZ; Dir Chicano studies, Univ Mich-Flint, 75-78 & 79-81; consult, Nat Inst Educ, 77-81, Nat Educ Asn, 78-81 & Nat Teacher Corps, 75-80; VP Acad Aff, Col St Mary, Omaha, NE, 98; Univ Arizona, Dept Hist, 01-. **MEMBERSHIPS** Nat Asn Chicano Studies; W Soc Sci Asn. **RESEARCH** Mexican immigration history; Mexicans and Mexican Americans in the Midwest 1900-1941; United States History 1918-45. **SELECTED PUBLICATIONS** Auth, A History of the People of Mexican Descent in Chicago Heights, Illinois, 1900-1975, PSC Press, 76; A history of Chicanos in Chicago Heights, Illinois, Aztlan, 78; A History of the Mexican American People: A Teacher's Guide, Univ Notre Dame, 79; The people of Mexican descent in Michigan: A historical overview, Blacks and Chicanos in Urban Michigan, Mich Hist Div, 79; Operation Wetback: The Mass Deportation of Mexican Undocumented Workers, 1954, Greenwood, 81; Midwest Mexicanos in the 1920's: Issues, questions & directions, Social Sci Quart, 82; Perspectives in Mexican American Studies, Volumes 1-7, 88-01; Mexicans In The Midwest, 1900-1932, Univ AZ, 98; ed, Perspectives in Mexican American Studies. **CONTACT ADDRESS** VP Acad Aff, Col of Saint Mary, 1901 S 72nd St, Omaha, NE 68124. **EMAIL** Jgarcia@csm.edu

GARCIA, MATT
DISCIPLINE HISTORY **EDUCATION** Claremont Graduate Sch, PhD, 96. **CAREER** Asst prof, Univ Ill Urbana Champaign. **RESEARCH** Chicano/Latino history; history of American West; popular culture and cultural criticism. **SELECTED PUBLICATIONS** Auth, Just put on that Padua Hills 'smile': The Padua Hills Theatre and The Mexican Players, 1931-1974, Calif Hist, 95; Adjusting the Focus: Padua Hills Theatre and Latino History, 96; Chicana/o history in a changing discipline, Humboldt J Social Relations, 96. **CONTACT ADDRESS** History Dept, Univ of Illinois, Urbana-Champaign, 52 E Gregory Dr, Champaign, IL 61820. **EMAIL** garcia2@staff.uiuc.edu

GARDELLA, ROBERT PAUL
PERSONAL Born 02/16/1943, Newark, NJ, m, 1970, 1 child **DISCIPLINE** CHINESE HISTORY **EDUCATION** Rice Univ, BA, 65; Univ Wash, MA, 68, PhD(hist), 76. **CAREER** Instr hist, Loyola Univ, La, 73-74; asst prof humanities, US Merchant Marine Acad, 77-. **HONORS AND AWARDS** Chiang Ching-Kuo Res Grant, 96-98. **MEMBERSHIPS** Asn Asian Studies; Soc Ch'ing Studies. **RESEARCH** Social and economic history of Ch'ing and modern China; regional history of southeast China; Chinese business hist. **SELECTED PUBLICATIONS** Auth, Harvesting Mountains: Fujian and the China Tea Trade 1757-1937, Univ Calif Press, 94; Squaring Accounts: Commercial Bookkeeping Methods and Capitalist Rationalism in Late Qing and Republican China, J Asian Studies, 92; From Treaty Ports to Provincial Status, Taiwan: A New History, ME Sharpe, 98; co-ed, Chinese Business History: Interpretive Trends and Priorities for the Future, ME Sharpe, 98. **CONTACT ADDRESS** Dept of Humanities, United States Merchant Marine Acad, 300 Steamboat Rd, Kings Point, NY 11024-1699. **EMAIL** Robert-Gardella@usmma.edu

GARDINIER, DAVID E.
PERSONAL Born 10/13/1932, Syracuse, NY, m, 1966, 3 children **DISCIPLINE** HISTORY OF AFRICA **EDUCATION** State Univ NYork Albany, AB, 53; Yale Univ, MAT, 54, PhD(hist), 60. **CAREER** Instr hist, Univ Del, 59-60; from instr to asst prof, Bowling Green State Univ, 60-65; res assoc, Ctr Int Studies, Ohio Univ, 65-66; assoc prof, 66-69, chmn dept, 69-75, Prof Hist, Marquette Univ, 69-99, African sect ed, Am Hist Rev, 64-90. **HONORS AND AWARDS** Chevalier dans

l'Ordre des Palmes Academiques, 95. **MEMBERSHIPS** AHA; African Studies Asn; Fr Colonial Hist Soc (vpres, 76-78, pres, 78-80). **RESEARCH** History of French-speaking Africa; equatorial Africa; colonialism. **SELECTED PUBLICATIONS** Auth, Education in the States of Equatorial Africa, A Bibliographical Essay, Africana J, No. 3, 72; Schooling in the States of Equatorial Africa, Can J African Studies, 12/74; Education in French Equatorial Africa, 1842-1945, Proc Fr Colonial Hist Soc, 78; The Beginnings of French Catholic Evangelization in Gabon, 1844-83, Fr Colonial Studies, No 2, 78; The Impact of French Education on Africa, 1817-1960, Proc Fr Colonial Hist Soc, 78; Education Souns la Tutelle in: Education au Cameroun, Univ Montreal, 82; Bibliographical Essay: Decolonization in French, Belgian, & Portuguese in Africa, In: Transfer of Power in Africa, Yale Univ, 82; auth, Gabon, Clio Press, 92; auth, The Peace-Corps in Cameroon, Am Hist Rev, Vol 0098, 93; Historical Dictionary of Gabon, Scarcrow Press, 94; co-auth, Political Reform in Francophone Africa, Westview, 97. **CONTACT ADDRESS** Dept of Hist, Marquette Univ, Milwaukee, WI 53201-1881.

GARDNER, BETTYE J.
PERSONAL Born Vicksburg, MS, s **DISCIPLINE** HISTORY **EDUCATION** Howard Univ, BA 1962, MA 1964; George Washington Univ, PhD 1974. **CAREER** Howard Univ, instructor 64-69; Social Sys Intervention Inc, sr rsch assoc 69; Washington DC Bd of Educ, consultant 69; Black History Calvert Ct MD, consultant; Washington Technical Inst, asst prof 69-71; Coppin State Coll, dean of arts & sciences 81-87, prof of history 82-, chairperson dept of history 88-90. **HONORS AND AWARDS** Moton Fellowship, Moton Institute, 1978-79; Danforth Assn, Danforth Foundation, 1980-86; Fellowship, Smithsonian, summer 1988. **MEMBERSHIPS** Mem NAACP, Org of Amer Historians, Assoc of Black Women Historians, Assoc for the Study of Afro-Amer Life & History; mem Natl Educ Assn; NCNW, 1980; editorial bd Journal of Negro History; exec counc Asso for the Study of Afro-Amer Life & Hist; vp, Association for Afro-American Life and History, 1993-95, natl pres, 1995-97; publ numerous articles, Educ Licensure Commission, Washington DC, chairperson; Bethune House Federal Commission. **CONTACT ADDRESS** History Dept, Coppin State Col, 2500 W North Ave, Baltimore, MD 21216.

GAREN, SALLY
PERSONAL Born 10/11/1947, Oak Ridge, TN, m, 1978, 2 children **DISCIPLINE** MEDIEVAL ART HISTORY **EDUCATION** Smith Col, BA, 68; Art Inst of Chicago, MFA, 70; Univ Chicago, MFA, 75, PhD, 85. **CAREER** Lect, DePaul Univ, 77-82; Art Hist teacher, The Madeira School, 90-98; teacher, Northern Va Community Col, 00-. **HONORS AND AWARDS** Smith Col, Alpha Awd in the Arts; Univ of Chicago: Cochrane Woods Travel Grant. **MEMBERSHIPS** Soc of Architectural Historians; the Textile Museum; The Pre-Columbian Soc of Washington, DC. **RESEARCH** Visigothic Period Spanish architecture and sculpture. **SELECTED PUBLICATIONS** Auth, book review of Jerrilyn Dodds, Architecture and Ideology in Early Medieval Spain, in JSAH, March 92; Santa Maria de Melque and Church Construction under Muslim Rule, J of the Soc of Architectural Historians, Sept 92. **CONTACT ADDRESS** 1625 Evers Dr, McLean, VA 22101-5010. **EMAIL** sgaren@aol.com

GARFINKLE, CHARLENE G.
PERSONAL Born 09/01/1955, Inglewood, CA, m, 1977, 1 child **DISCIPLINE** HISTORY OF ART AND ARCHITECTURE; 19TH CENTURY ART AND ARCHITECTURE OF UNITE **EDUCATION** Calif State Univ, BA, 77; Univ Calif Santa Barbara, MA, 86; Univ Calif Santa Barbara PhD, 96 **CAREER** Assoc lctr, Univ Calif Santa Barbara, 90-92; lctr, Univ Calif Santa Barbara, 90-97; instr, Santa Barbara City Col, current **HONORS AND AWARDS** Regents' Fel, 91, 93; Art Affiliates, Art Hist Grad Fel, 92; Newberry Libr Residence Fel, 91; Gen Affiliates, Grad Dissertation Fel, 91; Murray Roman Art Hist Fel, 89-91; **MEMBERSHIPS** Am Cult Assoc; Am Studies Assoc; Art Historians of Southern Calif; Assoc Historians Amer Art; Assoc Historians Nineteenth-Century Art; Assoc Independent Historians Art; Col Art Assoc; Interdisciplinary Nineteenth-Century Studies; Nat Coalition Independent Scholars; Native Amer Art Studies Assoc; Nineteenth-Century Studies Assoc; Soc Archit Hist; Soc for Historians of the Gilded Age & Progressive Era Western Assoc of Women Historians. **RESEARCH** Nineteenth Century American Art; History of American Women Artists; Nineteenth Century Expositions in the United States; Imagery of Nineteenth-Century American Women **SELECTED PUBLICATIONS** Auth, Lucia Fairchild Fuller's Lost Woman's Building Moral, American Art, NMAA, Smithsonian Institution, Winter 93; auth, "Becoming Visible: The 'Coming Woman" Stained Glass of the Woman's Building, World's Columbian Exposition," Stained Glass, summer 99; contribr, "Anne Whitney" and "Alice Rideout," Amer Ntl Biog, Oxford Univ, 99. **CONTACT ADDRESS** 1030 Kellogg Place, Santa Barbara, CA 93111. **EMAIL** arthistgar@aol.com

GARIEPY, MARGO R.
PERSONAL Born 12/14/1942, Evanston, IL **DISCIPLINE** ENGLISH, HISTORY **EDUCATION** N Ill Univ, BA, 66; MA, 71. **CAREER** Instructor, N Ill Univ, 69-72; Asst Prof, Kennedy-King Col, 72-87; Assoc Prof, Wright Col, 87-. **MEMBERSHIPS** AAUW; NCTE; TYCA; ALSC. **RESEARCH** Adult Learning Strategies; Great Books; Writing Across Curriculum. **CONTACT ADDRESS** Dept Eng, City Cols of Chicago, Wilbur Wright Col, 4300 N Narragansett Ave, Chicago, IL 60634-1591. **EMAIL** mgari17673@aol.com

GARLAND, MARTHA
PERSONAL Born 07/18/1942, Salem, IL, m, 1985, 2 children **DISCIPLINE** HISTORY **EDUCATION** Tulane Univ, BA, 64; Cornell Univ, MA, 66; Ohio State, PhD, 75. **CAREER** Asst Prof, 82-88, assoc prof, 88- , assoc dean, Col of Human, 93-96, actg dean, Arts and Sci, 96-97, VProvost, Undergrad Stud, 97- , Ohio State. **HONORS AND AWARDS** Phi Beta Kappa; Woodrow Wilson Fellow; Phi Kappa Phi; Commencement Speaker, Ohio State, Wint 94. **MEMBERSHIPS** Am Hist Asn; N Am Conf on British Studies; Social Hist Soc UK; Am Asn Higher Ed; Am Asn Col Univ. **RESEARCH** British social and cultural history, 19th and 20th centuries. **SELECTED PUBLICATIONS** Cambridge Before Darwin, CUP, 80. **CONTACT ADDRESS** Ohio State Univ, Columbus, 190 N Oval Mall, Columbus, OH 43210. **EMAIL** garland.1@osu.edu

GARRARD, MARY
DISCIPLINE ART HISTORY **CAREER** Prof, Am Univ. **RESEARCH** Italian Renaissance and feminist studies. **SELECTED PUBLICATIONS** Auth, Artemisia Gentileschi; Coauth, The Power of Feminist Art: The American Movement of the 1970's; Feminism and Art History: Questioning the Litany. **CONTACT ADDRESS** American Univ, 4400 Massachusetts Ave, Washington, DC 20016. **EMAIL** mdgarrard@aol.com

GARRETT, CLARKE W.
PERSONAL Born 02/26/1935, Evanston, IL, m, 1957, 3 children **DISCIPLINE** MODERN EUROPEAN HISTORY **EDUCATION** Carleton Col, BA, 56, Univ Wis, MS, 57, PhD(hist), 61. **CAREER** Asst prof hist, Wake Forest Col, 61-65; from asst prof to assoc prof, 65-73, prof, 73-81, Dana prof hist, 81-97, Prof Emer, 97-, Dickinson Col; Nat Endowment for Humanities grant, 70; Huntington Libr fel, 78; Am Philos Soc grant, 81, ACLS Fel 84-85; NEH Fel 91-92; Prof Emer of History. **MEMBERSHIPS** Western Soc French Hist **RESEARCH** European social and intellectual history, 1660-1800; history of popular religion. **SELECTED PUBLICATIONS** Contrib, The Family, Communes and Utopian Societies, Harper, 72; auth, Respectable Folly: Millenarianism and the French Revolution, Johns Hopkins Univ, 74; The spiritual odyssey of Jacob Duche, Proc Am Philos Soc, 75; co-auth, The Wolf and the Lamb: Popular Culture in France, Anma Libri, 77; auth, Women and witches: patterns of analysis, J Women Cult & Soc, 78; auth, "The Myth of the Counterrevolution in 1789" in French Hist Studies, 94; co-auth, Joseph Priestly in America, Carlisle, 94; auth, The Origins of the Shakers, Johns Hopkins Univ, 98. **CONTACT ADDRESS** 340 W Zia Rd. #A, Santa Fe, NM 87505-5723. **EMAIL** garrettc@dickinson.edu

GARRISON, LORA DEE
PERSONAL Born 10/18/1934, Cleburne, TX, 2 children **DISCIPLINE** AMERICAN INTELLECTUAL & SOCIAL HISTORY **EDUCATION** Fullerton State Col, BA, 68; Univ Calif, Irvine, MA, 69, PhD, 73. **CAREER** Asst prof, 72-80, Assoc Prof Am Hist, Livingston Col, Rutgers Univ, 80-. **RESEARCH** American intellectual history; women's history. **SELECTED PUBLICATIONS** Auth, Apostles of Culture: The Public Librarian and American Society, 1876-1920, Macmillan, 79; Mary Heaton Vorse, Temple Univ Press, 89. **CONTACT ADDRESS** Dept of Hist, Rutgers, The State Univ of New Jersey, New Brunswick, P O Box 5059, New Brunswick, NJ 08903-5059.

GARRISON, MARK
DISCIPLINE ART AND ARCHAEOLOGY OF ANCIENT WESTERN ASIA **EDUCATION** Univ OK, BA; Univ Ottawa, MA; Univ MI, PhD. **CAREER** Field dir, Tunisia, 90-92; Bilkent Uni excavations at Hacimusalar, Turkey, 95-; asst prof, 89-94; assoc prof, 94-00; prof, 00-. **RESEARCH** Archaeol of Roman North Africa. **SELECTED PUBLICATIONS** Co-auth, Seal Impressions on the Persepolis Fortification Tablets. Vol I: Images of Heroic Encounter; Persepolis Seal Studies. An Introduction with Provisional Concordances of Seal Numbers and Associated Documents on Fortification Tablets 1-2087. **CONTACT ADDRESS** Dept of Class, Trinity Univ, 715 Stadium Dr, San Antonio, TX 78212. **EMAIL** mgarrison@trinity.edu

GARTHWAITE, GENE RALPH
PERSONAL Born 07/15/1933, Mt. Hope, WI, d, 3 children **DISCIPLINE** NEAR EASTERN HISTORY, IRANIAN STUDIES **EDUCATION** St Olaf Col, BA, 55; Univ Calif, Los Angeles, PhD(hist), 69. **CAREER** Asst prof, 68-75, fac fel, 70-71, assoc prof hist, 75-83, prof hist, Dartmouth Col, 83-, Soc Sci Res Coun grant, 70-71; Am Philos Soc grants, 71-73; Am Coun Learned Soc grant, 78; Nat Endowment Humanities transl grant, 79-80; Jane & Raphael Berstein prof, 98-. **HONORS AND AWARDS** NEH Grant, 79-80, 89, 90, & 92. **MEMBERSHIPS** Am Oriental Soc; Soc Iranian Studies; MidE Studies Asn; Am Inst Iranian Studies. **RESEARCH** Eighteenth, nineteenth and twentieth century history of Iran; social history of Iran. **SELECTED PUBLICATIONS** Auth, Khan, Encyl of the Modern Islamic World, Oxford Univ Press, 95; Mirza Malkum Khan, Encycl of the Modern Islamic World, Oxford Univ Press, 95; Iran: Annotated Biliographic Guide, Guide to His Lit, Oxford Univ Press, 95; Reimagined Internal Frontiers: Tribes and Nationalism-Bakhtiyari and Kurds, Russia's Muslim Frontiers: New Directions in Cross-Cultural Analysis, Indiana Univ Press, 93; Popular Islamic Perceptions of Paradise Gained, Images of Paradise in Islamic Art, Univ of Texas Press, 91; Tribes, Encycl of Asian Hist IV, 88; Qajar Dynasty, Encycl of Asisian Hist III, 88. **CONTACT ADDRESS** Dept of History, Dartmouth Col, 6107 Reed Hall, Hanover, NH 03755-3506. **EMAIL** gene.r.garthwaite@dartmouth.edu

GARVIN, JAMES L.
PERSONAL Born 02/24/1943, Melrose, MA, m, 1969 **DISCIPLINE** ARCHITECTURAL HISTORY **EDUCATION** Wentworth Inst, MA 63; Univ New Hampshire, BA 67; Univ Delaware, MA 69; Boston Univ, PhD 83. **CAREER** Strawbery Banke Museum NH, cur 63-74; Portsmouth Athenaeum NH, curator 71-74; New Hamp Hist Soc, cur 76-87; NH State Hist Preservation Off, State Archit Hist, 87-. **HONORS AND AWARDS** Winterthur Fel; Spec Univ Fel BU; Newcomen Soc NA Hon Mem; Dist Alum Awd WIT; Pres Cit AIA; Dunfey Awd Excel Hum. **MEMBERSHIPS** SAH; APT; SIA; SPNEA; NSNA; Committee for New Eng Bibliography. **RESEARCH** Amererican architecture and other material culture; History of tools and technologies; New England history. **SELECTED PUBLICATIONS** Auth, Early White Mountain Taverns, The Grand Resort Hotels and Tourism in the White Mountains, Hist New Hampshire, 95; auth, Small Scale Brickmaking in New Hampshire, The Jour of the Soc Indust Archaeology, 94; auth, Portsmouth and Piscataqua: Social History and Material Culture, Hist New Hampshire, 71; auth, St. John's Church in Portsmouth: An Architectural Study, Hist New Hampshire, 73; auth, Historic Portsmouth: Early Photographs from the Collection of Strawbery Banke, Somersworth NH, NH Pub Co 74, 2nd ed, with rev by Susan Grigg NH, Peter E Randall for Strawbery Banke Museum, 95; auth, Ebenezer Clifford, Architect and Inventor, Old-Time New Eng, 75; Mail-Order House Plans and American Victorian Architecture, Winterthur Portfolio, 81; auth, The Old New Hampshire State House, Hist NH, 91. **CONTACT ADDRESS** New Hampshire Historic Preservation Office, 19 Pillsbury Street, Concord, NH 03302-2043. **EMAIL** jgarvin@nhdhr.state.nh.us

GASKELL, IVAN
PERSONAL Born 02/26/1955, Somerset, England, m, 1981, 1 child **DISCIPLINE** HISTORY OF ART **EDUCATION** Oxford Univ, England, MA; London Univ, England, MA; Cambridge Univ, England, PhD. **CAREER** Res fel & Acad Curatorial Asst, Warburg Inst, London Univ, 80-83; fel of Wolfson Col, Cambridge Univ, 83-91; Margaret S. Winthrop Cur, Fogg Art Museum, Harvard Univ Art Museums, 91- . **HONORS AND AWARDS** Vis scholar, Clark Art Inst, Williamstown, 98. **MEMBERSHIPS** Col Art Asn. **RESEARCH** 17th century Dutch art; 17th century European sculpture; 20th century photographic & time-based art; Philos of art; Museology. **SELECTED PUBLICATIONS** Auth, The Thyssen-Bornemisza Collection: Dutch and Flemish Painting, 90; coed, The Language of Art History, 91; Landscape, Natural Beauty and the Arts, 93; Explanation and Value in the Arts, 98, Vermeer Studies, 98; Nietzsche, Philosophy and the Arts, 98; Performance and Authenticity in the Arts, 99; Politics and Aesthetics in the Arts, 00; Vermeer's Wager: Speculations on Art Hist, Theory, and Art Museums, 00. **CONTACT ADDRESS** Fogg Art Museum, Harvard Univ, 32 Quincy St., Cambridge, MA 02138. **EMAIL** gaskell@fas.harvard.edu

GASMAN, DANIEL E.
PERSONAL Born 11/18/1933, New York, NY **DISCIPLINE** MODERN EUROPEAN & INTELLECTUAL HISTORY, HISTORY OF SCIENCE **EDUCATION** Brooklyn Col, BA, 55; Univ Chicago, PhD, 69. **CAREER** Instr hist, State Univ NY, Stony Brook, 60-66; from instr to asst prof, Yeshiva Univ, 66-70; asst prof, 70-72, assoc prof, 72-80; prof hist, John Jay Col & Grad Ctr, City Univ NY, 80-; Directeur D'etudes Ehess, Paris, 6/87; Res grant, City Univ NY, 72-73. **MEMBERSHIPS** HSS. **RESEARCH** Ger and Europ intellectual hist. **SELECTED PUBLICATIONS** Auth, The Scientific Origins of National Socialism, Macdonald, London, 71; Introd to Alfred Fried, Handbuch der Friedensbewegung, Garland, 72; Haeckel's Monism and the Birth of Fascist Ideology, Peter Lang, 98. **CONTACT ADDRESS** Dept of Hist, John Jay Col of Criminal Justice, CUNY, 445 W 59th St, New York, NY 10019-1104. **EMAIL** dgasman@jjay.cuny.edu

GASSTER, MICHAEL
PERSONAL Born 07/12/1930, New York, NY **DISCIPLINE** MODERN HISTORY **EDUCATION** City Col New York, BS, 51; Columbia Univ, MA, 53; Univ Wash, PhD, 62. **CAREER** Instr hist, Princeton Univ, 61-63; from asst prof to assoc prof, George Washington Univ, 63-66; assoc prof mod Chinese hist and chmn mod Chinese hist proj, Univ Wash, 66-70; Assoc Prof Hist, Livingston Col, Rutgers Univ, New Brunswick, 70-, Inter-

Univ fel field training in Chinese, 57-58; Ford Found foreign area training fel, 58-61; mem joint comt contemporary China and comt exchange with Asian Insts, Soc Sci Res Coun-Am Coun Learned Soc, 69-70. **HONORS AND AWARDS** Einstein Prize Am Diplomacy, Columbia Univ, 53. **MEMBERSHIPS** Asn Asian Studies; AHA; Soc Ch'ing Studies. **RESEARCH** Twentieth century Chinese thought and politics; comparative study of revolutions and modernization. **SELECTED PUBLICATIONS** Auth, Reform and revolution in China's political modernization, In: China in Revolution: The First Phase, 1900-1913, Yale Univ, 68; Chinese Intellectuals and the Revolution of 1911: The Birth of Modern Chinese Radicalism, Univ Wash, 69; China's Struggle to Modernize, Knopf, 72. **CONTACT ADDRESS** Dept of Hist, Rutgers, The State Univ of New Jersey, New Brunswick, PO Box 5059, New Brunswick, NJ 08903-5059.

GASTON, PAUL M.
PERSONAL Born 01/31/1928, Fairhope, AL, m, 1952, 3 children **DISCIPLINE** AMERICAN HISTORY **EDUCATION** Swathmore Col, BA, 52; Univ NC, MA, 55, PhD, 61. **CAREER** From instr to assoc prof, 57-71, prof Hist, 71-97, prof emer, Univ VA, 97; Am Coun Learned Soc fel, 61-62, 76-77; vis lectr, Johns Hopkins Univ, 63-64; NEH Summer fel, 83; Rockefeller Humanities fel, 83; vis prof, Univ Cape Town, 86; pres, Southern Regional Coun, 84-88; South African Human Sciences Res Coun, Overseas Res Scholar, 96. **HONORS AND AWARDS** Lillian Smith Awd, 70; Bethune-Roosevelt Awd, 78; Lamar lectr, 81; Outstanding Faculty Awd, State Coun of Higher Ed in VA, 94; Paul M. Gaston Internship, Southern Regional Coun-Univ of VA, 97. **MEMBERSHIPS** Southern Hist Asn; Orgn Am Historians; Southern Regional Coun. **RESEARCH** History of the South; race relations; comparative South-South Africa; utopian communities. **SELECTED PUBLICATIONS** Auth, The New South Creed, Knopf, 70; Women of Fair Hope, Georgia, 84; Man and Mission, Black Belt, 93; A Southerner in South Africa, Southern Changes, 86. **CONTACT ADDRESS** 810 Rugby Rd, Charlottesville, VA 22903. **EMAIL** pmg@virginia.edu

GATES, JOHN MORGAN
PERSONAL Born 11/06/1937, San Jose, CA, m, 1961, 2 children **DISCIPLINE** AMERICAN & MILITARY HISTORY **EDUCATION** Stanford Univ, AB, 59, MA, 60; Duke Univ, PhD, 67. **CAREER** Asst prof, 67-72, assoc prof, 72-78, prof hist, Col Wooster, 78- **HONORS AND AWARDS** Harold L Peterson Awd, Eastern Nat Park & Monument Asn, 80. **MEMBERSHIPS** AHA; Orgn Am Hist; Am Mil Inst. **RESEARCH** Revolutionary and irregular warfare. **SELECTED PUBLICATIONS** Auth, Schoolbooks and Krags: The United States Army in the Philippines, 1898-1902, Greenwood, 73; The alleged isolation of US Army officers in the late 19th Century, Parameters, Vol X, 80; The U.S. Army and Irregular Warfare, 98. **CONTACT ADDRESS** Dept of Hist, The Col of Wooster, 1189 Beall Ave, Wooster, OH 44691-2363. **EMAIL** jgates@acs.wooster.edu

GATEWOOD, WILLARD BADGETT
PERSONAL Born 02/23/1931, Pelham, NC, m, 1958, 2 children **DISCIPLINE** RECENT UNITED STATES HISTORY **EDUCATION** Duke Univ, AB, 53, MA, PhD(hist), 57. **CAREER** Asst prof hist, E Tenn State Univ, 57-58; asst prof, E Carolina Univ, 58-60; assoc prof, NC Wesleyan Col, 60-64; assoc prof, Univ of Ga, 64-70; Alumni Distinguisher Prof Hist, Univ Ark, Fayetteville, 70-98. **HONORS AND AWARDS** Michael Res Awd, Univ of Georgia, 68; Parks Excellence in Teaching Awd, Univ of Georgia, 70; Teacher of the Year, Univ of Arkansas, 78-79; Destinguished Res Awd, Univ of Arkansas, 80; Humanist of the Year, 81-82; Arkansiana Awd, 83; Virginia Ledbetter Prize, 94; Certificate of Merit, 96. **MEMBERSHIPS** AHA; Asn Studies Afro-Am Life & Hist, Orgn Am Hist; Southern Hist Asn; Historical Soc of North Carolina, Arkansas Historical Asn. **RESEARCH** African Americans; Progressive Era; South; the 1920's , United States. **SELECTED PUBLICATIONS** Auth, Controversy in the Twenties, 96; auth, Theodore Roosevelt and the Art of Controversy, 70; auth, Smoked Yankees, 71; Black Americans and the White Man's Burden, 75; auth, Slave and Freeman, 79; coauth, Governors of Arkansas, 81, 2nd ed, 96; auth, Free Man of Color, 82; auth, Aristocrats of Color: The Black Elite 1880-1920, 90; auth, The Arkansas Delta: Land of Paradox, 93; coauth, America Interpreted 2 vols, 97. **CONTACT ADDRESS** 1651 W Cleveland St., Fayetteville, AR 72701-3030. **EMAIL** wgatewood@earthlink.net

GAUSTAD, EDWIN SCOTT
PERSONAL Born 11/14/1923, m, 1946, 3 children **DISCIPLINE** AMERICAN RELIGIOUS HISTORY **EDUCATION** Baylor Univ, AB, 47; Brown Univ, AM, 48, PhD, 51. **CAREER** Instr relig, Brown Univ, 51-52; Am Coun Learned Soc scholar, 52-53; dean and prof relig and philos, Shorter Col, Ga, 53-57; assoc prof humanities, Univ Redlands, 57-65; assoc prof hist, 65-67, Prof Hist to Prof Emer, Univ Calif, Riverside, 67-. **HONORS AND AWARDS** Am Coun Learned Soc grant-in-aid, 63-64 and 72-73. **MEMBERSHIPS** Am Soc Church Hist; Am Studies Asn; Am Acad Relig; AHA; Orgn Am Historians. **SELECTED PUBLICATIONS** Ed, Religious Issues in American History, Harper, 68; co-ed, Religious Issues in Social Studies, Addison-Wesley, Vols I-III, 72-74; auth, Dissent in American Religion, Univ Chicago, 73; Religion in America: Its history and historiography, AHA, 73; ed, Rise of Adventism, Harper, 74; auth, Baptist Piety, Eerdmans, 78; George Berkely in America, Yale, 79; ed, Documentary History of Regligion in America, Vol I, Eerdmans, 82. **CONTACT ADDRESS** Dept of Hist, Univ of California, Riverside, Riverside, CA 92521.

GAUVREAU, J. MICHAEL
DISCIPLINE HISTORY **EDUCATION** Laurentian Univ, BA; Univ Toronto, MA, PhD. **RESEARCH** Social, intellectual, and religious Canadian hist; development of the social sciences in English Canada; cultural hist of the evangelical impulse from 1780 to 1870. **SELECTED PUBLICATIONS** Auth, The Evangelical Century: College and Creed in English Canada from the Great Revival to the Great Depression, 91. **CONTACT ADDRESS** History Dept, McMaster Univ, 1280 Main St W, Hamilton, ON, Canada L8S 4L9. **EMAIL** mgauvrea@mcmaster.ca

GAVINS, RAYMOND
PERSONAL Born 10/26/1942, Atlanta, GA, d, 2 children **DISCIPLINE** AMERICAN AND AFRO-AMERICAN HISTORY **EDUCATION** Va Union Univ, AB, 64; Univ Va, MA, 67, PhD(hist), 70. **CAREER** Asst prof, 70-76, Assoc prof 77-91, Prof Hist, Duke Univ, 92-, Instr hist and govt, Henrico County Pub Schs, Va, 65-66; minorities studies consult, Durham, NC pub schs, 71; Younger Humanist fel, Nat Endowment Humanities, 74-75. **MEMBERSHIPS** Am Hist Asn; Southern Hist Asn; Orgn Am Hist; Asn Studies Afro-Am Life & Hist. **RESEARCH** Black South, 1890s-1950s; 20th century Southern race relations; Southern Black intellectual history. **SELECTED PUBLICATIONS** Auth, "Perils and Prospect of Southern Black Leadership, 93; auth, "The Meaning of Freedom: Black North Carolina in the Nadir," 89; auth, "Fear, Hope and Struggle: Recasting Black North Carolina in the Age of Jim Crow," 98. **CONTACT ADDRESS** Dept of Hist, Duke Univ, Durham, NC 27708. **EMAIL** rgavins@acpub.duke.edu

GAWALT, GERARD WILFRED
PERSONAL Born 02/10/1943, Boston, MA, m, 1966, 3 children **DISCIPLINE** HISTORY **EDUCATION** Northeastern Univ, BA, 65; Clark Univ, MA, 68, PhD(Am hist), 69. **CAREER** Assumption Col, 67-68; Clark Univ, 68-69; Adj lectr, George Mason Univ, 73; George Wash Univ, 81, 82,85; Manuscript Historian, Libr of Cong, 91-; Hist Specialist Libr of Cong, 69-91; Adj prof, Salem State Col, 89; Wash Col, 95; Guest lectr, Col of Wva, 97. **HONORS AND AWARDS** NDEA grad fel, 65-68; Am counc of learned societies, fel, 79-80; Choice, bk of the yr, 79; Meritorious Service Awds, Libr of Cong, 88, 93 and 98; West Virginia Humanities Counc Lecture Grant, 97. **MEMBERSHIPS** Am Soc Legal Hist; Orgn Am Historians. **RESEARCH** Development of the professions in the nineteenth century; justice in the American Revolutionary Era; Continental Congress. **SELECTED PUBLICATIONS** auth, The Promise of Power: The Emergence of the Massachusetts Legal Profession, 1760-1840 (Westport, Ct), 79; auth, The New High Priests: Lawyers in Post-Civil War America (Westport, CT), 84; auth, James Monroe: Presidential and Biography, 93 and James Monroe: Presidential Planter, Ashlawn-Highland, 94; auth, Jefferson's Slaves: Crop Accounts at Monticello, 1805-1809, Journal of the Afro-American Historical and Genealogical Society, 94; auth, Justifying Jefferson: The Political Writings of John James Beckley, Library of Congress, 95; auth, Roads of Relocation and Renewal: James Monroe's Relations with Native Americans, Fredericksburg, Va: Monroe Museum, 98; coauth, Gathering History: Americana, Univ Press of New England and the Library of Congress, 99; auth, Correspondence of William Short and Thomas Jefferson, NDL, online publication, 99; auth, The Declaration of Independence: The Evolution of the Text Independence: The Evolution of the Text, reediting of book first edited by Julian Boyd in 1943 for the Library of Congress, Univ Press of New England and Library of Congress, 99; Joint-auth, Thomas Jefferson: Genius of Liberty Viking Press and Library of Congress, 00 **CONTACT ADDRESS** Libr of Cong, 6808 Quebec Ct., Springfield, VA 22152.

GEAGAN, DANIEL J.
DISCIPLINE HISTORY **EDUCATION** Boston Univ, BA; Johns Hopkins Univ, PhD. **RESEARCH** Ancient history. **SELECTED PUBLICATIONS** Auth, Roman Athens: Some Aspects of Life and Culture I. 86 B.C. - A.D. 267, 79; auth, Imperial Visits to Athens: the Epigraphical Evidence, 82. **CONTACT ADDRESS** History Dept, McMaster Univ, 1280 Main St W, Hamilton, ON, Canada L8S 4L9. **EMAIL** geagand@mcmaster.ca

GEALT, ADELHEID MEDICUS
PERSONAL Born 05/29/1946, Munich, Germany, m, 1969 **DISCIPLINE** HISTORY OF ART **EDUCATION** Ohio State Univ, BA, 68; Indiana Univ, MA, 73; Indiana Univ, PhD, 79 **CAREER** Registrar, Indiana Univ Art Museum, 72-76; adjunct assoc prof, Indiana Univ, 85-89; assoc scholar, Indiana Univ, 86; assoc prof, Henry Radford Hope School Fine Arts, 89-; curator Western Art, Indiana Univ Art Museum, 76-87; Interim/Acting Dir, Indiana Univ Art Museum, 87-89; Dir, Indiana Univ Art Museum, 89- **HONORS AND AWARDS** Ntl Endowment Humanities, 85; Amer Philos Soc Grant, 85; Ntl Endowment Arts, 83; Indiana Univ Res Development Grant, 86,89; Ntl Endowment Art Planning Grant, 82 **MEMBERSHIPS** Commissioner, Indiana Arts Comm, 97; Ntl Endowment Art, Museum Panelist, 91; Assoc Art Museum Directors, 90-; Brauer Museum Art, Valparaiso Univ; Institution Museum Libr Services, 96-98 **RESEARCH** European Art of 17th and 18th Century **SELECTED PUBLICATIONS** Auth, "Disegni di Giuseppe Bernardino Bison nelle collezione nordamericane," Giuseppe Bernardino Bison, pittore e disgegnatore, Cvici Musei, 97; coauth, Domenico Tiepolo: Master Draftsman, IU Press, 96; coauth, Giandomenico Tiepolo, Disegni dal mondo, Electra, 96 **CONTACT ADDRESS** Art Mus, Indiana Univ, Bloomington, East 7th St., Bloomington, IN 47405.

GEARY, PATRICK
PERSONAL Born 09/26/1948, Jackson, MI, m, 1970, 2 children **DISCIPLINE** HISTORY **EDUCATION** Spring Hill Col, AB, 70; Yale Univ, PhD, 74. **CAREER** Asst prof, Princeton Univ, 74-80; prof, Univ Wien, 83; Dir, Ecole des Hautes Etudes, 84, 90; assoc prof to prof, Univ Fla, 80-93; dir, UCLA, 93-98; prof, Univ Notre Dame, 98-00; prof, UCLA, 93-. **HONORS AND AWARDS** ACLS Fel; Guggenheim Fel; Fel, Medieval Acad of Am. **MEMBERSHIPS** Am Hist Asn; Medieval Acad of Am; Royal Hist Soc. **RESEARCH** Medieval European History. **SELECTED PUBLICATIONS** Auth, Furta Sacra: Thefts of Relics in the Central Middle Ages rev ed, Princeton Univ Press, 91; auth, Living with the Dead in the Middle Ages, Cornell Univ Press, 94; auth, Aristocracy in Provence: The Rhone Basin at the Dawn of the Carolingian Age, Univ Pa Press, 85; auth, Phantoms of Remembrance: Memory and Oblivion at the end of the first Millennium, Princeton Univ Press, 94; auth, Medieval Germany in America, German Hist Inst, 96; auth, Myths of Nations, Princeton Univ Press, in press. **CONTACT ADDRESS** Dept Hist, Univ of California, Los Angeles, 6265 Bunche, Box 951473, Los Angeles, CA 90095-1473. **EMAIL** geary@ucla.edu

GEBHARD, DAVID
PERSONAL Born 07/21/1927, Cannon Falls, MN, m, 1954, 2 children **DISCIPLINE** ARCHITECTURAL HISTORY **EDUCATION** Univ Minn, BA, 49, MA, 51, PhD(art hist), 58. **CAREER** Asst prof art hist, Univ NMex, 53-55; dir, Roswell Mus and Art Ctr, NMex, 55-59; Fulbright prof art hist, Istanbul Tech Univ, 59-61; dir, Art Mus and asst prof, 61-64, assoc prof, 64-68, Prof Archit Hist, Univ Calif, Santa Barbara, 68-, Cur, Archit Drawing Collection, 80-, Nat Park Serv grant, 58-59; NSF grant, 64-; Ford Found Near East Studies grant, 65-66; vis prof archit, Sch Environ Design, Univ Calif, Berkeley, 70, 72, 74 and 77; mem, Nat Archit Accrediting Bd, 81- **MEMBERSHIPS** Soc Archit Historians (2nd vpres, 76-78, 1st vpres, 78-80, pres, 80-82); hon mem Am Inst Archit. **RESEARCH** Ottoman Turkish vernacular house, 1500-1900; moderne in the United States, 1925-1942; history of drive-in architecture in the United States. **SELECTED PUBLICATIONS** Auth, The California Garden and the Landscape-Architects Who Shaped It, Calif Hist, Vol 0075, 96; California Gardens--Creating a New Eden, Calif Hist, Vol 0075, 96; The Gardens of California--4 Centuries of Design from Mission to Modern, Calif Hist, Vol 0075, 96; Buildings and Builders in Hispanic California, 1769-1850, Calif Hist, Vol 0075, 96. **CONTACT ADDRESS** 895 E Mountain Dr, Santa Barbara, CA 93108.

GEBHARD, ELIZABETH REPLOGLE
PERSONAL Born 03/25/1935, Oak Park, IL, m, 1957, 2 children **DISCIPLINE** CLASSICAL ARCHEOLOGY **EDUCATION** Wellesley Col, BA, 57; Univ Chicago, MA, 59, PhD(-classics), 63. **CAREER** Vis lectr Classics, Roosevelt Univ, 63-67; asst prof, 69-72, chmn dept, 77-79, Assoc Prof Classics, Univ Ill, Chicago Circle, 72-, Primary investr, Theater at Stobi, Stobi Excavations, 70-75; Cur and Dir, Isthmian Res Proj, Isthmia Mus, Greece, 76-; chmn archaeological studies comt, Univ Ill, Chicago, 78-80. **MEMBERSHIPS** Archaeol Inst Arn; Am Sch Class Studies at Athens; Am Philol Asn; Asn Field Archaeol; Am Sch Oriental Res. **RESEARCH** Field archaeology; architecture and history of Greek and Roman theatre; materials analysis and techniques of production of artifacts. **SELECTED PUBLICATIONS** Auth, Votives in the Archaic Temple of Poseidon at Isthmia, American J Archaeol, Vol 0098, 94; Seek the Welfare of the City--Christians as Benefactors and Citizens, J Relig, Vol 0076, 96. **CONTACT ADDRESS** Dept of Classics, Univ of Illinois, Chicago, at Chicago Circle, 1204 UH, Chicago, IL 60680. **EMAIL** lir@uic.edu

GEDALECIA, DAVID
PERSONAL Born 06/08/1942, New York, NY, m, 1967, 2 children **DISCIPLINE** CHINESE HISTORY **EDUCATION** Queens Col, CUNY, BA, 65; Harvard Univ, AM, 67; PhD, 71. **CAREER** Teaching fel, Harvard Univ, 69-70; Michael O. Fisher, prof hist, 71- , chemn, Int Educ Comt, 76-78, chr dept hist, 85-86, Col Wooster. **HONORS AND AWARDS** Phi Beta Kappa, 65; NDFL fel, Harvard, 65-71; Fencing fel, Harvard, 69-70, ACLS fel Int Philos Conf, Univ Hawaii, 82. **MEMBERSHIPS** Asn Asian Stud; Am Orient Soc; Asia Network; Columbia Univ Fac Sem. **RESEARCH** Chinese history and thought, mid-Imperial period (Sung-Yuan). **SELECTED PUBLICATIONS** Auth, The Philosophy of Wu Cheng: A Neo-Confucian

of the Yuau Dynasty, Ind Univ, 99; auth, Solitary Crane in a Spring Grove, Harrassowitz Verlag, 00. **CONTACT ADDRESS** Dept Hist, The Col of Wooster, 826 Country Club Dr, Wooster, OH 44691. **EMAIL** dgedalecia@wooster.edu

GEDMINTAS, ALEKSANDRAS
DISCIPLINE BALTIC STUDIES **EDUCATION** SUNY Binghamton, PhD, 79. **CAREER** SUNY Delhi, NY, 75-. **MEMBERSHIPS** Asn for the Advancement of Baltic Studies, Eastern Community Col Soc Sci Asn. **RESEARCH** American immigration, Thekaraim of Lithuania. **SELECTED PUBLICATIONS** Auth, "Organizational Development Among Binghamton, New York, Lithuanians," J of Baltic Studies, Vol 11, no 4 (80); auth, "The Cultural Components of Ethnic Identity Retention Among Binghamton, New York, Lithuanians," Lituanus, Vol 28, no 3 (82); rev of three Am ethnic group ethnographies, Anthopol & Humanism Quart, Vol 12, no 2 (87); auth, "An Interesting Bit of Identity: The Dynamics of Ethnicity," AMS Press, NY (89); auth, "A Cultural History of the Lithuanians in Binghamton," in the 50th Anniversary Commemorative Book of St Joseph's Lithuanian Parish (90); auth, "The Karaim of Lithuania: A Case of Ethnic Survival," J of Baltic Studies, Vol 28, no 4 (97); auth, "Lithuanian-Americans," reference article for the Macmillan Encyclopedia of American Ethnic Groups, **CONTACT ADDRESS** Dept Humanities & Soc Sci, SUNY, Col of Tech at Delhi, 2 Main St, Delhi, NY 13753. **EMAIL** gedminal@delhi.edu

GEEHR, RICHARD STOCKWELL
PERSONAL Born 05/06/1938, New Brunswick, NJ, m, 1961 **DISCIPLINE** AUSTRIAN SOCIAL & INTELLECTUAL HISTORY **EDUCATION** Middlebury Col, BA, 60; Columbia Univ, MA, 65; Univ Mass, Amherst, PhD, 73. **CAREER** Instr Ger & hist, Windham Col, 66-67; instr Western civilization, Keene State Col, 67; instr hist, Mark Hopkins Col, 67-68; instr Ger Greenfield Community Col, 67-68; teaching asst, Univ Mass, Amherst, 68-73; instr hist, Lake Mich Col, 73-74 & St Mary's Col, Md, 75-76; asst prof to prof, hist, Bentley Col, 77-. **HONORS AND AWARDS** Nat Endowment Humanities Younger Humanist res award, 74; Fulbright res grants, 69, 74, 76, 85, 86; Marion & Jasper Whiting Found grant, 80; Charles P McNear Jr Found grant, 82. **MEMBERSHIPS** AHA; Die Int Robert-Musil Gesellschaft; Historians Film Comt. **RESEARCH** Modern Austrian cultural and intellectual history; film and history. **SELECTED PUBLICATIONS** Auth, Adam Muller-Guttenbrunn and the Aryan Theater of Vienna: 1898-1903, The Approach of Cultural Fascism, Verlag Alfred Kummerle Goppingen, 73; auth, The Aryan theater of Vienna: The Career of Adam Muller-Guttenbrunn, Wiener Libr Bull, UK, 75; ed, Soviet History and Film, Ginn & Co, 80; I Decide Who is a Jew!, The Papers of Dr Karl Lueger, Univ Press Am, 82; auth, Karl Lueger: Mayor of Fin de Siecle Vienna, Wayne State, 90; auth, Letters from the Doomed, University Press of America, 91. **CONTACT ADDRESS** Dept of History, Bentley Col, Beaver & Foster Sts, Waltham, MA 02155. **EMAIL** rgeehr@bentley.edu

GEERKEN, JOHN HENRY
PERSONAL Born 10/11/1938, Colon, Panama, m, 1960, 4 children **DISCIPLINE** EUROPEAN HISTORY **EDUCATION** George Washington Univ, BA, 60; Yale Univ, MA, 61, PhD(hist), 67. **CAREER** From actg instr to instr hist, Yale Univ, 65-68; asst prof, 68-74, assoc prof, 74-82, Prof Hist, Scripps Col, 82-, Consult and res assoc, Ctr Medieval and Renaissance Studies, Univ Calif, Los Angeles, 75-. **MEMBERSHIPS** AHA; Renaissance Soc Am; Am Soc Legal Hist; Soc Ital Hist Studies. **RESEARCH** History and philosophy of law; Italian Renaissance. **SELECTED PUBLICATIONS** Auth, Machiavelli's Moses and Renaissance Politics, Journal Hist of Ideas, Vol 64, 99. **CONTACT ADDRESS** 1030 Columbia Ave, Claremont, CA 91711-3948. **EMAIL** jgeerken@scrippscol.edu

GEGGUS, D.
PERSONAL Born 11/19/1949, Romford, England, m, 1994, 1 child **DISCIPLINE** HISTORY **EDUCATION** Oxford Univ, BA, 71; London MA, York PhD, 79. **CAREER** Prof 82-, Univ Florida; res fel 80-82, Southampton Univ; jr res fel, 76-80, Oxford Univ. **HONORS AND AWARDS** Guggenheim Fel; Woodrow Wilson Fel; NEH Fel; NHC Fel. **MEMBERSHIPS** SHH; ACH; AHA. **RESEARCH** Caribbean History; Slavery. **SELECTED PUBLICATIONS** Auth, Slavery War and Revolution, Oxford, 82; coauth, A Turbulent Time, Bloomington, 97; coauth, French Revolution Research Collection, Witney, 93. **CONTACT ADDRESS** Dept History, Univ of Florida, Box 117320, Gainesville, FL 32611. **EMAIL** dgeggus@history.ufl.edu

GEIB, GEORGE WINTHROP
PERSONAL Born 10/31/1939, Buffalo, NY, m, 1973, 2 children **DISCIPLINE** AMERICAN HISTORY **EDUCATION** Purdue Univ, Lafayette, BA, 61; Univ Wis-Madison, MA, 63, PhD, 69. **CAREER** From instr to asst prof, 65-72, assoc prof, 73-78, Prof Hist, Butler Univ, 79-, Actg Dean, Liberal Arts, 87-89. **HONORS AND AWARDS** Phi Alpha Theta; Phi Kappa Phi; Best Book Awd, Ind Religious Hist Asn, 90; Sagomore of the Wabash, 97. **MEMBERSHIPS** OAH; SHEAR; Ind Hist Soc; Soc Mil Hist. **RESEARCH** Early national American history; urban history; military history; midwest regional. **SELECTED PUBLICATIONS** Auth, The William F Charters South Seas Collection: An Introduction, Irwin Libr, 70, rev ed, 94; coauth, Indiana's Citizen Soldiers, Ind Armory Bd, 80; auth, Indianapolis Hoosier's Circle City, Continental Heritage Press, 81; Lives Touched By Faith, 87; Indianapolis First, 90; contrib ed, Encyclopedia of Indianapolis, 94. **CONTACT ADDRESS** Dept of Hist, Butler Univ, 4600 Sunset Ave, Indianapolis, IN 46208-3443.

GEIGER, MARY VIRGINIA
PERSONAL Born 02/02/1915, Irvington, NJ **DISCIPLINE** PHILOSOPHY, HISTORY **EDUCATION** Col Notre Dame, Md, AB, 37; Cath Univ Am, MA, 41, PhD(hist, philos), 43. **CAREER** Instr hist, 38-56, PROF PHILOS, Col Notre Dame, MD, 56-. **HONORS AND AWARDS** DHL, Col Notre Dame, Md, 76. **MEMBERSHIPS** Am Cath Philos Asn; Am Hist Asn. **SELECTED PUBLICATIONS** Auth, Daniel Carroll II, One Man and His Descendants, 1730-1978, 78; Daniel Carroll, Signer of the Constitution, Cath Univ Am, 43; Genealogy of Charles Carroll of Carrollton, 98; articles in: Catholic Encyclopedia, McGraw, 67; Encyclopedia of American Catholic History, Glazier Shelley Book, Liturgical Press, 97. **CONTACT ADDRESS** Dept of Philosophy, Col of Notre Dame of Maryland, 4701 N Charles St, Baltimore, MD 21210-2404. **EMAIL** VGEIGER@NDM.EDU

GEIGER, REED G.
PERSONAL Born 08/14/1932, Cleveland, OH, m, 1962, 2 children **DISCIPLINE** EUROPEAN ECONOMIC HISTORY **EDUCATION** Col Wooster, BA, 54; Univ Minn, MA, 57, PhD(hist), 64. **CAREER** Instr, 61-64, asst prof, 64-75, Assoc Prof Hist, Univ Del, 75-. **MEMBERSHIPS** AHA; Econ Hist Asn. **RESEARCH** Early industrial revolution in Europe; European radicalism, especially in the 19th century. **SELECTED PUBLICATIONS** Auth, The Role of Transportation in the Industrial-Revolution--A Comparison of England and France, J Interdisciplinary Hist, Vol 0023, 93. **CONTACT ADDRESS** Dept of Hist, Univ of Delaware, Newark, DE 19711.

GEISON, GERALD LYNN
PERSONAL Born 03/26/1943, Savanna, IL, 2 children **DISCIPLINE** HISTORY OF SCIENCE AND MEDICINE **EDUCATION** Beloit Col, BA, 65; Yale Univ, MA, 67, PhD(hist of sci & med), 70. **CAREER** Res fel hist med, Univ Minn, 69-70; asst prof, 70-76, assoc dean col, 77-79, Assoc Prof Hist, Princeton Univ, 76-, Dir, Prog Hist Sci, 80-, Fel, Inst Hist Med, Med Sch, Johns Hopkins Univ, 72-73; Jonathan Dickinson Bicentennial preceptor, Princeton Univ, 74-77; Nat Endowment for Humanities fel, 75-76; NSF grant, 77-81. **MEMBERSHIPS** Hist Sci Soc; Am Asn Hist Med. **RESEARCH** Historical relationship between medical theory and medical practice; life and work of Louis Pasteur; history of physiology in the 19th century. **SELECTED PUBLICATIONS** Auth, Research Schools and New Directions in the Historiography of Science, Osiris, Vol 0008, 93; The Experimental Life Sciences in the 20th-Century, Osiris, Vol 0010, 95; auth, The Private Science of Louis Pasteur, Princeton, 95; Lords of the Fly--Drosophila Genetics and the Experimental Life, Isis, Vol 0087, 96; Pasteur and the Culture Wars, in Response to Perutz, Max--An Exchange, NY Rev of Bks, Vol 0043, 96. **CONTACT ADDRESS** Dept of Hist, Princeton Univ, Dickinson Hall, Princeton, NJ 08544. **EMAIL** gerry@princeton.edu

GELBER, STEVEN MICHAEL
PERSONAL Born 02/21/1943, New York, NY, m, 1990, 2 children **DISCIPLINE** AMERICAN SOCIAL & CULTURAL HISTORY **EDUCATION** Cornell Univ, BS, 65; Univ Wis-Madison, MS, 67, PhD, 72. **CAREER** Prof hist, Univ Santa Clara, 69. **MEMBERSHIPS** Orgn Am Hist; AHA. **RESEARCH** Am business thought; cult hist. **SELECTED PUBLICATIONS** Auth, Business Ideology and Black Employment, Addison-Wesley, 73; Black Men and Businessmen, Kennikat, 74; co-auth, New Deal Art: California, de Saisset Mus, 76; auth, California's new deal murals, Calif Hist, 79; Culture of the work place and the rise of baseball, J Social Hist, 82; Their hands are all out playing: business and amateur baseball, 185-1917, Jour Sports Hist, spring 84; The eye of the beholder: Images of California by Dorothea Lange and Russell Lee, Calif Hist, fall 85; Sequoia seminar: Th origins of religious sectarianism, Calif Hist, spring 90; Co-auth (with Martin Cook), Saving the Earth: The history of a middle-class millenarian movement, Univ Calif Press, 90; A job you can't lose: Work and hobbies in the Great Depression, J Social Hist, summer 91; Free market metaphor: The historical dyanics of stamp collecting, Comparative Studies in Society and Hist, 10/92; Do-it-yourself: Constructing, repairing and maintaining domestic masculinity, Am Quart, 3/97; Hobbies: Productive learning and the culture of work in America, Columbia Univ Press, 99. **CONTACT ADDRESS** Dept of Hist, Santa Clara Univ, 500 El Camino Real, Santa Clara, CA 95053-0285. **EMAIL** sgelber@scu.edu

GELFAND, ELISSA DEBORAH
PERSONAL Born 01/26/1949, New York, NY, 1 child **DISCIPLINE** FRENCH STUDIES, WOMEN'S STUDIES **EDUCATION** Barnard Col, BA, 69; Brown Univ, MA, 72, PhD, 75. **CAREER** Prof Eng, Ecole Active Bilingue, Paris, 73-75; asst prof, 75-81, assoc prof, 81-88, Prof French, Mount Holyoke Col, 88-, Dir, Women's Studies Prog, 82-84, 98-, Instr French, Alliance Ft Providence, RI, 71-73; instr English, Int House, Paris, 73; Andrew W Mellon fel interdisciplinary res, 79. **HONORS AND AWARDS** Dorothy Rooke McCulloch Chair in Romance Languages 92-; Faculty Research Fellowship, 88-89. **MEMBERSHIPS** Ed bd, Women in French Studies; Am Asn Tchr(s) Ft; MLA; Northeast Mod Lang Asn; Nat Women's Studies Asn; Women's Caucus Mod Lang. **RESEARCH** Feminist theory, women's and gender studies; prison lit; Interwar French Jewish writers: **SELECTED PUBLICATIONS** Auth, Alberline Sarrazin: A control case for femininity in form, Fr Rev, 12/77; A response to the void: Madame Roland's memoires particuliers and her imprisonment, Romance Notes, 79; translr, texts by B Groult, F Parturier & D Pogg,: In: New French Feminisms, Univ MA Press, 80; auth, Women prison writers in France: Twice criminal, Mod Lang Studies, 80-81; Imprisoned women: Toward a socio-literary feminist analysis, Yale Fr Studie, 81; Imagination in Confinement: Women Writers from French Prisons, Cornell Univ Press, 83; coauth, French Feminist Criticism: An Annotated Bibliography, Garland Press, 85; Albertine Sarvazin, Dictionary of Literary Biography, 89; Gender and Me Rise of te Novel, The French Review, 88; Resetting the Margins: The Outsider in French Literature and Culture, Critical Issues in Foreign Language Instruction, 91; Feminist Criticism, French, Encyclopedia of Contemporary Literary Theory, 93; Clara Malraux, Dictionaire literaire des femmes de langue francaise, 97. **CONTACT ADDRESS** Dept of French, Mount Holyoke Col, 50 College St, South Hadley, MA 01075-1461. **EMAIL** egelfand@mtholyoke.edu

GELFAND, LAWRENCE E.
PERSONAL Born 06/20/1926, Cleveland, OH, m, 1953, 3 children **DISCIPLINE** AMERICAN HISTORY **EDUCATION** Western Reserve Univ, BA, 49, MA, 50; Univ Wash, PhD, 58. **CAREER** Asst prof hist, Univ Hawaii, 56-58, Univ Wash, 58-59 and Univ Wyo, 59-62; from asst prof to assoc prof, 62-66, Prof Hist, Univ Iowa, 66-94, Rockefeller Found fel, 64-65; vis prof hist, Univ Wash, 74; prof emer, 94. **MEMBERSHIPS** AHA; Orgn Am Hist; Soc Historians Am Foreign Rels (pres, 82); Soc Am Archivists. **RESEARCH** History of American foreign relations; First World War and the Paris peace conference; U.S. relations with doctatorships during the 1920s and 1930s. **SELECTED PUBLICATIONS** Auth, The Inquiry: American Preparations for Peace 1917-1919, 63 & ed, A Diplomat Looks Back, 68, Yale Univ; ed, Essays on the History of American Foreign Relations, Holt, 72; Herbert Hoover: The Great War and Its Aftermath 1914-1923, Univ Iowa Press, 79. **CONTACT ADDRESS** Dept of Hist, Univ of Iowa, Iowa City, IA 52242. **EMAIL** lawrence:gelfand@uiowa.edu

GELLMAN, I.
PERSONAL Born 09/03/1942, Philadelphia, PA, m, 1989, 3 children **DISCIPLINE** HISTORY **EDUCATION** Univ Md, BA, 64; MA, 66; Ind Univ, PhD, 70. **CAREER** Prof, Morgan State Col, 74-77; from vpres to pres, VIP Properties, Inc., 77-89; vis prof, Univ of Calif at Irvine, 97-98; vis prof, Chapman Univ, 98-99; Allergan Chair of Modern Am Hist, Chapman Univ, 99-00. **HONORS AND AWARDS** Phi Alpha Theta; Omicron Delta Kappa. **MEMBERSHIPS** Soc of Historians of Am For Relations. **RESEARCH** Multivolume biography of Richard Nixon. **SELECTED PUBLICATIONS** Auth, Roosevelt and Batista: Good Neighbor Diplomacy in Cuba, 73; auth, Good Neighbor Diplomacy: United States Policies in Latin America, 79; auth, Secret Affairs: Franklin Roosevelt, Cordell Hull and Sumner Welles, 95; auth, The Contender: Richard Nixon--The Congress Years, 99. **CONTACT ADDRESS** Dept Hist, Chapman Univ, 333 N Glassell St, Orange, CA 92866-1011. **EMAIL** ifgellman@aol.com

GELLOTT, LAURA S.
DISCIPLINE HISTORY **EDUCATION** Marquette Univ, BA, 74, MA, 76; Univ Wis, PhD, 82. **CAREER** Assoc prof, Univ of WI, Parkside. **HONORS AND AWARDS** DAAD fel, 85 & 87; UW-Parkside Tchg Excellence Awd, 86. **RESEARCH** 20th century Austria; Women; Church-state issues. **SELECTED PUBLICATIONS** Publ in, Austrian Hist Yearbk, J Contemp Hist, Catholic Hist Rev; contrib to, Liberalism and Catholicism. **CONTACT ADDRESS** Dept of Hist, Univ of Wisconsin, Parkside, 900 Wood Rd, Molinaro 121, PO Box 2000, Kenosha, WI 53141-2000. **EMAIL** laura.gellott@uwp.edu

GENOVESE, EUGENE D.
PERSONAL Born 05/19/1930, Brooklyn, NY **DISCIPLINE** MODERN HISTORY **EDUCATION** Brooklyn Col, BA, 53; Columbia Univ, MA, 55, PhD(hist), 59. **CAREER** From instr to asst prof hist and econ, Polytech Inst Brooklyn, 58-63; from asst prof to assoc prof hist, Rutgers Univ, 63-67; prof, Sir George Williams Univ, 68-69; chmn dept, 69-76, Prof Hist, Univ Rochester, 69-, Soc Sci Res Coun fel, 68-69; fel, Ctr Advan Studies Behav Sci, Stanford, Calif, 72-73. **MEMBERSHIPS** Southern Hist Asn; Agr Hist Asn; fel Am Acad Arts & Sci; Orgn Am Historians (pres, 77-78). **RESEARCH** Southern and Afro-American history. **SELECTED PUBLICATIONS** Auth, The Political Economy of Slavery, Pantheon, 65; ed, The Slave Economy of the Old South: Economic and Social Essays

of U B Phillips, La State Univ, 68; co-ed, Slavery in the New World: A Reader in Comparative History, Prentice-Hall, 69; auth, The World the Slaveholders Made, 69, In Red and Black, 71 & Roll, Jordan, Roll, 74, Pantheon; From Rebellion to Revolution: Afro-American Slave Revolts in the Making of the Modern World, La State Univ Press, 79; coauth (with Elizabeth Fox-Genovese), Fruits of Merchant Capital: Slavery and Bourgeois Property in the Rise and Expansion of Capitalism, Oxford Univ Press (in press). **CONTACT ADDRESS** Dept of Hist, Univ of Rochester, Rochester, NY 14627.

GENTLES, IAN
PERSONAL Born 10/25/1941, Kingston, Jamaica **DISCIPLINE** HISTORY **EDUCATION** Univ Toronto, BA, 63, MA, 65; Univ London, PhD, 69. **CAREER** Asst to assoc prof, 69-93, dean students, 70-75, assoc prin acad affairs, 85-87, Prof Hist, Glendon Col, York Univ, 93-, dept ch, 93-; vis scholar, Corpus Christi Col, 82-83, vis fel, Clare Hall, Cambridge, 93. **HONORS AND AWARDS** Glendon Col Res Fel, 92-93; Vistiong Fel, Clare Hall, Cambridge, 93; Philip A Knachel Fel, Foger Shakespeare Lib, 96; Mayers Fel, Huntingtion Lib, San Marion, Ca, 97; Frederick A & Marion S Pottle Fel, Beinecke Lib, Yale Unvi, 97. **MEMBERSHIPS** Fel, Royal Hist Soc, 78-; ch, London House Asn Can, 84-87. **SELECTED PUBLICATIONS** Ed, Care of the Dying and Bereaved, 82; ed, A Time to Choose Life, 90; auth, The New Model Army in England, Ireland and Scotland 1645-1653, 92; coauth, Public Policy, Private Voices: The Euthanasia Debate, 92; auth, The New Model Army in england, Ireland and Scotland, 1645-1653, (Blackwell, Oxford and Cambridge, Mass, 92): 584; ed, Euthanasia and Assisted Suicide: the Current Debate, 95; coed, Soldiers, Writers and Statesmen of the English Revolution, Cambridge Univ Press, Cambridge, 98. **CONTACT ADDRESS** Glendon Col, York Univ, 2275 Bayview Ave, Toronto, ON, Canada M4N 3M6. **EMAIL** igentles@glendon.yorku.ca

GENTRY, JUDITH ANNE FENNER
PERSONAL Born 05/28/1942, Baltimore, MD, m, 1969, 1 child **DISCIPLINE** UNITED STATES CIVIL WAR & ECONOMIC HISTORY **EDUCATION** Univ Md, College Park, BA, 64; Rice Univ, PhD(hist), 69. **CAREER** Asst prof, 69-74, assoc prof hist, Univ La at Lafayette, 74-85, prof 85-, dir grad prog hist, 85-99. **HONORS AND AWARDS** Mary Hayes Ewing Publ Prize, Rice Univ, 71; Nat Endowment for Humanities res grants, 78 & 79; Fellow, Newberry Library Summer Institute in Quantitative History, 80; Univ of Southwestern La Foundation Outstanding Teacher Awd, 94; Fellow, La Historical Asn, 95. **MEMBERSHIPS** AHA; Orgn Am Historians; Southern Hist Asn; AAUP; Southern Asn Women Historians (vpres, 77-78, pres, 78-79); Louisiana Historical Asn, vice-pres, 90-91, pres, 91-92. **RESEARCH** United States Civil War finances. **SELECTED PUBLICATIONS** Auth, A Confederate Success in Europe: The Erlanger Loan, J Southern Hist, 5/70; The Louisiana State Lottery, in: Encyclopedia of Southern History, 79; ed, Eliminating Sex Bias in Vocational Education, Univ Southwestern La Printshop, 80; co-auth with James Dorman, Higher Education and Historical Literacy in Louisiana: An Analsis and Modest Proposal, La Hist, fall 83; An Historical Study of Women in the Southern Historical Association, 1934-1985, J Southern Hist, 5/86; A Private Fortune and the Democratic Process, La History, 87; 7 entries in Directory of Louisiana Biography, 88; Alexander Mouton, Governor of Louisiana and Pierre Derbigny, Arnaud Beauvais, and Jacques Dupre in Joseph G. Dawson The Louisiana Governors from Iberville to Edwards, 90; White Gold: The Confederate Government and Cotton in Louisiana, La Hist, 92; What if the Constitution as Written Had Provided for Equal Rights for Women and Men? in Herb Levine, What if the American Political System Were Different?, 92; The Erlanger Loan, in Encyclopedia of the Confederacy, 93; John A. Stevenson: Confederate Adventurer, La Hist, 94; George Eustis, Jr, in American National Biography, 99; Introduction to Vol 9 of the Jefferson Davis Papers, January- September 1863, 97. **CONTACT ADDRESS** Dept of Hist, Univ of Southwestern Louisiana, 200 Hebrard Blvd, Lafayette, LA 70504-2531. **EMAIL** jfggentry@louisiana.edu

GEORGE, CHARLES HILLES
PERSONAL Born 05/22/1922, Kansas City, MO, m, 1951, 1 child **DISCIPLINE** HISTORY **EDUCATION** Princeton Univ, PhD(hist), 50. **CAREER** Instr hist, Stanford Univ, 50-51 and Pomona Col, 51-52; asst prof, Colo Col, 52-53, Univ Rochester, 54-55 and Univ Wash, 56-57; from asst prof to assoc prof, Univ Pittsburgh, 57-61; Prof Hist, Northern Ill Univ, 61-, Soc Sci Res Coun fel, 55-56. **MEMBERSHIPS** Conf Brit Studies; Am Soc Reformation Res; Hist Asn England. **RESEARCH** Intellectual history of early modern Europe; English history; history of English bourgeoisie. **SELECTED PUBLICATIONS** Co-auth, Teh Protestant Mind of the English Reformation, Princeton Univ Pr, 61; ed, Revolution: Five Centuries of Europe in Conflict, Dell, 62, reissued as, Revolution: European Radicals from Hus to Lenin, Scott Foresman, 70. **CONTACT ADDRESS** Dept of Hist, No Illinois Univ, De Kalb, IL 60115.

GEORGE, EMERY EDWARD
PERSONAL Born 05/08/1933, Budapest, Hungary **DISCIPLINE** GERMANIC LANGUAGES, EAST EUROPEAN STUDIES **EDUCATION** Univ Mich, BA, 55, MA, 59, PhD(Ger), 64. **CAREER** Instr Ger, Univ Mich, 62-64; from instr to asst prof, Univ Ill, Urbana, 64-66; from asst prof to assoc prof, 66-75, off res admin res grant, 67-68, Prof Ger Lang and Lit, Univ Mich Ann Arbor, 75-, Assoc ed Russ lit, Triquarterly, 73-; found ed, Mich Ger Studies, 75-76; Fel, Int Acad Poets, England, 76-; Int Res and Exchanges Bd fel, 81. **HONORS AND AWARDS** Hopwood Awd in Poetry, 60. **MEMBERSHIPS** MLA; AM Soc Aesthet; Holderlin Ges; Poetry Soc Am; Int Poetry Soc. **RESEARCH** German literature of the Age of Goethe; English literature; Russian and Hungarian literataure. **SELECTED PUBLICATIONS CONTACT ADDRESS** Dept of Ger, Univ of Michigan, Ann Arbor, Ann Arbor, MI 48109.

GEORGE, PETER J.
DISCIPLINE HISTORY **EDUCATION** Univ Toronto, BA, MA, PhD; Univ Ottawa, DU. **CAREER** Assoc dean, Grad Studies, 74-79, dean, Fac of Soc Sci, 80-89, pres, McMaster Univ, 95-. **RESEARCH** The impacts of resource-based development on Aboriginal peoples, communities and the environment in Northern Ontario. **SELECTED PUBLICATIONS** Auth, Government Subsidies and the Construction of the Canadian Pacific Railway, 81; auth, The Emergence of Industrial America: Strategic Factors in American Economic Growth Since 1870, 82; auth, Ontario's Mining Industry 1870-1940; auth, Progress Without Planning: The Economic Development of Ontario 1870-1940, 87; co-auth, The Courts and the Development of Trade in Upper Canada, Bus Hist Rev, 86. **CONTACT ADDRESS** Office of the President, McMaster Univ, 1280 Main St W, 238 Gilmour Hall, Hamilton, ON, Canada L8S 4L8. **EMAIL** pgeorge@mcmaster.ca

GEPHART, RONALD MICHAEL
PERSONAL Born 09/29/1939, Dayton, OH, m, 1961, 2 children **DISCIPLINE** AMERICAN HISTORY **EDUCATION** Univ Nebr, BA, 63, MA, 65; Northwestern Univ, PhD(Am hist), 80. **CAREER** Lectr colonial and revolutionary Am, Northwestern Am, 68-69; sr bibliogr, 69-75, specialist Am hist, 75-81, Assoc Ed, Lett Deleg Congress 1774-1789, Libr Cong, 81-, Co-chmn, Libr Cong Task Force, subcomt bibliog role, Libr Cong, 75-76; consult, Ctr Hist Population Studies, Univ Utah, 77-79. **HONORS AND AWARDS** Thomas Jefferson Prize for hist editing, Soc for Hist in Fed Govt's, 98. **MEMBERSHIPS** Inst Early Am Hist & Cult; Va Hist Soc; Soc Hist Fed Govt; Asn for Documentary Editing. **RESEARCH** Historical bibliography; documentary editing; American colonial and revolutionary history. **SELECTED PUBLICATIONS** Auth, Revolutionary America, 1763-1789: A Biography, 2 vols, 84; auth, "Who Wrote the 'North American' Essays," William and Mary Quart, 54 (97). **CONTACT ADDRESS** Manuscript Div Libr of Cong, Washington, DC 20540. **EMAIL** rgep@loc.gov

GERATY, LAWRENCE THOMAS
PERSONAL Born 04/21/1940, St. Helena, CA, m, 1962, 2 children **DISCIPLINE** NEAR EASTERN ARCHEOLOGY, OLD TESTAMENT **EDUCATION** Pac Union Col, AB, 62; Andrews Univ, AM, 63, BD, 65; Harvard Univ, PhD(Near Eastern lang & lit), 72. **CAREER** Asst prof, 72-76, assoc prof, 76-80, PROF ARCHAEOL and HIST ANTIQ, ANDREWS UNIV, 80-, Ed, Andrews Univ Monographs, 72-; res grants, Ctr for Field Res, 76 and Nat Endowment for Humanities, 77; trustee, Am Ctr Orient Res, Amman, Jordon, 76-; cur, Andrews Univ Archaeol Mus, 76-; assoc ed, Andrews Univ Sem Studies, 77-. **MEMBERSHIPS** Am Schs Orient Res; Soc Bibl Lit; Am Inst Archaeol; Nat Asn Prof Hebrew; Asn Adventist Forums (pres, 72-73). **RESEARCH** Palestinian archaeology; semitic inscriptions; Old Testament exegesis. **SELECTED PUBLICATIONS** Auth, A Tribute to Horn, Siegfried, H.--March-17, 1908 November-28, 1993--In-Memoriam, Biblical Archaeol, Vol 0057, 94. **CONTACT ADDRESS** Theol Sem, Andrews Univ, Berrien Springs, MI 49104.

GERBER, DAVID
PERSONAL Born 09/28/1944, Chicago, IL, m, 1975, 2 children **DISCIPLINE** HISTORY **EDUCATION** Northwestern Univ, BA, 66; Princeton Univ, PhD, 71. **CAREER** Asst Instr, Princeton Univ, 70-71; Vis Schol, Flinders Univ of S Australia, 80; Prof, SUNY at Buffalo, 71-. **HONORS AND AWARDS** Ford Found Grants, 70-71; David Center Fel, 73; Fulbright Schol, Australia, 80; NEH Fel, 86-87; Gutman Prize for Soc Hist, 90; Myers Center Hon Mention for Human Rights, 87; Augspurger Prize for Local Hist, 97. **MEMBERSHIPS** Am Hist Assoc, Orgn of Am Hist, Immigration and Ethnic Hist Soc. **RESEARCH** American social history. **SELECTED PUBLICATIONS** Auth, Black Ohio and the Color Line, Univ Ill Pr, 76; ed, Anti-Semitism in American History, Univ Ill Pr, 86; auth, The Making of An American Pluralism: Buffalo, New York, 1825-1860, Univ Ill Pr, 89; auth, "Nativism, Anti-Catholicism and Anti-Semitism," in Encycl of Am Soc Hist, vol 3, (NY: Scribners, 93): 39-60; auth, "Anger and Affability: The Rise of a Repertory of Roles and Motives in the Life of a Disabled Veteran of world War II," J of Soc Hist 27 (93): 1-27; coath, "The Invention of Ethnicity," J of Am Ethnic Hist 12 (93-2): 3-41; auth, "Heroes and Misfits: Conflicting Representations of Disabled Veterans of World War II," in The Best Years of Our Lives, American Quart 46 (94): 545-574; ed, The Rise and Fall of a Frontier Entrepreneur: Benjamin Rathbun: Master Builder and Architect, Syracuse Univ Pr, 96; ed, Identity, Community and Pluralism: An American Reader, Oxford Univ Pr, 97; ed, Disabled Veterans in History, Univ Mich Pr, 00. **CONTACT ADDRESS** Dept Hist, SUNY, Buffalo, PO Box 604130, Buffalo, NY 14260-0001. **EMAIL** dagerber@buffalo.edu

GERBER, JANE SATLOW
PERSONAL Born 06/17/1938, New York, NY, m, 1964, 3 children **DISCIPLINE** JEWISH HISTORY, MIDDLE EASTERN STUDIES **EDUCATION** Wellesley Col, BA, 59; Radcliffe Col, MA, 62; Columbia Univ, PhD, 72. **CAREER** Instr Jewish hist, Stern Col, Yeshiva Univ, 71-72; asst prof, Lehman Col, 72-77; asst prof, 77-81, Assoc Prof Hist, Grad Ctr, City Univ New York, 81-, Bk rev ed, Jewish Social Studies J, 68-; mem off-campus fac, Sephardic Inst, Yeshiva Univ, 73-; Fac Res Found grant, City Univ New York, 74 and 75; ed, Shoah: Rev of Holocaust Studies and Commemorations, 78- **MEMBERSHIPS** Am Acad Jewish Res, Am Jewish Hist Soc, Am Asn Jewish Studies, Israel Hist Soc, Am Soc for Sephardic Studies. **RESEARCH** Jewish history in Muslim lands; Jews in Morocco; Sephardic history. **SELECTED PUBLICATIONS** Auth, The Jews of Spain, Macmillan, The Free Press, 92; auth, "The Jews of North Africa and the Middle East," in The Modern Jewish Expericence, ed J. Wertheimer, 93; auth, Sephardic Studies in the University, Assoc Univ Pr, 94; auth, "Toward and Understanding of the Term 'The Golden Age' as an Historical Reality" in The Culture of Spanish Jewry, ed Aviva Doron, Tel Aviv, 94; auth, Sephardi Entrepreneurs in Eretz-Israel--The Amzalak Family, 1816-1918, Jewish Quart Rev, Vol 0084, 94. **CONTACT ADDRESS** Graduate Sch and Univ Ctr, CUNY, 33 W 42nd St, New York, NY 10018. **EMAIL** gerberjs@aol.com

GERBER, LARRY G.
PERSONAL Born 10/27/1947, Los Angeles, CA, m, 1980, 1 child **DISCIPLINE** HISTORY **EDUCATION** Univ Calif Berkeley, BA, 68; MA, 69; PhD, 79. **CAREER** Instr, Univ Md, 79-80; Vis Asst Prof, Univ Ariz, 80-82; Vis Asst Prof, Brown Univ, 82-83; Assoc Prof, Auburn Univ, 83-. **HONORS AND AWARDS** Fel, NEH, 87; Fel, Ford Found, 68-73; Phi Beta Kappa. **MEMBERSHIPS** Am Hist Asn; Org of Am Hist; Am Asn of Univ Prof. **RESEARCH** Twentieth-Century History of American Public Policy. **SELECTED PUBLICATIONS** Auth, "United States and Canadian Industrial Conferences of 1919," Labor Hist, 91; auth, "National Industrial Recovery Act in Comparative Perspective," J of Policy Hist, 94; auth, "corporatism and State Theory," Soc Sci Hist, 97; auth, "Reaffirming the Value of Shared Governance," Academe, 97; auth, "Defending the Values of Academe Through Shared Governance," Academe, 01. **CONTACT ADDRESS** Dept Hist, Auburn Univ, Thach Hall, Auburn, AL 36849-5207. **EMAIL** gerbelg@auburn.edu

GERBERDING, RICHARD A.
PERSONAL Born 09/08/1945, Punxsutawney, PA, s **DISCIPLINE** HISTORY **EDUCATION** Univ Minn, BA, 67; Univ Manitoba, MA, 77; Oxford Univ, PhD, 83. **CAREER** PROF HIST, UNIV ALA, HUNTSVILLE **HONORS AND AWARDS** Am Philol Soc Awd Exc Teach Class, 96. **MEMBERSHIPS** Medieval Acad Am **RESEARCH** Frankish hist **SELECTED PUBLICATIONS** Auth, The Rise of the Carolingians and the Liber Historiae Francorum, Clarendon Press, 87; co-auth, Late Merovingian France, Manchester Univ Press, 97. **CONTACT ADDRESS** Dept of History, Univ of Alabama, Huntsville, Huntsville, AL 35899. **EMAIL** gerberdingr@email.uah.edu

GERLACH, DON R.
PERSONAL Born 06/09/1932, Harvard, NE, s **DISCIPLINE** AMERICAN HISTORY **EDUCATION** Univ Nebr, BSEd, 54, MA, 56, PhD, 61. **CAREER** Asst hist, Univ Nebr, 57-58, instr, 61-62; instr, Far East Div, Univ Md, 58-59; from asst prof to assoc prof, 62-72, Prof Hist, Univ Akron, 72-, Historiographer, Anglican Cath Church; Fulbright scholar, 56-57. **HONORS AND AWARDS** Fulbright Scholar, 1956-57; John Ben Snow Manuscript Prize. 1986. **MEMBERSHIPS** AHA; Orgn Am Hist; fel Royal Hist Soc. **RESEARCH** Early America until 1800, especially the revolutionary era. **SELECTED PUBLICATIONS** Auth, Philip Schuyler & The American Revolution in New York, 1733-1777, U of Nebr Press, 64; auth, Twenty Years of the "Promotion of Literature": The Regents of the University of the State of New York, 1784-1804, State U of NY Press, 74; auth, Proud Patriot: Philip Schuyler & The War of Independence, 1775-1783, Syracuse U Press, 87. **CONTACT ADDRESS** Dept of Hist, Univ of Akron, Akron, OH 44325.

GERLACH, JERRY
PERSONAL Born 11/22/1942, Lincoln, NE, m, 1967, 3 children **DISCIPLINE** GEOGRAPHY **EDUCATION** Univ Neb, BA, 64; MA, 68; Univ Okla, PhD, 74. **CAREER** Instructor, Wisc State Univ, 68-70; Teaching Asst, Univ Okla, 71-72; Instructor, Univ Wisc, 72-74; Asst Prof, William Paterson Col, 74-79; Asst Prof, Ut State Univ, 79-85; Lecturer, Univ Wisc, 85-86; Asst Prof, McNeese State Univ, 86-88; Prof, Winona State Univ, 88-. **HONORS AND AWARDS** Gamma Theta Upsilon; Fulbright Exchange Scholarship, 83-84. **MEMBERSHIPS** Nat Coun for Geog Educ; Asn of Am Geog; Soc for the

N Am Cultural Survey; WI Geog Soc. **SELECTED PUBLICATIONS** Auth, "The Prohibition Tavern: A Nebraska Study," Journal of the West, 91; auth, "Tourism and Its Impact in Costa del Sol, Spain," Focus, 91; co-auth, "Tubing the Apple River: A New Industry," focus, 93; auth, "Beer Drinking and Small Town River Festivals," Focus, 94. **CONTACT ADDRESS** Dept Geog, Winona State Univ, PO Box 5838, Winona, MN 55987.

GERLACH, LARRY REUBEN
PERSONAL Born 11/09/1941, Lincoln, NE, 1 child **DISCIPLINE** AMERICAN HISTORY **EDUCATION** Univ Nebr, Lincoln, BS, 63, MA, 65; Rutgers Univ, New Brunswick, PhD, 68. **CAREER** Asst prof to assoc prof, 68-76, prof hist, Univ Utah, 77-; vis asst prof hist, Col William & Mary, 70-71; vis bk rev ed, William & Mary Quart, 70-71; fel, NJ Hist Soc, 77; assoc dean, Col Humanities, Univ Utah, 82-. **HONORS AND AWARDS** William A Whitehead Awd, NJ Hist Soc, 73; Awd of Merit, Am Assn State & Local Hist, 77; Distinguished Achievement Awd, NJ Hist Comn, 80; Distinguished Teaching Awd, Univ Utah, 81. **MEMBERSHIPS** AHA; Org Am Hist; Am Assn State & Local Hist; Western Hist Assn; North Am Soc Study Sport Hist. **RESEARCH** Colonial America; the American Revolution; sports history. **SELECTED PUBLICATIONS** Ed, The American Revolution: New York as a Case Study, Wadsworth, 72; ed, New Jersey in the American Revolution, NJ Hist Comn, 75; auth, Prologue to Independence: New Jersey in the Coming of the American Revolution, Rutgers Univ, 76; auth, Connecticut Congressman: Samuel Huntington, 1731-1796, Am Revolution Bicentennial Comn Conn, 77; auth, The Men in Blue: Conversations with Umpires, Viking, 80; auth, Blazing Crosses in Zion: The Klu Klux Klan in Utah, Utah State Univ, 82. **CONTACT ADDRESS** Dept of History, Univ of Utah, 217 Carlson Hall, Salt Lake City, UT 84112-3124. **EMAIL** larry.gerlach@m.cc.utah.edu

GERLI, E. MICHAEL
PERSONAL Born 03/11/1945, San Jose, Costa Rica, m, 1966, 2 children **DISCIPLINE** SPANISH, HISPANIC STUDIES **EDUCATION** Univ Calif, BA, 68; Middlebury Col, MA, 69; Univ Calif at Los Angeles, PhD, 72. **CAREER** From asst prof to prof, Georgetown Univ, 72-00; vis prof, Univ Calif at Los Angeles, 80; vis prof, Univ Md, 86-87 & 90; vis prof, Johns Hopkins Univ, 91-92; vis prof, Univ Pa, 93; vis prof, Univ Va, 94; Commonwealth of Va Prof of Hispanic Studies, Univ Va, 00-. **HONORS AND AWARDS** Competitive Grants in Aid for Res, Georgetown Univ, 77, 84, 86, 88, & 89; res & travel grants, Am Philos Soc, 78; res & travel grants, ACLS, 81 & 89; res & travel grants, Comite Conjunto Hispano-Norteamericano, 83; NEH Sr Summer Stipend, 86 & 93; Comt for Cultural Coop Between U.S. Universities and Spain, 87, 90, 92, &95; NEH Sr Res Fel, 94. **MEMBERSHIPS** MLA, Asn Int de Hispanistas, Asn de Lit Hispanica Medieval, Am Asn of Res Historian on Medieval Spain, Int Courtly Lit Soc, Medieval Acad of Am. **RESEARCH** Medieval and Early Modern Iberian Literature and Culture. **SELECTED PUBLICATIONS** Auth, Alfonso Martinez de Toledo, 76; co-ed, Studies in Honor of Gerald E. Wade, 78; ed, Arcipreste de Talavera, 76, 81, & 87; ed, Triste deleytacion: An Anonymous Fifteenth-Century Castilian Romance, 82; ed, Milagros de Nuestra Senora, 85, 87, & 90; ed, La poesia cancioneril: Historia y texto, 90; co-ed, Hispanic Medieval Studies in Honor of Samuel G. Armistead, 92; auth, Refiguring Authority: Reading, Writing, and Rewriting in Cervantes, Univ Press of Kent, 95; co-ed, Studies on the Spanish Sentimental Romance, Tamesis, 97; co-ed, Poetry at Court in Trastamaran Spain: from the Cancionero de Baena To the Cancionero general, Ctr for medieval and Renaissance Studies, Univ Ariz Press, 98. **CONTACT ADDRESS** Dept Span, Ital, & Port, Univ of Virginia, 115 Wilson Hall, Charlottesville, VA 22903.

GERRISH, BRIAN ALBERT
PERSONAL Born 08/14/1931, London, England, m, 1955, 2 children **DISCIPLINE** RELIGION, HISTORY **EDUCATION** Cambridge Univ, BA, 52, MA, 56; Westminster Col, Eng, cert, 55; Union Theol Sem, STM, 56; Columbia Univ, PhD(philos relig), 58. **CAREER** From instr to assoc prof church hist, McCormick Theol Sem, 58-65; assoc prof hist theol, 65-68, prof hist theol and Reformation hist, 68-72, PROF HIST THEOL, DIVINITY SCH, UNIV CHICAGO, 72-, Am Asn Theol Schs fac fel, 6i-62; John Simon Guggenheim Mem Found fel, 70-72; CO-ED, J RELIG, 72-; Nat Endowment for Humanities fel, 80-81. **MEMBERSHIPS** Am Acad Relig; Am Soc Reformation Res; Am Soc Church Hist (pres, 79). **RESEARCH** Continental Protestant thought in the 16th and 19th centuries. **SELECTED PUBLICATIONS** Auth, Natural Religion and the Nature of Religion--The Legacy of Deism, J Relig, Vol 0073, 93; Religion and the Religions in the English Enlightenment, J Relig, Vol 0073, 93; Atheism from the Reformation to the Enlightenment, J Relig, Vol 0074, 94. **CONTACT ADDRESS** Univ of Chicago, 18541 Klimm Ave, Homewood, IL 60430.

GERSTEIN, LINDA GROVES
PERSONAL Born 04/03/1943, Gouverneur, NY, m, 1964, 2 children **DISCIPLINE** AFRICAN HISTORY **EDUCATION** State Univ NYork Col Geneseo, BS, 65; Syracuse Univ, PhD, 72. **CAREER** Asst prof, 67-80, chmn dept, 72-74, prof hist, Westfield State Col, 80-, Consult, NY State Prison Syst, 72; dir, Raymond Patterson Archives, 74-; res grant, Am Philos Soc, 79. **MEMBERSHIPS** AHAG African Studies Asn; Liberian Studies Asn. **RESEARCH** Slavery; slave trade; Liberia. **SELECTED PUBLICATIONS** Auth, Fernando Po and the Anti-Sierra Leonean Campaign: 1826-1834, Int J African Hist Studies, Vol 6, No 2; coauth, Curtin's Atlantic Slave Trade: An Analysis from Two Perspectives, Hist J Western Mass, Vol II, No 1; Immigrants to Liberia, 1843-1754, Inst Liberian Studies, 80; Simon Greenleaf and the Liberian Constitution of 1847, J Liberian Studies, 82. **CONTACT ADDRESS** Dept of Hist, Haverford Col, 370 Lancaster Ave, Haverford, PA 19041-1392. **EMAIL** lgerstei@haverford.edu

GERSTEL, SHARON E. J.
PERSONAL Born 06/14/1962 **DISCIPLINE** ART HISTORY **EDUCATION** Bryn Mawr Col, AB; NYork Univ, MA; PhD. **CAREER** Prof, Univ MD. **HONORS AND AWARDS** Samuel H Kress fel; two Dumbarton Oaks fel(s); grant, NEH; postdoc fel, J Paul Getty. **MEMBERSHIPS** Governing Board, Byzantine Studies Conference, Christian Archaeol Assn , Greece. **RESEARCH** Relationship between liturgical and extra-liturgical ceremony and monumental painting of medieval Byzantium. **SELECTED PUBLICATIONS** Auth, Beholding the Sacred Mysteries: Programs of the Byzantine Sanctuary. **CONTACT ADDRESS** Dept of Art Hist, Univ of Maryland, Col Park, 4229 Art-Sociology Building, College Park, MD 20742-1335. **EMAIL** sg113@umail.umd.edu

GERTEIS, LOUIS
PERSONAL Born 12/13/1942, Kansas City, MO, m, 1983, 4 children **DISCIPLINE** HISTORY **EDUCATION** Antioch Col, BA, 65; Univ Wis, MA, 66; PhD, 69. **CAREER** Prof **HONORS AND AWARDS** Research Fellow, Public Policy Research Centers, Univ of Missouri, St. Louis, 91- ; Stanley J. Kahrl visiting Fellow in Theatre History, Harvard Univ, 91; Principal Investigator, Information Technology Grants, Univ Missouri, St. Louis, 97, 1998; Board of Directors, Campbell House Museum, St. Louis, Missouri. **MEMBERSHIPS** American Historical Assoc; Missouri Conference on History; Organization of American Historians. **RESEARCH** Nineteenth century United States; slavery and emancipation; Civil War and reconstruction; democracy and race. **SELECTED PUBLICATIONS** Auth, From Contraband to Freedman: Federal Policy Toward Southern Blacks, 1861-1865, Greenwood, 73; Salmon P. Chase, Radicalism, and the Politics of Emancipation, 1861-1864, J Am Hist, 73; Slavery and Hard Times: Morality and Utility in American Antislavery Reform, Civil War Hist, 83; Morality and Utility in American Antislavery Reform, Univ NC, 87; Blackface Minstrelsy and the Construction of Race in Nineteenth Century America, Kent, 97. **CONTACT ADDRESS** History Dept, Univ of Missouri, St. Louis, 484 Lucas Hall, Saint Louis, MO 63121. **EMAIL** gerteis@umsl.edu

GERVERS, MICHAEL
PERSONAL Born 01/19/1942, Flaunden, England, m, 1967 **DISCIPLINE** MEDIEVAL SOCIAL AND ECONOMIC HISTORY **EDUCATION** Princeton Univ, BA, 64; Univ Poitiers, France, MA, 65; Univ Toronto, PhD(Medieval studies), 72. **CAREER** Asst prof Medieval hist, NY Univ, 72-75; asst prof Medieval art hist, Univ Toronto, 76, asst prof Medieval hist, Erindale Col, 76-77, Asst Prof Medieval Hist and Art Hist, Scarborough Col, Univ Toronto, 77-, Res assoc hist, Can Coun Killam Fel, 74-75. **MEMBERSHIPS** Medieval Acad Am; Col Art Asn; Essex Archaeol Soc; Societe Archeologique et Hist Charente; Arms & Armour Soc. **RESEARCH** Social and economic development of the Order of St John of Jerusalem in England; Medieval rock-cut churches of the Mediterranean world; historical ethnography; medieval economic and social history (military orders, monasticism), textual criticism; textile history and historical ethnography and computer assisted analysis of medieval property exchange documents. **SELECTED PUBLICATIONS** Auth, "The Cartulary of the Knight of St. John of Jerusalem Part I," (1982, and Part II (1996); ed, "The Second Crusade & the Cistercians," (1992). **CONTACT ADDRESS** Dept of History, Univ of Toronto, Sidney Smith Hall, 100 St George St, Rm 2074, Toronto, ON, Canada M5S 3G3. **EMAIL** gervers@chass.utoronto.ca

GETTLEMAN, MARVIN EDWARD
PERSONAL Born 09/12/1933, New York, NY, m, 1981, 4 children **DISCIPLINE** MODERN UNITED STATES HISTORY **EDUCATION** City Col New York, BA, 57; Johns Hopkins Univ, MA, 59, PhD(hist), 72. **CAREER** Lectr polit sci & hist, City Col New York, 59-62; lectr US econ hist, 62-63, from instr to asst prof, 63-68, assoc prof, 68-79, prof hist, 79-95, Prof Emer, Polytech Inst Brooklyn, 95- ; Consult, proj impact technol change on privacy in US, Asn Bar City New York, 64; Louis M Rabinowitz Found res grant, 68; Nat Endowment for Humanities fel, 73-74; Nat Hist Publ & Records Comn grant, 77-78; mem, Brooklyn Rediscovery Proj, 78-79; Exec Dir, Abraham Lincoln Brigade Arch, 97-98; Mem ed bd, Sci & Soc, 74-; Ed, The Vol, J of the Vet of the Abraham Lincoln Brigade, 97-98; Dir, Proj on the Comp Int Hist of Left Educ, 95-. **MEMBERSHIPS** AHA; Orgn Am Historians **RESEARCH** United States foreign policy in Asia; history of higher education; American Communist education. **SELECTED PUBLICATIONS** Auth, John Glenn: Hero and America, New Left Rev, 62; Vietnam: History, Documents, Opinions, Fawcett, US, 65, 2nd ed, Penguin, England, 66 & 3rd ed, New Am Libr/Signet, US, 70; The Dorr Rebellion: A Study in American Radicalism, 1833-1849, Random, 73, 2nd ed, Krieger, 80; Philanthropy and Social Control in Late 19th Century America, Societas, summer 75; auth, An Elusive Presence: John Finley & His America, Nelson-Hall, 79; co-ed, El Salvador: Central America in the New Cold War, Grove, 80; auth, The Johns Hopkins Seminary of History and Politics, 1877-1912, 5 v, Garland, 88-90; auth, "The New York Workers School, 1923-1944: Communist Education in American Society," in New Studies in the Politics and Culture of U.S. Communism, ed. M. Brown et al (New York: Monthly Rev Press, 93); coauth, Vietnam & America: Documented History, Grove-Atlantic, 95; ed, "Explorations in the History of Left Education in Nineteenth and Twentieth Century Europe," Paedagogica Historica 35 (99). **CONTACT ADDRESS** 771 West End Ave, New York, NY 10025.

GETTY, J. ARCH
PERSONAL Born 11/30/1950, Shreveport, LA, m, 1972, 1 child **DISCIPLINE** RUSSIAN HISTORY **EDUCATION** Univ Pa, AB, 72; Boston Col, MA, 73, PhD(hist), 79. **CAREER** Lectr hist, Boston Col, 77-80; Asst Prof Russ Hist, Univ Calif, Riverside, 80-, Managing ed, Russ Hist, 78-; sr fel, Russ Inst, Columbia Univ, 81. **MEMBERSHIPS** Am Asn Advan Slavic Studies. **RESEARCH** History of Soviet Communist Party; Russian Revolution; Stalin. **SELECTED PUBLICATIONS** Coauth, The Moscow Bolshevik Elite of 1917 in the Great Purges, 78 & The Moscow Bolshevik Cadres of 1917: A prosopographic analysis, 78, Russ Hist; auth, Party and purge in Smolensk 1933-37, Slavic Rev (in prep). **CONTACT ADDRESS** Dept of Hist, Univ of California, Riverside, Riverside, CA 92507.

GEYER, M.
PERSONAL Born 10/30/1947, Germany, m, 1991 **DISCIPLINE** HISTORY **EDUCATION** Albert Ludwigs Univ, PhD summa cum laud, 76, staatsexamew 72. **CAREER** Leipzig Univ, Leibniz Prof, 95-96; John F Kennedy Inst Berlin, vis prof, 93-94; Univ Chicago, prof, 86-; Univ Michigan Ann Arbor, asst prof, assoc prof, 77-86; Univ Bochum, guest prof, 84. **HONORS AND AWARDS** Woodrow Wilson Fel; St Anthony's Col Sr Res Fel; Stud des Deutschen Volkes Schshp; Grad Schshp Freiburg; APS Tvl Gnt; Ruth M Sinclair Awd; Dist Ser Awd U of M; Max-Planck-Inst Fel; Cen Euro Hist Con Group Article Prize. **MEMBERSHIPS** AHA; AHF; AM; CGCEH; CES; GSA; IISS; SCS; WHA; Karl Lamprecht Gesellschaft; Verein fur Geschichte der Weltsysteme. **RESEARCH** German and European History; History of Modern War and Violence; History of Globalization/World History. **SELECTED PUBLICATIONS** Auth, Germany or: The Twentieth Century as History, S Atlantic Quart, 97; Historians at the Beginning and End of the Twentieth Century, Comparative, 96; Global Violence and Nationalizing Wars in Eurasia and the Americas: The Geopolitics of War in the Mid-Nineteenth Century, Comp Stud in Soc and Hist, 96; The Politics of Memory in Contemporary Germany, in: Joan Copjec, ed, Radical Evil, London, NY, Verso, 96; Restorative Elites, German Society and the Nazi Pursuit of War, in: Fascist Italy and Nazi Germany: Comparison and Contrast, ed Richard Bessel, Cambridge, NY, Cambridge Univ Press, 96; Why Culture history? What Future? Which Germany? In: New German critique, 95; Great Men and Postmodern Raptures: Overcoming the Belatedness of German Historiography, coauth, in: German Studies Rev, 95. **CONTACT ADDRESS** Dept of History, Univ of Chicago, Chicago, IL 60637. **EMAIL** mgeyer@midway.uchicago.edu

GHAZZAL, ZOUHAIR
PERSONAL Born 08/06/1956, Bhamdoun, Lebanon, s **DISCIPLINE** HISTORY **EDUCATION** Sorbonne, PhD. **CAREER** Hist, Loyola Univ. **HONORS AND AWARDS** Rockefeller Fel, 91-92; NEH, 96-97. **RESEARCH** Islamic and Middle Eastern societies; legal and economic history. **SELECTED PUBLICATIONS** Auth, L'economie politique de Damas durant le XIXe siecle: Structures traditionnelles et capitalisme, Damascus, 93; auth, The Grammars of Adjudication: Judicial Decision Making in Fin-de-Siecle Ottoman Beirut and Beirut and Demascus, (in press). **CONTACT ADDRESS** Dept of Hist, Loyola Univ, Chicago, 820 N Michigan, Chicago, IL 60611. **EMAIL** zghazza@luc.edu

GHIRARDO, DIANE
DISCIPLINE ARCHITECTURAL HISTORY AND THEORY **EDUCATION** San Jose State Univ, BA, 73; Stanford Univ, MA, 76, PhD, 82. **CAREER** Prof, USC, 95-; vis prof, Rice Univ, 95; assoc prof, USC, 88-95; asst prof, USC, 84-88; vis prof, SCI-ARC, 86, 87 & 89; asst prof, TX A&M Univ, 83-84; lectr & tchg asst, Stanford Univ, 80-83. **HONORS AND AWARDS** Phi Kappa Phi Fac Recognition Awd, 97; Graham Found Awd, 96; fel, Am Acad, Rome, 87-88; Woodrow Wilson Post Doctoral fel, 87-88, declined; Univ Scholar, USC, 86; Fulbright fel, 76-77. **MEMBERSHIPS** ACSA; Col Art Asn; Soc Arch Hist. **SELECTED PUBLICATIONS** Auth, Architecture After Modernism, Thames & Hudson, 96; Mark Mack, Wasmuth Verlag, 94, monogr; Out of Site: A Social Criticism of Architecture, Bay Press, 91; Building New Communities: New Deal America & Fascist Italy, Princeton, UP, 89; The Case for

Letting Malibu Burn, Mortal City, 95; Eisenman's Bogus Avant-Garde, Progressive Arch, 94; Peter Eisenman: Il camouflage dell'avanguardia, Casabella 613, 94; Citta Fascista: Surveillance and Spectacle, J Mod Hist, 94. **CONTACT ADDRESS** School of Archit, Univ of So California, University Park Campus, Los Angeles, CA 90089. **EMAIL** admitusc@usc.edu

GIACUMAKIS, GEORGE
PERSONAL Born 07/06/1937, New Castle, PA, m, 1960, 4 children **DISCIPLINE** HISTORY **EDUCATION** Shelton Col, BA, 59; Brandeis Univ, MA, 61; PhD, 63. **CAREER** Prof, Calif State Univ, 63-79; pres & exec dir, Jerusalem Univ Col, 78-84; adj prof & dir, Calif State Univ-Fullerton, 85-. **HONORS AND AWARDS** Nat Defense For Lang Fel for Arabic and Islamic Studies, Brandeis Univ, 60-63; Sabbatical Grant and Res Fel, Isreal, 72. **MEMBERSHIPS** Am Sci Affiliation, Bibl Archeol Soc, Conf on Faith and Hist, Evangel Theol Soc, Hist Soc, Inst of Bibl Res, Middle East Inst. **SELECTED PUBLICATIONS** Auth, "The Ancient Kingdom of Alalah," The Bibl World: A Dict of Bibl Archaeol (Grand rapids, MI: Baker Book House, 68); auth, "The Isreali-Arab Conflict in the Middle East," Protest and Pol (Attic Press Inc, 68); auth, The Akkadian of Alalah, Mouton Publ (The Hague, Neth), 69; transl, New American Standard Bible, 71 & 77; auth, "Christian Attitudes Toward Isreal," The Cross and the Flag (Wheaton, IL: Creation House, 72); auth, "The Gate Below the Gate," Bull of the Near E Archaeol Soc (74); ed, Young's Bible Dictionary, Tyndale House Publ (Wheaton, IL), 84, 89 & 96; ed, International Standard Version of the Bible, Davidson Press, 99. **CONTACT ADDRESS** Dept Hist, California State Univ, Fullerton, 28000 Marguerite Pkwy, Mission Viejo, CA 92692-3635. **EMAIL** ggiacumakis@fullerton.edu

GIAMO, BENEDICT
PERSONAL Born 08/27/1954, Cleveland, OH **DISCIPLINE** HISTORY **EDUCATION** Baldwin-Wallace Col, BA, 76; New Sch for Soc Res, MA, 78; Emory Univ, PhD, 87. **CAREER** Chair & assoc prof, Univ Notre Dame. **HONORS AND AWARDS** Ralph Henry Gabriel Prize, Am Studies Asn, 88. **MEMBERSHIPS** Am Studies Asn. **RESEARCH** Homelessness, Literature & Culture, Intercultural Studies. **SELECTED PUBLICATIONS** Auth, On the Bowery: Confronting Homelessness in American Society, Univ Iowa Press, 89; auth, Beyond Homelessness: Frames of Reference, Univ Iowa Press, 92; auth, The Homeless of "Ironweed": Blossoms on the Crag, Univ Iowa Press, 96; auth, Kerouac, the Word and the Way: Prose Artist as Spiritual Quester, Southern Ill Univ Press, 00. **CONTACT ADDRESS** Dept Am Studies, Univ of Notre Dame, 303 O'Shaugnessy Hall, Notre Dame, IN 46556-5639. **EMAIL** giamo.1@nd.edu

GIBERT, JOHN C.
DISCIPLINE CLASSICAL HISTORY **EDUCATION** Yale, BA, 82; Harvard, PhD, 91. **CAREER** Asst Prof, 90-92, St Olaf Coll; Asst Prof, 92-, Univ of Colorado, Boulder. **MEMBERSHIPS** Amer Philos Assoc; Class Assoc of the Middle West and South. **RESEARCH** Greek Drama. **SELECTED PUBLICATIONS** Auth, Euripides Hippolytus Plays: Which Came First?, Classical Quarterly 47, pp 80-92, 97; Euripides Hercules 1351 and the Hero's Encounter with Death,, Classical Philology 92, pp 247-58, 97; Change of Mind in Greek Tragedy(Hypomnemata 108), Gottingen, 95; Review of Theseus, Tragedy and the Athenian Empire, by S. Mills, Bryn Mawr Classical Review, 98; Review of Collecting Fragments/Fragmente sammeln, ed, G Most, BMCR, 98; Review of Aristophanes' Birds, ed, N.Dunbar, BMCR 7, 96. **CONTACT ADDRESS** Dept Classics, Univ of Colorado, Boulder, Boulder, CO 80309-0348. **EMAIL** John.Gibert@colorado.edu

GIBSON, ANN EDEN
DISCIPLINE TWENTIETH-CENTURY AMERICAN AND CONTEMPORARY ART **EDUCATION** Univ of Del, PhD. **CAREER** Prof, ch. **SELECTED PUBLICATIONS** Auth, Issues in Abstract Expressionism: The Artist-Run Periodicals, UMI, 90; Abstract Expressionism: Other Politics, Yale Univ Press, 97; co-auth, Norman Lewis: The Black Paintings, The Studio Museum in Harlem, 98. **CONTACT ADDRESS** Dept of Art Hist, Univ of Delaware, Newark, DE 19716. **EMAIL** agibson@udel.edu

GIBSON, WALTER S.
PERSONAL Born 03/31/1932, Columbus, OH, m, 1972 **DISCIPLINE** ART HISTORY **EDUCATION** Ohio State Univ, BFA, 57, MA, 60; Harvard Univ, PhD, 69. **CAREER** Asst prof, 66-71; assoc prof, 71-78, act chair dept art, 70- 71, chair, 71-79, Andrew W. Mellow prof hum, 78-97, Prof Emer, 97-, Case Western Reserve Univ; Murphy Lectr, Univ Kans, Nelson- Atkins Mus ARt, 88; Clark vis prof, Williams Col, 89, 92. **HONORS AND AWARDS** Fulbright Scholarship, Rijksuniversiteit, Utrecht, 60-61; Guggenheim fel, 78-79; Fulbright res grant, Belgium, 84; fel, Netherlands Inst Adv Stud, 95-96. **RESEARCH** Dutch, Flemish painting **SELECTED PUBLICATIONS** Auth, Peter Bruegel the Elder: Two Studies, Franklin D. Murphy Lecture XI, Univ Kans, 91; auth, Hieronymus Bosch, Thames and Hudson, 73, Praeger, 73, reprint, 88, auth, Hieronymus Bosch; An Annotated Bibliography, G.K.H., 83; Gered, 74, Dutched, 74, Japed, 89, auth, "Mirror of the Earth,": The World Landscape in Painting, Prince, 89; auth, Bruegel, Thames & Hudson, Oxford, 77, reprint, 88, Dutched, 77, Japanese ed, 92; Spaned (El Bosco), 93, Fred (Jerome Bosch), 95, Finnished, Czecked, Hungarian ed, Rused, forthcoming; auth, Pleasant Places; The Rustic Landscape in Dutch Painting from Bruegel to Ruisdael, California, 00. **CONTACT ADDRESS** RR2., No. 461H, Pownal, VT 05261-9767. **EMAIL** wsgibson@together.net

GIEBELHAUS, AUGUST WILLIAM
PERSONAL Born 06/01/1943, Rahway, NJ, m, 1967, 2 children **DISCIPLINE** AMERICAN AND ECONOMIC HISTORY **EDUCATION** Rutgers Univ, BA, 64, MA, 70; Univ Del, PhD(hist), 77. **CAREER** Teacher hist, Union County Regional High Sch Dist, Springfield, NJ, 64-71; Hagley fel econ hist, Eleutherian Mills Hagley Found, 71-74 and 75-76; lectr, Univ Birmingham, UK, 74-75; asst prof hist, 76-80, Assoc Prof Hist, GA Inst Technol, 80-, Adj instr, Univ Col, Rutgers Univ, 69-71; asst ed, Technol and Cult, 77-78, assoc ed, 79-81; assoc, Hist Assoc Inc, Washington, DC, 80-. **MEMBERSHIPS** AHA; Econ Hist Asn; Nat Coun Pub hist; Orgn Am Historians; Soc Hist Technol. **RESEARCH** History of American business; energy history; petroleum industry. **SELECTED PUBLICATIONS** Auth, The rise of an independent major: The Sun Oil Company, 1876-1945, Vol 6, 77 & Teaching business history to engineers, Vol 8, 79, Bus & Econ Hist; Farming for fuel: The alchohol motor fuel movement of the 1930's, Agr Hist, 80; Business and Government in the Oil Indusry: A Case Study of Sun Oil, 1876-1945, Jai Press, 80; co-ed, Energy Transitions--Long-Term Perspectives, AAAS, 81; auth, Petroleum refining and transportation: Oil companies and economic development, In: Energy and Transport: Historical Perspectives on Policy Issues, Sage, 82. **CONTACT ADDRESS** Sch of Soc Sci Ga Inst of Technol, 225 North Ave N W, Atlanta, GA 30332-0002.

GIFFIN, FREDERICK CHARLES
PERSONAL Born 09/10/1938, Pittsburgh, PA, m, 1959, 2 children **DISCIPLINE** RUSSIAN HISTORY **EDUCATION** Denison Univ, BA, 60; Emory Univ, MA, 61, PhD(hist), 65. **CAREER** Vis instr hist, Agnes Scott Col, 63-64; from instr to asst prof, Southern Methodist Univ, 64-67; from asst prof to assoc prof, 67-74, asst dean, Grad Col, 70-72, Prof Hist, Ariz State Univ, 74-, Chmn Dept, 82-86. **HONORS AND AWARDS** Grad Coun of Humanities fel, Southern Methodist Univ, 66-67; Outstanding Educr Am Awd, 73 **RESEARCH** Russian factory legislation; Soviet-American relations. **SELECTED PUBLICATIONS** Auth, The formative years of the Russian factory inspectorate, 1882-1885, Slavic Rev, 12/66; The prohibition of night work for women and young persons: The Russian Factory Law of June 3, 1885, Can Slavic Studies, summer 68; co-ed, Against the Grain, New Am Libr, 71; auth, I I Yanzhul: Russia's first district factory inspector, Slavonic & East Europ Rev, 1/71; ed, Woman as revolutionary, New Am Libr, 73; auth, Six Who Protested, Kennikat, 77; ed, The Tongue of Angels, Susquehanna Univ Press, 88; auth, James Putnam Goodrich and Soviet Russia, Mid-Am, 10/89; An American Railroad Man East of the Urals, 1918-1922, The Hist, Summer 98. **CONTACT ADDRESS** Dept of History, Arizona State Univ, PO Box 872501, Tempe, AZ 85287-2501. **EMAIL** mfgiff@asu.edu

GIFFIN, PHILLIP E.
PERSONAL Born 05/30/1944, Maryville, TN, m, 1990, 1 child **DISCIPLINE** ECONOMICS; ECONOMIC HISTORY **EDUCATION** Univ Tex-Austin, BA; Tex Tech Univ, MA; Univ Tenn-Knoxville, PhD. **CAREER** Asst prof econ, Valdosta State Col, 72-76; prof econ, Univ Tenn-Chattanooga, 77-00. **HONORS AND AWARDS** Fulbright fel-Poland, 89-90. **MEMBERSHIPS** Asn Evolutionary Econ. **RESEARCH** History of economic thought, Economic history, Industrial economics. **SELECTED PUBLICATIONS** Auth, "Institutional Development in a Transitional Economy: The Case of Poland" Int J Soc Econ, pp 35-55, (94); auth, "The Origins of Capitalist Markets: Transition in Poland", J Econ Issues, pp 585-590, (95). **CONTACT ADDRESS** Dept Econ, Univ of Tennessee, Chattanooga, 615 McCallie Ave, Chattanooga, TN 37403-2504. **EMAIL** phillip-giffin@utc.edu

GIFFIN, WILLIAM WAYNE
PERSONAL Born 04/06/1938, Bellaire, OH, w, 2 children **DISCIPLINE** AMERICAN HISTORY **EDUCATION** Col Wooster, BA, 60; Ohio State Univ, BSEd, 62, MA, 63, PhD(hist), 68. **CAREER** Prof Ethnic Hist, Ind State Univ, 68- **MEMBERSHIPS** Orgn Am Hist; Ind Asn Hist. **RESEARCH** African-American history; immigration. **SELECTED PUBLICATIONS** Auth, Black insurgency in the Republican Party of Ohio, 1920-1932, Ohio Hist, 73; The Mercy Hospital controversy among Cleveland's Afro-American Civic Leaders, 1927" J Negro Hist, 76; Mobilization of Black militiamen in World War I: Ohio's Ninth Battalion, The Historian, 78; The Political Realignment of Black Voters in Indianapolis, 1924, Ind Mag Hist, 6/83; coauth, Centennial History of the Indiana General Assembly: Three Review Essays, Ind Mag Hist, 12/88; auth, Irish, In: Peopling Indiana: The Ethnic Experience, Ind Hist Soc, 96; auth, "Destruction of Deleware and Miami Towns in the Aftermath of the Battle of Tippecanoe: The Impact of Perspective on History," (Winnipeg, Canada: Univ of Manitoba, 00): 68-76. **CONTACT ADDRESS** Dept of Hist, Indiana State Univ, 210 N 7th St, Terre Haute, IN 47809-0002. **EMAIL** HIGIFFN@Ruby.indstate.edu

GIGLIO, JAMES N.
PERSONAL Born 03/28/1939, Akron, OH, m, 1965, 2 children **DISCIPLINE** HISTORY **EDUCATION** Kent State Univ, BA, 61; MA, 64; Ohio State Univ, PhD, 68. **CAREER** From asst prof to distinguished prof, Southwest Mo State Univ, 68-. **HONORS AND AWARDS** Distinguished Scholar, 88-98. **MEMBERSHIPS** Orgn of Am Historians, Soc for Historians of Am For Relations, Soc for Am Baseball Res. **RESEARCH** Twentieth-Century American Political History, Twentieth Century American Foreign Policy, History of Baseball. **SELECTED PUBLICATIONS** Auth, H. M. Daugherty and the Politics of Expediency, Kent State Univ Press, 78; coauth, Truman in Cartoon and Caricature, Iowa State Univ Press, 84; auth, The Presidency of John F. Kennedy, Univ Press of Kans, 91; auth, John F. Kennedy: A Bibliography, Greenwood Press, 95; auth, Stash: A Biography of Stanley F. Musial, Univ Mo Press, 01. **CONTACT ADDRESS** Dept Hist, Southwest Missouri State Univ, Springfield, 901 S National Ave, Springfield, MO 65804-0027. **EMAIL** jng890f@mail.smsu.edu

GILB, CORINNE LATHROP
PERSONAL Born 02/19/1925, Lethbridge, AB, Canada, m, 1945, 2 children **DISCIPLINE** HISTORY **EDUCATION** Univ Wash, BA, 46; Univ Calif, Berkeley, MA, 51; Radcliffe Col, PhD(Am civilization), 57. **CAREER** Researcher, Calif State Bar, 49-51; asst hist, Univ Calif, Berkeley, 50-52, head oral hist proj, 53-57; lectr hist, Mills Col, 57-61; prof humanities, San Francisco State Col, 64-67; Prof Hist, Wayne State Univ, 68-, Co-Dir Urban Studies and Spec Adv Law/Hist Prog, 76-, Res polit scientist labor mgt, Inst Indust Rels, 56-59 and Ctr Studies Law and Soc, 60-66; Soc Sci Res Coun grant, 58; Guggenheim fel, 67; spec consult, Interim Comt Revenue and Taxation, Calif Assembly, 63-64; dir, Planning Dept Detroit, 79. **MEMBERSHIPS** AHA; Orgn Am Historians; Int Soc Comp Study of Civilizations; Soc Am Legal Historians; Soc Sci Hist Asn. **RESEARCH** Comparative world cities; legal history; comparative United States and European history. **SELECTED PUBLICATIONS** Auth, Notebook of a 60s Lawyer--An Unrepentant Memoir and Selected-Writings, Mich Hist Rev, Vol 0018, 92, Layered Violence--The Detroit Rioters of 1943, J Am Ethnic Hist, Vol 0013, 94. **CONTACT ADDRESS** Dept of Hist, Wayne State Univ, Detroit, MI 48202.

GILBERT, ARLAN KEMMERER
PERSONAL Born 06/29/1933, Emmaus, PA, m, 1959, 3 children **DISCIPLINE** UNITED STATES HISTORY **EDUCATION** Susquehanna Univ, BA, 55; Univ Del, MA, 57. **CAREER** Asst prof, 60-64, chmn dept, 64-70, assoc prof, 64-88, prof us hist, Hillsdale Col, 88-98, William and Berniece Grewcock Prof Am Hist, 95-98, Prof Emer, 98-; Teaching asst hist, Univ Wis, 57-59; dir, Model UN assembly for high schs of Mich & Northern Ohio, 60-70. **RESEARCH** American economic history from the colonial period to the Civil War; United States constitutional history; sectionalism and the American Civil War. **SELECTED PUBLICATIONS** Auth, Oliver Evans Memoir on the Origin of Steam Boats and Steam Wagons, Del Hist, 56; auth, Gunpowder Production in post-Revolutionary Maryland, Md Hist Mag, 57; auth, Historic Hillsdale Col, 91; auth, "Hilldale Honor: The Civil War Experience," 94; auth, The Permanent Things, 98. **CONTACT ADDRESS** 33 E College St, Hillsdale, MI 49242-1298. **EMAIL** gilbertarlan@dmci.net

GILBERT, BENTLEY BRINKERHOFF
PERSONAL Born 04/05/1924, Mansfield, OH, m, 1968, 4 children **DISCIPLINE** HISTORY **EDUCATION** Miami Univ, BA, 49; Univ Cincinnati, MA, 50; Univ Wis, PhD(hist), 54. **CAREER** Instr hist, Univ Cincinnati, 54-55; from asst prof to assoc prof, Colo Col, 55-67; assoc prof, 67-69, Prof Hist, Univ Ill, Chicago Circle, 69-, Nat Inst Health res grant, 62-; consult, Hist Life Sci Studies Group, Nat Inst Health, 72-76; Royal Hist Soc fel, 73; John Simon Guggenheim Found fel, 73-74; exec secy, Conf Brit Studies, 74-78; ed, J Brit Studies, 78. **MEMBERSHIPS** AHA; Conf Brit Studies. **RESEARCH** Twentieth century British social and institutional history; life of David Lloyd George. **CONTACT ADDRESS** Dept of Hist, Univ of Illinois, Chicago, Chicago, IL 60680. **EMAIL** bgilbert@uic.edu

GILBERT, JAMES B.
PERSONAL Born 05/23/1939, Chicago, IL **DISCIPLINE** HISTORY **EDUCATION** Carleton Col, BA, 61; Univ Wis, MA, 63, PhD, 66. **CAREER** Asst prof, Univ Md, 66-68, assoc prof, 69-71, prof, 72-. **HONORS AND AWARDS** Carleton Col, Grad with Distinction, 61; Distinguished Scholar-Teacher, Univ Md, 76; Distinguished Univ Prof, Univ Md, 99-. **MEMBERSHIPS** OAH, AHA, ASA. **RESEARCH** American culture, 20th century. **SELECTED PUBLICATIONS** Auth, Writers and Partisans: A History of Literary Radicalism in America, John Wiley (68); auth, Designing the Industrial State: The Intellectuals and Industrial Alienation, 1880-1910, Johns Hopkins (78); auth, Work Without Salvation: America's Intel-

lectuals and Industrial Alienation, 1880-1910, Johns Hopkins (78); coauth with R. Jackson Wilson, et al, The Pursuit of Liberty, Random House (83); auth, A Cycle of Outrage: America's Reaction to the Juvenile Delinquent in the 1950s, Oxford (86); auth, Perfect Cities: Chicago's Utopias in the 1890s, Univ Chicago (91); co-ed, Mythmaking Frame of Mind, Wadsworth, 93; auth, Redeeming Culture: American Religion in an Age of Science, Univ Chicago (97). **CONTACT ADDRESS** Dept Hist, Univ of Maryland, Col Park, 2115 F S Key Hall, College Park, MD 20742-0001. **EMAIL** jg19@umail.umd.edu

GILDEMEISTER, GLEN A.
PERSONAL Born 05/08/1945, Racine, WI, m, 1968, 2 children **DISCIPLINE** HISTORY **EDUCATION** Univ Wis, BS, 68; Northern Ill Univ, MA, 72, PhD(hist), 77. **CAREER** Co-dir labor hist, Ohio Hist Soc, 75-77; Dir Hist, Northern Ill Regional Hist Ctr, 77- **MEMBERSHIPS** Soc Am Archivists; Midwest Archives Conf; Orgn Am Historians. **RESEARCH** Labor history; prison history; regional history. **SELECTED PUBLICATIONS** Auth, Preliminary guide to sources in Ohio labor history, 76 & Labor archives manual, 78, Ohio Hist Soc; The founding of the American Federation of Labor, Labor Hist, 78. **CONTACT ADDRESS** Libr, No Illinois Regional Historical Ctr, 1425 W Lincoln Hwy, De Kalb, IL 60115-2825.

GILDERHUS, MARK THEODORE
PERSONAL Born 11/15/1941, Rochester, MN, m, 1967 **DISCIPLINE** AMERICAN HISTORY **EDUCATION** Gustavus Adolphus Col, BA, 63; Univ Nebr, MA, 65, PhD(Am hist), 68. **CAREER** Asst prof, 68-73, assoc prof, 73-78, Prof Hist, Colo State Univ, 78-, Chmn, Dept Hist, 80- **MEMBERSHIPS** AHA; Orgn Am Hist; Conf Latin Am Hist; Soc Hist Am Foreign Rels. **RESEARCH** United States foreign relations, particularly with Latin America; recent United States; United States military history. **SELECTED PUBLICATIONS** Auth, The United States and Carranza, 1917: The question of DeJure recognition, The Americans, 71; Henry P Flethcer in Mexico: An ambassador's response to revolutionary nationalism, Rocky Mountain Soc Sci J, 73; Senator Albert B Fell and the plot against Mexico, NMex Hist Rev, 73; Carranza and the decision to revolt, 1913, The Americas, 76; Diplomacy and Revolution: US-Mexican Relations under Wilson and Carranza, Univ Ariz, 77; Diplomatic perspectives: Mexico, an early voice from the Third World, Soc Sci J, 78; Pan-Ameican Initiatives: The Wilson Presidency and Regional Integration, 1914-1917, Diplomatic Hist, 80. **CONTACT ADDRESS** Dept of Hist, Colorado State Univ, Fort Collins, CO 80523-0001.

GILDRIC, RICHARD P.
PERSONAL Born 04/18/1945, Norfolk, VA, m, 1966, 2 children **DISCIPLINE** HISTORY & PHILOSOPHY **EDUCATION** Eckerd Col, BA, 66; Univ Va, MA, 68, PhD, 71. **CAREER** Prof, Austin Peay State Univ, 70-. **HONORS AND AWARDS** Kenneth S. Lafaurette Prize. **MEMBERSHIPS** OIEAHC; OAH; AHA; AAUP **RESEARCH** Colonial America; early modern Britian. **SELECTED PUBLICATIONS** Auth, The Profane, The Civil & the Godly: The Reformation of Manners in Orthodox New England 1679-1749, 94. **CONTACT ADDRESS** Dept of History & Philosophy, Austin Peay State Univ, Clarksville, TN 37044. **EMAIL** gildrier@apsu01.apsu.edu

GILES, GEOFFREY JOHN
PERSONAL Born 08/08/1947, Bournemouth, England **DISCIPLINE** MODERN EUROPEAN HISTORY **EDUCATION** Univ London, BA Hons, 69; Univ Cambridge, cert educ, 70, PhD(hist), 75. **CAREER** Fel, Yale Univ, Yale Higher Educ Res Group, 75-76, res assoc, 76-78 and lectr hist, Yale Col, 76; vis asst prof, 78-79, Asst Prof Hist, Univ Fla, 79-, Vis fel, Silliman Col, Yale Univ, 76 and res affil, Yale Higher Educ Res Group, 78-80. **MEMBERSHIPS** AHA; Cambridge Hist Soc; Deut Ges fur Hochschulkunde; Soc Hist Soc; Western Asn Ger Studies. **RESEARCH** Modern Germany; history of European higher education. **SELECTED PUBLICATIONS** Auth, Der NSD-Studentenbund und der Geist der studentischen Korporationen, Deut Ges fur Hochschulkunde, Wuerzburg, 76; The structure of higher education in the German Democratic Republic, Higher Educ, Vol 7, 131-56; University government in Nazi Germany: Hamburg, Minerva, summer 78; The rise of the National Socialist Students Association and the failure of political education in the Third Reich, In: The Shaping of the Nazi State, London & NY, 78; Die Idee der politischen Universitaet, Hochschulreform nach der Machtergreifung, In: Erziehung und Schulung im Dritten Reich, Teil 2, Hochschule, Erwachsenenbildung, Stuttgart, 80; Die Verbaendepolitik des Nationalsozialistishcen Deutschen Studentenbundes, In: Darstellungen und Quellen zur Geschichte der deutschen Einheitsbewegung im neunzehnten und zwanzigsten Jahrhundert, Band XI, Heidelberg, 81. **CONTACT ADDRESS** Dept of Hist, Univ of Florida, P O Box 117320, Gainesville, FL 32611-7320.

GILFOYLE, TIMOTHY J.
DISCIPLINE HISTORY **EDUCATION** Columbia Univ, BA, 79, PhD, 87. **CAREER** Assoc prof; assoc ed, J Urban Hist; ed bd(s), The Encycl NY City, Yale Univ Press, 95, Mid-Am, & Stud in Sport and Leisure, Syracuse UP; John Simon Guggenheim Memorial Foun fel, 98-99; sr fel, Mus Am Hist & Smithsonian Inst, 97; NEH-Lloyd Lewis fel, Newberry Libr Chicago, 93-94. **HONORS AND AWARDS** Allan Nevins Prize, Soc Am Hist; Best Manuscript Prize, NY State Hist Asn. **MEMBERSHIPS** Bd dir(s), Chicago Metro Hist Edu Center. **RESEARCH** Late nineteenth-century Am city. **SELECTED PUBLICATIONS** Auth, City of Eros: New York City, Prostitution, and the Commercialization of Sex, 1790-1920, NY: W.W. Norton, 92; White Cities, Linguistic Turns, and Disneylands: New Paradigms in Urban History; articles in, Am Quart, Prospects, NY Hist, Miss Rev, & Chicago Hist. **CONTACT ADDRESS** Fine Arts Dept, Loyola Univ, Chicago, 6525 N. Sheridan Rd. 6525 North Sheridan Rd., Chicago, IL 6062660626. **EMAIL** tgilfoy@orion.it.luc.edu

GILJE, PAUL ARN
PERSONAL Born Brooklyn, NY, m, 1973, 1 child **DISCIPLINE** AMERICAN HISTORY **EDUCATION** Brooklyn Col, CUNY, BA, 74; Brown Univ, AM, 75; PhD, 80. **CAREER** Vis assoc prof, NYork Univ, Summer 85; from asst prof to Samuel Roberts Noble Found Presidential Prof, Univ of Okla, 80-. **HONORS AND AWARDS** Rockefeller Resident Fel, Johns Hopkins Univ, 87-88; fel, Ctr for the Hist of Freedom, Wash Univ, St. Louis, 91; Merrick Found Teaching Award, Univ of Okla, 93; Va Soc of Cincinnati Lectr, Wash and Lee Univ, 93; Kerr Hist Prize, NYork State Hist Soc, 97; Centennial Historian of the City of NYork, 99. **MEMBERSHIPS** Orgn Am Historians; Am Hist Soc; Soc Historians Early Repub; Inst Early Am Hist & Cult. **RESEARCH** Early America; social history; popular culture. **SELECTED PUBLICATIONS** Auth, The Road to Mobocracy: Popular Disorder in New York City, 1763 to 1834, Univ of NCar Press, 87; coed, New York in the Age of the Constitution, Fairleigh-Dickinson Univ Press, 92; coed, Keepers of the Revolution: Working Men and Women in New York During the Early Republic, Cornell Univ Press, 92; coed, American Artisans: Explorations in Social Identity, 1750-1850, Johns Hopkins Univ Press, 95; auth, Rioting in America, Ind Univ Press, 96; ed, Wages of Independence: Capitalism in the Early Republic, Madison House, 97. **CONTACT ADDRESS** Dept of Hist, Univ of Oklahoma, Norman, OK 73019. **EMAIL** pgilje@ou.edu

GILL, GERALD ROBERT
PERSONAL Born 11/18/1948, New Rochelle, NY, d **DISCIPLINE** HISTORY **EDUCATION** Lafayette Coll, AB 1966-70; Howard Univ, MA 1974, PhD 1985. **CAREER** City School Dist, New Rochelle NY, social studies teacher 1970-72; Inst for the Study of Educ Policy, research asst 1976-78, research fellow 1978-79; Tufts Univ, Department of History, Assoc Prof, 80-. **HONORS AND AWARDS** Massachusetts College Professor of the Year, 1995. **MEMBERSHIPS** Consult NAACP 1979; consult Ohio Hist Society 1980-85; Office of American Historians; American Hist Assn; Southern Hist Assn; Assn for the Study of Afro-American Life and History; Natl Assn for the Advancement of Colored People. **SELECTED PUBLICATIONS** Co-author: The Case for Affirmative Action for Blacks in Higher Ed 1978; author Meanness Mania 1980; author: The Rightward Drift in Amer in the State of Black America Natl Urban League 1981; co-editor: Eyes On the Prize Civil Rights Reader, 1991. **CONTACT ADDRESS** Dept of History, Tufts Univ, Medford, Medford, MS 02155.

GILL, GLENDA E.
PERSONAL Born 06/26/1939, Clarksville, TN **DISCIPLINE** THEATRE HISTORY **EDUCATION** Ala A & M Col, BS, 60; Univ Wis at Madison, MA, 64; Univ Iowa, PhD, 81. **CAREER** Tuskegee Univ, 82-83; assoc prof, Winston-Salem State Univ, 84-90; prof, Mich Technol Univ, 90-. **HONORS AND AWARDS** NEH Summer Fel, Univ Iowa, 74; Rockefeller Fel, 76 & 77; NEH Summer Fel, Yale Univ, 85; NEH Summer Fel, Univ NC Chapel Hill, 89; Summer Fel, Nat Portrait Gallery, The Smithsonian Inst, 90; NEH Summer Fel, Duke Univ, 91. **MEMBERSHIPS** MLA, Am Soc for Theatre Res, The Eugene O'Neill Soc. **RESEARCH** The African American in the performing arts--especially in non-traditional roles. **SELECTED PUBLICATIONS** Auth, No Surrender! No Retreat! African American Pioneer Performers of Twentieth-Century American Theater, St Martin's Press, 00. **CONTACT ADDRESS** Dept Humanities, Michigan Tech Univ, 1400 Townsend Dr, Houghton, MI 49931-1200.

GILL, J.
PERSONAL Born 05/19/1964, Spokane, WA, s **DISCIPLINE** HISTORY **EDUCATION** Whitworth Col, BA, 86; Univ Penn, MA, 88; PhD, 96. **CAREER** Asst Prof, Univ Findlay, 98-00; Asst Prof, Boise State Univ, 00-. **HONORS AND AWARDS** Fac Excellence Awd, 99. **MEMBERSHIPS** Org of Am Hist, Am Hist Asn. **RESEARCH** The 1960s; 20th Century American Religious History. **CONTACT ADDRESS** Dept History, Boise State Univ, 1910 Univ Dr, Boise, ID 83725. **EMAIL** jgill@boisestate.edu

GILLESPIE, ANGUS K.
PERSONAL Born 04/25/1942, Bryn Mawr, PA, m, 1986, 2 children **DISCIPLINE** AMERICAN STUDIES **EDUCATION** Yale Univ, BA, 64; Univ of Pa, PhD, 75. **CAREER** Asst prof, Rutgers- the State Univ of New Jersey, 75-81, assoc prof, 81-00. **HONORS AND AWARDS** Douglass Medal for Outstanding service to Douglass Col, Assoc Alumnae and Barbara A. Shailor, Dean of Douglass Col, May 98; New Jersey Folk Festival Lifetime Achievement Awd, May 99; Ernest E. McMahon Class of 1930 Awd, Rutgers Univ, May 99. **MEMBERSHIPS** Am Folklore Soc. **SELECTED PUBLICATIONS** Contribur (9 articles), American Folklore: An Encyclopedia, ed by Jan Harold Brunvand, NY: Garland Pub (96); auth, "Cranberries," in Rooted in American Soil, ed by Angus Gillespie and David Wilson, Knoxville: Univ of Tenn Press (99); co-ed with David Wilson, Rooted in American Soil: Plants in Symbol Story, Univ of Tenn Press (forthcoming); auth, Twin Towers: The Life of New York City's World Trade Center, Rutgers Univ Press,99. **CONTACT ADDRESS** Dept Am Studies, Rutgers, The State Univ of New Jersey, New Brunswick, 131 George St, New Brunswick, NJ 08901-1414. **EMAIL** angusgi@rci.rutgers.edu

GILLETTE, WILLIAM
PERSONAL Born 03/02/1933, Bridgeport, CT, m, 1971, 2 children **DISCIPLINE** HISTORY **EDUCATION** Georgetown Univ, BSFS, 55; Columbia Univ, MA, 56; Princeton Univ, PhD, 63. **CAREER** Instr, Ohio State Univ, 62-64; acting asst prof, Univ Conn, 65-66; asst prof, Brooklyn Col, CUNY, 66-67; assoc prof, Rutgers Univ, 67-81, prof, 81-. **HONORS AND AWARDS** Landry Prize, 79; Chastain Prize, 80; AASLH Merit award, 96; NJHC, Special Awd, 96; McCormick Prize, 97. **MEMBERSHIPS** Western Hist Asn, NJ Hist Soc, AAUP. **RESEARCH** Political history, U.S., Civil War and Reconstruction, U.S. western history. **SELECTED PUBLICATIONS** Auth, The Right to Vote: Poitics and the Passage of the Fifteenth Amendment, Baltimore: Johns Hopkins Univ Press (65, paperback, 69); auth, "Epilogue: The Black Voter and the White Historian: Another Look at Negro Suffrage, Republican Politics, and Reconstruction Historiography," in the paperback ed of The Right to Vote, (69): 166-190; auth, "Benjamin Curtis, John Campbell, Nathan Clifford, Noah Swayne, Samuel Miller," in Leon Friedman and Fred L. Israel, eds, The Justices of the United States Supreme Court, 1789-1969: Their Lives and Major Opinions, New York: R.R. Bowker, Vol II, (69): 893-1041; auth, "The Election of 1872," in Arthur M. Schlesinger, Jr, ed, History of American Presidential Elections, 1789-1968, New York: McGraw-Hill, Vol II (71): 1303-1330; auth, Retreat From Reconstruction, 1869-1879, Baton Rouge: La State Univ Press (79, paperback ed, 82); auth, Jersey Blue: Civil War Politics in New Jersey, 1854-1865, New Brunswick: Rutgers Univ Press (95, paperback ed, 99); auth, "New Jersey," in the Encyclopedia of the American Civil War, Denver: ABC-CLIO (forthcoming); auth, "Civil War," "Copperheads," "Charles S. Olden," "Joel Parker," in the Encyclopedia of New Jersey, New Brunswick: Rutgers Univ Press (forthcoming); auth, "Fifteenth Amendment," in The Oxford Companion to United States History, New York: Oxford Univ Press (forthcoming). **CONTACT ADDRESS** Dept Hist, Rutgers, The State Univ of New Jersey, New Brunswick, PO Box 5059, New Brunswick, NJ 08903-5059. **EMAIL** begillet@injersey.infi.net

GILLIARD, FRANK DANIEL
PERSONAL Born 02/13/1937, Jacksonville, FL **DISCIPLINE** ANCIENT HISTORY **EDUCATION** Univ Fla, BA, 57; Univ Calif, Berkeley, MA, 61, PhD(ancient hist), 66. **CAREER** From asst prof to assoc prof, 66-76, Prof Ancient Hist, Calif State Univ, Hayward, 76-, Chmn, Dept Hist, 80-83, Vis asst prof, Hunter Col, 68-69; Am Coun Learned Soc grant, 73. **MEMBERSHIPS** AHA. **RESEARCH** Late Roman Empire. **SELECTED PUBLICATIONS** Auth, Teleological development in the Athenaion Politeia, History, 71; The birth date of Julian the Apostate, Calif Studies Class Antiq, 71; Chaucer's attitute toward astrology, J Warburg Inst, 73; The apostolicity of gallic churches, Harvard Theol Rev, 75; auth, "The Senators of Sixth-Century Gaul," Speculum 54 (79): 685-97; auth, "Senatorial Bishops in the Fourth Century," Harvard Theological Review 77 (84): 153-75; auth, "The Problem of the Antisemitic Comma between 1 Thessalonians 2:14 and 15," New Testament Studies (89): 481-502; auth, "More Silent Reading in Antiquity: Non omne verbum sonabat," Journal of Biblical Literature 112 (93): 689-694; auth, "Paul and the Killing of the Prophets in 1 Thess. 2:15," Novum Testamentum 36, (94). **CONTACT ADDRESS** Dept of Hist, California State Univ, Hayward, 25800 Carlos Bee Bvd, Hayward, CA 94542-3001. **EMAIL** guillard@csuhayward.edu

GILLINGHAM, BRYAN R.
PERSONAL Born 04/12/1944, Vancouver, BC, Canada **DISCIPLINE** MUSIC, HISTORY **EDUCATION** Univ BC, BA, 66, BMus, 68; Toronto Conserv, ARCT, 69; King's Col (UK), MMus, 71; Univ Wash, PhD, 76. **CAREER** Instr, Herdman Col & Memorial Univ, 70-72; lectr, Mt Allison Univ, 72-73; lectr, Univ Alta, 75-76; guest lectr, Univ Ottawa, 77-79; asst prof, 76-80, assoc ch, 80-84, ch, 84-91, prof music, Carleton Univ, 86-; dir, inst mediaeval music, 85-. **HONORS AND AWARDS** Scholarly Achievement Awds, Carleton Univ, 84, 88; Res Achievement Awd, 91. **RESEARCH** Medieval, renaissance and baroque music, early opera, and various aspects of music theory and analysis. **SELECTED PUBLICATIONS** Auth, The Polyphonic Sequences in Codex Wolfenbuttel, 82; auth, Saint-Martial Mehrstimmigkeit, 84; auth, Medieval Polyphonic Sequences, 85; auth, Modal Rhythm, 86; auth, Medieval Latin Song: An Anthology, 93; auth, Indices to the Notre-Dame Fac-

similes, 94; auth, A Critical Study of Secular Medieval Latin Song, 95; co-ed, Beyond the Moon, 90. **CONTACT ADDRESS** School for Stud in Art and Cultural, Carleton Univ, 1125 Colonel By Dr, Ottawa, ON, Canada K1S 5B6. **EMAIL** bryan_gillingham@carleton.ca

GILLIS, JOHN R.
PERSONAL Born 01/13/1939, Plainfield, NJ, m, 1960, 2 children **DISCIPLINE** EUROPEAN HISTORY **EDUCATION** Amherst Col, BA, 60; Stanford Univ, PhD, 65. **CAREER** Instr, Stanford Univ, 64-65; asst prof, Princeton Univ, 66-71; assoc prof, 71-76, prof hist, Rurtgers Univ, 76, Vis fel hist, St Antony's Col, 69-70; vis prof, Princeton Univ, 82. **HONORS AND AWARDS** NEH Seminar fel, 79-80; Fellow Center for Advan Sutdy in Behavioral Sciences, 93-94. **MEMBERSHIPS** AHA; Am Asn Univ Prof. **RESEARCH** Europ soc hist, 1750-present; hist of family and marriage; Global hist. **SELECTED PUBLICATIONS** auth, The Prussian Bureaucracy in Crisis, Stanford Press, 71; Youth and History, Acad Press, 74; contribr, Crises of Political Development in Europe and the United States, Princeton, 78; For Better, For Worse: British Marriages, 1600-present, Oxford Press, 85; Commemovaticms: The Politics of National Identity, 94; A World of Their Own Making: Myth, Rotual, and the Quest for Family Values, Baric Books, 96. **CONTACT ADDRESS** Hist Dept, Rutgers, The State Univ of New Jersey, New Brunswick, PO Box 5059, New Brunswick, NJ 08903-5059. **EMAIL** gottgillis@cs.com

GILLMOR, CHARLES STEWART
PERSONAL Born 11/06/1938, Kansas City, MO, m, 1964, 2 children **DISCIPLINE** HISTORY OF SCIENCE **EDUCATION** Stanford Univ, BSEE, 62; Princeton Univ, MA, 66, Ph-D(hist of sci), 68. **CAREER** Ionospheric physicist GS-12, US Nat Bur Standards, 60-62; instr hist of sci, 67-68, asst prof, 68-72, assoc prof, 73-79, Prof Hist and Sci, Wesleyan Univ, 79-, Res grants, Am Coun Learned Soc, 71, Soc Sci Res Coun, 71-72 and NSF, 72-74; AAASNSF Chautauqua short course lectr, 73-74; NSF grants, 75-76 and 76-78; Fulbright-Hays Sr Res fel, Dept Physics, Cambridge Univ, England, 76; Visiting Scholar, National Aero & Space Admin (NASA) Washington DC, 80-81; NSF/CNRS Fellow, Planetary Physics, Paris, France 84-85; Hennebac Prof, Colorado School of Mines, 97; Visiting Prof, Electrical Engineering, Stanford Univ, 98-. **HONORS AND AWARDS** Fellow, American Physical Society. **MEMBERSHIPS** AAAS; Hist Sci Soc; Soc Hist Technol; Am Geophys Union; Am Phys Soc. **RESEARCH** History of physics and engineering, 18th century to present; quantitative measures of science growth; quantitative methods in historical research. **SELECTED PUBLICATIONS** Auth, "Covlants and The Evolution of Physics and Engineering in Eighteenth-Century France," Princeton U. Press, 71; ed, "The History of Geophysics," Vol. 1 84, Vol. 2 86, Vol. 4, 90, American Geophysical Union, Washingon, DC.; auth, "A History of Antarctic Science, Isis," Vol 0085, 94; coed, "Discovery of the Magnerosphere," The History of Geophysics, vol 7, 97, editors C. Stewart Gillmor and John R. Spreiter, American Geophysical Union, Washington DC.; **CONTACT ADDRESS** Dept of Hist, Wesleyan Univ, 238 Church St., Middletown, CT 06459-0002.

GILMORE, AL TONY
PERSONAL Born 06/29/1946, Spartanburg, SC, m **DISCIPLINE** HISTORY **EDUCATION** NC Central Univ, BA 1968, MA 1969; Univ of Toledo, PhD 1972. **CAREER** Howard Univ, prof of history; Univ of MD, prof of history; Natl Afro-Amer Museum Project, consultant director; ASALH, researcher; Natl Educ Assoc, sr policy analyst, currently. **MEMBERSHIPS** Bd dirs Assoc for the Study of Afro Amer Life & History 1977-88; consultant dir Natl Afro-American Museum Project Columbus OH 1979-82; mem Organization of Amer Historians, Amer Historical Assoc; Association for Study of African-American Life & History; pres, The Forum for the Study of Educ Excellence; board of directors, Quality Education for Minorities Project; National Council on Educating Black Children; consultant, California Commission on the Status of African-American Males. **SELECTED PUBLICATIONS** Author of several books "The Natl Impact of Jack Johnson" 1975, "Revisiting the Slave Community" 1979; book reviews and articles have appeared in Washington Post, New York Times, New Republic, American Scholar and others; lectured at over 40 colleges and univs including Harvard, Brown, UCLA, Morehouse and others; editor, African-American Males: The Struggle for Equality. **CONTACT ADDRESS** Sr Policy Analyst, National Education Association, 1201 16th St, NW, Washington, VT 20036.

GIMELLI, LOUIS B.
PERSONAL Born 10/08/1925, Oswego, NY, m, 1951, 2 children **DISCIPLINE** POLITICAL SCIENCE, HISTORY **EDUCATION** State Univ NYork Oswego, BS, 51; NYork Univ, MA, 54, PhD(hist), 64. **CAREER** Teacher elem and high schs, NY, 51-66; from assoc prof to prof hist, 66-76, Prof Hist and Philos, Eastern Mich Univ, 76-. **MEMBERSHIPS** AHA. **RESEARCH** Jacksonian era, especially New York state politics. **SELECTED PUBLICATIONS** Auth, Oswego, from Indian Pathway Through the French and Indian War, Oswego Hist Soc, 55. **CONTACT ADDRESS** Dept of Hist and Philos, Eastern Michigan Univ, Ypsilanti, MI 48197.

GIRARDOT, NORMAN J.
PERSONAL Born 04/19/1943, 2 children **DISCIPLINE** HISTORY OF RELIGIONS **EDUCATION** Col Holy Cross, BS, 65; Univ Chicago, MA, 72, PhD, 74. **CAREER** Ed asst, Hist Relig J, 68-70; asst prof Theol, Notre Dame Univ, 72-79; vis asst prof, Oberlin Col, 79-80; assoc prof & chmn, Relig Studies Dept, Lehigh Univ, 80-; prof, 89; Nat Endowment for Humanities fel, 83, 93-95; Chiang Ching-kuo fel, 93-95; Pacific Cult Found fel, 93-95; exec comt, Soc Study Chinese Relig, 75-78; Univ Distinguished Prof of Relig, 99; reader Univ Chicago Press, Univ Notre Dame Press, Scholars Press & Greenwood Press. **HONORS AND AWARDS** Phi Beta Kappa . **MEMBERSHIPS** Am Soc for the Study of Religion; Am Acad Relig; Asn Asian Scholars; Soc Study Chinese Relig; Amer Folk Art Society; International Assoc of the History of Religions; President, Society for the Study of Chinese Religions. **RESEARCH** Taoism; Chinese religion and myth; Western study of Asian religion; Visionary folkart; polular religion. **SELECTED PUBLICATIONS** Auth, The problem of creation mythology in the study of Chinese religion, Vol 15, 76 & co-ed, Current perspectives in the study of Chinese religions, Vol 17, 78, Hist Relig; auth, Returning to the Beginning and the arts of Mr Huntun in the Chuang Tzu, J Chinese Philos, Vol 5, 78; Chaotic order and benevolent disorder in the Chuang Tau, Philos East & West, Vol 28, 78; Taoism, In: Encycl of Bioethics, 78; co-ed, China and Christianity, Notre Dame Univ Press, 79; Imagination and Meaning: The Scholarly and Literary Worlds of Mircea Eliade, Seabury Press, 82; auth, Myth and Meaning in Early Taoism, Univ Calif Press, 82, rb, 89; trans, I Robinet's Tavist Meditation, SUNY, 93; auth, "Daoism and Ecology," Howard, 00; auth, "The Victorian Translation of China," California, 01. **CONTACT ADDRESS** Relig Studies Dept, Lehigh Univ, 9 W Packer Ave, #5, Bethlehem, PA 18015-3082. **EMAIL** njgo@lehigh.edu

GIRGIS, MONIR SAAD
PERSONAL Born 03/30/1923, Cairo, Egypt, w, 2 children **DISCIPLINE** AFRICAN STUDIES **EDUCATION** Clark Univ, PhD, 57. **CAREER** Prof, Edinboro Univ. **MEMBERSHIPS** AAG; EGS. **RESEARCH** Climate; political; Africa. **SELECTED PUBLICATIONS** Auth, Khamasin Winds and Wheat Production; auth, Land Reclamation in Egypt; auth, Mediterranean Africa. **CONTACT ADDRESS** Dept Geosciences, Edinboro Univ of Pennsylvania, 219 Meadville St, Edinboro, PA 16444-0001.

GISH, STEVEN D.
DISCIPLINE HISTORY **EDUCATION** Nwest Univ, BA, 85; Stan Univ, AM, 88; PhD, 94. **CAREER** Vis prof, J Mad Univ, 95-97; asst prof, Aub Univ, 97-. **MEMBERSHIPS** ASA; SAHS. **RESEARCH** Modern South Africa. **SELECTED PUBLICATIONS** Auth, Cultures of the World, Marshall Cavendish (NY), 96; auth, Alfred B Xuma: African, American, South African, NY Univ Press (NY), 00. **CONTACT ADDRESS** Dept History, Auburn Univ, PO Box 244023, Montgomery, AL 36124-4023. **EMAIL** sgish@mickey.aum.edu

GISOLFI, DIANA
PERSONAL Born 09/12/1940, New York, NY, d, 1963, 5 children **DISCIPLINE** ART HISTORY **EDUCATION** Radcliffe (Harvard), BA, Yale Grad Work; Univ Chicago, MA, PhD. **CAREER** Ch; prof. **HONORS AND AWARDS** Grants, Delmas Found, 96, Design, Candine Country; illusr, classic ground. **MEMBERSHIPS** Am Philosophical Soc, 89. **SELECTED PUBLICATIONS** Illus,Yale Univ Art Gallery Bulletin; Artibus et Historiae, Arte Veneta, Art Bulletin, Dictionary of Art, Renaissance Quart, Burlington Mag, encyclopedia of Italian renaissance and Mannerist Art; co-auth, The Rule, the Bible, and the Council: The Library of the Benedictine Abbey at Praglia, CAA Monograph series, 98. **CONTACT ADDRESS** Dept of Art Hist, Pratt Inst, 200 Willoughby Ave, Brooklyn, NY 11205. **EMAIL** dgisolfi@pratt.edu

GISPEN, KEES
DISCIPLINE GERMAN AND EUROPEAN HISTORY **EDUCATION** Univ CA, Berkeley, PhD, 81. **CAREER** Assoc prof, Univ MS, 83-; ed bd, Cent Europ Hist; exec secy and treas, Conf Gp for Cent Europ Hist, 97-. **RESEARCH** The changes in intellectual property rights of inventors, scientists and engineers in Germany between 1890 and 1960. **SELECTED PUBLICATIONS** Auth, New Profession, Old Order: Engineers and German Society, 1815-1914, Cambridge UP, 89. **CONTACT ADDRESS** Univ of Mississippi, Oxford, MS 38677. **EMAIL** hsgispen@olemiss.edu

GITTLEN, BARRY M.
PERSONAL Born Norfolk, VA **DISCIPLINE** NEAR EAST ARCHEOLOGY **EDUCATION** Wayne State Univ, PhB, 65; Univ Pa, PhD(Near East archeol), 77. **CAREER** Asst prof, 72-78, Assoc Prof Ancient Near East Studies, Baltimore Hebrew Col, 78-, Am Schs Orient Res fel archeol, 69-70; staff archaeologist, Ben Gurion Univ Excavation Tell esh-Shari'a, Israel, 74-75; field archaeologist joint exped to Cent Negev Highlands, 78-80 and Tell Miqne Exped, 82; vis prof, Towson State Univ. **MEMBERSHIPS** Am Orient Soc; Am Schs Orient Res; Archaeol Inst Am; Asn Jewish Studies; Israel Explor Soc. **RESEARCH** Trade in the Ancient Near East; Cypro-Palestinian relationships in the Bronze Age; the archaeology of Ancient Israel. **SELECTED PUBLICATIONS** Auth, Cypriote White Slip pottery in its Palestinian stratigraphic context, In: The Archaeology of Cyprus Recent Developments, Noyes, 75; The cultural and chronological implications of the Cypro-Palestinian trade during the Bronze Age, In: Basor 241, 81; Form and function in the new Late Bronze Age Temple at Lachish, In: Eretz Israel 16, 82; The massacre of the merchants near Akko, In: Iwry Feshschrift (in prep). **CONTACT ADDRESS** Baltimore Hebrew Univ, 5800 Park Heights Av, Baltimore, MD 21215-3932.

GIVENS, STUART R.
PERSONAL Born 04/01/1924, Honolulu, HI, m, 1947, 3 children **DISCIPLINE** MODERN HISTORY **EDUCATION** George Washington Univ, BA, 48; Stanford Univ, MA, 49, Ph-D(hist), 56. **CAREER** Coordr student activities & instr, 52-56, from asst prof to assoc prof, 56-65, chmn dept, 65-69, prof hist, Bowling Green State Univ, 65-, Univ Historian, 78-, Ed, Ohio Acad of Hist Newslett, 74-. **MEMBERSHIPS** AHA; Nat Educ Asn; Mid-West Brit Studies Asn; Asn Can Studies US; Can Hist Asn. **RESEARCH** Britain and the Commonwealth; Canada. **CONTACT ADDRESS** Dept of History, Bowling Green State Univ, 1001 E Wooster St, Bowling Green, OH 43403-0001.

GLAAB, CHARLES NELSON
PERSONAL Born 12/19/1927, Williston, ND, m, 1949, 2 children **DISCIPLINE** AMERICAN HISTORY **EDUCATION** Univ NDak, PhB, 51; MA, 52; Univ Mo, PhD, 58. **CAREER** Res assoc hist Kansas City proj, Univ Chicago, 56-58; asst prof hist, Kans State Univ, 58-60; from assoc prof to prof, Univ Wis-Milwaukee, 60-68, Prof Hist, Univ Toledo, 68-; ed, Urban Hist, Group Newsletter, 61-68; co-ed Northwest Ohio Quart, 95-. **HONORS AND AWARDS** Phi Beta Kappa; Am Asn State & Local Hist res grant, 61; Hist Kansas City Res Proj fel, 62. **MEMBERSHIPS** Orgn Am Historians; Am Hist Asn; Urban Hist Asn. **RESEARCH** Intellectual history; urban history; social history. **SELECTED PUBLICATIONS** Auth, Kansas City and the Railroads, State Hist Soc Wis, 62, 2nd ed, Univ Press of Kans, 93; auth, The American City: A Documentary History, Dorsey, 63; coauth, A History of Urban America, Macmillan, 67, 76, 83; auth, Factories in the Valley, State Hist Soc Wis, 69; Toledo: Gateway to the Great Lakes, Continental Heritage, 82. **CONTACT ADDRESS** Dept of Hist, Univ of Toledo, Toledo, OH 43606-3390. **EMAIL** cglaab@uoft02.utoledo.edu

GLAD, PAUL WILBUR
PERSONAL Born 08/15/1926, Salt Lake City, UT, m, 1948, 4 children **DISCIPLINE** HISTORY **EDUCATION** Purdue Univ, BS, 47; Ind Univ, MA, 49, PhD(hist), 57. **CAREER** Asst prof hist, Hastings Col, 50-55; assoc prof, Coe Col, 55-64 and Univ Md, 64-66; prof, Univ Wis-Madison, 66-77; Merrick Prof Hist, Univ Okla, 77-, Fulbright prof Am hist, Marburg, Ger, 61-62; Guggenheim Mem fel, 62-63; Am Philos Soc fel, 67; vis prof, Univ Okla, 71-72; fel, Nat Humanities Inst, Univ Chicago, 77-78. **MEMBERSHIPS** AHA; Orgn Am Historians. **RESEARCH** Recent American history; United States political and social history; Western history. **SELECTED PUBLICATIONS** Auth, Boileau, Gerald, J. and the Progressive-Farmer-Labor Alliance--Politics of the New-Deal, J Am Hist, Vol 0082, 95. **CONTACT ADDRESS** Dept of Hist, Univ of Oklahoma, W Lindsay, Rm 403A, Norman, OK 73019. **EMAIL** paul.w.glad-1@ou.edu

GLASCO, LAURENCE A.
PERSONAL Born 07/01/1940, Xenia, OH, m, 1969 **DISCIPLINE** AFRO-AMERICAN HISTORY **EDUCATION** Antioch Col, BA, 62; State Univ NYork Buffalo, MA, 65, PhD(hist), 73. **CAREER** Instr, 69-73, asst prof, 73-76, Assoc Prof Hist, Univ Pittsburgh, 76-. **MEMBERSHIPS** AHA; Orgn Am Historians; Asn Study of Afro-Am Life & Hist. **RESEARCH** Black middle class; ethnic mobility; family history. **SELECTED PUBLICATIONS** Auth, Computerizing the manuscript census, Hist Methods Newsletter, 69-70; Black & mulatto: Historical bases for Afro-American culture, Black Lines, 71; coauth, Occupation & ethnicity in five 19th century cities, Hist Methods Newsletter, 74; contribr, Ethnicity & occupation in the mid-19th century, In: Immigrants in Industrial America, Univ Va Press, 77; The life cycles & household structures of American ethnic groups, In: A Heritage of Her Own, Simon & Schuster Publs, 79; Migration & adjustment in the 19th century city, In: Family & Population in 19th Century America, Princeton Univ Press, 79; auth, Ethnicity & Social Structure: Irish, Germans and Native Born of Buffalo NY, 1850-1860, Arno Press, 80. **CONTACT ADDRESS** Hist Dept, Univ of Pittsburgh, 3p38 Forbes Quad, Pittsburgh, PA 15260-0001.

GLASRUD, BRUCE A.
DISCIPLINE HISTORY **EDUCATION** Luther Col, BA; Eastern NMex Univ, MA; Tex Tech Univ, PhD. **CAREER** Prof. **MEMBERSHIPS** Western Soc Sci Asn. **SELECTED PUBLICATIONS** Auth, African Americans in the West: A Bibliography of Secondary Sources, 98; William Henry Dean, Jr., 94; Martha Ostenso, Garland, 94. **CONTACT ADDRESS** Sul Ross State Univ, 1866 Southern Lane, Decatur, GA 30033-4097. **EMAIL** bglasrud@sulross.edu

GLASS, DOROTHY
DISCIPLINE ART HISTORY **EDUCATION** Johns Hopkins Univ, PhD. **CAREER** Fac, SUNY Buffalo. **HONORS AND AWARDS** Jane and Morgan Whitney Fellow, Metropolitan Museum of Art; Rome Prize, Am Acad Rome; Chancellor's Awd Excellence Tchg, SUNY Buffalo; exec comm, int ctr medieval art; coun, medieval acad am. **RESEARCH** Middle Ages; late Medieval Italy; the methodology of art hist. **SELECTED PUBLICATIONS** Auth, Crusade and Pilgrimage: Romanesque Portals in Western Tuscany, 97; Romanesque Sculpture in Campania: Patrons, Programs, and Style, Penn State P, 91; Italian Romanesque Sculpture: An Annotated Bibliography, GK Hall, 83. **CONTACT ADDRESS** Dept Art, SUNY, Buffalo, 202 Center for the Arts, Buffalo, NY 14260-6010.

GLASSBERG, DAVID
DISCIPLINE HISTORY **EDUCATION** Johns Hopkins Univ, PhD, 82. **CAREER** Assoc prof, Univ MA Amherst. **RESEARCH** Public hist; environmental hist. **SELECTED PUBLICATIONS** Auth, American Historical Pageantry: The Uses of Tradition in the Early Twentieth Century, 90. **CONTACT ADDRESS** Dept of Hist, Univ of Massachusetts, Amherst, Mass Ave, Amherst, MA 01003.

GLASSNER, MARTIN
PERSONAL Born 07/07/1932, Plainfield, NJ, m, 1955, 3 children **DISCIPLINE** POLITICAL SCIENCE, GEOGRAPHY **EDUCATION** Syracuse Univ, BA, 53; Cal State Univ, Fullerton, MA, 64; Claremont Grad Sch, PhD, 68. **CAREER** Lectr, Chapman Col, 64-65; asst prof, Cal State Poly Col, 65-67; asst prof, Univ Puget Sound, 67-68; asst prof, S Conn Univ, 68-95; prof, 93-95; prof emer, 95-. **HONORS AND AWARDS** Am Men Women Sci; Dict Intl Bio; Comm Leaders Noteworthy Am; Who's Who - Intl Auth Writers, Am Edu, World, East; Men of Achiev; Fac Schl Awd, 75; NGS, Res Gnt; CSU Res Gnts; Dist Alum Awd. **MEMBERSHIPS** AAG; MGSG; PGSG; Comm on Antarctica; CLAG; ILA; ISA; IGU; ASIL. **SELECTED PUBLICATIONS** Auth, NeptuneÛs Domain; A Political Geography Of The Sea, Unwin Hyman (London), 90; auth, Bibliography On Land-Locked States, Nijhoft (Dordrecht), 91; auth, Political Geography, John Wiley And Sons (NY), 92; auth, Bibliography On Land-Locked States, Nijhoft (Dordrecht), 95; auth, Political Geography, John Wiley And Sons (NY), 96; auth, "Bolivia's Orientation: Toward The Atlantic or the Pacific?" in Geopolitics of the Southern Cone and Antarctica, eds. Philip Kelly, Jack Child (Boulder And London: Rienner, 88), 154-169; auth, "Resolving The Problems Of Land-Lockedness," in Land-Locked States Of Africa And Asia, eds. Dick Hodder, et al (London: Frank Cass, 98), 197-208; auth, "Different Perspectives on the Law of the Sea," Political Geog Quart (91); auth, "The Frontiers of Earth -- and of Political Geography: The Sea, Antarctica and Outer Space," Polit Geog Quart (91); auth, "The Political Geography of the Sea," Canadian Geog (93); auth, "Recent Books on Marine Affairs," Ocean Devel Intl Law (93); auth, "Political Geography in the United Nations," Political Geog (94); auth, "The Tide Flows On," Ocean Yearbook 11 (94); auth, "New Books on Marine Affairs," Ocean and Coastal Manage (97); auth, "Navigating Difficult Waters," Ocean Yearbook 13 (98). **CONTACT ADDRESS** 742 Paradise Ave, Hamden, CT 06514.

GLATFELTER, RALPH EDWARD
PERSONAL Born 11/21/1939, Wenatchee, WA, m, 1966 **DISCIPLINE** HISTORY **EDUCATION** Whitman Col, BA, 63; Ind Univ, Bloomington, MA, 68, PhD(hist), 75. **CAREER** Exec dir alumni affairs, Whitman Col Alumni Asn, 63-65; instr, 70-75, asst prof, 75-79, Assoc Prof Hist, Ut State Univ, 79-; Dept Head, Hist dept, Ut State Univ, 85-95; Assoc Dean, Col of Humanities, Arts and Science, Ut State Univ, 95-. **MEMBERSHIPS** Am Asn Advan Slavic Studies; Asian Studies Asn; Western Soc Sci Asn. **RESEARCH** Nineteenth century Russian diplomatic history, Siberian history, History of Russian Emigres in China. **SELECTED PUBLICATIONS** Auth, The Portuguese in Shanghai, Macau, 99. **CONTACT ADDRESS** Col of Humanities, Arts and Soc Sci, Utah State Univ, 710 University Blvd, Logan, UT 84322-0700. **EMAIL** edwardg@hass.usu.edu

GLAZIER, IRA ALBERT
PERSONAL Born 08/12/1925, New York, NY, m, 1953, 1 child **DISCIPLINE** ECONOMIC HISTORY **EDUCATION** NYork Univ, BA, 48; Univ Chicago, MA, 51; Harvard Univ, PhD(hist & econ), 63. **CAREER** Instr econ hist, Ill Inst Technol, 50-51 and Ctr Int Affairs, Harvard Univ, 58-59; lectr hist, Northwestern Univ, 59-60; from instr to asst prof, Mass Inst Technol, 61-66; assoc prof, Boston Col, 66-67; Prof Econ Hist, Temple Univ, 69-, Old Dominion grant, 64; fac assoc, Columbia Univ, 70-; Fulbright-Hays res scholar, Bocconi Univ, Milan, 71; ed, Journal Europ Econ Hist, 72-; NATO Professorship, Univ Naples, NAtlantic Treaty Orgn, 78-79; Rockefeller grant, 80. **HONORS AND AWARDS** Widener Trust Awd, 81. **MEMBERSHIPS** AHA; Am Econ Asn; Royal Econ Soc; Econ Hist Soc; Econ Hist Asn. **RESEARCH** Foreign trade and industrialization; economic development of modern Europe; Soviet-Italian economic relations. **SELECTED PUBLICATIONS** Auth, The National-Integration of Italian Return Migration, 1870-1929, Am Hist Rev, Vol 0098, 93; Crossings--The Great Transatlantic Migrations, 1870-1914, Am Hist Rev, Vol 0099, 94. **CONTACT ADDRESS** Dept Hist, Temple Univ, 1115 W Berks St, Gladfelter Rm 913, Philadelphia, PA 19122-6006.

GLEASON, ABBOTT
DISCIPLINE HISTORY **EDUCATION** Harvard Col, BA, 61; Harvard Univ, PhD, 69. **CAREER** Teaching Fel, Harvard Univ, 64-68; Asst Prof to Prof, 68-93, Barnaby Conrad and Mary Critchfield Keeney Prof Hist, Brown Univ, 93-; Assoc, Russ Res Ctr, Harvard Univ, 68-79, 82-; Secy, Kennan Inst Advanced Russ Studies, Woodrow Wilson Int Ctr Schol, 80-82; Dir, Brown Univ, 99-00. **MEMBERSHIPS** Am Asn for the Advancement of Slavic Studies, World Slavic Congress. **SELECTED PUBLICATIONS** Auth, European and Muscovite: Ivan Kireevsky and the Origins of Slavophilism, 72; auth, Young Russian, 80; auth, Bolshevik Culture: Experiment and Order in the Russian Revolution, 85; auth, Shared Destiny: Fifty Years of Soviet-American Relations, 85; auth, Totalitarianism: The Inner History of the Cold War, 95; auth, Nikita Khrushchev: Fresh Perspectives on the Last Commnist, forthcoming, 00. **CONTACT ADDRESS** Brown Univ, 30 John St, Providence, RI 02906.

GLEASON, ELISABETH GREGORICH
PERSONAL Born 07/08/1933, Belgrade, Yugoslavia, m, 1954 **DISCIPLINE** EARLY MODERN HISTORY **EDUCATION** Univ Ill, Urbana, BA, 54; Ohio State Univ, MA, 56; Univ Calif, Berkeley, PhD(hist), 63. **CAREER** Instr hist, Univ Calif, Berkeley, 62-63; from asst prof to assoc prof, San Francisco State Col, 63-69; chmn dept, 75-80, Prof Hist, Univ San Francisco, 69-, Soc Relig Higher Educ fel, 66-67; vis prof, Stanford, 76 and Univ Calif, Berkeley, 79; Nat Endowment for Humanities fel, 80; Gladys K Delmas Found fel, 80. **MEMBERSHIPS** AHA; Am Soc Reformation Res; Renaissance Soc Am; Am Soc Church Hist; Soc for Ital Hist Study. **RESEARCH** Reformation history; 16th century Italian history; Venice. **SELECTED PUBLICATIONS** Auth, Sixteenth Century Italian Interpretations of Luther, Arch Reformation Hist, 69; On the nature of sixteenth century Italian evangelism: Scholarship, 1953-1978, Sixteenth Century J, IX: 3-25; ed & transl, Reform and reformation in sixteenth century Italy, In: American Academy of Religion Texts and Translations, Vol 4, Scholars Press, 81. **CONTACT ADDRESS** Dept of Hist, Univ of San Francisco, San Francisco, CA 94132.

GLEISSNER, STEPHEN
PERSONAL Born 06/27/1962, Wichita, KS, s **DISCIPLINE** ART HISTORY **EDUCATION** Northwestern Univ, PhD, 95. **CAREER** Independent art appraiser and historian **MEMBERSHIPS** Coll Art Assoc; Soc of Architectural Historians, Appraisers Assoc of Amer **RESEARCH** British 17th century art; arts and crafts architecture; decorative arts **SELECTED PUBLICATIONS** Auth, Journal of the History of Collections, Reassembling a Royal Art Collection for the Restored King of Great Britain, 94; Auth, Kings and Connoisseurs: Collecting Art in Seventeenth Century Europe, Review of Jonathan Brown, 97; Auth, Literature and History, Paper Bullets: Print and Kingship Under Charles II, Summer 97; **CONTACT ADDRESS** 115 S. Rutan, Wichita, KS 67218.

GLEN, ROBERT ALLAN
PERSONAL Born 11/05/1946, Sioux Falls, SD **DISCIPLINE** BRITISH AND EUROPEAN HISTORY **EDUCATION** Univ Wash, BA, 68; Univ Calif, Berkeley, MA, 69, PhD, 78. **CAREER** Instr hist, Univ Wis, Parkside, 75-77 & Univ Vt, 77-78; asst prof, 79-82, assoc prof 82-87, prof Hist, Univ New Haven, 87-; chair, Hist, Univ New Haven 83-87; 94-96; **MEMBERSHIPS** AHA; Hist Asn London; Econ Hist Soc; Social Hist Soc. **RESEARCH** British labor during the industrial revolution; history of English and Caribbean methodism; British urban history. **SELECTED PUBLICATIONS** Auth, The Milnes of Stockport and the export of English technology, Cheshire Hist, 79; The Manchester grammar school in the early nineteenth century, Trans Lancashire & Cheshire Antiquarian Soc, 79; Benjamin Franklin and a case of machine smuggling in the 1780's, Bus Hist, 81; auth, Urban Workers in the Early Industrial Revolution, 84; auth, Man or Beast? English Methodists as Animals in the 18th Centure Satiric Prints, Conneticut Review, 93; auth, Anatomy of a Religious Revival: The Stockport Methodists in the 1790s, Manchester Region Hist Review, 96; auth 'Audieu the delights of the stage': an anti-methodist song of 1746, notes and Queries, 99. **CONTACT ADDRESS** Dept of History, Univ of New Haven, 300 Orange Ave, West Haven, CT 06516-1999. **EMAIL** bobglen@charger.newhaven.edu

GLEN, THOMAS L.
DISCIPLINE ART HISTORY **EDUCATION** Princeton Univ, MA, PhD. **CAREER** Assoc prof, McGill, 75; ch, 85-92. **RESEARCH** 17th cent painting and sculpture; Rubens; van Dyck; Poussin; Velazquez. **CONTACT ADDRESS** Dept of Art History, McGill Univ, 853 Sherbrooke St W, Montreal, QC, Canada H3A 2T5. **EMAIL** tlglen@leacock.lan.mcgill.ca

GLENN, GEORGE D.
DISCIPLINE THEATRE HISTORY **EDUCATION** Univ IL, PhD. **CAREER** Prof, ch, grad prog, dept Theater, dir, Iowa Regents London prog, Univ Northern IA, 91/92. **MEMBERSHIPS** Pres, Mid-Am Theatre Conf. **SELECTED PUBLICATIONS** Publ in a variety of areas from nautical drama to the use of firearms on stage. **CONTACT ADDRESS** Dept of Theatre, Univ of No Iowa, Cedar Falls, IA 50614.

GLICK, THOMAS F.
PERSONAL Born 01/28/1939, Cleveland, OH, m, 1963, 2 children **DISCIPLINE** MEDIEVAL HISTORY **EDUCATION** Harvard Univ, BA, 60, PhD, 68; Columbia Univ, MA, 63. **CAREER** From asst prof to assoc prof hist, Univ Tex, Austin, 68-72; assoc prof, 72-79, prof hist, Boston Univ, 79-, Dir, Inst Medieval Hist, 98-. **HONORS AND AWARDS** Guggenheim Fel, 87-88; NSF Fel, 89-90; NEH Fel, 93-94; Sr Fel, Dibner Inst, 00-01. **MEMBERSHIPS** Hist Sci Soc; Soc Hist Technol. **RESEARCH** Medieval science and technology in Spain and the Islamic world. **SELECTED PUBLICATIONS** Auth, Islamic and Christian Spain in the Early Middle Ages, Princeton Univ Press, 79; From Muslim Fortress to Christian Castle, Manchester Univ Press, 95. **CONTACT ADDRESS** Dept of Hist, Boston Univ, 226 Bay State Rd, Boston, MA 02215-1403. **EMAIL** tglick@bu.edu

GLOSECKI, STEPHEN O.
PERSONAL Born 03/12/1952, Springfield, IL, m, 1981, 2 children **DISCIPLINE** ANGLO-SAXON ART AND CULTURE **EDUCATION** Univ of CA, PhD, 80. **CAREER** Dept Eng, Univ Ala **HONORS AND AWARDS** Fulbright Prof, 91-92. **RESEARCH** Anthropology, Literature, Folklore. **SELECTED PUBLICATIONS** Auth, Shamanism and Old English Poetry, Garland Press; Movable Beasts: The Manifold Implications of Early Germanic Animal Imagery, Garland Press; auth, "Greudel", BPR 21, Beowulf, 99; auth, "Beowulf and the Wills: Traces of Totemism?" PQ, 00; auth, "Skalded Epic: Make It Old" PN Review, 133 (00); auth, Encyclopedia of Medieval Folklore, ABC-CLIO, 00. **CONTACT ADDRESS** Univ of Alabama, Birmingham, 1400 University Blvd, Birmingham, AL 35294-1260.

GLUCK, CAROL
DISCIPLINE MODERN JAPANESE INTELLECTUAL HISTORY **EDUCATION** Wellesley Col, BA, 62; Columbia Univ, PhD, 77. **CAREER** George Sansom prof. **SELECTED PUBLICATIONS** Auth, Japan's Modern Myths: Ideology in the Late Meiji Period, 85; Showa: the Japan of Hirohito, 92; Asia in Western and World History, 97; auth, Past Obsessions: War and Memory in the Twentieth Century, forthcoming, 01. **CONTACT ADDRESS** Dept of Hist, East Asian Inst, 420 W 118th St, Rm 912, Mailcode 3333, New York, NY 10027. **EMAIL** cg9@columbia.edu

GLUECKERT, LEOPOLD
DISCIPLINE HISTORY **EDUCATION** Mt Carmel Col, BA, 65; Pontifical Gregorian Univ, BTh, 69; DePaul Univ, MS, 76; Loyola Univ, PhD, 89. **CAREER** Hist, Loyola Univ; prof, Lewis Univ. **RESEARCH** Modern European history. **SELECTED PUBLICATIONS** Auth, Between Two Amnesties: Former Polit Prisoners and Exiles in the Roman Revolution of 1848; Papal States: Before 1849, in Encycl of 1848 Revolution; Papal States: Exiles and Polit Prisoners, in Encycl of 1848 Revolution; Origins of Carmel in Kansas, Sword, 90; The World of Therese: France, Church and State in the Late 19th century, in Carmelite Stud, 90; rev, Saveno Fabriani, Catholic Hist Rev, 95. **CONTACT ADDRESS** Hist Dept, Lewis Univ, Romeoville, IL 60446-2200. **EMAIL** twitmeistr@aol.com

GNUSE, ROBERT
PERSONAL Born 12/04/1947, Quincy, IL, m, 1982, 3 children **DISCIPLINE** OLD TESTAMENT, HISTORY OF CHRISTIAN THOUGHT **EDUCATION** Concordia Sem Exile, MDiv, 74, STM, 75; Univ Chicago, STM, 75; Vanderbilt, MA, 78, PhD(Old Testament), 80. **CAREER** Asst prof Old Testament, Univ Va, 78-79; asst prof relig, NC Wesleyan Col, 79-80; ASST PROF OLD TESTAMENT, Assp prof Old Testament, Univ VA, 78-79; Asst Prof relig, NC, Wesleyan Col, 79-80; Asst Prof Old Testament, LOYOLA UNIV, 80-86; Asso Prof 86-90; Full Prof, 90-. **MEMBERSHIPS** Soc Bibl Lit; Cath Bibl Asn; Col Theol Soc; Am Schs Orient Res. **RESEARCH** World religions. **SELECTED PUBLICATIONS** Auth, You Shall Not Steal, Maryknoll, 85; auth, Authority of the Bible, Ramsy, NJ, 85; auth, Heilsgeschichte as Model for Biblical Theology, Lanhom, 89; auth, The Temple Experience of Jaddus in the 'Antiquities' of Josephus--A Report of Jewish Dream-Incubation, Jewish Quart Rev, Vol 0083, 93; Dreams in the Night--Scholarly Mirage or Theophanic Formula--The Dream-Report as a Motif of the So-Called Elohist Tradition, Biblische Zeitschrift, Vol 0039, 95, auth, Dreams and Deam Reports in the Writings of Josephus, Leidgw, 97; auth, Emergent Monotheism in Israel, Sheffield, Eng, 98. **CONTACT ADDRESS** Loyola Univ, New Orleans, 6363 St Charles Ave, New Orleans, LA 70118. **EMAIL** rkgnuse@loyno.edu

GOBEL, DAVID W.
PERSONAL Born 06/11/1958, Sierra Madre, CA, m, 1988, 2 children **DISCIPLINE** HISTORY OF ARCHITECTURE **EDUCATION** Princeton Univ, PhD 91; Univ VI, M arch, 88; Princeton Univ, MA 86; Texas Tech Univ, BArch 81. **CAREER** Savannah Col of Art and Design, prof 96-; Univ Oregon, adj asst prof 94-96; Portland State Univ, adj asst prof 93-94; Clackamas Comm Col, inst 93; Portland Comm Col, inst 92-93; Maryhurst Col, inst 91-93; Pacific NW Col, inst 92; Oregon Sch Arch, asst prof 90-91; Princeton Univ, asst inst, res asst, 86-88. **HONORS AND AWARDS** William G. Bowen Fel; Fulbright-Hays Fel; Stanley J. Seeger Fel; Princeton Univ Fels; Omicron Delta Kappa; Tau Sigma Delta. **MEMBERSHIPS** SAH; CAA; SSAH; ASHAHS. **RESEARCH** Renaissance and baroque arch and urbanism; hist of arch and theory. **SELECTED PUBLICATIONS** Auth, The Demise of the City Gate, The U of Penn Archi Jour, 98; Rev of Catherine Wilkinson-Zerner, Juan de Herrera: Architect to Philip of Spain, in: Jour of the Soc of Archi Historians, 95; Assoc ed, The Princeton Journal: Thematic Studies in Architecture, Princeton Arch Press, 89; Gates of Glory, Coll of Charles, 97; The Plan of St. Gall and the Representation of Architecture, Portland St U, 94. **CONTACT ADDRESS** Dept of Architectural History, Savannah Col of Art and Design, PO Box 3146, Savannah, GA 31402-3146. **EMAIL** dgobel@scad.edu

GOCKING, ROGER
PERSONAL Born 10/09/1943, Trinidad, s **DISCIPLINE** HISTORY **EDUCATION** Fairfield Univ, BA, 68; Stanford Univ, MA, 72; PhD, 81. **CAREER** Asst Prof, Mercy Col, 85-91; Fulbright Prof, Nat Univ of Lesotho, 91-92; Assoc Prof, Mercy Col, 92-. **HONORS AND AWARDS** Res grant, Stanford Univ, 73; Fulbright Teaching Awd, Univ Lesotho, 91; Teaching Excellence Awd, Mercy Col, 98. **MEMBERSHIPS** Am Alpine Club, NY African Studies Asn, African Studies Asn. **SELECTED PUBLICATIONS** Auth, Facing Two Ways: Ghana's Coastal Communities Under Colonial Rule, Univ Press of Am, 99; auth, "A Chieftaincy dispute and ritual Murder in Elmina, Ghana 1945-46", Journal of African History, forthcoming; auth, "The Tribunal System in Ghana's fourth Republic: An Experiment in Judicial Reintegration," African Affairs 99,)00): 47-71; auth, "colonial Rule and the 'Legal Factor' in Ghana and Lesotho," Africa, (97): 61-85; auth, "Ghana's Public Tribunals: An Experiment in Revolutionary Justice," African Affairs, (96): 197-223; auth, "Indirect Rule in the gold Coast: Competition for Office and the Invention of Tradition," Canadian Journal of African Studies, (94): 421-446; auth, "Afrocentricity: Implications for South Africa?," Africa Insight, (93): 42-46; auth, "British Justice and the Native Tribunals of the Southern Gold coast Colony," The Journal of African History, (93): 93-113; auth, "Listening to and Interpreting Africa for the New Millennium: The forty-Second annual Meeting of the African Studies Association," NY African Studies Asn Newsletter, (00): 4-6; auth, "Ghana: Casely Hayford, J.E. (1866-1930), Lawyer and Journalist," encyclopedia of African History, forthcoming; auth, "Ghana Colonial administration: Indirect Rule and 'Native Authority'." forthcoming. **CONTACT ADDRESS** Dept cultural Studies, Mercy Col, 555 Broadway, Dobbs Ferry, NY 10522-1134. **EMAIL** gocking@attglobal.net

GODBEER, R.
DISCIPLINE HISTORY **EDUCATION** Oxford Univ, BA, 84; Brandeis Univ, PhD, 89 **CAREER** Instr hist, U.C. Riverside, 89- **RESEARCH** Early America - cultural and religious; gender and sexuality **CONTACT ADDRESS** Univ of California, Riverside, Riverside, CA 92521.

GODBOLD, E. STANLY
PERSONAL Born 03/15/1942, SC, m, 1 child **DISCIPLINE** HISTORY **EDUCATION** Duke Univ, BA, 63; Southern Methodist Univ, BD, 66; Duke Univ, MA, 68, PhD, 70. **CAREER** Asst prof, hist, Univ Tenn, 69-70; assoc prof, Valdosta State Univ, 70-77; Prof Hist, Miss State Univ, 77-. **HONORS AND AWARDS** Thomas Wolfe Literary Awd, 91; MSU Alumni Awd, Graduate Teaching, 94; Hum Fac Awd, 95. **MEMBERSHIPS** South Hist Asn. **RESEARCH** South History **SELECTED PUBLICATIONS** Auth, Ellen Glasgow and the Woman Within, LSU Press, 72; auth, Christopher Gadsden and the American Revolution, Univ Tenn Press, 82; auth, Confederate Colonel and the Cherokee Chief: The Life of William Holland Thomas, Univ Tenn Press, 91. **CONTACT ADDRESS** Mississippi State Univ, PO Drawer H, Mississippi State, MS 39762. **EMAIL** esg@ra.msstate.edu

GODFREY, WILLIAM GERALD
PERSONAL Born 06/10/1941, Stratford, ON, Canada, m, 1967, 3 children **DISCIPLINE** NORTH AMERICAN AND CANADIAN HISTORY **EDUCATION** Univ Waterloo, BA, 63, MA, 66; Queen's Univ, PhD(hist), 74. **CAREER** Lectr hist, Notre Dame Univ Nelson, 65-67, asst prof, 67-68; asst prof, 70-77, Assoc Prof Hist, Mt Allison Univ, 77-, Head Dept, 80-, Dean men, Notre Dame Univ Nelson, 66-67. **MEMBERSHIPS** AHA; Can Hist Asn. **RESEARCH** Comparative colonial societies; 18th century trans-Atlantic world. **SELECTED PUBLICATIONS** Auth, Pursuit of Profit and Preferment in Colonial North America: John Bradstreet's Quest, Wilfrid Univ Pr (Waterloo, ON), 82. **CONTACT ADDRESS** Hist Dept, Mount Allison Univ, Sackville, NB, Canada E0A 3C0. **EMAIL** wgodfrey@mta.ca

GOEDICKE, HANS
PERSONAL Born 08/07/1926, Vienna, Austria **DISCIPLINE** EGYPTOLOGY **EDUCATION** Univ Vienna, PhD, 49. **CAREER** Res Assoc Egyptol, Brown Univ, 52-56; lectr, 60-62, from asst prof to assoc prof, 62-68, prof, 68-79, Chmn Near Eastern Studies, Johns Hopkins Univ, 79-, Howard fel, 56-57; tech asst, Unesco-Centre doc l'ancienne Egypte, Cairo, 57-58; asst, Univ Gottingen, 58-60; Am Philos Soc grant, 66; John Simon Guggenheim Mem fel, 66-67; mem, Am Res Ctr Egypt; dir archaeol exped, Giza, Egypt, 72 and 74 and Tell el Rataba, 77, 78 and 81; corresp mem, Ger Archaeol Inst, 74. **MEMBERSHIPS** Egypt Explor Soc, London. **RESEARCH** Egyptian historical and administrative inscriptions. **SELECTED PUBLICATIONS** **CONTACT ADDRESS** Dept of Near Eastern Studies, Johns Hopkins Univ, Baltimore, 3400 N Charles St, Baltimore, MD 21218.

GOETZMANN, WILLIAM HARRY
PERSONAL Born 07/20/1930, Washington, DC, m, 1953, 3 children **DISCIPLINE** AMERICAN STUDIES **EDUCATION** Yale Univ, BA, 52, PhD(Am studies), 57. **CAREER** Asst instr hist, Yale Univ, 55-57, from instr to assoc prof hist and Am studies, 57-64; from assoc prof to prof, 64-67, dir, Am studies prog, 65-81, Stiles Prof Am Studies, Univ Tex, 67-, Am Philos Soc grants, 59-60 and 63-64; Susan B Morse fel, 59-60; Soc Sci Res Coun fel, 62-63; Fulbright vis sr lectr, Cambridge Univ, 67-68; chief hist consult, US Nat Atlas Proj, 62-; Guggenheim fel award, 77-78; fel, Ctr Advan Studies in Behav Sci, 80-81. **HONORS AND AWARDS** Pulitzer Prize, 67; Francis Parkman Prize, Orgn Am Historians, 67; Golden Plate Awd, Am Acad Achievement, 68; lld, st edwards univ, 67. **MEMBERSHIPS** Am Studies Asn (pres, 75-76); Western Hist Asn; Soc Am Historians. **RESEARCH** American cultural history; history of the American West; history of science in America. **SELECTED PUBLICATIONS** Auth, Army Exploration in the American West, Yale Univ, 59; The mountain man as Jacksonian man, Am Quart, fall 63; When the Eagle Screamed, Wiley, 66; Exploration and Empire, 66 & The American Hegelians: An Intellectual Episode in the History of Western America, 73, Knopf; Time's American adventures: American historians and their writing since 1776, In: Social Science in America: The First Two Hundred Years, 76; The Mountain Man, Buffalo Hist Ctr, 78; coauth (with J Porter), West as Romantic Horizon, 81. **CONTACT ADDRESS** Am Studies Prog, Univ of Texas, Austin, 0 Univ of Texas, Austin, TX 78712-1026.

GOFF, JOHN S.
PERSONAL Born 06/20/1931, Los Angeles, CA, m, 1967, 2 children **DISCIPLINE** UNITED STATES HISTORY **EDUCATION** Univ Southern Calif, AB, 53, AM, 55, PhD(hist), 60; Ariz State Univ, JD, 74. **CAREER** Teaching asst Am civilization, Univ Southern Calif, 55-57; instr hist and polit sci, WTex State Univ, 57-60; chmn educ, philos and soc sci, 62-69, Insrt Hist and Polit Sci, Phoenix Col, 60-, Consult and examr, NCent Accrediting Asn, 70-; consult, Nat Endowment for Humanities, 73- **RESEARCH** Constitutional and legal history; Arizona history. **SELECTED PUBLICATIONS** Auth, Arizona Civilization, Hooper, 68; Robert Todd Lincoln, Univ Okla, 69; coauth, Arizona, Past and Present, Black Mountain, 70; auth, George W P Hunt and His Arizona, Socio-Tech Publ, 73; Arizona Territorial Officials, Vol 1, 75 & Vol 2, 78, Black Mountain. **CONTACT ADDRESS** Phoenix Col, 1202 W Thomas, Phoenix, AZ 85013.

GOFF, RICHARD D.
DISCIPLINE HISTORY **EDUCATION** Duke Univ, PhD. **CAREER** Prof and undergrad adv, Eastern Michigan Univ. **RESEARCH** US early national period, US old south. **SELECTED PUBLICATIONS** Coauth, The Twentieth Century, A Brief Global history; World History. **CONTACT ADDRESS** Dept of History and Philosophy, Eastern Michigan Univ, 701 Pray-Harrold, Ypsilanti, MI 48197.

GOFFART, WALTER A.
PERSONAL Born 02/22/1934, Berlin, Germany **DISCIPLINE** MEDIEVAL HISTORY **EDUCATION** Harvard Univ, AB, 55, AM, 56, PhD, 61. **CAREER** Lectr to assoc prof, 60-71, PROF MEDIEVAL HISTORY, UNIV TORONTO, 71-; vis asst prof, Univ Calif Berkeley, 65-66; vis fel, Inst Advan Stud, Princeton, 67-68; vis fel, Dumbarton Oaks Ctr Byzantine Stud, 73-74. **HONORS AND AWARDS** Connaught sr fel, 83; Can Coun leave fel, 67-68; Coun Learned Soc fel, 73-74; Guggenheim fel, 79-80; SSHRCC leave fel, 85-86, res grant, 90-92; Haskins Medal, Medieval Acad Am, 91; fel, Royal Soc Can, 96. **MEMBERSHIPS** Int Soc Anglo-Saxonists; Hagiography Soc; Can Soc Medievalists; Medieval Acad Am; Royal Hist Soc. **RESEARCH** Late Roman and early medieval history. **SELECTED PUBLICATIONS** Auth, Le Mans Forgeries, 66; auth, Caput and Colonate, 74; auth, Barbarians and Romans A.D. 418-584, 80; auth, The Narrators of Barbarian History (A.D. 550-800), 88; auth, Rome's Fall and After, 89; co-transl, The Origin of the Idea of Crusade, 78; ed bd, Speculum. **CONTACT ADDRESS** Dept History, Univ of Toronto, Toronto, ON, Canada M5S 1A1.

GOFFEN, RONA
DISCIPLINE ART HISTORY **EDUCATION** Columbia Univ, PhD. **CAREER** Prof, Rutgers Univ; Board of Governors Prof. **HONORS AND AWARDS** Fel, Am Council of Learned Soc, Itatti (Havard University Center for Italian Renaissance Studies), Guggenleim Foundation, National Humanities Center, Visitor, Institute for Advanced Study; asso ed, renaissance quart. **RESEARCH** Italian Medieval and Renaissance Art; contextual hist of Italian painting and sculpture from ca. 1250-1600, emphasizing Florence, Venice, and Rome; the definition of gender in rel to soc realities; "new critical" methologies regarding (self-) imagery and narrative. **SELECTED PUBLICATIONS** Auth, Piety and Patronage in Renaissance Venice: Bellini, Titian, and the Franciscans, New Haven and London, 86, paperback ed New Haven and London, 90, Ital ed, Venice, 91; Auth,Spirituality in Conflict: Saint Francis and Giotto's Bardi Chapel, Univ Park and London, 89; Giovanni Bellini, New Haven and London, 89, Ital ed, Milan, 90, second printing, 94; Auth, Titian's Women; New Haven and London, 97; Auth,Titian's Venus of Urbino; NY and Cambridge, 97, second printing, 00; Auth, Giovanni Bellini: Il Colore Ritrovato, 00. **CONTACT ADDRESS** Dept of Art Hist, Rutgers, The State Univ of New Jersey, Rutgers Col, Hamilton St., New Brunswick, NJ 08903. **EMAIL** rgoffen@compuserve.edu

GOHEEN, R. B.
DISCIPLINE HISTORY **EDUCATION** Univ Toronto, BA, 61;, Yale Univ, MA, 62, PhD, 67. **CAREER** Assoc prof. **RESEARCH** The relevance of social philosophic conceptions of consciousness, responsibility and power to historical analyses of political practice. **SELECTED PUBLICATIONS** Auth, "Peasant Politics? Village Community and the Crown in Fifteenth Century England," Amer Hist Rev 96, 91. **CONTACT ADDRESS** Dept of Hist, Carleton Univ, 1125 Colonel By Dr, 400 Paterson Hall, Ottawa, ON, Canada K1S 5B6.

GOINS, RICHARD ANTHONY
PERSONAL Born 03/01/1950, New Orleans, LA, m, 1990 **DISCIPLINE** HISTORY **EDUCATION** Yale Univ, BA (cum laude), History, 1972; Stanford Univ & Law School, JD, 1975. **CAREER** New Orleans Legal Assist Corp, mgr & staff attorney, 75-77; deputy dir, 77-78; exec dir, 78-81; Hon Adrian G Duplantier, law clerk, 82; Loyola Univ School of Law, asst prof, 81-84; Adams & Reese, asst attorney, 84-87; attorney, partner, 87-. **HONORS AND AWARDS** Stanford Univ, School of Law, Reginald Heber Smith Fellowship, 1975. **MEMBERSHIPS** Thomas More Inn of Court, barrister, 1988-; Loyola Univ Law School, adjunct prof, 1984-; Fed bar Assn, bd of dirs local chapter, 1992-; Merit Selection Panel for the Selection & Appointment of US Magistrate, 1992-96; Amer Bar Assn Conference of Minority Partners in Majority/Corporate Law Firm, 1990-; California State Bar, 1977-; Louisiana State Bar Assn, 1975-. **SELECTED PUBLICATIONS** Leadership Louisiana 1992 Participant; Practical Issues in Class Action Litigation, The Practical Litigator, Vol 6,# 1, Jan 1995, Author; Seminar Presenter, LA Public Retirement Seminar, Baton Rouge, LA 1989, 1990, topic: "Fiduciary Responsibilities of Trustees of Pension Plans;" Seminar Presenter, Recent Dev Seminar, Tulane Univ, New Orleans, LA, 1994, topic: "Recent Dev in Labor & Employment Law." **CONTACT ADDRESS** Adams & Reese, 4500 One Shell Sq, New Orleans, LA 70139.

GOIST, PARK DIXON
PERSONAL Born 09/07/1936, Seattle, WA, m, 1987, 1 child **DISCIPLINE** AMERICAN STUDIES, THEATRE **EDUCATION** Univ WA, BA, 58; Univ Rochester, PhD, 67. **CAREER** Instr hist, Colgate Univ, 63 & Kent State Univ, 63-64; from instr to asst prof, 66-71, assoc prof Am studies, Case Western Reserve Univ, 71, Nat Am Studies Fac, 77. **MEMBERSHIPS** Am Studies Asn; Gt Lakes Am Studies Asn. **RESEARCH** Am intellectual hist; Am urban and community studies; Am drama. **SELECTED PUBLICATIONS** Co-ed, The Urban Vision: Selected Interpretations of the Modern American Dity, Dorsey, 70; auth, City and community: the urban theory of Robert Park, Am Quart, spring 71; Seeing things whole: a consideration of Lewis Mumford, 11/72 & Patrick Geddes and the city, 1/74, J Am Inst Planners: Town, City and Community, 1890-1920's, Am Studies, spring 73; Community and self in the Midwest town: Dell's Moon-Calf, Mid America II, 75; From Main Street to State Street: Town, City and Community in America, Kennikat, 77; Oregon Trail Diary, Reserve, 4/81; auth, A Small Squall, Cleveland Play House, 94; auth, Partners, Harold Clorman Theatre, 96; auth, My Writer . My Actress, Hararo International Festival of the Arts (zimbabwe), 00. **CONTACT ADDRESS** Case Western Reserve Univ, 3021 Somerton Rd, Cleveland, OH 44118. **EMAIL** pdg8@aol.com

GOKHALE, BALKRISHNA GOVIND
PERSONAL Born 09/04/1919, Dwarka, India, m, 1943, 2 children **DISCIPLINE** HISTORY OF INDIA **EDUCATION** Univ Bombay, BA, 39, MA, 41, PhD, 46. **CAREER** Asst prof Indian hist & Pali-Buddhism, St Xavier's Col, Bombay, 42-54; vis lectr Indian hist, Bowdoin Col, 54-55; assoc prof Indian & Southeast Asian hist, Oberlin Col, 55-56; chmn dept hist, Sidhart Col, India, 56-59; vis lectr Indian hist, Univ Wash, 59-60; prof hist & dir Asian Studies Prog, 60-90, prof emeritus, Wake Forest Univ; Lectr & res guide hist & Pali, Univ Bombay, 48-

59. **MEMBERSHIPS** Am Orient Soc; Asn Asian Studies; AHA; fel Royal Asiatic Soc. **RESEARCH** History and civilization of India; Buddhism; Indian culture. **SELECTED PUBLICATIONS** Auth, Indian Thought Through the Ages, 60 & Samudragupta, 62, Asia; Asoka Maurya, Twayne, 66; Buddhism in Maharashtra, Popular Prakashan, 76; Surat in the XVIIth Century, Curzon, 78; Bharatavarsha, Sterling, 82; auth, Poona in the Eighteenth Century, Oxford, 88; auth, The Fiery Quill, Bowker, 98. **CONTACT ADDRESS** 1881 Faculty Dr, Winston-Salem, NC 27106.

GOLAHNY, AMY
PERSONAL Born Detroit, MI **DISCIPLINE** ART HISTORY **EDUCATION** Brandeis Univ, BA, 73; Williams Col-Clark Art Inst, MA, 75; Columbia Univ, Mphil, 77, PhD, 84. **CAREER** Curatorial asst, Philadelphia Museum Art, 78; asst prof, Chatham Col, 83-85; assoc prof, Lycoming Col, 85-. **MEMBERSHIPS** Am Asn Netherlandic Stud; Historians of Netherlandish Art. **RESEARCH** Rembrandt; Renaissance European art. **SELECTED PUBLICATIONS** Auth, Rubens Hero and Leander and its Poetic Progeny, 90; auth, Literature, Poetry, and the Visual Arts in the 17th Century, 96; auth, Pieter Lastman in the Literature: From Immortality to Oblivion, 96; auth, Rembrandts Approach to Italian Art: Three Variations, 99; auth, Lastmans Dido Sacrificing to Juno Identified, 99. **CONTACT ADDRESS** Art Dept, Lycoming Col, 700 College Pl, Williamsport, PA 17701. **EMAIL** golahny@lycoming.edu

GOLANY, GIDEON S.
DISCIPLINE URBAN DESIGN **EDUCATION** Hebrew University, Jerusalem, BA, 56, MA, 62; Inst for Soc Stud, The Hague, The Netherlands, DipCP, 65; Technion-Israel Inst of Tech, Haifa, Israel, MSc, 66; Hebrew Univ, Jerusalem, PhD, 66. **CAREER** Lecturer, Technion-Israel Inst of tech, 63-67; Lecturer, Cornell Univ, 67-68; Asn Prof, Va Polytechnic Inst & State Univ, 68-70; Ch of Grad Prog in Archit, Pa State Univ, 68-70; Sr Member Grad Sch Fac, 70-; Prof of Urban & Reg Planning, 70-87; Coord, China Progs, 84-89; Dir, PhD Prog, 86-89; Res Prof of Urban Des/Planning, 87-91; Distinguished Prof Urban Design, 91-; Aff Prof, Istanbul Tech Univ, Mid-E Tech Univ, Turkey, 96-. **HONORS AND AWARDS** Fulbright Res Awd for Japan, 90-91; Nat Endowment for the Arts Grant, 94; Creative Accomplishment & Res Grant, Pa State Univ, 94-95; Fulbright Res Awd for Turkey, 95-96; Finalist, Int Ach Awd, Pa State Univ, 96, 97; member, acad counc, babylonian jewry heritage cent, israel. **MEMBERSHIPS** Am Planning Asn; Asn of Engineers & Archit in Israel; Am Underground Space Asn; Int New-Towns Asn; Int Ctr for Arid & Semi-Arid Land Stud; Asn for Arid Land Stud. **RESEARCH** Urban design/planning; planning for developing society; new-town planning & design; urban design in arid zone; geo-space urban design. **SELECTED PUBLICATIONS** Auth, Ethics and Urban Design: Culture, Form and Environment, John Wiley & Sons, 95; auth, Babylonian Jewelry: Culture, Home and Neighborhood: Historical Appraisal, in review by press, 95; co-auth, Geo-Space Urban Design, John Wiley & Sons; 96; Japan Urban Environment, Elsevier Sci Ltd & Pergamon Press, 98; numerous multilingual publishings and book chapters. **CONTACT ADDRESS** Dept of Archit, Pennsylvania State Univ, Univ Park, 210 Engineering Unit C, University Park, PA 16802. **EMAIL** gxg3@email.psu.edu

GOLAS, PETER JOHN
PERSONAL Born 04/24/1937, Paterson, NJ, m, 1967, 2 children **DISCIPLINE** HISTORY **EDUCATION** Fordham Univ, AB, 58; Stanford Univ, MA, 64; Harvard Univ, PhD(hist & Far Eastern lang), 72. **CAREER** Asst prof, 73-76, assoc prof Hist, Univ Denver, 76-96, prof History, 96-. **HONORS AND AWARDS** Distinguished Scholar, Univ of Denver. **MEMBERSHIPS** Asn Asian Studies. **RESEARCH** Socio-economic history of Sung China; history of technology in China. **SELECTED PUBLICATIONS** Co-ed, Change in Sung China; Innovation or Renovation?, Heath, 59; coauth, On Contradiction in the Light of Mao Tse-tung's Essay on Dialectical Materialism, China Quart, 7-9/64; auth, Early Ch'ing Guilds, In: The City in Late Imperial China, Stanford Univ, 77; Rural China in the Song, J Asian Studies, 2/80; Science and Civilization in China, Vol 5, Pt 13, Mining, 98. **CONTACT ADDRESS** Dept of Hist, Univ of Denver, 2199 S University, Denver, CO 80210-4711. **EMAIL** pgolas@du.edu

GOLB, NORMAN
PERSONAL Born 01/15/1928, Chicago, IL, m, 1949, 3 children **DISCIPLINE** JEWISH HISTORY, HEBREW AND JUDEO-ARABIC STUDIES **EDUCATION** Roosevelt Col, BA, 48; Johns Hopkins Univ, PhD, 54. **CAREER** Warburg res fel Judaeo-Arabic studies, Hebrew Univ, Jerusalem, 55-57; vis lectr Semitic lang, Univ Wis, 57-58; from instr to asst prof Mediaeval Jewish studies, Hebrew Union Col, 58-63; from asst prof to prof Hebrew and Judeo-Arabic Studies, Univ Chicago, 63-88, Rosenberger Prof Jewish Hist and Civilization, 88-. **HONORS AND AWARDS** Adler res fel, Dropsie Col, 54-55; Am Philos Soc grants-in-aid, 59, 63 & 67; Am Coun Learned Soc grants-in-aid, 63 & 65; Guggenheim Mem Found fels, 64-65 & 66-67; vis fel, Clare Hall, Cambridge Univ, 70; Nat Endowment for Humanities grant, 70-72; Grand Medal of Honor of the City of Rouen, 85; Docteur Honoris Causa (Histoire), Univ of Rouen, 87; Medal of Haute Normandie, 87. **MEMBERSHIPS** Fel Am Acad Jewish Res; life mem, Clare Hall, Cambridge Univ, 80-; Soc de l'Histoire de France, 87-; Founder and vice-pres, Soc for Judeo-Arabic Studies, 84-. **RESEARCH** Jewish History, Hebrew and Judeo-Arabic Studies; Voting mem, Orient Inst, 61-. **SELECTED PUBLICATIONS** Auth, A Judaeo-Arabic Court Document of Syracuse, AD 1020, J Near Eastern Studies, 73; The Problem of Origin and Identification of the Dead Sea Scrolls, Proc Am Philos Soc, 80; Nature et destination du monument hebraique decouvert a Rouen, Proc Am Acad Jewish Res, 81; coauth (with Omeljan Pritsak), Khazarian Hebrew Documents of the Tenth Century, Cornell Univ Press, 82, trans to Russ, 97; auth, Les Juifs de Rouen au Moyen Age, Presses Univ de Rouen, 85; Who Wrote the Dead Sea Scrolls?, Scribner, 95, translated in Ger, Dutch, Port, Fr, Japanese; The Jews of Medieval Normandy, Cambridge Univ Press, 98; ed, Judeo-Arabic Studies, Harwood Acad Press, 97. **CONTACT ADDRESS** Univ of Chicago, Oriental Inst, 1155 E 58th St, Chicago, IL 60637-1540. **EMAIL** n-golb@uchicago.edu

GOLD, CAROL
DISCIPLINE MODERN SCANDINAVIA **EDUCATION** Univ Wis, PhD, 75. **CAREER** Univ Alaska **SELECTED PUBLICATIONS** Auth, Educating Middle Class Daughters, Museum Tusculanum Press & the Royal Library, 96. **CONTACT ADDRESS** Univ of Alaska, Fairbanks, PO Box 757480, Fairbanks, AK 99775-7480. **EMAIL** ffcg@aurora.alaska.edu

GOLD, PENNY SCHINE
PERSONAL Born 12/09/1947, Bridgeport, CT, m, 1973, 1 child **DISCIPLINE** HISTORY **EDUCATION** Univ Chicago, BA, 69; Stanford Univ, MA, 70, PhD(medieval studies), 77. **CAREER** Instr, Univ Cincinnati, 75-76; instr, 76-77, Asst Prof Hist, Knox Col, 83-91-, Monticello Col Found fel for Women, Newberry Libr, 79; mem teaching staff, Nat Summer Inst in Women's Studies, 81; vis asst prof, Univ Iowa, summer, 82; Prof, 91. **HONORS AND AWARDS** Nat Endowment for the Humanities Fellowship, 97-98. **MEMBERSHIPS** AHA; AAR (American Academy of Religion), AJS (Association for Jewish Studies), MJSA (Midwest Jewish Studies Association). **RESEARCH** Modern Jewish History. **SELECTED PUBLICATIONS** Auth, The Lady and The Virgin: Image, Attitude and Experience in Twelfth-Century France, Univ of Chicago Press, 85; auth, Men Helping Women, A Monastic Case-Study, Sociol of Relig, Vol 0054, 93; auth, "Making the Bible Modern: Translating Biblical Culture by Jewish American Children In the Early 20th Century," Sofar 13 (95): 43-63; The Language of Sex--5 Voices from Northern France around 1200, J Interdisciplinary Hist, Vol 0027, 96. **CONTACT ADDRESS** Dept of Hist, Knox Col, Illinois, 2 E South St, Galesburg, IL 61401-4938. **EMAIL** pgold@knox.edu

GOLDBERG, BARRY
DISCIPLINE LATE 19TH AND 20TH CENTURY SOCIAL HISTORY **EDUCATION** Columbia Univ, PhD. **CAREER** Assoc prof; assoc ch, undergrad stud, Fordham Univ. **RESEARCH** Ideological vision of immigration historians. **SELECTED PUBLICATIONS** Auth, Wage Slaves and White Niggers, Garland Press anthology, Critical Race Theory, 97; rev, Let Them Eat Multiculturalism, We Are All Multiculturalists Now, New Politics, 97; **CONTACT ADDRESS** Dept of Hist, Fordham Univ, 113 W 60th St, New York, NY 10023.

GOLDBERG, ROBERT A.
PERSONAL Born 08/16/1949, New York, NY, m, 2001, 2 children **DISCIPLINE** HISTORY **EDUCATION** Ariz State Univ, BA, 71; Univ Wisc-Madison, MA, 72; PhD, 77. **CAREER** Prof, Univ Utah, 77-. **MEMBERSHIPS** Org of Am Hist; W Hist Asn. **RESEARCH** 20th century America; American West. **SELECTED PUBLICATIONS** Auth, Barry Goldwater, Yale Univ Press, 95; co-ed, American Views: Documents in American History, Simon & Schuster, 98; auth, Enemies Within: The Idea of Conspiracy in Modern America, Yale Univ Press, under contract; auth, Enemies Within: The Culture of Conspiracy in Modern America, Yale Univ Press, 01. **CONTACT ADDRESS** Dept of Hist, Univ of Utah, 312 Carlson Hall, Salt Lake City, UT 84112. **EMAIL** bob.goldberg@m.cc.utah.edu

GOLDEN, RICHARD MARTIN
PERSONAL Born 06/14/1947, New York, NY, m, 1969, 3 children **DISCIPLINE** EARLY MODERN EUROPEAN HISTORY **EDUCATION** Vanderbilt Univ, BA, 69; Johns Hopkins Univ, MA, 72; Johns Hopkins, PhD(hist), 75. **CAREER** Instr, Clemson Univ, 74-75; Asst prof, Clemson Univ, 75-80; Assoc Prof, Clemson Univ, 80-83; Prof, Clemson Univ, 83-94, Prof and Chair, Hist, Univ N Texas 94-. **HONORS AND AWARDS** Fel, Nat Defense Educ Act, 70-73; Phi Beta Kappa; Nominee, Gov Prof of the Year Awd, 94; Professing Women Awd, 94 & 95; Regent's Faculty Lecturer, Univ N Texas, 97. **MEMBERSHIPS** Am Hist Assoc; Soc Fr Hist Studies. **RESEARCH** Early modern France; European witchcraft; European witch hunters: the Noailles family in 17th and 18th Century France. **SELECTED PUBLICATIONS** Ed, The Godly Rebellion: Parisian Cures and the Religious Fronde, 1652-1662, Chapel Hill: Univ Of North Carolina Press, 81; Ed, Church, State and Society under the Bourbon Kings of France, Lawrence, KS, Coronado Press, 82; Ed, The Huguenot Connection: The Edict of Nantes, Its Revocation, and Early French Migration to South Carolina, Boston, Dordrecht, and Lancaster: Kluwer Academic Publishers 88; Coed, Western Societies: Primary Sources in Social History, New York, St Martins Press, 93; Ed, The Social Dimension of Western Civilization, 99; Didactic Dialectic in the Teaching of Early Modern European Religious History in the United States: The Conflict between Cultural Heritage and Historical Accuracy, Mitteilungen der Internationale Gesellschaft fur Geschichtsdidaktik Vol 20/1 1999; Auth, American Perspectives on the European Witch Hunts, The Hist Teacher Vol 30/4, 97; Auth, Satan in Europe: The Geography of Witch-Hunts, Changing Identities in Early Modrn Europe, Wolfe, 97; **CONTACT ADDRESS** Dept of Hist, Univ of No Texas, PO BOX 310650, Denton, TX 76203-0650. **EMAIL** rmg@unt.edu

GOLDFIELD, DAVID
PERSONAL 2 children **DISCIPLINE** THE AMERICAN SOUTH HISTORY **EDUCATION** Univ MD, PhD, 70. **CAREER** Robert Lee Bailey Prof Hist, Univ NC, Charlotte. **RESEARCH** The Am South; the urban South. **SELECTED PUBLICATIONS** Auth, America's Changing Perceptions of Race, 1946-1996, in Cristina Giorcelli and Rob Kroes, eds, Living With America, 1946-1996, VU UP, Amsterdam, 97; Race, Region, and Cities: Interpreting the Urban South, LSU Press; coauth, The American Journey: A History of the United States, Prentice Hall. **CONTACT ADDRESS** Univ of No Carolina, Charlotte, Charlotte, NC 28223-0001. **EMAIL** drgoldfi@email.uncc.edu

GOLDIN, PAUL RAKITA
DISCIPLINE ASIAN STUDIES **EDUCATION** Univ Penn, BA, 92; MA, 92; Harvard Univ, PhD, 96. **CAREER** Asst prof, Univ Pa, 96-. **MEMBERSHIPS** AAS; SSEC; APA. **RESEARCH** Chinese philosophy and history. **SELECTED PUBLICATIONS** Auth, "Imagery of Copulation in Early Chinese Poetry: Chin Lit: Essays, Articles, Rev 21 (99): 35-66; auth, "Insidious Syncretism in the Political Philosophy of Huai-nan-tzu," Asian Philo 9 (99): 165-91; auth, auth, "Reading Po Chu-i," T'ang Studies 12 (94): 57-96; auth, "Some Old Chinese Words," J Am Oriental Soc 114 (94): 628-31; auth, "Job's Transgressions," Zeitschrift fur die alttestamentliche Wissenschaft 108 (96): 378-90; auth, "Reflections on Irrationalism in Chinese Aesthetics," Monumenta Serica 44 (96): 167-89; auth, "Changing Frontier Policy in the Northern Wei and Liao Dynasties," J Asian Hist 33 (99): 45-62; auth, "The View of Women in Early Confucionism," in The Sage and the Second Sex: Confucianism, Ethics, and Gender, ed. Chenyang Li (Chicago and La Salle, Ill: Open Court, 00); auth, "Chinese Classics and Chinese Modernity," in Classics and the Modern Curriculum, ed. Juana Celia Djelal, forthcoming; auth, "Some Commonplaces in the Shiji Biographies of Talented Men," in Studies on the Shiji: A Volume of Essays on Sima Qian, ed. Michael Puett, forthcoming. **CONTACT ADDRESS** Dept Asian Studies, Univ of Pennsylvania, 847 Williams Hall, Philadelphia, PA 19104-3805. **EMAIL** prg@mail.sas.upenn.edu

GOLDMAN, AARON L.
PERSONAL Born 05/10/1938, Chicago, IL, m, 1989 **DISCIPLINE** MODERN EUROPEAN & DIPLOMATIC HISTORY **EDUCATION** City Col New York, BA, 59; IN Univ, MA, 63, cert Russ area studies, 64, PhD(hist), 67. **CAREER** Instr hist, Univ Col, Univ MD, 63-64; assoc prof, 67-80, prof hist, San Jose State Univ, 80-, coordr Jewish Studies Prog, 80-84; Univ fel, San Jose State Univ, 74-75, fac grant, Off Sponsored Res & Proj Serv, 71,73 & 77-78. **MEMBERSHIPS** Conf Brit Studies; AHA, **RESEARCH** Modern European diplomatic history; British foreign policy 1930's; modern European Jewish history. **SELECTED PUBLICATIONS** Auth, The Link and the Anglo-German Review, SAtlantic Quart, summer 72; Claud Cockburn, The Week and the Cliveden Set, Jour Quart, winter 72; Defense Regulation 18B: Emergency Internment of Aliens and Political Dissenters in Great Britain during World War Two, J Brit Studies, spring 73; Sir Robert Vansittart's Search for Italian Cooperation against Hitler, 1933-36, J Contemp Hist, 7/74; Stephen King-Hall and the German Newsletter Controversy of 1939, Can J Hist, 8/75; Germans and Nazis: The Controversy over Vansittartism in Britain during the Second World War, J Contemp Hist, 1/79; Two Views of Germany: Nevise Henderson vs Vansittmas and the Foreign Office, Brit J Int Studies, 80; The Resurgence of Anti-Semitism in Britain during World War II, Jewish Social Studies, winter 84; Press Freedom in Britain During World War II, Journalism Hist, winter 97. **CONTACT ADDRESS** Dept Hist, San Jose State Univ, 1 Washington Sq, San Jose, CA 95192-0117.

GOLDMAN, BERNARD
PERSONAL Born 05/30/1922, Toronto, ON, Canada, m, 1944, 1 child **DISCIPLINE** ANCIENT NEAR EASTERN ART **EDUCATION** Wayne State Univ, AB, 46, AM, 47; Univ Mich, PhD(hist art), 59. **CAREER** Prof Hist of Art, Wayne State Univ, 60-, now retired; Am Coun Learned Soc fel, 68; dir press, Wayne State Univ, 74-; distinguished vis prof, Hope Col, 81-82. **MEMBERSHIPS** Archaeol Inst Am. **RESEARCH** Ancient Iranian art; ancient Judaic art. **SELECTED PUBLICATIONS** Auth, Nabataean/Syro-Roman Lunate Earrings, Israel Exploration J, 96. **CONTACT ADDRESS** Dept of Art and Art Hist, Wayne State Univ, 150 Community Art Bldg., Detroit, MI 48202.

GOLDMAN, JEAN
DISCIPLINE ART HISTORY **EDUCATION** Univ Chicago, PhD, 78. **CAREER** Instr, Univ PA; vis lectr, 89. **HONORS AND AWARDS** Kress fel; cur, inst contemp art, boston, 65-67; dir, rennaissance soc, 76-78 **SELECTED PUBLICATIONS** Ed, Centennial Essays, Art Inst Chicago; auth, Portraits, Art Inst Chicago; Masterpieces, Art Inst Chicago; pub(s), articles on old master drawings. **CONTACT ADDRESS** Dept of Art Hist, Sch of the Art Inst of Chicago, 37 S Wabash Ave, Chicago, IL 60603.

GOLDMAN, MERLE
PERSONAL Born 03/12/1931, New Haven, CT, m, 1953, 4 children **DISCIPLINE** HISTORY **EDUCATION** Sarah Lawrence Col, BA, 53; Radcliffe, MA, 57; Harvard Univ, PhD, 64. **CAREER** Prof, Boston Univ. **HONORS AND AWARDS** SSRC Awd; US State Dept Awd; Fel, RIIS; Postdoc Fel, Wang Inst; Guggenheim Fel. **SELECTED PUBLICATIONS** Auth, Literary Dissent in Communist China, Harvard Univ Press, 67; auth, China's Intellectuals: Advise and Dissent, Harvard Univ Press, 81; auth, Sowing the Seeds of Democracy in China: Political Reform in the Deng Xiaping Era, Harvard Univ Press, 94; co auth, China: A New History, Enlarged Edition, Belknap Press of Harvard Univ Press, 98. **CONTACT ADDRESS** Dept History, Boston Univ, 226 Bay State Rd, Boston, MA 02215. **EMAIL** mgoldman@fas.harvard.edu

GOLDMAN, STEVEN
PERSONAL Born 04/12/1941, Brooklyn, NY, m, 1968, 4 children **DISCIPLINE** HISTORICAL DEVELOPMENT AND THE SOCIAL RELATIONS OF MODERN SCIENCE AND TECHN **EDUCATION** PhD; Boston Univ. **CAREER** Prof, Lehigh Univ; Andrew W. Mellon Distinguished prof in the Humanities. **MEMBERSHIPS** APA; PSA; HSS; Sigma Xi; SPT; ISST. **RESEARCH** Medieval and Renaissance roots of modern science; philosophy of technology; contingency and necessity in western culture. **SELECTED PUBLICATIONS** ed, Science, Technology and Social Progress; ed, Competitiveness and American Society; coauth, Agile Competitors and Virtual Organizations; coauth, Cooperate to Compete; ed, Agility in Health Care. **CONTACT ADDRESS** Lehigh Univ, Bethlehem, PA 18015. **EMAIL** slg2@lehigh.edu

GOLDSCHMIDT, ARTHUR E., JR
PERSONAL Born 03/17/1938, Washington, DC, m, 1961, 2 children **DISCIPLINE** HISTORY **EDUCATION** Colby Col, AB, 59; Harvard Univ, AM, 61; PhD, 68. **CAREER** Acad Dean, NJ Scholars Prog, 85; Vis Lectr, Semester at Sea, 87; From Asst Prof to Emer Prof, Pa State Univ, 65-; **HONORS AND AWARDS** Phi Alpha Theta, Phi Beta kappa, Harvard GSAS Fel, 59-60; Nat Defense Foreign Lang Fel, 60-65; Fulbright Travel Grant, 63-64; Class of 1933 Awd for Outstanding contribution to Humanities, 72; Lib Arts Advising Awd, 76; AMOCO Found Teaching, 81. **MEMBERSHIPS** AHA, Middle E Studies Asn, Am Res Center in Egypt, World Hist Asn. **RESEARCH** Modern Egypt, general Middle East History, Sojourners in the Middle East. **SELECTED PUBLICATIONS** Auth, "Farouk I," and "Nahhas, Mustafa al-," in Political Leaders of the Contemporary Middle East and North Africa, ed. Bernard Reich (Westport, CT: Greenwood, 90); auth, The Memoirs and Diaries of Muhammad Farid, an Egyptian Nationalist Leader (1868-1919), Edwin Mellen Press (San Francisco), 92; auth, "Butrus Ghali Family," J of Am Res Center in Egypt 30 (93): 183-188; auth, A Historical Dictionary of Egypt, Scarecrow Press (Metuchen, NJ), 94; auth, entries on Egypt, Libya, and the Sudan, in AHA Guide to Historical Literature (NY: Oxford Univ Press, 95), I 546-548; auth, 72 entries in The Encyclopedia of the Modern Middle East (NY: Macmillan, 96); auth, "Van Dyck, Cornelius," in Am Nat Biog (NY,99), 208; auth, "Egypt-Modern History," in Encarta Encyclopedia (Microsoft Corp, 00); auth, "History," in Understanding the Contemporary Middle East, ed. Deborah Gerner (Boulder: Lynne Rienner Publ, 00); auth, Bibliography Dictionary of Modern Egypt (Boulder: Lynne Rienner Publ, 00). **CONTACT ADDRESS** Dept Hist, Pennsylvania State Univ, Univ Park, 108 Weaver Bldg., University Park, PA 16802-5500. **EMAIL** axg2@psu.edu

GOLDSTEIN, CARL
PERSONAL Born 06/24/1938, New York, NY, m, 2 children **DISCIPLINE** ART HISTORY **EDUCATION** Columbia Univ, PhD, 66. **CAREER** Visiting instr, Wheaton Col, 66; asst prof, Brown Univ, 66-71; ASSOC PROF, 71-80, PROF, 80-, UNIV OF NC. **HONORS AND AWARDS** S.H. Kress Fel, 65; Howard Found Fel, 70-71; Am Philos Soc Summer Grants, 77 & 82. **MEMBERSHIPS** Col Art Asn. **RESEARCH** Renaissance and Baroque art history. **SELECTED PUBLICATIONS** Auth, Visual Fact Over Verbal Fiction. A Study of the Carracci and the Criticism, Theory, and Practice of Painting in Renaissance and Baroque Italy, Cambridge Univ Press, 88; auth, Teaching Art. Academies and Schools from Vasari to Albers, Cambridge Univ Press, 96; auth, The Platonic Beginnings of the Academy of Painting and Sculpture in Paris, Academies of Art, Between Renaissance and Romanticism. Leids Kunsthistorisch Jaarboek, 89; auth, A New Role for the Antique in Academies, Antikenrezeption im Hochbarock, 89; auth, L'academie de Poussin, Nicolas Poussin 1594-1665, Musee du Louvre, 94; auth, Le musee imaginaire de l'acdemie au XVIIe et XVIIIe siecles, Les Musees en Europe a la veille de l'ouverture du Louvre, 95; auth, La fortune: Poussin et les academies au XIXe siecle, Colloque Poussin, 96; auth, Writing History, Viewing Art: The Question of the Humanist's Eye, Text and Image in the Renaissance: Antiquity Transumed, Cambridge Univ Press, forthcoming; auth, The Image of the Artist Reviews, Word and Image, 93. **CONTACT ADDRESS** Art Dept, Univ of No Carolina, Greensboro, Greensboro, NC 27412.

GOLDSTEIN, JONATHAN
PERSONAL Born 03/24/1947, Boston, MA, d **DISCIPLINE** HISTORY **EDUCATION** Univ Pa, PhD, History, 73. **CAREER** Prof. Of History, State Univ of West Georgia; Research Assoc, ohn K. Fairbank Center for East Asian Research, Harvard Univ. **HONORS AND AWARDS** Certificate of Commendation from American Association for State and Local History for the book Philadelphia and the China Trade, 78; Fulbright Fellowships: India , 89; Japan 90; NEH Fellowships: Harvvard University, 85; Columbia Univ 86; Univ of Massachusetts 87; Brown Universit. **MEMBERSHIPS** American Historical Assoc; Assoc for Asian Studies; Sino-Judaic Institute. **RESEARCH** Nineteenth and Twentieth Century East asian Internationa Relations; Sino-Judaica. **SELECTED PUBLICATIONS** Auth, pubs on East Asian international relations, and Jewish Diaspora in China; auth, "Philadelphia and the China Trade, 98; "America Views China," 91; "The Jews of China," 99; "China and Israel, 48-98;" auth, "A Fifty Year Retrospective," 99. **CONTACT ADDRESS** History Dept, State Univ of West Georgia, Carrollton, GA 30118.

GOLDSTEIN, LAURENCE ALAN
PERSONAL Born 01/05/1943, Los Angeles, CA, m, 1968, 2 children **DISCIPLINE** 20TH CENTURY **EDUCATION** Univ Calif, Los Angeles, BA, 65; Brown Univ, PhD, 70. **CAREER** From Asst Prof to Assoc Prof, 70-84, prof English, Univ of Mich Ann Arbor, 84-; Ed, Mich Quart Rev, 78-. **RESEARCH** Romantic poetry; film history; contemporary poetry. **SELECTED PUBLICATIONS** Auth, Familiarity and contempt: An essay on the star-presence in film, Centennial Rev, summer 73; Audubon and R P Warren, Contemp Poetry, winter 73; Ruins and Empire: The Evolution of a Theme in Augustan and Romantic Literature, Univ Pittsburgh, 77; Wordsworth and Snyder, Centennial Rev, winter 77; Kitty Hawk and the Question of American Destiny, Iowa Rev, winter 78; The Automobile and American Culture, Mich Quart Rev, fall 80 & winter 81; Lindbergh in 1927: The Response of Poets to the Poem of Fact, Prospects V, Burt Franklyn, 80; The Flying Machine and Modern Literature, Ind Univ Press, 87; The American Poet at the Movies: A Critical History, Univ Mich Press, 94; The Fiction of Arthur Miller, Mich Quart Rev, Fall 98; auth, Coruscating Glamour: Lynda Hull and the Movies, Iowa Rev, 99; auth, the Greatest Poem in the World, Southern Rev, 99. **CONTACT ADDRESS** Dept of English, Univ of Michigan, Ann Arbor, 505 S State St, Ann Arbor, MI 48109-1045. **EMAIL** lgoldste@umich.edu

GOLDTHWAITE, RICHARD A.
PERSONAL Born 06/06/1933, Marion, IN **DISCIPLINE** RENAISSANCE HISTORY **EDUCATION** Oberlin Col, BA, 55; Columbia Univ, MA, 57, PhD(hist), 65. **CAREER** From instr to asst prof hist, Kent State Univ, 62-68; asst prof, 68-73, Prof Hist, Johns Hopkins Univ, 73-, Assoc prof, Kent State Univ, 71-72. **MEMBERSHIPS** AHA; Renaissance Soc Am; Soc Ital Hist Studies. **RESEARCH** Italian Renaissance social and economic history; history of Florence; history of art patronage. **SELECTED PUBLICATIONS** Auth, Private Wealth in Renaissance Florence: A Study of Four Families, Princeton Univ, 68. **CONTACT ADDRESS** Dept of Hist, Johns Hopkins Univ, Baltimore, 3400 N Charles St, Baltimore, MD 21218-2680.

GOLDY, CHARLOTTE NEWMAN
PERSONAL Born 06/14/1949, New York, NY, m, 1988, 1 child **DISCIPLINE** MEDIEVAL HISTORY **EDUCATION** SUNY - Binghamton, BA, 71; MA, 73; PhD, 78 **CAREER** Instr hist, Jr Col Albany, 79-84; asst prof hist, 84-89, assoc prof, 89, dept chmn, Miami Univ, 95; **HONORS AND AWARDS** Phi Beta Kappa; Phi Kappa Phi. **MEMBERSHIPS** Soc Medieval Feminist Studies; Medieval Acad Am; Haskins Soc **RESEARCH** England in the High Middle Ages, especially Jewish and Christian family history. **SELECTED PUBLICATIONS** Auth, The Anglo-Norman Nobility in the Reign of Henry I: The Second Generation, 88. **CONTACT ADDRESS** Dept of History, Miami Univ, Oxford, OH 45056. **EMAIL** goldycn@muohio.edu

GOLINSKI, JAN
PERSONAL Born 04/09/1957, London, England **DISCIPLINE** HISTORY OF SCIENCE **EDUCATION** Univ Cambridge, BA, 79; Univ Cambridge, MA, 83; Univ Leeds, PhD, 84 **CAREER** Jnr Res Fel, Churchill Col, 86-90; asst prof, Univ NH, 90-94; assoc prof, Univ NH, 94- **HONORS AND AWARDS** Fel, Dibner Inst, MIT, 94; Outstanding Fac Awd, Univ NH, 98 **MEMBERSHIPS** Hist Sci Soc; Brit Soc Hist Sci; Amer Hist Assoc **RESEARCH** History of Chemistry & Meteorology; Science in British Society (17th-19th Century); Enlightenment; Historiography **SELECTED PUBLICATIONS** Auth, Science as Public Culture: Chemistry and Enlightenment in Britain, 1760-1820, Cambridge, 92; auth, Making Natural Knowledge: Constructivism and the History of Science, Cambridge, 98; co-ed, The Sciences in Enlightened Europe, Univ Chicago, 99. **CONTACT ADDRESS** History Dept, Univ of New Hampshire, Durham, Durham, NH 03824-3586. **EMAIL** jan.golinski@unh.edu

GOLLAHER, DAVID L.
PERSONAL Born 09/10/1949, Glendale, CA, m, 1982, 2 children **DISCIPLINE** HISTORY OF AMERICAN CIVILIZATION, HISTORY OF SCIENCE AND MEDICINE **EDUCATION** Univ Calif Santa Barbara, BA; Harvard Divinity School, MTS; Harvard Univ, PhD. **CAREER** Tchg fel History and Literature, Harvard Univ, 75-80; VP, Scripps Clinic and Res Found, 84-91; Grad School Pub Health, San Diego State Univ, 91-92; PRES CEO, CALIF HEALTHCARE INST, 93-; fel Natl Endowment for Hum, 93; Houghton Libr 50th Anniv Fel, 94. **HONORS AND AWARDS** Avery O Craven Prize, 96. **RESEARCH** History of Medicine. **SELECTED PUBLICATIONS** Voice for the Mad: The Life of Dorothea Dix, Free Press, 95; auth, Circumcision: A History of the World's Most Controversial Surgery, (Basic Books, 00) **CONTACT ADDRESS** California Health Care Inst, 1020 Prospect St, Ste 310, La Jolla, CA 92037. **EMAIL** gollaher@chi.org

GOLLEDGE, REGINALD G.
PERSONAL Born 12/06/1937, Dungog, Australia, m, 1976, 4 children **DISCIPLINE** GEOGRAPHY **EDUCATION** Univ New England, BA, 59, MA, 61; Univ Iowa, PhD, 66. **CAREER** Asst prof, Univ British Columbia, Vancouver, 65-66; asst prof, Ohio State Univ, 66-67; assoc prof, Ohio State Univ, 67-71; prof, Dept Geography, Univ Calif, Santa Barbara, 77-, chemn, 80-84. **HONORS AND AWARDS** Best Content Awd for J of Geography article, Nat Coun for Geographic Educ, 95; Inst of Australian Geographers Int Geographers Gold Medal, 98. **MEMBERSHIPS** Am Asn for the Advancement of Sci, Asn of Am Geographers, Regional Sci Asn Int, Inst of Australian Geographers, Am Psychol Soc. **RESEARCH** Behavioral geography, spatial cognition, cognitive maps, disaggregate travel behavior, geographic education. **SELECTED PUBLICATIONS** Coauth, Spatial Behavior: A Geographic Perspective, Guilford Press, NY (97); co-ed, Spatial and Temporal Reasoning in Geographic Information Systems, Oxford Press, NY (98); auth, Wayfinding Behavior: Cognitive Mapping and Other Spatial Processes, Johns Hopkins Univ Press, Baltimore, MD (99); auth, "Behavioral Geography (1999)," in Encyclopedia of Social Sciences (in press); coauth, "The Role of Cognitive Maps in Spatial Decision Making: Implications of the Past for the Future," and coauth, "Sex, Gender, and Cognitive Mapping," in Cognitive Mapping: Past, Present and Future, eds. R. Kitchin and S. Freundschuh (Routledge, London, in press). **CONTACT ADDRESS** Dept Geography, Univ of California, Santa Barbara, 552 Univ Rd, Santa Barbara, CA 93106. **EMAIL** golledge@geog.ucsb.edu

GOLOMBEK, LISA
PERSONAL Born 11/27/1939, Huntington, NY **DISCIPLINE** ISLAMIC ART & ARCHITECTURE **EDUCATION** Barnard Col, BA, 62; Univ Mich, MA, 63, PhD, 68. **CAREER** Asst prof, 68-72, assoc prof, 72-89, Prof Middle East & Islamic Stud, Univ Toronto, 89-; asst cur, 68-73, assoc cur, 73-80, Curator, Near Eastern & Asian Civilizations Dept, Royal Ontario Museum, 80-. **HONORS AND AWARDS** Fel, Royal Soc Can. **SELECTED PUBLICATIONS** Auth, The Timurid Shrine at Gazur Gah, 69; coauth, The Timurid Architecture of Iran and Turan, 2 vols, 88; coauth, Tamerlane's Tableware, 96; co-ed, Timurid Art and Culture, 92. **CONTACT ADDRESS** Near Eastern & Asian Civilizations Dept, Royal Ontario Mus, 100 Queens Park, Toronto, ON, Canada M5S 2C6. **EMAIL** lisag@rom.on.ca

GOMEZ-HERRERO, FERNANDO
PERSONAL Born 01/26/1969, Spain **DISCIPLINE** LATIN AMERICAN STUDIES **EDUCATION** Universidad de Salamanca, BA, 92; MA, 95; Wake Forest Univ, MA, 95; Duke Univ, PhD, 99. **CAREER** Asst prof, Stanford Univ, 99-. **HONORS AND AWARDS** Duke Univ Grants, 95-98; Fac Res Grant, Stanford Univ, 00, 01. **MEMBERSHIPS** MLA, IILI, LASA. **RESEARCH** Transatlantic literature, Latin American Studies of the colonial period (pre-1800), Early Modern Europe with a special emphasis on the Iberian peninsula. **SELECTED PUBLICATIONS** Auth, Good Places and Non-Places in Colonial Mexico: The Figure of Vasco de Quiroga (1470-1565), Univ Pr of Am, 01. **CONTACT ADDRESS** Stanford Univ, Pigott Hall 260-228, Stanford, CA 94305-2014. **EMAIL** fgomez@stanford. Edu

GONZALES, JOHN EDMOND
PERSONAL Born 09/17/1924, New Orleans, LA **DISCIPLINE** HISTORY **EDUCATION** La State Univ, BS, 43, MA, 45; Univ NC, PhD, 57. **CAREER** From asst prof to prof hist, 45-69, William D Mc Cain Prof, Univ Southern Miss, 69-, Distinguished Univ Prof Hist, 73-, Ed, J Miss Hist, 63-; mem bd dirs, Univ Press Miss, 70-. **MEMBERSHIPS** Southern Hist Asn. **RESEARCH** Southern history, especially Mississippi; American intellectual and social history. **SELECTED PUBLICATIONS** Auth, William Pitt Kellogg, Reconstruction Gover-

nor of Louisiana, 1873-1877, 46 & Henry Stuart Foote: A Republican Appointee in Louisiana, 60, La Hist Quart; Henry Stuart Foote: A Forgotten Unionist of the Fifties, Southern Quart, 64; Henry Stuart Foote: Confederate Congressman and Exile, Civil War Hist, 12/65; John Anthony Quitman in the United States House of Representatives, Southern Quart, 4/66; Thirty Years of the Journal of Mississippi History (1939-1969), J Miss Hist, 5/69; co-ed & contribr, A History of Mississippi (2 vols), 73 & Territorial and Early Statehood, In: Atlas of Mississippi, 74, Univ Press Miss; ed & contribr, A Mississippi Reader, Miss Hist Soc, 80. **CONTACT ADDRESS** Univ of So Mississippi, Hattiesburg, MS 39406.

GONZALES, MANUEL G.

PERSONAL Born 01/08/1943, Fresno, CA, m, 1969, 2 children **DISCIPLINE** HISTORY **EDUCATION** Univ CA, Santa Barb, BA 65, MA 67, PhD 72. **CAREER** Diablo Valley Col, instr hist 71; Univ CA, Berkeley, vis prof 93. **HONORS AND AWARDS** 5 NEH Fells; NDEA; TIT; FELL. **MEMBERSHIPS** CHS; SIHS; WHA; Nat Assn Chicana. **RESEARCH** Chicana Hist, modern Italian Hist **SELECTED PUBLICATIONS** Andrea Costa and the Rise of Socialism in the Romagna, Univ Press Of Amer, 80; The Hispanic Elite of the Southwest, TX Western Press, 89; Mexicanos: A History of Mexicans in the United States, IN Univ Press, 99. **CONTACT ADDRESS** Dept of Soc Sci(s), Diablo Valley Col, 321 Golf Club Rd, Pleasant Hill, CA 94523. **EMAIL** magonzal@dvc.edu

GONZALEZ, CATHERINE GUNSALUS

PERSONAL Born 05/20/1934, Albany, NY, m, 1973 **DISCIPLINE** HISTORICAL AND SYSTEMATIC THEOLOGY **EDUCATION** Beaver Col, BA, 56; Boston Univ, STB, 60, PhD(syst theol, hist doctrine), 65. **CAREER** From asst prof to assoc prof Bible and relig, WVa Wesleyan Col, 65-70, dir student relig life, 65-70; assoc prof hist theol, Louisville Presby Theol Sem, 70-73; assoc prof church hist, 74-78, PROF CHURCH HIST, COLUMBIA THEOL SEM, 78-, Mem comt on status of women, Gen Assembly, United Presby Church, 67-70, comt on baptism, 70-72; mem, Faith and Order Comn, Nat Coun Churches, 73-. **MEMBERSHIPS** Presby Hist Soc. **RESEARCH** Liturgical theology; women and theology; comparative systematic theology. **SELECTED PUBLICATIONS** Auth, Between Text and Sermon--Isaiah 43, 8-15, Interpretation-J Bible and Theol, Vol 0048, 94. **CONTACT ADDRESS** Dept of Church Hist, Columbia Theol Sem, PO Box 520, Decatur, GA 30031-0520.

GONZALEZ, DEENA J.

PERSONAL Born 08/25/1952, Hatch, NM **DISCIPLINE** HISTORY **EDUCATION** NM State Univ, BA, 74; Univ CA, Berkeley, MA, 76, PhD, 85. **CAREER** Assoc Prof of Hist and Chicano Studies, Pomona Col, 83-; vis assoc prof: Hist, Univ NM, 91-92, Chicano Studies, UCSB, 92, Chicano Studies, UCLA, 96-97. **HONORS AND AWARDS** Nat Res Council/ Ford Found fel, 87-88; Inst of Am Cultures fel, UCLA, 96-97. **MEMBERSHIPS** Am Hist Asn; Nat Asn of Chicano/a Studies; Org of Am Historians. **RESEARCH** Chicana hist; frontier, 19th century US hist; gay/lesbian hist. **SELECTED PUBLICATIONS** Auth, Series, co-ed with Antonia Castaneda, Chicano Identity Matters Series, Univ TX Press, 96-; La Tules of Santa Fe, forthcoming in Zaragonza Vargas, ed, Major Issues in Chicano History, Houghton-Mifflin, 98; The Unmarried Women of Santa Fe, in Zaragoza Vargas, Major Issues in Chicano History, Houghton-Mifflin, 98; The Travail of War: Women and Children in the Years After the US-Mexican War, Sept 98, printed at http://www.pbs.org/kera/usmexican war; On the Lives of Women and Children in the Aftermath of the US-Mexican War, in John Bloom, ed, The Treaty of Guadalupe-Hidalgo: Its Impact in New Mexico, 99; Chicana Studies: Paths and Detentions, commissioned by the Julian Samora Inst, MI State Univ, East Lansing, Inst Pubs, 99; Not Honey or Money: Chicana Body Politics, in Debra King, ed, The Body Politic, forthcoming, IN Univ Press, 99; Families and Different Cultural Traditions, commissioned by the AHA, pamphlet series, in Antonio Rios-Bustamante, Nell Painter, eds, Teaching Diversity: People of Color and Women of Color, Temple Univ Press, 99; Refusing the Favor: The Spanish-Mexican of Sante Fe, 1820-1880, Oxford U Pr, 99; Dictionary of Latinas in the US, Atte Publico Pr, 02. **CONTACT ADDRESS** Hist Dept, Pomona Col, Claremont, CA 91711. **EMAIL** dgonzalez@pomona.edu

GONZALEZ, EVELYN

DISCIPLINE HISTORY **EDUCATION** City Col NYork, BA, 75; Columbia Univ NYork, MA, 77, Mphil, 79, PhD, 93. **CAREER** Asst prof, William Paterson Univ 95-; adj lectr, Stevens Inst Technol, LaGuardia Community Col, Manhattan Col, Baruch Col & LaGuardia Community Col, 80-81; tchg asst, Columbia Univ, 77. **HONORS AND AWARDS** Ford Found fel, 75-80; Phi Beta Kappa, 75; Cromwell Medal, City Col NY, 75, Zimmerman Schol Awd Phi Alpha Theta, 75-76; Phi Alpha Theta Hist Hon Soc, 74. **SELECTED PUBLICATIONS** Auth, Seeds of Decay: The South Bronx Long Before the Sixties, J Urban Hist, 97; The Urban Decay Process: Housing, Crime, and Race in the South Bronx, City Sem, Columbia Univ, 98; Image, Poverty, and Decay: The South Bronx in the 1940s, Sch Mgt & Urban Policy of the New Sch for Soc Res, NY City, 96; Seeds of Decay: The South Bronx Before the Sixties, 26th Annual Meeting of the Urban Aff Asn, NY City, 96; Seven entries on the South Bronx: Mott Haven, Melrose, Morrisania, Claremont, Hunts Point, Crotona Park East, and Fort Apache, The Encycl NY City, New Haven, 95; The Development and Role of New York City's Community Boards, Urban Aff Roundtable of the Special Libr(s) Asn, 80th Annual Conf, NY City, 89; The Development of the Bronx and the Grand Concourse, Bronx Museum of the Arts' sem, 87. **CONTACT ADDRESS** Dept of History, William Paterson Col of New Jersey, 300 Pompton Rd, Atrium 210, Wayne, NJ 07470. **EMAIL** gonzaleze@wpunj.edu

GONZALEZ, JUSTO LUIS

PERSONAL Born 08/09/1937, Havana, Cuba, m, 1973, 1 child **DISCIPLINE** HISTORICAL THEOLOGY **EDUCATION** Union Theol Sem, Cuba, STB, 57; Yale Univ, STM, 58, MA, 60, PhD, 61. **CAREER** Prof, 61-68, dean, 68-69, Evangel Sem PR; assoc prof world Christianity, 69-77, Candler Sch Theol, Emory Univ; res & writing, 77-78; Ed, Apuntes; Journal Hispanic Theol, 79-; res fels hist theol, Yale Univ, 68 & 69; consult theol educ, Protestant Episcopal Church, 71-72 & 73-74; mem, Comn Faith & Order, Nat Coun Churches, 73-81; dir, 87-, Hispanic Sum Prog; exec dir, 96-, Hispanic Theol Initiative. **HONORS AND AWARDS** Hon degree, Divinas Letras, Seminario Evangelico de Puerto Rico, 94; Virgilio Elizondo Awd; Acad of Cath Hispanic Theologians in US, 91; Gold Medallion Bk Awd, Evangelical Christian Publ Assn, 93; Orlando Costas Awd, Latino Pastoral Action Ctr, 98. **RESEARCH** Patristics; liberation theology; contemporary Latin American theology. **SELECTED PUBLICATIONS** Auth, Mana: Christian Theology from a Hispanic Perspective, 90; auth, Faith and Wealth, Harper, 90; auth, Out of Every Tribe and Nation: Christian Theology at the Ethnic Roundtable, Abingdon, 92; auth, Santa Biblia: The Bible Through Hispanic Eyes, Abingdon, 96. **CONTACT ADDRESS** PO Box 520, Decatur, GA 30031. **EMAIL** jgonz02@emory.edu

GONZALEZ DE LEON, FERNANDO JAVIER

DISCIPLINE EUROPEAN HISTORY **EDUCATION** Rutgers Col, AB, 81; Univ Va, MA, 84; Johns Hopkins Univ, MA, 85, PhD, 92. **CAREER** Vis asst prof, Purchase Col, 90-91; vis asst prof, Bard Col, 91-92; asst to assoc prof, Springfield Col, 92-. **HONORS AND AWARDS** Rutgers Col: Dean's List, 78-81, Henry Rutgers Honors Scholar, 79-81, Phi Beta Kappa, 81; Univ Va, Coun of Advanced Studies, 83; Johns Hopkins Univ, Frederick Jackson Turner Res Fel, 84-85; Nat Hispanic Merit Scholarship, 85, 86, 87, 88; Hoghn F. Olin Postdoctoral Fel, Yale Univ, 94-95. **MEMBERSHIPS** Am Hist Asn, Soc for Spanish and Portuguese Hist Studies, Sixteenth Century Studies Conf, Renaissance Studies Soc. **RESEARCH** Early Modern Europe, Imperial Spain. **SELECTED PUBLICATIONS** Auth, "The Legal System of Colonial Latin America," & "Slavery in Latin America," in The Latino Encyclopedia, Richard and Rafael Chabrian, eds, NY: Marshall Cavendish (95); auth, "Doctors of the Military Discipline: Technica Expertise and the Paradigm of the Spanish Soldier in the Early Modern Period," in The Sixteenth Century Journal, XXVII, No 1 (spring 96): 61-85; auth, "Aristocratic Draft-Dodgers in 17th Century Spain," in History Today, Vol 46, No 7 (July 96): 14-21; coauth, "The Grand Strategy of Philip II and the Revolt of the Netherlands, 1559-1584, Reformation, Revolution and Civil War in France and the Netherlands, Amsterdam: Royal Netherlands Acad of the Arts and Scis (99): 215-232; coauth, "La Gran Estrategia de Felipe II," in Catedra Felipe II, Universidad de Valladolid, Spain (forthcoming); coauth, "Spain and the Dutch Revolt," in Graham Darby, ed, The Origins of the Dutch Revolt, London: UCL Press (forthcoming); auth, The Road to Rocrio. The Duke of Alba, the Count-Duke of Olivares and the Spanish Army of Flanders in the Eighty Years War, 1567-1659, Cambridge Univ Press (submitted). **CONTACT ADDRESS** Dept Soc Sci, Springfield Col, Massachusetts, 263 Alden St, Springfield, MA 01109-3707. **EMAIL** fgonzale@spfldcol.edu

GOOD, DAVID F.

DISCIPLINE HISTORY **EDUCATION** Wesleyan Univ, BA, 65; Univ Chicago, MBA, 67; Univ Pa, PhD, 72. **CAREER** Prof, Temple Univ, 74-90; Univ Minn Twin Cities, 90-. **RESEARCH** European economic history; economic development of Central and Eatern Europe since 1750. **SELECTED PUBLICATIONS** Auth, The Economic Rise of the Habsburg Empire, 1750-1914, Univ Calif, 84; ed, Economic Transformations in East and Central Europe, 94; co-ed, Nationalism and Empire: The Habsburg Empire and the Soviet Union, 92; Austrian Women in the Nineteenth and Twentieth Centuries, 96. **CONTACT ADDRESS** History Dept, Univ of Minnesota, Twin Cities, 614 Social Sciences Tower, 267 19th Ave. S, Minneapolis, MN 55455. **EMAIL** goodx001@tc.umn.edu

GOOD, IRENE LEE

PERSONAL Born 04/24/1958, Orinda, CA, 2 children **DISCIPLINE** ARCHAEOLOGY **EDUCATION** Boston Univ, BA, 85, MA, 86; Univ Penn, PhD cand, 99. **CAREER** Tchg asst, Boston Univ, 83-86; tchg asst, 88-89, guest lectr, 89, historic preservation, Univ Penn; guest lectr, 93-96, textiles; instr, Archaeology, Univ Penn, 96; guest lectr, Smithsonian Inst, 97. **HONORS AND AWARDS** Travel grant, West Indies, 84; Grad asst, Boston Univ, 84-85, 85-86; tchg asst, 88-89, res asst, 89-92, 96-98, Univ Penn; Univ Res Found Grant, 91-93; fel, Univ Penn, 91-93; dis fel, 93-94; Am Inst iranian Stud Dis Fel, 94; Cotsen Found Res Fel, 97. **MEMBERSHIPS** Am Anthrop Asn, NY Acad of Sci; AAAS. **RESEARCH** Bronze Age; Central Asia; technological innovation and social change; fiber use and weaving/textile technology; long distance exchange/ interaction. **SELECTED PUBLICATIONS** Coauth, Quseir al-Aadim, Egypt and the Potential of Archaological Pollen Analysis in the Near East, in J of Field Archaeol, 95; auth, On the Question of Silk in Pre-Han Eurasia, in Antiquity, 95; auth, Notes on a Textile Fragment from Hami, Xinjiang with Comments on the Significance of Twill, in J of Indo-European Stud, 95; auth, Bronze Age Textiles from the Tarim Basin: The Cherchen Evidence, in Bronze Age and Early Iron Age Peoples of Eastern Central Asia, Univ Penn Museum, 97; auth, Hard Evidence from Fuzzy Data: A Closer Look at Invisible Imports, in Fleeting Identities: Perishable Material Culture in Archaeological Research, Southern Ill, 98. **CONTACT ADDRESS** Dept of Anthropology, Univ of Pennsylvania, 33rd & Spruce Sts, Philadelphia, PA 19104. **EMAIL** igood@mail.sas.upenn.edu

GOOD, JANE E.

PERSONAL Born 03/24/1948, Akron, OH, d, 2 children **DISCIPLINE** HISTORY **EDUCATION** Wittenberg Univ, BA, 70; Brown Univ, MAT, 72; Am Univ, PhD, 79. **CAREER** Asst prof , 79-84, assoc prof, 84-89, asst dean, 89-94, Dir Acad Coun, US Naval Acad, 94-. **HONORS AND AWARDS** Dept of Navy, Meritorious Civilian Service Medal, 88, Superior Civilian Service Medal, 94. **MEMBERSHIPS** AHA, AAASS. **RESEARCH** Russian history, women in Navy. **SELECTED PUBLICATIONS** Auth, "Integration of Women in Brigade of Midshipman," (87); auth, Babushka: Life of E. K. Breshkovskara (90). **CONTACT ADDRESS** Dept Hist, United States Naval Acad, 121 Blake Rd, Annapolis, MD 21402-1300. **EMAIL** good@nadn.navy.mil

GOODE, JAMES

PERSONAL Born 05/29/1944, Hyannis, MA, m, 1972, 2 children **DISCIPLINE** HISTORY **EDUCATION** Georgetown Univ, BS, 66; Univ Mass, MA, 68; Mitchell Col, Australia, D Ed, 76; Indiana Univ, PhD, 84. **CAREER** Peace Corp, Iran, 68-71; instr, Univ Mashhad, Iran, 71-73; teach, Sacred Heart Sch, Australia, 74-78; ed asst, AHR, 80-84; lectr, Univ Georgia, 84-86; prof, Grand Valley State Univ, 86-; coord, MESP, Grand Valley State Univ, 97-. **HONORS AND AWARDS** Phi Kappa Phi, 91; NEH, 85, 88, 92; Fel, Nat Coun US-Arab Rel, 87, 90, 94; Fulbright Sr Lectr, 99-00. **MEMBERSHIPS** SHAFR; MESA; SIS; Mich Comt US-Arab Rel. **RESEARCH** US Foreign relations, Twentieth-Century Middle East; archeology and nationalism in the Middle East. **SELECTED PUBLICATIONS** Auth, United States and Iran 46-51: The Diplomacy of Neglect (89); auth, United States and Iran: In the Shadow of Musaddig (97); auth, "Reforming Iran During the Kennedy Years," Diplomatic History 15 (91); auth, "Samuel Benjamin: Unorthodox Observer of the Middle East," Islam and Christian-Muslim Relations (98); auth, "A Good Start: The First U.S. Mission to Iran, 1883-85," Muslim World 74 (84); auth, "A Liberal Iran: Casualty of the Cold War," Paths Not Taken (00). **CONTACT ADDRESS** Dept History, Grand Valley State Univ, 1 Campus Dr, Allendale, MI 49401-9401. **EMAIL** goodej@gvsu.edu

GOODFRIEND, JOYCE DIANE

PERSONAL Born 10/29/1940, New York, NY **DISCIPLINE** AMERICAN HISTORY **EDUCATION** Brown Univ, BA, 61; Univ Calif, Los Angeles, MA, 68, PhD(hist), 75. **CAREER** Vis asst prof, 72-76, Asst Prof Hist, Univ Denver, 76-, Dir Am Studies, 81-, Hist consult coun women's hist, Colo Women's Conf Int Women's Decade, 76-77; lectr, Denver Lilly Prog Continuing Educ for Col Teachers, 80. **MEMBERSHIPS** AHA; Orgn Am Historians; Immigration Hist Soc. **RESEARCH** American colonial history; history of women in America; history of ethnic groups in America. **SELECTED PUBLICATIONS** Coauth, Women in Colorado before the First World War, Colo Mag, summer 76; auth, Burghers and Blacks: The evolution of a slave society at New Amsterdam, NY Hist, 4/78; coauth, Lives of American Women: A History With Documents, Boston, Little, Brown, 81. **CONTACT ADDRESS** Dept of Hist, Univ of Denver, Denver, CO 80208.

GOODHEART, LAWRENCE

PERSONAL Born 06/29/1944, Washington, DC **DISCIPLINE** HISTORY **EDUCATION** Univ Rochester, BA, 66, MA, 68; SUNY Albany, MA, 72; Univ Conn, PhD, 79. **CAREER** Asst prof, Univ Conn, 90-93, assoc prof, 93-. **RESEARCH** 19th century US social and intellectual history. **SELECTED PUBLICATIONS** Auth, Abolitionist, Actuary Atheist: Elizar Wright and the Reform Impulse, Kent: Kent State Univ Press (90); co-ed, American Chameleon: Individualism in Trans-National Context, Kent: Kent State Univ Press (91); co-ed, Slavery in American Society, Boston: Houghton Mifflin (93); co-ed, The Abolitionists: Means, Ends, and Motivations, Boston: Houghton Mifflin (95). **CONTACT ADDRESS** Dept Hist, Univ of Connecticut, Hartford, 85 Lawler Rd, West Hartford, CT 06117-2620. **EMAIL** lawrence.goodheart@uconn.edu

GOODMAN, GRANT KOHN
PERSONAL Born 10/18/1924, Cleveland, OH **DISCIPLINE** JAPANESE HISTORY **EDUCATION** Princeton Univ, BA, 48; Univ Mich, MA, 49, PhD(hist), 55. **CAREER** Actg asst prof hist, Univ Wash, 55-56; instr Far Eastern hist, Univ Del, 56-58; asst prof, State Univ NY Col Fredonia, 58-62; Prof Hist, Univ Kans, 62-89, Fulbright lectr, Univ Philippines, 59-60; NDEA fac fel, Japan and Philippines, 64-65; preceptor, Int Honors Prog, 66-67; vis prof EAsian Hist, Sophia Univ, Japan, 70-71 and 80; vis prof Japan hist, Univ Col, Dublin, Ireland, 75; fel, Neth Inst Advan Study in Humanities and Soc Sci, 76-77; res grantee, Sumitomo Fund-Rockefeller Found, 76-78; Mid-Am State Univs Asn honor lectr, 81-82; mem, Am Adv Comt Japan Found, 81-. **MEMBERSHIPS** AHA; Asn Asian Studies; Asia Soc; Conf Asian Hist (pres, 71-72 & 76-89); Midwest Conf Asian Affairs (vpres, 73-74, pres, 74-75). **RESEARCH** Japanese Pan-Asianism; Tokugawa intellectual history; modern Philippine history. **SELECTED PUBLICATIONS** Auth, Experiment in Wartime Intercultural Relations: Philippine Students in Japan, 1943-1945, Cornell Univ, 62; Four Aspects of Philippine-Japanese Relations, 1930-1940, Yale Univ, 67; Davao: A Case Study in Japanese-Philippine Relations, Univ Kans East Asian Ser, 67; ed, The American Occupation of Japan: A Retrospective View, Univ Kans East Asian Ser, 68; From Bataan to Tokyo: Diary of a Filipino student in wartime Japan, 1943-44, Univ Kans East Asian Ser, 79; co-ed & contribr, The United States and Japan in the Western Pacific: Micronesia and Papua New Guinea, Westview Press, 80; ed, Japanese Cultural Policies in Southeast Asia During World War 2, Macmillan, 91; auth, Asian History: Markus Wiener, 3rd ed., 93; auth, Japan and the Dutch, Curzon, 00. **CONTACT ADDRESS** Univ of Kansas, Lawrence, PO Box 968, Lawrence, KS 66044. **EMAIL** plim@falcon.cc.ukans.edu

GOODMAN, PAUL
PERSONAL Born 03/01/1934, Brooklyn, NY **DISCIPLINE** HISTORY **EDUCATION** Cornell Univ, BS, 55; Harvard Univ, MA, 57, PhD, 61. **CAREER** Res assoc bus hist, Harvard Univ, 61-62; instr hist, Brooklyn Col, 62-65; from asst prof to assoc prof, 65-70, Prof Hist, Univ Calif, Davis, 70-, Soc Sci Res Coun grant-in-aid, 62-63; Am Philos Soc grant-in-aid, 64. **MEMBERSHIPS** AHA; Orgn Am Historians. **RESEARCH** Early American history to 1815; political history. **SELECTED PUBLICATIONS** Auth, Democratic-Republicans of Massachusetts, Politics in a Young Republic, Harvard Univ, 64; Ethics and enterprise: The values of a Boston elite, Am Quart, 67; The first American party system, Am Party Syst, 67; ed, Essays in American Colonial History, 67 & The Federalists vs the Democratic Republicans, 67, Holt; The American Constitution, Wiley, 70; coauth, USA: An American Record, Holt, 72; co-ed, Growth of American Politics, Oxford Univ, 72. **CONTACT ADDRESS** Dept of Hist, Univ of California, Davis, Davis, CA 95616.

GOODRICH, THOMAS DAY
PERSONAL Born 00/00/1927, New York, NY, m, 1988, 6 children **DISCIPLINE** NEAR EASTERN STUDIES, HISTORY **EDUCATION** Univ Calif, Santa Barbara, BA, 52; Columbia Univ, MA, 53, PhD, 68. **CAREER** Prof Hist, Indiana Univ PA, 67-86. **HONORS AND AWARDS** 3 Fulbright Res Awds; The Newberry Libr Summer Grant, Yale Univ Libr Res Grant. **MEMBERSHIPS** Mid East Studies Asn; Turkish Studies Asn; Hist of Cartography; CIEPO; World Hist Asn. **RESEARCH** Ottoman history; 16th century; map history. **SELECTED PUBLICATIONS** Auth, Ottoman Americana, 90; auth, Goodrich, Luther, Carrington (1894-1986)--A Bibliography, J Am Orient Soc, Vol 0113, 93. **CONTACT ADDRESS** Dept of Hist, Indiana Univ of Pennsylvania, Indiana, PA 15701. **EMAIL** ottomantom@cs.com

GOODSTEIN, JUDITH RONNIE
PERSONAL Born 07/08/1939, Brooklyn, NY, m, 1960, 2 children **DISCIPLINE** HISTORY OF SCIENCE **EDUCATION** Brooklyn Col, BA, 60; Univ Wash, PhD(hist), 69. **CAREER** Univ archivist, 68-, fac assoc, Calif Inst Technol, 82-, registrar, 89-. **MEMBERSHIPS** Hist Sci Soc, Sigma Xi. **RESEARCH** Italian science since 1860; 20th century science. **SELECTED PUBLICATIONS** Auth, Sir Humphry Davy: Chemical Theory and the Nature of Matter, Univ Wash, 69; Richard Chace Tolman, In: Dict of American Biography, Suppl 4, Scribner's, 74; Levi-Civita, Einstein and Relativity in Italy, Atti Rend Acc Naz Lincei, 75; ed, The Robert Andrews Millikan Collection at the California Institute of Technology, Guide to a Microfilm Edition, Archives, Calif Inst Technol, 77; Sci & Caltech in the Turbulent Thirties, Calif Hist, 81; co-ed, The Theodore von Karman Collection at the California Institute of Technology, Guide to the Original Collection and a Microfiche Edition, Archives, 81; coauth, Caltech's Throop Hall, Castle Press, 81; auth, The Rise and Fall of Vito Volterra's World, J Hist of Ideas, 45, 84; Millikan's School: A History of the California Institute of Technology, W. W. Norton, 91; coauth, Feynman's Last Lecture: The Motion of Planets Around the Sun, W. W. Norton, 96; auth, A Conversation with Hans Bethe, Physics in Perspective, 1, 99. **CONTACT ADDRESS** California Inst of Tech, 1201 E California, Pasadena, CA 91125-0002. **EMAIL** jrg@cco.caltech.edu

GOODWIN, G. F.
DISCIPLINE HISTORY **EDUCATION** Univ Va, BA, 65; Princeton Univ, PhD, 78. **CAREER** Assoc prof, Carleton Univ. **RESEARCH** The Democratic Party in the 1920s, J. B. Matthews; United States foreign and domestic politics in the 1920s and 1930s. **SELECTED PUBLICATIONS** Rev, "Power and Prominence in Washington, D.C.," Can Rev Amer Stud, Vol 16, 85. **CONTACT ADDRESS** Dept of Hist, Carleton Univ, 1125 Colonel By Dr, Ottawa, ON, Canada K1S 5B6. **EMAIL** history@carleton.ca

GOODWIN, JOANNE
DISCIPLINE HISTORY **EDUCATION** Univ Mich, PhD, 91. **CAREER** Assoc prof, Univ Nev Las Vegas. **RESEARCH** American women history; social history. **SELECTED PUBLICATIONS** Auth, Gender and the Politics of Welfare Reform, Univ Chicago, 97. **CONTACT ADDRESS** History Dept, Univ of Nevada, Las Vegas, 4505 Md Pky, Las Vegas, NV 89154.

GOOTENBERG, PAUL
PERSONAL Born 10/01/1954, Washington, DC, m, 1996, 1 child **DISCIPLINE** HISTORY **EDUCATION** Univ Chicago, BA, 78, PhD, 85; Univ Oxford, St. Anthony's Col, Mphil, 81. **CAREER** Vis asst prof hist, Univ Ill at Chicago, 85-86; mem, Sch of Soc Sci, Inst for Advan Study, 86-87; asst prof Latin Am His, Brandeis Univ, 87-90; vis scholar, Comt on Latin Am and Iberian Studies, Harvard Univ, 90; prof hist, SUNY at Stony Brook, 90-; vis prof, comt hist studies, The New Sch for Soc Res, 95; vis scholar, Russel Sage found, 96. **HONORS AND AWARDS** Rhodes Scholar, Oxford Univ; Searle Grad Fel, Univ Chicago; Int Doctoral Res Fel, Soc Sci Res Coun; Fulbright-Hays Diss Res Abroad Awd; Soc Sci Res Coun, Postdoctoral Awd; res fel for recent recipients of the PhD, Am Coun of Learned Soc; Best Article in Latin Am Studies Awd, NECLAS; John M. Olin Fac Fel Hist; Joseph T. Crescenti Best Article Prize, NECLAS; H.G. Davis Best Article Prize; Honorable Mention, NECLAS Best Article Awd; John Simon Guggenheim Mem Fel; Res Prize, Lindesmith Ctr/Open Soc Inst; Advan Res Awd, Soc Sci Res Coun. **MEMBERSHIPS** CLAH-Am His Asn; Latin Am Studies Asn. **RESEARCH** Latin American history 1400-1990; economic history and development; Andean history; Mexican history; colonial Latin America; historical polititical economics of Latin America; European expansion; Latin American-United States relations 1823-1973; drugs in history. **SELECTED PUBLICATIONS** Auth, Population and Ethnicity in Early Republican Peru: Some Revisions, Latin Am Res Review, 26/3, 91; auth, Imagining Development: Economic Ideas in Peru's Fictitious Prosperity of Guano' 1825-1840, Univ Calif Press, 93; aitj. Guano Industry, in Encyclopedia of Latin Am Hist & Culture, 95; auth Caudillismo, Encyclopedia of Soc Hist, 95; auth, Order(s) and Progress in Developmental Discourse: A Case of Nineteenth-Century Peru, Jorn of Hist Sociology, 8/2, 95; auth, Not So Liberal: Protecionist Peru, Latin America and the World Economy: Dependence and Beyond, 96; auth, On Salamanders, Pyramids, and Mexico's 'Growth-without-Change': Anachronistic Reflections on a Case of Bourbon New Spain, Colonial Latin Am Review, 5/1, 96; auth, Paying for Caudillos: The Politics of Emergency Finance in Peru, 1820-45, Liberals, Politics & Power: State Formation in 19th-Century Latin America, Univ Ga Press, 96; auth, Order(s) and Progress in Developmental Discourse: A Case of Nineteenth-Century Peru, in Institute for Latin Am Studies London, 98; ed, Cocaine: Global Histories, Routledge, 99; ed, "Cocaine: Global Histories," Paul Gootenberg, Routledge, (99). **CONTACT ADDRESS** Dept of History Social Behavioral Sciences Bldg, SUNY, Stony Brook, Stony Brook, NY 11794-4348. **EMAIL** paul.gootenberg@sunysb.edu

GORANSON, STEPHEN
PERSONAL Born 11/05/1950, Surrey, England **DISCIPLINE** RELIGION AND HISTORY **EDUCATION** Brandeis Univ, BA, 72; Duke Univ, PhD, 90. **CAREER** Wake Forest Univ; Univ NC Wilmington; NC State Univ; vis asst prof/vis scholar, Duke Univ, 98-. **SELECTED PUBLICATIONS** Auth, Essene Polemic in the Apocalypse of John, Legal Texts, Legal Issues, Proceedings of the Second Meeting of International Organization for Qumran Studies, Cambridge 1995: Published in Honour of Joseph M. Baumgarten, Cambridge, England, STJD, 23, Leiden, E. J. Brill, 97; auth, The Text of Revelation 22:14, New Testament Studies, 97; auth, 7 vs. 8--The Battle Over the Holy Day at Dura-Europos, Bible Rev, 96; auth, Inkwell, Ostracon with Maria Graffito, Sepphoris in Galilee: Crosscurrents of Culture, NC Mus of Art, 96; auth, The Exclusion of Ephraim in Rev. 7:4-8 and Essene Polemic Against Pharisees, Dead Sea Discoveries, 95; auth, Posidonius, Strabo, and Marcus Vipsanius Agrippa as Sources on Essenes, Jour of Jewish Studies, 94; auth, Sectarianism, Geography, and the Copper Scroll, Jour of Jewish Studies, 92; auth, Nazarenes and Ebionites, Anchor Bible Dict, 92; auth, Essenes: Etymology from 'asah, Revue de Qumran, 84; auth, Others and Intra-Jewish Polemic as Reflected in Qumran Texts, in: Dead Sea Scrolls After Fifty Years: A Comprehensive Assessment, vol. 2, Leiden: Brill, 99. **CONTACT ADDRESS** 706 Louise Cir., #30-J, Durham, NC 27705. **EMAIL** goranson@duke.edu

GORDON, ALLAN M.
PERSONAL Born 08/31/1933, Seminole, OK, m **DISCIPLINE** ART HISTORY **EDUCATION** BA 1955; MA 1962; PhD 1969. **CAREER** CSUS CA, prof art 69-; OH U, tchg flw 66-69; Prairie View Clg, asst prof 64-66. **HONORS AND AWARDS** Awd for distinguished publications in Art Criticism Fisk Univ 1974-75; fellow Natl Endowment for the Humanities 1979; Distinguished Alumni Natl Conf of Blacks in Higher Educ 1989; SMAC Fel for Visual Artists, 95; Certificate of Recognition and Commendation, Sacramento County Baord of Supervisors, 95; Proclamation issued by Major of Sacramento, 96. **MEMBERSHIPS** Mem Natl Conf of Artists; Clg Art Assc of Am Inc; mem Alpha Phi Alpha Frat; mem NAACP; bd dirs Crocker Art Gallery Assc Sacramento 1970-74; bd dirs Amistad II Exhib Recip; Awards Comm Chair, Sacramento Metropolitan Arts Commn; College Art Association of America. **SELECTED PUBLICATIONS** Auth, Forever Free: Art by African American Women, 1862-1980, J. Bontemps, Ill, 81; auth, Echoes of Our Past: The Narrative Artistry of Palmer C Hayden 1988; auth, "Lenox Avenue, 1938," Lenox Avenue, A Jour of Interartistic Inquiry, Vol 1, Columbia Col; auth, A Visual heritage, 1945 to 1980: Bay Area African American Arists, Triton Mus of Art, Santa Clara, Calif, 97; auth, "The Art Ensemble of Chicago as Performance Art," Lenox Avenue: A Jour of Artistic Inquiry, Vol 3, Columbia Col, 97. **CONTACT ADDRESS** Art Dept, California State Univ, Sacramento, Sacramento, CA 95819. **EMAIL** gordee1@aol.com

GORDON, AMY GLASSNER
PERSONAL Born 02/12/1942, Brooklyn, NY, m, 1964, 2 children **DISCIPLINE** HISTORY **EDUCATION** Conn Col, BA, 63; Univ Chicago, MA, 64, PhD(hist), 74. **CAREER** Lectr hist, City Col New York, 67-68; instr, 68-69, asst prof, 70-72 & 75-78, assoc prof to prof hist, Denison Univ, 78-; Dean of Col, Denison Univ, 87-92. **HONORS AND AWARDS** Newberry Library Research Fellowship, NEH Summer Seminar Grant, Research Grants from Denison Univ and Denison Univ Research Found. **MEMBERSHIPS** Soc Hist Discoveries. **RESEARCH** Sixteenth century French Protestant colonization; Protestant theology and the Amerindians in the 16th century; family in early modern Europe. **SELECTED PUBLICATIONS** Auth, Confronting Cultures: The Effect of the Discoveries on 16th Century French Thought, 76; Mapping La Popeliniere's Thought: Some Geographical Dimensions, Terrae Incognitae, 77; History and Anthropology, J Mod Hist, 78; coauth, History, Values, and Simulation, Simulation in Higher Educ, 79; The First Protestant Missionary Effort: Why Did It Fail?, Int Bulletin of Missionary Research, 84; Autres Temps, Autres Moeurs: French Attitudes to Cultures Revealed by the Discoveries, In: Asia and the West Exchanges, The Age of Exploration, 86. **CONTACT ADDRESS** Dept of Hist, Denison Univ, 1 Denison University, Granville, OH 43023-1359. **EMAIL** gordona@cc.denison.edu

GORDON, BERTRAM M.
PERSONAL Born 04/19/1943, Brooklyn, NY, m, 1991, 2 children **DISCIPLINE** MODERN EUROPEAN HISTORY **EDUCATION** Brooklyn Col, BA, 63; Rutgers Univ, MA, 64, PhD(hist), 69. **CAREER** Lectr hist, Brooklyn Col, 67-69; asst prof, 69-76, assoc prof, 76-81, Prof Hist, Mills Col, 81-, Actg Provost, 98-, Res grant, Am Philos Soc, 74; vis assoc prof, Calif State Univ, Dominguez Hills, 78-79. **HONORS AND AWARDS** Cert Merit, Western Soc French Hist, 75. **MEMBERSHIPS** AHA, Soc Fr Hist Studies, Western Soc Fr Hist, Assoc Int d'Histoire Contemporaine de l'Europe; Assoc Francaise de Recherche sur l'Histoire du Cinema; French Colonial hiat Soc. **RESEARCH** Fascism and collaboration in wartime france, 1940-1944; Fascism and youth; food in history; history of tourism. **SELECTED PUBLICATIONS** Auth, "Collaboration, Retribution, and Crimes against Humanity: the Touvier, Bousquet, and Papon Affairs," Contemporary French Civilization 19:2 (95): 250-274; auth, "Afterward: Who Are The Guitly and Should They Be Tried?" Memory, the holocaust, and French Justice, Hanover New Hampshire: Univ Press of New England, (96): 179-198; auth, "Ist Gott Franzosisch? Germans, Tourism, and Occupied France, 1940-1944," Modern and Contemporary France, NS4:3 (96): 287-298; auth, "Warfare and Tourism: Paris in World War II," Annals of Tourism Research 25:3 (98): 616-638; auth, "The Eyes of the Marcher, Paris, May 1968, Theory and Its Consequences," in Gerard Jan de Groot, ed., Student Protest from the 1960s to the Present, Harlow, Essex UK: Addison Wesley Longman (98): 39-53; auth, "Going Abroad to Taste: North Americans, France and the Continental Tour from the Late Nineteenth Century to the Present," Proceedings of the Western Society for French History: Selected Papers of the Annual Meeting, Greeley, Colorado: University Press of Colorado, (98): 156-170; auth, "World War II France Half a Century After: In Historical Perspective," in Richard J. Golsan, ed., Fascism's Return: Scandal, Revision, and Ideology, Lincoln: University of Nebraska Press, (98): 152-181; auth, "Right Wing Historiographical Models in France from World War I through World War II," in Stefan Berger, Mark Donovan, and Kevin Passmore, eds., Writing National Histories: Western Europe Since 1800, London: Routledge (98): 163-175; auth, "The Decline of a Cultural Icon: Francin in American Perspective," French Hist Studies 22:4 (99): 625-651; auth, "The Countryside and the City: Some Notes on the Collaboration Model during the Vichy Period," in Sarah Fishman, France at War:

Vichy and the Historians, Oxford: Berg (00): 145-160. **CONTACT ADDRESS** Mills Col, 5000 MacArthur Blvd, PO Box 9962, Oakland, CA 94613-1000. **EMAIL** bmgordon@mills.edu

GORDON, DANIEL
PERSONAL Born 01/14/1961, Massachusetts, m, 1995, 2 children **DISCIPLINE** HISTORY **EDUCATION** Univ Chicago, PhD, 90. **CAREER** Assoc prof, Univ MA Amherst, 95; asst prof, Harvard, 91-95, vis prof, Col de France, 00. **RESEARCH** European history. **SELECTED PUBLICATIONS** Auth, The Idea of Sociability in Pre-Revolutionary France, 94; Transl, Voltaire's Candide, 99; ed, Postmodernism and the Enlightenment, 00. **CONTACT ADDRESS** Dept of Hist, Univ of Massachusetts, Amherst, Mass Ave, Amherst, MA 01003.

GORDON, JACOB U.
PERSONAL Born 10/25/1939, Nigeria, m, 1962, 4 children **DISCIPLINE** HISTORY **EDUCATION** Bethune Cookman Col, BA, 62; Howard Univ, MA, 64; Mich State Univ, PhD, 69. **CAREER** Instr, Rust Col, 64-66; assoc prof, Albany State Univ, 67-70; prof, Univ of Kans, 70-. **HONORS AND AWARDS** Teacher of the Year, Rust Col, 64; Hamline Univ Fel, 65; Scholar of the Year, Albany State Univ, 69; Steeples Fac Awd, 98; Kans African-Am Affairs Commission's Outstanding Leadership Awd, 98. **MEMBERSHIPS** Phi Alpha Theta Nat Honor Soc in Hist; Am His Soc; Assoc for the Study of African-Am Life and Hist; Kans Hist Soc; Assoc of African Studies; Am Assoc for the Advan of Humanities. **RESEARCH** African and African-American History. **SELECTED PUBLICATIONS** Auth, "A Culturally Specific Approach to Ethnic Minority Young Adults", Substance Abuse Treatment: A Family systems Perspective", ed Edith Freeman, Sage Pub, (93): 71-99; auth, "Black Leadership in Gang Movement: New Directions", Free Inquiry in Creative Sociol 25.1 (97): 51-58; auth, A Systems Change Approach to Substance Abuse Prevention, Edwin Mellen Pr, (Lewiston, NY), 97; auth, The African American Male: An Annotated Bibliography, Greenwood, (Westport, CT), 99; auth, An American Journey: The Civil Rights Movement, College Enterprise, (Atlanta, GA), 99; coauth, Search for Equal Justice by African American Lawyers: A History of the National Bar Association, Vantage Pr, (NY), 99; ed, The African-American Male in American Life and Thought", ANNALS of Am Acad of Polit Sci and Soc Sci, (00); auth, Black Leadership for Social Change, Greenwood Pub, (Westport, CT), 00. **CONTACT ADDRESS** Dept African and Afro-Am, Univ of Kansas, Lawrence, 1 Univ of Kans, Lawrence, KS 66045-0001.

GORDON, JOHN W.
PERSONAL Born 12/31/1943, Montgomery, AL, m, 1997, 2 children **DISCIPLINE** HISTORY **EDUCATION** The Citadel, BA, 66; Duke Univ, MA, 70; PhD, 74. **CAREER** Asst prof to prof, The Citadel, 74-; vis prof, U.S. Military Academy, West Point, 78-84, 88-93. **HONORS AND AWARDS** NEH, 78-82; Daniel Awd for Outstanding Teaching, 79; Commander's Awd for Pub Serv, West Point, 84; Writing Awd, US Army War Col Found, 92; Fac Achievement Awd, 94; Citadel Develop Found Fac Fel, 97-00; Who's Who Among Am Teachers, 98. **MEMBERSHIPS** AAUP; Int Inst for Strategic Studies, Phi Alpha Theta; Phi Kappa Phi; Kappa Delta Pi; SC Hist Soc; Marine Corps Univ Found; Wash Light Infantry; Army and Navy Club of Wash, DC; Atlantic Counc of the US. **RESEARCH** U.S. and British 20th Centtury Military history, Colonial American Revolutionary War. **SELECTED PUBLICATIONS** Coed, The Citadel Conferences on War and Diplomacy, 78; auth, The Other Desert War: British Special Forces in North Africa, 1940-1943, Greenwood, (Westport, CT), 87; "Orde Wingate", Churchill's Generals, ed John Keegan, Weidenfeld & Nicolson (London), 91; South Carolina and the American Revolution (forthcoming). **CONTACT ADDRESS** Dept Hist, The Citadel, The Military Col of So Carolina, 171 Moultrie St, Charleston, SC 29409-0001. **EMAIL** gordonb@citadel.edu

GORDON, LEONARD ABRAHAM
PERSONAL Born 01/17/1938, New York, NY, m, 1 child **DISCIPLINE** INDIAN HISTORY **EDUCATION** Amherst Col, BA, 59; Harvard Univ, MA, 61, PhD, 69. **CAREER** Asst prof hist, Columbis Univ, 67-73; assoc prof, 73-78, prof, hist, story, Brooklyn Col, 78-; Fulbright-Hays sr res fel, India, 71-72; vis assoc prof hist, Columbia Univ, 73-74; sr res assoc, Southern Asian Inst, Columbia Univ, 74-; dir and vpres, Taraknath Das Found, 86-. **HONORS AND AWARDS** Watumull Prize, AHA, 74. **MEMBERSHIPS** AHA; Asn Asian Studies. **RESEARCH** History of 20th century India; comparative partitions. **SELECTED PUBLICATIONS** Auth, Brothers Against the Raj: A Biography of Indian nationalists Sarat and Subhas Chandra Bose, columbia, 90; co-ed, India Briefing 1992, Westview, 92; auth, Subhas Chandra Bose: la Violence Liberatrice, Calcutta 1905-1971, Editions Autrement, 97; auth, Asias in Enlightenment and Early British Imperial Thought, Asia in Western and World History: A Guide for Teaching, Sharpe, 97; auth, Studying the History of South Asians in America, Indian Archives, 97; auth, Wealth Equals Freedom? The Rockefeller and Ford Foundations in India, The Annals, 97. **CONTACT ADDRESS** 276 Riverside Dr, New York, NY 10025. **EMAIL** lrgoc@cunyvm.cuny.edu

GORDON, LEONARD H. D.
PERSONAL Born 08/08/1928, New York, NY, m, 1951, 2 children **DISCIPLINE** MODERN CHINESE HISTORY **EDUCATION** Ind Univ, AB, 50, MA, 53; Univ Mich, PhD(hist EAsia), 61. **CAREER** Far Eastern diplomatic historian, US Dept State, 61-63; asst prof EAsian hist, Univ Wis, 63-67, res asst prof hist, Grad Sch, 63; Assoc Prof Chinese Hist, Purdue Univ, West Lafayette, 67-; Ed China sect, Newsletter, Asn Asian Studies, 66-68, ed, 68-71; mem preliminary screening comt, Foreign Area Fel Prog Asia, Joint Comt Soc Sci Res Coun and Am Coun Learned Soc, 71-72, mem nat screening comt, 72-73, 73-74. **HONORS AND AWARDS** Award for Educational Excellence, Purdue University, 86. **MEMBERSHIPS** Asn Asian Studies **RESEARCH** History of modern China; diplomatic history of China, 19th and 20th centuries; history of United States-China relations. **SELECTED PUBLICATIONS** Co-auth, All Under Heaven: Sun Yat-sen and His Revolutionary thought, Stanford, CA: Hoover Institution Press, 91; co-ed, Bibliography of Sun Yat-sen in China's Republican Revolution, 1885-1925, Lanham, MD: University Press of America, First Edition: 1991: 1991, Second Edition, 1998. **CONTACT ADDRESS** Dept of Hist, Purdue Univ, West Lafayette, West Lafayette, IN 47907. **EMAIL** lhdgordon@alumni.indiana.edu

GORDON, LINDA
PERSONAL Born 01/19/1940, Chicago, IL **DISCIPLINE** HISTORY **EDUCATION** Swarthmore Col, BA, Magna cum laude, 61; Yale Univ, MA, 63, PhD, With Distinction, 70. **CAREER** Asst, assoc and full prof, Univ of MA/Boston, 68-84; visiting prof, spring 84, Univ of Amsterdam; prof, 84-, Florence Kelley Prof, 90, Vilas Dist Res Prof, 93, Univ of Wis, Madison; Prof, Hist, NYork Univ, 99-; Eugene Lang vis prof, Swarthmore Col, spring 01. **HONORS AND AWARDS** Univ of MA Outstanding Achievement Awd, 82-83; Guggenheim Fel 83-84; Inst for Research on Poverty, res awards, 89-90, 90-91, 91-92; Joan Kelley Prize of the /aha, 88; Florence Kelley Professorship, 90; Vilas Research Professorship, 93; Berkshire Prize, 94; Honorary doctorage, SUNY-Binghamton, 97; Kittrell Memorial Lecture, Cornell, 97; Russel Sage Found, 97-98; Eleanor Roosevelt Lecture, Vassar Coll, 98; Bancroft Prize, 00; Beveridge Prized, 00; Willa Carter Prize, 00. **SELECTED PUBLICATIONS** Auth, Heroes of Their Own Lives: The Politics and History of Family Violence, 88; Pitied but not Entitled: Single Mothers and the Origins of Welfare, 94, paperback; Teenage Pregnancy and Out-of-Wedlock Birth, Morality and Health, 97; Family Resilience and Family Violence, Promoting Resiliency in Families and Children at Risk, 97; US Women's History, The New American History, 97; Reflections on the Concept of Patriarchy, Radical History Review, spring 98; How Welfare Became a Dirty Word, Journal of International and Comparative Social Welfare, 98; auth, The Great Arizona Orphan Abduction, 99; coed, Dear Sisters: Dispatches from the Women's Liberation Movement, 00. **CONTACT ADDRESS** Dept of History, New York Univ, 53 Washington Sq S, New York, NY 10012. **EMAIL** Linda.gordon@nyu.edu

GORDON, LYNN DOROTHY
PERSONAL Born 11/25/1946, New York, NY, m, 1981, 2 children **DISCIPLINE** AMERICAN HISTORY, WOMEN'S STUDIES **EDUCATION** Columbia Univ, AB, 68; Univ Chicago, MA, 74, PhD, 80. **CAREER** Teacher social studies, Sweet Home Jr High Sch, 69-73; assoc master of arts prog, Univ Chicago, 74-77; instr educ, Bowdoin Col, 77-78; instr hist, Northern Ill Univ, 79-80; lectr, Princeton Univ, 80-82; from asst prof to assoc prof Educ & Hist, 82-98; Assoc Dean Warner Grad Sch Educ, Univ Rochester, 89-91. **HONORS AND AWARDS** Loewenstein-Wiener Fel Am Jewish Arch, 84; Spencer Found Fel, 91-92; Flora Stone Mather Vis Prof, Case W Reserve Univ, 96. **MEMBERSHIPS** Orgn Am Historians; Nat Women's Studies Asn; Hist Educ Soc (Pres 93); Women Historians Midwest; Berkshire Conf Women Hist. **RESEARCH** History of education and higher education; women's hist; ethnicity and immigration; 20th Century Am Hist. **SELECTED PUBLICATIONS** Auth, Coeducation on two campuses: Berkeley and Chicago 1890-1912, Woman's Being, Woman's Place, 79; Women and the anti-child labor movement in Illinois, Compassion and Responsibility, Univ Chicago, 80; Gender & Higher Education in the Progressive Era, Yale Univ, 90; Why Dorothy Thompson Lost Her Job, Hist Educ Quart, Fall, 94; Race, Class and the Bonds of Womanhood at Spelman Seminary, 1881-1923, Hist Higher Educ Annual, 89. **CONTACT ADDRESS** Dept History, Univ of Rochester, Rochester, NY 14627. **EMAIL** lngo@troi.cc.rochester.edu

GORDON, MARY MCDOUGALL
PERSONAL Born Toowoomba, Australia **DISCIPLINE** UNITED STATES HISTORY **EDUCATION** Univ Sydney, BA, 50; Radcliffe Col, MA, 52; Univ Pittsburgh, PhD(hist), 74. **CAREER** Asst prof, Carnegie-Mellon Univ, 74-75; asst prof, 75-79, Assoc Prof US Hist, Univ Santa Clara, 79-, Dir Women's Studies Prog, 80-, Table leader advan placement, Am Hist and Educ Testing Serv; Andrew Mellon fel, Am Asn Univ Women, 69. **MEMBERSHIPS** AHA; Orgn Am Historians; Nat Women's Studies Asn; fel Am Asn Univ Women. **RESEARCH** Nineteenth century social and intellectual history; history of education. **SELECTED PUBLICATIONS** Auth, Patriots and Christians: A Reassessment of Nineteenth-Century School Reformers, J Social Hist, summer 78; Overland to California in 1849: A Neglected Commercial Enterprise, Pac Hist Rev (in prep). **CONTACT ADDRESS** Dept of Hist, Santa Clara Univ, Santa Clara, CA 95053.

GORDON, MICHAEL DANISH
PERSONAL Born 01/04/1943, Chicago, IL, m, 1964, 2 children **DISCIPLINE** EUROPEAN HISTORY **EDUCATION** Univ Chicago, BA, 64, MA, 65, PhD(hist), 72. **CAREER** Asst prof, 68-72, assoc prof, 72-80, Prof Hist, Denison Univ, 80-, Chmn Dept, 77-, Yale Univ fel hist, 74. **MEMBERSHIPS** AHA; Soc Span and Port Hist Studies; Am Soc for Legal Hist; Selden Soc. **RESEARCH** European legal history; 16th and 17th century Spanish history; Renaissance political thought. **SELECTED PUBLICATIONS** Auth, Jean Bodin and the English ship of state, Bibliot Humanisme et Renaissance, 73; The Arbitristas: An historiographical and bibliographical survey, Newslett of Soc Span & Port Hist Studies, 74; The science of politics in 17th century Spanish thought, Il Pensiero Politico, 74; The decline of Spain, J Mod Hist, 75; Morality, reform and the empire in 17th century Spain, Il Pensiero Politico, 77. **CONTACT ADDRESS** Dept of Hist, Denison Univ, 1 Denison University, Granville, OH 43023-1359.

GORDON-SEIFERT, CATHERINE
PERSONAL Born 01/13/1954, Columbus, OH, m, 1986, 2 children **DISCIPLINE** HISTORY OF MUSIC **EDUCATION** Univ of MI, PhD, 94, MM, 83; IN Univ, MM, 80; Bowling Green St Univ, BM, 76 **CAREER** Facul, 96-98, Boston Conserv of Music; Asst Prof, 98-, Providence Col **HONORS AND AWARDS** Disting Svc Awd for Graduating Sr; alpha lambda delta **MEMBERSHIPS** Am Musicol Asn; Sonneck Soc **RESEARCH** Opera **CONTACT ADDRESS** Dept of Music, Providence Col, Providence, RI 02918. **EMAIL** cgordon@providence.edu

GOREN, ARTHUR
PERSONAL Born 02/15/1926, Chelsea, MA, m, 1954, 2 children **DISCIPLINE** UNITED STATES HISTORY **EDUCATION** Hebrew Univ, BA, 57; Columbia Univ, PhD, 66. **CAREER** Knapp prof. **HONORS AND AWARDS** Jewish Cultural Achievement Awd in Histol Studies, National Foundation of Jewish Culture, 98. **RESEARCH** American Jewish history. **SELECTED PUBLICATIONS** Auth, New York Jews and the Quest for Community: The Kehillah Experiment 1908-1922, 70, Dissenter in Zion: From the Writings of Judah L. Magnes, 82. **CONTACT ADDRESS** Dept of History, Columbia Col, New York, 2960 Broadway, New York, NY 10027-6902. **EMAIL** aag3@columbia.edu

GORHAM, DEBORAH
PERSONAL Born New York, NY **DISCIPLINE** HISTORY **EDUCATION** McGill Univ, BA, 59; Univ Wisconsin, MA, 63; Univ Ottawa, PhD, 82. **CAREER** Asst prof, 69-78, assoc prof, 78-88, prof Hist, Carleton Univ, 88-, dir, Pauline Jewett Inst Women's Studs 94-. **HONORS AND AWARDS** Carleton Univ Scholarly Achievement Awd, 82, 86; Arts Fac Bd Tchr Awd, 87; 3M Can Inc, 87. **MEMBERSHIPS** Can Comt Women's Hist; Can Hist Asn; Can Friends Peace Now; Temple Israel. **RESEARCH** Nineteenth-and twentieth-century women's hist, Britain and North Am. **SELECTED PUBLICATIONS** Ed, Janice Williamson and Deborah Gorham, eds., "Up and Doing: Canadian Women and Peace," Toronto: The Women's Press, (90): 262; auth, "The Education of Vera and Edward Brittain: Class and gender in a late-Victorain and Edwardian family," in History of Education Review, Australia, Vol. 20, No. 1, (91): 20-38; auth, "The friendships of women: Friendship, feminism and achievement in Vera Brittain's life and work in the interwar decades," The Journal of Women's History, Vol. 3, No. 2, (92): 4-69; auth, "No Longer an Invisible Minority: Women Physicians and Medical Practice in Late Twentieth-Century North America," Diane Dodd and Deborah Gorham, eds., in Caring and Curing: Historical Perspectives on Women and Healing in Canada, Ottawa: Univ of Ottawa Press, (94): 183-211; ed, Caring and Curing: Historical Perspectives on Women and Healing in Canada, with Dianne Dodd and Deborah Gorham, eds., Ottawa: Univ of Ottawa Press, (94): 218; auth, "Vera Brittain: A Feminist Life," Oxford, U.K. and Cambridge, U.S.A., Blackwell Publishers, (96): 330; auth, "Women's Hist: Founding a New Field," in Beverly Boutilier and Alison Prentice, Creating Historical Memory: English-Canadian Women and the Work of History, Vancouver: UBC Press, 97. **CONTACT ADDRESS** Dept of History, Carleton Univ, 1125 Colonel By Dr, Ottawa, ON, Canada K1S 5B6. **EMAIL** dgorham@ccs.carleton.ca

GORIN, ROBERT M., JR
PERSONAL Born 10/29/1948, New York, NY **DISCIPLINE** HISTORY **EDUCATION** Xavier Univ, OH, AB, 70, MA, 70; Hofstra Univ, MS, 74; Fordham Univ, MA, 78; Saint Louis Univ, PhD, 80; Johns Hopkins Univ, MS, 93. **CAREER** Soc studies teacher, Bellmore-Merrick Central High Sch District, 74-83; soc studies teacher, Rockville Center UFSD, 77-78; soc studies teacher, Manhasset UFSD, 83-; adjunct asst prof, Hofstra Univ, 86-. **HONORS AND AWARDS** Phi Alpha Theta; Fel, Soc for Values in Higher Ed; Who's Who Among America's Teachers; Who's Who in America; papers presented at the Nat Coun for the Soc Studies meetings; prof ethics comt, 82-92

Nat Coun for the Soc Studies, chair, 86; Institutes: Gettysburg Col, Harvard Univ, Oxford Univ, Yale Univ. **MEMBERSHIPS** Org Am Hists, Southern Hist Asn, Nat Coun for the Soc Studies, Long Island and New York State Couns. **RESEARCH** American Civil War-19th century Anglo-American politics. **SELECTED PUBLICATIONS** Author of various newsletter articles. **CONTACT ADDRESS** Dept Hist, Hofstra Univ, 1000 Fulton Ave, Hempstead, NY 11550-1030.

GORMAN, CARMA

DISCIPLINE ART HISTORY **EDUCATION** Carleton Col, BA, 91; Univ CA, Berkeley, MA, 94, PhD, 98. **CAREER** Asst prof, School of Art & Design, Southern IL Univ, Carbondale IL, 98-. **HONORS AND AWARDS** Mellon Dissertation-Year Fel, UCB Regents Intern-fellowship, 92-95; Henry Luce/ACLS fel in Am Art, 96-97; Winterthur Res Fel, 96; Robert Wark fel, Huntington Library, 97. **MEMBERSHIPS** Am Studies Asn; Soc of Architectural Historians; Col Art Asn; Vernacular Architecture Forum. **RESEARCH** Am art, architecture, and design. **SELECTED PUBLICATIONS** Auth, Fitting Rooms: The Dress Designs of Frank Lloyd Wright, Winterthur Porfolio 30:4, winter 95. **CONTACT ADDRESS** School of Art & Design, So Illinois Univ, Carbondale, Carbondale, IL 62901-4301. **EMAIL** cgorman@siu.edu

GORMAN, MICHAEL J.

PERSONAL Born 11/03/1955, MD, m, 1976, 3 children **DISCIPLINE** NEW TESTAMENT, EARLY CHURCH HISTORY AND THEOLOGICAL ETHICS **EDUCATION** BA, Gordon Col, 77; M Div, Princeton Theol Sem, 82; PhD, 89. **CAREER** Tchg fel, 81-85, instr, 86, Princeton Theol Sem; adjunct facul, 91-93, assoc dean, 93, assoc prof, 93-98, acting dean, 94-95, dean, 95-, prof, 98-, Ecumenical Inst of Theol, St Mary's Sem & Univ Baltimore. **MEMBERSHIPS** Soc of Bibl Lit. **RESEARCH** NT/early Christian ethics; Paul; Abortion; Non-violence. **SELECTED PUBLICATIONS** Auth, Texts and Contexts, 89, 97; Abortion and the Early Church, 82; auth, The Elements of Exegesis, 00; auth, Cruciformity: Paul's Narrative Spirituality of the Cross, 00. **CONTACT ADDRESS** Ecumenical Institute of Theology, St. Mary's Sem and Univ, 5400 Roland Av., Baltimore, MD 21210. **EMAIL** mgorman@stmarys.edu

GORMAN, VANESSA

DISCIPLINE ANCIENT GREEK AND ROMAN HISTORY **EDUCATION** BYU, BA, 85; Univ of PA, MA, 88; Univ Pa, PhD, 93. **CAREER** Vis asst prof, Southern Methodist Univ, 93-94; asst prof, Univ of NE-Lincoln, 94-00; assoc prof, Univ of NE-Lincoln, 00. **HONORS AND AWARDS** NE Research Council, fac summer research fellow for travel, 95; cert of recognition for contributions to students from the UNL Parents Assoc and the UNL Tchng Council, 96 & 97; Col of Arts and Sciences Distinguished Tchng Awd, 00. **MEMBERSHIPS** Am Philological Assoc; Assoc of Ancient Historians; The Classical Assoc of the Mid-West and South; The Archaeological Inst of Am. **RESEARCH** Archaic and Classical Greek history; Ancient Epic. **SELECTED PUBLICATIONS** Auth, Aristotle's Hippodamos, Historia, 95; auth, Vergilian Models for the Characterization of Scylla in the Ciris, Vergilius, 95; co-auth, The Tyrants around Thoas and Damasenor, Classical Quarterly, forthcoming; auth, Lucan's Epic Aristeia and the Hero and of the Bellum Civile, Classical Journal, forthcoming; auth, Miletos, the Ornament of Ionia: A History of the City to 400 BCE, forthcoming from the U of M Press. **CONTACT ADDRESS** Dept of History, Univ of Nebraska, Lincoln, 619 Oldfather Hall, Lincoln, NE 68588-0327. **EMAIL** vgorman@unlinfo.unl.edu

GORN, ELLIOTT J.

PERSONAL Born 05/03/1951, Los Angeles, CA, d, 1 child **DISCIPLINE** HISTORY **EDUCATION** Berkeley, BA, 73; Yale Univ, PhD, 83. **CAREER** Univ Alabama; Miami Univ, Ohio; assoc prof, Am Social and Cultural Hist, Purdue Univ. **HONORS AND AWARDS** Guggenheim fel; Newberry Lib fel; Stanford Hum Ctr fel. **RESEARCH** American social and cultural history. **SELECTED PUBLICATIONS** Auth, The Manly Art: Bare-Knuckle Prize Fighting in America, Cornell, 86; co-ed, Constructing the American Past, Addison, Wesley, Longman, 90, 94, 98, 01; coauth, A Brief History of American Sports, Hill & Wang, 93; co-ed, the Encyclopedia of American Social History, 3 v, Scribners, 93; ed, Muhammad Ali: The People's Champ, Illinois, 96; ed, The McGuffey Readers: Selections from the 1879 Edition, Bedford, 98; auth, Mother Jones: The Most Dangerous Woman in America, Hill and Wang, 01. **CONTACT ADDRESS** Dept of History, Purdue Univ, West Lafayette, West Lafayette, IN 47907. **EMAIL** egorn@sla.purdue.edu

GORRELL, DONALD KENNETH

PERSONAL Born 01/24/1928, Cleveland, OH, m, 1951, 3 children **DISCIPLINE** CHURCH HISTORY **EDUCATION** Miami Univ, BA, 49; Western Reserve Univ, MA, 51, PhD, 60; Yale Univ, BD, 55. **CAREER** Minister to students, Ohio State Univ, 55-60; asst prof, 60-68; Prof Church Hist, United Theol Sem, Ohio, 68-93; secy, Gen Comn Arch and Hist, United Methodist Church, 68-72, 76-80 and 80-84. **HONORS AND AWARDS** Am Asn Theol Sch fac fel, 65-66; fel, Case-Study inst, Mass, 72. **MEMBERSHIPS** AHA; Am Soc Church Hist; Orgn Am Historians; World Methodist Hist Soc. **RESEARCH** Social Gospel in the Progressive Era, 1900-1920; American church history; United Methodist Church history; Women in church history. **SELECTED PUBLICATIONS** Contribr, Encycl of World Biography, McGraw-Hill, 73 & Encycl of World Methodism, Abingdon, 74; auth, The Methodist Federation for social service and the social creed, 1/75, Methodist Hist; ed, Woman's Rightful Place, United Theol Sem, 80; auth, A New Impulse, In: Women in New Worlds, Abingdon, 81; auth, "Ride A Circuit or Let It Alone," Methodist Hist, (86); auth, The Age of Social Responsibility, Mercer 88; contribr, Dictionary of the Ecumenica Movement, Eerdmans 91; auth, "The Social Creed and Methodism Through Eighty Years, In: Perspectives on American Methodism," (Abingdon, 93); contribr, Historical Dictionary of Methodism, Scarecrow, 96. **CONTACT ADDRESS** United Theol Sem, 1810 Harvard Blvd, Dayton, OH 45406.

GORSE, GEORGE L.

PERSONAL Born 01/06/1949, Ithaca, NY, m, 1978 **DISCIPLINE** ART HISTORY **EDUCATION** Brown Univ, PhD 80, MA 73; John Hopkins Univ, BA 71. **CAREER** Pomona Col, prof, Viola Horton Prof, 93-, assoc prof, asst prof, 80-93; Univ Pennsylvania, inst 79-80. **HONORS AND AWARDS** NEH; ACLS fel; Inst Adv Stud Princeton; Villa I Tatti, Florence **MEMBERSHIPS** CAA; SAH; RSA; SCSC. **RESEARCH** Genoese medieval; renaissance and baroque studies; hist of cities and gdns, villas and palaces. **SELECTED PUBLICATIONS** Auth, A Classical Stage for the Nobility: the Strada Nuova in Sixteenth-Century Genoa, Art Bull, 97. **CONTACT ADDRESS** Dept of Art and Art History, Pomona Col, 333 N College Way, Claremont, CA 91711. **EMAIL** ggorse@pomona.edu

GORSUCH, EDWIN N.

PERSONAL Born 08/28/1939, Wauseon, OH **DISCIPLINE** MEDIEVAL HISTORY **EDUCATION** Bowling Green State Univ, BS, 62, MA, 64; Ohio State Univ, PhD(hist), 67. **CAREER** Asst prof, 67-71, Assoc Prof Hist, GA State Univ, 71-. **MEMBERSHIPS** AHA. **RESEARCH** Medieval intellectual and economic history. **SELECTED PUBLICATIONS** Auth, Mismanagement and ecclesiastical visitation of English monasteries, Traditio, 72. **CONTACT ADDRESS** Dept of Hist, Georgia State Univ, 33 Gilmer St SE, Atlanta, GA 30303-3080.

GOSSELIN, EDWARD ALBERIC

PERSONAL Born 02/12/1943, Rutland, VT, m, 1970, 2 children **DISCIPLINE** RENAISSANCE HISTORY & HISTORY OF SCIENCE **EDUCATION** Yale Univ, BA, 65; Columbia Univ, MA, 66, PhD(hist), 73. **CAREER** Asst prof, 69-74, assoc prof, 74-79, Prof Hist, Calif State Univ, Long Beach, 79-, Assoc, Danforth Found, 73-; dir, Ctr Medieval and Renaissance Studies, 80-83. **MEMBERSHIPS** AHA; Renaissance Soc Am; Am Soc Reformation Res; Medieval Acad Am. **RESEARCH** Sixteenth century intellectual history; medieval, Renaissance and Reformation commentaries on the Psalms; Hermetism and 16th and 17th century science. **SELECTED PUBLICATIONS** Auth, A Listing of the Printed Editions of Nicolaus of Lyra, Traditio, 70; coauth, Was Giordano Bruno a scientist? A scientist's view, Am J Physics, 1/73; Giordano Bruno, Sci Am, 4/73; Galileo and the long shadow of Bruno, Archives Int Hist Sci, 12/75; auth, David in Tempore Belli: Beza's David in the service of the Huguenots, Sixteenth Century J, 10/76; The King's Progress to Jerusalem, Undena, 76; co-ed, Giordano Bruno, The Ash Wednesday Supper, Archon, 77. **CONTACT ADDRESS** Dept of Hist, California State Univ, Long Beach, 1250 N Bellflower, Long Beach, CA 90840-0001.

GOSSIN, PAMELA

PERSONAL Born 10/13/1956, Lincoln, NE, m, 4 children **DISCIPLINE** HISTORY OF SCIENCE & ENGL LIT **EDUCATION** Univ Wis, PhD, 89. **CAREER** Asst prof. **HONORS AND AWARDS** Howard Foundation Fellowship in History of Science; NEH Summer Stipend; Dudley Observatory Research Grant; Rockefeller Fellowship in Interdisciplinary Humanities. **RESEARCH** History of science and literature and science; women and science; scientific biography and autobiography; popularization of science; rhetoric of science; astronomy and literature. **SELECTED PUBLICATIONS** Auth, Literature and Science: An Encyclopedic Companion, Garland; Literature and Astronomy; Literature & Science, Guide Hist Lit, 94; auth, "An Encyclopedia of Literature & Science," Greenwood, forthcoming; auth, "Thomas Hardy's Novel Universe: Astronomy, Cosmology & the Cosmic Heroines of his Major & Minor Fichon, Ashgate, forthcoming; auth, "Literauture & The Modern Physical Sciences," in vol 5 of Cambridge History of Science, sem; ed., Mary Jo Nye; auth, "All Danae to the Stars: 19th C. Rpresentations of Women in the Cosmos," Victorian Studies, 96; auth, "Living Poetics, Enacting the Cosmos: Diane Ackerman's Popularization of Astronomy in the Planet: A Pastoral," Women's Stables. **CONTACT ADDRESS** Dept of Literary & Historical Studies, Univ of Texas, Dallas, Richardson, TX 75083-0688. **EMAIL** psgossin@utdallas.edu

GOSSMAN, NORBERT JOSEPH

PERSONAL Born 02/21/1924, Ridgeway, IA, m, 1949, 4 children **DISCIPLINE** HISTORY **EDUCATION** Univ Iowa, BA, 47, MA, 48, PhD(hist), 52. **CAREER** Instr hist, Coe Col, 52-53 and Whitman Col, 53-54; asst prof, Wis State Col, Eau Claire, 54-55; from asst prof to assoc prof, 55-69, Prof Hist, Univ Detroit, 69-, Chmn Dept, 77-, Res grant, Univ Detroit, 56 and 58; Soc Sci Res Coun grant, 57-58, Nat Endowment Humanities, 76. **MEMBERSHIPS** AHA; Conf Brit Studies; AAUP. **RESEARCH** English history, especially the 19th century Victorian period. **SELECTED PUBLICATIONS** Auth, Political and Social Themes in the English Popular Novel 1815-1832, Public Opinion Quart, 56; Republicanism in Nineteenth Century England, Int Rev Soc Hist, 62; coauth, Readings in Western Civilization, Brown, 64; auth, British Aid to Polish, Italian and Hungarian Exiles, 1830-1870, South Atlantic Quart, 69; Definitions of and Recent Writings on Modern British Radicalism, Brit Studies Monitor, 73; Origins of Modern British Radicalism: The Case for the 18th Century, Int Labor & Working Class Hist, 75; co-ed, Biographical Dictionary of Modern British Radicals, Harvester, 79. **CONTACT ADDRESS** 12654 Beaverland, Detroit, MI 48223.

GOTTLIEB, CARLA

PERSONAL Born 07/16/1912, Cernauti, Austria **DISCIPLINE** HISTORY OF ART, ARCHEOLOGY **EDUCATION** Carolina Univ, Cernauti, Licenta, 34; Columbia Univ, PhD(art), 51. **CAREER** Asst hist of art, Bryn Mawr Col, 54-56; prof, New Sch Social Res, NY, 56-60; assoc prof art & chair dept, Ripon Col, 60-62; assoc prof hist of art, Univ IL, Urbana, 62-64, cataloguer, Francois L Schwarz Collection, NY & Paris, 65-70; Curator, Samuel J Lefrak Collection, 67-77., mem fac, sem in mod art, Sarah Lawrence Col, 58-59; sr researcher, Albright-Knox Art Gallery, Buffalo, NY, 71; vis prof, Carleton Univ, 72. **HONORS AND AWARDS** Travel and Research Grants: Univ Grant Carolina Univ, Cernauti 33; Univ Grant Columbia Univ NY, 52; Am Phil Soc, 53, 54; de Rothchild Found, 54; Am Asn Univ Women, 57-58; Univ IL, 63, 64; Colloquia: Am Council Learned Soc Participant Athens Greece, 60; UNAM participant Xalapa, Mexico, 77. **MEMBERSHIPS** AAUP; Auth Guild; Auth League Am; Yad Vashem, Jerusalem, Israel; Dorot Inc, NY, Programs for the Elderly; Oxford Medicare Advantage; Hamilton Senior Center, Project Find; Dem Congress Campaign Comm. **RESEARCH** Modern Art; aesthetics; iconology. **SELECTED PUBLICATIONS** Auth, Death and modern art, In: The Meaning of Death, McGraw, 59, 65; contrib, Harmony and discord in the visual arts, In: Acts IV International Congress of Aesthetics, Athens, 1960, Menas D Myrtides, Athens, 62; auth, Respiciens per fenestras: The symbolism of the Merode altarpiece, Oud Holland, 70; En ipse stat post parietem nostrum: The symbolism of the Ghent Annuniciation, Bull des Musees Royal des Beaux-Arts de Belgique, 70; Beyond Modern Art, Dutton, 74; Fanny Sanin, Profile, 77; From the Window of God to the Vanity of Man, Abaris, 78; Self-Portraiture: From Ancient Egypt to World War II, Dutton, 82; The Window as a Symbol in Western Painting: From Divinity to Doubt, Boian, 82; The Window in the Soap Bubble as Illustration of Psalm 26, Wallraf-Richartz-Jahrbuch vol 43, 82; The Bewitched Mirror Coloquio/Artes vol 71, 2d ser 28, 86; The Window as a Symbol in Western Painting: From Divinity to Doubt (in progress); Self-Portraiture: From Ancient Egypt to WWII (in progress); The Window in Painting: A Study of Its Morphology as a Basis for Motif Classification (in progress); Speech, God's Punishment for Man's Sin (in progress). **CONTACT ADDRESS** 246 W End Ave Apt 10B, New York, NY 10023.

GOTTSCHALK, PETER

DISCIPLINE HISTORY OF RELIGION **EDUCATION** Col of the Holy Cross, BA, 85; Univ Wis, MA, 89; Univ Chicago, PhD, 97. **CAREER** Asst prof, Southwestern Univ, 97- . **MEMBERSHIPS** AAR; AAS **RESEARCH** Narrative, identity, Hinuism, and Islam in South Asia; Time and space in religion. **CONTACT ADDRESS** Dept of Religions, Southwestern Univ, Box 6318, Georgetown, TX 78756. **EMAIL** gottschp@southwestern.edu

GOUGH, JERRY B.

DISCIPLINE EARLY BRITAIN HISTORY **EDUCATION** Cornell Univ, PhD, 71. **CAREER** Assoc prof, Washington State Univ. **RESEARCH** Chemistry and wine technology in the 18th century. **SELECTED PUBLICATIONS** Ed, The Plutonium Story: The Journals of Professor Glenn T. Seaborg 1939-1946, Battelle Press, 94. **CONTACT ADDRESS** Dept of History, Washington State Univ, 301 Wilson Hall, PO Box 644030, Pullman, WA 99164-4030. **EMAIL** gough@wsu.edu

GOULD, ELIGA H.

DISCIPLINE COLONIAL AND REVOLUTIONARY AMERICA, MODERN BRITAIN, HISTORY OF THE BRITISH **EDUCATION** Johns Hopkins Univ, PhD. **CAREER** Asst prof, assoc prof, Univ NH, 93-. **HONORS AND AWARDS** Charles Warren fel, Harvard Univ, 97-98; NEH; Fulbright-Hays; Huntington Libr fel; Clark Libr fel; Jamestown Prize of the Omohundro Inst of Early Am Hist and Cult. **RESEARCH** Civilizing nature. **SELECTED PUBLICATIONS** Auth, "To Strengthen the King's Hands: Militia Reform, Dynastic Legitimacy and Ideas of National Unity in England, 1745-60," Hist

J (91); auth, "American Independence and the Cosmopolitan Foundations of Britain's First Counterrevolution," Past and Present 154 (97); auth, "A Virtual Nation: Greater Britain and the Imperial Legacy of the American Revolution," American Historical Review (99); auth, "What is the Country? Patriotism and the Language of Popularity during the English Militia Riots of 1757," in The Country and the City Revisited: England and the Politics of Culture, 1560-1840, ed. Donna Landry, et al. (Cambridge Univ Press, 99); auth, The Persistence of Empire: British Political Culture in the Age of the American Revolution, Univ of North Carolina Press, 00. **CONTACT ADDRESS** Univ of New Hampshire, Durham, Durham, NH 03824. **EMAIL** ehg@christa.unh.edu

GOULD, LEWIS LUDLOW
PERSONAL Born 09/21/1939, New York, NY, m, 1970 **DISCIPLINE** AMERICAN POLITICAL HISTORY **EDUCATION** Brown Univ, AB, 61; Yale Univ, MA, 62, PhD(hist), 66. **CAREER** From instr to asst prof Hist, Yale Univ, 65-67; from asst prof to assoc prof, 67-76, prof Hist, Univ Tex, Austin, 76-83, chmn dept, 80-84, Eugene C Barker Centennial prof, American History, Univ Tex, Austin, 83-98; Fel, Nat Endowment for Humanities, 74. **HONORS AND AWARDS** Carr P Collins Prize, Tex Inst Letters, 74. **MEMBERSHIPS** AHA; Orgn Am Historians; Southern Hist Asn. **RESEARCH** American political history, 1880-1920; First Ladies. **SELECTED PUBLICATIONS** Auth, Wyoming: A Political History, 1868-1896, Yale Univ, 68; co-ed, The Black Experience in America: Selected Essays, 70 & auth, Progressives and Prohibitionists Texas Democrats in the Wilson Era, 73, Univ Tex; ed, The Progressive Era, Syracuse Univ, 74; co-auth, Photojournalist: The Career of Jimmy Har, Univ Tex, 77; auth, Reform and Regulation: American Politics, 1900-1916, Wiley, 78; The presidency of William McKinley, Kansas, 80; auth, Lady Bird Johnson and The Environment, 88; auth, 1968: The Election That Changed America, 93; ed, American First Ladies, 96; auth, The Presidency of Theodore Roosevelt, 91; The Life and Times of Frances Goff, 97; coed, Inside the Natchez Trace Collection, 99; auth, Lady Bird Johnson: Our Environmental First Lady, 99; auth, America in the Progressive Era, 1890-1914, 01. **CONTACT ADDRESS** 2602 La Ronde, Austin, TX 78731-5924.

GOUMA-PETERSON, THALIA
DISCIPLINE ANCIENT AND MEDIEVAL ART **EDUCATION** Mills Col; BA, 54, MA, 57; Univ Wis, PhD, 64. **CAREER** Prof emer, Col of Wooster. **HONORS AND AWARDS** Lifetime Achievement Awd (Women's Caucus For Art). **SELECTED PUBLICATIONS** Ed, auth, monograph on Flack, Harry N Abrams, 92; ed, Bibliography on Women in Byzantium; extensive pubs on Byzantine icons and wall paintings; auth, Monograph on Miriam Schapiro, Harry N. Abrams, 99. **CONTACT ADDRESS** 394 Edgemeer Pl, Oberlin, OH 44074. **EMAIL** tgoumapeterson@oberlin.net

GOVAN, SANDRA YVONNE
PERSONAL Born 07/28/1948, Chicago, IL, s **DISCIPLINE** ENGLISH; AFRICAN AMERICAN STUDIES **EDUCATION** Valparaiso University, Valparaiso, IN, BA, 1970; Bowling Green University, Bowling Green, OH, MA, 1972; Emory University, Atlanta, GA, PhD, 1980. **CAREER** Luther College, Decorah, IA, instructor, 72-75; University of Kentucky, Lexington, KY, assistant professor, 80-83; University of North Carolina, Charlotte, NC, associate professor, 83-. **HONORS AND AWARDS** Schomburg Scholar in Residence, NEH, Schomburg Center for Research in Black Culture, 1990-91; Outstanding Alumni Awd, Valparaiso University, 1982; National Fellowship Fund Awd, Ford Foundation, 1976-80; Emory University Fellowship, 1975. **MEMBERSHIPS** Member, Association for the Study of African American Life and History; member, Modern Language Association, 1980-; member, College Language Association, 1975-; member, Langston Hughes Society; dir, Ronald E McNair Postbaccalaureate Achievement Program. **RESEARCH** African-American Literature; Science Fiction. **SELECTED PUBLICATIONS** Essays contributed to: Erotique Noire, Sexual Politics, Langston Hughes: The Man, His Art & His Continuing Influence, Notable Black American Woman VI & VII, Notable Black American Man, My Soul is a Witness: African American Women's Spiritly, Fatner Songs: testimonies by African American Sons and Daughter, Novello Anthology: 10 Years of Graf American Writing. **CONTACT ADDRESS** Professor of English, Univ of No Carolina, Charlotte, Charlotte, NC 28223. **EMAIL** sygovan@email.uncc.edu

GOWANS, ALAN
PERSONAL Born 11/30/1923, Toronto, ON, Canada, m, 1948, 4 children **DISCIPLINE** HISTORY OF ART **EDUCATION** Univ Toronto, BA, 45, MA, 46; Princeton Univ, MFA, 48, PhD, 50. **CAREER** Instr hist art, Rutgers Univ, 48-49, asst prof, 50-53; asst prof, Middlebury Col, 53-54; dir, Fleming Mus, Vt, 54-56; from assoc prof to prof hist art, Univ Del, 56-66, chmn dept, 56-66; prof hist in art & chmn dept, Univ Victoria, BC, 66-81; Fel, Ctr for Adv Study, Nat Gallery of Art, Washington, DC, 81-, Vis prof art hist, Harvard Univ, 72-73; Univ Uppsala, 77-78 & George Washington Univ, 81-83. **MEMBERSHIPS** Soc Archit Hist (secy, 59-63, vpres, 69-71, pres, 71-74). **RESEARCH** Social function of arts, especially popular arts; cross-cultural studies of world civilization; American and Canadian architectural history. **SELECTED PUBLICATIONS** Auth The Comfortable House: Surburban Architecture in North American 1890-1930, MIT Press, 86; Sainte-Croix d'Orleans: A Major Monument too long neglected, Gazette des Beaux-Arts (Paris), 88; Pradigmatic Social Function in Anglican Church Architecture of the Fifteen Colonies, Studies in Art History , Johns Hopkins & Nat Gallery of Art, 89; Styles and Types of North American Architecture: Social Function and Cultural Expression, Harper Collins, 92; Fruitful Fields: Churches of the Aamerican Mission to Hawaii1820-1863, Honolulu: State Historic Preservation Office, 93. **CONTACT ADDRESS** 524-2020 F St NW, Washington, DC 20006.

GOWASKIE, JOSEPH M.
PERSONAL Born 09/27/1942, Menominee, MI, m, 1964, 1 child **DISCIPLINE** HISTORY **EDUCATION** St Norbert Col, BA, 64; Catholic Univ Am, MA, 66; PhD, 69. **CAREER** From asst prof to prof, Rider Univ, 71-. **HONORS AND AWARDS** Distinguished Teaching Awd, Rider Col, 76. **MEMBERSHIPS** Orgn of Am Historians. **RESEARCH** American Labor History. **SELECTED PUBLICATIONS** Auth, "From Conflict to Cooperation: John Mitchell and the Bituminous Coal Operators, 1898-1908," The Historian 38 (76): 669-688; auth, "Charisma in the Coal Fields: John Mitchell and the Anthracite Mine Workers, 1899-1902," Proceedings of the Canal Hist and Technol Symposium vol 4 (85); auth, "The Teaching of World History: A Status Report," The Hist Teacher 18 (85): 365-375; auth, "John Mitchell and the Anthracite Mine Workers: Leadership Conservatism and Rank-and-File Militance," Labor Hist 27 (Winter 85-86): 54-84; auth, "Deindustrialization: A Panel Discussion," Pa Hist 58 (91): 181-211; auth, Workers in New Jersey History, NJ Hist Comn, 96. **CONTACT ADDRESS** Dept Hist, Rider Univ, 2083 Lawrenceville Rd, Trenton, NJ 08648-3001.

GOWER, CALVIN WILLIAM
PERSONAL Born 11/14/1926, Delta, CO, m, 1962, 1 child **DISCIPLINE** AMERICAN HISTORY **EDUCATION** Western State Col, BA, 49; Univ SDak, MA, 50 Univ Kans, PhD(Western Am hist),59. **CAREER** From asst prof to assoc prof, 57-66; chmn dept, 62-70, Prof Am Hist, St Cloud State Univ, 66-. **MEMBERSHIPS** AHA; Orgn Am Historians; Western Hist Asn. **RESEARCH** Kansas territory and the Pikes Peak gold rush; the Civilian Conservation Corps, 1933-1942; forest conservation in Minnesota. **SELECTED PUBLICATIONS** Auth, Circles of Tradition--Fine-Arts in Minnesota, J the W, Vol 0032, 93. **CONTACT ADDRESS** Dept of Hist, St. Cloud State Univ, Saint Cloud, MN 56301.

GRABOWSKA, JAMES A.
DISCIPLINE MEDIEVAL STUDIES **EDUCATION** Northern State Univ, BS, 82; Univ OK, MA, 91; Univ MN; PhD, 96. **CAREER** Hist, Col St. Benedict. **HONORS AND AWARDS** Phi Kappa Phi, 90; M.J. Meixner Scholarship, 92; Herbert Garvin Scholarship, 93; Fulbright-Hays Scholarship, 94; Herbert Garvin and Bambenek Scholarship, 95; Dissertation Fel, 95. **MEMBERSHIPS** MLA, SCMLA. **SELECTED PUBLICATIONS** Auth, A Multimedia Critical Reader's Guide to Cervantes' Don Quixote, Pending, 97. **CONTACT ADDRESS** Col of Saint Benedict, Saint Joseph, MN 56374-2099. **EMAIL** jgrabowska@csbsju.edu

GRAD, BONNIE L.
PERSONAL Born 06/01/1949, New York, NY, m, 1980, 2 children **DISCIPLINE** ART HISTORY **EDUCATION** Cornell Univ, BA, 71; Univ Va, PhD, 77. **CAREER** Art instr, Cincinnati Art Mus, 67, 68; teaching asst, Univ Va, 73-74; collections asst, Graphic Arts Collection, Princeton Univ, 76-77; asst prof, 77-83, assoc prof, Clark Univ, 83-. **HONORS AND AWARDS** Fulbright-Hayes grant, 74-75; NEH grants, 80-83; Mellon and Higgins grants, Clark Univ, 84-95; Richard A. Florsheim Art Fund grant, 93-94; Seymour N. Logan Facul fel, Clark Univ, 92-94; vis scholar, Pollock-Krasner House and Studies Ctr, 94, 97. **MEMBERSHIPS** Col Art Asn; New England Fulbright Asn. **RESEARCH** Nineteenth and twentieth century art; Landscape painting; Georgia O'Keeffe. **SELECTED PUBLICATIONS** Auth, Georgia O'Keeffe, The Archives of Amer Art Jour, 98; auth, Robert Richenburg: Abstract Expressionist, 94; auth, Stuart Davis, Artibus et Historiae, 91; co-auth, Visions of City and Country: Prints and Photographs of Nineteenth Century France, 82; auth, Milton Avery, 81; auth, Charles Francois Daubigny, The Print Collector's Newsletter, 79. **CONTACT ADDRESS** 21 Willard Rd., Weston, MA 02493. **EMAIL** bonniegrad@aol.com

GRAEBNER, ALAN
PERSONAL Born 08/06/1938, Pittsburgh, PA, m, 1958 **DISCIPLINE** AMERICAN HISTORY **EDUCATION** Valparaiso Univ, BA, 59; Columbia Univ, MA, 61, PhD(hist), 65. **CAREER** Asst prof, Concordia Col, Morrhead, Minn, 64-69; Assoc Prof Hist, Col St Catherine, 69-. **RESEARCH** Women and the family in American history; health professions. **SELECTED PUBLICATIONS** Auth, Birth control and the Lutherans, J Soc Hist, summer 69; After Eve: The New Feminism, Augsburg, 72; Uncertain Saints, The Laity in the Lutheran Church-Mo Synod, 1900-1970, Greenwood, 75. **CONTACT ADDRESS** Dept of Hist, Col of St. Catherine, 2004 Randolph Ave, Saint Paul, MN 55105-1789.

GRAF, DANIEL WILLIAM
PERSONAL Born 09/20/1940, La Crosse, WI, m, 1967, 2 children **DISCIPLINE** MODERN EUROPEAN HISTORY **EDUCATION** Univ Wis-La Crosse, BS, 65; Univ Nebr, Lincoln, MA, 67, PhD(hist), 72. **CAREER** Asst hist Univ Nebr-Lincoln, 65-67, assoc, 68-69; asst prof, 70-80, Prof Hist, VA Weskeyan Col, 80-. **MEMBERSHIPS** AHA; Am Asn Advan Slavic Studies. **RESEARCH** Twentieth century Russian society and institutions; reign of Nicholas II and the revolutions of 1917. **SELECTED PUBLICATIONS** Auth, Military rule behind the Russian front, 1914-1917: The political ramifications, Jahrbuecher fuer Geschichte Osteuropas, 74. **CONTACT ADDRESS** Dept of Hist, Virginia Wesleyan Col, 1584 Wesleyan Dr, Norfolk, VA 23502-5599.

GRAF, DAVID FRANK
PERSONAL Born 12/03/1939, Detroit, MI, m, 1963, 2 children **DISCIPLINE** ANCIENT HISTORY (NEAR EAST, GREECE, ROME) **EDUCATION** Harding Col , BA, 65; McCormick Theological Seminary, BD (with honors), 70; Univ Mich, Near Eastern Languages, MA, 75, History, PhD, 79. **CAREER** Assoc ed, Biblical Archeol, Amer Schools Oriental Research, 80-82; visiting lecturer, Univ Mich, Dept Near Eastern Studies, 82-83, adjunct lecturer, Program on Studies in Religion, 84-86; adjunct asst prof, Montana State Univ, Dept History & Philos, 83-84; asst prof, 86-90, assoc prof, 90-95, prof, 95-, Univ Miami, Dept History. **HONORS AND AWARDS** Senior Fellow, Dumbarton Oaks, 93; summer res grant, NEH, 94; Amer Schools of Oriental Research Archeol Grant, 95; Phi Beta Delta Honor Soc for Intl Scholars, 97; life-time member, chap pres, 97-98, Phi Kappa Phi Honor Soc. **MEMBERSHIPS** Am Inst Archeol; Am Schools Oriental Research; Asn Ancient Historians; ARAM: Syro-Mesopotamian Soc. **RESEARCH** Greco-Roman Near East history, especially Roman Arabia; Roman roads; inscriptions; Greek-Persian relations. **SELECTED PUBLICATIONS** Auth, "Medism," Journal of Hellenic Studies, vol. 104, 84; co-auth, "The Roman East from the Chinese Perspective," Palmyra and the Silk Road: Les Annales Archeologiques Arabes Syriennes, vol. 42, 96; auth, "The Via Militarias in Arabia," Dumbarton Oaks Papers, vol 51, 97; "Camels, Roads, and Wheels in Late Antiquity," Donum Amicitiae, 97; "The Via Militarias and Limes Arabicus," Roman Frontier Studies 1995, 97; Rome and Its Arabian Frontier from the Nabataeans to the Saracens, 97; auth, "Camel, Roads, and Wheels," in Late Antiquity, Donum Amixitiae, 97; auth, "Town and Countryside in Roman Arabia during Late Antiquity," in Urban Centers and Rural Contexts in Late Antiquity, ed. T. Burns and J. Eadie, 01. **CONTACT ADDRESS** Dept of History, Univ of Miami, PO Box 248107, Coral Gables, FL 33124-4662. **EMAIL** Dgraf@miami.edu

GRAFF, HARVEY J.
PERSONAL Born 06/19/1949, Pittsburgh, PA, m **DISCIPLINE** HISTORY **EDUCATION** Nwestern Univ, BA, 70; Univ Toronto, MA, 71, PhD, 75. **CAREER** Instructor, Northwestern Univ, 73; Extramural Lecturer, 74-75; Asst to Assoc, Univ of Tex at Dallas, 75-98; Vis Adunct Prof, Loyola Univ, 80; Vis Prof, Simon Fraser Univ, 81, 82; Dir, Uiv of Tex at San Antonio, 98-. **HONORS AND AWARDS** Spencer Fel, Nat Acad of Educ, 79-82; Res Assoc, The New Library, 80-81; Res grants, Univ of Tex at Dallas, 83-85; Newberry Library, Short-term Fel, 85-86; Res Grants, Univ of Tex at Dallas, 87-89; Am Educational Studies Asn Critics Choice Awd, 87; Am Antiquarian Soc/Nat Endowment for the Humanities Fel, 88-89; Spencr Foundation Res Grants, 91-92; Univ of Tex at Dallas Special Fac Development Assignment for Res, 97-98; Univ of Tex at San Antonio Res and Travel Awd, 99-00. **MEMBERSHIPS** AM Antiquarian Soc **SELECTED PUBLICATIONS** Auth, Growing Up in American: Historical Experiences, Wayne State Univ Pr, 87; auth, The Literacy Myth: Cultural Integration and Social Structure in the Nineteenth Century, Transaction Publishers, 91; auth, Conflicting Paths: Growing Up in America, Harvard Univ Press, 95; auth, The Labyrinths of Literacy, Univ of Pittsburgh Pr, Composition, Literacy, and Culture Series, 95; auth, Dallas Public and Private by Warren Leslie (1964), coed with Patricia E Hill, Methodist Univ Pr, 98; auth, "Introduction" to Dallas Public and Private by Warren Leslie (1964), Southern Methodist Univ Pr, 98; auth, "Teaching Historical Understanding: Disciplining Historical Imagination with Historical Context," in The Social Worlds of Higher Education: Handbook for Teaching in a New Century, ed. Bernice A. Pesosolido and Ronald Amizade, Pine Forge Press/Sage Publications for the American Sociological Association, 99; auth, "Interdisciplinary Explorations in the History of Children, Adolescents, and Youth-for the Past, Present, and Future," Journal of American History, 99; auth, "Teaching and Historical Understanding: Discipling Historical Imagination with Historical Context," Interchange, 99; auth, "The Nineteenth-Century Origins of Our Times," in Literacy: A Critical Sourcebook, ed. Ellen Cushman, Eugene Kintgen, Barry Knoll and Mike Rose, Bedford/St. Martins Pr, 00. **CONTACT ADDRESS** Div of Behav & Cult Sci, Univ of Texas, San Antonio, 6900 N Loop 1604 W, San Antonio, TX 78249-0652. **EMAIL** hgraff@utsa.edu

GRAFTON, ANTHONY T.
PERSONAL Born 05/21/1950, New Haven, NY, M, 2 children **DISCIPLINE** HISTORY **EDUCATION** Univ of Chicago, BA, 71; MA, 72; PhD, 75. **CAREER** Instr, Cornell Univ, 74-

75; asst prof to Dodge prof, Princeton Univ, 75-. **HONORS AND AWARDS** LA Times Prize for Hist, 93. **MEMBERSHIPS** AHA; RSA. **RESEARCH** Renaissance Intellectual History. **CONTACT ADDRESS** Dept Hist, Princeton Univ, 130 Dickinson Hall, Princeton, NJ 08544-0001.

GRAHAM, GAEL N.
DISCIPLINE MODERN AMERICAN HISTORY **EDUCATION** Univ MI, PhD. **CAREER** Hist Dept, Western Carolina Univ **SELECTED PUBLICATIONS** Auth, Gender, Culture, and Christianity: American Protestant Mission Schools in China, 1880-1930, 95. **CONTACT ADDRESS** Western Carolina Univ, Cullowhee, NC 28723.

GRAHAM, HUGH DAVIS
PERSONAL Born 09/02/1936, Little Rock, AR, m, 1966, 2 children **DISCIPLINE** AMERICAN HISTORY **EDUCATION** Yale Univ, BA, 58; Stanford Univ, MA, 61, PhD(Am hist), 64. **CAREER** Instr US hist, Foothill Col, 63-64; from asst prof to assoc prof, San Jose State Col, 64-67; regional dir training & pub affairs, Peace Corps, 65-66; vis asst prof US hist, Stanford Univ, 67; assoc prof, Johns Hopkins Univ, 67-71; dean soc sci, 71-77, Prof hist, Univ MD Baltimore County, 72-91, Co-dir hist & comp task force, Nat Comn Causes & Prev Violence, 68-69; Guggenheim Found fel, 70-71; Holland M. McTyeire Prof Hist, Vanderbilt Univ 91-; Ch hist dept, Vanderbilt Univ, 94-96. **HONORS AND AWARDS** Chastain Awd, Southern Polit Sci Asn, 76; Moody Fel, 80; Fel, Woodrow Wilson Ctr, 85-86; Sen fel, Natl Endowment for the Hum, 89-90; Jury nominee, Pulitzer Prize in Hist, 91; G. Welsey Johnson Prize, 93. **MEMBERSHIPS** Southern Hist Asn; AHA; Am Pol Sci Asn. **RESEARCH** Am polit hist; civil rights; educ; immigration policy. **SELECTED PUBLICATIONS** Auth, Crisis in Print, Vanderbilt Univ, 67; Since 1954: Desegregation, Harper, 72; The Uncertain Triumph: Federal Education Policy in the Kennedy and Johnson Years, Univ of NC, 84; The Civil Rights Era: Origins and Development of National Policy, 1960-1972, Oxford Univ Press, 90; Civil Rights and the Presidency, Oxford Univ Press, 92; coauth, Southern Politics and the Second Reconstruction, Johns Hopkins Univ, 75; The Rise of American Research Universities, John Hopkins Univ, 97; ed, Huey Long, Prentice-Hall, 70; Violence, Johns Hopkins Univ, 71; American Politics and Government, Harper, 75; Civil Rights in the United States, PSU Press, 94; co-ed, Violence in America, US Govt Printing Off, 69; Southern Elections, La State Univ, 78; Violence in America, Sage, rev ed, 79; The Carter Presidency: Policy Choices in the Post-New Deal Era, Univ of KS, 98. **CONTACT ADDRESS** Dept of History, Vanderbilt Univ, PO Box 1802, Sta B, Nashville, TN 37235. **EMAIL** hugh.graham@vanderbilt.edu

GRAHAM, JOHN THOMAS
PERSONAL Born 03/28/1928, Brookfield, MO, m, 1968, 1 child **DISCIPLINE** MODERN EUROPEAN HISTORY **EDUCATION** Rockhurst Col, BA, 52; St Louis Univ, PhD, 57. **CAREER** From instr to asst prof Europ hist, St Ambrose Col, 57-62; asst prof, Gonzaga Univ, 62-66; asst prof, 66-74, assoc prof, 74-93, Prof, Mod Europ Hist, Univ MO-Kansas City, 96-99, prof emeritus 99-00-. **MEMBERSHIPS** Soc Sci Hist Asn; AHA; AAUP. **RESEARCH** Nineteenth and twentieth century Europe; history of crisis thought; intellectual history. **SELECTED PUBLICATIONS** Auth, Donoso Cortes: Utopian Romanticism and Political Realism, Univ Mo, 74; A Pragmatist Philosophy of Life: Ortega y Gasset, 94; Theory of History in Ortega y Gasset: The Dawn of Historical Reason, 97; Postmodernism and Interdisciplinarity: The Social Thought of Ortega y Gasset (in press). **CONTACT ADDRESS** Dept of Hist, Univ of Missouri, Kansas City, 203 Cockefair Hall, 1525 Rockh, Kansas City, MO 64110-2499.

GRAHAM, LOREN RAYMOND
PERSONAL Born 06/29/1933, Hymera, IN, m, 1955, 1 child **DISCIPLINE** RUSSIAN HISTORY, HISTORY OF SCIENCE **EDUCATION** Purdue Univ, BS, 55; Columbia Univ, MA, 60, PhD, 64; Purdue Univ, DHL, 86. **CAREER** Res engr, Dow Chem Co, 55; lectr hist, Ind Univ, 63-64, asst prof hist, 64-65, asst prof hist of sci, 65-66; from asst prof to assoc prof hist, Columbia Univ, 66-72, prof, 72-80; Prof of History of Science, Mass Institute of Technology, 80-; Prof of History of Science, Harvard Univ, 86-00; Am Philos Soc grant, 64; vis asst prof pub law & govt & sr fel, Russ Inst, Columbia Univ, 65-66; Fulbright-Hays grant, 66; mem, Inst Advan Studies, 69-70; Guggenheim fel, 69-70; res fel hist of sci, Harvard Univ, 72-73; consult, NSF, 75-76, NEH, 76-99; mem panel on eval sci exhanges, Nat Acad Sci, 75-77; Rockefeller Found Humanities fel 76-77; res fel, Prog Sci & Int Affairs, Harvard Univ, 76-77; adv ed, Isis, 76-91. **HONORS AND AWARDS** Nominated for National Book Awd, 73; Saxton Prize, Hist Sci Soc, 96; Follo Prize, Michigan Historical Society, 00. **MEMBERSHIPS** AHA; Hist Sci Soc, Am Asn Advan Slavic Studies (treas, 67-68); AAAS; Soc Hist Technol; Am Acad Arts & Sci; Am Philos Soc; Russ Acad Natural Scie, foreign mem; Russ Acad Humanitarian Sci, foreign mem. **RESEARCH** History of science; Russian history; Am Philos Soc; Member of Council, 98 **SELECTED PUBLICATIONS** Auth, A Soviet Marxist View of Structural Chemistry: The Theory of Resonance Controversy, Isis, 3/64; Quantum mech and dialectical materialism, Slavic Rev, 9/66; Cybernetics, in Science and Ideology in Soviet Society, Atherton, 67; The Soviet Academy of Sciences and the Communist Party, 1927-1932, Princeton Univ, 67; Science and Philosophy in the Soviet Union, Knopf, 72; ed, Review of US-USSR Interacademy Exchanges and Relations, Nat Acad Sci, 77; auth, Eugenics in Weimar Germany and Soviet Russia in the Twenties, Am Hist Rev, 12/77; Concerns about science and attempts to regulate scientific inquiry, Daedalas, spring 78; Between Science and Values, Columbia Univ, 81; Functions and Uses of Disciplinary History, Dovdeucht, 84; Red Star: The First Bolshevik Science Utopia, Ind Univ, 84; Science, Philosophy, and Human Behavior in the Soviet Union, Columbia Univ, 87; Science and the Soviet Social Order, Harvard Univ, 90; Science in Russia and the Soviet Union: A Short History, Cambridge Univ, 93; The Ghost of the Executed Engineer, Harvard Univ, 93; A Face in the Rock, Island Press, 95; What Have We Learned about Science and Technology from the Russian Experience?, Stanford Univ, 98 **CONTACT ADDRESS** Dept of Hist, Massachusetts Inst of Tech, Program on Science, Technology and Society, E51-163, Cambridge, MA 02139. **EMAIL** lrg@mit.edu

GRAHAM, PATRICIA ALBJERG
PERSONAL Born 02/09/1935, Lafayette, IN, m, 1955, 1 child **DISCIPLINE** AMERICAN HISTORY **EDUCATION** Purdue Univ, BS, 55, MS, 57; Columbia Univ, PhD(hist educ), 64. **CAREER** Teacher, High Sch, Va, 55-58; chmn dept hist, St Hilda's and St Hugh's Sch, NY, 58-60; lectr hist educ, Ind Univ, 64-65, asst prof, 65-66; dir educ prog and asst prof educ, Barnard Col, Columbia Univ, 65-68, assoc prof hist educ, 68-72, prof educ and dir educ prog, 72-74, from assoc prof to prof hist educ, Teachers Col, 68-74; prof educ, Harvard Univ, 74-79; dir, Nat Inst Educ, Dept Health, Educ and Welfare, 77-79; prof educ, 74-79, Charles Warren Prof Hist Educ, Harvard Univ, 79-, Dean Grad Sch Educ, 82-91; Spencer Fnd, pres, 91-00; John Simon Guggenheim Found fel and Radcliffe Inst fel, 72-73; dean, Radcliffe Inst and vpres, Radcliffe Col, 74-77; Woodrow Wilson Ctr fel, 81-82. **MEMBERSHIPS** AHA; Hist Educ Soc; Am Acad of Arts and Sciences; Am Philos Soc; Natl Acad of Education. **RESEARCH** History of education. **SELECTED PUBLICATIONS** Auth, Progressive Education: From Arcady to Academe, 67; auth, "Women in Academe," Science, 70; auth; Community and Class in American Education, 1865-1918, 74; auth, Women in Higher Education, 74; auth, SOS: Sustain Our Schools, 92; Battleships and Schools, Daedalus, Vol 0124, 95. **CONTACT ADDRESS** Graduate School of Education, Harvard Univ, Cambridge, MA 02138. **EMAIL** patricia_graham@harvard.edu

GRAHAM, RICHARD
PERSONAL Born 11/01/1934, Brazil, m, 1978, 3 children **DISCIPLINE** HISTORY **EDUCATION** Col Wooster, BA, 56; Univ Texas, Austin, MA, 57, PhD, 61. **CAREER** Asst prof, 61-68, Cornell Univ; Assoc prof, 68-70, Univ Utah; assoc prof, 70-73, prof, 73-86, F H Nalle Prof of History, 86-, Univ Texas, Austin. **RESEARCH** Independence of Latin Am; Brazilian hist, slavery & race; intl econ rels; econ liberalism in Brazil. **CONTACT ADDRESS** Dept of History, Univ of Texas, Austin, Austin, TX 78731-1163. **EMAIL** rgraham@mail.utexas.edu

GRAHAM, W. FRED
PERSONAL Born 10/31/1930, Columbus, OH, m, 1953, 4 children **DISCIPLINE** RELIGION, HISTORY **EDUCATION** Tarkio Col, BA, 52; Pittsburgh Theol Sem, BD, 55; Louisville Presby Sem, ThM, 58; Univ Iowa, PhD(relig), 65. **CAREER** From instr to asst prof relig, 63-65, from asst prof to assoc prof dept relig studies, 66-73, PROF RELIG, MICH STATE UNIV, 73-. **MEMBERSHIPS** Am Soc Church Hist; Calvin Studies Soc; Am Acad Relig; Soc 16th Century Studies. **RESEARCH** Reformation, particularly 16th century Geneva and Calvin; relationship between religion and social, economic and political life and thought; science and religion. **SELECTED PUBLICATIONS** Auth, An Uncounseled King--Charles-I and the Scottish Troubles, 1637-1641, Church Hist, Vol 0062, 93; Calvin, John Preaching, Church Hist, Vol 0063, 94; Where Shall Wisdom Be Found--Calvin Exegesis of Job from Medieval and Modern Perspectives, 16th Century J, Vol 0026, 95; Calvinism in Europe, 1540-1610--A Collection of Documents, Church Hist, Vol 0064, 95; Ecclesia-Reformata--Studies on the Reformation, Vol 2, 16th Century J, Vol 0026, 95; Humanism and Reform--The Church in Europe, England and Scotland, 1400-1643, Church Hist, Vol 0064, 95; Calvin, John Concept of the Law, Church Hist, Vol 0064, 95; Sin and the Calvinists--Morals Control and the Consistory in the Reformed Tradition, Cath Hist Rev, Vol 0082, 96; Politics, Religion, and Diplomacy in Early-Modern Europe--Essays in Honor of Jensen, de, Lamar, Church Hist, Vol 0065, 96; The Uses of Reform--Godly Discipline and Popular Behavior in Scotland and Beyond, 1560-1610, 16th Century J, Vol 0028, 97. **CONTACT ADDRESS** Dept of Relig Studies, Michigan State Univ, East Lansing, MI 48823.

GRAHAM, WILLIAM
PERSONAL Born 08/16/1943, Raleigh, NC, m, 1983, 1 child **DISCIPLINE** HISTORY OF RELIGION, ISLAMIC STUDIES **EDUCATION** Univ NC, BA, 66; Harvard Univ, AM, 70; PhD, 73. **CAREER** Lectr to Prof, Harvard Univ, 73-. **HONORS AND AWARDS** Woodrow Wilson Fel, 66; Danforth Fel, 66-73; Phi Beta Kappa, Univ NC, 64. **MEMBERSHIPS** AOS, AAR, MESA, ASSR, MEM. **RESEARCH** Islamic religion, Qur'an, Hadith. **SELECTED PUBLICATIONS** Auth, "'The Winds to Herald his Mercy': Nature as Token of God's Sovereignty and Grace in the Qur'an," in Faithful Imaging (Atlanta, GA: Scholars Pr, 95), 19-38; auth, "Politics and Religion in Islam in Historical Perspective: Some Reflections," in Future Dimensions (Vienna, Austria: 96), 22-23; auth, "Sahrif," in The Encycl of Islam, New Ed (97), 329-337; coauth, The Heritage of World Civilizations, Prentice Hall, 00; auth, "Basmalah," in Encycl of the Qur'an (Leiden: E J Brill, 00), forthcoming; auth, "Fatihah," in Encycl of the Qur'an (Leiden: E J Brill, 00), forthcoming. **CONTACT ADDRESS** Dept Lang, Harvard Univ, Semetic Museum, Cambridge, MA 02138. **EMAIL** wgraham@fas.harvard.edu

GRAHAM, WILLIAM C.
PERSONAL Born 04/16/1950, Duluth, MN **DISCIPLINE** HISTORICAL THEOLOGY **EDUCATION** Fordham Univ, PhD, 93. **CAREER** Assoc prof, Caldwell Col, NJ; dir, Caldwell Pastoral Ministry Inst. **HONORS AND AWARDS** Asst ed, Listening; columnist for Natl Cath Reporter. **MEMBERSHIPS** Am Acad Relig; Asn of Grad Prog in Ministry; New Jersey Consortium for Grad Prog in Theol; N Am Acad of Liturgy. **SELECTED PUBLICATIONS** Co-ed, Common Good, Uncommon Questions: A Primer in Moral Theology, Liturgical, 95; auth, Half Finished Heaven: The Social Gospel in American Literature, Univ Pr Am, 95; ed, More Urgent Than Usual: The Final Homilies of Mark Hollenhorst, Liturgical, 95; auth, Is There A Case Against St. Therese As Doctor of the Church? Sisters Today, 95; auth, Sadness of the City, in Legalized Gambling, Greenhaven, 98; auth, Up In Smoke: Preparation for Ash Wednesday, Mod Liturgy, 97/98; auth, Television, Resistance and Orthodoxy, Natl Cath Reporter, 98; auth, The Preacher and the Abortion Opponent, Celebration, 98; auth, Sacred Adventure: Beginning Theological Study, (UPA,99). **CONTACT ADDRESS** 5887 S Pike Lake Rd, Duluth, MN 55811. **EMAIL** wcgnycpl@aol.com

GRANATSTEIN, JACK L.
PERSONAL Born 05/21/1939, Toronto, ON, Canada **DISCIPLINE** HISTORY **EDUCATION** Royal Mil Col Kingston, BA, 61; Univ Toronto, MA, 62; Duke Univ, PhD, 66; Memorial Univ, DLitt, 93; Univ Calgary, LLD, 94. **CAREER** Hist, Directorate Hist, Nat Defence HQ, 64-66; prof history, 66-95, dir, Grad Hist Prog, 84-87; distinguished res prof hist emer, York Univ, 95-. **HONORS AND AWARDS** Killam Res Fel, 82-84, 91-93; Tyrrell Medal Can Hist 92; JW Dafoe Prize, 93; Univ BC Medal Can Biog, 93; Vimy Awd, Conf Def Asns Inst, 96; Off, Order Can, 97. **MEMBERSHIPS** Fel, Royal Soc Can; Can Inst Int Affairs; Orgn Stud Nat Hist Can. **SELECTED PUBLICATIONS** Auth, The Politics of Survival, 67; Peacekeeping: International Challenge and Canadian Response, 68; Marlborough Marathon, 71; co-ed, The Generals: The Canadian Army's Senior Commanders in the Second World War, 93; Empire to Umpire: Canadian Foreign Policy to the 1990s, 94; Victory 1945, 95; The Good Fight, 95; Yankee Go Home? Canadians and Anti-Americanism, 96; The Canadian 100: The Hundred Most Influential Canadians of the 20th Century, 97; Petrified Campus: Canada's Universities in Crisis, 97. **CONTACT ADDRESS** Hist Dept, York Univ, 4700 Keele St, Toronto, ON, Canada M3J 1P3.

GRANT, EDWARD
PERSONAL Born 04/06/1926, Canton, OH, m, 1951, 3 children **DISCIPLINE** HISTORY OF SCIENCE **EDUCATION** City Col New York, BSS, 51; Univ Wis, MA, 53; PhD(hist of sci), 57. **CAREER** Instr Europ hist and hist of sci, Univ Maine, 57-58; instr hist of sci, Harvard Univ, 58-59; from asst prof to full prof, 59-64, full prof to distinguished prof, 83, chmn, Dept Hist and Philos Sci, 73-79, 87-90, Prof Hist of Sci and Hist, 64-83, distinguished prof, 83-92, distinguished prof emeritus, 92-, Ind Univ, Bloomington, 64-, NSF res grants, 59-74; Am Coun Learned Soc grant, 61-62; vis asst prof, Univ Wis, 62; Guggenheim fel, 65-66; vis mem, Inst Advan Studies, 65-66; chmn US nat comt, Int Union Hist and Philos Sci, 68-69; mem adv bd, Speculum, J Mediaeval Acad Am, 72-75; Am Coun Learned Soc fel, 75-76; pres, Hist of Sci Soc, 85-86; Inst Advan Studies, 65-66, 83-84. **HONORS AND AWARDS** Fel, Am Acad of Arts and Sciences, 84-; George Sarton medal of the History of Science Soc, 92. **MEMBERSHIPS** Int Acad Hist Sci; Hist Sci Soc; fel Mediaeval Acad Am; AAUP. **RESEARCH** Ancient and medieval science; medieval cosmology; Medieval and Renaissance Aristotelianism. **SELECTED PUBLICATIONS** Auth, Physical Science in the Middle Ages, Wiley History of Science Series, John Wiley and Sons (NYork), 71; auth, translations, annotations, introductions, and "Brief Author Biographies," in A Source Book in Medieval Science, ed. Edward Grant (Camrbidge, MA, Harvard Univ Press, 74); auth, Much Ado About Nothing: Theories of Space and Vacuum From the Middle Ages to the Scientific Revolution, Cambridge Univ Press (Cambridge), 81; auth, Planets, Stars, & Orbs: The Medieval Cosmos, 1200-1687; Cambridge Univ Press (Cambridge), 81; auth, The Foundations of Modern Science in the Middle Ages: Their Religious, Institutional, and Intellectual Contexts, Cambridge Univ Press (Cambridge), 96. **CONTACT AD-**

DRESS Dept of Hist and Philos of Sci, Indiana Univ, Bloomington, 130 Goodbody Hall, Bloomington, IN 47405. **EMAIL** grant@indiana.edu

GRANT, GLEN
PERSONAL Born 02/23/1947, Los Angeles, CA, s **DISCIPLINE** AMERICAN STUDIES **EDUCATION** Univ Calif, Los Angeles, BA, 68; Univ Hawaii, M.Ed, 74, PhD, 82. **CAREER** Tchg asst, 72-82, instr, 92-, acad chemn, 98-, Hawaii tokai Int Col; educ specialist, Kapiolani Commun Col, 84-91; vice chancellor, Hawaii Tokai Intl Col, fall, 00-. **HONORS AND AWARDS** Excellence Tchg Awd, 79, Univ Hawaii; Living Treasure Hawaii's Multiculturalism, 96, City and County of Honolulu. **MEMBERSHIPS** Honolulu City & County, Comn on Cult & the Arts. **RESEARCH** Hawaii's multiculturalism; ethnic studies. **SELECTED PUBLICATIONS** Coauth, Kodomo No Tame Ni (For the Sake of the Children) The Japanese American Experience in Hawaii, 78; coauth, art, Race Relations in the Hawaiian Schools: The Haole Newcomer, 78; auth, art, Living Proof: Is Hawaii the Answer?, 93; auth, art, Hawaiians and Volcanoes, 96; coauth, An Unlikely Revolutionary: The Memoirs of Matsuo Takabuki, 98. **CONTACT ADDRESS** Hawaii Tokai Intl Col, 2241 Kapiolani Blvd, Honolulu, HI 96826. **EMAIL** ggrant@tokai.edu

GRANT, H. ROGER
PERSONAL Born 11/28/1943, Ottumwa, IA, m, 1966, 1 child **DISCIPLINE** HISTORY **EDUCATION** Simpson Col, BA, 66; Univ Mo, MA, 67, PhD, 70. **CAREER** From asst prof to assoc prof to prof, 70-96, Univ Akron; prof, chemn, Clemson Univ, 96-. **HONORS AND AWARDS** Woodrow Wilson Fel, 66; Woodrow Wilson Dissertation Fel, 68-69; Railroad Hist Book Awd; Railway and Locomotive Hist Society, 85. **MEMBERSHIPS** OAH; SHA; Lexington Group in Transportation Hist. **RESEARCH** Transportation history **SELECTED PUBLICATIONS** Auth, Erie Lackawanna: Death of an American Railroad, 1938-1992, 94; auth, Ohio's Railway Age in Postcards, 96; auth, The North Western: A History of the Chicago and North Western Railway System, 96; auth, Ohio in Historic Postcards: Self Portrait of a State, 97; auth, Railroads in the Heartland: Steam and Traction in the Golden Age of Postcards, 97. **CONTACT ADDRESS** 123 Hickory Ridge Rd, Central, SC 29603-9461. **EMAIL** ggrant@clemson.edu

GRANT, SHELAGH D.
PERSONAL Born 06/28/1938, Montreal, PQ, Canada **DISCIPLINE** HISTORY, CANADIAN STUDIES **EDUCATION** Univ Western Ont, Hosp Sick Children, RN, 60; Trent Univ, BA, 81, MA, 83. **CAREER** Tutor/lectr, 82-88, Adj Fac, History & Canadian Stud, Trent Univ, 88-; adv bd, The Northern Rev, 89-; ed adv bd, Arctic, 92-. **MEMBERSHIPS** Can Hist Asn; Am Hist Asn; Asn Can Stud; Can Inst Int Affairs; UN Asn Can; Brit Asn Can Stud; Champlain Soc. **SELECTED PUBLICATIONS** Auth, Sovereignty or Security? Government Policy in the Canadian North 1936-1950, 88; co-ed & contribur, Federalism in Canada and Australia, 89. **CONTACT ADDRESS** Can Stud, Trent Univ, Peterborough, ON, Canada K9J 7B8. **EMAIL** sgrant@terntu.ca

GRANTHAM, DEWEY WESLEY
PERSONAL Born 03/16/1921, Manassas, GA, m, 1942, 3 children **DISCIPLINE** HISTORY **EDUCATION** Univ Ga, AB, 42; Univ NC, MA, 47, PhD, 49. **CAREER** Asst prof hist, NTex State Col, 49-50 and Woman's Col Univ NC, 50-52; from asst prof to prof, 52-77, Holland N MCtyeire Prof Hist, Vanderbilt Univ, 77-, Fund Advan Educ fac fel, 55-56; chmn regional selection comt, Woodrow Wilson Nat Fel Prog, 57-59; Soc Sci Res Coun fac fel, 59, mem, Comt Fac Res Grants, 66-67; Guggenheim Mem Found fel, 60; mem advan placement exam comt Am hist, Col Entrance Exam Bd, 66-67; fel, Henry E Huntington Libr and Art Gallery, 68-69; mem, Regional Archives Adv Coun, Fed Arch and Records Ctr, 70-77; gen ed, Twentieth-Century America Series, Univ Tenn, 76-; Fulbright-Hays lectr, Univ Aix-en-Provence, 78-79; fel, Nat Humanities Ctr, 82-83. **HONORS AND AWARDS** Sydnor Awd, Southern Hist Asn, 59. **MEMBERSHIPS** AHA; Am Studies Asn; Orgn Am Historians; Southern Hist Asn, (pres, 67); Am Coun Learned Soc. **RESEARCH** Twentieth century American history; recent Southern history; modern Afro-American history. **SELECTED PUBLICATIONS** Auth, The Democratic South, Univ Ga, 63; ed, Following the Color Line, 64 & auth, The South and the Sectional Image, 67, Harper; ed, Theodore Roosevelt, Prentice-Hall, 70 & The Political Status of the Negro in the Age of FDR, Univ Chicago, 73; auth, Contemporary American history: The United States since 1945, AHA, 75; The United States Since 1945: The Ordeal of Power, McGraw-Hill, 76; The regional imagination: The south and recent American history, Vanderbilt Univ Press, 79; The contours of southern progressivism, Am Hist Rev, 12/81. **CONTACT ADDRESS** Dept of Hist, Vanderbilt Univ, Nashville, TN 37235.

GRATTON, BRIAN
PERSONAL Born 05/19/1946, Roswell, NM, m, 1988 **DISCIPLINE** HISTORY **EDUCATION** Univ NM, BA, 70; Boston Univ, PhD, 80. **CAREER** Asst prof to prof, Ariz State Univ, 83-. **HONORS AND AWARDS** Fel, GSA. **MEMBERSHIPS** Phi Beta Kappa; Phi Alpha Theta; Immigration Hist Soc; Org of Am Hist; Am Hist Asn; Econ Hist Asn; Soc Sci Hist Asn; Gerontol Soc; Population Asn of Am. **RESEARCH** Initial research interests in history of social security, retirement, and the elderly. Current research is focused on Hispanic immigration to the United States, 1880 to 2000. **SELECTED PUBLICATIONS** Auth, "A Triumph of Modern Philanthropy: Age Criteria in Labor Management: Pennsylvania Railroad, 1900," Bus Hist Rev, (90): 630-656; co-auth, "Industrialization, the Family Economy, and the Economic Status of the Elderly," Soc Sci Hist, (91): 337-362; co-auth, Old Age and the Search for Security: An American Social History, Ind Univ Press, 94; auth, "The Poverty of Impoverishment Theory: The Economic Well-Being of the American Elderly, 1890-1950," J of Econ Hist, (96): 39-61; co-auth, "Hispanics in the United States, 1850-1990: Estimates of Populations Size and National Origin," Hist Methods, (00): 137-153; co-auth, "Los efectos demograficos de la revolucion mexicana en Estados Unidos," Hist Mex, (00): 145-165. **CONTACT ADDRESS** Dept Hist, Arizona State Univ, MC 2501, Tempe, AZ 85287. **EMAIL** brian@asu.edu

GRATZ, DELBERT L.
PERSONAL Born 03/05/1920, Allen Co, OH, m, 1943, 4 children **DISCIPLINE** CHURCH HISTORY **EDUCATION** Bluffton Col, AB, 42; Ohio State Univ, MA, 45; Univ Bern, DPhil(hist), 50; Univ Mich, Ann Arbor, AMLS, 52. **CAREER** Librn, Mennonite Hist Libr and Col Libr and Prof Hist, Bluffton Col 50-, Scholar, Nordrhein-Westfalen Ministry of Educ, Bonn, Ger, 64; fel, Pro Helvetia, Zurich, Switz, 64-65; Ger Acad Exchange Serv fel, Bad Godesberg, 64-65; res scholar, Baptist Theol Sem, Zurich, 64-65 and 71-72; Fulbright travel grant, 71-72. **MEMBERSHIPS** Church Hist Soc; Am Soc Reformation Res; Swiss Am Hist Soc; Mennonite Hist Soc. **RESEARCH** Anabaptist and Mennonite research; genealogical research. **SELECTED PUBLICATIONS** Auth, The Bernese Anabaptists, Herald, 53; Records relating the Mennonite story, World Conf on Records, 69; The Swiss Menonnites of Allen and Putnam Counties, Ohio, Northwest Ohio Quart, 56; Manuscript materials in Europe that concern the Anabaptists, Mennonite Quart Rev, 67; A personal contact with Hans Landis, Mennonite Res J, 69-70. **CONTACT ADDRESS** Mennonite Hist Libr, Bluffton Col, Bluffton, OH 45817.

GRAUBARD, STEPHEN RICHARDS
PERSONAL Born 12/05/1924, New York, NY **DISCIPLINE** HISTORY **EDUCATION** George Washington Univ, AB, 45; Harvard Univ, AM, 46, PhD(hist), 52. **CAREER** From instr to asst prof hist and gen educ, Harvard Univ, 52-55, lectr hist, 60-63; Prof Hist, Brown Univ, 64-, Dir Studies, Assembly Univ Goals and Governance, 69-, Harvard Found grant, 56; managing ed, Daedalus, 60-61, ed, 61-; mem adv comt, Giovanni Agnelli Found, Italy, 70- **HONORS AND AWARDS** DHuL, Providence Col, 71. **MEMBERSHIPS** AHA; Coun Foreign Rels; Am Acad Arts and Sci. **RESEARCH** British labor history; history of the First World War; modern French social and intellectual history. **SELECTED PUBLICATIONS** Auth, British Labor and the Russian Revolution, 1917-1942; Burke, Disraeli and Churchill: The Politics of Perseverance; coauth, A New Europe?, Houghton, 65; coed, The Embattled University, Braziller, 70; Historical Studies Today, 72 & auth, Kissinger: Portrait of a Mind, 73, Norton. **CONTACT ADDRESS** Dept of Hist, Brown Univ, Providence, RI 02912.

GRAVES, JOHN W.
PERSONAL Born 06/25/1942, Little Rock, AR, s **DISCIPLINE** HISTORY, POLITICAL SCIENCE **EDUCATION** Univ Ark, BA, 64; MA, 67; Univ Va, PhD, 78. **CAREER** Grad teaching asst, Univ Ark, 65-66; instr, Univ Southwestern La, 66-68; grader, Univ Va, 70-72; instr, Southwest Tex State Univ, 72-77; lectr, St Edward's Univ, 77-85; prof, Henderson State Univ, 85-. **HONORS AND AWARDS** Stonewall Jackson memorial Scholar, Ark Hist Comn, 65-66; Grad Teaching Fel, Univ Ark, 65-66; George L. Seay Fel in Hist, Univ Va, 68-69; Fac Res Grant, Henderson State Univ, 86; Best Paper Awd, Ark Asn of Col Hist Teachers, 90; Arkansiana Awd, Ark Libr Asn, 91; State Res Grant, Ark Hist Preservation Prog of the Dept of Ark Heritage, 96. **MEMBERSHIPS** Ark Hist Advisory Coun, Ark Black Hist Advisory Comt, Woodward Lecture Comt, Soc for the Preservation of the Mosaic Templars of America Building, Phi Alpha Theta. **RESEARCH** U.S. Southern and Arkansas History, U.S. Race Relations, U.S. Urban and Black History, Gilded Age America. **SELECTED PUBLICATIONS** Rev, of "Opening Doors: Perspectives on Race Relations in Contemporary America," ed. by H. J. Knopke, Robert J. Norrell, and Ronald W. Rogers, J of Southern Hist (May, 94): 434-435; auth, "President's Report to the Membership," Ark Hist Quart 994): 90-94; rev, of "Carpenter from Conway: George Washington Donaghey as Governor of Arkansas, 1909-1913," by Calvin R. Ledbetter, Jr, Am Rev of Politics (Autumn, 94): 419-421; auth, "President's Report to the membership," Ark Hist Quart (95): 80-84; rev, of "Civil Obedience: An Oral History of School Desegregation in Fayetteville, Arkansas, 1954-1965," by Julianne Lewis Adams and Thomas A. DeBlack, Ark Hist Quart (95), 396-400; rev, of "Race and the City: Work, Community, and Protest in Cincinnati, 1820-1970," by Henry Louis Taylor, Jr, J of Southern Hist (95): 798-799; auth, "President's Report to the Membership," Ark Hist Quart (96): 95-106. **CONTACT ADDRESS** Dept Soc Sci, Henderson State Univ, 1100 Henderson St, PO Box 7793, Arkadelphia, AR 71999-0001.

GRAVES, PAMELA
DISCIPLINE HISTORY **EDUCATION** Univ Pitt, PhD. **CAREER** Asst prof, Eastern Michigan Univ. **RESEARCH** Modern Europe, Europe, labor, history of women. **SELECTED PUBLICATIONS** Auth, Labor Women, Women in British Working Class Politics, 1918-1939. **CONTACT ADDRESS** Dept of History and Philosophy, Eastern Michigan Univ, 701 Pray-Harrold, Ypsilanti, MI 48197.

GRAVES, STEVEN
PERSONAL Born 07/30/1966, Chillicotne, OH, m, 1998, 2 children **DISCIPLINE** GEOGRAPHY **EDUCATION** Oh State Univ, BA, 88; BsEd, 91; MA, 93; Univ Ill, PhD, 99. **CAREER** Assoc Prof, La Tech Univ, 99-. **RESEARCH** Popular Culture. **CONTACT ADDRESS** Dept Soc Sci, Louisiana Tech Univ, 305 Wisteria St, Ruston, LA 71270. **EMAIL** sgraves@latech.edu

GRAY, HANNA HOLBORN
PERSONAL Born 10/25/1930, Heidelberg, Germany, m, 1954 **DISCIPLINE** RENAISSANCE & REFORMATION HISTORY **EDUCATION** Bryn Mawr Col, AB, 50; Harvard Univ, PhD, 57. **CAREER** Instr hist, Bryn Mawr Col, 53-54; from instr to asst prof, Harvard Univ, 57-60; from asst prof to assoc prof, Univ Chicago, 61-72; dean arts & sci & prof hist, Northwestern Univ, 72-74; provost & prof hist, Yale Univ, 74-78, actg pres, 77-78; Prof Hist, 78-93, Harry Pratt Judson Distinguished Service Prof Hist, Univ Chicago, 93-, Pres 78-93, Pres Emer 93-; vis lectr, Harvard Univ, 63-64 & Northwestern Univ, 65 & 66; Ctr Advan Studies Behav Sci fel, 66-67; co-ed J Mod Hist, 66-70; vis assoc prof hist, Univ Calif, Berkeley, 70-71; trustee, Yale Univ, 71-74; dir bd dirs, Am Coun Learned Socs, 71-76; mem NEH, 72-77; trustee, Inst Advan Studies, 72-78, Carnegie Found Advan Teaching, 72-75 & Mayo Found, 74-86, Bryn Mawr Col, 77-97, Ctr Advan Studies Behav Sci, 77-, Mellon Found, 80- & Brookings Inst, 81-86; fel, Harvard Univ Corp; Chair, Howard Hughes Med Inst; Chair, Andrew W. Mellon Found; Bd of Regents, Smithsonian Inst; bd mem, Marlboro Sch of Music; mem bd dir, J.P. Morgan & Co, the Cummins Engine Co; mem, Secretary's Energy Advisory Bd, U.S. Dept Energy. **HONORS AND AWARDS** Newberry Libr fel, 60-61; Phi Beta Kappa; Radcliffe Graduate Medal, 76; Medal of Liberty Awd, 86; Presidential Medal of Freedom, 91; Charles Frankel Prize, NEH, 93; Jefferson Medal, Am Philos Soc, 93; Quantrell Awd for Excellence in Undergraduate Teaching, Univ Chicago, 96; M. Carey Thomas Awd, Bryn Mawr Col, 97; numerous other awards; sixty honors & awards from us & foreign univs & cols, 71-81. **MEMBERSHIPS** Renaissance Soc Am; fel Am Acad Arts & Sci; Am Philos Soc; Nat Acad Educ; Coun on For Relations of NY; honorary degrees from several colleges and universities, including Oxford, Yale, Brown, Columbia, Princeton, Duke, and Harvard. **RESEARCH** Renaissance intellectual history; historiography; Europe in the Renaissance and Reformation. **SELECTED PUBLICATIONS** Auth, Renaissance humanism: The pursuit of eloquence, in J Hist Ideas, 63; Valla's Encomium of St Thomas Aquinas and the Humanist Conception of Christian Antiquity, Studies Hist & Lit, Newberry Libr, 65; Machiavelli: The art of politics and the paradox of power, in The Responsibility of Power, Doubleday, 68. **CONTACT ADDRESS** Univ of Chicago, 1126 E 59th St., Chicago, IL 60637-1539. **EMAIL** h-gray@uchicago.edu

GRAY, RALPH D.
PERSONAL Born 10/13/1933, Otwell, IN, w, 1956, 3 children **DISCIPLINE** UNITED STATES HISTORY **EDUCATION** Hanover Col, BA, 55; Univ Del, MA, 58; Univ Ill PhD(hist), 62. **CAREER** Teaching asst, Univ Ill, 60-61; instr, Ohio State Univ, 61-64; from asst prof to assoc prof, Ind Univ Kokomo, 64-68; assoc prof, 68-72, Prof Hist, Ind Univ-Purdue Univ, Indianapolis, 72-98, Consult, Stellite Div, Cabot Corp, 71; ed, J Early Repub, 81-; Prof Emeritus, 98. **HONORS AND AWARDS** Thomas McKean Mem Cup Award, Antique Automobile Club Am, 79. **MEMBERSHIPS** Orgn Am Historians; Bus Hist Conf; Lexington Group; Soc Historians of Early Am Republic. **RESEARCH** Indiana history; 19th and 20th century transportation history; 19th and 20 century United States political and economic history. **SELECTED PUBLICATIONS** Auth, The National Waterway: A History of the Chesapeak and Delaware Cand, 67-94; auth, Alloys and Automobiles: A Life of Elwood Haynes, 79; auth, Indiana History: A Book of Readings, 94; auth, Structures in the Stream--Water, Science, and the Rise of the US-Army-Corps-of-Engineers, J Am Hist, Vol 0082, 95; We the People--Voices and Images of the New Nation, Publ Historian, Vol 0017, 95; Common Labor--Workers and the Digging of North-American Canals, 1780-1860, Am Hist Rev, Vol 0102, 97; auth, Public Ports for Indiana: A History of the Indiana Port Commission, 98. **CONTACT ADDRESS** Dept of Hist, Indiana Univ-Purdue Univ, Indianapolis, 425 Univ Blvd, Indianapolis, IN 46202. **EMAIL** rgray@iupui.edu

GRAY, SUSAN E.
PERSONAL Born 09/02/1952, Northampton, MA, m, 1988 **DISCIPLINE** HISTORY **EDUCATION** Earlham Col, AB, 74; Univ Chicago, MA, 80; PhD, 85. **CAREER** Vis Asst Prof, Middlebury Col, 86-91; Asst Prof to Assoc Prof, Ariz State Univ, 91-. **HONORS AND AWARDS** Fel, Harvard Univ, 90-

91; Fel, Nat Hist Pub and Records Commission, 95; NEH Fel, 97-98. **MEMBERSHIPS** Org of Am Hist; Am Hist Asn; Soc for Hist of the Early Am Republic; Agr Hist Soc; Am Soc for Ethnohist; W Hist Asn. **RESEARCH** Biography of a missionary couple who worked among a band of Odawa Indians in western Michigan for much of their adult lives. History of Michigan in the frontier period. **SELECTED PUBLICATIONS** Auth, The Yankee West: community Life on the Michigan Frontier, Univ of NC Press, 96; auth, The American Midwest: Essays on Regional History, Ind Univ Press, 01. **CONTACT ADDRESS** Dept Hist, Arizona State Univ, 2063 E La Jolla Dr, Tempe, AZ 85287-2501. **EMAIL** segray@asu.edu

GRAYBAR, LLOYD JOSEPH
PERSONAL Born 11/29/1937, Bellows Falls, VT **DISCIPLINE** AMERICAN HISTORY **EDUCATION** Middlebury Col, AB, 60; Columbia Univ, MA, 61, PhD, 66. **CAREER** From asst prof to assoc prof, 66-76, Prof Hist, Eastern KY Univ, 76-; Vis lectr, Univ NDak, 67; Am Philos Soc grant, 70; Earhart Found grant, 81. **MEMBERSHIPS** Orgn Am Historians; Immigration Hist Group; Am Mil Inst, Comt Hist 2nd World War. **RESEARCH** American social and urban history, 1877-1920; American nuclear testing, 1946-1950; Admiral Ernest J King and the United States Navy, 1900-1945. **SELECTED PUBLICATIONS** Auth, The whiskey war at Paddy's Run, Ohio Hist, winter 66; Albert Shaw's search for the ideal city, Historian, 5/72; Albert Shaw and the founding of the Review of Reviews: An Intellectual Biography, Univ Press Ky, 74; Admiral King's toughest battle, Naval War Col Rev, 2/79; American Pacific strategy after Pearl Harbor: The relief of Wake Island, Prologue, fall 80; The 1946 Atomic Bomb Tests, J Am Hist, 3/86; Ernest J King: Commander of the Two-Ocean Navy, in Quarterdeck & Bridge, Naval Inst Press, 97. **CONTACT ADDRESS** Dept of Hist, Eastern Kentucky Univ, 521 Lancaster Ave, Richmond, KY 40475-3102.

GRAYBILL, MARIBETH
DISCIPLINE ART HISTORY **EDUCATION** Col Wooster, BA, 71; Univ MI, MA, 75, PhD, 83. **CAREER** Assoc prof art hist; chr Asian studies. **RESEARCH** Japan painting and prints, espec in rel to vernacular narrative traditions. **SELECTED PUBLICATIONS** Auth, Nobuzane and Gotoba In in International Symposium on the Conservation and Restoration of Cultural Property: Periods of Transition in East Asian Art, Tokyo Nat Res Inst Cult Properties, 88; Buson as Heir to Saigyo and Nobuzane: A Study in Self-Fashioning, Kobijutsu, 89; Painting as Family Business: Portraits by Nobuzane and his Descendants, Bijutsu Kenku, 94. **CONTACT ADDRESS** Swarthmore Col, Swarthmore, PA 19081-1397. **EMAIL** mgraybi1@swarthmore.edu

GRAYSON, ALBERT K.
PERSONAL Born 04/01/1935, Windsor, ON, Canada **DISCIPLINE** NEAR EASTERN STUDIES **EDUCATION** Univ Toronto, BA, 55, MA, 58; Univ Vienna, 59-60; Johns Hopkins Univ, PhD, 62. **CAREER** Res asst, Orient Inst Univ Chicago, 62-63; asst prof hist, Temple Univ, 63-64; asst prof to assoc prof, 64-72, PROF NEAR EASTERN STUD, UNIV TORONTO, 72-. **HONORS AND AWARDS** Can Coun pre-doctoral fel, 59-61; Samuel S Fels Fund fel, 61-62; SSHRCC ed grant, 81-2001. **MEMBERSHIPS** Soc Mesopotamian Stud; Brit Sch Archaeol Iraq; Fondation Assyriologique Georges Dossin; Rencontre Assyriologique Int; Am Orient Soc. **SELECTED PUBLICATIONS** Auth, Assyrian and Babylonian Chronicles-Texts from Cuneiform Sources V, 75,; auth, Assyrian Royal Inscriptions I, 72, II 76; auth, Babylonian Historical-Literary texts - Toronto Semitic Texts and Studies III, 75; coauth, Papyrus and Tablet, 73; coauth, Royal Inscriptions on Clay Cones from Ashur Now in Istanbul, 84; coauth, Assyrian Rulers of the Third and Second Millenia BC - Royal Inscriptions of Mesopotamia: Assyrian Perids I, 87; coauth, Assyrian Rulers of the Early First Millenium BC I-II - Royal Inscriptions of Mesopotamia: Assyrian Periods II-III, 91, 96; coauth, Cambirdge Ancient History III, 92. **CONTACT ADDRESS** Near Eastern Stud, Univ of Toronto, 4 Bancroft Ave, Toronto, ON, Canada M5S 1A1. **EMAIL** kgrayson@chass.utoronto.ca

GREAVES, RICHARD L.
PERSONAL Born 09/11/1938, Glendale, CA, m, 1959, 2 children **DISCIPLINE** HISTORY **EDUCATION** Bethel Col, BA, 60; Berkeley Baptist Divinity Sch, MA, 62; Univ of London, PhD, 64. **CAREER** Assoc prof, Fla Memorial Col, 64-65; asst prof, William Woods Col, 65-66; asst prof, Eastern Wash State Col, 66-69; from asst prof to assoc prof, Mich State Univ, 69-72; from assoc prof to prof, Fla State Univ, 72-89; prof, London Ctr at Fla State Univ, 73; vis scholar, William Andrews Clark Memorial Libr at Univ Calif Los Angeles, 77; prof, Florence Ctr at Fla State Univ, 83 & 87; courtesy prof, Fla State Univ, 85-95; Robert O. Lawton Distinguished Prof of History, Fla State Univ, 89-; co-director of Ctr for British and Irish Studies, Fla State Univ, 91-92; chemn of dept of Hist, Fla State Univ, 93-. **HONORS AND AWARDS** Merriam Park Scholar, Bethel Col, 59-60; Awd for Academic Excellence, St Paul, Minn Jr Chamber of Commerce, 60; Salutatoria, Bethel Col Class of 1960; Knights Templar Scholar, 61-62; Regents' Grant, Univ Mo, 65; Outstanding Young Men of Am, 66; Walter D. Love Memorial Prize, Confr on British Studies, 70; Elected Fel, Royal Hist Soc, 81; Albert C. Outler Prize, Am Soc of Church Hist, 96; Professorial Excellence Awd, Fla State Univ, 97. **MEMBERSHIPS** Royal Hist Soc, Am Hist Asn, Am Soc of Church Hist, Baptist Hist Soc, Carolinas Symposium on British Studies, Historians of Early Modern Europe, N Am Confr on British Studies, Southern Confr on British Studies, Sixteenth-Century Studies Confr, Int John Bunyan Soc. **RESEARCH** Early Modern Britain. **SELECTED PUBLICATIONS** Coauth, Civilizations of the World: the Human Adventure, Harper and Row (New York, NY), 90; coauth, Civilizations of the West: The Human Adventure, Harper Collins (New York, NY), 92; coauth, Civilizations of the West: The Human Adventure Abridged Version, Harper Collins (New York, NY), 94; auth, God's Other Children: Protestant Nonconformists and the Emergence of Denominational Churches in Ireland 1660-1700, Stanford Univ Press, 97; auth, Dublin's Merchant-Quaker: Anthony Sharp and the Community of Friends 1643-1707, Stanford Univ Press, 98; auth, "Bunyan's Doctrine of Predestination: A Historical Perspective," The Recorder (forthcoming); auth, "Seditious Sectaries of 'Sober and Useful Inhabitants'? Changing Conceptions of the Quakers in Early Modern Britain," Albion (forthcoming). **CONTACT ADDRESS** Dept Hist, Florida State Univ, PO Box 3062200, Tallahassee, FL 32312-2446. **EMAIL** rgreaves@mailer.fsu.edu

GREAVES, ROSE LOUISE
PERSONAL Born 02/12/1925, Kansas City, KS, m, 1955 **DISCIPLINE** MODERN DIPLOMATIC & MIDDLE EASTERN HISTORY **EDUCATION** Univ Kans, BA, 46, MA, 47, PhD(hist), 52; Univ London, PhD(hist), 54. **CAREER** From asst instr to instr hist, Univ Kans, 47-51; asst lectr, Univ London, 54-56, res fel, Bedford Col, 56-57; res fel, Europ Ctr, Carnegie Found, 57-67; historian, Brit Petro Co, Ltd, London, 59-67; sr res fel & teaching asst hist & Islamic studies, Univ Toronto, 68; assoc prof hist, 69-73, Prof Hist, Univ Kans, 73-, Sr assoc mem Mid E hist, St Antony's Col, Oxford Univ, 73 & 74, Hilary & Trinity Terms; vis scholar, Wolfson Col, Cambridge Univ, 81; vis prof, U.S. Army, For Area Officers Course, Fort Bragg, NC, 84-87. **HONORS AND AWARDS** Fulbright Scholar, Eng, 52-54; Res Fel, Carnegie Found, Europ Ctr, 57-59; Am Philos Soc grant, 74; Fel, Am Asn for Univ Women, 75-76; multiple research grants, Univ Kans; Commander's Awd for Public Service, Special Warfare Center and School, Fort Bragg, NC, 87; Elected Kans Univ Women's Hal lof Fame, 91; Laurel Leaf Cluster, Commander's Awd for Public Service, USMA, West Point, 93. **MEMBERSHIPS** Fel Royal Hist Soc; Royal Soc Asian Affairs. **RESEARCH** Diplomatic relations of the great powers 19th and early 20th centuries; Middle East, especailly Persia, Afghanistan and India; oil. **SELECTED PUBLICATIONS** Auth, Persia and the Defence of India, 1884-1892, The Athlone Press, 59; British Policy in Persia, 1892-1903, 65, & Some Aspects of the Anglo-Russian Convention and its Working in Persia, 1907-1914, 68, Bull Sch Orient & African Studies; National Perceptions and Cultural Identities. The Hidden Infrastructure of the Petroleum Confrontation, A Report from the Center for Mediterranean Studies, Am Universities Field Staff; Profiles of the Third World, River City Publ, 86; The Cambridge History of Iran: Vol 7, From Nadir Shah to the Islamic Republic, Cambridge Univ Press, 91; Durand, Henry Mortimer, Encyclopaedia Iranica, 96; auth of a number of journal articles and book contributions. **CONTACT ADDRESS** Dept of Hist, Univ of Kansas, Lawrence, Lawrence, KS 66045-0001.

GREEN, CAROL HURD
PERSONAL Born 12/25/1935, Cambridge, MA, m, 1967, 2 children **DISCIPLINE** AMERICAN STUDIES **EDUCATION** Regis Col, BA, 57; Georgetown Univ, MA, 60; George Washington Univ, PhD(Am studies), 71. **CAREER** Instr English, Col Notre Dame, MD, 59-63; asst prof, Merrimack Col, 63-64; instr, Boston Col, 64-70; asst prof Am studies, Newton Col, 73-75; co-ed, Notable Am Women, Radcliffe Col, 76-80; assoc dean, col arts & sci, Boston Col, 81-. **HONORS AND AWARDS** Sr Fulbright Scholar, Palacky Univ, Czech Rep, 96-97. **MEMBERSHIPS** Am Studies Asn; Nat Women's Studies Asn. **RESEARCH** Literature and politics; American political trials; women's history. **SELECTED PUBLICATIONS** Auth, The Writer is a Spy: The Poetry of Ann Sexton and Maxine Kumin, Boston Rev of Arts, 73; co-ed, Journeys: Autobiographical Writings by Women, G K Hall, 79; Notable American Women: The Modern Period, Harvard Univ Press, 80; co-ed, American Women Writers: Supplement (Continuum), 94; coauth, American Women in the 1960's: Changing the Future, Twayne, 93; auth, The Suffering Body in M Garber and R Walkowitz, eds, Secret Agents, Routledge, 95. **CONTACT ADDRESS** Col of Arts & Scis, Boston Col, Chestnut Hill, 140 Commonwealth Ave, Chestnut Hill, MA 02167-3800. **EMAIL** green@bc.edu

GREEN, ELNA C.
DISCIPLINE U.S. HISTORY **EDUCATION** Wake Forest Univ, BA, 82; Wake Forest Univ, MA, 84; Tulane Univ, PhD, 92 **CAREER** Visiting asst prof, Tulane Univ, 92-93; asst prof, Sweet Briar Col, 93-98; assoc prof, Florida State Univ, 98- **HONORS AND AWARDS** Sweet Briar Grant-in-Aid of Res, 93, 96, 97; Amer Council Learned Soc Res Fel, 95; Mellon Res Fel, Virginia Historical Soc, 92; Patricia Harris Dissertation Fel, Tulane Univ, 90-92; **MEMBERSHIPS** Amer Historical Assoc; Orgn Amer Historians; Southern Hist Assoc; Southern Assoc Women Historians; Soc Welfare History Group **SELECTED PUBLICATIONS** Auth, "Ideals of Government, of Home, and of Women': The Ideology of Southern Antisuffragism," Hidden Histories of Women in the New South, Univ Missouri, 94; auth, "New Women," "True Daughters," and "Mad Women," Atlanta Hist, 96-97; auth, Southern Strategies: Southern Women and the Woman Suffrage Question, Univ North Carolina, 97; ed, Before the New Deal: Social Welfare in the South 1830-1930, Univ of Georgia Press, 99. **CONTACT ADDRESS** Dept of Hist, Florida State Univ, 1532 Grape St, Tallahassee, FL 32306-2200. **EMAIL** egreen@mailer.fsu.edu

GREEN, GEORGE D.
PERSONAL Born 09/17/1938, Fresno, CA, m, 1961, 4 children **DISCIPLINE** HISTORY **EDUCATION** Stanford Univ, PhD, 68. **CAREER** Assoc prof **RESEARCH** Political economy of twentieth-century America. **SELECTED PUBLICATIONS** Auth, Finance and Economic Development in the Old South: Louisiana Banking, 1804-1861, Stanford, 72. **CONTACT ADDRESS** History Dept, Univ of Minnesota, Twin Cities, 614 Social Sciences Tower, 267 19th Ave. S, Minneapolis, MN 55455. **EMAIL** green007@tc.umn.edu

GREEN, GEORGE N.
PERSONAL Born 04/27/1939, Rockdale, TX, m, 1972, 2 children **DISCIPLINE** AMERICAN HISTORY **EDUCATION** Univ Tex, Austin, BA, 61; Fla State Univ, MA, 62, PhD(hist), 66. **CAREER** Instr, Fla State Univ, 64-65 and Tex Woman's Univ, 65-66; from instr to asst prof, 66-72, Assoc Prof Hist, Univ Tex, Arlingotn, 72-, Younger Humanist res fel, Nat Endowment for Humanities, 70-71; coordr, AFL-CIO Fed Prison Prog, 73-74; grant, Tex Comt for Humanities, 77-78; Prof, 81-. **HONORS AND AWARDS** Outstanding Teacher in Liberal Arts, 82. **MEMBERSHIPS** Fellow, Tx St Hist Asn, 89; Board Member, 94; Southwestern Labor Hist Asn. **RESEARCH** Twentieth century political, and labor history of the United States, especially Texas. **SELECTED PUBLICATIONS** Auth, Establishment in Texas Politics, 79; auth, Hurst, Euless, & Bedford, 95; auth, North Richland Hills, 98. **CONTACT ADDRESS** Dept of Hist, Univ of Texas, Arlington, Arlington, TX 76019. **EMAIL** ggreen@uta.etu

GREEN, HARVEY
PERSONAL Born 09/15/1946, Buffalo, NY, m, 1980 **DISCIPLINE** HISTORY **EDUCATION** Univ Rochester, BA, 68; Rutgers Univ, MA, 70, PhD, 76. **CAREER** Chief hist, Strong Mus Rochester NY, 76-82; asst dir, 82-89, Prof of History, Northeastern Univ, 89-. **HONORS AND AWARDS** Rutgers Univ fel, 75; Fulbright prof hist, Univ Turku, Finland, 95; Bicentennial Prof Am Studies, Univ Helsinki, 99-2000. **MEMBERSHIPS** Am Studies Asn; Nat Coun Public Hist; Am Asn State & Local Orgn Am Hist; Am Hist Asn. **RESEARCH** US Cultural history, 1800-1950; Public history; American material culture; US literary history. **SELECTED PUBLICATIONS** Auth, Light of the Home: An Intimate View of the Lives of Women in Victorian America, Pantheon, 83; Fit for America: Health, Fitness, Sport, and American Society, 1830-1940, Pantheon, 86 & Johns Hopkins Univ Press, 88; The Uncertainty of Everyday Life, 1915-45, Harper, 92. **CONTACT ADDRESS** History Dept, Northeastern Univ, Boston, MA 02115. **EMAIL** hgreen@lynx.neu.edu

GREEN, JESSE DAWES
PERSONAL Born 02/09/1928, Chippewa Falls, WI, m, 1950, 3 children **DISCIPLINE** AMERICAN STUDIES, HISTORY OF ANTHROPOLOGY **EDUCATION** Reed Col, BA, 51; Univ Calif, Berkeley, MA, 57; Northwestern Univ, PhD(English), 72. **CAREER** Asst prof compos and lit, Univ Cincinnati, 64-68; prof to prof emer, Chicago State Univ, 68-. **HONORS AND AWARDS** Summer grant, National Endowment for Humanities, 76 and 81; fel, National Endowment for Humanities, 82-83. **RESEARCH** History of consciousness; literature and anthropology. **CONTACT ADDRESS** Dept of English, Chicago State Univ, Chicago, IL 60628. **EMAIL** j-green1@csu.edu

GREEN, LEAMON L., JR.
PERSONAL Born 06/28/1959, AL, m, 1996, 1 child **DISCIPLINE** ART **EDUCATION** Cleveland Inst Art; BFA, 82; Temple Univ, MFA, 85. **CAREER** Asst prof, Tx S Univ; 96- **HONORS AND AWARDS** Cosby Fel, 94; Creative Artist Prog Grant, 95; Project Artist, 98. **CONTACT ADDRESS** 1319 W 22nd St, Houston, TX 77008.

GREEN, MICHAEL KNIGHT
PERSONAL Born 12/26/1935, Spokane, WA, m, 1961, 2 children **DISCIPLINE** AMERICAN HISTORY **EDUCATION** Eastern Wash Univ, BA, 60; Univ Idaho, MA, 62, PhD(hist), 68. **CAREER** Asst prof Am hist, Pac Univ, 64-67; from Asst Prof to Assoc Prof, 67-80, Prof Eastern Wash Univ, 80-. **MEMBERSHIPS** Orgn Am Historians; Western Hist Asn. **RESEARCH** New Deal and post New Deal western history. **CONTACT ADDRESS** Dept of Hist, Eastern Washington Univ, M/S 27, Cheney, WA 99004-2496.

GREEN, THOMAS ANDREW
PERSONAL Born 03/18/1940, New York, NY, m, 1968 **DISCIPLINE** ANGLO-AMERICAN LEGAL HISTORY **EDUCATION** Columbia Univ, AB, 61; Harvard Univ, PhD(hist), 70, JD, 72. **CAREER** Asst prof hist, Bard Col, 67-69; asst prof law, 72-75, assoc prof, 75-77, Prof Law, Law Sch, Univ Mich, 77-, Prof Hist, Hist Dept, 80-. **HONORS AND AWARDS** NEH fel, Fel, Guggenheim fel **MEMBERSHIPS** AHA; Medieval Acad Am; Am Soc Legal Hist; Royal Hist Soc; Conf Critical Legal Studies. **RESEARCH** History of criminal law; history of legal and social theory; history of law in America, 1870-present. **SELECTED PUBLICATIONS** Auth, Societal concepts of criminal liability, Speculum, 72; The jury and the English law of homicide, Mich Law Rev, 76; co-ed, On the Law and Customs of England: Essays in Honor of S E Thorne, Univ NC Press, 81; auth, Art: Seditious libel, juries and the criminal law, Univ Calif, Los Angeles (in press). **CONTACT ADDRESS** Law Sch, Univ of Michigan, Ann Arbor, 625 S State St, Ann Arbor, MI 48109-1215. **EMAIL** tagreen@umich.edu

GREENBAUM, FRED
PERSONAL Born 11/06/1930, Brooklyn, NY, m, 1954, 2 children **DISCIPLINE** AMERICAN HISTORY **EDUCATION** Brooklyn Col, BA, 52; Univ Wis, MA, 53; Columbia Univ, PhD, 62. **CAREER** Lectr hist, Brooklyn Col, 58-59 & Queens Col, 60-61; from instr to assoc prof, 61-70, prof hist, Queensborough Community Col, 70-, lectr, Cooper Union, 61; mem, Prof Staff Cong. **MEMBERSHIPS** AHA; Orgn Am Historians. **RESEARCH** American progressive movement; the New Deal; labor history. **SELECTED PUBLICATIONS** Auth, John Dewey views Karl Marx, Soc Sci, 67; Progressivism: A Complex Phenomenon, New Politics, 68; The Progressive World of Gabirel Kolko, Social Studies, 69; co-ed, Readings in Western Civilization, Early Modern Period, McCutchan, 70; Fighting Progressive, A Biography of Edward P Costigan, Pub Affairs Press, 71; auth, Hiram Johnson and the New Deal, Pac Historian, 74; Robert Marion LaFollette, Twayne, 75; The Foreign Policy of Progressive Irreconcilables, In: Toward a New View of America, Burt Franklin, 77; Empire and Autonomy: The American and Netherland Revolutions, International Social Science Review, 89; Teddy Roosevelt Creates a Draft in 1912, in Theodore Roosevelt, Many Sided American, Heart of the Lakes Pub, 92; Ambivalent Friends, Progressive Era Politicians and Organized Labor, Labors Heritage, 94; American Nation, Whittier pub, 95; auth, Men Against Myths: The Progressive Response, Praeger, 00 . **CONTACT ADDRESS** Queensborough Comm Col, CUNY, 22205 56th Ave, Flushing, NY 11364-1432.

GREENBAUM, LOUIS SIMPSON
PERSONAL Born 02/14/1930, Chicago, IL, M, 1961, 3 children **DISCIPLINE** HISTORY **EDUCATION** Univ Wis, BA, 50, MA, 51; Harvard Univ, PhD, 55. **CAREER** From instr to assoc prof, 55-69, Prof Hist, Univ Mass, Amherst, 69-, Am Philos Soc fel, 63-64; NIH spec fel, 68-69, grant, 72-73; consult hist pop studies, Sch Pub Health, Harvard Univ, 68-72; mem, White House Conf Food, Nutrit and Health, 69. **MEMBERSHIPS** AHA; Soc Fr Hist Studies; Am Soc Church Hist; Am Asn Hist Med; Am Soc 18th Century Studies. **RESEARCH** Church history; 18th century Europe; history of medicine and public health in 18th century France. **SELECTED PUBLICATIONS** Auth, Jefferson, Thomas, the Paris Hospitals, and the University-of-Virginia, 18th-Century Stud, Vol 0026, 93; The End of an Elite--The French Bishops and the Coming of the Revolution, 1786-1790, Cath Hist Rev, Vol 0080, 94. **CONTACT ADDRESS** PO Box 9625, North Amherst, MA 01059. **EMAIL** greenbau@history.umass.edu

GREENBERG, BRIAN
PERSONAL Born 08/22/1946, Brooklyn, NY, m, 1970, 2 children **DISCIPLINE** HISTORY **EDUCATION** Hofster Univ, BA, 68; SUNY at Albany, MA, 71; Princeton Univ, PhD, 80. **CAREER** Coordr for Prog in Hist, 80-87; Assoc Prof, 86; Dept Hist, Univ of Del, 80-90; Chair in Am Soc Hist, Monmouth Univ, 90-; Chair Dept of Hist and Anthrop, Monmouth Univ, 99-. **HONORS AND AWARDS** Univ Fel, SUNY; Nat Defense Educ Act Fel; Phi Alpha Theta; Res Fel, Transformation Prospect, Philadephia Ctr for Early Am Studies, 90; Summer Stipend, Nat Endowment of Industrial Am for the Humanities, 92. **MEMBERSHIPS** AHA, Orgn of Am Historians, Am Center Hist Mus, NY Labor Hist Asn. **RESEARCH** American Labor and Social History. **SELECTED PUBLICATIONS** Auth, Worker and Community: Response to Industrialization in a Nineteenth-Century American City, Albany, New York, 1850-1884, State Univ of NY Press, 85; coauth, Upheaval in the Quiet Zone: A History of Hospital Worker's Union, Local 1199, Univ of Ill Press, 89; ed, special issue, The Public Historian. Public History and Labor History, (fall 89); auth, "Local 1199, Drug, Hospital, and Health Care Employees Union," "United Hospital Fund," and "Greater New York Hospital Association," in Encyclopedia of New York City (NY Hist Soc and Yale Univ Press, 95); auth, "Samuel Gompers and Trade Unionism in America," in American Reforms and Reformers (Greenwood Publ Group, 96); auth, "Andrew Carr Cameron," "William Sylvis," and "Tench Coxe," in American National Biography (Oxford Univ Press, 99); auth, "Battle of '59: Hospital Workers Go Out on Strike," NY Labor Hist Asn News Serv (Dec 99); coauth, "The Impact of Steelworkers in America The Nonunion Era," Labor Hist (fall 93), and in Steelworkers in America The Nonunion Era, ed. David Broody (Univ of Ill Press, 99). **CONTACT ADDRESS** Dept Hist, Monmouth Univ, 400 Cedar Ave, West Long Branch, NJ 07764-1804. **EMAIL** bgreenbe@monmouth.edu

GREENBERG, CHERYL
PERSONAL Born 08/13/1958, m, 1990, 2 children **DISCIPLINE** HISTORY **EDUCATION** Princeton Univ, AB, 80; Columbia Univ, MA, 81; MPhil, 83; PhD, 88. **CAREER** Asst Prof, Trinity Col, 86-92; Vis Assoc Prof, Harvard Univ, 96-97; From Assoc Prof to Prof, Trinity Col, 92-. **HONORS AND AWARDS** Phi Beta Kappa; Fel, Harvard Univ, 93-94; Fel, Harvard Univ, 96-97; Trinity Col Fac Res Grant, 97; Carlton C Qualey Mem Article Awd, J of Am Ethnic Hist, 97. **SELECTED PUBLICATIONS** Auth, "Or Does It Explode?" Black Harlem in the Great Depression, Oxford UP (91); auth, "Pluralism and Its Discontents," in Insider/Outsider: Am Jews and Multiculturalism (Univ Calif Pr, 98), 55-87; auth, "The Southern Jewish Community and the Struggle for Civil Rights," in African-Am and Jews in the Twentieth-Century (Univ Mo Pr, 98), 123-164; ed, A Circle of Trust: Remembering SNCC, Rutgers UP, 98; auth, Troubling the Waters: Black-Jewish Relations in the American Century, Princeton UP, forthcoming; auth, "Liberalisms," in Making Sense of the Twentieth-Century (Oxford UP, forthcoming); auth, "Harold Cruse on Blacks and Jews," in The Black Intellectual in Crisis (Routledge Pr, forthcoming). **CONTACT ADDRESS** Dept Hist, Trinity Col, Connecticut, 300 Summit St, Hartford, CT 06106-3100. **EMAIL** cheryl.greenberg@mail.trincoll.edu

GREENBERG, KENNETH
PERSONAL Born 11/02/1947, Brooklyn, NY, m, 1969, 3 children **DISCIPLINE** HISTORY **EDUCATION** Cornell Univ, BA, 68; Columbia Univ, MA, 70; Univ Wis, PhD, 76. **CAREER** Asst prof Hist, Alfred Univ, 75-77; prof Hist, Suffolk Univ, 78- ; Ch, Hist Dept, 89-present, Suffolk Univ. **HONORS AND AWARDS** Fel, Charles Warren Ctr, Hist Dept, 88; NEH fel, 88; fel in Law and Hist, Harvard Law Sch, 90-91; fel, assoc, W.E.B. DuBois Inst, Harvard Univ; NEH Summer Sem Anthrop and Hist, Northwestern Univ, 80; Va Found Human, Spring 98; Activity dir, fac develop, Title III Grant Suffolk Univ, 82-86; Amer Assn Col Quill grant, 86. **MEMBERSHIPS** Amer Hist Assn; Org Amer Historians; S Hist Assn; Amer Stud Assn. **RESEARCH** United States History; South; Slavery. **CONTACT ADDRESS** Chair, Dept of History, Suffolk Univ, B Ashburton Pl, Boston, MA 02108. **EMAIL** kgreenbe@acad.suffolk.edu

GREENBERGER, ALLEN JAY
PERSONAL Born 03/18/1937, Chicago, IL **DISCIPLINE** BRITISH IMPERIAL HISTORY **EDUCATION** Univ Mich, BA, 58, MA, 60, PhD(hist), 66. **CAREER** Instr, Smith Col, 65-66; from asst prof to assoc prof, 66-75, Prof Hist, Pitzer Col, 75-97; Prof Emer of Hist, 97-. **MEMBERSHIPS** Asn Asian Studies; Conf Brit Studies Res. **RESEARCH** Social and intellectual history of the British empire; social history of the British in India. **SELECTED PUBLICATIONS** Auth, Acts of Supremacy, The British-Empire and the Stage, 1790-1930, Albion, Vol 0024, 92; European Women and the 2nd British-Empire, Int Hist Rev, Vol 0015, 93. **CONTACT ADDRESS** Pitzer Col, 1050 N Mills Ave, Claremont, CA 91711-6101.

GREENE, DOUGLAS G.
PERSONAL Born 09/24/1944, Middletown, CT, m, 1966, 2 children **DISCIPLINE** HISTORY **EDUCATION** Univ S Fla, BA, 66; Univ Chicago, AM, 67; PhD, 72. **CAREER** Instr, Univ Mont, 70-71; Instr to Prof and Dir, Old Dominion Univ, 72-. **MEMBERSHIPS** Mystery Writers of Am. **RESEARCH** British Studies; Popular Culture **SELECTED PUBLICATIONS** Ed, Great classics of detection, Dover Pub, 00; ed, The Dead Hand and Other Uncollected Stories, Battered silicon Dispatch Box, 99; ed, The Detections of Miss Cusack, Battered Silicon Dispatch Box, 98; auth, "Colin Dexter," in Mystery Writers, Scribers, 98; ed, Detection by Gaslight, The Great Victorian and Edwardian Detective Stories, Dover Pub, 97; auth, John Dickson Carr: The Man Who Explained Miracles, Simon & Schuster, 95; auth, "Marsh's Miniatures: An Examination of Ngaio Marsh's Short Mystery Stories," in Ngaio Marsh, The Woman and Her Work, Scarecrow, 95. **CONTACT ADDRESS** Inst of Humanities, Old Dominion Univ, Norfolk, VA 23529. **EMAIL** dgreene@odu.edu

GREENE, JACK P.
PERSONAL Born 08/12/1931, Lafayette, IN, m, 1990, 2 children **DISCIPLINE** HISTORY **EDUCATION** NC Univ, AB, 51; Ind Univ, MA, 52; Duke Univ, PhD, 56. **CAREER** Instr, 56-59, Mich St Univ; asst, assoc prof, 59-65, Western Reserve; assoc prof, 65-66, Mich St Univ; Andrew W. Mellon Prof, 66-, John Hopkins Univ; dist prof, 90-92, Univ Calif, Irvine. **HONORS AND AWARDS** Fulbright, UK, 53-54; Guggenheim, 64-65; Inst for Advan Stud, 70-71, 85-86; Woodrow Wilson Intl Ctr, 74-75; Harmsworth Prof, Oxford, 75-76; Fulbright, Israel, 79; Ctr for Advan Stud Behavioral Sci, 79-80; Churchill Col Cambridge, 86; Fulbright, France, 86-87; Natl Hum Ctr, 87-88; Phi Beta Kappa LlD, Indiana, 77; Freeman Prof, Richmond, 96; Sweet Prof, Mich St, 97; Royal Hist Soc, 97. **MEMBERSHIPS** AHA; Org of Amer Hist; So Hist Assn. **RESEARCH** Early modern colonial British Amer. **SELECTED PUBLICATIONS** Auth, The Quest for Power: the Lower Houses of Assembly in the Southern Royal Colonies, 1689-1776, Norton & Co, 72; coauth, Colonial British America: Essays in the New History of the Early Modern Era, Johns Hopkins Univ Press, 84; auth, Encyclopedia of American Political History, Scribner's Sons, 84; auth, The Diary of Colonel Landon Carter of Sabine Hall 1752-1778, Va Univ Press, Va Hist Soc, 88; auth, Pursuits of Happiness: The Social Development of the Early Modern British Colonies and the Formation of American Culture, Univ NC Press, 88; auth, Peripheries and Center: Constitutional Development in the Extended Polities of the British Empire and the United States 1607-1789, Norton & Co, 90; coauth, The Blackwell Encyclopedia of the American Revolution, Oxford Basil Blackwell, 91; auth, Imperatives, Behaviors and Identities: Essays in Early American Cultural History, Univ Press Va, 92; auth, The Intellectual Construction of America: Exceptionalism and Identity from 1492-1800, Univ NC Press, 93; auth, Negotiated Authorities: Essays in colonial Political and Constitutional History, Univ Press Va, 94; auth, Explaining the American Revolution: Issues, Interpretations, and Actors, Univ Press Va, 95; auth, Interpreting Early America: Historiographical Essays, Univ Press Va, 96. **CONTACT ADDRESS** History Dept, Johns Hopkins Univ, Baltimore, 3400 N Charles St, Baltimore, MD 21218.

GREENE, JEROME ALLEN
PERSONAL Born 03/23/1942, Watertown, NY, m, 1975 **DISCIPLINE** AMERICAN INDIAN AND AMERICAN MILITARY HISTORY **EDUCATION** Black Hills State Col, BS, 68; Univ SDak, MA, 69. **CAREER** Instr Am Indian hist, Haskell Indian Jr Col, 71-73; Historian, Hist Preserv Div Nat Park Serv, 73-. **MEMBERSHIPS** Western Hist Asn; Coun Am Military Past; Col Mil Historians; Order Indian Wars; Nat Trust Historic Preservation. **RESEARCH** Indian Wars, 1865-1900; government-Indian relations; US Army uniforms and equipment, 1850-1902. **SELECTED PUBLICATIONS** Auth, The Custer Reader, NMex Hist Rev, Vol 0068, 93; Hokahey--A Good Day to Die--The Indian Casualties of the Custer Fight, Western Hist Quart, Vol 0026, 95; A Good Year to Die--The Story of the Great-Sioux-War, Southwestern Hist Quart, Vol 0100, 96; Custer--The Controversial Life of Custer, George, Armstrong, J Am Hist, Vol 0084, 97; Touched by Fire--The Life Death, and Mythic Afterlife of Custer, George, Armstrong, J Am Hist, Vol 0084, 97. **CONTACT ADDRESS** Denver Serv Ctr, National Park Services, 755 Parfet, Denver, CO 80225.

GREENE, JOHN C.
PERSONAL Born 03/05/1917, Indianapolis, IN, w, 1945, 3 children **DISCIPLINE** HISTORY **EDUCATION** Univ SD, BA, 38; Harvard Univ, MA, 39, PhD, 52. **CAREER** Prof, Emeritus, 87, Univ Connecticut; Prof, 63-67, Univ Kansas; vis Prof, 62-63, Univ Cal Berkeley; Assoc Prof, Prof, 56-62, Iowa State Univ; Asst Prof, 52-56, Univ Wisc; Instr, 48-52, Univ Chicago. **HONORS AND AWARDS** Harvard Soc of Fellows; Guggenheim Fel; Vis Schl Corpus Christi College. **MEMBERSHIPS** HSS; AAUP; ISHPSSS. **RESEARCH** History of Evolutionary Thought in the Western World; Early American Science; Historical Relations of Science and Religion. **SELECTED PUBLICATIONS** Auth, The Death of Adam: Evolution and Its Impact on Western Thought, Iowa State U Press, 59; auth, Darwin and the Modern World View, La, State Univ Press, 61; coauth, The Science of Minerals in the Age of Jefferson, in: Transaction in the American Philo Soc, 78; auth, American Science in the Age of Jefferson, Iowa State U Press, 84; Science Ideology and World View, Essays in the History of Evolutionary Ideas, U of Cal Press, 81; auth, Debating Darwin, Regina Books, 99. **CONTACT ADDRESS** 651 Sinex Ave., Apt. B215, Pacific Grove, CA 93950-4247.

GREENE, NATHANAEL
PERSONAL Born 04/04/1935, Providence, RI, m, 1980, 4 children **DISCIPLINE** HISTORY **EDUCATION** Brown Univ, AB, 57; Harvard Univ, AM, 58; PhD, 64; Foundation Nationale des Sciences Politiques, 61-62. **CAREER** Instructor, Asst Prof of History, Wesleyan Univ, 63-68; Assoc Prof of History, Wesleyan Univ, 68-74; Prof of History, 74; Vice President for Academic Affairs, 77-90. **HONORS AND AWARDS** Fulbright Fellow in France, 61-62; Fellow of Amer Council of learned Societies, 89-69; Guggenheim Fellow, 71-72. **MEMBERSHIPS** Society for French Historical Studies; Amer Historical Assoc. **RESEARCH** France and Spain in the 19th and 20th centuries. **SELECTED PUBLICATIONS** Auth, "Crisis and Decline: The French Socialist Party in the Popular Front Era;" auth, "From Versailles to Vichy: the Third French Republic; auth, "European Socialism since World War I;" auth, "Fascism: An Anthology." **CONTACT ADDRESS** Dept History, Wesleyan Univ, 238 Church Street, Middletown, CT 06459-3149. **EMAIL** ngreene@wesleyan.edu

GREENE, SANDRA E.
DISCIPLINE HISTORY **EDUCATION** Northwestern Univ, PhD, 81. **CAREER** Assoc prof. **SELECTED PUBLICATIONS** Auth, From Whence They Came: A Note on the Influence of West African Ethnic and Gender Relations on the Organizational Character of the 1733 St. John Slave Rebellion, 94;

Gender, Ethnicity and Social Change on the Upper Slave Coast: A History of the Anlo-Ewe, 96; Religion, History and the Supreme Gods of Africa: A Contribution to the Debate, Jour Relig Africa, 96; Sacred Terrain: Religion, Politics and Place in the History of Anloga, Int Jour African Hist Studies, 97; auth, "Family Concerns: Gender and Ethnicity in Pre-colonial West Africa," International Review of Social History, Supp. No. 7, 99; auth, "Cultural Zones in the Era of the Atlantic Slave Trade: Exploring the Yoruba Connection Among the Anlo-Ewe," Papers of the UNESCO Slave Route Project, Edited by Paul Lovejoy and Robin Law, London: Cussell Pub., 00. **CONTACT ADDRESS** Dept of History, Cornell Univ, Ithaca, NY 14853-2801. **EMAIL** seg6@cornell.edu

GREENE, THOMAS R.
PERSONAL Born 10/17/1933, New York, NY, m, 1958, 2 children **DISCIPLINE** MEDIEVAL HISTORY, ENGLISH LITERATURE **EDUCATION** St Francis Col, NYork, BA, 58; NYork Univ, MA, 61, PhD(medieval hist), 67. **CAREER** Asst prof II Hist, Newark State Col, 63-64; instr, 64-66, Asst Prof II Hist, Villanova Univ, 66-. **MEMBERSHIPS** AHA. **RESEARCH** Twelfth century church history. **CONTACT ADDRESS** Dept of Hist, Villanova Univ, Villanova, PA 19385.

GREENE, VICTOR ROBERT
PERSONAL Born 11/15/1933, Newark, NJ, m, 1957, 2 children **DISCIPLINE** AMERICAN HISTORY & STUDIES **EDUCATION** Harvard Univ, AB, 55; Univ Rochester, MA, 60; Univ Pa, PhD, 63. **CAREER** From asst prof to assoc prof hist, Kans State Univ, 63-71; assoc prof hist, 71-77, coordr ethnic studies, 76-78, prof hist, Univ Wis-Milwaukee, 77-, vis prof hist, Cleveland State Univ, 68-69; Warwick Univ, 90-; NE Normal Univ (China), 98-; Am Coun Learned Socs grant-in-aid, 70; Int Res & Exchanges Bd grant, 70-; fel, Nat Humanities Inst, 75-76; demonstration grant, Nat Endowment for Humanities, 77-78; Fulbright Award, Ger, 80-81. **HONORS AND AWARDS** Haiman Awd, Polish Am Hist Asn, 81; NEH Senior Fel, 87-88. **MEMBERSHIPS** AHA; Orgn Am Historians; Immigration and Ethnic Hist Soc; Am St Asn. **RESEARCH** American ethnic and labor history; popular culture. **SELECTED PUBLICATIONS** Auth, Origins of Slavic American Self-Consciousness, Church Hist, winter 66; The Slavic Community on Strike, Univ Notre Dame, 68; Slavic American Nationalism, In: American Contributions to 7th Congress of Slavists, Mouton, 73; For God and Country: Polish and Lithuanian Ethnic Consciousness, Soc Press, 75; Becoming American, In: Ethnic Frontier, Erdmans, 77; The Poles, In: Harvard Encycl of American Ethnic Groups, 80; Ethnic Groups and State Universities, In: American Education and the European Immigrant, 82; auth, Immigrant Leaders, Johns Hopkins Univ, 85; A Passion for Polka, Univ Calif, 92; Friendly Entertainers, In: Prospects, 95; A Holistic View of American Ethnic History, In: Polish American Studies, 98. **CONTACT ADDRESS** Dept of Hist, Univ of Wisconsin, Milwaukee, PO Box 413, Milwaukee, WI 53201-0413. **EMAIL** vicgre@uwm.edu

GREENEWALT, CRAWFORD HALLOCK
PERSONAL Born 06/03/1937, Wilmington, DE **DISCIPLINE** CLASSICAL ARCHAEOLOGY **EDUCATION** Harvard Univ, BA, 59; Univ Penn, PhD, 66. **CAREER** Asst Prof, Assoc Prof, Prof, 66 to 78-, Univ Cal Berkeley. **MEMBERSHIPS** APS; GAI; AAI. **RESEARCH** Interconnections between Greece and Anatolia Ancient Lydia, Sardis. **SELECTED PUBLICATIONS** Coauth, The Sardis Campaigns of 1994 and 1995, Amer J Archaeol, 98; auth, Croesus of Sardis and the Lydian Kingdom of Anatolia, in: Civilizations of the Ancient Near East, ed, JM Sasson, NY, Scribner's, 95; Sardis in the Age of Xenophon, in: Dans les des dix-mille, ed, P Briant, Toulouse, Toulouse Univ, 95; George Maxim Anossov Hanfmann, November 1911-13, March 1986, APS, 86. **CONTACT ADDRESS** Dept of Classics, Univ of California, Berkeley, Dwinelle Hall 7303, Berkeley, CA 94720.

GREENFIELD, GERALD M.
DISCIPLINE LATIN AMERICAN HISTORY, AMERICAN HISTORY **EDUCATION** SUNY at Buffalo, BA, 67; Brooklyn Col, MA, 69; IN Univ, Bloomington, PhD, 75. **CAREER** Prof & ch, Univ of WI, Parkside. **HONORS AND AWARDS** UW-Parkside, Outstanding Ser Awd, 96; UW-Parkside Outstanding Tchg Awd, 96; Am Philos Soc, 94 & 85; Southeastern Wis Educators Hall of Fame, 00. **RESEARCH** Brazilian hist. **SELECTED PUBLICATIONS** Ed, Latin American Urbanization: Historical Profiles of Major Cities, Greenwood Press, 94; co-ed, Latin American Labor Organizations, Greenwood Press, 87; coauth, Western Hemisphere, Silver Burdett & Ginn, 92; The Great Drought and Elite Discourse in Imperial Brazil, Hisp Amer Hist Rev, 92; co-ed, Those United States, International Perspectives on American History, 2 vols., Harcourt Brace College Publishers (Ft Worth, TX), 00; auth, The Realities of Images: Imperial Brazil and the Great Drought, Am Philos Soc (Philadelphia, PA), 01. **CONTACT ADDRESS** Dept of Hist, Univ of Wisconsin, Parkside, 900 Wood Rd, Molinaro 1, PO Box 2000, Kenosha, WI 53141-2000. **EMAIL** gerald.greenfield@uwp.edu

GREENHOUSE, WENDY
PERSONAL m, 2 children **DISCIPLINE** HISTORY OF ART **EDUCATION** Yale Univ, BA, 77; Simmons, MLS, 81; Yale Univ, PhD, 89. **CAREER** Instr Art Hist **RESEARCH** American Art; History of art in Chicago and region. **SELECTED PUBLICATIONS** Auth, "Benjamin West and Edward III: A Neoclassical Painter and Medieval History," Art Hist 8, 85; auth, "The American Portrayal Tudor and Stuart History, 1835-65," PhD diss, 89; coauth, The Art of Archibald J. Motley, Jr., Chicago Hist Soc, 91; auth, "The Landing of the Fathers: Representing the National Past, 1770-1860" in Picturing History: American Painting 1770-1930, Rizzoli, 93; coauth, Herman Menzel: A Rediscovered Regionalist, Chicago Hist Soc, 93; auth, "Imperilled Ideals: British Historical Heroines in Antebellum American History Painting" in Redefining American History Painting, Cambridge Univ Press, 95; "Daniel Huntington and the Ideal of Christian Art," Winterthur Portfolio 31, (96): no 2/3; auth, "'To Unify and Elevate': Midwestern Art Organizations, 1890-1930," in Mathias Alten: Journey of an American Painter, (Grand Rapids Art Museum, 98), and others. **CONTACT ADDRESS** 303 N Cuyler Ave, Oak Park, IL 60302-2302. **EMAIL** mtrenary@uic.edu

GREENLAND, DAVID E.
PERSONAL Born Bournemouth, Hampshire, England **DISCIPLINE** GEOGRAPHY **EDUCATION** Univ Birmingham, BS, 63; MS, 65; Univ Canterbury, PhD, 71. **CAREER** Res Asst, Birmingham, 63-64; Instructor, Univ Ga, 65-66; Lecturer, Univ Canterbury, 66-75; Visiting Asst Prof, Univ Calif, 75; Dir or Res Station, Univ Colo, 76-78; Assoc Prof to Prof and Chair, Univ Colo, 76-89; Prof, Univ Ore, 91-97; Prof, Univ NCar, 97-. **MEMBERSHIPS** Royal Meterol Soc; Am Meterol Soc; Am Geophysical Union; Asn of Am Geog; Pacific NW Sci Asn; Intl Mountain Soc. **RESEARCH** Climate and Vegetation; The Climate of the Pacific Northwest; Long-Term Ecological Research. **SELECTED PUBLICATIONS** Auth, "Spatial Surface Energy Budgets Over Alpine Tundra," Mountain Research and Development, (91): 339-351; co-auth, "Physical and Boundary Layer Climatology," Physical Geography, (91): 189-206; auth, "Spatial Energy Budgets in Alpine Tundra," Theoretical and Applied Climatology, (93): 229-239; auth, "Use of satellite based sensing in land surface climatology," Progress in Physical Geography, (94): 1-15; ed, El Nino and Long-Term Ecological Research Sites, Univ WA Press, 94; co-auth, "Changes in Climate and Hydrochemical responses in a high-elevation catchment, Rocky Mountains," Limology and Oceanography, (96): 939-946; co-auth, "Effects of Climate Change on Inland Waters of the Pacific Coastal Mountains and Western Great Basin of North America," Hydrological Processes, (97): 971-992; auth, "Climate," in A Synthesis of the Niwot Ridge Alpine Tundra Ecosystem, Oxford Univ Press, 99; auth, The Geography of Climate and Vegetation, Johns Hopkins Univ Press, forthcoming. **CONTACT ADDRESS** Dept Geog, Univ of No Carolina, Chapel Hill, Chapel Hill, NC 27599-3220.

GREENLEAF, RICHARD E.
PERSONAL Born 05/06/1930, Hot Springs, AR **DISCIPLINE** LATIN AMERICAN HISTORY **EDUCATION** Univ NMex, BA, 53, MA, 54, PhD(hist), 57. **CAREER** Asst prof hist and int rels, Univ Am, 57-60, assoc prof int rels and chmn dept, 60-62, from asst to assoc dean, Grad Sch, 57-62, prof hist and int rels, acad vpres and grad dean, 62-69; Prof Hist, Tulane Univ, 69-, Dir, Ctr Latin Am Studies, 70-, Univ Am fel, Spain, 62. **MEMBERSHIPS** AHA. **RESEARCH** Social and intellectual history of colonial Latin American and the Hispanic Southwest; modern Mexico. **SELECTED PUBLICATIONS** Auth, Life Between Judaism and Christianity in New-Spain, 1580-1606, Hispanic Am Hist Rev, Vol 0074, 94; A Violent Evangelism--The Political and Religious Conquest of the America, Am Hist Rev, Vol 0099, 94; Persistence of Native Values, the Inquisition and the Indians of Colonial Mexico, Americas, Vol 0050, 94. **CONTACT ADDRESS** Ctr for Latin Am Studies, Tulane Univ, 6823 St Charles Ave, New Orleans, LA 70118-5698.

GREENLEE, JAMES G. C.
PERSONAL Born 07/04/1945, Hamilton, ON, Canada **DISCIPLINE** HISTORY **EDUCATION** McMaster Univ, BA, 68, MA, 69, PhD, 75. **CAREER** Asst prof, McMaster Univ, 73-77; asst prof to assoc prof, 77-89, prof hist, Grenfell Col, Mem Univ Nfld, 89-. **MEMBERSHIPS** Hum Asn Can; Asn Atlantic Hist. **SELECTED PUBLICATIONS** Auth, Education and Imperial Unity, 88; auth, Sir Robert Falconer: A Biography, 88. **CONTACT ADDRESS** Grenfell Col, Mem Univ of Newfoundland, University Dr, Corner Brook, NF, Canada A2H 6P9. **EMAIL** jgreenlee@swgc.mun.ca

GREENOUGH, SARAH
DISCIPLINE ART HISTORY **EDUCATION** Univ Penn, BA 73; Univ N Mexico, MA 76, PhD 83. **CAREER** Nat Gallery of Art, cur of photo, 90-, res cur dept graphic arts 86-89, guest scholar 84-86, guest cur 79-84; Univ NMex, teaching assoc, inst, 77-80; Metro mus of Art, res 76-77; Univ NMex, grad asst 74-76. **HONORS AND AWARDS** IAAC Best Photog Ex Awd; 2 Bk of the Year Awds Marine Photo Wkshp; Focal Press Awd; Awd Dist Content and Design; ICP Photo Bk of the Year; Art Critics Awd; Centennial Awd; Silver Medal for Alfred Stieglitz: Photos and Writings; Popejoy Awd; Samuel H. Kress Awd; Nat Bk Awd; Beaumont Newhall fel; Samuel H Kress Fel; UNM Grad Fel. **MEMBERSHIPS** CAA; NEH Panel; WCP; Smithsonian Inst Adv Panel. **SELECTED PUBLICATIONS** Auth, Paul Strand, Aperture, 90; auth, Walker Evans: Subways and Streets, Nat Gallery of Art, 91; auth, Harry Callahan, Washington DC, Nat Gallery Art and Bullfinch Press, 96; Robert Frank: Moving Out, ed, coauth, Washington DC, Nat Gallery Art and Bullfinch Press, 94; auth, Modern Art and America: Alfred Stieglitz and His New York Galeries, Nat Gallery of Art, Bulfinch Press, 01. **CONTACT ADDRESS** Dept of Photographs, National Art Gallery, Washington, DC 20565.

GREENSHIELDS, MALCOLM
DISCIPLINE HISTORY **EDUCATION** Univ Saskatchewan, BA, 78; Sussex Univ, DPhil. **RESEARCH** European and French history; social history; criminality; religion and popular culture. **SELECTED PUBLICATIONS** Auth, An Economy of Violence in Early Modern France, Penn State, 95. **CONTACT ADDRESS** Dept of History, Univ of Lethbridge, 4401 University Dr W, Lethbridge, AB, Canada T1K 3M4. **EMAIL** greenshields@uleth.ca

GREENSPAN, ANDERS
PERSONAL Born 07/23/1963, Wynne Wood, PA, s **DISCIPLINE** HISTORY **EDUCATION** Brandeis Univ, BA, 85; Ind Univ, MA, 88; PhD, 92. **CAREER** Vis lectr to asst prof, Ind Univ, 92-94; vis lectr, Anderson Univ, 94; vis asst prof, bowling Green State Univ, 95; asst prof, Nmex State Univ, 95; asst prof, Long Island Univ, 96-. **HONORS AND AWARDS** Kohlmeier Teaching Fel, Ind Univ, 89, 91; Phi Alpha Theta, 91; Res Grant, Long Island Univ, 97; Phi Eta Sigma, 98. **MEMBERSHIPS** OAH, AHA. **RESEARCH** U.S. 20th Century, public. **SELECTED PUBLICATIONS** Auth, "How Philanthropy Can Alter Our View of the Past: A Look at Colonial Williamsburg", Voluntas V.2 (94):193-203; auth, "The Great Depression" in Events That Changed America in the Twentieth Century, eds. John E. Findling and Frank W. Thackeray, (CT: Greenwood Pr, 96), 47-59; auth, American History 2, The Col Network Inc., (In) 97; rev, of "The Orphan Trains and Riding the Rails", The Am Hist Rev, 103.3 (June 98) 1015-16. **CONTACT ADDRESS** Dept Hist, Long Island Univ, C.W. Post, 720 N Blvd, Greenvale, NY 11548-1319. **EMAIL** agreensp@liu.edu

GREENSPAN, EZRA
PERSONAL Born 02/02/1952, Perth Amboy, NJ, m, 1978, 3 children **DISCIPLINE** AMERICAN STUDIES **EDUCATION** Union Col NY, BA, 74; Brown Univ, MA, 75; PhD, 81. **CAREER** Jr Lectr, Tel Aviv Univ Isreal, 81-88; Instr, Middlesex Col,89-90; From Asst to Full Prof, Univ of SC, 90-00. **HONORS AND AWARDS** Fel for Univ Teachers, NEH; Best New J "Book History, Coun of Ed of Learned J, 99; English Dept Teaching Awd, Univ of SC, 99. **MEMBERSHIPS** MLA, Am Studies Asn, S Atlantic MLA, D.H. Lawrence Soc, Res Soc for Am Periodicals, Soc for the Hist of Authorship, Reading, and Publ, Phi Beta Kappa. **RESEARCH** History of the book, Nineteenth Century American literary history, Modern Jewish Literature. **SELECTED PUBLICATIONS** Auth, The Schlemiel Comes to America: A Reading of Jewish American Literature, 81; auth, Walt Whitman and the American Reader, 90; auth, Cambridge Companion to Whitman, 95; found co-ed, Book History, 98-; auth, George Palmer Putnam: Representative American Publisher, 00. **CONTACT ADDRESS** Dept English, Univ of So Carolina, Columbia, Columbia, SC 29208. **EMAIL** ezra.greenspan@sc.edu

GREENWALD, MAURINE WEINER
PERSONAL Born 05/24/1944, Chicago, IL, m, 1 child **DISCIPLINE** AMERICAN SOCIAL HISTORY **EDUCATION** Univ IL, Urbana, BA, 66; Brown Univ, PhD, 77. **CAREER** Instr hist, RI Col, 71-72; instr, 72-77, asst prof, 77-78, assoc prof hist, Univ Pittsburgh, 78. **HONORS AND AWARDS** Nat Defense Educ Act Title IV fel, Brown Univ, 67-71; Face Arts & Sci Res grant, 77, 82-89, 95-96, 98; Russell Sage Found grant, 93-94; Pittsburgh Center for Social Hist, 93-94; Chancellor's Distinguished Tchg Awd, 94; Henry Murray Center Res Expenses grant, 97. **MEMBERSHIPS** Orgn Am Historians, Coord Comt Women in Hist Profession, Am Historical Assn, Golden Key Honor Soc, hon mem, 96. **RESEARCH** Hist of women, work and family in the US during the 19th and 20th centuries. **SELECTED PUBLICATIONS** Auth, Women's History in America, In: American Women and American Studies, Am Studies Asn, 71; Women Workers and World War I: The American Railroad Industry, A Case Study, Jour Am Hist, Dec 75; Women, War and Work: The Impact of World War I on Women Workers in the United States, Greenwood Press, 80, paperback ed, Cornell Univ Press, 90; Women at Work Through the Eyes of Elizabeth Beardsley Butler and Lewis Wickes Hine (intro essay to reprint of Women and the Trades, 1909), Univ Pittsburgh Press, 84; Assessing the Past, Looking to the Future: A Report by the OAH committee on the Status of Women, Org of Am Hist Newsletter, 86; Working-class Feminism and the Family Wage Ideal: The Seattle Debate on Married Women's Right to Work, 1914-1920, Jour Am Hist, June 89; Women and Class in Pittsburgh, 1850-1920, In: City at the Point: Essays on the Social History of Pittsburgh (Samuel P Hayes, ed), Univ Pittsburgh Press, 89; Organized Labor and Women in Modern America, In: Women's Studies Encyclope-

dia, vol 3 (Helen Tierney, ed), Greenwood Press, 91; Women and Working-Class History in Pennsylvania, Pa Hist, winter 96; Visualizing Pittsburgh in the 1900s: Photographs and Sketches in the Service of Social Reform, In: Pittsburgh Surveyed: Social Science and Social Reform in the Early Twentieth Century, Univ Pittsburgh Press, 96 (co-ed with Margo Anderson); Elizabeth Beardsley Butler, In: American National Biography (John A Garraty, ed), Oxford Univ Press, 99. **CONTACT ADDRESS** Hist Dept, Univ of Pittsburgh, 3p01 Forbes Quad, Pittsburgh, PA 15260-0001. **EMAIL** greenwal@pitt.edu

GREER, ALLAN R.
PERSONAL Born 06/04/1950, New Westminster, BC, Canada **DISCIPLINE** HISTORY **EDUCATION** Univ BC, BA, 72; Carleton Univ, MA, 75; York Univ, PhD, 80. **CAREER** Asst prof, Univ Maine, 80-83; asst to assoc prof, 83-94, PROF HISTORY, UNIV TORONTO, 94-. **HONORS AND AWARDS** John A. Macdonald Awd, Can Hist Asn, 85; Alan Sharlin Prize, Soc Sci Hist Asn, 85; Priz Lionel-Groulx, Inst hist Am francaise; John Porter Awd, Cam Soc Anthrop Asn. **MEMBERSHIPS** Can Hist Asn; Inst hist Am francaise; Inst Early Am Hist Cultur. **RESEARCH** Social hist of Canada from the seventeenth to early nineteenth century, colonization of the Americas and the cultural encounter of natives nad Europeans. **SELECTED PUBLICATIONS** Auth, Peasant, Lord and Merchant: Rural Society in Three Quebec Parishes 1740-1840, 85; auth, The Patriots and the People: The Rebellion of 1837 in Rural Lower Canada, 93; auth, The People of New France, 97. **CONTACT ADDRESS** Univ Col, Univ of Toronto, 100 St. George St, Rm 2074, Toronto, ON, Canada M5S 3H7. **EMAIL** allan.greer@utoronto.ca

GREGG, EDWARD
PERSONAL Born 04/08/1945, Ashland, KS **DISCIPLINE** HISTORY **EDUCATION** Univ Kans, BA, 67; Univ London, MA, 68, PhD(hist), 72. **CAREER** Asst prof, 72-77, Assoc Prof Hist, Univ SC, 77-, Clark Libr, Univ Calif Los Angeles fel hist, 73; Inst Advan Study, Univ Edinburgh fel hist, 78; vis scholar hist, London Sch Econ, 78-79; vis prof, Univ Kans, 79-80. **MEMBERSHIPS** Fel Royal Hist Soc. **RESEARCH** Reign of Queen Anne; Jacobite Movement; reign of Louis XIV. **SELECTED PUBLICATIONS** Auth, Marlborough in exile, 1712-1714, Hist J, 72; Was Queen Anne a Jacobite?, Hist, 72; coauth, Biography by Amateurs, European Studies Rev, 74; auth, The education of princes, 1675-1725, 18th Century Studies, 80; Queen Anne, Routledge & Kegan Paul, 78. **CONTACT ADDRESS** Dept of Hist, Univ of So Carolina, Columbia, Columbia, SC 29208.

GREGO, RICHARD
PERSONAL Born 04/03/1963, New York, NY, m, 1987 **DISCIPLINE** HISTORY **EDUCATION** SUNY, BA, 85; Col of St. Rose, MA; SUNY, DA, 97 **CAREER** Adj Inst, 91-pres, Indian Rvr Com Col **MEMBERSHIPS** Am Philos Assoc **RESEARCH** Existentialism, History of Ideas; Comparative Philosophy of Religion **CONTACT ADDRESS** PO Box 3104, Fort Pierce, FL 34948.

GREGORY, FREDERICK
PERSONAL Born 12/03/1942, Honesdale, PA, m, 1967, 2 children **DISCIPLINE** HISTORY OF SCIENCE **EDUCATION** Wheaton Col, BS, 65; Gordon-Conwell Theol Sem, BD, 68; Univ Wis, MA, 70; Harvard Univ, PhD(hist sci), 73. **CAREER** Asst prof math and hist sci, Eisenhower Col, 73-78; Asst Prof Hist Sci, Univ Fla, 78-. **MEMBERSHIPS** Hist Sci Soc; Sigma Xi. **RESEARCH** German science in modern era; science and religion; 19th century science. **SELECTED PUBLICATIONS** Hist sci ed, The Eighteenth Century: A Current Bibliography, 18th Century Studies, 76-; auth, Scientific Materialism in 19th Century Germany, D Reidel, 77; Scientific vs dialectical materialism, Isis, 6/78. **CONTACT ADDRESS** Dept of Hist, Univ of Florida, 4131 Turlington Hall, Gainesville, FL 32611.

GREGORY, ROBERT G.
PERSONAL Born 05/16/1924, Denver, CO, m, 1955, 2 children **DISCIPLINE** HISTORY **EDUCATION** Univ Calif, Los Angeles, BA, 48, MA, 50, PhD, 56. **CAREER** Civilian historian, 15th Air Force, March AFB, 57; from asst prof to assoc prof hist, Wake Forest Col, 57-66; assoc prof, 66-71, Prof Hist, Syracuse Univ, 71-; Prof Emeritis, Fac training fel, Am inst Indian Studies, 62-63; humanities fel, cooperative prog humanities, Duke Univ, 64-65; Nat Sci Found award, 68-69, grant, 70-75; chmn, Asn African Studies Prog, 74-77. **MEMBERSHIPS** AHA; African Studies Asn; Asian Studies Asn. **RESEARCH** South Asians in Britain. **SELECTED PUBLICATIONS** Auth, Sidney Webb and East Africa: Labour's Experiment With Native Paramountcy, Univ Calif, 62; Churchill's administration of East Africa: A period of Indian disillusionment, 1906-1922, J Indian Hist, 8/66; coauth, A Guide to the Kenya National Archives, Prog Eastern African Studies, 69; auth, Africana archives and innovative teaching, Africana Libr J, spring 71; India and East Africa: A History of Race Relations Within the British Empire, 1890-1939, Clarendon, 72; auth, H S L Polak and the Indians Overseas Association, Vivekananda Kendra Patrika, spring 73; Co-operation and collaboration in colonial East Africa: The Asians' political role, 1890-1964, African Affairs, 4/81; Literary development in East Africa: The Asian contribution, 1955-1975, Res African Lit, winter 81; The Rise and Fall of Bhizanthropy in East Africa: The Asian Contribution, Transactions, 92; Quest for Equality: Asian Politics in East Africa, 1900-67, Orient Longman, 93; South Asians In East Africa: An Economic and Social History, 1890-1980, Westview, 93. **CONTACT ADDRESS** Dept of Hist, Syracuse Univ, 750 E Adams St, Syracuse, NY 13210-2399.

GRELE, RONALD J.
PERSONAL Born 06/08/1934, Naugatuck, CT, d, 4 children **DISCIPLINE** UNITED STATES HISTORY **EDUCATION** Univ Conn, BA, 59; Rutgers Univ, PhD, 78. **CAREER** Dir, Oral Hist Res Office (Ret) **MEMBERSHIPS** AHA; OAH; OHA; CPH. **RESEARCH** Historical methods; social history; oral history. **SELECTED PUBLICATIONS** Auth, Envelopes of Sound: The Art of Oral History, 85; A Student Generation in Revolt, 88; co-auth, The Urbanization of New Jersey, 64; ed, Multi-culturalism and Subjectivity in Oral History: An International Anthology, 92. **CONTACT ADDRESS** 90 Morningside Dr 3A, New York, NY 10027. **EMAIL** rgg@columbia.edu

GRENDLER, PAUL F.
PERSONAL Born 05/24/1936, m, 1962, 2 children **DISCIPLINE** HISTORY **EDUCATION** Oberlin Col, BA, 59; Univ Wis, Madison, MA, 61, PhD, 64. **CAREER** Instr, Univ Pittsburgh, 63-64; lectr, Univ of Toronto, 64-65, asst prof, 65- 69, assoc prof, 69-73, prof, 73-98, prof emer, 98-, Univ Toronto; vis prof, Univ NC, Chapel Hill, 91. **HONORS AND AWARDS** Fulbright Fellow, 62-63; Postdoctoral Fellow, Inst for Research in the Humanities, Univ Wis, Madison, 67-68; Canada Council Leave Fellow, 70-71; Am Council of Learned Societies Fellow, 71-72; I Tatti Fellow, Harvard, 70-72; Sr Fellow, Soc for the Humanities, Cornell Univ, 73-74; Guggenheim Mem Fellow, 78-79; Soc Sci and Humanities Research Council of Canada Leave Fellow, 79-80, 85-86, 88-89; Fellow, Woodrow Wilson Int Ctr for Scholars, Washington, D.C., 82-83; Fellow, National Humanities Cntr, Research Triangle Pk, NC, 88-90; Interpretive Research Grant, NEH, 89-92; Connaught Fellowship, Univ of Toronto, 97; Sr Scholar Citation for achievement, Soc for Italian Historical Studies, 98. **MEMBERSHIPS** Renaissance Soc of Am, 91-92; Am Cath Hist Assoc, 83-84; Erasmus of Rotterdam Soc; Am Hist Assoc; Soc for Italian Hist Studies. **RESEARCH** Italian Renaissance; Renaissance and Reformation Europe; Hist of Edu. **SELECTED PUBLICATIONS** Auth, Critics of the Italian World 1530-1560, 69; auth, The Roman Inquisition and the Venetian Press 1540-1605, 77; auth, Culture and Censorship in Late Renaissance Italy and France, 81; auth, Schooling in Renaissance Italy: Literacy and Learning 1300-1600, 89; auth, Books and Schools in the Italian Renaissance, 95; auth, The Universities of the Italian Renaissance, 01. **CONTACT ADDRESS** 110 Fern Ln, Chapel Hill, NC 27514-4206. **EMAIL** pgrendler@compuserve.com

GRENIER, JUDSON A.
PERSONAL Born 03/06/1930, Indianapolis, IN, m, 1954, 4 children **DISCIPLINE** UNITED STATES HISTORY **EDUCATION** Univ Minn, AB, 51; Univ Calif, Berkeley, MA, 51; Univ Calif, Los Angeles, PhD(hist), 65. **CAREER** News analyst, US Inform Agency, US Dept State, 52; instr jour, El Camino Col, 56-60, asst prof hist, 60-65; vis lectr, Univ Calif, Los Angeles, 65-66; from asst prof to assoc prof, 66-72, coordr, interdisciplinary studies, 67-68 and 70-72, chmn urban studies interdept prog, 68-72, chmn dept hist, 68-70, 88-89, Prof Hist, Calif State Univ, Dominguez Hills, 72-93, prof, emeritus, 93-, Reporter, Los Angeles Mirror News, 57-58; exec secy, Jour Asn Jr Col, 58-60; mem bd dirs, Los Angeles Welfare PLanning Coun, 67-70; Carnegie Found grant, 72-73; mem hist team, Los Angeles Bicentennial Comt, 73-76, Los Angeles 200, 78-81; scribe, Hist Guild Southern Calif, 73-76; senator, Acad Sen Calif State Univ and Col, 73-82, secy, 76-78, vchair, 79-80, mem exec comt, 76-80, mem, Comn Extended Educ, 77-80; assoc Los Angeles, County Mus, 75-; dir and vchair, Hist Soc Southern Calif, 79-82; Sec, CSU Emeritus and Retired Faculty Assn, 00- . **HONORS AND AWARDS** Distinguished Prof Awd, Calif State Univ, Dominguez Hills, 74; Huntington-Haynes Fellowship, 85; Newberry Fellowship 91; Carl Wheat Awd, 94. **MEMBERSHIPS** AHA; Orgn Am Historians; California Historical Society. **RESEARCH** The progressive era, 1898-1919; mass culture and the mass media; California and the West. **SELECTED PUBLICATIONS** History of the California State University, 81; California Legacy: The Watson-Dominguez Family, 87; Growing Together for a Century: TI & T and Southern California, 99; John Houston, California's First Controller and the Origins of State Government, 99. **CONTACT ADDRESS** Dept of Hist, California State Univ, Dominguez Hills, Carson, CA 90747. **EMAIL** judgrenier@earthlink.net

GRENNEN, JOSEPH EDWARD
PERSONAL Born 09/03/1926, New York, NY, m, 1950, 6 children **DISCIPLINE** ENGLISH LITERATURE, MEDIEVAL SCIENCE **EDUCATION** Col Holy Cross, BS, 47; Fordham Univ, MA, 54, PhD, 60. **CAREER** Instr, High Sch, NY, 47-50; educ adv, Troop Info and Educ Div, US Army, Ger, 50-55; from asst prof to assoc prof, 56-76, chmn dept, 65-71, PROF ENGLISH, FORDHAM UNIV, 76-, Ed, Thought, 78-80. **MEMBERSHIPS** Mediaeval Acad Am; MLA; AAUP. **RESEARCH** Middle English literature; modern criticism; history of science. **SELECTED PUBLICATIONS** Auth, The Making of Works, Jones, David and the Medieval Drama, Renascence-Essays on Values in Lit, Vol 0045, 93. **CONTACT ADDRESS** Dept of English, Fordham Univ, New York, NY 10458.

GRESSLEY, GENE M.
PERSONAL Born 06/20/1931, Frankfort, IN, m, 1952, 2 children **DISCIPLINE** HISTORY **EDUCATION** Ind Univ, MA, 56; Univ Ore, PhD(hist), 64. **CAREER** Asst state historian, Colo State Hist Soc, 52-54; res grant, 63, Dir Western Hist Res Ctr, Univ WYO, 60-, Res Prof Am Studies, Univ, 64-, Nat Endowment for Humanities fel, 66-67. **HONORS AND AWARDS** Edwards Awd, Agr Hist Soc, 59; Pelzer Awd C, Orgn Am Historians, 73. **MEMBERSHIPS** Orgn Am Historians; Agr Hist Soc; Bus Hist Soc; Pac Coast Br AHA. **RESEARCH** American economic history; historiography; 20th century American history. **SELECTED PUBLICATIONS** Auth, Horter, Henry, M.--Rocky-Mountain Empire Builder, Pacific Hist Rev, Vol 0062, 93; The Great Thirst--Californians and Water, 1770s-1990s, Pacific Hist Rev, Vol 0062, 93; The Depression and the Urban West-Coast, 1929-1933--Los-Angeles, San-Francisco, Seattle, and Portland, Montana-Mag of Western Hist, Vol 0043, 93; An Alpha and Omega of 20th-Century Mining History--A Review-Essay, NMex Hist Rev, Vol 0069, 94; Under an Open Sky--Rethinking America Western Past, Montana-Mag of Western Hist, Vol 0044, 94; Sutter, John and a Wider West, Ore Hist Quart, Vol 0096, 95; Colony and Empire--The Capitalist Transformation of the American-West, NMex Hist Rev, Vol 0071, 96; North-American Cattle-Ranching Frontiers--Origins, Diffusion, and Differentiation, Pacific Northwest Quart, Vol 0087, 96; Remaking the Agrarian Dream--New-Deal Rural Settlement in the Mountain West, NMex Hist Rev, Vol 0072, 97. **CONTACT ADDRESS** Univ of Wyoming, Laramie, WY 82071.

GREW, RAYMOND
PERSONAL Born 10/28/1930, San Jose, CA, m, 1952, 3 children **DISCIPLINE** MODERN EUROPEAN HISTORY **EDUCATION** Harvard Univ, AB, 51, AM, 52, PhD, 57. **CAREER** Tutor and teaching fel, Harvard Univ, 55-57; instr hist, Brandies Univ, 57-58; from instr to asst prof, Princeton Univ, 58-64, Rollins preceptor, 61-64; assoc prof, 64-68, dir, Ctr Western Europ Studies, 69-71 and 75-78, Prof Hist, Univ Mich, Ann Arbor, 68-, Fulbright fel, Italy, 54-55; Am Philos Soc grant, 62-63; Guggenheim fel, 68; chmn, Coun Europ Studies, 70-71, mem exec comt, 71-74 and 81-84; co-chair, Counc European Studies, 70, 84-87; ed, Comp Studies in Soc and Hist, 74-97; dir d'etudes, Ecoles des Hautes Etudes en Sciences Sociales, 76; ed, Comp Study Soc and Hist, 73-; dir, Univ Mich, Florence 73-75 and 81, 84, 96, 98. **HONORS AND AWARDS** First Annual Prize, Soc Ital Hist Studies, 57; Chester Higby Prize, AHA, 62; Unita d'Italia Prize, Ital Govt, 63; David Pinkey Prize, Soc Fr Hist Stud, 93; Career Achievement Citation, Soc. It Hist Studies, 00. **MEMBERSHIPS** AHA; Soc Fr Hist Studies (vpres, 66); Soc Ital Hist Studies (Pres, 90-98); Soc Sci Hist Asn. **SELECTED PUBLICATIONS** Auth, A Sterner Plan for Italian Unity, Princeton Univ, 63; coauth, The Western Experience, Knopf, 74-98; auth, Catholicism in Italy, in Modern Italy, NY Univ, 74; ed, Crises of Political Development in Europe and the United States, Princeton Univ, 78; auth, Picturing the People, J Interdisciplinary Hist, 86;auth, School, State and Society: Growth of Elementary Schooling in France, Univ Mich, 91; auth, On the Prospects of Global History, in Conceptualizing Global History, 93; auth, The Paradoxes of Italy's Nineteenth Century Political Cutlure, in Revolutions and Freedom, 96;auth, Seeking the Cultural Context of Fundamentalisms, in Religion, Ethnicity, and Self-Identity, 97; auth, Food in Global History, 00. **CONTACT ADDRESS** Dept of Hist, Univ of Michigan, Ann Arbor, Ann Arbor, MI 48109-1003. **EMAIL** rgrew@umich.edu

GREWAL, JYOTI
PERSONAL Born 09/21/1962, Patna, India, s **DISCIPLINE** HISTORY **EDUCATION** Delhi Univ, India, BA, 83; MA, 85; Univ Stony Brook NYork, PhD, 91. **CAREER** Asst prof, 91-97, assoc prof, 97-, Luther Col. **HONORS AND AWARDS** Freeman Found Res Grant to Study in Asia, 00; Paideia (NEH Funded Prog) res grant, 00; Anderson Grant for Col Fac Res, 94; Mumford Fel, 90-91, Federated Learning Community, Univ at Stony Brook. **MEMBERSHIPS** Am Hist Asn; Asn for Asian Studies, Inc.; ASIANetwork. **SELECTED PUBLICATIONS** Auth, "The United States and Japan in Siberia, 1918-1920: Co-Operation or Co-Optation?," Pakistan Jour of Am Studies (92); auth, "Pushing the Limits and Finding the Centre on the Margins," Diversity Digest (97); auth, "Indira Ghandi: Prime Minister of India," in Women in World History (98); auth, "Lakshmi Bai: Freedom Fighter Against the British Raj," in Women in World History (98); auth, "Nur Jahan: Empress of Mughal India," in Women in World History (98); auth, "Razia: Sole Queen of the Sultanate," in Women in World History (98); auth, "Remapping 'Asia': In the Words of Asian Women Authors," The Asian Exchange (00). **CONTACT ADDRESS** Dept of History, Luther Col, Decorah, IA 52101. **EMAIL** grewaljy@luther.edu

GRIBBIN, WILLIAM JAMES
PERSONAL Born 10/02/1943, Washington, DC, m, 1986, 4 children **DISCIPLINE** AMERICAN HISTORY **EDUCATION** Cath Univ Am, BA, 65, MA, 66, PhD(hist), 68. **CAREER** From instr to asst prof Am hist, Va Union Univ, 68-71; asst prof, DC Teachers Col, 72; specialist minority educ, Off Econ Opportunity, 73; legis asst, US Sen James L Buckley, 75-77; sr policy analyst, US Senate Republican Policy Comt, 77-81; dep dir, Off Legis Affairs, White House, 81-82, dep dir, Senate Republican Policy Comt, 82-89; asst to VPres for Legislative Affairs, 89-93; ed-in-chief Republican platforms, 84, 88, 92, 96, 00; Sr Policy Analyst, House Republican Policy Committee, 93-95; Counsellor to the U.S. Senate Majority Leader, 96- . **RESEARCH** American social and intellectual history; history of religion in the United States. **SELECTED PUBLICATIONS** Auth, "Rollin's Histories and American Republicanism, William and Mary Quart," 92; auth, "A Mirror to New England: The "Compendious History," New England Quart, 72; auth, Republicanism and Religion in the Early National Period, Historian, 11/72; The Churches Militant: The War of 1812 and American Religion, Yale Univ, 73; Anti-Masonry, Religious Radicalism and the Paranoid Style of the 1820's, Hist Teacher, 2/74; A Greater Than Lafayette is Here: Dissenting Views of the Last American Visit, SAtlantic Quart, summer 74; Republicanism, Reform, and the Sense of Sin in Ante Bellum America, Cithara, 12/74; A Matter of Faith: North America's Religion and South America's Independence, Americas, 4/75; ed, Emblem of Freedom: The American Family in the 1980's, 81; The Wealth of Families, 82, Am Family Inst; ed, The Family in the Modern World, 82; ed, The Family and the Flat Tax, 84. **CONTACT ADDRESS** Office of the Majority Leader, The Capitol, Room S-230, Washington, DC 20510.

GRIEB, KENNETH J.
PERSONAL Born 04/03/1939, Buffalo, NY, s **DISCIPLINE** LATIN-AMERICAN & AMERICAN HISTORY **EDUCATION** Univ Buffalo, BA, 60, MA, 62; Ind Univ, PhD(hist), 66. **CAREER** Resident lectr hist, Ind Univ South Bend, 65-66; asst prof hist, 66-70, assoc prof hist and int studies, 70-74, coordr Latin Am studies, 68-77, Prof Hist and Int Studies, Univ Wis-Oshkosh, 74-, Coordr Int Studies, 77-, Ed Newsletter, Midwest Asn Latin Am Studies, 72-77; dir, Interdisciplinary Ctr, 78-; John McNaughton Rosebush Univ Prof, Univ of Wis, 83-; SNC Corp Prof of international Relations, univ of Wis, 93-. **HONORS AND AWARDS** Doherty Found fel, 64-65; grantee univ of Wis, 66, 67-68, 71-71, 72-73, 74-75, 77, 80, 85; Chancellor's Citation for Leadership and Excellence, 91; Meritorious Service Awd, Helicopter Asn Int, 95; Wis State League of Women Voters tribute to Excellence Awd, 97; Regents teaching excellence award, Univ of Wis System Board of Regents, 98; Inspirational Teaching Awd, Order of Omega, 98; Oshkosh Area Chamber of Commerce citation for Excellence, 99. **MEMBERSHIPS** AHA; Conf Latin Am Hist; Latin Am Studies Asn; Soc Hist Am Foreign Rels; Midwest Asn Latin Am Studies (secy, protem, 71, pres, 72-73); Org of Am Hist; North Central Coun Latin Americanists (pres, 70-71); Soc for hist of Am foreign relations; Nat Comm of Int Studies and Prog Administrators; Int Studies Asn; United Nations Asn of the USA; Phi Alpha Theta; Sigma Iota Rho. **RESEARCH** United States relations with Latin America; Mexico since independence; the Caribbean and Central America in the 20th century. **SELECTED PUBLICATIONS** Auth, The United States and Huerta, Univ of Nebraska, 69; ed, Research Guide to Central America and the Caribbean, Univ of Wis, 85; auth, Central America in the Nineteenth and Twentieth Centuries: An Annotated Bibliography, GK Hall, 88; auth, Doheney, Edward, L. Petroleum, Power, and Politics in the United-States and Mexico, Pacific Hist Rev, Vol 0062, 93; Historical Dictionary of Costa-Rica, Americas, Vol 0049, 93; Political and Agrarian Development in Guatemala, Hisp Am Hist Rev, Vol 0073, 93; Washington, Somoza, the Sandinistas, State and Regime in United-States-Policy Toward Nicaragua, 1969-1981, Americas, Vol 0052, 95; Origins of Liberal Dictatorship in Central-America, Guatemala, 1865-1873, Hisp Am Hist Rev, Vol 0075, 95; Rural Guatemala--1760-1940, Historian, Vol 0058, 96; The Banana Men--American Mercenaries and Entrepreneurs in Central-America, 1880-1930, Hisp Am Hist Rev, Vol 0077, 97; Oil, Banks and Politics--The United-States and Postrevolutionary Mexico, 1917-1924, Pacific Hist Rev, Vol 0066, 97. **CONTACT ADDRESS** International Studies Program, Univ of Wisconsin, Oshkosh, Oshkosh, WI 54901.

GRIEDER, TERENCE
PERSONAL Born 09/02/1931, m, 1972, 4 children **DISCIPLINE** ART HISTORY **EDUCATION** Univ Colo, BA, 53; Univ Wisc Madison, MS, 56; Univ Penn, MA, 60, PhD, 61. **CAREER** David Bruton Jr Centennial Prof Art Hist, Univ TexAS Austin, 61- . **MEMBERSHIPS** Col Art Asn; Soc Am Archaeol; Inst Adean Studies **RESEARCH** South American archaeology and art history; Pre-Columbian art; Creative work in painting. **SELECTED PUBLICATIONS** Auth, Signs of an Ideology of Authority, Ancient Images, Ancient Thought: The Archaeology of Ideology, Univ Calgary, 92; Art in the Andes, Discovery: Research and Scholarship at the University of Texas at Austin, 92; A Global View of Central America, Reintrepreting Prehistory of Central America, Univ Press Colo, 93; Informe sobre estudios arquelogicos en Challuabamba, 95; Artist and Audience, Brown & Benchmark, 96; On Two Types of Andean Tombs.Arqueologica Peruana 2, Deutsch-Peruanishce Archaologische Gesellschaft, 97. **CONTACT ADDRESS** Art Dept, Univ of Texas, Austin, Fine Arts Bldg 2.110, Austin, TX 78712. **EMAIL** tgrieder@mail.utexas.edu

GRIFFIN, PAUL R.
PERSONAL Born Bridgeport, OH, m, 1970, 2 children **DISCIPLINE** HISTORY **EDUCATION** Wright State Univ, BA, 73; United Theol Sem, MDiv, 76; Emory Univ, PhD, 83. **CAREER** Asst prof to prof, Payne Theol Sem, 79-88; asst prof, chrmn, dept of relig, Special Asst to the Provost for community Outreach, Wright State Univ, 88-, assoc prof, 92-98, prof, 99-. **HONORS AND AWARDS** Robert E. and Mary Elizabeth Cramer Awd for Academic Excellence, United Theol Sem, 75; Fac development (1 year res and writing sabbatical), Wright State Univ, 97-98. **MEMBERSHIPS** Soc for Study of Black Relig, Am Acad of Relig, Am Hist Asn. **RESEARCH** Race and racism in America. **SELECTED PUBLICATIONS** Auth, The Struggles for a Black Theology of Education: The Pioneering Efforts of Post Civil War Clergy, Atlanta: Black Church Scholars Series, The Interdenominational Theol Center Press (93); auth, Seeds of Racism in the Soul of America, Pilgrim Press: Cleveland, Oh (in press). **CONTACT ADDRESS** African and African Am Studies, Wright State Univ, Dayton, 3640 Colonel Glenn Hwy, Dayton, OH 45435-0001. **EMAIL** paul.griffin@wright.edu

GRIFFIN, WILLIAM DENIS
PERSONAL Born 01/19/1936, New York, NY, m, 1960, 2 children **DISCIPLINE** MODERN EUROPEAN HISTORY **EDUCATION** Fordham Univ, AB, 57, MA, 59, PhD, 62. **CAREER** Lectr, Queens Col, NY, 62-65; from instr to asst prof, 65-71, Assoc Prof Mod Europ Hist, St John's Univ NY, 71-, Nat Endowment for Humanities res fel, 67-68; assoc ed, Studies in Burke and His Time, 70-75; chmn, Sem Irish Studies, Columbia Univ, 77-79; assoc ed, Dict of Irish Biog, 79-. **MEMBERSHIPS** AHA; Conf Brit Studies; Am Comt Irish Studies; Am Irish Hist Soc (secy-gen, 73-74); Am Soc 18th Century Studies. **RESEARCH** Anglo-Irish political and social history in the 18th and 19th centuries; the Irish overseas; revolutionary era in Europe and America. **SELECTED PUBLICATIONS** Co-ed, From Vienna to Vietnam, Kendall-Hunt, 69; auth, The Forces of the Crown in Ireland, 1798, In: Crisis in the Great Republic, Fordham Univ, 69; Irish Generals and Spanish Politics Under Fernando VII, Irish Sword, summer 71; The Irish in America, 73 & Ireland: A Chronology and Factbook, 73, Oceana; Canning and Wilberforce in 1824, Bull Inst Hist Res, London, 11/73; The Irish on the Continent in the 18th Century, In: Studies in 18th Century Culture, Univ Wis, 76; A Portrait of the Irish in America, Scribner's, 81. **CONTACT ADDRESS** Dept of Hist, St. John's Univ, 8150 Utopia Pky, Jamaica, NY 11439-0002.

GRIFFITH, DANIEL A.
PERSONAL Born 11/15/1948, Pittsburgh, PA, m, 1970, 2 children **DISCIPLINE** GEOGRAPHY **EDUCATION** Ind Univ Penn, BS, 70; MA, 72; Penn State Univ, MS, 85; Univ Toronto, PhD, 78. **CAREER** Teaching Asst, Ind Univ of Penn, 70-72; Teaching Asst, Univ Toronto, 72-75; Instructor, Ryerson Polytech Univ, 75-78; Asst Prof to Prof, SUNY, 78-88; Prof, Syracuse Univ, 88-. **HONORS AND AWARDS** Distinguished Geog of the Year, Penn Geog Soc, 99; Res Fel, Am Statistical Asn, 98; Second Prize, Besst Software 96; Fulbright Res Fel, 93; J. Warren Nystrom Awd, Asn of Am Geog, 80. **MEMBERSHIPS** Asn of Am Geog; Reg Sci Asn; Am Statistical Asn; fulbright Asn; NY Acad of Sci; Sigma Xi. **RESEARCH** Spatial Statistics; Quantitative/urban/economic geography; Applied statistics and statistical consulting. **SELECTED PUBLICATIONS** Auth, "Trade-offs associated with normalizing constant computational simplifications for estimating spatial statistical models," Journal of Statistical Computation and Simulation, (95): 165-183; auth, "Seasonal variation in pediatric blood lead levels in Syracuse, NY," environmental Geochemistry and Health, (96): 81-88; auth, "Spatial autocorrelation and eigenfunctions of the geographic weights matrix accompanying georeferenced data," The Canadian Geographer, (96): 351-367; auth, "Single spatial medion problem solutions for maps with hole in them that have been filled with estimated missing spatial data: explorations with urban census data," l'Espace Geographique, (97): 173-182; auth, "Developing user-friendly spatial statistical analysis modules for GIS: an example using Arc View," Computers, Environment and Urban Systems, (97): 5-29; auth, "Error propagation modeling in raster GIS: overlay operations," International Journal of Geographical Information systems, (98): 145-167; auth, "Provincial-level spatial statistical modeling of the change in per capita disposable family income in Spain, 1975-1983," Cybergeo, 98; auth, "On the quality of likelihood-based estimators in spatial autoregressive models when the data dependence structure is misspecified," Journal of Statistical Planning and Inference, (98): 153-174; auth, "A Tale of two swaths: urban childhood blood lead levels across Syracuse, NY" Annals, (98): 640-665; auth, "A variance stabilizing coding scheme for spatial link matrices," Environment and Planning, (99): 165-180. **CONTACT ADDRESS** Dept Geog, Syracuse Univ, 144 Eggers, Syracuse, NY 13244-1020. **EMAIL** griffith@maxwell.syr.edu

GRIFFITH, EZRA
PERSONAL Born 02/18/1942, m **DISCIPLINE** AFRICAN-AMERICAN STUDIES **EDUCATION** Harvard Univ BA 1963; Univ of Strasbourg, MD 1973. **CAREER** French Polyclinic Health Center, intern 1973-74; Albert Einstein Coll, chief res psych 1974-77; Ya;e Univ School of Medicine, asst prof 1977, assoc prof 1982-91, Professor of Psychiatry & African and African American Studies 1991-; Connecticut Mental Health Center, assoc dir 1986-89, director 1989-96; Dept of Psychiatry, Deputy Chairman, 96-. **HONORS AND AWARDS** Fellow, American Psychiatric Assn; mem & editorial bd, Hospital and Community Psychiatry; editor-in-chief, Yale Psychiatric Quarterly; Associate Editor, Diversity & Mental Health. **MEMBERSHIPS** Mem Black Psychs of Amer; Amer Psychiatric Assn; Amer Academy Psychiatry and Law; FALK Fellowship; traveling fellow Solomon Fuller Inst 1976; fellow WK Kellogg Found 1980; president, American Academy Psychiatry & Law, 1996-97. **CONTACT ADDRESS** Sch of Med, Yale Univ, 25 Park St, New Haven, CT 06519.

GRIFFITH, ROBERT
PERSONAL Born 10/17/1940, Atlanta, GA, m, 1960, 2 children **DISCIPLINE** HISTORY **EDUCATION** DePauw Univ, BA, 62; Univ Wis, Madison, MA, 64, PhD, 67. **CAREER** Instr, Univ Wisc, Kenosha, summer 66; asst prof, Univ Ga, 67-71; assoc prof, Univ Mass, Amherst, 71-77, prof, 77-89, chair, Dept Hist, 83-87; prof, Univ Md, Col Park, 89-95, Dean, Col of Arts and Humanities, 89-95; prof, Am Univ, 95-, Provost, 95-97. **HONORS AND AWARDS** Rector Scholar, DePauw Univ, 58-62; Phi Beta Kappa, 62; Woodrow Wilson Fel, 62-63; Univ Fel, Univ Wisc, 63-66; Frederick Jackson Turner Awd, Org of Am Hists, 70; Grantee, Harry S. Truman Library, 74; NEH Fel, 74; Tom L. Evans Fel, Harry S. Truman Library Inst, 78; John Simon Guggenheim Fel, 80-81. **MEMBERSHIPS** Am Hist Asn, Org of Am Hists, Am Studies Asn. **RESEARCH** The United States since 1945. **SELECTED PUBLICATIONS** Auth, The Politics of Fear: Joseph R. McCarthy and the Senate, Lexington, KY: Univ Press of Ky (70), 2nd ed, Amherst, Mass: Univ of Mass Press (87); auth, "Old Progressives and the Cold War," J of Am Hist (Sept 79): 334-347; auth, "Dwight D. Eisenhower and the Corporate Commonwealth," Am Hist Rev (Feb 82): 87-122; auth, "Forging Postwar America: Politics and Political Economy in the Age of Truman," in Michael J. Lacey, ed, The Truman Presidency, Cambridge Univ Press (89): 57-88; auth, major Problems in American History Since 1945, DC Heath (92, 2nd ed, 2000). **CONTACT ADDRESS** Dept Hist, American Univ, 4400 Mass Ave NW, Washington, DC 20016. **EMAIL** bgriff@american.edu

GRIFFITH, SALLY F.
PERSONAL Born 07/24/1952, Lusk, WY, m, 1980, 1 child **DISCIPLINE** HISTORY **EDUCATION** Radcliffe, AB, 74; Johns Hopkins, MA, 81, PhD, 85. **CAREER** Assoc prof, hist, Villanova Univ; current, Col Historian, Franklin and Marshall Col. **HONORS AND AWARDS** Allen Nevius Prize, 85. **MEMBERSHIPS** AHA, OAH, Historical Society. **RESEARCH** U.S. Cultural history institutional history. **SELECTED PUBLICATIONS** Auth, Home Town News: William Allen White and the Emporia Gazette, Oxford Univ Press, 89; ed, The Autobiography of William Allen White, Univ Press Kansas, 90; auth, Order, Discipline, and a Few Cannon: Benjamin Franklin, The Association, and the Rhetoric of Boosterism, Penn Mag of Hist and Bio 116, April 92; auth, A Total Dissolution of the Bonds of Society: Community Wealth and Regeneration in Mathew Carey's Short Account of the Malignant Fever, in A Melancholy Scene of Devastation, Phila Coll of Phys and Library Co of Phila, 97; auth, "Rituals of Incorporation in Antebellum Civic Life," Mid-America 82 (00);auth, Serving History in a Changing World: The Historical Society of Pennsylvania in the Twentieth Century, HSP, 01. **CONTACT ADDRESS** 532 Strathmore Rd, Havertown, PA 19083. **EMAIL** s_griffith@acad.fandm.edu

GRIFFITHS, NAOMI ELIZABETH SAUNDAUS
PERSONAL Born 04/20/1934, Hove, United Kingdom **DISCIPLINE** MODERN HISTORY **EDUCATION** Univ London, BA, 56, PhD(hist), 69; Univ NB, MA, 57. **CAREER** Lectr hist, 61-64, asst prof, 64-69, assoc dean, 75-79, Assoc Prof Hist, Carleton Univ, 69-, Dean, 79-, Pres, Acad Staff Asn, Carleton Univ, 71-72, bd of governors, 81-; ed, Can Asn Univ Teachers Monogr Ser, 72-. **MEMBERSHIPS** Can Hist Asn; AHA; Hist Asn, Eng. **RESEARCH** Acadian history; 17th century history; women's history. **SELECTED PUBLICATIONS** Auth,The Contexts of Acadian History, 1686-1784 (The 1988 Winthrop Pickard Bell Lectures in Maritime Studies), 92; auth, The Acadians: Creation of a People; auth, Penelope's Web: Some Perceptions of Women in European and Canadian Society. **CONTACT ADDRESS** Dept of Hist, Carleton Univ, 1125 Colonel By Dr, 400 Paterson Hall, Ottawa, ON, Canada K1S 5B6.

GRIGGS, JOHN W.
PERSONAL Born 10/05/1948, Three Rivers, MI, d **DISCIPLINE** SPANISH LITERATURE, SPANISH HISTORY **EDUCATION** Ariz State Univ, BA, 70, MA, 71, PhD, 83. **CAREER** Chemn, 71-, Glendale Comm Col. **MEMBERSHIPS** AATSP **RESEARCH** Spanish civil war; modern Spanish poetry, drama, novel. **CONTACT ADDRESS** Glendale Comm Col, Arizona, 6000 W Olive Ave, Glendale, AZ 85302. **EMAIL** jgriggs@gcmail.maricopa.edu

GRILL, JOHNPETER HORST
PERSONAL Born 09/24/1943, Munich, Germany, m, 1961, 2 children **DISCIPLINE** MODERN EUROPEAN HISTORY **EDUCATION** Univ Va, BA, 66, MA, 67; Univ Mich, Ann Arbor, PhD, 75. **CAREER** Lectr hist, Univ Mich, 74-75; from Asst Prof to Assoc Prof, 76-92, prof hist, Miss State Univ, 92-. **MEMBERSHIPS** AHA; Cath Hist Asn; Ger Studies Asn. **RESEARCH** Weimar and Nazi Germany; politics and society in Baden; European agriculture; Himmler's SS; racism; American South and Nazi Germany. **SELECTED PUBLICATIONS** Auth, "The Nazi Party's Rural Propaganda Before 1928, " Cent Europ Hist 15 (82): 149-185; auth, The Nazi Movement in Baden, 1920-1945, Univ NC Press, 83; auth, "The Local and Regional Studies on National Socialism: A Review", J of Contemp Hist 21 (86): 253-294; auth, "The Nazis and the American South in the 1930s: A Mirror Image?," J of Southern Hist 58 (92): 667-694; auth, "Robert Wagner: Der 'Herrenmensch' im Elsass," in DIE Braune Elite II, ed. R. Smelser, et al (93); Josef Stalin, In: Great Leaders/Great Tyrants: Opposing Views of People who have Influenced History, Greenwood Press, 95; Genocide, In: Survey of Social Science: Government and Politics Series, Salem Press, 95; Eugenics, In: The Twentieth Century: Great Events, Supplement, Salem Press, 96; German Officials Seize Plutonium, In: The Twentieth Century: Great Events, Supplement, Salem Press, 96; Racism, In: Encyclopedia of Contemporary Social Issues, Marshall Cavendish, 97; Goebbels, Joseph, In: The Encyclopedia of Propaganda, M.E. Sharpe, 98. **CONTACT ADDRESS** Dept of Hist, Mississippi State Univ, PO Box H, Mississippi State, MS 39762-5508. **EMAIL** jhg1@ra.msstate.edu

GRILLO, LAURA
PERSONAL Born 08/22/1956, New York, NY, m, 1998 **DISCIPLINE** HISTORY OF RELIGIONS **EDUCATION** Brown Univ, Ab, 78; Union Theol Sem NYork, MDiv, 86; Univ Chicago, PhD, 95. **CAREER** Asst prof, Millsaps Coll, 95-97; Sr Fel, Inst for Advanced Study of Rel, Univ Chicago, 97-98; Vis Asst Prof, Coll Wooster, 98-99; Adj Prof, Pacifica Grad Institute, 00; Vis Res Assoc, Univ Calif, Los Angeles, 99-00. **HONORS AND AWARDS** Charles M Ross Trust grants 80-84, 89-90; Joseph M Kitagawa Scholar, Awd in Hist of Rel, 87-88; Jr Fel, Inst for Advanced Study of Rel, 92-93; am Acad of Rel grant, 96; west African Res Asn grant, 97; Nat Endowment for Humanities grant, 97; Inst for Advanced Study of Rel, Univ Chicago Sr Fel, 97-98. **MEMBERSHIPS** Am Acad of Rel; African Studies Asn; West African Res Asn; Int Asn of Hist of Rel; am Asn Univ Prof. **RESEARCH** Method and theory of the Study of Religions; African Religions; Anthropology; Comparative Ethics; Philosophy of religion. **SELECTED PUBLICATIONS** Auth, African Traditional Religions, Encarta Encycl, 97; Divination in Contemporary Urban West Africa, Rel Study News, 98; The Body in African Religions, Purification, The Circle and African Religions, Encycl of Women and World Rel, forthcoming; Dogon: religionsgeschichtlich, Rel in Geschichte und Gegenwart, forthcoming. **CONTACT ADDRESS** 1320 Riviera Dr, Pasadena, CA 91107. **EMAIL** lsgrillo@earthlink.net

GRIM, JOHN A.
PERSONAL Born 10/07/1946, ND, m, 1978 **DISCIPLINE** HISTORY OF RELIGION **EDUCATION** St. John's Univ, BA, 68; Fordham Univ, MA, 75, PhD, 79. **CAREER** Adj lectr, Col of Mt St Vincent, 76-79; adj lectr, St Francis Col, 79; adj lectr, Col of New Rochelle, 79-80; vis prof, Fordham Univ, 79-80; vis prof, Maryknoll Grad Sch of Theol, 80-81; assoc prof, Elizabeth Seton Col, 77-87; Hum Div, Sarah Lawrence Col, 86-89; assoc prof, 89-98, Prof, Chair Relig Dept, Bucknell Univ, 98-; Coord, Forum on Relig and Ecology, 96-. **HONORS AND AWARDS** V.Kann-Rasmussen Awd, 98; Aga Khan Trust for Culture Grant, 98; Sacharuna Found Grant, 97; Laurance Rockefeller Found Grant, 97; Sr Fel, Center for the Study of World Religions, Harvard Univ, Spring 97. **SELECTED PUBLICATIONS** Auth, The Shaman: Patterns of Siberian and Ojibway Healing, Civilization of the Am Indian Series, Univ of Okla Press, 83, 87; Native North and South American Mystical Traditions, An Anthology of Mysticism, Univ of Calif Press, 00; An Awful Feeling of Loneliness: Native North American Mystical Traditions, Doors of Understanding: Conversations on Global Spirituality in Honor of Ewert Cousins, Franciscan Press, 97; A Comparative Study in Native American Philanthropy, Philanthropy and Culture: A Comparative Perspective, Indiana Univ Press, 97; Rituals Among Native Americans, Handbook in Anthrop of Relig, Greenwood Press, 97; co-ed, Worldviews and Ecology: Religion, Philosophy, and the Environment, Bucknell Univ Press, 93, Orbis Press, 94. **CONTACT ADDRESS** Dept of Relig, Bucknell Univ, Lewisburg, PA 17837. **EMAIL** grim@bucknell.edu

GRIMSTED, DAVID ALLEN
PERSONAL Born 06/09/1935, Cumberland, WI, m, 1960, 3 children **DISCIPLINE** AMERICAN CULTURAL HISTORY **EDUCATION** Harvard Univ, AB, 57; Univ Calif, Berkeley, MA, 58, PhD, 63. **CAREER** Actg instr, Am hist, Univ Calif, Berkeley, 62-63; asst prof, Bucknell Univ, 63-67; fel, Charles Warren Ctr, Harvard Univ, 67-68; Assoc Prof Am Hist, Univ MD, College Park, 68-, Nat Endowment for Humanities fel, 67-68. **HONORS AND AWARDS** Recipient of a Citation for Excellent Teaching, Univ Commencement, 88; Research grants from NEH, the Charles Warren Ctr at Harvard, ACLS, and an IREX grant to the former USSR. **MEMBERSHIPS** Am Studies Asn; Orgn Am Historians; AHA. **RESEARCH** Nineteenth century American cultural history; Jacksonian America. **CONTACT ADDRESS** Dept of Hist, Univ of Maryland, Col Park, 3434 30th St, NW, Washington, DC 20008. **EMAIL** dg33@umail.umd.edu

GRIMSTED, PATRICIA KENNEDY
PERSONAL Born 10/31/1935, Elkins, WV, d, 3 children **DISCIPLINE** RUSSIAN & EUROPEAN HISTORY **EDUCATION** Univ Calif, Berkeley, AB, 57, MA, 59, PhD, 64. **CAREER** Lectr, Bucknell Univ, 65-67; assoc prof hist, Am Univ, 70-72; Res Assoc, Ukrainian Res Inst & Russ Res Ctr, Harvard Univ, 74-, assoc, Russ Res Ctr, Harvard Univ, 67-68 and 74-97; Russ Inst, Columbia Univ, res assoc, 69-74; lectr, Univ Col, Univ Md, 68-70; vis res prof, Warsaw Univ, 77, 78, 79 & 81-82. **HONORS AND AWARDS** Radcliffe Inst Fel, 67-69; Russian Inst, Sr fel; Waldo Gifford Leland Prize, (Soc of Am Archivists), 73; Katherine Branson Sch, distinguished alumna award, 80; Cenko Prize for Ukrainian Bibliography, 83; Univ of Mich, Bentley Hist Library, fel, 88; Nat Endowment for the Humanities (NEH), res travel grant, 93 and multiple res resources grants; Kennan Inst for Advanced Russian Studies grant, 93-94; Am Counc of Learned Societies, Proj Grant, 93-94; Smith Richardson Found, 93-94, 94-95; Eurasia Found, 94-95; Open Soc Inst, 96-97; Int Res & Exchanges Bd (IREX), proj grants; U.S. Holocause Mem Mus, Sr Res Fel, 99-00; Cert of Commendation for Archives of Russia, Soc of Am Archivists, 00. **MEMBERSHIPS** AHA; Am Asn Advan Slavic Studies; Soc Am Archivists; Am Asn Baltic Studies; Int Coun on Arch. **RESEARCH** Soviet-area archival affairs; modern European diplomacy. **SELECTED PUBLICATIONS** Auth, The Odyssey of the Smolensk Archive: Phundered Communist Records for the Service of Anti-Communism, Univ of Pittsburgh, 95; auth, Arkhivy Rossii: Moskva-Sankt-Peterburg: Spravochnik-obozrenie I bibliograficheskii ukazatel, 97; auth, Archives of Russia Seven Years After: Purveyors of Sensations or Shadows Cast out to the Past, Cold War International History Project, 98; auth, "The Odyssey of the Petliura Library from Paris and Records of the Ukrainian National Republic (UNR) during World War II," Harvard Ukrainian Stuies 22 (99): 181-208; auth, "The Fate of the Petliura Library from Paris and Records of the Ukrainian National Republic (UNR) after World War II," Harvard Ukrainian Studies, (00); auth, "Bach Scores in Kyiv: The Long-Lost Music Archive of the Berlin Sing-Akademie Surfaces in Ukraine," Spoils of War International Newsletter 7 (00); auth, Archives of Russia: A Directory and Bibliographic Guide to Holdings in Moscow and St. Petersburg, M.E. Sharpe, 00; auth, Trophies of War and Empire: The Archival Heritage of Ukraine, World War II, and the International Politics of Restitution, Harvard Univ Press for the Ukrainian Res Inst, 00; auth, U.S. Restitution of Nazi Looted Cultural Treasures to the U.S.S.R., 1945-1959: Facsimile Documents from the National Archives of the United States, GPO, 00; auth, "Twice Plundered or Twice Save: Russia's Trophy Archives and Nazi Agencies of Plunder," Holocaust and Genocide Studies (01). **CONTACT ADDRESS** Ukranian Res Inst, Harvard Univ, 1583 Massachusetts Ave, Cambridge, MA 02138. **EMAIL** grimsted@fas.harvard.edu

GRINDE, DONALD ANDREW
PERSONAL Born 08/23/1946, Savannah, GA, m, 1997, 3 children **DISCIPLINE** HISTORY **EDUCATION** Georgia Southern Univ, BA, 66; Univ Delaware, MA, 68; Univ Delaware, PhD, 74 **CAREER** Prof & Dir, ALANA/Ethnic Studies, Univ Vermont, 95-; George Washington Carver Distinguished prof, Iowa State Univ; 95; prof, Californai Polytechnic State Univ, 91-95; Rupert Costo prof, Univ California Riverside, 89-91; prof, Calif Polytechnic State Univ, 88-89; prof, Gettysburg Col, 87-88 **HONORS AND AWARDS** Rockefeller fel, 94-95; Summer Res Grant, Rockefeller Archives, 90; Rupert Costo Professor Amer Indian Hist, 89-91; Eugene Crawford Mem Fel, 87-88; **MEMBERSHIPS** Amer Assoc Museums; Amer Hist Assoc; Amer Indian Hist Soc; Bus Hist Conf; New York State Amer Studies Assoc; Ontario Archaeol Soc; Southern Hist Assoc; **RESEARCH** American Indian History; U.S. People's of Color **SELECTED PUBLICATIONS** Coauth, Apocalypse de Chiokoyhikov, Chef des Iroquois, Laval Univ, 97; coauth, Debating Democracy: Native American Legacy of Freedom, Clearlight, 98; coauth, Encyclopedia of Native American Biography, Da Capo, 98; coauth, The Ecocide of Native America, Clear Light, 98; coauth, Exemplar of Liberty: native America and the Evolution of Democracy, Univ CA Press, 91. **CONTACT ADDRESS** Univ of Vermont, Burlington, VT 05405. **EMAIL** dgrinde@zoo.uvm.edu

GRITSCH, ERIC W.
PERSONAL Born 04/19/1931, Neuhaus, Austria, m, 1955 **DISCIPLINE** RELIGION, HISTORY **EDUCATION** Yale Univ, STM, 55, MA, 58, PhD(relig), 60; Univ Vienna, BD, 56. **CAREER** Instr Bible, Wellesley Col, 59-61; PROF CHURCH HIST, LUTHERAN THEOL SEM, GETTYSBURG, 61-, DIR INST LUTHER STUDIES, 70-, Asn Am Theol Schs fel, Univ Heidelberg, 67-68; rep scholar, Lutheran-Roman Cath Dialog in USA, 72-. **MEMBERSHIPS** Am Soc Church Hist; Am Soc Reformation Res; AAUP. **RESEARCH** German Reformation to 1900; European history of theology; Thomas Muenzer and Martin Luther. **SELECTED PUBLICATIONS CONTACT ADDRESS** Dept of Church History, Gettysburg Col, Gettysburg, PA 17325.

GROB, GERALD N.
PERSONAL Born 04/25/1931, New York, NY, m, 1954, 3 children **DISCIPLINE** AMERICAN HISTORY **EDUCATION** City Col New York, BSS, 51; Columbia Univ, AM, 52; Northwestern Univ, PhD, 58. **CAREER** From instr to prof Am hist and chmn dept hist, Clark Univ, 57-69; Prof Hist, Rutgers Univ, New Brunswick, 69-, Chmn Dept, 81-84, NIMH and Nat Libr Med res grants, 60-65 and 67-91; Nat Endowment Humanities sr fel, 72-73 and 89-90; Guggenheim fel, 80-81. **MEMBERSHIPS** Orgn Am Hist; Am Asn Hist Med. **RESEARCH** American social history; history of American psychiatry and medicine. **SELECTED PUBLICATIONS** Auth, Workers and Utopia, 61; auth, The State and the Mentally Ill, 66; Mental Institutions in America, 73; auth, Edward Jarvis and the Medical Wired of Nineteenth-Century America, 78; auth, Mental Illness and American Society, 1875-1940, 83; auth, The Inner World of American Psychiatry 1890-1940, 85; auth, From Asylum to Community, 91; auth, The Mad Among Us, 94. **CONTACT ADDRESS** Institute for Health, Rutgers, The State Univ of New Jersey, New Brunswick, New Brunswick, NJ 08901. **EMAIL** ggrob@rci.rutgers.edu

GROOS, ARTHUR
PERSONAL Born 02/05/1943, Fullerton, CA, m, 1979, 2 children **DISCIPLINE** GERMAN STUDIES **EDUCATION** Princeton Univ, BA, 64; Cornell Univ, MA, 66, PhD, 70. **CAREER** Asst prof, UCLA, 69-73; asst prof, Cornell Univ, 73-76, assoc prof, 76-82, prof, 82-, Dir, Medieval Studies, 74-79, 81-86, chair, dept of German, 86-91, 96-99. **HONORS AND AWARDS** Fulbright Sr Res Fel to Germany, 79-80; Guggenheim Fel; ASCAP Deems Taylor Prize, 93; Fel, Cornell Soc for the Humanities, 99; Alexander von Humboldt Res Prize, 99; founding co-ed, Cambridge Opera J, 89-; founding mem and Bd of Dirs, Centro Studi Giacomo Puccini (Lucca), 96-; founding ed, Studi pucciniani, 98-. **MEMBERSHIPS** Am Musicological Soc, Modern Lang Asn, Medieval Acad, Wolfram-von-Eschenbach Gesellschaft. **RESEARCH** Opera (German, Italian); postcolonial studies; medieval German literature; history of science. **SELECTED PUBLICATIONS** Auth, "Matthijs Jolles," Dichtkunst und Lebenskunst: Studien zum Problem der Sprache bei Friedrich Schiller, ed, Arthur Groos, Bonn: Bouvier (80); coauth, "Puccini: La boheme," Cambridge Opera Handbooks, Cambridge: Cambridge Univ Press (86); auth, "Magister Regis: Studies in Honor of Robert Earl Kaske, ed Arthur Groos, NY: Fordham Univ Press (86); coauth, Medieval Christian Imagery: A Guide to Interpretation, Toronto: Univ of Toronto Press (86); co-ed, Reading Opera, Princeton, NJ: Princeton Univ Press (88); auth, Romancing the Grail: Genre, Science, and Quest in Wolfram von Eschenbach's Parzival, Ithaca: Cornell Univ Press (95); co-ed, Studi pucciniani I, Lucca: Centro Studi Giacomo Puccini (98). **CONTACT ADDRESS** Dept German Studies, Cornell Univ, 183 Goldwin Smith Hall, Ithaca, NY 14853. **EMAIL** abg3@cornell.edu

GROPMAN, ALAN LOUIS
PERSONAL Born 02/04/1938, Medford, MA, m, 1960, 3 children **DISCIPLINE** MILITARY HISTORY, AFRICAN-AMERICAN STUDIES **EDUCATION** Boston Univ, AB, 59; Tufts Univ, MA, 70, PhD(hist), 75. **CAREER** Asst prof, US Air Force Acad, 70-74; instr, Univ Md, 76; instr hist, Air War Col, 77-78; Instr Hist, Nat War Col, 81-. **RESEARCH** Black military history; aviation history, World War II. **SELECTED PUBLICATIONS** Auth, Be bold, Air Force Mag, 7/72; Hidden history, Negro Heritage, 74; Why is there still a Cold War?, Air Univ Rev, 1-2/78; The Air Force Integrates 1945-1964, US Govt, 78; Evolution of war, Wash Post, 8/78; Airpower and the Airlift Evacuation from Kham Due, US Govt, 79; Three books for the fifties: Fans who still like Ike, Wash Star, 5/81; Eisenhower's lieutenants, Wilson Quart, 1/82. **CONTACT ADDRESS** 6015 Kerrwood St, Burke, VA 22015.

GROSS, DAVID
PERSONAL Born 11/05/1940, Kankakee, IL, m, 1965, 2 children **DISCIPLINE** HISTORY **EDUCATION** St Ambrose Col, BA, 62; Univ Wis-Mad, MA, 64, PhD, 69. **CAREER** Instr, Univ Wis, 68-69; asst prof, Univ Colo, 69-73; assoc prof, Univ Colo, 73-81; Prof, Hist, Univ Colo, 81-. **MEMBERSHIPS** Am Hist Asn **RESEARCH** Modern European Intellectual History **SELECTED PUBLICATIONS** The Past in Ruins: Tradition and the Critique of Modernity, Univ Mass Press, 92; auth, Lost Time: On Remembering and Forgetting in Late Modern Culture, Univ of Mass Press, 00. **CONTACT ADDRESS** Dept hist, Univ of Colorado, Boulder, Box 234, Boulder, CO 80309-0234.

GROSS, HANNS
PERSONAL Born 06/20/1928, Stockerau, Austria, m, 1991 **DISCIPLINE** EARLY MODERN EUROPEAN HISTORY **EDUCATION** Univ London, BA, 50; Univ Chicago, AM, 63, PhD(Hist), 66. **CAREER** Asst prof Hist, Southern Ill Univ, 66-67; from asst prof to assoc prof, 67-78, prof Hist, Loyola Univ Chicago, 78-. **MEMBERSHIPS** AHA; Conf Faith & Hist; Am Soc Legal Hist; Am Soc Eighteenth Century Studies; Soc Ital

Hist Studies. **RESEARCH** Central European history from 13th to 18th centuries, especially legal, constitutional, administrative and social history; history of the city of Rome in the 18th century; the European city in the preindustrial age; A cultural and intellectual hist of the relationship between Halle Pietism and the early germ enlightenment. **SELECTED PUBLICATIONS** Auth, Empire and Sovereignty: A History of the Public Law Literature in the Holy Roman Empire, 1599-1804, Univ Chicago, 73; Lupold of Bebenburg, National Monarchy and Representative Government in Germany, Il Pensiero Politico, 74; The Holy Roman Empire in modern times: Constitutional reality and legal theory, In: The Old Reich: Essays on German Political Institutions, 1495-1806, Etudes presentees a la commission internationale pour l'histoire des assemblees d'etats, 75; Pope Clement XIII In Frank Coppa, ed, Notable Popes A Biocritical Sourcebook, Greenwood Press, forthcoming. **CONTACT ADDRESS** Dept of History Loyola, Univ of Chicago, 6525 N Sheridan Rd, Chicago, IL 60626-5385. **EMAIL** hgross@wpo.it.luc.ed

GROSS, PAMELA
PERSONAL Born 08/12/1952, Buffalo, NY, s **DISCIPLINE** HISTORY **EDUCATION** SUNY Buffalo, BA, 76; MA, 78; PhD, 83. **CAREER** Assoc prof to prof, chair, Alucinia Col, 89-93; assoc prof, Adams State Col, 94-. **HONORS AND AWARDS** Teaching Awd, Alvernia Col. **MEMBERSHIPS** AHA; Conf of British Studies. **RESEARCH** Tudor England, Henry VIII and wives, Dukes of Somerset, Queen's Household. **SELECTED PUBLICATIONS** Auth, Jane, The Quene, A Study of Queen Jane Seymour, Third Wife of Henry VIII. **CONTACT ADDRESS** Dept Hist, Philos and Govt, Adams State Col, Alamosa, CO 81102. **EMAIL** pmgross@adams.edu

GROSS, RITA M.
PERSONAL Born 07/06/1943, Rhinelander, WI **DISCIPLINE** HISTORY OF RELIGIONS **EDUCATION** Univ Wis-Milwaukee, BA, 65; Univ Chicago, MA, 68, PhD(hist relig), 75. **CAREER** Instr theol, Loyola Univ, Chicago, 70-71; instr Indian rel, New Col, Fla, 71-73; instr, 73-75, asst prof, 75-80, ASSOC PROF EASTERN RELIG, UNIV WIS-EAU CLAIRE, 80-, Mem, rev bd relig, Anima; An Experiental J, 73- and Nat Endowment Humanities, 77-. **MEMBERSHIPS** Soc Values Higher Educ; Am Acad Relig; Women's Caucus Am Acad Relig. **RESEARCH** Hindu Theism, especially the Hindu Goddesses; Hindu inconography and mythology. **SELECTED PUBLICATIONS** Auth, Why Me--Methodological-Autobiographical Reflections of a Wisconsin Farm Girl Who Became a Buddhist Theologian when She Grew Up, J Feminist Stud in Relig, Vol 0013, 97; Toward a Buddhist Environmental Ethic: Religious Responses to Problems of Population, Consumption, and Degradation of the Global Environment, J Am Acad of Relig, Vol 0065, 97. **CONTACT ADDRESS** Dept of Philos and Relig Studies, Univ of Wisconsin, Eau Claire, Eau Claire, WI 54701.

GROSS, ROBERT A.
PERSONAL Born 02/17/1945, New Haven, CT, m, 1966, 3 children **DISCIPLINE** HISTORY & AMERICAN STUDIES **EDUCATION** Univ Penn, BA, 66; Columbia Univ, MA, 68; PhD, 76. **CAREER** Asst to prof, Am stud & hist, Amherst Col 76-88; current, Murden Prof, Am Stud & Hist & Dir, Am Stud, Col of Will & Mary and Bk Review ed, William and Mary Quarterly; chair, AAS Prog for the Hist the Book in Am Cult. **HONORS AND AWARDS** Bancroft Prize in Am Hist, 77. **MEMBERSHIPS** Am Antiquarian Soc; Mass Hist Soc; Soc of Am Hist. **RESEARCH** Social and Cultural History of the U.S., 1750-1860; New England and Transcendentalism; hisory of the book. **SELECTED PUBLICATIONS** Auth, Printing, Politics and the People, Worcester, 89; auth, Reading Culture, Reading Books, Procs. of the AAS 106, 96; auth, The Minutemen and Their World, 76; auth, Books and Libraries in Thoreau's Concord, Procs of AAS 97, 87; ed, In Debt to Shays: The Bicentennial of an Agrarian Rebellion, 93; auth, The Authority of the Word: Print and Social Change in America, 1607-1880, paper, AAS, 84. **CONTACT ADDRESS** Am Stud Prog, Col of William and Mary, PO Box 8795, Williamsburg, VA 23187-8795. **EMAIL** ragros@facstaff.wm.edu

GROSS-DIAZ, THERESA
DISCIPLINE HISTORY **EDUCATION** Northwestern Univ, PhD. **CAREER** Hist, Loyola Univ. **MEMBERSHIPS** Osc for the Study of the Bible in the Middle Ages. **RESEARCH** Medieval England; Biblical commentaries; schools; pilgrimage. **SELECTED PUBLICATIONS** Auth, From Iectio divina to the Lecture Room: The Psalms Commentary of Gilbert of Poitiers, Brill Publishers, 96; auth, Gilbert of Poitiers: Commentarius in Psalmos, Brepols Publishers, 99; auth, "The Culmination of a Tradition? Nicholas of Lyra on the Psalms," in The Biblical Commentaries of Nicholas of Lyra, ed. Leslie Smith and Philip Krey (Brill, 99); ed and contr, The Tradition of Psalms Commentary in the Latin Middle Ages, Brill Pyblishers, 00. **CONTACT ADDRESS** Dept of Hist, Loyola Univ, Chicago, 6525 N. Sheridan Rd., Chicago, IL 60626. **EMAIL** Tgross@wpo.it.luc.edu

GROTH, PAUL
PERSONAL Born 04/25/1949, Mayville, ND **DISCIPLINE** HUMAN GEOGRAPHY, HISTORIAN OF VERNACULAR ARCHITECTURE **EDUCATION** Univ Cal Berk PhD 83. **CAREER** Fac, Univ Cal Berk, Dept Arch, 83-, Dept Geog, 96-. **HONORS AND AWARDS** Smithsonian Fel; J. B. Jackson Book Prize; Abbott Lowell Cummings prize; Sr Fel, Townsend Humanities **MEMBERSHIPS** OAH; SAH; AAG **RESEARCH** Cultural Lands Hist; Urban Hist; Indian Reserv; 19 and 20th Cent; Housing. **SELECTED PUBLICATIONS** Auth, Living Downtown: The History of Residential Hotels in the US, UNW CA Press, 94; Understanding Ordinary Landscapes, with Todd Bessi, eds, New Haven, Yale Univ Press, 97. **CONTACT ADDRESS** Dept of Architecture, Univ of California, Berkeley, Berkeley, CA 94720-1800. **EMAIL** pgroth@uclink4.berkeley.edu

GROTHAUS, LARRY HENRY
PERSONAL Born 01/05/1930, Ft. Wayne, IN, m, 1954, 4 children **DISCIPLINE** UNITED STATES & AFRO-AMERICAN HISTORY **EDUCATION** Concordia Univ, Ill, BSEd, 54; Univ Mo-Columbia, MA, 59, PhD(Hist), 70. **CAREER** Assoc prof Soc Sci, St Paul's Col, 54-68; asst acad dean, 73-77; dean Arts and Sci, 89-94; prof Hist, Concordia Univ, Nebr, 68-98. **MEMBERSHIPS** Orgn Am Historians. **SELECTED PUBLICATIONS** Auth, Kansas City Blacks, Harry Truman and the Pendergast machine, Mo Hist Rev, 10/74. **CONTACT ADDRESS** Dept of History, Concordia Col, Nebraska, 800 N Columbia Ave, Seward, NE 68434-1556. **EMAIL** lgrochaus@seward.ccsn.edu

GROVER, DORYS CROW
PERSONAL Born 09/23/1921, Pendleton, OR, s **DISCIPLINE** AMERICAN STUDIES, BRITISH LITERATURE **EDUCATION** Ore State Univ, BA, 51; Wash State Univ, PhD(Am studies), 69. **CAREER** Ed, The Pendleton Record, 59-69; news mgr., KUMA Radio, 59-64; news writer, KCRL-TV, Reno, NV, 70-71; asst instr English, Wash State Univ, 64-69; prof, Drake Univ, 71-72; prof, english, Tex A&M Univ, Commerce, 72-93, emerita prof, 93-; Fac res grants, 72-76 and 81-82. **HONORS AND AWARDS** Southwest Heritage Awd, 77; Distinguished prof award, 90; Nat Education Award, 92; Sandburg Award, 79; Fort Concho Cent. Poetry Award, 89; Poetry Awards, 78-79, 85, 87-90, 93; Short story awards, 75, 88-89, 92. **MEMBERSHIPS** MLA; Western Lit Asn; Soc for Study of Midwest Lit; Tex Folklore Soc; Sherwood Anderson Soc; Melville Soc; James Branch Cabell Soc. **RESEARCH** American novel and novelists; Colonial American literature; Western literature. **SELECTED PUBLICATIONS** Auth, A Solitary Voice: Collection of Critical Essays, 73; auth, Vardis Fisher: The Novelist as Poet, Revisionist Press, 73; auth, "The Antelope Sonnets," Tex Quarterly (74); auth, "Garland's Emily Dickinson - A Case of Mistaken Identity," Am Lit (74); auth, "W.H.D. Koerner & Emerson Hough: A Western Collaboration," Montana Magazine (79); auth, John Graves, Boise State Univ Press, 90; auth, The Valley of Tutuilla, and Other Lines, 97; **CONTACT ADDRESS** 71330 Tutuilla Road, Pendleton, OR 97801. **EMAIL** dg88@ucinet.com

GROVES, NICHOLAS
PERSONAL Born 11/05/1945, Hyannis, MA, 2 children **DISCIPLINE** MEDIEVAL HISTORY **EDUCATION** Duke Univ, AB, 67; Univ Chicago, MA, 68, PhD, 83. **CAREER** De Andreis Seminary, 80-83; Assoc prof, St Thomas Seminary, 83-87; part-time, 87-91, Loyola Univ. **MEMBERSHIPS** Amer Acad of Relig; Soc for Buddhist Christian Studies. **RESEARCH** Medieval monastic hist; historical theology; Buddhist-Christian Studies. **CONTACT ADDRESS** 6455 N Sheridan Rd, #704, Chicago, IL 60626.

GRUBB, JAMES S.
PERSONAL Born 09/19/1952, m, 1976, 1 child **DISCIPLINE** HISTORY **EDUCATION** Univ Chicago, PhD. **CAREER** Prof, Univ MD Baltimore County. **RESEARCH** Renaissance and Reformation hist. **SELECTED PUBLICATIONS** Auth, Firstborn of Venice: Vicenza in the Early Renaissance; Provincial Families in the Renaissance: Private and Public Life in the Veneto. **CONTACT ADDRESS** Dept of Hist, Univ of Maryland, Baltimore County, 1000 Hilltop Circle, Baltimore, MD 21250. **EMAIL** grubb@umbc.edu

GRUBBS, DONALD HUGHES
PERSONAL Born 12/14/1936, Miami, FL, m, 1979, 3 children **DISCIPLINE** UNITED STATES HISTORY **EDUCATION** Univ FL, BA, 58, MA, 59, PhD, 63. **CAREER** Instr soc sci, Dade County Jr Col, 61-62; assoc prof hist, 63-73, Prof Hist, Univ of the Pac, 73- **RESEARCH** Agricultural, labor and New Deal history. **SELECTED PUBLICATIONS** Auth, Gardner Jackson, STFU and New Deal, Agr Hist, 4/68; Cry from the Cotton: The Southern Tenant Farmers Union and the New Deal, Univ NC, 71; Prelude to Chavez: NFLU in Calif, Labor Hist, fall 75; coauth, Racism: From Irrational to Functional, Rev Black Polit Econ, fall 75; Migrant Workers, in Encyclopedia of Southern Culture, pp 1401-1403, 89; Southern Tenant Farmers' Union, in Encyclopedia of Southern Culture, p 1427, 89. **CONTACT ADDRESS** Dept of Hist, Univ of the Pacific, Stockton, 3601 Pacific Ave, Stockton, CA 95211-0197.

GRUBER, CARLOS S.
DISCIPLINE HISTORY **EDUCATION** Brandeis Univ, BA, 55;Columbia Univ, MA, 59; PhD, 68. **CAREER** Prof, William Paterson Col, 82-, assoc prof, 77-82 & dept ch, 87-93; asst prof, Rutgers Univ, 72-75; asst prof, Stern Col for Women, Yeshiva Univ, 68-71. **HONORS AND AWARDS** NJ Hist Soc grant, 92; NJ Coun for the Humanities grant, 92; Japan Found grant, 91; Fulbright-Hays fel, Group Study Abroad, Japan, 90; Nat Sci Found, Summer Scholar's Awd, 86, 85 & 82; res grant, 82, 78-80; Nat Endowment for the Humanities, Col Tchr(s) fel, 85-86, Summer Stipend, 78, Younger Humanist fel, 71-72; Charles Thomson Prize, 82. **MEMBERSHIPS** AHA: ch, Local Arrangements Comt, 90 Annual Meeting; US Dept of State, Adv Comt on Hist Diplomatic Doc, rep AHA, 83-86; Berkshire Conf of Women Hist(s): Bd of Trustees, 81-85; ch, Bk Awd Comt, 79-81; Columbia Univ Sem on Amer Civilization: co-chr, 88-91; Orgn Amer Hist(s): Comt on the Status of Women in the Hist Prof, 86-89, ch, 88-89 Membership Comt NJ, 87-89. **SELECTED PUBLICATIONS** Auth, The Overhead System in Government-Sponsored Academic Science: Origins and Early Development, Hist Stud in the Phys and Biol Sci, 95; Jane Addams--Frauen werden Friedenmachen, Der Friedens Nobelpreis von 1901 bis heute, vol IV, Ed Pacis, Munich, 89; rev(s), The Best War Ever, Mil Hist Rev, 95; An Actor in Recent History, James B. Conant: Harvard to Hiroshima and the Making of the Atomic Bomb, Sci, 94; The Cold War and American Science: The Military-Industrial-Academic Complex at MIT and Stanford, Hist Educ Quart, XXX, 94; The Manhattan Story Retold, The Making of the Atomic Bomb, Sci, 87; Academic Freedom Under Pressure, No Ivory Tower: McCarthyism and the Universities, Sci, 87. **CONTACT ADDRESS** Dept of History, William Paterson Col of New Jersey, 300 Pompton Rd., Wayne, NJ 07470. **EMAIL** gruber@frontier.wilpaterson.edu

GRUBER, HELMUT
PERSONAL Born 07/20/1928, Austria **DISCIPLINE** MODERN EUROPEAN HISTORY **EDUCATION** City Col New York, BSS, 50; Columbia Univ, MA, 51, PhD(hist), 62. **CAREER** From instr to assoc prof hist, 56-75, head dept soc sci, 62-72, Prof Hist, Polytech Inst New York, 65-, Consult soc sci div, Univ Sask, 68; vis prof, NY Univ, 74-75 and Maison des sci de l'homme, Paris, 80; chmn univ sem hist working class, Columbia Univ, 75-. **MEMBERSHIPS** AHA; Int Tagung Historiker Arbeiterbewegung (executive mem, 81-84). **RESEARCH** Nineteenth and twentieth century intellectual history of Europe; history of modern Germany; history of international socialism and communism. **SELECTED PUBLICATIONS** Auth, Paul Levi and the Comintern, Survey: J Soviet & East Europ Studies, No 53, 64; Willi Munzenberg: Propagandist for and against the Comintern, Int Rev Soc Hist, Vol X, Part II, 65; Willi Munzenberg's German communist propaganda empire, 1921-1933, J Mod Hist, 9/66; International Communism in the Era of Lenin: A Documenatary History, Cornell Univ Press, 67, Fawcett World Libr, 67 & Doubleday, 72; coauth (with E B Leacock & L Menashe), Social Science Theory and Method: An Integrated Historical Introduction, NY Polytechnic Inst Press (8 vols), 67-68; auth, Soviet Russia Masters the Comintern: International Communism in the Era of Stalin's Ascendancy, Doubleday, 74; Die politisch-ethische Mission des deutschen Expressionismus, In: Begriffsbestimmung des literarischen Expressionismus, Wissenschaftliche Buchgesellschaft, Darmstadt, 76. **CONTACT ADDRESS** Dept of Soc Sci, Polytech Inst of New York, 6 Metro Tech Ctr, Brooklyn, NY 11201.

GRUBER, IRA
PERSONAL Born 01/06/1934, Philadelphia, PA, m, 1958, 3 children **DISCIPLINE** HISTORY **EDUCATION** Duke Univ, BA, 55; MA, 59; PhD, 61. **CAREER** Instr, Duke Univ, 61-62; Fel, Inst of Early Am Hist and Culture, 62-65; asst prof, Occidental Col, 65-66; from asst prof to Harris Masterson Jr Prof of Hist, Rice Univ, 66-; John F. Morrison Prof, U.S. Army Command and General Staff Col, 79-80; vis prof, U.S. Military Acad, 84-85 & 92-93. **HONORS AND AWARDS** Postdoctoral Fel, Inst of Early Am Hist and Culture, 62-65; Brown Awd for Superior Teaching, Rice Univ, 74; Victor Gordos Memorial Service Awd, Soc for Military Hist, 98. **MEMBERSHIPS** Am Hist Asn, Assocs of the Inst of EArly Am Hist and Culture, Soc for Military Hist, Southern Hist Asn. **RESEARCH** Theory and practice of Eighteenth-Century warfare. **SELECTED PUBLICATIONS** Auth, The Howe Brothers and the American Revolution, 72; coauth, Warfare in the Western World (2 vols), 96; ed, John Peebles' American War, Army Records Soc (Stroud, Gloucestershire), 98. **CONTACT ADDRESS** Dept Hist, Rice Univ, 6100 Main St, Houston, TX 77005-1892. **EMAIL** gruber@rice.edu

GRUDER, VIVIAN REBECCA
PERSONAL Born 01/07/1937, New York, NY, 1 child **DISCIPLINE** MODERN HISTORY **EDUCATION** Barnard Col, AB, 57; Harvard Univ, PhD Hist, 66. **CAREER** Teaching fel gen educ, Harvard Univ, 60-61 & 62-63; instr Hist, Douglass Col, Rutgers Univ, 63-64; lectr, Hunter Col, 64-65, instr, 65-67; asst prof, 67-69, assoc prof Hist, Queens Col, NY, 69-, Am Coun Learned Soc fel, 73-74. **HONORS AND AWARDS** PSC-CUNY Fullbright Travel Grant, 83-84; Res Grant, 83-84, 90-91, 92-96. **MEMBERSHIPS** AHA; Soc Fr Hist Studies; Int Soc Studies 18th Century; Am Soc 18th Century Studies; Int Comn Hist Rep & Parliamentary Insts. **RESEARCH** Eigh-

teenth century French history; the Assembly of Notables, 1787 and 1788. **SELECTED PUBLICATIONS** Auth, The Royal Provincial Intendants: A Governing Elite in Eighteenth Century France, Cornell Univ, 68. **CONTACT ADDRESS** Dept of History, Queens Col, CUNY, 6530 Kissena Blvd, Flushing, NY 11367-1597. **EMAIL** Gruder@QC.VAXA.ACC.QC.EDU

GRUEN, ERICH S.
PERSONAL Born 05/07/1935, Vienna, Austria, m, 1959, 3 children **DISCIPLINE** ANCIENT HISTORY **EDUCATION** Columbia Univ, BA, 57; Oxford Univ, MA, 60; Harvard Univ, PhD(Hist), 64. **CAREER** Instr Hist, Harvard Univ, 64-66; from asst prof to assoc prof, 66-72, prof Hist, Univ Calif, Berkeley, 72-, consult, Educ Develop Corp, 65-72; Nat Humanities fac fel, 68-70; Guggenheim fel, 69-70; 89-90; mem, Inst Advan Studies, Princeton, 73-74; vis fel, Merton Col, Oxford, 78; vis Distinguished Humanist, Univ Colo, 81; vis prof Princeton, 87-88; NEH fel 84-96; fel First Advan Studies Jerusalem, 96. **HONORS AND AWARDS** Disting Teaching Awd, U Calif, 87; Fel Am Academy of Arts & Sciences, 86-. **MEMBERSHIPS** AHA; Am Philol Asn. **RESEARCH** Roman history, Hellenistic history. **SELECTED PUBLICATIONS** Auth, The Last Generation of the Roman Republic, Univ Calif, 74; The origins of the Achaean War, J Hellenic Studies, 76; The Hellenistic World and the Coming of Rome, Univ Calif, 84; Studies in Green Culture & Roman Policy, Brill, 90; Culture & National Identity in Republican Rome, Cornell Univ, 92; Heritage & Hellenism, Univ Calif, 98. **CONTACT ADDRESS** Dept of History, Univ of California, Berkeley, 3229 Dwinelle Hall, Berkeley, CA 94720-2551.

GRUPENHOFF, RICHARD
DISCIPLINE FILM PRODUCTION, FILM HISTORY, SCREENWRITING **EDUCATION** Xavier Univ BA; Purdue Univ, MA; Ohio State Univ, PhD. **CAREER** Instr, 75-, ch, dept Radio-TV-Film, Rowan Col of NJ. **SELECTED PUBLICATIONS** Auth, The Black Valentino: The Stage and Screen Career of Lorenzo Tucker. **CONTACT ADDRESS** Rowan Univ, Glassboro, NJ 08028-1701. **EMAIL** grupenhoff@rowan.edu

GUARNERI, CARL J.
PERSONAL Born 07/15/1950, Yonkers, NY, m, 1974, 2 children **DISCIPLINE** HISTORY **EDUCATION** Univ Penn, BA, 72; Univ Michigan, MA, 74; Johns Hopkins Univ, PhD, 79. **CAREER** Instr, hist and cultural stud, Bates Col, 77-78; from asst prof to assoc prof, 79-93, prof, 93- , hist, Saint Mary's Col, Calif, visiting prof, Univ Paris VIII, Spring 00. **HONORS AND AWARDS** Phi Beta Kappa, 71; ACLS fel, 81-82; res fel, Charles Warren Ctr, Harvard Univ, 81-82; NEH summer stipend, 85; annual book award, Soc for Hist of the Early Am Republic, 92; Irvine Found curric grant, 93; dir, NEH Summer Seminars, 95, 98; USIA lectr, Brazil, 97. **MEMBERSHIPS** AHA; Org of Am Hist; Am Studies Asn; Soc for Hist of the Early Am Republic. **RESEARCH** Antebellum United States and the Civil War; United States intellectual and cultural history; comparative history. **SELECTED PUBLICATIONS** Auth, The Utopian Alternative: Fourieism in 19th c America, Cornell, 91; auth, U.S. Intellectual and Cultural History, 1815-1877, AHA Guide to Historical Literature, Oxford, 95; auth, Utopias, in, Fox, ed, A Companion to American Thought, Blackwell, 95; auth, C. Vann Woodward and the Comparative Approach to American History, Rev in Am Hist, 95; auth, Reconstructing the Antebellum Communitarian Movement: Oneida and Fourierism, J of the Early Republic, 96; auth, Out of Its Shell: Internationalizing the Teaching of American History, AHA Perspectives, 97; ed, America Compared: American History in International Perspective, Houghton Mifflin, 97; auth, Brook Farm, Fourierism, and the Nationalist Dilemma in American Utopianism, in Capper, ed, Transient and Permanent: Transcendentalism in Its Contexts, Univ Ma, 99. **CONTACT ADDRESS** Dept of History, Saint Mary's Col, California, Moraga, CA 94575. **EMAIL** cguarner@stmarys-ca.edu

GUBERTI-BASSETT, SARAH
DISCIPLINE ART HISTORY **EDUCATION** Smith Col, BA, 76; Univ Chicago, MA, 80; Bryn Mawr Col, PhD, 85. **CAREER** Asst prof, Wayne State Univ, 97-. **HONORS AND AWARDS** Whiting fel in the humanities, 84-58; Dumbarton Oaks fel, 89-90. **MEMBERSHIPS** Archaeol Inst of Amer; Byzantine Studies Conf; Col Art Asn; Intl Ctr for Medieval Art, Nat Comt for Byzantine Studies, Medieval Soc of Amer. **RESEARCH** Late antique & early Christian art & architecture. **SELECTED PUBLICATIONS** Auth, Historiae Custos: Sculpture & Tradition in the Baths of Zeuxippos, Amer Jour of Archaeol, 96; auth, Antiquities in the Hippodrome at Constantinople, Dumbarton Oaks Papers, 91. **CONTACT ADDRESS** Dept. of Art & Art History, Wayne State Univ, 150 Arts Bldg., Detroit, MI 48202.

GUDDING, GABRIEL
PERSONAL Born 06/16/1966, MN, 1 child **DISCIPLINE** AMERICAN STUDIES, CREATIVE WRITING (POETRY) **EDUCATION** Evergreen Col, BA, 94; Purdue Univ, MA, 97. **CAREER** Grad stud, Purdue Univ, 95-97; Grad stud, Cornell Univ, 98-. **HONORS AND AWARDS** The Nation "Discovery" Awd, 98. **MEMBERSHIPS** Poetry Society of America **RESEARCH** American poetry; history of science **SELECTED PUBLICATIONS** The Phenotype/Genotype Distinction and The Disappearance of the Body, Journal of the History of Ideas, John Hopkins Univ Press, July 96; The Wallace Stevens Jour, I See Your Hammer in the Horologe of Time and I Raise You a Westclock, Spring 97; The Iowa Review, One Petition Lofted into the Ginkgos, Fall 97; The Nation, The Parenthesis Inserts Itself into the Transcripts of The Committee on Un-American Activities, May 18, 1998; River Styx, The Bosun, August 1998; The Beloit Poetry Journal, The Footnote Reconnoiters the Piedmont. **CONTACT ADDRESS** Cornell Univ, 250 Goldwin Smith, Ithaca, NY 14850. **EMAIL** gwg6@cornell.edu

GUDMUNDSON, LOWELL
PERSONAL Born 11/10/1951, Grafton, ND, m, 1973, 2 children **DISCIPLINE** LATIN AMERICAN STUDIES, HISTORY **EDUCATION** Macalester Col, AB, 73; Stanford Univ, MA, 74; Univ Minn, PhD, 82. **CAREER** Asst Prof, Universidad Nacional (Costa Rica), 75-82; Asst Prof, Fla Int Univ, 82-85; Assoc Prof, Univ Okla, 85-91; Asst Prof, Mt Holyoke Col, 95-. **HONORS AND AWARDS** Nat Merit Schol, 69-73; Ford Found Fel, 78-80; Hon Mention, Robertson Prize, Conf on Latin Am Hist, AHA, 89; Fulbright Schol, Universidad de Costa Rica, 86, 91. **MEMBERSHIPS** AHA, Conf on Latin Am Hist. **RESEARCH** Social history and export agriculture in Latin America, coffee, Central America, Afro-American history. **SELECTED PUBLICATIONS** Auth, Costa Rica Before Coffee: Economy and Society on the Eve of the Export Boom, LSU Pr, 93; coauth, "Costa Rica: New Issues and Alignments," in Constructing Democratic Governance: Latin America and the Caribbean in the 1990s, John Hopkins Univ Pr (96): Part IV, 78-91; coauth, "Central American Historiography After the Violence," Latin Am Res Rev, 37:2 (97): 244-256; coauth, "Imagining the Future of the Subaltern Past: Fragments of Race, Class and Gender in Central America and the Hispanic Caribbean, 1850-1950," in Identity and Struggle at the Margins of the Nation-State: The Laboring Peoples of Central America and the Hispanic Caribbean, Duke Univ Pr (98): 335-364; coauth, "Historical Setting," in Costa Rica: A Country Study, Libr of Cong (forthcoming). **CONTACT ADDRESS** Dept Latin Am Studies-Hist, Mount Holyoke Col, 50 College St, South Hadley, MA 01075-1423. **EMAIL** igudmund@mtholyoke.edu

GUENTHER, KAREN
PERSONAL Born 08/25/1959, West Reading, PA, s **DISCIPLINE** HISTORY **EDUCATION** Stephen F Austin State Univ, BA, 80; Pa State Univ, MA, 83; Univ Houston, PhD, 94. **CAREER** Asst Prof, Mansfield Univ, 98-. **HONORS AND AWARDS** Travel Grant, Mansfield Univ Fac Prof Development Committee, Summer 99, Fall 99; Spring 00; Commonwealth Speakers Prog, Penn Human Coun, 00. **MEMBERSHIPS** Org of Am Hist, Penn Hist Asn. **RESEARCH** Early American History, Ethnic History, Religious History, Public History. **SELECTED PUBLICATIONS** Auth, "The World of Moses Boone: The Economic Activity of a Berks County Tanner in the 1780s," Historical Review of Berks County, forthcoming; auth, "A Crisis of Allegiance: Berks County, Pennsylvania Quakers and the War for Independence," Quaker History, forthcoming; auth, "The Religious Environment of Eighteenth-Century Berks County, Pennsylvania," Pennsylvania History, forthcoming; auth, "Berks County," in Beyond Philadelphia: The American Revolution in the Pennsylvania Hinterland, Penn State Univ Press, 98; auth, "Judge Roy's Playground: A History of Astroworld," East Texas Historical Journal, (98): 58-67; auth, "Social Control and Exeter Monthly Meeting of the Religious Society of Friends, 1737-1789: A Research Note," Pennsylvania History, (90): 150-163; auth, "Diverging Views of Life in Eighteenth-Century Pennsylvania: A Review Essay," Pennsylvania History, (99): 616-620. **CONTACT ADDRESS** Dept Hist, Mansfield Univ of Pennsylvania, 1 Mansfield Univ, Mansfield, PA 16933-1601. **EMAIL** kguenthe@mnsfld.edu

GUICE, JOHN DAVID WYNNE
PERSONAL Born 03/24/1931, Biloxi, MS, m, 1958, 2 children **DISCIPLINE** UNITED STATES COLONIAL HISTORY **EDUCATION** Yale Univ, BA, 52; Univ Tex, El Paso, MA, 53; Univ Colo, Phd(hist), 69. **CAREER** Assoc hist, Univ Colo, Denver Ctr, 67-69; from asst prof to assoc prof, 69-78, Prof Hist, Univ Southern Miss, 78-, Dir Am Studies Prog, 77-, Part-time instr hist Univ Tex, El Paso, 62-66. **HONORS AND AWARDS** Leroy R Hafen Awd, Colo Hist Soc, 77. **MEMBERSHIPS** Western Hist Asn; Orgn Am Historians. **RESEARCH** United States territorial history; old Southwest; frontier legal institutions. **SELECTED PUBLICATIONS** Auth, Moses Hallett--Territorial Chief Justice, Colo Mag, spring 70; On circuit in Montana territory with Justice Hiram Knowles--1870, Am J Legal hist, 10/72; The Rocky Mountain Bench: The Territorial Supreme Courts of Colorado, Montana and Wyoming, 1861-1890, Yale Univ, 73; contribr, The American Territorial System, Ohio Univ, 73; Indigenous prologue--a synthesis of Mississippi Indian History, In: Atlas of Mississippi, Univ Miss, 74; auth, Alabama planters in the Rockies, Colo Mag, winter 76; Cattle raisers of the Old Southwest: A reinterpretation, Western Hist Quart, 4/77; ed, The Confession of James Copeland, Univ Press Miss, 80. **CONTACT ADDRESS** Dept of Hist, Univ of So Mississippi, Hattiesburg, MS 39401.

GUIDORIZZI, RICHARD PETER
PERSONAL Born 09/26/1937, Brooklyn, NY, m, 1964, 4 children **DISCIPLINE** AMERICAN HISTORY **EDUCATION** St John's Univ, NYork, BA, 59, MA, 61, PhD, 68. **CAREER** From instr to asst prof, 62-68, chmn, Dept Hist & Polit Sci, 72-76, prof hist, Iona Col, 72-. **MEMBERSHIPS** Am Cath Hist Soc; AHA; AAUP; Am Assn State & Local Hist. **RESEARCH** United States diplomatic history; American political parites; immigrant history, oral history project. **CONTACT ADDRESS** Dept of Hist & Polit Sci, Iona Col, 715 North Ave, New Rochelle, NY 10801-1890.

GUILMAIN, JACQUES
PERSONAL Born 10/15/1926, Brussels, Belgium, m, 1961, 2 children **DISCIPLINE** ART HISTORY **EDUCATION** Queens Col, NYork, BS (biology), 48; Columbia Univ (art history), MA, 52, PhD (art history), 58. **CAREER** Vis asst prof, Stanford Univ, 58-59; vis asst prof, Univ Calif, 59-60; instr, Queens Col, CUNY, 60-63; from asst prof to prof art, SUNY, Stony Brook, 63-98; vis prof, Columbia Univ, 68, 72; chemn, dept art, SUNY, Stony Brook, 70-77; prof emer, SUNY, Stony Brook, 98-. **HONORS AND AWARDS** NEH, 81. **MEMBERSHIPS** Col Art Asn; Medieval Academy; Int Ctr for Medieval Art. **RESEARCH** Medieval art. **SELECTED PUBLICATIONS** Auth, "An Analysis of Some Ornamental Patterns in Hiberno-Saxon Manuscript Illumination in Relation to their Mediterranean Origins," in The Age of Migrating Ideas, Early Medieval Art in Northern Britain and Ireland, ed. R. M. Spearmand and J. Higgitt (Edinburgh: Nat Museums of Scotland, 93), 92-103; auth, "The Geometry of the Cross-Carpet Pages in the Lindifarne Gospels," Speculum LXII (87): 21-52; auth, "The Composition of the First Cross Page in the Lindisfarne Gospels: 'Square Schematism' and the Hiberno-Saxon Aesthetic," The Art Bulletin, LXVII (85): 535-547; auth, "On the Layout and Ornamentation of the Cross-Carpet Page of the Lindisfarne Gospels, folio 138v," Gesta XXIIV (85): 13-18; auth, "On the Chronological Development and Classification of Decorated Initials in Latin Manuscripts of Tenth-Century Spain," Bulletin of the John Rylands Univ Libr of Manchester LXIII (81): 369-401. **CONTACT ADDRESS** Art Dept, SUNY, Stony Brook, Stony Brook, NY 11794-5400.

GUILMARTIN, JOHN F.
PERSONAL Born 09/18/1940, Chicago, IL, m, 1988 **DISCIPLINE** HISTORY **EDUCATION** Princeton Univ, Phd, 71, MA, 69; United State Air Force Academy, Colorado Springs, 58-62; BS, in Engineering Sciences and History, 62. **CAREER** Instr to Assoc Prof, Dept of History, USAF Academy, 70-74; Adjunct Prof of History, Rtcc Univ, Houston, TX, 83-86; Sentor Secretary of the Navy Research Fellow, US Navel War Col, Newport RI, 86-87; Assoc Prof of History, The Ohio State Univ, Columbus, OH, 87-. **HONORS AND AWARDS** Charles Grosvenor Osgood Fellow, Princeton Univ, 69-70; Foreign Guest Lecturer of the Servico de Documentacao Geral da Marinha, The Historical Service of the Brazilian Navy, 78; Finalist, Ohio State Univ, Arts and Sciences Student Council Outstanding Teacher Awd, 94, one of ten Fac members so honored; Nominee, Ohio State Univ, Arts and Sciences Student Council Outstanding Teacher Awd, 93, on of fifty Fac members so honored; Rice University summa cum laude, for History 391a, History of Warfare and Technology Through the Sixteenth Century," Fall Semester, 83. **MEMBERSHIPS** Society for the History of Technology. **RESEARCH** Military History; maritime History; Early Modern Europe. **SELECTED PUBLICATIONS** Auth, "The Early Provisions of Artillery Armament on Mediterranean War Galleys," The Mariner's Mirror, Vol 59, No. 2, August, 73, 257-80; auth, "The Guns of the Santissimo Sacramento," Technology and Culture, Vol. 24, No. 4, October, 83, 559-601; auth, "Early modern naval ordnance and European penetration of the Caribbean: the operational dimension," The International Journal of National Archaeology and Underwater Exploration, 88, 17.1, 35-53; auth, "Ballistics in the Black Powder Era: a cursory examination of technical factors influencing the design of ordnance and the emergence of ballistics as an applied science," Royal Armouries, Conference Proceedings 1, Robert D. Smith, ed, HM Tower of London, England, 89, 73-98; "The logistics of Sixteenth Century Warfare at Sea: The Spanish Perspective," John Lynn, ed., Feeding Mars: Logistics in Western Warfare from the Middle Ages to the Present, Boulder, Colorodo; Westview Press, 93: 109-136; auth, "Guns and Gunnery," Richard unger, ed., Cogs, Caravels and Galleons: The Sailing Ship 1000-1650, in Conway's History of the Ship," Gardiner, series ed., London; Conway Maritifme Press, 94, 133-150; auth, "The Military Revolution: Orginis and First Tests Abroad,' Clifford J. Rogers, ed., The Military Revolution Debate: Readings on the Military Transformation of Early Modern Europe, Boulder, Colorado, Westview Press, 95, 299-333. **CONTACT ADDRESS** Dept History, Ohio State Univ, Columbus, 230 West 17th Ave, Columbus, OH 43210-1361. **EMAIL** guilmartini1@osu.edu

GUINN, PAUL
PERSONAL Born 10/30/1928, The Hague, Netherlands, m, 1971, 3 children **DISCIPLINE** MODERN HISTORY **EDUCATION** Swarthmore Col, BA, 50; Harvard Univ, MA, 51, PhD, 62. **CAREER** Analyst nat defense, Legis Ref Serv, Libr Cong, 55-56; instr hist, Simmons Col, 57-58; Univ Md Overseas Prog, UK, 59-60; exec ed, Int Studies Div, Inst Defense

Anal, 61-67; Assoc Prof Hist, SUNY Buffalo, 67-98, Instr mil hist, Air Univ, 53-54; instr hist, Univ Baltimore, 55-56; assoc prof and lectr hist and polit sci, George Washington Univ, 65-66; vis assoc prof, Grad Sch Pub and Int Affairs, Univ Pittsburgh, 66; adj assoc prof hist, NY Univ, 66-67. **HONORS AND AWARDS** George Louis Beer Prize, AHA, 65; Carnegie Endowment Int Peace vis res scholar, 66-67; Nat Endowment for Humanities sr fel, 71-72. **MEMBERSHIPS** AHA; SHAFR. **RESEARCH** Modern Europe; national security policy; international relations. **SELECTED PUBLICATIONS** Auth, British Politics and Foreign-Policy in the Age of Appeasement, 1935-39, Albion, Vol 0025, 93; auth, On Throwing Ballot in Foreign Policy: Poincare, the Entente and the Ruhr Occupation," European History Quarterly (88). **CONTACT ADDRESS** Dept of Hist, SUNY, Buffalo, Buffalo, NY 14260. **EMAIL** paulguinn@yahoo.com

GULLACE, NICOLETTA F.
DISCIPLINE MODERN BRITAIN, EUROPEAN SOCIAL HISTORY, WOMEN'S HISTORY **EDUCATION** Univ Calif, Berkeley, PhD. **CAREER** Asst prof, Univ NH, 95-. **HONORS AND AWARDS** Fulbright-Hays fel, UK; Mellon dissertation fel; Charlotte Newcombe fel; Olin postdoctoral fel in Mil and Strategic Hist; Hortense Cavis Shepherd Professorship, 99-02. **RESEARCH** Gender, popular culture, and political ideology; the cultural construction of warfare, particularly issues of propaganda, public opinion, and the rhetoric of international law. **SELECTED PUBLICATIONS** Auth, White Feathers and Wounded Men: Female Patriotism and the Memory of the Great War, J of Brit Stud; Women and the Ideology of War: Recruitment, Propaganda, and the Mobilization of Public Opinion in Britain, 1914-1918, Univ Calif, Berkeley; Sexual Violence and Family Honor: British Propaganda and International Law during the First World War, Am Hist Rev, 97. **CONTACT ADDRESS** Univ of New Hampshire, Durham, Durham, NH 03824. **EMAIL** nfg@hopper.unh.edu

GULLICKSON, GAY LINDA
PERSONAL Born 07/04/1943, Portland, OR **DISCIPLINE** WOMEN'S STUDIES, EUROPEAN HISTORY **EDUCATION** Pomona Col, BA, 65; Yale Univ, BD, 68, STM, 70; Univ NC, Chapel Hill, PhD(hist), 78. **CAREER** Teacher relig, Day Prospect Hill Sch, 69-72; asst prof hist, Skidmore Col, 78-81; Andrew Mellon fel, Univ Pittsburgh, 81-82; Asst Prof Hist, Univ MD, 82-, Teaching assoc, Danforth Found, 80-. **MEMBERSHIPS** AHA; Social Sci Hist Asn. **RESEARCH** The French textile industry; rural industrialization; sexual divisions of labor and women's work. **SELECTED PUBLICATIONS** Auth, Property, Production, and Family in Neckarhausen, 1700-1870, Soc Hist, Vol 0018, 93; The Land and the Loom--Peasants and Profit in Northern France, 1680-1800, J Econ Hist, Vol 0054, 94; Industry and Politics in Rural France--Peasants of the Isere, 1870-1914, Am Hist Rev, Vol 0100, 95; Art and the French Commune--Imagining Paris after War and Revolution, Am Hist Rev, Vol 0101, 96; The Flour War--Gender, Class, and Community in Late Ancien-Regime French Society, J Interdisciplinary Hist, Vol 0027, 96; European Women and Preindustrial Craft, J Interdisciplinary Hist, Vol 0028, 97. **CONTACT ADDRESS** Dept of Hist, Univ of Maryland, Col Park, 2115 Francis Scott Key Hall, College Park, MD 20742. **EMAIL** gg17@umail.umd.edu

GUNDERSEN, J.
PERSONAL Born 11/09/1946, Chicago, IL, m, 1969, 1 child **DISCIPLINE** HISTORY **EDUCATION** Monmouth Col, BA, 68; Col William & Mary, AM, 69; Univ Notre Dame, PhD, 72. **CAREER** Assoc fac, Ind Univ, 71-74; vis asst prof, Univ of Notre Dame, 72; vis asst prof, Vanderbilt Univ, 74-75; asst prof to prof, St. Olaf Col, 75-90; prof, Calif State Univ, San Marcos, 89-97; Dean, Elon Col, 97-00; Dean of Faculty, Chatham Col, 00- **HONORS AND AWARDS** NEH , 82; Phi Alpha Theta Fel, 89; Va Hist Soc Fel, 89; Alumni Achievement Awd, Monmouth Col, 98; Fulbright Prof, Finalnd, 96. **RESEARCH** Early American History, Women's History, Episcopal Church. **SELECTED PUBLICATIONS** Coauth, American History at a Glance, Harper & Row, 75; coauth, America: Changing Times, John Wiley & Sons, (NY), 79; coauth, America: Changing Times, a Brief Edition, John Wiley & Sons, 80; auth, Before the World Confessed: All Saints Parish, Northfield, and the Community, 1858-1985; Northfield Hist Soc, (Northfield, MN), 87; auth, The Anglican Ministry in Virginia, 1723-1776: a Study of a Social Class, Garland, (NY), 89; auth, "Women and the Parallel Church", Episcopal Women: Gender, Spirituality and Commitment in an American Mainline Denomination, ed Catherine Prelinger, Oxford Univ Pr, 92; auth, to Be Useful Unto the World: Women in Revolutionary America, Twayne Pub, 96; auth "Kith and Kin: Women's Networks in Colonial Virginia", The Devil's Lane: Sex and Race in the Early South, eds Catherine Clinton and Michele Gillespie, Oxford Univ Pr, 97; auth, "Women and Inheritance: Virginia and New York as a Case Study 1700-1860", Economic Wealth and Inheritance in America, eds Robert Miller and William McNamee, Plenum Pub, 98. **CONTACT ADDRESS** Acad Affairs, Chatham Col, Woodland Rd, Pittaburgh, PA 15232. **EMAIL** jgundersen@chatham.edu

GUNDERSHEIMER, W. L.
PERSONAL Born 04/07/1937, Frankfurt, Germany, m, 1963, 2 children **DISCIPLINE** HISTORY **EDUCATION** Amherst Univ, BA, 59; Harvard Univ, MA, 60, PhD, 63. **CAREER** Jr Fel, Soc Fels, Harvard Univ, 62-66; Asst Prof to Prof Hist, Univ Pa, 66-84, Dir, Ctr Ital Studies, 80-83, Dept Chair, 76-78; Dir, Folger Shakespeare Libr, 84-. **HONORS AND AWARDS** Order of the Star of Italian Solidarity, Am Philos Soc; Honorary doctorates from Amherst, Williams, Muhlensky, & Davidson Cols; Capitol Hill Community Achievement Awd; recipient of numerous fellowships and grants. **MEMBERSHIPS** Medieval Acad; Renaissance Soc Am; Am Hist Asn. **RESEARCH** 15th & 16th century Italian cultural and intellectual history. **SELECTED PUBLICATIONS** Auth, The Italian Renaissance, Prentice-Hall, 65, repr, Univ Toronto Press, 94; Life and Works of Louis LeRoy, Droz, 66; French Humanism, 1470-1600, Macmillan, 69, Harper & Row, 70; Art and Life at the Court of Ercole I d'Este: The 'De triumphis religionis' of Giovanni Sabadino degli Arienti, Droz, 72; Ferrara: The Style of a Renaissance Despotism, Princeton Univ Press, 73; Ferrara estense: Lo stile del potere, Modena, Edizioni Panini, 88; author of numerous articles and reviews. **CONTACT ADDRESS** Folger Shakespeare Libr, 201 E Capitol St. SE, Washington, DC 20003. **EMAIL** gundersheimer@folger.edu

GUNTHER, GERALD
PERSONAL Born 05/26/1927, Germany, m, 1949, 2 children **DISCIPLINE** AMERICAN CONSTITUTIONAL LAW AND HISTORY **EDUCATION** Brooklyn Col, AB, 49; Columbia Univ, MA, 50; Harvard Univ, LLB, 53. **CAREER** Law clerk, Judge Learned Hand, 53-54 and Chief Justice Earl Warren, 54-55; from assoc prof to prof law, Sch Law, Columbia Univ, 56-62; prof, 62-72, WILLIAM NELSON CROMWELL PROF LAW, SCH LAW, STANFORD UNIV, 72-, Res dir, Inter-Law Sch Comn Const Simplification, 57-58; Guggenheim fel, 62-63; Fulbright lectr, Ghana, 69; fel, Ctr Advan Studies Behav Sci, 69-70, vis prof const law, Harvard Law Sch, 72-73; Nat Endowment for Humanities fel, 80-81. **HONORS AND AWARDS** Distinguished Alumnus Awd, Brooklyn Col, 61. **MEMBERSHIPS** Fel Am Acad Arts & Sci; Am Philos Soc; AHA; Am Law Inst; Orgn Am Historians. **RESEARCH** Judicial biography. **SELECTED PUBLICATIONS** Auth, Learned Hand--Outstanding Copyright Judge--The 24th Annual Donald-C-Brace-Lecture, J Copyright Soc of USA, Vol 0041, 94; Objectivity and Hagiography in Judicial Biography--Transcript, NY Univ Law Rev, Vol 0070, 95; Contracted Biographies and Other Obstacles to Truth, NY Univ Law Rev, Vol 0070, 95; Members of the Warren-Court in Judicial Biography--Transcript, NY Univ Law Rev, Vol 0070, 95; Judge Hand, Learned: Examining the Life of an American Jurist--The Choices and Satisfactions of a Biographer, Proc of Am Philos Soc, Vol 0140, 96. **CONTACT ADDRESS** Sch of Law, Stanford Univ, Stanford, CA 94305.

GUPTA, BRIJEN KISHORE
PERSONAL Born 09/17/1929, Ferozpur, India, w, 3 children **DISCIPLINE** HISTORY, SOUTH ASIAN STUDIES **EDUCATION** Dayanand Col, India, BA, 52; Yale Univ, MA, 54; Univ Chicago, PhD, 58. **CAREER** Lectr hist & govt, 58-60, Southern Ill Univ; lectr Asian studies, 60-63, Victoria Univ, NZ; asst prof hist, 63-67, assoc prof, 67-69, Brooklyn Col; prof, 69-76, Univ Rochester; prof, 70-76, State Univ NY Col Brockport; sr fel & dir, res & develop, coun int & pub affairs, 76-; vis fel, 61-62, Inst Advan Studies, Australian Nat Univ; Carnegie Soc Sci Res Fund grant, NZ, 61-62; Am Philos Soc grant, 66-67; vis prof, Columbia Univ, 68-69; Swedenberg Found res grant, 71-72; Tarak Nath Das-Ram Mohan Roy lectr, Yale Univ, 75; NEH lectr, Univ Wis-Madison, 76; consult, UN Ctr Transnational Corps, 80-82. **MEMBERSHIPS** Indo-Brit Hist Soc. Overbrook fel, Yale Univ, 53-54; Found World Govt fel, 54-55; Univ & Asia Found fel, Univ Chicago,55-58; Rapporteur, Strategy for Peace Conf, Stanley Found, 77; NSF res grant, 78-80; Assn Asian Studies grant, 80-81 **RESEARCH** Indian science policy; comparative intellectual history; urban studies. **SELECTED PUBLICATIONS** Auth, Sirajuddaullah and the East India Company, 1756-57, E J Brill, 62 & 66; coauth, Indian and American Labor Legislations and Practices: A Comparative Analysis, Asia Publ House, 66; auth, India in English Fiction, 1800-1970, Scarecrow-Grolier, 73; art, The Working Class in Modern India, New Polit, 11/73; art, The Ethical System in Sankara and Swedenborg, Indian J Theol, 12/73; coauth, Learning About India: An Annotated Guide for the Nonspecialists, Univ NY Albany, 77; Small Business Development in the Inner City Area of Rochester, 2 vols, NY Coun on Int & Pub Affairs, 78; art, The Political Economy of North-South Relations: Studies in the Transfer of US Science and Technology, Nat Tech Info Serv, 81; auth, India, Amer Bibliographical Center and Clio Press, 84. **CONTACT ADDRESS** 226 Idlewood Rd, Rochester, NY 14618. **EMAIL** bgupta@frontiernet.net

GURA, PHILIP F.
PERSONAL Born 06/14/1950, Ware, MA, m, 1979, 3 children **DISCIPLINE** HISTORY, AMERICAN CIVILIZATION **EDUCATION** Harvard Univ, AB, 72; PhD, 77. **CAREER** Instr, Middlebury Col, 74-76; asst prof to prof, Univ of Colo, 76-87; prof, Univ of NC, 87-. **HONORS AND AWARDS** William S. Newman Distinguished Prof of Am Lit and Cult; NEH Fel; Am Antiquarian Soc Fel; Charles Warren Center Fel; Norman Foerster Prize, MLA; Frances Densmore Prize, Am Musical Instrument Soc. **MEMBERSHIPS** Mass Hist Soc; Am Antiquarian Soc, Colonial soc of Mass, Inst of Early Am Hist and Cult; MLA. **RESEARCH** Early American Literature and Culture, American Church History, History of American Music, American Studies. **SELECTED PUBLICATIONS** Auth, The Wisdom of Words: Language, Theology, and Literature in the New England Renaissance, Wesleyan Univ Pr, (Middletown, CT), 81; coed, Critical Essays on American Transcendentalism, Hall and Co, (Boston), 82; auth, A Glimpse of Sion's Glory: Puritan Radicalism in New England, 1620-1600, Wesleyn Univ Pr, (Middletown,CT), 84; ed, Memoirs of Stephen Burroughs, NE Univ Pr, (Boston), 88; auth, The Crossroads of American History and Literature, Pa State Univ Pr, (University Park), 96. **CONTACT ADDRESS** Dept English, Univ of No Carolina, Chapel Hill, 440 W Franklin St, Chapel Hill, NC 27599-2319. **EMAIL** gura@email.unc.edu

GUSTAFSON, DAVID
PERSONAL Born 01/25/1942, Cokate, MN, m, 1964, 2 children **DISCIPLINE** CHURCH HISTORY **EDUCATION** Hamline Univ, BA, 64; M. Div Lutheran School of Theol, 68; Luther Seminary, Th M, 73; Union Inst, PhD, 90. **CAREER** Lutheran Pastor, 68-98, Univ of St Thomas, St Paul, MN, 98-. **HONORS AND AWARDS** Concordia Hist Inst Book Awd, 94. **MEMBERSHIPS** ASCH, LHC, AAR, Sixteenth Century Soc. **RESEARCH** American Religious History. **SELECTED PUBLICATIONS** Lectr, The theme of Lutheran identity at the meeting of the Concordia Academy, St Paul, MN, 91; rev, of George M Marsden, Understanding Fundamentalism and Evangelicalism, The Lutheran Quarterly, 92; auth, Lutherans in Crisis: The Question of Identity in the American Republic, Minneapolis: Fortress Press, 93; rev, of William Lazareth and Peri Rasolondraibe, Lutheran Identity and Mission, Augsburg Fortress Book Newsletter, 94; auth, "A Quiet Week in the ELCa" Forum Letter, 95; auth, "The ELCA: Its Past, Present, and Future" Logia, Eastertide, 96; auth, "The ELCA and Ecumenism: Past, Present, and Future" Lectures in St Louis, MO, 97; auth, "The Church: Community of the Crucified or Community that Crucifies?" Lutheran Forum, 97; rev, of Francis McGrath, John Henry Newman: Universal Revelation, Church History, 98; auth, rev, of Karin Maag, ed, melanchthon in Europe: His Work and Influence Beyond Wittenberg, The Sixteenth Century Journal, 00. **CONTACT ADDRESS** 5220 Oakley St., Duluth, MN 55804. **EMAIL** DAGusto@aol.com

GUSTAFSON, MILTON ODELL
PERSONAL Born 11/20/1939, Minneapolis, MN, m, 1962, 2 children **DISCIPLINE** AMERICAN HISTORY **EDUCATION** Gustavus Adolphus Col, BA, 61; Univ Nebr, MA, 63, PhD, 66. **CAREER** Asst prof hist and int rels, Univ of the Americas, 66-67; diplomatic rec specialist, 67-71, Chief Diplomatic Br,71-88; Chief Civil Ref, 88-94; Sr Specialist Diplomatic Records, Nat Arch, 94-. **MEMBERSHIPS** Orgn Am Historians; AHA; Soc Hist Am Foreign Rels; Soc Am Archivists. **RESEARCH** United States diplomatic history. **CONTACT ADDRESS** 2706 Shawn Ct, Fort Washington, MD 20744. **EMAIL** milton.gustafson@arch2.nara.gov

GUTCHEN, ROBERT M.
PERSONAL Born 01/25/1932, Antwerp, Belgium, m, 1955, 3 children **DISCIPLINE** MODERN HISTORY **EDUCATION** Columbia Univ, BS, 55, MA, 57, PhD(hist), 66. **CAREER** Lectr hist, Long Island Univ, 58-61, from instr to asst prof, 61-64; instr English hist, 64-65, from asst prof to assoc prof, 65-76, actg chmn dept, 66-67, asst dean col arts and sci, 66-68, chmn, Dept Hist, 68-71, Prof Hist, Univ RI, 76-, Chairperson Dept, 77-, Am Coun Educ fel, acad admin internship prog, Ind Univ, 67-68. **MEMBERSHIPS** AHA; Conf Brit Studies; AAUP. **RESEARCH** Nineteenth century British administrative history; English poor laws. **SELECTED PUBLICATIONS** Auth, Local improvements and centralization in nineteenth century England, Hist J, 61; Computer analysis of admissions and discharges of paupers in union workhouses, Local Historian, 75; The government and misgovernment of Hitchin: The local board of health 1848-1873, Hertfordshire Past & Present, 76. **CONTACT ADDRESS** Dept of Hist, Univ of Rhode Island, Kingston, RI 02881.

GUTEK, GERALD LEE
PERSONAL Born 07/10/1935, Streator, IL, m, 1965, 2 children **DISCIPLINE** HISTORY OF EDUCATION **EDUCATION** Univ Ill, Urbana, BA, 57, MA, 59, PhD(educ), 64. **CAREER** From instr to asst prof educ, 63-68, assoc prof found of educ, 68-72, chmn dept found of educ, 69-72, Prof Hist and Found of Educ, Loyola Univ Chicago, 72-, Am Philos Soc res grant, 68; partic, Foreign Policy Asn Proj Modernization in India, 69. **MEMBERSHIPS** Hist Educ Soc; Philos Educ Soc; Nat Coun Social Studies; Orgn Am Historians. **RESEARCH** History of the Pestalozzian Movement in the United States; educational theory. **SELECTED PUBLICATIONS** Auth, Pestalozzi and Education, Random, 68; The Educational Theory of George S Counts, Ohio State Univ, 70; An Historical Introduction to American Education, Crowell, 70; A History of the Western Educational Experience, Random, 72; Philosophical Alternatives in Education, Merrill, 74; Joseph Neef: The Ameri-

canization of Pestalozzianism, Univ Ala, 78. **CONTACT ADDRESS** Found of Educ, Loyola Univ, Chicago, Chicago, IL 60611.

GUTHRIE, DANILLE TAYLOR
DISCIPLINE AFRO AMERICAN STUDIES **EDUCATION** Brown Univ, PhD, 84. **CAREER** Asst prof. **RESEARCH** African American literature and culture; black cultural studies; race ethnic studies; women's studies; native American literature; literature by American women of color; folklore and arts; black music. **SELECTED PUBLICATIONS** Auth, Conversations with Toni Morrison, Univ Miss, 94; Scholar In Residence-Rockerfeller Fellow at Integrative Studies Conference for Balck Musi Research, Columbia Col, 97; Who Are The Beloved?a Old and New Testaments, Old and New Communities of Faith in Toni Morrison's Beloved; Looking Beneath the Wings of Two Wings to Veil My Face (rev), Callalloo. **CONTACT ADDRESS** Dept of Minority Studies, Indiana Univ, Northwest, 3400 Broadway, Gary, IN 46408.

GUTIERREZ, RAMON A.
PERSONAL Born 04/19/1951, Albuquerque, NM **DISCIPLINE** LATIN AMERICAN HISTORY **EDUCATION** Univ New Mex, BA, 73; Univ Wisc Mad, MA, 75, PhD, 80. **CAREER** Assoc Chancellor, 96-, 82 to present, Univ California San Diego; 80-82, Pomona College; 74-80, Univ Wisc; 77-78, Inst Ntl de Antroplogia NM; 73-74, U Ntl del Altiplano Peru; 73, Cornell Univ; 72-73, UNM Andean Study Cen, Ecuador; 69-72, Univ New Mexico; 66-69, ST Pius HS NM; Consultant for numerous Institutions, Publications and TV Media; Grant Referee for numerous Foundations, Institutes and Councils; Journal Referee for numerous Reviews and Journals; Manuscript Referee for numerous Press Publications; Prize Referee on numerous committees and associations. **HONORS AND AWARDS** Ray A Billington Awd; Howard Francis Cline Prize; Caroline Bancroft Hist Prize; Herbert E Bolton Prize; Quincentennary of Discovery Prize; Alan Sharlin Prize; John Hope Franklin Awd; Bryce Wood Book Awd; Frederick Jackson Turner Prize; Jane A Rawley Prize; Herbert Herring Prize; AHAP-CB Best Book of the Year; AHACLAH Conference Prize; John D and Catherine MacArthur Foun Genius Prize; Herbert Herring Prize; Reginald Fisher Prize; Getty Cen HAH Sr Schl; Cushwa Cen SAC Fel; Rockefeller postdoc Fel; 2 CASBS Stanford Fel; 2 NEH Fel; Mellon Foun Fel; Haynes Foun Fel; Mex Mins Foreign Rel Fel; Danforth Grad Fel; Fulbright-Hayes Fel; NDEA Foreign Lang Fel; UNM Andean Stud Cen Schshp; Phi Beta Kappa Ntl Vis Prof; Paul Anthony Brick Lectr, U MO; UCSD Chanc Assoc Endowed Ch; PNM Ch Vis Prof U of NM; Stella Jo Morrisett Mem Lect U of OK; Ena H Thompson Dist Lectr, P College; neh ntl council mem, 94-2000; dept of interior, ntl pk ser adv bd mem, 95-99. **MEMBERSHIPS** ASA; OAH; UCHIAC; SHC; CCH; AAC; LSA; NMAH. **SELECTED PUBLICATIONS** Auth, American Society at the End of the Millennium, New Religious Movements, Columbia, U of Missouri Press, under review; Cuando Jesus llego las madres del maiz se fueron: Matrimonio sexualidad y poder en Nuevo Mexico, 1500-1846, Mexico, Fondo de la Cultrua Economica, 93; coed, Contested Eden: California Before the Goldrush, Berk, U of Cal Press, 98; ed, Mexican Home Alters, Albuquerque, U NM Press, 97; coauth, The Drama, of Diversity and Democracy: Higher Education and American Commitments, Wash DC, Assoc Amer Colleges and Univ's, 95; coauth, Liberal Learning and the Arts of Connection for the New Academy, Wash DC, Assoc of Amer College Univ, 95; coed, Encyclopedia of the North American Colonies, NY, Charles Scribner's and Sons, 93; auth, Charles Fletcher Lummis and the Orientalization of New Mexico, in: Hispanic Expressive Culture in New Mexico, ed, Francisco Lomeli, Albuquerque, U of NM Press, forthcoming; auth, Chicano History: Paradigm Shifts and Shifting Boundaries, in: Toward a New Paradigm for Chicano History, ed Refugio Rochin, Flint, Mich State U Press, forthcoming; auth, Hispanic Diaspora and Chicano Identity in the USA, in: Diversity of Knowledge and Unity of Science: The Case of Immigration and Diaspora's, ed VT Mudimbe, in press; auth, Crucifixion Slavery and Death: The Hermanos Penitentes of the Southwest, in: Over the Edge: Mapping Western Experiences, ed, Valerie Matsumoto, Blake Allmendinger, Berk, U of Cal Press, forthcoming; auth, Honor and Shame in the Barrio Streets: A Modern Code of Ethic, Cahiers Charles V, Paris, 97; The Hermanos Penitentes Their Alters Their History, Spirit Mag, 97; Introduction to Elsie Clews Parsons Pueblo Indian Religion, Lincoln, U of NE Press, 96; Historical and Social Science Research on Mexican Americans, in: Handbook of Research on Multicultural Education, ed, JA Banks, C McGee, NY, Macmillan Pub, 95. **CONTACT ADDRESS** Ethnic STDS. Dept, Univ of California, San Diego, 9500 Gilman Dr, P O Box 0522, La Jolla, CA 92093-0522. **EMAIL** rgutierrez@ucsd.edu

GUTMANN, JOSEPH
PERSONAL Born 08/17/1923, Wurzburg, Germany, m, 1953, 2 children **DISCIPLINE** ART HISTORY, ARCHEOLOGY **EDUCATION** Temple Univ, BS, 49; NYork Univ, MA, 52; Hebrew Union Col, Ohio, PhD(medieval Jewish hist & art), 60. **CAREER** Assoc prof Jewish art hist, Hebrew Union Col, Ohio, 60-69; Prof Medieval Christian Art, Wayne State Univ, 69-, Adj prof, Grad Sch, Univ Cincinnati, 61-66; mem adv bd, Wayne State Univ Press, 70-; Mem Found Jewish Cult grant, 71-72; fac grant-in-aid, Wayne State Univ, 71 and 73; consult, Spertus Mus Judaica, Ill, 71- and Choice Asn Col and Res Libr, 73; mem adv bd, Int Survey of Jewish Monuments of CAASAH, 77-. **MEMBERSHIPS** Art Asn Am; Cent Conf Am Rabbis; Soc Bibl Lit. **RESEARCH** Early Christian and byzantine art; medieval illuminated manuscripts; biblical archaeology. **SELECTED PUBLICATIONS** Auth, Jewish Ceremonial Art, Yoseloff, 68; ed, Beauty in holiness: Studies in Jewish customs and ceremonial art, 70 & No graven images: Studies in art and the Hebrew Bible, 71, KTAV; coauth, Die Darmstadter Pessach-Haggadah, Propylaen Verlag, Berlin, 71-72; ed, The Dura-Europos Synagogue: A re-evaluation, 73, The Temple of Solomon: Archaeological fact and Medieval tradition, In: Christian, Islamic and Jewish Art, 75 & The Image and the Word: Confrontations in Judaism, Christianity and Islam, 77, Scholars Press; Auth, Hebrew Manuscript Painting, George Braziller, 78. **CONTACT ADDRESS** Dept of Art/Art Hist, Wayne State Univ, Detroit, MI 48202.

GUTMANN, MYRON P.
PERSONAL Born 11/04/1949, Chicago, IL, m, 1970 **DISCIPLINE** HISTORY **EDUCATION** Columbia Univ, BA, 71; Princeton Univ, PhD(hist), 76. **CAREER** Res assoc demog, Univ Pa, 75-76; Asst Prof Hist, Univ Tex, Austin, 76-. **MEMBERSHIPS** AHA; Soc Sci Hist Asn; Pop Asn Am; Asn Hist Family. **RESEARCH** Economic and demographic history of early modern Europe; methodology of historic demography. **SELECTED PUBLICATIONS** Auth, Putting crisis in perspective: The impact of war on civilian populations, 77 & Reconstituting wandre: An example of semi-automatic family reconstitution, 77, Annales Demographie Hist; The future of record linkage in history, J Family Hist, 77. **CONTACT ADDRESS** Dept of Hist, Univ of Texas, Austin, Austin, TX 78712.

GUTTMANN, ALLEN
DISCIPLINE AMERICAN STUDIES **EDUCATION** Univ MN, PhD, 61. **CAREER** Prof, Amherst Col, 59; coed, Olympika. **SELECTED PUBLICATIONS** Auth, The Wound in the Heart: America and the Spanish Civil War, 62; From Ritual to Record: The Nature of Modern Sports, 78; Games and Empires, 94; The Erotic in Sports, 96. **CONTACT ADDRESS** Amherst Col, Amherst, MA 01002-5000.

GUTZKE, DAVID W.
PERSONAL Born 01/21/1949, Milwaukee, WI, m, 1982, 2 children **DISCIPLINE** HISTORY **EDUCATION** Univ Wis at Milwaukee, BA, 72; MA, 74; Univ Toronto, PhD, 82. **CAREER** From asst prof to prof, Southwest Mo State Univ, 85-; exec comt member, Soc Hist of Alcohol Rev, 86-; secy & treasurer, Soc Hist of Alcohol Rev, 88-92; rev ed, Soc Hist of Alcohol Rev, 93-. **HONORS AND AWARDS** Phi Alpha Theta, 72; Phi Alpha Phi, 74; NEH Travel to Collections, 87; Awd from Am Philos Soc, 90; Southwest Mo State Univ Found Fac Achievement Awd for Outstanding Scholar, 95. **MEMBERSHIPS** Am Hist Asn, N Am Confr on British Studies, Alcohol and Temperance Hist Group, Soc Hist Soc. **RESEARCH** Interwar Improved Public House Movement, Cultures of Drinking Since 1750, Mergers in the British Brewing Industry 1950s-1960s, Social and Economic History of English Publicans since 1840. **SELECTED PUBLICATIONS** Auth, "Rosebery and Ireland, 1898-1903: A Reappraisal," in Reactions to Irish Nationalism 1865-1914, ed. Alan O'Day (London: Hambledon Press, 87), 285-295; auth, Protecting the Pub: Brewers and Publicans Against Temperance, Royal Historical Soc (Woodbridge, Suffolk), 89; auth, "Rhetoric and Reality: The Political Influence of British Brewers, 1832-1914," Parliamentary Hist 9 (90): 78-115; auth, "Gentrifying the British Public House, 1896-1914," Int Labor and Working Class Hist 45 (94): 29-43; auth, "Gender, Class and Public Drinking in Britain during the First World War," in The Changing Face of Drink: Substance, Imagery, and Behaviour, eds. Jack S. Blocker, Jr. and Cheryl Krasnick Warsh (Ottawa: Les Publications Histoire sociale, 97), 291-319; auth, Alcohol in the British Isles from Roman Times to 1996: An Annotated Bibliography, Greenwood Press (Westport, CT), 96. **CONTACT ADDRESS** Dept Hist, Southwest Missouri State Univ, Springfield, 901 S National Ave, Springfield, MO 65804-0027. **EMAIL** davidgutzke@mail.smsu.edu

GUY, DONNA JAY
PERSONAL Born Cambridge, MA **DISCIPLINE** HISTORY **EDUCATION** Brandeis Univ, BA, 67; Ind Univ, AM, 69, PhD, 73. **CAREER** Instr hist, 72-73, asst prof, 73-80, Assoc Prof to Prof Hist, Univ ARIZ, 80-. **HONORS AND AWARDS** Foreign Area fel, 70-72; Midwest Consortium for Int Activ fel, 70-71; Fulbright Hays res grant, 78; Fulbright Hays sr lectr, Great Britain, 82-83. **MEMBERSHIPS** AHA; Latin Am Studies Asn; Conf Latin Am Hist. **RESEARCH** Argentine economic history; entrepreneurial history, womens history. **SELECTED PUBLICATIONS** Auth, Argentine Sugar Politics: Tucuman and the Generation of Eighty, Center for Latin American Studies, 80; auth, Sex and Danger in Buenos Aires: Prostitution, Family, and Nation in Argentina, Univ of Nebraska Press, 91; coauth, Sex and sexuality in Latin America, New York Univ Press, 97; coauth, Contested Ground: Comparative Frontiers on the Northern and Southern Edges of the Spanish Empire, Univ of Arizona Press, 98; coauth, Feminisms and Internationalism, Blackwell, 99. **CONTACT ADDRESS** Dept of Hist, Univ of Arizona, 1 University of Az, Tucson, AZ 85721-0001. **EMAIL** dguy@earthlink.net

GUYOTTE, ROLAND L.
PERSONAL Born 03/22/1946, Chicago, IL, m, 1982 **DISCIPLINE** HISTORY **EDUCATION** Brown Univ, AB, 67; Northwestern Univ, MA, 69; PhD, 80. **CAREER** Instr to prof, Univ of Minn Morris, 69-; dir of general educ, Univ of Minn Morris, 89-91; vice chemn div of soc sci, Univ of Minn Morris, 95-. **HONORS AND AWARDS** William Randolph Hearst Fel, Northwestern Univ, 72-73; Horace T. Morse-Alumni Awd for Outstanding Contributions to Undergrad Educ, 82; Harry Pratt Memorial Awd, Ill Hist Soc, 92; Acad of Distinguished Teachers, Univ of Minn, 99. **MEMBERSHIPS** Am Hist Asn, Org of Am Historians, Filipino Am Nat Hist Soc, Am Asn of Univ Professors. **RESEARCH** U.S. history, history of higher education, immigration history, biography and autobiography. **SELECTED PUBLICATIONS** Auth, "Celebrating Rizal Day," Celebrations in North American Ethnic Communities, 95; auth, "Filipinos, Ethnicity and Race in 20th Century Chicago," Amerasia J (98); auth,, "Preface," The Experimental College, 00 **CONTACT ADDRESS** Div of Soc Sci, Univ of Minnesota, Morris, 600 E 4th St, Morris, MN 56267-2132. **EMAIL** guyottrl@mrs.umn.edu

GUZMAN, GREGORY G.
PERSONAL Born 12/25/1939, Stevens Point, WI, m, 1964, 3 children **DISCIPLINE** ANCIENT & MEDIEVAL EUROPEAN HISTORY **EDUCATION** Wis State Univ, Stevens Point, BS, 63; Univ Pittsburgh, MA, 64; Univ Cincinnati, PhD(hist), 68. **CAREER** From asst prof to full prof, 67-77, prof hist, Bradley Univ, 77-, NDEA Fulbright-Hays grant, Southeast Asia, 70; fel, Intercult Studies Prog, East-West Ctr, 72. **HONORS AND AWARDS** Awd for Professional Excellence, Bradley Univ, 77. **MEMBERSHIPS** Midwest Medieval Conf; Medieval Acad Am. **RESEARCH** Thirteenth century papal missions to the Mongols; Simon of Saint-Quentin; Vincent of Beauvais and his encyclopedia; Speculum Historiale. **SELECTED PUBLICATIONS** Auth, The Cambron Manuscript of the Speculum Historiale, Manuscripta, XIII: 95-104; Simon of Saint-Quentin and the Dominican Mission to the Mongol Baiju: A Reappraisal, Speculum, LXVI: 232-249; Simon of Saint-Quentin as Historian of the Mongols and Seljuk Turks, Medievalia et Humanistica, new ser, 3:155-178; coauth, Origins of Tomorrow (2 vols), Holbrook, 73; auth, The Encyclopedist Vincent of Beauvais and his Mongol Extracts from John of Plano Carpini and Simon of Saint-Quentin, Speculum, XLIX: 287-307; A Growing Tabulation of Vincent of Beauvaus' Speculum Historiale Manuscripts, Scriptorium, XXIX: 122-125; ed, Vincent of Beauvais Newsletter, 76-; Were the Barbarians a Negative or Positive Factor in Ancient & Medieval History, in The Historian, L, 558-72, 88; Vincent of Beauvais' Epistola actoris ad regem Ludoricum: A Critical Analysis and a Critical Editiom, in Vincent Beauvais: Intentious et Receptious d'une oevre encyclopedique au Moyen Age, ed by M. Paulmia-Foucart, S. O. Lusignam, & A. Nadeau, Paris & Montreal, 1990, pp 57-85; Report of Mongol Cannabilism in the Thirteenth-Century Latin Source: Oriental Fact or Western Fiction?, in Discovering New Worlds: Essays on Medieval Exploration and Immigration, ed by Scott D. Westrem, NY, 91, pp 31-68; The Testimony of Medieval Dominicain Concerning Vincent Beauvain, in Latin et Compilator: Vincent de Beauvain, frere precheur un intellectuel et son milieu au XIIIe riecle, ed by S. Lusignam & M. Paulmier-Foucart, Royarmt, 96, pp 303-326; European Clerical Envoys to the Mongols: reports of Western Merchants in Eastern Europe and Central Asia, 1231-1255, in Journal of Medieval Hist, XXII, 53-69, 96, Assoc ed, Medieval Travel, Trade, & Exploration: An Encyclopedia (525-1492), Garland Press, NY, 00. **CONTACT ADDRESS** Dept of Hist, Bradley Univ, 1501 W Bradley Ave, Peoria, IL 61625-0002. **EMAIL** ggg@bumail.bradley.edu

GWYN, ALEXANDRA
PERSONAL Born 05/17/1935, St. John's, NF, Canada **DISCIPLINE** HISTORY **EDUCATION** Dalhousie Univ, BA, 55; DLitt(hon), Memorial Univ Nfld, 91. **CAREER** Infor off, Nat Gallery Can, 57-61; freelance journalist & auth, 61-; Ottawa ed, Saturday Night Mag, 75-80. **HONORS AND AWARDS** Found Arts & Lett awards, 77, 78, 94; Nat Mag Awds, 79, 85; Gov Gen Awd Non-fiction, 84; Nfld & Labrador Arts Coun Hall Honour, 96. **MEMBERSHIPS** Dir, PEN Can, 93-. **SELECTED PUBLICATIONS** Auth, The Private Capital: Ambition and Love in the Age of Macdonald and Laurier, 84; auth, Tapestry of War: A Private View of Canadians in the Great War, 92. **CONTACT ADDRESS** 300 Carlton St, Toronto, ON, Canada M5A 2L5.

GWYN, JULIAN
PERSONAL Born 03/30/1937, Birmingham, England, m, 1961, 5 children **DISCIPLINE** MODERN HISTORY **EDUCATION** Loyola Col Montreal, BA, 56; McGill Univ, MA, 58; Oxford Univ, BLitt, 61, DPhil(hist), 71. **CAREER** Lectr, 61-63, from asst prof to assoc prof, 63-78, Prof Hist, Univ Ottawa, 78-, Sessional lectr, Carleton Univ, 71-72; Can Coun fel, 71-73 and 75-77; asst ed, Hist Sociale-Social Hist, 72-. **MEMBERSHIPS** Soc Nautical Res. **RESEARCH** Eighteenth century British and Irish history; American colonial and economic history; British history; the colonial era of American History; preconfederation Nova Scotia and British Imperial History. **SELECTED PUBLICATIONS** Ed, American Manuscripts in the Gage Papers, 71; ed, The Royal Navy in North America, 1736-

52, 73; auth, The Enterprising Admiralm. The Personal Fortune of Admiral Sir Peter Warren, 74; co-ed, La Chute de Louisbourg, 1745, 78; ed, Nova Scotia Naval Office Shipping Lists, 1730-1820, 82; auth, Excessive Expectations Maritime Commerce and the Economic Development of Novia Scotia, 1740-1870, 98. **CONTACT ADDRESS** Dept of Hist, Univ of Ottawa, Seraphin Marion, 147 Seraphin-Marion, Ottawa, ON, Canada K1N 6N5.

GYTHIEL, ANTHONY P.
PERSONAL Born 10/17/1930, Poperinge West-Flanders Belguim, Germany **DISCIPLINE** WESTERN CIVILIZATION I, THE MIDDLE AGES, THE RENAISSANCE, THE REFORMATION. **EDUCATION** Univ Detroit, PhD, 71. **CAREER** Dept Hist, Wichita State Univ **HONORS AND AWARDS** Regents award for excellence in tchg; Wichita State Univ, 76; Emory Lindquist excellence in hon(s), 92; John Barrier distinguished tchg award; summer grants 93, (6) NEH; internal grants (7), Wichita State Univ. **RESEARCH** Trinitarian experience and vision in biblical and patristic tradition. **SELECTED PUBLICATIONS** Transl, seven bk(s) that deal with the theology of the early Christian East. **CONTACT ADDRESS** Dept of Hist, Wichita State Univ, 1845 Fairmont, Wichita, KS 67260-0062. **EMAIL** gythiel@gateway.net

GYUG, RICHARD F.
DISCIPLINE MEDIEVAL LITURGY, RELIGION AND SOCIETY **EDUCATION** Univ Toronto, PhD. **CAREER** Chair; assoc prof, Fordham Univ. **SELECTED PUBLICATIONS** Auth, Missale ragusinum: The Missal of Dubrovnik, 90; The Diocese of Barcelona during the Black Death: The Register 'Notule communium' 15, 94. **CONTACT ADDRESS** Dept of Hist, Fordham Univ, 441 E Fordham Rd, Bronx, NY 10458. **EMAIL** gyug@fordham.edu

H

HAAR, JAMES
PERSONAL Born 07/04/1929, St. Louis, MO **DISCIPLINE** HISTORY OF MUSIC **EDUCATION** Harvard Univ, BA, 50, PhD(music), 61; Univ NC, MA, 54. **CAREER** From instr to asst prof music, Harvard Univ, 60-67; assoc prof, Univ Pa, 67-69; prof, NY Univ, 69-78; W R Kenan JR Prof Music, Univ NC, 78-, Villa I Tatti fel music, 65; Am Coun Learned Soc fel, 73. **MEMBERSHIPS** Am Musicol Soc (vpres, 72-74, pres, 76-78); Renaissance Soc Am. **RESEARCH** Italian Madrigal; history of theory; humanism and music. **SELECTED PUBLICATIONS** Ed, Chanson & Madrigal, 1480-1530, Harvard Univ, 64; auth, The Note Nere Madrigal, J Am Musicol Soc, 65; Pace non Troro: A study in literary and musical parody, Musica Disciplina, 66; Classicism & mannerism in 16th century music, Int Rev Music Aesthet & Sociol, 70; Pythagorean harmony of the Universe, In: Dictionary of the History of Ideas, 73; Some remarks on the Missa la sol fa re mi, Josouin des prez, 76; Chromaticism & false relations in 16th century music, J Am Musicol Soc, 77; co-ed, The Duos of Gero, Broude Bros, 78. **CONTACT ADDRESS** Dept of Music, Univ of No Carolina, Chapel Hill, Chapel Hill, NC 27514.

HAARBAUER, DON WARD
PERSONAL Born 09/17/1940, Charleroi, PA, m, 1964, 2 children **DISCIPLINE** THEATRE HISTORY **EDUCATION** Univ Ala, Tuscaloosa, BS, 62, MA, 65; Univ Wis, Madison PhD(theatre), 73. **CAREER** Asst prof speech & theatre, 68-73, asst dean sch humanities, 73-75, asst prof theatre, 73-77, chmn performing arts, 73-81, assoc prof, 77-80, prof theatre, Univ Ala, Birmingham, 80-, assoc dean sch arts & humanities, 81-, dir, Horn in the West, Boone, NC, 67-71. **MEMBERSHIPS** Southeastern Theatre Conf (admin vpres, 77-79, vpres, 79-80, pres, 80-81). **RESEARCH** Pre-twentieth century English theatre. **SELECTED PUBLICATIONS** Auth, The Birmingham theatres of Frank O'Brien, Southern Theatre, summer 77. **CONTACT ADDRESS** Univ of Alabama, Birmingham, 301 Humanities Bldg, Birmingham, AL 35294-1260. **EMAIL** whaar@uab.edu

HAAS, ARTHUR G.
DISCIPLINE HISTORY **EDUCATION** Univ Chicago, PhD. **CAREER** Prof emer, Hist, Univ Tenn. **SELECTED PUBLICATIONS** Auth, Metternich, Reorganization and Nationality 1813-1818, Univ Tennessee. **CONTACT ADDRESS** Dept of History, Univ of Tennessee, Knoxville, 915 Volunteer Blvd, 6th Fl Dunford Hall, Knoxville, TN 37996.

HAAS, JAMES M.
PERSONAL Born 09/16/1927, Milwaukee, WI, m, 1959, 1 child **DISCIPLINE** ENGLISH HISTORY **EDUCATION** Marquette Univ, BA, 50; Univ Ill, AM, 55, PhD, 60. **CAREER** Instr hist, Univ Dayton, 59-61; from asst prof to assoc prof English hist, 61-75, Prof Hist, Southern Ill Univ, Edwardsville, 75-95, Am Philos Soc res grant, 70. **MEMBERSHIPS** Conf Brit Studies. **RESEARCH** Nineteenth-century English economic history. **SELECTED PUBLICATIONS** Auth, 18th-Century, Am Hist Rev, Vol 0100, 95; Traffic and Politics--The Role of Transportation in the Industrial-Revolution--A Comparison of England and France, Albion, Vol 0024, 92, The Origins of Railway Enterprise, the Stockton-and-Darlington Railway, 1821-1863, Albion, Vol 0026, 94; auth, A Management Odyssey: The Royal Dockyards, 1714-1914, Durham, MD, 94; Bristol and the Atlantic Trade in the the Construction and Management of Rochester-Bridge, Ad-43-1993, Albion, Vol 0027, 95. **CONTACT ADDRESS** Dept of Hist, So Illinois Univ, Edwardsville, Edwardsville, IL 62026.

HAAS, PETER J.
PERSONAL Born 11/29/1947, Detroit, MI, m, 1971, 3 children **DISCIPLINE** RELIGIOUS HISTORY, JUDAISM **EDUCATION** Hebrew Union Col, MA, 74; Brown Univ, PhD, 80. **CAREER** Asst prof to assoc prof, Vanderbilt Univ, 80-99; prof, Case Western Reserve Univ, 00-. **MEMBERSHIPS** AAR; SBL; MJSA; CCAR. **RESEARCH** Jewish Moral Discourse, Science and Religion. **SELECTED PUBLICATIONS** Auth, Morality After Auschwitz; auth, Responsa: Literary History of a Rabbinic Genre. **CONTACT ADDRESS** Dept Relig, Case Western Reserve Univ, Cleveland, OH 44106. **EMAIL** pjh7@po.cwru.edu

HAASE, DONALD P.
PERSONAL Born 03/20/1950, Cincinnati, OH, m, 1972, 3 children **DISCIPLINE** COMPARATIVE LITERATURE, GERMAN STUDIES **EDUCATION** Univ Cincinnati, BA, 72; MA, 73; Univ NC Chapel Hill, PhD, 79. **CAREER** Vis asst prof, Miami Univ, 78-81; asst prof to assoc prof, Wayne State Univ, 81-; Chair, 89-. **HONORS AND AWARDS** President's Awd for Excellence in Teaching; NEH Summer Stipend; Ger Acad Exchange Serv Fel. **MEMBERSHIPS** MLA; Am Assoc of Teachers of Ger; Bruder Grimm-Gesellschaft. **RESEARCH** Folktale, Fairytale, European Romanticism, Reception Studies, Children's Literature, Exile and Holocaust. **SELECTED PUBLICATIONS** Ed, the Reception of Grimm's Fairy Tales, 93; ed, Marvels and Tales: Journal of Fairy-Tale Studies 97-. **CONTACT ADDRESS** Dept Ger and Slavic Lang, Wayne State Univ, 443 Manoogian, Detroit, MI 48202. **EMAIL** d.haase@wayne.edu

HABEL, DOROTHY METZGER
DISCIPLINE ART HISTORY **EDUCATION** Univ Mich, PhD, 77. **CAREER** Assoc prof, Art Hist, Univ Tenn. **HONORS AND AWARDS** Alumni Outstanding Tchg Awd, 85; Fac Tchg Awd, 82, 84, 87; Fac Develop Awd, 91; res grant, Graham Found for Advanced Studies in the Visual Arts, 91. **SELECTED PUBLICATIONS** Auth, "Architects and Clods: The Emergence of Planning in the Context of Palace Architecture in Seventeenth-Century Rome," Pa State Univ, 93; auth, "The Projected Palazzo Chigi al Corso and S. Maria in Via Lata: The Palace-Church Component of Alexander VIIs Program for the Corso," 91; auth, "Alexander VII and The Private Builder," Jour Soc Archit Hist, 90. **CONTACT ADDRESS** Sch of Art, Univ of Tennessee, Knoxville, Knoxville, TN 37996. **EMAIL** dhabel@utk.edu

HABER, CAROLE
DISCIPLINE AMERICAN HISTORY, MEDICAL, SOCIAL, AND FAMILY HISTORY, VICTORIAN CULTURE **EDUCATION** Univ PA, PhD, 79. **CAREER** Prof, ch, dept Hist, Univ NC, Charlotte; exec bd, Behav and Soc Sci Sect, Gerontological Soc Am; prof, ch, dept history, Univ Delaware. **MEMBERSHIPS** Gerontological Soc Am. **RESEARCH** Old age; insanity; death. **SELECTED PUBLICATIONS** Auth, Witches, Widows, Wives and Workers: The Historiography of Elderly Women in America, in Jean M. Coyle, ed, Handbook on Women and Aging, Greenwood Press. **CONTACT ADDRESS** Dept of Hist, Univ of Delaware, 237 John Munroe Hall, Newark, DE 19716. **EMAIL** chaber@udel.edu

HABER, SAMUEL
PERSONAL Born 05/05/1928, New York, NY, m, 1949, 3 children **DISCIPLINE** UNITED STATES HISTORY **EDUCATION** Univ Calif, AB, 52, MA, 53, PhD, 61. **CAREER** Asst prof US Hist, Univ Del, 61-65; asst prof, 65-67, from assoc prof to prof US History, Univ Calif, Berkeley, 67-95; prof grad school, 95-. **HONORS AND AWARDS** NEH Sr Fel, 75-76; Proj 87 Award, July-December 78; Davis Ctr Fel, January-June 79; vis lectureship, Hebrew Univ, Jerusalem, May 85; Humanities Res Grant, 86-7. **RESEARCH** American intellectual history. **SELECTED PUBLICATIONS** Auth, Efficiency and Uplift, Univ Chicago, 64; contribr, The professions and higher education, an historical analysis, In: Higher Education and the Labor Market, 73; The Quest for Authority and Honor in the American Professions, 1750-1900, Univ Chicago, 91; rev. "The Taming of the Jew: A review of Jews in the American Academy, 1900-1940," by Susan Klingenstein in Reviews in American History 21 (Dec 93): 677-680; rev, "The Conundrum of Class" by Martin J. Burke in Journal of the Early Republic, (Fall 96); rev, "The True Professional Ideal, in America: A History," by Bruce A. Kimball in Contemporary Sociology, 22, (July 93): 590-1; auth, "History of Professions in America," Encyclopedia of American Social History, ed. Mary K. Clayton, (Charles Scribners' Sons, 93). **CONTACT ADDRESS** Dept of History, Univ of California, Berkeley, 3229 Dwinelle Hall, Berkeley, CA 94720. **EMAIL** zanvil@socrates.berkeley.edu

HABOUSH, JA-HYUN KIM
DISCIPLINE EAST ASIAN STUDIES **EDUCATION** Ewha Woman's Univ, BA, 67; Univ of Mich, MA, 70; Columbia Univ, PhD, 78. **CAREER** Res assoc, Columbia Univ, 82-83; lectr, Barnard Col, Columbia Univ, 83-84; assoc prof, Univ of Ill, 88-96; prof, Univ of Ill, 96-; vis prof, Barnard Col, Columbia Univ, 97. **HONORS AND AWARDS** Summer Res Grant, International Cultural Soc of Korea, 84; Summer Travel Graant, Univ of Ill Res Bd, 86; Res Grant, The Nat Endowment for the Humanities, 88-89; Summer Travel Grant, Univ of Ill Res Bd, 90; Res Grant, 91; Conference Grant, 92; Workshop Grant, 94; Short Term Travel Grant, 94; Summer Travel Grant, Univ of Ill Res Bd, 95; Grand Prize of the Korean Culture and Arts Found Korean Lit Translation Awd. **MEMBERSHIPS** Am Hist Asn; Asn for Asian Studies. **RESEARCH** Cultural and intellectual history and literature of late Choson and early modern Korea; gender and women's narratives. **SELECTED PUBLICATIONS** Co-ed, The Rise of Neo-Confucianism in Korea, New York: Columbia Univ Press, 85; auth, A Heritage of Kings: One Man's Monarchy in the Confucian World, New York: Columbia Univ Press, 88; auth, "The Censorial Voice in Chosen Korea: A Tradition of Institutionalized Dissent," Han-Kuo hsueh-bao, (93): 11-19; auth, "Academies and Civil Society in Chosen Korea," in La societe civile face a l' Etat: dans traditions chinoise, japonaise, coreenne et vietnamienne, ed. Leon Vandermeersch, (Paris: Ecole Francaise d'Extreme-Orient, 94): 383-392; auth, "Dreamland: Korean Dreamland: Korean Dreamscapes as an Alternative Confucian Space," in Das Andere China, ed. Helwig Schmidt-Glintzer, (Wiesbaden, Germany: Harrassowitz, 95): 659-70; auth, "Filial Emotions and Filial Vlues: Changing Patterns in the Discourse of Filiality in Late Choson Korea," Harvard Journal of Asiatic Studies, 55.1, (95): 129-177; auth, The Memoirs of Lady Hyegyong: The Autobiographical Writings of A Crown Princess of Eighteenth-Century Korea, Berkeley: Univ of Calif Press, 96; auth, "Sigong ul nomnadun mannam," (Encounter beyond space and time) in Readers' Today, (97): 22-25; auth, "Constructing the Center: The Ritual Controversy and the Search for a New Identity in Seventeenth-Century Korea," 99; co-ed, Culture and the State in Late Choson Korea, Cambridge: Harvard Univ, 99. **CONTACT ADDRESS** Dept East Asian Languages and Cultures, Univ of Illinois, Urbana-Champaign, 618 S Mathews, Urbana, IL 61801. **EMAIL** jhaboush@uiuc.edu

HACKENBURG, MICHAEL
DISCIPLINE HISTORY **EDUCATION** Wichita St Univ, BA, 69; Univ Calif, Berkeley, MLS, 73, PhD, 83. **CAREER** Asst prof, librnshp, Univ Chicago; current, Partner, Bolerium Books, San Francisco. **MEMBERSHIPS** Am Antiquarian Soc **RESEARCH** Subscription publishing; Underground Railroad; Robert Sears of NY. **SELECTED PUBLICATIONS** Auth, Hawking Subscription Books in 1870: A Salesman's Prospectus from Western Pennsylvania, PBSA 78, 84; ed & auth, The Subscription Publishing Network in Nineteenth- Century America, in Getting the Books Out: Papers of the Chicago Conference on the Book in the 19th-Century America, Lib Congress, 87. **CONTACT ADDRESS** Bolerium Books, 2141 Mission, Ste 300, San Francisco, CA 94110.

HACKETT, DAVID ANDREW
PERSONAL Born 01/29/1940, Rensselaer, IN, m, 1974, 3 children **DISCIPLINE** EUROPEAN HISTORY **EDUCATION** Earlham Col, BA, 62; Univ Wis, MA, 65, PhD(hist), 71. **CAREER** Asst prof hist, Kans State Col, Pittsburg, 68-71; asst prof hist, 71-, chemn, Univ Tex, El Paso, 96- **HONORS AND AWARDS** Chancellor's Awd for Outstanding Teaching; Fulbright, Univ Munich, 67-68; Fulbright, Ger, 80 & 93; DAAD Fellowship, 84. **MEMBERSHIPS** AHA; Western Ger Studies Asn. **RESEARCH** Germany-Weimar & Nazi period; electoral behavior; Holocaust. **SELECTED PUBLICATIONS** Ed & transl, The Buchenwald Report, Westview Press, 95; ed, Der Buchenwald Report, C.H. Beck, 96; Buchenwald: Symbol and Metaphor for the Changing Political Culture of East Germany, Stud in GDR Culture and Soc, Univ Press Am, 96. **CONTACT ADDRESS** Dept of History, Univ of Texas, El Paso, 500 W University Ave, El Paso, TX 79968-0532. **EMAIL** dhackett@utep.edu

HACKETT, DAVID H.
DISCIPLINE AMERICAN RELIGIOUS HISTORY, SOCIOLOGY OF RELIGION **EDUCATION** Emory Univ, PhD, 86. **CAREER** Assoc prof. **RESEARCH** Gender and American culture, American catholicism. **SELECTED PUBLICATIONS** Auth, Religion and American Culture: A Reader, Routledge, 95; Gender and Religion in American Culture, 1870-1930, Rel and Amer Cult, 95; The Silent Dialogue: Zen Letters to a Trappist Monk, Continuum, 96. **CONTACT ADDRESS** Dept of Relig, Univ of Florida, 226 Tigert Hall, Gainesville, FL 32611. **EMAIL** dhackett@religion.ufl.edu

HACKMANN, WILLIAM KENT
PERSONAL Born 08/12/1937, Denver, CO, m, 1960, 2 children **DISCIPLINE** ENGLISH AND MODERN EUROPEAN HISTORY **EDUCATION** Yale Univ, BA, 59; Univ Mich, MA, 62, PhD(hist), 69. **CAREER** Chm, Univ of Iowa, 84-85, 93-94, sec of Fac Council, 95-. **MEMBERSHIPS** Conf Brit Studies; AHA; Selden Soc Brit Mus Soc; Am Soc Eighteenth-Century

Studies. **RESEARCH** High politics in eighteenth-century England; for the period 1788-1833 studies the effort of the West India interest in the British House of Commons to block legislation. **CONTACT ADDRESS** Dept of Hist, Univ of Idaho, Administration Bldg 315, Moscow, ID 83844. **EMAIL** hackmann@uidaho.edu

HACKNEY, SHELDON

PERSONAL Born 12/05/1933, Birmingham, AL, m, 1957, 3 children **DISCIPLINE** HISTORY **EDUCATION** Vanderbilt Univ, BA, 55; Yale Univ, MA, 63, PhD, 66. **CAREER** Instr, Princeton Univ, 65-66, asst prof to prof, 66-75, provost, 72-75; Pres and prof, Tulane Univ, 75-81; Pres and prof, Univ Pa, 81-93; chairman, Nat Endowment of the Humanities, 93-97; prof, Univ Pa, 97-. **HONORS AND AWARDS** Bereridgre Prize, Am Hist Asn; Sydnor Prize, Southern Hist Asn. **MEMBERSHIPS** Am Hist Asn, Southern Hist Asn, Org of Am Hists. **RESEARCH** U.S., history of the South, 1960s, American identity. **SELECTED PUBLICATIONS** Auth, Populism to Progressivism in Alabama, Princeton Press (69); auth, One America Indivisible, GPO (77). **CONTACT ADDRESS** Dept Hist, Univ of Pennsylvania, 3401 Walnut St, Philadelphia, PA 19104-6228. **EMAIL** shackney@history.upenn.edu

HADDAD, GLADYS

PERSONAL Born 09/12/1930, Cleveland, OH, s **DISCIPLINE** AMERICAN STUDIES **EDUCATION** Allegheny Col, BA, 52; Case Western Reserve Univ, MA, 61; Lake Erie Col, BFA, 74; Case Western Reserve Univ, PhD, 80. **CAREER** Prof, dean, exec asst to pres, Lake Erie Col, 63-89; prof, dir, Western Reserve Studies Symposia, Case Western Reserve Univ, 91-. **HONORS AND AWARDS** Biographical entries in Who's Who in the Midwest, 79-,Who's Who of Am Women, 79-, Two Thousand Notable Am Women, 93-,Who's Who in Am Educ, 95-,Who's Who in the World, 95-; Grad Alumni Res Grant, Case Western Reserve Univ, 79; Nat Forum: Am Coun on Educ Nat Idnetification Progr for the Advancement of Women in Higher Educ, 81; Rockefeller Res Grant, 83; Am Asn for State and Local Hist Cert of Commendation Awd for Western Reserve Studies Symposium/ Western Reserve Studies: A J of Regional Hist and Cult, 88; Am Asn for State and Local Hist Grant-in Aid for Anthology of Western Reserve Lit, 88; Northern Ohio Live Achievement Awd, 91; Nat Endowment for the Hums, Vassar Col, 93; Flora Stone Mather Alumnae Asn Grant, 94; Nat Television Broadcasting Silver Telly Highest Awd for Documentary Video Samuel Mather: Vision, Leadership, Generosity, 95; Case Western Reserve Univ Fel, 96; Ohio Hums Coun Grant for film script, 96. **MEMBERSHIPS** Am Studies Asn; Great Lakes Am Studies Asn; Ohio Hist Soc. **RESEARCH** Regional Studies: History, literature, and art; Women's Studies: biography. **SELECTED PUBLICATIONS** Auth, Ohio's Western Reserve: A Regional Reader, Kent State Univ Press, 88; auth, Anthology of Western Reserve Literature, Kent State Univ Press,92; auth, Samuel Mather: Vision, Leadership, Generosity, a Video Documentary, Dedication-Samuel Mather Pavilion, Univ Hospitals, 94; Samuel and Flora Stone Mather: Partners in Philanthropy, a Video Documentary, Western Reserve Studies Symposium, 95; Laukhoff's Book Store: Cleveland's Literary and Artistic Landmark, in Cleveland's Artistic Heritage, Cleveland's Artists Found, 96; Laukhoff's Book Store of Cleveland: An Epilogue, Northern Ohio Bibliophilic Soc, 97; Flora Stone Mather: A Legacy of Stewardship, aVideo Documentary, Col of Arts and Scis, Case Western Reserve Univ, 97; rev, Converting the West: A Biography of Narcissa Whitman, The Western Hist Soc Quart, XXIII, 92; auth, " Education of Girls and Women" Encyclopedia of the United States In the Nineteenth Century, Scribaers Sons, 00. **CONTACT ADDRESS** Interdisciplinary Centers and Programs, Case Western Reserve Univ, Cleveland, OH 44106-7120. **EMAIL** qmh3@po.cwru.edu

HADDAD, MAHMOUD

DISCIPLINE MODERN MIDDLE EASTERN HISTORY **EDUCATION** Amer Univ Beirut, BA, 70; Columbia Univ, PhD, 89. **CAREER** Assoc prof. **RESEARCH** Modern Islamic nationalism. **SELECTED PUBLICATIONS** Auth, The Rise of Arab Nationalism Reconsidered, Intl Jour Middle Eastern Stud, 94. **CONTACT ADDRESS** Dept of Hist, Columbia Col, New York, 2960 Broadway, New York, NY 10027-6902.

HADDAD, ROBERT MITCHELL

PERSONAL Born 10/01/1930, New York, NY, m, 1964, 4 children **DISCIPLINE** ISLAMIC HISTORY **EDUCATION** Univ Pittsburgh, BS, 52; Univ Mich, MA, 54; Harvard Univ, PhD(hist, Mid Eastern studies), 65. **CAREER** Lectr nonwestern studies, Amherst, Smith, Mt Holyoke Cols & Univ Mass, 60-63; lectr hist, 63-65, asst prof, 65-68, assoc prof hist & relig, 68-73, prof hist & relig, 73- 82; Sophia Smith Prof hist & prof relig, 82-93, Sophia Smith Prof Hist & Prof Relig Emer, 93- , Smith Col; pres, Am Univ Beirut, 93-96. **HONORS AND AWARDS** Soc Sci Res Coun grant, 66-67 **MEMBERSHIPS** Mid E Studies Asn N Am; AAUP. **RESEARCH** Syrian Christianity in the Muslim era; Greater Syria in the Ottoman period. **SELECTED PUBLICATIONS** Syrian Christians in Muslim Society: An Interpretation, Princeton Univ, 70; auth, "The Ottoman Empire in the Contempory Middle East," in Aftermath of Empire, Smith College Studies in History, (Northampton, MA, 75); auth, "Iconoclasts and Mu'tazila: the Politics of Anthropumorphism,"The Greek Orthodox Theological Review, Vol. 27, 82; auth,The Conversion of Eastern Christians to the Unia, in Gervers, ed, Conversion and Continuity: Indigenous Christian Communities in Islamic Lands, Eighth to Eighteenth Centuries, Pontifical Inst of Mediaeval Stud in Toronto, 90; auth, Constantinople over Antioch, 1516-1724: Patriarchal Politics in the Ottoman Era, in, J of Ecclesiastical Hist, 90. **CONTACT ADDRESS** Dept of History, Smith Col, Northampton, MA 01060. **EMAIL** rhaddad@sophia.smith.edu

HADDEN, SALLY E.

PERSONAL Born, NC, m, 1994 **DISCIPLINE** HISTORY **EDUCATION** Univ NC, BA, 84; Harvard Univ, MA, 85, PhD, 93; Harvard Law Sch, JD, 89. **CAREER** Asst prof, 93-95, Univ Toledo; asst prof, 95-, Fl St Univ. **HONORS AND AWARDS** Mark DeWolfe Howe Fund res grant, 90, 91; Charles Warren Center for Amer His res grant, 90, 91; Va Hist Soc Res Fel, 91; Josephine de Karman Found Dissertation Fel, 92-93; res assoc, Univ Toledo, 93-94; Harry Frank Guggenheim Dissertation Fel, 92-93; Kate B & Hall J Peterson Fel, 94; Archie K Davis Fel, 97; W B H Dowse Fel, 98; phi beta kappa **MEMBERSHIPS** AHA; ASLH; OAH; SHA. **RESEARCH** Legal & constitutional hist; colonial Amer; the South. **SELECTED PUBLICATIONS** Auth, James Madison, in Statesmen Who Changed the World, Greenwood Press, 93; auth, The War of 1812, Events that Shaped Nineteenth-Century America, Greenwood Press, 97; art, Redefining the Boundaries of Public History: Mystic Seaport Goes Online and On Board with Amistad, OAH Newsletter, 98; auth, Judging Slavery: Thomas Mann and State V. Mann, in Local Matters: Race and Criminal Justice..Thomas Ruffin and State v. Mann: Race and Criminal Justice in the American South, 1800-1900, Univ Ga Press, 01; art, Colonial and Revolutionary Era Slave Patrols in Virginia, Lethal Imagination: Violence and Brutality in American History, NY Univ Press, 99. **CONTACT ADDRESS** Dept of History, Florida State Univ, Tallahassee, FL 32306-2200. **EMAIL** shadden@mailer.fsu.edu

HADDOCK, GREGORY

PERSONAL Born 05/09/1968, Fairfax, VA, m, 1990, 2 children **DISCIPLINE** GEOGRAPHY **EDUCATION** Mary Washington Col, BA, 90; Univ Idaho, MS, 93, Doctor Philos, 96. **CAREER** Instr and PhD candidate, Univ Idaho, 94-96; asst prof, Northwest Missouri State Univ, 96-. **MEMBERSHIPS** Am Asn Univ Profs, Nat Coun for Geographic Ed, Asn of Am Geographers. **RESEARCH** Spatial analysis and programming/ modeling in geographic information systems teaching web-based teaching. **SELECTED PUBLICATIONS** Coauth with P. Jankowski, "A Visual Programming Environment for Spatial Modeling," Transactions in GIS, Vol 1, 177-188 (3). **CONTACT ADDRESS** Dept Geography & Geology, Northwest Missouri State Univ, 800 University Dr, Maryville, MO 64468. **EMAIL** haddock@mail.nwmissouri.edu

HAFNER, J.

DISCIPLINE GEOGRAPHY, ASIAN STUDIES **EDUCATION** Miami Univ, Ohio, BA, 63; Univ Mich, MA, 65, PhD, 70. **CAREER** Prof, Univ Mass, Amherst, 86-, chair, Asian Studies Prog, 99-. **MEMBERSHIPS** Asn Asian Studies, Inc.; Siam Soc; Asn Am Geographers. **SELECTED PUBLICATIONS** Auth, "Agriculture and Rural Development," Ch. 6, and "Thailand: Nation in Transition," Ch 14, in Southeast Asia: Development and Diversity, T. Leinbach and R. Ulack, eds, Prentice-Hall, 2000. **CONTACT ADDRESS** Dept Geosci, Univ of Massachusetts, Amherst, Amherst, MA 01003. **EMAIL** hafner@geo.umass.edu

HAFTER, DARYL MASLOW

PERSONAL Born 01/17/1935, Elizabeth, NJ, m, 1957, 2 children **DISCIPLINE** MODERN EUROPEAN HISTORY **EDUCATION** Smith, Col, BA, 56; Yale Univ, MA, 58, PhD(Fr hist), 64 **CAREER** Lectr, 68-69, asst prof, 69-76, assoc prof, 76-81, Prof Hist & Philos, Eastern Mich Univ, 81-; Res grant, Am Philos Soc, 75; consult, Nat Endowment for Humanities, 77-; NSF grant, 84, 86. **HONORS AND AWARDS** Pres, Soc for the Hist of Technology, 01-03. **MEMBERSHIPS** Soc Hist Technol; Women Historians Midwest; AHA; Fr Hist Asn **RESEARCH** French eighteenth century; women's history; history of technology. **SELECTED PUBLICATIONS** Auth, Philippe de Lasalle: From Mise-en-carte to Industrial Design, Winterthur Portfolio XII; ed, European Women and Preindustrial Craft, Ind Univ Press, 95; Female masters in the Ribbonmaking Guild of Eighteenth Century Rouen, French Hist Studies, winter 97; auth, " Measuring Cloth by the Elbow and a Thumb: Resistance to Numbers in France of the 1780's," in Culture and Control, ed. Miriam R. Levin (London: Horwood, 99); auth, "Women in Underground Business of Eighteenth-Century Lyon, " (Enterprise & Soc, Spring, 01). **CONTACT ADDRESS** Dept of Hist, Eastern Michigan Univ, 701 Pray Harrold, Ypsilanti, MI 48197-2201. **EMAIL** his_hafter@online.emich.edu

HAGAN, KENNETH JAMES

PERSONAL Born 02/20/1936, Oakland, CA, m, 1964, 3 children **DISCIPLINE** AMERICAN DIPLOMATIC AND NAVAL HISTORY **EDUCATION** Univ Calif, Berkeley, AB, 58, MA, 64; Claremont Grad Sch, PhD(hist), 70. **CAREER** Instr hist, Claremont Men's Col, 68-69; asst prof, Kans State Univ, 69-73; asst prof, 73-77, Assoc Prof Hist, US Naval Acad, 77-. **MEMBERSHIPS** AHA; Orgn Am Historians; Soc Historians Am Foreign Rels; Am Mil Inst; NAm Soc Oceanic Hist. **RESEARCH** US Naval and diplomatic history; American foreign relations and naval history; Soviet-American naval strategy. **SELECTED PUBLICATIONS** Auth, How Navies Fight--The United-States-Navy and Its Allies, Int Hist Rev, Vol 0017, 95; 100 Years of Sea Power--The United-States-Navy, 1890-1990, Int Hist Rev, Vol 0017, 95. **CONTACT ADDRESS** Dept of Hist, United States Naval Acad, Annapolis, MD 21402.

HAGAN, WILLIAM THOMAS

PERSONAL Born 12/19/1918, Huntington, WV, m, 1943, 4 children **DISCIPLINE** AMERICAN HISTORY **EDUCATION** Marshall Univ, BA, 41; Univ Wis, PhD, 50. **CAREER** From asst prof to prof hist, NTex State Univ, 50-65; prof, 65-75, distinguished prof hist, State Univ NY Col, Fredonia, 75-88; prof History, Univ Okla, 89-95; Adv comt, Newberry Libr Ctr Indian Hist, 72-86; bd eds, Western Hist Quart, 73-78; ed consult, Ariz & West, 78-84. **HONORS AND AWARDS** W Hist Asn Prize, 89 **MEMBERSHIPS** Orgn Am Historians; Am Hist Asn; Am Soc Ethnohistory (pres, 63); Western His Asn. **SELECTED PUBLICATIONS** Auth, The Sac and Fox Indians, Univ Okla, 58 & 80; American Indians, Univ Chicago, 61 & 79 & 93; The Indian in American History, Am Hist Asn, 63 & rev ed, 71; Indian Police and Judges, 71 & United States-Comanche Relations, Yale Univ, 76; The Indian Rights Association, Univ Arizona, 85; Quanah Parker, Comanche Chief, Univ Okla, 93; Theodore Roosevelt and Six Friends of the Indian, Univ Okla, 97. **CONTACT ADDRESS** 2542 Cypress Ave, Norman, OK 73072. **EMAIL** Whagan5281@AOL.com

HAGEDORN, NANCY

PERSONAL Born 09/16/1958, Cincinnati, OH, s **DISCIPLINE** HISTORY **EDUCATION** Univ of Cincinnati, BA, 81; Col of William & Mary, PhD, 95. **CAREER** Teaching Fel, Col of William & Mary, 85-86; Staff Historian, Cincinnati Hist Soc, 88-89, Lect, Univ Cincinnati, 88-89; Asst Prof, St Johns Univ, 96-00; Asst Prof, Ind State Univ, 00-. **HONORS AND AWARDS** Jamestown Fel, Jamestown-Yorktown Found, 86-87; Newberry Libr short-term Fel, 87-88; Hon Mention, Kerr Kist Prize, NY St Hist Asn, 96; Fel, Seminar for the Hist of the Atlantic World, Harvard Univ, 97; Kate B. and Hall J. Peterson Fel, Am Antiquarian Soç, 98, 88. **MEMBERSHIPS** Am Soc for Ethnohistory, Orgn of Am Historians, Am Hist Asn. **RESEARCH** Early American history, Early American Ethnohistory, Atlantic World, 1500-1800. **SELECTED PUBLICATIONS** Auth, "A Friend to go Between Them: The Interpreter as Cultural Broker During Anglo-Iroquois Councils, 1740-1770," Ethnohistory 35 (Winter, 88): 60-80; coauth, Tools: Working Wood in Eighteenth-Century America, Wallace Gallery Decorative Arts Ser (Colonial Williamsburg Found, 93); auth, "Faithful, Knowing and Prudent: Andrew Montour as Interpreter and Cultural Broker, 1740-1772," in Between Indian and White Worlds: The Cultural Broker, ed. Margaret Connell Szasz (Univ of Okla, 94); auth, Brokers of Understanding: Interpreters as Agents of Cultural Exchange in Colonial New York, New York History LXXVI (95): 379-408; auth, "Tools for Sale: The Marketing and Distribution of English Woodworking Tools in England and America," in Eighteenth-Century Woodworking Tools: Papers Presented at a Tool Symposium, (Colonial Williamsburg Found, 97): 37-54; auth, "Communications," in American Eras: Early American Civilizations and Exploration to 1600, (Detroit: Gale Res, 98): 77-101 **CONTACT ADDRESS** Dept Hist, Indiana State Univ, Terre Haute, IN 47809. **EMAIL** hihagedo@ruby.indstate.edu

HAGEN, KENNETH G.

PERSONAL Born 07/02/1936, Minneapolis, MN, m, 1958 **DISCIPLINE** HISTORY **EDUCATION** Augsburg Col, AB, 58; Harvard Divinity Sch, STB, 61; Harvard Univ, ThD, 67. **CAREER** Teaching fel, Harvard Divinity Sch, 63-65; asst prof, Concordia-Moorhead, 65-67; from vis asst prof to prof, 67-; vis prof Univ of San Francisco, 71; prof, Universitetet I Oslo, 90. **HONORS AND AWARDS** Grants, Harvard Divinity Sch, 58-63; Rockefeller Doctoral Fel in Relig, 63-65; Lutheran World Federation Grant, Int Luther Res Congress, 66; Res Grants, Marquette Univ, 68-70, 75-77, & 93; Summer Fac Fel, Marquette Univ, 70, 74, & 85; Newberry Libr Grant, 70; Newberry Libr Fel, 76; Am Philos Soc Grant, 77; Sr Fulbright-Hays Fel, 79-80; Wolfenbuttel Libr Grant, 82; Marshall Fund, Norway-America Asn, 82 & 84; Distinguished Alumnus Citation, Augsburg Col, 82; Guest of the Libr, Wolfenbuttel, 85; Resident Scholar, Inst for Ecumenical and Cultural Res, 94-95. **MEMBERSHIPS** Norwegian Acad of Sci and Letters, **RESEARCH** Am Soc of Church Hist, Am Soc of Reformation Res, Fulbright Alumni Asn, Luther-Gesellschaft, Luther Acad, Sixteenth-Century Studies Confr. **SELECTED PUBLICATIONS** Ed, Reformation Texts With Translation (1350-1650) Vol 3, Marquette Univ Press, (Milwaukee, WI), 96 & 98; auth, "Luther on Atonement Reconfigured," Concordia Theol Quart 61 (97): 251-276; auth, "The Bible in the Churches: How Various Christians Interpret the Scriptures, Marquette Univ Press (Milwaukee, WI), 98; Auth, "Luther, Martin (1483-1546)," in Historical Handbook of Major Biblical Interpreters, ed. Donald K. McKim (IL: InterVarsity Press, 98), 212-220; ed & contribur, Luther Digest: An Annual Abridgment of Luther Studies Vol 6, The

Luther Acad (St. Louis, MO), 98; ed & contribur, Luther Digest: An Annual Abridgment of Luther Studies Vol 7, The Luther Acad (St. Louis, MO), 99; auth, "Luther's So-Called Judenschriften: A Genre Approach," Archiv fur Reformationsgeschichte 90 (99): 130-158. **CONTACT ADDRESS** Dept Theol, Marquette Univ, PO Box 1881, Milwaukee, WI 53201-1881. **EMAIL** ak@gdinet.com

HAGEN, WILLIAM WALTER
PERSONAL Born 10/24/1942, Butte, MT, m, 1961, 2 children **DISCIPLINE** MODERN EUROPEAN HISTORY **EDUCATION** Harvard Univ, BA, 65; Univ Chicago, MA, 67, PhD(hist), 71. **CAREER** Asst prof, 70-77, Assoc Prof Hist, Univ Calif, Davis, 77-. **MEMBERSHIPS** AHA; Am Asn Advan Slavic Studies; Western Slavic Asn. **RESEARCH** Polish-German-Jewish nationality conflict in Prussian Poland 1772-1918; nineteenth century German social history; social and political history of Poland and Hapsburgh Empire. **SELECTED PUBLICATIONS** Auth, National solidarity and organic work in Prussian Poland 1815-1914, J Mod Hist, 3/72; The impact of economic modernization on traditional nationality relations in Prussian Poland, 1815-1914, J Social Hist, spring 73; The partitions of Poland and the crisis of the old regime in Prussia 1772-1806, Cent Europ Hist, 6/77. **CONTACT ADDRESS** Dept of Hist, Univ of California, Davis, Davis, CA 95616-5200.

HAGER, HELLMUT
PERSONAL Born 03/27/1926, Berlin **DISCIPLINE** ITALIAN AND GERMAN BAROQUE AND ROCOCO ARCHITECTURE **EDUCATION** Bonn University, Dr Phil. **CAREER** Prof, Pa State Univ, 71-, Hd dept Art Hist, 72-96. **HONORS AND AWARDS** Fel, Instit Arts and Humanistic Stuc; Evan Pugh Professor. **RESEARCH** Italian architects Carlo Fontana, Filippo Juvarra, and the school of Bernini. **SELECTED PUBLICATIONS** Coauth, Loyola Historia y Arquitectura, 91; Carlo Fontana: The Drawings at Windsor Castle, London; Filippo Juvarra e il concorso di modelli del 1715 bandito da Clemente XI per la nuova sacrestia di S. Pietro; ed and crit intro; Carlo Fontana, Utilessimo trattato dell'Acque Correnti (Rome, 1696); Rome, 99; contrib, The Triumph of the Baroque: Architecture in Europe 1600-1750, catalogue of the exhibition, ed by Henry A. Millon, Turin, 99, essays pgs 431-432, 568-570, 577-578. **CONTACT ADDRESS** Pennsylvania State Univ, Univ Park, 229 Arts Bldg., University Park, PA 16802. **EMAIL** axc6@psu.edu

HAGGIS, DONALD
DISCIPLINE CLASSICAL ARCHAEOLOGY **EDUCATION** Wayne State Univ, AB, 82, MA, 85; Univ MN, PhD, 92. **CAREER** Asst prof, Univ NC, Chapel Hill; assoc mem, Am Schl Class Stud, Athens, 89-92, Schl Archaeol, Athens, 90-91. **RESEARCH** Archaeol of bronze age Crete; early iron age Greece; early state soc. **SELECTED PUBLICATIONS** Auth, East Crete in the Middle Minoan Period: A Pre-State Society, Am J of Archaeol 98, 94; An Early Minoan I Pottery Assemblage from East Crete, Am J of Archaeol 99, 95; Archaeological Survey at Kavousi, East Crete: Preliminary Report, Hesperia 65, 96; The Port of Tholos in Eastern Crete and the Role of a Roman Horreum along the Egyptian 'Corn Route,' Oxford J of Archaeol 15, 96; Excavations at Kalo Khorio, East Crete, Am J of Archaeol 100, 96; coauth, Aspects of Vernacular Architecture in Postpalatial and Early Iron Age Crete, Am J of Archaeol 98, 94. **CONTACT ADDRESS** Univ of No Carolina, Chapel Hill, Chapel Hill, NC 27599. **EMAIL** dchaggis@email.unc.edu

HAHM, DAVID EDGAR
PERSONAL Born 09/30/1938, Milwaukee, WI, m, 1964, 4 children **DISCIPLINE** CLASSICAL LANGUAGES, ANCIENT PHILOSOPHY, INTELLECTUAL HISTORY **EDUCATION** Northwestern Col, BA, 60; Univ Wis-Madison, MA, 62, PhD(classics), 66. **CAREER** Asst prof class lang, Univ Mo-Columbia, 66-69; from asst prof to assoc prof class, 69-78, Prof Classics, Ohio State Univ, 78-, Fel, Ctr Hellenic Studies, Wash, DC, 68-69. **MEMBERSHIPS** Am Philol Asn; Am Philos Asn; Hist Sci Soc; Class Asn Midwest & South. **RESEARCH** Ancient philosophy and science, Greek literature. **SELECTED PUBLICATIONS** Auth, The origins of Stoic cosmology, Columbus, 77; auth, "A neglected Stoic argument for human responsibility," Illinois Classical Studies 17, (92): 23-48; auth, "Galen and Chrysippus on the soul: argument and refutation in the 'De placitis, bks. 2-3," Bulletin of the Hist of Medicine 73, (99): 302-3; auth, "Plato, Carneades and Cicero's Philus, (Cicero, Rep. 3.8-31)," Classical Quarterly ns. 49, (99): 167-83. **CONTACT ADDRESS** Dept of Greek & Latin, Ohio State Univ, Columbus, 230 N Oval Mall, Columbus, OH 43210-1335. **EMAIL** hahm.1@osu.edu

HAHN, ROGER
PERSONAL Born 01/05/1932, Paris, France, m, 1955, 2 children **DISCIPLINE** HISTORY OF SCIENCE **EDUCATION** Harvard Univ, BA, 53, MAT, 54; Ecole Pratique des Hautes Etudes, Paris, dipl, 55; Cornell Univ, PhD, 62. **CAREER** Instr hist, Univ Del, 60-61; from instr to assoc prof, 61-74, Prof Hist, Univ Calif, Berkeley, 74-, Spec Asst to Dir Sci Affairs, Bancroft Libr, 71-, adv ed, Isis, 71-76, Hist Sci, 72-, Soc Studies Sci, 74- & Eighteenth Century Studies, 76-80; Am Coun Learned Soc fel, 73-74; Pres, Am Soc for Eighteenth Century Studies, 82-83. **HONORS AND AWARDS** Fulbright scholar, 54-55, 83-84; NSF fels, 59-60 & 64-65; Bk-of-the-Year Award, Pac Coast Br, AHA, 72; Chevalier Palmes Academiques, 77; officer, 88. **MEMBERSHIPS** AHA; Hist Sci Soc; Soc Fr Hist Studies, fel AAAS; corresp mem Int Acad Hist Sci; Pres, American Society for Fifthteenth Century Studies, 82-83. **RESEARCH** Eighteenth century science; history of scientific institutions; French history. **SELECTED PUBLICATIONS** Auth, L'Hydrodynamique au 18e siecle, Palais Decouverte, Paris, 65; Laplace as a Newtonian Scientist, W A Clark Libr, 67; The Anatomy of a Scientific Institution: The Paris Academy of Sciences, 1666-1803, Univ Calif, 71; Scientific research as an occupation in 18th century France, Minerva, 75; New directions in the social history of science, Physis, 75; L'autobiographie de Lacepede retrouvee, Dix-huitieme Siecle, 75; Laplace and the Mechanistic Universe, God and Nature, 86; The Meaning of the Mechanistic Age, The Boundaries of Humanity, 91; The Ideological and Institutional Difficulties of a Jesuit Scientist in Paris, R J Boscovich, 93. **CONTACT ADDRESS** Dept of Hist, Univ of California, Berkeley, 3229 Dwinelle Hall, Berkeley, CA 94720-2550. **EMAIL** rhahn@socrates.berkeley.edu

HAHNER, JUNE EDITH
PERSONAL Born 07/08/1940, New York, NY **DISCIPLINE** LATIN AMERICAN HISTORY **EDUCATION** Earlham Col, AB, 61; Cornell Univ, MA, 63, PhD, 66. **CAREER** Foreign Area Fel Prog fel, Brazil & Cornell Univ, 64-66; asst prof Latin Am hist, Tex Technol Col, 66-68; asst prof, 68-72, assoc prof, 72-80, Prof Latin Am Hist, State Univ NY Albany, 80-; NEH fel, 71 & 82-83; Rockefeller Found fel, 86-87; ; mem, ed bd, The Americas, 74-92 and Latin Am Res Review, 94-96; Co-Pres, comm Women in Hist, 98-2000 **HONORS AND AWARDS** NECLAS Book Prize, 87; Fulbright fel, 80. **MEMBERSHIPS** Latin Am Studies Asn; Conf Latin Am Hist; AHA; Int Conf Group Mod Portugal. **RESEARCH** Urban change and politics in Brazilian empire and republic; women in Latin America; Brazilian armed forces in Brazil. **SELECTED PUBLICATIONS** Auth, Civilian Military Relations in Brazil, 1889-1898, Univ SC, 69; The Brazilian Armed Forces and the overthrow of the monarchy: Another perspective, Americas, 10/69; A molestia do Imperador e as interpretacoes da queda do Imperio, Rev Inst Hist Geog Brasileiro, 10-12/71; Floriano Peixoto: Brazil's iron marshal: A reevaluation, The Americas, 6/74; ed, Women in Latin American History: Their Lives and Views, Univ Calif, Los Angeles, 76, rev ed, 80; auth, Jacobinos vs Galegos: Urban radicals vs Portuguese immigrants in Rio de Janeiro in the 1890's, J Inter Am Studies & World Affairs, 5/76; Women and work in Brazil, 1850-1920, in Essays Concerning the Socioeconomic History of Brazil and Portuguese India, Univ Fla, 77; ed, A Mulher No Brasil, Editora Civilisacao Brasileira, 78; The Nineteenth-Century feminist press and women's rights in Brazil, in Latin American Women, A Historical Perspective, Greenwood, 78; auth, Feminism, women's rights, and the suffrage movement in Brazil, 1850-1932, Latin Am Res Rev, 80; auth, A Mulher Brasileira e Suas Lutas Sociais e Politicas, 1850-1937, Brasiliense, 81; Women's place in politics and economics in Brazil since 1964, Luso-Brazilian Rev, 82; Researching the history of Latin American women: Past and future directions, Inter-Am Rev of Bibliog, 83; Recent research on women in Brazil, Latin Am Res Rev, 85; Poverty and Politics. The Urban Poor in Brazil, 1870-1920, Univ NM, 86; Women's work in Brazil. Recent researach and publications, Inter-Am Rev of Bibliog, 88; La historiografia de la mujer. Problemas y perspectivas, in Seminario de Estudios sobre la Mujer, Min de Cultura de CR, 89; Emancipating the Female Sex. The Struggle for Women's Rights in Brazil, 1850-1940, Duke, 90; Educacao e ideologia: Profissionais liberais na America latina do seculo XIX, Estudos Feminista 5, 94; Recent tendencies in the historiography of women in Latin America, Noticia Bibliografica e Historica, 96; Educacao e ideologia. Profissionais pioneiras na Amerca Latina do Seculo SIX, in Educacao na America Latina, EDUSP, 96; Women in Brazil, rev ed, Latin Am Inst, Univ NM, 98; ed, Women through Women's Eyes. Latin American Women in Nineteenth-Century Travel Accounts. **CONTACT ADDRESS** Dept of Hist, SUNY, Albany, 1400 Washington Ave, Albany, NY 12222-1000. **EMAIL** hahner@csc.albany.edu

HAIKEN, ELIZABETH
DISCIPLINE HISTORY **EDUCATION** Univ Ca, PhD. **CAREER** Asst prof, Hist, Univ Tenn; asst prof, Hist, Univ Brit Colum. **RESEARCH** U.S. history; history of medicine. **SELECTED PUBLICATIONS** Auth, Venus Envy: A History of Cosmetic Surgery, Johns Hopkins Univ 97. **CONTACT ADDRESS** Dept Hist, Univ of British Columbia, 1873 E Mall, Ste 1297, Vancouver, BC, Canada V6T 1Z1.

HAINES, GERALD KENNETH
PERSONAL Born 05/19/1943, Detroit, MI, m, 1969 **DISCIPLINE** UNITED STATES DIPLOMATIC HISTORY **EDUCATION** Wayne State Univ, BA, 65, MA, 67; Univ Wis, Madison, PhD(diplomatic hist), 73. **CAREER** Teacher social studies, Detroit Pub Schs, 65-67; instr Am hist, Wayne County Community Col, 73-74; Archivist Am Hist, Nat Arch, 74-81; vis assoc prof, Univ Tex, San Antonio, 81-82. **MEMBERSHIPS** Orgn Am Historians; AHA; Soc Historians Am Foreign Rels; Soc Am Archivists; Soc Hist Fed Govt. **RESEARCH** US-Latin American relations; US-Asian relations. **SELECTED PUBLICATIONS** Auth, Who gives a damn about medieval walls? The Roberts Commission and efforts to save European Art during World War II, Prologue, summer 76; Citing Department of State Records, Newsletter Soc Historians Am Foreign Rels, spring 77; Under the eagles' wing: The Franklin Roosevelt administration forges an American hemisphere, Diplomatic Hist, fall 77; The Franklin D Roosevelt administration interprets the Monroe Doctrine, Australian J Polit Hist, fall 78; Ideological myopia, The US & A Japanese Monroe Doctrine 1931-1941, Prologue, summer 81; co-ed (with J Samuel Walker), American Foreign Relations: A Historiographical Review, 81; In The American Image, The US & Brazil, 1945-1954, US & Third World, 82. **CONTACT ADDRESS** 202 N Highland, Arlington, VA 22201.

HALBERSLEBEN, KAREN I.
DISCIPLINE HISTORY **EDUCATION** SUNY Buffalo, BA, 79; MA, 83; PhD, 87. **CAREER** Assoc prof, SUNY Oswego; VP for acad affairs, Buena Vista Univ, 98-. **HONORS AND AWARDS** NEH Summer Fellow, 90; Am Coun on Educ Fel, 96. **RESEARCH** Mod Brit hist; Europ women's hist. **SELECTED PUBLICATIONS** Auth, Women's Participation in the Brit Antislavery Movement 1824-1865, Mellen, 93; Elizabeth Pease: One Woman's Vision of Peace, Justice and Human Rights, Quaker Hist, 95; Epilogue to Play "Seneca Falls, 1848: All Men and Women are Created Equal," Willson, 84. **CONTACT ADDRESS** Dept Acad Affairs, Buena Vista Univ, PO Box 2011, Storm Lake, IA 50588. **EMAIL** halbersk@bvu.edu

HALE, CHARLES ADAMS
PERSONAL Born 06/05/1930, Minneapolis, MN, m, 1952, 4 children **DISCIPLINE** LATIN AMERICAN HISTORY **EDUCATION** Amherst Col, BA, 51; Univ Minn, MA, 52; Univ Strasbourg, dipl, 53; Columbia Univ, PhD(Latin Am hist), 57. **CAREER** Instr soc sci, Univ NC, 56-57; asst prof hist, Lehigh Univ, 57-63 and Amherst Col, 63-66; from asst prof to assoc prof, 66-70, chmn dept, 77-80, Prof Hist, Univ Iowa, 70-97, Soc Sci Res Coun and Am Coun Learned Soc Latin-Am study grant, 62-63, 65-66 and 76-77; Nat Endowment for Humanities fel, 69-70, 92; Guggenheim Found fel, 73-74; adv ed, Hisp Am Hist Rev, 77; Prof Emeritus, 97-. **HONORS AND AWARDS** Robertson Prize, Conf Latin Am Hist, 66, Conf Prize, 74, Mexican Order of the Aztec Eagle, 83; Bolton Prize, 90; Honorary President, X Conference of Mexican and US Historians, 99. **MEMBERSHIPS** Conf Latin Am Hist; AHA; Latin Am Studies Asn. **RESEARCH** Mexico; Latin American social and political thought. **SELECTED PUBLICATIONS** Auth, Mexican Liberalism in the Age of Mora, 1821-1853, Yale Univ Press, 68; auth, Political and Social Ideas in Latin America, 1870-1930, Cambridge History of Latin America, Vol. 4 85; auth, The Transformation of Liberalism in Late Nineteenth Century Mexico, Princeton Univ Press, 89; auth, FrankTannenbaum and the Mexican-Revolution, Hisp Am Hist Rev, Vol 0075, 95. **CONTACT ADDRESS** 250 Black Springs Circle, Iowa City, IA 52240. **EMAIL** charles-hale@uiowa.edu

HALES, PETER BACON
PERSONAL Born 12/13/1950, Pasadena, CA, 2 children **DISCIPLINE** ART HISTORY **EDUCATION** Haverford Col, BA, 72; Univ of Tx at Austin, MA, PhD, 80. **CAREER** Lectr, Calif State Univ, 80; ASST PROF TO PROF, UNIV OF ILL AT CHICAGO. **HONORS AND AWARDS** Amoco Teaching Awd, 84; Univ of Ill Teaching Awd, 90; Focus/Infinity Artist's Grant, 87-88; Nat Endowment for the Humanities Fel, 87; Herbert Hoover Prize, 98; Ill Arts Coun Grant, 83. **MEMBERSHIPS** Am Studies Asn. **RESEARCH** American cultural landscape; history of photography. **SELECTED PUBLICATIONS** Coauth, The Perfect City: Photographs and Meditations, Johns Hopkins Univ Press, 94; auth, Atomic Spaces: Living on the Manhattan Project, Univ of Ill Press, 97; auth, Topographies of Power: The Forced Spaces of the Manhattan Project, Mapping Am Culture, Univ of Iowa Press, 92; auth, Life Presents the Atomic Bomb, Looking at Life, Smithsonian Inst Press, 99; auth, Surveying the Field: Artists Make Art History, Artjournal, 95; auth, Discipline/Survey, Artjournal, 95; auth, The Mass Aesthetic of Holocaust: American Media Construct the Atomic Bomb, Yearbook of the Japanese Asn for Am Studies, 96. **CONTACT ADDRESS** Art Hist Dept, M/C 201, Univ of Illinois, Chicago, 935 W. Harrison St., Chicago, IL 60607. **EMAIL** pbhale@uic.edu

HALEY, EVAN W.
PERSONAL Born 08/02/1954, Tacoma, WA, m, 1987, 1 child **DISCIPLINE** HISTORY **EDUCATION** Dartmouth Col, AB, 77; Columbia Univ, PhD, 86. **CAREER** Vis Asst Prof, 87-89, Univ of Oregon; Vis Asst Prof, 90-, Franklin & Marshall Col; Asst Prof, 90-96, Assoc Prof, 96-, McMaster Univ. **HONORS AND AWARDS** Fulbright-Hays Scholar, Spain, 84-85. **MEMBERSHIPS** Amer Philological Asn; Archeol Inst of Amer; Assoc of Ancient Hist **RESEARCH** Roman Social Economic and Political History; Pioneers of the Roman Empire. **SELECTED PUBLICATIONS** Migration and Economy in Roman Imperial Spain, Univ of Barcelona Press, 91; A Palace of Maximianus Herculius at Corduba?!, Zeitschrift fur Papyrologie und Epigraphik, 94; Rural Settlement in the Conventus Astigitanus, (Baetica) Under the Flarians, Pheonix, 96. **CONTACT ADDRESS** McMaster Univ, Dept of Classics, Hamilton, ON, Canada L8S 4M2. **EMAIL** haleyev@mcmaster.ca

HALL, DAVID D.
PERSONAL m, 2001, 3 children **DISCIPLINE** HISTORY **EDUCATION** Harvard Univ, BA, 58; Yale Univ, PhD, 64. **CAREER** Prof, hist, Univ Boston; current, Prof Am Rel Hist, Harvard Divinity Sch. **HONORS AND AWARDS** Co-winner, Merle Curti Prize, 91 **MEMBERSHIPS** Am Antiquarian Soc **SELECTED PUBLICATIONS** Auth, A World of Wonders: The Mentality of the Supernatural in Seventeenth Century New England, in Seventeenth Century New England, Boston, 84; auth, Worlds of Wonder, Days of Judgment: Popular Religious Belief in Early New England, Knopf, 89; auth, The Faithful Shepherd: A History of the New England Ministry in the Seventeenth Century, Chapel Hill, 72; auth, Puritanism in Seventeenth Century Massachusetts, 68; co-ed, Saints and Revolutionaries: Essays on Early American History, 83; auth, Witch-hunting in New England, 1638-1692: A Documentary History, Boston, 90; auth, The Uses of Literacy in New England, 1600-1850, in Printing and Society in Early America, AAS, 83; auth, Cultures of Print: Essays in the History of the Book, Univ MA Pr, 96. **CONTACT ADDRESS** Harvard Divinity Sch, Harvard Univ, Cambridge, MA 02138. **EMAIL** david_hall@harvard.edu

HALL, FREDERICK A.
PERSONAL Born 07/02/1944, Niagara-on-the-Lake, ON, Canada **DISCIPLINE** HISTORY OF MUSIC **EDUCATION** McGill Univ, BMus, 69; Univ Toronto, MA, 70; PhD 78. **CAREER** ASSOC PROF SCHOOL OF ART, DRAMA AND MUSIC, MCMASTER UNIV, 72-, chmn, 80-86, assoc dean, Hum, 88-96, acting dean, Hum, 96-97. **SELECTED PUBLICATIONS** Ed, Songs I to English Texts, 85; Songs IV to English Texts, 93; co-ed, Musical Canada: Words and Music Honouring Helmut Kallmann, 88; The Romantic Tradition, 92; contribur, Encyclopedia of Music in Canada; The Canadian Encyclopedia; Dictionary of Canadian Biography, vols XIII & XIV; Studies in Eighteenth Century Culture; Canadian Music: Issues of Hegemony and Identity. **CONTACT ADDRESS** Sch of Art, Drama & Music, McMaster Univ, 1280 Main St W, Hamilton, ON, Canada L8S 4M2. **EMAIL** hallfa@mcmaster.ca

HALL, GWENDOLYN MIDLO
PERSONAL Born 06/27/1929, New Orleans, LA, m, 1956, 3 children **DISCIPLINE** CARIBBEAN AND LATIN AMERICAN HISTORY **EDUCATION** Univ Am, BA, 62, MA, 63; Univ Mich, PhD(hist), 70. **CAREER** Instr hist, Elizabeth City State Col, 65; lectr Afro-Am studies, Univ Mich, 69; res asst, Mich Hist Collections, 70; asst prof, 71-73, Assoc Prof Hist, Rutgers Univ, 73-92; Full prof Hist, 92-96; Emerita, 96. **MEMBERSHIPS** Asn Caribbean Historians. **RESEARCH** Comparative slavery; race relations. **SELECTED PUBLICATIONS** Auth, Africans in colonial Louisiana: The Development of Afao-Creole Culture in the Eighteenth Century, LSU Press, 92; auth, Africa and Africans in the Making of the Atlantic World, 1400-1680, J Am Hist, Vol 0080, 93; Cultivation and Culture--Labor and the Shaping of Slave Life in the America, J Southern Hist, Vol 0060, 94; American Slavery--1619-1877, Am Hist Rev, Vol 0100, 95; African-Americans at Mars-Bluff, South-Carolina, Southern Cult, Vol 0001, 95; Our Rightful Share--The Afro-Cuban Struggle for Equality, 1886-1912, Am Hist Rev, Vol 0101, 96; Maroon Heritage--Archaeological, Ethnographic, and Historical Perspectives, Hisp Am Hist Rev, Vol 0076, 96; Slave Cultures and the Cultures of Slavery, Am Hist Rev, Vol 0102, 97; Slavery, the Civil-Law and the Supreme-Court of Louisiana, African Am Rev, Vol 0031, 97; auth, Databases for the study of Afro-Louisiana History and Genealogy, 1720-1820, La State Press, 00. **CONTACT ADDRESS** 1300 Dante St., New Orleans, LA 70118. **EMAIL** ghall1929@aol.com

HALL, JACQUELYN DOWD
PERSONAL Born 01/14/1943, Pauls Valley, OK **DISCIPLINE** AMERICAN HISTORY **EDUCATION** Rhodes Col, BA, 65; Columbia Univ, MA, 67, PhD, 74. **CAREER** Instr Am hist, Columbia Univ, summer, 71; instr, 73-74, asst prof, 74-79, assoc prof hist, 79-88, Julia Cherry Spruill Prof of Hist, 89-,Univ NC, Chapel Hill; dir, Southern Oral History Prog, 73-. **HONORS AND AWARDS** Lillian Smith Awd, Southern Regional Coun, 79; Francis B Simkins Awd, Southern Hist Asn, 79-80; Merle Curti Social History Awd, 86-87; Albert J. Beveridge Awd; Philip Taft Labor History Prize; Lyndhurst Prize, 89; UNC distinguished teaching award, 97. **MEMBERSHIPS** Orgn Am Historians; Oral Hist Asn; Southern Hist Asn; Am Stud Asn; S Asn of Women Hist; Am Hist Asn; Soc of Am Hist; Univ NC Press Bd Gov; Ctr for the Study of the Am South, exec bd. **RESEARCH** Women in United States history; labor history; history of the United States south. **SELECTED PUBLICATIONS** Auth, Class, A Companion to American Thought, Kloppenberg, 95; contribur, What We See and Can't See in the Past: A Round Table, J of Am Hist, 97; auth, O Delight Smith: A Labor Organizer's Odyssey, Forgotten Heroes from America's Past: Inspiring Portraits from Our Leading Historians, Free Press, 98; auth, Open Secrets: Memory, Imagination, and the Refashioning of Southern Identity, Am Q, 98; auth, You Must Remember This: Autobiography as Social Critique, J of Am Hist, 98. **CONTACT ADDRESS** History Dept, Univ of No Carolina, Chapel Hill, Chapel Hill, NC 27514. **EMAIL** jhall@email.unc.edu

HALL, LARRY JOE
PERSONAL Born 10/22/1937, Heavener, OK, m, 1959, 3 children **DISCIPLINE** AMERICAN LITERATURE & STUDIES **EDUCATION** Oklahoma City Univ, BA, 59; Garrett Theol Sem, MDiv, 62; NTex State Univ, MA, 70, PhD(Am Lit), 74. **CAREER** Asst prof, 74-81, from assoc prof to prof English, Okla Baptist Univ, 81-86. **HONORS AND AWARDS** Distinguished Teaching Awd, 88. **MEMBERSHIPS** MLA; Am Studies Asn; Midcontinent Am Studies Assn; Conf on Christianity and Lit. **RESEARCH** Myth criticism and the contemporary novel. **SELECTED PUBLICATIONS** Auth, "Three Consciousnesses in Wright Morris's Plains Song," Western American Literature 31.4, 97: 291-320; auth, "Slothrop's Progress: A Christian Ironist Reading of Gravity's Rainbow," Christianity and Literature 41.2, 92: 159-178. **CONTACT ADDRESS** Oklahoma Baptist Univ, 500 W University, Shawnee, OK 74801-2558. **EMAIL** joe_hall@mail.okbu.edu

HALL, LINDA
DISCIPLINE MODERN LATIN AMERICA, MODERN MEXICO **EDUCATION** Columbia Univ, PhD, 76. **CAREER** Prof, dir, Lat Am Stud prog, Univ NMex. **HONORS AND AWARDS** Phi Alpha Theta; NEH; Ctr for US Mex Stud, Univ Calif, San Diego, Huntington Libr; Fulbright. **MEMBERSHIPS** Am Hist Asn. **RESEARCH** Modern Mexico; US Latin relations, Women in Latin Amer. **SELECTED PUBLICATIONS** Auth, Alvaro Obregon: Power and Revolution in Mexico, 81; coauth, Revolution on the Border: The United States and Mexico, 1910-1920, 88; auth, Oil, banks, and Politics: The United States and Post-Revolutionary Mexico, 95. **CONTACT ADDRESS** Univ of New Mexico, Albuquerque, Albuquerque, NM 87131. **EMAIL** lbhall@unm.edu

HALL, MICHAEL
PERSONAL Born 11/01/1960, Philadelphia, PA, m, 1985, 3 children **DISCIPLINE** HISTORY **EDUCATION** Ohio Univ, PhD, 96. **CAREER** Asst Prof of History, Armstrong Atlantic State Univ, 97. **MEMBERSHIPS** ATWS; LASA; SHAFR; AHA; SECOLAS. **RESEARCH** NS/Latin American Relations. **SELECTED PUBLICATIONS** Auth, "Sugar and Power in the Dominican Republic," Greenwood, 00. **CONTACT ADDRESS** Dept History, Armstrong Atlantic State Univ, 11935 Abercorn St, Savannah, GA 31419-1909. **EMAIL** hallmich@mail.armsrong.edu

HALL, MICHAEL G.
PERSONAL Born 01/08/1926, Princeton, NJ, m, 1972, 4 children **DISCIPLINE** HISTORY **EDUCATION** Princeton Univ, BA (magna cum laude), 49; Johns Hopkins Univ, PhD, 56. **CAREER** Asst Prof, 59-64, Assoc Prof, 64-70, Prof, 70-, Chemn, Dept of Hist, Univ of Tex, 76-80; sr fulbright lectr, Pakistan, 94-95; advisory coun, Omohundro Inst of Early Am Hist and Culture, 90-92. **HONORS AND AWARDS** C.O. Joline Prize, Princeton Univ; book of the year Awd, Confr on Christianity & Lit, 88. **MEMBERSHIPS** Am Antiquarian Soc; Mass Hist Soc; Colonial Soc of Mass. **RESEARCH** Early America; Native America; world history. **SELECTED PUBLICATIONS** Auth, Edward Randolph and the American Colonies 1676-1703, Chapel Hill, 60; The Last American Puritan: The Life of Increase Mather, Weslayn Univ Press, 88; ed, The Autobiography of Increase Mather, Am Antiquarian Society, 62; co-ed, The Glorious Revolution in America, Chapel Hill, 63; Science and Society in the United States, 66. **CONTACT ADDRESS** Dept of Hist, Univ of Texas, Austin, Austin, TX 78712. **EMAIL** mghall@mail.utexas.edu

HALL, MITCHELL K.
PERSONAL Born 04/12/1955, Anderson, IN, m, 1975 **DISCIPLINE** HISTORY **EDUCATION** Univ Kentucky, Phd, 87; MA, 80, BA, 77. **CAREER** Prof of History, Central Michigan Univ, 95-; Co-Exec. Editor, Peace & Change, 00-; Book Review Editor, Michigan Historical Review, 96-00; Assoc Prof of History, Central Michigan Univ, 91-95; Assist Prof of History, Central Michigan Univ, 89-91; Vis Asst Prof of History, Indiana Univ/Purdue Univ at Indianapolis, 87-89; Instr of History, Univ of Kentucky, 81-86. **HONORS AND AWARDS** Central Michigan Univ, Research Professorship, 94-95; Central Michigan Univ, Summer Fel, 90. **MEMBERSHIPS** Amer Historical Assoc; Organization of Amer Historians; Peace History Society; Society for Historians of Amer Foreign Relations. **RESEARCH** Vietnam Antiwar Movement. **SELECTED PUBLICATIONS** Auth, "The Vietnam War," London: Longman Publishers, 99; auth, "Unsell the War: Vietnam and Antiwar Advertising," The Historian 58, Autumn 95: 69-86; auth, "CALCAV and Religious Opposition to the Vietnam War," in Melvin Small and William D. Hoover," eds, Give Peace A Chance: Exploring the Vietnam Antiwar Movement, Syracuse, NY: Syracuse University Press, 92: 35-52; auth, "Because of Their Faith: CALCAV and Religious Opposition to the Vietnam War," New York: Columbia University Press, 90; auth, "A Withdrawal from Peace: The Historical Response to War of the Church of God," Anderson, Indiana, Journal of Church and State 27, Spring 85: 301-314; auth, "A Crack In Time: The Response of Students at the Univ of Kentucky to the Tragedy at Kent State," May 70, The Register of the Kentucky Historical Society 83, Winter 85: 36-63; auth, "A Time For War: The Church of God's Response to Vietnam," Indiana Magazine of History, 79, December 83: 285-304. **CONTACT ADDRESS** Dept of History, Central Michigan Univ, Mount Pleasant, MI 48859-0001. **EMAIL** mitchell.hall@cmich.edu

HALL, TIMOTHY D.
DISCIPLINE HISTORY **EDUCATION** Grace Univ, BA, 70; Dallas Theol Sem, ThM, 84; Univ Chicago, MA, 86; Northwestern Univ, PhD, 91. **CAREER** Res asst prof, Northwestern Univ, 91-92; vis asst prof, Colgate Univ, 92-93; assoc prof, Cen Mich Univ, 93-. **HONORS AND AWARDS** Charlotte W Newcombe Fel. **MEMBERSHIPS** AHA; OAH; OIEAHC. **RESEARCH** Colonial American culture and religious history; history of the Atlantic world to 1800. **SELECTED PUBLICATIONS** Auth, Contested Boundaries: Itinerancy and the Reshaping of the Colonial American Religious World (Durham, Duke Univ Press, 94); coauth, "Structuring Provincial Imagination: The Rhetoric and Experience of Social Change in Eighteenth Century New England," Am Hist Rev (98): 1411-39. **CONTACT ADDRESS** Dept History, Central Michigan Univ, 100 Preston Rd, Mount Pleasant, MI 48859-0001.

HALL, VAN BECK
PERSONAL Born 09/03/1934, Charleston, WV, m, 2 children **DISCIPLINE** AMERICAN HISTORY **EDUCATION** Oberlin Col, AB, 56; Univ Wis, MS, 61, PhD(hist), 64. **CAREER** Asst prof, 64-71, Assoc Prof Hist, Univ Pittsburgh, 71- , dept chm, 91-92. **MEMBERSHIPS** AHA; Orgn Am Historians. **RESEARCH** Political economy of Virginia, 1790-1830; politics in the United States, 1790-1830. **SELECTED PUBLICATIONS** Auth, Politics Without Parties: Massachusetts 1780-1791, Univ Pittsburgh, 72; A Fond Farewell to Henry Adams in Human Dimensions of Nation Building, Hist Soc Wis, 76; auth, Appalachian Politics, in Mitchell, ed, Appalachian Frontiers, Tennessee, 90. **CONTACT ADDRESS** 5854 Douglas St, Pittsburgh, PA 15217.

HALLER, JOHN S., JR
PERSONAL Born 07/22/1940, Pittsburgh, PA, m, 1968, 2 children **DISCIPLINE** HISTORY **EDUCATION** Georgetown Univ, BA, 62; John Carroll Univ, MA, 64; Univ Md, PhD, 68. **CAREER** Prof and Assoc Dean, Ind Univ, 68-80; Assoc VP to Acting VP, Calif State Univ, 80-86; Vice Chancellor and Special Consult, Univ Colo, 86-90; VP, S Ill Univ, 90-. **MEMBERSHIPS** Am Asn for the Hist of Med. **CONTACT ADDRESS** Dept Hist, So Illinois Univ, Carbondale, 1400 Douglas Dr, Carbondale, IL 62901. **EMAIL** jhaller@notes.siu.edu

HALLER, MARK HUGHLIN
PERSONAL Born 12/22/1928, Washington, DC, s **DISCIPLINE** HISTORY, CRIMINAL JUSTICE **EDUCATION** Wesleyan Univ, BA, 51; Univ of MD, MA, 54; Univ of Wis, PhD, 59. **CAREER** Instr & asst prof of Hist, Univ of Chicago, 59-68; ASSOC PROF & PROF OF HIST & CRIMINAL JUSTICE, 68-, TEMPLE UNIV. **MEMBERSHIPS** Am Hist Assoc, Org of Am Historians; Am Soc of Criminology; Law & Soc Asn. **RESEARCH** Hist of the Am City; Hist of Crime and Criminal Justice. **SELECTED PUBLICATIONS** Auth, Eugenics; Hereditarian Attitudes in American Thought, 63; auth, "Urban Cirme and Cirminal Justice: Th eCHicago Case: Journal of American History, 70; auth, "Bootleggers as Businessmen: From City Slums to City Builders," in David Kyvig, ed., Law, Alcohol, an dORder: Perspectives on National Prohibition, 85; auth, "Illegal Enterprise: A Theoretical and Historical Interpretation," Criminology, 90; auth, "Policy Gambling, Entertainment, and the Emergence of Black Politics: Chicago from 1900 to 1940," Journal of Social History, 91. **CONTACT ADDRESS** Dept of History, Temple Univ, Philadelphia, PA 19122. **EMAIL** hallerm@vm.temple.edu

HALLION, RICHARD PAUL
PERSONAL Born 05/17/1948, Washington, DC, m **DISCIPLINE** HISTORY OF SCIENCE **EDUCATION** Univ Md, BA, 70, PhD, 75. **CAREER** Mus cur, Nat Air and Space Mus, Smithsonian Inst, 74-80; assoc prof gen admin, Univ Col, Univ Md, 80-82; Air Force Historian, 82-; Adj assoc prof hist, Univ Md, 75-82, lectr, Dept Aerospace Eng, 76-82; vis fel, Silliman Col, Yale Univ, 77; mus consult, Toshihiko Sakow Assoc Inc, 79-; consult and auth, Time-Life Bks, 79-82. **HONORS AND AWARDS** Am Inst Aeronaut and Astronaut, Hist Manuscript Awd, 76 and Young Engineer and Scientist Awd, 79; Robert H Goddard Awd, Nat Space Club, 79; AIAA Distinguished Lectr, 82-83; Lt. Col. Roy Mase Trophy, 85; Citation of Honor, Air Force Asn, 85; Meritorious Civilian Serv Medal, U.S. Air Force, 86; Commander's Awd for Public Serv, U.S. Army, 88; Ira Eaker Awd, Air Univ, 90; Aviation Space Writers Asn Premier Awd for defense aviation coverage, 93. **MEMBERSHIPS** Air Force Hist Found; Air Force Asn; Int Footprint Asn; Nat Aviation Club; Int Order of Characters; Mil Operations Res Soc; Precision Strike Asn; Nat Asn of Scholars. **RESEARCH** History of aviation, especially aerodynamics and flight testing; military history, especially 20th century development of military technology; United States social and cultural history since 1945. **SELECTED PUBLICATIONS** Auth, NASA Engineers and the Age of Apollo, Pub Historian, Vol 0016, 94; Untitled, J Am Hist, Vol 0082, 95; Race to the Moon--America Duel with the Soviets, J Am Hist, Vol 0081, 95. **CONTACT ADDRESS** Off Af Historian, United States Air Force Acad, Bolling AFB, Washington, DC 20330.

HALPERN, PAUL G.
PERSONAL Born 01/27/1937, New York, NY, s **DISCIPLINE** HISTORY **EDUCATION** Univ Va, BA, 58; Harvard Univ, AM, 61; PhD, 66. **CAREER** Instr to prof, Fla State Univ, 65- . **HONORS AND AWARDS** Phi Beta Kappa; Woodrow Wilson fel; Phi Eta Sigma; Fel Royal Hist Soc, 93. **MEMBERSHIPS** Am His Asn; Navy Rec Soc; Naval Rev; US Naval Inst; Royal Hist Soc; Royal US Inst; Naval His Found; Soc Army Hist Res; Soc Mil Hist. **RESEARCH** Naval history, Modern Europe (France & Italy), World War I. **SELECTED PUBLICATIONS** Auth, The Mediterranean Naval Situation, 71; auth, The Naval War in the Mediterranean, 1914-1918, 87; auth, A Naval History of World War I, 94; auth, Anton Haus: Osterreich-Ungarus Grossadmiral, 98; ed, The Keys Papers, 3 vol, 72-81; ED, The Royal Navy in the Mediterranean, 1915-1918, 87. **CONTACT ADDRESS** Dept Hist, Florida State Univ, 3103 Brandemere Dr, Tallahassee, FL 32306. **EMAIL** phalpern@mailer.fsu.edu

HALTMAN, KENNETH
DISCIPLINE ART HISTORY **EDUCATION** Wesleyan, BA, 80; Yale Univ, MA, 85, PhD, 92. **CAREER** Asst Prof, Art Hist & Am Stud, Mich State Univ. **MEMBERSHIPS** Am Antiquarian Soc **SELECTED PUBLICATIONS** Auth, "Private Impressions and Public Views: The Long Expedition Sketchbooks of Titian Ramsay Peale, 1819-1820," Yale Univ Art Gallery Bull, 89; auth, "Between Science and Art: Titian Ramsay Peale's Long Expedition Sketches, Newly Discovered at the State Historical Society of Iowa," Palimpsest: Jour of Iowa State Hist Soc 74, 93; auth, "Titian Ramsay Peale: Specimen Portraiture, or Natural History as Family History," in The Peale Family: Creation of a Legacy, 1770-1870, Abbeville Press with Natl Port Gall, 96; auth, "The Poetics of Geologic Reverie: Figures of Source and Origin" in Samuel Seymour's Landscapes of the Rocky Mountains, Huntingon Library Q, Fall 97; auth, entries in Reader's Encyclopedia of the American West, Yale Univ Press; auth, Earth and Reveries of Will, Gaston Bachelard, Jose Corti, 97; auth, Figures in A Western Landscape: Expeditionary Art and Science in the Early Republic, Princeton Univ Press. **CONTACT ADDRESS** Michigan State Univ, 113 Kresge Art Ctr, East Lansing, MI 48824-1119. **EMAIL** haltman@pilot.msu.edu

HALTTUNEN, KAREN
DISCIPLINE HISTORY **EDUCATION** Brown Univ, BA, 73; Yale Univ, PhD, 79. **CAREER** Assoc prof, hist & Am cult, Northwestern Univ; current, Prof Hist, Univ Calif Davis. **MEMBERSHIPS** Am Antiquarian Soc **SELECTED PUBLICATIONS** Auth, "Domestic Differences: Competing Narratives of Womanhood in the Murder Trial of Lucretia Chapman," in The Culture of Sentiment: Race, Gender, and Sentimentality in 19th Century America, Oxford Univ Press, 92; auth, "Early American Narratives: The Birth of Horror", in The Power of Culture: Critical Essays in American History, Univ Chicago Press, 93; auth, Murder Most Foul! The Killer and the American Gothic Imagination, Harvard Univ Press, 98; auth, Confidence Men and Painted Women: A Study of Middle-Class Culture in America, 1830-1870, 83; auth, "Gothic Imagination and Social Reform: The Haunted Houses of Lyman Beecher, Henry Ward Beecher, and Harriet Beecher Stowe," in New Essays on Uncle Tom's Cabin, 86; auth, "The Domestic Drama of Louisa May Alcott," Feminist Studies 10, 84. **CONTACT ADDRESS** Dept of Hist, Univ of California, Davis, Davis, CA 95616.

HALVORSON, PETER L.
PERSONAL Born 09/07/1940, Berlin, NH, m, 1 child **DISCIPLINE** GEOGRAPHY **EDUCATION** Dartmouth Col, BA, 62; Univ Cincinnati, MA, 65; PhD, 70. **CAREER** Asst prof, Univ Northern Colo, 68-70; from asst prof to prof, Univ Conn, 70-. **MEMBERSHIPS** AAUP, Am Geog Soc, Asn of Am Geog. **RESEARCH** American Religion. **SELECTED PUBLICATIONS** Coauth, Atlas of American Religion: The Denominational Era, 1776-1990, Alta Mira Press (Walnut Creek, CA), 00. **CONTACT ADDRESS** Dept Geog, Univ of Connecticut, Storrs, 354 Mansfield Rd, Storrs, CT 06269-9000.

HAM, DEBRA NEWMAN
PERSONAL Born 08/27/1948, York, PA, m, 1989, 2 children **DISCIPLINE** HISTORY, AFRICAN-AMERICAN HISTORY **EDUCATION** Howard Univ, BA, 70; Boston Univ, MA, 71; Howard Univ, PhD, 84. **CAREER** African-Am Hist specialist, Nat Archives, 70-86; African-Am Hist specialist, Library of Congress, 86-95; prof Hist, Morgan State Univ, 95-. **RESEARCH** Africa; African, American and public history. **SELECTED PUBLICATIONS** Auth, Black History, A Guide to Civilian Records in the National Archives (84); ed, The African-American Mosaic: A Library of Congress Resource Guide (93); ed, The African-American Odyssey: A Library of Congress Exhibit (98). **CONTACT ADDRESS** Dept Hist, Morgan State Univ, 1700 E Cold Spring Ln, Baltimore, MD 2151-0001. **EMAIL** dham@moac.morgan.edu

HAM, F. GERALD
PERSONAL Born 04/13/1930, Toms River, NJ, m, 1953, 4 children **DISCIPLINE** AMERICAN HISTORY **EDUCATION** Wheaton Col, Ill, AB, 52; Univ Ky, MA, 55, PhD(hist), 62. **CAREER** Assoc curator arch, WVa Univ Libr, 58-64; State Archivist, State Hist Soc, WIS, 64-90, Lectr Am hist, WVa Univ, 62-63, asst prof, 63-64; Prof Emer, Univ Wis Libr Sch, 67-91. **HONORS AND AWARDS** National Historical Publication and Records Commission, Distinguished Service Awd, 97; Society of American Archivists, Fellows Posner Prize, 85; Waldo Gifford Leland Pr, 97. **MEMBERSHIPS** Fel Soc Am Archivists (exec secy, 68-72, vpres, 72-73, pres, 73-74). **RESEARCH** American social and religious history; American archival institutions and practices; 19th century communitarian experiments. **SELECTED PUBLICATIONS** Auth, Is the Past Still Prologue--History And Archival Education, Am Archivist, Vol 0056, 93. **CONTACT ADDRESS** 3527 Tallyho Ln, Madison, WI 53705. **EMAIL** fgham@facstaff.wisc.edu

HAMALAINEN, PEKKA KALEVI
PERSONAL Born 12/28/1938, Finland, m, 1965, 4 children **DISCIPLINE** EUROPEAN HISTORY **EDUCATION** IN Univ, AB, 61, PhD, 66. **CAREER** Actg asst prof hist, Univ CA, Santa Barbara, 65-66, asst prof, 66-70; assoc prof, 70-76, Prof Hist, Univ WI-Madison, 76-, Chmn Western Europ Area Studies Prog, 77-, fac res grants, Univ CA, Santa Barbara, 66-69; Ford Found grant, 67-68; fac res grants, Univ WI-Madison, 71-; Am Philos Soc res grant, 73-74; mem, Nat Screening Comt, Fulbright-Hays Prog, 74-75; Am Coun Learned Socs fel, 76-77, res grant, 78; cons Dept of State, DC, 91-; Chair, Grad Educ Comm, Univ Wis, 96-97. **HONORS AND AWARDS** Vilas Associate, 96. **MEMBERSHIPS** AHA; Soc Advan Scand Studies. **RESEARCH** North European hist, twentieth century European hist; Finnish hist. **SELECTED PUBLICATIONS** Auth, Kielitaistelu Suomessa, 1917-1939, Werner Soderstrom Osakeyhtio, 68; Nationnalitetskampen och sprakstriden i Finland, 1917-1939, Holger Schildts Forlag, 69; In Time of Storm: Revolution, Civil War and the Ethnolinguistic Issue in Finland, State Univ NY, 78; Luokka ja Kieli vallankumouksen suomessa, Suomen Hist Seura, 78; Uniting Germany: Actions and Reactions, 94. **CONTACT ADDRESS** Dept of Hist, Univ of Wisconsin, Madison, 455 North Park St, Madison, WI 53706-1483.

HAMBLY, GAVIN RICHARD GRENVILLE
PERSONAL Born 07/04/1934, Sevenoaks, England, m, 1990, 2 children **DISCIPLINE** MIDDLE EASTERN HISTORY, HISTORY OF INDIA **EDUCATION** Cambridge Univ, BA, 58, MA & PhD(hist), 62. **CAREER** Lectr, Brit Coun, Tehran, Iran, 61-63, dir studies, Ankara, Turkey, 64-66, asst rep, New Delhi, India, 66-68; from asst prof to assoc prof hist of India, Yale Univ, 68-75; Prof Hist, Univ Tex, Dallas, 75-, Dean Sch Arts & Humanities, 77-84, Smuts Mem Fund Commonwealth Study res grant, Cambridge Univ, 63-64; res grants, Soc Sci Res Coun, 70 & Nat Endowment for Humanities, 71 & fel, 76-77. **MEMBERSHIPS** Egypt Exploration Society; Brit Inst Persian Studies. **RESEARCH** Mughal and British rule in India; Iranian civilization and its spread in India and Central Asia; Indian and Iranian urban and cultural history. **SELECTED PUBLICATIONS** ed, Central Asia, 66; Auth, Cities of Mughul India, 68; contr, Comparative History of Civilizations in Asia, 77; contr, The Cambridge Economic History of India, 82; auth, Delhi through the Ages, 86, and the Encyclopedia Iranica; coed, The Cambridge History of Iran, vol. 7, 91; ed., Women in the Medieval Islamic World, 98. **CONTACT ADDRESS** Sch of Arts & Humanities, Univ of Texas, Dallas, Box 830688, Richardson, TX 75083-0688.

HAMBY, ALONZO LEE
PERSONAL Born 01/13/1940, Humansville, MO, m, 1967 **DISCIPLINE** HISTORY **EDUCATION** Southeast Mo State Col, BA, 60; Columbia Univ, MA, 61; Univ Mo, PhD(hist), 65. **CAREER** From Asst prof to Distinguished Prof Hist, Ohio Univ, 65-; dir grad studies, dept hist, Ohio Univ, 78-80, 87-88, 95-98; mem, Ohio Hist Records Preserv Adv Bd, 78-80; Fac Senate, Ohio Univ, 80-83; Univ Compensation Comt, Ohio Univ, 80-82; chmn, dept hist, Ohio Univ, 80-83; Col Arts and Sci Staffing Advisory Comt, Ohio Univ, 83-84, 87-89; Univ Grad Coun, Ohio Univ, 93-96, **HONORS AND AWARDS** Woodrow Wilson Fel, 60-61; Nat Defense Educ Act Fel, 62-64; Univ Mo Wilson Fel, 64-65; Harry S. Truman Libr Inst grants, 64, 66, 67, 69; Am Philos Soc grant, 67; Ohio Univ Res Coun grants, 67, 76, 83; Ohio Univ Baker Fund awards, 69, 86; Nat Endowment for Humanities fel, 72-73; Evans fel, Harry S Truman Libr Inst, 73-74; David D Lloyd Prize, Harry S. Truman Inst, 74; First Book Awd, Phi Alpha Theta, 74; Publ Awd, Ohio Acad Hist, 74; Phi Beta Kappa, Lambda of Ohio, honorary membership, 77; SE Mo State Univ Outstanding History Alumnus, 85; NEH Summer Fel, 85; Harry S. Truman Library Inst Sr Fel, 86-87; Col of Liberal Arts Alumni Merit Awd, 90; Fel, Woodrow Wilson Int Ctr for Schol, 91-92; Herbert Hoover Book Awd, 96; Harry S. Truman Book Awd, 96; Ohio Acad of Hist Distinguished Serv Awd, 98. **MEMBERSHIPS** AHA; Orgn Am Historians,; Southern Hist Asn; Soc Historians Am Foreign Rels. **RESEARCH** United States history, 1607-present; Twentieth-century America; American Historiography; contemporary history. **SELECTED PUBLICATIONS** Ed, The New Deal, Analysis and Interpretation, Weybright & Talley, 69, 2nd ed, Longman, 80; auth, The Liberals, Truman and FDR as symbol and myth, J Am Hist, 3/70; The vital center, the Fair Deal, and the quest for a liberal political economy, Am Hist Rev, 6/72; Beyond the New Deal: Harry S Truman and American Liberalism, Columbia Univ, 73; ed and contribr, Harry S. Truman and The Fair Deal, Heath, 74; auth, The clash of perspectives.., In: The Truman Period as a Research Field, 2nd ed, Univ Mo, 74; The Imperial Years: The United States Since 1939, Weybright & Talley, 76; co-ed & contribr, Historian, Archivists, and Access to The Papers of Recent Public Figures, Orgn Am Historians, 78; auth, Liberalism and Its Challengers: F.D.R. to Reagan, Oxford Univ Press, 85, 2nd ed, 92; Man of the People: A Life of Harry S. Truman, Oxford Univ Press, 95; numerous articles and book reviews published or forthcoming in scholarly journals or magazines and essay collections, and pieces for encyclopedias and other reference works. **CONTACT ADDRESS** Dept of History, Ohio Univ, Athens, OH 45701-2979. **EMAIL** hambya@ohiou.edu

HAMDANI, ABBAS HUSAYN
PERSONAL Born 08/11/1926, Surat, India, m, 1961, 2 children **DISCIPLINE** MIDDLE EASTERN HISTORY, ISLAMIC CIVILIZATION **EDUCATION** Univ Bombay, BA, 45, LLB, 47; Univ London, PhD, 50. **CAREER** Prof Islamic hist, SM & Islamia Cols, Univ Karachi, 51-62; prof Arabic studies, Am Univ Cairo, 62-69; vis lectr hist, Univ Wis-Madison, 69-70, Prof Hist, Univ Wis-Milwaukee, 70-; Chmn, Comt Mid Eastern and NAfrican Studies, Univ Wis-Milwaukee, 72-. **HONORS AND AWARDS** NEH res fel, Am Res Ctr Egypt, 74-75, 78-79, 88-89; Fulbright Fel, India, 92, Egypt, 96-97. **MEMBERSHIPS** Fel Mid E Studies Asn NAm; Am Orient Soc; Am Inst Res in Yemen. **RESEARCH** Fatimid movement and caliphate; South Arabian history; medieval Islamic social history; Islamic background to the Voyages of Discovery. **SELECTED PUBLICATIONS** Auth, Islamic Fundamentalism, Mediterranean Quart, Fall 93; Islam and Politics: Egypt, Algeria and Tunisia, The Digest of Middle Eastern Studies, Summer 94; A Time-Table for Palestinian-Israeli Peace, The Digest of Middle Eastern Studies, Winter 94; An Overview of the Current Status of the Muslim countries of the Former Soviet Union, Islamic Studies, Vol 33, 94; A Critique of Casanova's Dating of the Rasa' il Ikhwan al Safa', In: Essays in Medieval Isma' ili History and Thought, Cambridge Univ Press, 95; author of numerous other articles. **CONTACT ADDRESS** Dept of Hist, Col Lett & Sci, Univ of Wisconsin, Milwaukee, PO Box 413, Milwaukee, WI 53201-0413.

HAMELIN, MARCEL
PERSONAL Born 09/18/1937, Saint-Narcisse, PQ, Canada, m, 1962, 3 children **DISCIPLINE** HISTORY **EDUCATION** Univ Laval, LL, 61, DL, 72. **CAREER** Prof hist, 66-, dept ch, 68-70, vice dean grad stud, 72-74, dean arts, 74-90, Rector and Vice Chancellor, Univ of Ottawa, 90-01. **MEMBERSHIPS** Asn canadienne-francaise pour l'avancement des sciences; Can Hist Asn; Royal Soc Can; vice pres, Inter-Am Orgn Higher Educ; dir, Canada-US Fulbright Prog. **SELECTED PUBLICATIONS** Auth, Les premieres annees du parlamentarisme quebecois: 1867-1878, 75; coauth, Les moeurs electorales dans le Quebec, de 1791 a nos jours, 62; coauth, Apercu de la politique canadienne au XIXe siecle, 65; coauth, Confederation 1867, 66; coauth, Les elections provinciales dans le Quebec, 69; ed, Les memoires de l'honorable Raoul Dandurand, 67; ed, Les debats de l'Assemblee legislative de la province de Quebec 1867-1870, vol I-IV, 74; ed, Les debats de l'Assemblee legislative de la province de Quebec 1871-1875, vol V-VIII, 76; ed, Les debats de l'Assemblee legislative de la province de Quebec 1875-1878, vol IX-XI, 77. **CONTACT ADDRESS** Univ of Ottawa, 550 Cumberland, Ottawa, ON, Canada K1N 6N5.

HAMEROW, THEODORE STEPHEN
PERSONAL Born 08/24/1920, Warsaw, Poland, m, 1954, 2 children **DISCIPLINE** MODERN HISTORY **EDUCATION** City Col New York, BA, 42; Columbia Univ, MA, 47; Yale Univ, PhD, 51. **CAREER** Instr hist, Wellesley Col, 50-51 & overseas prog, Univ Md, 51-52; from instr to assoc prof, Univ Ill, 52-58; assoc prof, 58-61, chmn dept, 73-76, Prof emer, Univ Wis-Madison, 61-, Consult ed, Dorsey Press, 61-70. **HONORS AND AWARDS** Fulbright scholar & Soc Sci Res Coun fel, 62-63. **MEMBERSHIPS** AHA, Conf Group Cent Europ Hist. **RESEARCH** Modern European history; modern Germany; the 19th century. **SELECTED PUBLICATIONS** Auth, Restoration, Revolution, Reaction: Economics and Politics in Germany, 1815-1871, Princeton Univ, 58; coauth, A History of the World, Rand McNally, 60; auth, Otto von Bismarck: A Historical Assessment, Heath, 62; ed, Reflections and Reminiscences, Harper, 68; The Social Foundations of German Unification, 1858-1871 (2 vols), Princeton Univ, 69 & 72; History of Europe, Rand McNally, 69; The Age of Bismarck, Harper, 73. **CONTACT ADDRESS** Univ of Wisconsin, Madison, 455 N Park St, Madison, WI 53706.

HAMILTON, VICTOR PAUL
PERSONAL Born 09/26/1941, Toronto, ON, Canada, m, 1965, 4 children **DISCIPLINE** OLD TESTAMENT STUDIES, ANCIENT NEAR EASTERN HISTORY **EDUCATION** Houghton Col, BA, 63; Asbury Theol Sem, BD, 66, ThM, 67; Brandeis Univ, MA, 69, PhD, 71. **CAREER** From asst prof to assoc prof, 71-85, prof Old Testament, Asbury Col, 85-. **MEMBERSHIPS** Soc Bibl Lit; Evangelical Theol Soc. **RESEARCH** Old Testament languages. **SELECTED PUBLICATIONS** Auth, The Shepherd Psalm: Psalm 23, Asbury Seminarian, 72; Handbook on the Pentateuch, Baker, 82; Genesis Chapters 1-17,

Eerdmans, 92; Genesis, Chapters 18-50, Eerdmans, 95. **CONTACT ADDRESS** 1 Macklem Dr, Wilmore, KY 40390-1198. **EMAIL** victor.hamilton@asbury.edu

HAMILTON, VIRGINIA V.
PERSONAL Born Kansas City, MO **DISCIPLINE** UNITED STATES HISTORY **EDUCATION** Birmingham-Southern Col, AB, 41, MA, 61; Univ Ala, PhD(hist), 68. **CAREER** Asst prof hist, Univ Montevallo, 51-55; asst to pres, Birmingham-Southern Col, 55-65; lectr, 65-69, from asst prof to assoc prof, 69-75, Prof Hist, Univ Ala, Birmingham, 75-, Chairperson Dept, 75- **HONORS AND AWARDS** Awd of Merit, Am Asn State & Local Hist, 73. **MEMBERSHIPS** Southern Hist Asn; Soc Am Historians; AHA; Orgn Am Historians; Am Asn State & Local Hist. **RESEARCH** Southern politics since 1900. **SELECTED PUBLICATIONS** Auth, Unheard Voices--The 1st Historians of Southern Women, J S Hist, Vol 0060, 94. **CONTACT ADDRESS** Dept of Hist, Univ of Alabama, Birmingham, Birmingham, AL 35294.

HAMLIN, CHRISTOPHER S.
DISCIPLINE HISTORY **EDUCATION** Antioch Col, BA, 74; Univ Wis, MA, 77, PhD, 82. **CAREER** Assoc fel, Joan B. Kroc Inst for Intl Peace Stu, prof. **RESEARCH** History of technology; history of medicine. **SELECTED PUBLICATIONS** Auth, What Becomes of Pollution? Adversary Science and the Controversy on the Self-Purification of Rivers in Britain, 1850-1900, 87; A Science of Impurity: Water Analysis in Nineteenth-Century Britain, 90; Concepts of Predisposing Causes in the Early Nineteenth Century Public Health Movement, 92; Reflexivity in Technology Studies: Toward a Technology of Technology (and Science)?, 92; Between Knowledge and Action: Themes in the History of Environmental Chemistry, 93; Environmental Sensibility in Edinburgh, 1839-1840: the 'Fetid Irrigation' Controversy, 94; Public Health and Social Justice in the Age of Chadwick: Britain 1800-1854, 98; co-auth, Deep Disagreement in U.S. Agriculture: Making Sense of Policy Conflict, 93. **CONTACT ADDRESS** History and Philosophy of Science Dept, Univ of Notre Dame, Notre Dame, IN 46556. **EMAIL** Christopher.S.Hamlin.1@nd.edu

HAMM, MICHAEL FRANKLIN
PERSONAL Born 08/29/1943, Ithaca, NY, m, 1963, 2 children **DISCIPLINE** RUSSIAN HISTORY, EAST & EUROPE, MODERN EUROPEAN HISTORY **EDUCATION** Macalester Col, BA, 65; Ind Univ, Bloomington, AM, 67, PhD, 71. **CAREER** Asst prof, 70-76, assoc prof, 76-86, Prof hist Centre Col, 86-, Ewing T Boles Prof Hist, 93-, ch, Div Soc Sci, 91-95, ch, Hist Prog, 84-89, 95-99; Am Philos Soc fel, Helsinki, 73; res fel, Int Res & Exchanges Bd, IREX, 76-77; Nat Endowment for Hum grant, 78 & 81. **HONORS AND AWARDS** IREX & Fulbright grants, USSR, 76-77, 86; Phi Beta Kappa, 89; Antonovych Found Prize, Most Outstanding Work on Ukraine, 95, for Kiev: A Portrait (Princeton, 93). **MEMBERSHIPS** Am Asn Slavic Studies. **RESEARCH** Russ urban and soc hist; conservation issues. **SELECTED PUBLICATIONS** Auth, Liberalism and the Jewish question; the progressive bloc, Russ Rev, 4/72; Liberal politics in wartime Russia: an analysis of the progressive bloc, Slavic Rev, 74; ed, The City in Russian History, Univ Ky, 76; coauth, The breakdown or urban modernization: a prelude to the revolutions of 1917, In: City in Russ Hist; auth, The modern Russian city: an historiographical analysis, J Urban Hist, 77; Riga's municipal election of 1913: A study in Baltic urban politics, Russ Rev, 4/80; Khar'kov's progressive Duma, 1910-1914: A study in Russian municipal reform, Slav Rev, spring 81; The City in Late Imperial Russia, Ind Univ Press, 86; Kiev: A Portrait, 1800-1917, Princeton Univ Press, 93; Teaching in Almaty, Kazakstan: Autumn 1995, ISRE Newsletter on Russian & Eurasian Educ, spring 96; Kishinev: The Character and Development of a Tsarist Frontier Town, Nationalities Papers, 3/98, ed, Moldova - The Forgotten Republic, Nationalities Papers, 3/98. **CONTACT ADDRESS** Centre Col, 600 W Walnut St, Danville, KY 40422-1394. **EMAIL** hamm@centre.edu

HAMM, THOMAS D.
PERSONAL Born 01/08/1957, New Castle, IN, m, 1984 **DISCIPLINE** HISTORY **EDUCATION** Butler Univ, BA, 79; Ind Univ, MA, 81, PhD, 85. **CAREER** Vis asst prof, Ind Univ-Purdue Univ, 85-87; Arch, Prof Hist, Archivist, Earlham Col, 87-. **HONORS AND AWARDS** An Soc Church Hist Brewer Prize, 87. **MEMBERSHIPS** AHA; OAH; SHEAR; SAA; AAUP; Am Soc Church Hist. **RESEARCH** Am rel hist; antebellum reform; Quakerism. **SELECTED PUBLICATIONS** Auth, The Transformation of American Quakerism, Ind Univ Press, 88; auth, George Fox and the Politics of Late Nineteenth-Century Quaker Historiography, in New Light on George Fox, 1624-1691: A Collection of Essays, Sessions, 94; auth, Hicksite Quakers and the Antebellum Nonresistance Movement, Church Hist 63, Dec 94; auth, Quakers and African Americans, in Encyclopedia of African American Culture and History, Macmillan, 89; auth, Gurneyites and Hicksites, 1871-1917, in Quaker Crosscurrents: Three Hundred Years of Friends in the New York Yearly Meetings, Syracuse Univ Press, 95; auth, God's Government Begun: The Society for Universal Inquiry and Reform, 95, Indiana Univ Press; auth, Earlham College: A History, 1847- 1997, Ind Univ Press, 97. **CONTACT ADDRESS** Lilly Libr, Earlham Col, Richmond, IN 47374. **EMAIL** tomh@earlham.edu

HAMMERMEISTER, KAI
PERSONAL Born 07/15/1967, Gottingen, Germany **DISCIPLINE** GERMAN STUDIES **EDUCATION** Univ Va, MA, 92, PhD, 95. **CAREER** Instr, Univ Va, 95-96; asst prof, Ohio State Univ, 98-. **MEMBERSHIPS** MLA **RESEARCH** German intellectual history; literary theory; aesthetics; hermeneutics. **SELECTED PUBLICATIONS** Auth, art, Inventing History: Toward a Gay Holocaust Literature, 96; auth, art, Pragmatismus als Anti-Asthetik, 96; auth, art, Literature between Social Change and the Valuation of Tradition, 99; auth, Hans-Georg Gadamer, 99. **CONTACT ADDRESS** Dept of Germanic Languages and Literatures, Ohio State Univ, Columbus, 1841 Millikin Rd, 314 Cunz Hall, Columbus, OH 43210. **EMAIL** hammermeister.2@osu.edu

HAMMOND, MASON
PERSONAL Born 02/14/1903, Boston, MA, m, 1935, 3 children **DISCIPLINE** ROMAN HISTORY, LATIN LITERATURE **EDUCATION** Harvard Univ, AB, 25; Oxford Univ, BA, 27, BLitt, 30. **CAREER** From instr to Pope prof, 28-73, Emer Pope Prof, Latin Lang & Lit, Harvard Univ, 73-, From instr to prof, Radcliffe Col, 28-42; prof in charge class studies, Am Acad Rome, 37-39 & 55-57, vis prof, 51-52 & 63; actg dir, Villa I Tatti, Harvard Ctr Renaissance Studies, Florence, Italy, 72 & 73; vis prof classics, Univ Wis-Madison, 74; emer trustee, Am Acad Rome & St Mark's Sch; trustee, Isabella Stewart Gardner Mus, Boston. **HONORS AND AWARDS** LHD, St Bonaventure Univ, 78. **MEMBERSHIPS** Am Philol Asn; Archaeol Inst Am; Am Acad Arts & Sci; hon mem Ger Archaeol Inst. **RESEARCH** Roman history; Latin literature. **SELECTED PUBLICATIONS** Auth, The Augustan Principate, 33 & Russell, 68, co-ed, Plautus, Menaechmi, 33 & rev ed, 68, auth, City-State and World State, etc, 51 & Biblo & Tannen, 66, Harvard; The Antonine Monarch, Am Acad Rome, 57; coauth, From Aeneas to Augustus, 62 & 2nd ed, 67, ed, Plautus, Miles, 63 & rev ed, 69, coauth, The City in the Ancient World, 72 & auth, Latin: A Historical and Linguistic Handbook, 76, Harvard. **CONTACT ADDRESS** Harvard Univ, Widener Libr H, Cambridge, MA 02138.

HAMMOND, NORMAN
PERSONAL Born 07/10/1944, Brighton, England, m, 1972, 2 children **DISCIPLINE** ARCHAEOLOGY **EDUCATION** Cambridge Univ, BA, 66; MA, 70; PhD, 72; Univ Bradford, DSc, 99. **CAREER** Res fel, Center of Latin Am Studies Cambridge Univ, 67-75; sen lectr, Univ Bradford, 75-77; vis prof, Univ Calif Berkeley, 77; vis prof to prof, Rutgers Univ, 77-88; prof, Boston Univ, 88-. **HONORS AND AWARDS** Dumbarton Oaks Fel, 88; Vis Fel, Worcester Col, 89; Vis Fel, Cambridge Univ, 91, 97; ACLS Fel, 92; Rockefeller Found Residency, Bellagio Study Ctr, 97; Corresponding Fel, Brit Acad, 98; Society Medal, Soc of Antiquaries of London, 01; Brit Archaeol Awd, 94, 98. **MEMBERSHIPS** Prehist Soc; Soc of Antiquaries of London; Archaeol Inst of Am, Soc for Am Archaeol. **RESEARCH** Mesoamerican archaeology, especially Maya civilization; South Asian archaeology, especially Afghanistan; History of archaeology; British Colonial funerary monuments. **SELECTED PUBLICATIONS** Auth, Cuello: An Early Maya Community in Belize, Cambridge Univ Press, 91. **CONTACT ADDRESS** Dept Archaeol, Boston Univ, 675 Commonwealth, Ste 347, Boston, MA 02215. **EMAIL** ndch@bu.edu

HAMRE, JAMES S.
PERSONAL Born 10/28/1931, Montevideo, MN, m, 1957, 2 children **DISCIPLINE** RELIGION IN AMERICAN HISTORY **EDUCATION** Augsburg Col, BA, 53; Luther Theol Sem, Minn, BTh, 57; Univ Chicago, MA, 59; Univ Iowa, PhD(-Relig), 67. **CAREER** Prof Religion & Philosophy to prof emeritus, Waldorf Col, Iowa, 67-; visiting lectr, Luther Theo Sem, MN, spring 76; vis lectr, Augsburg Col, MN, spring 81; vis lectr, District College, Volda, Norway, spring 95. **HONORS AND AWARDS** Endowment for Humanities, 74, 87; Regents Outstanding Fac Awd, Waldorf Col, 84; Holmen Fac Achievement Awd, Waldorf Col, 92. **MEMBERSHIPS** Norwegian-American Historical Association. **RESEARCH** Life and thought of Georg Sverdrup; Norwegian immigrant experience; American religious history. **SELECTED PUBLICATIONS** Auth, Georg Sverdrup concerning Luther's principles in America, Concordia Hist Inst Quart, 70; Georg Sverdrup's concept of theological education in the context of a free church, Lutheran Quart, 70; A Thanksgiving Day Address by Georg Sverdrup, Norweg-Am Studies, 70; The Augsburg Triumvirate and the Kvartal-Skrift, Luther Theol Sem Rev, 72; Georg Sverdrup and the Augsburg Plan of Education, Norweg-Am Studies, 74; John O Evjen: Teacher, theologian, biographer, 74 & Georg Sverdrup's Errand into the Wilderness: Building the Free and Living Congregation, 80, Concordia Hist Inst Quart; Norwegian immigrants respond to the common school: A case study of American values and the Lutheran Tradition, Church Hist, 81; auth, Georg Sverdrup: Educator, Theologian, Churchman, 86; The Creationist-Evolutionist Debate and the Public Schools, Journal of Church and State, 91. **CONTACT ADDRESS** Dept of Religion & Philosophy, Waldorf Col, 106 S 6th St, Forest City, IA 50436-1713. **EMAIL** hamrej@Waldorf.edu

HAMSCHER, ALBERT NELSON
PERSONAL Born 08/19/1946, Philadelphia, PA, m, 1997 **DISCIPLINE** EARLY MODERN & FRENCH HISTORY **EDUCATION** Pa State Univ, BA, 68; Emory Univ, MA, 70, PhD, 73. **CAREER** From Asst Prof to Assoc Prof, 72-86, prof hist, Kans State Univ, 86-. **HONORS AND AWARDS** Nat Endowment for Humanities fel, 76, 80-81, 87, 88-89; Am Philos Soc res grant, 77; mem, Inst for Advanced Study, 88-89. **MEMBERSHIPS** Soc Fr Hist Studies. **RESEARCH** Seventeenth century France; administrative history; history of law. **SELECTED PUBLICATIONS** Auth, The Parlement of Paris After the Fronde, 1653-1673, Univ Pittsburgh, 76; The Conseil Prive and the Parlements in the Age of Louis XIV: A Study in French Absolutism, Am Philos Soc, 87; author of numerous articles. **CONTACT ADDRESS** Dept of Hist, Kansas State Univ, 208 Eisenhower Hall, Manhattan, KS 66506-1002. **EMAIL** aham@ksu.edu

HANAK, WALTER KARL
PERSONAL Born Trenton, NJ, w, 1959, 4 children **DISCIPLINE** BYZANTINE & MEDIAEVAL SLAVIC HISTORY **EDUCATION** Univ Tex Austin, BA, 57; Ind Univ, Bloomington, MA, 65, PhD(hist), 73. **CAREER** Instr hist, Univ Tex Austin, 59-60, asst archivist, 60-63; teaching asst hist, Ind Univ, Bloomington, 67; instr, Univ Va, 67-70; from asst prof to assoc prof, 70-78, Prof Hist, Shepherd Col, 78-, Ed, Byzantine Studies/Etudes Byzantines, 72-; mem, US Nat Comt Byzantine Studies. **MEMBERSHIPS** Medieval Acad Am; Asn Int des Etudes Byzantines. **RESEARCH** History of the Byzantine Empire, 700-1000; history of the Kievan Russia, 860-1240; history of the Great Moravian Empire and Bohemia/Moravia to 1200. **SELECTED PUBLICATIONS** Auth, "The Infamous Svjatoslav: Master of Duplicity in War and Peace?" Peace and War in Vyzantium: Essays in Honor of George T Dennis, The Catholic Univ of America Press, (95): 135-151; auth," Byzantine, Western, and Muscovite Sources on the Fall (1453) of Constantinople and Its Conqueror, Mehmet II," Twenty-First Annual Byzantine Studies Conference, Abstract of Papers, (95): 9-12, New York Univ and Metropolitan Museum of Art, NY, NY, (95): 34; auth, " The Great Moravian Empire: An Argument for a Northern Location," Medievalia Historica Bohemica, no 4, (95): 7-24; auth, "Photios and the Slavs, 885-867." Papers, 18th International Byzantine Congress, Moscow, 91 vol I Shepherdstown: Byzantine Studies Press, (96): 222-232; auth, corr ed, Papers, 18th International Byzantine Congress, Moscow, 91, 4 vols, Shepherdstown: Byzantine Studies Press, 96; auth, " Byzantine, Latin, and Muscovite Sources on the Fall of Constantinople (1453) and Its Conqueror, Mehmet II," Eastern Churches Journal 3/2 (96): 53-68; auth, Nestor-Iskander, The Tale of Constantinople (Of Its Origin and Conquest by thr Turks in 1453), The Troitse-Sergeevaja Lavra Ms, New Rochelle, NY: Athens & Moscow; 98. **CONTACT ADDRESS** Dept of Hist, Shepherd Col, Pox Box 3210, Shepherdstown, WV 25443-3210. **EMAIL** walterhanak@mail.shepherdcollege.edu

HANAWALT, BARBARA A.
PERSONAL Born 03/04/1941, New Brunswick, NJ **DISCIPLINE** HISTORY **EDUCATION** Douglass Col, BA, 63; Univ Mich, MA, 64, PhD, 70. **CAREER** Instr, San Fernando Valley State Col, 70-72; vis asst prof, Univ So Calif, 72; vis asst prof, Univ Oregon, 72-73; asst prof, 74-78, assoc prof, 78-84, prof, 84-87, dir, Criminal Justice Consortium, 85-87, Indiana Univ; prof, 87-98, dir Center for Medieval Stud, 91-97, Univ Minn; King George III Prof British Hist, 99- , Ohio State Univ. **HONORS AND AWARDS** Phi Beta Kappa; Woodrow Wilson fel, 63-64, dissertation fel, 66-68; AAUW fel, 68-69; ACLS fel, 75-76; Am Philos Soc grant, 71, 78; NEH sr res fel, 79-80; NEH fel and mem, School for Hist Stud, Inst for Advanced Stud, Princeton, NJ, 82-83; Fulbright travel grant, 88-89; Guggenheim fel, 88-89; fel, Wissenschaftskolleg zu Berlin, 90-91; fel, Royal Hist Soc, 94- ; Scholar-of-the-College, Univ Minn, 95-98; NEH res fel, 97-98; fel, Natl Hum Ctr, 97-98. **MEMBERSHIPS** Am Hist Asn; Royal Hist Soc; British Stud Asn; Medieval Acad of Am; Social Sci Hist Asn; Past and Present Soc. **RESEARCH** Medieval history including history of crime, children, family and women, peasants, urban history, law. **SELECTED PUBLICATIONS** Auth, Growing Up in Medieval London: The Experience of Childhood in History, Oxford, 93; auth, Of Good and Ill Repute: Gender and Social Control in Medieval England, Oxford, 98; coauth, The Western Experience, McGraw Hill, 7th ed, 98; auth, An Illustrated History of the Middle Ages, Oxford, 99. **CONTACT ADDRESS** Dept of History, Ohio State Univ, Columbus, 230 West 17th St, Columbus, OH 43210. **EMAIL** hanawalt.4@osu.edu

HANCHETT, TOM
PERSONAL Born 01/16/1956, Chicago, IL, m, 1 child **DISCIPLINE** URBAN HISTORY; HISTORIC PRESERVATION **EDUCATION** Cornell Univ, BA, 78; Univ Chicago, MA, 86; Univ North Carolina, PhD, 93 **CAREER** Asst prof, Youngstown State Univ, 95-98; asst prof, Cornell Univ, 98- **HONORS AND AWARDS** Catherine Bauer Wurster Prize, 95-97; Mellon Postdoctoral Teaching Fel, 94-95; Best Dissertation Urban Hist, 93; Best Dissertation Southern Studies, 92-93; First Place Hist Book Awd, 87 **MEMBERSHIPS** Soc Amer City & Regional Planning Hist; Soc Archit Historians; Nat Trust Historic Preservation; Urban Hist Assoc; Orgn Amer Historians **RESEARCH** Forces shaping the built environment in the US during 19th and

20th Centuries **SELECTED PUBLICATIONS** Auth, Sorting Out the New South City: Race, Class and Urban Development in Charlotte, 1875-1975, UNC, 98; auth, "US Tax Policy and the Shopping Center Boom of the 1950s and 1960s," Amer Historical Rev, 96; auth, "Roots of the 'Renaissance:' Federal Incentives to Urban Planning, 1941-1948," Planning the Twentieth Century American City, Johns Hopkins, 96 **CONTACT ADDRESS** Dept City & Reg Planning, Cornell Univ, Ithaca, NY 14853-6701. **EMAIL** twh3@cornell.edu

HANCHETT, WILLIAM
PERSONAL Born 05/25/1922, Evanston, IL, m, 1945, 2 children **DISCIPLINE** UNITED STATES HISTORY **EDUCATION** Southern Methodist Univ, BA, 48; Univ Calif, MA, 49, PhD, 52. **CAREER** Asst prof US hist, Univ Colo, 54-55 & Colo State Univ, 55-56; Prof US Hist, San Diego State Univ, 56- **RESEARCH** Lincoln; Lincoln's assassination; Civil War and Reconstruction. **SELECTED PUBLICATIONS** Auth, Irish, Charles G Halpine in Civil War America, Syracuse Univ, 70; Booth's Diary, J Ill State Hist Soc, 2/79; The EisenschemI Thesis, Civil War Hist, 9/79; The War Department and Booth's Abduction Plot, Lincoln Herald, winter 80. **CONTACT ADDRESS** Dept of Hist, San Diego State Univ, San Diego, CA 92115.

HAND, SAMUEL B.
PERSONAL Born 08/20/1931, New York, NY, m, 1957, 3 children **DISCIPLINE** UNITED STATES HISTORY **EDUCATION** NYork Univ, BA, 52; Syracuse Univ, PhD, 60. **CAREER** Asst prof hist, Slippery Rock State Col, 60-61; from instr to assoc prof, 61-70, chmn dept, 74-76, Prof Hist, Univ Vt, 70-, Ed, Oral Hist Rev, 73-79. **HONORS AND AWARDS** Stephen Greene Awd, Stephen Greene Press, 76; Grad Fac Teacher of the Year, Univ Vt; Harvey Kantor Oral Hist Awd; Ben B. Lane Awd. **MEMBERSHIPS** AHA; Orgn Am Historians; Oral Hist Asn. **RESEARCH** Recent political history; Vermont history; oral history. **SELECTED PUBLICATIONS** Auth, Advise and Counsel, a political biography of Samuel I Rosenman; auth, State of Nature, Readings in Vermont History; auth, Vermont Voices. **CONTACT ADDRESS** Dept of Hist, Univ of Vermont, Burlington, VT 05401.

HANDLIN, OSCAR
PERSONAL Born 09/29/1915, Brooklyn, NY, m, 1937, 3 children **DISCIPLINE** AMERICAN HISTORY **EDUCATION** Brooklyn Col, AB, 34; Harvard Univ, AM, 35, PhD, 40. **CAREER** From instr to prof, 39-72, Carl H Pforzheimer Univ Prof Hist, Harvard Univ, 72-, Vchmn, US Bd Foreign Scholar, 62-65, chmn, 65-66; dir, Charles Warren Ctr Study Am Hist, 65-72; dir, Harvard Univ Libr, 79- **HONORS AND AWARDS** Pulitzer Prize, 52; Dunning Prize, AHA, 41; littd, brooklyn col, 72, oakland univ, 68; lld, colby col, 62, univ cincinnati, 81; lhd, hebrew union col, 67, northern mich univ, 69, seton hall univ, 72 & boston col, 75, univ lowell, 80. **MEMBERSHIPS** AHA; Nat Acad Educ; Nat Educ Asn; Am Acad Arts & Sci; Am Jewish Hist Soc (vpres, 73-). **RESEARCH** Social and economic history; commonwealth. **SELECTED PUBLICATIONS** Auth, The Bill-Of-Rights in its Context, Am Scholar, Vol 0062, 93; Being Jewish--The Endless Quest, Am Scholar, Vol 0066, 97; A Career at Harvard, Am Scholar, Vol 0065, 96; The 'Unmarked Way', Am Scholar, Vol 0065, 96. **CONTACT ADDRESS** Harvard Univ, Widener 783, Cambridge, MA 02138. **EMAIL** lilioscar@aol.com

HANDSMAN, RUSSELL G.
DISCIPLINE HISTORY **EDUCATION** Franklin & Marshall, BA, 70; Am Univ, PhD, 76. **CAREER** Ind Sch. **MEMBERSHIPS** Am Antiquarian Soc **RESEARCH** John Milton Earle, Mass Indians **CONTACT ADDRESS** 5 Periwinkle St, Saunderstown, RI 02874-2711.

HANE, MIKISO
PERSONAL Born 01/16/1922, Hollister, CA, m, 1948, 2 children **DISCIPLINE** ASIAN HISTORY **EDUCATION** Yale Univ, BA, 52, MA, 53, PhD, 57. **CAREER** Instr Japanese, Yale Univ, 49-53; Fulbright res grant, Japan, 57-58; asst prof hist, Univ Toledo, 59-61; from asst prof to prof, 61-75, Szold Distinguished Serv Prof Hist, Knox Col, 75-92, Fulbright grant, Univ Mysore, India, 63; Japan Found res fel, 73; Nat Endowment Humanities res grant, 79-80. **MEMBERSHIPS** AHA; Asn Asian Studies. **RESEARCH** Modern Japanese history. **SELECTED PUBLICATIONS** Auth, coauth, Cultures in Transition, Follett, 73; Studies in the intellectual History of Tokugawa Japan (transl, Maruyama, Nihon Seijishisoshi Kenkyu), Univ Tokyo, 74; Peasants, Rebels and Outcastes, Panthenon, 82; auth, Emperor Hirohito and His Chief Aide, the Honjo Diary, 1933-1936, Univ Tokyo, 82; auth, Modern Japan, A Historical Survey, Westview, 86; auth, Reflections on the Way to the Gallows, Rebel Women in Prewar Japan, Univ Calif, 88; auth, Premodern Japan, A Historical Survey, Westview, 90; auth, The Age of Hirohito, Free Press, 95; auth, Eastern Phoenix: Japan Since 1945, Westview, 96; auth, Japan, A Short Cultural History, Oneworld, 00. **CONTACT ADDRESS** Dept of Hist, Knox Col, Illinois, Galesburg, IL 61401. **EMAIL** mhane@knox.edu

HANEY, RICHARD CARLTON
PERSONAL Born 11/01/1940, Stoughton, WI **DISCIPLINE** TWENTIETH CENTURY UNITED STATES HISTORY **EDUCATION** Univ Wis-Whitewater, BEd, 63; Univ Wis-Madison, MS, 64, PhD(Am hist), 70; post-PhD (Military Hist Program), USMA West Point, 89. **CAREER** Teacher hist, Monroe High Sch, Wis, 64-66; prof hist, Univ Wis-Whitewater, 66-, Publ ed on six-vol hist of Wis proj, Wis State Hist Soc, 70; coordr student internship prog, Old World Wis Outdoor Ethnic Mus, Univ Wis-Whitewater, 76-80. **HONORS AND AWARDS** Disabled Student Serv Teaching Awd, 87; Teaching Excellence Awd, Wis Asn for Promotion of Hist, 91. **MEMBERSHIPS** Vestlandslag. **RESEARCH** State, local and regional history; political history; ethnic immigrant history. **SELECTED PUBLICATIONS** Auth, A case study of the midwestern Ku Klux Klan of the 1920's: Whitewater, Wis, 10/69 & JFK's Catholic vote in the 1960 Wisconsin presidential primary: A reassessment, 10/70, Paper Wis Asn Teachers Col Hist; The rise of Wisconsin's New Democrats: A Political Realignment in the Mid-Twentieth Century, Wis Mag Hist, winter 74-75; A Concise History of the Modern Republican Party of Wisconsin: 1925-1975, Kramer & Republican Party Wis, 76; Wallace in Wisconsin: The Presidential Primary of 1964, Wis Mag Hist, summer 78; auth, From Black Earth to Liverpool: Transatlantic Observations by George W Bate, Wis Mag Hist, autumn 81; William Jennings Bryan: Orator was a force in American life for three decades, Cameo Speech Quart, autumn 81; auth, Campus Cornerstones at UW-Whitewater: Biographical Sketches of People for Whom Buildings and Facilities are Names, 97. **CONTACT ADDRESS** Dept of Hist, Univ of Wisconsin, Whitewater, 800 W Main, Whitewater, WI 53190-1790. **EMAIL** haneyr@mail.uww.edu

HANFT, SHELDON
PERSONAL Born 08/06/1939, New York, NY, m, 1961, 3 children **DISCIPLINE** HISTORY **EDUCATION** NY Univ, BA, 61; NY Univ, MA, 66; NY Univ, PhD, 69. **CAREER** Teacher, Eli Whitney Voc High Sch, 61-69; From Asst Prof to Prof, Appalachian St Univ, 69-. **HONORS AND AWARDS** Sheldon Hanft Annual Travel Awd, Carolinas' Symp on Brit Studies. **MEMBERSHIPS** SJHS, SHS, AHS. **RESEARCH** Early modern Britain. **SELECTED PUBLICATIONS** Co-ed, "The Anglo-Scottish Waas 1513-1561," Magill's Military Hist, 97; auth, "Mordecai's Female Academy," Am Jewish Hist vol LXXIX (97): 72-93. **CONTACT ADDRESS** Dept Hist, Appalachian State Univ, 238 Whitener Hall, Boone, NC 28608-0001. **EMAIL** hanfts@appstate.edu

HANKINS, THOMAS LEROY
PERSONAL Born 09/09/1933, Lawrence, KS, m, 1960, 2 children **DISCIPLINE** HISTORY OF SCIENCE **EDUCATION** Yale Univ, BS, 56; Harvard Univ, MAT, 58; Cornell Univ, PhD(hist), 64. **CAREER** Instr physics, Phillips Acad, 56-60; asst prof, 64-69, assoc prof, 69-75, Prof Hist, Univ Wash, 75- **HONORS AND AWARDS** Zeitlin-Verbrugge Prize, Hist Sci Soc, 80; Sarton Medal, 00. **MEMBERSHIPS** Hist Sci Soc; AHA; Am Soc Eighteenth Century Studies. **RESEARCH** History of mechanics; the French enlightenment; scientific biography. **SELECTED PUBLICATIONS** Auth, The influence of Malebranche on the science of mechanics during the 18th century, J Hist Ideas, 67; The reception of Newton's second law of motion in the 18th century, Arch Int d'Hist Sci, 1-6/67; Jean d'Alembert: Science and the Enlightenment, Clarendon, 71; Triplets and triads: Sir William Rowan Hamilton on the metaphysics of mathematics, Isis, 77; In defense of biography, His Sci Soc, Vol 17, 79; Sir William Rowan Hamilton, Johns Hopkins Univ Press, 80; auth, Science and the Enlightenment, Cambridge, 85; coauth, Instruments and the Imagination, Princeton Univ Press, 95. **CONTACT ADDRESS** DP-20 Dept of Hist, Univ of Washington, Seattle, WA 98195. **EMAIL** hankins@u.washington.edu

HANLEY, SARAH
PERSONAL Born, NY **DISCIPLINE** HISTORY **EDUCATION** Univ Pittsburgh, BA, 67; Univ IA, MA, 70, PhD, 75. **CAREER** Instr, 69-70, vis asst prof, 75-76, Coe Col; asst, 77, assoc prof, 82, asst chair and dir, 84-85, prof, 87, fac dean, 87-90, Univ IA. **HONORS AND AWARDS** Fel, 90-91, William Koren, Jr. Prize 90; Nat Hum Ctr; Seminar Fel, 93, Univ Bielefeld; Fel, 93-94, John Simon Guggenheim Memorial Found; Fel, 97, Camargo Found; Fel, 98, Huntington Libry; Mary Parker Follett Awd, 98, Am Political Science Asn; Soc for French Hist Studies. **MEMBERSHIPS** Soc French Hist Studies; Am Hist Asn; Soc French Hist Studies; Western Soc French Hist; Social Science Hist; Am Soc Legal Hist. **RESEARCH** Early modern France, 1500-1800, political culture, society, law, and litigation, critical theory and interpretation. **SELECTED PUBLICATIONS** Auth, The Lit de Justice of the Kings of France: Constitutional Ideology in Legend, Ritual, and Discourse, Princeton Univ Press, 83; Le Lit de Justice des Rois de France: L'Ideologie Constitutionnelle dans la Legende, le Rituel, et le Discours, Aubier, 91; auth, "Les droits des femmes et la loi salique, Paris: Indigo & Cote-femmes, 94; auth, "Mapping Rulership in the French Body Politic: Political Identity, Public Law, and The King's One Body," Hist Reflections, 97; "Social Sites of Political Practice in France: Lawsuits, Civil Rights, and the Separation of Powers in Domestic and State Government, 1500-1800," Am Hist Rev, 97; "The Politics of Identity and Monarchic Governance in France: The Debate over Female Exclusion," Women Writers and the Early Modern British Political Tradition, Hilda L. Smith, ed, 98 **CONTACT ADDRESS** Dept of History, Univ of Iowa, Iowa City, IA 52242. **EMAIL** sarah-hanley@uiowa.edu

HANNA, MARTHA
DISCIPLINE HISTORY **EDUCATION** Georgetown Univ, PhD, 89. **CAREER** Instr, 88, asst prof, 89-96, assoc prof, Univ Colo, 96-. **SELECTED PUBLICATIONS** Auth, The Mobilization of Intellect: French Scholars and Writers during the Great War, Harvard, 96; Metaphors of Malaise and Misogyny in the Rhetoric of the Action francaise, Hist Reflections, 94; The Catholic Construction of the Great War, W Soc French Hist, 94; Metaphors of Malaise and Misogyny in the Rhetoric of the Action francaise, Hist Reflections, 94; Natalism, Homosexuality, and the Controversy over Corydon, Oxford, 96. **CONTACT ADDRESS** History Dept, Univ of Colorado, Boulder, Boulder, CO 80309. **EMAIL** hanna@spot.colorado.edu

HANNON, BRUCE M.
PERSONAL Born 08/14/1934, Ivesdale, IL, m, 1956, 3 children **DISCIPLINE** GEOGRAPHY **EDUCATION** Univ IL Urbana, BS, 56; MS, 65; PhD, 70. **CAREER** Proj eng, Quantum Chemical, 56-65. **HONORS AND AWARDS** Limits to Growth, Club of Rome First Prize, 75; Jubilee Prof Lib Arts 7 Sci, Univ of IL Urbana. **RESEARCH** Modeling ecological and economic systems. **SELECTED PUBLICATIONS** Auth, "Accounting in Ecological Systems", Ecol Econ: the Sci and Management of Sustainability, ed R. Costanza, Columbia Univ Pr, (91): 234-252; auth, Empirical Cyclic Stabilization of an Oyster Reef System", J Theo Biol 149 (91): 507-519; coauth, "Modeling Monkeys: A comparison of computer generated and empirical measures", Int J Primatology 14.6 (93): 827-852; coauth, "A physical view of sustainability", Ecol Econ 8 (93): 253-268; auth, "Sense of Place: geographic discounting by people, animals and plants, Ecol Econ 10 (94): 157-174; coauth, Dynamic Modeling, Springer-Verlag, (NY), 94; coauth, Dynamic Biological Systems, Springer-Verlag, (NY), 96, coauth, Modeling Dynamic Economic Systems, Springer-Verlag, (NY), 96; auth, "How might nature value man?", Ecol Econ 25.3 (96): 265-280. **CONTACT ADDRESS** Dept Geog, Univ of Illinois, Urbana-Champaign, 607 S Mathews Ave, Urbana, IL 61801. **EMAIL** b-hannon@uiuc.edu

HANSEN, BERT
PERSONAL Born 02/05/1944, Chicago, IL, s **DISCIPLINE** HISTORY **EDUCATION** Columbia Col, AB, 65; Princeton Univ, PhD, 74. **CAREER** Asst Prof, SUNY 74-79; Fac Fel, Harvard Univ, 78-79; Asst Prof, Univ Toronto, 79-84; Member, Sch of Hist Studies, 84-85; Coordinator of Med Humanities, NY Univ, 85-87; Asst to the Pres, Res Foundation of CUNY, 89-91; Asst to the Pres to Assoc Prof, Baruch Col, 91-. **HONORS AND AWARDS** Scholar Incentive Awd, CUNY, 99; Eugene Lang Jr Fac Res Fel, Baruch Col, 98; Laurance D. Redway Awd, Med Soc of the State of NY, 86; Mellon foundation Fel, Harvard Univ, 78-79. **MEMBERSHIPS** Am Asn for the Hist of Medicine; Am Hist Asn; Hist of Sci Soc; Org of Am Hist. **RESEARCH** History of medicine and public health in the United States. **SELECTED PUBLICATIONS** Auth, Nicole Oresme and the Marvels of Nature: A Study of His 'De causis mirabilium' with Critical Edition, Translation, and commentary, Toronto, 85; auth, "The complementarity of Science and Magic before the Scientific Revolution," American Scientist, (86): 128-136; auth, "Western European Bookish Magic," The Dictionary of the Middle Ages, (87), 31-40; auth, "New York City epidemics and History for the Public," in AIDS and the Historian, (Bethesda, 91), 21-28; auth, "La reponse americaine a la victoire de Pasteur contra la rage: Quand la medecine fait pour la premiere fois la 'une'," in L'Institut Pasteur: Contributions a son histoire, (Paris, 91): 89-102; auth, "American Physicians' 'Discovery' of Homosexuals, 1880-1900: A New Diagnosis in a Changing Society," in Framing Disease: Studies in Cultural History, (Rutgers Univ Press, 92), 104-133; auth, "The Image and Advocacy of Public Health in American Caricature and Cartoons from 1860 to 1900," American Journal of Public Health, (97): 1798-1807; auth, "American Physicians' 'Discovery' of Homosexuals, 1880-1900: A New Diagnosis in a Changing Society," in Framing Disease: Studies in Cultural History 3rd ed, (Univ WI Press, 97), 13-31; auth, "America's First Medical Breakthrough: How Popular Excitement about a French Rabies Cure in 1885 Raised New Expectations of Medical Progress," Am Hist Review, (98): 373-418; auth, "New Images of a New Medicine: Visual Evidence for Widespread Popularity of Therapeutic Discoveries in America after 1885," Bulletin of the History of Medicine, (99): 62-678. **CONTACT ADDRESS** Dept Hist, Baruch Col, CUNY, 17 Lexington Ave, New York, NY 10010-5518. **EMAIL** Bert_Hansen@baruch.cuny.edu

HANSEN, BOB
DISCIPLINE THEATRE HISTORY, DRAMATIC LITERATURE **EDUCATION** Univ MN, BA; FL State Univ, MA; Univ MN, PhD. **CAREER** Instr, ch, dept Theatre, mng dir, Huron Playhouse, Bowling Green State Univ; instr, 86-, hd, dept, Broadcasting/Cinema and Theatre, Univ NC, Greensboro. **MEMBERSHIPS** NC Theatre Asn; USITT-Ohio; Am Theatre Asn; Southeastern Theatre Conf; Nat Asn Sch Theatre. **SE-**

LECTED PUBLICATIONS Auth, Scenic and Costume Design for the Ballets Russes, UMI Res Press. CONTACT ADDRESS Univ of No Carolina, Greensboro, Greensboro, NC 27412-5001. EMAIL rchansen@dewey.uncg.edu

HANSEN, DEBRA GOLD
PERSONAL Born 09/16/1953, Orange, CA, m, 1977 **DISCIPLINE** HISTORY **EDUCATION** Calif State Univ Fullerton, BA, 75; MA, 79; MA Libr and Information Sci, 83; Univ Calif Irvine, PhD, 88. **CAREER** Ed, Oral Hist Program, Calif State Univ Fullerton, 75-79; freelance indexer for acad presses, 80-93; hist bibliogr, ref librn, Honnold Libr, Claremont Coll Calif, 84-89; asst coordr biblogr instructions, Pomona Coll Claremont Calif, 88-89; archivist, Anaheim Public Libr Calif, 89-90; instr, Calif State Univ Fullerton, 90; aasst prof, San Jose Univ calif, 89-95; assoc dir, School of Libr and Infor Sci, San Jose Univ Calif, 95-. **HONORS AND AWARDS** Grad with Honors, Calif State Univ Fullerton, 75; Joint recipient of Robert G Athearn Awd Western Hist Asn, 92; Contemporary Authors; Who's Who in the West, 96-97. **RESEARCH** Nineteenth Century American Social History; Women's History; Family and Ethnic History. **SELECTED PUBLICATIONS** Auth, The Boston Female Anti-Slavery Society and the Limits of Gender Politics, The Abolitionist Sisterhood: Antislavery and Women's Political Culture, 94; coauth, Interactive Video and Female Learning: Imlications for a Feminized Profession, Feminist Collections, 96. **CONTACT ADDRESS** San Jose State University - University Library, California State Univ, Fullerton, Box 4150, Fullerton, CA 92834-4150. **EMAIL** Dhansen@wahoo.sjsu.edu

HANSEN, JULIE
DISCIPLINE ARCHAEOLOGY **EDUCATION** Univ MN, MA, 75, PhD, 80. **CAREER** Asst prof, 85-93, assoc prof, 93-, chmn, dept of archaeol, 95-, Boston Univ. **HONORS AND AWARDS** NEH Univ Tchrs Fel; NMERTP Fel to Acor, Amman; Fulbright Fel. **MEMBERSHIPS** Archaeol Inst of Am; Am Schools of Oriental Res; Soc of Am Archaeol; Soc of Ethnobiology; Soc of Economic Botany. **RESEARCH** East Mediterranean prehistory; palaeoethnobotany. **SELECTED PUBLICATIONS** Auth, The Palaeoethnobotany of Franchthi Cave, IN Univ Press, 91; auth, L'Agricula del Neolitic Antic a L'Egeu, Cota Zero, 93; auth, Beyond the Site: Palaeoethnobotany in Regional Perspective, Beyond the Site: Reg Stud in the Aegean Area, Univ Press Am, 94; auth, Preliminary Report on the Plant Remains (1986, 1988-1991), Fouilled Recentes a Khirokitia (Chypre) 1988-91, Ed Recherche sur les civilisations, ADPF, 94; auth, Ethnobotany, and Paleobotany, Oxford Encycl of Archaeol in the Near East, 96. **CONTACT ADDRESS** Dept of Archaeology, Boston Univ, 675 Commonwealth Ave, Boston, MA 02215. **EMAIL** jmh@bu.edu

HANSEN, KLAUS JUERGEN
PERSONAL Born 11/29/1931, Kiel, Germany, m, 1959, 4 children **DISCIPLINE** AMERICAN HISTORY **EDUCATION** Brigham Young Univ, BA, 57, MA, 59; Wayne State Univ, PhD, 63. **CAREER** Instr hist, Eastern Mich Univ, 63 & Ohio State Univ, 63-65; asst prof, Utah State Univ, 65-68; assoc prof, 68-78, Prof Hist, Queen's Univ, Ont, 78-, Consult, Am Heritage Dictionary, Houghton Mifflin, 69; Queen's res awards, 69-70 & 72-73; vis fel, Yale Univ, 74-75; Can Coun fel, 74-75. **HONORS AND AWARDS** Awd of Merit, Am Asn State & Local Hist, 68; Book Awd, Mormon Hist Asn, 68. **MEMBERSHIPS** AHA; Orgn Am Historians; Am Studies Asn; Am Soc Church Hist; Can Asn Am Studies. **RESEARCH** American cultural history; American race relations; American religion. **SELECTED PUBLICATIONS** Auth, Quest for Empire, Michigan State, 67; auth, Mormonism and the American Experience, Chicago, 81; auth, When Truth Was Treason: German Youth in Opposition to Hitler, Illinois, 95. **CONTACT ADDRESS** Dept of Hist, Queen's Univ at Kingston, Kingston, ON, Canada K7L 3N6.

HANSEN, PETER H.
PERSONAL Born 10/31/1961, New Haven, CT, m, 1988, 2 children **DISCIPLINE** HISTORY **EDUCATION** Carleton Col, BA, 84; Harvard Univ, MA, 86, PhD, 91. **CAREER** Tchng fel, 86-88, Harvard Univ; vis mem, 88-90, Inst for Hist Res, Univ London; adj asst prof, 91-92, Lehman Col, CUNY; vis fel, 95-96, Clare Hall, Cambridge Univ; vis fel, 98, Australian Nat Univ, Hum Res Centre; asst prof, 92-98, dir of int stud, 95-, assoc prof, 98-, Worchester Polytechnic Inst. **HONORS AND AWARDS** Phi Beta Kappa, 84; NYC Urban fel, 84-85; Krupp Found Fel in European Stud, 88-89; Bowdoin Grad Diss Prize, Harvard Univ, 91; Nat Endowment for the Hum, travel to collections grant, 93; Royal Geographical Soc, Inst of British Geographers, Young Res Award, 96; Nat Endowment for the Hum, fel for Col Tchrs, 95-96. **MEMBERSHIPS** Am Hist Asn; North Am Conference on British Studies; North East Conference on British Studies; World Hist Asn; Soc for Cinema Studies; Royal Hist Soc, fel; Royal Geographical Soc, Inst British Geographers, fel; Clare Hall, Cambridge, life member. **SELECTED PUBLICATIONS** Auth, Albert Smith, the Alpine Club, and the Invention of Mountaineering in Mid-Victorian Britain, J of Brit Stud 34, 95; auth, Mountaineering, in Twentieth-Century Britain: an Encycl, Garland, 95; auth, International Education and Sustainable Development: An American Experience in Bangkok, Venice, and Guayaquil, The Environmentalist 15, 95; auth, Vertical Boundaries, National Identities: Victorian Mountaineering on the Frontiers of Europe and the Empire, 1868-1914, J of Imperial and Commonwealth Hist, 24, 96; auth, The Dancing Lamas of Everest: Cimema, Orientalism, and Anglo-Tibetan Relations in the 1920's, Am Hist Rev, 1010, 96; Der tibetische Horizont, Tibet im Kino des Fruhen 20, Jahrhunderts, in Mythos Tibet: Wahrnehmungen, Projektionen, Phantasien, ed Thierry Dodin and Heinz Rather, DuMont, 97; auth, Debate: Tenzing's Two Wrist-Watches: the Conquest of Everest and Late Imperial Culture in Britain, 1921-1953: Comment, Past and Present, 157, 97; auth, Partners: Guides and Sherpas in the Alps and Himalayas, 1850s-1950s, Voyages and Visions: Towards a Cultural History of Travel, 98; auth; Confetti of Empire the Conquest of Everest in Nepal, India, Britian and New Zealand. Comparative Studies in Society and History 42, (00): 307-332; contrib, New Dictionary of National Biography, Oxford Univ Press. **CONTACT ADDRESS** Dept of Humanities and Arts, Worcester Polytech Inst, 100 Institute Rd, Worcester, MA 01609-2280. **EMAIL** phansen@wpi.edu

HANSON, CARL AARON
PERSONAL Born 11/02/1946, Washington, DC, m, 1969 **DISCIPLINE** PORTUGUESE ECONOMIC HISTORY **EDUCATION** Univ Denver, BA, 68, MA, 69; Univ NMex, PhD(hist), 78; IN Univ, MLS, 88. **CAREER** Asst prof hist, Grad Ctr, Univ NMex, Santa Fe, 79; vis scholar Hist, Univ NMex, Albuquerque, 80-; Head Bibliographer, Trninity Univ, San Antonio, 89-96. **MEMBERSHIPS** Soc Span & Port Hist Studies; Int Conf Group Mod Port; AHA; Conf Latin Am Hist. **RESEARCH** Early modern Portugal; European economic history; history of science, cosmology. **SELECTED PUBLICATIONS** Auth, Economy and Society in Baroque Portugal, 1668-1703 (Minneapolis: Univ of MN Press), 81. **CONTACT ADDRESS** Univ of New Mexico, Albuquerque, 701 Ridgecrest SE, Albuquerque, NM 87108. **EMAIL** chanson@unm.edu

HANSON, CHARLES PARKER
DISCIPLINE HISTORY **EDUCATION** Harvard Univ, AB, 82; Univ Calif at Berkeley, MA, 89, PhD, 93. **CAREER** Asst Prof, Hist, Doane Coll. **MEMBERSHIPS** Am Antiquarian Soc **SELECTED PUBLICATIONS** Auth, A Necessary Virtue: The Reconfiguration of Religious Differences in Revolutionary New England, Univ Press of Va. **CONTACT ADDRESS** Dept of Hist, Doane Col, 1014 Boswell Ave, Crete, NE 68333. **EMAIL** chanson@doane.edu

HANYAN, CRAIG
DISCIPLINE HISTORY **EDUCATION** Yale Univ, BA; Harvard Univ, AM, PhD. **CAREER** Prof. **HONORS AND AWARDS** Presidential Released Time award, 96. **RESEARCH** New York politics and society in the early national period. **SELECTED PUBLICATIONS** Auth, King George, Queen Caroline and the Albany Regency, NY Hist; De Witt Clinton and the Rise of the People's Men, McGill-Queen's UP, 96. **CONTACT ADDRESS** Dept of Hist, Brock Univ, 500 Glenridge Ave, Saint Catharines, ON, Canada L2S 3A1. **EMAIL** chanyan@spartan.ac.brocku.ca

HAO, YEN-PING
DISCIPLINE HISTORY **EDUCATION** Harvard Univ, PhD. **CAREER** Lindsay Young prof. **SELECTED PUBLICATIONS** Auth, The Comprador in Nineteenth Century China: Bridge Between East and West, Harvard; Commercial Revolution in Nineteenth-Century China: The Rise of Sino-Western Mercantile Capitalism, Univ Ca Pr. **CONTACT ADDRESS** Dept of History, Knoxville, TN 37996.

HAPKE, LAURA
PERSONAL Born 01/04/1946, New York, NY, m **DISCIPLINE** ENGLISH; AMERICAN STUDIES **EDUCATION** Brandeis Univ, BA, 67; Univ of Chicago, MA, 69; City Univ of NYork, PhD, 74. **CAREER** Tchg fel, 72-74; adjunct instr, Queens Col, 78-81; instr, Nassau Comm Col, 78-81; from asst prof to prof Eng, Pace Univ, 81-91. **HONORS AND AWARDS** NEH awards, 80, 81; Choice Outstanding Acad Book Awd, 92. **MEMBERSHIPS** PMLA; ASA; NYLNA. **RESEARCH** Labor lit; Women's studies; American & Victorian lit and cult. **SELECTED PUBLICATIONS** Auth, Girls Who Went Wrong: Prostitutes in American Fiction, 1885-1917, Bowling Green Univ, 89; Tales of the Working Girl: Wage - Earning Women in American Literature, 1890-1925, Twayne/Macmillan, 92; The Ideology of the Salvation Army, The Eighteen Nineties: An Ecyclopedia of British Literature, Art and Culture, ed George Cevasco, Garland, 93; A Wealth of Possibilities: The Worker, the Text, and the Composition Classroom, Women's Studies Quarterly, 94; Homage to Daniel Horwitz, Liberating Memory: Working Class Intellectuals and Their Work, ed Janet Zandy, Rutgers Univ, 95; Daughters of the Great Depression: Women, Work, and Fiction in the American 1930s, Univ Georgia, 95. **CONTACT ADDRESS** Dept of English, Pace Univ, New York, Pace Plaza, New York, NY 10038-1502. **EMAIL** lhapke@tiac.net

HARBISON, CRAIG
PERSONAL Born 04/19/1944, Baltimore, MD, m, 1966, 2 children **DISCIPLINE** ART HISTORY **EDUCATION** Princeton Univ, PhD, 72. **CAREER** Prof, 74-. **RESEARCH** Study of social origins and functions of sixteenth-century Flemish still-life painting; history of the iconographic method; sixteenth-century northern artists in Italy; sexuality and gender issues in northern Renaissance art. **SELECTED PUBLICATIONS** Auth, Sexuality and Social Standing in Jan van Eyck's Arnolfini Double Portrait, Renaissance Quarterly, 90; The Play of Realism, London (rev), Reaktion Bk, 91; Meaning in Venetian Renaissance art: the issues of artistic ingenuity and oral tradition, Art Hist, 92; Miracles Happen: Image and Experience in Jan van Eyck's Madonna in a Church, Princeton, 93; The Sexuality of Christ in the Early Sixteenth Century in Germany, Princeton, 94; The Mirror of the Artist: Northern Renaissance Art in its Historical Context, Abrams, 95. **CONTACT ADDRESS** Art History Dept, Univ of Massachusetts, Amherst, 325 Bartlett Hall, Amherst, MA 01003. **EMAIL** craighar@arthist.umass.edu

HARBUTT, FRASER J.
DISCIPLINE HISTORY **EDUCATION** Univ Otago, BA, 60, LLB, 60; Univ Auckland, LLM, 67; Univ Calif Berkeley, PhD, 76. **CAREER** Assoc prof **HONORS AND AWARDS** Stuart L. Bernath Mem Bk Prize, Soc Hist Am For Rel, 86. **RESEARCH** International history; United States diplomatic and political history; US-Soviet relations. **SELECTED PUBLICATIONS** Auth, The Iron Curtain: Churchill, America and the Origins of the Cold War. **CONTACT ADDRESS** Dept History, Emory Univ, 221 Bowden Hall, 561 Kilgo Cir, Atlanta, GA 30322-1950. **EMAIL** fharbut@emory.edu

HARCAVE, SIDNEY SAMUEL
PERSONAL Born 09/12/1916, Washington, DC, w, 1947 **DISCIPLINE** HISTORY **EDUCATION** City Col New York, BS, 37; Univ Chicago, PhD(hist), 43. **CAREER** Foreign affairs analyst, Foreign Broadcast Intelligence Serv, 42-44; res analyst, Off Strategic Serv, 44-45 & US Dept State, 45-46; instr hist, Univ Wyo, 46-47; asst prof, Champlain Col, State Univ NY, 47-50 & 51-53; from asst prof to assoc prof, 53-57, chmn dept, 56-59 & 60-65, div soc sci, 56-59, dir Russ & East Europ Prog, 70-73, prof, 57-81, Emer Prof Hist, State Univ NY, Binghamton, 81-, Hon fel, Yale Univ, 46; Soc Sci Res Coun fel, 46, grant-in-aid, 57; res assoc, Russ Res Ctr, Harvard Univ, 50-51; consult, Ford Found, 56-59; Inter-Univ Comt Travel Grants travel grant, 57 & mem final selection comt, Soviet exchange prog, 62; vis prof, Univ Mich, 62. **MEMBERSHIPS** AHA **RESEARCH** Russian and modern European history. **SELECTED PUBLICATIONS** Auth, Russia: A History, Lippincott, 1st ed, 52, 4th ed, 59, 6th ed, 68; Structure and Functioning of the Lower Party Organs of the Soviet Union, US Air Force 54; The Revolution of 1848, Russ Rev, 7/55; coauth, The Transformation of Russian Society, Harvard Univ, 60; ed, Readings in Russian History, Crowell, 62; auth, Years of the Golden Cockerel, Macmillan, 68; The Russian Revolution of 1905, Collier, 70; auth, The Hessen Redaction of the Witte Memoirs, Jahrbucher fur Geschichte Osteuropas 36, 88; trans, ed, The Memoirs of Count Witte, M. E. Sharpe, 90. **CONTACT ADDRESS** 20 Fuller Hollow Rd, Binghamton, NY 13903.

HARDIN, JOHN ARTHUR
PERSONAL Born 09/18/1948, Louisville, KY, m, 1973, 1 child **DISCIPLINE** HISTORY **EDUCATION** Bellarmine College, BA 1970; Fisk Univ, MA 1972; Univ of Michigan, PhD 1989. **CAREER** Univ of Louisville, lecturer 1972-84; KY State Univ, asst prof 1976-84, area coord 1978-80; Univ of KY, visiting asst prof 1980-81; Eastern WA Univ, asst prof 1984-90, assoc prof 1990-91; Western KY University, assoc professor, 91-97, assistant dean, Potter College of Arts, Humanities and Social Sciences, 97-. **HONORS AND AWARDS** Lenihan Awd for Comm Serv Bellarmine Col 1969; Three Univ Fellowship Fisk Univ 1970-72; J Pierce Scholarship Univ of MI Dept of History 1976; Distinguished Alumni Gallery Bellarmine Col 1979-80; Pres Awd, Natl Council For Black Studies-Region X (1987); **MEMBERSHIPS** Mem exec comm KY Assoc of Teachers of History 1976-80, 1991-; state dir Phi Beta Sigma Frat Inc 1981-83; club pres Frankfort Kiwanis Club 1983-84; mem KY Historic Preservation Review Bd 1983-84, Publ Advisory Comm Kentucky Historical Soc 1983-84, Natl Council on Black Studies 1984-, KY Historical Soc 1984-; NAACP, 1984-; editorial advisory board member, Filson Club History Quarterly, 1989-92; life member, Phi Beta Sigma, 1980-; member, KY Oral History Commission, 1995-03; member, Phi Alpha Theta History Honor Society. **SELECTED PUBLICATIONS** author, Onward and Upward: A Centennial History of Kentucky State University 1886-1986, author, Fifty Years of Segregation: Black Higher Education in Kentucky, 1904-1954. **CONTACT ADDRESS** Potter College of Arts, Humanities & Social Sciences, Western Kentucky Univ, 1 Big Red Way, Bowling Green, KY 42101-3576. **EMAIL** john.hardin@wku.edu

HARDIN, STEPHEN L.
PERSONAL Born 01/13/1953, McKinney, TX, m, 1991, 2 children **DISCIPLINE** HISTORY **EDUCATION** Southwest Tex State Univ, BA, 76; MA, 85; Tex Christian Univ, PhD, 89. **CAREER** Sr res fel, Tex State Hist Asn, 88-90; Chief Historian, Old San Antonio Road Project, State Dept of Highways and Public Transportation, 90-91; instr, The Victoria Col, 91-; paid consult for "The Real West" documentary series, Arts and En-

tertainment Network; paid consult for "The Alamo," American Heritage Magazine and the Arts and Entertainment Network. **HONORS AND AWARDS** T.R. Fehrenbach Awd, 94; Summerfield G. Roberts Awd, 94; listed in Men of Achievement, Int Biog Ctr; Westerners Int Co-Founders Book Awd, 94; Certificate of Merit, Am Asn for State and Local Hist, 95; listed in Who's Who in the S and Southwest, 95-96; Kate Broocks Bates Awd, 96; listed in Who's Who Among America's Teachers, 96; fel of the Grady McWhiney Res Found, 98. **MEMBERSHIPS** Tex State Historical Asn, Phi Alpha Theta, Int Hist Honor Soc, Western Hist Asn, Am Military Inst, Company of Military Historians, Alamo Battlefield Asn, The Hist Soc. **RESEARCH** Military History, Texas, Old South, Spanish Borderlands. **SELECTED PUBLICATIONS** Auth, The Texas Rangers, Osprey Pub Co. (London, Eng), 91; auth, Texian Iliad: A Military History of the Texas Revolution 1835-1836, Univ of Tex Press (Austin, TX), 94; auth, Lone Star: The Republic of Texas, Discovery Enterprises, Ltd. (Carlisle, MA), 98. **CONTACT ADDRESS** Dept Soc Sci, Victoria Col, 2200 E Red River St, Victoria, TX 77901-4442. **EMAIL** slhardin@vc.cc.tx.us

HARDING, VINCENT
PERSONAL Born 07/25/1931, New York, NY, m **DISCIPLINE** HISTORY **EDUCATION** City Coll NYork, BA 1952; Columbia, MS 1953; Univ of Chgo, MA 1956; PhD 1965. **CAREER** Seventh Day Adventist Church Chicago, sply pastor 55-57; Woodlawn Mennoite Church Chicago, lay assoc pastor 57-61; Mennonite Central Com Atlanta, southern rep 61-64; Spelman Coll Atlanta, asst prof History, dept chmn History Social Sciences 65-69; Martin Luther King Jr Center, dir 68-70; Institute of Black World, Atlanta, GA, dir 69-74; Blackside, Inc, Boston, MA, academic adviser to "Eyes on the Prize" documentary, 85-90; Iliff School of Theology, professor, 81-. **HONORS AND AWARDS** Kent fellow Soc Rel in Hghr Edn; Honorary Doctorate, Lincoln University, Swarthmore Coll, 1987; Member, Howard Thurman Trust, 1990; Humanist of the Year, Colorado Council of the Humanities, 1991. **SELECTED PUBLICATIONS** Must walls divide, 1965; There Is a River, 1981; Hope and History, 1990; contrib ed, mem, ed bd, Concern Christianity & Crisis Christian Country; also poems, short stories, articles, sermons to professional pubs. **CONTACT ADDRESS** Relig, Social Change, Iliff Sch of Theol, 2201 S University Blvd, Denver, CO 80210.

HARDWICK, SUSAN WILEY
PERSONAL Born 05/09/1945, Greensburg, PA, m, 1987, 3 children **DISCIPLINE** GEOGRAPHY **EDUCATION** Slippery Rock State Univ, Pa, BS, 68; Calif State Univ, Chico, MA, 76; Univ Calif, Davis, PhD, 86. **CAREER** Instr and chair, Dept Earth Scis, Cosummes River Col, Sacramento, Ca, 74-86; asst and assoc prof to prof, Calif State Univ, Chico, 86-97; prof of Geography and assoc Dir, Gilbert M. Grosvenor Center for Geographic Educ, Southwest Tex State Univ, San Marcos, 97-. **HONORS AND AWARDS** Prof Achievement Awd, Calif State Univ, Chico, 91, 94; Distinguished Univ Educ Awd, Nat Coun for Geographic Educ, 94; Outstanding Teaching Awd, Calif State Univ, Chico, 94; Outstanding Professor Awd, Calif State Univ, Chico, 95; Statewide Outstanding Prof Awd, Calif State Univ System, 95; nominee, Outstanding Prof of the United States, Carnegie Found, 97; Outstanding Fac Service Awd, Southwest Tex State Univ Grad Forum, 99; Tex Telecommunications Infrastructure Fund grant, 99; U.S. Dept of Educ Fund for the Improvement of Post-Secondary Educ, 98-2001; Nat Sci Found, advisory bd mem, 98-2001. **MEMBERSHIPS** Int Geographical Union, Commission on Geographic Educ, Lisbon and Oporto, Portugal; Int Coun on Open and Distance Learning, Melbourne, Australia; Tex Int Educ Exchange; Tahoe-Baikal Inst; Int Asn for the Scholarly Study of Russian Old Ritualism in the U.S. and Russia; Int Geography Honor Soc, Gamma Theta Upsilon; Asn of Am Geographers; Nat Coun for Geographic Educ; Nat Coun for the social Studies; Education 2000: The Nat Geography Standards Project; Nat Assessment of Educ Progs; Nat Geographic Soc; The Soc of Women Geographers; Nat Coun for the Social Studies; The Nat Honor Soc of Phi Kappa Phi; Golden Key Nat Honor Soc; Nat League of Am Penwomen. **SELECTED PUBLICATIONS** Auth, "Going the Distance: Post-Graduate Educational Reform in Geographic Education," Open Praxis: The Int J of Distance Learning, Vol 1 (98): 18-22; co-ed with Fred Shelley, invited co-eds of special issue "Gender in Geographic Education" in The J of Geography (2000); coauth, "Teaching Courses Internationally," The J of Geography in Higher Educ (2000); coauth, "Understanding Gender and Sex Differences in Geographic Education," The J of Geography (2000); auth, "Humanizing the Technology Landscape Through a Collaborative Pedagogy," The J of Geography in Higher Educ (2000); auth, "California's Emerging Russian Homeland," Chapter in Homelands in the United States, R. Nostrand and L. Estaville, eds, Baltimore: The Johns Hopkins Univ Press (2000); auth, "Russian Acculturation in Sacramento," Chapter in Race, Space, and Place, K. Berry, ed, Reno: Univ of Nevada Press (2000); auth, "Contextualizing Research on Local Landscapes through Geographic Fieldwork," Chapter in Looking at the Land, Darrell Napton, ed, Placitas, N Mex: The Center for Am Places (2000); auth, Mythic Galveston: Re-Inventing People and Place on the Texas Gulf Coast, Baltimore: The Johns Hopkins Univ Press (2000). **CONTACT ADDRESS** Dept Geography and Planning, Southwest Texas State Univ, 601 Univ Dr, San Marcos, TX 78666. **EMAIL** SH19@swt.edu

HARDY, B. CARMON
PERSONAL Born 12/24/1934, Vernal, UT, m, 1954, 5 children **DISCIPLINE** HISTORY **EDUCATION** Wash State Univ, BA, 57; Brigham Young Univ, MA, 59; Wayne State Univ, PhD, 63. **CAREER** Asst prof, Brigham Young Univ, 61-66; Asst Prof to Full Prof, 66-98, Prof Emeritus, Calif State Univ, 98-. **RESEARCH** American Constitutional history; American intellectual history; history of religion. **SELECTED PUBLICATIONS** Auth, Solemn Covenant: Mormonism's Polygamous Passage, Univ of Ill Press, 92; The Sonora, Sinaloa and Chihuahua Railroad, Jahrbuch Fur Geschichte Von Staat, Mirtshcaft Und Gesellschaft Lateinamericas, 75; The Schoolboy God: A Mormon American Model, J of Religious Hist, 76; The Third Amendment, The Bill of Rights: A Lively Heritage, Va State Libr and Archives, 87; Early Mormon Polygamy in Mexico and Canada: A Legal and Historiographical Review, Univ of Alberta Press, 90. **CONTACT ADDRESS** History Dept, California State Univ, Fullerton, Fullerton, CA 92634.

HARDY, CHARLES, III
PERSONAL Born 12/31/1951, Norwalk, CN, m, 1975, 2 children **DISCIPLINE** HISTORY **EDUCATION** Temple Univ, BA, 76; PhD, 89. **CAREER** Vis instr to adj prof, Temple Univ, 82-89; asst prof to prof, West Chester Univ, 90-; fac, Columbia Univ, 95-98; fac, Scribe Video Center, 97-; adj prof, Univ of the Arts, 00. **HONORS AND AWARDS** Public Radio Prog Awd, Corp for Pub Broadcasting, 83; Audio Fels, Pa Coun on the Arts, 84, 88, 90; Red Ribbon Educ Prog, Am Film and Video Asn, 90; Sara Leeds Miller Doctoral Awd, Temple Univ, 90; Fel, Salzburg Sem, 95; Biennial Nonprint Media Awd, Oral Hist Asn, 99. **MEMBERSHIPS** Am Soc for Environ Hist; Assoc of Independents in Radio; Oral Hist Assoc; Org of Am Hist. **RESEARCH** Aural history, American civil religion, regional environmental history. **SELECTED PUBLICATIONS** Auth, Philadelphia All the Time: Sounds of the Quaker City, 1896 to 1947, Spinning Disc Prod, (Rydal, PA), 92; prod, Charles Hardy's Popular Culture Show, WUHY, 80-84; prod, I Remember When: Times Gone But Not Forgotten, WHYY-FM, 83; prod, Goin' North: Tales of the Great Migration, Am Public Radio, 94; prod, Stories from the Collection, Columbia Univ Oral Hist Res Office, 98; auth, All Aboard for Philadelphia, Hist Soc of Pa, 97; coprod, I Can almost See the Lights of Home: A Field Trip to Harlan County, Kentucky, Jour of Multimedia Hist, Vol 2, 99. **CONTACT ADDRESS** Dept Hist, West Chester Univ of Pennsylvania, 700 S High St, West Chester, PA 19383-0003. **EMAIL** chardy@wcupa.edu

HARE, JOHN ELLIS
PERSONAL Born 04/30/1933, Toronto, ON, Canada, m, 1954, 7 children **DISCIPLINE** SOCIAL HISTORY & LITERATURE OF FRENCH CANADA **EDUCATION** Laval Univ, BPhilos, 55, MA, 56 & 62, PhD(ling), 70. **CAREER** Instr educ & English, LavalUniv, 59-66; asst prof, 66-71, assoc prof, 71-80, Prof Can Studies, Univ Ottawa, 80- **HONORS AND AWARDS** Marie Tremaine Medal, Can Bibliog Soc, 73. **RESEARCH** Social and cultural history of French Canada. **SELECTED PUBLICATIONS** Coauth, Les Imprimes dans le Bas-Canada, 1801-1810, Montreal, P.U.M., 67; auth, La Pensee socio-politique au Quebec, 1784-1812, Ottawa, Editions de l'Universite d'Ottawa, 77; coauth, Histoire de la ville de Quebec 1608-1871, Montreal, Boreal/Musee canadien des civilisations, 87. **CONTACT ADDRESS** Dept of Can Studies, Univ of Ottawa, Pavillon Simard, local 200, C P 450, Succ A, Ottawa, ON, Canada K1N 6N5.

HARGREAVES, MARY WILMA MASSEY
PERSONAL Born 03/01/1914, Erie, PA, m, 1940 **DISCIPLINE** HISTORY **EDUCATION** Bucknell Univ, AB, 35; Radcliffe Col, MA, 36, PhD, 51. **CAREER** Res asst, Baker Libr, Bus Sch, Harvard Univ, 37-39; res-ed/co-ed, proj dir, Henry Clay Papers, 52-79; asst prof, 64-69, assoc prof, 69-73, prof, 73-84, Prof Emer, 84- , Univ KY, 73-; Brookings Inst fel, 39-40; Phi Beta Kappa; Phi Alpha Theta; Sigma Tau Delta; Hallam prof, 75-77. **HONORS AND AWARDS** Saloutos Awd, 94 **MEMBERSHIPS** Agr Hist Soc (pres, 75-76); Orgn Am Historians; AHA: Southern Hist Asn; Econ Hist Asn; SHEAR; KHS. **RESEARCH** Agricultural history of the Northern Great Plains; dryland agriculture; land utilization. **SELECTED PUBLICATIONS** Auth, Dry Farming in the Northern Great Plains, Harvard Univ, 57; Presidency of John Quincy Adams, Kansas, 85; Dry Farming in the Northern Great Plains, Readjustment Years, 1920-1990, Kansas, 93; assoc ed, Papers of Henry Clay, Univ Ky, Vols I, II & III, 59, 61 & 63; co-ed, Vols IV, V & VI, 72, 73 & 81; auth, The Durum Wheat Controversy, 68, Women in the agricultural settlement of the Northern Plains, 76, Land-use planning in response to drought: Experience of the thirties, 76 & Dry-farming movement in retrospect, 77, Agr Hist; Rural Education in the Northern Plains Frontier, Jour of West, 79; auth, "Dry Farming Alias Scientific Farming," Agricultural History, 48. **CONTACT ADDRESS** 237 Cassidy Ave, Lexington, KY 40502-2303.

HARLAN, LOUIS R.
PERSONAL Born 07/13/1922, Clay Co, MS, m, 1947, 2 children **DISCIPLINE** AMERICAN HISTORY **EDUCATION** Emory Univ, BA, 43; Vanderbilt Univ, MA, 48; Johns Hopkins Univ, PhD, 55. **CAREER** From asst prof to assoc prof hist, ETex State Col, 50-59; from assoc prof to prof, Univ Cincinnati, 59-66; vis prof, 66-67, Prof Hist, Univ MD, College Park, 67-. Am Coun Learned Soc fel, 63-64; Guggenheim fel, 75; Walter Lynwood Fleming lectr southern hist, La State Univ, 77; Ctr for Advan Study in Behav Sci fel, 80-81. **HONORS AND AWARDS** Bancroft Prize, Am Coun Learned Soc, 73. **MEMBERSHIPS** AHA; Orgn Am Historians; Southern Hist Asn; Asn Study Afro-Am Life & Hist; fel Soc Am Hist. **RESEARCH** Recent United States history; Afro-American history; Southern history since 1865. **SELECTED PUBLICATIONS** **CONTACT ADDRESS** Dept of Hist, Univ of Maryland, Col Park, College Park, MD 20742.

HARMOND, RICHARD PETER
PERSONAL Born Bronx, NY **DISCIPLINE** AMERICAN HISTORY & HISTORY OF SCIENCE **EDUCATION** Fordham Univ, BA, 51; Columbia Univ, MA, 54, PhD(hist), 66. **CAREER** Assoc prof hist, St John's Univ, NY, 57-. **MEMBERSHIPS** Orgn Am Historians; Soc Hist Technol. **RESEARCH** Social history; local history. **SELECTED PUBLICATIONS** Coauth, Long Island As America: A Documentary History, Kennibat Press, 77; Auth, The Recollections of Nathaniel S. Prime, J Long Island Hist, 81; Technology in the Twentieth Century, Kendall Hunt, 83; Counting Board, Altar and Vista: The Bradys and Inisfada, New York Irish, 87; Robert Roosevelt and the Early Conservation Movement, Theodore Roosevelt Assoc Journal XIV, 88; JP Morgan, St James Guide to Bio, St James Press, 91; Robert Cushman Murphy: Environmental Issues on Long Island, Long Island Hist J, Vol. VIII, 95; co-ed, A Biographical Dictionary of North American Environmentalists and Naturalists, Greenwood Press, 97; coauth, "Literary Environmentalists Before Silent Spring, 1945-1960," in Patrick Murphy, ed, Literaturer of Nature, Fitzroy Dearborn, 98. **CONTACT ADDRESS** Dept of History, St. John's Univ, 8000 Utopia Pky, Jamaica, NY 11439-0002.

HARNER, JOHN P.
PERSONAL Born 01/06/1963, Miami, OK, m, 1989, 1 child **DISCIPLINE** GEOLOGY **EDUCATION** Penn State Univ, BS, 86; Ariz State Univ, MA, 93; Ariz State Univ, PhD, 96. **CAREER** Asst Prof, Univ Colo, 97-. **MEMBERSHIPS** Asn of Am Geog. **RESEARCH** Cultural landscape, Mexico, urban geography. **SELECTED PUBLICATIONS** Auth, Historical-Cultural Continuity Between Sonora and Arizona, J of Cult Geog 15(2) (95): 17-33; auth, Continuity Amidst Change: Undocumented Mexican Migration to Arizona, The Prof Geog 47(4) (95): 399-411; coauth, Human Geography in Action, John Wily & Sons (New York), 98; auth, "Dependency and Development in the Copper Mining Region of Sonora, Mexico," Yearbk, Conf of Latin Americanist Geog 24 (98): 17-30; auth, "The Mexican Community in Scottsdale, Arizona," Yearbk, Conf of Latin Americanist Geog 25 (00). **CONTACT ADDRESS** Dept Geog, Univ of Colorado, Colorado Springs, 1420 Austin Bluffs, Colorado Springs, CO 80918. **EMAIL** jharner@mail.uccs.edu

HARNETTY, PETER
PERSONAL Born 06/06/1927, Brighton, England, m, 1956, 1 child **DISCIPLINE** MODERN INDIAN HISTORY **EDUCATION** Univ BC, BA, 53; Harvard Univ, AM, 54, PhD(hist), 58. **CAREER** From instr hist to assoc prof, 58-71, head, Dept Asian Studies, 75-81, Prof Hist & Asian Studies, Univ BC, 71-, Can Coun sr fel, 64-65 & 71-72; Nuffield Found fel, 64-65; assoc ed, Pac Affairs, 66-69 & 78-; pres, Shastri Indo-Can Inst, 70-71; Soc Sci & Humanities Res Coun of Can sr fel, 80-81. **MEMBERSHIPS** Asn Asian Studies; Econ Hist Asn; Can Soc Asian Studies; Hist Asn. **RESEARCH** India; modern; social and economic history. **SELECTED PUBLICATIONS** Auth, Imperialism and Free Trade: Lancashire and India in the Mid-Nineteenth Century. **CONTACT ADDRESS** Dept of Asian Studies, Univ of British Columbia, 3026 W 24th Ave, Vancouver, BC, Canada V6N 2K2. **EMAIL** harnetty@interchange.ubc.ca

HARP, STEPHEN L.
PERSONAL Born 05/06/1964, La Grange, IN, m, 1989, 2 children **DISCIPLINE** HISTORY **EDUCATION** Manchester Col, BA, 86; Ind Univ, MA, 88; MA, 88; PhD, 93. **CAREER** Ed asst, Am Hist Rev, 92-93; Asst prof to assoc prof, Univ Akron, 93-. **HONORS AND AWARDS** DAAD Fel, 90-91; Spencer Found Fel, 94, 97; NEH Fel, 99-00. **MEMBERSHIPS** AHA; Soc for Fr Hist Studies; W Soc for Fr Hist; Phi Alpha Theta, Hist of Educ soc. **RESEARCH** History of Education, Nationalism, Regionalism, Tourism, Consumerism, Cultural History. **SELECTED PUBLICATIONS** Auth, Learning to be Loyal: Primary Schooling as Nation Building in Alsace and Lorraine, 1850-1940, N Il Univ Pr, 98; auth, Marketing Michelin: A Cultural History of Twentieth-Century France, (forthcoming). **CONTACT ADDRESS** Dept Hist, Univ of Akron, 302 Buchtel Mall, Akron, OH 44325-0001. **EMAIL** sharp@uakron.edu

HARPER, KATHERINE
PERSONAL Born Detroit, MI **DISCIPLINE** ART HISTORY **EDUCATION** UCLA, PhD, Ancient India and Hindu goddesses. 77. **CAREER** Prof. **RESEARCH** Art History of Zen Buddhism, Islamic Art and the Arts of Prehistory from Europe to Ancient India, Art Hist of India. **SELECTED PUBLICA-**

TIONS Published widely on the subject of Ancient Goddesses including a book entitled, "The Iconography of the Saptamatrikas: Seven Hindu Goddesses of Spiritual Transformation, " (Lewiston, New York: The Edwin Mellen Press, 1989; ed, The Roots of Tantra, Albany State Univ, NY press, 01. **CONTACT ADDRESS** Dept of Art and Art History, Loyola Marymount Univ, 7900 Loyola Blvd, Los Angeles, CA 90045. **EMAIL** kharper@lmumail.lmu.edu

HARRELL, DAVID E.
PERSONAL Born 02/22/1930, Jacksonville, FL, m, 5 children **DISCIPLINE** HISTORY **EDUCATION** David Lipscomb Col, BA, 54; Vanderbilt Univ, MA, 58; PhD, 62. **CAREER** Teaching fel, Vanderbilt Univ, 56-60; asst to assoc prof, E Tenn State Univ, 61-66; assoc prof, Univ of Okla, 66-67; assoc prof, Univ of Ga, 67-70; prof, Univ of Ala, 70-90; Daniel F Breeden Eminent Scholar, Auburn Univ, 90-. **HONORS AND AWARDS** Phi Beta Delta; Phi Alpha Theta; McClung Awd, 66; Author's Awd, Miss Hist Rev, 69; Ramsdell Awd Comm, 76-77; Fulbright Lectr, India, 76-77; Rockefeller lectr, 84; Lyceum lectr, 86; Hubert Humphrey Fel, 94-95; Special Ambassadorial Citation, US Ambassador to India, 95; Distinguished US Info Agency Lectr, 96; Who's Who in the World. **MEMBERSHIPS** AHA; Org of Am Hist; Southern Hist Assoc; Am Soc of Church Hist; Am Acad of Relig; Fulbright Alumni Assoc; Disciples of Christ Hist Soc. **RESEARCH** American Religious History of the Twentieth century, American charismatic, pentecostal, fundamental religious movements, revivalists, World charistmatic, fundamentalist religious leaders. **SELECTED PUBLICATIONS** Auth, Quest for a Christian America: A Social History of the Disciples of Christ, Disciples of Christ Hist Soc, (Nashville), 66; auth, White Sects and Black Men in the Recent South, Vanderbilt Univ Pr, (Nashville), 71; auth, The Social Sources of Division in the Disciples of Christ: A Social History of the Disciples of Christ, Publishing Sys, (Athens, GA), 73; auth, All Things Are Possible: The Healing and Charismatic Revivals in Modern America, Ind Univ Pr, (Bloomington), 75; auth, Oral Roberts: An American Life, Ind Univ Pr, (Bloomington), 85; auth, Pat Robertson: A Personal, Religious and Political Portrait, Harper and Row, (San Francisco), 87; auth, "Christian Primitivism and Modernization in the Stone-Campbell Movement", The Primitive Church in the Modern World, Univ of IL Pr, (95): 109-120; auth, "Pentecost at Prime Time", Christian Hist XV.1, (96): 52-54; auth, "The Disciples of Christ - Churches of Christ Tradition", Caring and Curing, eds Ronald L Numbers and Darrell W Admundsen, Johns Hopkins Univ Pr, (Baltimore, 98): 376-396; auth, The Churches of Christ in the Twentieth Century: Homer Hailey's Personal Journey of Faith, Univ of Ala Pr, (Tuscaloosa), 00. **CONTACT ADDRESS** Dept Hist, Auburn Univ, 310 Thach Hall, Auburn, AL 36849-5207. **EMAIL** harrede@auburn.edu

HARRIGAN, PATRICK JOSEPH
PERSONAL Born 07/26/1941, Detroit, MI, m, 1966, 1 child **DISCIPLINE** MODERN HISTORY **EDUCATION** Univ Detroit, AB, 63; Univ Mich, AM, 64, PhD(hist), 70. **CAREER** Lectr hist, Univ Mich, 68-69; asst prof, 69-75, assoc prof, 75-82, Prof Hist, Univ Waterloo, 82-, Res fel, Shelby Cullom Davis Ctr Hist Studies, Princeton Univ, 71-72. **MEMBERSHIPS** Fr Hist Soc; Can Asn Univ Teachers. **RESEARCH** Social history, French education and the Church in the 19th century; and Canadian schooling. **SELECTED PUBLICATIONS** Auth, Mobility, Elites, and Education in French Society of the Second Empire, Waterloo: Wilfrid Laurier UP, 80; coed, with D.N. Bakers, eds., The Making of Frenchmen, Waterloo: Historical Reflections Press, 80; coauth, School, State and Society: The Growth of Elementary Schooling in Nineteenth-Century France, Ann Arbor: University of Michigan Press, 91; auth, The Development of a Corps of public School Teachers in Canada 1870-1980, History of Education Quarterly, 32, 92, 483-522; auth, The Detroit Tigers: Club and Community, 1945-1995, Toronto: UTP, 97; auth, Women Teachers and the Schooling of Girls in France: Recent Historiographical Trends, French Historical Studies, 21.4, 593-610. **CONTACT ADDRESS** Dept of History, Univ of Waterloo, 200 University Ave W, Waterloo, ON, Canada N2L 3G1. **EMAIL** harrigan@watarts.uwaterloo.ca

HARRINGTON, ANN M.
DISCIPLINE HISTORY **EDUCATION** Claremont, PhD, 77. **CAREER** Hist, Loyola Univ. **RESEARCH** 19th-20th century Japanese history. **SELECTED PUBLICATIONS** Auth, Japan's Hidden Christians, Chicago: Loyola UP, 93; Women and Higher Education in the Japanese Empire, J Asian Hist, 87; Meiji Imperialism: Not Based on Preordained Design in Japan Examined: Perspectives on Modern Japanese History, Honolulu: Univ Hawaii Press, 83. **CONTACT ADDRESS** Fine Arts Dept, Loyola Univ, Chicago, 6525 N. Sheridan Rd., Chicago, IL 60626. **EMAIL** aharri1@orion.it.luc.edu

HARRINGTON, DANIEL JOSEPH
PERSONAL Born 07/19/1940, Arlington, MA **DISCIPLINE** BIBLICAL STUDIES, JEWISH HISTORY **EDUCATION** Boston Col, BA, 64, MA, 65; Harvard Univ, PhD(Oriental lang), 70; Weston Sch Theol, BD, 71. **CAREER** PROF NEW TESTAMENT, WESTON JESUIT SCH THEOL, 72-; Vis lectr Old Testament, Harvard Divinity Sch, 72-; ed, New Testament Abstracts, 72-; pastoral assoc, St Agnes Church, Mass, 72-; coordr, New Testament Colloquium, Boston, 77-; trustee, Holy Cross Col, Mass, 78- **MEMBERSHIPS** Cath Bibl Asn of Am, pres 85-86; Soc Bibl Lit; Soc New Testament Studies. **SELECTED PUBLICATIONS** Auth, The Gospel According to Matthew, Collegeville: Liturgical, 83; The Gospel According to Mark, NY: Sadlier, 83; The Gospel According to Luke, NY: Sadlier, 83; Pentecost 2, Series B, Philadelphia: Fortress, 85; The New Testament: A Bibliography, Wilmington: Glazier, 85; Targum Jonathan of the Former Prophets, Wilmington: Glazier, 87; The Maccabean Revolt: Anatomy of a Biblical Revolution, Wilmington: Glazier, 88; John's Thought and Theology: An Introduction, Wilmington: Glazier, 90; The Gospel of Matthew, Collegeville: Liturgical, 91; Paul on the Mystery of Israel, Collegeville: Liturgical, 92; How to Read the Gospels, Hyde Park, NY: New City Press, 96; Wisdom Texts from Oumran, London: Routledge, 96; Paul's Prison Letters, Hyde Park, NY: New City Press, 97; Romans. The Good News According to Paul, Hyde Park, NY: New City Press, 98; and author of many other articles in directories, encyclopedias, scholarly journals, and other publications; auth, Who Is Jesus?, Franklin, WI: Sheed & Ward, 99; auth, Invitation to the Apocrypha, Grand Rapids, MI: Erdmans, 99; auth, Why Do We Suffer?, Franklin, WI: Sheed & Ward, 00. **CONTACT ADDRESS** Bibl Studies Dept, Weston Jesuit Sch of Theol, 3 Phillips Place, Cambridge, MA 02138-3495. **EMAIL** dharrington@wjst.edu

HARRINGTON, JESSE DREW
PERSONAL Born 11/21/1933, Tallahassee, AL **DISCIPLINE** ANCIENT & AMERICAN HISTORY **EDUCATION** Samford Univ, BA, 57; Univ Ky, MA, 63, PhD(hist), 70. **CAREER** Instr, Georgetown Col, 65-68; Prof Hist, Western KY Univ, 68- **MEMBERSHIPS** Asn Ancient Historians; Am Philol Asn; AHA. **RESEARCH** Comparative study of slavery in the ancient world and the antebellum South; early Roman Empire; Greek history and historiography. **SELECTED PUBLICATIONS** Auth, Cassius Dio as a military historian, Acta Classica, Vol XX, 77; William L Burton: Cypress millionaire and philanthropist, La Hist (in prep); The battle of Actium: A study in historiography, Ancient World (in prep). **CONTACT ADDRESS** Dept of Hist, Western Kentucky Univ, Bowling Green, KY 42101.

HARRINGTON, KEVIN
PERSONAL Born 07/14/1944, Rochester, NY, m, 1968 **DISCIPLINE** HISTORY OF ARCHITECTURE **EDUCATION** Colgate Univ, BA 67; Cornell Univ, MA 74, PhD 81. **CAREER** IL Inst Technology, inst, asst prof, assoc prof, prof, 78-. **HONORS AND AWARDS** Graham Foun Fel; 4 NEH Gnts. **MEMBERSHIPS** SAH; CAA; VAF; ACSA; NTHP; CAC. **RESEARCH** Chicago architecture and urbanism; Mies Van der Rohe. **SELECTED PUBLICATIONS** Auth, Chicago's Famous Buildings, co-ed, 4th ed, Chicago IL, Univ Chicago Press, 93; forthcoming, Mies Vander Rohe's design of the IIT Campus, 5th edition, and an electronic version of Chicago's famous buildings; auth, Changing ideas in architecture in the Encyclopedie, 1750-1776, Voll Res Press (Ann Arbor, MI), 85. **CONTACT ADDRESS** IIT Center, Illinois Inst of Tech, Chicago, IL 60616. **EMAIL** kevinhar@charlie.iit.edu

HARRIS, ANN SUTHERLAND
PERSONAL Born 11/04/1937, Cambridge, England, d, 1 child **DISCIPLINE** ART HISTORY **EDUCATION** Univ London, Courtauld Inst, BA, 61; PhD, 65. **CAREER** Asst lectr, Art Dept, Univ of Leeds, 64-65; asst lectr, Barnard & Columbia Col; asst prof, Dept of Art & Archeol, 66-71, adjunct prof, Columbia Univ, 80; vis lectr, Dept of Art Hist, Yale Univ, 72-73; asst prof, Art Dept, Hunter Col, CUNY, 71-73; from asst prof to assoc prof, Art Dept, SUNY at Albany, 73-77; vis assoc prof, Inst of Fine Arts, NYU, 74; Arthur Kittredge Watson Chair for Acad Affairs, Metropolitan Museum of Art, 77-81; part-time member of liberal arts fac, Juilliard School, 78-83; Amon Carter Distinguished vis prof of Art Hist, Univ Tx at Arlington, 82; Mellon prof of Art Hist, Univ Pittsburgh, 84-; adjunct prof, Art Dept, Carnegie-Mellon Univ, 89; Eleanor Tufts Distinguished vis prof, Southern Methodist Univ, 93. **HONORS AND AWARDS** Guggenheim Found Fel, 70-71; Ford Found Fac Fel, 75-76; Andrew W. Mellon Fel, Metropolitan Museum of Art, 77; Mademoiselle Magazine Woman of the Year, 77; NEA Museum Professional Fel, 81; Honorary Doctor of Arts, Eastern Mich Univ, 81; Pittsburgh YWCA Woman of the Year in the Arts, 86; Sr Res Fel, Nat Endowment for the Humanities, 81-82; guest scholar, J. Paul Getty Museum, 88; Honorary Doctor of Humanities, Atlanta Col of Art, 90. **MEMBERSHIPS** Col Art Asn; Women's Caucus for Art. **RESEARCH** Italian and French 16th and 17th century painting, drawing sculpture; women artists 1150-1800 and post 1950; images of women. **SELECTED PUBLICATIONS** Andrea Sacchi, Princeton, 77; selected drawings of G. L. Bernjni, New York, 77; coauth, The Collections of the Detroit Institute of Arts: Italian, French and English Drawings and Watercolors, Hudson Hills Press, 92; auth, Cool Waves and Hot Blocks: The Art of Edna Andrade, Pa Acad of the Fine Arts, 93; The Katalan Collection of Italian Drawings, 95-96; Nicolas Poussin dessinateur, Nicolas Poussin 1594-1665, Galeries nationales du Grand Palais, 94-95; Ludovico, Agostino, Annibale: ..l'abbiam fatta tutti noi, Academia Clementina, Atti e memorie, Nuova Serie, 94; Domenichino's Caccia di Diana: Art and Politics in Seicento Rome, Shope Talk, Studies in Art Hist for Seymour Slive, Harvard Univ, 95; Le mariage mystique de Sainte Catherine: attribution, commanditaire, iconographie, Nicolas Poussin (1594-1665), Actes du colloque..Octobre, 1994, 96; Artemisia Gentileschi: The Literate Illiterate or Learning from Example, Docere, Delectare, Movere: Affetti e Rettorica nel Linguaggio Artistico nel Primo Barocco Romano, Rome and the Biblioteca Hertziana, 97; Guido Reni's First Thoughts, Master Drawings Vol 36, 98. **CONTACT ADDRESS** Univ of Pittsburgh, Frick Fine Arts Bldg, Pittsburgh, PA 15260. **EMAIL** asht@pitt.edu

HARRIS, J. WILLIAM
DISCIPLINE HISTORY **EDUCATION** Johns Hopkins Univ, PhD. **CAREER** Assoc prof to prof, 85-, ch, dept Hist, Univ NH. **HONORS AND AWARDS** Nat Hum Ctr fel; Charles Warren Ctr fel, Harvard Univ; Fulbright lectr, Ital, 97. **RESEARCH** Comparative social history of three Southern regions in the era of segregation. **SELECTED PUBLICATIONS** Auth, Plain Folk and Gentry in a Slave Society, 85; ed, Society and Culture in the Slave South, 92; auth, Deep Souths: Delta, Piedmont, and the Sea Island Society in the Age of Segregation (forthcoming). **CONTACT ADDRESS** Univ of New Hampshire, Durham, Durham, NH 03824. **EMAIL** jwharris@christa.unh.edu

HARRIS, JAMES F.
PERSONAL Born 09/29/1940, Cleveland, OH, m, 1963, 2 children **DISCIPLINE** MODERN EUROPEAN & GERMAN HISTORY **EDUCATION** Loyola Univ, Ill, BA, 62; Univ Wis, MS, 64, PhD(hist), 68. **CAREER** Instr hist, Univ Wis, 66-67; lectr, 67-68, Asst Prof Hist, Univ MD, College Park, 68- **MEMBERSHIPS** AHA **RESEARCH** German liberalism; the second empire in Germany, 1848-1914. **CONTACT ADDRESS** Dept of Hist, Univ of Maryland, Col Park, College Park, MD 20740. **EMAIL** jharris@deans.umd.edu

HARRIS, JANICE HUBBARD
PERSONAL Born 03/30/1943, Los Angeles, CA, m, 1966, 2 children **DISCIPLINE** BRITISH FICTION; WOMEN'S STUDIES; POST COLONIAL STUDIES **EDUCATION** Stanford Univ, AB, 65; Brown Univ, PhD, 73. **CAREER** Instr English, Tougaloo Col, 69-73; from asst prof English to prof, 75-, assoc dean arts sci, 83-84, dir univ honors prog, 82-86, dir women's studies, 95-99, Univ Wyo. **HONORS AND AWARDS** Danforth Teaching fel, 81. **MEMBERSHIPS** MLA; Nat Women's Studies Asn; Women's Caucus Mod Lang. **RESEARCH** Modern British fiction; women's studies; Post-Colonial Literatures. **SELECTED PUBLICATIONS** Auth, D H Lawrence and Kate Millett, Mass Rev, summer 74; Our mute, inglorious mothers, Midwest Quart, 4/75; Insight and experiment in D H Lawrence's early short fiction, Philol Quart, summer 76; Sexual antagonism in D H Lawrence's early leadership fiction, Mod Lang Studies, spring 77; The moulting of the plumed serpent, Mod Lang Quart, 3/79; Bushes, bears and the beast in the jungle, Studies in Short Fiction, spring 81; Gayl Jones' Corregidora, Frontiers, Vol 3; Feminist Representations of Wives and Work: An Almost Irreconcilable' Edwardian Debate, Women's Stud, 93; Challenging the Script of the Heterosexual Couple: Three Marriage Novels by May Sinclair, Papers on Lang & Lit, 93; Wifely Speech and Silence: Three Marriage Novels by H G Wells, Stud in Novel, 94; Edwardian Stories of Divorce, Rutgers Univ, 96. **CONTACT ADDRESS** Dept English, Univ of Wyoming, PO Box 3353, Laramie, WY 82071-3353. **EMAIL** jharris@vwyo.edu

HARRIS, JOSEPH E.
PERSONAL Born 07/02/1929, Rocky Mount, NC, m, 1958, 2 children **DISCIPLINE** AFRICAN HISTORY **EDUCATION** Howard Univ, BA, 52, MA, 56; Northwestern Univ, PhD(hist), 65. **CAREER** Prof hist, 75- , distinguished prof, 92- , Howard Univ. **HONORS AND AWARDS** Rockefeller Found fel, 72-74; Woodrow Wilson Ind Ctr for Scholars fel, 81-82; fel Nat Hum Ctr, 83; vis fel Ctr for Hum and Soc Sci, Williams Col, 89; res award, Black Management Forum, 92; James Kwegir Aggrey Medal awarded by Phelps-Stokes Fund, 94; Outstanding Author award, Howard Univ, 95; Troyer Steele Anderson Prize awarded by Am Hist Asn, 95; Howard Univ Scholar-in-Residence, Cape Town, 97; Caseley Hayford Awd by the African Heritage Studies Assoc, 94. **MEMBERSHIPS** UNESCO, Int Sci Comt for the Slave Route Project to Promote Intercultural Cooperation; Nat Mus of African Art, Smithsonian Inst; West African Res Asn; World Found for the Preservation of Goree, Senegal; Goree Hist Trust Soc; Hist Asn of Kenya; Coun of For Rel; Asn for the Study of Afro-American Life and Hist; Int African Stud Asn. **RESEARCH** African history; the African diaspora. **SELECTED PUBLICATIONS** Auth, The African Presence in Asia: Consequences of the East African Slave Trade, Northwestern Univ Press, 71; auth, East African Slave Trade and Repatriation in Kenya, Dept of History, Howard Univ, 74; auth, East African Slave Trade and Repatriation in Kenya, Dept of History, Howard Univ, 74; auth, Pillars in Ethiopian History: The William Leo Hansberry African History Notebook, Howard Univ Press, 77, (cloth), Howard Univ Press, 81, (paper editor); auth, Abolition and Repatriation in Kenya, East African Literature Bureau, Nairobi, Kenya, 77; auth, Recollections of James Juma Mbotela, East African Publishing House, Nairobi, Kenya, 77; auth, Africa and Africans as Seen By Classical Writ-

ers: The William Leo Hansberry African History Notebook, Howard Univ Press, 77 (cloth), Howard Univ Press, 81, (paper); auth, Repatriates and Refugees in a Colonial Society: The Case of Kenya, Howard Univ Press, 81; Rev, Eurasia and Africa: The Growth of Civilization to AD 200, Rand McNally, 91; rev, Africa in 1815 and the Partition of Africa, Rand McNally, 92; auth, Scope of the Dispersion to 1873, and, Return Movements and Outreach Activities to 1945, African Diaspora Map Series, Rand McNally, 90, 92; auth, Africans and Their History, New American Library, rev eds, 87, 98; ed and contrib, Global Dimensions of the African Diaspora, Howard Univ, rev ed, 93; auth, African-American Reactions to War in Ethiopia, 1936-1941, Louisiana, 94; auth, African-American Reactions to War in Ethiopia, 1936-1941, Louisiana State Univ Press, 94; auth, Global Dimensions of the African Diaspora, Howard Univ Press, 96. **CONTACT ADDRESS** Dept of History, Howard Univ, 2400 6th St NW, Washington, DC 20059-0002.

HARRIS, LAURILYN J.
DISCIPLINE THEATRE HISTORY AND DRAMATURGY **EDUCATION** Ind Univ, BA; Univ Iowa, MA, PhD. **CAREER** Prof & dir Grad Stud, Washington State Univ. **SELECTED PUBLICATIONS** Publ in, Theatre Res Int; Theatre Hist Stud; J Creative Behavior; Theatre J; Notable Women in the Amer Theatre; Theatre Annual; Theatre Southwest; Amer Theatre Companies; Stud in Amer Drama; Nineteenth Century Theatre Res; Confronting Tenn Williams' Streetcar Named Desire. **CONTACT ADDRESS** Dept of Music and Theater, Washington State Univ, Pullman, WA 99164-5300.

HARRIS, LESLIE M.
DISCIPLINE HISTORY **EDUCATION** Columbia Univ, BA, 88; Stanford Univ, MA, 89, PhD, 95. **CAREER** Asst prof **RESEARCH** Pre-Civil War African-American; American labor and social history. **SELECTED PUBLICATIONS** Auth, Creating the African-American Working Class in New York City, 1626-1863. **CONTACT ADDRESS** Dept History, Emory Univ, 221 Bowden Hall, 561 Kilgo Cir, Atlanta, GA 30322-1950. **EMAIL** lharr04@emory.edu

HARRIS, MICHAEL D.
PERSONAL Born Cleveland, OH, m, 2 children **DISCIPLINE** ART **EDUCATION** Bowling Green St Univ, BS, 71; Howard Univ, MFA, 79; Yale Univ, MA, 89, MPhil, 91, PhD, 96. **CAREER** Teacher, 71-73, Cleveland Pub Sch; artist-in-res, 77, Dougherty Co Public Sch; artist-in-res, gallery dir, 80-81, Neighborhood Arts Center, Atlanta; adj prof, 80-82, Atlanta Jr Col; adj prof, 84-85, Ga St Univ; tech svc ed, 88-90, Yale Univ; adj prof, 92, Wellesley Col; asst prof, 81-93, Morehouse Col; asst prof, 93-95, Ga St Univ Atlanta; asst prof, 95-, Univ NC Chapel Hill. **HONORS AND AWARDS** Artist Initiated Grant, 81, 83; Coors Found Grant, 84; Bronze Jubilee Awd, 85; Mayor's Fel, Atlanta, 87; Charles Dana Faculty Improvement Fel, 88-89; Foreign Lang Area Stud Fel, 89; Patricia Roberts Harris Fel, 89-92; Foreign Res Grant, 91-92; Nat Endow for the Humanities Faculty Grand Study Fel, 92; Andrew W Mellon Pre-Dissertation Fel, 93; art work purchased for Hartsfield Int Airport, 95. **MEMBERSHIPS** ACASA; CAA. **RESEARCH** Contemporary African art; African Amer art. **SELECTED PUBLICATIONS** Auth, Beyond Aesthetics: Visual Activism in Ile-Ife, the Yoruba Artist: New Theoretical Perspective on African Arts, Smithsonian Inst Press, 94; auth, Hand Me Downs: Innovation Within a Tradition, Afro-Amer Cultural Center, 95; auth, Crosscurrents: Ile-Ife, Washington, DC and the TransAfrican Artist, African Arts, 97; art, The Past is Prologue but is Parody and Pastiche Progress?: A Conversation, Int Rev of African Amer Art, 97; auth, Memories and Memorabilia, Art and Identity: Is Aunt Jemima Really a Black Woman, Third Text, 98. **CONTACT ADDRESS** Dept of Art, Univ of No Carolina, Chapel Hill, Box 3405, Chapel Hill, NC 27599-3405. **EMAIL** mharris1@email.unc.edu

HARRIS, MICHAEL WESLEY
PERSONAL Born 11/09/1945, Indianapolis, IN, d **DISCIPLINE** HISTORY, AFRICAN-AMERICAN STUDIES **EDUCATION** Ball State University, Muncie, IN, 1963-66; Andrews University, Berrien Springs, MI, BA, 1967; Bowling Green State University, Bowling Green, OH, MM, 1968; Harvard University, Cambridge, MA, PhD, 1982. **CAREER** Oakwood College, Huntsville, AL, instructor of music/German, 68-71; Univ of Tenn-Knoxville, Knoxville, TN, asst prof of religious studies, 82-87; Temple Univ, Philadelphia, PA, visiting asst prof of religious studies, 87-88; Wesleyan Univ, Middletown, CT, assoc prof of history, 88-91; Univ of Iowa, Prof, History and African-American World Studies, currently. **HONORS AND AWARDS** Rockefeller Humanities Fellowship, Rockefeller Foundation, 1985-86; Research Fellowship, Smithsonian Institution, 1979-80; National Fellowships Fund Dissertation Fellowship, 1976-77; Board of Editors, History and Theory, 1990-92. **MEMBERSHIPS** Member, board of directors and co-chair of program committee, National Council of Black Studies, 1988-90; council member, American Society of Church History, 1990-93; member, American Historical Association, 1978-; member, American Studies Association, 1987-. **SELECTED PUBLICATIONS** Author: The Rise of Gospel Blues: The Music of Thomas A Dorsey in the Urban Church, Oxford University Press, 1992. **CONTACT ADDRESS** History & African-American World Studies, Univ of Iowa, 205 Schaeffer Hall, Iowa City, IA 52242.

HARRIS, P. M. G.
DISCIPLINE AMERICAN COLONIAL HISTORY **EDUCATION** Columbia Univ, PhD. **CAREER** Assoc prof, Temple Univ. **HONORS AND AWARDS** Res grant, Nat Inst for Ment Hea, Nat Sci Found, Am Coun of Learned Soc, NEH. **RESEARCH** The evolution of the Am colonies. **SELECTED PUBLICATIONS** Auth, Of Two Minds, Falsely Sundered: Faith and Reason, Duality and Complexity, 'Art' and Science in Perry Miller and in Puritan New England, Am Quart, 82; The Demographic Development of Colonial Philadelphia in Some Comparative Perspective, in Susan Klepp, ed, The Demographic History of the Philadelphia Region, 1600-1860, 89; Economic Growth in Demographic Perspective: The Example of the Chesapeake, 1607-1775, in John J. McClusker, et al, eds, Lois Green Carr: The Chesapeake and Beyond -- A Celebration, Md Dept of Housing and Commun Develop, May 92; Inflation and Deflation in Early America 1634-1860: Patterns of Change in the British-American Economy, Soc Sci Hist, Vol 20, No 4, 96. **CONTACT ADDRESS** Temple Univ, Philadelphia, PA 19122.

HARRIS, PAUL
PERSONAL Born 04/11/1954, Rochester, NY, d, 2 children **DISCIPLINE** HISTORY **EDUCATION** State Univ of NY at Binghamton, BA, 76; Univ of Mich, MA, 80; PhD, 86. **CAREER** Minn State Univ Moorhead, 86-. **HONORS AND AWARDS** Phi Beta Kappa; Phi Kappa Phi; Charlotte Newcombe Fel, 82-83; Fulbright Lecturer,Germany, 84-85. **MEMBERSHIPS** Org of Am Hist. **RESEARCH** History of foreign missions, religion and social reform, political thought in the age of democratic revolutions. **SELECTED PUBLICATIONS** Auth, Nothing but Christ: Rufus Anderson and the Ideology of Protestant Foreign Missions, Oxford Univ Pr, 99. **CONTACT ADDRESS** Dept Hist, Moorhead State Univ, 1104 7 Ave S, Moorhead, MN 56563-0001. **EMAIL** harrispa@mnstate.edu

HARRIS, ROBERT DALTON
PERSONAL Born 12/24/1921, Jamieson, OR **DISCIPLINE** EUROPEAN HISTORY **EDUCATION** Whitman Col, BA, 51; Univ Calif, Berkeley, MA, 53, PhD(hist), 59. **CAREER** Teaching asst, Univ Calif, Berkeley, 56-58, assoc soc sci, 58-59; from instr to assoc prof, 59-74, Prof to Prof Emer Hist, Univ Idaho, 74-. **MEMBERSHIPS** AHA; Soc Fr Hist Studies. **RESEARCH** France in the 18th century and revolutionary era. **SELECTED PUBLICATIONS** Auth, Necker's Compte Rendu of 1781; a reconsideration, 6/70 & French finances and the American war, 6/76, J Mod Hist; Necker Reform Statesman of the Ancien Regime, Univ Calif Press, 79; The Reform of the Ancien Regime in France, In: Problems in European History, Moore Publ Co, 79. **CONTACT ADDRESS** Dept of Hist, Univ of Idaho, Moscow, ID 83843. **EMAIL** roberth@uidaho.edu

HARRIS, ROBERT L., JR.
PERSONAL Born 04/23/1943, Chicago, IL, m, 1964, 3 children **DISCIPLINE** HISTORY **EDUCATION** Roosevelt University, Chicago, IL, BA, 1966, MA, 1968; Northwestern University, Evanston, IL, PhD, 1974. **CAREER** St Rita Elementary Sch, Chicago, IL, 6th grade teacher, 65-68; Miles College, Birmingham, AL, instructor, 68-69; Univ of Illinois, Urbana, IL, asst prof, 72-75; Cornell University, Ithaca, NY, director, 86-91, assistant to associate professor, beginning 1975, associate professor, currently, special assistant to the provost, 94; Vice Provost, 00-. **HONORS AND AWARDS** Teaching Afro-Amer History, American Historical Assn, 1992; Black Studies in the United States, The Ford Foundation, 1990; Rockefeller Humanities Fellow, SUNY at Buffalo, 1991-92; WEB DuBois Fellow, Harvard Univ, 1983-84; Ford Foundation Fellow, 1983-84; National Endowment for the Humanities Fellow, 1974-75. **MEMBERSHIPS** President, Assn for the Study of Afro-Amer Life & Hist, 1991-92; chair/membership comm, American Historical Assn, 1989-94; chair/program comm, American Historical Assn, 1995; member/bd of directors, New York Council for the Humanitites, 1983-87; member/editorial bd, Journal of Negro History, 1978-96; member/editorial bd, Western Journal of Black Studies, 1990-; National Advisory Board, The Society for History Education, 1996-; General Editor, Twayne African American History Series, 1990-. **RESEARCH** African Am Thought and Culture; Historiography; Leaders and Movements. **SELECTED PUBLICATIONS** Auth, Black Studies in the United States, The Ford Foundation, 90; auth, Teaching Afro-Am History; auth, Am Historical Asn, 92. **CONTACT ADDRESS** Africana Studies & Research Center, Cornell Univ, 310 Triphammer Rd, Ithaca, NY 14850.

HARRIS, SUSAN KUMIN
PERSONAL Born 08/29/1945, Baltimore, MD, m, 1968 **DISCIPLINE** AMERICAN LITERATURE & STUDIES **EDUCATION** Antioch Col, BA, 68; Stanford Univ, MA, 72; Cornell Univ, PhD(English), 77. **CAREER** ASSOC PROF ENGLISH, QUEENS COL, 77- **MEMBERSHIPS** MLA. **RESEARCH** Mark Twain studies; women's studies (American, 19th century); rhetoric. **SELECTED PUBLICATIONS** Auth, This peace, this deep contentment's images of temporal freedom in the writings of Mark Twain, Essays in Lit, fall 80; Narrative structure in Mark Twain's Joan of Arc, J Narrative Technique, winter 82; Mark Twain's Escape from Time: A Study of Patterns and Images, Univ Mo Press, 82; Mark Twain's good and bad women, Prospects (in prep). **CONTACT ADDRESS** Dept of English, Queens Col, CUNY, Flushing, NY 11367.

HARRIS, WILLIAM C.
PERSONAL Born 02/07/1933, Mt Pleasant, AL, m, 1960, 3 children **DISCIPLINE** UNITED STATES HISTORY **EDUCATION** Univ Ala, AB, 54, MA, 59, PhD(hist), 65. **CAREER** From asst prof to assoc prof hist, Millsaps Col, 63-68; assoc prof, 69-76, Prof Hist, NC State Univ, 76-, Nat Endowment for Humanities younger scholar's fel, 68-69. **HONORS AND AWARDS** Mayflower Cup, 88; Jefferson Davis Awd, 88; Lincoln Prize, Second Place, 98. **MEMBERSHIPS** Southern Hist Asn; Abraham Lincoln Assn; Abraham Lincoln Institute; Society of Civil War Historians. **RESEARCH** History of southern reconstruction; the middle period in United States history; Abraham Lincoln; North Carolina during the Civil War. **SELECTED PUBLICATIONS** Levy Pope Walker: Confederate Secretary of War, 62; Presidential Reconstruction in Mississippi, 67; The Day of the Carpetbagger: Republican Reconstruction in Mississippi, 79; William Woods Holden: Firebrand of North Carolina Politics, 87; North Carolina and the Coming of the Civil War, 87; North Carolina and the Coming of the Civil War, 88; Lincoln Loyalists--Union Soldiers From the Confederacy, Southwestern Hist Quarterly, Vol 0097, 93; Political Culture in the 19th Century South Mississippi, 1830-1900, Civil War Hist, Vol 0042, 96; Multiparty Politics in Mississippi, 1877-1902, Am Hist Rev, Vol 0102, 97; With Charity for All: Lincoln and the Restoration of the Union, 97 . **CONTACT ADDRESS** Dept of Hist, No Carolina State Univ, Raleigh, NC 27695-8108. **EMAIL** william-harris@ncsu.edu

HARRIS, WILLIAM VERNON
PERSONAL Born 09/13/1938, Nottingham, England, m, 1 child **DISCIPLINE** ANCIENT HISTORY **EDUCATION** Oxford Univ, BA, 61, MA, 64, PhD, 68. **CAREER** Lectr ancient hist, Queen's Univ Belfast, 64-65; from instr to assoc prof, 65-76, prof hist Columbia Univ, 76-95; Shepherd prof hist 95; Am Coun Learned Soc fel, 70-71; Herodotus fel & mem, Inst Advan Study, NJ, 70-71 & 78; foreign mem, Inst Etruscan & Ital Studies, Florence, Italy, 73; vis fel, Corpus Christi Col, Oxford, 75; Nat Endowment for Humanities fel, 78; res, Am Acad Rome, 78; dir, Nat Endowment for Humanities summer sem Col Teachers, 79 & 81; vis fel, All Souls Col, Oxford, 83; Chair, Hist Dept, Columbia Univ, 88-94. **HONORS AND AWARDS** Guggenheim Fel, 82-83; Fellow, Soc of Antiquarians (London), 84; Foreign Mem, Finnish Acad of Science, 88-; Foreign Mem, Academic Europea, 94; prof invite, Ecole Normale Aes Haute Etude, (Paris), 89; Gray Lecturer, Univ of Cambridge, 98; Fellow National Humanities Ctr, 98. **MEMBERSHIPS** AHA Am Philol Asn; Archaeol Inst Am; Asn Ancient Historians. **RESEARCH** Cultural & social history of Greece & Rome. **SELECTED PUBLICATIONS** Auth, Rome in Etruria and Umbria, Oxford Univ, 71; ed, Columbia Studies in the Classical Tradition (ser), Brill, Leiden, 76-; ed, Columbia Studies in Classical Tradition, 79-; auth, War and Imperialism in Republican Rome, Oxford Univ, 79; Towards a Study of the Roman Slave Trade, Memoirs of the American Academy in Rome, 80; Ancient Literary, Harvard UP, 89; ed, The Transformation of Urbs Roman in Late Antiquity, 99; contribr, Cambridge Ancient History, Vols VIII and XI, 2nd ed. **CONTACT ADDRESS** Dept Hist, Columbia Univ, 2960 Broadway, New York, NY 10027-6900. **EMAIL** wvh1@columbia.edu

HARRIS-CLINE, DIANE
DISCIPLINE CLASSICAL ARCHAEOLOGY **EDUCATION** Stanford Univ, BA, 83; Princeton Univ, MA, 86; PhD, 91. **CAREER** Vis instr, Portland State Univ, 90-91; Asst prof, Calif State Univ, 91-94; Assoc prof, Calif State Univ, 94-96; Vis Assoc prof, Univ Cincinnati, 94-95; Asst prof, Univ Cincinnati, 95-. **HONORS AND AWARDS** URC Fac Res Grant, 96; Fac Dev Grant, 96; Globalization Initiative Grant, 96; Semple Fund, Summer Res Grant, 96; Institute for Aegean Prehistory for Semple Symposium April 1997, 95-6; Samuel H. Kress Found, 96-7; Archaeological Institute of Am, Regional Symposia Grant for Semple Symposium April 1997; 96-7; Gertrude Smith Professor of the Summer Session of the Am School of Classical Studies in Athens, 97; Visiting Scholar, Stanford Univ, Dept of Classics, 97-98. **RESEARCH** Greek art and archeology; ancient history; Greek epigraphy; mythology. **SELECTED PUBLICATIONS** Auth, "Aias and Eurysakes on a Fourth-Century Honorary Decree from Salamis," with Dr. Carol Lawton, ZPE 80, (90): 109-115, pl. 2; auth, "The Treasures of the Parthenon: Greek or Persian?" Classical Asn of the Pacific Northwest Bulletin 22: 8, (91); auth, "Bronze Statues on the Athenian Acropolis," AJA 95, (91): 296; auth, "Bronze Statues on the Athenian Acropolis: The Evidence of a Lycurgan Inventory," AJA 96, (92): 637-652; auth, "Thucydides 2.13.4 and the Inventory Lists," Horos 8, 91, (93): 75-82; auth, "Freedom of Information and Accountability: The Inventory Lists of the Parthenon," chapter 13 in Rituals Finance, Politics, Athenian Democratic Accounts, Oxford Univ Press, (94): 213-225; auth, "A Question of Standards: Metrology and the Parthenon Treasures," The Ancient History Bulletin 11.1, (97): 30-36; auth, "The Archaeology of Greek Epigraphy," Preatti XI Congresso Internazionale di Epigrafia Greca e Latina, Rome: Edizioni Quasar (97): 191-194; auth, The Inventory Lists of the Parthenon Treasures, Univ Microfilms Int, 91; auth, The Treasures of the Parthenon and the Erechtheion, Oxford Monographs on Classical Archaeology, Oxford Univ Press, 95; . **CONTACT ADDRESS** Dept of Classics, Univ of Cincinnati, PO Box 210226, Cincinnati, OH 45210-0226. **EMAIL** diane.harris@uc.edu

HARRISON, CAROL
DISCIPLINE MODERN HISTORY **EDUCATION** La State Univ, BA, 90; Oxford Univ, DPhil, 93. **CAREER** Asst prof, hist, Auburn Univ, 93-97; asst prof, hist, Kent State Univ, 97-. **HONORS AND AWARDS** Eccles Res Fellow, Tanner Human Ctr, Univ Utah 96-97; Rhodes Scholar, 90-93. **MEMBERSHIPS** Am Hist Asn, Soc French Hist Stud; West Soc French Hist. **RESEARCH** Modern Europe, France, cultural and gender history. **SELECTED PUBLICATIONS** The Unsociable Frenchman: Associations and Democracy in Historical Perspective, The Tocqueville Rev, 17, 96, 37-56. **CONTACT ADDRESS** Kent State Univ, Bowman Hall, Kent, OH 44242. **EMAIL** charris1@kent.edu

HARRISON, CYNTHIA
PERSONAL Born 10/29/1946, Brooklyn, NY **DISCIPLINE** HISTORY **EDUCATION** Brooklyn Col, BA, 66; Columbia Univ, MS, 67 PhD, 82. **CAREER** Project 87, Amer Hist Assoc, 82-88; chief, Hist Off, Fed Judicial Center, 88-94; assoc prof, George Washington Univ, 95- . **HONORS AND AWARDS** Res Fel, Brookings Inst, 79-80; CETA Dissertation Grant, US Dept of Labor, 78-79; Lyndon Baines Johnson Found Grant, 78; Eleanor Roosevelt Inst Grant, 77; Harry S. Truman Inst Grant, 77; Columbia Univ Readership, 74-75; Columbia Univ Scholar, 66-67; NYS Regents' Scholar, 63-66; Dir Awd, Fed Judicial Center, 92. **MEMBERSHIPS** Amer Hist Assoc; Org of Amer Hist; Coord Comm for Women in the Hist Prof/Conf Group in Women's Hist; Amer Polit Sci Assoc. **SELECTED PUBLICATIONS** Auth, On Account of Sex: The Politics of Women's Issues, 1945 to 1968, Univ Calif Berkeley Press, 88, 89; Women, Gender, Values, and Public Policy, in Democracy, Social Values, and Public Policy, Greenwood Press, 98; A Revolution But Half Accomplished, Columbia Univ Press, forthcoming; Constitutional Equality for Women: Losing the Battle or Winning the War?, in Time to Reclaim: American Constitutional History at the Millennium, forthcoming. **CONTACT ADDRESS** 3707 Harrison St NW, Washington, DC 20015-1815. **EMAIL** harrison@gwu.edu

HARRISON, GEORGE WILLIAM MALLORY
PERSONAL Born 07/29/1951, Milwaukee, WI, m, 1988, 1 child **DISCIPLINE** ARCHAEOLOGY **EDUCATION** John Hopkins, PhD, 85. **CAREER** Assoc Prof, Chair of Classics, 85-, Xavier Univ, Cincinnati. **HONORS AND AWARDS** Teacher of Year, Northeast Normal (China) 99. **MEMBERSHIPS** AIA, Poe Society. **RESEARCH** Archaeology of Roman Empire in the East; Plutarch Seneca. **SELECTED PUBLICATIONS** Auth, Romans and Crete, 94; ed, Oxford Moralia Papers(Plutarch), 95; Seneca in Production, 00. **CONTACT ADDRESS** 3788 Ault Park Ave, Cincinnati, OH 45208-1704. **EMAIL** Harrison@xavier.xu.edu

HARRISON, LOWELL HAYES
PERSONAL Born 10/23/1922, Russell Springs, KY, m, 1948 **DISCIPLINE** HISTORY **EDUCATION** Western Ky State Col, AB, 46; NYork Univ, MA, 47, PhD, 51. **CAREER** Instr hist, NY Univ, 47-50, asst dir foreign student ctr, 50-51; assoc prof, W Tex State Col, 52-57, prof & head dept, 57-67, chmn div soc sci, 61-67; res prof history, W Ky Univ, 67-88, Fulbright fel, London Sch Econ, 51-52; Southern Fel fac res grant, 59; co-ed, Panhandle-Plains Hist Rev, 59-68. **HONORS AND AWARDS** Fac Excellence Awd, WTex State Univ, 65; Fac Awd, Minnie Stevens Piper Found, 66; Fac Res Awd, Western Ky Univ, 71. **MEMBERSHIPS** Nat Hist Soc; Orgn Am Historians; Southern Hist Asn; Soc Historians Early Am Republic; Filson Club Hist Soc; Kentucky Hist Soc. **RESEARCH** Southern history; United States history, 1789-1865; Kentucky history. **SELECTED PUBLICATIONS** Auth, John Breckinridge, Jeffersonian Republican Filson Club Hist Soc, 69; auth, The Civil War in Kentucky, Univ Pr Ky, 75; auth, George Rogers Clark and the War in the West, Univ Pr Ky, 76; co-ed, A Kentucky Sampler, Univ Pr Ky, 77; co-ed, Antislavery Movement in Kentucky, Univ Press Ky, 78; ed, Kentucky's Governors, Univ Pr Ky, 85; auth, Western Kentuck University, Univ Pr Ky, 87; auth, Kentucky's Road to Statehood, Univ Pr Ky, 92; coauth, A New History of Kentucky, Univ Pr Ky, 99; auth, Lincoln of Ky, Univ Pr Ky, 00. **CONTACT ADDRESS** 704 Logan Ave, Bowling Green, KY 42101.

HARRISON, PATRICIA G.
PERSONAL Born 01/02/1937, Monticello, AR, m, 1960, 3 children **DISCIPLINE** HISTORY **EDUCATION** Henderson State Univ, BSE, 59; southern Methodist Univ, MA, 64; Univ Wisc, doctoral Prog, 64-67; Tulane Univ, PhD, 94. **CAREER** Adj Prof, Eastfield Col, 72-74; Adj Prof, Richland Col, 72-74; Adj Prof, Univ S Ala, 76-86; Assoc Prof and chair, Spring Hill Col, 79-. **HONORS AND AWARDS** Selley Fel, Tulane Univ, 93-94; Mitchell Fac Grant, Spring Hill Col, 89. **MEMBERSHIPS** Am Hist Asn, N Am Conf on British Studies, Southern Conf on British Studies, Southern Asn for Women Hist, Southern Hist Asn. **RESEARCH** Connections between the British and American woman suffrage movements. **SELECTED PUBLICATIONS** Auth, connecting Links: the British and American Woman Suffrage Movements, 1900-1914, Greenwood Press, 00; auth, "Riveters, Volunteers and WACS: Women in Mobile during World War II," in History of Women in the United States: Historical Articles on Women's Lives and Activities, Univ Pub of Am, 92; auth, "Riveters, Volunteers and WACS: Women in Mobile during World War II, Gulf Coast Historical Review, 86; auth, "The Development of Gulf Shores, Alabama: an Interview with Erie Hall Meyer," Gulf Coast Historical Review, 86. **CONTACT ADDRESS** Dept Hist, Spring Hill Col, 4000 Dauphin St, Mobile, AL 36608-1780.

HARRISON, TIMOTHY P.
PERSONAL Born 08/13/1965, Ft. Wayne, IN, m, 1989, 2 children **DISCIPLINE** ARCHAEOLOGY **EDUCATION** Wheaton Col, BA, 87; Univ Chicago, MA, 91, PhD, 95. **CAREER** Lectr, Oriental Inst, 93-94, lectr, The College, 94-95, res assoc, 95-97, Univ of Chicago; asst prof, 97-, Univ of Toronto. **HONORS AND AWARDS** White-Levy Found Pub Awd, 97-98, Sr Post-Doct Res Fel, NMERTA Program, 96-97, Stuart Taye Tchng Awd, The College, Univ of Chicago, 94. **MEMBERSHIPS** Amer Anthropological Asn; Amer Schools of Oriental Res; Archaeological Inst of Amer. **RESEARCH** Near Eastern Archaeology; emergence of early civilizations; urbanism; ethnicity; exchange networks; ceramic analysis; spatial analysis; archaeological method/theory. **SELECTED PUBLICATIONS** Art, The Early Umayyad Settlement at Tabariyah A Case of Yet Another Misr, Jour of New Eastern Stud, 92; art, Economics with an Entrepreneurial Spirit Early Bronze Trade with Late Predynastic Egypt, Biblical Archaeologist, 93; art, Madaba Region Early Bronze Age Survey, Amer Jour of Archaeology, 94; art, A Sixth-Seventh Century Ceramic Assemblage from Madaba Jordan, Annual of the Dept of Antiquities of Jordan (ADAJ), 94; art, The Surface Survey, pp 18-23 in Madaba Cultural Heritage, Amer Center of Oriental Res, 96; art, The History of Madaba, pp 1-17 in Madaba Cultural Heritage, Amer Center of Oriental Res, 96; art, Tell Madaba Excavations 1996, Liber Annuus, 96; art, Field D The Lower Southern Terrace pp 99-175, Madaba Plains Project III The 1989 Season at Tell el-'Umeiri and Vicinity, Andrews Univ Press, 97; art, Investigations of Urban Life in Madaba Jordan, Biblical Archaeologist, 97; coauth, Tell Madaba, Amer Jour of Archaeology, 97; art, Intrasite Spatial Analysis and the Settlement History of Madaba, Stud in the History and Archaeology of Jordan, 97; art, Shifting Patterns of Settlement in the Highlands of Central Jordan During the Early Bronze Age, Bull of the Amer Schools of Oriental Res, 97; art, Retrieving the Past Essays on Archaeological Research and Methodology in Honor of Gus W van Beek, Biblical Archaeologist, 97. **CONTACT ADDRESS** Dept of Near and Middle Eastern Civ, Univ of Toronto, 4 Bancroft Ave, Toronto, ON, Canada M5S 1C1. **EMAIL** tim.harrison@utoronto.ca

HARROLD, STANLEY
PERSONAL Born 10/16/1940, Morristown, NJ, m, 1975, 1 child **DISCIPLINE** HISTORY **EDUCATION** AlleghenyCol, BA, 68; Kent State Univ, MA, 70, PhD, 75. **CAREER** Asst prof to prof, SC State Univ, 76-. **HONORS AND AWARDS** Res Fel, Univ of SC, 88; NEH Fel, 91-92, 96-97; SC State Univ Fac Grant, 95-96. **MEMBERSHIPS** Org of Am Hist; Soc for Hist of the Early Republic; Southern Hist Assoc; Phi Alpha Theta; Soc for Civil War Hist; SC Hist Soc. **RESEARCH** The antislavery movement, nineteenth-century American reform, antebellum sectional conflict, the border South, and race relations. **SELECTED PUBLICATIONS** Auth, The Abolitionists and the South, 1831-1861, Univ Pr of Ky, (Lexington), 95; auth, "Freeing the Weems Family: A New Look at the Underground Railroad", Civil War Hist 42, (96): 289-306; coed, Antislavery Violence: Sectional, Racial, and Cultural Conflict in Antebellum America, Univ of Tenn Pr, (Knoxville), 99; coauth, The African American Odyssey, Prentice Hall, (Lower Saddle River, NJ), 00; auth, American Abolitionists, Addison Wesley Longman, (forthcoming); auth, "On the Borders of Slavery and Race: Charles T Torrey and the Underground Railroad", J of the Early Republic 20, (forthcoming). **CONTACT ADDRESS** Dept Hist and Govt, So Carolina State Univ, 300 College St NE, Orangeburg, SC 29117-0001. **EMAIL** sharrold@scsu.edu

HARSHBARGER, TERRY L.
PERSONAL Born 11/16/1941, Champaign, IL, d, 6 children **DISCIPLINE** GEOGRAPHY **EDUCATION** Purdue Univ, MS, 70; PhD, 74; Ind State Univ, MA, 96. **CAREER** Asst prof, Purdue Univ, 65-79; prof, Univ of IL, 79-93; assoc prof, Parkland Col, 95-. **HONORS AND AWARDS** Who's Who in Aviation; Fel, Purdue Univ; Sigma Xi Awd, Indiana State Univ. **MEMBERSHIPS** IL Geog Soc. **RESEARCH** Historical Geography, Academic Assessment, Interface of Arts and Sciences with Technology. **SELECTED PUBLICATIONS** Auth, "Troubleshooting Aircraft", Instructional Microcomputing Newsletter, 5.8 (90):2; auth, Physiographic Aviation Hazards in the Aspen and Leadville Areas of Colorado, Ind State Univ, 96; auth, "Use of the Geobrief for Academic Assessment", Bull of the IL Geog Soc, XLI.2 (99):26-36. **CONTACT ADDRESS** Dept Soc Sci, Parkland Col, 2400 W Bradley Ave, Champaign, IL 61821-1899. **EMAIL** tharshbarger@parkland.cc.il.us

HART, DARRYL GLENN
DISCIPLINE CHURCH HISTORY, THEOLOGICAL BIBLIOGRAPHY **EDUCATION** Temple Univ, BA, 79; Westminster Theol Sem, MAR, 81; Harvard Univ, MTS, 83; Johns Hopkins Univ, MA, 85, PhD, 88. **CAREER** Tchg asst, Johns Hopkins Univ, 85-88; post-dr fel, lectr, Divinity Sch, Duke Univ, 88-89; dir, Inst Stud of Amer Evangelicals, Wheaton Cole, 89-93; assoc prof, Westminster Theol Sem, 93-. **HONORS AND AWARDS** Co-ed, Dictionary of the Presbyterian and Reformed Tradition in America, 91-; bk rev ed, Fides et Historia 92-96; ed, Westminster Theol Jour, 96-; **MEMBERSHIPS** Historical Society; Amer Historical Assoc; Organization of Amer Historians; Amer Society of Church History. **RESEARCH** American Presbyterianism; Religion and Higher Education; Secularism. **SELECTED PUBLICATIONS** Auth, J. Gresham Machen and the Crisis of Conservative Protestantism in Modern America; The Troubled Soul of the Academy: American Learning and the Problem of Religious Studies, Rel and Amer Cult, 92; The Legacy of J. Gresham Machen and the Identity of the Orthodox Presbyterian Church, Westminster Theol Jour 53, 92; auth, The University Gets Religion: Religious Studies and American Higher Education, 99. **CONTACT ADDRESS** Westminster Theol Sem, Pennsylvania, PO Box 27009, Philadelphia, PA 19118. **EMAIL** dhart@wts.edu

HART, JOHN MASON
PERSONAL Born 02/14/1935, Los Angeles, CA, m, 1957, 2 children **DISCIPLINE** HISTORY **EDUCATION** UCLA, PhD, 70. **CAREER** Asst Prof, Univ North Dakota, 69-73; Assoc Prof, 73-78, Prof, 78-, Univ Houston **HONORS AND AWARDS** SSRC/ACLS Post Doctoral Research, 75; Conference Prize, 75; Herring Prize, 81; Johnson Prize, 88; Visiting research Fel, UCSD, 88; NEH Senior Univ Research Fel, 91; Shelby Cullom Davis Fel, Princeton, 91; Johnson Prize, 00; Distinguished Res Awd, Univ Houston, Humanities, Fine Arts, and Communications, 00. **MEMBERSHIPS** Amer Historical Assoc. **RESEARCH** Mexico **SELECTED PUBLICATIONS** Auth, Anarchism and the Mexican Working Class, 1860-1931, 78; auth, Revolutionary Mexico: The Coming and Process of the Mexican Revolution, 10th Anniv Ed, 98; Auth, Border Crossings: Mexican and Mexican American Workers, 98; auth, Empire and Revolution: The Americans in Mexico since the Civil War, 00; auth, Empire and Revolution: The Americans in Mexico since the Civil War, 00. **CONTACT ADDRESS** Dept of History, Univ of Houston, Houston, TX 77204-3785. **EMAIL** jhart@uh.edu

HARTGROVE, JOSEPH DANE
PERSONAL Born 02/12/1947, Winston-Salem, NC, m, 1978 **DISCIPLINE** RUSSIAN & AMERICAN HISTORY **EDUCATION** Duke Univ, AB, 69; Univ NC, Chapel Hill, PhD(hist), 75. **CAREER** Archivost, Diplomatic Br, Nat Archives, 76-**MEMBERSHIPS** AHA; Am Asn Advan Slavic Studies; Soc Historians Am Foreign Rels. **RESEARCH** Russian-American relations; the Russian Revolution and Civil War; Russian military and naval history. **SELECTED PUBLICATIONS** Ed, The United States and Russia: The Beginning of Relations, 1765-1815, US Govt Printing Off, 80. **CONTACT ADDRESS** Diplomatic Br Nat Archives Eighth & Pennsylvania A, Washington, DC 20408.

HARTMAN, MARY SUSAN
PERSONAL Born 06/25/1941, Minneapolis, MN, m, 1966 **DISCIPLINE** HISTORY **EDUCATION** Swarthmore Col, BA, 63; Columbia Univ, MA, 64, PhD, 70. **CAREER** Instr, hist, 68-69, asst prof, 69-75, assoc prof, 75-82, acting dean, 81-82, dean, 82-94, prof, history, 82-, dir, Inst for Women's Leadership, 94-, Douglass Col, Rutgers Univ. **HONORS AND AWARDS** Magna Cum Laude; Phi Beta Kappa, 63; Woodrow Wilson Fel, 63-64; Columbia Univ grant, 64-65; Fulbright Fel to France, 65-66; NEH, sum grant, 72; Rutgers Univ Fac Leave Grant, 74, 77, 85; Hannah G. Solomon Awd; NJ Chapter of the Natl Coun of Jewish Women, 93; Girl Scout Awd, Delaware-Rarian Girl Scout Council Women of Distinction Awd, 93; Women of the Year, Hispanic Women's Task Force of NJ, 93; Woman of Achievement, Middlesex County Comm on the Status of Women, 93; NJ Women of the Year, NJ Woman Magazine, 93; NJ Woman of Achievement, 96. **MEMBERSHIPS** Amer Hist Asn; Berkshire Conf of Women Historians; Amer Asn of Univ Women; NJ Coalition for Women's Education; Women's Col Coalition; Chmn, Public Leadership Ed. Network. **RESEARCH** French & English social and political history; women's history. **SELECTED PUBLICATIONS** Auth, Victorian Murderesses: A True History of Thirteen Respectable French English Women Accused of Unspeakable Crimes, Jeremy Robson, 85; art, The Hall-Mills Murder Case: The Most Fascinating Unsolved Homicide in America, Jour Rutgers Univ Libraries, 84; art, Mills Students Provide Eloquent Testimony to the Value of Women's Colleges, Point of View ed, Chronicle of Higher Ed, 90; art, Leadership: The Agenda for Women, NJ Bell Jour, Vol 14, 91; art, The Sacrilege Law of 1825 in France: A Study in Anticlericalism and Mythmaking, Jour of Modern History, Vol LXLIV, 92; Auth, Talking Leadership: conversations With Powerful Women, Rutgers Univ Press, 99. **CONTACT ADDRESS** Inst for Women's Leadership, Rutgers, The State Univ of New Jersey, New Brunswick, 162 Ryders Lane, New Brunswick, NJ 08901-8555. **EMAIL** msh@rci.rutgers.edu

HARTMANN, SUSAN
PERSONAL Born 05/03/1940, St Louis, MO, d, 1 child **DISCIPLINE** HISTORY **EDUCATION** Washington Univ, BA, 61; Univ Mo, MA, 63; PhD, 66. **CAREER** Asst Prof to Prof,

Univ Mo, 66-86; Vis Assoc Prof, Boston Univ, 71-72; Program Officer, NEH, 78-79; Dir, Center for women's Studies Ohio State Univ, 86-92; Prof, Ohio State Univ, 86-. **HONORS AND AWARDS** Rockefeller Foundation Fel, 73-74; NEH Fel, 83; Am Coun of Learned Soc Fel, 94-95; Exemplary Fac Awd, Ohio State Univ, 95; Distinguished Fac Service Awd, Ohio State Univ, 98. **MEMBERSHIPS** Org of Am Hist, Am Hist Asn, Am Studies Asn, Nat Women's Studies Asn. **RESEARCH** US 20th Century history; Social movements; Public policy; Women's history. **SELECTED PUBLICATIONS** Auth, The American Promise: A History of the United state, St Martin's Press, 99; auth, The Other Feminists: Activists in the Liberal Establishment, Yale Univ Press, 98; auth, From Margin to Mainstream: American Women and Politics since 1960, Alfred A Knopf, 89; auth, The Home Front and Beyond: American Women in the 1940s, Twayne Pub, 82; auth, Truman and the 80th Congress, Univ Mo Press, 71. **CONTACT ADDRESS** Dept Hist, Ohio State Univ, Columbus, 230 W 17th Ave, Columbus, OH 4321-1361. **EMAIL** Hartmann.1@osu.edu

HARTSHORNE, THOMAS LLEWELLYN

PERSONAL Born 06/28/1935, Madison, WI, m, 1958 **DISCIPLINE** AMERICAN HISTORY **EDUCATION** Univ Wis, BA, 55, PhD(hist), 65. **CAREER** From instr to asst Prof hist, Kent State Univ, 62-66; asst prof, 66-69, Assoc Prof Hist, Cleveland State Univ, 69. **MEMBERSHIPS** Orgn Am Historians; Am Studies Asn; Pop Cult Asn. **RESEARCH** American popular culture; American intellectual history; recent American history. **SELECTED PUBLICATIONS** Auth, The Distorted Image: Changing Conceptions of the American Character Since Turner, Case Western Reserv Univ, 68; Recent Interpretations of the American Character, Am Studies Int, winter 75; From Catch 22 to Slaughterhouse V: The Decline of the Political Mode, South Atlantic Quart, winter 78; Tom Wolfe on the 1960's, The Midwest Quart, winter 82. **CONTACT ADDRESS** Dept of Hist, Cleveland State Univ, 1983 E 24th St, Cleveland, OH 44115-2440.

HARVEY, PAUL

DISCIPLINE MODERN AMERICAN HISTORY **EDUCATION** Okla Baptist Univ, BA, 83; Univ Calif, Barkely, PhD, 92. **CAREER** Lectr, Univ Calif, Berkeley, 92; vis prof, Colo Col, 91, 93; asst prof, 96-; fac ch, 97. **HONORS AND AWARDS** Postdoc tchg fel, Valparaiso Univ, 93-94, 94-95; postdoc fel, Yale Univ, 95-96. **MEMBERSHIPS** Mem, Amer Hist Assn; S Hist Assn; Amer Acad Rel; Amer Soc Church Hist; Org Amer Hist. **SELECTED PUBLICATIONS** Auth, Redeeming the South: Religious Cultures and Racial Identities Among Southern Baptists, 1865-25, Univ NC, 97; Sweet Homes, Sacred Blues, Religious Orders: The Search for the Meaning of Southern Religious History, Rel Stud Rev, 97;The Ideal of Professionalism and the Southern Baptist Ministry, 1870-20, Rel and Amer Cult, 95; Sweet Home Alabama: Southern Popular Culture and the American Search for Community, Southern Cult, 95; Yankee Faith and Southern Redemption: Southern Baptist Ministers and the Public World, 1850-1890, Rel and the Amer Civil War, Oxford Univ Press, 98; The Holy Spirit Come to Us and Denied the Negro Taking a Second Place: Richard H. Boyd and Black Religious Activism in Nashville, Tennessee, 1895-20, Tenn Hist Quart, 96; Easily Centered: the Reformed Tradition and American Religious History, Amer Hist, 95; The Politicization of White and Black Southern Baptist Missionaries, Amer Baptist Quart, 94; Southern Baptist Missionaries and the Expansion of Evangelical Protestantism, CrossRoads: A Jour of S Stud, 94; The Importance of Being Elvis: Fame, Religion and the Color Line in 50s America, Cresset, 95; rev, Southern Baptists and the Social Gospel: White Religious Progressivism in the South, 1895-20, Fides et Hist, 95. **CONTACT ADDRESS** Dept of Hist, Univ of Colorado, Colorado Springs, PO Box 7150, Colorado Springs, CO 80933-7150. **EMAIL** pharvey@mail.uccs.edu

HARZER, EDELTRAUD

PERSONAL Born, Czech Republic, m, 1987 **DISCIPLINE** ASIAN STUDIES **EDUCATION** Charles Univ, Prague, Prom Filolog, 70; PhD, Univ Wash, 86. **CAREER** Stanford Univ, 92-93; Ind Univ, 93-96; Univ of Tex, 98-. **HONORS AND AWARDS** Indo-Czech Exchange Awd, Am Inst of Indian Studies; NEH. **MEMBERSHIPS** Am Oriental Soc; Assoc for Asian Studies; Am Acad of Relig; Am Lit Transl Assoc. **RESEARCH** Classical Studies of India and Modern Indian Philosophy and Literature. **CONTACT ADDRESS** Center for Asian Studies, Univ of Texas, Austin, Austin, TX 78712-1013.

HASKELL, THOMAS LANGDON

PERSONAL Born 05/26/1939, Washington, DC, m, 1966, 2 children **DISCIPLINE** AMERICAN SOCIAL & INTELLECTUAL HISTORY **EDUCATION** Princeton Univ, BA, 61; Stanford Univ, PhD(hist), 73. **CAREER** From instr to asst prof, 70-77, Assoc Prof US Hist, Rice Univ, 77-, Fel, Nat Humanities Inst, Yale Univ, 75-76; vis mem, Inst Advan Study, Princeton Univ, 78-79; fel, Rockefeller Found, 78-79. **MEMBERSHIPS** AHA; Orgn Am Historians. **RESEARCH** History of social thought in the 19th and 20th centuries; intellectual consequences of modernization; attitudes toward criminal responsibility. **SELECTED PUBLICATIONS** Auth, The Emergence of Professional Social Science: The American Social Science Association and the Nineteenth Century Crisis of Authority, Urbana: University of Ill Press, 77; ed, The Authority of Experts: Historical and Theoretical Essays, Bloomington: Indiana Univ Press, 84; contrib, The Antislavery Debate, ed. Thomas Bender, Includes Capitalism and the Origins of the Humanitarian Sensibility, parts I and II, and Convention and Hegemonic Interest in the Debate Over Antislavery: A Reply to Davis and Ashworth, as well as rejoinders and counter-replies from Davis and Ashworth, Berkeley: Univ of California Press, 92; co-ed, The Culture of the Market: Historical Essays, Cambridge Univ Press, 93; auth, "Justifying the Rights of Academic Freedom in the Era of Power/Knowledge," in Legal Rights: Historical and Philosophical Perspectives, eds. Austin Sarat and Thomas R. Kearns, Ann Arbor: Univ of Mich Press (96); auth, "The New Aristocracy," New York Review of Books, XLIV, no. 19 (97): 47-53; auth, "Farewell to Fallibilism: Robert Berkhofer's Beyond the Great Story and the Allure of the Postmodern," History and Theory 37 (98): 347-367; auth, Objectivity is not Neutrality: Explanatory Schemes in History, Johns Hopkins, Univ Press, 98; auth, "Responsibility, Conventions, and the Role of Ideas in History," in Objectivity is not Neutrality: Explanatory Schemes in History, John Hopkins Univ Press, (98); auth, "Redrawing the Boundaries of Permissible Speech," Texas Law Review, vol. 77 (99): 807-824. **CONTACT ADDRESS** Dept of Hist, Rice Univ, Houston, TX 77251. **EMAIL** thaskell@rice.edu

HASNATH, SYED A.

PERSONAL Born 01/02/1944, Bangladesh, m, 1975, 1 child **DISCIPLINE** GEOGRAPHY **EDUCATION** Rajshahi Univ, BA; Bangladesh Univ, MPP; Univ Wales, MSc; Boston Univ, PhD. **CAREER** Lectr, Bangladesh Univ, 72-75; asst prof, BUET, 76-81; sr consul, UN dev proj, 81-82; adj asst prof, mast lectr, Boston Univ, 93-. **HONORS AND AWARDS** Boston Univ Dean Dis Scholar, Teach Fel, UN Dev Prog Fel, Jawaharlal Nehru Univ Fel. **MEMBERSHIPS** AAG, ARSA, CUS, Probini Found for Needy and Orphaned. **RESEARCH** Urbanization, infrastructure and development; international trade, globalization, environment and development; political economy of third world development; environmental security in South Asia. **SELECTED PUBLICATIONS** Auth, "Consequences of Squatters Removal," Ekistics 267 (78); "Sites and Services in Dhaka: A Critique," Pub Admin and Dev (82); auth, "The Practice and Effects of Development Planning in Bangladesh," Pub Admin and Dev (87); co-auth, "Public Construction in the United States: An Analysis of Expenditure," Annals of Reg Sci 24 (90); auth, "Choice in India's Building Sector: An Introduction to a Regional Model," Modeling and Simul 18 (90); co-auth, "Public Construction Expenditures in the United States: Are There Structural Breaks in the 1921-1987 Periods?," Econ Geo 67 (91); co-auth, "The Effect of Infrastructure on Invention: Innovative Capacity, and Dynamics of Public Construction in Investment," Tech Forecast and Soc Change 44 (93): 333-358; co-auth, "The Public Trial of an Alien War Criminal: An Essay on the Revival of Bengali Nationalism," in Bengal Studies: Essays in Economy, Society, and Culture, ed. S.G. Dastidar, (NY: SUNY Press, 95); co-auth, "Trafficking in Bangladesh Women and Girls," Geo Rev 90 (00); auth, "Communal Difference and Social Tension in South Asia," in Contestable Difference: A Global Dilemma, eds. Lata Chatterjee and A. Anderson (forthcoming). **CONTACT ADDRESS** Dept Geog, Boston Univ, 675 Commonwealth Ave, Stone Science Bldg., Boston, MA 02215. **EMAIL** hasnath@bu.edu

HASSING, ARNE

PERSONAL Born 04/02/1943, Umtali, Rhodesia, m, 1966, 2 children **DISCIPLINE** RELIGION, HISTORY **EDUCATION** Boston Univ, BA, 64; Garrett-Evangel Theol Sem, MDiv, 68; Northwestern Univ, PhD(relig), 74. **CAREER** Asst Prof Humanities, Northern Ariz Univ, 73 **HONORS AND AWARDS** Jesse Lee Prize, Gen Comn Arch & Hist, United Methodist Church, 77. **MEMBERSHIPS** Am Soc Church Hist; Am Acad Relig; Soc Advan Scand Study; World Methodist Hist Soc. **RESEARCH** History of religion in Scandinavia; religion and modern culture; history of Christianity in the American Southwest. **SELECTED PUBLICATIONS** Auth, Norway's organized response to emigration, Norweg-Am Studies, 72; Methodism in Norway: The social and cultural relation between the Evangelical minority and the state church, Methodist Hist, 74. **CONTACT ADDRESS** Dept of Humanities, No Arizona Univ, Box 6031, Flagstaff, AZ 86011-0001.

HASSING, RICHARD F.

DISCIPLINE HISTORY AND PHILOSOPHY OF SCIENCE **EDUCATION** Cornell Univ, PhD. **CAREER** Philos, Catholic Univ Am. **RESEARCH** Atistotle; hist of physics & philos of nature. **SELECTED PUBLICATIONS** Auth, The Use and Non-Use of Physics in Spinoza's Ethics; The Southwestern Jour Philos 11, 80; Wholes, Parts, and Laws of Motion; Nature and System 6, 84; Thomas Aquinas on Physics VII;1 and the Aristotelian Science of the Physical Continuum, Catholic Univ Press, 91; Animals versus the Laws of Inertia; Rev Metaphysics 46, 92, Introduction, and Modern Natural Science and the Intelligibility of Human Experience, Catholic Univ Press, 97; The Exemplary Career of Newton's Mathematics, The St John's Rev 44, 97. **CONTACT ADDRESS** Catholic Univ of America, 620 Michigan Ave Northeast, Washington, DC 20064. **EMAIL** hassing@cua.edu

HASSRICK, PETER H.

PERSONAL Born 04/27/1941, Philadelphia, PA, m, 1963, 2 children **DISCIPLINE** ART HISTORY, HISTORY **EDUCATION** Univ CO, Boulder, BA (Hist, minor Classics), 63; Univ Denver, MA (Art Hist), 69. **CAREER** Instr, TX Christian Univ, Fort Worth, 74-75; Curator of Collections, Amon Carter Museum, Fort Worth, TX, 69-75; Curator, Buffalo Bill Hist Center, Whitney Gallery of Western Art, Cody, WY, 76-96; Dir, Buffalo Bill Hist Center, Cody, WY, 76-96; Dir, The Georgia O'Keefe Museum, Santa Fe, NM, 96-97; Dir, Charles M. Russell Center for The Study of Art of the American West and Charles Marion Russell Endowed Chair, Art Hist at The Univ OK, Norman, 98-. **HONORS AND AWARDS** Leadership Awd, Yellowstone Nat Park, 89; WY Governor's Art Awd, 89; Who's Who in America, 95-; ma thesis: artists employed on the united states government expeditions to the trans-mississippi west before 1850. **RESEARCH** Am 19th-20th century art. **SELECTED PUBLICATIONS** Auth, Frederic Remington: Paintings, Drawings, and Sculpture in the Amon Carter Museum and the Sid W. Richardson Foundation Collections, Harry Abrams, Inc., 73; chief coord and ed, Amon Carter Museum of Western Art, Catalogue of the Collection 1972, Amon Carter Museum, 73; The American West Goes East, Am Art Rev, 75; The Artists, Buffalo Bill and the Wild West, The Brooklyn Museum, 81; Intro, Alfred Jacob Miller: Artist on the Oregon Trail, Amon Carter Museum, 82; The Rocky Mountains: A Vision for Artists in the Nineteenth Century, with Patricia Trenton, Univ OK Press, 83; Intro, American Frontier Life: Early Western Paintings and Prints, Abbeville Press, 87; co-auth with Michael Shapiro and others, Frederic Remington: The Masterworks, Harry N. Abrams, 88; Charles Russell, Harry N. Abrams, 89; Western Art Museums: A Question of Style or Content, Montana, summer 92; with Melissa Webster, Frederic Remington: A Catalogue Raisonne in 2 vols with CD-ROM, Buffalo Bill Hist Center, 96; Frederic Remington's Studio: A Reflection, Antiques, Nov 94; Georgia O'Keefe's West, Antiques, Nov 97; ed and auth with others, The Georgia O'Keefe Museum, Harry N. Abrams, Inc., 97; auth, "Intro," in The American West: Out of Myth, Into Reality, Miss Museum of Art, Jackson, in cooperation with Trust for Mueum Exhibitions, 00; auth, "Intro," in Unending Frontier, Art of the West, Grand Rapids Art Museum in cooperation with the Charles M. Russell Center, Univ Okla, 00. **CONTACT ADDRESS** 520 Parrington Oval, Room 202, Norman, OK 73019. **EMAIL** hassrick@ou.edu

HATA, DONALD TERUO

PERSONAL Born Los Angeles, CA, m, 1966 **DISCIPLINE** HISTORY **EDUCATION** Univ So Calif, BA, 62, MA, 64, PhD, 70. **CAREER** Vis instr his, Occidental Coll, 67-68; adj inst, LA Cty probation dept staff training, 72-75; asst prof hist, 70-73, assoc prof, 73-74, Prof, Hist, 74-. **HONORS AND AWARDS** Lyle Gibson Distinguished Teaching Awd, Calif State Univ, Dominguez Hills, 77; Awd of Merit, Calif Hist Soc, 80; Board of Trustees systemwide outstanding prof award, Calif State Univ, 90; Outstanding prof award, Asn Students, Inc, Calif State Univ, Dominguez Hills, 98. **MEMBERSHIPS** Amer hist asn; org of Amer historians, Asn for Asian Studies; Calif Hist Soc; Hist Soc of So Calif; LA Conservancy; Asian Amer Studies Asn **RESEARCH** Hist of Asian Calif; hist of multicultural, race, ethnicity and gender relations in Los Angeles; unexplored dimensions of the evacuation and incarceration of persons of Japanese ancestry in United States during WWII. **SELECTED PUBLICATIONS** Coauth, Asian-Pacific Angelinos: Model Minorities and Indipensable Scapegoats, in: 20th Century Los Angeles: Power, Promotion, and Social Conflict, Regina Books, 2nd ed, 91; coauth, Thinking Historically in the classroom, American Hist Asn perspectives, 95; coauth, Japanese Americans and World War II, Exclusion, Internment and Redress, 2nd ed, Harlan Davidson, 95. **CONTACT ADDRESS** Dept of Hist, California State Univ, Dominguez Hills, 1000 E. Victoria St, Carson, CA 90747. **EMAIL** DHATA@DHVX20.CSUDH.EDU

HATA, NADINE ISHITANI

PERSONAL Born Honolulu, HI, m, 1966 **DISCIPLINE** HISTORY **EDUCATION** Univ Hawaii, BA, 63; Univ Mich, Ann Arbor, MA 65; Univ of Southern Calif, PhD, 83. **CAREER** Asst prof hist, Calif State Univ, Long Beach, 67-68; lectr, Calif State Univ, Dominguez Hills, 69-70; Prof Hist, El Camino Col, 70-; Acting VP-instruction, El Camino Col, 92-93; VP-Aca Affairs, El Camino Col, 93-. **HONORS AND AWARDS** Vice ch, 74-81, member, 73-85, Calif State Advisory Comt, U.S. Commission on Civil Rights; Nat Advisory bd to the Hist Teacher, 84-; Scholarly Advisory Coun, Japanese Am Nat Museum, 89-; Distinguished Humanities Educator, Community Col Asn, 99; Fellows Award, Hist Soc of Southern Calif, 00. **MEMBERSHIPS** Am Hist Asn; Org of Am Historians; Asn for Asian Studies; Calif Hist Soc; Hist Soc of So Calif, LA Conservancy; Community Coll Humanities Asn; Asian Am Studies Asn. **RESEARCH** History of Asian and Pacific Americans in LA, Calif and the west coast; historic preservation in Calif; hist of multicultural, race, ethnicity and gender relations in LA. **SELECTED PUBLICATIONS** , Coauth, Asian-Pacific Angelinos: Model Minorities and Indispensable Scapegoats, in: 20th Century Los Angeles: Power, Promotion and Social Conflict, Regina Books 2nd ed, 91; The Historic Preservation Movement in California, 1940-1976, California State Dept of parks and Rec, 92; coath, Thinking Historically in the Classroom, Amer Hist

Asn, Perspective, 95; coath, Japanese Americans and World War II, Exclusion, Internment, and Redress, 2nd ed, Harlan Davidson, 95; ed, Community College Historians in the United States, Organization of American Historians, 99; Coauth, "Justice Delayed But Not Denied?" in: Alien Justice, Wartime Internment in Australia and North America, (Univ of Queensland Press, 00). **CONTACT ADDRESS** El Camino Col, 16007 Crenshaw Boulevard, Torrance, CA 90506. **EMAIL** Nhata@elcamino.cc.ca.us

HATCH, GEORGE
DISCIPLINE EARLY CHINA **EDUCATION** Yale Univ, BA, 59; Univ Wash, PhD, 72. **CAREER** Instr to assoc prof, Wash Univ, 68-. **SELECTED PUBLICATIONS** Transl, Yonezawa Yoshiho and Kawakita Michiaki, Arts China, Iii: Paintings In Chinese Museums, New Collection, Kodansha Int, 70; Contribr, Sung Bibliographies, Ostasiatische Studien, 76; A Sung Bibliography, Chinese Univ Profess, 78; Su Hsun's Profagmatic Statecraft, Ordering The World: Approfoaches To State And Society In Sung Dynasty China. **CONTACT ADDRESS** Washington Univ, 1 Brookings Dr, Saint Louis, MO 63130.

HATCH, NATHAN O.
PERSONAL Born 05/17/1946, Chicago, IL, m, 3 children **DISCIPLINE** HISTORY **EDUCATION** Wheaton Coll, BA, 68; Univ Wash, MA, 72, PhD, 74. **CAREER** From asst prof to prof, hist, Univ Notre Dame, 75-96; vice-president, Graduate Studies and Res, Univ Notre Dame, 89-96; provost, Univ Notre Dame, 96-; The Andrew V. Tackes Prof of Hist, Univ Notre Dame, 99-. **HONORS AND AWARDS** Post-doctoral Fel, The Johns Hopkins Univ, 74-75; Charles Warren Fel, Harvard Univ, 77-78; Paul Fenlon Teaching Awd for Arts and Letters, Sorin Hall, Univ Notre Dame, 81; Albert C. Outler Prize in Ecumenical Church Hist, for "The Democratization of Am Christianity," Am Soc of Church Hist, 88; Book Prize, for "The Democratization of Am Christianity," Soc for Historians of the Early Am Republic, 89; John Hope Franklin Publication Prize, for "The Democratization of Am Christianity," 90; Phi Beta Kappa, 96; appointed by President Clinton to the Nat Counc on the Humanities, 00. **MEMBERSHIPS** Am Antiquarian Soc **SELECTED PUBLICATIONS** Auth, The Sacred Cause of Liberty: Republican Thought and the Millenium in Revolutionary New England, Yale Univ Pr, 77; auth, "The Christian Movement and the Demand for a Theology of the People," Jour of Am Hist, 80; co-ed, The Bible in America, 82; coauth, The Search for Christian Am, Crossway Books, 82; co-ed, Jonathan Edwards and the American Experience, Oxford, 88; ed, The Professions in American History, Univ Notre Dame, 88; The Democratization of American Christianity, Yale Univ Press, 89. **CONTACT ADDRESS** Univ of Notre Dame, 300 Main Bldg, Notre Dame, IN 46556.

HATCH, ROBERT A.
DISCIPLINE HISTORY OF SCIENCE **EDUCATION** Univ Wis, BS, 70, MA, 72, PhD, 78. **CAREER** Asst prof, hist of sci, Univ Fla, 78-83; assoc prof 83-; Ed, hist of sci sect, The Eighteenth Century: A Current Bibliography, Am Soc Eighteenth Century Studies, 81-98. **HONORS AND AWARDS** Finalist Univ Teacher of the Yr, 96; CLAS Teacher of the Yr, 96; Mahon Teaching Awd, 96; TIP Teaching Awd, 93, 96, 00. **MEMBERSHIPS** Hist Sci Soc; Soc Fr Hist Studies; Midwest Junto for Hist Sci; Southern Asn Hist Sci & Technol; Southern Hist Asn; British Soc Hist Sci. **RESEARCH** Seventeenth-century science; French science; correspondence networks in the Scientific Revolution. **SELECTED PUBLICATIONS** Auth, The Collection Boulliau, (BN, FF 13019-13059): An Inventory, Am Philos Soc, 82. **CONTACT ADDRESS** Dept of History, Univ of Florida, PO Box 117320, Gainesville, FL 32611-7320. **EMAIL** ufhatch@ufl.edu

HATFIELD, DOUGLAS WILFORD
PERSONAL Born 05/22/1939, Baton Rouge, LA, m, 1966, 1 child **DISCIPLINE** MODERN EUROPEAN HISTORY **EDUCATION** Baylor Univ, BA, 60; Univ Ky, MA, 61, PhD(hist), 69. **CAREER** Instr, Univ Tenn, Knoxville, 64 & Rhodes Col, 65-66; asst prof, Baylor Univ, 66-67; asst prof, 67-70, assoc prof, 70-79, prof hist, 80-, dir, interdisciplinary humanitites, 85-, JJ McComb prof hist, 89-, Rhodes Col, vis lectr, Memphis Acad Arts, 68-74; mem, Inst Hist Res, Univ London, 73; vis fel, Princeton Theol Sem, 80, 83. **HONORS AND AWARDS** Sears Interdisciplinary Teaching Awd; Diehl Soc Fac Service Awd, 94. **MEMBERSHIPS** Phi Beta Kappa; Phi Alpha Theta. **SELECTED PUBLICATIONS** Auth, Kulturkampf: The Relationship of Church and State and the Failure of German Political Reform, J Church & State, Vol 23, No 3; German Protestantism and the Kulturkampf, Red River Valley Hist J, Vol 5, No 4; Reform in the Prussian Evangelical Church and the Concept of the Londesherr, J Church & State, Vol 24, 3; Coauth, Celebrating the Humanities: A Half-Century of the Search Course at Rhodes College, Vanderbilt Press, 96. **CONTACT ADDRESS** Dept of History, Rhodes Col, 2000 N Parkway, Memphis, TN 38112-1690. **EMAIL** hatfield@rhodes.edu

HATHAWAY, JANE
DISCIPLINE HISTORY **EDUCATION** Univ Tex, BA, 82, MA, 86; Princeton Univ, PhD, 92. **CAREER** From asst prof to assoc prof, 92-, Ohio State Univ. **HONORS AND AWARDS** Turkey Fel, Am Res Inst, 88-89, 90, 93, 97; Fulbright Fel, 88-89; Whiting Fel, 91-92; SSRC postdoctoral Fel, 93-94; **MEMBERSHIPS** Middle East Stud Asn; Am Hist Asn; Turkish Stud Asn; Am Oriental Soc; World Hist Asn. **RESEARCH** Ottoman empire; Ottoman Egypt. **SELECTED PUBLICATIONS** Auth, The Politics of Households in Ottoman Egypt, 97; auth, art, The Grand Vizier and the False Messiah: The Sabbatai Sevi Controversy and Ottoman Reform in Egypt, 97; auth, art, Eunuchs, Ghulams, Janissaries, Slavery in the Ottoman Empire, 98; auth, art, Egypt in the Seventeenth Century, 98; auth, art, Mamluk Households' and Mamluk Factions' in Ottoman Egypt: A Reconsideration, 98; auth, art, Cerkes Mehmed Bey: Rebel, Traitor, Hero?, 98. **CONTACT ADDRESS** Dept of History, Ohio State Univ, Columbus, 230 W 17th Ave, Columbus, OH 43210. **EMAIL** hathaway.24@osu.edu

HATHEWAY, JOSEPH G.
PERSONAL Born 08/20/1949, Los Angeles, CA, m **DISCIPLINE** MODERN EUROPEAN HISTORY **EDUCATION** Claremont McKenna Col, BA, 71; Diploma, Cert Achievement, Defense Lang Inst, Presidio Monterey, Federal Republic Germany, 72, 73; Monterey Inst Int Stud, MA, 79; Univ Wis, Madison, PhD, 92. **CAREER** Tchg asst, 82-84, reader, 83-, Univ Wis, Madison; adj prof, Cardinal Stritch Col, 87-93; adj prof, Lakeland Col, 95; instr, lectr, asst prof, 91-, Edgewood Col, Madison. **HONORS AND AWARDS** Chicago Resource Ctr Grant, 84; Ameritech Awd, 94; **MEMBERSHIPS** Soc Hist Gilded Age and Progressive Era; Soc German-American Stud; Max Kade Inst; Council European Stud; Gay & Lesbian Caucus Am Hist Asn; Am Hist Asn. **SELECTED PUBLICATIONS** Auth, art, The Pre-1920 Origins of the Nazi Party, 94; auth, art, The Puritan Covenant Revisited: Anti-Modernism and the Contract with America, 95; auth, art, Gay Liberation Front, 96; auth, art, Anti-Modernism and the Contract With America, 97; auth, In Perfect Formation: SS Ideology and the SS-Junkerschule-Tolz, 99; auth, Gulily as Charged, 01. **CONTACT ADDRESS** 1000 Edgewood College Dr., Stoughton, WI 53589. **EMAIL** hatheway@edgewood.edu

HATHORN, BILLY B.
PERSONAL Born 05/05/1948, Natchitoches, LA, m, 1975, 2 children **DISCIPLINE** HISTORY **EDUCATION** LA Tech, BA; Northwestern State Univ, MA, 80; Texas AM, PhD, 83. **CAREER** Vis asst prof, Tex Tech Univ, 83-84; Campbellsville Col, 84-88; Laredo Comm Col, 88-. **HONORS AND AWARDS** Alex Bealer Awd, GHS, 89. **MEMBERSHIPS** Phi Kappa Phi. **RESEARCH** US Political history. **SELECTED PUBLICATIONS** Auth, A Study Guide: The American Nation, by John Garraty, 91, 00; **CONTACT ADDRESS** Dept Social Behavioral Science, Laredo Comm Col, 1 West End Washington, Laredo, TX 78040-4395.

HATTAWAY, HERMAN MORELL
PERSONAL Born 12/26/1938, New Orleans, LA, m, 1961 **DISCIPLINE** UNITED STATES & MILITARY HISTORY **EDUCATION** La State Univ, Baton Rouge, BA, 61, MA, 63, PhD(hist), 69. **CAREER** Asst prof, 69-73, assoc prof, 73-81, prof Hist, Univ Mo, Kansas City, 81-, vis asst prof hist, La State Univ, Baton Rouge, 72; vis prof, military art, USMA West point, 90-91; prof Religion Studies, Univ Mo, Kansas City, 96-. **HONORS AND AWARDS** Jefferson Davis award, 76, 86. **MEMBERSHIPS** Southern Hist Asn. **RESEARCH** Civil War Reconstruction; generalship; Jefferson Davis new south: United Confederate veterans. **SELECTED PUBLICATIONS** Auth, Some Aspects of Tudor Military History, Brit Army Quart & Defence J, 4/69; Clio's Southern Soldiers: the United Confederate Veterans and History, La Hist, summer 71; General Stephen D Lee, Univ Miss, 76; coauth, How the North Won: A Military Analysis of the Civil War, Univ Ill, 82; Shades of Blue and Gray, Univ Mo Press, 97. **CONTACT ADDRESS** Dept of Hist, Univ of Missouri, Kansas City, 5100 Rockhill Rd, Kansas City, MO 64110-2499.

HATZENBUEHLER, RONALD LEE
PERSONAL Born 06/09/1945, Dallas, TX, m, 1970, 3 children **DISCIPLINE** HISTORY **EDUCATION** Southwestern at Memphis, BA, 67; Kent State Univ, MA, 69, PhD(hist), 72. **CAREER** From asst prof to chmn dept, 72-77, Assoc Prof Hist, Idaho State Univ, 77-82; prof Hist, 82-. **HONORS AND AWARDS** Distinguished Teacher Awd, Idaho State Univ, 95. **MEMBERSHIPS** Orgn Am Historians; Inst Early Am Hist & Cult; Soc Historians Am Foreign Relations; Southern Hist Soc; Soc Sci Hist Asn. **RESEARCH** United States early National Period; United States diplomacy; quantitative methods. **SELECTED PUBLICATIONS** Coauth, Congress Declares War: Rhetoric, Leadership, and Bartizenship in Early America, Kent State Univ Press, 83; auth, Principle and Interest-- Thomas Jefferson and the Problem of Debt, Virginia Magazine of History and Biography, Vol 0104, 96; Western Rivermen, 1763-1861--Ohio and Mississippi Boatmen and the Myth of the Alligator Horse, NMex Hist Rev, Vol 0068, 93; Answering the Call: The First Inaugural Addresses of Thomas Jefferson and William Jefferson Clinton in S.C. Bills and E.T. Smith, eds., The Romance of History: Essays in Honor of Lawrence S. Kaplan, (Kent State Univ Press, 97): 53-67; auth, "Growing Weary in Well-Being Thomas Teffason's Life among the Virginia Gentry, Virginia Magazine of History and Biography, vol 0101, 5-36; auth, Assessing the Meaning of Mosaiacre: Boston (1770) and Kent State (1970), Peace and Change, vol 0021, 208-220. **CONTACT ADDRESS** Dept of Hist, Idaho State Univ, Pocatello, ID 83209. **EMAIL** hatzrona@atsisn.edu

HAUBEN, PAUL J.
PERSONAL Born 07/02/1932, Brooklyn, NY **DISCIPLINE** EARLY MODERN EUROPEAN HISTORY **EDUCATION** Brooklyn Col, BA, 58; Princeton Univ, PhD(hist), 63. **CAREER** Instr hist, Lafayette Col, 60-63; vis lectr, Univ Calif, Davis, 63-64; asst prof, Portland State Col, 64-65 & Mich State Univ, 65-69; assoc prof, 69-74, Prof Hist, Univ of The Pac, 74-, Assoc Dean, Col Pac, 80-, Am Philos Soc grants-in-aid, 64-66. **RESEARCH** Early modern Spain; reformation; aspects of 18th century Spain. **SELECTED PUBLICATIONS CONTACT ADDRESS** Dean's Office, Univ of the Pacific, Stockton, Stockton, CA 95211.

HAUPTMAN, LAURENCE MARC
PERSONAL Born 05/18/1945, New York, NY, m, 1970, 2 children **DISCIPLINE** UNITED STATES HISTORY **EDUCATION** NYork Univ, BA, 66; MA, 68; PhD(Am hist), 71. **CAREER** From instr to assoc prof, 71-82, prof, 82-99, dist prof, Hist, SUNY, New Paltz, 99- . **HONORS AND AWARDS** Peter Doctor Mem Awd, Peter Doctor Fel Found of Iroquois Indiands, 87, 98; NYS-UUP Aws for Excel in Tchg, 91; Excel in Res Awd, NYork State Bd of Regents, 92; John Ben Snow Book Prize, 99. **MEMBERSHIPS** Am Hist Asn; Org Am Hists; West Hist Asn; Am Soc for Ethnohist; NYork State Hist Asn. **RESEARCH** American Indian-white relations; the frontier in American history; American diplomatic history. **SELECTED PUBLICATIONS** Auth, The Iroquiois and the New Deal, 81; auth, The Iroquois Struggle for Survival, 86; auth, Formulating American Indian Policy in New York State, 88; ed, The Pequots in Southern New England, 90; auth, The Iroquois Indians in the Civil War: From Battlefield to Reservation, 93; auth, Tribes & Tribulations, 95; auth, Between Two Fires: American Indians in the Civil War, 95; ed, A Seneca Indian Sergeant in the Civil War, 95; ed, The Oneida Indian Journey: from New York to Wisconsin, 98; auth, Conspiracy of Interests: The Iroquois Dispossession and the Rise of New York State, 99. **CONTACT ADDRESS** Dept of Hist, SUNY, New Paltz, 75 S Manheim Blvd, New Paltz, NY 12561-2400. **EMAIL** lmhaupt@atglobal.net

HAUSE, STEVEN C.
PERSONAL Born 09/15/1942, Fort Wayne, IN, m, 1992 **DISCIPLINE** MODERN EUROPEAN HISTORY **EDUCATION** Northwestern Univ, BS, 64; WA Univ, AM, 66, PhD, 69 . **CAREER** Asst prof, 69-80, assoc prof hist, Univ MO, St Louis, 80-87, Res assoc int studies, Univ MO, St Louis, 70-72 & 82-85, Fellow, 86-, Prof, 87. **HONORS AND AWARDS** Phi Alpha Theta Best First Bk, 85; MO Conference on Hist, Distinguished Bk Awd, 85 and 88; UM-St Louis Chancellor Awd for Excellence in Tchg, 96. **MEMBERSHIPS** AHA; Soc French Hist Studies; Western Soc French Hist; Soc Hist; Soc Hist Mod; Southern Hist Asn. **RESEARCH** Polit and soc hist of the French Third Republic; women's rights in mod France. **SELECTED PUBLICATIONS** The Evolution of Social History, French Hist Studies, 96; Anti-Protestant Rhetoric in the Early Third Republic, French Hist Studies, 89; More Minerva Than Mars: The French Womans Rights Campaign and the First World War, IN Margaret Higonnet et al, Behind the Lines Gender and Discourse in the Two World Wars, Yak UP, 86; Western Civilization, with William Maltby, Wadsworth, 98; Feminisms of the Belle Epoque, with Jennifer Waelti-Walters, Neb UP, 95; Hubertine Auckrt: The French Suffagette, Yak UP, 87; Women's Suffrage and Social Politics in the French Third Republic, Princeton UP, with Anne R Kenney, 84; The development of the Catholic women's suffrage movement in France, Cath Hist Rev, 81; The limits of suffragist behavior: Legalism & militancy in France, Am Hist Rev, 81. **CONTACT ADDRESS** Dept Hist, Univ of Missouri, St. Louis, 8001 Natural Bridge, Saint Louis, MO 63121-4499. **EMAIL** schause@umslvma.umsl.edu

HAUSER, STEPHEN
PERSONAL Born 01/13/1952, Menomonee Falls, WI, m, 1980 **DISCIPLINE** HISTORY **EDUCATION** Carroll Col, BA, 74; Marquette Univ, MA, 75; Marquette Univ, PhD, 80. **CAREER** Instr, Milwaukee Area Technic Col, 81-; Instr, Marquette Univ, 88-; Instr, Lakeland Col, 89-; Instr, Mt Senario Col, 87-. **HONORS AND AWARDS** Brookfield Libr Recognition Awd, 98; Phi Alpha Theta; Who's Who in the Midwest, 94-95; Pi Sigma Alpha; Pi Gamma Mu. **MEMBERSHIPS** MCHS, WLHS, Waukesha Co Hist Soc, Menomonee Falls Hist Soc, Elmbrook Hist Soc. **RESEARCH** History of Milwaukee, third parties in 20th-Century presidential campaigns, history of Wisconsin, the Socialist movement in Milwaukee history. **SELECTED PUBLICATIONS** Auth, "A Statistical History of the American Independent Party in Presidential Elections 1968-1992," in Bull Moose Quart, vol 20, no 4 (95); auth, "Homer, Bill and the Theocratic Party," in The Keynoter Quart, vol 96, no 2 (96); coauth, Following the Trail: A Pictorial History of Blue Mound Road, Heritage House Publ (MS: 98); auth, "Frank Zeidler: Heartland Socialist," in The Keynoter Quart, vol 98, no

3 (98); auth, "Not of this Earth: The Story of the Universal Party," in The Keynoter Quart, vol 98, no 1 (98); auth, "George Lincoln Rockwell and the Presidential Election of 1964," in The Bull Moose Quart, vol 24, no 2 (99). **CONTACT ADDRESS** Dept Hist, Marquette Univ, PO Box 1881, Milwaukee, WI 53201-1881.

HAUSER, WILLIAM BARRY
PERSONAL Born 05/02/1939, Washington, DC, d, 3 children **DISCIPLINE** ASIAN HISTORY, JAPANESE HISTORY, ASIAN-AMERICAN HISTORY **EDUCATION** Univ Chicago, SB, 60; Yale Univ, MA, 62, PhD(hist), 69. **CAREER** Lectr hist, Univ Mich, Ann Arbor, 67-69, asst prof, 70-74; asst prof, 74-77, assoc prof, 77-83, Prof Hist, Univ Rochester, 83-, Chmn Dept, 79-85, Nat Endowment for Humanities younger humanist fel, 71-72; Japan Found fel, 76; Mellon Found Fac fel, Univ Rochester, 77; Nat Endowment Humanities fel, 82-83. **MEMBERSHIPS** Asn Asian Studies. **RESEARCH** Economic and social change in Tokugawa Japan; Japanese local history; Asian women's history; Asian Am hist, lit. **SELECTED PUBLICATIONS** Auth, Kinsei Osaka ni okeru shogyo kiko no henshitsu katei--Osaka wata tonya no baai, Shakai Keizai Shigaku, 70; Economic Institutional Change in Tokugawa Japan--Osaka and Kinai Cotton Trade, Cambridge Univ, 74; The diffusion of cotton processing and trade in the Kinai region in Tokugawa, Japan, J Asian Studies, Vol XXXIII, 74; The Early Development of Osaka and Rule by Status, Miyamoto Mataji sensei koki kinen ronbunshu, Kindai Keizai no rekishiteki kiban, 77; Osaka: A commercial city in Tokugawa Japan, Urbanism Past & Present (transl, Sasaki Gin'ya, Sengoku Daimyo Rule and Commerce), 78; Japan Before Tokugawa: Political Consolidation and Economic Growth, 1500-1650, Princeton Univ, 81; Burghers, In: Japan Handbuch, Wiesbaden: Frank Steiner Verlag, 81; auth, Woman and War: The Japanese Film Image, in Recreating Japanese Women, 1600-1945, Univ Calif, 91; auth, Why so Few? Female Household Heads in Early Modern Osaka, J Fam Hist, II, 4, 86; auth, Fires on the Plain: The Human Costs of the Pacific War, in Reforming Japanese Cinema, Univ Tnchana, 92; auth, Tokugawa Japan, in Asia in Western and World History, ME Sharpe, 97; ed, The Bakufu in Japanese History, with Jeffrey P. Mass, Stanford, 85. **CONTACT ADDRESS** Dept of Hist, Univ of Rochester, 500 Joseph C Wilson, Rochester, NY 14627-9000.

HAVRAN, MARTIN JOSEPH
PERSONAL Born 11/12/1929, Windsor, ON, Canada, m, 1958, 1 child **DISCIPLINE** HISTORY **EDUCATION** Univ Detroit, PhB, 51; Wayne State Univ, MA, 53; Western Reserve Univ, PhD(hist), 57. **CAREER** Res assoc Can hist, Essex County Hist Asn, Windsor, Ont, 52-53; instr to assoc prof English hist, Kent State Univ, 57-68; assoc prof, 68-72, chemn dept hist, 74-79, dir, Self-Study Prog, 84-86, prof English hist, Univ Va, 72-, Consult, Scott, Foresman & Co Publ, 64-70; vis assoc prof, Northwestern Univ, 67-68; mem bd overseers, Case Western Reserve Univ, 76-79. **HONORS AND AWARDS** Whittaker Hist Prize, Wayne State Univ, 53; Alumni Distinguished Prof Awd, 86; Raven Soc Distinguished Fac Awd, 87; Distinguished Teacher Awd, 64, 66, 92; Omicron Delta Fac Awd for Teaching, 97; Arthur Stodser Distinguished Fac Awd, 97. **MEMBERSHIPS** AHA; North Am Conf Brit Studies (pres, 79-81); Am Cath Hist Asn (pres, 82); Asn Can Studies in US; fel Royal Hist Soc. **RESEARCH** Tudor and Stuart England; the English Reformation; history of Canada. **SELECTED PUBLICATIONS** Auth, Catholics in Caroline England, Stanford Univ & Oxford Univ, 62; co-ed, Readings in English History, Scribner, 67; coauth, England: Prehistory to the Present, Doubleday & Praeger, 68; Caroline Courtier: The Life of Lord Cottington, Macmillan, London & Univ SC, 73. **CONTACT ADDRESS** Corcoran Dept of Hist, Univ of Virginia, 205 Randall Hall, Charlottesville, VA 22903-3244. **EMAIL** mjh6f@virginia.edu

HAW, JAMES A.
PERSONAL Born Charleston, MO **DISCIPLINE** HISTORY **EDUCATION** Univ Va, PhD, 72. **CAREER** Prof. **RESEARCH** American Colonial history; American Revolution. **SELECTED PUBLICATIONS** Co-auth, Stormy Patriot: the Life of Samuel Chase, 80, auth, John and Edward Rutledge of South Carolina, 97. **CONTACT ADDRESS** Dept of History, Indiana Univ-Purdue Univ, Fort Wayne, 2101 Coliseum Blvd, Fort Wayne, IN 46805. **EMAIL** haw@ipfw.edu

HAWES, JOSEPH
PERSONAL Born 05/09/1938, Fort Davis, TX, m, 1989, 2 children **DISCIPLINE** HISTORY **EDUCATION** Rice Univ, AB, 60; Okla State Univ, MA, 62; Univ Tex, PhD, 69. **CAREER** Asst Prof, Ind Univ Southeast, 69-71; asst prof, Kans State Univ, 71-73; assoc prof to prof, dept hd, Kans State Univ 73-84; prof, Univ Memphis, 84-present. **HONORS AND AWARDS** Phi Alpha Theta and Phi Kappa Phi; Outstanding Academic Book, Choice Mag, 93; Outstanding Fac Member, Univ Col, 95-96. **MEMBERSHIPS** AHA; Orgn Am Historians; Southern Hist Asn; Hist Educ Society; Am Studies Asn; Am Asn of Univ Prof. **RESEARCH** History of childhood in the United States. **SELECTED PUBLICATIONS** Auth, Children in Urban Society, Oxford Univ Press, 71; ed, Law and Order in American History, Kennikat Press, 73; co-ed, American Childhood, Greenwood Press, 85; co-ed, American Families, Greenwood Press, 85; co-ed, Growing Up in America, Univ Ill Press, 85; auth, The Children's Rights Movement, Twayne Publ, 91; co-ed, Children in Historical and Comparative Perspective, Greenwood Press, 91; auth, Children Between the Wars, Twayne Publ, 97. **CONTACT ADDRESS** Univ of Memphis, Campus Box 526120, Memphis, TN 38152-6120. **EMAIL** jhawes@memphis.edu

HAWKINS, HUGH DODGE
PERSONAL Born 09/03/1929, Topeka, KS **DISCIPLINE** AMERICAN HISTORY **EDUCATION** DePauw Univ, AB, 50; Johns Hopkins Univ, PhD(hist), 54. **CAREER** Instr hist, Univ NC, 56-67; instr Am studies, 57-59, from asst prof to assoc prof hist & Am studies, 59-69, prof, 69-75, Anson D Morse Prof Hist & Am Studies, Amherst Col, 75-; Fulbright lectr, Goettingen, WGer, 73-74; vis assoc, Ctr Studies in Higher Educ, Univ Calif, Berkeley, 78-79 & 82-83; Fulbright Lectr, Hamburg, Ger, 93-94. **HONORS AND AWARDS** Moses Coit Tyler Prize, AHA, 59; Guggenheim fel, 61-62; Nat Endowment Humanities fel, 82-83. **MEMBERSHIPS** AHA; Orgn Am Historians; Hist Educ Soc; Mass Hist Soc. **RESEARCH** Social and intellectual history; race in American history. **SELECTED PUBLICATIONS** Auth, Pioneer: A History of the Johns Hopkins University, 1874-1889, Cornell Univ, 60; The Emerging University and Industrial America, 70 & The Abolitionists: Means, Ends and Motivations, 2nd ed, 72, Heath; auth, Between Harvard and America: The Educational Leadership of Charles W Eliot, Oxford Univ, 72; ed, Booker T Washington and His Critics: Black Leadership in Crisis, 2nd ed, Heath, 74; coauth, Education at Amherst Reconsidered: The Liberal Studies Program, Amherst Col Press, 78; auth, Transatlantic discipleship: Two American biologists and their German mentor, Isis, Vol LXXI, 80; University Identity: The Teaching and Research Functions, In: The Organization of Knowledge in Modern America, 1860-1920, Johns Hopkins Univ, 79; Edward Jones, Marginal Man, In: Black Apostles at Home and Abroad, G.K. Hall, 82; Banding Together: The Rise of National Associations in American Higher Education, 1887-1950, Johns Hopkins Univ, 92; The University, In: Encyclopedia of the United States in the Twentieth Century, Vol IV, Scribner's, 96. **CONTACT ADDRESS** Dept of Am Studies, Amherst Col, Amherst, MA 01002-5000. **EMAIL** hhawkins@amherst.edu

HAWLEY, ELLIS WAYNE
PERSONAL Born 06/02/1929, Cambridge, KS, m, 1953, 3 children **DISCIPLINE** HISTORY **EDUCATION** Univ Wichita, BA, 50; Univ Kans, MA, 51; Univ Wis, PhD(hist), 59. **CAREER** Instr hist, NTex State Univ, 57-58, from asst prof to prof, 58-68; prof, Ohio State Univ, 68-69; Prof Hist, Univ Iowa, 69-, Hist consult, Pub Paper of Hoover Presidency Proj, Off Fed Reg, 73-78, Dept Chair, 86-89; Emer, 94-. **HONORS AND AWARDS** Ellis W. Hawley book Prize established by Orgn of Am Historians, 97. **MEMBERSHIPS** AHA; Orgn Am Historizans; AAUP; Southern Historical Asn; State Historical Soc of Iowa. **RESEARCH** Recent United States history. **SELECTED PUBLICATIONS** Auth, The politics of the Mexican labor issue, 1950-65, Agr Hist, 7/66; The New Deal and the Problem of Monopoly, Princeton Univ, 66; coauth, Herbert Hoover and the Crisis of American Capitalism, Schenkman, 73; auth, Herbert Hoover, the Commerce Secretariat, and Vision of an Associative State: 1921-1928, J Am Hist, 6/74; The Great War and the Search for a Modern Order, St Martin's Press, 79; ed & coauth, Herbert Hoover as Secretary of Commerce, Univ Iowa Press, 81; coauth, Regulation in Perspective: Historical Essays, Harvard Business Sch, 81; coed & coauth, Federal Social Policy in Modern America: The Historical Dimension, Penn State, 88; coauth, The New Deal and Its Legacy, Greenwood, 89; coauth, Always with US: A History of Private Charity and Public Welfare, Rowman & Littlefield, 98. **CONTACT ADDRESS** Dept of Hist, Univ of Iowa, Iowa City, IA 52242. **EMAIL** e-hawley@worldnet.att.net

HAY, CARLA H.
PERSONAL Born 11/12/1942, Louisville, KY, m, 1966 **DISCIPLINE** HISTORY **EDUCATION** Spalding Univ, BA, 64; Univ of Ky, PhD, 72. **CAREER** Lectr, Cardinal Stritch Col, 67-73; from instr to assoc prof, Marquette Univ, 70-. **HONORS AND AWARDS** Univ of Ky Haggin Fel, 64 & 65; NEH Summer Fel, 76. **MEMBERSHIPS** Am Hist Asn, N Am Confr on British Studies, AAUP, Am Soc for Eighteenth-Century Studies. **RESEARCH** Eighteenth-Century British History, Women's History. **SELECTED PUBLICATIONS** Auth, James Burg: Spokesman for Reform in Hanoverian England, 79; ed, Studies in Eighteenth-Century Culture (vols 21-24), 91-95; ed, The Past as Prologue: Essays to Celebrate the Twenty-Fifth Anniversary of ASECS, 95; auth, "John Sawbridge and Popular Politics in Late Eighteenth-Century Britain," The Historian (90); auth, "Catharine Macaulay and the American Revolution," The Historian (94). **CONTACT ADDRESS** Dept Hist, Marquette Univ, PO Box 1881, Milwaukee, WI 53201-1881. **EMAIL** carla.hay@marquette.edu

HAY, MELBA PORTER
PERSONAL Born 03/16/1949, Somerset, KY, m, 1977 **DISCIPLINE** AMERICAN HISTORY **EDUCATION** Univ Ky, BA, 71, MA, 73, PhD, 80. **CAREER** Instr Am Hist, 74-78, Asn Ed Papers of Henry Clay, Univ Ky, 80-87; ed & dir, Papers of Henry Clay, 87-91; Division Manager of Research and Publications, Kentucky Historical Society, 91- . **MEMBERSHIPS** Southern Hist Asn; Kentucky Hist Soc; Kentucky Coun Arch. **RESEARCH** United States political history; women's history; Southern history. **SELECTED PUBLICATIONS** Auth, Madeline McDowell Breckinridge: Her Role in the Kentucky Women Suffrage Movement, 1908-1920, 10/74 & ed, The memoirs of Charles Henry Daily, 4/78, Regist Ky Hist Soc; contribr, James D Dole, Suppl VI, Frederick Hale, Supple VII & Owen Brewster, Suppl VII, Dict Am Biog, Scribners; The Election of 1824, Running for President, NY, 94; Suffragist Triumphant: Madeline McDowell Breckinridge and the Nineteenth Amendment, The Register, 95; Letitia Tyler and Julia Gardiner Tyler, American First Ladies: Their Lives and Their Legacies, Lewis Gould, 96; Compromiser or Conspirator? Henry Clay and the Graves-Cilley Duel, A Mythic Land Apart: Reassessing Southerners and Their History, Westport, CT, 97. **CONTACT ADDRESS** 126 Buckwood Dr, Richmond, KY 40475. **EMAIL** melba.hay@mail.state.ky.us

HAY, ROBERT PETTUS
PERSONAL Born 10/23/1941, Eagleville, TN, m, 1966 **DISCIPLINE** AMERICAN HISTORY **EDUCATION** Mid Tenn State Univ, BS, 62; Univ Ky, PhD(Am hist), 67. **CAREER** Lectr hist, Univ Ky, 66-67; asst prof, 67-71, asst chmn dept, 75, chmn dept & dir grad study, 75-79, Assoc Prof Hist, Marquette Univ, 71-, Res grant, Marquette Univ, 68; Nat Endowment for Humanities fel, 69-70; assoc hist ed, USA Today, 80- **MEMBERSHIPS** Southern Hist Asn; Orgn Am Historians; AAUP; Soc Historians of the Early Am Republic. **RESEARCH** American intellectual history; American nationalism; Jeffersonian and Jacksonian democracy. **SELECTED PUBLICATIONS** Auth, Providence and the American Past, Ind Mag Hist, 6/69; The Glorious Departure of the American Patriarchs: Contemporary Reactions to the Deaths of Jefferson and Adams, J Southern Hist, 11/69; The Liberty Tree: A Symbol for American Patriots, Quart J Speech, 12/69; George Washington: American Moses, Am Quart, winter 69; Charles Carroll and the Passing the Revolutionary Generation, Md Hist Mag, spring 72; The American Revolution Twice Recalled: Lafayette's Visit and the Election of 1824, Ind Mag Hist, 3/73; And Ten Dollars Extra, for Every Hundred Lashes any Person Will Give Him, to the Amount of Three Hundred: A Note on Andrew Jackson's Runaway Slave Ad of 1804 and on the Historian's Use of Evidence, Tenn Hist Quart, winter 77; Alexis de Tocqueville and His America: 150 Years Later, USA Today, 11/81. **CONTACT ADDRESS** Dept of Hist, Marquette Univ, Milwaukee, WI 53233.

HAYCOCK, RONALD G.
PERSONAL Born 06/30/1942, Ingersoll, ON, Canada **DISCIPLINE** MILITARY HISTORY **EDUCATION** Wilfrid Laurier Univ, BA, 68; Univ Waterloo, MA, 69; Univ Western Ont, PhD, 76. **CAREER** Lectr, Waterloo Lutheran Univ, 69-71; instr, Wilfrid Laurier Univ & Univ Western Ont, 72-75; lectr to assoc prof, 75-87, prof, Royal Military Col Canada, 87-, head hist dept, 90-93. **HONORS AND AWARDS** Moncado Prize Mil Hist, Am Soc Mil Hist, 79. **MEMBERSHIPS** Soc Mil Hist; past pres Can Mil Hist Gp, Can Hist Asn, 83-92; ed bd, Ont Hist, 82-; ed bd, War and Society, 83-. **SELECTED PUBLICATIONS** Auth, Image of the Indian, 72; auth, Sam Hughes, 86; auth, Clio and Mars in Canada, 95; ed, Regular Armies and Insurgency, 79; co-ed, Men, Machines and War, 88; co-ed, The Cold War and Defense, 90; co-ed, Canada's Defense, 93. **CONTACT ADDRESS** Dean of Arts, Royal Military Col, PO Box 17000, Kingston, ON, Canada K7K 7B4. **EMAIL** haycock-r@rmc.ca

HAYCOX, STEVE
PERSONAL Born 07/19/1940, Ft Wayne, IN, d **DISCIPLINE** HISTORY, GEOGRAPHY **EDUCATION** Seattle Univ, BA, 66; Univ Ore, MA, 67; Univ Ore, PhD, 71. **CAREER** From Asst Prof to Prof, Univ Alaska, 70-. **HONORS AND AWARDS** Chancellor's Awd for Distinguished Serv; Distinguished Teaching Awd, Univ Alaska. **MEMBERSHIPS** WHA, Pac Northwest Historians Conf, ASEH. **RESEARCH** Alaskan history, American West. **SELECTED PUBLICATIONS** Auth, "Economic Development and Indian Land Rights in Modern Alaska: The 1947 Tongass Timber Act," Am Forests: Nature, Culture and Polit (97); auth, "The Road to Success? Principles and Interests: The Permanent Fund and Alaska's Future," Frame of Ref (98): 3-5; auth, "Fenced In: Cross-Border Perspectives in Alaska Hist," Columbia (98): 3-6; auth, The Law of the Land: A History of the Office of the Attorney General and the Department of Law in Alaska, St of Alaska (Juneau, AK), 98; auth, "A New Face: Implementing Law in the New State of Alaska," Western Legal Hist 11 (98): 1-21; auth, "A View From Above: Alaska and the Great Northwest," in The Pac Northwest: A Region in Transition (Corvallis: Ore St UP, forthcoming); auth, "The Political Power of a Rhetorical Paradigm," in Land in the Am West: Private Claims and the Common Good (Seattle: Univ Wash Pr, forthcoming). **CONTACT ADDRESS** Dept Hist & Geog, Univ of Alaska, Anchorage, 3211 Providence Dr, Anchorage, AK 99508-4614.

HAYDEN, ALBERT A.
PERSONAL Born 09/18/1923, Cape Girardeau County, MO, m, 1954, 2 children **DISCIPLINE** BRITISH HISTORY **EDUCATION** Univ Ill, BA, 50, Bucknell Univ, MA, 52; Univ Wis, PhD, 59. **CAREER** From instr to prof hist, Wittenberg Univ, 59-94; managing ed, Study Brit Hist & Cult. **HONORS AND AWARDS** Fel, Int Biographical Asn; fel, Am Biographical Institute. **MEMBERSHIPS** AHA; NAm Conf British Studies; Midwest Conf British Studies. **RESEARCH** British imperial history; 19th century Britain. **SELECTED PUBLICATIONS** Rev, Lord Curzon--The Last of the British Moghuls, Historian, Vol 0057, 94; rev,Gladstone's Imperialism in Egypt--Techniques of Domination/, Historian, Vol 0059, 96; rev, Capitalism, Culture, and Decline in Britain 1750-1990, Historian, Vol 0056, 94; rev, Joseph Chamberlain--Entrepreneur in Politics, Historian, Vol 0058, 95. **CONTACT ADDRESS** 1329 Eastgate Rd, Springfield, OH 45503.

HAYDEN, DOLORES
PERSONAL Born 03/15/1945, New York, NY, m, 1975, 1 child **DISCIPLINE** ARCHITECTURE **EDUCATION** Mount Holyoke Col, MA, 66; Harvard Univ, M Archit; Dipl English Studies, Cambridge Univ. **CAREER** Asst/Assoc Prof, MIT, 73-78; Prof, Univ Calif, Los Angeles, 79-91; Prof, Yale Univ, 91-. **HONORS AND AWARDS** Phi Beta Kappa; Bardwell Fel; Guggenheim Fel; Rockefeller Humanities Fel; ACLA/Ford Fel; Radcliffe Grad Medal. **MEMBERSHIPS** Urban Hist Asn. **RESEARCH** Housing, Historic preservation, History of American built environment, Los Angeles, Suburbs, Feminist theory of space. **SELECTED PUBLICATIONS** Auth, The Grand Domestic Revolution, MIT Press, 81; auth, The Power of Place: Urban Landscapes as Public History, MIT Press, 95; auth, A history of Feminist Design for American Homes, Neighborhoods, Cities. **CONTACT ADDRESS** Dept Archit, Yale Univ, PO Box 208242, New Heaven, CT 06520-8242. **EMAIL** dolores.hayden@yale.edu

HAYDEN, JAMES MICHAEL
PERSONAL Born 06/04/1934, Akron, OH, m, 1961, 3 children **DISCIPLINE** MODERN EUROPEAN HISTORY **EDUCATION** John Carroll Univ, MA, 58; Loyola Univ, Ill, PhD, 63. **CAREER** From instr to asst prof hist, Univ Detroit, 61-66; from asst prof to assoc prof, 66-74, Prof Hist, Univ Sask, 74-, Ed, Can J Hist, 70-73. **MEMBERSHIPS** Soc Fr Hist Studies; Can Hist Asn; Western Soc Fr Hist. **RESEARCH** Early modern European history, especially social, institutional and religious; France; late 16th-early 17th centuries. **SELECTED PUBLICATIONS** Auth, France and the Estates General of 1614, (Cambridge 74); auth, So Much To Do So Little Time: The Writings of Hilda Neatby (Vancouver 83); auth, Seeking a Balance: The University of Saskatchewan, 1907-1982, Vancouver 84. **CONTACT ADDRESS** Dept of Hist, Univ of Saskatchewan, 9 Campus Dr., Saskatoon, SK, Canada S7N 5A5. **EMAIL** hayden@sask.usask.ca

HAYDEN, JOHN K.
PERSONAL Born 05/10/1962, New York, NY, m, 1992, 2 children **DISCIPLINE** HISTORY **EDUCATION** Georgetown Univ, BA, 84; Univ Va, MA, 88; PhD, 91. **CAREER** Lectr, Piedmont Va Community Col, 88-92; asst dean of the fac of arts & sci, Univ Va, 91-92; from asst prof to assoc prof, Southwestern Okla State Univ, 92-. **MEMBERSHIPS** AAUP. **RESEARCH** Late Medieval & Tudor England. **CONTACT ADDRESS** Dept Soc Sci, Southwestern Oklahoma State Univ, Weatherford, 100 Campus Dr, Weatherford, OK 73096-3001.

HAYES, FLOYD WINDOM, III
PERSONAL Born 11/03/1942, Gary, IN, m **DISCIPLINE** HISTORY **EDUCATION** Univ of Paris, Cert d'Etudes 1964; NC Central Univ, BA (Cum Laude) 1967; Univ of CA Los Angeles, MA (w/Distinction) 1969; Univ of MD, PhD 1985. **CAREER** Univ of CA Los Angeles, instruction specialist, 69-70; Princeton Univ, lecturer dept of pol exec sec Afro-Amer studies, 70-71; Swarthmore Coll, vstg lecturer dept of history, 71; Univ of MD, asst coord Afro-Amer studies, 71-73, instructor, 71-77; Cornell Univ, instructor Africana studies, 77-78; Close Up Found, prog instructor, 79-80; Howard Univ, res asst, res fellow inst for the study of ed policy, 80-81, 81-85; US Equal Employment Oppor Com, special asst to chmn, 85-86; San Diego State Univ, asst prof Africana studies, 86-. **HONORS AND AWARDS** Outstanding Young Men of Amer 1977; Phi Delta Kappa Professional Educ Frat Howard Univ Chap 1982. **MEMBERSHIPS** Consultant Union Township Sch System 1971, Comm Educ Exchange Prog Columbia Univ 1972, MD State Dept of Educ 1973-75; mem Early Childhood Educ Subcomm FICE US Dept of Educ 1986. **SELECTED PUBLICATIONS** "The Future, A Guide to Information Sources," World Future Soc 1977; "The African Presence in America Before Columbus," Black World July 1973; "Structures of Dominance and the Political Economy of Black Higher Education," Institute for the Study of Educational Policy Howard Univ 1981; "The Political Economy, Reaganomics, and Blacks," The Western Journal of Black Studies 1982; "Politics and Education in America's Multicultural Society," Journal of Ethnic Studies 1989; "Governmental Retreat and the Politics of African American Self-Reliant Development," Journal of Black Studies 1990. **CONTACT ADDRESS** San Diego State Univ, Dept of Africana Studies, San Diego, CA 92182.

HAYES, JACK
PERSONAL Born 08/13/1944, Danville, VA, m, 1966, 2 children **DISCIPLINE** HISTORY, UNITED STATES HISTORY **EDUCATION** Hampden-Sydney Col, BA, 66; Va Polytech Inst, MA, 68; Univ SC, PhD, 72; Averett Col, BS, 89. **CAREER** Dir Continuing Ed, Univ SC, 72-74; asst to full prof, Averett Col, 74-; Archival Consult, Dibrell Bros, Inc, 90-91; adjunct prof, Grad Sch, VPI and SU. **HONORS AND AWARDS** Sem for Hist Adminr Fel, Colonial Williamsburg, 67; Westmoreland Davis Memorial Found Fel, 67-68; Outstanding Young Man of Am, 76; Who's Who in the South and Southwest, since 91; Who's Who in Am, since 2000; Lewis P. Jones Res Fel. SC Library, 98. **MEMBERSHIPS** Southern Hist Asn, Asn for the Preservation of Va Antiquities. **RESEARCH** Twentieth century U. S., southern history. **SELECTED PUBLICATIONS** Auth, A History of Averett College, Averett Col Press (83); auth, Dan Daniel and the Persistence of Conservatism in Virginia, Mercer Univ Press (98); articles or entries in the Directory of Virginia Biography. **CONTACT ADDRESS** Dept Soc Sci, Averett Col, 420 W Main St, Danville, VA 24541-3612. **EMAIL** jhayes@averett.edu

HAYES, JEFFREY R.
PERSONAL Born 08/29/1946, Portsmouth, VA, m, 1988, 3 children **DISCIPLINE** ART HISTORY **EDUCATION** Wake Forest Univ, BA, 67; Johns Hopkins Univ, MLA, 72; Univ Md, PhD, 82. **CAREER** Instr, Trinity Col, 76-77; instr, Univ Md, 77-80; lectr, Smithsonian Inst, 81; asst prof, 82-88; assoc prof, 88-96; assoc prof, 88-96; prof, 96-. **HONORS AND AWARDS** Smithsonian Fellowship, 1980-82; NEH Research Awd, 1984; American Philosophical Society Fellowship, 1988. **RESEARCH** American painting and sculpture; folk and nonacademic art. **SELECTED PUBLICATIONS** Auth, Oscar Bluemner, Cambridge, 91; Foreword, 96; Use to Beauty: The Artful Decoy, 96; Oscar Julius (FLORIANUS) Bluemner, 95; Carl Mckenzie: Life and Art of a Southern Highlander, 94; Artworks by Carl McKenzie in the Exhibition, 94; Oscar Bluemner 1867-1938, Providence, Rhode Island, 1923, 94; Common Ground/Uncommon Vision, 1993; Signs of Inspiration: Prophet William Blackman, 1999. **CONTACT ADDRESS** Dept of Art History, Univ of Wisconsin, Milwaukee, PO Box 413, Milwaukee, WI 53201. **EMAIL** jhayes@csd.uwm.edu

HAYES, ZACHARY JEROME
PERSONAL Born 09/21/1932, Chicago, IL **DISCIPLINE** HISTORY OF CHRISTIAN THEOLOGY **EDUCATION** Quincy Col, BA, 56; Univ Bonn, Ger, ThD, 64. **CAREER** Lectr syst theol, St Joseph Sem, Ill, 64-68; assoc prof, 68-74, Prof Hist Of Theol, Cath Theol Union, Chicago, 74. **HONORS AND AWARDS** Res grant, Asn of Theol Schs, 77, res scholar, 78, Scholar-in-Residence, 84, 91; J.C. Murray Awd, CTSA, 85; LittD, Quincy Univ, 85; littd, st bonaventure univ, 74. **MEMBERSHIPS** Cath Theol Soc Am; Soc for Sci Study Relig. **RESEARCH** Mediaeval philos and theol; contemp theological developments, particularly in Christology. **SELECTED PUBLICATIONS** Auth, The General Doctrine of Creation in the Thirteenth Century, Schoningh, 64; transl, The Theology of History in St Bonaventure, Franciscan Herald, 71; What Manner of Man? Sermons on Christ by St Bonaventure, Franciscan Herald, 64; The meaning of Convenientia in the metaphysics of St Bonaventure, Franciscan Studies, 74; Incarnation and creation in the theology of St Bonaventure, In: Studies Honoring Ignatius Brady, Franciscan Inst, 76; Christology and metaphysics, J of Relig, 78; Disputed Questions on the Trinity, Franciscan Inst, 79; The Hidden Center, Paulist, 81; Visions of a Future, Glazier, 89; Disputed Questions on the Knowledge of Christ, Franciscan Inst, 92; Reduction of the Arts to Theology, Franciscan Inst, 96; A Window to the Divine, Franciscan Press, 96; auth, Bonaventure: Mystical Writings, 99; auth, The Gift of Being, 00. **CONTACT ADDRESS** Catholic Theol Union at Chicago, 5401 S Cornell Ave, Chicago, IL 60615-6200. **EMAIL** zach@ctu.edu

HAYNER, LINDA K.
PERSONAL Born 09/11/1946, Jackson, MI, s **DISCIPLINE** HISTORY **EDUCATION** Western Mich Univ, BA, 68, MA, 70; Vanderbilt Univ, PhD, 82. **CAREER** Prof, Bob Jones Univ, 71-; Chair, Hist Dept, 92- **HONORS AND AWARDS** Bob Jones Univ Alumni Asn Hon Life Member; univ fel, wmu, 68-69; teach fel, hist dept, vanderbilt, 74-75; ethel macwilson scholarship, 75. **MEMBERSHIPS** SC Hist Asn; SC Comn Hum Scholars Forum; SE Renaissance Conf. **RESEARCH** Tudor-Stuart **SELECTED PUBLICATIONS** Auth, "Biblical Christianity: Its Relationship to the Humanities," SCCH Proceedings, 83; "The Responsibilities of the Parishes of England for the Poor, 1640-1660," SCHA Journal, 83; The Foundling, 97. **CONTACT ADDRESS** 211 Batesview #127, Greenville, SC 29607. **EMAIL** lhayner@bju.edu

HAYNES, EDWARD S.
PERSONAL Born 10/16/1948, Roanoke, VA, m, 1994, 3 children **DISCIPLINE** MODERN SOUTH ASIAN AND MIDDLE EASTERN HISTORY AND CIVILIZATION **EDUCATION** Duke Univ, BA; MA; Jawaharlal Nehru Univ, Mphil; Duke Univ, PhD. **CAREER** Tchng Asst and Course Coord South Asian Civilization, Duke Univ, 75; Vis Instr, Kansas State Univ, 75-76; Vis Scholar South Asian Studies, Skidmore Col, 76-77; Adj Asst prof, State Univ NY, 77-78; Asst Prof, Univ of Northern Iowa, 78-80; Occasional Tchng, Dept History, Duke Univ, 84-87; Asst Prof, 87-92; Assoc Prof, 92; Winthrop Col/Univ, 87-. **HONORS AND AWARDS** AIIS Senior Research Fels; Joseph Malone Fels; ndea title vi grad fel in hindi-urdu; 72; am inst indian studies summer hindi fel; 1973 shell companies foundation rés fel; 73-74; am inst indian studies; supplementary res grant; 73-74; neh summer seminar fel; 80; am inst indian studies senior res fel; 8 **MEMBERSHIPS** Industrial Workers of the World IU 620. **RESEARCH** Modern Southern Asian and Middle Eastern history and civilization. **SELECTED PUBLICATIONS** Auth, "Comparative Industrialization in Nineteenth and Twentieth Century India: Alwar State and Gurgaon District," in South Asia 3(2) (80): 25-42; coed, Guide to Buddhist Religion, G. K. Hall, 81; coed, Guide to Islam, G. K. Hall, 83; coauth, " Changes in the Land and Human Productivity in Northern India, 1870-1970," in Agricultural History 60 (85):523-548; coed, Guide to Chinese Religion, G. K. Hall, 85; auth, "Computers and Non-Roman Script Languages," in Overseas Research Bulletin 1 (87):3-10; auth, "Patawallas of Paramountcy: Professional Nureaucratic Subversion of the Indian Princely States," in Indo-British Review: A Journal of History 15(2) (88):123-138; auth, "The British Alteration of the Political System of Alwar State: Lineage Patrimonialism, Indirect Rule, and the Raijput Jagir System in an Indian Princely State, 1775-1920," in Studies in History 5(1) (89):27-71; auth, "The Political Role of the Armed Forces of the Indian States after World War 1," in Journal of Asian History 24(1) (90):30-56; auth, "Patronage for the Arts and the Rise of the Alwar State," in The Idea of Rajasthan: Explorations in Regional Identity (2), ed. Karine Schomer, Joan L. Erdman, Deryck O. Lodrick, and Lloyd Rudolph (Delphi: Manohar, 94), 265-289. **CONTACT ADDRESS** Winthrop Univ, 346 Bancroft Hall, Rock Hill, SC 29733-0001. **EMAIL** haynese@winthrop.edu

HAYNES, JOHN EARL
PERSONAL Born 11/22/1944, Plant City, FL, m, 1971, 3 children **DISCIPLINE** HISTORY **EDUCATION** Fla State Univ, BA, 66; Univ Minn, MA, 68, PhD, 78. **CAREER** 20th century polit hist, manuscript div, Libr of Congress, 87-. **HONORS AND AWARDS** Magna cum laude with honors, hist, Fla State Univ, 66. **MEMBERSHIPS** Phi Beta Kappa; Phi Alpha Theta; The Hist Soc. **RESEARCH** Communism; Anti-communism; Liberalism; Labor. **SELECTED PUBLICATIONS** Auth, Communism and Anti-communism in the United States: An Annotated Guide to Historical Writings, Garland Publ, 87; coauth, with Harvey Klehr, The American Communist Movement: Storming Heaven Itself, Twayne Publ, 92; coauth, with Harvey Klehr and Fridrikh Firsov, The Secret World of American Communism, Yale Univ Press, 95; auth, Red Scare or Red Menace? American Communism and Anticommunism in the Cold War Era, Ivan Dee, 96; coauth, with Harvey Klehr and Kyrill Anderson, The Soviet World of American Communism, Yale Univ Press, 98; Ed, Calvin Coolidge and the Coolidge Era: Essays on the History of the 1920s, Libr of Congress and Univ Press of New England, 98; coauth, with Harvey Klehr, Venona: Decoding Soviet Espionage in America, Yale Univ Press, 00. **CONTACT ADDRESS** Manuscript Div, Library of Congress, Washington, DC 20540-4689. **EMAIL** jhay@loc.gov

HAYNES, KEITH A.
PERSONAL Born 07/09/1951, Beloit, WI, m, 1977, 1 child **DISCIPLINE** HISTORY **EDUCATION** Northern Ill Univ, PhD, 81. **CAREER** Vis asst prof, hist, Univ Vermont, 84-85; assoc prof hist, 85-90, chemn Dept of Hist and Polit Sci, 90-98, College of Saint Rose. **MEMBERSHIPS** Conf of Latin Am Hist; Latin Am Stud Asn. **RESEARCH** Latin America; Mexico; United States foreign policy. **SELECTED PUBLICATIONS** Auth, Imperialism, Ultraimperialism, and Postimperialism: International Relations and the Periodization of Corporate Capitalism, Radical Hist Rev, 93; contribur, Beede, ed, The War of 1898 and U.S. Interventions, 1898-1934: An Encyclopedia, Garland, 94; auth, The Mexican Revolution as a Province of Postimperialism, in, Becker, ed, Postimperialism and World Politics, Praeger, 99; auth, A History of Latin American, 6th ed. Houghton-Mifflin, 00; coauth, "with Benjamin Keen, "Captialism and the Periodsation of International Relations," in Peter Cain and Mark Harrison, eds. Imperialism: Critical Concepts, Routledge, 00. **CONTACT ADDRESS** Col of Saint Rose, 432 Western Ave, Albany, NY 12203. **EMAIL** haynesk@mail.strose.edu

HAYS, JO N.
DISCIPLINE HISTORY **EDUCATION** Univ Chicago, PhD, 70. **CAREER** Hist, Loyola Univ. **RESEARCH** History of science and Med, especially British. **SELECTED PUBLICATIONS** Auth, The Burdens of Disease: Epidemics and Human Response in Western History, Rutgers UP, 98; essay rev on med in, Fr & Indust Revolutions, Perspectives in Biol & Med 33, 90; res articles in, Anns of Sci, Brit J for Hist of Sci; Metropolis and province; Pa Mag of Hist; Perspectives in Biol & Med. **CONTACT ADDRESS** Fine Arts Dept, Loyola Univ, Chicago, 6525 N. Sheridan Rd., Chicago, IL 60626. **EMAIL** jhays@wpo.it.luc.edu

HAYS, ROSALIND CONKLIN
PERSONAL Born 12/01/1940, Chicago, IL, m, 1966, 2 children **DISCIPLINE** MEDIEVAL BRITISH HISTORY **EDUCATION** Univ Chicago, BA, 60, MA, 61, PhD(hist), 64; MBA Rosary College, 86; Dominican Univ, MLIS, 98. **CAREER** Instr hist, Wells Col, 64-66; asst prof, 66-68, Assoc Prof Hist, Hist, Rosary Col, 68-; prof, Dominican Univ, 94-. **HONORS AND AWARDS** Mother Evelyn Murphy Awd ; Sears Awd , Phi Beta Kappa, Phi Alph Theta. **MEMBERSHIPS** AHA; AAUP; Medieval Acad; Medieval and Renaissance Drama Soc: Coordinating Council of Women in the Historical Profession. **RESEARCH** Medieval English social history of the 13th through the 15th centuries; Tudor social history; the Crusades. **SELECTED PUBLICATIONS** Coed, Records of Early English Drama: Dorset Cornwall; auth, "'Lot's Wife or 'The Burning of Sodom': The Tudor Corpus Christi Play at Sherborne, Dorset," Research Opporunities in Renaissance Drama Vol 33, 0094; auth, " Dorset Church Houses and the Drama," Research Opportunities in Renaissance Drama, Vol 0031, 92; auth, " Castiglione's Courtier and Neo-Platonic Thought: The Influence of Plato's Theoetetus, Sophist and Statesman," Italiana 88, Rosary College Italian Studies Vol 0004, 90; auth, The Widening Gate--Bristol and the Atlantic Economy, 1450-1700, Ethnohistt, Vol 0040, 93. **CONTACT ADDRESS** Dept Hist, Dominican Univ, 7900 W Division, River Forest, IL 60305-1099. **EMAIL** haysrosc@email.dom.edu

HAYS, SAMUEL PFRIMMER
PERSONAL Born 04/05/1921, Coydon, IN, m, 1948, 4 children **DISCIPLINE** HISTORY **EDUCATION** Swarthmore Col, BA, 48; Harvard Univ, MA, 49, PhD, 53. **CAREER** Instr hist, Univ Ill, 52-53; from asst prof to assoc prof, State Univ Iowa, 53-60; prof & chmn dept, 60-73, Distinguished Serv Prof Hist, Univ Pittsburgh, 73-, Mem bd dirs, Harry S Truman Libr Inst, 57-70; mem, Soc Sci Res Coun, 66-72; chmn comt, Am Soc Polit, Woodrow Wilson Int Ctr Scholars, 80- ; Fulbright lectr Aus, 70; Harmsworth Prof Am Hist, Oxforc Univ, 83-84; Lectr Acad Sinica, Taiwan, 87; fel Forest Hist Soc, 80. **HONORS AND AWARDS** Penn Distinguished Hum Awd, 91; Hist Makers Awd, Hist Soc W. Penn, 93; Career Achievement Awd, Am Soc Environ Hist, 97; Distinguished Service Awd, Organization of American Historians, 99. **MEMBERSHIPS** Orgn Am Historians; Social Sci Hist Asn; Am Asn Environ Hist. **RESEARCH** Social analysis of American politics; urbanization; the politics of environmental conservation. **SELECTED PUBLICATIONS** Auth, The Response to Industrialism, Univ Chicago, 57; Conservation and the Gospel of Efficiency, Harvard Univ, 58; American Political History as Social Analysis, Univ Tenn, 80; Politics and Society: Beyond the Political Party, In: The Evolution of American Electoral Systems, Greenwood Press, 81; The Structure of Environmental Politics Since World War II, J Social Hist, summer 81; Political Choice in Regulatory Administration, In: Regulation in Perspective: Historical Essays, Harvard Univ Press, 81; ed City at the Point, Univ Pitt Press, 85; coauth Beauty, Health and Permanence: Environmental Politics in the United States, 1955-1985, Cambridge Univ Press, 87; Response to Industrialism, 95; Explorations in Environmental History, Univ Pitts Press, 98. **CONTACT ADDRESS** Dept of Hist, Univ of Pittsburgh, 1421 Wightman St., Pittsburgh, PA 15217. **EMAIL** sph1+@pitt.edu

HAYS, WILLARD MURRELL
PERSONAL Born 07/26/1928, Lewisburg, TN, m, 1964, 2 children **DISCIPLINE** AMERICAN HISTORY **EDUCATION** Va Mil Inst, BA, 51; Univ Tenn, MA, 58, PhD(hist), 71. **CAREER** Teaching asst, Univ Tenn, 57-58, instr eve sch, 58-59; instr hist, West Tex State Col, 59-61; from asst prof to assoc prof, 61-75, Prof Hist, VA Mil Inst, 75- **MEMBERSHIPS** AHA; Orgn Am Historians. **RESEARCH** American revolution; 19th century United States history; American thought. **SELECTED PUBLICATIONS** Auth, Andrew Johnson's reputation, 2 parts, Publication, ETenn Hist Soc, 59 & 60. **CONTACT ADDRESS** Dept Hist, Virginia Military Inst, Lexington, VA 24450.

HAYSE, MICHAEL
PERSONAL Born 02/24/1961, Louisville, KY, m, 1989 **DISCIPLINE** HISTORY **EDUCATION** Dartmouth Col, Ba, 84; Univ Md, MA, 88; Univ NCar, PhD, 95. **CAREER** Instructor, Miami Univ of Oh, 93-95; Adj Asst Prof, Drexel Univ, 95-96; Asst Prof, Richard Stockton Col, 96-. **HONORS AND AWARDS** Fulbright Summer Sem, 98; Diss Res Grant, DAAD, 90-91. **MEMBERSHIPS** AHA; GSA; SHA. **RESEARCH** 20th Century German History; History and Memory; Memorials; Holocaust. **CONTACT ADDRESS** Dept Arts & Humanities, Richard Stockton Col, PO Box 195, Pomona, NJ 08240-0195. **EMAIL** haysem@stockton.edu

HAYWOOD, C. ROBERT
PERSONAL Born 08/27/1921, Fowler, KS, m, 1942, 3 children **DISCIPLINE** UNITED STATES HISTORY **EDUCATION** Univ Kans, AB, 47, MA, 48; Univ NC, PhD, 56. **CAREER** From instr US hist to dean, Southwestern Col, 48-66; dean, Col Arts & Sci, Millikin Univ, 66-69; prof hist, vpres acad affairs & dean, 69-81, VPres & Provost, Washburn Univ, 81- **MEMBERSHIPS** Orgn Am Historians; Southern Hist Soc; Am Conf Acad Deans. **SELECTED PUBLICATIONS CONTACT ADDRESS** Acad Affairs, Washburn Univ of Topeka, Topeka, KS 66621.

HAYWOOD, GEOFFREY
PERSONAL Born 08/26/1952, Auckland, New Zealand, m, 1982, 2 children **DISCIPLINE** HISTORY **EDUCATION** Auckland Univ, BA; Auckland Univ, MA; Columbia Univ, PhD. **CAREER** Lect, Univ Pa, 90-92; Asst Prof, Beaver Col, 92-. **HONORS AND AWARDS** SIHS Awd, 90. **MEMBERSHIPS** AHA, Soc for Italian Hist Studies. **RESEARCH** Mod European hist. **SELECTED PUBLICATIONS** Auth, Failure of a Dream: Sidney Sonrino and the Rise and Fall of Liberal Italy 1847-1922, 99. **CONTACT ADDRESS** Dept Hist, Beaver Col, 450 S Easton Rd, Glenside, PA 19038-3215. **EMAIL** haywood@beaver.edu

HE, CHANSHENG
PERSONAL Born 12/17/1958, China, m, 1986, 2 children **DISCIPLINE** GEOGRAPHY **EDUCATION** Northwest Agr Univ, BS, 82; MS, 85; Mich State Univ, PhD, 92. **CAREER** Res spec, Mich State Univ, 90-92; vis asst prof, Mich State Univ, 92-94; asst prof, St Cloud State Univ, 94-95; asst prof, assoc prof, Western Michigan Univ, 95-. **HONORS AND AWARDS** Thoman Fel; AWRA Bst Stud Paper Awd; ILP Awd; Deans Appr List; Res Dev Awd, WMU. **MEMBERSHIPS** AWRA; AAG; CPGIS. **RESEARCH** Assessment of land use on watershed hydrology, nonpoint source modeling, scaling, GIS, remote sensing, and GPS applications, and comparative analysis of Sino-US water resources policies. **SELECTED PUBLICATIONS** Coauth, "The Development of Water Resources Policy and Management in the United States," Resour Sci 20 (98): 71-77 (in Chinese); coauth, "Nonpoint Source Pollution Control and Management in the United States," Envir Sci 19 (98): 101-106 (in Chinese); coauth, "A Preliminary Analysis of Animal Manure Distribution in Michigan for Nutrient Utilization," J Am Water Resou Asn 34 (98): 1-14; auth, "Assessing Regional Crop Irrigation Requirements and Streamflow Availability for Irrigation Development in Saginaw Bay, Michigan," Geog Ana 31(99):169-186; auth, "Incorporating Soil Associations into Linear Programming Models for Development of Irrigation Scenarios," Geog Ana 31(99): 236-248; auth, "Use of Hydrologic Budget and Chemical Data for Groundwater Assessment," J Water Resou Plan Manag 125 (99): 234-238; coauth, "Environmental and Economic Concerns in the Saginaw Bay Watershed: Results of A Survey of Environmental Professionals," Great Lakes Geog 6 (99): 40-50; auth, "Hydrological and Biological Indicators into Watershed Management," Land Urb Plan (in press); coauth, "A conceptual Framework for Integrating Hydrological and Biological Indicators into Watershed Management," Landscp Urb Plan (in press). **CONTACT ADDRESS** Dept Geography, Western Michigan Univ, 1201 Oliver St, Kalamazoo, MI 49008. **EMAIL** he@wmich.edu

HEAD, LAURA DEAN
PERSONAL Born 11/03/1948, Los Angeles, CA, s **DISCIPLINE** AFRICAN-AMERICAN STUDIES **EDUCATION** San Francisco State Coll, BA 1971; Univ of MI, MA 1974, PhD 1978. **CAREER** Univ of CA Riverside, 73-76; Urban Inst for Human Develop, project dir 1978-80; Far West Lab for Educ Rsch & Develop, project dir 1980-81; San Francisco State Univ, prof black studies 1978-. **HONORS AND AWARDS** Minority Fellowship Prog Amer Psych Assn, 76-77; Meritorious Promise Awd San Francisco State Univ, 84. **MEMBERSHIPS** Chair of bd Marin City Multi-Serv Inst 1978-; chair Black Child Develop Inst 1978-81; Comm on School Crime CA State Dept of Educ 1981; bd of dir Oakland Men's Project 1988-; Committee to Organize the 20th Anniversary Commemoration of the 1968 San Francisco State University Student Strike 1988. **CONTACT ADDRESS** Professor of Black Studies, San Francisco State Univ, 1600 Holloway Ave, San Francisco, CA 94132.

HEAD, THOMAS F.
DISCIPLINE MEDIEVAL FRANCE **EDUCATION** Harvard Univ, BA, MA, 78, PhD, 85. **CAREER** Asst prof, Sch Theol Claremont, 85-89; Asst prof, Pomona Col, 89-90; Assoc prof, Yale Univ, 90-94; Asst prof, Washington Unive, 94-. **SELECTED PUBLICATIONS** Auth, Monks And Their Enemies: A Comparative Approfoach Speculum, 91; The Peace God: Social Violence And Religious Response In France Around The Year One Thousand, Cornell Univ, 92; Soldiers Christ: Saints And Saints' Lives From Late Antiquity And The Early Middle Ages, Pa State Univ, 94; Contribr, Dictionary The Middle Ages, 82-89; Lexicon Des Mittelalters, 80-; An Encyclopedia Continental Women Writers, 91; The Orlanais, 950-1130; Hagiographies, 94; Medieval France: An Encyclopedia, 95, Harper's Dictionary Religion, 96; Encyclopedia Medieval Women, 96. **CONTACT ADDRESS** Washington Univ, 1 Brookings Dr, Saint Louis, MO 63130.

HEADLEY, JOHN M.
PERSONAL Born 10/23/1929, New York, NY **DISCIPLINE** EARLY MODERN EUROPEAN HISTORY **EDUCATION** Princeton Univ, BA, 51; Yale Univ, PhD, 60. **CAREER** Instr hist, Univ Mass, 59-61; res assoc, St Thomas More Proj, Yale Univ, 61-62; instr hist, Univ BC, 62-64; from instr to assoc prof, 64-70, Prof Hist, Univ NC, Chapel Hill, 70-, Chmn, Southeastern Inst Medieval & Renaissance Studies, 67; Guggenheim fel, 74. **MEMBERSHIPS** Am Soc Reformation Res (vpres, 78-80); Renaissance Soc Am; AHA. **RESEARCH** Historiography and church history in the Reformation Period; intellectual history. **SELECTED PUBLICATIONS** Auth, The 16th-Century Venetian Celebration of the Earths Total Habitability--The Issue of the Fully Habitable World for Renaissance Europe, J World Hist, Vol 0008, 97; Spain Struggle for Europe, 1598-1668, Sixteenth Century J, Vol 0027, 96; Nuptial Arithmetic--Marsilio Ficino 'Commentary on the Fatal Number in Book-VIII of Platos Republic', Renaissance Quarterly, Vol 0049, 96; The Burden of European Imperialisms, 1500-1800, Int Hist Rev, Vol 0018, 96; Spain Asian Presence, 1565-1590--Structures and Aspirations, Hisp Am Hist Rev, Vol 0075, 95; Isabel The Queen--Life and Times, Sixteenth Century J, Vol 0026, 95; auth, Tommaso Campanella and the Transformation of the World, Princeton, 97. **CONTACT ADDRESS** Dept of Hist, Univ of No Carolina, Chapel Hill, Chapel Hill, NC 27599-3195. **EMAIL** headley@email.unc.edu

HEADRICK, ANNABETH
DISCIPLINE ART HISTORY **EDUCATION** Colo Col, BA, 85; MA Univ Tex Austin, MA, 91; PhD 96. **CAREER** Achaeol lab asst, Espey, Houston and Assoc, 93; lab dir, camp mgr, K'axob archaeol project, 92; Valley archaeol proj, 95; lab dir, Belize, 95; asst instr, tchg asst, Univ Tex, 90-93; vis instr, Colo Col, 94-95; vis asst prof, Baylor Univ, 95-96; asst prof, Western State Col, 96; asst prof, Vanderbilt Univ. **MEMBERSHIPS** Col Art Assn; Soc Am Archaeol; Am Anthropol Assn. **SELECTED PUBLICATIONS** Co-founder, ed, contrib auth, Free Food For Thought, Univ Tex Art; co-auth, The Teotihuacan Trinity: Mythological Justification of Power, Narratives of Power: Monumental Architecture in Mesoamerica; Iconographic Expression in the Agrarian Context, The Genesis of Ancestor Veneration; Maya Help You? When Mesoamerica Beckons, Artists and Scientists Answer the Call, The Edge, 93. **CONTACT ADDRESS** Anthrop Dept, Vanderbilt Univ, 2301 Vanderbilt Place, VU Station B, Box 356050, Nashville, TN 37235-7703. **EMAIL** annabeth.headrick@vanderbilt.edu

HEADRICK, DANIEL RICHARD
PERSONAL Born 08/02/1941, Bay Shore, NY, m, 1992, 3 children **DISCIPLINE** WORLD HISTORY **EDUCATION** Swarthmore Col, BA, 62; Johns Hopkins Sch Advan Int Studies, MA, 64; Princeton Univ, MA & PhD(hist), 71. **CAREER** From instr to asst prof hist, Tuskegee Inst, 68-75, dir freshman study prog, 73-75; assoc prof soc sci, Roosevelt Univ, 75-, fel, Shelby Cullom Davis Ctr Hist Study, 72; viss scholar in World Hist, Pacific Univ, 00. **HONORS AND AWARDS** Guggenheim Fel, 94-95; Alfred P. Sloan Fel, 98. **MEMBERSHIPS** AHA; Soc Hist Technol. **RESEARCH** World Hist; Hist of Technology and International Realtions; Hist of Information Systems. **SELECTED PUBLICATIONS** Auth, Spain and the Revolutions of 1848, Europ Studies Rev, 4/76; The Tools of Imperialism: Technology and the Expansion of the European Colonial Empires in the Nineteenth Century, J Mod Hist, Vol 51, No 2; Canovas del Castillo y el Conde-Duque de Olivares, Historia-16, 2/80; The Tools of Empire: Technology and European Imperialism in the Nineteenth Century, Oxford Univ Press, 81; Ejercito y Politica en Espana, 1866-1898, Ed Tecnos, 81; The Tentacles of Progress: Technology Transfer in the Age of Imperialism, 1850-1940, Oxford Univ Press, 88; The Invisible Weapon: Telecommunications and International Politics, 1851-1945, Oxford Univ Press, 91; The Earth and its Peoples: A Global History, Houghton Mifflin, 97; auth, When Information Came of Age: Technologies of Knowledge in the Age of reason and Revolution, 1700-1850, (New York: Oxford Univ Press, 00). **CONTACT ADDRESS** Roosevelt Univ, 430 S Michigan Ave, Chicago, IL 60605-1394. **EMAIL** dheadric@roosevelt.edu

HEALEY, ROBERT MATHIEU
PERSONAL Born 06/01/1921, New York, NY, m, 1953, 1 child **DISCIPLINE** CHURCH, HISTORY **EDUCATION** Princeton Univ, BA, 42; Yale Univ, MFA, 47, BD, 55, MA, 56, PhD(relig), 59. **CAREER** Instr English, Mercersburg Acad, 42-44 & Rensselaer Polytech Inst, 48-52; assoc prof commun, 56-63, from assoc prof to prof Am church hist, 63-74, chnin div hist & theol, 68-70, interim acad dean, 70-71, Prof Church Hist, Theol Sem, Univ Dubuque, 74-, Mem comt relig & pub educ, Nat Coun Churches, 58-62; consult, Nat Studies Conf Church & State, Ohio, 64; theologian in residence, Am Church in Paris, 65-66; mem bd dirs, Asn Theol Fac Iowa, 67-71 & 76-80; consult Gen Coun, United Presby Church USA, 71-72; resident scholar, Ecumenical Inst Advan Theol Studies, Israel, 73-74; pres, Asn Fac & Theol Educ Prof Theol Sem, Univ Dubuque, 73-77; vis prof, Univ Edinburgh, 80-81; Asn Theol Schs in US & Can basic res grant, 80-81. **MEMBERSHIPS** Am Soc Church Hist; Am Acad Relig; Presby Hist Soc. **RESEARCH** Relationships of church, state and education in the United States and in France; Andrew Melville (1545-1622), and Scottish reformation; Judaism in American religious history. **SELECTED PUBLICATIONS** Auth, The Mainstream Protestant Decline--The Presbyterian Pattern, Church Hist, Vol 0064, 95; The Organizational Revolution--Presbyterian and American Denominationalism, Church Hist, Vol 0064, 95; The Language of Liberty 1660-1832--Political Discourse and Social Dynamics in the Anglo-American World, Church Hist, Vol 0066, 97; John Duns-Scotus, Doctor of the Church, J Ecumenical Studies, Vol 0030, 93; Waiting For Deborah-- John Knox, And 4 Ruling

Queens, Sixteenth Century J, Vol 0025, 94. **CONTACT ADDRESS** Dept of Hist & Theol Theol Sem, Univ of Dubuque, Dubuque, IA 52001.

HEATH, JIM FRANK
PERSONAL Born 04/09/1931, Clarendon, TX, m, 1975, 2 children **DISCIPLINE** MODERN UNITED STATES HISTORY **EDUCATION** Univ NMex, BBA, 53, MA, 55; Stanford Univ, PhD(hist), 67. **CAREER** From asst prof to assoc prof, 67-74, dean undergrad studies, 77-81, Prof Hist, Portland State Univ, 74-, Am Coun Learned Soc grant-in-aid, 73-74; Danforth teaching assoc, 70. **MEMBERSHIPS** Orgn Am Historians; Am Comt Hist 2nd World War. **RESEARCH** The Kennedy and Johnson administration; United States domestic history during World War II. **SELECTED PUBLICATIONS** Auth, John F Kennedy and the Business Community, Univ Chicago, 69; Domestic America during World War II--research opportunities for historians, J Am Hist, 9/71; American war mobilization and the use of small manufacturers, 1939-1943, Bus Hist Rev, autumn 72; Decade of Disillusionment: The Kennedy-Johnson Years, Ind Univ, 75. **CONTACT ADDRESS** Dept of Hist, Portland State Univ, Portland, OR 97207.

HEATH, KINGSTON W.
DISCIPLINE ARCHITECTURAL HISTORY **EDUCATION** Brown Univ, PhD. **CAREER** Assoc prof, Univ NC, Charlotte. **SELECTED PUBLICATIONS** Auth, False-Front Architecture on Montana's Urban Frontier, in Perspectives in Vernacular Architecture, III ,eds, Thomas Carter and Bernard L. Herman, 89; Crossing the Vemacular Threshold: The Transformation of the American HouseTrailer from a Standardized Consumer Product to a Vehicle for Regional Exploration, The Harvard Archit Rev, 10, 93; Timber Frame, III, Balloon Frame, in the Dictionary of Art, MacMillan Publ Ltd, 93. **CONTACT ADDRESS** Univ of No Carolina, Charlotte, Charlotte, NC 28223-0001. **EMAIL** kwheath@email.uncc.edu

HECK, MARLENE
DISCIPLINE ART HISTORY **EDUCATION** Univ Tex Austin, BA; Univ VA, MAH; Univ PA, MA, PhD. **CAREER** Sr letr. **RESEARCH** Archit hist, soc hist, material cult studies, Islamic art & archit. **SELECTED PUBLICATIONS** Auth, Building Status: Virginia's Winged Pavilion Dwellings, in Shaping Communities: Perspectives in Vernacular Architecture VI, Univ TN P, 97; var other articles. **CONTACT ADDRESS** Dartmouth Col, 3529 N Main St, Ste. 207, Hanover, NH 03755. **EMAIL** marlene.heck@dartmouth.edu

HEDREEN, GUY
PERSONAL Born 12/12/1958, Dallas, TX, m, 1985, 2 children **DISCIPLINE** CLASSICAL ARCHAEOLOGY **EDUCATION** Bryn Mawr Col, PhD 88, MA 83; Pomona Col, BA cum laude 81. **CAREER** Williams Col, ch, assoc prof, asst prof, act dir, 90 to 98-; Middlebury College, asst prof, 89-90; Franklin and Marshall Col, vis asst 88-89; Bryn Mawr Col, tchg asst, 83-84. **HONORS AND AWARDS** NEH Sr Fel; Rome Prize Fel; Whiting Fel; BMC Fel; Kress Fel; Samuel and Lucy Chew Fel; Asstshp BMC. **MEMBERSHIPS** ASCS at Athens; AIA; CAA. **SELECTED PUBLICATIONS** Auth, Capturing Troy: The Narrative Functions of Landscape in Arabic and Early Classical Greek Art, forthcoming; Univ Michigan Press; auth, Sliens in Attic Black-figure Vase-painting: Myth and Performance, Univ Michigan Press, 92; auth, Image Text and Story in the Recovery of Helen, Classical Antiquity, 96; auth, Narrative art, I.3. Greece and Rome, in: The Dictionary of Art, ed Jane Turner, NY, 96; auth, Sir Lawrence Alma-Tadema's Women of Amphissa, The Jour of the Walters art Gallery, 96; Silens Nymphs and Maenads, Jour of Hellenic Studies, 94; **CONTACT ADDRESS** Dept of Art, Williams Col, Williamstown, MA 01267.

HEDRICK, CHARLES W., JR.
PERSONAL 2 children **DISCIPLINE** GREEK AND ROMAN HISTORY **EDUCATION** Univ Penn, PhD, 84. **CAREER** Instr, Buffalo Univ, NY; Prof, Univ Calif, Santa Cruz. **SELECTED PUBLICATIONS** Ed, The Decrees of the Demotionidai, 90; co-edr, The Birth of Democracy: an Exhibition, 93; Demokratia, 96. **CONTACT ADDRESS** Dept of Hist, Univ of California, Santa Cruz, 1156 High St, Santa Cruz, CA 95064.

HEFFRON, PAUL THAYER
PERSONAL Born 11/05/1920, Newton, MA, m, 1963 **DISCIPLINE** POLITICAL SCIENCE; AMERICAN HISTORY **EDUCATION** Boston Col, AB, 42, MA, 47; Fordham Univ, PhD, 51. **CAREER** Assoc prof Am govt, Boston Col, 50-66; Historian, Libr of Cong, 66-. **MEMBERSHIPS** AHA; Am Polit Sci Asn; Am Soc for Legal Hist; Orgn Am Historians; Supreme Court Hist Soc. **RESEARCH** American constitutional law; American presidency: twentieth century political history. **SELECTED PUBLICATIONS** Auth, Theodore Roosevelt and the appointment of Mr Justice Moody, Vanderbilt Law Rev, 3/65; Secretary Moody and naval administrative reform, Am Neptune, 1/69; William Moody: Profile of a Public Man, Supreme Court Hist Soc Yearbk, 80. **CONTACT ADDRESS** Manuscript Div Libr of Cong, Washington, DC 20540.

HEIBRON, JOHN L.
PERSONAL Born 03/17/1934, San Francisco, CA, m, 1995 **DISCIPLINE** PHYSICS; HISTORY **EDUCATION** Univ of Cal-Berkeley, BA, 55, MA, 58, PhD, 64. **CAREER** Asst Prof, Univ of PA, 64-67; Asst prof, Assoc prof, prof, 67-94, Vice Chancellor, 90-94, Prof Emer, 94-, Univ Cal-Berkeley; Sr Research Fel, Museum of the History of Science, Worcester Col, Oxford, 96-. **HONORS AND AWARDS** Laurea in Phil, Univ of Bologna; Berkeley Citation; George Sarton Medal. **MEMBERSHIPS** Royal Swedish Acad of Sci; Amer Phil Soc; Amer Acad of Arts and Sciences; Academic internationale d'histoire des sciences; History of Science Soc; British Soc for the History of Science. **RESEARCH** History of the Physical Sciences **SELECTED PUBLICATIONS** coed, The Quantifying Spirit in the 18th Century, 90; auth, Weighing Imponderables and other Quantitative Science around 1800, 93; Geometry Civilized: History, Culture and Technique, 98; The Sun in the Church: Cathedrals as Big Science Facilities, 99; coauth, Science and Technology in the 20th Century, forthcoming; Ernest Rutherford, forthcoming. **EMAIL** jlheilbron@ohst7.berkeley.edu

HEILBRON, JOHN L.
PERSONAL Born 03/17/1934, San Francisco, CA, m, 1995 **DISCIPLINE** HISTORY OF SCIENCE **EDUCATION** Univ Calif, Berkeley, AB, 55; MA, 58; PhD, 64. **CAREER** Asst dir, Sources Hist Quantum Physics, 61-64; asst prof hist & philos sci, Univ Pa, 64-67; from asst prof to assoc prof, 67-73; prof hist, Univ Calif, Berkeley, 73-94; prof emer, 94-, Dir, Off For Hist of Sci & Technol, 73-94; vice chancellor, 90-94; Ed, Historical Studies in the Physical Sciences, 79-; sr res fel, Oxford Museum for Hist of Sci, 96-. **HONORS AND AWARDS** Andrew Dickson White prof at large, Cornell Univ, 85-91; Fairchild Scholar, Calif Inst of Technol, 85-91; for mem, Royal Swedish Acad of Scis, 87; Am Acad of Arts and Scis, 88; Berkeley citation, 94; hon doctorate in philo, Univ of Bologna, 88; Univ of Pavia, 00; Univ of Uppsala, 00; mem, Am Philos Soc, 90; Sarton medalist, Hist of Sci Soc, 93; Koyre medallist, Int Acad of the Hist of Sci, 00. **MEMBERSHIPS** Hist Sci Soc; Brit Soc Hist Sci. **RESEARCH** History of physical science and its institutions since the Renaissnce. **SELECTED PUBLICATIONS** Auth, Electricity in the Seventeenth and Eighteenth Centuries. A Study of Early Modern Physics, 79, 99; auth, Elements of Early Modern Physics, 82; auth, Physics at the Royal Society during Newton's Presidency, Los Angeles, 83; auth, The Dilemmas of an Upright Man, Max Planck as Spokesman for German Science, Berkeley, 86, 00; coauth, Lawrence and His Laboratory: A History of the Lawrence Berkeley Laboratory, Vol 1, Berkeley, 89; auth, Weighing Imponderables and Other Quantitative Science Around 1800, Berkeley, 93; auth, Geometry Civilized: History, Culture, and Technique, Oxford, 98; auth, The Sun in the Church, Cathedrals as Solar Observatories, Cambridge, 99; auth, Rutherford, a Force of Nature, 01; ed, Oxford Companion to the History of Modern Science (forthcoming). **CONTACT ADDRESS** April House, Shilton, Burford, England OX18 4AB. **EMAIL** john.heilbron@dial.appleinter.net

HEINEMANN, RONALD
PERSONAL Born 07/24/1939, Flushing, NY, m, 1962, 2 children **DISCIPLINE** HISTORY **EDUCATION** Dartmouth College, BA, 61; Univ Virginia, MA, 67, PhD, 68. **CAREER** Squires Prof Hist, 68-, Hamden-Sydney College. **HONORS AND AWARDS** Phi Beta Kappa; Cabell and Fuqua Awds for Excell in Teaching; Mettauer and Wilson Awds for Excell in Research. **MEMBERSHIPS** OAH; SHA; VHS; AAUP. **RESEARCH** 20th Century US and Virginia History. **SELECTED PUBLICATIONS** Auth, Depression and New Deal in Virginia; The Enduring Dominion, 83; Harry Byrd of Virginia, 96. **CONTACT ADDRESS** Box 122, Hampden-Sydney, VA 23943. **EMAIL** rheinemann@hsc.edu

HEINZ, VIRA I.
DISCIPLINE MODERN WESTERN CIVILIZATION **EDUCATION** Conception Sem Col, 81-85; Divinity Sch Univ Chicago, MA, 87, PhD, 93. **CAREER** Lang fel, Amer Inst Indian Stud, Calcutta, 89-90; assoc prof. **MEMBERSHIPS** Mem, Amer Hist Assn; Org Amer Historians; Soc Historians Amer For Rel; Univ Calif Hist Assoc; NATO Assoc Lyman L Lemnitzer Ctr NATO Stud; Ger Hist Inst; Ohio Acad Hist; Assn Asian StudInc; Amer Inst Contemp Ger Stud. **RESEARCH** Nineteenth-century Bengali texts. **SELECTED PUBLICATIONS** Auth, Kali's Child: The Mystical and the Erotic in the Life and Teachings of Ramakrishna, Univ Chicago Press, 95. **CONTACT ADDRESS** Rel, Hist, Philos, Classics Dept, Westminster Col, Pennsylvania, New Wilmington, PA 16172-0001.

HEISS, MARY ANN
PERSONAL Born 01/25/1961, Cleveland, OH, m, 1997 **DISCIPLINE** HISTORY **EDUCATION** Miami Univ, BA, 83, MA, 84; Ohio State Univ, PhD, 91. **CAREER** Asst prof, 92-98, assoc prof, 98- , Kent State Univ. **MEMBERSHIPS** Am Hist Asn; Org Am Historians; Soc Historians Am Foreign Rel. **RESEARCH** US foreign relations. **SELECTED PUBLICATIONS** Empire and Nationhood: The United States, Great Britain, and Iranian Oil, 1950-1954, NY, Columbia Univ Press, 97; Coed, NATO in the Post-Cold War Era: Does It Have a Future, NY, St Martin's Press, 95. **CONTACT ADDRESS** Dept of History, Kent State Univ, PO Box 5190, Kent, OH 44242-0001. **EMAIL** mheiss@kent.edu

HEISSER, DAVID C. R.
PERSONAL Born 10/22/1942, Charleston, SC **DISCIPLINE** HISTORY, LIBRARY SCIENCE **EDUCATION** Col of Charleston, BS, 64; Univ NC, Chapel Hill, MA, 67, PhD, 72; Columbia Univ, MS, 75. **CAREER** Assoc prof, Head of Reference, Tufts Univ Library, 78-89; assoc prof & Government Documents Librarian, Univ Miami, 89-92; asst prof & Walterboro Librarian, Univ SC, Salkehatchie, 92-95; Asst Prof & Reference/Documents Librarian, The Citadel, 95-. **HONORS AND AWARDS** Fulbright fel; Woodrow Wilson fel; res grant, Cushwa Center for the Study of American Catholicism. **MEMBERSHIPS** Am Library Asn; Special Libraries Asn; SC Library Asn; SC Hist Soc; Am Cath Hist Asn. **RESEARCH** Government information; hist of SC; emblematica & symbolism. **SELECTED PUBLICATIONS** Auth, Marketing US Government Depository Libraries, Government Pubs Rev 13, 86; with Peter Hernon, GPO Regional Depositories, The Reference Librarian 32, 91; South Carolina's Mace and Its Heritage, House of Representatives of SC, 91; The State Seal of South Carolina: A Short History, SC Dept of Archives and Hist, 92; Warrior Queen of Ocean: The Story of Charleston and Its Seal, SC Hist Mag 93, 92; Jean Mayer: A Bibliography, 1948-1993, Tufts Univ Library, 98; Bishop Lynch's Civil War Pamphlet on Slavery, Cath Hist Rev 84, 98; Federal Depository Program at the Crossroads: The Library Administrator's Perspective, Government Information Quart 16, 99. **CONTACT ADDRESS** Daniel Library, The Citadel, The Military Col of So Carolina, Charleston, SC 29409. **EMAIL** David.Heisser@Citadel.edu

HEITZENRATER, RICHARD
PERSONAL Born 11/09/1939, Dover, NJ, m, 1962, 3 children **DISCIPLINE** CHURCH HISTORY **EDUCATION** Duke Univ, AB; BD; PhD. **CAREER** Assoc prof, Center Col of Ky, 69-77; prof, S Methodist Univ, 77-98; prof, Duke Univ. **HONORS AND AWARDS** Kearns Fel, 67-68; Dempster Fel, 68-69; ACLS Fel, 75-76; Distinguished Teaching Awd, 76; Distinguished Service Awd, 99. **MEMBERSHIPS** Am Soc of Church Hist; Wesley Hist Soc. **RESEARCH** John and Charles Wesley, Early Methodism, History of Books and Printing. **SELECTED PUBLICATIONS** Auth, Wesley and the People Called Methodists; auth, Mirror and Memory: Reflections on Early Methodism; auth, The Elusive Mr. Wesley; auth, Diary of an Oxford Methodist; coed, The Works of John Wesley: Journal and Diaries. **CONTACT ADDRESS** Divinity School, Duke Univ, PO Box 90964, Durham, NC 27708-0964. **EMAIL** rheitz@duke.edu

HELD, BEVERLY ORLOVE
DISCIPLINE HISTORY **EDUCATION** Univ of Penn, BA, 72; MA, 74, PhD, 87. **CAREER** Lect, Hist, San Francisco State Univ. **MEMBERSHIPS** Am Antiquarian Soc **CONTACT ADDRESS** 1340 Lombard St. No. 304, San Francisco, CA 94109.

HELD, JOSEPH
PERSONAL Born 10/14/1930, Budapest, Hungary, m, 1954, 2 children **DISCIPLINE** MODERN EUROPEAN HISTORY **EDUCATION** Rutgers Univ, AB, 62, MA, 63, PhD, 68. **CAREER** Asst mod Europ hist, Rutgers Univ, 62-65; instr, Newark Col Eng, 66; asst prof Hungarian & E Europ studies, 66-68, asst prof hist & Hungarian studies, 68-70, dir, E Europ Soviet Studies, 76, Assoc Prof Hist & Hungarian Studies, Univ Col, Rutgers Univ, New Brunswick, 70-, Chmn Dept, 74-, Int Res & Exchanges Bd, Soc Sci Res Coun fel, 71-72. **MEMBERSHIPS** AHA; Am Asn Advan Slavic Studies. **RESEARCH** Social, political and economic history; Hungarian society in the early 15th century. **SELECTED PUBLICATIONS** Auth, Hungary: Iron Out of Wood, In: Current Changes in Soviet Type Economies, Int Publ, 68; co-ed, Intellectual and Social Developments in the Habsburg Empire from Maria Theresa to World War I Essays in honor of Robert A Kann, East Europ Quart, East Europ Monogr Ser, 74; Revolt of Babolna, 1437-1438, Slavic Rev, 77; The Modernization of Agriculture: Rural Transformation in Hungary, 1848-1948, East Europ Quart Press, 80. **CONTACT ADDRESS** Dept of Hist, Rutgers, The State Univ of New Jersey, New Brunswick, 84 College Ave, New Brunswick, NJ 08903.

HELGUERA, J. LEON
PERSONAL Born 10/29/1926, New York, NY, m, 1950, 3 children **DISCIPLINE** LATIN AMERICAN HISTORY **EDUCATION** Univ of Americas, Mex, BA, 48; Univ NC, MA, 51, PhD(Latin Am hist & polit sci), 58. **CAREER** Actg instr hist, Univ Tenn, 55; actg asst prof, Lynchburg Col, 56 & Univ NC, Ft Bragg, 56; actg instr, NC State Col, 57, instr, 57-59, from asst prof to assoc prof, 59-63; assoc prof, 63 & 68, Prof Latin Am Hist, Vanderbilt Univ, 68-, US res rep, John Boulton Found Caracas, Venezuela, 58-; US consult, Simon Bolivar Biog Proj Venezuelan Govt & Bolivarian Soc of Venzuela, 63; vis sr fel, St Antony's Col, Oxford Univ, 72-73. **HONORS AND AWARDS** Order of Andres Bello, Venezuelan Govt, 71. **MEMBERSHIPS** Conf Latin Am Hist; Southeastern Conf Latin Am Studies; Southern Hist Asn; corresp mem Centro de Estudios Montaneses, Santander; Gran Colombianist Comt. **RESEARCH** Colombian and Venezuelan history, the national period since 1830; foreigners in the independence movement of Northern South America, 1810-1830; social-economic history

of Southwestern Colombia in the 19th century. **SELECTED PUBLICATIONS CONTACT ADDRESS** Vanderbilt Univ, Sta B, Box 1606, Nashville, TN 37235.

HELLER, HENRY

PERSONAL Born 07/17/1938, New York, NY, 2 children **DISCIPLINE** FRENCH RENAISSANCE HISTORY **EDUCATION** Univ Mich, BA, 59; Cornell Univ, PhD(hist), 69. **CAREER** Lectr, 63-66, asst prof, 66-69, assoc prof, 69-79, Prof Hist, Univ Manitoba, 79-, Can Coun fels & grants, 71, 72 & 78-79. **MEMBERSHIPS** Can Cath Hist Soc (vpres, 69); Can Hist Asn; AHA; Renaissance Soc Am; Am Soc Reformation Res. **RESEARCH** French Renaissance and Reformation; early modern Europe. **SELECTED PUBLICATIONS** auth, Iron and Blood: Civil Wars in Sixteenth-Century France, 91; auth, Labour, Science and Technology in France, 1500-1620 (Cambridge Studies in Early Modern History), 96. **CONTACT ADDRESS** Dept of Hist, Univ of Manitoba, 403 Fletcher Argue Bldg, Winnipeg, MB, Canada R3T 5V5. **EMAIL** heller@cc.umanitoba.ca

HELLER, RITA

PERSONAL Born 07/23/1938, New York, NY, m, 1960, 2 children **DISCIPLINE** HISTORY **EDUCATION** Bryn Mawr Col, BA, 59; Columbia Univ, MA, 61; Rutgers Univ, PhD, 86. **CAREER** Adj Instr, Bergen Community Col, 68-80; asst prof to assoc prof, County Col of Morris, 88-. **HONORS AND AWARDS** Dept of Labor Diss Grant; Bevier Fel, Rutgers Univ; NEH Media Grant; CINE Golden Eagle, 86; Broadcast Awd, 87; CINE Golden Eagle and Directors Choice Awd, Black Maria Film Festival, 99; Cert of Commendation, Am Asn for State and Local Hist, 99. **MEMBERSHIPS** Am Assoc for State and Local Hist; Nat Coun for Hist Educ; Advocate for NJ Hist; NJ Studies Acad Alliance. **RESEARCH** New Jersey Local History; documentary film; American social history. **CONTACT ADDRESS** Dept Hist and Govt, County Col of Morris, 214 Center Grove Rd, Randolph, NJ 07869-2007. **EMAIL** rheller@ccm.edu

HELLIE, RICHARD

PERSONAL Born 05/08/1937, Waterloo, IA, m, 1998, 2 children **DISCIPLINE** RUSSIAN HISTORY **EDUCATION** Univ Chicago, AB, 58, AM, 60, PhD, 65. **CAREER** Asst prof Russ hist, Rutgers Univ, 65-66; asst prof, 66-71, assoc prof, 71-80, prof Russ hist, Univ of Chicago, 80-, **HONORS AND AWARDS** Herbert Baxter Adams Prize, AHA, 72; Guggenheim fel, 73-74; Nat Endowment for Humanities fel, 78-79 & 82-83. **MEMBERSHIPS** Am Soc Legal Hist, Hist Early Mod Europe, Am Asn Slavic Studies, The Historical Soc. **RESEARCH** Early modern Russian social, institutional, economic, and legal history. **SELECTED PUBLICATIONS** Auth, Slavery in Russia, 1450-1725, Chicago: The Univ of Chicago Pr, 82; ed, The Plow, the Hammer, and the Knout: Essays in Eighteenth-Century Russian Economic History, by Arcadius Kahana, The Univ of Chicago Pr, 85; ed, Ivan the Terrible: A Quarcentenary Celebration of His Death, Irvine: Charles Schlacks Publisher, 87; auth, The Ulozhenie (Law Code) of 1649, Charles Schlacks Publisher, 88; ed, The Frontier in Russian History, CharlesSchlacks Publisher, 95; auth, "Russian Clothing and Its International Context: 1600-1725," In Drevnerusskaia kul'tura v mirovom noiabria 97; auth, "Why Did the Muscovite Elite Not Rebel?", In a Festschrift issue of Russian History, 98; auth, Kholopstvo v Rossii 1450-1725, Academia, 98; auth, The Economy and Material Culture of Russia 1600-1725, The Univ of Chicago Pr, 99; auth, Thoughts on the Absencd of Elite Resistance in Muscovy," Kritika, Explorations in Russian and Eurasian History, 00. **CONTACT ADDRESS** Dept of Hist, Univ of Chicago, 1126 E 59th St, Chicago, IL 60637-1587. **EMAIL** hell@midway.uchicago.edu

HELLY, DOROTHY O.

PERSONAL Born 02/02/1931, Torrington, CT, m, 1956, 1 child **DISCIPLINE** MODERN BRITISH HISTORY **EDUCATION** Smith Col, AB, 52; Radcliffe Col, AM, 53, PhD, 61. **CAREER** Ed, Col Dept, Ginn & Co, Boston, 57-59; sr ed, Col Dept, Holt, Rinehart & Winston, Inc, NY, 61-63; instr, 63-69, asst prof, 69-80, assoc prof, 80-87, prof hist, 87-, assoc dean, Sch Gen Studies, 77-84, Hunter Col; mem, Berkshire Conf Women Historians, 69-, co-chmn prog comm, 84-87; co-chair, Prog Comm, 4th Intnatl Interdisciplinary Congress on Women, 87-90; pres, MidAtlantic Conf on Brit Studies, 96-99 **HONORS AND AWARDS** CUNY fac res grant, 68; Ford Found grant, 92-94; Hunter Col Pres Fac Incentive and Tchg grant, 96-97; AAUW awards, 97; res assoc, Queen Elizabeth House, oxford Univ, 98; mem, steering comt, seminar, Women Writing Women's Lives, 98- ; sr assoc mem, St Antony's Col, Oxford Univ, 90-91; co-chair, Columbia Seminar on Women & Soc, 98-99. **MEMBERSHIPS** AHA; fel Royal Geog Soc; Northeast Conf Victorian Studies; Inst Res Hist; Mid-Atlantic Conf Brit Studies. **RESEARCH** British imperialism and British antislavery. **SELECTED PUBLICATIONS** Ed, Family History, Haworth, 85; auth, Livingstone's Legacy: Horace Waller and Victorian Mythmaking, Ohio, 87; co-ed, Gendered Domains: Rethinking Public and Private in Women's History, Cornell, 92; co-auth, "Crusader for Empire: Flora Shaw/Lady Lugard," in Western Women and Imperialism, eds N. Chauduri & M. Strobel (Ind Univ Pr, 92); co-auth, Women's Realities, Women's Choices: An Introduction to Women's Studies, Oxford, 95; coauth, Journalism as Active Politics: Flora Shaw, The Times, and South Africa, The South African War, Manchester, 98. **CONTACT ADDRESS** 91 Central Park W, New York, NY 10021. **EMAIL** DOHelly@aol.com

HELMER, STEPHEN

PERSONAL Born 08/31/1944, Cleveland, OH, m **DISCIPLINE** ART HISTORY; ARCHITECTURE AND CITY DESIGN **EDUCATION** Principia Col, BA, 66; Cornell Univ, PhD, 80. **CAREER** Asst Prof Art Hist, Principia Col, 96-. **MEMBERSHIPS** Soc Archit Hist. **RESEARCH** History of city design; history of architecture. **SELECTED PUBLICATIONS** Auth, Gammage Auditorium and the Baghdad Opera Project: Two Late Designs by Frank Lloyd Wright, The Frank Wright Newsletter, vol 3, 80; Hitler's Berlin: A New Look at the Plan of Nazi Masterbuilder, Albert Speer, Archetype, Fall 80; Totaliarianism and the Modern Planning Tradition: Nazi Berlin Revisited, Planning Hist Bull, no 2, 82; Hitler's Berlin: The Speer Plans for Reshaping the Central City, UMI Res Press, 85. **CONTACT ADDRESS** Principia Col, Elsah, IL 62028. **EMAIL** SHD@PRIN.EDU

HELMHOLZ, R. H.

PERSONAL Born 07/01/1940, Pasadena, CA **DISCIPLINE** HISTORY, LAW **EDUCATION** Princeton Univ, AB, 61; Harvard Univ, LLB, 65; Univ Calif, Berkeley, MA, 66, PhD(hist), 70; Trinity Col, Dublin, LLD(h.c.), 92. **CAREER** Asst Prof Hist to Prof Law and Hist, Washington Univ, St. Louis, 70-81; Prof Law, 81-84, Ruth Wyatt Rosenson Prof Law, Univ Chicago, 84-; co-ed, Comparative Studies in Continental and Anglo-Am Legal Hist, 97-; assoc ed, New Dictionary of Nat Biography, 98-. **HONORS AND AWARDS** Fulbright Schol, Univ Kent, 68-69; Royal Hist Soc, Fel, 78-; Guggenheim Fel, 86-87; Cambridge Univ, Maitland Lectr and Vis Fel Commoner, Trinity Col, 86-87; Am Acad of Arts and Sci, Fel, 91-; Alexander von Humboldt Found, Res Prize, 92-93; Medieval Acad of Am, Fel, 97-; All Souls Col, Oxford, vis fel, Michaelmas term, 98. **MEMBERSHIPS** Selden Soc; Am Soc Legal Hist; Royal Hist Soc. **RESEARCH** Legal history. **SELECTED PUBLICATIONS** Auth, Canonical Defamation, Vol 15, Am J Legal Hist, 72; Marriage Litigation in Medieval England, Cambridge Univ, 74; Assumpsit and fidei laesio, Law Quart Rev, Vol 91, 75; Writs of prohibition and ecclesiastical sanctions, Minn Law Rev, 76; Support Orders, Church Courts and the Rule of Filius Nullius, Va Law Rev, Vol 63, 77; Early Enforcement of Uses, Columbia Law Rev, Vol 79, 79; Canon Law and English Common Law, London, 83; Select Cases on Defamation to 1600, Seldon Soc, Vol 101, 85; Canon Law and the Law of England, London, 87; Roman Canon Law in Reformation England, Cambridge, 90; coauth, Notaries Public in England since the Reformation, London, 91; ed and contribur, Canon Law in Protestant Lands, Berlin, 92; auth, The Spirit of Classical Canon Law, Athens, Ga, 96; coauth, The Privilege against Self-Incrimination: its Origins and Development, Chicago, 97. **CONTACT ADDRESS** Law Sch, Univ of Chicago, 1111 E 60th St., Chicago, IL 60637-2702. **EMAIL** dick_helmholz@law.uchicago.edu

HELMREICH, ERNST CHRISTIAN

PERSONAL Born 08/26/1902, Crescent City, IL, m, 1932, 2 children **DISCIPLINE** HISTORY **EDUCATION** Univ Ill, AB, 24, AM, 25; Harvard Univ, PhD, 32. **CAREER** Instr hist & govt, Purdue Univ, 24-26; asst hist, Radcliffe Col, 27-29 & 30-31; from instr to prof hist & govt, 31-59, Thomas Brackett Reed prof, 59-72, Emer Thomas Brackett Reed Prof Hist & Polit Sci, Bowdoin Col, 72-, Prof, Fletcher Sch Law & Diplomacy, 43-44. **MEMBERSHIPS** AHA **RESEARCH** Modern European and diplomatic history; Church and state in Germany. **SELECTED PUBLICATIONS** Auth, Twisted Cross--The German Christian Movement in the Third-Reich, Cath Hist Rev, Vol 0083, 97. **CONTACT ADDRESS** Bowdoin Col, 6 Boody St, Brunswick, ME 04011.

HELMREICH, JONATHAN ERNST

PERSONAL Born 12/21/1936, Brunswick, ME, 3 children **DISCIPLINE** MODERN EUROPEAN HISTORY **EDUCATION** Amherst Col, AB,58; Princeton Univ, MA, 60, PhD(hist), 61. **CAREER** Asst instr, Princeton Univ, 61; US Int Educ Exchange scholar, Free Univ Brussels, 61-62; from asst prof to assoc prof, 62-72, dean instr, 66-81, sec of fac, 91-93, prof hist, 72-88, prof emeritus, 88-, col historian, Allegheny Col, 98-. **HONORS AND AWARDS** BA degree magna cum laude; Phi Beta Kappa; Raymond P Shafer Awd for Distinguished Community Service. **MEMBERSHIPS** AHA; Phi Beta Kappa; Phi Alpha Theta; Rotary Int; Meadville Lit Union. **RESEARCH** Nineteenth and 20th century European diplomacy; modern Belgium. **SELECTED PUBLICATIONS** Auth, Is There an Honors Inflation?, Col & Univ, 77; A Prayer for the Spirit of Acceptance, Hist Mag Protestant Episcopal Church, 12/77; From Paris to Cannes: Belgium's Fight for Priority Reparation Payments, Studia Diplomatica, 12/80; The Serbs: A Warning from a Past Contributer, Contemp Rev, 93; US Foreign Policy and the Belgian Congo in the 1950s, Historian, winter 96; Historic Ties, Allegheny 17, fall/winter 97; Installation of a King, Allegheny, spring 98; Brand Whitlock, The United States in the First World War: An Encycl, Garland, 95; co-ed, The Civil War Diaries of Seth Waid III, Crawford County Hist Soc, 93; The Lake as it Was: An Informal History and Memoir of Conneaut Lake, Crawford County Hist Soc, 94; Place Names of Crawford County, Crawford County Hist Soc, 96, 98; ed, Pioneer Life in Crawford County, Pennsylvania, Crawford County Hist Soc, 96; Motering to Conneaut Lake: A Memoir by Bronson B. Luty, Pittsburgh History, spring 97; auth, Belgium and Europe: A Study in Small Power Diplomacy, 76; auth, Gathering Rare Ores: The Diplomacy of Uranium Acquisition, 86; auth, United States Relations with Belgium and the Congo 1940-1960, 98; coauth, Rebirth: A History of Europe Since World War II, 1st ed, 92, 2nd ed, 00. **CONTACT ADDRESS** Dept of History, Allegheny Col, 520 N Main St, Meadville, PA 16335-3902. **EMAIL** jhemrei@alleg.edu

HELMREICH, PAUL CHRISTIAN

PERSONAL Born 07/13/1933, Brunswick, ME, m, 1956, 3 children **DISCIPLINE** HISTORY **EDUCATION** Amherst Col, BA, 55; Harvard Univ, MA, 57, PhD(hist), 64. **CAREER** From instr to assoc prof, 57-74, chm dept, 68-75, prof hist, 74-99, Col Historian, 85-; Prof Emer, 99- Wheaton Col, MASS; lectr current events, Katherine Gibbs Sch, 65-78; vis assoc prof Rhode Island Col, 69; vis prof, Brown Univ, 70; consult, Hist Prog, Roger Williams Col, 71 and Bentley Col, 90; trustee's adv comt humanities, Southeastern Mass Univ, 79-82. **HONORS AND AWARDS** NEH summer stipend fel, 67; Prentice Prof, 82-85. **MEMBERSHIPS** AHA; New Eng Hist Asn; AAUP. **RESEARCH** Diplomatic history of Europe 1918-1939; New England higher education for women; 19th and 20th centuries. **SELECTED PUBLICATIONS** Auth, From Paris to Sevres: The Partition of the Ottoman Empire at the Peace Conference of 1919-1920, Ohio State, 74; auth, The Diary of Charles G Lee in the Andersonville and Florence Prison Camps, 1864, Conn Hist Soc Bull, 76; auth, Italy and the Anglo-French Repudiation of the 1917 St Jean de Maurienne Agreement, J Mod Hist, 77; auth, Wheaton College, 1834-1912: The Seminary years, Wheaton, 85; auth, Switzerland, Americana Annual, Grolier, 68-99; auth, Lucy Larcom at Wheaton, New England Q, 91. **CONTACT ADDRESS** Dept of History, Wheaton Col, Massachusetts, Norton, MA 02766. **EMAIL** phelmrei@wheatonma.edu

HELMS, JOHN DOUGLAS

PERSONAL Born 06/29/1945, Union County, NC, s **DISCIPLINE** AMERICAN HISTORY **EDUCATION** Univ NC, Chapel Hill, AB, 67; Fla State Univ, MA, 70, PhD(hist), 77. **CAREER** Archivist, Nat Arch & Rec Serv, 73-81; historian, Soil Conserv Service, 81-94; historian, Natural Resources Conserv Service, 94-. **HONORS AND AWARDS** Fel, Smithsonian Inst, 72-73, 78-79; Agricultural Hist Soc, pres, 99-00; Soc for Hist in the Federal Government, exec council, 97-99. **MEMBERSHIPS** Agr Hist Soc; Orgn Am Historians; Southern Hist Asn; Forest Hist Soc; Soil and Water Conserv Soc **RESEARCH** Agricultural history; conservhistory; Southern United States. **SELECTED PUBLICATIONS** Auth, "Technological Methods for Boll Weevil Control," Agr Hist, 79; auth, "Revision and Reversion: Changing Cultural Control Practices," The Cotton Boll Weevil, 80; auth, "Walter Lowdermilk's Journey: Forester to Land Conservationist," Environmental Review, 84; auth, "Conserving the Plains: The Soil Conservation Service in the Great Plains," Agr Hist, 90; auth, Readings in the Hist of the Soil Conserv Service, Washington, DC: Soil Conserv Service, 92. **CONTACT ADDRESS** Natural Resources Conserv Service, PO Box 2890, Washington, DC 20013-1890. **EMAIL** douglas.helms@usda.gov

HEMAND, JOST

PERSONAL Born 04/11/1930, Kassel, Germany, m, 1956 **DISCIPLINE** GERMAN LITERATURE, HISTORY, PHILOSOPHY **EDUCATION** Univ Marburg, Ger, PhD, 55. **CAREER** From Asst Prof to Vilas Res Prof, Univ Wis, 58-. **HONORS AND AWARDS** ACLS Fel, 63; Vilas Res Prof, 67; Mem of Saxon Acad, 85. **RESEARCH** German Culture 1750 to the Present, German-Jewish History, Comparative Arts, Fascism and Exile. **SELECTED PUBLICATIONS** Auth, Judentum und deutsche Kultur, 96; auth, A Hitler Youth to Poland, 97; auth, Deutsche Diditer bunde, 98; auth, Formen des Eses tu der Kunst, 00. **CONTACT ADDRESS** Dept German, Univ of Wisconsin, Madison, 1230 Linden Dr, Van Hise Hall, Madison, WI 53706-1525.

HEMPHILL, C. DALLETT

PERSONAL Born 01/26/1959, Philadelphia, PA, m, 2 children **DISCIPLINE** HISTORY **EDUCATION** Brandeis Univ, PhD; Princeton, AB. **CAREER** Prof, Ursinus Col. **HONORS AND AWARDS** NEH grant. **MEMBERSHIPS** AHA. **RESEARCH** American history before the Civil War. **SELECTED PUBLICATIONS** Published several articles and reviews on early American culture; auth, Bowing to Necessities: A History of Manners in America, 1620-1860, New York: Oxford Univ Press, 99. **CONTACT ADDRESS** Ursinus Col, Collegeville, PA 19426-1000. **EMAIL** dhemphill@ursinus.edu

HENCH, JOHN BIXLER

PERSONAL Born 02/21/1943, Colorado Springs, CO, m, 1966, 2 children **DISCIPLINE** AMERICAN HISTORY **EDUCATION** Lafayette Col, AB, 65; Clark Univ, AM, 68, PhD, 79.

CAREER Asst prof hist, Mankato State Col, 70-73; ed publ, 73-77, res & publ officer, 77-81, asst dir res & publ, 81-84, Am Antiquarian Soc; assoc dir res & publ, 84-89, dir res & publ, 89-96, vice pres for acad public progs, 96- ed, 73-96, Proc Am Antiquarian Soc & Early Am Imprints Ser; proj dir, NAm Imprints Prog, 79-89; affil prof hist, 92-, Clark Univ. **MEMBERSHIPS** Am Printing Hist Assn, AHA, Orgn Am Historians, Assn Bibliog Hist, Soc of the Hist of Authorship, Reading and Publishing, Am Studies Asn. **RESEARCH** American printing and publishing history; United States early national period; American Revolution. **SELECTED PUBLICATIONS** Ed, Three Hundred Years of the American Newspaper, Am Antiquarian Soc, 91; co-ed, Under It's Generous Dome: The Collections and Programs of the American Antiquarian Society, Am Antiquarian Soc, 92; ed, Serendipity and Synergy: Collection Development, Access, and Research Opportunities at the American Antiquarian Society in the McCorison Era, Am Antiquarian Soc, 93; auth, Toward a History of the Book in America, Publ Research Quart, 94. **CONTACT ADDRESS** Am Antiquarian Soc, 185 Salisbury St, Worcester, MA 01609. **EMAIL** jhench@mwa.org

HENDEL, KURT KARL
DISCIPLINE REFORMATION HISTORY **EDUCATION** Concordia Sr Col; Concordia Sem; Ohio State Univ, PhD. **CAREER** Dir, MA prog; prof. **HONORS AND AWARDS** Fulbright scholar, Univ Gottingen. **MEMBERSHIPS** Am Hist Asn; Am Soc of Church Hist; The Sixteenth Century Studies Confernece. **RESEARCH** Sixteenth-century reformer, Johannes Bugenhagen; Luther and Lutheran Theology. **SELECTED PUBLICATIONS** Auth, various articles on Reformation and general church history; The Doctrine of the Ministry: The Reformation Heritage, Currents in Theology and Mission. **CONTACT ADDRESS** Dept of Reformation History, Lutheran Sch of Theol at Chicago, 1100 E 55th St, Chicago, IL 60615. **EMAIL** khendel@lstc.edu

HENDERSON, ALEXA BENSON
PERSONAL Born 01/08/1944, Elberton, GA, m, 1967 **DISCIPLINE** AMERICAN HISTORY **EDUCATION** Fort Valley State Col, BS, 65; Atlanta Univ, MA, 66; Ga State Univ, PhD(hist), 75. **CAREER** Instr soc sci, Savannah State Col, 66-67; assoc prof, 67-79, Prof Hist, Clark Col, 79-, Partic soc sci, Inst Ser Educ, 67-74; adj prof, Atlanta Univ, 78-81; consult historian, Nat Park Serv; fel, Col Teachers, Nat Endowment Humanities, 82-83. **MEMBERSHIPS** Asn Study Afro-Am Life Hist; Southern Hist Asn; Asn Gen & Liberal Studies. **RESEARCH** Afro-American history; business history; urban history. **SELECTED PUBLICATIONS** Auth, Richard Wright and the National-Negro-Bankers-Association--Early Organizing Efforts Among Black Bankers, 1924-1942, Penn Magazine Hist Biography, Vol 0117, 93. **CONTACT ADDRESS** Clark Atlanta Univ, 204 Chestnut St SW, Atlanta, GA 30314.

HENDERSON, DWIGHT F.
PERSONAL Born 08/14/1937, Austin, TX, m, 1966, 1 child **DISCIPLINE** HISTORY **EDUCATION** Univ Tex Austin, BA, 59; MA, 61; PhD, 66. **CAREER** Asst to assoc prof, Ind Univ Ft Wayne, 66-80; prof, Univ of Tex San Antonio, 80-. **HONORS AND AWARDS** Fulbright Program 93. **MEMBERSHIPS** Org of Am Hist; S Hist Assoc; Omohundro Inst of Early Am Hist and Cult; Soc for Hist of the Early Am Republic; Counc of Col of Arts and Sci. **RESEARCH** U.S. legal and constitutional history, Environment History of U.S. with emphasis on the Southwest. **SELECTED PUBLICATIONS** Auth, Courts for a New Nation, Pub Aff Pr, 70; auth, Courts, Congress and Criminals - the Development of Federal Criminal Law, 1801-1829, Greenwich Pr, 85. **CONTACT ADDRESS** Col of Soc and Behav Sci, Univ of Texas, San Antonio, 6900 N Loop 1604 W, San Antonio, TX 78249-0651. **EMAIL** dhenderson@utsa.edu

HENDERSON, H. JAMES
PERSONAL Born 09/03/1927, Wobourn, MA, m, 1952, 4 children **DISCIPLINE** HISTORY **EDUCATION** Boston, AB, 50; Columbia Univ, MA, 57, PhD, 62. **CAREER** Retired Prof, Hist, Oklahoma State Univ. **HONORS AND AWARDS** Phi Beta Kappa **MEMBERSHIPS** Am Antiquarian Soc **RESEARCH** Early National U.S. Political Culture. **SELECTED PUBLICATIONS** Auth, "The Structure of Politics in the Continental Congress," Kurtz and Hutson, eds, Essays on the American Revolution, (73); auth, "The First Party System," Vaughan and Billias, eds, Perspectives on Early American History: Essays in Honor of Richard B. Morris, (73); auth, Party Politics in the Continental Congress, 74; auth, "Taxation and Political Culture: Massachusetts and Virginia, 1760-1800," Will & Mary Quart, Vol xlvii, 90. **CONTACT ADDRESS** 163 Spring St, Marshfield, MA 02050. **EMAIL** hjamesh27@aol.com

HENDERSON, JOHN B.
DISCIPLINE HISTORY AND RELIGIONS OF CHINA **EDUCATION** Univ Calif, Berkeley, PhD, 77. **CAREER** Prof Hist and Relig Stud, La State Univ. **SELECTED PUBLICATIONS** Auth, The Development and Decline of Chinese Cosmology, Columbia, 84; Auth, Scripture, Canon, and Commentary: A Comparison of Confucian and Western Exegesis, Princeton, 91; Auth, The Construction of Orthodoxy and Heresy, SUNY, 98. **CONTACT ADDRESS** Dept of History, Louisiana State Univ and A&M Col, Baton Rouge, LA 70803. **EMAIL** jbhende@lsu.edu

HENDERSON, LINDA
PERSONAL Born 01/22/1948, Warren, PA, m, 2 children **DISCIPLINE** 20TH-CENTURY ART **EDUCATION** Yale Univ, PhD, 75. **CAREER** Prof; Univ TX at Austin, 78-; curator, Mod Art, Mus of Fine Arts, Houston, 74-77. **HONORS AND AWARDS** Guggenheim fell, 88-89; Vasari awd, Dallas Mus Art; Robert W. Hamilton Author Awd; Academy of Distinguished Teachers, Univ of Texas; Who's Who in Am Art. **RESEARCH** Interdisciplinary study of modernism; rel of mod art to fields such as geometry; sci and technol; mystical and occult philos. **SELECTED PUBLICATIONS** Auth, The Fourth Dimension and Non-Euclidian Geometry in Modern Art, Princeton, 83; Duchamp in Context: Science and Technology in the 'Large Glass' and Related Works, Princeton Press, 98. **CONTACT ADDRESS** Dept of Art and Art Hist, Univ of Texas, Austin, Austin, TX 78712.

HENDON, DAVID WARREN
PERSONAL Born 09/11/1947, Atlanta, GA **DISCIPLINE** HISTORY **EDUCATION** Vanderbilt Univ, BA, 69; Emory Univ, MA, 74, PhD(hist), 76. **CAREER** Asst Prof Hist, Baylor Univ, 77-, Managing ed, Cent European Hist, 76-77, assoc ed, 78-; exchange prof, Seinan Gakuin Univ, Japan, 80-81. **MEMBERSHIPS** AHA; Conf Group Cent European Hist; Western Asn Ger Studies. **RESEARCH** Agrarian politics; political Catholicism. **SELECTED PUBLICATIONS** Auth, Notes on Church-State Affairs, J Church State, Vol 0038, 96. **CONTACT ADDRESS** Dept of Hist, Baylor Univ, Waco, Waco, TX 76703.

HENDRICK, IRVING GUILFORD
PERSONAL Born 08/30/1936, Los Angeles, CA, m, 1996, 3 children **DISCIPLINE** HISTORY OF EDUCATION **EDUCATION** Whittier Col, AB, 58, MA, 60; Univ Calif, Los Angeles, EdD, 64. **CAREER** Teacher, jr high sch, Calif, 59-62; asst prof educ, Flint Col, Univ Mich, 64-65; from asst prof to assoc prof, 65-74, prof educ, 74-, assoc dean, sch educ, 75-, Univ Calif, Riverside; Ex officio mem, Calif Comn Teacher Prep & Licensing, 77-. **MEMBERSHIPS** Hist Educ Soc; Am Educ Res Assn; Nat Soc for Study Educ. **RESEARCH** History of education in the United States; history of minority group education in the United States; history of teacher education and certification requirements. **SELECTED PUBLICATIONS** Auth, The Development of a School Integration Plan in Riverside, California, Riverside Sch Study, 68; auth, The Education of Non-Whites in Clifornia, 1849-1970, R & E Res Assocs, 75; art, Federal Policy Affecting the Education of Indians in California, Hist Educ Quart, summer 76; auth, California Education, Boyd & Fraser, 80. **CONTACT ADDRESS** Sch of Educ, Univ of California, Riverside, 900 University Ave, Riverside, CA 92521-0001. **EMAIL** irving.hendrick@ucr.edu

HENDRICKS, J. EDWIN
PERSONAL Born 10/19/1935, Pickens Co, SC, m, 1958, 3 children **DISCIPLINE** AMERICAN HISTORY **EDUCATION** Furman Univ, BA, 57; Univ Va, MA, 59, PhD, 61. **CAREER** Asst prof, 61-66; Assoc Prof, 66-75; Prof Hist, Wake Forest University, 75-; Chair, 95-00; dir hist pres prog, Wake Forest University, 73-; restoration consultant, 73-; American Philosophical Society res grant, 69, 70; R J Reynolds res leave, 72, 87. **HONORS AND AWARDS** NC Sons of the American Revolution, William R. Davie Awd, 81; Kiwanis International, Outstanding Club President, 88; Wake Forest University, Community Service Awd, 90. **MEMBERSHIPS** Southern Historical Association; Historical Society of North Carolina, NC Literary and Historical Association; National Trust for Hist Preservation. **RESEARCH** Local and institutional history; historic preservation; temperance movement; Revolutionary and early national US hist. **SELECTED PUBLICATIONS** Coauth, "Liquor and Anti-Liquor in Virginia, 1619-1919," 1967; auth, "Charles Thomson and the Making of the a Nation, 1729-1823," 79; ed, "Forsyth, the History of a County on the March, 76; auth, "Wake Forest University School of Law," "One Hundred Years of Legal Education," 94; auth, "Seeking Liberty and Justice: A History of the North Carolina Bar Association," 99. **CONTACT ADDRESS** Dept of Hist, Wake Forest Univ, P O Box 7806, Winston-Salem, NC 27109. **EMAIL** hendrije@wfu.edu

HENGGELER, PAUL R.
PERSONAL Born 02/02/1955, Wantagh, NY, m **DISCIPLINE** HISTORY **EDUCATION** State Univ NY at Cortland, BA, 77; Bowling Green State Univ, MA, 85; PhD, 89. **CAREER** From asst prof to assoc prof, Univ Tex Pan Am, 92-. **MEMBERSHIPS** Phi Kappa Phi, The Hist Soc. **RESEARCH** Modern U.S. Presidency, Cesar Chavez and the United Farm Workers Union, 1960s Political Culture, Kennedy/Johnson Administrations. **SELECTED PUBLICATIONS** Auth, In His Steps: Lyndon Johnson and the Kennedy Mystique, Dee, 91; auth, The Kennedy Persuasion: The Politics of Style Since JFK, Dee, 95. **CONTACT ADDRESS** Dept Hist & Philos, Univ of Texas, Pan American, 1201 W University Dr, Edinburg, TX 78539-2909. **EMAIL** henggeler@panam.edu

HENIG, GERALD S.
PERSONAL Born 10/09/1942, New York, NY, m, 1972, 3 children **DISCIPLINE** HISTORY **EDUCATION** Brooklyn Col, BA, 64; Univ Wis, MA, 65; City Univ NYork, PhD (hist), 71. **CAREER** Res asst, CUNY, 65-68; lectr hist, Hunter Col, 68-69; asst prof, 70-75, assoc prof hist, 75-79, prof hist 79-, Calif State Univ, Hayward, 75- **HONORS AND AWARDS** Arthur Rosenberg Awd in Hist, 64; Outstanding Prof Awd, Ca State Univ, 83; Pi Kappa Delta Awd for Best Lectr, Ca State Univ, 79, 83, 85, 90. **MEMBERSHIPS** AHA; Orgn Am Historians. **RESEARCH** US political and social history, 1850-1876; Maryland political and social history, 1850-1865; California Jewish history. **SELECTED PUBLICATIONS** Auth, Henry Winter Davis, The Encycl of the United States Congress, Macmillan, 94; To Dwell Together in Freedom: The Jews in America, 87; The Jacksonian Attitude Toward Abolitionism in the 1830s, Tenn Hist Quart, spring 69; ed, Give My Love to All: The Civil War Letters of George S Rollins, Civil War Times Illus, 11/72; auth, Henry Winter Davis and the Speakership Contest of 1859-1860, Md Hist Mag, spring 73; Henry Winter Davis: Antebellum and Civil War Congressman From Maryland, Twayne, 73; A Neglected Cause of the Sioux Uprising, Minn Hist, fall 76; ed, A Marylander's Impressions of Europe During the Summer of 1854, Md Hist Mag, summer 77; Soldiering is One Hard Way of Serving the Lord: The Civil War Letters of Martin D Hamilton, Ind Mil Hist J, 10/77; auth, Civil War Firsts: The Legacies of America's Bloodiest Conflict, 01. **CONTACT ADDRESS** Dept of History, California State Univ, Hayward, 25800 Carlos Bee Bvd, Hayward, CA 94542-3001. **EMAIL** ghenig@csuhayward.edu

HENNING, RANDALL
DISCIPLINE POLITICS AND INSTITUTIONS OF ECONOMIC POLICY MAKING **EDUCATION** Stanford Univ, BA; Tufts Univ, PhD. **CAREER** Prof, Am Univ. **RESEARCH** International and comparative political economy;International economic organizations; European integration; Exchange rate policy making, and macroeconomic conflict and cooperation. **SELECTED PUBLICATIONS** Auth, Currencies and Politics in the United States, Germany and Japan, Inst Int Econ, 94; coauth Global Economic Leadership and the Group of Seven, Inst Int Econ, 96. **CONTACT ADDRESS** American Univ, 4400 Massachusetts Ave, Washington, DC 20016.

HENRETTA, JAMES A.
DISCIPLINE HISTORY **EDUCATION** Swarthmore Col, BA, 62; Harvard Univ, MA, 63; PhD, 68; Oxford Univ, MA, 91. **CAREER** Asst lecturer, Sussex Univ, 66-68; Asst prof, Princeton Univ, 68-71; Prof, Univ Calif, 73-78; Vis Prof, Columbia Univ, 79; Prof, Boston Univ, 78-85; Burke Prof, Univ Md, 85-; Prof, Oxford Univ, 91-92. **HONORS AND AWARDS** Phi Beta Kappa, 62; Paul Hyland Harris Fel, Harvard Univ, 63-65; Fulbright Sen Scholar, Australia, 72; Charles Warren Fel, Harvard Univ, 75-76; NEH Fel, Am Antiquarian Soc, 85; ACLS Res Fel, 84-85 **SELECTED PUBLICATIONS** Auth, Salutary Neglect: Colonial Administration under the Duke of Newcastle, Princeton Univ Press, 72; auth, The Evolutions of American Society, 1700-1815: An Interdisciplinary Analysis, 73; co-auth, America's History, The Dorsey Press, 87, 2nd ed, Worth Pub, 93, 3rd ed, Worth Pub, 97, 4th ed, Bedford Books, 00; auth, Evolution and Revolution: American Society, 1600-1820, D.C. Heath & Co., 87; auth, The Origins of American Capitalism, Northeastern Univ Press, 91; co-ed, The Transformation of Early American History: Society, Authority, and Ideology, 91; co-auth, America: A concise History, Bedford Books, 97. **CONTACT ADDRESS** Dept Hist, Univ of Maryland, Col Park, 2115 F S Key Hall, College Park, MD 20742-0001. **EMAIL** jh53@umail.umd.edu

HENRIKSSON, ANDERS H.
PERSONAL Born 12/09/1948, Rochester, NY, m, 1971 **DISCIPLINE** HISTORY **EDUCATION** Univ Rochester, BA, 71; Univ Toronto, MA, 72; PhD, 78. **CAREER** Asst prof, Shepherd Col, 85-91; assoc prof, 91-97; prof, 97-. **HONORS AND AWARDS** NEH; IREX; Can Council; Deutchen Akad Austanschdierst Grants. **MEMBERSHIPS** AHAA; AASS; CAS; AABS. **RESEARCH** Late Imperial Russia; modern Baltic States. **SELECTED PUBLICATIONS** Auth, The Tsar's Loyal Germans, East Euro Monographs (Boulder and NY), 83. **CONTACT ADDRESS** Dept History, Shepherd Col, PO Box 3210, Shepherdstown, WV 25443. **EMAIL** ahenriks@shepherd.edu

HENRY, ERIC PUTNAM
PERSONAL Born 03/15/1943, Greensboro, NC, m, 1976, 3 children **DISCIPLINE** CHINESE LITERATURE & HISTORY **EDUCATION** Amherst Col, BA, 72; Yale Univ, Mph, 76, PhD, 79. **CAREER** Vis asst prof Chinese lang & lit, Dartmouth Col, 80-82; Lectr Chinese Lang, Univ NC, 82- . **MEMBERSHIPS** Asn Asian Studies; Warring States Project. **RESEARCH** Chinese drama and fiction; Chinese legendary history; Chinese social history; Vietnamese lang, lit, and hist. **SELECTED PUBLICATIONS** Auth, Chinese Amusement: The Lively Plays of Li Yu, Shoe String Press, 80; auth, "The Motif of Recognition in Early China,: Harvard Journal of Asiatic Stud, 47:1, 87; auth, "Chu-ko Liang in the Eyes of His Contemporaries," Harvard Journal of Asiatic Stud 52.2, 92; auth,

"Junzi Yue Varsus Zhongni Yeu in Zuo Zhuan," Harvard Journal of Asiatic Stud 59.1, 99; auth, "The Social Significance of Nudity in Early China," Fashion Theory 3.4, 99. **CONTACT ADDRESS** Asian Studies Curric, Univ of No Carolina, Chapel Hill, Campus Box 3267, Chapel Hill, NC 27514. **EMAIL** henryhme@bellsouth.net

HENRY, GRAY
PERSONAL 2 children **DISCIPLINE** COMPARATIVE RELIGION, ART HISTORY **EDUCATION** Sarah Lawrence, BA, 65; Univ Mich, MA, 80; doctoral work, Univ Kent, Canterbury. **CAREER** Teach, Fordham Univ, Dalton Sch, 66-68; teach, Azhar Acad, Cairo Am Col, 70-78; lect, Cambridge Univ, 88; instr, Bellarmine Col, 91-92; instr, Center Col, 93; Dir, Found Pub House: Islamic Texts Soc, Quinta essentia, Founs Vitae, 80-. **SELECTED PUBLICATIONS** Ed, Merton and Sufism: The Untold Story; narrator, Cairo, 1001 Years of Islamic Art and Architecture; Production, Islam: A Pictorial Essay in Four Parts, video, 86; ed, Islam in Tebet, 97; Production, the Ornaments of Lhasa: Islam in Tabet, 97; **CONTACT ADDRESS** 49 Mockingbird Valley Dr, Louisville, KY 40207. **EMAIL** grayh101@aol.com

HENWOOD, JAMES N. J.
PERSONAL Born 04/17/1932, Upper Darby, PA **DISCIPLINE** AMERICAN & MODERN EUROPEAN HISTORY **EDUCATION** West Chester State Col, BSEd, 54; Univ PA, AM, 58, PhD, 75. **CAREER** Tchr, high sch, PA, 58-66; assoc prof, 66-75, prof hist, East Stroudsburg Univ, 75; bk rev ed, Railroad Hist, and National Railway Bulletin. **MEMBERSHIPS** Orgn Am Historians; AHA; Nat Railway Hist Soc; Steamship Hist Soc Am; Railway & Locomotive Hist Soc. **RESEARCH** Twentieth century Am hist; railroad and maritime hist. **SELECTED PUBLICATIONS** Auth, Team teaching, Pa Sch J, 3/68; A Short Haul to the Bay, Greene, 69; A Cruise on the USS Sabine, Am Neptune, 4/69; Experiment in relief: The CWA in Pennsylvania, Pa Hist, 1/72; coauth, Monroe County, An Area in Transition, Pa Heritage, 10/84; Laurel Line: An Anthracite Region Railway, Interurban Press, 86; auth, Country Carrier of the Poconos: The Delaware Valley Railroad, Railroad Hist 174; contribr, Railroads in the Age of Regulation, 1900-1980; contribr, American National Biography, Oxford, 98; auth, "The Ocean City Electric Railroad: A Seashore Toonerville Trolley," Natl Railway Bulletin, vol 63, no 4 (98). **CONTACT ADDRESS** Dept of Hist, East Stroudsburg Univ of Pennsylvania, 200 Prospect St, East Stroudsburg, PA 18301-2999.

HEPBURN, SHARON ROGER
PERSONAL Born New York, NY, m, 1995, 2 children **DISCIPLINE** HISTORY **EDUCATION** SUNY Geneseo, BA, 87; SUNY Buffalo, MA, 92; PhD, 95. **CAREER** Asst prof, Radford Univ, 95-. **MEMBERSHIPS** AHA. **RESEARCH** African American 19th Century, Slavery. **SELECTED PUBLICATIONS** Auth, "Following the North Star: Canada as a Haven for 19th Century American Blacks", Mich Hist Rev 25.2 (Fall 99). **CONTACT ADDRESS** Dept Hist, Radford Univ, PO Box 6941, Radford, VA 24142-6941. **EMAIL** shepburn@runet.edu

HERBER, CHARLES JOSEPH
PERSONAL Born 07/04/1930, Allentown, PA, m, 1957 **DISCIPLINE** MODERN EUROPEAN HISTORY **EDUCATION** Dickinson Col, AB, 52; Univ Calif, Berkeley, MA, 57, PhD(hist), 65. **CAREER** Asst prof, 60-65, chmn dept, 71-73, assoc prof Europ hist, 65- , chemn dept, 83-84, George Washington Univ. **HONORS AND AWARDS** Woodrow Wilson fel, 55-56. **MEMBERSHIPS** AHA; Conf Group Cent Europ Hist; AAUP; Ger Stud Asn. **RESEARCH** Politics of peace in time of war, 1916-1918; German history in the modern era; the age of Austrian Baroque. **SELECTED PUBLICATIONS** Auth, Economic and social aspects of Austrian Baroque architecture, Eighteenth-Century Life, 6/77; auth, Eugenio Pacelli's Mission to germany and the Papal Peace Proposals of 1917, Cath Hist Rev, 79; co-auth, Conflict and Stability: Modern Europe, 1870-1970, Lexington, MA, 83; auth, Secular Implications of Religious Building Construction, in, Sangallensia in Washington, New York, 93; auth, Regulation or Disequilibration: Intervention in Economic and Social Matters in Late Eighteenth-Century German Lands, in, Consortium on Revolutionary Europe, 1750-1850: Selected papers, 1995, Tallahassee, 95. **CONTACT ADDRESS** Dept of History, The George Washington Univ, 2035 H St NW, Washington, DC 20052-0001. **EMAIL** cherber@gwu.edu

HERBERT, EUGENIA WARREN
PERSONAL Born 09/08/1929, Summit, NJ, m, 1953, 3 children **DISCIPLINE** HISTORY **EDUCATION** Wellesley Col, BA, 51; Yale Univ, MA, 53, PhD(hist), 57. **CAREER** Asst prof, 78-80, assoc, 80-85, E. Nevius Rodman prof hist, 85-97, E. Nevius Rodman Prof Hist Emer, Mount Holyoke Col, 97-, Stevens traveling fel hist, Wellesley Col, 68-69; book rev ed, African Studies Review, 97-. **HONORS AND AWARDS** Winship Book Awd, Boston Globe, 76. **MEMBERSHIPS** African Studies Asn; Hist Metal Soc; Royal Geog Soc. **RESEARCH** History of copper in Africa; historical roles of women in Africa. **SELECTED PUBLICATIONS** Auth, Alcune istituzioni commerciali anseatiche del medioevo, Rivista di Storia del Diritto Italiano, 55; coauth, Artists and anarchism: unpublished letters of Pissarro, Signac and others, Burlington Mag, 60; auth, The Artist and Social Reform, Yale Univ, 61; Aspects of the use of copper in pre-colonial West Africa, J African Hist, 73; Portuguese adaptation to trade patterns, Guinea to Angola, 1443-1640, African Studies Rev, 74; Smallpox inoculation in Africa, J African Hist, 75; coauth, The Private Franklin, W W Norton, 75; contribr, Timbuktu: a case study of the role of legend in history, West African Culture Dynamics, Mouton, 78; auth, Red Gold of AFrica: Copper in Precolonial History and Culture, Univ Wis Press, 84; auth, Iron, Gender and Power: Rituals of Transformation in African Societies, Indiana Univ Press, 93; co- ed, Social Approaches to an Industrial Past: The Archaeology and Anthropology of Mining, Routledge, 98. **CONTACT ADDRESS** Dept of Hist, Mount Holyoke Col, South Hadley, MA 01075. **EMAIL** eherbert@mtholyoke.edu

HERBERT, SANDRA SWANSON
PERSONAL Born 04/10/1942, Chicago, IL, m, 1966, 2 children **DISCIPLINE** HISTORY OF SCIENCE **EDUCATION** Wittenberg Univ, BA, 63; Brandeis Univ, MA, 65, PhD, 68. **CAREER** Asst prof, 73-78, assoc prof, 78-86, prof, 86-, Univ Maryland; vis asst prof, 76, vis assoc prof, 84, Princeton Univ. **CONTACT ADDRESS** Dept of History, Univ of Maryland, Baltimore, 1000 Hilltop Circle, Baltimore, MD 21250. **EMAIL** herbert@umbc.edu

HERLAN, RONALD WALLACE
PERSONAL Born 03/19/1942, Buffalo, NY, m, 1966, 2 children **DISCIPLINE** MODERN EUROPEAN & BRITISH HISTORY **EDUCATION** Houghton Col, BA, 64; State Univ NYork, Buffalo, MA, 67, PhD(hist), 73. **CAREER** Asst prof, 70-80, assoc prof hist, State Univ NY Col Brockport, 79-, State Univ NY Res Found grant-in-aid, 74 & 77 & fac res fel, 76-77; Willmott Found Grant, 87. **MEMBERSHIPS** Conf Brit Studies; Past & Present Soc; Hist Film Comt; London Rec Soc. **RESEARCH** Tudor-Stuart England; English poor relief; historical demography; local hist. **SELECTED PUBLICATIONS** Auth, Social articulation and the configuration of parochial poverty in London on the eve of the restoration, 4/76, Poor relief in the London parish of Antholin's budge row, 1638-1664, 4/77 & Poor relief in the London Parish of Dunstan in the west during the English revolution, 10/77, Guildhall Studies London Hist; Relief of the poor in Bristol from late Elizabethan times until the Restoration Era, Proc Am Philos Soc, Vol 126, 82; Local History materials in Drake Memorial Library, SUNY Col Brockport: An annotated bibliography with index of names and places, 1988; Hillside Cemetery. 125 Years, 92. **CONTACT ADDRESS** Dept of History, SUNY, Col at Brockport, 350 New Campus Dr, Brockport, NY 14420-2956. **EMAIL** rherlan@brockport.edu

HERMAN, BERNARD L.
DISCIPLINE ART HISTORY **EDUCATION** Col William and Mary, BA, 73; Univ Pa, PhD, 78. **CAREER** Lectr, Amer stud prog, 77-80; res assoc, 81-85; asst dir, Ctr Hist Arch and Engg, 84-85; asst prof, dept hist, 81-89; asst prof, Col Urban Aff and Pub Policy, 85-89; sr policy sci, 85-93; assoc prof, dept hist, 89-98; prof, dept hist, 98-; assoc prof, Col Urban Aff and Pub Policy, 89-98; prof, Col Urban Aff and Pub Policy, 98-; assoc dir, Ctr Hist Arch and Engg, 85-; assoc prof, 93-98; prof, 98-. **HONORS AND AWARDS** Abbott Lowell Cummings award, Vernacular Arch Forum, 87, 93; excellence in tchg, Univ Del, 92; Fred Kniffen prize, Pioneer Amer Soc, 92; Univ Del gen res grant, 95; summer res fel, NEH, 95; res fel, NEH, 96-97; ch, evaluation comm, univ delaware seaford hist soc, 92-93; bk rev recognition, ny times. **MEMBERSHIPS** Mem, Vernacular Arch Forum; Soc Hist Archaeol. **RESEARCH** Folklore and folklife. **SELECTED PUBLICATIONS** Co-auth, A Land and Life Remembered: Americo-Liberian Folk Architecture, Univ Ga Press, 88; Everyday Architecture of the Mid-Atlantic: Looking at Buildings and Landscapes, Johns Hopkins Univ Press, 97; auth, Architecture and Rural Life in Central Delaware: 1700-00, Tenn Univ Press, 87; The Stolen House, Va Univ Press, 92; ed, Historical Archaeology and the Study of American Culture, Tenn Univ Press, 96; rev(s), North Carolina Architecture by Catherine Bishir, Jour Soc Arch Hist, 94; Back of the Big House by John Vlach, SC Hist Mag, 94; The Old Village and the Great House: An Archaeological and Historical Example of Drax Hall Plantation, St. Anne's Bay, Jamaica by Douglas V. Armstrong, Jour Amer Folklore, 95; Housing Culture: Traditional Architecture in an English Landscape by Matthew Johnson, Amer Anthrop, 95. **CONTACT ADDRESS** Dept of Art Hist, Univ of Delaware, 162 Ctr Mall, Newark, DE 19716.

HERMAN, GERALD HARVEY
PERSONAL Born 09/13/1944, Brooklyn, NY, m, 1965, 2 children **DISCIPLINE** CONTEMPORARY HISTORY **EDUCATION** Hunter Col, BA, 65; Northeastern Univ, MA, 67. **CAREER** Instr, 65-71, asst prof hist, Northeastern Univ, 71, Spec Asst to the Provost, 78-88, Spec Asst to the Univ Counsel, 88, Actg Chmn Dept Hist, 98-99; Dir, Ctr for Interdisciplinary Stud, 99; hist consult, WGBH-Boston, 76-; fac develop officer, Northeastern Univ, 77. **HONORS AND AWARDS** Mellon Found grant, 73-74; OH State Awd for Excellence in Educational, Informational, and Public Affairs Broadcasting, 80; Northeastern Univ Excellence in Tchg Awd, 83; "Reaching for New Standards: Partnerships Take the Lead" Awd, Am Asn Higher Educ, 92. **MEMBERSHIPS** AHA; Hist Sci Soc; Film Comt. **RESEARCH** Contemp philos of hist; tchg of hist; Romanticism; media in hist. **SELECTED PUBLICATIONS** Ed, World War I: The Destroying Fathers Confirmed, Northeastern Univ, 72; auth, Making multimedia lectures for classroom use: A case history, Film & Hist, 12/72; coauth, To Know Thyself, Northeastern Univ, 73; A mediated instructional model to assure student competence in the history of Western civilization, Int J Instrnl Media, 76-77; auth, An integration of teacher and technology in a western civilization program, Soc Hist Educ Network News Exchange, fall 77; For God and Country: Khartoum as an Object Lesson for Global Policemen, Film & Hist, 79; coauth, Wien 1910, Film & Hist, 83; Media and History, In: The Craft of Public History, 83; World History on the Screen, 90, repr, 95; co-prodr, Public History Today, 90; auth, The Pivotal Conflict, 92; coauth, U.S. History on the Screen, 94; auth, The Great War Revisioned, In: Hollywood's World War I, 97. **CONTACT ADDRESS** Dept of Hist, Northeastern Univ, 360 Huntington Ave, Boston, MA 02115-5000. **EMAIL** G.Herman@nunet.neu.edu

HERMAN, PHYLLIS
PERSONAL Born 03/20/1946, Los Angeles, CA, m, 1973, 1 child **DISCIPLINE** HISTORY **EDUCATION** UCLA, PhD, 79. **CAREER** Calif State Univ Northridge, lectr, asst prof, 75-. **HONORS AND AWARDS** Calif State Univ, Gold Key Society Awd. **MEMBERSHIPS** AAR, AAUW, SCICSA. **RESEARCH** Hinduism; women and religion. **SELECTED PUBLICATIONS** Auth, Relocating Ramarajya, Int Jour Hindu Studies, 98. **CONTACT ADDRESS** Dept of Religious Studies, California State Univ, Northridge, 18111 Nordhoff St, Northridge, CA 91330-8316. **EMAIL** phyllis.k.herman@csum.edu

HERMANSEN, MARCIA
PERSONAL Born Montreal, PQ, Canada **DISCIPLINE** ARABIC AND ISLAMIC STUDIES **EDUCATION** Univ Waterloo, BA, 74; Univ Chicago, PhD, 82. **CAREER** assoc prof relig studies, 82-97, San Diego Univ; vis prof, 85-86, McGill Univ; assoc prof theology, 97-, Loyola Univ Chicago. **HONORS AND AWARDS** Amer Research Ctr in Cairo Award for Post-Doctoral Research, 86; Fulbright, US Dept of Educ Faculty Research Abroad Award, Pakistan, 89-90; Fulbright Lectureship in Islamic Studies, Malaysia, 94; San Diego Historical Soc, Award for Best paper on San Diego Religious History, 94; Fel, Inst for the Advanced Study of Religion, Univ Chicago Divinity School, 95; Sr Fel, Rutgers Univ Ctr for Historical Analysis, 96-97; Ethics Fel, Loyola Univ Chicago, 01. **MEMBERSHIPS** Chr, Study of Islam Sect, Am Acad of Religion; Middle East Studies Asn. **RESEARCH** Arabic and Islamic Studies; hist of religions. **SELECTED PUBLICATIONS** Auth, The Muslim Community of San Diego, Muslim Communities in America, 94; Shah Wali Allah of Delhi's Hujjat Allah al-Baligha (The Conclusive Argument from God), 96; The Study of Visions in Islam, Religion 27, 97; Mystical Visions as Good to Think: Examples from Pre-Modern South Asian Sufi Thought, Religion 27, 97; Religion and Literature in Muslim South Asia, Muslim World, 97; In the Garden of American Sufi Movements: Hybrids and Perennials, New Trends and Developments in the World of Islam, 97; Women, Men, and Gender in Islam, The Muslim Almanac: A Reference Work on the History, Faith, Culture, and Peoples of Islam, 96. **CONTACT ADDRESS** Theology Dept, Loyola Univ, Chicago, 6525 N Sheridan Rd, Crown Ctr., Chicago, IL 60626. **EMAIL** mherman@orion.luc.edu

HERR, RICHARD
PERSONAL Born 04/07/1922, Guanajuato, Mexico, m, 1968, 4 children **DISCIPLINE** HISTORY **EDUCATION** Harvard Col, AB, 43; Univ Chicago, PhD, 54. **CAREER** Instr to asst prof, Yale Univ 52-29; asst to assoc to prof Prof Emer, Univ Calif, Berkeley, 55-. **HONORS AND AWARDS** Bronze medal, Col de France, Paris, 85; Clare Hall, Cambridge, Eng, vis life member, 85-, Chancellor's fel, Univ Calif, Berkeley, 87-90; Comendador, Order of Isabel La Catolica, Spain, 88; Fel, Am Acad Arts & Sci, 90; Am Hist Asn Gershoy Prize for Rural Change and Royal Finances in Spain, 90; The Berkeley Citation, Univ Calif-Berkeley, 91, Am Philos Soc. **MEMBERSHIPS** Inst for Hist Stud; Soc for Spanish and Portuguese Hist Stud; Asn de Hist Demografica; Asn de Hist Economica. **RESEARCH** History of modern Spain, history of agriculture, modern history of group identities. **SELECTED PUBLICATIONS** Ed & contr, Themes in the Rural History of the Western World, Iowa State Univ Press, 93; ed & contr, The New Portugal: Democracy and Europe, Univ Calif, Intl and Area Stud, 93; auth, "The Constitution of 1812 and the Spanish Road to Parliamentary Monarchy," in Revolution and the Meanings of Freedom in the Nineteenth Century, Stanford Univ Press, 96; "El principio de la virtud y la critica politica: los origenes de la Monarquia constitucional en Francia y Espana," in Sociedad Espanola de Estudios del Siglo XVIII, El Mundo hispancio en el siglo de las luces, 96; auth, "Centralism and Provincialism in the Spanish Rising against Napoleon," in Andre Burguiere et al, eds, L'Histoire grande ouverte: Homamages a Emmanuel Le Roy Laudrie (97): 163-69; auth, "Jouvellanos y la desamortizacion de Carlos IV," in Jovellanos, ministro de Gracia y Justicia, Exposicion organizada por la Fundacion "La Caixa", Barcelona, Funcacion "La Caixa" (98): 105-113; auth, "La Guerra del 98

vista en un marco universal," in Fundacion BBV, Imagenes del 98, Bilbao, Fundacion BBV (99): 33-47; auth, "Algunas observaciones sobre la historia contemporanes de Espana," Albert Carreras et al. Eds, Doctor Jordi Nadal; La industrializacio i el desenvolupament economic d' Espanya, Barcelona Univ de Barcelona Col leccio Homenatges (99): 253-62; auth, "Flow and Ebb, 1700-1833" in Raymond Carr, ed, Spain: A History, Oxford, Oxford Univ Press (00): 173-204. **CONTACT ADDRESS** 1541 Hawthorne Terr, Berkeley, CA 94708-1805. **EMAIL** rherr@socrates.berkeley.edu

HERREN, MICHAEL W.
PERSONAL Born 12/15/1940, Santa Ana, CA **DISCIPLINE** CLASSICS, MEDIEVAL STUDIES **EDUCATION** Claremont Men's Col, BA, 62; Pontif Inst Medieval Stud, MSL, 67; Univ Toronto, PhD, 69. **CAREER** High sch tchr, Calif, 62-64; asst to assoc prof, 69-78, PROF HUMANITIES AND CLASSICS, YORK UNIV, 78-, ch hum, 82-85; grad fac medieval stud, Univ Toronto, 90-. **HONORS AND AWARDS** Assoc fel, Clare Hall, Cambridge Univ, 74; SSHRCC leave fel, 80-81, 87-88; Alexander von Humboldt res fel, Munich, 81-82; Atkinson Col res fel, 86-87; sr res fel, class, King's Col London, 87-88; DAAD fel, 92; Killam res fel, 95-97. **MEMBERSHIPS** Medieval Acad Am; Medieval Latin Asn Am; Soc Promotion Eriugenian Stud; Soc Hiberno-Latin Stud. **RESEARCH** Classics and medieval studies. **SELECTED PUBLICATIONS** Auth, Hisperica Famina I: The A-Text, 74, II: Related Poems, 87; auth, Aldhelm: The Prose Works, 79; auth, Johannis Scotti Eriugenae Carmina, 93; ed, Insular Latin Studies, 82; ed, The Sacred Nectar of the Greeks, 88; ed, J Medieval Latin, 91-; comp, Latin Letters in Early Christian Ireland, 96. **CONTACT ADDRESS** York Univ, 4700 Keele St, North York, ON, Canada M3J 1P3. **EMAIL** aethicus@yorku.ca

HERRING, GEORGE C.
PERSONAL Born 05/23/1936, Blacksburg, VA, m, 1995, 2 children **DISCIPLINE** HISTORY **EDUCATION** Roanoke Coll, BA, 57; Univ Vir, MA, 62; PhD, 65. **CAREER** Asst prof, Ohio Univ, 65-69; assoc prof, 70-80; prof, 80-, alum prof, 90-, Univ Ken. **HONORS AND AWARDS** NEH, 76; Fulbright Awd, 90; Guggenheim Fel, 97; Dist Prof, 88; Sturgill Awd, 96. **MEMBERSHIPS** AHA; SHAFR. **RESEARCH** US Foreign relations; Vietnam War. **SELECTED PUBLICATIONS** Auth, Aid to Russia: Strategy, Diplomacy, The Origins of the Cold War, Columbia Univ Press (NY), 73; auth, America's Longest War: The United States and Vietnam, 1950-1975, John Wiley (NY) 1st ed, 79; Knopf, (NY), 2nd ed, 85; McGraw-Hill (NY), 3rd ed, 96; auth, The Secret Diplomacy of the Vietnam War: The Negotiating Volumes of the Pentagon Papers, Univ Tex Press (Austin), 83; auth, LBJ and Vietnam: A Different Kind of War, Univ Tex Press (Austin), 94. **CONTACT ADDRESS** Dept History, Univ of Kentucky, 500 S Limestone St, Lexington, KY 40506-0001. **EMAIL** gherrin@pop.uky.edu

HERRON, CAROLIVIA
PERSONAL Born Washington, DC, s **DISCIPLINE** ENGLISH, AFRICAN-AMERICAN STUDIES **EDUCATION** Eastern Baptist College, BA, English lit, 1969; Villanova University, MA, English, 1973; University of Pennsylvania, MA, comparative lit & creative writing, 1983, PhD, comparative lit & lit theory, 1985. **CAREER** Harvard University, asst professor, African-American Studies and Comparative Literature, 86-90; Mount Holyoke College, assoc prof, English, 90-92; Hebrew College, visiting scholar, 94-95; Harvard University, visiting scholar, 95. **HONORS AND AWARDS** US Information Service, Fulbright Post-Doctoral Research Awd, 1985; NEH, Visit to Collections Awd, 1987; Radcliffe College, Bunting Institute Fellowship, 1988; Yale University, Beineke Library Fellowship, 1988; Folger Shakespeare Library, Post-Doctoral Research Awd, 1989. **MEMBERSHIPS** Classical Association of New England, 1986-93. **SELECTED PUBLICATIONS** Author: Thereafter Johnnie, novel, 1991; Selected Works of Angelina Weld Grimke, 1991. **CONTACT ADDRESS** Random House, 201 E 50th St, New York, NY 10022.

HERRUP, CYNTHIA
PERSONAL Born 03/10/1950, Miami Beach, FL **DISCIPLINE** HISTORY, LAW **EDUCATION** Northwestern Univ, PhD, 82. **CAREER** Asst prof, Univ of Mich, 81-84; Asst Prof, 84-88, Assoc Prof, 88-91, Prof of Law, Duke Univ, 91-; vis prof, Birkbeck Col, Univ of London, 98- ; ed, J of Brit Studies, 91-96. **HONORS AND AWARDS** Distinguished vis, Centre for British Studies, Univ of Adelaide, 98; fel, Royal Hist Soc, 86-; Walter D. Love Prize, North Am Confr on British Studies, 86; NEH/Folger Shakespeare Libr Fel, 96-97; John Simon Guggenheim Fel, 89-90; NEH Fel for Univ Teachers, 88-89; ACLS Recent Recipients of the PhD Awd, 84; Fletcher Jones Found Dist Fel, Henry E. Huntington Lib, 00-01. **MEMBERSHIPS** Am Hist Asn; Am Soc for Legal Hist; North Am Confr on British Studies. **RESEARCH** Early modern Britain; legal hist; social hist. **SELECTED PUBLICATIONS** Auth, Crimes Most Dishonorable: Sex, Law, and the 2nd Earl of Castlehaven, Oxford Univ Press, 99; The Common Peace: Participation and the Criminal Law in Seventeenth-Century England, Cambridge Univ Press, 87; The Pluck Bright Honour from the Pale-Fac'd Moon: Gender and Honor in the Castlehaven Story, Transactions of the Royal Hist Soc, 96; The Patriarch at Home. The Trial of the Earl of Castlehaven for Rape and Sodomy, Hist Workshop J, 96; Law and Morality in Seventeenth-Century England, Past & Present, 85; auth, Finding the Bodies, GLQ, 99. **CONTACT ADDRESS** Dept of Hist, Duke Univ, Box 90719, Durham, NC 27708. **EMAIL** cherrup@duke.edu

HERSEY, GEORGE LEONARD
PERSONAL Born 08/30/1927, Cambridge, MA, m, 1953, 2 children **DISCIPLINE** HISTORY OF ART **EDUCATION** Harvard Univ, BA, 51; Yale Univ, MFA, 54, MA, 61, PhD(hist of art), 64. **CAREER** From instr to asst prof art, Bucknell Univ, 54-59, actg chmn dept, 58-59; from instr to prof hist of art, Yale Univ, 63-; dir grad studies, 68-71; dir spec prog humanities, Yale Col, 75-76; mem adv board Conn Preservation Trust, 77-79; mem Conn State Commn Capitol Restoration, 77-79; lectr, Princeton Univ, Columbia Univ, others; mem adv board: J of Pre-Raphaelite and Aesthetic Studies; art exhibition co-orgnr, The Taste of Angels: Neapolitan Paintings in North America, 1650-1750, Yale Univ Art Gallery and other museums, 87-88. **HONORS AND AWARDS** Recipient Monticello Prize, 61; Fulbright scholar, Italy, 62; Am Philos Soc fel, Italy, 62; Morse fel, Yale Univ, 66-67; Schepp fel, Florence, Italy, 72. **MEMBERSHIPS** Renaissance Soc Am; Col Art Asn; Soc Archit Historians, dir, 71-73; Victorian Soc (US and Gr Brit), dir chapt; Dunky Club. **RESEARCH** Italian Renaissance art; Victorian art. **SELECTED PUBLICATIONS** Auth, J C Loudon and Architectural Associationism, Archit Rev, 68; The Arch of Alfonso in Naples and its Pisanellesque Design, Master Drawings, 69; Alfonso II and the Artistic Renewal of Naples, 1485-1495, Yale Univ, 69; Associationism and Sensibility in Eighteenth-Century Architecture, 18th Century Studies, spring 71; High Victorian Gothic: A Study in Associationism, Johns Hopkins Univ, 72; The Aragonese Arch at Naples, 1443-1475, Yale Univ, 73; auth, Poggioreale: Notes on a Reconstruction, and an Early Replication, Architectura, 73; Pythagorean Palaces: Architecture and Magic in the Renaissance, Cornell Univ, 76; Architecture, Poetry, and Number in the Royal Palace at Caserta, 83; co-ed, Architectura, 71-; ed, Yale Publs in History of Art, 74-. **CONTACT ADDRESS** Dept Hist of Art, Yale Univ, New Haven, CT 06520-0000. **EMAIL** george.hersey@yale.edu

HERSHKOWITZ, LEO
PERSONAL Born 11/21/1924, New York, NY, m, 1953, 2 children **DISCIPLINE** HISTORY **EDUCATION** Hunter Col, BA, 50; Columbia Univ, MA, 54; NYork Univ, PhD(hist), 60. **CAREER** From instr to assoc prof, 60-70, prof Hist, Queens Col, NY, 70-. **MEMBERSHIPS** AHA; Am Jewish Hist Soc. **RESEARCH** New York City history. **SELECTED PUBLICATIONS** Auth, Native American Democratic Association in New York City, 1/62 & Loco Foco party of New York, 7/62, NY Hist Soc Quart; Troublesome Turk: An Illustration of Judicial Process in New Amsterdam, NY Hist, 10/65; ed, Wills of Early New York Jews, 67 & co-ed, Letters of the Franks Family, 68, Am Jewish Hist Soc; auth, Tweed's New York: Another Look, Doubleday, 76. **CONTACT ADDRESS** Dept of Hist, Queens Col, CUNY, 6530 Kissena Blvd, Flushing, NY 11367-1597.

HERTZBERG, ARTHUR
PERSONAL Born 06/09/1921, Poland, m, 1950, 2 children **DISCIPLINE** HISTORY **EDUCATION** Johns Hopkins Univ, AB, 40; Jewish Theol Sem Am, MHL, 43; Columbia Univ, PhD, 66. **CAREER** Instr, Temple Emanuel, 56-85; Adjunct Prof, Columbia Univ, 60-88; Prof, Dartmouth Col, 85-91; Vis Prof, NYork Univ, 91-. **MEMBERSHIPS** Am Hist Soc, Israeli Host Soc. **SELECTED PUBLICATIONS** Auth, Jewish Polemics, Columbia Univ Pr, 92; auth, Judaism, 2ndd Ed, Touchstone, 92; auth, At Home Only With God, Aperture, 93; auth, The Zionist Idea, Jewish Publ Soc, 97; auth, The Jews in America, Columbia Univ Pr, 97; coauth, Jews: The Essence and Character of a People, HarperCollins (San Francisco, CA), 98. **CONTACT ADDRESS** Dept Hist, New York Univ, 83 Glenwood Rd, Englewood, NJ 07631. **EMAIL** ah3@is.nyu.edu

HERVEY, NORMA J.
PERSONAL Born 10/28/1935, Akron, OH, m, 1955, 6 children **DISCIPLINE** HISTORY **EDUCATION** Univ Akron, BA, 56; SUNY, Geneseo, MLS, 72; St Bonaventure Univ, MA, 80; Univ Minn, PhD, 91. **CAREER** Instr, asst prof, 70-80, Bonaventure Univ; assoc prof, 80-81, Univ Arkansas; assoc prof, 81-88, Gustavus Adolphus Col; vis prof, 94-95, Palackeho Univ, Czech Rep; prof, 88-, Luther Col. **HONORS AND AWARDS** Fulbright scholar 01; Czech Republic; Research grants: James J. Hill Foundation, 85, 86; Blandin Foundation, 85; Anderson Sabbatical leave Awd, 94; NEH Awd, profit dir, 91-94. **MEMBERSHIPS** Fellow Easter Europe Institute; Organization of American Historians; American Historical Assn; AAUP; ALA. **RESEARCH** Ethnicity, human rights, peace stud, comm stud; soc & econ hist. **SELECTED PUBLICATIONS** Auth, Genesis of a Library: From the Broom Closet to the Bootstacks, Global Reach, Local Touch, Chicago: ALA, 98; Birth of a Community, Phd dissertation U of Minnesota, 90; auth, Ethnic Issues in Eastern Europe, Haven International Review, 93; auth, History and Geography of the Greater Glamour Legion, ed for Palaeheho University, 95; auth, Teaching Overseas, Loch Haven International Review, 96. **CONTACT ADDRESS** Luther Col, 700 College Drive, Decorah, IA 52101. **EMAIL** herveynj@luther.edu

HERZSTEIN, ROBERT EDWIN
PERSONAL Born 09/26/1940, New York, NY, s **DISCIPLINE** HISTORY **EDUCATION** NY Univ, BA, 61; MA, 63; PhD, 64. **CAREER** Asst prof, MIT, 66-72; assoc prof to prof, Univ SC, 72-. **HONORS AND AWARDS** Founders Day Awd, NY Univ; Russell Awd, Univ of SC. **MEMBERSHIPS** German Studies Assoc; Hist Soc; Soc for Hist of Am For Relations. **RESEARCH** WW II, Holocaust, American Foreign Policy and Politics after 1919. **SELECTED PUBLICATIONS** Auth, Western Civilization, Houghton Mifflin, 75; auth, The War That Hitler Won; Goebbels and the Nazi Media Campaign, Putnam, 78; auth, Adolf Hitler and the German Trauma: An Interpretation of the Nazi Phenomenon 1913-1945, Putnam, 80; auth, When Nazi Dreams Come True: The Third Reich's Internal Struggle Over the Future of Europe After a German Victory, Sphere, 82; auth, Waldheim: The Missing Years, Wm Morrow, (Arbor House), 88; auth, Roosevelt and Hitler: Prelude to War, Paragon House, 89; auth, "Newsfilm and Documentary as Sources for Factual Information", Image as Artifact: The Historical Analysis of Film and Television, ed John O'Connor, AHA, 90; auth, "The Career of Dr Kurt Waldheim, 1938-1948: Sources in the National Archives", Historians and Archivists: Essays in Modern German History and Archival Policy, ed George O Kent, George Mason Univ Pr, 91; auth, Henry R Luce: A Political History of the Man Who Created the American Century, Scribner's, 94; auth, "Luce, Marshall and China: The Parting of the Ways in 1946", George C Marshall's China Mediation Mission, December 1945-January 1947, ed Larry I Bland, George C Marshall Found, 98. **CONTACT ADDRESS** Dept Hist, Univ of So Carolina, Columbia, Columbia, SC 29225. **EMAIL** robert-herzstein@sc.edu

HESS, GARY R.
PERSONAL Born 03/23/1937, Pittsburgh, PA, m, 1966, 1 child **DISCIPLINE** AMERICAN HISTORY **EDUCATION** Univ Pittsburgh, AB, 59; Univ VA, MA, 62, PhD(Hist), 65. **CAREER** From instr to assoc prof, 64-72, prof Hist, Bowling Green State Univ, 72-, chmn dept, 73-81, 85-93-; act dean, Col Arts & Sciences, 81-82; disting research prof, 88-; Nat Endowment for Humanities res fel, 78-79. **HONORS AND AWARDS** Pres, Soc for Historians of Am Foreign Relations, 91; Olscamp Research Awd, Bowling Green State Univ, 88; John M Burns Vis Prof, Univ of Hawaii, 93. **MEMBERSHIPS** AHA; Soc Hist Am Foreign Rels; Orgn Am Historians. **RESEARCH** United States foreign policy in South and Southeast Asia; United States diplomacy in World War II; United States foreign policy in early Cold War. **SELECTED PUBLICATIONS** Auth, Sam Higginbottom of Allahabad: Pioneer of Point Four to India, Univ VA, 67; American agricultural missionaries and efforts at economic improvement in India, Agr Hist, 1/68; The Hindu in America: Immigration and naturalization policy and India, 1917-1946, Pac Hist Rev, 2/69; American Encounters India, 1941-1947, Johns Hopkins Univ, 71; Franklin Roosevelt and Indochina, J Am Hist, 9/72; ed, America and Russia: From Cold War Confrontation to Coexistence, Crowell, 73; auth, The Iranian Crisis of 1945-46 and the Cold War, Polit Sci Quart, 4/74; United States policy and the origins of the French-Viet Minh War, 1945-46, Peace & Change, Summer-Fall 75; auth, The United States' Emergence as a Southwest Asian Power, Columbus Univ, 87; The Unending Debate: Historians & the Vietnam War, Diplomatic History, Spring, 94; auth, Vietnam and the United States: Origin and Legacy of War, Twayne, 1900, rev. edition, 98; auth, The United States at War, 1941-1945, Harlan Davidson, 86, rev. edition 87. **CONTACT ADDRESS** Dept of History, Bowling Green State Univ, 1001 E Wooster St, Bowling Green, OH 43403-0001. **EMAIL** ghess@bgnet.bgsu.edu

HESSE, C.
PERSONAL Born 07/24/1956, Berkeley, CA, m, 1999 **DISCIPLINE** HISTORY **EDUCATION** Univ Calif Santa Cruz, BA, 78; Princeton Univ, MA, 82; PhD, 86. **CAREER** Lectr, Princeton Univ, 86-87; asst prof, Rutgers Univ, 87-89; asst prof to prof, Univ Calif Berkeley, 89-. **HONORS AND AWARDS** Bourse Chateaubriand, 84; Whiting Found Fel, 85; Henry Rutgers Res Fel, 87-88; Koren Prize, Soc for French Hist Studies; NEH Fel, Inst for Adv Studies, Princeton, 92-93; Chevalier, Order des Palmes Academiques, 93; Guggenheim Fel, 98-99; Mellon Fel, Nat Humanities Ctr, 00-01. **MEMBERSHIPS** Am Hist Asn; Soc for French Hist Studies. **RESEARCH** Modern French History; History of Women; History of the Book. **SELECTED PUBLICATIONS** Auth, Publishing and Cultural Politics in Revolutionary Paris, 1789-1815, Calif, 91; auth, Culture and Identity in Early Modern Europe, 1500-1800, Mich 93; auth, Future Libraries, Calif, 94; auth, Human Rights in Political Transitions: Gettysburg to Bosnia, Zone, 99; auth, The Other Enlightenment: How French Women Became Modern, Princeton, 01. **CONTACT ADDRESS** Dept Hist, Univ of California, Berkeley, 3229 Dwinelle Hall, Berkeley, CA 94720. **EMAIL** shesse@socrates.berkeley.edu

HETHERINGTON, NORRISS SWIGART
PERSONAL Born 01/30/1942, Berkeley, CA, m, 1966, 2 children **DISCIPLINE** HISTORY OF SCIENCE **EDUCATION** Univ of Calif, Berkeley, BA, 63, MA (astronomy), 65, MA (hist), 67; Indiana Univ, PhD, 70. **CAREER** Res aid, Univ of Calif Forest Products Laboratory, 59; res asst, Univ of Calif Space Sci Laboratory, 63-66; res asst, Lick Observatory, 64;

instr, San Mateo Col, 67; instr, Agnes Scott Col, 67-68; asst prof, Atkinson Col, York Univ, 70-72; asst prof, 72-76, chm, Program in History and Philos of Sci, 73-74, staff, Western Civilization Senior Honors, 75-76, Univ Kansas; visiting fel, Henry E. Huntington Libr, 73; asst prof, Razi Univ, 76-77; visiting scholar, hist and philos of sci, Cambridge Univ, 77-78; visiting assoc prof, Univ of Ok, 81; RES ASSOC, OFFICE FOR THE HIST OF SCI AND TECH, UNIV OF CALIF, 78-; DIR, INST FOR THE HIST OF ASTRONOMY, 88-. **HONORS AND AWARDS** Robert H. Goddard Hist Essay Awd, 74. **MEMBERSHIPS** Berkeley Sci Historians; Hist Comn, Int Astronomical Union; Inst for the Hist of Astronomy; ed advisory board, Cosmos and Culture; ed advisor, The Oxford Companion to the History of Science and Its Uses. **RESEARCH** History of cosmology; U.S. science, technology, & society. **SELECTED PUBLICATIONS** Auth, Hubble's Cosmology: A Guided Study of Selected Texts, Pachart Pub House, 96; auth, Converting an Hypothesis into a Research Program: T.C. Chamberlin, his Planetesimal Hypothesis, and its Effect on Research at the Mount Wilson Observatory, The Earth, the Heavens, and the Carnegie Inst of Washington: Historical Perspectives after Ninety Years, History of Geophysics, 93; auth, Isaac Newton and Adam Smith: Intellectual Links between Natural Science and Economics, Action and Reaction: Proceedings of a Symposium to Commemorate the Tercentenary of Newton's Principia, 93; auth, Plato and Eudoxus: Instrumentalists, Realists, or Prisoners of Themata?, Studies in Hist and Philos of Sci, 96; auth, Early Greek Cosmology: A Historiographical Review, Culture and Cosmos, 97; ed & contribur, Encyclopedia of Cosmology: Historical, Philosophical, and Scientific Foundations of Modern Cosmology, Garland Pub, 93; auth, Cosmology: Historical, Literary, Philosophical, Religious, and Scientific Perspectives, Garland Pub, 93. **CONTACT ADDRESS** Office for History of Science and Technology, Univ of California, Berkeley, 543 Stephens Hall, Berkeley, CA 94720. **EMAIL** norriss@ohst7.berkeley.edu

HETTINGER, MADONNA
DISCIPLINE HISTORY **EDUCATION** St Francis Univ, AB, 77; Ind Univ, MA, 79, PhD, 86. **CAREER** Assoc prof. **RESEARCH** Women's writing and women's performance in the Renaissance. **SELECTED PUBLICATIONS** Auth, Defining the Servant, The Work of Work, Cruithne Press, 94. **CONTACT ADDRESS** Dept of Hist, The Col of Wooster, Wooster, OH 44691.

HEWLETT, RICHARD GREENING
PERSONAL Born 02/12/1923, Toledo, OH, m, 1946 **DISCIPLINE** HISTORY OF TECHNOLOGY **EDUCATION** Univ Chicago, MA, 48, PhD, 52. **CAREER** Intel specialist, 51-52, US Air Force, Wash DC; prog analyst, 52-57, chief hist, 57-75, US Atomic Energy Comn, Wash, DC; chief hist, US Energy Res & Develop Admin, 75-77; chief hist, US Dept Energy, 77-80; sr vice pres, sr hist, 80-, chmn, 90-98, History Assoc, Inc, Rockville MD; Regents Lect, Uiv Calif, 82; historiographer, Wash Natl Cathedral & Episcopal Diocese of Wash, 78-. **HONORS AND AWARDS** David D Lloyd Prize, Truman Libr Inst, 70; Dist Serv Awd, US Atomic Energy Comn, 73; Richard W. Leopold Prize, orgn Am Hist, 90; Henry Adams Prize, Soc Hist in Fed Govt, 90; Franklin D Roosevelt Awd, Soc Hist in Fed Govt, 93. **MEMBERSHIPS** AHA; Orgn Am Historians; Soc Hist Technol; Am Nuclear Soc Hist Sci Soc; Soc Hist in Fed Govt; Natl Coun on Public Hist; Hist Soc Episcopal Church. **RESEARCH** History of science and technology; history of the Episcopal Church. **SELECTED PUBLICATIONS** Coauth, The New World, 1939-1946, Vol I, 62 & Atomic shield, 1947-1952, Vol II, Atomic Energy Commission History, Pa State Univ, 69; auth, Nuclear Navy, 1939-1962, Univ Chicago, 74; auth, Atoms for Peace and War, 1953-1962, vol III, Univ Calif, 89; auth, Jessie Ball DuPont, Univ Fla, 92. **CONTACT ADDRESS** 7909 Deepwell Dr, Bethesda, MD 20034. **EMAIL** rghewlett@compuserve.com

HEWSEN, ROBERT
DISCIPLINE RUSSIAN AND BYZANTINE HISTORY **EDUCATION** Univ Md, BA; Georgetown Univ, PhD, 67. **CAREER** Instr, Rowan Col of NJ. **HONORS AND AWARDS** Cofounder, Soc for the Stud of Caucasia. **MEMBERSHIPS** Pres, Soc for the Stud of Caucasia. **RESEARCH** History of the Caucasis. **SELECTED PUBLICATIONS** Published several books and numerous articles on the history of the Caucasus, especially Armenia. **CONTACT ADDRESS** Rowan Univ, Glassboro, NJ 08028-1701.

HEYCK, THOMAS WILLIAM
PERSONAL Born 09/17/1938, Beaumont, TX, m, 1964, 2 children **DISCIPLINE** HISTORY **EDUCATION** Rice Inst, BA, 60; Rice Univ, MA, 62; Univ Tex, Austin, PhD(hist), 69. **CAREER** Asst prof, 68-73, Assoc Prof Hist, Northwestern Univ, 73-, Assoc Dean, 80-, Am Coun Learned Socs fel Brit hist, 74-75; Prof, 82; Prof., 82; NEH Fellow 84-85. **HONORS AND AWARDS** Harold H. and Virginia Anderson Prof, 89-92; Charles Deering McCormick Professor of Teaching Excellence, 98-00. **MEMBERSHIPS** AHA; Midwest Conf Brit Studies; Midwest Victorian Studies Asn. **RESEARCH** Modern British history; intellectual history; history of Ireland. **SELECTED PUBLICATIONS** Auth, The Decline of Christianity in 20th-Century Britain, Albion, Vol 0028, 96; Englishness and the Study of Politics--The Social and Political-Thought of Ernest Barker, Am Hist Rev, Vol 0101, 96; A Moralist in and out of Parliament-- John Stuart Mill, at Westminster, 1865-1868, Am Hist Rev, Vol 0098, 93; auth, Transformation of Intellectual Life in Victorian England; Coom Helm, 82; auth, The Peoples of The British Isles: A New History, Vol II, 1688-1870-Present, Wadsworth, 92. **CONTACT ADDRESS** Dept of Hist, Northwestern Univ, Evanston, IL 60208. **EMAIL** twh982@nwu.edu

HEYING, CHARLES
PERSONAL Born 11/15/1945, West Union, IA, m, 1967, 3 children **DISCIPLINE** URBAN STUDIES **EDUCATION** Creighton Univ, BA, 67; Iowa State Univ, MCRP, 88; Univ NC, PhD, 95. **CAREER** Asst prof, Portland State Univ, 95-. **HONORS AND AWARDS** ARNOVA Dissertation Awd, 96. **MEMBERSHIPS** W Polic Sci Asn, Am Polic Sci Asn, Am Asn of Univ Prof, ARNOVA, Urban Affairs Asn. **RESEARCH** Civic elites, Civic engagement, Sustainable economies, Nonprofit organizations. **SELECTED PUBLICATIONS** Auth, "Antigrowth politics or piecemeal resistance? Citizen opposition to Olympic-related economic growth," Urban Affairs Review, 00; auth, "Autonomy vs. solidarity: Liberal, totalitarian, and communitarian traditions," Administrative Theory and Praxis, (99): 39-50; auth, "Watershed management and community building: A case study of Portland's community Watershed Stewardship program," Administrative Theory and Praxis, (99): 88-102; auth, "Civic elites and corporate delocalization: An alternative explanation for declining civic engagement," American Behavioral Scientist, (97): 656-667; auth, "Second order cultural effects of civil rights in southern nonprofit organizations: The Atlanta YMCAs," Nonprofit and Voluntary Sector Quarterly, (96): 174-179. **CONTACT ADDRESS** Dept Urban Studies, Portland State Univ, PO Box 751, Portland, OR 97207. **EMAIL** heyingc@pdx.edu

HEYRMAN, CHRISTINE L.
PERSONAL Born Boston, MA **DISCIPLINE** HISTORY **EDUCATION** Macalester, BA, 71; Yale Univ, PhD, 76. **CAREER** Asst prof, hist, Univ Calif Irvine; current, Prof, Hist, Univ Delaware. **MEMBERSHIPS** OAH; Southern Hist Assn. **SELECTED PUBLICATIONS** Auth, A Model of Christian Charity: The Rich and the Poor in Colonial New England, 1630-1730, 77; auth, "Spectres of Subversion, Societies of Friends: Dissent and the Devil in Provincial Essex County, Massachusetts," in Saints and Revolutionaries: Essays in Early American History, Nortin, 83; auth, Commerce and Culture: The Maritime Communities of Colonial Massachusetts, 1690-1750, Norton, 84; coauth, Nation of Nations: A Narrative History of the American Republic, McGraw-Hill, 90, 94; auth, Southern Cross: The Beginnings of the Bible Belt, Knopf, 97. **CONTACT ADDRESS** Dept of Hist, Univ of Delaware, Newark, DE 19716. **EMAIL** cheyrman@udel.edu

HIBBARD, CAROLINE MARSH
PERSONAL Born 04/01/1942, Boston, MA **DISCIPLINE** ENGLISH HISTORY **EDUCATION** Wellesley Col, BA, 64; Oxford Univ, BA, 66; Yale Univ, PhD(hist), 75. **CAREER** Sessional lectr hist, Queen's Univ, 72-73; lectr, 73-75, asst prof, 75-81, assoc prof hist, Univ Ill, Urbana, 81-. **HONORS AND AWARDS** Article Prize, Berkshire Conf, 81; NEH Scholar Newberry, 88-89; Newberry Library/Brit. Acad. Fellowship summer 09; Fellow, Royal Historical Soc, 90. **MEMBERSHIPS** Am Cath Hist Asn; Conf Brit Studies; Cath Rec Soc, Gt Brit; AHA; Soc for Court Studies; Sixteenth Century Studies Society. **RESEARCH** Early Stuart English history; English Catholic history; early modern Europe. **SELECTED PUBLICATIONS** Auth, Early Stuart Catholicism: Revisions and Re-Revisions, J Mod Hist, 80; The Contribution of 1639, Recusant Hist, 82; Charles I and the Popish Plot, Chapel Hill, 83; Role of a Queen Consort: Household and Court of Henrietta Maria, 1625-42, in Court at the Beginning of the Modern Age, ed R. Asch, London, 91; Theatre of Dynasty, in Stuart Court and Europe, ed R.M. Smuts, Cambridge, 96. **CONTACT ADDRESS** Dept of Hist, Univ of Illinois, Urbana-Champaign, 810 S Wright St, Urbana, IL 61801-3611. **EMAIL** hibbardc@uiuc.edu

HICKEY, DAMON
PERSONAL Born 10/30/1942, Houston, TX, m, 1967, 1 child **DISCIPLINE** HISTORY **EDUCATION** Rice Univ, BA, 65; Princeton Theol Sem, MDiv, 68; Univ NC-Chapel Hill, MSLS, 75; Univ NC-Greensboro, MA, 82; Univ SC-Columbia, PhD, 89. **CAREER** Assoc Libr Dir, 75-91, Curator, Friends Hist Collect, 82-91, Guilford Col; Dir Libr, Col Wooster, 91-. **HONORS AND AWARDS** Ethel W. Twiford Religious Hist Book Awd, for "Sojourners No More," North Carolina Soc of Historians, Inc, 98. **MEMBERSHIPS** Org Am Hist; South Hist Asn; NC Hist Soc; NC Friends Hist Soc; Friends Hist Asn; Am Soc Church Hist; Am Libr Asn, Acad Libr Asn Ohio. **RESEARCH** American religious history, southern history, history of late 19th-century United States. **SELECTED PUBLICATIONS** Sojourners No More: The Quakers in the New South, 1865-1930, Greensboro, NC, Friends Hist Soc, 67. **CONTACT ADDRESS** The Col of Wooster, Libraries, Wooster, OH 44691. **EMAIL** dhickey@wooster.edu

HICKEY, DONALD ROBERT
PERSONAL Born 03/03/1944, Berwyn, IL, m, 1981 **DISCIPLINE** HISTORY **EDUCATION** Univ Ill, Urbana, BA, 66, PhD(hist), 72. **CAREER** Vis lectr hist, Univ Ill, Urbana, 72-73; vis asst prof, Univ Colo, 73-75; lectr, Univ Calif, Santa Barbara, 76-77; vis asst prof hist, Tex Tech Univ, 78; from asst prof to prof hist, Wayne State Col, 78-, John F Morrison Prof of Military History, U.S. Army Command and General Staff College, 91-92; Visiting Prof of Stragegy, Naval War College, 95-96. **HONORS AND AWARDS** Phi Beta Kappa, 66, American Military Institute's Best Book Awd, 90, National Historical Society's Book Prize, 90, Finalist, Nebraska State College Teaching Excellence Awd, 86,91,93, Burlington Northern Awd, 91,93, Commander's Awd for Public Service, U.S. Army Command and General Staff College, 92, Phi Gamma Mu Outstanding Faculty Member, 93. **MEMBERSHIPS** Soc Historians Early Am Repub; Society for Military History. **RESEARCH** American Early National, American Military history. **SELECTED PUBLICATIONS** Auth, The War of 1812: A Forgotten Conflict, Univ of Iillinois Press, 89; auth, Nebraska Movements: Glimpses of Nebraska's Past, Univ of Nebraska Press, 92; auth, The War of 1812: A Short History, Univ of Illinois Press, 95; auth, The War of 1812: A ShortHistory, U of Illinois Press, 95. **CONTACT ADDRESS** Div of Soc Sci, Wayne State Col, 1111 Main St, Wayne, NE 68787-1172. **EMAIL** dhickey@wscgate.wsc.edu

HICKEY, MICHAEL C.
PERSONAL Born 07/22/1960, Itasca, IL, m **DISCIPLINE** HISTORY **EDUCATION** Northern IL Univ, BA, 81, MA, 83, PhD, 93. **CAREER** Asst Prof, Assoc Prof, 92 to 96-, Bloomsburg Univ; Instr, 90-92, Univ Minn; Instr, 85,90, N IL Univ. **HONORS AND AWARDS** U IL REEC Res Lab Assoc 85, 98; 4 BU Res Gnts; Kennan Inst Adv Stud; NEH; Hayter Endow Res Gnt; NIU Grad Diss Fel; Fulbright-Hays Fel; NIU Haynes outstanding Stud Awd; NIU Hist Res Prize; NIU Hist Fel. **MEMBERSHIPS** AHA; AAASS; MASA; SSA; DE Valley Sem Russ Hist; CO U Sem Slavic Hist and Cult; Wildman Stud Grp Hist Russ Labor. **RESEARCH** 19th and 20th Century Russia. **SELECTED PUBLICATIONS** Auth, Urban Zemliachestva and Rural Revolution: Petrograd and the Smolensk Countryside in 19171, The Sov and Post Sov Rev, 98; auth, Gorod Smolensk v 1917 godu: Revoliusiia kak politicheskii protsess problemy I istochniki, in: E V Kodin ed, Stalinizm v Rossiiskoi provintsii sbornik statei, Smolensk, Smolensk Pedagogical Univ, 99; Russian Migrant Laborers in Helsinki on the Eve of World War one: A Res Note, J Baltic Stud, 96; Revolution on the Jewish Street: Smolensk 1917, J Social Hist, 98; Peasant Autonomy Soviet Power and Land Distribution in Smolensk Province, November 1917-May 1918, Revolution Russ, 96; Local Govt and State Authority in the Provinces: Smolensk Feb-Jun 1917, Slavic Rev, 97; Discourses of Public Identity and Liberalism in the February Revolution: Smolensk 1917, The Russian Rev, 96. **CONTACT ADDRESS** Dept of History, Bloomsburg Univ of Pennsylvania, 400 East Second St, Bloomsburg, PA 17815. **EMAIL** hickey@planetx.bloomu.edu

HICKS, DAVID L.
PERSONAL Born 08/12/1927, Kansas City, MO, m, 1947, 1 child **DISCIPLINE** EARLY MODERN EUROPEAN HISTORY **EDUCATION** Columbia Univ, AB, 49, AM, 50, PhD(hist), 59. **CAREER** Historian, US Air Force, 54-60; instr hist, Columbia Col, 60-62; asst prof, 62-65, Assoc Prof Hist, NY Univ, 65- **RESEARCH** Siena; Italian political and social history in the late Middle Ages and Renaissance. **SELECTED PUBLICATIONS** Auth, Sienese society in the Renaissance, Comp Study Soc & Hist, 7/60; The education of a prince: Lodovic il Moro and the rise of Pandolfo Petrucci, Study in Renaissance, 61; coauth, European History in a World Perspective, Heath, 64, rev ed, 75; auth, The Sienese state in the Renaissance, In: From Renaissance to Counter-Reformation, Random, 65; auth, sources of wealth in Renaissance Siena: business men and land owners, Bulletino senese di storia patria, 93/86; auth, from democracy to oligarchy: the transformation of the Siene government in the Renaissance Duquesne History Forum, 89; auth, the Sienese oligarchy and the rise of Pandolfo Petrucci, La Toscana al tempo di Lorenzo di Medici, 96. **CONTACT ADDRESS** Dept of Hist, New York Univ, 53 Washington Sq S, New York, NY 10011. **EMAIL** david.hicks@nyu.edu

HICKS, L. EDWARD
PERSONAL Born 06/05/1946, Dyersburg, TN, m, 1968, 2 children **DISCIPLINE** HISTORY **EDUCATION** Claremont McKenna Col, BA 68; Claremont Grad Univ, MA 71; Grad Study: Ed, Admin, Calif State Univ and Claremont Grad Univ 71-76, relig, Harding Grad Sch Relig, 82-85; Univ Memphis, PhD 90. **CAREER** Faulkner Univ, prof, assoc prof, full prof, ch hum fine arts, ch soc behav sci, fac rep pres cab bd dir's, 91-97; Christian Bros Univ, instr 90-91; Univ Memphis, teach asst 85-87; BD Hicks Ent Inc, vpres, pres, 76-91; Fullerton Jr Col, adj instr 70-76; Buena Park HS, tchr, coach, asst Dept hd, hd varsity bb coach, var fb off coord, 70-76; Fullerton Union HS, tchr, coach, 68-70; Claremont McKenna Col, grad tchg asst, 68-69. **HONORS AND AWARDS** Phi Alpha Theta; Outstanding Grad Stud; AUSCS Res Awd; Belle McWilliams Endow Res Gnt; Who's Who Amg Amer Univ Profs; NAIA All Amer CMC. **MEMBERSHIPS** AAUP; ASCH; AHA; AAH; BAS; CFH; NEAS; OAH; SCS; SHA. **SELECTED PUBLICA-**

TIONS Auth, Sometimes in the Wrong But Never in Doubt: George S. Benson and the Education of the New Religious Right, Knoxville, The U of Tenn Press, 95; Donald C. Swift, Religion and The American Experience, 1765-1997, Armonk NY, ME SHarpe Inc, 97, rev, Hist Rev of New Books, 98; auth, George Stuart Benson, Dict of Arkansas Biography, Fort Smith, AR Univ Press, 98; auth, Martin E Marty, Modern Amer Religion, vol 3 Under God Indivisible 1941-1960, Chicago, U of Chicago Press, 96, rev, Hist Rev of New Books, 97; auth, Diana Hochstedt Butler, Standing Against the Whirlwind: Evangelical Episcopalians in Nineteenth Century America, NY Oxford U Press, 95, rev, Hist Rev New Bks, 96; auth, Randy J. Sparks, On Jordan's Stormy Banks: Evangelicalism in Mississippi, 1773-1876, Athens GA, U of GA Press, 94, rev, Hist of New Bks Rev, 95. **CONTACT ADDRESS** Dept of Social and Behavioral Sciences, Faulkner Univ, 5345 Atlanta Hwy, Montgomery, AL 36109-3398. **EMAIL** ehick@faulkner.edu

HIGASHI, SUMIKO
PERSONAL Born 08/05/1941, Los Angeles, CA, m, 1980, 2 children **DISCIPLINE** HISTORY **EDUCATION** Univ Ca, BA, PhD. **CAREER** Prof. **RESEARCH** Am film history; Am cultural history; Film criticism. **SELECTED PUBLICATIONS** Auth, Cecil B. DeMille and American Culture: The Silent Era, Univ Ca, 94; auth, Antimodernism as Historical Representation in a Consumer Culture, Routlege, 96; auth, Postmodernism versus Illusionist Narrative as History: Walker and Mississippi Burning, Princeton Univ, 95; Night of the Living Dead: A Horror Film about the Horrors of the Vietnam Era, Rutgers, 90; Melodrama, Realism, and Race: World War II News Reels and Propaganda Film, Cinema Jour, 98; Rethinking Film as American History, 98. **CONTACT ADDRESS** 140 Sconset Ln, Guilford, CT 06437. **EMAIL** rjsmth@att.net

HIGBEE, MARK
DISCIPLINE HISTORY **EDUCATION** Columbia Univ, PhD. **CAREER** Asst prof, Eastern Michigan Univ. **RESEARCH** US, African-American. **SELECTED PUBLICATIONS** Publ in, J Negro Hist; Ind mag Hist. **CONTACT ADDRESS** Dept of History and Philosophy, Eastern Michigan Univ, 701 Pray-Harrold, Ypsilanti, MI 48197. **EMAIL** his_higbee@online.emich.edu

HIGGINBOTHAM, R. DON
PERSONAL Born 05/22/1931, Fresno, CA, m, 1980, 3 children **DISCIPLINE** HISTORY **EDUCATION** Wash Univ, AB, 53; MA, 54; Duke Univ, PhD, 58. **CAREER** Instr, Duke Univ, 57-58; Instr, William & Mary Univ, 58-59; Instr, Longwood Col, 59-60; Asst Prof, La State Univ, 60-67; From Assoc Prof to Prof, Univ NC, 70-. **HONORS AND AWARDS** NY Revolution Roundtable Awd for best bk on Am Revolution, 71; R D W Connor Awd for best article on phase of NC Hist, 72; Outstanding Civilian Serv Medal, US Army, 76; Pres Southern Hist Asn, 91-92; Pres Soc Hist of the Early Republic, 94-95. **MEMBERSHIPS** AHA, SHA, Orgn of Am Historians, Soc for Historians of the Early Republic. **RESEARCH** Colonial and Revolutionary American history. **SELECTED PUBLICATIONS** Auth, Daniel Morgan, 61; auth, War of American Independence, 71; auth, Atlas of the American Revolution, 74; ed, Papers of James Iredell, 76; ed, Reconsiderations on the Revolutionary War, 78. **CONTACT ADDRESS** Dept Hist, Univ of No Carolina, Chapel Hill, Chapel Hill, NC 27599-2319. **EMAIL** higginbo@email.unc.edu

HIGGINS, HANNAH
DISCIPLINE ART HISTORY **EDUCATION** Univ Chicago, PhD. **CAREER** Assoc prof. **SELECTED PUBLICATIONS** Auth, pubs in New Art Examiner. **CONTACT ADDRESS** Art Hist Dept, Univ of Illinois, Chicago, S Halsted St, PO Box 705, Chicago, IL 60607.

HIGGINSON, JOHN
DISCIPLINE HISTORY **EDUCATION** Univ MI, PhD, 79. **CAREER** Prof, Univ MA Amherst. **RESEARCH** Hist of South Africa; comp labor hist. **SELECTED PUBLICATIONS** Auth, A Working Class in the Making: The Union Miniere du Haut-Katanga and the African Mineworkers 1907-1949, Univ Wis, 89; Liberating the Captives: Watchtower as an Avatar of Colonial Revolt in Southern Africa and Katanga Province, Belgian Congo, 1907-1941, Jour Soc Hist. **CONTACT ADDRESS** Dept of Hist, Univ of Massachusetts, Amherst, Mass Ave, Amherst, MA 01003.

HIGGS, CATHERINE
DISCIPLINE HISTORY **EDUCATION** Yale Univ, PhD, 93. **CAREER** Assoc prof, Hist, Univ Tenn. **RESEARCH** Hist of mod S Africa. **SELECTED PUBLICATIONS** Auth, The Ghost of Equality: The Public Lives of D.D.T. Jabavu of South Africa 1885-1959, Ohio Univ Pr, 97; auth, "Travel with a Purpose: A South African at Tuskegee, 1913," J of African Travel Writing, forthcoming. **CONTACT ADDRESS** Dept of History, Univ of Tennessee, Knoxville, 915 Volunteer Blvd, 6th Fl, Dunford Hall, Knoxville, TN 37996-4065. **EMAIL** chiggs@utk.edu

HIGHAM, JOHN
PERSONAL Born 10/26/1920, Jamaica, NY, m, 1948, 4 children **DISCIPLINE** HISTORY **EDUCATION** Johns Hopkins Univ, AB, 41; Univ Wis, AM, 42, PhD(hist), 49. **CAREER** Asst ed, Am Mercury, 45-46; from instr to asst prof hist, Univ Calif, Los Angeles, 48-54; from assoc prof to prof, Rutgers Univ, 54-60; prof, Univ Mich, Ann Arbor, 60-68, Tyler univ prof, 68-71 & 72-73, chmn prog Am cult, 69-71; prof, 71-80, Vincent prof hist, 73-89, Prof Emeritus, 89-, Johns Hopkins Univ; Fund Advan Educ fel, 55-56; vis assoc prof, Columbia Univ, 58-59; vis fel, Coun Humanities, Princeton Univ, 60-61; fel, Ctr Advan Studies Behav Sci, 65-66; Commonwealth Fund lectr Am hist, Univ Col, London, 68; sr fel, Mich Soc Fels, 70-73; vis scholar, Phi Beta Kappa, 72-73; mem, Inst Advan Studies, 73-74; consult ed, Comp Studies Soc & Hist, 74-; Ecole des Hautes Etudes en Sciences Sociales, Paris, directeur d'etudes, 81-82. **HONORS AND AWARDS** Dunning Prize, AHA, 56. **MEMBERSHIPS** Orgn Am Historians (vpres, 72-73, pres, 73-74); hon mem New Soc Letts, Sweden; Am Antiq Soc; AHA; Immigration Hist Soc (pres, 79-82). **RESEARCH** American immigration and ethnic history; American cultural and intellectual history since 1830. **SELECTED PUBLICATIONS** Auth, Strangers in the Land, Rutgers Univ, 55; coauth & ed, Reconstruction of American History, Hutchinson & Co, 62; coauth, History: Humanistic Scholarship in America, Prentice-Hall, 65; auth, From Boundlessness to Consolidation: The Transformation of American Culture, 1848-1860, Clements Libr, 69; Writing American History, Ind Univ, 70; Send These to Me: Jews and Other Immigrants in Urban America, Atheneum, 75; ed, Ethnic Leadership in America, Johns Hopkins Univ, 78; ed, Civil Rights and Social Wrongs: Black-White Relations Since World War II, Pa State Univ Press, 97. **CONTACT ADDRESS** Dept of Hist, Johns Hopkins Univ, Baltimore, 3400 N Charles St, Baltimore, MD 21218. **EMAIL** jhigham@jhu.edu

HIGHAM, ROBIN
PERSONAL Born 06/20/1925, London, England, m, 1950, 4 children **DISCIPLINE** HISTORY **EDUCATION** Harvard Univ, AB cum laude, 50, PhD, 57; Claremont Grad Sch, MA, 53. **CAREER** Instr Eng & hist, 50-52, Webb Sch, Calif; instr hist, 54-57, Univ Mass; asst prof, 57-63, Univ NC; assoc prof, 63-66, prof mod Brit & mil hist, 66-98, Kans St Univ; Soc Sci Res Coun Natl Security Policy res fel, 60-61; historian, 60-66 & 75-79, Brit Overseas Airways Corp; adv ed, 67-, Technol & Cult; ed, 68-88, Mil Affairs; ed, 70-88, Aerospace Historian; grad fac lectr, 71, Kans St Univ; mil adv, 70-75, Univ Ky Press; ed, 76-85, Bd Int Comn on Mil Hist; ed, J of the West, 77-, mem and pres archives comt ICMH, 90-00; Advisory Editor, Greenwood Press, 90-. **HONORS AND AWARDS** Se Morison Prize, AMI 85; Korea Goremor's Aviation Honor Award, 00. **MEMBERSHIPS** Am Aviation Hist Soc; Soc Hist Technol; Am Mil Inst; Orgn Am Historians; RAFHS. **RESEARCH** Modern British; military aviation, and technological history. **SELECTED PUBLICATIONS** Auth, Air Power: A Concise History, Macdonald's, London, 72 & St Martin's, NY, 73; ed, Civil Wars in the Twentieth Century, 72-98 Intervention or Abstention: The Dilemma of US Foreign Policy, Univ Ky, 74; co-ed, A Guide to the Sources of US Military History, Archon Bks, 75-98; co-ed, Flying Combat Aircraft of the USAAF-USAF, 75 & Flying Combat Aircraft II, Iowa State Univ, 78; auth, Soviet Aviation and Air Power, Westview, 78; auth, Diary of a Disaster: British Aid to Greece 1940-1941, UP Kentucky, 86; auth, The Bases of Air Strategy: Building Airfields for the RAF 1915-1945, Airlife, 98; co-ed, Russian Aviation & Air Power, Cass, 98. **CONTACT ADDRESS** President, Sunflower Univ, Box 1009, Manhattan, KS 66506-1000. **EMAIL** rhigham@sunflower-unv-press.org

HIGONNET, PATRICE
DISCIPLINE HISTORY **EDUCATION** Harvard Univ, BA, 58; Oxford Univ, BA, 60; Harvard Univ, PhD, 65. **CAREER** Prof, fr hist, Harvard Univ. **SELECTED PUBLICATIONS** Auth, Goodnen Beyond Virtue, Harvard Univ Press, 98. **CONTACT ADDRESS** Harvard Univ, Cambridge, MA 02138.

HILDEN, PATRICIA PENN
PERSONAL Born Burbank, CA, m, 1987, 3 children **DISCIPLINE** HISTORY **EDUCATION** Univ Calif, BA, 65; MA, 77; Univ Cambridge, MA, PhD, 81. **CAREER** Asst to assoc prof, Emory Univ, 82-95; prof, Univ of Calif, 95-. **HONORS AND AWARDS** Soc Sci Res Counc, 81; Centre Nat de Recherche Scientifique Res Fel, 82-83; ACLS Humanities Fel, 83-84; Visiting Fel, Oxford, 83-84; Outstanding Teacher Awd, Emory Col, 85; Fulbright Found Awd, 85-86; ACLS Grant, 88; Historian Prize, Berkshire Conf of Women Hist, 92; Mentor of the Year, 97. **MEMBERSHIPS** AHA, Am Studies Assoc, Wordcraft Circle of Native Am Scholars, Writers, Storytellers, Native Writers Circle of the Am. **RESEARCH** The History of the Racialization of the Western U.S., 1800-present, North Americans Indians Enslaved in the Caribbean, 1630-1750, History of women of Color in the U.S., Feminist Theory. **SELECTED PUBLICATIONS** Auth, Working Women and Socialist Politics in France, 1880-1914, Clarendon Pr, (Oxford), 86; auth, Women, Work and Politics: Belgium, 1830-194, Clarendon Pr, (Oxford), 93; auth, When Nickels Were Indians, Smithsonian Inst Pr, (Washington, DC), 95; auth, "The Rhetoric and Iconography of Reform: Women Coal Miners in Belgium, 1840-1914," Hist Jour, (91): 411-36; auth, "Ritchie Valens Is Dead: E Pluribus Unum," As We Are Now, ed W.S. Penn, Univ of Calif, (Berkeley, 98): 219-52; auth, "Readings from the Red Zone: Cultural Studies, History, Anthropology," Am Lit Hist, (98): 524-43; auth, "Performing Indian in the National Museum of the American Indian," Soc Identities 5.2 (99): 161-83; auth, "Race for Sale: Narratives of Possession in Two Ethnic Museums," TDR: The Drama Rev, (00); auth, "til Indian Voices Wake Us," Towards a Geography of a Soul: New Perspectives on Kamau Brathwaite, ed Timothy Reiss, Africa World Pr, (London, 01): 403-30. **CONTACT ADDRESS** Dept of Ethnic Studies, Univ of California, Berkeley, 506 Burrows Hall, 2570, Berkeley, CA 94720-2570. **EMAIL** hilden@uclink4.berkeley.edu

HILDERBRAND, ROBERT CLINTON
PERSONAL Born 08/24/1947, Marshalltown, IA, m, 1986, 1 child **DISCIPLINE** UNITED STATES HISTORY, AMERICAN FOREIGN RELATIONS **EDUCATION** Univ Iowa, BA, 69, MA, 74, PhD(hist), 77. **CAREER** Asst prof hist, Univ SDak, 77-78; asst prof, Univ NC, 78-79; asst prof, Univ Mo, 79-80; asst prof, 80-87, Prof Hisy, Univ SDak, 87-. **HONORS AND AWARDS** Univ Teacher of the Year Awd, 84, 92. **MEMBERSHIPS** AHA; Soc Historians Am Foreign Rels; Phi Beta Kappa. **RESEARCH** Management of United States public opinion in foreign affairs; creation of United Nations; World War II. **SELECTED PUBLICATIONS** Auth, Power and the People: Executive Management of Public Opinion in Foreign Affairs, 1897-1921, Univ NC Press, 81; The Press Conferences of Woodrow Wilson, Princeton Univ Press, 85; Dumberton Oaks: The Origins of the United Nations and the Search for Postwar Security, Univ NC Press, 90. **CONTACT ADDRESS** Dept of Hist, Univ of So Dakota, Vermillion, 414 E Clark St., Vermillion, SD 57069-2390. **EMAIL** rhilderb@usd.edu

HILES, TIMOTHY
DISCIPLINE ART HISTORY **EDUCATION** Pa State Univ, PhD, 92. **CAREER** Assoc prof, Art Hist, Univ Tenn **HONORS AND AWARDS** Francis E. Hyslop Mem Fel, Pa State Univ, 90; Creative Ach Awd, Pa State Univ, 90-91; Scholarly Activities Res Incentive Fund Awd, Univ Tenn, 94, 95; Reproduction and Rights Expense Awd, Univ Tenn, 94; Dept of Art Excel in Tchg Awd, 97; Kurka Fac Awd, Univ Tenn, 98. **SELECTED PUBLICATIONS** Auth, "Morris Louis," 20th-Century Supplement, Encycl of World Biog (92); auth, "Hector Guimards Paris Metro Stations," The Int Dict of Architects & Architecture (93); auth, "Keith Haring," 20th-Century Supplement, Encycl of World Biog (94); auth, Thomas Theodore Heine: Fin-de-siecle Munich and the Origins of Simplicissimus, Lang (NY), 96; auth, "Klimt, Nietzsche and the Beethoven Frieze," in Nietzsch, Philosophy and the Arts: Cambridge Studies in Philosophy and the Arts, Cambridge Univ Pr (Cambridge), 98. **CONTACT ADDRESS** Sch of Art, Univ of Tennessee, Knoxville, Knoxville, TN 37996. **EMAIL** thiles@utk.edu

HILL, ALLAN G.
PERSONAL Born 09/16/1944, Bangor, Ireland, m, 1968, 2 children **DISCIPLINE** DEMOGRAPHY **EDUCATION** Durham Univ, BA, 66; PhD, 69; Princeton Univ, Dipl Demog, 75; Harvard, MA, 91. **CAREER** Adelot Prof, Harvard Sch Public Health. **RESEARCH** Birth interval dynamics in the MRC Main Study Area, The Gambia, Assessment of the impact of insecticide-treated bed-nets on the mortality and morbidity of young children in The Gambia, The fertility, mortality and nutritional status of selected pastoral and agro-pastoral communities of the western Sahel. **SELECTED PUBLICATIONS** Auth, "L'Enquete pilote sur la mortalite aux jeunes ages dans cinq maternites de la ville de Bamako, Mali," in Estimations de la mortalite du jeunne enfant pour guider les actions de sante dans les pays en developpement (Editions INSERM, Paris, 86), 107-129; auth, "Introduction," in Health interventions and mortality change in developing countries, J of Bioscience supplement 10, ed. Allan G. Hill and D.F. Roberts (Cambridge: Parkes Found, 89); auth, "Demographic responses to food shortages in the Sahel," in Rural Development and population: institutions and policy, ed. G. McNicoll and M.Cain, supplement to Vol 15 of Pop and Develop Rev (Oxford: Oxford Univ Press,90), 168-192; coauth, co-ed, "Advantages and limitations of large-scale health interview surveys for the study of health and its determinants," in Health transition: methods and measures (Australian Nat Univ, 91); auth, "African demographic regimes, past and present," in Africa Thirty years on, ed. Douglas Rimmer (Heinemann Educational for the Royal African Soc, 91); auth, "Making better use of demographic data and health statistics in Primary Health Care," in Mortality and society in sub-Saharan Africa, ed. E van de Walle, G. Pison and M. Sala-Diakanda (Oxford: Clarendon Press, 92); auth, Effects of health programs on child mortality in sub-Saharan Africa, Nat Res Coun, Nat Acad Press (Wash DC), 93; coauth, "A Critical analysis of the design, results and implications of the mortality and use of health services surveys," Int J of Epidemiology 22 (93): 73-80; coauth, "A malaria control trial using insecticide-treated bed nets and targeted chemoprophylaxis in a rural area of The Gambia, West Africa, " "Mortality and morbidity from malaria in the study area," "The impact of the interventions on mortality and morbidity from malarian," in Transactions of the Royal Society of Tropical Medicine and Hygiene 87 supplement 2.2 (93): 87, 13-17; 37-44; coauth, "Constructing natural fertility: the use of

Western contraceptive technologies on rural Gambia," Pop and Develop rev 20-1 (94): 81-113. **CONTACT ADDRESS** Dept Pop Studies, Harvard Univ, 677 Huntington Ave, Boston, MA 02115.

HILL, BENNETT DAVID
PERSONAL Born 09/27/1934, Baltimore, MD, s **DISCIPLINE** HISTORY **EDUCATION** Princeton Univ, AB 1956; Harvard Univ, AM 1958; Princeton Univ, PhD 1963. **CAREER** University of Western Ontario, London CN, asst prof, 62-64; Univ of Ill, Urbana, asst and assoc prof, 64-78, dept of history, prof, 75-81, chm, 78-81; Benedictine Monk of St Anselm's Abbey, Washington District of Columbia, 80-; Univ of Maryland, visiting prof, 84-87; Roman Catholic priest ordained, 85; Georgetown University visiting prof, 87-. **HONORS AND AWARDS** Flw Amer Cncl of Learned Soc 1970-71. **MEMBERSHIPS** Consltnt Natl Endowmnt for the Humanities 1978, Woodrow Wilson Natl Fdtn 1982; bd of dir American Benedictine Review; Princeton Club of Washington. **SELECTED PUBLICATIONS** Author, English Cistercian Monasteries and Their Patrons in the Twelfth Century, 1970; Church and State in the Middle Ages, 1970; co-author, A History of Western Society, 1979, 6th edition, 1990, 6th edition, 1998; A History of World Societies, 4th edition, 1991, 5th edition, 1999. **CONTACT ADDRESS** History Dept, Georgetown Univ, 604 ICC Bldg, Washington, DC 20057.

HILL, CHRISTOPHER V.
PERSONAL Born 04/14/1953, Salt Lake City, UT, m, 1974, 2 children **DISCIPLINE** HISTORY **EDUCATION** Univ Ut, BA, 80; Univ Va, MA, 82, PhD, 87. **CAREER** Assoc prof, Lock Haven Univ Pa, 90-93; assoc prof to chair, Col Univ, Colorado Springs, 93-; Prof/Chmn, 99-. **HONORS AND AWARDS** First Aldo Leopold Award, Amer Soc for Environ Hist, 93; J. William Fulbright, Senior Res Fel, 99-00. **MEMBERSHIPS** Assoc Asian Stud; Amer Soc Environ Hist. **RESEARCH** Colonial India; global environ hist. **SELECTED PUBLICATIONS** Auth, River of Sorrow: Environment and Agrarian control in Riparian North India, 1770-1994, Assoc Asian Stud Monograph, 97; art, Ideology and Public Works: Managing the Mahanadi River in Colonial North India, Capitalism, Nature, Socialism, 95; art, Philosophy and Reality in Riparian South India: British Famine Policy and Migration in Colonial North India, Modern Asian Stud, 91; art, Water and Power: Riparian Legislation and Agrarian Control in Colonial Bengal, Environmental History Review, 90. **CONTACT ADDRESS** Dept of History, Univ of Colorado, Colorado Springs, Colorado Springs, CO 80918-3733. **EMAIL** chill@mail.uccs.edu

HILL, EUGENE DAVID
PERSONAL Born 02/25/1949, New York, NY, m, 1987 **DISCIPLINE** RENAISSANCE LITERATURE, INTELLECTUAL HISTORY. **EDUCATION** Columbia Univ, BA, 70; Princeton Univ, PhD(English), 80. **CAREER** Instr, 78-80, asst prof Eng, Mt Holyoke Col, 80-86; from assoc prof to prof Eng, 86-94. **MEMBERSHIPS** Renaissance Soc Am. **RESEARCH** John Milton, John Donne, Thomas Kyd. **SELECTED PUBLICATIONS** Auth, The trinitarian allegory of the moral play of Wisdom, Mod Philol, 75; The place of the future, Sci Fiction Studies, 82; Parody and History in Arden of Feversham, Huntington Library Quarterly, 93. **CONTACT ADDRESS** Dept of English, Mount Holyoke Col, 50 College St, South Hadley, MA 01075-6421.

HILL, JOHN
DISCIPLINE ASIAN HISTORY **EDUCATION** Okla Baptist Col, BA, Duke Univ, MA, PhD. **CAREER** Assoc prof. **RESEARCH** Evolution of Indian nationalism, Muslim politicization, British famine and agricultural policy. **SELECTED PUBLICATIONS** Ed, The Congress and Indian Nationalism: Historical Perspectives, Curzon Press, 91. **CONTACT ADDRESS** Dept of Hist, Concordia Univ, Montreal, 1400 de Maisonneuve Blvd W, Montreal, QC, Canada H3G 1W8. **EMAIL** hillj@vax2.concordia.ca

HILL, LAMAR MOTT
PERSONAL Born 02/23/1938, New York, NY, m, 1960, 2 children **DISCIPLINE** HISTORY **EDUCATION** Kenyon Col, AB, 60; Western Reserve Univ, MA, 65; Univ London, PhD(hist), 68. **CAREER** Asst prof hist, 68-73, asst vice chancellor acad affairs, 76-77, Assoc Prof Hist, Univ Calif, Irvine, 73-, Inst Hist Res, London, res fel hist, 68; Nat Endowment Humanities fel hist, 73-74; consult, Gen Educ Proficiency, Educ Testing Serv, 76-77. **MEMBERSHIPS** AHA; Historians Early Mod Europe; Conf Brit Studies; Selden Soc; fel Royal Hist Soc. **RESEARCH** Tudor-Stuart English history; social structure of Tudor-Stuart politics; English law and administration. **SELECTED PUBLICATIONS** Auth, The Two-Witness Rule in English treason trials, Am J Legal Hist, 68; The admiralty circuit of 1591: Some comments on the relations between central government and local interests, Hist J, 71; ed, Sir Julius Caesar's journal of Salisbury's first two months and twenty days as Lord Treasurer: 1608, Bull Inst Hist Res, 72; contribr, County government in Caroline England, In: The Origins of the English Civil War, Macmillan, 73; auth & ed, The Ancient State, Authorite, and Proceedings of the Court of Requests by Sir Julius Caesar, Cambridge Univ, 75; auth, Government and governance: Continuity and discontinuity in Elizabethan politics, Albion, 78; The Decline of Tudor Monarchy: Essays in the Structure of Change, Macmillan, (in press); contribr, Biographical Dictionary of British Radicals in the Seventeenth Century, Harvester, (in press). **CONTACT ADDRESS** Dept of Hist, Univ of California, Irvine, Irvine, CA 92717.

HILL, PATRICIA
DISCIPLINE NINETEENTH-CENTURY U.S. CULTURAL HISTORY **EDUCATION** Col Wooster, BA; Harvard Univ, MTS; Harvard Univ, PhD. **CAREER** Wesleyan Univ. **SELECTED PUBLICATIONS** Auth, The World Their Household: The American Woman's Foreign Mission Movement And Cultural Transformation, 1870-1920. **CONTACT ADDRESS** Wesleyan Univ, Middletown, CT 06459. **EMAIL** phill@wesleyan.edu

HILL, PETER PROAL
PERSONAL Born 10/04/1926, Concord, MA, m, 1953, 1 child **DISCIPLINE** AMERICAN DIPLOMATIC & EARLY NATIONAL HISTORY **EDUCATION** Tufts Univ, AB, 48; Boston Univ, MA, 54; George Washington Univ, PhD(hist), 66. **CAREER** From instr to assoc prof, 60-74, Prof Hist, George Washington Univ, 74-96. **HONORS AND AWARDS** Fel, Camargo Foundation, Cassis, France, 75-76. **MEMBERSHIPS** AHA; Soc Fr Hist Study; Soc Historians Am Foreign Rels. **RESEARCH** Federalist era diplomacy; Franco-American relations. **SELECTED PUBLICATIONS** Auth, Footnote to XYZ, Md Hist Mag, 3/67; auth, Third parties in a two-party system, New Repub, 7/68; auth, William Van Murray, Federalist Diplomat: The Shaping of Peace with France, 1797-1801, Syracuse Univ, 71; auth, Prologue to the quasi war: commercial stresses in Franco-American relations, 1794-96, J Mod Hist, 3/77; auth, La suite imprevue de l'alliance: l'ingratitude americaine, 1783-1798, In: La Revolution americaine et l'Europe, Centre Nat de la Rech Sci, 79; auth, A Masked Acquisition, In: French Designs on Cumberland Island, 1794-95, Ga Hist Quart, Vol LXIV, No. 3; auth, French Perceptions of The Early American Republic, 1783-1793, American Philosophical Society, 88; auth, America and France--2 Revolutions, J Am Hist, Vol 0081, 94. **CONTACT ADDRESS** Dept of Hist, The George Washington Univ, Washington, DC 20052. **EMAIL** pphill@gwu.edu

HILLGARTH, JOCELYN NIGEL
PERSONAL Born 09/22/1929, London, England, m, 1966 **DISCIPLINE** MEDIEVAL HISTORY **EDUCATION** Cambridge Univ, BA, 50, MA, 54, PhD(hist), 57. **CAREER** Sr res fel hist, Warburg Inst, London, 59-62; mem, Inst Advan Studies, 63-64; vis lectr, Univ Tex, Austin, 64-65; lectr, Harvard Univ, 65-66, asst prof, 66-70; Guggenheim fel, 67-68; from assoc prof to prof, Boston Col, 70-77; from prof to prof emer, Pontif Inst Mediaeval Studies, 77-; Am Coun Learned Soc fel, 76-77; Lady Davis vis prof, Hebrew Univ, Jerusalem, fall 80. **MEMBERSHIPS** Mediaeval Acad Am; Soc Span & Port Hist Studies. **RESEARCH** Medieval Spain; medieval intellectual and church history. **SELECTED PUBLICATIONS** Ed., Christianity and Paganism, 350-750: The Conversion of Western Europe, January 86; auth, The Mirror of Spain, 1500-1700: The Formation of a Myth, - February 01; auth, The conversion of Western Europe, 350-750; auth, The problem of a Catalan Mediterranean empire 1229-1327, auth, Ramon Lull and Lullism in Fourteenth-Century France; auth, The Spanish Kingdoms, 1250-1516: 250-1410 Precarious Balance; auth, Spanish Kingdoms, 1250-1516; auth, Visigothic Spain, Byzantium, and the Irish; auth, Who read Thomas Aquinas? **CONTACT ADDRESS** Pontifical Inst of Mediaeval Studies, 39 Queens' Park Crescent E, Toronto, ON, Canada M5S 2C4.

HILLMER, GEORGE NORMAN
PERSONAL Born 11/24/1942, Niagara Falls, ON, Canada **DISCIPLINE** HISTORY **EDUCATION** Univ Toronto, BA, 66; MA 67; Cambridge Univ, PhD, 74. **CAREER** Lectr to adj prof, 72-89, prof Hist, Carleton Univ, 90-; hist, Directorate Hist Dept Nat Defence, 72-90; vis prof, Leeds Univ (Eng), 78-79. **HONORS AND AWARDS** Commonwealth Scholar, 68-70; IODE, Univ London, Mackenzie King & Can Counc Fels, 70-72; Queen's Silver Jubilee Medal, 77; Carleton Excellence Tchg Awd, 94; Marston LaFrance Fel, 95; Prime Minister's Publ Awd, Japan, 97. **MEMBERSHIPS** Can Hist Asn **RESEARCH** The Anglo-Canadian "Alliance," 1919-1939: Great Britain and the Birth of Canadian Foreign Policy. **SELECTED PUBLICATIONS** Auth, For Better or For Worse: Canada and the United States to the 1990s, with J.L. Granatstein, Toronto: Copp Clark Pitman, (91): 334; ed, Making a Difference? Canada's Foreign Policy in a Changing World Order, Toronto: Lester Publishing, with John English, (92): 236; auth, Documents relatifs aux relations exterieures de Canada/Documents on Canadian External Relations, vol. XIII: 1947, with Donald Page, Ottawa: Affairs exterieures et Commerce exterieur Canada/ External Affairs and International Trade Canada, (93): 1654; ed, "Canadian Peacekeeping and the Road Back to 1945," in Fabrizio Ghilardi, ed., Canada e Italia: Prospettive di Cooperazione, (Pisa and Milan: Centro Interuniversitario di Studi sul Canada, 94): 145-159; auth, Empire to Umpire: Canada and the World to the 1990s, with J.L. Granatstein, Toronto: Copp Clark Longman, (94): 373; co-ed, A Country of Limitations: Canada and the World in 1939 / Un pays dans la gene; le Canada et le monde ed 1939, with Robert Bothwell, Roger Sarty and Claude Beauregard, Ottawa: Canadian Committee for the History of the Second World War/Comite canadien d'Histoire de la Deuxieme Guerre mondiale, (96): 295; ed, Pearson: The Unlikely Gladiator, McGill-Queen's Univ Press, (forthcoming 99). **CONTACT ADDRESS** Dept of History, Carleton Univ, 1125 Colonel By Dr, Ottawa, ON, Canada K1S 5B6. **EMAIL** nhillmer@ccs.carleton.ca

HILSON, ARTHUR LEE
PERSONAL Born 04/06/1936, Cincinnati, OH, m, 1982 **DISCIPLINE** AMERICAN STUDIES **EDUCATION** Wheaton College, Springfield Christian Bible Seminary, Wheaton, IL, bachelor of theology; Andover Newton Theological Seminary, Newton Center, MA, MDiv; University of Massachusetts, Amherst, MA, MEd, 1974, EdD, 1979. **CAREER** Human Resources Development Center, Newport, RI, human relations consultant, 73; Univ of Mass at Amherst, MA, admin asst to dean of grad affairs, School of Education, 73-75, dept head, Veterans Assistance and Couseling Services, 76-78, dept head, Univ Placement Services, 78-87, exec dir, Public Safety, 87-92; Univ of NH, Faculty, American Studies for Student Affairs, 93-; New Hope Baptist Church, Pastor, 91-. **HONORS AND AWARDS** Developed and faciliated over 100 workshops on human/race relations and multicultural communications; Kellogg Fellow, Kellogg Foundation, 1973-74. **MEMBERSHIPS** Member, Phi Delta Kappa; member, American Personnel Officers Assn; member, Eastern College Personnel Officers Assn; member, College Placement Council; member, NAACP; bd member, American Veterans Committee; chairman, Natl Assn of Minority Veterans Program Administrators; bd member, Natl Assn of Veterans Program Administrators; bd member, interim director, Veterans Outreach Center of Greenfield, MA; member, Intl Assn of Campus Law Enforcement Administrators; member, Intl Assn of Chiefs of Police; chairman, United Christian Foundation; charter president, Amherst NAACP; member, bd of dirs, Western Massachusetts Girl Scouts; member, bd of dirs, United Way of Hampshire County; School Bd, elected mem. **CONTACT ADDRESS** New Hope Baptist Church, 263 Peverly Hill Rd, Portsmouth, NH 03801.

HILTON, KATHLEEN C.
PERSONAL Born Tacoma, WA **DISCIPLINE** SOCIAL HISTORY **EDUCATION** Seattle Univ, BEd, cum laude, 69; Carnegie Mellon Univ, MA, 82, PhD, 87. **CAREER** Assoc prof, hist, coordr, Soc Stud educ prog, Univ NC, Pembroke. **HONORS AND AWARDS** Univ Awd for Teaching Excellence, 98. **MEMBERSHIPS** AHA; OAH; SAWH; NCSS. **RESEARCH** Progressive Era adolescent socialization patterns; women's hist. **SELECTED PUBLICATIONS** Auth, Domesticity, in Encycl of Soc Hist, Garland Press. 94; Both in the Field, Each With a Plow: Race Gender, and Women's Work in the Rural South, 1907-1929, in Hidden Histories of Women in the New South, Unvi Mo Press, 94. **CONTACT ADDRESS** Univ of No Carolina, Pembroke, Pembroke, NC 28372-1510. **EMAIL** kch@papa.uncp.edu

HILTS, VICTOR L.
PERSONAL Born 11/01/1937, Great Falls, MT, m, 1965 **DISCIPLINE** HISTORY OF SCIENCE **EDUCATION** Harvard Univ, AB, 59, PhD, 67. **CAREER** Asst prof, 65-71, chmn dept, 77-81, 87-90 & 91-94, assoc prof, 71-85, Prof Hist Sci, Univ Wis-Madison, 85-. **MEMBERSHIPS** Hist Sci Soc; AAAS; Midwest J Hist Sci. **SELECTED PUBLICATIONS** Auth, Statistics and social science, in Foundations of Method, Ind Univ, 73; Guide to Francis Galton's English Men of Science, Am Philos Soc, 75; Allis exterendum: Or, origins of the statistical society of London, Isis, 78; Statist and Statistician, Arno Press, 81; Obeying the laws of hereditary descent: Phrenological views on inheritance and eugenics, J Hist Behav Sci, 82; Enlightentment view, in Transformation and Tradition in the Sciences, Cambridge Univ Press, 84; Towards the social organism: Herbert Spencer and William B Carpenter on the analogical method, in The Natural Sciences and the Social Sciences, Kluwer Acad Press, 94. **CONTACT ADDRESS** Dept of Hist of Sci, Univ of Wisconsin, Madison, 1180 Observatory Dr, Madison, WI 53706-1393.

HILTY, JAMES
DISCIPLINE TWENTIETH CENTURY UNITED STATES POLITICAL HISTORY **EDUCATION** Univ MO, Columbia, PhD. **CAREER** Assoc prof, Temple Univ; prof. **RESEARCH** Hist of the US Presidency: Twentieth Century United States Political Hist; Quantitative Analysis of Hist Data. **SELECTED PUBLICATIONS** Auth, "John F. Kennedy: An Idealist without Illusions," Forum Series in Hist, 76; ed, "Senatorial Papers and the New Political History," Senataors Papers, 79; coauth, "Prologue: The Senate Voting Record of Harry S Truman," Journal of Interdisciplinary Hist, 73; ed, "John F. Kennedy and Robert F. Kennedy," in Leaders of the World, 93; auth, Robert Kennedy: Brother Protector, 97. **CONTACT ADDRESS** Temple Univ, Philadelphia, PA 19122. **EMAIL** jwhilty77@aol.com

HILWIG, STUART
PERSONAL Born 07/12/1968, Salem, MA, s **DISCIPLINE** HISTORY **EDUCATION** Vanderbilt Univ, BA, 91; Ohio State

Univ, MA, 94; PhD, 00. **CAREER** Grad teaching assoc, Ohio State Univ, 95-00; asst prof, Adams State Col, 00-. **HONORS AND AWARDS** Grant, DAAD, 98; Ruth Higgins Summer Fel, 98; FLAS, 96-97. **MEMBERSHIPS** Phi Kappa Phi. **RESEARCH** Post-1945 Italy and Germany; Oral History; Political and Cultural History. **SELECTED PUBLICATIONS** Auth, "Le reazioni della stampa e dei politici agli studenti nel Sessantotto," in Per il sessantotto: Bollettino di ricerche e memorie, bibliografie, critiche e documentazione su avvenimenti, culture, pratiche alternative e ideologie attorno al 1968, (Spring 98), 2-12; auth, "The revolt against the Establishment: Students versus the Press in West Germany and Italy," in The World Transformed, (Cambridge, 98), 321-349; auth, The End of Consensus: The Student Revolts of the 1960s," in Exploring the European Past: Text and Images, (Ohio State Univ Press, 01); auth, "Are you calling me a fascist? A Contribution to the Oral History of the Italian Student Rebellion in 1968," J of Contemporary Hist, (forthcoming). **CONTACT ADDRESS** Dept Hist, Adams State Col, 208 Edgemont Blvd, Alamosa, CO 81102. **EMAIL** sjhilwig@adams.edu

HIMMELBERG, ROBERT F.
PERSONAL Born 07/16/1934, Kansas City, MO, m, 1958, 3 children **DISCIPLINE** AMERICAN POLITICAL ECONOMIC HISTORY **EDUCATION** Penn State Univ, PhD. **CAREER** Prof of History. **RESEARCH** Study of the Democratic party in Congress during the Republican Era. **SELECTED PUBLICATIONS** Auth, The Great Depression and American Capitalism, D C Heath, 68; Co-auth, Herbert Hoover and the Crisis of American Capitalism, Cambridge, Schenckman, 74; The Origins of the National Recovery Administration: Business, Government and the Trade Association Issue, 1921-1933, Fordham UP, 76, revised, 93; ed, Business and Government in America Since 1870, 94; co-ed, Historians and Race: Autobiography and the Writing of History , 96. **CONTACT ADDRESS** Dept of Hist, Fordham Univ, Bronx, NY 10458. **EMAIL** himmelberg@fordham.edu

HIMMELFARB, GERTRUDE
PERSONAL Born 08/08/1922, New York, NY, m, 1942, 2 children **DISCIPLINE** MODERN HISTORY **EDUCATION** Brooklyn Col, BA, 42; Univ Chicago, MA, 44, PhD, 50. **CAREER** Prof hist, 65-78, exec officer, 74-79, distinguished prof, Grad Sch & Univ Ctr, 78-87, prof emeritus, 87- , City Univ NY; Res & writing, 52-; **HONORS AND AWARDS** Jefferson Lecture, NEH, 91; Templeton Found Awd for Outstanding Book, 97; fels, Am Asn Univ Women, 51-52, Am Philos Soc, 53-54, Guggenheim Found, 55-56 & 57-58 & Rockefeller Found, 62-63 & 63-64; Nat Endowment for Humanities sr fel, 68-69; Am Coun Learned Socs fel, 72-73; mem, Presidential Adv Comt Econ Role of Women, 72-; Woodrow Wilson Int Ctr fel, 76-77; Rockefeller Found Humanities fel, 80-81; littd, smith col, 77, jewish theol sem & lafayette col, 78; lhd, rhode island col, 76. **MEMBERSHIPS** Fel Am Acad Arts & Sci; Soc Am Historians; fel Royal Hist Soc; British Acad; Am Philos Soc. **RESEARCH** Nineteenth century English history; modern intellectual history; social history. **SELECTED PUBLICATIONS** Auth, Lord Acton: A Study in Conscience and Politics, Univ Chicago, 52; Darwin and the Darwinian Revolution, Doubleday, 59; ed, T S Malthus, On Population, Mod Libr, 60; J S Mill, Essays on Politics and Culture, Doubleday, 62; auth, Victorian Minds, Knopf, 68; contribr, The Victorian City, Routledge & Kegan Paul, 73; auth, On Liberty and Liberalism, Knopf, 74; ed, On Liberty, Penquin, 74; auth, The Idea of Poverty, Knopf, 84; auth, Marriage and Morals Among the Victorians, Knopf, 86; auth, The New History and the Old, Harvard, 87; auth, Poverty and Compassion, Knopf, 92; auth, On Looking Into the Abyss, Knopf, 94; auth, The De-Moralization of Society, Knopf, 95; ed, Alexis de Tocqueville, Memoir on Pauperism, Ivan Dee, 97. **CONTACT ADDRESS** Dept of History, Graduate Sch and Univ Ctr, CUNY, 365 Fifth Ave, New York, NY 10016-4309.

HINCKLEY, TED C.
PERSONAL Born 10/04/1925, New York, NY, m, 1948, 2 children **DISCIPLINE** HISTORY **EDUCATION** Claremont Men's Col, BA, 50; Northwest Mo State Col, BS, 51; Univ Kansas City, MA, 53; Ind Univ, PhD(hist), 61. **CAREER** Instr hist, Barstow Sch, 51-53; instr & asst to pres, Claremont Men's Col, 53-55; headmaster, St Katharine's Sch, 55-57; assoc prof US hist, 63-67, Prof Hist, San Jose State Univ, 67-, Am Philos Soc grants, 62 & 66; Danforth assoc, 62; lectr, Nat Endowment for Humanities, 67 & 76; Am Asn State & Local Hist grant, 69; Huntington Libr grant, 71; dir, Sourisseau Acad Calif State & Local Hist, 71-73. **HONORS AND AWARDS** Distinguished Teaching Awd, Calif State Cols, 67, Outstanding Professor Awd, 81. **MEMBERSHIPS** AHA; Orgn Am Historians; Presby Hist Soc: Western Hist Asn. **RESEARCH** Pacific Basin, 1500-1941; Alaska, 1867-1897; 19th century United States. **SELECTED PUBLICATIONS CONTACT ADDRESS** Dept of Hist, San Jose State Univ, San Jose, CA 95192.

HINDMAN, E. JAMES
PERSONAL Born 01/09/1943, Lubbock, TX, m, 1964, 2 children **DISCIPLINE** HISTORY **EDUCATION** Tex Tech Univ, BA, 66; MA, 68; PhD, 72. **CAREER** Lamar Univ, 70-72; Sul Ross State Univ, 72-86; Eastern N Mex Univ, 86-88; dean, Col Lib Arts Univ N Colo, 88-91; assoc VP of Academic Affairs, Middle Tenn State Univ, 91-95; provost and VP to president, Angelo State Univ, 95-. **HONORS AND AWARDS** Who's Who in the West, 22nd edition; Tex Tech Dept of His Distinguished Grad, 00. **MEMBERSHIPS** Tex State Hist Asn, Soc of Hist of Am For Rel, Am Asn of Higher Educ. **RESEARCH** US Foreign Policy, Mexico. **SELECTED PUBLICATIONS** Auth, "The General Arbitration Treaties of William Howard Taft," The Historian (73); auth, "Confustion o conspiraction? Estados Unidos frente a Obregon," Historia Mexican (75). **CONTACT ADDRESS** Dept Hist, Angelo State Univ, San Angelo, TX 76909-0001. **EMAIL** president@angelo.edu

HINDMAN, SANDRA L.
DISCIPLINE MEDIEVAL MANUSCRIPTS, EARLY PRINTED BOOK **EDUCATION** Cornell Univ, PhD. **CAREER** Prof, Ch Art History dpt, Northwestern Univ. **RESEARCH** Gothic art, women in medieval art and society. **SELECTED PUBLICATIONS** Auth, Sealed in Parchment: Rereadings of Knighthood in the Illuminated Manuscripts of Chretien de Troyes, Univ Chicago Press, 94; Christine de Pizan's "Epistre Othea": Painting and Politics at the Court of Charles VI; ed, Printing the Written Word: The Social History of Books, c.1450-1520. **CONTACT ADDRESS** Dept of Art History, Northwestern Univ, 1801 Hinman, Evanston, IL 60208.

HINDS, HAROLD E., JR
PERSONAL Born 01/21/1941, Portland, OR, m, 1962, 1 child **DISCIPLINE** HISTORY, LATIN AMERICAN HISTORY **EDUCATION** Univ Ore, BA, 65; Vanderbilt Univ, MA, 67, PhD, 76. **CAREER** Instr, Univ Minn-Morris, 70-76, asst prof, 77-80, assoc prof, 80-87, prof, 87-; Dir, Latin Am Studies, Univ Minn-Morris, 72-; assoc mem and adjunct lectr, The Center for Latin Am, Univ of Wisc-Milwaukee, 77-. **HONORS AND AWARDS** Nat Defense Ed Act (Title IV) Fel in Latin Am Studies, 65-68; Best paper, North Central Coun of Latin Americanists, 74; Russel Nye Awd for best article in the J of Popular Culture, 79; vis scholar, Univ of Chicago-Univ of Ill, 82. **MEMBERSHIPS** Latin Am Studies Asn, Popular Culture Asn, Conf on Latin Am Hist, Nat Genealogical Soc. **RESEARCH** 19th century Columbia, 20th century Mexico, family history, Latin American popular culture. **SELECTED PUBLICATIONS** Auth, Studies in Latin American Popular Culture (81-98); auth, Not Just for Children: The Mexican Comic Book in the Late 1960s and 1970s (92); auth, Handbook of Latin American Popular Culture (85); auth, Popular Culture Theory and Methodology: A Basic Introduction (in press). **CONTACT ADDRESS** Dept Soc Sci, Univ of Minnesota, Morris, 600 E 4th St, Morris, MN 56267-2132. **EMAIL** hindshe@cda.mrs.umn.edu

HINE, WILLIAM CASSIDY
PERSONAL Born 10/16/1943, Dodge City, KS **DISCIPLINE** UNITED STATES HISTORY **EDUCATION** Bowling Green State Univ, BS, 65; Univ Wyo, MA, 67; Kent State Univ, PhD, 79. **CAREER** From Instr to Assoc Prof, 67-83, prof hist, SC State Univ, 83-; Vis prof, Idaho State Univ, 80. **MEMBERSHIPS** Orgn Am Historians; Southern Hist Asn; Asn Study Afro-Am Life Hist. **RESEARCH** United States reconstruction; United States African-American; black higher education. **SELECTED PUBLICATIONS** Contribr, Dr Benjamin A Boseman Jr: Charleston's black physician-politician, in Southern Black Leaders During Reconstruction, Univ Ill Press, 6/82; auth, Black politicians in reconstruction Charleston, J of Southern Hist, 11/83; South Carolina State College, Agr Hist, Spring 91; South Carolina's Challenge to Civil Rights, Agr and Human Values, Winter 92; Civil Rights and Campus Wrongs, SC Magazine of Hist, 10/96; Thomas E. Miller and the Early Years of South Carolina State University, Carologue, Winter 96; encyclopedia articles in Black Women in America: An Historical Encyclopedia, Encyclopedia of the Confederacy, and American National Biography; coauth, The African-American Odyssey, Prentice Hall, 00. **CONTACT ADDRESS** So Carolina State Univ, 300 College St NE, Box 7207, Orangeburg, SC 29117-0001. **EMAIL** WHINE@scsu.edu

HINES, THOMAS S.
PERSONAL Born 10/28/1936, Oxford, MS, 2 children **DISCIPLINE** HISTORY **EDUCATION** Univ Mississippi, BA, 58, MA, 60; Univ Wis, Madison, PhD, 71. **CAREER** Prof Hist & Arch, UCLA, 68-; vis prof, Sch of Arch & Am Stud Prog, Univ Texas, 74-75; Fulbright prof, Am Stud, Univ Exeter, Eng, 84-84. **HONORS AND AWARDS** John H. Dunning Prize, Am Hist Asn, 76; NEH Fel, 78-79; Fulbright Fel, 84-85; Guggenheim Fel, 87-88; Am Acad Arts, Scis, 94; Getty Scholar, 96-97. **SELECTED PUBLICATIONS** Auth, Burnham of Chicago: Architect and Planner, 74; auth, Richard Neutra and the Search for Modern Architecture, 82; auth, "The Search for Frank Lloyd Wright: History, Biography, Autobiography," Jour Soc Arch Hist, 95;auth, William Faulkner and the Tangible Past: The Architecture of Yoknapatawpha, Univ Calif Press, 96; auth, "The Blessing and the Curse: The Achievement of Lloyd Wright," in The Architecture of Lloyd Wright," Thames and Hudson, 98; auth, and the Architecture of Reform, 00. **CONTACT ADDRESS** Dept of History, Univ of California, Los Angeles, 405 Hilgard Ave, Los Angeles, CA 90024. **EMAIL** hines@history.ucla.edu

HINSLEY, CURTIS M.
DISCIPLINE HISTORY **EDUCATION** Princeton Univ, BA, 67; Univ Wis Madison, MA, 71, PhD, 76. **CAREER** Assoc prof, hist, Colgate Univ; current, Regents' prof of hist, N. Ariz. **HONORS AND AWARDS** Phi Kappa Phi. **MEMBERSHIPS** Am Antiquarian Soc **RESEARCH** History american anthropology and archaeology; history of science in america. **SELECTED PUBLICATIONS** Auth, Savages and Scientists: The Smithsonian Institution and the Development of American Anthropology, 1846-1910, Smithsonian Inst Press, 81; auth, Zunis and Brahmins: Cultural Ambivalence in the Gilded Age, in History of Anthropology 6: Romantic Motives: Essays on Anthropological Sensibility, 169-207; auth, Revising and Revisioning the History of Archaeology: Reflections on Region and Context, in Tracing Archaeology's Past: The Historiography of Archaeology, So Ill Univ Press, 89; auth, Collecting Cultures and Cultures of Collecting: The Lure of the American Southwest, 1880-1915, in Museum Anthropology 16, 92; auth, In Search of the New World Classical, in Collecting the Pre-Columbian Past, Dumbarton Oaks, 93; auth/ed, The Southest in the American Imagination, U of Az Press, 96. **CONTACT ADDRESS** Dept of Applied Indigenous Studies, No Arizona Univ, Flagstaff, AZ 86011-5020. **EMAIL** curtis.hinsley@nau.edu

HINSON, E. GLENN
PERSONAL Born 07/27/1931, St. Louis, MO, m, 1956, 2 children **DISCIPLINE** CHURCH HISTORY **EDUCATION** Washington Univ; BA 54; Southern Baptist Theological Seminary; BD, ThD, 57,62; Oxford Univ; D Phil 74. **CAREER** Southern Baptist Theological Sem; prof, 62-92, prof of spirituality, John Loftis Prof of church hist, 92-99; Wake Forest Univ; prof 82-84. **HONORS AND AWARDS** Johannes Quasten Medal; Cuthbert Allen Awd; 2 ATS Fell; Prof of the Year SBTS. **MEMBERSHIPS** ASCH; AAR; IPS; EIS; NAPS; NABPR; ITMS. **RESEARCH** Early Christianity and Spirituality. **SELECTED PUBLICATIONS** Auth, Love At the Heart of Things: A Biography of Douglas V. Steer, Pendle Hill Pub, 98; The Early Church, Abingdon, 96; The Church Triumphant: A History of Christianity up to 1300, Mercer Univ, 95; A Serious Call to a Contemplative Lifestyles, rev, ed, Smith & Helwys 93. **CONTACT ADDRESS** Dept of Church History, So Baptist Theol Sem, 3400 Brook Rd, Richmond, VA 23227.

HIRSCH, ARNOLD RICHARD
PERSONAL Born 03/09/1949, Chicago, IL, m, 1971, 2 children **DISCIPLINE** AMERICAN & URBAN HISTORY **EDUCATION** Univ Ill, Chicago Circle, BA, 70, MA, 72, PhD(US hist), 78. **CAREER** Asst prof US hist, Univ Ill, Chicago Circle, 78; Asst Prof US & Urban Hist, Univ New Orleans, 79-, Vis lectr Urban hist, Univ Mich, 79. **MEMBERSHIPS** AHA; Orgn Am Historians. **RESEARCH** Urban politics and policy; race relations; immigration and ethnicity. **SELECTED PUBLICATIONS** Auth, Race and housing: Violence and communal protest in Chicago, 1940-1960, In: The Ethnic Frontier, William B Eerdmans Publ Co, Inc, 77; Sunbelt in the swamp: New Orleans and the rising south, 1945-1980, In: Sunbelt Cities, Univ, Texas Press (in press); Making the Second Ghetto: Race and Housing in Chicago, 1940-1960, Cambridge Univ Press (in press). **CONTACT ADDRESS** Dept Hist, Univ of New Orleans, 2000 Lakeshore Dr, New Orleans, LA 70148-0001.

HIRSCH, SUSAN E.
DISCIPLINE HISTORY **EDUCATION** Univ Mich, PhD, 74. **CAREER** Hist, Loyola Univ. **HONORS AND AWARDS** Phi Beta Kappa, 66; NEH fel, Newberry Library, 87-88; Sr Fulbright Scholar, Univ of Munich, 01. **MEMBERSHIPS** Organization of Am Hist, Am Hist Asn, Social Sci Hist Asn, Urban Hist Asn, Labor and Working Class Hist Asn, Coordinating Coun for Women in Hist. **RESEARCH** Labor; work; soc structure. **SELECTED PUBLICATIONS** Auth, Roots of the American Working Class: The Industrialization of Crafts in Newark, 1800-1860, Philadelphia: Univ Pa Press, 78; coauth, A City Comes of Age: Chicago in the 1890s, Chicago Hist Soc, 90; co-ed, The War in American Culture: Society and Consciousness during World War II, Univ Chicago Press, 96. **CONTACT ADDRESS** Dept of Hist, Loyola Univ, Chicago, 6525 N Sheridan Rd, Chicago, IL 60626. **EMAIL** shirsch@orion.it.luc.edu

HIRSCHMANN, DAVID
DISCIPLINE RURAL DEVELOPMENT **EDUCATION** Univ Witwatersrand, Johannesburg, BA, LLB, MA, PhD. **CAREER** Prof, Am Univ. **RESEARCH** Development management; Decentralization; Women and development, Democracy. **SELECTED PUBLICATIONS** Auth, Women Farmers in Malawi, UCLA, 84; Changing Attitudes of Black South Africans toward the United States, E. Mellen Press, 89. **CONTACT ADDRESS** American Univ, 4400 Massachusetts Ave, Washington, DC 20016.

HIRSCHMANN, EDWIN A.
PERSONAL Born 09/03/1932, Baltimore, MD, m, 1995 **DISCIPLINE** HISTORY **EDUCATION** Johns Hopkins Univ, BA, 54; Penn State Univ, MA, 64; Univ Wisc, MA, 68, PhD, 72. **CAREER** History prof, Towson Univ. **MEMBERSHIPS** Am Hist Asn, Asn for Asian Studies, AAUP. **RESEARCH** Victorian India. **SELECTED PUBLICATIONS** Auth, 'White

Mutiny': The Ilbert Bill Crisis in India and the Genesis of Indian Nationalism. **CONTACT ADDRESS** Dept Hist, Towson State Univ, 8000 York Rd, Baltimore, MD 21252-0001.

HIRSH, RICHARD FREDERIC
PERSONAL Born New York, NY **DISCIPLINE** HISTORY OF SCIENCE & TECHNOLOGY **EDUCATION** Middlebury Col, BA, 74; Univ Wis-Madison, MA, 76, PhD(hist sci), 79, MS (physics), 80. **CAREER** Asst prof hist sci, Univ Md, 79; fel, Lilly Found, Univ Fla, 79-80; Asst Prof Hist, VA Polytech Inst & State Univ, 80-91,;prof, VA Polytech Inst State Univ, 91-. **HONORS AND AWARDS** Henry Schuman Prize, Hist Sci Soc, 76; Hist Manuscript Awd, Am Inst Aeronaut & Astronaut, Physics, 80. **MEMBERSHIPS** Hist Sci Soc; Soc Hist Technol. **RESEARCH** History of electric power industry; science, technology and public policy. **SELECTED PUBLICATIONS** Auth, Glimpsing An Invisible Universe, 83; Technology and Transformation in the American Electric Utility Industry, 89; auth, Momentum Shifts in the American Electric Utility System--Catastrophic Change, or No Change At All, Tech Cult, Vol 0037, 96; Wolf Creek Station--Kansas Gas and Electric Company in the Nuclear Era, Tech Cult, Vol 0037, 96; Electrifying Eden--Portland-General-Electric, 1889-1965, J West, Vol 0032, 93; Power Loss: The Origins of Deregulation and Restructuring In the American Electric Utility System, 99. **CONTACT ADDRESS** Dept of Hist, Virginia Polytech Inst and State Univ, Blacksburg, VA 24061. **EMAIL** rhirsh@vt.edu

HIRST, DEREK M.
DISCIPLINE EARLY-MODERN BRITAIN **EDUCATION** Cambridge Univ, BA, 69; PhD, 74. **CAREER** Hist, Washington Univ; William Eliot Smith, prof of history, 92; chair, History Dept, 98- . **HONORS AND AWARDS** Nat Endowment Hum sr fel, Folger Library, 79; Guggenheim fel, 81-82; Vis sr res fel, Gonville & Caius College, 81-82; fel, royal hist socy, trinity hall; dir studies history, 74-75; asst prof to prof, washington univ, 75-; clark lect, univ calif, 83; codir, folger inst seminar,91. **SELECTED PUBLICATIONS** Auth, The Lord Profotector, Oliver Cromwell And The English Revolution, Longmans, 90; The Political Context Literature In The 1650s, The Seventeenth-Century, 90; Liberty, Revolution And Beyond, Parliament And Liberty From The Reign Elizabeth To The Civil War, Stanford Univ Profess, 91; The Failure Godly Rule In The English Republic, Past And Profesent, 91; Coauth, High Summer At Nunappleton, 1651: Andrew Marvell And Lord Fairfax's Occasions, Histl Jour, 93; The Rupturing The Cromwellian Alliance English Historical Rev, 93; 'The English Republic And The Meaning Britain,' Jour Mod Hist, 94; 'Milton And The Drama Justice,' The Theatrical City,Cambridge Univ Profess, 95; 'British Isles 1450-1800', Aha Guide To Histl Lit, Oxford, 95; Locating the 1650's History, 96; Coauth, Fatherhood and Longing: Andrew Marvell and the Toils of Patriarchy Elit, 99; England in Conflict 1603-1660: Kingdom, Community, Commonwealth (Edward Arnold/Oxford UP, 99); coed, Writing and Political Engagement in 17th Century England (Cambridge U.P.), 00. **CONTACT ADDRESS** Washington Univ, 1 Brookings Dr, Saint Louis, MO 63130. **EMAIL** dmhirst@artsci.wustl.edu

HIRT, PAUL W.
PERSONAL Born 07/22/1954, Detroit, MI, m, 1982 **DISCIPLINE** HISTORY, AMERICAN WEST ENVIRONMENTAL HISTORY **EDUCATION** Univ Ariz, PhD, 91. **CAREER** Assoc prof, Washington State Univ. **HONORS AND AWARDS** Rockefeller Found fel, Univ Kansas, 93. **MEMBERSHIPS** AHA, WHA, ASEH. **RESEARCH** Public lands, environmental policy, forests, energy, western landscapes. **SELECTED PUBLICATIONS** Auth, A Conspiracy of Optimism: Management of the National Forests Since World War II, Univ Nebr Press, 94 & Timber Dreams: Fifty Years of National Forest Planning, Inner Voice, 94; auth, Terra Pacifica: People and Place in the Northwest States and Western Canada, WSU Press, 98; Northwest Lands, Northwest Peoples: Readings in Environmental History, Univ of WA Press, 99. **CONTACT ADDRESS** Dept of History, Washington State Univ, 301 Wilson Hall, PO Box 644030, Pullman, WA 99164-4030. **EMAIL** forrest@mail.wsu.edu

HISE, GREG
DISCIPLINE HISTORY OF ARCHITECTURE, ARCHITECTURE **EDUCATION** Univ CA, Berkeley, AB (Architecture, with honors), 80-84, PhD (Hist of Arch), 87-92. **CAREER** Asst prof, School of Urban Planning and Development, Univ Southern CA, 92-98, assoc prof, School of Policy, Planning, and Development, 98-; vis assoc, Div of Humanities and Social Sciences, Cal Tech, 97-98. **HONORS AND AWARDS** John Reps Prize, Soc of Am City & Regional Planning Hist, 93; Spiro Kostof Book Prize for Architecture and Urbanism, Soc of Architectural Historians, for Magnetic Los Angeles, 98. **SELECTED PUBLICATIONS** Auth, Home Building and Industrial Decentralization in Los Angeles: The Roots of the Postwar Urban Region, J of Urban Hist, Feb 93; Building the World of Tomorrow: Regional Visions, Modern Community Housing and America's Postwar Urban Expansion, Center: A J for Architecture in Am, 93; The Airplane and the Garden City: Regional Transformations during World War II, in Donald Albrecht, ed, World War II and the American Dream: How Wartime Building Changed a Nation, MIT Press with the Nat Building Museum, 95; From Roadside Camps to Garden Homes: Housing and Community Planning for California's Migrant Workforce, 1935-41, in Elizabeth Cromley and Carter L Huggins, eds, Gender, Race, and Shelter: Perspectives in Vernacular Architecture V, Univ TN Press, 95; Building Design as Social Art: The Public Architecture of William Wurster, 1935-1950, in Marc Treib, ed, An Everyday Modernism: The Houses of Willaim Wurster, UC Press with SFMOMA, 95; ed, Rethinking Los Angeles, with Michael J Dear and H Eric Schockman, Sage Pub, 96; Magnetic Los Angeles: Planning the Twentieth-Century Metropolis, Johns Hopkins Univ Press, 97; auth, Eden by Design: The 1930 Olmsted-Bartholomew Plan for the Los Angeles Region, UC Pr, 00; auth, "Nature's Workshop": Industry and Urban Expension in Los Angeles, 1900-1950 J of Historical Geo, 01. **CONTACT ADDRESS** School of Policy, Planning, and Development, Univ of So California, 315 Lewis Hall, Los Angeles, CA 90089-0626.

HITCHCOCK, JAMES
PERSONAL Born 02/13/1938, St Louis, MO, m, 1986, 4 children **DISCIPLINE** HISTORY **EDUCATION** St Louis Univ, AB, 58; Princeton Univ, MA, 62; PhD, 65. **CAREER** Prof, St Louis Univ, 71-. **HONORS AND AWARDS** Woodrow Wilson Fel; NEH Fel. **MEMBERSHIPS** AHA; NAS; HS; Fell Cath Scholars. **RESEARCH** Religion and Society; History of Crime. **SELECTED PUBLICATIONS** Auth, Catholicism and Modernity, 78; auth, The Recovery of the Sacred, 73; auth, The Pope and the Jesuits, 84; auth, Years of Crisis, 85. **CONTACT ADDRESS** Dept History, St. Louis Univ, 221 North Grand Blvd, Saint Louis, MO 63103-2006. **EMAIL** hitchcpj@slu.edu

HITCHENS, MARILYNN JO
PERSONAL Born 12/14/1938, w, 1974, 2 children **DISCIPLINE** HISTORY **EDUCATION** Miami Univ, BA, 60; Univ Colo, MA, 75, PhD, 79. **CAREER** Research/Writer, US Congress, 68-70; Teacher Russ & Hist, Jefferson County Schools, 70-95; Instr World & Russ Hist, Univ Colo, 94-98; International Legal Res, Holme Roberts & Owen LLP, 95-. **HONORS AND AWARDS** Phi Beta Kappa; Int Analyst, CH2M Hill. **MEMBERSHIPS** Am Hist Asn; World Hist Asn. **RESEARCH** World history. **SELECTED PUBLICATIONS** Auth, Germany, Russia and the Balkans: Prelude to the Nazi-Soviet Non-Aggression Pact; SATII World History; Aspen World History Handbooks I & II; Discovering World History; Discovering Nation States; Essays in World History; Readings in World History. **CONTACT ADDRESS** 720 Josephine, Denver, CO 80206. **EMAIL** mhitchen@carbon.cudenver.edu

HITCHINS, KEITH
PERSONAL Born 04/02/1931, Schenectady, NY **DISCIPLINE** MODERN HISTORY **EDUCATION** Union Col, NYork, AB, 52; Harvard Univ, AM, 53, PhD(Hist), 64. **CAREER** Instr Hist, Wake Forest Univ, 58-60 & 62-64, asst prof, 64-65; asst prof, Rice Univ, 66-67; assoc prof, 67-69, prof Hist, Univ Ill, Urbana Champaign, 69-, Am Coun Learned Soc grant, 65-66, res fel, Hungary & Rumania, 69-70; mem, Nat Screening Comt Fulbright-Hays Awards for Poland, Rumania & Yugoslavia, 66-68; mem East Europ adv comt, Coun Int Exchange of Scholars, 70-79; mem East Europ screening comt, Int Res & Exchange Bd, 72-75, res fel for Hungary, 73. **HONORS AND AWARDS** Honorary Member, Romanian Academy, 91; Doctor honoris causa, U of Cluj, 91, Univ Sibiu, 93. **RESEARCH** Southeastern Europe; Habsburg monarchy; the Caucasus. **SELECTED PUBLICATIONS** Auth, The Rumanian National Movement in Transylvania, 1780-1849, Harvard Univ, 69; ed, Rumanian Studies, E J Brill, Leyden Vol I, 70, Vol II, 71-72, Vol III, 73-75, Vol IV, 76-79; coauth, Corespondenta lui Ioan Ratiu cu George Baritiu, 70, auth, Studii privind istoria moderna a Transilvaniei, 70 & Cultura si nationalitate in Transilvania, 72, Dacia; The Nationality Problem in Austria-Hungary, 74 & ed, Studies in Eastern European Social History, Vol 1,77, Vol II, 81, E J Brill, Leyden; auth, Orthodoxy and Nationality: Andreiu Saguna and the Rumanians of Transylvania, 1846-1873, Harvard Univ, 77; Hungarica, 1961-1974, Historische Zeitschrift, Sonderheft 9; auth, Rumania, 1866-1947, Oxford, 94; auth, The Romanians, 1774-1866, Oxford, 96; Mit si realitate in istoriografia romaneasca, Enciclopedica, 97; auth, A Nation Discovered, Bucharest, 99; auth, A Nation Affirmed, Bucharest, 99. **CONTACT ADDRESS** Dept of History, Univ of Illinois, Urbana-Champaign, 810 S Wright St, Urbana, IL 61801-3611.

HIXSON, WALTER L.
PERSONAL Born 10/18/1955, Louisville, KY, m, 1994, 2 children **DISCIPLINE** HISTORY **EDUCATION** Univ of Ky, BA, 78; W Ky Univ, MA, 81; Univ of Colo, PhD, 86. **CAREER** Prof & Chair , Dept of History, Univ of Akron, 98-; Prof, at Akron, 89-; Mellon Vis Asst Prof, Northwestern Univ, 87-89. **HONORS AND AWARDS** Bernath Prize; Society for Historians of American Foreign Relations; Fulbright lecturer, Kazan State Univ, 90-91. **MEMBERSHIPS** Society for Historians of American Foreign Relations. **RESEARCH** Cold War History; US, Foreign Policy; Crime and Culture. **SELECTED PUBLICATIONS** Auth, "George F. Kennan: Cold War Iconclast," Columbia Univ Press, 89; auth, "Red Storm Rising: Tom Clancy Novels as Representations of Reagan Era National Security," Diplomatic History, 17, Fall 93: 599-613; auth, Witness to Disintegration: Provincial Life in the Last Year of the USSR," Univ Press of New England, 93; auth, "Nuclear Weapons and US Cold War Diplomacy," Modern American Dipomacy, 2nd ed., eds. John M. Carroll and George C. Herring, Scholarly Resources, 96; auth, "Charles A. Lindbergh, Lone Eagle," Longman, 96; auth "The Vindication os 'X': Reassessing Kennan After the Cold War," The Historian 59, Summer, 97: 849-58; auth, "Parting the Curtain: Propaganda, Culture, and the Cold War, 1945-1961, St. Martin's Press, 97; auth, "Murder, Cultture, and Injustice: Four Sensational Crimes in American History, Univ of Akron Press, 00. **CONTACT ADDRESS** Dept History, Univ of Akron, 302 Buchtel Mall, Akron, OH 44325-0001. **EMAIL** whixson@uakron.edu

HOAK, DALE E.
PERSONAL Born 12/12/1941, Springfield, OH, m, 1968, 2 children **DISCIPLINE** HISTORY **EDUCATION** Col Wooster, BA, 63; Univ Pittsburgh, BA, 64; Univ Cambridge, PhD, 71. **CAREER** Lecturer, Chatham Col, 65-67; instr, Carnegie-Mellon Univ, 66-67; asst prof, Fla Atl Univ, 71-75; assoc prof to chancellor prof, Col of William & Mary, 75-. **HONORS AND AWARDS** Outstanding Fac Awd, Virginia, 97; Fel, Royal Hist Soc; Visiting Res Fel, Cambridge, 81; assoc Fel, Cambridge, 72. **MEMBERSHIPS** Am Hist Asn, Renaissance Soc of Am, Sixteenth-Cent Studies Conf, N Am Conf on Brit Studies. **RESEARCH** Tudor Government and political culture. **SELECTED PUBLICATIONS** Auth, The World of William & Mary: Anglo-Dutch Perspectives on the Revolution of 1688-89, Stanford Univ Press, 96; ed, Tudor Political Culture, Cambridge Univ Press, 95; ed, The King's Council in the Reign of Edward VI, Cambridge Univ Press, 76; auth, "The Anglo-Dutch Revolution of 1688-89," The World of William & Mary, (96); auth, "The Iconography of the Crown Imperial," Tudor Political Culture, (95): 52-103; auth, "The Secret History of the Tudor Court: the King's Coffers and the King's Purse, 1542-53," Journal of British Studies, (87): 208-231; auth, "Mary I's Privy Council," Revolution Reassessed, (86): 87-115; auth, "Art, Culture, and Mentality in Renaissance Society: Hans Baldung Grien's Bewitched Groom (1544)," Renaissance Quarterly, (85): 488-510; auth, "The Great European Witch Hunts, 1400-1700," American Journal of Sociology, (83): 1270-1274. **CONTACT ADDRESS** Dept Hist, Col of William and Mary, PO Box 8795, Williamsburg, PA 23187-8795. **EMAIL** dehoak@wm.edu

HOBERMAN, LOUISA SCHELL
PERSONAL Born 06/01/1942, Boston, MA, m, 1968 **DISCIPLINE** LATIN-AMERICAN HISTORY **EDUCATION** Radcliffe Col, BA, 63; Columbia Univ, MA, 66, PhD(hist), 72. **CAREER** Instr hist, Univ Calif Exten, Berkeley, 70; asst prof, Pomona Col, 72-76; asst prof hist, Wesleyan Univ, 76-80; RES & WRITING, 80-, Vis scholar, Inst Latin Am Studies, Univ Texas, Austin, 79-80; Mary I Bunting Inst Radcliffe Col fel, 77-78. **MEMBERSHIPS** Conf Latin Am Hist; AHA; Latin Am Studies Asn; Women's Coalition Latin Americanists; Nat Coun on Pub Hist. **RESEARCH** Business history **SELECTED PUBLICATIONS** Auth, Latin American female archetypes as portrayed in the historical literature, Revista/Rev Interam, fall 74; Bureaucracy and disaster: Mexico City and the flood of 1629, J Latin Am Studies, fall 74; Merchants in seventeenth century Mexico City: A preliminary portrait, Hispanic Am Hist Rev, 76; Hispanic American political theory as a distinct tradition, J Hist of Ideas, spring 80; Technological change in a traditional society: The case of the Desague in colonial Mexico, Technol & Culture, 7/80; Enrico Martinez: Printer and Engineer, Survival and Struggle in Colonial America, Univ Calif, 81. **CONTACT ADDRESS** 2637 West 49th St, Austin, TX 78731.

HOBGOOD-OSTER, LAURA
PERSONAL Born 09/18/1964, Indiana, m, 1995 **DISCIPLINE** HISTORICAL THEOLOGY **EDUCATION** St Louis Univ, PhD, 97; Vanderbilt Univ, Mdiv, 89; James Madison Univ, BA, 85. **CAREER** Asst Prof of Rel, 98-, Southwestern Univ; Lectr/Instr of Rel Studies, 97-98, Cal State Univ. **HONORS AND AWARDS** Pres Fellow, 94-97, St Louis Univ; Faculty Merit Scholar, 88-89, Vanderbilt Univ. **MEMBERSHIPS** AAR **RESEARCH** Christianity in America, Theology of Nature, Gnostic Christianity, Women and Religion. **SELECTED PUBLICATIONS** Auth, As Heaven and Earth Combine: Perceptions of Nature in American Shakerism, Esoteric Studies, 98; She Glanceth From Earth to Heaven: The Phenomenon of Love Mysticism Among Women in Antebellum Virginia and Maryland, Univ Press of the South, 98; Mary Magdalene, Gnostic Revealer, Koinonia Journal, Princeton Seminary Graduate Forum 96; Sexuality-One of God's Gifts, A Year in the Life, St Louis, Chalice Books, 93; Building Self Esteem, Christian Children's Fellowship Manual, Chalice Books, 92; ed, The Sabbath Journal of Judith Lomax, Scholar Press, Texts and Translations Series, forthcoming; **CONTACT ADDRESS** Southwestern Univ, 1001 E University, Georgetown, TX 78626. **EMAIL** hoboster@southwestern.edu

HOBSBAWM, ERIC
DISCIPLINE HISTORY **EDUCATION** Cambridge Univ, PhD, 51. **CAREER** Prof Pol and Soc Emeritus and sr lctr grad

fac. **RESEARCH** Comp polit, soc, and economic hist. **SELECTED PUBLICATIONS** Auth, Nations and Nationalism Since 1780, 90; Echoes of the Marseillaise, 90; The Age of Empire 1875-1914, 89; The Age of Capital 1848-1875, 75; Industry and Empire, 68; The Age of Revolution 1789-1848, 62. **CONTACT ADDRESS** Eugene Lang Col, New Sch for Social Research, 66 West 12th St, New York, NY 10011.

HOBSON, CHARLES FREDERIC
PERSONAL Born 03/27/1943, Mobile, AL, m, 1969, 2 children **DISCIPLINE** UNITED STATES HISTORY **EDUCATION** Brown Univ, BA, 65; Emory Univ, MA, 66, PhD(hist), 71. **CAREER** Instr hist, Ga State Univ, 70-72; asst ed, Papers of James Madison, Univ Va, 72-73, assoc ed, 73-77, co-ed, 77-79; Ed, Papers of John Marshall,Omohundro Inst Early Am Hist & Culture, Williamsburg, 79-; lectr, Col William & Mary, 79-. **HONORS AND AWARDS** Assoc for Documentery Editing, 95-96 **MEMBERSHIPS** Southern Hist Asn; Am Soc Legal Hist; Asn Doc Ed; Soc Historians Early Am Repub. **RESEARCH** Revolution and early national period; 18th century Virginia. **SELECTED PUBLICATIONS** Auth, " The Viginia Plan of 1787: A Note on the Original Text," Quarterly Journal of the Library of Congress 37, (80): 201-214; " The Recovery of British Debts in the Federal Circuit Court of Virginia, 1790 to 1797," Virginia Magazine of History and Biography 91, (84): 176-200; auth, " The Negative on State Laws: James Madison, the Constiution, and the Crisis of Republican Government," William and Mary Quarterly, 3rd ser 36 (79): 215-235; ed, The Papers of John Marshall vols 5,6,7,8,9, Univ of North Carolina Press, 87. 90, 93, 95, 98; coed, The Papers of James Madison vols, 9,10, Univ of Chicago Press, 75, 77, vols 11, 12, 13, Univ Press of Virginia, 77, 79, 81; auth, The Great Chief Justice: John Marshall and the Rule of Law , Univ Press of Kansas, 96; auth, " A Nation of States: Federalism in the Framing of the Constitution, " Our Perculiar Security: The Written Constitution and Limited Government, Lanham, MD: Rowman & Littlefield Publishers, Inc (93): 97-109; auth, " John Marshall and His Papers," Journal of Supreme Court Hisory 1996, vol 2, (96: 30-35; auth, " John Marshall and the Fairfax Litigation: The Background of Martin V Hunter's Lessee," Journal of Supreme Court History 1996, vol2 (96): 36-50; auth, " John Marshall," American Nationa Biography, New York, (99): 14, 564-570; auth, The Great Chief Justice: John Marshall and the Rule of Law, Univ Press of Kansas 96. **CONTACT ADDRESS** Papers of John Marshall, Col of William and Mary, P O Box 8781, Williamsburg, VA 23187. **EMAIL** efhobs@mail.wm.edu

HOBSON, WAYNE K.
PERSONAL Born 07/01/1941, Moscow, ID, m, 1966, 2 children **DISCIPLINE** AMERICAN STUDIES, HISTORY **EDUCATION** Univ Ore, BA, 65; Reed Col, MAT, 66; Stanford Univ, MA, 69, PhD(hist), 77. **CAREER** Asst prof, 73-78, Assoc Prof, 78-86, Prof Am Studies, Calif State Univ, Fullerton, 86-. **MEMBERSHIPS** Am Studies Asn; Orgn Am Historians. **RESEARCH** American social and cultural history; late 19th and early 20th centuries; cultural history of image and reality of crime and violence in America. **SELECTED PUBLICATIONS** Auth, New-Deal Justice--The Life of Stanley Reed of Kentucky, Am Hist Rev, Vol 0101, 96; The Quest for Authority and Honor in the American Professions, 1750-1900, Am Studies Int, Vol 0031, 93. **CONTACT ADDRESS** Dept of Am Studies, California State Univ, Fullerton, Fullerton, CA 92834. **EMAIL** hobson@fullerton.edu

HOCHMAN, JIRI
PERSONAL Born 03/06/1926, Prague, Czechoslovakia, m, 1963, 2 children **DISCIPLINE** HISTORY **EDUCATION** Ohio State Univ, PhD, 80. **CAREER** Vis Prof, 74-77, from Assoc Prof to Prof, 83-95, Prof Emeritus Hist, Ohio State Univ, 95-. **HONORS AND AWARDS** Czechoslovakia Press Prize, 64; Am Pen Club, 84. **MEMBERSHIPS** Czechoslovakia Hist Conf. **RESEARCH** European history. **SELECTED PUBLICATIONS** Auth, The Soviet Union and the Failure of Collective Security, 1934-1938, Cornell Univ Press, 84; coauth, Hope Dies Last, An Autobiography of Alexander Dubcek, Kodansha Amerrica, 93; auth, Historical Dictionary of the Czech State, Scarecrow Press, 98. **CONTACT ADDRESS** 103 Putter Dr., Palm Coast, FL 32164. **EMAIL** jirhoch@pcfl.net

HOCHSTADT, STEVE
PERSONAL Born 08/30/1948, New York, NY, m, 1978, 2 children **DISCIPLINE** EUROPEAN HISTORY **EDUCATION** Brown Univ, BA, 71, PhD, 83. **CAREER** PROF HIST, CHAIR HIST DEPT, BATES COL, 79-. **HONORS AND AWARDS** Grant, Memorial Foundation for Jewish; grant, Dimmer-Bergstrom Fund; grant, Holocaust Educational Foundation; grant , Lucious N Littauer Foundation. **MEMBERSHIPS** American Historical Assn, Social Science History Assn, Sino-Judaic Institute. **RESEARCH** Migration in Germany, Holocaust, Jewish refugees in Shanghai **SELECTED PUBLICATIONS** Auth, " Social History and Politics: A Materialist View, " Social History, v 7, Jan 82: 75-83; auth, " Migration in Preindustrial Germany," Central European History, v 16, Sept 83: 195-224; auth, " The Socioeconomic Determinants of Increasing Mobility in Nineteenth-Century Germany," Historical Social Research--Historische Sozialforschung, v 22, 97: 254-274; auth, Mobility and Modernity: Migration in Germany 1820-1989, Ann Arbor: Univ of Mich Press, 99; auth, " Vertreibung aus Deutschland und Uberleben in Shanghai: judische NS-Vertriebene in China," IMIS-Beitrage, Institut fur Migrationsforschung und Interkulturelle Studien, Universitat Osnabruck,, vol, 12,99: 51-67; auth, " The Unspoken Purposeds of Service-Learning: Teaching the Holocaust," in Ira Harkavy and Bill M. Donovan, eds, Connecting Past and Present: Connecting Past and Present: Concept and Models for Service-Learning in History (Washington, DC: American Assoc for Higher Education, 00: 189-197. **CONTACT ADDRESS** History Dept, Bates Col, Lewiston, ME 04240. **EMAIL** shochsta@bates.edu

HOCKLEY, ALLEN
DISCIPLINE ART HISTORY **EDUCATION** Univ Victoria, BA; Univ British Columbia, MA; Univ Toronto, PhD. **CAREER** Asst prof, Dartmouth Col. **HONORS AND AWARDS** Ed, E Asia Forum, 90-92). **RESEARCH** Japanese prints, early photography in Asia, Buddhist art. **SELECTED PUBLICATIONS** Auth, Harunobu and the Megane-e Tradition, Ukiyo-e guijutsu, 891; Harunobu's Relationship with Hiraga Gennai, Andon, 89. **CONTACT ADDRESS** Dartmouth Col, 3529 N Main St, Ste. 207, Hanover, NH 03755. **EMAIL** allen.hockley@dartmouth.edu

HODDESON, LILLIAN
PERSONAL Born 12/20/1940, New York, NY **DISCIPLINE** HISTORY **EDUCATION** Barnard Col, NY, AB, 61, Columbia Univ, NY, MA, 63, Columbia Univ, NY, Ph.D, 66. **CAREER** Asst Prof, Barnard Col, 67-70, Asst Prof, Rutgers Univ, 71-77, Historian, Fermi National Accelerator Lab, 78-, Sr Research Physicist, Univ of Illinois, 80-, Historian, Los Alamos National Lab Hist, 84-. **HONORS AND AWARDS** A.P Sloan Fond, 80, Nat Sci Found Grant, 67-70, 74, 89-93, 92-95, 95-99, Am Coun of Learned Soc Study Fel, 74-75, AT&T Found, 93-94, AT&T Bell Labs, 94-97. **RESEARCH** History of twentieth century science and technology, oral history. **SELECTED PUBLICATIONS** Ed, The Birth of Particle Physics, (New York, Cambridge Univ Press), 83; ed, Out of the Crystal Maze: A History of Solid State Physics 1900-1960, Oxoford Univ Press, 92; auth, "Mission Change in the Large Laboratory: the Los Alamos Implosion Program," Big Science, (93), 265-290; auth, "The Discovery of Spontaneous Fission in Plutonium During World War II," Hist Studies in the Physical and Biological Sci, (93), 279-300; auth, "The Mirage of the World Accelerator for World Peace and the Origins of the SSC," Hist Studies in the Physical and Biological Sci, (93), 101-124; coauth, Critical Assembly: A History of Los Alamos During the Oppenheimer Years 1943-1945, New York, Cambridge Univ Press, 93; auth, "Research on Crystal Rectifiers During World War II, and the Invention of the Transistor," Hist and Tech Vol 11, (94), 121-130; auth, " A New Frontier in the Chicago Suburbs: Settling Fermi National Accelerator Laboratory 1963-1972," Illinois Hist Journal, (95), 2-18. **CONTACT ADDRESS** History Dept, Univ of Illinois, Urbana-Champaign, 810 S. Wright St, Gregory Hall, Urbana, IL 61801. **EMAIL** hoddeson@uiuc.edu

HODGE, ROBERT WHITE
PERSONAL Born 10/03/1939, Grand Rapids, MI **DISCIPLINE** UNITED STATES HISTORY **EDUCATION** Cent Mich Univ, BS, 61, MA, 63; Mich State Univ, PhD(US foreign rels), 68. **CAREER** From instr to asst prof, 66-72, assoc prof, 72-79, Prof Hist, Beloit Col, 79-, Vis prof, Univ Nottingham, 73. **MEMBERSHIPS** AHA; Orgn Am Historians. **RESEARCH** United States diplomatic history in the twentieth century. **SELECTED PUBLICATIONS CONTACT ADDRESS** Dept of Hist, Beloit Col, 700 College St, Beloit, WI 53511-5595.

HODGES, JAMES A.
DISCIPLINE HISTORY **EDUCATION** N Ala Univ, BS, 55; Vanderbilt Univ, MA, 59, PhD, 63. **CAREER** Michael O Fisher prof. **RESEARCH** Study on textile unionism in the modern South. **SELECTED PUBLICATIONS** Auth, articles in Tenn Histl Quart; auth, Encycl S Hist; auth, New Deal Labor Policy and the Southern Cotton Textile Industry, 1933-1941, Univ Tenn Press, 86. **CONTACT ADDRESS** Dept of Hist, The Col of Wooster, Wooster, OH 44691.

HODGINS, BRUCE W.
PERSONAL Born 01/29/1931, Kitchener, ON, Canada, m, 1958, 2 children **DISCIPLINE** CANADIAN & COMMONWEALTH HISTORY **EDUCATION** Univ Western Ont, BA, 53; Queen's Univ, Ont, MA, 55; Duke Univ, PhD(hist), 65. **CAREER** Chmn dept hist, Prince of Wales Col, 55-58; 61-62; lectr, Univ Western Ont, 62-64, asst prof, 64-65; from asst prof to assoc prof, 65-72, Prof Hist, Trent Univ, 72-, Chmn, Dept Hist, 80-, Spec adv federalism, Govt P E I, 57-58, prov archivist, 61-62; mem, Nat Exec Coun, UN Asn in Can, 61-62 & 65-, vchmn, Nat Admin Comt, 66-67, chmn, 67-68, Nat Policy Coun, 68-; vis fel hist, Australian Nat Univ, 70. **HONORS AND AWARDS** Can Centennial Medal, 67; Ont Hist Cruikshank Awd, 68. **MEMBERSHIPS** Can Hist Asn; Asn for Cancer Studies. **RESEARCH** Canadian politics, 1841-1873 and 1956 to the present; French Canadian society; Canadian North. **SELECTED PUBLICATIONS** Ed., Canadiens, Canadians and Quebecoi's (Canada: Issues & Options), Paperback June 74; ed., The Canoe in Canadian Cultures; et al Paperback July 99; coauth, Canoeing North into the Unknown: A Record River Travel 1874-1974, Gwyneth Hoyle, Paperback February 97; coed, Changing Parks: The History Future and Cultural Context of Parks and Heritage Landscapes, by John Marsh, (editor), Bruce Hodgins, (editor) Paperback - December 97; coauth, Nastawgan: The Canadian North by Canoe and Snowshoe, by Bruce W. Hodgins, Margaret Hobbs, Hardcover - June 85; auth, John Sandfield Macdonald, 1812-1872; coed, Nastawgan: The Canadian North by Canoe and Showshoe, by Bruce W Hodgins, Margaret Hobbs, (editor); auth, Paradis of Temagami: the story of Charles Paradis, 1848-1926: northern priest, colonizer, and rebel," by Bruce W. Hodgins; coauth, The Temagami Experience: Recreation, Resources, and Aboriginal Rights in the Northern Ontario Wilderness, by Bruce W. Hodgins, Jamie Benidickson. **CONTACT ADDRESS** Dept of Hist, Trent Univ, 1600 W Bank Dr, Peterborough, ON, Canada K9J 7B8. **EMAIL** bhodgins@trentu.ca

HOEFLICH, MICHAEL H.
PERSONAL Born 01/11/1952, New York, NY, m, 1986 **DISCIPLINE** LAW, HISTORY **EDUCATION** Haverford Col, BA, 73; MA, 73; Cambridge Univ, MA, 76; Yale Law Sch, JD, 79. **CAREER** Res fel, Clare Col at Cambridge Univ, 75-77; tax assoc, Cravath, Swaine & Moore, 79-81; from asst prof to prof, Univ of Ill at Ubana-Champaign, 84-88; dean & prof, Syracuse Univ, 88-94; dean, prof & Courtesy Prof of Hist, Univ of Kans Sch of Law, 94-97; dean, Courtesy Prof of Hist, and John H. & John M. Kane Distinguished Prof of Law, Univ of Kans Sch of Law, 97-. **HONORS AND AWARDS** Fulbright Fel, 73; Sr Studentship, Clare Col at Cambridge, 74; NEH Travel Awd, 85; Surrency Prize, Am Soc for Legal Hist, 85; NEH Summer Stipend, 88; grant, Delmas Found, 95-96; Phillips Fel, Am Philos Soc, 95-96; grant, Kans Bar Found; vis res fel, Univ of Aberdeen, 00. **MEMBERSHIPS** ABA, NYSBA, Kans Bar Asn, Wichita Bar Asn. **RESEARCH** Legal History. **SELECTED PUBLICATIONS** Coauth, Property Law & Legal Education, Univ of Ill Press, 88; ed, The Gladsome Light of Jurisprudence, Learning the Law in England and the United States in the 18th & 19th Centuries, Greenwood Press (Westport, CT), 88; coauth, Cases & Materials on Federal Taxation of Deferred Compensation, Commerce Clearing House (Chicago, IL), 89; coauth, Der Einfluss deutscher Emigranten auf die Rechtsentwicklung in den USA und in Deutschland, JCB Mohr, 93; auth, Roman & Civil Law & the Development of Anglo-American Jurisprudence in the Nineteenth Century, Univ of Ga Press, 97; ed, Lex et Romanitas. Essays in Honor of Alan Watson, Robbins Inst Press, forthcoming. **CONTACT ADDRESS** Sch of Law, Univ of Kansas, Lawrence, 202 Green Hall, Lawrence, KS 66045.

HOENG, PETER
PERSONAL Born 03/05/1960, s **DISCIPLINE** GERMAN LITERARY HISTORY & CULTURE **EDUCATION** Univ Siegen, MA, 88; Univ Wis, PhD, 94. **CAREER** From asst prof to assoc prof, Univ Tenn, 94-. **HONORS AND AWARDS** Fac Res Awd, Univ Tenn, 95, 96, & 99; Promising Young Scholar Awd, Univ Tenn, 99. **MEMBERSHIPS** Asn of Teachers in Ger, Soc for Eighteenth-Century Studies, Ger Studies Asn. **RESEARCH** German Literature and Culture since the Eighteenth-Century, Beethoven's Intellectual Life, Ger Jewish Culture, Censorship, Authors: Schiller, Goethe, Tabori, Bernhard. **SELECTED PUBLICATIONS** Ed, Embodied Projections on History: George Tabori's Theater Work, 98; auth, Die Sterne, Die Zensur. Das Vaterland: Geschichte Und Theater Im Spaten 18. Jahr Hun Dert, 00. **CONTACT ADDRESS** Ger & Slavic Lang, Univ of Tennessee, Knoxville, 1345 Circle Park, Knoxville, TN 37996-0001. **EMAIL** hoeyng@utk.edu

HOEVELER, J. DAVID
PERSONAL Born 07/31/1943, Bridgeport, CT, m, 1972, 2 children **DISCIPLINE** HISTORY **EDUCATION** Lehigh Univ, BA, 65; Univ Ill-Urbana Champaign, PhD, 71. **CAREER** From asst prof to prof, Univ Wis, 71-. **MEMBERSHIPS** Org Am Hist; Am Soc for 18th Cent Stud **RESEARCH** American thought & culture. **SELECTED PUBLICATIONS** Watch on the Right: Conservative Intellectuals in the Reagan Era, Univ Wis Press, 92; The Postmodernist Turn: American Thought and Culture in the 1970s, Twayne Publ, 96. **CONTACT ADDRESS** Dept History, Univ of Wisconsin, Milwaukee, PO Box 413, Milwaukee, WI 53201. **EMAIL** jdh2@csd.uwm.edu

HOEY, LAWRENCE R.
DISCIPLINE ART HISTORY **EDUCATION** Univ Rochester, BA, 73; Univ Chicago, MA, 74, PhD, 81. **CAREER** Asst prof, 81-88; assoc prof, 88-99. **HONORS AND AWARDS** Prof 99-. **MEMBERSHIPS** Soc Antiquaries London; British Archaeol Asn; Soc Archit Hist; Int Center Medieval Art; AVISTA. **SELECTED PUBLICATIONS** Auth, A Problem in Romanesque Aesthetics: The Articulation of Groin and Early Rib Vaults in the Larger Churches of England and Normandy, 96; Style, Patronage, and Artistic Creativity in Kent Parish Church Architecture in the Early English Period, 96; The 13th-Century Choir and Transepts of Rievaulx Abbey, 95; Stone Vaults in English Parish Churches in the Early Gothic and Decorated Periods, 94; Pier Design in Early Gothic Architecture in East-Central Scotland c.1170-1250, 94. **CONTACT ADDRESS** Dept of Art History, Univ of Wisconsin, Milwaukee, PO Box 413, Milwaukee, WI 53201. **EMAIL** lhoey@uwm.edu

HOFF, JOAN
PERSONAL Born 06/27/1939, Butte, MT, d **DISCIPLINE** U.S. HISTORY **EDUCATION** Univ MT, BA 57; Cornell Univ, MA, 60; Univ Calif, PhD, 66. **CAREER** Prof Calif State Univ, 67-76; Sr Prof Ariz State Univ, 76-81; Kathe Tappe Vernon Vis prof, Dartmouth, 80; vis prof, Univ Va, 81; prof, Ind Univ, 81-97; co-ed/co-founder, The Journal of Women's History 88-96; pres and CEO, Ctr for Study of the Presidency, 95-96; ed, Pres Stu Qrt, 95-97; dir, Contemp Hist Inst, prof, Ohio Univ 97-. **HONORS AND AWARDS** Fel, Soc of Am Historians; Visiting James Pinckney Harrison Prof of History, College of William and Mary, 00-01; USIS Fac Lectr Warsaw Univ; Mary Ball Washington Ch, Univ Col, Dublin; Hon Doctorate, MT State Univ. **MEMBERSHIPS** OAH, SNAFR, Peace Hist Soc. **RESEARCH** Modern Presidency; U.S. 20th century for policy and politics; U.S. women's legal history. **SELECTED PUBLICATIONS** Auth, Law, Gender, and Injustice: A Legal History of U.S. Women from the American Revolution to the Present, NY Univ Press 91; auth, Herbert Hoover: Forgotten Progressive Waveland Press, 92; auth, Nixon Reconsidered, Basic Books, 94; co-ed, Voices of Irish Women: Past and Present, Ind Univ Press 95; co-ed; auth, The Cooper's Wife Is Missing: A Tale of Ritual Murder in late-Nineteenth Century Ireland, Basic Books, 00. **CONTACT ADDRESS** Contemporary History Inst, Ohio Univ, Brown House, Athens, OH 45701. **EMAIL** joanhoff1@aol.com

HOFFECKER, CAROL E.
PERSONAL Born 12/29/1938, Wilmington, DE **DISCIPLINE** AMERICAN HISTORY **CAREER** Asst prof hist, Sweet Briar Col, 63-66; coordr Hagley Fel Prog, Hagley Mus, Univ Del, 70-73; asst prof, 70-75, assoc prof, 75-81, prof hist, 82-, Univ Del. **HONORS AND AWARDS** Francis Alison Prof; Richards Prof; Medal of Distinction, Univ Del; Del Women's Hall of Fame. **MEMBERSHIPS** Orgn Am Historians; AHA. **RESEARCH** History of Delaware; urban history. **SELECTED PUBLICATIONS** Auth, U.S. District Court for Delaware, 92; auth, Beneath Thy Guiding Hand: A History of Women at the University of Delaware, 94; auth, Honest John Williams, U.S. Senator From Delaware, 00. **CONTACT ADDRESS** Dept of History, Univ of Delaware, Newark, DE 19711. **EMAIL** Carol.Hoffecker@mvs.udel.edu

HOFFECKER, J. F.
PERSONAL Born 12/16/1952, London, England; m, 1985, 2 children **DISCIPLINE** ARCHAEOLOGY **EDUCATION** Univ Chicago, anthropology 86; Yale Univ, archaeology 75. **CAREER** Argonne National Laboratory, environ scientist, 84-98; Univ of Colorado, Inst of Arctic and Alpine Research, 98-. **HONORS AND AWARDS** Dist Performance Awd ANL. **MEMBERSHIPS** SAA **RESEARCH** Stone age archaeology of Russia; early prehistory of Alaska. **SELECTED PUBLICATIONS** Auth, Neanderthal Ecology in the northwestern Caucasus: Faunal remains from the Borisovskoe Gorge sites, coauth, in: Quaternary Paleozoology in the Northern Hemisphere, eds J.J. Saunders B.W. Styles G. Baryshnikov, IL State Museum Scientific Papers, 98; Un site Micoquien Est-European du Caucases du Nord, resultsats preliminaires de l'etude de la grotte Mezmaiskaya, les fouilles des annees 1987-1993, coauth, L'Anthropologie, Paris, 98; The Archaeology of the European Neanderthals: East and west, The Rev of Archaeology, 97; The Last Neanderthals, London, Weidenfield and Nicolson, 97; Introduction to the Archaeology of Beringia, in: American Beginnings, ed FH West, Chicago, UCP, 96; Zooarchaeology and palaeoecology of Mezmaiskaya Cave, Northwestern Caucasus, coauth, Jour of Arch Sci, 96; Mousterian hunters of the NW Caucasus: Preliminary results of recent investigations, coauth, Jour of Field Arch, 94. **CONTACT ADDRESS** Dept of Environmental Assessment, Argonne National Laboratory, 7876 South Niagara Way, Englewood, CO 80112. **EMAIL** JFHoffeck@aol.com

HOFFECKER, W. ANDREW
DISCIPLINE CHURCH HISTORY **EDUCATION** Dickinson Col, BA; Gordon-Conwell, MDiv; Brown Univ, PhD. **CAREER** Prof, Grove City Col; prof; Reformed Theol Sem. **HONORS AND AWARDS** Captain, US Army. **MEMBERSHIPS** Evangel Theol Soc. **RESEARCH** Princeton Theology; C.S. Lewis; Worldview. **SELECTED PUBLICATIONS** Auth, Piety and the Princeton Theologians; ed, Building a Christian World View. **CONTACT ADDRESS** Dept of Church History, Reformed Theol Sem, Mississippi, 5422 Clinton Blvd, Jackson, MS 39209-3099. **EMAIL** ahoffecker@rts.edu

HOFFER, PETER CHARLES
PERSONAL Born 08/03/1944, Brooklyn, NY, m, 1970, 1 child **DISCIPLINE** AMERICAN HISTORY **EDUCATION** Univ Rochester, AB, 65; Harvard Univ, MA, 66, PhD(hist), 70. **CAREER** Asst prof hist, Ohio State Univ, 70-77; vis asst prof hist, Univ Notre Dame, 77-78; asst prof, 78-82, assoc prof hist, Univ GA, 82-86, prof, 86, research prof, 93-. **HONORS AND AWARDS** Grants, Nat Endowment for Humanities, 75, 90, Am Philos Soc, 77, Colonial Williamsburg Found, 78, Project '87, 79 & Am Bar Found, 80; Golieb Fellow, N.Y.O. Law School, 92, 95, 96; Lyans Visiting Prof, Brooklyn Col, 93-94. **MEMBERSHIPS** AHA; Orgn Am Historians; Inst Early Am Hist & Cult; Am Soc Legal Hist. **RESEARCH** Early American legal and constitutional history. **SELECTED PUBLICATIONS** Coauth, Murdering Mothers, Infanticide in England and New England, 1558-1803, NY Univ Press, 81; Criminal Proceedings in Colonial Virginia, the Richmond County, Virginia, Record, 1711-1754, Am Legal Rec Ser, Am Hist Asn, Vol 10, 82; coauth, Impeachment in America, 1635-1805, Yale Univ Press, 84; auth, Revolution and Regeneration, Univ of GA Press, 81; auth, The Law's Conscience, Univ of NC Press, 90; auth, Law and People in Colonial America, John Hopkins Univ Press, 1st ed, 92, 2nd ed, 98; auth, The Devil's Disciples: M..of the Salem Witchcraft Trials, John Hopkins Univ Press, 96; auth, The Salem Witchcraft Trials: A Legal History, Univ Press of Kansas, 97; co-auth, Reading and Writing in American History, Houghton-Miffin, 2nd ed, 98. **CONTACT ADDRESS** Dept of Hist, Univ of Georgia, 202 LeConte Hall, Athens, GA 30602-1603. **EMAIL** pchoffer@arches.uga.edu

HOFFER, PETER T.
PERSONAL Born 05/27/1942, Providence, RI, s **DISCIPLINE** GERMAN STUDIES **EDUCATION** Columbia Univ, BA, 64; Tufts Univ, MA, 65; Univ Pa, PhD, 75. **CAREER** Instr, asst prof, Lincoln Univ, 71082; asst prof to assoc, prof, Univ Sci, 82. **HONORS AND AWARDS** Psych Cen, Fel Assoc. **MEMBERSHIPS** MLA; AATG; GSA; Fulbright Asn. **RESEARCH** History of psychoanalysis; applied psychoanalysis; history of science; intellectual history; modern German literature; translation. **SELECTED PUBLICATIONS** Auth, Monograph: Klaus Mann, GK Hall, 78; transl, Sigmund Freud: A Phylogenic Fantasy: Overview of the Transference Neuroses (Harvard Univ Pr, 1987); transl, The Correspondence of Sigmund Freud and Sandor Ferench (Harvard Univ Pr, 1993, 1996, 2000). **CONTACT ADDRESS** 151 Bishop Ave, Apt L14, Secane, PA 19018. **EMAIL** p.hoffer@usip.edu

HOFFMAN, ANNE
DISCIPLINE MODERN EUROPEAN FICTION, JEWISH LITERARY HISTORY **EDUCATION** Columbia Univ, PhD. **CAREER** Prof, Fordham Univ. **RESEARCH** Lit and psychoanalysis, feminist theory, contemp critical theory. **SELECTED PUBLICATIONS** Auth, A Book That Was Lost and Other Stories, Schocken Bk(s), 95. **CONTACT ADDRESS** Dept of Eng Lang and Lit, Fordham Univ, 113 W 60th St, New York, NY 10023.

HOFFMAN, DANIEL
PERSONAL Born 01/07/1957, Hamilton, OH, m, 1987 **DISCIPLINE** ANCIENT AND CHURCH HISTORY **EDUCATION** Miami Univ, PhD, BS Ed; Trinity Evangelical Divinity School, MA; Moody Bible Inst, BA. **CAREER** Asst Prof of Hist, 94-, Lee Univ of Cleveland; Tchr, Dept Chr, 86-94, Soc Stud, Charlotte Christian School. **HONORS AND AWARDS** John Stephenson Fellowships; Who's Who in Amer Tchr; Lee Univ Faculty Res Grants. **MEMBERSHIPS** NAPS, ASOR, The Conf on Faith and Hist. **RESEARCH** Gnosticism; Women in the Early Church; Karak Region of Jordan during the Roman Era. **SELECTED PUBLICATIONS** Auth, The Status of Women and Gnosticism in Irenaeus and Tertullian, Studies in Women and Religion 36, Lewiston NY, Edwin Mellen, 95; Bathe, Jewish and Prisons in: A Dictionary of Biblical Manners and Customs, eds, RK Harrison, M Wilson, S Carroll & E Yamauchi, Grand Rapids, Zondervan, forthcoming; Walter Bauer, Suetonius, in: Encyclopedia of Historians and Historical Writing, ed, K Boyd, London, Fitzroy Dearborn, 97; Phoenix, The Anchor Bible Dictionary, ed, DN Freedman, NY, Doubleday, 92. **CONTACT ADDRESS** Dept of Behavioral and Social Science, Lee Col, Tennessee, Box 3450, Cleveland, TN 37320-3450. **EMAIL** dhoffman@leeuniversity.edu

HOFFMAN, DONALD STONE
PERSONAL Born 12/10/1936, Albany, NY, m, 1963, 2 children **DISCIPLINE** MODERN GERMAN HISTORY **EDUCATION** Syracuse Univ, AB, 58; Univ Del, PhD(hist), 69. **CAREER** Lectr hist, Univ Western Ont, 65-69, asst prof, 69-71; assoc prof, 71-77, Prof Hist, Edinboro Univ PA, 71-, Coordr Acad Res, 73-, Mem publ comt, Can Coun, 68-71; Can Coun res award, 69. **MEMBERSHIPS** AHA; Conf Group Cent Europ Hist. **RESEARCH** Germany in the 19th century; railway history; economic history of Europe. **SELECTED PUBLICATIONS** Auth, Science and the American Dream, In: The American Fabric, Edinboro, 73; The Real Cost of Industrial Progress, In: Regional Public Affairs, 10/75; ConRail and America's National Needs, In: Regional Public Affairs, 4/75; The Preservation of America, In: The American Fabric, Dubuque, Iowa, 76; Obstacles to Modern Nationalism: Myth and Nineteenth Century German Particularism, Sind J Hist & Polit Sci, winter 77; Some Perspectives on Architecture, The Edinboro Rev, 12/77; The Arts and Politics of College Administration, Analytical Review of Kenneth E Eble, The Art of Admin, 78 & The Edinboro Rev, 12/78; German Railways in the 1850's: Did They Aid Unification?, Sind J Hist & Polit Sci, winter 80. **CONTACT ADDRESS** Dept of Hist, Edinboro Univ of Pennsylvania, Edinboro, PA 16444. **EMAIL** dhoffman@edinboro.edu

HOFFMAN, PAUL
DISCIPLINE HISTORY OF EARLY MODERN PHILOSOPHY **EDUCATION** UCLA, PhD. **CAREER** Assoc Prof, Univ Calif, Riverside. **RESEARCH** Moral psychology; Philosophy of mind. **SELECTED PUBLICATIONS** Coauth, "Alternative Possibilities: A Reply to Lamb," Jour Philos 91, 94; "Responses to Chappell and Watson," Philos Stud 77, 95; "Strength and Freedom of Will: Descartes and Albritton," Philos Stud 77, 95; "The Being of Leibnizian Phenomena," Studia Leibnitiana 28, 96; "Descartes on Misrepresentation," Jour Hist of Philos 34, 96. **CONTACT ADDRESS** Dept of Philos, Univ of California, Riverside, 1156 Hinderaker Hall, Riverside, CA 92521-0209. **EMAIL** phoffman@ucrac1.ucr.edu

HOFFMAN, PETER C. W.
PERSONAL Born 08/13/1930, Dresden, Germany **DISCIPLINE** HISTORY **EDUCATION** Univ Stuttgart; Univ Tubingen; Univ Zurich; Northwestern Univ; Univ Munich, PhD, 61. **CAREER** Prof History, McGILL Univ, 70-, William Kingsford Prof, 88-. **HONORS AND AWARDS** Mem, Royal Soc Can. **MEMBERSHIPS** Ger Stud Asn; Deutsche Schillergesellschaft; Bibliothekgesellschaft; Can Comt Hist Second World War; Wurttembergischer Geschichts- und Altertumsverein. **SELECTED PUBLICATIONS** Auth, "Claus Schenk Graf von Stauffenberg und seine Bruder," Deutsche Verlags-Anstalt: Stuttgart, (92), 672; auth, "Tedeschi contro il nazismo, La Resistenza in Germania," Bologna, Societa editrice il Mulino, (94), 187; auth, Stauffenberg. A Family History, 1905-1944," Cambridge, New York, Melbourne, Cambridge University Press, (95), 424; auth, "Stauffenberg und der 20. Juli 1944," Munich, C.H. Beck Verlag, (98), 104; auth, "Wurm, D. Theophil (1868-1953) in Modern Germany," Vol. II, (98), 1098-99; auth, "Moltke, Hellmuth James von (1907-44), in Modern Germany," (New York & London: Garland Publishing Inc., 98), 665-666; auth, "Hammerstein-Equord, Kurt von (1878-1943)," (New York & London: Garland Publishing Inc., 98), 433; auth "Introduction," in Hans Bernd Gisevius, to the Bitter End, 1933-44, 7-24; ed, "Socialism," in Andrew Chandler, The Moral Imperative, Boulder, Colorado, and Cumnor Hill, Oxford: Westview Press, (98), 73-104; auth, "Stauffenberg und der 20." Juli 1944," Verlag C.H. Beck, Munich, (98), 104. **CONTACT ADDRESS** Dept of History, McGill Univ, 855 Sherbrooke St W, Montreal, QC, Canada H3A 2T7. **EMAIL** hoffman@leacock.lan.mcgill.ca

HOFFMAN, PIOTR
DISCIPLINE HISTORY OF PHILOSOPHY AND CONTINENTAL PHILOSOPHY **EDUCATION** Univ Paris, Sorbonne, PhD, 70. **CAREER** Prof, Univ Nev, Reno. **RESEARCH** Ontological implications of the political philosophies of Hobbes, Locke, and Rousseau. **SELECTED PUBLICATIONS** Auth, The Anatomy of Idealism, Kluwer/Martinus Nijhoff, 82; The Human Self and the Life and Death Struggle, Univ Fla, 83; Doubt, Time, and Violence, Univ Chicago, 86; Violence in Modern Philosophy, Univ Chicago, 89; The Quest for Power: Hobbes, Descartes and the Emergence of Modernity, Hum Press, 96. **CONTACT ADDRESS** Univ of Nevada, Reno, Reno, NV 89557.

HOFFMAN, RONALD
PERSONAL Born 02/10/1941, Baltimore, MD, m, 1965, 2 children **DISCIPLINE** HISTORY **EDUCATION** George Peabody Coll, BA, 64; Univ Wisconsin, MA, 65; PhD, 69. **CAREER** From asst prof to prof, Univ Md, 69-95; prof, Coll of William and Mary, 93-; dir, Omohundro Inst of Early Am Hist and Culture, 93-; ed, Charles Carroll of Carrollton Papers. **HONORS AND AWARDS** Nat Endowment for Humanities Grant, 78; Nat Hist Publ and Records Comn Grant, 80-; E Harold Hugo Memorial Book Prize; Va Found for the Humanities Grant. **MEMBERSHIPS** Am Hist Asn; Org of Am Hist; Soc for the Hist of the Early Repub. **RESEARCH** Irish History; American History. **SELECTED PUBLICATIONS** Numerous publications on American and Irish history, 69-; auth, A Spirit of Dissension: Economics, Politics, and the Revolution in Maryland, 73; coauth, The Pursuit of Liberty: A History of the American People, 83; auth, Princes of Ireland, Planters of Maryland, A Carroll Saga, 1500-1782, 00. **CONTACT ADDRESS** Omohundro Inst of Early American History and Culture, Box 8781, Williamsburg, VA 23187-8781. **EMAIL** leach2@wm.edu

HOFFMAN, STEVEN J.
PERSONAL Born 10/28/1959, Ft. Belvoir, VA, m, 1 child **DISCIPLINE** HISTORY **EDUCATION** Georgia State Univ, BA, 85; MHP, 87; Carnegie Mellon Univ, PhD, 93. **CAREER** Hist, SE Missouri St Univ; consulting ed, Jour of the Asn for Histand Computing, 98-. **HONORS AND AWARDS** Fel for graduate study, Carnegie Mellon Univ, 87-90; res grant, Carnegie Mellon Univ, hist dept, spring 90; Mellon Res fel, Virigina Hist Soc, summer 93; Historic resources survey grant, Historic Preservation Commission, Cape Girardeau, Missouri, 96, 97, 98, 99. **MEMBERSHIPS** Am Asn for Hsit and Computing, exec board, 99-; Missouri Downtown Asn, board mem, 98-; MO-RARE, secretary, 98-; Nat Asn for African American Heritage Preservation, Missouri chapter, secretary, 97-98; Missouri African American Heritage Preservation Taskforce, vice chair, 96-97; Martin Luther King, Jr. Celebration Planning Comm, cochair, 97-98, 96-97; "Black Women: Achievements Agaisnt the Odds," Univ Mus Exhibit, planning comm, 95-96; mem, planning comm, AFRITECH 95: AN ELECTRONIC CON-

FERENCE. **RESEARCH** American social history; urban history; African American history; suburbanization. **SELECTED PUBLICATIONS** Auth, review, "Richard Harris, Unplanned Suburbs: Toronto's American Tragedy 1900-1950," Journal of Social Hist 31 (98), 711-712; auth, review, "Ronald H. Bayor, Race & the Shaping of Twentieth-Century Atlanta," in Journal of Social Hist 31 (98): 975-977; auth, "Mt. Lebanon," in American Cities and Suburbs: An Encyclopedia, ed. Neil Larry Shumsky (NY, Garland Publishing, 99); auth, Behind the Facade: Race, Class and Power in the City-Building Process, Richmond, Virginia, 1870-1920, forthcoming; auth, "Creating the Electronic Classroom: A Practical Guide," Journal for Social Education (forthcoming); auth, "The Decline of the Port of Richmond: The Richmond Chamber of Commerce and the U.S. Army Corps. Of Engineers," The Virigina Magazine of Hist and Biography (forthcoming); auth, Progressive Public Health Administration in the Jim Crow South: A Case Study of Richmond, Virginia, 1907-1920, forthcoming; coauth, "Reinventing the American History Survey," in History.Edu: Essays in Teaching, Writing, and Researching History, ed. Dennis Trinkle (M.E. Sharpe, forthcoming). **CONTACT ADDRESS** Dept of Hist, Southeast Missouri State Univ, 1 University Plz, Mail Stop 2960, Cape Girardeau, MO 63701. **EMAIL** shoffman@semovm.semo.edu

HOFFMANN, DAVID
PERSONAL Born 05/31/1961, Springfield, OH, m, 2000 **DISCIPLINE** HISTORY **EDUCATION** Columbia Univ, MA, 86; Mphil, 87; PhD, 90; Lawrence Univ, BA, 83. **CAREER** Assoc Prof, Ohio State Univ, 97-; Asst Prof, 94-97; vis Asst Prof, Cornell Univ, 94-96; Co-Editor, The Russian Review, 94-. **HONORS AND AWARDS** Postdoctoral fellowships, Stanford Univ; Harvard Univ; Kennan Institute; National Council for Eurasian; East European Research. **MEMBERSHIPS** Amer Assoc for the Advancement of Slavic Studies. **RESEARCH** Twentieth-century Russian Social; Cultural History. **SELECTED PUBLICATIONS** Auth, "Metropolis: Social Identities in Moscow, 1929-1941, Ithaca: Cornell Univ Press, 94; ed, "Russian Mdernity: Politics, Knowledge, Practices,New York: St. Martin's Press, 00. **CONTACT ADDRESS** Dept History, Ohio State Univ, Columbus, 230 West 17th Ave, Columbus, OH 43210-1361. **EMAIL** hoffmann.218@osu.edu

HOFFMANN, DONALD
PERSONAL Born 06/24/1933, Springfield, IL, m, 1958, 5 children **DISCIPLINE** ART HISTORY **EDUCATION** Univ Chicago **CAREER** Reporter to art and archit critic, The Kansas City Star, 56-90; police reporter, The Illinois State Register, 54-56; office, City News Bureau of Chicago, 54. **HONORS AND AWARDS** NEA fel, 74; NEH grant, 70; asst ed, J of the Soc of Archit Historians, 70-71. **MEMBERSHIPS** Soc Archit Historians; Art Inst of Chicago (Life). **RESEARCH** Architecture; photography. **SELECTED PUBLICATIONS** Auth, Frank Lloyd Wright's Dana House, 96; Understanding Frank Lloyd Wright's Archit, 95; Frank Lloyd Wright's Fallingwater, 2nd rev ed, 94; Frank Lloyd Wright's Hollyhock House, 93. **CONTACT ADDRESS** 6441 Holmes St., Kansas City, MO 64131.

HOFSOMMER, DON L.
PERSONAL Born 04/10/1938, Fort Dodge, IO, m, 1965, 3 children **DISCIPLINE** HISTORY **EDUCATION** Univ N Iowa, BA, 60; MA, 66; Okla State Univ, PhD, 73. **CAREER** Instr, Univ of N Ioewa, 65-66; instr, Lea Col, 66-70; assoc prof, Wayland Col, 73-81; Vis prof, Univ of Mont, 86-87; exec dir, Augustana Col, 87-89; prof, St Could State Univ, 89-. **HONORS AND AWARDS** Excellence In Teaching Awd, SCSU, 92; Sr Achievement Awd in Railroad Hist, 95. **MEMBERSHIPS** Lexington Group, W Hist Assoc, Org of Am Hist, State Hist Soc of Iowa. **RESEARCH** Railroad history of the United States and Canada. **SELECTED PUBLICATIONS** Auth, Prairie Oasis, 75; auth, Katy Northwest, 76; auth, Southern Pacific, 1901, 85; coauth, The Great Northern Railroad, 88; auth, The Quanah Route, 91; coauth, St. Louis Union Station, 94; auth, Grand Trunk Corporation, 95. **CONTACT ADDRESS** Dept Hist, St. Cloud State Univ, 720 - 4th Ave S, Saint Could, MN 56301-4442.

HOFSTRA, WARREN R.
PERSONAL Born 05/12/1947, New York, NY, m, 1979, 2 children **DISCIPLINE** EARLY AMERICAN HISTORY, SOCIAL, MATERIAL CULTURE **EDUCATION** Washington Univ, BA, 69; Boston Univ, MA, 74; Univ Virginia, PhD, 85. **CAREER** Proj dir, 86-; instr, 76-85; asst prof, 85-90; assoc prof, 90-95; Shenandoah Univ, prof, 95-. **HONORS AND AWARDS** DuPont Fel; Vir Found Hum, res Fel; Ben Belchic Awd; MESDA Res Fel; Mednick Fel; James R and Mary B Wilkins Awd; NEH, 92, 94; Mellon Fel. **MEMBERSHIPS** OAH; AHA; SHA; SHS; VHS; ASEH; VAF. **RESEARCH** Early American social and cultural history; material culture; landscape. **SELECTED PUBLICATIONS** Auth, "Ethnicity and Community Formation on the Shenandoah Valley Frontier, 1730-1800." in Diversity and Accommodation: Essays on the Cultural Composition of the Virginia Frontier, ed. Michael J Puglisi (Knoxville: Univ Tenn Press, 97); ed, George Washington and the Virginia Backcountry, Madison House (Madison, Wis, 98); auth, "'The Extension of His Majesties Dominions': The Virginia Backcountry and the Reconfiguration of Imperial Frontiers." J Am Hist 84 (98): 1281-1312; auth, Epilogue: Interdisciplinary Dialogues on the Southern Colonial Backcountry, 1893-97." In The Southern Colonial Backcountry: Interdisciplinary Perspectives on Frontier Communities, ed. David C Crass, Richard D Brooks, Steven Smith, Martha Zierden (Knoxville: Univ Tenn Press, 98); auth, A Separate Place: The Formation of Clarke County, Virginia, White Post Virginia, 1986, Madison House (Madison Wis), 99; coauth, "Native American Settlement within the Middle and Upper Drainage of Opequon Creek, Frederick County, Virginia," Quart Bul Archeo Soc Vir 54 (99): 154-65; coauth, "'A Murder. . of Horrible and Savage Barbarity': The Death of Robert Berkeley and the Burden of Race in the Southern Past,." J South Hist 65 (99): 41-76; auth, "Reconstructing the Colonial Environment of the Upper Chesapeake Watershed," in Discovering the Chesapeake: The History of a Watershed Ecosystem, ed. Philip D Curtin (Baltimore: Johns Hopkins Univ Press, forthcoming); co-ed, After the Backcountry: Rural Life in the Great Valley of Virginia, 1800-1900, Univ Tenn Press (Knoxville), forthcoming; auth, "From Farm to Mill to Market: The Historical Archaeology of an Emerging Grain Economy in the Shenandoah Valley of Virginia," in After the Backcountry: Rural Life in the Great Valley of Virginia, 1800-1900, ed. Kenneth E Koons, Warren R Hofstra (Knoxville: Univ Tenn Press, forthcoming). **CONTACT ADDRESS** Dept Social, Behavioral Science, Shenandoah Univ, 1460 University Dr, Winchester, VA 22601. **EMAIL** whofstra@su.edu

HOGAN, HEATHER
PERSONAL Born 09/20/1949, Mineola, NY, m, 1975, 1 child **DISCIPLINE** RUSSIAN HISTORY **EDUCATION** BA, Northwestern Univ, 71; Univ of MI, MA, 76, PhD, 81. **CAREER** Prof, 86-present, Oberlin Col. **HONORS AND AWARDS** NDFL,IREX,NEH, Culpepper. **MEMBERSHIPS** AHA, AWSS **RESEARCH** Imperial, Soviet, post-Soviet hist. **SELECTED PUBLICATIONS** Forging Revolution: Metalworkers, Managers and the State in St. Petersburg, 1890-1914, IN Univ Press, 93. **CONTACT ADDRESS** Dept of Hist, Oberlin Col, Rice Hall 307, Oberlin, OH 44074. **EMAIL** heather.hogan@oberlin.edu

HOGAN, LAWRENCE DANIEL
PERSONAL Born 06/01/1944, Stamford, CT, m, 1968, 3 children **DISCIPLINE** HISTORY **EDUCATION** Fairfield Univ, BA; Univ Conn, MA; Indiana Univ, PhD. **CAREER** Consul/curator, 98, Middlesex County Hist Museum. **HONORS AND AWARDS** New Jersey Historical Comm, Awd of Recog, outstanding svc. **MEMBERSHIPS** Garden St Immigration History Consortium. **RESEARCH** History of Black Baseball in New Jersey. **SELECTED PUBLICATIONS** Auth, A Black National News Service: The Associated Negro Press and Claude Barnett, 1919-1945; auth, Afro-American History as Immigration History: the Anguillians of Perth Amboy, Give Me Your Tired, Your Poor..? Voluntary Black Migration to The United States, 86. **CONTACT ADDRESS** Union County Col, Cranford, NJ 07016. **EMAIL** hogan@hawk.ucc.edu

HOGAN, MICHAEL J.
DISCIPLINE HISTORY **EDUCATION** Univ of N Iowa, BA, 65; Univ of Iowa, MA, 67; PhD, 74. **CAREER** Asst prof to assoc prof, Miami Univ, 77-86; prof, Ohio State Univ, 86-; chair, 93-00; dean, 00-. **HONORS AND AWARDS** Woodrow Wilson Fel, Woodrow Wilson Int Center for Scholars, 81; Res Fel, Am Philos Soc, 84; Seed Grant, Ohio State Univ, 88; Ohio Acad of Hist Book Awd, 88; Quincy Wright Book Prize, Int Studies Assoc, 88; George Louis Beer Book Prize, AHA, 88; Louis Martin Sears Distinguished Prof, Purdue Univ, 89; Univ Distinguished Scholar Awd, Ohio State Univ, 90; Distinguished Alumni Awd, Univ of N Iowa, 91. **MEMBERSHIPS** AHA; Org of Am Hist; Soc for Hist of Am For Rel. **RESEARCH** History of American foreign relations, national security studies, Cold War studies. **SELECTED PUBLICATIONS** Auth, Informal Entente: The Private Structure of Cooperation in Anglo-American Economic Diplomacy, 1918-1928, Univ of Miss Pr (Columbia), 77; auth, The Marshall Plan: America, Britain, and the Reconstruction of Western Europe, 1947-1952, Cambridge Univ Pr, (NY), 87; coed, Explaining the History of American Foreign Relations, Cambridge Univ Pr (NY), 91; ed, The End of the Cold War: Its Meaning and Implications, Cambride Univ Pr (NY), 92; ed, America in the World: The Historiography of American Foreign Relations since 1941, Cambridge Univ Pr (NY), 95; ed, Hiroshima in History and Memory, Cambridge Univ Pr (NY), 96; auth, A Cross of Iron: Harry S. Truman and the Origins of the National Security State, 1945-1954, Cambridge Univ Pr (NY), 98; ed, The Ambiguous Legacy, U.S. Foreign Relations in the "American Century", Cambridge Univ Pr (NY), 99; ed, Paths to Power: The Historiography of American Foreign Relations to 1941, Cambridge Univ Pr (NY), 00. **CONTACT ADDRESS** Dept Hist, Ohio State Univ, Columbus, 230 W 17th Ave, Columbus, OH 43210-1361.

HOGAN, PATRICIA
DISCIPLINE HISTORY **EDUCATION** St Francis Xavier Univ, BA, 64; Univ Toronto, Pontif Inst Medieval Studs, LMS, 67, PhD, 71. **CAREER** Asst prof, 70-75, assoc prof, 75-94, Prof, St Francis Xavier Univ, 95-. **HONORS AND AWARDS** Pontif Inst Medieval Studs Fel, 65-67; Ont Grad Fel, 67-69; Can Coun Doctoral Fel, 69-70. **SELECTED PUBLICATIONS** Auth, Medieval Villainy: A Study in the Meaning of Crime and Social Control in a Medieval Village, in Studs in Medieval and Renaissance Hist, 87; auth, Clays, Culturae and The Cultivator's Wisdom-Management Efficiency at Fourteenth-Century Wistow, in Brit Agricultural Hist Rev, 88; auth, The Slight to Honor-Slander and Wrongful Prosecution in Five English Medieval Villages, in Studs in Medieval and Renaissance History, 91. **CONTACT ADDRESS** Dept of History, St. Francis Xavier Univ, Antigonish, NS, Canada B2G 2W5. **EMAIL** phogan@stfx.ca

HOGLUND, A. WILLIAM
PERSONAL Born 09/04/1926, Baltimore, MD **DISCIPLINE** AMERICAN HISTORY **EDUCATION** Cornell Univ, BA, 49; Univ Wis, MA, 50, PhD, 57. **CAREER** Asst prof Am hist, Muskingum Col, 57-61; from asst prof to assoc prof, 61-68, Prof Am Hist to Prof Emer, Univ Conn, 68-, Trustee, The Balch Inst Ethnic Studies, 75- **MEMBERSHIPS** AHA; Orgn Am Historians; Am Studies Asn; Agr Hist Soc; Immigration Hist Soc. **RESEARCH** General study of immigration, George F. Warren, intellectual response to the exodus from the farms of New York, reform and radicalism. **SELECTED PUBLICATIONS** Auth, Finnish Immigrants in America, 1880-1920, Univ of Wis Press, 60; auth, Immigrants and their Children in the United States: A Bibliography of Doctoral Dissertations, 1885-1982, Garland Publ, 86; auth, "Training for the Class Struggle: Finnish Immigrants and Workers' Education, 1899 to World War II," in Nordics in America: The Future of Their Past, ed. Odd S. Lovoll (Norwegian-Am Hist Asn, 93), 47-60. **CONTACT ADDRESS** Dept of Hist, Univ of Connecticut, Storrs, Storrs, CT 06268. **EMAIL** hoglund@uconnvm.uconn.edu

HOHENDAHL, PETER U.
PERSONAL Born 03/17/1936, Hamburg, Germany, m, 2 children **DISCIPLINE** GERMAN STUDIES **EDUCATION** Univ Hamburg, PhD, 64. **CAREER** Asst prof Ger, PA State Univ, 65-68; assoc prof, WA Univ, 68-69, prof, 70-77, chmn dept, 72-77; Prof Ger & Comp Lit, Cornell Univ, 77-, Chmn Dept, 81-86; Jacob Gould Shurman Prof Ger & Comp Lit, 85-; Merton vis prof, Free Univ Berlin, 76; Distinguished vis prof, OH state Univ, 87. **HONORS AND AWARDS** Choice Outstanding Acad Bk Awd, 96. **MEMBERSHIPS** MLA; Am Asn Tchr(s) Ger; Ger studies Asn; Heinnoh Heine soc; AHA. **RESEARCH** Theory of lit; 18th and 19th century Europ lit; mod Ger lit. **SELECTED PUBLICATIONS** Auth, Literaturkritik und Offentlichkeit, Piper, 74; auth, Der europaische Roman der Empfindsamikeit, Athenaion, 77; The Institution of Criticism, Cornell Univ Press, 82; Building a National Literature, The Case of Germany, 1830-1870, 89; Reappraisals: Shifting Alignments in Postwar Critical Theory, 91; Geschichte Opposition Subersion: Studien zur Literatur des 19 Jahrhunderts, 93; Prismatic Thought: Theodore W. Adorno, 95. **CONTACT ADDRESS** Dept of Ger Studies, Cornell Univ, 193 Goldwin Smith Hall, Ithaca, NY 14853-3201. **EMAIL** puh1@cornell.edu

HOHLFELDER, ROBERT L.
PERSONAL Born 09/21/1938, Brooklyn, NY **DISCIPLINE** HISTORY **EDUCATION** Bowdoin Col, BA, 60; Univ Ind, MA, 62; PhD, 66. **CAREER** From asst prof to prof, 69-, dept ch, 89-91, Univ Colo. **SELECTED PUBLICATIONS** Auth, Ancient Paphos Beneath the Sea: A Survey of the Submerged Structures, Univ Cyprus, 95; ICOMOS Goes to Sea, 95; Evidence for a Lighthouse at Nea Paphos?, Univ Cyprus, 95. **CONTACT ADDRESS** History Dept, Univ of Colorado, Boulder, Boulder, CO 80309. **EMAIL** Hohlfeld@spot.Colorado.edu

HOIDAL, ODDVAR KARSTEN
PERSONAL Born 07/26/1938, Alesund, Norway, m, 1966, 1 child **DISCIPLINE** HISTORY **EDUCATION** San Diego State Col, BA, 61; Univ Southern CA, PhD, 70. **CAREER** Asst prof, 67-71, assoc prof, 71-80, Prof Hist, San Diego State Univ, 80-; Res scholar hist, Fulbright-Hayes, 71-72. **HONORS AND AWARDS** Phi Beta Kppa, 99. **MEMBERSHIPS** Soc Advan Scandinavian Studies; Norwegian Hist Asn; Am Hist Asn; Soc of Hist of Scandinavia, bd member. **RESEARCH** Modern Norwegian history; Scandinavian history; modern European history. **SELECTED PUBLICATIONS** Auth, Vidkun Quisling's Decline as a Political Figure in Prewar Norway, J Mod Hist, 9/71; Quisling's Position at the Norwegian Legation in Moscow, June 1927-December 1929, Historisk Tidsskrift, 74; Hjort, Quisling, and Nasjonal Samling's Disintegration, fall 75 & Okonomisk Verneplikt and Nordiske Folkereisning: Two Predecessors of Nasjonal Samling, fall 77, Scand Studies; The unwelcomed exile: Leon Trotsky's failure to receive asylum in Norway, 1929, Scand Studies, winter 80; Norsemen and the North American forests, J Forest Hist, 10/80; Quisling and the Agrarian Party in the spring of 1933, Historisk Tidsskrift, 78; Quisling: A Study in Treason, Oslo: The Norwegian Univ Press, 89; Betrayal and Rescue: The Fate of the Jews in Scandinavia during World War II, in Michalczyk, John J., ed, Resistors, Rescuers and Refugees: Historical and Ethical Issues, Kansas City: Sheed & Ward, 97. **CONTACT ADDRESS** Dept of Hist, San Diego State Univ, 5500 Campanile Dr, San Diego, CA 92182-8147. **EMAIL** hoidal@mail.sdsu.edu

HOLBERT, RAYMOND
PERSONAL Born 02/24/1945, Berkeley, CA, m, 1984, 3 children **DISCIPLINE** ART HISTORY **EDUCATION** Univ Calif, BA, 70, MA, 72, MFA, 74. **CAREER** Instr, chemn, City Col San Francisco. **MEMBERSHIPS** Col Art Asn; Org African Art Stud. **RESEARCH** International imagery in art history. **CONTACT ADDRESS** 50 Phelan St, San Francisco, CA 94112. **EMAIL** rholbert@ccsf.cc.ca.us

HOLBO, PAUL S.
PERSONAL Born 07/10/1929, Wildrose, ND, m, 1962, 2 children **DISCIPLINE** AMERICAN HISTORY **EDUCATION** Yale Univ, BA, 51; Univ Chicago, MA, 55, PhD, 61. **CAREER** From instr to prof Am & Latin Am hist, 59-75, actg dean, Col Lib Arts, 73-74, assoc dean, 70-73, Prof Hist, Univ Ore, 75-, Lectr, Univ Chicago, 56-58; examr, Col Entrance Exam Bd, 65-71, chmn test develop Am hist, 81-; chief reader, adv placement, Am Hist Educ Testing Serv, Princeton, NJ, 68-71; found & interim ed, J Diplomatic Hist, 76. **HONORS AND AWARDS** Binkley-Stephenson Awd, Orgn Am Historians, 69. **MEMBERSHIPS** AHA; Orgn Am Historians; Soc Historians Am Foreign Rels. **RESEARCH** American diplomatic and political history; historiography of American foreign relations; United States foreign relations in the Gilded Age. **SELECTED PUBLICATIONS CONTACT ADDRESS** Dept of Hist, Univ of Oregon, Eugene, OR 97403.

HOLCOMBE, LEE
PERSONAL Born Spartanburg, SC **DISCIPLINE** HISTORY **EDUCATION** Mt Holyoke Col, BA, 49; Columbia Univ, MA, 50, PhD(hist), 62. **CAREER** Instr hist & govt, Queens Col, NC, 50-51, Westlake Sch, Calif, 51-52 & Quinnipiac Col, Conn, 61-62; lectr hist, Univ Conn, Groton, 67-73; asst prof hist, Univ Conn, Storrs, 73-74; Assoc Prof Hist, Univ SC, Spartanburg, 75-. **MEMBERSHIPS** AHA; Conf Brit Studies; Southern Asn Women Historians. **RESEARCH** Nineteenth century British history; women's history. **SELECTED PUBLICATIONS** Auth, Lady Inspectors, the Campaign for a Better Workplace, 1893-1921, Albion, Vol 0024, 92. **CONTACT ADDRESS** Dept of Hist, Univ of So Carolina, Spartanburg, Spartanburg, SC 29303.

HOLIFIELD, E. BROOKS
PERSONAL Born 01/05/1942, Little Rock, AR, m, 1963, 2 children **DISCIPLINE** HISTORY, RELIGION **EDUCATION** Hendrix Col, BA, 63; Yale Divinity Sch, BD, 66; Yale Grad Sch, MA, 68, PhD, 70. **CAREER** Asst prof, Candler Sch of Theol and Grad Div of Relig, Emory Univ, 70-75, assoc prof, 75-80, prof, 80-84, chair, Dept Hist Studies, Grad Div, 77-79, Dir, Grad Div of Relig, 79-83, Charles Howard Candler Prof of Am Church Hist and Assoc Member of the Dept of Hist, 84-. **HONORS AND AWARDS** Woodrow Wilson Fel, 63; Danforth Fel, 63-70; Yale Steering Fel, 69; NEH Res Fel, 76-77, 83-84, 91-92; Pew fel, 98-99; Louisville Inst Fel, 98-99. **MEMBERSHIPS** Am Acad of Relig, Am Soc of Church Hist, Am Hist Asn. **RESEARCH** American religious history. **SELECTED PUBLICATIONS** Auth, The Covenant Sealed: The Development of Puritan Sacramental Theology in Old and New England, 1570-1720, New Haven: Yale Univ Press (74); auth, The Gentlemen Theologians: American Theology and Southern Culture, 1795-1860, Durham: Duke Univ Press (78); auth, A History of Pastoral Care in America: From Salvation to Self-Realization, 1570-1970, Nashville: Abingdon Press (83); auth, Health and Medicine in the Methodist Tradition, NY: Crossroad Press (86); auth, Era of Persuasion: American Thought and Culture 1521-1680, Boston: Twayne Pubs (89). **CONTACT ADDRESS** Sch of Theol, Emory Univ, 1364 Clifton Rd NE, Atlanta, GA 30322-1061. **EMAIL** eholifi@emory.edu

HOLLAND, ANTONIO F.
PERSONAL Born 12/05/1943, Petersburg, VA, m, 1975, 2 children **DISCIPLINE** HISTORY **EDUCATION** Northeastern Univ, BA, 67, MA, 69; Univ Mo, Columbia, PhD, 84. **CAREER** Military svc, 68-70; from inst to prof hist & soc scis, Lincoln Univ, 70-; lt col, Mo Army Nat Guard, 78-; head dept, soc & beh scis, Lincoln Univ, 86-. **HONORS AND AWARDS** Lawrence Prize, Boston Public Schs, Lewis Athenton fel, Hist dept, Univ Mos, 83,84; Martin Luther King Jr Awd, Ctr Mo, 99; Nat Teach fel; Phelps-Stokes Fund Fel to West Africa; NEH rev. **MEMBERSHIPS** Asn Stud Afro-Am Life, Hist; So Hist Asn; Mo Hist Soc; Mo Folklore Soc; Mo Nat Guard Asn. **RESEARCH** African-Am hist; Mo hist. **SELECTED PUBLICATIONS** Co-auth, Missouri's Black Heritage, Univ Mo Press, 93; auth, Education over Politics: Nathan B Young at Florida A & M College, 1901-1923, Ag Hist, 65:2. **CONTACT ADDRESS** 306 W El Cortez Dr, Columbia, MO 65203.

HOLLAND, JAMES C.
PERSONAL Born 11/03/1935, Baltimore, MD, m, 1968 **DISCIPLINE** HISTORY **EDUCATION** Univ of Maryland, BA, 59, MA, 65; Catholic Univ of America, PhD, 68. **CAREER** From asst prof to assoc prof, Albertus Magnus Col, New Haven, CT; from assoc prof to prof, Shepherd Col, Shepherdstown, WV. **MEMBERSHIPS** Am Cath. Hist Asn **RESEARCH** Victorian England; History of Ideas; Old South and the American Civil War. **SELECTED PUBLICATIONS** Auth, A Capital in Search of a Nation, 86; The Legacy of an Education, 97; coauth, Lord Acton: The Decisive Decade, 1864-1874, 70; The Correspondence of Lord Acton and Richard Simpson, 3 vols, 71-75; The Correspondence of Lord Acton and Mr. Gladstone, forthcoming. **CONTACT ADDRESS** Dept of History, Shepherd Col, Shepherdstown, WV 25443.

HOLLI, MELVIN G.
PERSONAL Born 02/22/1933, Ishpeming, MI, m, 1961, 2 children **DISCIPLINE** HISTORY **EDUCATION** Suomi Col, Certificate of Arts, 54; North Mich Univ, BA, 57; Univ Mich, MA, 58; PhD, 66. **CAREER** Prof, Univ Ill, 65-. **HONORS AND AWARDS** NEH Sen Fel, 70; Fulbright Prof, Finland, 78, 89; Nat Woodrow Wilson Fel, 57-58; Book Awd, Soc of Midland, 81, Book Prize, 84. **MEMBERSHIPS** Org of Am Hist, URBAN Hist Asn, Swedish Am Hist Soc. **RESEARCH** Political, Ethnic, Urban History. **SELECTED PUBLICATIONS** auth, The American Mayor: The Best and Worst Big City Leaders, 99; auth, A View from Chicago's City Hall: Mid-Century to Millennium, 99; auth, Ethnic Chicago: A Multi-cultural Portrait, 95; auth, Restoration: Chicago Elects another Daley, 95. **CONTACT ADDRESS** Dept Hist, Univ of Illinois, Chicago, 601 S Morgan St, Chicago, IL 60607-7042. **EMAIL** mholli@uic.edu

HOLLIDAY, VIVIAN LOYREA
PERSONAL Born 02/25/1935, Manning, SC **DISCIPLINE** CLASSICS, ANCIENT HISTORY **EDUCATION** Winthrop Col, AB, 57; Univ Mo, MA, 59; Univ NC, PhD(classics), 61. **CAREER** Instr classics, 61-63, from asst prof to assoc prof, 63-69, Aylesworth Prof Classics, Col Wooster, 69-, Dean Fac, 77-85, mem managing comt, Am Sch Class Studies, Athens, 67. **MEMBERSHIPS** Am Philol Asn; Am Inst Archaeol. **RESEARCH** Republican Rome; comparative literature; modern Greek literature. **SELECTED PUBLICATIONS** Auth, Pompey in Cicero's Letters and Lucan's Civil War, Mouton, The Hauge, 69; Kazantzakis, Odyssey, Neo-Hellenika, Vol III, 78; Job Satisfaction for the Faculty, Academic Job Satisfaction: Varieties and Values, 80; Classical and Modern Narratives of Leadership, (pub 1999). **CONTACT ADDRESS** Dept of Classics, The Col of Wooster, 1189 Beall Ave, Wooster, OH 44691-2363. **EMAIL** IN%vholliday@acs.wooster.edu

HOLLINGER, DAVID A.
PERSONAL Born 04/25/1941, Chicago, IL, m, 1967, 2 children **DISCIPLINE** HISTORY **EDUCATION** La Verne Col, BA, 63; Univ Calif-Berkeley, MA, 65; PhD, 70. **CAREER** Lectr to assoc prof, SUNY Buffalo, 69-77; prof, Univ Mich, 77-92; prof, Univ Cal Berkeley, 92-. **HONORS AND AWARDS** Guggenheim Fel, 83; CASBS Fel, 84-85; Merle Curtis Fel, Univ Wis, 99; Harmsworth Prof, Univ Oxford, 01-02. **MEMBERSHIPS** AHA; OAH; HSS. **RESEARCH** US intellectual history; 20th century. **SELECTED PUBLICATIONS** Auth, Morris R Cohen and the Scientific Ideal (75); auth, In the American Province (85); auth, Postethnic America (95); auth, Science, Jews and Secular Culture (96). **CONTACT ADDRESS** Dept History, Univ of California, Berkeley, 3229 Dwinelle Hall, Berkeley, CA 94720-2550.

HOLLINGSWORTH, JOSEPH ROGERS
PERSONAL Born 07/26/1932, Anniston, AL, m, 1957 **DISCIPLINE** HISTORY **EDUCATION** Emory Univ, BA, 54; Univ Chicago, PhD, 60. **CAREER** Instr soc sci, Univ Chicago, 57-59; asst prof hist, Univ Ill, Urbana, 60-64; assoc prof, 64-69, partic mem, Law Sch, 66-70, Prof Hist, Univ Wis-Madison, 69-, Chairperson Prog Comp World Hist, 77-, **HONORS AND AWARDS** Honorary Doctorate, Univ of Uppsala (Sweden); Andrew Mellon fel, 62-63; Am Coun Learned Soc fel, 66-67; Nat Endowment for Humanities grant, 67-68; Rockefeller Fund vis prof hist, Univ Ibadan, 69-71; fel, Prog Law Sci & Med, Yale Univ & German Marshall Found, 75-76; Inst Res Poverty, Univ Wis, 75-; fel, Woodrow Wilson Int Ctr Scholars, 77; Commonwealth Fund fel, 77; fel, Am Scand Found, 81. **MEMBERSHIPS** AHA; Orgn Am Historians; Am Sociol Asn; Am Polit Sci Asn. **RESEARCH** Comparative historical politics; American social history; comparative public policy. **SELECTED PUBLICATIONS** Auth, Cages of Reason--The Rise of the Rational State in France, Japan, The United-States, and Great-Britain, J Am Hist, Vol 0082, 95. **CONTACT ADDRESS** Dept of Hist, Univ of Wisconsin, Madison, Madison, WI 53706. **EMAIL** hollingsjr@aol.com

HOLLIS, DANIEL W.
PERSONAL Born 11/02/1942, Talladega, AL, m, 1966, 2 children **DISCIPLINE** HISTORY **EDUCATION** Univ Ga, BA, 64; Auburn Univ, MA, 68; Vanderbilt Univ, PhD, 72. **CAREER** Asst prof, prof, Jacksonville State Univ, 71-. **HONORS AND AWARDS** Fac Schl Lectr, JSU, 96-97. **MEMBERSHIPS** NACBS; SCBS; Phi Alpha Theta. **RESEARCH** England; Ireland; Intellectual. **SELECTED PUBLICATIONS** Auth, An Alabama Newspaper Tradition (Univ AL Press, 83); auth, The Media in America (ABC-Clio Press, 95); auth, World History Companion to Utopian Movements (ABC-Clio Press, 98); auth, History of Ireland, Greenwood Press, forthcoming. **CONTACT ADDRESS** Dept History, Jacksonville State Univ, 700 Pelham Rd, Jacksonville, AL 36265-1602. **EMAIL** dhollis@jscc.jsu.edu

HOLLOWAY, R. R.
PERSONAL Born 08/15/1934, Newton, MA, m, 1960, 2 children **DISCIPLINE** ARCHAEOLOGY **EDUCATION** The Roxbury Latin Sch, 52; Amherst Col, AB, 56; Univ Pa, MA, 57; Princeton Univ, MA and PhD, 60. **CAREER** Vis asst prof, Princeton Univ, 62-63; asst prof, Univ NC, Chapel Hill, 63-64; asst prof, Brown Univ, 64, assoc prof, 67, prof, 69, Elisha Benjamin Andrews Prof, 90-. **HONORS AND AWARDS** Phi Beta Kappa, 55; Amherst Col, AB, summa cum laude, 56; Archaeol Inst of Am Gold Medal, 95; L.H.D., Amherst Col, 76; Doctor Philos et Literarum Honoric Causa, Cath Univ of Louvain, 97. **MEMBERSHIPS** German Archeol Inst, Royal Numismatic Soc of Belgium, Royal Numismatic Soc (London), Inst of Prehistory and Protohistory (Italy), Nat Inst of Etruscan and Italic Studies (Italy). **RESEARCH** Research Ancient Numismatics, Ancient art, Italian prehistory. **SELECTED PUBLICATIONS** Auth, The Archaeology of Ancient Sicily, Routledge, London (91); auth, The Archaeology of Early Rome and Latium, Routledge, London (94); auth, Ustica I, The Results of the Excavations of the Regione Siciliana, Soprintendenza ai Beni Culturali ed Ambientali Provincia di Palermo in collaboration with Brown Univ in 1990 and 1991, with Susan S. Lukesh and other contributors, Archaeologia Transatlantica XIV, Providence and Louvain (95); auth, catalogue of the Classical Colelection, Museum of Art, Rhode Islamd,School of Design, Ancient Greek Coins, Archaeologia Transatlantica XV, Providence aand Louvain-la-Neuve (98); auth, "Hand of Daedalus", lectures delivered at Washington Univ, (http://www.brown.edu/Departments/Old_World_Archaeology_and_Art/Publications/). **CONTACT ADDRESS** Center for Old World Archaeol and Art, Brown Univ, PO Box 1837, Providence, RI 02912. **EMAIL** r_holloway@brown.edu

HOLLOWAY, THOMAS HALSEY
PERSONAL Born 06/24/1944, Enterprise, OR, m, 1963, 2 children **DISCIPLINE** LATIN AMERICAN HISTORY **EDUCATION** Univ Calif, Santa Barbara, BA, 68; Univ Wis-Madison, MA, 69, PhD(Latin Am hist), 74. **CAREER** Asst prof, 74-80, assoc prof, 80-91, prof, Cornell Univ, 91-, Dir, Latin Am Studies Prog, Cornell Univ, 82-87 **MEMBERSHIPS** Conf Latin Am Hist; Latin Am Studies Asn. **RESEARCH** History of Brazil. **SELECTED PUBLICATIONS** Auth, The Brazilian Coffee Valorization of 1906, State Hist Soc Wis, 75; Immigrants on the Land: Coffee and Society in Sao Paulo, 1886-1934, Univ NC Press, 80; auth, Policing Rio De Janerio: Repression and Resistance in a 19th Century City, Stanford Univ, 93. **CONTACT ADDRESS** Dept of Hist, Cornell Univ, Mcgraw Hall, Ithaca, NY 14853-0001.

HOLLY, MICHAEL ANN
PERSONAL 2 children **DISCIPLINE** ART HISTORY, VISUAL AND CULTURAL STUDIES **EDUCATION** Cornell Univ, PhD, 81. **CAREER** Ch & prof, Univ of Rochester; Dir of Research, Clark Art Institute, 00-. **HONORS AND AWARDS** Getty Summer Inst on Visual and Cult Stud, 98; Ailsa Bruce Mellon sr fel, Ctr for Advanced Study in the Visual Arts, Nat Gallery of Art, DC, 96-97; Guggenheim fel, 91-92; ACLS grant, 89 & NEH Summer Inst grants (dir), 87, 89. **RESEARCH** Art historiography and criticism; intellectual hist of the hist of art; ancient, medieval and renaissance art. **SELECTED PUBLICATIONS** Auth, Past Looking: Historical Imagination and the Rhetoric of the Image, Ithaca, Cornell UP, 96; Iconography and Iconology, Milan: Jaca Publ, 92 & Panofsky and the Foundations of Art History, Ithaca, Cornell UP, 84; ed, The Subjects of Art History: Historical Objects in Contemporary Perspectives, NY: Cambridge UP, 98; Visual Culture: Images and Interpretation, Hanover, UP New Eng for Wesleyan UP, 94 & Visual Theory: Painting and Interpretation, NY, Harper & Row, 90. **CONTACT ADDRESS** Sterling and Francine Clark Art Inst, Williamstown, MA 01267. **EMAIL** mholly@clark.williams.edu

HOLMES, BLAIR R.
PERSONAL Born 06/29/1942, Driggs, ID, m, 1965, 6 children **DISCIPLINE** HISTORY **EDUCATION** Brigham Young Univ, BA, 66; Univ of Colo, MA, 68, PhD, 72. **CAREER** Asst prof to assoc prof, Brigham Young Univ, 71-99. **RESEARCH** Social history; Austrian empire. **SELECTED PUBLICATIONS** Auth, When Truth Was Treason: German Youth Against Hitler, Univ of Ill Press, 95. **CONTACT ADDRESS** Brigham Young Univ, 406 KMB, Provo, UT 84602. **EMAIL** Blair_Holmes@byu.edu

HOLMES, LARRY E.
DISCIPLINE HISTORY **EDUCATION** McPherson Col, BA; Eastern NMex Univ, MA; Univ Kans, PhD. **CAREER** Prof, Univ South Al. **SELECTED PUBLICATIONS** Auth, The Kremlin and the Schoolhouse: Reforming Education in Soviet Russia, 1917-1931, Ind UP, 91; auth, Sotsial'naia istoriia Rossii: 1917-1941 (Russian Social History, 1917-1941), Rostov State Univ Press, 94; auth, Stalin's School: Moscow's Model School No. 25, 1931-1937, Univ of Pitts, 99. **CONTACT ADDRESS** Dept of History, Univ of So Alabama, 344 Humanities, Mobile, AL 36688-0002. **EMAIL** lholmes@jaguar1.usouthal.edu

HOLMES, STEVEN J.
PERSONAL Born 10/21/1960, San Francisco, CA, s **DISCIPLINE** HISTORY **EDUCATION** Harvard Univ, PhD, 96; Harvard Div Sch, MTS, 87; Univ of Notre Dame, MA, 83 **CAREER** Lect, 96-00, Harvard Univ **RESEARCH** Environmental Biography and Autobiography; History of American Attitudes toward Nature. **SELECTED PUBLICATIONS** Auth, The Young John Muir: An Environmental Biography, University of Wisconsin Press, 99 **CONTACT ADDRESS** 170 Walter St #1, Roslindale, MA 02131. **EMAIL** 76463.1165@compuserve.com

HOLMES, WILLIAM F.
PERSONAL Born 10/31/1937, Greenwood, MS, m, 1965, 2 children **DISCIPLINE** HISTORY **EDUCATION** Univ Notre Dame, BA, 59; Univ Del, MA, 61; Rice Univ, PhD(hist), 64. **CAREER** Asst prof hist, Univ Tex, Arlington, 64-67; assoc prof, 68-79, Prof Hist to Prof Emer, Univ Ga, 79-. **HONORS AND AWARDS** Nat Endowment for Humanities fel, 67-68 & 77-79; Am Philos Soc fel, 68. **MEMBERSHIPS** Orgn Am Historians; Southern Hist Asn (secy-treas, 86-) **RESEARCH** History of the American South. **SELECTED PUBLICATIONS** Auth, The White Chief: James Kimble Vardaman, La State Univ, 70; Whitecapping: Agrarian violence in Mississippi, Mid-Am, 4/73; The demise of the Colored Farmers' Alliance, J Southern Hist, 75; A History of Georgia, Univ Ga, 77; Moonshining and Collective Violence: Georgia, 1889-1895, J Am Hist, 80; Labor Agents and the Georgia Exodus, 1899-1900, S Atlantic Quart, 80; Populism: In Search of Context, Agr Hist, Fall 90; Charivari: Race, Honor, and Post Office Politics, Sharon, Georgia, 1890, Ga Hist Quart, Winter 96. **CONTACT ADDRESS** Dept of Hist, Univ of Georgia, 202 LeConte Hall, Athens, GA 30602-1602. **EMAIL** wfholmes@arches.uga.edu

HOLOKA, JAMES P.
PERSONAL Born 01/19/1947, Rochester, NY, m, 1968, 3 children **DISCIPLINE** CLASSICS AND ANCIENT HISTORY **EDUCATION** Univ Rochester, BA, 69; SUNY-Binghamton, MA, 72; Univ Mich, PhD, 74. **CAREER** Teaching asst/fel, 69-72; lectr, Eastern Mich Univ, 74-76; from asst prof to prof, Eastern Mich Univ, 76-. **HONORS AND AWARDS** Rackham Prize Fel, Univ Mich, 73-74; NEH Summer Stipend, 76; Distinguish Fac Award for Excellence in Teaching and Commitment to Students, 80; Scholarly Recognition Award, 91. **MEMBERSHIPS** Am Philol Asn; Class Asn of the Mid West and South; Cen Intl d'Etudes Homeriques. **RESEARCH** Greek and Roman epic, lyric, and satire; Ancient history; Women in antiquity; Comparative literature and literary theory. **SELECTED PUBLICATIONS** Auth, "Homeric Originality: A Survey," 78; "Homer Studies 1971-1977," 79; "Looking Darkely: Reflections on Status and Decorum in Homer," 83; "Homer Studies 1978-1983 Pt. 1," 90; "Homer Studies 1978-1983 Pt. 2," 90; "Homer, Oral Poetry Theory and Comparative Literature: Major Trends and Controversies in Twentieth-Century Criticism," 91; World History, 91; "Nonverbal Communication in the Classics: Research Opportunities," 92; Lives and Times: A World History Reader, 95; trans, Homer: His Art and His World, 96; Co-auth, A Survey of Western Civilization, 97; auth, Marathon and the Myth of the Same-Day March 97, 00. **CONTACT ADDRESS** Foreign Language Dept, Eastern Michigan Univ, 7685 Paint Creek Dr, Ypsilanti, MI 48197. **EMAIL** fla_holoka@online.emich.edu

HOLSINGER, M. PAUL
PERSONAL Born 01/31/1938, Philadelphia, PA, m, 1958, 4 children **DISCIPLINE** AMERICAN & CANADIAN HISTORY **EDUCATION** Duke Univ, AB, 59; Univ Denver, MA, 60, PhD(hist), 64. **CAREER** From instr to asst prof hist, Ore State Univ, 62-67; asst prof Am thought & lang, Mich State Univ, 67-69; assoc prof, 69-76, Prof Hist, Ill State Univ, 76-, Eppley prof hist, Culver Mil Acad, Ind, 65-66. **HONORS AND AWARDS** Louis Knott Koontz Prize, Pac Hist Quart, 69. **MEMBERSHIPS** Southern Hist Asn; Asn Can Studies US. **RESEARCH** American legal and constitutional history; Canadian studies; environmental history. **CONTACT ADDRESS** Dept of Hist, Illinois State Univ, Campus Box 4420, Normal, IL 61790-4420. **EMAIL** mpholsi@ilstu.edu

HOLT, FRANK L.
PERSONAL Born, VA, m, 1975, 1 child **DISCIPLINE** ANCIENT HISTORY **EDUCATION** Lynchburg Col, BA, 76; Univ Virginia, MA, 78; PhD, 84. **CAREER** From asst prof to prof, Univ of Houston, 82-. **HONORS AND AWARDS** Aristotle Prize, Greece; Alexander the Great Medal, Macedonian Asn; Craddock Prize, Southwestern Hist Asn; Univ Teaching Awd; Master Teacher of the Humanities Awd. **MEMBERSHIPS** Am Numismatic Soc, Asn of Ancient Historians, Inst of Balkan Studies. **RESEARCH** Alexander the Great, Hellenistic East, numismatics. **SELECTED PUBLICATIONS** Auth, "Response to Stanley Burnstein," in Hellenistic Hist and Culture, ed. Peter Green (CA: Univ of Calif Press, 93): 54-64; auth, "Alexander the Great and Hellenism," Macedonian Life 28 (95): 1-2; auth, Alexander the Great and Bactria: The Formation of a Greek Frontier in Central Asia, E.J. Brill (New York, NY), 95; auth, "The Autobiography of a Coin," Aramco World 45 (97): 10-15; ed, The Greeks in Bactria and India, Ares Press (Chicago, IL), 85, rev 97; auth, "Nimesis in Metal: The Fate of Greek Culture on Bactrian Coins," in The Expanded Eye, eds. Frances Titchener and Richard Moorton (CA: Univ of Calif Press, 97): 93-104; auth, "Alaxender the Great Today: In the Interests of Historical History," Hist Bull 13.3 (99): 111-117; auth, Thundering Zeus: The Making of Hellenistic Bactria, Univ of Calif Press (Berkeley, CA), 99; auth, "The Roman Millennium," Aramco World 51 (00): 26-29; auth, "A Journey into the Mind of Alaxender the Great," Aramco World (forthcoming); auth, "Weighing the Evidence for Early Hellenistic Bactria," Vadim Masson Festschrift (forthcoming); **CONTACT ADDRESS** Dept Hist, Univ of Houston, Univ Houston, Houston, TX 77204-3785. **EMAIL** histm@pop.uh.edu

HOLT, MICHAEL FITZGIBBON
PERSONAL Born 07/08/1940, Pittsburgh, PA, m, 1967, 3 children **DISCIPLINE** AMERICAN HISTORY **EDUCATION** Princeton Univ, AB, 62; Johns Hopkins Univ, PhD(hist), 67. **CAREER** Actg instr hist, Yale Univ, 65-67, from asst prof to assoc prof, 67-73; Vis assoc prof, Stanford Univ, 73-74; Assoc prof, Univ Va, 74-79; NEH sr fel, 76-77; Prof Hist, Univ Va, 80-; fel, Stanford Center, 81-82; fel, National Humanities Center, 87-88. **HONORS AND AWARDS** Pitt Prof of Am Hist and Institutions, Cambridge Univ, 93-94; Second prize in Lincoln competititon, 00. **MEMBERSHIPS** Orgn Am Historians; AHA; SHA **RESEARCH** United States political history 1840-1860. **SELECTED PUBLICATIONS** Auth, Nativism and Slavery--The Northern Know Nothings and the Politics of the 1850s, Am Hist Rev, Vol 0098, 93; auth, Political Parties and American Political Development from the Age of Jackson to the Age of Lincoln, LSU, 92; auth, The Rise and Fall of the American Whig Party, 99. **CONTACT ADDRESS** Dept of Hist, Univ of Virginia, 1 Randall Hall, Charlottesville, VA 22903-3244. **EMAIL** mfh6p@virginia.edu

HOLT, PHILIP
DISCIPLINE ANCIENT GREECE AND ROME **EDUCATION** Stanford Univ, PhD, 76. **CAREER** Assoc prof; Univ WY, 87-. **RESEARCH** Greek myth and drama; Greek and Roman epic poetry. **SELECTED PUBLICATIONS** Publ in, scholarly jour in NAm & Europe. **CONTACT ADDRESS** Dept of Mod and Class Lang(s), Univ of Wyoming, PO Box 3964, Laramie, WY 82071-3964. **EMAIL** PHOLT@UWYO.EDU

HOLTMAN, ROBERT BARNEY
PERSONAL Born 08/26/1914, Kenosha, WI, m, 1952, 2 children **DISCIPLINE** MODERN EUROPEAN HISTORY **EDUCATION** Univ Wis, BS & AM, 35, PhD, 41. **CAREER** Instr, Western Wash Col Educ, 41-42; from asst prof to assoc prof, 46-61, assoc dean grad sch, 70-74, Prof Hist, LA State Univ, Baton Rouge, 61-, Am Philos Soc res grant, 67; mem bd consult, Hist Teachers Asn, 67-71. **MEMBERSHIPS** AHA; Southern Hist Asn; Soc Fr Hist Studies (vpres, 66-67, treas, 74); Soc Mod Hist, France. **RESEARCH** Nineteenth and 20th century France; Napoleonic and Hitlerian wartime propaganda. **SELECTED PUBLICATIONS** Auth, Napoleon Integration of Europe, J Modern Hist, Vol 0066, 94; Legitimism and the Reconstruction of French Society, 1852-1883, J Modern Hist, Vol 0067, 95; Bonapartism and Revolutionary Tradition in France--The Federes of 1815, Am Hist Rev, Vol 0097, 92. **CONTACT ADDRESS** Dept of Hist, Louisiana State Univ and A&M Col, Baton Rouge, LA 70803.

HOLUB, RENATE
PERSONAL Born 10/06/1946, Germany, 1 child **DISCIPLINE** ITALIAN STUDIES **EDUCATION** Univ Wisc, PhD, 83. **CAREER** Univ Cal-Berkeley. **MEMBERSHIPS** Am Philos Asn; Am Sociol Asn; Intl Assoc of Sociology. **RESEARCH** Social theory; European studies. **SELECTED PUBLICATIONS** Auth, Antonio Grauesci: Beyond Naxism and Postmodernism, 92. **CONTACT ADDRESS** Intnatl & Area Studies, Univ of California, Berkeley, 317 Campbell Hall, Berkeley, CA 94720-2300. **EMAIL** rholub@socrates.berkeley.edu

HOLZ, ROBERT K.
PERSONAL Born 11/03/1930, Kaukekee, IL, m, 1951, 1 child **DISCIPLINE** GEOGRAPHY **EDUCATION** Southern Ill Univ, BA, 58; MA, 59; Mich State Univ, PhD, 63. **CAREER** Instr, Mich State Univ, 61-62; From Asst Prof to Prof, Univ of Tex at Austin, 62-99. **HONORS AND AWARDS** Group Achievement Awd, NASA, 74; Eric Zimmerman Regents Prof, 92-99; Remote Sensing specialty Group Medal, Aag, 98. **MEMBERSHIPS** Asn of Am Geogr, Am Soc of Photogrammetry. **RESEARCH** Middle East and North Africa, Remote Sensing of the Environment, Cartography-Map Reading and Interpretation. **SELECTED PUBLICATIONS** Auth, "The Surveillant Science," in 1st and 2nd ed Remote Sensing of the Environment; chapter in Manual of Remote Sensing, 1st and 2nd ed. **CONTACT ADDRESS** Dept Geog, Univ of Texas, Austin, 0 Univ of Tex, Austin, TX 78712.

HOMAN, GERLOF DOUWE
PERSONAL Born 08/28/1929, Appingedam, Netherlands, m, 1953, 3 children **DISCIPLINE** MODERN EUROPEAN HISTORY **EDUCATION** Bethel Col, Kans, BA, 54; Univ Kans, MA, 56, PhD, 58. **CAREER** Assoc prof hist, Cent State Col, Okla, 58-63; vis assoc prof, Univ Okla, 63-64; assoc prof, Kans State Col Pittsburg, 64-68; assoc prof, 68-72, prof to prof emer, Ill State Univ, 72-, Chmn Dept, 76- **MEMBERSHIPS** AHA; Soc Fr Hist Studies. **RESEARCH** The French Revolution and Napoleon; the Netherlands in French Revolution and Napoleon Era; Netherlands-American relations and the Indonesian revolution. **SELECTED PUBLICATIONS** Auth, Jean-Francois Reubell, director, Fr Hist Studies, fall 60; Constitutional reform in the Kingdom of the Netherlands, Historian, 5/66; Jean Francois Reubell, Nijhoff, 71; The Staatsbewind and Freedom of the Press, Tijdschrift voor Geschiedenis, 76. **CONTACT ADDRESS** Dept of Hist, Illinois State Univ, Normal, IL 61790. **EMAIL** ghoman@ilstu.edu

HOMEL, MICHAEL W.
PERSONAL Born Chicago, IL **DISCIPLINE** HISTORY **EDUCATION** Grinnell Col, BA; Univ Chicago, MA, PhD. **CAREER** Prof, Eastern Michigan Univ. **RESEARCH** US 20th-Century, US urban. **SELECTED PUBLICATIONS** Auth, Down From Equality: Black Chicagoans and the Public Schools, 1920-1941; Southern Cities, Southern Schools; The Politics of Public Education in Black Chicago, 1910-1941, J Negro Educ 65, 76; Race and Schools in Nineteenth-Century Chicago, Integrated Educ 12, 74; The Lilydale School Campaign of 1936: Direct Action in the Verbal Protest Era, J Negro Hist 59, 74; contribur, Biographical Dictionary of American Mayors, 1820-1980. **CONTACT ADDRESS** Dept of History and Philosophy, Eastern Michigan Univ, 701 Pray-Harrold, Ypsilanti, MI 48197. **EMAIL** his_homel@online.emich.edu

HOMER, FRANCIS X. J.
PERSONAL Born 07/30/1941, Scranton, PA, s **DISCIPLINE** HISTORY **EDUCATION** Univ Scranton, AB, 64; Univ Va, MA, 66; PhD, 71. **CAREER** Instr, Univ Va, 67; from instr to prof, Univ Scranton, 68-. **HONORS AND AWARDS** Woodrow Wilson Fel, 64. **MEMBERSHIPS** AHA, AAUP, Northeast Asn of Pre-Law Advisors. **RESEARCH** Modern European History. **SELECTED PUBLICATIONS** Auth, Germany and Europe in the Era of the Two World Wars, Univ Pr of Va, 84. **CONTACT ADDRESS** Dept Hist, Univ of Scranton, 800 Linden St, Scranton, PA 18510-4501. **EMAIL** Homerf1@uofs.edu

HOMER, WILLIAM I.
PERSONAL Born 11/08/1929, Merion, PA, m, 1986, 1 child **DISCIPLINE** ART HISTORY **EDUCATION** Princeton Univ, BA, 51; Harvard Univ, MA, 54; PhD, 61. **CAREER** Asst dir, Art Museum, Princeton Univ, 56-57; cur, Princeton Univ, 56-57; cur, Mus Amer Art, Ogunquitime, 55, 56, 58; asst prof, Princeton Univ, 61-64; lectr, 59-61; instr, 55-59; assoc prof, Cornell Univ, 64-66,; ch, 88-93; act ch, 86-87; ch, 66-81; prof, 66-84; H. Rodney Sapp prof, 84-99. **HONORS AND AWARDS** Jr fel, Princeton Univ, 62-63; fel, Amer Coun Learned Soc, 64-65; John Simon Guggenheim Memorial fel, 72-73; NEH fel, 80-81; Univ Del Francis Alison Fac award, 80; distinguished fac lectureship, 81; fel, 85-86; Delaware Hum Forum, res fel, 88-89. **MEMBERSHIPS** Mem, Col Art Assn Am; Pictorial Photogr Am; Photog Soc Philadelphia. **RESEARCH** Amer Art, History of Photography. **SELECTED PUBLICATIONS** Auth, Seurat and the Science of Painting, MIT Press, 64, repr ed, 85; Robert Henri and His Circle, Cornell Univ Press, 69, second ed, 88; Alfred Stieglitz and the American Avant-Garde, Little, Brown, 77; Alfred Stieglitz and the Photo-Secession, Little, Brown, 83; Thomas Eakins: His Life and Art, Abbeville Press, 92; Preface, Randall C. Griffin, Thomas Anshutz: Artist and Teacher, Wa Univ Press, 94; Robert Henri as a Portrait Painter, Valerie Leeds, My People: The Portraits of Robert Henri, Orlando Museum of Art, 94, 95; The Watercolors of Abraham Walkowitz, Abraham Walkowitz (1878-65): Watercolors from 05 through 20 and Other Works on Paper, Zabriskie Gallery, 94, 95; Unheralded Genius: Karl Struss, Photographer, New York to Hollywood: The Photography of Karl Struss, Amon Carter Mus and Albuquerque, Nmex Univ Press, 95; Karl Struss, Photographer: Unheralded Genius, Amer Art Rev, 95; Charles Demuth: Flowers, 150 Years of Philadelphia Still-Life Painting, The Schwarz Gallery, 97; Collaborative Efforts: Genesis and Fulfillment, The Gist of Drawing, Delaware Art Museum, 97; Whitman, Eakins, and The Naked Truth, Walt Whitman Quart Rev, 97; Visual Culture: A New Paradigm, Amer Art, 98. **CONTACT ADDRESS** Dept of Art Hist, Univ of Delaware, Newark, DE 19716.

HOMZE, EDWARD L.
PERSONAL Born 10/13/1930, Canton, OH, m, 1959, 2 children **DISCIPLINE** MODERN & GERMAN HISTORY **EDUCATION** Bowling Green State Univ, BA, 52, MA, 53; Pa State Univ, PhD(Europ hist), 63. **CAREER** Asst prof Europ hist, Kans State Teachers Col, 61-65; assoc prof, 65-71, prof Europ Hist, Univ Nebr, Lincoln, 71-, Nat Found Arts & Humanities fel, 68. **MEMBERSHIPS** AHA. **RESEARCH** Twentieth century Europe; modern Germany. **SELECTED PUBLICATIONS** Auth, Foreign Labor in Nazi Germany, Princeton Univ, 67; coauth, Germany: The Divided Nation, 70 & Willy Brandt, 74, Nelson; auth, Arming the Luftwaffe, Univ Nebr, 76. **CONTACT ADDRESS** History Dept, Univ of Nebraska, Lincoln, PO Box 880327, Lincoln, NE 68588-0327. **EMAIL** ehomze@unl.edu

HONDROS, JOHN L.
DISCIPLINE HISTORY **EDUCATION** Univ NC, AB, 59; Vanderbilt Univ, MA, 63, PhD, 69. **CAREER** Prof. **RESEARCH** Origins of the Cold War. **SELECTED PUBLICATIONS** Auth, Greece in the 1940s: A Nation in Crisis, New Eng UP; Occupation and Resistance: The Greek Agony, 1941-1944, Pella Pub Co, 83. **CONTACT ADDRESS** Dept of Hist, The Col of Wooster, Wooster, OH 44691.

HONEY, MAUREEN
PERSONAL Born 10/25/1945, Memphis, TN **DISCIPLINE** AMERICAN STUDIES, WOMEN'S STUDIES **EDUCATION** Mich State Univ, BA, 67; MA, 70; PhD, 79. **CAREER** Instr, Mich State univ, 77-79; from asst prof to prof, Univ Nebr, 79-. **HONORS AND AWARDS** Distinguished Teaching Awd, 91. **MEMBERSHIPS** Am Studies Asn, Am Culture Asn, Edith Wharton Soc, Melus. **RESEARCH** Women in World War II, American Women's Literature, Harlem Renaissance, Popular Fiction (1890-1930). **SELECTED PUBLICATIONS** Auth, Creating Rosie the Riveter: Class, Gender, and Propaganda During World War II, Univ Mass Press, 84; auth, Shadowed Dreams: Women's Poetry of the Harlem Renaissance, Rutgers Univ Press, 89, 96, & 99; auth, Breaking the Ties that Bind: Popular Stories of the New Woman, 1915-1930, Univ Okla Press, 92 & 98; auth, "Introduction," in The Job by Sinclair Lewis (NE: Univ Nebr Press, 94); ed, Bitter Fruit: African American Women in World War II, Univ Mo Press, 99; co-ed, Texts and Contexts of the Harlem Renaissance: A Multi-Genre Anthology, forthcoming. **CONTACT ADDRESS** Dept English, Univ of Nebraska, Lincoln, PO Box 880333, Lincoln, NE 68588-0333. **EMAIL** mhoney1@unl.edu

HONEY, MICHAEL
PERSONAL Born 04/25/1947, Lansing, MI, m **DISCIPLINE** HISTORY **EDUCATION** Howard Univ, MA, 78; Northern Ill Univ, PhD, 88. **CAREER** Wesleyan Univ, 87-88; Univ of Puget Sound, 88-89; Stanford Univ, 89-90; Univ Washington, 90-. **HONORS AND AWARDS** Stanford Humanities Ctr Fel, 89-90; James A. Rawley Prize, Org of Am Hists, 93; Charles Syndor Awd, Southern Hist Asn, 93; Nat Humanities Ctr Fel, 95-96. **MEMBERSHIPS** OAH, SHA. **RESEARCH** Labor, civil rights, African American history. **SELECTED PUBLICATIONS** Auth, Southern Labor and Black Civil Rights: Organizing Memphis Workers, Ill (93); auth, Black Workers Remember, An Oral History, Calif (99). **CONTACT ADDRESS** Dept Liberal Arts, Univ of Washington-Tacoma, 1900 Commerce St, Tacoma, WA 98402-3112. **EMAIL** mhoney@u.washington.edu

HONEYCUTT, DWIGHT A.
PERSONAL Born 10/17/1937, Bessemer, AL, m, 1960, 3 children **DISCIPLINE** CHURCH HISTORY **EDUCATION** Mercer Univ, BA; Midwestern Baptist Sem, BD; Intl Baptist Theol Sem, Switzerland, ThM; New Orleans Baptist Theol Sem, ThD. **CAREER** Instr, Intl Baptist Theol Sem, Cali, Colombia, 77; vis prof, New Orleans Baptist Theol Sem; Midwestern Baptist Theol Sem, 87-88; prof, 88; William A. Carleton prof, Golden Gate Baptist Theol Sem, 92-. **HONORS AND AWARDS** Assoc secy, missionary personnel, S Baptist For Mission Bd, 72. **MEMBERSHIPS** AAR, Am Soc of Church History. **SELECTED PUBLICATIONS** Pub(s), Theol Educator; Bolotin Teologico de ABITHA; El Heraldo; Dialogo Teologica; Jour Church and State; SBC Quart Rev. **CONTACT ADDRESS** Golden Gate Baptist Theol Sem, 201 Sem Dr, Mill Valley, CA 94941-3197. **EMAIL** dhoneycutt@ggbts.edu

HOOD, DAVID CROCKETT
PERSONAL Born 04/21/1937, Tulsa, OK, d, 2 children **DISCIPLINE** ANCIENT HISTORY **EDUCATION** Univ Calif, Santa Barbara, BA, 61; Univ Southern Calif, PhD(Hist), 67. **CAREER** Asst prof Hist, Wichita State Univ, 65-66; from asst prof to assoc prof, 66-75, prof hist, Calif State Univ, Long Beach, 75-. **HONORS AND AWARDS** So Calif Classical Assoc; chmn, Academic Senate, 9a5-98; chmn, Friends of Ancient Hist in So Calif, 82. **MEMBERSHIPS** Soc Prom Hellenic Studies; Am Philol Asn; Soc Prom Roman Studies. **RESEARCH** Roman historiography. **SELECTED PUBLICATIONS** Ed, The Rise of Rome: How to Explain It?, Heath, 70. **CONTACT ADDRESS** Dept of History, California State Univ, Long Beach, 1250 N Bellflower, Long Beach, CA 90840-1601. **EMAIL** dhood@csulb.edu

HOOGENBOOM, ARI
PERSONAL Born 11/28/1927, Richmond Hill, NY, m, 1949, 3 children **DISCIPLINE** AMERICAN HISTORY **EDUCATION** Atlantic Union Col, AB, 49; Columbia Univ, AM, 51, PhD, 58. **CAREER** Lectr Am hist, Columbia Univ, 55-56; from instr to asst prof hist, TX Western Col, 56-58; from instr to asst prof, PA State Univ, 58-62, from assoc prof to prof Am hist, 62-68; chmn dept, 68-74, prof hist, Brooklyn Col, City Univ NY, 68-98, Emeritus 98-, Am Philos Soc grants-in-aid, 59, 60; Guggenheim fel, 65-66. **HONORS AND AWARDS** Fulbright Awd, Ger, 91-92. **MEMBERSHIPS** AHA; Orgn Am Historians. **RESEARCH** Post Civil War Am hist; Am bureaucratic hist; the Am Civil War. **SELECTED PUBLICATIONS** Auth, The Pendleton Act and the Civil Service, American Hist Rev, 59; Outlawing the Spoils: A History of the Civil Service Reform Movement, 1865-1883, Univ IL, 61; Thomas A Jenckes and Civil Service reform, Miss Valley Hist Rev, 3/61; Gustavus Fox and the relief of Fort Sumter, Civil War Hist, 12/63; coauth, The Enterprising Colonials: Society on the Eve of the Revolution, Argonaut, Inc, 65; co-ed, The Gilded Age, 67 & An Interdisciplinary Approach to American History (2 vols), 73, Prentice-Hall; coauth, A History of Pennsylvania, McGraw, 73, 2nd ed, PA State Univ Press, 80; A History of the ICC: From Panacea to Palliative, Norton, 76; The Presidency of Rutherford B. Hayes, Univ Press of KS, 88; Rutherford B. Hayes: Warrior and President, Univ Press of KS, 95. **CONTACT ADDRESS** Dept of Hist, Brooklyn Col, CUNY, 2901 Bedford Ave, Brooklyn, NY 11210-2813.

HOOGENBOOM, HILDE
DISCIPLINE RUSSIAN STUDIES **EDUCATION** Williams Col, BA, 81; Columbia, BA, 89; MPhil, 92; PhD, 96 **CAREER** Lecturer, Princeton Univ, 90-91; lecturer, Columbia Univ, 89-95; vis asst prof, Col Wooster, 95-97; asst prof, Stetson Univ, 97-. **HONORS AND AWARDS** Fel, Nat Humanities Ctr, 00; Steton Univ Fac Prof Dev Grant, 98-00; IRES Short-Term Travel Grant, 96-98; NEH Summer Seminar for Col Teachers, 96; ACLS Travel Grant to Intl Conf, 96; Col of Wooster Fac Dev Grant, 96; USIA Reg Scholar Exchange Fel, 95; Harriman Inst, Jun Fel, 91-95; Pepsico Travel Grant, 93-94; IREX Indep Res Grant, 92-93; IREX for Teachers of Russian Grant, 91. **MEMBERSHIPS** AAASS, AWSS, AATSEEL, Friends of RGESAND. **RESEARCH** Russian women, writes, Autobiography. **SELECTED PUBLICATIONS** Auth, Biographies of Elizaveta Kul'man and representations of female Poetic Genius, Univ Helsinki, 00; auth, The Importance of Being Provincial: Nineteenth-Century Russian Women Writers and the Countryside, Penn State Univ, 00; auth, "The Famous White Box: The Creation of Mariia Bashkirtseva and her Diary," Studies in Russian and European Literature: Gender and Sexuality in Russian Civilization, Harwood Acad Pub, (forthcoming); auth, Vladimir Karenine and her Biography of George Sand: One Russian Woman Writer Responds to Sand," George Sand Papers: Conference Proceedings, 1996, (98): 177-187; auth, "The Society Tale as Pastiche: Mariia Zhukova's Heroines Move to the Country," in Studies in slavic Literature and Poetics: The Society Tale in Russian Literature, Amsterdam, (98): 85-97; auth, "Vera Figner and Revolutionary Autobiographies: The Influence of Gender on Genre," in Women in Russia and Ukraine, Cambridge, (96): 78-93; auth, Identity and Realism: Russian Women Writers in the Nineteenth Century, (forthcoming); auth, Mapping the Feminine: Russian Women and Cultural Difference, (forthcoming); auth, Catherine the Great's Many Memoirs, or the Mind of a Chevalier, (forthcoming); auth, "Biblio9graphers and the Order of Russian Women Writers," Mapping the Feminine: Russian Women and Cultural Difference, (forthcoming). **CONTACT ADDRESS** Dept For Lang, Stetson Univ, De Land, 421 N Woodland Blvd, Deland, FL 32720. **EMAIL** hhoogenb@stetson.edu

HOOPER, PAUL F.
PERSONAL Born 07/31/1938, Walla Walla, WA, m, 1960, 1 child **DISCIPLINE** HISTORY, AMERICAN STUDIES **EDUCATION** Eastern Wash Univ, BA, 61; Univ of Haw, MA, 65; PhD, 72. **CAREER** Res Dir, Asia Training Ctr--USAID, 67-69; minority res dir, Haw State House of Representatives, 69-72; am studies fac, Univ of Haw, 72-; exec asst to managing dir, City and County of Honolulu, 85-86; prof & chair of am studies, Univ of Haw, 88-. **HONORS AND AWARDS** NDEA Fel, 62-63; East-West Center Fel, 63-66; Fulbright Sr Lectureship, China, 83-84; Japan Soc for the Promotion of Sci Fel, 99. **MEMBERSHIPS** Am Asn for Univ Professors, Am Studies Asn, Fulbright Asn. **RESEARCH** American-Asian-Pacific Relations, Hawaiian History and Politics, Institute of Pacific Relations History. **SELECTED PUBLICATIONS** Auth, Elusive Destiny: The Internationalist Movement in Modern Hawaii, Unvi Press of Hawaii (Honolulu, HI), 80; ed, Building a Pacific Community, East-West Center (Honolulu, HI), 82; ed, Remembering the Institute of Pacific Relations: The Memoirs of William L. Holland, Ryukei Shyosha (Tokyo, Japan), 95. **CONTACT ADDRESS** Dept Am Studies, Univ of Hawaii, Manoa, 1890 E West Road, Honolulu, HI 96822-2318. **EMAIL** hooper@hawaii.edu

HOOPES, JAMES E.
PERSONAL Born 05/16/1944, Pittsburgh, PA, m, 1975, 2 children **DISCIPLINE** HISTORY **EDUCATION** Bowling Green State Univ, BA, 65; Univ Wis, MA, 69; Johns Hopkins, PhD, 73. **CAREER** Prof, Babson Col, 75-. **HONORS AND AWARDS** Guggenheim Fel; NEH Fel; Fulbright Sen Lectr. **MEMBERSHIPS** AHA, HS, OAH. **RESEARCH** Business history and intellectual history. **SELECTED PUBLICATIONS** Ed, Peirce on Signs: Writings on Semiotic by Charles Sanders Peirce, 91; rev, "The Promise of Pragmatism" by John Patrick Diggins, Intellectual Hist Newsletter (95); auth, "Organization," in Examining Bus Process Re-Engineering (London: Kogan Page, 95); coauth, "Anthony Giddens and Charles Sanders Peirce: History, Theory and a Way Out of the Linguistic Cul-de-Sac," J of the Hist of Ideas (95); auth, Community Denied: The Wrong Turn on Pragmatic Liberalism, Cornell UP (Ithaca, NY), 98; auth, "The History of Ideas," Encycl of Am Cult and Intellectual Hist, Scribners (00); rev, "Dorothea Dix: New England Reformer" by Thomas J Brown, Am Studies Europe (forthcoming). **CONTACT ADDRESS** Dept Hist, Babson Col, PO Box 57310, Babson Park, MA 02457-0310. **EMAIL** hoopes@babson.edu

HOOVER, DWIGHT W.
PERSONAL Born 09/15/1926, Oskaloosa, IA, m, 1954, 3 children **DISCIPLINE** AMERICAN INTELLECTUAL HISTORY **EDUCATION** William Penn Col, BA, 48; Haverford Col, MA, 49; State Univ Iowa, PhD, 53. **CAREER** Prof, chmn dept & head div soc sci, Bethune-Cookman Col, 53-55 & 58; asst prof gen studies, Kans State Univ, 58-59; from asst prof to assoc prof soc sci, 59-67, Prof Hist, Ball State Univ, 67-, Consult urban hist, Nat Endowment for Humanities, 71-72 & pub progs, 76-77; prof hist sociol, Univ Va, 77-78. **MEMBERSHIPS** AHA; Orgn Am Historians; Am Studies Asn; AAUP. **RESEARCH** Intellectual origins of racism; recent historiography; urban history, particularly of Muncie, Indiana. **SELECTED PUBLICATIONS** Auth, Venice West--The Beat Generation in Southern California, J West, Vol 0032, 93. **CONTACT ADDRESS** Dept of Hist, Ball State Univ, Muncie, IN 47306. **EMAIL** 00dwhoover@bsu.edu

HOOVER, HERBERT THEODORE
PERSONAL Born 03/09/1930, Millville, MN, m, 1957, 2 children **DISCIPLINE** AMERICAN FRONTIER & INDIAN HISTORY **EDUCATION** NMex State Univ, BA, 60, MA, 61; Univ Okla, PhD, 66. **CAREER** Asst prof hist, ETex State Univ, 65-66; assoc prof, 67-74, grad adv, 71-76, prof hist, Univ S Dak, Vermillion, 74-, mem SDak Comt on Humanities, NEH, 75-78; fel, Newberry Libr, Chicago, 77; dir, SDak Oral Hist Ctr, 77-78; adv panelist, Res Div, NEH, 77-78; NEH res award, 78-81. **HONORS AND AWARDS** Western America Award, Augustana Ctr for Western Studies, 84; Chair, Rhodes Schol S Dakota State Selection Comt, 91-98. **MEMBERSHIPS** Western Hist Asn; Orgn Am Historians. **RESEARCH** American frontier; American Indian history; oral history. **SELECTED PUBLICATIONS** Coauth, To Be An Indian, Holt, 71; The Practice of Oral History, Microfilming Corp of Am, 75; auth, The Chitimacha People, Indian Tribal Series, 75; Yankton Sioux tribal claims against the United States, 1917-1975, in Western Hist Quart, 76; The Sioux: A Critical Bibliography, Ind Univ Press, 79; Bibliography of the Sioux, Scarecrow Press, 80; The Yankton Sioux, Chelsea House Publ, 88; South Dakota Leaders, Univ Publ Assoc, 89; Yanktonai Sioux Images: The Watercolors of John Saul, Augustana Col Ctr for Western Studies, 93; South Dakota History: An Annotated Bibliography, Greenwood Press, 93; The Sioux and Other Native American Cultures of the Dakotas: An Annotated Bibliography, Greenwood Press, 93; "South Dakota" entries in Encycl Am 76-, Wordmark Encycl 81, Encycl Brittanica 90, Dict Am Hist 96, Encarta Encycl 96; author of numerous other journal articles and book chapters. **CONTACT ADDRESS** Dept of Hist, Univ of So Dakota, Vermillion, 414 E Clark St., Vermillion, SD 57069-2390. **EMAIL** hhoover@usd.edu

HOOVER, WILLIAM DAVIS
PERSONAL Born 04/25/1941, Columbus, OH, m, 1964, 3 children **DISCIPLINE** JAPANESE HISTORY **EDUCATION** Muskingum Col, BA, 63; Univ Mich, Ann Arbor, MA, 65; PhD, 73. **CAREER** From Instr to Assoc Prof, 68-85, prof hist, Univ Toledo, 85, Chmn Dept, 79-94. **HONORS AND AWARDS** Japan Found Res Fel, Tokyo, 95-96; Fulbright Res Fel, Japan, 77-78. **MEMBERSHIPS** Asn Asian Studies; AHA; SHAFR. **RESEARCH** Meiji Japan; Pacificism in Japan history; social, cultural and intellectual exchange with Japan; US-Japanese relations. **SELECTED PUBLICATIONS** Auth, "Crisis Resolution in Early Meiji Diplomatic Relations: The Role of Godai Tomoatsu," Journal of Asian History 9.1 (75): 57-81; auth, "From Xenophone to Business Leader, Shibusawa Eiichi," in Great Historical Figures of Japan, ed. Japan Cultural Institute (Tokyo, 78), 284-295; auth, "Shibusawa Eiichi: nihon jitsugyokai no so," in Shihonshugi no senkusha, vol 6 (Britannica, Tokyo, 83), 175-224; regional ed, Biographical Dictionary of Modern Peace Leaders, Greenwood Press (Westport, CT), 85; auth, "Gilbert Bowles," "Kashiwagi Gien," "Kawai Michi," Kiryu Yuyu," "Saito Takao," and "Yabe Kiyoshi," Biographical Dictionary of Modern Peace leaders (Greenwood Press, Westport, CT, 85), 103-104, 490-492, 494-495, 511-512, 832-833, 1039-1040; coed, Give Peace A Chance, Exploring the Vietnam Antiwar Movement, Syracuse Univ Press, 92; auth, "The Japanese Journalist KoKo Kawakami Evaluates International Organizations in Early Showa Japan," Waseda Univ SSR 35 (96): 14-49; **CONTACT ADDRESS** 2801 W Bancroft St, Toledo, OH 43606-3390. **EMAIL** whoover@utoledo.edu

HOPKINS, FRED
PERSONAL Born 11/19/1935, Staten Island, NY, m, 1961, 2 children **DISCIPLINE** HISTORY **EDUCATION** Gettysburg Col, BA, 56; Univ of Md, MEd, 64, PhD, 69. **CAREER** Anne Arundel County Public High Sch, 59-70; Assoc prof, Univ Baltimore, 70-71; Adj Fac, Univ Baltimore, 71-92; Prof, Univ Baltimore, 93-. **HONORS AND AWARDS** Phi Beta Kappa. **MEMBERSHIPS** Inst of Nautical Archaeol; Md Hist Soc; North Am Soc of Oceanic Hist. **SELECTED PUBLICATIONS** Auth, Tom Boyle, Master Privateer, Tidewater Press, 76; Coauth, War on the Patuxent, 1814, Calvert Marine Museum Press, 81. **CONTACT ADDRESS** Univ of Baltimore, 1420 N. Charles Street, Baltimore, MD 21201.

HOPKINS, RICHARD JOSEPH
PERSONAL Born 10/25/1939, Deposit, NY, m, 1961, 2 children **DISCIPLINE** AMERICAN URBAN & SOCIAL HISTORY **EDUCATION** Univ Rochester, BA, 61; Emory Univ, MA, 65, PhD(hist), 72. **CAREER** Instr hist, Univ Wis, Milwaukee, 68-69; instr, 69-72, Asst Prof Hist, Ohio State Univ, 72- **MEMBERSHIPS** AHA; Orgn Am Historians; Southern Hist Asn **RESEARCH** American urbanization, especially occupational and residential mobility. **SELECTED PUBLICATIONS** Auth, Occupational and geographic mobility in Atlanta, Georgia, 1870-1896, J Southern Hist, 68; Status, mobility, and the dimensions of change in a Southern city: Atlanta, 1870-1910, In: Cities in American History, Knopf, 72; Are Southern cities unique? Persistence as a clue, Miss Quart, 73. **CONTACT ADDRESS** Dept of Hist, Ohio State Univ, Columbus, 230 W 17th Ave, Columbus, OH 43210.

HOPKINS, THOMAS J.
PERSONAL Born 07/28/1930, Champaign, IL, m, 1956, 4 children **DISCIPLINE** HISTORY OF RELIGIONS **EDUCATION** Col William & Mary & Mass Inst Technol, BS, 53; Yale Univ, BS, 58, MA, 59, PhD, 62. **CAREER** From instr to assoc prof, 61-72, Prof Relig, 72-96, EMER PROF RELIG STU, 96-, FRANKLIN & MARSHALL COL, 61- ; Dir India Studies prog, Cent Pa Consortium, 71-75; chmn group Indian philos & relig, Coun Intercult Studies & Prog, 72-77; chr AAR Asian Relig/Hist Relig Sect, 75-80; co-chr AAR Comp Stud Relig Section, 80-87. **MEMBERSHIPS** Asn Asian Studies; Am Orient; Am Soc Study Relig. **RESEARCH** Indian history; phenomenology of religion. **SELECTED PUBLICATIONS** Auth, The social teaching of the Bhagavata Purana, In: Krishna: Myths, Rites and Attitudes, East-West, 66; The Hindu Religious Tradition, Dickenson, 71; Contribr, Six Pillars: Introduction to the Major Works of Sri Avrobindo, Conchocheague Assoc, 74; contrib Hare Krishna, Hare Krishna, Grove Press, 83; Krishna Consciousness in the West, Bucknell Univ Press, 89; Death and Afterlife: Perspectives of World Religions, Greenwood Press, 92. **CONTACT ADDRESS** 323 N West End Ave, Lancaster, PA 17603. **EMAIL** tjhopkins@supernet.com

HORD, FREDERICK LEE
PERSONAL Born 11/07/1941, Kokomo, IN, d, 3 children **DISCIPLINE** BLACK STUDIES **EDUCATION** Ind State Univ, BS, 63, MS, 65; Union Grad School, PhD, 87. **CAREER** Asst prof English, Wabash Col, 72-76; lectr, Howard Univ, 84-87; Dir Ctr Black Cult & Res, W Va Univ, 87-88; dir, Black Studies & full prof, Knox Col, 88-. **HONORS AND AWARDS** ACM grant for Blacks-Jews Relationships; Ed bd, Jour of Black Stud; First Poets Series Awd; Who's Who Among Black Am. **MEMBERSHIPS** Nat Asn Black Cult Ctrs; Nat Coun Black Studies; ILL Comm Black Concerns Higher Educ. **RESEARCH** African American literature; black philosophy; black psychology; history of black intellectuals; black culture centers. **SELECTED PUBLICATIONS** Auth, Reconstructing Memory, 91; auth, Life Sentences: Freeing Black Relationships, Third World Press, 94; auth, I Am Because We Are: Readings in Black Philosophy, Univ of Mass Press, 95; auth, "Black Culture Centers, Unity and Color Lines," Nommo (97); auth, "Black Students and Cultural Pigmentation," Nommo (98); auth, Africa to Me, 99; auth, The Rhythm of Home: Selected Poems, forthcoming. **CONTACT ADDRESS** Black Studies Dept, Knox Col, Illinois, 2 E South St, Galesburg, IL 61401-4999. **EMAIL** fhord@knox.edu

HORGAN, PAUL
PERSONAL Born 08/01/1903, Buffalo, NY **DISCIPLINE** MODERN HISTORY **CAREER** Librn, NMex Mil Inst, 26-42, asst to pres, 47-49; adj prof English, 67-71, dir, 62-67, Auth in Residence, Wesleyan Univ, 67-, Emer Prof English, 71-, Guggenheim fels, 46, 50, 59; lectr, Grad Sch Lett, Univ Iowa, 46; mem bd mgr & exec comt, Sch Am Res, 63-; mem Nat Coun on Humanities, 66-72; hon fel, Saybrook Col, Yale, 66-, lectr English, 70; scholar in residence, Aspen Inst Humanistic Studies, 68, 71 & 73. **HONORS AND AWARDS** Harper Prize, 33; Pulitzer Prize in Hist, 55 & 77; Bancroft Prize hist, 55; Campion Awd, 57; littd, wesleyan univ, 56, southern methodist univ, 57, univ notre dame, 58, boston col, 59, nmex state univ, 61, col holy cross, 63, univ nmex, 63, lincoln col, ill, 68, st bonaventure univ, 70, loyola col, md, 70 & lasalle col, 71; lhd, canisius col, 60, **MEMBERSHIPS** AHA; Cath Hist Asn (vpres, 57, pres, 58); Nat Inst Arts & Lett; Soc Am Historians; life fel Am Acad Arts & Sci. **RESEARCH** Southwest United States history; United States biography; English literature criticism. **SELECTED PUBLICATIONS** Auth, Things As They Are, 65, Songs After Lincoln, 65, The Peach Stone, 67, Everything to Live For, 68, Whitewater, 70, ed, Maurice Baring Restored, 70, auth, Encounters with Stravinsky, 72, Approaches to Writing, 73, Lamy of Santa Fe, 77 & Mexico Bay, 82, Farrar, Strauss. **CONTACT ADDRESS** Wesleyan Univ, Middletown, CT 06457.

HORN, JOHN STEPHEN
PERSONAL Born 05/31/1931, San Juan Bautista, CA, m, 1954, 2 children **DISCIPLINE** POLITICAL SCIENCE, U.S. HISTORY **EDUCATION** Stanford, AB, 53; PhD, 58; Harvard, MPA, 55. **CAREER** Admin asst, U.S. Secretary of Labor James P. Mitchell, 59-60; legislative asst to U.S. Senator Thomas H. Kuchel, 60-66; sr fel, The Brookings Inst, 66-69; Dean of Grad Studies, The Am Univ, Washington, DC, 69-70; Pres, Calif State Univ, 70-88, prof, 71-95, Trustee Prof of Political Sci, 88-95; U.S. Representative, 93-, member of Congress, 103rd, 104th, 105th, 106th. **HONORS AND AWARDS** Stanford, AB with Great Distinction, 58. **RESEARCH** Political theory, public administration, political parties, Constitutional law, 19th and 20th century U. S. history. **SELECTED PUBLICATIONS** Auth, The Cabinet and Congress (selected for White House Library); auth, Unused Power: The Work of the Senate Committee on Appropriations; coauth with Edmund Beard, Congressional Ethics-The View From the House. **CONTACT ADDRESS** U.S. Representative, House of Representatives, 2331 Rayburn, Washington, DC 20515-0538.

HORN, MARTIN
DISCIPLINE HISTORY **EDUCATION** Univ Western Ontario, BA; McMaster Univ, MA; Univ Toronto, PhD. **RESEARCH** Economics; power. **SELECTED PUBLICATIONS** Art, International Hist Rev; art, Guerres Mondiales et Conflits Contemporains. **CONTACT ADDRESS** History Dept, McMaster Univ, 1280 Main St W, Hamilton, ON, Canada L8S 4L9. **EMAIL** mhorn@mcmaster.ca

HORNSBY, ALTON
PERSONAL Born 09/03/1940, Atlanta, GA, m, 1965, 2 children **DISCIPLINE** HISTORY **EDUCATION** Morehouse Col, BA, 61; Univ Texas, MA, 62, PhD, 69. **CAREER** Instr, hist, 62-65,Tuskegee Inst; asst prof, actng chmn, dept hist, 68-71, assoc prof, chmn, dept hist, 71-74, prof, 74-, Fuller E. Callaway Prof of History, 89-, Morehouse Col. **HONORS AND AWARDS** Woodrow Wilson Fel, 61-62; S Ed Found Fel, 66-68; Univ Fel, Univ Texas, 69; S Fel Fund Fel, 78-79; United Negro Col Fund Hum Fel, Sum, 81; NEH Fel for Col Tchrs, 81-82; Amer Coun of Learned Soc Grant-in-aid, Sum, 82; United Negro Col Fund Dist Scholar, 82-83; Morehouse Col Fac Res Grant, 71-73; Alpha Phi Alpha Tchr of the Year, Morehouse Col, 71-72; Danforth Found Assoc, 78-81; Rockefeller Hum Fel, 77-78; Phi Alpha Theta; Phi Beta Kappa; WEB Du Bois Awd, 89; Fuller E Callaway Prof of Hist, 89. **MEMBERSHIPS** Assn for Stud for Afro-Amer Life & Hist; Assn of Soc & Behav Sci; Georgia Assn of Hist; Atlanta Hist Soc; Org of Amer Hist; Assn of St and Local Hist; Natl Coun for Black Stud; St Comm on Life & Hist of Black Georgians; So Conf on Afro-Amer Stud; So Hist Assn. **SELECTED PUBLICATIONS** Ed & intro, In The Cage: Eyewitness Accounts of the Freed Negro in Southern Society 1877-1929, Chicago, 71; auth, The Black Almanac, Woodbury, 77; auth, The Negro in Revolutionary Georgia, Atlanta, 72; auth, The City Too Busy to Hate: Atlanta Businessmen and Desegregation, in So Businessmen & Desegregation, Baton Rouge, 82; auth, Georgia, The Black Press in the South, Westport, 83; auth, The Black Revolution, Black History, and Professor Franklin, The Atlanta Univ Ctr Sampler, 72; auth, Black History in a Vacuum, The Black Collegian, 72; art, The Freedman's Bureau Schools in Texas, S Hist Quart, 73; art, The Colored University Issue in Texas Politics: Prelude to Sweatt vs. Painter, J Negro Hist, 76; art, The Negro in Atlanta Politics, 1961-1973, Atlanta Hist J, 77. **CONTACT ADDRESS** Dept of History, Morehouse Col, 223 Chestnut SW, Atlanta, GA 30314.

HORNSTEIN, SHELLEY
DISCIPLINE ART HISTORY **EDUCATION** Univ des Sciences Humaines de Strasbourg, LL, 76, Diplome des Etudes Approfondies, DEA, 76, ML, 78, PhD, 81. **CAREER** Lectr, 82, instr, 83-84, Laval Univ; coordr, visual arts, 87-89, ch, fine arts, 88-90, assoc Prof Atkinson Col, York Univ, 88-, assoc dean, 90-92, ch, Fine Arts, 95-. **MEMBERSHIPS** Art Gallery York Univ; Ctr Feminist Res, York Univ. **SELECTED PUBLICATIONS** Curator, The Wedding: A Ceremony, or Thoughts about an Indecisive Reunion Revisited, Art Gallery of York Univ (AGYU), Accompanying illustrated catalogue, 90; auth, "The Architecture of the First Montreal Teaching Hospitals of the 19th Century," in The Journal of Canadian Art History, Vol XIII/2 and XIV/1, (91): 12-25; auth, "Art Nouveau as Surface Described," in Visual and Verbal Crossings 1890-1980, eds. J.D. Hunt, Theo d'Haen & S.A. Varga, (Amsterdam/Atlanta: 90); auth, Of Identities and Nationalism, or, Longing to Belong, ACS Bulletin AEC, 18, 2-3, (96): 22-50; auth, Musing on Time and Space for Lyl Rye in Exhibition Caatalogue for Lyla Rye, Glendon Galerie, York Univ; auth, Of Identities and Nationalism seen from near and far, vol. 1, 98; auth, Nothing to See: Private Mourning in Public Art, in Memory and Oblivion, (Dordrechct, The Netherlands: Kluwer Academic Publishers, 99); auth, "Architectural Memory and Strasbourg National Identity," Strasbourg between Germany and France, Starsbourg, 99; auth, "Ornament, Boundaries and Mourning, after Auschwitz: Charlotte Salomon and Chantal Akerman say Kaddish," in Charlotte Salomon, ed. Monica Bohm-Duchen, (Royal Academy of Art, London with Cornell Univ Press, 00); auth, "Fugitive Places," Art Journal, 00. **CONTACT ADDRESS** Dept of Fine Arts, York Univ, North York, ON, Canada M3J 1P3. **EMAIL** shelley@yorku.ca

HOROWITZ, DANIEL
PERSONAL Born 03/23/1938, New Haven, CT, m, 1963, 2 children **DISCIPLINE** AMERICAN STUDIES; HISTORY **EDUCATION** Yale Col, BA, 60; Pembroke Col, 60-61; Harvard Univ, PhD, 67. **CAREER** Asst prof to prof, Scripps Col, 73-88; prof and Dir Am Studies Prog, Smith Col, 89- . **HONORS AND AWARDS** NEH fel, 73; Nat Human Ctr fel, 84-85; NEH fel for Col Teachers, 95; Hon Vis Fel, Schlesinger Libr, Radcliffe Col, 96-98; Constance Rourke Prize, Am Studies Asn, 97. **MEMBERSHIPS** ASA; AHA; OAH. **RESEARCH** History of consumer culture; social criticism. **SELECTED PUBLICATIONS** Auth, The Morality of Spending: Attitudes Toward the Consumer Society in America, 1875-1940; auth, Vance Packard and American Social Criticism, 94; Betty Friedan and the Making of the Feminine Mystique: The American Left, The Cold War, Modern Feminism, 98. **CONTACT ADDRESS** American Studies Program, Smith Col, Northampton, MA 01063. **EMAIL** dhorowit@smith.edu

HOROWITZ, DAVID A.
PERSONAL Born 08/17/1941, Bronx, NY, m, 1996 **DISCIPLINE** HISTORY **EDUCATION** Antioch Col, BA, 64; Univ of Minn, PhD, 71. **CAREER** INSTR TO PROF OF HISTORY, PORTLAND STATE UNIV, 68-. **MEMBERSHIPS** Historical Soc. **RESEARCH** 20th century U.S. cultural and political history. **SELECTED PUBLICATIONS** Ed & annotator, Inside the Klavern: The Secret History of a 1920 Klu Klux Klan, Southern Ill Univ Press, 99; coauth, On the Edge: The U.S. in the 20th Century, West/Wadsworth, 98; auth, The Normality of Extremism: The Ku Klux Klan Revisited, Soc, 98; auth, Beyond Left and Right: Insurgency and the Establishment, Univ of Ill Press, 97; auth, An Alliance of Convenience: Independent Exhibitors and Purity Crusaders Battle Hollywood 1920-1940, Historian, 97; auth, Senator Borah's Crusade to Save Small Business from the New Deal, Historian, 93; auth, The Cross of Culture: La Grande, Oregon in the 1920s, Ore Hist Quart, 93. **CONTACT ADDRESS** Dept of Hist, Portland State Univ, Portland, OR 97207.

HOROWITZ, JOEL
PERSONAL Born 06/18/1949, New York, NY, m, 1975, 2 children **DISCIPLINE** HISTORY **EDUCATION** Univ Pa, AB, 71; Univ Calif, PhD, 79. **CAREER** Prof, St Bonaventure Univ, 89-. **HONORS AND AWARDS** Tibesar Prize, Conf on Latin Am hist, 91; Fulbright Res Schol, St Bonaventure Univ, 84, 93. **RESEARCH** Argentina, 20th-century, labor, radical party. **SELECTED PUBLICATIONS** Auth, "The Impact of Pre-1943 Labor Union Traditions on Peronism," J of Latin Am Studies (83): 101-116; auth, La Formacion del Sindicalismo Peronista, ed by Juan Carlos Tore (Buenos Aires: Legasa, 88): 99-118; auth, "Ideologias Sindicales y Politicas Estatales en la Argentina 1930-1943," Desarollo Economico (94): 275-296; auth, "Occupational Community and the Creation of a Self-Styled Elite: Railroad Workers in Argentina," The Americas (85): 55-81; auth, "The Industrialists and the Rise of Juan Peron, 1943-1946: Some Implications for the Conceptualization of Populism," The Americas (90): 199-218; auth, Argentine Unions, the State and the Rise of Peron 1930-1945, Inst of Int Studies, Univ Calif (Berkeley, CA), 90; auth, "Argentina's Failed General Strike of 1921: A Critical Moment in the Radicals' Relations with Unions," Hisp Am Hist Rev (95): 57-79; auth, "Populism and Its Legacies in Argentina," in Populism in Latin Am, Univ Ala Pr (Tuscaloosa, AL), 99; coauth, "History: 19th and 20th-Centuries: Argentina, Paraguay and Uruguay," Handbook of Latin Am Studies, no 56, prepared for the Hisp Div of the Libr Congress, Univ Tex Pr (Austin, TX: 99): 420-456; auth, "Bosses and Clients: Municipal Employment in the Buenos Aires of the Radicals 1916-1930," J of Latin Am Studies (99): 617-644. **CONTACT ADDRESS** Dept Hist, St. Bonaventure Univ, Saint Bonaventure, NY 14778-2400. **EMAIL** jhorowit@sbu.edu

HOROWITZ, MARYANNE CLINE
PERSONAL Born 06/29/1945, Boston, MA, m, 1968, 3 children **DISCIPLINE** RENAISSANCE HISTORY **EDUCATION** Brown Univ, AB, 65; Harvard Univ, MAT, 66; Univ Wis-Madison, MA, 68, PhD, 70. **CAREER** Instr govt, 70-71, res assoc, 71-73, Cornell Univ; asst prof polit, Ithaca Col, 72-73; asst prof, 73-80, assoc prof, 80-88, Prof Hist, Occidental Col, 88-, chair, women's studies, 77-79, 82-85, chair, hist dept, 88-91; assoc, Center for Medieval & Renaissance Studies, Univ Calif Los Angeles, 88-; vis fac, Divinity Sch, Harvard Univ, 79-80, hist, UCLA, 92; reader, Huntington Libr, Warburg Inst, Getty Center. **HONORS AND AWARDS** Mellon Found 79, 98, 99; Ford fel, 90, 91; NEH Summer, 71, 86, 90; ACLS Travel, 84; Haynes, 74, 77; Jacques Barzun Awd in Cultural History, Am Philos Society, 99. **MEMBERSHIPS** AHA; AAR; APSA; Renaissance Soc Am (exec bd, 86-98); Sixteenth Century Studies Conf (counc 77-80); WAWH; CAA. **RESEARCH** Moral, educational, and political ideas and images. **SELECTED PUBLICATIONS** Auth, The Image of God in Man - Is Woman Included?, J Hist Biol, 76; auth, "Aristotle and Woman", Harvard Theological Review, 79; Marie de Gournay, Ed of the Essaies of Michel de Montaigne, Sixteenth Century J, 86; Renaissance Rereadings: Intertext and Context, 88; Drogue medicinale ou vieux conte, in Montaigne et l'histoire, 89; Politics of Gender in Early Modern Europe, 89; Race, Gender and Rank: Early Modern Ideas of Humanity, 91; Playing with Gender: A Renaissance Pursuit, 91; Race, Class, and Gender in Nineteenth-Century Culture, 91; Bodin and Judaism, Il pensiero politico, 97; Seeds of Virtue and Knowledge, Prince-

ton, 98. **CONTACT ADDRESS** Dept of Hist, Occidental Col, 1600 Campus Rd, Los Angeles, CA 90041-3314. **EMAIL** horowitz@oxy.edu

HORSMAN, REGINALD
PERSONAL Born 10/24/1931, Leeds, England, m, 1955, 3 children **DISCIPLINE** HISTORY **EDUCATION** Univ Birmingham (England), BA, 52, MA, 55; Ind Univ, PhD, 58. **CAREER** From instr to prof, 58-73, Distinguished Prof Hist, Univ Wis-Milwaukee, 73; Distinguished Prof Emeritus, 99-. **HONORS AND AWARDS** Guggenheim Fel, 65; Kiekhofer Awd for Excellence in Teaching, Univ Wis, 61; Univ Wis Alumni Awd for Teaching Excellence, 95. **MEMBERSHIPS** Org Am Hist; Soc Am Hist; Soc Hist Early Am Republic (pres 87-88); State Hist Soc Wis. **RESEARCH** 19th century American history; race and expansion; War of 1812; American Indian policy; medical history. **SELECTED PUBLICATIONS** Auth, The Causes of the War of 1812, Univ Pa Press, 62; auth, "Matthew Elliott: British Indian Agent," Wayne State Univ Press, 64; auth, Expansion and American Indian Policy, 1783-1812, Mich State Univ Press, 67, paperback ed, Okla State Univ Press, 93; auth, The War of 1812, Alfred Knopf, Inc/Eyre & Spottiswood, Ltd, 69; auth, The Frontier in the Formative Years, 1783-1815, Holt, Rhinehart, and Winston, Inc, 70; auth, Race and Manifest Destiny: The Origins of American Racial Anglo-Saxonism, Harvard Univ Press, 81; auth, The Diplomacy of the New Republic, 1776-1815, Harlan Davidson, Inc, 85; auth, "Dr. Nott of Mobile: Southerner, Physician, and Racial Theorist," Louis State Univ Press, 87; auth, Frontier Doctor: William Beaumont, America's First Great Medical Scientist, Univ Mo Press, 96; auth, "The New Republic: The United States of America, 1789-1875," Longman, 00. **CONTACT ADDRESS** Dept Hist, Univ of Wisconsin, Milwaukee, PO Box 413, Milwaukee, WI 53201. **EMAIL** horsman@csd.uwm.edu

HORSTMAN, ALLEN
PERSONAL Born 08/01/1968, Seymour, IN, 2 children **DISCIPLINE** HISTORY, LAW **EDUCATION** Purdue Univ, BS, 65; Harvard Law Sch, LLB, 68; Univ Calif, Berkeley, PhD, 77. **CAREER** Prof hist, Albion Col, 77-. **MEMBERSHIPS** AHA; Am Bar Asn; Conf Brit Studies. **RESEARCH** English legal history; American legal history. **SELECTED PUBLICATIONS** Auth, Victorian Divorce, Croom Helm, London, and St. Martins, NY. **CONTACT ADDRESS** Dept of History, Albion Col, 611 E Porte St, Albion, MI 49224. **EMAIL** ahorstman@albion.edu

HORTON, JAMES O.
PERSONAL Born 03/28/1943, Newark, NJ, m, 1964, 1 child **DISCIPLINE** AMERICAN STUDIES **EDUCATION** Brandeis Univ, PhD, 73. **CAREER** Prof, George Wash Univ, 77-. **HONORS AND AWARDS** Sr Fulbright Prof, Ger, 88-89; Carnegie Found Awd; CASE Prof of Year Awd; Trachtenberg Dist Teach Awd; Appt Nat Pk Sys Adv Bd, 93, Chair, 96. **MEMBERSHIPS** OAH; AAHA. **RESEARCH** African American history; 19th Century social history; public history. **SELECTED PUBLICATIONS** Auth, Free People of Color: Interior Issues in African American Community, Smithsonian Inst Press, (93); coauth, In Hope of Liberty: Free Black Culture and Community in the North, 1700-1865, Oxford Univ Press (97); co-ed, The History of the African American People, Smithmark Pub (95); coauth, Von Benin Nach Baltimore: Geschichte der African Americans, Hamburger Ed (Germany), 99; auth, Hard Road to Freedom: The African America Story, Rutgers Univ Press, 00; auth, "Presenting Slavery: The Perils of Telling American's Racial Story," Pub Hist (99); auth, "Flight to Freedom: One Family and the Story of the Underground Railroad," in African American History Month Handbook & Guide, ed. Bernard Powers (Asn Study of African Am Life and History, 99); auth, "Making Free: African Americans and the Civil War," Civil War Landscape (99); auth, "The Underground Railroad: Personal Stories," History Matters (99); auth, "Race in America's National Identity: A Challenge for Public History," in Negotiations of America's National Identity, eds, Roland Hagenbuchle, Josef Raab (Stauffenburg Verlag, 00); coauth, "Manhood and Womanhood in a Slave Society," in Major Problems in African-American History, eds. Thomas Holt, Elsa Barkley Brown (Houghton Mifflin, 00); auth, "Defending the Manhood of the Race," in Hope and Gory: Essays on the '~Legacy of the 54th Massachusetts Regiment, eds. Martin Blatt (Univ Massachusetts Press, forthcoming). **CONTACT ADDRESS** Dept American Studies, The George Washington Univ, 2108 G St NW, Washington, DC 20052. **EMAIL** horton@gwu.edu

HORTON, LOREN NELSON
PERSONAL Born 03/16/1933, Hopeville, IA, m, 1957 **DISCIPLINE** UNITED STATES HISTORY **EDUCATION** Univ Northern Iowa, BA, 55, MA, 60, PhD, 78. **CAREER** Teacher hist. Toledo Pub Schs, 55-57; Cedar Falls Comm Schs, 60-62; Shimer Coll, 63; St. Katharine's Sch, 63-68; Palmer Jr Coll, 65-73: Hist Spec, State Hist soc of Iowa, 72-96; Inst. Iowa Wesleyan Coll, 89-00. **HONORS AND AWARDS** Outstanding Educr, NEA, 72. **MEMBERSHIPS** Am Culture Assoc, Am Assoc Mus, Am Assoc St & Local Hist, Assoc Gravestone Studies. **RESEARCH** 19th cent social history; U.S. Frontier history; town planning and architecture; urbanization process; Victorian customs. **SELECTED PUBLICATIONS** Auth, Census Data for Iowa, 73; auth, The Character of the Country, 76; auth, The Worlds Columbian Exposition, J West, Vol 0033, 94; Nebraska Moments--Glimpses of Nebraska Past, J West, Vol 0034, 95; auth, Men With Splendid Hearts, 96; auth, A Richer Dust Concealed, 00. **CONTACT ADDRESS** 3367 Hanover Ct, Iowa City, IA 52240.

HORWARD, DONALD D.
PERSONAL Born 01/09/1933, Pittsburgh, PA, m, 1958 **DISCIPLINE** MODERN HISTORY **EDUCATION** Waynesburg Col, BA, 55; Ohio Univ, MA, 56; Univ Minn, PhD, 62. **CAREER** Asst, Ohio Univ, 55-56; asst, Univ Minn, 56-58, fac adv & coun, 58-61; from instr to assoc prof, 61-70, chmn dept, 72-75, Prof Hist, Fla St Univ, 70-, Mem, Defesa Nacional, Port, 65-; Am rep, Comt Honor, Soc Chateau Imperial Pont-de-Briques, 66-68; Calouste Gulbenkian Found award, Port, 67 & 72, fel, 76; mem bd dirs, Consortium Revolutionary Europe, 1750-1850, 71-; Am Coun Learned Socs travel grant, 76; Dir, Inst on Napoleon and the French Revolution, 90; Ben Weider Eminent Scholar Chair in Napleonic History, Fl St Univ, 98. **HONORS AND AWARDS** Standard Oil Ind Teaching Awd, 67; Calouste Gulbenkian Fnd Awd, 78, 80, 82, 84, 86, 87, 89; French Min of Culture; Edwin P. Conquest Chair in Human, Va Milit Inst, 84; Chair of Milit Hist, US Milit Acad, 86-87; Chair of Milit Aff, US Marine War Col, 93, 95, 96, 97, 98, 99, 00; Chair of Milit Stu, US Marine Sch of Advan Warfighting, 94; Excel in Teach, 88, 93, 95, 98; Distinguished Teach Prof, 90; Chavalier, Palmes Academiques; Officier, Palmes Academiques, 91; Grand Off, Ordem da Infante Dom Henrique, 92; Outstand Civil Svc Medal, US Army; Medal of Merit, Ohio Univ; Mancado Prize, Soc of Mil Hist, 89. **MEMBERSHIPS** AHA; Soc Fr Hist Studies; Soc Mod Hist France; Soc Army Hist Res; Inst Napoleon; Portuguese Acad Hist; British Hist Soc Portugal; Soc Litteraire et Historique de la Brie; Int Napoleonic Soc, Napoleonic All; Soc Mil Hist **RESEARCH** Napoleon; the Peninsular Wars; French Revolution. **SELECTED PUBLICATIONS** Auth, "Napoleon and the Transformation of Warfare," in Selected Readings in Military History (Dubuque, Iowa, 95), 67-118; auth, "Napoleon in Iberia: The Twin Sieges of Ciudad odrigo and Almeida, 1810," Napoleonic Library Series (London, 95); coauth, Warfare in the Western World, D.C. Heath (Lexington, MA), 96; auth, "Andre Massena, Prince d'Essling, in the Age of Revolution," Napoleonic Scholarship, The Jour of the Int Napoleonic Soc 1 (97): 5-22; auth, "Napoleon's Great Competitor: Massena," 27th Consortium, Selected Papers, 1997 (Tallahassee, FL, 97); auth, "Massena in Italy: The Rise of a Marshal (1796-1800)," L'Europa Scopre Napoleone 1793-1804 (Alessandria, Italy, 99), 785-805; ed, Proceedings, Consortium on Revolutionary Europe, 74, 80, 86, 89, 94, 95, 96, 97, 98, 99, 00; auth, "Andre Massena in the Age of Revolution," Napoleonic Historical Review of Georgia (00); auth, "French Failure in the Peninsula - Logistics and Strategy: A Case Study," Selected Papers, 1999 (Talahassee, FL, 00). **CONTACT ADDRESS** Dept of History, Florida State Univ, 429 Bellamy Hall, Tallahassee, FL 32306. **EMAIL** dhorward@mailer.fsu.edu

HORWITZ, HENRY GLUCK
PERSONAL Born 08/02/1938, New York, NY, d, 1 child **DISCIPLINE** EARLY MODERN ENGLISH HISTORY; ENGLISH LEGAL HISTORY **EDUCATION** Haverford Col, BA, 59; Oxford Univ, DPhil(English hist), 63; J.D., Univ of Iowa, 82 **CAREER** From asst prof to assoc prof, 63-68, prof hist, Univ Iowa, 70-. **HONORS AND AWARDS** Nat Endowment for Humanities younger scholar award, 69; Guggenheim fel, 78; NEH Senior Fel, 00. **RESEARCH** Later seventeenth and eighteenth century English political and legal history. **SELECTED PUBLICATIONS** Auth, Revolution Politicks: The Career of Daniel Finch, 2nd Earl of Nottingham, Cambridge Univ, 68; ed, The Parliamentary Diary of Narcissus Luttrell, Clarendon, 72; auth, Parliament, Policy and Politics in the Reign of William III, Manchester Univ, 77; Chancery Equity Records and Proceedings 1600-1800, HMSO, 95; auth, Exchegver Equity Records and Proceedings 1649-1841, PRO, 01. **CONTACT ADDRESS** Dept of Hist, Univ of Iowa, 280 Schaeffer Hall, Iowa City, IA 52242-1409. **EMAIL** henry-horwitz@uiowa.edu

HOSTETLER, THEODORE J.
PERSONAL Born 02/07/1951, Canton, OH, m, 1975, 3 children **DISCIPLINE** LIBRARY SCIENCE, HISTORY **EDUCATION** Univ of IA, MA, 74; Bluffton Col, BA, 73 **CAREER** Libr Dir, 93-, Randolph-Macon Woman's Col; Head Access Svcs, 89-93, Univ of CA; Head Access Svcs, 79-89, Syracuse Univ; Head Circulation, 78-79 Univ of S FL **HONORS AND AWARDS** ALA, Univ of CA Achievement Awd, 92 **MEMBERSHIPS** VLA; ALA **RESEARCH** Reference; Undergraduate educ exp **SELECTED PUBLICATIONS** Auth, Introduction, 95; Coauth, Issue of Library Trends **CONTACT ADDRESS** Lipscomb Libr, Randolph-Macon Woman's Col, Lynchburg, VA 24503. **EMAIL** thostetler@rmwc.edu

HOULD, CLAUDETTE
PERSONAL Born 00/00/1942, Montreal, PQ, Canada **DISCIPLINE** ART HISTORY **EDUCATION** Univ Montreal, BA, 65, LL, 69, MA, 71; Ecole des Hautes Etudes en Sciences sociales (Paris), PhD, 90. **CAREER** Tchr, 60-71; cur, Montreal Mus Fine Arts, 75-76; Prof Art History, Univ Quebec Montreal, 76-, dir dept, 79-81, 83-89. **HONORS AND AWARDS** Prix d'excellence, Asn Musees can, 89; Medaille argent du Bicentenaire de la Revolution francaise, 89; Prix Publication, Asn Musees Que, 90. **MEMBERSHIPS** Soc d'histoire de l'art francais; Am Soc Eighteenth Century Stud; Conseil int des musee; Asn d'art des universites can. **SELECTED PUBLICATIONS** Auth, Repertoire des livres d'artistes au Quebec 1900-1982, 82; auth, Repertoire des livres d'artistes au Quebec 1981-90, 93; ed, Iconographie et image de la Revolution francaise, 90; co-ed, Code d'ethique de l'estampe originale, 82. **CONTACT ADDRESS** Art History Dept, Univ of Quebec, Montreal, Montreal, QC, Canada H3C 3J7. **EMAIL** hould.claudette@uqam.ca

HOUSER, CAROLINE
DISCIPLINE ART HISTORY **EDUCATION** Mills Col, BA; Harvard Univ, MA, PhD. **CAREER** Dir, Archaeol Prog. **RESEARCH** Golden Greek and Graeco-Roman statues. **SELECTED PUBLICATIONS** Auth, a catalogue Dionysos & His Circle to accompany an exhibition she curated at Harvard Univ; bk on, a monument in the Athenian Agora; 2 bk(s) on, the large bronze sculptures of ancient Greece. **CONTACT ADDRESS** Dept of Art, Smith Col, Hillyer Hall 318, Northampton, MA 01063. **EMAIL** chouser@sophia.smith.edu

HOVANEC, EVELYN ANN
PERSONAL Born 12/23/1937, Uniontown, PA **DISCIPLINE** ENGLISH, FOLKLORE, HISTORY AND LORE OF COAL MINERS **EDUCATION** Duquesne Univ, BEd, 62, MA, 66; Univ Pittsburgh, PhD, 73. **CAREER** Teacher social studies & English, Pittsburgh pub jr high schs, 62-66; ASSOC prof English, PA State Univ, Fayette, 66-85 and 92-00, dir Acad Aff, PA State, McKeesport 85-92. **HONORS AND AWARDS** PSF Awd for Pub Svc, 94; PSM Awd for Svc, 89; PSF Awd for Teach Excel, 97; PSF Min Stu Org Fac Awd, 98. **MEMBERSHIPS** Nat Coun Teachers English; Col English Asn; MLA. **RESEARCH** Mining literature and lore; mythology; Henry James. **SELECTED PUBLICATIONS** Auth, 3 poems, Earth & You, 72; coauth, Making the humanities human, WVa Rev Educ Res, fall 73; auth, Horses of the Sun (2 poems), In: Cathedral Poets II, Boxwood, 76; coauth, Patch/Work Voices: The Culture & Lore of a Mining People, Harry Hoffman, 77; auth, Coal culture & communities, Pa Oral Hist Newslett, 77; The Sea (poem), In: Strawberry Saxifrage, Nat Soc Publ Poets, 77; coauth, Making the Humanities Human, West VA Review of Educ Res 1, 46-47, 73; auth, A Mythological Approach to Tomorrow, Assoc of Teach Educ Review 3, 78; auth, Reader's Guide to Coal Mining Fiction and Selected Prose Narratives, Bul of Biblio, 41-57, Sept, 86; auth, Marie Belloc Lowndes, An Encyclopedia of British Women Writers, Garland, 297-298, 88. **CONTACT ADDRESS** Pennsylvania State Univ, Fayette, PO Box 519, Uniontown, PA 15401-0519. **EMAIL** eah2@psu.edu

HOVENDICK, KELLY B.
PERSONAL Born 12/18/1970, Hanover, PA, m, 1996, 1 child **DISCIPLINE** HISTORY; ANTHROPOLOGY; LIBRARY SCIENCE **EDUCATION** E NM Univ, BS, 94; Univ Az, MA, 99. **MEMBERSHIPS** Amer Libr Assoc **RESEARCH** Gender & libr sci; technophobia. **CONTACT ADDRESS** E.S. Bird Libr, Syracuse Univ, Reference Dept, Room 210, Syracuse, NY 13244-2010. **EMAIL** kbhovend@library.syr.edu

HOWARD, ANGELA
DISCIPLINE FAR EASTERN ART **EDUCATION** NYork Univ, PhD. **CAREER** Assoc prof, Rutgers, The State Univ NJ, Univ Col-Camden. **RESEARCH** Buddhist art of southwest China; Central Asian Buddhist art. **SELECTED PUBLICATIONS** Auth, The Imagery of the Cosmological Buddha, E.J. Brill, Leiden, 86; Tang Buddhist Sculpture of Sichuan: Unknown and Forgotten, The Mus of Far Eastern Antiq, Stockholm 60, 88; In Support of a New Chronology for the Kizil Mural Paintings, in Arch of Asian Art 44, 91; Buddhist Cave Sculpture of the Northern Qi Dynasty: Shaping a New Style, Formulating New Iconographies, in Arch of Asian Art 49, 96; Buddhist Monuments of Yunnan: Eclectic Art of a Frontier Kingdom, in Arts of the Song and Yuan, Hearn, M. and Smith, J. eds, The Metropolitan Mus of Art, NY, 96; The Dharani Pillar of Kunming, Tunnan. A Legacy of Esoteric Buddhism and Burial Rites of the Bai People in the Kingdom of Dali (937-1253), in Artibus Asiae 57, 1/2, 97. **CONTACT ADDRESS** Dept of Art Hist, Rutgers, The State Univ of New Jersey, New Brunswick, Voorhees Hall, 71 Hamilton St, New Brunswick, NJ 08903.

HOWARD, THOMAS A.
PERSONAL Born 11/20/1967, Tuscaloosa, AL, m, 1994, 1 child **DISCIPLINE** HISTORY **EDUCATION** Univ Alabama, BA, 90; Univ of VA, 96, PhD. **CAREER** Lilly fel and lect, Hist and Humanities, Valparaiso Univ, 97-. **HONORS AND AWARDS** DAAD grant, 94-95; AAR grant, 97. **MEMBERSHIPS** AHA, AAR, German Studies Asn. **RESEARCH** Modern Germany; European intellectual hist. **SELECTED PUBLICATIONS** Auth, Religion and Rise of Historicism, Cambridge, UP, forthcoming. **CONTACT ADDRESS** Dept of Hist, Gordon Col, Massachusetts, Wenham, MA 01984. **EMAIL** thoward@gordon.edu

HOWARD, THOMAS CARLTON
PERSONAL Born 07/27/1938, Miami, FL, m, 1962, 2 children **DISCIPLINE** BRISTISH & AFRICAN HISTORY **EDUCATION** Washington & Lee Univ, AB, 60; Fla State Univ, MA, 62, PhD(hist), 65. **CAREER** Asst prof, 66-77, Assoc Prof Hist, VA Polytech Inst & State Univ, 77-, Dir, NDEA Inst Advan Studies Hist, 67-68; vis prof African hist, Univ Wis-Madison, 69-70; Nat Endowment for Humanities fel, 72-73; Am Philos Soc fel, 72-73. **MEMBERSHIPS** AHA; Southern Asn Africanists; African Studies Asn; Royal African Soc; Southeastern Regional Sem African Studies. **RESEARCH** African history; English history; imperial history. **SELECTED PUBLICATIONS** **CONTACT ADDRESS** Dept of Hist, Virginia Polytech Inst and State Univ, Blacksburg, VA 24061.

HOWARTH, THOMAS
PERSONAL Born 05/01/1914, Wesham, England **DISCIPLINE** ARCHITECTURE, HISTORY **EDUCATION** Univ Glasgow, PhD, 49. **CAREER** Lectr, Glasgow Sch Archit & Glasgow Sch Art, 39-46; lectr to sr lectr, Univ Manchester, 46-58; dir, sch archit, 58-67, dean, 67-74, prof emer, Univ Toronto, 82-; campus planner, Glendon Col & adv to bd, York Univ, 60-87; campus planner, Laurentian Univ, 61-87. **HONORS AND AWARDS** Annual Bk Awd, Soc Archit Hist (US); Alice Davis Hitchcock Medal, 53; Rockefeller res scholar, 55-56; Killam sr res scholar, 78. **MEMBERSHIPS** Can Soc Decorative Arts; Royal Ont Mus; Charles Rennie Makintosh Soc Glasgow. **SELECTED PUBLICATIONS** Auth, Charles Rennie Mackintosh and the Modern Movement, 52, 77, 90; auth, RAIC College of Fellows, 62, 77; auth, Two Cultures Two Cities, 76; contribur, A History of Architecture on the Comparative Method, 61; contribur, Chambers Encyclopedia; contribur, Encyclopedia Britannica; contribur, Macmillan's Encyclopedia of Architecture. **CONTACT ADDRESS** Dept of Archit, Landscape and Design, Univ of Toronto, 230 College St, Toronto, ON, Canada M5T 1R2.

HOWE, DANIEL
PERSONAL Born 01/10/1937, Ogden, UT, m, 1961, 3 children **DISCIPLINE** HISTORY **EDUCATION** Harvard Col, AB, 59; Oxford Univ, MA, 62; Univ Calif at Berkeley, PhD, 66. **CAREER** Instr to Assoc Prof, Yale Univ, 66-73; Assoc Prof to Prof and Dept Chair, Univ Calif at Los Angeles, 73-87; Harmsworth Vis Prof, Univ Oxford, 89-90; Rhodes Prof, St Catherine's Col, 92-. **HONORS AND AWARDS** Brewer Prize, Am Soc of Church Hist, 69; Douglas Adair Prize, 87; Binkley-Stephenson Awd, Org of Am Hist, 91; Fel , Charles Warren Ctr for Studies in Am Hist, Harvard Univ, 70-71; Fel, NEH, 75-76; Fel, John Simon Guggenheim Found, 84-85; Res Fel, Henry E. Huntington Libr, 91-92, 94; Fel, Soc of Am Hist; Hewitt Lectr, Cath Univ of Am, 91; Carl Becker Lectr, Cornell Univ, 94; Wade Lectr, Ky Wesleyan Col, 99; Cardozo Lectr, Yale Univ, 01. **MEMBERSHIPS** AHA; OAH; SHEAR; OIEAHC; BrANCH. **RESEARCH** History of the United States before the Civil War; American Intellectual History; American Religious History. **SELECTED PUBLICATIONS** Auth, "The Evangelical Movement and Political Culture in the North during the Second Party System," J of Am Hist, 91; auth, "The Market Revolution and the Shaping of Identity in Whig-Jacksonian America," in The Market Revolution: Social Political, and Religious Expression, 1800-1880, (Univ Va Press, 96); auth, Making of the American Self: Jonathan Edwards to Abraham Lincoln, Harvard Univ Press, 97; auth, "Religion, Voluntarism, and Personal Identity in Antebellum America," in New Directions in American Religious History, (Oxford Univ Press, 97); auth, "The United State and the Revolutions of 1848," in The Revolutions in Europe, 1848-1849, (Oxford Univ Press, 00). **CONTACT ADDRESS** Dept Hist, Univ of California, Los Angeles, 6265 Bunche, PO Box 951473, Los Angeles, CA 90095-1473. **EMAIL** howe@history.ucla.edu

HOWE, JOHN MCDONALD
PERSONAL Born 03/13/1947, Alameda, CA, m, 1974, 3 children **DISCIPLINE** MEDIEVAL HISTORY **EDUCATION** Univ San Francisco, BA, 69; Univ Calif, Los Angeles, MA, 71, CPhil, 73, PhD, 79. **CAREER** Res asst, Ctr Medieval & Renaissance Studies, Univ Calif, Los Angeles, 71-72 & 76-77; teaching fel hist, Univ Calif, Los Angeles, 73-75; teacher social studies, Harvard School, spring 80; vis asst prof relig studies, Ariz State Univ, spring, 81; asst prof, 81-88, assoc prof, 88-98, Prof Hist, Tex Tech Univ, 98-. **HONORS AND AWARDS** TTU fac award, Creative Excellence Teaching, 88; TTU Pres Excellence Teaching, 95; TTU fac sen pres, 96-97. **MEMBERSHIPS** Medieval Acad Am AHA; Archeol Inst Am; Am Cath Hist Asn. **RESEARCH** Medieval hagiography; medieval mysticism; medieval technology. **SELECTED PUBLICATIONS** Auth, The Nobility's Reform of the Medieval Church, Am Hist Rev, 88; Church Reform and Social Change in Eleventh-Century Italy, 97. **CONTACT ADDRESS** Dept Hist, Texas Tech Univ, Lubbock, TX 79409-1013. **EMAIL** john.howe@ttu.edu

HOWE, JOHN R.
PERSONAL Born 09/23/1935, Dayton, OH, m, 1958, 2 children **DISCIPLINE** HISTORY **EDUCATION** Yale Univ, PhD, 62. **CAREER** Prof, Emeritus. **HONORS AND AWARDS** John Simon Huggenheim Fel; Fel, Charles Warner Center, Harvard Univ. **RESEARCH** American political history; early American history. **SELECTED PUBLICATIONS** Auth, The Changing Political Thought of John Adams, the Role of Ideology in the American Revolution, From the Revolution to Jackson. **CONTACT ADDRESS** History Dept, Univ of Minnesota, Twin Cities, 614 Social Sciences Tower, 267 19th Ave. S, Minneapolis, MN 55455. **EMAIL** howex002@tc.umn.edu

HOWELL, MARTHA
PERSONAL m, 1974, 2 children **DISCIPLINE** SOCIAL HISTORY OF NORTHERN EUROPE **EDUCATION** Georgetown Univ, BS, 66; Columbia Univ, PhD, 79. **CAREER** Ch dept; prof. **RESEARCH** Urban society, economy, culture and gender. **SELECTED PUBLICATIONS** Auth, Women, Production, and Patriarchy in Late Medieval Cities, 86; The Marriage Exchange:Property, Social Place and Gender in Cities of the UN Countries, 1300-1550 (1998). **CONTACT ADDRESS** Dept of Hist, Columbia Col, New York, Columbia University, Mail Code: 2512, New York, NY 10027-6902. **EMAIL** mch4@columbia.edu

HOWELL, SARAH MCCANLESS
PERSONAL Born 08/09/1930, Morristown, TN, d, 1954, 1 child **DISCIPLINE** UNITED STATES SOCIAL & INTELLECTUAL HISTORY **EDUCATION** Vanderbilt Univ, BA, 52, MAT, 54, MA, 67, PhD, 70. **CAREER** From asst prof to prof emerita, Mid Tenn State Univ, 70-. **HONORS AND AWARDS** Fac res grant, Mid Tenn State Univ, 72. **MEMBERSHIPS** Orgn Am Historians; Am Studies Asn. **RESEARCH** Social and intellectual changes of late 19th century United States; Tenn hist; intellectual conflicts of the 1920's. **SELECTED PUBLICATIONS** Auth, The editorials of Arthur S Colyar, Nashville prophet of the New South, Tenn Hist Quart, fall 68; Jesse Wills and the Conflicts of the 1920s, Tenn Hist Quart, spring 88; James I. Vance: Transformations in Religion and Society, 1922-32, Tenn Hist Quart, spring 90; articles on Vance, black leader Charles S. Johnson, and film director Delbert Mann in forth coming Tennessee Encyclopedia. **CONTACT ADDRESS** Dept of Hist, 700 Crescent Rd, Nashville, TN 37205-1918. **EMAIL** SallyMH@aol.com

HOXIE, FREDERICK E.
DISCIPLINE HISTORY **EDUCATION** Brandeis Univ, PhD, 77. **CAREER** Prof, Univ Ill Urbana Champaign, 98. **HONORS AND AWARDS** Pres, Am Soc Ethnohist. **RESEARCH** American Indian communities in the twentieth century. **SELECTED PUBLICATIONS** Auth, A Final Promise: The Campaign to Assimilate the Indians, 1880-1920, 84; Parading Through History: The Making of the Crow Nation in America, 1805-1935, 95; ed, Encyclopedia of North American Indians, 96; auth, Talking back to Civilization: Indian From the Progressive Era, 01; ed, "The American Indians," Time-Life; coed, "American Indian History," Camgridge Studie. **CONTACT ADDRESS** History Dept, Univ of Illinois, Urbana-Champaign, 810 S Wright, 446F Gregory Hall, MC 466, Urbana, IL 61801. **EMAIL** hoxie@uiuc.edu

HOXIE, RALPH GORDON
PERSONAL Born 03/18/1919, Waterloo, IA, m, 1997 **DISCIPLINE** HISTORY POLITICAL SCIENCE **EDUCATION** Univ Northern Iowa, BA, 40; Univ Wis, MA, 41; Columbia Univ, PhD, 50. **CAREER** Asst to provost, Columbia Univ, 48-49; asst prof hist, ed studies, Soc Sci Found & asst to chancellor, Univ Denver, 50-53; proj assoc, Bicentennial, Columbia Univ, 53-54; dean col lib arts & sci, Long Island Univ, 54-55, dean, C W Post Col, 55-60, provost, 60-62, pres col, 62-68; pres dep, Mitchel Col, 55-60, vpres univ, 62, chancellor, 64-68; Founder, Pres, Chm Emery, Ctr for Study of Presidency, 69-97: Vis lectr numerous univs & cols; consult col training & develop progs & educ policies; adv mil educ progs, US Air Force, Brig Gen, ret; mem adv coun, Robert A Taft Inst Govt; dir, Greater NY Coun Foreign Studies; secy, Comn Govt Rev Nassau County; co-chmn, Nassau-Suffolk Conf Christians & Jews; pub mem, US State Dept Selection Bd, 69. **HONORS AND AWARDS** Legion of Merit; Distinguished Serv Medal, City New York; Gold Medal, Paderewski Found; Korean Cult Medal; Gold Medal, Univ Northern Iowa, 65; LLD, Chungang Univ, Korea, 65; LHD, Gannon Univ, 88; Wesley Col, 89; Univ N Iowa, 90; Shepherd Col, 92; Teikyo Post Univ, 94; Long Island Univ, 95; Fitchburg State Col, 97; Alumni Achievement Awd, Columbia Univ, 97; lld, chungang univ, korea, 65; littd, d'youville col, 66. **MEMBERSHIPS** Am Soc Pub Admin; AHA; Acad Polit Sci; Am Polit Sci Asn. **RESEARCH** History of education; American presidency; American foreign policy. **SELECTED PUBLICATIONS** Ed, Frontiers for Freedon, 52; ed, Presidential Studies Quart, 1970-1995; The Presidency of the 1970's, 73; contrib, The Coattailless Landslide, Tex Western, 74; Power and the Presidency, Scribner's, 76; auth, Command Decision and the Presidency, Reader's Digest, 77; coauth, Organizing and Staffing the Presidency, 80; Presidency and Information Policy, 81; contribr, The Presidency and National Security Policy, 84; Encycl Britannica, World Book Encycl, Greenwood Encycl of American Institutions. **CONTACT ADDRESS** 208 E 75th St, New York, NY 10021. **EMAIL** rghoxie@aol.com

HOYT-O'CONNOR, PAUL E.
PERSONAL Born 04/01/1960, Brooklyn, NY, m, 1987, 1 child **DISCIPLINE** PHILOSOPHY; HISTORY **EDUCATION** Fordham Univ, BA, 92; Boston Col, PhD, 92. **CAREER** Asst prof, 94- , Spalding Univ. **MEMBERSHIPS** APA; Amer Catholic Philos Assn; Kentucky Philos Assn **RESEARCH** Social and political philos; Ethical theory. **SELECTED PUBLICATIONS** Auth, Lonegan and Bellah: Social Science in Public Philosophy, American Catholic Philosophy Quarterly, 95; auth, Progress Without End, International Philosophical Quarterly, 98. **CONTACT ADDRESS** Dept of Philos, Spalding Univ, 851 S 4th St, Louisville, KY 40203.

HOZESKI, BRUCE WILLIAM
PERSONAL Born 02/28/1941, Grand Rapids, MI, m, 1967, 1 child **DISCIPLINE** ENGLISH LITERATURE, HISTORY OF LANGUAGE, MEDIEVAL BRITISH LITERATURE **EDUCATION** Aquinas Col, BA, 64; Mich State Univ, MA, 66, Ph-D(medieval English lit), 69. **CAREER** Grad asst English, Mich State Univ, 64-69; instr, Lansing Community Col, 68-69; Prof English, Ball State Univ, 69-, Chair, University Senate, 96-, Dir Grad Programs in English, 98-01; Exec Secy and Treas of Lambda Iota Tau, The Nat Honor Soc for Lit, 90-; founder and president, Int Soc of Hildegard von Bingen Studies, 84-89, lifetime mem of exec coun; mem Bd of Dir, Christian Ministries of Delaware County, 97-03. **HONORS AND AWARDS** Outstanding Faculty Service Awd, 99-00. **MEMBERSHIPS** AAUP; MLA; Midwest Mod Lang Asn; NCTE; Medieval Acad Am. **RESEARCH** Medieval English literature; medieval drama; Hildegard of Bingen. **SELECTED PUBLICATIONS** Auth, Hildegard of Bingen's Ordo Virtutum: The earliest discovered liturgical morality play, Am Benedictine Rev, 75; A mathematical error in Jonathan Swift's A Modest Proposal, Am Notes & Queries, 76; The parallel patterns in Hrotsvitha of Gandersheim, a tenth century German playwright, and in Hildegard of Bingen, a twentieth century German playwright, Annuale Mediaevale, 78; The parallel patterns in Prudentia's Psychomachia and Hildegarde of Bingen's Ordo Virtutum, 14th Century, English Mystics Newslett, 82; Hildegard of Bingen's Scivias, 86; Hildegard von Bingen's Mystical Visions, 95; Hildegard of Bingen: The Book of the Rewards of Life: Liber Vitae Meritorum, 97; regular contribr to An Annotated Chaucer Bibliography - Studies in the Age of Chaucer, 91-present. **CONTACT ADDRESS** Dept of English, Ball State Univ, 2000 W University, Muncie, IN 47306-0460. **EMAIL** 00bwhozeski@bsuuc.edu

HSU, CHO-YUN
PERSONAL Born 07/10/1930, Amoy, China, m, 1969, 1 child **DISCIPLINE** CHINESE HISTORY **EDUCATION** Nat Taiwan Univ, BA, 53, MA, 56; Univ Chicago, PhD, 62. **CAREER** Assoc prof hist, Nat Taiwan Univ, 62-65, prof & chmn dept, 65-70; prof hist & sociol, Univ Pittsburgh, 70-, Univ, prof, 79-, asst res fel hist, Inst Hist & Philol, Acad Sinica, 56-62, assoc res fel, 62-67, res fel, 67-; Johns Burns Prof, Univ Hawaii, 96; Seman Prof, Duke Univ, 99; Univ Prof Emeritus, Univ Pittsburgh, 99-;Fulbright fel, Off Educ, Dept Health, Educ & Welfare, 77-78. **MEMBERSHIPS** AHA; Asn Asian Studies; Chinese Hist Soc; Bd Dir Chiang Ching-Kuo Found, 89-; China Times Found, 87-. **RESEARCH** Peasant life and rural economy; 19th century China; comparative social history. **SELECTED PUBLICATIONS** Auth, Ancient China in trasition, Stanford Univ, 65; auth, The farming technique in Chou China, 72, Bull Inst Hist & Philol; I-lan in the 19th century, Bull Inst Ethnol, 73; co-ed, History of ancient China series, Acad Sinica, 73-; auth, Urbanization and commercial development in the Chou period, Bull Inst Hist & Philol, 78; The founding of Eastern Chou, Bull Acad Sinica, 78; Han Agriculture, Univ Wash, 80; Western Chou Civilization, Yale Univ, 88. **CONTACT ADDRESS** Dept Hist, Univ of Pittsburgh, 3M38 Forbes Quad, Pittsburgh, PA 15260-0001. **EMAIL** hsusun@yahoo.com

HSU, GINGER CHENG-CHI
DISCIPLINE CHINESE ART AND CULTURE **EDUCATION** Univ Calif-Berkeley, PhD. **CAREER** Prof, Art Hist, Univ Calif, Riverside. **SELECTED PUBLICATIONS** Auth, "Anhui Merchant Culture and Patronage," Shadows of Mt Huang, 81; Merchant Patronage of the Eighteen Century Yangchow Painting, 89; Zheng Xie's Price List: Paintings as a Source of Income, Yangzhou, 91; The Drunken Demon Queller, 96; Incarnations of the Blossoming Plum, 96. **CONTACT ADDRESS** Dept of Art Hist, Univ of California, Riverside, 1156 Hinderaker Hall, Riverside, CA 92521-0209.

HSU, KYLIE
PERSONAL Born 07/03/1957, Taiwan **DISCIPLINE** APPLIED LINGUISTICS, CHINESE STUDIES **EDUCATION** Univ Mich, BA, 80; Cal State Univ, Northridge, MA, 94; Univ Calif at Los Angeles, PhD, 96. **CAREER** Instr, Univ Mich, 76-80; res, admin asst, Am GNC Corp, 80-86; exec vpres, 86-93; instr, Univ Calif, Los Angeles, 94-95; dir, pres asst, Pacific States Univ, 96-97; asst prof, Cal State Univ, LA, 97-; assoc cen dir, 99-. **HONORS AND AWARDS** Who's Who in World, Am, Am Women; 2000 Outstand Scholars; 1000 World Leaders of Influence; Inn Inst Awd; Pres Fel Res Grant; St Cal Fel; ALT Scholar; Bausch & Lomb Hon Sci Awd; Dept Edu Scholar; James B Angell Scholar; Martin Luther King Scholar; Nat

Deans List; Olive M Roosenraad Mem Scholar; Regents Alumni; Vieta Vogt Woodlock Scholar; WK Kellogg Found Scholar. **MEMBERSHIPS** AAAL; ACTFL; AAS; ROCLING; ALT; CIBER; CLIC; CLTA; IACL; IBA; IPA; LASSO; LSA; MLA; ROCMELLA; TESOL. **RESEARCH** Contextual analysis of written and spoken discourse; language and cultural socialization; heritage language pedagogy; intercultural communication. **SELECTED PUBLICATIONS** Auth, A Discourse Analysis of Temporal Markers in Written and Spoken Mandarin Chinese: The Interaction of Semantics, Syntax, and Pragmatics, Edwin Mellen Press (Lewiston, NY), 98; auth, "Business Chinese through the world wide web," Global Bus Lang 4 (99): 122-135; rev of, Heinle & Heinle's Complete Guide to TOEFL Test: Practice Tests by Bruce Rogers, CATESOL NL 30 (98): 20-22; auth, "Joint attention in a father-child-mother triad: A Chinese-American case study," Issues in Applied Ling 7 (96): 77-90; rev of "Culture and Language Learning in Higher Education," Issues in Applied Ling 6 (95): 112-116; rev of, "Second-Language Classroom Interaction; Questions and Answers in ESL Classes," Issues in Applied Ling 6 (95): 155-157; auth, "How do Immigrant Chinese parents in the U.S. help their children to acquire literacy," in Literacy Instruction in English for Bilingual Students (Northridge: Cal St Univ, 94): 112-127. **CONTACT ADDRESS** Dept Modern Languages, Lit, California State Univ, Los Angeles, 5151 State University Dr, Los Angeles, CA 90032-8112.

HUANG, RAY
PERSONAL Born 06/25/1918, Changsha, China, m, 1966, 3 children **DISCIPLINE** CHINESE HISTORY **EDUCATION** Univ Mich, BA, 54, MA, 57, PhD(hist), 64. **CAREER** Asst prof hist, Southern Ill Univ, 64-66; vis assoc prof, Columbia Univ, 66-67; assoc prof, State Univ NY, 67-71, prof, 71-80. Am Coun Learned Soc fel, 66 & 72; Harvard Univ res fel, 70-71; Nat Sci Found grant, 73; Guggenheim fel, 75. **MEMBERSHIPS** PEN **RESEARCH** Social-economic history of China; Ming Dynasty in China; History of science in China. **SELECTED PUBLICATIONS** Auth, Kai-Shek Chiang and His Diary as a Historical Source--Proposals for the Revision of Modern Chinese History, Chinese Studies Hist, Vol 0029, 96. **CONTACT ADDRESS** Dept of Hist, SUNY, New Paltz, New Paltz, NY 12561.

HUBBARD, NANCY
DISCIPLINE ARCHITECTURE **EDUCATION** Univ Ill, BA, 68; Northwestern Univ, PhD, 84. **CAREER** Lectr, Univ Chicago, 77-84; instr, Northeastern Ill Univ, 86-87; asst prof, 88-93; assoc prof, 93-. **HONORS AND AWARDS** Phalin/Field Enterprises Prize Res, 77. **MEMBERSHIPS** AIA; Soc Archit Hist; Col Asn; Asn Preservation Tech. **RESEARCH** Criticism; historic preservation; professional practice and legal issues in architecture. **SELECTED PUBLICATIONS** Auth, Dollars for Design: A Case Study of Design Review in a Facade Rebate Program, Univ Cinn, 92; Landscape in Civil War Cemeteries, 92. **CONTACT ADDRESS** Sch of Architecture and Urban Planning, Univ of Wisconsin, Milwaukee, PO Box 413, Milwaukee, WI 53201. **EMAIL** nanhub@uwm.edu

HUBBARD, WILLIAM H.
DISCIPLINE HISTORY **EDUCATION** Columbia Univ, PhD. **CAREER** Prof emer, Concordia Univ. **RESEARCH** Social and economic history of German-speaking Europe in the nineteenth century. **SELECTED PUBLICATIONS** Auth, Familiengeschichte, Munich, 83; Auf dem Weg zur Grossstadt, Graz 1857-1914, Vienna, 84; Sozial- und Wirtschaftsgeschichte Europas im 20 Jahrhundert, Munich, 86; editions in English, 89; Spanish, 92; Japanese, 92; ed, Making a Historical Culture: Norwegian Historiography, Oslo, 95. **CONTACT ADDRESS** Dept of Hist, Concordia Univ, Montreal, 1455 de Maisonneuve W, Montreal, QC, Canada H3G 1M8.

HUBBELL, JOHN THOMAS
PERSONAL Born 11/23/1934, Okay, OK, m, 1958, 2 children **DISCIPLINE** UNITED STATES HISTORY **EDUCATION** Northeastern State Col, BA, 59; Univ Okla, MA, 61; Univ Ill, PhD(hist), 69. **CAREER** Ed, Civil War Hist, Univ Iowa, 65-68; asst prof, 68-74, assoc prof hist, Kent State Univ, 74-, Ed, Civil War Hist, Kent State Univ, 68-99; prof Hist, Kent State Univ, 81-; dir, Kent State Univ Press, 85-. **HONORS AND AWARDS** Distinguished Teaching Awd, 80; Ohioanna Library Assoc, Awd for Editorial Excellence, 96. **MEMBERSHIPS** Southern Hist Asn. **RESEARCH** Civil War and Reconstruction. **SELECTED PUBLICATIONS** Auth, Three Georgia Unionists and the Compromise of 1850, Ga Hist Quart, 9/67; The desegregation of the University of Oklahoma, 1946-1950, J Negro Hist, 10/72; The Douglas Democrats and the Election of 1860, Mid-Am, 4/73; ed, Battles Lost and Won; Essays from Civil War History, Greenwood, 75; co-ed, Biographical Dictionary of the Union: Northern Leaders of the Civil War, Greenwood Press, 95. **CONTACT ADDRESS** Kent State Univ, PO Box 5190, Kent, OH 44242-0001. **EMAIL** jhubbell@kent.edu

HUBER, DONALD L.
PERSONAL Born 09/19/1940, Columbus, OH, m, 3 children **DISCIPLINE** CHURCH HISTORY **EDUCATION** Capital Univ, BA, 62; Evangel Lutheran Theol Sem, BD, 66; Duke Univ, PhD, 71; Univ Mich, MALS, 73. **CAREER** Instr, ELTS, 69-72; librarian, ELTS, 73-78; librarian, Trinity Lutheran sem, 78-91; sec fac, 78-80; act dean Acad Aff, 84-85; guest lectr, Luther Sem, Adelaide, Australia, 86-87; prof, Trinity Lutheran Sem, 88-; archiv, Trinity Lutheran Sem, 91-; Acad Dean, Trinity Lutheran Sem, 00-. **MEMBERSHIPS** Am Sic of Church Hist, Lutheran Hist Conf. **SELECTED PUBLICATIONS** Auth, The Rise and Fall of Lane Seminary: An Antislavery Episode, 95; auth, Teddy, Rah! Theodore Roosevelt and German-Americanism, Timeline, Ohio Hist Soc, 96; auth, Red, White, and Black: The Wyandot Mission at Upper Sandusky, Timeline XIII, 96; auth, Luther A. Gottwald, John H. Tietjen, Dictionary of Heresy Trials in Amer Christianity, Greenwood, 97; auth, The Prophet Joseph In Ohio, Timeline, 99; auth, funk and Wagnalls, Timeline, 99; World Lutheranism: a select Bibliography for English Readers, 00. **CONTACT ADDRESS** Hist, Theol, Soc Dept, Trinity Lutheran Sem, 2199 E Main St, Columbus, OH 43209-2334. **EMAIL** dhuber@trinity.capital.edu

HUDDLE, THOMAS S.
PERSONAL Born 01/20/1955, Bath, ME, m, 1998 **DISCIPLINE** HISTORY **EDUCATION** Univ Ill Urbana Champaign, BS, 77, AM, 83, MD, 85, PhD, 88. **CAREER** Internal med residency, Univ Wisc Madison, 86-89; fel, general internal med, Univ Penn, 89-91; asst prof, med, Univ Ala Birmingham, 91-98. **MEMBERSHIPS** Amer Asn Hist of Med; Hist Sci Soc; Amer Col Physicians. **RESEARCH** History of American medical education. **SELECTED PUBLICATIONS** Competition and Reform at the Medical Department of the University of Pennsylvania 1847-1877, Jour of the Hist of Med and Allied Sci, 51, 251-92, Jul, 96; rev, Medical Lives and Scientific Medicine at Michigan, 1891-1969, Univ Mich Press, Jour of General Internal Med, 11, 65-66, 96; Osler's Clinical Clerkship: Origins and Interpretations, Jour of the Hist of Med and Allied Sci, 49, 483-503, 94; rev, A History of Education in Public Health, Health that Mocks the Doctor's Rules, NY, Oxford Univ Press, Jour of General Internal Med, 9, 240, 94; rev, Beyond Flexner: Medical Education in the Twentieth Century, Jour of General Internal Med, 8, 287-88, 93; auth, Basic Science and the Undergraduate Medical Curriculum, Perspectives in Bio and Med, 36, 550-64, Summer, 93; auth, Looking Backward: The 1871 Reforms at Harvard Medical School Reconsidered, Bull of the Hist of Med, 65, 340-365, 91; rev, The Caring Physician: The Life of Dr. Francis W. Peabody, Boston, Harvard Univ Press, Jour of General Internal Med, 8, 287-88, 92; rev, In Sickness and in Wealth: American Hospitals in the Twentieth Century, NY, Basic Books, Jour of General Internal Med, 6, 271, 91; essay rev, Educating Competent and Humane Physicians, Ind Univ Press, Jour of General Internal Med, 7, 129-130, 91; auth, Science, Practice and the Reform of American Medical Education, Univ Ill, 88. **CONTACT ADDRESS** Med-Gen Med, Univ of Alabama, Birmingham, 1530 3rd Ave S, Birmingham, AL 35294-0001. **EMAIL** thuddle@uas.edu

HUDSON, BENJAMIN T.
PERSONAL Born Bethseda, MD, m, 2 children **DISCIPLINE** HISTORY **EDUCATION** Penn State Univ, BA; Univ Col Dublin, MA; Univ Oxford, PhD. **CAREER** Assoc Prof, Pa State Univ; Chemn, Medieval Studies, Pa State Univ. **HONORS AND AWARDS** Vis Fel, Inst for Arts and Humanistic Studies-Univ of Edinburgh; Sir John Rhys Prize in Celtic Oxford; Scholar, Dublin Inst for Advan Studies. **MEMBERSHIPS** Medieval Acad, Soc for Advan of Scand Studies, Celtic Studies Asn of N Am, hagiography Soc. **RESEARCH** Middle Ages. **SELECTED PUBLICATIONS** co-ed, Crossed Paths: the Celtic Dimension to the European Middle Ages, Univ Press of Am, 91; auth, Kings of Celtic Scotland, Greenwood Press (Wesport and London), 94; auth, "William the Conqueror and Ireland, " Irish Hist Studies 29 (94): 145-158; auth, "Kings and Church in early Scotland," Scottish Hist rev 73(94): 145-170; auth, "Knutr and Viking Dublin," Scand Studies 66(94): 319-335; auth, The Prophecy of Berchan, Greenwood Press (Wesport and London), 96; auth, "The Language of the Scottish Chronicle and its European Context," Scottish Gaelic Studies 18 (98): 57-73; auth, "The Scottish Chronicle," Scottish Hist Rev 77 (98): 129-161; auth, "Time is Short: the eschatology of the early Gaelic Church," in Last Things, ed. C. Bynum and P. Freedman (Univ of Penn, 00): 101-123; auth, "The Changing Economy of Irish Sea Province," in Britain and Ireland 900-1300, ed. Brendan Smith (Cambridge, 99): 39-66. **CONTACT ADDRESS** Dept Hist, Pennsylvania State Univ, Univ Park, 108 Weaver Bldg, University Park, PA 16802-5500. **EMAIL** bth1@psu.edu

HUDSON, HERMAN C.
PERSONAL Born 02/16/1923, m **DISCIPLINE** AFRICAN-AMERICAN STUDIES **EDUCATION** Univ MI, BA1945; Univ MI, MA 1946; Univ MI, PhD 1961. **CAREER** IN U, prof 78; Afro-Am Affairs, dean, minority achievers program, currently; Dept of AfroAm Studies IN U, chmn, 70-72; Dept of Applied Linguistics IN U, chmn, 69-70; IN U, asso prof, 68-69; Univ MI, ind reading, 67-68; TC Columbia Univ English Prgm in Afghanistan, asst prof, dir, 61-67; VA State Coll, consult, 60; NC Coll, asst prof, 59-60; Univ Puerto Rico, asst prof, 57-59; Univ MI, tchng fellow, 53-57; FL A&M U, instr, 46-51. **HONORS AND AWARDS** Publs; "The Black Studies Prgm Strategy & Structure" 1971; "From Paragraph to Theme" 1972; "From Paragraph to Essay" 1975; "How To Make It In Coll" 1977; "The Black Composer Speaks" 1978. **CONTACT ADDRESS** Minority Achievers Program, Indiana Univ, Bloomington, Memorial Hall West 003A, Bloomington, IN 47405.

HUDSON, LEONNE M.
PERSONAL Born 07/23/1954, Andrews, SC, m, 1991, 1 child **DISCIPLINE** HISTORY **EDUCATION** Voorhees Col, BA, 76; Kent St Univ, MA, 78, PhD, 90. **CAREER** Dir, proj Upward Bound, Williamsburg Tech Col, 79-81; assoc prof, Kent St Univ, 91- . **HONORS AND AWARDS** Phi Alpha Theta; Omicron Delta Kappa; Alpha Kappa Mu; Alpha Chi; Prof of Excellence Award, Kent State Univ, 95; Prof of Distinction Award, Kent State Univ, 96. **RESEARCH** Civil War, Old South, African American. **SELECTED PUBLICATIONS** Auth, The Odyssey of a Southerner: The Life and Time of Gustavus Woodson Smith, Mercer Univ Press, 98; A Confederate Victory at Grahamville: Fighting at Honey Hill, SC Hist Mag, 93; Gustavus W. Smith and the Battle of Seven Pines, Confederate Verteran Mag, 93; Valor at Wilson's Wharf, Civil War Times Illustrated, 98; Robert E. Lee, in Leaders of the American Civil War, Greenwood Press, 98. **CONTACT ADDRESS** Dept of Hist, Kent State Univ, PO Box 5190, Kent, OH 44242-0001. **EMAIL** lhudson@kent.edu

HUDSON, ROBERT
DISCIPLINE HISTORY AND PHILOSOPHY OF SCIENCE AND EPISTEMOLOGY **EDUCATION** W Ontario Univ, PhD. **CAREER** Dept Philos, Concordia Univ **RESEARCH** Contemporary experimental microbiology. **SELECTED PUBLICATIONS** Pub(s), in Synthese; Stud in Hist and Philos of Sci. **CONTACT ADDRESS** Dept of Philos, Concordia Univ, Montreal, 1455 de Maisonneuve W, Montreal, QC, Canada H3G 1M8. **EMAIL** hudsonr@alcor.concordia.ca

HUDSON, ROBERT VERNON
PERSONAL Born 08/29/1932, Indianapolis, IN, 2 children **DISCIPLINE** HISTORY OF MASS COMMUNICATION **EDUCATION** Ind Univ, Bloomington, BS, 54; Univ Ore, MS, 66; Univ Minn, Minneapolis, PhD(mass commun), 70. **CAREER** Sports writer, Indianapolis Stars, 51; City ed, News-Sentinel, Rochester, Ind, 54; staff corresp, United Press, Indianapolis, 54-56; reporter, Chicago Daily News, 56-57 & Fairchild Publ, Chicago, 57-58; serv exec, Pub Rels Bd, Chicago, 58-59; publ asst, Traffic Inst & Transp Ctr, Northwestern Univ, 60-61, news bur mgr, 61-63, info serv dir, 63; asst dir, News Bur, Ariz State Univ, 63-65; asst prof, 68-73, asst chmn, Sch Joun, 72-74, asst dean, Col Commun Arts, 74, assoc prof to prof Jour, Mich State Univ, 73-98, prof emeritus, 98-; freelance writer, 49-; staff writer, Traffic Dig & Rev, 60-61; TV prod-writer-anchorman, Phoenix, Ariz, 64-65; prof jour & head dept, Calif Polytech State Univ, San Luis Opispo, 75-76. **MEMBERSHIPS** Jack London Soc; Am Lit Asn. **RESEARCH** Biography; mass media history; The First Amendment; Literary Journalism; Will Irwin; Jack London. **SELECTED PUBLICATIONS** Coauth, Johnson's Information Strategy for Vietnam: An Evaluation, autumn 68, auth, Will Irwin's Pioneering Criticism of the Press, summer 70 & FoI Crusade in Perspective: Three Victories for the Press, spring 73, Jour Quart; Will Irwin's Crusade for the League of Nations, Jour Hist, autumn 75; The English roots of Benjamin Franklin's jour, Jour Hist, autumn 76; Non-indigenous Influences on Benjamin Franklin's Jour: Newsletters to Newspapers: Eighteenth-Century Jour, WVa Univ, 77; auth, The Writing Game: A Biography of Will Irwin, Iowa State Univ Press, 82; auth, Irwin, William Henry in: Biographical Dictionary of Internationalists, Greenwood, 83; auth, Will Irwin, in: American Newspaper Journalists, 1901-1925, Gale, 84; auth, Mass MediaL A Chronological Encyclopedia of Television, Radio, Motion Pictures, Magazines, Newspapers, and Books in the United States, Garland Publ, 87. **CONTACT ADDRESS** Michigan State Univ, 5420 Wild Oak Dr, East Lansing, MI 48823-7218.

HUEBNER, TIMOTHY
PERSONAL Born 10/13/1966, Orlando, FL, m, 1999 **DISCIPLINE** HISTORY **EDUCATION** Univ Miami, BA, 88; Univ Fla, MA, 90; PhD, 93. **CAREER** Vis asst prof, Univ Miami, 93-94; vis asst prof, Fla Int Univ, 94-95; asst prof, Rhodes Col, 95-. **HONORS AND AWARDS** Andrew Mellon Res Fel, 92; Archie Davis Fel, 93; NEH Summer Inst, Harvard Univ, 97. **MEMBERSHIPS** Orgn of Am Historians, Southern Hist Asn, Am Soc for Legal Hist, Tenn Hist Asn. **RESEARCH** U.S. South, Nineteenth-Century, Constitutional/Legal History. **SELECTED PUBLICATIONS** Auth, The Southern Judicial Tradition: State Judges and Sectional Distinctiveness, 1790-1890, Univ Ga Press (Athens, GA), 99. **CONTACT ADDRESS** Dept Hist, Rhodes Col, 2000 N Pkwy, Memphis, TN 38112-1624.

HUEL, RAY
DISCIPLINE HISTORY **EDUCATION** Univ Regina, BA; MA; Alberta Univ, PhD. **RESEARCH** Canadian and French Canadian history. **SELECTED PUBLICATIONS** Auth, pubs on moutaineering in the Canadian Rockies, French minorities in western Canada, anti Catholicism and Francophobia in Saskatchewan and the Metis and Oblate missionaries in western Canada. **CONTACT ADDRESS** Dept of History, Univ of Lethbridge, 4401 University Dr W, Lethbridge, AB, Canada T1K 3M4. **EMAIL** huel@uleth.ca

HUESTON, ROBERT FRANCIS
PERSONAL Born 08/25/1941, Darby, PA **DISCIPLINE** UNITED STATES HISTORY **EDUCATION** Col of the Holy Cross, AB, 63, Univ Notre Dame, MA, 65, PhD, 72. **CAREER** From instr to asst prof, 68-76, assoc prof hist, Univ Scranton, 76. **MEMBERSHIPS** Am Cath Hist Soc; Hist Soc PA; The Hist Soc. **RESEARCH** Hist of Am immigration; Am Cath Hist. **SELECTED PUBLICATIONS** Auth, Noah Webster's linguistic nationalism, Bull Hist Teacher's Club, Notre Dame Univ, 12/65-1/66; The Catholic Press and Nativism, 1840-1860, ser on Irish Americans, Arno, 76. **CONTACT ADDRESS** Dept of Hist, Univ of Scranton, Scranton, PA 18510-0000.

HUFBAUER, KARL G.
PERSONAL Born 07/07/1937, San Diego, CA, m, 1960, 3 children **DISCIPLINE** HISTORY **EDUCATION** Stanford Univ, BS, 59; Oxford Univ, Diploma, 61; Univ Calif, PhD, 70. **CAREER** Asst Prof to Prof Emeritus, Univ Calif, 66-; Contract Historian, NASA, 94-91; Director, Scandinavian Study Center, 97-99. **HONORS AND AWARDS** Eugene Emme Awd, Am Astronautical Soc, 91. **MEMBERSHIPS** Hist of Sci Soc. **RESEARCH** History of Astronomy & Astrophysics; 19th and 20th Centuries; Interdisciplinarity in the physical sciences. **SELECTED PUBLICATIONS** Auth, The Formation of the German Chemical Community, 1720-1795, U C Press, 82; auth, Exploring the Sun: Solar Science since Galileo, JHU Press, 91. **CONTACT ADDRESS** Dept Hist, Univ of California, Irvine, Irvine, CA 92697.

HUFF, CAROLYN BARBARA
PERSONAL Born 04/30/1943, Maryville, TN **DISCIPLINE** UNITED STATES HISTORY, BLACK STUDIES **EDUCATION** Maryville Col, BA, 65; Univ NC, Chapel Hill, MA, 66, PhD(hist), 69. **CAREER** Asst prof, 69-75, assoc prof, 75-80, prof hist, Lenoir Rhyne Col, 80-, chmn dept, 72-, Danforth Found fel, Atlanta Univ, 71-72. **HONORS AND AWARDS** Bost Distinguished Professor Awd. **MEMBERSHIPS** Orgn Am Historians. **RESEARCH** Nineteenth century United States social history; the abolitionist crusade; African history, the apartheid system in South Africa. **SELECTED PUBLICATIONS** Auth, The Black Experience in Catawba County, various reviews. **CONTACT ADDRESS** Dept of Hist, Lenoir-Rhyne Col, 743 6th St N E, Hickory, NC 28601-3976. **EMAIL** huff_c@LRC.edu

HUFF, PETER A.
PERSONAL Born 11/01/1958, Atlanta, GA, m, 1994, 1 child **DISCIPLINE** HISTORICAL THEOLOGY **EDUCATION** Mercer Univ, BA, 80; Southern Baptist Theol Seminary, MDiv, 84; St Louis Univ, PhD, 94. **CAREER** Asst Prof, Univ Puget Sound, 94-95; Asst Prof Theol, St. Anselm Col, 95-; chair, dept of theology, St. Anselm Col, 00-. **HONORS AND AWARDS** Phi Beta Kappa. **MEMBERSHIPS** Am Acad Relig; Am Soc Church Hist; Col Theol Soc. **RESEARCH** Religion in American culture; religion and literature; catholic studies. **SELECTED PUBLICATIONS** Co-ed, Knowledge and Belief in America: Enlightenment Traditions and Modern Religious Thought, Cambridge Univ Press, 95; auth, With the Body of This World: Allen Tate's Quarrel with Modern Gnosticism, Fides et Hist, 95; New Apologists in America's Conservative Catholic Subculture, Horizons, 96; Allen Tate and the Catholic Revival: Trace of the Fugitive Gods, Isaac Hecker Studies in Religion and American Culture, Paulist Press, 96; John Locke and the Prophecy of Quaker Women, Quaker Hist, 97. **CONTACT ADDRESS** Theology Dept, Saint Anselm Col, 100 Saint Anselm Dr., Manchester, NH 03102. **EMAIL** pehuff@anselm.edu

HUFFMAN, JAMES LAMAR
PERSONAL Born 10/17/1941, Plymouth, IN, w, 1964, 2 children **DISCIPLINE** MODERN JAPANESE HISTORY **EDUCATION** Ind Wesleyan Univ, Ind, AB, 63; Northwestern Univ, Evanston, MSJ, 64; Univ Mich, Ann Arbor, MA, 67, PhD, 72. **CAREER** Reporter, Minneapolis Tribune, 64-66; asst prof hist, Univ Nebr, Lincoln 72-75; asst prof, Marion Col, Ind 75-77; from Asst Prof to Assoc Prof, 77-87, H. Orth Hirt, prof hist, Wittenberg Univ, 87-; sr translr-ed consult, Japan Interpreter, 74-75; Am Advisory Comt, Japan Found, 95-. **HONORS AND AWARDS** Fulbright-Hayes res grant; Fulbright-Hayes res grant, 74-75; Tokyo, 83-84; Japan Found res grant, Tokyo, 94-95. **MEMBERSHIPS** Asn Asian Studies; Midwest Japan Sem (chmn, 78-81); Editorial Board, 99-. **RESEARCH** The press and modernization in 19th century Japan; comparative press history; Edward H House and early American images of Japan. **SELECTED PUBLICATIONS** Auth, Politics of the Meiji Press: Life of Fukuchi Genichiro, Univ Hawaii, 80; auth, "Freedom and the Press in Meiji-Taisho Japan," Transaction of the Asiatic Society of Japan, 84; auth, "Edward Howard House in the Service of Meiji Japan," Pacific Historical Review, 87; auth, "Japan's First Newpaper Law," American Asian Review, 89; Creating a Public: People and Press in Meiji Japan, Univ Hawaii, 97; auth, "Commercialization and the Changing World of the Mid-Meiji Press," New Directions in the Study of Meiji Japan, 97; ed, Modern Japan: An Encyclopedia of History, Culture, and Nationalism, Garland, 98; auth, "Edward H. House: Questions of Meaning and Influences," Japan Forum, 00. **CONTACT ADDRESS** Dept of Hist, Wittenberg Univ, PO Box 720, Springfield, OH 45501-0720. **EMAIL** jhuffman@wittenberg.edu

HUFFMAN, JAMES RICHARD
PERSONAL Born 05/08/1944, Liberal, KS, m, 1965, 2 children **DISCIPLINE** ENGLISH, AMERICAN STUDIES **EDUCATION** Harvard Col, BA, 66; MI State Univ, MA, 67; PhD, 70. **CAREER** Asst prof Eng & Am lit, 70-75, assoc prof Eng, 75-85, prof eng, State Univ NY Col, Fredonia, 85, Dir Am Studies, 74-, Assoc prof, UER Des Pays Anglophones, Univ Paris III, Sorbonne Nouvelle, Paris, 76-77. **MEMBERSHIPS** Am Cult Asn; Popular Cult Asn. **RESEARCH** Am lit; popular cult; psychology and cult. **SELECTED PUBLICATIONS** Auth, Jesus Christ Superstar: Popular art and unpopular criticism, J Popular Culture, fall 72; The cuckoo clocks in Kesey's Nest, Mod Lang Studies, spring 77; A psychological redefinition of Styron's Confessions of Nat Turner, Literary Rev, winter 81; A psychological critique of American culture, Am J Psychoanalysis, 82; Murray Krieger and the impasse in contextualist poetics, In: Murray Krieger and Contemporary Critical Theory (Bruce Henriksen, ed), Columbia Univ, 86; Coauth (with Julie L Hoffman), Sexism and cultural lag: The rise of the jailbait song, 1955-1985, J Popular Culture, fall 87; Young Man Johnson, The Am J of Psychoanalysis, 9/89; A Norreyan approach to American literature, In: Dionysius in Literature: Essays on Literary Madness (Branimis M Rieger, ed), Bowling Green Univ Popular Press, 94. **CONTACT ADDRESS** American Studies Dept., SUNY, Col at Fredonia, Fredonia, NY 14063. **EMAIL** james.huffman@fredonia.edu

HUGGARD, CHRIS
PERSONAL Born 05/15/1962, Muskegon, MI, m, 1988 **DISCIPLINE** HISTORY **EDUCATION** Univ Ark, BSEd, 84; MA, 87; Univ NM, PhD, 94. **CAREER** Assoc Prof, NW Ark Cmty Col, 95-. **MEMBERSHIPS** Am Soc of Environmental Hist; Am Hist Asn; Org of Am Hist; W Hist Asn; Mining Hist Asn. **RESEARCH** 20th Century Environmental History, Wilderness, Mining and the Environment. **SELECTED PUBLICATIONS** Auth, Forests Under Fire: A Century of Ecosystem Mismanagement in the Southwest, Univ AR Press, 01; Ed, Mining History Journal, 94-00. **CONTACT ADDRESS** Dept Soc & Beh Sci, Northwest Arkansas Comm Col, 1 Col Dr, Bentonville, AR 72712-5091. **EMAIL** chuggard@nwacc.cc.ar.us

HUGHES, ANDREW
PERSONAL Born 08/03/1937, London, England **DISCIPLINE** MUSIC, HISTORY **EDUCATION** BA, Bmus, MA, Dphil. **CAREER** Lectr, Queen's Univ (Belfast), 62-64; asst prof, Univ Ill, 64-67; assoc prof, Univ N Carolina, 67-69; prof, Univ Toronto, 69-. **HONORS AND AWARDS** Henry Hadow scholar, Oxford, 55; John Lowell Osgood Mem Prize, Oxford, 58; Guggenheim fel, 73-74; fel, Trinity Col, Univ Toronto, 80; Killam res fel, 93-95. **MEMBERSHIPS** Am Musicol Soc; Medieval Acad Am. **RESEARCH** Medieval liturgy, plainsong and other music, and liturgical manuscripts. **SELECTED PUBLICATIONS** Auth, Manuscript Accidentals: Ficta in Focus, 72; auth, A Bibliography of Medieval Music, 74, 2nd ed, 80; auth, Medieval Manuscripts for Mass and Office, 81, 86; auth, Style and Symbol: Medieval Music 800-1453, 89; auth, Late Medieval Liturgical Offices: Resources for Electronic Research: Texts, 94; auth, Late Medieval Liturgical Offices: Resources for Electronic Research: Sources and Chants, 96; ed, Fifteenth Century Liturgical Music, 68; co-ed, The Old Hall Manuscript, 69, 73. **CONTACT ADDRESS** Ctr Medieval Stud, Univ of Toronto, Toronto, ON, Canada M5S 1A1.

HUGHES, J. DONALD
PERSONAL Born 06/05/1932, Santa Monica, CA, m, 1964, 2 children **DISCIPLINE** HISTORY **EDUCATION** Univ Calif, LA, AB, 54; Boston Univ, STB, 57; PhD, 60. **CAREER** Asst prof, Calif W Univ, 61-66; prof, Pierce Col, Greece, 66-67; vis prof, Univ of Colo, 86-87, 90-91; asst prof to prof, Univ of Denver, 67-; Chair, 00-01. **HONORS AND AWARDS** Phi Beta Kappa; Alumni Fel, Bost Univ, 57; Phi Alpha Theta; Danforth Asn, 65085; Burlington N Fac Achievement Awd, Univ of Denver, 85; Charles A. Lindbergh Grant, 87; John Evans Prof, Univ of Denver, 94; Distinguished Serv Awd, Am Soc for Environ Hist, 00. **MEMBERSHIPS** Am Soc for Environ Hist; C.G. Jung Soc of Colo; Am Inst of Archaeol; Forest Hist Soc; World Histo Assoc; AHA; Assoc of Ancient Hist; Egyptian Studies Soc; Int Psychohistorical Assoc. **RESEARCH** World Environmental History, Ancient Environmental History, Sacred Groves. **SELECTED PUBLICATIONS** Auth, Pan's Travail: Environmental Problems of the Ancient Greeks and Romans, Johns Hopkins Univ Pr, (Baltimore), 94; auth, "Ecology and Development as Narrative Themes of World History", Environ Hist Rev, 19 (95): 1-16; auth, "The Effect of Knowledge of Indian Biota on Ecological Thought", Indian Jof Hist of Sci 30.1 (95): 1-12; auth, "The Hunters of Euboea: Mountain Folk in the Classical Mediterranean", Mountain Res and Develop 16.2 (96): 91-100; auth, "Francis of Assisi and the Diversity of Creation", Environ Ethics 18.3 (96): 311-320; auth, "Ancient Forests: The Idea of Forest Age in the Greek and Latin Classics", in Australia Ever-Changing Forests III: Proceedings of the Third Nat Conf on Australian Forest Hist, ed John Dargavel, Australian Nat Univ, (97): 3-10; coauth, "The Sacred Groves of South India: Ecology, Traditional Communities and Religious Change", Social Compass 44.3, (97): 413-427; auth, "Early Ecological Knowledge of India from Alexander and Aristotle to Arian", in Nature and the Orient: The Environ Hist of S and SE Asia, ed Richard H. Grove, Vinita Damodaran and Satpal Sangwan, Oxford Univ Pr, (Delhi, 98), 70-86; auth, "Environmental History - World", in A Global Encycl of Hist Writing, ed David R. Woolf, Garland Pub, (NY, 98), 288-291; ed, The Face of the Earth: Environment and World History, Sharpe (Armonk, NY), 00. **CONTACT ADDRESS** Dept Hist, Univ of Denver, 2020 S Race St, Denver, CO 80210-4711. **EMAIL** dhughes@du.edu

HUGHES, JUDITH MARKHAM
PERSONAL Born 02/20/1941, New York, NY, m, 1964, 1 child **DISCIPLINE** HISTORY **EDUCATION** Swarthmore Col, BA, 62; Harvard Univ, MA, 63, PhD(hist), 70; Clinical Assoc, San Diego Pschoanalytic Inst, 91-. **CAREER** Asst prof soc studies, Harvard Univ, 70-75; assoc prof hist, 75-84, prof hist, Univ Calif, San Diego, 84-. **HONORS AND AWARDS** Phi Beta kappa; Woodrow Wilson Fel, 62-63; Nat Endowment of the Humanities Fel, 74. **RESEARCH** History of psychoanalysis. **SELECTED PUBLICATIONS** Auth, To the Maginot Line: The Politics of French Military Preparation in the 1920's, Harvard Univ, 71; Emotion and High Politics: Personal Relations at the Summit in Late Nineteenth-Century Britain and Germany, Univ Calif Press, 83; Reshaping the Psychoanalytic Domain: The Work of Melanie Klein, W R D Fairbairn and D W Winnicott, Univ Calif Press, 89; From Freud's Consulting Room: The Unconscious in a Scientific Age, Harvard Univ Press, 94; Fruedian Analysts/Feminist Issues, Yale Univ Press, 99. **CONTACT ADDRESS** Dept of History, Univ of California, San Diego, 9500 Gilman Dr, La Jolla, CA 92093-0104. **EMAIL** jhughes@ucsd.edu

HUGHES, KEVIN L.
PERSONAL Born 11/12/1969, Baltimore, MD, m, 1995, 1 child **DISCIPLINE** HISTORY OF CHRISTIANITY **EDUCATION** Univ Chicago, PhD, 97. **CAREER** Asst Prof , theology and Religious Studies, Villanova Univ, 00-. **HONORS AND AWARDS** Phi Beta Kappa, 90; Pres Scholar, Villanova Univ, 87-91; Dist Stud Award (Relig Studies), Villanova Univ, 91; summa cum laude, Villanova Univ, 91; Valedictorian, Villanova Univ, 91; Century Fel, Univ Chicago, 91-95; jr fel, Inst for Advanced Stud of Relig, 95-96. **MEMBERSHIPS** Am Soc of Church Hist; AAR; Soc of Bibl Lit. **RESEARCH** Theology, religion, and culture of the Middle Ages; history of biblical exegesis; apocalypticism. **SELECTED PUBLICATIONS** Auth, Visionary Exegesis: Vision, Text and Interparetation in Hildegard's Scivias," Am Benedictine Rev 50:3, 99; coauth, Augustine and Liberal Education, London: Ashgate, 00; auth, The Arts Reputed Liberal: Augusine on the Perils of Liberal Education, " Augustine and Liberal education, London: Ashgate, 00; auth, Faith Handed On: Church History, Chicago: Loyola Univ Press, 2nd ed, (01), 1st print 2000. **CONTACT ADDRESS** Dept of Theology and Reoigius Studies, Villanova Univ, 800 Lancaster Ave, Villanova, PA 19085. **EMAIL** kevin.hughes@villanova.edu

HUGHES, RICHARD T.
PERSONAL Born 02/21/1943, Lubbock, TX, m, 1963, 1 child **DISCIPLINE** CHRISTIAN HISTORY **EDUCATION** Harding Univ, BA (Bible), 65; Abilene Christian Univ, MA (Christian history), 67; Univ IA, PhD (Christian history), 72. **CAREER** Asst prof, relig div, Pepperdine Univ, 71-76; assoc prof and prof, Dept of Religious Studies, Southwest MO State Univ, 77-82; prof, history dept, Abilene Christian Univ, 83-88; prof, relig div, 88-94, Distinguished Prof, Religion Division, Pepperdine Univ, 94-. **HONORS AND AWARDS** Outstanding Alumnus, Col of Arts and Sciences, Harding Univ, 86; Faculty Person of the Year, Seaver Col, Pepperdine Univ, 92-93; Distinguished Alumnus, Col of Biblical and Family Studies, Abilene Christian Univ, 96. **MEMBERSHIPS** Am Soc Church Hist; Am Academy Relig. **RESEARCH** 19th century Am relig, especially restorationist movements; religion and higher ed in the US. **SELECTED PUBLICATIONS** Co-auth with Leonard Allen, Illusions of Innocence, Chicago, 88; Ed, The Primitive Church in the Modern World, Univ IL Press, 95; auth, Reviving the Ancient Faith: The Story of Churches of Christ in America, Eerdmans, 96; co-ed with Wm. B. Adrian, Models for Christian Higher Education, Eerdmans, 97. **CONTACT ADDRESS** Religion Division, Pepperdine Univ, 24255 Pacific Coast Hwy, Malibu, CA 90263. **EMAIL** rhughes@pepperdine.edu

HUGHES, THOMAS PARKE
PERSONAL Born 09/13/1923, Richmond, VA, m, 1948, 3 children **DISCIPLINE** HISTORY OF SCIENCE **EDUCATION** Univ Va, BME, 47; MA, 50; PhD, 53. **CAREER** Instr eng English, Univ Va, 52-54; asst prof mod Europ hist, Sweet Briar Col, 54-56; from asst prof to assoc prof, Wash & Lee Univ, 56-63; assoc prof hist, Mass Inst Technol, 63-66; vis assoc prof, Johns Hopkins Univ, 66-69; prof hist technol, Inst Technol, Southern Methodist Univ, 69-73; chmn dept hist & sociol sci, 77-81, Prof to Prof Emer Hist of Technol, Univ Pa, 73-; adv ed, Technol & Cult, Soc Hist Technol, 60-; vis prof hist tech, Univ Wis, 63; vis scholar, Univ Ctr Va, 66; mem hist adv comt, Atomic Energy Comn, 73-77 & NASA, 73-79; mem, US Comt, Int Union for Hist & Philos of Sci, 74-, chmn, 75-77; chmn hist adv comn comt, NASA, 77-79; coun mem, Hist Sci Soc, 77-. **HONORS AND AWARDS** Fulbright res grant, Ger, 58-59; fel, Ctr Recent Am Hist, Johns Hopkins Univ, 66-68; Am Coun Learned Soc fel, Smithsonian Inst, 68; Tex Inst Lett

Bk Awd, 72; Dexter Prize, Soc Hist Technol, 72; Nat Sci Found grant, 73-74; Rockefeller Found humanities grant, 76; fel, Forschung Inst, Univ Bielefeld, 79. **MEMBERSHIPS** Hist Sci Soc; Soc Hist Technol. **RESEARCH** History of technology and science in the modern West; biography of inventors, engineers and entrepreneurs; history of invention and discovery. **SELECTED PUBLICATIONS** Ed, The Development of Western Technology, Macmillan, 64; Selections from Smiles' Lives of the Engineers, Mass Inst Technol, 66; auth, Technological Momentum .., Past & Present, 69; Elmer Sperry: Inventor and Engineer, Johns Hopkins Univ, 71; ENIAC: Invention of a Computer, Technikgeschichte, 6/75; ed, Changing Attitudes Toward American Technology, Harper, 75; auth, Thomas Edison: Professional Inventor, Sci Mus, London, 76; Electrification of America, Technol & Cult, Vol 20, 79; Ideologie fur Ingenieure, Technikgeschichte, Vol 48, 81. **CONTACT ADDRESS** Dept of Hist & Sociol of Sci, Univ of Pennsylvania, Philadelphia, PA 19174.

HUHTA, JAMES KENNETH
PERSONAL Born 08/27/1937, Ashtabula, OH, m, 1958, 2 children **DISCIPLINE** HISTORY, HISTORIC PRESERVATION **EDUCATION** Baldwin-Wallace Col, BA, 59; Univ NC, Chapel Hill, MA, 63, PhD(Am colonial & revolutionary hist), 65. **CAREER** Res asst hist, Univ NC, Chapel Hill, 60-62 & 63-65; asst ed, NC Colonial Rec Proj, 62-63; from asst prof to assoc prof, 65-73, asst vpres acad affairs, 76-79, Prof Hist & Dir Hist Preserv Prog, Middle Tenn State Univ, 73-90, Instr hist, NC State Univ, 63-65; bd trustees, Comt Preserv Services, 77-79; reviewer, Nat Heritage Trust Task Force, US Dept Interior, 77-78; nat bd mem, Preserv Action, 77-82, chmn nominating comt, 81, vpres southern region, 81-82; chmn, Nat Coun Preserv Educ, 78-81; dir, Mid-South Humanities Proj, Nat Endowment Humanities, 78-83; reviewer & panelist consult, Nat Endowment Humanities, 78-; mem bd adv, Ctr Study Southern Hist & Culture, Univ Mississippi, 79-, Boston/ Newton Local Hist Collaborative, 80-, Hiram Regional Studies Proj, 81- & Nat Trust Hist Preserv, 81-; chmn, Comt Historic Preserv, 81 & Comt Public Hist, 82; comt archit conserv, Nat Conserv Adv Coun, Smithsonian Inst, 81-. **MEMBERSHIPS** Orgn Am Historians, Soc Hist Archaeol, Asn Preserv Technol; Am Asn State & Local Hist, Soc Archit Historians, MTSU Ctr for His Preservation, 84; National Trust for Historic Preservation, 88-91, Am Asn for State and Local History, 86-90, ICOMOS, Ed Board, Public Historian, 89-92, Nat Heritage Area on the Civil War in Tennessee, 94-, National Council for Public History, Advisory Coun for His Preservation, 95, Alliance of Nat Heritage Areas, 96-. **RESEARCH** Historic preservation textbook; grant support alternatives for historic preservation; use of community cultural heritage resources for the teaching of history. **SELECTED PUBLICATIONS** Auth, Instructor's Manual for Teaching American History (2 vols), Ronald, 68; coed, The Regulators in North Carolina, 1759-1776: A Documentary History, NC State Dept Arch & Hist, 71; auth, Tennessee and the American Revolution Bicentennial, Tenn Hist Quart, 72; co-ed, Preservation: Toward an Ethnic for the 1980's, Preserv Press of the Nat Trust Hist Preserv, 80; contribr, Historic Preservation in Small Towns: A Manual of Practice, Am Asn State & Local Hist, 80. **CONTACT ADDRESS** Dept of Hist, Middle Tennessee State Univ, Murfreesboro, TN 37132-0001. **EMAIL** jhuhta@mtsu.edu

HULL, HENRY LANE
PERSONAL Born 10/05/1942, Washington, DC **DISCIPLINE** RUSSIAN & EUROPEAN HISTORY **EDUCATION** Georgetown Univ, BA, 64, MA, 69, PhD(Russ hist), 70. **CAREER** Intern hist, Smithsonian Inst, 65; lectr hist, Georgetown Univ, 67-70; Relm Found fel, 70-71; asst prof, 71-77, chmn Int Studies Comt, 75-76, Assoc Prof Hist, Univ Ala, Huntsville, 77-, Chmn Int Studies Comt, 81-, Mem acad adv coun, Charles Edison Mem Youth Fund, 72-; mem, Nat Captive Nations Comt, 79- **MEMBERSHIPS** Am Asn Advan Slavic Studies; Am Cath Hist Asn; Consortium on Revolutionary Europe; Southern Conf Slavic Studies. **RESEARCH** Soviet diplomacy of the 1920's and 1930's; Russian religious history; papal history. **SELECTED PUBLICATIONS** Auth, American relief administration, 75 & Catholic relief mission, John Baptist Cieplak, 77, Mod Encycl Russ & Soviet Hist; Decembrists revisited, Proc Consortium Revolutionary Europe, 77; Joseph E Davies, Mod Encycl Russ & Soviet Hist, 78; Mikhail Frunze, Ekaterina Furtseva, 79; Peace of Portsmouth, Mod Encycl Russ & Soviet Hist, 82. **CONTACT ADDRESS** Dept of Hist, Univ of Alabama, Huntsville, Huntsville, AL 35807.

HULL, N. E. H.
PERSONAL Born 08/27/1949, New York, NY, m, 1970, 2 children **DISCIPLINE** LAW, HISTORY **EDUCATION** Ohio State, Univ, BA, 74; Columbia Univ, PhD, 81; Univ of Georgia, JD, 85. **CAREER** Assoc prof, 87-93, prof, 93-97, distinguish prof of law and hist, 97-present, Rutgers Univ. **HONORS AND AWARDS** Scribes Book Awd for 1998; Erwin Surrency Prize of Amer Soc for Legal Hist, 99. **MEMBERSHIPS** ABA, New Jersey Bar Assn; AHA; ASLA; OAH **RESEARCH** Amer Legal and Jurisprudential Hist **SELECTED PUBLICATIONS** Auth, Vital Schools of Jurisprudence: Roscoe Pound, Wesley Newcomb Hohfeld, and the Promotion of an Academic Jurisprudential Agenda, 1910-1919, Journal of Legal Education, 95; The Romantic Realist: Art, Literature and the Enduring Legacy of Karl Llewellyn's Jurisprudence, 40 American Journal of Legal History, 96; Roscoe Pound & Karl Llewellyn: Searching for an American Jurisprudence, 97; Back to the Future of the Institute: William Draper Lewis's Vision of the ALI's Mission During Its First Twenty-Five Years and The Implications for the Institute's Seventy-Fifth Anniversary, 98. **CONTACT ADDRESS** Sch Law-Camden, Rutgers, The State Univ of New Jersey, Camden, 217 N. Fifth St., Camden, NJ 08102-1203. **EMAIL** nehhul@crab.rutgers.edu

HULL, RICHARD W.
PERSONAL Born 08/29/1940, Hackensack, NJ, 2 children **DISCIPLINE** AFRICAN HISTORY **EDUCATION** Rutgers Univ, BA, 62; Columbia Univ, MA, 64; prof cert African studies, 65; PhD, 68. **CAREER** Assoc prof to prof, African Hist, NY Univ, 68-; pres, African Consults, Inc. **MEMBERSHIPS** African Studies Asn. **RESEARCH** Race relations in Southern Africa; architecture in pre-colonial Africa. **SELECTED PUBLICATIONS** Auth, Munyakare: African Civilization before the Batuuree, Wiley, 72; auth, African Cities and Towns before the European Conquest, Norton, 77; auth, American Enterprise in South Africa, NYU Press, 90. **CONTACT ADDRESS** Dept of Hist, New York Univ, 53 Wash Sq S, New York, NY 10012. **EMAIL** rwh1@is.nyu.edu

HULSE, CLARK
PERSONAL Born 01/01/1947, Pittsburgh, PA, m, 1969, 2 children **DISCIPLINE** ENGLISH, ART HISTORY **EDUCATION** Williams Col, BA, 69; Claremont Grad Sch, MA, 70, PhD(English), 74. **CAREER** Instr, 72-74, asst prof, 74-80, assoc prof, 80-90, prof, English and Art Hist,, 90-, interim dean, graduate college, 99-, Univ Ill Chicago, Acting Dir Center for Renaissance Studies, Newberry Libr, 86, 95, Visiting prof Art History, Northwestern Univ, 92. **HONORS AND AWARDS** Nat Endowment Humanities Newberry Libr fel, 79; Guggenheim fel, 87; Pres, Spencer Society, 90; British Academy Exchange fel, 93. **MEMBERSHIPS** MLA; Renaissance Soc Am, College Art Assoc. **RESEARCH** Sixteenth-century literature and visual culture; Shakespeare. **SELECTED PUBLICATIONS** Auth, Metamorphic Verse: The Elizabethan Minor Epic, 81; Stella's Wit: Penelope Devereux as reader of Sidney's Sonnets, in Rewriting the Renassaince: The Discourses of Sexual Difference in Early Modern Europe, 86; Shakespear's Sonnets and the Art of the Face, John Donne Jour, Vol 5, 86; Spenser, Bacon and the Myth of Power, in The Historical Renaissance: New Essays on Literature and History, 88; The Significance of Titian's Pastoral Scene, J. Paul Getty Museum Jour, Vol 17, 89; The Rule of Art: Literature and Painting in the Renaissance, 90; Dead Man's Treasure: The Cult of Thomas More, in The Production of English Renaissance Culture, 94; Early Modern Visual Culture: Representation, Race and Empire, 2000; Tudor Aesthetics, in Cambridge Companion to English Literature 1500-1600, 2000. **CONTACT ADDRESS** Dept of English, Univ of Illinois, Chicago, 601 S. Morgan, Chicago, IL 60607. **EMAIL** chulse@uic.edu

HULSE, JAMES W.
PERSONAL Born 06/04/1930, Pioche, NV, m, 1962, 2 children **DISCIPLINE** MODERN EUROPEAN HISTORY **EDUCATION** Univ Nev, BA, 52, MA, 58; Stanford Univ, PhD, 62. **CAREER** Asst prof Hist, Cent Wash State Col, 61-62; from asst prof to assoc prof, 62-70, prof Hist, Univ Nev, Reno, 70-97; prof Emeritus, 97-; Danforth Assoc, 81-. **HONORS AND AWARDS** Grace A Griffen chemn hist, 92-98; Disting Fac Awd, 96. **MEMBERSHIPS** AHA; Am Asn Advan Slavic Studies. **RESEARCH** European socialism; modern Communism and Russia; intellectual history. **SELECTED PUBLICATIONS** Auth, The Forming of the Communist International, Stanford Univ, 64; The Nevada Adventure: A History, Univ Nev, 65, 5th ed, 81; Revolutionists in London, Oxford Univ, 70; The University of Nevada: A Centennial History, Univ Nev, 74; The Reputations of Socrates: The Afterlife of a Gadfly, Peter Lang, 95; The Silver State: Nevada's Heritage Reinterpreted, Univ Nev, 91, 98. **CONTACT ADDRESS** Dept of History, Univ of Nevada, Reno, Reno, NV 89557-0001. **EMAIL** Jhulse@unr.edu

HULTS, LINDA
DISCIPLINE RENAISSANCE AND BAROQUE ART **EDUCATION** Ind Univ, BA, 71; Univ NC, PhD, 78. **CAREER** Assoc prof. **SELECTED PUBLICATIONS** Auth, The Print in the Western World: An Introductory History, Univ Wis Press, 96. **CONTACT ADDRESS** Dept of Art, The Col of Wooster, Wooster, OH 44691.

HUME, RICHARD L.
PERSONAL Born 11/09/1939, Prescott, AZ, m, 1961, 1 child **DISCIPLINE** JEFFERSONIAN JACKSONIAN AMERICA, THE CIVIL WAR, RECONSTRUCTION **EDUCATION** Univ Wash, PhD, 69. **CAREER** Prof, Washington State Univ. **MEMBERSHIPS** Southern Hist Asn; Orgn Am Historians. **SELECTED PUBLICATIONS** Co-ed, God Made Man, Man Made the Slave: The Autobiography of George Teamoh, Mercer UP, 90; publ in, J Amer Hist; J Southern Hist & Virginia Mag Hist and Biog. **CONTACT ADDRESS** Dept of History, Washington State Univ, 301 Wilson Hall, Pullman, WA 99164-4030. **EMAIL** rhume@wsu.edu

HUMPHREYS, LEONARD A.
PERSONAL Born 09/09/1924, Troy, NY, m, 1948, 3 children **DISCIPLINE** HISTORY **EDUCATION** U.S.M.A, BS, 45; Stanford Univ MA, 60, PhD, 75. **CAREER** Prof emer, Univ Pacific, 61-. **HONORS AND AWARDS** Order of the Pacific, Univ Pacific. **RESEARCH** Japan, Military. **SELECTED PUBLICATIONS** Auth, The Way of the Heavenly Sword: The Japanese Army in the 1920s, Stanford. **CONTACT ADDRESS** Hist Dept, Univ of the Pacific, Stockton, Pacific Ave, PO Box 3601, Stockton, CA 95211.

HUMPHREYS, MARGARET
PERSONAL Born 12/06/1955, New Orleans, LA, m, 2000 **DISCIPLINE** HISTORY **EDUCATION** Univ Notre Dame, BA, 76; Harvard Univ, MA, 77, PhD, 83; Harvard Medical School, MD, 87. **CAREER** Lect, instr, Harvard Univ, 87-93; staff physician, Harvard Comm Health Plan, 90-93; assoc prof, history & medicine, Duke Univ, 93-. **HONORS AND AWARDS** Phi Beta Kappa, 76; Sigma Xi, 79. **MEMBERSHIPS** Am Asn Hist Med; Soc for Gen Internal Med; Am Hist Asn; Hist for Sci Soc. **RESEARCH** Hist med; US public health. **SELECTED PUBLICATIONS** Auth, "Kicking a Dying Dog: DDT and the Demise of Malaria in the American South, 1942-1952," Isis 87, 96; "Yellow Fever Since 1793: History and Historiography," in A Melancholy Scene of Devastation: The Public Response to the 1793 Philadelphia Yellow Fever Epidemic, 97; essays on "Chlorosis," "Dengue," "Malaria," "Tuberculosis," "Typhoid Fever," and "Yellow Fever," in Plague, Pox and Pestilence in History, 97; "Water Won't Run Uphill:The New Deal and Malaria Control in the American South, 1933-1940," Parassitologia 40, 98; biographies of "James Lawrence Cabell," "Jerome Cochran," Henry Rose Carter," "John Maynard Woodworth," and "Stanford Emerson Chaille," in American National Biography, 99; ed, Journal of the History of Medicine, 99. **CONTACT ADDRESS** Dept of History, Duke Univ, Box 90719, Durham, NC 27708. **EMAIL** meh@duke.edu

HUNDERT, EDWARD J.
PERSONAL Born 05/28/1940, New York, NY, m, 1967, 1 child **DISCIPLINE** MODERN & INTELLECTUAL HISTORY **EDUCATION** City Col New York, BA, 61; NY Univ, MA, 63; Univ Rochester, PhD(hist), 69. **CAREER** Asst hist, Univ Rochester, 63-65; asst prof, Univ Calgary, 66-68; asst prof, 68-71, Assoc Prof Hist, Univ BC, 71-, Can Coun res grants, 69-71, fel, 72-73 & leave fel, 78-79. **MEMBERSHIPS** AHA; Past & Present Soc, England; Am Philos Asn; Soc Study Hist Philos; Conf for Study of Polit Thought. **RESEARCH** Development of the work ethic; psychoanalysis and history; relationship of the social sciences and history. **SELECTED PUBLICATIONS** Auth, The Enlightenment's 'Fable': Bernard Manderville and the Discovery of Society, Cambridge, 95. **CONTACT ADDRESS** Dept of Hist, Univ of British Columbia, Vancouver, BC, Canada V6T 1W5. **EMAIL** hundert@home.com

HUNDLEY, NORRIS CECIL
PERSONAL Born 10/26/1935, Houston, TX, m, 1957, 2 children **DISCIPLINE** HISTORY **EDUCATION** Mt. San Antonio Col, AA, 56; Whittier Col, AB, 58; UCLA, PhD, 63. **CAREER** Instr, Univ of Houston, 63-64; Asst Prof of Am Hist, 64-69, Assoc Prof, 69-73, Prof, 73-, UCLA; chemn, exec comt, Inst of Am Cultures, 76-93; chemn, Univ prog on Mex, 81-94; acting dir, 89-90, dir, 90-94, Latin Am Center; mem, exec comt, Univ of Calif Consortium on Mex and the U.S., 81-86; mem, adv comt, Calif water atlas project, Calif Office Planning and Res, 77-79; Whitsett Lecturer, 00. **HONORS AND AWARDS** Awd of Merit, Calf Hist Soc, 79; Am Philos Soc grantee, 64 & 71; Ford Found Grantee, 68-69; Univ of Calif Water Resources grantee, 72, 91, 00; Acad Grantee, 72; Winter Awd, 73, 79; NEH Grantee, 83-89; Hewlett Found Grantee, 86-89; Univ of Calif Regenis Fac Fel in Humanities, 75; Guggenheim Fel, 78-79; Hist Soc of Southern Calif Fel, 96-. **MEMBERSHIPS** Am Hist Asn, Western Hist Asn, Orgn Am Hist, Pacific Coast Branch, 94-95. **SELECTED PUBLICATIONS** Managing ed, Pacific History Review, 68-97; auth, Water and the West: ed, The American Indian, 74; The Colorado River Compact and the Politics of Water in the American West, 75; ed, The Chicano, 75; ed, The Asian American, 76; co-ed, Golden State series, 78-; coauth, The California Water Atlas, 79; California: History of a Remarkable State, 82; auth, The Great Thirst: Californians and Water, 1770s-1990s, 92; auth, The Great Thrist: Californians and Water-A History, 00. **CONTACT ADDRESS** Dept of History, Univ of California, Los Angeles, Los Angeles, CA 90095. **EMAIL** hundley@history.ucla.edu

HUNGERFORD, CONSTANCE CAIN
DISCIPLINE ART HISTORY **EDUCATION** Wellesley Col, BA; Univ CA Berkeley, MA; PhD. **CAREER** Prof, Swarthmore Col. **RESEARCH** 19th century French painting. **SELECTED PUBLICATIONS** Numerous articles and essays on Jean-Louis-Ernest Meissonier (1815-1891), and contributions to the catalog for "Ernest Meissonier--Retrospective," an exhibition curated for the Musee des Beaux-Arts, Lyons, France; auth, Ernest Meissonier: Master in His Genre, Cambridge, 99. **CONTACT ADDRESS** Swarthmore Col, Swarthmore, PA 19081-1390. **EMAIL** chunger1@swarthmore.edu

HUNT, BRUCE J.
PERSONAL Born 06/23/1956, Walla Walla, WA, m, 1992, 2 children **DISCIPLINE** HISTORY OF SCIENCE **EDUCATION** Univ Wash, BA & BS, 79; Johns Hopkins Univ, PhD, 84. **CAREER** From asst prof to assoc prof, Univ Tex at Austin, 85-. **HONORS AND AWARDS** Teaching Excellence Awd, Univ Tex, 89; Vis Fel, Cambridge Univ Clare Hall, 89-90. **MEMBERSHIPS** Hist of Sci Soc, British Soc for the Hist of Sci. **RESEARCH** History of Physics, History of Technology. **SELECTED PUBLICATIONS** Auth, The Maxwelleans, Cornell Univ Press, 91. **CONTACT ADDRESS** History Dept, Univ of Texas, Austin, Campus Mail Code B7000, Austin, TX 78712. **EMAIL** bjhunt@mail.utexas.edu

HUNT, JAMES
PERSONAL Born Socorro, NM, m **DISCIPLINE** AMERICAN HISTORY, HISTORICAL, POLITICAL AND INTERNATIONAL STUDIES **EDUCATION** Univ Wash, BA, MA, PhD, 73. **CAREER** Tchg, Univ Wash; Core prog; Cent Amer Stud/Serv prog; prof, Whitworth Col, 73-. **HONORS AND AWARDS** Burlington Northern award for teaching excellence; grants, FIPSE, NEH, Wash Comm for Hum. **RESEARCH** Latin American Colonial History. **SELECTED PUBLICATIONS** Publ, articles on the faith journeys of Frederick Douglass and Jane Addams. **CONTACT ADDRESS** Dept of Hist, Whitworth Col, 300 West Hawthorne Rd, Mail Stop 1103, Spokane, WA 99251. **EMAIL** jhunt@whitworth.edu

HUNT, MICHAEL H.
PERSONAL Born 12/19/1942, Pearsall, TX, m **DISCIPLINE** HISTORY **EDUCATION** Georgetown Univ, BS, 65; Yale Univ, MA, 67; PhD, 71. **CAREER** Teaching Asst to Asst Prof, Yale Univ, 67-78; Assoc Prof, Colgate Univ, 78-80; Assoc Prof to Prof, Univ NCar, 80-. **HONORS AND AWARDS** Fel, UNC Inst for Arts and Humanities, 99; UNC W.N. Reynolds competitive leave, 98; Grant, Committee for Intl Relations Study, 92; Grant, Fairbank Center for E Asian Studies, 91; Fel, Woodrow Wilson Intl Center for Scholars, 90-91; Res Awd, Soc for Hist of Am For Relations, 89; NEH Grant, 85; Stuart L Bernath Memorial Book Awd, SHAFR, 84; NEH Fel, Yale Univ, 79-80; Stuart L Bernath Memorial Awd, SHAFR, 74; Phi Beta Kappa, 65. **MEMBERSHIPS** AHA; AAS; SHAFR; Org of Am Hist. **RESEARCH** Cold War Asia; The Vietnam War; The World since 1945. **SELECTED PUBLICATIONS** Auth, Frontier Defense and the Open Door: Manchuria in Chinese-American Relations, 1895-1911, Yale Univ Press, 73; auth, The Making of a Special Relationship: The United States and China to 1914, Columbia Univ Press, 83; auth, Ideology and US Foreign Policy, Yale Univ Press, 87; auth, "The Long Crisis in US Diplomatic History: Coming to Closure," Diplomatic History, (92): 115-140; auth, The Genesis of Chinese Communist Foreign Policy, Columbia Univ Press, 96; auth, Crises in US Foreign Policy: An International History Reader, Yale Univ Press, 96; auth, Lyndon Johnson's War: America's Cold War Crusade in Vietnam, 1945-1968, Hill and Wang, 96. **CONTACT ADDRESS** Dept Hist, Univ of No Carolina, Chapel Hill, Chapel Hill, NC 27599-3195. **EMAIL** mhhunt@email.unc.edu

HUNT, RICHARD ALLEN
PERSONAL Born Jersey City, NJ **DISCIPLINE** HISTORY **EDUCATION** Rutgers Univ, BA, 64; Univ Pa, MA, 65, PhD(hist), 73. **CAREER** Historian, US Mil Assistance Command, Vietnam, 70-71; Historian, US Army Ctr Mil Hist, 71-, Univ Pa teaching fel, 65-67. **MEMBERSHIPS** AHA; French Hist Studies; Soc Historians Am Foreign Rels; US Comn Miltary Hist. **RESEARCH** Vietnam war; American foreign policy; France. **SELECTED PUBLICATIONS CONTACT ADDRESS** United States Army Center of Mil Hist, Pulaski Bldg, Washington, DC 20314.

HUNT, RICHARD M.
PERSONAL Born 10/16/1926, Pittsburgh, PA, m, 1955, 3 children **DISCIPLINE** HISTORY, SOCIOLOGY **EDUCATION** Yale Univ, BA, 49; Columbia Univ, MA, 51; Harvard Univ, PhD, 60. **CAREER** Sr Lectr Social Studies & Univ Marshal, Harvard Univ, Vice Chair, Am Coun on Ger, New York; founding chair, Am Russian Young Artists Orch. **MEMBERSHIPS** AHA. **RESEARCH** Nazi German history; 20th century European intellectual history; contemporary sociological theory. **SELECTED PUBLICATIONS** Auth, Surviving the Swastika--Scientific-Research in Nazi Germany, J Interdisciplinary Hist, Vol 0026, 95; The Logic of Evil--The Social Origins of the Nazi Party, 1925-1933, J Interdisciplinary Hist, Vol 0028, 97. **CONTACT ADDRESS** Harvard Univ, Marshal's Office, Wadsworth Home, Cambridge, MA 02138. **EMAIL** marshal@harvard.edu

HUNT, WILLIAM RAYMOND
PERSONAL Born 08/01/1929, Seattle, WA, m, 1963, 2 children **DISCIPLINE** EARLY MODERN HISTORY **EDUCATION** Seattle Univ, BSS, 51; Univ Wash, LLB, 58, MA, 66, PhD(hist), 67. **CAREER** From asst prof to assoc prof, 67-74, Prpf Hist, Univ Alaska, Fairbanks, 74-, Head Dept, 71- **RESEARCH** Travel and exploration; crime and roguery; Arctic. **SELECTED PUBLICATIONS** Auth, Travelers and travel literature of the 19th century, Explorers J, 9/68. **CONTACT ADDRESS** Dept of Hist, Univ of Alaska, Fairbanks, Fairbanks, AK 99701.

HUNTER, GARY
PERSONAL Born 09/23/1946, Coatesville, PA, m, 1969, 3 children **DISCIPLINE** HISTORY **EDUCATION** Lincoln Univ, BA, 69; Atlanta Univ, MA, 70; Univ Mich, PhD, 77. **CAREER** Inst, Fisk Univ, 70-71; vis prof, Univ Calabar, 81-83; Rowan Univ, 74-. **HONORS AND AWARDS** NAACP Citizenship Awd; New Jersey Black Educators Awd for Teaching. **MEMBERSHIPS** Am Hist Asn; African Hist Asn. **RESEARCH** African American and African history. **SELECTED PUBLICATIONS** Auth, Neighborhoods of Color: African American Communities of South Jersey, 90. **CONTACT ADDRESS** Dept of History, Rowan Univ, Glassboro, NJ 08028. **EMAIL** hunter@rowan.edu

HUNTER, JOHN
DISCIPLINE RENAISSANCE ART HISTORY **EDUCATION** Wayne State Univ, BPh, 65, MA, 71; Univ Mich, MA, 77, PhD, 83. **CAREER** Edu cur, Detroit Inst Arts; assoc prof, ch; instr, 82-. **RESEARCH** Study of portraits of renaissance cardinals. **SELECTED PUBLICATIONS** Auth, monograph of the sixteenth-century Roman painter Girolamo Siciolante da Sermoneta (Girolamo Siciolante: Pittore da Sermoneta, Rome, 96; publ, articles on renaissance topics, The Art Bulletin, Romisches Jarhbuch fur Kunstgeschichte, Master Drawings, Storia dell'Arte. **CONTACT ADDRESS** Dept of Art, Cleveland State Univ, 83 E 24th St, Cleveland, OH 44115.

HUNTER, LESLIE G.
PERSONAL Born 09/26/1941, Meadville, PA, m, 1969, 4 children **DISCIPLINE** HISTORY **EDUCATION** Univ Ariz, BA, 64; MA, 66; PhD, 71. **CAREER** Asst prof, 69-74, assoc prof, 74-81, prof, 81-98, Regents prof, 98-, Texas A&M Univ-Kingsville; Chair dept hist, Tex A&M Univ-Kingsville, 86-90, 91-96. **HONORS AND AWARDS** Top Ten Teacher, 72; Bicentennial Comn Res Grant, 75; NEH Fel, 77; Alumni Asn Distinguished Teaching Prof, 90; Minnie Stevens Piper Prof, 97; Regents Prof, 98. **MEMBERSHIPS** SMRC, STHA, Tex Coun for Soc Studies, TFA, TACT. **RESEARCH** American frontier, 19th-Century United States, use of computers to research and teach history. **SELECTED PUBLICATIONS** Rev ed of History Computer Review, 88-; auth, Historic Kingsville, Texas, vol 1, Kingsville Hist Develop Board (Kingsville, TX), 94; auth, Historic Kingsville, Texas, vol 2, Kingsville Hist Develop Board (Kingsville, TX), 97; ed., Journal of South Texas, 98; Co-chair Ranching Heritage Symposium, 98; auth, Texas A&M University-Kingsville: College History Series, 00. **CONTACT ADDRESS** Dept Hist, Texas A&M Univ, Kingsville, 700 University Blvd, MSC #166, Kingsville, TX 78363-8202. **EMAIL** kflgh00@tamuk.edu

HUNTER, PHYLLIS A.
DISCIPLINE HISTORY, AMERICAN STUDIES **EDUCATION** Harvard Univ, BA, 65; So Flor, MA, 90; Will & Mary, PhD, 96. **CAREER** Asst Prof, Hist, NC at Greensboro. **MEMBERSHIPS** Am Antiquarian Soc **SELECTED PUBLICATIONS** Auth, Ship of Wealth: Massachusetts Merchants, Foreign Goods, and the Transformation of Anglo-America, 1670-1760; reviews in Va Mag Hist and Biog and Gender and Hist. **CONTACT ADDRESS** Hist Dept, Univ of No Carolina, Greensboro, 219 McIver, Greensboro, NC 27412-5001. **EMAIL** pwhunter@fagan.uncg.edu

HUNTING, MARY ANNE
PERSONAL Born 07/26/1957, Grand Rapids, MI, s **DISCIPLINE** HISTORY OF DECORATIVE ARTS **EDUCATION** BA, Vanderbilt Univ, MDA, Parsons School of Design. **CAREER** Asst ed, The Magazine Antiques, 90-94; freelance writer, antiques, 94-98. **MEMBERSHIPS** Show Catalogue. **RESEARCH** 19th century interiors and decorative arts. **CONTACT ADDRESS** Board of Managers, Eastside House Settlement, 337 Alexander Ave., Bronx, NY 10454-5250. **EMAIL** mhunt6994@aol.com

HUPCHICK, DENNIS P.
PERSONAL Born 09/03/1948, Monongahela, PA, m, 1976, 2 children **DISCIPLINE** HISTORY **EDUCATION** Univ Pittsburgh, Ba, 70, MA, 72, PhD, 83. **CAREER** ASSOC PROF, HIST, WILKES UNIV, 90-. **HONORS AND AWARDS** Fulbright res scholar Bulgaria, 89; Wilkes Univ Fac Lect award, 94; Int Res, Exch Bd Res Exch Scholar, Bulgaria, 76-77; NDFL-VI Lang gel, Univ Pittsburgh, 77-78, 75-76, 74-75; dir, wilkes univ e european, rus stud prog **MEMBERSHIPS** Bulgarian Studies Asn; Am Asn Adv Slavic Stud. **RESEARCH** Hist Bulgaria, Balkans, Ottoman Emp, Byzantine Emp, East Europe. **SELECTED PUBLICATIONS** Co-auth, A Concise Historical Atlas of Eastern Europe, St. Martin's Press, 96; auth, Conflict and Chaos in Eastern Europe, St. Martin's Press, 95; auth, Culture and History in Eastern Europe, St. Martin's Press, 94; auth, The Bulgarians in the Seventeenth Century: Slavic Orthodox Society under Ottoman Rule, McFarland and Cr., 93; co-ed, Hungary's Historical Legacies, Eastern European Monographs, 00; co-ed, Bulgaria, Past & Present: Transitions & Turning Points, vol 9 of Balkanistica, 96; ed, The Pen and the Sword, Eastern European Monographs, 88. **CONTACT ADDRESS** History Dept, Wilkes Univ, Wilkes-Barre, PA 18766. **EMAIL** dhupchi@wilkes.edu

HUPPERT, GEORGE
PERSONAL Born 02/02/1934, Tesin, Czechoslovakia, m, 1956, 5 children **DISCIPLINE** HISTORY **EDUCATION** Univ Calif Berkeley, PhD, 62. **CAREER** Prof, 65-, Univ Il Chicago. **HONORS AND AWARDS** Guggenheim Fel; NEH Fel, ACLS Fel; Bronze Medal, Col de France. **MEMBERSHIPS** Hist Soc; Soc for French Hist Stud. **RESEARCH** Renaissance France **SELECTED PUBLICATIONS** Auth, The Idea of Perfect History: Historical Erudition and Historical Philosophy in Renaissance France, Univ Il Press, 70; auth, Les Bourgeois Gentilshommes: An Essay on the Definition of Elitesin Renaissance France, Univ Chicago Press, 77; auth, Public Schools in Renaissance France, Univ Il Press, 84; auth, After the Black Death: A Social History of Early Modern Europe, Ind Univ Press, 98; auth, Il Mulino, Bologna, Italy, 90; auth, The Style of Paris: Renaissance Origins of the French Enlightenment, Ind Univ Press, 99. **CONTACT ADDRESS** 832 Seventeenth St, Wilmette, IL 60091. **EMAIL** huppert@uic.edu

HURLEY, ALFRED FRANCIS
PERSONAL Born 10/16/1928, Brooklyn, NY, m, 1953, 5 children **DISCIPLINE** MODERN HISTORY **EDUCATION** St John's Univ, NYork, BA, 50; Princeton Univ, MA, 58, PhD, 61. **CAREER** US Air Force, 50-80, retired Brig. Gen., USAF; from instr to asst prof, 58-62, res assoc, 62-63, actg head dept, 66-67, prof hist, US Air Force Acad, 66-80, head dept, 67-80, chmn humanities div, 77-80; vpres admin affairs, 80-82, Prof Hist, Univ of N Tex, 81-, Pres, N Tex State Univ, 82-, Chancellor, Tex Col of Osteopathic Medicine, 82-, dir, Am Comt Hist 2nd World War, 73-80; trustee, Am Mil Inst, 73-81; dir, US Comn Mil Hist, 75-80; fel, Eisenhower Inst Hist res, Smithsonian Inst, 76-77; trustee, Air Force Hist Fedn, 80-; Pres, Univ of N Tex and Chancellor, Tex Col of Osteopathic Medicine, 88; Pres, Univ of N Tex, Chancellor, Univ of N Tex Health Sci Ctr of Fort Worth, 93; Chancellor, Univ of N Tex System, 00. **HONORS AND AWARDS** Guggenheim fel, 71-72. **MEMBERSHIPS** AHA; Orgn Am Historians **RESEARCH** Modern military and diplomatic history. **SELECTED PUBLICATIONS** Auth, Carl Spaatz, and the Air War in Europe, Am Hist Rev, Vol 0100, 95. **CONTACT ADDRESS** 828 Skylark, Denton, TX 76201. **EMAIL** hurley@unt.edu

HURLEY, ANDREW J.
PERSONAL Born 06/19/1961, New York, NY **DISCIPLINE** HISTORY **EDUCATION** Johns Hopkins Univ, BA, MA, 83; Northwestern Univ, PhD, 88. **CAREER** Asst prof, Rhodes Col, 88-91; assoc prof, Univ Mo St. Louis, 91-. **RESEARCH** Urban history, environmental history, 20th century United States, the effects of consumer culture on the urban landscape in the post WWII era. **SELECTED PUBLICATIONS** Auth, Creating Ecological Wastelands: Oil Pollution in New York City, 1870-1900, J of Urban Hist, 94; Environmental Inequalities: Class, Race, and Industrial Pollution in Gary, Indiana, 1945-1980, Univ of NC Press, 95; Fiasco at Wagner Electric: Environmental Justice and Urban Geography, Environmental Hist, 97; From Hash House to Family Restaurant: The Transformation of the Diner and Post-War II Consumer Culture, J of Amer Hist, 97; ed, Common Fields: An Environmental History of St. Louis, Mo Hist Soc Press, 97; auth, Chasing the American Dream: A History of Diners, Bowling Alleys and Trailer Parks, Basic Bks, 01. **CONTACT ADDRESS** Dept of History, Univ of Missouri, St. Louis, 8001 Natural Bridge Rd, Saint Louis, MO 63121. **EMAIL** ahurley@umsl.edu

HURLEY, DAVID
DISCIPLINE MUSIC HISTORY AND OBOE **EDUCATION** Univ Mich, BA, 80; Univ Chicago, MA, PhD, 90, 91. **CAREER** Asst prof, 96- **RESEARCH** Seventeenth- and eighteenth-century music, G. Fl handel. **SELECTED PUBLICATIONS** Publ, articles and rev(s), The Jour of Musicol Res, The Mus Quart. **CONTACT ADDRESS** Dept of Mus, Pittsburg State Univ, 1701 S Broadway St, Pittsburg, KS 66762. **EMAIL** dhurley@pittstate.edu

HURLEY, FORREST JACK
PERSONAL Born 08/28/1940, Ft. Worth, TX, m, 1961, 3 children **DISCIPLINE** AMERICAN SOCIAL HISTORY, HISTORY OF PHOTOGRAPHY **EDUCATION** Austin Col, BA, 62; Tulane Univ, MA, 66, PhD(hist), 71. **CAREER** Instr, 66-71, asst prof, 71-76, assoc prof, 76-81, PROF HIST, MEMPHIS STATE UNIV, 81-; Humanist in residence, Int Mus Photog George Eastman House, Rochester, 74-75; vis prof, Austin Col, summer, 80. **HONORS AND AWARDS** Young Humanist Awd, Nat Endowment for the Humanities, 72, BiCentennial Awd, 74-75; Lyndhurst Prize, 90, for distinguished and original writing on photography and culture. **MEMBERSHIPS** Southern Hist Asn; Soc Hist Technol. **RESEARCH** History of photography as a social force in American culture; southern regional social and cultural history; history of technology. **SELECTED PUBLICATIONS** Auth, Portrait of a Decade, LA State Univ Press, 72; Russell Lee: Photographer, Morgan & Morgan, 78; ed, Industry and the Photographic Image, Dover, 80; coauth, Tennessee Traditional Singers, Univ TN Press, 80; co-ed, Southern Eye: Southern Mind--A Photographic Inquiry, Memphis Acad of the Arts, 81; Marion Post Wolcott: A Photographic Journey, Univ NM Press, 89. **CONTACT ADDRESS** Hist Dept, Univ of Memphis, 3706 Alumni St, Memphis, TN 38152-0001. **EMAIL** jhurley@cc.memphis.edu

HURTADO, A. L.
PERSONAL Born 10/19/1946, Sacramento, CA, m, 1980 **DISCIPLINE** HISTORY **EDUCATION** Calif State Univ, Sacramento, BA, 69, MA, 74; Univ Calif, Santa Barbara, PhD, 81. **CAREER** Indiana Univ-Purdue Univ, Indianapolis, 83-86; Ariz State Univ, 86-98; Univ Okla, 98-. **HONORS AND AWARDS** Billington Prize, Best Book in Frontier History, OAH, 89; Bolton Awd, Koontz Prize, Bolton-Kinnaird Awd, and Paladin Prize for scholarly articles. **MEMBERSHIPS** Am Hist Asn, Org of Am Hists, Western Hist Asn, Am Soc for Ethnohistory. **RESEARCH** American West, American Indians. **SELECTED PUBLICATIONS** Auth, Indian Survival on the California Frontier (88); co-ed, Major Problems in American Indian History; auth, Intimate Frontiers: Sex, Gender, and Culture in Old California (99). **CONTACT ADDRESS** Dept Hist, Univ of Oklahoma, 455 W Lindsey St, Norman, OK 73019-2000. **EMAIL** Ahurtado@ou.edu

HUSSAIN, AMIR
PERSONAL Born 10/31/1965, Llyalpur, Pakistan, w, 1989 **DISCIPLINE** ISLAMIC STUDIES **EDUCATION** Univ Col, Univ of Toronto, BSc, 87; MA, 90; PhD, 00. **CAREER** Asst prof, 97-; instr, McMaster Univ, 94-97, Univ of Waterloo, 94-97; Lectr Humanities, Univ of Toronto, 94-95; teaching asst, Univ of Toronto, 89-95. **HONORS AND AWARDS** Arbor Awd, Univ of Toronto, 98; doctoral fellowship, soc sci and humanities res coun of can 91-93; reuben wells leonard mem scholar, 83-87 **MEMBERSHIPS** Amer Acad of Religion; Can Soc for the Study of Religion; Middle East Studies Asn **RESEARCH** Islamic Studies; Religion and literature; Christianity. **SELECTED PUBLICATIONS** Coauth, Trying to Profess Religion Globally: North, South, East and West, 98; auth, The Concept of Law in Islam, 97; auth, Salman Rushdie and The Satanic Verses, 97; coauth, Islam, 94; **CONTACT ADDRESS** Dept of Religious Studies, California State Univ, Northridge, Northridge, CA 91330-8316.

HUSTON, JAMES ALVIN
PERSONAL Born 03/24/1918, Fairmount, IN, m, 1983, 2 children **DISCIPLINE** HISTORY **EDUCATION** Ind Univ, Ab, 39, AM, 40; NYork Univ, PhD, 47. **CAREER** From instr to prof hist, Purdue Univ, 46-72; Prof Hist & Dean, Lynchburg Col, 72-84; Dir, Honors Prog, Lynchburg Col, 89-92; King prof maritime hist, US Naval War Col, 59-60; NATO fel, 63-64; prof foreign affairs, Nat War Col, 66-67, dir Europ studies, 71-72. **HONORS AND AWARDS** Phi Beta Kappa; Dept of the Army Medal. **MEMBERSHIPS** AHA; Am Mil Inst; Inst Strategic Studies, Eng; London Inst World Affairs. **RESEARCH** National security policy; United States military history. **SELECTED PUBLICATIONS** Auth, The Sinews of War, 66; auth, One for All, 84; auth, Outposts and Allies, 88; auth, Logistics of Liberty, 91; auth, Guns and Butter, Powder and Rice; auth, Out of the Blue, 99; auth, Across the Face of France, 99; auth, Counterpoint; auth, Biography of a Battalion; auth, Combat History of the 134th Infantry. **CONTACT ADDRESS** 300 Langhorne Ln., Lynchburg, VA 24501. **EMAIL** hustonjam@aol.com

HUSTON, RICHARD P.
DISCIPLINE HISTORY **EDUCATION** Greenville Col, BA, 78; Asbury Sem, MDiv, 86; Univ Calif, Los Angeles, Phd, 93. **CAREER** Assoc prof, Aldersgate Col, 92-94; DEPT CHAIR, HIST, GREENVILLE COL, 94-. **CONTACT ADDRESS** 315 E College Ave, Greenville, IL 62246. **EMAIL** rhuston@greenville.edu

HUTCHESON, JOHN A., JR.
PERSONAL Born 07/18/1944, Winston-Salem, NC, m, 1967, 2 children **DISCIPLINE** HISTORY **EDUCATION** Univ NC at Chapel Hill, AB, 66; MA, 68; PhD, 73. **CAREER** Instr, Univ NC at Chapel Hill, 73-74; from asst prof to prof, Dalton Col, 74-. **MEMBERSHIPS** Am Hist Asn, Southern Hist Asn, Southern Confr on British Studies, Cariolinas Symposium on British Studies, World Hist Asn, Ga Asn of Historians. **RESEARCH** Modern Britain, especially Conservative Party since 1880 & Naval History since 1870. **SELECTED PUBLICATIONS** Auth, Leopold Mause and the National Review, 1893-1914, Garland, 89. **CONTACT ADDRESS** Div of Soc Sci, Dalton Col, 213 College Dr, Dalton, GA 30720-3745. **EMAIL** jhutcheson@em.daltonstate.edu

HUTCHISON, JANE CAMPBELL
PERSONAL Born 07/20/1932, Washington, DC **DISCIPLINE** ART HISTORY **EDUCATION** Western Md Col, BA, 54; Oberlin Col, MA, 58; Univ Wis, PhD, 64. **CAREER** From instr to assoc prof, 63-75, chmn dept, 77-80, Prof Art Hist, Univ Wis-Madison, 75-; Consult, NEH, 71-. **HONORS AND AWARDS** Elected Print Counc Am, 94; Trustee Alumni Awd, Western Md Col; Major grant, DAAD, ACLS, Fulbright. **MEMBERSHIPS** Col Art Asn Am; Mediaeval Aead Am; Mid-Am Col Art (secy, 69-70); AAUP; Midwest Art Hist Soc (treas, 81-83); Hist Netherlandish Art (treas, 94-99); Am Asc Netherlandis Studies. **RESEARCH** Fifteenth century German graphics; fifteenth century Flemish, Dutch and German portraiture; seventeenth century Flemish and Dutch low-genre p ainting. **SELECTED PUBLICATIONS** Auth, The housebook master and the folly of the wise man, Art Bull, 3/66; The Housebook Master, Collectors Ed, Van Nostrand, 72; 17th Century Dutch and Flemish Paintings from Private Collections, exhib catalogue, E lvehjem Art Ctr, 75; The housebook master and the Mainz Marienleben, Prin t Rev: A Tribute to Wolfgang Stechow, 2/76; Der vielgefeierte Durer, in Deutsche Feiern, Athenaion, Wiesbaden, 77; Early German Artists: Master E S-Schongauer, The Illustrated Bartsch 8, 80; Early German Artists: Wenzel von Qlmutz-Monogrammists, The Illustrated Bartsch 9, 81; Albrecht Durer : A Biography, Princeton Univ Press, 90; Albrecht Durer: Eine Biographie, Campus Verlag, 94; auth, Albrecht Durer: A Guide to Research, Garland/Taylor of Francis, 00. **CONTACT ADDRESS** Elvehjem Art Museum, Univ of Wisconsin, Madison, 2261 Regent, Saint Madison, WI 53705. **EMAIL** jchutchi@facstaff.wisc.edu

HUTCHISON, WILLIAM ROBERT
PERSONAL Born 05/21/1930, San Francisco, CA, m, 1952, 4 children **DISCIPLINE** AMERICAN HISTORY **EDUCATION** Hamilton Col, BA, 51; Oxford Univ, Fulbright Scholar, BA, 53, MA, 57; Yale Univ, PhD(hist), 56. **CAREER** Instr hist, Hunter Col, 56-58; from assoc prof to prof hist & Am studies, Am Univ, 58-68; ed consult, UNESCO, 62-69; vis assoc prof hist, Univ Wis, 63-64; Charles Warren prof Hist Relig in Am, Harvard Univ, 68-; mem Am studies adv comt, Am Coun Learned Soc, 68-71; mem, ed board, Am Quart, 70-73; Master Winthrop House, 74-79; mem, ed board, J of Ecclesiastical Hist, 84-91. **HONORS AND AWARDS** Egleston Prize, Yale Univ, 56; Brewer Prize, Am Soc Church Hist, 57; Guggenheim fel, 60-61; Am Philos Soc grant, 62, 65; res fel, Charles Warren Ctr, Harvard Univ, 66-67; Nat Rel Book Awd, 76; Fulbright sr res grant, Free Univ, Berlin, 76; Asn Theol Schs grants, 71, 79; Fulbright distinguished lectr Am hist, India, 81, Indonesia, 93; Fulbright Regional Reasearch grant, W Europe, 87; Olaus Petri Lecturer, Uppsala Univ, Sweden, 96; ma, harvard univ, 68. **MEMBERSHIPS** AHA; Am Studies Asn; Am Soc Church Hist (pres, 81); Orgn Am Historians; Unitarian-Universalist Hist Soc; Am Acad Relig. **RESEARCH** American intellectual history; American religious history; comparative cultural history. **SELECTED PUBLICATIONS** Auth, Transcendentalist Ministers: Church Reform in the New England Renaissance, Yale Univ, 59; Liberal Protestantism and the End of Innocence, Am Quart, summer 63; ed, American Protestant Thought: The Liberal Era, Harper, 68; contribr, UNESCO History of the Scientific and Cultural Development of Mankind, Laffont, Paris, Vol V, 69; auth, Cultural Strain and Protestant Liberalism, Am Hist Rev, 71; The Americanness of the Social Gospel: an Inquiry in Comparative History, Church Hist, 9/75; The Modernist Impulse in American Protestantism, Harvard Univ, 76; Errand to the World: American Protestant Thought and Foreign Missions, Univ of Chicago, 87; ed, Between the Times: The Travail of the Protestant Establishment in America, 1900-1960, Cambridge Univ, 89; co-ed with H. Lehman, Many are Chosen: Divine Election and Western Nationalism, Fortress, 94. **CONTACT ADDRESS** Harvard Univ, Widener N, Cambridge, MA 02138-1994. **EMAIL** whutchis@fas.harvard.edu

HUTTENBACH, HENRY R.
PERSONAL Born 10/15/1930, Worms, Germany, 5 children **DISCIPLINE** HISTORY **EDUCATION** Gonzaga Univ, BA, 51; Univ WA, PhD(hist), 61. **CAREER** Instr hist, Univ Seattle, 56-59; asst prof, E TX State Univ, 60-61; asst prof, LA State Univ, 61-66; from asst prof to assoc prof, 66-78, prof hist, City Col New York, 78-; US State Dept Cult Exchange Scholar, Moscow State Univ, 64-65 & 75. **MEMBERSHIPS** AHA; Am Asn Advan Slavic Studies; Asn Jewish Studies; Asn for the Study of Nationalities. **RESEARCH** 15th and 16th century Russian history; contemporary German Jewish history; genocide. **SELECTED PUBLICATIONS** Contribr, Russian Expansionism, Rutgers Univ Press, 72; The Emigration Book of Worms, Koblenz, 74; The Destruction of the Jewish Community of Worms, 1933-1945, New York, 81. **CONTACT ADDRESS** Dept Hist, City Col, CUNY, 160 Convent Ave, New York, NY 10031-9198.

HUTTON, JOHN
DISCIPLINE NINETEENTH-CENTURY EUROPEAN AND AMERICAN ART **EDUCATION** Northwestern Univ, PhD. **CAREER** Assoc prof, Truman State Univ. **SELECTED PUBLICATIONS** Pub(s), relationship of art and soc. **CONTACT ADDRESS** Dept of Art Hist, Trinity Univ, 715 Stadium Dr, San Antonio, TX 78212. **EMAIL** jhutton@trinity.edu

HUTTON, PATRICK H.
PERSONAL Born 03/16/1938, Trenton, NJ, m, 1991, 5 children **DISCIPLINE** MODERN EUROPEAN HISTORY **EDUCATION** Princeton Univ, AB, 60; Univ Wis, MA, 64, PhD, 69. **CAREER** From Instr to Assoc Prof, 68-82, Prof Hist, Univ Vt, 82-, Chair, Dept Hist, 92-99. **HONORS AND AWARDS** Kent fel, 65-68; Am Coun Learned Socs grant-in-aid, 74-75; UVM bicentennial fel, 88; Sr Fulbright research fel, France, 95-96. **MEMBERSHIPS** Soc Values Higher Educ; Soc Fr Hist Studies; Am Hist Asn; Fulbright Asn. **RESEARCH** French history; European intellectual history; historiography. **SELECTED PUBLICATIONS** Auth, The Cult of the Revolutionary Tradition, Univ Calif Press, 81; History as an Art of Memory, Univ Press New Eng, 93; ed, Historical Dictionary of the Third French Republic, 1870-1940, Greenwood Press, 86; co-ed, Technologies of the Self: A Seminar with Michael Foucault, Univ Mass Press, 88; ed, Vico for Historians, special issue of Historical Reflections XXII/3, 96. **CONTACT ADDRESS** Dept Hist, Univ of Vermont, Burlington, VT 05405-0164. **EMAIL** phutton@polyglot.uvm.edu

HUZAR, ELEANOR GOLTZ
PERSONAL Born 06/15/1922, St. Paul, MN, m, 1950 **DISCIPLINE** ANCIENT HISTORY **EDUCATION** Univ Minn, BA, 43; Cornell Univ, MA, 45, PhD(hist), 49. **CAREER** Instr hist, Stanford Univ, 48-50; from instr to asst prof classics, Univ Ill, 51-55; assoc prof hist, Southeastern Mo State Col, 55-59; assoc prof classics, Carleton Col, 59-60; from asst prof to assoc prof, 60-70, Prof Hist, Mich State Univ, 70-, Chmn Prog Class Studies, 64-. **MEMBERSHIPS** AHA; Am Philol Asn; Class Asn Mid W & S; Asn Ancient Historians; Archaeol Inst of Am. **RESEARCH** Relations between the Roman Republic and Egypt; the Fall of the Roman Republic; Greek athletics. **SELECTED PUBLICATIONS** Auth, Philhellenism and Imperialism--Ideological Aspects of the Roman Conquest of the Hellenistic World from the 2nd Macedonian War to the War Against Mithridates, Am Hist Rev, Vol 0097, 92. **CONTACT ADDRESS** Dept of Hist, Michigan State Univ, East Lansing, MI 48824.

HYATT, IRWIN T., JR.
DISCIPLINE HISTORY **EDUCATION** Emory Univ, BA, 57, MA, 58; Harvard Univ, PhD, 69. **CAREER** Assoc prof **RESEARCH** East Asian history, especially modern Chinese history and Sino-American relations. **SELECTED PUBLICATIONS** Auth, Ordered Lives Confess. **CONTACT ADDRESS** Dept History, Emory Univ, 1380 Oxford Rd NE, Atlanta, GA 30322-1950.

HYER, PAUL V.
PERSONAL Born 06/02/1926, Ogden, UT, m, 1948, 8 children **DISCIPLINE** ASIAN HISTORY, CULTURE **EDUCATION** Brigham Young Univ, BA, 51; Univ Calif, Berkeley, MA, 53, PhD, 60. **CAREER** Asst prof to prof, 58-66, Coordr, Asian Studies Prog, 61-67, Prof hist & Asian Studies, Brigham Young Univ, 66-; res, Toyo Bunko on Mongolia & China border lands, 63-64, Academia Sinica, 66-67; ed, Mongolia Soc Bull, 69; vis prof, Chengchi Univ, 71-72; vis prof, Inner Mongolia Univ, 81; vis prof, Foreign Affairs Col and Central Univ for Nationalities, Beijing, 97-99. **HONORS AND AWARDS** Maeser Awd for Excellence in Res. **MEMBERSHIPS** Asn of Asian Studies; Mongolia Soc; Int Altaistic Conf. **RESEARCH** Modern Mongolian & Tibetan history; Japanese expansion. **SELECTED PUBLICATIONS** Ed, Papers of the CIC Far Eastern Language Institute, Univ of Mich, 63; The Cultural Revolution in Inner Mongolia, China Quart, 68; articles in: Encycl Americana, 70; Hu Shih: The Diplomacy of Gentle Persuasions, The Diplomats in Crisis, Am Bibliog Ctr, 74; The Mongolian Nation Within the People's Republic of China, Case Studies on Human Rights and Fundamental Freedoms, The Hague, 75; The Chin-tan-tao Movement: A Chinese Revolt in Mongolia, Altaica, Helsinki, 77; Mongolian Stereotypes and Images, J Mongolian Studies, 78; Mongolia's Culture and Society, Praeger's Westview, 79. **CONTACT ADDRESS** Kennedy Center for Int Studies, Brigham Young Univ, HRCB, Provo, UT 84602-0002. **EMAIL** prhyer@byu.edu

HYERS, M. CONRAD
PERSONAL Born 07/31/1933, Philadelphia, PA, m, 1955, 3 children **DISCIPLINE** COMPARATIVE MYTHOLOGY & HISTORY OF RELIGIONS **EDUCATION** Carson-Newman Col, BA, 54; Eastern Theol Sem, BD, 58; Princeton Theol Sem, ThM, 59, PhD(phenomenol relig), 65. **CAREER** From instr to assoc prof hist relig, Beloit Col, 65-77; assoc prof, 77-81, Prof Hist Relig, Gustavus Adolphus Col, 81-97, Prof Emer, 97-. **HONORS AND AWARDS** Humanities develop grant, 69; Assoc Col Midwest non-Western studies fel, East-West Ctr, 70; Nat Found Humanities fel, 70-71; Fund Studies Great Relig fel, 71; Nat Found Humanities res fel, 75-76. **MEMBERSHIPS** Am Acad Relig **RESEARCH** A phenomenological study of the mythological motifs of Paradise Lost, fall and degeneration; a phenomenological study of the nature and function of comedy and humor in relation to the sacred; interfaith relations. **SELECTED PUBLICATIONS** Auth, Holy Laughter: Essays on Religion in the Comic Perspective, Seabury, 69; The Dialectic of the Sacred and the Comic, Cross Currents, winter 69; The Ancient Ch'an Master as Clown Figure and Comic Midwife, Philos East & West, winter, 69-70; The Comic Perspective in Zen Literature and Art, Eastern Buddhist, 72; Zen and the Comic Spirit, Rider, London, 73; The Chickadees: A Contemporary Zen Fable, Westminster, 74; The Comic Vision and the Christian Faith, Pilgrim, 81; The Meaning of Creation: Genesis and Modern Science, John Knox, 84; And God Created Laughter, The Bible as Divine Comedy, John Knox, 86; Once-Born, Twice-Born Zen, The Soto and Rinzai Schools of Japan, Hollowbrook, 89; The Laughing Buddha, Hollowbrook, 90; The Spirituality of Comedy, Comic Heroism in a Tragic World, Transaction Publ, 96. **CONTACT ADDRESS** 2162 Harbor View Drive, Dunedin, FL 34698.

HYMAN, HAROLD MELVIN
PERSONAL Born 07/24/1924, New York, NY, m, 1946, 3 children **DISCIPLINE** UNITED STATES HISTORY **EDUCATION** Univ Calif, BA, 48; Columbia Univ, MA, 50, PhD, 52. **CAREER** Asst prof hist, Earlham Col, 52-55; vis asst prof, Univ Calif, Los Angeles, 55-56, from assoc prof to prof, 57-63; prof, Univ Ill, 63-68; William Hobby Prof Am Hist, Rice Univ, 68-, Fund for Repub fel, 56; assoc prof, Ariz State Univ, 56-57; Soc Sci Res Coun res award, 59; Nat Endowment for Humanities sr fel hist & law, 70-71; juror, Pulitzer Prize Selection Jury, 72 & 77; Fulbright sr lectr, Univ Tokyo & Keio Univ, 73; Meyer vis distinguished prof, NY Univ Sch Law, 82- **HONORS AND AWARDS** Beveridge Awd, AHA, 52; Hillman Awd, 59. **MEMBERSHIPS** AHA Orgn Am Historians. **RESEARCH** Civil War, legal and constitutional histories; legal history of cities; civil-military relationships. **SELECTED PUBLICATIONS** Coauth, Stanton: The Life and Times of Lincoln's Secretary of War, New York: Alfred A Knopf, 62, History Book Club, 62, reprinted Greenwood Press, 81; auth, Soldiers and Spruce: Origins of the Loyal Legion of Loggers and Lumbermen: The Army's Labor Union of World War I, Institute of Industrial Relations: University of California Press, 63; auth, A More Perfect Union: The Impact of the Civil War and Reconstruction on the Constitution, New York: Knopft, 73, Sentry edition 83, 75, reprinted, Civil War Times Illustrated, 73; auth, Union and Confidence: The 1860's , New York, Crowell, 76; coauth, Equal Justice Under Law: Constitutional History, 1833-1880, New York, Harper & Row, 82, " New American Nation" series, 83; auth, Quiet Past and Stormy Present? War Powers In American History, American Hist Assoc, 86; auth, American Singularity: The 1787 Northwest Ordinance, the 1862 Homestead-Morrill Acts, and the 1944 GI Bill, (the 1985 Richard B. Russell Lectures at the Univ of Georgia, Univ of Georgia Press, 86; auth, The Reconstruction Justice of Salmon P Chase, Ret Turner and Texas v White Lawerence, Kans, Univ Press of Kansas, 97; auth, Craftsmanship and Character: A History of Houston's Vinson & Elkins Law Firm, 1917-1990s, Athens, GA, The University of Georgia Press, 98. **CONTACT ADDRESS** Dept of Hist, Rice Univ, Houston, TX 77001. **EMAIL** hyman@rice.edu

HYSER, RAYMOND M.
PERSONAL Born 01/31/1955, Akron, OH, m, 1990, 3 children **DISCIPLINE** HISTORY **EDUCATION** Ga Southern Col, BS, 77; Ga Southern Col, MA, 79; Fla State Univ, PhD, 83. **CAREER** Instr, Ga Southern Col, 79-80; From Asst Prof to Prof, James Madison Univ, 83-. **HONORS AND AWARDS** Outstanding Book Awd, 91. **MEMBERSHIPS** VSHT, OAH, SHA, SHGAPE. **RESEARCH** American business history, Gilded Age, Progressive Era. **SELECTED PUBLICATIONS** Coauth, "'A Crooked Death': Coatesville Pennsylvania and the Lynching of Zachariah Walker," Pa Hist 54 (87): 85-102; auth, "Frank Armstrong 1871-1954," Dict of Va Biog (Richmond: Va St Libr and Archives, 91); coauth, "The Industrial Age 1876-1919," A Guide to the Hist of Pa (Westport, CT: Greenwood Pr, 93); coauth, "Assessment with a Human Face: Developing a Meaningful System of Program Assessment," OAH Newsletter 26 (98): 8-9; auth, "Is a 3 Really a C?: The Reliability of the Advanced Placement United States History Test for College Credit," The Hist Teacher 32 (99): 223-236; coauth, "Voices of the American Past: Documents in United states History, Second Edition," Two Vols (Ft Worth, TX: Harcourt Col Publ, forthcoming). **CONTACT ADDRESS** Dept Hist, James Madison Univ, 800 S Main St, Harrisonburg, VA 22807-0001.

I

IACOVETTA, FRANCA
PERSONAL Born 09/14/1957, Toronto, ON, Canada **DISCIPLINE** CANADIAN HISTORY **EDUCATION** York Univ, BA, 80, MA, 81, PhD, 88. **CAREER** Postdoctoral fel, Univ Guelph, 88-89; Canada res fel, SSHRCC, 89-90; prof Canadian Hist, Univ Toronto, 90-. **HONORS AND AWARDS** Hilda Neatby Prize, 86; Univ Toronto Jr Connaught Res fel, 91; Floyd Chalmers Awd Ont hist, 92; Toronto Hist Bd Awd Merit, 92. **MEMBERSHIPS** Can Hist Asn. **RESEARCH** Comparative migration and Comparatie gender hist; women's and gender hist, immigrants and minorities, working-class hist and ethnic left, moral/sexual regulation and juvenile delinquency, and diaspora studies. **SELECTED PUBLICATIONS** Auth, Such Hardworking People, 92; co-ed, Gender Conflicts, 92; co-ed, Social History of Canada (ser), 92-94; co-ed, Studies in Gender and History (ser), 94-; co-ed, Teaching Women's History, 95; co-ed, Themes in Social History (ser), 96-; chief ed, A Nation of Immigrants: Women, Workers & Communities in Canadian History 1840s-1960s, 97; auth, On the case: Explorations in Social History; auth, Becoming a Historian; auth, Enemies within: Italian and Other Wartime Internees in canada and Beyond; auth, Making Model Citizens in Cold War Canada. **CONTACT ADDRESS** Dept of History, Univ of Toronto, Sidney Smith Hall, 100 St George St, Rm 2074, Toronto, ON, Canada M5S 3G3. **EMAIL** iacovetta@banks.scar.utoronto.ca

IGGERS, GEORG G.
PERSONAL Born 12/07/1926, Hamburg, Germany, m, 1948, 3 children **DISCIPLINE** HISTORY **EDUCATION** Univ Richmond, BA, 44; Univ Chicago, AM, 45; PhD, 51. **CAREER** Instr, Univ Akron, 48-50; assoc prof, Philander Smith Col, 57-63; assoc prof, Dillard Univ, 63-65; assoc prof, Roosevelt Univ, 65; prof to prof emeritus, 65-. **HONORS AND AWARDS** Guggenheim; NEH; Fulbright; Woodrow Wilson Centre Fel; GDR, 90-92; Alexander von Humboldt Res Prize. **MEMBERSHIPS** Intl Commission for the Hist and theory of Historiography, AHA, German Studies Asn. **RESEARCH** Comparative historiography. **SELECTED PUBLICATIONS** Auth, German Conception of History, 1968, 4th ed, Deutsche Geschichtswicsenschaft, 97; auth, New directions in European Historiography, 1975-1986, Geschichtswissenschaft, 93; co-ed, Geschichtswissenschaft der DDR als Forschurgeproblem, Historische Zeitschrift, Sonderband, 98. **CONTACT ADDRESS** Dept Hist, SUNY, Buffalo, PO Box 604130, Buffalo, NY 14260-0001. **EMAIL** iggers@acsu.buffalo.edu

ILARDI, VINCENT
PERSONAL Born 05/15/1925, Newark, NJ, m, 1 child **DISCIPLINE** RENAISSANCE HISTORY **EDUCATION** Rutgers Univ, AB, 52; Harvard Univ, AM, 53, PhD, 58. **CAREER** Instr hist, Carnegie Inst Technol, 56-57; instr, 57-59, from asst prof to assoc prof, 60-69 prof hist, Univ Mass, Amherst, 69-95; Vis Prof Hist, Yale Univ, 90-00. **HONORS AND AWARDS** Fulbright res scholar, Italy, 59-60; Am Philos Soc res grant, 60-63; Rockefeller Found res grant, 61-63, int res grant, 63-64; chm, Fulbright Nat Screening Comt for Greece & Italy, 63-64; Guggenheim fel, 70-71; Nat Endowment for Humanities res grant, 76-85. **MEMBERSHIPS** Renaissance Soc Am; Am Soc Reformation Res; Mediaeval Acad Am. **RESEARCH** Renaissance political and diplomatic history; origins of modern diplomatic institutions and of modern nationalism; history of eyeglasses. **SELECTED PUBLICATIONS** Auth, France and Milan: The Uneasy "Alliance, 1452-1466, in Gli Sforza a Milano e in Lombardia e i Loro Rapporti con gli State Italiani ed Europei, 1450-1535, 82; auth, The Banker-Statesman and the Condottiere-Prince: Cosimo de' Medici and Francesco Sforza, 1450-1464, In; Florence and Milan: Comparisons and Relations, 89; auth, Crosses and Carets: Renaissance Patronage and Coded Letters of Recommendation, Am Hist Rev, 87; auth, Renaissance Florence: The Optical Capital of the World, J of Europ Econ Hist, 93; auth, The First Permanent Embassy Outside Italy: The Milanese Embassy at the French Court, 1464-1483, in Politics, Religion and Diplomacy in Early Modern Europe, 94; auth, Towards the Tragedia d'Italia: Ferrante and Galeazzo Maria Sforza, Friendly Enemies and Hostile Allies, and, The Ilardi Microfilm Collection of Renaissance Diplomatic Documents, ca1450-ca1500, Index, In, Abulafia, ed, The French Descent Into Renaissance Italy, 1494-95, 95, and Studies in Italian Renaissance Diplomatic History, London, 86. **CONTACT ADDRESS** 238 N Main St, Sunderland, MA 01375. **EMAIL** ilardi@history.umass.edu

ILLICK, JOSEPH E.
PERSONAL Born 11/15/1934, Bethlehem, PA, m, 1956, 3 children **DISCIPLINE** COLONIAL AMERICAN HISTORY, PSYCHOHISTORY **EDUCATION** Princeton Univ, BSE, 56; Univ Pa, MA, 58, PhD, 63. **CAREER** Asst instr civil eng, Univ Pa, 56-58, asst instr hist, 58-61; instr, Kalamazoo Col, 61-62; instr, Lafayette Col, 62-63; from asst prof to assoc prof, 63-71, prof hist, San Francisco State Univ, 71-, Bk ed, The Am West, 66-70; prof, San Francisco Psychoanal Inst, 74-75 & 78-79. **MEMBERSHIPS** AHA **RESEARCH** Colonial Pennsylvania; American biography; psychohistory; Childhood Studies. **SELECTED PUBLICATIONS** Auth, William Penn the Politician, Cornell Univ, 65; The Pennsylvania grant: a re-evaluation, Pa Mag Hist & Biog, 62; ed, America and England, 1558-1776, Appleton, 70; auth, Bibliographic essay, In: Anglo-American Political Relations, 1675-1775, Rutgers Univ, 70; Robert Proud, In: The Colonial Legacy, 71 & Anglo-American Child Rearing in Seventeenth Century, In: History of Childhood, 74, Harper; Colonial Pennsylvania: A History, Scribner, 76; At Liberty, Univ of Tenn, 89. **CONTACT ADDRESS** Dept of Hist, San Francisco State Univ, 1600 Holloway Ave, San Francisco, CA 94132-1740. **EMAIL** illick@sfsu.edu

IMHOLT, ROBERT JOSEPH
PERSONAL Born 05/22/1946, Cincinnati, OH, m, 1973, 3 children **DISCIPLINE** HISTORY **EDUCATION** Washington & Lee Univ, BA, 67; Univ Ky, MA, 69, PhD, 74. **CAREER** From instr to assoc prof, 71-81, prof hist & chemn dept, 82-, Albertus Magnus Col. Ed, NEHA News, newsletter New Eng Hist Asn, 77-83. **MEMBERSHIPS** Orgn Am Historians; Southern Hist Asn; New Eng Hist Asn. **RESEARCH** Timothy Dwight; early American Republic. **CONTACT ADDRESS** Dept of History, Albertus Magnus Col, 700 Prospect St, New Haven, CT 06511-1189. **EMAIL** imholt@albertus.edu

INGALLS, ROBERT PAUL
PERSONAL Born 05/19/1941, New York, NY, m, 1967, 2 children **DISCIPLINE** HISTORY **EDUCATION** Purdue Univ, BA, 63; Columbia Univ, MA, 65, PhD(hist), 73. **CAREER** Asst cur, Herbert Lehman Papers, Columbia Univ, 67-68 & 72-74; asst prof, 74-78, Assoc Prof Hist, Univ South Fla, 78-88, prof, 89-, Chmn, Hist Dept, 79-82, 89-95, Adj asst prof hist, Hunter Col, City Univ NY, 67-74; consult, Impeachment Inquiry Staff of House Comt Judiciary, 74. **HONORS AND AWARDS** Nat Endowment for the Humanities Fel, 84-85. **MEMBERSHIPS** Orgn Am Historians; Southern Hist Asn **RESEARCH** American labor history during the 1930's; anti-labor vigilantism in the South. **SELECTED PUBLICATIONS** Auth, No Crooked Death--Coatesville, Pennsylvania, and the Lynching of Walker, Zachariah, Pa Mag Hist and Biography, Vol 0117, 93; Stories of Scottsboro, Amer Hist Rev, Vol 0100, 95; Untitled--Reply, Amer Hist Rev, Vol 0101, 96; Twice the Work of Free Labor--The Political-Economy of Convict Labor in the New South, J Southern Hist, Vol 0063, 97; auth, Urban Vigilantism in the New South: Tampa, 1882-1936, Univ Pr of FL,93. **CONTACT ADDRESS** Dept of Hist, Univ of So Florida, 4202 Fowler Ave, Tampa, FL 33620-9951. **EMAIL** ingalls@chuma1.cas.usf.edu

INGHAM, JOHN NORMAN
PERSONAL Born 03/15/1939, Green Bay, WI, m, 1961, 3 children **DISCIPLINE** AMERICAN URBAN & SOCIAL HISTORY **EDUCATION** Univ Wis-Milwaukee, BA, 63; Univ Pittsburgh, MA, 64, PhD(hist), 73. **CAREER** Lectr hist, Carnegie-Mellon Univ, 67-68; instr, Univ Bridgeport, 68-70; from asst prof to assoc prof, State Univ NY Col Brockport, 70-77, coordr, Annual Conf Social & Polit Hist, 71-77; Assoc Prof Hist, Univ Toronto, 77-. **HONORS AND AWARDS** Wallace K Ferguson Prize, Can Hist Asn, 80. **MEMBERSHIPS** Orgn Am Historians; Urban Hist Group **RESEARCH** American urban upper classes; urban history; social history. **SELECTED PUBLICATIONS** Auth, The Iron Barons: A Social Analysis of an American Elite, 1887, 1965, 78; auth, A Biographical Dictionary of African American Business Leaders, 4 vols, 83; auth, Comtemporary Business Leaders, 90; auth, Making Iron and Steel: The Independent Mills of Pittsburgh, 1850-1920, 91; auth, African-American Business Leaders: A Biographical Dictionary, 94. **CONTACT ADDRESS** Dept of Hist, Univ of Toronto, 100 St George St, Sidney Smith Hall Rm 2074, Toronto, ON, Canada M5S 3G3. **EMAIL** jingham@artsci.utoronto.ca

INGLE, HAROLD NORMAN
PERSONAL Born 09/20/1938, m, 1969 **DISCIPLINE** RUSSIAN & EUROPEAN HISTORY **EDUCATION** Johns Hopkins Univ, BA, 64, MA, 65; Univ Calif, Davis, PhD(hist), 72. **CAREER** Lectr Europ hist, Univ New S Wales, 70-73; Res & Writing, 73- **MEMBERSHIPS** Am Hist Asn; Am Asn Advan Slavic Studies; Acad Polit Sci; Orgn Am Hist; AAAS. **RESEARCH** International history. **SELECTED PUBLICATIONS** Auth, Late Soviet Culture--From Perestroika to Novostroika, Can Slavonic Papers-Revue Canadienne des Slavistes, Vol 0035, 94. **CONTACT ADDRESS** 780 D St #C, Arcata, CA 95521.

INGLE, HOMER LARRY
PERSONAL Born 10/09/1936, Greensboro, NC, m, 1958, 2 children **DISCIPLINE** RECENT UNITED STATES HISTORY **EDUCATION** Wake Forest Col, BA, 58; Am Univ, MA, 61; Univ Wis, PhD(hist), 67 **CAREER** Asst prof hist, Wilmington Col, 61-63; asst prof, Presby Col, 64-67; asst prof, 67-69, assoc prof, 69-84, prof hist, 84-97, Prof Emer, Univ Tenn, Chattanooga, 97-; Danforth fel Black studies, Yale Univ, 69-70; Fulbright fel hist, Univ Cape Coast, 73-74. **HONORS AND AWARDS** Pres, Friends Hist Soc (London), 97. **MEMBERSHIPS** Orgn Am Historians **RESEARCH** Populism; Nixon; Quakerism. **SELECTED PUBLICATIONS** Coauth, American History: A Brief View, Little, 78; Quakers in Conflict: The Hicksite Reformation, Univ Tenn Press, Knoxville, 86, 2nd ed, Pendle Hill Publ, 98; First among Friends: George Fox and the Creation of Quakerism, Oxford Univ Press, 94. **CONTACT ADDRESS** 1106 Collins Circle, Chattanooga, TN 37411. **EMAIL** lingle@bellsouth.net

INGLES, ERNIE B.
PERSONAL Born 12/30/1948, Calgary, AB, Canada **DISCIPLINE** BIBLIOGRAPHY, HISTORY **EDUCATION** Univ Calgary, BA, 70, MA, 73; Univ BC, MLS, 75. **CAREER** Head, Rare Bks & Spec Coll, Univ Calgary, 74-84; univ librn, Univ Regina, 84-90; dir librs, 90-95, Assoc Vice Pres Learning Systems, Univ Alberta, 95-. **HONORS AND AWARDS** Marie Tremaine Medal Bibliog; Ruth Cameron Medal; Int Lib Sci Honour Soc, 74. **MEMBERSHIPS** Can Libr Asn; Bibliog Soc Can; Can Asn Col Univ Librs; Can Asn Res Librs. **SELECTED PUBLICATIONS** Auth, Canada: The Printed Record, 81, 82, 83, 84; auth, Canada: World Bibliography Series, 90; auth, Bibliography of Canadian Bibliographies, 94. **CONTACT ADDRESS** Univ of Alberta, University Hall 3-16, Edmonton, AB, Canada T6G 2J9. **EMAIL** ernie.ingles@ualberta.ca

INGRAM, EARL GLYNN
DISCIPLINE HISTORY **EDUCATION** La Polytech Univ, BA, 62; Auburn Univ, MA, 63; Univ GA, PhD, 73. **CAREER** Asst prof hist, 66-73, assoc prof hist, 73-, La Tech Univ. **MEMBERSHIPS** Autrey House Mus Comt, 91-; Autrey House Restoration Comt, 85-92; N La Hist Asn, 79-80. **RESEARCH** Europ hist; Brit hist. **SELECTED PUBLICATIONS** Auth, Huey P. Long: A Synopsis, With a Selected Bibliography of Works on Huey P. Long and His Era, McGinty, 94; Dictionary

of Louisiana Biography, La Hist Asoc, 88; North Louisiana: An Historical Overview, Ruston, 84. **CONTACT ADDRESS** Dept of Hist, Louisiana Tech Univ, PO Box 3178, Ruston, LA 71272.

INGRAM, NORMAN
DISCIPLINE HISTORY OF MODERN FRANCE **EDUCATION** Univ Alberta, BA; Univ Toronto, MA; Univ Edinburgh, PhD, 88. **CAREER** Assoc prof, Concorrdia Univ. **HONORS AND AWARDS** Killam Post-Doc fel; Can res fel, Univ Alberta, 88-92. **RESEARCH** History of modern Fance and of peace movements. **SELECTED PUBLICATIONS** Auth, The Politics of Dissent: Pacifism in France, 1919-1939, Clarendon Press, 91. **CONTACT ADDRESS** Dept of Hist, Concordia Univ, Montreal, 1455 de Maisonneuve W, Montreal, QC, Canada H3G 1M8. **EMAIL** ingram@vax2.concordia.ca

INGRAO, CHARLES WILLIAM
PERSONAL Born 03/15/1948, New York, NY, m, 1971, 2 children **DISCIPLINE** EUROPEAN HISTORY **EDUCATION** Wesleyan Univ, BA, 69; Brown Univ, MA, 71, PhD(hist), 74. **CAREER** Asst prof, 76-82, assoc prof Hist, Purdue Univ, 82-87, prof 87-, Alexander von Humboldt Found fel, Institut fur Europaische Geschichte, Mainz, 80-82; Senior Fulbright Fel, Vienna 00; editor, The Austrian History Yearbook, 95-. **MEMBERSHIPS** Soc Austrian Habsburg History. **RESEARCH** Eighteenth century central Europe; early modern and modern central Europe **SELECTED PUBLICATIONS** Auth, In Quest and Crisis: Emperor Joseph I and the Habsburg Monarchy, Purdue Univ, 79; Guerilla Warfare in Early Modern Europe: The Kuruc War, In: War and Society in East Central Europe, Vol I, Brooklyn Col Studies, 79; Empress Wilhelmine Amalia and the Pragmatic Sanction, Mitteilungen des Osterreichischen Staatsarchivs, 81; Kaiser Josef I, Styria Verlag, rev ed, 82; Austrian Strategy and Geopolitics in the Eighteenth Century, In: War and Society in East Central Europe, Vol II, Brooklyn Col Studies, 82; Barbarous Strangers: Hesse-Cassel and the American Revolution, Am Hist Rev, Vol 87, 82; The Problem of Enlightened Absolutism and the German States, J of Modern History, Vol 58, 86; The Pragmatic Sanction and the Theresian Succession: A Reevaluation, Etudes Danubiennes, Vol 9, 93; The Hessian Mercenary State, Cambridge Univ, 87; The Habsburg Monarchy 1618-1815, Cambridge Univ, 94; ed, State and Society in Early Modern Austria, Purdue Univ, 94; ed, A Guide to East Central European Archives [Austrian History Yearbook, Vol XXIX/2], 98; auth, Understanding Ethnic Conflict in Central Europe, In: Nationalities Papers, Vol 27, 99; auth, The Habsburg Monarchy, 1618-1815, Cambridge Univ, 94, 2nd ed. 00; **CONTACT ADDRESS** Dept of Hist, Purdue Univ, West Lafayette, West Lafayette, IN 47907-1358. **EMAIL** cingrao@purdue.edu

INMAN, BEVERLY J.
PERSONAL Born 06/17/1944, Cedar Rapids, IA, s **DISCIPLINE** GERMAN, HISTORY **EDUCATION** Coe Col, BA, 66; Univ Iowa, MA, 69; PhD, 84; EdS, 88. **CAREER** Teaching asst, Univ Wash, 66-67; teaching asst, Univ Iowa, 71-73, 74-75, & 83-84; teacher, Geschwister-Scholl-Schule, 73-74; instr, Quincy Univ, 75-76; assoc ed, Univ Iowa, 78-83; instr, Kirkwood Community Col, 82-83; asst prof, Winona State Univ, 84-85; instr, Iowa State Univ, 86; instr, Univ Memphis, 89-93; instr, Talladega Col, 93-95; instr, Kirkwood Community Col, 96-. **HONORS AND AWARDS** Grant, NDEA Ger Lang Inst of Northwestern Univ, 65; Fulbright Ger Studies Sem, 76; Fel, DAAD Sem, Cornell Univ, 91; Berlin Sem, Loyola of Md & European Acad for Urban Affairs, 94; Teagle Found, 94. **MEMBERSHIPS** MLA, AATG, Fulbright Alumni, GSA. **RESEARCH** Interdisciplinary German Studies: Late Nineteenth- and Early Twentieth-Century German Regional and Heimat Literature, Folklore, Cultural Studies, Nineteenth- and Twentieth-Century German History, Reformation, Higher Education: liberal arts, humanities, international and general education. **SELECTED PUBLICATIONS** Auth, "The Influence of the Kulturkampf on Austro-Bavarian Heimatliterature," SCHATZ-KAMMER 7.2 (86). **CONTACT ADDRESS** Kirkwood Comm Col, PO Box 2068, Cedar Rapids, IA 52406-2068. **EMAIL** bjinman@juno.com

IOFFE, GRIGORY
DISCIPLINE GEOGRAPHY **EDUCATION** Moscow State Univ, USSR, MA, 74; USSR Acad Scis, Moscow, PhD, 80. **CAREER** Sr Researcher, Inst of Geog, Acad of Scis, Moscow, USSR, 86-88, Dept Chair, 88-89; asst prof, Radford Univ, 90-94, assoc prof, 94-96, tenured assoc prof, 96-. **HONORS AND AWARDS** Res Grants, Radford Univ, 94, 98, 99; Nat Coun for Eurasian and East European Res Grants, 95-96, 97-98, 99-2001. **MEMBERSHIPS** Asn of Am Geogrs, Am Asn for the Advancement of Slavic Studies, Geog Soc of the USSR. **SELECTED PUBLICATIONS** Coauth, Territorial Structure of the Economy in the Regions of Old Colonization, Moscow, Nauka (95, in Russian); coauth, "Demographic and Migratory Responses to Agrarian Reform in Russia," J of Communist Studies and Transition Politics, Vol 13, No 4 (97): 54-78; rev of book by Kathryn Stoner-Weiss The Political Economy of Russian Regional Governance, Post-Soviet Geography and Economics, Vol 38, No 10 (97): 619-623; coauth, Continuity and Change in Rural Russia, Boulder, Westview Press (97); coauth, "Environs of Russian Cities: The Case Study of Moscow, Europe-Asia Studies, Vol 50, No 8 (98): 1325-1356; co-ed and contribr, Population Under Duress: The Geodemography of Post-Soviet Russia, Boulder, Westview Press (99); coauth, The Environs of Russian Cities, Lewiston: Edwin Mellon Press (forthcoming, April 2000). **CONTACT ADDRESS** Dept Geography, Radford Univ, PO Box 6938, Radford, VA 24142. **EMAIL** gioffe@runet.edu

IPSEN, CARL
DISCIPLINE HISTORY **EDUCATION** Univ Calif, Berkeley, BA, 85; MA, 87; MA, 91; PhD, 92. **CAREER** Asst Prof, Ind Univ, 94-. **HONORS AND AWARDS** Phi Beta Kappa, 84; Berkeley Sci Historians Awd, 88; Fulbright Grant, 90; Marraro Prize for Best Book, AHA, 97; Res Grant, APA, 98; Mellon Prize, Am Acad Rome, 98-99; Outstanding Jr Fac Awd, 99-00; Res Grant, Ind Univ, 00. **MEMBERSHIPS** NIH, AAR, APA, AHA, SIHS, ASMI. **RESEARCH** Political and social demography of Italy, Italian history. **SELECTED PUBLICATIONS** Auth, "Population Policy in the Age of Fascism: A Commentary on Recent Writings," Pop and Develop Rev 24 (98); auth, "The Annunziata Scandal of 1897 and Foundling Care in Liberal Italy," J of Mod Ital Studies, vol 4, no 1 (99); auth, "Legal Infanticide: Foundling Mortality and its Measurement in Turn-of-the-Century Italy with Special Reference to the Casa Dell' Annunziata of Naples," Popolazione e storia (forthcoming). **CONTACT ADDRESS** Dept Hist, Indiana Univ, Bloomington, 1020 E Kirkman Ave, Ballantine Hall 542, Bloomington, IN 47405-7103. **EMAIL** cipsen@indiana.edu

IRELAND, ROBERT
PERSONAL Born 09/16/1937, Lincoln, NB, m, 1959, 3 children **DISCIPLINE** HISTORY **EDUCATION** Univ of Nebr, BA, 59; MA, 65; Stanford Univ, PhD, 67. **CAREER** Asst prof to prof, Univ Ky, 67-. **HONORS AND AWARDS** Outstanding prof, Col Arts; Great Teacher, Univ of Ky; Distinguished Teacher, Col Arts Sciences; Outstanding Faculty Advisor, Univ of Ky. **MEMBERSHIPS** Orgn Am Historians; Am Soc for Legal Hist; Ky Hist Soc; Or State Bar Assn; Phi Beta Kappa. **RESEARCH** American Legal History **SELECTED PUBLICATIONS** Auth, The County Courts in Antebellum Kentucky, 72; auth, The County in Kentuckyy His, 76; auth Little Kingdoms; the Counties of Kentuckyy, 1850-1891, 77; authThe Kentucky State Constitution: A Reference Guide, 99. **CONTACT ADDRESS** Dept Hist, Univ of Kentucky, 550 S Limestone St, Lexington, KY 40506-0001. **EMAIL** rmirel00@pop.uky.edu

IRISH, SHARON
PERSONAL Born 11/12/1952, Seattle, WA, m, 1982, 2 children **DISCIPLINE** ART HISTORY **EDUCATION** Univ of NMex, BA, 76; Northwestern Univ, MA, 82, PhD, 85. **CAREER** Grad Coll Scholar, 86-, Univ of IL, Urbana. **MEMBERSHIPS** CAA, SAH, SHT. **RESEARCH** American architecture & public sculpture, history of civil engineering. **SELECTED PUBLICATIONS** Auth, Cass Gilbert Architect, Modern Traditionalist, NY, Monacelli Press, 99; Cass Gilbert in Practice 1884-1934, in: Cass Gilbert Ten Projects, NY, NY Hist Soc, 00; Memorial, Carl W Condit 1914-1997, in: Technology and Culture, 97; What Might a Polluted Creek Teach Us about Architecture? in: Design for the Environment/ Proceedings of the 1995 ACSA West Central Regional Conference, 95; Physical Spaces and Public Life, in: Nordic J of Arch Research, 94; West Hails East, Cass Gilbert in Minnesota, in: Minnesota Hist, 93. **CONTACT ADDRESS** 608 West Iowa St, Urbana, IL 61801-4036. **EMAIL** s-irishl@uiuc.edu

IRSCHICK, EUGENE FREDERICK
PERSONAL Born 08/15/1934, Kodaikanal, m, 1998, 5 children **DISCIPLINE** HISTORY, ANTHROPOLOGY, PHILOSOPHY **EDUCATION** Gettysburg Col, AB, 55; Univ Pa, AM, 59; Univ Chicago, PhD(hist), 64. **CAREER** Instr Indian civilization & Carnegie Corp teaching internship, Univ Chicago, 60-61; asst prof hist, 63-69, assoc prof, 69-78, Prof Hist, Univ Calif Berkeley, 78-, Am Inst Indian Studies grant, 67-68 & 79; Fulbright res fel, Institute for the International Exchange of Persons, 80. **HONORS AND AWARDS** Walmull Prize, 69. **MEMBERSHIPS** Asn Asian Studies; Am Hist Asn; Am Philosophical Soc, 82; Humanities Institute, 85; Am Institute of Indian Studies, 85-6; Fulbright, Institute for the International Exchange of Persons, 89; Fulbright, Institute for the International Exchange of Persons, 93; Am Institute of Indian Stud, 93; Fulbright-Hays Fel, 96. **RESEARCH** South Asian history; social change; peasant culture and economy; critical stud, postcolonialism. **SELECTED PUBLICATIONS** Auth, "Peasant Survival Stratagies and Rehearsals for Rebellion in Eighteenth Century South India," Peasant Studies, Vol. 9:4, (82): 215-241; auth, "Gandhian non-violent Protest," Economic and Political Weekly, (86): 1276-1285; auth, Tamil Revivalism in the 1930s, Madas: Crea, 86; auth, "Order and Disorder in Colonial South India," Modern Asian Studies, (89): 459-492; auth, Dialogue and History: Constructing South India, 1795-1895, Berkeley: Univ of Calif Press, 94; auth, The Nation and its Fragments--Colonial and Postcolonial Histories, Int Hist Rev, Vol 0017, 95; Gandhi,Mahatma--Nonviolent Power in Action, J Interdisciplinary Hist, Vol 0026, 95; Caste, Nationalism and Communism in South-India, Malabar, 1900-1948, J Interdisciplinary Hist, Vol 0027, 96; Hindu Nationalists in India--The Rise of the Bahratiya-Janata Party, J Church and State, Vol 0038, 96; The Origins of Industrial Capitalism in India--Business Strategies and the Working Classes in Bombay, 1900-1940, J Interdisciplinary Hist, Vol 0027, 97. **CONTACT ADDRESS** Univ of California, Berkeley, 3229 Dwinelle MC2550, Berkeley, CA 94720. **EMAIL** irschick@socrates.berkeley.edu

IRVINE, B. J.
PERSONAL Born 07/13/1943, Indianapolis, IN **DISCIPLINE** ART HISTORY **EDUCATION** Univ Ind, PhD. **CAREER** Adj assoc prof. **HONORS AND AWARDS** Gros Louis Special Recognition Awd, Off for Women's Affairs, Tchng Excellence Recognition Awd, Intl Projects, Pres Coun on Intl Prog, Indiana Univ; vis scholar, Nanjing Arts Inst, PRC. **MEMBERSHIPS** Art Libraries Soc/North Am; Ad Bd, AERBibliographies Mod. **RESEARCH** Art libraries in PRC (China). **SELECTED PUBLICATIONS** Auth, pubs on art libraries in China, women in academic librarianship. **CONTACT ADDRESS** Dept of History and Art, Indiana Univ, Bloomington, 300 N Jordan Ave, Bloomington, IN 47405. **EMAIL** irvine@indiana.edu

IRWIN, JOHN THOMAS
PERSONAL Born 04/24/1940, Houston, TX **DISCIPLINE** AMERICAN LITERATURE, HISTORY OF IDEAS **EDUCATION** Univ St Thomas, BA, 62; Rice Univ, MA & PhD, 70. **CAREER** Supvr pub affairs libr, Ling-Temco-Vought, NASA Manned Spacecraft Ctr, 66-67; asst prof Eng, Johns Hopkins Univ, 70-74; Ed, Ga Rev, Univ GA, 74-77; Prof Lit & English, 77-84, Decker Prof in the Humanities, The Writing Seminars, Johns Hopkins Univ, 84-, Chmn Dept, 77-96; ed, Johns Hopkins Fiction and Poetry Series, 79. **HONORS AND AWARDS** Danforth fel, Rice Univ, 70; Guggenheim fel, 91; Christian Gauss Prize, Phi Beta Kappa, 94; Scaglione Prize in Comparative Lit, MLA, 94. **MEMBERSHIPS** MLA; Asn of Literary; Scholars & Critics; Poe Studies Asn; Faulkner Soc. **RESEARCH** Mod Am poetry; 19th century Am novel; 20th century Am novel. **SELECTED PUBLICATIONS** Coauth, The structure of Cleanness: Parable as effective sign, Medieval Studies, 73; auth, Doubling and Incest/Repetition and Revenge, Johns Hopkins Univ, 75, expanded ed, Johns Hopkins Pr, 96; The Heisenberg Variations, Univ Ga, 76; American Hieroglyphics, Yale Univ Press, 80; The Mystery to a Solution, Johns Hopkins Press, 94; Just Let Me Say This About That, Overlook Press, 98. **CONTACT ADDRESS** Johns Hopkins Univ, Baltimore, 3400 N Charles St, Baltimore, MD 21218-2680.

IRWIN, JOYCE LOUISE
PERSONAL Born 11/04/1944, Joplin, MO, m, 1980 **DISCIPLINE** REFORMATION & POST-REFORMATION THOUGHT, HISTORY OF CHRISTIANITY **EDUCATION** Wash Univ, AB, 66; Yale Univ, MA, 68, MPhil, 69, PhD(relig studies), 72. **CAREER** Asst prof hist, Univ Ga, 70-77; ASST PROF PHILOS & RELIG, COLGATE UNIV, 77-82. **MEMBERSHIPS** Am Soc Reformation Res; Am Acad Relig; Am Soc Church Hist. **RESEARCH** Theology and music; women in religion. **SELECTED PUBLICATIONS** Auth, Crautwald and Erasmus--A Study in Humanism and Radical Reform in 16th-Century Silesia, Renaissance Quart, Vol 0047, 94; The Radical Reformation, Renaissance Quart, Vol 0047, 94. **CONTACT ADDRESS** Colgate Univ, 13 Oak Dr, Hamilton, NY 13346.

IRWIN, RAYMOND D.
PERSONAL Born 07/12/1966, Marysville, OH, m, 1990, 2 children **DISCIPLINE** HISTORY, RELIGION **EDUCATION** Ohio State Univ, BA, 88; PhD, 96. **CAREER** Res assoc to teaching assoc, 90-96; instr to director, Just Inst, 96-. **HONORS AND AWARDS** Eugene Roseboom Prize, Ohio State Univ; Travel grant, Ohio State Univ, Alumni Res Awd, Ohio State Univ, Tuition Fel, Univ Minn. **RESEARCH** Early American historiography, Religion and government in seventeenth-century America. **SELECTED PUBLICATIONS** Auth, Books on Early American History and Culture: An Annotated Bibliography, 1991-1995, Greenwood Pub: Westport, 00; auth, "A Study in Schism: Sabbatarian Baptists in England and America, 1665-1672," American Baptist Quarterly, (94): 237-248; auth, "Cast Out from the 'City Upon a Hill': Antinomian Exiles in Rhode Island, 1638-1650," Rhode Island History, (94): 3-19; auth, "A Man for All Eras: The Changing Historical Image of Roger Williams, 1636-1993," Fides et Historia (94): 6-23. **CONTACT ADDRESS** 5295 Olentangy River Rd, Columbus, OH 43235. **EMAIL** irwin@just-inst.org

IRWIN, ROBERT
PERSONAL Born 06/20/1961, Regina, m, 1987, 2 children **DISCIPLINE** HISTORY **EDUCATION** Univ Saskatchewan, BA, 85; MA, 88; Univ Alberta, PhD, 95. **CAREER** Lectr, Univ Alberta, 95-98; asst prof, Univ Alaska at Fairbanks, 98- **HONORS AND AWARDS** SSHRC Doctoral Fel. **MEMBERSHIPS** Carolina Hist Asn. **RESEARCH** Environmental History, Agricultural History, Native History, Northern History. **SELECTED PUBLICATIONS** Auth, "Farmers and Managerial Capitalism," Agricultural Hist (96); auth, "Breaking the Shackles of the Metropolitan Thesis," J of Canadian Studies (97). **CONTACT ADDRESS** Dept Hist, Univ of Alaska, Fairbanks, PO Box 756460, Fairbanks, AK 99775-6460. **EMAIL** ffrsi@uaf.edu

IRWIN, ROBERT MCKEE
PERSONAL Born 05/21/1962, PA **DISCIPLINE** LATIN AMERICAN STUDIES **EDUCATION** Univ Penn, BA, 84; NYU, MA, 99. **CAREER** Vis asst prof, asst prof, Tulane Univ, 99-. **HONORS AND AWARDS** Tulane Univ Sen Comm on Res Fel, 01; Stone Cen for Latin Am Stud Fac Grnt, 00, 01; Culpepper Grnt web instr dev, 01; Dean's Dis Fel, 98-99; Res Fel , 97; NYU MacCracken Fel, 94-98; Tulane Univ Newcomb Col, Mortar Bd Awd Outst Teach 00-01. **MEMBERSHIPS** MLA, LASA, Inst Nac Lit Iberoamericana. **RESEARCH** Gender and sexuality studies; Mexican and Latin American cultural studies; cultural studies of the Americas; border studies. **SELECTED PUBLICATIONS** Co-ed, Hispanisms and Homosexualities, Duke UP (98); auth, "Altamirano's Studs: Male Beauty in 19th Century Mexican Literature," Nomada (00); co-ed, "As Invisible as He Is: The Queer Enigma of Xavier Villaurrutia," in En el ambiente (WI UP, 00); auth, "La Pedo Embotellado: Sexual Roles and Play in Salvador Novo's La estatua de sal," Stud in the Lit Imagination (00); auth, "The Famous 41: The Scandalous Birth of Modern Mexican Homosexuality," GLQ (00); auth, "La homosexualidad cosmica mexicana: Espejos de diferencia racial en Xavier Villaurrutia," Revista Iberoamericana (98); auth, "El Periquillo Sarniento y sus cuates: El 'extasis misterioso' del ambiente homosocial en el siglo diecinueve," Lit Mex (99); co-ed, "The Legend of Jorge Cuesta: The Perils of Alchemy and the Paranoia of Gender" in Hispanisms and Homosexualities (Duke UP, 98). **CONTACT ADDRESS** Dept of Span and Portuguese, Tulane Univ, 302 Newcomb, New Orleans, LA 70118. **EMAIL** rirwin@tulane.edu

ISAAC, EPHRAIM
PERSONAL Born 05/29/1936, Nedjio, Ethiopia, m **DISCIPLINE** HISTORY, PHILOLOGY **EDUCATION** Concordia Coll, BA 1958; Harvard Univ Div School, BD 1963; Harvard Univ, PhD 1969. **CAREER** Harvard Univ, instr, 68-69, lecturer, 69-71, assoc prof, 71-77; Hebrew Univ, visiting prof, 77-79; Inst for Advanced Study Princeton, fellow, 79-80; Princeton Theol Sem/Hunter Coll, visiting prof, 80-81; Bard Coll, visiting prof, 81-83; Lehigh Univ, visiting prof of religion Princeton Univ, visiting prof, 83-85; Institute of Semitic Studies, dir, 85. **HONORS AND AWARDS** Second Prize Ethiopian HS Matric Awd 1954; Ethiopian Natl Prize for literacy (Humanity) 1967; Outstanding Educators of Amer 1972; Fellow Endowment for the Humanities 1979; NEH Rsch Grant 1976-77; Harvard Univ Faculty Fund Rsch Grants; Concordia Coll Scholarships 1956-58; Univ Coll of Addis Ababa Fellowship 1954-56. **MEMBERSHIPS** Dir general Natl Literacy Campaign of Ethiopia 1966-72; bd mem Amer Assn for Ethiopian Jews 1973-; pres Ethiopian Student Assn in North Amer 1959-62; vice chmn Ethiopian Famine Relief Comm 1984-; bd mem African Studies Heritage Assoc 1969-73; chmn Comm for Ethiopian Literacy 1963-68; treas Harvard Graduate Student Assoc 1962-65; chorale dir Harvard Graduate Chorale 1962-64. **SELECTED PUBLICATIONS** Ethiopic Book of Enoch, Doubleday, 1983; A History of Religions in Africa, Oxford. **CONTACT ADDRESS** Inst of Semitic Studies, 9 Grover Ave, Princeton, NJ 08540-3601.

ISAAC, GORDON L.
PERSONAL Born Seattle, WA, m **DISCIPLINE** ADVENT CHRISTIAN STUDIES, CHURCH HISTORY **EDUCATION** Seattle Pacific Univ, BA; Western Evangel Theol Sem, MDiv; Luther Theol Sem, MTh; Marquette Univ, PhD. **CAREER** Berkshire asst prof, Gordon-Conwell Theol Sem, 97-. **HONORS AND AWARDS** Dir, Ctr Advent Christian Stud. **MEMBERSHIPS** Mem, Sixteenth Century Soc; Amer Soc Church Hist. **RESEARCH** Theology of Martin Luther, history of exegesis, Trinitarian theology, the Early Church Fathers. **SELECTED PUBLICATIONS** Assoc ed, Luther Digest. **CONTACT ADDRESS** Gordon-Conwell Theol Sem, 130 Essex St, South Hamilton, MA 01982. **EMAIL** gisaac@gcts.edu

ISAACMAN, ALLEN
DISCIPLINE HISTORY **EDUCATION** City Coll, New York, BA; Univ Wis, MA, PhD. **CAREER** Chemn, Am Council of Learned Societies/Soc Sci Res Council Joint Africa Comm, 80-88; dir, MacArthur Prog on Peace and Intl Coop, 88-; prof, 65-. **HONORS AND AWARDS** Melville Herkovits Awd, 73. **RESEARCH** Pre-Colonial southern and central Africa. **SELECTED PUBLICATIONS** Auth, Mozambique: The Africanization of a European Institution: The Zambesi Prazos, 1750-1902, 73; The Tradition of Resistance in Mozambique: A Luta Continua and Mozambique: From Colonialism To Revolution, 1900-1982; Cotton Is the Mother of Poverty: Peasants, Work, and Struggle in Colonial Mozambique; co-ed, Cotton, Colonialism and Social History in Colonial Africa. **CONTACT ADDRESS** History Dept, Univ of Minnesota, Twin Cities, 614 Social Sciences Tower, 267 19th Ave. S, Minneapolis, MN 55455. **EMAIL** isaac001@tc.umn.edu

ISAACS, HAROLD
PERSONAL Born 12/19/1936, Newark, NJ, m, 1974, 2 children **DISCIPLINE** HISTORY **EDUCATION** Univ Ala, BS, 58; MA, 60; PhD, 68. **CAREER** Teaching fel, Univ Ala, 59-62; instr, Memphis State Univ, 62-65; asst to full prof, Ga SW State Univ, 65-. **HONORS AND AWARDS** Graduate Teaching Fel, Univ Ala, 59-62; Nat Endowment for the Humanities, 78; Teacher of the Year, Ga SW Col, 81-82; Fac Development grants, Ga SW State Univ, 91-99. **MEMBERSHIPS** Asn of Third World Studies, World Hist Org, Latin Am Studies Asn, Ga Asn of Hist. **RESEARCH** Mexico, Central America and US Foreign policy in the Third World. **SELECTED PUBLICATIONS** Ed, "Historical and Contemporary Third World Issues," Journal of Third World Studies, 95; ed, "National Development, Imperialism, and Religion in the Third World," Journal of Third World Studies, 96; ed, "Third World Political, Economic and Intellectual Developments," Journal of Third World Studies, 96; ed, "The Third World on the Brink of the 21st Century," Journal of Third World Studies, 97; ed, "Third World Developments: Past and Present," Journal of Third World Studies, 97; ed, "Rethinking Development: The Role of the Third World in the New World Order," Journal of Third World Studies, 98; ed, "Political, Economic, and Social Issues in the Third World," Journal of Third World Studies, 98; ed, "Rhetoric Versus Reality: The Challenge of Policy Implementation," Journal of Third World Studies, 99; ed, "Third World Development on the Eve of the New Millennium: Problems and Prospects," Journal of Third World Studies, 99; ed, "Interdisciplinary Approaches to Third World Studies," Journal of Third World Studies, 00. **CONTACT ADDRESS** Dept Hist & Pol Sci, Georgia Southwestern Col, 800 Wheatley St, Americus, GA 31709-4376. **EMAIL** hisaacs@canes.gsu.edu

ISEMINGER, GORDON LLEWELLYN
PERSONAL Born 02/22/1933, DeSmet, SD, m, 1958, 3 children **DISCIPLINE** MODERN EUROPEAN HISTORY **EDUCATION** Augustana Col, SDak, BA, 59; Univ SDak, MA, 60; Univ Okla, PhD(Europ hist), 65. **CAREER** From asst prof to assoc prof hist, 62-73, Prof Hist, Univ N Dak, 73-. **HONORS AND AWARDS** Standard Oil Ind Outstanding Teacher Awd, Univ NDak, 68. **RESEARCH** Late nineteenth century British diplomatic history; nineteenth-century British social history; immigration history. **SELECTED PUBLICATIONS** Rev, Family, Church, and Market--A Mennonite Community in the Old and the New Worlds, 1850-1930, J Amer Hist, Vol 0081, 94; auth, The Quartzite Border: Surveying and Marking the North Dakota-South Dakota Boundary, 1891-1892, Center for Western Studies, Augustana College (Sioux Falls, SD), 88. **CONTACT ADDRESS** Dept of Hist, Univ of No Dakota, PO Box 8096, Grand Forks, ND 58202-3681.

ISENBERG, NANCY G.
DISCIPLINE HISTORY, AMERICAN STUDIES **EDUCATION** Rutgers, BA, 78; Univ Wis, MA, 83, PhD, 90. **CAREER** Asst Prof, Hist, Univ N Iowa. **HONORS AND AWARDS** Faculty Awd for Outstanding Scholarship, Univ of N. Iowa 00-01. **MEMBERSHIPS** Am Antiquarian Soc **SELECTED PUBLICATIONS** Auth, "Eleanor Roosevelt: Joseph Lash's Eternal Mother," Bio 10, 87. **CONTACT ADDRESS** Dept of Hist, Univ of No Iowa, 319 Seerley Hall, Cedar Falls, IA 50614-0701.

ISENBERG, SHELDON ROBERT
PERSONAL Born 10/21/1941, Fall River, MA **DISCIPLINE** HISTORY OF JUDAISM & EARLY CHRISTIANITY **EDUCATION** Columbia Univ, AB, 62; Harvard Univ, MA, 65, PhD (relig), 69. **CAREER** Asst prof relig, Duke Univ, 68-69 & Princeton Univ, 69-73; asst prof relig, 73-76, ASSOC PROF RELIG, CTR JEWISH STUDIES, UNIV FLA, 76-, Assoc Dir Ctr, 73-, Soc Relig Higher Educ cross-disciplinary fel, 72-73. **MEMBERSHIPS** Asn Jewish Studies; Soc Values Higher Educ; Am Acad Relig; Soc Bibl Lit. **RESEARCH** Judaism in Greco-Roman Palestine; Biblical text criticism; historical method from social psychological and social anthropoligical perspectives. **SELECTED PUBLICATIONS** Auth, An anti-Sadducee polemic in the Palestinian Targum tradition, Harvard Theol Rev, 70; On the Jewish-Palestinian origins of the Peshitta to the Pentateuch, J Bibl Lit, 71; Millenarism in Greco-Roman Palestine, Relgion, 74; Temple and Torah in Palestinian Judaism, In: Christianity, Judaism, and Other Grego-Roman Cults, E J Brill, 75; coauth, Bodies, natural and contrived: The work of Mary Douglas, Relig Studies Rev, 77; auth, Some uses and limitations of social scientific methodology in the study of early Christianity, Proc Soc Bibl Lit, 80. **CONTACT ADDRESS** Ctr for Jewish Studies, Univ of Florida, PO Box 118020, Gainesville, FL 32611. **EMAIL** sri@religion.ufl.edu

ISETT, CHRISTOPHER
DISCIPLINE HISTORY **EDUCATION** Univ Mich, BA, 85, MA, 90; Univ Calif Los Angeles, PhD, 98. **CAREER** Asst prof **RESEARCH** Asian history. **SELECTED PUBLICATIONS** Auth, Sugar Manufacture and the Agrarian Economy of Nineteenth-Century Taiwan, Modern China, 94. **CONTACT ADDRESS** History Dept, Univ of Minnesota, Twin Cities, 614 Social Sciences Tower, 267 19th Ave. S, Minneapolis, MN 55455. **EMAIL** isett003@tc.umn.edu

ISHERWOOD, ROBERT M.
PERSONAL Born 04/18/1935, Waynesburg, PA, m, 1959, 2 children **DISCIPLINE** EARLY MODERN EUROPEAN HISTORY **EDUCATION** Allegheny Col, BA, 57; Univ Chicago, MA, 59, PhD(hist), 64. **CAREER** Asst prof hist, Univ NH, 64-67; asst prof, 67-71, Assoc Prof Hist, Vanderbilt Univ, 71-; Prof of History, 76-. **MEMBERSHIPS** AHA; Soc Hist Studies, France; Am Soc 18th Century Studies; Soc Fr Etude XVIIIe Siecle. **RESEARCH** Politics and culture in the reign of Louis XIV; music and ideas in the French Enlightenment; popular entertainment in 18th century Paris. **SELECTED PUBLICATIONS** Auth, Farce and Fantasy: Popular Culture in Eighteenth-Century France, NY, Oxford Univ Press, 86, pafer, 89; auth, Music and the French Enlightenment--Reconstruction of a Dialog, 1750-1764, Amer Hist Rev, Vol 0099, 94. **CONTACT ADDRESS** Dept of Hist, Vanderbilt Univ, Nashville, TN 37240.

ISRAEL, FRED L.
PERSONAL Born 02/08/1934, New York, NY **DISCIPLINE** AMERICAN HISTORY **EDUCATION** City Col New York, BS, 55; Columbia Univ, MA, 56, PhD, 59. **CAREER** From instr to assoc prof, 56-74, prof hist, City Col NY, 74. **MEMBERSHIPS** AHA; Orgn Am Historians **RESEARCH** Contemp Am hist. **SELECTED PUBLICATIONS** Auth, Nevada's Key Pittman, 63 & War Diary of Breckinridge Long, 65, Univ Nebr; ed, State of the Union Messages of the Presidents, 1789-1966, 66 & Major Peace Treaties of Modern History, 1648-1967, 68-00, Chelsea House; co-ed, History of American Presidential Elections, McGraw, 71; auth, "American Presidential Elections, 1789-1996, Congressional Quarterly, 97; auth, The Presidents, 1789-1993, 8 vols, Grolier, 98; coed, Presidential Documents, Routledge, 00; auth, The Inaugural Addresses of Presidents, Chelsea House, 01. **CONTACT ADDRESS** Dept of Hist, City Col, CUNY, 160 Convent Ave, New York, NY 10031-9198. **EMAIL** fredlisr@epix.net

ISRAEL, MILTON
PERSONAL Born 07/27/1936, Hartford, CT **DISCIPLINE** HISTORY **EDUCATION** Trinity Col (Hartford), BA, 58; Univ Mich, MA, 59, PhD, 65. **CAREER** Lectr 64, assoc prof, 72, assoc ch dept, 72-74, vice provost, 74-79, dir, ctr South Asian stud, 81-91, prof History, Univ Toronto, 90-. **HONORS AND AWARDS** Fulbright fel, India, 63-64; Int Stud fel (Univ Toronto), India, 70-71; Shastri Inst fel, 80-81. **MEMBERSHIPS** Multicultur Hist Soc Ont; Shastri-Indo Can Inst; Asn Asian Stud; Can Ethnic Stud Adv Comt; Heritage Can. **RESEARCH** Nationalism, communications and the hist of the Indian press, migration and Indian settlement in North Am. **SELECTED PUBLICATIONS** Auth, Communications and Power, Propaganda and the Press in the Indian Nationalist Struggle 1920-1947, 94; auth, In the Further Soil: A Social History of Indo-Canadians in Ontario, 94; ed, Pax Britannica, 68; ed, Islamic Society and Culture: Essays in Honor of Professor Aziz Ahmad, 83; ed, National Unity: The South Asian Experience, 83; ed, Nehru and the Twentieth Century, 91; co-ed, Religion and Society in Maharashtra, 87; co-ed, City, Countryside and Society in Maharashtra, 88; co-ed, Sikh History and Religion in the Twentieth Century, 88; auth, Communications and Power, Propaganda and the Press in the Indian Nationalist Struggle 1920-1947, 94; auth, In the Further Soil, A Social History of Indo-Canadians in Ontario, 94. **CONTACT ADDRESS** Univ of Toronto, 100 St. George St, Rm 2074, Toronto, ON, Canada M5S 3G3. **EMAIL** milton.israel@utoronto.ca

ISSEL, WILLIAM HENRY
PERSONAL Born 04/27/1940, San Francisco, CA, 4 children **DISCIPLINE** AMERICAN POLITICS, SOCIETY, CULTURE **EDUCATION** San Francisco State Col, BA, 63, MA, 64; Univ Pa, AM, 66, PhD(Am civilization), 69. **CAREER** Prog assoc & ed, Inst Serv Educ, Rutgers Univ, 67-68; from instr to assoc prof hist, 68-76, prof hist & urban studies, San Francisco State Univ, 76-, coordr Am studies, 77-78, sr lectr, Fulbright-Hays grant, Am Studies Resources Ctr, Polytech Cent London, 78-79. **HONORS AND AWARDS** Phi Beta Kappa Alumni Member, 90; Univ Merit Awd, 94, 96. **MEMBERSHIPS** AHA; Orgn Am Historians; Urban Hist Asn. **RESEARCH** Business, Labor, Religion, and Urban Politics and Policy. **SELECTED PUBLICATIONS** Auth, "Teachers and Educational Reform during the Progressive Era," Hist Educ Quart (summer 67); Modernization to Philadelphia School Reform, 1882-1905, Pa Mag Hist & Biog, 7/70; History, Social Science and Ideology, Hist Teacher, 11/75; School Reform Ideology in Industrial Pennsylvania, 1880-1910, J Social Hist, summer 79; coauth, San Francisco: Presidio, Port and Pacific Metropolis, Boyd & Fraser, 81; Class and Ethnic Conflict in San Francisco Political History, Labor Hist, summer 77; The Politcs of Public School Reform in Pennsylvania, 1880-1911, Pa Mag Hist & Biog, 1/78; auth, Social Change in the U.S., 1945-1983, 85; co auth, San Francisco, 1865-1932: Politics, Power, and Urban Development, Univ of Ca, 86; Business and Urban Policy in San Francisco and Los Angelos, 1890-1932, Pacific Historical Review, Nov 88; Business Power and Political Culture in San Francisco, 1900-1940, Journal of Urban History, Nov 89; Liberalism and Urban Policy in San Francisco from the 30's to the 60's, Western Historical Quart, Nov 91; auth, "Environmentalism, Politics, and the San Francisco Freeway Revolt", Pacific Hist Rev, Nov (99). **CONTACT ADDRESS** Dept of Hist, San Francisco State Univ, 1600 Holloway Ave, San Francisco, CA 94132-1740. **EMAIL** BI@sfsu.edu

ISSER, NATALIE K.
PERSONAL Born 07/12/1927, Philadelphia, PA, m, 1947, 4 children **DISCIPLINE** MODERN EUROPEAN HISTORY

EDUCATION Univ PA, BA, 47, MA, 48, PhD(hist), 62. **CAREER** Asst prof, 63-75, Assoc prof Hist, PA State Univ, Ogontz Campus, 75-85; Prof Hist, PA State Univ, Abington Col, 85-95, Emer prof Hist, PA State Univ, Abington Col, 95-. **MEMBERSHIPS** AHA; Soc Fr Hist Studies. **RESEARCH** Public opinion during the Second Empire, France; anti-semitism during the Second Empire. **SELECTED PUBLICATIONS** Auth, The Second Empire and the Press, Nijhoff, 74; Antisemitism During the Second French Empire, 90; coauth, AmSchools and Melting Pot, 86. **CONTACT ADDRESS** Dept of History, Pennsylvania State Univ, Abington-Ogontz, Abington, PA 19001. **EMAIL** Nxi1@psu.edu

IVERS, LOUISE H.
PERSONAL Born 05/30/1943, CT, d **DISCIPLINE** ART HISTORY **EDUCATION** Boston Univ, BFA, 64; Univ Nmex, MA 67; PhD, 75. **CAREER** Chair Art Dept, 86-91 and 96-00; assoc, prof, Calif State Univ Dominguez Hills, 71-. **HONORS AND AWARDS** Univ Fellowship, Univ of New Mexico, 66-68; 69-70; Junior Consultantship in American Studies, Univ of New Mexico, 68; Teaching Assistantship, Dept of Art, Univ of New Mexico, 70-71; Del Amo Foundation Fellowship for Travel to Spain, Del Amo Foundation, Los Angeles, Calif, 77; Outstanding Contributor of Merit, Southwest Heritage, Volume 8, for publication of The Montezuma Hotel, 80; Affirmative Action Faculty Development Awd for Research, Calif State Univ Dominguez Hills, 84; Univ Foundation Awd, Calif State Univ Dominguez Hills; Honorable Mention, Long Beach Art Assoc Open juried Photographic Exhibition, 88; Sunbird Grant, Getty Center for Education in the Arts and Calif State Univ, 89; Women's Architectural League grant for publication of Cecil Schilling Catalogue, 94; RSCAAP Research Awd, Calif State Univ Dominguez Hills, 99. **MEMBERSHIPS** Society of Architectural Historians. **RESEARCH** Architecture of US and Latin Amer. **SELECTED PUBLICATIONS** Auth, "The Pride of Las Vegas: the Charles Ilfeld Building, 1882-1891," New Mexico Architecture, 12, (March-April, 70): 15-19; auth, "Picture Writing from Ancient Southern Mexico Norman," Line drawings in Mary Elizabeth Smith, Univ of Oklahoma, 73; auth, "The Montezuma Hotel at Las Vegas Hot Springs, New Mexico," Journal of the Society of Architetural Historians, XXXIII, (October, 74): 306-13; auth, "The Hotel Castaneda, Las Vegas, New Mexico," The Masterkey, 51, (July-September, 77), 85-100; auth, "The Montezuma Hotel," The Greater Llano Estacado Southwest Heritage, 8 (Spring, 78), 20-31; auth, "Indigenous Dwellings of Mexico," The Masterkey, 53, (April-June, 79), 62-70; auth, "Portfolio of Photographs," The Clouds, May 80; auth, "Long Beach junk Yard," The Clouds, July 80; auth, "Modernistic Architecture in Long Beach, California, 1928-1937, and Decorative Arts of the Thirties, Carson: California State Univ Dominguez Hills, 85, auth, "Cecil Schilling, Long Beach Architect," Southern California Quarterly LXXIX, (Summer, 97): 171-204. **CONTACT ADDRESS** Dept Art, California State Univ, Dominguez Hills, 1000 East Victoria St., Carson, CA 90747-0001. **EMAIL** livers@dhvx20.csudh.edu

IZENBERG, GERALD NATHAN
PERSONAL Born 06/30/1939, Toronto, ON, Canada, m, 1963, 2 children **DISCIPLINE** HISTORY **EDUCATION** Univ Toronto, BA, 61; Harvard Univ, AM, 62, PhD, 69. **CAREER** Asst prof hist of ideas, Brandeis Univ, 68-75; assoc prof hist, WA Univ, 76-91; Nat Endowment for Hum res fel, Boston Univ, 75-76; prof, WV, 90; Fellowship, Institute for Advanced Study, 01-02. **HONORS AND AWARDS** W.U. Alumni Awd for Teaching 96. **MEMBERSHIPS** AHA, American Psychoanalytic Assoc. **RESEARCH** Mod Europ intellectual hist; methodology; psychohist. **SELECTED PUBLICATIONS** Auth, Psychohistory and intellectual history, History & Theory, 75; The Existentialist Critique of Freud: The Crisis of Autonomy, Princeton Univ, 76; Die Aristokratisierung der burgerlichen Kultur im 19 Jahrhundert In: Legitimationskrisen des deutschen Adels 1200-1900, 79; Seduced and Abandoned: The Rise and Fall of Freuds Seduction Theory, The Cambridge Companion to Freud, Cambridge, 92; Impossible Individuality: Romanticism, Revolution and The Origins of Modern Selfhood 1787-1802, Princeton, 92; Modernism and Masculinity: Mann, Wedekind & Kandinsky Through World War I, Chicago, 00. **CONTACT ADDRESS** Dept of Hist, Washington Univ, 1 Brookings Dr, Saint Louis, MO 63130-4899. **EMAIL** onizenbe@artsci.wustl.edu

J

JABLON, HOWARD
PERSONAL Born 12/21/1939, Brooklyn, NY, m, 1961, 2 children **DISCIPLINE** UNITED STATES DIPLOMATIC & RECENT HISTORY **EDUCATION** Hofstra Col, BA, 61; Rutgers Univ, MA, 62, PhD, 67. **CAREER** From asst prof to assoc prof, 66-75, prof hist, Purdue Univ, 75. **HONORS AND AWARDS** Phi Alpha Theta; Hofstra Honors; NEH Summer Fel - Symposium, Yale Univ, 74; Resident Humanist Series, Univ Wis extension, 75; Humanist-in-Residence, Ind Libr Asn, 79; Fel, Berlin Seminar, AHA & West Berlin Govt, 82. **MEMBERSHIPS** AHA; Orgn Am Historians; Soc Study Am Foreign Fels; Soc Hist Am For Rels; Conf Peace Res Hist. **RESEARCH** US New Deal diplomatic and twentieth century hist. **SELECTED PUBLICATIONS** Auth, FDR and Spanish Civil War, Social Studies, 2/65; State Department and collective security, 1933-34, Historian, 2/71; Cordell Hull, His Associates and Relations with Japan 1933-1936, Mid-Am, 7/74; Crossroads of Decision, Univ Press Ky, 83; General David M. Shoup: Warrior & War Protestor, J Mil Hist, 96; Diaries of Michael & Patterson Lewark, Oregon-Calif Trails Asn, Fall 98. **CONTACT ADDRESS** Dept of Hist, Purdue Univ, No Central, 1402 S U S Hwy 421, Westville, IN 46391-9542. **EMAIL** hjablon@purduenc.edu

JACKLIN, THOMAS M.
DISCIPLINE MODERN AMERICA **EDUCATION** Allegheny Col, BA; Northern Ariz Univ, MA; Johns Hopkins Univ, PhD. **CAREER** Vis fel, Univ Baltimore, 79-80; Asst prof, Univ Baltimore, 80-; Dir, Interdisciplinary Studies Prog, Univ Baltimore, 83-91; Dir, Hist prog, Univ Baltimore, 91-94, 96-97; Dir, Public hist, Univ Baltimore, 95-96. **MEMBERSHIPS** Org Am Hist; Nat Coun Public Hist; Baltimore Hist Res Gp; Frederick Jackson Turner Soc; Lexington Gp Transportation Hist; Railway & Locomotive Hist Soc; B&O Hist Soc; Nat Railway Hist Soc; Soc Industiral Archeology. **SELECTED PUBLICATIONS** Auth, The Civic Awakening: Social Christianity and the Usable Past, Mid-Am, LXIV, 82; auth, History in the Roundhouse, Md Hum, 95; auth, Railroading and American Life in the Nineteenth Century, America's Great Road, 96. **CONTACT ADDRESS** Univ of Baltimore, 1420 N. Charles Street, Baltimore, MD 21201.

JACKMAN, JARRELL C.
PERSONAL Born 12/05/1943, Kenosha, WI, m, 1998, 1 child **DISCIPLINE** GERMAN AND AMERICAN STUDIES **EDUCATION** UCLA, BA, 66; Cal State Univ, MA, 69; Univ Cal, SB, PhD, 77. **CAREER** Exec Dir, 81-, Santa Barbara Trust for Hist Preservations. **HONORS AND AWARDS** Fulbright Fel; U of Cal Fel; DAAD; Spanish Min Cult Res Gnt. **MEMBERSHIPS** CMSA; SBDO; SBHA; SCIF; SMRC; CHS. **RESEARCH** German History and Literature; Spanish Colonial History. **SELECTED PUBLICATIONS** Coed, Santa Barbara Presido Area 1840-present, Univ California, Santa Barbara CA, 93; Presidos of the Big Bend Area, by James E Ivey, in: Public Historian, 92; Felipe de Goicoechea: Santa Barbara Presidio Commandante, in: The Spanish Beginnings in CA, UCSB, 90, pub, Anson Luman Press, Santa Barb, 93. **CONTACT ADDRESS** Santa Barbara Trust for Historic Preservation, 123 E. Canon Perdido, PO Box 388, Santa Barbara, CA 93102. **EMAIL** sbthp@rain.org

JACKMAN, SYDNEY W.
PERSONAL Born 03/25/1925, Fullerton, CA **DISCIPLINE** ENGLISH HISTORY **EDUCATION** Univ Wash, BS, 46, MA, 47; Harvard Univ, AM, 48; PhD(hist), 53. **CAREER** Tutor hist, Harvard Univ, 49-52; instr, Phillips Exeter Acad, 52-56; from instr to assoc prof, Bates Col, 56-64; assoc prof, 64-65, Prof Hist, Univ Victoria, BC, 65-, Rockefeller res grant, 61-62; Am Philos Soc Penrose fel, 64; mem fac bd hist & assoc Clare Hall, Cambridge Univ, 70-71; vis fel, Australian Nat Univ, 75; mem bd dirs, Humanities Res Coun Can, 77; vis scholar, Trinity Hall, Cambridge Univ, 77-78. **MEMBERSHIPS** Am Antiq Soc; fel Soc Antiq London; fel Royal Soc Antiq Ireland; fel Royal Hist Soc; Royal Soc Tasmania. **RESEARCH** British history, 17th century to end of 19th century; American colonial history; imperial history. **SELECTED PUBLICATIONS** Auth, Higgins, Andrew, Jackson and the Boats that Won the War, Amer Neptune, Vol 0056, 96. **CONTACT ADDRESS** 1065 Deal St, Victoria, BC, Canada V8S 5G6.

JACKS, PHILIP
PERSONAL Born 06/10/1954, St. Louis, MO, m, 1990, 2 children **DISCIPLINE** HISTORY OF ART **EDUCATION** Univ Chic, PhD, 81; Cornell Univ, BA, 76. **CAREER** Asst prof, Yale Univ, 88-92; assoc prof, Yale Univ, 93-96; vis assoc prof, Univ Mich, 96-97; asst prof Fine Arts & Art History, George Washington Univ, 97. **HONORS AND AWARDS** Univ Facilitating Fund Fel George Washington Univ, 98; Getty Grant Prog, 96; FW Hilles Awds, 92, 95; Ntl Endowment Humanities, 93/94; Gladys Krieble Delmas Found Fel, 87, 96; Morse Jr Fac Fel, Yale Univ, 90-91; Samuel H Kress Instn Fel, 81-83; Fulbright-Hays Fel to Italy, 81-82 **MEMBERSHIPS** Spiro Kostof Award Committee, 97-99; Soc Archit Historians. **RESEARCH** Italian Renaissance Architecture and Urbanism. **SELECTED PUBLICATIONS** Coauth, The Spinelli of Florence: Fortunes of a Renaissance Merchant Family, Penn State, 00; Vasari's Florence: Artists and Literati at the Medicean Court, Cambridge Univ Pr, 98; Vasari's Florence: Artists and Literati at the Medicean Court, exhibition catalogue, Yale Univ Art Gallery, 94; The Antiquarian and the Myth of Antiquity: The Origins of Rome in Renaissance Thought, Cambridge Univ Pr, 93. **CONTACT ADDRESS** Dept of Fine Arts & Art History, The George Washington Univ, 801 22nd St, Washington, DC 20052. **EMAIL** pjacks@gwu.edu

JACKSON, CARL THOMAS
PERSONAL Born 03/24/1934, Santa Rita, NM, m, 1955, 3 children **DISCIPLINE** UNITED STATES INTELLECTUAL & SOCIAL HISTORY, WORLD HISTORY **EDUCATION** Univ NMex, BA, 56; Univ Calif, Los Angeles, PhD(hist), 64. **CAREER** From instr to assoc prof, 62-73, prof US Hist, Univ Tx, El Paso, 73-, Dean of Lib Arts, 89-96; chr, Hist Dept, 81-84. **HONORS AND AWARDS** Ralph Henry Gabriel Prize in American Studies, 79; Teaching Excellence Awd, Amoco Found, 81; Fulbright Sr Lect Awd, 99-00. **MEMBERSHIPS** Orgn Am Historians; Am Hist Asn; World Hist Asn. **RESEARCH** Influence of Asian thought upon American culture; Asian religions in the United States; meeting of East and West. **SELECTED PUBLICATIONS** Auth, The Meeting of East and West: The Case of Paul Carus, J Hist Ideas, 1-3/68; The Orient in Post-Bellum American Thought: Three Pioneer Popularizers, Am Quart, spring 70; Oriental Ideas in American Thought, In: Dict of the History of Ideas, Vol III, Scribner's, 73; The New Thought Movement and the 19th Century Discovery of Oriental Philosophy, J Popular Cult, winter 75; The Oriental Religions and American Thought, Nineteenth Century Explorations, Greenwood Press, 81; The Orient in American transcendentalism: The Later Phase, South Asian Rev, 7/81; Theodore Parker and the Orient, Amer Transend Q., fall 81; Zen, Mysticism, and Counter-culture: The Pilgramage of Alan Watts, Indian J of Amer Stud, Jan 84; The Influence of Asia upon Amer Thought: A Bibliographical Essay, Amer Stud Interntts, Apr. 84; D.T.Suzuki in America, Zen Stud, Jul 87; The Counterculture looks East: Beat Writers and Asian religion, Amer Stud, Spring 89; Vedanta for the West: The Ramakrishna Movement in the United States, Indiana Univ Press, 94. **CONTACT ADDRESS** Dept of Hist, Univ of Texas, El Paso, 500 W University Ave, El Paso, TX 79968-0532. **EMAIL** cjackson@utep.edu

JACKSON, CARLTON LUTHER
PERSONAL Born 01/15/1933, Blount Co, AL, m, 1954, 4 children **DISCIPLINE** UNITED STATES HISTORY **EDUCATION** Birmingham-Southern Col, BA, 58, MA, 59; Univ GA, PhD, 63; Oxford Univ, cert, 66. **CAREER** Tchr, Birmingham Univ Sch, AL, 57-59; asst prof hist, AL Col, 59-60; tchg asst, Univ GA, 60-61; from Asst Prof to Assoc Prof, 61-67, Prof Hist, 67-96, Univ Distinguished Prof, Western KY Univ, 96-; Fulbright vis lectr, Bangalore Univ & lectr, 16 univs & cols, India, 71-72 & Univ Islamabad, 74-75; US Info Agency lectr, Greece, Iran & India, 72; vis prof, Pahlavi Univ, 78 & Univ Graz, 81; lectr, US Int Commun Agency tour in Ger, 80. **HONORS AND AWARDS** Fulbright Lectr, Univ Dhaka, Bangladesh, 85; Fulbright Centennial Chair Am Studies, Univ Helsinki, Finland, 89-90; Fulbright Selection Comt, Scandinavia, 91-94; dipl (am studies), john f kennedy univ, 76. **MEMBERSHIPS** Am Culture Asn. **RESEARCH** Presidential powers, vetoes; biog; Am studies. **SELECTED PUBLICATIONS** Auth, Presidential Vetoes, 1792-1945, Univ GA, 67; Bronson Alcott's Temple, PHP-Int, Japan, 4/71; Pulitzer Prize winning novels as social history, J Hist Studies, Univ Mysore, 3/72; Come drink the brew and sing a fine song (short story), Southern Humanities Rev, 6/72; coauth, US History Textbook (8th and 9th grades), Laidlaw, 74; auth, Zane Grey, Twayne, 73; Apostle of Nonconformity: A Life of J I Rodale, Pyramid, 74; The Great Lili, Strawberry Hill, 78; The Dreadful Month, Popular Press; Hounds of the Road, Popular Press; Picking up the Tab: The Life and Movies of Martin Rhitt, Popular Press; ed, Befriending, The American Samaritans, Popular Press; A Social History of the Scottish-Irish, Madison Bks; Forgotten Tragedy: The Sinking of HMT Rohna, Naval Inst Press. **CONTACT ADDRESS** Dept of Hist, Western Kentucky Univ, 1 Big Red Way St, Bowling Green, KY 42101-3576. **EMAIL** carlton.jackson@wku.edu

JACKSON, JOE C.
PERSONAL Born 04/24/1911, Gene Autrey, OK, 1 child **DISCIPLINE** HISTORY, GOVERNMENT **EDUCATION** Univ Okla, BSEd, 34, EdM, 40, EdD(hist, govt), 50. **CAREER** Instr speech, hist & govt, Sulphur High Sch, 34-37; vprin, Bristow High Sch, 37-40; dean, Bristow Jr Col, 40-44; prin, Bristow Jr High Sch, 44-48; assoc prof hist & govt, 48-51, dean col, 51-59, prof hist & polit sci, 51-76, Emer Prof Hist & Polit Sci, Cent State Univ, 76-, VPres Acad Affairs, 69-. **MEMBERSHIPS** NEA **RESEARCH** History of the Southwest. **SELECTED PUBLICATIONS** Auth, Born to Wander--Autobiography of Ball, John, Oregon Hist Quart, Vol 0096, 95. **CONTACT ADDRESS** Academic Affairs, Central State Univ, Oklahoma, Edmond, OK 73034.

JACKSON, KENNELL A., JR.
PERSONAL Born 03/19/1941, Farmville, VA **DISCIPLINE** HISTORY **EDUCATION** Hampton Inst VA, BA; King's Coll Cambridge Univ England; UCLA, PhD. **CAREER** Stanford Univ Dept of History, asst prof, 69-78, assoc prof, 79-; **HONORS AND AWARDS** Woodrow Wilson Scholar 1962; John Hay Whitney Scholar Univ Ghana 1963; Fulbright Scholar, Cambridge Univ, 1964-65; Foreign Areas Fellow, Kenya, 1965-68; Lloyd W Dinkelspiel Serv Undergrad Educ, Stanford Univ, 1972; Fellow, Society for the Humanities, Cornell Univ, 1997-98; Univ Fellow, Stanford Univ; Allan V Cox Awd, Fostering Undergrad Research; chair, African-American Studies, 1980-89. **SELECTED PUBLICATIONS** Publications: "America is Me: The Most Asked and Least Understood Questions About Black American History," Harper Collins. **CONTACT ADDRESS** Dept History, Stanford Univ, Palo Alto, CA 94305.

JACKSON, KENNETH T.
PERSONAL Born 07/27/1939, Memphis, TN, m, 1962, 2 children **DISCIPLINE** UNITED STATES HISTORY **EDUCATION** Univ Memphis, BA, 61; Univ Chicago, PhD, 66. **CAREER** Jacques Barzun prof; Columbia Univ, 68. **HONORS AND AWARDS** Barcroft Prize; Parkman Prize. **MEMBERSHIPS** History Asn, 94-95, Society of Am Historians, 98-00; Organization of American Historians, 00-01. **SELECTED PUBLICATIONS** Auth, The Ku Klux Klan in the City 1915-1930, 67; Cities in American History, 72; Crabgrass Frontier: The Suburbanization of the United States, 85; co-auth, Silent Cities: The Evolution of the American Cemetery, 90; ed, The Encyclopedia of New York City, 95. **CONTACT ADDRESS** Dept of History, Columbia Col, New York, 2960 Broadway, New York, NY 10027-6902. **EMAIL** ktj1@columbia.edu

JACKSON, RICHARD A.
PERSONAL Born 05/09/1937, Minneapolis, MN, m **DISCIPLINE** HISTORY **EDUCATION** North Park Col, 55-57; Free Univ of Berlin, 58-59; Univ of Minn, BA, 60, MA, 63; PhD, 67. **CAREER** Instr, Creighton Univ, 64; Instr, 65-67, Asst Prof, 67-70, Assoc Prof, 70-94, Prof, Univ of Houston, 94-; exchange prof, 79-80, vis prof, Univ of Strasborg, 80-83. **HONORS AND AWARDS** Grant, Am Philos Soc, 69 & 74; Fel, 70-71, grant, 75, Am Coun of Learned Soc; travel grant, Coun for Int Exchange of Scholars, 75; Docteur h.c. es Lettres et Sciences Humaines, Univ de Relms, 75; summer stipend, 85, grant, NEH, 94-95. **MEMBERSHIPS** Medieval Acad of Am; Soc de l'Histoire de France; Societet Nationale des Antiquaires de France; MAJESTAS. **RESEARCH** Ceremonial coronation; kingship; France 1300-1600. **SELECTED PUBLICATIONS** Auth, Vive le Roi!, Univ of NC, 84; Manuscripts, Texts, and Enigmas of Medieval French Coronation Ordines, Viator, 92; Who Wrote Hincmar's Ordines, Viator, 94; Ordines Coronationis Franciae, 2 vols, Univ of Pa, 95, 00; Le pouvoir monarchique dans la ceremonie du sacre et couronnement des rois de France, Representation, pouvoir et royaute, 95; joint ed, European Monarchy, Franz Steiner Verlag, 84; Majestas 1-7, 93-99. **CONTACT ADDRESS** Dept of Hist, Univ of Houston, 4800 Calhoun, Houston, TX 77024-3785. **EMAIL** rjackson@uh.edu

JACKSON, ROBERT H.
PERSONAL Born 12/31/1955, Alameda, CA, m, 1977, 3 children **DISCIPLINE** HISTORY **EDUCATION** Univ Calif State, BA, 80; Univ Ariz, MA, 82; Univ Calif, PhD, 88. **CAREER** Asst prof, Tex Southern Univ, 90-98; asst prof, SUNY Col at Oneonta, 98-. **HONORS AND AWARDS** Book Race, Caste, and Status cited as an outstanding academic book for 1999 by Choice Mag. **RESEARCH** Latin American history, Native American history, historical demography. **SELECTED PUBLICATIONS** Auth, Missions of Baja California, Garland Pubs (91); auth, Regional Markets and Agrarian Transformation in Bolivia, Univ of New Mex Press (94); auth, Indian Population Decline: The Missions of Northwestern New Spain, 1687-1840, Univ of New Mex Press (94); coed with Erick Langer, The New Latin American Mission History, Univ of Nebr Press (95); coauth with Ed Castillo, Indians, Franciscans, and Spanish Colonization, Univ of New Mex Press (95); ed, "Indians, Peasants, The Church, and Liberal Reformers, " in Spanish Americans, Univ of New Mex Press (97); ed, New Perspectives on Borderlands History, Univ of New Mex Press (98); auth, Race, Caste, and Status: Indians in Colonial Spanish America, Univ of New Mex Press (99); auth, From Savages to Subjects: Missions in the History of the American Southwest, M. E. Sharpe (2000). **CONTACT ADDRESS** Dept Hist, SUNY, Col at Oneonta, PO Box 4015, Oneonta, NY 13820-4015. **EMAIL** Jacksorh@oneonta.edu

JACKSON, W. SHERMAN
PERSONAL Born 05/21/1939, Crowley, LA, m **DISCIPLINE** HISTORY **EDUCATION** So Univ, AB 1962; NC Central Univ, MA 1962-63; OH State Univ, PhD 1969. **CAREER** Alcorn Coll Lorman MS, instr, 63-64; Central State Univ, instr, 66-68; Univ of Lagos Nigeria, sr fulbright lecturer, 72-73; Amer Constitutionalism Miami Univ, prof, 69-. **MEMBERSHIPS** History ed NIP Mag 1969-71; assoc ed NIP Mag 1971-75; ed consult Pentagon Ed Testing Svc; pres, founder Assoc for Acad Advancement 1969-; pres Oxford NAACP 1979-; consult NEH. **CONTACT ADDRESS** Miami Univ, 241 Irvin, Oxford, OH 45056.

JACKSON, WILLIAM TURRENTINE
PERSONAL Born 04/05/1915, Ruston, LA **DISCIPLINE** AMERICAN HISTORY **EDUCATION** Tex Western Col, AB, 35; Univ Tex, AM, 36, PhD, 40. **CAREER** Instr hist, Univ Calif, Los Angeles, 40-41; from instr to assoc prof, Iowa State Col, 41-42, 43-47; asst prof, Univ Chicago, 47-49; from asst prof to assoc prof, 50-56, chmn dept, 59-60, Prof Hist, Univ Calif, Davis, 56-, Vis prof Am hist, Univ Glasgow, Scotland, 49-50; res grants, Rockefeller Found, Fulbright award, Huntington Libr, Am Hist Res Ctr, Am Philos Soc & Soc Sci Res Coun; Am Asn State & Local Hist award, 56; Guggenheim fel, 57-58; consult, Governor's Calif Hist Comn, 64-66; Fulton Found lectr, Univ Nev, 64; Guggenheim fel, 65; hist consult, Wells Fargo Bank, 65-82; Nat Sci Found grant, 68-73; Inst Humanities award, 71-72; Huntington Libr res fel, 72; Am Coun Learned Soc grant-in-aid, 72; Calif Coun for Humanities, 75-80; Walter Prescott Webb lectr, Univ Tex, 76; mem coord bd, Calif Water Resources Ctr, 77-81; distinguished Am specialist lectr for western Europe, Dept State, 78; consult, US Army Corp Engrs, Tetra Tech, Inc & Teknekron, Inc; Am Historical Asn rep, Nat Arch, 81- **MEMBERSHIPS** AHA; Orgn Am Historians; Western Hist Asn (pres, 76-77). **RESEARCH** The West in American history, especially trans-Mississippi western frontier influences; European contribution to economic development of the West; environmental history. **SELECTED PUBLICATIONS** Auth, When Grass was King: Report of the Range Cattle Study, Univ Colo Press, 56; Treasure Hill, Univ Ariz, 63; Twenty Years on the Pacific Slope, Yale Univ, 65; The Enterprising Scot, Unlv Edinburgh, 68; The California Gold Rush Diary of a German Sailor, Howell-North, 69; coauth, Lake Tahoe Water: A Chronicle of Conflict Affecting the Environment, Inst Govt Affairs, 72; Historical Survey of the New Melones Reservoir Project Area, 76; The Sacramento-San Joaquin Delta and the Implementation of Water Policy: An Historical Perspective, 77. **CONTACT ADDRESS** Dept of Hist, Univ of California, Davis, Davis, CA 95616-5200.

JACOB, JAMES R.
PERSONAL Born 08/28/1940 **DISCIPLINE** HISTORY **EDUCATION** Cornell Univ, PhD, 69. **CAREER** Prof, John Jay Col, 71-. **RESEARCH** Science, Religion, Ethics and Reform. **SELECTED PUBLICATIONS** Auth, The Scientific Revolution: Aspirations and Achievements, 1500-1700, Humanity Books, 98. **CONTACT ADDRESS** Dept Hist, John Jay Col of Criminal Justice, CUNY, 445 W 59 St, New York, NY 10019-1104. **EMAIL** jjacob1067@aol.com

JACOBS, DAVID M.
PERSONAL Born 08/10/1942, Los Angeles, CA, m, 1963, 2 children **DISCIPLINE** HISTORY **EDUCATION** Univ Calif, BA, 66; Univ Wis, MA, 68; PhD, 73. **CAREER** Assoc prof to asst prof, Temple Univ, 75-. **HONORS AND AWARDS** Distinguished Teaching Awd, Col of Lib Arts, 99; Hedri Foundation Awd, Univ Bern Switzerland, 97. **MEMBERSHIPS** Org of Am Hist, Soc for Sci Exploration. **RESEARCH** Unidentified Flying Objects, American Popular Culture **SELECTED PUBLICATIONS** Auth, UFOs and Abductions: Challenging the Borders of Knowledge, Univ Press of Kansas; auth, The Threat, Simon & Schuster, 98; auth, Secret Life, Simon & Schuster, 92; auth, The UFO Controversy in America, Ind Univ Press, 75. **CONTACT ADDRESS** Dept Hist, Temple Univ, 1115 West Berks St, Philadelphia, PA 19122-6006. **EMAIL** djacobs@temple.edu

JACOBS, DONALD MARTIN
PERSONAL Born 05/17/1937, Cambridge, MA, m, 1967, 1 child **DISCIPLINE** UNITED STATES & AFRICAN-AMERICAN HISTORY **EDUCATION** Brown Univ, BA, 59; Boston Univ, MA, 62, PhD(hist), 68. **CAREER** Asst prof hist, Bridgewater State Col, 66-69; assoc prof, 72-78, Prof Hist, Northeastern Univ, 78-; Lectr Afro-Am hist, Boston Univ, 70-71. **MEMBERSHIPS** AHA; Orgn Am Hist; Asn Study Afro-Am Life & Hist; New England Hist Asn. **RESEARCH** Nineteenth century pre-Civil War Black history; antebellum reform in America; Civil War and Reconstruction. **SELECTED PUBLICATIONS** Ed, Afro-American History: A Bibliography, Northeastern Univ, 70; auth, The 19th Century Struggle over Segregated Education in the Boston Schools, J Negro Educ, winter 70; David Walker: Boston Race Leader, 1825-1830, Essex Inst Hist Collections, 1/71; William Lloyd Garrison's Liberator and Boston's Blacks, New Eng Quart, 6/71; coauth, America's Testing Time: 1848-1877, Allyn & Bacon, 73; ed, Antebellum Black Newspapers, Greenwood, 76; ed, Index to the American Slave, Greenwood, 81; ed, Courage and Conscience: Black and White Abolitionists in Boston, Bloomington, IN: Univ IN Press, 93. **CONTACT ADDRESS** Dept of Hist, Northeastern Univ, 360 Huntington Ave, Boston, MA 02115-5000.

JACOBS, LYNN F.
DISCIPLINE NORTHERN RENAISSANCE ART **EDUCATION** Princeton Univ, BA; NYork Univ, MA, PhD. **CAREER** Univ Ark. **HONORS AND AWARDS** Col Art Asn Porter Prize. **SELECTED PUBLICATIONS** Auth, The Marketing and Standardization of South Netherlandish Carved Altarpieces: Limits on the Role of the Patron, Art Bull, 89, The Inverted "T"-Shape in Early Netherlandish Altarpieces: Studies in the Relationship Between Painting and Sculpture, Zeitschrift fur Kunstgeschichte, 91; The Master of Getty Ms. 10 and 15th Century Manuscript Illumination in Lyon, J. Paul Getty Mus Jour, 93; The Commissioning of Early Netherlandish Carved Altarpieces: Some Documentary Evidence, Princeton, 94; . **CONTACT ADDRESS** Dept of Art, Univ of Arkansas, Fayetteville, Fayetteville, AR 72701.

JACOBS, MARGARET D.
PERSONAL Born 01/31/1963, San Pedro, CA, m, 1992, 2 children **DISCIPLINE** HISTORY **EDUCATION** Stanford, AB, 86; Univ Calif, Davis, MA, 92, PhD, 96. **CAREER** Asst prof, NMex State Univ, 97-. **HONORS AND AWARDS** Gaspar Perez de Villagra Awd for outstanding book by an individual for 1999 from NMex Hist Soc. **MEMBERSHIPS** Am Hist Asn, Coord Coun on Women in Hist, Western Asn of Women's Hists, Western Hist Asn. **RESEARCH** Cross-cultural relations between women, US women's history, Native American history. **SELECTED PUBLICATIONS** Auth, "Making Savages of Us All: White Women, Pueblo Indians, and the Controversy Over Indian Dances in the 1920s," Frontiers: A J of Women Studies, 17:3 (97): 178-209; auth, "Resistance to Rescue: The Indians at Bahapki and Mrs. Annie E. K. Bidwell," in Writing the Range: Race, Class, and Culture in the Women's West, ed Susan Armitage and Elizabeth Jameson, Norman: Univ Okla Press (97); auth, "Shaping a New Way: White Women and the Movement to Promote Pueblo Indian Arts and Crafts, 1900-1935," J of the Southwest, 40, no 2 (summer 98): 187-215; auth, "International Federation for Research in Women's History (IFRWH), Report on the Conference, Melbourne, Australia, June 30-July 1, 1998," CCWH Newsletter (the newsletter of the Coordinating Council on Women in History), 29, no 4 (Oct 98): 10-13; auth, Engendered Encounters: Feminism and Pueblo Cultures, 1879-1934, Lincoln: Univ Nebr Press (99); auth, "Clara True: Female Moral Authority and American Indians in the Age of Assimilation," in The Human Tradition in the American West, ed Benson Tong and Regan Ann Lutz, Wilmington, DE: Scholarly Resources (forthcoming). **CONTACT ADDRESS** Dept Hist, New Mexico State Univ, MSC 3H, PO Box 3001, Las Cruces, NM 88003-8001. **EMAIL** marjacob@nmsu.edu

JACOBS, SYLVIA M.
PERSONAL Born 10/27/1946, Mansfield, OH, m, 1980, 2 children **DISCIPLINE** HISTORY **EDUCATION** Wayne State Univ, BS, 69; MBA, 72; Howard Univ, PhD, 75. **CAREER** Asst Prof, Univ of Ark at Pine Bluff, 75-76; From Assoc Prof to Prof, NC Central Univ, 76-. **HONORS AND AWARDS** Fel for Col Teachers, Nat Endowment for the Humanities, 84-85; Summer Inst, Nat Endowment for the Humanities, 88; Rockefeller Found Res Fel Prog for Minority-Group Scholars, 87-88. **MEMBERSHIPS** African Studies Asn, AHA, Asn for the Study of Am Life and Hist, Asn of Black Women Historians, Southern Hist Asn. **RESEARCH** African Americans in Africa. **SELECTED PUBLICATIONS** Auth, The African Nexus: Black American Perspectives on the European Partitioning of Africa, 1880-1920, Greenwood Press (Westport, CT), 81; ed, coauth, Black Americans and the Missionary Movement in Africa, Greenwood Press (Westport, CT), 82; co-ed, Encyclopedia of African-American Education, Greenwood Publ Group Inc (Westport, CT), 97. **CONTACT ADDRESS** Dept Hist, No Carolina Central Univ, 4109 Cobscook Dr, Durham, NC 27707-3129. **EMAIL** sjacobs@wpo.nccu.edu

JACOBS, TRAVIS B.
PERSONAL Born 04/22/1939, New York, NY, d, 2 children **DISCIPLINE** AMERICAN HISTORY **EDUCATION** Princeton Univ, AB; Columbia Univ, MA, PhD. **CAREER** Prof, 65-; Fletcher D. Proctor prof Amer Hist, 92. **RESEARCH** Am Historical Assoc; Organization of Am Historians; Society for Historians of Am Foreign Relations; Vermont Historical Assoc. **SELECTED PUBLICATIONS** Auth, America and the Winter War, 39-40; Navigating the Rapids, 18-71; Middlebury College Bicentennial General Catalogue; Eisenhower at Columbia: Ik's Univ Crusade, 1948-53. **CONTACT ADDRESS** Dept of History, Middlebury Col, Middlebury, VT 05753. **EMAIL** tjacobs@middlebury.edu

JACOBSEN, NILS
PERSONAL Born 04/09/1948, Hamburg, Germany **DISCIPLINE** HISTORY **EDUCATION** Univ Calif Berkeley, MA, 73, PhD, 82. **CAREER** Asst to assoc prof, Univ of Illinois, 85-. **HONORS AND AWARDS** Mabelle McLeod Lewis Memorial Fund Dissertation Fel; Tinker Field Res Grant; Univ Scholar, Univ of Illinois, 94-97. **RESEARCH** Latin American history; politics and society in nineteenth century Peru. **SELECTED PUBLICATIONS** Auth, Mirages of Transition: The Peruvian Altiplano, 1780-1930, Univ Calif, 93. **CONTACT ADDRESS** History Dept, Univ of Illinois, Urbana-Champaign, 52 E Gregory Dr, Champaign, IL 61820. **EMAIL** njacobse@uiuc.edu

JACOBSEN, THORKILD
PERSONAL Born 06/07/1904, Copenhagen, Denmark, m, 1966, 4 children **DISCIPLINE** ASSYRIOLOGY **EDUCATION** Univ Copenhagen, MA, 27, Dr Phil(Assyriol), 39; Univ Chicago, PhD(Syriac), 29. **CAREER** Field Assyriologist, Orient Inst, Univ Chicago, 29-37, res assoc Assyriol, 37-42, from asst prof to prof soc insts, 42-62, chmn dept Near Eastern lang & lit & dir Orient Inst, 46-48, dean div humanities, 48-51; Prof Assyriol, Harvard Univ, 63-74. Haskell lectr, Oberlin Col, 52; Am Coun Learned Soc lectr hist relig, 66-67; Guggenheim fel, 68-69. **HONORS AND AWARDS** MA, Harvard Univ, 63. **MEMBERSHIPS** Am Philos Soc; Am Acad Arts & Sci; corresp mem Royal Danish Acad Arts & Sci, Brit Acad; Am Soc Studies Relig. **RESEARCH** Ancient Mesopotamian languages; archaeology; civilization. **SELECTED PUBLICATIONS** Auth, The Historian and the Sumerian Gods, J Amer Oriental SOC, Vol 0114, 94. **CONTACT ADDRESS** E Washington Rd, Bradford, NH 03221.

JACOBSON, PAUL KENNETH
PERSONAL Born 06/21/1946, Bayonne, NJ, m, 1968, 2 children **DISCIPLINE** PHILOSOPHY, INTELLECTUAL HIS-

TORY **EDUCATION** Seton Hall Univ, AB, 67; Duquesne Univ, MA, 70, PhD(philos), 75. **CAREER** Instr philos, St Peter's Col, 70-71; asst prof, Marywood Col, 72-77; assoc prof philos, 77-85, prof philos, 85-, dean, col of arts and sci, 87-98, assoc vp acad affairs, 82-87, dir honors prog, 78-79, registrar, St Ambrose Univ, 77-. **HONORS AND AWARDS** NDEA Fel, 68-70. **MEMBERSHIPS** Am Philos Asn; Soc Phenomenol & Existential Philos; Merleau-Ponty Circle US; Consult/evaluator, 91-, team chemn, 95-, accrditation rev coun, 96-00, North Central Asn of Col and Schools. **RESEARCH** Phenomenology; epistemology; philosophical anthropology. **SELECTED PUBLICATIONS** Auth, Plato's theory of Anamnesis, 66 & Longinus's conception of the sublime, 67, Bayley Rev; One more new botched beginning: Review of Merleau-Ponty's La Prose du Monde, 72 & Dirty work: Gurwitsch on the phenomenological theory of science and constitutive phenomenology, 76, Res Phenomen; The return of Alcibiades: An approach to the meaning of sexuality through the works of Freud and Merlear-Ponty, Philos Today, 78. **CONTACT ADDRESS** Dept Philosophy, St. Ambrose Univ, 518 W Locust St, Davenport, IA 52803-2898. **EMAIL** pjacobsn@saunix.sau.edu

JACOBY, KARL
PERSONAL Born 05/29/1965, Boston, MA, m, 1997 **DISCIPLINE** HISTORY **EDUCATION** Brown Univ, BA, 87; Yale Univ, PhD, 97. **CAREER** Visiting Asst Prof, Oberlin Col, 97-98; Asst Prof, Brown Univ, 98-. **RESEARCH** Women and Environment; History. **CONTACT ADDRESS** Dept Hist, Brown Univ, Box N, Providence, RI 02912-9100. **EMAIL** Karl_Jacoby@brown.edu

JACOWAY, ELIZABETH
PERSONAL Born 06/16/1944, Little Rock, AR **DISCIPLINE** AMERICAN HISTORY **EDUCATION** Univ Ark, BA, 66; Univ NC, MA, 68, PhD(hist), 74. **CAREER** Asst prof behav studies, Univ Fla, 72-75; asst prof hist, 75-78, Assoc Prof Hist, Univ Ark, 78-, Nat Endowment Humanties fel hist, 76; Am Philos Soc grant-in-aid, 77. **MEMBERSHIPS** Southern Hist Asn; Oral Hist Asn. **RESEARCH** New South; race relations; civil rights. **SELECTED PUBLICATIONS** Auth, Down From the Pedestal--Gender and Regional Culture in a Lady-Like Assault on the Southern Way of Life, Ark Hist Quart, Vol 0056, 97. **CONTACT ADDRESS** Dept of Hist, Univ of Arkansas, Little Rock, Little Rock, AR 72204.

JAEGERS, MARVIN
PERSONAL Born 04/03/1916, New Albany, IN, m, 1945, 2 children **DISCIPLINE** HISTORY **EDUCATION** Ind Univ, BS, 49; MS, 49. **CAREER** Teacher, Cash Grande Union High Sch, 50-57; teacher, N Eugene High Sch, 57-68; vis prof, Univ Ore, 63-66; from asst prof to assoc prof, 68-00. **HONORS AND AWARDS** William Robertson Coe Fel, Stanford Inst of Am Hist, 60; John Hat Fel, Harvard Univ, 60-61; Teacher of the Year, Eugene, Ore Sch district 4J, 66. **MEMBERSHIPS** Orgn of Am Historians, NEA, Ore Educ Asn. **RESEARCH** Testing/Evaluation. **SELECTED PUBLICATIONS** Auth, Tests for History of a Free People, McMillan, 81. **CONTACT ADDRESS** Dept Soc Sci, Lane Comm Col, 4000 E 30th Ave, Eugene, OR 97405-0640.

JAENEN, CORNELIUS JOHN
PERSONAL Born 02/21/1927, Cannington Manor, SK, Canada, m, 1949, 9 children **DISCIPLINE** HISTORY **EDUCATION** Univ Man, BA, 47, MA, 50, BEd, 58; Univ Bordeaux, dipl, 48; Univ Ottawa, PhD, 63. **CAREER** Hist master, St John's-Ravenscourt, Winnipeg, 48-52; lectr hist, Haile Sellassie Inst, Ethiopia, 52-55; asst prof, Mem Univ, 58-59; from asst to assoc prof, Univ Winnipeg, 59-67; chmn dept, 70-72, prof Hist, Univ Ottawa, 67-, Consult, Fortress Louisbourg Nat Hist Park, 68-72; mem Can comn, UNESCO, 70-72; consult, Fed Dept Secy State, Ottawa, 71- & Fed Dept Indian Affairs, 80- **HONORS AND AWARDS** Ronsard Medal, 47; Gold Medal Educ, 58; Ste Marie Prize in Can Hist, Ont Ministry Cult, 74; Book Prize, Fr Colonial Hist Soc, 76; lld, univ winnipeg, 81. **MEMBERSHIPS** Can Hist Asn Soc Fr Hist Studies (vpres, 71-72); Soc Hist Am Fr; Can Ethnic Studies Asn (pres, 71-73); Fr Colonial Hist Soc. **RESEARCH** Franco-Amerindian Relations, New France, Canadian History: Native Peoples, Religious and Educational Aspects, Ethnic Studies. **SELECTED PUBLICATIONS** Auth, Friend and Foe, 76; auth, Role of the Church in New Frane, 76; auth, The French Relationship with the Native Poeples of New Frnace, 5; auth, Emerging Identities, 86; auth, Canada, A North American Nation, 89; uath, History of the Canadian Peoples, vol. 1: Beginnings to 1867, 93; auth, Les Franco-Ontariens, 93; auth, The French Regime in the Upper Country of Canada, 96. **CONTACT ADDRESS** Dept of Hist, Univ of Ottawa, 155 Seraphin-Marion, Ottawa, ON, Canada K1N 6N5.

JAFFE, DAVID P.
DISCIPLINE HISTORY **EDUCATION** Harvard Univ, BA, 76; MA, 80, PhD, 82. **CAREER** Teach fell, Harvard Univ, 81-82; asst prof, Prof, Hist, City Coll NY, 88-. **MEMBERSHIPS** Am Antiquarian Soc **SELECTED PUBLICATIONS** Auth, "'One of the Rural Sort': Portrait-Makers in Rural America, 1760-1860," in Rural America: 1780-1900, Essays in Soc Hist, Chapel Hill, 86; auth, "The Village Enlightenment in the Rural North," Wm & Mary Quart 47, 90;auth, "Peddlers of Progress and the Transformation of the Rural North, 1760-1860," Jour of Am Hist 78, 91; auth, "The Age of Democratic Portraiture: Artisan-entrepreneurs and the Rise of Consumer Goods," in Meet Your Neighbors: New England Portraits, Painters, & Society, 1790-1850, 92. **CONTACT ADDRESS** Dept of Hist, City Col, CUNY, 138th and Convent Ave, New York, NY 10031. **EMAIL** dpjhist@mail.humanities.ccny.cuny.edu

JAFFE, LORNA S.
DISCIPLINE HISTORY **EDUCATION** Tulane, BA, 63; Yale Univ, MA, 65, PhD, 82. **CAREER** Tchg Fellow, Yale Univ, 66-68; Instr, 68-71, Acad Advisor, 71-72, Temple Univ; Historian, US Army Materiel Command, 84-85; Hist, SE Asia Branch, Hist Div, US Army Ctr of Mil Hist, 85-87; Hist, Joint Staff Hist Div, 87-93; Deputy Chief, Joint Staff Hist Branch, Joint Hist Office, 93-. **HONORS AND AWARDS** Phi Beta Kappa; Woodrow Wilson Fellow. **MEMBERSHIPS** Soc for Hist of Am Foreign Relations; Soc for Hist in the Fed Govt; US Commission on Mil Hist; Dept of Defense Sr Professional Women's Asn. **RESEARCH** 20th century European and US diplomatic history; contemporary national security policy; Joint Staff. **SELECTED PUBLICATIONS** Auth, The Decision to Disarm Germany: British Policy towards Postwar German Disarmament, 1914-1919, Allen & Unwin, 85; auth, Abolishing War? Military Disarmament at the Paris Peace Conference, 1919, Arms Limitation and Disarmament, Praeger, 92; auth, The Development of the Base Force, 1989-1992, Joint Hist Office, 93; co-auth, The Chairmanship of the Joint Chiefs of Staff, Joint Hist Office, 95. **CONTACT ADDRESS** Joint History Office, Office of the Ch of the Joint Chiefs of Staff, Washington, DC 20318-9999.

JAGODZINSKI, CECILE M.
PERSONAL Born 10/15/1951, Buffalo, NY **DISCIPLINE** HISTORY **EDUCATION** Canisius Col, BA, 78; SUNY Buffalo, MLS, 79; Univ Chicago, CAS, 85; Northwestern Univ, MA, 88; Univ Ill Urbana-Champaign, PhD, 96. **CAREER** Libr, Buffalo and Erie County Publ Libr, 79-80; asst libr, Quincy Col, 80-83; cataloger, Northwestern Univ Law Libr, 83-86; Manager, Am Med Assoc, 86-88; catalog ed, head, coordinator of Collection Mgmt, Ill State Univ, 88-. **HONORS AND AWARDS** Fel, Univ Ill Urbana Champaign, 92. **MEMBERSHIPS** Am Libr Assoc, MLA, Assoc of Col and Res Libr, Renaissance English Text Soc, Soc for Hist of Authorship, Reading and Publ. **RESEARCH** History of books and reading, Seventeenth-Century British Literature, Library history, Library collection development and acquisitions. **SELECTED PUBLICATIONS** Auth, "Liberty," Am Mass Market Mag: Hist Guides to the World's Periodicals and Newspapers, Greenwood, (90); auth, "Mrs Steuart Erskine," Brit Travel Writers, 1910-1939, Dict of Lit Biog v195 (Gale Group, 98); auth, Privacy and Print: Reading and Writing in Seventeenth Century England, Unv Pr of Va, 99; auth, "Florence Farmborough," Brit Travel Writers 1910-1939, Dict of Lit Biog v204, (Gale Group, 99); auth, "Beryl Bainbridge" and "Julia O'Faolain," Brit Novelists Since 1960, Dict of Lit Biog v231, (Gale Group, 01). **CONTACT ADDRESS** Milner Libr, Illinois State Univ, Campus Box 8900, Normal, IL 61790-8900. **EMAIL** cmjagod@ilstu.edu

JAHER, FREDERIC COPLE
PERSONAL Born 03/17/1934, Beverly, MA **DISCIPLINE** HISTORY **EDUCATION** City Col New York, BA, 55; Harvard Univ, MA, 57, PhD, 61. **CAREER** Instr hist, City Col New York, 61-64; asst prof, Long Island Univ, 64-65; asst prof, Univ Chicago, 65-68; assoc prof, 68-78, Prof Hist, Univ Ill, Urbana, 78-, Am Philos Soc grant, 67; Am Philos Soc res fel, Ctr Advan Studies, Univ Ill, 71-72. **HONORS AND AWARDS** The Newcomen Awd in Business History, Am Newcomen Soc, 76. **MEMBERSHIPS** AHA; Orgn Am Historians; Am Studies Asn **RESEARCH** American social and intellectual history. **SELECTED PUBLICATIONS** Auth, Doubters and Dissenters, Free Press, 64; Businessman and gentleman: Nathan and Thomas Gold Appleton, an exploration in intergenerational history, Explor Entrepreneurial Hist, fall 66; coauth & ed, America in the Age of Industrialism, Free Press, 68; Nineteenth century elites in Boston and New York, J Social Hist, fall 72; coauth & ed, The Rich, the Welborn and the Powerful, Univ Ill, 72; coauth, The Chicago business elite: 1830-1930, a collective profile, Bus Hist Rev, autumn 76; The Urban Establishment, Univ Ill Press, 82; auth, A Scapegoat in the New Wilderness, Harvard Univ Press, 94. **CONTACT ADDRESS** Dept of History, Univ of Illinois, Urbana-Champaign, 810 S Wright St, Urbana, IL 61801-3611. **EMAIL** f-jaher@uiuc.edu

JAIMES-GUERRERO, MARIANA
PERSONAL Born 09/10/1946, Mesa, AZ, s, 2 children **DISCIPLINE** AMERICAN HISTORY, HIGHER EDUCATION AND PUBLIC POLICY **EDUCATION** AZ State Univ, BA, 71, MA, 78, EdD, 90. **CAREER** Vis prof, Cornell Univ, Soc for the Humanities, 91-92; vis prof, School of Justice Studies, AZ State Univ, 94-95; Assoc Prof, Women's Dept, Humanities Col at San Francisco State Univ, 95-. **HONORS AND AWARDS** Humanities fel, Australian Nat Univ, 96; Humanities fel, Cornell Univ, Soc for the Humanities, 91-92. **MEMBERSHIPS** Amer Academy Relig; World Philos Congress; Native Amer Methodist Assoc. **RESEARCH** Indigenous perspectives and experiences; Native women and cancer control res; impact of peoples, cultures, and ecology. **SELECTED PUBLICATIONS** Auth, The State of Native America, SEP, 92; numerous articles in academic journals; several works in progress; brd, Aboriginal Voices; reviewer brd, Journal of American Indian Education, CIE at ASU, Tempe, AZ. **CONTACT ADDRESS** College of Humanities, San Francisco State Univ, 1600 Holloway Ave., Room 363, San Francisco, CA 94132. **EMAIL** guerrero@athena.sfsu.edu

JAKLE, JOHN ALLAIS
PERSONAL Born 05/16/1939, Terre Haute, IN, m, 1957, 2 children **DISCIPLINE** HISTORICAL & SOCIAL GEOGRAPHY **EDUCATION** Western Mich Univ, BBA, 61; Southern Ill Univ, MA, 63; Ind Univ, PhD(geog), 67. **CAREER** Asst prof, Univ Maine, 65-66; instr, Western Mich Univ, 66-67; asst prof, 67-70, Assoc Prof Geog, Univ Ill, Urbana, 70-. **MEMBERSHIPS** Pioneer Am Soc; Asn Am Geog; AHA **RESEARCH** History of American built environment; vernacular architecture. **SELECTED PUBLICATIONS** Auth, Beautiful Machine--Rivers and the Republican Plan, 1755-1825, J Amer Hist, Vol 0080, 93; The Mountainous West--Explorations in Historical Geography, Pacific Northwest Quart, Vol 0088, 97. **CONTACT ADDRESS** Dept of Geog, Univ of Illinois, Urbana-Champaign, 607 S Mathews Ave, Urbana, IL 61801-3601. **EMAIL** j_jakle@uiuc.edu

JALAL, AYESHA
DISCIPLINE SOUTH ASIAN HISTORY **EDUCATION** Wellesley Univ, BA, 78; Cambridge Univ, PhD, 83. **CAREER** Assoc prof. **SELECTED PUBLICATIONS** Auth, The Sole Spokesman: Jinnah, the Muslim League, and the Demand for Pakistan, 85; The State of Martial Rule: the Origins of Pakistan's Political Economy of Defense, 90; Democracy and Authoritarianism in South Asia: a Comparative and Historical Perspective, 95. **CONTACT ADDRESS** Dept of History, Columbia Col, New York, 2960 Broadway, New York, NY 10027-6902.

JAMES, FELIX
PERSONAL Born 11/17/1937, Hurtsboro, AL, m, 1985 **DISCIPLINE** HISTORY **EDUCATION** Fort Valley State Coll, Fort Valley, GA, BS, 1962; Howard Univ, Washington, DC, MA, 1967; Ohio State Univ, Columbus, PhD, 1972; New Orleans Baptist Theological Seminary, New Orleans, Masters of Arts in Christian Education, 1991. **CAREER** Columbia Public Schools, Columbia, SC, instructor of social studies, 62-64; Howard Univ, Washington, DC, reserve book librarian, 65-67; Tuskegee Inst, Tuskegee, AL, instructor of history, 67-70; Southern IL Univ, Carbondale, asst prof of history, 72-74; Southern Univ in New Orleans, chairman of history dept, 74-75, prof of history, 79-; Salvation Baptist Church, pastor and moderator; Mt Zion Miss Bapt, assoc, currently. **MEMBERSHIPS** Assn for the Study of Afro-Amer Life and History, state direc, 1973-, co-chair of program comm, 1979-80, member of exec bd; member, New Orleans Martin Luther King Steering Comm, 1977-; member, faculty coun, Southern Univ in New Orleans, 1980-85; vice-chair of arrangement comm, ASBS Annual Meeting in New Orleans, 1983; member of exec bd, Louisiana Historical Assn, 1984-86; member of advisory bd, Annual City-Wide Black Heritage Celebration, 1985-; commr, New Orleans Bicentennial Comm, 1987-91; consultant, Ethnic Minorities Cultural Center, Univ of N Iowa, 1988; senior warden, DeGruy Lodge, Prince Hall Free and Accepted Masons, 1989; member, bd of direcs, S Christian Leadership Conf, 1983-; worshipful master, DeGruy Lodge No 7, Prince Hall Free & Accepted Masons, 1991-; Illustrious Comman of Kadosh, Eureka Consistory, No 7-Masons. **SELECTED PUBLICATIONS** Author of The American Addition: History of a Black Community, Univ Press of Amer, 1978; contributor to Dict of Amer Negro Biography, 1982, Dict of Louisiana Biography, 1986, Black Leadership in the 20th Century, 1989, Edn of the Black Adult in the US, 1989, and Twentieth Century Black Leaders, 1989. **CONTACT ADDRESS** Dept of History, So Univ, New Orleans, 6400 Press Dr, New Orleans, LA 70126. **EMAIL** fjames@suno.edu

JAMES, FRANK A., III
DISCIPLINE CHURCH HISTORY **EDUCATION** Oxford Univ, PhD. **CAREER** Instr, Ctr for Medieval and Renaissance Stud, affil Keble Col, Oxford Univ; assoc prof, Reformed Theol Sem. **HONORS AND AWARDS** Transl, ch, Ed Comm of the Peter Martyr Lib. **SELECTED PUBLICATIONS** Auth, Peter Martyr Vermigli: Praedestinatio Dei in the Thought of an Italian Reformer; ed/transl, Selected Works of Peter Martyr Vermigli: Theological Treatises; co-ed, Via Augustini: Augustine in the Later Middle Ages, Renaissance and Reformation; gen ed, Peter Martyr Lib; sr ed, Library of Classical Protestant Theology Texts on CD-ROM; consult ed, The Blackwell Encycl of Medieval, Renaissance and Reformation Christian Thought. **CONTACT ADDRESS** Dept of Church Hist, Reformed Theol Sem, Florida, 1231 Reformation Dr, Oviedo, FL 32765. **EMAIL** fjames@rts.edu

JAMES, HAROLD
PERSONAL Born 01/19/1956, Bedford, United Kingdom, m, 1991, 2 children **DISCIPLINE** HISTORY **EDUCATION** Cambridge Univ, BA, 78, PhD, 81. **CAREER** Peterhouse,

Cambridge, lectr, 78-86; Princeton Univ, prof hist, 86-. **HONORS AND AWARDS** Fin Times Global Bus Book of the Year Awd, 96. **MEMBERSHIPS** AHA; Econo Hist Asn. **RESEARCH** Econo Hist; Hist of Germany **SELECTED PUBLICATIONS** The German Slump, Politics and Economics, 1924-1936, OUP, 86; A German Identity, Weidenfeld, Nicolson, 89; International Monetary Cooperation Since Bretton Woods, OUP and Intl Monetary Fund, 96; The Deutsche Bank, 1870-1995, Co auth C H Beck, 95. **CONTACT ADDRESS** Dept History, Princeton Univ, 129 Dickson Hall, Princeton, NJ 08544. **EMAIL** hjames@princeton.edu

JAMES, WINSTON
DISCIPLINE UNITED STATES HISTORY **EDUCATION** Leeds Univ, BA, 78; London Sch Econ, PhD, 93. **CAREER** Asst prof. **RESEARCH** Caribbean and African-American history. **SELECTED PUBLICATIONS** Auth, Holding Aloft the Banner of Ethiopia: Caribbean Radicalism in America 1900 to 1932, 97; co-auth, Inside Babylon: The Caribbean Diaspora in Britain, 93. **CONTACT ADDRESS** Dept of History, Columbia Col, New York, 2960 Broadway, New York, NY 10027-6902.

JAMESON, ELIZABETH
DISCIPLINE WESTERN AMERICA, U.S. SOCIAL, WOMEN'S HISTORY **EDUCATION** Univ Mich, PhD. **CAREER** Assoc prof, Univ NMex. **RESEARCH** Women's and gender history; labor history. **SELECTED PUBLICATIONS** Auth, Building Colorado: The United Brotherhood of Carpenters and Joiners in the Centennial State, 84; coed, The Women's West, 87. **CONTACT ADDRESS** Univ of New Mexico, Albuquerque, Albuquerque, NM 87131.

JAMESON, JOHN R.
PERSONAL Born 05/30/1945, Annapolis, MD, m, 1968, 2 children **DISCIPLINE** US HISTORY **EDUCATION** Austin Col, BA, 67; Tex A&M Univ at Commerce, MA, 70; Univ Toledo, PhD, 74. **CAREER** Asst prof, Washington State Univ, 79-84; assoc prof, Washington State Univ, 84-88; assoc prof, Kent State Univ, 88-97; prof and chair, Kent State Univ, 97-. **RESEARCH** U.S. 20th century; environmental; public. **SELECTED PUBLICATIONS** Auth, "The Quest for a National Park in Texas", in West Texas Historical Asn Yearbook, vol. 50, 74; auth, Big Bend National Park: The Formative Years, Texas Western Press, 80; auth, "The National park System in the United States: An Overview with a Survey of Selected Government Documents and Archival Materials", in Government Publications Review, vol. 7A, 80; auth, "Walter Prescott Webb, Public Historian", in Public Historian, vol. 7, 85; auth, "From Dude Ranches to Haciendas: Master Planning at Big Bend National Park, Texas", in Forest and Conservation History, vol. 38, 94; auth, The Story of Big Bend National Park, Univ Texas Press, 96. **CONTACT ADDRESS** Department of History, Kent State Univ, PO Box 5190, Kent, OH 44242-0001. **EMAIL** jjameson@kent.edu

JANISKEE, ROBERT L.
PERSONAL Born 12/30/1942, Bay City, MI, m, 1964, 2 children **DISCIPLINE** GEOGRAPHY **EDUCATION** Univ Illinois, Phd, 74; Western Mich Univ, MA, 69, BA, 64. **CAREER** Prof, Univ of South Carolina, 72-. **HONORS AND AWARDS** Asn Am Geographers Roy Wolfe Awd. **MEMBERSHIPS** Assoc of Amer Geographers. **RESEARCH** Travel and Tourism; Special Events; Festivals. **SELECTED PUBLICATIONS** Auth, "Climbing," In The Theater of Sport, by Janiskee, R., edited by Karl Raitz, Baltimore: The Johns Hopkins University Press, 95: 382-409; auth, "The Temporal Distribution of America's Community Festivals," Festival Management and Event Tourism: An International Journal 3 96: 129-137; auth, "Oktoberfest--American Style," by Janiskee, R., Festival Management & Event Tourism: An International Journal 3, 96: 197-199; auth, "Myrtle Beach: Crowded Mecca by the Sea," In Snapshots of the Carolinas: Landscapes and Cultures, Washington, D.C.: Association of American Geographers, 96: 217-220; auth, "Community Festivals in the Carolinas," In Snapshots of the Carolinas: Landscapes and Cultures, by Janiskee, R., Edited by G. Gordon Bennett, Washington, DC: Association of American Geographers, 57-61; auth, "Historic Houses and Special Events," by Janiskee, R., Annals of Tourism Research 23, 2, 96: 398-414; auth, "Managing for Low-Impact Recreation and Ecotourism in South Carolina's ACE Basin," by Janiskee, R. and P. Chirico, , In Proceedings of the 1996 Northeastern Recreation Research Symposium, by Janiskee, R., Edited by Walker F. Kuentzel, USDA Forest Service General Technical Report NE-232, Radnor, PA: USDA Forest Service, Northeastern Forest experiment Station, 97: 293-295; auth, "Rural Festivals and Community Reimaging," In Tourism and Recreation in Rural Areas, by Janiskee, R., and P.L. Drews, Edited by Richard W. Butler, C. Michael Hall, and John Jenkins, Chichester, England: John Wiley, 98: 157-175. **CONTACT ADDRESS** Dept Geography, Univ of So Carolina, Columbia, Columbia, SC 29225-0001. **EMAIL** janiskee@sc.edu

JANKOWSKI, JAMES PAUL
PERSONAL Born 07/17/1937, Buffalo, NY, m, 1965, 2 children **DISCIPLINE** MODERN AND MIDDLE EAST HISTORY **EDUCATION** Univ Buffalo, BA, 59; Univ Mich, MA, 63, PhD(hist), 67. **CAREER** From instr to assoc prof, 66-78, Prof Hist, IV Colorado, Boulder, 78. **HONORS AND AWARDS** Nat Endowment for Humanities grant, summer, 69; res fel, Am Res Ctr in Cairo Egypt, 74-75; res fel, Inst for Advan Studies, Hebrew Univ Jerusalem, 82. **MEMBERSHIPS** AHA; fel Mid East Studies Asn N Am; World Hist Assoc. **RESEARCH** Twentieth century Egypt; modern Arab history. **SELECTED PUBLICATIONS** Coauth, The Middle East: A Social Geography, Duckworth, England & Aldine-Atherton, 70; auth, The Egyptian Blue Shirts and the Egyptian Wafd, 1935-1938, Mid East Studies, 1/70; Egypt's Young Rebels: Young Egypt, 1933-1952, Hoover Inst, 75;Nationalism in Twentieth Century Egypt, Middle East Rev, 79; Egyptian Responses to the Palestine Problem in the Interwar Period, Int J Mid East Studies, 80; The Government of Egypt and the Palestine Question, 1936-1939, Mid East Studies, 81; coauth, Redefining the Egyptian Nation, 1930-1945, Cambridge Univ, 95; coauth, Egypt, Islam, and the Arabs: The Search for Egyptian Nationhood, 1900-1930, Oxford Univ, 86; coed, Rethinking Nationalism in the Arab Middle East, Columbia Univ, 97; auth, Egypt: A Short History, Oxford: Oneworld Pub, 00. **CONTACT ADDRESS** Dept of History, Univ of Colorado, Boulder, Box 234, Boulder, CO 80309-0234. **EMAIL** james.jankowski@colorado.edu

JANKOWSKI, PIOTR
PERSONAL Born 01/06/1956, Poznaii, Poland, m, 2 children **DISCIPLINE** GEOGRAPHY **EDUCATION** Poznaii School, MS, 79; Univ Wash, PhD, 89. **CAREER** Comp consultant, Univ Wash, 85-89; asst prof to assoc prof, Univ Idaho, 89-. **HONORS AND AWARDS** Fulbright, Univ Wash, 84; Outstanding Fac Awd, Univ Idaho, 94. **MEMBERSHIPS** AAG, RSA. **RESEARCH** Participatory Geog Inf Sys, Group Decision Analysis. **SELECTED PUBLICATIONS** Auth, "Tradeoff Approach to spatial Decision Making," in GIS and Multiple Criteria Decision Making: a Geographic Information Science Perspective, London, 99; auth, "Spatial Understanding and Decision Support system: A Prototype for Public GIS," Transactions in GIS, (97): 73-84; auth, "Spatial Group Choice: A Spatial Decision Support Tool for Collaborative Decision Making," International Journal of Geographical Information Systems, (97): 577-602; auth, "Enhanced Adoptive Structuration Theory: a theory of GIS-supported Collaborative Decision Making," Geographical Systems, (97): 225-257; auth, "Integrated Nonpoint Source Pollution Modeling System," in GIS and Environmental Modeling: Progress and Research Issues, (96): 209-211; auth, "GIS and environmental decision making to aid smelter reclamation planning," Environment and Planning A, (96): 5-19; auth, "Spatial Decision Support System for Health Care Practitioners: Selecting a Location of Health Care Practice," Geographical Systems, (96): 279-299; auth, "Graphical modeling system supporting dynamic processing in a raster GIS," computers, Environment, and Urban Systems, (96): 391-407; auth, "Integrating GIS and Multiple Criteria Decision Making Methods," International Journal of Geographical Information Systems, (95): 252-273;auth, "Integration of GIS-based suitability analysis and multicriteria evaluation in a spatial decision support system for site selection," Environment and Planning B, (94): 323-340. **CONTACT ADDRESS** Dept Geog, Univ of Idaho, 375 S Line St, Moscow, ID 83844-0001. **EMAIL** piotrj@uidaho.edu

JANSEN, VIRGINIA
PERSONAL m **DISCIPLINE** ART HISTORY AND ARCHITECTURAL HISTORY **EDUCATION** Smith Col, AB, 64; Univ Calif Berkeley, MA, 67; Univ Calif Berkeley, PhD, 75. **CAREER** Tchg asst, Franzosisches Gymnasium, Berlin, Ger, 64-65; assoc cur, Montreal Mus of Fine Arts, Montreal, Que, 67-68; instr, div of fine arts, Foothill Col, Los Altos Hills, Calif, 72-73; vis lectr, dept of design, Univ of Calif, Davis, fall, 72; lectr, dept of fine arts, Univ Santa Clara, Santa Clara, Calif, 73-75; asst prof, 75-83, assoc prof, 83-93, prof, art hist, Univ of Calif, Santa Cruz. **HONORS AND AWARDS** Graham Found for Advan Studies in the Fine Arts, 93; Favorite Prof Awd, Student Alum Asn, Univ Calif Santa Cruz, 93; Univ Calif Pres Res Fel in the Humanities, 89; Amer Coun of Learned Soc, grant-in-aid, 86; NEH Summer Inst: The Tech of Hist Archit, dir Robert Mark, Princeton Univ, 86; Elliott Prize, Medieval Acad of Amer, Superposed Wall Passages and the Triforium Elevation of St. Weburg's, Chester, 81; Amer Philos Soc, res grant from Penrose Fund, 81; Nat Endowment for the Humanities, summer stipend, 79; Facul Res grants, Univ Calif Santa Cruz; instr improvement grants, 76-78, 80, 91, 94-96; dean's descretionary award, 92-93; Regents' Jr Facul Fel, Univ Calif Santa Cruz, 78, 80-81; Humanities Fel Summer Stipend, Univ Calif Santa Cruz, 76; Mabelle McLeod Lewis Memorial Fund Grant, 70-71; Univ Calif Regents' Intern Fel for PhD studies, Univ Calif Berkeley, 68-72; NDEA Fel, Title IV, Univ Calif Berkeley, 66-67. **MEMBERSHIPS** Soc of Archit Hist; The Medieval Acad of Amer; Col Art Asn; The Brit Archaeol Asn; Soc Francaise d'Archeol; The Intl Ctr of Medieval Art; Asn Villard de Honnecourt for the Interdisciplinary Study of Medieval Tech, Sci and Art; Medieval Asn of the Pacific. **RESEARCH** Medieval architecture, both ecclesiastical and secular, particularly Gothic, in cultural context; Urbanism in the Middle Ages. **SELECTED PUBLICATIONS** Auth, Salisbury Cathedral and the Episcopal Style in the Early Thirteenth Century, Medieval Art and Archit at Salisbury, Brit Archaeol Asn Conf Transactions XVII, ed Thomas Cocke and Laurence Keen, 32-39, 96; Medieval Service Architecture: Undercrofts, Medieveal Archit and its Intellectual Context: Studies in Honour of Peter Kidson, ed Eric Fernie and Paul Crossley, London, The Hambledon Press, 73-79, 90; Dying Mouldings, Vertical Springer Blocks and Hollow Chamfers in Thirteenth Century Architecture, Jour of the Brit Archaeol Asn, CXXXV, 35-54, 82; Superposed Wall Passages and the Triforium Elevation of St. Werburg's, Chester, Jour of the Soc of Archit Hist, XXXVIII, 223-243, 79; Lambeth Palace Chapel, the Temple Choir, and Southern English Gothic Architecture of c. 1215-1240, Eng in the Thirteenth Cent, proceed of the 1984 Harlaxton Symposium, ed W. M. Ormrod, Grantham, Lincolnshire, Eng, 95-99, 85; The Design and Building Sequence of the Eastern Arm of Exeter Cathedral, c 1270-1310: A Qualified Study, Medieval Art and Archit at Exeter Cathedral, Brit Archaeol Asn Conf Transactions XI ed Francis Kelly, 35-56, 91; Architectural Remains of King John's Abbey, Beaulieu, Hampshire, Studies in Cistercian Art and Archit, II, ed Meredith Lillich, 76-114, 84. **CONTACT ADDRESS** Cowell College, Univ of California, Santa Cruz, Santa Cruz, CA 95064. **EMAIL** goth@cats.ucsc.edu

JANSON, ANTHONY F.
PERSONAL Born St. Louis, MO, m, 1968, 1 child **DISCIPLINE** ART HISTORY **EDUCATION** Columbia Univ, BA; NYork Univ, MA; Harvard Univ, PhD. **CAREER** Instr, SUNY, Buffalo; instr, Col Charleston; cur, Indianapolis Mus of Art, John and Mable Ringling Mus of Art, Sarasota, NC Mus of Art; vis prof, 94-, ch, dept Art and Theater, Univ NC, Wilmington, 96-98. **RESEARCH** American 19th-century painting. **SELECTED PUBLICATIONS** Author of numerous articles on a wide range of art, from the Renaissance to the present day. **CONTACT ADDRESS** Univ of No Carolina, Wilmington, Wilmington, NC 28403-3297. **EMAIL** ajanson@uncwil.edu

JANSON, CAROL
DISCIPLINE ART HISTORY **EDUCATION** Univ Minn, BA, BFA, 76; MA, 80; PhD, 82. **CAREER** Dept Art, Western Wash Univ **MEMBERSHIPS** Mem, Hist Netherlandish Art; Sixteenth Century Soc; Col Age Assn. **SELECTED PUBLICATIONS** Auth, Artists' Confraternities and Craftsmen's Guild, Dutch History in Art, Gouda as an Artistic Center, Dutch Art from 1475 to 1990: An Encyclopedia, Garland Press, 96; Pieter Bruegel, Encycl Reformation, Oxford Univ Press, 95; Public Places, Private Lives: The Reformed Church as Historical Monument; The Public and Private--Dutch Culture of the Golden Age, Univ Delaware Press, 98. **CONTACT ADDRESS** Dept of Art, Western Washington Univ, Bellingham, WA 98225-9068. **EMAIL** janson@cc.wwu.edu

JANSON-LA PALME, BAYLY
PERSONAL Born 07/31/1943, Baltimore, MD, m, 1997 **DISCIPLINE** HISTORY **EDUCATION** Randolph-Macon Woman's Col, AB, 65; Univ Va, MA, 67; Univ Md, PhD, 79 **CAREER** Curator Manuscripts, Maryland Historical Soc, 67-69; prof, Catonsville Comm Col, 69-95 **MEMBERSHIPS** Maryland Historical Soc; Res Soc for Amer Periodicals **RESEARCH** 18th and 19th century Maryland History **SELECTED PUBLICATIONS** Auth, "William Wilkins Glenn," Encyclopedia of American Biography, Oxford, 96; auth "Tax Assessor's Portrait of a County," History Trails, 96; auth, "Rakes, Nippers, and Tongs, Oystermen in Antebellum St. Mary's County," Maryland Hist Mag, 93 **CONTACT ADDRESS** 7 Byford Ct, Chestertown, MD 21620.

JANSSON, MAIJA
PERSONAL Born Philadelphia, PA, m, 1985, 2 children **DISCIPLINE** HISTORY **EDUCATION** Temple Univ, BA, 64; MA, 65; PhD, 85. **CAREER** Cen dir, Yale Univ, 97-. **MEMBERSHIPS** RHS; CBS; JHS; Int Comm Hist Rep Parli Inst. **SELECTED PUBLICATIONS** Ed, Two Diaries of the Long Parliament, St Martin's Press (NY), 84; ed, Proceedings in Parliament 1614 (House of Commons), APS, 88; co-ed, Proceedings in Parliament 1614: House of Lords, Yale Univ Press, 96; co-ed, Proceedings in Parliament 1614: Appendixes and Indexes, Yale Univ Press, 96; co-ed, England and the North: Anglo-Russian Relations 1560-1614, the Ziuzin Embassy, APS, 94; co-ed, "Remembering Marston Moor," in Political Cultural and Cultural Politics in Early Modern England, ed. S Amussen and MA Kishlansky (Manchester Univ Press, 95); auth, "Dues Paid," Parliamentary Hist 15 (96): 215-220. **CONTACT ADDRESS** Dept History, Yale Univ, PO Box 208324, New Haven, CT 06520-8324. **EMAIL** maija.jansson@yale.edu

JARRELL, RICHARD A.
PERSONAL Born 08/29/1946, Connersville, IN **DISCIPLINE** HISTORY OF SCIENCE **EDUCATION** Indiana Univ, AB, 67; Univ Toronto, MA, 69, PhD, 72. **CAREER** Prof Hist, York Univ, 70-; vis lectr, Univ Toronto, 76-78; founding ed, Scientia Canadensis, 76-88; co-founder, Can Sci & Technol Hist Asn, 80; Atkinson Col Res Fel, 84-85. **MEMBERSHIPS** Ed Board, soc Studies of sci; meme of hist comm of the Am Astronomical Soc, Can Astronomical Soc and the Astronomical Soc of th Pacific. **RESEARCH** History of Canadian science, especially astrononmy, science and education and science and the state; 19th century Irish and Brithsh scientific/technical education. **SELECTED PUBLICATIONS** Auth, Science, Technology and Canadian History, 80; Critical Issues in the History of Canadian Science, Technology & Medicine, 83; The Cold

Light of Dawn, 88; Science, Technology and Medicine in Canada's Past, 91; Building Canadian Science, 92; Dominions Apart, 95; auth, ed, Dominions Apart: Reflections on the Culture of Science and Technology in Cancda and Australia 1850-1945, Toronto: Canadian Science and Technology Historical Association, 95; auth, " The Formative Years of Candian Radio Astronomy," J of the Royal Astronomical Soc of Can, (97): 20-27; auth, "Some Aspects of the Evolution of Agricultural and Technical Education in nineteenth-Century Ireland," in Peter J Bowler and Nicholas Whyte, Sci and Soc in Irelandc, The Soc Context of Sci and Technology in Ireland, (Belfast: Institute of Iresh Studies, 97): 101-117; auth, visionary of bureacrat?: T.H. Huxley, the Dept of Sci and Arts and Sci Teaching for the Working Class, (Annals of Sci 55, 98): 219-240. **CONTACT ADDRESS** Dept of History, York Univ, 4700 Keele St, North York, ON, Canada M3J 1P3.

JARVIS, CHARLES AUSTIN

PERSONAL Born 12/21/1941, Easton, MD, d, 2 children **DISCIPLINE** UNITED STATES HISTORY **EDUCATION** DePauw Univ, BA, 63; Univ MoColumbia, MA, 64, PhD(hist), 70. **CAREER** Asst prof, 69-73, Assoc Prof Hist, Dickinson Col, 73-88, prof, 88-; Nat Endowment for Humanities fel, Univ Mich, 75-76; dir, Dickinson Ctr Europ Studies, Bologna, Italy, 78-80, vis prof, Univ of Malaga, Spain, 96; ed, Whittier Newsletter. **HONORS AND AWARDS** ODK Excellence in Teaching Awd, 95. **MEMBERSHIPS** AHA; Orgn Am Historians; Southern Hist Asn **RESEARCH** United States history, 19th century; United States diplomatic history; Afro-American history. **SELECTED PUBLICATIONS** Auth, Jefferson, Thomas, Passionate Pilgrim--The Presidency, the Founding of the University, and the Private Battle, Pennsylvania Magazine of History and Biography, Vol 0117, 93; The Political-Philosophy of Jefferson, Thomas, Pa Mag Hist and Biography, Vol 0117, 93; auth, "John Quincy Adams Ambassador to Russia," Modern Encyclopedia of Russian, Soviet, and Eurasian History, Vol 1, 95; auth, "John Greenleaf Whittier and the Trial of Anthony Burns," rev of Alber J. von Frank, The Trials of Anthony Burns: Freedom and Slavery in Emerson's Boston, Whittier Newsletter, No 30, 98. **CONTACT ADDRESS** Dept of Hist, Dickinson Col, 1 Dickinson College, Carlisle, PA 17013-2897. **EMAIL** jarvisc@dickinson.edu

JARVIS, JOSEPH ANTHONY

PERSONAL Born 04/05/1939, Queens, NY, m, 1966, 2 children **DISCIPLINE** AMERICAN HISTORY **EDUCATION** St John's Univ, NYork, BA, 60; Columbia Univ, MA, 61; NYork Univ, PhD, 70. **CAREER** Instr hist, St John's Univ, NY, 61-65; asst prof, State Univ NY Col Potsdam, 65-67; assoc prof, E Stroudsburg State Col, 67-, Kellogg fel pub affairs leadership prog, Pa State Univ, 73-75. **MEMBERSHIPS** AHA; ASCUF **RESEARCH** New York City politics, 1880-1890; urban American history. **CONTACT ADDRESS** Dept of Hist, East Stroudsburg Univ of Pennsylvania, 200 Prospect St, East Stroudsburg, PA 18301-2999. **EMAIL** JJarvis@esu.edu

JARVIS, MICHAEL J.

PERSONAL Born 07/21/1968, East Stroudsburg, PA, m, 1995, 1 child **DISCIPLINE** HISTORY **EDUCATION** Rutgers Univ, BA, 89; Col William and Mary, MA, 93, PhD, 98. **CAREER** Tchg asst, 92-94, 98, lectr, 94, 98, Col William and Mary; asst prof, Long Island Univ, 98-. **HONORS AND AWARDS** Henry Rutgers Scholar, 88-89, Rutgers Univ; Albert O. Vietor Fel, 96, John Carter Brown Library. **MEMBERSHIPS** Am Hist Asn **RESEARCH** Colonial Bermuda; the atlantic world; maritime history in age of sail. **SELECTED PUBLICATIONS** Auth, art, The Henry Tucker House: 280 Years of Bermudian Social History, 94; auth, art, The Fastest Vessels in the World: The Origin and Evolution of the Bemuda Sloop, 95; auth, art, The Long, Hot Summer of 1863, 96; auth, art, The Vingboons Chart of the James River, circa 1617, 97; auth, art, Bemuda's Architectural Heritage: Saint George's, 98. **CONTACT ADDRESS** Dept of History, Col of William and Mary, PO Box 8795, Williamsburg, VA 23187-8795.

JASHEMSKI, WILHELMINA F.

PERSONAL Born 07/10/1910, Yory, NE, m, 1945 **DISCIPLINE** ANCIENT HISTORY **EDUCATION** York Col, AB, 31; Univ Nebr, AM, 33; Univ Chicago, PhD, 42. **CAREER** Teacher, Walthill High Sch, 34-35; mem fac Latin, Greek & hist, Ind Cent Col, 35-37, 38-40; mem fac hist, Lindenwood Col Women, 42-45; from asst prof to assoc prof, 46-65, prof, 65-80, fel, Dumbarton Oaks, 80-81, distinguished scholar-teacher, 82, Emer Prof Greek & Roman Hist, Univ MD, College Park, 80-, Sr Fel & Proj Dir, Univ MD, Dumbarton Oaks, 81-, Biomed sci support grant, 67-68; Nat Endowment for Humanities sr fel, 68-69 & res grants, 72-78. **HONORS AND AWARDS** Tatiana Warscher Awd for Archaeol Res, Am Acad Rome, 68; Bradford Williams Awd, Am Soc Landscape Architects, 77; dr humanities, univ nebr, 80. **MEMBERSHIPS** Soc Prom Roman Studies; Archaeol Inst Am; Am Philol Asn; Int Asn Classical Archaeol. **RESEARCH** Roman provinces; ancient gardens of pompeii and the Roman Empire. **SELECTED PUBLICATIONS** Auth, Excavations in the Gardens in the House of Bacchus and Ariadne and in the East Temple at Thuburbo-Majus, Amer Jf Archaeol, Vol 0098, 94; Roman Gardens in Tunisia--Preliminary Excavations in the House of Bacchus and Ariadne and in the East Temple at Thuburbo Maius, Amer J Archaeol, Vol 0099, 95. **CONTACT ADDRESS** Dept of Hist, Univ of Maryland, Col Park, 415 Pershing Dr Silver, College Park, MD 20742. **EMAIL** wj26@umail.umd.edu

JAY, MARTIN EVAN

PERSONAL Born 05/04/1944, New York, NY, m, 1974, 2 children **DISCIPLINE** MODERN EUROPEAN INTELLECTUAL HISTORY **EDUCATION** Union Col, NYork, BA, 65; Harvard Univ, PhD(hist), 71. **CAREER** Asst prof, 71-75, assoc prof, 75-80, prof Hist, 80-97, SIDNEY HELLMAN EHRMAN PROF, UNIV CA, BERKELEY, 97-; Sr assoc mem, St Antony's Col, 74-75; Col internationale de philosophie, 84-85;Sr assoc member, Clare Hall, Cambridge, 89; Sr fel, Stanford Humanities Center, 97-98; Guggenheim Found fel, 74-75; Nat Endowment for Humanities fel, 79-80; sr ed, Theory and Society, 80-; Rockefeller Found fel, 84-85; ACLS fel, 89-90; Univ CA Presidential fel in the Humanities, 93-94; regular columnist, Salmagundi, 87-. **HONORS AND AWARDS** Herbert Baxter Adams Prize, AHA, 73; Am Academy of Arts and Sciences, 96. **MEMBERSHIPS** AHA; Soc for Exile Studies. **RESEARCH** Twentieth century European intellectual history; history of Marxist theory; history of German exiles to Am; visual culture. **SELECTED PUBLICATIONS** Auth, The Dialectial Imagination: A History of the Frankfurt School and the Institute of Social Research, 1923-1950, Little, Brown, 73, 2nd ed, Univ CA Press, 96; Marxism and Totality, Univ CA Press, 84; Adorno, Harvard, 84; Permanent Exiles, Columbia Univ Press, 85; Finde-siecle Socialism, Routledge, 89; Force Fields, Routledge, 93; Downcast Eyes, Univ CA Press, 93; Cultural Semantics, Univ MA Press, 98; Ed: An Unmastered past, Univ CA Press, 87; The Weimar Republic Sourcebook, Univ CA Press, 94; Vision in Context, Routledge, 97. **CONTACT ADDRESS** Dept of Hist, Univ of California, Berkeley, 3229 Dwinelle Hall, Berkeley, CA 94720-2551. **EMAIL** martjay@socrates.berkeley.edu

JEFFERSON, ALPHINE W.

DISCIPLINE HISTORY **EDUCATION** Univ Chicago, AB, 73; Duke Univ, MA, 75, PhD, 79. **CAREER** Assoc prof. **RESEARCH** Blacks and Jews in Chicago. **SELECTED PUBLICATIONS** Auth, Contemporary Diaspora and the Future, Africana Stud; auth, articles in African-American history. **CONTACT ADDRESS** Dept of Hist, The Col of Wooster, Wooster, OH 44691.

JEFFERSON, CARTER

PERSONAL Born 07/12/1927, Dallas, TX, m, 1955, 1 child **DISCIPLINE** HISTORY **EDUCATION** George Washington Univ, BA, 49; Southern Methodist Univ, MA, 55; Univ Chicago, PhD, 59. **CAREER** Instr hist, Wayne State Univ, 58-59 & Univ Mich, 59-62; from asst prof to assoc prof, Rutgers Univ, 62-69; Prof Hist, Univ Mass, Boston, 69-80. **MEMBERSHIPS** AHA; Soc Fr Hist Studies; Soc Mod Hist France; Hist Educ Soc. **RESEARCH** European political and social history. **CONTACT ADDRESS** 6 Cazenove St, Boston, MA 02116. **EMAIL** carterj98@hotmail.edu

JEFFREY, DAVID LYLE

PERSONAL Born 06/28/1941, Ottawa, ON, Canada **DISCIPLINE** ENGLISH LITERATURE, ART HISTORY **EDUCATION** Wheaton Col, Ill, BA, 65; Princeton Univ, MA, 67, PhD(English), 68. **CAREER** Asst prof, Univ Victoria, BC, 68-69 & Univ Rochester, 69-72; assoc prof English & chmn dept, Univ Victoria, BC, 73-78; chmn dept, 78-81, Prof English, Univ Ottawa, 78-, Gen ed, Dict Biblical Tradition in English Lit, 77-; Can Coun leave fel, 77-78; adj prof, Regent Col, 78-, **HONORS AND AWARDS** Bk of Year Awd, Conf Christianity & Lit, 75; Solomon Katz Distinguished Lectr in Humanities, Univ Wash, 77. **MEMBERSHIPS** MLA; Conf Christianity & Lit; Mediaeval Acad Am; Asn Can Univ Teachers English; Am Acad Relig & Soc Biblical Lit. **RESEARCH** Medieval, modern and biblical literature. **SELECTED PUBLICATIONS** Ed, Dictionary of Biblical Tradition in English Literature, 93; auth, People of the Book: Christian Identity and Literary Culture, 96; co-ed, Rethinking the Future of the University (University of Ottawa Press Mentor Series), by David Lyle Jeffrey and Dominic Manganiello, 98; auth, English Spirituality in the Age of Wyclif; ed, A Burning and a Shining Light: English Spirituality in the Age of Wesley; ed, The Law of Love: English Spirituality in the Age of Wycliff. **CONTACT ADDRESS** Dept of English, Univ of Ottawa, Arts Bldg, 70 Laurier, Ottawa, ON, Canada K1N 6N5.

JEFFREY, JULIE ROY

PERSONAL Born 03/20/1941, Boston, MA, m, 1963, 2 children **DISCIPLINE** AMERICAN HISTORY **EDUCATION** Radcliffe Col, FA, 62; Rice Univ, PhD, 72. **CAREER** Asst prof, 72-80, assoc prof, 80-84, Prof Am Hist, Goucher Col, 84-; Dir, Historic Preservation, 76-84, Comnr, Comn Historic & Archit Preservation Baltimore City, 77-86 & Nat Historic Recs & Publ Comn, 79-84; Newberry Libr fel, 79. **HONORS AND AWARDS** Elizabeth Connolly Todd Prof 89-94; Am Counc Educ fel 87-88; Fulbright sr lectr, 92; Sudler Awd, 92; NEH Awd 95-96. **MEMBERSHIPS** Orgn Am Historians; Am Hist Asn; Coordinating Comt Women Hist Profession; Soc Hist Early Republic. **RESEARCH** American reform; American women in the nineteenth century; architecture and social roles. **SELECTED PUBLICATIONS** Coauth, An experiment in combat simulation: The battle of Cambrai, J Interdisciplinary Hist, winter 72; auth, The southern alliance and women: Another look at equal rights to all, special privileges to none, Feminist Studies, fall 75; coauth, Historical preservation projects, Newberry Papers in Family & Community Hist, 1/78; auth, Education for Children of the Poor: A Study of the Origins and Implementation of the Elementary andSecondary Education Act of 1975, Ohio State Univ, winter 78; auth, Beautiful walls for Baltimore, in Baltimore Museum of Fine Arts Catalogue, Baltimore Museum, spring 78; Buildings in and out of the classroom, Teaching Hist, spring 79; Frontier Women: Women in the Trans Mississippi West, 1840-1880, Hill & Wang, spring 79; The other half of the calling: Methodist clergy wives on the trans-Mississipi frontier, in Women in the Methodist Tradition, Abingdon Press, fall 81; co-auth, The American People: A History of a Nation and a Society, Longman, 4th ed, 87; The Making of a Missionary: Narcissa Whitman and Her Vocation, Idaho Yesterdays, summer 87; There Is Some Splendid Scenery: Women's Responses to the Great Plains Landscape, Great Plains Quart, spring 88; Narcissa Whitman: The Significanceof a Missionary's Life, Mont Mag of Western Hist, spring 91; Empty Harvest at Waiilatpu: The Mission Life of Narcissa Whitman, Columbia Mag of Northwest Hist, fall 92; Converting the West: A Biography of Narcissa Whitman, Univ Okla, 92, 94; The Great Silent Army of Abolitionism: Ordinary Women in the Abolitionist Movement, Univ NC, 98; The Heathen Are Far Different from What You Imagine: Narcissa Whitman's Conflict between Imagination and Reality, in Terra Pacifica: People and Place in the Northwestern States and Canada, Wash State Univ Press, 98. **CONTACT ADDRESS** Dept of Hist, Goucher Col, 1021 Dulaney Vlly Rd, Baltimore, MD 21204-2780. **EMAIL** riezler@aol.com

JEFFREY, KIRK

PERSONAL Born 09/05/1944, Washington, DC, m, 1965, 2 children **DISCIPLINE** AMERICAN HISTORY **EDUCATION** Harvard Univ, BA, 66; Stanford Univ, MA, 67, PhD(hist), 72. **CAREER** From instr to asst prof, 70-77, Assoc Prof Hist, Carleton Col, 77-, Am Coun Learned Soc grant-in-aid, 73; fac fel, Newberry Libr Sem Humanities, 73-74. **MEMBERSHIPS** Orgn Am Hist; Am Studies Asn **RESEARCH** Nineteenth century American cultural history; history of the family; history of women. **SELECTED PUBLICATIONS** Auth, The family as utopian retreat from the city, Soundings, 3/72; Marital experience, career, & feminine ideology in nineteenth-century America, Feminist Studies, 75; Varieties of family history, Am Archivist, 10/75; coauth, Women's history in the high school, Hist Teacher, 11/77. **CONTACT ADDRESS** Dept of Hist, Carleton Col, Northfield, MN 55057.

JEFFREY, THOMAS EDWARD

PERSONAL Born 09/05/1947, Chelsea, MA **DISCIPLINE** HISTORY **EDUCATION** Cath Univ Am, AB, 69, MA, 70, MSLS, 73, PhD(hist), 76. **CAREER** Microfiche ed hist, Papers Benjamin Henry Latrobe, Md Hist Soc, Baltimore, 74-77; Assoc Ed, Thomas A Edison Papers, Rutgers Univ, 79-, Consult hist ed, Nat Hist Publ & Records Comn, 77. **MEMBERSHIPS** Southern Hist Asn; Orgn Am Historians; Asn Doc Ed. **RESEARCH** Antebellum US politics; North Carolina history. **SELECTED PUBLICATIONS** Ed, The Microfiche Edition of the Papers of Benjamin Henry Latrobe, 76 & The Guide and Index to the Microfiche Edition of the Papers of Benjamin H Latrobe, 76, James T White & Co; auth, The Papers of Benjamin Henry Latrobe: Problems and possibilities of editing historical documents on microfiche, J Micrographics, 11/76; The Papers of Benjamin Henry Latrobe: New approaches to the micropublication of historical records, Microform Rev, 3/77; Internal improvements and political parties in Antebellum North Carolina 1836-1860, NC Hist Rev, spring 78; Thunder from the mountains: Thomas Lanier Clingman and the end of Whig supremacy in North Carolina, NC Hist Rev, fall 79; Free suffrage, revisited: Political parties and constitutional reform in Antebellum North Carolina, NC Hist Rev, winter 82; The progressive paradigm of antebellum North Carolina politics, Carolina Comments (in press). **CONTACT ADDRESS** Thomas Edison Papers, Rutgers, The State Univ of New Jersey, New Brunswick, 16 Seminary Place Van Dyck Hall Rm 113, New Brunswick, NJ 08901-1108. **EMAIL** taep@rci.rutgers.edu

JEFFRIES, JOHN W.

PERSONAL Born 04/06/1942, Oxford, MS, m, 1964, 2 children **DISCIPLINE** HISTORY **EDUCATION** Yale Univ, PhD. **CAREER** Prof, Univ MD Baltimore County. **RESEARCH** Twentieth century Am; Am polit and policy hist. **SELECTED PUBLICATIONS** Auth, Testing the Roosevelt Coalition and Wartime America: The World War II Homefront; publ(s) on polit(s) and policy of the Franklin D. Roosevelt era; World War II American homefront. **CONTACT ADDRESS** Dept of Hist, Univ of Maryland, Baltimore County, Hilltop Circle, Baltimore, MD 21250. **EMAIL** jeffries@umbc.edu

JEFFRIES, LEONARD

DISCIPLINE AFRICAN-AMERICAN STUDIES **EDUCATION** PhD. **CAREER** New York State Commission on Education, Task Force on Deficiency Correction in Curriculum Regarding People of Color, former consultant, former member; City College of New York, Dept of African American Studies, chairman, until 1992, professor, currently. **SELECTED PUBLICATIONS** Task Force's final report entitled, "A Cirriculum of Inclusion". **CONTACT ADDRESS** Department of African-American Studies, City Col, CUNY, 138th & Covant St, Rm 4150, New York, NY 10031.

JEFFRIES, ROSALIND R.
PERSONAL Born 06/24/1936, New York, NY, m, 1965 **DISCIPLINE** ART HISTORY **EDUCATION** Hunter Coll, BA 1963; Columbia Univ, MA, 1968; Yale Univ, PhD, 1990. **CAREER** Bishop's Bible Col Church of God in Christ, New York, NY, assistant professor, 91; Jersey City State Col, Jersey City, assistant professor, currently; School of Visual Arts, New York, NY, senior teaching faculty, currently; City Univ NY, art hist, artist, prof 1972-; San Jose St Univ, asst prof 1969-72; Brooklyn Museum, lectr 1969; Group Seminars, Africa, co-ldr 1966-72; US Govt USIS, Abidjan, & Ivory Cst, W Africa, dir exhib 1965-66. **HONORS AND AWARDS** Listed, Black Artists On Art; Afro-am Artist; Arts Achievement Awd, President of Senegal, 1986. **MEMBERSHIPS** Lectr, univs, colls & comm cntrsnum one-woman art shows; cat writer, Museums; mem, Coll Arts Assn; CA St Art Historians; Nat Conf Artists; board of directors, Kem-Were Science Consortium, 1986-; director of art & culture, Association for the Study of African Classical Civilizations, 1986-; member, Blacklight Fellowship, Black Presence in the Bible, 1991-. **SELECTED PUBLICATIONS** Negro in Music & Art 1969; African Arts Mag, UCLA 1974; Enstooled as Queen Mother, Ashantehene Traditional Government of Ghana, 1988. **CONTACT ADDRESS** City Col, CUNY, 138 St & Convent Ave, New York, NY 10031.

JEGEDE, DELE
PERSONAL Born 04/19/1945, Nigeria, m, 1975, 4 children **DISCIPLINE** ART HISTORY **EDUCATION** Ahmadu Bello Univ, Zaria, Nigeria, BA, 73; Ind Univ Bloomington, MA, 81, PhD, 83. **CAREER** Assoc prof, Ind St Univ Terre Haute **HONORS AND AWARDS** Fulbright Scholar-in-residence, Spelman Col, 87-88; ACASA Traveling Awd, Art & Archaeology in Africa Program, 92; Ind St Univ res grant, 95; Smithsonian Sr Post-doctoral res grant, 95 **MEMBERSHIPS** African Stud Assoc; Arts Coun of African Stud Assoc; Col Art Assoc; Midwest Art Hist Soc. **SELECTED PUBLICATIONS** Auth, Recent Offerings in Contemporary African Art, rev essay, Res in African Lit, 94; Contemporary Art in Post-Colonial Africa, in An Inside Story: African Art of Our Time, Setagaya Art Museum, 95; The Essential Emokpae, in Seven Stories About Modern Art in Africa, Whitechapel, 95; New Currents, Ancient Rivers Contemporary African Artists in a Generation of Change, in African Arts, 96; On Scholars and Magicians: A Review of Contemporary Art of Africa, in Issues in Contemporary Art, 98. **CONTACT ADDRESS** Dept of Art, Indiana State Univ, Terre Haute, IN 47809. **EMAIL** arjeged@ruby.indstate.edu

JELAVICH, BARBARA
PERSONAL Born 04/12/1923, Belleville, IL, m, 1944, 2 children **DISCIPLINE** HISTORY **EDUCATION** Univ Calif, AB, 43, AM, 44, PhD, 48. **CAREER** From asst prof to assoc prof, 62-64, Prof Hist, Ind Univ, Bloomington, 67-, Am Asn Univ Women Palmer fel & Harnach grant, Deutscher Akademikerinnenbund, 60-61; Rockefeller Found fel, 63-64; Nat Endowment for Humanities grant & Am Coun Learned Soc res grant, 69-70, 76-77; Off Educ Am Coun Learned Soc fel, 77-79. **RESEARCH** European and Russian diplomatic history; Balkan history. **SELECTED PUBLICATIONS** Auth, Destruction of Russia as a Major Power--British Military Goals in the Crimean War, Amer Hist Rev, Vol 0099, 94. **CONTACT ADDRESS** Dept of Hist, Indiana Univ, Bloomington, Bloomington, IN 47401.

JELKS, EDWARD BAKER
PERSONAL Born 09/10/1922, Macon, GA, m, 1944, 1 child **DISCIPLINE** ARCHAEOLOGY, HISTORICAL ARCHAEOLOGY **EDUCATION** Univ Tex, BA, 48, MA, 51, PhD(anthrop), 65. **CAREER** Archaeologist, Smithsonian Inst, 50-53; archaeologist, Nat Park Serv, 63-56, supvry archaeologist, 56-58; dir, Tex Archaeol Salvage Proj, Univ Tex, 58-65, lectr anthrop, 63-65; assoc prof, Southern Methodist Univ, 65-68; Prof Anthrop & Dir Midwestern Archeol Res Ctr, Ill State Univ, 68-83, Dir, Signal Hill, Nfld Proj, Can Govt, 65-67; dir excavations, Ft Lancaster, San Saba, Ft Leaton & Washington-on-the-Brazos, Tex Hist Sites Prog, State Tex, 65-69; fel, Smithsonian Inst, 68; collabr improv soc sci teaching, US Off Educ, 70-72; dir, Archaeol Surv Mackinaw River & Cent Ill River Valleys, Ill Hist Sites Prog & Const Island Proj, US Mil Acad, 71-72. **HONORS AND AWARDS** Jc Harrington Medal in Historical Archaeology. **MEMBERSHIPS** Fel AAAS; Soc Am Archaeol; Soc Hist Archaeol (pres, 68); Soc Prof Archeologists (pres, 76). **RESEARCH** North American archaeology; historical archaeology. **SELECTED PUBLICATIONS** Coauth, Handbook of Texas Archaelogy, Bull of the Teas Archeological Soc, Vol 25, 54; ed, Historical Dictionary of North American Archaelolgy, Greenwood Press, 88; auth, The Founding Meeting of the Society-For-Historical-Archaeology, 67, Hist Arch, Vol 0027, 93. **CONTACT ADDRESS** 605 N School St, Normal, IL 61761. **EMAIL** ebjelks@ilstu.edu

JENKINS, A. LAWRENCE
PERSONAL Born 08/02/1959, Spain, m **DISCIPLINE** ART HISTORY **EDUCATION** Harvard Univ, BA, 81; Inst of Fine Arts, MA, 85, PhD, 95. **CAREER** Asst prof, Univ New Orleans, Dept of Fine Arts, 94-. **HONORS AND AWARDS** NEH fel, 97-98. **MEMBERSHIPS** CAA; SAH; Renaissance Soc of Am. **RESEARCH** Italian Renaissance architecture; fifteenth century; Sienese art of the Renaissance. **SELECTED PUBLICATIONS** Co-ed, Pratum Romanum: Richard Krautheimer zum 100 Geburstag, Ludwig Reichert Verlag, 97; rev, Massimo Bulgarelli, All'ombra Delle Volte: Architettura del Quattrocento a Firenze e Venezia, Jour of Soc of Archit Hist, 97; auth, Pius II and His Loggia in Siena, in, Pratum Romanum: Richard Krautheimer zum 100 Geburstag, Ludwig Reichert Verlag, 97; auth, Caterina Piccolomini and the Palazzo delle Papesse in Siena, in Wilkins, ed, Beyond Isabella: Secular Women Patrons of Art in Renaissance Italy, Thomas Jefferson, 99. **CONTACT ADDRESS** Dept of Fine Arts, Univ of New Orleans, New Orleans, LA 70148. **EMAIL** aljfa@uno.edu

JENKINS, ELLEN JANET
PERSONAL Born 11/19/1952, Austin, TX, d **DISCIPLINE** HISTORY **EDUCATION** Univ Tex, BA, 77; N Tex Univ, MA, 83; PhD, 92. **CAREER** Teacher, Garland Independent Sch Dist, 77-81; Grad Teaching Fel, N Tex Univ, 82-87; Res Asst, Oxford Univ, 84-; Asst Prof, Univ Ark, 92-97; Asst Prof, Ark Technol Univ, 97-. **HONORS AND AWARDS** Fac Res Grants, 93-, 94, 96; Grant, Ark Humanities coun/Nat Endowment of the Humanities; Phi Alpha Theta. **MEMBERSHIPS** St Cross Asn, Southern Hist Asn, Ark Asn of Col Hist Teachers, Popular Cult Asn, Nat Soc Sci Asn, Southwest Soc Sci Asn. **RESEARCH** England 1870-1920, World War I. **SELECTED PUBLICATIONS** Auth, "Center Point April 1939, Drew Co Hist J 9 (94): 27-32; auth, "Alice James," Great Live From History: American Women," Salem Pr (95): 971-975; rev, Churchill and the Politics of War 1940-1941, by Sheila Lawlor in Teaching Hist (95), 103; auth, "FDR's Tree Army: Monticello and the Civilian Conservation Corps," Drew Co Hist J 10 (95): 36-39; auth, "Pre-World War I British Propaganda," Encycl of Propaganda, M E Sharpe, Inc (97): 286-288; auth, "J P Morgan and Company, the Allies and the Commercial Agency Agreement," forthcoming. **CONTACT ADDRESS** Dept Soc Sci, Arkansas Tech Univ, 215 W O St, Russellville, AR 72801-2222. **EMAIL** jan.jenkins@mail.atu.edu

JENKINS, JENNIFER L.
DISCIPLINE MODERN EUROPE **EDUCATION** Stanford Univ, BA, 88; Univ Mich, MA, 91, PhD, 97. **CAREER** Hist, Washington Univ. **HONORS AND AWARDS** Krupp Found Intern Profog fel, Stanford Univ, 87; Regents Fel, Univ Mich, 89-92; Mellon Candidacy Fel, Univ Michigan, 92; Germanistic Socy Am Dissertation Grant, 92-93; Rackham Profedoctoral Fel, Univ Michigan, 94-95; Dissertation Res Grant, Nat Endowment Hum, 95-96; James Bryant Conant Fel, Center for Euro Studies, Harvard Univ, 98-99. **SELECTED PUBLICATIONS** Coauth, The Kaiserreich in the 1990s: New Research, New Agendas, New Directions German History, 91; Die Kulturreformbewegung um 1900 am Beispiel Hamburgs Materialien Jugendliteratur Und Medien Heft 30, 93; Collaborative paper, Postmodernism and Television: Speaking of Twin Peaks, Full of Secrets: Critical Approaches To Twin Peaks, Wayne State Univ Press, 94; auth, "The Kitsch Collections and The Spirit in the Furniture: Cultural Reform and National Culture in Germany," Social History, 21, 2, (96): 123-141. **CONTACT ADDRESS** Dept of History, Washington Univ, 1 Brookings Dr, Campus Box 1062, Saint Louis, MO 63130. **EMAIL** jjenkins@artsci.wustl.edu

JENKINS, VIRGINIA SCOTT
DISCIPLINE AMERICAN STUDIES, HISTORY **EDUCATION** Wheaton Col, BA, 73; George WA Univ, PhD, 91. **RESEARCH** Material cult studies. **SELECTED PUBLICATIONS** Auth, " Early Nineteenth Century Road Food: What People Ate When They Traveld in the United States," Mid-Atlantic Almanack 2, (93); auth, " A Green Velvety Carpet: the Front Lawn in America," Journal of Am Culture, (94); auth, the lawn: A History of An American Obsession, Smithsonian Inst Press, 94; auth, "Slipping Up: Bananas and American Humor," Columbia Journal of Am Studies, (98); auth, "Fairway Living," Princton Architectrue Press, (98). **CONTACT ADDRESS** Am Stud Dept, Univ of Maryland, Col Park, College Park, MD 20742. **EMAIL** vjenkins@mnsinc.com

JENSEN, DE LAMAR
PERSONAL Born 04/22/1925, Roseworth, ID, m, 1951, 5 children **DISCIPLINE** MODERN EUROPEAN HISTORY **EDUCATION** Brigham Young Univ, AB, 52; Columbia Univ, AM, 53, PhD, 57. **CAREER** Teacher, high sch, Idaho, 47-48; instr of Western civilization, NY Univ, 54-57; from instr to assoc prof, 57-66, chmn dept, 67-72, Prof to Prof Emer Hist, Brigham Young Univ, 66-; newsletter ed, Historians Early Mod Europe, 65-; consult ed, Forums in hist ser, Forum Press, 72-; ed exec, Biog Dictionary Early Mod Europ, 73- **HONORS AND AWARDS** Fac res fel, Brigham Young Univ, 63; Rockefeller Found res grant early mod diplomacy in Europe, 64-65; Nat Endowment for Humanities res grant, 70-71. **MEMBERSHIPS** AHA; Renaissance Soc Am; Am Soc Reformation Res; Hist Asn, Eng. **RESEARCH** Early modern diplomatic history; Renaissance and Reformation; European thought. **SELECTED PUBLICATIONS** Auth, Machiavelli: Cynic, Patriot, or Political Scientist?, 60 & The Expansion of Europe: Motives, Methods, and Meanings, 67, Heath; The artist in Renaissance society, Western Humanities Rev, autumn 62; Diplomacy and Dogmatism: Bernardino de Mendoza and the French Catholic League, Harvard Univ, 64; Franco-Spanish diplomacy and the Armada, In: From the Renaissance to the Counter-Reformation, Random, 65; Confrontation at Worms, Brigham Young Univ, 73; Power politics and diplomacy, 1500-1650, In: The Meaning of the Renaissance and Reformation, Houghton, 73. **CONTACT ADDRESS** Dept of Hist, Brigham Young Univ, Provo, UT 84602. **EMAIL** dlj2@email.byu.edu

JENSEN, JOAN MARIA
PERSONAL Born 12/09/1934, St. Paul, MN **DISCIPLINE** UNITED STATES HISTORY **EDUCATION** Univ Calif, Los Angeles, BA, 57, MA, 59, PhD(hist), 62. **CAREER** Teaching asst, Univ Calif, Los Angeles, 59-61; from asst prof to assoc prof hist, US Int Univ, 62-71; asst prof, 76-78, assoc prof, 78-82, Prof Hist, NMex State Univ, 82-93, prof emerita, 94-, Vis asst prof hist, Ariz State Univ, 74-75; vis lectr hist, Univ Calif, Los Angeles, 75-76; vis prof, Univ of Wisconsin, Madison, 87. **HONORS AND AWARDS** Fulbright, Univ of Bremen, Ger, 88; Fulbright, Lady Shri Ram Col, Delhi, India, 92; vis distinguished prof, Univ of Central Florida, 98. **MEMBERSHIPS** Orgn Am Historians; AHA; Coord Comt Women in Hist Professions; Agricultural Hist Soc. **RESEARCH** United States intelligence and internal security in the 20th century; women in American labor history; Asian immigration. **SELECTED PUBLICATIONS** Auth, Lossening the Bonds, 86; auth, Passage from India, 88; auth, Promise to the Land, 91; auth, One Foot on the Rookies, 95; The Death of Rosa--Sexuality in Rural America, Agr Hist, Vol 0067, 93. **CONTACT ADDRESS** Dept of Hist, New Mexico State Univ, Las Cruces, NM 88003. **EMAIL** jjensen@nmsu.edu

JENSON, CAROL ELIZABETH
PERSONAL Born 11/27/1939, Albert Lea, MN, m, 1976 **DISCIPLINE** AMERICAN CONSTITUTIONAL HISTORY **EDUCATION** St Olaf Col, BA, 61; Brown Univ, MA, 63; Univ Minn, Minneapolis, PhD(hist), 68. **CAREER** Instr Hist, Gogebic Community Col, 63; instr, Dakota State Col, 63-64; ref librn, Chicago Hist Soc, 64; asst prof hist, 68-72, assoc prof, 72-79, Prof Hist, Univ Wis-La Crosse, 79-, Nat Endowment for Humanities fel, 77-78. **HONORS AND AWARDS** Solon J Buck Awd, Minn Hist Soc Writing Awd, 73. **MEMBERSHIPS** Orgn Am Historians; Am Civil Liberties Union; AHA; Am Soc Legal Hist; Women Historians Midwest. **RESEARCH** American civil liberties in the twentieth century; women's history; women and the law. **SELECTED PUBLICATIONS** Auth, Promise to the Land--Essays On Rural Women, J West, Vol 0032, 93. **CONTACT ADDRESS** Dept of Hist, Univ of Wisconsin, La Crosse, La Crosse, WI 54601.

JETT, STEPHEN C.
PERSONAL Born 10/12/1938, Cleveland, OH, m, 1995, 1 child **DISCIPLINE** GEOGRAPHY **EDUCATION** Princeton Univ, AB, 60; Johns Hopkins Univ, PhD, 64 **CAREER** Prof Textiles, Univ Calif Davis, 96-; prof Geography, Univ Calif Davis, 79-; assoc prof Geography, Univ Calif Davis, 72-79; asst prof Geography, Univ Calif Davis, 64-72; instr Geography, Ohio State Univ, 63-64. **HONORS AND AWARDS** Navajo Wildlands Top 50 Bks of Yr, 97 **MEMBERSHIPS** Amer Assoc Advancement Science, Assoc Amer Geographers, Amer Geographical Soc, Soc Amer Archaeology, Explorers Club. **RESEARCH** Culture-Historical Geography; Navajo Indians; Pre-Columbian Transoceanic Influences; Material Culture; Sacred Places; Placenames **SELECTED PUBLICATIONS** "Dyestuffs and Possible Early Southwestern Asian/South American Contacts," Across before Columbus? Evidence for Transoceanic Contact with the Americas prior to 1492, NEARA Publications, 98; "Resist-Dyeing as a Possible Ancient Transoceanic Transfer," Mormons, Scripture, and the Ancient World: Studies in Honor of John L. Sorenson, 98; "Place-Naming, Environment, and Perception among the Canyon de Chelly Navajo of Arizona," The Professional Geographer, 97 **CONTACT ADDRESS** Div of Textiles and Clothing, Univ of California, Davis, 1 Shields Ave, Davis, CA 95616.

JEWSBURY, GEORGE FREDERICK
PERSONAL Born 11/26/1941, Colchester, IL, m, 1964, 3 children **DISCIPLINE** RUSSIAN & EAST EUROPEAN HISTORY **EDUCATION** Mankato State Col, BA, 62; Univ Wash, MA, 65, PhD(hist), 70; Univ Bucharest, dipl Romanian studies, 68. **CAREER** From instr to asst prof, 67-76, Assoc Prof Hist, Okla State Univ, 76-, Fulbright teaching fel, Univ Nancy, 71-72. **MEMBERSHIPS** Am Asn Advan Slavic Studies; Fulbright Alumni Asn; Am Asn southeastern Europ Studies. **RESEARCH** Russian activities in the Danubian principalities; Russia in the nineteenth century; French Emigres in Russia. **SELECTED PUBLICATIONS** Auth, The Russian Army in the Danubian Principalities: 1806-1812, Southeastern Europ, 75; A Soviet view of modern art, Cimarron Rev, 4/75; Russian students in Nancy, France: 1905-1914, Jahrbucher fur Geschichte Osteuropas, 75; The Russian Annexation of Bessarabia: 1774-

1828, A Study of Imperial Expansion, In: East Europ Monogr, No 15, Columbia Univ, 76; The Allied Military Occupation of Meurthe-et-Moselle: January-April, 1814, Mil Affairs, 2/77; coauth, Civilization Past and Present, Scott, Foresman and Co, 5th ed, 76 and 8th ed (2 vols), 81; auth, Nationalism in the Danubian Principalities: 1800-1825: A Reconsideration, East Europ Quart, Vol 13, 79; Comte de Langeron and His Role in Russia's Wars against the Porte and France, 1805-1814, Proc of Tenth Consortium on Revolutionary Europe, Vol 1, 80. **CONTACT ADDRESS** Dept of Hist, Oklahoma State Univ, Stillwater, 501 Life Sciences W, Stillwater, OK 74078. **EMAIL** gfcdj@ao.com

JEZIERSKI, JOHN V.
PERSONAL Born 04/05/1943, Cleveland, OH, m, 1966, 2 children **DISCIPLINE** HISTORY, HISTORICAL GEOGRAPHY **EDUCATION** John Carroll Univ, AB 65; IN Univ, MA, 67; PhD, 71. **CAREER** Prof, Saginaw Valley State Univ, 70-. **HONORS AND AWARDS** Earl Warrick Awd for Excellence in Res, 00; Fletcher Jones Foundation Fel, 99; Who's Who Among Am Teachers, 96; Fel, Can Govt Fac Res Prog, 86. **MEMBERSHIPS** Hist Soc of Mich. **RESEARCH** History of Photography, Michigan and Great Lakes Regional History. **SELECTED PUBLICATIONS** Auth, "Dangerous Opportunity: Glenalvin J. Goodridge and Early Photography in York, Pennsylvania," Pennsylvania History, (97): 310-332; auth, "Henry G. Peabody and the Detroit Publishing Company in British Columbia,: BC Studies: The British Columbian Quarterly, (99): 77-84; auth, Enterprising Images: The Goodridge Brothers, African American Photographers, 1847-1922, Detroit, 00. **CONTACT ADDRESS** Dept History, Saginaw Valley State Univ, Brown Hall 307, University Center, MI 48710. **EMAIL** jvjez@svsu.edu

JICK, LEON ALLEN
PERSONAL Born 10/04/1924, St. Louis, MO, m, 1959, 4 children **DISCIPLINE** JEWISH HISTORY **EDUCATION** Washington Univ, BA, 47; Hebrew Union Col, MA, 54; Columbia Univ, PhD(Am immigration hist), 73. **CAREER** Asst prof, 66-69, dean col, 69-71, dir contemp Jewry, Inst for Jewish Life, 71-73, prof, 69-80, Schneider Prof Am Jewish Studies, Brandeis Univ, 80-, Trustee, Boston Hebrew Col, 72-76. **MEMBERSHIPS** Asn for Jewish Studies (pres, 70-72); Am Jewish Hist Soc; Inst for Contemp Jewry, Jerusalem; Acad Jewish Studies; Boston Hebrew Col. **RESEARCH** American Jewish history, Holocaust **SELECTED PUBLICATIONS** Auth, The Teaching of Judaism in American Universities, 70; The American system of the Synogogue, 74; Uses and Abuse of the Holocaust in the American Jewish Public, Yad Vashbein Annual XIII, 81; The Reformation of Zionism, 97; Method in Madness - An Analysis of for the Nazi Extermination Policy, Modern Jewish Thought, 90; The Transformation of Jewish Social Work, Journal of Jewish Communal Service, Winter, Spring, 98-99; Wise, Isaac, Meyer--Shaping American Judaism, Amer Jewish Arch, Vol 0046, 94; Comments on the Washington Hebrew Congregation Article--Response, Amer Jewish Hist, Vol 0084, 96. **CONTACT ADDRESS** Near Eastern and Judaic Studies, Brandeis Univ, 415 South St, Waltham, MA 02454. **EMAIL** mljick@aol.com

JIMENEZ, RANDALL
PERSONAL Born 10/24/1943, San Francisco, CA, m, 1985, 5 children **DISCIPLINE** HISTORY, GEOGRAPHY **EDUCATION** San Jose State Univ, BA, 65; MA, 68; Univ Calif, EdD, 74. **CAREER** San Jose State Univ, 68-74; Loyola Univ, 74-79; Community Services Agency, 79; San Jose State Univ, 89-. **HONORS AND AWARDS** Teacher of the Year, Santa Clara county, 99. **MEMBERSHIPS** Nat Asn of Chicana and Chicano Studies; Calif Faculty Asn. **RESEARCH** Curriculum Development and Teaching styles in Chicana/o studies. **SELECTED PUBLICATIONS** Auth, Voices of Matalalan: A Novel, chusma House, 95; auth, Muchos Boletos Pero No Tren, Historical Sci Pub; auth, Aztec Prophesy, Hist Sci Pub, 00; auth, Chicano Paradigms, H8st Sci Pub., 00. **CONTACT ADDRESS** Dept Hist & Geog, West Valley Col, 14000 Fruitvale Ave, Saratoga, CA 95070-5640.

JITENDRA, ASHA K.
DISCIPLINE 17TH AND 18TH CENTURY BRITISH AMERICA **EDUCATION** BA, Univ Madras,76; MS, Purdue Univ, 86; PhD, Univ Ore, 91. **CAREER** Res asst, Univ Oregon, 89-91; Asst prof, Texas Tech Univ, 91-93; Asst prof, 93-97, special ed, Lehigh Univ. **MEMBERSHIPS** Ed bd, Remedial & Spec Ed, 1995-; ed bd, Ed & Treatment of Children, 96-. **SELECTED PUBLICATIONS** Auth, "Let's learn contractions!" Teaching Exceptional Children 29 (97): 16-19; auth, "Aligning the basal curriculum and assessment in elementary mathematics: The experimental development of curriculum-valid survey tests," Diagnostique 22 (97): 101-127; auth, "A descriptive analysis of mathematics curricula materials from a pedagogical perspective: A case study of fractions," Remedial and Special Education 18 (97): 66-81; co-auth, "A dynamic curriculum-based language assessment: Identifying the academic needs of students who are linguistically diverse with special needs," Preventing School Failure 42 (98): 182-185; co-auth, "Effects of mathematical word problem solving by students at risk or with mild disabilities," J of Educational Research 91 (98): 345-356; co-auth, "Effects of a direct instruction main idea summarization program and self-monitoring on reading comprehension of middle school students with learning disabilities," Reading and Writing Quaterly: Overcoming Learning Difficulties 14 (98): 379-396; co-auth, "The effects of instructionin solving mathematical word problems for students with learning problems: A meta-analysis," The J of Special Educsation 32 (99): 207-225; co-auth, "Teaching middle school students with learning disabilities to solve multistep word problems using a schema-based approach," Remedial and Special Education 20 (99): 50-64; co-auth, "A case study of subtraction analysis in basal mathematics programs: Adherence to important instructional design criteria," Learning Disabilities Research & Practice 14 (99): 69-79; co-auth, "Advanced story map instruction: Effects on the reading comprehension of students with learning disabilities," J of Special Education 33 (99): 2-17. **CONTACT ADDRESS** Col of Educ, Special Educ Prog, Lehigh Univ, Iacocca Hall, 111 Research Dr., Bethlehem, PA 18015. **EMAIL** AKJ2@lehigh.edu

JODZIEWICZ, THOMAS W.
PERSONAL Born 03/07/1944, Alburquerque, NM, m, 1967, 2 children **DISCIPLINE** HISTORY **EDUCATION** Providence Col, AB; Tufts Univ, MA; Col William and Mary, PhD. **CAREER** Dept ch; prof, Dallas Univ. **RESEARCH** Early American history, particularly New England and American Catholic. **SELECTED PUBLICATIONS** Auth, A Curious Soaking Rain to Night Thanks Be to God: Gershom Bulkeley's 1710 Diary, Conn Hist Soc, Bul LVI, 91, 93; An Unexpected Coda for the Early American Captivity Narrative: A Letter from a Romish Priest, Cath Hist Rev LXXXI, 95. **CONTACT ADDRESS** Dept of History, Univ of Dallas, 1845 E Northgate Dr, Braniff 244, Irving, TX 75062-4736. **EMAIL** tjodz@acad.udallas.edu

JOHANNINGSMEIER, CHARLES
PERSONAL Born 11/27/1959, Lafayette, IN, m, 1989, 2 children **DISCIPLINE** AMERICAN STUDIES, ENGLISH **EDUCATION** Haverford Col, BA, 81; Ind Univ, MA, 88; PhD, 93. **CAREER** Instr, State Univ NYork at Cortland, 92-98; asst prof, Univ Nebr at Omaha, 98-. **HONORS AND AWARDS** Bibliog Soc of Am Fel, 94; CN Bibliog Soc of England Fel, 94. NEH Summer Stipend, 97. **MEMBERSHIPS** Res Soc for Am Periodicals; Soc for the Hist of Authorship Reading; Soc for Textual Scholar. **RESEARCH** Newspapers and Fiction, American Regionalism. **SELECTED PUBLICATIONS** Auth, Fiction and the American Literary Marketplace: The Role of Newspaper Syndicates in America, 1860-1900, Cambridge UP, 97. **CONTACT ADDRESS** Dept English, Univ of Nebraska, Omaha, 6001 Dodge St, Omaha, NE 68182-0001.

JOHANNSEN, ROBERT W.
PERSONAL Born 08/22/1925, Portland, OR, m, 1949, 2 children **DISCIPLINE** HISTORY **EDUCATION** Reed Col, BA, 48; Univ of Wash, MA, 49; PhD, 53. **CAREER** Univ of Wash, 53-54; Univ of Kans, 54-59; Univ of IL Urbana-Champaign, 59-. **HONORS AND AWARDS** Pelzer Prize, Miss Valley Hist Assoc, 52; Koontz Prize, AHA, 53; Awd of Merit, Am Assoc of State and Local Hist, 61; Guggenheim Fel, 67-68; Fel, Soc of Am Hist, 74; Francis Parkman Prize for Lit Distinction in the Writing of Hist, 74; University Scholar, Univ of IL, 90-93. **RESEARCH** Early American history, Nineteenth Century (1820s-1860), Civil War and Reconstruction. **SELECTED PUBLICATIONS** Auth, Frontier Politics and the Sectional Conflict, Univ of Wash Pr, (Seattle), 55; auth, Stephen A Douglas, Oxford Univ Pr, (NY), 73; auth, To the Halls of the Montezumas: The Mexican War in the American Imagination, Oxford Univ Pr, 85; auth, The Frontier, The Union, and Stephen A. Douglas, Univ of IL Pr, (Urbana), 89; Auth, Lincoln, the South, and Slavery: The Political Dimension, La State Univ Pr, (Baton Rouge), 91; auth, "La Joven America y la guerra con Mexico", Historia Mexicana, XLVII (97): 261-284; auth, "Introduction", and "The Meaning of Manifest Destiny", Manifest Destiny and Empire: American Antebellum Expansionism, eds Sam W. Hayes and Christopher Morris, Tex A&M Univ Pr, (College Station), 97. **CONTACT ADDRESS** Dept Hist, Univ of Illinois, Urbana-Champaign, 810 S Wright St, Urbana, IL 61801-3611. **EMAIL** rjohanns@uiuc.edu

JOHANSEN, BRUCE ELLIOTT
PERSONAL Born 01/30/1950, San Diego, CA **DISCIPLINE** AMERICAN HISTORY, CROSS-CULTURAL COMMUNICATIONS **EDUCATION** Univ Wash, BA, 72, PhD(comm), 79; Univ Minn, MA, 75. **CAREER** Staff writer, Seattle Times, 70-76; teaching assoc newswriting, Univ Wash, 76-79; grant coord, El Centro de la Raza, 80-81; asst to full prof Commun, Robert T. Reilly Diamond Prof, Univ Nebr, Omaha, 82-, co-ord Native American Studies, Univ of Nebr at Omaha, 98-, consult, El Centro de la Raza, 76-, Seattle Times, 77, Ford Found, 77 & Nat Endowment for Humanities, 81-. **HONORS AND AWARDS** Univ of Omaha's Awd for Outstanding Research or Creative Activity, 97.RG **RESEARCH** American Revolutionary history; American Indian history and contemporary issues; Chicano history and contemporary issues. **SELECTED PUBLICATIONS** Auth, The Reservation Offensive, In: Essential Sociology, Scott, Foresman & Co, 79; coauth (with Roberto Maestas), Wasi'chu: The Continuing Indian Wars, Monthly Rev Press, 79, Span transl, Fondo Cultura y Economica, Mexico City, 62 & Arabic transl, Hindi, Beruit; auth, Black Hills uranium rush, In: America's Energy: Reports from the Nation on 100 Years of Struggles for the Democratic Control of Our Resources, Pantheon, 81; The Forgotten Founders: Benjamin Franklin, the Iroquois and the Rationale for American Revolution, Gambit, 82; coauth (with Roberto Maestas), El Pueblo: The Gallegos Family's American Journey, 1503-1980, Monthly Rev Press, 82; Exemplar of Liberty: Native America and the Evolution of Democracy, with Dr. Donald A. Grinde, Jr., Los Angelos: American Indian Study Center, UCLA, 91; Life and Death in Mohawk Country, Golden, Co: North American Press/ Fulcrum Pubs, 93; Eccocide of Native America: Ecology, Economics, and the Environment, with Donald A. Grinde, Jr., Santa Fe, NM: Clear Light Pubs, 95; Native American Political Systems and the Evolution of Democracy: An Annotated Bibliography, Westport, Conn: Greenwood Press, 96; So Far From Home: Manila's Santo Tomas Internment Camp, 1942-1945, Omaha: NE: PBI Press (self-published), 96; The Encyclopedia of Native American Biography, with Donald A. Grinde, Jr., New York: Henry Holt, 97; Debating Democracy: The Iroquois Legacy of Freedom, Santa Fe: Clear Light Pubs, 98; The Encyclopedia of Native American Legal Tradition, Westport, Conn: Greenwood Press, 98; The Encyclopedia of Native American Economic History, Westport, Conn: Greenwood Press, est 99; The Haudeosaunee (Iroquois) Encyclopedia, Westport, Conn: Greenwood Press, 99; Native American Political Systems and the Evolution of Democracy; An Annotated Bibliography, Vol II, Westport, Conn: Greenwood Press, 99; The Shapers of the Great Debates: Native Americans, Land, Spirit, and Power, Wesrport, Conn: Greenwood Press, 00; The Global Warming Desk Reference, Greenwood (Westport, CT), forthcoming. **CONTACT ADDRESS** Dept of Commun, Univ of Nebraska, Omaha, 6001 Dodge St, Omaha, NE 68182-0002. **EMAIL** bruce.johansen@unomaha.edu

JOHANSON, HERBERT A.
PERSONAL Born 01/10/1934, Jersey City, NJ, m, 1983, 2 children **DISCIPLINE** CONST LAW, AND LEGAL HISTORY **EDUCATION** Columbia Univ, AB, 55, MA, 61, PhD, 65; NYork Law Sch, LLB, 60. **CAREER** Ernest F. Hollings prof Const Law, Univ of SC. **HONORS AND AWARDS** Am Council of Learned Soc(s) Fel, 74-75; Inst for Humane Studies Fellow, 81-85; Univ of South Carolina Educational Found, Res Awd for Professional Schools, 00. **MEMBERSHIPS** Am Soc for Legal Hist, 74-75, 99-02; Am Historical Assoc, The Historical Soc, Am Law Inst. **RESEARCH** The Supreme Court under John Marshall; History of Criminal Justice; English and American Constitutional Thought, 17th to19th century. **SELECTED PUBLICATIONS** Auth, casebk on Amer legal and const hist & textbk on the hist of criminal justice; auth, Foundations of Power: John Marshall, 1801-15, vol 2, History of the United States Supreme Court, with George L. Haskins, 81; coauth, History of Criminal Justice, 2nd editon, 95; auth, The Chief Justiceship of Johnn Marshall, 98. **CONTACT ADDRESS** School of Law, Univ of So Carolina, Columbia, Law Center, Columbia, SC 29208. **EMAIL** hjohnson@law.law.sc.edu

JOHN, JAMES J.
PERSONAL Born 07/25/1928, Long Prairie, MN, w, 1952, 6 children **DISCIPLINE** LATIN, MEDIEVAL HISTORY **EDUCATION** Univ Notre Dame, BA, 48, MA, 50, MMS, 51, DMS-(mediaeval studies), 59. **CAREER** Asst paleography, Inst Advan Studies, 51-61, res assoc, 62-64; Prof Paleography & Medieval Hist, Cornell Univ, 65-, Vis lectr, Princeton Univ, 59, Bryn Mawr Col & Fordham Univ, 61-62; consult, Free Libr Philadelphia, 60-65; fel, Inst Res Humanities, Univ Wis, 64-65; Am Philos Soc grant, 69-70; Am Coun Learned Soc grant, 69-70, fel, 72-73; mem, Inst Advan Studies, 69-70 & 72-73; Nat Endowment for Humanities grant, 72-73; vis prof, State Univ NY Binghamton, 74. **HONORS AND AWARDS** Member, Comite Intl de Paleographie Latine, 79. **MEMBERSHIPS** Am Cath Hist Asn; Mediaeval Acad Am **RESEARCH** Medieval intellectual history; Latin paleography. **SELECTED PUBLICATIONS** The Ex-Libris in 'Codices Latini Antiquiores' Scriptorium, Vol 50, 96; auth, "Latin Paleography," in Medieval Studies: An Introduction, ed James M. Powell, 2nd rev ed, (Syracuse: Syracuse Univ Press, 92) 3-81; coauth, "Addenda to Codices Latini Antiquiores (II)," Mediaeval Studies, Vol 54 (92): 286-307; auth, "The Named (and Namable) Scribes in Codices Latini Antiquiores," in Scribi e colofoni: Le sottoscrizioni di copiste dalle origini all'avvento della stampa, ed Emma Condello and Giuseppe DeGregorio (Spoleto, 95) 107-121. **CONTACT ADDRESS** Dept of Hist, Cornell Univ, McGraw Hall Rm 450, Ithaca, NY 14853-0001. **EMAIL** jjj2@cornell

JOHN, RICHARD R.
PERSONAL Born Lawrence, MA, m, 1996, 1 child **DISCIPLINE** HISTORY **EDUCATION** Harvard Univ, BA, 81; MA, 83, PhD, 89. **CAREER** Instr, hist, lit & social studies, Harvard Univ, 89-91; asst prof, Col of William and Mary; Assoc Prof, Hist, Univ Ill at Chicago. **HONORS AND AWARDS** Allan Nevins Prize, Herman E Kroos Prize; Vis Prof, Ecole des Hautes Etudes en Sciences Sociales (EHESS), Paris, spring 01; Univ Scholar, Univ Ill at Chicago, 99-02 (the highest honor awarded to scholars at UIC); Fel, Woodrow Wilson Int ctr for scholrs, 98-99; Newcomen-Harvard Prize for the best essay in the Bus His Rev, 97; Phi Beta Kappa. **MEMBERSHIPS** Am

Antiquarian Soc; SHEAR; Bus hist conf: Am Hist Assoc; Orgn of Am Historians. **SELECTED PUBLICATIONS** Auth, "Taking Sabbatarianism Seriously: The Postal System, the Sabbath, and the Transformation of American Political Culture," Jour of the Early Repub, 90; auth, "American Historians and the Concept of the Communications Revolution," in Information Acumen: The Understanding and Use of Knowledge in Modern Business, Routledge, 94; auth, Spreading the News: The American Postal System from Franklin to Morse, Harvard Univ Press, 95; auth, "Champions, Critics, and Skeptics: Alfred D. Chandler's The Visible Hand, Organizational Innovation, and the Stages of American Economic Development," Bus Hist Rev, 97; auth, "The Lost World of Bartleby the Ex-Officeholder: Variations on a Venerable Literary Form," (New England Quarterly, 97), 631-641; auth, "Governmental Institutions as Agents of Change: Rethinking American Political Development in the Early Republic, 1787-1835," (Studies in American Political Development, 97), 347-380; auth, "Elaborations, Revisions, Dissents: Alfred D. Chandler, Jr.'s, The Visible Hand after Twenty Years." (Business History Review, 97), 151-200; auth, "Hiland Hall's 'Report on Incendiary Publications': A Forgotten Nineteenth-Century Defense of the Constitutional Guarantee of the Freedom of the Press" Am Jour of Legal Hist; auth, "The Illusion of the Ordinary: John Lewis Krimmel's, Village Tavern and the Democratization of Public Life in the Early Republic" (Pennsylvania History, 98), 87-96; auth, "The Politics of Innovation," (Daedalus, 98), 187-214; auth, "Le Debat sur la Telegraphie Publique aux Etas-Unis," (Reseaux, 99), 391:411; auth, "Recasting the Information Infrastructure for the Industrial Age," In "A Nation Transformed by Information: How Information Has Shaped the United from Colonial Times to the Present," (New York: Oxford University Press, 00), 55-105. **CONTACT ADDRESS** Dept of Hist, Univ of Illinois, Chicago, 601 S Morgan St, Chicago, IL 60607-7049. **EMAIL** rjohn@uic.edu

JOHNSON, ARTHUR L.
PERSONAL Born 11/15/1933, Natick, MA, m, 1960, 2 children **DISCIPLINE** AMERICAN & CANADIAN HISTORY **EDUCATION** Kenyon Col, BA, 55; Univ Maine, MA, 66, PhD(Am hist), 71. **CAREER** Instr hist, Univ Maine, 67-68; asst prof, 68-73, assoc prof, State Univ NY Col Potsdam, 73-. **MEMBERSHIPS** Org Am Historians; Can Hist Asn; Asn Can Studies US; Steamship Hist Soc Am; Railway and Locomotive Hist Soc. **RESEARCH** East Coast steamship lines; United States and Canada. **SELECTED PUBLICATIONS** Auth, Historic Night Line Revived, Steamboat Bill, spring 72; The International Line: A History of the Boston-Saint John Steamship Service, Am Neptune, 4/73; Steam Navigation Between Boston and the Maritimes, Abstrs for Colloquium on Maritime Provinces Hist, 72; From Eastern State to Evangeline, Am Neptune, 7/74; No Firebell in the Night, Steamboat Bill, fall 74; The Transportation Revolution on Lake Ontario, Ont Hist, 12/75; The Boston-Halifax Steamship Lines, Am Neptune, 10/77; The Montreal Secondary: Origins and History, Railroad Hist, Spring 98. **CONTACT ADDRESS** Dept of Hist, SUNY, Col at Potsdam, 44 Pierrepont Ave., Potsdam, NY 13676-2299. **EMAIL** johnsoal@potsdam.edu

JOHNSON, BOBBY HAROLD
PERSONAL Born 11/09/1935, Overton, TX, m, 1959, 2 children **DISCIPLINE** AMERICAN & JOURNALISM HISTORY **EDUCATION** Abilene Christian Col, BA, 58; Univ Okla, MA, 62, PhD(hist), 67. **CAREER** From asst prof to assoc prof, 66-77, Prof Hist, Stephen F Austin State Univ, 77-, Dir, Off Univ Info, Stephen F Austin State Univ, 79-82. **MEMBERSHIPS** Orgn Am Historans; Western Hist Asn **RESEARCH** American West, especially Oklahoma territory; history of American journalism; history of aviation. **SELECTED PUBLICATIONS** Auth, Booster attitudes of some newspapers in Oklahoma territory--the land of the fair god, autumn 65 & Reports of the governors of Oklahoma territory, winter 66-67, Chronicles Okla; Singing Oklahoma's praises: boosterism in the Soonerland, Great Plains J, fall 71; coauth, Wiley Post, his Winnie Mae, and the World's First Pressure Suit, Smithsonia, 71; auth, The Coushatta People Indian Tribal Series, 76; Doctors, druggists and dentists in the Oklahoma Territory, 1889-1907, Ariz & the West, summer 77. **CONTACT ADDRESS** Dept of Hist, Stephen F. Austin State Univ, Box 13013, Nacogdoches, TX 75962.

JOHNSON, CHARLES
PERSONAL Born Chicago, IL, m, 1998 **DISCIPLINE** HISTORY **EDUCATION** Mich State Univ, BA, 81; Western Mich Univ, MA, 88; PhD, 97. **CAREER** Asst prof, Valdosta State Univ, 97-. **HONORS AND AWARDS** Ger Hist Inst Res Fel, 95; DAAD-Goethe Inst Fel, 99. **MEMBERSHIPS** Soc for Ger Am Studies; Soc for Hist of Am For Rel; Soc for Hist of the Gilded Age and Progressive Era. **RESEARCH** US Diplomatic and Cultural History, German-American and Irish-American studies, German history, Film Studies, German. **SELECTED PUBLICATIONS** Auth, "The National German-American Alliance: The Rise and Fall of an Ethnic Organization", Schatzkammer: Der deutschen Sprache, Dichtung und Geschichte XXIII 1.2 (97): 57-68; auth, "Nicaraguan Intervention, August 4 - November 1912", encycl of N Am Hist Vol 6, Salem Pr, (Pasadena, CA), 99; auth, "The Webster-Ashburton Treaty", Encycl of N Am Hist Vol 10, Salem Pr, (Pasadena, CA), 99; auth, Culture at Twilight: The National German-American Alliance, 1901-1918, Peter Lang, (NY/Bern), 99; auth, "Kemal Atatürk", Dict of World Biography, Vol 1, Salem Pr, (Pasadena, CA), 00. **CONTACT ADDRESS** Dept Hist, Valdosta State Univ, 1500 N Patterson St, Valdosta, GA 31698-0100. **EMAIL** ctjohnso@valdosta.edu

JOHNSON, CHRISTOPHER HOWARD
PERSONAL Born 11/22/1937, Washington, IN, m, 1960, 2 children **DISCIPLINE** MODERN EUROPEAN SOCIAL HISTORY **EDUCATION** Wabash Col, BA, 60; Univ Wis-Madison, MA, 62, PhD(Hist), 68. **CAREER** Instr Hist, Univ Wis Ctr-Wausau, 65-66; from instr to asst prof, 66-75, assoc prof, 75-79, prof Hist, Wayne State Univ, 79-, Leverhulme vis fel, Univ E Anglia, UK, 70-71; Nat Endowment for Humanities younger humanist fel, 74-75; Guggenheim fel, 81-82. **HONORS AND AWARDS** Fac Recognition Awd, Bd Govs, Wayne State Univ, 76, 89, 96; Prof of the Year, Wayne State Univ, 97; Acad of Scholars, Wayne State, 98. **MEMBERSHIPS** AHA; Soc Fr Hist Studies. **RESEARCH** Eighteenth/Nineteenth century French social and cultural history; working class US history. **SELECTED PUBLICATIONS** Auth, Etienne Cabet and the problem of class antagonism, Int Rev Social Hist, 66; Communism and the working class before Marx: The Icarian experience, Am Hist Rev, 71; Utopian Communism in France: Cabet and the Icarians, 1839-1851, Cornell Univ, 74; The Revolution of 1830 in French economic history, In: 1830 in France, New Viewpoints, 75; Economic change and artisan discontent: the Tailors' history, 1800-1848, In: Revolution and Reaction: 1848 and the Second French Republic, Croom Helm, 75; Patterns of proletarianization: Parisian tailors and Lodeve woolen workers, In: Consciousness and Class Experience in Nineteenth Century Europe, Holmes and Meier, 79; Maurice Sugar: Law, Labor, and the Left in Detroit, 1912-1950, Wayne State Univ Press, 89; Capitalism and the State: Capital Accumulation and Proletarianization in the Languedocian Woolens Industry, In the Workplace before the Factory, Cornell, 93; The Life and Death of Industrial Languedoc, 1700-1920: The Politics of Deindustrialization, Oxford U Press, 95. **CONTACT ADDRESS** Dept of History, Wayne State Univ, 3094 Faculty Admin Bldg, Detroit, MI 48202-3919. **EMAIL** aa4307@wayne.edu

JOHNSON, CURTIS
DISCIPLINE 19TH CENTURY AMERICAN SOCIAL AND RELIGIOUS HISTORY **EDUCATION** Univ Minn, PhD, 85. **CAREER** Dept Hist, Mt. St. Mary's Col **SELECTED PUBLICATIONS** Auth, Redeeming America: Evangelicals and the Road to Civil War. **CONTACT ADDRESS** Dept of History, Mount Saint Mary's Col and Sem, 16300 Old Emmitsburg Rd, Emmitsburg, MD 21727-7799. **EMAIL** johnson@msmary.edu

JOHNSON, DALE
PERSONAL Born 10/10/1954, Lapeer, MI, m, 1983, 1 child **DISCIPLINE** HISTORY, RELIGION **EDUCATION** Cedarville Col, BA, 76; Covenant Theol Sem, MA, 84; Fla Atlantic Univ, MA, 88; Georgia State Univ, PhD, 95. **CAREER** Adj Prof, Erskine Theol Sem; Assoc Prof, Southern Wesleyan Univ, 87-. **HONORS AND AWARDS** Max Beltz Awd, Covenant Theol Sem, 83; English Speaking Union Scholar's Fel, Oxford Univ, 87; SC Governor's Distinguished Prof Awd, 91, 98; Summer Fel, Univ SC, 98. **MEMBERSHIPS** Am Soc of Church Historians, Calvin Studies Soc. **RESEARCH** English and Scottish Reformations, American religious history, second great awakening, Nineteenth-Century revivals. **SELECTED PUBLICATIONS** Auth, "The Sixties in America," in The Encycl of the U S Supreme Ct; auth, "Prophet in Scotland: The Prophetic Self Image of John Knox," The Calvin Theol J, vol 3 (98). **CONTACT ADDRESS** Dept Soc Sci, So Wesleyan Univ, PO Box 1020, Central, SC 29630-1020. **EMAIL** dwjohnson@hotmail.com

JOHNSON, DAVID ALAN
PERSONAL Born 03/16/1950, Altadena, CA, m, 1981, 2 children **DISCIPLINE** AMERICAN HISTORY & STUDIES **EDUCATION** Univ Calif, Irvine, BA, 72; Univ Pa, MA, 73, PhD, 77. **CAREER** Lectr Am civilization, Univ Pa, 76-77, hist, San Diego State Univ, 77-78, & Univ Calif, Los Angeles, 78-79; asst prof, 79-82, assoc prof, 82-92, Prof Hist, Portland State Univ, 92-, fac asst to Univ pres, 92-93, chair, hist dept, 93-96; Planning analyst, Univ Pa, 76-77; consult, Acad & Financial Planning, Univ Southern Calif, 79; dir, Grad Prog Pub Hist, Portland State Univ, 79-82; managing ed, Pacific Hist Rev, 96-. **HONORS AND AWARDS** Haynes Found res fel, Huntington Libr, 94; Burlington Northern Teach Awd, Portland State Univ, 92; Pacific Coast Br, Am Hist Asc Book Awd, 92. **MEMBERSHIPS** Orgn Am Historians; Am Studies Asn; Soc Sci Hist Asn; AAUP. **RESEARCH** American social and intellectual history; American West; history of violence in American. **SELECTED PUBLICATIONS** Ed, American Culture and the American Frontier & auth, Vigilance and the law: The moral authority of popular justice in the far West, in American Culture and the American Frontier, Am Quart (spec issue), winter 81; Founding the Far West: California, Oregon, Nevada, 1840-1890, Univ Calif Press, 92. **CONTACT ADDRESS** Portland Historical Review, Portland State Univ, 487 Cramer Hall, Portland, OR 97207-0751. **EMAIL** johnsonda@pdx.edu

JOHNSON, DAVID C.
PERSONAL Born 02/26/1946, Seattle, WA, s **DISCIPLINE** HISTORY, GEOGRAPHY **EDUCATION** Univ Washington, PhD, 76. **CAREER** Assoc Prof, Univ of La at Lafayette, 74. **MEMBERSHIPS** Population Asn of Am (PAA), Asn of Am Geographers (AAG), National Council for Geographic Educ (NCGE). **RESEARCH** Urban, economic, and regional geography, demography. **SELECTED PUBLICATIONS** Auth, "Municipal Services," Chapter Five in Outer Continental Shelf Impacts, Morgan City, Louisiana, 76-77; auth, "Population Profiles: A Useful Technique in Teaching Urban Geography," The Mississippi Geographer, 6 (78); auth, "Natural Decreases in Population Among Louisiana Parishes," The Louisisan Economy 17 (80); auth, "Age Waves in Cities," Social Sciences Journal, 17 (80); auth, "Louisiana: A Geography, with H. Bullamore and O. Abington, Dept of Geography/Urban & Regional Planning, Univ of Southwestern Louisiana, Lafayette, LA, 93; auth, "Analyzing Neighborhood Age Mix," Population Today, 25 (97); auth, "Population Stuctures within the Dallas-Fort Worth Region," Geographic Perspectives on the Texas Region, ed. Donald Lyons and Paul Hudak, Asn of Am Geographers, Washington DC (97): 37-45; auth, "A Classification of Cities," National Social Science Perspectives Journal, 98; auth, "Geography of Louisiana, with Elaine Yodis, McGraw-Hill, New York, NY, 98; auth, "Distribution of the Urban Elderly," National Social Science Journal, 10 (98): 31-38. **CONTACT ADDRESS** Dept History & Geography, Univ of Louisiana, Lafayette, PO Box 43531, Lafayette, LA 70504. **EMAIL** theprof2@aol.com

JOHNSON, DAVID R.
PERSONAL Born 12/20/1942, Rockford, IL **DISCIPLINE** HISTORY **EDUCATION** Univ Ill, BA, 65; Univ Chicago, MA, 66; PhD, 72. **CAREER** Asst prof, Univ New Orleans, 70-75; from asst prof to prof, Univ Tex at San Antonio; assoc vpres for fac affairs, Univ Tex at San Antonio, 97-. **HONORS AND AWARDS** NEH Travel Grant, 85 & 88; NEH Summer Sem, 87; UTSA Distinguished Achievement Awd for Teaching Excellence, 94. **MEMBERSHIPS** Am Hist Asn, Urban Hist Asn. **RESEARCH** Crime, Law Enforcement, Urban Economic Development. **SELECTED PUBLICATIONS** Auth, Policing the Urban Underworld, Temple Univ Press (Philadelphia, PA), 79; auth, American Law Enforcement: A History, Forum Press (St. Louis, MO), 81; ed, The Politics of San Antonio, Univ Nebr Press (Lincoln, NE), 83; auth, Illegal Tender. Counterfeiting and the Secret Source, 95. **CONTACT ADDRESS** Dept Behav Sci, Univ of Texas, San Antonio, 6900 N Loop 1604 W, San Antonio, TX 78249-1130. **EMAIL** djohnson@utsa.edu

JOHNSON, DONALD ELLIS
PERSONAL Born 04/07/1918, Plaistow, NH, m, 1942, 3 children **DISCIPLINE** HISTORY, INTERNATIONAL RELATIONS **EDUCATION** Mass State Col Fitchburg, BSEd, 40; Clark Univ, AM, 41, PhD(hist & int rels), 53. **CAREER** From instr to assoc prof, 46-66, head dept hist, 68-74, Prof Hist, Worcester Polytech Inst, 66-, Head Dept Humanities, 74-, Vis lectr US dipl hist, Col Holy Cross, 68; abstractor, Hist Abstr. **MEMBERSHIPS** AHA; AAUP **RESEARCH** Local United States Colonial history; Worcester in the war for independence. **SELECTED PUBLICATIONS** Coauth, Pioneer Class, LaVigne, 66. **CONTACT ADDRESS** 16 Lowell Ave, Holden, MA 01520.

JOHNSON, ERIC A.
PERSONAL Born 05/09/1948, Salem, MA, m, 1988, 2 children **DISCIPLINE** HISTORY **EDUCATION** Brown Univ, BA, 70; Univ Stockholm, Grad Dip, 71; Univ Pa, MA, 72; PhD, 76. **CAREER** Asst to prof, Central Mich Univ, 76-; vis prof, Univ of Strathclyde, 88-89; vis prof, Univ of Cologne, 89-95. **HONORS AND AWARDS** Fulbright Fel, 89-90; NEH Fel, 92-95; Nat Sci Found Fel, 92-95; Alexander Von Humboldt Found Fel, 94-96; Inst for Advan Study Fel, 95-96; Shorlin Awd for Outstanding Book, 96; Nethlands Inst for Advan Study Fel, 98-99. **MEMBERSHIPS** AHA; Soc Sci Hist Assoc. **RESEARCH** Modern German history, the history of crime, law and violence. **SELECTED PUBLICATIONS** Auth, The Civilization of Crime: Violence in Town and Country Since the Middle Ages, Univ of IL Pr, (Urbana, IL), 94; AUTH, Urbanization and Crime: Germany 1871-1914, Cambridge Univ Pr, (NY), 95; auth, Nazi Terror: The Gestapo, Jews and Ordinary Germans, Boric Books, (NY), 00. **CONTACT ADDRESS** Dept Hist, Central Michigan Univ, Powens Hall, Mount Pleasant, MI 48859-0001. **EMAIL** eric.a.johnson@cmich.edu

JOHNSON, HAROLD BENJAMIN
PERSONAL Born 11/17/1931, Hastings, NE, s **DISCIPLINE** HISTORY **EDUCATION** Cambridge Univ, BA, 53, MA, 60; Univ of Chicago, PhD, 63. **CAREER** Instr, 61-63, Univ of Chicago; Asst Prof, 69-72, Assoc Prof, 72-81, Scholar in Res, 81-, Univ of Virginia. **HONORS AND AWARDS** SSRC Fel 64-65, 68-69; Ford Found Fel, 65-66. **MEMBERSHIPS** Amer Hist Assoc; Soc for the History of Discoveries; Yale Library Assoc; Friends of the Univ of Arizona Library; Amer Friends of the Univ of Arizona **RESEARCH** Medieval, Early Modern Portugal; Colonial Brazil. **SELECTED PUBLICATIONS** Portrait of a Portuguese Parish Santa Maria de Alvarenga in 1719, Lisboa, 83; The Settlement of Brazil 1500-1580, Cambridge Hist of Latin Amer, 84; CoAuth, O Imperio Luso-Brasileiro 1500-

1620, Lisbon, 92; Distribuicao de Rendimentos numa Aldeia Medieval Portuguesa, Ler Historia, 97. **CONTACT ADDRESS** PO Box 89669, Tucson, AZ 85752. **EMAIL** mvesgate@aol.com

JOHNSON, HERBERT A.
PERSONAL Born 01/10/1934, Jersey City, NJ, m, 1983, 2 children **DISCIPLINE** AMERICAN LEGAL AND CONSTITUTIONAL HISTORY **EDUCATION** Columbia Univ, AB, 55; MA, 61; PhD, 65; NY Law Sch, LLB, 60. **CAREER** Lectr and asst prof, Hunter Col of CUNY, 64-67; from assoc ed to ed, The Papers of John Marshall, Inst of Early Am Hist and Culture, 67-77; from prof to Ernest F. Hollings Prof, Univ of SC, 77-. **HONORS AND AWARDS** Schiff Fel, Columbia Univ, 63-64; ACLS Fel, 74-75. **MEMBERSHIPS** Am Soc for Legal Hist, Am Hist Asn, Am Law Inst. **RESEARCH** John marshall and the Marshall Court, History of Criminal Justice, Early Air Force History 1907-1918. **SELECTED PUBLICATIONS** Auth, American Legal and Constitutional History: Cases and Materials, Austin & Winfield (San Francisco, CA), 94; coauth, History of Criminal Justice 2nd edition, Anderson Pub Co. (Cincinnati, OH), 95; auth, The Chief Justiceship of John Marshall 1801-35, Univ of SC Press (Columbia, SC), 97 & 98. **CONTACT ADDRESS** Sch of Law, Univ of So Carolina, Columbia, Columbia, SC 29208. **EMAIL** johnsonh@sc.edu

JOHNSON, JAMES M.
PERSONAL Born 06/28/1947, Montezuma, GA, m, 1969, 2 children **DISCIPLINE** HISTORY **EDUCATION** USMA, BS, 69; Duke Univ, MA, 77; PhD, 80; US Naval War Col, MA, Natl Security & Strategic Scholar, 95. **CAREER** Off, field artillery, 69-99, Colonel, 91, US Army; instr, asst prof, 77-80, assoc prof, 87-94, prof, 94-99, USMA. **RESEARCH** Colonial and Amer revolutionary hist; hist of the US Army. **CONTACT ADDRESS** 214 Wilson Rd, West Point, NY 10996. **EMAIL** yj5648@usma.edu

JOHNSON, JAMES PEARCE
PERSONAL Born 08/20/1937, Birmingham, AL, m, 1959, 2 children **DISCIPLINE** AMERICAN HISTORY **EDUCATION** Duke Univ, AB, 59; Columbia Univ, MA, 62, PhD(hist), 68. **CAREER** From instr to assoc prof, 66-80, chmn dept, 72-78, PROF HIST, BROOKLYN COL, 80-99, retired; Danforth fellow, 61-67; Mem, Bd Educ, Westfield, NJ, 72-75; assoc, Danforth Found, 77; consult var NJ & Brooklyn pub high Schs, 77-. **HONORS AND AWARDS** Louis Pelzer Awd, Orgn Am Historians, 66. **RESEARCH** Psychohistory; twentieth century American politics. **SELECTED PUBLICATIONS** Auth, Drafting the NRA Code of Fair Competition for the Bituminous Coal Industry, J Am Hist, 12/66; The Fuel Crisis, Largely Forgotten, of 1918, Smithsonian, 12/76; Westfield: From Settlement to Suburb, Westfield Bicentennial Comt, 77; The Wilsonians as War Managers, Prologue: J Nat Archives, winter 77-78; How Mother Got Her Day, Am Heritage, 4/79; Nixon's Use of Metaphor: The Real Nixon Tapes, Psychoanalytic Rev, summer 79; The Assassination in Dallas: A Search for Meaning, Psychoanalytic Rev, summer 79; The Politics of Soft Coal: From the First World War to the New Deal, Univ IL Press, 79; New Jersey: History of Ingenuity and Industry, Windsor Pubs, 87; with Timothy B. Benford, Righteous Carnage: The John E. List Murders, Scribner, 91. **CONTACT ADDRESS** 716 Clark St, Westfield, NJ 07090.

JOHNSON, JERAH W.
PERSONAL Born 05/21/1931, GA, s **DISCIPLINE** HISTORY **EDUCATION** Emory Univ, BA, 52; Univ NCar, MA, 54; PhD, 63. **CAREER** Instr, Univ of NCar, 54-56, 58-59; instr to prof, Univ of New Orleans, 59-. **HONORS AND AWARDS** Fulbright Fel, 56-58; Outstanding Educators of Am, 70-80; Ford Found Venture Grant, 74; Hub Cotton Fel, 85. **MEMBERSHIPS** AHA, SHA, La Hist Assoc. **RESEARCH** Early New Orleans, Architectural History, Jazz History. **SELECTED PUBLICATIONS** Auth, The Age of Recovery: The Fifteenth Century, Cornell, 70; auth, Africa and the West, Holt, 74; auth, UNO Prisons, 83; auth, "Colonial New Orleans," Creole New Orleans, ed Hirsh and Logston, La State Univ, (97); auth, "Vernacular Architecture of the South," Plain Folk of the South Revisited, ed Folk, La State Univ, (97). **CONTACT ADDRESS** Dept Hist, Univ of New Orleans, 2000 Lakeshore Dr, New Orleans, LA 70148-0001.

JOHNSON, JOHN W.
PERSONAL Born 04/09/1946, Minneapolis, MN, m, 5 children **DISCIPLINE** HISTORY **EDUCATION** St Olaf Col, BA, 68; Univ of Minn, MA, 70; PhD, 74. **CAREER** From instr to asst prof, Skidmore Col, 73-76; from asst prof to prof, Clemson Univ, 76-88; prof and head of dept of hist, Univ of Northern Iowa, 88-. **HONORS AND AWARDS** Phi Beta Kappa, 68; NEH summer Fel, 75; NEH summer stipend, 81; summer fel, SC Comt for the Humanities, 83; Outstanding Book Awd, Am Libr Asn and Choice, 93; Thomas Jefferson Awd, Soc for Hist in the Federal Govt, 94; honorary member, Golden Key, 95; Benjamin F. Shambaugh Awd, State Historical Soc of Iowa, 98. **MEMBERSHIPS** Orgn of Am Historians, Am Soc for Legal Hist, Am Studies Asn, Phi Alpha Theta, Soc for Hist in the Fed Govt. **RESEARCH** U.S. legal/constitutional history, Twentieth-Century U.S. history. **SELECTED PUBLICATIONS** Auth, "Adaptive Jurisprudence: Some dimensions of Early Twentieth Century American Legal Culture," The Historian 40 (77): 16-35; auth, American Legal Culture 1908-1940, Greenwood Pub, 81; auth, Insuring Against disaster: The Nuclear Industry on Trial, Mercer Univ Press, 86; auth, "Commercial Nuclear Power and the Price-Anderson Act: An Overview of a Policy in Transition," J of Policy Hist 2 (90):213-232; auth, The Dimensions of Non-Legal Evidence in the American Judicial Process, Garland Pub, 90; auth, Historic U.S. Court Cases 1690-1990: An Encyclopedia, Garland Pub, 92; auth, "'Dear Mr. Justice': Public Correspondence with Members of the U.S. Supreme Court," J of Supreme Court Hist 2 (97): 101-112; auth, The Struggle for Student Rights: Tinker v. Des Moines and the 1960s, Univ Press of Kans, 97. **CONTACT ADDRESS** Dept Hist, Univ of No Iowa, 319 Seerley Hall, Cedar Falls, IA 50614-0701. **EMAIL** john.johnson@uni.edu

JOHNSON, JUDITH R.
DISCIPLINE TWENTIETH CENTURY UNITED STATES, AND LATIN AMERICAN HISTORY **EDUCATION** BS, MA, PhD. **CAREER** Asst prof **RESEARCH** Oral history projects; reform movements with emphasis on the New Deal, and Civil Rights. **SELECTED PUBLICATIONS** Auth, The Penitentiaries in Arizona, Nevada, New Mexico, and Utah From 1900 to 1980, 97; John Weinzirl: A Personal Search for the Conquest of Tuberculosis; Kansas in the Grippe, The Spanish Influenza Epidemic of 1918. **CONTACT ADDRESS** Dept of Hist, Wichita State Univ, 1845 Fairmont, Wichita, KS 67260-0045. **EMAIL** jjohnson@twsu.edu

JOHNSON, LEROY RONALD
PERSONAL Born 01/25/1944, Smithville, GA, d **DISCIPLINE** HISTORY **EDUCATION** Univ of Caen France, Licence-es Lettres Ancient & Medieval History 1966-69; The Sorbonne Univ of Paris, Maitrise-es Lettres Medieval History 1971; Univ of MI, PhD African History 1981. **CAREER** Inst St Jean-Eudes France, dir & teacher 1969-70; Inst St Joseph Paris, dir & teacher 1970-72; MI State Univ, instructor 1973-77; Univ of FL, asst prof history 1977-78; Bryn Mawr Coll, lecturer African Hist; Towson State University, asst prof of history; Moorhead State University, assoc prof, dept of humanities, currently. **HONORS AND AWARDS** French govt scholarship Caen, Paris France 1967-68, 1971-72; Natl Defense Foreign Lang Fellowship MI State Univ 1972-73; Rackham Fellowship Univ of MI 1973-75. **MEMBERSHIPS** Reg officer French Fed of Basketball Coaches 1964-72; hon mem African Students Assoc France 1966-72, West Indian Students Assoc France 1966-72; lecturer Ctr for Afro-Amer & African Studies Univ of MI 1978-79; sr lecturer history Univ of Lagos Nigeria 1982-83; lecturer history Bryn Mawr Coll 1983-86. **CONTACT ADDRESS** Humanities & Multicultural Studies Dept, Moorhead State Univ, Moorhead, MN 56560.

JOHNSON, LLOYD
PERSONAL Born 08/13/1955, Dunn, NC, s **DISCIPLINE** HISTORY **EDUCATION** Campbell Univ, BA, 77; Campbell Univ, MEd, 78; E Carolina Univ, MA, 85; Univ SCar, PhD, 95. **CAREER** Teaching Asst, Univ SCar, 90; Asst Prof to Assoc Prof, Campbell Univ, 91-. **HONORS AND AWARDS** Fel, NEH Summer Inst, 98; Prof of the Year Awd, Campbell Univ, 99-00; Who's Who Among Am Teachers, 95, 00. **MEMBERSHIPS** Am Hist Asn, S Hist Asn, NC Literary & Hist Asn. **RESEARCH** Colonial South; African-American; Religion. **SELECTED PUBLICATIONS** Auth, The Frontier in the Colonial South: South Carolina Backcountry, 1736-1800, Greenwood Press, 97. **CONTACT ADDRESS** Dept Govt & Hist, Campbell Univ, PO Box 356, Buies Creek, NC 27506-0356. **EMAIL** johnson@mailcenter.campbell.edu

JOHNSON, OWEN V.
PERSONAL Born 02/22/1946, Madison, WI, m, 1969, 2 children **DISCIPLINE** EAST EUROPEAN MEDIA AND HISTORY, HISTORY OF JOURNALISM **EDUCATION** Washington State Univ, BA, 68; Univ Mich, MA, 70, cert Russ & East Europ studies & PhD(hist), 78. **CAREER** Lect East Europ hist, Univ Mich, 78-79; asst prof journalism, Southern Ill Univ, Carbondale, 79-80; Asst Prof, 80-87, Assoc Prof Journalism, Ind Univ, 87-, Adjunct Prof Hist, 97-, Dir, Russ & East Europ Inst, 91-95; Producer, ed & reporter, WUOM, Ann Arbor & WVGR, Grand Rapids, 69-77. **HONORS AND AWARDS** Am Philos Soc grant, 79; Int Res & Exchanges Bd res grant, Czech, 82; ACLS Conf grant, 83; Head, Hist Div, Asn Educ in Journalism, 85-86; Stanley Pech Awd, Czechoslovak Hist Conf, 87-88; Nat Coun Soviet & East Europe Res Grant, 88-90; Excellence in Jour Award, Wash State Univ. **MEMBERSHIPS** AHA; Am Asn Advan Slavic Studies; Asn Educ Jour and Mass Commun; Czechoslovak Hist Conf; OAH; Slovak Studies Asn (pres 88-90). **RESEARCH** The theory and practice of journalism in the Central and Eastern Europe, international communications. **SELECTED PUBLICATIONS** Auth, Slovakia 1918-1938: Education and the Making of a Nation, Columbia Univ Press/East Europ Monographs, 85; Whose Voice?: Freedom of Speech and the Media in Central Europe, In: Creating a Free Press in Eastern Europe, Univ Ga, 93; coauth, Mass Media and the Velvet Revolution, In: Media and Revolution: Comparative Perspectives, Univ Press Ky, 95; Professional Roles of Russian and U.S. Journalists: A Comparative Study, Journalism & Mass Commun Quart, Autumn 96; auth, The Media and Democracy in Eastern Europe, In: Communicating Democracy, Lynne Rienner, 98; contribr, Journalism and the Education of Journalists in the New East/Central Europe, Hampden Press (in press); coauth, Eastern European Journalism: Past, Present, and Future, 99. **CONTACT ADDRESS** School of Jour, Indiana Univ, Bloomington, Bloomington, IN 47405. **EMAIL** johnsono@indiana.edu

JOHNSON, PAUL B.
PERSONAL Born 06/07/1921, Paw Paw, MO, m, 1947 **DISCIPLINE** AMERICAN & BRITISH HISTORY **EDUCATION** Univ Chicago, AB, 42, PhD(hist), 54. **CAREER** Instr hist, Denison Univ, 47-49; lectr Europ hist, Univ Chicago, 49-52; from asst prof to assoc prof, 52-62, Prof Am Hist, Roosevelt Univ, 62-, Sr Fulbright lectr, Univ Edinburgh, 66-67; lectr Brit hist, Univ Ill, Chicago Circle, 74. **MEMBERSHIPS** Midwest Conf Brit Studies (secy, 70-). **RESEARCH** British housing, planning and reform, 1900-1949. **SELECTED PUBLICATIONS** Auth, Citizens Participation in Urban Renewal, Hull-House, 60; Land Fit for Heroes, Univ Chicago, 68; War, reform and hope: British Labour's perceptions, in: Im Gegenstrom, Peter Hammer, 77. **CONTACT ADDRESS** Dept of Hist, Roosevelt Univ, 600 S Michigan Ave, Chicago, IL 60605-1901.

JOHNSON, PAUL E.
DISCIPLINE HISTORY **EDUCATION** Univ Calif Berkeley, BA, 65; UCLA, MA, 68, PhD, 75. **CAREER** Guest lect, hist, Princeton; current, Prof, Hist, Univ Utah. **MEMBERSHIPS** Am Antiquarian Soc **SELECTED PUBLICATIONS** Auth, A Shopkeeper's Millenium: Society and Revivals in Rochester, New York, 1815- 1837, Hill & Wang, 78; auth, "The Modernization of Mayo Greenleaf Patch: Land, Family, and Marginality in New England, 1766-1818," New Eng Quart 55, 82; auth, "Drinking, Temperance, and the Construction of Identity in Nineteenth-Century America," Soc Sci Info 25, 86; auth, "Art and the Language of Progress in Early Industrial Paterson: Sam Patch at Clinton Bridge, Am Quart, Dec 88; auth, "Democracy, Patriarchy, and American Revivals, 1780-1830," Jour of Soc Hist 24, 91; auth, "The Market Revolution," in Encyclopedia of Am Soc Hist, Charles Scribner's Sons, 93; African-American Christianity: Essays in History, Univ Calif Press, 94; coauth, The Kingdom of Matthias: A Story of Sex and Salvation in Nineteenth-Century America, Oxford Univ Press, 94. **CONTACT ADDRESS** Dept of Hist, Univ of Utah, Salt Lake City, UT 84112.

JOHNSON, PENELOPE DELAFIELD
PERSONAL Born 03/02/1938, New York, NY, m, 1957, 2 children **DISCIPLINE** MEDIEVAL HISTORY, WOMEN'S HISTORY **EDUCATION** Yale Univ, BA, 73, MPhil, 76, PhD, 79. **CAREER** Teaching asst history, Yale Univ, 74-75, lectr, 77; asst prof hist, NY UNIV, 79-. **HONORS AND AWARDS** Phi Beta Kappa, Summa Cum Laude, Yale Univ, 73; ACLS Fel, 81; NEH Summer Fel, 81; ACLS Fel 85-86; Rockefeller Fel 85-86; NYU Research Challenge Grant, 89; Great Teacher Awd, NYU, 92; Golden Dozen Reach Awd, NYU, 90/97. **MEMBERSHIPS** AHA; Medieval Acad Am; Soc Archeol Sci et Lit du Vendomois; New England Hist Asn. **RESEARCH** Medieval religious women; medieval monasticism; medieval mysticism. **SELECTED PUBLICATIONS** Auth, Virtus: Transition from classical Latin to the De civitate Dei, Augustinian Studies, 75; Pious legends & historical realities: The foundation myths of la Trinite, Bonport & Holyrood, Rev Benedictine, 81; Prayer, Patronage & Power: The Abbey of la Trinite, Vendome, 1032-1187, NY Univ, 81; auth, "Family Involvement in the Lives of Medieval nuns and Monks," Monks, Nuns, and Friars in Mediaeval Society, Louvain: Peeters, 89; auth, "Agnes of burgundy: an eleventh-Century wooman as Monastic Patron," The J of Medieval Hist 15, (89), 93-104; Equal in Monastic Profession: Religious Women in Medieval France, Chicago Univ, 91; auth, "the Cloistering of Medieval Nuns: Release or Repression, Reality or Fantasy?" Womens Hist, Essays from the 7th Berkshire Conference on the Hist of Women, Cornell Univ Press, 91; auth, "La theorie de la cloture et l' activite reelle des moniales francaises du Xie au XIIIe siecle," Les religieuses dans le cloitre et dans le monde, 4 CERCOR: Travaux et recherches, St. Etienne: l' Unversite de Saint-Etienne, (94), 491-505; Priere, Patronage et pouvoir: l'abbaye de la Trinite de Vendome (1032-1187), Cherche-Lune, 97; auth, "Suicide and its Prevention in Later Medieval France," The Proceedings of the Western Society for Frech Studies 26, (00), 184-191. **CONTACT ADDRESS** Dept Hist, New York Univ, 53 Washington Sq South, New York, NY 10012-4556. **EMAIL** penny.johnson@nyu.edu

JOHNSON, PHIL BRIAN
DISCIPLINE LATIN AMERICAN HISTORY **EDUCATION** Univ Minn, BA 63; Tulane Univ, MA, 66, PhD(hist), 71. **CAREER** Assoc prof, 68-80, Prpf Hist, San Francisco State Univ, 80-, Dir Latin Am Studies, Monterey Inst Foreign Studies, 68-71; Dept of Health, Educ, Welfare res grant, 75; contribr ed, New Scholar, 75- **MEMBERSHIPS** Pac Coast Coun Latin Am Studies; Latin Am Studies Asn; AHA; Southern Hist Asn. **RESEARCH** Ruy Barbosa; waste disposal in Latin America; teaching innovation in Latin American area studies. **SELECTED PUBLICATIONS** Auth, Stevenson, Robert, Louis, Smithsonian, Vol 0026, 95. **CONTACT ADDRESS** Dept of Hist, San Francisco State Univ, San Francisco, CA 94132.

JOHNSON, RICHARD RIGBY
PERSONAL Born 07/06/1942, Tunbridge Wells, England, m, 1976, 1 child **DISCIPLINE** AMERICAN HISTORY **EDUCATION** Oxford Univ, BA, 64; Univ Calif, Berkeley, MA, 65, PhD(hist), 72. **CAREER** Instr hist, Univ Calif, Berkeley, 68-69 & 71-72; from asst prof to prof hist, Univ Wash, 72-; lect hist, Oxford Univ, 87-92; chair dept hist, Univ Wash, 92-97. **HONORS AND AWARDS** Rotary Found fel, 64-65; William Andrews Clark Libr fel, 76; fel, Nat Endowment for the Humanities, Huntington Libr, March-September 85; vis fel, Clare Hall, Cambridge Univ, 85-86; vis fel, St. Catherine's Col, Oxford Univ, 97-98; Huntington Libr fel, June-July, 98. **MEMBERSHIPS** AHA; Orgn Am Historians. **RESEARCH** Colonial America; Anglo-American political relations. **SELECTED PUBLICATIONS** Auth, Adjustment to Empire: The New England Colonies, 1675-1715, Rutgers Univ Pr (Newark, NJers), 81; auth, John Nelson, Merchant Adventurer: A Life Between Empires, Oxford Univ Pr (NYork), 91; articles in William and Mary Quarterly and Journal of Am Hist. **CONTACT ADDRESS** Dept of Hist, Univ of Washington, PO Box 353560, Seattle, WA 98195-3560. **EMAIL** rrj@u.washington

JOHNSON, RICHARD RONALD
PERSONAL Born 09/24/1937, Santa Rita, NM **DISCIPLINE** ANCIENT HISTORY **EDUCATION** Univ Calif, Los Angeles, BA, 60, PhD(hist), 68. **CAREER** From instr to asst prof, 66-70, Assoc Prof Hist, Univ Houston, 70-. **MEMBERSHIPS** Am Soc Papyrologists; Hellenic Soc; Soc Promotion Roman Studies; Medieval Acad Am. **RESEARCH** Classical palaeography; Roman Empire; Early Byzantine history. **SELECTED PUBLICATIONS** Auth, Ancient and Medieval accounts of the Invention of Parchment, Calif Studies Class Antiq, 70; Bicolor Membrana, Class Quart, 73. **CONTACT ADDRESS** Dept of Hist, Univ of Houston, Houston, TX 77004.

JOHNSON, ROBERT E.
PERSONAL Born 08/07/1943, New York, NY **DISCIPLINE** RUSSIAN & EAST EUROPEAN STUD **EDUCATION** Antioch Col, BA, 65; Cornell Univ, PhD, 75. **CAREER** Fac mem hist, Erindale Col, 71-, mem grad fac, 79-, dir, Ctr Russian & East European Stud, Univ Toronto, 89-; vis scholar, Russian Inst Hist, 83, 91; proj dir, Archives of the Stalin Era, 94-. **RESEARCH** Economic and demographic hist of rural Russia, Statistics in hist. **SELECTED PUBLICATIONS** Auth, "Family Life in Moscow during NEP," in Russia in the Era of NEP: Explorations in Soviet Culture and Society, ed. Sheila Fitzpatrick, Alexander Rabinowitch and Richard Stites, (Bloomington: Indiana Univ Press, 91); auth, "Introduction: The Soviet Census of 1937," Russian Studies in Hist, vol. 31, no. 1, (92): 3-9; auth, "Hist by Numbers," in Hist Anew: Innovations in the Teaching of Hist Today, ed. Robert Blackey, (Lapham, MD: Univ Publishing Associates, 92); auth, Contadini e Proletari: La classe laavoratrice moscovita alla fine dell'800 (Bologna: societe editrice il Mulino, 93); auth, "Krestianskoe khoziaistvo I semeinye sturktury v Kostrome: novye voprosy I stary dannye," in Rossiia v XX veke, Istoriki mira sporiat, ed. I.D. Koval'chenko and A.N. Sakharov, (Moscow: Nauka, 94): 115-24; auth, "Family Life-cycles and Economic Stratification: A Case-Study in Rural Russia," Journal of Social History, vol. 30, no. 3, (97): 705-31 **CONTACT ADDRESS** Robarts Libr, Univ of Toronto, 100 St. George St Rm 2074, Toronto, ON, Canada M5S 3G3. **EMAIL** johnson@chass.utoronto.ca

JOHNSON, ROGER A.
PERSONAL Born 09/07/1930 **DISCIPLINE** HISTORY, THEOLOGY **EDUCATION** Northwestern Univ, BA, 52; Yale Divinity Sch, BD, 55; Harvard Divinity Sch, ThD, 66. **CAREER** Elisabeth Luce Moore Prof of Christian Studies, Wellesley Col, 59-. **RESEARCH** Philosophical origins of demythologizing; existentialist theology and philosophy; psychoanalysis and theology. **CONTACT ADDRESS** 7 Apleby Rd., Wellesley, MA 02181. **EMAIL** rjohnson@mediaone.net

JOHNSON, RONALD MABERRY
PERSONAL Born 10/15/1936, Kansas City, MO, m, 1965, 3 children **DISCIPLINE** AMERICAN SOCIAL & CULTURAL HISTORY **EDUCATION** Col Emporia, BA, 61; Univ Kans, MA, 65; Univ Ill, Urbana, PhD(Am social & intellectual hist), 70. **CAREER** Asst prof Afro-Am hist, Cleveland State Univ, 69-72; asst prof urban & Afro-Am hist, 72-76, assoc prof Am Hist, Georgetown Univ, 76-86, prof Am Hist, Georgetown, 86-, dir Am Studies, 79-85, 89-. **MEMBERSHIPS** ASA; AHA; Orgn Am Historians. **RESEARCH** Social and cultural history; history of race relations; educational history. **SELECTED PUBLICATIONS** Auth, Schooling the Savage: Andrew S Draper and Indian Education, Phylon, 3/74; coauth, Forgotten Pages: Black Literary Magazines in the 1920s, J Am Studies, 12/74; auth, Politics and Pedagogy: The 1892 Cleveland School Reform, Ohio Hist, autumn 75; Captain of Education: Andrew S Draper, 1848-1913, Societas, summer 76; Black History and White Students: Broadening Cultural Horizons, Negro Educ Rev, 1/77; coauth, Away from Acommodation: Radical Editors and Protest Journalism, J Negro Hist, 10/77; Propaganda and Aesthetics: Literary Politics of Afro-American Magazines in the Twentieth Century, Univ Mass Press, 79, rev ed, 92. **CONTACT ADDRESS** Dept of Hist, Georgetown Univ, 1421 37th St N W, Washington, DC 20057-0001. **EMAIL** johnson2@gusun.georgetown.edu

JOHNSON, RONALD WILLIAM
PERSONAL Born 07/29/1937, Rockford, IL, 1 child **DISCIPLINE** HISTORY OF ART, PSYCHOLOGY **EDUCATION** Calif State Univ, San Diego, AB, 59; MA, 63; Univ Calif, Berkeley, MA, 65, PhD, 71. **CAREER** Asst prof art hist, Univ Iowa, 70-73; prof art hist, Humboldt State Univ, 74-. **HONORS AND AWARDS** Nat Defense Travelling Fel, 67; Kress Fel, 69-70; Nat Endowment for the Humanities Summer Seminar, 76; Nat Endowment for the Humanities Summer Seminar, 80; President's Merit Awd, (H.S.U.), 85. **MEMBERSHIPS** Col Art Asn Am. **RESEARCH** Late 19th and early 20th century art history. **SELECTED PUBLICATIONS** Auth, Picasso's Old Guitarist and the Symbolist Sensibility, Artforum XIII, 12/74; Dante Rossetti's Beata Beatrix and the New Life, Art Bull, 12/75; Poetic Pathways to Dada: Marcel Duchamp and Jules Laforgue, 5/76, Picasso's Parisian Family and the Saltimbanques, 1/77, Vincent van Gogh and the Vernacular: His Southern Accent, 6/78, Arts Mag; Picasso's Demoiselles d'Avignon and the Theatre of the Absurd, 10/80 & Whistler's Musical Modes: Symbolist Symphonies, 4/81, Arts Mag; auth, "The Early Picasso & Spanish Literature," National Gallery, Washington, DC, 96. **CONTACT ADDRESS** Humboldt State Univ, 1 Harpst St, Arcata, CA 95521-8299. **EMAIL** rwj1@axe.humboldt.edu

JOHNSON, TIMOTHY D.
PERSONAL Born 06/06/1957, Anniston, AL, m, 1978, 3 children **DISCIPLINE** HISTORY **EDUCATION** Univ Ala, BS, 79; MA (educ), 82; MA (hist), 82; PhD, 89. **CAREER** Declassification archivist, US Air Force Hist Res Center, 88-91; assoc prof, Lipscomb Univ, 91-. **HONORS AND AWARDS** Mellon Res Fel, Va Hist Soc, 94. **MEMBERSHIPS** S Hist Asn, Soc for Military Hist, Tenn Hist Asn. **RESEARCH** US Army, Civil War, Mexican War. **SELECTED PUBLICATIONS** Auth, Winfield Scott: The Quest for Military Glory, Univ Press of Kans, 98. **CONTACT ADDRESS** Dept Hist and Govt, Lipscomb Univ, 3901 Granny White Pike, Nashville, TN 37204-3903. **EMAIL** tim.johnson@lipscomb.edu

JOHNSON, TROY R.
PERSONAL Born 02/29/1940, Wichita Falls, TX, m, 1960, 6 children **DISCIPLINE** HISTORY **EDUCATION** San Diego State Univ, BA, 86; Univ Calif, MA, 91; PhD, 93. **CAREER** Vis Asst Prof, to Vis Assoc Prof, Univ Calif, 93-99; Prof, Calif State Univ, 94-. **SELECTED PUBLICATIONS** Co-auth, Roots of Red Power: The Untold Story, Univ Neb Press, forthcoming; auth, Distinguished Native American Religious Practitioners and Healers, Orxy Press, forthcoming; co-auth, Native American Nationalism, W.W. Norton Inc, forthcoming; auth, assoc ed, Native North American Almanac, Gale Research, 001; co-auth, Red Power: The American Indians fight for Freedom, Univ Neb Press, 99; ed, Contemporary Political Issues of the American Indian, AltaMira Press, 99; auth, "The state and the American Indian: Who Gets the Indian Child?," Wicazo Sa Review, 99; auth, "Helplessness, Hopelessness, and Despair: Identifying the Precursors to Indian Youth Suicide," American Indian Culture and Research Journal, 99; auth, "American Indian Activism and Transformation," in American Indian Activism: Alcatraz to the Longest Walk, Univ Ill Press, 97; auth, "Roots of Contemporary Native American Activism," American Indian Culture and Research Journal, 96 **CONTACT ADDRESS** Dept Hist, California State Univ, Long Beach, 1250 N Bellflower Blvd, Long Beach, CA 90840-0006. **EMAIL** trj@csulb.edu

JOHNSON, WALKER C.
PERSONAL Born 07/24/1935, Stevens Point, WI, m, 1958, 3 children **DISCIPLINE** ARCHITECTURE, HISTORY **EDUCATION** Univ Wisc, BS, hist, 58; Univ of Illinois, BArch, 66. **CAREER** Adj prof, Univ VA, 87-88. **HONORS AND AWARDS** Fel, AIA. **MEMBERSHIPS** AIA; SAH; APT. **RESEARCH** Architectural history; building pathology & restoration. **SELECTED PUBLICATIONS** Auth, Twentieth Century Building Materials, Terrazzo, Natl Park Svc, McGraw-Hill, 95. **CONTACT ADDRESS** Johnson-Lasky Architects, 22 West Monroe St, Ste 1601, Chicago, IL 60603. **EMAIL** jlarch@ibm.net

JOHNSON, WILLIAM M.
PERSONAL Born 10/24/1939, Columbia, MO **DISCIPLINE** ART HISTORY **EDUCATION** Univ Missouri, BA, 60, MA, 62; Princeton Univ, MFA, 64, PhD, 65. **CAREER** Lectr to assoc prof, 65-76, prof Fine Art, Univ Toronto, 77-. **HONORS AND AWARDS** Fulbright fel, 60-61; Guggenheim fel, 78-79; Prix Bernier Acad Beaux-Arts, Inst France, 82. **MEMBERSHIPS** Am Soc Eighteenth Stud; Renaissance Soc Am; Soc hist de l'art francais. **RESEARCH** 18th century Fr prints and painting. **SELECTED PUBLICATIONS** Auth, French Lithography: The Restoration Salons 1817-1824, 77; auth, French Royal Academy of Painting and Sculpture: Engraved Reception Pieces 1673-1789, 82; auth, Art History: Its Use and Abuse, 88; auth, Hugues-Adrien Joly: Lettres a Karl-Heinrich von Heinecken 1772-1789, 88; coauth, Estienne Jodelle, Le Recueil des Inscriptions 1558, 72; coauth, The Paris Entries of Charles IX and Elisabeth of Austria 1571, 74; coauth, The Royal Tour of Charles IX and Catherine de Medici 1564-1566, 79; ed, Ontario Association of Art Galleries Art Gallery Handbook, 82; auth, "Les servitudes de la gravure, I. Le Bas de Madame de Pompadour: Depenses et protocole autour de l'estampe dedicacee au XVIIIe siecle," Nouvelles de l'estampe, (98): 5-51. **CONTACT ADDRESS** Dept of Fine Art, Univ of Toronto, 100 St. George St, Toronto, ON, Canada M5S 1A1.

JOHNSON, YVONNE
PERSONAL Born 12/17/1945, Muskogee, OK, 2 children **DISCIPLINE** HISTORY **EDUCATION** Univ Ark, BSEd, 67; Univ Colo, MA, 74; Univ Tex, PhD, 92. **CAREER** Instructor, Collin county Cmty Col, 88-94; Asst Prof to Assoc Prof, Central Mo State Univ, 94-. **HONORS AND AWARDS** Excellence in Teaching Awd, NISOD, 92; NEH Fel, Univ Kans, 93; NEH Fel, Johns Hopkins Univ, 97; NEH Fel, Va Foundation for the Humanities, 98. **MEMBERSHIPS** Nat Asn for African Am Studies, S Asn of Women Hist, Am Asn of Univ Women. **RESEARCH** Women's History; African American History; Death and Burial Practices (US and Africa). **SELECTED PUBLICATIONS** Auth, The voices of African American Women, Peter Lang, Inc, 98; auth, "Leadbelly" and "James Brown", in Encyclopedia of Popular Musicians, Salem Press, 99; auth, "Robert Thompson VanHorn", and "Russell and Clara Stover," in Dictionary of Missouri Biographies, Univ of Mo Press, 99. **CONTACT ADDRESS** Dept History, Central Missouri State Univ, Warrensburg, MO 64093. **EMAIL** yjohnson@cmsu1.cmsu.edu

JOHNSON-ODIM, CHERYL
DISCIPLINE HISTORY **EDUCATION** Northwestern Univ, PhD, 78. **CAREER** Hist, Loyola Univ. **MEMBERSHIPS** Ed bd(s), Hist Encycl Chicago Women, J Women's His, Nat Women's Stud Asn J. **RESEARCH** Women's history; African; African American history. **SELECTED PUBLICATIONS** Auth, monograph For Women and the Nation: Funmilayo Ransome-Kuti of Nigeria, Univ Ill Press, 97; Lady Oyinkan Abayomi, Nigerian Women in Historical Perspective, Nigeria: Sankore Press, 92; Common Themes, Different Contexts: Third World Women and Feminism, Ind UP, 91; co-ed, Expanding the Boundaries of Women's History, Ind UP, 92; guest ed on special issue of Nat Women's Stud Asn J on, Global Perspectives on Gender, 96. **CONTACT ADDRESS** Liberal Educ Dept, Columbia Col, Illinois, 600 S Michigan Ave, Chicago, IL 60605. **EMAIL** cjohnson-odim@popmail.colum.edu

JOHNSTON, CAROLYN
DISCIPLINE HISTORY **EDUCATION** Univ Ca, PhD. **CAREER** Prof. **RESEARCH** American intellectual history; history of radical and working class movements; history of women in America. **SELECTED PUBLICATIONS** Auth, Jack London: An American Radical, 84; Sexual Power: Feminism and the Family, 92. **CONTACT ADDRESS** Dept of History, Eckerd Col, 54th Ave S, PO Box 4200, Saint Petersburg, FL 33711.

JOHNSTON, CHARLES MURRAY
PERSONAL Born 04/01/1926, Hamilton, ON, Canada, m, 1953, 4 children **DISCIPLINE** MODERN HISTORY **EDUCATION** McMaster Univ, BA, 49; Univ Pa, MA, 50, PhD(hist), 54. **CAREER** From lectr to assoc prof, 53-66, Prof Hist, McMaster Univ, 66-, Can Coun res grants, 60, 61 & 63, res fel for overseas studies, 63-64, 75-76, 82-83; consult, Ont Centennial Ctr Sci & Technol, 64-65; mem, Archaeol & Hist Sites Bd, Ont, 65-70; mem, Soc Sci Res Coun Can, 67-71; Ont Prov Govt res grant for biog of E C Drury, 72. **MEMBERSHIPS** Can Hist Asn; Can Asn Am Studies. **RESEARCH** British imperial, Canadian and Ontario history. **SELECTED PUBLICATIONS** Auth, The Chiefs, Warriors and Cadets of Academe--Recent Writings on Canadian Higher-Education, Acadiensis, Vol 0022, 92; Mcquesten, Thomas, Baker, Public-Works, Politics, and Imagination, Can Hist Rev, Vol 0074, 93; The British Abroad--The Grand Tour in the 18th-Century, Historian, Vol 0056, 94; Matters of Mind-- Univ in Ontario, 1791-1951, Dalhousie Rev, Vol 0075, 95. **CONTACT ADDRESS** Dept of History, McMaster Univ, 1280 Main St W, Hamilton, ON, Canada L8S 4M4.

JOHNSTON, ROBERT H.
DISCIPLINE HISTORY **EDUCATION** Univ Toronto, BA; Yale Univ, MA, PhD. **HONORS AND AWARDS** Humanities Bk Prize, 90. **RESEARCH** Russian exile migrant communties. **SELECTED PUBLICATIONS** Auth, New Mecca, New Babylon, Paris and the Russian Exiles 1920-1945, 88; auth, Soviet Foreign Policy 1918-1945, 91. **CONTACT ADDRESS** History Dept, McMaster Univ, 1280 Main St W, Hamilton, ON, Canada L8S 4L9. **EMAIL** johnstrh@mcmaster.ca

JOHNSTON, WILLIAM M.
PERSONAL m, 1987, 2 children **DISCIPLINE** HISTORY **EDUCATION** Harvard Univ, PhD, 65. **CAREER** Prof, Univ MA Amherst. **HONORS AND AWARDS** Austrian Hist Prize, 69. **RESEARCH** Mod Europe; intellectual hist of relig(s). **SELECTED PUBLICATIONS** Auth, In Search of Italy: Foreign Writers in Northern Italy, 87; Celebrations, 91; Recent Reference Books in Religion, 96. **CONTACT ADDRESS** Dept of Hist, Univ of Massachusetts, Amherst, Mass Ave, Amherst, MA 01003. **EMAIL** wmjohnston@start.com.au

JOINER, BURNETT
PERSONAL Born 11/10/1941, Raymond, MS, m **DISCIPLINE** AFRICAN-AMERICAN STUDIES **EDUCATION** Utica Jr Coll, AA 1962; Alcorn State Univ, BS 1964; Bradley Univ, MA 1968; Univ of SC, PhD 1975. **CAREER** Oliver School Clarksdale, MS, principal 1968-71; York School Dist #1, asst supt of schls 1971-73; SC Coll Orangeburg, SC, asst prof 1974-75; Atlanta Univ Atlanta, GA, exec dir/assoc prof 1975-80; Grambling State Univ, exec academic dean and prof, 84-91; Lemonte-Owens College, Pres, 91-. **MEMBERSHIPS** Mem Ouachita Valley Boy Scouts 1982-; charter mem Grambling Lion's Club 1983-; consultant US Dept Educ 1983-85; commr LA Learning Adv Commn 1984-85; commr LA Internship Commn 1984-85; mem Natl Inst of Education Study Group on Teacher Edn; chaired special comm in Coll of Educ Univ of SC on student advisement; past mem Curriculum Comm Sch of Educ at SC State Coll; mem Ruston-Lincoln C of C; vice chairperson Comm on Social Concerns Lewis Temple Church; conducted numerous workshops and seminars for more than 50 schools, agencies and community groups; mem of the bd of dir Teacher Ed Council for State Coll and Univ, American Assoc of Coll for Teacher Ed; mem of the Governor's Internship Commission and Learning Adv Commission. **SELECTED PUBLICATIONS** Publications, "The Teacher Corps Policy Board; Three Perspectives on Role and Function" 1979; "A Documentation Primer; Some Perspectives from the Field" 1979; "New Perspectives on Black Education History" Book Review for the Journal of Negro History in progress; "Identifying Needs and Prioritizing Goals Through Collaboration" 1978; "Education That Is Multicultural; A Process of Curriculum Development" 1979; "The Design, Implementation and Evaluation of a Pre-Service Prototype Competency-Based Teacher Education Model" 1975; "Maximizing Opportunities for Professional Improvement" 1983; Improving Teacher Education: A Conscious Choice, co-author. **CONTACT ADDRESS** LeMoyne-Owen Col, 807 Walker Ave, Memphis, TN 38126.

JOINER, DOROTHY
DISCIPLINE ART **EDUCATION** Emory Univ, PhD; Fr lit, 73; Ph.D., Emory Univ, 82, Art hist. **CAREER** Prof. **MEMBERSHIPS** CAA; SECAC. **RESEARCH** Renaissance art; contemporary art. **SELECTED PUBLICATIONS** Auth, Hieronymus Bosch's Temptation of Saint Anthony and the Hieros Gamos, Duke, 85; A New Methodology for Bosch, Emory Univ, 89; Figurative Art and Portaiture, Macon, 88. **CONTACT ADDRESS** Art Dept, State Univ of West Georgia, Carrollton, GA 30118. **EMAIL** djoiner@westga.edu

JOINER, HARRY M.
PERSONAL Born 08/30/1944, Paducah, KY, m, 1968, 4 children **DISCIPLINE** HISTORY **EDUCATION** DePauw Univ, BA, 65; Univ Ky, MA, 66; PhD, 71; Dip Grad, Inst Int Studies, Switzerland, 69. **CAREER** Prof, Athens State Univ, 69-. **HONORS AND AWARDS** Patterson School Fel, Univ of Ky. **MEMBERSHIPS** Acad of Int Bus; Acad of Int Bus Educ; Int Studies Assoc; Ala Polit Sci Assoc. **RESEARCH** American foreign policy, international relations, international commerce. **SELECTED PUBLICATIONS** Auth, Exporting and Importing, Southern Textbooks, 70; auth, American Foreign Policy - The Kissinger Era, Strode Pub, auth, Communism Today, Southern Textbooks, 80; auth, Alabama Then and Now, Southern Textbooks, 96; auth, American Foreign Policy: 1776-1945, Southern Textbooks, 00. **CONTACT ADDRESS** Dept Arts and Sci, Athens State Univ, 302 N Beaty St, Athens, AL 35611-1902. **EMAIL** joinehm@athens.edu

JONAITIS, ALDONA
PERSONAL Born 01/27/1948, New York, NY, s **DISCIPLINE** ART HISTORY **EDUCATION** SUNY, BA, 69; Columbia Univ, MA, 73, PhD, 77. **CAREER** Lecturer, Asst Prof, Assoc Prof, Prof, SUNY Stony Brook, 73-89; Ch, Dept Art, SUNY, 81-84; Assoc Provost, SUNY, 84-86; V Provost for Undergrad Stud, SUNY, 86-89; VP for Public Progs, Am Mus of Nat Hist, 89-93; Adjunct Prof of Art Hist & Archaeol, Columbia univ, 90-93; Prof Anthrop, Univ Alaska, Fairbanks, 93-; Dir, Univ of Alaska Mus, 93-. **MEMBERSHIPS** Otsego Inst for Native Am Art, Founding Bd member, 96-; Native Am Art Stud Asn (founding member, pres 93-95). **RESEARCH** NW Coast Indian Art. **SELECTED PUBLICATIONS** Auth, Traders of Tradition: The History of Haida Art, Robert Davidson: Eagle of the Dawn, 1st ed, The Vancouver Art Gallery, 3-23, 93; co-auth, Power, History and Authenticity: The Mowachaht Whaler's Washing Shrine, Eloquent Obsessions: Writing Cultural Criticism, Duke Univ Press, 157-84, 94; auth, Introduction, Eagle Transforming: The Art of Robert Davidson, Univ Washington Press, 1-11, 94; ed, A Wealth of Thought: Franz Boas on Native American Art, Univ Wash Press, 3-37, 306-337, 95; auth, The Beauty and the Magic of His Horse, Heritage, 4-15, spring/summer 97; ed, Looking North: Art from the University of Alaska Museum, Univ Wash Press/.Univ Alaska Mus, 13-43, 98; The Yuquot Whalers' Shrine: A Study of Representation, Univ Wash Press, in press. **CONTACT ADDRESS** Univ of Alaska, Fairbanks, 907 Yukon Dr, Fairbanks, AK 99775. **EMAIL** ffaj@uaf.edu

JONAS, MANFRED
PERSONAL Born 04/09/1927, Mannheim, Germany, m, 1952, 4 children **DISCIPLINE** AMERICAN HISTORY **EDUCATION** City Col New York, BS, 49; Harvard Univ, AM, 50, PhD, 59. **CAREER** Mil Intel analyst, US Dept of Defense 51-54; vis prof Northamerican Hist ; Free Univ Berlin 59-62; assoc prof hist, Widener Col 62-63; from asst to assoc porf 63-67;dir grad mod lit and hist studies 64-74; chm div soc sci 71-74; chm dept, 70-81; prof hist 67-80; Washington Irving prof mod lit and hist studies 80-86; John Bigelow prof hist 86-96; Union Col NY letr, City Col New York,50, Exten Div, Univ MD 54, Northeastern Univ 58; consult, Choice: 64-89; dir , NDEA Inst Advan Study Hist 66-68; consult, US Office of Educ 67; Dr otto Salgo vis prof Am studies, Eotvos Lorand Univ Budapest 83-84; FRN Scholar-in-Residence, New York Univ 91; adj grad prof hist, State Univ New York, Albany 90-94; emer, 96-. **HONORS AND AWARDS** res fel, Charles Warren Ctr Studies Am Hist 70-78; Sr Fulbright-Hays lectr hist, Univ Saarland, 73; Phi Beta Kappa; **MEMBERSHIPS** AHA; Orgn Am Historians; Soc Historians Am Foreign Rels; AAUP; NY State Col Proficiency Exam Comm Am Hist; **RESEARCH** US diplomatic history, German-American relations, isloationism, ideas and politics. **SELECTED PUBLICATIONS** Auth, Isolationism in America, 1935-1941, Cornell Univ, 66 Imprint, 90; auth, The United States and Germany, Cornell Univ, 84; Deutschland und die USA im Kaaiserreich, 1890-1918 in Deutschland und die USA, 1890-1985, Heidleberg German-American Institute, 86; auth, Allies of a Kind: The United States and Germany 1945-1962 in Proceedings of the American Historical Assoc, 86, Univ Microfilms; auth, Continuity and Change in American Law in Search for American Values, National Library Budapest, 90; ed, Die Unabhangigkeitserklarung der Vereingten Staaten, Hans Pfeiffer, 65; auth, American Foreign Relations in the Twentieth Century, Crowell, 67; coed, Roosevelt and Churchill: Their Secret Wartime Correspondence, Sat Rev/Dutton, 75, Barrie & Jenkins, 75, Mondatore, 77, Dacapo 90; auth, New Opportunities in a New Nation, Union Col, 82; gen ed, The Politics and Strategy of World War II, 9 vols, DaCapo, 76-77. **CONTACT ADDRESS** Dept of Hist, Union Col, New York, Schenectady, NY 12308. **EMAIL** jonasm@union,edu

JONES, AMELIA
PERSONAL Born 07/14/1961, Durham, NC, m, 1987, 2 children **DISCIPLINE** ART HISTORY **EDUCATION** Harvard Univ, BA, 83; Univ PA, MA, 87; UCLA, PhD, 91. **CAREER** Instr, UCLA, 89; instr, Art Ctr Col of Design, 90-91; assoc prof, Univ CA, Riverside, 91-; instr, USC, 92; exec ed, Los Angeles Ctr Photog Studies, 95-98. **HONORS AND AWARDS** Elizabeth Agassiz Scholarship, Harvard Univ; Deans Fel, 86-87, Univ PA; Dickson Fel, 89-91, UCLA; Affirmative Action Career Development Awd, 93, Distinguished Humanist Achievement Awd, 93-94, Univ CA, Riverside; Postdoctoral Fel, 94-95, Am Coun Learned Soc; Group Fel, 95, Graham Found; Best Exhibition Catalogue, third place, 95-96, Int Asn Art Critics; NEH fel, 00; Guggenhein Foundation fel, 00. **MEMBERSHIPS** Col Art Asn; Educ Publications Committee; Ctr For Photographic Studies; Asn Art Historians. **RESEARCH** Contemporary art and theory; 20th century European and Am art; feminist art theory; history and theory of photog. **SELECTED PUBLICATIONS** Auth, Postmodernism and the En-Gendering of Marcel Duchamp, Cambridge, England and New York, Cambridge Univ Press, 94; ed, coauth, Sexual Politics: Judy Chicago's Dinner Party in Feminist Art History, Los Angeles and Berkeley, Univ of Cali Press and Los Angeles UCLA/ Hammer Museum of Art, 96; auth, coauth, coed, " In Between " issue of Framework, Los Angeles, 98; auth, Body Art/Performing the Subject, Minneapolis, Univ of Minn Press, 98; coed, coauth, Performing the Body/Performing the Text, an anthropology of texts on performance and body art, London and New York, Routledge Press, 99; auth, " Every man knows where and how beauty give him pleasure': Beauty Discourse and the Logic of Aesthetics," Aesthetics and Difference, Oxford, Oxford Univ Press, forthcoming, 00; auth, " Paul McCarhty's Inside Out Body and the Desublination of Masculinity," New York, New Museum of Contemporary Art, forthcoming, 00; auth, " Performing the Other Self: Cindy Sherman Poses he Subject," Interfaces: Visualizing and Performing Women's Lives, Ann Arbor, Univ of Mich Press, forthcoming, 00; auth, " Postmodernism and the Arts," Encyclopedia of American Cultural and Intellectual History , New York, Macmillan Publishing , forthcoming, 01. **CONTACT ADDRESS** Dept of Art History, Univ of California, Riverside, 339 S Orange Dr, Los Angeles, CA 90036-3008. **EMAIL** jonessher@aol.com

JONES, BARNEY LEE
PERSONAL Born 06/11/1920, Raleigh, NC, m, 1944, 5 children **DISCIPLINE** AMERICAN CHURCH HISTORY, BIBLICAL LITERATURE **EDUCATION** Duke Univ, BA, 41, PhD(Am Christiani y), 58; Yale Univ, BD, 44. **CAREER** Instr Bible, Duke Univ, 48-50, chaplain, 53-56, asst dean, Trinity Col, 56-64, assoc prof relig, 64-72, PROF RELIG, 72-80. **MEMBERSHIPS** Soc Relig Higher Educ; Am Soc Church Hist. **RESEARCH** Colonial American church history, particularly New England area; Charles Chauncy, 1707-1782. **SELECTED PUBLICATIONS** Auth, John Caldwell, critic of the Great Awakening in New England, in: A Miscellany of American Christianity, Duke Univ, 63. **CONTACT ADDRESS** 2622 Pickett Rd, Durham, NC 27705.

JONES, BEVERLY WASHINGTON
PERSONAL Born 12/13/1947, Durham, NC, m, 1970, 3 children **DISCIPLINE** AMERICAN & AFRO-AMERICAN HISTORY **EDUCATION** NC, Cent Univ, BA, 70, MA, 71; Univ NC Chapel Hill, PhD(Am hist), 80. **CAREER** Teacher US hist, Guy B Phillips Jr High Sch, 71-72; instr hist, 72-76, asst prof, 76-80, prof hist, NC Cent Univ, 80-; Consult, Nat Endowment Humanities, 75-76, reviewer, 77-78; vis assoc, Univ NC Chapel Hill, 80-. **MEMBERSHIPS** Orgn Black Women Historians; Asn Study Afro-Am Life & Hist; Orgn Am Historians. **RESEARCH** Black women's history; labor history, especially labor concerns of tobacco workers and domestics; psycho history, motivational concepts of Black leaders. **SELECTED PUBLICATIONS** Auth, Mary Church Terrell and the National Association of Colored Women, 1896-1901, J Negro Hist (in press); Mary Church Terrell: A new woman, Negro Hist Bull (in press); Before Montgomery and Greensboro: The desegregation movement in the District of Columbia, Phylon (in press). **CONTACT ADDRESS** 1801 Fayetteville St, Durham, NC 27707-3129. **EMAIL** Bjones@wpo.nccu.edu

JONES, CHRISTOPHER P.
PERSONAL Born 08/21/1940, Chislehurst, England **DISCIPLINE** CLASSICS, ANCIENT HISTORY **EDUCATION** Oxon (Oxford), BA, 61, MA, 67; Harvard, PhD, 65. **CAREER** Lect, 65-66, Univ Toronto; asst prof, 66-68, assoc prof, 68-75, prof, 65-92, prof of class & hist, 92-97, George Martin Lane Prof of Classics & Hist, 97-, Harvard Univ. **HONORS AND AWARDS** Fel, Royal Soc of Canada; Corresp mem, Ger Archaeol Inst, 92; fel, Am Numismatic Soc, 93; The Am Philos Soc, 96; fel, Am Acad of Arts & Sci, 98. **MEMBERSHIPS** APA; Bd of Sr Fellows, Byzantine Stud, Dumbarton Oaks Res Lib & Collection, Harvard Univ; Class Asn of Canada; Inst for Advanced Stud, Princeton, Sch of Hist Stud; Soc for the Promotion of Hellenic Stud; Soc for Promotion of Roman Stud. **RESEARCH** Greek lit of the Roman period; Hellenistic and Roman hist; Greek epigraphy. **SELECTED PUBLICATIONS** Auth, Philostratus: Life of Apollonius of Tyana, Penguin Books, 71; auth, Plutarch and Rome, Oxford Univ Press, 71, 72; auth, The Roman World of Dio Chrysostom, Harvard Univ Press, 78; auth, Culture and Society in Lucian, Harvard Univ Press, 86; coed, Louis Robert, Le Martyre de Pionios, pretre de Smyrne, mis au point et complete par G. W. Bowersock et C. P. Jones, Dumbarton Oaks Res Lib & Collection, Wash, 94; auth, Kinship Diplomacy in the Ancient World, Harvard Univ Press, forthcoming 99. **CONTACT ADDRESS** Dept of Classics, Harvard Univ, 226 Boylston Hall, Cambridge, MA 02138. **EMAIL** cjones@fas.harvard.edu

JONES, EDWARD LOUIS
PERSONAL Born 01/15/1922, Georgetown, TX, m, 1964 **DISCIPLINE** HISTORY **EDUCATION** Univ of WA, BA (2) 1952, BA 1955; Univ of Gonzaga, JD 1967. **CAREER** Hollywood Players Theatre, prod, dir 1956-58; Roycroft Leg Theatre, prod, dir 1958-59; WA State Dept of Publ Asst, soc worker 1958; Seattle Water Dept, cost acctg clerk 1960-61; State of WA, atty gen office 1963-66; Seattle Oppty Indust Ctr, suprv 1966-68; Univ of WA, asst dean a&s 1968-, lecturer. **HONORS AND AWARDS** Moot Court Contest, First Place, 1953. **MEMBERSHIPS** Consult State Attny Gen Adv Comm on Crime, State Supr of Counseling; vice pres WA Comm on Consumer Interests, Natl Council on Crime & Delinquency; bd mem Natl Acad Adv & Assn; ed NACADA Jrnl; mem Natl Assn of Student Personnel Admin, The Amer Acad of Pol & Soc Sci, The Smithsonian Assn; historical advisor, Anheuser Busch. **SELECTED PUBLICATIONS** Author: Profiles in African Heritage, Black Zeus, 1972; Tutankhamon, King of Upper & Lower Egypt, 1978; Orator's Workbook, 1982; The Black Diaspora: Colonization of Colored People, 1989; co-author, Money Exchange Flashcards, Currency Converters, 1976; From Rulers of the World to Slavery, 1990; President Zachary Taylor and Senator Hamlin: Union or Death, 1991; Why Colored Americans Need an Abraham Lincoln in 1992; Forty Acres & a Mule: The Rape of Colored Americans, 1995. **CONTACT ADDRESS** Ethnic Cultural Ctr, HH-05, Univ of Washington, 3931 Brooklyn Ave, NE, Seattle, WA 98195.

JONES, ELWOOD HUGH
PERSONAL Born 05/06/1941, SK, Canada, m, 1964, 2 children **DISCIPLINE** HISTORY **EDUCATION** Univ Sask, BA, 62; Univ Western Ont, MA, 64; Queen's Univ, Ont, PhD(hist), 71. **CAREER** Archivist, Pub Arch Can, 64-67; lectr hist, 69-70, asst prof, 70-75, assoc prof, 75-81, Prof Hist, Trent Univ, 81-, Dir, Can Hist Asn, 70-73, dir, Nat Archival Appraisal Bd, 71-. **MEMBERSHIPS** Can Hist Asn; Orgn Am Historians; Inst Early Am Hist & Cult; Inst Fr-Am Hist; Can Church Hist Soc (pres, 78-). **RESEARCH** Canada; political and religious development, nineteenth century; urban history. **SELECTED PUBLICATIONS** Co-ed, A letter on the Reform Party, 1860: Sandfield Macdonald and the London Free Press, Ont Hist, 65; Union List of Manuscripts in Canadian Repositories, Queen's Printer, 68; auth, Ephemeral compromise: the Great Reform Convention revisited, J Can Studies, 68; contribr, Illustrated Historical Atlas of Peterborough County 1825-1875, Hunter Rose, 75; St John's Peterborough, the Sesquicentennial History of an Anglican Parish 1826-1976, Peterborough St John's Church, 76; auth, Localism and Federalism in Upper Canada to 1865, in: Early Canadian and Australian Federalism, Waterloo,

78; coauth, Toronto Waterworks 1840-1877: Continuity and change in 19th century Toronto politics, Can Hist Rev, 79; auth, The Church in the Backwoods: Anglican missionaries in the Peterborough area, J Can Church Hist Soc, 81. **CONTACT ADDRESS** Dept of Hist, Trent Univ, 1600 West Bank Dr, Peterborough, ON, Canada K9J 7B8. **EMAIL** ejones@trentu.ca

JONES, GREGORY

PERSONAL Born 07/15/1957, Murray, KY, m, 1995, 2 children **DISCIPLINE** GEOGRAPHY **EDUCATION** Univ Va, BA, 93; Univ Va, PhD, 98. **CAREER** Teaching Asst, Univ Va, 93, 96; Instr, Univ Va, 95-97; Asst Prof, Southern Ore Univ, 97-. **HONORS AND AWARDS** Undergrad Student of the Year Awd, 92-93; Grad Student of the Year Awd, 94-95; Grad Teaching Asst of the Year Awd, 94-95; Governor's Fel, Univ Va, 94-95; duPont Fel, Univ VA, 94-95; Dean's Reserve Fel, Univ Va, 95-96; Governor's Fel, Univ Va, 96-97; Moore Res Awd, Univ Va, 96; AMS Global Change Studies Awd, 96; Sigma Xi, 99. **MEMBERSHIPS** Int Soc of Biometeorology, AAG, AMS, Am Soc of Enology and Viticult. **RESEARCH** Climatology, hydrology, biosphere and atmosphere interactions, climate change, quantitative methods in spatial and temporal analysis. **SELECTED PUBLICATIONS** Coauth, "Climatology of Nor'easters and the 30 kPa Jet," J of Coastal Res 11:4 (95): 1210-1220; coauth, "The Atlantic Subtropical High," J of Climate 10:4 (97): 728-744; coauth, "A Synoptic Climatology of Tornadoes in Virginia," Physical Geog 18:5 (97): 383-407; coauth, "Using a Synoptic Climatological Approach to Understand Climate/Viticulture Relationships," Int J of Climatology (99); coauth, "Empire der Preisbildung bei Crus Classe des Bordelais - Determinanten, Sensitivitaten und Prognosen," Die Wein-Wissenschaft 53 (98): 136-149; auth, "Relationships Between Grapevine Phenology, Composition and Wine Quality for Bordeaux, France," Arboreta Phaenologica 42 (99): 3-7; coauth, "A Pollution Climatology of the Rogue Valley, Oregon," Atmospheric Environ (99). **CONTACT ADDRESS** Dept Geog, Southern Oregon Univ, 1250 Siskiyou Blvd, Ashland, OR 97520. **EMAIL** gjones@sou.edu

JONES, HOUSTON GWYNNE

PERSONAL Born 01/07/1924, Caswell Co, NC **DISCIPLINE** UNITED STATES HISTORY **EDUCATION** Appalachian State Teachers Col, BS, 49; Peabody Col, MA, 50; Duke Univ, PhD(hist), 65. **CAREER** Prof hist & polit sci, Oak Ridge Mil Inst, 50-53; prof & chmn dept, WGa Col, 55-56; state archivist, NC Div Arch & Hist, 56-68, dir, 68-72, state historian & dir, 72-74; Cur, NC Collection, 74-93, Davis Research Historian, 94- , Univ NC Libr, Chapel Hill; Adj prof hist, NC State Univ, 66-73; arch consult, State Calif, 66, State Fla, 67 & State Va, 68; chmn, America's Four Hundredth Anniversary Comt, 77-80; adj prof hist, Univ NC, 74-90; comnr, Nat Hist Publ & Rec Comn, 79-83; ed, NC Hist Rev, 68-74 & NCaroliniana Soc Imprints, 78- . **HONORS AND AWARDS** Leland Prize, Soc Am Archivists, 67 & 81; Awd of Merit, Am Asn State & Local Hist, 68; Crittenden Mem Awd, NC Lit & Hist Asn, 77; Awd of Distinction, AASLH, 89. **MEMBERSHIPS** Fel Soc Am Archivists (treas, 61-67, pres, 68-69); AHA; Orgn Am Historians; Am Asn State & Local Hist (secy, 78-82); Nat Trust Hist Preserv. **RESEARCH** History of North Carolina; archival administration in the United States; Arctic history and Inuit culture. **SELECTED PUBLICATIONS** Auth, Bedford Brown: State Rights Unionist, 55; Guide to State and Provincial Archival Agencies, 1961, Soc Am Archivists, 61; For History's Sake, Univ NC, 66; The Records of a Nation, Atheneum, 69; Archival training in American universities, 4/68 & The Pink Elephant Revisited, 10/80, Am Archivist; Local Government Records, Am Asn State & Local Hist, 80; N Carolina Illustrated, Univ NC Press, 84; N. Carolina Hist: A Bibliography, Greenwood, 95. **CONTACT ADDRESS** Library, Univ of No Carolina, Chapel Hill, Campus Box 3930, Chapel Hill, NC 27514-8890. **EMAIL** hgjones@email.unc.edu

JONES, HOWARD

PERSONAL Born 10/21/1940, Lebanon, TN, m, 1962, 2 children **DISCIPLINE** AMERICAN FOREIGN POLICY **EDUCATION** Ind Univ, BS, Educ, 63, MA, Hist, 65, PhD, Hist, 73. **CAREER** Vis asst prof, univ Nebr, 72-74; res prof & ch, Hist, Univ Ala, 74-. **HONORS AND AWARDS** Recipient of both John F. Burnum Distinguished Fac Awd for teaching and res and the Frederick Moody Blackmon; Sara McCorkle Moody Awd for bringing recognition to the Univ; A Hist Book Club Selection and winner of the Phi Alpha Theta Book Awd; received the Phi Alpha Theta Book Awd and was nominated for the Pulitzer Prize and Stuart L. Bernath Book Awd. **MEMBERSHIPS** South Hist Asn; Soc Historians Am For Relations; Org Am Historians; Am Hist Asn; Phi Alpha Theta **RESEARCH** American foreign policy; Civil War; Vietnam War; Cold War; pre-Civil War. **SELECTED PUBLICATIONS** Auth, "A New Kind of War," America's Global Strategy and the Truman Doctrine in Greece, 89; auth, Union in Peril: The Crisis over British Intervention in the Civil War, 92; Prologue to Manifest Destiny: Anglo-American Relations in the 1840s, 97; Quest for Security: A History of US Foreign Relations, 96; Abraham Lincoln and a New Birth fo Freedom: The Union and Slavery in the Diplomacy of the Civil War; auth, Mutiny on the Amistad: The Saga of a Slave Revolt and Its Impact on American Abolition, Law, and Diplomacy, 97. **CONTACT ADDRESS** Dept Hist, Univ of Alabama, Tuscaloosa, PO Box 870212, University, AL 35486. **EMAIL** Hjones@TenHoor.as.ua.edu

JONES, JACQUELINE

DISCIPLINE HISTORY **EDUCATION** Univ Del, BA, 70; Univ Wis, MA, 72, PhD, 76. **CAREER** Truman Prof, Am Civilization, Brandeis Univ. **MEMBERSHIPS** Am Antiquarian Soc **SELECTED PUBLICATIONS** Auth, Soldiers of Light and Love: Northern Teachers and Georgia Blacks, 1865-73, 80; auth, Labor of Love, Labor of Sorrow; Black Women, Work and the Family: From Slavery to the Present, Basic, 85; auth, American Work: Black and White Labor Since 1600, Norton, 85; auth, The Dispossessed: America's Underclasses form the Civil War to the Present, Basic, 92. **CONTACT ADDRESS** Dept of Hist, Brandeis Univ, Waltham, MA 02254.

JONES, JAMES HOWARD

PERSONAL Born 03/22/1943, Bauxite, AR, m, 1965, 3 children **DISCIPLINE** AMERICAN HISTORY **EDUCATION** Henderson State Teachers Col, BA, 64; East Tex State Univ, MA, 66; Ind Univ, PhD(hist), 73. **CAREER** Teacher Am hist, Carlisle Pub High Sch, 64-65; instr, Henderson State Teachers Col, 66-68; prog officer, Nat Endowment Humanities, 73-81; Assoc Prof Am Hist, Univ Houston, 81-, Sr res scholar, Kennedy Inst Ethics, Georgetown Univ, 75; consult ed, Free Press, 82- **HONORS AND AWARDS** Best Bks 81 Awd, NY Times Bk Rev, 81. **MEMBERSHIPS** AHA; Orgn Am Historians; Southern Hist Asn. **RESEARCH** United States history since 1900; social history of medicine. **SELECTED PUBLICATIONS** Auth, Racism in Medicine, In: The Encycl of Bioethics, Free Press, Vol IV, 78; Alan Gregg, In: The Dict of American Biography, Vol VI, 80; Bad Blood: The Tuskegee Syphilis Experiment, Free Press, 81; George Washington Carver, In: The Encycl of Social Reformers, H W Wilson, 82. **CONTACT ADDRESS** Dept of Hist, Univ of Houston, 4800 Calhoun, Houston, TX 77024-3785.

JONES, JERRY W.

PERSONAL Born 12/10/1964, CA, m, 1989, 2 children **DISCIPLINE** HISTORY **EDUCATION** Ambassador Univ, BA, 88; Tex A & M Univ, MS, 92; Univ N Tex, PhD, 95. **CAREER** Asst prof, Univ Central Tex, 96-99; asst prof, Tarleton State Univ, 99-. **HONORS AND AWARDS** Listed in Who's Who Among Am Teachers, 97. **MEMBERSHIPS** Soc for Military Hist. **RESEARCH** Naval History. **SELECTED PUBLICATIONS** Auth, U.S. Battleship Operations in World War I, United States Navel Inst, 98. **CONTACT ADDRESS** Dept Soc & Behav Sci, Tarleton State Univ, PO Box 1416, Killeen, TX 76540-1416. **EMAIL** jjones@tarleton.edu

JONES, KENNETH PAUL

PERSONAL Born 03/15/1937, Brooklyn, NY, 3 children **DISCIPLINE** HISTORY **EDUCATION** Univ MO, Kansas City, BA, 59; Columbia Univ, MIA, 61; Univ Wis, Madison, PhD, 70. **CAREER** Instr hist, Mansfield State Univ; 61-65, teaching asst, Univ Wis, Madison, 65-66, instr, Rock County Ctr, 66-69; assoc prof, 70-80, Prof Hist, 80-, Assoc Vice Chancellor for Academic Affairs and Dean of Graduate Studies, 97-, Univ Tenn, Martin; Guest prof, Johannes Gutenberg Univ, Mainz, 74-75; screening comt grad study USA, Deutscher Akademischer Austauschdienst, 74-75; Fulbright jr lectr, Coun Int Exchange Persons, 74-75; Deutscher Akademischer Austauschdienst travel study grant, summer 78. **HONORS AND AWARDS** Wilson Scholarship (UMKC), 55-59; Columbia Univ Fel, 59-61; Ford Found Dissertation Completion Grant, 68-69; US Dept of State Scholar-Diplomat Seminar, March 71; UTM Fac Res grants, 72, 78, 84, 87; Fulbright Lecturer, Mainz Univ, GER, 74-75; German Academic Exchange Service, Research Grant, summer 78; NEH Summer Seminar, Yale Univ, 74; NEH Travel to Collections Grant, 84; Who's Who in Am Ed, 92-; Dict of Int Biography, 93-; member, nat steering comm, pod network in higher ed, 83-86; tn conf of grad schools, pres, 93-94, vice pres, 92-93; tn asn of inst res: pres, 95-96; vice pres, 94-95. **MEMBERSHIPS** AHA Conf Group Cent Europ Hist; Soc Historians Am Foreign Rels; AAHE; AAUP; POD Network in Higher Ed; Phi Kappa Phi; Phi Alpha Theta; Am Hist Asn; AHA Comm on Hist in the Classroom; Soc for Hist Ed. **RESEARCH** The diplomacy of the Ruhr Crisis, 1923-1924; German-American relations, 1919-1933. **SELECTED PUBLICATIONS** Auth, Discord and Collaboration: Choosing an Agent General for Reparations, Diplomatic Hist, spring 77; Stresemann, the Ruhr Crisis, and Rhenish Separatism: A Case Study of Westpolitik, Europ Studies Rev, 7/77; US Diplomats in Europe, 1919-1941, Santa Barbara: ABC-Clio Press, 81, rev paperback ed, 83; book revs in the Am Hist Rev, Choice, History, and The Hist Teacher; book-length manuscript on The Diplomacy of the Ruhr Crisis: Germany and the West, 1922-24, in prep. **CONTACT ADDRESS** Admin Bldg, Rm 312, Univ of Tennessee, Chattanooga, 554 University St, Martin, TN 38238-5001. **EMAIL** kpjones@utm.edu

JONES, LAIRD

DISCIPLINE WORLD HISTORY, AFRICAN HISTORY **EDUCATION** Carleton Col, BA, 82; MSU, MA, 85, PhD, 92. **CAREER** Grad tchg asst, MSU, 83-87, 89-91; asst prof Hist, Lock Haven Univ Pa, 91-. **HONORS AND AWARDS** Nat rsrc lang fel, MSU, 83-87; net rsrc summer lang fel, Kenya, 85; res stipend, MSU, 87; Hinman fel , MSU, 87-88; Fulbright-Hayes doctoral dissertation abroad fel, Tanzania, 87-88; doctoral writing fel, MSU, 91; fac develop grant, LHU, 92; alternative workload leave, LHU, 1998. **MEMBERSHIPS** African Stud Asn; Can African Stud Asn; NY African Stud Asn; Phi Beta Delta-Honor Soc for Int Scholars; Tanzania Stud Asn; World Hist Asn. **RESEARCH** German trading house branch activities in early colonial East Africa. **SELECTED PUBLICATIONS** Auth, Commercial Politics and the Overstocking Crisis in Mwanza Province, 1927-35, African Econ Hist, 95; Rev of Cotton, Colonialism, and Social History in Sub-Saharan Africa, eds Allan Issacman and Richard Roberts, in H-AFRICA, 96. **CONTACT ADDRESS** Lock Haven Univ of Pennsylvania, Lock Haven, PA 17745. **EMAIL** ljones@eagle.lhup.edu

JONES, LARRY EUGENE

PERSONAL Born 02/16/1940, El Dorado, KS, m, 1988, 2 children **DISCIPLINE** MODERN EUROPEAN & GERMAN HISTORY **EDUCATION** Univ Kans, BA, 61, MA, 63; Univ Wis, PhD(hist), 70. **CAREER** Asst prof, 68-73, assoc prof, 74-79, Prof Hist, Canisius Col, 80-, Res fel, Alexander von Humboldt-Stiftung, Univ Bochum, W Ger, 75-77. **HONORS AND AWARDS** Fels from the ACLS, 83-84; NEH, 88-89; Nat Humanities Ctr, 88-89; Ger Marshall Fund, 90-91; Woodrow Wilson Int Ctr for Scholars, fall 91; Oishei Distinguished Teaching Professorship, Canisius Col, 99-. **MEMBERSHIPS** AHA, Ger Studies Asn. **RESEARCH** German history, 1918-1945; history of Marxism, Holocaust. **SELECTED PUBLICATIONS** Auth, In the Twilight of the Liberal Era: Max Weber and the Crisis of German Liberalism, 1914-20, Cent Europ Hist, 89; auth, German Liberalism and the Alienation of the Younger Generation in the Weimar Republic, in In Search of a Liberal Germany: Studies in the History of German Liberalism from 1789 to the Present, New York, 90; auth, The Greatest Stupidity of My Life: Alfred Hugenberg and the Formation of the Hitler Cabinet, January 1933, J Cont Hist, 92; auth, Generational Conflict and the Problem of Political Mobilization in the Weimar Republic, in Elections, Mass Politics, and Social Change in Germany: New Perspectives, New York, 92; auth, The Limits of Collaboration: Edgar Jung, Herbert von Bose, and the Origins of the Conservative Resistance to Hitler, 1933-34, in Between Reform, Reaction, and Resistance: Studies in the History of German Conservatism from 1789 to 1945, Providence, R.I., 93; auth, Liberalism and the Challenge of the Younger Generation: The Young Liberal Struggle for a Reform of the Weimar Party System, 1928-30, in Politische Jugend in der Weimarer Republik, Bochum, 93; auth, Nazis, Conservatives, and the Establishment of the Third Reich, Tel Aviver Jahrbuch fur deutsche Geschichte, 94; auth, Carl Friedrich von Siemens and the Industrial Financing of Political Parties in the Weimar Republic, in Von der Aufgabe der Freiheit, Berlin 95; auth, Hindenburg and the Conservative Dilemma in the 1932 Presidential Elections, Germ Studies Rev, 97; auth, Catholic Conservatives in the Weimar Republic: The Politics of the Rhenish-Westphalian Aristocracy, 1918-1933, German Hist 00. **CONTACT ADDRESS** Dept of Hist, Canisius Col, 2001 Main St, Buffalo, NY 14208-1098. **EMAIL** jones@canisius.edu

JONES, LEANDER CORBIN

PERSONAL Born 07/16/1934, Vincent, AR, m, 1962, 3 children **DISCIPLINE** BLACK AMERICANA STUDIES, COMMUNICATIONS **EDUCATION** Univ of AR at Pine Bluff, AB 1956; Univ of IL, MS 1968; Union Graduate Institute, PhD 1973. **CAREER** Chicago Public Schools, English teacher 1956-68; Peace Corps Volunteer, English teacher 1964-66; City Colls of Chicago, TV producer 1968-73; Meharry Medical Coll, media specialist 1973-75; Western Michigan Univ, assoc prof Black Amer studies, 75-89, prof 1989-. **HONORS AND AWARDS** "Roof Over My Head" TV Series WDCN Nashville 1975; acted in and directed several plays Kalamazoo 1979-86; exec producer & host for TV series "Fade to Black" 1986. **MEMBERSHIPS** Mem Kappa Alpha Psi 1953-; mem exec comm DuSable Mus African Amer History 1970-; designer of programs in theatre andTV for hard-to-educate; pres TABS Ctr 1972-; mem AAUP 1973-; mem Natl Council of Black Studies 1977-, MI Council of Black Studies 1977-, Popular Culture Assoc 1978-; chmn Comm Against Apartheid 1977-; mem South African Solidarity Org 1978-; mem MI Org African Studies 1980-; commander Vets for Peace Kalamazoo 1980-; pres Black Theatre Group of the Kalamazoo Civic Players 1980-83; bd of dirs Kalamazoo Civic Players 1981-83, MI Commn on Crime and Delinquency 1981-83; pres Corbin 22 Ltd 1986; Lester Lake Corp, secretary of the bd, 1992. **SELECTED PUBLICATIONS** Author "Africa Is for Reel," Kalamazoo 1983. **CONTACT ADDRESS** Prof, Black Amer Studies, Western Michigan Univ, Kalamazoo, MI 49008. **EMAIL** jonesl@umich.edu

JONES, LOUIS CLARK

PERSONAL Born 06/28/1908, Albany, NY, m, 1932, 3 children **DISCIPLINE** HISTORY, LITERATURE **EDUCATION** Hamilton Col, BA, 30; Columbia Univ, MA, 31, PhD(Eng lit), 42. **CAREER** From instr to assoc prof English & Am lit, NY State Col Teachers, Albany, 34-46; dir, 46-72, Emer Dir, NY State Hist Asn & Farmers Mus, 72-; Prof Am Folk Art, Cooperstown Grad Prog, State Univ NY Col Oneonta, 73-, Guggenheim fel, 46; mem, NY Coun on Hist Sites, 54-58, NY Coun on Arts, 60-72 & NY State Hist Trust, 66-72; dir, Coopertown

Grad Prog, State Univ NY col Oneonta, 64-72; Nat Endowment for Humanitics rcs grant, 72-73. **HONORS AND AWARDS** Awd of Distinction, Am Asn State & Local Hist, 70; Katherine Coffee Prize, 81; lhd, hamilton col, 62. **MEMBERSHIPS** Am Asn Mus (vpres, 52-68); Am Asn State & Loal Hist (vpres, 50-57); fel Am Folklore Soc. **RESEARCH** Eighteenth century social history; New York state folklore; folklore of the supernatural; American folk art. **SELECTED PUBLICATIONS** Auth, Clubs of the Georgian Rakes, Columbia Univ, 42; Spooks of the Valley, Houghton, 48; Things that Bump in the Night, Hill & Wang, 59; ed, Growing up in the Cooper Country, Syracuse Univ, 65; Murder at Clearry Hill, 82; Three Eyes on the Past, Syracuse Univ Press, 82. **CONTACT ADDRESS** 11 Main St, Box 351, Cooperstown, NY 13326.

JONES, MARCUS E.
PERSONAL Born 01/07/1943, Decatur, IL, m, 1983, 9 children **DISCIPLINE** AFRICAN AMERICAN STUDIES **EDUCATION** S Il Univ, BA, 65; PhD, 78; Chicago State Univ, MA 69. **CAREER** Assoc prof and Chair, Morris Brown Col, 78-85; vis prof, Valdosta State Univ, 86-87; assoc prof, Claflin Univ, 90-. **HONORS AND AWARDS** NEH Fel, 79, 80, 85, 90; Who's Who Among African Ams, 1988-200; Who's Who Among Am Teachers, 94, 00; Fulbright Res Scholar, Egypt, 95. **MEMBERSHIPS** Nat Assoc African Am Studies; Assoc for the Study of Class African Civilizations. **RESEARCH** AIDS; Black Social Problems; Black Migration and Urbanization. **SELECTED PUBLICATIONS** Auth, Black Migration in the United States with Emphasis on Selected Central Cities, Century Twenty One Pub, (Saratoga, CA), 80; auth, A Preliminary View of Current Practice in Transit Station Planning and Impact Assessment Techniques, Univ of Va, 81; coauth, Lower Socio-Economic and Minority Households in Camden County, Georgia, Atlanta Univ, 87; auth "Black Fatherhood in North America: Historical, Sociological, and Spiritual Perspectives", Proceedings of the Nat Assoc of African Am Studies, Vol 2, (98): 994-1007; auth, "The Changing Roles of Egyptian Women: Pre-Socialists Post-Socialists Eras", Proceedings of the Nat Assoc of African Am Studies, Vol 2, (98):1008-1024. **CONTACT ADDRESS** Dept Social Science, Claflin Col, 400 College St, Orangeburg, SC 29115. **EMAIL** marcusjones@claflin.edu

JONES, NICHOLAS FRANCIS
PERSONAL Born 08/22/1946, Los Angeles, CA, m, 1971, 4 children **DISCIPLINE** ANCIENT HISTORY, CLASSICAL PHILOLOGY **EDUCATION** Univ Southern Calif, BA, 68; Univ Calif, Berkeley, MA, 72, PhD(classics), 75. **CAREER** Instr, 75-76, asst prof 76-81, assoc, 82-97, Prof Classics, Univ Pittsburgh, 97-. **HONORS AND AWARDS** Fulbright Fel, 72-73; Am Coun of Learned Societies Fel, 79; Nat Endowment for the Humanities Fel, 84-85; Inst for Advanced Study, Princeton, visitor, 84-85. **MEMBERSHIPS** Am Philol Asn; Archaeol Inst Am; Asn Ancient Historians. **RESEARCH** Greek and Roman hist; classical philol. **SELECTED PUBLICATIONS** Auth, Public Organization in Ancient Greece, Am Philos Soc, 87; auth, Ancient Greece: State and Society, Prentice Hall, 97; auth, The Associations of Classical Athens. The Response to Democracy, Oxford Univ Press, 99. **CONTACT ADDRESS** Dept of Classics, Univ of Pittsburgh, 1518 Cathedral, Pittsburgh, PA 15260-0001. **EMAIL** nfjones@pitt.edu

JONES, NORMAN L.
PERSONAL Born 04/27/1951, Twin Falls, ID, m, 1994 **DISCIPLINE** HISTORY **EDUCATION** Idaho State Univ, BA, 72; Univ Colo, MA, 74; Cambridge Univ, PhD, 78. **CAREER** Prof & Ch, Dept Hist, Utah State Univ. **HONORS AND AWARDS** Mellon Fel, Harvard Univ, 81-2; Whitefield Prize for the Best Book in Stud in Hist Series, 82; Vis Fellow, Institut d'Histoire de la Reformation, Univ de Geneve, SWI, 85; NZL V Chancellors' Casual Vis, 8/94; Fowler Hamilton Vis Res Fellow, Christ Church, Oxford Univ, 98. **RESEARCH** 16th cent Britain; Parliamentary hist; Reformation Europe. **SELECTED PUBLICATIONS** Auth, Faith by Statute: Parliament and the Settlement of Religion, 1559, Royal Hist Soc, 82; co-ed, Interest Groups and Legislation in Elizabethan Parliaments: Essays Presented to Sir Geoffrey Elton, Parliamentary Hist, 8:2, 89; auth, God and the Moneylenders, Usury and Law in Early Modern England, Basil Blackwell, 89; co-ed, The Parliaments of Elizabethan England, Basil Blackwell, 90; auth, The Birth of the Elizabethan Age, England in the 1560s, Blackwell Pubs, 93, 95; auth, The English Reformation, Religion and Culture Adaptation, Blackwell Pubs, (forthcoming, 01). **CONTACT ADDRESS** Dept Hist, Utah State Univ, Logan, UT 84322-0710. **EMAIL** njones@wpo.hass.usu.edu

JONES, PAUL HENRY
PERSONAL Born 06/28/1949, Richmond, VA, m, 1976, 2 children **DISCIPLINE** HISTORICAL THEOLOGY **EDUCATION** Yale Univ, BA, 72; Brite Div Sch, Tex Christian Univ, MDiv, 78; Vanderbilt Univ, MA, 84, PhD, 88. **CAREER** Dean of the Chapel, prof, prog dir Rel, Transylvania Univ, 85- ; tchg asst, Vanderbilt Univ, 81-83. **HONORS AND AWARDS** Alpha Omicron Pi Awd for tchg excellence, 98, Transylvania Univ; Bingham Awd excellence tchg, 97, Transylvania Univ; T.A. Abbott Awd fac excellence, Div higher educ, Christian Church, 97; John H. Smith fel, Vanderbilt Univ; Theta Phi Hon Soc, Fac Bk Awd (s) in New Testament, Hebrew Bible, Rel ed, and Christian Board of Publ Awd (s) for scholastic excellence at Brite Div Sch. **MEMBERSHIPS** AAR, NAAL. **SELECTED PUBLICATIONS** Auth, An Eidetics of the Eucharist, Mid-stream: An Ecumenical Jour, Jan 91; Worship as Identity Formation, Lexington Theol Quart, April 91; Tarry at the Cross: A Christian Response to the Holocaust, Perspectives, March 92; The Meaning of the Eucharist: Its Origins in the New Testament Texts, Encounter, Spring 93; Christ's Eucharistic Presence: A History of the Doctrine, NY, Peter Lang Publ, 94; Making a Differnce is Imperative, The Disciple, Aug 94; We Are How We Worship: Corporate Worship as a Matrix for Christian Identity Formation, Worship, July 95; Worship and Christian Identity, The Disciple, Dec 96; Disciples at Worship: From Ancient Order to Thankful Praise, in Christian Faith Seeking Historical Understanding, Macon, GA, Mercer UP, 97; coauth, 500 Illustrations: Stories from Life for Preaching and Teaching, Nashville, Abingdon Press, 98; auth, "Christian Worship for Secular People," The Christian Ministry (99). **CONTACT ADDRESS** Dept of Religion, Transylvania Univ, 300 N. Broadway, Lexington, KY 40508. **EMAIL** pjones@transy.edu

JONES, PETER D. A.
PERSONAL Born 06/09/1931, Hull, England **DISCIPLINE** ECONOMIC HISTORY **EDUCATION** Univ Manchester, Eng, BA, 52, MA, 53; London Sch Econ, PhD, 63. **CAREER** Asst lectr Am hist & insts, Dept Am Studies, Univ Manchester, 57-58; vis asst prof econ & hist, Tulane Univ, 59-60; from asst prof to prof hist, Smith Col, 60-68; Prof Hist to Prof Emer, Univ Ill, Chicago, 68-; Am Specialist, US Dept State, 76-, Danforth teaching fel, 63; ed in hist & soc sci, Pegasus, New York, 66-68; mem hist comt, Grad Rec Exam, Educ Testing Serv, Princeton Univ, NJ, 66-70; vis prof US hist, Univ Hawaii, 72, 76; vis prof Am hist, Univ Warsaw, 73-74; mem Am studies comt, Am Coun Learned Soc, 73-; vis prof, Univ Dusseldorf, 74-75. **MEMBERSHIPS** AHA; Econ Hist Asn; Econ Hist Soc; Am Econ Asn; Conf Brit Studies. **RESEARCH** United States social and economic history; comparative history; foreign affairs. **SELECTED PUBLICATIONS** Auth, Economic History of the US since 1783, Routeledge, 56, coauth, The Christian Socialist Revival, 1877-1914: Religion, Class, and Social Conscience in Late-Victorian England, Princeton Univ, 68; The Robber Barons Revisited, Heath, 68; auth, Since Columbus: Pluralism and Poverty in the History of the Americas, Heinemann, London, 75; The USA: A History of its People and Society (2 vols), Dorsey, 76; co-ed, The Ethnic Frontier: Group Survival in Chicago and the Midwest, Eerdmans, 77; Ethnic Chicago, Eerdmans, 81; Biographical Dict of American Mayors, Greenwood Press, 82. **CONTACT ADDRESS** Dept of Hist, Univ of Illinois, Chicago, 1021 Univ Hall, Chicago, IL 60607.

JONES, ROBERT EDWARD
PERSONAL Born 01/11/1942, Wilkes-Barre, PA, m, 1966, 2 children **DISCIPLINE** RUSSIAN HISTORY **EDUCATION** Lafayette Col, BA, 63; Cornell Univ, PhD(hist), 68. **CAREER** Asst prof, 68-73, assoc prof, 73-80, Prof Hist, Univ Mass, Amherst, 80-. **MEMBERSHIPS** Am Asn Advan Slavic Studies. **RESEARCH** Eighteenth century Russia 1650-1850. **SELECTED PUBLICATIONS** Auth, Urban planning and the development of provincial towns in Russia, 1762-1796, in: The Eighteenth Century in Russia, Clarendon, 73; The Emancipation of the Russian Nobility, 1762-1785, Princeton Univ, 73; Jacob Sievers, Enlightened Reform, and the development of a Third Estate in Russia, Russ Rev, 10/77; auth, Provincial Development in Russia, Catherine II and Jacob Sievers, Rutgers U Press, 84; auth, "The Opposition to War and Expansion in Late Eighteenth century Russia," Jahrbucher fur Geshchichte Osteuropas 32, (84): 34-51; auth, "Getting the Goods to St. Petersburg, Water Transport from the Interior, 1709-1811," Slavic Review 43, (84): 413-433; auth, "The Charter to the Nobility of 1785: a Legislative Landmark?" Canadian-American Slavic Studies 23, (89): 1-16; auth, "Runway Peasants and Russian Motives for the Partitions of Poland," in Hugh Ragsdale, ed. Imperial Russian Foreign Policy, Cambridge U Press, (91): 210-228; auth, "The Nobility and Russian Foreign Policy," Cahiers du monde russe et sovietique, (93): 159-169; auth, "Opening a Window on the South, Russia and the Black Sea, 1695-1792," in Maria di Salvo and Lindsey Hughes, eds., A Window on Russia, La Fenice Edizioni, (96): 123-131; auth, "Morals and Markets: the Conflict of Traditional Values and Liberal Ideas in the Economic thought of Catherin II, " Jahrbucher fur Geschichte Osteuropas 45, (97): 526-540; auth, "Catherine the Great and the Russian Nobility," in Eckhard Hubenr and Jan Kusbar, eds., Russlan ZurZeit Katharinas II, Bohlau Verlag, (98): 103-114; auth, "Why St. Petersburg?" in Lindsey Hughes, ed., Peter the Great and the West New Perspectives, Palgrave Press, (01): 189-205. **CONTACT ADDRESS** Dept of Hist, Univ of Massachusetts, Amherst, 612 Herter Hall, Amherst, MA 01003. **EMAIL** rejones@history.umass.edu

JONES, ROBERT FRANCIS
PERSONAL Born 03/10/1935, Philadelphia, PA, m, 1959, 5 children **DISCIPLINE** AMERICAN HISTORY **EDUCATION** La Salle Col, BA, 56; Univ Notre Dame, MA 58, PhD, 67. **CAREER** Teacher, high sch, Pa, 60-61; instr hist, Sch Bus, 61-65, asst prof, Fordham Col, 65-76, assoc prof, 76-93, prof hist, Fordham Col and Grad Sch, Fordham Univ, Am Philos Soc grants, 69-71 & 80-81. **HONORS AND AWARDS** NYork State Soc of the Cincinnati Distinguished Prof, 99-. **MEMBERSHIPS** Orgn Am Historians; Inst Early Am Hist & Cult. **RESEARCH** Early national period in United States history, political and commercial. **SELECTED PUBLICATIONS** Auth, "Naval Thought of Benjamin Stoddert, First Secretary of the Navy, 1798-1801," Am Neptune, 1/64; ed, The Formation of the Constitution, Holt, 71; auth, "William Duer and the Business of Government in the Era of the American Revolution," William & Mary Quart, 7/75; contribr, Power and the Presidency, Scribner, 76; auth, George Washington: A Biography, Twayne, 79; "George Washington and the Politics of the Presidency," Presidential Studies Quart, 1/80; auth, Economic Opportunism and the Constitution in New York: the Example of William Duer, New York History, 87; auth, The King of the Alley: The Career of William Duer, Politician, Entrepreneur, and Speculator, 1768-1799, Memories of American Philosophical Society, 92; ed, Astorian Adventure: The Journal of Alfred Seton, 1811-1815, Fordham, 93; auth, Annals of Astoria: the Log Headquarters of the Pacific Fur Company on the Columbia River, 1811-1813, Fordham. **CONTACT ADDRESS** Dept of History, Fordham Univ, 441 E Fordham Rd, Bronx, NY 10458-5191. **EMAIL** rjones@fordham.edu

JONES, WILBUR DEVEREUX
PERSONAL Born 09/28/1916, Youngstown, OH, m, 1943, 2 children **DISCIPLINE** HISTORY **EDUCATION** Youngstown Col, AB, 40; Western Reserve Univ, AM, 47, PhD(hist), 49. **CAREER** Instr hist, Western Reserve Univ, 47-49; from instr to assoc prof, 49-61, Prof Hist, Univ GA, 62-. **RESEARCH** Nineteenth century British history; Anglo-American relations; ancient history. **SELECTED PUBLICATIONS** Auth, Lord Derby and Victorian Conservatism, Oxford: Blackwell, 56; auth, Lord Aberdeen and the Americas, Athens, U. of GA, Press, 58; auth, Civilization Through the Centuries, Boston: Ginn, 60; auth, The Confederate Rams at Birkenhead, Tuscaloosa: Conferederate Publishing Co., 61; auth, Prosperity Robindon, London: Macmillan, 67; auth, The Peelites, 1846-1857, Columbus: Ohio St. U. Press, 72; auth, The American Problem in British Diplomacy, 1841-61, London: Macmillan, 74; auth, Venus and Sothis: How the Ancient Near East was Rediscovered, Chicago: Nelson; Hall, 82; auth, Dir, Our World Today, 1954-1964; auth, Make Believe Ballroom + Roadhouse Musicians of the 1930s, A Personal Account, Amer Heritage, Vol 0045, 94 **CONTACT ADDRESS** 420 S Milledge Ave, Athens, GA 30605.

JONES, WILLIAM J.
PERSONAL Born 07/04/1932, London, England **DISCIPLINE** HISTORY **EDUCATION** Univ Col, London, BA, 54, PhD, 58, DLitt(hon), 84. **CAREER** Hist Parliament Trust, Westminster, 57-61; fac mem to prof, 61-91, ch hist, 75-77, PROF EMER HISTORY, UNIV ALBERTA, 92-; vis prof, Univ Calif Davis, 65-66; vis assoc prof, Univ Calif Berkeley, 67. **HONORS AND AWARDS** Guggenheim fel, 68; fel, Royal Hist Soc, 73; fel, Royal Soc Can, 82. **MEMBERSHIPS** Econ Hist Soc; Selden Soc; Past Present Soc; N Am Conf Brit Stud; Hist Asn; Am Soc Legal Hist. **SELECTED PUBLICATIONS** Auth, The Elizabethan Court of Chancery, 67; auth, Politics and the Bench, 71; auth, The Foundations of English Bankruptcy, 79; contribur, History of Parliament 1559-1601, 3 vols, 82-83. **CONTACT ADDRESS** Dept of History and Classics, Univ of Alberta, Edmonton, AB, Canada T6G 2H4.

JORAVSKY, DAVID
PERSONAL Born 09/09/1925, m, 1949, 2 children **DISCIPLINE** MODERN HISTORY **EDUCATION** Univ Pa, BA, 47; Columbia Univ, MA, 49, Russ Inst, cert, 49, PhD, 58. **CAREER** Instr hist, Cornell Univ, 53, Marietta Col, 53-54 & Univ Conn, 54-58; from asst prof to assoc prof, Brown Univ, 58-66; Prof Hist, Northwestern Univ, Evanston, 66-, Chmn Dept, 80-, Res grants-in-aid, Am Acad Arts & Sci & Am Philos Soc, Brown Univ, 58-61; NSF & Am Coun Learned Soc, Russ Res Ctr, Harvard Univ, 61-72; mem screening comt, Foreign Area Fel Prog, 62-63; NSF & Am Coun Learned Soc res grants, 69-70 & 73-74; fel, Woodrow Wilson Ctr, Smithsonian Inst, 77-78. **HONORS AND AWARDS** Pfizer Prize, Hist Sci Soc, 71. **MEMBERSHIPS** AHA; Hist Sci Soc; Am Asn Advan Slavic Studies. **RESEARCH** Russian intellectual history; history of science; history of communism. **SELECTED PUBLICATIONS** Auth, Soviet Marxism and Natural Science, 1917-32, Columbia Univ, 61; The Vavilov Brothers, Slavic Rev, 9/65; The Lusenko Affair, Harvard Univ, 70; ed, Let History Judge: The Origins and Consequences of Stalinism, Knopf, 72; auth, The head on Jung's pillow, NY Rev Bk, 9/72; Lamarckism, In: Dictionary of History of Ideas, Scribner, 73. **CONTACT ADDRESS** Dept of History, Northwestern Univ, 1881 N Sheridan Rd, Evanston, IL 60208.

JORDAN, DAVID P.
PERSONAL Born 01/05/1939, Detroit, MI, m, 1988, 1 child **DISCIPLINE** HISTORY **EDUCATION** Univ of Mich, BA, 61; Yale Univ, MA, 62; PhD, 66. **CAREER** Asst prof hist, Brooklyn Col, 66-68; asst prof, 68-71; assoc prof, 71-79, Prof Hist, Univ Ill, Chicago Circle, 79-. **HONORS AND AWARDS** Shirley A Bill Teaching Awd; NEH Fel. **RESEARCH** French Revolution, Napoleon, Paris, Edward Gibbon, Urban History. **SELECTED PUBLICATIONS** Auth, Gibbon and his Roman

Empire, Univ Ill, 71; The Kings Trial, Univ Calif Press, 79; Auth,The Revolutionary Career of Maximilien Robespierre, The Free Press, 85; Auth, Transforming Paris, Free Pr, 95. **CONTACT ADDRESS** Dept Hist, Univ of Illinois, Chicago, 852 S Morgan St, #723, Chicago, IL 60607-7042. **EMAIL** dpj@uic.edu

JORDAN, DONALD A.
PERSONAL Born 06/06/1936, Chicago, IL, m, 1963, 3 children **DISCIPLINE** ASIAN HISTORY **EDUCATION** Allegheny Col, BA, 58; Univ Pittsburgh, MA, 63; Univ Wis, PhD(E Asian hist), 67. **CAREER** Asst prof, 67-74, dir summer inst China, 72-75, dir, Southeast Asia Studies Ctr, 77-81, Assoc Prof E Asian Hist, Ohio Univ, 74-, Nat Endowment for Humanities fel, 82. **MEMBERSHIPS** Asn Asian Studies; Nat Educ Asn; Mid-west China Sem; Tri-state China Sem. **RESEARCH** Republican China; Sino-Japanese relations. **SELECTED PUBLICATIONS** Rev, Amer Hist Rev, Vol 0098, 93; rev, Amer Hist Rev, Vol 0100, 95; auth, The Northern Expedition, China's National Revolution; auth, Chinese Boycotts Versus Japanese Bombs, The Failure of China's Revolutionary Diplomacy in 31; auth, China's Trin bg Fire, the Shamghai War of 32. **CONTACT ADDRESS** Dept of Hist, Ohio Univ, 110 Bentley Hall, Athens, OH 45701-2979. **EMAIL** jordand@ohio.edu

JORDAN, ERVIN L.
PERSONAL Born 00/00/1954, Norfolk, VA, m, 1985 **DISCIPLINE** HISTORY **EDUCATION** Norfolk State Col, BA cum laude 73; Old Dominion Univ, MA 79. **CAREER** Univ Virginia, asst prof, assoc curator, assoc prof, cur, 81 to 96-; Piedmont Virginia Comm Col, adj fac, 93-. **HONORS AND AWARDS** Sergeant Kirkland Awd; Cert of Hon Civil War Rnd Table; Outstanding Alumnus; VFH; Floyd W Crawford Awd; H. H. Clay Humane Awd; Who's Who in the South; Who's Who in the World; Phi Kappa Phi; member of the advisory comm on african-amer interpretation at monticello; appointed to the bd of trustees of the va museum of natural hist and the state historical advisory bd; has been the subject of numerous television, radio and newspaper interviews; a **MEMBERSHIPS** SHA; NAAAS; ASAALH; SAA; MARAC. **RESEARCH** Civil war hist; afro/amer history; southern history; amer hist. **SELECTED PUBLICATIONS** Auth, Black Confederates and Afro-Yankees in Civil War Virginia. A Nation Divided: New Studies in Civil War History, ed, James I. Robertson Jr, Charlottesville and London, U press of VA, 95; Jamestown Virginia, 1607-1907: An Overview, Jamestown Virtual Website, 98; Battlefield and Home Front: African Americans and the Civil war, 1860-1865, in: The African American Odyssey: An Exhibition at the Library of Congress, ed, Debra Newman Ham, Washington, Library of Congress, 98; Slave Laws in Virginia, by Philip J. Schwarz, Athens and London, U of GA press, rev in: the Jour of Amer Hist, 97; Hearts at Home: Southern Women in the Civil War, coauth, Charlottesville, U of VA Print and Press, 97; George Washington: A Hero for American Students?, coauth, The Social Studies, 97. **CONTACT ADDRESS** Library, Univ of Virginia, Charlottesville, VA 22903.

JORDAN, JIM
DISCIPLINE ART HISTORY **EDUCATION** Univ IA, BA, MFA; Inst Fine Arts NYork Univ, PhD. **CAREER** Prof, Dartmouth Col. **RESEARCH** Art of the first half of the 20th century, espec abstract art. **SELECTED PUBLICATIONS** Auth, Paul Klee and Cubism, Princeton UP, 84; Graphic Legacy of Paul Klee (exh cat), 83; var other articles; coauth, The Paintings of Arshile Gorky, NY UP, 82. **CONTACT ADDRESS** Dartmouth Col, 3529 N Main St, Ste. 207, Hanover, NH 03755. **EMAIL** jim.jordan@dartmouth.edu

JORDAN, PHILIP D.
PERSONAL Born 11/23/1940, Copaigue, NY, m, 1968, 2 children **DISCIPLINE** HISTORY **EDUCATION** Alfred Univ, BA, 63; Univ Rochester, MA, 65; Univ Iowa, PhD, 71. **CAREER** TA, Univ of Iowa, 66-68; asst prof to prof, Western State Col of Colo, 69-85; assoc prof to prof, Hastings Col, 85-. **HONORS AND AWARDS** NEY Summer Sem, 80, 86; Dorothy Weyer Creigh Distinguished Prof, 89. **MEMBERSHIPS** AHA; Am Soc of Church Hist; Hist of Sci Soc; Org of Am Hist; Phi Alpha Theta; AAUP. **RESEARCH** American Intellectual History, History of Religion in America, History of Science - John William Draper. **SELECTED PUBLICATIONS** Auth, "The Evangelical Alliance and American Presbyterians, 1867-1873", J of Presby Hist 51 (Fall 73): 390-26; auth, "Call for the Washington Conference", The Social Gospel: Religion and Reform in Changing America, eds Ronald C. White, Jr and C. Howard Hopkins, Temple Univ Pr, (Philadelphia, 76): 202-05; auth, "Cooperation Without Incorporation - America and the Presbyterian Alliance, 1870-1880", J of Presby Hist, 55 (Spring 77): 13-35; auth, "Immigrants, Methodists and a Conservative Social Gospel, 1865-1908", Methodist Hist, XVII (Oct 78): 16-43; auth, The Evangelical Alliance for the United States of America, 1847-1900: Ecumenism, Identity and the Religion of the Republic, Vol 7, Studies in Am Relig, Edwin Mellen Pr, (NY and Toronto), 82; auth, Josiah Strong and a Scientific Social Gospel", Iliff Rev, XLII (Winter 85): 21-31. **CONTACT ADDRESS** Dept Hist, Hastings Col, PO Box 269, Hastings, NE 68902-0269.

JORDAN, ROBERT WELSH
PERSONAL Born 12/20/1936, Miami Beach, FL, m, 1962, 1 child **DISCIPLINE** PHILOSOPHY, PHILOSOPHY OF HISTORY **EDUCATION** Univ Houston, BS, 57; New Sch Social Res, MA, 70. **CAREER** Asst prof, 70-82, ASSOC PROF PHILOS, CO STATE UNIV, 82-. **MEMBERSHIPS** Husserl Circle; Soc Phenomenol & Existential Philos; Am Soc Value Inquiry. **RESEARCH** Twentieth century Continental philosophy; German philosophy since Kant; philosophy of history and social science. **SELECTED PUBLICATIONS** Auth, Vico and Husserl: History and Historical Science, In: Giambattista Vico's Science of Humanity, John's Hopkins Univ Press, 76; Vico and the Phenomenology of the Moral Sphere, Social Res, Vol 43, 76; Das transzendentale Ich als Seiendes in der Welt, Perspecktiven Philos, Vol 5, 79; Das Gesetz, die Anklage und Klc Prozess: Franz Kafka und Franz Brentano, Jahrbuch deutschen Schillerges, Vol 24, 80; auth, intro to & transl of Husserl's Inaugeral Lecture at Freiburg im Breisgau (1917): Pure Phenomenology, its Method and its Field of Investigation, In: Husserl: The Shorter Works, Univ Notre Dame Press, 80; Extended Critical Review of Edmind Husserl's Vorlesungen uper Ethik and Wertlehre, 1908-1914, ed by Ullrich Melle (Husserliana, vol 28), Dordrecht, Boston, London: Kluwer Academic Pubs, 88, in Husserl Studies 8, 92; Phenomenalism, Idealism, and Gurwisch's Account of the Sensory Noema, in To Work at the Foundations, J. C. Evans and R. W. Stufflebeam, eds, Kluwer Academic Pubs, 97; The Part Played by Value in the Modification of Open into Attractive possibilities, Ch 5 oh Phenomenology of Values and Valuing, J. G. Hart and Lester Embree, eds, Kluwer Academic Pubs, 97; Hartmann, Nicolai, in Encyclopedia of Phenomenology, Lester Embree, gen ed, Kluwer Academic Pubs, 97; Value Theory in Encyclopedia of Phenomenology, Lester Embree, gen ed, Kluwer Academic Pubs, 97. **CONTACT ADDRESS** Dept of Philos, Colorado State Univ, Fort Collins, CO 80523-0001. **EMAIL** rjordan@vines.colostate.edu

JORDAN, WILLIAM C.
PERSONAL Born 07/04/1948, Chicago, IL, m, 1970, 4 children **DISCIPLINE** HISTORY **EDUCATION** Ripon Col, AB, 69; Princton Univ, PhD, 73. **CAREER** Asst prof to prof, Princeton Univ, 75-. **HONORS AND AWARDS** Haskins Medal, Medieval Acad of Am. **MEMBERSHIPS** Am Hist Asn, Medieval Acad of Am. **RESEARCH** High Middle Ages. **SELECTED PUBLICATIONS** Coed, Order and Innovation in the Middle Ages: Essays in Honor of Joseph r. Strayer, Princeton Univ Press, 76; auth, Louis IX and the Challenge of the Crusade: A Study in Rulership, Princeton Univ Press, 79; auth, From Servitude to Freedom: Manumission in the Senonais in the Thirteenth Century, Univ of Penn Press, 86; auth, The French Monarchy and the Jews from Philip Augustus to the Last Capetians, Univ of Penn Press, 89; auth, Women and credit in Pre-Industrial and Developing Societies, Univ of Penn Press, 93; auth, The Great Famine: Northern Europe in the Early Fourteenth Century, Princeton Univ Press, 96; ed, The Middle Ages: An Encyclopedia for Student, Scribner's, 96; ed, The Middle Ages: A Watts Guide for Children, Franklin Watts, 00. **CONTACT ADDRESS** Dept History, Princeton Univ, 130 Dickinson Hall, Princeton, NJ 08544-0001. **EMAIL** wchester@princeton.edu

JOSEPH, HARRIET D.
PERSONAL Born 01/16/1947, Wichita Falls, TX, d, 1 child **DISCIPLINE** LATIN AMERICAN HISTORY **EDUCATION** Southern Methodist Univ, BA, 67; Univ North Tex, MA, 71, PhD, 76. **CAREER** Instr, Tex Southmost Col, 76-92; prof, Univ of Tex at Brownsville/Tex Southmost Col, 92-. **HONORS AND AWARDS** Res Enhancement Grants, Univ Tex, Brownsville, 94-95, 95-96; Awded Exceptional Merit (top ten percent of fac), Univ Tex, Brownsville, 98-99; Piper Prof nominee for Univ of Tex, Brownsville, 98-99. **MEMBERSHIPS** Phi Beta Kappa, Tex State Hist Asn, Tex Oral Hist Asn, Southwestern Coun of Latin Am Studies, Brownsville Hist Asn, South Tex Hist Asn. **RESEARCH** Texas during Spanish period (1500-1821); Jewish history in Brownsville, Texas in the twentieth century. **SELECTED PUBLICATIONS** Co-ed, Papers of the Second Annual Palo Alto Conf, U. S. Dept of the Interior (97); coauth with Dr. Donald Chipman, Notable Men and Women of Spanish Texas, Univ Tex Press; coauth with Dr. Donald Chipman, "Los Latinos," contract with Univ Tex Press at Austin (forthcoming 2001). **CONTACT ADDRESS** Dept Soc Sci, Univ of Texas, Brownsville, 83 Fort Brown St, Brownsville, TX 78520-4956. **EMAIL** hdjoseph@utb1.utb.edu

JOSLIN, KATHERINE
DISCIPLINE AMERICAN LITERATURE, AMERICAN STUDIES **EDUCATION** Northwestern Univ, PhD. **CAREER** Prof, English, W Mich Univ. **HONORS AND AWARDS** Western Mich Univ Alum; Fulbright Summer Inst for Intl Edu Grants. **MEMBERSHIPS** Am Asn for the Study of Lit and Environ; Am Studies Asn; Great Lakes Am Studies Asn; Edith Wharton Soc; Modern Lang Asn. **RESEARCH** Edith Wharton, literary criticism, Jane Addams as a writer, progressive era writers. **SELECTED PUBLICATIONS** Auth, Wretched Exotic: Essays on Edith Wharton in Europe, Peter Lang, 93; auth, Edith Wharton, in Women Writers Series, Macmillan Publs Limited & St. Martin's Press (London & NY), 91. **CONTACT ADDRESS** Dept of English, Western Michigan Univ, Sprau Tower, Kalamazoo, MI 49008. **EMAIL** joslin@wmich.edu

JOUKOWSKY, MARTHA SHARP
PERSONAL Born 09/02/1936, Cambridge, MA, m, 1956, 3 children **DISCIPLINE** NEAR EASTERN ARCHAEOLOGY **EDUCATION** Amer Univ Beirut, Lebanon, MA, 72; Univ Paris Sorbonne, PhD, 82. **CAREER** Prof, Brown Univ, 97-; assoc prof, Brown Univ, 88-97; asst prof, Brown Univ, 87-88. **MEMBERSHIPS** Archaeol Inst Amer; Amer Schools of Oriental Res; Amer Center Oriental Res. **RESEARCH** Near Eastern Archaeology **SELECTED PUBLICATIONS** Early Turkey: An Introduction to the Archaeology of Anatolia from Prehistory through the Lydian Period, Kendall-Hunt, 96; The Great Temple at Petra," Amer Jour Archaeol, 98; Re-Discovering Elephants at Petra! Ancient Egyptian and Mediterranean Studies: In Memory of William A. Ward, Brown Univ, 98. **CONTACT ADDRESS** Dept of Archaeology, Brown Univ, Box 1921, Providence, RI 02912. **EMAIL** martha_joukowsky@brown.edu

JOY, MARK S.
PERSONAL Born 03/10/1954, Maryville, MO, m, 1975, 3 children **DISCIPLINE** AMERICAN HISTORY **EDUCATION** Central Christian Col, BA, 76; E NM Univ, MA, 83; Ks St Univ, MA, 85, PhD, 92. **CAREER** Vis prof, 88-89, Washburn Univ; asst prof to assoc prof, 91-, Jamestown Col. **HONORS AND AWARDS** Best paper W Hist, 84; Phi Alpha Theta **MEMBERSHIPS** Conf on Faith & Hist; Amer Soc of Church Hist; Org Amer Hist. **RESEARCH** Relig in Amer, espec primitivists & restorationist groups **SELECTED PUBLICATIONS** Auth, Caleb May: Kansas Territorial Pioneer and Politician, Prairie Scout, 85; art, Missions to Native Americans, Protestant, Dictionary of Christianity in American, Inter-Varsity Press, 90; art, Riggs, Stephen Return, The Blackwell Dictionary of Evangelical Biography, 1760-1830, Basil Blackwell Ltd, 95. **CONTACT ADDRESS** 6045 College Ln, Jamestown, ND 58405. **EMAIL** joy@jc.edu

JOYCE, DAVIS D.
PERSONAL Born 06/19/1940, Greenwood, AR, m, 1975, 5 children **DISCIPLINE** HISTORY **EDUCATION** Eastern NM Univ, BS, 61; NM State Univ, MA, 63; Univ OK, PhD, 68. **CAREER** Asst to assoc prof, Hist, Univ Tulsa, 66-83; vis prof, American studies, Univ Keele (England), 81; Soros Prof Am studies, Kossuth Univ (Hungary), 94-96; assoc prof to prof Hist, East Central Univ, 87-. **HONORS AND AWARDS** Nat Endowment for the Humanities grants, 71, 76, 80, 83, 88, 90, 92; McCasland Awd for Excellence in Teaching OK Hist, OK Heritage Asn, 97. **MEMBERSHIPS** OK Hist Soc; OK Asn of Prof Hist; Am Asn of Univ Profs. **RESEARCH** Am historiography; OK hist. **SELECTED PUBLICATIONS** Auth, A History of the United States by Edward Channing, ed, Univ Press Am, 93; An Oklahoma I Had Never Seen Before: Alternative Views of Oklahoma History, ed, Univ OK Press, 94; United States History: A Brief Introduction for Hungarian Students, with Tibor Glant, Kossuth Univ Press, 96. **CONTACT ADDRESS** Dept of History, East Central Univ, Ada, OK 74820. **EMAIL** djoyce@mailclerk.ecok.edu

JOYCE, JOYCE A.
DISCIPLINE AFRICAN AMERICAN STUDIES **EDUCATION** Valdosta State Col, BA, 70; Univ Ga, MA, 72; PhD, 79. **CAREER** Coordinator and Chairperson, Black Studies Dept Chicago State Univ, 96-97; Chair African Am Studies, Temple Univ, 97-. **HONORS AND AWARDS** Am Book Awd for Literary Criticism, 95. **RESEARCH** Black Studies; Literary Criticism, Womanism; black Women Spirituality. **SELECTED PUBLICATIONS** Auth, Ijala: Sonia Sanchez and the African Poetic Tradition, Third World Press, 96; auth, Warriors, Conjurers, and Priests: Defining African-centered Literary Criticism, Third World Press, 94; co-ed, The New Cavalcade: an anthology of African American Writing from 1760 to the Present, Vol II, Univ Press, 92; co-ed, The New Cavalcade: an anthology of African American Writing from 1760 to the Present, Vol I, Univ Press, 91; auth, Native son: Richard Wright's Art of Tragedy, Univ Iowa Press, 86. **CONTACT ADDRESS** African-American Studies, Temple Univ, 1115 W Berks St, Philadelphia, PA 19122-6006. **EMAIL** jjoyce@astro.temple.edu

JOYCE, ROSEMARY A.
PERSONAL Born 04/07/1956, Lackawanna, NY, m, 1984 **DISCIPLINE** ANTHROPOLOGY, ARCHAEOLOGY **EDUCATION** Cornell Univ, AB, 78; Univ Ill, Urbana-Champaign, PhD, 85. **CAREER** Asst curator, 85-94, asst dir, 86-89, Peabody Museum, Harvard Univ; asst prof, 89-91, assoc prof, 91-94, anthrop, Harvard Univ; dir, Phoebe Hearst Museum of Anthropology, 94-99, assoc prof, anthrop, Univ Calif Berkeley, 94. **HONORS AND AWARDS** Resident fellowships: Bunting Inst, Radcliffe Coll, Harvard Univ, 92-93; Stanford Univ Center Study Behavioral Scis, 98 (deferred); Univ Calif Humanities Research Inst, spring 99; research grants: Getty Grant Program; Wenner-G Fren Found Anthrop Research; Heinz Charitable Fund; Nat Sci Foundation; Nat Endowment for the Humanities; Fulbright-Hays Prog, Fam SI. **MEMBERSHIPS** Soc Amer Archeol; Amer Anthrop Assn; Coun Museum Anthrop; Amer Assn Museums. **RESEARCH** Archaeology of Central America and Mesoamerica; the archaeology of gender; ceramic analysis; Maya writing; the anthropology of representation and identity; museum anthropology. **SELECTED PUBLICATIONS**

Coauth, Encounters with the Americas: The Latin American Gallery of the Peabody Museum, 95; auth, "The Construction of Gender in Classic Maya Monuments," in Gender in Archaeology: Essays in Research and Practice, 96; co-ed, Women in Prehistory: North American and Mesoamerica, 97; co-ed, Social Patterns in Pre-Classic Mesoamerica, 98; auth, "Performing the Body in Prehispanic Central America," RES: Anthropology and Aesthetics, spring 98. **CONTACT ADDRESS** Dept Anthropology, Univ of California, Berkeley, Kroeber Hall, #3710, Berkeley, CA 94720-3710. **EMAIL** rajoyce@uclink.berkeley.edu

JUDD, JACOB
PERSONAL Born 07/16/1929, New York, NY, m, 1951, 2 children **DISCIPLINE** AMERICAN HISTORY **EDUCATION** NYork Univ, BA, 50, MA, 53, PhD, 59. **CAREER** Instr hist & polit sci, Sch Com, NY Univ, 55-56; res assoc Am hist, Sleepy Hollow Restorations, 56-63; from asst prof to assoc prof, 63-78, Prof Am Hist, Lehman Col, 78-98, Lectr, Sch Gen Studies, Hunter Col, 58-59, 62-63, Grad Div, 62; George N Shuster grant, 67-68; res coord, Sleepy Hollow Restorations, 69-89; assoc, Columbia Univ Sem Early Am Hist, 70-; Nat Endowment for Humanities res grant, 75-76; Grad Fac, Grad Ctr, City Univ New York, 79-98; Prof Emeritus, 98. **MEMBERSHIPS** Am Asn State & Local Hist; Am Studies Asn; AHA; Orgn Am Historians. **RESEARCH** American Colonial history; development of urbanism; the Hudson Valley in American history. **SELECTED PUBLICATIONS** Ed, The Van Cortlandt Family Papers, 4 Vols, Sleepy Hollow Press, 76-86. **CONTACT ADDRESS** Dept of Hist, Lehman Col, CUNY, 250 Bedford Park Blvd W, Bronx, NY 10468-1589. **EMAIL** I.j.judd@prodigy.net

JUDD, RICHARD
PERSONAL Born 02/23/1947, Cheboygan, MI, m, 1975, 1 child **DISCIPLINE** HISTORY **EDUCATION** Calif State Univ, BA, 70; MA, 72; PhD, 79. **CAREER** Res fel , asst to full prof, Univ Maine, 80-. **HONORS AND AWARDS** Ralph Hday Awd, 89. **MEMBERSHIPS** Am Soc for Environmental Hist, Org of Am Hist. **RESEARCH** New England Environmental History. **SELECTED PUBLICATIONS** Auth, Common Lands, Common People: The Origins of Conservation in Northern New England, Cambridge, 97; auth, Maine: The Pine Tree State from Prehistory to the Present, Orono, 95; auth, socialist Cities: Municipal Politics and the Grass-roots of American Socialism, Albany, 89; auth, Aroostook: A Century of Logging in Northern Maine, 1832-1931, Orono, 89, auth, "Searching for the Roots of the Conservation Movement: Fish Protection in New England, 1865-1900," Transactions of the Fifty-Seventh North American Wildlife and Natural Resources Conference, (92): 717-723; auth, "A Man for all Seasons: Frank John Dixie Barnjum, Conservationist, Pulpwood Embargoist and Speculator," Acadiensis: Journal of the History of the Atlantic Region, (91): 129-144; auth, The Coming of the Clean Water Acts in Maine, 1941-1961," Environmental Review, (90): 50-73; auth, "Grass-Roots Conservation in Eastern Coastal Maine: Monopoly and the Moral Economy of Weir fishing, 1893-1911," Environmental Review, (88): 80-103. **CONTACT ADDRESS** Dept History, Univ of Maine, 5774 Stevens Hall, Orono, ME 04469-5774. **EMAIL** richard_judd@umit.maine.edu

JUDGE, EDWARD H.
PERSONAL Born 06/07/1945, Detroit, MI, m, 1970, 4 children **DISCIPLINE** RUSSIAN AND SOVIET HISTORY **EDUCATION** Univ of Detroit, BA, 67; Univ Mich, MA, 69, PhD, 75. **CAREER** Asst prof hist, SUNY Plattsburgh, 77-78; asst to prof of hist, LeMoyne Col, 78- . **HONORS AND AWARDS** IREX USSR Young Scholar Exchange, 76-77; NEH res and travel grant, 86, 90, 93; NEH summer sem grant, 86; LeMoyne Scholar of the year, 84; J.T. Georg endowed professorship, 97-00; Le Moyne Teacher of the Year, 99; Matteo Ricci Awd for Achievement in Diversity, 00. **MEMBERSHIPS** Am Asn for Advanc of Slavic Stud; Central NY Russian Hist. **RESEARCH** Hist of late Imperial Russia; hist of the Cold War. **SELECTED PUBLICATIONS** Auth, Plehve: Repression and Reform in Imperial Russia, 1902-1904, Syracuse Univ, 83; auth, Easter in Kishinev: Anatomy of a Pogrom, NY Univ, 92; coauth, Modernization and Revolution: Dilemmas of Progress in Late Imperial Russia, East European Monographs, 92; coauth, A Hard and Bitter Peace: A Global History of the Cold War, Prentice-Hall, 96; coauth, The Cold War: A History Through Documents, Prentice-Hall, 99. **CONTACT ADDRESS** Dept of History, Le Moyne Col, 1419 Salt Springs Rd, Syracuse, NY 13214. **EMAIL** judge@mail.lemoyne.edu

JUHNKE, JAMES CARLTON
PERSONAL Born 05/14/1938, Newton, KS, m, 1963, 2 children **DISCIPLINE** AMERICAN HISTORY **EDUCATION** Bethel Col, Kans, AB, 60; Ind Univ, MA, 64, PhD, 68. **CAREER** Asst prof, 66-71, assoc prof, 73-77, prof hist, Bethel Col, Kans, 77-, Dir, Mennonite Libr & Arch, 73-75; co-ed, Mennonite Life, 75-80; 89-95, 00-. **MEMBERSHIPS** AHA; Asn Am Historians; Conf Faith & Hist. **RESEARCH** American Mennonite history; conscientious objection in World War I; modern Christian missions. **SELECTED PUBLICATIONS** Co-ed, Voices Against War, Bethel Col, 73; auth, The Victories of Nonresistance, Fides et Hist, fall, 74; A People of Two Kingdoms, Faith and Life, 75; Mob Violence and Kansas Mennonites in 1918, Kans Hist Quart, autumn 77; A People of Mission, A History of General Conference Mennonite Overseas Missions, Faith and Life Press, 79; General Conference Mennonite Missions to the American Indians in the Late Nineteenth Century, Menn Quart Rev, 4/80; Gustav H Enss, Mennonite Alien, Mennonite Life, 12/81; Dialogue With a Heritage: Cornelius H. Wedel and the Beginnings of Bethel College, Bethel Col, 87; Vision, Doctrine, War: The Mennonite Experience in America 1890-1930, Herald Press, 89; co-ed, Nonviolent America: History Through the Eyes of Peace, Bethel Col, 93; Creative Crusader: Edmund G. Kaufman and Mennonite Community, Bethel Col, 94; auth, "Shaping Religious Community Through Martyr Memories," Menn Quart Rev, 99. **CONTACT ADDRESS** Dept of Hist, Bethel Col, Kansas, 300 E 27th St, North Newton, KS 67117-8061. **EMAIL** jjuhnke@bethelks.edu

JUMONVILLE, NEIL TALBOT
PERSONAL Born 10/07/1952, Portland, OR, m, 1998 **DISCIPLINE** HISTORY **EDUCATION** Reed Col, BA, 77; Columbia Univ, MA, 79; Harvard Univ, AM, 83, PhD, 87. **CAREER** Teaching fel, resident tutor, lectr, 82-90, Harvard Univ; asst prof to assoc prof to prof, 90-, Fl St Univ; Wm. Warren Rogers Prof, Flordia State Univ, 00. **HONORS AND AWARDS** Reed Col Faculty commendation for Acad Excellence, 75, 76; Phi Beta Kappa, 77; Univ Teaching Awd, Fl St Univ, 94. **MEMBERSHIPS** Amer Hist Assoc; Org of Amer Hist; Signet Soc. **RESEARCH** US intellectual & cultural hist; Amer historiography; Amer stud, twentieth century US. **SELECTED PUBLICATIONS** Auth, Critical Crossing: the New York Intellectuals in Postwar America, Univ Calif Press, 91; art, The New York Intellectuals' Defense of the Intellect, Queen's Quart, 90; auth, The Origin of Henry Steele Commager's Activist Ideas, His Teacher, 96; auth, Henry Steele Commager: Midcentury Liberalism and the History of the Present, Univ NC Press, 99. **CONTACT ADDRESS** Dept of History, Florida State Univ, Tallahassee, FL 32306-2200. **EMAIL** njumonvi@mailer.fsu.edu

JUNNE, GEORGE
PERSONAL Born 05/10/1943, Philadelphia, PA, d **DISCIPLINE** AFRICAN STUDIES **EDUCATION** Univ Mich, BFA, 72; MA, 78; PhD, 88. **CAREER** Lectr, Univ Colo Boulder, 88-; asst to assoc prof, Univ of N Colo, 94-. **MEMBERSHIPS** WSSA; SVP; NAES; Phi Delta Kappa. **RESEARCH** Black in the U.S. West, African Muslims in the New World, Social and Cultural Transformations in Cuba. **SELECTED PUBLICATIONS** Auth, Afro-Americans History: A Chronicle of People of African Descent in the United States, Kendall/Hunt, (Dubuque), 96; auth, The Black West - A Bibliography, Africana Studies Occasional Paper Series 2, Spring 99; auth, Blacks in the American West and Beyond - America, Canada and Mexico: A Selectively Annotated Bibliography, Greenwood Pr, (Westport, CT), 00. **CONTACT ADDRESS** Dept African Studies, Univ of No Colorado, Greeley, CO 80639. **EMAIL** ghjunne@aol.com

JURICEK, JOHN T.
PERSONAL Born 05/17/1938, Chicago, IL, d, 1963, 2 children **DISCIPLINE** HISTORY **EDUCATION** Univ Chicago, BA, 59, MA, 62, PhD, 70. **CAREER** Assoc prof **HONORS AND AWARDS** Younger Humanist Fel, NEH, 71-72; Fel, Nat Humanities Institute, New Haven, 75-76; NEH Demonstration Grant, 77. **RESEARCH** American colonial history; the Indian in American history. **SELECTED PUBLICATIONS** Ed, Early American Indian Documents: Treaties and Laws, 1607-1789; auth, "American Usage of the Word 'Frontier' From Colonial Times to Frederick Jackson Turner," Proc Am Philos Soc, CX (66): 10-34; auth, "English Territorial Claims in North Am under Elizabeth and the Early Stuarts," Terrae Incognitae, VII (75): 7-22. **CONTACT ADDRESS** Dept History, Emory Univ, Atlanta, GA 30322-2350. **EMAIL** jjurice@emory.edu

JUSDANIS, GREGORY
DISCIPLINE CLASSICAL LITERATURE, AESTHETICS **EDUCATION** McMaster Univ, BA, 78; Birmingham Univ, PhD, 83. **CAREER** Asst prof to assoc prof to prof, Ohio State Univ, 87-. **HONORS AND AWARDS** Guggenheim Fel, 92; Woodrow Wilson, 94. **MEMBERSHIPS** MLA; MGSA. **RESEARCH** Nationalism; Greek literature; globalization; aesthetics. **SELECTED PUBLICATIONS** Auth, The Poetics of Cavafy, Eroticism, Texuality, History, Princeton, 87; auth, Belated Modernity and Aesthetics, Culture, Inventing National Lit, 91; auth, The Necessary Nation, Princeton, 01. **CONTACT ADDRESS** Dept Classics, Ohio State Univ, Columbus, 230 N Oval Mall, 414 University Hall, Columbus, OH 43210.

K

KACZYNSKI, BERNICE M.
DISCIPLINE HISTORY **EDUCATION** Univ Pittsburgh, BA; Yale Univ, MA, PhD. **HONORS AND AWARDS** Assoc ed, Jour Medieval Latin. **RESEARCH** Intellectual hist of late Antiquity and the early Middle Ages. **SELECTED PUBLICATIONS** Auth, Greek in the Carolingian Age: The St. Gall Manuscripts, 88. **CONTACT ADDRESS** History Dept, McMaster Univ, 1280 Main St W Rm 619 Chester New Hall, Hamilton, ON, Canada L8S 4L9. **EMAIL** kaczynb@mcmaster.ca

KADISH, GERALD E.
PERSONAL Born 05/16/1932, New York, NY, m, 1983 **DISCIPLINE** HISTORY **EDUCATION** Hunter Col, BA, 59; Univ Chicago, MA, 62; PhD, 64. **CAREER** Instr, State Univ NY, 63-64; Asst Prof, State Univ NY, 64-67; Assoc Prof, State Univ NY, 67-95; Prof, State Univ NY, 95-. **HONORS AND AWARDS** Chancellor's Awd for Excellence in Teaching, State Univ NY. **MEMBERSHIPS** Int Assoc of Egyptologists, Am Res Ctr in Egypt, Soc for the Study of Egyptian Antiq. **RESEARCH** Ancient Egypt, history, religion, literature. **SELECTED PUBLICATIONS** Auth, "British Museum Writing Board 5645: The Complaints of Kha-Kheper-Re-senebu," J of Egyptian Archaeol, 59 (73): 77-90; auth, "The Sacatophagous Egyptian," The J of the Soc for the Study of Egyptian Antiq IX (79): 203-217; auth, "Seasonality and the Name of the Nile," J of the Am Res Ctr in Egypt XXV (88): 185-194; auth, "Observations on Time in Ancient Egyptian Culture," Papers on Ancient Greek and Islamic Philos, III, Inst for Global Cult Studies (93); auth, "Observations on Time and Work-Discipline in Ancient Egypt," in Studies in Hon of William Kelly Simpson, II (96), 439-449; ed, Oxford Encyclopedia of Ancient Egypt, 96-00. **CONTACT ADDRESS** Dept Hist, SUNY, Binghamton, PO Box 6000, Binghamton, NY 13902-6000.

KAEGI, WALTER EMIL
PERSONAL Born 11/08/1937, New Albany, IN, m, 1969, 2 children **DISCIPLINE** HISTORY **EDUCATION** Haverford Coll, BA, 59; Harvard Univ, MA, 60, PhD, 65. **CAREER** Teach fel, 61-63, Harvard; Asst Prof, 65-69, Assoc Prof, 69-74, Prof, 74-, vote mem Oriental Instr, 97-, Univ of Chicago. **HONORS AND AWARDS** Harv Fel, Dum Oaks/Harv Fel, IRH Fel, ACLS Fel, SHS Fel, IAS Fel, NEH Fel, Guggenheim Fel, NHC Fel, 2 Fulbright Fel, SSRC Mid East Fel. **MEMBERSHIPS** Mid-east Medievalists, SAHS, USNCBS, MAA. **RESEARCH** Byzantine & Islamic history, seventh century & early Islamic conquests, Byzantino-Arabica history. **SELECTED PUBLICATIONS** Auth, Byzantium and the Decline of Rome, Princeton, Princeton Univ Press, 68; Byzantine Military Unrest 471-843, An Interpretation, Amsterdam & Las Palmas, AM Hakkert, 81; Byzantium and the Early Islamic Conquests, Cambridge Eng, Cambridge Univ Press, 92; Byzantine Logistics, Problems and Perspectives, in: The Feeding of Mars, ed J A Lynn, Boulder, Westview Press, 93; The Capability of the Byzantium Army for Military Operations in Italy, in: Teodorico e i Goti, ed, A Carile, Ravenna Longo Editore, 95; auth, "Egypt on the Eve of the Muslim Invasion," in Cambridge Hist of Egypt, 98. **CONTACT ADDRESS** Dept of History, Univ of Chicago, 1126 E 59th St, Chicago, IL 60637-1539. **EMAIL** kwal@midway.uchicago.edu

KAEUPER, RICHARD WILLIAM
PERSONAL Born 06/20/1941, Richmond, IN, m, 1965 **DISCIPLINE** MEDIEVAL HISTORY **EDUCATION** Capital Univ, BA, 63; Princeton Univ, MA, 65, PhD, 67. **CAREER** Lectr hist, Kenyon Col, 67-68; asst prof, IL State Univ, 68-69; asst prof, 69-73, assoc prof hist, Univ Rochester, 73, chmn dept, 77, Am Philos Soc grant, 71; res grant, Guggenheim Found, 78; R T French vis prof, Worcester Col Oxford, 79-80. **HONORS AND AWARDS** H.F. Gugeneim grt, 89-91. **MEMBERSHIPS** AHA; Mediaeval Acad Am; fel Royal Hist Soc. **RESEARCH** Medieval Britain and continental Europe; chivalry and issues of public order and religion in northwestern Europe. **SELECTED PUBLICATIONS** Auth, Bankers to the Crown: The Riccardi of Lucca and Edward I, Princeton Univ, 73; The Role of Italian Financiers in the Conquest of Wales, Welsh Hist Rev, 73; The Frescobaldi of Florence and the English Crown, Studies Medieval & Renaissance Hist, 73; Royal Finance and the Crisis of 1297, In: Order and Innovation in the Middle Ages, Princeton Univ, 76; Law and Order in Fourteenth Century England, Speculum, 79, An Historians Reading of the Tale of Gamelyn, 83; War, Justice and Public Order, Clarendon Press, Oxford, 88; Chivalry and Violence in Medieval Europe, Clarendon Press, Oxford, (99); co auth, The Book of Chivalry of Geoffroide Charny, Univ PA Press, 96, 2nd ed (99); auth, "Chivalry: Fantasy and Fear," Writing & Fantasy, Longman, (99); auth, "The Social Meaning of Chivalry in Romance," Cambridge Companion to Medieval Romance Cambridge University Press, (00); auth, "Violence in Medieval Society," edited with introduction, Boydell and Brewer, (00). **CONTACT ADDRESS** Dept of Hist, Univ of Rochester, 441 Rush Rhees Library, Rochester, NY 14627-0055. **EMAIL** rkpr@mail.rochester.edu

KAFKER, FRANK ARTHUR
PERSONAL Born 12/18/1931, New York, NY, m, 1953, 2 children **DISCIPLINE** MODERN EUROPEAN HISTORY **EDUCATION** Columbia Col, BA, 53; Columbia Univ, MA, 54, PhD(hist), 61. **CAREER** From instr to assoc prof hist, Corning Community Col, 58-62; from asst Prof to assoc Prof, 62-72, Prof, Hist, Univ Cincinnati, 72-98; Prof Emeritus, 98--. **HONORS AND AWARDS** Fulbright Fellow, 54-55, American Philosophical Society Fellow, 78, Rieveschal Awd for Dis-

tinguished Scolarship, University of Cincinnati, 91; Camargo Foundation Fellow, 93. **MEMBERSHIPS** AHA, Soc for Fr Hist Studies (Co-Editor, 85-92 French Historical Studies), Society for 18th Century French Studies (President, 95-97), American Society for 18th Century Studies; Societe Diderot; British Society for 18th Century Studies, 18th century Scottish Studies Society, Societe francaise d'etude du xviii siecle. **RESEARCH** France and Scotland, 1715-1815; Diderot and the Encyclopedists; the history of encyclopedias, especially the Encyclopedie and the early editions of the Encyclopedia Britannica. **SELECTED PUBLICATIONS** Auth, "The Encyclopedists as a Group: A Collective Biography of the Authors of the Encyclopedie," vo. 342, Studies on Voltaire and the 18th Century, (Oxford: Voltaire Foundation, 96; coauth, "The Encyclopedists as Individuals: A Biographical Dictionary of the Authors of the Encyclopedie," Vol. 257, auth, "Studies on Voltaire and the 18th Century," Oxford: Voltaire Foundation, 88; ed., "Notable Encyclopedias of the 17th and 18th Centuries: Nine Predecessors of the Encyclopedies," Vol. 1194, Studies on Voltaire and the 18th Century, Oxford: Voltaire Foundation, 81; Ed., "Notable Encyclopedias of the Late Eighteenth Century: Eleven Successors of the Encyclopedie, Vol. 315; auth, "Studies on Voltaire and the 18th Century," Oxford: Voltaire Foundation, 94; coed, "The French Revolution: Conflicting Interpretations," Random, 64 4th ed. Krieger, 89; coed, "Napoleon and His Times: Selected Interpretations," Krieger, 89. **CONTACT ADDRESS** Dept of Hist, Univ of Cincinnati, 31 Brimmer St., Apt. 4, Boston, MA 02108. **EMAIL** fkafker@msn.com

KAGAN, RICHARD C.
PERSONAL Born 06/24/1938, Los Angeles, CA, m, 1962, 2 children **DISCIPLINE** ASIAN HISTORY **EDUCATION** Univ Calif, Berkeley, BA, 60, MA, 63; Univ Pa, PhD(hist), 69. **CAREER** Instr hist, Boston State Col, 69-71; res assoc, Ctr Chinese Studies, Univ Mich, Ann Arbor, 71-72; asst prof hist, Grinnell Col, 72-73; from assoc prof to prof, Hamline Univ, 73-. **MEMBERSHIPS** AHA; Asn Asian Studies. **RESEARCH** Communist Revolution; Shamanism in China; political and economic development of Taiwan. **SELECTED PUBLICATIONS** Auth & ed, "Introduction," in The China Lobby in American Politics (Harper and Row, 74); auth, "Autobiography of Ch'en Tu-hsiu," The China Q, 72; auth, "Public Health in China," J of the Hellenic Diaspora (July 75): 51-57; auth, "From Revolutionary Iconoclasm to national Revolution: Ch'en tuhsiu and the Chinese Communist Movement" in China in the 1920s: Nationalism and Revolution, eds F. Gilbert Chan and Thomas H. Etzold (NY: New Vewpoints), 55-72; auth, "The Chinese Approach to Shamanism," in Chinese Sociol & Anthrop (Summer 80), 1-135; coauth, "The Taiwanese Tang-ki: THe Shaman as Community Healer and Protector," Asian Studies in Sociol (NY: Praeger, 82); coauth, "The Chinese Labor Movement from 1915-1949," Int Soc Sci Rev (Spring 83), 67-87; coauth, Human Rights in the Democratic People's Republic of Korea, Asia Watch and the Minnesota Lawyers Int Human Rights Committee, 88; auth, "Japan's Global Human Rights Policy," ed East Asian Studies, Univ of Calif Berkeley, 97. **CONTACT ADDRESS** Dept of Hist, Hamline Univ, 1536 Hewitt Ave, Saint Paul, MN 55104-1284. **EMAIL** ariel@umn.edu

KAGAN, RICHARD LAUREN
PERSONAL Born 09/18/1943, Newark, NJ, m, 1983, 1 child **DISCIPLINE** EARLY MODERN HISTORY **EDUCATION** Columbia Univ, AB, 65; Cambridge Univ, PhD, 68. **CAREER** Asst prof hist, Ind Univ, Bloomington, 68-72; asst prof, 72-74; assoc prof, 74-79; prof hist, Johns Hopkins Univ, 79-, fel, Shelby Cullom Davis Ctr Hist Studies, NJ, 69-70; US Dept Health, Educ & Welfare Comt Basic Res Educ res grant, 71-72; Herodotus fel, Inst Advan Study, Princeton, 76-77; US-Span Joint Comt res grant, 80. **HONORS AND AWARDS** John Simon Guggenheim Fel, 82; Quincentenary Fel, US-Spanish Joint Comm, 91-92; Sr Research Fel, The Getty Trust, 93-95; Collab Proj Grant, NEH, 94-97; Knight Comdr, Order of Isabel the Catholic; Catedra Foundacion Banco Bilbao Vizcaya, 99; Beca Sabatico, Universidad Complutense de Madrid, 00. **MEMBERSHIPS** AHA; Soc Span & Port Hist Studies; Ctr for Advan Study in Visual Arts, Wash, DC. **RESEARCH** Early modern Spain; history of European education; history of law; colonial Latin America; history of cartography. **SELECTED PUBLICATIONS** Auth, Universities in Castile, 1500-1700, Past & Present, 70; auth, Students and Society in Early Modern Spain, Johns Hopkins Univ, 74; auth, Universities in Castille 1500-1810, Universities in Society: Studies in The History of Higher Education, Princeton Univ, 74; auth, Law students and legal careers in eighteenth-century France, Past & Present, 75; auth, Lawsuits and Litigants in Castile, 1500-1700, Univ NC, 81; auth, The Toledo of El Greco, El Greco et Toledo, 82; auth, Spanish Cities of the Golden Age, 89; auth, Lucrecia's Dreams: Politics & Prophecy in Sixteenth Century Spain, 90; auth, Spain, Europe and the Atlantic World, Cambridge Univ, 95; auth, Prescott's Paradigm: American Historical Scholarship and the Decline of Spain, Am Hist Rev, April 96; auth, "Urbs and Civitas in Sixteenth and Seventeenth Century Spain," in Envisioning the City; Six Studies in Urban Cartography, ed. David Buisseret (Univ of Chicago Press, Chicago, 98), 73-108; auth, "A World Without Walls: City and Town in Spanish America, 1500-1700," in The Walled Tradition, ed. Jim Tracy (Cambridge Univ Press, 00), 117-150; auth, Urban Images of the Hispanic World, 1943-1793, Yale, 00. **CONTACT ADDRESS** Dept of Hist, Johns Hopkins Univ, Baltimore, 3400 N Charles St, Baltimore, MD 21218-2680. **EMAIL** Kagan@jhu.edu

KAHAN, ALAN S.
PERSONAL Born 07/24/1959 **DISCIPLINE** HISTORY **EDUCATION** Princeton Univ, BA, 80; Univ Chicago, PhD, 87. **CAREER** Mellon asst prof, Rice Univ, 88-92; asst prof, hist, Fla Intl Univ, 92-94; assoc prof, hist, Fla Intl Univ, 95-. **HONORS AND AWARDS** NEH Transl Grant, 95-96. **RESEARCH** European liberalism; Tocqueville; Burckhardt; J.S. Mill. **SELECTED PUBLICATIONS** Auth, Alexis de Tocqueville, The Old Regime and the Revolution, a new transl, The Univ of Chicago Press, vol 1, 98; Aristocratic Liberalism: The Social and Political Thought of Jacob Burckhardt, John Stuart Mill and Alexis de Tocqueville, Oxford Univ Press, 92; articles, Defining Opportunism: The Political Writings of Eugene Spuller, Hist of Polit Thought, winter, 94; Liberalism and Realpolitik in Prussia, 1830-52: The Case of David Hansemann, German Hist, oct, 91; Guizot et le modele anglais, in Francois Guizot et la culture politique de son temps, Paris, Gallimard, 91; The Victory of German Liberalism?, Rudolf Haym, Liberalism and Bismarck, Cent Europ Hist, mar, 90; Tocqueville's Two Revolutions, Jour of the Hist of Ideas, oct, 85. **CONTACT ADDRESS** History Dept, Florida Intl Univ, Miami, FL 33199. **EMAIL** kahana@fiu.edu

KAHN, B. WINSTON
DISCIPLINE ASIAN STUDIES & HISTORY **EDUCATION** Nat Taiwan Univ, BA, 55; Univ Minn, MA, 59; Univ Penn, PhD, 69. **CAREER** Lectr, Rutgers Univ, 65-66; asst prof, Ariz St Univ, 66-78; assoc prof, 78-. **HONORS AND AWARDS** Fulbright res Awd; Japan Found Staff Grant. **MEMBERSHIPS** AAS; SJS; JPRI; AASA FAA. **RESEARCH** Modern Japanese history; US Japanese relations; International history; Asian American experience. **SELECTED PUBLICATIONS** Ed, "US Japan Trade in the 80s: Problems and Prospects," Asian Affairs (85); auth, "Changing Attitude Toward Cultural Interchange in Postwar Japan,: Asia Pac Rev 6 (99): 65-77; auth, "Hani Motoko (1873-1957) and the Education of Japanese Women," The Hist 59 (97): 391-401. **CONTACT ADDRESS** Dept of History, Arizona State Univ, MC 2501, Tempe, AZ 85287. **EMAIL** bwkahn@asu.edu

KAHN, CHARLES H.
PERSONAL Born 05/29/1928, New Iberia, LA, m, 1988, 2 children **DISCIPLINE** HISTORY OF PHILOSOPHY **EDUCATION** Univ Chicago, BA, 46, MA, 49; Columbia Univ, PhD, 58. **CAREER** From instr to assoc prof Greek & Latin, Columbia Univ, 57-65; assoc prof, 65-68, chmn dept, 75-78, PROF PHILOS, UNIV PA, 68-, Univ Chicago exchange fel to Univ Paris, 49-50; Cutting traveling fel, Columbia Univ, 55-56; Am Coun Learned Soc res fel, 63-64; co-ed, Arch Geschichte Philos, 65-79; mem managing comt, Am Sch Class Studies in Athens, 70-99, vis prof, 74-75; Nat Endowment for Humanities fel, 74-75. **HONORS AND AWARDS** Guggenheim Fellow 79-80; ACLS Research Fellow, 85; NEH Research Fellow, 90-91. **MEMBERSHIPS** Am Philos Asn; Soc Ancient Greek Philosophers (pres, 76-78). **RESEARCH** Greek philosophy, especially Presocratics, Plato and Aristotle; political philosophy. **SELECTED PUBLICATIONS** Auth, Anaximander and the Orignis of Greek Cosmology, Columbia Univ Press, 1960, 250 pp. Translation into Modern Gree, 82. Reprinted by Hackett Pub, 94; auth, The Verb "Be in Ancient Greek, Reidel, Dordrecht, 1973 (Vol. 16, Foundations of Language Supplementary Series, ed JWM Verhaar): The Verb "Be" and its Synonyms, part 6, 486 pp.; auth, The Art and Thought of Heraclitus: An edition of the fragments with translation and commentary, Cambridtge Univ Pres, 99 (paperback, 81), 356 pp.; auth, Pitagora e I pitagorici (Instituto della encicolpedia Italiana, 1993). Italian translation of Pythagoras and the Pythagoreans, 100-page monograph; auth, Plato and the Socratic Dialogue, Cambridge Univ Press, (96): 431. **CONTACT ADDRESS** Dept of Philos/CN, Univ of Pennsylvania, 433 Logan Hall, Philadelphia, PA 19104. **EMAIL** chcon@sas.upenn.edu

KAHN, DAVID
PERSONAL Born 02/07/1930, New York, NY, d, 2 children **DISCIPLINE** MODERN HISTORY **EDUCATION** Bucknell Univ, AB, 51; Oxford Univ, PhD, 74. **CAREER** Reporter, Newsday, 55-63; Auth, 63-65; Ed, Iternational Herald Tribune, Paris, 65-67; Auth, 67-75; Jour, 75-79. **MEMBERSHIPS** Am Hist. Assoc; Intern Assoc ofr Cryptologic Research; Am Cryptogram Assoc. **RESEARCH** Hist of Intelligence; Hist of Cryptology. **SELECTED PUBLICATIONS** Auth, Hitler's Spies: German Military Intelligence in World War II, Macmillan, 78; auth, Kahn on Codes: Secrets of the New Cryptology, 84; auth, Seizing the Enigma: The Race to Crack the German U-Boat Codes, 1939-1943, Houghton Mifflin, 91; coed, "Cryptologia quarterly," articles on cryptology in journals, encylopedia, and magazines. **CONTACT ADDRESS** 120 Wooleys Lane, Great Neck, NY 11023. **EMAIL** davidkahn1@aol.com

KAHN, JONATHAN
PERSONAL Born 08/06/1958, Cambridge, MA **DISCIPLINE** HISTORY **EDUCATION** Yale Univ, BA, 80; Boalt Hall Sch of Law, JD, 88; Cornell Univ, PhD, 92. **CAREER** Asst Prof, Bard Col, 92-98 **HONORS AND AWARDS** Mellon Fel; Order of the Caif; Sage Fel; Yee Fel **MEMBERSHIPS** AHA; APSA; OAH; SHGAGE; ASLH **RESEARCH** U.S political culture; legal studies **CONTACT ADDRESS** Bard Col, 13 Hollis St, Cambridge, MA 02140. **EMAIL** kahn@bard.edu

KAISER, DANIEL HUGH
PERSONAL Born 07/20/1945, Philadelphia, PA, m, 1968, 2 children **DISCIPLINE** RUSSIAN HISTORY **EDUCATION** Wheaton Col, Ill, AB, 67; Univ Chicago, AM, 70, PhD(Russ hist), 77. **CAREER** Instr hist, King's Col, NY, 68-71; asst prof, Trinity Col, Ill, 71-73; vis asst prof, Russ hist, Univ Chicago, 77-78; asst prof hist, Grinnell Iowa Coll, 79-84; assoc prof, 84-86; prof hist, 86-; Joseph F Rosenfield prof social studies, 84-; chemn dept hist, 89-90, 96-98; Lectr & tour dir, Smithsonian Inst tours to USSR, 76-; vis prof, UCLA, 96. **HONORS AND AWARDS** Mem adv bd Soviet Studies in History, 79-85; editl bd Slavic Rev, 96; Fel Nat Endowment Humanities, 79, 92-93, 00, John Simon Guggenheim Meml Found, 86; Fulbright-Hays Fac Research Abroad Found, 86. **MEMBERSHIPS** AHA; Am Assn Advan Slavic Studies; Early Slavic Studies Assn, vp, 95-97, pres 97-99; Slavonic and East European Medieval Studies Group, UK; Study Group on 18th Century Russia, UK; 18th Century Russian Studies Assn. **RESEARCH** Russian and comparative law; Russian and comparative family history; Historical climatology. **SELECTED PUBLICATIONS** Trans ed, The Laws of Rus Tenth to Fifteenth Centuries, Charles Schlacks Jr, Publisher, 92; co-ed, with Gary Marker, Reinterpreting Russian History 860-1860s, Oxford Univ Press, 94; The Growth of the Law in Medieval Russia, Princeton Univ Press, 80; ed, The Worker's Revolution in Russia, 1918, Cambridge Univ Press, 87. **CONTACT ADDRESS** Dept of History, Grinnell Col, Grinnell, IA 50112-1690. **EMAIL** kaiser@grinnell.edu

KAISER, KEVIN ROBERT
PERSONAL Born 03/17/1964, Oakland, CA, s **DISCIPLINE** BIBLICAL STUDIES, NEAR EASTERN ART AND ARCHAEOLOGY **EDUCATION** San Jose State Univ, BA, 87; Grad Theol Union, Berkeley, MA, 90; Univ Calif, Berkeley, C. phil. 98, PhD, expected 01. **CAREER** Mus dir, Bade Inst Bibl Arch, Berkeley CA, 90-98. **HONORS AND AWARDS** Phi Kappa Phi; ASOR summer travel grant; Univ Calif, Berkeley summer fel. **MEMBERSHIPS** ASOR. **RESEARCH** Archaeology; history; Near Eastern languages. **CONTACT ADDRESS** 14328 Cuesta Ct., Sonora, CA 95370. **EMAIL** krkaiser@aol.com

KAISER, THOMAS ERNEST
PERSONAL Born 06/10/1947, New York, NY, m, 1975, 1 child **DISCIPLINE** HISTORY **EDUCATION** Univ Mich, BA, 68; Harvard Univ, PhD, 76. **CAREER** Asst prof, 76-80, assoc prof, 80-94, prof hist, 94-, Univ Ark, Little Rock; Univ Ark, Little Rock fac res grant, 77; Am Coun Learned Soc grant-in-aid, 78. **HONORS AND AWARDS** Article Awd, Southeastern Am Soc 18th-Century Studies, 81. **MEMBERSHIPS** Am Soc 18th Century Studies; Soc French Hist Studies. **RESEARCH** Eighteenth-century French political and cultural history. **SELECTED PUBLICATIONS** Auth, Property, Sovereignth, the Declaration of the Rights of Man, and the Tradition of French Jurisprudence, The French Idea of Freedom: The Old Regime and the Declaration of Rights of 1789, Stanford, 94; auth, Madame de Pompadour and the Theaters of Power, French Hist Stud, 96; auth, The Drama of Charles Edward Stuart, Jacobite Propaganda, and French Political Protest, 1745-1750, Eighteenth-Century Stud, 97; auth, Louis le Bien-Aime and the Rhetoric of the Royal Body, From the Royal to the Republican Body: Incorporating the political in Seventeenth and Eighteenth Century France, California, 98; auth, Enlightenment, Public Opinion and Politics in the Work of Robert Darnton, The Darnton Debate: Books and Revolution in the Eighteenth Century, Oxford, 98; art, The Evil Empire: Constructing Turkish Despotism in Eighteenth-Century French Political culture, J of Modern Hist, 99. **CONTACT ADDRESS** Dept of History, Univ of Arkansas, Little Rock, 2801 S University Ave, Little Rock, AR 72204-1099. **EMAIL** tekaiser@ualr.edu

KAISER, WALTER C., JR.
PERSONAL Born 04/11/1933, Folcroft, PA, m, 1957, 4 children **DISCIPLINE** BIBLICAL ARCHAEOLOGY **EDUCATION** Wheaton Col, AB, 55, BD, 58; Brandeis Univ, MA, 62, PhD, 73. **CAREER** Instr, 58-60, asst prof of Bible, 60-64, actg dir of archaeol & Near Eastern stud, 65-55, Wheaton Col; asst prof, 66-70, assoc prof, 70-75, chmn dept of OT, 75-79, sr vice pres, acad dean, 80-92, sr vice pres of Distance Learning, 92-93, Trinity Evangel Divin Schl; Coleman M Mockler Dist Prof of OT, 93-96; pres, 97-, Gordon Conwell Theol Sem. **HONORS AND AWARDS** Danforth Tchr Stud grant. **MEMBERSHIPS** Evangel Theol Soc; Inst of Bibl Res; Near Eastern Archaeol Soc; Soc of Bibl Lit. **RESEARCH** Old Testament Theol; Israel, history and archaeology; ethics. **SELECTED PUBLICATIONS** Auth, The Journey Isn't Over: The Pilgrim Psalms (120-134) for Life's Challenges and Joys, Baker 93; coauth, An Introduction to Biblical Hermeneutics: The Search for Meaning, Zondervan, 94; auth, The Book of Leviticus: Introduction, Commentary and Reflections, New Interpreter's Bible, Abingdon, 94; auth, Proverbs: Wisdom for Everyday Life, Zondervan, 95; auth, Psalms: Heart to Heart with God, Zondervan, 95; auth,

The Messiah in the Old Testament, Zondervan, 95; auth, Hard Sayings of the Bible, InterVarsity, 96; auth, A History of Israel, Broadman & Holman, 98; auth, The Christian and the "Old" Testament, US Ctr for World Mission, 98; auth, An Urgent Call For Revival and Renewal in Our Times: Sixteen Revivals in the Old and New Testament with a Study Guide, Broadman & Holman, 99; auth, Are the Old testament Documents Reliable?, InterVarsity, 99. **CONTACT ADDRESS** Gordon-Conwell Theol Sem, 130 Essex St, South Hamilton, MA 01982. **EMAIL** wckaiser@gcts.edu

KALANTZIS, GEORGE
PERSONAL Born 04/18/1967, Athens, Greece **DISCIPLINE** HISTORY OF CHRISTIANITY **EDUCATION** Univ IL, BS, 90; Northeastern IL Univ, MS, 93; Moody Grad Sch, MABS, 93; Garrett-Evangelical Theol Sem, MTS, 94; Northwestern Univ, PhD, 97. **CAREER** Assoc, pastor, ed, Hellenic Christ Prog, Greek Free Church, 92-; adj fac, Moody Bible Inst, 95-96; asst prof, Garrett-Evangelical Theol Sem, 96-. **HONORS AND AWARDS** Hartman Fel; Ernest W. Saunders End Doct Fel; Ester Y. Armstrong Schl; Teach Gnt, Wabash Cen; Doct Schl, Garrett-Evangelical Theol Sem; Schl, Grad Sch Northwestern Univ; Schl, Hellenic Christian Prog; Schl, Northeastern IL Univ, Schl Moody Bible Inst. **MEMBERSHIPS** NAPS; ASOR; ASCH; SBL; ETS. **RESEARCH** Development of early Christological models, esp Antioch from the fourth to the sixth century by Diodore of Tarsus, Theodore of Mopsuestia, and Nestorius of Constantinople; classical Graeco-Roman and early Christian philosophical understandings of anthropology and biblical hermeneutics as shown in the works of Origen, Tertullian, and the Cappadocians; Byzantine archaeology and architecture in Palestine. **SELECTED PUBLICATIONS** Auth, "Ephesus: A Roman, Jewish, and Christian Metropolis in the First and Second Centuries C.E.," Jian Dao: A J of Bible and Theol 7 (97): 103-119; auth, A translation of the critical text of the Greek New Testament into Modern Greek, 00. **CONTACT ADDRESS** Dept Christianity, Garrett-Evangelical Theol Sem, 2121 Sheridan Rd, Evanston, IL 60201-2926. **EMAIL** george-kalantzis@northwestern.edu

KALAS, ROBERT
PERSONAL Born 09/06/1949, New York City, NY, m, 4 children **DISCIPLINE** WESTERN CIVILIZATION, FRENCH SOCIAL HISTORY **EDUCATION** NYork Univ, PhD **CAREER** Dept Hist, Mt. St. Mary's Col **RESEARCH** Roles of widows within noble families in 16th and 17th century France. **SELECTED PUBLICATIONS** Publ on, structure of the nobility in 16th and 17th century France **CONTACT ADDRESS** Dept of History, Mount Saint Mary's Col and Sem, 16300 Old Emmitsburg Rd, Emmitsburg, MD 21727-7799. **EMAIL** kalas@msmary.edu

KALE, STEVEN D.
PERSONAL Born 03/10/1957, Los Angeles, CA, w, 1991, 1 child **DISCIPLINE** MODERN EUROPEAN HISTORY **EDUCATION** Univ Wis, Madison, PhD, 87. **CAREER** Assoc prof, Wash State Univ. **MEMBERSHIPS** Western Soc for Fr Hist; Soc for Fr Hist Studies; Am Hist Asn. **RESEARCH** History of modern France. **SELECTED PUBLICATIONS** Auth, Legitimism and the Reconstruction of French Society, 1852-1883, La State UP, 92. **CONTACT ADDRESS** Dept of Hist, Washington State Univ, 301 Wilson Hall, PO Box 644030, Pullman, WA 99164-4030. **EMAIL** kale@wsu.edu

KALIPENI, EZEKIEL
PERSONAL Born 02/04/1954, Mchinji, Malawi, m, 1984, 5 children **DISCIPLINE** GEOGRAPHY **EDUCATION** Univ Malawa, B Soc Sci, 79; Univ NC Chapel Hill, MA, 82; PhD, 86. **CAREER** Lectr, Univ of Malawi, 86-88; vis asst prof, Univ of NC, 88-91; vis asst prof, Colgate Univ, 91-94; asst prof to assoc prof, Univ of IL Urbana, 94-. **HONORS AND AWARDS** Grant, Rockegeller Found; Grant, Nat Sci Found, Grant, Int Develop Res Ctr, Canada; Outstanding Member of Fac, Panhellenic Asn of Univ of IL; Fel, Ctr for Advan Study. **MEMBERSHIPS** Assoc of Am Geogr; African Studies Assoc; African Assoc of Polit Sci; Am Geog Soc. **RESEARCH** Medical Geography, Population Studies, Environmental Issues, Health Care, Africa. **SELECTED PUBLICATIONS** Ed, Population Growth and Environmental Degradation in Southern Africa, Lynne Rienner Pub, (Boulder, CO), 94; coed, "AIDS, Health Care Systems and Culture in Sub-Saharan Africa: Rethinking and Re-Appraisal", African Rural and Urban Studies 3.2, Mich State Univ Pr, (East Lansing), 96; coed, Issues and Perspectives on Health Care in Contemporary Sub-Saharan Africa, Edwin Mellen Pr, (Lewiston, NY), 97; auth, "Population Pressure, Social change, Culture and Malawi's Pattern of Fertility Transition", African Studies Rev 40.2, (97): 173-208; coauth, "The Refugee Crisis in Africa and Implications for Health and Disease: A Political Ecology Approach", Soc Sci and Med 46.12, (98): 1637-1653; coed, Sacred Spaces and Public Quarrels: African Economic and Cultural Landscapes, Africa World Pr, (Trenton, NJ), 99; auth, "The spatial Context of Lilongwe's Growth and Development in Malawi", Sacred Spaces and Public Quarrels: African Economic and Cultural Landscapes, eds, E. Kalipeni and P. Zeleza, Africa World Pr, (99): 73-108;coauth, "Environmental change in the Blantyre Fuelwood Project Area in Malawi: A Political Ecology Perspective", Politics and the Life Sci 18.1 (99): 37-54; auth, "Health and disease in Southern Africa: A Comparative and Vulnerability Perspective", Soc Sci and Med 50.7, (00): 965-984; auth, "Health and Society in Southern Africa", Southern Africa: Reconciliation and Development?, eds York Bradshaw and Philip Ndegwa, Ind Univ Pr, (forthcoming); coed, HIV/AIDS in Africa: Mapping the Issues, Blackwell Pub, (forthcoming). **CONTACT ADDRESS** Dept Geog, Univ of Illinois, Urbana-Champaign, 607 S Mathews Ave, Urbana, IL 61801.

KALLGREN, DANIEL C.
PERSONAL Born 08/23/1963, Hendricks, MN, m, 2 children **DISCIPLINE** HISTORY **EDUCATION** Gustavus Adolphus Col, BA, 86; Univ Minn, MA, 91; PhD, 95. **CAREER** Asst prof, Univ of Wis Marinette, 95-. **HONORS AND AWARDS** Univ of Wis Marinette Fac of the Year, 98, 99. **MEMBERSHIPS** AHA; Soc Sci Hist Assoc. **RESEARCH** 19th and 20th Century American Social History, Historical Geography. **SELECTED PUBLICATIONS** Auth, "Race, Place and Poverty in the Pattern of Southern School Attendance, 1850-1950, Hist Geog 27, (99): 167-192; auth, "Technology and Student-Center Learning: The University of Wisconsin Student History Network Project", the Hist Teacher, 33.1 (Nov 99): 41-54. **CONTACT ADDRESS** Dept Soc Sci, Univ of Wisconsin, Marinette, 750 W Bay Shore St, Marinette, WI 54143-4253. **EMAIL** dkallgre@uwc.edu

KALLMAN, THEODORE
PERSONAL Born 11/03/1945, New York, NY, m, 1985, 2 children **DISCIPLINE** US HISTORY **EDUCATION** Oglethorpe Univ, BA, 68; Mich State Univ, MA, 69; Ga State Univ, PhD, 87. **CAREER** Lectr, Oglethorpe Univ, 89-94; Instr, San Joaquin Delta Col, 95-. **HONORS AND AWARDS** Nat Defense Educ Act Fel, 69-72; Res Grant, Radcliffe Col, 94-95; New Educ Awd, San Joaquin Delta Col, 98. **MEMBERSHIPS** WHA, Orgn of Am Historians, Soc for Utopian Studies. **RESEARCH** United States cultural and intellectual history, African-American history, progressivism, utopian socialism. **SELECTED PUBLICATIONS** Auth, "African-American Life in Atlanta 1847-1864," Atlanta Hist (forthcoming). **CONTACT ADDRESS** Dept Soc Sci, San Joaquin Delta Col, 5151 Pacific Ave, Stockton, CA 95207-6304. **EMAIL** tkallman@sjdccd.cc.ca.us

KALMAN, LAURA
PERSONAL Born 03/19/1955, Los Angeles, CA, m, 1984 **DISCIPLINE** HISTORY **EDUCATION** Pomona Col, BA, 74; UCLA, JD, 77; Yale Univ, PhD, 82. **CAREER** Asst prof, Univ Calif Santa Barbara, 82-85; assoc prof, 85-91; prof, 91-. **HONORS AND AWARDS** Golieb Res Fel, NYU Law School, 81-82; Am Coun of Learned Soc Fel, 84-85; Am Bar Found Fel, 84-85; Visiting Res Fel, Am Bar Found, 86-87; Littleton-Griswold Prize, Am Hist Asoc, 91; Charles Warren Res Fel, 94-95. **MEMBERSHIPS** Am Hist Asoc; Am Soc for Legal Hist; Orgn of Am Hist. **RESEARCH** Recant American legal and political history. **SELECTED PUBLICATIONS** Auth, Legal Realism at Yale, 1927-1960, 86; auth, Abe Fortas: A Biography, 90; auth, The Strange Career of Legal Liberalism, 96. **CONTACT ADDRESS** Dept. of History, Univ of California, Santa Barbara, Santa Barbara, CA 93106. **EMAIL** kalman@humanitas.ucsb.edu

KALOUDIS, GEORGE
PERSONAL Born 01/03/1952, Greece, m, 1975, 2 children **DISCIPLINE** HISTORY **EDUCATION** Panteios Sch Polit Sci, BA, 74; Calif St Univ, MA, 76; Univ Kan, MA, 81; PhD, 81. **CAREER** From Instr to Assoc Prof, Rivier Col, 85--. **HONORS AND AWARDS** Who's Who in the East; Who's Who in Am; Who's Who Among Am Teachers; Instr of the Year, 84-85, 85-86; Carnegie Found Awd, 94. **MEMBERSHIPS** APSA, NEPSA, NEHA, PSA, VFP, ISA. **RESEARCH** History of the United Nations, history of Cyprus, Greek history. **SELECTED PUBLICATIONS** Auth, "The Evolving United Nations: Is There a Hope?" Veterans for Peace J 27 (94): 17-18; auth, "The New Globalism and the Global Citizen," Peace Rev: A Transnational Quart 7:3/4 (95); auth, "Cycles in the Life of the United Nations," Transnational Perspectives (96); auth, "Cyprus: The Unresolved Conflict," Crossings: Bi-Communal Cypriot J (96); auth, "The Evolution of the United Nations in the Global Transformation," Rivier Insight 3 (96): 55-64; auth, "The Search for Global Order," The Int J on World Peace, XV.1 (98): 3-21; auth, Modern Greek Democracy: The End of a Long Journey? UP of Am, forthcoming; auth, "Cyprus: The Enduring Conflict," The Int J of World Peace (forthcoming). **CONTACT ADDRESS** Dept Hist, Rivier Col, 420 S Main St, Nashua, NH 03060-5043. **EMAIL** gkaloudis@rivier.edu

KALVODA, JOSEF
PERSONAL Born 01/15/1923, Czechoslovakia, m, 1956 **DISCIPLINE** HISTORY, POLITICAL SCIENCE **EDUCATION** Hunter Col, BA, 56; Columbia Univ, MA, 57, PhD, 60. **CAREER** From instr to assoc prof polit sci & hist, St Joseph Col, Conn, 57-61; assoc prof, Col for Women, Univ San Diego, 61-64, prof, 64-77; assoc prof govt, La State Univ, 66-68; Prof Polit Sci & Hist, St Joseph Col, Conn, 68-. **MEMBERSHIPS** AAUP; Am Asn Advan Slavic Studies; Am Polit Sci Asn. **RESEARCH** East central Europe; international relations; comparative government. **SELECTED PUBLICATIONS** Auth, Titoism, 58; auth, Czechoslovakia's Role in Soviet Strategy, 78; auth, The Genesis of Czechoslovakia, 86; auth, Z boju o zitrek, Fighting for Tomorrow, vol.I, 95; auth, Z boju o zitrek, Fighting for Tomorrow, vol.II, 96; auth, Genese Ceskoslovenska, The Genesis of Czechoslovakia, 98; auth, Z boju o zitrek, vol.III, Historicke eseje, Fighting for Tomorrow, Historical Essays, 98. **CONTACT ADDRESS** 9 Greenwood Dr, Avon, CT 06001-4115.

KAMACHI, NORIKO
DISCIPLINE HISTORY **EDUCATION** Harvard Univ, MA, 72; PhD, 72. **CAREER** Asst Prof to Prof, Univ Mich, 71-. **MEMBERSHIPS** Asn for Asian Studies. **RESEARCH** Modern Chinese History. **SELECTED PUBLICATIONS** Auth, Reform in China: Huang Tsun-hsien and the Japanese Model, Harvard UnivPress,71; auth, Japanese Culture and Customs, Greenwood Publ, 99. **CONTACT ADDRESS** Dept Soc Sci, Univ of Michigan, Dearborn, 4901 Evergreen Rd, Dearborn, MI 48128-2406.

KAMAU, MOSI
PERSONAL Born 05/05/1955, Chicago, IL, s **DISCIPLINE** AFRICAN-AMERICAN STUDIES **EDUCATION** Univ of Minnesota, BFA 1979; Florida State Univ, MFA 1983; Temple Univ, PhD, African-Amer Studies, 1989-. **CAREER** Tutle Contemporary Elem School, pottery instructor, 77-78 Talbot Supply Co Inc, welder 1979-80; Florida State Univ, asst preparator 1980-81; Williams Foundry, foundryman 1981-82; St Pauls Coll, asst prof of art 1984-89. **HONORS AND AWARDS** Intl Exchange Scholarship from Univ of Minnesota to Univ of Ife Ile, Ife Nigeria 1976-77; Sculpture/$5000 Natl Endowment of the Arts, Visual Arts, Washington DC 1984-85. **MEMBERSHIPS** Natl Council of Black Studies; African American Assn of Ghana; African Heritage Assn. **CONTACT ADDRESS** Saint Paul's Col, PO Box 901, Lawrenceville, VA 23868.

KAMBER, RICHARD
DISCIPLINE AESTHETICS **EDUCATION** Claremont Grad Sch, PhD, 75. **CAREER** Philos, Col NJ. **HONORS AND AWARDS** Dean, Arts & Scis. **SELECTED PUBLICATIONS** Auth, On the Nonexistence of Literary Ideas, Philos & Lit, 79; A Modest Proposal for Defining a Work of Art, British Journal Aesthetics, 93. **CONTACT ADDRESS** The Col of New Jersey, PO Box 7718, Ewing, NJ 08628-0718.

KAMHI, MICHELLE MARDER
PERSONAL Born 06/09/1937, New York, NY, m, 1987, 1 child **DISCIPLINE** ART HISTORY **EDUCATION** Barnard Coll, BA, 58; Hunter Coll CUNY, MA, 70. **CAREER** Ed, Columbia Univ Press 66-70; freelance ed and writer, 71-84; assoc ed, Aristos, 84-91; Co-ed, Aristos, 92-. **HONORS AND AWARDS** Fulbright scholar, Univ Paris, 58-59. **MEMBERSHIPS** Am Philos Asn; Am Soc for Aesthetics; Asn for Art History; Asn of Literary Scholars and Critics. **RESEARCH** Philosophy of Art. **SELECTED PUBLICATIONS** Auth, Limiting What Students Shall Read: Books and Other Learning Materials in Our Schools, 81; Censorship vs Selection: Choosing Books for Schools, Am Educ, 82; auth, Books Our Children Read, Documentary, Films, Inc, 84; Today's 'Public Art': Rarely Public, Rarely Art, Aristos, 88; The Misreading of Literature: Context, Would-Be Censors, and Critics, Aristos, 86; coauth, Ayn Rand's Philosophy of Art: A Critical Introduction, Aristos, 91-92; What Art Is: The Esthetic Theory of Ayn Rand, Open Court, 00. **CONTACT ADDRESS** Aristos, Radio City Station, PO Box 1105, New York, NY 10101.

KAMINSKI, JOHN PAUL
PERSONAL Born 01/16/1945, Bridgeton, NJ, m, 1967, 2 children **DISCIPLINE** AMERICAN HISTORY **EDUCATION** Ill State Univ, BS, 66, MS, 67; Univ Wis-Madison, PhD(US hist), 72. **CAREER** Dir, Ctr Study Am Constitution, Univ Wis-Madison, 81-, Assoc ed, Doc Hist Ratification Constit & Bill of Rights, 69-80, prin investr & co-ed, 80. **MEMBERSHIPS** Orgn Am Historians; Asn Doc Ed. **RESEARCH** United States Constitution; American Revolution. **SELECTED PUBLICATIONS** Assoc ed, Constitutional Documents and Records 1776-1787, 76. **CONTACT ADDRESS** Dept of Hist, Univ of Wisconsin, Madison, Ctr for the Study of the Am Constitution, 455 N Park St, 3211 Humanities, Madison, WI 53706-1483. **EMAIL** jpkamins@faestaff.wisc.edu

KAMMAN, WILLIAM
PERSONAL Born 03/23/1930, Geneva, IN, m, 1957, 3 children **DISCIPLINE** UNITED STATES DIPLOMATIC HISTORY **EDUCATION** Ind Univ, AB, 52, PhD(hist), 62; Yale Univ, MA, 58. **CAREER** Assoc prof, 62-69, prof hist, N Tx State Univ, 69-, chmn dept, 77-89, 93-94, assoc dean of A&S, 96-97, 98-, interim dean of A&S, 97-98. **MEMBERSHIPS** AHA; Orgn Am Historians; Soc Hist Am Foreign Rels, exec sec-treas, 85-89. **RESEARCH** United States Foreign policy in the 1920's and 1930's. **SELECTED PUBLICATIONS** Auth, A Search for Stability: United States Diplomacy Toward Nicaragua, 1925-1933, Univ Notre Dame, 68; contribr, Makes of American Diplomacy, 74 & Encycl of American Foreign Poli-

cy, 78, Scribner's; Encyclopedia World Biography, McGraw Hill, 73; 20th Century Encyl World Biography, Jack Heraty & Assoc, 87, 92; The War of 1898 and U.S. Intervention, 1898-34: An Encyl, Garland, 94. **CONTACT ADDRESS** Dept of Hist, Univ of No Texas, PO Box 310650, Denton, TX 76203-0650. **EMAIL** Kamman@UNT.EDU

KAMMEN, MICHAEL

PERSONAL Born 10/25/1936, Rochester, NY, m, 1961, 2 children **DISCIPLINE** HISTORY **EDUCATION** PhD. **CAREER** Prof. **HONORS AND AWARDS** Pulitzer Prize, 73; The Francis Parkman Prize, 87; Henry Adams Prize, 87; Nat Bk Awd, Popular Cult Asn, 96; pres, org am hist, 95-96. **MEMBERSHIPS** Am Academy of Arts and Science, Am Historical Asn, Organization of Am Historians, 95-96, Am Studies Asn, NY State Historical Asn, 81-94. **RESEARCH** U.S. cultural history; historical relationship between government and culture in the U.S. **SELECTED PUBLICATIONS** Auth, Mystic Chords of Memory; The Transformation of Tradition in American Culture, 91; Selvages and Biases: The Fabric of History in American Culture, 87; A Machine That Would Go of Itself: The Constitution in American Culture, 86. **CONTACT ADDRESS** Dept of History, Cornell Univ, Ithaca, NY 14853-2801. **EMAIL** mgk5@cornell.edu

KAMOCHE, JIDLAPH GITAU

PERSONAL Born 12/01/1942, Kabete, Kenya, m **DISCIPLINE** HISTORY **EDUCATION** Amherst Col, BA 1967; Univ of MA, MA 1969; State Univ of NYork at Buffalo, PhD 1977. **CAREER** African & Afro-Amer Studies Univ of OK, asst prof of History dir 1977-; State Univ Coll Buffalo, asst prof History 1972-77; African & Afro-Amer, dir; State Univ Coll Buffalo, stud 1970-72. **HONORS AND AWARDS** Recipeint inst of intl Educ Fellowship NY 1968-69; author Afro-am Life & Hist 1977; recipient coll of arts research fellowship Univ of OK 1979-80. **MEMBERSHIPS** Mem Several African & Afro-am Studies Orgns 1970-80; past vice pres Assn of Black Personnel Univ of OK 1978-79. **SELECTED PUBLICATIONS** author articles & book reviews in several scholarly journs 1977-; author "Umoja" 1980. **CONTACT ADDRESS** Department of History, Univ of Oklahoma, 455 W Lindsey, Norman, OK 73019.

KANE, STANLEY G.

PERSONAL Born 04/03/1938, Shanghai, China, m, 1959, 1 child **DISCIPLINE** PHILOSOPHY OF RELIGION, HISTORY OF PHILOSOPHY, ENVIRONMENTAL PHILOSOPHY **EDUCATION** Barrington Col, BA; Brown Univ, AM; Harvard Univ, PhD. **CAREER** Prof, Miami Univ **RESEARCH** Philosophy of religion, Environmental Philosophy. **SELECTED PUBLICATIONS** Publ on, problems of God and evil; nature of God; nature of religious lang; Anselm's theory of free will; Aquinas' doctrine of the soul and personal identity; 17th century mechanism phylos & histl roots of the env crisis. **CONTACT ADDRESS** Dept of Philosophy, Miami Univ, Oxford, OH 45056. **EMAIL** kanegs@muohio.edu

KANG, SOO Y.

PERSONAL Born 07/24/1964, Seoul, Korea, s **DISCIPLINE** ART HISTORY **EDUCATION** Univ So Calif, BA, 85; Univ Calif, Berkeley, MA, 89; Univ Calif, Santa Barbara, PhD, 94. **CAREER** Lectr, Univ Calif, Santa Barbara, 95; lectr, Santa Barbara City Col, 95; asst prof Art Hist, Chicago State Univ, 95- . **MEMBERSHIPS** Col Art Asn; Lancanian Soc, Chicago. **RESEARCH** Modern art; feminist art, religious art of the Twentieth Century. **SELECTED PUBLICATIONS** Auth, The Political Dimension of Rouault's Art, Cummer Stud, 96; auth, Voicing Post-Modern Women, Una Kim exhibition catalogue, Seoul, 98-99; auth, Rouault in Perspective; Contextual and Theoretical Study of His Art, International Scholars, 00. **CONTACT ADDRESS** 600 N McClung Ct, 3908A, Chicago, IL 60611. **EMAIL** bisyk@csu.edu

KANG, WI JO

PERSONAL Born 03/10/1930, Chinju, Korea, m, 1961, 4 children **DISCIPLINE** HISTORY OF RELIGIONS, MISSIONS **EDUCATION** Concordia Sem, BA, 57, 1313, 60; Univ Chicago, MA, 62, PhD, 67. **CAREER** Instr hist of relig, Columbia Univ, 64-66; asst prof, Valparaiso Univ, 66-68; assoc prof, Concordia Sem, 68-74 & Christ Sem-Seminex, 74-78; vis prof, Yonsei Univ, Korea, 78-79; Prof of Mission, Wartburg Sem, 80-98, prof emer, 98-. **MEMBERSHIPS** Am Acad Relig; Am Hist Soc; Int Soc Buddhist Studies; Am Soc Missiology; Am Soc Church Hist. **RESEARCH** History of religions in Asia; history of Christian missions in East Asia; world religions and politics. **SELECTED PUBLICATIONS** Auth, Korean Religions Under the Japanese Government (in Japanese), Seibunsha, Tokyo, 76; In Search of Light (in Korean), 76 & Religion and Politics of Korea Under Japanese Rule (in Korean), 77, Christian Lit Soc Korea, Seoul; The secularization of Korean Buddhism, Actes du XXIXe Cong Int des Orient Paris L'Asiatheque, 77; Religious response to Japanese rule, Ctr for Korean Studies, Kalamazoo, Mich, 77; co-ed, Christian Presence in Japan, Seibunsha, Tokyo, 81; auth, Christianity under the government of Chung Hee Park, Missiology: Int Rev, 81; Christianity in China, Currents in Theol & Mission, 82; auth, Christ and Caesar in Modern Korea: A History of Christianity and Politics, SUNY Press, 97. **CONTACT ADDRESS** 9980 Farthing Dr, Colorado Springs, CO 80906. **EMAIL** wjcjkang@aol.com

KANIPE, ESTHER SUE

PERSONAL Born 03/22/1945, Rockingham, NC **DISCIPLINE** EUROPEAN & WOMEN'S HISTORY **EDUCATION** Univ NC, Greensboro, BA, 67; Univ Wis, MA, 70, PhD(hist), 76. **CAREER** Instr hist, Grinnell Col, 73-75; asst prof, Lawrence Univ, 75-76; asst prof, 76-82, Assoc Prof Hist, Hamilton Col, 82-, Nat Endowment for the Humanities fel hist, Brown Univ, 80-81; consult, Nat Endowment for the Humanities, 81-; prof of hist, Marjorie and Robert W. McEwen, 91. **MEMBERSHIPS** AHA; Soc French Hist Studies. **RESEARCH** Modern French social history; World War I. **SELECTED PUBLICATIONS** Auth, Women and Medicine in the French Enlightenment--The Debate Over Maladies Des Femmes, J Hist Sexuality, Vol 0004, 94. **CONTACT ADDRESS** Dept of Hist, Hamilton Col, New York, 198 College Hill Rd, Clinton, NY 13323-1292. **EMAIL** ekanipe@hamilton.edu

KANTOWICZ, EDWARD ROBERT

PERSONAL Born 06/20/1943, Chicago, IL, m, 1967, 2 children **DISCIPLINE** UNITED STATES HISTORY **EDUCATION** St Mary of the Lake Sem, BA, 65; Univ Chicago, MA, 66, PhD(hist), 72. **CAREER** Asst prof, 69-75, Assoc Prof Hist, Carleton Univ, 75-, Fel, Can Coun, 75-76. **RESEARCH** Immigration to the United States; American Catholic history; American urban history. **SELECTED PUBLICATIONS** Auth, Research Guide toAmerican Historical Biography, J Amer Hist, Vol 0079, 93; Research Guide toAmerican Historical Biography, Vol 4, J Amer Hist, Vol 0079, 93; Research Guide toAmerican Historical Biography, Vol 5, J Amer Hist, Vol 0079, 93; Unmeltable Ethnics--Politics and Culture in American Life, J Amer Ethnic Hist, Vol 0016, 97. **CONTACT ADDRESS** 509-1701 Kilborn, Ottawa, ON, Canada K1H 6M8.

KAO, ARTHUR MU-SEN

DISCIPLINE ART HISTORY **EDUCATION** Nat Taiwan Univ, BA, 67; Univ Chinese Culture, MA, 70; Univ Kans, MA, 74, MPh, 75, PhD, 79. **CAREER** Instr, Chinese Univ Hong Kong, 79-85; assoc prof, Kent State Univ, 85-89; PROF, 89-, DIR, SCH ART, SAN JOSE STATE UNIV. **CONTACT ADDRESS** Sch Art and Design, San Jose State Univ, 1 Washington Sq, San Jose, CA 95192.

KAPLAN, ABRAM

PERSONAL Born 04/15/1963, Ann Arbor, MI, m, 1993, 2 children **DISCIPLINE** GEOGRAPHY **EDUCATION** Univ North Carolina at Chapel Hill, Phd, Dept City and Regional Planning; Univ Wisconsin, Land Resources Program, Institute for Environmental Studies, MS, 89; Univ Wisconsin, Energy Analysis and Policy Program, Institute for Environmental Studies, Certificate, 89; Oberlin Col, AB, 85. **CAREER** Anne Powell Riley Dir and Assoc Prof, Environmental Studies Program, Denison Univ, 99-; Instr, Alternative Dispute Resolution component of the US Geological Survey's Leadership Development Program, 98-; Anne Powell Riley Dir and Asst Prof, Environmental Studies Program, Denison Univ, 94-99; Vis Scholar, Dept of City and Regional Planning, Univ of North Carolina at Chapel Hill, 98. **HONORS AND AWARDS** Honored as Educator of the Year by the Ohio Alliance for the Environment, 98; Awd for Distinguished Service in the Field of Environmental Education, recognizing individuals, organizations, and businesses which have made significant contributions to environmental education. **MEMBERSHIPS** Urban & Regional Information Systems Assoc; Amer Society for Photogrammetry & Remote Sensing; Assoc of Collegiate Schools of Planning; National Assoc of Environmental Professionals; Amer Planning Assoc; Environmental Design Research Assoc; Amer Solar Energy Society; Amer Assoc of Geographers. **RESEARCH** Decision making processes and the role of experience among Ohio Amish farmers; Utility commercialization of photovoltaics: first steps in a diffusion strategy; Development of a pattern language for proactive environmental decision-making; The teaching and doing of environmental problem-solving: rethinking models of change. **SELECTED PUBLICATIONS** Auth, "Generating Interest in Photovoltaics Among Electric Utility Managers," Proceedings of the American Solar Energy Society, Solar 94, Conference, San Jose, CA, 94: 133-138; auth, "Working with Muni Managers on Solar Power: Knowledge and Familiarity in Decision-Making," Public Power, July/August, 96; auth, "Environmental Laboratory: Participation and Education in a Green Campus Renovation Renovation Project," Environmental Design Research Association Conference, May 97; auth, "Integrating the Undergraduate Experience: A Course on Environmental Dispute Resolution," Negotiation Journal, 14:4, October, 98, 367-377; auth, "Educating a Building: Green Renovation & the Liberal Arts," In preparation for Afield Orion; auth, "Generating Interest, Generating Power: Commercializing Photovoltaics in the Utility Sector," Energy Policy, 27:6, 99: 317-329; auth, "From Passive to Active about Scholar Electricity: Innovation Decision Process and Photovoltaic Interest Generation," Technovation, 19:8, 99: 467-481; auth, "Teaching Environmental Problem Solving: Perspective, Tools, and Action," In preparation for Environmental Practice; auth, "Building a Sense of Community: An Empirical Study of Neighborhood Interactions," In preparation for the Journal of Planning Education and Research, With G. Milliken, first author; auth, "Adaptive Farming Decisions: Lessons from the Amish," Presented at "The role of Culture in the Agriculture of the 21st Century" Conference, With S. Kishel, first author, in preparation for submission to Agriculture and Human Values. **CONTACT ADDRESS** Dept Geography & Geology, Denison Univ, Granville, OH 43023. **EMAIL** kaplan@denison.edu

KAPLAN, BENJAMIN J.

PERSONAL Born 01/31/1960 **DISCIPLINE** HISTORY **EDUCATION** Yale Univ, BA, 81; Harvard Univ, MA, 83, PhD, 89. **CAREER** Tutor, tchg fel, Harvard Univ, 84-86, 88; asst prof, Brandeis Univ, 89-96; from asst prof to assoc prof, 96-, Univ IA. **HONORS AND AWARDS** Harold K. Gross Prize, 90; Harold J. Grimm Prize, 95; Roland Bainton Prize, 96; Philip Schaff Prize, 97; Frederick Solmnsen Fel, 97, Univ WI; Fel, Woodrow Wilson International Center for Scholars, 99-00. **RESEARCH** Tolorance/interlorance in early modern Europe, the Dutch Golden Age. **SELECTED PUBLICATIONS** Auth, Dutch Particularism and the Calvinist Quest for "Holy Uniformity," 91; auth, "Hubert Duifhuis and the Nature of Dutch Libertinism," 92; auth, art, Remnants of the Papal Yoke: Apathy and Opposition in the Dutch Reformation, 94; auth, art, Confessionalism and Popular Piety in the Netherlands, 95; auth, Calvinists and Libertines: Confession and Community in Utrecht, 1578-1620, 95; auth, art, Possessed by the Devil? A Very Public Dispute in Utrecht, 96; auth, Confessionalism and Its Limits: Religion in Utrecht, 1600-1650, 97; auth, "A Clash of Values: The Survival of Utrecht's Confraternities After the Reformation and the Debate Over their Dissolution," 00. **CONTACT ADDRESS** Dept of History, Univ of Iowa, 280 Schaeffer Hall, Iowa City, IA 52242. **EMAIL** benjamin-kaplan@uiowa.edu

KAPLAN, DAVID H.

DISCIPLINE GEOGRAPHY **EDUCATION** Univ Wis Madison, PhD, 91. **CAREER** Asst Prof, Univ of St. Thomas, 92-95; Asst Prof to Assoc Prof, Kent State Univ, 95-. **RESEARCH** Nationalism, Ethic Segregation. **SELECTED PUBLICATIONS** Auth, "Two Nations in Search of a State: Canada's Ambivalent Spatial Identities," Annals of the Asn of Am Geogr 84-4 (Dec 94): 587-608; auth, "Differences in Migration Determinants for Linguistic Groups in Canada," The Prof Geogr 47-2 (May 95): 115-125; coauth, "Minneapolis/St. Paul in Global Economy," Urban Geog 17-1 (Jan 96): 44-59; auth, "What is Measured in Measuring the Mortgage Market," The Prof Geog 48-4 (Nov 96): 356-367; auth, "The Creation of an Ethnic Economy: Indochinese Business Expansion in Saint Paul," Econ Geog 73-2 (Apr 97): 214-233; auth, "The Spatial Structure of Urban Ethnic Economies," Urban Geog 1906 (Sept 98): 489-501; coauth, Segregation in Cities, Resource Publ in Geog Ser of the Asn of Am Geogr; in auth, "The Uneven Distribution of Employment Opportunities: Neighborhood and Race in Cleveland, Ohio, " J of Urban Affairs 21-2 (Summer 99): 189-212; auth, "Territorial Identities and Geographic Scale", in Nested Identities: Nationalism, Territory, and Scale, ed. G. Herb and D. Kaplan Lanham, MD: Rowman & Littlefield, 99), 31-49; auth, "Conflict and Compromise among Borderland Identities in Northern Italy, " Tijdschrift voor Economische en Sociale Geografie 91-1 (Winter 00): 44-60. **CONTACT ADDRESS** Dept Geog, Kent State Univ, PO Box 5190, Kent, OH 44242-0001.

KAPLAN, EDWARD HAROLD

PERSONAL Born 01/09/1936, New York, NY, m, 1957, 2 children **DISCIPLINE** CHINESE HISTORY & LANGUAGE **EDUCATION** Georgetown Univ, BS, 60; Univ Iowa, MA, 63, PhD, 70. **CAREER** Instr hist, Univ Del, 64-68; from lectr to asst prof, 68-74, assoc prof hist, Western Wash Univ 74-; Ed, Studies on East Asia, WWC CEAS, 94-. **MEMBERSHIPS** Asn Asian Studies; Am Orient Soc; AHA. **RESEARCH** Sung history; Chinese economic history. **SELECTED PUBLICATIONS** Transl & ed, Maxims for the Well Governed Household, Occasional Papers No 1, Prog EAsian Studies, 71 & An Economic History of China, by Chou Chin-sheng, Occasional Papers No 7, 74, Western Wash Univ; A Monetary History of China, East Asian Res Aids and Translations, no 5, Western Wash Univ Ctr East Asian Studies, 94; . **CONTACT ADDRESS** Dept of Hist, Western Washington Univ, M/S 9056, Bellingham, WA 98225-9056. **EMAIL** kaplan@cc.wwu.edu

KAPLAN, HERBERT HAROLD

PERSONAL Born 06/05/1932, New York, NY **DISCIPLINE** HISTORY **EDUCATION** Brooklyn Col, AB, 54; Columbia Univ, AM, cert prof E Cent Europe, 56, PhD(hist), 60. **CAREER** From instr to assoc prof, 60-70, Prof Hist, Ind Univ, Bloomington, 70-, Am Coun Learned Soc grant, 61; Inter-Univ Comt Travel Grants grant, Moscow State Univ, 64-66; Ger Acad Exchange Serv vis scholar fel, Ger, 68; Guggenheim Mem Found fel, 70-71; off Ind Univ rep, Anglo-Am Conf Historians, London, 72; Russ & E Europ Inst cross cult fel, Ind Univ, 73-74; consult, Slavic Rev, 74-; Pres Coun Int Prog grant, Ind Univ, 78. **MEMBERSHIPS** AHA; Am Asn Advan Slavic Studies; Am Soc Eighteenth Century Studies. **RESEARCH** Russian commerce with Great Britain during the second half of the 18th century; social and economic management of landed estates in 18th century Russia; history of the Polish-Lithuanian Commonwealth from 1569-1795. **SELECTED PUBLICATIONS** Auth, The First Partition of Poland, Columbia Univ, 62; Russia and the Outbreak of the Seven Years' War, Univ Calif, 68. **CONTACT ADDRESS** Dept of Hist, Indiana Univ, Bloomington, Bloomington, IN 47401.

KAPLAN, LAWRENCE SAMUEL
PERSONAL Born 10/28/1924, Cambridge, MA, m, 1948, 2 children **DISCIPLINE** HISTORY **EDUCATION** Colby Col, BA, 47; Yale Univ, MA, 48, PhD(hist), 51. **CAREER** Lectr hist, Univ Bridgeport, 50; historian, US Dept Defense, 51-54; from instr to prof, 54-77, Univ Prof Hist, Kent State Univ, 77-, Dir, Ctr NATO Studies, 79-, Fulbright lectr Am hist, Univ Bonn, 59-60 & Univ Louvain, 64-65; Am Philos Soc grant, 67 & 69 & vis res scholar US hist, Univ London, 69-70; fel, Woodrow Wilson Int Ctr Scholars, 74; consult, Historian Off, Off Secy Defense, 75-80; vis prof, Europ Univ Inst, Florence, Italy, 78; NATO res fel, 80-81. **MEMBERSHIPS** AHA; Orgn Am Historians; Soc Hist Am Foreign Rels (secy-treas, 74-79, pres, 81); Am Studies Asn; Soc Historians Early Am Repub. **RESEARCH** American diplomatic history; American politico-military history. **SELECTED PUBLICATIONS** Auth, Jefferson and France, Yale Univ, 67 & Greenwood, 80; ed, Recent American Foreign Policy, Dorsey, 68, rev ed, 72; auth, Colonies into Nation, Macmillan, 72; contribr, The Korean War and US foreign relations: The case of NATO, In: The Korean War: A 25-Year Perspective, Regents Press Kans, 77; ed, The American Revolution and A Candid World, Kent State Univ, 77; coauth, Culture and Diplomacy: The American Experience, Greenwood, 77; auth, A Community of Interests: NATO and the Military Assistance Program, 1948-1951, US Govt Printing Off, 80; co-ed, NATO after thirty years, Scholarly Resources, 81. **CONTACT ADDRESS** Dept of Hist, Kent State Univ, Kent, OH 44242.

KAPSCH, ROBERT J.
PERSONAL Born 07/25/1942, Elizabeth, NJ, s **DISCIPLINE** AMERICAN STUDIES, ENGINEERING & ARCHITECTURE **EDUCATION** Univ Md, PhD, 93; Cath Univ Amer, PhD, 83; George Washington Univ, MA, 78; MS, 74; Rutgers Univ, BS, 64. **CAREER** Special Asst to Dir, Ntl Park Service, 95-; Chief, Historic Amer Buildings Survey/Historic Amer Engineering Record, Ntl Park Service, 80-95; Program Manager, Dept Housing & Urban Develop, 78-80; Amer Polit Sci Assoc Congressional Fel, 77-78. **HONORS AND AWARDS** US Dept Interior Meritorious Service Medal, 93; Ntl Park Service First Vail Partnership Awd, 94; Amer Inst Architects Honorary Membership Awd, 94. **MEMBERSHIPS** Amer Soc Civil Engineers; Amer Inst Architects; Soc Industrial Archeol; Soc Archit Historians; Washington Historical Soc; US Capitol Historical Soc; Ntl Trust for Historical Preservation. **RESEARCH** Historic Architecture and Engineering of US **SELECTED PUBLICATIONS** Auth, Building the Infrastructure of the New Federal City, 1793-1800, Civil Engineering History, Engineers Make History, Proceedings of the First National Symposium on Civil Engineering History, 96; auth, Blacks and the Construction of the White House, 1793-1800, Amer Vision Mag, 95; auth, A Labor History of the Construction and Reconstruction of the White House, 1793-1817, Univ Maryland, 93, auth, Benjamin Wright and the Design and Construction of the Monocacy Aqueduct, Canal History and Technology Proceedings, 00; The Rehabilitation of the Monocacy Aqueduct of the Chesapeake and Ohio Canal National Park, Internaitonal Conference, Preservation of the Engineering Heritage-Gdansk Outlook 2000, 00; American Canals as a source of Revitalization: The Chesapeake and Ohio Canal as a case study, The Millennium Link Conference, Edinburgh, 00. **CONTACT ADDRESS** Dept of National Park Service, 15220 DuFief Dr, North Potomac, MD 20878. **EMAIL** bobhist@erols.com

KARAMANSKI, THEODORE J.
PERSONAL Born 08/01/1953, Chicago, IL **DISCIPLINE** HISTORY **EDUCATION** Loyola, PhD, 80. **CAREER** Act grad prog dir; pres, Nat Coun Publ Hist, 89-90. **HONORS AND AWARDS** Graduate Faculty Member of the Year, Loyola U. 94 **RESEARCH** 19th century Frontier history; midwest public history. **SELECTED PUBLICATIONS** Auth, Fur Trade and Exploration, Okla, 83; Rally Round the Flag: Chicago and the Civil War, Nelson Hall, 92; Deep Woods Frontier: a History of Logging in Northern Michigan, Wayne State Press, 89; ed, Ethics and Public History: An Anthology, Krieger, 90; auth, Schooner Passage: Sailing Ships and the Lake Michigan Frontier Detroit: Wayne State U Press, 00, Maritime Chicago, London: Arcadia Press, 00. **CONTACT ADDRESS** Fine Arts Dept, Loyola Univ, Chicago, 6525 N. Sheridan Rd., Chicago, IL 60626. **EMAIL** tkarama@wpo.it.luc.edu

KARAMUSTAFA, AHMET T.
PERSONAL Born 11/15/1956, Turkey, m, 1986, 3 children **DISCIPLINE** HISTORY; RELIGIOUS STUDIES **EDUCATION** Hamilton Col NYork, BA, 78; McGill Univ Can, MA, 81; PhD, 87. **CAREER** Asst prof, Wash Univ, 87-94; acting chair, Wash Univ, 94; dir, Center for the Study of Islamic Socs and civilizations, Wash Univ, 94-97; Assoc Prof, Wash Univ, 94-; dir, Relig Studies Program, 99-. **HONORS AND AWARDS** Phi Beta Kappa, 78; Grad magna cum laude, Hamilton Coll, 78; Dean's List, McGill Univ, 87. **MEMBERSHIPS** Am Acad of Rel; Am Res Inst in Turkey; Middle E Studies Asn; Soc for Iranian Studies; Turkish Studies Asn. **RESEARCH** Premodern Islamic intellectual traditions. **SELECTED PUBLICATIONS** Auth, God's Unruly Friends: Dervish Groups in the Islamic Later Middle Period, 1200-1550, 94; Vahidid's Menakib-I Hvoca-I Cihan ve Nefice-I can: critical Edition and Analysis, 93; asst ed, The History of Cartography, cartography in the Traditional Islamic and South Asian Societies, 92. **CONTACT ADDRESS** Dept of Hist, Washington Univ, CB 1062, One Brookings Dr, Saint Louis, MO 63130. **EMAIL** akaramus@artsci.wustl.edu

KARAVITES, PETER
PERSONAL Born 04/05/1932, Patras, Greece, m, 1966, 2 children **DISCIPLINE** HISTORY **EDUCATION** Univ of Chic, MA, 59; Loyola in Chic, PhD, 71. **CAREER** Teachers asst, Loyola Univ, 64-70; Appalachian State Univ, 71-77; prof, Bridgewater State Col, 78-99. **HONORS AND AWARDS** Schmidt Schol, 69-70; NEH Summer Schol; Inst for Adv Study, Princeton. **MEMBERSHIPS** AHH, AHEPA. **RESEARCH** Early Greek History, Hymnology, Book Reviews. **SELECTED PUBLICATIONS** Auth, Capitulation and Greek Interstate Relations; auth, Promise Giving and Treaty-Making; auth, Homer and the Near East; auth, Evil, Freedom, and the Road to Perfection in Clement of Alexandria. **CONTACT ADDRESS** Dept History, Bridgewater State Col, 131 Summer St, Bridgewater, MA 02325-0001. **EMAIL** pk470@gis.net

KARCHER, CAROLYN LURY
PERSONAL Born 02/25/1945, Washington, DC, m, 1965 **DISCIPLINE** AMERICAN LITERATURE & STUDIES **EDUCATION** Johns Hopkins Univ, MA, 67; Univ Md, PhD(Am studies), 80. **CAREER** Asst Prof English, Temple Univ, 1981-1988, assoc prof, 1988-1995, prof, 1995- **MEMBERSHIPS** MLA; Am Studies Asn; Melville Soc. **RESEARCH** Nineteenth and early 20th century American literature; women's studies; slavery. **SELECTED PUBLICATIONS** Auth, Shadow over the Promised Land: Slavery, Race, and Violence in Melville's America, 1980; The First Woman in the Republic: A Cultural Biography of Lydia Maria Child, 1994; Reconceiving 19th-Century American Literature--The Challenge of Women Writers, Amer Lit, Vol 0066, 1994; Margaret Fuller and Lydia Maria Child: Intersecting Careers, Reciprocal Influences, Essays on Margaret Fuller, ed. Fritz Fleischman, 2000; ed., HOBOMOK and Other Writings on Indians by Lydia Maria Child, 1986; An Appeal in Favor of that Class of Americans Called Indians by Lydia Maria Child, 1996; A Lydia Maria Child Reader, 1997; Hope Leslie by Catharine Maria Sedgwick, 1998. **CONTACT ADDRESS** Dept of English, Temple Univ, 1114 W Berks St, Philadelphia, PA 19122-6029.

KARDON, PETER F.
PERSONAL m, 1991 **DISCIPLINE** MEDIEVAL STUDIES **EDUCATION** Dartmouth Col, AB, 70; Univ Chi, MA, 75; PhD, 84. **CAREER** Acad aff assoc, dir, NYU, 84-88; dir, John Simon Guggenheim Found, 88-; adj prof, NYU, 86-. **HONORS AND AWARDS** Dartmouth James B. Reynolds Scholar, 70-71; Fulbright-Hays Fel, 73-74; Georges Lurcy Fel, 76-77; Whiting Fel, 78-79; Winner of Medieval Acad of Am Comp "Papers by Young Scholars," 77; NYU CAS, "Golden Dozen" Dis Teach Awd, 96. **MEMBERSHIPS** MLA; MAA; IAS. **RESEARCH** Old French literature (esp. Chretien de Troyes), Arthurian literature in Old French, Middle High German, Middle Welsh, and Middle English. **CONTACT ADDRESS** John Simon Guggenheim Mem Found, 90 Park Ave., New York, NY 10011. **EMAIL** pk@gf.org

KARETZKY, STEPHEN
PERSONAL Born 08/29/1946, Brooklyn, NY, m, 1985 **DISCIPLINE** HISTORY **EDUCATION** Queens Col, BA, 67; Columbia Univ, MA, 69, PhD, 78; Calif St Univ, MA, 91. **CAREER** Asst prof, 74-76, Buffalo, 77-78, Geneseo, SUNY; assoc prof, 78-81, Haifa Univ, Israel; ed, 81-82, Shapolsky, Staimatzky Pub NY; assoc prof, 82-85, Calif St Univ, San Jose; sr ed, 86-86, Shapolsky Pub, NY; lib dir & assoc prof, 86-, Felician Col, Lodi NJ. **HONORS AND AWARDS** Who's Who in Amer; Who's Who in the World; 2nd place, Book of the Year, Amer Soc Info Science, 83. **MEMBERSHIPS** Am Historical Asn, Organization of Am Historians; Am Soc for Info Science. **RESEARCH** U.S. History **SELECTED PUBLICATIONS** Auth, Reading Research and Librarianship: A History and Analysis, 82; auth, The Cannons of Journalism, 84; auth, The Media's Coverage of the Arab-Israeli Conflict, 89; auth, Not Seeing Red: American Librarianship and the Soviet Union 1917-1960, 98. **CONTACT ADDRESS** Felician Col, 262 S Main St, Lodi, NJ 07644.

KARGON, ROBERT
PERSONAL Born 10/18/1938, Brooklyn, NY, m, 1962, 2 children **DISCIPLINE** HISTORY OF SCIENCE **EDUCATION** Duke Univ, BS, 59; Yale Univ, MS, 60; Cornell Univ, PhD (hist), 64. **CAREER** Asst prof hist, Univ Ill, 64-65; from asst prof to assoc prof, 65-72, prof, 72-77, Willis K Shepard Prof Hist of Sci, Johns Hopkins Univ, 77-, Chmn Dept, 72-, Am Philos Soc grant, 71-72; Nat Endowment for Humanities grant, 72-73, fel, 76-77; Nat Sci Found grant, 75-79. **MEMBERSHIPS** Hist of Sci Soc. **RESEARCH** History of physics of the 17th and 19th centuries; social history of science; American science. **SELECTED PUBLICATIONS** Auth, Atomism in England: From Hariot to Newton, Clarendon, 66; Newton, Barrow and the Hypothetical Physics, Centaurus, 66; Model and analogy in Victorian science, J Hist of Ideas, 69; co-ed, Victorian Science, Doubleday, 70; auth, The testimony of nature, Albion, 71; Science in Victorian Manchester, Johns Hopkins Univ, 77; Temple to science: Cooperative research and the birth of Caltech, Hist Studies Phys Sci, No 8, 77; The Rise of Robert Millikan, Cornell Univ, 82. **CONTACT ADDRESS** Dept of Hist of Sci, Johns Hopkins Univ, Baltimore, 3400 N Charles St, Baltimore, MD 21218-2680. **EMAIL** kargon@jhu.edu

KARKHANIS, SHARAD
PERSONAL Born 03/08/1935, Khopoli, India **DISCIPLINE** POLITICAL SCIENCE, AMERICAN GOVERNMENT **EDUCATION** Bombaby Libr Asn, diploma, 56; Univ of Bombay, BA, 58; Rutgers State Univ, MLS, 62; Brooklyn Col, CUNY, MA, 67; NYork Univ, PhD, 78. **CAREER** Librn, U.S. Infor Service Libr, 55-58; librn trainee, Leyton Public Libr, 58-59; librn trainee, Montclair Public Libr, 59-60; librn, East Orange Pub Libr, 60-63; librn, Brooklyn Col Libr, 63-64; prof of Libr & Political Sci, Kingsborough Community Col, CUNY, 64-. **HONORS AND AWARDS** Distinguished Service Awd, Asian/Pacific Am Librn Asn, 89; Taraknath Das Awd, NY Univ Grad School, 77; Certificate of Appreciation by the Libr Asn of the City Univ of NY, 73. **MEMBERSHIPS** Am Libr Asn, 64-; Asian/Pacific Am Libr Asn, 80-. **RESEARCH** Press and politics of India; Judaism in America. **SELECTED PUBLICATIONS** Auth, Jewish Heritage in America: An Annotated Bibliography, Garland Pub, 88; Indian Politics and the Ride of the Press, Vikas Pub, 81. **CONTACT ADDRESS** Kingsborough Comm Col, CUNY, 2001 Oriental Blvd, Brooklyn, NY 11235. **EMAIL** skarkhanis@kbcc.cuny.edu

KARL, BARRY D.
PERSONAL Born 07/24/1927, Louisville, KY, m, 1957, 2 children **DISCIPLINE** UNITED STATES HISTORY **EDUCATION** Univ Louisville, BA, 49; Univ Chicago, MA, 51; Harvard Univ, PhD(Am civilization), 60. **CAREER** Head tutor hist & lit, Harvard Univ, 60-62; asst prof, 62-63, prof hist, Wash Univ, 63-68; prof hist, Brown Univ, 68-71; Prof Am Hist, Univ Chicago, 71-, Mem, Joint Comt Res Philanthropy, 75-; chmn dept hist, Univ Chicago, 76-; Norman & Edna Freehling Prof Social Sci & Am Hist, 77-; Bloomberg prof of Philanthropy at Harvard Univ, 96-98. **HONORS AND AWARDS** Bloomberg Prof of Philanthropy, Harvard Univ, 96-98. **MEMBERSHIPS** The Organization of American Historians **RESEARCH** Social science and public policy in the twentieth century; public administration; philanthrony. **SELECTED PUBLICATIONS** Auth, Executive Reorganization and Reform in the New Deal, 63; auth, Charles E. Merriam and the Study of Politics, 73; auth, Public Administration and America History: a Century of Professionalism, 76; auth, The Uneasy State, 83; auth, Foundations and Universities in Historical Perspective, 91; auth, Struggles for Justice--Social-Responsibility and the Liberal State, J Southern Hist, Vol 0059, 93; Science Policy and Politics, Rev(s) in Amer Hist, Vol 0023, 95; The Rich Man and the Kingdom--Rockefeller, John, D., Jr, and the Protestant Establishment, J Rel, Vol 0077, 97; auth, Foundations and the Future of Philanthropy, 98. **CONTACT ADDRESS** Dept of Hist, Univ of Chicago, Chicago, IL 60637. **EMAIL** bdkx@wchicago.edu

KARLSEN, CAROL F.
DISCIPLINE HISTORY **EDUCATION** Univ of Maryland, BA, 70; NYork Univ, MA, 72; Yale Univ, PhD, 80. **CAREER** Assoc Prof, Hist, Univ Mich. **MEMBERSHIPS** Am Antiquarian Soc **RESEARCH** American women, early American social and cultural history. **SELECTED PUBLICATIONS** Co-ed, The Journal of Esther Edwards Burr, 1754-1757, Yale Univ Press, 84; auth, The Devil in the Shape of a Woman: Witchcraft in Colonial New England, Norton, 87, Vintage, 89; auth, The Salem Witchcraft Outbreak of 1692, Oxford Univ Press, 98. **CONTACT ADDRESS** Dept of Hist, Univ of Michigan, Ann Arbor, 1029 Tisch Hall, 555 S State St, Ann Arbor, MI 48109-1003. **EMAIL** ckarlsen@umich.edu

KARMAN, JAMES
PERSONAL Born 08/12/1947, Moline, IL, m, 1968 **DISCIPLINE** ENGLISH, LITERATURE, ART, RELIGION **EDUCATION** Augustana Col, BA, 69; Univ Iowa, MA, 71; Syracuse Univ, PhD, 76. **CAREER** Postdoctoral fel, Syracuse Univ, 76-77; ast prof, 77-84, asoc prof, 84-87, prof coord, 87-, Calif St Univ, Chico. **HONORS AND AWARDS** Res fel, Nat Endowment Hum, 98-99; Book Club of California grnt, 99. **MEMBERSHIPS** Robinson Jeffers Tor House Found; Robinson Jeffers Asn; MLA; Col Art Asn; Am Acad Relig; Asn for Documentary Editing; Soc for Textua Scholar. **RESEARCH** Art; religion; literature; twentieth century history and culture; life and work of Robinson Jeffers. **SELECTED PUBLICATIONS** Ed, Critical Essays on Robinson Jeffers, GK Hall, 90; auth, Robinson Jeffers: Poet of California, rev., Story Line, 95; ed, Of Una Jeffers, Story Line, 98. **CONTACT ADDRESS** Dept of English, California State Univ, Chico, Chico, CA 95929-0830. **EMAIL** Jkarman@csuchico.edu

KARS, MARJOLEINE
DISCIPLINE HISTORY **EDUCATION** Duke Univ, PhD. **CAREER** Asst prof, Univ MD Baltimore County. **RESEARCH** Am women's hist; popular cult and relig in the eighteenth century. **SELECTED PUBLICATIONS** Auth, publ(s) on tchg. **CONTACT ADDRESS** Dept of Hist, Univ of Maryland, Baltimore, Hilltop Circle, PO Box 1000, Baltimore, MD 21250. **EMAIL** kars@umbc7.umbc.edu

KARSTEN, PETER
DISCIPLINE HISTORY **EDUCATION** Yale Univ, BA, 60; Univ Wis, PhD, 68. **CAREER** Asst to assoc prof, Univ Pittsburgh, 67-77, prof, Dept Hist, Joint Appt, Dept Sociol, 77-; consult, Hudson Inst, 73-80; Co-Dir (with Peter Stearns of CMU), Pittsburgh Center for Soc Hist, 85-98. **HONORS AND AWARDS** Am Philos Soc grants, 68, 70; Am Coun of Learned Socs Fel, 72-73; Phi Alpha Theta Best Book Awd, 73; Mary Ball Washington Prof of Am Hist, Univ Col, Dublin, 79-80; Guest prof, Augsburg Univ, 88; Co-Dir (with Peter Stearns of CMU), NEH Summer Inst on Recent Cultural Hist for High School Teachers, 90; Fulbright Res Fel, Alexander Turnbull Library, Wellington, New Zealand, 92; Surrency (Best Article) Prize of the Am Soc for Legal Hist, 92; Fel, Centre for Interdisciplinary Studies of Property Rights, Sch of Law, Univ of Newcastle, NSW, Australia, 99-. **RESEARCH** Legal history; law and society; military and society. **SELECTED PUBLICATIONS** Co-ed with John Modell, Theory, Method & Practice in Social and Cultural History, NYU (92); auth, "Heart" versus "Head": Judge-made Law in Nineteenth Century America, Univ of NC Press (97); auth, "The Coup d'Etat and Civilian Control of the Military in Competitive Democracies," in To Sheathe the Sword, ed John Lovell, Greenwood Press (97); auth, "Supervising the 'Spoiled Children of Legislation': Judicial Judgements of Quasi-Public Corporations in the Nineteenth Century," 41 Am J of Legal Hist (97); auth, "Cows in the Corn, Pigs in the Garden, and 'The Problem of Social. Costs': 'High' and 'Low' Legal Cultures and Resolution of Animal Trespass Disputes in the British Diaspora Lands of the 17th, 18th and 19th Centuries," 32 Law & Soc Rev (98): 63-92; ed, The Military and Society, a five volume set of essays, Vol 1: Raising Military Forces: Recruitment, Enlistment, Conscription, Vol 2: Training and Socialization, Vol 3: Motivation, Morale, Mutiny, Vol 4: Civil-Military Relations and Coups, Vol 5: The State-Society-Military Symbiosis, Garland Press (98). **CONTACT ADDRESS** Dept Hist, Univ of Pittsburgh, Pittsburgh, PA 15260. **EMAIL** pjk2@pitt.edu

KASSAM, ZAYN
DISCIPLINE HISTORY OF RELIGIONS **EDUCATION** McGill Univ, PhD, 95. **CAREER** Assoc prof, Pomona Col, 95-. **HONORS AND AWARDS** Wig Awd for Distinguished Teaching, 98. **MEMBERSHIPS** Am Acad of Rel; Middle East Studies Asn; Soc for Iranian Studies; North Am Asn for the Study of Rel; Asian Studies Asn. **RESEARCH** Islamic Philosophy, Comparative Studies in Philosophy, Mysticism, Gender in the Islamic World. **CONTACT ADDRESS** Religious Studies, Pomona Col, 551 N College Ave, Claremont, CA 91711. **EMAIL** zkassam@pomona.edu

KASSON, JOHN FRANKLIN
PERSONAL Born 10/20/1944, Muncie, IN, m, 1968, 2 children **DISCIPLINE** AMERICAN HISTORY **EDUCATION** Harvard Univ, BA, 66; Yale Univ, PhD, 71. **CAREER** Asst prof, 71-76, assoc prof, 76-81, prof hist, 81-, Univ NC, Chapel Hill; NEH fel, 74; Rockefeller Humanities fel, 80-81; Nat Humanities Ctr fel, 80-81; Humanities Inst Fel, Univ Calif, Davis, 87-88; Guggenheim fel, 99. **HONORS AND AWARDS** Soc of Am Historians, 91; Bowman & Gordon Gray Professorship for inspirational tchng, 93-96; Bank of Am Honors Prof, 01-04. **MEMBERSHIPS** Am Studies Assn; AHA; OAH. **RESEARCH** Modes of American cultural expression; technology and American culture; the popular arts. **SELECTED PUBLICATIONS** Auth, Civilizing the Machine: Technology and Republican Values in America, 1776-1900, Grossman/ Viking, 76 & Penguin, 77; auth, Amusing the Million: Coney Island at the Turn of the Century, Hill & Wang, 78; auth, Rudeness and Civility: Manners in Nineteenth-Century Urban America, Hill & Wang, 90; auth, Houdini, Tarzan, and the Perfect Man: The White Male Body and the Challenge of Modernity in America, New York: Hill and Wang, 01. **CONTACT ADDRESS** Dept of Hist, Univ of No Carolina, Chapel Hill, Chapel Hill, NC 27599. **EMAIL** jfkasson@email.unc.edu

KASSOW, SAMUEL D.
PERSONAL Born 10/03/1946, Stuttgart, Germany **DISCIPLINE** RUSSIAN HISTORY **EDUCATION** Trinity Col, BA, 66; London Sch Econ, MsC, 68; Princeton Univ, PhD(hist), 76. **CAREER** Asst prof, 76-78, Assoc Prof Hist, Trinity Col, 78-. **MEMBERSHIPS** Am Asn Advan Slavic Studies; Asn Jewish Studies. **RESEARCH** Modern Russian history; modern European history; East European Jewish history. **SELECTED PUBLICATIONS CONTACT ADDRESS** Dept of Hist, Trinity Col, Connecticut, 300 Summit St, Hartford, CT 06106-3186.

KATER, MICHAEL H.
PERSONAL Born 07/04/1937, Zittau, Germany **DISCIPLINE** HISTORY **EDUCATION** Univ Toronto, BA, 59, MA, 61; Univ Heidelberg, PhD, 66. **CAREER** Lectr, Univ Maryland, 65-66; asst prof to prof, 67-91, Distinguished Res Prof Hist, Atkinson Col, York Univ, 91-; Jason A. Hannah vis prof hist med, McMaster Univ, 85-86; Jason A. Hannah vis prof hist med, Univ Toronto, 97-98. **HONORS AND AWARDS** Can Coun leave fel, 73-74; Guggenheim fel, 76-77; Killam sr fel, 78-79, 79-80, 93-94, 94-95; SSHRCC leave fel, 82-83; Atkinson res fel, 84-85; York Walter L. Gordon fel, 90-91; Am Hist Asn First Prize, central Europ hist, 72; Konrad Adenauer res award, 90-91; Jason A. Hannah Medal, 91. **SELECTED PUBLICATIONS** Auth, Das 'Ahnenerbe' der SS 1935-1945, 74; auth, Studentenschaft und Rechtsradikalismus in Deutschland 1918-1933, 75; auth, The Nazi Party: A Social Profile of Members and Leaders 1919-1945, 83; auth, Doctors Under Hitler, 89; auth, Different Drummers: Jazz in the Culture of Nazi Germany, 92; auth, The Twisted Muse: Musicians and Their Music in the Third Reich, 3rd ed, 97; auth, Composers of the Nazi Era: Eight Portraits, New York/Oxford: Oxford UP, 99. **CONTACT ADDRESS** Dept of History, York Univ, 4700 Keele St, North York, ON, Canada M3J 1P3. **EMAIL** mkater@yorku.ca

KATES, GARY R.
PERSONAL Born 11/09/1952, Los Angeles, CA, m, 1978, 2 children **DISCIPLINE** HISTORY **EDUCATION** Pitzer Col, BA, 74; Univ Chicago, MA, 75; PhD, 78. **CAREER** Vis Asst prof, Pitzer Col, 78-79; Asst prof to Full Prof and Interim Dean, Trinity Univ, 80-. **HONORS AND AWARDS** Nancy Lyman Roelker Mentor Awd, 00. **MEMBERSHIPS** Am Hist Asn, soc for French Hist Studies, Western soc for French Hist, Am Soc for eighteenth Century Studies. **RESEARCH** 18th Century France. **SELECTED PUBLICATIONS** Auth, Monsieur d'Eon is a Woman: A Tale of Political Intrigue and sexual masquerade, Basic Books, 95; auth, The Cercle Social, the Girondins, ad the French Revolution, Princeton Univ Press, 85; ed, The French Revolution: Recent Debates and New Controversies, Routledge press, 98. **CONTACT ADDRESS** Dept Hist, Trinity Univ, 715 Stadium Dr, San Antonio, TX 78212-3104. **EMAIL** gkates@trinity.edu

KATSAROS, THOMAS
PERSONAL Born 02/21/1926, New York, NY, m, 1971 **DISCIPLINE** HISTORY, AREA STUDIES **EDUCATION** NYork Univ, BA, 53, MA, 56, MBA, 58, PhD(area studies), 63; Int Bus, 75. **CAREER** Asst prof soc studies, State Univ NY, 63-65; from asst prof to assoc prof hist, Univ New Haven, 65-70, prof & chmn dept, 70-80, assoc Dean, Business School, Univ New Haven, 84-95, PROF AND CHAIR, HISTORY DEPT, 96-, DIR OF UNIV NEW HAVEN PRESS AND DIR OF BUSINESS RESEARCH, 96-. **MEMBERSHIPS** AHA **RESEARCH** Anglo-Soviet relations during World War II; the welfare state. **SELECTED PUBLICATIONS** Coauth, The Western Mystical Tradition, Col & Univ Press, 69; auth, Early Modern Science and Mysticism, Essays in Arts & Sciences, spring 72; coauth, American Transcendentalism: Its Mystical and Philosophical Origins, Col & Univ Press, 75; A Brief History of the Western World, 78 & Capitalism: A Cooperative Venture, 81, Univ Press Am; auth, The Development of the Welfare State in the Western World, Univ Press Am, 95. **CONTACT ADDRESS** 11 Carriage Dr, North Haven, CT 06574. **EMAIL** mharvey@chargernewhaven.edu

KATZ, ESTHER
PERSONAL Born 08/14/1945, Belgium **DISCIPLINE** HISTORY **EDUCATION** Hunter Col, BA, 69; NY Univ, MA, 73; NY Univ, PhD, 80. **CAREER** Ed and Dir, Margaret Sanger Papers Proj, 85-; Adj Assoc Prof, NYork Univ, 93-. **HONORS AND AWARDS** Fel, NHPRC, 86; Grant-in-Aid, ACLS, 89; grant, Jacob and Bessye Blaufarb Libr Am Labor Movement, 90-91; Grant, Independent Television Serv, 91-92. **MEMBERSHIPS** AHA, OAH, BCWH, CCWHP, ADE, ACLS. **RESEARCH** United States women's history, history of sexuality, history of the birth control movement. **SELECTED PUBLICATIONS** Auth, The Margaret Sanger Papers: The Smith College Collections Series with printed reel guide, Univ Publ of Am, 95; auth, The Margaret Sanger Papers: The Smith College Collections Series with printed reel guide, UP of Am, 97; auth, "Margaret Sanger," for Am Nat Biog, Oxford UP (99); auth, Margaret Sanger and 'The woman Rebel'," Electronic ed, Model Editions Partnership (99); coauth, "Editing in the New Millennium: Review of Mary-Jo Kline, A Guide to Documentary Editing, 2nd ed," Documentary Editing, vol 21, no 2 (99): 29-32; auth, "Reel Guide and Index to the Complete Margaret Sanger Papers Microfilm, Integrated Three-Series Edition," Univ Publ of Am (forthcoming); auth, The Selected Letters and Writings of Margaret Sanger (4 vol book ed), Ind Univ Pr, forthcoming. **CONTACT ADDRESS** Dept Hist, New York Univ, 53 Washington Sq S, New York, NY 10012. **EMAIL** esther.katz@nyu.edu

KATZ, IRVING
PERSONAL Born 09/24/1932, New York, NY, 2 children **DISCIPLINE** AMERICAN POLITICAL & JEWISH HISTORY **EDUCATION** City Col NYork, BA, 54; NYork Univ, MA, 59, PhD(hist), 64. **CAREER** Res assoc bus hist, Harvard Univ, 61-64; asst prof, 64-68, assoc prof, 68-81, Prof Hist, Ind Univ, Bloomington, 81-. **HONORS AND AWARDS** Am Philos Soc res grant, 68. **MEMBERSHIPS** AHA; Orgn Am Historians; Am Jewish Hist Soc. **RESEARCH** American political history; immigration and labor history; investment banking. **SELECTED PUBLICATIONS** Auth, August Belmont: A Political Biography, Columbia Univ Press, 68; auth, "August Belmont's Cuban Acquistion Scheme," Mid-Am, 68; auth, "Henry Lee Higginson vs Louis Dembitz Brandeis," New England Quart, 68; contrib, Investment Banking in America: A History, Harvard Univ Press, 70. **CONTACT ADDRESS** Dept of Hist, Indiana Univ, Bloomington, Ballantine Rm 742, Bloomington, IN 47405. **EMAIL** ikatz@indiana.edu

KATZ, MICHAEL B.
PERSONAL Born 04/13/1939, Wilmington, DE **DISCIPLINE** AMERICAN SOCIAL HISTORY **EDUCATION** Harvard Univ, BA, 61, MAT, 62, EdD, 66. **CAREER** Res asst hist educ, Harvard Univ Grad Sch Educ, 64-65, instr & res assoc, 65-66; from asst prof to prof hist educ, Univ Toronto & Ont Inst Studies in Educ, 66-74; prof hist & educ, York Univ, 74-78; Prof Educ & Hist, Univ PA, 78-, Vis mem, Inst Advan Studies, 73-74; Guggenheim fel, 77-78. **HONORS AND AWARDS** Albert C Corey Awd, Am & Canadian Hist Asns, 78. **MEMBERSHIPS** Orgn Am Historians; Hist Educ Soc (pres, 75-76); Can Hist Asn; Am Hist Soc; Soc Sci Hist Asn. **RESEARCH** Nineteenth century social history; history of social structure; history of the family. **SELECTED PUBLICATIONS CONTACT ADDRESS** Dept of History, Univ of Pennsylvania, 3401 Walnut St 352B, Philadelphia, PA 19104. **EMAIL** mkatz@sas

KATZ, STANLEY NIDER
PERSONAL Born 04/23/1934, Chicago, IL, m, 1960, 2 children **DISCIPLINE** AMERICAN LEGAL AND CONSTITUTIONAL HISTORY, HISTORY OF PHILANTHROPY **EDUCATION** Harvard Univ, AB, 55, MA, 59, PhD(Am colonial hist), 61. **CAREER** From instr to asst prof hist, Harvard Univ, 61-65, Allston Burr sr tutor, Leverett House, 63-65; from asst prof to assoc prof hist, Univ Wis-Madison, 65-70; prof legal hist, Law Sch, Univ Chicago, 70-78; prof, Princeton Univ, 78-86; President, Am Council of Learned Societies, 86-97; Prof Public adnd International Affairs, 97-, Woodrow Wilson School, 82-, Res fel, Charles Warren Ctr, Harvard Univ, 66-67, fel law and hist, Law Sch, 69-70; Am Bar Asn fel legal hist, 66-67; Am Coun Learned Soc fel, 69-70; Editing on Oliver Wendell Holmes, History of the U.S. Supreme Court, 77-, 77-; Vis Meme, Inst Advan Study, 81-82. **HONORS AND AWARDS** LLD, Stockton State Col, 81, DHL, Univ of Pugit Sound, 94; C.W. Post, LIU, 97, Sacred Heart Univ, 97, Ohio State Univ, 98. **MEMBERSHIPS** VP res, 97-00, AHA Orgn Am Historians; Am Soc Legal Hist (pres, 78-80); Am Studies Asn; Selden Soc. **RESEARCH** Anglo-Am legal and constitutional, history of philanthropy. **SELECTED PUBLICATIONS** Auth, "Influences on Public Policies in the United States," in W. McNeil Lowry, ed., The Arts and Public Policy, Prentice-Hall (84): 23-37; auth, "The Strange Birth and Unlikely History of Constitutional Equality," The Journal of American History, vol 75, no. 3 (88): 747-762; ed, Constitutionalism and Democracy: Transitions in the Contemporary World, Oxford Univ Press, New York, 93; auth, Constitutionalism in East Central Europe: Some Negative Lessons from the American Experience, German Historical Institute, Annual Lecture Series no. 7, Washington, DC, 94; auth, "Do Disciplines Matter? History and the Social Sciences," Social Science Quarterly, vol 76, no. 4 (95): 863-877; auth, "Restructuring for the Twenty-First Century," in Nicholas H. Farnham and Adam Yarmolinsky, eds, Rethinking Liberal Education, Oxford Univ Press, New York (96): 77-90; coauth, with Warren F. Ilchman and Edward L. Queen, II, eds, Philanthropy in the World's Traditions, Indiana Univ Press, 98; auth, Can Liberal Education Cope?, The Journal of Graduate Liberal Studies, vol 4 no 1 fall (98): 1-10. **CONTACT ADDRESS** Woodrow Wilson School, Princeton Univ, Robertson Hall 428, Princeton, NJ 08544. **EMAIL** snkatz@princeton.edu

KATZMAN, DAVID MANNERS
PERSONAL Born 10/25/1941, New York, NY, m, 1965, 2 children **DISCIPLINE** AMERICAN STUDIES, ETHNIC STUDIES, AMERICAN HISTORY **EDUCATION** Queens Col, NYork, BA, 63; Univ Mich, Ann Arbor, PhD (hist), 69. **CAREER** Prof, 78-90, Prof and Chair Am Studies, Univ Kans, 90-, assoc dean, col lib arts & scis & dir honors prog, 80-87, Ford Found fel, 75-76; vis prof mod hist, Univ Col Dublin, Ireland, 76-77; assoc ed, Am Studies, 77-; Guggenheim fel, 79-80, vis prof eco hist, Univ Birmingham, Eng, 84-85, Ed Bd, Regents Press of Kansas, 83-86; dir, NEH Sumer Seminars for Col Teachers, 90, 92, 94, 96; dir and commissioner, Nat Commission on Social Stud, 88-92; elected member, Professional Comm., AHA, 88-91; contributing ed, Perspectives (AHA), 89-92, 95-97; vis prof Am Stud, Univ Tokushima, Japan, 94, vis prof hist & Am Studies, Hong Kong Univ, 95, NEH fel, 94-95; ed, Am Stud, 98-. **HONORS AND AWARDS** Certificate of Commendation, Am Asn State & Local Hist, 74; Philip Taft Labor History Prize, 79; Byron Caldwell Smith Award, Humanistic Scholarship, 80. **MEMBERSHIPS** AHA; Orgn Am Historians; Am Jewish Hist Soc; Immigrant Hist Soc; Am Studies Asn. **RESEARCH** Race and Ethnicity; African Am culture. **SELECTED PUBLICATIONS** Auth, Ann Arbor: Depression City, Mich Hist, 12/66; Black Slavery in Michigan, Midcontinent Am Studies J, fall 70; contribr, Perspectives in Geography II: Geography of the Ghetto, Northern Ill Univ, 72; auth, Before the Ghetto: Black Detroit in the Nineteenth Century, Univ Ill,

73; coauth, Three Generations in 20th Century America, Dorsey, 77, rev ed, 82; auth, Seven Days a Week: Women and Domestic in Industrializing America, Oxford Univ, 78 & Univ Ill, 81; coauth, A People & A Nation, Houghton Mifflin, 82, 86, 90, 94, 98; co-ed, Plain Folk: The Life Stories of Undistinguished Americans, Univ Ill, 82; co-ed, Technical Knowledge in American Culture, Univ Ala, 96; contr, La storia americana e le scienze sociali, Inst della Enciclopedia Italiana, 96; auth, A People & Nation, 01. **CONTACT ADDRESS** Dept of Hist, Univ of Kansas, Lawrence, Lawrence, KS 66045-0001. **EMAIL** dkatzman@ku.edu

KATZNELSON, IRA
DISCIPLINE UNITED STATES HISTORY **EDUCATION** Columbia Univ, BA, 66; Cambridge Univ, PhD, 69. **CAREER** Ruggles prof. **RESEARCH** Comparative politics; political theory. **SELECTED PUBLICATIONS** Auth, Black Men, White Cities, 73; City Trenches: Urban Politics and the Patterning of Class in the United States, 81; Liberalism's Crooked Circle: Letters to Adam Michnik, 96; co-auth, Schooling for All, 85; co-ed, Working Class Formation: Nineteenth-century Patterns in Western Europe and the United States, 88; Paths of Emancipation, 95. **CONTACT ADDRESS** Dept of History, Columbia Col, New York, 2960 Broadway, New York, NY 10027-6902.

KAUFFMAN, GEORGE B.
PERSONAL Born 09/04/1930, Philadelphia, PA, m, 1969, 2 children **DISCIPLINE** HISTORY OF SCIENCE **EDUCATION** Univ Pa, BA, 51; Univ Fla, PhD(chem), 56. **CAREER** Instr, Univ Tex, 55-56; asst prof, 56-61, assoc prof, 61-66, Prof Chem, Calif State Univ, Fresno, 66-, Res mem, Oak Ridge Nat Lab, 55; res chemist, Humble Oil and Refining Co, 56 and Gen Elec Co, 57 and 59; Exec comt, Am Chem Soc, 70-73, guest lectr, Coop Lect Tours, 71; Guggenheim fel, 72; Contrib Ed, J Col Sci Teaching, 73-& Hexagon, 80-; ed, Hist Chem Series, Am Chem Soc, 75-81; vis scholar, Univ Calif, Berkeley, 76 and 77 and Univ Puget Sound, 78; consult, Educ Testing Serv and Am Col Testing Prog; contrib scholar, Isis Critical Bibliog Hist Sci. **HONORS AND AWARDS** Outstanding Prof, Calif State Univ and Col Syst, 73; Col Chem Teacher Awd, Mfg Chemists Asn, 76; Lev Aleksandrovich Chugaev Mem Dipl and Bronze Medal, Acad Sci USSR, 76; Dexter Awd, Am Chem Soc, 78. **MEMBERSHIPS** AAAS; Am Chem Soc; Hist Sci Soc; Soc Hist Alchemy and Chem; Strindberg Soc. **RESEARCH** Hist of chemistry; translation of chemical classics; biographies of famous chemists. **SELECTED PUBLICATIONS** Auth, The Central Science: Essays on the Uses of Chemistry, 84; auth, Frederick Soddy (1877-1956): Early Pioneer in Radiochemistry, 86; auth, Aleksandr Porfirevich Borodin: A Chemist's Biography, 88; auth, Coordination Chemistry: A Century of Progress, 94; auth, Classics in Coordination Chemistry, 95; auth, Metal and Nonmetal Biguanide Complexes, 99. **CONTACT ADDRESS** 1609 E Quincy Ave, Fresno, CA 93720-2309.

KAUFMAN, BURTON I.
PERSONAL Born 11/26/1940, Boston, MA, m, 1966 **DISCIPLINE** AMERICAN HISTORY **EDUCATION** Brandeis Univ, BA, 62; Rice Univ, MA, 64; PhD(hist), 66. **CAREER** From asst prof Am hist to assoc prof hist, La State Univ, New Orleans, 66-73; assoc prof, 73-77, Prof Hist, Kans State Univ, 77- **MEMBERSHIPS** Orgn Am Historians; Newcomen Soc; Soc Hist Am Foreign Rel. **RESEARCH** Am foreign policy. **SELECTED PUBLICATIONS** Report Of The Working Group On Conflicts-Of-Interest, Fordham Law Rev, Vol 64, 96. **CONTACT ADDRESS** Virginia Polytech Inst and State Univ, 100 Virginia Tech, Blacksburg, VA 24061-0002.

KAUFMAN, MARTIN
PERSONAL Born 12/06/1940, Boston, MA, m, 1968, 3 children **DISCIPLINE** HISTORY OF MEDICINE, AMERICAN HISTORY **EDUCATION** Boston Univ, AB, 62; Univ Pittsburgh, MA, 63; Tulane Univ, PhD(hist), 69. **CAREER** Instr hist, Worcester State Col, 68-69; from asst prof to assoc prof, 69-76, Prpf Hist, Westfield State Col, 76- . **HONORS AND AWARDS** Ed dir, Hist J Mass, 72-; dir, Inst Mass Studies, 80-98. **MEMBERSHIPS** Am Asn Hist Med; Orgn Am Historians. **RESEARCH** History of American medical education; unorthodox practitioners; women and minorities in medicine. **SELECTED PUBLICATIONS** Auth, The American Antivaccinationists and Their Arguments, Bull Hist Med, 67; Homepathy in America, Johns Hopkins Univ, 71; coauth, Body-Snatching in the Midwest, Mich Hist, 71; co-ed, The Ethnic Contribution to the American Revolution, Westfield Bicentennial Comt, 76; auth, American Medical Education, The Formative Years, Greenwood, 76; The Admission of Women to Nineteenth Century American Medical Societies, Bull Hist Med, 76; The University of Vermont College of Medicine, Univ Vt, 79. **CONTACT ADDRESS** Dept of History, Westfield State Col, 577 Western Ave, Westfield, MA 01085-2501.

KAUFMAN, SUZANNE
PERSONAL Born 09/22/1965, New York, NY, s **DISCIPLINE** MODERN EUROPEAN HISTORY **EDUCATION** Wesleyan Univ, BA, 87; Rutgers Univ, MA, 92, PhD, 96. **CAREER** Vis Asst Prof, Miami Univ, 96-97; Asst Prof, Ga State Univ, 97-98; Asst Prof Hist, Loyola Univ - Chicago, 98-. **HONORS AND AWARDS** Chateaubriand Dissertation Res Fel, 92-93; NEH Dissertation Grant, 94-95. **MEMBERSHIPS** Am Acad Relig; Am Hist Asn; Soc Fr Hist Studies. **RESEARCH** Modern European social and cultural history; modern France; history of religion & popular culture; history of women & gender. **SELECTED PUBLICATIONS** Auth, Influence of Christianity on women in France, The Feminist Companion to French Literature, Greenwood Press, 99. **CONTACT ADDRESS** History Dept, Loyola Univ, Chicago, 6525 N Sheridan Rd., Chicago, IL 60640. **EMAIL** SKaufma@luc.edu

KAUFMANN, FRANK
PERSONAL Born 12/23/1952, New York, NY, m, 1982, 3 children **DISCIPLINE** CHURCH HISTORY **EDUCATION** Vanderbuilt Univ, PhD 85. **CAREER** adj prof, Pace Univ; adj prof, Univ Theol Sem; founder, dir, The Common-Good Project. **HONORS AND AWARDS** Vanderbilt Univ Schshp; F U Berlin Schshp; Sr Res Fel, Center for Ethics, Relig, and International Relations. **MEMBERSHIPS** AAr **RESEARCH** Religion and society; New religions; Inter religious dialogue. **SELECTED PUBLICATIONS** Auth, Religion and Peace in the Middle East, New Era Books (NYork), 87; auth, The Foundations of Modern Church History, Lang Publ (NYork), 89; ed, Dialogue and Alliance, Quart J; ed, Newsletter of the Interreligious Federation for World Peace, quart; sr ed consul, Today's World, monthly; ed, Christianity in the Americas, Paragon Publ (NYork), 98; auth, ed, Religion and the Future of South African Societies. **CONTACT ADDRESS** Inter Religious Federation, Pace Univ, New York, 4 West 43rd St, New York, NY 10036. **EMAIL** fortl@pipeline.com

KAUFMANN, THOMAS DACOSTA
PERSONAL Born 05/07/1948, New York, NY, m, 1999, 1 child **DISCIPLINE** ART HISTORY **EDUCATION** Harvard Univ, PhD, 77. **CAREER** Asst to full prof, Princeton Univ, 77-. **HONORS AND AWARDS** Guggenheim, Fel; Getty, Fel. **MEMBERSHIPS** Col Art Asn, Polish Acad of Sci, Royal Flemish Acad, Deutscher Kunsthistoriker Verband, Renaissance Soc of Am. **RESEARCH** Art of central Europe; Latin America; Historiography; Art & science; Geography of art. **SELECTED PUBLICATIONS** Auth, Cloister, Court, and City. The Art and Culture of Central Europe, 1450-1800, London, Univ Chicago Press, 95; auth, Empire of Curiosity, Tokyo, Kousakusha, 95; auth, The Mastery of Nature, Aspects of Art, Science and Humanism in the Renaissance, Princeton Univ Press, 93; article, Archduke Albrecht as an Austrian Habsburg and Prince of the Empire, Albrecht and Isabella, Brussels, Sept, 98; rev, Dazwischen. Kulturwissenschaft auf Warburgs Spuren (Saecula Spiritalia 29), Winckelmann and the Notion of Aesthetic Education, The Absolute Artist; The Historiography of a Concept, Past Looking. Historical Imagination and the Rhetoric of the Image, Art Bull, lxxx.no 3, 581-85, Sept, 98; article, Planeten im kaiserlichen Universum. Prag und die kunst an den deutschen Furstenhofen zur Zeit Rudolfs II, Hofkunst der Spatrenaissance. Braunschweig - Wolfenbuttel und das kaiserliche, Prag um 1600, Braunschweig, 9-19, 98; article, The Adoration of the Shepherds, Master Paintings, London-NY, Colnaghi, no 7, 98; article, Lessons of History, The New York Times, A18, 4 May, 98; article, Gothico More Nondum Visa: The Modern Gothic Architecture of Jan Blazej Santini Aichl, Artes atque humaniora. Studia Stanislao Mossakowski sexagenario dicata, Warsaw, 317-331, 98; article, Caprices of Art and Nature: Arcimboldo and the Monstrous, Kunstform Capricccio. Von der Groteske zur Spieltheorie der Moderne, Verlag der Buchhandlung Walther Konig, 33-51, 97; article, Kunst und Alchemie, Moritz der Gelerhrte--ein Renassancefurst in Europa, Lemgo, Minerva, 370-77, 97; article, Architecture and Sculpture, Schubert's Vienna, Yale Univ Press, 143-73, 97. **CONTACT ADDRESS** Dept. of Art and Archaeology, Princeton Univ, McCormick Hall, Princeton, NJ 08840. **EMAIL** tkaufman@princeton.edu

KAWAMURA, NORIKO
PERSONAL Born 09/20/1955, Japan, m, 1988 **DISCIPLINE** HISTORY **EDUCATION** Keio Univ Tokyo, BA, 78; Univ Wash, MA, 82; PhD, 89. **CAREER** Asst Prof, Va Mil Inst, 89-92; Asst Prof, Wash State Univ, 92-. **MEMBERSHIPS** Soc for Historians of Am For Relations, Orgn of Am Historians, Japan Asn of Int Relations. **RESEARCH** U.S.-Japanese relations from World War I to World War II. **SELECTED PUBLICATIONS** Auth, "Wilsonian Idealism and Japanese Claims at the Paris Peace Conference," Pac Hist Rev 66 (Nov 97): 503-526; auth, Turbulence in the Pacific: Japanese-U.S. Relations during World War I, Praeger (Westport, CT), 00. **CONTACT ADDRESS** Dept Hist, Washington State Univ, PO Box 644030, Pullman, WA 99164-4030. **EMAIL** nkawamura@wsu.edu

KAWASHIMA, YASUHIDE
PERSONAL Born 10/22/1931, Nagasaki, Japan **DISCIPLINE** AMERICAN LEGAL & ASIAN HISTORY **EDUCATION** Keio Univ, Japan, LLB, 54, LLM, 56; Univ Calif, Santa Barbara, BA, 61, MA, 63, PhD(hist), 67. **CAREER** From instr to asst prof, 66-73, assoc prof, 73-80, Prof Am Hist, Univ Tex, El Paso, 80-, Colonial Williamsburg Found grant-in-aid, 70; fel, John Carter Brown Libr, Brown Univ, 71; Soc Sci Res Coun res training fel, 71-72; Charles Warren fel, Am legal hist, Harvard Law Sch, 71-72; Am Philos Soc res grant, 73; Huntington Libr fel, 80; Japan Found Professional fel, 81-82. **MEMBERSHIPS** AHA; Orgn Am Historians; Asn Asian Studies; Western Hist Asn; Am Soc Legal Hist. **RESEARCH** Indian-white relations; early Am legal history; history of Am-Japanese legal relations. **SELECTED PUBLICATIONS** Auth, Racial Fault Lines--The Hist Origins of White Supremacy in California, Am Hist Rev, Vol 101, 96; auth, Frontier and Pioneer Settlers--A Study of the Am Westward Movement, J Am Hist, Vol 83, 96; auth, Exemplar of Liberty--Native Am and the Evolution of Democracy, Am Hist Rev, Vol 98, 93; auth, The New-Deal and Am Capitalism--From a Viewpolnt of Popular Movements, J Am Hist, Vol 81, 94; auth, Am Holocaust--The Conquest of the New-World, Western Hist Quart, Vol 25, 94; auth, Essays on English Law and the Am Experience, J Am Hist, Vol 82, 95; auth, Civil-Law in Qing and Republican China, Am J Legal Hist, Vol 40, 96; auth, The New-Deal and Am Democracy--The Political-Process of the Agricultural Policy, J Am Hist, Vol 81, 94; auth, The Fox Wars--The Mesquakie Challenge to New France, Am Hist Rev, Vol 100, 95. **CONTACT ADDRESS** Dept of Hist, Univ of Texas, El Paso, 500 W University Ave, El Paso, TX 79968-0001. **EMAIL** ykawashi@miners.utep.edu

KAWIN, BRUCE FREDERICK
PERSONAL Born 11/06/1945, Los Angeles, CA **DISCIPLINE** FILM HISTORY; MODERN LITERATURE **EDUCATION** Columbia Univ, AB, 67; Cornell Univ, MFA, 69, PhD, 70. **CAREER** Asst prof English, Wells Col, 70-73; lectr English & Film, Univ Calif, Riverside, 73-75; specialist, Ctr for Advan Film Studies, Am Film Inst, 74; assoc prof, 75-80, prof English & Film, Univ Co, Boulder. **MEMBERSHIPS** MLA; SCS. **RESEARCH** Narrative theory; relations between literature and film. **SELECTED PUBLICATIONS** Auth, Slides (poem), Angelfish, 70; Telling It Again and Again: Repetition in Literature and Film, Cornell Univ, 72, repr Univ Press Co, 89; Faulkner and Film, Ungar, 77; Me Tarzan, you junk, Take One, 78; Mindscreen: Bergman, Godard and First-Person Film, Princeton Univ, 78; ed, To Have and Have Not--The Screenplay, Univ Wis, 80; The Mind of the Novel: Reflexive Fiction and the Ineffable, Princeton Univ, 82; Faulkner's MGM Screenplays, Univ Tenn, 82; How Movies Work, MacMillan, 87, repr Univ Ca Press, 92; co-auth, A short History of the Movies, 5th ed, MacMillan, 92; 6th ed, Allyn & Bacon, 96; 7th ed Allyn & Bacon, 99. **CONTACT ADDRESS** Dept of English, Univ of Colorado, Boulder, Box 226, Boulder, CO 80309-0226. **EMAIL** bkawin@aol.com

KAY, THOMAS O.
DISCIPLINE HISTORY **EDUCATION** Wheaton Col, AB, 53; Univ Chicago, MA, 54, PhD, 74. **CAREER** ASSOC PROF, 75-, CHAIR HIST, 80, COORD INTERDISC & GEN STUD, 89-, WHEATON COL; **CONTACT ADDRESS** History Dept, Wheaton Col, Illinois, Wheaton, IL 60187. **EMAIL** Thomas.O.Kay@wheaton.edu

KAYE, FRANCES WELLER
PERSONAL Born 04/04/1949, Englewood, NJ, m, 1973 **DISCIPLINE** AMERICAN STUDIES AND AMERICAN LITERATURE **EDUCATION** Cornell Univ, BA, 70, MA, 72, PhD(Am studies), 73. **CAREER** Vis asst prof Am studies, Univ Iowa, 76-77; asst prof English, 77-80, Assoc Prof English, Univ Nebr-Lincoln, 81-, Assoc Ed, Great Plains Quart, 80- **RESEARCH** Great Plains studies; Aman studies; Canadian literature. **SELECTED PUBLICATIONS** Auth, Hamlin Garland & Frederick Philip Grove as self-conscious chroniclers of the pioneers, Can Rev Am Studies, 79; Bringing a symphony orchestra to Albion, Nebraska, Prairie Schooner, 81; The 49th Parallel and the 98th Meridian, Mosaic, 81; The Past is Prologue, 81 & Desert Places, 82, Prairie Schooner. **CONTACT ADDRESS** Dept of English, Univ of Nebraska, Lincoln, P O Box 880333, Lincoln, NE 68588-0333.

KAYE, HARVEY JORDAN
PERSONAL Born 10/09/1949, Englewood, NJ, m, 1973, 2 children **DISCIPLINE** HISTORY OF CULTURE **EDUCATION** Rutger Univ, BA, 71; Univ London, MA 73; La St Univ, PhD 76. **CAREER** Inst, hist & sociology, La St Univ, 74, 75; asst prof social sci, St. Cloud St Univ, 77-78; from asst prof to assoc prof, Univ Wisc, 78-86, Ben & Joyce Rosenberg Prof of Social Change & Develop & Dir, Ctr for Hist & Social Change, 86- . **HONORS AND AWARDS** Honors Res Student in Hist, Rutger Col, 70-71; Fel, La St Univ, 74-75 & 75-76; postdoctoral fel, Lilly Endowment, 78-79; Nat Endowment for the Humanities Fel, 81 & 83; Visiting Fel, Inst for Advanced Res in the Humanities, Univ Birmingham, Engl, 87; Ed & Executor, George Rude Lit Estate, 88-; Endowed Chair, Rosenberg Professorship, 90-; Bd of Dir, Wisc Hist Soc, 81-; Deutscher Memorial Lect, London Sch of Econ, 94; Teaching Awd, St. Cloud St Univ, 77-78; Awd for Excellence in Scholarship, UWGB Founders Assn, 85; Isaac Deutscher Memorial Prize, 93; scholarship, columbia univ, 77. **MEMBERSHIPS** Amer Historical Assn; Amer Studies Assn; Org of Amer Historians. **RESEARCH** Amer History; politics; ideas; intellectuals; critics and radicals. **SELECTED PUBLICATIONS** Auth, British Marxist Historians: An Introductory Analysis, Polity Press/ Blackwell, 84; auth, The Powers of the Past: Reflections on the Crisis and the Promise of History, Simon & Schuster & Univ Minn, 91; auth, The Education of Desire: Marxists and the Writing of History, Routledge, 92; auth, Why Do Ruling Classes

Fear History? and Other Questions, St Martin's/Macmillan, 96; auth, Thomas Paine-A Young People's Biography, Oxford Univ, 99; ed History, Classes and Nation-States: Selected Writings of VG Kiernan, Polity Press/Blackwell, 88; ed Face of the Crowd: Selected Essays of George Rude, Simon & Schuster & Humanities Press, 88; ed, Poets, Politics and the People: Selected Writings of VG Kiernan, Verso, 89; co-ed, EP Thompson: Critical Perspectives, Polity Press & Temple Univ, 90; co-ed, American Radical, Routledge, 94; ed, Imperialism and Its Contradictions: Selected Writings of VG Kiernan, Routledge, 95; ed, Ideology and Popular Protest, Univ NCar, 95; series co-ed, American Radicals, Routledge, 92-98. **CONTACT ADDRESS** Dept of Social Change & Develop, Univ of Wisconsin, Green Bay, Green Bay, WI 54301. **EMAIL** kayeh@uwgb.edu

KAYE, JOEL
DISCIPLINE MEDIEVAL HISTORY **EDUCATION** Univ Pa, Phd, 91. **CAREER** Asst prof, Bernard Col. **SELECTED PUBLICATIONS** The Impact of Money on the Emergence of Scientific Thought, Jour Medieval Hist, 88; Economy and Nature in the Fourteenth Century: Money, Market Exchange, and the Emergence of Scientific Thought, 97. **CONTACT ADDRESS** Dept of Hist, Columbia Col, New York, 2960 Broadway, New York, NY 10027-6902.

KAZEMZADEH, FIRUZ
PERSONAL Born 10/27/1924, Moscow, USSR, m, 1959, 3 children **DISCIPLINE** RUSSIAN HISTORY **EDUCATION** Stanford Univ, BA, 46, MA, 47; Harvard Univ, PhD(hist), 51. **CAREER** Res fel, Hoover Inst, 49-50; consult publ, US Dept State, 51-52; head Soviet affairs unit, Info Dept, Radio Free Europe, 52-54; res fel, Russian Res Ctr and Ctr Mid Eastern Studies, Harvard Univ, 54-56, instr hist and lit, 55-56; from instr to assoc prof, 56-67, chmn coun Russ and E Europ Studies, 68-69, dir grad studies hist, 75-76, master Davenport Col, 76-81, Prof Hist, Yale Univ, 67-, Morse fel, 58-59; Ford fac grant Int studies, 66-67. **MEMBERSHIPS** AHA; Am Asn Advan Slavic Studies; Soc Iranian Studies. **RESEARCH** Russian imperial history; foreign relations; modern Persian history. **SELECTED PUBLICATIONS** Nationalism and Hist--The Politics of Nation Building in Post-Soviet Armenia, Azerbaijan and Georgia, Slavic Rev, Vol 54, 95; The Soviet Socialist Republic of Iran, 1920-1921--Birth Of The Trauma, Am Hist Rev, Vol 102, 97. **CONTACT ADDRESS** Dept of Hist, Yale Univ, New Haven, CT 06520.

KAZIN, ALFRED
PERSONAL Born 06/05/1915, Brooklyn, NY, m, 1952, 2 children **DISCIPLINE** AMERICAN STUDIES **EDUCATION** City Col New York, BSS, 35; Columbia Univ, MA, 38. **CAREER** Tutor English, City Col New York, 39-42; lectr English and gen lit, New Sch Social Res, 41-42, 48-49, 51, 52-53, 58-63; vis lectr, Harvard Univ, 53; Neilson res prof, Smith Col, 54-55; prof Am Studies, Amherst Col, 55-58; distinguished prof English, State Univ NY, Stony Brook, 63-73; vis prof English, Univ Notre Dame, 78-79. Vis lectr, Ger, Eng, France, Sweden and Norway; vis lectr, Black Mountain Col, 44; Berg prof, NY Univ, 57-58; vis prof, Univ PR, 59; Gauss lectr, Princeton Univ, 62; Gallagher prof, City Col New York, 63; Beckman prof, Univ Calif, Berkeley, 63; Distinguished Prof English Lit, City Univ NY, 73-; Nat Endowment Humantiies, sr fel, 77-78; Ctr for Advancec Study Behavioral Scis, fel, 77-78. **HONORS AND AWARDS** MA, Amherst Col, 56; LittD, Adelphi Univ, 64, Univ New Haven, 76. **MEMBERSHIPS** Am Acad Arts and Sci; Nat Inst Arts and Lett. **RESEARCH** Am literature; English literature; modern European literature. **SELECTED PUBLICATIONS** Auth, On Native Grounds, 42, A Walker in the City, 51 & The Inmost Leaf, 55, Harcourt; Contemporaries, 62; Starting Out in the thirties, 65 & Bright Book of Life: American Novelists & Storytellers from Hemingway to Mailer, Little Brown, 73; New York Jew, Knopf, 78. **CONTACT ADDRESS** Dept of English, Univ of Notre Dame, Notre Dame, IN 46556.

KEALEY, EDWARD J.
PERSONAL Born 08/01/1936, New York, NY **DISCIPLINE** MEDIEVAL HISTORY **EDUCATION** Manhattan Col, BA, 58; Johns Hopkins Univ, MA and PhD, 62. **CAREER** From asst prof to assoc prof, 62-73, adv grad studies, 64-69, Prpf Hist, Col Holy Cross, 73-, Chmn Hist Dept, 80-, Lectr pub speaking and parliamentary law, Labor Rels and Res Ctr, Univ Mass, 69-76; Nat Endowment for Humanities fel, 76; Holy Cross Col fac fel, 72 and 78-79; Am Philos Soc fel, 80. **MEMBERSHIPS** AHA; Am Cath Hist Asn; Conf Brit Hist; Soc Values Higher Educ; Medieval Acad Am. **RESEARCH** Medieval history, England and France in the 12th century; European and Am archaeology; pre-Columbian Am. **SELECTED PUBLICATIONS** **CONTACT ADDRESS** Dept of Hist, Col of the Holy Cross, Worcester, MA 01610.

KEALEY, GREGORY S.
PERSONAL Born 10/07/1948, Hamilton, ON, Canada **DISCIPLINE** HISTORY **EDUCATION** Univ Toronto, BA, 70; Univ Rochester(Mass) MA, 71, PhD, 77. **CAREER** Asst prof, 74-79, assoc prof hist, Dalhousie Univ, 79-81; assoc prof, 81-83, prof hist, 83-, univ res prof, 92-, DEAN GRAD STUD, MEMORIAL UNIV NFLD, 97-; vis prof, Univ Alta, 84; vis prof, Univ Guelph, 85; Univ Sydney, Univ New Eng, Griffith Univ, 93; scholar res, Laurentian Univ, 96. **HONORS AND AWARDS** Maurice Cody Memorial Prize, Univ Toronto, 70; Sir John A Macdonald Prize, Can Hist Asn, 80; AB Corey Prize, Can & Amer Hist Asns, 84; Pres Awd Outstanding Res, Memorial Univ Nfld, 85. **MEMBERSHIPS** Royal Hist Soc; Can Hist Asn; Can Comt Labour Hist; Asn Can Stud; Can Asn Learned Jour. **SELECTED PUBLICATIONS** Auth, Toronto Workers Respond to Industrial Capitalism, 1867-1892, 80; Workers and Canadian History, 95; co-auth, Dreaming of What Might Be, 82; Labour and Hibernia, 93; ed, Labour/Le Travail, 76-97; McClelland & Stewart Social History Series, 80-96; Oxford Univ Press Social History Series, 96-. **CONTACT ADDRESS** Grad Stud, Mem Univ of Newfoundland, Saint John's, NF, Canada A1C 5S7. **EMAIL** gkealey@morgan.ucs.mun.ca

KEALEY, LINDA
PERSONAL Born Rochester, NY **DISCIPLINE** HISTORY **EDUCATION** Univ Toronto, BA, 69, BLS, 70, MA, 74, PhD, 82. **CAREER** Vis asst prof, 80-81, asst prof, 81-86, ASSOC PROF HISTORY, MEMORIAL UNIV NEWFOUNDLAND 86-, head dept, 94-. **MEMBERSHIPS** Royal Hist Asn; Can Women's Studs Asn; Can Res Inst Advan Women. **SELECTED PUBLICATIONS** Auth, A Not Unreasonable Claim: Women and Reform in Canada, 1880s-1920s, 79; auth, Canadian Socialism and the Women Question 1900-14, in Labour/Le Travail, 84; auth, The Status of Women in the Historical Profession in Canada, 1989 Survey, in Can Hist Rev, 91. **CONTACT ADDRESS** History Dept, Mem Univ of Newfoundland, Saint John's, NF, Canada A1C 5S7. **EMAIL** lkealey@morgan.ucs.mun.ca

KEARNEY, MILO
PERSONAL Born 01/10/1938, Kansas City, MO, m, 1970, 2 children **DISCIPLINE** HISTORY **EDUCATION** Univ Tex at Austin, BSc, 62; Univ Calif at Berkeley, MA, 66; PhD, 70. **CAREER** Wissenschaftlicher asst, Goethe Univ, 69; prof, Univ of Tex at Brownsville, 70-; fulbright prof, Inst Technol, Matamoros, 92-93. **HONORS AND AWARDS** Woodrow Wilson Fel, 65-66; Minnie Stevens Piper Teaching Awd, 82; Univ of Tex Chancellor's Teaching Awd, 92; Fulbright Scholar, 92-93. **MEMBERSHIPS** International Soc for the comparative Study of Civilizations, Nat Soc Sci Asn, Am studies Asn of Tex. **RESEARCH** Medieval culture, Mexican-American border studies. **SELECTED PUBLICATIONS** Auth, Boom and Bust: The Historical Cycles of Matamoros and Brownsville, Eakin, 91; auth, The Role of Swine Symbolism in Medieval Culture: Blanc Sanglier, Mellen, 91; auth, Border Cuates: A History of the U.S.-Mexican Twin Cities, Eakin, 95. **CONTACT ADDRESS** Dept Hist, Univ of Texas, Brownsville, 80 Fort Brown, Brownsville, TX 78520-4964.

KEBEDE, ASHENAFI AMDE
PERSONAL Born 05/07/1938, Addis Ababa, Ethiopia, d, 1964 **DISCIPLINE** AFRICAN-AMERICAN STUDIES **EDUCATION** University of Rochester, BA, 1962; Wesleyan University, MA, 1969, PhD, 1971. **CAREER** US Peace Corps, counselor/teacher, summer 1962; Ethiopian Ministry of Education, director/teacher, 62-68; Wesleyan University, instructor, 68-71; Queens College, CUNY, assistant professor, 71-75; Brandeis University, assistant professor, 76-80; Florida State University, Center for African-American Culture, professor/director, 80-. **HONORS AND AWARDS** Haile Selassie Foundation, Outstanding Young Ethiopian Scholar, 1958; UNESCO, UNESCO Expert to Sudan, 1979; Institute for International Education, Senior Fulbright Scholar to Israel, 1986-87. **MEMBERSHIPS** Ethiopian National Music Committee, president, 1963-71; International Music Council, UNESCO, 1964-69; Society for Ethnomusicology, 1964-90; Florida Arts Council for African-American Affairs, executive director, 1982-90; Ethius, Inc, executive director, 1989-. **SELECTED PUBLICATIONS** Founded Ethiopia's Institute of Music, 1963; first African to conduct the Hungarian State Orchestra in Budapest, 1967; commissioned by UNESCO, wrote the syllabus for Sudan's Institute of Music, Dance and Drama, 1979; numerous books, monograms, articles and compositions in Black Perspectives in Music, Musical Quarterly, Ethnomusicology. **CONTACT ADDRESS** Center for African-American Culture, Florida State Univ, 210 S Woodward Ave, B-105, Tallahassee, FL 32306.

KEBRIC, ROBERT BARNETT
PERSONAL Born 04/30/1946, Palo Alto, CA, m, 1971 **DISCIPLINE** ANCIENT HISTORY **EDUCATION** Univ Southern Calif, AB, 68; Binghamton Univ, MA, 71, PhD (ancient hist), 72. **CAREER** From instr to asst prof, 73-77, vchmn dept, 77-79, Assoc Prof Hist, Univ Louisville, 77-, prof, 83-. **HONORS AND AWARDS** Woodrow Wilson Fel, 68. **MEMBERSHIPS** Asn Ancient Historians; Soc for Hellenic Studies; Soc for Roman Studies; Friends of Ancient Hist. **RESEARCH** Greek history; Roman history; classical culture and literature; Olympic Games; Gerontology; history in film; humor. **SELECTED PUBLICATIONS** Auth, A note on Duris in Athens, Class Philol, No 69, 74; Duris of Samos: Early ties with Sicily, Am J Archaeol, No 79, 75; Herodotus: A source for Duris on Egypt, J Am Res Ctr in Egypt, No 12, 75; Lucan's snake episode: A historical model, Latomus, No 35, 76; Implications of Alcibiades relationship with Endius Mnemosyne, No 29, 76; In the Shadow of Macedon: Duris of Samos, Franz Steiner Verlag, 77; auth, The Paintings in the Cnidian Lesche at Delphi an and their Historical Context, E.J. Brill, 83; auth, Historical Context, E.J. Brill , 83; auth, Historical consultant for Time-Life's when Rome Ruled the World, 97; auth, Greek People, Mayfield Publishing Co. (now McGraw/Hill) 3rd ed. 01; Roman People, Mayfield Publishing Co., 01; Various other essays, entries, and reviews. **CONTACT ADDRESS** Dept of Hist, Univ of Louisville, Louisville, KY 40292. **EMAIL** rbkebr01@athena.louisville.edu

KEDDIE, NIKKI R.
PERSONAL Born 08/30/1930, New York, NY **DISCIPLINE** MIDDLE EAST HISTORY **EDUCATION** Radcliffe Col, BA, 51; Stanford Univ, MA, 51; Univ Calif, PhD(hist), 55. **CAREER** Res historian, Univ Calif, 55-56; instr hist, Univ Ariz, 57; from instr to asst prof, Scripps Col, 57-61; from asst prof to assoc prof, 61-71, Prof Hist, Univ Calif, Los Angeles, 71-, Soc Sci Res Coun Near and Mid E fel, 59-60, 76; Guggenheim Mem Found Fel, 63-64; vis prof hist, Univ Paris, 3, 76-78; Rockefeller fel, 80-82; Woodrow Wilson fel, 82. **HONORS AND AWARDS** Fellow, American Academy of Arts & Sciences **MEMBERSHIPS** Asn Asian Studies; Mid East Inst; Mid East Studies Asn. **RESEARCH** Middle East; intellectual and social history. **SELECTED PUBLICATIONS** Auth, Roots of Revolution: An Interpretive History of Modern Iran, 81; Iran and the Muslim World: Resistance and Revolution, 95; Qajar Iran and the Rise of Reza Khan, 99. **CONTACT ADDRESS** Dept of Hist, Univ of California, Los Angeles, Los Angeles, CA 90095.

KEE, HOWARD CLARK
PERSONAL Born 07/28/1920, Beverly, NJ, m, 1951, 3 children **DISCIPLINE** RELIGION, HISTORY **EDUCATION** Bryan Col, BA, 40; Dallas Theol Sem, ThM, 44; Yale Univ, PhD(relig), 51. **CAREER** Instr relig thought, Univ Pa, 51-53; from asst prof to prof New Testament, Drew Univ, 53-67; Rufus Jones prof hist relig, Bryn Mawr Col, 68-77; prof New Testament, 77-82, William Goodwin Aurelio Prof Biblical Studies and Dir Grad Div Relig Studies, Sch Theol, Boston Univ, 82-, Vis prof relig, Princeton Univ, 55-56; mem bd managers and chmn transl comt, Am Bible Soc, 58-; Am Asn Theol Schs fel, Marburg, Ger, 59-60; Guggenheim Found fel archaeol, Jerusalem, 66-67; ed, Soc Bibl Lit Dissertation Ser; Bd Adv, Yale Univ Inst Sacred Music, 79- **MEMBERSHIPS** Soc Relig Higher Educ; Soc Bibl Lit; Am Acad Relig; Aaup; Soc New Testament Studies. **RESEARCH** Hist and literature of early Christianity; archaeology of the Hellenistic and early Roman periods; social setting of early Christianity in the Graeco-Roman world. **SELECTED PUBLICATIONS** Auth, Jesus in History, Harcourt, 69, 2nd ed, 77; translr, W G Kummel, The New Testament: The History of the Investigations of its Problems, Abingdon, 71; auth, The Origins of Christianity: Sources and Documents, 72; Community of the New Age: Studies in Mark, Westminister, 77; translr, Introduction to the New Testament, 17th ed, Abingdon, 77; Christianity (Major World Religions ser), Argus, 79; Christian Origins in Sociological Perspective, Westminster, 80; Understanding the New Testament, 4th ed (in press). **CONTACT ADDRESS** Sch of Theol, Boston Univ, Boston, MA 02215.

KEEFE, SUSAN ANN
PERSONAL Born 05/21/1954, RYE, NY **DISCIPLINE** MEDIEVAL INTELLECTUAL HISTORY **EDUCATION** Univ Pa, BA, 75; Univ Toronto, MA, 76, PhD(medieval studies), 81. **CAREER** Mellon Instr Hist, Calif Inst Technol, 81- **MEMBERSHIPS** Medieval Acad Am; Medieval Asn Pac; AHA; Inst Relig Life. **RESEARCH** Carolingian liturgical expositions; manuscript evidence for the teaching and celebration of Christian initiation in the early Middle Ages. **SELECTED PUBLICATIONS** Liturgy and Sacramental Theology in History, Speculum-A J Medieval Studies, Vol 68, 93; Law and Liturgy in the Latin Church, 5th-12th Centuries, Cath Hist Rev, Vol 82, 96; Liturgy and Sacramental Theology in History, Speculum-A J Medieval Studies, Vol 68, 93. **CONTACT ADDRESS** Duke Univ, Durham, NC 27706.

KEEFE, THOMAS M.
PERSONAL Born 12/25/1933, Chicago, IL **DISCIPLINE** MODERN GERMANY **EDUCATION** St Mary's Col, Minn, BA, 56; Univ Denver, MA, 57; Loyola Univ, Ill, PhD(hist), 66. **CAREER** Asst prof hist, St Mary's Col, Minn, 63-64; lectr, Sch Bus, Loyola Univ, Ill, 64-65; from instr to asst prof, 65-71; Assoc Prof Hist, St Joseph's Univ, PA, 71- **MEMBERSHIPS** AHA; Am Cath Hist Asn; Conf Group Cent Europ Hist; Hist Asn, Eng; Soc Hist Educ. **RESEARCH** Germany, 19-1939; Am press; nativism. **SELECTED PUBLICATIONS** Germany Rude Awakening--Censorship in the Land of the Brothers Grimm, Historian, Vol 55, 93; Hecker, Isaac--An American-Catholic, Church Hist, Vol 64, 95. **CONTACT ADDRESS** 25 Old Lancaster Rd, Bala-Cynwyd, PA 19004.

KEELER, MARY FREAR
PERSONAL Born 01/01/1904, State College, PA, m, 1938, 1 child **DISCIPLINE** HISTORY **EDUCATION** Pa State Univ, AB, 24; Yale Univ, MA, 29, PhD(hist), 33. **CAREER** Instr hist, Univ Wyo, 29-31; instr, NJ Col Women, 31-32; from instr to asst prof, Pa State Univ, 33-38; lectr, Vassar Col, 52-53 &

Wellesley Col, 53-54; lectr hist, 54-58, prof, 58-71, dean fac, 54-69, Emer Dean Fac, Hood Col, 69-; Exec Ed Parliamentary Debates, Yale Ctr Parliamentary Hist, 74-, Am Asn Univ Women fel, 35-36; sr fel, Folger Shakespeare Libr, 71-72; res assoc hist, Yale Univ, 74-76; consult, Yale Ctr Parliamentary Hist, 76-; co-ed, Commons Debates 1628, Yale Univ, 77-83. **HONORS AND AWARDS** AAUW Fel, 35-36; Am Phil Soc grant, 72-73. **MEMBERSHIPS** AHA; Conf Brit Studies; fel Royal Hist Soc; Berkshire Conf Women Historians; Soc Hist Discoveries. **RESEARCH** History of Parliament; English and modern European history; Elizabethan explorations. **SELECTED PUBLICATIONS** Auth, The Long Parliament, 1640-1641, Am Philos Soc, 54; ed, Bibliography of British History, Stuart Period, Clarendon, 2nd ed, 70; Sir Francis Drake's West Indian Voyage, 1585-1586, Hakluyt Soc, 81. **CONTACT ADDRESS** 302 W 12th St, Frederick, MD 21701.

KEEN, BENJAMIN

PERSONAL Born 04/25/1913, m, 1937, 4 children **DISCIPLINE** LATIN AMERICAN HISTORY **EDUCATION** Muhlenberg Col, AB, 36; Lehigh Univ, MA, 39; Yale Univ, PhD(hist), 41. **CAREER** Instr hist, Yale Univ, 43-45; asst prof, Amherst Col, 45-46; assoc prof, WVa Univ, 46-56; prof hist, Jersey City State Col, 56-59; Prof Hist, Northern Ill Univ, 59-. **MEMBERSHIPS** Conf Latin Am Hist; AHA. **RESEARCH** Pre-Columbian Am; social history of colonial Latin Am; historiography of colonial Latin Am. **SELECTED PUBLICATIONS** Auth, Quetzalcoatl & Guadalupe, Univ Chicago Pr, 76, 87; auth, Aztec Image in Western Though, Rutgers Univ Pr, 90; auth, Life of the Admiral Christopher Columbus by His Son Ferdinand, Rutgers Univ Pr, 92; auth, Life & Labor in Ancient Mexico, Univ of Okla Pr, 94; auth, History of Latin America, Houghton Mifflin, 95, rev ed 00; auth, Latin American Civilization, 95; auth, Essays in the Intellectual History of Colonial Latin America, Westview Pr, 98. **CONTACT ADDRESS** Dept of Hist, 2216 Calle Cacique, Santa Fe, NM 87501.

KEENE, JENNIFER D.

DISCIPLINE HISTORY **EDUCATION** George Wash Univ, BA, 84; Carnegie Mellon Univ, PhD, 91. **CAREER** Asst prof, Univ of Redlands. **HONORS AND AWARDS** Albert J. Beveridge Res Grant, Am Hist Asn, 97; Fulbright Sr Scholar Award, 98-99; Graves Award in the Humanities, 00-01. **RESEARCH** Am Diplomatic Hist; Civil War and Reconstruction; Am Political Hist; War and Society; World War I, African-American Hist; Am Social Hist. **SELECTED PUBLICATIONS** Auth, Intelligence and Morale in the Army of a Democracy: The Genesis of Military Psychology During the First World War, Military Psychol, 94; Between Mutiny and Obedience: The Case of the French Fifth Infantry Division during World War I (rev), J Social Hist, 95; auth, "Uneasy Alliances: French Military Intelligence and the American Army during the First World War," Intelligence and National Security, 13, no 1, (98): 18-36; auth, "W.E.B. Du Bois and the Wounded World: Seeking Meaning in the First World War for African-Americans," Peace & Change, 26, no. 2, (01): 135-52; auth, The United States and the First World War, Seminar Series in Hist, London: Longman, 00; auth, Doughboys, the Great War, and the Remaking of America, Baltimore, MD: Johns Hopkins Univ Press, 01. **CONTACT ADDRESS** History Dept, Univ of Redlands, 1200 E Colton Ave, Box 3090, Redlands, CA 92373-0999. **EMAIL** keene@jasper.uor.edu

KEEP, JOHN L. H.

PERSONAL Born 01/21/1926, Orpington, m, 1948 **DISCIPLINE** RUSSIAN HISTORY **EDUCATION** Univ London, BA, 50, PhD(Russ hist), 54. **CAREER** Lectr Russ and reader hist, Univ London, 54-70; Prof Hist, Univ Toronto, 70-, Vis assoc prof hist, Univ Wash, 64-65. **MEMBERSHIPS** Can Asn Slavists; Am Asn Advan Slavic Studies. **RESEARCH** Social history of Russian army; Russian revolution. **SELECTED PUBLICATIONS** Co-ed, Contemporary History in a Soviet Mirror, Praeger (New York, NY), 64; auth, Power to the People, E Europ Mono, 95; auth, Last of the Empires: A History of the Soviet Union 1945-1991, Oxford Univ Pr (Oxford), 95; coauth, The Making of Modern Russia: From Kiev Rus' to the Collapse of the Soviet Union, 97. **CONTACT ADDRESS** Dept Hist, Univ of Toronto, 100 St George St, Sidney Smith Hall Rm 2074, Toronto, ON, Canada M5S 3G3.

KEHL, JAMES ARTHUR

PERSONAL Born 02/16/1922, Pittsburgh, PA, m, 1972, 1 child **DISCIPLINE** HISTORY **EDUCATION** Univ Pittsburgh, BA, 44, MA, 47; Univ Pa, PhD, 54. **CAREER** Lectr hist, 46-47, from instr to assoc prof, 47-65, admin asst dept, 55-58, admin asst to chancellor, 58-60, asst dean soc sci, 60-65, dean col arts & sci, 65-69, prof hist, 65-92, prof emeritus, 92-, Univ Pittsburgh; instr, Carnegie Mellon Univ, 46-47. **HONORS AND AWARDS** Distinguished Alumnus Awd, Univ Pittsburgh; Meritorious Service Awd, Phi Alpha Theta. **RESEARCH** Pennsylvania history; history of American political parties. **SELECTED PUBLICATIONS** Auth, Ill Feeling in the Era of Good Feeling, Western Pennsylvania Political Battles, 1815-1825, Univ Pittsburgh; art, Defender of the Faith: Orphan Annie and the Conservative Tradition, SAtlantic Quart, 77; art, A Bull Moose Responds to the New Deal, Pa Mag of Hist & Biog, 64; art,The Unmaking of a President, 1889-1892, Pa Hist, 72; art,The Delegate Convention: Agent of the Democratic Process, SAtlantic Quart, 73; art, Albert Gallatin: Man of Moderation, WPa Hist Mag, 78; art, Boss Rule in the Gilded Age: Matt Quay of Pennsylvania, Univ Pittsburgh, 81; art, White House or Animal House, SAtlantic Quart, 80; auth, When Civilians Manned the Ships: Life in the Amphibious Fleet During World War II, Brandylane, 97. **CONTACT ADDRESS** 5057 Brownsville Rd, Pittsburgh, PA 15236.

KEHOE, DENNIS P.

DISCIPLINE ROMAN IMPERIAL HISTORY, LITERATURE **EDUCATION** Dartmouth Col, AB, 73-77; Oxford Univ, Magdalen Col, BA, 77-79; Univ Mich, PhD, 79-82. **CAREER** Prof, Tulane Univ. **RESEARCH** Roman Social and Economic History; Roman law; Papyrology. **SELECTED PUBLICATIONS** Auth, The Economics of Agriculture on Roman Imperial Estates in North Africa, HYPOMNEMATA 89, Vandenhoeck und Ruprecht, 88; auth, Management and Investment on Estates in Roman Egypt during the Early Empire, Papyrologische Texte und Abhandlungen 40, Habelt, 92; auth, Legal Institutions and the Bargaining Power of the Tenant in Roman Egypt, Archv fur Papyrusforschung 41, 95; auth, Roman-Law Influence on Louisiana's Landlord-Tenant Law: The Question of Risk in Agriculture, Tulane Law Rev 70, 96; auth, Investment, Profit, and Tenancy: The Jurists and the Roman Agrarian Economy, Univ Mich Press, 97. **CONTACT ADDRESS** Dept Class Stud, Tulane Univ, 6823 St Charles Ave, New Orleans, LA 70118. **EMAIL** kehoe@tulane.edu

KEIGHTLEY, DAVID NOEL

PERSONAL Born 10/25/1932, London, England, m, 1965, 2 children **DISCIPLINE** CHINESE HISTORY **EDUCATION** Amherst Col, BA, 53; NYork Univ, MA, 56; Columbia Univ, PhD(Chinese hist), 69. **CAREER** ed, Early China, 75-; vis prof, Peking Univ, spring 81; asst prof, 69-75, assoc prof, 75-79, prof, Univ Calif Berkeley, 79-98; assoc ed, J Asian Studies, 81-. **HONORS AND AWARDS** Fels, Humanities Res Inst, Univ Calif, Berkeley, 72-73; fel, Am Counc Learned Socs, 75-76; Guggenheim fel, 78-79; MacArthur Fel, 86-91. **MEMBERSHIPS** Asn Asian Studies; Soc Study Early China; Am Orient Soc. **RESEARCH** Ancient Chinese history; oracle bone inscriptions; Shang religion. **SELECTED PUBLICATIONS** Auth, Akatsuka Kiyoshi and the study of early China: A study in historical method, Harvard J Asiatic Studies, 6/82; The late Shang state: When, where, and what?, In: Origins of Chinese Civilizations, Calif, 83; Late Shang Divination: The Magico-Religious Legacy, In: Explorations in Early Chinese Cosmology, J of the Am Acad of Relig Studies, 84; Archaeology and Mentality: The Making of China, Representations, Spring 87; Shang Divination and Metaphysics, Philos East and West, 10/88; Clean Hands and Shining Helmets: Heroic Action in Early Chinese and Greek Culture, In: Religion and Authority, Univ Mich Press, 93; A Measure of Man in Early China: In Search of the Neolithic Inch, Chinese Sci 12, 94-95; Art, Ancestors, and the Origins of Writing in China, Representations, Fall 96; The Shang: China's First Historical Dynasty, In: The Cambridge History of Ancient China, Cambridge Univ Press, 99; auth, The Ancestral Landscape, 00. **CONTACT ADDRESS** Dept of History, Univ of California, Berkeley, 3229 Dwinelle Hall, Berkeley, CA 94720-1742. **EMAIL** keightle@socrates.berkeley.edu

KEILLOR, ELAINE

DISCIPLINE BAROQUE AND CLASSICAL PERIODS, ETHNOMUSICOLOGY **EDUCATION** Univ Toronto, BA, MA, PhD. **CAREER** Lectr, York Univ, 75-76; instr, Queen's Univ, 76-77; asst prof, 77-82, assoc prof, 82-95, prof, Carleton Univ, 95-. **HONORS AND AWARDS** Chappell Medal, 58; Merit Awd, Fac Arts, Carleton Univ, 81; Canadian Women's Mentor Awd, 99; principal investigator, the can mus heritage soc; coch, another organized res unit. **MEMBERSHIPS** Can Musical Heritage; Am Musicol Soc; Int Musicol Soc; Soc Ethnomusicol; Can Univ Music Soc; Can Soc Traditional Music. **RESEARCH** Canadian music. **SELECTED PUBLICATIONS** Auth, monograph John Weinzweig and His Music: The Radical Romantic of Canada, 94; **CONTACT ADDRESS** Dept of Mus, Carleton Univ, 1125 Colonel By Dr, Ottawa, ON, Canada K1S 5B6. **EMAIL** elaine_keillor@carleton.ca

KEITER, ROBERT B.

PERSONAL Born 07/05/1946, Bethesda, MD, m, 1976, 2 children **DISCIPLINE** LAW; HISTORY **EDUCATION** Northwestern Univ, JD 72; Washington Univ, BA 68. **CAREER** Univ Utah Col Law, Wallace Stegner prof, dir, 93-; Wallace Stegner Cen Land Resource Environ, prof, James I. Farr prof, 93-98, Univ Wyoming College of Law, assoc prof, interim dean, prof, Winston S. Howard dist prof, 78-93; vis prof, Boston Col, 85; Southwestern Univ, assoc prof, 76-78; Idaho Legal Aid, managing att, 75-76; Appalachian Res Def Fund, Reginald Heber Smith Fel, 72-74. **HONORS AND AWARDS** Omicron delta Kappa; Phi Kappa Phi; Sr Fulbright Sch **MEMBERSHIPS** ABA; State Bars of Wyoming, Idaho, West Virginia; RMMLF Trustee; NPCA trustee. **RESEARCH** Nat Resources Law and Policy; Constitutional Law. **SELECTED PUBLICATIONS** Auth, Reclaiming the Native Home of Hope: Community Ecology and the West, ed, Univ Utah Press, 98; Visions of the Grand Staircase-Escalante: Examining Utah's Newest National Monument, co-ed, Wallace Stegner Cen Utah Museum Natural Hist, 98; The Greater Yellowstone System: Redefining America's Wilderness Heritage, coed, Yale Univ Press, 91; Ecosystems and the Law: Toward an Integrated Approach, Ecolo Apps, Preserving Nature in the National Parks: Law Policy and Science in a Dynamic Environment, rev, Denver U L, 97; Ecological Policy and the Courts: Of Rights, Processes, and the Judicial Role, Human Ecolo Rev, 97; Greater Yellowstone's Bison: The Unraveling of an Early American Wildlife Conservation Achievement, Jour of Wildlife Mgmt, 97; Law and Large Carnivore Conservation in the Rocky Mountains of the Us and Canada, coauth, Conservation Biology, 96. **CONTACT ADDRESS** College of Law, Univ of Utah, 332 S. 1400 E. Front, Salt Lake City, UT 84112. **EMAIL** keiterb@law.utah.edu

KELLEHER, PATRICIA

DISCIPLINE HISTORY **EDUCATION** Univ Wis, Madison, PhD. **CAREER** Asst prof, Univ NH, 95-. **HONORS AND AWARDS** Soc Sci Res Coun fel; Nat Sci Found fel; Newberry Libr fel, Chicago. **RESEARCH** Gender dynamics in 18th- and 19th-century Ireland and among Irish immigrants in North America. **SELECTED PUBLICATIONS** Coauth, Women, Social Institutions and Social Change, in Irish Women and Irish Immigration, ed. Patrick O'Sullivan, 95. **CONTACT ADDRESS** Univ of New Hampshire, Durham, Durham, NH 03824.

KELLER, CLAIR WAYNE

PERSONAL Born 01/00/1932, Fargo, ND, m, 1959, 2 children **DISCIPLINE** COLONIAL HISTORY **EDUCATION** Univ Wash, BA, 57, MA, 62, PhD(hist), 67. **CAREER** Teacher soc studies, Lake Wash High Sch, 57-59 and Sammamish High Sch, 60-66; instr hist, Univ Wash, 66-67; chmn dept soc studies, Interlake High Sch, Wash, 67-69; assoc prof, 69-80, Prof Hist and Educ, Iowa State Univ, 80-. **MEMBERSHIPS** Nat Coun Soc Studies; AHA; Orgn Am Historians; Soc Hist Educ. **RESEARCH** Pennsylvania government, 1701-1740; life and times of George Washington; ratification of the 27th Amendment. **SELECTED PUBLICATIONS** Auth, "The County Commission System, 1712-1740," Pennsylvania Magazine of History and Biography 93 (69); auth, Involving Students in the New Social Studies, Little Brown and Company, 74; coauth, Freedom's Trail, Boston: Houghton-Mifflin Co, 79; auth, "The Rise of Representation: Electing County Officeholders in Colonial Pennsylvania," Social Science History, 79; auth, "Improving High School History Teaching," Against Mediocrity: The Humanities in America's High School, edited by Chester E. Finn, Jr., eds. Diane Ravitch and Robert T. Fancher, Homes & Meier: New York, 84; coauth, Lessons on the Federalist Papers, Social Studies Development Center, Indiana University, 86; auth, "Enhancing the Expository Approach to Teaching History," The Social Studies, 88; auth, "The Failure to Provide a Constitutional Guarantee on Representation: Rejecting the First Proposed Constitutional Amendment," Journal of the Early Republic 13 (93).; auth, "Comparing the Original and Revised Standards for History," The History Teacher, 30/3 (97): 306-338. **CONTACT ADDRESS** Dept of Hist, Iowa State Univ of Science and Tech, Ames, IA 50010. **EMAIL** ckeller@iastate.edu

KELLER, KENNETH WAYNE

PERSONAL Born 10/29/1943, St. Louis, MO, m **DISCIPLINE** AMERICAN HISTORY **EDUCATION** Wash Univ, AB, 65; Yale Univ, MPhil, 68, PhD(hist), 71. **CAREER** From instr to asst prof hist, OH Univ, 70-74; asst prof, OH State Univ, 74-81; assoc prof, 81-87, prof, Mary Baldwin Col, 87-. **HONORS AND AWARDS** Phi Beta Kappa. **MEMBERSHIPS** AHA; Orgn Am Historians; Soc Historians Early Am Repub. **RESEARCH** United States early national history; frontier; American colonial history. **SELECTED PUBLICATIONS** Auth, The Philadelphia Pilots' Strike of 1792, Labor Hist, winter 77; Alexander McNair and John B C Lucas: The Background of Early Missouri Politics, Bull Mo Hist Soc, 7/77; contribr, The Reader's Encycl of the American West, 77; The Encycl of Southern History, 79; coauth, Tenancy and Assetholding in Late Eighteenth Century Washington County, Pennsylvania, Western PA Hist Mag, 1/82; coauth, Rural Pennsylvania in 1800: A Portrait from the Septennial Census, PA Hist, 4/82; coauth, New Jersey Wealth-holding and the Republican Congressional Victory of 1800, NJ Hist, 82; auth, Rural Politics and the Collapse of Pennsylvania Federalism, Trans Am Philos Soc, 82; Cultural Conflict and Early Nineteenth Century Pennsylvania Politics, PA Mag of Hist and Biog, Oct 86; From the Rhineland to the Virginia Frontier: Flax Production as a Commercial Enterprise, VA Mag Hist and Biog, July 90; What is Distinctive About the Scotch-Irish?, in Robert Mitchell, ed, Appalachian Frontiers, 91; Origins of Ulster--Scots Emigration to America, 1600-1800: A Survey of Recent Research, Am Presbyterians, summer 92; The Outlook of Rhinelanders on the Virginia Frontier, in Michael Puglisi, ed, Diversity and Accomodation; Merchandising Nature: The H J Weber and Sons Nursery, MO Hist Rev, April 95; Cyrus McCormick, The Inventor as Creator of Controversy, Proceedings of the Asn for Living History Farms and Museums, 97. **CONTACT ADDRESS** Mary Baldwin Col, Staunton, VA 24401. **EMAIL** kkeller@cit.mbc.edu

KELLER, MORTON
PERSONAL Born 03/01/1929, Brooklyn, NY, m, 1951, 2 children **DISCIPLINE** AMERICAN HISTORY **EDUCATION** Univ Rochester, BA, 50; Harvard Univ, MA, 52, PhD, 56. **CAREER** Instr hist, Univ NC, 56-58; from asst prof to assoc prof hist, Univ Pa, 58-64; prof hist, Brandeis Univ, 64-, Guggenheim fel, 59-60; Soc Sci Res Coun auxiliary res award, 59-60; fel, Harvard Ctr Studies Hist Liberty in Am, 60-61; Nat Sci Found soc sci res grant, 62; Am Philos Soc res award, 62; vis lectr, Harvard Univ, 63-64; res fel, Charles Warren Ctr Studies Am Hist, 67-68; mem US deleg, UNESCO Gen Conf, 68; lib arts fel, Harvard Law Sch, 70-71; sr fel, Nat Endowment for Hum, 74-75; resident scholar, Bellagio Study & Res Ctr, 76; Commonwealth Fund Lectr Am Hist, Univ Col, London, 79; Harmsworth prof Am hist, Oxford Univ, 80-81. **MEMBERSHIPS** Soc Am Historians; Am Acad Arts & Sci. **RESEARCH** Am polit, institutional and legal hist. **SELECTED PUBLICATIONS** Auth, The Life Insurance Enterprise, 1885-1910: A Study in the Limits of Corporate Power, Harvard Univ, 63; Affairs of State: Public Life in Late Nineteenth Century America, Harvard Univ, 77; Regulating a New Economy, Harvard Univ, 90; Regulating a New Society, Harvard Univ, 94. **CONTACT ADDRESS** Dept of Hist, Brandeis Univ, 415 South St, Waltham, MA 02154-2700. **EMAIL** keller@binah.cc.brandeis.edu

KELLER, WILLIAM
PERSONAL Born 01/27/1920, Newark, NJ **DISCIPLINE** EUROPEAN HISTORY **EDUCATION** Seton Hall Univ, AB, 43; Cath Univ Am, STL, 47; Fordham Univ, AM, 61. **CAREER** Lectr relig, Seton Hall Univ, 51-56, asst prof social studies, 56-61, dir grad info off, 60-79, assoc prof hist, 61-79. NJ Cath Rec Comn, 76- **RESEARCH** Ancient Greece and Rome, early church; Eighteenth century England and Ireland; Renaissance reformation. **SELECTED PUBLICATIONS** Auth, Sir Edmund Plowden and the Province of New Albion, 1632-1650, Hist Rec & Studies; contribr, Ledger of death, Vol I & Anti-Semitism in Soviet Russia, Vol II, The Bridge. **CONTACT ADDRESS** 104 Clark Glen, Ridge, NJ 07028.

KELLEY, BROOKS MATHER
PERSONAL Born 08/18/1929, Lake Forest, IL, m, 1980, 3 children **DISCIPLINE** AMERICAN HISTORY **EDUCATION** Yale Univ, BA, 53, Univ Chicago, MA, 56, PhD, 61. **CAREER** From instr to asst prof hist, 61-67, lectr, 68, cur hist manuscripts, libr & univ archivist, 64-66, dir res, Off Univ Develop, 67, res assoc, 68-73, res fel 73-75, res affiliate hist, Yale Univ, 75-; Writer Am hist, 70-, Vis prof hist, Brown Univ, 69-70. **MEMBERSHIPS** AHA, Orgn Am Historians. **RESEARCH** Educ hist; 19th century Am history. **SELECTED PUBLICATIONS** Auth, Simon Cameron and the senatorial nomination of 1867, 10/63 & Fossildom, old fogeyism, and red tape, 1/66, Pa Mag Hist & Biog; Yale, A History, Yale Univ, 74; New Haven Heritage, New Haven Preservation Trust, 74; coauth (with Daniel J Boorstin), A History of the United States, Ginn & Co, 81. **CONTACT ADDRESS** 91 Andrews Rd, Guilford, CT 06437. **EMAIL** brooks.kelley@aya.yale.edu

KELLEY, DONALD B.
PERSONAL Born 10/04/1937, Charleston, WV, m, 1961, 3 children **DISCIPLINE** AMERICAN INTELLECTUAL HISTORY **EDUCATION** Wheeling Col, BA, 60; Univ Miss, MA, 62; Tulane Univ, PhD, 65. **CAREER** Asst prof, 65-69, dir honors prog, 67-72, Assoc Prof Hist, Villanova Univ, 69-, Vis prof, Univ Kent, 72-73. **MEMBERSHIPS** AHA; AAUP; Southern Hist Asn. **RESEARCH** Am colonial history; Am Quaker history. **SELECTED PUBLICATIONS** The Papers Washington, George, Revolutionary-War Series, Vol 4, April-June 1776, Pa Mag Hist Biog, Vol 118, 94. **CONTACT ADDRESS** Dept of Hist, Villanova Univ, Villanova, PA 19085. **EMAIL** donald.kelley@villanova.edu

KELLEY, DONALD R.
PERSONAL m, 1979, 3 children **DISCIPLINE** EUROPEAN HISTORY **CAREER** James Westfall Thompson Prof Hist, Rutgers, 91- ; exec ed, J of the Hist of Ideas. **HONORS AND AWARDS** Davis Center, Princeton Univ, 87-88; Woodrow Wilson Center, 92-93; Princeton Inst Advanced Stud, 96-97. **MEMBERSHIPS** Am Philos Soc. **SELECTED PUBLICATIONS** Auth, The Human Measure; Social Thought in the Western Legal Tradition, Harvard, 90; auth, Renaissance Humanism, Twayne, 91; auth, the Writing of History and the Study of Law, Variorum, 97; ed, History and the Disciplines: The Reclassification of Knowledge in Early Modern Europe, Rochester, 97; auth, Faces of History: Historical Inquiry from Herodotus to Herder, Yale, 98. **CONTACT ADDRESS** Dept of History, Rutgers, The State Univ of New Jersey, New Brunswick, 88 Col Ave, New Brunswick, NJ 08901. **EMAIL** dkelley@rci.rutgers.edu

KELLEY, JOHN T.
DISCIPLINE HISTORY **EDUCATION** Amherst, BA, 70; Harvard Univ, MA, 71, PhD, 77, MD, 79. **CAREER** Teach fell, hist, Harvard Univ; current, V.P. & Dir of Med Aff, Strat Prdt Plan & Marketplace, HBO & CO. **MEMBERSHIPS** Am Antiquarian Soc **RESEARCH** Am almanacs **SELECTED PUBLICATIONS** Auth, Practical Astronomy During the Seventeenth Century: A Study of Almanac-Makers in America and England, Garland Press, 91. **CONTACT ADDRESS** 5 Country View Rd, Malvern, PA 19355. **EMAIL** john.kelly@hboc.com

KELLEY, MARY
DISCIPLINE HISTORY **EDUCATION** Mt Holyoke, BA, 65; New York Univ, MA, 70; Univ Iowa, PhD, 74. **CAREER** Prof, Wheelock Prof, Hist, Dartmouth Coll. **MEMBERSHIPS** Am Antiquarian Soc **SELECTED PUBLICATIONS** Auth, Private Woman, Public Stage: Literacy Domesticity in Nineteenth-Century America, Oxford Univ Press, 84; coauth, The Units of Sisterhood: The Beecher Sisters on Human Rights and Women's Sphere, Univ NC Press, 88; "'Vindicating the Equality of Female Intellect': Women and Authority in the Early Republic," Prospects: An Ann of Am Cult Stud 17, 92; ed, The Power of Her Sympathy: The Autobiography and Journal of Catherine Maria Sedgwick, Northeastern Univ Press, 93; ed, The Portable Margaret Fuller, Viking, 94; auth, "Designing a Past for the Present: Women Writing Women's History in Nineteenth-Century America," Procs of the AAS 105, 95; auth, "Reading Women/Women Reading: The Making of Learned Women in Antebellum America," Jour of Am Hist LXXXIII, Sept 96. **CONTACT ADDRESS** Dept of Hist, Dartmouth Col, Hanover, NH 03755. **EMAIL** mary.c.kelley@dartmouth.edu

KELLNER, GEORGE
DISCIPLINE AMERICAN IMMIGRATION; URBAN HISTORY; AMERICA, 1815-77 **EDUCATION** Hiram Col, BA; Univ MO, Columbia, MA, PhD. **CAREER** Instr, RI Col. **RESEARCH** Immigration; urban hist; RI hist. **SELECTED PUBLICATIONS** Auth, Providence: A Century of Greatness, 1832-1932, RI Hist; coauth, Rhode Island: The Independent State. **CONTACT ADDRESS** Rhode Island Col, Providence, RI 02908.

KELLOGG, FREDERICK
PERSONAL Born 12/09/1929, Boston, MA, w, 1954, 1 child **DISCIPLINE** HISTORY **EDUCATION** Stanford Univ, AB, 52; Univ Southern Calif, MA, 58; Ind Univ, PhD, 69. **CAREER** Instr to assoc prof, Boise State Univ, 62-67; instr to assoc prof, 67-. **HONORS AND AWARDS** Hon Member, Institutul de istorie "Alexandru D. Xenopol" Romania, 91; Cert of Recognition, Soc for Romanian Studies, 93; Nicholae Iorga Prize, Romanian Acad, 97. **MEMBERSHIPS** AHA; Am Assoc for Advan of Slavic Studies; Soc for Romanian Studies. **RESEARCH** Modern Romanian History. **SELECTED PUBLICATIONS** Auth, A History of Romanian Historical Writing, Charles Schlachs, Jr. Pub, (Bakersfield, CA), 90; auth, The Road to Romanian Independence, Purdue Univ Pr, (West Lafayette), 95; auth, O istorie a istoriografiei romane, Inst **CONTACT ADDRESS** Dept Hist, Univ of Arizona, PO Box 210027, Tucson, AZ 85721-0027. **EMAIL** kellogg@u.arizona.edu

KELLUM, BARBARA
DISCIPLINE VISUAL CULTURE OF THE ANCIENT ROMAN WORLD **EDUCATION** Univ Southern CA, AB, AM; Univ MI, AM; Harvard Univ, PhD. **CAREER** Art, Smith Col. **HONORS AND AWARDS** Initiated, Dept's crse in Art Hist Methods and Film & Art Hist. **RESEARCH** Aspect of life in ancient Roman and Etruscan times. **SELECTED PUBLICATIONS** Publ on, res interest. **CONTACT ADDRESS** Dept of Art, Smith Col, Hillyer Hall 317, Northampton, MA 01063. **EMAIL** bkellum@julia.smith.edu

KELLY, ALFRED HERBERT
PERSONAL Born 02/22/1947, Detroit, MI, m, 1977, 1 child **DISCIPLINE** EUROPEAN INTELLECTUAL & GERMAN HISTORY **EDUCATION** Univ Chicago, BA, 69; Univ Wis, MA, 71 & PhD(hist), 75. **CAREER** Vis asst prof hist, Va Commonwealth Univ, 76-77; adj asst prof, Univ Richmond, 77-78; mem fac, Shimer Col, 80-81; from Asst Prof to Prof, 81-93, Edgar B. Graves prof hist, Hamilton Col, 93-. **MEMBERSHIPS** AHA; Ger Studies Asn. **RESEARCH** Cultural impact of Darwinism; German working class culture; philosophy of history; war memory; nationalism. **SELECTED PUBLICATIONS** Auth, The Descent of Darwin: The Popularization of Darwinisim in Germany, 1860-1914, Univ NC Press, 81; ed & transl, The German Worker: Working-Class Autobiographies from the Age of Industrialization, Univ Calif Press, 87. **CONTACT ADDRESS** Hist Dept, Hamilton Col, New York, 198 College Hill Rd., Clinton, NY 13323-1292. **EMAIL** akelly@hamilton.edu

KELLY, CATHIE
DISCIPLINE RENAISSANCE AND BAROQUE ART AND ARCHITECTURE **EDUCATION** Pa State Univ, PHD, 80. **CAREER** Instr, Univ Nev, Las Vegas, 80. **HONORS AND AWARDS** Outstanding Tchr of the Yr Awd, Univ Nev, Las Vegas. **RESEARCH** Rome. **SELECTED PUBLICATIONS** Published in architectural history journals, as well as in collected essay volumes. **CONTACT ADDRESS** Univ of Nevada, Las Vegas, Las Vegas, NV 89154.

KELLY, DAVID H.
PERSONAL Born 11/10/1942, Chicago, IL, m, 1992, 2 children **DISCIPLINE** HISTORY **EDUCATION** Univ Chicago, BA, 65; Ind Univ, MA, 68, PhD, 76. **CAREER** Bibliographic res, Univ Wi, 70-74; hist to adjunct to prof, D'Youville Col, 75-. **MEMBERSHIPS** OAH; AHA. **RESEARCH** Social & institutional history **SELECTED PUBLICATIONS** Coauth, Women's Education in the Third World: An Annotated Bibliography of Published Research, 89; ed, Women's Education: a Selected Bibliography of Published Works, International Handbook of Women's Education, Greenwood Press, 89; auth, Women in Higher Education: A Select International Bibliography, St Univ NY, Buffalo, 90; ed, International Feminist Perspectives on Educational Reform, the Work of Gail Kelly, 96; ed, French Colonial Education by Gail Kelly, AMS, 00. **CONTACT ADDRESS** 131 Greenfield, Buffalo, NY 14214.

KELLY, THOMAS
DISCIPLINE HISTORY **EDUCATION** Univ Ill, PhD, 64. **CAREER** Prof **RESEARCH** Greek history. **SELECTED PUBLICATIONS** Auth, A History of Argos To 500 B.C., 77. **CONTACT ADDRESS** History Dept, Univ of Minnesota, Twin Cities, 614 Social Sciences Tower, 267 19th Ave. S, Minneapolis, MN 55455. **EMAIL** kelly004@tc.umn.edu

KEMENY, P
PERSONAL Born 12/13/1960, Morristown, NJ, m, 1983, 1 child **DISCIPLINE** AMERICAN RELIGIOUS HISTORY **EDUCATION** Wake Forest, BA, 83; Westminster Sem, MAR, 86, MDiv, 87; Duke Univ, ThM, 88; Princeton Sem, PhD, 95. **CAREER** Vis fel, ctr stud (s) Amer Rel, Princeton Univ, 95-96; asst prof, Rel, Calvin Col, 96- . **HONORS AND AWARDS** Woodrow Wilson awd, 97 **MEMBERSHIPS** AAR; HEQ; AHA; ASOH; Conf Earth Hist. **CONTACT ADDRESS** Dept of Relig and Philos, Grove City Col, 100 Campus Dr, Grove City, PA 16127-2104.

KEMP, HENRIETTA J.
DISCIPLINE GERMAN, HISTORY, LIBRARY SCIENCE **EDUCATION** Univ Iowa, BA, 66; Univ Pittsburgh, MLS, 71. **CAREER** LIBR, 81-, SUPERV, FINE ARTS COLLECT, 89-, LUTHER COL. **CONTACT ADDRESS** Library, Luther Col, 700 College Dr, Decorah, IA 52101. **EMAIL** kempjane@luther.edu

KENEZ, PETER
PERSONAL Born 04/05/1937, Budapest, Hungary, m, 1959 **DISCIPLINE** RUSSIAN HISTORY **EDUCATION** Princeton Univ, BA, 60; Harvard Univ, MA, 62, PhD, 67. **CAREER** From asst prof to assoc prof, 66-75, prof hist, Univ CA, Santa Cruz,75, Int Res & Exchange Bd studies grant in USSR, 69-70; nat fel, Hoover Inst, 73-74. **RESEARCH** Russ revolution and civil war; hist of the Russ Army. **SELECTED PUBLICATIONS** Auth, The volunteer army and Georgia, Slavonic Rev, 70; Civil War in South Russia, 1918, 71 & Coalition politics in the Hungarian Soviet Republic, In: Revolution in Perspective, 72, Univ CA; A profile of the pre-revolutionary officer corps, Calif Slavic Studies, 73; Civil War in South Russia, 1919-1920, Univ CA, 76; The birth of the propaganda state: Soviet methods of mobilization, 1917-29, Cambridge Univ, 85; Co-ed (with Abbott Gleason and Richard Stites), Bolsheviks culture, Ind Univ, 85; Cinema in Soviet society, 1917-1953, Cambridge Univ, 92; Varieties of fear, Am Univ, 95; A history of the Soviet Union from the beginning to the end, Cambridge Univ, 99. **CONTACT ADDRESS** Dept of Hist, Univ of California, Santa Cruz, 1156 High St, Santa Cruz, CA 95064-0001.

KENFIELD, JOHN F., III
DISCIPLINE ART HISTORY **EDUCATION** Princeton Univ, PhD. **CAREER** Assoc prof, Rutgers Univ. **RESEARCH** Greek sculpture with emphasis on the Hellenistic and archaic periods, espec Western Greece or Magna Graecia (Southern Italy and Sicily). **SELECTED PUBLICATIONS** Auth, The Mosaics and Wall Paintings in The Palatial Late Roman Villa at Castle Copse, Great Bedwyn, Wiltshire, Ind UP, 97; An East Greek Master Coroplast at late Archaic Morgantina, Hesperia, 90; A Modelled Terracotta Frieze from Archaic Morgantina: Its East Greek and Central Italic Affinities, Deliciae Fictiles, 93; The Case for a Phokaian Presence at Archaic Morgantina as Evidenced by the Site's Archaic Architectural Terracottas, Varia Anatolica III, 93; High Classical and High Baroque in the Architectural Terracottas of Morgantina, Hesperia Suppl, 94. **CONTACT ADDRESS** Dept of Art Hist, Rutgers, The State Univ of New Jersey, Rutgers Col, Hamilton St., New Brunswick, NJ 08903.

KENNEDY, DANE KEITH
PERSONAL Born 05/30/1951, Bonne Terre, MO, m, 1974, 1 child **DISCIPLINE** BRITISH & COMMONWEALTH HISTORY **EDUCATION** Univ Calif, Berkeley, BA, 73, MA, 75, PhD(Brit hist), 81. **CAREER** Prof And Ch Brit Hist, Univ Nebr-Lincoln, 81-00; prof and Elmer Louis Keyser Chair in Hist, George Washington Univ, 00-. **HONORS AND AWARDS** Fel, Royal Hist Soc; Distinguished Teaching Awd, Univ Nebr, 89. **MEMBERSHIPS** Am Hist Asn; Conf Brit Studies; World Hist Asn. **RESEARCH** British colonialism in Africa and India. **SELECTED PUBLICATIONS** Auth, Islands of White: Settler Society & Culture in Kenya and Southern Rhodesia, 1890-1939, Duke Univ Press, 87; The Magic Mountains: Hill Stations and the British Raj, Berkeley: Univ Calif Press, 96, Delhi: Oxford Univ Press, 96; numerous articles in: J of Mod Hist; J of Brit Studies; Int J of African Hist Studies;

Albion; South Asia; Clio; J of Imperial and Commonwealth Hist; The Nation; and others. **CONTACT ADDRESS** History Dept, The George Washington Univ, Washington, DC 20052. **EMAIL** dkennedy@unlinfo.unl.edu

KENNEDY, DAVID M.
PERSONAL Born 07/22/1941, Seattle, WA, m, 1970, 3 children **DISCIPLINE** HISTORY **EDUCATION** Stanford, BA, 63; Yale, MA, 64; PhD, 68. **CAREER** Harmsworth prof, Oxford Univ, 95-96; asst to full prof, Stanford Univ, 67- . **HONORS AND AWARDS** ACLS fel, 71-72; Guggenheim fel, 75-76; Dean's Awd Outstanding Teaching, 88; Bancroft Prize, 71; Francis Parkman Prize, 00; Pulitzer Prize, 00. **MEMBERSHIPS** Orgn Am Hist; Am Hist Asn; Soc Am Hist. **RESEARCH** American history. **SELECTED PUBLICATIONS** Auth, Birth Control in America: The Career of Margaret Sanger, (70); auth, Over Here: The First World War & American Society, (80); auth, Freedom from Fear: The American People in Depression & War, 1929-1945, (00). **CONTACT ADDRESS** Dept Hist, Stanford Univ, Bldg 200, Stanford, CA 94305. **EMAIL** DMK@stanford.edu

KENNEDY, JAMES C.
PERSONAL Born 09/02/1963, Orange City, IA, m, 1994, 2 children **DISCIPLINE** HISTORY **EDUCATION** Georgetown Univ, BSc, 86; Calvin Col, MA, 88; Univ Iowa, 95. **CAREER** Lectr, Northwestern Col, 90-91; asst prof, Hope Col, 97-. **HONORS AND AWARDS** Fulbright Scholar, Neth; Lilly Fel, Valparaiso Univ, 95-97; Res Fel, Hope Col. **MEMBERSHIPS** AHA **RESEARCH** Pre-history of euthanasia in the Netherlands. **SELECTED PUBLICATIONS** Auth, Nieuw Babylon in aanbouw: Nederland in de Jaren Zestig, Boom (Amsterdam, Neth), 95. **CONTACT ADDRESS** Dept Hist, Hope Col, 280 W 12th St, Holland, MI 49423. **EMAIL** kennedy@hope.edu

KENNEDY, JANET
PERSONAL Born 06/18/1948, Baltimore, MD **DISCIPLINE** MODERN ART **EDUCATION** Columbia Univ, PhD. **CAREER** Prof **RESEARCH** Turn-of-the-century Russian art; Reception of Russian Art **SELECTED PUBLICATIONS** Auth, Mir iskustva, 77; Shrovetide Revelry: Alexandre Benois's Contribution to Petrushka; Line of Succession: Three Productions of Tchaikovsky's Sleeping Beauty; auth, "Shrovetide Revelry" appeared in Petrushka: Sources and Contexts, edited by Andrew Wachtel, "Lines of Succession" appeared in Tchaikovsky and His World, edited by Leslie Kearney; auth, "The World of Art and Other Turn-of-the-Century Russian Art Journals, 1898-1910" in Defining Russian Graphic Arts, edited by Alla Rosenfeld. **CONTACT ADDRESS** Dept of History and Art, Indiana Univ, Bloomington, 300 N Jordan Ave, Bloomington, IN 47405. **EMAIL** kennedy@indiana.edu

KENNEDY, LAWRENCE W.
PERSONAL Born 08/04/1952, Riverside, CA, m, 1974, 2 children **DISCIPLINE** HISTORY **EDUCATION** Boston Col, BA, polit sci, 75, MA, hist, 78, PhD, hist, 87. **CAREER** St Sebastian's Country Day Sch, 75-76; Boston Col HS, teacher, 76-85; Univ Mass, Northeastern univ, Tufts univ, adjunt faculty, 87-92; Boston Redel Auth, consult histn, 87-92; Boston col, lectr, 87-92; asst prof, 92-98; Univ Scranton, assoc prof, 98-. **HONORS AND AWARDS** Outstanding Fac Mem Awd, 98; Alph Sigma Nu, 98; Phi Alpha Theta, 93; Who's Who in the East, 96-00; Intl Writ and Auth's Who's Who, 97. **MEMBERSHIPS** Am Cath Hist Asn; NEHA; OAH; Soc of Hist of the Gilded Age and Progress Era; Urban Hist Asn. **RESEARCH** Boston; urban; ethnic; religious hist; planning hist and architectural **SELECTED PUBLICATIONS** Boston: A Topographical History, co auth Walter Muir Whitehill, 3d ed, Cambridge MA, Harvard Univ Press, 00; Planning the City upon a Hill: Boston since 1630, Amherst MA, Univ Mass Press, 92; pp bk 94; Boston's First Irish Mayor: Hugh O' Brien, 1885-1889, in: Mass Politics: Selected Hist Essays, Westfield MA, Inst Mass Stud, 98; numerous other articles. **CONTACT ADDRESS** Dept History, Univ of Scranton, 800 Linden St, Scranton, PA 18510. **EMAIL** lawrence.kennedy@uofs.edu

KENNEDY, RICK
PERSONAL Born 03/22/1958, Olatle, KS, m, 1979, 3 children **DISCIPLINE** HISTORY **EDUCATION** Univ Calif, Santa Barbara, BA, 80; MA, 83; PhD, 87. **CAREER** Asst lectr, Col of William and Mary, 86; asst lectr, Univ of Calif Santa Barbara, 86-87; lectr, Santa Barbara City Col, 87; asst prof to assoc prof, Ind Univ Southeast 87-96; vis asst prof, to prof, Point Loma Nazarene Col, 95-. **RESEARCH** Intellectual and Cultural History of Early America. **SELECTED PUBLICATIONS** Auth, "John Henry Newman, Henry Adams, and Albert Einstein: Mining History for Lasting Values", Thresholds I (85): 66-79; auth, "Thomas Brattle: A Mathematician-Architect in the Transition of the New England Mind, 1690-1700", Winterthur Portfolio 24 (89): 231-245; auth, "Thomas Brattle and the Provincialism of New England Science, 1690-1720", New England Quarterly 63, (90): 584-600; auth, "The Alliance Between Puritanism and Cartesian Logic at Harvard", J of the Hist of Ideas 51 (90): 549-572; auth, "The Application of Mathematics to Christian Apologetics in Pascal's Pensees and Arnauld's The Port-Royal Logic", Fides et Historia 23 (91): 37-52; auth, "Miracles in the Dock: A Critique of the Historical Profession's Special Treatment of Alleged Spiritual Events", Fides et Historia 26, (94): 7-22; auth, Aristotelian and Cartesian Logic at Harvard: Morton's System of Logick and Brattle's Compendium of Logick, Univ Pr of Va, 95; auth, "Faith and History: Toward a Better Understanding of Balancing of Likelihoods", Fides et Historia 29 (97): 66-73; coauth, "In Usum Pupillorum: Student-Transcribed Texts at Harvard College Before 1740", Proceedings of The Am Antiquarian Soc 109, 99; coauth, "Increase Mather's Catechismus Logicus: A Translation and the Role of a late Ramist Catechism in Harvard's Curriculum", Proceedings of the Am Antiquarian Soc 109, 99. **CONTACT ADDRESS** Dept Hist and Govt, Point Loma Nazarene Col, 3900 Lomaland Dr, San Diego, CA 92106-2810. **EMAIL** rkennedy@ptloma.edu

KENNEDY, THOMAS C.
DISCIPLINE HISTORY **EDUCATION** Univ SC, PhD. **CAREER** Prof. **RESEARCH** 19th and 20th Century Britain; imperialism. **SELECTED PUBLICATIONS** Auth, Female Friends and the Pacifist Impulse, Univ Toronto, 96; Comments on Military/Civilian Relations in Britain and Germany, Univ Tex, 90; auth, British Quakerism, 1860-1920: The Transformation of a Religious Community, Oxford Univ Press, forthcoming; auth, "What Hath Manchester Wrought? Change in the British Society of Friends, 1895-1920," Jrnl of the Friends Historical Soc, 57/3 (96). **CONTACT ADDRESS** History Dept, Univ of Arkansas, Fayetteville, 409 Old Main, Fayetteville, AR 72701. **EMAIL** tkennedy@comp.uark.edu

KENNEDY, THOMAS L.
PERSONAL Born 05/09/1930, Newark, NJ, w, 3 children **DISCIPLINE** CHINESE AND EAST ASIAN HISTORY **EDUCATION** Columbia Univ, PhD, 68. **CAREER** Prof, Washington State Univ. **HONORS AND AWARDS** Assoc for Asian Studies; Historical Society for Twentieth Century China; Second Marine Divison Association; late 19th and 20th century modernization and social history. **SELECTED PUBLICATIONS** Auth, Testimony of a Confucian Women: The Autobiography of Mrs. Nie Zeng Jifen, 1852-1942, Univ Ga Press, 93; Li Translator: Testimony of A Confucian Woman, Univ of GA Press, 93; Hung-chang and the Kiangnan Arsenal, 1860-1865, Li Hung-chang and China's Early Modernization," Sichuan Univ Press, PRC, 94; auth, "Confucian Feminist," American Philosophical Society, 01. **CONTACT ADDRESS** Dept of History, Washington State Univ, 301 Wilson Hall, PO Box 644030, Pullman, WA 99164-4030. **EMAIL** kennedyt@wsunix.wsu.edu

KENNEDY, W. BENJAMIN
PERSONAL Born 04/15/1938, Tifton, GA, m, 1959, 3 children **DISCIPLINE** MODERN EUROPEAN HISTORY **EDUCATION** Georgetown Col, AB, 60; Univ NC, MA, 62; Univ Ga, PhD, 66. **CAREER** From instr to assoc prof, 62-76, from actg head dept to head dept, 67-71, prof hist, State Univ of Western Goergia, 76- . **MEMBERSHIPS** AHA; Soc Fr Hist Studies. **RESEARCH** Military history in the French Revolution; 18th century Europe. **SELECTED PUBLICATIONS** Auth, Without any guarantee on our part: The French Directory's Irish policy, In: Proceedings of the Consortium on Revolutionary Europe, Univ Fla, 73; ed, Siege of Savannah in 1779, Beehive, 74; The Irish Jacobins, Studia Hibernica, Dublin, 76; The French are on the sea: Irish, French and British reactions to the abortive bantry expedition in 1796, Proceedings Western Soc Fr Hist, 77; auth, Biographical sketches of William Duckett, William Jackson, Edward John Lewines, Henry Sheares, Matthew Tone, In: Biographical Dictionary of Modern British Radicals, Harvester, 79; Conspiracy tinged with blarney: Wolfe Tone and other Irish emissaries to Revolutionary France, Proceedings of the Consortium on Revolutionary Europe, Univ Ga, 80. **CONTACT ADDRESS** 617 Scataway Rd., Hiawassee, GA 30546.

KENNY, KEVIN
PERSONAL Born 07/11/1960, London, England, m, 1992, 1 child **DISCIPLINE** HISTORY **EDUCATION** Univ Edinburgh UK, BA, MA 87; Columbia Univ, MA 89, MPhil 90, PhD 94. **CAREER** CUNY, City Col, adj instr, 93-94; Columbia Univ, vis asst prof, 95; Univ Texas Austin, asst prof, 94-99; assoc prof, Boston Col, 99-. **HONORS AND AWARDS** Whiting Foun Fel; Albert J Beveridge Res Grant; Res Grants, Irish Am Cultural Inst, 95, 99; Junior Fac Fel, British Studies Sem, Univ of Tex, 96-99; Bancroft Dissertation Awd, 95; Styskal Res Fel, City Univ of New York Grad Ctr, 91-92 **MEMBERSHIPS** AHA; OAH; ASA. **RESEARCH** US Labor and Immigration; Irish studies. **SELECTED PUBLICATIONS** Auth, Making Sense of the Molly Maguires, NY, Oxford U Press, 98; The American Irish: A Concise History Since 1700, Addison Wesley Longman, 01; Development of the Working Classes, Blackwell Companion to Nineteenth-Century America, Blackwell, 99; co-auth, Ethnicity and Immigration in The New American History, rev ed, Temple Univ Press, 97, pamphlet in series, The New American History, AHA; The Molly Maguires in Popular Culture, Jour of Amer Ethnic Hist, 95; The Molly Maguires and the Catholic Church, Labor Hist, 95. **CONTACT ADDRESS** Dept of Hist, Boston Col, Chestnut Hill, 140 Commonwealth Ave., Chestnut Hill, MA 02467-3930. **EMAIL** kennyka@bc.edu

KENSETH, JOY
DISCIPLINE ART HISTORY **EDUCATION** Hiram Col, BA; Harvard Univ, MA, PhD. **CAREER** Prof, Dartmouth Col. **RESEARCH** Sculpture of Bernini; painting of Caravaggio; the art of dying in Roman Baroque sculpture. **SELECTED PUBLICATIONS** Auth, The Age of the Marvelous (exh cat), 91; Bernini's David, excerpts of studies p ubl in Basic Design: Systems, Elements, Application, Prentice Hall, 83; var a rticles. **CONTACT ADDRESS** Dartmouth Col, 3529 N Main St, Ste. 207, Hanover, NH 03755. **EMAIL** joy.kenseth@dartmouth.edu

KENT, ROBERT B.
DISCIPLINE GEOGRAPHY AND PLANNING **EDUCATION** Univ Calif, Davis, BA, 73, MA, 76; Syracuse Univ, PhD, 83. **CAREER** Prof, Geography and Planning, Univ Akron, 94-. **HONORS AND AWARDS** Fulbright Scholar, Argentina, 93-94; Chair, Conf of Latin Americanist Geographers, 94-96. **MEMBERSHIPS** Conf of Latin Americanist Geographers, Asn of Am Geog. **RESEARCH** Human geography of Latin America, cartography/GIS, regional planning. **SELECTED PUBLICATIONS** Auth, "Peru," in Latin American Urbanization: Historical Profiles of Major Cities, ed by Gerald M. Greenfield, Westport, CN: Greenwood Press (94): 446-467; co-ed, Regional Development and Planning for the 21st Century, Aldershot, UK: Ashgate Pub (98); auth, "Currents of change: Urban planning and regional development," in Regional Development and Planning for the 21st Century, Aldershot, UK: Ashgate Pub (98); auth, "Circular and rectangle folk silos in the Andes of Southern Bolivia," Espacio y Desarrollo, 10 (98): 141-150; coauth with Abigail Byer Smith, "Map use in comprehensive city plans," Applied Geographical Studies, 3, 1 (99): 45-62; auth, "The Puerto Rican residential landscape of Lorain, Ohio," Yearbook, Conf of Latin Am Geographers 25 (99): 45-60; coauth with Richard E. Klosterman, "GIS and mapping: Pitfalls for planners," J of the Am Planning Asn (forthcoming 2000). **CONTACT ADDRESS** Dept Geography and Planning, Univ of Akron, Akron, OH 44325-5005. **EMAIL** rkent@uakron.edu

KENT, SUSAN
PERSONAL Born 05/09/1952, Cincinnati, OH **DISCIPLINE** HISTORY **EDUCATION** Suffolk Univ, BS, 78; Brandeis Univ, MA, 81; PhD, 84. **CAREER** Asst to assoc prof, Univ of Fla, 88-93; assoc to prof, Univ of Colo, 93-. **HONORS AND AWARDS** NEH Fel, 93-94; Fel, Inst for Advan Study, 93-94. **MEMBERSHIPS** AHA, N Am Conf of British Studies, Berkshire Conf on Womens Hist. **RESEARCH** British history (18th century - present), gender, World War I and interwar period. **SELECTED PUBLICATIONS** Auth, Sex and Suffrage in Britian, 1860-1914, Princeton, 87; auth, Making Peace: The Reconstruction of Gender in Interwar Britian, Princeton, 93; auth, Gender and Power in Britain, 1640-1990, Routledge, 99. **CONTACT ADDRESS** Dept Hist, Univ of Colorado, Boulder, Hellems Bldg Rm 204, 234 UCB, Boulder, CO 80309. **EMAIL** susan.kent@colorado.edu

KENZER, ROBERT C.
PERSONAL Born 02/11/1955, Chicago, IL, m, 1976, 1 child **DISCIPLINE** HISTORY **EDUCATION** Univ of Calif Santa Barbara, BA, 76; Harvard Univ, MA, 77; PhD, 82. **CAREER** Instr, Harvard Univ, 81-82; asst prof to assoc prof, Brigham Young Univ, 82-93; asst prof to prof, Univ of Richmond, 93- . **HONORS AND AWARDS** Brigham Young Univ Alumni Assoc, Hist Teacher of the Year, 84, 86, 87; Archie K. Davis Res Fel, NC Soc, 88; Donald B. Hoffman Awd for Best Phi Alpha Theta Fac Advisor, 88; Albert J. Beveridge Res Grant, AHA, 88. **MEMBERSHIPS** AHA; Orgn of Am Hist; S Hist Assoc; Soc of Civil War Hist; Museum of the Confederacy, Va Hist Soc. **RESEARCH** Civil War and Reconstruction Era, American South. **SELECTED PUBLICATIONS** Auth, Kinship and Neighborhood in a Southern Community: Orange County, North Carolina, 1849-1881, Univ of Tenn Pr, 87; auth, The Black Businessman in the Postwar South: North Carolina, 1865-1880, Bus Hist Rev 63 (Spring 89):61-87; auth, Enterprising Southerners: Black Economic Success in North Carolina, 1865-1915, Univ Pr of Va, 97; auth, "South, Black Business, 1860-1880" in Encycl of African Am Bus Hist, ed, Juliet E.K. Walker, Greenwood Pr, 99; coed, Enemies of My Country: New Perspectives on Unionists in the Civil War South, Univ of Ga Pr (forthcoming). **CONTACT ADDRESS** Dept Hist, Univ of Richmond, 28 Westhampton Way, Richmond, VA 73173. **EMAIL** rkenzer@richmond.edu

KEPLER, JON S.
PERSONAL Born 12/05/1939, Tulsa, OK, m, 1967, 3 children **DISCIPLINE** HISTORY **EDUCATION** Univ Tulsa, BA, 62, MA, 66; Univ London, London Sch Economics and Political Sci, RFS, 69-70; Univ Kans, PhD, 72. **CAREER** Archivist, Dwight D. Eisenhower Presidential Library, 72-75; assoc prof, Marymount Col of Kans, 75-86; assoc prof, Mo Western State Col, 86-. **HONORS AND AWARDS** F. B. Pariott Fel, Univ Tulsa, 63; NDEA Title IV Fel, Univ Kans, 67-70. **MEMBERSHIPS** Am Hist Soc. **RESEARCH** English maritime and economic history in the Medieval and Early Modern Periods. **SELECTED PUBLICATIONS** Auth, "Fiscal Aspects of the English Carrying Trade during the Thirty Years War," EcHR (72); auth, "The Effects of the Battle of Sluys upon the Administration of English Naval Impressment, 1340-43," Speculum

(73); auth, The Exchange of Christendom: The International Entrepot at Dover, 1622-1651, Leicester (76); auth, "Estimates of the Volume of Direct Shipments of Tobacco and Sugar from the Chief English Plantations to European Markets, 1620-1669," J of European Economic History (99). **CONTACT ADDRESS** Dept Soc Sci, Missouri Western State Col, 4525 Downs Dr, Saint Joseph, MO 64507-2294. **EMAIL** kepler@griffon.mwsc.edu

KERBER, LINDA KAUFMAN
PERSONAL Born 01/23/1940, New York, NY, m, 1960, 2 children **DISCIPLINE** AMERICAN HISTORY **EDUCATION** Barnard Col, AB, 60; NYork Univ, MA, 61; Columbia Univ, PhD, 68. **CAREER** Instr hist, Stern Col, Yeshiva Univ, 63-67, asst prof, 68; instr, San Jose State Col, 69-70; vis asst prof, Stanford Univ, 70-71; assoc prof, 71-75, prof hist, Univ IA, 75-, May Brodbeck Prof Lib Arts & Prof Hist, 85; Penrose Fund grant; Am Philos Soc, 71-72; fel, National Endowment for Humanities, 76, 83, 94; mem ann prize comt, Am Quart, 76-78; biog jury, Pulitzer Prize, 77-78; J S Guggenheim Found, Nat Humanities Center, Rockefeller Found Residency, Bellagio. **HONORS AND AWARDS** Phi Beta Kappa Nat Vis Scholar, 98-99; Joan Kelly Memorial Prize, Littleton Griswold Prize. **MEMBERSHIPS** AHA; Orgn Am Historians, Pres, 96-97; Am Studies Asn, pres 88-89; Am Acad Arts & Sci; PEN/American Center; Soc Am Historians; Berkshire Conf Women Hist; Am Soc Legal Hist. **RESEARCH** US; women's hist; US Legal history. **SELECTED PUBLICATIONS** Auth, Federalists in Dissent: Imagery and Ideology in Jeffersonian America, Cornell Univ, 70, paperback, 80; Women of the Republic: Intellect and ideology in revolutionary America, Univ NC Press, 80, 2nd paperback, W W Norton, 86, 3rd paperback, UNC Press, 97; co-ed (with Jane Sherron De Hart), Women's America: Refocusing the Past, Oxford Univ Press, 82, 5th ed, 00; co-ed (with Emory Elliott, A Walton Litz and Terence Martin), American Literature: An Anthology, 2 vol, Prentice-Hall, 91; co-ed (with Alice Kessler-Harris and Kathryn Kish Sklar), U S History as Women's History: New Feminist Essays, UNC Press, 95; Toward an Intellectual History of Women: Essays by Linda K Kerber, UNC Press, 97; No Constitutional Right to Be Ladies: Women and the Obligations of Citizenship, Hill and Wang, 9/98. **CONTACT ADDRESS** Dept of Hist, Univ of Iowa, 280 Schaeffer Hall, Iowa City, IA 52242-1409. **EMAIL** linda-kerber@uiowa.edu

KERN, GILBERT RICHARD
PERSONAL Born 12/05/1932, Detroit, MI, 6 children **DISCIPLINE** CHURCH & AMERICAN HISTORY **EDUCATION** Findlay Col, AB, 54; Winebrenner Theol Sem, BD, 58; Univ Chicago, MA, 60, PhD, 68. **CAREER** From lectr to prof church hist, Winebrenner Theol Sem, 60-70, pres, 63-70; Prof Relig, 70-75, Prof Hist, 75-98, Professor Emeritus, The Univ of Findlay, 98-; Lectr Hist, Winebrenner Theol Sem, 72-84. **HONORS AND AWARDS** Dist Alumni Awd, Univ Findlay, 89. **MEMBERSHIPS** Am Soc Church Hist; Am Hist Asn. **RESEARCH** Nineteenth century Am church. **SELECTED PUBLICATIONS** Auth, John Winebrenner: 19th Century Reformer, Cent Publ House 74; Findlay College: The first one hundred years, 82. **CONTACT ADDRESS** Dept Hist, Univ of Findlay, 1000 N Main St, Findlay, OH 45840-3695. **EMAIL** kern@lucy.findlay.edu

KERN, ROBERT
DISCIPLINE IBERIAN HISTORY, MODERN EUROPE **EDUCATION** Univ Chicago, PhD. **CAREER** Prof emer, Univ NMex. **HONORS AND AWARDS** Grant, Harkness Found, NEH, Am Philos Soc. **RESEARCH** Western U.S. labor. **SELECTED PUBLICATIONS** Auth, Caciquismo and the Luso-Hispanic World, 72; Liberals, Reformers, and Caciques in Restoration Spain, 74; Red Years/Black Years: The Political History of Spanish Liberalism, 78; The Labor History of New Mexico, 83; Building New Mexico, 84; The Regions of Spain, 95; coauth, European Women on the Left, 82; Historical Dictionary of Modern Spain, 1700 to Present, 90. **CONTACT ADDRESS** Dept of Hist, Univ of New Mexico, Albuquerque, Albuquerque, NM 87131-1181.

KERN, STEPHEN R.
PERSONAL Born 01/28/1943, Los Angeles, CA, m, 1983, 2 children **DISCIPLINE** HISTORY **EDUCATION** Univ Calif, Berkeley, BA, 64; Columbia Univ, PhD, 70. **CAREER** Preceptor, Columbia Univ, 66-68; asst prof, Northern Ill Univ, 70-77, asst prof and adminr, NIU Salzburg Prog, fall 71, assoc prof, 77-84, prof, 84-. **HONORS AND AWARDS** Rockefeller Fel, 77-78; Honorary Res Fel, Harvard Univ, Center for European Studies, 77-78; NEH Fel, 98-99. **RESEARCH** Modern European intellectual history; time, space, vision, causality, crime. **SELECTED PUBLICATIONS** Auth, Anatomy and Destiny: A Cultural History of the Human Body, Bobbs-Merrill: New York (75); auth, The Culture of Time and Space 1880-1918, Harvard Univ Press: Cambridge, MA (83); auth, The Culture of Love: Victorians to Moderns, Harvard Univ Press: Cambridge, MA (92); auth, Eyes of Love: The Gaze in French and English Paintings and Novels, 1840-1900, Reaktion Books: London (96). **CONTACT ADDRESS** Dept Hist, No Illinois Univ, 1425 W Lincoln Hwy, Dekalb, IL 60115-2828. **EMAIL** skern@elnet.com

KERR, KATHEL AUSTIN
PERSONAL Born 08/29/1938, St. Louis, MO, m, 1967, 3 children **DISCIPLINE** RECENT AMERICAN HISTORY **EDUCATION** Oberlin Col, AB, 59; Univ Iowa, MA, 60; Univ Pittsburgh, PhD, 65. **CAREER** Asst prof, 65-72, assoc prof hist, Ohio State Univ, Columbus, 72-; prof hist, Ohio State Univ, Columbus, 84; Fulbright lectr, Univ Tokyo & Waseda Univ, Japan, 73. **HONORS AND AWARDS** Sr Fulbright Lectr, Univ Tokyo, Waseda Univ, Japan, 73; Sr Fulbright Lectr, Univ Hamburg, Germany, 82-83. **MEMBERSHIPS** Am Hist Asn; Business Hist Conf; Ohio Acad of Hist; Ohio Hist Soc; Alcohol & Temperance Hist Group; Orgn Hist. **RESEARCH** American political and business history. **SELECTED PUBLICATIONS** Auth, Organized for Prohibition: An New History of the Anti-Saloon League, Yale University, 85; auth, Local Businesses: Exploring Their History, American Association State and Local History, 90; auth, BF Goodrich: Traditions and Transformations, Ohio State University, 96. **CONTACT ADDRESS** Dept of History, Ohio State Univ, Columbus, 230 W 17th Ave, Columbus, OH 43210-1361. **EMAIL** kerr.6@osu.edu

KERR-RITCHIE, JEFFREY R.
DISCIPLINE HISTORY **EDUCATION** Kingston Polytech, BA, 84; Univ Pa, MA, 87; Univ Pa, PhD, 93. **CAREER** Teaching Asst, Univ Pa, 86-90; Asst Prof, Wesleyan Univ, 92-. **HONORS AND AWARDS** Fulbright-Hays, 85; WEB De Bois Awd for Acad Excellence, Univ Pa, 88; Fel, Va Hist Soc, 92; Ford Grants for Res, 96; Meigs Grant for Res, 97; Caleb T Winchester Teaching Awd, Psi Upsilon, Wesleyan Univ, 99. **SELECTED PUBLICATIONS** Auth, "Emancipation from the Communist Manifesto," Nature, Soc, Thought 10:4 (99): 523-538; auth, Freed People in the Tobacco South, Virginia 1860-1900, Univ NC Pr (Chapel Hill, NC), 99; auth, "The Atlantic Basin in the Era of the Slave Trade," in Encycl of African Hist (London: Fitzroy Dearborn Publ, 00-01); auth, "African Americans," in Encycl of Contemp Am Cult (London: Routledge, 00-01. **CONTACT ADDRESS** Dept Hist, Wesleyan Univ, Middletown, CT 06459-0002. **EMAIL** jkerrritchie@wesleyan.edu

KERSEY, HARRY A.
DISCIPLINE HISTORY **EDUCATION** Univ Ill, PhD. **CAREER** Prof. **MEMBERSHIPS** Am Philos Soc; Am Asn State Local Hist. **RESEARCH** Southeastern Native American history; Florida history. **SELECTED PUBLICATIONS** Auth, Pelts, Plumes and Hides: White Traders Among the Seminole Indians 1870-1930; An Assumption of Sovereignty: Social and Political transformation Among the Florida Seminoles 1953-1979, 96. **CONTACT ADDRESS** History Dept, Florida Atlantic Univ, 777 Glades Rd, Boca Raton, FL 33431.

KESELMAN, THOMAS A.
PERSONAL Born 12/21/1948, Perth, NJ, m, 1973, 3 children **DISCIPLINE** HISTORY **EDUCATION** Univ MI, Ann Arbor, PhD 79. **CAREER** Univ Notre Dame, asst prof 79-84, assoc prof 85-91, prof 92. **HONORS AND AWARDS** John Gilmart Shea Prize; NEH Fell; Guggenheim Fell. **MEMBERSHIPS** AHS; Soc for Fr Hist Stud; WSFH; ACHS; ASCH. **RESEARCH** Mod France; Modern Europe, Religious Hist. **SELECTED PUBLICATIONS** Death and Afterlife in Modern France, Prin, Prin Univ Press, 93; Miracles and Prophecies in Nineteenth Century France, New Brunswick, NJ, Rutgers Univ Press, 83; Belief in History: Innovative Approaches to European and American Religion, Notre Dame, Univ Notre Dame, 91; The Perraud Affair: Clergy, Church, and Sexual Politics in Fin-de-Siecle France, Journal of Modern Hist, 98; Religion as Enduring Theme in French Cultural Conflict, in: Memory, History and Critique: Europea Identity at the Millennium, eds, Frank Brinkhuis and Sascha Talmor, Cambridge, MIT Press, 97. **CONTACT ADDRESS** Dept of Hist, Univ of Notre Dame, Notre Dame, IN 46656. **EMAIL** thomas.a.kselman.1@nd.edu

KESSELMAN, AMY
PERSONAL Born 06/01/1944, New York, NY, s **DISCIPLINE** HISTORY **EDUCATION** Cornell Univ, PhD, 85. **CAREER** SUNY New Paltz, 81-. **HONORS AND AWARDS** Gustaves Myers Awd, 91. **RESEARCH** Women's History. **SELECTED PUBLICATIONS** Auth, Women: Images and Realities, A Multicultural Anthology, Mayfield. **CONTACT ADDRESS** Dept Hist, SUNY, New Paltz, 75 S Manheim Blvd, New Paltz, NY 12561-2400.

KESSLER, ANN VERONA
PERSONAL Born 01/28/1928, Aberdeen, SD **DISCIPLINE** MODERN & CHURCH HISTORY **EDUCATION** Mt Marty Col, BA, 53; Creighton Univ, MA, 57; Univ Notre Dame, PhD, 63. **CAREER** Teacher elem schs, 47-49, 57-59 & Mt Marty High Sch, 52-56; from instr to assoc prof, 62-73, acad dean, 63-65, head dept hist, 68-77, Prof Hist, Mt Marty Col, 73-98, Professor Emeritus, 98-; mem, Am Benedictine Acad, 67-98; mem, Fulbright Scholar Selection Comt, 77, 79. **HONORS AND AWARDS** Teaching Excellence and Campus Leadership Awd, Sears-Roebuck Found, 91. **MEMBERSHIPS** Am Acad Polit & Soc Sci; AHA; Am Polit Sci Asn. **RESEARCH** Fate of religious orders in France since the revolution; modern church-state controversies; monastic history and biography of Benedictines. **SELECTED PUBLICATIONS** Auth, French Benedictines under stress, fall 66 & Political legacy to the religions in France: Laic laws of the Third Republic, 12/69, Am Benedictine Rev; Post-Revolution Restoration of French Monasticism, SDak Soc Sci Asn J, fall 77; Founded on Courage, Inspired with Vision: Mt Marty Col, In: From Idea to Institution, 89; First Catholic Bishop of Dakota: Martin Marty, In: South Dakota Leaders, 89; Benedictine Men and Women of Courage, 96. **CONTACT ADDRESS** Mount Marty Col, Yankton, 1105 W 8th St, Yankton, SD 57078-3724. **EMAIL** akessler@rs6.mtmc.edu

KESSLER, HERBERT LEON
PERSONAL Born 07/20/1941, Chicago, IL, m, 1976, 1 child **DISCIPLINE** ART HISTORY **EDUCATION** Univ Chicago, BA, 61; Princeton Univ, MFA, 63, PhD(art hist), 65. **CAREER** From asst prof art & col to prof art & New Testament & early Christian lit, Univ Chicago, 65-76, assoc chmn, Dept Art, 68-69, chmn, 73-76, univ dir of fine arts, 75-76; Prof Hist Art & Chmn Dept, 76-98, Charlotte Bloomberg Prof, Johns Hopkins Univ, 84-98, Dean, Krieger Sch of Arts and Sci, 98-99; mem, Int Ctr Medieval Studies, 71-; mem bd dirs, 74-76; Richard Krautheimer Guest Prof, Bibliotheca Hertziana, Rome, 96-97. **HONORS AND AWARDS** Nat Endowment for Humanities fel, 67; Herodotus fel, Inst Advan Study, Princeton, 69-70; Guggenheim fel, NY, 72-73; fel, Am Acad Learned Soc, 79-80 & Am Philos Soc, 80; sr fel, Dumbarton Oaks, Wash, 80-86; Fel, Am Acad Rome, 84-85; Fel, Medieval Acad of Am, 91; Fel, Am Acad Arts and Sci, 95-. **MEMBERSHIPS** Col Art Asn Am; Mediaeval Acad Am. **RESEARCH** Carolingian manuscript illumination; early Christian art; medieval art. **SELECTED PUBLICATIONS** Auth, French and Flemish Illuminated Manuscripts from Chicago Collections, Newberry Libr, 69; ed, Studies in Classical and Byzantine Manuscript Illumination, Univ Chicago, 71; auth, The Illustrated Bibles From Tours, Princeton Univ, 77; coauth, The Cotton Genesis, Princeton Univ Press, 86; The Frescoes of the Dura Synagogue and Christian Art, Dumbarton Oaks Studies XXVIII, Dumbarton Oaks, 90; auth, Studies in Pictorial Narrative, Pindar Press, 94; coauth, The Poetry and Paintings in the First Bible of Charles the Bald, Recentiores: Later Latin Texts and Contexts, Univ Mich Press, 97; The Holy Face and the Paradox of Representation, Villa Spelman Studies, vol 6, 98; auth, Rome 1300: On the Path of the Pilgrim, Yale Univ Press, 00; auth, Spiritual Seeing: Picturing God's Invisibility in Medieval Art, Univ of Penn Press, 00. **CONTACT ADDRESS** Sch Arts and Sci, Johns Hopkins Univ, Baltimore, 3400 N Charles St, Baltimore, MD 21218-2680. **EMAIL** herbkessler@earthlink.net

KESSLER-HARRIS, ALICE
PERSONAL Born 06/02/1941, Leicester, England, m, 1982, 3 children **DISCIPLINE** HISTORY **EDUCATION** Goucher Col, AB, 61; Rutgers Univ, MA, 63; PhD, 68. **CAREER** Vis fac, Sarah Lawrence Col, 74-76; Dir, Women's Hist Prog, 75-76; Vis Sr Lecturer, Univ Warwick, 79-80; Vis Prof, SUNY, 85; Asst Prof, Hofstra Univ, 68-74; Assoc Prof, Hofstra Univ, 74-81; Prof Hist, Hofstra Univ, 81-88; Prof Hist, Temple Univ, 88-90; Prof Hist, Rutgers Univ, 90-99; Prof II, 94; Dir Women's Stud, 90-95; prof, Hist, Columbia Univ, 99-. **HONORS AND AWARDS** NEH Fellow, 76-77, 85-86; Fellow, Rockefeller Found, 88-89; Fellow, Guggenheim Mem Found, 89-90; Res Assoc, Ctr for Stud of Soc Change, 89-90; Vis Fellow, Swed Coll for Adv Stud in the Soc Sci, 91; Doctor of Laws, Honoris causa, Goucher Col, 91; Vis Fellow, Inst for Soc Res, Oslo, 94-95; Dr of Philos, honoris causa, Uppsala Univ, Sweden, 95; Fulbright Awd, Aus & N Zealand, 95; Fellow, Swedish Coll for Adv Stud in Soc Sci, 97. **MEMBERSHIPS** Soc Am Hist; Am Hist Asn; Org of Am Hist; Am Stud Asn; Berkshire Conf of Women Hist; Columbia Univ Seminar in Am Civ; Columbia Univ Seminar on Women in Soc; ACLU. **RESEARCH** History; women's studies. **SELECTED PUBLICATIONS** Auth, Women Have Always Worked: An Historical Overview, Feminist Press, 81; auth, Out to Work: A History of Wage-Earning Women in the United States, Oxford Univ Press, 82; coed, Faith of a Woman Writer: Essays in Twentieth Century Literature, Greenwood, 88; coed, Perspectives on American Labor History: The Problem of Synthesis, Northern Ill Univ Press, 90; auth, A Woman's Wage: Historical Meanings and Social Consequences, Univ Press of KY, 90; auth, "Designing Women and Old Fools: The Construction of the Social Security Amendments of 1939," in US History as Womens' History, ed. Kerber, Kessler-Harris, and Sklar (Univ NC Press, 95), 87-106; coed, Protecting Women: Labor Legislation in Europe, Australia, and the United States, 1880-1920, Univ of Ill Press, 95; coed, U.S. History as Women's History, Univ of NC Press, 95; auth, "'A Principle of Law but not of Justice:' Men, Women, and Income Taxes in the United States, 1913-1948," S Calif Rev of Law and Women's Studies 6 (97): 331-360; auth, "In the Nation's Image: The Gendered Limits of Social Citizenship in the Depresssion Era," Journal of Am Hist 86 (99): 1251-1279. **CONTACT ADDRESS** Columbia Univ, 610 West 116th St. #92, New York, NY 10027. **EMAIL** AK571@columbia.edu

KESSNER, THOMAS
PERSONAL Born 12/20/1946, Germany, m, 1967, 6 children **DISCIPLINE** HISTORY **EDUCATION** Brooklyn Col, City Univ NYork, BA, 67; Columbia Univ, MA, 68, PhD(hist), 75. **CAREER** Prof Hist, Grad Ctr, City Univ New York, 91-. **HONORS AND AWARDS** Phi Beta Kappa; Am Coun Learned Soc fel hist, 76; Nat Endowment for Humanities fel

hist, 76-77; City Univ Inst New Hist fel hist, 76; consult ethnic heritage, NY City Bd Educ Community Dist 22, 78-79; assoc dir, Hist & Humanities Prog, City Univ New York Grad Ctr, 81-; consult, Select Pres Comn Refugee & Immigration Policy & Harvard Encycl Am Ethnic Groups; Rockefeller Found res fel; Distinguished Alumnus Medal, Brooklyn Col, 89; CUNY PSC-BHE Res Awd, 82-87, 91, 95-97; CUNY Fac Excellence Awd, 90-96. **MEMBERSHIPS** Am Jewish Hist Soc; Orgn Am Historians; Immigrant Hist Soc. **RESEARCH** American urban history; American immigrant history; Jewish history. **SELECTED PUBLICATIONS** Auth, Gershom Mendes Seixas: A Jewish Minister, Am Jewish Hist Soc, 6/69; The Golden Door: Italian and Jewish Immigrant Mobility in New York City, 1880-1915, Oxford Univ, 1/77; coauth, Immigrant Women at Work, J Ethnic Hist, 12/77; auth, New York's Immigrants in Prosperity and Depression, In: Ravitch and Goodenow, Educating an Urban People, 81; Repatriation in American History, Report of Select Comn Refugee & Immigration Policy, 81; Today's Immigrants, Their Stories: A New Look at the Newest Americans, Oxford Univ Press, 81; Jobs, Ghettos and the Urban Economy, Am Jewish Hist, 81; auth, Fiorello H. La Guardia and the Making of Modern New York, McGraw Hill, 89; auth, Capital Metropolis: New York's Rise to Dominance, 1869-1898, Simon and Schuster, forthcoming. **CONTACT ADDRESS** Graduate School and University Center, City Univ, 365 Fifth Ave, New York, NY 10016. **EMAIL** tkessner@cuny.edu

KETCHAM, RALPH LOUIS
PERSONAL Born 10/28/1927, Berea, OH, m, 1958, 2 children **DISCIPLINE** AMERICAN STUDIES **EDUCATION** Allegheny Col, AB, 49; Colgate Univ, MA, 52; Syracuse Univ, PhD, 56. **CAREER** Res assoc polit sci, Univ Chicago, 56-60, assoc ed, Papers of James Madison, 56-60; from assoc prof to prof Am studies, 63-68, prof Am Studies, Polit Sci & Hist, Syracuse Univ, 68-, Res assoc hist & assoc ed, Papers of Benjamin Franklin, Yale Univ, 61-63, lectr, 62-63; lectr Am civilization, Tokyo Univ, 65; vis prof, Univ Tex, 67-68; vis prof Am hist, Univ Sheffield, 71-72; Fulbright lectr, India, 74; scholar-in-residence, Aspen Inst for Humanistic Studies, 75-76; Fulbright lectr, Netherlands, 87; vis prof, Public Affairs, George Mason Univ, 91; vis prof, Am Hist, Massey Univ, NZ, 98. **HONORS AND AWARDS** Hon DLitt, Allegheny Col, 85; CASE Prof of the Year, 87; Maxwell Prof of Citizenship and Public Aff, 94. **MEMBERSHIPS** Orgn Am Hist; Am Studies Asn. **RESEARCH** American intellectual history and political theory; American revolutionary and early national period. **SELECTED PUBLICATIONS** Auth, Presidents above Party: The First American Presidency, 1789-1829, Univ North Carolina, 84; auth, Individualism and Public Life: A Modern Dilemma, Blackwell, 87; auth, Framed for Posterity: The Enduring Philosophy of the Constitution, Univ Kansas, 93. **CONTACT ADDRESS** Maxwell Sch, Syracuse Univ, Syracuse, NY 13244. **EMAIL** rketcham@syr.edu

KETCHERSID, WILLIAM L.
PERSONAL Born 02/22/1943, Rockhood, TN, m, 1966, 4 children **DISCIPLINE** HISTORY **EDUCATION** Tenn Wesleyan Col, BA, 65; Univ Tenn, MA, 66; Univ Ga, PhD, 77. **CAREER** Bryan Col, 66-69; TA, Univ of Ga, 70-73; Bryan Col, 73-79; 84-. **HONORS AND AWARDS** Teacher of the Year, Bryan Col, 69; Teacher of the Year, Bryan Col, 79; Outstanding Teacher in Appalachia, Univ Ky, 87. **MEMBERSHIPS** S Hist Assoc. **RESEARCH** American Civil War, United States Presidency. **CONTACT ADDRESS** Dept Humanities, Bryan Col, PO Box 7616, Dayton, TN 37327. **EMAIL** ketcheb@bryan.edu

KETT, JOSEPH FRANCIS
PERSONAL Born 03/11/1938, Brooklyn, NY, m, 1965, 2 children **DISCIPLINE** AMERICAN HISTORY, HISTORY OF EDUCATION **EDUCATION** Holy Cross Col, AB, 59; Harvard Univ, MA, 60, PhD (hist), 64. **CAREER** Instr hist, Harvard Univ, 65-66; from asst prof to assoc prof, 66-76, prof hist, Univ VA, 76 , mem panel on youth, President's Sci Adv Coun, 71-72, chair, hist dept, 85-90. **MEMBERSHIPS** Orgn Am Hist. **RESEARCH** American social and intellectual history; history of education. **SELECTED PUBLICATIONS** Auth, The Formation of the American Medical Profession, Yale Univ, 68; Adolescence and youth in nineteenth century America, J Interdisciplinary Hist, 71; Growing up in rural New England, 1800-1840, in: Anonymous Americans, Prentice-Hall, 72; Rites of Passage: Adolescence in America, 1790 to the Present, Basic Bk, 77; The perils of precocity, in: Turning Points, Univ Chicago Press, 78; The Adolescence of Vocational Education, Stanford Univ Press, 82; The Pursuit of Knowledge Under Difficulties: From Self Improvement to Adult Education in America, 1750-1990, Stanford Univ Press, 94; co-auth, The Enduring Vision: A History of the American People, Houghton Mifflin, 96; Dictionary of Cultural Literacy, 93. **CONTACT ADDRESS** Dept of History, Univ of Virginia, 1 Randall Hall, Charlottesville, VA 22903-3244. **EMAIL** jfk9v@virginia.edu

KETTNER, JAMES HAROLD
PERSONAL Born 10/04/1944, Greenville, OH **DISCIPLINE** AMERICAN HISTORY **EDUCATION** Harvard Univ, AB, 66, PhD(hist), 73; Univ Sussex, BA, 68. **CAREER** Actg asst prof, 73-74, lectr, 74-77, asst prof to assoc prof, 77-90, Prof Hist, Univ Calif, Berkeley, 90-; Mem, Joint Comt Proj 87, Am Hist Asn/Am Polit Sci Asn, 78-80. **HONORS AND AWARDS** Jamestown Prize, Inst Early Am Hist & Cult, 75. **MEMBERSHIPS** AHA; Orgn Am Historians; Am Soc Legal Hist; Asn Marshall Scholars Alumni. **RESEARCH** American colonial & early national periods; American legal history. **SELECTED PUBLICATIONS** Auth, The development of American citizenship in the Revolutionary Era: the idea of volitional allegiance, Am J Legal Hist, 7/74; Subjects or citizens? A note on British views respecting the legal effects of American independence, Va Law Rev, 6/76; The Development of American Citizenship, 1608-1870, Univ NC, 78; Persons or Property? The Pleasants Slaves in the Virginia Courts, 1792-1799, In: Launching the Extended Republic: The Federalist Era, Univ Va, 96. **CONTACT ADDRESS** Dept of History, Univ of California, Berkeley, 3229 Dwinelle Hall, Berkeley, CA 94720-2551.

KEUCHEL, EDWARD F.
PERSONAL Born 09/20/1934, Kansas City, KS, m, 1967, 2 children **DISCIPLINE** HISTORY **EDUCATION** Rockhurst Col, BS, 56; Univ KS, MA, 61; Cornell Univ, PhD, 70. **CAREER** Instr, hist, OH State Univ, 65-68; asst prof, 68-74, assoc prof, 74-81, Prof, History, FL State Univ, 81-. **MEMBERSHIPS** FL Hist Soc; Southern Hist Soc; Oral Hist Asn. **RESEARCH** FL hist; US military hist. **SELECTED PUBLICATIONS** Co-auth, Civil War Marine: A Diary of the Red River Expedition, 1864, 75; co-auth, American Economic History: From Abundance to Constraint, 81; auth, A History of Columbia County Florida, 81; Florida: Enterprise Under the Sun, 90; Family, Community, Business Enterprise: The Millers of Crescent City, Florida, 97. **CONTACT ADDRESS** Dept of Hist, Florida State Univ, Tallahassee, FL 32306-2200. **EMAIL** ekeuchel@mailer.fsu.edu

KEVERN, JOHN
DISCIPLINE CHURCH HISTORY **EDUCATION** Univ Paris-Sorbonne, Dipl Sup, 74; Univ Ill, BA, 75; Gen Theol Sem, MDiv, 80; Univ Chicago Divinity Sch, PhD, 97. **CAREER** Asst prof, Cooke Ch of Hist Theol, Bexley Hall Sem, 92-; dean, Bexley Hall Sem, 96. **SELECTED PUBLICATIONS** Auth, The Future of Anglican Theology, Anglican Theol Rev 75th Anniversary Ed, 94; Form in Tragedy: A Study in the Methodology of Hans Urs von Balthasar, In Communio, 94; The Fullness of Catholic Identity, In The Anglican Cath, 96; The Trinity and the Search for Justice, Anglican Theol Rev, 97. **CONTACT ADDRESS** Hist, Theol, Soc Dept, Trinity Lutheran Sem, 2199 E Main St, Columbus, OH 43209-2334. **EMAIL** jkevern@trinity.capital.edu

KEVLES, DANIEL JEROME
PERSONAL Born 03/02/1939, Philadelphia, PA, m, 1961, 2 children **DISCIPLINE** AMERICAN HISTORY, HISTORY OF SCIENCE **EDUCATION** Princeton Univ, BA (physics), 60, PhD(hist), 64. **CAREER** From asst prof to assoc prof, 64-78, exec officer humanities, 78-81, prof hist, 78-86, J.O. and Juliette Koepfli Prof of Humanities, 86-, Calif Inst Technol; chair of the Caltech fac, 95-97; Old Dom fel, Calif Inst Technol, 66-67; consult, Ranger Hist Proj, Jet Propulsion Lab, 72-77; Am Coun Learned Soc grant-in-aid, 73; vis res fel, Univ Sussex, 76; vis prof, Univ Pa, 79; fel, Charles Warren Ctr, Harvard Univ, 81-82; mem coun, Hist Sci Soc, 80-82; Am Inst of Physics, Adv Comm on the Hist of Physics, 84-, chair, 93-94; assoc ed, HSPS: Historical Studies in the Physical and Biological Sciences, 86-; fel, Center for Advanced Study in the Behavioral Sciences, Stanford, Calif, 86-87; Educational Advisory Board, Guggenheim Found, 86-90, 90-94; Directeur d'Etudes, Ecoles des Hautes Etudes en Sciences Sociales, Paris, April 91; vis comm, Hist of Sci Dept, Harvard, 95-; Chair, Selection Comm for Hist and Philos of Sci, James S. McDonnell Centennial Fels, 97-98; Adv Council, Nat Inst of General Medical Sciences, 98-01; DeCamp porf, Princeton Univ, spring 99; Consulting Bk Review ed, Am Scientist, 99-; Fel Selection Comm, The Center for Scholars and Writers, NYork Public Libr, 99-; Nat Res Council/Nat Acad of Sciences, Panel on Sci, Tech, and the Law, 00-; vis prof, Yale Univ, 00-01; "Editorial Board," The American Experience in the Twentieth Century. **HONORS AND AWARDS** Woodrow Wilson fel, 61-62; Nat Sci Found fel, 62-64; Nat Sci Found fel, Oxford, 60-61; Nat Hist Soc Prize, 79; Page One Awd, 84; Nat Sci Found grant, 65, 73-74 & 78-80; fel panel, Nat Sci Found, 78; Nat Hist Soc Bk Prize in Am Hist, 79; Nat Endowment Humanities sr fel, 81-82; Guggenheim fel, 82-83; Watson Davis Prize, Hist of Sci Soc, 99. **MEMBERSHIPS** Orgn Am Hist; Am Asn Hist Medicine; Am Hist Asn; Hist Sci Soc; Am Asn for the Advancement of Sci (fel); Am Acad of Arts and Sciences; Am Philos Soc; Soc of Am Historians (fel); Phi Beta Kappa; P.E.N.; Author's Guild. **RESEARCH** The social and political history of modern science, especially in the United States; history of physics, genetics and eugenics. **SELECTED PUBLICATIONS** Auth, The Physicists: The History of a Scientific Community in Modern America, Alfred A. Knopf, 78; auth, In the Name of Eugenics: Genetics and the Uses of Human Heredity, Alfred A. Knopf, 85; coed, The Code of Codes: Scientific and Social Issues in the Human Genome Project, Harvard University Press (Cambridge), 92; auth, The Baltimore Case: A Trial of Politics, Science, and Character; Norton, 98. **CONTACT ADDRESS** Div of Humanities & Soc Sci, California Inst of Tech, Mail Code 228-77, Pasadena, CA 91125. **EMAIL** kevles@its.caltech.edu

KEYLOR, WILLIAM ROBERT
PERSONAL Born 08/15/1944, Sacramento, CA, m, 1968, 2 children **DISCIPLINE** MODERN EUROPEAN HISTORY **EDUCATION** Stanford Univ, BA, 66; Columbia Univ, MA, 67, cert & PhD, 71. **CAREER** Lectr mod hist, Rutgers Univ, Newark, 68-69; lectr Am studies, Univ Paris, Vincennes, 69-70; instr mod hist, Rutgers Univ, 70-72; asst prof, 72-75, assoc prof, 75-79, Prof Mod Hist, Boston Univ, 80-; Vis assoc prof , Mass Inst Technol, 79-80. **HONORS AND AWARDS** Chevalier de L'Ordre National du Merite (France); Fulbright Fel; Guggenheim Fel. **MEMBERSHIPS** Soc Fr Hist Studies; AHA. **RESEARCH** Modern French history; European diplomatic history; Franco-American relations since 1919. **SELECTED PUBLICATIONS** Auth, Academy and Community: The Foundation of the French Historical Profession, Harvard Univ, 75; co-ed, From Parnassus: Essays in Honors of Jacques Barzun, 76 & auth, Clio on trial: Charles Peguy as historical critic, in From Parnassus: Essays in Honor of Jacques Barzun, 76, Harper & Row; Jacques Bainville and the Renaissance of Royalist History in Twentieth Century France, La State Univ, 79; Prohibition Diplomacy: An Incident of Franco-American Misunderstanding, French Civilization, spring 81; The Twentieth Century World: An International History, 3rd ed, 96; ed, The Legacy of the Great War: Peacemaking, 1919, 97. **CONTACT ADDRESS** Dept of Hist, Boston Univ, 226 Bay State Rd, Boston, MA 02215-1403. **EMAIL** wrkeylor@bu.edu

KEYSSAR, ALEXANDER
DISCIPLINE HISTORY **EDUCATION** Harvard Col, BA, 69; Harvard Univ, PhD, 77. **CAREER** Tutor, Harvard Univ, 71-73; instr, Fed State County, Municipal Employees, NY, 74; asst prof, Mass Inst Tech, 76-77; asst prof, Brandeis Univ, 77-85; vis scholar, Russel Sage Fdn, 85-86; asst prof, 86-87, assoc prof, 87-91, Duke Univ; guest dir d'Edtudes, L'Ecole Hautes Etudes Scis Soc, Paris, 91-95; prof, Mass Inst Tech, 91-93; prof, Duke Univ, 92-97; PROF HIST, PUB POLICY, DUKE UNIV, 97. **CONTACT ADDRESS** History Dept, Duke Univ, 223 Carr Bldg, Durham, NC 27708.

KHAN, YOSHMITSU
PERSONAL Born, Japan, m, 2 children **DISCIPLINE** ASIAN STUDIES, JAPAN **EDUCATION** Sophia Univ, Tokyo, Hist and Govt; Seton Hall Univ, Asian Studies; Pa State Univ, Educ Theory and Policy, 94. **CAREER** Asst Prof, Union Col, 93-. **MEMBERSHIPS** Asn of Asian Studies. **RESEARCH** Japanese History, Japanese Moral Education. **SELECTED PUBLICATIONS** Auth, Japanese Moral Education, Past and Present, Assoc Univ Presses, 98. **CONTACT ADDRESS** Dept Mod Lang, Union Col, New York, 807 Union St, Schenectady, NY 12308-3103.

KHODARKOVSKY, MICHAEL
PERSONAL Born 02/12/1955, Kiev, Uktaine, m, 1 child **DISCIPLINE** HISTORY **EDUCATION** Univ Chicago, PhD, 87. **CAREER** Assoc prof, Loyola Univ-Chicago, 91-; NEH, 96; Fulbright-Hays, 83; Woodrow Wilson Ctr, 92-93; NCREER, 97. **RESEARCH** Russian Imperial and Early Modern History. **SELECTED PUBLICATIONS** Where Two Worlds Met: The Russian State and the Kalmyk Nomads, 1600-1771 (Ithaca and London: Cornell Univ Press, 92); Of Religion and Empire: Missions and Religious Conversion in the Russian Empire, Robert Geraci and Michael Khodarkovsky eds. (Ithaca and London: Cornell Univ Press, 00. **CONTACT ADDRESS** 726 W Melrose St, Chicago, IL 60657. **EMAIL** mkhodar@orion.it.luc.edu

KHOURY, PHILIP S.
PERSONAL Born 10/15/1949, Washington, DC, m, 1980 **DISCIPLINE** HISTORY **EDUCATION** Trinity Col, BA, 71; Harvard Univ, PhD, 80. **CAREER** From asst prof to prof and dean, Mass Inst of Technol, 81-. **HONORS AND AWARDS** Pi Gamma Mu, 71; T.J. Watson Fel, 71; Nat Defense Foreign Langs Fels, 71-72, 73-74, 77-78; St Antony's Col Assoc, Univ of Oxford, 74-75, 76-77; Fulbright Scholar, 76-77; Soc Sci Res Coun Post-doctoral Fel, 83-84; Mellon Fel, 84-85; Class of 1922 Career Develop Prof, M.I.T., 84-86; G. Louis Beer Prize, AHA, 87; Navas Awd, M.I.T., 90, 92; Pres, Middle East Studies Asn of North Am, 98. **MEMBERSHIPS** Brit Soc for Middle Eastern Studies; Middle East Inst; Am Asn for the Advancement of Sci; Middle East Studies Asn. **SELECTED PUBLICATIONS** Auth, Urban Notables and Arab Nationalism, 83; Syria and the French Mandate, 87; coed, Tribes and State Formation in the Middle East, 90; Recovering Beirut: Urban Design and Post-war Reconstruction, 93; The Modern Middle East: A Reader, 93. **CONTACT ADDRESS** Dean's Office, Massachusetts Inst of Tech, 77 Mass Inst of Tech, E51-255, Cambridge, MA 02139. **EMAIL** khoury@mit.edu

KICKLIGHTER, JOSEPH ALLEN
PERSONAL Born 08/14/1945, Macon, GA, S **DISCIPLINE** HISTORY **EDUCATION** Univ the South, BA 67; Emory Univ, MA, 70, PhD(medieval hist), 73. **CAREER** Instr social studies, Woodward Acad, 73-75; from Asst Prof to Assoc Prof, 75-91, Prof Hist, Auburn Univ, 91-. **MEMBERSHIPS** Mediaeval Acad Am; AHA. **RESEARCH** Anglo-French relations in the High and Late Middle Ages; Medieval French royal institutions; the Papacy in the late Middle Ages. **SELECTED PUBLICATIONS** Auth, La Carriere de Beraud de Got, Annales du

Midi, 73; An unknown brother of Pope Clement V, Mediaeval Studies, 76; French jurisdictional supremacy in Gascony: One aspect of the ducal government's response, J Medieval Hist, 79; Les monasteres de gascogne et le conflit Franco-Anglais, 1270-1327, Annales du Midi, 79; English Bordeaux in Conflict: the Execution of Pierre Vigier de la Rouselle and its Aftermath, J Medieval Hist, 83; The Parlement of Paris, Dictionary of the Middle Ages, 87; Arnaud Caillau: Maire de Bordeaux et officier d'Edouard II, Annales du Midi, 87; The Nobility of English Gascony: the Case of Jourdain de l'Isle, J Medieval Hist, 87; English Legal Representatives at the Parlement of Paris, 1259-1337, In: Documenting the Past: Essays in Honor of G.P. Cuttino, 89; The Abbey of Sainte-Croix de Bordeaux versus the King of England/Duke of Aquitaine Phillipps Charter 6 in the John Rylands Library, Bulletin of the John Rylands Library, 90; English Gascony, The Parlement of Paris and the Origins of the Hundred Years War, 1330-1337, Sewanee Medieval Studies, 90; Appeal, Negotiation and Conflict: The Evolution of an Anglo-French Legal Relationship during the Hundred Years War, Proceedings of the Western Soc for Fr Hist, 90. **CONTACT ADDRESS** Dept of History, Auburn Univ, Auburn, AL 36849. **EMAIL** kicklja@auburn.edu

KICZA, JOHN EDWARD
PERSONAL Born 07/29/1947, Northhampton, MA, m, 1980, 2 children **DISCIPLINE** LATIN AMERICAN & SOCIAL HISTORY **EDUCATION** Amherst Col, BA, 69; Univ Mass, MA, 73; Univ Calif, Los Angeles, PhD(hist), 79. **CAREER** Instr hist, Univ Santa Clara, 77-78; asst prof, Loyola Marymount Univ, 79-80; from asst prof to prof, 80-88, Edward R. Meyer Distinguished Professor Hist, Wash State Univ, 96-99. **MEMBERSHIPS** AHA; Conf Latin Am Hist; Latin Am Studies Asn; Pac Coast Coun Latin Am Studies. **RESEARCH** Social history of Latin America; race relations in the history of the Americas; colonial Mexico. **SELECTED PUBLICATIONS** Auth, Colonial urban social history: The case of Mexico, Proc Rocky Mt Coun Latin Am Studies, 79; The Pulque Trade of Late Colonial Mexico City, The Americas, 10/80; Mexican demographic history of the nineteenth century, Statist Abstract Latin Am, 81; Women and business life in late colonial Mexico City, J Univ Autonoma Metropolitana, Azcapotzalco, 81; The great families of Mexico: Elite maintenance and business, Hisp Am Hist Rev, 8/82; Colonial Entrepreneurs: Families and Business in Bourbon Mexico City, Univ NMex Press, 83; auth, The Social and Ethnic Historiography of Colonial Latin America: The Last Twenty Years, William and Mary Quart, 3rd series, July 88; auth, Patterns in Early Spanish Overseas Expansion, William and Mary Quart, 3rd series, April 92; ed, The Indian in Latin American History: Resistence, Resilience, and Acculturation, Schol Resources, 2nd 00; auth, The Social and Political Position of Spanish Immigrants in Bourbon America and the Origins of the Independence Movements, Colonial Latin Am Rev, 4:1, 95; auth, The Native Peoples and Civilizations of the Americas Before Contact, Washington DC: Am Hist Asn Essays on Global and Comparitive Hist, 98. **CONTACT ADDRESS** Dept of Hist, Washington State Univ, PO Box 644030, Pullman, WA 99164-4030. **EMAIL** jekicza@wsu.edu

KIDWELL, CLARA SUE
PERSONAL Born 07/08/1941, Tahlequah, OK **DISCIPLINE** HISTORY OF SCIENCE **EDUCATION** BA, letters, 62; MA, history of science, 63; PhD, history of science, 70. **CAREER** Instr history, Kansas City Art Inst, 68-69; instr social sci, Haskell Jr Coll, 70-72; asst prof Amer Indian Studies, Univ Minnesota, 72-74; assoc to full prof Native Amer Studies, Univ Calif Berkeley, 74-93; asst dir cultural resources, Natl Museum Amer Indian, Smithsonian Inst, 93-95; prof history, dir Native Amer Studies, Univ Oklahoma, 95-. **HONORS AND AWARDS** Rockefeller Found Fel, 75-76; summer res fel, Smithsonian Inst, 84; Newberry Library Summer Res Fel, 84; Humanities Res Inst Fellowship, Univ Calif Irvine, spring 92. **MEMBERSHIPS** Amer Hist Assn; Org Amer Historians; Amer Soc Ethnohistory. **RESEARCH** History of Choctaw Indians; Amer Indian science and technology. **SELECTED PUBLICATIONS** Auth, "Choctaws and Missionaries in Mississippi Before 1830," American Indian Culture and Research Journ, vol XI, no 2, 87; auth, "Systems of Knowledge," in America in 1492, 91; auth, "Indian Women as Cultural Mediators," Ethnohistory, spring 92; auth, "Choctaw Women as Cultural Mediators," Ethnohistory, spring 92; auth, "Choctaw Women and Cultural Persistence in Mississippi," in Negotiators of Change: Historical Perspectives on Native American Women, 95; auth, Choctaws and Missionaries in Mississippi 1818-1918, 95. **CONTACT ADDRESS** 455 W Lindsey, Rm 804, Norman, OK 73019. **EMAIL** cskidwell@ou.edu

KIECKHEFER, RICHARD
PERSONAL Born 06/01/1946, Minneapolis, MN, m, 1986, 2 children **DISCIPLINE** RELIGION, HISTORY **EDUCATION** Saint Louis Univ, BA, 68; Univ Tex Austin, MA Philos, 70; PhD Hist, 72. **CAREER** Instr, Univ Tex Austin, 73-74; lectr, 74; asst prof, Philips Univ, 75; asst prof, 75-79; assoc prof, 79-84, Prof, Northwest Univ, 84-. **HONORS AND AWARDS** Tchg citation from Council for Advancement and Support of Education, 82, 83; Nat Endowment for the Humanities Fel, 87-88; Guggenheim Found Fel, 92-93; Fel of Medieval Acad Of Am, 98. **MEMBERSHIPS** Medieval Acad Of Am; Am Soc of Church Hist; An Acad of Rel; Societas Magica. **RESEARCH** Late medieval religious culture-including mystical theology, magic and witchcraft, and church in relation architecture to parish religion. **SELECTED PUBLICATIONS** Auth, The holy and the unholy: sainthood, witchcraft, and magic in late medieval Europe, J of Medieval And Renaissance Studies, 94; The specific rationality of medieval magic, Am Hist Rev, 94; Forbidden Rites: A Necromancer's manual of the fifteenth Century, 98; The office of inquisition and medieval heresy: the transition from personal to institutional jurisdiction, J of Ecclesiastical Hist, 95; Avenging the blood of children: anxiety over child victims and the origins of the European witch trials, the Devil, Heresy and Witchcraft in the Middle Ages: Essays in Honor of Jeffrey B Russel, 98; The Devils' contemplative: the Liber iuratus, the Liber visionum, and Christian appropriation of Jewish occultism, Conjuring Spirits: Texts and Traditions of Medieval Ritual magic, 98; auth, Magic in the Middle Ages, new ed, Cambridge U.PR. 00. **CONTACT ADDRESS** Dept of Religion, Northwestern Univ, 1940 Sheridan Rd, Evanston, IL 60208-4050. **EMAIL** kieckhefer@northwestern.edu

KIEFT, DAVID
DISCIPLINE HISTORY **EDUCATION** Univ Calif Berkeley, PhD, 66. **CAREER** Assoc prof, Univ Minn, 66- . **RESEARCH** Diplomatic history; German history. **SELECTED PUBLICATIONS** Auth, Belgium's Return to Neutrality, 72. **CONTACT ADDRESS** History Dept, Univ of Minnesota, Twin Cities, 614 Social Sciences Tower, 267 19th Ave. S, Minneapolis, MN 55455. **EMAIL** kieft001@tc.umn.edu

KIESWETTER, JAMES KAY
PERSONAL Born 03/08/1942, Dodge City, KS **DISCIPLINE** FRENCH & MODERN EUROPEAN HISTORY **EDUCATION** Univ Colo, Boulder, BM, 63, MA, 65, PhD(hist), 68. **CAREER** From asst prof to assoc prof, 68-76, prof hist, Eastern Wash Univ, 76-, Nat Endowment for Humanities summer stipend, 69; Am Philos Soc grant, 69. em exam comt, Educ Testing Serv Col Level Exam Prog, 72-. **MEMBERSHIPS** AHA; Soc Fr Hist Studies; Western Soc Fr Hist. **RESEARCH** French Restoration; French Revolution and Napoleon; 19th century European diplomatic history. **SELECTED PUBLICATIONS** Auth, French diplomacy at the congresses of Troppau and Laiback, Can J Hist, 9/69; ed, Documents Illustrative of the Origin, Development and Application of Metternich's Intervention Policy at the Congresses of Troppau and Laiback, Eastern Wash State Col, 70; auth, Metternich and the Bourbon succession 1819-1820, E Europ Quart, 9/72; France and the American Revolution, Historians Bicentennial Newslett, 3/75; Etienne-Denis Pasquier: The Last Chancellor of France, Am Philos Soc, 77; War and American Society 1914-1975, Geront Uses Hist, Fed Admin Aging, 81. Auth, The Imperial Restoration, The Historian, November 82; auth, 109 articles in: Historical Dictionary of France from the 1815 Restoration to the Second Empire, Greenwood Press, 87; auth, articles on Napoleon I, and French Revolutionary-Napoleonic Wars, In: International Military and Defence Encyclopedia, Pergamon-Brassey, 93; auth, articles on French Revolutionary-Napoleonic Wars, and Napoleon I, In: Brassey's Encyclopedia of Military History and Biography, Brassey, 94. **CONTACT ADDRESS** Dept of Hist, Eastern Washington Univ, M/S 27, Cheney, WA 99004-2496.

KIGER, JOSEPH CHARLES
PERSONAL Born 08/19/1920, Covington, KY, m, 2 children **DISCIPLINE** HISTORY **EDUCATION** Birmingham-Southern Col, AB, 43; Univ Ala, MA, 47; Vanderbilt Univ, PhD, 50. **CAREER** Instr hist, Univ Ala, 50 & Wash Univ, 50-51; dir res, House Select Comt Investigate Found, 52-53; staff assoc, Am Coun Educ, 53-55; asst dir, Southern Fel Fund, 55-58; assoc prof hist, Univ Ala, 58-61; chm dept, 69-74, Prof Hist, Univ Miss, 61-, Guggenheim fel, 60-61; Rockefeller grant, 61; consult on philanthropists, Dictionary of American Biography, 68-; Am Coun Learned Soc grant, 80. **MEMBERSHIPS** AHA; Org Am Historians; Southern Hist Asn. **RESEARCH** Intellectual and social history; history of philanthropy; history of educational and research institutions. **SELECTED PUBLICATIONS** Auth, Operating Principles of the Larger Foundations, Russell Sage, 54; coauth, Sponsored Research Policy of Colleges and Universities, Am Coun Educ, 54; Am Learned Societies, Pub Affairs, 63; Inovation in Education, In: Foundation Support of Educational Innovation by Learned Societies, Councils and Institutes, Columbia Univ, 64; Disciplines and American Learned Societies, In: Encyclopedia of Education, MacMillan, 71; Frederick P Keppel, In: Dictionary of American Biography, 73 & Learned Societies, In: Dictionary of American History, 76, Scribner's; ed, Research Institutions and Learned Societies, Greenwood, 82. **CONTACT ADDRESS** Dept of History, Univ of Mississippi, University, MS 38677.

KILLEN, LINDA
PERSONAL Born 04/02/1945, Washington, DC, s **DISCIPLINE** DIPLOMATIC HISTORY **EDUCATION** Univ N Carolina, PhD 75, MA 71; Univ Wisconsin Madison, BA honors 66. **CAREER** Radford Univ, prof 76-; Univ N Carolina CH, lectr 75-76. **HONORS AND AWARDS** SCHEV Outstanding Tchg Awd nom; Fulbright Res Gnt; Woodrow Wilson Gnt; Radford Foun Gnt; Donald Dedmon Awd for Excell; photo exhibition, flossie martin gallery 98, local black history **MEMBERSHIPS** SHAFR; VSHT; NRVHS; RHF. **RESEARCH** Diplomatic; Local. **SELECTED PUBLICATIONS** Auth, Variations on New World Order: Eastern Europe as a Factor in Past present and Future US-Soviet/Russian Relations, The Soviet and Post-Soviet Rev, 95; auth, Testing the Peripheries: US Econ Relations with Interwar Yugoslavia, Boulder, E Euro Mono Series, 94; auth, Life At Pepper's Ferry, 1826-1865, taken from ledger accounts, compiled and ed, 97; auth, Radford's Early Black Residents 1880-1925, compiled, 97; auth, Freedmen's Bureau: Reports of Charles S. Schaeffer 1866-1868, ed, 97; These People live in a Pleasant Valley: A History of Slave and Freedmen in Nineteenth Century Pulaski County, Radford, A&S Occasional Pub, 96; auth, The Wharton's Town: New River Depot 1870-1940, A&S Occasional Pub, 94. **CONTACT ADDRESS** Dept of History, Radford Univ, Radford, VA 24142. **EMAIL** lkillen@runet.edu

KILMER, ANNE DRAFFKORN
PERSONAL Born 06/01/1931, Chicago, IL, d, 1 child **DISCIPLINE** ANCIENT NEAR EASTERN HISTORY & LITERATURE **EDUCATION** State Univ Iowa, BA, 53; Univ Pa, PhD(Assyriol), 59. **CAREER** Res asst assyriol, Orient Inst, Chicago, 57-63; vis lectr, 63-64, from asst prof to assoc prof, 65-72, chmn, Dept Near Eastern Studies, 70-72, 89-91, 97-00; dean humanities, Col Lett & Sci, 72-76 & 80-82, chmn, Berkeley Academic Senate, 91-92; prof Near Eastern Studies, Univ Calif, Berkeley, 72-, Guggenheim fel, 61-63; Am Asn Univ Women res fel, 64-65; Humanities Inst res grant & fel, Univ Calif, Berkeley, 67, 69, 70, 76, 79 & 82; Nat Endowment for Humanities res grant studies in Ancient music, Univ Calif, Berekeley, 76-77. **MEMBERSHIPS** Am Schs Orient Res; Am Orient Soc. **RESEARCH** Ancient Mesopotamian music, games and entertainment; Sumero-Akkadian lexical texts; Sumero-Akkadian literature and mythology. **SELECTED PUBLICATIONS** Coauth, Materialien zum Sumerischen Lexikon, Vol VIII/1, 60 & Vol VIII/2, 63, Pontif Bibl Inst; auth, The Mesopotamian Concept of Overpopulation and its Solution as Reflected in the Mythology, Orientalia, 72; Symbolic gestures in Akkadian Contracts from Alalakh and Ugarit, J Am Oriental Soc, 74; auth, The Cult Song with Music from Ancient Ugarit: Another Interpretation, Rev Assyriologie, 74; coauth, Sounds from Silence: Recent Discoveries in Ancient Near Eastern Music (bk and 12 inch stereo rec), Bit Enki Publ, 76; Note on overlooked word play in Akkadian Gilgamesh, In: Zikir Shumim, Leiden, 82; Musik, Reallexikon der Assyriologie VIII, pp. 463-482, 95; Fugal Features of Atrahasis: The Birth Theme, Mesopotamian Poetic Language: Sumerian and Akkadian, Proceedings of the Groningen Group for the Study of Mesopotamian Literature, Vol 2, Styx Publications, pp 127-139, 96. **CONTACT ADDRESS** Dept of Near Eastern Studies, Univ of California, Berkeley, 250 Barrows Hall, Berkeley, CA 94720-1941. **EMAIL** adkilmer@socrates.berkeley.edu

KILPINEN, JON T.
PERSONAL Born 06/03/1966, Detroit, MI, m, 1989, 2 children **DISCIPLINE** GEOGRAPHY **EDUCATION** Valparaiso Univ, BA, 88; Univ TX, Austin, MA. 90; PhD, 94. **CAREER** Instr, Valaparaiso Univ, 92-94; asst prof, 94-00; assoc prof, 00-. **HONORS AND AWARDS** Fred B Kniffen Bk Awd. **MEMBERSHIPS** AAG. **RESEARCH** North American culture; historical geography. **SELECTED PUBLICATIONS** Auth, "Traditional Fence Types of Western North America," Pioneer Am Sco Tran 15 (92): 15-22; auth "The Mountain Horse Barn: A Case of Western Innovation," Pioneer Am Sco Tran 17 (94): 25-32; auth, "Cultural Diffusion and the Formation of the Western Cultural Landscape: Roofed Single-Crib Outbuilding," Pioneer Am Soc Tran 18 (95): 9-15; coauth, The Mountain West: Interpreting the Folk Landscape, Johns Hopkins Univ Press (Baltimore, MD), 97; co-ref art, "Square Notching in the Log Carpentry Tradition of Pennsylvania Extended," Penn Folklife 40 (1990): 2-18; "Material Folk Culture of the Rocky Mountain High Valleys," Material Culture 23 (91): 25-41; auth, "Finnish Cultural Landscapes in the Pacific Northwest," Pacific Northwest 86 (94): 25-34; auth, "The Front-Gabled Log Cabin and the Role of the Great Plains in the Formation of the Mountain West's Built Landscape," Great Plains Quart 15 (95): 19-31; auth, "The Mountain Horse Barn: A Case of Western Innovation," in Baseball, Barns, and Bluegrass: A Geography of American Folklife, ed. George 0 Carney (Lanham, MD: Rowman & Littlefield, 98); auth, "Rocky Mountains," in The Oxford Companion to United States History, ed. Paul Boyer (NY, Oxford Univ Press, forthcoming). **CONTACT ADDRESS** Dept Geography, Valparaiso Univ, 651 College Ave, Valparaiso, IN 46383. **EMAIL** jon.kilpinen@valpo.edu

KIM, HYUNG KOOK
DISCIPLINE RURAL DEVELOPMENT **EDUCATION** Lewis and Clark Col, BA; Korea Univ, BS; John Hopkins Univ, PhD. **CAREER** Prof, Am Univ. **HONORS AND AWARDS** Dir, Ctr Asian Studies, Am Univ. **RESEARCH** Japan and the United States and Contemporary Korea and East Asia. **SELECTED PUBLICATIONS** Auth, The Division of Korea and the Alliance-Making Process: Internationalization of Internal Conflict and Internalization of International Struggle, Univ Press Am, 95. **CONTACT ADDRESS** American Univ, 4400 Massachusetts Ave, Washington, DC 20016.

KIM, YOUNG HUM
PERSONAL Born 12/19/1920, Korea, m **DISCIPLINE** HISTORY, POLITICAL SCIENCE **EDUCATION** Schinheung Univ, Korea, BA, 53; Bradley Univ, BS, 55; Univ Southern CA, MA, 56, PhD, 60. **CAREER** Instr, Inchon Commerce Inst, Korea, 48-50; res assoc Soviet studies, Sch Int Rel, 60-61; from asst prof to assoc prof, 61-70, prof hist & polit sci, US Int Univ, CA, 70, Asst dir, Soviet-Asian Studies Ctr, Univ Southern CA. **MEMBERSHIPS** AHA; Am Polit Sci Asn; Asn Asian Studies; Am Acad Polit & Social Sci; Coun For Rel. **RESEARCH** US diplomatic hist. **SELECTED PUBLICATIONS** Auth, East Asia's Turbulent Century, Appleton, 66; Patterns of Competitive Coexistence: USA vs USSR, Putnam, 66; Struggle Against History: US Foreign Policy in an Age of Revolution, Simon & Schuster, 68; The Central Intelligence Agency: Problems of Secrecy in a Democracy, Heath, 68; Twenty Years of Crisis: The Cold War Era, Prentice-Hall, 68; American Frontier Activities in Asia: Nelson-Hall, 81; Ideology vs National Interests, USA Today, 85; Centennial History of American Diplomacy in Asia, Shinku Cultural Press, Korea, 88; Women Liberation Issue in Korea, Jeonju Univ Press, Korea, 88; War of No Return: The Korean War, 2 vol, Kwiin Publ, Korea, 88; U S-Asian Relations in the 20th Century, Edwin Mellen Press, 96. **CONTACT ADDRESS** Dept of Hist & Polit Sci, US Int Univ, 10455 Pomerado Rd, San Diego, CA 92131-1717. **EMAIL** ykim1@san.rr.com

KIMBALL, JEFFREY P.
PERSONAL Born 12/14/1941, New Orleans, LA, m, 1963, 2 children **DISCIPLINE** HISTORY **EDUCATION** Univ New Orleans, BA, 63; Queens Univ, MA, 64; La State Univ, PhD, 69. **CAREER** Instr to prof, Miami Univ, 68-. **HONORS AND AWARDS** Moncado Awd, 69; Eleazer Wood Lectr, Bowling Green State Univ, 83; Mershon Ctr Fel, 87; Norwegian Nobel Inst Sr Fel, 95; Norman Thomas Mem Lectr, 97; Ohio Acad of Hist book Awd, 98; Robert H Ferrell Book Prize, 98. **MEMBERSHIPS** Hist soc; Ohio Acad of Hist; Peace Hist Soc; Soc for Hist of Am For Relations. **RESEARCH** The Nixon presidency, Nixon-Kissinger foreign policy, The Vietnam War, War and society. **SELECTED PUBLICATIONS** Auth, "The Stab-in-the-Back Legend and the Vietnam War", Armed Forces and Soc 14, (88): 433-458; Ed, To Reason Why: The Debate About the Causes of American Involvement in the Vietnam War, McGraw Hill, (NY), 90; coauth, "The United States", Encyclop of Arms Control and Disarmament, ed Richard Dean Burns, Charles Scribner's Sons, (NY, 93): 253-276; auth, "Peace with Honor: Richard Nixon and the Diplomacy of Threat and Symbolism", Shadow on the White House: Presidents and the Vietnam War, 1945-1975, ed David L. Anderson, Univ of Kans Pr, (93): 152-183; auth, "Alternatives to War in History", Mag of Hist 8, (94): 5-9; auth, "How Wars End: The Vietnam War", Peace and Change: A J of Peace Res 20, (95): 181-200; auth, Nixon's Vietnam War, Univ Pr of Kans, (Lawrence), 98; auth, "War", Scribner's Am Hist and Culture on CD-ROM, Macmillan Libr Ref, 98; auth, "Ernest Gruening", Am Nat Biography, Vol 9, eds J.A. Garraty, M.C. Carnes, Oxford Univ Pr, (99): 683-684. **CONTACT ADDRESS** Dept Hist, Miami Univ, Upham Hall, Rm 354, Oxford, OH 45056-1879. **EMAIL** kimbaljp@muohio.edu

KIMBALL, WARREN
PERSONAL Born 12/24/1935, Brooklyn, NY, m, 1959, 3 children **DISCIPLINE** HISTORY **EDUCATION** Villanova Univ, BA, 58; Georgetown Univ, MA, 65; PhD, 68. **CAREER** Teacher, U S Naval Acad, 61-65; Instr, Georgetown Univ, 65-67; Instr, Univ Ga, 67-70; From Asst Prof to Prof, Rutgers Univ, 70-. **HONORS AND AWARDS** Sen Fulbright Fel, Univ Madrid, 75-76; Sen Fulbright Fel, 90; Vis Fel & Sen Mellon Res Fel, Univ Cambridge, 97; Archives by-Fel, Churchill Col-Cambridge, 98. **MEMBERSHIPS** Soc for Historians of Am For Relig, AHA. **SELECTED PUBLICATIONS** Auth, The Juggler: Franklin Roosevelt as Wartime Statesman, Princeton UP (Princeton), 91; ed, America Unbound: World War II and the Making of a Super-Power, St Martin's Pr (New York, NY), 92; co-ed, Allies at War: The American, British and Soviet Experience in the Second World War, St Martin's Pr (New York, NY), 94; auth, Forged in War: Roosevelt, Churchill and the Second World War, William Morrow Publ (New York, NY), 97. **CONTACT ADDRESS** Dept Hist, Rutgers, The State Univ of New Jersey, Newark, 175 University Ave, Newark, NJ 07102-1803. **EMAIL** wkimball@andromeda.rutgers.edu

KIMES, DON
PERSONAL Born 11/18/1953, Oil City, PA, m, 1978, 3 children **DISCIPLINE** ART **EDUCATION** Westminster Col, BA, 75; Brooklyn Col, MFA, 80. **CAREER** Prog dir, 80-85, NY Stud Sch; artistic dir, 86-, Chautaugua Inst; dir, 98-, Int Inst Art & Archit, Corciano, Italy; prof, chair, 88-, Amer Univ. **HONORS AND AWARDS** US Dept of Interior Awd; Eisenhower Found Awd, 86; Camerata di Todi, Italy, 94-95; Mellon Grant, 96; Artiste in the Manicomium, 96. **RESEARCH** Painting, drawing, sculpture, printmaking. **SELECTED PUBLICATIONS** Exhibitor, Claudia Carr Gallery, New York City, 99; exhib, Kennedy Museum of Art, Oh Univ, Athens, Oh, 99; exhib, E J Vaughn Assoc, NYC, 00; exhib, Kouros Gallery, NYC, 97; exhib, America House, Munich, 97; exhib, Galleria Rocca Paolina, Perugia Italy, 96; exhib Corcoran Museum, 95; exhib, National Academy of Sciences, 92. **CONTACT ADDRESS** 902 Gilbert Rd, Rockville, MD 20851. **EMAIL** drmusky@aol.com

KIMMEL, RICHARD H.
PERSONAL Born Dayton, OH **DISCIPLINE** ANTHROPOLOGY AND ARCHAEOLOGY **EDUCATION** Univ NC, anthrop, MA, 78. **CAREER** Archaeol, US Army Corps of Engineers. **MEMBERSHIPS** Soc for Hist Archaeol; Southeastern Archaeol Conf. **RESEARCH** Mid-Atlantic and southeast U.S. historical archaeology, ecology and climate. **SELECTED PUBLICATIONS** Papers, Notes on the Cultural Origins and Functions of Sub-Floor Pits, Hist Archaeol, 27, 3, 102-113, 93; Estimating Magnetic Anomaly Sampling Fractions in Underwater Archaeology: Resolving Funding and Date Limitations, Underwater Archaeol Proceedings: Soc for Hist Archaeol Conf, 90-93, 90; Mitigating the Federal Review Process: A Preliminary Formulation of Data Contexts for the Ecological Interpretation of Small Craft, Underwater Archaeol Proceedings: Soc for Hist Archaeol Conf, 64-70, 89; Introduction to the Symposium: Current Research and Management Perspectives on Confederate Maritime Trade, Underwater Archaeol Proceedings: Soc for Hist Archaeol Conf, 19, 85. **CONTACT ADDRESS** US Army Corps Engineers, Environmental Resources Branch, PO Box 1890, Wilmington, NC 28402-1890.

KINDIG, EVERETT W.
PERSONAL Born 10/05/1936, Kansas City, KS, m, 1966, 2 children **DISCIPLINE** HISTORY **EDUCATION** Stanford Univ, BA, 58; MA, 63; PhD, 75. **CAREER** Teaching Asst, Stanford, 59-61; lecturer, San Jose State Univ, 71-72; vis asst prof, Santa Clara Univ, 71-72; asst prof, 71-85; assoc prof, Midwestern State Univ, 85-. **HONORS AND AWARDS** Hardin Foundation Research Grant. **MEMBERSHIPS** Phi Alpha Theta; Missouri Historical Society; Ft. Belknap Historical Soceity; Pi Sigma Alpha. **RESEARCH** Politics; Early National Period, Culture and Economics; 20th Century Higher Education. **SELECTED PUBLICATIONS** Auth, The Better Part of a Century: A History of Midwestern State University" Midwestern State Univ Press, 00; auth "Midwestern State Univ, The New Handbook of Texas, 96; auth, "Journalist Hooper Warren, Illinois Historical Journal, Autusm, 86. **CONTACT ADDRESS** Dept Humanities, Midwestern State Univ, 3410 Taft Blvd, Wichita Falls, TX 76308-2095. **EMAIL** everett.kindig@nexus.mwsu.edu

KING, ANTHONY D.
DISCIPLINE ART HISTORY **EDUCATION** Brunel Univ, PhD, 83. **CAREER** Prof, SUNY Binghamton. **RESEARCH** Soc production of building form; urbanism and colonialism; world syst and postcolonial theory; ethnic archit and develop. **SELECTED PUBLICATIONS** Auth, Re-Presenting the City: Ethnicity, Capital and Culture in the 21st Century Metropolis, Macmillan Educ and NY UP, 96; The Bungalow, The Production of a Global Culture, 2d ed, Oxford UP, 95;. Writing Colonial Space, in Comparative Studies Soc Hist, 95; Vernacular, Transnational, Postcolonial, Casabella, 95; The Times and Spaces of Modernity (Or Who Needs Postmodernism?) in Global Modernities, Sage, 95. **CONTACT ADDRESS** SUNY, Binghamton, PO Box 6000, Binghamton, NY 13902-6000. **EMAIL** adking@binghamton.edu

KING, H. ROGER
PERSONAL Born 05/12/1935, Plainville, CT, m, 1962, 2 children **DISCIPLINE** HISTORY **EDUCATION** Vanderbilt Univ, PhD. **CAREER** Prof and grad adv, Eastern Michigan Univ. **RESEARCH** US colonial period, US revolutionary war. **SELECTED PUBLICATIONS** Auth, Cape Cod and Plymouth Colony in the Seventeenth Century. **CONTACT ADDRESS** Dept of History and Philosophy, Eastern Michigan Univ, 701 Pray-Harrold, Ypsilanti, MI 48197. **EMAIL** roger.king@emich.edu

KING, JOHN O.
DISCIPLINE HISTORY **EDUCATION** Princeton univ, AB, 65; Univ Wis, PhD, 76. **CAREER** Asst prof, hist, Univ Mich; current, Ind Sch. **MEMBERSHIPS** Am Antiquarian Soc **SELECTED PUBLICATIONS** Auth, "Demonic New World and Wilderness Land: The Making of America," Prospects: The Ann of Am Cult Stud 7, 82; auth, The Iron of Melancholy, Wesleyan Univ Press, 83; auth, "On the Effectual Work of the Word: William James and the Practice of Puritan Confession," Texas Stud in Lang & Lit 25, 85. **CONTACT ADDRESS** 419 Second St, Ann Arbor, MI 48103.

KING, MARGARET L.
PERSONAL Born 10/16/1947, New York, NY, m, 1976, 2 children **DISCIPLINE** HISTORY **EDUCATION** Sarah Lawrence Col, BA, 67; Stanford Univ, MA, 68; PhD, 72. **CAREER** Asst Prof to Full Prof, Brooklyn Col, 72-. **HONORS AND AWARDS** Helen & Howard R Marraro prize, Am Hist Asn, 96; Tow Awd for Distinction in Scholarship, Brooklyn Col, 95; Favorite Teacher, Brooklyn Col, 93; Grant, Am Philos Soc, 91; NEH Fel, 87; NEH summer stipend, 84; Am Philos Grant, 79; Am Coun of Learned Soc Fel, 78; Gladys Krieble Delmas Foundation Grant, 78; Danforth Foundation Fel, 72; Woodrow Wilson Fel, 68. **MEMBERSHIPS** Renaissance Soc of Am, Am Hist Asn, Hist Soc. **RESEARCH** Renaissance Italy especially Venice, humanism, women. **SELECTED PUBLICATIONS** auth, Venetian Humanism in an Age of Patrician Dominance, Princeton Univ Press, 86; auth, Western Civilization: A Social and Cultural History, Prentice Hall, 00; auth, The Death of the Child Valerio Marcello, Univ Chicago Press, 94; auth, Women of the Renaissance, Univ Chicago Press, 91; ed, Her Immaculate Hand: Selected Works by and about the Women Humanists of Quattrocento Italy, Binghamton, 92. **CONTACT ADDRESS** Dept Hist, Brooklyn Col, CUNY, 2901 Bedford Ave, Brooklyn, NY 11210-2813. **EMAIL** margking@att.uet

KING, PETER
PERSONAL Born New York, NY **DISCIPLINE** CLASSICS, ANCIENT HISTORY **EDUCATION** Fordham Univ, MA; Univ NC, JD; PhD. **MEMBERSHIPS** Am Philol Asn. **RESEARCH** Roman Law, History and Society; Latin Language. **CONTACT ADDRESS** Dept Class, Temple Univ, 213 E 84th St, New York, NY 10028. **EMAIL** pking002@astro.temple.edu

KING, PETER JOHN
DISCIPLINE AMERICAN HISTORY **EDUCATION** Cambridge Univ, BA, 57, MA, 61; Univ Ill, PhD, 61. **CAREER** Prof. **RESEARCH** Eighteenth-century American intellectual history. **SELECTED PUBLICATIONS** Auth, Utilitarian Jurisprudence in America: The Influence of Bentham and Austin on American Legal Thought in the 19th Century, Garland, 86. **CONTACT ADDRESS** Dept of Hist, Carleton Univ, 1125 Colonel By Dr, 400 Patterson Hall, Ottawa, ON, Canada K1S 5B6. **EMAIL** pking@ccs.carleton.ca

KING, RICHARD D.
PERSONAL Born 09/16/1950, Chicago, IL, s **DISCIPLINE** HISTORY **EDUCATION** Mich State Univ, BA, 72; MA, 74; Univ Ill, PhD, 83. **CAREER** Instructor to Assoc Prof, Ursinus Col, 88-. **MEMBERSHIPS** Am Asn for the Adv of Slavic Studies. **RESEARCH** Russia, 1855-1917. **SELECTED PUBLICATIONS** Auth, Sergei Kirov and the Struggle for Soviet Power in the Terer Region, 1917-1918, Garland Pub, 87. **CONTACT ADDRESS** Dept Hist, Ursinus Col, 601 E Main St, Collegeville, PA 19426-2562. **EMAIL** rking@ursinus.edu

KING, WALTER JOSEPH
PERSONAL Born 01/10/1943, Leominster, MA, m, 1964, 1 child **DISCIPLINE** HISTORY **EDUCATION** Univ Mich, BA, 67, MA, 69, PhD(hist), 77. **CAREER** Asst prof, Upper Iowa Univ, 76-80; prof hist & philos, Northern State Univ, 80-, adj lectr hist, Univ Northern Iowa, 77. **HONORS AND AWARDS** Distinguished South Dakota Regental Professor, 90; Burlington Northern Excellence-in-Research Awd, 86; Outstanding Faculty Member, 84. **MEMBERSHIPS** AHA; Social Hist Soc England; Conf on British Studies; NAm Nietzsche Soc. **RESEARCH** Illegal behavior in early modern England; causes of change in history. **SELECTED PUBLICATIONS** Auth, Punishment for Bastardy in Early Seventeenth-Century England, Albion, 9/78; Modern European History, Univ Press, 78; Vagrancy and Local Law Enforcement: Why be a Constable in Stuart Lancashire?, The Historian, 2/80; Leet Jurors and the Search for Law and Order: Galling Persecution or Reasonable Justice?, Social Hist, 11/80; Regulation of Ale Houses in Stuart Lancashire: An Example of Discretionary Administration of the Law, Trans of the Hist Soc of Lancashire and Cheshire, 80; Out-of-Court Settlements in 17th Century England: Can Historians of Crime Trust Quantification?, 81 & Is Crime normal? Attitudes Toward Crime Since About 1500, 82, The Northern Soc Sci Rev; Untapped Resources for Social Historians: Court Leet Records, Journal Of Social History, spring 82; Early Stuart Courts Leet: Still Needful and Useful, Histoire Sociale-Social History, Nov 92; The Holocaust: Questions and Implications for Christianity, Journal of Ethnical Studies, Jan-March 92; How High is Too High? Disposing of Dung in Seventeenth-Century Prescot, Sixteenth-Century Journal, fall 92. **CONTACT ADDRESS** Dept of Hist & Philos, No State Univ, 1200 S Jay St, Aberdeen, SD 57401-7198. **EMAIL** kingw@northern.edu

KING-HAMMOND, LESLIE
PERSONAL Born 08/04/1944, Bronx, NY, d, 1 child **DISCIPLINE** ART HISTORY **EDUCATION** Queens College CUNY, BA 1969; Johns Hopkins Univ, MA 1973, PhD 1975. **CAREER** Performing Arts Workshops of Queens, New York, NY, chair dept of art, 69-71; Haryou-Act, Inc, Harlem, NY, pogram writer, 71; MD Institute, College of Art, Lecturer 1973-, Dean of Grad Studies 1976-; Corcoran School of Art, lecturer 1977, visiting faculty 1982; Howard Univ, Dept of African Studies, doctoral supervisor, 77-81; Civic Design Commission Baltimore City, commissioner 1983-87; Afro-Amer Historical & Cultural Museum, art consultant, 90-96; Philip Morris Scholarships for Artists of Color, Project Dir, 85-. **HONORS AND AWARDS** Horizon Fellowship, 1969-73; Kress Fellowship, John Hopkins Univ, 1974-75; Guest curator, Montage of Dreams Deferred, Baltimore Museum of Art 1979; published Celebrations: Myth & Ritual in Afro-American Art, Studio Museum in Harlem, 1982; Mellon Grant for Faculty Research, MD Institute, College of Art, 1984; guest curator, The Intuitive Eye, MD Art Place 1985; Trustee Awd for Excellence in Teaching 1986; co curator, Woman of the Year 1986, Women's Art Caucus, 1986; Mellon Grant for faculty research, 1987. **MEMBERSHIPS** Panelist, Natl Endowment for the Humanities 1978-80; panelist Natl Endowment for the Arts 1980-82; mem bd Baltimore School for the Arts 1984-; mem, Natl Conf of Artist; Col-

lege Art Association; mem bd Community Foundation of Greater Baltimore 1984-87; consult MD Arts Council 1985-; mem bd Art Commission, Baltimore City, Office of the Mayor, 1988; bd of drs, CAA, 1991-99, pres, 1996-98; bd, Alvin Ailey Dance Theatre Found of Maryland, 1990-93; bd of overseers, School for the Arts, Baltimore, 1996-99. **SELECTED PUBLICATIONS** Curator, 18 Visions/Divisions, Eubie Blake Cultural Center and Museum, 1988; co curator, Art as a Verb: The Evolving Continuum, 1988; curator, Black Printmakers and the WPA, Lehman Gallery of Art, 1989; coordinated Hale Woodruff Biennial, Studio Museum in Harlem, 1989; Masters, Makers and Inventors, Artscape, 1992; MCAC, 1992; Tom Miller Retrospective, Baltimore Museum of Art & Maryland Art Place, 1995; Hale Woodruff Biennale, Studio Museum in Harlem, 1994; Co-curator, Three Generations of African-American Women Sculptors, African-American Historial and Cultural Museum, Philadelphia, Equitable Gallery, NY, The Smithsonian, 1996-98; Exhibiting Artist, Artist-Scholar: In Search of A Balance, Ctr for African American History & Culture; The Smithsonian, 1997. **CONTACT ADDRESS** Maryland Inst, Col of Art, 1300 W Mt Royal Ave, Baltimore, MD 21217. **EMAIL** lkingha@mica.edu

KINGDON, ROBERT MCCUNE
PERSONAL Born 12/29/1927, Chicago, IL **DISCIPLINE** HISTORY **EDUCATION** Oberlin Col, AB, 49; Columbia Univ, MA, 50, PhD, 55. **CAREER** From instr to asst prof hist, Univ Mass, 52-57; from asst prof to pr of hist, State Univ Iowa, 57-65; Prof Hist, Univ Wis, Madison, 65-98, Dir, Inst Res Humanities, 75-87; Vis instr, Amherst Col, 53-54; Am Coun Learned Soc fel, 60-61; vis prof, Stanford Univ, 64 & 80; mem, Inst Advan Studies, 65-66; pres bd, Center Reformation Res, 67-; Guggenheim Found fel, 69-70; ed-in-chief, Sixteenth-Century J, 73-97; Folger Shakespeare Libr sr fel, 73-74; mem, Inst Res Humanities, 74-98; Pres bd, Center Reformation Res, 00. **HONORS AND AWARDS** Docteur es lettres, honoris causa, Univ Geneva, 86; Recipient of Festschrift, Essays Presented to Robert M. Kingdon, Sixteenth Century Essays and Studies, Sixteenth Century J, 87; Alexander von Humboldt Res Awd, Germany, 92-94; Fel, Inst Advan Studies, Hebew Univ, Jerusalem, 98; Honorary degree of Doctor of Humanities, Oberlin College, 99. **MEMBERSHIPS** Am Soc Reformation Res (secy-treas, 63-69, pres, 70-71); AHA; Am Soc Church Hist (pres, 80); Renaissance Soc Am; Int Fed Renaissance Socs & Insts (secy-treas, 67-89). **RESEARCH** History of the Calvinist Reformation and Catholic Reformation; business history of early printing industry. **SELECTED PUBLICATIONS** Auth, Geneva and the Coming of the Wars of Religion in France, 1555-1563, Librarie E Droz, Geneva, 56; The Plantin Breviaries, Biblio d'Humanisme et Renaissance, 60; coed, Registres de la Compagnie des Pasteurs de Geneve au Temps de Calvin, Librairie Droz, Geneva, 62 & 64; The Execution of Justice in England & A Defense of English Catholics, Cornell Univ, 65; auth, Geneva and the Consolidation of the French Protestant Movement, 1564-1572, Droz, Geneva & Univ Wis, Madison, 67; ed, Du Droit des Magistrats, Droz, 71; Transition and Revolution: Problems and Issues of European Renaissance and Reformation History, Burgess, 74; The Political Thought of Peter Martyr Vermigli, Libr E Droz, Geneva, 80; Church and Society in Reformation Europe, Variorum, London, 85; Myths about St Bartholomew's Day Massacres, 1572-1576, Harvard Univ Press, 88; auth, "Registres du Consitoire. . .vol. I," English Translation by Eerdmans, Grand Rapids, MI, 00. **CONTACT ADDRESS** Inst for Res in the Humanities, Univ of Wisconsin, Madison, 1401 Observatory Dr, Madison, WI 53706. **EMAIL** rkingdon@facstaff.wisc.edu

KINGHORN, KENNETH CAIN
PERSONAL Born 06/23/1930, Albany, OK, m, 1955, 4 children **DISCIPLINE** CHURCH HISTORY **EDUCATION** Ball State Univ, BS, 52; Asbury Theol Sem, BD, 62; Emory Univ, PhD, 65. **CAREER** From prof church hist to Dean Sch Theol, Asbury Theol Sem, 65-. **MEMBERSHIPS** Am Soc Church Hist. **RESEARCH** Wesley studies; Protestant Reformation; spiritual formation. **SELECTED PUBLICATIONS** Auth, Dynamic Discipleship, Fleming H Revell, 73; Fresh Wind of the Spirit, 75, Gifts of the Spirit, 76 & Christ Can Make You Fully Human, 79, Abingdon; Discovering Your Spiritual Gifts, 81 & A Celebration of Ministry, 82, Francis Asbury Publ Co; The Gospel of Grace, Abingdon, 92; auth, The Heritage of American Methodism, Abingdon, 99. **CONTACT ADDRESS** Dept of Church Hist, Asbury Theol Sem, 204 N Lexington Ave, Wilmore, KY 40390-1199. **EMAIL** ken_kinghorn@asburyseminary.edu

KINKLEY, JEFFREY CARROLL
PERSONAL Born Urbana, IL, m, 1981, 1 child **DISCIPLINE** HISTORY **EDUCATION** Univ Chicago, BA, 69; Harvard Univ, MA, 71, PhD, 77. **CAREER** Lectr, Harvard Univ, Hist, 77-79; asst prof, St Johns Univ, 79; assoc prof, 86; instr, Rutgers Univ, 92; PROF, ST JOHNS UNIV, 93-; vis prof, Columbia Univ, Asian Lang & Cult, 97. **MEMBERSHIPS** Asn Asian Stud; Am Hist Asn; Am Asn Chinese Comparative Lit **RESEARCH** History & literature of modern China. **SELECTED PUBLICATIONS** Auth, After Mao: Chinese Literature and Society, 78-81 ed., Harvard 85; auth, The Odyssey of Shen Congwen, Stanford Univ Press, 87; auth, Hsiao Chien Traveller Without a Map, trans, Hutchinson, 90; ed, Chen Xuezhao, Surviving the Storm, M.E. Sharpe, 90; coed, Modern Chinese Writers: Self-Portrayals M.E. Sharpe, 92; Shen Congwen bixia de Zhongguo Shehui yu Wenhua, East China Normal UP, 94; Shen Congwen. Imperfect Paradise: Stories by Shen Congwen, Univ Hawaii, 95; Chinese Justice, the Fiction: Law and Literature in Modern China, Stanford Univ Press, 00; Escape from the Law: Crime, Law and Literature in Post-Mao China. **CONTACT ADDRESS** Hist Dept, St. John's Univ, Jamaica, NY 11439. **EMAIL** kinkleyj@stjohns.edu

KINNEAR, MICHAEL S. R.
PERSONAL Born 08/13/1937, Saskatoon, SK, Canada **DISCIPLINE** HISTORY **EDUCATION** Univ Sask, BA, 60; Univ Oregon, MA, 61; Oxford Univ, DPhil, 65. **CAREER** PROF HISTORY, UNIV MANITOBA, 65-. **HONORS AND AWARDS** Can Coun scholar, leave fel; Woodrow Wilson fel; IODE scholar; SSHRC leave fel. **RESEARCH** Elections: Canada, historical electoral geography, the United States and Great Britain. **SELECTED PUBLICATIONS** Auth, The British Voter, 68, 81; auth, The Fall of Lloyd George, 73, 74; auth, Gleanings and Memoranda 1893-1968, 75; coauth, A History of the Vote in Canada, 97. **CONTACT ADDRESS** History Dept, Univ of Manitoba, 356 University College, Winnipeg, MB, Canada R3T 2M8. **EMAIL** michael_kinnear@umanitoba.ca

KINSELLA, DAVID
PERSONAL Born 12/09/1961, Detroit, MI, m, 1993, 1 child **DISCIPLINE** WORLD POLITICS **EDUCATION** Univ Calif, Irvine BA; Yale Univ, MA, Mphil, PhD. **CAREER** Asst prof; Univ Miss; Asst Prof, Am Univ. **HONORS AND AWARDS** Mershon postdoctoral fel, Ohio State Univ. **MEMBERSHIPS** American Political Science Assoc; International Studies Assoc; Peace Science Society. **RESEARCH** World politics, international relations theory, national security, arms trade. **SELECTED PUBLICATIONS** Contribur, Am Jour Pol Sci; Intl Studies Quart, Jour Conflict Resolution; auth, World Politics: The Menu to Choice, 6th ed. **CONTACT ADDRESS** American Univ, 4400 Massachusetts Ave, Washington, DC 20016. **EMAIL** kinsell@american.edu

KINSER, SAMUEL
PERSONAL Born 06/04/1931, Davenport, IA, m, 3 children **DISCIPLINE** MODERN HISTORY **EDUCATION** Carleton Col, BA, 53; Cornell Univ, PhD(hist), 60. **CAREER** Asst prof hist, Wash State Univ, 60-65; assoc prof, 65-70, prof hist, Northern Ill Univ, 70-, Newberry Libr grants-in-aid, 64 & 69; Am Philos Soc grant, 64-65 & 79; Weil Found fel, 64; Am Coun Learned Soc grant-in-aid, 65; Inst Res in Humanities fel, Madison, Wis, 68-69; vis prof, Ecole des hautes etudes en sciences sociales, Paris, 83. **HONORS AND AWARDS** Inst for Adv Studs in Humanities Fel, Univ of Edinburgh, 79; Nat Endowment for Humanities Fel, 93-94; Presidential Res Prof, North Ill Univ, 94-98. **RESEARCH** The relation of ideology and style to social and psychological formation in the Renaissance period; the emergence of concepts of historical process, social science and culture; folk and popular culture in Europe and the Americas. **SELECTED PUBLICATIONS** Auth, D'Aubigne and the Murder of Concini: Complaintes du sang du grand Henry, Studies Philol, 65; auth, The Works of Jacques-Auguste de Thou, Nijhoff, The Hague, 66; ed, Memoirs of Philippe de Commynes, Univ SC, Vols I & II, 69 & 73; auth, Ideas of Temporal Change and Cultural Process in France, 1470-1535, In: Renaissance Studies in Honor of Hans Baron, Florence, Italy & De Kalb, Ill, 71; auth, Annaliste paradigm?, The Geohistorical Structuralism of Fernand Braudel, Am Hist Rev, 81; auth, "Presentation and Representation: Carnival at Nuremberg, 1450-1550," Representations (86); auth, Carnival American Style, Mardi Gras at new Orleans and Mobile, Univ Chicago Press, Chicago, 90; auth, Rabelais's Carnival: Text, Context, Metatext, Univ Cal Press, Berkeley, 90; coauth, "Amerindian Masking in Trinidad's Carnival," Drama Review (98); auth, "Danser la conquete: Michoacan, Mexique 1586," in Creaolisations dans les contextes coloniaux et post-coloniaux (Quebec, 01). **CONTACT ADDRESS** Dept of History, No Illinois Univ, 1425 W Lincoln Hwy, De Kalb, IL 60115-2825. **EMAIL** sakinser@aol.com

KINSEY, WINSTON LEE
PERSONAL Born 03/07/1943, Lampasas, TX, m, 1964, 3 children **DISCIPLINE** AFRICAN HISTORY; WORLD CIV; AGRICULTURE **EDUCATION** Baylor Univ, BA, 64, MA, 65; Tx Tech Univ, PhD, 69. **CAREER** Teacher social studies, Tx City Independent Schs, 65-66; asst prof, 69-74, asst dean, Col Arts & Sci, 77-81, assoc prof hist to full prof, 74-91, Appalachian State Univ, 74-. **HONORS AND AWARDS** Inducted: Col of Outstanding Teachers, Col of Arts and Sciences, ASU, 99. **MEMBERSHIPS** African Studies Asn; SE Reg Sem N African St; AHA; Agr Hist Soc; Asn Hist NC. **RESEARCH** Recent Ghana; recent Africa; Texas agriculture, Agriculture in Western NC. **SELECTED PUBLICATIONS** Auth, Black Americans and the African Republic of Ghana, Faculty Publications, Appalachian State Univ, 70; The Immigrant in Texas Agriculture During Reconstruction, Agricultural History, 1/79. **CONTACT ADDRESS** Dept Hist, Appalachian State Univ, 1 Appalachian State, Boone, NC 28608-0001. **EMAIL** KinseyWL@appstate.edu

KIPLE, KENNETH FRANKLIN
PERSONAL Born 01/29/1939, Waterloo, IA, m, 1974, 4 children **DISCIPLINE** LATIN AMERICAN AND AMERICAN HISTORY **EDUCATION** Univ S FL, BA, 65; Univ FL, PhD, 70. **CAREER** Instr soc sci, Univ Fla, 69-70; asst prof, 70-77, assoc prof, 78-80, prof hist, Bowling Green State Univ, 81-94, Joint Soc Sci Res Coun & Am Coun Learned Soc grant, 77-79, distin prof, 94. **HONORS AND AWARDS** Natl inst health, natl lib meds - pub grant 98-99, OH coun for human gra, 92, natl lib med extralmurals prog gra, 91-92, Guggenheim mem found gra, 90-91, natl endow human fell, 88, Earhart found gra, 87, milbank mem fund gra, 86. **MEMBERSHIPS** Conf Latin Am Hist; AHA; Southern Hist Asn, Am Asn Hist Med. **RESEARCH** Slavery in the Am; Spain and Portugal; med hist; Hist food nutrit. **SELECTED PUBLICATIONS** Auth, Slave Nutrition, Disease and Infant Mortality in the Caribbean, J Interdisciplinary Hist, Vol XI, No 2, autumn 80; The African Connection: Slavery, Disease and Racism, Phylon, Vol XLI, fall 80; Another Dimension to the Black Diaspora: Diet, Disease and Racism, Cambridge Univ Press, 81; ed, The Caribbean Slave: A Biologiacal History, Cambridge univ Press, 84; The African Exchange: Toward a Biological History of Black People, Duke Univ Press, 88; The Cambridge World history of Human Disease, Cambridge Univ Press, 93; Plague, Pox, Pestilence: Disease in History, Weidenfeld and Nicolson in London, Barnes and Nobel in NY, 97; co-ed, Biological Consequences of the European Expansion, Variouvum (London), 97; co-ed, The Cambridge World Hist of Food, 2 vol, New York and Cambridge, 00. **CONTACT ADDRESS** Dept of Hist, Bowling Green State Univ, Bowling Green, OH 43403-0001.

KIRBY, ALEC
PERSONAL Born 07/24/1962, Royal Oak, MI, s **DISCIPLINE** HISTORY **EDUCATION** Muskingum Col, BA, 84; MA, 86, PhD, 92, George Washington Univ. **CAREER** Lectr in History and Govt, 91-97; Sr. Lectr, Univ Wisconsin-Stout, 97-; Asst Prof of History and Government, Univ of Wisconsin-Stout, 99-. **MEMBERSHIPS** Amer Historical Assoc. **RESEARCH** 20th century political history **CONTACT ADDRESS** Box 72, Menomonie, WI 54751. **EMAIL** kirbya@uwstout.edu

KIRBY, JACK TEMPLE
PERSONAL Born Portsmouth, VA, s, 2 children **DISCIPLINE** HISTORY **EDUCATION** Old Dominion Coll, BA, 63; Univ Va, MA, 64; PhD, 65. **CAREER** Asst prof, 65-69; assoc prof, 69-74; prof, 74-88; WE Smith prof, 88-, Miami Univ. **HONORS AND AWARDS** Fulbright Sr Lectr, NAH, Univ Genoa, 99. **MEMBERSHIPS** OAH; ASA; SHA; ASEH; VHS. **RESEARCH** Environmental; rural cultures; American South. **SELECTED PUBLICATIONS** Auth, Poquoson: A Study in Rural Landscape and Society (NC, 95); auth, The Counterculture South (GA, 00); auth, "Designs Necessary and Sublime," Harvard Design Mag (00): 41-46. **CONTACT ADDRESS** Dept History, Miami Univ, Oxford, OH 45056-1602. **EMAIL** kirbyjt@muohio.edu

KIRBY, TORRANCE W.
PERSONAL Born 07/04/1955, Red Deer, AB, Canada, m, 1980, 2 children **DISCIPLINE** RENAISSANCE & REFORMATION **EDUCATION** Dalhousie Univ,BA; MA, Oxford Univ, DPhil, 88. **CAREER** Commonwealth Schol, Christ Church, Oxford, 80-84; Fel, King's Col, Nova Scotia, 84-89; Tutor, St. John's Col, 89-96; Mem, Princeton Ctr Theol Inquiry, 96-; Prof Church Hist, Mc McGill Univ, 97-. **HONORS AND AWARDS** Univ Medal in Classics, Dalhousie, 77; Killam Fel, Dalhousie, 77-79. **MEMBERSHIPS** Am Acad Relig; Soc Christian Ethics; Sixteenth Century Studies Conf; Atlantic Theol Conf. **RESEARCH** Richard Hooker, Peter Martyr Vermigli, Reformation and Neoplatonism, Patristic Studies. **SELECTED PUBLICATIONS** Auth, Richard Hooker's Doctrine of the Royal Supremacy, Leiden, New York, Copenhagen and Cologne: E.J. Brill, 90; auth, "Richard Hooker as an Apologist of the Magisterial Reformation in England," Richard Hooker and the Construction of Christian Community, Tempe, AZ: Medieval and Renaissance Texts and Studies, (97); 219-233, auth, "Richard Hooker," The Oxford Dictionary of the Christion Church 3rd ed, Oxford University Press, (97); auth, " Praise as the Soul"s Overcoming of Time in the Confessions of St. Augustine," Pro Ecclesia: A Journal of Catholic and Evangelical Theology vol 6, (97), 333-350; auth, "Richard Hooker's Theory of Natural Law: Magisterial reform and the Question Orthodoxy," Animus vol 3, (98); auth, "the Neoplatonic Logic of Procession and Return," Richard Hooker's Discourse on Law, Animus vol 4, (99). **CONTACT ADDRESS** 3520 University St., Montreal, QC, Canada H3A 2A7. **EMAIL** tkirby@wilson.lan.mcgill.ca

KIRKPATRICK, DIANE MARIE
PERSONAL Born 06/28/1933, Grand Rapids, MI **DISCIPLINE** HISTORY OF ART **EDUCATION** Vassar Col, BA, 55; Cranbrook Acad Art, MFA, 57; Univ Mich, Ann Arbor, MA, 65, PhD, 69. **CAREER** Manuscript & layout ed, Fideler Publ Co, Mich, 57-58; serv club dir, US Army Europe, Ger, 58-60; dir children's educ art hist & appreciation, Grand Rapids Art Mus, Mich, 61-63; lectr hist of art, 68-69, instr, 69-70, asst prof, 72-74, dir, Prog in Film Video Studies, 77-78, assoc prof,

Prof, 82- , Hist of Art, Univ Mich, Ann Arbor, 74- , Sr fel, Mich Soc Fels, 73-78; Nat Endowment for grant to spec exhibs, 92. **HONORS AND AWARDS** Thurman Prof Hist of Art, 97; Time-Warner Media Develop Awd, 95-99; H R Bloch Fund Spec Awd Course Develop, 97-98. **MEMBERSHIPS** Col Art Asn Am. **RESEARCH** Twentieth century Western art; movies; popular culture. **SELECTED PUBLICATIONS** Auth, Eduardo Paolozzi, Studio Vista, 70; The Creation of Art (10 TV progs), Univ Mich TV Ctr, 74-75; An interview with film pioneer Frank Goldman, Cinegram, 77; Sonia Sharidan: Mind and machine, Afterimage, 78; Imaging and the machine, In: Chicago: The City and Its Artists 1945-1978, Univ Mich Mus Art, 78; The Artistic Vision of Jim Pallas, Detroit Inst Arts, 78; Making Waves: Recent Art, Science, and Technology Interactions in Chicago, Evanston Art Ctr, 86; Gardners Art Through the Ages, Harcourt, Brace, Jovanovitch, 90; Time and space in the Work of Laszlo Moholy-Nagy, Hungarian Stud Rev, 89; The Artists of the IG: Backgrounds and Continuities, The Independent Group: Postwar Britain and the Aesthetics of Plenty, MIT Press, 90; La Fotografia e la Nuova Tecnologia, Fotologia, 92; In-Visibility: Art and Disability, Mich Quart Rev, 98. **CONTACT ADDRESS** Dept of Hist of Art, Univ of Michigan, Ann Arbor, 519 S State St, Ann Arbor, MI 48109-1357. **EMAIL** dianek@umich.edu

KIRSHNER, ALAN MICHAEL
PERSONAL Born 02/01/1938, New York, NY, m, 1977, 3 children **DISCIPLINE** LATIN-AMERICAN HISTORY **EDUCATION** Hofstra Univ, BA, 59; City Col New York, MA, 63; NYork Univ, PhD(Hist), 70. **CAREER** Asst prof Hist, Univ WFla, 69-71; assoc prof, 71-76, prof Hist, Ohlone Col, 76-. **RESEARCH** Mexico, 1930-1935; marginal groups in Western civilization; masculinity. **SELECTED PUBLICATIONS** Auth, A Setback for Tomas Garrido Canabal's Desire to Eliminate the Church in Mexico, J Church & State, Autumn 71; Closing Phases of Global Exploration: The Evolution of the Early Works of Halford J Mackinder, Community Col Soc Sci Quart, Spring 72; Tomas Garrido Canabal y el Movimiento de los Camisas Rojas, Sep-Setentas, 76; Teaching the History Survey Course: Looking to the 1980's--The Need to Introduce Popular Culture, Popular Culture Methods, 6/77; Heretical Interpretations of Western Civilization: A Teaching Method, Community Col Soc Sci Asn, Fall 77; Masculinity in an Historical Perspective: Readings and Discussions, Univ Press Am, 77; Masculinity in American Comics, In: Men in Difficult Times, Prentice-Hall, 81; Tomas Garrido Canabal and the Repression of Religion in Tabasco, In: Religion in Latin American Life and Literature, Baylor Univ Press, 81; In the Course Of Human Events: Essays in American Government, Simon & Schuster, 98. **CONTACT ADDRESS** Dept of History, Ohlone Col, 43600 Mission Blvd, Fremont, CA 94539-5884. **EMAIL** AKirshner@ohlone.cc.ca.us

KIRSHNER, JULIUS
PERSONAL Born 07/12/1939, New York, NY, m, 1965, 1 child **DISCIPLINE** MEDIEVAL & RENAISSANCE HISTORY **EDUCATION** Pace Col, BA, 61; Vatican Paleog & Diplomatic Sch, dipl paleog & diplomatics, 69; Am Acad Rome, dipl, 69; Columbia Univ, PhD, 70. **CAREER** Instr hist, Pace Col, 63-65; Lectr hist, City Col New York, 64-65; asst prof, Bard Col, 65-70; from Asst Prof to Assoc Prof, 70-83, prof hist, Univ of Chicago, 83-. **HONORS AND AWARDS** Herodotus fel, Inst Advan Studies, 72-73; I Tatti fel, 78-79; Nat Endowment Humanities fel, 78-79. **MEMBERSHIPS** Medieval Acad Am; Renaissance Soc Am. **SELECTED PUBLICATIONS** Auth, Papa Eugenio IV e il Monte Comune, Arch Storico Ital, 69; The Moral Theology of Public Finance, Archivum Fratrum Praedicatorum, 70; Civitas Sibi Faciat Civem: Bartolus of Sassoferrato's Doctrine on the Making of a Citizen, Speculum, 73; The Dowry Fund and the Marriage Market in Early Quattrocento Florence, J Mod Hist, 78; Between Nature and Culture: An Opinion of Baldus of Perugia on Venetian Citizenship as Second Nature, J Medieval and Renaissance Studies, 79; co-ed, University of Chicago Readings in Western Civilization, Univ Chicago Press, 9 vols, 86-87; ed, Italy, 1530-1630, Longman, 88; coauth, A Grammar of Signs: Bartolo da Sassoferrato's Tract on Insignia and Coats of Arms, Studies in Comparative Legal Hist, Publ of The Robbins Collection in Relig and Civil Law, Univ Calif, 94; ed and contribr, The Origins of the State in Italy, 1300-1600, Univ Chicago Press, 96. **CONTACT ADDRESS** Dept of Hist, Univ of Chicago, 1126 E 59th St, Chicago, IL 60637-1539.

KISER, JOY
DISCIPLINE ART HISTORY, LIBRARY AND INFORMATION SERVICES **EDUCATION** Univ Akron, BA, 88; Case Western Reserve Univ, MA, 90; Kent State Univ, MLIS, 94. **CAREER** HEAD LIBR, CLEVELAND MUS NAT HIST; med libr Wooster Community Hosp. **CONTACT ADDRESS** Cleveland Mus of Nat Hist, Harold Terry Clark Lib, 1 Wade Oval Dr, Univ Cir, Cleveland, OH 44106-1767. **EMAIL** jkiser@cmnh.org

KITAO, T. KAORI
PERSONAL Born 01/30/1933, Tokyo, Japan **DISCIPLINE** ART HISTORY **EDUCATION** Univ CA, BA; MA; Harvard Univ, PhD. **CAREER** Fac, RI Sch Design, 63-66; fac, Swarthmore Col, 66; Chp, 75-81; William R. Kenan, Jr. Prof Art Hist, present. **HONORS AND AWARDS** VP Int Soc Comp Study of Civs, 80-83. **RESEARCH** Renaissance and Baroque art and archit; Am archit; cinema, design, and visual semiotics; material cult as hist of ideas; Bernini's archit. **SELECTED PUBLICATIONS** Auth, Oval and Circle in the Square of St. Peter's; scholarly articles in the Art Bulletin and the Journal of the Society of Architectural Historians; writings also on Japanese gardens **CONTACT ADDRESS** Swarthmore Col, Swarthmore, PA 19081-1397. **EMAIL** tkitao1@swarthmore.edu

KITCHEL, MARY JEAN
PERSONAL Born New York, NY **DISCIPLINE** PHILOSOPHY, MEDIEVAL STUDIES **EDUCATION** Rice Univ, BA, 64; Pontif Inst Mediaeval Studies, MSL, 68; Univ Toronto, PhD, 74. **CAREER** Asst prof philos, Univ St Thomas, TX, 68-69; asst prof, Emmanuel Col, MA, 69-74; loan asst, Student Financial Aid, Houston Community Col Syst, 76-77; asst prof, 77-79, assoc dean extended educ, 80-82, Assoc Prof Philos, Univ St Thomas, TX, 79-88, Prof Phil, 88-, Dean Acad Serv, 90-93, Dept Ch Phil, 96-, Asst prof church hist, St Mary's Sem, TX, 68-69; res assoc philos & text ed, Pontif Inst Mediaeval Studies, Toronto, 73-75; Nat Endowment for Hum grant, 79. **HONORS AND AWARDS** Piper Professorship, 90; Sears-Roebuck Found Awd, 90 **MEMBERSHIPS** Am Cath Philos Asn. **RESEARCH** Ed and analysis of texts of Walter Burley; philos psychol, philos of hum person; medl ethics. **SELECTED PUBLICATIONS** Auth, The De potentis animae of Walter Burley, 71, Walter Burley's Doctrine of the Soul: Another view, 77 Mediaeval Studies; Walter Burley and radical Aristotelanism, Proc World Cong on Aristotle (in press). **CONTACT ADDRESS** Dept of Philos, Univ of St. Thomas, Texas, 3800 Montrose, Houston, TX 77006-4696. **EMAIL** kitchel@stthom.edu

KITCHEN, MARTIN
PERSONAL Born 12/21/1936, Nottingham, England **DISCIPLINE** HISTORY **EDUCATION** Univ London, BA, 63, PhD, 66. **CAREER** Fac mem, 66-76, prof Hist, Simon Fraser Univ, 76-. **SELECTED PUBLICATIONS** Auth, British Policy Towards the Soviet Union, 1939-1945, London: MacMillan, 86; auth, The Origins of the Cold War, London: MacMillan, 88; auth, Europe Between the Wars, London: Longman, 88; auth, A World in Flames: A Short History of the Second World War in Europe and Asia 1939-1945, London: Longman, 90; auth, "Nazi Germani at War," London: Longmans, 94; auth, Empire and After: A Short History of the British Empire and Commonwealth Nazi Germany at War, Centre for Distance Education, SFU, 94; auth, The Cambridge History of Germany, Cambridge Univ Press, 96. **CONTACT ADDRESS** Dept of History, Simon Fraser Univ, 8888 Univ Dr, Burnaby, BC, Canada V5A 1S6. **EMAIL** martin_kitchen@sfu.ca

KITTELSON, JAMES
DISCIPLINE CHURCH HISTORY **EDUCATION** St. Olaf Col, Phi Beta Kappa grad, 63; Stanford Univ, MA, 64, PhD, 69. **CAREER** Instr, Ohio State Univ, 71; vice-ch, Ohio State Univ, 74-77; ch, grad stud, Ohio State Univ, 89-91; vis grad prof, Luther Northwestern Theol Sem, 92; Concordia Univ. 97; prof, 97-; dir, Lutheran Brotherhood Res Prog. **HONORS AND AWARDS** Pres, bd of the Sixteenth Century Stud (s) Conf; exec comm, Coun Amer Soc for Reformation Res; Soc for Reformation Res; bd of dir(s), Ctr for Reformation Res. **SELECTED PUBLICATIONS** Auth, Luther the Reformer: The Story of the Man and His Career, 86; sr ed, Oxford Encycl of the Reformation, 96. **CONTACT ADDRESS** Dept of Church History, Luther Sem, 2481 Como Ave, Saint Paul, MN 55108. **EMAIL** jkittels@luthersem.edu

KITTERMAN, DAVID HAROLD
PERSONAL Born 04/01/1940, Denver, CO, m, 1964, 3 children **DISCIPLINE** MODERN EUROPEAN HISTORY **EDUCATION** Univ Utah, BA, 64, MA, 66; Univ Wash, PhD(Europ hist), 72. **CAREER** Instr hist, Utah State Univ, 69-70; asst prof, 70-78, Assoc Prof Hist, Northern Ariz Univ, 78-. **MEMBERSHIPS** AHA; Western Soc Sci Asn; Asn Ger Studies (pres, 76-78). **RESEARCH** Twentieth century German social, cultural and intellectual history; World War II and World War I history; modern Russian history. **SELECTED PUBLICATIONS** **CONTACT ADDRESS** Dept of Hist, No Arizona Univ, Flagstaff, AZ 86001.

KIVELSON, VALERIE
DISCIPLINE HISTORY **EDUCATION** Harvard Univ, AB, 80; San Francisco State Univ, MA, 82; Stanford Univ, PhD, 88. **CAREER** Assoc Prof, Univ Mich. **HONORS AND AWARDS** IREX Fel; NEH Fel; Fulbright-Hays Fel; Arthur F Thurman Awd. **MEMBERSHIPS** AHA, ESSA, AAASS, WAAASS. **RESEARCH** Early modern Russia, cartography, witchcraft, Russian orthodoxy. **SELECTED PUBLICATIONS** Auth, "Patrolling the Boundaries: Witchcraft Accusations and Household Strife in Seventeenth-Century Moscovy," Harvard Ukrainian Studies, 29 (95): 302-323; auth, "Political Sorcery in Sixteenth-Century Muscovy," in Cult Identity in Muscovy 1359-1584 (Moscow: Slavica Publ, 97), 267-283; auth, Autocracy in the Provinces: Russian Political Culture and the Gentry in the Seventeenth-Century, Stanford UP (Stanford), 97; auth, "Kinship Politics/Autocratic Politics: A Reconsideration of Eighteenth-Century political Culture," in Imperial Russia: New Hist for the Empire (Bloomington: Ind UP, 98), 5-3; auth, "The Souls of the Righteous in a Bright Place: Landscape and Orthodoxy in Seventeenth-Century Russian Maps," Russ Rev, 58 (99): 1-25; auth, "Cartography, Autocracy and State Powerlessness: The Uses of Maps in Early Modern Russia," Imago Mundi, 51 (99): 83-105. **CONTACT ADDRESS** Dept Hist, Univ of Michigan, Ann Arbor, 435 S State St, Tisch Hall, Ann Arbor, MI 48109-1003. **EMAIL** vkivelso@umich.edu

KLAASSEN, WALTER
PERSONAL Born 05/27/1926, Laird, SK, Canada, m, 1952, 3 children **DISCIPLINE** HISTORY, THEOLOGY **EDUCATION** McMaster Univ, BA, 54; McMaster Divinity Sch, BD, 57; Oxford Univ, DPhil(hist theol), 60. **CAREER** Assoc prof Bible, Bethel Col, Kans, 60-62, chmn dept Bible and relig, 62-64; assoc prof Bible and relig, 64-70, assoc prof hist, 71-73, Prof Hist, Conrad Grebel Col, Univ Waterloo, 73-; Can Coun grants, 70-73 and 78-79. **MEMBERSHIPS** Am Soc Church Hist; Can Soc Church Hist; Mennonitischer Geschichtsverein; NAm Comt for Doc Free Church Origins (secy, 71). **RESEARCH** Just war theory; dissent in the 16th century; unilateral peace initiatives in history. **SELECTED PUBLICATIONS** Jesus, A Crucified Pharisee, J Ecumenical Studies, Vol 0029, 92; Homosexuality in the Church in Both Sides of the Debate, J Ecumenical Studies, Vol 0033, 96. **CONTACT ADDRESS** Conrad Grebel Col, Univ of Waterloo, 200 Westmount Rd, Waterloo, ON, Canada N2L 3G6.

KLANG, DANIEL M.
PERSONAL Born 09/12/1934, San Francisco, CA, m, 1967 **DISCIPLINE** MODERN EUROPEAN HISTORY **EDUCATION** Univ Calif, Berkeley, BA, 59; Princeton Univ, PhD(hist), 63. **CAREER** Asst prof, 63-70, Assoc Prof Hist, Univ BC, 70-. **MEMBERSHIPS** AHA **RESEARCH** Western Europe, 1600-1918. **SELECTED PUBLICATIONS** Auth, , Political Science and Revolution in Works of Fabbroni,Giovanni 1752-1822, Intellectual and Civil Servant in Lorraine, J Mod Hist, Vol 0064, 92; Culture, Intellectuals and Circulation of Ideas in the 18th Cent, J Modern Hist, Vol 0064, 92; 18th-Century Reform, Vol 5, Italy of the Enlightenment, Pt 2, The Republic of Venice, 1761-1797, Engl Hist Rev, Vol 0109, 94. **CONTACT ADDRESS** Dept of Hist, Univ of British Columbia, Vancouver, BC, Canada V6T 1W5.

KLAREN, PETER FLINDELL
PERSONAL Born 10/18/1938, Summit, NJ, m, 1963, 1 child **DISCIPLINE** LATIN AMERICAN HISTORY **EDUCATION** Dartmouth Col, AB, 60; Univ Calif, Los Angeles, MA, 64, PhD(hist), 68. **CAREER** Asst prof hist, Wash State Univ, 68-70; adj asst prof, Dartmouth Col, 71-72; asst prof, 72-75; assoc prof, 75-79, prof hist, George Washington Univ, 79-, Soc Sci Res Coun fel, 73-74; fel, Andrew Mellon Found, Aspen Inst Humanistic Studies, 75-76 & Am Philos Soc, 76-77. **HONORS AND AWARDS** Trachtenberg Teaching Prize, GWU, 95. **MEMBERSHIPS** AHA; Latin Am Studies Asn. **RESEARCH** Late 19th and early 20th century social and economic history of Latin America; Peru. **SELECTED PUBLICATIONS** Auth, Las Haciendas Azucareras y los Origines del Apra, Inst Peruvian Studies, Lima, 70 & 2nd ed, 76; Modernization, Dislocation and Aprismo: Origins of the Peruvian Aprista Party, 1870-1932, Univ Tex, 73; contrib, The social and Economic Consequences of Modernization in the Peruvian Sugar Industry, 1860-1940, In: Land and Labour in Latin America: Essays in the Development of Agrarian Capitalism, Cambridge Univ, 77; Orgins of Modern Peru, 1880-1930, In: Vol V, Cambridge History of Latin America, Cambridge Univ Press, 86; contrib, Historical Background, Peru: A Country Study, ed by Rex Hudson, Washington, 93; co-ed; Promise of Change, Theories of Development in Latin America, Westview Press, 86; auth, Peru: Society and Nationhood in the Andes, Oxford Univ Press, 00. **CONTACT ADDRESS** Dept of Hist, The George Washington Univ, 2035 H St N W, Washington, DC 20052-0001. **EMAIL** klaren@gwu.edu

KLASSEN, PETER JAMES
PERSONAL Born 12/18/1930, AB, Canada, m, 1959, 3 children **DISCIPLINE** EARLY MODERN EUROPEAN HISTORY **EDUCATION** Univ BC, BA, 55; Univ Southern Calif, MA, 68, PhD(hist), 62. **CAREER** Prin, Fraser Lake Sch, BC, Can, 53-54; lectr hist, Univ Southern Calif, 58-60, admin supvr, Dept Gen Studies, 60-62; head dept hist and cur arch, Pac Col, 62-66; from asst prof to assoc prof, 66-69, chmn dept, 69-74, dir conflict resolution prog, 73-75, Prof Hist, Calif State Univ, Fresno, 69-, Dean, Sch Soc Sci, 80-97; Dir, Int Programs, 93-. **MEMBERSHIPS** AHA; Am Soc Church Hist; Am Soc Reformation Res; Renaissance Soc Am. **RESEARCH** The Reformation; western civilization; Mennonite history. **SELECTED PUBLICATIONS** Auth, The Economics of Anabaptism, 1525-1560, 64; auth, Europe in the Reformation, 79; auth, The Reformation: Change and Stability, 80; auth, A Homeland For Strangers, 89. **CONTACT ADDRESS** Dept of Hist, California State Univ, Fresno, Fresno, CA 93710. **EMAIL** peterk@csu.fresno.edu

KLAUSNER, CARLA LEVINE
PERSONAL Born 11/09/1936, Kansas City, MO, m, 1963, 3 children **DISCIPLINE** MIDDLE EASTERN HISTORY, MEDIEVAL HISTORY **EDUCATION** Barnard Col, Columbia Univ, AB, 58; Radcliffe Col, AM, 60; Harvard Univ, PhD (Mid E hist), 63. **CAREER** Teaching asst Islamic insts, Harvard Univ, 61-62; from lectr to prof Mid E hist and civilization, Univ Mo Kansas City, 64-. **HONORS AND AWARDS** Shelby Storck Awd, Univ MoKansas City, 77. **MEMBERSHIPS** AHA; MidE Studies Asn NAm. **RESEARCH** Islamic civilization and modern Middle East history; medieval and contemporary Jewish history; medieval European civilization. **SELECTED PUBLICATIONS** Auth, The Seljule Vezivate, Harvard Univ Pr (Cambridge), 73; coauth, A Concise Hist of the Arab-Israeli Conflict, Prentice Hall (NYork), 4th ed, 98. **CONTACT ADDRESS** Dept of Hist, Univ of Missouri, Kansas City, 5100 Rockhill Rd, Kansas City, MO 64110-2499. **EMAIL** klausnenc@umkc.edu

KLEBER, BROOKS EDWARD
PERSONAL Born 04/15/1919, Trenton, NJ, w, 1946 **DISCIPLINE** MILITARY HISTORY **EDUCATION** Dickinson Col, PhB, 40; Univ Pa, MA, 48, PhD, 57. **CAREER** Historian, US Army Chem Corps Hist off, 50-59, asst chief, 59-63; chief historian, US Continental Army Command, 63-73; chief historian, US Army Training and Doctrine Command, 73-80; Dep Chief Historian, US Army Ctr Mil Hist, 80-. **HONORS AND AWARDS** Infinity OCS Hall of Fame **MEMBERSHIPS** Society of Military Historians **RESEARCH** POW and military history. **SELECTED PUBLICATIONS** Chemicals in Combat: US Army in WWII. **CONTACT ADDRESS** 440 Summer Dr, Newport News, VA 23606.

KLEIMOLA, ANN
DISCIPLINE MEDIEVAL RUSSIAN HISTORY **EDUCATION** Univ Mich, PhD, 70. **CAREER** Prof, Univ Nebr, Lincoln. **HONORS AND AWARDS** NEH Inst, 94. **SELECTED PUBLICATIONS** Auth, Justice in Medieval Russia, Am Philos Soc, 75; coed, Culture and Identity in Muscovy, 1359-1584, Moscow, 97. **CONTACT ADDRESS** Univ of Nebraska, Lincoln, 635 Oldfather Hall, Lincoln, NE 68588-0327. **EMAIL** akleimola1@unl.edu

KLEIN, BERNARD
PERSONAL Born 10/15/1928, Czechoslovakia, m, 1961, 2 children **DISCIPLINE** MODERN & JEWISH HISTORY; THE NAZI HOLOCAUST **EDUCATION** Rabbi, Torah Vodaath Talmudical Sem, 53; Brooklyn Col, BA, magna cum laud, 54; Columbia Univ, MA, 56, PhD, 62. **CAREER** Lectr hist, Brooklyn Col, 58-61 & City Col New York, 64; from instr to assoc prof, 65-69, chmn, Div Behav & Soc Sci, 68-70, chmn, Dept Hist & Polit Sci, 70-71, chmn, Dept Hist & Philos, 72-79, Prof Hist, Kingsborough Community Col, 69-, Chmn Dept Soc Sci, 79-95, Chmn Dept Hist, Philos & Polit Sci, 95-; Lectr, Long Island Univ, 60; consult, Nat Curric Res Inst, Am Asn Jewish Educ, 65-67; mem educ coun, Fed Jewish Philanthropists, pres, 67-69; pres, Jewish Fac Asn, City Univ New York, 79-. **HONORS AND AWARDS** Phi Beta Kappa, 54; Fel, Conf Material Claims Jews against Ger, 57-58, 59-60; Fel, Res Found State Univ NY, 71; Chemn & Coordr of Annual Interdisciplinary Conferences on the Holocaust at the Hebrew Univ, Jerusalem, Israel. **MEMBERSHIPS** AHA **RESEARCH** German international policy during the Nazi Period; the right-radical movements in Hungary during the inter-war period; Jewish history and the Nazi Holocaust. **SELECTED PUBLICATIONS** Auth, Rudolf Kasztner and the Hungarian Rescue Effort, in Perspective, Vol I, 59; The Judenrat, Jewish Social Studies, 1/60; New developments in Jewish school curricula, Am Asn Jewish Educ, 65 & in Jewish Education Register and Directory, 65; The decline of a Sephardic community in Transylvania, Studies in Honor of M J Benardete, 65; Hungarian politics and the Jewish question, 4/66 & Anti-Jewish demonstrations in Hungarian universities, 1932-1936: Their role in the struggle for political power between Istvan, Bethlen, and Gyula Gombos, 82, Jewish Soc Studies, 82; Hungarian politics and the Jewish question, in Hostages of Modernization: Studies on Modern Antisemitism, 1870-1933/39, Walter de Gruyer, 93. **CONTACT ADDRESS** Dept Hist, Philos & Polit Sci, Kingsborough Comm Col, CUNY, 2001 Oriental Blvd, Brooklyn, NY 11235-2333. **EMAIL** bklein@kbcc.cuny.edu

KLEIN, CECELIA F.
PERSONAL Born 06/05/1938, Pittsburgh, PA **DISCIPLINE** ART HISTORY **EDUCATION** Oberlin Col, BA, 60; MA, 67; Columbia Univ, PhD, 72. **CAREER** Asst Prof, Oakland Univ, 72-76; Asst Prof to Prof, UCLA, 76-. **HONORS AND AWARDS** Fel, Samuel H. Kress Found, 64-65; Fel, NDEA Title IV, 65-68; Fel, Ails Mellon , Ctr for Adv Study in the Visual Arts, 86; Fel, Dumbarton Oaks, 92; Res Grant, UCLA, 97-;Distinguished Teaching of Art Hist Awd, Col Art Asn, 00. **MEMBERSHIPS** Col Art Asn; Asn for Latin Am Art; Soc for Am Archaeol; Am Anthropol Asn; Am Soc for Ethnohist. **RESEARCH** The political functions of Aztec art; Gender ideology in Aztec art; Body symbolism in Aztec art; Historiography and theory of Pre-Columbian and 'Primitive' art. **SELECTED PUBLICATIONS** Auth, "Teocuitlatl, 'Divine Excrement: The Significance of 'Holy Shit' in Aztec Mexico," Art J, (93): 39-64; auth, "Fighting with Feminity: Gender and War in Aztec Mexico," in Gendering Rhetorics: Postures of Dominance and Submission in Human History, (SUNY, 94), 107-146; auth, "Wild Woman in Colonial Mexico: An Encounter of European and Aztec Concepts of the Other," in Reframing the Renaissance: Studies in the Migration of Visual Culture, (Yale Univ Press, 95), 244-263. **CONTACT ADDRESS** Dept Art Hist, Univ of California, Los Angeles, 100 Dodd Hall, 405 Hilgard Ave, Los Angeles, CA 90095. **EMAIL** cklein@ucla.edu

KLEIN, DENNIS B.
PERSONAL Born 05/28/1948, Cleveland, OH, m, 1979, 3 children **DISCIPLINE** HISTORY, JEWISH HISTORY **EDUCATION** Hobart Col, BA, 70; Univ Rochester, MA, 72, PhD, 78. **CAREER** Dorst Teaching Fel, New York Univ, 81-84; Dir, ADL Holocaust Studies, 84-93; assoc prof and Jewish Studies Dir, Kean Univ, 96-. **HONORS AND AWARDS** Phi Beta Kappa, 70; Hobart Col, BA, cum laude, 70; Fulbright-Hays Diss Fel, Vienna, 74-75; Post-doctoral Fel, Harvard Univ, 79-81; New York State Governor's Awd in Ed, 87; Awds: Nat Endowment for the Humanities, Nat Acad of Ed; listed: Who's Who in the East, Who's Who in Am Cols and Univs, Dict of Int Biog. **MEMBERSHIPS** Am Hist Soc, Asn for Jewish Studies. **RESEARCH** Central European history, Jewish history, history and psychology. **SELECTED PUBLICATIONS** Auth, American Deeds-Jewish Dreams: A Study of the American Jewish Movement, 1916-1955, Waltham, MA: Am Jewish Hist Soc (80); auth, Jewish Origins of the Psychoanalytic Movement, New York: Praeger (81), Univ Chicago Press (85); founding ed, Dimensions: A J of Holocaust Studies, 85-; coauth with J. M. Muffs, The Holocaust in Books and Films: A Selected Annotated List, New York: Hippocrene (86); auth, "The Fate of Holocaust Literature," Handbook of Holocaust Literature, ed Saul Friedman, Westport, CT: Greenwood Press (93); ed, Hidden History of the Kovno Ghetto, in collaboration with the U.S. Holocaust Memorial Museum, Little, Brown (Bulfinch, 97); auth, "Holocaust, " Encyclopedia of Historians and Historical Writing, London and Chicago: Fitzroy Dearborn (99); auth, "Dimensions Magazine: Wrestling with Memory," Encyclopedia of Genocide, Jerusalem: Hebrew Univ Inst on the Holocaust and Genocide (forthcoming); rev, "Thinking About the Holocaust," German Politics and Soc (forthcoming); auth, "Myth of the Hidden Jew," Holocaust and Genocide Studies (forthcoming). **CONTACT ADDRESS** Dept Hist, Kean Col of New Jersey, Union, NJ 07083. **EMAIL** dbklein1@juno.com

KLEIN, HERBERT S.
DISCIPLINE LATIN AMERICAN HISTORY **EDUCATION** Univ Chicago, BA, 57, PhD, 63. **CAREER** Prof. **SELECTED PUBLICATIONS** Slavery in the Americas, A Comparative History of Cuba and Virginia, 67; Origenes de la Revolucion Nacional Boliviana: La Crisis de la generacion del Chaco, 68, 93; Parties and Political Change in Bolivia, 1880-1952, 69; The Middle Passage: Comparative Studies in the Atlantic Slave Trade, 78; Bolivia: The Evolution of a Multi-Ethnic Society, 82; African Slavery in Latin America and the Caribbean, 86; Haciendas y Ayllus, Rural Society in the Bolivian Andes in the 18th- and 19th-century, 93. **CONTACT ADDRESS** Dept of Hist, Columbia Col, New York, 2960 Broadway, New York, NY 10027-6902.

KLEIN, IRA N.
PERSONAL Born 12/07/1931, New York, NY, m, 1966, 3 children **DISCIPLINE** MODERN EUROPEAN & ASIAN HISTORY **EDUCATION** Columbia Univ, BS, 56, MA, 60, PhD, 68. **CAREER** Lectr contemporary civilization, Queens Col, NY, 67-68; asst prof mod Europ hist, 68-72, assoc prof mod europ & asian hist, Am Univ, 72-, Nat Endowment for Humanities fel, 72 & 75-76; Ford-Rockefeller fel, Population Policy, 77-78. **HONORS AND AWARDS** Outstanding Tchr Col Arts & Sci Am Univ, 91-92; Distinguished Serv, Nat Gold Key Soc, 93; Outstanding Commun Serv, Stud Life, Am Univ, 94 & 96. **RESEARCH** Modern European diplomacy; British imperialism in Asia; development of modern India. **SELECTED PUBLICATIONS** Auth Imperialism Ecology & Presence Indian Econ Soc ist Rev, 94; Plague & Popular Responses in India, Jour Indian Hist, 98; Materialism, Modernization & Mutiny in India, Mod Asian Study. **CONTACT ADDRESS** Dept Hist, American Univ, 4400 Mass Ave NW, Washington, DC 20016-8200.

KLEIN, LAWRENCE E.
DISCIPLINE HISTORY **EDUCATION** Johns Hopkins Univ, PhD, 83. **CAREER** Assoc prof, Univ Nev Las Vegas. **SELECTED PUBLICATIONS** Auth, Britain History; Early Modern Europe; Cultural History; Shaftesbury and the Culture of Politeness, Cambridge, 94. **CONTACT ADDRESS** History Dept, Univ of Nevada, Las Vegas, 4505 Md Pky, Las Vegas, NV 89154.

KLEIN, MARTIN A.
PERSONAL Born 04/09/1934, New York, NY, m, 1963, 2 children **DISCIPLINE** AFRICAN HISTORY **EDUCATION** Northwestern Univ, BA, 55; Univ Chicago, MA, 59, PhD(hist), 64. **CAREER** Instr hist, Univ RI, 61-62; asst prof, Univ Calif, Berkeley, 65-70; assoc prof, 70-79, Prof Hist, Univ Toronto, 79-; Mem, Comt Comp Studies New Nations, Univ Chicago, 64-65; vis assoc prof, Louvanium Univ, Kinshasa, 68-69. **MEMBERSHIPS** AHA; African Studies Asn. **SELECTED PUBLICATIONS** Ed, Breaking the Chains: Slavery, Bondage, and Emancipation in Modern Africa and Asia, by Martin A. Klein, 93; co-ed, Slavery and Colonial Rule in Africa (Studies in Slave and Post-Slave Societies and Cultures), by Suzanne Miers and Martin A. Klein, 98; auth, Slavery, and Colonial Rule in French West Africa (African Studies Series No 94), by Martin Klein, 98; co-ed, Women and Slavery in Africa, by Claire C. Robertson, 98; auth, Peasants in Africa; Historical and Contemporary Perspectives (Sage Series on African Modernization and Development; v. 4), by Martin A. Klein. **CONTACT ADDRESS** Dept of Hist, Univ of Toronto, 100 St George St, Sidney Smith Hall Rm 2074, Toronto, ON, Canada M5S 3G3. **EMAIL** mklein@chass.utoronto.ca

KLEIN, MAURICE N.
PERSONAL Born 03/14/1939, Memphis, TN, m, 1995, 4 children **DISCIPLINE** HISTORY **EDUCATION** Knox Col, BA, 60; Emory Univ, MA, 61; PhD, 65. **CAREER** Instr to prof, Univ of RI, 64-. **RESEARCH** U.S. History since Civil War. **SELECTED PUBLICATIONS** Auth, The Life and Legend of Jay Gould, Johns Hopkins Univ Pr, 86; auth, Union Pacific: The Birth, 1862-1893, Doubleday & Co, 87; auth, Union Pacific: The Rebirth, 1894-1969, Doubleday & Co, 90; auth, The Flowering of Third America, Ivan Dee, 93; auth, Unfinished Business: The Railroad in American Life, Univ Pr New England, 94; auth, Days of Defiance: Sumter, Secession and the Road to the Civil War, Knopf, 97; auth, The Life and Legend of E.H. Harriman, Univ of NC. **CONTACT ADDRESS** Dept History, Univ of Rhode Island, Kingston, RI 02881. **EMAIL** mauryk@uri.edu

KLEIN, MICHAEL EUGENE
PERSONAL Born 07/30/1940, Philadelphia, PA **DISCIPLINE** ART HISTORY **EDUCATION** Rutgers Col, BA, 62; Columbia Univ, MA, 65, PhD, 71. **CAREER** Lectr, Douglass Col, 69-70; asst prof, State Univ NY Col Brockport, 71-73 & Univ SC, 73-77; asst prof, 77-81, assoc prof art hist, Western KY Univ, 81, Vis cur, Hirshhorn Mus & Sculpture Garden, Smithsonian Inst, 75. **MEMBERSHIPS** Col Art Asn Am. **RESEARCH** Twentieth century Am painting; 19th century Eng painting. **SELECTED PUBLICATIONS** Auth, John Covert's Time: Cubism, Duchamp, Einstein--a quasi-scientific fantasy, Art J, summer 74; John Covert and the Arensberg Circle: Symbolism, cubism and protosurrealism, Arts Mag, 5/77; John Covert's studios in 1916 and 1923: Two views into the past, Art J, fall 79. **CONTACT ADDRESS** Dept of Art, Western Kentucky Univ, 1 Big Red Way St, Bowling Green, KY 42101-3576.

KLEIN, MILTON M.
PERSONAL Born 08/15/1917, New York, NY, m, 1963, 2 children **DISCIPLINE** AMERICAN HISTORY **EDUCATION** City Col New York, BSS, 37, MSEd, 39; Columbia Univ, PhD, 54. **CAREER** Lectr hist, Columbia Univ, 54-58; Chmn dept hist, Long Island Univ, 58-62; Dean col lib arts and sci, 62-66; Dean grad studies, State Univ NY Col Fredonia, 66-69; Prof hist, 69-77, Alumni Distinguished Serv prof, 77-84, Lindsay Young Prof Hist, Univ Tenn, Knoxville, 80-84;Prof Emeritus, 85-; Ford Found fel, 55-56; Lilly fel, Clements Libr, Ann Arbor, Mich, 61; Fulbright lectr, Univ Canterbury, NZ, 62; Am Philos Soc res grant, 73; Adv Ed, 18th Century Studies, 75-81, 92-95; Walter E Meyer vis prof, NY Univ Sch Law, 76-77; Ed Board, New York History, 73-00. **HONORS AND AWARDS** Kerr Hist Prize, NY State Hist Asn, 75, Articles, 92; Prize, Am Soc for 18th-Century Studies, 76. **MEMBERSHIPS** Orgn Am Historians; AAUP; Am Hist Asn; Am Soc Legal Hist (secy, 75-77, vpres, 78-79, pres, 80-82); Southeast Am Soc 18th Century Studies. **RESEARCH** American colonial history; New York history; American legal history. **SELECTED PUBLICATIONS** Auth, The Politics of Divesity: Essays in the History of Colonial New York, (Port Washington, NY, 63); Gen. Ed., A History of the American Colonies, 13 vols, (New York, 73-86); ed, Courts and Law in Early New York (Port Washington, NY, 76); ed, New York: The Centennial Years, 1676-1976 (Port Washington, NY, 76); ed, The Twilight of British Rule in Revolutionary America: The New York Letter Book of General James Robertson,. 1780-1783 (Cooperstown, NY, 83); auth, "Origins of the Bill of Rights in Colonial New York," New York History, 72, 91; ed, Encyclopedia of the North America Colonies (New York, 93); auth, TheTwilight of British Rule in Revolutionary America: The New York Letter Book of General James Robertson, 1780-1783; ed, The Republican Synthesis Revisited Essays in Honor of George Billias; ed, North America in Colonial Times (New York, 98); auth, "The First Impeachment, Tennessee Bar Journal, 25, 99; auth, "John Jay and the Revolution," New York History, 71, 00. **CONTACT ADDRESS** Dept of Hist, Univ of Tennessee, Knoxville, Knoxville, TN 37996. **EMAIL** mklein@utk.edu

KLEIN, OWEN
DISCIPLINE THEATRE HISTORY; IMPROVISATION **EDUCATION** Villanova, MA; Ind Univ, PhD. **CAREER** Adj assoc prof. **SELECTED PUBLICATIONS** Pub (s), Theatre Hist in Can and 19th century Theatre Res; contrib ed, Oxford Companion to Canadian Drama and Theatre. **CONTACT ADDRESS** Dept of Dramatic Art, Univ of Windsor, 401 Sunset Ave, Windsor, ON, Canada N9B 3P4.

KLEIN, R.
PERSONAL Born 12/27/1926, Cincinnati, OH, m, 1954, 2 children **DISCIPLINE** HISTORY **EDUCATION** Kenyon Univ, AB, 50; Cornell Univ, MBA, 52; Uiv Chicago, AM, 69; PhD, 83. **HONORS AND AWARDS** Who's Who Am. **CONTACT ADDRESS** Dept Hist, Loyola Univ, Chicago, 6525 N Sheridan Rd, Chicago, IL 60626-5344.

KLEINBAUER, W. EUGENE
PERSONAL Born 06/15/1937, Los Angeles, CA, 2 children **DISCIPLINE** MEDIEVAL HISTORY, ART HISTORY **EDUCATION** Univ Calif, Berkeley, BA, 59, MA, 62; Princeton Univ, PhD(Hist of Art), 67. **CAREER** Asst prof Hist of Art, Univ Calif, Los Angeles, 65-71, assoc prof, 72; chmn, Dept Fine Arts, 73-76, assoc prof, 73-77, prof Hist of Art, Ind Univ, Bloomington, 77-, Nat Endowment for the Humanities fel, 76-77; Zacks vis prof, Hebrew Univ, Jerusalem, 78; Frederic L Morgan prof, U of Louisville, 96; ed, Int Ctr Medieval Art, Gesta, 80-83. **HONORS AND AWARDS** Am Philosophical Soc Travel Grant, 69; Distinguished Teaching Awd, Grad Students' Asn, Univ of Calif at Los Angeles, 70; Nat Endowment for the Humanities Fel for Independent study and res, 76-77; Int Res and Exchange Bd, Travel Grant to U.S.S.R., 78; Am Coun of Learned Societies, Travel Grant to Greece, 80; I.U. President's Coun on the Humanities Grants, 80, 87; I.U. President's Awd for Distinguished Teaching, 99; I.U. Grad Sch-Col of Arts and Sci Alumni; Asn Distinguished Teaching Awd, 88; Samuel H. Kress Found Travel Grant to Jerusalem, 96. **MEMBERSHIPS** Col Art Asn; Mediaeval Acad Am; Int Ctr Medieval Art; Midwest Art Hist Soc; Archaeol Inst Am. **RESEARCH** Byzantine art; early medieval art. **SELECTED PUBLICATIONS** Auth, Modern Perspectives in Western Art History, Holt, Rinehart & Winston, 71; Origins and functions of aisled Tetraconch churches in Syria and Mesopotamia, Dumbarton Oaks Papers, 27: 89-114; ed, Art of Byzantium and Medieval West: Selected Studies by Ernst Kitzinger, Ind Univ Press, 76; Aedita in Turribus: Superstructure of S Lorenzo, Milan, Gesta, 15: 1-9; Tradition and Innovation in The Design of Zvartnots, Acad Sci Armenian, 81; Ornts in the Mosaic Decoration of the Rotunda at Thessaloniki, Cahiers archeologiques, Vol 30, 82; coauth, Research Guide to the History of Western Art, Am Libr Asn, 82; Early Christian and Byzantine Architecture, 92; auth, Saint Sophia at Constantinople: Singulariter in Mundo, 99. **CONTACT ADDRESS** Dept of Art History, Indiana Univ, Bloomington, Bloomington, IN 47405. **EMAIL** kleinbau@indiana.edu

KLEINE-AHLBRANDT, WM. LAIRD
PERSONAL Born 06/17/1932, Cincinnati, OH, m, 1995, 3 children **DISCIPLINE** HISTORY **EDUCATION** Univ Cincinnati, BA, 54; MA, 59; Univ de Geneve, Dr es Sciences politiques, 62. **CAREER** U.S. Air Force, 54-58; instr, Richmond Prof Inst, 62-63; asst prof to assoc prof, Purdue Univ, 63-. **HONORS AND AWARDS** Chevalier, Order des palmes academique. **RESEARCH** Modern European history. **SELECTED PUBLICATIONS** Auth, The Policy of Simmering: A Study of British Policy during the Spanish Civil War, 1936-1939, Martinus Nijhoff (The Hague), 63; ed, Appeasement of the Dictators, Crisis Diplomacy, Hold, Rinehart and Winston (NY), 70; transl, of La Tosca (The Drama behind the Opera) by Victorien Sardou, Studies in the Hist and Interpretation of Music 19, Edwin Mellen Pr, (Lewiston/Queenston), 90, auth, Twentieth-Century European History, West Pub Co, (St. Paul/NY), 93; auth, Europe Since 1945: From Conflict to Community, West Pub Co, (Minneapolis/St Paul), 93; auth, The Burden of Victory, France, Britain and the Enforcement of the Treaty of Versailles, 1919-1925, Univ Pr of Am (Lanhan/NY), 95; auth, Bitter Prerequisites, A Faculty for Survival from Nazi Terror, Purdue Univ Pr, (W Lafayette, IN), 00. **CONTACT ADDRESS** Dept Hist, Purdue Univ, West Lafayette, West Lafayette, IN 47907.

KLEINER, FRED S.
PERSONAL Born 04/29/1948, New York, NY, m, 1972, 1 child **DISCIPLINE** ART HISTORY, ARCHAEOLOGY **EDUCATION** Univ Penn, BA, 68; Columbia Univ, MA, 69; PhD, 73. **CAREER** Asst prof, Univ of Va, 75-78; asst prof to prof, Boston Univ, 78-. **HONORS AND AWARDS** Grant, Am Philos Soc, 71, 80; Grant, Am Counc of Learned Soc, 78, 82; Guggenheim Fel, 88-89; Boston Univ Col Teaching Awd, 99, 00; Text and Acad Authors Asn Texty Book Prize, 01; Text and Acad Authors Asn McGuffey Book Prize, 01. **MEMBERSHIPS** Archaeol Ins of Am, Col Art Assoc, Am Numismatic Soc, Text and Acad Authors Assoc. **RESEARCH** Greek, Etruscan and Roman art, architecture, archaeology, and numismatics. **SELECTED PUBLICATIONS** Auth, Greek and Roman Coins in the Athenian Agora, Princeton, 75; auth, The Early Cistophoric Coinage, New York, 77; auth, Mediaeval and Modern Coins in the Athenian Agora, Princeton, 75; auth, The Arch of Nero in Rome. A Study of the Roman Honorary Arch before and under Nero, Rome, 85; coauth, Gardner's Art Through the Ages, 10th ed, Fort Worth, 96, coauth, Gardner's Art Through the Ages, 11th ed, Fort Worth, 01. **CONTACT ADDRESS** Art Hist Dept, Boston Univ, 725 Commonwealth Ave, # 302, Boston, MA 02215. **EMAIL** fsk@bu.edu

KLEINFELD, GERALD R.
PERSONAL Born 11/08/1936, New York, NY **DISCIPLINE** GERMAN STUDIES & HISTORY **EDUCATION** NYork Univ, BA, 56, PhD, 61; Univ Mich, MA, 57. **CAREER** Vis instr hist, Bates Col, 61-62; from asst prof to assoc prof, 62-77, Prof Hist, Ariz State Univ, 77-; Asst Dean Off-Campus Instr, 77-; Vis asst prof, State Univ NY Col Fredonia, 67-68; ED, Ger Studies Rev, 77-01, Exec Dir, German Studies Asn, 78-. **HONORS AND AWARDS** Grand merit cross 99 Ger; Order of merit, First Class 82, Ger/ **MEMBERSHIPS** AHA; Conf Group Cent Europ Hist; Am Comt Hist 2nd World War; Western Asn Ger Studies; Coun Ger Studies Mod Lang Asn; Ger Studies Asn. **RESEARCH** German-American relations, German politics and society. **SELECTED PUBLICATIONS** Coauth, Hitler's Spanish Legion, Southern Ill Univ, 78; auth, Germans New Politics, 98; auth, Power Shift in Germany, 00; **CONTACT ADDRESS** Ger Studies, Arizona State Univ, Box 873204, Tempe, AZ 85287-3204. **EMAIL** kleinfeld@asn.edu

KLEJMENT, ANNE
PERSONAL Born 04/27/1950, Rochester, NY **DISCIPLINE** HISTORY **EDUCATION** Nazareth Col Rochester, BA, 72; State Univ NY at Binghamton, MA, 74; PhD, 81. **CAREER** Instr, Vassar Col, 78-79; adminr, Cornell Univ NYork Hist Resources Ctr, 79-81; asst prof, State Univ NYork Col at Plattsburgh, 81-83; coord of women's studies, State Univ NYork Col at Plattsburgh, 82-83; prof, Univ St Thomas, 83-. **HONORS AND AWARDS** Sr Muriel Ford Lectr, Briarcliff Col; Burlington Northern Awd for Res, Univ St Thomas; Pax Christi USA Book Awd. **MEMBERSHIPS** OAH, Peace Hist Soc, Am Catholic Hist Asn. **RESEARCH** Dorothy Day and Catholic Worker Movement, U.S. Catholic Social History. **SELECTED PUBLICATIONS** Auth, The Berrigans: A Bibliography, Garland, 79; coauth, Dorothy Day and "The Catholic Worker": A Bibliography and Index, Garland, 86; co-ed American Catholic Pacifism: The Influence of Dorothy Day and the Catholic Worker Movement, Praeger, 97. **CONTACT ADDRESS** Dept Hist, Univ of St. Thomas, Minnesota, 2115 Summit Ave, Saint Paul, MN 55105-1048.

KLEPAK, HAL
DISCIPLINE HISTORY **EDUCATION** McGill Univ, BA; London Univ, MA, PhD. **CAREER** Prof, Royal Milit Col. **MEMBERSHIPS** Canadian Found for the Ams (FOCAI) **RESEARCH** Latin American security issues; Canadian foreign and defense policy; conventional strategy. **SELECTED PUBLICATIONS** Auth, Canada and Latin American Security, 1996; Natural Allies? Canadian and Mexican Views on International Security, 1996. **CONTACT ADDRESS** Dept Hist, Royal Military Col, PO Box 17000, Kingston, ON, Canada K7K 7B4. **EMAIL** klepak_h@rmc.ca

KLEPPER, DEEANA
PERSONAL Born 12/01/1959, Chicago, IL, m, 2 children **DISCIPLINE** HISTORY **EDUCATION** Northland Col, BA, 83; Northwestern Univ, MA, 88; PhD, 95. **CAREER** Asst prof, Williams Col, 99-00; asst prof, Boston Univ, 00-. **HONORS AND AWARDS** Rome Prize Fel, 89-90; Diss Fel, Northwestern Univ, 92-93; Fel, Univ of Pa, 01-02. **MEMBERSHIPS** Medieval Acad of Am, AHA, Am Acad of Relig, Assoc for Jewish Studies, Am Soc of Church Hist, Soc for Values in Higher Educ. **RESEARCH** Christian approaches to Jews and Jewish traditions in the later Middles Ages, comparative Bible exegesis in social context, history of the mendicant orders. **SELECTED PUBLICATIONS** Auth, "The Dating of Nicholas of Lyra's Quaestio de adventu Christi," Archivum Franciscanum Historicum 86, (93): 297-312; auth, "Nicholas of Lyra and Franciscan Interest in Hebrew Scholarship," Nicholas of Lyra: the Senses of Scripture, eds Philip Krey and Lesley Smith, Brill (Leiden, 00); auth, From Exegesis to Polemic: Nicholas of Lyra's Struggle with Jewish Tradition. **CONTACT ADDRESS** Dept Relig, Boston Univ, 745 Commonwealth Ave, Boston, MA 02215. **EMAIL** dklepper@bu.edu

KLINE, RONALD R.
PERSONAL Born 04/21/1947, Oswego, KS, m, 1976, 5 children **DISCIPLINE** HISTORY OF SCIENCE & TECHNOLOGY **EDUCATION** Univ Wisc-Madison, PhD, 83. **CAREER** Dir, IEEE Ctr for Hist of Elec Eng, 84-87; Asst Prof, Hist & Tech, 87-93, Assoc Prof, 93-, Cornell Univ. **HONORS AND AWARDS** Soc for Hist of Tech, IEEE Life embers Prize in Elec Hist, 88; Soc of Nat Asn Pubs, Best Editorial or Column, 92; Soc for Tech Commun, 1st Place Awd of Distinction for editorial excellence, 97, editing prize-winning paper, 96; Cornell Col of Eng, recognized for exemplary tchng, 96; assoc ed for hist, ieee transactions on educ, 88-94; ed bd, ieee spectrum, 89-91; ed, ieee tech & soc magazine, 95-97; advisory ed, isis, 96-98, tech & culture, 98-00. **MEMBERSHIPS** IEEE Soc on Soc Implications of Tech, (pres 91-92); Soc for the Hist of Technol; Hist of Sci Soc. **RESEARCH** History of urban technology in rural life; history of engineering; history of information technology. **SELECTED PUBLICATIONS** Auth, Stienmetz: Engineer and Socialist, Johns Hopkins Stud in the Hist of Tech, Johns Hopkins Univ Press, 92; auth, Construing Technology as Applied Science: Public Rhetoric of Scientists and Engineers in the United States, 1880-1945, Isis, 86, 194-221, 95; auth, Ideology and the New Deal Fact Film Power and the Land, Public Understanding of Science, 6, 19-30, 97; auth, Ideology and Social Surveys: Reinterpreting the Effects of Laborsaving Technology on American Farm Women, Tech & Culture, 38, 355-385, 97; auth, Consumers in the Country: Technology and Social Change in Rural America, Johns Hopkins Univ Press, 00. **CONTACT ADDRESS** Cornell Univ, 394 Rhodes Hall, Ithaca, NY 14850. **EMAIL** rrk1@cornell.edu

KLING, BLAIR B.
DISCIPLINE HISTORY **EDUCATION** Univ of Calif, BA, 50; MA, 55; Univ Pa, PhD, 60. **CAREER** Emer; asst prof, Univ of Ill, 62-67; assoc prof, Univ of Ill, 67-76; prof, Univ of Ill, 76-. **HONORS AND AWARDS** Fulbright Grant, 57-58; ACLSS Grant, 70; Am Institute of Indian Studies Fel, 84-85; **RESEARCH** Modern South Asian business and entrepreneurial history; industrialization; urban history. **SELECTED PUBLICATIONS** Auth, The Blue Mutiny: The Indigo Disturbances in Bengal, 1859-1862, Univ of Pa Press, 66; auth, Partner in Empire: Dwarkanth Tagore and the Age of Enterprise in Eastern India, Univ of Calif Press, 76; auth, The Age of Partnership: Europeans in Asia Before Dominion, Univ Press of Hawaii, 79; auth, "The Tatas and the Tagores," in Shaping Bengali Worlds, Public and Private, ed. Tony K. Stewart, (Michigan State Univ, 89): 168-172; auth, "Rabindranath's Bonfire," in Rabindranath Tagaore Commemorative Voume, ed. Bhabatosh Datta, (Visva-Bharati Press, West Bengal, 90): 41-52; auth, "Gandhi, Nonviolence, and The Holocaust," Peace and Change, Vol. 16, No. 2, (91): 176-196. **CONTACT ADDRESS** History Dept, Univ of Illinois, Urbana-Champaign, 52 E Gregory Dr, Champaign, IL 61820. **EMAIL** b-kling@staff.uiuc.edu

KLING, DAVID
PERSONAL Born 04/21/1950, Mora, MN, m, 1985, 4 children **DISCIPLINE** HISTORY OF CHRISTIANITY, RELIGION IN AMERICAN LIFE **EDUCATION** Trinity Col, IL, BA, 72; Northern IL Univ, 76; Univ Chicago, PhD, 85. **CAREER** Asst prof hist, Palm Beach Atlantic Col, 82-86; Univ administration, Univ Miami, 86-93; asst prof of relig studies, 93-95, assoc prof, Univ Miami, 95-. **HONORS AND AWARDS** Kenneth Scott Latourette Prize in Religion and Modern Hist (Best Book Manuscript), 92. **MEMBERSHIPS** Am Academy of Relig; Am Soc of Church Hist. **RESEARCH** Revivalism in Am; biblical texts in hist of Christianity. **SELECTED PUBLICATIONS** Auth, A Field of Divine Wonders: The New Divinity and Village Revivals in Northwestern Connecticut, 1792-1822, PA State Univ Press, 93; For Males Only: The Image of the Infidel and the Construction of Gender in the Second Great Awakening in New England, J of Men's Studies 3, May 95; twenty-five entries in The Blackwell Dictionary of Evangelical Biography, 1730-1860, ed Donald M Lewis, 2 vols, Blackwell Pubs, 95; The New Divinity and Williams College, 1793-1836, Religion and American Culture: A Journal of Interpretation 6, summer 96; By the Light of His Example: New Divinity Schools of the Prophets and Theological Education in New England, 1750-1825, in American Theological Education in the Evangelical Tradition, eds D G Hart and R Albert Mohler, Jr, Baker Books, 96; Smyth, Newman, in Dictionary of Heresy Trials in American Christianity, ed George H Shriver, Greenwood Press, 97; New Divinity Schools of the Prophets, 1750-1825: A Case Study in Ministerial Education, History of Ed Quart 37, summer 97. **CONTACT ADDRESS** Dept of Relig Studies, Univ of Miami, PO Box 248264, Miami, FL 33124. **EMAIL** dkling@miami.edu

KLOOSTER, WILLEM
PERSONAL Born 09/10/1962, Groningen, The Netherlands, s **DISCIPLINE** HISTORY **EDUCATION** Univ Groningen, The Neth, MA, 87; Univ Leiden, The Neth, PhD, 95. **CAREER** Asst Prof, Univ of Southern Maine, 98-. **HONORS AND AWARDS** Fulbright Fel, 95-96; Alexander O. Vietor Memorial Awd Fel, John Carter Brown Libr, 96; Charles Warren Fel, Harvard Univ, 97-98; Leab Exhib Catalogue Awd, Am Libr Asn, 99. **MEMBERSHIPS** AHA, Oah, Soc for Netherlandic Hist. **RESEARCH** Early modern Europe, Atlantic history. **SELECTED PUBLICATIONS** Auth, "Winds of Change. Colonization, Commerce, and Consolidation in the Seventeenth-Century Atlantic world," De Halve Maen: Magazine of the Dutch Colonial Period in Am 70-3 (97): 53-58; auth, "Berbice Slave Revolt (1763-1764)," "Slavery in the Dutch Caribbean," "Piezas de Indias," "Dutch-Portuguese Wars in West Africa (1620-55)," "Dutch West India Company (1621)," in Historical Encyclopedia of World Slavery, ed. Junius Rodriguez (Santa Barbara: ABC Clio, 97); auth, "Contraband Trade by Curacao's Jews With Countries of Idolatry, 1660-1800," Studia Rosenthalia 31-1/2 (97): 58-73; auth, The Dutch in the America, 1600-1800, The John Carter Brown Libr (Providence), 97; auth, Illicit Riches. Dutch Trade in the Caribbean, 1648-1795, KITLW Press (Leiden), 98; coauth, "The Dutch Atlantic, 1600-1800: Expansion Without Empire," Itinerary. Europ J of Overseas Hist XXIII-2 (99): 48-69; coauth, "Forced African Settlement. The Basis of Freed Settlement, Africa and its Trading Conditions," in New Societies: The Caribbean in the Lang Sixteenth Century ed. P.C. Emmer and German Carrera Damas (London: UNESCO Publ, Macmillan Educ, 99); auth, "The Jews in Suriname and Curacao," in The Jews and the Expansion of Europe to the West, 1400-1800, ed. Paolo Bernardini and Norman Fiering (NY and Oxford: Berghahn, 99); auth, "Failing to Square the Circle: The West India Company's Volte-Face in

1638-39," De Halve Maen: Magazine of the Dutch Colonial Period in Am 73 (00). **CONTACT ADDRESS** Dept Hist, Univ of So Maine, PO Box 9300, Portland, ME 04104-9300.

KLOTTER, JAMES
PERSONAL Born 01/17/1947, Lexington, KY, m, 1966, 3 children **DISCIPLINE** HISTORY **EDUCATION** Univ KY, PhD, 75; Eastern KY Univ, Doct of Humane Letters, 97; Union Col, Doct of Letter, 98. **CAREER** Asst ed to ed, Register of the KY Hist Soc, 73-88; asst dir to exec dir, KY Hist Soc, 88-90; prof, Georgetown Col, 98-. **HONORS AND AWARDS** Governor's Outstanding Kentuckian Awd, 98. **MEMBERSHIPS** Am Hist Asn, Org of Am Historians, Southern Hist Asn, Oral hist Asn, Public Hist, KY Historical Soc. **RESEARCH** souther History, post civil-war, history of the family, Applachian history, Kentucky. **SELECTED PUBLICATIONS** Auth, "The Black South and White Appalachia," Jaournal of american History 66 (80); auth, William Goebel: The Politics of Wrath, Univ Press of KY, 77; auth, The Breckinridges of Kentucky, Univ Press of KY, 86; auth, Our Kentucky: A Study of the Bluegrass State, Univ Press of KY, 92; auth, Kentucky: Portrait in Paradox, 1900-1950, 96; auth, A New History of Kentucky, Univ Press, 97; auth, Kentucky: Decades of Discord, 1865-1900, Kentucky Historical Soc, 77; auth, "Moving Kentucky into the 21st Century: Where do we go from here?" Register of the Kentucky Historical Society, 99. **CONTACT ADDRESS** Dept History, Georgetown Col, 400 E Col St, Georgetown, KY 40324-1628. **EMAIL** james_klotter@georgetowncollege.edu

KLUNDER, WILLARD CARL
PERSONAL Born Chicago, IL, m, 1986, 3 children **DISCIPLINE** POLITICAL HISTORY **EDUCATION** St. Olaf Col; Univ Ill, MA, PhD. **CAREER** Vis profships, Ind Univ; Univ Cincinnati; assoc prof, Wichita State Univ, 86-. **HONORS AND AWARDS** Asst ed, Jour Early Republic. **MEMBERSHIPS** SHEAR; OAH. **RESEARCH** Antebellum political history. **SELECTED PUBLICATIONS** Ed, transcriber, The Story of My Life, by Frederick Finnup, Finney County Hist Soc; auth, Lewis Cass and the Politics of Moderation, 1782-1866, Kent State Univ Press, 96. **CONTACT ADDRESS** Dept of Hist, Wichita State Univ, 1845 Fairmont, Wichita, KS 67260-0062. **EMAIL** klunder@twsu.edu

KNAFLA, LOUIS A.
PERSONAL Born 07/27/1935, Bakersfield, CA, m, 1965, 1 child **DISCIPLINE** EARLY MODERN HISTORY **EDUCATION** Claremont Mens Col, BA, 57; Univ Calif, Los Angeles, MA, 61, PhD (Tudor-Stuart English), 65. **CAREER** Lectr Brit hist, Calif State Col, Long Beach, 64-65; from asst prof to asoc prof, 65-77, asst chmn to chmn dept, 68-69, Prof Hist, Univ Calgary, 77-; Ed, Can Soc Legal Hist, 71-73; Can Coun res grants, 70-71, 73-75 and 79-82, leave fel, 75; chmn, Law Lib Arts Minor, 76-80; Killam resident fel, 77; Assoc Ed, Criminal Justice Hist, 81-. **MEMBERSHIPS** AHA; Renaissance Soc Am; Am Soc Legal Hist; Can Soc Legal Hist (pres, 73-78); fel Royal Hist Soc. **RESEARCH** England in the 16th and 17th centuries; history of English law; history of Canadian law, crime and criminal justice. **SELECTED PUBLICATIONS** Auth, Fundamental Authority in Late Medieval English Law, Hist Polit Thought, Vol 0013, 92. **CONTACT ADDRESS** Dept of Hist, Univ of Calgary, 2500 Univ Dr NW, Calgary, AB, Canada T2N 1N4. **EMAIL** knafla@ucalgary.ca

KNAPP, ARTHUR BERNARD
PERSONAL Born 09/06/1941, Akron, OH **DISCIPLINE** ARCHAEOLOGY AND ANCIENT HISTORY **EDUCATION** Univ Akron, BA, 67; Univ Calif, Berkeley, MA, 76, PhD(ancient hist and mediter archaeol), 79. **CAREER** Teaching asst archaeol and ancient hist, 73-75, assoc, 75-76, actg instr, 76-79, Lectr Archaeol and Ancient Hist, Univ Calif, Berkeley, 79-; Instr, Extension Div, Univ Calif, Berkeley, 76-77. **MEMBERSHIPS** Archaeol Inst Am; Am Orient Soc; Asn Field Archaeol; Soc Am Archaeol; Am Schs Orient Res. **RESEARCH** Trade and interaction in eastern Mediterranean prehistory; island archaeology, especially in the Mediterranean; method and theory in archaeology. **SELECTED PUBLICATIONS** Auth, Gordion Excavation Final Reports, Vol 3, The Bronze-Age J Hellenic Studies, Vol 0112, 92; Thalassocracies in Bronze-Age Eastern Mediterranean Trade in Making And Breaking A Myth, World Archaeol, Vol 0024, 93; The Prehistory of Cyprus in Problems and Prospects, J World Prehistory, Vol 0008, 94; Provenance Studies and Problem Solving On Bronze-Age Cyprus, American J Archaeol, Vol 0098, 94; Volatile Bodies in Bodies Evidence On Prehistoric Cyprus, American J Archaeol, Vol 0100, 96; Recent Excavations In Israel in A View to the West, Reports on Kabri, J Am Orient Soc, Vol 0117, 97 **CONTACT ADDRESS** Dept of Near East Studies, Univ of California, Berkeley, Berkeley, CA 94720.

KNAPP, ROBERT C.
PERSONAL Born 02/12/1946, m, 1974, 2 children **DISCIPLINE** ANCIENT HISTORY, CLASSICS **EDUCATION** Cent MI Univ, BA, 68; Univ PA, PhD, 73. **CAREER** Vis asst prof classics, Colby Col, 73; asst prof of hist, Univ of Utah, 73-74; asst prof, 74-80, Assoc Prof Classics, Numismatics, Univ CA, Berkeley, 80-87; Prof 87. **HONORS AND AWARDS** Am Council of Learned Societies Fellowship, 82-83. **MEMBERSHIPS** Asn Ancient Historians; Am Philol Asn; Archaeological Institute of Am Fellow; Royal Numismatic Society. **RESEARCH** Roman Spain; Roman Cult Studies. **SELECTED PUBLICATIONS** Auth, Aspects of the Roman Experience in Iberia, 206-100 BC, Anejos IX Hisp Antiqua, 77; The date and purpose of the Iberian denarii, Numis Chronicle, 77; The origins of provincial prosopography in the West, Ancient Soc, 78; Cato in Spain, 195-194 BC, In: Studies in Latin Literature and Roman History II, C Deroux, Brussells, 80; La epigrafia y la historia de la Cordoba romana, Annario, de Filologia, 80; Festus 262L and Praefecturae in Italy, Athenaeum, 80; L Axius Naso and Pro legato, Phoenix, 81; Roman Cordoba, Univ Calif press, 83; Latin Inscriptions from Central Spain, Univ Calif, 92; Mapping Ancient Iberia: Progress and Perspectives, intro, ed (and contribution, Ptolemy Mapping Baetica, pp 29-36) Classical Bulletin, special issue, 96; auth, Finis Rei Publicae, Eyewitneses to the End of the Roman Republic, with P. Baughn, Focus Publishing, 99; ed, Barrington Atlas of the Greek and roman World, ed. By R.J. A Talbert, Princeton, 00. **CONTACT ADDRESS** Dept Class, Univ of California, Berkeley, 7233 Dwinelle Hall, Berkeley, CA 94720-2520. **EMAIL** RCKNAPP@SOCRATES.Berkeley.edu

KNAPP, RONALD G.
PERSONAL Born 08/15/1940, Pittsburgh, PA, m, 1968, 3 children **DISCIPLINE** CULTURAL GEOGRAPHY **EDUCATION** Stetson Univ, BA, 62; Univ of Pittsburgh, PhD, 68. **CAREER** SUNY exchange prof, Nanyang Univ, 71-72; asst prof, 68-71, assoc prof, 71-78, prof, 78-98, Distinguished prof, State Univ of NY, NEW PALTZ, 98-. **HONORS AND AWARDS** Woodrow Wilson Nat Fel, 62-63; ACLS/Mellon Found Postdoctoral Fel for Advanced Training in Chinese Studies, 78; Summer Seminar, 79, Fel, Nat Endowment for the Humanities, 84 & 94; Nat Geographic Soc Comt for Res and Exploration Grant, 87; Nat Geographic Soc Comt for Res and Exploration, 80; Chiang Ching-kuo Found, 96. **MEMBERSHIPS** Asn of Am Geographers; Asn for Asian Studies; Vernacular Archit Forum; Int Asn for the Study of Traditional Environments; NY Conf on Asian Studies. **RESEARCH** The cultural and historical geography of China, especially the frontier settlement and the evolution of cultural landscapes; Chinese vernacular architecture; Chinese folk symbols and household ornamentation. **SELECTED PUBLICATIONS** Auth, China's Traditional Rural Architecture, Univ of Hawaii Press, 86; auth, China's Vernacular Architecture, Univ of Hawaii Press, 89; auth, The Chinese House, Oxford Univ Press, 90; auth, Chinese Bridges, Oxford Univ Press, 93; auth, Popular Rural Architecture, Handbook of Chinese Popular Culture, Greenwood Pub Group, 94; auth, China's didactic landscapes: the folk tradition and the built environment, History and Culture of Vernacular Architecture, South China Univ of Tech, 95; auth, Chinese Villages as Didactic Texts, Landscape, Culture, and Power in Chinese Soc, Inst of East Asian Studies, Univ of Calif, 98; auth, The Shaping of Taiwan's Landscapes, Taiwan: A Hist 1600-1994, M.E. Sharpe, 98; auth, China's Living Houses: Folk Beliefs, symbols and Household Ornamentation, Univ of Hawaii Press, 99; auth, China's Walled Cities, Oxford Univ Press, 00; auth, China's Old Dwellings, Univ of Hawaii Press, 00. **CONTACT ADDRESS** Dept of Geography, SUNY, New Paltz, New Paltz, NY 12561-2499. **EMAIL** knappr@newpaltz.edu

KNAPP, THOMAS A.
DISCIPLINE HISTORY **EDUCATION** Catholic Univ, PhD. **CAREER** Hist, Loyola Univ. **RESEARCH** Modern European history. **SELECTED PUBLICATIONS** Auth, Joseph Karl Wirth, Badische Biographien 2, 82. **CONTACT ADDRESS** Fine Arts Dept, Loyola Univ, Chicago, 6525 N. Sheridan Rd., Chicago, IL 60626. **EMAIL** tknapp@wpo.it.luc.edu

KNEELAND, TIMOTHY W.
PERSONAL Born 11/25/1962, Buffalo, NY, m, 1988, 4 children **DISCIPLINE** HISTORY **EDUCATION** Univ Buffalo, BA, 87, MA, 89; Univ Okla, MA, 93, PhD, 96. **CAREER** Asst prof, Greenville Col, 96-00; asst prof, Nazareth Col, 00-. **HONORS AND AWARDS** Reinhard Fel, 98; Who's Who in Am Ed, 98, 99. **MEMBERSHIPS** Hist Soc, Org of Am Hists, Hist of Sci Soc. **RESEARCH** American intellectual history, American science. **SELECTED PUBLICATIONS** Auth, "Science an Overview," Encyclopedia of American Studies (2000); auth, Pushbutton Psychiatry: A History of Electroconvulsive Therapy, Greenwood Press (forthcoming). **CONTACT ADDRESS** Dept Hist, Nazareth Col of Rochester, 4245 E Ave, Rochester, NY 14618. **EMAIL** Kneelands-1@Juno.com

KNEESHAW, STEPHEN
PERSONAL Born 10/04/1946, Tacoma, WA, m, 1969, 3 children **DISCIPLINE** AMERICAN HISTORY, HISTORY OF EDUCATION **EDUCATION** Univ Puget Sound, BA, 68; Univ Colo, Boulder, MA, 69; PhD, 71. **CAREER** Instr, Univ Colo, 71-72; asst to prof and chair, Col of the Ozarks, 72-; ed of Teaching Hist: A J of Methods, 76-. **HONORS AND AWARDS** Phi Alpha Theta; Mu Sigma Delta; Nat Man-of-the-Year for Sigma Nu Frat, 68; Who's Who in Am Cols and Univs, 68; Outstanding Educators in Am, 75; Outstanding Young Men of Am, 79, 82; NEH Fel in State and Community Hist, Newberry Lib, Chicago, 79; Vis Scholar, Univ Puget Sound, 82, 89; Distinguished Fac Awd, Col of the Ozarks, 85; nominee for CASE Nat Prof of the Year, 86; Wye Fel, Wye Fac Inst, 89; Who's Who Among Am Teachers, 94, 96, 98; West Point ROTC Fel in Military Hist, 96; Outstanding Americans, 97-98. **MEMBERSHIPS** Am Hist Asn, Org of Am Hists, Soc of Hists of Am Foreign Relations, Nat Comn for Hist Educ. **RESEARCH** 20th century American Diplomatic History, especially World War II and Vietnam, and history educations, including teaching methods and computer-based methods and materials. **SELECTED PUBLICATIONS** Auth, In Pursuit of Peace: The American Reaction to the Kellogg-Briand Pact, 1928-1929, New York: Garland Pub (91); auth, "Hugh Simons Gibson," in The Encyclopedia of U.S. Foreign Relations, Lakeview, Ct: Am Reference Pub Co (96); auth, "The Internet, Email, and the Environment," OAH Mag of Hist, 10 (96); auth, "Using Reader Response to Improve Student Writing in History," OAH Mag of Hist, 13 (99); auth, "Some Thoughts on American Education and on American Teachers," Teaching History, 24 (99); auth, "Teaching History at Twenty-Five Years," Teaching History, 25 (spring 2000); auth, "History Websites on the Internet and WWW," in The History Highway 2000 (2000); auth, "Teaching History with Technology," in History.Edu (2000). **CONTACT ADDRESS** Dept Humanities, Col of the Ozarks, Point Lookout, MO 65726. **EMAIL** kneeshaw@cofo.edu

KNEPPER, GEORGE W.
PERSONAL Born 01/15/1926, Akron, OH, m, 1949, 2 children **DISCIPLINE** HISTORY **EDUCATION** Univ Akron, BA, 48; Univ Mich, MA, 50, PhD(hist), 54. **CAREER** Asst adv men, 48-49, from instr to assoc prof hist, 54-65, head dept, 59-62, dean Col Lib Arts, 62-72, vpres acad affairs, 72, Prof Hist, Univ Akron, 65-; Dir Educ Res and Develop Ctr, 72-. **MEMBERSHIPS** AHA; Orgn Am Historians. **RESEARCH** American Colonial and Revolutionary history; state and local history; history of higher education. **SELECTED PUBLICATIONS** **CONTACT ADDRESS** 1189 Temple Trails, Stow, OH 44224.

KNIGHT, FRANKLIN WILLIS
PERSONAL Born 01/10/1942, Manchester, Jamaica, m, 1965, 3 children **DISCIPLINE** LATIN AMERICAN HISTORY **EDUCATION** Univ Col West Indies, BA, 64; Univ Wis, Madison, MA, 65, PhD, 69. **CAREER** From instr to assoc prof hist, State Univ NYork, Stony Brook, 68-73; assoc prof, 73-77, Prof hist, Johns Hopkins Univ, 77-91, Stulman Prof, 91-, Mem joint comt Latin Am studies, Soc Sci Res Coun & Coun Learned Socs, 71-73; Nat Endowment for Hum fel, 77-78; Ctr Advan Study in Behav Sci fel, 77-78. **HONORS AND AWARDS** Hum Awd, Black Acad Arts & Lett, 70. **MEMBERSHIPS** Assoc of Caribbean Historians; Conf of Latin Am Hist; The Hist Soc; Latin Am Studies Asn (pres, 98-2000). **RESEARCH** Late colonial and early nat Latin Am hist; Am slave sys(s); Caribbean region. **SELECTED PUBLICATIONS** Auth, Slave Society in Cuba During the Nineteenth Century, Univ Wis, 70; A colonial response to the glorious revolution in Spain, In: La Revolucion de 1868.., Americas, 70; Cuba, In: Neither Slave nor Free, Johns Hopkins, 72; Slavery, In: Encycl Americana, 73; African Dimension in Latin American Societies, Macmillan, 74; The Caribbean: The Genesis of a Fragmented Nationalism, Oxford Univ, 90; Atlantic Port Cities, Tenn, 91; Slave Societies in Caribbean, UNESCO, 97. **CONTACT ADDRESS** Dept of Hist, Johns Hopkins Univ, Baltimore, 3400 N Charles St, Baltimore, MD 21218-2680. **EMAIL** fknight@jhu.edu

KNIGHT, ISABEL FRANCES
PERSONAL Born 11/24/1930, Los Angeles, CA **DISCIPLINE** MODERN EUROPEAN HISTORY **EDUCATION** Univ Calif, Los Angeles, BA, 51, MA, 58; Yale Univ, PhD (hist), 64. **CAREER** Instr hist, Yale Univ, 61-64; lectr, 64-72, Assoc Prof to Assoc Prof Emer Hist, Pa State Univ, Univ Park, 72-. **HONORS AND AWARDS** Am Coun Learned Socs interdisciplinary studies fel, 70-71. **MEMBERSHIPS** AHA; Conf on Utopian Studies. **RESEARCH** Intellectual history of psychoanalysis; social criticism; Utopian thought. **SELECTED PUBLICATIONS** Auth, The Geometric Spirit, Yale Univ, 68; Utopian Dream as Psychic Reality, Studies 18th Century Cult, 77; Alienation, Eros, and Work, 78, Reclaiming the Wasteland, 80 & The Feminist Scholar and the Future of Gender, 81, Alternative Futures. **CONTACT ADDRESS** Dept of Hist, Pennsylvania State Univ, Univ Park, University Park, PA 16802. **EMAIL** ifk@psu.edu

KNIPE, DAVID MACLAY
PERSONAL Born 11/25/1932, Johnstown, PA, m, 3 children **DISCIPLINE** HISTORY OF RELIGION, SOUTH ASIAN STUDIES **EDUCATION** Cornell Univ, AB, 55; Union Theol Sem, MA, 58; Univ Chicago, MA, 65, PhD(hist relig), 71. **CAREER** Lectr, 67-69, from instr to asst prof, 69-73, assoc prof, 73-79, Prof South Asian Studies, Univ Wis-Madison, 79-; Sr res fel, Am Inst Indian Studies, 71-72, and 80. **MEMBERSHIPS** Am Acad Relig; Asn Asian Studies; Am Soc Study Relig. **RESEARCH** Vedic religion; Hinduism Jainism; methodology and religion. **SELECTED PUBLICATIONS** Auth, The heroic theft: Myths from Rgveda IV and the Ancient- Near East, 5/67 & One fire, three fires, five fires: Vedic symbols in transition, 8/72, Hist Relig; In the image of fire: Vedic experiences of heat, Motilal Banarsidass, Delhi, 75; Religious encounters with death: Essays in the history and anthropology of religion, Pa

State Univ, 77; Exploring the religions of South Asia, A series of fifteen color video productions, WHA-TV, 74 & 75; Vedas, Vedic Hinduism, Sacrifice and 26 other articles, In: The Abingdon Dict of Living Religions, Abingdon, 81; coauth, Focus on Hinduism: Audio-visual resources for teaching religion, Chambersburg, Anima, 2nd ed 81. **CONTACT ADDRESS** Dept of S Asian Studies, Univ of Wisconsin, Madison, 1220 Linden Drive, Madison, WI 53706-1557.

KNOBEL, DALE THOMAS

PERSONAL Born 09/14/1949, East Cleveland, OH, m, 1971, 2 children **DISCIPLINE** AMERICAN HISTORY **EDUCATION** Yale Univ, BA, 71; Northwestern Univ, PhD(hist), 76. **CAREER** Instr hist and Am cult, Northwestern Univ, 76-77; asst prof Hist, Tex Am Univ, 77-; Info Syst consult, G D Searle and Co, 76-77. **HONORS AND AWARDS** Fac Distinguished Achievement Award. **MEMBERSHIPS** Organization for Am Historians; Immigration Hist Soc; Soc fo Historians of the Early Am Republic; Am Conference on Irish Studies; Am Studies Asn; Social Science Hist Asn; Tes State Historical Asn; Nat hist Honorary; Phi Alpha Theta; Honor Soc of Phi Kappa Phi; Ph Beta Delta Honor Soc for international scholars; Honorary fac member of the Golden Key Nat Honorary Soc. **RESEARCH** Am intellectual and cultural hist; Am immigration and ethnic hist; race relations. **CONTACT ADDRESS** Dept of Hist, Denison Univ, 100 S Rd, Granville, OH 43023.

KNOLL, PAUL W.

PERSONAL Born 12/25/1937, Spokane, WA, m, 1960, 2 children **DISCIPLINE** HISTORY **EDUCATION** Lewis and Clark Col, BA, 60; Univ Colo, MA, 61, PhD, 64. **CAREER** Prof, Purdue Univ, 64-69; Prof, Univ Southern Calif; Asst prof, Purdue Univ, 64-69; assoc prof, Univ of So. Cal, 80-. **HONORS AND AWARDS** Kosciuszko Foundation prize, Prof, Univ Southern Calif, 69-. **RESEARCH** Medieval & Renaissance periods in European history; history & civilization of the western Slavs. **SELECTED PUBLICATIONS** Auth, The Rise of the Polish Monarchy, Piast Poland in East Central Eurpoe, 1320-1370; auth, The Rise of the Polish Monarchy, Piast Polant in East Central Europe, 1320-1370; coauth, St. Stanislaw, Bishop of Cracow. **CONTACT ADDRESS** Dept of History, Univ of So California, University Park Campus, Los Angeles, CA 90089. **EMAIL** knoll@usc.edu

KNOPOFF, L.

PERSONAL Born 07/01/1925, Los Angeles, CA, m, 1961, 3 children **DISCIPLINE** PHYSICS; GEOPHYSICS **EDUCATION** Calif Inst of Technol, PhD, 49. **CAREER** Univ Calif, 50-; Prof, Univ Calif. **HONORS AND AWARDS** Gold Medal of Royal Astron Soc; Medal of Seismological Soc Am; Wiechert Medal of Ger Geophysical Soc; Guggenheim Fel; Fel, Am Asn for the Advan of Sci; Fel, Am Geophysical Union; Honorary member, Seismological Soc of Am; Honorary member, Phi Beta Kappa. **MEMBERSHIPS** Nat Acad Sci; Am Acad Arts and Sci; Am Philos Soc. **RESEARCH** Earthquake Physics; Earthquake Prediction; Fracture Mechanics; Elasticity Theory; Systematic musicology; Compex Systems; Elastic Wave propagation; Structure of the interior of the earth. **SELECTED PUBLICATIONS** More than 350 scientific papers and other publications, including co-editing of 6 books. **CONTACT ADDRESS** Physics Dept, Univ of California, Los Angeles, Los Angeles, CA 90095. **EMAIL** knopoff@physics.ucla.edu

KNOTT, ALEXANDER W.

PERSONAL Born 10/14/1938, Chicago, IL, m, 1963, 2 children **DISCIPLINE** HISTORY **EDUCATION** Univ Colo, BA, 61, MA, 63, PhD, 68. **CAREER** Asst prof, Univ Northern Colo, 68-74, assoc prof, 74-. **MEMBERSHIPS** Soc for Historians of Am Foreign Relations; Org of Am Hists. **RESEARCH** U.S. Diplomatic History. **SELECTED PUBLICATIONS** Coauth with G. S. Rowe, "Power, Justice and Foreign Relations in the Confederation Period: The Marbois-Longchamps Affair, 1784-1786," Pa Mag of Hist and Biography, CIV (July 80): 275-307; co-ed with Clifford L. Egan, Essays in Twentieth Century American Diplomatic History Dedicated to Daniel M. Smith, Baltimore: Univ Press Am (82); coauth with G. S. Rowe, "The Longchamps Affair (1784-1786), the Law of Nations, and the Shaping of Early American Foreign Policy," Diplomatic Hist, X (summer 86): 199-220Rev of "The Second World War in Sight and Sound," by John Sylvester, NY: Ardsley House Pubs, Inc (98); auth, Warmaking and American Democracy: The Struggle over Military Strategy, 1700 to the Present, by Michael D. Pearlman, Lawrence: Univ. of Kans Press (99), Red River Quart (in press). **CONTACT ADDRESS** Dept Hist, Univ of No Colorado, 501 20th St, Greeley, CO 80639-0001. **EMAIL** awknott@bentley.unco.edu

KNOWLES, RALPH L.

PERSONAL Born 12/09/1928, Cleveland, OH, m, 1955, 3 children **DISCIPLINE** ARCHITECTURE **EDUCATION** NC State Univ, BA, 54; Mass Inst Tech, MA, 59. **CAREER** Auburn Univ, 59-63; USC, 63-94; adj prof, Univ Haw, 99. **HONORS AND AWARDS** Grand Nat Awd, 62; Awd for Teaching Excellence, Univ of southern Calif, 70; Am Inst of Archit, Medal for Res, 74; Nat endowment for the arts, 80; Phi Kappa Phi Honor soc, 83; Phi Kappa Phi Book Awd, 83; Fulbright Teaching Fel, 93; am col Schools of Archit, 95; USC Torch and Tassel, Fac of the Month, 96; USC distinguised, Emeritus Awd, 00; Grant-in-Aid, Auburn Univ, 60; container Corpoartion of am, 61-62; Graham Foundation Fel, 62-63; Nat endowment for the Arts, 67-80; Los Angeles Dept of Water and Power, 68; Albert c. Martin and Asoc, Los angeles, 79; solar Energy Res Inst, 79-81; nat endowment for the Arts, 84-85; Lujk Ctr Res Inst, 94. **RESEARCH** Passive solar design. **SELECTED PUBLICATIONS** Auth, "The solar Envelope: Its meaning for urban growth and form," Proceeding of the Millennium conference on Passive and Low Energy Architecture, Cambridge, 00; auth, The Interstitium: a zoning strategy for seasonally adaptive architecture," Proceedings of the Environmental Design research association, San Francisco, 00; auth, "Advanced Technical Education in the New Millennium: The Academy of Architectural Sciences, a New Post Graduate virtual University," Proceedings of the Association of Collegiate Schools of Architecture, Montreal, 99; auth, Sun Rhythm Form, MIT Press, 81; auth, Energia E Forma, Padua, 81; auth, Solar Envelope concepts: Moderate Density Building Applications, SERI, 79; auth, Sun, USC, 1976; auth, Energy and Form: An Ecological Approach to Urban Growth, MIT Press, 74. **CONTACT ADDRESS** School of Archit, Univ of So California, Univ Park Mc-0291, Los Angeles, CA 90089-001. **EMAIL** rknowles@usc.edu

KNOWLTON, ROBERT JAMES

PERSONAL Born 01/16/1931, Akron, OH, m, 1958, 2 children **DISCIPLINE** LATIN AMERICAN HISTORY **EDUCATION** Miami Univ, BA, 53; Western Reserve Univ, MA, 59; State Univ lowa, PhD(hist), 63. **CAREER** Asst, State Univ lowa, 59-61; from instr to assoc prof, 62-72, Prof Hist, Univ Wis, Stevens Point, 72-93; Emeritus, 93-; Improvement leave, Univ Wis, 66-67 and 71; Assoc, Latin Am Ctr, Univ Wis, Milwaukee, 72; Mem Policy Comt, 74-; chmn policy comt, 77-82. **MEMBERSHIPS** AHA; Latin Am Studies Asn; Conf Latin Am Hist; MidW Asn Latin Am Studies; N Cent Coun Latin Americanist (pres, 68-69). **RESEARCH** Mexican history, 19th century; expropriation of corporate property in 19th century Mexico and Colombia. **SELECTED PUBLICATIONS** Auth, "Church Property and the Mexican Reform, 1856-1910," Northern Illinois University Press, 76; auth, "Los bienes del clero y la Reforma mexicana, 1856-1910," translated by Juan Jose Utrilla, Fondo de Cultura Economica, Mexico, 85; contrib, "Dealing in Real Estate in Mid-Nineteenth Century Jalisco," The Guadalajara Region," Liberals, the Church and Robert H. Jackson, University of New Mexico Press, Albuquerque, 97; auth, "Clerical Response to the Mexican Reform, 1855-1875," The Catholic Historical Review, vol. L, no. 4, January 65; auth, "Some Practical Effects of Clerical Opposition to the Mexican Reforma mexican, 1856-1910," translated by Juan Jose Utrilla, Fondo de Cultura Economica, Mexico, 85; contr. "Dealing in Real Estate in Mid-Nineteenth Century Jalisco," The Guadalajar Region," Liberals, the Church and Indian Peasants: Corporate Lands and the Challenge of Reform in Nineteenth-Century Spanish America, edited by Robert H. Jackson, University of New Mexico Press, Albuquerque, 97; auth, "Clerical Response to the Mexican Reform, 1855-1875," The Catholic History Review, vol. L, no. 4, January 65; auth, "Some Practical Effects of Clerical Opposition to the Mexican Reform 1856-1860," The Hispanic American Historical Review, vol. Xlv, no. 2, May 65; auth, "Expropriation of Church Property in Nineteenth-Century Mexico and Colomiba: A Comparison," The Americas, vol. Xxv, no. 4, April 69; auth, "La iglesis mexicana y la reforma: respuesta y resultados," Historia Mexican, vol. Xviii, no. 4, abril-junio, 69; auth, "La individualizacion de la propiedad corporativa civil en el siglo xix--notas sobre Jolisco," Historia Mexicana, vol. Xxviii, no. 1, 78; auth, "La division de las tierras de los pueblos durante el siglo xix: el caso de Michoacan," Historia Mexicana, vol. Xl, no. 1, 90; auth, "El ejido mexicano en el siglo xix," Historia Mexicana, vol. Xlviii, no. 1, julio-septiembre 98. **CONTACT ADDRESS** Dept of Hist, Univ of Wisconsin, Stevens Point, Stevens Point, WI 54481.

KNYSH, ALEXANDER D.

PERSONAL Born 09/28/1957, Russia, m, 1979, 1 child **DISCIPLINE** ARABIC AND ISLAMIC STUDIES **EDUCATION** State Univ Leningrad, MA, PhD. **CAREER** Prof, Univ of Exeter, 97-98; prof, Univ of Mich, 98-. **HONORS AND AWARDS** Mem, Inst for Advan Study, Princeton, 91-92; Fel, Rockefeller Fel, Wash Univ; 92-93. **MEMBERSHIPS** Middle East Studies Assoc; Am Oriental Soc. **RESEARCH** Islamic studies, Russian history, Arabian peninsula. **SELECTED PUBLICATIONS** Auth; Ibn Arabi in the Later Islamic Tradition; SUNY Pr, 98; auth; Islamic Mysticism: A short history; Leiden, 00. **CONTACT ADDRESS** Dept Near East, Univ of Michigan, Ann Arbor, 105 S State St, Ann Arbor, MI 48109-1285. **EMAIL** alknysh@umich.edu

KODITSCHEK, THEODORE

PERSONAL Born 05/19/1951, Elizabeth, NJ, d, 1 child **DISCIPLINE** HISTORY **EDUCATION** Rutgers Univ, AB, 73; Princeton Univ, MA, 75; PhD, 81. **CAREER** Asst prof, Univ of Calif Irvine, 81-87; asst to assoc prof, Univ of Miss, 89-. **HONORS AND AWARDS** Herbert Baxter Adams Prize, AHA, 91; Robert Livingston Schuyler Prize, AHA, 91. **MEMBERSHIPS** AHA, Conf on British Studies. **RESEARCH** Modern British Social History, Historiography, History of European Social Thought. **SELECTED PUBLICATIONS** Auth, Class Formation and Urban Industrial Society: Bradford, 1750-1850, Cambridge Univ Pr, 90. **CONTACT ADDRESS** Dept Hist, Univ of Missouri, Columbia, 101 Read Hall, Columbia, MO 65211-7500. **EMAIL** kodit@missouri.edu

KOELSCH, WILLIAM ALVIN

PERSONAL Born 05/16/1933, Morristown, NJ, s **DISCIPLINE** AMERICAN HISTORY & GEOGRAPHY **EDUCATION** Bucknell Univ, ScB, 55; Clark Univ, AM, 59; Univ Chicago, PhD(hist), 66. **CAREER** Vis asst prof geog, Clark Univ, 63; from instr to asst prof hist, Fla Presby Col, 63-67; asst prof, 67-69, assoc prof, 69-81, univ archivist, 72-82, prof hist & geog, Clark Univ, 81-98, univ historian, 82-90, comnr, Mass Arch Adv Comn, 74-96; registrar-historiographer, Episcopal Diocese of Mass, 92-98; corresp mem, Int Geog Union Comn, 75-. **HONORS AND AWARDS** Prof Emeritus, 98-. **MEMBERSHIPS** Hist Educ Soc; Am Geog Soc; Orgn Am Historians. **RESEARCH** History of geography and related fields; history of American higher education. **SELECTED PUBLICATIONS** Auth, A Propound Through Special Erudition?: Justin Winsor as Historian of Discovery, Proc Am Antiquarian Soc, 4/83; Coauth, Psychoanalysis Arrives in America, Am Psychologist, 85; contribur, The Episcopal Diocese of Massachusetts, Boston, 84; Aspects of Antiquity in the History of Education, Lax, 92; Geographers: Biobibliographical Studies, 79. **CONTACT ADDRESS** 3310 First Ave, Apt 3C, San Diego, CA 92103.

KOENIGER, A. CASH

PERSONAL Born 03/16/1949, Little Rock, AZ, m, 1980 **DISCIPLINE** HISTORY **EDUCATION** Wash and Lee Univ, AB, 71; Vanderbilt Univ, MA, 74; PhD, 80. **CAREER** Instr, Murray State Univ, 79-80; Asst Prof, Miss State Univ, 80-81; Asst Prof, Univ S Miss, 81-86; Assoc Prof to Prof, Va Military Inst, 86-. **MEMBERSHIPS** S Hist Asn. **RESEARCH** United States history: Old South, Sectional controversy and Civil War, Twentieth century, especially 1900-1940, especially South; American South; US political history. **SELECTED PUBLICATIONS** Auth, "Ken Burns's The Civil War: Triumph or Travesty?", Journal of Military History, (910;: 225-233; auth, "Climate and Southern Distinctiveness," Journal of Southern History, (88): 21-44; auth, "The New Deal and the States: Roosevelt versus the Byrd Organization in Virginia," Journal of American History, (82): 876-896; auth, "The Politics of Independence: Carter Glass and the Elections of 1936," South Atlantic Quarterly, (81): 95-106; auth, "Carter Glass and the National Recovery Administration," South Atlantic Quarterly, (75): 349-364; auth, "Carter Glass," in Encyclopedia of the United States Congress, Simon and Schuster, 95; auth, "Carter Glass," in Encyclopedia USA, Academic International Press, in press. **CONTACT ADDRESS** Dept Hist, Virginia Military Inst, Lexington, VA 24450-0304. **EMAIL** koenigerac@mail.vmi.edu

KOENIGSBERG, LISA M.

DISCIPLINE AMERICAN STUDIES **EDUCATION** Johns Hopkins, BA, 79; MA, 79, PhD, 88. **CAREER** PhD Cand In AM Stud, Yale Univ. **MEMBERSHIPS** Am Antiquarian Soc **SELECTED PUBLICATIONS** "Emblem for an Era: Selected Images of America Victorian Womanhood from the Yale University Community, 1837-1911," Yale exhibition, 82; auth, "Renderings from Worcester's Past: Nineteenth-Century Architectural Drawings at the American Antiquarian Soc," Procs of the AAS 96, 86. **CONTACT ADDRESS** Landmarks Preserv Comm, City of New York, 225 Broadway, New York, NY 10007.

KOENKER, DIANE P.

DISCIPLINE HISTORY **EDUCATION** Grinnell Col, AB, 69; Univ of Mich, AM, 71; Univ of Mich, PhD, 76 **CAREER** Vis lectr in history, Univ of Ill at Urbana-Champaign, 75; asst to assoc prof, Temple Univ, 76-83; asst prof, Univ of Ill at Urbana-Champaign, 83-86; assoc prof, Univ of Ill at Urbana-Champaign, 86-88; dir, Russian and East European Ctr, Univ of Ill at Urbana-Champaign, 90-96; prof of hist, Univ of Ill at Urbana-Champaign, 88-; editor, Slavic Review, 96-. **HONORS AND AWARDS** NEH Individual Fel, 83-84; NEH Res Rel, 84-85; Fulbright-Hays Fac Res Awd for USSR, 89; Vis Fel, Australian Nat Univ, 89; Midwest Univ Consortium for International Affairs (MUCIA) Exchange Fel with Moscow State Univ, 91; IREX Short-Term Travel Grants, 93, 98; International Res and Exchanges Board (IREX) Exchange with Russian Acad of Sci, 93; Fulbright-Hays Fac Res Awd, 93; Nat Endow for the Humanities (NEH) Collaborative Projects Grant, 94-95; Univ of Ill Res Board Grants, 83-00; Univ of Ill Ctr for Advanced Study Assoc, 96-97; Dept of hist George S. and Gladys W. Queen Excellence in Teach Awd in Hist, 96-97; LAS Teach Acad Mentor, 99-00; ed, slavic rev. **MEMBERSHIPS** Am His Assoc; Am Assoc for the Advancement of Slavic Studies; Midwest Workshop of Russ Historians; Assoc of Women in Slavic Studies. **RESEARCH** Society in Soviet Russia. **SELECTED PUBLICATIONS** Auth, Moscow Workers and the 1917 Revolution, Princeton, N.J., Princeton University Press, 81; ed, Tret'ya Vserossiskaya Konferentsiya Professional'nykh Soyuzov, 1917, Stenograficheskii otchet, editor with introduction, notes, and index, London, Kraus-Thomson Organization, 82; auth, Strikes and Revolution in Russia, 1917, with William G. Rosenberg, (Princeton, N.J., Princeton University Press, 89; ed, Party, State, and Society in the Russian Civil War: Explorations in Social History editor with William G. Rosenberg and Ronald Grigor Suny, Bloomington, Ind., Indiana University Press, 89; ed and trans, Notes of a Red Guard, by Edward Dune, Urbana, Ill., University of Illinois Press, 93; auth, "Men against Women on the Shop Floor in Early Soviet Russia: Gender and Class in the Socialist Workplace," American Historical Review, (December 95): 1438-64; auth, "Factory Tales: Narratives of Industrial Relations in the Transition to NEP," Russian Review, (July 96): 384-411; auth, Revelations from the Russian Archives: Documents in English Translation Washington, D.C., Library of Congress, 97; auth, "The Trade Unions," in Critical Companion to the Russian Revolution 1917-1922, and Edward Acton, Vladimir Cherniaev, and William G. Rosenberg, eds., London, Edward Allen, 97, pp. 446-56; auth, "Gazeta Trud o trudovykh konfliktakh v Rossii v 1920-e gg." The Newspaper Trud on Labor Conflicts in Russia in the 1920s, in Trudovye konflikty v Sovetskoi Rossii: 1918-1928 gg., Iu. I. Kir'ianov, V. Rozenberg, and A.N. Sakharov, eds., Moscow, Editorial URSS, 98, 169-79. **CONTACT ADDRESS** History Dept, Univ of Illinois, Urbana-Champaign, 309 Gregory hall, mc 466, 810 S Wright, Urbana, IL 61801. **EMAIL** koenker@ysidro.econ.uiuc.edu

KOEPKE, ROBERT L.

PERSONAL Born 06/17/1932, Arcadia, IA, m, 1960 **DISCIPLINE** MODERN HISTORY **EDUCATION** Univ Iowa, BA, 59; Stanford Univ, MA, 61, PhD(hist), 67. **CAREER** Instr hist, Stanford Univ, 63-65; instr, 65-67, Asst Prof Hist, Simon Fraser Univ, 67-. **MEMBERSHIPS** AHA; Soc Fr Hist Studies. **RESEARCH** Modern French history. **SELECTED PUBLICATIONS** Auth, Cooperation, Not Conflict, Parisian Bureaucracy and the Third-Republic, Ministry-of-Education in Cures and Primary-School, Inspectors in July-Monarchy France, Church Hist. Vol 0064, 95. **CONTACT ADDRESS** 5017 Howe Sound Lane W, Vancouver, BC, Canada V7W 1L3. **EMAIL** robert_koepke@sfu.ca

KOERPER, PHILLIP ELDON

PERSONAL Born 06/23/1941, Ironton, OH, m, 1964, 2 children **DISCIPLINE** BRITISH HISTORY, EUROPEAN HISTORY **EDUCATION** Fla Southern Col, BA, 67; Univ Ga, MA, 68, PhD (hist), 71. **CAREER** Assoc Prof, 69-83, Prof Brit Europ Hist, Jacksonville State Univ, 83-. **HONORS AND AWARDS** English Speaking Union res grant, 70. **MEMBERSHIPS** Southeastern Conf Latin Am Studies; AHA; Int Churchill Soc. **RESEARCH** British Empire; modern Britain; early modern Europe. **SELECTED PUBLICATIONS** Auth, Cable Imbroglio in the Pacific, Hawaiian J Hist, 75; Ernest Belfort Bax, William Pember Reeves, David James Shakleton & H R L Sheppard, In: Biographical Dictionary of Modern British Radicals, Vol III, 78; Classics in Western Civilization, 2 vols, Ginn & Co, 86-87; author of numerous journal articles/entries. **CONTACT ADDRESS** Dept of Hist Col of Letters & Sci, Jacksonville State Univ, 700 Pelham Rd N, Jacksonville, AL 36265-1602.

KOERTGE, NORETTA

PERSONAL Born 10/07/1935, Olney, IL **DISCIPLINE** PHILOSOPHY OF SCIENCE, HISTORY OF SCIENCE **EDUCATION** Univ Ill, BS, 55, MS, 56; London Univ, PhD(philos of sci), 69. **CAREER** Instr chem, Elmhurst Col, 60-63; head chem sect, Am Col for Girls, Instanbul, Turkey, 63-64; lectr philos of sci, Ont Inst for Studies Educ, 68-69; asst prof, 70-73, assoc prof, 74-81, Prof Hist and Philos of Sci, Ind Univ, Bloomington, 81-; Editor-in-Chief, Phil of Sci, 99-. **HONORS AND AWARDS** Fellow of Amer Assoc Adv Sci. **MEMBERSHIPS** Philos Sci Asn. **RESEARCH** Theories of scientific method; historical development of philosophy of science; Poppers philosophy of science. **SELECTED PUBLICATIONS** Auth, A House Built on Sand, professing Feminism, Philosophy and Homosexuality. **CONTACT ADDRESS** Indiana Univ, Bloomington, 130 Goodbody Hall, Bloomington, IN 47401. **EMAIL** koertge@indiana.edu

KOFAS, JON

PERSONAL Born 09/29/1953, Greece, m, 1974, 1 child **DISCIPLINE** HISTORY **CAREER** Lecturer, Loyola Univ, 80-87; vis asst prof, Marquette Univ, 87-89; vis asst prof, Univ Wis, 89-92; asst prof to full prof, Ind Univ Kokomo, 92-. **HONORS AND AWARDS** Claude Rich Excellence in Teaching Awd, 98; Teaching Excellence Recognition Awd, 97; Fac Colloquium on Excellence in Teaching, Ind Univ, 94; Excellence in Teaching Awd, 92; hewlett Foundation Fac Fel, 93; Chancellor's Grant incentive fund, 93; In Univ Kokomo res grant, 95; In Univ President's coun, 96; Ind Univ Kokomo summer grant, 96. **RESEARCH** International political economy, US diplomatic, Interamerican relations, Balkans. **SELECTED PUBLICATIONS** Auth, "US Foreign Policy and the World Federation of Trade Unions, 1944-1948," Diplomatic History, (forthcoming); auth, "The IMF, the World Bank, and US Foreign Policy in Ecuador, 1956-1966, Latin American Perspectives, (forthcoming); auth, "Stabilization and Class Conflict: The State Department, the IMF, and the IFRD in Chile, 1952-58," The International History Review, (99): 352-385; auth, "Growth by Debt: Foreign Borrowing and Dependent Capitalism in Chile, 1958-1970," Journal of Third World Studies, (99): 101-135; auth, "The Politics of Foreign Debt: IMF, World Bank, and US Foreign Policy in Chile, 1946-1952," Journal of Developing Area, (97): 26; auth, "US Foreign Policy and the Latin American Foreign Debt during the Early Cold War, 1945-53," Journal of Developing Area, (97): 23; auth, Foreign Debt and Underdevelopment: US-Peru Economic Relations, 1930-1970, Univ Press of Am: Lanham, 96; auth, "Politics of Conflict and Containment: Ecuador's Labor Movement and US Foreign Policy, 1944-1963," Journal of Third World Studies, (96): 61; auth, "The Politics of Austerity: The IMF and US Foreign Policy in Bolivia, 1956-1964," Journal of Developing Area, (95): 23; auth, Developmentalism and Hemispheric Integration: US-Chile Economic Relations, 1938-1945," International Third World Studies Journal & Review, (95): 18. **CONTACT ADDRESS** Dept Soc & Beh Sci, Indiana Univ, Kokomo, PO Box 9003, Kokomo, IN 46904-9003. **EMAIL** jkofas@iuk.edu

KOGINOS, MANNY T.

PERSONAL Born 03/12/1933, New Castle, PA, m, 2 children **DISCIPLINE** AMERICAN DIPLOMATIC HISTORY **EDUCATION** Bowling Green State Univ, BA, 54; Am Univ, MA, 60, PhD, 66. **CAREER** Instr Am hist, Ohio Wesleyan Univ, 64-65; asst prof, Purdue Univ, 65-67; assoc prof Am Hist, State Univ NY Col Buffalo, 67-. **HONORS AND AWARDS** NY State grant-in-aid, 68-69; vis prof Am hist, Didesbury Col, Univ Manchester, England, 71-72; vis prof, Univ Hawaii, Hilo, 81-82; vis prof, Kansai Univ of For Studies, Osaka, Japan, 86. **MEMBERSHIPS** AHA; Orgn Am Historians; Soc Hist Am Foreign Rels; Western Hist Asn. **RESEARCH** American-Far Eastern and American-Japanese relations. **SELECTED PUBLICATIONS** Auth, The Panay Incident: Prelude to War, Purdue Univ, 67. **CONTACT ADDRESS** Dept of Hist, SUNY, Buffalo, 1300 Elmwood Ave, Buffalo, NY 14222-1095.

KOHL, BENJAMIN GIBBS

PERSONAL Born 10/26/1938, Middletown, DE, m, 1961, 2 children **DISCIPLINE** MEDIEVAL AND RENAISSANCE HISTORY **EDUCATION** Bowdoin Col, AB, 60; Univ Del, MA, 62; Johns Hopkins Univ, PhD(hist), 68. **CAREER** Instr hist, Johns Hopkins Univ, 65-66; from instr to asst prof, 66-74, assoc prof, 74-81; Prof Hist, Vassar Col, 81-01, prof emer, 01, Assoc, Columbia Univ Colloquium Renaissance, 80-00; Rome prize fel post-classical humanistic studies, Am Acad Rome, 70-71. **HONORS AND AWARDS** Fel, Royal Historical Soc (London), 80. **MEMBERSHIPS** Mediaeval Acad Am; Renaissance Soc Am; Dante Soc Am; Soc Ital Hist Studies; Am Hist Assoc (life). **RESEARCH** Renaissance history; history of Venice. **SELECTED PUBLICATIONS** Auth, Renaissance Humanism, 1300-1550, A Bibliography of Materials in English, Garland, 85; coed, Major Problems in the History of the Italian Renaissance, Houghton Miflin, 95; auth, Padua Under the Canara, 1318-1405, Johns Hopkins UP, 98; auth, The Records of the Venetian Senato on Disk, 1335-1400, CD-ROM, NY: Italica Press, 00; auth, Cultures and Politics in Early Renaissance Padua, Ashgate, 01. **CONTACT ADDRESS** PO Box 166, Betterton, MD 21610. **EMAIL** kohlinmd@dmv.com

KOHLER, ERIC DAVE

PERSONAL Born 10/24/1943, Cincinnati, OH, m, 1968 **DISCIPLINE** MODERN EUROPEAN HISTORY, GERMAN HISTORY **EDUCATION** Brown Univ, AB, 65; Stanford Univ, MA, 67, PhD (hist), 71. **CAREER** Asst prof hist, Calif State Univ, Humbolt, 70-71; asst prof, 71-78, Assoc Prof Hist, Univ Wyo, 78-. **MEMBERSHIPS** AHA; Conf Group Cent Europ Hist. **RESEARCH** Prussian state in the Weimar Republic; European labor history; national socialism. **SELECTED PUBLICATIONS** Auth, Weimar Prussia, 1925-1933 in the Illusion of Strength, Ger Studies Rev, Vol 0016, 93; The German Bourgeoisie in Essays on the Social-History of the German Middle-Class From the Late 18th-Century to the Early-20th-Century, Ger Studies Rev, Vol 0016, 93; Himmler Auxiliaries, The Volksdeutsche-Mittelstelle and the German National Minorities of Europe, 1933-1945, Ger Studies Rev, Vol 0017, 94; Red Vienna, Experiment in Working-Class Culture, 1919-1934, Ger Studies Rev, Vol 0018, 95; German Social-Democracy and the Rise of Nazism, Ger Studies Rev, Vol 0018, 95; National-Socialist Leadership and Total War, 1941-1945 Ger Studies Rev, Vol 0018, 95; Medicine and Health-Policy in the Nazi Period in German Ger Studies Rev, Vol 0019, 96. **CONTACT ADDRESS** Dept of Hist, Univ of Wyoming, P O Box 3198, Laramie, WY 82071-3198.

KOHLER, SUE A.

PERSONAL Born 11/27/1927, Grand Rapids, MI, w, 1953, 3 children **DISCIPLINE** HISTORY; HISTORY OF ART **EDUCATION** Univ Mich, BA, 49, MA, 50. **CAREER** Asst to cur, Mus of Cranbrook Acad of Art, 51-53; archit hist, US Comn of Fine Arts, 74-. **HONORS AND AWARDS** Phi Beta Kappa; Phi Kappa Phi. **MEMBERSHIPS** Soc of Archit Hist; Nat Trust for Hist Preserv; Victorian Soc in Amer; Class Amer; Nat Building Mus; Hist Soc of Wash DC. **RESEARCH** 19th and 20th century American architecture. **SELECTED PUBLICATIONS** Auth, chapt, The Grand American Avenue, Amer Archit Found, 94; auth, The Commission of Fine Arts: A Brief History, 1910-1995, The Comn of Fine Arts, 95; co-auth, Sixteenth Street Architecture, vol 2, The Comn of Fine Arts, 88; co-auth, Sixteenth Street Architecture, vol 1, The Comn of Fine Arts, 78; co-auth, Massachusetts Avenue Architecture, vol 2, The Comn of Fine Arts, 75. **CONTACT ADDRESS** US Commission of Fine Arts, National Building Museum, Suite 312, 441 F. Str N.W., Washington, DC 20001. **EMAIL** Sue_Kohler@ios.doi.gov

KOHLS, WINFRED A.

PERSONAL Born 07/07/1929, Yingtak, China, m, 3 children **DISCIPLINE** MODERN EUROPEAN HISTORY **EDUCATION** Augustana Col, SDak, AB, 51; Univ Calif, Berkeley, MA, 59, PhD (hist), 67. **CAREER** Instr hist, Univ Md, Overseas Br, 57-58; from asst prof to assoc prof, 63-72, chmn dept, 73-78, Prof Hist, Moravian Col, 72-; Emeritus, 01; Participant, Soviet-Am Inter-Univ Cult Exchange, 68-69; Adj Prof Hist, Lehigh Univ, 69-; sr res fel, Alexander von Humboldt Found, Ger and vis res prof, Univ Marburg, 72-73; Bk Rev Ed, Russian Histhistoire Russe, 75-; Am Ed, Unitas Fratrum, 76-93; res fel, Kennan Inst Advan Russ Res, Washington, DC, 78. **HONORS AND AWARDS** Re-Invitied Alex V. Hurboldt Fellow, 78-79; Lindback Found Awd Distinguished Teaching. **MEMBERSHIPS** AHA; Am Asn Advan Slavic Studies. **RESEARCH** Russian history, 19th century; history of Russian education; German Colonies in Russia; German history, post World War I. **SELECTED PUBLICATIONS** Auth, Among Others: Chapters in the History of Foreign Colonization in Russia, The Sarepta Crisis in Its Historical Context, Russ Hist-Histoire Russe, Vol 0020, 93. **CONTACT ADDRESS** Dept of Hist, Moravian Col, 1200 Main St, Bethlehem, PA 18018-6650. **EMAIL** winkohls@fast.net

KOHLSTEDT, SALLY GREGORY

PERSONAL Born 01/30/1943, Ypsilanti, MI, m, 1966, 2 children **DISCIPLINE** HISTORY OF SCIENCE AND TECHNOLOGY **EDUCATION** Valparaiso Univ, BA, 65; Mich State Univ, MA, 66; Univ Ill, Urbana, PhD, 72. **CAREER** Simmons Col, Dept of Hist, Syracuse Univ, Dept of Hist, 75-88, acting ch, 80-81; women's studies dir, 80-81; Fulbright vis prof, Univ of Melbourne, spring, 83; visiting prof, Cornell Univ, spring, 89; assoc dean, Inst of Tech, 89-95; vis prof, Amer-Inst, Univ of Munich, spring, 97; prof, Prog in Hist of Sci and Tech; dir, Ctr for Advan Feminist Studies. **HONORS AND AWARDS** Mortar bd; Valparaiso Univ; Nat Sci Found, res funding, summer, 69, 78-79, 93-94, 95; conference funding, 84, 95; Smithsonian Inst Pre-Doctoral Fel, 70-71; Syracuse Univ Facul Res Grant, 76, 82; Amer Philos Soc Res Grant, 77; Amer Antiquarian Soc, Haven Res Fel, oct, 82, mem, 84; Woodrow Wilson Ctr Fel, fall, 86; Smithsonian Inst Sr Fel, spring, 87; Hist of Sci Soc Plenary Lectr, 88; Univ of Minn Facul Res Grant, 90, 97-98; UMN TEL award: Outstanding Computer Aided Course Project, 98. **MEMBERSHIPS** Am Asn for the Advan of Sci; Am Hist Asn; Hist of Sci Soc; Intl Congress for the Hist of Sci; Orgn of Am Hist; Am Hist Asn; Hist of Sci Soc, Pres, 94-96; Bd of Dir, 98-02. **RESEARCH** Science in America; Women, gender and science; Science in public culture, including museums and amateur associations. **SELECTED PUBLICATIONS** Auth, The Formation of the American Scientific Community: The American Association for the Advancement of Science, Urbana, Univ Ill Press, 76; ed, with Margaret Rossiter, Historical Writing on American Science, Osiris, 2nd series, 1, 85; ed, The Origins of Natural Science in the United States: The Essays of George Brown Goode, Wash, Smithsonian Inst Press, 91; ed, with R. W. Home, International Science and National Scientific Identity: Australia between Britain and America, Holland, Kluewer Acad Publ, 91; ed, with Barbara Laslett, Helen Longino and Evelyn Hammonds, Gender and Scientific Authority, Chicago, Univ Chicago Press, 96; ed, with Helen Longino, Women, Gender and Science: New Directions, Osiris, 12, Chicago, Univ Chicago Press, 97; ed, History of Women in the Sciences, Chicago, Univ Chicago Press, 97; coauth, The Establishment of Science in America, New Brunswick, Rutgers Univ Press, 00 **CONTACT ADDRESS** Univ of Minnesota, Twin Cities, 123 Pillsbury Hall, 318 Pillsbury Dr., Minneapolis, MN 55455. **EMAIL** sgk@umn.edu

KOHN, RICHARD HENRY

PERSONAL Born 12/29/1940, Chicago, IL, m, 1964, 2 children **DISCIPLINE** AMERICAN MILITARY HISTORY **EDUCATION** Harvard Univ, AB, 62; Univ Wis-Madison, MS, 64, PhD, 68. **CAREER** Asst prof hist, City Col New York, 68-71; asst prof, Rutgers Univ, New Brunswick, 71-75, assoc prof, 75-83; prof, 83-84; Visiting prof military hist, US Army Military Hist Inst, US Army War Col, 80-81; Chief, Office of Air Force Hist, 81-91; Adjunct Prof, Nat War Col, 85-90; Vis Scholar in Strategic Studies, Johns Hopkins Univ, 91; Prof of Hist, Univ of North Carolina at Chapel Hill, Assoc Prof, 91-93. **HONORS AND AWARDS** Nat Endowment for Humanities bicentennial grant, 70-71; Am Philos Soc res grant, 70-71; Binkley-Stephenson Prize, Orgn Am Historians, 73; Am Coun Learned Soc fel, 77-78; Dept of Army: Certificates of Appreciation for Patriotic Civilian Service, 81, 86; Air Force Historical Foundation: President's Awd, 87; Dept of Air Force, Organizational Excellence Awd, 90; Decoration for Exceptional Civilain Service, 91; Univ of North Carolina at Chapel Hill: Institute for the Arts and Humanities Faculty Fel, 95-96; Society for Military History: Victory Gondos Memorial Service Awd, 96; Smith-Richardson Foundation Res Grants, 97, 98-00. **MEMBERSHIPS** Am Mil Inst, AHA, Orgn Am Historians, Inter-Univ Sem on Armed Forces and Soc, Air Force Historical Found, Soc for Military History. **RESEARCH** American miitary policy, strategy, war-making, presidential war leadership, civil-military relations. **SELECTED PUBLICATIONS** Ed, The United States Military under the Constitution of the United States, 1789-1989, New York Press, 91; auth, History and the Culture Wars in the Case of the Smithsonian-Institution Enola-Gay Exhibition, J Am Hist, Vol 0082, 95; Untitled, J Am Hist, Vol 0083, 96; The Practice of Military History in the Us Government in the Department of Defense, J Military History, Vol 0061, 97; auth, The Exclusion of Black Studies from the Medal of Honor in World War II: The Study Commissioned by the United State Army to Investigate Racial Bias in the Awarding of the Nation's Highest Military Decoration, McFarland Publishers, 97; auth, "Grand Army of the Republicans," The New Republic (97): 22-24; auth, "An Officer Corps for the Next Century," Joint Forces Quarterly (98): 76-80; auth, "Civil-Military Relations: Civilian Control of the Military," in John Whiteclay Chambers II, Oxford Companion to American Military History, Oxford Press (99): 122-125; auth, "The Gap: Soldiers, Civilians, and Their Mutual Misunderstanding," The National Interest (00): 29-37; auth, "The Political Trap for the Military, " Raleigh, NC News and Observer, 00. **CONTACT ADDRESS** Univ of No Carolina, Chapel Hill, 402 Hamilton Hall, CB No. 3200, Chapel Hill, NC 27599-3200. **EMAIL** rhkohn@unc.edu

KOHUT, THOMAS A.
PERSONAL Born 03/11/1950, Chicago, IL, m, 1975, 2 children **DISCIPLINE** HISTORY **EDUCATION** Oberlin Col, BA, 72; Univ of Minn, MA, 75, PhD, 83; Cinn Psychoanalytic Inst grad, 84. **CAREER** Fac, Cinn Psychoanalytic Inst, 84-; asst prof to prof, Williams Col, 84-; Sue and Edgar Wachenheim III Prof of Hist, 95-; Dean, 00-. **HONORS AND AWARDS** DAAD Grant, Fed Rep Ger, 78-79; IREX Grant, Ger Dem Rep, 79; Univ of Minn Fel, 80-81; Fulbright Scholar, 87-88; Grant, Kohler Found, Fed Rep Ger, 96. **MEMBERSHIPS** AHA; Ger Studies Assoc. **RESEARCH** Modern European cultural, intellectural, and social history. **SELECTED PUBLICATIONS** Auth, "Kaiser Wilhelm and his Parents: An Inquiry into the Psychological Roots of German Policy Towards England Before the First World War", Kaiser Wilhelm II: New Interpretations, (Cambridge: Cambridge Univ Pr 82), 63-89; auth, "Mirror Image of the Nation: An Investigation of Kaiser Wilhelm II's Leadership of the Germans", The Leader: Psychohistorical Essays, (New York: Plenum Pr, 85), 179-229; auth, "Psychohistory as History", The Am Hist Rev 91, (86): 336-354; auth, "Empathizing with Nazis: Reflections on Robert Jay Lifton's the Nazi Doctors", The Psychohistory Rev 16, (87): 33-50; auth, Wilhelm II and the Germans: A Study in Leadership, Oxford Univ Pr, (New York) 91; coauth, "Sterben wie eine Ratte, die der Bauer ertappt. Letzte Briefe aus Stalingrad", Stalingrad: Ereignis, Wirkung, Symbol, (Munich and Zurich: Piper Verlag 92) 456-71; auth, "Commentary on Robert Jay Lifton's 'Reflections on Aum Shinrikyo' and on the 25th Anniversary of the Group for the Use of Psychology in History", The Psychohistory Rev 25, (97):234-239; auth, "The Creation of Wilhelm Busch as a German Cultural Hero, 1902-1908", Enlightenment, Culture and Passion: Essays in Honor of Peter Gay, (Stanford: Stanford Univ Pr), 00; auth, "Pladoyer fur eine historisierte Psychoanalyse", Psychotherapie in Zeiten der Veranderung - Historische, kulturelle und gesellschaftliche Hintergrunde einer Profession, (Berlin: Westdeutsche Verlag) 00; auth, "Wilhelm Busche: Die Erfindung eines literarischen Nationalhelden, 1902-08", Zeitschrift fur Literaturwissenschaft und Linguistik (forthcoming). **CONTACT ADDRESS** Dept History, Williams Col, 880 Main St., Williamstown, MA 01267-2600. **EMAIL** thomas.a.kohut@williams.edu

KOISTINEN, PAUL ABRAHAM CARL
PERSONAL Born 03/27/1933, Wedena, MN, m, 1961, 2 children **DISCIPLINE** AMERICAN HISTORY **EDUCATION** Univ CA, Berkeley, AB, 56, MA, 59, PhD (hist), 64. **CAREER** From asst prof to prof hist, Calif State Univ Northridge, 63-; vis scholar, US Military Acad, 79 & US Air Force Acad, 82. **HONORS AND AWARDS** Res grants, CA State Univ, Northridge, 65-66, 68-70, 72-73, 76-78 & 79-00; res fel, Charles Warren Ctr Studies Am Hist; res fel, Harvard Univ, 74-75; res fel, Am Coun Learned Soc, 75; NEH, 88. **MEMBERSHIPS** AHA; Orgn Am Historians; Am Comt Hist 2nd World War; Conf Peace Res in Hist; Inter-Univ Sem Armed Forces & Soc. **RESEARCH** American political, economic and military history. **SELECTED PUBLICATIONS** Auth, The Industrial-Military Complex in Historical Perspective: World War I, Bus Hist Rev, winter 67; The Industrial-Military Complex in Historical Perspective: the Interwar Years, J Am Hist, 3/70; Mobilizing the World War II Economy: Labor and the Industrialmilitary Alliance, Pac Hist Rev, 11/73; The Hammer and the Sword: Labor, the Military, and Industrial Mobilization, 1920-1945, Arno Press, 79; The Military-Industrial Complex: A Historical Perspective, Praeger, 80; Warfare and Power Relations in America: Mobilizing the World War II Economy, in Home Front and War in the 20th Century, ed James Titus, Air Force Academy, 84; Towards A Warfare State: Militarization in America During the Period of the World Wars, in Militarization of the Western World, ed John Gillis, Rutgers, 89; The Political Economy of Warfare in America, 1865-1914, in Anticipating Total War? The United States and Germany, 1871-1914, ed Stig Forster, Cambridge, 98; assoc ed, American National Biography, 89-98; Beating Plowshares into Swords: The Political Economy of American Warfare, 1606-1865, KS, 96; Mobilizing for Modern War: The Political Economy of Am Warfare, 1865-1919, 97; Planning War, Pursuing Peace: The Political Economy of American Warfare, 1920-1939, KS, 98 -- the above three volumes are part of a 5 vol study of the political economy of warfare in America (vol 4 will cover WWII, vol 5, the Cold War years). **CONTACT ADDRESS** Dept Hist, California State Univ, Northridge, 18111 Nordhoff St, Northridge, CA 91330-8200.

KOLB, ROBERT A.
PERSONAL Born 06/17/1941, Fort Dodge, IA, m, 1965, 1 child **DISCIPLINE** HISTORY **EDUCATION** Concordia Sr Col, BA, 63; Concordia Sem, MDiv, 67; STM, 68; Univ Wis, MA, 69; PhD, 73. **CAREER** Director, Center for Reformation Res, 72-77; prof, Concordia Col, 77-93; director, prof, Concordia Sem, 93-. **MEMBERSHIPS** Soc for Reformed Res; Sixteenth Century Studies Conf. **RESEARCH** Reformation, Confessionalization. **SELECTED PUBLICATIONS** Auth, Speaking the Gospel Today, A Theology for Evangelism, Concordia Pub House, (St Louis), 84; auth, For All the Saints, Changing Perceptions of Martyrdom and Sainthood in the Lutheran Reformation, Mercer Univ Pr, (Macon, GA), 87; auth, Confessing the Faith, Reformers Define the Church, 1530-1580, Concordia Pub House, (St Louis), 91; auth, Teaching God's Children His Teaching, a Guide to the Study of Luther's Catechism, Crown Pub, (Hutchinson, MN), 92; auth, The Christian Faith, a Lutheran Exposition, Concordia Pub House, (St Louis), 93; auth, Luther's Heirs Define His Legacy, Studies on Lutheran Confessionalization, Variorum (Aldershot, Hampshire), 96; auth, Martin Luther as Prophet, Teacher and Hero: Images of the Reformer, 1520-1620, Baker Books, (Grand Rapids), 99; auth, "Luther on the Two Kinds of Righteousness. Reflections on His Two-Dimensional Definition of Humanity at the Heart of His Theology", Lutheran Quarterly 13 (99): 449-466; auth, "Patristic Citation as Homiletical Tool in the Vernacular Sermon of the German Late Reformation", Die Patrisik in der Bibelexegese des 16 Jahrhunderts, ed David C Steinmetz, Harrassowitz, (Wiesbaden, 99): 151-179; auth, "Altering the Agenda, Shifting the Strategy: The Grundfest of 1571 as Philippist Program for Lutheran Concord", Sixteenth Century J 30, (99): 705-726. **CONTACT ADDRESS** Dept Systematic Theol, Concordia Sem, 801 De Mun Ave, Saint Louis, MO 63105-3168. **EMAIL** kolbr@csl.edu

KOLKO, GABRIEL
PERSONAL Born 08/17/1932, Paterson, NJ, m, 1955 **DISCIPLINE** AMERICAN HISTORY **EDUCATION** Kent State Univ, BA, 54; Univ Wis, MS, 55; Harvard Univ, PhD (hist), 62. **CAREER** Soc Sci Res Coun fel, 63-64; assoc prof hist, Univ Pa, 64-68; prof hist, State Univ NY, Buffalo, 68-70; Prof Hist to Dist Res Prof Emer, York Univ, 70-. **HONORS AND AWARDS** Guggenheim Found fel, 66-67; Inst Policy Studies fel, 67-68; Am Coun Learned Soc fel, 71-72. **MEMBERSHIPS** AHA; Orgn Am Historians. **RESEARCH** American political and economic history since 1876; American diplomatic history in the 20th century. **CONTACT ADDRESS** Dept of Hist, York Univ, 4700 Keele St, Toronto, ON, Canada M3J 1P3.

KOLLANDER, PATRICIA A.
PERSONAL Born 09/17/1959, Cleveland, OH, m, 1995, 2 children **DISCIPLINE** MODERN EUROPEAN HISTORY **EDUCATION** Col Wooster, BA, 81; Brown Univ, MA, 86; PhD, 92. **CAREER** Instr, Col Wooster, 89-90; asst prof, Fla Atlantic Univ, 91-96; assoc prof, 96-. **HONORS AND AWARDS** FAU Res Fel; Ger Acad Diss Gnt; Fulbright Stud Gnt. **MEMBERSHIPS** AHA; GSA; Phi Alpha Theta. **RESEARCH** German liberalism in the 19th century; Hohenzollern family; Bismarchian politics and diplomacy; German-Yugoslav relations in the 20th century. **SELECTED PUBLICATIONS** Auth, Frederick III: Germany's Liberal Emperor, Greenwood Press, 95; auth, "Bismark, Crown Prince Frederick William and the Hohenzollern Candidacy Revisited," Euro Rev Hist (97); auth, "politics for the Defence? : Bismark, Battenberg and the Cartel of 1887," Ger Hist (95); auth, "Empress Frederick: Last Hope for a Liberal Germany?," Histn (99); auth, "Malevolent Partnership or Blatant Opportunism? : Croat-German Relations, 1919-1941," in Germany and Eastern Europe: Cultural Identities and Cultural Realities, ed. K Bullivant (99). **CONTACT ADDRESS** Dept History, Florida Atlantic Univ, PO Box 3091, Boca Raton, FL 33431-0991. **EMAIL** kollande@fau.edu

KOLLAR, NATHAN RUDOLPH
PERSONAL Born 07/20/1938, Braddock, PA, m, 1972, 2 children **DISCIPLINE** RELIGIOUS STUDIES, HISTORY **EDUCATION** St Bonaventure Univ, BA, 60; Cath Univ Am, STL, 64, STD, 67; Univ Notre Dame, MA, 68. **CAREER** Instr theol, Whitefriars Hall, 64-67; asst prof, Washington Theol Coalition, 68-71; asst prof relig studies, St Thomas Univ, 71-74; assoc prof, 74-82, Prof Relig Studies, St John Fisher Col, 82-; Chmn Dept, 79-; prof, St Bernards Institute, 86-; sr lectr, grad school of ed, Univ of Rochester, 89-; assoc ed, Explorations, 84-. **HONORS AND AWARDS** Trustees Awd, St John Fishe, 91; Lilly Grant, 96-97; Louisville Inst Research Grant, 98. **MEMBERSHIPS** Am Acad Relig; Col Theol Soc; Soc Sci Study Relig; Can Soc Study Relig; Forum for Death Educ and Coun. **RESEARCH** "Values, Leadership and Religion." **SELECTED PUBLICATIONS** Auth, "The Death of National Symbols: Roman Catholism in Quebec," Ethinicity, Nationality, and Religious Experience, Lanham, MD: Univ Press of America, 95; auth, "Doing It Together: Changing Pedagogies," Teaching Theology nad Religion , 99. **CONTACT ADDRESS** St. John Fisher Col, Rochester, NY 14618. **EMAIL** kollar@sjfc.edu

KOLLMANN, NANCY SHIELDS
PERSONAL Born 09/09/1950, Brockton, MA, m, 1976 **DISCIPLINE** RUSSIAN & EUROPEAN HISTORY **EDUCATION** Middlebury Col, BA, 72; Harvard Univ, MA 74, PhD(hist), 80. **CAREER** Teaching fel Russ and Europ hist, Harvard Univ, 75-80 and lectr, 80-82; Asst Prof Hist, Stanford Univ, 82-; Allston Burr sr tutor, Harvard Univ, 80-82. **MEMBERSHIPS** AHA; Am Asn Advan Slavic Studies. **RESEARCH** Musovite political history, 15th-17th centuries; muscovite social history; Polish-Lithuanian history. **SELECTED PUBLICATIONS** Auth, The bozar clan and court politics: The founding of the moscovite political system, Cahiers du monde russe et societique, 82; The seclusion of elite moscovite women, Russ Hist (in press). **CONTACT ADDRESS** Dept of Hist, Stanford Univ, Stanford, CA 94305-1926.

KOLMER, ELIZABETH
PERSONAL Born 12/11/1931, Waterloo, IL **DISCIPLINE** AMERICAN HISTORY **EDUCATION** St Louis Univ, BS, 61, MA, 62; PhD, 65. **CAREER** From lectr to asst prof, 64-73, coordr Am Studies Prog, 69-81, assoc prof, 73-80, prof hist, 80, prof Am studies, St Louis Univ, 81- **MEMBERSHIPS** Mid America Am Studies Asn. **RESEARCH** Feminist movement; The Shakers; St. Louis history; women in religion. **SELECTED PUBLICATIONS** Auth, Nineteenth century woman's rights movement: Black and white, Negro Hist Bull, 12/72; McGuffey readers: Exponents of American classical liberalism, J Gen Educ, 76; Religious women and the Women's Movement, Am Quart, 78; Nationalism in eighteenth century American schoolbooks, 79 & Domestic economy: The whole duty of woman, 81, Am Studies; The Sisters of St. Mary & The Sick Poor of St. Louis, Soc Justice Rev, 11-12/82; Religious Women in the United States Since 1950, Michael Glazier, Inc, 84; Blessed are the Peacemakers: The Shakers as Pacifists, in Locating the Shakers, Univ Exeter Press, 90; A New Heaven and a New Earth: The Progressive Shakers and Social Reform, Hungarian J English and Am Studies (forthcoming 98). **CONTACT ADDRESS** Dept of Am Studies, Saint Louis Univ, 221 N Grand Blvd, Saint Louis, MO 63103-2097. **EMAIL** kolmere@slu.edu

KOM, AMBROISE
PERSONAL Born, Cameroon, m, 3 children **DISCIPLINE** FRANCOPHONE STUDIES **EDUCATION** Universite de la Sorbonne Nouvelle, Paris III, Doctorat d'Etat es lettres, 81. **CAREER** Eleanor Howard O'Leary prof; dir, Presence Francophone, International Journal of lang and lit. **RESEARCH** Literary production and its institutions; Colonial education and creativity; Francophonie; Imperialism and African cultures. **SELECTED PUBLICATIONS** Auth, Education et democratie en Afrique, le temps des illusions, Paris: l'Harmattan, 96; Le Cas Chester Himes, Paris: Nouvelles du Sud, 94; George Lamming et le destin des Caraibes, Montreal: Didier, 86; Le Harlem de Chester Himes, Sherbrooke: Naaman, 78; et al, Dictionnaire des oeuvres litteraires de langue francaise en Afrique au Sud du sahara, vol 2, 79-89, San Francisco, Bethesda, London: Int Scholars Publ, 96; Dictionnaire des oeuvres litteraires de langue francaise en Afrique au Sud du Sahara, Vol 1, des Origines a 78, San Francisco, Bethesda, London: Int Scholars Publ, 96; Mongo Beti, 40 ans d'ecriture, 60 ans de dissidence, Presence Francophone 42, 93 & Litteratures africaines, Paris: Silex, 87; auth, La Malediction francophone, Cle/Lit Verlag, Yaounde/Hamburg, 00. **CONTACT ADDRESS** Dept of Modern Languages and Literatures, Col of the Holy Cross, 1 College St, PO Box 89A, Worcester, MA 01610-2395. **EMAIL** akom@holycross.edu

KONIG, DAVID THOMAS
PERSONAL Born 01/22/1947, Baltimore, MD, 2 children **DISCIPLINE** EARLY AMERICAN AND LEGAL HISTORY **EDUCATION** NYork Univ, AB, 68; Harvard Univ, AM, 69, PhD(hist), 73. **CAREER** From asst prof to prof hist, Washington Univ, 73-; dir, Nat Endowment for Humanities summer sem, 80; Fulbright sr lectr, Italy, 81-82. **RESEARCH** American legal development; colonial through Jacksonian America; science and witchcraft. **SELECTED PUBLICATIONS** Auth, Law and Soc in Puritan Mass, 79; auth, A Summary View of the Law of British America, William Mary Quart, Vol 0050, 93; Devising Liberty, 95. **CONTACT ADDRESS** Dept of Hist, Washington Univ, 1 Brookings Dr, Saint Louis, MO 63130-4899.

KONISHI, HARUO
PERSONAL Born 12/20/1932, Tokyo, Japan, m, 1984 **DISCIPLINE** GREEK HISTORIOGRAPHY **EDUCATION** Int Christian Univ, BA, 56; Univ Penn, MA, 60; Univ Liverpool, PhD, 66. **CAREER** Asst prof, assoc prof, prof, Univ New Brunswick, 67-98. **MEMBERSHIPS** Class Asn of Canada; Am Philol Asn. **RESEARCH** Grek epic; Greek history; Greek drama. **SELECTED PUBLICATIONS** Auth, Thucydides' Method in the Episodes of Pausanias and Themistocles, Am J of Philol, 70; auth, Thucydides History, Tokyo, 76; auth, The Composition of Thucydides' History, Am J Philol, 80; auth, Thucydides History as a Finished Piece, Liverpool Class

Monthly, 87; auth, Agamemnon's Reasons for Yielding, Am J Philol, 89; auth, The Plot of Aeschylus Oresteia: A Literary Commentary, Amsterdam, 91; auth, Did Thucydides Write a History? PEDILAVIUM, 97. **CONTACT ADDRESS** 86 Burnham Ct, Fredericton, NB, Canada E3B 5T7. **EMAIL** konishi@unb.ca

KONVITZ, JOSEF WOLF
PERSONAL Born 07/27/1946, New York, NY, m, 1969, 2 children **DISCIPLINE** EUROPEAN URBAN HISTORY **EDUCATION** Cornell Univ, BA, 67; Princeton Univ, MA, 71, PhD(hist), 73. **CAREER** Asst prof, 73-78, Assoc Prof Hist, Mich State Univ, 78-; Newberry Libr fel, 76; Nat Endowment for Humanities fel, 79-80. **MEMBERSHIPS** AHA; Soc French Hist Studies. **RESEARCH** Urban history; history of cartography; early modern Europe. **SELECTED PUBLICATIONS** Auth, Megalopolis, Introduction, J Urban Hist, Vol 0019, 93; The Widening Gate in Bristol and the Atlantic Economy, 1450-1700, J Urban Hist, Vol 0019, 93; Brides of the Sea in Port Cities of Asia From the 16th-20th Centuries, J Urban Hist, Vol 0019, 93; Atlantic Port Cities in Economy, Culture, and Society in the Atlantic World, 1650-1850, J Urban Hist, Vol 0019, 93; The Crises of Atlantic Port Cities, 1880 To 1920, Comparative Studies in Society and History, Vol 0036, 94; Urban Rivalries in the French-Revolution, J Interdisciplinary Hist, Vol 0025, 94; Small Towns in Early-Modern Europe, J Interdisciplinary Hist, Vol 0027, 97; Maps and Civilization, Cartography in Culture and Society, Technology and Culture, Vol 0038, 97; The Assassination of Paris, J Urban Hist, Vol 0023, 97; Building Paris in Architectural Institutions and the Transformation of the French Capital, 1830-1870, J Urban Hist, Vol 0023, 97. **CONTACT ADDRESS** Dept of Hist, Michigan State Univ, East Lansing, MI 48824.

KOOI, CHRISTINE
DISCIPLINE HISTORY **EDUCATION** Col St Rose, BA, 87; Yale Univ, MA, 88; MPhil, 90; PhD, 93. **CAREER** Vis asst prof, Univ Louisville, 93-94; asst prof, La State Univ, 94-. **HONORS AND AWARDS** Carl S. Meyer Prize, Sixteenth-Century Studies Confr, 93. **MEMBERSHIPS** Sixteenth-Century Studies Confr, Soc for Reformation Res. **RESEARCH** Early Modern Netherlands, Reformation. **SELECTED PUBLICATIONS** Auth, Liberty and Religion: Church and State in Leiden's Reformation, 1572-1620, Brill, 00. **CONTACT ADDRESS** Dept Hist, La State Univ at Baton Rouge, Baton Rouge, LA 70803-0104.

KOONZ, CLAUDIA
DISCIPLINE HISTORY **EDUCATION** Univ Wis Madison, BA, 62; Columbia Univ, MA, 64; Rutgers Univ, PhD, 69. **CAREER** Prof, Duke Univ. **HONORS AND AWARDS** Nat Bk Awd, 87; Berkshire Conf Bk Awd; Winship-Boston Globe Awd. **RESEARCH** Twentieth century European history; Women's history; Genocide. **SELECTED PUBLICATIONS** Co-ed, Becoming Visible: Women in European History, 87; auth, Women , the family, and Politics in Nazi Germany, St. Martin's, 87; auth, The Nazi Conscience, Harvard Univ Press, 02. **CONTACT ADDRESS** Dept of Hist, Duke Univ, Carr Bldg, Box 90719, Durham, NC 27706. **EMAIL** ckoonz@acpub.duke.edu

KOOT, GERARD M.
PERSONAL Born 11/17/1944, Netherlands, m, 1967, 2 children **DISCIPLINE** EUROPEAN HISTORY **EDUCATION** Assumption Col, Mass, BA, 67; State Univ NYork, Stony Brook, MA; 69, PhD(hist), 72. **CAREER** Chancellor prof of hist, 72-, Univ of Mass, Dartmouth; Kress fel, Harvard Univ, 72; NEH fel, 85, 95. **MEMBERSHIPS** AHA; Conf Brit Studies; Soc Hist Econ Thought. **RESEARCH** History of British economic throught and policy; neo-mercantilist British economic thought and policy; domestic impact of late 19th century British imperialism. **SELECTED PUBLICATIONS** Auth, "H.S. Foxwell and the English Historical School of Economics," Journal of Economic Issues XI (77): 561-586; auth, "The Emergence of Economic History in England," History of Political Economy 12 (80): 174-205; auth, "An Alternative to Marshall: Historical Economies at the Early London School of Economics," Atlantic Economic Journal X (82): 3-17; auth, "Sir John Seeley (1834-1895)," in Biographical Dictionary of Modern British Radicals I (London, Harvester Press, 82); auth, "H.S. Foxwell," in The New Palgrave: A Dictionary of Economic Theory and Doctrine I (Baltimore, Johns Hopkins Univ Press, 86); auth, English Historical Economics, 1870-1926: The Rise of Economic History and Neomercantilism, Cambridge Univ (Cambridge), 87; auth, "Historians and Economist: The Study of Economic History in Britain, ca 1920-1950," History of Political Economy 23.4 (93): 641-675; auth, "Historical Economics and the Revival of Mercantilist Thought in Britain, 1870-1920," in Mercantilist Economies, ed. Lars Magnusson (London, Kluwer Academic, 94), 187-219; coauth, "L.L. Price, Memories and Notes on British Economists, 1881-1947," History of Political Economy 28 (96): 633-662; auth, "William Cunningham," in The New Dictionary of National Biography (Oxford, Oxford Univ, forthcoming). **CONTACT ADDRESS** Dept of Hist, Univ of Massachusetts, Dartmouth, 285 Old Westport Rd, North Dartmouth, MA 02747-2300.

KOPF, DAVID
PERSONAL Born 03/12/1930, Paterson, NJ, m, 1955, 2 children **DISCIPLINE** MODERN SOUTH ASIAN HISTORY **EDUCATION** NYork Univ, BA, 51, MA, 56; Univ Chicago, PhD(hist), 64. **CAREER** Asst prof S Asian Hist, Univ Mo, 64-67; assoc prof, 67-76, Prof S Asian Hist, Univ Minn, Minneapolis, 73-; S Asian ed, Newsletter of Asn Asian Studies, 65-68, res coun grant, 66; Univ Minn Off Int Prog Grants, 68- and travel grant to participate Rammohun Roy Bi-Centenary Symp, Jawaharlal Nehru Arch, New Delhi, 72; sr fel, Am Inst Indian Studies, Calcutta, 69-71; Trustee, Am Inst Indian Studies, Univ PA, 71-; Ford Found vis prof fel, Inst Bangladesh Studies, Rajshahi Univ, Bangladesh, 75; Guggenheim fel, Genesis of Hinduism, Bengal, 79-80. **HONORS AND AWARDS** Watumull Prize, AHA, 69; Travel Grant, China Center, Univ of Minn, 93; McMillan grant, London, 95; Bush Sabbatical grant, 96-97. **MEMBERSHIPS** AHA Asn Asian Studies, Bengal Studies Group; Int Soc for the Comp Study of Civilizations; World Hist Asn; Asn of Genocide Scholars. **RESEARCH** Socio-religious modernism and search for modern identity in Bengal under the British focused on history of Brahmo Samaj movement and community; comparative history of Asian civilizations; translation of selected works in contemporary Bangaldeshi literature. **SELECTED PUBLICATIONS** Coauth, The Holocaust and Strategic Bombing: Genocide and Total War in the 20th Century, Westview, 95; auth, Scatches on Kali's Mind, Contemp World Fiction, 96. **CONTACT ADDRESS** Dept of Hist, Univ of Minnesota, Twin Cities, 267 19th Ave S, 614 Soc Sci Bldg, Minneapolis, MN 55455.

KOPPES, CLAYTON R.
PERSONAL Born 09/24/1945, Lincoln, NE **DISCIPLINE** HISTORY **EDUCATION** Bethel Col, Kans, AB, 67; Emory Univ, Atlanta, MA, 68; Univ Kans, PhD(hist), 74. **CAREER** Coordr curric, Independent Study Ctr, Univ Kans, 70-72; sr res fel hist, Calif Inst Technol, 74-78; Asst Prof Hist, Oberlin Col, 78-; US Steel Found fel, 68-70. **MEMBERSHIPS** Orgn Am Historians; Am Hist Asn, Forest Hist Soc; Am Asn Soc Environ Hist. **RESEARCH** American political history 20th century; international oil policy. **SELECTED PUBLICATIONS** Auth, The Kansas Trial of the IWW, 1917-1919, Labor Hist, summer 75; The Industrial Workers of the World and County-Jail Reform in Kansas, 1915-1920, Kans Hist Quart, spring 75; Captain Mahan, General Gordon and the Origins of the Term Middle East, Middle Eastern Studies, 1/76; What To Show the World: The Office of War Information and Hollywood, 1942-1945, J Am Hist, 6/77; From New Deal to Termination: Liberalism and Indian Policy, 1933-1953, Pac Hist Rev, 11/77; The Jet Propulsion Laboratory and the Beginning of American Exploration of Space, J British Interplanetary Soc, 8/81; JPL and the American Space Program, 1936-1976, Yale Univ Press, 82; The Good Neighbor Policy and the Nationalization of Mexican Oil: A Reinterpretation, J Am Hist, 82. **CONTACT ADDRESS** Dept of Hist, Oberlin Col, OH 44704.

KORNBERG, JACQUES
PERSONAL Born 08/10/1933, Antwerp, Belgium, m, 1965, 3 children **DISCIPLINE** MODERN INTELLECTUAL HISTORY **EDUCATION** Brandeis Univ, BA, 55; Harvard Univ, PhD(hist), 64. **CAREER** Instr hist, Stanford Univ, 64-67; asst prof intellectual hist mod Europe, 68-71, Assoc Prof Intellectual Hist Mod Europ, Univ Toronto, 71-; Can Coun fel, 69-70. **MEMBERSHIPS** AHA **RESEARCH** Nineteenth and 20th century European social thought; theories of Wilhelm Dilthey; modern Jewish History. **SELECTED PUBLICATIONS** Ed, At the Crossroads: Essays on Ahad Ha'Am, by Jacques Kornberg, 83; auth, Theodor Herzl: From Assimilation to Zionism (Jewish Literature and Culture), by Jacques Kornberg, 93; auth, Elusive Prophet in Haam, Ahad and The Origin of Zionism, Am Hist Rev, Vol 0100, 95; Vienna, The 1890s in Jews in the Eyes of Their Defenders The Verein-Zur-Abwehr-Des-Antisemitismus, Cent European Hist, Vol 0028, 95; On Modern Jewish Politics, J Interdisciplinary History, Vol 0026, 96. **CONTACT ADDRESS** Dept of Hist, Univ of Toronto, 100 St George St, Sidney Smith Hall Rm 2074, Toronto, ON, Canada M5S 3G3. **EMAIL** kornberg@chass.utoronto.ca

KORNBLITH, GARY J.
PERSONAL Born 11/14/1950, Chicago, IL, m, 1980, 3 children **DISCIPLINE** HISTORY **EDUCATION** Amherst Col, BA, 73; Princeton Univ, MA, 75, PhD, 83. **CAREER** Acting dir of Computing, Oberlin Col, 95-96; prof, Hist, Oberlin Col, 97; dir, Oberlin Ctr for Technologically Enhanced Teaching, 97-00. **HONORS AND AWARDS** Special Article Awrd in Business Hist, Newcomen Soc, 85; Historical Collections Prize, Essex Institute, 85; Service to Education Awd, Oberlin Ohio Education Asn, 98. **MEMBERSHIPS** AHA, OAH, SHAER, OIEAHC. **RESEARCH** Joseph T. Buckingham; Social History of Oberlin, Ohio. **SELECTED PUBLICATIONS** Auth, "The Rise of the Mechanic Interest and the Campaign to Develop Manufacturing in Salem, 1815-1830," Essex Inst Coll 121, 85; auth, "Self-Made Men: The Development of Middling- Class Consciousness in New England," Mass Rev 26, 85; auth, "Cementing the Mechanic Interest": Origins of the Providence Association of Mechanics and Manufacturers," Jour of the Early Rep 6, 88; auth, "The Artisanal Response to Capitalist Transformation," Jour of the Early Rep 10, 90; coauth, "The Making and Unmaking of an American Ruling Class, " in Beyond the American Revolution: Explorations in the History of American Radicalism, No Ill Univ Press, 93; auth, "Artisan Federalism: New England Mechanics and the Political Economy of the 1790s," in Launching the "Extended Republic": The Federalist Era, UPV, 96; auth, "Becoming Joseph T. Buckingham: The Struggle for Artisanal Independence in Early Nineteenth-Century Boston," in American Artisans: Explorations in Social Identity, Johns Hopkins Univ Press; auth, "Dynamic Syllabi for Dummies: Posting Class Assignments on the World Wide Web," J of Am Hist 84 (98): 1447-1453; ed and coauth, The Industrial Revolution in America, Houghton Mifflin Co, 98; auth, "Hiram Hill: House Carpenter, Lumber Merchant, Self-Made Man," in The Human Tradition in Antebellum America, ed. Michael A. Morrison (Scholarly Resources, 00). **CONTACT ADDRESS** Hist Dept, Oberlin Col, 10 N Professor St, Oberlin, OH 44074. **EMAIL** gary.kornblith@oberlin.edu

KORNBLUTH, GENEVRA
DISCIPLINE ART OF MEDIEVAL WESTERN EUROPE **EDUCATION** Pomona Col, AB; Univ NC, MA, PhD. **CAREER** Prof, Univ MD. **HONORS AND AWARDS** Fel, Ctr Advan Stud in the Visual Arts; visitorship, Sch Hist Stud; Inst Advan Stud, Princeton; support, Millard Meiss Publ Fund, Col Art Asn; J Paul Getty postdoc fel; Dumbarton Oaks summer fel; Adv bd, Int Ctr of Medieval Art; ed, ICMP Newsletter. **SELECTED PUBLICATIONS** Auth, Engraved Gems of the Carolingian Empire. **CONTACT ADDRESS** Dept of Art and Archeol, Univ of Maryland, Col Park, 4210 Art-Sociology Building, College Park, MD 20742-1335. **EMAIL** gkornblu@deans.umd.edu

KORR, CHARLES P.
PERSONAL Born 07/31/1939, Philadelphia, PA, m, 1963 **DISCIPLINE** HISTORY **EDUCATION** Univ Calif, Los Angeles, BA, 61, MA, 65, PhD, 69. **CAREER** Inst, Stanford Univ, 67-70; asst prof, 70-76, assoc prof, 76-86, Univ Mo, St Louis; asst to mayor, City St Louis, 77-81; vis prof, Univ WEstern Cape, S Africa, 93; chair dept hist, 92- 95, dir, ctr hum, 95-97, PROF HIST, UNIV MO, ST LOUIS, 86-. **HONORS AND AWARDS** Batts Happy Lecture, 98; Follow-up Report Historical Society, 76. **MEMBERSHIPS** North American Society for Sport History; American Historical Association, International Council for Study of History of Sports and others. **RESEARCH** Social History of Sports: Britain, Europe and US; Politics of Sports in South America; Unionism in Sports. **SELECTED PUBLICATIONS** West Hem United: The Making of a Football Club (1986) numerous articles dealing with political, social, and economic aspects of sports. **CONTACT ADDRESS** Dept of History, Univ of Missouri, St. Louis, Saint Louis, MO 63121. **EMAIL** cpkorr@umsl.edu

KORS, ALAN CHARLES
PERSONAL Born 07/18/1943, Jersey City, NJ, m, 1975, 1 child **DISCIPLINE** INTELLECTUAL AND EARLY MODERN HISTORY **EDUCATION** Princeton Univ, BA, 64; Harvard Univ, MA, 65, PhD(hist), 68 **CAREER** Asst Prof, 68-74, Assoc Prof Hist, Univ PA, 74-; Am Coun Learned Soc res fel hist, 75-76; bk rev ed, Am Soc 18th Century Studies, 76-78; adv ed, 18th Century Life, Eastern Soc Am Soc 18th Century Studies. **HONORS AND AWARDS** Lindback Found Awd, 75. **MEMBERSHIPS** Am Soc 18th Century Studies; AHA; Eastern Soc Am Soc 18th Century Studies. **RESEARCH** French enlightenment; origins and development of materialism in early modern France; philosophy and revolution. **SELECTED PUBLICATIONS** Co-ed, Witchcraft in Europe 1100-1700, Univ Pa, 72; auth, D'Holbach's Coterie: An Enlightenment in Paris, Princeton Univ, 76; contribr, The Marquis de Chastellux, In: Abroad in America: Visitors to the New Nation, 1776-1914, Addison-Wesley, 76; auth, The myth of the coterie Holbachique, Fr Hist Studies 3/76; Bernard Plongeron's Theologie et Politique .., 3/76 & Keith Baker's Condorcet, 12/76, J Modern Hist. **CONTACT ADDRESS** Dept of Hist, Univ of Pennsylvania, 3401 Walnut St, Philadelphia, PA 19104-6228.

KORTEPETER, C. MAX
PERSONAL Born 05/27/1928, Indianapolis, IN, m, 1957, 6 children **DISCIPLINE** MIDDLE EAST HISTORY & POLITICS **EDUCATION** Harvard Univ, BA, 50, McGill Univ, MA, 54; Univ London, PhD(hist), 62; Rytgers Univ, M.Sc., 89. **CAREER** Instr sci, Robert Col, Istanbul, 50-53; Prof, Russ hist, U.S. Army, 54-56;lectr Islamic studies, Univ Toronto, 61-64, from asst prof to assoc prof, 64-67; Sr fel, Am Res Inst, Turkey, 66-67, bd mem & secy, 69-71; vis prof, Princeton Univ, 71-72; dir, Princeton Mid E Syst, 76-; Am Res Ctr Egypt sr fel, 78; Assoc prof hist & near eastern lang, NY Univ, 67-96. **MEMBERSHIPS** Turkish Studies Asn; J of Middle East Politics; Am Vets of For Wars; Middle East Studies Asn. **RESEARCH** Turko-Slavic hist; hist of the Ottoman Emp; gen Islamic hist. **SELECTED PUBLICATIONS** Auth, Ottoman Imperialism during the Reformation: Europe and the Caucasus, 72, NY Univ; auth, The origins and Nature of Turkish power, Fakueltesi Tarih Arastirmalari Dergisi, Ankara Univ, 72, The Ottoman Turks: Nomad Kingdom to World Empire, 91; Co-auth, The Human Experience, Columbus, 85; Co-ed, The Transformation of Turkish Culture: The Ataturk Legacy, Princeton, 86; ed, Literature and Society: The Modern Middle East, 73; ed, Oil and Economic Geography, 93; auth, "The Cowboy Mythos and Its

Origins in the Middle East," Inst Univ Sci (Naples, Italy), 01; auth, "Did the Ottomans Obtain Enlightenment Through Military Reform?" Balkan Studies, 01; auth, "The Ambassadorship of General Lew Wallace to Ott. Turkey," Festschrift for Talat Halman (Istanbul, 01). **CONTACT ADDRESS** PO Box 39, New Russia, NY 12964. **EMAIL** cmaxkortepeter@post.harvard.edu

KORTH, PHILIP ALAN
PERSONAL Born 08/06/1936, Fairmont, MN, m, 1963, 3 children **DISCIPLINE** AMERICAN STUDIES **EDUCATION** Univ Minn, BA, 61, MA, 65, PhD(Am studies), 67. **CAREER** Asst prof, 67-70, assoc prof, 70-77, Prof Am Thought and Lang, Mich State Univ, 77-; Proj dir, Rockefeller Found res grant, 72-75. **MEMBERSHIPS** Am Studies Asn; Orgn Am Historians; Nat Educ Asn. **RESEARCH** American cultural history; American labor history; American literature 1865-1940. **SELECTED PUBLICATIONS** Auth, The American yeoman vs progress, NDak Hist, 70; The ideological heritage of student radicals, Univ Col Quart, 70; Politics in American studies, Am Examr, 73; The autolite strike, Labor Hist, 75; Hemingway's Deception, Eberly Mich J. **CONTACT ADDRESS** Dept of Am Thought and Lang, Michigan State Univ, East Lansing, MI 48823.

KOSCHMANN, JULIEN VICTOR
PERSONAL Born 12/30/1942, Fairbanks, AK, m, 1964, 3 children **DISCIPLINE** JAPANESE HISTORY **EDUCATION** Int Christian Univ, Tokyo, BA, 65; Sophia Univ, Tokyo, MA, 71; Univ Chicago, PhD Hist, 80. **CAREER** Transl & assoc ed, Japan Interpreter, 71-76; lectr Social Sci, Univ Chicago, 78-80; asst prof Japanese Hist, Cornell Univ, 80-, instr Asian Studies, Sophia Univ, Tokyo, 75-76. **MEMBERSHIPS** Asn Asian Studies. **RESEARCH** Thought and action in the domain of Mito, late Tokugawa period; post-World War II Japanese intellectual and social history; 20th century intellectual history. **SELECTED PUBLICATIONS** Ed, Authority and the Individual in Japan: Citizen Protest in Historical Perspective, Univ Tokyo Press, Tokyo, 78; auth, The debate on subjectivity in postwar Japan: Foundations of modernism as a political critique, Pac Affairs, Winter 81; co-ed (with Tetsuo Najita), Conflict in Modern Japanese History: The Neglected Tradition, Princeton Univ Press, 82; Revolution and Subjectivity in Postwar Japan, Univ of Chicago Press, 96. **CONTACT ADDRESS** Dept of History, Cornell Univ, Mcgraw Hall, Ithaca, NY 14853-0001. **EMAIL** jvk1@cornell.edu

KOSHKIN-YOURITZIN, VICTOR
PERSONAL Born 12/20/1942, New York, NY **DISCIPLINE** ART HISTORY **EDUCATION** Williams Col, BA (Cum Laude), 64; N Y Univ, MA, 67. **CAREER** Instr, Vanderbilt Univ, Nashville Tn, 68-69; instr, Tulane Univ, 69-72; asst prof to assoc prof to prof, Univ Ok, 72- . **HONORS AND AWARDS** Univ of Al Alumni Assoc Baldwin Awd for Excellence , Undergraduate teaching, 87; Univ Ok Stud Assoc Awd, outstanding faculty member, 89, 94; Governor's Arts and Education Awd, 92; Honorable citation, Ok St House of Rep, 93; David Ross Boyd Distinguished Prof in Art Hist, Univ Ok, 97; NEH panel, 84 panelist, MMA/Getty, Prog Art on Film, 87; neh panel, 84; panelist, prog on film. **MEMBERSHIPS** Trustee; Mabee-Gerrer Museum of Art; Koussevitzky Recordings Soc, Inc. **SELECTED PUBLICATIONS** Auth, The Irony of Pegas, Gazette des Beaux-Arts, 76; auth, Oklahoma Treasures: Paintings, Drawings, and Watercolors from Public and Private Collections, The Ok Art Center, 86; Koussevitzky: Missing in Action, Los Angeles Times, 88; coauth, American Watercolors from The Metropolitan Museum of Art, Abrams in Assoc with Amer Federation of Arts, 91; Twentieth-Century Russian Drawings from a Private Collection, Ar Arts Center, 97, auth, Paintings by Glenda Green: A Focus on the Oklahoma Years, Mabee-Gerrer Museum of Art, 1998. **CONTACT ADDRESS** 1721 Oakwood Dr, Norman, OK 73069. **EMAIL** vky@ou.edu

KOSLOFSKY, CRAIG
DISCIPLINE HISTORY **EDUCATION** The Univ of Warwick, Coventry, England, Study Abroad, 84; Duke Univ, Durham, North Carolina, AB, 85; Eberhard-Karls-Universitat Tubingen, Germany, Graduate Exchange Fel, 89; Freie Universitat Berlin, German Acad Exchange, 92; The Univ of Mich, Ann Arbor, PhD, 94, MA, 90. **CAREER** Asst prof, Millersville Univ of Penn, res fel, Max-Planck-Institut fur Geschichte, Gottingen, Germany, 94-95; asst prof, Univ of Ill, Urbana-Champaign, 97-. **HONORS AND AWARDS** Charlotte W. Newcombe Doctoral Dissertation fel, awarded by the Woodrow Wilson Nat fel found, 93-94; Max-Planck-Institut fur Geschichte, Gottingen, Germany, 96; Millersville Univ of Penn, Fac Grants Com, 96; Univ of Ill, Campus res Board, awarded funds for one graduate res asst, 97-98; Univ of Ill, office of instructional resources, rated "outstanding" on the university-wide "Incomplete list of teachers ranked as excellent by their students" academic year 97-98; Univ of Ill, Campus res Board, awarded one semester of leave from teaching and one graduate res assistantship, 98-99; Univ of Ill, International Prog and Studies, awarded a William and Flora Hewlett International res grant, 00; Univ of Ill, Ill Prog for res in the Humanities, awarded a fac fel for the 00-01, program on cities; Center 17th & 18th Century Studies, Univ of Calif, Los Angeles, vis scholar, 00-01; Natt Endow for the hum, 00-01. **MEMBERSHIPS** Am hist assoc; Am soc for eighteenth century studies; Sixteenth century studies conf; Soc for reformation res; Fruhe Neuzeit Interdisziplinar; Ill medieval assoc. **RESEARCH** Ritual and religion in early modern Germany; the night as experiences in early modern Europe; cultural transformation between the late Middle Ages and the Reformation; the history of daily life; the body in early modern Europe; the history of Christianity. **SELECTED PUBLICATIONS** Auth, "Separating the Living from the Dead: Wessel Gansfort and the Death of Purgatory," Essays in Medieval Studies 10, (1994): 129-143; auth, "Die Trennung der Lebenden von den Toten: Friedhofverlgungen und die Reformation in Leipzig 1536," In Memoria als Kultur, edited by Otto Gerhard Oexle, Veroffentlichungen des Max-Planck-Instituts fur Geschichte 121, Gottingen: Vandenhoeck & Ruprecht, (95): 335-386; auth, "Honour and Violence in German Lutheran Funerals in the Confessional Age," Social History 20, 3, (95): 315-337; auth, "Von der Schande zur Ehre: Nachtliche Begrabnisse im lutherischen Deutschland, 1650-1700," from Disgrace to Distinction: Nocturnal Burial in Lutheran Germany, 1650-1700, Historische Anthropologie 5, 3, (97): 350-369; auth, "Pest' - 'Gift' - Ketzerei': Konkurrierende Konzepte von Gemeinschaft und die Verlegung der Friedhofe (Leipzig 1536)," In Kulturelle Reformation: Sinnformationen in Umbruch 1400-1600, ed by Bernhard Jussen and Craig Koslofsky, Veroffentlichungen des Max-Planck-Instituts fur Geschichte 145, Gottingen: Vandenhoeck & Ruprecht, (98): 131-149; auth, "Sakularisierung und der Umgang mit der Leiche des Selbstmorders im fruhmodernen Leipzig," In Im Zeichen der Krise, Religiositat im Europa des 17, Jahrhunderts, edited by Hartmut Lehmann and Anne-Charlott Trepp, Veroffentlichungen des Max-Planck-Instituts fur Geschichte 152, Gottingen: Vandenhoeck & Ruprecht, 99; auth, "Kulturelle Reformation: Sinnformationen im Umbruch 1400-1600,' edited with an introduction by Bernhard Jussen and Craig Koslofsky, Veroffentlichungen des Max-Planck-Instituts fur Geschichte 145, Gottingen: Vandenhoeck & Ruprecht, 99; auth, "The Reformation of the Dead: Death and Ritual in Early Modern Germany, 1450-1700," Early Modern History: Society and Culture, London and New York; Macmillan Press/St. Martin's Press; auth, "The Establishment of Street Lighting in Eighteenth Century Leipzig: From Court Society to the Public Sphere?" In 'Jedem das Seine.' Grenzziehungen und Grenzuberschreitungen im fruhneuzeitlichen Leipzig, edited by Barbara Hoffmann and Heide Wunder, Manuscript completed, forthcoming, 00. **CONTACT ADDRESS** History Dept, Univ of Illinois, Urbana-Champaign, 810 South Wright St., Urbana, IL 61801. **EMAIL** koslof@staff.uiuc.edu

KOSTELANETZ, RICHARD
PERSONAL Born 05/14/1940, New York, NY **DISCIPLINE** AMERICAN CULTURE **EDUCATION** Brown Univ, AB, 62; Columbia Univ, MA, 66. **CAREER** Co-founder and president, Assembling Press, 70-82; Contrib Ed, NY Arts J, 80-; prog assoc thematic studies, John Jay Col Criminal Justice, 72-73; sr staff, Univ Indiana Writers Conf, 76; vis prof, Am Studies and English, Univ Tex, Austin, 77; co-ed, Precisely: A Critical Jour, 76-; Sole proprietor, Archaeol Editions, 78-. **HONORS AND AWARDS** Res and Writing, 62-; Guggenheim fel, 67-68; Pulitzer Fel, 65; Guggenheim Fel, 67; Best Books of 1976 by the American Inst of Graphic Arts, Nat Endowment for Arts grant, 76; Ludwig Vogelstein Foundation, 80; CCLM Editors Fel, 81; NEA Visual arts senior fel, 85; Fel, New Assoc of Sephardi/Mizrahi Artists and Writers Int, 00-02. **RESEARCH** Experimental literature, particularly in North America; arts and artists in America; criticism of avant- garde arts, particularly literature. **SELECTED PUBLICATIONS** Auth, Avant Garde American Radio Art, North Am Rev, Vol 0278, 93; Flood in a Novel in Pictures, Am Book Rev, Vol 0014, 93; The Roaring Silence in Cage, John, A Life, Notes, Vol 0049, 93; Caxon, Caxton, a Predating, A Definition, and a Supposed Derivation, Notes and Queries, Vol 0040, 93; Not Wanting to Say Anything About Cage, John 1912-92, Chicago Rev, Vol 0038, 93; Grrrhhhh, Amn Book Rev, Vol 0014, 93; The Phenomenology of Revelation, Am Book Rev, Vol 0014, 93; Minimal Audio Plays, Western Hum Rev, Vol 0048, 94; It Too Shall Pass, Modern Languages Association Rev, Am Book Rev, Vol 0016, 94; Hysterical Pregnancy , North Am Rev, Vol 0279, 94; The Boulez-Cage Correspondence, Am Book Rev, Vol 0016, 95; Literary Video, Visible Language, Vol 0029, 95; Postmodern American Poetry in a Norton Anthology, Am Book Rev, Vol 0016, 95; Preface to Solos, Duets, Trios, and Choruses Membrane Future, Midwest Quart-A J Contemporary Thought, Vol 0037, 95; A Poetry-Film Storyboard in Transformations, Visible Lang, Vol 0030, 96; Anarchist Voices in an Oral-History of Anarchism in America, Am Book Rev, Vol 0017, 96; Interview With Schwartz, Tony, American Horspielmacher, Perspectives New Mus, Vol 0034, 96; Conservative Subversion, Am Book Rev, Vol 0017, 96; Format And Anxiety, Am Book Rev, Vol 0017, 96; The Year of the Hot Jock and Other Stories, Am Book Rev, Vol 0019, 97; A Star in the Family, Am Book Rev, Vol 0019, 97; Newsreel, Am Book Rev, Vol 0019, 97; Jim Dandy, Am Book Rev, Vol 0019, 97; The File on Stanley Patton Buchta, Am Book Rev, Vol 0019, 97; Roar Lion Roar and Other Stories, Am Book Rev, Vol 0019, 97; The Steagle, Am Book Rev, Vol 0019, 97; The Winner of the Slow Bicycle Race, Am Book Rev, Vol 0018, 97; Willy Remembers, Am Book Rev, Vol 0019, 97; Foreign Devils, Am Book Rev, Vol 0019, 97; auth, Political Essays, Autonomedia, 99; auth, Thirty Years of Visible Writing, BGB, 00; auth, More On Innovative Music(ian)s, Fallen Leaf-Scarecrow, 01. **CONTACT ADDRESS** Prince St, PO Box 444, New York, NY 10013. **EMAIL** rkostelanetz@bigfoot.com

KOSTO, ADAM
DISCIPLINE MEDIEVAL HISTORY **EDUCATION** Yale Univ, BA, 89; Harvard Univ PhD, 96. **CAREER** Asst prof. **SELECTED PUBLICATIONS** Rev, Pierre Bonnassie, From Slavery to Feudalism in South-Western Europe, Cambridge, 91; Parergon 26, 96; Paul Freedman, The Origins of Peasant Servitude in Medieval Catalonia, Cambridge, 92, Paragon 26, 96. **CONTACT ADDRESS** Dept of Hist, Columbia Col, New York, 2960 Broadway, New York, NY 10027-6902.

KOSZTOLNYIK, ZOLTAN JOSEPH DESIDERIUS
PERSONAL Born 12/15/1930, Heves, Hungary, m, 1966, 2 children **DISCIPLINE** MEDIEVAL HISTORY **EDUCATION** St Bonaventure Univ, BA, 59; Fordham Univ, MA, 61; NYork Univ, PhD, 68. **CAREER** From instr to asst prof, 67-72, assoc prof, 72-81, Prof Hisy, Tex A&M Univ, 81-; Guest Prof, Dept of Medieval History/Janus Pannonius Univ, Pecs, Hungary, 99 . **HONORS AND AWARDS** Univ Fund Organized Res grants, Tex A&M Univ, 70 & 72; Phi Kappa Phi, 79; Distinguished Teaching Awd, TAMU/Col Lib Arts, 95. **MEMBERSHIPS** Mediaeval Acad Am; AHA; Am Cath Hist Asn. **RESEARCH** Church and state in Hungary in the reign of the Arpads, 9th century to 1301; intellectual eleventh century Hungary, Gerard of Csanad; intellectual twelfth century Germany, Gerhoch of Reichersberg. **SELECTED PUBLICATIONS** Auth, Five eleventh century Hungarian kings: their policies and their relations with Rome (EEM-Columbia UP, 81; auth, from Coloman the Learned to Bela III, 1095-1196: Hungarian domestic policy and its impact uponfoteign affairs (EEM-Columbia UP, 87); auth, "In the European mainstream: Hungarian churchmen and 13th century synods," Catholic Historical Revie, 70 (93): 413ff; auth, Eventuelle spanische (Leon-aragonosche) und westliche Wirkingen in der Zusammenstellung der Landtage wahrend Regierugszeit Andreas' III, Aetas, 94; Early Hungarian towns and town life in the record of western chronicles, Specimina nova Universitatis de Iano Pannonio nominate, 95; Hungary in the Thirteenth Century, EEM-Columbia Univ Press, 96; auth, "The question of belonging: religious politics over Pannonia at the time of Magyars' arrival in the 890's," Citkthara: Essays in Judaeo-Christian Tradition, 37-II, (98): 22ff; auth, "German political developments in the background of tenth-early eleventh centur Hungarina history," Acta historica Szegediensis, 109 (99): 413ff; auth, "Similarities between King St. Stephen of Hungary's Law Code and the Laws of Jaroslav the Wise of Kiev," in Hungary's historical legacies, ed D.P. Hupchick et al (EEM-Columbia UP, 00), 45-54. **CONTACT ADDRESS** Dept of Hist, Texas A&M Univ, Col Station, College Station, TX 77843-4236. **EMAIL** z-kosztolnyik@tamu.edu

KOUMOULIDES, JOHN A.
PERSONAL Born 08/23/1938, Athens, Greece **DISCIPLINE** MODERN HISTORY, ANCIENT EUROPEAN HISTORY **EDUCATION** Montclair State Col, BA, 60, MA, 61; Univ Md, PhD, 67. **CAREER** Asst prof ancient hist & 19th century Europ, 63-65, 67-68, Austin Peay State Univ; res studies hist, Cambridge Univ, 65-67; from asst prof to assoc prof ancient hist, 68-75, prof hist 75-, adm of Greek Studies prof, Ball State Univ; **HONORS AND AWARDS** Res grants, 69-71, 74 & 79; Am Coun Learned Soc travel grants, 69, 71 & 74; vis fel, Fitzwilliam Col, Cambridge Univ, 71-72; Am Philosophical Soc res grants, 73 & 81; Fulbright-Hays sr res scholar, Greece, 77-78, 87-88; vis tutor, Campion Hall, Oxford, England, 80-81; guest Scholar, Woodrow Wilson Int Cen for Scholars, 82; Fulbright-Hays Sr Res Scholar, Greece, 87-88; vis fel, Wolfson Coll, Oxford, 83-84; dis vis fel, Fitzwilliam Col, Cambridge, 89-90; Archon Chartophylax of the Ecumenical Patriarchate, Ecumenical Patriarch Dimitrios I, 79; Golden Cross of the Mitropolis of Dimitriados, 91; Honorary Mem, The Soc for the Promotion of Hellenic Studies, UK, 93; Corresponding Mem, The Academy of Athens, 93; Commander of the Order of Phoenix, Greece, 97; Paul Harris Fel of The Rotary Found of Rotary Int, 97 **MEMBERSHIPS** AHA; Hist Assn, Eng; Soc Promotion Hellenic Studies; Archaeol Inst Am; Mod Greek Studies Asn; AAUP. **RESEARCH** Ancient history; Neo-Hellenic history; 19th century European history. **SELECTED PUBLICATIONS** Auth, Hellenic Perspectives: Essays in the History of Greece, Univ Press Am, 80; auth, The Monastery of Tatarna: History and Treasures, 91; auth, The Good Idea: Democracy in Ancient Greece, 95; auth, Greece: The Legacy, 98; auth, Cyprus: The Legacy--Historic Landmarks that Influenced the Arts of Cyrus Late Bronze Age to A.D. 1600, 99 **CONTACT ADDRESS** Dept of Hist, Ball State Univ, 2000 W University, Muncie, IN 47306-0002.

KOUSSER, JOSEPH MORGAN
PERSONAL Born 10/07/1943, Lewisburg, TN, m, 1968, 2 children **DISCIPLINE** HISTORY **EDUCATION** Princeton Univ, AB, 65; Yale Univ, MPhil, 68, PhD(hist), 71. **CAREER** From instr to prof hist & soc, Calif Inst Technol, 69-; consult, 76; vis instr, Univ Mich, 80; vis prof, Harvard Univ, 81-82; Harold Vyvyan Harmsworth Prof, Oxford Univ, 84-85; vis prof, Claremont Grad Univ, 93. **HONORS AND AWARDS** Nat Endowment for Humanities res grant, 74-75, 81-83; Graves Found

fel, 76; Guggenheim fel, 85-86; Woodrow Wilson Center fel, 85-86; Lillian Smith Awd, Southern Regional Council, 99. **MEMBERSHIPS** Orgn Am Historians; Soc Sci Hist Asn; Southern Hist Assoc. **RESEARCH** Quantitative history; Southern United States history; American political history. **SELECTED PUBLICATIONS** Auth, Ecological Regression and the Analysis of Past Politics, J Interdisciplinary Hist, autumn 73; The Shaping of Southern Politics, Yale Univ, 74; The New Political History: A Methodological Critique, Rev Am Hist, 3/76; Separate But Not Equal: The First Supreme Court Case on Racial Discrimination in Education, 80 & Progressivism for Middle-Class Whites Only: The Distribution of Taxation and Expenditures for Education in North Carolina, 1800-1910, 80, J Southern Hist; Quantitative Social Scientific History, In: The Past Before Us: Contemporary Historical Writing in the US, Cornell Univ Press, 80; Making Separate Equal: The Integration of Black and White School Funds in Kentucky, J Interdisciplinary Hist, 79; coauth (with Gary W Cox), Turnout and Rural Corruption: New York as a Test Case, Am J Polit Sci, 81; Estimating the Partisan Consequences of Redistricting Plans - Simply, Legislative Studies Q, 96; Ironies of California Redistricting, 1971-2001, In: Governing the Golden State: Politics, Government, and Public Policy in California, U of CA Press, 97; Reapportionment Wars: Party, Race, and Redistricting in California, 1971-92, Agathon Press, 98; Colorblind Injustice: Minority Voting Rights and the Undoing of the Second Reconstruction, U North Carolina, 99. **CONTACT ADDRESS** Div of Humanities & Social Sciences 228-77, California Inst of Tech, 1201 E California, Pasadena, CA 91125-7700. **EMAIL** kousser@hss.caltech.edu

KOVALEFF, THEODORE PHILIP
PERSONAL Born 02/08/1943, New York, NY, m, 1977, 2 children **DISCIPLINE** MODERN AMERICAN AND LEGAL AND ECONOMIC HISTORY **EDUCATION** Columbia Univ, BA, 64, MA, 66; NYork Univ, PhD, 72. **CAREER** From instr to asst prof hist, St John's Univ, NY, 69-75; lectr hist, 75-77, Barnard Col; dir admis, sch law, 77-80, asst dean, Sch Law, Columbia Univ, 77-92, hist adv, Westinghouse Broadcasting Co, 72-80; moderator & producer, Nighttalk, WOR radio, New York City; adv bd, The Antitrust Bull, 88-; ed bd, Presidential Stud Q, 91-; anal, small banks/thrifts, national securities, 96-. **HONORS AND AWARDS** NY Univ Founder's Day Awd, 73; Borough Pres Certificate of Service, 77; Borough Pres Citation for Service to the Commun, 83; City of NY Certification of Appreciation, 87; Ted Kovaleff Day proclaimed by Borough Pres Ruth Messinger, Jan 18, 1996, in recognition of service to Manhattan. **MEMBERSHIPS** AHA; Orgn Am Historians; AAUP; Bus Hist Conf. **RESEARCH** Diplomatic history; antitrust. **SELECTED PUBLICATIONS** Coauth, Poland and the Coming of World War II, Ohio, 77; auth, Business and Government During the Eisenhower Administration, Ohio, 80; auth, The Antitrust Impulse, Sharpe, 94; ed, J of Reprints for Antitrust Law and Econ, 94; ed, The Antitrust Bull, 94; auth, Interview with Anne Bingaman, The Antitrust Bull, 94. **CONTACT ADDRESS** 454 Riverside Dr, New York, NY 10027. **EMAIL** kovaleff@dirksco.com

KOVALIO, JACOB
DISCIPLINE MODERN JAPANESE DIPLOMATIC AND POLITICAL HISTORY **EDUCATION** Tel-Aviv Univ, BA, 69, Univ Pittsburgh, MA, 72, PhD, 81. **CAREER** Assoc prof, Carleton Univ. **RESEARCH** Asia-Pacific politics, international relations, and nationalism. **SELECTED PUBLICATIONS** Ed, "Gendai Nihonron," Modern Japanese Studies, ch. 7, in Hiroaki Kato ed., Nyumon gendai chiiki kenkyu, An Introduction to Area Stud, (Kyoto, Showado, 92): 163-190; ed, Japan in Focus, (Ottawa/Toronto: APRRC/Captus Univ Press, 94): 320; ed, "A.J. Toynbee and Japan," in Jacab Kovalio ed., Japan in Focus, (APRRC/Captus, 94): 294-306; auth, "Old and new clash in recent Japanese politics," APRRC Newsletter, vol. 5, No. 2, (94): 1-3; auth, "Japanese antisemitism in the 1990s," Antisemitism Worldwide 1994, Tel Aviv Univ Press, (95): 35-55; ed, "Japan - a security profile," in W.A. Herrmann ed., Security Challenges in Asia, Bandung, 96; ed, "Japan - a security profile," in Wilfried Hermann ed., Asia's Security Challenges, Nova Science Publishers, Commack (98): 227-239; ed, "A Glimpse at antisemitism in Japan and Asia Pacific," in R. Stauber, D. Porat, eds., Antisemitism Worldwide, Tel-Aviv: Tel Aviv Univ Press, (98): 281-290. **CONTACT ADDRESS** Dept of Hist, Carleton Univ, 1125 Colonel By Dr, Ottawa, ON, Canada K1S 5B6. **EMAIL** jacob_kovalio@carleton.ca

KOWALESKI, MARYANNE
PERSONAL Born 07/08/1952, Chicago, IL **DISCIPLINE** HISTORY **EDUCATION** Univ of Mich, AB, 74; Pontifical Inst of Medieval Studies, MSL, 78; Univ of Toronto, MA, 76; PhD, 82. **CAREER** Asst prof to prof, Fordham Univ, 82-. **HONORS AND AWARDS** Fulbright Scholar, 78, 79, NEH Grant, 86, 87-88, 89; ACSL Grant, 83, 87; Am Philos Soc Grant, 83, 95; Grants, Fordham Univ; Undergrad Teacher of the year, 95; Hon Res Fel, Univ of London, 96; Fel, Shelby Cullon Davis Center, Princeton, 98; SSHRC. **MEMBERSHIPS** Royal Hist Soc; **RESEARCH** Women's History, Medieval England, Medieval towns and trade, Medieval women and family. **SELECTED PUBLICATIONS** Coed, Women and Power in the Middle Ages, Univ of Ga Pr, (Athens), 88; ed, transl, The Local Customs According to the Port of Exeter, 1266-1321; Devon and Cornwall Record Soc 36, 93; auth, Local Markets and Regional Trade in Medieval Exeter, Cambridge Univ Pr, 95; Auth, "The Grain Trade in Fourteenth-Century Exeter", The Salt of Common Life: Essays in Honor of J Ambrose Raftis, ed Edwin DeWindt, Medieval Inst Pr, (Kalamazoo, 96): 1-52; auth, "Assize of Weights and Measures", Medieval France: An Encyclopedia, ed WW Kibler et al, Garland Pub, 95; auth, "Singlewomen in Medieval and Early Modern Europe: The Demographic Perspective", Singlewomen in the European Past, eds JM Bennett and A Froide, Univ of Pa Pr, (Philadelphia, 99): 38-81, 325-44; auth, "Port Towns in Medieval England and Wales", The Urban History of England, ed David Palliser, Cambridge Univ Pr, (forthcoming); auth, "The Duchy of Cornwall Havener's Accounts, 1337-1356", Devon and Cornwall Record Soc, (forthcoming); auth, "The Consumer Economy", A Social History of England 1200-1600, ed Rosemary Horrox and Mark Romrod, Cambridge Univ Pr, (forthcoming). **CONTACT ADDRESS** Dept Hist, Fordham Univ, 441 E Fordham Rd, Bronx, NY 10034. **EMAIL** kowaleski@fordhaml.edu

KRAEHE, ENNO EDWARD
PERSONAL Born 12/09/1921 **DISCIPLINE** HISTORY **EDUCATION** Univ Mo, AB, 43, AM, 44; Univ Minn, PhD, 48. **CAREER** From asst prof to prof hist, Univ Ky, 48-64; prof hist, Univ NC- 64-68; prof, 68-71, Commonwealth prof, 71-77, William W Cororan Prof Hist, Univ VA, 77-; Fulbright res scholar, Austria, 52-53; specialist, US Dept State, Ger, 53; vis assoc prof, Univ Tex, 55-56; Guggenheim fel, 60-61; Am Coun Learned Soc fel, 69; screening comt, Sr Fulbright-Hays Prog, 70-73; Nat Endowment for Humanities res grant, 73-74; chmn Europ sect, Soc Hist Asn, 75; Nat Endowment for Humanities fel, 80. **MEMBERSHIPS** AHA; Southern Hist Asn; Conf Group Cent Europ Hist. **RESEARCH** Modern European history; Central Europe; diplomatic history. **SELECTED PUBLICATIONS** Auth, Metternich's German Policy, Princeton Univ, 63; Ideologie et raison d'etat dans la politique allemande de Metternich 1812-1820, Rev Hist Mod et Contemporaine, 1-12/66; ed, The Metternich Controversy, Holt, 71. **CONTACT ADDRESS** Dept of Hist, Univ of Virginia, 216 Randall Hall, Charlottesville, VA 22903.

KRAFT, JAMES P.
DISCIPLINE AMERICAN HISTORY, LABOR-BUSINESS **EDUCATION** Univ S Calif, PhD, 90. **CAREER** ASSOC PROF, UNIV HAWAII, MANOA, PRESENTLY. **CONTACT ADDRESS** History Dept, Univ of Hawaii, Manoa, 2530 Dole St, Honolulu, HI 96822.

KRAFT, ROBERT ALAN
PERSONAL Born 03/18/1934, Waterbury, CT, m, 1955, 4 children **DISCIPLINE** HISTORY OF WESTERN RELIGION **EDUCATION** Wheaton Col, IL, BA, 55, MA, 57; Harvard Univ, PhD, 61. **CAREER** Asst lectr New Testament studies, Univ Manchester, 61-63; from asst prof to assoc prof relig thought, 63-76, acting chmn dept, 72-73, 92, Prof Relig Studies, Univ PA, 76-, Chmn Grad Studies, 73-84, 96-, Chmn Dept, 77-84; Vis lectr, Lutheran Theol Sem, Philadelphia, 65-66; ed, Monogr ser, Soc Bibl Lit, 67-72 & Pseudepigrapha ser, 73-78; task force on scholarly publ, Coun Studies Relig, 71-72. **HONORS AND AWARDS** Fels, Guggenheim, 69-70 & Am Coun Learned Soc, 75-76. **MEMBERSHIPS** Soc Bibl Lit; Int Orgn Septuagint & Cognate Studies; NAm Patristic Soc; Studiorum Nov Testamenti Societas; Am Soc Papyrologists. **RESEARCH** Judaism in the Hellenistic era, especially Greek-speaking Judaism; Christianity to the time of Constantine, espec the second century; computers and Ancient lit. **SELECTED PUBLICATIONS** Auth, Was There a Messiah-Joshua Tradition at the Turn of the Era?, RKMESSIA ARTICLE on the IOUDAIOS Electronic Discussion Group, 6/10/92; Philo's Text of Genesis 2.18 (I will make a helper), on the IOUDAIOS Electronic Discussion Group, 6/10/93; The Pseudepigrapha in Christianity, In: Tracing the Threads: Studies in the Vitality of Jewish Pseudepigrapha, SBL Early Judaism and Its Literature 6, Scholars, 94; coauth, Jerome's Translation of Origen's Homily on Jeremiah 2.21-22 (Greek Homily 2; Latin 13), Revue Be/ne/dictine 104, 94; auth, The Use of Computers in New Testament Textual Criticism, In: The Text of the NT in Contemporary Research, Studies and Documents 46, 95; Scripture and Canon in Jewish Apocrypha and Pseudepigrapha, In: Hebrew Bible/Old Testament: The History of its Interpretation, I: From Beginnings to the Middle Ages (Until 1300), 1: Antiquity, Vandenhoeck & Ruprecht, 96; author of numerous other articles. **CONTACT ADDRESS** Relig Studies, Univ of Pennsylvania, Logan Hall, Philadelphia, PA 19104-6304. **EMAIL** kraft@ccat.sas.upenn.edu

KRAHMALKOV, CHARLES R.
PERSONAL Born 06/06/1936, New York, NY, m, 1968, 2 children **DISCIPLINE** ANCIENT NEAR EAST HISTORY **EDUCATION** Univ Calif, Berkeley, AB, 57; Harvard Univ, PhD, 65. **CAREER** Asst prof Near E lang and lit, Univ Mich, 65-66; asst prof, Univ Calif, Los Angeles, 67-68; asst prof, 68-71, assoc prof, 71-79, Prof Near East Lang and Lit, Univ Mich, Ann Arbor, 80-. **RESEARCH** Early Northwest Semitic philology; Egyptology; Biblical exegesis. **SELECTED PUBLICATIONS** Auth, "'When He Drove Out Yrirachan': A Phoenician (Punic) Poem, ca. A.D. 350," Bulletin of American Schools of Oriental Research 294 (94): 69-82; auth, "Egyptian Roads and the Biblical Conquest," Biblical Archaeology Review (94): 54-79; auth, "phoenician Language" in Encyclopedia of the World's Major Languages, New England Publishing Associates, forthcoming; auth, "Phoenicia" in Eerdmans Dictionary of the Bible, forthcoming. **CONTACT ADDRESS** Dept of Near East Studies, Univ of Michigan, Ann Arbor, 2068 Frieze Bldg, Ann Arbor, MI 48109-1285. **EMAIL** crkrah@umich.edu

KRAMER, ARNOLD PAUL
PERSONAL Born 08/15/1941, Chicago, IL, m, 2 children **DISCIPLINE** MODERN EUROPE, GERMAN HISTORY **EDUCATION** Univ Wis-Madison, BS, 63, MS & cert Russ area studies, 65, PhD(mod Ger), 70; Univ Vienna, dipl, 64. **CAREER** Fac preceptor, Parsons Col, 65-68; asst prof mod Europe, Russ & Ger hist, Rockford Col, 70-74; assoc prof, 74-79, Prof Mod Ger Hist, Tex A&M Univ, 79-, Am Coun Learned Soc grant & Am Philos Soc grant, 72; Nat Endowment for Hum grant, 75; prin investr, Ctr for Energy & Mineral Resources, Tex A&M Univ, 76-; vis prof, Rice Univ, 80; Nat Sci Found, 82; vis prof Tubingen Univ, 93-94. **HONORS AND AWARDS** Grants from Holocaust Educational Found; Texas A&M Distinguished Teaching Awd, 83; Dir, A&M Study Abroad, Germany, 89-91; Texas A&M Distinguished Teaching Awd, 89, 00; Sr Fulbright Fel, 92-93; Dir, A&M Study Abroad, France, 96, 97, 99; Phi Beta Delta, Nat Fac Awd, 99; Dir, A&M Study Abroad, Poland, 00,01. **MEMBERSHIPS** Historians Second World War; Soc Hist Am For Rels; Western Asn Ger Studies. **RESEARCH** International brigades in Spanish Civil War; heavy industry in Nazi Germany; Germany Prisoners of War in the US during World War II. **SELECTED PUBLICATIONS** Auth, Die Internierten Deutschen, 99; auth, Deutsche Kriegsgefangen in Amerika 1942-1946, 95; auth, Undue Process: The Untold Story of America's German Enemy Aliens, 97; auth, Hitler's Last Soldier in Am, 85; auth, Nazi Prisoners of War in Am, 79, 85, 95; auth, The Forgotten Friendship, 74. **CONTACT ADDRESS** Dept of History, Texas A&M Univ, Col Station, College Station, TX 77843. **EMAIL** apkrammer@aol.com

KRAMER, CARL EDWARD
PERSONAL Born 05/22/1946, New Albany, IN **DISCIPLINE** AMERICAN HISTORY **EDUCATION** Anderson Col, AB, 68; Roosevelt Univ, AM, 70; Univ Louisville, MS, 72; Univ Toledo, PhD(Am hist), 80. **CAREER** Pop analyst, US Bur Census, 70-71; res planner, Louisville and Jefferson County Planning Comn, 71-72; archit historian, Louisville Hist Landmarks and Preserv Dist Comn, 77-79; Pres, Kentuckiana Hist Serv, 81-; Adj Lectr Hist, Inst Community Develop, Univ Louisville, 76- and Ind Univ Southeast, 78-. **MEMBERSHIPS** AHA; Orgn Am Historians; Community Develop Soc; Am Soc Pub Admin. **RESEARCH** Urbanization and land development; urban imagery; urban politics and planning. **SELECTED PUBLICATIONS** Coauth (with Richard T Shogren), Population Report, Louisville and Jefferson County 1970-1990, Louisville & Jefferson County Planning Comn, 72; auth, Two centuries of urban development in central and southern Louisville, In: Louisville Survey: Central and South Report, Hist Landmarks & Preserv Dist Comn, 78; Fortunes of war, Louisville, 1/78; Images of a developing city: Louisville, 1800-1830, Filson Club Hist Quart, 4/78; The notorious James B Brown, Louisville, 1/79; A history of eastern Louisville, In: Louisville Survey: East Report, Hist Landmarks & Preserv Dist Comn, 80; The origins of the subdivision process in Louisville, 1772-1932, In: An Introduction to the Louisville Region, Am Geogr, 80; coauth (with Raymond L Spann), The violent life and death of Chief Frank M Thomas, Filson Club Hist Quart (in prep). **CONTACT ADDRESS** 210 Ettles Lane No 112, Clarksville, IN 47130.

KRANZBERG, MELVIN
PERSONAL Born 11/22/1917, St. Louis, MO, m, 1943, 2 children **DISCIPLINE** HISTORY OF SCIENCE **EDUCATION** Amherst Col, AB, 38; Harvard Univ, AM, 39, PhD, 42. **CAREER** Instr and tutor, Harvard Univ, 46; instr, Stevens Inst Technol, 46-47; asst prof hist, Amherst Col, 47-52; from assoc prof to prof, Case Western Reserve Univ, 52-72; Callaway Prof Hist of Technol, GA Inst Technol, 72-; Assoc economist, off Price Admin, 42-43; consult, Opers Res off, Johns Hopkins Univ, 51-52; ed, Technol and Cult, Soc Hist Technol, 59-; vpres, Int Comt Coopin Hist of Technol, 65-68; chmn hist adv comt, NASA, 66-69; mem panel on technol assessment, Nat Acad Sci, 69-71, mem comt on surv of mat sci and eng, 71-73; mem adv panel, Prog on Sci, Technol and Values, Nat Endowment for Humanities, 75-77; chmn adv panel, Div Policy Res and Anal, NSF, 77-80; chmn comt on sci, eng and public policy, AAAS, 78-80. **HONORS AND AWARDS** Leonardo da Vinci Medal, Soc Hist Technol, 68; Roe Medal, Am Soc Mech Engrs, 80; lhd, denison univ, 67; littd, neward col eng, 68 and northern mich univ, 72; dr english, worcester polytech inst, 81. **MEMBERSHIPS** AHA; AAAS (vpres, 65-66); Soc Hist Technol (secy, 58-74); Soc Fr Hist Studies (vpres, 58-59); Sigma Xi (pres, 79-80). **RESEARCH** History of technology; innovation and technology transfer; technology assessment. **SELECTED PUBLICATIONS** Auth, Glennan, T.Keith, 1905-95, Memorial, Technol Cult, Vol 0037, 96. **CONTACT ADDRESS** Dept of Soc Sci, Georgia Inst of Tech, Atlanta, GA 30332.

KRAUSE, CORINNE AZEN
PERSONAL Born 03/03/1927, Pittsburgh, PA, m, 1948, 4 children **DISCIPLINE** HISTORY, SOCIOLOGY **EDUCATION** Univ Mich, BA, 48; Carnegie-Mellon Univ, MA, 66; Univ Pittsburgh, PhD(hist), 70. **CAREER** Teacher, Chatham Col, Carnegie-Mellon Univ and Univ Pittsburg, Greensburg; proj dir, Women, Ethnicity, and Mental Health Oral Hist Study, Am Jewish Comt, 75-78; Res and Writing, 78-; Proj dir, Roots and Branches, exhibit Pittsburghs Jewish hist. **MEMBERSHIPS** Inst Res Hist; Orgn Am Historians; Am Jewish Hist Soc; AHA; Oral Hist Soc. **RESEARCH** Womens history in United States; United States Jewish history; Latin American history. **SELECTED PUBLICATIONS** Auth, "Mexico, Another Promised Land," Am Jewish Hist Qtly LXI (72): 325-341; auth, "Positivist Liberalism in Mexico," Jrnl of Inter-American Stud and Wrld Affairs LVIII (76): 475-494; auth, "Italian, Jewish, and Slavic Grandmothers in Pittsburgh: Their Economic Roles," Frontiers II, (77): 18-28; auth, "Urbanization Without Breakdown: Italian, Jewish, and Slavic Immigrant Women in Pittsburgh, 1900-1945," Jrn of Urban Hist (78): 291-306, reprinted in Immigrant Women, ed Maxine Schwartz Seller, (Philadelphia: Temple Univ Press, 81); auth, Isaac W. Frank, Idustrialist and Civic Leader, Historical Soc of Western Penn (Pittsburgh), 84; auth, Los Judios in Mexico: Una Historia con Enfasis en el Periodo de 1857 a 1930, Universidad Iberoamericana (Mexico), 87; auth, Refractories: The Hidden Industry, A History of Refractories in the United States, 1860 to 1985, Am Ceramic Soc (Cincinnati), 87; auth, Grandmothers, Mothers, and Daughters: Oral Histories of Three Generations of Ethnic American Women, Twayne Publishing Company (Boston), 91; auth, Immigrant Family Patterns in Demography, Fertility, Housing, Kinship, and Urban Life, Vol 11, of American Immigration and Ethnicity, J Am Ethnic Hist, Vol 0013, 94. **CONTACT ADDRESS** 7 Darlington Ct, Pittsburgh, PA 15217. **EMAIL** ckrause@bellatlantic.net

KRAUSE, LINDA R.
DISCIPLINE ARCHITECTURE **EDUCATION** Temple Univ, BA; Western Reserve Univ, MA, 70; Yale Univ, M.Phil, 75; Ph.D, 80. **CAREER** Instr, Yale Univ, 76-66; vis asst prof, Dartmouth Col, 78-83; vis asst prof, Sch of the Art Inst of Chicago, 84-85; asst prof, Sch of the Art Inst of Chicago, 85-88; assoc prof, Univ of Wis-Milwaukee, 93-. **HONORS AND AWARDS** Fel, Ctr for Twentieth Century Stud, 91-92. **MEMBERSHIPS** Chic Archit Club; The Col Art Asn; The Soc of Archit Historians; The Midwest Art Hist Soc. **RESEARCH** Diverse aspects of the built environment of Victorian London; Victorian Commercial street architecture and urban design; Victorian creation of an urban esthetic that challenged the dominant Baroque principles announced in Haussmann's Second Empire Paris. **SELECTED PUBLICATIONS** Auth, Milwaukee: In Praise of the Commonplace, Inland Architect, July/August, 90; auth, The New Brutalism: Frampton Reconsidered, Circa, Sep/Oct, 90; auth, Detours On the Roads Not Taken, Architecture Chicago: The Chicago Chapter of the American Institute of Architects, Nov, (90); auth, The Image of the House of Images, Vol IV: Landscape, Ethnoscape, Proceedings of the 12th International Association of People-Environment Studies Conference, Maramaras, Greece, (92); coed, Commercial Sites: Early Victorian Development of Cannon Street, In Debra Mancoff and D.J. Trela, eds, Victorian Urban Settings: Essay on the Nineteenth-Century City and Its Contexts, New York and London: Garland Publishing, (96). **CONTACT ADDRESS** Dept Archit, Univ of Wisconsin, Milwaukee, PO Box 413, Milwaukee, WI 53201. **EMAIL** lrkrause@uwm.edu

KRAUT, ALAN M.
PERSONAL Born 10/06/1946, Bronx, NY, m, 1973, 1 child **DISCIPLINE** HISTORY **EDUCATION** Hunter Col, BA, 68; Cornell Univ, MA, 71, PhD, 75. **CAREER** Asst prof, 74-78, Assoc Prof Am Hist, Am Univ, 78-. **MEMBERSHIPS** AHA; Orgn Am Historians; Southern Hist Asn; Social Sci Hist Asn; Immigration Hist Soc. **RESEARCH** Nineteenth century United States political and social history; immigration and ethnic history; Civil War and reconstruction. **SELECTED PUBLICATIONS CONTACT ADDRESS** Dept of Hist, American Univ, 4400 Mass Ave NW, Washington, DC 20016-8200.

KRAUT, BENNY
PERSONAL Born 12/24/1947, Munich, Germany, m, 1972, 3 children **DISCIPLINE** MODERN JEWISH HISTORY, MODERN JUDAISM **EDUCATION** Yeshiva Univ, BA, 68; Brandeis Univ, MA, 70, PhD(Jewish hist), 75. **CAREER** Vis asst prof Judaica, Vassar Col, 75-76; Assoc Prof Judaica, Univ Cincinnati, 76-. **MEMBERSHIPS** Orgn Am Historians; Asn Jewish Studies; World Union Jewish Studies. **RESEARCH** Development of American Judaism; religious and theological responses to the Holocaust; Jewish-Christian relations in American history. **SELECTED PUBLICATIONS** Auth, The approach to Jewish law of Martin Buber and Franz Rosenzweig, Tradition, Vol XII, 72; Perspectives on the drug issue, In: Judaism and Drugs, Hermon Press, 73; A unique American apostate, Columbia Libr Columns, 5/78; From Reform Judaism to Ethical Culture: The Religious Evolution of Felix Adler, Hebrew Union Col Press, 79; Francis E Abbott: Perceptions of a 19th century religious radical on Jews and Judaism, Studies Am Jewish Experience, spring 81; The role of the Jewish academic in Jewish affairs, Occasional Papers, 81; Faith and the Holocaust, Judaism, spring 82; Judaism triumphant: Isaac Mayer Wise on unitarianism and liberal Christianity, Asn Jewish Studies Rev, 82. **CONTACT ADDRESS** Judaic Studies, Univ of Cincinnati, P O Box 210169, Cincinnati, OH 45221-0169.

KREKIC, BARISA
PERSONAL Born 10/14/1928, Dubrovnik, Croatia, m, 1 child **DISCIPLINE** MEDIEVAL HISTORY, BYZANTINE HISTORY **EDUCATION** Univ Belgrade, BA, 51; Serbian Acad Arts and Sci, PhD(medieval hist), 54. **CAREER** Asst Byzantine hist, Byzantine Inst, Belgrade, 51-56; from asst prof to prof medieval hist, Univ Novi Sad, 56-70; prof, Ind Univ, Bloomington, 68-69; Prof Southeast Europ Hist, Univ Calif, Los Angeles, 70-; Res teacher, Nat Ctr Sci Res, Paris, 57, 58 and 60; mem, Yugoslav Nat Comt Byzantine Studies, 66-70; US Nat Comt Byzantine Studies, 71-; prof hist, Dumbarton Oaks Byzantine Ctr, Harvard Univ, 75-76. **MEMBERSHIPS** AHA; Am Asn Advan Slavic Studies. **RESEARCH** Medieval Balkans; Byzantine history; Italian cities. **SELECTED PUBLICATIONS** Auth, Debrovnik (Ragusa) et le Levant au Moyen Age, Paris, EPHE-Sorbome, 61; auth, Dubrovik in the 14th and 15th Centuries, Norman, Univ of Okla Pr, 72; auth, Dubrovik, Italay and the Balkans in the Late Middle Ages, London, Variorum, 80; auth, Dubrovik: A Mediteranean Urban Soc, 1300-1600, Aldershot-Brookfield, Ashgate/Variorum, 97. **CONTACT ADDRESS** Dept of Hist, Univ of California, Los Angeles, Los Angeles, CA 90024.

KREMER, GARY R.
PERSONAL Born 09/03/1948, Jefferson City, MO, m, 1968, 2 children **DISCIPLINE** AMERICAN HISTORY **EDUCATION** Lincoln Univ, BA, 71, MA, 72; American Univ, PhD(hist), 78. **CAREER** Asst Prof Hist, Lincoln Univ, 72-; Dir, Black Hist Sites Proj, 78-. **MEMBERSHIPS** Orgn Am Historians; Southern Hist Asn; Inst Study of Early Am Life and Hist. **RESEARCH** History of prisons; black history; social history. **SELECTED PUBLICATIONS CONTACT ADDRESS** Dept of Soc Sci, Lincoln Univ, Missouri, Jefferson City, MO 65101.

KREMM, DIANE NEAL
PERSONAL Born 08/18/1947, SC **DISCIPLINE** HISTORY **EDUCATION** Winthrop Col, BA, 69; Clemson Univ, MA, 71; Kent State Univ, PhD, 76. **CAREER** Instr, Kent State Univ, 75-76; lectr, Sangamon State Univ, 77; from asst prof to prof, Univ of Cent Okla, 77-. **HONORS AND AWARDS** Distinguished Scholar, Univ of Cent Okla, 94. **MEMBERSHIPS** Soc of Civil War Historians, SC Hist Asn, Phi Alpha Theta, Okla Asn of Prof Historians. **RESEARCH** Presidential reconstruction in Arkansas, Arkansas in the Civil War. **SELECTED PUBLICATIONS** Coauth, "Loyal Government on Trial: The Union Versus Arkansas," South Studies: An Interdisciplinary J of the S (86); auth, "Treason or Patriotism? Union Peace Societies in Arkansas During the Civil War," J of Confederate Hist (88); auth, "Seduction, Accommodation, or Realism? Tabbs Gross and the Arkansas Freeman," Ark Hist Quart (89); coauth, "What Shall We Do With The Negro? The Freeman Bureau in Texas," E Tex Hist J (89); coauth, "An Experiment in Collective Security: The Union Army's Use of Armed Colonies in Arkansas," Mil Hist of the SW (90); coauth, "The King of Revolution is the Bayonet: General Thomas C. Hindman's Proposal to Arm the Slaves," J of Confederate Hist 7 (91); coauth, "Crisis of Command: The Hindman/Pike Controversy Over the Defense of the Trans-Mississippi District," Chronicles of Okla (92); coauth, Lion of the South: General Thomas C. Hindman, Mercer Univ Press, 93. **CONTACT ADDRESS** Dept Hist & Geog, Univ of Central Oklahoma, 100 N Univ Dr, Edmond, OK 73034-5207. **EMAIL** dkremm@ucok.edu

KREN, GEORGE M.
PERSONAL Born 06/03/1926, Linz, Austria, m, 1 child **DISCIPLINE** MODERN EUROPEAN HISTORY **EDUCATION** Colby Col, BA, 48; Univ Wis, MA, 49, PhD, 60. **CAREER** Instr hist, Oberlin Col, 58-59; asst prof, Elmira Col, 59-60; from instr to asst prof, Lake Forest Col, 60-65; assoc prof, 65-77, Prof Hist, Kans State Univ, 77-; Contrib ed, J Psychohist, 75-. **RESEARCH** European intellectual and cultural history; 19th and 20th century Germany; historiography and psychohistory; Holocaust. **SELECTED PUBLICATIONS** Co-ed, Varieties of Psychohistory, Springer Publ, 76; auth, Psychohistory in the university, J Psychohist, winter 77; The SS: A Social and Psychohistorical Analysis, In: Int Terrorism in the Contemporary World, Greenwood Press, 78; Psychohistorical Interpretation of National Socialism, German Studies Rev, 5/78; The Jew the Image as Reality, J Psychohist, 78; The Literature of the Holocaust, Choice, 1/79; Psychohistory and the Holocaust, J Psychohist, winter 79; coauth, The Holocaust and the Crisis of Human Behavior, Holmes & Meier, 80. **CONTACT ADDRESS** Dept of History, Kansas State Univ, 208 Eisenhower Hall, Manhattan, KS 66506-1000. **EMAIL** kreng@ksu.edu

KRENTZ, PETER MARTIN
PERSONAL Born 07/11/1953, St. Louis, MO, m, 1981 **DISCIPLINE** ANCIENT HISTORY **EDUCATION** Yale Univ, BA, 75, MA, 76, PhD, 79. **CAREER** Prof Classics & Hist, Davidson Col, 79-. **MEMBERSHIPS** Asn Ancient Historians; Am Philol Asn; Class Asn Can. **RESEARCH** Greek political and military history; Greek orators; Greek epigraphy. **SELECTED PUBLICATIONS** Auth, The Thirty at Athens, Cornell Univ Press, 82; Xenophon, Hellenika, I-II.3.10, Aris & Phillps, 89; Xenophon, Hellenika, I.3.11-IV.2.8, Aris & Phillips, 95 **CONTACT ADDRESS** Dept Classics, Davidson Col, PO Box 1719, Davidson, NC 28036-1719. **EMAIL** pekrentz@davidson.edu

KRESS, LEE BRUCE
PERSONAL Born 06/19/1941, Baltimore, MD, m, 1968, 1 child **DISCIPLINE** LATIN AMERICAN & AMERICAN HISTORY **EDUCATION** Johns Hopkins Univ, BA, 63; Columbia Univ, MA & cert Latin Am Studies, 67, PhD(hist), 72. **CAREER** Instr hist & polit, Baltimore Col of Com, 69-71; from instr to asst prof hist, Univ Md, 71-73; from asst prof to assoc prof hist, Rowan Univ, 73-, Res grants, NJ Comt for Humanities, 74 & Glassboro State Col, 77-78 & 79; instr & consult, Pace Prog, Old Dominion Univ, 76-78; adj instr, Camden County Col, 77-. **MEMBERSHIPS** Conf Latin Am Hist; AHA; Latin Am Studies Asn; Inter-Am Coun; Middle Atlantic Conf on Latin Am Studies; Soc for Military Hist; Western Front Assoc; Great War Soc; Soc for the Hist of Am Foreign Relations. **RESEARCH** Latin American history, Argentine and Mexico; American history, diplomatic and military. **SELECTED PUBLICATIONS** Auth, Centralism and federalism in Latin America, J Int & Comp Studies, 73; Argentine liberalism and the church, The Americas, 74; Development of Spanish-speaking community in New Jersey, NJ Hist, 77; co-ed, Terrorism in the Contemporary World, Greenwood, 78. **CONTACT ADDRESS** Dept of History, Rowan Univ, 201 Mullica Hill Rd, Glassboro, NJ 08028-1702. **EMAIL** lbkress@rowan.edu

KREY, GARY DE
PERSONAL m, 1 child **DISCIPLINE** BRITAIN, EARLY MODERN EUROPE **EDUCATION** Princeton, PhD, 78. **CAREER** History, St. Olaf Col. **SELECTED PUBLICATIONS** Area: seventeenth-century London. **CONTACT ADDRESS** St. Olaf Col, 1520 St Olaf Ave, Northfield, MN 55057. **EMAIL** dekrey@stolaf.edu

KREY, PHILIP D. W.
DISCIPLINE EARLY; MEDIEVAL CHURCH HISTORY **EDUCATION** Univ Mass/Boston, BA, 72; Lutheran Theol Sem at Gettysburg, MDiv, 76; Cath Univ Am, MA, 85; Univ Chicago, PhD, 90. **CAREER** Dean; prof-. **HONORS AND AWARDS** Fulbright fel, Univ Munich, 89; co-founder, soc stud of the bible in the middle ages. **SELECTED PUBLICATIONS** Auth, transl, medieval Franciscan's Revelation Commentary - Nicholas of Lyra; co-ed, Sources of Medieval Christian Thought, Cath UP. **CONTACT ADDRESS** Dept of History and Systematic Theology, Lutheran Theol Sem at Gettysburg, 7301 Germantown Ave, Philadelphia, PA 19119 1794. **EMAIL** Pkrey@ltsp.edu

KRICK, ROBERT KENNETH
PERSONAL m, 1980, 2 children **DISCIPLINE** AMERICAN HISTORY **EDUCATION** Pac Union Col, BA, 65; San Jose State Col, MA, 67. **CAREER** Chief historian, Ft McHenry Nat Monument, 67-69; supt, Ft Necessity Nat Battlefield, 69-72; chief historian, Fredericksburg and Spotsylvania Nat Mil Park, 72-. **HONORS AND AWARDS** Douglas Southall Freeman Awd, best work in Southern History, 91; Richard Barksdale Harwell Awd, best Civil War book of 1990. **RESEARCH** The Army of Northern Virginia, 1862-1865. **SELECTED PUBLICATIONS** Auth, Stonewall Jackson at Cedar Mountain, Univ NC Press, 90; auth, Lee's Colonels, 4th ed. Morningside, (92); auth, Conquering the Valley: Stonewall Jackson at Port Republic, Morrow, 96; auth, "The Smoothbore Volley that Doomed the Confederacy," in Chancellorsville, the Battle and Its Aftermath, ed, Gary W. Gallagher, Univ NC Press, 96. **CONTACT ADDRESS** PO Box 1327, Fredericksburg, VA 22402. **EMAIL** sfg49@starpower.net

KRIEGER, DANIEL
PERSONAL Born 08/13/1940, Toledo, OH, m, 1963 **DISCIPLINE** HISTORY **EDUCATION** Univ Calif, PhD, 73. **CAREER** prof, Cal Poly State Univ, 71-; chair, Univ Res Comt, 89-98. **HONORS AND AWARDS** NEH, Newberry Lib Fel, 78. **MEMBERSHIPS** AHA, Conf on British Studies, Calif Comt for the Promotion of Hist **RESEARCH** California & regional history, British travel accounts and diaries of the American west. **SELECTED PUBLICATIONS** Auth, Looking Back into the Middle Kingdom: An Interpretive History of San Luis Obispo County and the Central Coast, Windsor, 88; auth, War Comes to the Middle Kingdom, vol 1 (91), vol 2 (00). **CONTACT ADDRESS** California Polytech State Univ, San Luis Obispo, 1 Grand Ave, San Luis Obispo, CA 93407-9000. **EMAIL** dkrieger@calpoly.edu

KRIEGER, LEONARD
PERSONAL Born 08/28/1918, Newark, NJ **DISCIPLINE** MODERN EUROPEAN HISTORY **EDUCATION** Rutgers Univ, AB, 38; Yale Univ, AM, 42, PhD, 49. **CAREER** Polit analyst, US Dept State, 46; asst instr, Yale Univ, 46-47, from instr to prof hist, 48-62; univ prof, Univ Chicago, 62-69; prof, Columbia Univ, 69-72; Univ Prof Hist, Univ Chicago, 72-; Fel, Ctr Advan Studies Behav Sci, 56-57; mem, Inst Advan Study,

63 and 69-70; Ed, Classics European Historians, Univ Chicago, 67-; vis comt for dept hist, Harvard Univ, 70-73; Mem Counc, Am Acad Arts and Sci, 75-; Mem Univ Counc and Chmn Vis Comt for Grad Sch, Yale Univ, 76-. **HONORS AND AWARDS** Soc Sci Res Counc demobilization awards, 46-48. **MEMBERSHIPS** AHA; Am Acad Arts and Sci; Am Soc Polit and Legal Philos; Int Soc Hist Ideas; Am Philos Soc. **RESEARCH** Intellectual history; philosophy of history. **SELECTED PUBLICATIONS** Auth, Teaching Professional Judgment, Wash Law Rev, Vol 0069, 94. **CONTACT ADDRESS** Dept of Hist, Univ of Chicago, Chicago, IL 60637.

KRIMSKY, SHELDON
PERSONAL Born 06/26/1941, New York, NY, m, 1970, 2 children **DISCIPLINE** PHILOSOPHY, HISTORY OF SCIENCE **EDUCATION** Brooklyn Col, BS, 63; Purdue Univ, MS, 65; Boston Univ, PhD(philos), 70. **CAREER** Urban & environ policy: prof, 90-; assoc prof, 83-90; assit prof, 80-82; Prog Urban, Social & Env Policy, acting dir, 78-80; assoc dir, 75-78; res assoc, Boston Univ, 73-75; assit prof, Univ of South Fla, 70-73. **HONORS AND AWARDS** NDEA Fel; Distinguished Alumnus, Boston Univ fel; Am Asn for the Advancement of Sci; Fel, Hastings Center. **MEMBERSHIPS** AAAS. **RESEARCH** Biotechnology; science and society; bioethics; chemicals and health; environmental ethics; environmental policy; risk management. **SELECTED PUBLICATIONS** Auth, Regulating Recombinant DNA Research in Controversy: Politics of Technical Decisions, Sage, 78; auth, The Role of the Citizen Court in the Recombinant DNA Debate, Bull Atomic Scientists, 10/78; coauth, Recombinant DNA research: The Scope and lLimits of Regulation, The Am J Pub Health, 12/79; auth, Genetic Alchemy: The Social History of the Recombinant DNA Debate, MIT Press, 82; auth, Patents for Life Forms sui generis: Some New Questions for Science Law and Society, Recombinant DNA Tech Bull, 4/81; coauth, Environmental Hazards, Auburn House Publ Co, 88; auth, Social Theories of Risk, Praeger, 92; auth, Biotechnics and Society, Praeger, 92; coauth, Agricultural Biotechnology and the Environment, Univ Ill Press, 96; auth, The Profit of Scientific Discovery and its Normative Implications, Chicago Kent Law Review 75 (99): 15-39; auth, Hormonal Choas, John Hopkins Univ Press, 00. **CONTACT ADDRESS** Dept of Urban Environ Policy, Tufts Univ, Medford, 97 Talbot Ave, Medford, MA 02155-5555. **EMAIL** sheldon.krimsky@tufts.edu

KRINSKY, CAROL HERSELLE
PERSONAL Born 06/02/1937, New York, NY, m, 1959, 2 children **DISCIPLINE** HISTORY OF ART **EDUCATION** Smith Col, BA, 57; New York Univ, MA, 60, PhD, 65. **CAREER** Instr, 65-77, prof, New York Univ, 78-. **HONORS AND AWARDS** Phi Beta Kappa; ACLS grant; NEA grant; Arnold Brunner Awd of NY City Chapter, Am Inst of Architects; Nat Jewish Book Awd. **MEMBERSHIPS** Soc of Architectural Hist (pres, 84-86); Col Art Asn; Int Survey of Jewish Monuments; Int Center for Medieval Art; Urban History Asn. **RESEARCH** Architectural history; 15th century Netherlandish painting. **SELECTED PUBLICATIONS** Auth, Vitruvius de Architectura, Como, 1521, Munich: Wilhelm Fink Verlag, 69; Rockefeller Center, NY: Oxford Univ Press, 78; Synagogues of Europe, NY: Cambridge, Architectural History Found/MIT Press, 85; Gordon Bunshaft of Skidmore Owings and Merrill, NY: Cambridge, 88; Contemporary Native American Architecture, NY: Oxford Univ Press, 96; numerous articles, book reviews, book chapters, and introductions to books. **CONTACT ADDRESS** New York Univ, 303 Main, 100 Washington Sq SE, New York, NY 10003-6688. **EMAIL** chk1@as2.nyu.edu

KRISTOF, JANE
PERSONAL Born 05/25/1932, Chicago, IL, m, 1956, 1 child **DISCIPLINE** ART HISTORY **EDUCATION** Columbia Univ, PhD, 72; Univ Chicago, MA, 56, BA, 50. **CAREER** Lectr, Instr, Asst Prof, Assoc Prof, Prof, 73 to 92-, Portland State Univ, Instr, 72-73, Mount Hood Comm College; Lectr, 70-71, Univ Waterloo, ON CA. **MEMBERSHIPS** CAA; RSA; NWRS; CLA; SCS; INCS; AHNCA. **SELECTED PUBLICATIONS** Auth, The Feminization of Piety in Nineteenth Century Art, in: Reinventing Christianity: Nineteenth Century Contexts, ed, Linda Woodward Ashgate, forthcoming; Rouault and the Catholic Revival in France, in: Through a Glass Darkly: Essays in the Religious Imagination, ed, John Hawley, Fordham Univ Press, 96; Mary Stevenson Cassatt in Great Lives from History: American Women, Salem Press, 95; Blacksmiths Weavers and Artists: Images of Labor in Nineteenth Century Contexts, 93. **CONTACT ADDRESS** Art Dept, Portland State Univ, Portland, OR 97207. **EMAIL** kristofj@pdx.edu

KRODEL, GOTTFRIED G.
PERSONAL Born 07/14/1931, Redwitz, Germany, m, 1956, 1 child **DISCIPLINE** CHURCH HISTORY **EDUCATION** Univ Erlangen, ThD, 55. **CAREER** Instr church hist, Univ Chicago, 56-59; from asst prof to assoc prof relig, Concordia Col, Moorhead, Minn, 59-65; assoc prof hist and church hist, 65-71, Prof Hist and Church Hist, Valparaiso Univ, 71-. **MEMBERSHIPS** Am Soc Church Hist; Am Soc Reformation Res; AHA; Renaissance Soc Am; Luther Ges. **RESEARCH** History of Christian thought; Renaissance and humanism; constitutional history of 16th century Germany. **SELECTED PUBLICATIONS** **CONTACT ADDRESS** Dept of Hist, Valparaiso Univ, Valparaiso, IN 46383.

KROEBER, CLIFTON BROWN
PERSONAL Born 09/07/1921, Berkeley, CA, m, 1944, 4 children **DISCIPLINE** HISTORY **EDUCATION** Univ Calif, AB, 43, MA, 47, PhD, 51. **CAREER** Asst prof hist, Univ Wis, 51-55; from asst prof to assoc prof, 55-64, Norman Bridge Prof Hisp Am Hist, Occidental Col, 64-. **MEMBERSHIPS** AHA Latin Am Studies Asn. **RESEARCH** Latin American history. **SELECTED PUBLICATIONS** Auth, Violence, Resistance, and Survival in the America in Native-Americans and the Legacy of Conquest, Pacific Hist Rev, Vol 0064, 95; Theory and History of Revolution, J World Hist, Vol 0007, 96. **CONTACT ADDRESS** Occidental Col, 1600 Campus Rd, Los Angeles, CA 90041.

KROG, CARL EDWARD
PERSONAL Born 03/02/1936, Cedar Rapids, IA, m, 1962, 3 children **DISCIPLINE** HISTORY **EDUCATION** Univ Chicago, BA, 58, MA, 60; Univ Wis, Madison, PhD(hist), 71. **CAREER** Instr hist and geog, Concordia High Sch, Wis, 59-63; instr hist, Univ-Cent High Sch, Wis, 65-66; from instr to asst prof, 66-75, Assoc Prof Hist, Univ Wis Ctr, Marinette, 75-95; Instr hist, Univ Wis, Green Bay, Marinette Campus, 69-72. **MEMBERSHIPS** State Hist Soc of Wis SHSW. **RESEARCH** Great Lakes regional history. **SELECTED PUBLICATIONS** Auth, "Carl E. Krogs and Wm. R. Tanner Herbert Hoover and the Republican Era: A Reconsideration," University Prew of America, 84. **CONTACT ADDRESS** 720 Edwin, Marinette, WI 54143. **EMAIL** ckrog@uwcmail.uwc.edu

KROLL, JOHN HENNIG
PERSONAL Born 02/12/1938, Washington, DC, d, 3 children **DISCIPLINE** GREEK ARCHEOLOGY, ANCIENT NUMISMATICS **EDUCATION** Oberlin Col, BA, 59; Harvard Univ, MA, 61, PhD(class archaeol), 68. **CAREER** Excavation numismatist, Agora Excavation, Athens, Greece, 70-74; asst prof, to assoc prof, to prof Classics, Univ Tex, Austin, 74-93. **HONORS AND AWARDS** Nat Endowment for Humanities fel, 81; ACLS Fell, 86. **MEMBERSHIPS** Archaeol Inst Am; Am Numis Soc Am Sch Class Studies Athens; Soc Ancient Historians; Am Philol Asn. **RESEARCH** Greek coinage; Athenian government and monuments. **SELECTED PUBLICATIONS** Auth, Athenian Bronze Allotment Plates, Harvard Univ, 72; Greek Coins: The Athenian Agore, vol 26, 93. **CONTACT ADDRESS** Dept of Classics, Univ of Texas, Austin, Austin, TX 78712-1026. **EMAIL** jKroll@utxvms.cc.utexas.edu

KROSS, JESSICA
PERSONAL Born 09/20/1943, New York, NY **DISCIPLINE** HISTORY **EDUCATION** Brandeis Univ, BA, 65; Univ Mich, MA, 69, PhD(hist), 74. **CAREER** Asst prof, Southwest Mo State Univ, 74-75; Asst Prof Hist, Univ SC, 75-. **MEMBERSHIPS** AHA; Orgn Am Historians; Econ Hist Asn; Social Sci Hist Asn. **RESEARCH** Colonial America; social history; American Revolution. **SELECTED PUBLICATIONS** Auth, Local justice: The Town Court of Newtown New York 1662-1691, NY Hist, 78. **CONTACT ADDRESS** Dept of Hist, Univ of So Carolina, Columbia, Columbia, SC 29208.

KRUMAN, MARC WAYNE
PERSONAL Born 12/13/1949, Brooklyn, NY, m, 1977, 1 child **DISCIPLINE** AMERICAN HISTORY **EDUCATION** Cornell Univ, BS, 71; Yale Univ, MA and MPhil, 73; PhD(hist), 78. **CAREER** Instr, 75-78, Asst Prof Hist, 78-, Wayne State Univ, ch, dept hist; Andrew W Mellon fac fel, Harvard Univ, 80-81; vis asst prof hist, Harvard Univ, 81. **MEMBERSHIPS** AHA; Orgn Am Historians; Southern Hist Asn. **RESEARCH** American political history; 19th century American history; Southern history. **SELECTED PUBLICATIONS** Auth, "The Presidency of Jackson, Andrew," J Am Hist (94). **CONTACT ADDRESS** Dept of Hist, Wayne State Univ, 222 6 Faculty/Admin Bldg, Detroit, MI 48202. **EMAIL** aa1277@wayne.edu

KRUPP, E. C.
PERSONAL Born 11/18/1944, Chicago, IL, m, 1968, 1 child **DISCIPLINE** PHYSICS ASTRONOMY **EDUCATION** Pomona Col, BA 66; UCLA, MA 68, PhD 72. **CAREER** Griffith Observatory, Curator 72-74, Director 74. **HONORS AND AWARDS** Am Inst Physics, best writer; Bruce Medal, W Am Astron; Astro Soc of Pacific, Klumpke Roberts Awd. **MEMBERSHIPS** Astron Soc of the Pacific; AAS; Intl Astron Union. **RESEARCH** Ancient and pre-historic Astron; celestial component of belief systems. **SELECTED PUBLICATIONS** Skywatchers, Shamans & Kings: Astronomy and the Archaeology of Power, 97; Beyond the Blue Horizon: Myths and Legends of the Sun, Moon , Stars and Planets, 91; Archaeolastronomy and the Roots of Science, 84; numerous bks, papers and articles. **CONTACT ADDRESS** Griffith Observatory, 2800 East Observatory Rd, Los Angeles, CA 90027. **EMAIL** eckrupp@earthlink.net

KRUPPA, PATRICIA STALLINGS
PERSONAL Born 10/02/1936, Corpus Christi, TX, m, 1975, 1 child **DISCIPLINE** BRITISH HISTORY **EDUCATION** Univ Houston, BA, 58; Columbia Univ, MA, 59, PhD(Brit hist), 68. **CAREER** Instr hist, Towson State Col, 61-64; instr, 67-80, Assoc Prof Hist and Dir Womens Studies, Univ Tex, Austin, 80-; Asst dean col social and behav sci, Univ Tex, Austin, 71-73. **MEMBERSHIPS** AHA **RESEARCH** Anglo-American history; history of popular religion in the 19th century; womens history. **SELECTED PUBLICATIONS** **CONTACT ADDRESS** 101 E 31st S St, Austin, TX 78705.

KRUTY, PAUL
PERSONAL Born 12/10/1952, Chicago, IL, m, 1984 **DISCIPLINE** ART HISTORY, ARCHITECTURAL HISTORY **EDUCATION** Univ Chicago, BA, 74; Univ Wisc, Milwaukee, MA, 84; Princeton Univ, PhD, 89. **CAREER** Asst prof, Univ Ill, Urbana-Champaign, 89-95, assoc prof, 95-. **HONORS AND AWARDS** Graham Found grants, 90, 96. **MEMBERSHIPS** Soc of Archit Hists, Nat Trust for Hist Preservation, Walter Burley Griffin Soc (Australia), Walter Burley Griffin Soc of Am. **RESEARCH** Modern architecture, American architecture, Frank Lloyd Wright and the Prairie School. **SELECTED PUBLICATIONS** Auth, "Heurtley to Bluemner: Early Impressions of Frank Lloyd Wright," Ill Hist J, 86 (summer 93): 85-92; auth, "The Gilbert Cooley House, 1925: Walter Burley Griffin's last American Building," Fabrications [Arch Hists, Australia & New Zealand], 6 (June 95): 8-23; auth, "Wright, Spencer, and the Casement Window," Winterthur Portfolio 30 (summer/autumn 95): 103-127; auth, Walter Burley Griffin in America, photographs by Mati Maldre, text by Paul Kruty, Urbana: Univ ILL Press (96); auth, "A New Look at the Illinois Architects' Licensing Law," Ill Hist J, 90 (Autumn 97): 154-66; coauth with Paul E. Sprague, Two American Architects in India: Walter B. Griffin and Marion M. Griffin, 1935-1937, Urbana: Sch of Archit, Univ Ill (97); auth, "Chicago 1900: the Griffins Come of Age," and "Creating a Modern Architecture for India," in Anne Watson, ed, Beyond Architecture: Marion Mahony and Walter Burley Griffin; America, Australia, India, Sydney: Powerhouse Pub (98): 10-25, 138-159; coauth with Ronald E. Schmitt, George G. Elmslie: Architectural Ornament from the Edison and Morton Schools, Hammond, Indiana, Urbana: Sch of Archit, Univ Ill (98); auth, Frank Lloyd Wright and Midway Gardens, Urbana: Univ Ill Press (98); auth, "Art for Building: Mural Painting in the Prairie School," in Susan Weininger, ed, Thinking Modern: Painting in Chicago, 1910-1940, Evanston, Ill: Block Gallery, Northwestern Univ (2000). **CONTACT ADDRESS** Sch of Archit, Univ of Illinois, Urbana-Champaign, 117 Buell Hall, MC-621, Champaign, IL 61820-6921. **EMAIL** p-kruty@uiuc.edu

KRUZE, ULDIS
PERSONAL Born 03/11/1944, Riga, Latvia, m, 1970 **DISCIPLINE** HISTORY **EDUCATION** Yale Univ, BA, 66; Northwestern Univ, MA, 68; Ind Univ, PhD, 76. **CAREER** Asst Prof Hist, Univ San Francisco, 77-; Res scholar, Ctr Chinese Studies, Univ Calif, Berkeley, 76-. **MEMBERSHIPS** Asn Asian Studies; Comt Concerned Asian Scholars. **RESEARCH** Modern Chinese and Japanese history. **SELECTED PUBLICATIONS** Trans, An Economic History of the Major Capitalist Countries (Kang Fau, et al), M E Sharpe, 92. **CONTACT ADDRESS** Dept of Hist, Univ of San Francisco, 2130 Fulton St, San Francisco, CA 94117-1080. **EMAIL** kruzeu@usfca.edu

KRYSIEK, JAMES STEPHEN
PERSONAL Born 01/29/1954, Milwaukee, WI **DISCIPLINE** HISTORY **EDUCATION** York Univ, MA; Marquette Univ, PhD. **CAREER** Fac, Mt Saint Mary's, 88-. **MEMBERSHIPS** ACSUS; ACQS. **RESEARCH** Nineteenth-century commercial relations between British North America and the United States. **SELECTED PUBLICATIONS** Publ on Anglo-Dutch relations during the 1820s and New Perspectives on the Belgian Rev. **CONTACT ADDRESS** Dept of History, Mount Saint Mary's Col and Sem, Emmitsburg, MD 21727-7799. **EMAIL** krysiek@msmary.edu

KUBLER, CORNELIUS C.
PERSONAL Born 05/05/1951, Basel, Switzerland, m, 1976, 1 child **DISCIPLINE** ASIAN STUDIES **EDUCATION** Cornell Univ, BA, 72; MA, 75; PhD, 81; Nat Taiwan Univ, MA, 78. **CAREER** Dept chair, dir, linguist, Foreign Ser Inst, 80-91; prof, Williams Coll, 91-. **HONORS AND AWARDS** Fulbright Fel; Tuttle Lang Gnt Gnd Prize; Dept of State Superior Hon Awd. **MEMBERSHIPS** CLTA; AAS; LSA. **RESEARCH** Chinese language and linguistics. **SELECTED PUBLICATIONS** Coauth, Read Chinese Signs, Cheng & Tsui Co, 93; auth, Listening Comprehension in Chinese: Performing 'Comic Dialogs', Far Eastern Pub, 95; coauth, "NFLC Guide for Basic Chinese Language Programs, Pathway to Advanced Skills," Nat Foreign Lang Resource Cen, Ohio State Univ, (Columbus), 97; auth, "Jiao Waiji Renshi Huayuwen Ying Shuyide Wenti," World of Chinese Lang 86 (97): 67-74; auth, "Study Abroad as an Integral Part of the Chinese Language Curriculum", J Chinese Lang Teach Asn 3 (97): 15-31; auth, "A Framework for Basic Chinese Language Programs," J Chinese Lang Teach Asn 3 (97): 41-49; auth, "Recommendations of the U.S. National Task Force on Basic Chinese," CHUN 13 (97): 105-112. **CONTACT ADDRESS** Dept Asian Studies, Williams Col, 880 Main St, Williamstown, MA 01267. **EMAIL** ckubler@williams.edu

KUBY, MICHAEL
PERSONAL Born 08/15/1958, Philadelphia, PA, m, 1983, 2 children **DISCIPLINE** GEOGRAPHY **EDUCATION** Univ Chicago, AB, 80; Boston Univ, PhD, 88. **CAREER** Asst Prof to Assoc Prof, Ariz State Univ, 88-. **HONORS AND AWARDS** Applied Geography Citation Awd, 93; Franz Edelman Management Sci Achievement Awd, 94f. **MEMBERSHIPS** Asn of Am Geog. **RESEARCH** Transportation; Energy; Environment; Models; Geographic education; Tourism. **SELECTED PUBLICATIONS** Co-auth, "Modeling Spatial Impacts of Siting a NIMBY Facility," Transportation Research Record, (92): 133-140; co-auth, "Technological Change and the Concentration of the U.S. Liner Port System: 1970-1988," Economic Geography, (92): 272-289; co-auth, "The Hub Network Design Problem with Stopovers and Feeders: The Case of Federal Express," Transportation Research, (93): 1-12; co-auth, "Planning China's Coal and Electricity Delivery System," Interfaces, (95): 48-68; co-auth, "Proactive Optimization: A Multiobjective Technology Location Model for Designing Toxic Waste Systems," Location Science, (96), 167-185; co-auth, "The Implications of Structural Change, Reform and congestion for Freight Traffic in China," Asian Profile, (97): 1-21; co-auth, "A New Approach to Paleoclimatic Research Using Linear Programming," Palaeogeography, (97): 269-290; co-auth, "Supply side-Demand side Optimization and cost-Environment tradeoffs for China's coal and Electricity Delivery System," energy Policy, (97): 313-326. **CONTACT ADDRESS** Dept Geog, Arizona State Univ, PO Box 870104, Tempe, AZ 85287. **EMAIL** mikekuby@asu.edu

KUCZYNSKI, MICHAEL
DISCIPLINE MEDIEVAL STUDIES **EDUCATION** St Joseph's Univ, BA, 79; Univ NC, PhD, 87. **CAREER** Instr, 88. **SELECTED PUBLICATIONS** Auth, A Classical Allusion in Gulliver's Travels, The Explicator, 83; A New Manuscript of Nicholas of Lynn's Kalendarium, Oxoniensia, 86; Gower's Metaethics, John Gower: Recent Readings, Kalamazoo: The Medieval Inst, 89; A Fragment of Richard Rolle's Form of Living in MS Bodley 554, Bodleian Lib Record, 94; Prophetic Song: The Psalms as Moral Discourse in Late Medieval England, Univ Pa Press, 95. **CONTACT ADDRESS** Dept of Eng, Tulane Univ, 6823 St Charles Ave, New Orleans, LA 70118.

KUEHL, JOHN WILLIAM
PERSONAL Born 11/18/1941, Wausau, WI, m, 1966, 2 children **DISCIPLINE** AMERICAN HISTORY **EDUCATION** St Olaf Col, BA, 63; Univ Wis, Madison, MA, 64, PhD(hist), 68. **CAREER** Asst prof, 68-73, Assoc Prof Hist, Old Dominion Univ, 73-; Chmn Dept Hist, 81-87. **RESEARCH** American early national period; history of American thought. **SELECTED PUBLICATIONS** Auth, Justice, Republican Energy, and the Search for Middle Ground James Madison and the Assumption of State Debts, Va Mag Hist Biog, Vol 0103, 95. **CONTACT ADDRESS** Dept of Hist, Old Dominion Univ, Norfolk, VA 23508.

KUEHN, D. D.
PERSONAL Born 11/25/1952, Bismarck, ND, m, 1990 **DISCIPLINE** ARCHAEOLOGY; GEOARCHAEOLOGY **EDUCATION** Texas A&M Univ, PhD, 95. **CAREER** Assoc dir Ctr for Ecol Archaeol and adj asst prof, anthrop, Texas A&M Univ, 95-98; geoarchaeological consult, 95- ; asst prof, dept of sociol and anthrop, Luther Col, 98- . **HONORS AND AWARDS** Outstanding Student Research Paper Awd, Geol Soc Am, 93; dissertation award, 94; Interdisciplinary Research Initiative award, 94-96. **MEMBERSHIPS** Soc of Am Archaeol; Am Anthrop Asn; Soc for African Archaeol; Geol Soc Am; Olains Anthrop Soc. **RESEARCH** Geoarchaeology, stratigraphy, soils, site formation in archaeology; paleoenvironmental reconstruction; hunter-gatherer archaeology; arid landa; U.S. Great Plains, Midwest, Southwest, East Africa, Chile. **SELECTED PUBLICATIONS** Auth, Landforms and Archaeological Site Location in the Little Missouri Badlands: A New Look at Some Well Established Patterns, Geoarchaeology: An Int J, 93; auth, The Aggie Brown Member of the Oahe Formation: A Late Pleistocene/Early Holocene Marker Horizon in Western North Dakota, Current Res in the Pleistocene, 96; auth, A Geoarchaeological Assessment of Bison Kill Site Preservation in the Little Missouri Badlands, Plains Anthrop, 97; auth, Late Quaternary Vegetation and Climate Change in the North American Great Plains: Evidence from Stable Carbon Isotopic Composition of Paleosol Organic Carbon, Isotope Techniques in the Study of Environmental Change, 98; auth, Late Wisconsin-Age Proboscideans from Southern New Mexico, Texas J of Sci, forthcoming; auth, Stratigraphy and Non-Cultural Site Formation at the Shurmai Rockshelter, GnJm1, North-Central Kenya, Geoarchaeology: an Int J, forthcoming. **CONTACT ADDRESS** Dept of Sociology and Anthropology, Luther Col, 700 College Dr, Decorah, IA 52101. **EMAIL** kuehndav@luther.edu

KUEHN, MANFRED
DISCIPLINE THE HISTORY OF EARLY MODERN PHILOSOPHY **EDUCATION** McGill Univ, PhD. **CAREER** Prof, Purdue Univ. **RESEARCH** 18th century philosophy; Immanuel Kant, Hume, Reid. **SELECTED PUBLICATIONS** Auth, Scottish Common Sense in Germany, 1768-1800. **CONTACT ADDRESS** Dept of Philos, Purdue Univ, West Lafayette, 1080 Schleman Hall, West Lafayette, IN 47907-1080.

KUETHE, ALLAN JAMES
PERSONAL Born 02/01/1940, Waverly, IA, m, 1962, 4 children **DISCIPLINE** LATIN AMERICAN HISTORY **EDUCATION** Univ Iowa, BA, 62; Univ Fla, MA, 63, PhD(Latin Am hist), 67. **CAREER** Asst prof Latin Am hist, 67-72, assoc prof, 72-80, Prof Hist, Tex Tech Univ, 80-. **MEMBERSHIPS** AHA; Conf Latin Am Hist; InterUniv Sem Armed Forces and Soc. **RESEARCH** Bourbon reforms in eighteenth century New Granada and Cuba. **SELECTED PUBLICATIONS** Auth, The pacification campaign on the Riohacha Frontier, 1772-1779, Hisp Am Hist Rev, 70; The status of the Free Pardo in the disciplined militia of New Granada, J Negro Hist, 71; La batalla de Cartagena de 1741: Nuevas perspectivas, Historiografia y Bibliografia Americanistas, 74; Anastasio Zejudo en Nueva Granada, Boletin de Historia y Antiguedades, 77; Military Reform and Society in New Granada, Univ Press Fla, 78; Social Mobility in the Reformed Army of Colonial New Granada, Armed Forces & Soc, 79; La introduccion del sistema de milicias disciplinadas en America, Revista de Historia Militar, 79; The Development of the Cuban Military as a Socio-Political Elite, 1763-1783, The Hisp Am Hist Rev, 81. **CONTACT ADDRESS** Dept of Hist, Texas Tech Univ, Lubbock, TX 79409-0001.

KUHLMAN, ERIKA
PERSONAL Born 01/04/1961, Billimas, Canada, m, 1999 **DISCIPLINE** HISTORY, AMERICAN STUDIES **EDUCATION** Univ Mont, BA, 83; MA, 87; Wash State Univ, PhD, 95. **CAREER** Vis Instr, Univ of Mont, 89-91; Vis Prof, Idaho State Univ, 96-98; Adj Prof, Wash State Univ, 98-. **RESEARCH** Women's history. **SELECTED PUBLICATIONS** Auth, Petticoats and White Feathers, Greenwood Press, 97; auth, Famous Women in World History, Facts on File, forthcoming 01. **CONTACT ADDRESS** Dept Hist, Washington State Univ, Pullman, WA 99164-4030. **EMAIL** erika@completebbs.com

KUHN, GARY G.
PERSONAL Born 07/22/1937, St. Paul, MN **DISCIPLINE** LATIN AMERICAN HISTORY **EDUCATION** Univ MN, BA, 59, MA, 61, PhD, 65. **CAREER** Assoc Prof Hist to Prof Emeritus, Univ WI, La Crosse, 65-. **MEMBERSHIPS** Conf Latin Am Hist; NCent Coun Latin Americanists; Am Aviation Hist Soc. **RESEARCH** Latin American aeronautical hist; 19th century Central America; Latin American Aviation Historical Society. **SELECTED PUBLICATIONS** Auth, United States Maritime Influence in Central America, 1863-1865, Am Neptune, Vol XXXII No 4, 72; Liberian Contract Labor in Panama, 1887-1897, Liberian Studies J, 75. **CONTACT ADDRESS** 23-D Crusader Ave. E., West Saint Paul, MN 55118-4456. **EMAIL** ggkuhn@earthlink.net

KUISEL, RICHARD F.
PERSONAL Born 10/17/1935, Detroit, MI, m, 1960, 2 children **DISCIPLINE** MODERN EUROPEAN HISTORY **EDUCATION** Univ Mich, AB, 57; Univ Calif, MA, 59, PhD, 63. **CAREER** Instr Western civilization, Stanford Univ, 61-63; asst prof 20th century Europe, Univ Ill, 63-67; asst prof Mod Fr hist, Univ Calif, Berkeley, 67-70; assoc prof, 70-80, Prof Mod Fr Hist, State Univ NY Stony Brook, 80-; Am Coun Learned Soc fel, 76-77; Lehrman Inst fel, 76-78; nat selection comt, Soc Sci Res Coun, 76-78. **HONORS AND AWARDS** William Koren Prize, Soc Fr Hist Studies, 70. **MEMBERSHIPS** AHA; Soc Fr Hist Studies; Conf Group Fr Politics; Inst Fr Studies; Cent Int Univ dEtudes Europeennes. **RESEARCH** Modern French history; 20th century European history; economic policy. **SELECTED PUBLICATIONS CONTACT ADDRESS** Dept of Hist, SUNY, Stony Brook, Stony Brook, NY 11790.

KUKLA, REBECCA
DISCIPLINE HISTORY OF MODERN PHILOSOPHY, SOCIAL PHILOSOPHY, GENDER THEORY **EDUCATION** Univ Toronto, BA, 90; Univ Pittsburgh, PhD, 95. **CAREER** Asst prof, Univ NMex. **RESEARCH** The writing of Jean-Jacques Rousseau. **SELECTED PUBLICATIONS** Published in The Brit J for Psihol of Sci, Metaphilosophy, J of Speculative Philos, J of Brit Soc for Phenomenol, Poznan Stud, Eidos, and Anal, as well as contributing chapters to volumes on Rousseau, Feminist Theory, and Popular Cult. **CONTACT ADDRESS** Univ of New Mexico, Albuquerque, Albuquerque, NM 87131. **EMAIL** rkukla@ccs.carleton.ca

KUKLICK, BRUCE
PERSONAL Born 03/13/1941, Philadelphia, PA, m, 1982, 4 children **DISCIPLINE** HISTORY **EDUCATION** Univ Pa, BA, 63, MA, 66, PhD(Am civilization), 68; Bryn Mawr Col, MA, 65. **CAREER** From instr to asst prof philos, Am Studies Prog, Yale Univ, 68-72; Assoc Prof to Prof, 72-96, Nichols Prof Hist, Univ PA, 96-; ed, Am Quart, 74-83; Walt Whitman Prof, groningen, 92; guest prof Leuven, 96. **HONORS AND AWARDS** Am Coun Learned Soc fel, 73; Guggenheim fel, 76-77; fel, Ctr Advan Study Behav Sci, 78-79; Rockefeller Humanities fel, 82; NEH Fel, 93. **MEMBERSHIPS** Orgn Am Historians. **RESEARCH** Diplomatic history; American philosophy; philosophy of history; intellectual history; Am Philosophical Asn; Editorial bds: Journal of hist of ideas; journal of the history of philosophy; religion and am culture. **SELECTED PUBLICATIONS** Auth, The mind of the historian, Hist & Theory, 69; History as a way of learning, Am Quart, 70; Myth and symbol in American studies, Am Quart, 72; United States and the Division of Germany, Cornell Univ, 72; Josiah Royce, Bobbs, 72; Rise of American Philosophy, Yale Univ, 77; Churchmen and Philosophies, Yale, 85; The Good Ruler, Rutgers, 88; To Everything a Season, Princeton, 91; Puritans in Babylon, Princeton, 96. **CONTACT ADDRESS** Dept of History, Univ of Pennsylvania, 3401 Walnut St, Philadelphia, PA 19104-6228. **EMAIL** bkuklick@sas.upenn.edu

KULCZYCKI, JOHN
PERSONAL Born 04/27/1944, Milwaukee, WI, m, 1971 **DISCIPLINE** HISTORY **EDUCATION** Col of the Holy Cross, BS, 61; Columbia Univ, MA, 66; PhD, 73. **CAREER** Instr to asst prof, CUNY, Brooklyn, 72-75; res fel, Columbia Univ, 75-78; asst prof to prof, Univ of IL Chicago, 78-. **HONORS AND AWARDS** ACLS Grants, 68, 73, 77-78, 80, 87, 95; Herbert H Lehman Fel, 67-69; Kosciuszko Found Awd, 69-71, 73; Univ IL Chicago Grants, 80, 87, 88, 89-90, 93, 98; NEH Grant, 89. **MEMBERSHIPS** AHA; Am Assoc for the Advan of Slavic Studies; Polish Inst of Arts and Sci in Am. **RESEARCH** Modern Polish History. **SELECTED PUBLICATIONS** Auth, "A Trade Union for Polish Miners in the Ruhr: Alter Verband, Gewerkverein and Zjednoczenie Zawodowe Polski", Sozialgeschichte des Bergbaus im 19 und 20 Jahrhundert, ed Klaus Tenfeld, CH Book, (92): 609-622; auth, "Democratization and Nationalism in Contemporary Poland", Totalitarianism and the Challenge of Democracy, ed Andrzej W Jablonski and Wojciech Piasecki, Wydawnichtwo Univ Wrochlawskiego, (Wroclas, 92); 65-72; auth, "The Foreign Worker and the German Labor Movement: Xenophobia and Solidarity in the coal Fields of the Ruhr, 1871-1914, Berg Pub, (Oxford), 94; auth, "The First Migrants' Miner Associations in the Ruhr", Essays in Russian and East European History: Festschrift in Honor of Edward C Thaden, ed Leo Schelbert and Nick Ceh, East Europ Monographs, (Boulder, CO, 95); 101-115; auth, "Rural Transformation in Poland after 1945: The Polanization of the Recovered Lands", The Transformation of the Systems of East-Central Europe Rural Societies before and after 1989, ed Shingo Minamizuka, Tiberias BT, (Hungary, 96): 83-93; auth, The Polish Coal Miners' Union and the German Labor Movement in the Ruhr, 1902-1934: National and Social Solidarity, Berg, (Oxford, NY), 97; auth, "Working-Class Nationalism among Polish Migrants in the Ruhr Region", National Identities and Ethnic Minorities in Eastern Europe: Selected Papers from the Fifth World Congress of Central and East European Studies, Warsaw, 1995, ed Ray Taras, St Martins Pr, (98): 122-130; auth, "Language, National Identity, and Nationalism", Discourse on Multilingual Cultures: Popular Cultures, Societies and Art, ed Yuich Midzunoe, Taga Shuppan (Tokyo, 99): 389-394; auth, "Who's a Pole? Polish Nationality Criteria in the Recovered Lands, 1945 - 1951", Can Rev of Studies in Nationalism, (forthcoming); auth, The National Identity of the Natives of Poland's Recovered Lands, 1945 - 1956, (forthcoming). **CONTACT ADDRESS** Dept Hist, Univ of Illinois, Chicago, 601 S Morgan St, Chicago, IL 60607-7042. **EMAIL** kul@uic.edu

KULIKOWSKI, MARK
DISCIPLINE HISTORY **EDUCATION** SUNY Binghamton, BA; MA; PhD. **CAREER** Assoc prof, SUNY Oswego. **RESEARCH** 20th century Russ Am For Policy. **SELECTED PUBLICATIONS** Auth, articles, bk revs on Russ and East Europe, 79-. **CONTACT ADDRESS** Dept Hist, SUNY, Oswego, 427 Mahar Hall, Oswego, NY 13126.

KULIKOWSKI, MICHAEL
DISCIPLINE HISTORY **EDUCATION** Rutgers Col, BA, 91; Univ Toronto, MA, 92; Pont Inst Mediev stud, MSL, 96; Univ Toronto, PhD, 98. **CAREER** Vis asst prof, Wash-Lee Univ, 98-99; vis asst prof, Smith Col, 99-. **MEMBERSHIPS** AHA; MAA; RSBSC. **RESEARCH** Institutional and legal history of the early middle ages. **SELECTED PUBLICATIONS** Auth, "Two Councils of Turin," J Theol Stud 47 (96): 159-68; auth, "Gallo-Roman Poetry and the End of Antiquity," Ruminator 1 (96): 13-20; auth, "An English Abridgement of the Hispania of Autun at Antwerp," Feitschrift der Savigny-Stiftung fur Rechtsgeschichte, Kanonistische Abteilung 83 (97): 198-208; auth, "The Epistula Honorli, Again," Festschrift far Papyrologie und Epigraphik 122 (98): 247-52; auth, "Litterae, Legati, Nuntil: Communications in the Historia Roderici,is Latornus: Revue detudes latines 57 (98): 900-908; auth, "The Notitia Dignita turn as a Historical Source," in press, Historia (00); auth, "Barbarians in Gaul, Usurpers in Britain," forthcoming, Britannia 31(00); auth, "The Career of the Comes Hispaniarum Asterius, forthcoming, Phoenix (00). **CONTACT ADDRESS** Dept History, Smith Col, 98 Green St, Northampton, MA 01063-1000. **EMAIL** mkulikow@sophia.smith.edu

KUMMINGS, DONALD D.
PERSONAL Born 07/28/1940, Lafayette, IN, m, 1987, 2 children **DISCIPLINE** ENGLISH, AMERICAN STUDIES **EDUCATION** Pur Univ, BA, 62; MA, 64; Ind Univ, PhD, 71. **CAREER** Teach assoc, Pur Univ, 63-64; instr, Adrian Coll, 64-66; assoc instr, Ind Univ, 66-70; asst prof, Univ Wis, 70-75; assoc prof, 75-85; prof, 85-. **HONORS AND AWARDS** Prof of Year, Carnegie Found, 97; Reg Teach Excell Awd; Stella C Gray Dist Teach Awd, 77, 90; Posner Poet Prize, CWW, 90;

MEMBERSHIPS AAP; ALA; MLAA; WWA; WWBA; WFP. **RESEARCH** Walt Whitman; American poetry and poetics; Nineteenth-Century American literature; American short stories. **SELECTED PUBLICATIONS** Auth, "The Poetry of Democracies: Tocqueville's Aristocratic View," Comp Lit Stud 11 (74): 306-319; auth, "The Issue of Morality in James's The Golden Bowl," Ariz Quart 32 (76): 381-391; auth, "Walt Whitman's Vernacular Poetics," Can Rev Am Stud 7 (76): 119-131; auth, "Williams Paterson: The Vernacular Hero in the Twentieth Century," Am Poet 4 (86): 2-21; auth, Walt Whitman, 1940-1975: A Reference Guide, G K Hall (Boston), 82; auth, The Open Road Trip: Poems, Geryon Press (NY), 89; ed, "Approaches to Teaching Whitman's 'Leaves of Grass'," MLA (90); co-ed, Walt Whitman: An Encyclopedia, Garland Pub (NY and London), 98. **CONTACT ADDRESS** Dept English, Univ of Wisconsin, Parkside, PO Box 2000, Kenosha, WI 53141-2000. **EMAIL** d-p.kummings@worldnet.att.edu

KUNIHOLM, BRUCE ROBELLET

PERSONAL Born 10/04/1942, Washington, DC, d, 2 children **DISCIPLINE** HISTORY **EDUCATION** Dartmouth Col, BA, 64; Duke Univ, MA, 72, MAPPS & PhD, 76. **CAREER** Instr English, Robert Acad, Robert Col, Turkey, 64-67; from lectr policy sci & hist to prof, Duke Univ, 75-; mem, policy planning staff, Dept State, 79-80; dir, Terry Sanford Inst Pub Policy, 89-94; chemn dept, Duke Univ, 89-94; vis prof, Int Rels Koc U, Istanbul, 95-96; vice provost for acad and int affairs, Duke Univ, 96-; dir, Center for Int Studies, Duke Univ, 99- **HONORS AND AWARDS** Phi Beta Kappa; Stuart L Bernath Prize, Nat Endowment Humanities Int Affairs fel, Coun Foreign Rel, 78-79; Soc Historians Am Foreign Rel, 81; Decorated Bronze Star with V device; Distinguished Tchg award, Duke Univ, 89; res grant Harry S Truman Libr, 84; Duke Univ Res Coun, 85-86; Ctr Soviet and East European Stud grant, 91; Fulbright fel, Turkey, 86-87; sr fel Nobel Inst, 94. **MEMBERSHIPS** AHA; Orgn Am Historians; Soc Historians Am Foreign Rel; Middle East Inst; Coun Foreign Relations; Middle East Stud Asn; Int Inst Strategis Stud. **RESEARCH** Cold War; Arab-Israeli problem; United States policy in Persian Gulf; US-Turkish relations. **SELECTED PUBLICATIONS** Auth, The Origins of the Cold War in the Near East: Great Power Conflict and Diplomacy in Iran, Turkey, and Greece, Princeton Univ, 80, 94; auth, The Persian Gulf and United States Policy, 84; auth, The Palestine Problem and United States Policy, 86. **CONTACT ADDRESS** Office Provost, Duke Univ, PO Box 90006, Durham, NC 27706-0006. **EMAIL** Bruce.Kuniholm@duke.edu

KUNIHOLM, PETER IAN

PERSONAL Born 09/30/1937, Washington, DC, m, 1959, 2 children **DISCIPLINE** CLASSICAL ARCHAEOLOGY **EDUCATION** Brown Univ, AB, 58; Vanderbilt Univ, AM, 63; Univ Pa, PhD(class archaeol), 77. **CAREER** Instr English, Worcester Acad, Mass, 60-62; instr, house master, dean and dir athletics, Robert Col, Istanbul, Turkey, 62-68; instr, house master and dir athletics, Verde Valley Sch, Ariz, 68-70; fel, Am Res Inst, Turkey, 73-76, dir class archaeol, 74-76; Asst Prof Classics and Cur Class Antiq, Cornell Univ, 76-; Res fel classics, Cornell Univ, 77-78; from assoc prof to prof, 89-, history of art and archaeol, Cornelll Univ. **MEMBERSHIPS** Archaeol Inst Am; Am Inst Nautical Archaeol; Am Res Inst Turkey; Am Orient Soc; Brit Inst of Archaeol Ankara. **RESEARCH** Aegean dendrochronology and dendroclimatology; the Greek Dark Ages. **SELECTED PUBLICATIONS** Auth, Dendrochronology, Am J Archeol, Vol 0099, 95; The Absolute Chronology of the Aegean Early Bronze Age, Archeology, Radiocarbon and History, Am J Archeol, Vol 0100, 96. **CONTACT ADDRESS** Dept of Classics, Cornell Univ, 35 Goldwin Smith Hal, Ithaca, NY 14853-0001. **EMAIL** pik3@cornell.edu

KUNNIE, JULIAN

DISCIPLINE AFRICAN STUDIES **EDUCATION** United Theol Col, BD, 81; Pacific School of Relig, MA, 84; Grad Theol Union, Univ Calif, Berkeley, ThD, 90. **CAREER** Asst prof, theol, 90-94, chair, Intercultural Stud Program, 91-94, Valparaiso Univ; dir African Stud, asst prof relig, Kalamazoo Col, 94-96; assoc prof and acting dir African American Stud, Univ Arizona, 96- . **HONORS AND AWARDS** Lilly Found grant, 91; Newhall Fel, 87-88, 89-90; eight academic prizes from United Theol Col for academic excellence; Awd of Merit, 85; res grants, 90, 94; Kellogg Found grant 94, 96; Hum Res Initiative Grant, 96. **MEMBERSHIPS** Chemn, Indigenous Religious Traditions Sect, Am Acad of Relig; chemn, Ad Hoc Comm on African Study Abroad, Univ Ariz; African Stud Asn; Am Acad Relig/ Soc Bibl Lit; Asn for Study of Afro-American Life and Hist; Ed Advisory Board, Collegiate Press; Nat Coun for Black Stud; Nat Asn of Black Cultural Stud Centers; Southern African Asn for Culture and Develop Stud; Peace and Justice Comn; South African Asn for Literacy and Educ; Int Asn of Black Prof in Int Affairs; UMTAPO Center, S Africa. **RESEARCH** Systematic theology and philosophy; global religions; indigenous religions; ancient and contgemporary African religions; African politics; religions and society; Black religion and society in the United States; Black theologies; Third World liberation theologies; womanist and feminist theologies. **SELECTED PUBLICATIONS** Auth, Doing Social Analysis in Black Theology in Post-Apartheid Society in South Africa, in, Perspectives in Mission and Theology from South Africa: Signs of the Times, Mellen Research University, 93; auth, Models of Black Theology: Issues in Class, Culture, and Gender, Trinity, 94; auth, Black Churches in South Africa and the United States: Similarities and Differences, in, Afro-Christianity at the Grassroots, Brill, 94; auth, The Life, Thought, and Works of Desmond Tutu, in, The New Handbook of Christian Theologians, Abingdon, 96. **CONTACT ADDRESS** African Studies, Univ of Arizona, Martin Luther King Bldg, Room 305, PO Box 210128, Tucson, AZ 85721-0128. **EMAIL** jkunnie@u.arizona.edu

KUNZLE, DAVID M.

PERSONAL Born 04/17/1936, Birmingham, England, m, 1985, 2 children **DISCIPLINE** ART HISTORY **EDUCATION** Gonville and Caius Col, BA, 57; MA; London Univ, PhD, 64. **CAREER** Lectr, Nat Gallery; prof, Univ Calif, 62-64; prof, Unit Toronto, 64-65; prof, Santa Barbara, 65-73; prof, UCLA, 77-. **HONORS AND AWARDS** NEH, 66; ACLS, 77. **MEMBERSHIPS** CAA **RESEARCH** Intersection of art and politics; Popular art; Art of protest. **SELECTED PUBLICATIONS** Auth, Posters of Protest; auth, History of the Comic Strip (two vols: 1450-1825, 1826-1896); auth, Fashion and Fetishism; auth, Dagobert und Donald Duck; auth, Murals of Revolutionary Nicaragua; auth, Che Guevara, Icon Myth and Message; auth, From Criminal to Courtier: The Soldier in Netherlandish Art 1550-1670, (forthcoming). **CONTACT ADDRESS** Dept Art Hist, Univ of California, Los Angeles, 6265 Bunche, Box 951473, Los Angeles, CA 90095-1473. **EMAIL** kunzle@humnet.ucla.edu

KUO, LENORE

PERSONAL Born New York, NY **DISCIPLINE** METAPHYSICS, ETHICS AND THE HISTORY OF PHILOSOPHY **EDUCATION** Univ Wis, Madison, BA, MA, PhD. **CAREER** Assoc prof Philos and Women's Stud, Univ Nebr, Omaha, 85-. **RESEARCH** Social policy analysis. **SELECTED PUBLICATIONS** Published on topics as diverse as surrogate mothering, corruption in bureaucracy and recent U.S. attempts to require women to use Norplant (a form of birth control) as a condition of probation. **CONTACT ADDRESS** Univ of Nebraska, Omaha, Omaha, NE 68182.

KUPPERMAN, KAREN

DISCIPLINE HISTORY **EDUCATION** Univ Mo, BA, 61; Harvard Univ, MA, 62; Cambridge Univ, PhD, 78. **CAREER** Mellon Fac Fel, Harvard Univ, 80-81; Univ Conn, 78-95; Prof, New York Univ, 95-. **HONORS AND AWARDS** Albert A Beveridge Awd, Am Hist Asn, 95; Times-Mirror Foundation Distinguished Fel, Huntington Library, 95-96; Distinguished Alumna, Univ Mo, 92; NEH Fel, John Carter Brown Library, 89; Binkley-Stephenson Awd, Org of Am Hist, 80. **MEMBERSHIPS** Am Antiquarian Asn, Am Hist Asn, Am Soc for Ethnohistory, Asn of Caribbean Hist, Colonial Soc of Mass, Forum for European Expansion and Global Interaction, N England Hist Asn, OIEAHC, Org of Am Hist, Soc of Am Hist. **RESEARCH** Early modern Atlantic history, colonialism in seventeenth-century North America, American Indian history, ethnohistory. **SELECTED PUBLICATIONS** Auth, Indians and English: Facing Off in Early America, 00; auth, Major Problems in American Colonial History, 2nd ed, Boston, 00; auth, "Presentment of Civility: English Response to American Self-Presentation, 1580-1640," William and Mary Quarterly, (97): 193-228; auth, "A continent revealed: assimilation of the shape and Possibilities of North America's East Coast, 1524-1610," in North American Exploration, Univ Neb Press, 96; auth, "The founding Years of Virginia--and the United states," Virginia Magazine of History and Biography, (96): 103-112; auth, "The Beehive as a Model for Colonial Design," in America in European Consciousness, (95): 272-292; auth, "Scandinavian colonists confront the New world," New Sweden in America, Univ of Delaware Press, 95; auth, America in European consciousness, Chapel Hill, 95; auth, Providence Island, 1630-1641: The Other Puritan Colony, Cambridge, 93; auth, Roanoke: the abandoned colony, Totowa, NJ, 84. **CONTACT ADDRESS** Dept Hist, New York Univ, 53 Washington Square S, New York, NY 10012-1098. **EMAIL** karen.kupperman@nyu.edu

KURLAND, JORDAN EMIL

PERSONAL Born 07/18/1928, Boston, MA, m, 1947, 4 children **DISCIPLINE** HISTORY **EDUCATION** Boston Univ, AB, 49, AM 50; Columbia Univ, cert, 52. **CAREER** Instr hist, Univ NC, Greensboro, 54-57, asst prof hist and Russ, 57-65; staff assoc, 65-67, assoc secy, 67-69, Assoc Gen Secy, Am Asn Univ Profs, 69-; Instr and admin asst, Russ Inst, Columbia Univ, 55-56; Inter-Univ Comt Travel Grants exchange fel, 59-60; reserve off res and anal, US Info Agency, 60-; asst prof hist, Ind Univ, 62. **MEMBERSHIPS** AHA; Conf Slavic and East Europ Hist; Neth-Am Inst; Am Asn Advan Slavic Studies; Am Asn Teachers Slavic and East Europ Lang. **RESEARCH** Russian history and language; diplomatic history. **SELECTED PUBLICATIONS** Auth, Compromised Campus in the Collaboration of Universities With the Intelligence Community, 1945-1955, Slavic Rev, Vol 0052, 93. **CONTACT ADDRESS** General Secy, American Assn of Universities, Washington, DC 20036.

KURODA, TADAHISA

DISCIPLINE EARLY AMERICAN HISTORY **EDUCATION** Yale Col, BA; Columbia Univ, MA, PhD. **CAREER** Prof, Skidmore Col. **HONORS AND AWARDS** Winner, essay contest sponsored by, NY State Hist Asn & NY State Bicentennial Comn. **RESEARCH** Early national US hist. **SELECTED PUBLICATIONS** Auth, New York and the First Presidential Election, New York History LXIX, 88; The Origins of the Twelfth Amendment: The Electoral College in the Early Republic, Westport: Greenwood Press, 94; coauth, The United States: Creating the Republic, in Establishing Democracies, Boulder: Westview Press, 96. **CONTACT ADDRESS** Dept of Hist, Skidmore Col, 815 North Broadway, Saratoga Springs, NY 12866. **EMAIL** tkuroda@skidmore.edu

KURTZ, MICHAEL L.

PERSONAL Born 08/26/1941, New Orleans, LA, m, 1966, 1 child **DISCIPLINE** HISTORY **EDUCATION** Tulane Univ, PhD, 71. **CAREER** Prof of Hist & Govt, SE La Univ, 67-; Dean of Grad Sch, SE La Univ, 97-. **HONORS AND AWARDS** L Kemper Williams Prize for Best Manuscript (83) & Best Book (90) in La Hist. **MEMBERSHIPS** La Hist Asn; Southern Hist Asn; Org of Am Hist; Phi Alpha Theta; Author's Guild. **RESEARCH** JFK assassination; recent US history; recent Louisiana history. **SELECTED PUBLICATIONS** Coauth, Louisiana: A History, 3rd ed, 96; ed, Louisiana Since the Longs, 99; auth, Crime of the Century: The Kennedy Assassination From a Historian's Perspective, 2nd ed, 93; auth, Oliver Stone, JFK, and History, 00. **CONTACT ADDRESS** Grad School, Southeastern Louisiana Univ, SLU 10809, Hammond, LA 70402. **EMAIL** mkurtz@selu.edu

KUSHNER, HOWARD I.

DISCIPLINE HISTORY OF MEDICINE **EDUCATION** Rutgers Univ, AB, 65; Cornell Univ, MA, 68, PhD, 70. **CAREER** Prof & dir, MA in Liberal Arts & Science, San Diego State Univ; vis scholar, Univ Calif, San Diego, 94-; past Jennifer Allen Simons prof, Simon Fraser University's Harbour Ctr in Vancouver, BC; adj prof, Simon Fraser Univ; res on childhood movements disorders, Brown Univ Med School's Child Neuro-Psychiatric Develop Clinic and at the Neuropsychiatric Clinic at Children's Hospital, Univ BC, 94-; ed adv bd, J Hist NeuroSci; sci consult, Discovery Network's tv ser World of Wonder; John Adams Prof of Graduate Studies, San Digeo State Univ, 99-. **HONORS AND AWARDS** Nat Endowment for the Humanities, Sci, and Technol grant, $108,000, 94-96; San Diego State Univ Alumni Asn awd for Outstanding Fac Contrib to the Univ, 95; Univ Prof Performance awd(s), 96 and 97; Nat C Robertson Distinguished Prof of Science & Society, Emory Uni, 00. **RESEARCH** Historical and clinical aspects of Gilles de la Tourette's syndrome and associated neuropsychiatric disorders. **SELECTED PUBLICATIONS** Auth, American Suicide: A Psychocultural Exploration, Rutgers UP, 91; Chinese Translation San Min Book Co, Ltd., Taipei, Taiwan, 97; auth, Freud and the Diagnosis of Gilles de la Tourette's Illness, History of Psychiatry, (March 98): 1-25; auth, From Gilles de la Tourette's Disease to Tourette Syndrome, CNS Spectrums, (Feb 99): 24-35The Cursing Brain The Histories of Tourette Syndrome, Harvard UP, 99; auth, French Translation of A Cursing Brain, Paris: Institute d' Edition SanfiSynelabo, 01. **CONTACT ADDRESS** Dept of History, San Diego State Univ, 5500 Campanile Dr, San Diego, CA 92182. **EMAIL** hkushner@mail.sdsu.edu

KUSHNER, JAMES ALAN

PERSONAL Born 04/14/1945, Philadelphia, PA, m, 1970, 3 children **DISCIPLINE** LAW, CONSTITUTIONAL HISTORY, URBAN PLANNING **EDUCATION** Univ Miami, BBA, 67; Univ Md, LLB & JD, 68. **CAREER** Adj prof housing law, Univ Mo-Kansas City, 73; vis lectr, Univ Calif, Berkeley, 74-75; assoc prof, 75-78, Prof Law, Southwestern Univ, Calif, 78-; Consult, Am Bar Asn, 74-76; vis lectr, Univ Va, 81; vis prof, UCLA, 83 & 93. **HONORS AND AWARDS** Irving D. and Florence Rosenberg Prof, 00. **MEMBERSHIPS** Am Asn Law Schs. **RESEARCH** Race and Law; urban housing and planning. **SELECTED PUBLICATIONS** Auth, Apartheid in America, Carrollton Press, 80; Urban Transportation Planning, Urban Law & Policy, Vol 4, 81; Housing & Community Development (with Mandelker et al), Michie/Bobbs-Merrill, 81, 2nd ed, 89, 3rd ed, 99; The Reagan Urban Policy: Centrifugal Force in the Empire, UCLA J Environ Law & Policy, 82; Non-Owner Rights in Real Property and the Impact on Property Taxes, Urban Law & Policy, 85; Government Discrimination, West, 88; DMS: The Development Monitoring System is the Latest Technique for Subdivision Review and Growth Management, Zoning and Planning Law Report, 88; Unfinished Agenda: The Federal Fair Housing Enforcement Effort, Yale Law & Pol Review, 88; Substantive Equal Protection: The Rehnquist Court and the Fourth Tier of Judicial Review, Mo Law Rev, 88; The Fair Housing Amendments Act of 1988: The Second Generation of Fair Housing, Vanderbilt Law Rev, 89; Subdivision Law and Growth Management, West, 91; Property and Mysticism: The Legality of Exactions as a Condition for Public Development Approval in the Time of the Rehnquist Court, J Land Use & Environ Law, 92; Vested Development Rights, in 1992 Zoning and Planning Law Handbook, 92; A Tale of Three Cities: Land Development and Planning for Growth in Stockholm, Berlin, and Los Angeles, Urban Lawyer, 93; Growth Management and the City, Yale Law & Pol Rev, 94; Fair Housing: Discrimination in Real Estate, Community Development and Revitalization, 2nd ed, West, 95; Growth for the Twenty-First Century: Tales from Bavaria and the Vienna Woods -- Comparative Images of Urban Planning in Munich, Salzburg, Vienna, and the United States, Southern Calif Interdisciplinary Law J, 97; co-auth, Land Use Regulation: Cases and Materials, Aspen Law and Business, 99; co-auth, Housing and Community Development: Cases and Materials, 3rd ed, Carolina Acad Press, 99. **CONTACT ADDRESS** Southwestern Univ Sch of Law, 675 S Westmoreland Ave, Los Angeles, CA 90005-3905. **EMAIL** jkushner@swlaw.edu

KUSMER, KENNETH L.
PERSONAL Born 06/19/1945, Cleveland, OH, d **DISCIPLINE** HISTORY **EDUCATION** Oberlin Col, AB, 68; Kent State Univ, MA, 70; Univ Chicago, AM, 80; PhD, 80. **CAREER** From asst prof to prof, Temple Univ, 76-; vis assoc prof, Univ Pa, 84-85; Bancroft Prof of Am Hist, Univ Goettingen, 87-88. **HONORS AND AWARDS** Nominating Board, OAH, 86-88; Advisory Board, Balch Inst for Ethnic Studies, 85-; Board of Editors, J of Urban Hist, 98-03. **MEMBERSHIPS** OAH, AHA, Southern Hist Asn, Urban Hist Asn, Immigration Hist Soc. **RESEARCH** U.S. Social History, Afriecan American History, Ethnic History, History since 1865. **SELECTED PUBLICATIONS** Auth, A Ghetto Takes Shape: Black Cleveland, 1870-1930, Univ Ill Press (Urbana, IL), 76; ed, Black Communities and Urban Development in America, 1720-1990, Garland, 91; auth, "African Americans in the City since World War II," J of Urban Hist 21 (95); auth, "Toward a Comparative History of Racism and Xenophobia in the United States and Germany, 1865-1933," in Bridging the Atlantic: Germany and the United States in Modern Times, eds. Hermann Wellenreuther and Elisabeth Glaser (Cambridge, England: Cambridge Univ Press, 00); auth, Down and Out, On the Road: The Homeless in American Society, 1820-1970, Oxford Univ Press, in press. **CONTACT ADDRESS** Dept Hist, Temple Univ, 1115 W Berks St, Philadelphia, PA 19122-6006. **EMAIL** kkusmer@nimbus.temple.edu

KUTLER, STANLEY I.
PERSONAL Born 08/10/1934, Cleveland, OH, m, 1956, 4 children **DISCIPLINE** AMERICAN HISTORY **EDUCATION** Bowling Green State Univ, BA, 56; Ohio State Univ, PhD, 60. **CAREER** Teaching asst hist, Ohio State Univ, 58-59; vis instr, Ohio Wesleyan Univ, 59; instr, Pa State Univ, 60-62; asst prof, San Diego State Col, 62-64; from asst prof to assoc prof, 64-70, prof hist, 70-80, E Gordon Fox Prof Am Hist & Insts, Univ Wis-Madison, 80-, Am Philos Soc res grant, 61 & 63; Am Coun Learned Soc fel, 67-68; Russell Sage residency law & soc sci, 67-68; Guggenheim fel, 71-72; ed, Rev Am Hist, 73-; Fulbright lectr, Japan, 76-77. **MEMBERSHIPS** Orgn Am Historians; AHA; Am Soc Legal Hist. **RESEARCH** American legal and constitutional history. **SELECTED PUBLICATIONS** Auth, Ex Parte McCardle: Judicial Impotence?, in Am Hist Rev, 4/67; ed, Dred Scott Decision, Houghton, 67; Supreme Court and the Constitution, Norton, 68 & 77; auth, Judicial Power and Reconstruction Politics, Univ Chicago, 68; Privilege and Creative Destruction, Norton, 71 & 78; co-ed, New Perspectives on American Past (2 vols), Little, 71 & 74; auth, Looking for America (2 vols), Norton, 76 & 79; The American Inquisition: Justice and Injustice in the Cold War, Hill & Wang, 82; The Wars of Watergate, Norton, 92; Abuse of Power, The Free Press, 97. **CONTACT ADDRESS** Dept of Hist, Univ of Wisconsin, Madison, 455 North Park St, Madison, WI 53706-1483. **EMAIL** sikutler@facstaff.wisc.edu

KUTOLOWSKI, JOHN FRANCIS
PERSONAL Born 11/18/1931, Lynn, MA, m, 1971, 2 children **DISCIPLINE** MODERN EUROPEAN HISTORY **EDUCATION** Univ Mass, BA, 53; Univ Chicago, PhD, 66. **CAREER** Asst prof hist, Univ Dayton, 62-66; asst prof, 66-70, assoc prof hist, State Univ NY Col, Brockport, 70-. **MEMBERSHIPS** AHA; Polish Inst Arts & Sci Am. **RESEARCH** Victorian England; history of modern war. **SELECTED PUBLICATIONS** Auth, British Economic Interests and the Polish Insurrection of 1861-1864, The Polish Review, XXIX, 84; auth, Victorian Provincial Businessmen and Foreign Affairs: The Case of the Polish Insurrection, 1863-64, Northern History, XXI, 85; Auth, The West and Poland: Essays on Governmental and Public Relations to the Polish National Movement, 1861-64, Columbia Univ Pr, 00. **CONTACT ADDRESS** Dept of History, SUNY, Col at Brockport, 350 New Campus Dr, Brockport, NY 14420-2914. **EMAIL** jkut@frontiernet.net

KUTOLOWSKI, KATHLEEN SMITH
PERSONAL 2 children **DISCIPLINE** AMERICAN HISTORY **EDUCATION** Gettysburg Col, BA, 64; Cornell Univ, MA, 66; Univ Rochester, PhD(hist), 73. **CAREER** Instr, 70-73, asst prof, 73-81, assoc prof hist, State Univ NY Col Brockport, 81-. **HONORS AND AWARDS** Chancellor's Awd for Excellence in Teaching, State Univ NY, 77; NEH Fel, 84-85. **MEMBERSHIPS** Orgn Am Historians; Soc Historians Early Am Republic. **RESEARCH** Nineteenth century American social and political history. **SELECTED PUBLICATIONS** co-Auth, Commission and Canvasses: Politics and the Militia in Western New York, 1803-1845, 1/82; Freemasonry and Community in The Early Republic: The Case for Antimasonic Anxieties, American Quarterly, 82; Antimasonry Reexamined: Social Bases of the Grassroots Party, Journal of American History, 84; auth, The Social Composition of Political Leadership: Genesee County, New York, 1821-1860 (New York: Garland Publishing, Inc., 89). **CONTACT ADDRESS** Dept of History, SUNY, Col at Brockport, 350 New Campus Dr, Brockport, NY 14420-2914. **EMAIL** kkutolow@brockport.edu

KUTULAS, JUDY
PERSONAL Born 02/22/1953, San Francisco, CA, m, 1986, 2 children **DISCIPLINE** US HISTORY, AMERICAN STUDIES, WOMENS STUDIES **EDUCATION** Univ Cal, BA, 75; Univ Calif at Los Angeles, MA, 77; PhD, 86. **CAREER** Loyola Univ, 86; Univ St Thomas, 87; asst, assoc prof, St Olaf, 89-. **HONORS AND AWARDS** ACLS Gnt; NEH Trv Gnt; Newberry Lib Fel. **MEMBERSHIPS** AHA; OAH; PCA; ASA. **RESEARCH** 20th Century American liberals and radicals; media; gender. **SELECTED PUBLICATIONS** Auth, The Long War: The Intellectual People's Front and Anti-Stalinism, 1930-1940, Duke Univ Press (95). **CONTACT ADDRESS** Dept History, St. Olaf Col, 1520 St Olaf Ave, Northfield, MN 55057-1574. **EMAIL** kutulas@stolaf.edu

KUZDALE, ANN E.
PERSONAL Born 01/01/1958, Dunkirk, NY, s **DISCIPLINE** HISTORY AND MEDIEVAL STUDIES **EDUCATION** Boston Col, MA, hist, 80; Harvard Univ, MTS, church hist, 85; Univ Toronto, PhD, medieval studies (hist), 95. **CAREER** Instr, Trent Univ, Peterborough, Ont, 96; asst prof, Chicago State Univ, 96-. **HONORS AND AWARDS** Pontifical Inst of Medieval Studies res assoc, 95-96. **MEMBERSHIPS** AHA; AAR; Cath Hist Asn; North Amer Patristics Soc; Ital Hist Soc; Hagiography Soc. **RESEARCH** Late antiquity; Early middle ages; Hagiography; Papacy. **SELECTED PUBLICATIONS** Book rev, Jour of the Amer Acad of Relig, v 66, 191-194, spring, 98. **CONTACT ADDRESS** History Dept., Chicago State Univ, 9501 S. King Dr., Chicago, IL 60628-1598. **EMAIL** ae-kuzdale@csu.edu

KUZMIC, PETER
PERSONAL Born 06/26/1946, Nuskova, Slovenia, m, 1973, 3 children **DISCIPLINE** WORLD MISSIONS, EUROPEAN STUDIES **EDUCATION** S Calif Col, BA; Wheaton Col Grad Sch, MA; Univ Zagreb, MTh, DTh. **CAREER** Dir, Evangel Theol Sem, Osijek, Croatia; ch, Theol Commn of World Evangel Fel, 86; Eva B. and Paul E. Toms Distinguished prof, Gordon-Conwell Theol Sem, 93-. **HONORS AND AWARDS** Hon DD degree award, Asbury Theol Sem, 92; co-founder, ch, coun evangelical christians of (former) yu; pres, protestant evangel coun croatia; founding pres, agape and new europe vision.; founding exec, coun evangel christians of yu. **MEMBERSHIPS** Mem, Lausanne Comm for World Evangelization, AAR, SBL, FEET, Rotary Club, Helsinki Committee for Human Rights. **RESEARCH** Hermeneutics, Gospel and Culture. **SELECTED PUBLICATIONS** Pub(s), On The Influence of Slavic Bible Translations Upon Slavic Literature, Language and Culture; auth, The Gospel of John and Biblical Hermeneutic; ed, Izvori. **CONTACT ADDRESS** Gordon-Conwell Theol Sem, 130 Essex St, South Hamilton, MA 01982. **EMAIL** pkuzmia@gcts.edu

KUZMINSKI, ADRIAN
PERSONAL Born 02/21/1944, Washington, PA, m, 1966, 2 children **DISCIPLINE** HISTORY, PHILOSOPHY **EDUCATION** Amherst Col, BA, 66; Univ of Rochester, PhD, 73. **CAREER** Prof of Hist, 71-80, Univ of Hawaii; Res Scholar in Philos, 96-, Hartwick Coll. **HONORS AND AWARDS** Fulbright and Wilson Fellow. **MEMBERSHIPS** APA **RESEARCH** Consciousness, political economy. **SELECTED PUBLICATIONS** The Soul, Peter Lang Pub, NY, 94. **CONTACT ADDRESS** RD #1, Box 68, Fly Creek, NY 13337. **EMAIL** adrian@clarityconnect.com

KUZNICK, PETER J.
PERSONAL Born Brooklyn, NY, d, 1 child **DISCIPLINE** HISTORY **EDUCATION** Rutgers Univ, PhD, 84. **CAREER** Dir, Nuclear Studies Inst, 95-; assoc prof, hist, Amer Univ, 86-. **HONORS AND AWARDS** Woodrow Wilson fel; Smithsonian Postdoctoral fel; NEH summer fel. **MEMBERSHIPS** AHA; OAH. **RESEARCH** U.S. cultural history; Recent American history; Nuclear history; Radicalism; History and film. **SELECTED PUBLICATIONS** Auth, Beyond the Laboratory: Scientists as Political Activists in 1930s America, Univ Chicago Press, 87; coed, Rethinking Cold War Culture. **CONTACT ADDRESS** Dept. of History, American Univ, Washington, DC 20016. **EMAIL** kuznick@american.edu

KUZNIEWSKI, ANTHONY JOSEPH
PERSONAL Born 01/28/1945, Carthage, MO **DISCIPLINE** AMERICAN HISTORY, CHURCH HISTORY **EDUCATION** Marquette Univ, AB, 66; Harvard Univ, AM, 67, PhD(hist), 73; Loyola Univ Chicago, MDiv, 80. **CAREER** Teaching fel hist, Harvard Univ, 68-72; asst prof, Col Holy Cross, 74-76 and Loyola Univ Chicago, 80-81; Asst Prof Hist, Col Holy Cross, 81-; Res tutor hist, Kirkland, House Harvard Col, 70-72; Vis lectr, Loyola Univ Chicago, 76-77. **HONORS AND AWARDS** Oscar Halecki Awd, Polish Am Hist Asn and Am Hist Asn, 81. **MEMBERSHIPS** Polish Am Hist Asn (pres, 82-83); Am Cath Hist Asn; Orgn Am Historians. **RESEARCH** Polish immigrants in the United States; the religious life of Polish Americans; the interaction of various Catholic immigrant groups in the United States. **SELECTED PUBLICATIONS** Auth, Boot straps or book learning?: Reflections on the education of Polish Americans, Polish Am Studies, 75; Polish Catholics in America, In: Catholics in America, Nat Conf Cath Bishops, 76; Milwaukee's Poles, 1866-1918: The rise and fall of a model community, Milwaukee Hist, 1/78; The Catholic Church in the life of the Polish Americans, In: Poles in America: Bicentennial Essays, Worzalla Publ Co, 78; Faith and Fatherland: The Polish Church War in Wisconsin, 1896-1918, Univ Notre Dame Press, 80. **CONTACT ADDRESS** Dept of Hist, Col of the Holy Cross, Worcester, MA 01610.

KWOK, D. W. Y.
PERSONAL Born 09/03/1932, Shanghai, China, m, 1954, 2 children **DISCIPLINE** CHINESE HISTORY **EDUCATION** Brown Univ, BA, 54; Yale Univ, PHD, 59. **HONORS AND AWARDS** Tan Kah Kee Chair in Hist, Nanyang Technol Univ, Singapore, 98; Hon Prof, State Comn on Educ, China. **MEMBERSHIPS** Asn Asian Studies; AHA. **RESEARCH** Mod Chinese intellectual hist; early mod Chinese hist; late Ming thought. **SELECTED PUBLICATIONS** Auth, Scientism in Chinese Thought, 1900-1950, Yale Univ, 65; Anarchism and traditionalism, J Inst Chinese Studies, Univ Hong King, 12/71; contrib, Chinas grosse wandlung, C H Beck, 72; Die Sohne des Drachen, List Verlag, Munich, 74; Chinas Handbuch, Bertelsmann, Dusseldorf, 74; Ming Biographical Dictionary, Columbia Univ, 76; Mao Tsetung and Populism, Centre Asian Studies, Univ Hong Kong, 79; coauth, Cosmology, Ontology, and Human Efficacy, Univ Hawaii, 93; ed & transl, Turbulent Decade, Univ Hawaii, 96; auth, The Urbane Imagination, Kendall/Hunt, 97. **CONTACT ADDRESS** Dept of Hist, Univ of Hawaii, Manoa, 2530 Dole St, Honolulu, HI 96822-2303. **EMAIL** dkwok@hawaii.edu

KYLE, DONALD G.
PERSONAL Born 06/26/1950, Westmount, QC, Canada, m, 1980, 2 children **DISCIPLINE** HISTORY **EDUCATION** York Univ, BA, 73; McMaster Univ, MA, 74; Univ Toronto, BEd, 77; McMaster, PhD, 81. **CAREER** Lecturer, Univ Winnipeg, 80-81; Vis Asst Prof, Univ Saskatchewan, 81-84; Asst Prof to Prof and Chair, Univ Tex, 84-. **HONORS AND AWARDS** Golladay Liberal Arts Teaching Awd, 00; Acad of distinguished Teachers, 99; Chancellor's Awd for Excellence in teaching, 90; Soc Sci and Humanities Res Coun of Canada Fel, 80; Canada Coun Fel, 79; Dalley Fel, McMaster Univ, 74-76 **MEMBERSHIPS** Am Hist Asn, N Am Soc for Sport History, Classical Asn of Canada, Archaeol Inst of Am, Asn of Ancient Hist. **RESEARCH** Greek and Roman history, Ancient sport. **SELECTED PUBLICATIONS** Auth, "Inside the Roman Arena," Archaeology Odyssey, (00): 14-25; auth, Spectacles of Death in Ancient Rome, Routledge Press, 98; auth, "Games, Prizes and Athletes in Greek Sport: Patterns and Perspectives," classical Bulletin, (98): 103-127; auth, "The First 100 Olympiads: A Process of Decline or democratization?," Nikephoros, (97): 53-75; auth, "Gifts and glory: Panathenaic and Other Greek Athletic Prizes," in Worshipping Athena: Panathenaia and Parthenon, 96; auth, "Winning at Olympia," Archaeology, (96): 26-37, 75; auth, "Philostratus, Repechage, Running and Wrestling: The Greek Pentathlon ?Again," Journal of Sport History, (95): 60-65. **CONTACT ADDRESS** Dept Hist, Univ of Texas, Arlington, Box 19529, Arlington, TX 76019. **EMAIL** kyle@uta.edu

KYTE, GEORGE WALLACE
PERSONAL Born 03/01/1918, Berkeley, CA **DISCIPLINE** HISTORY **EDUCATION** Univ Calif, AB, 40, MA, 41, PhD, 43. **CAREER** Assoc res analyst, res br, off Strategic Serv, 43-45; from instr to assoc prof hist, Lehigh Univ, 46-66; assoc prof, 66-68, Prof Hist to Prof Emer, Northern Ariz Univ, 68-. **MEMBERSHIPS** AHA; Orgn Am Historians; Conf Brit Studies; Conf Early Am Hist. **RESEARCH** Anglo-American colonial history in the 18th century; British Empire history and Anglo-American colonial history; American colonial history, especially the War for American Independence. **SELECTED PUBLICATIONS** Auth, Bouligny,Francisco in A Bourbon Soldier in Spanish Louisiana, Am, Vol 0051, 94. **CONTACT ADDRESS** Dept of Hist, No Arizona Univ, Box 5718, Flagstaff, AZ 86011.

KYVIG, DAVID E.
PERSONAL Born 03/08/1944, Ames, IA, m, 1988, 2 children **DISCIPLINE** HISTORY **EDUCATION** Kalamazoo Col, BA, 66; Northwestern Univ, PhD, 71. **CAREER** Archivist, Nat Archives and Records Service, 70-71; asst prof and dir of Am Hist Res Center, Univ of Akron, 71-79; vis asst prof, Kalamazoo Col, 72; asssoc prof of hist and consult archivist, Univ of Akron, 79-85; prof, Univ of Akron, 85-99; fulbright prof, Univ of Tromso, 87-88; prof to presidential res prof, N Ill Univ, 99-. **HONORS AND AWARDS** Phi Beta Kappa, Kalamazoo Col, 66; Newberry Libr Fel, 79; ACLS Fel, 80-81; NEH Summer Stipend, 86; Ohio Acad of Hist Pub Awd, 97; Henry Adams Prize, Soc for Hist in the Federal Govt, 97; Bancroft Prize in Am Hist, 97; Presidential Res Professorship, N Ill Univ, 00-.

MEMBERSHIPS Alcohol and Temperance Hist Group, Am hist Asn, Am Soc for Legal Hist, Dirksen Congressional Center Board of Trustees, Nat Coun of Public Hist, Ohio Acad of Hist, Org of Am Historians, Soc for Hist in the Federal Govt. **RESEARCH** Twentieth century United States history with a focus on constitutional amendments, national prohibition, the New Deal, and recent America. **SELECTED PUBLICATIONS** Ed, FDR's America, Forum Press (St. Louis, MO), 76; coauth, Your Family History: A Handbook for Research and Writing, Harlan Davidson (Arlington Hights, IL), 78; auth, Repealing National Prohibition, Univ of Chicago Press (Chicago, IL) 79, Kent State Univ Press (Kent, OH), 00; coauth, Nearby History: Exploring the Past Around You, Am Asn for State and Local Hist (Nashville, TN), 82; ed, Law, Alcohol, and Order: Perspectives on National Prohibition, Greenwood Press (Westport, CT), 85; coauth, New Day/New Deal: A Bibliography of the Great American Depression 1929-1941, Greenwood Press (Westport, CT), 88; ed, Reagan and the World, Greenwood Press (Westport, CT), 90, Praeger (New York, NY), 90. **CONTACT ADDRESS** Dept Hist, No Illinois Univ, 1425 W Lincoln Hwy, Dekalb, IL 60115-2828. **EMAIL** kyvig@niu.edu

L

LA FORTE, ROBERT SHERMAN

PERSONAL Born 09/08/1933, Frontenac, KS, m, 1959, 3 children **DISCIPLINE** UNITED STATES HISTORY & BIBLIOGRAPHY **EDUCATION** Kans State Col Pittsburg, BSE & MS, 59; Univ Tex, Austin, MLS, 68; Univ Kans, PhD(hist), 66. **CAREER** From instr to asst prof hist, East Tex State Univ, 64-67; from asst prof to assoc prof, 68-74, prof hist, N Tex State Univ, 77-00, prof emer, 00-, dept chair, 89-93, Univ Archivist, 75-85, Higher Educ Act fel, 67-68. **HONORS AND AWARDS** UNT Pres Teaching Awd, 92; Shelton Teaching Awd, 94; 'Fessor' Graham Awd, 95. **MEMBERSHIPS** The Hist Soc. **RESEARCH** Nineteenth and Twentieth century United States; History of Kansas. **SELECTED PUBLICATIONS** Auth, Leaders in Reform, Kansas' Progressive Republicans, Univ Kans, 74; Down the Corridor of Years, A Centennial History of U.N.T., 1890-1990, UNT Press, 89; co-ed, Remembering Pearl Harbor, SR Books, 91; co-ed, Building the Death Railway, SR Books, 93; co-ed, With Only the Will to Live, SR Books, 94. **CONTACT ADDRESS** Dept of Hist, Univ of No Texas, PO Box 310650, Denton, TX 76203-0650. **EMAIL** cb36@jove.unt.edu

LACCETTI, SILVIO R.

PERSONAL Born 01/14/1941, Teaneck, NJ **DISCIPLINE** MODERN EUROPEAN HISTORY, URBAN STUDIES **EDUCATION** Columbia Univ, AB, 62, MA, 63, PhD(Europ hist), 67. **CAREER** From instr to full prof, 65-01, Prof Humanities, Stevens Inst Technol, 88-; Spec adv, Hudson County Dist Atty Off, 68-70; educ consult, NJ Regional Drug Abuse Agency, 70; exec dir, N Bergen Drug Prog, Inc, 70-72; planning consult, N Hudson Mayon's Coun, 71-72; prof dir, Citizenship Inst, 74-76; chmn, Hudson Bicentennial Cong, 74-76; gen ed, Pub Policy Series, Commonwealth Books; Danforth Teaching Assoc, 78-; NJ Master Fac prog, 89-91; Stevens Teacher of the Year, 90, 93; Embroidery Ind. Assistance Proj, 95-01; Com Sems, 98-00; Brownfields Commissioner, 98-01. **MEMBERSHIPS** AAUP **RESEARCH** Drug abuse education; municipal studies; international politics; regional econ; embroidery industry, leadership studies. **SELECTED PUBLICATIONS** Co-ed, The City in Western Civilization, Vol I, In: Cities in Civilization, Speller, 71; auth, Drug Dilemma, J Forum Contemp Hist, 1/73; Dialogue on Drugs, Exposition, 74; ed, New Jersey Colleges and Vocational Schools, 77, Casebook in New Jersey Studies, 78 & contribr, Major Development Plans for New Jersey, In: Casebook for New Jersey Studies, 78, Wm Wise; NJ Profiles in Public Policy, Commonwealth, 90; auth, Embroidery Industry in the Global Economy. **CONTACT ADDRESS** Dept of Humanities Stevens, Stevens Inst of Tech, 1 Castle Point Ter, Hoboken, NJ 07030-5991.

LACEY, BARBARA E.

DISCIPLINE HISTORY **EDUCATION** Smith Coll, BA, 58; Univ Conn, MA, 71; Clark, PhD, 82. **CAREER** Prof, Hist, St. Joseph Coll. **MEMBERSHIPS** Am Antiquarian Soc **SELECTED PUBLICATIONS** Auth, "The World Hannah Heaton: Autobiography an 18th Century Connecticut Farm Woman," Wm & Mary Quart 45, 88; auth, "Gender, Piety and Secularization in Connecticut Religion, 1720-1775," Jour of Soc Hist, Summer 91; auth, "Visual Images of Blacks in Early American Imprints," Wm & Mary Quart 53, 96. **CONTACT ADDRESS** Dept of Hist & Pol Sci, Saint Joseph Col, 1678 Asylum Ave, West Hartford, CT 06117. **EMAIL** blacey@sjc.edu

LACEY, JAMES

PERSONAL Born 10/15/1933, New York, NY, m, 1958, 2 children **DISCIPLINE** AMERICAN STUDIES **EDUCATION** St Peter's Col, AB, 55; Boston Col, MA, 58; NYork Univ, PhD(Am civilization), 68. **CAREER** From instr to asst prof English, St Francis Col, NY, 58-68; assoc prof, 68-71, Prof Am Lit and Am Studies, Eastern Conn State Col, 71-, Ger Acad Exchange Serv res grant, Am Inst, Univ Munich, 65-66; Dir, Univ Honors Program, 93-. **MEMBERSHIPS** MLA; Am Studies Asn; Aaup; Vice President, Northeast Region of the National Collegiate Honors Council, NE-NCHC, 99-00; Pres, NE-NCHC, 00-01. **RESEARCH** American literature and history; Henry David Thoreau in German criticism, 1881-1965. **SELECTED PUBLICATIONS** Auth, The 1994 American Studies Conference in Tubingen, Amer Stud Int, Vol 0032, 94; The 1995 American Studies Conference in Hamburg, Amer Stud Int, Vol 0033, 95. **CONTACT ADDRESS** Dept of English, Eastern Connecticut State Univ, 83 Windham St, Willimantic, CT 06226-2211. **EMAIL** lacey@mail.ecsu.ctstateu.edu

LACHAN, KATHARINE

PERSONAL Born Ottawa, ON, Canada **DISCIPLINE** PRINTS, DRAWINGS **EDUCATION** Univ Toronto, BA, 68, MA, 71; Univ London, Courtauld Inst, PhD, 82. **CAREER** Cur asst, European dept, ROM, 68-69; cur asst, 69-71, asst cur, 71-76, Curator, Prints & Drawings, Art Gallery Ont 76-; fac mem, Art Hist, Univ Toronto, 92-. **HONORS AND AWARDS** J. Paul Getty Trust, Scholar, 87; Awd Merit, Ryerson Polytechnic Inst, 91. **MEMBERSHIPS** Can Museum Asn; Master Print and Drawing Soc Ont; Massey Col, Univ Toronto; Print Coun Am; William Soc Can; Opera Atelier; Toronto Hist Board. **SELECTED PUBLICATIONS** Auth, The Etchings of James McNeil Whistler, 84; auth, Whistler's Etchings and the Sources of His Etching Style, 87; coauth, The Earthly Paradise: Arts and Crafts by William Morris and His Circle of Friends from Canadian Collections, 93. **CONTACT ADDRESS** Art Gallery of Ontario, 317 Dundas St W, Toronto, ON, Canada M5S 1A1.

LADD, DORIS

PERSONAL Born 12/17/1933, Los Angeles, CA, 1 child **DISCIPLINE** HISTORY **EDUCATION** Stanford Univ, AB, 55, MA, 56 & 63, PhD(Hist), 70. **CAREER** Teacher Span & Biol, High Schs, Calif, 56-59; teacher English, USIA Schs, Lucca, Italy, 59, Madrid, 60-63; instr Hist, Col Notre Dame, Belmont, 70; asst prof Hist, Univ Hawaii, Manoa, 70-, asst prof Hist, Univ Tex, Austin, 74-76. **HONORS AND AWARDS** Bolton Prize, Conf Latin Am Hist, AHA, 77. **MEMBERSHIPS** Conf Latin Am Hist; AHA. **RESEARCH** Mexico; social & economic history; women. **SELECTED PUBLICATIONS** Coauth, Simon Bolivar and Spanish American Independence, Anvil, 68; auth, The Mexican Nobility at Independence, Univ Tex, 76; contribr, The Solitude of Self by Elizabeth Cady Stanton, Press Pacifica, 78; The Making of a Strike, 88. **CONTACT ADDRESS** Dept of History, Univ of Hawaii, Manoa, 2530 Dole St, Honolulu, HI 96822-2303.

LADEWIG, JAMES L.

DISCIPLINE MUSIC HISTORY, MUSICOLOGY, MUSIC APPRECIATION **EDUCATION** Northwestern Univ, BM, 71; Univ CA, Berkeley, MA, 73, PhD, 78. **CAREER** Prof; Univ RI, 85-; taught at, Vassar Col & Wellesley Col; vis scholar, Harvard Univ; past ed, nat Newletter, Am Musicol Soc. **HONORS AND AWARDS** Am Coun Learned Soc & URI Found, grants. **MEMBERSHIPS** Am Musicol Soc; Soc for 17th-century Music & Renaissance Soc Am; past pres, New Eng Chap, Am Musicol Soc. **RESEARCH** Renaissance and Baroque eras; instrumental and keyboard music of Italy. **SELECTED PUBLICATIONS** Publ on, Variation canzona, Frescobaldi, Luzzaschi I Bach; in, J Musicol, Frescobaldi Stud & Studi Musicali; completed ed, 30-vol series Italian Instrumental Music of the 16th and Early 17th Centuries: Previously Unpubl Full Scores of Major Works from the Renaissance and Early Baroque, New York & London: Garland Publ. **CONTACT ADDRESS** Dept of Music, Univ of Rhode Island, 8 Ranger Rd, Ste. 1, Kingston, RI 02881-0807.

LAEL, RICHARD LEE

PERSONAL Born 09/16/1946, NC, m, 1987, 2 children **DISCIPLINE** HISTORY, US DIPLOMATIC HISTORY **EDUCATION** Lenoir-Rhyne Col, BA, 68; Univ NC, Chapel Hill, MA, 72, PhD, 76. **CAREER** Instr, NC State Univ, 75-77, vis asst prof, 77-78; asst prof, 78-84, assoc prof, 84-90, prof, Westminster Col, 91-, chair, Div of Humanities, 98-. **HONORS AND AWARDS** MO Conference of Hist Distinguished Book Awd for The Yamashita Precedent, 83. **MEMBERSHIPS** Org Am Historians; Soc for Historians of Am Foreign Relations; Phi Alpha Theta (Hist Honor Soc). **RESEARCH** War crimes; Latin America; local hist. **SELECTED PUBLICATIONS** Auth, The Yamashita Precedent: War Crimes and Command Responsibility, 82; co-auth with Dr Linda Killen, Versailles and After: An Annotated Bibliography of American Foreign Relations, 1919-1933, 83; auth, Arrogant Diplomacy: US Policy Toward Columbia, 1903-1922, 87; The Rating Game in American Politics: An Interdisciplinary Approach, ed Ann McLaurin and William Pederson, 87; The War of 1989 and US Interventions, 1898-1934, ed Benjamin Beede, 94; articles in the following journals: Diplomatic History, 78; Mid-America, 79; Business History Rev, 82. **CONTACT ADDRESS** Dept of History, Westminster Col, Missouri, 501 Westminster Ave, Fulton, MO 65251-1299. **EMAIL** laelr@jaynet.wcmo.edu

LAFEBER, WALTER

PERSONAL Born 08/30/1933, Walkerton, IN, m, 1955, 2 children **DISCIPLINE** AMERICAN HISTORY **EDUCATION** Hanover Col, BA, 55; Stanford Univ, MA, 56; Univ Wis, PhD, 59. **CAREER** Asst prof Am hist, 59-63, from assoc prof to prof, 63-68, chmn dept, 68-69, Noll prof hist, Cornell Univ, 68-, Soc Sci Res Coun grant, 63-64; Am Philos Soc grant, 67-68; Guggenheim Fel, 90; mem adv comt, Hist Div, US Dept of State, 71-74; commonwealth lectr, Univ London, 73; Edmundson lectr, Baylor Univ, 80. **HONORS AND AWARDS** Clark Teaching Awd, Col Arts & Sci, Cornell Univ, 66; Albert J Beveridge Awd, AHA, 62; Bancroft Prize, 98; Hawley Prize, 98, Weiss Presidential teaching Fel, 94-99. **MEMBERSHIPS** AHA; Orgn Am Historians; Soc Historians Foreign Rels; Soc of Am Historians. **RESEARCH** American diplomatic history. **SELECTED PUBLICATIONS** Auth, The New Empire: An Interpretation of American Expansion, 1860-1898, Cornell Univ, 63; John Quincy Adams and American Continental Empire, Quadrangle, 65; America, Russia, and the Cold War, 67, rev ed, 72, 76, 80, 85, 91, 93, 97, & The United States and the Cold War: 20 Years of Revolution and Response, 69, Wiley; coauth, Creation of the American Empire, Rand McNally, 73, rev ed, 76; The American Century, Wiley, 75, rev ed, 79.97; auth, The Panama Canal: The Crisis in Historical Perspective, Oxford Univ, 78, 89; The Third Cold War, Baylor Univ, 81; auth, Inevitable Revolutions: The U.S. in Central America, 83, 92; The American Search for Opportunity 1865-1912, 93; The Clash: the United States and Japan Throughout History, 97; auth, Michael Jordan and the New Global Capitalism, 99. **CONTACT ADDRESS** Dept of History, Cornell Univ, Mcgraw Hall, Ithaca, NY 14853-0001. **EMAIL** wlf3@cornell.edu

LAFONTANT, JULIEN J.

PERSONAL Born Port-au-Prince, Haiti, m **DISCIPLINE** FRENCH, BLACK STUDIES **EDUCATION** SUNY Binghamton, MA (distinction) 1974, PhD 1976. **CAREER** Exec Mansion Morovia Liberia, translator 1961-63; Ivory Coast Embassy Monrovia Liberia, translator 1963-66; Cuttington Coll Suakoko Liberia, asst prof 1966-72; SUNY Binghamton, teaching asst 1972-76; Univ of NE Lincoln, asst prof 1976-77; Acting Chair Black Studies UNO, asst prof 1977-78; Univ of NE, assoc prof 1978-82, full prof French Chair Black Studies UNO 1983-85; full prof French and Black Studies 1986-98; full prof french, 98-. **HONORS AND AWARDS** Great Teacher Awd Univ of NE Omaha 1982. **MEMBERSHIPS** Fr Review; Nineteenth Century Fr Studies. **SELECTED PUBLICATIONS** book on Montesquieu; book entitled Understanding A Culture; several articles dealing with the Black exper in general and the French encounter with Blacks. **CONTACT ADDRESS** Dept of Foreign Languages, Univ of Nebraska, Omaha, Omaha, NE 68182-0001. **EMAIL** julien_lafontant@unomaha.edu

LAGEMANN, ELLEN CONDLIFFE

PERSONAL Born 12/20/1945, New York, NY, m, 1969, 1 child **DISCIPLINE** AMERICAN AND WOMEN'S HISTORY **EDUCATION** Smith Col, AB, 67; Columbia Univ, MA, 68, PhD(hist and educ), 78. **CAREER** Asst prof, 78-81, Assoc Prof Hist and Educ, Teachers Col, Columbia Univ, 81-, Res Assoc, Inst Philos and Politics Educ, 78-. **HONORS AND AWARDS** Outstanding res award, Nat Soc of Fund Raising Executives for The Politics of Knowledge: The Carnegie Corporation, Philanthropy, and Public Policy, 89; Critics' Choice Award, Am Educational Studies Asn, for Private Power for the Public Good: A History of the Carnegie Found for the Advancement of Teaching; Outstanding Mentor Award, Spencer Found, 94. **MEMBERSHIPS** Hist Educ Asn; AHA; Orgn Am Historians; Coord Comt Women Hist Professions; Am Educ Res Asn. **RESEARCH** History of philanthropy; Twentieth century history of education; Contemporary education policy. **SELECTED PUBLICATIONS** Coed, Brown v. Board of Education: The Challenge for Today's Schools, Teachers Col Press, 96; auth, "From Discipline-Based to Problem-Centered Learning," in Education and Democracy: Reimagining Liberal Learning (Col Board, 97); auth, "A Subjective Necessity: Being and Becoming an Historian of Education," in Learning from Our Lives: Women, Research, and Autobiography (Teachers Col Press, 97); coed, Issues in Education Research: Problems and Possibilities, Jossey-Bass, 99; ed, Philanthropic Foundations: New Scholarship, New Possibilities, Indiana Univ Press, 99; auth, John Dewey's Defeat: The Problem of Scholarship in Education, Univ of Chicago Press (forthcoming). **CONTACT ADDRESS** Dept of Humanities and Social Sciences, New York Univ, 70 Washinton Square South, New York, NY 10012. **EMAIL** ec11@is.nyu.edu

LAGRAND, JAMES B.

PERSONAL Born 11/18/1968, Cambridge, MA, m, 1990, 2 children **DISCIPLINE** HISTORY **EDUCATION** Calvin Col, BA, 90; Ind Univ, MA, 92; PhD, 97. **CAREER** Asst prof, Messiah Col 97-. **HONORS AND AWARDS** Teaching Excellence Awd, Ind Univ, 97; Scholarship Grant, Messiah Col, 99; Scholar Chair, Messiah Col, 00-02. **MEMBERSHIPS** AHA; Org of Am Hist; W Hist Assoc; Conf on Faith and Hist. **RESEARCH** Twentieth-Century U.S., American Indian. **SELECTED PUBLICATIONS** Rev, "Manifest Manners", by Gerald Vizenor, W Hist quart 27, (96): 87; rev, of "Native Americans and Wage Labor", by Alice Littlefield and Martha C. Knack, Mich Hist Rev 22.2 (96): 211-212; auth, "The Changing 'Jesus Road': Protestants Reappraise American Indian Missions in the 1920s and 1930s", W Hist Quart 27 (96): 479-504; rev, of "The Cherokees and Christianity", by William G. McLoughlin, J of Appalachian Studies 3.1 (97): 161-163; auth, "Whose Voices Count? Oral Sources and Twentieth-Century American Indian History", Am Indian Cult and Res J 21.1 (97): 73-105; rev, of "American Indian Quotations", by Howard J. Langer, Am Indian Cult and Res J 21.4 (97): 293-296; auth, Indian Metropolis: Native Americans in Chicago, 1945-1975 (forthcoming). **CONTACT ADDRESS** Dept Hist and Govt, Messiah Col, Grantham, PA 17027. **EMAIL** jlagrand@messiah.edu

LAHAIE, SCOTT

PERSONAL Born 01/10/1961, Tulsa, OK, m, 1985, 2 children **DISCIPLINE** THEATRE HISTORY **EDUCATION** Sam Houston State Univ, BFA, 85; Baylor Univ, MA, 96; MFA, 00. **CAREER** Stage director to artistic director, Keller Theater, Germany, 83-93; multimedia dev, lectr, Baylor Univ, 96-. **HONORS AND AWARDS** Best Director of a Play Awd, Europ Tournament of Plays, 88; Best Lighting for a Play Awd, 92. **MEMBERSHIPS** IIR, ICSA, SSSA, SWGA. **RESEARCH** Bertolt Brecht, Irwin Piscator, and the theatre of the Weimar Republic, The German Playwright Heinz Coubier, Ira Adridge and the acting traditions of the 19th century, Genre criticism and the fiction of C.S. Lewis, Hypertext theory and the new literature, Applied Technology in the Arts and Humanities. **SELECTED PUBLICATIONS** Cotransl, The Beloved, by Heinz Coubier, (Will Meisel Verlag, 90); rev, of "The Outrageous Idea of Christian Scholarship," by George Marsden, Jour of Interdisciplinary Studies, (98); rev, of "Reclaiming the Soul," by Jeffrey H. Boyd, Jour of Interdisciplinary Studies, (00); auth, 'Ira Aldridge: In Search of Recognition," Jour of African Studies, forthcoming. **CONTACT ADDRESS** Baylor Univ, Waco, PO Box 97262, Waco, TX 76707. **EMAIL** scot_lahaie@baylor.edu

LAIRD, WALTER ROY

DISCIPLINE MEDIEVAL HISTORY **EDUCATION** Concordia Univ, BA, 76; Univ Toronto, MA, 78, PhD, 83. **CAREER** Assoc prof, Carleton Univ. **RESEARCH** Medieval and renaissance Aristolelianism, Impact in the Middle Ages and Renaissance. **SELECTED PUBLICATIONS** Auth, Patronage of Mechanics and Theories of Impact in Sixteenth-Century Italy, Patronage and Institutions: Science, Technology, and Medicine at the European Court, 1500-1750, Woodbridge, Suffolk: Boy dell-Brewer, 91; Archimedes Among the Humanists, Isis, 82, 91. **CONTACT ADDRESS** Dept of Hist, Carleton Univ, 1125 Colonel By Dr, Ottawa, ON, Canada K1S 5B6. **EMAIL** roy_laird@carleton.ca

LAITOS, JAN GORDON

PERSONAL Born 05/06/1946, Colorado Springs, CO **DISCIPLINE** LAW, AMERICAN LEGAL HISTORY **EDUCATION** Yale Univ, BA, 68; Law Sch, Univ Colo, JD, 71; Law Sch, Univ Wis, SJD, 74. **CAREER** Law clerk, Colo Supreme Ct, 71-72; atty, Off Legal Coun, US Dept of Justice, 74-76; Prof Law, Law Sch, Univ Denver, 76-, Sr legal adv, Solar Energy Res Inst, 78-81; consult, Colo State Dept of Natural Resources, 79-80, US Dept of Interior, 79-80 and US Dept of Energy, 80-81. **MEMBERSHIPS** Natural resources law; energy law. **RESEARCH** Auth, Causation and the Unconstitutional Conditions Doctrine--Why the City of Tigards Exaction Was a Taking, Denver Univ Law Rev, Vol 0072, 95; National Parks and the Recreation Resource, Denver Univ Law Rev, Vol 0074, 97. **CONTACT ADDRESS** Law Sch, Univ of Denver, Denver, CO 80208.

LAKER, JOSEPH ALPHONSE

PERSONAL Born 03/17/1941, Indianapolis, IN, m, 1987 **DISCIPLINE** HISTORY, JAPANESE STUDIES **EDUCATION** Marian Col, BA, 63; IN Univ, MA, 67, PhD, 75. **CAREER** Instr hist, St Olaf Col, 67-70; asst prof, 74-80, assoc prof, 80-94, Prof Hist, Wheeling Col, 94-; NEH Summer Seminar, Brown Univ, 79; Fulbright/Hays Summer Seminar, Korea, 87; co-dir, NEH Summer Inst for High Sch Tchr(s), summer 95. **MEMBERSHIPS** Asn Asian Studies; Econ Hist Asn; Bus Hist Asn. **RESEARCH** The develop of the Japan beer industry; mod Japan economic and soc hist; Japan Colonialism. **SELECTED PUBLICATIONS** Encyclopedia of World War II, Cord Publ, 78; Oligopoly at home and expansion abroad: The develop of the Japan beer industry, 1907-1937, Proc Second Int Symp Asian Studies, 80; coauth, Tchr Outreach in Japanese Studies, Educ About Asia, fall 96. **CONTACT ADDRESS** Wheeling Jesuit Col, 316 Washington Ave, Wheeling, WV 26003-6243. **EMAIL** lakerj@wju.edu

LAL, VINAY

PERSONAL Born 04/19/1961, New Delhi, India, m, 1996, 1 child **DISCIPLINE** HISTORY **EDUCATION** Johns Hopkins Univ, BA, 82; MA, 82; Univ Chicago, PhD, 92. **CAREER** Lectr, Univ Chicago, 92; Lectr, Columbia Univ, 92-93; Vis Fel, New Delhi, 93, 94; Asst Prof, UCLA, 93-. **HONORS AND AWARDS** Best Diss in the Humanities Div, Univ Chicago, 92; Marc Galler Awd; William R. Kenan Fel, Columbia Univ, 92-93; Sen Fel, Am Inst for Indian Studies, 95; Fel, NEH, 96; Second Joseph Asanbe Mem Lect, Austin Peay State Univ, 98; Fel, Japan Soc for the Promotion of Sci, 99; Fel, World Acad of Arts and Sci, 01. **MEMBERSHIPS** World Future Studies Fed; Form on Globalization; Intl Network for Cult Alternatives to Develop. **RESEARCH** Indian history, 1750-present; Popular Indian culture; Indian Diaspora; Comparative colonial histories; Historiography (especially of South Asia); Politics of knowledge; Politics of culture; Contemporary North-South political relations. **SELECTED PUBLICATIONS** Auth, South Asian Cultural Studies: A Bibliography, Delhi, 96; ed, Dissenting Knowledges, Open Futures: The Multiple Selves and Strange Destinations of Ashis Nandy, Oxford Press, 00; ed, Special Issue of J "Emergences", Vol 10, 00; auth, The Dialiectic of Civilization and Nation-State: Essays in Indian History and Culture, in press; auth, The Empire of Knowledge: Culture and Plurality in the Global Economy, Pluto Press, forthcoming. **CONTACT ADDRESS** Dept Hist, Univ of California, Los Angeles, 6265 Bunche, Box 951473, Los Angeles, CA 90095-1473. **EMAIL** vlal@history.ucla.edu

LALONDE, GERALD VINCENT

PERSONAL Born 05/18/1938, Bellingham, WA, m, 1969, 2 children **DISCIPLINE** CLASSICS, ANCIENT HISTORY **EDUCATION** Univ Wash, BA, 62, MA, 64, PhD(classics), 71. **CAREER** Instr classics, Univ Wash, 68-69; from instr to asst prof, 69-74, assoc prof, 74-79, Prof Class, Grinnell Col, 80. **MEMBERSHIPS** Archaeol Inst Am; Am Philol Asn; Brit Class Asn. **RESEARCH** Greek epigraphy, history and archaeology. **SELECTED PUBLICATIONS** Auth, A fifth century Hieron southwest of the Athenian Agora, 68 & A Boiotien decree in Athens, 77, Hisperia. **CONTACT ADDRESS** Dept of Classics, Grinnell Col, P O Box 805, Grinnell, IA 50112-0805.

LAM, TRUONG BUU

PERSONAL Born 03/23/1933, Tan-An, Vietnam, d, 1 child **DISCIPLINE** MODERN HISTORY, SOUTHEAST ASIA **EDUCATION** Cath Univ Louvain, D(hist), 57. **CAREER** Asst prof hist, Univ Saigon & Univ Hue, 57-64; res assoc, E Asian Res Ctr, Harvard Univ, 64-65, Southeast Asia Studies, Yale Univ, 65-66 & Southeast Asia Prog, Cornell Univ, 66-71; assoc prof hist, State Univ NY Stony Brook, 71-72; assoc prof hist, Univ Hawaii, Manoa, 72-, dir, Inst Hist Res, Saigon, 57-64; Soc Sci Res Coun grant, 66-69; adj asst prof, State Univ NY, Stony Brook, 68-71; res fel, Inst Southeast Asian Studies, Singapore, 77-78; dir, SE Asia Res Ctr, Univ Hawaii, 85-86; Dir, Hanoi Center, Council on International Educational Exchange (CIEE), 91-1993. **RESEARCH** Tributary systems in China and Vietnam; impact of the West on Southeast Asia; Vietnamese nationalism. **SELECTED PUBLICATIONS** Auth, Patterns of Vietnamese Response to Foreign Intervention, 1858-1900, Yale Southeast Asia Studies, 67; Tributary Versus Intervention, a Case-Study in Vietnamese History, 1789-1792, Chinese World Order, 68; A Vietnamese Viewpoint, In: The Pentagon Papers, Vol V, Quadrangle, 71; Japan and the Disruption of the Vietnamese Nationalist Movement, In: Aspects of Vietnamese History, Univ Hawaii, 72; auth, Revolution, ISEAS, Singapore, 84; coauth, An Annotated Bibliography of the VAN-SU-DIA, 85; Colonialism Experience, Michigan U Press, 2000. **CONTACT ADDRESS** Dept of Hist, Univ of Hawaii, Manoa, 2530 Dole St, Honolulu, HI 96822-2303. **EMAIL** lamb@hawaii.edu

LAMAR, HOWARD ROBERTS

PERSONAL Born 11/18/1923, Tuskegee, AL, m, 1959, 2 children **DISCIPLINE** AMERICAN HISTORY **EDUCATION** Emory Univ, BA, 45; Yale Univ, MA, 45, PhD(Am hist), 51. **CAREER** Instr hist, Univ Mass, 45-46 and Wesleyan Univ, 48-49; from instr to assoc prof, 49-64, chmn dept, 67-70, Prof Hist, Yale Univ, 64-; Dean, 79-; Pres, Yale Univ, 92-93. **HONORS AND AWARDS** Morse fel, 53-54; Am Coun Learned Soc fel, 59-60; Soc Sci Res Coun fel, 60-61; DHumL, Emory Univ, 75; Hon Degree, Yale Univ, 93; Hon Degree, Univ Nebr, 94. **MEMBERSHIPS** AHA; Orgn Am Historians; Western Hist Asn (pres, 72). **RESEARCH** American frontier history; family history; comparative history. **SELECTED PUBLICATIONS** Auth, "Sutter, John, Augustus, Wilderness Entrepreneur," California Hist 73 (94); "Coming into the Mainstream at Last--Comparative Approaches to the History of the American West," J West 35 (96); "The Dust Rose Like Smoke--the Subjugation of the Zulu and the Sioux," Ethnohist 44 (97); Auth, Dakota Territory, 1861-1865, A Study of Frontier Politics, Yale Univ Press, 56, 2nd ed, NDak Regional Pr, 97; auth, The Far Southwest, 1850-1912: A Political History of the Territories of Arizona, Colorado, New Mexico and Utah, Yale Press, 66, 2nd ed, Univ of NMex Pr, 00; ed, New Encyclopedia of the American West, Yale Univ Press, 98; coed, History of the American Frontier Series, Univ of NMex Press, 76-. **CONTACT ADDRESS** Dept of Hist Studies, Yale Univ, 237 Hall of Grad, New Haven, CT 06520-8324.

LAMARCHE, JEAN

PERSONAL Born 04/29/1945, Manchester, NH, m, 1996 **DISCIPLINE** ARCHITECTURE **EDUCATION** Lawrence Technol Univ, BS, 81; Univ Michigan, ArchD, 95. **CONTACT ADDRESS** 6456 Hamilton Dr, Derby, NY 14047. **EMAIL** lamarche@ap.buffalo.edu

LAMARRE, THOMAS

DISCIPLINE EAST ASIAN STUDIES **EDUCATION** Univ Chicago, PhD. **CAREER** Asst prof, McGill Univ. **RESEARCH** Cultural and intellectual Japanese history. **SELECTED PUBLICATIONS** Auth, Science, History, and Culture in the Late Meiji Period, New Directions in the Study of Meiji Japan, ed. Helen Hardacre, E.J. Brill, 97; auth, "Diagram, Inscription, Sensation," Deleuze and Expression, special edition of Literary Res/Recherche litteraire 24, (97): 669-94; auth, The Order of the Senses: Poetry, Calligraphy, and Cosmology in Heian Japan, Durham: Duke Univ Press, 98. **CONTACT ADDRESS** East Asian Studies Dept, McGill Univ, 845 Sherbrooke St, Montreal, QC, Canada H3A 2T5. **EMAIL** tlamarre@leacock.lan.mcgill.ca

LAMBERT, BYRON C.

PERSONAL Born 04/19/1923, Delta, OH, m, 1949, 1 child **DISCIPLINE** CHRISTIAN DOCTRINE; HISTORY OF CULTURE **EDUCATION** Univ Buffalo, BA, 45, MA, 46; Butler Univ sch Rel, BD, 50; Univ Chicago, PhD, 57. **CAREER** Assoc prof English, Milligan Col, 57-60; dean, assoc prof English, Simpson Col, 60-62; dean, 62-65, campus dean, 65-71, assoc prof Hum, 71-75, assoc dean, Col ed, 71-75, Fairleigh Dickinson Univ; Prof Philos, 75-85, actg dean, Arts and Sci, 82-83, acting Provost, Madison Campus, 81. **HONORS AND AWARDS** Fairleigh Dickinson Univ, Campus Achieve Awd, 74; Pres James A. Garfield Awd, Emmanuel Sch Rel, Tenn, 98. **MEMBERSHIPS** Amer Philos Asn; Soc Christian Philso; Disciples of Christ Hist Soc. **RESEARCH** C.S. Lewis; Paul Elmer More; Christian theology, sacraments, Holy Spirit. **SELECTED PUBLICATIONS** Auth, The Essential Paul Elmer More, 72; The Rise of the Anti-Mission Baptist, 80; The Recovery of Reality, 80; The Restoration of the Lord's Supper and the Sacramental Principle, 92; Experience-Different Semantic Worlds, Wasleyan Theol Jour, Spring 95; Shifting Frontiers and the Invisible Hand, Disciplina, Fall 95; The Middle Way of Frederick Doyle Kershner, 98; The Regrettable Silence of Paul Elmer More, Modern Age, Fall 98; C.S. Lewis and the Moral Law, Stone-Campbell Jour, Fall 98. **CONTACT ADDRESS** 300 North Perry St, Hagerstown, IN 47346. **EMAIL** phybylam@infocom.com

LAMBERT, LYNDA J.

PERSONAL Born 08/27/1943, PA, m, 1961, 5 children **DISCIPLINE** ART, LITERATURE **EDUCATION** Slippery Rock Univ Pa, BFA, MA; WV Univ, MFA **CAREER** Instr, Commun Col of Beaver Co, Monaca, Pa, 85-88; instr, Slippery Rock Univ Pa, 90; teaching asst, WV Univ, 89-91; exec dir, Hoyt Inst, New Castle, Pa, 92-96, asst prof, Geneva Col, Beaver Falls, Pa, present. **MEMBERSHIPS** Assoc Artists of Pittsburgh; Assoc for Integrative Stud; Group A; Amer Assoc of Museums; Inst of Museum Svcs; Nat Assoc of Women Artists Inc; Pa Rural Arts Alliance, Women's Caucus for Art; Cal Art Assoc; Handweaver's Guild of Amer. **RESEARCH** Viking glass; African Amer art & lit; African art; ancient art. **SELECTED PUBLICATIONS** Auth, MacLennan, Rosalind, Abstract art exhibition invites interpretation, Butler Eagle, 95; MacLennan, Rosalind, Painter, sculptor complement each other, Butler Eagle, 95; Mabin, Connie, Artists painting Aliquippa portrait as a city of pride, Beaver Valley Times, 95; Marcello, Patricia Cornin, Parade of 25 Successful women for 1996, Successful Women Mag, 96; Wilson, Gladys Blews, Painter chooses unusual medium for her prints, Beaver Valley Times, 96. **CONTACT ADDRESS** 104 River Rd, Ellwood City, PA 16117. **EMAIL** llambert@geneva.edu

LAMBERT, RICHARD THOMAS

PERSONAL Born 03/28/1943, Rochester, NY, m, 1978, 3 children **DISCIPLINE** HISTORY OF PHILOSOPHY, LOGIC, ETHICS **EDUCATION** St Bernard's Col, BA, 65; Univ Notre Dame, PhD, 71. **CAREER** Asst prof, 70-80, philos dept chmn, 77-82, assoc prof 80-, prof philos, Carrol Col, Mont, Dir, Summer, 81-82, Dir, Continuing Educ, 81-85, Exchange prof philos, Loras Col, 76-77. **HONORS AND AWARDS** NY State Regents Scholar, 61-65; NDEA Grad Fel, 66-70; Exec Comt, Delta Epsilon Sigma, 90-94, vpres & pres, 94-98. **MEMBERSHIPS** Int Berkeley Soc; Am Cath Philos Asn; Am Philos Asn; Delta Epsilon Sigma. **RESEARCH** Berkeley; Aquinas; Camus. **SELECTED PUBLICATIONS** Auth, Berkeley's use of the relativity argument, Idealistic Studies, 10: 107-121; Albert Camus and the paradoxes of expressing a relativism, Thought, 56: 185-198; A textual study of Aquinas' comparison of the intellect to prime matter, New Scholasticism, Vol 56; Berkeley's commitment to relativism, Berkeley: Critical and Interpretive Essays, Univ Minn Press, 82; Habitual knowledge of the soul in St Thomas Aquinas, Mod Schoolman, 40: 1-19; The literal intent of Berkeley's Dialogues, Philos & Lit, 6: 165-171; Nonintentional experience of oneself in Thomas Aquinas, New Scholasticism, 59: 253-275; Teaching Camus's The Plague in an introductory philosophy course, Approaches to Teaching Camus's The Plague, MLA, 85; transl, Thomas Aquinas, Disputed Question on the Soul's Knowledge of Itself, Clearinghouse for Medieval Philos Transl, 87; Conferring honors in a democratic society, Delta Epsilon Sigma Jour, 33: 59-60; President's report to the membership, Delta Epsilon Sigma Jour, 43: 77-78; Ethics column, Helena Independent Record, 90. **CONTACT ADDRESS** Carroll Col, Montana, 1601 N Benton Ave, Fac Box 49, Helena, MT 59625-0002. **EMAIL** rlambert@carroll.edu

LAMBERTI, MARJORIE
PERSONAL Born 09/30/1937, New Haven, CT **DISCIPLINE** HISTORY **EDUCATION** Smith Col, BA, 59; Yale Univ, PhD, 65. **CAREER** Prof, Middlebury Col, 64-; Charles A. Dana Prof, Middlebury Col, 84-. **HONORS AND AWARDS** Phi Beta Kappa, 59; NEH Fel, 68-69, 81-82; Inst for Advanced Study Fel, 92-93; Woodrow Wilson Fel, 97-98. **SELECTED PUBLICATIONS** Auth, "Liberals, Socialists, and the Defense Against Antisemitism in the Wilhelminian Period", Leo Baeck Inst Year Book 25, 78; auth, Jewish Activism in imperial Germany. The Struggle for Civil Equality, Yale Univ Pr, (New Haven), 78; auth, "From Coexistence to Conflict - Zionism and the Jewish Community in Germany, 1897-1914", Leo Baeck Inst Year Book 27, 82; auth, State, Society, and the Elementary School in Imperial Germany, Oxford Univ Pr, (NY), 89; auth, "Elementary School Teachers and the Struggle Against Social Democracy in Wilhelmine Germany", Hist of Educ Quarterly, Spring 92; auth, "Radical Schoolteachers and the Origins of the Progressive Education Movement in Germany, 1900-1914", Hist of Educ Quarterly, Spring 00. **CONTACT ADDRESS** Dept History, Middlebury Col, 0 Middlebury Col, Middlebury, VT 05753-6200. **EMAIL** lamberti@middlebury.edu

LAMIRANDE, EMILIEN
PERSONAL Born 05/22/1926, St-Georges de Windsor, Canada **DISCIPLINE** HISTORY OF CHRISTIANITY **EDUCATION** Univ Ottawa, BA, 49, LPh, 50, MA, 51, LTh, 55; Univ Innsbruck, DTh, 60; Union Theol Sem, NY, STM, 65;. **CAREER** Assoc prof theol, Univ Ottawa, 60-65; prof, St Paul Univ, Ont, 65-70, dean fac theol, 67-69; chmn dept, 72-74, Prof Relig Studies, Univ Ottawa, 70-. **MEMBERSHIPS** Am Acad Relig; Can Cath Hist Asn; Can Theol Soc (vpres, 67-70); Asn Can d'Estudes Patristiques (vpres, 79-). **RESEARCH** Early Christianity; North African Church; ecclesiology. **SELECTED PUBLICATIONS** Auth, Sulpician Priests in Canada--Major Figures in Their History, Stud in Rel-Sciences Religieuses, Vol 0022, 93; Body of the Church, Body of Christ--Sources for the Ecclesiology of the Communion, Stud in Rel-Sciences Religieuses, Vol 0022, 93; Writings of the Reformation Fathers, Stud in Rel-Sciences Religieuses, Vol 0025, 96; The Aggiornamento and Its Eclipse--Free Thinking in the Church and in the Faithful, Stud in Rel-Sciences Religieuses, Vol 0025, 96. **CONTACT ADDRESS** Dept of Relig Studies, Univ of Ottawa, Ottawa, ON, Canada K1H 8M5.

LAMM, ALAN K.
PERSONAL Born 03/01/1959, Wilson, NC, m **DISCIPLINE** HISTORY, RELIGION **EDUCATION** Univ NC at Greensboro, BA, 81; Duke Univ, Masters Divinity, 87; MTh, 88; Univ SC, PhD, 95. **CAREER** Chaplain asst, U.S. Army, 81-84; adj prof, Mount Olive Col, 88-90; Chaplain & Army Historian, U.S. Army Reserve, 89-97; adj instr, Wayne Community Col, 89-90; adj instr, Midlands Technical Col, 90-93; instr, Orangeburg-Calhoun Technical Col, 93-95; U.S. Army Historian, U.S. Army Reserve Command, 96; instr, Trident Technical Col, 96-97; assoc prof, Mount Olive Col, 97-. **MEMBERSHIPS** Orgn of Am Historians, Soc for Military Hist, NC Literary and Hist Asn, Coun on Am Military Past, Army Hist Found. **RESEARCH** Nineteenth- and Twentieth-Century American History, Religious History, Military History, African American History. **SELECTED PUBLICATIONS** Rev, of "The Unwept: Black American Soldiers and the Spanish-American War," by John W. Bailey, NC Hist Rev (April 99); auth, Five Black Preachers in Army Blue, 1884-1901: The Buffalo Soldier Chaplains, Edwin Mellen Press (Lewiston, NY), 98; auth, "Buffalo Soldier Chaplians of the Old West," The J of America's Military Past Vol XXVI (99): 25-40; rev, of "The Life and Works of General Charles King, 1844-1933: Martial Spirit," by John W. Baily, The J of America's Military Past (forthcoming); auth, "General Wesley Merritt" and "Black Army Chaplains in the Civil War," Encyclopedia of the American Civil War, ABC-Clio Pub, forthcoming; rev, of "Southern Unionist Pamphlets and the Civil War," edited by Jon L. Waklyn, The J of Military Hist (forthcoming). **CONTACT ADDRESS** Dept Soc Sci, Mount Olive Col, 634 Henderson St, Mount Olive, NC 28365-1263. **EMAIL** lamm1084@aol.com

LAMMERS, DONALD N.
PERSONAL Born 04/27/1930, Chicago, IL, m, 1952, 3 children **DISCIPLINE** ENGLISH HISTORY **EDUCATION** Cornell Univ, AB, 52; Stanford Univ, MA, 53, PhD, 60. **CAREER** Actg instr hist Western civilization, Stanford Univ, 59-60; asst prof hist, Univ Ariz, 60-67; assoc prof, Mich State Univ, 67-71 and Univ Waterloo, 71-73; assoc prof, 73-78, Prof Hist, Mich State Univ, 78-, Chmn Dept, 80-, Jr fel, Ctr Advan Studies Behav Sci, 64-65. **MEMBERSHIPS** Conf Brit Studies. **RESEARCH** British foreign and imperial relations since 1900. **SELECTED PUBLICATIONS** Auth, Winning the Peace--British Diplomatic Strategy, Peace Planning, and the Paris Peace Conference, 1916-1920, Amer Hist Rev, Vol 0098, 93; The Spoils of War--the Politics, Economics, and Diplomacy of Reparations, 1918-1932, J Mod Hist, Vol 0065, 93; British Policy and European Reconstruction After the 1st World War, J Mod Hist, Vol 0065, 93; Portrait of an Appeaser--Hadow, Robert, First Secretary in the British Foreign Office, 1931-1939, Int Hist Rev, Vol 0019, 97. **CONTACT ADDRESS** Dept of Hist, Michigan State Univ, East Lansing, MI 48824.

LAMPLUGH, GEORGE RUSSELL
PERSONAL Born 05/20/1944, Wilmington, DE, m, 1967, 2 children **DISCIPLINE** AMERICAN AND EUROPEAN HISTORY **EDUCATION** Univ Del, BA, 66; Emory Univ, MA, 71, PhD(hist), 73. **CAREER** Teaching asst hist, Emory Univ, 70-71, teaching assoc, 72-73; instr, Ga Inst Technol, spring 73; teacher hist, The Westminster Sch, 73-, Vis asst prof, Emory Univ, summer 75; chr, hist dept, The Westminster Sch, 89-96; interim chr, hist dept, The Westminster Sch, 99-00. **MEMBERSHIPS** Orgn Am Historians; Soc Historians of the Early Am Repub; Southern Hist Asn. **RESEARCH** Factions and parties in Georgia, 1776-1837; development of political parties in early National United States; southern history. **SELECTED PUBLICATIONS** Auth, Politics on the Periphery: Factions and Parties in Ga, 1783-1806, Univ of Delaware Press, 86. **CONTACT ADDRESS** Dept of Hist, Westminster Sch, Atlanta, GA 30327. **EMAIL** georgelamplugh@westminster.net

LANDAU, ELLEN G.
PERSONAL Born 02/27/1947, m, 1970, 2 children **DISCIPLINE** EUROPEAN AND AMERICAN MODERN ART **EDUCATION** Cornell Univ, BA; George Washington Univ, MA, Delaware, PhD, 81. **CAREER** Guest curator, Library Congress traveling exhib; kunstmuseum Bern, Switzerland. **HONORS AND AWARDS** Fel, Am Coun Learned Societies; Rockefeller Found, National Mus Am Art , Smithsonian Institution, John S. Diekhoff Awd; dept chair, art hist. **SELECTED PUBLICATIONS** Auth, Jackson Pollock, Harry N. Abrams, Pub, 89; auth, Lee Krasner: A Catalogue Raisonne, Harry N. Abrams, 95. **CONTACT ADDRESS** Case Western Reserve Univ, 10900 Euclid Ave, Cleveland, OH 44106. **EMAIL** exl3@po.cwru.edu

LANDAU, NORMA BEATRICE
PERSONAL Born 09/13/1942, Toronto, ON, Canada **DISCIPLINE** ENGLISH HISTORY **EDUCATION** Univ Toronto, BA, 64, MA, 65; Univ Calif, Berkeley, PhD(hist), 74. **CAREER** Lectr hist, Duke Univ, 72-74; vis lectr, Univ Calif, Los Angeles, 75-76; prof of hist, UC, Davis, 76-. **HONORS AND AWARDS** Honorable mention, John Ben Snow Prize (North American Conference on British Studies), 85; Surrency Prize (Am Soc for Legal Hist), 00; honorable mention, Sutherland Prize (Am Soc for Legal Hist), 00 **MEMBERSHIPS** Conf Brit Studies. **RESEARCH** English history, 1660-1832; legal and political history; Am Soc for Legal Hist **SELECTED PUBLICATIONS** Auth, The Justices of the Peace, 1679-1760, Univ Calif Press, 84; articles in Continuity and Change, Agricultural Hist Review, Historical Journal, Bulletin of the Institute of Historical Research; articles in: London Journal; Law and History; rev, Albion; Eighteenth-Century Studies. **CONTACT ADDRESS** Dept of Hist, Univ of California, Davis, Davis, CA 95616-5200. **EMAIL** nblandau@ucdavis.edu

LANDAU, SARAH BRADFORD
PERSONAL Born 03/27/1935, Raleigh, NC, m, 1959, 2 children **DISCIPLINE** ART HISTORY **EDUCATION** Univ NC Greensboro, BFA, 57; NYork Univ, MA, 59, PhD, 78. **CAREER** Instr, 71-73, 76-78, asst prof, 78-84, assoc prof, 84-96, prof, fine arts, 96-, NY Univ; mem, 87-96, com v chmn, 93-96, NY City Landmarks Preservation Comm. **HONORS AND AWARDS** Am Inst of Archit Intl Archit bk award, 97; Victorian Soc in Am bk award, 97; Lucy G. Moses award for preservation leadership, 97; designated a Contennial Historian of City of New York, 99; Metropolitan Chapter, Victorian Soc. In Am bk and exhibition award. **MEMBERSHIPS** Col Art Asn; Soc of Archit Hist; Victorian Soc of Am. **RESEARCH** History of Am archit; hist of 19th to early 20th century NYC archit. **SELECTED PUBLICATIONS** Ed, The Grand American Avenue 1850-1920, Pomegranite Artbks & Am Archit Found, 94; coauth, Rise of the New York Skyscraper, 1865-1913, Yale Univ Press, 96; auth, Potter & Robertson 1875-1880, Long Island Country Houses & their Archit, 1860-1940, WW Norton, 97; auth, George B Post, Architect: Picturesque Designer and Determined Realist, Monacelli Press, 98; auth, New-York Historical Soc guestt curator, exhibition on arch. Of George B. Post, 98-99. **CONTACT ADDRESS** Dept of Fine Arts, New York Univ, 100 Washington Sq E, New York, NY 10003-6688. **EMAIL** sarah.landau@nyu.edu

LANDER, JACK ROBERT
PERSONAL Born 02/15/1921, Hinckley, England **DISCIPLINE** MEDIEVAL ENGLISH HISTORY **EDUCATION** Cambridge Univ, BA, 42, MA, 45, MLitt, 50. **CAREER** From lectr to sr lectr hist, Univ Ghana, 50-63; assoc prof, Dalhousie Univ, 63-65; Prof Hist, Univ Western Ont, 65-, Leverhulme res fel, 59-60. **MEMBERSHIPS** AHA; Hist Asn, Eng; Royal Hist Soc. **RESEARCH** Italian Renaissance; late medieval and early modern England. **SELECTED PUBLICATIONS** Auth, Lordship, Kingship and Empire--the Idea of Monarchy, 1400-1525, Albion, Vol 0025, 93; Richard of England, Hist Today, Vol 0044, 94; Richard III--a Medieval Kingship, Hist Today, Vol 0044, 94; Gaunt, John--the Exercise of Princely Power in 14th-Century Europe, Amer Hist Rev, Vol 0099, 94; From Personal Duties Towards Personal Rights, Late-Medieval and Early Modern Political Thought, 1300-1600, Albion, Vol 0027, 95; Crown, Government and People in the 15th-Century, Albion, Vol 0029, 97. **CONTACT ADDRESS** Dept of Hist Soc Sci Ctr, Univ of Western Ontario, London, ON, Canada N6A 3K7.

LANDON, MICHAEL DE LAVAL
PERSONAL Born 10/08/1935, St. John, NB, Canada, m, 1959, 2 children **DISCIPLINE** MODERN HISTORY **EDUCATION** Oxford Univ, BA, 58, MA, 61; Univ Wis, MA, 62, PhD, 66. **CAREER** From asst prof to assoc prof, 64-72, prof hist, Univ Miss, 72-00; prof emer, Univ Miss, 00-, Am Philos Soc res grant, 66-67. **MEMBERSHIPS** Fel Royal Hist Soc Gt Brit; Conf Brit Studies; AHA; Am Soc Legal Hist. **RESEARCH** 17th century England; English legal history; MS legal history. **SELECTED PUBLICATIONS** Auth, The position of the public schools in postwar Britain, Soc Studies, 10/67; The Bristol Artillery Company and the Tory triumph in Bristol, 1679-1684, Proc Am Philos Soc, 4/70; The Triumph of the Lawyers, Univ Ala, 70; Burke on the law and the legal profession, Enlightenment Essays, winter 70; Fact and fiction in Bacon's Henry VII, Univ Miss, 71; Serjeant Maynard's family, Devon & Cornwall, 75-76; The learned Glynne and Maynard--Two characters dashed out of Samuel Butler's Hudibras, Proc Am Philos Soc, 6/76; auth, The Honor and Dignity of the Profession, Univ Miss, 79; auth, Erin and Britannia, Nelson Hall, 81. **CONTACT ADDRESS** Dept of History, Univ of Mississippi, P.O. Box 1848, University, MS 38677-1848. **EMAIL** hslandon@olemiss.edu

LANDOW, GEORGE PAUL
PERSONAL Born 08/25/1940, White Plains, NY, m, 1966, 2 children **DISCIPLINE** ENGLISH LITERATURE, DIGITAL CULTURE, ART HISTORY **EDUCATION** Brandeis Univ, MA, 62; Princeton Univ, AB, 61, MA, 63, PhD(English), 66; Brown Univ, MA, 72. **CAREER** Instr English, Columbia Univ, 65-68, asst prof, 69-70; vis assoc prof, Univ Chicago, 70-71; assoc prof, 71-78, Prof English & Artist Hist, Brown Univ, 78-; Fel, Soc for Humanities, Cornell Univ, 68-69; Guggenheim Found fels, 73 & 78; consult lit & art, Museum Art, RI Sch Design, 76-79; vis fel, Brasenose Col, Oxford Univ, 77; fac fel, Brown Univ Inst for Res in Information and Scholarship (IRIS), 85-92; NEA, 84-85; NEH Summer Inst, Yale, 88, 91; British Academy vis prof, Univ of Lancaster, vis res fel, Electronics and Computer Science, Univ of Southampton (UK), vis prof Univ of Zimbabwe, 97: IL SU, 98; Distinguished vis prof, Nat Univ of Singapore, 98; Dean, Univ Scholars Prog; Prof, Nat Univ of Singapore, 00-. **HONORS AND AWARDS** Gustave O Arldt Award, Coun Grad Schs US, 72; .EDUCOM/NCRIPTAL award innovative courseware in the humanities, 90; many awards for websites. **MEMBERSHIPS** ACM; Tennyson Soc; Trollope Soc. **RESEARCH** Hypertext and digital culture; Victorian British poetry and nonfiction; Victorian painting and visual arts; theology and literature; MLA; Univ Coun Board of trustees; NUS, 00-, Bovenring Board Singapore UP, 01. **SELECTED PUBLICATIONS** Auth, Your Good Influence on Me: The Correspondence of John Ruskin and W H Hunt, John Rylands Libr, England, 76; William Holman Hunt and Typological Symbolism, Yale Univ, 79; ed, Approaches to Victorian Autobiography, Ohio Univ, 79; Victorian Types, Victorian Shadows: Biblical Typology and Victorian Literature, Art and Thought, Routledge & Kegan Paul, 80; Images of Crisis: Literary Iconology 1750 to the Present, Routledge & Kegan Paul, 82; Ruskin, Oxford Univ Press, 85; ed with others, Pre-Raphaelite Friendship, UMI, 85; ed, Ladies of Shalott: A Victorian Masterpiece and its Contexts, Brown, 86; Elegant Jeremiahs: The Sage from Carlyle to Mailer, Cornell, 86; ed with P. Delany, Hypermedia and Literary Studies, MIT, 91; Hypertext: The Convergence of Contemporary Critical Theory and Technology, Johns Hopkins, 92; ed with P. delany, Digital Word: Text-Based Computing in the Humanities, MIT, 93; Hyper/Text/Theory, Johns Hopkins, 94; Hypertext 2.0, Johns Hopkins, 97. **CONTACT ADDRESS** Dept of English and Digital Culture, Nat Univ of Singapore, Singapore 119260. **EMAIL** george@landow.com/uspdean@nus.edu.sg

LANDSMAN, NED C.
PERSONAL Born 09/30/1951, New York, NY, m, 1982 **DISCIPLINE** AMERICAN AND SCOTTISH HISTORY **EDUCATION** Columbia Univ, BA, 73; Univ Pa, PhD(hist), 79. **CAREER** Asst Prof Hist, State Univ NY, Stony Brook, 79-, Assoc ed, Papers of William Penn, 79; Am Coun Learned Soc res fel, 80. **MEMBERSHIPS** Orgn Am Historians. **RESEARCH** Scottish colonization of North America; transatlantic influences in American social development. **SELECTED PUBLICATIONS CONTACT ADDRESS** Dept Hist, SUNY, Stony Brook, 100 Nicolls Rd, Stony Brook, NY 11794-0002.

LANE, BARBARA MILLER
PERSONAL Born 11/01/1934, New York, NY, m, 1956, 2 children **DISCIPLINE** EUROPEAN HISTORY **EDUCATION** Univ Chicago, BA, 53; Barnard Col, BA, 56; Radcliffe Col, MA, 57; Harvard Univ, PhD, 62. **CAREER** Tutor hist and lit, Harvard Univ, 60-61; from lectr to Andrew W. Mellon Prof Emer of Humanities, Bryn Mawr Col, 62-; Katherine McBride Prof Emer, Bryn Mawr Col, 99-; dir, Growth and Struct of Cities prog, Bryn Mawr, 71-89; vis prof archit, Columbia Univ, 89; vis examr, Univ Helsinki, 91; vis lectr, Technische Univ Berlin, 91. **HONORS AND AWARDS** Am coun learned soc fel, 67-68; John Simon Guggenheim Found fel, 77-78; CASVA fel, 83; Lindback Found award for Distinguished teaching, 1988; Phi Beta Kappa; Wissenschaftskolleg zu Berlin fel, 90-91; Univ Helsinki Medal of Honor, 1996; NEH Senior fel for Univ Teachers, 98 **MEMBERSHIPS** Am Hist Asn; Soc Archit His-

torians; Conf Group for Central European Hist; Col Art Asn; Nat Screening Comt at Inst of Int Educ, 99-01; Archit Hist Found, 88-; Berlin Stradtforum, 91-96 **RESEARCH** Modern Germany; architectural history; Italian and German urban history. **SELECTED PUBLICATIONS** Auth, Architecture and Politics in Germany, Harvard Univ Pr, 68, 85; auth, Die Moderne und die Politik in Deutschland zwischen 1919 und 1945, Mod Archit in Deutsch vol 2, 94; auth, Interpreting Nazi Architecture, Rome, 1998; auth, National Romanticism and Modern Architecture in Germany and the Scandinavian Countries, Cambridge Univ Press, 2000; auth, Urban Ideals in the Later Twentieth Century, work in progress. **CONTACT ADDRESS** Growth and Structure of Cities Program, Bryn Mawr Col, 101 N Merion Ave, Bryn Mawr, PA 19010-2899. **EMAIL** blane@brynmawr.edu

LANE, EVELYN STAUDINGER
DISCIPLINE ART HISTORY **EDUCATION** Wellesley Col, BA, 77; MA, 80; Brown Univ, PhD, 87. **CAREER** Asst Prof Art, Wheaton Coll **MEMBERSHIPS** CAA; Medieval Acad of Amer; ICMA; Corpus Vitrearum Medii Aevi. **RESEARCH** Gothic Art and Architecture; Medieval Stained Glass **CONTACT ADDRESS** 11 Pine Needle Rd., Wayland, MA 01778. **EMAIL** elane@wheatonma.edu

LANE, ROGER
PERSONAL Born 01/17/1934, Providence, RI, m, 1974, 3 children **DISCIPLINE** AMERICAN HISTORY **EDUCATION** Yale Univ, BA, 55; Harvard Univ, PhD, 63. **CAREER** From asst prof to assoc prof, 63-76, prof hist, 76-81, Benjamin R. Collins Prof Am Hist, Haverford Col, 81-; res prof, 99. **HONORS AND AWARDS** Bancroft Award, 87; Urban Hist Asn Best Book Award, 92. **MEMBERSHIPS** AHA; OAH; SSHA. **RESEARCH** History of 19th century police forces; local government and American criminal patterns; black urban hist; middle class social hist in 20th century. **SELECTED PUBLICATIONS** Auth, Policing the City: Boston 1822-1885, Harvard Univ, 67; Violent Death in the City: Suicide, Accident & Murder in 19th Century Philadelphia, Harvard Univ, 79; Roots of Violence in Black Philadelphia, Harvard Univ, 80; William Dorsey's Philadelphia & Ours, CY Revel, 91; Murder in America: A History, Ohio State, 97. **CONTACT ADDRESS** Dept of Hist, Haverford Col, 370 Lancaster Ave, Haverford, PA 19041-1392. **EMAIL** rlane@haverford.edu

LANG, BEREL
PERSONAL Born 11/13/1933, Norwich, CT, m, 1972, 2 children **DISCIPLINE** HISTORY, PHILOSOPHY **EDUCATION** Yale Univ, BA, 54; Columbia Univ, PhD, 61. **CAREER** Prof, Univ of CO, 61-84; prof, SUNY Albany, 84-97, prof, Trinity Col, 97-. **HONORS AND AWARDS** Fel, NEH;Fel, ACLS; Fel, Univ of Pa; Bauugardt Fel, APA: Remarque Fel, NYU. **MEMBERSHIPS** APA; MLA; Am Soc for Aesthetics; Assoc for Jewish Studies; Thoreau Soc. **RESEARCH** Political Philosophy, Aesthetics, Holocaust Studies. **SELECTED PUBLICATIONS** Auth, Hiidegger's Silence, Cornell Univ Pr, 96; auth, The Future of the Holocaust, Cornell Univ Pr, 99; ed, Race and Racism in Theory and Practice, Rowman and Littlefield, 00. **CONTACT ADDRESS** Dept Humanities, Trinity Col, Connecticut, 300 Summit St., Hartford, CT 06106-3100. **EMAIL** berel.lang@trincoll.edu

LANG, WILLIAM
PERSONAL Born 11/05/1942, Portland, OR, m, 1991, 3 children **DISCIPLINE** HISTORY **EDUCATION** Willamette Unv, BA, 64; Washington Univ, 64; Univ Delaware, PhD, 73. **CAREER** Assoc Prof, Carroll Col, 71-78; Editor, Montana Historical Society, 78-89; Assoc Prof, Washington State Univ, 90-94; Prof, Portland State Univ, 94-. **HONORS AND AWARDS** Montana Humanities Awd, 88. **MEMBERSHIPS** Western History Assoc; AMA-PCB; Oregon Historical Society; Washington State Historical Society; Amer Society for Environmental History. **RESEARCH** Environmental History; Pacific Northwest History; Columbia River. **SELECTED PUBLICATIONS** Auth, "Confederacy of Ambition: William Winlock Miller and The Making of Washington Territory, Univ of Washington Press 96; "Great River of the West: Essays on the Columbia River," with Robert C. Carriker, Univ of Washington Press, 99. **CONTACT ADDRESS** Dept History, Portland State Univ, PO Box 751, Portland, OR 97207-0751. **EMAIL** langw@pdx.edu

LANGDON, JOHN W.
PERSONAL Born 04/23/1947, Utica, NY, m, 1970, 2 children **DISCIPLINE** HISTORY **EDUCATION** Le Moyne Col, BA, 67; Syracuse Univ, PhD, 73. **CAREER** Prof, Le Moyne Col, 71-. **HONORS AND AWARDS** Kevin G O'Connell Distinguished Teaching Awd; Teacher of the Year, Le Moyne Col, 89; Alpha Sigma Nu, Phi Alpha Theta, Pi Gamma Mu, Nat Defense Fel. **MEMBERSHIPS** Soc for French Hist Studies, Conference Group on Central European History. **RESEARCH** 19th and 20th Century European diplomatic and military history. **SELECTED PUBLICATIONS** Auth, July 1914: The Long Debate, 1918-1990, Berg Pub, 91; auth, A Hard and Bitter Peace: A Global History of the Cold War, Prentice-Hall, 96; auth, The Cold War: A History Through Documents, Prentice-Hall, 99. **CONTACT ADDRESS** Dept History, Le Moyne Col, 1419 Salt Springs Rd, Syracuse, NY 13214-1302. **EMAIL** langdon@maple.lemoyne.edu

LANGER, ERICK DETLEF
PERSONAL Born 05/22/1955, Richland, WA, m, 1978, 4 children **DISCIPLINE** HISTORY **EDUCATION** Univ Wash, BA, 77; Stanford Univ, MA, 79, PhD, 84. **CAREER** Vis lectr, Ctr Lat Am Stud, Univ Calif, Los Angeles, 84; vis fac, Univ Pittsburgh, 85; vis prof, Univ Catolica Salta, Argentina, 88; asst prof, Carnegie Mellon Univ, 84-90; adj assoc prof, Univ Pittsburgh, 90-98; adj assoc prof, 94-98, assoc prof hist, 90-98, Carnegie Mellon Univ; ASSOC PROF HIST, GEORGETOWN UNIV, 99-. **HONORS AND AWARDS** Fulbright-Hays fel, 81; Inter-Am Fdn fel, 81; Soc Sci Res Counc fel, 81; James Alexander Robertson Mem prize best article, hon men, 85; NEH summer stipend, 85; Albert J. Beveridge res grant, 88; Am Philos Soc res grant, 88; Rocky Mountain Council Lat Am Stud, McGann Prize Best Article, 88; Fulbright res award, 88; Fulbright Lect award, Inst Nac Antropol, 90; Soc Sci Res Counc res grant, 92; Oversears Ministries Stud Ctr res grant, 94; Fulbright Lect. Res, 00. **MEMBERSHIPS** Soc Geo Hist Tarija; Am Soc Ethnohistory; Phi Alpha Theta; Soc Boliviana Hist; Conf Lat Am Hist; Soc Geo Hist Sucre; Lat Am Stud Asn; AHA. **RESEARCH** Lat Am hist, 19th, 20th cent; Andean peasants; econ dev Andes; Lat Am frontier hist; Cath missions Lat Am. **SELECTED PUBLICATIONS** Auth, "What About Our Church's Children?" America vol 169, (93); Co-ed, The New Latin American Mission History, Univ Neb Press, 95; auth, "Return to the Mountain of Love, " Cross Currents vol 46, (96), auth, Foreign Cloth in the Lowland Frontier: Commerce and Consumption of Textiles in Bolivia, 1830-1930, The Allure of the Foreign: The Role of Imports in Post-Colonial Latin America, Univ Mich Press, 97; auth, Indigenas y exploradores en el Gran Chaco: Relaciones indio-blancas en la Bolivia del siglo XIX, Archivo y Biblioteca Nacionales de Bolivia Anuario 1996, Editorial Tupac Katari, 97; auth, The Barriers to Proletarianization: Bolivian Mine Labour, 1826-1918, Peripheral Labour? Studies in the History of Partial Proletarianization, Cambridge Univ Press, 97; auth, "Una vision historica de Bolivia en el siglo XX," Bolivia en el siglo XX, (la Paz: Harvard club, 99); co-auth, Experiencing World History, NY Univ Press, 00. **CONTACT ADDRESS** Dept of History, Georgetown Univ, Washington, DC 22207-3401. **EMAIL** langere@gunet.georgetown.edu

LANGLEY, HAROLD D.
DISCIPLINE HISTORY **EDUCATION** Catholic Univ, BA, 50; Univ Penn, MA, 51, PhD, 60. **CAREER** Assoc cur, Mus Hist & Tech, to cur, Smithsonian Inst; current, cur nav hist emer, Nat Mus of Am Hist, Smithsonian Inst; adj prof, hist, Catholic Univ. **HONORS AND AWARDS** John Lyman Book Awd; res grant, Am Antiquarian Soc; Victor Gondos Awd, Soc for Military Hist, 90; K. Jack Bauer Awd, North Am Soc for Oceanic Hist, 99. **MEMBERSHIPS** Orgn of Am Historians; Soc of Historians of the Early Am Republic; North Am Soc for Oceanic Hist; Soc for Military Hist; Soc of Historians of Am For Relations; Am Asn for the Hist of Med; Wash Soc for the Hist of Med; The Hist Soc. **RESEARCH** Peace of Ghent **SELECTED PUBLICATIONS** Auth, "Military Educ and Training," in the Encyclopedia of the Am Military, ed John E. Jessup and Louise B. Ketz (NYork, 94); auth, "William Beanes," "Med, Naval," and "The Star Spangled Banner," in Encyclopedia of the War of 1812, ed David S. and Jeanne T. Heidler (Santa Barbara, 97); auth, "Shipboard Life," in The Confederate Navy: The Ships, Men and Orgn, 1861-1865, ed William N. Skill, Jr. (London, 97); auth, "Dewey, Sampson and the Courts: The Rise and Fall of Prize and Bounty Money," New Interpretations in Naval Hist, ed William M. McBride (Annapolis, 98). **CONTACT ADDRESS** 2515 N Utah St, Arlington, VA 22207. **EMAIL** HDLgrog@aol.com

LANGLEY, LESTER DANNY
PERSONAL Born 08/07/1940, Clarksville, TX, m, 1962, 2 children **DISCIPLINE** HISTORY **EDUCATION** WTex State Univ, BA, 61, MA, 62; Univ Kans, PhD(hist), 65. **CAREER** Asst prof hist, Tex A&M Univ, 65-67 & Cent Wash State Col, 67-70; from Assoc Prof to Prof, 70-88, Res Prof Hist to Res Prof Emer, Univ Ga, 88-. **MEMBERSHIPS** AHA; Orgn Am Historians; Conf Latin Am Hist; Soc Hist Am Foreign Rel. **RESEARCH** Latin American history; inter-American relations; history of the Americas. **SELECTED PUBLICATIONS** Ed, United States, Cuba, and the Cold War, Heath, 70; co-ed, United States & Latin America, Addison-Wesley, 71; auth, Senator Kennedy on United States Foreign Policy in Latin America, Rev Interam, fall 72; The Diplomatic Historians: Bailey & Bemis, Hist Teacher, fall 72; Cuba, Forum, 73; Struggle for the American Mediterranean: US-European Rivalry in Gulf Caribbean, Ga Univ, 76; The Jacksonians and the Origins of Inter-American Distrust, Inter-Am Affairs, Vol 30; The US, Latin America, and the Panama Canal, Forum, 78; The US and the Caribbean in the 20th Century, Ga Univ, 80, 82, 85, & 89; The Banana Wars, Kentucky, 83; Central America: The Real Stakes, Crown, 85; MexAmerica: Two Countries, One Future, Crown, 88; America and the Americas: The United States in the Western Hemisphere, Univ Ga, 89; Mexico and the United States, Twayne, 91; coauth, The Banana Men, Kentucky, 94; auth, The Americas in the Age of Revolution, 1750-1850, Yale, 96. **CONTACT ADDRESS** Dept of History, Univ of Georgia, 202 LeConte Hall, Athens, GA 30602-1602. **EMAIL** llangley@athens.net

LANGMUIR, GAVIN INCE
PERSONAL Born 04/02/1924, Toronto, ON, Canada **DISCIPLINE** HISTORY **EDUCATION** Univ Toronto, BA, 48; Harvard Univ, AM, 49, PhD(hist), 55. **CAREER** Instr hist, Harvard Univ, 55; from asst prof to assoc prof, 55-77, Prof Hist, Stanford Univ, 77-. **MEMBERSHIPS** Am Hist Asn; Asn Jewish Studies; Eccles Hist Soc; Medieval Acad Am; Medieval Asn Pac; Royal Historical Soc. **RESEARCH** Medieval political, legal and institutional history; formation of anti-Semitism. **SELECTED PUBLICATIONS** Auth, History, Religion, and Antisemitism, 90; auth, Toward a Definition of Antisemitism, 90; auth, "The Faith of Christians and Hostility to Jews," Studies in Church History (92); auth, "The Tortures of the Body of Christ," Christendom and Its Discontents (96); auth, "Continuities, Discontinuities, and Contingencies of the Holocaust, The Fate of European Jews, 1939-1945, Continuity or Contingency?,"Studies in Contemporary Jewry (97). **CONTACT ADDRESS** Dept of Hist, Stanford Univ, 585 Salvatierra St., Stanford, CA 94305. **EMAIL** glang@stanford.edu

LANGSAM, MIRIAM ZELDA
PERSONAL Born 02/09/1939, Brooklyn, NY **DISCIPLINE** AMERICAN INTELLECTUAL AND SOCIAL HISTORY **EDUCATION** Brooklyn Col, BA, 60; Univ Wis, MS, 71, PhD(hist), 67. **CAREER** Resident lectr, 64-67, asst prof, 67-72, assoc prof, 72-81, Prof Hist, Ind Univ, Indianapolis, 81-, Lilly fel, 75; dir, Honors Prog and prof hist, Ind Univ-Purdue Univ at Indianapolis. **MEMBERSHIPS** AHA; Orgn Am Historians. **RESEARCH** Nineteenth century social history; urban and penal history. **SELECTED PUBLICATIONS** Auth, Children West: A History of the Placing-Out system of the New York Children's Aid Society, 1853-1890, State Hist Soc Wis, 64. **CONTACT ADDRESS** Indiana Univ-Purdue Univ, Indianapolis, 4125 Ashbourne Ln, Indianapolis, IN 46202.

LANGSAM, WALTER E.
PERSONAL Born 06/24/1935, Manhattan, NY, d, 1 child **DISCIPLINE** ARCHITECTURAL HISTORY **EDUCATION** Miami Univ, BA, 60; Yale Univ, MA 68; work towards PhD. **CAREER** Prod ed, Prentice-Hall, 60-64; arts ed, Yale Univ Pr, 65-66; asst prof, Art History, Univ Louisville, 70-74; asst dir, Kentucky Heritage Comn, 74-78; hist preserv asst, Lexington-Fayette Co Hist Comn, 78-82; Hist Preserv Off, Kovington KY, 82-85; adj asst prof, architecture, Univ of Cincinnati, 85- . **HONORS AND AWARDS** Ohioana Lib Prize, 98; Architectural Found of Cincinnati Awd, 98, 99. **MEMBERSHIPS** Archit Found Cincinnati; Cincinnati Preservation Asn; Historic Southwest Ohio; Historic Northern Kentucky Found; Ohio River Valley Chapter of Victorian Soc in Am; Founder and pres, Isaiah Rogers/Ohio River Valley Chapter of Soc of Archit Hist. **RESEARCH** Cincinnati architecture; American art, architecture, interior design history; historic preservation; British architecture. **SELECTED PUBLICATIONS** Auth, Louisville Mansions from the Civil War to World War II, in Mag Antiques, 74; auth, Introduction, in The Kentucky Governor's Mansion, A Restoration, by Seale, Harmony House, 84; co-auth, Historic Architecture of Bourbon County, Kentucky, Ky Heritage Council, 85; auth, Great Houses of the Queen City: 200 Years of Historic and Contemporary Architecture and Interiors in Cincinnati and Northern Kentucky, Museum Ctr at Union Terminal, 97; auth, Architecture Cincinnati: A Guide to Nationally Significant Buildings and Their Architects in the Greater Cincinnati Area, 99. **CONTACT ADDRESS** 2355 Fairview Ave, Cincinnati, OH 45219. **EMAIL** walter.langsam@uc.edu

LANKEVICH, GEORGE J.
PERSONAL Born 04/23/1939, New York, NY, m, 1965, 2 children **DISCIPLINE** AMERICAN HISTORY **EDUCATION** Fordham Col, BSS, 59; Columbia Univ, MA, 60, PhD(Am hist), 67. **CAREER** From instr to assoc prof, 64-75, Prof Hist, Bronx Community Col, 75-, City Univ New York fac res fel, 68. **MEMBERSHIPS** AAUP; AHA; Orgn Am Historians. **SELECTED PUBLICATIONS CONTACT ADDRESS** Dept of Hist, Bronx Comm Col, CUNY, Bronx, NY 10453.

LANKFORD, NELSON DOUGLAS
DISCIPLINE HISTORY **EDUCATION** Univ Richmond, BA, 70; Ind Univ, Bloomington, MA, 72, PhD(hist), 76. **CAREER** Coordr, Ind Univ-Hist New Harmony Inst, 76-77; researcher, Centennial Hist of Ind Gen Assembly, 77-78; Asst Ed, Am Hist Rev, 78-. **MEMBERSHIPS** AHA **RESEARCH** Victorian social history; British imperial and commonwealth history; US business history. **SELECTED PUBLICATIONS** Auth, of Locks and Picklocks, Va Mag Hist and Biog, Vol 0103, 95. **CONTACT ADDRESS** 4901 Evelyn Byrd Rd, Richmond, VA 23225-3101.

LANSEN, OSCAR
DISCIPLINE 20TH CENTURY WORLD, HOLOCAUST **EDUCATION** Katholieke Unversiteit Nijmegen, PhD, 88. **CAREER** Lectr, Univ NC, Charlotte. **RESEARCH** World War II; war and soc. **SELECTED PUBLICATIONS** Auth, Welkom Yankee Bevrijders: Soldiers and Civilians During the Liberation of the Netherlands 1944-1945, in William Shetter, ed, Publ of the Am Asn for Netherlandic Stud, UP of Am; Gerhard Durlacher's Verzameld Werk, USHMM, Holocaust and Genocide Stud, Oxford UP. **CONTACT ADDRESS** Univ of No Carolina, Charlotte, Charlotte, NC 28223-0001.

LANSKY, LEWIS
PERSONAL Born 04/08/1938, Buffalo, NY, 1 child **DISCIPLINE** HISTORY **EDUCATION** Univ Rochester, BA, 60; State Univ NY at Buffalo, MS, 62; Case Western Reserve Univ, PhD, 76. **CAREER** Prof, Monroe Community Col, 62-67, 71-. **HONORS AND AWARDS** Grant, Overstreet Fund at CWRU; Univ Fel, Case Western Reserve Univ, 69-71; Sabbatical Leave, 99-00. **MEMBERSHIPS** AHA, Orgn of Am Historians. **RESEARCH** Great Depression, New Deal, Political economy, 1920's-1990's. **SELECTED PUBLICATIONS** Auth, "Buffalo and the Great Depression, 1929-1933," in An American Historian: Essays to Honor Selig Adler, ed. Milton Plesur (Buffalo, NY: State Univ of NY at Buffalo, 80). **CONTACT ADDRESS** Dept Hist and Govt, Monroe Comm Col, 1000 E Henriette Rd, Rochester, NY 14623-5701. **EMAIL** llansky@monroecc.edu

LANT, CHRISTOPHER
PERSONAL Born 02/22/1961, Albany, NY, m **DISCIPLINE** GEOGRAPHY **EDUCATION** SUNY Albany, BA, 83; Univ Iowa, MA, 85; PhD, 88. **CAREER** Asst prof to prof, Southern IL Univ Carbondale, 88-. **HONORS AND AWARDS** First Prize, PhD Student Paper Competition, Asn of Am Geog, 85; Norman and Ruth Berg Fel, Soil and Water Conserv Soc, 96. **MEMBERSHIPS** Assoc of Am Geog; Am Water Res Assoc; IL Register of Expert Witnesses, Int Water Res Assoc; Soil and Water Conserv Soc. **RESEARCH** Water resource management, watershed management, U.S. agricultural conservation and wetlands policy, political ecology, sustainable development. **SELECTED PUBLICATIONS** Coauth, "Conflicting Attitudes of Local People and Conservation Officials in Kenya", Nat Res and Soc 8, (95): 133-144; coauth, "The 1990 Farm Bill and Water Quality in Corn Belt Watersheds: Conserving Remaining Wetlands and Restoring of Farmed Wetlands", J of Soil and Water Conserv 50.2 (95): 201-205; coauth, "Enrollment of Filter Strips and Recharge Areas in the CRP and USDA Easement Programs", J of Soil and Water Conserv 50.2 (95): 193-200; coauth, "The Role of NIMBY Groups in 22 Sanitary Landfill Sitings in Illinois", Environ Prof, 17.3 (95): 243-250; coauth, "A Political Ecology Approach to Wildlife Conservation in Kenya", Environ Values 5, (96): 335-47; coauth, "WQIP: An Assessment of its Chances for Acceptance by Farmers: Survey Results", J of Soil and Water Conserv 51.6 (96): 494-498; auth, "The Influence of Social and Agricultural Trends on Water Quality: Implications for Future Policies", Influence of Social Trends in Agricultural Natural Resources, eds F. Clearfield and S.E. Kraft, 98; coauth, The Effect of Mitigation Banking on the Achievement of No-Net-Loss", Environ Management 23.3 (99): 333-345; auth, "Introduction: Human Dimensions of Watershed Management", J of the Am Water Res Assoc 35.3, (99): 483-486. **CONTACT ADDRESS** Dept Geog, So Illinois Univ, Carbondale, Carbondale, IL 62901-4514. **EMAIL** clant@siu.edu

LAPIDUS, IRA M.
PERSONAL Born 06/09/1937, New York, NY, m, 1983, 1 child **DISCIPLINE** HISTORY **EDUCATION** Harvard Univ, AB, 58, PhD, 64. **CAREER** Prof, hist, Univ Calif Berkeley, 65-94; chair, Ctr for Middle Eastern Studies, Univ Calif Berkeley, 79-94; pres, Middle East Studies Asn, 83-84. **HONORS AND AWARDS** Mem, Amer Philos Soc; Guggenheim fel; SSRC fel. **MEMBERSHIPS** Middle East Studies Asn; Urban Hist Asn. **RESEARCH** Islam; Middle East history; Urban history. **SELECTED PUBLICATIONS** ed, Middle Eastern Cities, Univ of Calif Pr, (Berkeley), 69; auth, Muslim Cities in the Later Middle Ages, Harvard Univ Pr, 67, 2nd ed, Cambridge Univ Pr, 84; auth, "Contemporary Islamic Movements in Historical Perspective," in Policy Papers No 18, Inst of International Stud, Univ of Calif, (Berkeley), 84; auth, Islam, Politics and Social Movements, Berkeley, Univ of Calif Press, 88; auth, A History of Islamic Societies, Cambridge Univ Pr, 88; ed, Islam Politics and Social Movements, Univ of Calif Pr, (Berkeley), 88; article, Islamism, Encycl Ital, 100-114, 96; article, State and Relgion in Islamic Societies, Past and Present, 151, 3-27, 96; article, A Sober Survey of the Islamic World, Orbis, 391-404, 96; Article, Islamic Revival and Modernity: The Contemporary Movements and the Historical Paradigms, Jour of the Econ and Soc Hist of the Orient, 38, 444-460, 97. **CONTACT ADDRESS** 2671 Shasta Rd., Berkeley, CA 94708. **EMAIL** ilapidus@uclink4.berkeley.edu

LAPOMARDA, VINCENT ANTHONY
PERSONAL Born 02/28/1934, Portland, ME **DISCIPLINE** UNITED STATES HISTORY, AMERICAN DIPLOMACY, AMERICAN RELIGIOUS HISTORY **EDUCATION** Boston Col, AB, 57, MA, 58, STL, 65; Boston Univ, PhD, 68. **CAREER** Teacher English, hist, Latin & relig, Boston Col High Sch, 58-61; asst prof, 69-74, assoc prof hist, Col of the Holy Cross, 74-, Dir, The Jesuits of Holy Cross Col, Inc, 71-87, secy, 72-87, mem educ policy comt, Col of the Holy Cross, 72-74, dir Washington internship prog, 74-75, coordr, Holocaust Collection, Col of the Holy Cross, 79-, dir, Italian Am Collection, Col of the Holy Cross; chmn comt hist memorials, Int Order Alhambra, 81-; state historian, Mass Knights of Columbus, 81-. **HONORS AND AWARDS** Coe Fel, 59; Phi Alpha Theta, 66; Batchelor Fel, 69, 70; Knight of Holy Sepulchre, 87; Alhambran of the Year, 87; Fac Service Awd, Col of the Holy Cross, 95. **MEMBERSHIPS** AHA; Am Cath Hist Asn; Orgn Am Historians; Am Ital Hist Asn. **RESEARCH** Jesuits in history; Italian Americans; The Holocaust. **SELECTED PUBLICATIONS** Auth, The Jesuit Heritage in New England, Worcester, 77; The Knights of Columbus in Massachusetts, Needham, 82, 2nd ed, Norwood, 92; The Jesuits and the Third Reich, Lewiston, 89; The Order of Alhambra, Baltimore, 94; The Boston Mayor Who Became Truman's Secretary of Labor, NY, 95; Charles Nolcini, Worcester, 97; author of numerous journal articles, letters, and reviews. **CONTACT ADDRESS** Col of the Holy Cross, 1 College St, Worcester, MA 01610-2322. **EMAIL** vlapomar@holycross.edu

LAPP, RUDOLPH MATHEW
PERSONAL Born 08/19/1915, Chicago, IL, m, 1943 **DISCIPLINE** AMERICAN HISTORY **EDUCATION** Roosevelt Univ, Chicago, BA, 48; Univ Calif, Berkeley, MA, 52, PhD(Am hist), 56. **CAREER** Emer Prof Am Hist, Col San Mateo, 55-. **HONORS AND AWARDS** Nat Endowment Humanities fel, 72-73. **MEMBERSHIPS** Southern Hist Asn, Study Negro Life and Hist, Calif Hist Soc. **RESEARCH** African Am Hist in Calif. **SELECTED PUBLICATIONS** Auth, Parallel Communities-African Americans in California East Bay, 1850-1963, PAC HIST REV, Vol 0064, 95. **CONTACT ADDRESS** Col of San Mateo, 1787 Wolfe Dr, San Mateo, CA 94402.

LAPSANSKY, EMMA J.
PERSONAL Born 04/19/1945, Washington, DC, d, 3 children **DISCIPLINE** HISTORY **EDUCATION** Univ Pa, BA, 68; MA, 69; PhD, 75 **CAREER** Prof of History and Curator, Special Collections Haverford Col, 95; Assoc Prof of History and Curator, Special Collections Haverford Col, 90; Vis Lecturer, History Princeton Univ, 90; Adjunct Prof, Univ of Pa, 88-95; Asst/then Assoc Prof, Temple Univ 73-90; Assoc Dean, Temple Univ, 84-86. **HONORS AND AWARDS** Am Council of Learned Societies, Fellow, 83. **MEMBERSHIPS** NEH Summer Institute, 96; Organization of American Historians, 95-96; Friends' Historical Association, 90. **RESEARCH** Family and community life, especially in antebellum cities; architecture, material culture and community planning; religion and popular culture in nineteenth-century America; Quaker history; the American West; historical interpretation for popular audiences. **SELECTED PUBLICATIONS** Auth, Neighborhoods in Transition: William Penn's Dream and Urban Reality, Garland Press, 94; auth, "Making it Home:" The Black Presence in Pennsylvania, Pennsylvania Historical and Museum Commission, 90; auth, "The World the Agitators Made: The Counterculture of Agitation in Urban Philadelphia, in The Abolitionist Sisterhood: Women's Political Culture in Antebellum America, ed. Jean Fagan Yellin and John C. Van Horne (94); auth, "Discipline to the Mind: The Banneker Institute of Philadelphia, 1854-1872", Pennsylvania Magazine of History and Biography (93); auth, "Feminism and Freedom: Black Women's Strategies in Nineteenth-Century Philadelphia," Pennsylvania of Magazine of History and Biography, (89). **CONTACT ADDRESS** Dept History, Haverford Col, 370 Lancaster Ave, Haverford, PA 19041-1336.

LAQUEUR, THOMAS WALTER
PERSONAL Born 09/06/1945, Istanbul, Turkey **DISCIPLINE** HISTORY **EDUCATION** Swarthmore Col, BA, 67; Princeton Univ, MA, 69, PhD(hist), 73. **CAREER** Instr social sci, Concord Col, 68-69; asst prof, 73-80, Assoc Prof Hist, Univ Calif, Berkeley, 80-, Nat Endowment for Humanities fel, 76. **MEMBERSHIPS** AHA **SELECTED PUBLICATIONS** Auth, Religion and Respectability: Sunday Schools and Working Class Culture, 1780-1850, Yale Univ, 76. **CONTACT ADDRESS** Dept of Hist, Univ of California, Berkeley, 3229 Dwinelle Hall, Berkeley, CA 94720-2551.

LAREBO, HAILE
PERSONAL Born 01/29/1949, Wagabata, Ethiopia, m, 1986, 3 children **DISCIPLINE** HISTORY **EDUCATION** BD; STL; PhD. **CAREER** asst prof, Morehouse Univ. **MEMBERSHIPS** AHA, African Studies ASN. **RESEARCH** European imperialism, religion in Africa **SELECTED PUBLICATIONS** Auth, The Building of an Empire: Italian Land Policy and Practice in Ethiopia 1935-1941, Clarendon Press/Oxford Univ Press, 94. **CONTACT ADDRESS** Dept Hist, Morehouse Col, 830 Westview Dr SW, Atlanta, GA 30314-3773. **EMAIL** hlarebo@morehouse.edu

LAREW, KARL G.
PERSONAL Born 12/09/1936, Ithaca, NY, m, 1972 **DISCIPLINE** EUROPEAN AND MILITARY HISTORY **EDUCATION** Univ Conn, BA, 59; Yale Univ, MA, 60; PhD, 64. **CAREER** Part time fac, Univ Conn, S Conn State Col, Univ MD, 60-66; 1st Lieut US Army Intell, 64-66; asst prof, Towson Univ, 66; assoc prof, 69; prof 73-. **HONORS AND AWARDS** Phi Beta Kappa; Phi Alpha Theta; Dist Serv Awd, Fac Advis Awd, 88; Merit Awd, Towson Univ, 87. **MEMBERSHIPS** AHA; AAUP; WFA; US Army Sig Corp Reg Assoc. **RESEARCH** World War II; WWI; Korean War; historical methodology; popular culture. **SELECTED PUBLICATIONS** Auth, Civil War Soldier, Gateway (Baltimore), 75; auth, "Great Britain and the Greco-Turkish War, 1919-1922," The Historian (73); auth, "Operation Sea Lion Revisited," in New Interpretations in Naval History: Selected Papers from the Ninth Naval History Symposium, eds. William R Roberts, Jack Sweetman (Annapolis: Naval Inst Press, 91); auth, "The Royal Navy in the Battle of Britain," The Historian (92); auth, "Planet Women: the Image of Women in Planet Comics," The Historian (97). **CONTACT ADDRESS** Dept History, Towson State Univ, 8000 York Rd, Baltimore, MD 21252-0001. **EMAIL** klarew@towson.edu

LARIVIERE, RICHARD WILFRED
PERSONAL Born 01/27/1950, Chicago, IL, m, 1971, 1 child **DISCIPLINE** INDIAN STUDIES **EDUCATION** Univ IA, BA, 72; Univ PA, PhD(Sanskrit), 78. **CAREER** Vis lectr Sanskrit, Univ PA, 78-79; vis asst prof, Univ IA, 80-81; asst prof, 82-85, prof Sanskrit, 86-89, Ralph B Thomas Regents Prof, Univ Tx, Austin, 90-, assoc vice-pres for int progs, Dean, College of Liberal Arts, Univ TX, 95-; Fel, Fulbright-Hays, 76-77, Am Inst Indian Studies, 76-77 & 80, Soc Sci Res Coun, 79 & Nat Endowment for Humanities, 79-83; panelist, National Endowment for Humanities, 80; bd of dirs, HCL/Perot Systems, NU, Amsterdam, 95-. **HONORS AND AWARDS** CESMEO Prize, 89; Gonda Lect, Royal Dutch Academy, 94; Prof-College de France, Paris, 96-97; Am Coun of Learned Socs delegate to int academic union, Paris, 95-. **MEMBERSHIPS** Am Orient Soc; Asn Asian Studies; Royal Asiatic Soc; Bhandarkar Orient Res Inst; Asiatic Soc Bengel. **RESEARCH** Classical Indian culture and philosophy; classical and modern Hindu law; history of religions. **SELECTED PUBLICATIONS** Auth, The Indian Supreme Court and the Freedom of Religion, J Const & Parliamentary Studies, 75; A Note on the Kosadivya, Adyar Libr Bull, 76; Madhyamamimamsa--The Sankarsakanda, Wiener fur die Kunde Sudasiens, 81; Ordeals in India and Europe, J Am Orient Soc, 81; The Divy tattva of Raghunandana Bhattacarya: Ordeals in Hindu Law, Manohar, New Delhi, 81; The Judicial Wager in Hindu Law, Ann Bhandarkar Orient Res Inst, 81; Asedha and Akrosa--Arrest in the Sarasvativilasa, Festschrift J D M Derret, 82; A Compilation of Pitamaha Verses Found in Two Manuscripts from Nepal, Studien zur Indologie & Iranistik, 85. **CONTACT ADDRESS** College of Liberal Arts, Univ of Texas, Austin, Main 101, Austin, TX 78712. **EMAIL** rwl@uts.cc.utexas.edu

LARKIN, JACK
PERSONAL Born 06/26/1943, Evergreen Park, IL, m, 1970, 2 children **DISCIPLINE** AMERICAN SOCIAL HISTORY AND MATERIAL CULTURE **EDUCATION** Harvard Col, AB, 65; Brandeis Univ, MA, 68; Museum Management Inst, J. Paul Getty Trust, 95. **CAREER** From coord to asst dir to res hist to chief hist to dir res, 71-, Old Sturbridge Village. **HONORS AND AWARDS** Am Quarterly Awd, 82; Finalist & Distinguished Mention, 89; PEN, 89; Mem Am Antiquarian Society, 94; President's Awd, 96; Kidger Awd, 99. **MEMBERSHIPS** Org Am Hist: Asn Am Museums; Am Asn State Local Hist. **RESEARCH** Social history; historical ethnography and material culture of rural New England, 1780-1860; public history and museums. **SELECTED PUBLICATIONS** Auth, art From 'Country Mediocrity' to Rurual Improvement: Transforming the Solvenly Countryside in the Early Republic, 95; coauth, Northern Comfort: New England's Early Quilts 1780-1850, 98; auth, art, Episodes from Daily Life: "The Life and Writings of Minerva Mayo by herself" as an Exercise in Microhistory, 00. **CONTACT ADDRESS** Director of Research, Collections & Library, Old Sturbridge Village, 1 Old Sturbridge Village Rd, Sturbridge, MA 01566-1138. **EMAIL** jlarkin@osv.org

LARKIN, JANET
PERSONAL Born 03/08/1961, Canada, m, 1992 **DISCIPLINE** HISTORY **EDUCATION** Univ Buffalo, PhD, 92. **CAREER** Asst Prof, Keuka Col, 92-. **MEMBERSHIPS** OAH, ARLS. **RESEARCH** Niagara borderland. **SELECTED PUBLICATIONS** Auth, The Origins of the Erie and Wetland Canals Along the Niagara Borderland, ARCS, 94; Auth, "Overcoming Niagara: The Internal Improvements Program in Western New York and Upper Canada, Essay (forthcoming). **CONTACT ADDRESS** Dept Soc Sci, Keuka Col, PO Box 98, Keuka Park, NY 14478-0098. **EMAIL** jlarkin@mail.keuka.edu

LAROCCA, JOHN JOSEPH
PERSONAL Born 06/01/1946, New York, NY **DISCIPLINE** HISTORY **EDUCATION** Fordham Univ, BA, 69; Rutgers Univ, MA, 71, PhD(hist), 77. **CAREER** Asst prof History, 77-81, from assoc prof to prof History, chmn dept, Xavier Univ, 81-87. **HONORS AND AWARDS** Midwest Conf on Brit Studies; Ecclesiastical Hist Soc, Gr Brit; Cath Record Society, Gr Brit. **MEMBERSHIPS** AHA; Cath Rec Soc; Conf Brit Studies. **RESEARCH** Elizabethan and Jacobean Recusancy; reformation. **SELECTED PUBLICATIONS** Auth, Time, death and the next generation: The early Elizabethan Recusancy Policy, 1558-1574, Albion (in press); The Recusant Rolls for London and Middlesex Counties, 1603-1625, The Catholic Record Society, Spring, 1996; Jacobean Recusant Rolls for Middlesex: an Abstract in English, trans and ed Catholic Record Society Publications, Record Series, Vol 76, Hampshire, 97. **CONTACT ADDRESS** Dept of History, Xavier Univ, Ohio, 3800 Victory Pky, Cincinnati, OH 45207-1092. **EMAIL** larocca@admin.xu.edu

LAROUCHE, MICHEL
PERSONAL Born 01/25/1951, PQ, Canada, m, 1973, 1 child **DISCIPLINE** HISTORY OF ART **EDUCATION** Univ Que, Montreal, BA, 73; Univ Montreal, BA, 73, MA, 75, PhD(-French), 80. **CAREER** Prof film, Col Bois-de-Boulogne, 73-75 and Col Andre-Laurendeau, 75-80; Prof Film, Art Hist Dept, Univ Montreal, 80-, Prof, art hist dept, Univ Que, Montreal, 75-80. **MEMBERSHIPS** Univ Art Asn of Can; Film Studies Asn of Can. **RESEARCH** The film style of Alexandro Jodorowsky; the experimental film; the animated film. **SELECTED PUBLICATIONS** Ed., Le Cinema Aujourd Hui: Film, Theories, Nouvelles Approches, (Essai No 8), (editor), Paperback (October 89); auth, Alexandro Jodorowsky: Cineaste Panique. **CONTACT ADDRESS** Histoire de l'art, Univ de Montreal, CP 6128 succ Centre-Ville, Montreal, QC, Canada H3C 3J7. **EMAIL** larouchm@histart.umontreal.ca

LARSEN, GRACE H.
PERSONAL Born 12/04/1920, Pomona, CA, m, 1943, 2 children **DISCIPLINE** AMERICAN HISTORY **EDUCATION** Univ Calif, Berkeley, AB, 42, MA, 45; Columbia Univ, PhD, 55. **CAREER** Lectr Europ hist, Rutgers Univ, 47-49, US hist, 52-55; from asst specialist to assoc specialist agr econ, Univ Calif, Berkeley, 55-66; assoc prof hist, 66-71, chmn dept hist, 67-70, acad dean, 70-80, Prof Hist, Holy Names Col, Calif, 71-, Lectr, Bryn Mawr Col, 49-50 and Swarthmore Col, 49-51; Huntington Library grant; Nat Endowment Humanities summer grant. **MEMBERSHIPS** AHA; Agr Hist Soc. **RESEARCH** American colonial history; agricultural history; women on the land. **SELECTED PUBLICATIONS** Auth, The Economics and Structure of the Citrus Industry--Comment on Papers by Moses, H.,Vincent and Tobey, Robert and Wetherell, Charles, Calif Hist, Vol 0074, 95. **CONTACT ADDRESS** Holy Names Col, 3500 Mountain Blvd, Oakland, CA 94619.

LARSEN, LAWRENCE H.
PERSONAL Born 01/18/1931, Racine, WI, m, 1963, 2 children **DISCIPLINE** AMERICAN HISTORY **EDUCATION** Lawrence Col, BS, 53; Univ Wis, MS, 55, PhD, 62. **CAREER** Asst hist, Univ Wis, 55-57, 58-59, instr hist, Exten Ctr, 57-58; asst archivist, State Hist Soc Wis, 59-61; instr hist, Carroll Col, 61-62; asst prof, Wis State Col, Oshkosh, 62-64; asst prof to assoc prof, 64-69, actg chmn dept, 65-66, Prof Hist, Univ MO-Kansas City, 69-, Instr, Univ Wis, 61, specialist, Exten Div, 62. **MEMBERSHIPS** Orgn Am Historians. **RESEARCH** 20th Century U.S.; urban history; legal history. **SELECTED PUBLICATIONS** Auth, The President Wore Spats, a Biography of Glenn Frank, 65; coauth, Factories in the Valley: Neenah-Menasha, 1870-1915, 69; co-ed, Aspects of American History, 1776-1970 (2 vols), Kendall-Hunt, 70, Urban Crisis in Modern America, Heath, 71 & The Eisenhower Administration, 1953-1961: A Documentary History, Random, 71; auth, The Urban West at the End of the Frontier, Regents Press of Kans, 78; coauth, The Gate City: A History of Omaha, Pruett Publ Co, 82; auth, Wall of Flames, North Dakota St Univ, 84; auth, the Rise of the Urban South, Univ Press of Kent, 85; auth, The Urban South: A History, Univ Press of Kent, 90; coauth, The University of Kansas Medical Center: A Pictoral History, Univ Press of Kans, 92; auth, Federal Justice in Western Missouri: The Judges, the Cases, the Times, Univ of MO, 94; coauth, The Gate City: A History of Omaha, enlarged ed, Univ of Neb 97; coauth, Pendergast!, Univ of MO, 97. **CONTACT ADDRESS** Dept of History, Univ of Missouri, Kansas City, 5100 Rockhill Rd, Kansas City, MO 64110-2499. **EMAIL** larsenl@umkc.edu

LARSON, BRUCE LLEWELLYN
PERSONAL Born 01/10/1936, Hawley, MN **DISCIPLINE** AMERICAN HISTORY **EDUCATION** Concordia Col Moorhead, BA, 59; Univ NDak, MA, 61; Univ Kans, PhD(hist), 71. **CAREER** Instr hist, Concordia Col, 62-63; from asst prof to assoc prof, 65-76, Prof Hist, Mankato State Univ, 76-, Elmer L and Eleanor J Andersen Found fel grant, 72-73; narrator and consult, TV Documentary on Charles a Lindbergh, KTVI, Mo, 77. **MEMBERSHIPS** AHA; Orgn Am Historians; Agr Hist Soc; Swed Pioneer Hist Soc; Am Aviation Hist Soc. **RESEARCH** Midwest and Scandinavian-American politics; Lindbergh history; Minnesota history. **SELECTED PUBLICATIONS** Auth, Kansas and the Panay Incident, 1937, Kans Hist Quart, autumn, 65; Lindbergh of Minnesota: A Political Biography, Harcourt Brace Jovanovich, 73; The Early Life of Charles A Lindbergh, Sr, 1859-1883, Swed Pioneer Hist Quart, 10/73; contribr, Swedes in Minnesota Politics, In: The Swedes in Minnesota, T S Denison & Co, 76; auth, Lindbergh's Return to Minnesota, 1927, Minn Hist, winter 70, reprinted in Am Aviation Hist Soc J, spring, 77; contribr, Kansas and the Nonpartisan League: The response to the affair at Great Bend, 1921, In: Essays on Kansas History in Honor of George L Anderson, Coronado, 77; Swedish Americans and Farmer-Labor Politics in Minnesota, In: Perspectives on Swedish Immigration, Swed Pioneer Hist Soc & Univ Minn, 78. **CONTACT ADDRESS** Dept of Hist, Mankato State Univ, Mankato, MN 56001.

LARSON, JOHN L.
PERSONAL Born 03/06/1950, Eagle Grove, IN, m, 2 children **DISCIPLINE** HISTORY **EDUCATION** Luther Col, BA, 72; Brown Univ, AM, 76; PhD, 81. **CAREER** Lecturer, Earlham Col, 79-83; Director, Conner Prairie, 79-83; Asst Prof to Assoc Prof, Purdue Univ, 83-. **HONORS AND AWARDS** NEH Summer Fel, 92; Center for Humanistic Studies, Purdue Univ, 89-90; am Asn for State and Local Hist Grant, 88; Ind Committee for the Humanities summer Fel, 88; Am Bar Foundation Legal Hist Grant, 86; NEH Summer Grant, 86; John E Rovensky Fel, 78-79. **MEMBERSHIPS** Soc for Hist of Early am Republic, Ind Hist Soc. **RESEARCH** United States, early republic: public policy, economic development, legal and political culture, westward movement, slavery and race. **SELECTED PUBLICATIONS** Auth, "Internal Improvement: Public Works and the Promise of Popular Government in the Early United States, Univ NC Press, forthcoming; auth, Bonds of Enterprise: John Murray Forbes and Western Development in America's Railway Age, 1813-1898, Harvard Univ Press, 84; auth, "Wisdom Enough to Improve Them: Government, Liberty, and Inland Waterways in the Rising American Empire," in Launching the Extended Republic, US Capitol Historical Society, 96; auth, "Jefferson's Union and the Problem of Internal Improvements," in Jeffersonian Legacies," Univ Press of Va, 93; auth, "Liberty By Design: Freedom, Planning, and John Quincy Adams's 'American System'," in The State and Economic Knowledge: Reflections on the American and British Experience, Cambridge Univ Press, 90; auth, "Ruins and Old Routes: Tracking the Remains of Indiana's 1836 Internal Improvement Program," Traces, (90): 37-47; auth, "To Try to Make a State of It: the Mammoth Internal Improvements Bill in Indiana," Indiana Academy of Social Sciences Proceedings, (87): 77-84; auth, "A Bridge, a Dam, a River: Liberty and Innovation in the Early Republic," Journal of the Early Republic, (87): 351-375; auth, "Bind the Republic Together," The National Union and the Struggle for a System of Internal Improvements," Journal of American History, (87): 363-387; auth, "Agent of Empire: William Conner on the Indiana Frontier," Indiana Magazine of History, (84): 301-328. **CONTACT ADDRESS** Dept Hist, Purdue Univ, West Lafayette, West Lafayette, IN 47907. **EMAIL** larsonjl@purdue.edu

LARSON, ROBERT H.
PERSONAL Born 03/03/1942, New York, NY, 3 children **DISCIPLINE** MODERN EUROPEAN HISTORY **EDUCATION** The Citadel, BA, 63; Univ Va, MA, 68, PhD, 73. **CAREER** Instr, 69-72, asst prof, 72-79, assoc prof mod Europ hist, 79-88, prof 88-98, Shangraw Prof of Hist, Lycoming Col. **HONORS AND AWARDS** Templer Medal, Soc for Army Hist Res, Eng, 84. **MEMBERSHIPS** AHA **RESEARCH** Military history of 19th- and 20th-century Europe. **SELECTED PUBLICATIONS** Auth, "B.H. Liddell Hart: Apostle of Limited War," Military Affairs, 4/80; auth, The British Army and the Theory of Armored Warfare, 1918-1940, Delaware, 84; coauth, Williamsport: From Frontier Village to Regional Center, Windsor, 84. **CONTACT ADDRESS** History Dept, Lycoming Col, 700 College Pl, Williamsport, PA 17701-5192. **EMAIL** larson@lycoming.edu

LARSON, ROBERT WALTER
PERSONAL Born 03/20/1927, Denver, CO, 2 children **DISCIPLINE** UNITED STATES HISTORY **EDUCATION** Univ Denver, AB, 50, Am, 53; Univ NMex, PhD(US hist), 61. **CAREER** Instr hist, pub schs, Colo, 50-56, supv teacher, 56-58; assoc prof, 60-68, Prof Hist, Univ Northern Colo, 68-, Hist consult, Britannica Jr Encycl, 69-; ed consult, NMex Hist Rev, 76-. **HONORS AND AWARDS** Distinguished Scholar Awd, Univ Northern Colo, 77. **MEMBERSHIPS** AHA; Orgn Am Historians; Western Hist Asn. **RESEARCH** Southwestern history, especially New Mexico; Progressive period during the administrations of Theodore Roosevelt and William Howard Taft; Western populism. **SELECTED PUBLICATIONS** Auth, Taft, Roosevelt, and New Mexico Statehood, Mid-Am, 4/63; New Mexico's Quest for Statehood, 1846-1912, Univ NMex, 68; Profile of a New Mexico Progressive, NMex Hist Rev, 7/70; Students, Populists, and a Sense of History, Colo Mag, winter 71; New Mexico Populism, Colo Assoc Univ, 74; The White Caps of New Mexico: A Study of Ethnic Militancy in the Southwest, Pac Hist Rev, 5/75; Populism in the Mountain West: A Mainstream Movement, Western Hist Quart, 4/82. **CONTACT ADDRESS** Dept of Hist, Univ of No Colorado, Greeley, CO 80639.

LARSON, STEPHANIE L.
PERSONAL Born 11/17/1968, St Paul, MN, m, 2000 **DISCIPLINE** HISTORY **EDUCATION** Univ Minn, BA, 92; Univ Tex, MA, 01. **CAREER** Asst Instr, Univ Tex, 96-98, 99-00. **HONORS AND AWARDS** Fel, Univ Tex, 00-01; Steven Res Fel, Am Sch of Class Studies, 98-99; Fulbright Fel, 97-98; Thomas Seymour Fel, Am Sch of Class Studies, 98-99; P.E.O. Scholar, 99-00. **MEMBERSHIPS** Am Philol Asn; Class Asn of the Mid W and S **RESEARCH** Ancient Greek history and culture; archaic Greek literature and culture; Boiotia; Ancient religion and magic; Hellenistic poetry; The Ancient Near East. **CONTACT ADDRESS** Dept Hist, Univ of Texas, Austin, 1500 Mark Thomas Dr, Monterey, CA 93940. **EMAIL** slarson68@hotmail.com

LARSON, TAFT ALFRED
PERSONAL Born 01/18/1910, Wakefield, NE, m, 1992 **DISCIPLINE** HISTORY **EDUCATION** Univ Colo, AB, 32, AM, 33; Univ Ill, PhD, 37. **CAREER** From instr to prof hist, 36-69, William Robertson Coe Prof Am Studies, 69-75, Emer Prof Am Studies, Univ Wyo, 75-; Mem House Rep, Wyo State Legis, 76-, Vis prof, Columbia Univ, 50-51; mem US Nat Comn for UNESCO, 63-66. **HONORS AND AWARDS** Who's Who in Am, 54-; LLD Univ of Wyo, 75. **MEMBERSHIPS** Western Hist Asn (pres, 70-71), Wyo House Rep, 76-83. **RESEARCH** Western American history; Wyoming history; history of woman suffrage. **SELECTED PUBLICATIONS** Auth, Who's who in Amer, 54. **CONTACT ADDRESS** 2052 N 7th, No 22, Laramie, WY 82072.

LASKA, VERA
PERSONAL Born 07/21/1928, Kosice, Czechoslovakia, m, 1949, 2 children **DISCIPLINE** HISTORY **EDUCATION** Univ of Chicago, PhD. **CAREER** Prof, Regis Col, 66-; Dir, Regis Col, 69-75, 75-88. **HONORS AND AWARDS** Outstanding Teachers of Am, 72; Kidger Awd for Excellence in Hist, 84; George Washington Honor Medal in Commun, 90; Fulbright Prof, 93. **MEMBERSHIPS** AHA; New England Hist Assoc; New England Hist Teachers Assoc; Nat Assoc of Foreign Student Affairs. **RESEARCH** World War II, women's studies, holocaust studies. **SELECTED PUBLICATIONS** Auth, Remember the Ladies, Outstanding Women of the Am Revolution, 76; auth, Czechs in America, 1633-1977, 78; auth, Franklin and Women, 79; auth, Benjamin Franklin the Diplomat, 82; auth, Nazism, Resistance & Holocaust, 85; auth, Women in the Resistance & Holocaust, 83, 88; auth, Two Loves of Benjamin Franklin, Prague, 94. **CONTACT ADDRESS** Dept History, Regis Col, Massachusetts, 50 Woodchester Dr, Weston, MA 02493.

LASLETT, JOHN HENRY MARTIN
PERSONAL Born 05/07/1933, Watford, England, m, 1959, 2 children **DISCIPLINE** AMERICAN AND COMPARATIVE SOCIAL HISTORY **EDUCATION** Oxford Univ, BA, 57, DPhil(hist), 62. **CAREER** Asst lectr polit theory and insts, Univ Liverpool, 61-62; assoc prof soc sci, Univ Chicago, 63-64 and Am hist, 64-68; assoc prof, 68-75, Prof Hist, Univ Calif, Los Angeles, 75-, Willett res award, Univ Chicago, 64; Soc Sci Res Coun res fel, 70-71; Am Coun Learned Soc fac award, 70-71; vis prof hist, Ctr Study Social Hist, Univ Warwick, 73-74; fel, Inst Ind Relations, Univ Calif, Los Angeles, 81-82. **MEMBERSHIPS** AHA **RESEARCH** Comparative Euro-American history; immigrant history; mining history. **SELECTED PUBLICATIONS** Auth, The Workingman in American Life, Houghton, 68; Labor and the Left: A Study of Socialist and Radical Influences in the American Labor Movement, 1881-1924, Basic Bks, 70; coauth, Failure of a Dream? Essays in the History of American Socialism, Doubleday & Anchor, 74, 2nd ed, Univ Calif Press (in press); Reluctant Proletarians: A Short Comparative History of American Socialism, Univ Calif Press (in press). **CONTACT ADDRESS** Dept of Hist, Univ of California, Los Angeles, Los Angeles, CA 90024.

LASS, WILLIAM EDWARD
PERSONAL Born 11/27/1928, Beresford, SD, m, 1955, 2 children **DISCIPLINE** AMERICAN HISTORY **EDUCATION** Univ SDak, BA, 51, MA, 54; Univ Wis, PhD, 60. **CAREER** Asst prof hist, Southwestern State Col, 57-60; from asst prof to assoc prof, 60-66, chmn dept, 73-80, Prof Hist, Mankato State Univ, 66-, Dir, Southern Minn Hist Ctr, 69-, Nebr Hist Soc Woods fel Nebr hist, 61-63; Minn Hist Soc pub affairs fel, 71-72. **MEMBERSHIPS** Western Hist Asn; Orgn Am Historians; Am Asn State and Local Hist. **RESEARCH** Frontier transportation; Minnesota history. **SELECTED PUBLICATIONS** Coauth, Stanley J Morrow, Frontier Photographer, 56 & auth, History of Steamboating on the Upper Missouri, 62, Univ Nebr; The Removal from Minnesota of the Sioux and Winnebago Indians, 12/63 & Ginseng Rush in Minnesota, summer 69, Minn Hist; Steamboating on the Missouri: Its Significance on the Northern Great Plains, J West, 1/67; From the Missouri to the Great Salt Lake: An Account of Overland Freighting, Nebr State Hist Soc, 72; Minnesota: A Bicentennial History, States and the Nation Ser, Norton, 77; Minnesota's Boundary With Canada: Its Evolution Since 1783, Minn Hist Soc, 80. **CONTACT ADDRESS** Dept of Hist, Mankato State Univ, Mankato, MN 56001.

LATEINER, DONALD
PERSONAL Born 06/01/1944, New Rochelle, NY, m, 1976, 2 children **DISCIPLINE** CLASSICAL STUDIES, ANCIENT HISTORY **EDUCATION** Univ Chicago, BA, 65; Cornell Univ, MA, 67; Stanford Univ, MA, 70, PhD(classics), 72. **CAREER** Lectr hist, San Francisco State Col, 68-69; acting asst prof classics, Stanford Univ, 71-72; asst prof class studies, Univ PA, 72-79; asst prof, 79-82, Assoc Prof Humanities-Classics, 82-85, prof, 85-92, JOHN WRIGHT PROF GREEK & HUMANITIES, OH WESLEYAN UNIV, 93-. **HONORS AND AWARDS** Am School of Classical Studies @ Athens, Seymour fel, 69-70; Center for Hellenic Studies, Washington, D.C., vis Sr Scholar, 99. **MEMBERSHIPS** Am Philol Asn; Am Asn Ancient Historians; Archaeol Inst Am; Friends Ancient Hist. **RESEARCH** Greek epic; nonverbal behaviors in ancient lit; Greek historiography; Latin elegy; Greek oratory. **SELECTED PUBLICATIONS** Auth, The Speech of Teutiaplus, Greek, Roman & Byzantine Studies, 75; Tissaphernes and the Phoenician fleet, Trans Am Philol Asn, 76; Obscenity in Catullus, Ramus, 77; No

Laughing Matter: A Literary Tactic in Herodotus, Trans Am Philol Asn, 77; An Analysis of Lysias' Defense Speeches, Rivista Storica dell' Antichita, 81; The Historical Method of Herodotus, Toronto, 89; The Failure of the Ionian Revolt, Historia, 82; Mimetic Syntax: Metaphor from World Order, Am J of Philol, 90; Sardonic Smile, Nonverbal Behavior in Homeric Epic, Ann Arbor, 95; auth, "Abduction Marriage in Heliodorus' Aethiopica," GRBS (97). **CONTACT ADDRESS** Dept of Humanities-Classics, Ohio Wesleyan Univ, 61 S Sandusky St, Delaware, OH 43015-2398. **EMAIL** dglatein@cc.owu.edu

LATHAM, MICHAEL E.
DISCIPLINE AMERICAN HISTORY **EDUCATION** UCLA, PhD, **CAREER** Asst prof, Fordham Univ. **RESEARCH** Intellectual hist. **SELECTED PUBLICATIONS** Co-ed, Knowledge and Postmodernism in Historical Perspective, Routledge, 95; auth, Modernization as Ideology: American Social Science and "Nation Building" in the Kennedy Era, North Carolina, 00. **CONTACT ADDRESS** Dept of Hist, Fordham Univ, 441 E Fordham Rd, Bronx, NY 10458.

LATNER, RICHARD BARNETT
PERSONAL Born 03/04/1944, New York, NY, m, 1974 **DISCIPLINE** AMERICAN HISTORY **EDUCATION** Swarthmore Col, BA, 65; Univ Wis, MA, 67, PhD(hist), 72. **CAREER** Asst prof hist, Univ Mich, 70-74; assoc ed Mich hist, Mich Hist Div Dept State, Mich, 74-75; asst prof, 75-78, Assoc Prof Hist, Newcomb Col, Tulane Univ, 78-, Dir Am Studies, 80-, Nat Endowment Humanities fel, 79-80. **MEMBERSHIPS** Orgn Am Historians; Southern Hist Asn; Am Studies Asn. **RESEARCH** Jacksonian political history; political issues involving slavery. **SELECTED PUBLICATIONS** Auth, A new look at Jacksonian politics, J Am Hist, 3/75; coauth, Perspectives on Antebellum pietistic politics, Rev Am Hist, 3/76; auth, The nullification crisis and Republican subversion, J Southern Hist, 2/77; The Eaton Affair reconsidered, Tenn Hist Quart, fall 77; The kitchen cabinet and Andrew Jackson's advisory system, J Am Hist, 9/78; The Presidency of Andrew Jackson: White House Politics, 1829-1837, Univ Ga, 79. **CONTACT ADDRESS** Dept of Hist, Tulane Univ, 6823 St Charles Ave, New Orleans, LA 70118-5698.

LATTIMORE, STEVEN
PERSONAL Born 05/25/1938, Bryn Mawr, PA **DISCIPLINE** CLASSICS, CLASSICAL ARCHEOLOGY **EDUCATION** Dartmouth Col, AB, 60; Princeton Univ, MA, 64, PhD(class archaeol), 68. **CAREER** Instr class archaeol, Dartmouth Col, 64; instr Greek, Haverford Col, 65-66; asst prof classics and class archaeol, Intercol Ctr Class Studies, Rome, 66-67; asst prof, 67-74, Assoc Prof Classics, Univ Calif, Los Angeles, 74-, Guggenheim Found fel, 75-76. **MEMBERSHIPS** Archaeol Inst Am; Am Philol Asn. **RESEARCH** Classical sculpture; Greek literature; mythology. **SELECTED PUBLICATIONS** Auth, The bronze apoxyomenos from Ephesos, Am J Archaeol, 72; Battus in Theocritus' fourth Idyll, Greek, Roman & Byzantine Studies, 73; A Greek pediment on a Roman temple, Am J Archaeol, 74; The Marine Thiasos in Greek Sculpture, Archaeol Inst Am, 76. **CONTACT ADDRESS** Dept of Classics, Univ of California, Los Angeles, Los Angeles, CA 90024.

LAUBER, JACK M.
PERSONAL Born 10/08/1934, Archbold, OH, m, 1964, 2 children **DISCIPLINE** MODERN HISTORY **EDUCATION** Bowling Green State Univ, BSEd, 59, MA, 60; Univ Iowa, PhD(Russ hist), 67. **CAREER** Instr Russia and western civilization, Ohio State Univ, 64-67; asst prof, 67-69, assoc prof, 69-77, Prof Russ Hist, Univ Wis-Eau Claire, 77-. **MEMBERSHIPS** Conf Slavic and East Europ Hist; Am Asn Advan Slavic Studies; Am Soc 18th Century Studies. **RESEARCH** Russian socioeconomic history of the 18th century; Russian revolutionary history of the 19th century. **CONTACT ADDRESS** Dept of Hist, Univ of Wisconsin, Eau Claire, Eau Claire, WI 54701.

LAUREN, PAUL GORDON
PERSONAL Born 02/17/1946, Seattle, WA, m, 1967, 2 children **DISCIPLINE** HISTORY **EDUCATION** Wash State Univ, BA, 68; Stanford Univ, MA, 69, PhD(Hist & Polit Sci), 73. **CAREER** Asst prof, 74-77, from assoc prof to prof Hist, Univ Mont, 78-82; Regents prof, 91-; Peace fel Hist, Hoover Inst & Stanford Univ, 73-74; vis asst prof Hist, Stanford Univ, 74; vis assoc prof Hist, Stanford Univ, 79 & 82; Rockefeller Found Humanities fel, 80. **HONORS AND AWARDS** Disting Expert, UN, 90; CASE Prof of Year, Montana, 91; Harris Fel, Rotary Int, 94; Sen Fulbright Scholar, 94; Disting Am Scholar, Fulbright, 97. **MEMBERSHIPS** AHA; Int Studies Asn. **RESEARCH** International human rights, diplomatic history; national security and peace research; the Cold War. **SELECTED PUBLICATIONS** Auth, Diplomats and Bureaucrats, Hoover Institution Press, 76; Human Rights in History: Diplomacy and Racial Equality, In: Diplomatic History, 78; ed, Diplomatic History: New Approaches, Free Press Macmillan, 79; Crisis Management: History and Theory, In: International History Review, 79; Crisis Management: An Assessment, J Conflict Resolution, 80; Destinies Shared, Westview, 89; Kokka to Jinshuhenken, TBS Britannica, 95; Power and Prejudice, 2nd ed, HarperCollins, 96; Between Pandemonium and Order, In: Am Behavioral Scientist, 96; The Evolution of International Human Rights: Visions Seen, Univ Penn Press, 98. **CONTACT ADDRESS** Dept of History, Univ of Montana, Missoula, MT 59812-0001.

LAURENCE, RICHARD ROBERT
PERSONAL Born 04/22/1937, Knoxville, TN, m, 1961, 3 children **DISCIPLINE** MODERN EUROPEAN HISTORY **EDUCATION** Univ Tenn, AB, 59; Univ Vienna (Austria), 59-60 (Fulbright scholar); Stanford Univ, MA, 62, PhD(hist & Humanities), 68. **CAREER** From instr to asst prof, 66-76, Assoc Prof Humanities, Mich State Univ, 76-82, prof humanities, 82-89; prof history, 89-, Austrian govt res fel, 64-65; Nat Endowment for Humanities Inst, 79-90. **MEMBERSHIPS** AHA; Peace Hist Asn Ger Studies Asn. **RESEARCH** 19th-20th century Austria: political and cultural history; history of pacifism and internationalism. **SELECTED PUBLICATIONS** Coauth & co-ed, A Review and Assessment of General Education and the University College, Mich State Univ, 77; The peace movement in Austria, 1867-1914, In: Doves and Diplomats: Foreign Offices and Peace Movements in Europe and America in the Twentieth Century, Greenwood Press, 78; The Viennese Press and the Peace Movement, 1899-1914, Mich Acad, fall 80; contribr, Biographical Dict of Internationalists, 83 & Biographical Dict of Modern Peace Leaders, 85, Greenwood Press; auth, "Rudolf Grossman and Anarchist Autimilitarism in Austria before World War I," Peace and Change: A Journal of Peace Research, XIV (89); auth, "Bertha von Suttner and the Peace Movement in Austria to World War I," Austrian History Yearbook, XXIII (92). **CONTACT ADDRESS** Dept of Humanities, Michigan State Univ, 301 Morrill Hall, East Lansing, MI 48824-1036. **EMAIL** laurenc3@msu.edu

LAURENT, JANE KATHERINE
PERSONAL Born 08/03/1947, Gainesville, FL, m, 1982, 2 children **DISCIPLINE** RENAISSANCE & EUROPEAN SOCIAL HISTORY **EDUCATION** Univ Ga, BA, 68, MA, 70; Brown Univ, PhD, 76. **CAREER** Adj prof, Univ Fla, 76-79; Asst prof, 79-85, Assoc Prof Hist, Univ NC Charlotte, 79-. **MEMBERSHIPS** AHA; Renaissance Soc Am; Southeastern Medieval-Renaissance Asn; Southern Hist Asn. **RESEARCH** Political history of Renaissance city-states; agricultural history: 1300-1600. **SELECTED PUBLICATIONS** Auth, The signory and its supporters: The este of Ferrara, J Medieval Hist, 77; Feudalesimo e la signoria, Arch Storico Ital, 79; The exiles and the signory: The case of Ferrara, J Medieval & Renaissance Studies, 81; Patterns of agrarian control in fourteenth century Ferrara, Peasant Studies, 82. **CONTACT ADDRESS** Hist Dept, Univ of No Carolina, Charlotte, 9201 University City, Charlotte, NC 28223-0002. **EMAIL** jklauren@email.uncc.edu

LAURENT, PIERRE HENRI
PERSONAL Born 05/15/1933, Fall River, MA, m, 1958, 4 children **DISCIPLINE** HISTORY **EDUCATION** Colgate Univ, AB, 56; Boston Univ, AM, 60; PhD, 64. **CAREER** Instr, Boston Univ, 61-64; asst prof, Sweet Briar Col, 64-66; vis prof, Univ Wisc, 66-67; asst prof, Tulane Univ, 67-68; assoc prof, 68-69; assoc prof Tufts Univ, 70-75; prof, 75-; Fulbright Prof, Col Europe, 98. **HONORS AND AWARDS** NATO Res Fel; NEH; Paul-Henri Spaak Fel; IIE Res Fel; Fulbright Res Schl; Lincoln-Filene Cen Fel; **MEMBERSHIPS** AHA; NEHA; ECSA; AAUP. **RESEARCH** Twentieth Century European Integration Movement; Transatlantic relations. **SELECTED PUBLICATIONS** Auth, "Widening Europe: The Dilemmas of Community Success," Annals Am Acad Political Soc Sci 531 (94): 124-140; auth, The European Community: To Maastricht and Beyond, Acad of Political and Soc Sci (Philadelphia), 94; coauth, The State of the European Union: Deepening and Widening, Lynne Rienner (Boulder), 98; coauth, NATO and the European Union: Confronting the Challenges of European Security and Enlargement, Kent State Univ Press (Kent), 99; coauth, "The Unique Relationship: The EC/ACP Connection," in The External Relations of the European Community: The International Response to 1992, ed. J Redmond (London and NY: Macmillan, 92); auth, "The United States, The European Union and the Visegrad States," in Transformation and Integration in Europe, eds. A Zielinska-Glebocka, A Stepniak (Gdansk: Univ Gdansk Press, 94); auth, "The Diplomacy of Junktim: Paul-Henri Spaak and European Integration," Personalities, War and Diplomacy, eds. TG Otte, C Pagedas (London: F Cass, 97); auth, "Creating the Euro-Atlantic System: NATO Expansion and Enlargement," in The New Europe and Germany, ed. D.B. Marshall (Columbia: Univ SC Press, 97); auth, "The Move To A Multi-Speed Europe," in The State of the European Union: Deepening and Widening, eds. PH Laurent, M Maresceau (Boulder: Lynne Rienner, 98); auth, "European-American Security Cooperation and Conflict, 1955-1995," in La Communaute Europenne de Defense, Lecons pour Demain? ed. Michel Dumoulin (Bruxelles: Peter Lang/Eurocho, 00); auth, "Belgium, Britain and the United States," in The Marshall Plan and Small Nations, eds. H Pharo, K Burk (London: Cambridge Univ Press, 00); auth, "NATO and the EU," in NATO After Fifty, eds. V Papacosma, S Kay (Wilmington: Scholarly Resour, 00); auth, "Creating the ESDI," in The European Union Agenda, eds. D Woods, J Ellensby (Columbia: Univ MO Press, 00). **CONTACT ADDRESS** Dept History, Tufts Univ, Medford, East Hall, Medford, MA 02155-5500. **EMAIL** plaurent@emerald.tufts.edu

LAURIE, BRUCE
PERSONAL Born 03/01/1943, Elizabeth, NJ, m, 1 child **DISCIPLINE** U.S. HISTORY **EDUCATION** Rutgers Univ, BA, 65; Univ Pittsburgh, MA, 67, PhD, 71. **CAREER** From asst prof to prof, Univ of Mass., 71-. **HONORS AND AWARDS** Phi Beta Kappa **MEMBERSHIPS** Orgn of Am Hists; Am Hist Asn; Soc Sci Hist Asn. **RESEARCH** U.S. Labor & Politics. **SELECTED PUBLICATIONS** Auth, Working People of Philadelphia, 1800-1850, 80; Artisans into Workers: Labor in Nineteenth Century America, 89; coauth, Labor Histories, 98. **CONTACT ADDRESS** Dept of History, Univ of Massachusetts, Amherst, MA 01003. **EMAIL** Laurie@History.umass.edu

LAURITSEN, FREDERICK MICHAEL
PERSONAL Born 03/10/1938, Montevideo, MN, m, 1968, 2 children **DISCIPLINE** ANCIENT HISTORY **EDUCATION** Univ Minn, Minneapolis, BA, 61, MA, 65, PhD(hist), 73. **CAREER** Librn, Winona State Col, 65-67 & Univ Iowa, 67-69; from asst prof to assoc prof, 69-80; prof hist, Eastern Wash Univ, 80-, Mem, Brit Inst Archaeol Ankara, 68-; numis consult, Cheney Cowles State Mem Mus, Spokane, 74-. **MEMBERSHIPS** Archaeol Inst Am; Am Numis Soc; Am Orient Soc; fel Royal Numis Soc. **RESEARCH** Numismatics; cuneiform studies. **SELECTED PUBLICATIONS** Auth, Rare nineteenth-century Latin American periodicals, Bks Iowa, 11/69. **CONTACT ADDRESS** Dept of Hist, Eastern Washington Univ, M/S 27, Cheney, WA 99004-2496. **EMAIL** fredlauritsen@signa.com

LAUSHEY, DAVID MASON
PERSONAL Born 01/30/1934, Colonial Heights, VA, m, 1958, 3 children **DISCIPLINE** HISTORY OF MODERN INDIA **EDUCATION** Univ Va, BSEd, 61, MA, 63, PhD(hist of India), 69. **CAREER** Asst prof hist, Midwestern Univ, 65-68; asst prof, 68-76, Assoc Prof Hist, GA State Univ, 76-. **MEMBERSHIPS** Asn Asian Studies. **RESEARCH** Terrorism and Marxism in Bengal. **SELECTED PUBLICATIONS** Auth, Sarat Chandra Bose and Bangladesh, Mod Rev, 72; The Shree Sangha and the Bengal Volunteers, J Indian Hist, 72; coauth, Tampering with the Temporal Order, Hist Teacher, 72; Bengal Terrorism and the Marxist Left, Firma K L Mukhopadhyay, 75. **CONTACT ADDRESS** Dept of Hist, Georgia State Univ, Atlanta, GA 30303.

LAUX, JAMES MICHAEL
PERSONAL Born 11/04/1927, La Crosse, WI, m, 1952, 3 children **DISCIPLINE** HISTORY **EDUCATION** Univ Wis, BS, 50; Univ Conn, MA, 52; Northwestern Univ, PhD, 57. **CAREER** Instr hist, Wis State Col, La Crosse, 55-57; from asst prof to assoc prof, 57-69, Prof Hist, Univ Cincinnati, 69-, Prof Emeritus, 89-; Vis assoc prof, Northwestern Univ, 66-67; vis prof hist, Ohio State Univ, 69. **MEMBERSHIPS** AHA; Soc Fr Hist Studies; Soc Automotive Historians. **RESEARCH** France since 1789; French economic history; auto and aviation history. **SELECTED PUBLICATIONS** Auth, In First Gear, McGill-Queen's, 76; auth, "The European Automobile Industry, Twayne," 92; trans, "The Right Wing in France," Univ. Pa, 66; coed, "The French Revolution: Conflicting Interpretations," Random, 68, Krieger, 89; Krieger, 89; coauth, "La Revolution," Univ NC Press, 82; auth, "The Rise and Fall of Armand Deperdussing," French Historical Studies, Spring 73; auth, "The Rise and Fall of Armand Deperdussin," French Historical Studies, Spring 73; auth, "Gnome et Rhone in 1915-1918, L'Autre Front, Editions Ouvrieres, 77; coauth, "Steaming through New England with Locombile," Journal of Transport History, 9/79. **CONTACT ADDRESS** Dept of Hist, Univ of Cincinnati, 100 South Tremain, No. A-4, Mount Dora, FL 32757.

LAVRIN, ASUNCION
PERSONAL Born Havana, Cuba, m, 2 children **DISCIPLINE** HISTORY **EDUCATION** Radcliffe Col, BA, 57; Harvard Univ, PhD, 63. **CAREER** Prof, Howard Univ, 76-95; Prof, Ariz State Univ, 95-. **HONORS AND AWARDS** J.A. Robertzon Prize, 67; NEH Grant, 80-81; Woodrow Wilson Cent for Intl Scholar, 84-85; Eng Soc Sci Res Coun Awd, 85; Benjamin Meaker Prof, Univ Bristol; NEH Grant, 93; Arthur P. Whitaker Prize, 96; Harold E. Davis Mem Prize, 99; John Simon Guggenheim Fel, 01. **MEMBERSHIPS** Am Hist Asn; Conf on Latin Am Studies; Mid Atlantic Coun on Latin Am Studies. **RESEARCH** Gender Studies; Colonial Latin America; Women's History: Latin America; The National Period; Church and Religion in Colonial Mexico. **SELECTED PUBLICATIONS** Auth, "Women in Twentieth Century Latin American Society," in Cambridge History of Latin America, Vol VI, (94): 483-544; auth, Women, Feminism and Social Change: Argentina, Chile, and Uruguay, 1890-1949, Univ Nebr Press, 95; auth, "International Feminisms: Latin American Alternatives," Gender and History, (98): 519-534; auth, "Indian Brides of Christ: Creating New Spaces for Indigenous Women in New Spain," Mexican Studies/Estudios Mexicanos, (99): 225-260; auth, "Women in Colonial Mexico," in The Oxford History of Mexico, (Oxford Univ Press, 00), 245-273. **CONTACT ADDRESS** Dept Hist, Arizona State Univ, MC 2501, Tempe, AZ 85287.

LAW, RON
DISCIPLINE HISTORY **EDUCATION** Univ St Thomas, BA, 74; Tex Christian Univ, MA, 78; PhD, 90. **CAREER** Assoc Prof, Tarrant County Col, 82-90; Prof, San Jacinto Col South, 93-. **HONORS AND AWARDS** Nat Fel fund Scholar;

Who's Who Among Am Teachers, 98, 99. **MEMBERSHIPS** SW Soc Sci Asn, E Tex Hist Asn, Nat Educ Asn, Tex Cmty Col Teachers Asn, Tex State Teachers Asn, Tex Faculty Asn. **RESEARCH** Late nineteenth, twentieth century US history; African-American history; Brazil. **SELECTED PUBLICATIONS** Co-ed, Our Legacy: Articles and Documents in American History, 2 Vols. **CONTACT ADDRESS** Dept Soc & Beh Sci, San Jacinto Col, South, 13735 Beamer Rd, Houston, TX 77089-6009.

LAWES, CAROLYN J.
DISCIPLINE HISTORY **EDUCATION** Univ Calif at Santa Clara, BA, 80; Univ Calif at Davis, MA, 84; PhD, 92. **CAREER** Assoc instr, hist, Univ Calif at Davis; current, Asst Prof, Hist, Old Dominion Univ. **MEMBERSHIPS** Am Antiquarian Soc **SELECTED PUBLICATIONS** Auth, "Trifling with Holy Time: Women and the Formation of the Calvinist Church of Worcester, Massachusetts," Rel & Am Cult, Winter 98. **CONTACT ADDRESS** Dept of Hist, Old Dominion Univ, Norfolk, VA 23529-0091.

LAWHEAD, WILLIAM F.
PERSONAL m, 2 children **DISCIPLINE** HISTORY OF PHILOSOPHY, PHILOSOPHY OF RELIGION **EDUCATION** Wheaton Col, BA; Univ TX, Austin, PhD. **CAREER** Prof, Univ MS, 80-. **RESEARCH** History of philosophy, God and time. **SELECTED PUBLICATIONS** Auth, The Voyage of Discovery: A History of Western Philosophy, Wadsworth Publ Co, 96; auth, The Philosophical Journey, Mayfield Publ Co, 00. **CONTACT ADDRESS** Univ of Mississippi, Oxford, MS 38677. **EMAIL** wlawhead@olemiss.edu

LAWSON, DARREN P.
PERSONAL Born 08/18/1964, Asheboro, NC, m, 1988, 1 child **DISCIPLINE** FINE ARTS **EDUCATION** Bob Jones Univ, BA, 86; MA, 88; Univ Kan, PhD, 96. **CAREER** Grad Asst, Bob Jones Univ, 86-88; Fac, Bob Jones Univ, 88-93; Grad Teaching Asst, Univ Kan, 93-96; From Assoc Prof to Prof, Bob Jones Univ, 96-. **HONORS AND AWARDS** Outstanding Grad Teaching Asst Awd, Univ Kan, 96; Employee Merit Awd, Bob Jones Univ, 97; Pac Bell Knowledge Network Learning Appln Awd, 97. **MEMBERSHIPS** Int Commun Asn, Nat Commun Asn, Am Soc for Training and Develop. **SELECTED PUBLICATIONS** Auth, "Netiquette: Understanding and Using Electronic Mail," in Handbk of Bus Commun (97); auth, "Electronic Mail: Attributes, Guidelines and Educational Applications," Balance, 17 (98). **CONTACT ADDRESS** Dept Fine Arts, Bob Jones Univ, 1700 Wade Hampton Blvd, Greenville, SC 29614-1000. **EMAIL** dplawson@bju.edu

LAWTON, CAROL
PERSONAL Born 03/21/1949, Cumberland, MD, m, 1984 **DISCIPLINE** ART HISTORY **EDUCATION** Vassar Col, BA, 71; Univ Pittsburgh, MA, 72; Princeton Univ, MA, 75, Phd, 84. **CAREER** Instr to asst prof to assoc prof, chair, curator, 80-, Lawrence Univ; vis assoc prof, UC Berkeley, 86; Elizabeth Whitehead vis prof, Amer Sch of Classical Stud, Athens, 99-00. **HONORS AND AWARDS** NDEA Title IV Fel, 71-73; Kress Found Fel, 74; Vanderpool Fel, Amer Sch Athens, 77; Lawrence Univ Young Teacher Awd, 82; Amer Philos Soc Grant, 85, 94; J Paul Getty Postdoctoral Fel, 87-88; NEH Sr Fel, 95-96; Solow Found Summer Res Fel, 98; Freshman Stud Teaching Awd, 98. **MEMBERSHIPS** Archaeol Inst of Amer; Col Art Assoc. **RESEARCH** Greek sculpture, classical archaeol. **SELECTED PUBLICATIONS** Auth, An Attic Document Relief in the Walters Art Gallery, J of the Walters Art Gallery, 93; auth, Four Document Reliefs from the Athenian Agora, Hesperia, 95; ed, Bearers of Meaning: the Ottilia Buerger collection of Ancient and Byzantine Coins, Lawrence Univ Press, 95; auth, Attic Document Reliefs: Art and Politics in Ancient Athens, Oxford Univ Press, 95; auth, Votive Reliefs and Popular Religion in the Athenian Agora: the Case of Asklepios and Hygieia, Proceedings of the XVth Int Cong of Classical Archaeol, Amsterdam, 98. **CONTACT ADDRESS** Art Dept, Lawrence Univ, Appleton, WI 54912. **EMAIL** clawton@lawrence.edu

LAY, SHAWN
PERSONAL Born 12/12/1953, Raceland, LA, m, 1983, 4 children **DISCIPLINE** HISTORY **EDUCATION** Univ Texas at El Paso, BA, 80, MA, 84; Vanderbilt Univ, PhD, 93. **CAREER** Vis Lecturer, SUNY Buffalo, 88-92; Vis Prof, Univ of Georgia, 93-96; Assoc Prof of History, Coker Col, 96-. **HONORS AND AWARDS** C.L. Sonnichsen Book Awd, 84; Outstanding Honors Prof, Univ of Georgia, 96. **MEMBERSHIPS** Amer Historical Assoc; Organization of Amer Historians. **RESEARCH** Amer Race Relations; Urban and Social History. **SELECTED PUBLICATIONS** Auth, "War, Revolution, and the Ku Klux Klan," 85; auth, "The Invisible Empire in the West, 92; auth, "Hooded Knights on the Niagara," 95. **CONTACT ADDRESS** Dept History & Philosophy, Coker Col, 300 E Col Ave, Hartsville, SC 29550-3742. **EMAIL** slay@pascal.coker.edu

LAYMAN, RICHARD
PERSONAL m, 1973, 2 children **DISCIPLINE** ENGLISH, AMERICAN LITERATURE, AMERICAN SOCIAL HISTORY **EDUCATION** Ind Univ, BA, 71; Univ Louisville, MA, 72; Univ SC, PhD, 75. **CAREER** Manly Inc, VPres, 83-; Bruccoli, Clark, Laymen, VPres, 76-. **SELECTED PUBLICATIONS** Numerous. **CONTACT ADDRESS** Bruccoli Clark Layman, Inc, 2006 Sumter St, Columbia, SC 29201. **EMAIL** rlayman@BCL-Manly.com

LAYTON, EDWIN THOMAS
DISCIPLINE HISTORY **EDUCATION** Univ Calif Los Angeles, PhD. **CAREER** Prof, Univ Minn, 75- . **HONORS AND AWARDS** Dexter Prize, 71; pres, soc hist tech, 85-86; pres, am asn advancement sci, 89-91. **RESEARCH** History of the engineering profession in France, England, and America; impact of Newtonian science on technology and invention in America; impact of technology on society and its ethical implications. **SELECTED PUBLICATIONS** Auth, Revolt of the Engineers, Social Responsibility and the American Engineering Profession, John Hopkins, 86; ed, Mirror Image Twins, the Communities of Science and Technology in 19th-Century America, Harper and Row, 73; co-ed, The Dynamics of Science and Technology, Reidel, 78. **CONTACT ADDRESS** History Dept, Univ of Minnesota, Twin Cities, 614 Social Sciences Tower, 267 19th Ave S, Minneapolis, MN 55455. **EMAIL** layto001@tc.umn.edu

LAZZERINI, EDWARD JAMES
PERSONAL Born 09/14/1943, Hartford, CT, m, 1966, 1 child **DISCIPLINE** HISTORY **EDUCATION** Trinity Col, BA, 65; Fordham Univ, MA, 67; Univ Wash, PhD(hist), 73. **CAREER** Asst prof, 73-80, Assoc Prof Hist, Univ New Orleans, 80-. **MEMBERSHIPS** Am Asn Advan Slavic Studies; AHA; Asn Studies Nationalities. **RESEARCH** Late Imperial Russian history; history of the Russian Islamic community. **SELECTED PUBLICATIONS** Auth, Gadidism at the turn of the twentieth century: A view from within, Cahiers du Monde Russe et Sovietique, 4-6/75; coauth, The Chinese World, Forum 78. **CONTACT ADDRESS** Dept of Hist, Univ of New Orleans, New Orleans, LA 70148.

LE BRETON, MARIETTA
PERSONAL Born 03/26/1936, New Orleans, LA, s **DISCIPLINE** HISTORY **EDUCATION** La State Univ, BS, 58; MA, 63; PhD, 69. **CAREER** From Instr to Prof, Northwestern State Univ, 63-; Head Hist Dept, Northwestern State Univ, 80-83. **HONORS AND AWARDS** Fel, Sem for Hist Admin, 60; Gibson Throphy for Outstanding Teaching, DAR, 76; Outstanding Teaching Awd, Northwestern State Univ; Phi Kappa Phi; Phi Alpha Theta. **MEMBERSHIPS** La Hist Asn, Southern Hist Asn, N La Hist Asn. **RESEARCH** Louisiana History, Early 19th Century, Western America. **SELECTED PUBLICATIONS** Auth, "Bayan Dorcheat," Revers and Bayans of La, 68; auth, "The Burr Conspiracy," Readings in La Hist, 78; auth, "The Acadians," in Harvard Encyclopedia of American Ethnic Groups (80); auth, Northwestern State University: A History, 85. **CONTACT ADDRESS** Dept Soc Sci, Northwestern State Univ of Louisiana, 350 Sam Sibley Rd, Natchitoches, LA 71497-0001.

LE GOFF, T. J. A.
PERSONAL Born 12/12/1942, Vancouver, BC, Canada **DISCIPLINE** HISTORY **EDUCATION** Univ BC, BA, 65; Univ Col London, PhD, 70. **CAREER** Lectr to asst prof, 69-73, Assoc Prof Hist, York Univ, 73-; lectr, Univ Reading (UK), 79-80; vis prof, Univ Laval, 83; ; vis prof, Col France, 91. **HONORS AND AWARDS** WK Ferguson Prize, Can Hist Asn, 84;vis fel, Balliol Col, Oxford, 83-84; Keith Matthews Prize, Can Nautical Res Soc, 87; fel, Royal Hist Soc, 95. **MEMBERSHIPS** Soc Fr Hist Stud; Soc d'hist moderne et contemporaine; Can Hist Asn. **SELECTED PUBLICATIONS** Auth, Vannes and its Region: A Study of Town and Country in Eighteenth Century France, 81; ed bd, Fr Hist Stud, 81-83; ed bd, Fr Hist, 86-; ed bd, Histoire sociale/Social History, 87-91; auth, "Les caisses d'amortissement en France 1749-1783," Minsistere de l'Economie et des Finanaces, comite pour l'Histoire economique et finaciere de la France, L'Administration des finaces sous l'Ancien Regime, (Paris, 97): 177-196; auth, Maps and commentaries in S. Bonin and C. Langlois," Atlas de la Revolution Francaise vol 10 Economie, (Paris: Ed de l'Ecole des Hautes Etudes en Sci Soc, 97): 61, 62, 68, 1810-1813. **CONTACT ADDRESS** Dept of History, York Univ, 4700 Keele St, North York, ON, Canada M3J 1P3. **EMAIL** tjal@yorku.ca

LE SUEUR, JAMES
PERSONAL Born 05/03/1963, Grand Junction, CO **DISCIPLINE** HISTORY **EDUCATION** Univ Mont, BA, 86; Univ Chicago, MA, 90; PhD, 96. **CAREER** Assoc prof, Univ La Verne. **HONORS AND AWARDS** Lurey Fel; Mellon Fel; NEH Fel. **MEMBERSHIPS** Soc for French Hist Studies, Western Soc for French Hist, Am Hist Asn. **RESEARCH** Twentieth-Century France, Intellectual History, Algerian History. **SELECTED PUBLICATIONS** Ed & contribur, Journal, 1955-1962: Reflections on the French-Algerian War, Univ Nebr Press, 00; ed, The Decolonization Reader, Routledge, forthcoming; ed, The Decolonization Sourcebook, Routledge, forthcoming; ed & contribur, July 14 Assassination, forthcoming; ed, Uncivil War: Intellectuals, Violence, and Identity Politics During the Decolonization of Algeria, 1954-1962, Univ Pa Press, forthcoming. **CONTACT ADDRESS** Dept Hist & Polit Sci, Univ of La Verne, 1950 3rd St, La Verne, CA 91750-4401. **EMAIL** lesueurj@ulv.edu

LEAB, DANIEL JOSEF
PERSONAL Born 08/29/1936, Berlin, Germany, m, 1964, 3 children **DISCIPLINE** AMERICAN HISTORY **EDUCATION** Columbia Univ, BA, 57, MA, 61, PhD(hist), 69. **CAREER** From instr to asst prof hist, Columbia Univ, 66-74, assoc dean, Columbia Col, 69-71, asst dean fac, univ, 71, spec asst, exec vpres and provost, 73-74; assoc prof, 74-79, prof Hist, Seton Hall Univ, 79-, dir, Am Studies, 74-, Consult, Atomic Energy Comn, 72-73; contrib ed, Columbia Jour Rev, 74-78 and Atlas World Press Rev, 74-78; ed, Labor Hist, 74-; Fulbright Sr lectureship, Univ Cologne, Ger, 76; mem exec comt, Univ Sem, 76-; Nat Endowment for Humanities fel, 81. **MEMBERSHIPS** AHA; Orgn Am Historians; Labor Hist; Hist Film Comt; Soc for Cinema Studies; International Asn for Media and Hist; Historians of Am Communism. **RESEARCH** Twentieth century United States social and political history; labor history; media history. **CONTACT ADDRESS** Seton Hall Univ, So Orange, South Orange, NJ 07079. **EMAIL** leabdani@shu.edu

LEAMON, JAMES SHENSTONE
PERSONAL Born 12/09/1930, Melrose, MA **DISCIPLINE** AMERICAN COLONIAL HISTORY **EDUCATION** Bates Col, BA, 55; Brown Univ, PhD, 61. **CAREER** Inst hist, Wartburg Col, 60-61; asst prof, Lebanon Valley Col, 61-64; from asst prof to assoc prof, 64-77, Prof Hist, Bates Col, 77-. **MEMBERSHIPS** Orgn Am Historians; Coun for NE Hist Archaeol; Maine Hist Soc; New Eng Hist Asn; Soc Hist of Early Republic. **RESEARCH** American Colonial history; American revolution; Maine history; historical archaeology. **SELECTED PUBLICATIONS** Auth, Governor Fletcher's recall, William & Mary Quart, 10/63; The Stamp Act crisis in Maine: the case of Scarborough, Maine Hist Soc Newslett, winter 72; Maine's Swedish Pioneers, Swedish Pioneer Hist Quart, 4/75; co-ed, Maine in the Revolution: a readers guide, Maine Hist Soc Quart, spring 76; auth, The Search for Security: Maine After Penobscot, Maine Hist Soc Quart, Winter 82; co-ed and auth, Maine in the Early Republic: From Revolution to Statehood, 88; auth, In Shay's Shadow: Separation and Ratification of the Constitution in Maine, In: In Debt to Shays, 93; Revolution Downeast: The War for American Independence in Maine, 93; King William's War (1689-1697), In: Colonial Wars of North America, 1512-1763: An Encyclopedia, 96. **CONTACT ADDRESS** Dept of Hist, Bates Col, Lewiston, ME 04240-6018. **EMAIL** jleamon@Bates.edu

LEARS, T. J. JACKSON
PERSONAL Born 07/26/1947, Annapolis, MD, m, 1969, 1 child **DISCIPLINE** AMERICAN HISTORY & LITERATURE **EDUCATION** Univ Va, BA, 69; Univ NC, Chapel Hill, MA, 73; Yale Univ, PhD, 78. **CAREER** Instr Am studies, Yale Univ, 77-79; Asst Prof US Hist, Univ MO, Columbia, 79-; prof, Rutgers Univ. **MEMBERSHIPS** Am Studies Asn. **RESEARCH** American advertising; literary modernism; cultural impact of modernization. **SELECTED PUBLICATIONS** Auth, Making Fun of Popular Culture, Amer Hist Rev, 92. **CONTACT ADDRESS** Dept of Hist, Rutgers, The State Univ of New Jersey, New Brunswick, 16 Seminary Place, New Brunswick, NJ 08901. **EMAIL** tjlears@rci.rutgers.edu

LEARY, DAVID E.
PERSONAL Born 05/05/1945, Los Angeles, CA, m, 1972, 3 children **DISCIPLINE** HISTORY & PHILOSOPHY OF PSYCHOLOGY **EDUCATION** San Luis Rey Col, CA, BA, 68; San Jose State, CA, MA, 71; Univ Chicago, IL, PhD, 77. **CAREER** Vis asst prof of Psychology, Graduate Theol Union, Berkeley, CA, 71-72; instr Psychol, Holy Names Col, Oakland, CA, 72-74; instr psychol, San Francisco State Univ Ext Services and Univ CA Ext Services, 73-74; instr of Psychol, Univ Chicago, 75; asst prof of the History and Philos of Psychol, Univ NH, Durham, 77-81, co-dir, grad prog in the Theory and History of Psychol, 77-89, assoc prof Psychol & Humanities, 81-87; fel, Center for Advanced Study in the Behavioral Sciences, Stanford, CA, 82-83, co-dir, summer inst on the Hist of Social Scientific Inquiry, 86; assoc prof Humanities, Cambridge Univ Summer prog, 84; Chairperson, Dept of Psychol, 86-89, prof of Psychol, Hist, and the Humanities, Univ NH, Durham, 87-89; prof of Psychology, dean of Arts and Sciences, Univ Richmond, VA, 89-. **HONORS AND AWARDS** San Luis Rey College Memorial Fund Scholarship, 63-68; Special Honors, PhD dissertation, 77; Univ NH Merit Awd, 78, 82; Asn of Am Pubs Awd, 85; Phi Beta Kappa, 87; numerous grants, fellowships, and stipends from the NEH, Univ NH, Nat Sci Found, Mellon Found, and others. **MEMBERSHIPS** Am Asn of Higher Ed; Am Conf of Academic Deans (member of the bd, 93-2000, chair of the bd, 98-99); Am Hist Asn; Am Psychol Asn (Pres, Div of History of Psychology; 83-84, Pres, Div of Theoretical and Philos Psychol, 94-95); Am Psychol Soc; Asn of Am Colleges and Universities; Cheiron: Int Soc for the History of the Behavioral and Social Sciences; Forum for the Hist of Human Science; Hist of Science Soc; Soc for the Hist of Science in Am. **RESEARCH** The intellectual, social, and cultural history of psychology, with a special focus on the relations between psychology and the humanities (eg, literature, philoso-

phy, and religion) and the other sciences. **SELECTED PUBLICATIONS** Auth, An Introduction to the Psychology of Guilt, Lansford Co, 75; A Century of Psychology as Science, co-ed with Sigmund Koch, MacGraw-Hill, 85 (recipient of the Asn of Am Pubs Award, 85), 2nd ed reissued with a new postscript, Am Psychol An, 92; Metaphors in the History of Psychology, Cambridge Univ Press, 90, paperback, 94; William James, the Psychologist's Dilema, and the Historiography of Psychology: Cautionary Tales, Hist of Human Sciences, 8, 95; Naming and Knowing: Giving Forms to Things Unknown, Social Res 62, 95; William James and the Art of Human Understanding, in Ludy T Benjamin, Jr, ed, A History of Psychology: Original Sources and Contemporary Research, 2nd ed, McGraw-Hill, 97 (reprinted from 92); Sigmund Koch (1917-1996), co-auth with Frank Kessel and William Bevan, Am Psychologist 53, 98; numerous other publications. **CONTACT ADDRESS** Dean of Arts and Sciences, Univ of Richmond, Richmond, VA 23173. **EMAIL** dleary@richmond.edu

LEARY, JAMES PATRICK
PERSONAL Born 08/19/1950, Rice Lake, WI **DISCIPLINE** FOLKLORE, AMERICAN STUDIES **EDUCATION** Univ Notre Dame, AB, 72; Univ NC, MA, 73; Ind Univ, PhD(folklore), 77. **CAREER** Asst Prof Folklore, Univ KY, 77-. **MEMBERSHIPS** Am Folklore Soc; Maledilta Soc. **RESEARCH** Folk narrative; ethnic folklore; folklore of the upper midwest. **SELECTED PUBLICATIONS** Auth, Images of Loggers + Recent Videos on Historic Lumbering, J Amer Folklore, Vol 0106, 93. **CONTACT ADDRESS** Dept Folklore, Univ of Wisconsin, Madison, 1155 Observatory Dr, Madison, WI 53706-1319.

LEARY, WILLIAM M.
PERSONAL Born 05/06/1934, Newark, NJ, m, 1978, 1 child **DISCIPLINE** HISTORY **EDUCATION** Wayne State Univ, BA, 63; Princeton Univ, MA, 65; PhD, 66. **CAREER** Res assoc, Princeton Univ, 68-68; asst prof, San Diego State Univ, 68-69; assoc prof, Univ of Victoria, 69-73; prof, Univ of Ga, 73-. **HONORS AND AWARDS** Woodrow Wilson Fel, 63; Fulbright-Hays, China, 74-75; Thailand, 79-80; Jalonik Memorial Distinguished Lecture, Univ of Tex Dallas, 82; Charles A. Lindbergh Chair, Nat Air and Space Museum, 96-97. **MEMBERSHIPS** Soc for Mil Hist. **RESEARCH** Aeronautical history, intelligence history, military history. **SELECTED PUBLICATIONS** Auth, Perilous Missions: Civil Air Transport and CIA Covert Operations in Asia, 84; auth, Aerial Pioneers: The U.S. Air Mail Service, 1918-1927, 85; auth, Porject Coldfeet: Secret Mission to a Soviet Ice Station, 96; auth, Under Ice: Waldo Lyon and the Development of the Arctic Submarine, 99. **CONTACT ADDRESS** Dept Hist, Univ of Georgia, Leconte Hall, Athens, GA 30602-1602. **EMAIL** wleary@arches.uga.edu

LEAVITT, JUDITH WALZER
PERSONAL Born 07/22/1940, New York, NY, m, 1966, 2 children **DISCIPLINE** AMERICAN MEDICAL HISTORY **EDUCATION** Antioch Col, BA, 63; Univ Chicago, MA, 66, PhD(hist), 75. **CAREER** Instr hist C W Post Col, 68-70; asst prof, 75-80, Assoc Prof Med Hist and Women's Studies, Univ Wis, Madison, 80-, Chairperson, Hist Med, 81-. **MEMBERSHIPS** Am Asn Hist Med; Orgn Am Historians; AHA; Am Pub Health Asn. **RESEARCH** US public health history; US urban history, 19th century; US women's health history. **SELECTED PUBLICATIONS** Auth, Politics and Public Health: Smallpox in Milwaukee, 1894-1895, Bull Hist Med, 50: 553-568; co-ed, Sickness and Health in America: Readings in the History of Medicine and Public Health, Univ Wis press, 78; contribr, Preventive Medicine and Public Health, Univ Calif, 79; coauth, Women in University of Wisconsin Medical School, In: University Women, Univ Wis, 80; auth, The Wasteland: Garbage and Sanitary Reform in the American City, J Hist Med & Allied Sci, 35: 431-452; Birthing and Anesthesia: The Debate over Twilight Sleep in America, Signs, 6: 147-164; Health in Urban Wisconsin: From Bad to Better, In: Wisconsin Medicine: Historical Perspectives, Univ Wis Press, 81; The Healthiest City: Milwaukee and the Politics of Health Reform, Princeton Univ Press, 82. **CONTACT ADDRESS** Univ of Wisconsin, Madison, 1300 Univ Ave, Madison, WI 53706.

LEBEAU, BRYAN
PERSONAL Born 07/23/1947, North Adams, MA, m, 1967, 1 child **DISCIPLINE** HISTORY **EDUCATION** North Adams St Col, BA, 70, MA 71; Penn St Univ, PhD, 82 **CAREER** Assoc Prof, Creighton Univ **HONORS AND AWARDS** Creighton Univ Awd for Teaching, 87; Creighton Univ Awd for Service, 90; Creighton Univ Awd for Collaboration, 95; Creighton Univ Awd for Res, 98, Creighton Univ Distinguished Service Awd, 00. **MEMBERSHIPS** Am Hist Assoc; Am Studies Assoc; Org of Amer Historians **RESEARCH** Religious History; Early American Culture **SELECTED PUBLICATIONS** Auth, Jonathan dickinson and the Formative Years of American Presbyterianism, UP of Kentucky, 97; Auth, History of the Salem Witch Trials, Prentice Hall, 98; auth, Religion in America to 1865, Edinburgh, 00. **CONTACT ADDRESS** Dept of Hist, Creighton Univ, 2500 California Plaza, Omaha, NE 68178. **EMAIL** blbeau@creighton.edu

LEBLANC, PHYLLIS
PERSONAL Born Moncton, NB, Canada **DISCIPLINE** HISTORY **EDUCATION** Univ Moncton, BA, 76, MA, 78; Univ Ottawa, PhD, 89. **CAREER** Policy Adv & Hist Res, Dept of Indian Affairs & Northern Dev, 84-88; asst prof, hist, Univ Winnipeg, 88-90; assoc prof, 90-95, prof Hist Univ Moncton, 95-. **HONORS AND AWARDS** Can Coun Special MA Scholar, 76; Scholar in Residence, Ctr Louisiana Studs, Univ South-Western Louisiana, 95-96. **MEMBERSHIPS** Gorsebrook Inst Atlantic Can Studs; Asn Can Studs; Can Hist Soc. **SELECTED PUBLICATIONS** Auth, L'ideologie nationale et l'integration des francophones dans un contexte urbain: le cas de Moncton, N-B, 1900-1929, in Moncton, 1871-1929: changements socio-economiques dans une ville ferroviaire, with Daniel Hickey, (Moncton, Editions d'Acadie, 90); auth, Le travail, les chemins de fer et les transformations economiques a Moncton, 1870-1941, Egalite 31, 92; auth, L'elaboration d'une vision uniforme de croissance dans une communaute urabaine: les elites francophones et anglophones de Moncton, 1870 a 1940, Egalite, 94; auth, The Vatican and the Roman Catholic Church in Atlantic Canada: Policies Regarding Ethnicity and Language, 1878-1922, in Peter C. Kent et John Pollard, Pappal Diplomacy in the Modern Age, (Westport, Praeger, 95). **CONTACT ADDRESS** Dept of History, Univ of Moncton, 165, boulevard Hebert, Edmundston, NB, Canada E3V 2S8. **EMAIL** leblanpc@umoncton,ca

LEBOVICS, HERMAN
PERSONAL Born 09/06/1935, Nagy Szollosa, Czechoslovakia **DISCIPLINE** MODERN EUROPEAN HISTORY **EDUCATION** Univ Conn, BA, 57; Yale Univ, MA, 58, PhD(hist), 65. **CAREER** Instr Europ hist, Brooklyn Col, 62-65; vis asst prof, Oberlin Col, 65-66; asst prof, 66-69, Assoc Prof Europ Hist, State Univ NY, Stony Brook, 69-. **MEMBERSHIPS** AHA; Conf Group Cent Europ Hist; Soc Fr Hist Studies. **RESEARCH** German social and intellectual history of the late 19th century; French social and intellectual history of the late 19th century; comparative history. **SELECTED PUBLICATIONS** Auth, Agrarians vs industrializers, Int Rev Social Hist, 67; Social Conservatism and the Middle Classes in Germany, 1914-1933, Princeton Univ, 69. **CONTACT ADDRESS** Dept of Hist, SUNY, Stony Brook, 100 Nicolls Rd, Stony Brook, NY 11794-0002.

LECKIE, SHIRLEY A.
PERSONAL Born 06/15/1937, Claremont, NH, m, 1975, 3 children **DISCIPLINE** AMERICAN HISTORY **EDUCATION** Univ Mo-Kansas City, BA, 67; MA, 69; Univ Toldeo, PhD. **CAREER** Dir of Adult Lib Studies, Univ Toledo, 73-80; asst dean of continuing educ, 80-81; assoc dean of continuing educ, Millsaps Col, 81-82; dir of continuing educ, Univ NC-Asheville, 83-85; asst prof, Univ Central Fla, 85-88; assoc prof, 88-95; prof, 95- . **HONORS AND AWARDS** Evans Bigraphy Awd, 93; Julian J. Rothbam Prize, 93. **MEMBERSHIPS** Western Hist Asoc; Southern Hist Asoc; Orgn of Am Hist. **RESEARCH** Women in American history; urban history; Western history; military history. **SELECTED PUBLICATIONS** Co-auth with William H. Leckie, Unlikely Warriors: General Benjamin H. Grierson and His Family, 84; ed, The Colonel's Lady on the Western Frontier: The Correspondence of Alice Kirk Grierson, 89; auth, Custer's Luck Runs Out, Montana, 93; auth, Elizabeth Bacon Custer and the Making of a Myth, 93; auth, Gender as a Force in History and Biography: The Custer Myth through the Prism of Domestic Ideals, North Dakota History, 97; auth, Angie Debo: Pioneering Historian, Univ of Oaklahoma Press, 00. **CONTACT ADDRESS** History Dept., Univ of Central Florida, Orlando, FL 32816. **EMAIL** sleckie@pegasus.cc.ucf.edu

LEDFORD, KENNETH F.
PERSONAL Born 08/17/1953, Gulfport, MS, m, 1977, 2 children **DISCIPLINE** HISTORY; LAW **EDUCATION** Univ NC, BA, 75, JD, 78; Johns Hopkins Univ, MA, 84, PhD, 89. **CAREER** Adjunct asst prof history, Univ MD, 88-89; vis asst prof history, Johns Hopkins Univ, 89, lectr Paul H. Nitze School Adv Int Studies, 88-91, Johns Hopkins Univ; res fel/ed, German Hist Inst, 89-91; asst prof history & law, 91-97, Assoc Prof History & Law, 97-, Case Western Reserve Univ; German Marshall Fund US res fel, 98-99; Fulbright fel, 97-98; ed bd Law Hist Rev, 96-; DAAD fel, 85-86; Mellon Found fel, 82-84; John Motley Morehead fel Univ NC, 75-78; Phi Beta Kappa, 74; Phi Eta Sigma, 72. **HONORS AND AWARDS** John Snell Mem Essay Prize S Hist Asn, 83; Seymour W Wurfel Prize Int Law Univ NC, 78. **MEMBERSHIPS** Am Hist Asn; Am Soc Legal Hist; Conf Grp Cent Europ Hist; S Hist Asn; Ger Stud Asn; Law Soc Asn; VA State Bar. **RESEARCH** German social history; German and European legal history; history of Central European professions; history of the German Burgertum; historiography of Germany. **SELECTED PUBLICATIONS** Conflict within the Legal Professions: Simultaneous Admission and the German Bar 1903-1927, German Professions, 1800-1950, Oxford Univ Press, 90; Lawyers, Liberalism, and Procedure: The German Imperial Justice Laws of 1877-79, Central European History, 93; "German Lawyers and the State in the Weimar Republic," Law and History Review, 95; "Identity, Difference, and Enlightenment Heritage: Comment on The Right to Be Punished," Law and History, 98; Lawyers and the Limits of Liberalism: The German Bar in the Weimar Republic, Lawyers and the Rise of Western Political Liberalism, Clarendon Press, 98; From General Estate to Special Interest: German Lawyers 1878-1933, Cambridge Univ Press, 96. **CONTACT ADDRESS** Dept of History, Case Western Reserve Univ, Cleveland, OH 44106-7107. **EMAIL** KXL15@po.cwru.edu

LEE, ANTHONY A.
PERSONAL Born 08/05/1947, m, 1979, 3 children **DISCIPLINE** HISTORY **EDUCATION** Univ of Calif, Los Angeles, BA, 68, MA, 74, CPhil 76. **CAREER** Instr, Cypress Col, 92-98; El Camino Col, 96-00; Oxnard Col, 92; Ventura Col, 91; online courses for NetNoir, 94-96; W LA GI, 98-00. **HONORS AND AWARDS** Grad Advan Prog Fel, UCLA, 72-75; ford found, nat fels fund awards, 74-75, 75-76; ndea, title vi, 73-74, 74-75; rackham fel, univ of mich, ann arbor, 68-69; regents' sch, ucla 64-68. **MEMBERSHIPS** Soc for Scholarly Publ. **RESEARCH** Baha'i Studies; African Religions; African American History; AHA; AAR. **SELECTED PUBLICATIONS** Ed, Studies in Baha'I History, 82-00. **CONTACT ADDRESS** 1600 Sawtelle Blvd, No 10, Los Angeles, CA 90025. **EMAIL** Member1700@aol.com

LEE, DAVID DALE
PERSONAL Born 08/05/1948, Cincinnati, OH **DISCIPLINE** AMERICAN HISTORY **EDUCATION** Miami Univ, BA, 70; Ohio State Univ, MA, 71, PhD(hist), 75. **CAREER** Asst prof, 75-81, Assoc Prof Hist, Western KY Univ, 81-, Nat Endowment for Humanities summer sem, 79, summer grant, 82; Hoover Libr Asn grant, 82. **HONORS AND AWARDS** Fac Excellence Awd, Western Ky Univ, 81. **MEMBERSHIPS** Orgn Am Historians; Southern Hist Asn. **RESEARCH** American South in the twentieth century; The United States in the 1920s and 1930s. **SELECTED PUBLICATIONS** Auth, Jesse Waugh, West Virginian, W Va Hist, 1/74; The Attempt to Impeach Governor Henry Horton, Tenn Hist Quart, summer 75; Merchandising and Politics in the 1920s, W Tenn Hist Soc Papers, 76; The Triumph of Boss Crump: The Tennessee Gubernatorial Election of 1932, Tenn Hist Quart, winter 76; The South and the American Mainstream: The Election of Jimmy Carter, Ga Hist Quart, spring 77; Tennessee in Turmoil: Politics in the Volunteer State, 1920-1932, Memphis State Univ Press, 79; The Emergence of the Imperial Presidency, In: America's Heritage in the Twentieth Century, Forum Press, 78; Appalachia on Film: The Making of Sergeant York, In: The South and Film, Univ Press Miss, 81. **CONTACT ADDRESS** Dept of Hist, Western Kentucky Univ, 1 Big Red Way St, Bowling Green, KY 42101-3576.

LEE, GEORGE ROBERT
PERSONAL Born 09/17/1933, Dawn, MO, m, 1964, 2 children **DISCIPLINE** HISTORY **EDUCATION** Northeastern State Col, BA, 54; Univ Okla, MA, 59; Johns Hopkins Univ, cert, 70. **CAREER** Teacher social studies, Wichita Pub Schs, 55-56; teacher hist, Oswego Pub Schs, Kans, 56-57 & Sterling Pub Schs, Colo, 57-61; instr, Lamar Jr Col, 61-62; from asst prof to prof hist, 62-98, Prof Emeritus Hist, Culver-Stockton Col, 98-. **MEMBERSHIPS** State Hist Soc Mo. **RESEARCH** Southern history and slavery. **SELECTED PUBLICATIONS** Auth, Slavery and Emancipation in Lewis County, Mo, Mo Hist Rev, 4/71; The Beaubiens of Chicago, Lee, 73; Carl Johann, Culver-Stockton Col, 75; James Shannon's Search for Happiness, Mo Hist Rev, 10/78; Conf Refugees, Encycl Southern Hist, La State Univ Press, 79; Culverton-Stockton College, the First 130 Years, Culverton-Stockton Col, 84; Decisions that Shaped America, Mark Twain, 93; China and the United States, Mark Twain, 94; World War II, Mark Twain, 95; Holocaust, Mark Twain, 98; auth, Slavery North of St. Louis, LCHS, 00. **CONTACT ADDRESS** Dept of History, Culver-Stockton Col, 1 College Hill, Canton, MO 63435-1299.

LEE, JEAN B.
PERSONAL Born Milwaukee, WI **DISCIPLINE** HISTORY **EDUCATION** Univ Va, PhD, 84. **CAREER** Asst prof, Col of Wm & Mary, 84-86; 89-91; asst prof, Univ Wisc, Madison 87-89; 92-95, assoc prof, Univ Wisc-Madison,95-. **HONORS AND AWARDS** NEH, Mellon fel; fel Wintenthur Mus & Libr; fel Va Hist Soc; fel David Libr Am Revolution; fel Inst Early Am Hist & Cult; fel, Am Assoc Univ Women. **MEMBERSHIPS** Am Hist Soc; Orgn Am Hist; S Hist Asn; S Asn Women Hist. **RESEARCH** American revolution; early national period; the South to 1835. **SELECTED PUBLICATIONS** Auth, The Problem of Slave Community in the Eighteenth-Century Chesapeake, Wm and Mary Quart, 86; The Price of Nationhood: The American Revolution in Charles County, W W Norton, 94; Experiencing the American Revolution, Taking Off the White Gloves: Annual Addresses of the S Asn Women Hist, Univ Mo Press, 98; auth, Touchstone of American Identities: Memory and the Revolution, 1775-1825, A Rhetorical History of the United States, Univ Mic Press, 00. **CONTACT ADDRESS** History Dept, Univ of Wisconsin, Madison, 455 N Park St., Madison, WI 53706.

LEE, LOYD ERVIN
PERSONAL Born 07/16/1939, Broadway, OH, m, 1963, 2 children **DISCIPLINE** MODERN EUROPEAN HISTORY **EDUCATION** Ohio State Univ, BA, 61; Cornell Univ, PhD, 67. **CAREER** Tchng asst hist, 62-64, Cornell Univ; asst prof, 65-67, Ark Agric, Mech & Norm Col; asst prof, 67-71, assoc

prof, 71-80, prof hist, 80-, SUNY, New Paltz. **HONORS AND AWARDS** Phi Beta Kappa, 61; Woodrow Wilson Fellow, 61-64; Jakob Schurmann Gould Fellow, 64-65; Woodrow Wilson Teaching Fellow, 65-67; SUNY Research Foundation Grant, 68; SUNY Research Foundation Fellowship, 69; National Endowment for the Humanities Award, 69; SUNY Research Foundation Fellowship, 81; NYS/UPP Professional Development research grant, July-August 89; NYS/UUP Faculty Development Award, 93; Chancellor's Award for Excellence in Teaching, 93. **MEMBERSHIPS** AHA; Am Comt Hist Second World War. **RESEARCH** Modern German History, World History, World War Two. **SELECTED PUBLICATIONS** Auth, The Politics of Harmony. Civil Service, Liberalism and Social Reform in Baden, 1800-50; auth, The War Years: A Global History of the Second World War, 89; auth, World War Two. Crucible of the Contemporary World. Commentary and Readings, 91; auth, Afro-Eurasian Worlds, 1500-1800, World Hist, The Am Hist Assn Guide to Hist Lit, Oxford Univ Press, 95; auth, The Rise of an Interdependent World, Asia in World Hist & Western Hist: A Guide for Col Tchrs, M E Sharpe, 97; auth, World War II in Europe, Africa, and the Americas, with General Sources, A Handbook of Literature and Research, Greenwood Pub, 97; auth, World War II in Asia and the Pacific and the War's Aftermath, with General Themes, A Handbook of Literature and Research, Greenwood Pub, 98; auth, World War II, Greenwood Pub, 99. **CONTACT ADDRESS** JFT814, 75 South Manheim Blvd, New Paltz, NY 12561. **EMAIL** leel@newpaltz.edu

LEE, MAURICE D., JR

PERSONAL Born 09/04/1925, Buffalo, NY, w, 1948, 2 children **DISCIPLINE** HISTORY **EDUCATION** Princeton Univ, AB, 45; MA, 48; PhD, 50. **CAREER** From instr to asst prof, Princeton Univ, 49-59; from assoc prof to prof, Univ Ill, 59-66; from prof to prof emeritus, Rutgers Univ, 60-. **HONORS AND AWARDS** Woodrow Wilson Fel, 46; Guggenheim Fel, 56; David Berry Prize, Royal Hist Soc, 58; Fulbright Res Fel, 61; Honorary LLD, Univ St Andrews, 94. **MEMBERSHIPS** AHA, Scottish Hist Soc, Scottish Medievalists, Royal Hist Soc. **RESEARCH** Sixteenth- and Seventeenth Century British History (primarily Scottish). **SELECTED PUBLICATIONS** Auth, Government by Pen: Scotland under King James VI and I, 80; auth, The Road to Revolution: Scotland under Charles I, 1625-1637, 85; auth, Great Britain's Solomon: James VI and I in his Three Kingdoms, 90; auth, The Heiresses of Buccleuch: Marriage, Money, and Politics in Seventeenth-Century Britain, 96. **CONTACT ADDRESS** Dept Hist, Rutgers, The State Univ of New Jersey, New Brunswick, PO Box 5059, New Brunswick, NJ 08903-5059.

LEE, PATRICIA-ANN

PERSONAL Born East Orange, NJ **DISCIPLINE** ENGLISH HISTORY **EDUCATION** Kean Col Union, BS; Columbia Univ, MA & PhD, 66. **CAREER** Asst prof hist, Newark State Col, 66-67; asst prof, 67-71, prof hist, Skidmore Col, 71, Ch Hist Dept. **MEMBERSHIPS** AHA; Conf Brit Studies. **RESEARCH** Tudor-Stuart English hist, espec the early Stuart Period. **SELECTED PUBLICATIONS** Auth, Play and the English Gentleman in the Early Seventeenth Century, Historian, 5/69; Some English Academies: An Experiment in Renaissance Education, Hist Educ Quart, fall 70; Reflections of Power, Margaret Fayou and the Dark Side of Queenship, Renaissance Quart, summer 89; A Bodye Politique to Governe: Aylmer, Knox and the Debate on Queenship, The Historian, winter 90; England: An Unfinished Revolution, In: Establising Democracies, Westview Press, 96; Mistress Stagg's Petitioners: February 1642, The Historian, winter 98. **CONTACT ADDRESS** 815 N Broadway, Saratoga Springs, NY 12866-1698. **EMAIL** plee@skidmore.edu

LEE, ROY ALTON

PERSONAL Born 05/24/1931, White City, KS, m, 1963, 2 children **DISCIPLINE** HISTORY **EDUCATION** Kans State Teachers Col, BS, 55, MS, 58; Univ Okla, PhD, 62. **CAREER** Teacher, high sch, Kans, 55-57; asst, Kans State Teachers Col, 57-58 and Univ Okla, 58-61; ; asst prof Am hist, Cent State Col, Okla, 61-66; assoc prof, 66-69, chmn dept, 70-73, Prof US Hist, Univ SDak, Vermillion, 69-. **HONORS AND AWARDS** Harry S Truman Libr Inst res grant, 61. **MEMBERSHIPS** Orgn Am Historians. **RESEARCH** Recent American history; United States constitutional history. **SELECTED PUBLICATIONS** Auth, Kaiser, Henry, J.--Builder in the Modern American West, J West, Vol 0032, 93; Campus Wars--the Peace Movement at American State-Universities in the Vietnam Era, Historian, Vol 0056, 93; United States Labor-Relations, 1945-1989--Accommodation and Conflict, Labor Hist, Vol 0035, 94; Truman in Retirement--a Former President View the Nation and the World, J Amer Hist, Vol 0081, 95; Introduction + Labor in the West, J West, Vol 0035, 96. **CONTACT ADDRESS** Dept of Hist, Univ of So Dakota, Vermillion, Vermillion, SD 57069.

LEE, SHERMAN E.

DISCIPLINE ART HISTORY **EDUCATION** Western Reserve Univ, PhD. **CAREER** Adj prof, Univ NC, Chapel Hill. **RESEARCH** Far Eastern art. **SELECTED PUBLICATIONS** Auth, Japanese Decorative Style, Cleveland Mus Art, 61; Chinese Landscape Painting, Cleveland Mus Art, 62; Reflections of Reality in Japanese Art, Cleveland Mus of Art, 83; History Far Eastern Art, Abrams, 62, 73, 82, 84, 94. **CONTACT ADDRESS** Univ of No Carolina, Chapel Hill, Chapel Hill, NC 27599.

LEE, TA-LING

PERSONAL Born 01/24/1934, Nanking, China, m, 1958, 1 child **DISCIPLINE** CHINESE & AMERICAN HISTORY **EDUCATION** Chung Hsing Univ, Taiwan, BA, 58; NYork Univ, MA, 61, PhD(hist), 67 **CAREER** News ed, Chinese Info Serv, NY, 58-67; transl Chinese & English, UN, 67-68; asst prof hist, Youngstown State Univ, 68 & 69; asst prof, 69-73, assoc prof, 73-78, Prof Hist, Southern Conn State Univ, 78-; Vis fac fel, Yale Univ, 78 & 80 **MEMBERSHIPS** AHA; Asn Asian Studies; Am Asn Chinese Studies **RESEARCH** Chinese Revolution of 1911; cultural revolution in China; modern Chinese politcs **SELECTED PUBLICATIONS** auth, Foundations of Chinese Revolution, 1905-1912, St. John's Univ Press, 70; coauth, The Revenge of Heaven, Putnam 72; Chen Tien-hua, Torment of a Revolutionary Nationalist, in: Sun Yat-sen and China, St. John's Uuniv Press, 74; auth, The Study of American History, Trends and Dynamics, in: Essays on America, Tankang Univ Press, 77; coauth, Human Rights in the People's Republic of China, Westview Press, 88; coauth, Reform in Reverse, Univ Md Sch Law, 88; coauth, One Step forward, One Step Backward, Univ Md Sch Law, 89; co-auth, Failure of a Democracy Movement, Univ Md Sch Law, 91; contrib, Historical Dictionary of Revolutionary China, 1839-1976, Greenwood Press, 92; co-auth, A Quantitative Analysis of Judicial Practice and Human Rights in the People's Republic of China, East Asia Res Ins, 92; co-auth, Tiananmen Aftermath, Univ Md Sch Law, 92; Chinese Intellectuals after Tiananmen, in: Forces of Change in Contemporary China, Univ SC Press, 93; co-auth, The Bamboo Gulag, Univ Md Sch Law, 94; American Policy Toward China and Japan: The East Asian giants, in: American in the Twenty-first Century: Opportunities and Challenges, Prentice-Hall, 96; co-auth, To Cope with a Bad Global Image: Human Rights in the People's Republic of China, 1993-1994, Univ Press Am, 97. **CONTACT ADDRESS** Dept of Hist, So Connecticut State Univ, 501 Crescent St, New Haven, CT 06515-1330.

LEEB, ISIDORE LEONARD

PERSONAL Born 10/11/1934, Philadelphia, PA, m, 1960 **DISCIPLINE** MODERN EUROPEAN HISTORY **EDUCATION** Univ Pa, BA, 55; Columbia Univ, PhD(hist), 70. **CAREER** Lectr contemp civilization, Queens Col, NY, 60-62; lectr hist, Yeshiva Univ, 62-63 and Brooklyn Col, 63-64; from instr to asst prof, 64-69, Assoc Prof Hist, Polytech Inst New York, 69-, Head Dept Soc Sci, 71-, Nat Endowment for Humanities fel, 70-71. **MEMBERSHIPS** Werkgroep 18e EEUW, Neth; Nederlands Hist Genoot; AHA. **RESEARCH** Historiography and political theory in the Dutch Republic; 18th century intellectual history; theory and practice of imperialism. **SELECTED PUBLICATIONS** Coauth, Social science theory and method: An integrated historical introduction, Vol VII, 68; auth, The Ideological Origins of the Batavian Revolution: History and Politics in the Dutch Republic, 1747-1800, Martinus Nijhoff, The Hague, 73. **CONTACT ADDRESS** Polytech Inst of New York, 6 Metro Tech Ctr, Brooklyn, NY 11201.

LEES, ANDREW

PERSONAL Born 11/15/1940, New York, NY, m, 1965, 2 children **DISCIPLINE** HISTORY **EDUCATION** Amherst Col, BA, 63; Harvard Univ, MA, 64, PhD(hist), 69. **CAREER** Instr hist, Amherst Col, 68-69, asst prof, 69-74; asst prof, 74-76, assoc prof, 76-85, prof hist, Rutgers Univ, Camden, 85-; mem Ger Acad Exchange Serv, 79, 87, 94; fel col teachers, NEH, 81-82; member, Inst for Advanced Study, 95. **MEMBERSHIPS** AHA; Conf Group Cent Europ Hist; Urban Hist Asn. **RESEARCH** Nineteenth and 20th century European intellectual and social history; modern Germany; modern England. **SELECTED PUBLICATIONS** Auth, Revolution and Reflection: Intellectual Change in Germany During the 1850's, Martinus Nijhoff, 74; co-ed, The Urbanization of European Society in the Nineteenth Century, Heath, 76; Critics of Urban Society in Germany, 1854-1914, J Hist Ideas, 79; Historical Perspectives on Cities in Modern Germany, J Urban Hist, 79; The Metropolis and the Intellectual, In: Metropolis, 1890-1940, Mansell, 82; Cities Perceived: Urban Society in European and American Thought, 1820-1940, Columbia Univ Press, 85; Social Reform, Social Policy and Social Welfare in Modern Germany, J Social Hist, 89; Berlin and Modern Urbanity in German Discourse, 1845-1945, J Urban Hist, 91; Das Denken uber die Grobstadt um 1900, Berichte zur Wissenschaftsgeschichte, 92; State and Society, in Imperial Germany, Greenwood, 96. **CONTACT ADDRESS** Dept Hist, Rutgers, The State Univ of New Jersey, Newark, 311 N 5th St, Camden, NJ 08102-1461. **EMAIL** alees@camden.rutgers.edu

LEES, LYNN HOLLEN

PERSONAL Born 10/06/1941, Akron, OH, m, 1965, 2 children **DISCIPLINE** MODERN EUROPEAN HISTORY **EDUCATION** Swarthmore Col, AB, 63; Harvard Univ, AM, 64, PhD(hist), 69. **CAREER** Lectr hist, Mt Holyoke Col, 68-69, asst prof, 69-73; from Asst Prof to Assoc Prof, 74-86, Prof Hist, Univ PA, 86-. **HONORS AND AWARDS** Howard Found fel, Brown Univ, 72-73; fel, Shelby Cullom Davis Ctr, Princeton Univ, 75-76; Am Coun Learned Soc fel, 78-79; mem W Europ fel screening comt, Soc Sci Res Coun, 76-78; Guggenheim fel, 78-79; John Ben Snow Prize, 82; Ford Grant, Am Coun of Learned Soc, 85-86; NEH Fel, 93; Rotary Found Fel, 95-96. **MEMBERSHIPS** AHA; Soc Sci Hist Asn; World Hist Asn; N Am Conf on Brit Studies. **RESEARCH** Urban history; 19th century European social history; history of British Empire. **SELECTED PUBLICATIONS** Auth, Patterns of Lower-Class Life: Irish Slum Communites in Nineteenth Century London, In: Nineteenth Century Cities, Yale Univ, 69; The Metropolitan Type: London and Paris compared, In: The Victorian City: Images and Reality, Routledge & Kegan Paul, 73; coauth, The people of June, 1848, In: Annales: Economies, Societes, Civilisation, 74; co-ed, The Urbanization of European Society, Heath, 76; The Irish Countryman Urbanized: A Comparative Perspective on the Famine Migration, J Urban Hist, 77; auth, Exiles of Erin: Irish Migrants in mid-Nineteenth Century London, Cornell Univ & Manchester Univ 78; coauth, The Making of Urban Europe, 1000-1950, Harvard Univ Press, 95; auth, The Solidarities of Strangers: The English Poor Laws and the People, 1900-1948, Cambridge Univ Press, 98. **CONTACT ADDRESS** Dept of History, Univ of Pennsylvania, 3401 Walnut St, Philadelphia, PA 19104-6228. **EMAIL** lhlees@history.upenn.edu

LEFF, MARK H.

DISCIPLINE HISTORY **EDUCATION** Univ of Chic, PhD, 78; Univ of Chic, MA, 72; Brown Univ, BA, 70. **CAREER** Assoc prof, 90-; asst prof, 86-90; Univ of Ill at Urbana-Champaign; asst prof, Washington Univ, 77-85. **HONORS AND AWARDS** Nat Endow for the hum summer stipend, 80; Andrew W. Mellon fac fel in the hum, Harvard Univ, 85; Andrew W. Mellon fac fel in hist, Harvard Univ, 85-86; George and Gladys Queen Awd for Excellence in Teaching in History, 90; Elected member, Nat Acad of Social Insurance, 90; William F. Prokasy Awd for Excellence in Undergraduate Teaching, 91; UI res board released time award, 90; UI res board released time award, 90; UI list of fac ranked as excellent by their students, 87-94; fac fel of prog for study of cultural values and ethics, 94-95. **RESEARCH** Twentieth century United States; public policy. **SELECTED PUBLICATIONS** Auth, "Consensus for Reform: The Mothers'-Pension Movement in the Progressive Era," Social Service Review, September 73, pp. 397-417; auth, "The Politics of Ineffectiveness: Federal Firearms Legislation, 1919-1938," Annals of the Academy of Political and Social Science, May 82, pp. 48-62; auth, "Taxing the 'Forgotten Man': The Politics of Social Security Finance in the New Deal," Journal of American History, September 83, pp. 359-81; auth, "Historical Perspectives on Old Age Insurance: The State of the Art on the Art of the State," in Edward Berkowitz, ed., Social Security after Fifty, 87, pp. 29-53; auth, "Speculating in Social Security Futures: The Perils of Payroll Tax Financing, 1939-1950," in Social Security: The First Half Century, 88, pp. 243-78; auth, "World War II, American Style: The Mystiue of Home Front Sacrific," Swords and Plowshares, October 89, 8-10; auth, "The Politics of Sacrifice on the American Home Front in World War II," Jounrnal of American History, March 91, pp. 1296-1318; auth, "Strange Bedfellows: The Utility Magnate as Politician," in James Madison, ed., Wendell Willkie, 92, pp. 22-46; auth, "Home Front Mobilization in World War II: American Political Images of Civic Responsibility," in Roger Kanet, ed., Peacekeeping and Warmaking: Esssays in Honor of Jeremiah D. Sullivan, 95, pp. 277-97; auth, "Revisioning U.S. Political History," American Historical Review, June 95, pp. 829-53. **CONTACT ADDRESS** History Dept, Univ of Illinois, Urbana-Champaign, 431 Gregory Hall, Urbana, IL 61801. **EMAIL** m-leff@staff.uiuc.edu

LEFFLER, MELVYN P.

PERSONAL Born 05/31/1945, New York, NY, m, 1968, 2 children **DISCIPLINE** HISTORY **EDUCATION** Cornell Univ, BS, 66; Ohio State Univ, PhD, 72. **CAREER** From asst prof to asoc prof, Vanderbilt Uiv, 72-86; prof, Univ Va, 86-; chair hist dept, Univ Va, 90-95; Edward R. Stettinius Prof of Am Hist, Univ Va, 93-; Dean of Col and Grad Sch of Arts & Sci, Univ Va, 97-. **HONORS AND AWARDS** Bernath Article Prize, 84; Ferrell Priz, 93; Hoover Prize, 93; Bancroft Prize, 93; Nobel Fel, 98. **MEMBERSHIPS** Am Hist Asn, Orgn of Am Historians, Soc for Historians of Am For Relations. **RESEARCH** U. S. Foreign Relations, Cold War, Morality and Foreign Policy, U. S. Economic Foreign Policy. **SELECTED PUBLICATIONS** Auth, Specter of Communism; auth, A Preponderance of Power: National Security, the Truman Administration, and the Cold War; auth, The Elusive Quest: America's Pursuit of European Stability and French Security, 1919-1933. **CONTACT ADDRESS** Dept Hist, Univ of Virginia, Randall Hall, Charlottesville, VA 22903. **EMAIL** mpl4j@virginia.edu

LEGAN, MARSHALL SCOTT

PERSONAL Born 02/17/1940, Louisville, MS, m, 1961, 2 children **DISCIPLINE** HISTORY OF THE SOUTH **EDUCATION** Miss State Univ, BS, 61, MA, 62; Univ Miss, PhD(hist), 68. **CAREER** Teacher social studies, Ackerman High Sch, 62-63; asst prof, 68-75, Assoc Prof Hist, Northeast LA Univ, 75-, Dept Head Hist and Govt, 75-, Abstractor, Am Hist and Life, ABC-Clio Press. **MEMBERSHIPS** Southern Hist Asn; Railway and Locomotive Hist Soc. **RESEARCH** Railroad history; medical history. **SELECTED PUBLICATIONS** Auth, Hydropathy in America: A Nineteenth Century Panacea, Bull Hist Med, 5/71; Mississippi and the Yellow Fever Epidemics of

1878-1879, J Miss Hist, 8/71; Disease and the Freedmen in Mississippi During Reconstruction, J Hist Med & Allied Sci, 7/73; Popular Reactions to the New Madrid Earthquakes, 1811-1812, Filson Club Hist Quart, 1/76; The Disappearance of Bronze John in Mississippi, J Miss Hist, 2/76; Railroad Sentiment in North Louisiana in the 1850's, La Hist, spring 76. **CONTACT ADDRESS** Dept of Hist and Govt, Northeast Louisiana Univ, 700 University Ave, Monroe, LA 71209-9000.

LEGGE, ELIZABETH
DISCIPLINE ART HISTORY **EDUCATION** Univ Toronto, BA, 73; Mt Allison Univ, studio art, 73-74; Cambridge Univ, BA, 76; Courtauld Inst, Univ London, MA, 79, PhD, 86. **CAREER** Lectr, 79-81, asst prof, 85-87, Univ Winnipeg; cur, Winnipeg Art Gallery, 79-81; Univ art cur, 88-, asst prof Fine Art, Univ Toronto, 96-. **HONORS AND AWARDS** Joseph Henderson Memorial Awd, Trinity Col, Univ Toronto, 69-73; Rainmaker Prize, Girton Col, Cambridge Univ, 76; Commonwealth Scholar, 81-84; SSHRC Res Grant, Taemaker Preze for First Class Degree, Cambridge Univ, 99-02. **MEMBERSHIPS** Inst Contempory Culture, ROM. **RESEARCH** Surrealism, contemporary art. **SELECTED PUBLICATIONS** Auth, Posing Questions: Max Ernst's Oedipus Rex and the Implicit Sphinx, in Arts Mag, 86; auth, Max Ernst: The Psychoanalytic Sources, 89; auth, Thirteen Ways of Looking at a Virgin: Picabia's La Sainte Vierge, in Word and Image, 96; auth, Of loss and leaving: Vera Fenkel's the body missing," Canadian Art, 96; auth, "Taking it as Red: Michael Snow and Wittgenstein," Journal of Canadian Art Hist, 18, (97): 68-91; auth, "ne le dire qu'a demi: Max Ernst and Emblems," Word and Image, 00. **CONTACT ADDRESS** Dept of Fine Arts, Univ of Toronto, 100 St. George St, Toronto, ON, Canada M5E 1A1. **EMAIL** eliz.legge@utoronto.ca

LEGON, RONALD
DISCIPLINE GREEK HISTORY **EDUCATION** Cornell Univ, PhD, 66. **CAREER** Instr, CUNY, 65-66; Asst prof, CUNY, 66-67; Asst prof, Univ Ill, 67-70; assoc prof, Univ Ill, 70-82; Vis assoc prof, Univ Chicago, 82; Prof, Univ Ill, 82-92; Vis prof, Univ Chicago, 83-94; Prof, Univ Baltimore, 92-. **SELECTED PUBLICATIONS** Auth, The Political History of a Greek City-State to 336 B.C., Cornell Univ Press, 81; auth, Thucydides and the Case for COntemporary History, Essays in Honor of Donald Kagan, 97. **CONTACT ADDRESS** Univ of Baltimore, 1420 N. Charles Street, Baltimore, MD 21201.

LEGUIN, CHARLES A.
PERSONAL Born 06/04/1927, Macon, GA, m, 1953 **DISCIPLINE** HISTORY **EDUCATION** Emory Univ, PhD(hist), 56. **CAREER** Instr hist, Syracuse Univ, 49-50; asst prof, Mercer Univ, 52-55; instr, Emory Univ, 55-56; asst prof, Univ Idaho, 56-59; from asst prof to assoc prof, 59-68, Prof Hist, Portland State Univ, 68-, Vis assoc prof, Emory Univ, 62-63. **MEMBERSHIPS** AHA; Soc Fr Hist Studies; Soc Mod Hist, France. **RESEARCH** French revolution. **SELECTED PUBLICATIONS** Auth, Roland de la Platiere and the universal language, Mod Lang Rev, 4/60; Jean-Marie Roland and 18th century French economy, Am J Econ & Sociol, 1/63. **CONTACT ADDRESS** Dept of Hist, Portland State Univ, Portland, OR 97207.

LEHMAN, CYNTHIA L.
PERSONAL Born 11/25/1968, Sunbury, PA, s **DISCIPLINE** AFRICAN AMERICAN STUDIES **EDUCATION** Temple Univ, MA, 95, PhD, 97. **CAREER** Asst prof, Eastern Ill Univ, 97-. **HONORS AND AWARDS** Phi Alpha Theta (Int Hist Honor Soc). **MEMBERSHIPS** AHA; AAUW; NCBS; NCA. **RESEARCH** African-American/Native American history & culture; curriculum revision. **SELECTED PUBLICATIONS** The Social and Political Views of Charles Chestnutt: Reflections on his Major Writings, J of Black Studs, 1/96. **CONTACT ADDRESS** 2003 S 12th St #16, Charleston, IL 61920. **EMAIL** cfcll1@eiu.edu

LEHMANN, CLAYTON M.
DISCIPLINE HISTORY **EDUCATION** Augustana Col, BA, 78; Univ Md, MA, 80; Univ Chicago, PhD, 86. **CAREER** Adj prof, Mont State Univ, 86-87; from asst to assoc prof, Univ SDak, 88-. **MEMBERSHIPS** AIA; Am Philos Asn; ASOR; AAAH. **RESEARCH** Greek history; Greek and Roman epigraphy; 16th Century Europe. **SELECTED PUBLICATIONS** Auth, Observations on the Latin Dedicatory Inscriptions from Caesarea Maritima, Bibl Archeol Today, 90; auth, Xenoi, Proxenoi, and Early Greek Traders, Helios, 94; auth, The Combined Caesarea Expeditions: The Excavation of Caesarea's Byzantine City Wall, 1989, Annual Am Sch Oriental Res, 94; auth, The City and the Text, Caesarea Maritima: Retrospective After Two Millennia, 96. **CONTACT ADDRESS** Dept of History, Univ of So Dakota, Vermillion, Vermillion, SD 57069-2390. **EMAIL** clehmann@usd.edu

LEHMBERG, STANFORD E.
PERSONAL Born 09/23/1931, m, 1962, 1 child **DISCIPLINE** HISTORY **EDUCATION** Univ Kansas, BA, 53, MA, 54; Cambridge Univ, PhD, 56. **CAREER** Prof, Univ Texas Austin, 56-69; prof, Univ Minn Twin Cities, 69-99; dept chair, 78-85; prof emer, 99-. **HONORS AND AWARDS** Fulbright Scholar, 54-56; Guggenheim Fellow, 65-66, 85-86. **MEMBERSHIPS** Fellow Royal Hist Soc; Fellow Soc of Antiquaries of London; AHA; Conf Br Sts. **RESEARCH** History of England during Tudor and Stuart periods. **SELECTED PUBLICATIONS** Auth, Sir Thomas Elyot, Tudor Humanist, TX, 60; auth, Sir Walter Mildmay and Tudor Government, TX, 64; auth, The Reformation Parliament, 1529-1536, Cambridge, 70; auth, The Later Parliaments of Henry VIII, 1536-1547, Cambridge, 77; auth, The Reformation of Cathedrals: Cathedrals in English Society 1485-1603, Princeton, 88; auth, The Peoples of the British Isles from Prehistoric Times to 1688, Wadsworth, 92; Cathedrals under Siege: Cathedrals in English Society 1600-1700, Penn State, 96; co-auth, The University of Minnesota, 1946-2000, Minnesota, 01. **CONTACT ADDRESS** 1005 Calle Largo, Santa Fe, NM 87501. **EMAIL** lehmberg@earthlink.net

LEHUU, ISABEL
DISCIPLINE HISTORY **EDUCATION** Paris-Sorbonne, BA, 78; MA, 79; Ecole des Hautes Etudes en Sciences Sociales, Paris, DEA, 83; Cornell, MA, 87, PhD, 92. **CAREER** Asst Prof, Hist, Univ. DU Quebec. **MEMBERSHIPS** AM Antiquarian Soc **SELECTED PUBLICATIONS** Auth, "Sentimental Figures: Reading Goley's Lady's Book in Antebellum America" in The Culture of Sentiment: Race, Gender, and Sentimentality in 19-Century America, Oxford Univ Press, 92; auth, "Une Tradition de Dialogue: L'histoire Culturelle et Intellectuelle," in Chantiers d'Histoire Americaine, Belin, 94; auth, "Ephemeral Myriads of Books": The Work of Popular Reading in America, 1830-1860, Univ NC Press. **CONTACT ADDRESS** Dept d'Histoire, Univ of Quebec, Montreal, succ. Centre-ville, Montreal, QC, Canada H3C 3PB. **EMAIL** lehuu.isabelle@uqam.ca

LEIBSOHN, DANA
DISCIPLINE ART HISTORY **EDUCATION** Bryn Mawr, BA; Univ CO, MA; UCLA, PhD. **CAREER** Act, Lat Am Stud Progr, Smith Col & 5 Col Native Am Stud Comt; post-doctoral fel, Getty Ctr. **RESEARCH** Indigenous visual cult after the Span conquest of Mexico, particularly on maps, histories, and modes of writing. **SELECTED PUBLICATIONS** Publ on, maps and indigenous bk(s) from colonial Mexico. **CONTACT ADDRESS** Dept of Art, Smith Col, Hillyer Hall 312, Northampton, MA 01063. **EMAIL** dleibsoh@julia.smith.edu

LEICHTY, ERLE VERDUN
PERSONAL Born 08/07/1933, Alpena, MI, m, 1963 **DISCIPLINE** ASSYRIOLOGY **EDUCATION** Univ Mich, BA, 55, MA, 57; Univ Chicago, PhD(Assyriol), 60. **CAREER** From res asst to res assoc Assyriol, Orient Inst, Univ Chicago, 60-63; from asst prof to assoc prof ancient hist, Univ Minn, 63-68; assoc prof Assyriol, 68-71, prof Assyriol, Univ Pa, 71-97, Clark Research prof of Assyriol, Univ Pa, 98-, Cur Akkadian Lang & Lit, Univ Mus, 68-95, Guggenheim fel, 64-65; ed, Expedition, 70-73 & J Cuneiform Studies, 72-91; ed, Occasional Publications of the Babylonian Fund, 76-; ed, for the Ancient Near East, The Am Hist Asn's Guide to Historical Literature, Oxford, 95; Curator of Tablet collections, Univ Museum, Univ Pa, 96-. **HONORS AND AWARDS** Fel, Am Numismatic Soc, 56; alternate Fulbright to England, 62-63; Fulbright to England, 63-64 (declined); annual prof of the Baghdad Schools of the American Schools of Oriental Research, 63-64 (declined); fel of the Guggenheim Foundation, 64-65; trustee, Institute of Semitic Studies, Princeton, NJ, 85-90. **MEMBERSHIPS** Am Orient Soc; Archaeol Inst Am; Am Schs Orient Res; Assoc of Current Anthropology; British School of Archaeology in Iraq. **RESEARCH** Ancient Near Eastern history. **SELECTED PUBLICATIONS** Auth, A Bibliography of the Kuyunjik Collection of the British Museum, Trustees Brit Mus, 64; The Omen Series Shumma Izbu, J J Augustin, 69; A Remarkable Forger, 70 & Demons and Population Control, 71, Expedition; Two Late Commentaries, Arch fur Orientforsch, 73; The Fourth Tablet of Erimhaus, Alter Orient und Altes Testament, 75; Literary Notes, Essays on the Ancient Near East in Memory of J. J. Finkelstein, 77; A Collection of Recipes for Dyeing, Alter Orient und Altes Testament-Sonderreihe 203, 79; The Curator's Write: The Summerian Dictionary, Expedition 24, 82; An Inscription of Ashur-etel-ilani, Journal of the American Oriental Soc, 83; Bel-epush and Tammaritu, Anatolian Studies 33, 83; A Legal Text from the Reign of Tiglath-Pileser III, American Oriental Series 67, 87; Omens from Doorknobs, Journal of Cuneiform Studies 39, 87; Catalogue of Babylonian Tablets in the British Museum, vol 6, London, 86, vol 7, London, 87, vol 8, London, 88; Ashurbanipal's Library at Ninevah, Syro-Mesopotamian Studies Bulletin, 88; Making Dictionaries, Humanities 9/3, 88; Guaranteed to Cure, A Scientific Humanist, Studies in Memory of Abraham Sachs, 89; Feet of Clay, Dumue2-dub-ba-a, Studies in Honor of Ake W. Sjoberg, 89; Esarhaddon's 'Letter to the Gods," Ah, Assyria.., Studies in Assyrian History and Ancient Near Eastern Historiography presented to Hayim Tadmor, Scripta Hierosolymitana 33, 90; A Tamitu from Nippur, Lingering Over Words, Studies in Ancient Near Eastern Literature in Honor of William L. Moran, 90; Sheep Lungs, The Tablet and Scroll, Near Eastern Studies in Honor of William W.Hallo, 93; Ritual, Sacrifice, and Divination in Mesopotamia, Ritual and Sacrifice in the Ancient Near East, OLA 55, 93; The Origins of Scholarship, Die Rolle der Astronomie in den Kulturen Mesopotamiens, Grazer Morgenlandishe Studies 3, 93; The Distribution of Agricultural Tools in Mesopotamia, Sulma IV, 93; Esarhaddon, King of Assyria, Civilizations of the Ancient Near East, 2, 95; Section 5: Ancient Near East, Guide to Historical Literature, 95; Angurinnu, Weiner Zeitschrift fur die Kunde des Morgenlandes 86, 96; Divination, Magic, and Astrology, Assyria 1995, 97; qabutu, sahu, and me-gati, Oelsner Fs, in press; An Old Babylonian Chronicle, Grayson FS, in press; The Fifth Tablet of Summa Izbu, CTMMA 2, in press. **CONTACT ADDRESS** Dept Orient Studies, Univ of Pennsylvania, 255 S 36th St, Philadelphia, PA 19104-3805.

LEIGHTEN, PATRICIA
DISCIPLINE ART HISTORY **EDUCATION** Rutgers Univ, PhD. **CAREER** Prof, Duke Univ. **RESEARCH** Late nineteenth and early twentieth-century art and the hist of photography. **SELECTED PUBLICATIONS** Auth, Re-Ordering the Universe: Picasso and Anarchism, 1897-1914; Anarchism and Audience in Avant-Guerre Paris; co-auth, Cubism and Culture. **CONTACT ADDRESS** Dept of Art and Art Hist, Duke Univ, 107B East Duke Building, PO Box 90764, Durham, NC 27708. **EMAIL** leighten@duke.edu

LEIMAN, SID ZALMAN
PERSONAL Born 11/03/1941, New York, NY **DISCIPLINE** HISTORY, RELIGION **EDUCATION** Brooklyn Col, BA, 64; Mirrer Yeshivah, BRE, 64; Univ Pa, PhD(Orient studies), 70. **CAREER** Lectr Jewish hist and lit, Yale Univ, 68-70, from asst prof to assoc prof relig studies, 70-78; prof Jewish hist and dean, Vervard Revel Grad Sch, Yeshiva Univ, 78-81; Prof and Chmn Dept Judaic Studies, Brooklyn Col, 81-, Nat Found Jewish Cult res grant, 67-68; Morse fel, Yale Univ, 71-72; vis scholar Jewish law and ethics, Kennedy Inst Ethics, Georgetown Univ, 77-78; Mem Found Jewish Cult res grant, 81-82. **MEMBERSHIPS** Am Schs Orient Res; Soc Bibl Lit; Am Acad Relig; Asn Jewish Studies; Am Jewish Hist Soc. **RESEARCH** Jewish history; Jewish ethics; Biblical studies. **SELECTED PUBLICATIONS** Auth, Horowitz, Jacob on the Study of Scripture--From the Pages of 'Tradition', Tradition-J Orthodox Jewish Thought, Vol 0027, 92; From the Pages of Tradition--Friedman, David of Karlin--the Ban on Secular Study in Jerusalem, Tradition-J Orthodox Jewish Thought, Vol 0026, 92; Dwarfs on the Shoulders of Giants + the Study of Torah Despite a Theology of Generational Regression, Tradition-J Orthodox Jewish Thought, Vol 0027, 93; Carlebach, Joseph, Wuerzburg and Jerusalem--a Conversation Between Bamberger, Seligmann, Baer and Salant, Shmuel, Tradition-J Orthodox Jewish Thought, Vol 0028, 94; Ha Kohen Kook, Abraham, Isaac--Invocation at the Inauguration of the Hebrew-University--Excerpt From the Pages of Tradition April-1, 1925, Tradition-J Orthodox Jewish Thought, Vol 0029, 94; Rabbi Schwab,Shimon + Respone on the Torah and Derekh-Eretz Movement Concerning Jewish Education--a Letter Regarding the Frankfurt Approach--From the Pages of 'Tradition', Tradition-J Orthodox Jewish Thought, Vol 0031, 97. **CONTACT ADDRESS** Dept of Judaic Studies, Brooklyn Col, CUNY, Brooklyn, NY 11367.

LEIREN, TERJE IVAN
PERSONAL Born 05/14/1943, Stamneshella, Norway, m, 1967, 2 children **DISCIPLINE** SCANDINAVIAN HISTORY **EDUCATION** Calif State Univ, Los Angeles, BA, 66, MA, 70; North Tex State Univ, PhD(hist), 78. **CAREER** Lectr hist and English, Lindaas Gymnas, Knarvik, Norway, 75-76; res asst and lectr mod Europ hist, Univ Oslo, 76-77; Asst Prof, Scand Hist, Univ Wash, 77-, Lectr, Univ Oslo, summers; assoc ed, Scand Studies. **HONORS AND AWARDS** Knight, Royal Norwegian Order of Merit, 96. **MEMBERSHIPS** Soc Advan Scand Studies; Norweg-Am Hist Asn; AHA; Soc Historians of Scand. **RESEARCH** Norwegian history: 19th and 20th centuries: nationalism in Norway and the establishment of modern Norwegian monarchy, 1905; Scandinavian immigration. **SELECTED PUBLICATIONS** Auth, Norwegian independence and British opinion: January to August, 1814, Scand Studies, summer 75; American press opionion and Norwegian independence, 1905, Norweg-Am Studies, 77; Republikanarane: 1906, Syn og Segn, 6/79; Sigurd Ibsen and origins of national monarchy in Norway, Scand Studies, fall 79; Halvdan Koht's American, In: Makers of An American Immigrant Legacy, 80; auth, Marcus Thrane: Norwegian Radical in America, 87; auth, "Marcus Thrane and the Chicago Fire," Scand Journal of Hist, (90); ed, "Sigurd Ibsen and Ringeren," Scand Studies, (99); ed, Stage and Screen, 00; auth, "Pilgrimage and Propaganda," Norweg-Am Studies, (00). **CONTACT ADDRESS** Dept of Scand Studies, Univ of Washington, Box 353420, Seattle, WA 98195-3420. **EMAIL** leiren@u.washington.edu

LEITH, JAMES A.
PERSONAL Born 10/26/1931, Toronto, ON, Canada, m, 1956, 2 children **DISCIPLINE** MODERN EUROPEAN HISTORY **EDUCATION** Univ Toronto, BA, 53, PhD(hist), 60; Duke Univ, MA, 55. **CAREER** Lectr hist, Univ Sask, 58-61; from lectr to assoc prof, 61-68, head dept, 68-73, Prof Hist, Queen's Univ, Ont, 68-, Can Coun fels, 61, 65, 68, 70, 75, 76 and 77; vis prof, Cornell Univ, 64; R H McLaughlin res prof, 65-66; vis prof, Oxford Univ, 70-71 and Australian Inst Advan Studies, 74-75; French govt fel, 74. **MEMBERSHIPS** Soc Fr Hist Studies; Soc Mod Hist France; AHA; Can Hist Asn; Can Soc 18th Century Studies. **RESEARCH** Eighteenth century French

cultural and intellectual history, especially ideas about education and mass indoctrination. **SELECTED PUBLICATIONS** Auth, Space and Revolution: Projects for Monuments Squares, and Public Buildings in France, 1789-1799, coed, Iconographie et Image de la Revolution Francaise. **CONTACT ADDRESS** Dept of Hist, Queen's Univ at Kingston, Kingston, ON, Canada K7L 3N6.

LEMAHIEU, DAN LLOYD
PERSONAL Born 05/09/1945, West Bend, WI, m, 1980, 1 child **DISCIPLINE** BRITISH HISTORY **EDUCATION** Lawrence Univ, BA, 67; Harvard Univ, MA, 68, PhD(hist), 73. **CAREER** Prof Hist, Lake Forest Col, 80-; visiting professor, U.S. Michigan, 83-84, Harvard University, 92-93. **HONORS AND AWARDS** Rockefeller Found humanities fel, 78-79. **MEMBERSHIPS** AHA; NAm Conf Brit Studies. **RESEARCH** British culture, History of Communication; 20th century. **SELECTED PUBLICATIONS** The Mind, William Daley, Nebraska 76, 215 pages; A Culture for Democracy: Mass Communications and The Cultivated Mind, Oxford, 88, 333 pages. **CONTACT ADDRESS** Dept of Hist, Lake Forest Col, 555 N Sheridan Rd, Lake Forest, IL 60045-2399.

LEMAY, HELEN RODNITE
PERSONAL Born 03/05/1941, New York, NY, 1 child **DISCIPLINE** MEDIEVAL INTELLECTUAL HISTORY **EDUCATION** Bryn Mawr Col, AB, 62; Columbia Univ, MA, 65, PhD(medieval hist), 72. **CAREER** Asst medieval hist, Columbia Univ, 64-67; instr hist, 70-71, asst prof, 71-76, Assoc Prof Hist, State Univ NY Stony Brook, 76-. **MEMBERSHIPS** Int Soc Neoplatonic Studies; Soc Pour L'Etude de la Philos Medievale; Soc Italian Hist Studies. **RESEARCH** Medieval sexuality in medical and astrological literature; Twelfthcentury school of Chartres. **SELECTED PUBLICATIONS** Auth, Platonisms in the twelfth-century School of Chartres, Acta II: The Twelfth Century, 75; Science and theology at Chartres: the case of the supracelestial waters, Brit J Hist Sci, 10: 226-236; Guillaume de Conches division of philosophy in the Accessus ad Macrobium, Mediaevalia, I: 115-129; Some thirteenth and fourteenth century lectures on female sexuality, Int J Womens Studies, I: 391-400; Arabic influence on Medieval attitudes toward infancy, Clio Medica: Acta Academiae Int Hist Medicinae, Vol 13, No 1; The stars and human sexual response: Some medieval scientific views, Isis, 71: 127-137; William of Saliceto on human sexuality, Viatory 12: 165-181; Homosexuality in the middle ages, Rev Essay Cross Currents, 30: 352-360. **CONTACT ADDRESS** Dept of Hist, SUNY, Stony Brook, 100 Nicolls Rd, Stony Brook, NY 11794-0002.

LEMAY, RICHARD
PERSONAL Born 06/30/1916, Montreal, PQ, Canada, m, 1971, 1 child **DISCIPLINE** MEDIEVAL EUROPEAN INTELLECTUAL HISTORY **EDUCATION** Univ Montreal, BA, 36, Lic, 40 and 46; Columbia Univ, PhD (hist), 58. **CAREER** Teacher relig educ, Ecole Normale Jacques Cartier, Montreal, 40-41; foreign corresp UN, Le Devoir Newspaper, 47-49; lectr medieval hist, Columbia Univ, 56-58; asst prof hist, Am Univ Beirut, 58-65; sr researcher medieval hist, Nat Ctr Sci Res, Paris, 65-70; assoc prof hist, 70-75, Prof Hist, Ctiy Col and Grad Sch, City Univ New York, 75-, Assoc dir, Ecole Pratique des Hautes Etudes, Paris, 63; lectr, Ctr Higher Studies Medieval Civilization, Poitiers, France, 73. **RESEARCH** Arabic background of medieval European science; Arabic and Latin astrology in the Middle Ages; Renaissance philosophy. **SELECTED PUBLICATIONS** Ed, P Pomponatii Libri quinque De Fato .., Thesaurus Mundi, Lugano, Switz, 57; auth, Abu Ma'shar and Latin Aristotelianism .., Am Univ Beirut, 62; Le Nemrod de l'Enfer de Dante et le liber Nemroth, Studi Danteschi, Florence, 63; Dans l'Espagne du XIIe siecle: les traductions de l'Arabe au Latin, 9-10/63 & A propos de l'origine Arabe de l'art des troubadours, 9-10/ 65, Annales Economies Societes Civilisations, Paris; The teaching of astronomy in medieval universities, principally at Paris in the fourteenth century, Manuscripta, 11/76; The Hispanic origin of our present numeral forms, Viator, 77; Gerard of Cremona, In: Dictionary of Scientific Biography, Scribner, 78. **CONTACT ADDRESS** Dept of Hist, City Univ, New York, NY 10021.

LEMELLE, TILDEN J.
PERSONAL Born 02/06/1929, New Iberia, LA, m **DISCIPLINE** AFRICAN-AMERICAN STUDIES **EDUCATION** Xavier Univ New Orleans, AB 1953, MA 1957; Univ of Denver, PhD 1965. **CAREER** Grambling Coll LA, asst prof 1957-63; Fordham Univ NY, assoc prof, 66-69; Ctr Intl Race Rel Univ Denver, prof, dir 1969-71; Hunter Clge NY, prof & acting dean 1971-, provost, vice pres, currently; Amer Com on Africa, treas 1973-; Univ of the District of Columbia, past pres. **HONORS AND AWARDS** John Hay Whitney Fellow NY 1963-65; The Black Coll Praeger NY 1969; Hon Consul-Senegal Denver CO 1969-71; Race Among Nations Heath-Lexington MA 1971. **MEMBERSHIPS** Trustee Africa Today Assoc Inc 1967-; bd office pres Amer Comm on Africa 1973-; trustee New Rochelle Bd of Educ 1976-;mem Cncl on Foreign Rel 1978-; trustee Social Sci Found 1979-; trustee Africa Fund 1979-; trustee Intl League for Human Rights 1980-; trustee Nurses Educ Fund 1984-; Council For International Exchange of Scholars, Fulbright, 1991-. **SELECTED PUBLICATIONS** Editor/publ Africa Today 1967-; **CONTACT ADDRESS** Univ of the District of Columbia, 4200 Connecticut Ave NW, Washington, DC 20008.

LEMIEUX, GERMAIN
PERSONAL Born 01/05/1914, Cap-Chat, PQ, Canada **DISCIPLINE** HISTORY, FOLKLORE **EDUCATION** Univ Laval, BA, 35, MA, 56, PhD, 61; York Univ, LLD(hon), 77; Univ Ottawa, LittD(hon), 78; Univ Laurentienne, LittD(hon), 84. **CAREER** Prof, Col Sacre-Coeur, Sudbury, 41-44, 49-50, 51-53, 56-59; prof Univ Laurentienne, 61-65; prof, Univ Laval, 66-69; prof dep folklore, 70-80, dir, Center for Franco-ontarian Folklore, Univ Sudbury. **HONORS AND AWARDS** Prix Champlain, 73; Medaille Luc-Lacourciere, 80; Prix du Nouvel-Ontario, 83; Carnochan Awd, Ont Hist Soc, 83; mem, l'Ordre Can, 84; Medaille Marius-Barbeau, 86; mem, l'Ordre de l'Ontario, 92; commandeur, l'Ordre des Palmes, 96. **SELECTED PUBLICATIONS** Auth, Chansonnier franco-ontarien, 2 vols, 74, 76; auth, Les vieux m'ont conte, 33 vols, completee 91; ed, Les jongleurs du billochet, 72; ed, Le four de glaise, 82; ed, La vie paysanne (1860-1900), 82. **CONTACT ADDRESS** Dept of Folklore (French), Univ of Sudbury, 935 Ramsey Lake Rd, Sudbury, ON, Canada P3E 2C6.

LEMIEUX, LUCIEN
PERSONAL Born 04/30/1934, St-Remi, PQ, Canada **DISCIPLINE** HISTORY, RELIGION **EDUCATION** St-Jean Col, BA, 54; Univ Montreal, LTh, 58; Gregorian Univ, DHist, 65. **CAREER** Prof hist, St-Jean Col, 65-68; asst prof church hist, Univ Montreal, 67-73, Assoc Prof, 73-79. Mem, Centre Hist Relig Can, 67-. **HONORS AND AWARDS** Prix Litteraire Du Quebec, 68. **MEMBERSHIPS** Can Soc Theol. **RESEARCH** Religious history of citizens of Quebec, 1760-1840. **SELECTED PUBLICATIONS** Auth, Leger, Paul, Emile--Evolution of his Philosophy, 1950-1967, Revue D Histoire De L Amerique Francaise, Vol 0048, 95; The Seminaire-De-Quebec From 1800 to 1850, Revue D Histoire De L Amerique Francaise, Vol 0049, 96. **CONTACT ADDRESS** Dept of Theol, Univ of Montreal, Montreal, QC, Canada H3C 3J7.

LEMIRE, BEVERLY
DISCIPLINE HISTORY **EDUCATION** Univ Guelph, BA, 79, MA, 81; Balloil Col, Oxford Univ, DPhil, 85. **CAREER** Instr, Wilfred Laurier Univ, 85; instr, Univ Guelph, 85; asst prof, Univ Lethbridge, 86-87; Assoc Prof History Univ New Brunswick 87-. **HONORS AND AWARDS** Killam Res Fel, 99. **SELECTED PUBLICATIONS** Ed, Research in Material History Bulletin 31, 90; auth, Fashion's Favourite: The Cotton Trade and the Consumer in Britain 1660-1800, Oxford Univ Press, 91; auth, Dress, Culture and Commerce: The English Clothing Trade before the Factory 1660-1800, Macmillan, 97; auth, Havoverian Britain: An Encyclopaedia, Garland Press, 97; auth, From Family Firms to Corporate Capitalism: Essays in Business and Industrial History in Honour of Peter Mathias, Oxford Univ Press, 98; auth, The Cambridge History of Western Textiles, Cambridge, 99; auth, The Encyclopedia of European social History, Charles Scribner's Sons, 00. **CONTACT ADDRESS** Dept of History, Univ of New Brunswick, Fredericton, Tilley Hall, RM 120, Fredericton, NB, Canada E3B 5A3. **EMAIL** lmre@unb.ca

LEMKE, WERNER ERICH
PERSONAL Born 01/31/1933, Berlin, Germany, m, 1959, 3 children **DISCIPLINE** OLD TESTAMENT, ANCIENT HISTORY **EDUCATION** Northwestern Univ, BA, 56; NPark Theol Sem, BD, 59; Harvard Univ, ThD(Old Testament), 64. **CAREER** Asst prof Bibl interpretation & lectr ancient hist, NPark Col & Theol Sem, 63-66; assoc prof, 66-69, actg dean, 73-74, Prof Old Testament Interpretation, Colgate Rochester Divinity Sch, 69-, Archaeol fel, Hebrew Union Col, Jerusalem, 69-70; prof, W F Albright Inst Archaeol Res Jerusalem, 72-73; vis prof in relig studies, Univ Rochester, 70, 74, 77. **MEMBERSHIPS** Colloquium Old Testament Res (secy-treas, 69-); Soc Bibl Lit; Am Schs Orient Res. **RESEARCH** Hebrew; Old Testament interpretation; ancient Near Eastern languages, literatures and history. **SELECTED PUBLICATIONS** Auth, The snyoptic problem in the chronicler's history, Harvard Theol Rev, 10/65; Nebuchadrezzar, my servant, Cath Bibl Quart, 1/66; Magnalia Dei: The Mighty Acts of God, Essays on the Bible and Archaeology presented to G Ernest Wright, Doubleday, 76; The way of obedience: I Kings 13 and the structure of the Deuteronomistic history, In: Magnalia Dei, Doubleday, 76; The near and distant God, J Bibl Lit, 12/81; Revelation through history in recent Biblical theology, Interpretation, 1/82; auth, "Theology, OT" in Anchor Bible Dictionary, Doubleday, 92; auth, "The Harper Collins Study Bible," Harper Collins, 93. **CONTACT ADDRESS** Colgate Rochester Divinity Sch/ Bexley Hall/Crozer Theol Sem, 1100 S Goodman St, Rochester, NY 14620-2530. **EMAIL** wlemke@crds.edu

LEMKE-SANTANGELO, GRETCHEN
DISCIPLINE HISTORY **EDUCATION** BA, 86, MA, 88, San Francisco State Univ; Duke Univ, PhD, 93. **CAREER** Dir of Women's Studies, St. Mary's, 95-97; Asst Prof, 93-97, Assoc Prof, 97-, St. Mary's Col. **HONORS AND AWARDS** Wesley Logan Prize; Am Hist Asn, 97. **SELECTED PUBLICATIONS** Auth, Abiding Courage: African American Women in the East Bay Community, Univ of Ncar Press, 96. **CONTACT ADDRESS** Dept of History, Saint Mary's Col, California, Moraga, CA 94575.

LEMMON, SARAH MCCULLOH
PERSONAL Born 10/24/1914, Davidsonville, MD **DISCIPLINE** HISTORY **EDUCATION** Madison Col, BS, 34; Columbia Univ, AM, 36; Univ NC, PhD, 52; Meredith Col, BA, 91; ord, Episcopal Deacon, 95. **CAREER** Acad supvr, 40-43, Oldfields Sch Girls; assoc prof, 43-47, La Grange Col; from asst prof to assoc prof, 47-63, prof hist, 63-, head dept hist & polit sci, 62-, dean cont educ & spec progs, 77-84, Meredith Col; chmn, 77-81, NC Hist Comn. **MEMBERSHIPS** Southern Hist Assn; Soc Am Historians. **RESEARCH** Eugene Talmadge of Georgia; North Carolina history; Episcopal Church history. **SELECTED PUBLICATIONS** Auth, Parson Pettigrew of the " Old Church," UNC Press, 70; auth, Frustrated Patriots, NC and the War of 1812, UNC Press, 73; ed, The Pettigrew Papers vol I 1685-1818, 71, vol 2, 1819-1843, NC State Dept Arch & Hist, 81; co-ed, The Episcopal Church in North Carolina 1701-1959, Episcopal Diocese of NC, 87; auth, Candido Portinari, The Protest Period, Latin American Art, 91; **CONTACT ADDRESS** Box 2001, Southern Pines, NC 28388-2001.

LEMMONS, RUSSELL
PERSONAL Born 07/21/1962, Camp Le Jeune, NC, m, 1985, 1 child **DISCIPLINE** HISTORY **EDUCATION** Franklin Col, BA, 84; Miami Univ, MA, 86; PhD, 91. **CAREER** NMex Highlands Univ, 91-93; Jacksonville State Univ, 93-. **HONORS AND AWARDS** Fulbright Fel, 88-89; NEH Grant, 95, 99; DAAD Grant, 96. **MEMBERSHIPS** Ger Studies Asn. **RESEARCH** Modern Germany. **SELECTED PUBLICATIONS** Auth, Goebbels and Der Angritt, Univ Press of Ky (Lexington, KY); auth, Holocaust Chronicle, Publ Int (Chicago, IL), 00. **CONTACT ADDRESS** Dept Hist and For Lang, Jacksonville State Univ, 700 Pelham Rd N, Jacksonville, AL 36265-1602. **EMAIL** rlemmons@jsucc.jsu.edu

LEMON, ROBERT S., JR.
PERSONAL Born 10/01/1938, Pittsburg, KS, m, 1967, 2 children **DISCIPLINE** ART HISTORY **EDUCATION** Univ Mo at KC, BA; Ohio Univ, MA, PhD. **CAREER** Asst, assoc prof, 73-87, prof, art hist & art dept chmn, 87-99, Rollins Col; Dept chmn, Marshall Univ, 99-01; prof, art hist **MEMBERSHIPS** Pres, Southeastern Col Art conf, 97-00. **RESEARCH** N Amer Indian art, 20th century art. **SELECTED PUBLICATIONS** Auth, The Figurative Pretext: Photo-Realist Painters and the New French Novel. **CONTACT ADDRESS** Rollins Col, PO Box 2684, Winter Park, FL 32789. **EMAIL** rlemon@rollins.edu

LEMONS, J. STANLEY
PERSONAL Born 06/14/1938, Louisville, KY, w **DISCIPLINE** HISTORY **EDUCATION** William Jewell Col, AB, 60; Univ Rochester, MA, 62; Univ Missouri, PhD, 67. **CAREER** Instr, Ohio State, 65-67; vis prof, SW Tex State Univ, 79-80; asst prof, 67-71; assoc prof, 71-76; prof, 76-; Rhode Island Coll. **HONORS AND AWARDS** Am Philosophical Society Grant, 74; Am Assoc for State & Local History, Awd of Merit, 81; Mary Tucker Thory Professorship for Scholarship, 87-88; Paul Maurner Professorship for Excellence in Teaching, 98-99; RI Historic Preservation Commission Awds, 86-89. **MEMBERSHIPS** OAH; ASA; AHA; NEHA. **RESEARCH** Cultural history; women's history; Rhode Island history. **SELECTED PUBLICATIONS** Auth, The Woman Citizen: Social Feminism in the 1920s, Univ Illinois Press (Urbana), 73; Univ Press Virginia (90); auth, The First Baptist Church in America, Charitable Baptist Soc (Providence), 88, revision forthcoming; coauth, The Elect: Rhode IslandÜs Women Legislators, 1922-1990, League of RI Hist Soc (Providence), 90; coauth, "The Independent Woman: Rhode Island's First Woman Legislator," RI Hist 49 (91): 3-11; auth, "The Automobile Comes to Rhode Island," RI Hist 52 (94): 71-93. **CONTACT ADDRESS** Dept History, Rhode Island Col, 600 Mount Pleasant Ave, Providence, RI 02908-1924.

LENAGHAN, MICHAEL J.
PERSONAL Born Oak Park, IL, m, 1982 **DISCIPLINE** HISTORY, GOVERNMENT **EDUCATION** Georgetown Univ, BS, 65; Grad Sch Govt, MA, 69; Va Polytech Inst & State Univ, CAGS, 75; Va Polytech Inst & State Univ, EdD, 78. **CAREER** Intern, Am Red Cross, 65-66; Exec Dir, Pax Romana Secretariat for N Am, 66-68; Dir, Nat Asn of Partners of the Americas, 70-71; Assoc Adminr, Univ DC, 71-75; Sen Professional Staff, Am Red Cross, 75-86; Pres, The Lenaghan Group, 86-88; Pres, Am Humanics Found, 88-91; Fac, Miami-Dade Community Col, 92-. **HONORS AND AWARDS** Kiwanas DC Urban Fel, 73-78; Fel, Georgetown Univ, 95-96; Educ Innovator of the Year, 96; Fel, Southern Methodist Univ, 97; Educ of the Year, Univ Mich, 98; Fel, Kettering Found, 95-00. **MEMBERSHIPS** FPSA, WFS, APSA, S Fla Cult Coalition, NCCA. **RESEARCH** Application of "multiple intelligences," theory to college student course success, negotiating styles in non-violent conflict resolution, American political economy, inter-cultural communication patterns as a barrier to consensus decision-making. **SELECTED PUBLICATIONS** Coauth, Give the Gang Our Best, Marknoll Publ (Ossining, NY), 65; coauth,

Human Rights and the Liberation of Man, Notre Dame Pr (South Bend, IN), 68; auth, The Social Environment: An Anthology, Prentice-Hall Publ, 96; coauth, The Social Environment, Forbes Publ, 00. **CONTACT ADDRESS** Dept Hist & Govt, Miami-Dade Comm Col, 11380 NW 27th Ave, Miami, FL 33167-3418.

LENIHAN, JOHN H.
DISCIPLINE HISTORY **EDUCATION** Seattle Univ, BA, 63; Univ Wash, MA, 66; Univ Md, PhD, 76. **CAREER** Asst prof to assoc prof, Texas A&M Univ, 77-. **HONORS AND AWARDS** Teacher-Scholar Awd, Tex A&M Univ, 88; Distinguished Teaching Awd, 94. **MEMBERSHIPS** Popular Cult Assoc, Org of Am Hist. **RESEARCH** American Film and Culture. **SELECTED PUBLICATIONS** Auth, Showdown: Confronting Modern American in the Western Film, Univ of Ill Pr, (Urbana), 80; auth, "Classics and Social Commentary: Postwar Westerns, 1946-1960," Jour of the West XXII.4 (83): 34-42; auth, "Films and the American Frontier," OAH Newsletter, (84); auth, "The Kid from Texas: The Movie Heroism of Audie Murphy," NMex Hist Rev 61.4, (86): 329-340; auth, "The Western Heroism of Randolph Scott," Shooting Stars, ed Archie P. McDonald, Ind Univ Pr, (Bloomington, 87): 42-59; auth, "Western Film and the American Dream: The Cinematic Frontier of Sam Peckinpah," The Frontier Experience and the American Dream, ed David Morgen, Tex A&M Univ Pr, (College Station, 89): 226-35; auth, "Movie Images of Electoral Politics," Beyond the Stars II: Plot Conventions in American Popular Film, ed Paul Loukides and Linda Fuller, Bowling Green State Univ Pr, (Bowling Green, 91): 77-90; auth, "Superweapons from the Past," Beyond the Stars III: The Material World in American Popular Film, ed Paul Loukides and Linda Fuller, Bowling Green Univ Pr, (Bowling Green, 93): 164-174; auth, "Hollywood Laughs at the Cold War, 1947-1961," Hollywood As Mirror: Changing Views of Outsiders and Enemies in American Movies, ed Robert Brent Toplin, Greenwood Pr, (CT: Westport, 93): 139-55; auth, "Westbound: Feature Films and the American West," Wanted Dead of Alive: The American West in Popular Culture, ed Richard Aquila, Univ of Ill Pr, (Urbana, 96): 109-134. **CONTACT ADDRESS** Dept Hist, Texas A&M Univ, Col Station, College Station, TX 77843-4236. **EMAIL** j-lenihan@tamu.edu

LENIOR, TIMOTHY
PERSONAL Born 02/07/1948 **DISCIPLINE** HISTORY **EDUCATION** St Mary's Col, BA, 70; Indiana Univ, PhD, 74. **CAREER** Asst prof, Univ of nore Dame, 74-78; res assoc, Univ Calif Berkley, 78-79; asst prof, 78-83, assoc prof, 83-86, Univ Ariz; assoc prof, Hebrew Univ of Jerusalem, 85-87; Julian Bers Assoc Prof, Univ Penn, 86-87; dir, Center for Hist and Philos of Science, Tech and Med, The Hebrew Univ of Jerusalem, 85-87; assoc prof, 87-93, chair, Program in Hist and Philos of Sci, 90-92, prof, Stanford Univ, 93-. **HONORS AND AWARDS** Indiana Univ Fel, 71; NSF Traineeship, 71-72; NDEA Fel, 73-74; Deutscher Akademischer Austauschdienst Fel, 74-75; NATO PostDoc Fel in Science, 75-76; NSF Res Grant, 78-80; Univ AZ Humanities Counc Grant, 81; Alexander von Humboldt-Stiftung Fel, 82-84; Zeitlin-Ver Brugge Prize, Hist of Science Soc, 82; NSF Res Grant, 82-84; Univ AZ Soc Sciences Res Inst Grant, 85; John Simon Guggenheim Fel, 87-88; Inst Advanced Studies Fel, Berlin, 87-88; John W. Hagerty Dist Lectr, St Mary's Col, 90; Natl Science Found Res Grant, 89-90; Bing Innovative Tchng Grant, Stanford Univ, 94; Provost's Res Fund Awd, Stanford Univ, 94; Stanford Humanities Center Fel, 94-95; GastProf, Graduierten Kolleg, Deutsches Museum Munich, 94; Natl Science Found Res Grant, 94; Alfred P. Sloan Found Grant, 97-99; Bing Fel for Excel in Tchng, 98. **MEMBERSHIPS** History of Science Soc; West Coast History of Science Soc, Pres, 89-91; Amer Asn For the Advancement of Science; Soc for the History of Technology; Soc for Social Stud of Science; Gesellschaft fur Wissenschaftsgeschichte. **RESEARCH** Intro of computing into biomedicine, 1960's-1980's, esp, development of computational chemistry and molecular graphics; constructing a multi-media database "siliconbase", for the history of silicon valley; history of the development of nuclear med as a medical specialty from WW II through recognition as a med board specialty. **SELECTED PUBLICATIONS** Auth, The Gottingen School and the Development of transcendental Naturphilosophie in the Romantic Era, Stud in the History of Biology Vol 5, Johns Hopkins Univ Press, 81; auth, Models and Instruments in the Development of Electrophysiology 1945-1912, Hist Stud in the Physical Sciences Vol 17, Univ CA Press, 87; coed, Practice, Context, and the Dialogue between Theory and Experiment, Science in Context Vol 2, 88; auth, The Strategy of Life: Teleology and Mechanics in Nineteenth Century German Biology, Univ Chicago, 89; auth, Politik im Tempel der Wissenschaft: Forschung und Machtausubung im deutschen Kaiserreich, Campus Verlag, 92; auth, Instituting Science: Essays on Discipline and the Culture of Science, Stanford Univ Press, 97; ed, Inscribing Science, Stanford Univ Press, 97. **CONTACT ADDRESS** Dept of History, Stanford Univ, Building 200-033, Stanford, CA 94305-2024. **EMAIL** Tlenior@leland.stanford.edu

LENK, RICHARD WILLIAM
PERSONAL Born 08/29/1936, Hackensack, NJ **DISCIPLINE** HISTORY **EDUCATION** Fairleigh Dickinson Univ, NJ, BA, 59; NYork Univ, PhD(hist), 69. **CAREER** Lectr hist, Long Island Univ, 64-65 & Brooklyn Col, 65-67; asst prof, 69-73, assoc prof, 73-80, prof 80-97, PROF EMERITUS, BERGEN COMMUNITY COL, 98-. **MEMBERSHIPS** Am Hist Soc; Orgn Am Historians; Archaeol Inst Am. **RESEARCH** American history; ancient history; New Jersey history. **CONTACT ADDRESS** Dept of Social Sci, Bergen Comm Col, 400 Paramus Rd, Paramus, NJ 07652-1595.

LENZ, RALPH D.
PERSONAL Born 08/13/1944, Flint, MI, m, 1983, 1 child **DISCIPLINE** GEOGRAPHY **EDUCATION** Concordia River Forest, BA, 66; Eastern MI Univ, MA, 69; Rutgers Univ, PhD, 77. **CAREER** Instr, Univ of Southwestern Louisiana, 75-75; Prof, Wittenberg Univ, 76-00. **MEMBERSHIPS** Asn of Am Geograhers, Am Geographical Society. **RESEARCH** Urban Geography, Southeast Asia. **SELECTED PUBLICATIONS** Auth, "A Note on the Role of Bose-Einstein Statistics in Point Pattern Analysis," Geographical Analysis 9 (77): 422-428; auth, "Redundancy as an Index of Change in Point Pattern Analysis," Geographical Analysis 11 (79)L 374-388; auth, "Urban Systems and Regional Development Strategies in India," in Discovery of Regions, Robert T. Norman and S. Rajgopal, eds. (Coimbatore, India, 79); auth, "Geographical and Temporal Changes Among Robberies in Milwaukee," George F. Rengert, eds, Monsey, N.Y.: Criminal Justice Press (86): 97-115; auth, "Disease Correlates within Jakarta Kampuns," with Amrul Munif, Jaumat Dulhajah, and Salim Usman, Ilmu dan Budava 9 (87): 688-699; auth, "Jakarta Kampung Morbidity Variations: Some Policy Implications," Social Science and Medicine 26 (88): 641-649; auth, "Family Planning within Jakarta Kampungs," with Amrul Munif, Jaumat Dulhajah, and Mimien Rachmat, Ilmu dan Budaya 14 (91): 47-60; auth, "On Resurrecting Tourism in Vietnam," Focus 43 (93): 1-6; auth, "Springfield Socioeconomic Profile," 97; auth, "Housing in Springfield and Clark County," 97; rev, "The Japanese City, ed. P.P. Karan and K. Stapleton, forthcoming in Journal of Geography. **CONTACT ADDRESS** Dept Geography, Wittenberg Univ, PO Box 720, Springfield, OH 45501. **EMAIL** rlenz@wittenbert.edu

LEONARD, ANGELA
PERSONAL Born 06/26/1954, Washington, DC, s **DISCIPLINE** HISTORY **EDUCATION** Harvard Univ, AB, 76; Vanderbilt Univ, MLS, 82; George Wash Univ, MPhil, 87; PhD, 94. **CAREER** Librarian. Howard Univ, 84-89; Teaching Asst, George Washington Univ, 86-90; Lecturer, Bowdoin Col, 90-91; Asst Prof, Dickinson Col, 92-94; Asst Prof, Bucknell Univ, 94-95; Vis Prof, Johns Hopkins Univ, 98; Asst Prof, Loyola Col, 96-. **HONORS AND AWARDS** Smithsonian Internship; Dissertation and Minority Fel, Fac Teaching & Res Grant, Loyola Col, Shriver Foundation Grant, Edward Birch Education Grant. **MEMBERSHIPS** Am Studies Asn, ALA, OAH, MLA AHA, Semiotics Soc of Am. **RESEARCH** African-Atlantic Diaspora; The discourse of jazz; the propaganda of colonization; Typography of violence **SELECTED PUBLICATIONS** Ed, Daniel J Boorstin: A comprehensive Bibliography Greenwood Press, in press; auth, "Review of Nat turner Before the Bar of Judgment: fictional Treatments of the Southampton Slave Insurrection," Journal of southern History, forthcoming; auth, "The Instability and Invention of Racial Categories in the Haverhill Gazette (MA), 1824-1827," Semiotics, forthcoming; auth, "Ebenezer Elliott," The New dictionary of National Biography, Oxford Univ Press, forthcoming; auth, "Review of slave counterpoint: Black culture in the eighteenth-Century Chesapeake & Lowcountry," Maryland Historical Magazine, (99): 105-109; auth, "The topography of violence in John Greenleaf Whittier's 'Antislavery Poems,'" American Journal of Semiotics, (98): 41-58; auth, "Exploratory Notes on the Wonders of Jazz: Take One," Semiotics, 98; rev, of "The Evils of Necessity: Robert Goodloe Harper and the Moral dilemma of slaver," by Eric Robert Papenfuse, Maryland Historical Magazine, (97): 390-393; auth, "Subverting Traditions: Ebenezer Elliott's corn law Rhymes," Semiotics, 96; auth, "Two Worldviews: corn Law protest in the Sheffield Independent, 1825-1835," in Worldmaking, Peter Lang, 96. **CONTACT ADDRESS** Dept Hist, Loyola Col, 4501 N Charles St, Baltimore, MD 21210-2601. **EMAIL** aleonard@loyola.edu

LEONARD, ELIZABETH D.
PERSONAL Born 03/17/1957, New York, NY, d, 2 children **DISCIPLINE** HISTORY **EDUCATION** Univ Cal, Riverside, PhD, 92. **CAREER** Asst prof, Colby Col, 92-98; assoc prof, dir woman's studies, 98-. **HONORS AND AWARDS** Mem Adv Bd Fordham Univ Press Series, 96-; Mem Adv Coun Lincoln Prize, 99-; Res Fel, Harriet S, George C Wiswell Jr, 99-. **MEMBERSHIPS** Org Am Hist; AHS; Phi Beta Kappa. **RESEARCH** Women in the civil war. **SELECTED PUBLICATIONS** Auth, Yankee Women: Gender Battles in the Civil War, Norton (94); auth, "Civil War Nurse, Civil War Nursing: Rebecca Usher of Maine," Civil War History (95); auth, All the Daring of the Soldier: Women of the Civil War Armies, Norton (99); ed, Memoirs of a Soldier, Nurse and Spy: A Woman's Adventures in the Union Army (N IL Univ Press, 99); auth, "Mary Surratt and the Plot to Assassinate Lincoln," in The Experience of War, ed. Joan E Cashin (John Hopkins Univ Press, forthcoming); auth, Lust for Revenge: Mary Surratt and the Abraham Lincoln Assassination, Norton (forthcoming). **CONTACT ADDRESS** Dept Hist, Colby Col, 150 Mayflower Hill Dr, Waterville, ME 04901-4799. **EMAIL** edleonar@colby.edu

LEONARD, HENRY BEARDSELL
PERSONAL Born 11/08/1938, Boston, MA, m, 1960, 2 children **DISCIPLINE** AMERICAN HISTORY **EDUCATION** Harvard Univ, AB, 60; Univ Calif, Berkeley, MA, 61; Northwestern Univ, PhD, 67. **CAREER** Asst prof, 67-77, Assoc Prof Hist, Kent State Univ, 77-, chmn, 92-96; prof emer, 96-. **MEMBERSHIPS** AHA; Orgn Am Historians. **RESEARCH** American immigrant history. **SELECTED PUBLICATIONS** Auth, Louis Marshall and Immigration Restriction, 1906-1924, Am Jewish Arch, 4/72; Ethnic Conflict and Episcopal Power: The Diocese of Cleveland, 1847-1870, Cath Hist Rev, 7/76; Ethnic Cleavage and Industrial Conflict: The Cleveland Rolling Mill Company Strikes of 1882 and 1885, Labor Hist, fall 79. **CONTACT ADDRESS** Dept of Hist, Kent State Univ, PO Box 5190, Kent, OH 44242-0001.

LEONARD, THOMAS CHARLES
PERSONAL Born 10/17/1944, Detroit, MI, m, 1969, 2 children **DISCIPLINE** AMERICAN HISTORY **EDUCATION** Univ Mich, Ann Arbor, BA, 66; Univ Calif, Berkeley, PhD(hist), 73. **CAREER** Asst prof hist, Columbia Univ, 73-76; asst prof, 76-80, Prof Jour & Assoc Dean, Univ Calif, Berkeley, 80-00; Univ Librn, Univ of Calif Berkeley, 01-. **MEMBERSHIPS** Orgn Am Historians. **RESEARCH** Role of war in American culture; the expose as a form of journalism and social criticism; propaganda; notoriety. **SELECTED PUBLICATIONS** Auth, Red, White, and the Army Blue: Anger and Empathy in the American West, Am Quart, 5/74; George Creel, Walter Duranty, Hegley Farson, John T Flynn & Robert Wagner, In: Dict Am Biog, Suppls V-VII, Scribner's, 77-81; Above the Battle: War-Making in America from Appomattox to Versailles, Oxford Univ, 78; News for a Revolution: The expose in America, 1768-1773, J Am Hist, 6/80; auth, The Power of the Press: The Birth of American Political Reporting, Oxford, 86; auth, News for All: America's Coming-of-Age with the Press, Oxford, 95. **CONTACT ADDRESS** Univ of California, Berkeley, 245 Doe Library, Berkeley, CA 94720. **EMAIL** toml@socrates.berkeley.edu

LEONARD, THOMAS M.
PERSONAL Born 11/08/1937, Elizabeth, NJ, m, 1968, 6 children **DISCIPLINE** HISTORY, PHILOSOPHY **EDUCATION** Mt St Mary's Col, BS, 59; Georgetown Univ, MA, 63; Am Univ, PhD, 69. **CAREER** From Instr to Assoc Prof, St Joseph Col, 62-73; From Assoc Prof to Prof, Univ N Fla, 73-. **HONORS AND AWARDS** Phi Alpha Theta; Phi Kappa Phi; Two Thousand Men Achievement Awd; Outstanding Educr Awd; Outstanding Young Men of Am Awd; Am Hist Asn Awd, 85; NEH Fel, 85, 89; Fulbright Fel, 90; Andrew W Mellon Found Res Awd, 94; U S Information Serv Awd, 94. **MEMBERSHIPS** ATWS, BSA, CLAH, LASA, NASSH, SHAFR, SCLAS. **RESEARCH** United States relations with Latin America, Central America. **SELECTED PUBLICATIONS** Auth, Central America and the United States: The Search for Stability, Univ Ga Pr, 91; auth, Panama and the United States: Guide to Issues and Sources, Regina Books, 93; auth, Guide to Archival Material in the United States on Central America, Greenwood Pr, 94; auth, "The Quest for Central American Democracy Since 1945," in Democracy in Latin Am, Westview Publ (98); auth, Castro and the Cuban Revolution, Greenwood Pr, 99; auth, "The New Pan Americanism in United States-Central American Relations 1933-1954," in Beyond the Ideal: Pan Americanism in Inter-American Affairs (Greenwood Pr, forthcoming). **CONTACT ADDRESS** Dept Hist & Philos, Univ of No Florida, 4567 St Johns Bluff Rd S, Jacksonville, FL 32224-2646. **EMAIL** tleonard@unf.edu

LEONARD, VIRGINIA WAUGH
PERSONAL Born Willimantic, CT, m **DISCIPLINE** LATIN AMERICAN & AMERICAN HISTORY **EDUCATION** Univ Calif, Berkeley, BA, 63; Hofstra Univ, MA, 67; Univ Fla, Gainesville, PhD(hist), 75. **CAREER** Teacher social studies, Colegio Lincoln, Buenos Aires, 70; instr world hist, NY Inst Technol, 73-75; biblingual teacher social studies, Seward Park High Sch, New York City, 75-77; prof Hist, Western Ill Univ, 77-; Task force on women, Latin Am Studies Asn, 82-83. **HONORS AND AWARDS** Peter Guilday Prize, Am Cath Hist Asn, 79. **MEMBERSHIPS** AHA; Latin Am Studies Asn; Orgn Am Historians; Midwest Asn Latin Am Studies; NCent Coun Latin Americanists. **RESEARCH** Church-state relations in education in Argentina; women's history; U.S. Navy and suppression of slavery. **SELECTED PUBLICATIONS** Auth, Education and the church-state clash in Argentina, Cath Hist Rev, 1/80; Politicians, Pupils, and Priests, Peter Lang Press, 89; Back to the Future: Haiti in 1915 and 1994, Low Intensity Conflict and Law Enforcement, Winter 97. **CONTACT ADDRESS** Dept Hist, Western Illinois Univ, 1 University Cir, Macomb, IL 61455-1390. **EMAIL** virginia_leonard@ccmail.wiu.edu

LEONTOVICH, OLGA
PERSONAL Born 10/09/1954, Volgograd, Russia, m, 1978, 2 children **DISCIPLINE** AMERICAN STUDIES **EDUCATION** Moscow Inst Foreign Lang, Certificate Higher Education, 77; Kandidat (equiv to PhD), 87. **CAREER** Instr, Volgograd Pedagogical Univ, 77-83; asst prof, Moscow Inst of For Lang, 83-87; assoc prof, Volgograd Pedagogical Univ, 90-99; vis prof, Ramapo Col, 99-. **MEMBERSHIPS** Am Studies Asn

(USA), Am Studies Asn (Russia), Nat Comm Asn, Psychol for Soc Responsibility, Volgograd Asn of Citizen Diplomacy. **RESEARCH** Intercultural Communication between Americans and Russians, Reflection of American mentality, values and national character in language. **SELECTED PUBLICATIONS** Auth, Dictionary of US Life and Culture, Volgograd: Stanitsa-2, 98. **CONTACT ADDRESS** Dept Am Studies, Ramapo Col of New Jersey, 505 Ramapo Valley Rd, Mahwah, NJ 07430-1623. **EMAIL** olgaleo@vspu.ru

LEOSHKO, JANICE
DISCIPLINE ART AND ART HISTORY **EDUCATION** OH State Univ, PhD. **CAREER** Asst prof; Univ TX at Austin, 93-; assoc curator art Indian and Southeast Asian, Los Angeles County Museum of Art, 7 yrs. **HONORS AND AWARDS** Co-curating, int loan exhibition, Romance of the Taj Mahal. **MEMBERSHIPS** Past pres, Am Coun Southern Asian Art. **RESEARCH** Ways in which relig imagery developed in South Asia. **SELECTED PUBLICATIONS** Ed & contrib vol, Bodhgaya, the Site of Enlightenment. **CONTACT ADDRESS** Dept of Art and Art Hist, Univ of Texas, Austin, 2613 Wichita St, FAB 1.110, Austin, TX 78705.

LEPLIN, JARRETT
PERSONAL Born 11/20/1944, Houston, TX **DISCIPLINE** HISTORY AND PHILOSOPHY OF SCIENCE **EDUCATION** Amherst Col, BA, 66; Univ Chicago, MA, 67, PhD(philos), 72. **CAREER** Instr philos, Ill Inst Technol, 67-70 and Univ Md Baltimore County, 70-71; asst prof, 71-76, Assoc Prof Philos, Univ NC, Greensboro, 76-. **MEMBERSHIPS** Am Philos Asn; Hist Sci Asn; AAAS; Brit Soc Hist Sci; Philos Sci Asn. **RESEARCH** Scientific methodology; theory comparison, philosophy of space and time. **SELECTED PUBLICATIONS** Auth, Kitcher, Philip the Advancement of Science--Science Without Legend, Objectivity Without Illusion, Philos of Sci, Vol 0061, 94. **CONTACT ADDRESS** Dept of Philos, Univ of No Carolina, Greensboro, Greensboro, NC 23412.

LEPORE, JILL
PERSONAL 1 child **DISCIPLINE** HISTORY **EDUCATION** Tufts, BA, 87; Univ Mich, MA, 90; Yale Univ, MA, 92; MPhil, 93; PhD, 95. **CAREER** Asst Prof, Hist, Boston Univ. **HONORS AND AWARDS** Ralph Henry Gabriel Prize, ASA, 95; Bancroft Prize, 89; Ralph Waldo Emerson Awd, 98. **MEMBERSHIPS** Am Antiquarian Soc. **SELECTED PUBLICATIONS** Auth, "Dead Men Tell No Tales: John Sassamon and the Fatal Consequences of Literacy," Am Quart 46, 94; auth, The Name of War: King Philip's War and the Origins of American Identity, Knopf, 98. **CONTACT ADDRESS** Dept of Hist, Boston Univ, 226 Bay State Rd, Boston, MA 02215. **EMAIL** jlepore@bu.edu

LERNER, BARRON H.
PERSONAL Born 09/27/1960, Boston, MA, m, 1990, 2 children **DISCIPLINE** HISTORY **EDUCATION** Columbia Univ MD 86; Univ Washington PhD 96. **CAREER** Columbia Univ, asst prof 93-; Presbyterian Hosp, asst att phys 93-; Univ Washington, inst 91-93; Columbia Univ, inst 89-91; Presbyterian Hosp, asst phys 89-91. **HONORS AND AWARDS** Rbt Wood Johnson Foun Sch 97-2001; Richard Shryock Medal; Phi Beta Kappa; Summa Cum Laude; Jos Garrison Parker prize; Arnold P. Gold award **MEMBERSHIPS** AAHM; ASBH; SGIM; SHHV; OAH. **RESEARCH** History of bioethics, tuberculosis, and cancer. **SELECTED PUBLICATIONS** Auth, The Breast Cancer Wars: Hope, Fear and the Pursuit of a Cure in Twentieth-Century America, NY: Oxford Univ Press, 01; auth, Contagion and Confinement: Controlling Tuberculosis Along the Skid Road, Baltimore MD, John Hopkins Univ Press, 98; Fighting the war on breast cancer: debates over early detection, 1945 to present, Ann Intern Med, 98; Nonadherence in tuberculosis treatment: predictors and consequences in New York City, coauth, Amer Jour Med, 97; Can stress cause disease? Revisiting the tuberculosis research of Thomas Holmes, 1949-61, Ann Intern Med, 96; Temporarily detained: tuberculosis alcoholics in Seattle, 1949-60, Am Jour Pub Health, 96; Knowing when to say goodbye: Final Exit and Suicide among the elderly, Suicide and Life Threatening Behavior, 95. **CONTACT ADDRESS** Dept of History, Columbia Univ, 630 West 168th Street, Box 11, New York, NY 10032. **EMAIL** BHL5@columbia.edu

LERNER, ROBERT E.
PERSONAL Born 02/08/1940, New York, NY, m, 1963, 2 children **DISCIPLINE** HISTORY **EDUCATION** Univ Chicago, BA, 60; Princeton Univ, MA, 62; PhD, 64. **CAREER** Instr, Princeton Univ, 63-64; Asst Prof, Western Res Univ, 64-67; From Asst Prof to Prof, Northwestern Univ, 67-. **HONORS AND AWARDS** Guggenheim Fel, ACLS, Inst for Advan Study, Woodrow Wilson Ctr; Fel, Medieval Acad of Am. **MEMBERSHIPS** Medieval Acad of Am. **RESEARCH** Medieval Europe. **SELECTED PUBLICATIONS** Auth, The Age of Adversity, 68; auth, The Heresy of the Free Spirit, 72; auth, The Powers of Prophecy, 83; coauth, Western Civilizations, 13th Ed, 98; auth, The Feast of Saint Abraham, 00. **CONTACT ADDRESS** Dept Hist, Northwestern Univ, 202 Harris, Evanston, IL 60208-0001. **EMAIL** rlerner@northwestern.edu

LERNER, WARREN
PERSONAL Born 07/16/1929, Boston, MA, m, 1959, 3 children **DISCIPLINE** RUSSIAN HISTORY, HISTORY OF SOCIALISM, EAST EUROPE **EDUCATION** Boston Univ, BS, 52; Columbia Univ, cert and MA, 54, PhD, 61. **CAREER** Asst prof hist, Roosevelt Univ, 59-61; from asst prof to assoc prof, 61-72, Prof Hist, Duke Univ, 72-, Nat Endowment for Humanities sr fel, 74-75; mem exec coun, Conf Slavic and E Europ Hist, 78-80, pres, 87-. **MEMBERSHIPS** Am Asn Advan Slavic Studies. **RESEARCH** History of Russia and east Europe; Soviet history; history of socialism and communism. **SELECTED PUBLICATIONS** Auth, Karl Radek and the Chinese Revolution, In: Essays in Russian and Soviet History, Columbia Univ, 63; The unperson in communist historiography, Satlantic Quart, fall 66; co-ed, The Soviet World in Flux, Southern Regional Educ Bd, 67; auth, Karl Radek: The Last Internationalist, Stanford Univ, 70; Attempting a revolution from without: Poland in 1920, Studies Soviet Union, 12/71; ed, Studies in the Development of Soviet Foreign Policy, Duke Univ, 73; auth, Poland in 1920: A Case Study in decision making under Lenin, S Atlantic Quart, summer 73; The caged lion: Trotsky's writings in exile, Studies Comp Communism, spring/summer 77; A History of Socialism and Communism in Modern Times: Theorists, Archivists and Humanists, Prentice-Hall, 82, 2nd ed, 94; auth, Lenin--a New Biog, Historian, Vol 0059, 97. **CONTACT ADDRESS** Dept of Hist, Duke Univ, Box 90719, Durham, NC 27708. **EMAIL** wlearner@duke.edu

LEROY, PERRY EUGENE
PERSONAL Born 03/17/1930, New York, NY **DISCIPLINE** AFRICAN HISTORY **EDUCATION** Univ Conn, BA, 52; Ohio State Univ, MA, 53, PhD, 60. **CAREER** Asst prof Latin Am, Memphis State Univ, 60-61; asst prof Latin Am and mod imperialism, 61-66, assoc prof, 66-68, from Prof to prof emer, African and Latin Am Hist, Morehead State Univ, 68-. **MEMBERSHIPS** AHA; NEA **RESEARCH** Latin America, Africa and colonial America. **SELECTED PUBLICATIONS** Auth, Discipline in the NW Militia During the War of 1812, Ohio Anthony Wayne Bd; Discipline and Humanity, Academe, 59. **CONTACT ADDRESS** Dept of Hist, Morehead State Univ, Morehead, KY 40351.

LESCH, JOHN EMMETT
PERSONAL Born 11/24/1945, Vallejo, CA, m, 1980, 2 children **DISCIPLINE** HISTORY OF SCIENCE AND MEDICINE **EDUCATION** Univ Mich, AB, 68; Univ London, MSc, 71; Princeton Univ, PhD(hist), 77. **CAREER** Asst Prof Hist, Univ Calif, Berkeley, 77-84; Assoc Prof, 84-96; Prof, 96-. **HONORS AND AWARDS** John Simon Guggenheim Memorial Foundation Fel, 88-89. **MEMBERSHIPS** Hist Sci Soc, West Coast Hist Sci Soc, Am Inst Hist Pharm, Am Asn for the Hist of Medicine. **RESEARCH** History of physiology, 19th century; history of chemotherapy, 20th century. **SELECTED PUBLICATIONS** Auth, Science and Medicine in France: The Emergence of Experimental Physiology 1790-1855 (Cambridge, Mass and London, England: Harvard Univ Pr, 84); auth, "Systematics and the geometrical spirit," in Tore Frangsmyr, ed J.L. Heibron and Robin E. Rider, The Quantifying Spirit in the Eighteenth Century (Berkely and Los Angeles: Univ of Calif Pr, 1990), 73-111; auth, "Chemistry and biomedicine in an industrial setting: the invention of the sulfa drugs," ed Seymour H. Mauskopf, Chemical Sciences in the Modern World (Philadelphia: Univ PA Pr, 93), 158-215; auth, Krebs, Hans, Vol 1, the Formation of a Scientific Life 1900-1933, Amer Hist Rev, Vol 0100, 95; Krebs,Hans, Vol 2, Architect of Intermediary Metabolism 1933-1937, Amer Hist Rev, Vol 0100, 95; Quantification and the Quest for Medical Certainty, Isis, Vol 0087, 96; auth, "The discovery of M&B 693 (Sulfapyridine)," ed Gregory J. Hiby and Elaine C. Stroud, The Inside Story of Medicines: A Symposium (Madison, WI: American Institue of the His of Pharmacy, 97), 101-119; auth, The German Chemcial Industry in the Twentieth Century (Dordrecht, Boston, London: Kluwer Academic Publishers), 00. **CONTACT ADDRESS** Dept of Hist, Univ of California, Berkeley, 3229 Dwinelle Hall, Berkeley, CA 94720-2551.

LESESNE, HENRY H.
PERSONAL Born 01/11/1968, Spartanburg, SC, m, 1992, 2 children **DISCIPLINE** HISTORY **EDUCATION** Duke Univ, BA, 90; Univ S C, MA, 95; PhD, 98. **CAREER** Res Asst Prof, Univ S C, 99-. **HONORS AND AWARDS** George C Rogers Jr. Fel, Univ S C, 98-99. **MEMBERSHIPS** Am Hist Asn, S Hist Asn, SC Hist Asn. **RESEARCH** American South. **CONTACT ADDRESS** Dept History, Univ of So Carolina, Columbia, Columbia, SC 29225. **EMAIL** hlesesne@sc.edu

LESHKO, JAROSLAV
DISCIPLINE ART HISTORY **EDUCATION** Columbia Univ, BA, MA, MPhil, PhD. **CAREER** Art, Smith Col. **HONORS AND AWARDS** Curated an exhibition of, Kokoschka's prints, 87-88. **RESEARCH** Vienna ca 1900, specifically the works of the Austrian Expressionist, Oskar Kokoschka. **SELECTED PUBLICATIONS** Auth, a catalogue, Orbis Pictus-the Prints of Oscar Kokoschka; Jacques Hnizdousky, a catalogue of paintings and prints, Ukrainian Mus NY, 95-96. **CONTACT ADDRESS** Dept of Art, Smith Col, Hillyer Hall 313, Northampton, MA 01063.

LESKO, LEONARD HENRY
PERSONAL Born 08/14/1938, Chicago, IL, m, 1966 **DISCIPLINE** EGYPTOLOGY **EDUCATION** Loyola Univ Chicago, AB, 61, MA, 64; Univ Chicago, PhD(Egyptol), 69. **CAREER** Instr Latin and Greek, Quigley Prep Sem S, Chicago, 61-64; res asst, Orient Inst, Univ Chicago, 64-65; actg instr Egyptology, Univ Calif, Berkeley, 66-67, actg asst prof, 67-69, from asst prof to assoc prof, 69-72, dir, Near Eastern Studies Ctr, 73-75, chmn dept Near Eastern studies, 75-77 and 79-81, prof, 77-82, chmn prog ancient hist and archaeol, 78-79; Wilbur Prof Egyptology and Chmn Dept, Brown Univ, 82-, **HONORS AND AWARDS** FIAT Fac fel, Turin, 90; NEH Hum Inst, 94-95; RI Comt Hum Grant, 98; Nat Endowment for Humanities younger humantist fel, 70-71; Am Coun Learned Soc award, 73-74; Nat Endowment for Humanities proj grant, 75-79. **MEMBERSHIPS** Egypt Explor Soc; Am Orient Soc; Am Res Ctr Egypt; Fondation Egyptol Reine Elisabeth, Brussels; Int Asn Egyptologists. **RESEARCH** Ancient Egyptian religious literature; Egyptian literature history and language. **SELECTED PUBLICATIONS** Auth, The Ancient Egyptian Book of Two Ways, Berkeley, 72; auth, Glossary of the Late Ramesside Letters, Berkeley, 75; auth, King Tut's Wine Cellar, Berkeley, 77; auth, Index of the Spells on Egyptian Middle Kingdom Coffins and Related Documents, Berkeley, 79; auth, A Dictionary of Late Egyptian, 5 vols, Berkeley & Providence, 82-90; auth, Egyptological Studies in Honor of Richard A. Parker, Hanover & London, 86; co-auth, Religion in Ancient Egypt, Ithaca, 91; ed, Pharoah's Workers: The Villagers of Deir al-Medina, Ithaca, 94; co-ed, Exodus: Egyptian Evidence, Winona Lake, 97; ed, Ancient Egyptian and Mediterranean Studies in Memory of William A. Ward, Providence, 98. **CONTACT ADDRESS** Dept of Egyptology, Brown Univ, Box 1899, Providence, RI 02912. **EMAIL** leonard_lesko@brown.edu

LESSER, GLORIA
PERSONAL Born Montreal, PQ, Canada **DISCIPLINE** ART HISTORY, DESIGN **EDUCATION** Chicago Sch Interior Design, Dipl, 63; Concordia Univ, BA, 77, MFA, 83. **CAREER** Sch tchr, 56-60; substitute tchr, 60-78; Prof Art History & Interior Design, Champlain Regional Col, 84-. **MEMBERSHIPS** Can Soc Decorative Arts; Interior Designers' Soc Que; Interior Designers Can. **SELECTED PUBLICATIONS** Auth, Ecole du Meuble 1930-50: Interior Design and Decorative Art in Montreal, 89; auth, The Homes and Furnishings of R.B. Angus, Montreal in Living in Style, 93; auth, Sources and Documents: R.B. Angus Collection, Paintings, Watercolours and Drawings, in J Can Art Hist, No 1, 94; auth, Carl Poul Peterson: Master Danish-Canadian Silversmith, in Material Hist Rev, 43, 96. **CONTACT ADDRESS** 4870 Cote des Neiges, E-305, Montreal, QC, Canada H3V 1H3.

LESSER, JEFFREY
DISCIPLINE HISTORY **EDUCATION** Brown Univ, BA, MA; NYork Univ, PhD. **CAREER** Assoc prof, Conn Col, 90-; assoc dir, Res Ctr Int Stud and Liberal Arts. **HONORS AND AWARDS** Best bk prize, New Eng Coun Latin Amer Stud; Natl Endowment for the Hum grant; Fulbright Comn, grant; North-South Ctr grant; Mellon Initiative for Multiculturalism Across the Curric grant; Amer Coun Learned Soc grant. **RESEARCH** Latin American history; Brazilian history; Modern Jewish history; Ethnic history; Immigration history. **SELECTED PUBLICATIONS** Auth, Welcoming the Undesirables: Brazil and the Jewish Question, 94; Jewish Colonization in Rio Grande do Sul, 1904-1925; Neither Slave nor Free, Neither Black nor White: The Chinese in Early Nineteenth Century Brazil, 94; Immigration and Shifting Concepts of National Identity in Brazil during the Vargas-Era, 94. **CONTACT ADDRESS** Dept of History, Connecticut Col, 270 Mohegan Ave, New London, CT 06320. **EMAIL** jhles@conncoll.edu

LESSOFF, ALAN H.
PERSONAL Born 02/24/1959, Boston, MA, m, 1987, 1 child **DISCIPLINE** HISTORY **EDUCATION** Columbia Univ, BA, 81; Cambridge Univ England, BA, 83; Johns Hopkins Univ, MA, 85; PhD, 90. **CAREER** Asst prof, Dickinson Col, 90-92; from asst prof to assoc prof, Tex A & M Univ Corpus Christi, 92-. **HONORS AND AWARDS** Fulbright jr lectr, Germany, 96-97. **MEMBERSHIPS** AHA, Orgn of Am Historians, Urban Hist Asn, Soc for Historians of the Gilded Age and Progressive Era. **RESEARCH** US and comparative urban history, US political/social history, 1850-1930. **SELECTED PUBLICATIONS** Auth, The Nation and It's City: Politics, "Corruption," and Progress in Washington, DC, 1861-1902 (Baltimore, MD), 94; coauth, Legacy: A History of the Art Museum of South Texas (Corpus Christi, TX), 97. **CONTACT ADDRESS** Dept Humanities, Texas A&M Univ, Corpus Christi, 6300 Ocean Dr, Corpus Christi, TX 78412-5503. **EMAIL** alessoff@falcon.tamucc.edu

LEVACK, BRIAN PAUL
PERSONAL Born 04/06/1943, New York, NY, m, 1966, 2 children **DISCIPLINE** ENGLISH HISTORY **EDUCATION** Fordham Col, BA, 65; Yale Univ, MA, 67, PhD(hist), 70. **CAREER** From instr to asst prof, 69-74, assoc prof, 74-94, John Green Regents Prof Hist, Univ Tx, Austin, 94-; . **HONORS AND AWARDS** Guggenheim fel, 75-76; Scholar-in-residence, Washington and Lee Univ School of Law, 94. **MEMBER-**

SHIPS AHA; Conf Brit Studies; Am Soc Legal Hist; Stair Soc; Sixteenth Century Studies Conference. **RESEARCH** Early modern British history; English legal history; Scottish history. **SELECTED PUBLICATIONS** Auth, The Civil Lawyers in English, 1603- 1641: A Political Study, Oxford, 73; The Formation of the British State: England, Scotland, and the Union, 1603-1707, Oxford, 87; Law, Sovereignty and the Union, in Scots and Britons, Cambridge, 94; The Great Witch Hunt, in Handbook of European History in the Later Middle Ages, Renaissance and Reformation, 1400-1600, vol 2, Brill, 95; The Witch in Baroque Personae, Chicago, 95; The Witch Hunt in Early Modern Europe, London: Longman, 2nd ed, 95; Possession, Witchcraft and the Law in Jacobean England, Washington and Lee Law Rev 52, 96; Possession and Exorcism, Oxford Encyclopedia of the Reformation, 96; State-Building and Witch Hunting in Early Modern Europe, in Witchcraft in Early Modern Europe: Studies in Culture and Belief, Cambridge, 96; Law in The History of the University of Oxford, Vol IV: The Seventeenth Century, Oxford, 97; co-auth, Witchcraft and Magin in Europe: The Eighteenth and Nineteenth Centuries, London, 99. **CONTACT ADDRESS** Dept Hist, Univ of Texas, Austin, Austin, TX 78712-1026. **EMAIL** levack@mail.utexas.edu

LEVENTHAL, FRED MARC
PERSONAL Born 05/17/1938, New York, NY, m, 1967, 1 child **DISCIPLINE** MODERN BRITISH HISTORY **EDUCATION** Harvard Univ, AB, 60, PhD, 68. **CAREER** Instr hist, Harvard Univ, 67-69; from Asst Prof to Assoc Prof, 69-84, Prof Hist, Boston Univ, 84-; Co-ed, Twentieth Century British History, 95-; res fel, Inst Advan Studies in Humanities, Univ Edinburgh, 74; vis prof, Univ Kent-Canterbury, 78-79; vis prof, Univ Sydney, 86; vis fel, St. Catherine's Col, Oxford Univ, 97; vis prof, Harvard Univ, 99, 01. **HONORS AND AWARDS** Recipient of numerous grants from NEH, American Coun Learned Soc, Am Philos Soc, and others. **MEMBERSHIPS** NAm Conf Brit Studies (pres 97-99); AHA; Fel, Royal Hist Soc. **RESEARCH** 20th century British culture and politics. **SELECTED PUBLICATIONS** Auth, Respectable Radical: George Howell and Victorian Working Class Politics, Harvard Univ, 71; ed, Trade Unionism New and Old, Harvester, 73; auth, H N Brailsford and the New Leader, J Contemp Hist, 1/74; chap, In: Edwardian radicalism: Aspects of British Radicalism, 1900-14, Routledge & Kegan Paul, 74; chap, In: Essays in Labour History 1918-1939, Croom Helm, 77; The Last Dissenter: H.N. Brailsford and His World, Clarendon Press, 85; Arthur Henderson, Manchester Univ Press, 89; ed, Twentieth-Century Britain: An Encyclopedia, Garland Publ, 95; author of several book chapters and journal articles; co-ed, Singular Contintuities: Tradition, Nostalgia, and Identity in Modern British Culture, Stanford Univ Press, 00; co-ed, Anglo-American Attitudes: From Revolution to Partnership, Ashgate Publ, 00. **CONTACT ADDRESS** Dept of Hist, Boston Univ, 226 Bay State Rd, Boston, MA 02215-1403. **EMAIL** fleventh@bu.edu

LEVERING, RALPH BROOKS
PERSONAL Born 02/27/1947, Mt. Airy, NC, m, 1967, 2 children **DISCIPLINE** HISTORY **EDUCATION** Univ NC, BA, 67; Princeton Univ, MA, 69, PhD, 72. **CAREER** Asst to assoc prof, 72-81, Western MD Col; assoc prof, 81-86, Earlhan Col,; assoc to full prof, 86-, Davidson Col. **HONORS AND AWARDS** Phi Beta Kappa, 67; NEH fel, 76-77. **MEMBERSHIPS** Soc of Hist of Am Foreign Relations; AHA; Org of Am Hist; Peace Hist Soc. **RESEARCH** US foreign relations since 1939; public opinion and US foreign policy. **SELECTED PUBLICATIONS** Auth, American Opinion and the Russian Alliance, 1945-1972, Univ NC Press, 76; auth, The Public and American Foreign Policy, 1918-1978, William Morrow, for the Foreign Policy Asn, 78; co-auth, The Kennedy Crises: The Press, the Presidency, and Foreign Policy, Univ NC Press, 83; auth, The Cold War: A Post-Cold War History, Harlan Davidson, 94; auth, Citizen Action for Global Change: The Neptune Group and Law of the Sea, Syracuse Univ Press, 99. **CONTACT ADDRESS** History Dept, Davidson Col, PO Box 1719, Davidson, NC 28036. **EMAIL** ralevering@davidson.edu

LEVERNIER, JAMES ARTHUR
PERSONAL Born 07/26/1949, Highland Park, IL **DISCIPLINE** ENGLISH, AMERICAN STUDIES **EDUCATION** Marquette Univ, BA, 71; Univ Pa, MA, 73; PhD, 75. **CAREER** Asst prof, 76-80, Assoc Prof English, Univ Ark, Little Rock, 80-, Dir, Am Studies, 78-. **MEMBERSHIPS** MLA; Children's Lit Asn; Am Studies Asn. **RESEARCH** Early American literature; native American studies; folklore. **SELECTED PUBLICATIONS** Co-ed, The Indians and Their Captives, Greenwood Press Contrib Am Studies, 77; auth, The captivity narrative as regional, military and ethnic history, 77; Introd to Increase Mather's An Essay for the Recording of Illustrious Providences, Scholars Facsimiles & Reprints, 77; Calvinism and transcendentalism in the poetry of Jones Very, ESQ: J Am Renaissance, 78; ed, Soldiery Spiritualized: Nine Sermons Preached Before the Artillery Companies of New England, 1672-1772, Scholars Facsimiles & Reprints, 80; coauth, Structuring Paragraphs: A Guide to Effective Writing, St Martins Press, 81; co-ed, Sermons and Cannonballs: Eleven Sermons on Military Events of Historic Significance During the French and Indian Wars, 1689-1760, Scholars' Facsimiles & Reprints, 82; The captivity narrative as children's literature, Markham Rev (in press). **CONTACT ADDRESS** Univ of Arkansas, Little Rock, 2801 S University Ave, Little Rock, AR 72204-1000.

LEVESQUE, GEORGE AUGUST
PERSONAL Born 06/08/1936, West Warwick, RI, S **DISCIPLINE** UNITED STATES & AFRO-AMERICAN HISTORY **EDUCATION** Brown Univ, AB, 62; Harvard Law Sch, LLB, 65; Brown Univ, AM, 69; State Univ NYork Binghamton, PhD(hist), 76. **CAREER** Asst dean men, Univ Ottawa, 64-66; asst prof US hist, State Univ NY Morrisville, 66-71; teaching fel urban hist, State Univ NY Binghamton, 71-72; Nat Endowment for Humanities-Charles Warren fel ethnic studies, Harvard Univ, 72-73; Fulbright scholar Afro-Am hist, Anglo-Am Sect, Univ Montpellier, 73-74; teaching fel, State Univ NY Binghamton, 74-75; asst prof hist, Ill State Univ, 75-77; asst prof Afro-Am studies, Ind State Univ, Terre Haute, 77-78, assoc prof, 78-81; assoc prof Afro-Am studies, 81-94, Am Coun Learned Soc grant-inaid, 77; consult, Nat Endowment for Humanities, 78-81; T Wistar Brown fel, Haverford Col, 79-80; sr Fulbright award, Univ Yaounde, CAmoon, 78-79 & John F Kennedy Prof, US Hist, Free Univ Berlin, 82-83; Univ Prof, Afro-Amer Studies, Univ Ctr, State Univ NY, Albany, 94. **HONORS AND AWARDS** Littleton-Griswold Res Grant, Am Hist Asn, 91-92; DuBois Inst Res Fel, Harvard univ, 87. **RESEARCH** Afro-American history, 1750-1865; 18th and 19th century American social-urban history; antebellum reform. **SELECTED PUBLICATIONS** Auth, Black Abolitionists in the Age of jackson, J Black Studies, 12/70; Inherent Reformers-Inherited Orthodoxy: Black Baptists in Boston, J Negro History, 9/75; LeRoi Jones' Dutchman: Myth & Allegory, Obsidian, 79; auth, Coventry (R.I.): The Colonial Years, 1741-1783 (Univ Press of New England, 81); Politicians in Petticoats: Interracial Sex and Leg, Politics in Antebellum Massachusetts, New England J Black Studies, 83; Slavery in the Ideology & Politics of the Revolutionary Generation, Canadian Rev, Am Studies, 87; auth, Forging Freedom: Free Blacks in Urban Amer (Oxford U.P., 90); auth, Black Boston: African-Amer Life & Culture in Urban America, 1750-1860 (Garland Press, 94); Slave Names and Naming Practices, Dictionary of Afro-Am Slavery, 88 & 97; auth, Boston's Black Brahmin: Dr. John S. Rock (Harvard Univ Press, 00). **CONTACT ADDRESS** Dept of African-Am Studies, SUNY, Albany, 1400 Washington Ave, Albany, NY 12222-1000.

LEVI, DARRELL ERVILLE
PERSONAL Born 11/14/1940, San Francisco, CA, m, 1963, 2 children **DISCIPLINE** HISTORY **EDUCATION** Univ Calif, Berkeley, BA, 63; Univ Calif, Davis, MA, 69; Yale Univ, PhD(hist), 74. **CAREER** Asst prof, 74-79, Assoc Prof Hist, Fla State Univ, 79-, Fla State Univ prof development grant, 78. **MEMBERSHIPS** Conf Latin Am Hist, Latin Am Studies Asn. **RESEARCH** Social history of Brazil; history of Puerto Rico; Latin American nationalism. **SELECTED PUBLICATIONS** Auth, The Prado family, European culture & the rediscovery of Brazil, Revista Hist, 75; Brazilian nationalism: an introduction, Can Rev Studies Nationalism, 76; A Familia Prado, Cultura 70, 77; Brazilian Nationalism: Perspectives, Problems, Perplexities, 78 & Nationalism in Central America, Panama and Belize: Some Views of the 1970's, 80, Can Rev Studies in Nationalsm. **CONTACT ADDRESS** Dept of Hist, Florida State Univ, 600 W College Ave, Tallahassee, FL 32306-1096.

LEVIN, DAVID J.
DISCIPLINE PERFORMANCE STUDIES, GERMANIC STUDIES, CINEMA STUDIES **EDUCATION** Brown Univ, BA, 82; Univ Cal, Berk, MA, 86; PhD, 92. **CAREER** Asst prof, Columbia Univ, 92-98; vis asst prof, Univ Chicago, 97; assoc prof, 98-. **HONORS AND AWARDS** SSRC Postdoc Fel, Berlin; Coun Res Hum, Colum Univ. **MEMBERSHIPS** MLA; AATC; AMS; SCS. **RESEARCH** Opera; theater; cinema; interdisciplinary performance studies. **SELECTED PUBLICATIONS** Co-ed, Opera Through Other Eyes, Stanford Univ Press (Stanford, CA), 94; auth Richard Wagner, Fritz Lang, and the Nibelungen: The Dramaturgy of Disavowal, Princeton Univ Press, 98; auth, "Taking Liberties with Liberties Taken: On the Aesthetic Politics of Helke Sander's Liberators take Liberties," MIT Press 72 (95): 65-77; auth, "Staging a Reading/Reading a Staging: Die Meistersinger von Nurnberg in Performance," Cambridge Opera J 9 (97), 47-71; auth, "Are We Sisters Yet? The Rhetoric of Reconciliation in Percy Adlon's Bagdad Caf¤," in Triangulated Visions: Gender, Race, and New German Cinema, ed. I Majer-OÛSickey (SUNY Press, 98); auth, "War of the White Roses: Resistance, Reification, and Community," in The Nasty Girl, The White Rose, and Five Last Days, Germanic Rev 73 (98): 86-100. **CONTACT ADDRESS** Dept Germanic Lang, Literature, Univ of Chicago, 1050 East 59th St, Chicago, IL 60637-1559. **EMAIL** dlevin@midway.uchicago.edu

LEVIN, DAVID S.
PERSONAL Born 05/30/1933, New York, NY, m, 1959, 2 children **DISCIPLINE** UNITED STATES HISTORY **EDUCATION** Hunter Col, BA, 57; Columbia Univ, MA, 60, PhD(hist), 69. **CAREER** From instr to asst prof hist, Adelphi Univ, 63-69; asst prof hist & asst dean fac, Dowling Col, 69-70; asst prof hist, John Jay Col Criminal Justice, 70-73; prof hist & chemn soc sci, Mercer County Comm Col, 73-; dean Arts, Communication & Engineering Technology, 83-; Chmn East Mid-Atlantic regional selection comt, Danforth Assoc Prog, 72-75; co-dir, Community Col Intern Prog, Princeton Univ, 75-; consult, Mid-Career Fels Prog, NJ Consortium on Community Cols, 77-. **MEMBERSHIPS** AHA; Orgn Am Historians; AAUP. **RESEARCH** Stock market regulation; Great Depression and the New Deal. **CONTACT ADDRESS** Dept of Soc Sci, Mercer County Comm Col, PO Box B, Trenton, NJ 08690-0182. **EMAIL** levind@mccc.edu

LEVIN, EVE
PERSONAL Born 03/28/1954, Chicago, IL **DISCIPLINE** HISTORY **EDUCATION** Mount Holyoke Col, BA, 75; Ind Univ, MA, 76, PhD, 83. **CAREER** Ohio State Univ, asst prof, 83-90, assoc prof ed, 90-. **HONORS AND AWARDS** Phi Beta Kappa, IREX/Fulbright-Hays, 81-82, 90; ACLS post-doctoral fel, 86-87; Heldt Prize for best translation in Slavic Women's Studies, 97; Nat Coun for Eurasian and East European Res Grant, 01. **MEMBERSHIPS** AAASS; Early Slavic Studies Asn; AHA; Medieval Acad Am; Asn Women Slavic Studies. **RESEARCH** Russian and Balkan hist, 900-1750. **CONTACT ADDRESS** Dept of History, Ohio State Univ, Columbus, 106 Dulles Hall, 230 W 17th Ave, Columbus, OH 43210. **EMAIL** levin.2@osu.edu

LEVIN, WILLIAM R.
PERSONAL Born 10/22/1948, Newton, MA, m, 1981, 2 children **DISCIPLINE** ART HISTORY **EDUCATION** Northwestern Univ, BA; Univ Mich, MA and PhD. **CAREER** Fac, Mankato State Univ; from asst prof to assoc prof, Centre Col, 83-. **HONORS AND AWARDS** Phi Beta Kappa. **MEMBERSHIPS** Int Cong Med Studies; SE Col Art Conf; Col Art Asn. **RESEARCH** History and art of Late-Medieval and Early Renaissance philanthropic institutions in Italy; works of art dealing with the concept of charity. **SELECTED PUBLICATIONS** Auth, Images of Love and Death in Late Medieval and Renaissance Art Univ Mich P, 76. **CONTACT ADDRESS** Centre Col, 600 W Walnut St, Danville, KY 40422. **EMAIL** levin@centre.edu

LEVINE, BRUCE C.
PERSONAL Born 02/23/1949, New York, NY **DISCIPLINE** U.S. HISTORY **EDUCATION** Univ Mich, BA, 71; Univ Rochester, MA, 73; PhD, 80. **CAREER** Director, Am Soc Hist Proj, CUNY, 81-86; adj prof, Columbia Univ, 85; asst prof, Univ of Cincinnati, 86-97; prof, Univ of Calif Santa Cruz, 97-. **HONORS AND AWARDS** Phi Beta Kappa, 71; Herbert H. Lehman Fel, 72-75; ACLS Grant, 83; Charles Phelps Taft Memorial Fund Grants, 87, 89, 91, 92, 96; Univ of Cincinnati Res Fel, 95, 98; Fac Develop Grant, Univ of Cincinnati, 95-96; Univ of Calif Res Grant, 98; Excellence in Teaching Awd, Univ of Calif, 98-99. **RESEARCH** Social and political history of the U.S.'s Civil War era. **SELECTED PUBLICATIONS** Coed, Work and Society: A Reader, Wayne State Univ, (Detroit), 77; auth, Who Built America? Working People and the Nation's Economy, Politics, Culture & Society, Pantheon Books (NY), 90; auth, Half Slave and Half Free: The Roots of Civil War, Hill & Want, (NY), 92; auth, The Spirit of 1848: German Immigrants, Labor Conflict, and the Coming of the Civil War, Univ of IL Pr, (Urbana and Chicago); 92; auth, The Migration of Ideology and the Contested Meaning of Freedom: German America in the Mid Nineteenth Century, Ger Hist Inst 7, (Washington, DC), 93. **CONTACT ADDRESS** Merrill Col Fac Serv, Univ of California, Santa Cruz, 1156 High St, Santa Cruz, CA 95064-1077. **EMAIL** blevine@cats.ucsc.edu

LEVINE, DANIEL
PERSONAL Born 12/31/1934, New York, NY, m, 1954, 2 children **DISCIPLINE** AMERICAN HISTORY **EDUCATION** Antioch Col, BA, 56; Northwestern Univ, MA, 57, PhD, 61. **CAREER** Asst prof hist, Earlham Col, 60-63; from asst prof to assoc prof, 63-72, Prof Hist, Bowdoin Col, 72-; Fulbright sr lectr hist, Univ Copenhagen & Aarhus, 69-70; Guggenheim fel, Denmark, 72-73; Fulbright sr lectr, Munich, 79-80. **MEMBERSHIPS** AHA; Orgn Am Historians. **RESEARCH** American intellectual history since the Civil War; modern Danish social history; comparative social welfare history. **SELECTED PUBLICATIONS** Auth, Varieties of Reform Thought, State Hist Soc Wis, 64; John Dewey, Randolph Bourne and the legacy of liberalism, Antioch Rev, summer 69; Jane Addams and the Liberal Tradition, State Hist Soc Wis, 71; Den ideologiske baggrnd for Dansk social-lovgivning, 1890-1933, Scandia, Oslo, 73; Conservation & tradition in Danish social welfare legislation, 1890-1933, Comp Studies Soc & Hist, 78; Social Democrats, socialism and social insurance: Germany and Denmark, 1918-1933, Comparative Soc Res, vol 6, 83; Poverty and Society, Rutgers, 88; A single standard of civilization, Ga Hist Quart, spring 97; Bayard Rustin and the Civil Rights Movement, New Brunswick: Rutgers Univ. Press, 00. **CONTACT ADDRESS** Dept of Hist, Bowdoin Col, 9900 College Station, Brunswick, ME 04011-8499. **EMAIL** dlevine@polar.bowdoin.edu

LEVINE, DAVID OSCAR
PERSONAL Born 08/16/1955, Middletown, NY, m, 1981, 2 children **DISCIPLINE** HISTORY OF AMERICAN CIVILIZATION **EDUCATION** Univ PA, BA, Magna Cum Laude with Distinction, 76; Harvard Univ, MA, History, 78, PhD, Hist and Am Civilization, 81. **CAREER** Visiting asst prof, dept hist, Univ Calif, Los Angeles, 81-87; exec dir, Touch Am Hist Foundation, 87-. **RESEARCH** Hist Am Edu **SELECTED PUBLICATIONS** The American College and the Culture of Aspira-

tion, Cornell Univ Press, 86. **CONTACT ADDRESS** Touch Am History, 4201 Via Marina, Marina del Rey, CA 90292. **EMAIL** levzach@earthlink.net

LEVINE, PETER D.
PERSONAL Born 06/23/1944, Brooklyn, NY, m, 1965, 1 child **DISCIPLINE** AMERICAN HISTORY **EDUCATION** Columbia Col, BA, 65; Columbia Univ, MA, 66; Rutgers Univ, PhD, 71. **CAREER** From instr to assoc prof, 69-84, prof Am hist, MI State Univ, 84. **RESEARCH** Hist of sport in Am. **SELECTED PUBLICATIONS** Auth, The Behavior of State Legislative Parties in the Jacksonian Era: New Jersey, 1829-44, J Am Hist, 12/75; Fairleigh Dickinson Univ, J Am Hist, 77; Draft Evasion in the North During the Civil War, 1863-1865, J Am Hist, 3/81; A.G. Spalding & the Rise of Baseball, Oxford Univ Press, 85; Ellis Island to Ebbets Field, Sport & the American Jewish Experience, Oxford Univ Press, 92; coauth, Idols of the Game, A Sporting History of 20th Century America, Turner, 95. **CONTACT ADDRESS** Dept of Hist, Michigan State Univ, 301 Morrill Hall, East Lansing, MI 48824-1036. **EMAIL** levinep@pilot.msu.edu

LEVINE, ROBERT M.
PERSONAL Born 03/26/1941, New York, NY, 2 children **DISCIPLINE** LATIN AMERICAN HISTORY **EDUCATION** Colgate Univ, AB, 62; Princeton Univ, AM, 64, PhD, 67. **CAREER** From asst prof hist to assoc prof, State Univ NY Stony Brook, 66-78, prof, 78-80; prof hist, Univ Miami, 80-, Dir, Latin Am Studies, Chmn comt, Brazilian studies, Conf Latin Am Hist, Hisp Found, 70-71; chmn sem Latin Am, Columbia Univ, 72-73; sr Fulbright-Hays lectr, Brazil, 73 & 80. **MEMBERSHIPS** AHA; Latin Am Studies Asn; Hisp Am Hist Soc; Conf Latin Am Hist. **RESEARCH** Mod Brazil; mod Latin Am. **SELECTED PUBLICATIONS** Auth, The Vargas Regime, Columbia Univ, 70; Pernambuco and the Brazilian Federation, 1889-1937, Stanford Univ, 74; Vale of Tears, Univ CA, 92; Father of the Poor?, Cambridge Univ, 98; Brazilian Legacies, Sharpe, 98; Cuban Miami, Rutgers, 00. **CONTACT ADDRESS** Dept of Hist, Univ of Miami, PO Box 248107, Miami, FL 33124-4662. **EMAIL** rml326@altavista.com

LEVINE, SURA
DISCIPLINE ART HISTORY **EDUCATION** Univ MI, BA; Univ Chicago, MA, PhD. **CAREER** Assoc prof, Hampshire Col. **HONORS AND AWARDS** Whiting Fellowship in the Humanities, Fullbright and Hays Dissertation Grant, Social Science Research Council **MEMBERSHIPS** College Association; American Association of Museums. **RESEARCH** Soc hist of 19th and 20th century Europ and Am art. **SELECTED PUBLICATIONS** Auth, Politics and the Graphic Art of the Belgian Avant-Garde; Belgian Art Nouveau Sculpture; Print Culture in the Age of the French Revolution; Constantin Meunier: A Life of Labor; Constantin Meunier's Monument au travail; Hommage a Constantin Meunier's. **CONTACT ADDRESS** Hampshire Col, Amherst, MA 01002.

LEVINE, VICTORIA LINDSAY
PERSONAL Born 09/08/1954, Palo Alto, CA, m, 1982, 2 children **DISCIPLINE** ETHNOMUSICOLOGY, AMERICAN INDIAN STUDIES **EDUCATION** San Francisco State Univ, BMUS, BA, 77; MA, 80; Univ Ill Urbana, PhD, 90. **CAREER** W.M. Keck Foundation dir of the Hulbert Center for Southwestern Studies; Assoc prof, Colorado Col. **HONORS AND AWARDS** John D. & Catherine T. McArthur prof, 91-93; Am Council of Learned Soc Sr Fellow, 94-95; Ida Halpern Fellow and Awd, 99. **MEMBERSHIPS** Soc for Ethnomusicology; Col Music Soc; Soc for Am Music. **RESEARCH** Am Indian musics & cultures; Latino musics & cultures; Balinese music. **SELECTED PUBLICATIONS** Auth, pubs on Ethnomusicology, American Indian Musical Cultures, Music of the American Southwest, and Latino Music of the US; co-auth, book on Choctaw Indian Music; co-ed; Catalogue of Music in the Ruben Cobos Collection of New Mexican Folklore. **CONTACT ADDRESS** Music Dept, Colo Col, 14 E Cache La Poudre St, Colorado Springs, CO 80903. **EMAIL** vlevine@coloradocollege.edu

LEVINSON, BERNARD M.
PERSONAL Born S Porcupine, ON, Canada **DISCIPLINE** NEAR EASTERN STUDIES **EDUCATION** York Univ, Toronto, BA, 74; McMaster Univ, Ontario, MA, 78; Brandeis Univ, PhD, 91. **CAREER** Vis lectr, Hebrew and relig stud, Middlebury Col, 83, 84; tchg fel, Brandeis Univ, 86-87; Stroum Fel Advanc Jewish Stud, Univ Wash, 87-88; instr relig, Penn State Univ, 88-90; asst prof Near Eastern Lang and Cult, adj asst prof Relig Stud, Jewish Stud, Indiana Univ, 90-97; Berman Family Chair Jewish Stud and Hebrew Bible, assoc prof Classical and Near Eastern Stud, Univ Minn, 97- . **HONORS AND AWARDS** First Class Honors, 74; dInt Sem on Bibl and Ancient Near Eastern Law, 92; fac res grant, Middle Eastern Stud Prof, 94; IU Summer Fac Fel, 95; Soc of Bibl Lit res grant, 96; Int Fel in Jewish Stud, memorial Found, 96; Littauer Found res grant, 96; Center for Judaic Stud, Univ Penn, sem, 97; Stanford Hum Ctr, 97; mem, Inst for Advanc Stud, Sch of Soc Sci, Princeton, 97. **MEMBERSHIPS** Am Acad Relig; Am Oriental Soc; Asn for Jewish Stud; Can Soc for Bibl Stud; Jewish Law Asn; Soc of Bibl Lit; World Union of Jewish Stud. **RESEARCH** Biblical and ancient Near Eastern law; religion; hermeneutics. **SELECTED PUBLICATIONS** Ed and contribur, Theory and Method in Biblical and Cuneiform Law: Revision, Interpolation and Development, Sheffield Academic, 94; auth, But You Shall Surely Kill Him! The Text-Critical and Neo-Assyrian Evidence for MT Deuteronomy 13:10, in Braulik, ed, Bundesdokument und Gesetz: Studien zum Deuteronomium, Herder, 95; auth, Deuteronomy and the Hermeneutics of Legal Innovation, Oxford, 97; co-ed, Gender and Law in the Hebrew Bible and the Ancient Near East, Sheffield Academic, 98. **CONTACT ADDRESS** Univ of Minnesota, Twin Cities, 9 Pleasant St. SE, 330 Folwell Hall, Minneapolis, MN 55455. **EMAIL** levinson@tc.umn.edu

LEVY, BARRY
DISCIPLINE HISTORY **EDUCATION** Cornell Univ, BA, 68; Univ Penn, PhD, 76. **CAREER** Assoc Prof, Hist, Univ Mass Amherst. **MEMBERSHIPS** Am Antiquarian Soc **SELECTED PUBLICATIONS** Auth, Girls and Boys: Poor Children and the labor Market in Colonial Maschusetts, Pennsylvania Hist, Vol 64, (97), 287-307; auth, Quakers and the American Family: British Settlement in the Deleware Valley, 1650- 1785, Oxford Univ Press, 98. **CONTACT ADDRESS** Dept of Hist, Univ of Massachusetts, Amherst, Herter Hall, Amherst, MA 01002. **EMAIL** bjl@history.umass.edu

LEVY, DARLINE G.
PERSONAL Born 03/02/1939, New York, NY, m, 1965, 2 children **DISCIPLINE** HISTORY **EDUCATION** Barnard Col, BA, 60; Harvard Univ, PhD, 68. **CAREER** Instr, Carnegie-Mellon Univ, 65-66; asst prof, Rutgets Univ, 70-71; asst prof, Hunter Col, 71-73; asst prof, Barnard Col, 73-80; asst to assoc prof, NYork Univ, 80-. **HONORS AND AWARDS** Fulbright Awd, France, 60-61; Woodrow Wilson Fel, 61-62, 64; Radcliffe Inst Scholar 69-71; ACLS Res Fel, 83-84; Fulbright Res Awd, 83-84; Rockefeller Found Conf Grant, 85; Am Philos Soc Res Grant, 97-98. **MEMBERSHIPS** Am Soc for Eighteenth Century Studies; Northeast Am Soc for Eighteenth Century Studies; AHA; Soc for French Hist Studies. **SELECTED PUBLICATIONS** Coed, Women in Revolutionary Paris, 1789-1795. Selected Documents Translated with Notes and Commentary, Univ of IL Pr, 79; auth, The Ideas and Careers of Simon-Nicolas-Henri Linguet: A Study in Eighteenth-Century French Politics, Univ of IL Pr, 80; coed, Women and Politics in the Age of the Democratic Revolution, Univ of Mich Pr, 90; coauth, "Women and Militant Citizenship in Revolutionary Paris", Rebel Daughters: Women and the French Revolution, eds Sara E. Melzer, Leslie W. Rabine, Oxford Univ Pr, (92): 79-101; auth, "Women's citizenship in Action, 1791: Setting the Boundaries", The Meaning of Citizenship in the French Revolution, ed Renee Waldinger, Philip Dawson, Isser Woloch, Greenwood Pr, (93): 169-184; auth, "The Press and Politics", Proceedings of the Consortium on Revolutionary Europe, (96): 588-590; auth, "Linguet et la creation d'une sphere publique oppositionnelle", Politeia, Revue de theorie politique et de philosophie pratique, nos. 102 (98): 15-29; auth, "A Political Revolution for Women? The Case of Paris", Becoming Visible: Women in European History, ed R. Bridenthal, S. Stuart, M. Weisner-Hanks, Houghton-Mifflin, (98): 264-292. **CONTACT ADDRESS** Dept Hist, New York Univ, 19 University Pl, New York, NY 10003-4556.

LEVY, DAVID W.
PERSONAL Born 05/06/1937, Chicago, IL, m, 1969, 2 children **DISCIPLINE** HISTORY **EDUCATION** Univ Ill, BA, 59; Univ Chicago, MA, 61; Univ Wis, PhD, 67. **CAREER** Grad asst, Univ Wis, 61-62; instr, Ohio State Univ, 64-67; asst to full prof, 67- , Univ Okla. **HONORS AND AWARDS** Phi Beta Kappa; AMOCO Distinguished Teaching Awd; Regents Awd Super Teaching; Student Asn Awd Outstanding Teacher Univ Okla; Danforth Teaching Assoc; Sam K. Viersen Pres Prof; David Ross Boyd Prof. **MEMBERSHIPS** Orgn Am Hist. **RESEARCH** American intellectual history, American legal and constitutional history, The Progressive movement, Vietnam. **SELECTED PUBLICATIONS** Auth, The Letters of Louis D. Brandeis (7 vol); auth, Herbert Croly of the New Republic, Princeton, (85); auth, The Debate over Vietnam, Johns Hopkins, (91, 95); auth, FDR's Fireside Chats, Okla, (95). **CONTACT ADDRESS** Dept Hist, Univ of Oklahoma, 455 W Lindsey St, Norman, OK 73019-2000. **EMAIL** dwlevy@ou.edu

LEVY, EUGENE DONALD
PERSONAL Born 12/04/1933, Los Angeles, CA, m, 1960, 2 children **DISCIPLINE** AMERICAN SOCIAL HISTORY **EDUCATION** Univ Calif, Riverside, AB, 56; Yale Univ, MA, 60, PhD, 70. **CAREER** Actg instr hist & Am studies, Yale Univ, 62-65; asst prof, 65-71, assoc prof hist, Carnegie-Mellon Univ, 71-95; NEH jr fac fel, 71-72; Am Coun Learned Soc res grant, 72; Pa Humanities Coun grant, 81. **MEMBERSHIPS** Orgn Am Historians; Am Assn State & Local Hist. **RESEARCH** Afro-American history; ethnic American history; industrial America. **SELECTED PUBLICATIONS** Art, Ragtime and Race Pride, J Popular Cult, winter 68; co-ed, In Search of America, Dryden, 72; auth, James Weldon Johnson: Black Leader, Black Voice, Univ Chicago, 73; art, Is the Jew a White Man? Press Reaction to the Leo Frank Case, Phylon, 6/74; coauth, America's People, Harper & Row, 82; art, High Bridge Low Bridge, Places, Summer, 93; art, The Aesthetics of Power: High Voltage Transmission Systems and the American Landscape, Technology and Cultures, 6/97. **CONTACT ADDRESS** Dept of History, Carnegie Mellon Univ, 5000 Forbes Ave, Pittsburgh, PA 15213-3890. **EMAIL** elil@andrew.cmu.edu

LEVY, IAN CHRISTOPHER
PERSONAL Born 02/24/1967, New York, NY **DISCIPLINE** HISTORICAL THEOLOGY **EDUCATION** Univ of New Mexico, BA, 89; Vanderbilt, MA, 91; Marquette Univ, PhD, 97. **CAREER** Marquette Univ, tchg asst, 94-96, Nashotah House Episcopal Sem, adj prof, 97; Marquette Univ, adj prof, 97-, Carroll Col, adj prof, 98-; Visiting Asst. Prof, Marquette Univ; Ed Assoc, Luther Digest; Ed with Reformation Texts in Translation. **HONORS AND AWARDS** Phi Beta Kappa, Marquette Univ, Schmitt fell. **MEMBERSHIPS** MAA, MAMW, SBL, ASCH **RESEARCH** Medieval Theol; esp biblical interpretations and sacraments. **SELECTED PUBLICATIONS** Auth, John Wyclif and Augustinian Realism, in: Augustiniana, 98; Biographical Dictionary of Christian Theologians, contributing auth, eds P. Carey, J. Lienhard, Greenwood Pub Co, 00; auth, Was John Wyclif's Theology of the Eucharist Donatistic? in: Scottish Jour of Theol, forthcoming; auth, "Christus qui Mentiri Non Potest: John Wyclif's Rejection of Transubstantiation Recherche de Theologie et Philosophie Medievale, 99. **CONTACT ADDRESS** Dept of Theology, Marquette Univ, 5400 W Washington Blvd, Milwaukee, WI 53208. **EMAIL** ian.levy@marquette.edu

LEVY, JOHN M.
PERSONAL Born 05/05/1935, New York, NY, m, 1968, 2 children **DISCIPLINE** URBAN AFFAIRS **EDUCATION** Oberlin Col, AB, 56; City Univ NY, MA, 70; NY Univ Grad Sch Public Affairs (Wagner Sch), PhD, 79. **CAREER** Prof, Va Polytechnic Inst & State Univ. **MEMBERSHIPS** Am Planning Asn. **RESEARCH** Urban Planning, Public Policy. **SELECTED PUBLICATIONS** Auth, Essential Microeconomics for Public Policy Analysis, Praeger, 95; auth, Contemporary Urban Planning 5th ed, Prentice-Hall, 00; auth, Urban America: Processes & Problems, Prentice-Hall, 00. **CONTACT ADDRESS** Dept Urban Planning, Virginia Polytech Inst and State Univ, Architecture Annex, Blacksburg, VA 24061.

LEVY, LEONARD WILLIAMS
PERSONAL Born 04/09/1923, m, 1944, 2 children **DISCIPLINE** HISTORY **EDUCATION** Columbia Univ, BA, 47, MA, 48, PhD(hist), 51. **CAREER** Res asst hist, Columbia Univ, 50-51; instr Am civilization, Brandeis Univ, 51-54, from asst prof to prof hist, 54-70, Earl Warren prof Am consitutional hist, 57-70, chmn dept hist, 67-68, assoc dean fac and dean grad sch, 58-63, dean fac, 63-66, chmn grad prog hist, 66-67, 69-70; William W Clary prof hist, 70-74, Andres W Mellon All-Claremont Prof Humanities and Hist, Claremont Grad Sch, 74-, Chmn Grad Fac Hist, Claremont Cols, 70-90, Guggenheim fel, 57-58; sr res fel, Ctr Study Hist Liberty Am, Harvard Univ, 61-62; mem, Nat Comn Law and Social Action, Am Jewish Cong, 62-67; mem, US Bicentennial Comn Am Revolution, 67-68; Am Bar Found fel legal hist, 73-74; Nat Endowment for Humanities sr fel, 74; bicentennial speaker, City St Louis, 76; consult ed, Encycl Britannica; Pulitzer Prize juror and chmn. **HONORS AND AWARDS** Pulitzer Prize in hist, 69; Gaspar Bacon lectr, Boston Univ, 72; Sheldon Elliott lectr, Law Sch, Univ Southern Calif, 72. **MEMBERSHIPS** Am Acad Polit and Soc Sci; Am Soc Legal Hist; Orgn Am Historians; Am Antiq Soc; Inst Early Am Hist and Cult. **RESEARCH** History of the Bill of Rights; American legal and constitutional history; history of religion. **SELECTED PUBLICATIONS** Auth, Blasphemy: Verbal Offense against the Sacred, from Moses to Salman Rushdie, Knopf, 93; coed, Encyclopedia of the American Presidency, Simon & Schuster, 94; auth, Seasoned Judgments: The American Constitution, Rights, and History, Transaction Publ, 95; auth, A License to Steal: The Forfeiture of Property, Univ of NCar Press, 96; auth, Origins of the Bill of Rights, Yale Univ Press, 99; auth, The Palladium of Justice: Origins of Trial by Jury, I.R. Dee, 00; auth, Ranters Run Amok and Other Adventures in the History of Law, I.R. Dee, 00. **CONTACT ADDRESS** Dept of Humanities and Hist, Claremont Graduate Sch, Claremont, CA 91711.

LEVY, RICHARD S.
PERSONAL Born 05/10/1940, Chicago, IL, m, 1967 **DISCIPLINE** GERMAN AND EUROPEAN HISTORY **EDUCATION** Univ Chicago, BA, 62; Yale Univ, MA, 64, PhD(hist), 69. **CAREER** Instr-asst hist, Univ Mass, Amherst, 66-70; asst prof, 70-76, Assoc Prof Hist, Univ Ill, Chicago Circle, 76-. **MEMBERSHIPS** Ger Studies Asn. **RESEARCH** German anti-Semitism; the German Empire, 1871-1918. **SELECTED PUBLICATIONS** Auth, Modernity Within Tradition--the Social History of Orthodox Jewry in Imperial Germany, Historian, Vol 0056, 94; Art, Ideology, and Economics in Nazi Germany--the Reich Chambers of Music, Theater, and the Visual Arts, Ger Stud Rev, Vol 0018, 95; auth, "A Lie and a Libel: The 'Protocols of the Elders of Zion' in Recent Hist," in Representation of Jews Through the Ages, ed. L. J. Greenspoon, (Omaha: Creighton Univ Pr, 96), 231-243; auth, "Antisemitism, 1871-1923," in Modern Germany: An Encyclopedia of Hist, People,

and Culture, 1871-1900, ed. Dieter K. Buse and Juergen C. Doeer (Garland, 98), I:33-35. **CONTACT ADDRESS** Dept of Hist, Univ of Illinois, Chicago, 913 University Hall/601 S Morgan, M/C 198, Chicago, IL 60607-7109. **EMAIL** rslevy@uic.edu

LEWARNE, CHARLES PIERCE

PERSONAL Born 08/16/1930, Kirkland, WA, m, 1956, 3 children **DISCIPLINE** UNITED STATES HISTORY **EDUCATION** Western Wash State Col, BA and BA in Ed, 55; Univ Calif, Berkeley, MA, 58; Univ Wash, PhD(hist), 69. **CAREER** Teacher hist, Battle Ground Sch Dist, Wash, 55-57; Teacher Hist, Edmonds Sch Dist 15, 58-, Part-time instr hist, Everett Community Col, 62-65 and Edmonds Community Col, 67. **MEMBERSHIPS** Orgn Am Historians; Western Hist Asn; NEA; Nat Hist Communal Soc Asn. **RESEARCH** Late 19th century communitarian movement; PACIFIC Northwest history; radicalism in the PACIFIC Northwest. **SELECTED PUBLICATIONS** Auth, Utopias on Puget Sound, 1885-1915, 75, 95; coauth, Washington : A Centennial History , 88; auth, Washington State, 86. 93; auth, Carstensen, Vernon 1907-1992, Pac Northwest Quart, Vol 0084, 93; Spokane and the Inland Empire--an Interior Pacific-Northwest Anthology, Ore Hist Quart, Vol 0094, 93; Washington Comes of Age--the State in the National Experience, Ore Hist Quart, Vol 0095, 94; The Pacific Northwest--an Interpretive History, Pac Northwest Quart, Vol 0088, 97. **CONTACT ADDRESS** 20829 Hillcrest Pl, Edmonds, WA 98020.

LEWENSTEIN, BRUCE V.

PERSONAL Born 09/18/1957, Palo Alto, CA, m, 1983, 3 children **DISCIPLINE** HISTORY OF SCIENCE **EDUCATION** Univ Chicago, BA 80; Univ Penn, MA 85; PhD 87. **CAREER** Cornell Univ, asst prof, assoc prof, 87-. **HONORS AND AWARDS** STC Distinguished Technical Communication, 86; Golden Key Teaching Awd, 99. **MEMBERSHIPS** Am Assoc for Advancement of Sci; Natl Assoc of Sci Writers; History of Sci Soc; Soc for Social Stud of Sci. **RESEARCH** Science communication. **SELECTED PUBLICATIONS** Ed, When Science Meets the Public, 92; co-auth, The Establishment of American Science, 99. **CONTACT ADDRESS** Dept of Communication, Cornell Univ, Ithaca, NY 14853. **EMAIL** blv1@cornell.edu

LEWIN, LINDA

PERSONAL Born 05/07/1941, Baltimore, MD **DISCIPLINE** LATIN AMERICAN HISTORY **EDUCATION** Univ Calif, Berkeley, AB, 63; Columbia Univ, MA, 68, PhD(hist), 75. **CAREER** From instr to asst prof hist, John Jay Col, City Univ New York, 71-76; asst prof, Princeton Univ, 76-82; Asst Prof Hist, Univ Calif, Berkeley, 82-, Vis res scholar, Boston Col Law Sch, 80-81. **HONORS AND AWARDS** Best article prize Latin Am hist, Conf Latin Am Hist, AHA, 80. **MEMBERSHIPS** Conf Latin Am Hist; Latin Am Studies Asn. **RESEARCH** Brazilian family history and family law; oligarchical politics in Brazil's Old Republic; history of the Brazilian northeast. **SELECTED PUBLICATIONS** Auth, Oral tradition and elite myth: The legend of Antonio Silvino in Brazilian popular culture, J Latin Am Lore, winter 79; The oligarchical limitations of social banditry in Brazil: The case of the good thief Antonio Silvino, Past & Present, 2/79; Some historical implications of kinship organization for family-based politics in the Brazilian northeast, Comp Studies Soc & Hist, 4/79. **CONTACT ADDRESS** Hist Dept, Univ of California, Berkeley, 3229 Dwinelle Hall, Berkeley, CA 94720-2551.

LEWIS, ANDREW WELLS

PERSONAL Born 09/05/1943, Savannah, GA, m, 1970, 2 children **DISCIPLINE** MEDIEVAL HISTORY **EDUCATION** Dartmouth Col, BA, 66; Univ Chicago, MA, 67; Harvard Univ, PhD(hist), 73. **CAREER** Vis asst prof hist, Univ Md College Park, 73-74; cur medieval collections, Stanford Univ Libr, 74-75; vis lectr hist, Univ Western Ont, 75-76; vis asst prof, Southern Ill Univ, Edwardsville, 76; Mellon fel, St Louis Univ, 77; asst prof, 77-80, Assoc Prof Hist, Southwest MO State Univ, 80-, Am Philos Soc grant, 75. **MEMBERSHIPS** Mediaeval Acad Am; AHA. **RESEARCH** Medieval France, 900-1328; medieval social history. **SELECTED PUBLICATIONS** Auth, Successions onttoniennes et robertiennes, Un essai de comparaison, and Observations sur la frontiere franco-normande, in le roi de France et son royaume autour de I an Mil, Picard, 92; auth,The Career of Philip the Cleric, Younger Brother of Louis VII: Apropos of an Unpublished Charter, Tradittio 0050,95; auth, Continuity and Change in capetian Kingship: Observations on the Acesson of Lous IX, De Boeck Univ, 96. **CONTACT ADDRESS** Dept of Hist, Southwest Missouri State Univ, Springfield, Springfield, MO 65802.

LEWIS, ARNOLD

PERSONAL Born 01/13/1930, New Castle, PA, m, 1958, 3 children **DISCIPLINE** ART HISTORY **EDUCATION** Univ Wis, PhD 62, MA 54; Allegheny Col, BA 52. **CAREER** Wells Col, instr 62-64; Col of Wooster, asst prof, 64-96, emeritus prof, 96-. **HONORS AND AWARDS** Nat Trust Fel; Fulbright Gnt; SAH Founder's Awd; SAH Western Reserve Bk Awd; SAH Dir; Jacques Barzun Bk Awd. **MEMBERSHIPS** CAA; SAH. **RESEARCH** 19th Century Architecture. **SELECTED PUBLICATIONS** Auth, Am Victorian Architecture, NYork, Dover Pr, 75; auth, Wooster in 1876, Wooster, College of Wooster, 76; auth, American Country Houses of the Gilded Age, NY, Dover Press, 83; coauth, The Opulent Interiors of the Gilded Age, NYork, Dover Pr, 87; auth, The Disquieting Progress of Chicago, in: Amer Pub Architecture: Euro Roots and Native Expressions: Papers in Art Hist from the Penn State Univ, 88; auth, Imaging the Real, Lee Waisler-Mostra Retrospectiva 1968-1988, Ferrara, Galleria Civica d'Arte Moderna, 88, with Beth Irwin Lewis; auth, An Early Encounter With Tomorrow: Europeans Chicago's Loop and the World's Columbian Exposition, Urbana, Univ IL Press, 97. **CONTACT ADDRESS** The Col of Wooster, 614 Kieffer St, Wooster, OH 44691. **EMAIL** alewis@acs.wooster.edu

LEWIS, DAVID LANIER

PERSONAL Born 04/05/1927, Bethalto, IL, m, 1953, 4 children **DISCIPLINE** BUSINESS HISTORY **EDUCATION** Univ Ill, BS, 48; Boston Univ, MS, 55; Univ Mich, MA, 56, Ph-D(hist), 59. **CAREER** Reporter, Edwardsville Intelligencer, Ill, 48; state ed, Alton Telegraph, 48-50; ed publ, Ford Motor Co, 50-51; press rel rep, Borden Co, 52; supvr, Indust Arts Awards, Ford Motor Co, 52-55; pub rel staff exec, Gen Motors Corp, 59-65; assoc prof, 65-68, Prof Bus Hist, Univ Mich, 68-, Contrib ed, Model T Times, 71-, V-8 Times, 71-, Horseless Carriage, 72-, Model A News, 72- and Old Car Illustrated, 76-; consult indust properties, Div Hist, Mich Dept State, 73-; assoc ed, Cars and Parts, 73-; feature ed, Bulb Horn, 74-; trustee, Nat Automotive Hist Collection, 75- **HONORS AND AWARDS** Cuqnot Awd, Soc Automotive Historians, 77; Duryea Awd, Antique Automobile Club Am, 77; Awd of Merit, Mich Hist Soc, 77. **MEMBERSHIPS** AHA; Econ Hist Asn; Soc Automotive Historians (dir, 74-, pres, 82-). **RESEARCH** Henry Ford; auto history; entrepreneurial history. **SELECTED PUBLICATIONS** Auth, International public relations, in: Handbook of Public Relations, McGraw, 60; Automobile industry, Collier's Encycl, 67; Automobile industry, Collier's Encycl Year Bk, annually, 68-; The Square Dancing Master, Am Heritage, 72; Milton Snavely Hershey, Dict of Am Biog, 73; The Public Image of Henry Ford, Wayne State Univ, 76; guest ed, Mich Quart Rev, fall 80 and winter 81. **CONTACT ADDRESS** Grad Sch of Bus Admin, Univ of Michigan, Ann Arbor, 435 S State St, Ann Arbor, MI 48109-1003.

LEWIS, DAVID LEVERING

DISCIPLINE AFRICAN-AMERICAN HISTORY **EDUCATION** London Sch of Econ and Polit Sci, PhD, 62. **CAREER** Prof, Martin Luther King, Jr Univ Prof, Rutgers, State Univ NJ, Livingston, 94-. **RESEARCH** African-American history; conceptions of race and racism; the dynamics of European colonialism, especially in Africa. **SELECTED PUBLICATIONS** Auth, W.E.B. Du Bois: Biography of a Race, 1868-1919 Vol I, Henry Holt and Co, 93; The Portable Harlem Renaissance Reader, Viking, 94; The Harlem Renaissance, in Robert O'Meally and Jack Salzman, eds, Encyclopedia of African-American Culture and History, Macmillan, 94; Rev of Carter G. Woodson: A Life in Black History, by Jacqueline Goggin, J of Am Hist, 94; Khartoum, in Past Imperfect: History According to Hollywood, Henry Holt, 95; W.E.B. Du Bois: A Reader, Henry Holt and Co, 95. **CONTACT ADDRESS** Dept of Hist, Rutgers, The State Univ of New Jersey, New Brunswick, 16 Seminary Place, New Brunswick, NJ 08901-1108.

LEWIS, DAVID RICH

PERSONAL Born 04/13/1957, Ogden, UT, m, 1990, 2 children **DISCIPLINE** HISTORY **EDUCATION** Ut St Univ, BS, 79; Univ Toronto, MA, 80; Univ Wi Madison, MA, 83, PhD, 88. **CAREER** Asst prof to assoc prof, Ut St Univ, 88- ; coed, W Hist Quart, 92- . **HONORS AND AWARDS** Bert M. Fireman Prize, W Hist Assoc, 84; Pre-doctoral Fel, D'Arcy McNickle Center for the Hist of the Amer Indian, Newberry Libr, Chicago, Il, 85-86; Honors Prof, Ut St Univ Honors Prog, 96-97; Res of the Year, Col of Humanities, Arts, & Soc Sci, Ut St Univ, 97. **MEMBERSHIPS** W Hist Assoc; Org of Amer Hist; Amer Soc for Ethnohistory; Amer Soc for Environ Hist. **RESEARCH** Native American, American West, Environment, Utah. **SELECTED PUBLICATIONS** Auth, Major Problems in the History of the American West, Houghton Mifflin, 97; Neither Wolf Nor Dog: American Indians, Environment and Agrarian Change, Oxford Univ Press, 94, 97; Sins of the Fathers (and Mothers): Utah, Past and Present, SLC Mag of the Mountainwest, 99; Great Basin and Rocky Mountain Indians, in American Heritage Encyclopedia of American History, Henry Holt & Co, 98; Native Americans: The Original Westerners, in The Rural West Since World War II, Univ Press Ks, 98. **CONTACT ADDRESS** Dept of History, Utah State Univ, 0710 Old Main Hill, Logan, UT 84322-0710. **EMAIL** dlewis@hass.usu.edu

LEWIS, DOUGLAS

PERSONAL Born 04/30/1938, Centreville, MS, w, 1969 **DISCIPLINE** HISTORY OF ART; HISTORY OF ARCHITECTURE ITALIAN RENAISSANCE **EDUCATION** Yale Col, BA, 59 & 60; Univ Cambridge, BA, 62, MA, 63; Yale Univ, MA, 63, PhD, 67. **CAREER** Lectr, Bryn Mawr Col, 67-68; curator of sculpture, Nat Gallery Art, 68-; vis prof, Univ Calif Berkeley, 70 & 79; adj prof, Johns Hopkins Univ, 73-77; prof lectr, Georgetown Univ, 80-93; lectr in univ honors, Univ Maryland College PK, 88-. **HONORS AND AWARDS** Mellon fel, Clare Col, 60-62; Chester Dale fel, Amer Acad Rome, 64-65; Rome Prize fel, AAR, 65-66; David E Finley fel, Nat Gallery Art, 65-68; Ailsa Mellon Bruce Cur Sabbatical fel, Nat Gallery Art, 97-87. **MEMBERSHIPS** Col Art Asn; Asn Art Hist; Soc Archit Hist; Nat Trust Hist Preserv; Amer Acad Rome. **RESEARCH** Italian Renaissance; Baroque art & architecture 1300-1800. **SELECTED PUBLICATIONS** contribur & ed, Essays in Art and Architecture in Memory of Carolyn Kolb: Artibus et Historiae, 97; auth, Longhena and His Patrons: The Creation of the Venetian Baroque, 97; The Last Gems: Italian Neoclassical Gem Engravings and Their Impressions, Engraved Gems, Survivals and Revivals, Stud in the Hist Art, 97. **CONTACT ADDRESS** National Gallery of Arts, 4th St at Constitution Ave NW, Washington, DC 20565-0001. **EMAIL** m.beck@nga.gov

LEWIS, JAMES A.

PERSONAL Born 07/29/1942, Galion, OH, m, 1969, 3 children **DISCIPLINE** HISTORY **EDUCATION** Ohio State Univ, BA, 64; Northern Ill, MA, 68; Duke Univ, PhD, 75. **CAREER** From asst prof to assoc prof to prof, 72-, WCU. **HONORS AND AWARDS** Daniel Creigton Sossomon Endowed Chemn, WCU, 88-92; Spain in Am Quincontennial Prize, Spanish Ministry of Culture, 88. **MEMBERSHIPS** SLAH; SECOLAS; Asn Carribean Hist; SC Hist Soc. **RESEARCH** Colonial Latin America; Spanish Carribean; Am revolution. **SELECTED PUBLICATIONS** Coauth, Guide to Cherokee Documents in Foreign Archives, 83; auth, The Final Campaign of the American Revolution: Rise and Fall of the Spanish Bahamas, 91; auth, Neptune's Militia: The Frigate South Carolina during the American Revolution, 99. **CONTACT ADDRESS** Dept of History, Western Carolina Univ, Cullowhee, SC 28723. **EMAIL** lewis@wcu.edu

LEWIS, JAMES F.

PERSONAL Born 06/21/1937, m, 1958, 3 children **DISCIPLINE** HISTORY OF RELIGIONS **EDUCATION** Bethel Col, BA, 60; Bethel Theol Sem, BD, 63; Univ Iowa, PhD, 76. **CAREER** Asst prof and dept chair, world relig, Union Bibl Sem, Pune, Maharashtra, India, 77-81; assoc prof and dept chair, world relig, St. Bonifacius, 81-94; assoc prof, world relig, Wheaton Col, 94-. **MEMBERSHIPS** Evang Theol Soc; Asn of Asian Studies; Amer Acad of Relig. **RESEARCH** Religion in Vietnam; Religion in Modern India. **SELECTED PUBLICATIONS** Co-auth, Religious Traditions of the World, Zondervan, 91. **CONTACT ADDRESS** 501 College Av., Wheaton, IL 60187. **EMAIL** james.f.lewis@wheaton.edu

LEWIS, JAN ELLEN

PERSONAL Born 07/10/1949, St. Louis, MO, m, 1 child **DISCIPLINE** AMERICAN HISTORY & STUDIES **EDUCATION** Bryn Mawr Col, BA, 71; Univ Mich, MA(Am studies), 72, MA(hist), 74, PhD(hist), 77. **CAREER** Asst prof to assoc prof, 77-94, Prof Hist, Rutgers Univ, Newark, 94-, chair, 87-93, graduate dir, 94-, grad fac, Rutger Univ, New Brunswick, 89-; vis prof hist, Princeton Univ, fall 95. **HONORS AND AWARDS** NEH fel, independent study and res, 85-86; Sr fel, Philadelphia Center Early Am Studies, spring 88; fel, Center Hist Freedom, Wash Univ, spring, 91. **MEMBERSHIPS** Am Hist Asn; Orgn Am Historians; Am Studies Asn; Southern Hist Asn; Soc Historians of Early Am Repub **RESEARCH** American history to 1865; Southern history; history of the family and women. **SELECTED PUBLICATIONS** Auth, Domestic Tranquility and the Management of Emotion among the Gentry of Pre-Revolutionary Virginia, Willliam & Mary Quart, 1/82; The Pursuit of Happiness: Family and Values in Jefferson's Virginia, Camabridge Univ Press, 83, paperbk ed, 85; The Republican Wife: Virtue and Seduction in the Early Republic, William and Mary Quart, 87; co-auth, Sally Has Been Sick: Pregnancy and Family Limitation among Virginia Gentry Women, 1780-1830, Jour Soc Hist, 88; Mother's Love: The Construction of an emotion in Nineteenth-Century America, In: Social History and Issues in Consciousness: Some Interdisciplinary Connections, NY Univ Press, 89; Mother's as Teachers: Reconceptualizing the Role of the Family as Educator, In: Education and the American Family: A Research Synthesis, NY Univ Press, 89; Motherhood and the Construction of the Male Citizen in the United States, 1750-1850, In: Constructions of Self, Rutgers Univ Press, 92; The Blessings of Domestic Society: Thomas Jefferson's Family and the Transformation of American Politics, In: Jeffersonian Legacies, Univ Press Va, 93; Southerners and the Problem of Slavery in Political Discourse, In: Devising Liberty: Preserving and Creating Freedom in the New American Republic, Stanford Univ Press, 95; Of Every Age, Sex & Condition: The Representation of Women in the Constitution, Jour Early Republic, 95; co-auth, American Synecdoche: Thomas Jefferson as Image, Icon, Character, and Self, Am Hist Rev, 2/98; ed & contribr, Those Scenes for which Along My Heart Was Made: Affection and Politics in the Age of Jefferson and Hamilton, In: An Emotional History of the United States, NY Univ Press, 98; auth, "Politics and the Ambivalence of the Private Sphere: Women in Early Washington, D.C.," Donald Kennon, ed., A Republic for the Ages, University Press of Virginia, 99; auth, "Jefferson, the Family, and Civic Education," in James Gilreath, ed., Thomas Jefferson and the Education of a Citizen, Library of Congress, 99); coed & contr,

Sally Hemings and Thomas Jefferson: History, Memory, and Civic Culture, University Press of Virginia, 1999); "Sex and the Married Man: Benjamin Franklin and His Families," in Larry Tise, ed., Benjamin Franklin and Women, Pennsylvania State University Press, 00; coauth, Making a Nation: The United States and Its People, Prentice Hall, 01. **CONTACT ADDRESS** Dept of Hist, Rutgers, The State Univ of New Jersey, Newark, 175 University Ave, Newark, NJ 07102-1897. **EMAIL** janlewis@andromeda.rutgers.edu

LEWIS, JOHANNA M.
PERSONAL Born 01/18/1961, Baltimore, MD, m, 1984 **DISCIPLINE** PUBLIC HISTORY **EDUCATION** Salem Col, AB, 83; Wake Forest Univ, MA, 85; Col William & Mary, PhD, 91. **CAREER** From asst prof to prof, Univ Ark at Little Rock, 91-. **HONORS AND AWARDS** Fac Excellence Awd in Service, UALR Col of Arts, Humanities, & Soc Sci, 98. **MEMBERSHIPS** Orgn of Am Historians, Southern Asn of Women Historians, Am Asn of Museums, Southern Hist Asn. **RESEARCH** Public History, Material Culture, Colonial History. **SELECTED PUBLICATIONS** Auth, Artisans in the North Carolina Back Country, Univ Press of Ky (Lexington, KY), 95. **CONTACT ADDRESS** Dept Hist, Univ of Arkansas, Little Rock, 2801 S Univ Ave, Little Rock, AR 72204-1000. **EMAIL** jmlewis@ualr.edu

LEWIS, NATHANIEL
DISCIPLINE AMERICAN LITERATURE AND IMAGES OF THE WEST **EDUCATION** Harvard Univ, PhD. **CAREER** Eng, St. Michaels Col. **SELECTED PUBLICATIONS** Area: cult of the Am West. **CONTACT ADDRESS** Saint Michael's Col, Winooski Park, Colchester, VT 05439. **EMAIL** nlewis@smcvt.edu

LEWIS, SAMELLA
PERSONAL Born 02/27/1924, New Orleans, LA, m, 1948 **DISCIPLINE** ART HISTORY **EDUCATION** Hampton Inst, BS 1945; OH State Univ, MA 1948, PhD 1951; Postdoctoral studies, Tung Hai Univ, NYork Univ, Univ of Southern CA. **CAREER** Art Hist Scripps Coll, prof; LA Co Museum of Art; Coordinator of Educ, CA State Univ; Univ State of NY; FL A&M Univ; Morgan State Univ; Hampton Inst. **HONORS AND AWARDS** Permanent collections, Baltimore Museum Art, VA museum fine arts, palm springs museum, high Mus Atlanta; Delta Sigma Theta Scholarship, Dillard Univ; Art Scholarship Hampton Inst; Amer Univ Fellowship OH State; Fulbright Fellowship Chinese Studies; NDEA Fellowship; NY Ford Found Grant; Honorary Doctorate, Chapman Coll, 1976; Fellowships, Fulbright Found, Ford Found. **MEMBERSHIPS** Mem, Expansion Arts Panel, NEA 1975-78; pres Contemp Crafts Inc; bd mem Museum African Amer Art; Art Educ Black Art Intl Quarterly Natl Conf of Artists; Coll Art Assn of Amer; Pres, Oxum Intl, 1988-; Dir/founder, Museum of African Amer Art, 1976-80. **SELECTED PUBLICATIONS** Published, Art African Amer, 1978; "Black Artist on Art," volumes I & II, 1969-71; "Art: African Amer", 1978. **CONTACT ADDRESS** Intl Review of African American Art, 3000 Biscayne Blvd, Ste 505, Miami, FL 33137.

LEWIS, T.
PERSONAL Born 03/04/1940, Hartford, CT, m, 1964, 2 children **DISCIPLINE** GEOGRAPHY **EDUCATION** Central CT State Univ, BS, 64; Clark Univ, CAGS, 67; Rutgers Univ, PhD, 78. **CAREER** Teacher, Penney High School, 64-68; Asst Prof to Prof of Geography and Social Science, 69-97; Chiar, 92-97; Assoc Prof, Univ of CT, 97-. **HONORS AND AWARDS** For Teaching: From the State of Ct and the National Council for Geographic Education, Fo Service: From the New England, St. Lawrence Valley Geographic Society, For Scholarship: From the Society of Arch. Historians, listed in Who's Who in Am Educ. **MEMBERSHIPS** Asn of Am Geographers, National Council for the Social Studies, CT Academy of Science, CT Council for the Social Studies, Steamship Historical Society of NA. **RESEARCH** Historical/Cultural Geography, Rail and Marine Transportation, Geographic Education. **SELECTED PUBLICATIONS** Auth, "Connecticut," The Columbia Gazetteer of the World, SB Cohen ed., Columbia Univ Press, 98; rev, Connecticut, Maine, Massachusetts, Rhode Island, ed. JH Lang (New York: Simon and Shuster, 94, Connecticut History, 99; auth, "Cape Cod Canal" and "The Waterfront" in Encyclopedia of New England Culture, Yale Univ Press, 00; auth, "Travel Through Time in Southern New England: A New View". **CONTACT ADDRESS** Dept Geography U-148, Univ of Connecticut, Storrs, 354 Mansfield Rd, Storrs, CT 06269-9000. **EMAIL** tlewis6895@aol.com

LEWIS, THOMAS T.
PERSONAL Born 10/21/1941, Paris, TX, m, 1968, 2 children **DISCIPLINE** HISTORY **EDUCATION** Okla Christian Univ, BA, 63; Southern Methodist Univ, MA, 65; Univ Okla, PhD, 70. **CAREER** Asst prof, Eastern Ky Univ, 69-71; prof, chair, Mount Senario Col, 71-. **HONORS AND AWARDS** Tchr of the Year, 90-91, 93-94; fulbright lectr, 73-74, univ metz. **MEMBERSHIPS** Am Hist Asn; Western Society for French Hist. **RESEARCH** History of law; constitutional history; US ethnic history. **SELECTED PUBLICATIONS** Auth, Carl Popper's Situational Logic; auth, Authoritarian Attitudes and Personality's; auth, Alternative Psychological Interpretations of Woodrow Wilson; ed, Supreme Court Encyclopedia, Salem Press (Pasadena), 00. **CONTACT ADDRESS** Mount Senario Col, 1500 College Ave W, Ladysmith, WI 54848. **EMAIL** tlewis@mscsf.edu

LEWIS, WALTER DAVID
PERSONAL Born 06/24/1931, Towanda, PA, m, 1954, 3 children **DISCIPLINE** AMERICAN HISTORY **EDUCATION** Pa State Univ, BA, 52, MA, 54; Cornell Univ, PhD(hist), 61. **CAREER** Instr pub speaking, Hamilton Col, 54-57; fel coord, Eleutherian Mills-Hagley Found, 59-65; assoc prof hist, State Univ NY Buffalo, 65-71, prof, 71, dir undergrad sem hist, 65-67, dir honors prog hist, 65-70; Hudson Prof Hist and Engineering, Auburn Univ, 71-, Instr, Univ Del, 59-61, lectr, 61-65; grants-in-aid, Eleutherian Mills Hist Libr, 70-72; Nat Endowment for Humanities grant, 74; dir, Proj Technol, Human Values and Southern Future, Auburn Univ, 74-78; exec coproducer film, About US: the Changing American South, 75-77; Delta Air Lines Found res grants, 75-78; fel, Nat Humanities Inst, Univ Chicago, 78-79. **MEMBERSHIPS** Soc Hist Technol; Bus Hist Conf; G A Henty Soc England. **RESEARCH** History of technology; American social and intellectual history; business history. **SELECTED PUBLICATIONS** Auth, From Newgate to Dannemora: The Rise of the Penitentiary in New York, 1796-1848, Cornell Univ, 65; coed, Economic Change in the Civil War Era, Eleutherian Mills-Hagley Found, 65; auth, Industrial Research and Development, In: Vol II, Technology in Western Civilization, Oxford Univ, 67; The Reformer as Conservative: Protestant Counter-Subversion in the Early Republic, In: The Development of an American Culture, Prentice-Hall, 70; The Early History of the Lackawanna Iron and Coal Company: A Study in Technological Adaptation, Pa Mag Hist & Biog, 10/72; On Nature, Technology, and Humanity, Eng Educ, 4/75; Iron and Steel in America, Hagley Mus, 76; coed, The Southern Mystique: Technology and Human Values in a Changing Region, Univ Ala, 77. **CONTACT ADDRESS** Dept of Hist, Auburn Univ, Auburn, AL 36849.

LEYENDECKER, LISTON EDGINGTON
PERSONAL Born 01/19/1931, Laredo, TX, m, 1963, 2 children **DISCIPLINE** AMERICAN WESTWARD MOVEMENT **EDUCATION** Univ N Mex, BA, 58; Univ Denver, MA, 61, PhD(Am studies), 66. **CAREER** Instr Am hist, Del Mar Col, 63-64, instr Am Hist & Western Civilization, 64-65; Dep State Historian, State Hist Soc Colo, 65-66; instr & acting chmn Dept Am Hist & Western Civilization, Arapahoe Jr Col, 66-67, instr & chmn Dept Am & Colo Hist, 67-68; from asst prof to assoc prof Am & Colo Hist, 68-78, prof Hist, Colo State Univ, 78-99, researcher & consult, Hist Georgetown Loop Mining Area prof, Colo State Univ, 69-99, dir, Georgetown Soc, Inc, 78-. **HONORS AND AWARDS** Harris T Guard Awd, Colo State Univ, 75. **MEMBERSHIPS** Western Hist Asn; Mining History Assn, Historic Georgetown; Colo Hist Soc. **RESEARCH** Mining in 19th century Colorado; preservation and restoration in Colorado; later 19th century United States. **SELECTED PUBLICATIONS** Auth, The History of Rufugio County Hospital, Jack Bonner Co, 65; Colorado and the Paris Universal Exposition, 1867, Colo Mag, Winter 69; contribr, The restoration of Black Hawk and Central City: the preliminary pains, panics and problems, In: Western American History in the Seventies, Educ Media & Info Systs, 73; auth, Washington Hall: Gilpin County's Oldest Courthouse (booklet), Colo State Univ Coop Exten Serv, 75; Georgetown: Colorado's Silver Queen, 1859-1876 (booklet), Centennial Publ, 77; Georgetown 1878: One Year in the Life of Colorado's Silver Queen, The Georgetown/Silver Plume National Historic Landmark District Journal, Feb 97; Palace Car Prince: A Biography of George Mortimer Pullman, University Press of Colorado, 98. **CONTACT ADDRESS** Dept of History, Colorado State Univ, Fort Collins, CO 80523-0001.

LEYERLE, BLAKE
PERSONAL Born 08/16/1960, Boston, MA, s **DISCIPLINE** HISTORY OF CHRISTIANITY **EDUCATION** Duke Univ, PhD 91. **CAREER** Univ Notre Dame, asst prof, assoc prof, 91 to 98-. **MEMBERSHIPS** NAPS; AAR. **RESEARCH** Social Hist of Early Christianity; John Chrysostom; Pilgrimage; Monasticism. **SELECTED PUBLICATIONS** Auth, Meal Customs in the Greco-Roman World, Passover and Easter: The Liturgical Structuring of a Sacred Season, eds, Paul Bradshaw, Lawrence A. Hoffman, Univ Notre dame Press, forthcoming; Appealing to Children, The Jour of Early Christian Studies, 97; auth, Landscape as Cartography in Early Christian Pilgrimage Narratives, Jour of Amer Acad Relig, 96; auth, Clement of Alexandria on the Importance of Table Etiquette, The Jour of Early Christian Studies, 95; auth, John Chrysostom on Almsgiving and the Use of Money, Harv Theol Rev, 94; auth, John Chrysostom on the Gaze, The Jour of Early Christian Studies, 93. **CONTACT ADDRESS** Dept of Theology, Univ of Notre Dame, 327 O'Shaughnessy Hall, Notre Dame, IN 46556. **EMAIL** Leyerle@nd.edu

LI, BING
PERSONAL Born 02/05/1954, Beijing, China, m, 1988, 2 children **DISCIPLINE** HISTORY **EDUCATION** Nankai Univ, BA, 82; Carnegie Mellon Univ, MA, 85; PhD, 91. **CAREER** Res fel, China Acad of Soc Sci, 82-84; vis lectr, China Acad of Soc Sci, 91; vis scholar, Taiwan Univ, 94; asst prof & dir of asian studies, Phillips Univ, 91-93; asst prof & assoc dir of Western Pacific Inst, Univ of Central Okla, 93-98; adj prof, Okla City Univ, 96-; assoc prof & assoc dir of Western Pacific Inst, Univ of Okla, 98-. **HONORS AND AWARDS** Higher Educ Grant, Luce Found, 91; Res Funding, Nat Reunification Asn, 94; Funding, Woodrow Wilson Int Ctr for Scholars, 96; UCO Fac Merit-Credit Awd for Res, 97; UCO Distinguished Scholar Awd, 98; UCO Hauptman Res Fel Awd, 98; Res Grant, U.S. Defense Intelligent Agent, 99-00. **RESEARCH** Ed Board of Modern China Studies, Sino-American Int Strategic Res Soc, UCO Western Pacific Inst, ed of Am J of China Stdies. **SELECTED PUBLICATIONS** Co-ed, Social-Economic Transition and Cultural Reconstruction in China, Univ Press of Am, 98; co-ed, Korea and Regional Geopolitics, Univ Press of Am, 99; auth, "PLA Attacks and Amphibious Operations during the Taiwan Straits Crises," U.S. Navy Dept, (99); coauth, "The Death of the Emperor: Kim Il-song and North Korea's China Policy," Am J of China Studies vol 1 (99): 134-155; coauth, U.S. Diplomacy and U.S.-China Relations, CASS Press, 00; coauth, Asia's Crisis and New Paradigm, Univ Press of Am, 00; co-ed & trans, "Chinese Generals Remember the Korean War, Univ Press of Kans, 00; coauth, "North Korea's Last Secret War: An Inside Story of Pyongyang's Strategic Thinking and New Foreign Policy Making," in Asian Crisis in the United States (Univ Press of Am, 00). **CONTACT ADDRESS** Dept Hist & Geog, Univ of Central Oklahoma, 100 N University Dr, Edmond, OK 73034-5207. **EMAIL** bli@ucok.edu

LI, CHU-TSING
PERSONAL Born 05/26/1920, Canton, China, m, 2 children **DISCIPLINE** ART HISTORY **EDUCATION** Univ Nanking, BA, 43; State Univ Iowa, MA, 49, PhD(Art hist), 55. **CAREER** Instr and cur prints and slides, Art Dept, State Univ Iowa, 54-55; actg asst prof fine arts, Oberlin Col, 55-56; from instr to prof hist of art, Univ Iowa, 56-66; chmn dept, 72-78, prof, 66-78, Judith Harris Murphy Distinguished Prof Hist of Art, Univ Kans, 78-, Ford Found training and res fel Orient art, Harvard Univ and Princeton Univ, 59-60; Am Coun Learned Soc and Soc Sci Res Coun res grants Chinese art, Far East, 63-64; Fulbright-Hays Ctr fac fel, 68-69; vis prof fine arts, Chinese Univ Hong Kong, 72-73; dir, Nat Endowment for Humanities summer sem on Chinese art hist, 75 and 78; res cur orient art, William Rockhill Nelson Gallery Art, 66- **MEMBERSHIPS** Col Art Asn Am; Asn Asian Studies; Midwest Art Hist Soc; Asia Soc. **RESEARCH** History of Yuan Dynasty painting; contemporary Chinese art; history of Kwangtung painting. **SELECTED PUBLICATIONS** Auth, Recent Studies on Zhao Mengfu Painting in China, Artibus Asiae, Vol 0053, 93. **CONTACT ADDRESS** Dept of Art Hist, Univ of Kansas, Lawrence, Lawrence, KS 66045.

LIBBY, JUSTIN
PERSONAL Born 12/04/1937, Cincinnati, OH, m, 1965, 2 children **DISCIPLINE** HISTORY **EDUCATION** Univ Cincinnati, BA, 65; MA, 66; Mich State Univ, PhD, 71. **CAREER** Assoc Prof, Ind Univ, 69-. **HONORS AND AWARDS** Res Fels, Ind Univ. **MEMBERSHIPS** U S Naval Inst, Naval Intelligence Professionals, Marine Corp Asn, Soc for Military Hist. **RESEARCH** Diplomatic relations between the United States and Japan, the Naval-Marine war in the Pacific 1941-1945. **SELECTED PUBLICATIONS** Auth, "The Search for a Negotiated Peace: Japanese Diplomats Attempt to Surrender Japan Prior to the Bombing of Hiroshima and Nagasaki," World Affairs 156 (93): 35-45; auth, "Rendezvous with Disaster: There Never Was a Chance for Peace in American-Japanese Relations 1941," World Affairs 158 (96): 137-147; auth, "Pan Am Gets a Pacific Partner," Naval Hist 13 (99): 24-28. **CONTACT ADDRESS** Dept Hist, Indiana Univ-Purdue Univ, Indianapolis, 1100 W Michigan St, Indianapolis, IN 46202-5208. **EMAIL** jhlibby@iupui.edu

LIBO, KENNETH HAROLD
PERSONAL Born 12/04/1937, Norwich, CT **DISCIPLINE** JEWISH AMERICAN STUDIES **EDUCATION** Dartmouth Col, BA, 59; Hunter Col, MA, 68; City Univ NYork Grad Ctr, PhD(Eng), 74. **CAREER** Asst prof Eng, City Col, City Univ NY, 71-78; ED, Jewish Daily Forward, 78-; Natl Museum of Am Jewish Hist, 86-89; Museum of Jewish Heritage, 89-92. **HONORS AND AWARDS** Nat Bk Awd, Am Acad & Inst Arts & Lett, 77. **MEMBERSHIPS** Gomez Foundation **RESEARCH** Jewish immigration; Lower East Side; Am Jewish Hist. **SELECTED PUBLICATIONS** Auth, World of Our Fathers, Harcourt Brace Jovanovich, 76; How We Lived, Richard Marek Publ, 79; We Lived There Too, St. Martin's Press, 84; All in a Life Time, John Loeb Publishers, 96; auth, "One Seixao-Kursheedts: Champions of Early American Judaism, American Jewish Historical Society, 00. **CONTACT ADDRESS** 365 W 20th St, New York, NY 10011. **EMAIL** kenlibo@aol.com

LIDDLE, WILLIAM D.
PERSONAL Born 08/31/1937, Nashville, TN, m, 1958, 2 children **DISCIPLINE** HISTORY **EDUCATION** George Peabody Col, BA, 59; Claremont Grad School, MA, 61, PhD, 70. **CAREER** Vis asst prof, Univ of Tenn, summer 74; Instr to Prof, 62-99, Dir of Grad Studies, Dept of Hist, Southwest Tes

State Univ, 95-. **HONORS AND AWARDS** Woodrow Wilson Nat Fel, 59-60; presidential scholar, 81, honors prof of the Year, Southwest Tex State Univ, 97. **MEMBERSHIPS** AAUP; Org of Am Historians; Southern Hist Asn; Soc of Historians of the Earlly Republic; Am Soc for 18th Century Studies; Asn of the Omohundro; Inst of Early Am Hist and Culture; Tex Fac Asn. **RESEARCH** Eighteenth-Century America; intellectual history of the Eighteenth-Century. **SELECTED PUBLICATIONS** Auth, Virtue and Liberty: An Inquiry into the Role of the Agrarian Mythin the Rhetoric of the American Revolutionary Era, South Atlantic Quart, 78; A Patriot King or None: Lord Bolingbroke and the American Renunciation of George III, J of Am Hist, 79; Edmund S. Morgan, The Dictionary of Literary Bio. **CONTACT ADDRESS** Dept of Hist, Southwest Texas State Univ, San Marcos, TX 78666. **EMAIL** wl01@swt.edu

LIDTKE, VERNON LEROY
PERSONAL Born 05/04/1930, Avon, SD, m, 1951 **DISCIPLINE** MODERN EUROPEAN HISTORY **EDUCATION** Univ OR, BA, 52, MA, 55; Univ CA, Berkeley, PhD, 62. **CAREER** Instr, High Sch, OR, 53-55; assoc soc sci, Univ CA, Berkeley, 60-62; from asst prof to assoc prof Europ hist, MI State Univ, 62-68; assoc prof, 68-73, chmn dept hist, 75-79, prof Europ hist, Johns Hopkins Univ, 73-, Nat Endowment for Hum younger scholar fel, 69-70; fel, Davis Ctr Hist Studies, Princeton Univ, 74-75; vis scholar, Humboldt Universitat, Berlin, Ger Democratic Repub, 5-6/86; fel, Wissenschaftskolleg zu Berlin (Inst Advan Study, Berlin), 87-88; fel, Max-Planck-Instut fur Geschichte, Gottingen, summer 96; mem exec coun, Conf Group Ger Polit, 75-80; chmn, Conf Group Central Europ Hist, 86; pres, Friends Ger Hist Inst, 91-94; chair, Mod Europ Sect, Am Hist Assoc, 92. **HONORS AND AWARDS** Awd for Excellence in Tchg, Johns Hopkins Univ, 4/97; Eugene Asher Distinguished Teaching Awd, Am Hist Assoc, 99; **MEMBERSHIPS** AHA; Conf Group Cent Europ Hist (secy-treas, 72-74); Conf Group Ger Polit. **RESEARCH** Mod Ger; Europ soc movements; popular cult of Central Europe. **SELECTED PUBLICATIONS** Auth, The Outlawed Party: Social Democracy in Germany, 1878-1890, Princeton Univ, 66; Revisionismus, Sowjetsystem und Demokratische, Ges, 71; contribr, Kultureller Wandel im 19 Jahrhundert, Vandenhoeck & Ruprecht, 73; auth, Naturalism and socialism in Germany, Am Hist Rev, 2/74; contribr, Storio del Marxismo Contemporaneo, Feltrinelli, 74; auth, Songs and politics: An exploratory essay on Arbeiterlieder in the Weimar Republic, Archiv fur Sozialgeschichte, 74; Lieder der deutschen Arbeiterbewegung, 1864-1914, Geschichte und Gesellschaft, 79; Social class and secularization in Imperial Germany: The working classes, In: Yearbook of the Leo Baeck Institute, Vol XXV, 80; Songs and Nazis: Political music and social change in Twentieth-Century Germany, In: Essays on Culture and Society in Modern Germany, Tex A M Press, 82; The Alternative Culture: Socialist Labor in Imperial Germany, Oxford Univ Press, 85; Recent literature on worker's culture in Germany and England, In: Arbeiter und Arbeiterbewegung im Vergleich, Berichte zur internationalen historischen Forschung, Historische Zeitschrift, Oldenbourg Verlag, 86; Twentieth-Century Germany: The cultural, social, and political context of the work of Oskar Schlemmer, In: Oskar Schlemmer, Baltimore Mus Art, 86; Burghers, workers and problems of class relationships 1870 to 1914: German comparative perspective, In: Arbeiter und Burger im 19 Jahrhundert, Varianten ihres Verhaltinisses im europaischen Vergleich, Oldenbourg Verlag, 86; Cahtolics and politics in Nineteenth-Century Germany, Central Europ Hist, 3/86; Museen und die Zeitgenossische Kunst in der Weimarer Republik, In: Sammler, mazene und Mussen, Kunstforderung in Deutschland im 19 un 20 jahrhundert, Bohlau Verlag, 93; The Socialist labor movement, In: Imperial Germany: A Historigraphical Companion, Greenwood Press, 96. **CONTACT ADDRESS** Dept of Hist, Johns Hopkins Univ, Baltimore, 3400 N Charles St, Baltimore, MD 21218-2680. **EMAIL** lidtke@jhu.edu

LIEBERMAN, STEPHEN JACOB
PERSONAL Born 03/21/1943, Minneapolis, MN **DISCIPLINE** ASSYRIOLOGY, LINGUISTICS **EDUCATION** Univ Minn, BA, 63; Harvard Univ, PhD(Near Eastern lang), 72. **CAREER** From asst prof to assoc prof Near Eastern studies, New York Univ, 71-75; res specialist, Sumerian Dict, Univ Mus, Univ Pa, 76-79; Assoc Prof Assyriol and Semitic Ling, Dropsie Univ, 82-, Fel Mesopotamian civilization, Baghdad Ctr Comt, Am Schs Orient Res, 70-71; Nat Endowment for Humanities fel, 75-76; Guggenheim fel, 79-80; Inaugural fel, Found for Mesopotamian Studies, 80- **MEMBERSHIPS** Am Orient Soc; AHA; Archaeol Inst Am; Ling Soc Am; NAm Conf Afro-Asiatic Ling. **RESEARCH** Sumerian and Akkadian languages and cultures; Semitic linguistics; Mesopotamian history. **SELECTED PUBLICATIONS** Auth, Bar Ilan Studies in Assyriology Dedicated to Artzi, Pinhas, J Amer Oriental Soc, Vol 0112, 92. **CONTACT ADDRESS** Dept Assyriol and Semitic Ling, Dropsie Univ, Philadelphia, PA 19132.

LIEBERSOHN, HARRY
DISCIPLINE HISTORY **EDUCATION** New Col, BA, 73, Princeton Univ, MA,75; PhD, 79. **CAREER** Prof, Hist, Univ Ill. **RESEARCH** European cultural and intellectual history; history of the social sciences. **SELECTED PUBLICATIONS** Auth, Fate and Utopia in German Sociology 1870-1923, MIT Press, 88; auth, Gemeinschaft und Gesellschaft, in Lars Clausen and Carsten Schluter, 91; auth, Introduction in Crossing Cultrues: Essays in the Displacement of Western Civilization, Tucson and London, 92; auth, "Troeltsch's Social Teachings and the Protestant Social Congress," Friedrich Wilhelm Graf and Trutz Rendtorff, Gutersloh: Mohn, (93), 241-257; auth, " Weber's Historical Concept of National Identity," Hartmut Lehmann and Guenther Roth, Farewell to the Protestant Ethic, New York: Cambridge, (93),123-131; auth, " Selective Affinities: Three Generations of German Intellectuals," Rediscovering Hist: Culture, Politics, and the Psyche, (93), 30-39; auth, "Discovering Indigenous Nobility: Tocqueville, Chamisso, and Romantic Travel Writing," Am Hist Rev, (94), 746-766; auth, Aristocratic Encounters: European Tavelers and North Amercan Indians, Cambridge Univ Press, 98; auth, "Images of Monarchy: Kamehameha I and the Art of Louis Choris," Double Vision: Art hist and Colonial Hist in the Pacific, (99), 44-64. **CONTACT ADDRESS** History Dept, Univ of Illinois, Urbana-Champaign, 810 S Wright St, 309 Gregory Hall, Champaign, IL 61820. **EMAIL** hliebersohn@cs.com

LIEDL, JANICE
DISCIPLINE HISTORY **EDUCATION** Purdue Univ, BA, 85; Univ of Toronto, MA, 86; PhD, 91. **CAREER** Assoc prof. **SELECTED PUBLICATIONS** Co-ed, Love and Death in the Renaissance, Ottawa: Dovehouse Press, 91; auth, "The Penitent Pilgrim: William Calverley and the Pilgrimage of Grace," The Sixteenth Century Journal 25:3, (94): 585-594. **CONTACT ADDRESS** Dept of History, Laurentian Univ, 935 Ramsey Lake Rd, Sudbury, ON, Canada P3E 2C6. **EMAIL** jliedl@nickel.laurentian.ca

LIENHARD, JOSEPH T.
PERSONAL Born 05/07/1940, Bronx, NY, s **DISCIPLINE** HISTORICAL THEOLOGY **EDUCATION** Fordham Univ, BA, MA,; Woodstock Col, PhL, BD, STM; Freiburg Dr Theol Habil. **CAREER** Prof, 90, Fordham Univ. **RESEARCH** Augustine's late works. **SELECTED PUBLICATIONS** Auth, The Bible, the Church, and Authority: The Canon of the Christian Bible, Hist and Theol, Collegeville, 95; transl, Gospel according to Luke, Origen: Homilies on Luke; Fragments on Luke, Wash, 96. **CONTACT ADDRESS** Dept of Theol, Fordham Univ, 441 E Fordham Rd, New York, NY 10458. **EMAIL** lienhard@fordham.edu

LIFKA, MARY L.
PERSONAL Born 10/31/1937, Oak Park, IL, s **DISCIPLINE** HISTORY **EDUCATION** Mundelein Col, BA, 60; Loyola Univ, MA, 65; Univ Mich, PhD, 74. **CAREER** High School teacher, Bellarmine-Jefferson High School, 60-65; assoc instr, Clarke Col, 65-76; assoc prof, Mundelein Col, 76-84; prof, Col of St Teresa, 84-89; prof, Lewis Univ, 89-. **HONORS AND AWARDS** Danforth Found, Ford Found, Rackham grants, 70-74; SPID and Title IV grants, 80; Cadero Excellence in Scholarship Awd, 98. **MEMBERSHIPS** Am Hist Asn, Phi Alpha Theta. **RESEARCH** Cognition and history teaching-learning, modern Europe, history of women. **SELECTED PUBLICATIONS** Auth, "Jihad vs McWorld," Salt, 24 (spring 96): 23; auth, "Convergence versus Diffusion," Listening: A J of Religion and Culture, 33 (spring 98): 83-89; ed, Listening: A J of Relig and Culture, 33 (spring 98); rev of Women and Political Insurgency: France in the Mid-Nineteenth Century by David Berry in the Historian, 60 (summer 98): 894-895; auth, "Primary Documents in Teaching European History," Proceedings of Am Hist Asn 2000, Ann Arbor: UMC (forthcoming 2000); ed, A History of Mundelein College, Chicago: Loyola Univ Press-Wild Onion Books (forthcoming 2001). **CONTACT ADDRESS** Dept Hist, Lewis Univ, 500 S Independence Blvd, Romeoville, IL 60446-2231. **EMAIL** lifkama@lewisu.edu

LIFSHITZ, FELICE
PERSONAL Born 09/21/1959, New York, NY, m, 1994, 1 child **DISCIPLINE** MEDIEVAL HISTORY **EDUCATION** Barnard Col, BA, 81; Columbia Univ, MA, 83; MPhil, 84; PhD, 88. **CAREER** Preceptor, Columbia Univ, 84-86; vis asst prof, Trinity Col, 88-89; vis fel, Pontif Inst of Medieval Studies, 93; from asst prof to prof, Fla Int Univ, 95-; guest researcher, Univ of Freiburg, 97; guest prof, Univ of Frankfurt, 98; guest researcher, Austrian Acad of Sci, 99. **HONORS AND AWARDS** Alexander von Humboldt Stiftung Fel; State of Fla Teaching Incentive Prog Awd for Excellence in Teaching; Pontif Inst of Medieval Studies Vis Fel; Columbia Univ President's Fel; Columia Univ Traveling Fel. **MEMBERSHIPS** Medieval Acad of Am; Int Ctr of Medieval Art, Soc for Medieval Feminist Scholar, Int Soc for Intellectual Hist, Hagiography Soc, Arbeitskreis fur Hagiographische Fragen, Haskins Soc. **RESEARCH** Historiography and Representations of the Past, Religion, Women, Gender. **SELECTED PUBLICATIONS** Auth, "Dudo's Historical Narrative and the Norman Succession of 996," J of Medieval Hist 20 (94): 101-120; auth, "Beyond Positivism and Genre: hagiographical Texts as Historical Narrative," Viator 25 (94): 95-113; auth, "The Migration of Neustrian Relics in the Viking Age: The Myth of Voluntary Exodus, the Reality of Coersion and Theft," Early Medieval Europe 4 (95): 175-192; auth, The Norman Conquest of Pious Neustria: Historiographic Discourse and Saintly Relics (684-1090), Pontifical Inst of Mediaeval Studies Press, 95; auth, "Is Mother Superior? Towards a History of Feminine Amtscharisma," in Medieval Mothering (The New Middle Ages 3), eds. Bonnie Wheeler and John Carmi Parsons (NY: Garland Pub, 96), 117-138; auth, "The Politics of Historiography: The Memory of Bishops in Eleventh-Century Rouen," Hist and memory 10 (98): 118-137; auth, "La Normandie carolingienne. Essai sur la continuite, avec utilisation de sources negliges," Annales de Normandie 48 (98): 505-524; auth, "Bede's Martyrologium: Translation and Historical Introduction," in Medieval Hagiography: A Sourcebook, ed. Thomas Head (NY, 00), 169-198. **CONTACT ADDRESS** Dept Hist, Florida Intl Univ, Miami, FL 33199-0001. **EMAIL** lifshitz@fiu.edu

LIGHTMAN, BERNARD V.
PERSONAL Born 04/30/1950, Toronto, ON, Canada, m, 1975, 2 children **DISCIPLINE** HISTORY **EDUCATION** York Univ, BA, 73; MA, 74; Brandeis Univ, PhD, 79. **CAREER** Asst Prof, Queen's Univ, 79-83; Asst Prof, Univ Ore, 83-87; Asst Prof to Prof, York Univ, 87-. **MEMBERSHIPS** Hist of Sci Soc; Can Soc for the Hist and Philos of Sci. **RESEARCH** History of Victorian Science. **SELECTED PUBLICATIONS** Co-ed, Victorian Faith in Crisis, Macmillan, 90; ed, Victorian Science in Context, Univ Chicago Press, 97. **CONTACT ADDRESS** Dept Humanities, York Univ, 4700 Keele St, Toronto, ON, Canada L3T 4X3. **EMAIL** lightman@yorku.ca

LIGHTNER, DAVID LEE
PERSONAL Born 05/13/1942, Bethlehem, PA **DISCIPLINE** AMERICAN HISTORY **EDUCATION** Pa State Univ, BA, 63; Univ Pa, AM, 64; Cornell Univ, PhD, 69. **CAREER** From instr to asst prof, Univ Ill, Chicago, 69-70; asst prof, St Olaf Col, 70-74; res asst, Inst of Soc Hist, CUNY, 74-75; vist asst prof, Univ Conn, Storrs, 75-77; from asst to assoc prof, Univ Alberta, 77-. **MEMBERSHIPS** AHA; Orgn Am Historians; Econ Hist Asn; Can Asn Univ Teachers. **RESEARCH** American economic history; labor and business; nineteenth century. **SELECTED PUBLICATIONS** Auth, Labor on the Illinois Central Railroad, 1852-1900: The Evolution of an Industrial Environment, in Dissertations in American Economic History, ed Stuart Bruchey, Arno Pr/NY Times (New York, NY), 77; auth, "Abraham Lincoln and the Ideal of Equality," in American Vistas, 1607-1877, ed Leonard Dinnerstein and Kenneth T. Jackson, 6th ed (NY: Oxford univ Pr, 91) 326-341; auth, "Managing Madness," Can Rev of Am Studs, 26 (Winter 96): 147-158; auth, "Ten Million Acres for the Insane: The Forgotten Collaboration of Dorothea L. Dix and William H. Bissell," Ill Hist J 89 (Spring 96): 17-34; auth, "William Henry Bissell," Am Nat Biog, 99; auth, Asylum, Prison, and Poorhouse: The Writings and Reform Work of Dorothea Dix in Illinois, Southern Ill Univ Pr (Carbondale, Ill) 99. **CONTACT ADDRESS** Dept Hist & Classics, Univ of Alberta, 2-28 Henry Marshall Tory Bldg, Edmonton, AB, Canada T6G 2H4. **EMAIL** david.lightner@ualberta.ca

LIGHTNER, ROBERT P.
PERSONAL Born 04/04/1931, Cleona, PA, m, 1952, 3 children **DISCIPLINE** THEOLOGY, MODERN HISTORY **EDUCATION** Baptist Bible Col, Sem, 55; Dallas Theol Sem, ThM, 59, ThD, 64; Southern Methodist Univ, MLA, 72. **CAREER** Instructor, 59-61; Asst Prof, Chairman, 63-66; Assoc Prof, 67-68; Asst Prof, 68-74; Assoc Prof, 74-84; Prof, 84-98; Prof Emer, 98-; Adjunct Prof, 84-. **HONORS AND AWARDS** Who's Who in Am Educ, 70; Outstanding Educators of Am, and Community Leaders of Am; Outstanding Alumnus of the Year 2000 Baptist Bible Col; started churches in ny and ar; pastor and interim pastor in ny, pa, ar, ok, la, and tx; mission trips to paraguay, venezuela, and peru. **MEMBERSHIPS** Grace Evangelical Soc; Conservative Theol Soc; Pre-Trib Study Group. **RESEARCH** Pre-millennial, A-millennial, and post-millennial theology. **SELECTED PUBLICATIONS** Auth, The Toungues Tied, Speaking in Tongues and Divine Healing; The Death Christ Died: A Case for Unlimited Atonement; Prophecy in the Ring; Truth for the Good Life; James: Apostle of Practical Christianity; The God of the Bible; The Saviour and the Scriptures; Triumph though Tragedy; Neo-Liberalism; Neo-Evangelicalism Today; Church-Union: A Layman's Guide; The God of the Bible and other gods; Last Days Handbook; author of numerous other publications and articles. **CONTACT ADDRESS** 324 Clear Springs Dr, Mesquite, TX 75150-0000.

LIGIBEL, THEODORE J.
PERSONAL Born 07/31/1949, Toledo, OH, m, 1977, 1 child **DISCIPLINE** HISTORIC PRESERVATION **EDUCATION** Univ Toledo, BA, 72; Bowling Green State Univ, MA, 81; Bowling Green State Univ, PhD, 95. **CAREER** Res assoc, Univ Toledo, 85-91; assoc prof, prof, East Michigan Univ, 91-; dir, 99-. **HONORS AND AWARDS** Who's Who Am Edu; HSM Merit Awd; Ohio Sen Resolu. **MEMBERSHIPS** NTHP; VAF; Phi Kappa Phi; PAS. **RESEARCH** Historic preservation; cultural landscapes; recent past; historic architecture. **SELECTED PUBLICATIONS** Auth, "Utilizing Library Resources: A Bibliographic Essay," in Public History: An Introduction, Kneger Pub, 86; auth, "Finding Common Ground: Whole Places New Possibilities," Forum 6 (92); coauth, "Lights Along the River: Landmark Architecture of the Maumee River Valley," Maumee Val Hist Soc (83); coauth, Island Heritage: A Guided Tour to Lake Erie's Bass Islands, Ohio State Univ Press (Columbus, OH), 87; auth, "Clark Lake Images of a Michigan Tradition," Clark Lake Hist Preser Comm (91); auth, The

Toledo ZooÛs First One Hundred Years: A Century of Adventure, Donning Co Pub (Vir Beach, VA), 99. **CONTACT ADDRESS** Dept Geography, Eastern Michigan Univ, 233 Strong Hall, Ypsilanti, MI 48197. **EMAIL** ted.ligibel@emich.edu

LIGO, LARRY L.
DISCIPLINE ART HISTORY **EDUCATION** Muskingum Col, AB; Princeton Sem, BD; Univ NC Chapel Hill, PhD. **CAREER** Prof, Davidson Col. **RESEARCH** 19th-century Europ painting; Edouard Manet; early 20th-century painting and sculpt (1890-1945); the hist of photography; mod archit. **SELECTED PUBLICATIONS** Auth, The Concept of Function in 20th Century Architectural Criticism; articles in Arts Magazine and Gazette des Beaux-Arts. **CONTACT ADDRESS** Dept Art, Davidson Col, 102 N Main St, PO Box 1719, Davidson, NC 28036. **EMAIL** laligo@davidson.edu

LIGON, DORIS HILLIAN
PERSONAL Born 04/28/1936, Baltimore, MD, m, 1955, 2 children **DISCIPLINE** AFRICAN HISTORY, ART HISTORY **EDUCATION** Morgan State Univ, BA Sociology (Summa Cum Laude) 1978, MA Art Hist/Museology 1979; Howard Univ, PhD courses African Hist. **CAREER** Natl Museum of African Art Smithsonian Inst, docent (tour guide), 76-88; Morgan State Univ, art gallery rsch asst 78-79; Howard Cty MD School Syst, Consultant African Art & Culture 80-; MD Museum of African Art, Founder/Exec Dir 80-. **HONORS AND AWARDS** Goldseeker Fellowship for Graduate Studies MSU 1978-79; Phi Alpha Theta (Natl History Hon Soc); Alpha Kappa Mu; Nirmaj K Sinha Awd for highest honors in Sociology 1978. **MEMBERSHIPS** Mem Assn Black Women Historians, African-American Museums Assn; charter mem Eubie Blake Cultural Center 1984; charter mem Columbia (MD) Chap Pierians Inc 1983; mem Morgan State Univ Alumni; mem NAACP; mem Urban League; mem Arts Council of the African Studies Assn. **CONTACT ADDRESS** African Art Museum of Maryland, 5430 Vantage Point Rd., POB 1105, Columbia, MD 21044. **EMAIL** africanantmuseum@erols.com

LILLIBRIDGE, GEORGE DONALD
PERSONAL Born 07/20/1921, Mitchell, SD, m, 1943, 4 children **DISCIPLINE** AMERICAN HISTORY **EDUCATION** Univ SDak, AB, 42; Univ Wis, MA, 48, PhD(hist), 51. **CAREER** Instr hist, State Univ NY Teachers Col Albany, 50-52; from asst prof to assoc prof, 52-65, Prof Hist, Calif State Univ, Chico, 65-, Chmn Dept, 73-. **MEMBERSHIPS** AHA; Orgn Am Historians. **RESEARCH** The American impact abroad. **SELECTED PUBLICATIONS** Auth, Beacon of Freedom, the Impact of American Democracy on Great Britain, Univ Pa, 55, A S Barnes, 61; The American impact abroad, Am Scholar, winter 65-66; The American Image: Past and Present, Heath, 68; Images of American Society: A History of the United States (2 vols), Houghton Mifflin, 76. **CONTACT ADDRESS** Dept of Hist, California State Univ, Chico, Chico, CA 95929.

LIMBAUGH, RONALD H.
DISCIPLINE HISTORY **EDUCATION** Col ID, BA, 60, MA, 62, PhD, 67. **CAREER** Prof, Univ Pacific. **SELECTED PUBLICATIONS** Auth, John Muir's Stickeen, Univ Alaska; Lessons of Nature, Univ Alaska. **CONTACT ADDRESS** Hist Dept, Univ of the Pacific, Stockton, Pacific Ave, PO Box 3601, Stockton, CA 95211.

LIMERICK, PATRICIA NELSON
DISCIPLINE HISTORY **EDUCATION** Univ Calif Santa Cruz, BA, 72; Yale Univ, PhD, 80. **CAREER** Lectr, Univ Calif, 70-71; vis asst prof, 71-73, asst prof, 73-78, assoc prof, Univ Colo, 78-. **SELECTED PUBLICATIONS** Auth, The Adventures of the Frontier in the Twentieth Century, Univ Calif, 94; Turnerians All: The Hope for a Helpful History in an Intelligible World, Am Hist Rev, 95; Reason and Region, Johns Hopkins, 95; The Shadows of Heaven Itself, Norton, 97. **CONTACT ADDRESS** History Dept, Univ of Colorado, Boulder, Boulder, CO 80309. **EMAIL** limerick@stripe.colorado.edu

LIN, YU-SHENG
PERSONAL Born 08/07/1934, Mukden, China, m, 1966, 2 children **DISCIPLINE** CHINESE INTELLECTUAL HISTORY **EDUCATION** Nat Taiwan Univ, AB, 58; Univ Chicago, PhD, 70. **CAREER** Vis asst prof hist, 66-67, acting asst prof, 67-68, Univ Va; asst prof, Univ Ore, 68-69; Soc Sci Res Coun & Am Coun Learned Soc res fel, EAsian Res Ctr, Harvard Univ, 69-70; asst prof, 70-75, assoc prof, 75-81, prof hist & E Asian lang & lit Univ Wis, Madison, 81-. **MEMBERSHIPS** Life Member, Academia Sinica, 94-. **RESEARCH** The Chinese Ideas of Political Order from the Neolithic Age to the End of Mao: A comparative approach **SELECTED PUBLICATIONS** Auth, From the Perspective of Civil Society (in Chinese), Taipei: Linking Publishing Co, 98 **CONTACT ADDRESS** Dept of History, Univ of Wisconsin, Madison, 455 North Park St, Madison, WI 53706-1483. **EMAIL** ylin1@facstaff.wisc.edu

LINDBERG, DAVID C.
PERSONAL Born 11/15/1935, Minneapolis, MN, m, 1959, 2 children **DISCIPLINE** HISTORY OF SCIENCE **EDUCATION** Wheaton Col, BS, 57; NWestern Univ, MS, 59; Ind Univ, PhD, 65. **CAREER** Asst Prof, Univ Mich, 65-67; Asst Prof to Hilldale Prof, Univ Wis, 67-, Dir, Inst Res Humanities, 87-93. **HONORS AND AWARDS** Guggenheim Fel, 77-78; Fel, Medieval Acad Am; Fel, Am Acad Arts & Sci; Fel, Int Acad Hist Sci; Watson Davis Bk Prize of the Hist Sci Soc, for: "The Beginnings of Western Science.."; Sarton Medal of the Hist of Science Soc, (for lifetime scholarly achievement), 99. **MEMBERSHIPS** Hist Sci Soc (pres 94-95); British Soc Hist Sci; Medieval Acad Am; Renaissance Soc Am. **RESEARCH** Medieval and early modern science. **SELECTED PUBLICATIONS** Auth, Theories of Vision from al-Kindi to Kepler, Univ Chicago Press, 76; auth, Roger Bacon's Philosophy of Nature, Claredon Press, 83; co-ed, God and Nature: Historical Essays on the Encounter between Christianity and Science, Univ of Calif Press, 86; auth, The Beginnings of Western Science: The European Scientific Tradition in Philosophical, Religious, and Institutional Context, 600 B.C. - A.D. 1450, Univ Chicago Press, 92; auth, Roger Bacon and the Origins of Perspectiva in the Middle Ages: A Critical Edition and English Translation of Bacon's Perspectiva, with Introduction and Notes, Clarendon Press, 96; coed, The Cambridge History of Science, 8 vols, Cambridge Univ Press (forthcoming); auth, Science and the Christian Tradition: Twelve Case Histories, Univ Chicago Press (forthcoming). **CONTACT ADDRESS** History Dept, Univ of Wisconsin, Madison, 5038 Marathon Dr., Madison, WI 53705. **EMAIL** dclindbe@facstaff.wisc.edu

LINDEMANN, ALBERT S.
PERSONAL Born 05/19/1938, Santa Monica, CA, m, 1963, 2 children **DISCIPLINE** MODERN EUROPEAN HISTORY **EDUCATION** Pomona Col, BA, 60; Harvard Univ, MA, 62, PhD(hist), 68. **CAREER** Instr hist Western civilization, Stanford Univ, 65-66; asst prof, 69-73, Assoc Prof Hist, Univ Calif, Santa Barbara, 73-; Full Prof, 82-00. **HONORS AND AWARDS** Distinguished Teacher, UCSB Academic Senate Awd, 93. **MEMBERSHIPS** AHA **RESEARCH** History of Anti-semitism. **SELECTED PUBLICATIONS** Auth, The Red Years: Bolshevison vs. European Socialism, 1919-21; UC Press, 74; auth, A History of European Socialism, Yale Univ Press, 83; auth, The Jew Accused, Cambridge Univ Press, 91; auth, On Socialists and the Jewish Question After Marx, Cent Europ Hist, Vol 0025, 92; Jews and the German State--the Political History of a Minority, 1848-1933, Cent Europ Hist, Vol 0026, 93; Marxist Intellectuals and the Working Class Mentality in Germany, 1887-1912, Cent Europ Hist, Vol 0027, 94; The British Labor Party and the German Social Democrats, 1900-1931--a Comparative Study, Cent Europ Hist, Vol 0029, 96; Esau's Tears: Modern Anti-Semitism & The Rise of the Jews (Cambridge Univ Press 97); Anti-Semitism Before the Holocaust (Longman, 00). **CONTACT ADDRESS** Dept of Hist, Univ of California, Santa Barbara, 552 University Rd, Santa Barbara, CA 93106-0001. **EMAIL** lindeman@humanities.ucsb.edu

LINDENFELD, DAVID FRANK
PERSONAL Born 01/25/1944, Bethlehem, PA **DISCIPLINE** GERMAN HISTORY, EUROPEAN INTELLECTUAL HISTORY **EDUCATION** Princeton Univ, AB, 65; Harvard Univ, MAT, 66; Univ Chicago, PhD, 73. **CAREER** Lectr, Univ Chicago, 69; asst prof, Ohio State Univ, 72-74; asst prof, 74-80, assoc prof, 80-97, prof hist, LA State Univ, 97-. **MEMBERSHIPS** Am Hist Assoc, German Stud Assoc, World Hist Assoc. **RESEARCH** Theory and philosophy of history. **SELECTED PUBLICATIONS** Contribr, Jenseits von Sein und Nichtsein, Akad Druck-und Verlagsanstalt, 72; auth, Oswald Kulpe and the Wurzburg School, J Hist Behav Sci, 78; The Transformation of Positivism, Alexius Meinong and European Thought 1880-1920, Univ Calif, 80; On Systems and Embodiments as Categories for Intel History, Hist & Theory, 88; The Myth of the Older German Historical School of Economics, Cent Europ Hist, 93; The Practical Imagination, The German Sciences of State in the Nineteenth Century, Univ Chicago, 97; The Prevalence of Irrational Thinking in the Third Reich, Cent Europ Hist, 98. **CONTACT ADDRESS** Dept Hist, Louisiana State Univ and A&M Col, Baton Rouge, LA 70803. **EMAIL** hylind@lsu.edu

LINDENMEYER, KRISTE A.
PERSONAL Born 04/11/1955, Cincinnati, OH, m, 1978, 3 children **DISCIPLINE** HISTORY **EDUCATION** Univ Cincinnati, BA, 85; MA, 87; PhD, 91. **CAREER** Adj Asst Prof, Univ Cincinnati, 91; Adj Assoc Prof, Vanderbilt Univ, 97-98; Asst Prof to Assoc Prof, Tenn Tech Univ, 91-00; Assoc Prof, Univ Md, 00-. **HONORS AND AWARDS** Outstanding Fac Teaching Awd, Tenn Technol Univ, 94-95; Innovative Teaching Awd, Tenn Technol Univ, 98-99; Innovation Awd, Tenn Board of Regents distance Educ committee, 99-00; Res Sabbaticals, Tenn Technol Univ, 00; Best Book, Univ of Cincinnati Hist Dept Prize, 99. **MEMBERSHIPS** Org of Am Hist, Am Hist Asn, Soc for Hist of the Gilded Age and Progressive Era, H-Net **RESEARCH** US public policy; Women; Childhood; Adolescence. **SELECTED PUBLICATIONS** Auth, A Right to Childhood: The Us Children's Bureau and Child Welfare, 1912-1946, Univ Ill Press, 97; ed, Ordinary women, Extraordinary Lives: Women in American History, Scholarly Resources, forthcoming; co-ed, Reach or Breach?: The State and society in the US, Greenwood Press, forthcoming; co-auth, The American Challenge, Longman Pub, forthcoming; auth, "When government Became Children's Advocate," in Connect for Kids Website, Benton Foundation, 99; auth, "Women's Christian Temperance Union and Women's Missionary Union," in Tennessee Encyclopedia of History and Culture, Tenn Hist Soc, 98; auth, "Winning the War, But Losing the Peace: the US Children's Bureau and Child Welfare During World War II," Queen City Heritage, (96): 34-47; auth, "Child Labor," in Encyclopedia of the United States in the Nineteenth Century, Scribner and Sons, forthcoming; auth, "Children and the Law," in Encyclopedia of Chicago History, forthcoming; auth, "Adolescence," in The Family in the United States, Colonial Times to the present: An Encyclopedia, forthcoming; auth, "Children's Bureau," in The Family in the United State, Colonial Times to the Present: An Encyclopedia, forthcoming. **CONTACT ADDRESS** Dept Hist, Tennessee Tech Univ, 1000 N Dixie Ave, Cookeville, TN 38505-0001. **EMAIL** klindenmeyer@tntech.edu

LINDENMEYR, ADELE
PERSONAL Born 09/16/1949, New York, NY, s, 1 child **DISCIPLINE** HISTORY **EDUCATION** Univ Penn, BA, 71, Princeton Univ, PhD, 80. **CAREER** Asst prof, Carnegie Mellon Univ, 80-86; prof, Villanova Univ, 87-. **HONORS AND AWARDS** Am Philos Soc Research grant,98; Heldt Prize, 96; Heldt Prize, 93; Nat Edowment for the Humanities grant, 93; Am Counof Learned Soc Fel, 91-92; Kennan Inst for Adv Russian Studies, 92; Nat Endowment for the Humanities, 91; Intl Res and Exchanges Board, res grant, 76-77; Woodrow Wilson Nat Fel, 71-72; Phi Beta Kappa, royal Soc of Arts, Silver Medal, 71; Goddard Awd, Univ Penn, 71. **MEMBERSHIPS** Am Hist Asn. **RESEARCH** Russian history, Women's history, Modern European social and cultural history. **SELECTED PUBLICATIONS** Auth, "Trends in the Writing and Teaching of History in the United States Since the 1960s," in Politoloiia I mezhdunarodnye otnosheniia v sovremennoi vyschei shkole, Novgorod, (99): 133-141; auth, "From Repression to Revival: Philanthropy in Twentieth-Century Russia," in Philanthropy in the World's Traditions, Indiana Univ Press, (98): 309-331; auth, "Daughters, Wives, Partners: Women of the Moscow Merchant Elite," Merchant Moscow: Images of Russia's Vanished Bourgeoisie, Princeton Univ Press, (97): 95-108; auth, Poverty is Not a Vice: Charity, Society and the State in Imperial Russia, Princeton Univ Press, 96; auth, "The Rise of Voluntary Associations During the Great Reforms: The Case of Charity," Russias's Great Reforms, 1855-1881: New Perspectives, Ind Univ Press, (94): 264-279; auth, "Maternalism and Child Welfare in Late Imperial Russia," Journal of Women's History, (93): 114-125; auth, "Public Lives, Privtae Virtues: women in Russian Charity, 1752-1914," Signs: Journal of Women in Culture and Society, (93): 562-591; auth, "The Ethos of Charity in Imperial Russia," Journal of Social History, (90): 679-694; auth, "Voluntary Associations and the Russian Autocracy: The Case of Private Charity," The Carl Beck Papers in Russian and East European Studies, 90. **CONTACT ADDRESS** Dept Hist, Villanova Univ, 800 E Lancaster Ave, Villanova, PA 1985-163. **EMAIL** adele.lindenmeyr@villanova.edu

LINDER, ROBERT DEAN
PERSONAL Born 10/06/1934, Salina, KS, m, 1957, 4 children **DISCIPLINE** EUROPEAN HISTORY, HISTORY OF CHRISTIANITY **EDUCATION** Emporia State Univ, BS, 56; Cent Baptist Theol Sem, MDiv, MRE, 58, Univ IA, MA, 60, PhD, 63. **CAREER** Instr western civilization, Univ IA, 58-61; asst prof hist, William Jewell Col, 63-65; from asst prof to assoc prof, 65-73, prof KS State Univ, 73-, Sr res fel, The Centre for the Study of Christianity, Macquarie Univ, Sydney, Australia, 95-, Ed, Fides et Historia, Conf Faith & Hist, 68-78; Mayor, Manhattan, KS, 71-72, 78-79; Dir, Relig Studies Prog, KS State Univ, 79-82. **HONORS AND AWARDS** KS State Univ Distinguished Tchg Awd, 68; Phi Kappa Phi Outstanding Scholar, 1980; Sr Fac Awd for Res Excellence, Inst for Soc & Behav Res, KS State Univ, 97. **MEMBERSHIPS** AHA; Am Soc Church Hist; Am Soc Reformation Res (secy, 71-79); Renaissance Soc Am; Rocky Mountain Soc Sci Asn; Conf Faith & Hist. **RESEARCH** Reformation and Renaissance hist; hist of Christianity; Australian relig hist. **SELECTED PUBLICATIONS** Auth, The Political Ideas of Pierre Viret, Droz, Geneva, 64; co-ed, Protest and Politics: Christianity and Contemporary Politics, Attic, 68; coauth, Calvin and Calvinism: Sources of Democracy?, Heath, 70; ed, God and Caesar: Case Studies in the Relationship between Christianity and the State, Conf Faith & Hist, 71; co-ed, The Cross and the Flag, Creation House, 72; coauth, Politics and Christianity, InterVarsity, 73; co-ed, The Eerdman's Handbook to the History of Christianity, Eerdmans, 77; coauth, Twilight of the Saints: Biblical Christianity and Civil Religion in America, InterVarsity, 78; coauth, Civil Religion and the Presidency, Zonervan, 88; co-ed, The Dictionary of Christianity in America, InterVarsity, 90; co-ed, The History of Christianity, Fortress, 90; co-ed, A Concise Dictionary of Christianity in America, InterVarsity, 95; auth, The Long Tragedy: Australian Evangelical Christians and the Great War, 1914-1918, Open Book Pub, 00. **CONTACT ADDRESS** Dept of Hist, Kansas State Univ, 208 Eisenhower Hall, Manhattan, KS 66506-1002. **EMAIL** rdl@ksu.edu

LINDGREN, C. E.
PERSONAL Born 11/20/1949, Coeburn, VA, s **DISCIPLINE** MEDIEVAL HISTORY, HISTORY OF EDUCATION **EDU-**

CATION Univ Miss, MEd, 77, EdS, 93; Coll of Preceptors, MPhil, 93; UNISA, DEd, 98. **CAREER** Dir, Delta Hills Educ Asn, 76-80; dir, Educ consultants of Oxford, 81-; chm, Hist & Phil of Educ, Greenwitch Univ, 98-; Dean, College of Arts and Humanities, 99-; Faculty Am Military Univ. **HONORS AND AWARDS** Robert A. Taft Fel; EDPA Fel; hon fel, World Jnana Sadhak Soc; assoc IIPS, knighthood, Order of Isnatias of Antioch (Catholic). **MEMBERSHIPS** Royal Soc Arts; Royal Asiatic Soc; Col of Preceptors; Royal Hist Soc; Am Acad Relig; Medieval Acad of Am; PSA; Hist of Ed Soc. **RESEARCH** Egyptology; medieval history; Qu Gong; metagogics; religion. **CONTACT ADDRESS** 10431 Hwy51, Courtland, MS 38620. **EMAIL** lindgren@panola.com

LINDGREN, JAMES
PERSONAL Born 09/03/1950, Elmhurst, IL, m, 1978, 2 children **DISCIPLINE** HISTORY **EDUCATION** William & Mary Col, PhD, 84. **CAREER** Prof, State Univ NYork (SUNY), 94-. **HONORS AND AWARDS** Phi Beta Kappa; Alpha of Va; G Wesley Johnson Prize. **MEMBERSHIPS** Orgn of Am Historians, Nat Coun on Public Hist. **RESEARCH** History of American Historic Preservation, history of museums, historical sites. **SELECTED PUBLICATIONS** Auth, Preserving Historic New England: Preservation, Progressivism and the Remaking of Memory, Oxford UP (New York, NY), 95; auth, "'That Every Mariner May Possess the History of the World': A Cabinet for the East India Marine Society of Salem," New Eng Quart 68 (95): 179-205; auth, "'The Rising Granduer of a Nation and the Decay of Its Virtue': Historic Preservation at the Fin de Siecle," in Fin-de-Siecle: Comparisons and Perspectives (New York: Peter Lang Publ, 96); Auth, "'A New Departure in Historic, Patriotic Work': Personalism, Professionalism and Conflicting Concepts of Material Culture in the Late Nineteenth and Early Twentieth Centuries," The Public Historian 18 (96): 41-60; auth, "'Let Us Idealize Old Types of Manhood': The New Bedford Whaling Museum 1903-1941," New Eng Quart 72 (99): 163-206; auth, "Historic Sites and Preservation Movements," in Encycl of New Eng Cult (New Haven: Yale UP, 00); **CONTACT ADDRESS** Dept Hist, SUNY, Col at Plattsburgh, 101 Broad St, Plattsburgh, NY 12901-2637. **EMAIL** LINDGRJM@PLATTSBURGH.EDU

LINDGREN, RAYMOND ELMER
PERSONAL Born 02/10/1913, Kansas City, KS, m, 1940, 3 children **DISCIPLINE** HISTORY **EDUCATION** Univ Calif, AB, 35, AM, 40, PhD, 43. **CAREER** Asst prof, Occidental Col, 42-45; assoc prof hist, Vanderbilt Univ, 45-52; vis lectr, Univ Wis, 52-54; from assoc prof to prof, Occidental Col, 54-61, chmn dept, 55-61; prof, 61-80, Emer Prof Hist, Calif State Univ, Long Beach, 80-, Vis lectr, Univ Minn, 49-50; Fulbright res grant, Norway, 50-51; Gustaf V fel, 50-51; prof and resident dir, Calif State Cols, Int Prog, Sweden, 67-69; Rockefeller Found fel, Villa Servelloni Conf Ctr, 73; sub-ed, Scandinavia, Am Hist Rev Knight, Order of the NStar, Sweden. **HONORS AND AWARDS** Gustav Adolf Medal, Uppsala Univ, 80. **MEMBERSHIPS** AHA; Norweg Hist Soc; Danish Hist Soc; Swedish Hist Soc. **RESEARCH** Scandinavian history; 18th century Europe; immigration in the southwest United States. **SELECTED PUBLICATIONS** Coauth, Origins and Consequences of World War II, Dryden, 48; auth, Norway-Sweden: Union Disunion and Scandinavian Integration, 59 & coauth, Political Community and the North Atlantic Area, 57, Princeton Univ. **CONTACT ADDRESS** Dept of Hist, California State Univ, Long Beach, 1250 Bellflower Blvd, Long Beach, CA 90840.

LINDLEY, TERRY
PERSONAL Born 01/15/1950, Forth Worth, TX, m, 1971, 2 children **DISCIPLINE** HISTORY **EDUCATION** Tex A&M, BA, 72; Univ New Orleans, MA, 75; Tex Christian Univ, PhD, 85. **CAREER** Instr, Tarrant Co Jr Col, 85-86; Asst/Assoc Prof, Union Univ, 86-. **HONORS AND AWARDS** Lynne E. May, Jr Study Grant, 99; Pew Summer Res Grant, 00. **MEMBERSHIPS** Soc of Historians of Am For Rel, Soc of Church Hist, Southern Baptist Hist Soc. **RESEARCH** Southern Baptist and Vietnam, The Jesus Movement, Fundamentalism and Evengelicism. **SELECTED PUBLICATIONS** Auth, "The 1998 SBC Opposition to Isreal: The J. Frank Norris Factor," Baptist Hist and Heritage XXII (Oct 87): 23-33. **CONTACT ADDRESS** Dept Hist and Govt, Union Univ, 1050 Union Univ Dr, Jackson, TN 38305-3656. **EMAIL** tlindley@uu.edu

LINDNER, RUDI PAUL
PERSONAL Born 07/17/1943, Stockton, CA, m **DISCIPLINE** MEDIEVAL HISTORY **EDUCATION** Harvard Col, AB, 65; Univ Wis-Madison, MA, 67; Univ Calif, Berkeley, PhD(hist), 76. **CAREER** Jr fel hist, Ctr Byzantine Studies, Dumbarton Oaks, 72-74; Instr, Tufts Univ, 74-77; Prof Hist, Univ Mich, Ann Arbor, 77-; vis prof, John Cabot Univ, Rome, 93; vis prof, Hebrew, Univ of Jerusalem, 02. **HONORS AND AWARDS** Fulbright Fel, 92-93. **RESEARCH** Byzantine, Turkish and Inner Asian history. **SELECTED PUBLICATIONS** Auth, The challenge of Kilij Arslan IV, In: Studies in Honor of George C Miles, Syracuse Univ, 74; Nomadism, horses and Huns, Past & Present, 8/81; What was a tribe?, Comp Studies Soc & Hist, 10/82; Stimulus and justification in early Ottoman history, In: Byzantium and Islam, Holy Cross Univ, 82; Nomads and Ottomans in medieval Anatolia, Ind Univ, 82; auth, "Icons Among the Iconoclasts," in the Iconic Page (Univ of Mich Pr, 88); auth, Explorations in Ottoman Prehistory, Univ of Mich Pr, 01. **CONTACT ADDRESS** Hist Dept, Univ of Michigan, Ann Arbor, 435 S State St, Ann Arbor, MI 48109-1003.

LINDO-FUENTES, HECTOR
PERSONAL Born 10/18/1952, El Salvador **DISCIPLINE** HISTORY **EDUCATION** Univ Chicago, PhD. **CAREER** Prof, Fordham Univ. **HONORS AND AWARDS** Dir, interdisciplinary prog, Latin Am Stud Lincoln Ctr campus; co-dir, interdisciplinary prog, latin am stud lincoln ctr campus. **MEMBERSHIPS** Latin Am Studies Asn. **RESEARCH** The evolution of the state in the nineteenth century and the polit economy of educ in Central Am. **SELECTED PUBLICATIONS** Auth, Weak Foundations: The Economy of El Salvador in the Nineteenth Century, 90; co-auth, Central America 1821-1871: Liberalism Before Reform, 95; Historia de El Salvador, 94. **CONTACT ADDRESS** Dept of Hist, Fordham Univ, 113 W 60th St, New York, NY 10023. **EMAIL** hlindo@atsaol.com

LINDSTROM, DIANA
PERSONAL Born 09/09/1944, Jamestown, NY, 1 child **DISCIPLINE** HISTORY **EDUCATION** Alfred Univ, BA, 66; Univ Del, MA, 69, PhD(hist), 74. **CAREER** Asst prof hist, 71-77, Assoc Prof Hist and Women's Studies, Univ Wis, Madison, 78-, Am Coun Learned Soc fel hist, 76 and Reg Econ Hist Res, 78-79. **HONORS AND AWARDS** Allan Nevins Prize Econ Hist, Columbia Univ, 74. **MEMBERSHIPS** Econ Hist Asn; Agr Hist Soc; Bus Hist Soc. **RESEARCH** American economic 1815-1860; American domestic trade. **SELECTED PUBLICATIONS** Contribr, The Structure of the Cotton Economy of the Antebellum South, Agr Hist Soc, 70; auth, Demand, markets and economic development, J Econ Hist, 3/75; coauth, Urban growth and economic structure in Antebellum America, Res Econ Hist, 6/78; auth, Economic Development in the Philadelphia Region, 1810-1850, Columbia Univ, 78. **CONTACT ADDRESS** Dept of Hist, Univ of Wisconsin, Madison, 455 North Park St, Madison, WI 53706-1483.

LINDUFF, KATHERYN MCALLISTER
PERSONAL Born 10/16/1941, Beaver, PA **DISCIPLINE** ART HISTORY, ARCHEOLOGY **EDUCATION** Dickinson Col, BA, 63; Univ Pittsburgh, MA, 66, PhD(art hist), 72. **CAREER** Instr art hist, Univ Wis-Madison, 69-72; asst dean, Col Arts and Sci, 73-74, asst prof, 72-79, Assoc Prof Art Hist, Univ Pittsburgh, 79-, Assoc cur, Jay C Leff Collections, 71-76; Full Prof, Art Hist, Anthropology, 79. **MEMBERSHIPS** Asn for Asian Studies; Am Orient Soc; Archaeol Inst Am; Early China Soc; Col Art Asn; Soc for Am Archaeol Anthrop Asn; E Asian Archaeol Network. **RESEARCH** Ancient Chinese art and archaeology; art and archaeology of Central Asia; prehistoric art of the Old World and Asia. **SELECTED PUBLICATIONS** Auth, Zhon Civilization, 79; auth, Art Past/Art Present, 90, 94, 97, 01; auth, The Beginnings of Chinese Metallurgy, 00; auth, Zhukaigou, Steppe Culture and the Rise of Chinese Civilization, Antiquity, Vol 0069, 95; **CONTACT ADDRESS** Dept of Art Hist, Univ of Pittsburgh, 104 Frick Fine Arts, Pittsburgh, PA 15260-7601. **EMAIL** lindufft@pitt.edu

LINENTHAL, EDWARD TABOR
PERSONAL Born 11/06/1947, Boston, MA, m, 1974, 1 child **DISCIPLINE** RELIGIOUS STUDIES, AMERICAN HISTORY **EDUCATION** Western Mich Univ, BA, 69; PACIFIC Sch Relig, MDiv, 73; Univ Calif, Santa Barbara, PhD(relig studies), 79. **CAREER** Lectr Am relig, Univ Calif, Santa Barbara, 78-79; Asst Prof Relig Studies, Univ Wis-Oshkosh, 79-, asst ed bk rev sect, Relig Studies Rev, 81-. **MEMBERSHIPS** Am Soc Church Hist; Am Acad Relig. **RESEARCH** Religion and war; religion and American culture; history of religions. **SELECTED PUBLICATIONS** Auth, From hero to anti-hero: The transformation of the warrior in modern America, Soundings, spring 80; Nostalgia for clarity: The memory of Patton, Studies Popular Cult, spring 82; Ritual drama at the Little Big Horn: The persistence and transformation of a national symbol, J Am Acad Relig (in press); The Warrior as a Symbolic Figure in America, Edwin Mellen Press (in press). **CONTACT ADDRESS** Dept of Relig, Univ of Wisconsin, Oshkosh, 800 Algoma Blvd, Oshkosh, WI 54901-8601.

LING, HUPING
DISCIPLINE HISTORY **EDUCATION** Shanxi Univ, Ba, 82; Univ Ore, MA, 87; Miami Univ, PhD, 91. **CAREER** Teacher, High School Shanxi, 74-78; asst prof, Shanxi Univ, 82-85; vis scholar, Georgetown Univ, 85; grad asst, Univ Ore, 86-87; teaching fel to instr, Miami Univ, 89-91; asst prof, Truman Univ, 91-96; vis prof, Wash Univ, 98-99; assoc prof, Turman State Univ, 96-. **HONORS AND AWARDS** Sabbatical leave grant, Truman Univ, 98-99; Who's Who Among america's Teachers, 98; Fel, Am Asn of Univ Women Educ foundation, 95-96; Fac res summer grant, Truman, Univ, 92, 94, 95, 96, 97; Jepson Fel grant, Truman Univ, 93-94; Memorial Awd, Miami Univ, 91; Miami Student Recognition Awd, Miami, 90, 91; Graduate achievement fund, Miami Univ, 89; Teaching Fel, Miami Univ, 88-91; Loretta Shower rossman Scholarsip, Univ Ore, 86, 87; Scholar orientation Prog of Am Studies, 87; Shanxi Educ commission Scholarship, 85-87. **MEMBERSHIPS** Asn for Asian Studies, Asn for Asian-Am Studies, am Hist Asn, Chinese Asn for Am Studies. **RESEARCH** Asian American studies, Immigration and ethnicity, Women's studies. **SELECTED PUBLICATIONS** Auth, "Isolated Assimilation: Chinese Women in the Midwest," The Middle Ground: women and the Transcendence of Domesticity in the Midwest, (forthcoming); auth, "Hop Alley: Myth and Reality of the St. Louis Chinatown," The New Missouri History, (forthcoming); auth, "Family and Marriage of Late-Nineteenth and Early-Twentieth Century Chinese Immigrant Women," Journal of American Ethnic History, (00); auth, "Chinese Female Students and the Sino-US Relations," New Studies on Chinese Overseas and China, Holland (00); auth, "Debate Over Affirmative Action," Chinese American forum, (99): 33-35; auth, "A Study of the Motives for Immigration of Chinese Women in the Late-Nineteenth and Early-Twentieth Century," American Studies, (99); 95-121; auth, "Reflections on My Recent Visits to China," St Louis Chinese News, 99; auth, Jinshan Yao: A History of Chinese American Women, Beijing, 99; auth, "Chinese American Professional and Business Women in a Midwest Small Town," Ethnic Chinese at Turn of Century, 98. **CONTACT ADDRESS** Dept Soc Sci, Truman State Univ, 100 E Normal St, Kirksville, MO 63501-4200. **EMAIL** hling@truman.edu

LINK, ARTHUR S.
PERSONAL Born 08/08/1920, New Market, VA, m, 1945, 4 children **DISCIPLINE** AMERICAN HISTORY **EDUCATION** Univ NC, AB, 41, AM, 42, PhD, 45; Oxford Univ, MA, 58. **CAREER** Instr, NC State Col, 43-44; from instr to asst prof, Princeton Univ, 45-49; from assoc prof to prof hist, Northwestern Univ, 49-60; Harmsworth prof, Oxford Univ, 58-59; prof hist, 60-65, Edwards prof Am hist, 65-76, George H Davis Prof Am Hist, Princeton Univ, 76-, Dir Wilson Papers, 60-, Rosenwald, Guggenheim and Rockefeller fel, 41-42, 44-45, 50-51, 62-63; mem Inst Advan Studies, 49, 54-55; Shaw lectr diplomatic hist, Johns Hopkins Univ, 56; mem, Nat Hist Publ Comn, 68-72. **HONORS AND AWARDS** Julian P Boyd Awd, Asn Doc Ed, 81; littd, bucknell univ, 61, univ nc, 62, washington and lee univ, 65; lhd, wash col, 62; dhum, davidson col, 65. **MEMBERSHIPS** AHA: Southern Hist Asn (vpres, 67-68; pres, 68-69); Orgn Am Historians; Am Philos Soc; Asn Doc Ed (pres, 79-80). **RESEARCH** United States history since 1890; the Wilson era. **SELECTED PUBLICATIONS CONTACT ADDRESS** Princeton Univ, Firestone Libr, Princeton, NJ 08544.

LINT, GREGG LEWIS
PERSONAL Born 12/21/1943, South Bend, IN, m, 1971 **DISCIPLINE** DIPLOMATIC HISTORY **EDUCATION** Central Mich Univ, BA, 65, Ma, 68; Mich State Univ, PhD(diplomatic hist), 75. **CAREER** Teacher, Benton Harbor Public Sch, Mich, 65-67 and Durand Public Sch, Mich, 68-70; instr diplomatic hist and arch, Mich State Univ, 74-75; asst ed, 75-78, Assoc Ed, Adams Papers, 78-. **MEMBERSHIPS** Soc Historians Am Foreign Rel; AHA; Orgn Am Historians; Asn Doc Editing. **RESEARCH** American foreign policy and the law of nations, 1776-1815; John Adams. **SELECTED PUBLICATIONS** Auth, The American Revolution and the Law of Nations, In: Diplomatic History, 77; contribr, The American Revolution and A Candid World, Kent State Univ, 77; coed, Papers of John Adams, Vol I & II, 77 & Vol III & IV, Harvard Univ, 79. **CONTACT ADDRESS** Adams Papers Mass Hist Soc, 1154 Boylston St, Boston, MA 02215.

LINTELMAN, JOY
PERSONAL Born 10/16/1957, Fairmont, MN, m, 1984, 3 children **DISCIPLINE** HISTORY **EDUCATION** Gustavus Adolphus Col, BA, 80; Univ Minn, MA, 83, PhD, 91. **CAREER** Tchg asst Hist Dept, 82-84, instr Hon Div, 86, instr Hist Dept, 88, instr Dept Independent Study, 84-91, Univ Minn; instr Hist Dept, Macalester Col, 88; ASSOC PROF HIST DEPT, CONCORDIA COL, 89-; diss fel, 87-88, Stout fel, 85-86, NW Area Stud For Lang fel, 84-85, Grad School fel, 81-82, Un iv Minn; Fulbright res scholar, 86-87; Lilly Lorenzen scholar, 86-87; Bush Fac Grant, Native Am Pedag, 94-95, Gender & Technol, 95-96; Nils William & Dagmar Olsson Scholar Fund, 97; Concordia Emigrant Inst grant, 97; Swedish Emigrant Inst Grant, 97. **MEMBERSHIPS** Am Hist Asn; Orgn Am Hist; Soc Sci Hist Asn; Immigration Hist Soc; Swed Am Hist Soc; Minn Hist Soc. **RESEARCH** Immigration; Women; Children; Native Americans. **SELECTED PUBLICATIONS** Auth On My Own: Single, Swedish, and Female in Turn-of-the-Century Chicago, Swedish-American L ife in Chicago: Cultural and Urban Aspects of an Immigrant People, 1850-1930, Univ Ill Press, 92; She did not whimper of complain: Case Records and Swedish American Working Class Women in Minneapolis, 1910-1930, Swed Am Hist Quart, 94; Making Service Serve Themselves: Immigrant Women and Domestic Service in N America, 1820-1930, Cambridge Univ Press, 95; An 'In-Progress' Report: The Crow Seminar and Teaching Indian History, Essays from Teaching and Writing Local and Reservation History: The Crows, Newberry Library, 95. **CONTACT ADDRESS** Concordia Col, Minnesota, 901 S 8th St, Moorhead, MN 56562. **EMAIL** lintelma@cord.edu

LIPE, WILLIAM DAVID
PERSONAL Born 05/05/1935, Struggleville, OK, m, 1962, 3 children **DISCIPLINE** ARCHAEOLOGY **EDUCATION** Univ Okla, BA 57; Yale Univ, PhD(anthrop), 66. **CAREER** Res asst archaeol, Univ Utah, 58-60; instr anthrop, Univ Okla, 63-64; actg asst prof, State Univ NY Binghamton, 64-66, from asst prof to assoc prof, 66-72, actg chmn dept anthrop, 69-70, Nat Geog Soc res grant, 69-70; asst dir, Mus Northern Ariz, 72-76; assoc prof, 76-79, Prof Anthrop, Wash State Univ, 79-, NSF res grants, 72-76; Wash State Univ fac res grant, 77. **MEMBERSHIPS** Fel AAAS; fel Am Anthrop Asn; Soc Am Archaeol. **RESEARCH** Cultural adaptation to the environment; prehistory of Indians of Southwestern United States. **SELECTED PUBLICATIONS** Auth, 1958 Excavations, Glen Canyon Area, 60 & coauth, 1959 Excavations, Glen Canyon Area, 60, Univ Utah Anthrop Papers; auth, Anasazi communities in the Red Rock Plateau, In: Reconstructing Prehistoric Pueblo Society, Univ NMex, 70; coauth, Human settlement and resources in the Cedar Mesa area, Southeast Utah, In: Distribution of Prehistoric Population Aggregates, Prescott Col, 71; auth, A conservation model for American archaeology, Kiva, 74; co-ed, Proceedings of the 1974 Cultural Resource Management Conference, Mus Northern Ariz, 74; coauth, Regional sampling: A case study from Cedar Mesa, Utah, In: Sampling in Archaeology, Univ Ariz, 75; auth, The Southwest, In: Ancient Native Americans, Freeman, 77. **CONTACT ADDRESS** Dept of Anthrop, Washington State Univ, P O Box 644910, Pullman, WA 99164-4910.

LIPPMAN, EDWARD
PERSONAL Born 05/24/1920, New York, NY, m, 1942, 2 children **DISCIPLINE** HISTORY OF MUSIC **EDUCATION** City Col NYork, BS, 42; NYork Univ, MA, 45; Columbia Univ, PhD(musicol), 52. **CAREER** From instr to assoc prof, 54-69, Prof Music, Columbia Univ, 69-, Guggenheim fel, 58-59; Columbia Univ Coun Res Humanities grants, 60, 63, 65; Am Coun Learned Soc fel, 67-68; lectr, Bryn Mawr Col, 72-73. **HONORS AND AWARDS** Harriet Cohen Int Music Awd, 54. **MEMBERSHIPS** Intenational Musicol Soc; Am Musicol Soc; Am Soc for Aesthetics. **RESEARCH** Philosophy and aesthetics of music; 19th century history of music; ancient Greek conceptions of music. **SELECTED PUBLICATIONS** Auth, Musical Thought in Ancient Greece, 64; auth, A Humanistic Philosophy of Music, 77; auth, Musical Aesthetics: A Historical Reader, 3v., 85; auth, A History of Western Musical Aesthetics, 92; auth, Wagner and Beethoven--Wagner, Richard Reception of Beethoven, Opera Quart, Vol 0009, 93; auth, The Philosophy and Aesthetics of Music, 99. **CONTACT ADDRESS** Dept of Music, Columbia Univ, New York, NY 10027. **EMAIL** eval424@aol.com

LIPSETT-RIVERA, SONYA
DISCIPLINE HISTORY **EDUCATION** Univ Ottawa, BA, 82; Tulane Univ, MA, 84, PhD, 88. **CAREER** Assoc prof. **HONORS AND AWARDS** Hon(s) Degree adv. **RESEARCH** Late colonial and early national Mexico. **SELECTED PUBLICATIONS** Auth, Indigenous Communities and Water Rights in Colonial Puebla: Patterns of Resistance, The Americas, 48:4, 92; "Water and Bureaucracy in Colonial Puebla de los Angeles," Jour Latin Amer Stud, 25:1, 93; coauth, Columbus Takes on the Forces of Darkness: Film and Historical Myth in 1492: The Conquest of Paradise, Based on a True Story, Latin Amer Hist at the Movies, Delaware, Scholarly Resources Press, 97; ed, The Faces of Honor: Sex, Shame and Violence in Colonial Latin America, Albuquerque: Univ of New Mexico Press, 98; ed, "A Slap in the Face of Honor: Social Transgression and Women in Late-Colonial Mexico," (Albuquerque: Univ of New Mexico Press, 98); auth, "De Obra y Palabra: Patterns of Insults in Mexico, 1750-1856," The Americas 54"4, (98): 221-224; auth, "Introduction: Children in the History of Latin America," Journal of Family History 23:3, (98): 221-224; auth, "Outsiders into Insiders: the Doctrine of Prior Appropriation and Indigenous Communities in Puebla, Mexico," Oklahoma City Univ Law Review 23:1-2, (98): 93-114. **CONTACT ADDRESS** Dept of Hist, Carleton Univ, 1125 Colonel By Dr, Ottawa, ON, Canada K1S 5B6. **EMAIL** sonya_lipsett-rivera@carleton.ca

LISIO, DONALD J.
PERSONAL Born 05/21/1934, Oak Park, IL, m, 2 children **DISCIPLINE** HISTORY **EDUCATION** Knox Col, BA, 56; Ohio Univ, MA, 58; Univ Wis, PhD, 65. **CAREER** Grad asst, Ohio Univ, 56-57; instr, Univ Maryland, 59-60; asst prof, Coe Col, 64-69; assoc prof, 69-74; prof, 75-; Henrietta Arnold Prof, 80-. **HONORS AND AWARDS** Charles L Lynch, Outstand Teach Awd; NEH, 69, 84; ACLS Fel; USIPR Fel; CASE Outstand Teach Awd; Mortar Bd, Outstand Prof; Geo Olmsted Fel; Who's Who in Am; William F Vilas Res Fel. **MEMBERSHIPS** AHA; OAH; Phi Alpha Theta; Phi Gamma Mu; Phi Kappa Phi. **RESEARCH** The presidency and Herbert Hoover; 1927 Geneva Naval Arms Control Conference; 1930 London Naval Conference; 1932 Geneva Federal Arms Control Conference. **SELECTED PUBLICATIONS** Auth, "A Blunder Becomes Catastrophe: Hoover, the Legion, and the Bonus Army," reprinted in The Dissonance of Change: 1929 to the Present, ed. Paul W Glad (NY: Random House, 70): 25-44; and Herbert Hoover Reassessed (US Government Printing Office: Washington, DC, 81): 188-206; auth, The President and Protest: Hoover: Conspiracy and the Bonus Riot, Univ Missouri Press (Columbia), 74; auth, "U S: Bread and Butter Politics," in Steve Ward, ed., The War Generation: Veterans of the First World War (Kennekat Press, 75); auth, "The Rout of the 1932 Bonus Army From Washington: Guide and Documents," Prima Fiche Series, Scholarly Resources (82); auth, Hoover, Blacks, and Lily-Whites: A Study of Southern Strategies, Univ North Carolina Press (Chapel Hill), 85; auth, "Bonus Amy," in The Encyclopedia of the United States Congress (New York: Simon and Schuster, 94); auth, The President and Protest: Hoover, MacArthur, and the Bonus, Fordham UP (NY), 94. **CONTACT ADDRESS** Dept History, Coe Col, 1220 1st Ave NE, Cedar Rapids, IA 52402-5008. **EMAIL** dlisio@coe.edu

LISS, PEGGY K.
PERSONAL Born 10/03/1927, Philadelphia, PA, d, 2 children **DISCIPLINE** LATIN AMERICAN HISTORY **EDUCATION** Beaver Col, BA, 61; Univ Pa, Ma, 62, PhD(hist), 65. **CAREER** Lectr, Swarthmore Col, 66-70; Lectr, Univ of Pa, 67; Lectr, Case Western Reserve Univ, 72; Lectr, Hiram Col, 73-75; Dir, Proj on Historical Documents for Bahamas, Grenada, St. Lucia, and St. Vincent, Under the auspices of the Organization of Am States, 84-85; Originator, Producer, Series Historian, additional writing, The Buried Mirror: Reflections on Spain and the New World, a documentary television series produced by Malone-Gill Productions; and sponsored by the Smithsonian Institution and SOGETEL (Madrid), 85-91; Vis Fel, 83-93. **HONORS AND AWARDS** Carnegie-Ford Foundations Fel to study Latin Am nationalism in a sem directed by Arthur P. Whitaker, 63-64; Am Philos Soc grant-in-aid to study the ideology of Span empire in Mex, 70; Am Philos Soc grant-in-aid to prepare a paper on the US Declaration of Independence and Latin Am, presented at the IV Int Conf on the Enlightenment, Yale Univ, 75; Atlantic Empires chosen as one of the best academic books of 1983 by Choice; Guggenheim Fel to complete Isabel the Queen, 90-91; Res grants, the Prof for Cultural Cooperation between Spain's Ministry of Cult and Us Universities, for A SEARCH FOR ISABEL, 93-94; Planning grant, Nat Endowment for the Humanities, for the documentary television prog, A SEARCH FOR ISABEL, 93; Scripting grant, Nat Endowment for the Humanities, for a documentary television prog, A SEARCH FOR ISABEL, 94; Scripting grant, Nat Endowment for the Humanities and Corp for Public Broadcasting, for a documentary television series, A HISTORY OF TOMORROW, 98. **MEMBERSHIPS** Conf Latin Am Hist. **RESEARCH** Spain in America; the Americas from 1713 to 1826; Isabel I of Spain. **SELECTED PUBLICATIONS** Co-ed, Man, State and Society in Latin American History, Praeger, 72; auth, Mexico Under Spain, 1521-1556: Society and the Origins of Nationality, Univ of Chicago Press, 75; auth, "Mexico en el siglo XVIII: Algunas interpretaciones e algunos problemas," Historia Mexicana 27 (77): 273-315; auth, Atlantic Empires: The Network of Trade and Revolution, 1713-1826, Johns Hopkins Univ Press, 83; auth, "Creole, the North American Example, and the Spanish American Economy, 1760-1810," in Jacques Barbier and Allen Kuethe, eds., The North American Role in the Spanish Imperial Economy, 1760-1819, Manchester Univ Press, (84); auth, "The Impact of the Treaty of Paris on Spanish America," in The Treaty of Paris (1783) in a Changing States System, Papers from a Conference, Woodrow Wilson International Center for Scholars and University Press of America (85): 145-61; auth, "Revolutionary Language and the Breakup of Empire," in a festschrift for Charles Gibson, ed by William Taylor and Richard Garner, Pa. State Univ (86); co-ed, Atlantic Port Cities, 1650-1850, Univ of Tenn. Pres, 91; auth, Isabel the Queen: Life and Times, Oxford Univ Press, 92; auth, "Isabel of Castile and Fernando of Aragon," in The Columbus Encyclopedia, Simon & Schuster (92). **CONTACT ADDRESS** 501 D St SE, Washington, DC 20003.

LISS, SHELDON BARNETT
PERSONAL Born 11/03/1936, Philadelphia, PA, m, 1959, 2 children **DISCIPLINE** LATIN AMERICAN HISTORY **EDUCATION** Am Univ, AB, 58, PhD(hist), 64; Duquesne Univ, MA, 62. **CAREER** Exec, pvt indust, 59-61; asst prof hist and co-chmn Latin Am Studies, Ind State Univ, 64-66; vis asst prof hist, Univ Notre Dame, 66-67; assoc prof, 67-69, dir doctoral studies, 69-70, Prof Hist, Univ Akron, 69-, Consult, Latin Am Inst, 65- and US Peace Corps, Latin Am, 66; adv, US Comt Panamanian Sovereignty, 76-77; consult, Nat Sci Found, 80 and Ohio Endowment Humanities, 80- **MEMBERSHIPS** AHA; Conf Latin Am Hist; Latin Am Studies Asn; Pan-Am Inst Geog and Hist; Soc Iberian and Latin Am Thought. **RESEARCH** Inter-American diplomacy; 20th century political history of Latin America; Marxist political and social thought in Latin America. **SELECTED PUBLICATIONS** Auth, A Century of Disagreement: The Chamizal Conflict 1864-1964, Univ Wash, 65; The Canal: Aspects of United States-Panamanian Relations, Univ Notre Dame, 67; contribr, Investigaciones Contemporaneas Sobre Historia de Mexico, Nat Univ Mex, Col Mex & Univ Tex, 71; co-ed, Man, State, and Society in Latin American History, Praeger, 72; contribr, Foreign Policies of Latin America: An Analysis, Johns Hopkins Univ, 75; Panama: Sovereignty for a Land Divided, EPICA, 76; auth, Diplomacy and Dependency: Venezuela, The United States, and the Americas, Doc Publ, 78; contribr, Political Parties in the Americas, Greenwood Press, 82. **CONTACT ADDRESS** Dept of Hist, Univ of Akron, Akron, OH 44325.

LITCHFIELD, ROBERT BURR
PERSONAL Born 08/16/1936 **DISCIPLINE** EUROPEAN HISTORY **EDUCATION** Harvard Univ, AB, 58; Princton Univ, AM, 61, PhD(hist), 66. **CAREER** Prof Hist, Brown Univ, 86-. **MEMBERSHIPS** AHA **RESEARCH** Italy, 16th-19th centuries, old regime, revolutionary period and early 19th century; economic and social history. **SELECTED PUBLICATIONS** Auth, Emergency of a Bureaucracy. The Floretine Patricians, 1530-1790, Princeton, 86; auth, Feuds and Clans--the Genoese State in the Society of Fontanabuona, Amer Hist Rev, Vol 0098, 93; The Continuity of Feudal Power--the Caracciolo Di Brienza in Spanish Naples, Cath Hist Rev, Vol 0079, 93; The English Translation of 'Settecento Riformatore' and its Anglo-American Reception, Rivista Storica Italiana, Vol 0108, 96; Siena and the Sienese in the 13th Century, J Urban Hist, Vol 0023, 97; Turin 1564-1680--Urban Design, Military Culture, and Creation of the Absolutist Capital, J Urban Hist, Vol 0023, 97; A Provincial Elite in Early-Modern Tuscany--Family and Power in the Creation of the State, J Interdisciplinary Hist, Vol 0028, 97; Civic Politics in the Rome of Urban-Viii, J Urban Hist, Vol 0023, 97. **CONTACT ADDRESS** Dept of Hist, Brown Univ, 142 Angell St, Providence, RI 02912-9127. **EMAIL** robert_litchfield@brown.edu

LITOFF, JUDY BARRETT
PERSONAL Born 12/23/1944, Atlanta, GA, d, 1966, 2 children **DISCIPLINE** HISTORY **EDUCATION** Emory Univ, BA, 67, MA, 68; Univ Maine, PhD(hist), 75-. **CAREER** Assoc Prof Hist, Bryant Col, 75-, hist consult for many documentary films, Bd. Of Trustees, RI Hist Society, 99-; Chair, Goff Council for Ingenuity and Enterprise Studies, 99-; Project Dir., U.S. State Dept Grant, Minsk, Belarus, 97-00; RI Com for Humanities, 82-86; Bd of Overseers, Moses Brown School, 84-93. **HONORS AND AWARDS** James Madison Prize, 94, Bryant Col Research/Publication Awd. 97; Bryant Col Herstory Awd, 96; Bryant Col Distinguished Faculty Member Awd, 89; Bryant Col Faculty Federation Distinguished Faculty Member Awd, 88. **MEMBERSHIPS** AHA; Orgn Am Historians; Southern Historical Assn; RI Hist Soc; Coordinating Com on Women in the Hist Profession; Southern Assn; Women Historians; Phi Kappa Phi; Phi Alpha Theta. **RESEARCH** Am Women's History; Women and World War II. **SELECTED PUBLICATIONS** Auth, "What Kind of World Do We Want," 00; auth, "Dear Poppa," 97; "American Women in a World at War," 97; auth, "European Immigrant Women," 94; auth, "We're In This War Too," 94; auth, "Dear Boys," 91; auth, "Since You Went Away," 91; auth, "Miss You," 90; auth, "American Midwife Debate," 86; auth, "American Midwives," 78. **CONTACT ADDRESS** Bryant Col, 1150 Douglas Pike, Smithfield, RI 02917-1291. **EMAIL** jlitoff@bryant.edu

LITTLE, DOUGLAS JAMES
PERSONAL Born 05/24/1950, Lincoln, NE, m, 1974, 2 children **DISCIPLINE** AMERICAN HISTORY **EDUCATION** Univ Wis-Madison, BA, 72; Cornell Univ, MA, 75, PhD(hist), 78 **CAREER** Asst Prof To Prof Am Hist, Clark Univ, 78-, Dean of the College and Assoc Provost, 00; vis prof Am Hist, Cornell Univ, 88-89. **HONORS AND AWARDS** Bernath Article Prize, Soc Historians Am Foreign Rel, 81. **MEMBERSHIPS** AHA; Orgn Am Historians; Soc Historians Am Foreign Rel **RESEARCH** American foreign relations with the Middle East; multinational corporations. **SELECTED PUBLICATIONS** Auth, Twenty years of turmoil: ITT, the State Department, and Spain 1924-1944, Bus Hist Rev, 79; Malevolent Neutrality: The United States, Great Britain, and the Origins of the Spanish Civil War, Cornell Univ Press, 85; New frontier on the Nile: JFK, Nasser, and Arab nationalism, Jour Am Hist, 88; Cold War and covert action: The United States and Syria 1945-1958, Middle East Jour, 93; Gideon's band: America and the Middle East since 1945, Diplomatic Hist, 94; His finest hour? Eisenhower, Lebanon, and the 1958 crisis in the Middle East, Diplomatic Hist, 96. **CONTACT ADDRESS** Dept Hist, Clark Univ, 950 Main St, Worcester, MA 01610-1473. **EMAIL** dlittle@clarku.edu

LITTLE, ELIZABETH A.
PERSONAL Born 09/25/1926, Mineola, NY, m, 1953, 4 children **DISCIPLINE** ARCHAEOLOGY, ANTHROPOLOGY **EDUCATION** Wellesley Col, BA (Physics, Durant Scholar with high honors), 48; MIT, D Phil (Physics), 54; Univ MA, MA (Anthropology), 85. **CAREER** Nantucket Hist Asn Archaeological Field Dir, 76-77; coord, MA Hist Commission survey grant, 78-79, res dir, 79-84, curator of Prehistoric Artifacts, Nantucket Historical Association, 85-95; MA Archaeological Soc, trustee, 79-96, pres, 84-86, ed of the Bul of the MA Archaeological Soc, 86-96; res assoc, R S Peabody Museum of Archaeology, Philips Academy, Andover, MA; res fel, Archaeology, Nantucket Hist Asn. **HONORS AND AWARDS** Phi Beta Kappa, Sigma Xi, IBM fel, 47-54; Preservation Awds, MA Hist Commission, 79, 88. **MEMBERSHIPS** Soc for Am Archaeology; Soc for Archaeological Sciences. **RESEARCH** Radiocarbon dating; stable isotope studies of prehistoric diet; ethnohistory. **SELECTED PUBLICATIONS** Auth, Radiocarbon Age Calibration at Archaeological Sites of Coastal Massachusetts and Vicinity, J of Archaeological Science, 93; with Margaret J Schoeninger, The Late Woodland Diet on Nantucket Island and the Problem of Maize in Coastal New England, Am Antiquity, 95; Daniel Spotso: A Sachem at Nantucket Island, Massa-

chusetts, circa 1691-1741, in Northeastern Indian Lives, 1632-1816, R S Grumet, ed, Univ MA Press, 96; Analyzing Prehistoric Diets by Linear Programming, with John D C Little, J of Archaeological Science, 97. **CONTACT ADDRESS** 37 Conant Road, Lincoln, MA 01773. **EMAIL** ealittle@alum.mit.edu

LITTLE, JOHN IRVINE

PERSONAL Born 01/06/1947, Thetford Mines, PQ, Canada, m, 1978 **DISCIPLINE** CANADIAN HISTORY **EDUCATION** Bishop's Univ, BA, 68; Univ NB, Ma, 70; Univ Ottawa, PhD, 77. **CAREER** Lectr Can hist, Univ PEI, 74-75 and St Thomas Univ, 75-76; from asst prof to prof, Simon Fraser Univ, 76- . **RESEARCH** Nineteenth century Quebec--social, economic, political; late 19th century Canadian political. **SELECTED PUBLICATIONS** Auth, Nationalism, Capitalism and Colonization in Nineteenth-Century Quebec: The Upper St. Fancis District, McGill-Queens Univ Pr (Montreal, QC) 89; auth, Crofters and Habitants: Settler Society, Economy and Culture in a Quebec Township, 1848-81, McGill-Queen's Univ Pr (Montreal, QC) 91; auth, The Child Letters: Public and Private Life in a Canadian Merchant-Politician'[s Family, 1841-1845, McGill-Queen's Univ Pr (Montreal, QC) 95; auth, "School Reform and Community Control in the 1840's: A Case Study form the Eastern Townships," Hist Suds in Educ 9 (97): 153-164; auth, "State Formation and Local Reaction in the Eastern Townships: A Brief Overview," in Espace et culture, eds Serge Courville and Normand Seguin (Ste Foy: Les Presses de l'Universite Laval, 95); auth, "A Moral Engine of Such Incalculable Power: The Temprance Movement in the Eastern Townships, 1830-52," J of Eastern Township Studs 11(Fall 97): 5-38; auth, State and Society in Transition: The Politics of Institutional Reform in the Eastern Townships, 1838-1852, McGill-Queen's Univ Pr (Montreal, QC) 97; auth "Labouring in a Great Cause: Marcus Child as Pioneer School Inspector in Lower Canada's Eastern Townships, 1852-59, " Hist Studs in Educ 10 (98): 85-115; auth, "Contested Land: Squatters and Agents in the Eastern Townships of Lower Canada," Can Hist Rev 80 (99): 318-412. **CONTACT ADDRESS** Dept Hist, Simon Fraser Univ, 8888 University Dr., Burnaby, BC, Canada V5A 1S6. **EMAIL** john_little@sfu.ca

LITTLE, MONROE HENRY

PERSONAL Born 06/30/1950, St Louis, MO, m **DISCIPLINE** HISTORY **EDUCATION** Denison Univ, BA 1971 (magna cum laude); Princeton Univ, MA 1973, PhD 1977. **CAREER** MIT, instructor 1976-77, asst prof 1977-80; Indiana Univ-Purdue Univ, Indianapolis, asst prof 1980-81, asst prof dir afro-amer studies 1981-. **HONORS AND AWARDS** Elected Omicron Delta Kappa Men's Leadership Honorary 1971; Fellowship Rockefeller Fellowship in Afro-Amer Studies 1972-75. **MEMBERSHIPS** Mem Amer Historical Assn; mem Organization of American Historians; mem Natl Urban League; mem Assoc for Study of Afro-Amer Life & History; consultant Educ Develop Ctr 1980; consultant CSR Inc US Dept of Labor 1981; consultant Black Women in the Mid-West Project Purdue Univ 1983. **CONTACT ADDRESS** Indiana Univ-Purdue Univ, Indianapolis, Indianapolis, IN 46206.

LITTLEFIELD, DANIEL C.

PERSONAL Born 09/29/1941, Dennison, TX, m **DISCIPLINE** UNITED STATES HISTORY **EDUCATION** Calif State Univ, AB, 64; Johns Hopkins Univ, MA, 72; PhD, 77. **CAREER** Instr, CUNY, 73-77; asst prof, Va Commonwealth Univ, 77-78; asst to assoc prof, La State Univ, 78-88; assoc prof to prof, Univ of IL, Urbana, 88-99; Carolina prof, Univ of SC, 99-. **HONORS AND AWARDS** Gilman Fel, Johns Hopkisn Univ; NEH; Ford Found, Nat Res Coun. **MEMBERSHIPS** S Hist Assoca; Orgn of Am Hist; AHA; Hist Soc; SC Soc. **RESEARCH** Colonial American Slavery, the slave trade, race relations in colonial America, comparative race relations. **SELECTED PUBLICATIONS** Auth, Race and Slaves: Ethnicity and the Slave Trade in Colonial South Carolina, La State Univ, 81; Rice and the Making of South Carolina: An Introductory Essay, 95; Blacks, John Brown, and a Theory of Manhood, Univ Va, 95. **CONTACT ADDRESS** Dept Hist, Univ of Illinois, Urbana-Champaign, 52 E Gregory Dr, Champaign, IL 61820. **EMAIL** dlittle@staff.uiuc.edu

LITTLEFIELD, DANIEL F.

PERSONAL Born 05/23/1939, Salina, OK **DISCIPLINE** NATIVE AMERICAN LITERATURE & HISTORY **EDUCATION** Oklahoma State Univ, PhD. **CAREER** Lit and Am Native Press Arch Dir, Univ of Ark at Little Rock. **HONORS AND AWARDS** Phi Beta Kappa; Oklahoma Hist Hall of Fame. **SELECTED PUBLICATIONS** auth, Africans and Seminoles; auth, Africans and Creeks; auth, The Cherokee Freedmen; auth, The Chicksaw Freedmen; auth, Alex Posey: Creek Poet, Journalist, and Humorist; auth, Seminole Burning; co-auth, A Bibliography of Native American Writers; co-auth, A Bibliography of Native Writers: A Supplement; co-auth, American Indian and Alaska Native Newspapers and Periodicals, 1826-1924; co-auth, American Indian and Alaska Native Newspapers and Periodicals, 1925-70; co-auth, American Indian and Alaska Native Newspapers and Periodicals, 1971-1985; ed, The Life of Okah Tubbee; co-ed, The Fus Fixico Letters; co-ed, Kemaha: The Omaha Stories of Francis LaFlesche; co-ed, Tales of the Bark Lodges; co-ed, Native American Writing in the Southeast: An Anthology. **CONTACT ADDRESS** Univ of Arkansas, Little Rock, 2801 S University Ave., Little Rock, AR 72204-1099. **EMAIL** dflittlefiel@ualr.edu

LITTMAN, ROBERT J.

PERSONAL Born 08/23/1943, Newark, NJ, m, 1966, 3 children **DISCIPLINE** ANCIENT HISTORY, CLASSICS **EDUCATION** Columbia Univ, BA, 64, PhD(class philol), 70; Oxford Univ, BLitt, 68. **CAREER** Instr hist, Rutgers Univ, 67-68; instr classics, Brandeis Univ, 68-70; asst prof, 70-75, assoc prof, 75-79, Prof Classics, Univ Hawaii, Manoa, 79-, Herodotus fel and vis mem, Inst Advan Study, Princeton, 77. **MEMBERSHIPS** Am Philol Asn; Am Hist Asn; Soc Prom Hellenic Studies, Friends Ancient Hist. **RESEARCH** Greek history; historiography; Greek literature. **SELECTED PUBLICATIONS** Auth, Epidemiology of the Plague of Athens, Transactions of the American Philol Asn, Vol 0122, 92; Athens, Persia and the Book of Ezra, Transactions of the Amer Philol Asn, Vol 0125, 95; Kinship and Politics in Athens, 90; Jewish History in 100 Nutshells, 96. **CONTACT ADDRESS** Dept of Europ Lang and Lit, Univ of Hawaii, Manoa, 1890 E. West Rd., Honolulu, HI 96822-2362. **EMAIL** littman@hawaii.edu

LITWACK, LEON F.

PERSONAL Born 12/02/1929, Santa Barbara, CA, m, 1952, 2 children **DISCIPLINE** UNITED STATES HISTORY **EDUCATION** Univ Calif, BA, 51, MA, 52, PhD, 58 **CAREER** From instr to assoc prof hist, Univ Wis-Madison, 58-65; assoc prof, 65-71, prof, 71-87 A F & May T Morrison Prof Hist, Univ Calif, Berkeley 87-, Soc Sci Res Coun fac fel, 61-62; Guggenheim fel, 67-68; humanities res fel, Univ Calif, Berkeley, 76 & 80; Fulbright lectr, Moscow State Univ, 80, Beijing Univ, China, 82, Univ Helsinki, 90, Univ Sydney, Australia, 91; lectr Am hist, Peking Univ, 82. **HONORS AND AWARDS** Distinguished Teaching Award, Univ Calif, Berkeley, 71; Francis Parkman Prize, Soc Am Historians, 79; Pulitzer Prize in Hist, 80; Am Book Award, History, 81; Pres, Orgn Am Hist, 86-87; Am Acad Arts & Sci, 87. **MEMBERSHIPS** AHA; Orgn Am Historians; Southern Hist Asn; Am Antiq Soc; Soc Am Hist **RESEARCH** African Am History and Race Relations. **SELECTED PUBLICATIONS** Auth, North of Slavery: The Negro in the Free States, 1789-1860, Univ Chicago, 61; ed, American Labor Movement, Prentice-Hall, 62; auth, The emancipation of the Negro abolitionist, In: The Antislavery Vanguard, Princeton Univ, 65; co-ed, Reconstruction: An Anthology of Revisionist Writings, La State Univ, 69; auth, Free at last, In: Anonymous Americans, Prentice-Hall, 71; co-ed, To Look for America (film), Nat Educ TV, 72; coauth, The United States, 4th ed, 76 & 5th ed, 82, Prentice-Hall; auth, Been in the Storm So Long, The Aftermath of Slavery, Knopf, 79; Trouble in Mind: Black Southerners in the Age of Jim Crow, Knopf, 98. **CONTACT ADDRESS** Dept of Hist, Univ of California, Berkeley, 3229 Dwinelle Hall, Berkeley, CA 94720-2551.

LITWICKI, ELLEN M.

PERSONAL Born 07/15/1955, Chicago, IL **DISCIPLINE** HISTORY **EDUCATION** Northern Ariz Univ, BA, 76; Ariz State Univ, MBA, 80; Univ Va, MA, 85; PhD, 92. **CAREER** Vis Instr/Vis Asst Prof, Univ of Utah, 90-92; Asst Prof to Assoc Prof, SUNY Col at Fredonia, 92-. **RESEARCH** Orgn of Am Historians, Am Studies Asn. **SELECTED PUBLICATIONS** Auth, "'The Inauguration of the People's Age': The Columbian Quadrucentennial and American Culture," The Md Historian (Spring/Summer 89); auth, "From Patron to Patria: The Nationalization of Mexicano Culture in Late Nineteenth-Century Tucson," Canon, the J of the Rocky Mountain Am Studies Asn 4 (Fall 98): 31-56; auth, "'Our Hearts Burn with Ardent Love for Two Countries': Ethnicity and Assimilation at Chicago Holiday Celebrations, 1876-1918," J of Am Ethnic Hist (forthcoming); auth, American's Public Holidays, 1865-1920, Smithsonian Inst Press (Washington, DC), forthcoming. **CONTACT ADDRESS** Dept Hist, SUNY, Col at Fredonia, Fredonia, NY 14063-1143. **EMAIL** litwicki@fredonia.edu

LIVEZEANU, I.

PERSONAL Born 10/18/1952, Bucharest, Romania **DISCIPLINE** EASTERN EUROPEAN HISTORY **EDUCATION** Swarthmore, BA, 74; Univ Mich, MA, 79; Univ Mich, PhD, 86. **CAREER** Asst prof, Colby Col, 87-91; **HONORS AND AWARDS** Phi Beta Kappa; FLAS-Russian; FLAS-Polish, IREX, ACLS Dissertation Fel; Mellon Post Doc, Univ Calif Berkeley; book award, Amer Romanian Acad; Heldt book prize. **MEMBERSHIPS** AAASS; Asn of Women in Slavic Studies; Soc for Romanian Studies; Asn for Jewish Studies; Asn for the Study of Nationalities. **RESEARCH** Culture; nationalism; Jews; intellectuals; identity. **SELECTED PUBLICATIONS** Auth, Defining Russian at the Margins, Russian Rev 95; A Jew from the Danube, Shvut: Jewish Problems in the USSR and Eastern Europe, 93; Moldavia, 1917-1990: Nationalism and Internationalism Then and Now, Armenian Rev, 90; Between State and Nation: Romania's Lower Middle Class Intellectuals in the Interwar Period, Splintered Classes: The European Lower Middle Classes in the Age of Fascism, 90; Fascists and Conservatives in Romania: Two Generations of Nationalists, Fascists and Conservatives in Europe, 90; Excerpts from a Troubled Book: An Episode in Romanian Literature, Cross Currents: A Yearbook of Central European Culture, 84; Urbanization in a Low Key and Linguistic Change in Soviet Moldavia Parts 1 and 2, Soviet Studies, 81; Cultural Politics in Greater Romania: Regionalism, Nation Building, and Ethnic Struggle, 1918-1930, Cornell Univ Press, 95; Cultura se Nationalism in Romania Mare, 1918-1930, Ed Humanitas, 98. **CONTACT ADDRESS** Univ of Pittsburgh, 3P01 Forbes Quadrangle, Pittsburgh, PA 15260. **EMAIL** irinal@pitt.edu

LIVINGSTON, DONALD W.

DISCIPLINE HISTORY OF MODERN PHILOSOPHY **EDUCATION** WA Univ, PhD, 65. **CAREER** Prof, Philos, Emory Univ. **HONORS AND AWARDS** Nat Endowment Hum fel, 78-79. **RESEARCH** History of modern philosophy (especially Hume and the Scottish Enlightenment), philosophy of history, political philosophy **SELECTED PUBLICATIONS** Auth, Hume's Philosophy of Common Life; auth, Philosophical Melancholy and Delirium; Coed Hume, A Re-evaluation; Liberty in Hume's "History of England"; Hume as Philosopher of Society, Politics, and History **CONTACT ADDRESS** Emory Univ, Atlanta, GA 30322-1950. **EMAIL** dliving@emory.edu

LIVINGSTON, JOHN W.

DISCIPLINE OTTOMAN EMPIRE AND MODERN ARAB STATES **EDUCATION** Princeton Univ, PhD, 68. **CAREER** Post Doctoral Res Fel, Harvard Univ, 68-70; William Paterson Col, 87-; Temple Univ, Pa, 86-87; Amer Univ, Beirut, 70-85; Univ Fla, Orlando, 85-86. **HONORS AND AWARDS** Fulbright Scholar, 63; Am Philos Soc award for res, 96. **MEMBERSHIPS** Middle Eastern Stud Asn. **RESEARCH** Ottoman Empire; Modern Arab States. **SELECTED PUBLICATIONS** Auth, "Ali Bey al-Kabir of Egypt and the Jews," Middle Eastern Studies (London, 72); auth, "The Makula: An Islamic Conical Sundial," Centaurus Int Magazine of the Hist of Mathematics, Sci, and Technology (Copenhagen, 72); auth, "Nasir al-Din al-Tadhkirah: A Category of Islamic Astronomical Literature," Centaurus (Copenhagen, 72); auth, "Evliyya Celebi on Surgical Operations in Vienna," Al-Abhath: Studies in Arabic and Islamic Culture (The Am Univ of Beruit, Lebanon, 73); auth, "Ali Bey al-Kabir and the Re-opening of the Red Sea Trade Route in the Eighteenth Century," Acts of the Twenty-Ninth Orientalists Congress (Sorbonne, Paris, 74); auth, "Science and the Occult in the Thinking of Ibn Qayyim al-Jawziyya," Journal of Am Oriental Soc 112 (92): 598-610; auth, "Shaykh Muhammad Abduh and the Legitimation of Western Science," J Middle East Stud (93); auth, "Shaykhs, Jabarti, and Attar: A Study of Science and Islam in Nineteenth Century Egypt," Studia Islamica (93); auth, "Shaykh Rifa'a Rafi'i al-Tahtawi and the Islamic Response to Western Science, Der Islam; Science and the Occult in the Thinking of Ibn Qayyim al- Jawziyya," J Amer Orient Soc (92); auth, "Bonaparte and Shaykh Bakri," Studia Islamica, fasicule 80 (94). **CONTACT ADDRESS** Dept of History, William Paterson Col of New Jersey, 300 Pompton Rd., Atrium 210, Wayne, NJ 07470. **EMAIL** Livingstonj@wpunj.edu

LLOYD, ELISABETH A.

PERSONAL Born 03/03/1956 **DISCIPLINE** HISTORY, PHILOSOPHY OF SCIENCE **EDUCATION** Queen's Univ, 74-75; Univ Colo-Boulder, BA, Sci/Polit Theory, 76-80; Princeton Univ, PhD, 80-84. **CAREER** Vis instr, Exper Stud, Univ Colo-Boulder, 80; vis scholar, Genetics, Harvard Univ, 83-84; vis lectr, Philos, Univ Calif-San Diego, 84-85; asst prof, Philos, Univ Calif-San Diego, 85-88; asst prof, Univ Calif-Berkeley, 88-90; assoc prof, Univ Calif-Berkeley, 90-97; prof, Philos, Univ Calif-Berkeley, 97-; PROF, BIOL, IND UNIV, 98-; visiting prof, Harvard, 98; prof, History & phil of sci dept, Ind Univ, 98-. **MEMBERSHIPS** Nat Endow Hum; Nat Sci Found; Am Philos Asn; Philos Sci Asn; Int Soc Hist, Philos, & Soc Stud of Biol **SELECTED PUBLICATIONS** The Structure and Confirmation of Evolutionary Theory, Princeton UP 94; co-edr, Keywords in Evolutionary Biology, Harvard Univ Press, 92; "The Anachronistic Anarchist," Philosophical Studies 81, APA West Div Sympos, 96; "Science and Anti-Science: Objectivity and its Real Enemies," Feminism, Science, and the Philosophy of Science, Kluwer, 96; "Feyerabend, Mill, and Pluralism," Philosophy of Science, Supplemental Issue: PSA 96 Symposium Papers, 97. **CONTACT ADDRESS** Hist & Philos Sci Dept, Indiana Univ, Bloomington, Goodbody Hall 130, Bloomington, IN 47405-2401. **EMAIL** ealloyd@indiana.edu

LLOYD, JENNIFER

PERSONAL Born 04/01/1939, United Kingdom, d, 2 children **DISCIPLINE** HISTORY, WOMEN'S STUDIES **EDUCATION** Cambridge Univ, BA, 61; Univ London, Post Graduate Certificate in Educ, 62; Cambridge Univ, MA, 66; State Univ NY at Brockport, MA, 87; Univ Rochester, PhD, 92. **CAREER** Asst prof & dir women's studies, State Univ NY at Brockport, 96-. **HONORS AND AWARDS** Eileen Power Prize, Gimton Col, 59; George Queen Awd for Teaching, Stat Univ NY at Brockport, 86 & 97; W. Wayne Dedman Awd, State Univ NY at Brockport, 86; Wilson S. Coates & Hilda M. Altschule Prize, Univ Rochester, 88 & 90. **MEMBERSHIPS** Am Hist Asn, Nat Women's Studies Asn, N Am Confr on British Studies, Berkshire Confr of Women's Historians. **RESEARCH** Nineteenth-Century British Women's History. **SELECTED PUBLICATIONS** Auth, "Cultivating Lilies: Ruskin and Women," J of British Studies, 95; auth, "Strains in the Ideas of Compasionate Marriage in Victorian England: The Failed Marriage of Effie

Gray and John Ruskin," J of Women's Hist, 99. **CONTACT ADDRESS** Dept Hist, SUNY, Col at Brockport, 350 New Campus Dr, Brockport, NY 14410-2997. **EMAIL** jlloyd@brockport.edu

LO, WINSTON W.
PERSONAL Born 04/12/1938, China, m, 1967, 2 children **DISCIPLINE** HISTORY **EDUCATION** Harvard Univ, PhD, 70. **CAREER** Prof of Hist, Fla State Univ, 88-. **MEMBERSHIPS** Asn of Asian Studies. **RESEARCH** Chinese intellectual & institutional history (Song through the Qing period). **SELECTED PUBLICATIONS** Auth, Life and Thought of Yeh Shih, Chinese Univ of Hong Kong Press, 74; Szechwan in Sung Times, The Univ of Chinese Culture Press, Taipei, 82; An Introduction to the Civil Service of Sung China, Univ of Hawaii Press, 87. **CONTACT ADDRESS** Dept of Hist, Florida State Univ, Tallahassee, FL 32306. **EMAIL** wlo@mailer.fsu.edu

LOADER, COLIN T.
DISCIPLINE HISTORY **EDUCATION** Univ Calif Los Angeles, PhD, 74. **CAREER** Assoc prof, Univ Nev Las Vegas. **RESEARCH** German history; European intellectual history; 19th century Europe. **SELECTED PUBLICATIONS** Auth, The Intellectual Development of Karl Mannheim: Culture, Politics and Planning, Cambridge, 85. **CONTACT ADDRESS** History Dept, Univ of Nevada, Las Vegas, 4505 Md Pky, Las Vegas, NV 89154.

LOCKARD, CRAIG ALAN
PERSONAL Born 10/20/1942, Ft Madison, IA, m, 1970, 2 children **DISCIPLINE** ASIAN AND WORLD HISTORY **EDUCATION** Univ Redlands, BA, 64; Univ Hawaii, MA, 67; Univ Wis, PhD(hist), 73. **CAREER** Instr hist, Univ Bridgeport, 69-70; vis asst prof, State Univ NY Stony Brook, 72-73 and State Univ NY Buffalo, 73-74; asst prof, 75-79, Assoc Prof Hist and Social Change, Univ Wis-Green Bay, 79-, Fulbright-Hays sr lectr, Univ Malaya, 77-78, grant, 77-78; fel, Univ Ky, 80; Am Ethnic Studies Coord Comt grant, 80-81; Univ Wis-Green Bay Outstanding Scholar Award, 81. **MEMBERSHIPS** Asn for Asin Studies; Borneo Res Coun; Royal Asiatic Soc; African Studies Asn. **RESEARCH** Modern Southeast Asian history especially Malaysia and Indonesia; overseas Chinese and Indonesians; comparative Third World socioeconomic history. **SELECTED PUBLICATIONS** Auth, Chinese leadership and power in Sarawak, 9/71 & 1857 Chinese rebellion in Sarawak, 9/78, J Southeast Asian Studies; Javanese as emigrant, Indonesia, 4/71; Repatriation movements among Javanese in Surinam, Caribbean Studies, 4/78; Patterns of social development in modern Southeast Asian cities, J Urban Hist, 11/78; Global history, modernization and world-system approach, Hist Teacher, 4/81; From Kampong to City: Social History of Kuching, Malaysia, Univ Malaya, 82. **CONTACT ADDRESS** Dept of Hist and Social Change, Univ of Wisconsin, Green Bay, Green Bay, WI 54302.

LOENGARD, JANET SENDEROWITZ
PERSONAL Born 06/21/1935, Allentown, PA, m, 1964, 2 children **DISCIPLINE** MEDIEVAL EUROPEAN HISTORY **EDUCATION** Cornell Univ, BA, 55; Harvard Univ, LLB, 58; Columbia Univ, MA, 64; PhD(hist), 70. **CAREER** Instr hist, Rutgers Univ, Newark, 69-70; asst prof, City Col New York, 70-71; asst prof, 71-74; assoc prof, 74-83; prof, hist, 83-, Moravian Col; lectr, law, Rutgers Law School, Newark, 89-94; Am Soc for Legal Hist, bd dirs, 78-80, 86-88; Bk Review ed, Am Jour of Legal Hist, 81-88. **HONORS AND AWARDS** NEH summer stipend, 78; gave J.H. Becker Lecture, Cornell Univ, 91; mem, Council of the Selden Soc, 94-. **MEMBERSHIPS** Conf Brit Studies; Am Soc Legal Hist; AHA; Medieval Acad Am; Selden Soc. **RESEARCH** Medieval English legal history; English legal history. **SELECTED PUBLICATIONS** Auth, "The Assize of Nuisance: Origins of an Action at Common Law," Cambridge Law Journal 37 (78); auth, "An Elizabethan Lawsuit: John Brayne, His Carpenters, and the Building of the Red Lion Theatre," Shakespeare Quarterly 34.3 (83); auth, "Of the Gift of her Husband: Dower in England c. 1200," in Women of the Medieval World, ed. Julius Kirshner and Suzanne Wemple (Oxford and NYork, Basil Blackwell, 85); auth, "Legal History and the Medieval Englishwoman: A Fragmented View," Law and History Review 4.1 (86); auth, London Viewers and their Certificates, 1500-1558, London Record Society, 89; auth, "Rationabilis Dos: Calculating the Widow's 'Fair Share' in the Earlier Thirteenth Century," in Wife and Widow in Medieval England, ed. Sue Sheridan Walker (Ann Arbor, Univ of Mich Press, 94); auth, "Common Law for Margery: Separate but not Equal," in Virgins, Viragos, Alewives, and Queens, ed. Linda Mitchell (NYork, Garland Press, 99). **CONTACT ADDRESS** Dept of Hist, Moravian Col, 1200 Main St, Bethlehem, PA 18018-6650. **EMAIL** loengardj@moravian.edu

LOERKE, WILLIAM
PERSONAL Born 08/13/1920, Toledo, OH, m, 1944, 7 children **DISCIPLINE** CLASSICAL ARCHAEOLOGY, ART HISTORY (ANCIENT-MEDIEVAL) **EDUCATION** Oberlin Col, BA, 42; Princeton Univ, MFA, 48; PhD, 56. **CAREER** Instr-asst prof, Brown Univ, 48-58; assoc prof, Bryn Mawr Col, 58-64; Prof of Art Hist, Univ Pittsburgh, 65-71, chmn Frick Fine Arts Dept, 65-68; Prof Byzantine Art, Harvard Univ at Dumbarton Oaks, Washington, DC, 71-88, dir, Center for Byzantine Studies, 71-78; vis prof, Hist of Architecture at School of Architecture, The Cath Univ of Am, Washington, DC, 78-88; lect in Hist of Architecture, The Cath Univ, Washington, DC, 88-91; lect in Hist of Architecture, School of Architecture, Univ MD, College Park, 91-93. **HONORS AND AWARDS** Miller scholar, Oberlin, 38-42; Phi Beta Kappa, Oberlin, 42; Jr fel, Princeton, 46-48; Fulbright res scholar at Am Academy Rome, 52-53; Danforth Teacher fel, 55-56. **MEMBERSHIPS** Med Academy of Am; Soc of Archit Historians; Soc of Fellows-Am Academy Rome; College Art Asn; Bd of Advisers, Center for Advanced Studies in the Visual Arts (CASVA), Nat Gallery, Washington, DC, 71-73, 81-83, 98-99. **RESEARCH** Roman Imperial Architecture (Pantheon); Early Christian Art. **SELECTED PUBLICATIONS** Auth, with G Cavallo and J Gribomont, Codex Purpureus Rossanensis, Commentarium, Salerno/Graz, 87; A Rereading of the Interior Elevation of Hadrian's Rotunda, JSAH, XLIX, 1, 90; contrib, Oxford Dictionary of Byzantium, Oxford Press, NYC, 91; Incipits and Author Portraits in Greek Books: Some Observations, in Byzantine East, Latin West, Art Historical Studies in Honor of Kurt Weitzmann, Princeton, 95; contrib, Dictionary of Early Christian Art & Archaeology, forthcoming. **CONTACT ADDRESS** 227 Gralan Rd, Catonsville, MD 21228. **EMAIL** bloerke@aol.com

LOFGREN, CHARLES AUGUSTIN
PERSONAL Born 09/08/1939, Missoula, MT, m, 1986 **DISCIPLINE** AMERICAN HISTORY **EDUCATION** Stanford Univ, AB, 61, AM, 62, PhD, 66. **CAREER** Instr hist, San Jose State Col, 65-66; Vis asst prof, Stanford Univ, 68-69; from asst prof to assoc prof, 66-76, prof his, Claremont McKenna Col, 76-, mem Claremont Grad Univ, Claremont Cols, 67-, Chmn Hist Claremont McKenna Col, 70-73, 76-80, Chmn Gov Dept, 84-86, 88-90, Crocker Prof Am Hist and Pol, 76. **MEMBERSHIPS** AHA; Orgn Am Historians; Am Soc Legal Hist. **RESEARCH** Am constitutional hist. **SELECTED PUBLICATIONS** Auth, Mr Truman's war: A debate and its aftermath, Rev Polit, 4/69; Warmaking under the constitution: The original understanding, Yale Law J, 3/72; United States vs Curtiss-Wright Export Corporation: An historical reassessment, Yale Law J, 11/73; Missouri vs Holland in historical perspective, Supreme Ct Rev, 75; Compulsory military service under the Constitution: The original understanding, William & Mary Quart, 1/76; National League of Cities versus Usery: Dual Federalism Reborn, Claremont J Pub Affairs, 77; contrib, Constitutional government in America, Carolina Acad Press, 80; To regulate commerce: Federal power under the Constitution, This Constitution, 86; Government from reflection and choice: Constitutional essays on war, foreign relations and federalism, Oxford Univ, 86; contr, The framing and ratification of the Constitution, Macmillan, 87; The original understanding of original intent?, Constitutional Commentrary, winter 88; auth, The Plessy Case: A legal-constitutional interpretation, Oxford Univ, 88; Madisonian limitations, Rev Am Hist, 3/92; contr, Benchmarks: Great constitutional controversies in the Supreme Court, Center for Ethics and Public Policy, 95; auth, Claremont pioneers: The founding of CMC, Gould Center, Claremont McKenna Col, 96. **CONTACT ADDRESS** Dept of Hist, Claremont McKenna Col, Pitzer Hall-850 Columbia, Claremont, CA 91711-6420. **EMAIL** clofgren@mckenna.edu

LOGAN, JOANNE
PERSONAL Born 08/14/1954, Boston, MA, m, 1986, 3 children **DISCIPLINE** GEOGRAPHY, HORTICULTURE, CLIMATOLOGY **EDUCATION** Univ Conn, BA, 72; Univ Nebr, MS, 81; PhD, 84. **CAREER** Asst Prof, Univ of Nebr, 84-87; Asst Prof/Assoc Prof, Univ of Tenn, 87-. **HONORS AND AWARDS** Sigma Xi, 84; Outstanding Teacher, NACTA; Outstanding Teacher, TACTA, W.S. Overton Fac Merit Awd. **MEMBERSHIPS** Am Soc of Horticultural Sci, Am Meteorological Soc, Tenn Geog Infor Coun. **RESEARCH** Applied Climatology. **SELECTED PUBLICATIONS** Coauth, "Mathematical formulas for calculating the base temperature in heat unit systems," Agr and Forest Meteorology 74 (95): 61-74; auth, "Using the Internet as a Multimedia tool in K-16 Classroom, " J Natural Res Life Sci Educ 25-2 (96): 111-112; coauth, "Evaluation of the Early Soybean Production System," Tenn Agr Sci 184 (98): 11-13; coauth, "A Comparison of Early (ESPS) and recommended soybean production systems in Tennessee," J of Prod Agr 11 (98): 319-325; caouth, "Photosynthesis and water-use rate of switchgrass varieties," in Switchgrass as a biofuels crop for the upper Southeast: Variety trials and cultural improvements (Blacksburg, VA: Va Polytech Inst State Univ, 99); coauth, Microclimates, peach bud phenology and freeze risks in a topographically diverse orchard, Hort Tech, in press. **CONTACT ADDRESS** Univ of Tennessee, Knoxville, 369 Plant Sciences, PO Box 1071, Knoxville, TX 37901-1071. **EMAIL** loganj@utk.edu

LOGAN, SAMUEL TALBOT, JR.
DISCIPLINE CHURCH HISTORY **EDUCATION** Princeton Univ, BA, 65; Westminster Theol Sem, MDiv, 68; Emory Univ, PhD, 72. **CAREER** Tchg asst, Emory Univ, 69; instr, DeKalb Jr Col, 70; dir, Dept Amer Stud, Barrington Col, 70-79; asst prof, 70-1978; prof, Barrington Col, 78-79; prof, Westminster Theol Sem, 79-. **SELECTED PUBLICATIONS** Auth, Academic Freedom at Christian Institutions, Christian Scholar's Rev; Shoulders to Stand On, Decision, 93; Theological Decline in Christian Institutions and the Value of Van Til's Epistemology, Westminster Theol Jour, 95; ed, The Preacher and Preaching: Reviving the Art in the Twentieth Century. **CONTACT ADDRESS** Westminster Theol Sem, Pennsylvania, PO Box 27009, Philadelphia, PA 19118. **EMAIL** slogan@wts.edu

LOGAN, WENDELL
DISCIPLINE AFRICAN-AMERICAN MUSIC **EDUCATION** Fla A&M Univ, BS, 62; S Ill Univ, MM, 64; Univ Iowa, PhD 68. **CAREER** Ball State Univ, 67-69; Fla A&M, 68-70; Western Ill Univer, 70-73; Prof; Oberlin, 73, ch, jazz studies prog. **HONORS AND AWARDS** NEA grants, 73, 78, 85, 96; ASCAP awards, 80-96; Ohio Arts Coun grants, 84, 85, 93; Guggenheim award, 90; Cleveland Arts Prize, 91; fel, Rockefeller Study Ctr, Italy, 94; ascap awards, 86-90. **SELECTED PUBLICATIONS** Publ in, Perspectives of New Music , The Black Perspective in Music , NUMUS West, Black Music Res Jour and Field Magazine. **CONTACT ADDRESS** Dept of Mus, Oberlin Col, Oberlin, OH 44074.

LOGSDON, JOSEPH
PERSONAL Born 03/12/1938, Chicago, IL, m, 1960, 2 children **DISCIPLINE** UNITED STATES HISTORY **EDUCATION** Univ Chicago, AB, 59, MA, 61; Univ Wis, PhD(hist), 66. **CAREER** From instr to asst prof hist, La State Univ, New Orleans, 64-69; assoc prof hist and urban studies, Lehigh Univ, 69-71; assoc prof, 71-72, Prof Hist, Univ New Orleans, 73-, Chair, 80-, La State Univ res coun grant and Am Philos Soc grant, 68; Danforth fel black study, 70-71 and Danforth assoc, 72-. **MEMBERSHIPS** AHA; Asn Study Negro Life and Hist. **RESEARCH** Reconstruction; nineteenth century liberalism; Black history. **SELECTED PUBLICATIONS** Auth, The Civil War-Russian Version .., Civil War Hist, 12/62 Coauth, Twelve Years a Slave, La State Univ, 68; An Illinois Carpetbagger Looks at the Southern Negro, J Ill State Hist Soc, 69; contribr, Seven on Black, Lippincott, 70; auth, Horace White: Nineteenth Century Liberal, Greenwood, 72; Black Reconstruction Revisited, Rev Am Hist, 12/73; contribr, Biographical Dictionary of American Mayors, Greenwood, 81. **CONTACT ADDRESS** Dept of Hist, Univ of New Orleans, New Orleans, LA 70148.

LOHMANN, CHRISTOPH KARL
PERSONAL Born 10/06/1935, Berlin, Germany, m, 1961, 2 children **DISCIPLINE** ENGLISH, AMERICAN STUDIES **EDUCATION** Swarthmore Col, BA, 58; Columbia Univ, MA, 61; Univ Pa, PhD(Am civilization), 68. **CAREER** Asst prof, 68-73, assoc prof, 73-81, Prof English, Ind Univ, Bloomington and Assoc Dean Fac, 81-, Assoc ed, a Selected Edition of W D Howells, Ind Univ, 72-; Fulbright Comn sr res fel, Fed Repub Ger, 76-77. **MEMBERSHIPS** MLA; Am Studies Asn. **RESEARCH** Nineteenth century American literature; American studies. **SELECTED PUBLICATIONS** Auth, The burden of the past in Hawthorne's American romances, SAtlantic Quart, winter 67; The agony of the English romance, Nathaniel Hawthorne J, 72; Jamesian irony and the American sense of mission, Tex Studies Lit & Lang, 74; coauth, Commentary on Henry James Letters, Nineteenth-Century Fiction, 9/76; coed, Selected Letters of W D Howells, vols I-V, Twayne, 82; E L Doctorow's Historical Romances, The Contemporary American Novel, Adler Foreign Books, 82. **CONTACT ADDRESS** Dept of English, Indiana Univ, Bloomington, Bloomington, IN 47401.

LOHOF, BRUCE ALAN
PERSONAL Born 02/29/1940, Billings, MT, m, 1964, 2 children **DISCIPLINE** AMERICAN STUDIES **EDUCATION** Stetson Univ, BA, 63, MA, 65; Syracuse Univ, PhD(Am studies), 68. **CAREER** Instr hist, Maria Regina Col, 66-68; asst prof Am studies, Heidelberg Col, 68-71, assoc prof, 71-72; asst prof hist and coordr Am studies, 72-75, chmn, Dept Hist, 75-76, Assoc Prof Hist, Univ Miami, 75-, Vis prof, Bowling Green State Univ, 72; Fulbright-Hays sr scholar and dir, Am Studies Res Centre, India, 76-78. **MEMBERSHIPS** Am Studies Asn; Orgn Am Historians; Popular Cult Asn. **RESEARCH** American studies; American history; popular culture. **SELECTED PUBLICATIONS** Auth, The Deeper Meaning of Marlboro, on Commercialization of a Metaphor, Neue Rundschau, Vol 0105, 94. **CONTACT ADDRESS** Univ of Miami, Box 248194, Coral Gables, FL 33124.

LOMAX, JOHN PHILLIP
PERSONAL Born 05/09/1952, Omaha, NE, d, 2 children **DISCIPLINE** HISTORY, CRIMINAL JUSTICE, POLITICAL SCIENCE **EDUCATION** Nebraska Wesley Univ, BA, 74; Univ Chicago, MA, 75; Univ Kansas, PhD, 87. **CAREER** Vis Instr of History, Univ of Nebr at Omaha, 86-87; Lecturer in History, Univ of Tex at Austin, 87-88; Asst Prof of History, Oh Northern Univ, 88-93; Assoc Prof of History, 93-00; Prof of History, 00-. **HONORS AND AWARDS** Fulbright-Hays Junior Fellow, 84-85. **MEMBERSHIPS** American Historical Assoc, Medieval Academy of America, Society for Medieval Canon Law. **RESEARCH** Medieval Politics and Law. **SELECTED PUBLICATIONS** Auth, "A Canonistic Reconsideration of the Crusade of Frederick II," Monumenta Iuris Canonici 9: 206-226; auth, "Frederick II, his Saracens, and the Papacy, " in Medieval Christian Perceptions of Islam (Garland, 96); auth, "Spolia as property," Res Publica Litterarum 20: 83-94. **CONTACT ADDRESS** Dept History, Political Science, and Criminal Justice, Ohio No Univ, 525 S Main St, Ada, OH 45810-6000. **EMAIL** j-lomax@onu.edu

LONDON, HERBERT
PERSONAL Born 03/06/1939, New York, NY, m, 1976, 3 children **DISCIPLINE** MODERN HISTORY **EDUCATION** Columbia Univ, BA, 60, MA, 61; NYork Univ, PhD(social studies), 66. **CAREER** Instr Am hist, New Sch Social Res, 63-64 & social studies, NY Univ, 65-66; Fulbright res scholar polit sci, Australian Nat Univ, 66-67; from asst prof to assoc prof, 67-73, dir exp progs, 72-73, Prof Social Studies, NY Univ, 73-, Dean, Gallation Div, 76-92; Consult, 69-97, Hudson Inst, Pres, 97-; host, Myths That Rule America, Nat Broadcasting Co TV. **HONORS AND AWARDS** Martin Luther King Humanitarian Awd; Ellis Island Medal of Honor; Peter Shaw Awd for Exemplary Writing. **MEMBERSHIPS** Popular Cult Asn; AHA; Polit Sci Asn; Nat Asn of Scholars. **RESEARCH** Popular culture; contemporary American history; Australia Policy. **SELECTED PUBLICATIONS** Co-ed, Education in the Twenty-First Century, Interstate Press, 69; auth, Non-White Immigration and the White Australia Policy, NY Univ, 70; Fitting In: Crosswise at Generation Gap, Grosset, 74; The Overheated Decade, NY Univ, 76; The Seventies: Counterfeit Decade, 79 & Myths That Rule America, Univ Press Am, 81; auth, Why are They Lying to Our Children, Stein and Day, 86; auth, From the Empire State to the Vampire State, UPA, 94. **CONTACT ADDRESS** New York Univ, 113 University Pl, New York, NY 10003. **EMAIL** hili@is.2.nyu.edu

LONG, JEROME HERBERT
PERSONAL Born 00/00/1931, Little Rock, AR, m, 1959, 2 children **DISCIPLINE** HISTORY OF RELIGIONS **EDUCATION** Knox Col, AB, 56; Univ Chicago Divinity Sch, BD, 60, MA, 62, PhD(hist of relig), 73. **CAREER** From instr to assoc prof relig, Western Mich Univ, 64-70; vis assoc prof, 70-71, Assoc Prof Relig, Wesleyan Univ, 71-, Mem, Comt on Reorgn of Curric of Relig Dept, Western Mich Univ, 65-67, mem, African Studies Comt, 65-70, secy, 66-67, mediator, Black Am Studies Prog, 68-70; mem, African Studies Comt, Wesleyan Univ, 74-75, chmn, 75-76, chmn, Search Comt for Dir for Ctr for Afro-Am Studies and interim curric coordr, Ctr for Afro-Am Studies, 75-76; Vis Scholar, Inst African Studies, Legon, Ghana, West Africa, Univ Ghana, 77-. **RESEARCH** Prehistoric and primitive religions; historical approaches to religion and culture; religions of African peoples. **SELECTED PUBLICATIONS** Auth, Symbol and reality among the Trobriand Islanders, in: Essays in Divinity, Vol 1: the History of Religion, Univ Chicago, 69. **CONTACT ADDRESS** Wesleyan Univ, Middletown, CT 06457.

LONG, JOHN WENDELL
PERSONAL Born 11/30/1939, Hartford, CT, m, 1961, 1 child **DISCIPLINE** MODERN EUROPEAN HISTORY **EDUCATION** Univ Mass, Amherst, BA, 61; Columbia Univ, MA and cert, 65, PhD(hist), 72. **CAREER** Lectr hist, Manhattan Sch Music, 64-70; asst prof, 70-76, Assoc Prof Hist, Rider Col, 76-, Vis prof, Trenton State Col, 72; res assoc, Russ and E Europ Ctr, Univ Ill, 73; assoc Danforth Found, 74-; vis scholar, Kennan Inst Advan Russ Studies, Smithsonian Inst, 80. **MEMBERSHIPS** AHA; Am Asn Advan Slavic Studies; AAUP; Soc Hist Educ. **RESEARCH** History of Russia; modern history of Eastern Europe; modern history of Western Europe. **SELECTED PUBLICATIONS** Auth, The Russian Naval Museum, Slavic Rev, 6/71; Using the sources, Soviet Studies, 7/74; coauth, the Church and the Russian Revolution, St Vladimir's Theol Quart, 9/76; T G Masaryk and the Strategy of Czechoslovak Independence, Slavonic and E Europ Rev, 1/78; American Jews and the Root Mission to Russia in 1917, Am Jewish Hist, 3/80; auth, American Intervention in Russia: the North Russian Expedition, 1918-1919, Diplomatic Hist, 2/82. **CONTACT ADDRESS** Dept of Hist, Rider Univ, 2083 Lawrenceville, Lawrenceville, NJ 08648-3099.

LONG, R. JAMES
PERSONAL Born 12/15/1938, Rochester, NY, m, 1974, 3 children **DISCIPLINE** HISTORY OF MEDIEVAL PHILOSOPHY **EDUCATION** Pontif Inst Med Studies, LMS, 66; Univ Toronto, PhD(Medieval studies), 68. **CAREER** From asst prof to assoc prof, 69-78, prof philos, Fairfield Univ, 78-, Fulbright scholar medieval philos, Fulbright Comn, US Govt, 68-69; Can Coun fel philos, 68-69; Am Coun Learned Socs & Am Philos Soc grant-in-aid, 77; Nat Endowment for Humanities scholarly publ grant, 79; vis fac fel, Yale Univ, 82-83, dir hon prog, 82-91; liason faculty, program in Greek and Roman Studies, Ffld univ, 81-. **HONORS AND AWARDS** Fellow of Massey Col, Toronto, 65-68; Province of Ontario Graduate Fellowships, 66-68; Canada Council Doctoral Fellowship, 67-68; Fulbright Scholarship, Italy and U.K., 68-69; Canada Council Postdoctoral Fellowship, 69; NEH Summer Stipend, 74; Am Council of Learned Socs Grant-in-Aid, 77; Am Philos Soc Grant, 77; Assoc of Clare Hall, Cambridge Univ, 77; NEH Scholarly Publications Grant, 79; NEH Summer Seminar for College Teachers, Fordham Univ, 81; Yale Visiting Faculty Fellowship, 82-83; NEH Summer Seminar for College Teachers, Yeshiva Univ, 84; Am Philos Soc Grant, 84; Fairfield Univ Summer Stipends, 86, 89, 92; NEH Summer Seminar for College Teachers, Columbia Univ, 87; NEH Summer Stipend, 88; Warren W. Wooden Citation, PMR Conference, 89; NEH Editions/Texts Grant, ed of Richard Fishacre's Sentences-Commentary, 1-2, $130,000, 92-94; Yale Visiting Fellowship, Philosophy Dept, 96-98. **MEMBERSHIPS** Medieval Acad Am; Am Cath Philos Asn (life member); Soc Textual Scholarship; Soc Medieval & Renaissance Philos, secrt-treas, 91-; Catholic Comm on Intellectual and Cultural Affairs; Consociatio cultorum historiae Ordinis Praedicatorum; International Soc for Napoleanic Studies; Societe Internationale pour l'Etude de la Philosophie Medievale. **RESEARCH** Early thirteenth-century philosophy, particularly Oxford; 13th-century science, particularly medicine and botany; works of Richard Fishacre. **SELECTED PUBLICATIONS** Auth, Utrum iurista vel theologus plus proficiat ad regimen ecclesie . . ., 68; The Science of Theology according to Richard Fishacre: Ed of the Prologue to his Commentary on the Sentences, 72, Mediaeval Studies; In Defense of the Tournament: an ed of Pierre Dubois' De torneamentis . . ., 73; A Note on the Dating of MS Ashmole 1512, 74, Manuscripta ; Richard Fishacre and the Problem of the Soul, Mod Schoolman, 75; Richard Fishacre's Quaestio on the Ascension of Christ: An Edition, Mediaeval Studies, 78; ed, Bartholomaeus Anglicus, On the Properties of Soul and Body, Toronto Medieval Latin Texts IV, 79; auth, Botany in the High Middle Ages: An introduction, Res Publica Litterarum, 81; The Virgin as Olive-Tree: A Marian Sermon of Richard Fishacre and Science at Oxford, Archivum Fratrum Praedicatorum 52: 77-87, 82; Alfred of Sareshel's Commentary on the Pseudo-Aristotelian De plantis: A Critical Edition, Mediaeval Studies 47: 125-67, 85; The Question "'Whether the Church Could Better be Ruled by a Good Canonist than by a Theologian' and the Origins of Ecclesiology, Proceedings of the PMR Conference 10: 99-112, 85; Richard Fishacre, Dictionnaire de Spiritualite 13, cols 563-65, 87; Richard Fishacre's Way to God, A Straight Path: Studies in Medieval Philosophy and Culture, Essays in Honor of Arthur Hyman, eds Ruth Link-Salinger et al, 174-82, Washington, D.C.: The Catholic Univ of Am Press, 88: with Joseph Goering, Richard Fishacre's Treatise De fide, spe, et caritate, Bull de Philos Medievale 31: 103-11, 89; Adam of Buckfield and John Sackville: Some Notes on Philadelphia Free Library MS Lewis European 53, Traditio 45: 364-67, 89-90; The Reception and Interpretation of the Pseudo-Arostolian De Plantis at Oxford in the Thirteenth Century, Knowledge and the Sciences in Medieval Philosophy (proceedings of the Eighth Intnl Congress of Medieval Philos: S.I.E.P.M, eds Reijo Tyorinoja, Anja I. Lehtinen, & Dagfinn Follesdal: Annuals of the Finnish Soc for Missiology and Ecumenics, 55, pp 111-23, Helsinki, 90; The Moral and Spiritual Theory of Richard Fishacre: Edition of Trinity Col, MS 0.1.30, Archivum Fratrum Praedicatorum 60, 5-143, 90; The Anonymous Peterhouse Master and the Natural Philosophy of Plants, Traditio 46: 313-26, 91; Richard Fishacre, Medieval Philosophers, ed Jeremiah Hackett, Dictionary of Literary Biography, vol 115, pp 195-200, Detroit: Bruccoli Clark Layman, Inc, 92; A Thirteenth-Century Teaching Aid: An Edition of the Bodleian Abbreviatio of the Pseudo-Aristolian De Plantis, in Aspectus et Affectus: Essays and Editions in Grosseteste and Medieval Intellectual Life in Honor of Richard C. Dales, ed Gunar Freibergs with an intro by Richard Southern, AMS Studies in the Middle Ages: no 23: 87-103, New York: AMS Press, 93; Richard Fishacre's Super S. Augustini librum de haeresibus adnotationes: An Edition and Commentary, Archives d'histoire doctrinale et litteraire du moyen age 60: 207-79, 93; Botany, in Medieval Latin: An Introduction and Bibliographical Guide, ed F.A.C. Mantello and A.G. Rigg, 401-05, Washington, D.C.: The Catholic Univ of America Press, 96; Richard Fishacre's Treatise De libero arbitrio, Moral and Political Philosophies in the Middle Ages, proceedings of the 9th Itnl congress of Medieval Philos, ed B. Carlos Bazan, Eduardo Andujar, Leonard Sbrocchi, 2: 879-91, Ottawa, 17-22, Aug 92, Ottawa: Legas, 95; with Margaret Jewett, A Newly Discovered Witness of Fishacre's Sentences-Commentary: Univ of Chicago MS 156, Traditio 50: 342-45, 95; The Reception and Use of Aristotle by the Early English Dominicans, Aristotle in Britain During the Middle Ages, ed John Marenbon, pp 51-56, Turnhout (Belgium): Brepols, 96; Roger Bacon on the Nature and Place of Angels, Vivarium 35/2: 266-82, 97; Richard Fishacre, in the New Dictionary of National Biography, (in press); Adam de Buckfield, ibid; Geoffrey de Aspale, ibid; The Cosmic Christ: The Christology of Richard Fishacre, OP, Christ Among the Medieval Dominicans, UND Press (in press); Of Angels and Pinheads: The Contributions of the Early Oxford Masters to the Doctrine of Spiritual Matter, Franciscan Studies, Essays in Honor of Girard Etzkorn, ed Gordon A. Wilson and Timothy B. Noone, 56: 237-52, 98; The First Oxford Debate on the Eternity of the World, Recherches de Philosophie et Theologie Medievale 65/1: 54-98, 98; with Timothy B. Noone, Fishacre and Rufus on the Metaphysics of Light: Two Unedited Texts, Melanges Leonard Boyle (in press); The Role of Philosophy in Richard Fishacre's Theology of Creation, proceedings of the 10th Inl Congress of Medieval Philosophy, Erfurt, 25-30 August 97: 571-78, in press; auth, "Fischacre and Rufus on the Metaphysics of Light: Two Unedited Texts," Roma, magistra mundi, Itineraria culturae medievalis, Melanges offerts au Pere L.E. Boyle a l'occasion de son 75 anniversire, Textes et Etudes du moyen age, with Timothy B. Noone, (Louvain-la-Neuve: Federation Internationale des Instituts d' Etudes Medievales, 98), 517-48; auth, "Richard Fishacre," Lexikon fur Theologie and Kirche 8, 99, 1171; auth, "The Integrative Theology of Richard Fishacre OP," New Blackfriars 80 no 941/42 (99): 354-60; auth, "Scholastic Texts and Orthography: A Response to Roland Hissette," Bulletin de Philosophie Medieval 41 (99), in press. **CONTACT ADDRESS** Dept of Philos, Fairfield Univ, 1073 N Benson Rd, Fairfield, CT 06430-5195. **EMAIL** long@fair1.fairfield.edu

LONG, ROGER D.
DISCIPLINE HISTORY **EDUCATION** Univ Calif, Los Angeles, PhD. **CAREER** Prof, Eastern Michigan Univ. **RESEARCH** Britain, British Empire, Canada, South Asia. **SELECTED PUBLICATIONS** Ed, The Man on the Spot: Essays on British Empire History; auth, "The Creation of Pakistan: An Annotated Bibliography." **CONTACT ADDRESS** Dept of History and Philosophy, Eastern Michigan Univ, 701 Pray-Harrold, Ypsilanti, MI 48197. **EMAIL** his_long@online.emich.edu

LONG, RONALD WILSON
PERSONAL Born 04/05/1937, Pittsburgh, PA, m, 1965, 2 children **DISCIPLINE** UNITED STATES HISTORY **EDUCATION** Waynesburg Col, BA, 64; Univ GA, PhD, 68. **CAREER** Asst prof, 68-74, assoc prof, 74-82, prof hist, WVA Univ Inst Technol, 82. **MEMBERSHIPS** Southern Hist Asn; Inst Early Am Hist & Cult. **RESEARCH** Am colonial hist; Am soc and intellectual hist; Hist of technol. **SELECTED PUBLICATIONS** Auth, The Presbyterians in the Whiskey Rebillion, J Presby Hist, 3/65; Malcolm X, In: Encyclopedia of Contemporary Social Issues, 96; Gerhard Domagk, In: Biographical Encyclopeida of Science, 97; Daniel Blain, In: Dictionary of Virginia Biography, 98. **CONTACT ADDRESS** Hum Div, West Virginia Univ Inst of Tech, 405 Fayette Pike, Montgomery, WV 25136-2436.

LONGFELLOW, DAVID LYMAN
PERSONAL Born 01/25/1949, Washington, DC **DISCIPLINE** EUROPEAN HISTORY **EDUCATION** Univ Va, AB, 70; Johns Hopkins Univ, MA, 72; PhD(hist), 80. **CAREER** Instr Europ hist, Hollins Col, 74-79, asst prof, 79-81; Asst Prof French Hist, Baylor Univ, 81-, Lectr, Roanoke Col, 75-81. **MEMBERSHIPS** AHA; Soc Fr Hist Studies; Western Soc Fr Hist; Western Hist Asn; AAUP. **RESEARCH** French artisanal politics and organization, 18th century; French Revolution, social, economic and political; Western European artisanal politics and organization, 18th and 19th centuries. **SELECTED PUBLICATIONS** Auth, Silk weavers and the social struggle in Lyon during the French Revolution, 1789-1794, Fr Hist Studies, spring 81; Artisanal labor movements and the French Revolution: The example of the silk weavers of Lyon, Vol 8, 81 & Jacobin economics? Reverchon and Dupuy's proposed reorganization of the Lyon silk industry in 1794, Vol 9, 82, Proc Western Soc Fr Hist; 7 articles in Dict of French History 1815-1859, Greenwood Press (in press). **CONTACT ADDRESS** Dept of Hist, Baylor Univ, Waco, Waco, TX 76798.

LOOMIE, ALBERT J.
PERSONAL Born 07/29/1922, New York, NY **DISCIPLINE** MODERN EUROPEAN HISTORY **EDUCATION** Loyola Univ, Ill, BA, 44; W Baden Col, PhL, 46; Fordham Univ, MA, 49; Woodstock Col, STL, 53; Univ London, PhD(Tudor hist), 57. **CAREER** From instr to assoc prof, 58-69, chmn dept, 78-81, Prof Hist, Fordham Univ, 69-93, Emeritus, 93-, Am Philos Soc grants, 64 and 71; Guggenheim fel, 65; Huntington Libr grantee, 67-; Folger Libr grants, 61, 62 and 70. **HONORS AND AWARDS** Award of Merit, Am Asn State and Local Hist, 54. **MEMBERSHIPS** Fel Royal Hist Soc; Am Cath Hist Asn; Renaissance Soc Am; Conf Brit Studies. **RESEARCH** Anglo-Spanish relations, 1580-1630; Tudor-Stuart history; Spain in the 16th and 17th centuries. **SELECTED PUBLICATIONS** Auth, English polemics at the Spanish Court: Joseph Creswell's Letter to the Ambassador from England, The English and the Spanish Texts of 1606, Fordham Univ Press, (93): 210; auth, Spain and the Early Stuarts, 1585-1655, Collected Studies Series: C522, Varriorum Press Aldershot, Hampshire, England, (96): 290; auth, "Spanish Secret Diplomacy at the Court of James I", Sixteenth Century Essays & Studies vol 27, (94): 231-244; auth, "Fr. Joseph Creswell's Information for Phillip II Archduke Ernest, ca., Aug 94" Recusant History, vol 22, (95): 465-481; auth, "A lost Crucifixion by Rubens", The Bulington Magazine, vol 138, (96): 734-739; auth, "The destruction of Ruben's "Crucifixion" in the Queen's Chapel, Somerset House", The Burlington Magazine, vol 140, (98): 680-682. **CONTACT ADDRESS** Loyola Hall, Fordham Univ, Bronx, NY 10458.

LOOS, JOHN LOUIS
PERSONAL Born 03/09/1918, Friend, NE, m, 1951, 2 children **DISCIPLINE** HISTORY **EDUCATION** Univ Nebr, AB, 39, MA, 40; Wash Univ, PhD, 53. **CAREER** Asst prof hist, Evansville Col, 48-51, instr, Wash Univ, 51-53; from instr to assoc prof, 55-66, Prof Hist, LA State Univ, Baton Rouge, 66-, Chmn Dept, 63- **MEMBERSHIPS** AHA; Orgn Am Historians; Western Hist Asn. **RESEARCH** Biog of William Clark, 1770-1838; Western American history; business history. **SELECTED PUBLICATIONS** Auth, Davis, Edwin, Adams--Obituary, J Southern Hist, Vol 0061, 95. **CONTACT ADDRESS** Dept of Hist, Louisiana State Univ and A&M Col, Baton Rouge, LA 70803.

LOPATA, ROY HAYWOOD
PERSONAL Born 02/26/1949, Bronx, NY, m, 1970, 2 children **DISCIPLINE** AMERICAN HISTORY **EDUCATION** Am Hist, BA, 70; Univ Del, MA, 72, PhD(hist), 75. **CAREER** Admin aide, 75-76, admin asst, 76-77, Planning Dir, City of

Newark, 77-, Asst prof, Hist Dept, Univ Del, 74-77. **MEMBERSHIPS** Nat Coun on Pub Hist, Amer Liver Found, Amer Planning Asn; Int City Management Asn. **RESEARCH** American urban and business history; urban planning and management. **SELECTED PUBLICATIONS** Auth, The Dome of the United States Capitol--an Architectural History, Public Historian, Vol 0017, 95. **CONTACT ADDRESS** PO Box 390, Newark, DE 19711.

LOPEZ, JOSE JAVIER

PERSONAL Born 02/19/1969, Puerto Rico, m, 1994, 2 children **DISCIPLINE** GEOGRAPHY **EDUCATION** Univ Puerto Rico, BA, 91; Ind State Univ, PhD, 98. **CAREER** Asst prof, Minn State Univ, 98-. **HONORS AND AWARDS** Benjamin Moulton Awd; Ed, Invest, Atlas Minn; Geog Grad Prog, Coord. **MEMBERSHIPS** AAG; NCGE. **RESEARCH** Quantitative techniques; economic geography; Latin America. **SELECTED PUBLICATIONS** Ed, Atlas of Minnesota, Cen for Rural Policy, Mankato (00); auth, "Assault," in Atlas of Crime, Onyx Press (00); auth, "The Geography of Crime in Puerto Rico: A Cross-Municipality Study of Murders and Manslaughter, 1983 to 1991," in Homines (00). **CONTACT ADDRESS** Dept Geography, Minnesota State Univ, Mankato, 7 Armstrong Hall, Mankato, MN 56001. **EMAIL** jose.lopez@mnsu.edu

LORA, RONALD GENE

PERSONAL Born 08/10/1938, Bluffton, OH, m, 1975, 4 children **DISCIPLINE** AMERICAN HISTORY **EDUCATION** Bluffton Col, BS, 60; Ohio State Univ, PhD, 67. **CAREER** Instr hist, Bluffton Col, 64-66; from asst prof to assoc prof Am hist, 67-75, prof hist, Univ Toledo, 75-; res leave, Univ Toledo, 73-74, 82, 89, 98. **HONORS AND AWARDS** Outstanding Teacher Awd, Univ Toledo, 76 & Ohio Academy of Hist, 87; Master Teacher, Univ Toledo, 93-95; pres, Ohio Acad of Hist, 97-98. **MEMBERSHIPS** Orgn Am Historians; AHA; Southern Hist Asn; Ohio Acad Hist. **RESEARCH** Recent American history; American intellectual history; nineteen-sixties. **SELECTED PUBLICATIONS** Ed, America in the 60's, Wiley, 74; ed, Conservative Press in the Eighteeth - and Nineteenth - Century America, Greenwood , 99; ed, Conservative Press in Twentieth Century America, Greenwood, 99; ed, The American West, Univ of Toledo, 80; auth, Conservative Minda in America, Rand McNelly,71, reprint, Greenwood, 79; auth, Education: Schools as crucible in Cold War America, Reshaping America, Ohio State Univ Press, 82; auth, Education, Public Policy and the State, American Choices, Ohio State, 86; auth, Jeffersonianism on Trial, For the General Welfare, 89; art, Russell Kirk: The Conservative Mind Three and One-Half Decades Later, Modern Age, 90. **CONTACT ADDRESS** Dept of History, Univ of Toledo, 2801 W Bancroft St, Toledo, OH 43606-3390. **EMAIL** rlora@utoledo.edu

LORENCE, JAMES J.

PERSONAL Born 11/18/1937, Racine, WI, m, 1960, 2 children **DISCIPLINE** HISTORY **EDUCATION** Univ Wisc, BS, 60, MS, 64, PhD, 70. **CAREER** Chemn, Univ Wisc Col Senate, 76-77, 85-86; chemn, dept hist, Univ Wisc Col, 78-81; from asst prof to prof, Univ Wisc, 81-. **HONORS AND AWARDS** Emil Steiger Awd for Excellence in Tchg, 70; State Historical Society Awd of Merit, 78, 95; AASLH Comendation, 78; Hesseltine Awd, 90; Carnegie- CASE Awd, 94; Beveridge Family Tchg Prize, 98; Kenneth Kingery Awd, 99; member, univ wisc, system tchr ed task force, 84. **MEMBERSHIPS** AHA; OAH; SHAFR; IAMHIST; SHE; SHSW; HFC; MCHS; WLHS **RESEARCH** US, 1900-; Great Depression; labor history; film history; US foreign relations. **SELECTED PUBLICATIONS** Coauth, Woodlot and Ballot Box: Marathon County in the Twentieth Century, 77; auth, Organized Business and the Myth of the China Market: The American Asiatic Association, 1898-1937, 81; auth, art, The Foreign Policy of Hollywood, 93; auth, Gerald J. Boileau and the Progressive-Farmer-Labor Alliance: Politics of the New Deal, 94; auth, Organizing the Unemployed: Community and Union Activists in the Industrial Heartland, 96; auth, Suppression of Salt of the Earth: How Hollywood, Big Labor, and Politicians Blacklisted a Movie in Cold War Am, 99. **CONTACT ADDRESS** Dept of History, Univ of Wisconsin Ctr, Marathon County, 518 S 7th Ave, Wausau, WI 54401. **EMAIL** jlorence@uwc.edu

LOREY, CHRISTOPH R.

DISCIPLINE GERMAN STUDIES **EDUCATION** Asst prof, assoc prof, Univ NBruns, 94-. **CAREER** Editor, The International Fiction Rev, 95-; Mem Ed Advisory Committee, J Can Lesbian Gay Study Asn, 98-00; Mem Ed Bd, Torquere, 00-. **RESEARCH** German culture and civilization; Queer theory; Gay and Lesbian literature; German enlightenment and classicism. **SELECTED PUBLICATIONS** Auth, Lessings Familienbild im Wechselbereich von Gesellschaft and Individuum, Bouvier (Bonn), 92; auth, "'Alles Ist so Schon, Dab es Fast zu Schon Ist': Die Sozialkritischen Motive in Adalbert Stifters Roman Der Nachsommer," Ger Quart 66 (94): 477-89; auth, "Glaube und Zweifel, Luge and Wahrheit, Genialitat and Einfalt: Georg Buchners Dantons Tod und Bertolt Brechts Leben des Galilei," Deuts Vierteljahr Lit Geistes 68 (94): 251-77; co-ed, "Die Schuld-Verhaltnisse in Hartmanns Iwein," in Analogon Rationis: Festschrift fur Gerwin Marahrens Zum 65, Geburtstag (Edmonton: Pub by the Eds, 94): 19-47; co-ed, Analogon Rationis: Festschrift fur Gerwin Marahrens zum 65, Geburtstag 95; auth, Die Ehe im Klassischen Werk Goethes, Rodopi Pr, 95; auth, "Zur Innen- und Aubenperspektive in Stephan Hermlin's Erzahlung Die Kommandeuse," J Ger Studies 33 (97): 134-48; co-ed, Queering the Canon: Defying Sights in German Literature and Culture, Camden House, 98; auth, "Warum es sinnvoll and notwendig ist, die Lesbenliteratur zu kanonisieren. Ein Beitrag zur Neuorientierung der deutschen Literaturgeschichtsschreibung," in Erinnern and Wiederentdecken: Tabuisierung and Enttabuisierung der mannlichen and weiblichen Homosexualitdt in Wissenschaft and Kritik, eds. Dirck Linck, Wolfgang Popp, Annette Runte (Berlin: Verlag rosa Winkel, 99): 149-168; co-auth, A New Guide to Reading German, Captus Pr, 00. **CONTACT ADDRESS** Dept Culture Lang Studies, Univ of New Brunswick, Fredericton, Carleton Hall Rm 334, PO Box 4400, Fredericton, NB, Canada E3B 5A3. **EMAIL** lorey@unb.ca

LORIMER, DOUGLAS

DISCIPLINE CANADIAN SOCIAL HISTORY **EDUCATION** British Columbia, PhD. **CAREER** Prof **RESEARCH** Science and secularization of Victorian images of race; continuities and discontinuities in the hist of scientific racism; antiracist voices in late-Victorian England; historical approaches to racism and anti-racism. **SELECTED PUBLICATIONS** Auth, Colour, Class and the Victorians: English Attitudes to the Negro in the Mid-Nineteenth Century, Leicester Univ Press, 78; auth, "Theoretical Racism in late Victorian Anthropology, 1870-1900," Victorian Studies 31, (88): 405-30; auth, "Nature, Racism and late Victorian Science," Canadian Journal of History 25, (90): 369-85; auth, "Black Resistance to Slavery and Racism in Eighteenth-Century England," in Essays on the History of Blacks in Britian, ed. I. Duffield and J. Gundara, (London: Avebury, 92): 58-80. **CONTACT ADDRESS** Dept of History, Wilfrid Laurier Univ, 75 University Ave W, Waterloo, ON, Canada N2L 3C5. **EMAIL** dlorimer@mach1.wlu.ca

LORIMER, JOYCE

DISCIPLINE EUROPEAN TRADE; SETTLEMENT IN GUAYANA **EDUCATION** Liverpool, PhD. **CAREER** Prof **RESEARCH** European trade and settlement in Guayana, (the region now incorporating the lower Amazon, Cayenne, Surinam, Guayana, and south-eastern Venezuela) between 1550 and 1670. **SELECTED PUBLICATIONS** Auth, English and Irish Settlement on the River Amazon, 1550-1646 , Hakluyt Soc & Cambridge UP, 90; co-ed, "The Reluctant Go-Between: John Ley's survey of aboriginal settlement on the Guayana coastline, 1597-1601," in The European Outthrust and Encounter, ed., P. E.H. Hair and C. Clough, (Liverpool: Liverpool Univ Press, 94); auth, "The Failure of the English Guiana Ventures, 1595-1667, and James I's Foreign Policy," Journal of Imperial and Commonwealth Hist 21. **CONTACT ADDRESS** Dept of History, Wilfrid Laurier Univ, 75 University Ave W, Waterloo, ON, Canada N2L 3C5. **EMAIL** jlorimer@mach1.wlu.ca

LOSADA, LUIS ANTONIO

PERSONAL Born 01/07/1939, New York, NY, m, 1966 **DISCIPLINE** CLASSICS, ANCIENT HISTORY **EDUCATION** Hunter Col, AB, 60; Columbia Univ, MA, 62, PhD(Greek and Latin), 70. **CAREER** From lectr to asst prof classics, 68-74, Assoc Prof Classics, Lehman Col, 74-, Chmn Dept Class and Orient Lang, 73-, Assoc mem, Univ Sem Class Civilization, Columbia Univ, 72-. **MEMBERSHIPS** Am Philol Asn; Petronian Soc; Am Inst Archaeol. **RESEARCH** Greek history and numismatics; the teaching of classical languages. **SELECTED PUBLICATIONS** Auth, The Aetolian indemnity of 189 and the Agrinion hoard, Phoenix, 65; coauth, The time of the shield signal at Marathon, Am J Archaeol, 70; auth, Fifth columns in the Peloponnesian War: How they worked and the defense against them, Klio, 72; The Fifth Column in the Peloponnesian War, E J Brill, 72. **CONTACT ADDRESS** Lehman Col, CUNY, Bronx, NY 10468.

LOSS, ARCHIE KRUG

PERSONAL Born 01/31/1939, Hanover, PA, m, 1967, 3 children **DISCIPLINE** MODERN LITERATURE, ART HISTORY, AMERICAN POPULAR CULTURE **EDUCATION** Millersville State Univ, BS, 60; Pa State Univ, MA, 66, PhD(English), 70. **CAREER** Asst prof English, Behrend Col, Pa State Univ, 70-72; asst prof, Wayne State Univ, 72-76; Assoc Prof English and Head Div Arts and Humanities, Behrend Col, PA State Univ, 76-; prof of Eng and Am Stud, 86. **MEMBERSHIPS** James Joyce Found; Soc for Commercial Archaeology. **RESEARCH** Modern literature, modern art, and popular culture. **SELECTED PUBLICATIONS** Auth, Pop Dreams: Music, Movies, and the Media in the 1960s, 99. **CONTACT ADDRESS** School of Humanities and Social Sciences, Pennsylvania State Univ, Erie, The Behrend Col, Station Rd, Erie, PA 16563. **EMAIL** akl1@psu.edu

LOTCHIN, ROGER W.

PERSONAL Born 01/31/1935, Shelbyville, IL, m, 1958, 1 child **DISCIPLINE** HISTORY **EDUCATION** Millikin Univ, BA, 57; Univ Chicago, MA, 61. **CAREER** Prof, Univ NC at Chapel Hill, 66-. **MEMBERSHIPS** Urban Hist Asn, Western Hist Asn, The Hist Asn. **RESEARCH** Twentieth-Century California Cities, California & Southern Cities in World War II, World War II, Twentieth-Century U.S. West. **SELECTED PUBLICATIONS** Auth, San Francisco, 1846-1856: From Hamlet to City, 74, 79, & 97; ed, The Martial Metropolis: U.S. Cities in War & Peace, Praeger, 84; Fortress California, 1910-1961: From Warfare to Welfare, 92; ed, The Way We Really Were: The Golden State in the Second Great War, 00. **CONTACT ADDRESS** Dept Hist, Univ of No Carolina, Chapel Hill, CB #3195, Hamilton Hall, Chapel Hill, NC 27599-3195. **EMAIL** rlotchin@email.unc.edu

LOTZ, DAVID WALTER

PERSONAL Born 07/01/1937, Houston, TX, m, 1965 **DISCIPLINE** CHURCH AND EARLY MODERN EUROPEAN HISTORY **EDUCATION** Concordia Sr Col, BA, 59; Concordia Theol Sem, MDiv, 63; Wash Univ, MA, 64; Union Theol Sem, STM 65, ThD, 71. **CAREER** Instr relig, Concordia Sr Col, 63-64; from instr to assoc prof, 68-76, Washburn Prof Church Hist, Union Theol Sem, 76-, Lectr church hist, Woodstock Col, NY, 71-74 and Gen Theol Sem, New York, 74-; consult, Inter-Lutheran Comn Worship, 73-74; theol consult, Atlantic Dist, Lutheran Church-Mo Synod, 74-. **MEMBERSHIPS** AHA; Am Acad Relig; Am Soc Church Hist; Am Soc Reformation Res; Am Cath Hist Asn. **RESEARCH** Reformation history and theology; 19th century religious thought; historiography. **SELECTED PUBLICATIONS** Auth, Christ Person and Life Work in the Theology of Ritschl,Albrecht With Special Attention to Munus Triplex, J Rel, Vol 0073, 93; The Harvest of Humanism in Central Europe--Essays in Honor of Spitz, Lewis, W, 16th Century J, Vol 0025, 94. **CONTACT ADDRESS** Dept of Church Hist, Union Theol Sem, New York, 3061 Broadway, New York, NY 10027-5710.

LOUD, PATRICIA CUMMINGS

PERSONAL Born Beaumont, TX, m, 3 children **DISCIPLINE** FINE ARTS **EDUCATION** Univ TX, Austin, BFA; Radcliffe Col, AM; Harvard Univ, PhD. **CAREER** Kimbell Art Museum, Fort Worth, TX, 81-, currently curator of Architecture and Museum Archivist. **HONORS AND AWARDS** Honorary memberships, AIA Fort Worth and TX Soc of Architects; 1998 John G Flowers Awd by TSA for excellence in promotion of architecture through the media. **MEMBERSHIPS** Col Art Asn; Soc of Architectural Hist. **SELECTED PUBLICATIONS** Auth, The History of the Kimbell Art Museum, in Pursuit of Quality: The Kimbell Art Museum, An Illustrated History of the Art and Architecture, Kimbell Art Museum, 87; The Critical Fortune, (The Kimbell Art Museum), Design Rev, winter, 87; The Art Museum of Louis I Kahn, Dule Univ Museum of Art, 89; Louis I Kahn musei, Electra, 91; Yale Univ Art Gallery, Kimbell Art Museum, and Yale Center for British Art, in Louis I Kahn: In the Realm of Architecture, David Brownlee, David G de Long, Museum of Contemporary Art and New York: Rizzoli, 91; Louis I Kahn's Kimbell Art Museum, in The Construction of the Kimbell Art Museum, Accademia di architettura dell'Universita della Svizzera italiana, Mendrisio, and Milan: Skira, 97. **CONTACT ADDRESS** Kimbell Art Mus, 3333 Camp Bouie Blvd, Fort Worth, TX 76107-2792. **EMAIL** ploud@kimballmuseum.org

LOUGEE, ROBERT WAYNE

PERSONAL Born 05/04/1919, Reading, MA, m, 1941, 3 children **DISCIPLINE** EUROPEAN HISTORY **EDUCATION** Brown Univ, AB, 41, PhD(hist), 52. **CAREER** Asst hist, Brown Univ, 47-49; from instr to assoc prof, 49-62, dean col libr arts and sci, 71-74, head dept, 60-69, Prof Hist, Univ Conn, 62-, Am Philos Soc grants, 56 and 65. **MEMBERSHIPS** AHA; New England Hist Asn (pres, 76-77). **RESEARCH** Modern German history; European social and intellectual movement, 1850-1914. **SELECTED PUBLICATIONS** Auth, Enlightenment, Revolution, and Romanticism--the Genesis of Modern German Political Thought, 1790-1800, Amer Hist Rev, Vol 0098, 93. **CONTACT ADDRESS** Dept of Hist, Univ of Connecticut, Storrs, Storrs, CT 06268.

LOUGEE-CHAPPELL, CAROLYN

PERSONAL Born 02/02/1942, MI, m, 1963, 2 children **DISCIPLINE** HISTORY **EDUCATION** Smith Col, AB; Univ Mich, PhD. **CAREER** Prof to Assoc Dean and Dept Chair, Stanford Univ, 73-. **HONORS AND AWARDS** Phi Beta Kappa; Dinkelspiel Awd; Dean's Awd for Distinguished Teaching. **RESEARCH** Early Modern France, Women's History, Family History. **SELECTED PUBLICATIONS** Auth, Le Paradis des fammes, 77. **CONTACT ADDRESS** Dept Hist, Stanford Univ, Bldg 200, Stanford, CA 94305-2024. **EMAIL** lougee@leland.stanford.edu

LOUIS, JAMES PAUL

PERSONAL Born 05/13/1938, Brooklyn, NY, d, 3 children **DISCIPLINE** TWENTIETH CENTURY UNITED STATES **EDUCATION** Colgate Univ, AB, 60; Harvard Univ, AM, 62; PhD, 68. **CAREER** From inst to asst prof, 64-74, asst dean, 74-81, assoc prof hist, Kent State Univ, 74-, assoc dean, Col Arts & Sci, 81-87; assoc provost fac affairs, 87-. **MEMBERSHIPS** Academy of Academic Personnel Administrators. **RESEARCH** Woman suffrage and the fight for the nineteenth amendment, 1913-1920; the progressive movement and progressive reform. **SELECTED PUBLICATIONS** Auth, The

Roots of Feminism: a Review Essay, Civil War Hist, 6/71; auth, "Josephine Jewell Dodge, Mary Garret Hay & Sue Shelton White," in Notable American Women, 1607-1950, (3 vols), 71; auth, "Ruth Hanna McCormick Simms," in Dictionary of American Biography, (3rd suppl), 73; auth, intro to F Chambers, Black Higher Education in the United States, 78. **CONTACT ADDRESS** Off Fac Affairs Exec Office, Kent State Univ, PO Box 5190, Kent, OH 44242-0001. **EMAIL** jlouis@kent.edu

LOUISA, ANGELO
PERSONAL Born 10/12/1951, Bridgeville, PA, m, 1976 **DISCIPLINE** HISTORY **EDUCATION** Saint Vincent Col, BA, 73; Duquesne Univ, MA, 75; Univ Minn, PhD, 85. **CAREER** Instr, Univ of Minn, 79; fac mem, MetropolitanState Univ, 82-87; instr, Concordia Col, 83; instr, Lakewood Community col, 85; asst prof, Metropolitan State Univ, 87-88; lectr to asst prof, Univ of Nebr Ohama, 97-; lectr, Creighton Univ, 99-. **HONORS AND AWARDS** Phi Alpha Ttheta, 71; Phi Kappa Phi, 78; McMillan Grant, Univ of Minn, 79; Leadership and Serv Awd, Univ of Minn, 80; Outstanding Young Men of America, 81; Omicron Delta Kappa, 82; Pi Gamma Kappa, 82; Oustanding Teacher Awd, Metropolitan State Univ, 86. **MEMBERSHIPS** Soc for Am Baseball Res; Pi Gamma Mu; AHA; Omicron Delta Kappa; Phi Kappa Phi; Phi Alpha Theta. **RESEARCH** Tudor-Stuart England, early modern Europe and sports history. **SELECTED PUBLICATIONS** Auth, "Albert von Hohenzollern", "Charles IV, Duke of Alencon", "Archibald Campbell, 1st Marquis and 8th Earl of Argyll", "Archibald Campbell, 9th Earl of Argyll", "Pierre de Montesquiou, Count d'Artagnan", The Harper Encyclopedia of Military Biography, Harper Collins, (NY), 92; auth, "Chris Evert", "Christy Mathewson", "Cy Young", The encyclopedia of Sport in American Culture, ABC-CLIO Books, (Santa Barbara), (forthcoming), auth, "Robert Aldrich", "Gilbert Bourne", "John Capon", "Henry Morgan", New Dictionary of National Biography, Oxford Univ Pr, (Oxford), (forthcoming). **CONTACT ADDRESS** Dept Hist, Univ of Nebraska, Omaha, 6001 Dodge St, Omaha, NE 68182-0001. **EMAIL** Angelo_Louisa@unomaha.edu

LOUNSBURY, CARL
PERSONAL Born 01/05/1952, St. Paul, MN, m, 1 child **DISCIPLINE** AMERICAN STUDIES **EDUCATION** Univ NC, BA, 74; George Washington Univ, MA, 77, PhD, 83. **CAREER** Archit Hist, Colonial Williamsburg Fdn, 82-. **SELECTED PUBLICATIONS** Auth, Architects and Builders in North Carolina: A History of the Practice of Building; auth, An Illustrated Glossary of Early Southern Architecture and Landscape; auth, The Architecture of the Charleston County Courthouse. **CONTACT ADDRESS** Archit Res Dept, Colonial Williamsburg Foundation, PO Box 1776, Williamsburg, VA 23187. **EMAIL** clounsbury@cwf.org

LOUNSBURY, MYRON
DISCIPLINE AMERICAN HISTORY & STUDIES **EDUCATION** Duke Univ, BA, 61; Univ PA, MA, 62, PhD, 66. **CAREER** Am Stud Dept, Univ Md **RESEARCH** Investigating film cult in NY City between 1940 and 1970. **SELECTED PUBLICATIONS** Auth, Flashes of Lightning: The Moving Picture in the Progressive Era, Jour Pop Cult, 70; The Origins of American Film Criticism, 1909-1939, Arno Press, 73; Against the American Game: The MStrenuous Life' of Willard Huntington Wright, Prospects: An Annual of Amer Cult Stud, 80; The Gathered Light: History, Criticism and the Rise of the American Film, Quart Rev of Film Stud, 80; The Progress and Poetry of the Movies: A Second Book of Film Criticism by Vachel Lindsay, Scarecrow Press, 95. **CONTACT ADDRESS** Am Stud Dept, Univ of Maryland, Col Park, Taliaferro Hall, Rm 2119, College Park, MD 20742-8821. **EMAIL** ml36@umail.umd.edu

LOUNSBURY, RICHARD CECIL
PERSONAL Born 01/03/1949, Yorkton, SK, Canada **DISCIPLINE** CLASSICAL LANGUAGES, CLASSICAL TRADITION, AMERICAN INTELLECTUAL HISTORY **EDUCATION** Univ Calgary, BA, 70; Univ Tex, Austin, MA, 72, PhD(classics), 79. **CAREER** Lectr classics, Univ Witwatersrand, 79-81; asst prof, Univ Victoria, 81-82; Prof Classics & Comp Lit, Brigham Young Univ, 82- **RESEARCH** Roman literature of the early Empire; classical rhetoric; intellectual history of the American South. **SELECTED PUBLICATIONS** Auth, The death of Domitius in the Pharsalia, Trans Am Philol Asn, 75; History and motive in book seven of Lucan's Pharsalia, Hermes, 76; Restoring the generous past: Recent books of rhetoric and criticism, Mich Quart Rev, 79; contribr, Intellectual Life in Antebellum Charleston, Tennessee, 86; auth, The Arts of Suetonius: An Introduction, peter Lang, 87; ed, Louisa S. McCord: Political and Social Essays, Univ Press of Virginia, 95; ed, Louisa S. McCord: Poems, Drama, Biography, Letters, Univ Press of Virginia, 96; ed, Louisa S. McCord: Selected Writings, Univ Press of Virginia, 97. **CONTACT ADDRESS** Dept of Humanities Classics & Comp Lit, Brigham Young Univ, 3010 Jhkb, Provo, UT 84602-0002. **EMAIL** richard_lounsbury@byu.edu

LOUTHAN, HOWARD
DISCIPLINE HISTORY **EDUCATION** Emory Univ, BA, 86, MA 90, Princeton Univ, PhD, 94. **CAREER** Asst prof, 94-. **RESEARCH** Early modern cultural and intellectual history; Renaissance and Reformation history. **SELECTED PUBLICATIONS** Auth, Reforming a Counter-reform Court: Johannis Crato and the Austrian Habsburgs, 94; A Reappraisal of J. A. Comenius's The Labyrinth of the World in Light of his Subsequent Writings on Educational Reform, 96; Religion and Gender in Late Medieval England, 96; The Quest for Compromise: Peace Makers in Counter-Reformation Vienna, 97. **CONTACT ADDRESS** History and Philosophy of Science Dept, Univ of Notre Dame, Notre Dame, IN 46556. **EMAIL** Howard.Louthan.2@nd.edu

LOVE, JOSEPH L.
PERSONAL Born 02/28/1938, Austin, TX, m, 1978, 4 children **DISCIPLINE** LATIN AMERICAN HISTORY **EDUCATION** Harvard Univ, AB, 60; Stanford Univ, MA, 63; Columbia Univ, PhD(hist), 67. **CAREER** From instr to prof hist, Univ Ill, Urbana-Champaign, 66-; dir, Latin Am Studies, Univ Ill, Urbana-Champaign, 93-99; chemn, Brazilian Studies Comt, Univ Ill, Urbana-Champaign, 73; mem, Bolton Prize Comt, 73-74; mem, Gen Comt, Conf Latin Am Hist, 81-83. **HONORS AND AWARDS** Conf Prize, Conf Latin Am Hist, 71; Latin Am Hist Prize, Southwest Soc Sci Asn, 77; sr res assoc, St Anthony's Col, Oxford Univ, 82; NEH, SSRC, IREX, Fulbright, and Guggenheim Fellowships; Vis Schol, Univ Sao Paulo, 89-90; Vis Schol, Inst Ortega y Gasset, Madrid, 95-96. **MEMBERSHIPS** AHA; Conf Latin Am Hist; Latin Am Studies Asn. **RESEARCH** Regional politics and economics in 19th and 20th century Brazil; history of economic ideas and policies in Latin America and Eastern Europe. **SELECTED PUBLICATIONS** Auth, Rio Grande do Sul and Brazilian Regionalism, Stanford Univ, 71; co-ed, Quantitative Social Science Research on Latin America, Univ Ill, 73; auth, Sao Paulo in the Brazilian Federation, Stanford Univ, 80; co-ed, Guiding the Invisible Hand: Economic Liberalism and the State in Latin American History, Praeger, 88; auth, Crafting the Third World: Theorizing Underdevelopment in Rumania and Brazil, Stanford Univ, 96. **CONTACT ADDRESS** Dept of History, Univ of Illinois, Urbana-Champaign, 810 S Wright St, Urbana, IL 61801-3611. **EMAIL** j-love2@uiuc.edu

LOVEJOY, DAVID SHERMAN
PERSONAL Born 11/30/1919, Pawtucket, RI, m, 1941, 1 child **DISCIPLINE** AMERICAN HISTORY **EDUCATION** Bowdoin Col, BS, 41; Brown Univ, AM, 47, PhD(Am civilization), 54. **CAREER** Fac Am hist and lit, Marlboro Col, 50-53; asst prof Am hist, Mich State Univ, 54-55 and Brown Univ, 55-59; vis asst prof, Northwestern Univ, 59-60; from asst prof to assoc prof, 60-65, Prof Am Hist, Univ Wis-Madison, 65-, Fulbright lectr, Univ Aberdeen, 64-65; Guggenheim fel, 67-68; coun mem, Inst Early Am Hist and Cult, Va, 75-78. **MEMBERSHIPS** AHA; Orgn Am Historians. **RESEARCH** American colonial history, American Revolution. **SELECTED PUBLICATIONS** Auth, Williams, Roger and Fox, George, the Arrogance of Self Righteousness, New Eng Quart-Hist Rev New Eng Life and Letters, Vol 0066, 93; Satanizing the American-Indian, New Eng Quart-Hist Rev of New England Life and Letters, Vol 0067, 94; Between Hell and Plum Island--Sewall, Samuel and the Legacy of the Witches, 1692-1697, New Eng Quart-Hist Rev of New Eng Life and Letters, Vol 0070, 97. **CONTACT ADDRESS** Dept of Hist, Univ of Wisconsin, Madison, Madison, WI 53706.

LOVEJOY, PAUL E.
PERSONAL Born 05/06/1943, Girard, PA, m, 1977, 3 children **DISCIPLINE** AFRICAN HISTORY **EDUCATION** Clarkson Col, BS, 65; Univ Wis, MS, 67, PhD(hist), 73. **CAREER** Dist Res Prof, York Univ, 71-, Hon lectr, Ahmadu Bello Univ, Nigeria, 75-76. **MEMBERSHIPS** African Studies Asn; Can Asn African Studies; Can Hist Asn. **RESEARCH** African economic and social, African diaspora, slavery. **SELECTED PUBLICATIONS** Auth, 'Pawns will Live when Slaves is Apt to Dye': Credit, Risk and Trust at Old Calabar in the Era of the Slave Trade, David Richardson, American Historical Review, 104:2, (99): 332-55; auth, Les origenes de los esclavos en as Americas Perspectivas Methodologicas, Revista de Historia, (99): 36; auth, Cerner les identites au sein de la diaspora afticaine, Fislam et l'esclavage aux Ameriques, Cahiers des Anneaux de la Memoire, 1, (99): 249-78. **CONTACT ADDRESS** Dept of Hist, York Univ, Toronto, ON, Canada M3J 1P3. **EMAIL** plovejoy@yorku.ca

LOVELAND, ANNE C.
PERSONAL Born 12/23/1938, Jamaica, NY, m **DISCIPLINE** HISTORY **EDUCATION** Univ of Rochester, BA, 60; Cornell Univ, MA, 63, PhD, 68. **CAREER** Instr to prof, Dept of Hist, La State Univ, 64-93, chair, 93-96, T. Harry Williams Prof of Am Hist, 93-. **HONORS AND AWARDS** Phi Beta Kappa; Francis Mackemie Awd, 80-82; U.S. Army M. H. I. Grant, 86; Willie Lee Rose Prize, 87; Inst for Study of Am Evangelicals Grant, 89; Distinguished Res Master Awd, 98. **MEMBERSHIPS** Southern Hist Asn, Org of Am Hists, Southern Asn of Women Hists. **RESEARCH** Evangelical religion in the U.S.; religion, ideology, and morality in the U.S. Army; megachurch architecture. **SELECTED PUBLICATIONS** Auth, Emblem of Liberty: The Image of Lafayette in the American Mind, Baton Rouge: LSU Press (71); auth, Southern Evangelicals and the Social Order, 1800-1860, Baton Rouge: LSU Press (80); auth, "American Perceptions of Lafayette," Laurels, 55 (winter 84-85): 155-70; auth, Lillian Smith: A Southerner Confronting the South, Baton Rouge: LSU Press (86); coauth with Stanley J. Idzerda and Marc H. Miller, Lafayette, Hero of Two Worlds: The Art and Pageantry of His Farewell Tour of America, 1824-1825, NY: The Queens Museum (89); auth, American Evangelicals and the U.S. Military, 1942-1993, Baton Rouge: LSU Press (96); auth, "A Religious Perspective on Writing and Teaching History," Reviews in Am Hist, 25 (Dec 97): 692-97; auth, "Later Stages of the Recovery of American Religious History," in Darryl Hart and Harry Stout, eds, New Directions in American Religious History, NY: Oxford Univ Press (97); auth, "Prophetic Ministry and the Military Chaplaincy during the Vietnam Era," in Lewis Perry and Karen Halttunen, eds, Moral Problems in American Life, Ithaca: Cornell Univ Press (98); auth, "Character Education in the U.S. Army, 1947-1977," J of Military Hist, 64 (July 2000): 1-25. **CONTACT ADDRESS** Dept Hist, La State Univ Baton Rouge, 0 La State Univ, Baton Rouge, LA 70803-0104. **EMAIL** hylove@lsumvs.sncc.lsu.edu

LOVERIDGE-SANBONMATSU, JOAN
PERSONAL Born 07/05/1938, Hartford, CT, m, 1964, 2 children **DISCIPLINE** RHETORIC AND COMMUNICATION; BRITISH AND IRISH HISTORY. **EDUCATION** Univ Vermont, BA, 60; Ohio Univ, MA, 63; Penn State Univ, PhD, 71. **CAREER** Tchg asst, Commun Stud, Ohio Univ, 62-63; instr Commun Stud & ESL, Penn State Univ, 66-67; vis asst prof Commun Stud, RIT, 71; adj prof Commun Stud, Monroe Commun Col, 72-76; asst prof Commun Stud & Womens Stud, SUNY Brockport, 63-77; Prof Commun Stud & Women,s Stud, SUNY Oswego, 77-98; Co-coord, Women's Studies Prog, 78-80 & 82; Prof emer, 99; instr Intensive Eng Summer Prog, 92-. **HONORS AND AWARDS** Postdoctoral fel Multicult Womens Summer Inst, Univ of IL at Chicago, 83; Trailblazer Higher Educ Awd, Nat Orgn Women, Cent NY State, 87; Womens Ctr Awd Extraordinary Commitment Womens Issues, 96, Womens Ctr Awd Outstanding Dedication to Womens Ctr, 98, SUNY Oswego ; SUNY Oswego Intensive Eng Prog, 95, 96; SEED Awd, 98; Am Red Cross Overseas Asn Pres Citation Awd Soc Change, 98; research grant, PA State Univ, 70; research grants SUNY Oswego, 78, 91, 92, 94, 95, 96; Working Life grantee, 85, 87, 93, 94, 98; Coalition for Peace Edu Awd. **MEMBERSHIPS** Nat Commun Asn; Nat Womens Stud Asn; E Commun Asn; NY State Speech Asn; Soc Int Educ, Trng & Res; Am Red Cross Overseas Asn; Speech Commun Asn Puerto Rico. **RESEARCH** Japanese American women interned at Poston in World War II; Womens studies, English as a second language; Rhetoric and social change poet selected. **SELECTED PUBLICATIONS** contrib-auth, Multicultural Dilemnas of Language Usage, Why Don't You Talk Right, Multicultural Commun Perspectives, Kendall Hunt, 92; Benazir Bhutto: Feminist Voice for Democracy in Pakistan, Howard Jour Commun, 94; Helen Broinowski, Caldicott: pediatrician, peace activist, catalyst for the nuclear disarmament movement, Women Public Speakers in the United States, Greenwood Press, 94; coauth Feminism and Womans Life, Minerva Publ Co, 95. **CONTACT ADDRESS** 23 McCracken Dr, Oswego, NY 13126. **EMAIL** sanbonma@oswego.edu

LOVETT, BOBBY L.
PERSONAL Born 01/19/1943, Memphis, TN, m, 1984, 5 children **DISCIPLINE** HISTORY **EDUCATION** Ark A.M. and N State Col, BA, 67; Univ Ark, MA, 69; PhD, 78. **CAREER** Asst prof, Eureka col; prof, Tenn State Univ, 73-; Dean, Col of Arts and Sci, Tenn State Univ, 89-00. **HONORS AND AWARDS** Fel, U.S. Dept of Educ, 67-69; Distinguished Public Service Awd, 96; Res Support Awd, 00. **MEMBERSHIPS** Southern Hist Asn, Asn for Study of Negro Life and Hist, Org of Am Hist, Tenn Hist Soc, Ark Hist Soc. **RESEARCH** American, urban, and African American history. **SELECTED PUBLICATIONS** Auth, The Story of R.H. Boyd and the National Baptist Publishing Board, 93; coauth, Profiles of African Americans in Tennessee, 96; auth, The African American History of Nashville, Tennessee 1780-1930: Elites and Dilemmas, 99; contribur, The Art of William Edmondson, 00. **CONTACT ADDRESS** Dept Hist, Geog, Polit Sci, Tennessee State Univ, 3500 John A Merritt Blvd, Nashville, TN 37209-1500. **EMAIL** blovett@tnstate.edu

LOVIN, CLIFFORD R.
DISCIPLINE HISTORY **EDUCATION** Davidson Col, BA 57; Univ NC, Chapel Hill, MA 62, PhD, 65. **CAREER** Asst, 66-69, assoc, 69-72, PROF, 72-, W CAROLINA UNIV; dir, Mountain Heritage Ctr, W Carolina Univ, 77-81; dean, col arts scis, W Caroline Univ, 87-93. **SELECTED PUBLICATIONS** Auth, A School for Diplomats: The Paris Peace Conference of 1919, 97. **CONTACT ADDRESS** Dept of History, Western Carolina Univ, Cullowhee, NC 28723. **EMAIL** lovin@wpoff.wcu.edu

LOVIN, HUGH TAYLOR
PERSONAL Born 12/10/1928, Pocatello, ID, m, 1956, 1 child **DISCIPLINE** COLONIAL AND RECENT AMERICAN HISTORY **EDUCATION** Idaho State Col, BA, 50; Wash State Univ, MA, 56; Univ Wash, PhD(hist), 63. **CAREER** Instr hist, Mil Br, Univ Alaska, 57-61; asst prof, Southwestern Ore Col,

63-64 and Kearney State Col, 64-65; assoc prof, 65-67, chmn dept, 68-71, Prof Hist, Boise State Univ, 68-93; emer, 93-. **RESEARCH** United States, 1900-1940; American labor history. **SELECTED PUBLICATIONS** Auth," Water Arid Land, and Visions of Advancement on the Snake River Plain," Idaho Yesterdays, vol 35, (91): 3-18; auth," Idaho's White Elephant: The King Hill Tracts and the United State Reclamation Service," Pacific Northwest Quarterly, vol 83; (92): 12-21; auth, " The Farwell Trust Company of Chicago and Idaho Irrigation Finance," Idaho Yesterdays, vol 38, (94): 7-17; auth, " The Fight for an Irrigation Empire in the Yellowstone River Valley," Pacifid Northwest Quarterly, vol 89. (98)" 188-201; auth, "Yellowstone National Part, Jackson Hole and the Idaho Irrigation Frontier," Idaho Yesterdays, vol 43, (00): 13-24. **CONTACT ADDRESS** Dept Hist, 1310 S Gourley, Boise, ID 83725.

LOVOLL, ODD SVERRE
PERSONAL Born 10/06/1934, Sande In Sunnmore, Norway, m, 1958, 2 children **DISCIPLINE** AMERICAN HISTORY **EDUCATION** Univ of Bergen, Bergen, Norway, Basic Examination in Norwegian lang and lit, 61; Univ of Oslo, Oslo, Norway, Basic and Intermediate Examinations in History, 65-67; Univ NDak, MA, 69; Univ Minn, Minneapolis, PhD(Am hist), 73. **CAREER** Instr Norweg, Univ NDak, 67-70; teaching asst, Univ Minn, 70-71; from Instr to Prof of Norwegian and History, King Olav V Prof, Scandinavian-Am Studies, St Olaf Col, 71-; publ ed, Norweg-Am Hist Asn, 80-; prof hist, Univ of Oslo, 95-; Guest Prof of Am Hist at the Univ of Trondheim and Univ of Oslo, fall 93. **HONORS AND AWARDS** Phi Alpha Theta; Awd of Merit for A Folk Epic, the State Hist Soc of Wis, 76; Norweg Govt res grant, 77-78; Knight's Cross of the Royal Order of Merit, 86; Awd of Superior Achievement for A Century of Urban Life, Ill State Hist Soc, 89; inducted member, The Norweg Acad of Sci and Letters, 89-; The Am-Norway Heritage Fund Awd, 90; Alf Mjoen Awd "Honored Emigrants", 96. **MEMBERSHIPS** Soc Advan Scand Studies; Norweg-Am Hist Asn. **RESEARCH** European migration to America, primarily Scandinavian; American ethnic studies; Scandinavian history. **SELECTED PUBLICATIONS** Auth, A Century of Urban Life: The Norwegians in Chicago before 1930, The Norweg-Am Hist Asn, 88; coauth, Den store Chicagoreisen, Oslo, Universitetsforlaget, 88; ed, Nordics in America: The Future of Their Past, Norweg-Am Hist Asn, 93; auth, Det lofterike landet, En norskamerikansk historie, Universitetsforlaget, 97; The Promise Fulfilled: A Portrait of Norwegian Americans Today, Univ Minn Press, 98; Loftet infridd, Et norskamerikansk samtidsbilde, Vett & Viten (Oslo), 99; The Promise of America: A Norwegian American History, Univ of Minn Press, 99; author of numerous other journal articles and book chapters. **CONTACT ADDRESS** History Dept, St. Olaf Col, 1520 St Olaf Ave., Northfield, MN 55057-1099. **EMAIL** loroll@stolaf.edu

LOWE, BENNO P.
PERSONAL Born Baltimore, MD **DISCIPLINE** HISTORY **EDUCATION** Western Md Coll, BA, 78; Univ Missouri-Columbia, MA, 80; GeoTown Univ, PhD, 90. **CAREER** Asst prof, Baron Univ, 90-93; asst prof, Fla Atlantic Univ, 93-96; assoc prof, 96-. **HONORS AND AWARDS** Dist Teach Awd; Scholar in Res; NEH Fel. **MEMBERSHIPS** AHA; SCSC; NACBS; PHS. **RESEARCH** Political culture of Tudor England, mainly between 1530 and 1560. **SELECTED PUBLICATIONS** Auth, Imaging Peace: A History of Early English Pacifist Ideas, 1340-1560, Penn St Press, 97. **CONTACT ADDRESS** Dept History, Florida Atlantic Univ, PO Box 3091, Boca Raton, FL 33431-0991. **EMAIL** bplowe@fau.edu

LOWE, DONALD M.
PERSONAL Born 12/27/1928, Shanghai, China, 2 children **DISCIPLINE** HISTORY **EDUCATION** Yale Univ, BA, 50; Univ Chicago, MA, 51; Univ Calif, Berekley, PhD(hist), 63. **CAREER** Asst prof hist, Duquesne Univ, 58-63 and Univ Calif, Riverside, 63-68; assoc prof, 68-72, Prof Hist, Univ Calif, San Francisco, 72-, Ford Found fel, 55-57; Fulbright-Hays grant, 64; Soc Sci Res Coun grant, 66-67. **MEMBERSHIPS** AHA; Asn Asian Studies; Soc Phenomenol and Existential Philos. **RESEARCH** Marxist thought; historiography; phenomenology. **SELECTED PUBLICATIONS CONTACT ADDRESS** Dept of Hist, San Francisco State Univ, San Francisco, CA 94132.

LOWE, EUGENE Y., JR.
PERSONAL Born 08/18/1949, New York, NY, m, 4 children **DISCIPLINE** RELIGION; CHURCH HISTORY **EDUCATION** Princeton Univ, AB, 71; Union Theol Sem, M Div, 78; Union Theol Sem, PhD, 87. **CAREER** Res assoc and consult, Andrew W. Mellon Found, 93-97; lectr, dept of relig, Princeton Univ, 93-95; dean of students, Princeton Univ, 83-93; assoc provost, Northwestern Univ, 95-99, asst to the pres, 99-. **HONORS AND AWARDS** Phi Beta Kappa; Protestant fel; fund for Theol Educ, 76-77; Harold Willis Dodds Prize, Princeton Univ, 71; grad fel, Episcopal Church Found, 78-81. **MEMBERSHIPS** Amer Acad of Relig; Amer Soc of Church Hist; Lilly Seminar on Relig and Higher Educ. **RESEARCH** Religion in American History, Higher Education Policy. **SELECTED PUBLICATIONS** Auth, Mordecai Kaplan, Twentieth-Century Shapers of American Popular Religion, 210-217, Greenwood, 89; auth, Racial Ideology, Encycl of Amer Social Hist, 335-346, Charles Scribner's Sons, 93; auth, From Social Gospel to Social Science at the University of Wisconsin, The Church's Public Role: Retrospect and Prospect, 233-251, Eerdmans, 93; auth, Walter Righter, Dict of Heresy Trials in American Christianity, Greenwood Press, 320-326, 97; ed, Promise and Dilemma: Perspectives in Racial Diversity and High Education, Princeton Univ Press, 99. **CONTACT ADDRESS** Office of the Provost, Northwestern Univ, Crown Center 2-154, Evanston, IL 60208.

LOWE, RICHARD GRADY
PERSONAL Born 07/05/1942, Eunice, LA, m, 1992, 3 children **DISCIPLINE** AMERICAN HISTORY **EDUCATION** Univ Southwestern La, BA, 64; Harvard Univ, AM, 65; Univ Va, PhD(hist), 68. **CAREER** Asst prof to regents prof hist, Univ N Tex, 68-. **MEMBERSHIPS** Southern Hist Asn; Va Hist Soc; Tex State Hist Asn; La Hist Asn; Soc of Civil War Historians. **RESEARCH** Civil War and Reconstruction; Southern United States; quantitative history. **SELECTED PUBLICATIONS** Auth, Massachusetts and the Acadians, William & Mary Quart, 4/68; Virginia's Reconstruction Convention, 10/72 & The Republican Party in Antebellum Virginia, 7/73, Va Mag Hist & Biog; coauth, Wealthholding and Political Power in Antebellum Texas, Southwestern Hist Quart, 7/75; The Slavebreeding Hypothesis, J Southern Hist, 8/76; Slavery and the Distribution of Wealth in Texas, J Am Hist, 9/76; Wealth and Power in Antebellum Texas, Tex A&M Univ, 77; auth, Planters and Pain, Folk, SMU Press, 87; Republicans and Reconstruction in Virginia, Univ Va, 91; The Texas Overland Expedition of 1863, Ryan Place, 93; The Freedmen's Bureau and Local Black Leadership, J Am Hist, 12/93; The Freedmen's Bureau and Local White Leaders in Virginia, J Southern Hist, 8/98; auth, A Texas Cavalry Officer's Civil War, La State Univ, 99. **CONTACT ADDRESS** Dept of Hist, Univ of No Texas, PO Box 310650, Denton, TX 76203-0650. **EMAIL** lowe@unt.edu

LOWE, STEPHEN
PERSONAL Born 06/03/1966, Garden City, MI, m, 1990, 2 children **DISCIPLINE** HISTORY **EDUCATION** Olivet Nazarene Univ, BA, 88; Ohio Univ, MA, 91; PhD, 93. **CAREER** Assoc Prof, Olivet Nazarene Univ, 93-. **MEMBERSHIPS** Org of Am Hist; Popular Cult Assoc; N Am Soc for Sport Hist. **RESEARCH** American Sports History. **SELECTED PUBLICATIONS** Auth, "The Kid on the Sandlot: Public Policy, Congress, and Organized Baseball, 1951", 3 Nine: J of Baseball Hist and Soc Policy Perspectives (95): 218-35; auth, The Kid on the Sandlot: Congress and Professional Sports, 1910-1992, Popular Pr, (Bowling Green), 95; auth, "Jerry Travers" and "Jimmy Demaret", Am Nat Biography, Oxford Univ Pr, (NY), 99; auth, "Change, Continuity, and Golf's Battle of the Century", 26 J of Sport Hist, (99); auth, "Demarbelizing Bobby Jones", Ga Hist Quarterly, (00); auth, Sir Walter and Mr Jones: Walter Hagen, Bobby Jones, and the Rise of American Golf, Sleeping Bear Pr, (Chelsea, MI), (forthcoming). **CONTACT ADDRESS** Dept Soc Sci, Olivet Nazarene Univ, PO Box 592', Kankakee, IL 60901-0592. **EMAIL** slowe@olivet.edu

LOWE, WILLIAM J.
DISCIPLINE MODERN IRISH HISTORY **EDUCATION** Michigan State Univ, BA; Univ Dublin, Trinity Col, PhD. **CAREER** Dean, Col Liberal Arts, prof, 91-. **HONORS AND AWARDS** Fulbright scholar, Ireland. **RESEARCH** Irish plice in the period before 1922. **SELECTED PUBLICATIONS** Pub(s), book and series of articles on Irish immigration in Victorian England. **CONTACT ADDRESS** Dept of Hist, Univ of Detroit Mercy, 4001 W McNichols Rd, PO BOX 19900, Detroit, MI 48219-0900.

LOWENSTEIN, STEVEN MARK
PERSONAL Born 02/26/1945, New York, NY, m, 1974, 2 children **DISCIPLINE** JEWISH HISTORY, EUROPEAN HISTORY **EDUCATION** City Col New York, BA, 66; Princeton Univ, MA, 69, PhD(hist), 72. **CAREER** Asst archivist & res assoc, YIVO Inst, 73-75; archivist, Leo Baeck Inst, 75-79; prof, Univ Of Judaism, 79-, Archivist, United Jewish Appeal, 75-77. **MEMBERSHIPS** AHA; Asn Jewish Studies; Soc Am Archivists. **RESEARCH** Modernization of German Jewry; Yiddish dialectology; Jewish folk traditions; social history of early modern France. **SELECTED PUBLICATIONS** Auth, The Rural Community and the urbanization of German Jewry, Cent Europ Hist, 80; The 1840's and the creation of the German Jewish Religious Reform movement, In: Revolution and Evolution, 1848, German Jewish History, 81; Voluntary and involuntary fertility limitations in nineteenth century Bavarian Jewry, In: Modern Jewish Fertility, 81; The Jewish Cultural Tapestry, International Jewish Folk Traditions, Oxford University Press, 00; The Berlin Jewish Community 1770-1830: Enlightenment, Family, & Crisis, Oxford Univ Press, 94; The Mechanics of Change: Essays in German Jewish Social History, Scholars Press, 92; Frankfurt on the Hudson: The German Jewish Community of Washington heights 1933-1983, Wayne State Univ Press, 89; 4 chapters in German-Jewish History in Modern Times, Vol 3: Integration in Dispute 1871-1918, Columbia Univ Press, 98. **CONTACT ADDRESS** Univ of Judaism, 15600 Mulholland Dr, Los Angeles, CA 90077-1599. **EMAIL** as155@lafn.org

LOWERY, BULLITT
PERSONAL Born 06/17/1936, New York, NY, m, 1974, 2 children **DISCIPLINE** HISTORY **EDUCATION** Transylvania Univ, AB, 56; Duke Univ, MA, 59; PhD, 63. **CAREER** US Marine Corp, 57-58; vis prof, Wylie Col, 68; legislat aide, 76; assoc prof, prof, Univ N Tex, 64-. **HONORS AND AWARDS** Lexington Comm Fel; Grad Scholar and Fel; NEH, 76, 80. **MEMBERSHIPS** AHA; SMH; WHA. **RESEARCH** Diplomacy and leadership of World War I. **SELECTED PUBLICATIONS** Coauth, The Red Virgin: The Memoirs of Louise Michel, Univ Ala Press, 80; auth, The Causes and Consequences of World War I, Univ Tamkang Press (Tamshui, Taiwan), 96; auth, Armistice 1918, Kent St UP, 96, 99. **CONTACT ADDRESS** Dept Hist, Univ of No Texas, PO Box 310650, Denton, TX 76203-0650.

LOWRY, BULLITT
PERSONAL Born 06/17/1936, New York, NY, m, 1974, 2 children **DISCIPLINE** MODERN EUROPEAN HISTORY **EDUCATION** Transylvania Col, AB, 56; Duke Univ, AM, 59, PhD, 63. **CAREER** Asst prof hist, Converse Col, 60-64; assoc prof to prof hist, Univ of North Texas, 64-; vis prof, Wiley Col, 68; res asst, US Congress, 78; prof and dir, TX-London semester, 89, 90. **HONORS AND AWARDS** Nat Endowment for Humanities grant, 76; John Ben Shepperd Awd, TX Hist Comm, 88; Foreign assoc member, Royal Inst of Int Affairs, 90-; Chairs lecturer, Tamkang Univ, Taiwan, 96. **MEMBERSHIPS** AHA; Soc for Military Hist; Eur His Sect of Southern Hist Asn. **RESEARCH** Modern European diplomatic and military history; nineteenth century European radicalism. **SELECTED PUBLICATIONS** Auth, Music under Stalin, fall 67 & The Historian and his Politics, spring 68, Arlington Quart; Pershing and the Armistice, J Am Hist, 9/68; El indefendible Penon: Inglaterra y la permuta de Gibraltar por Ceuta de 1917 a 1919, Revista Polit Int, 77; co-auth & trans, The Red Virgin: The Memoirs of Louise Michel, Univ AL Press, 81; coauth, World History, West Pub Co, 91; auth, War Experience and Armistice Conditions, in Facing Armageddon, ed, H Cecil and P H Liddle, Leo Cooper/Pen and Sword, 96; The Causes and Consequences of World War I, Tamkang Univ Press, 96; Armistice 1918, Kent State Univ Press, 96. **CONTACT ADDRESS** Dept Hist, Univ of No Texas, PO Box 310650, Denton, TX 76203-0650. **EMAIL** blowry@unt.edu

LOWTHER, LAWRENCE LELAND
PERSONAL Born 07/29/1927, Centralia, WA, m, 1947, 2 children **DISCIPLINE** COLONIAL AMERICAN HISTORY **EDUCATION** Univ Wash, BA, 52, MA, 59, PhD(Hist), 64. **CAREER** Assoc prof Am Hist, Gen Beadle State Col, 64-65; from asst prof to assoc prof, 65-74, prof Colonial & Revolutionary Am Hist, Cent Wash Univ, 74-, Col participant, Tri Univ Proj Elem Educ-Soc Sci, Univ Wash, 69-70; retired, prof emeritus, 92. **MEMBERSHIPS** AHA; Orgn Am Historians; Nat Coun Soc Studies. **RESEARCH** Colonial Rhode Island. **SELECTED PUBLICATIONS** Auth, Town and colony in early 18th century Rhode Island, Newport Hist, 7/64; coauth, History in the high school: A brief survey of Washington State, Pac Northwest Quart, 7/68; auth, Collingwood and historical inquiry, Univ Wash Col Educ Rec, 5/70; coauth, Education, Censorship and Teachers: Essays on the Centennial of Central Washington Univ, Central Washington Univ, Ellensbury, WA, 93. **CONTACT ADDRESS** Dept of History, Central Washington Univ, 400 E 8th Ave, Ellensburg, WA 98926-7502. **EMAIL** lowtherl@cwu.edu

LOZOVSKY, NATALIA
PERSONAL Born 03/11/1957, Moscow, Russia **DISCIPLINE** HISTORY **EDUCATION** Lomonosov Moscow State Univ, MA, 80; Inst Hist Sci and Technol, PhD, 89; Univ Colo, PhD, 97 **CAREER** Instr, Univ Colo at Boulder, 97-. **HONORS AND AWARDS** Bernadotte E. Schmitt Grant, Am Hist Asn, 95; NEH Summer Stipend; Am Philos Soc Res Grant; Nat Sci Found Res Grant. **MEMBERSHIPS** Am Hist Asn; Medieval Acad of Am. **RESEARCH** Medieval Intellectual History. **SELECTED PUBLICATIONS** Auth, "A.A. Fortunatov and His Works in the History of Medieval School and Pedagogy," in School and Pedagogical Thought in Medieval Western Europe, (Moscow, 90), 34-44; auth, "The Explanation of Geographical Material in the Commentary by Remigius of Auxerre," Studi Medievali, (93): 563-572; auth, "Carolingian Geographical Tradition: Was it Geography?" Early Medieval Europe, (96): 25-43; auth, The Earth is Our Book: Early Medieval Geographical Knowledge in the Latin West, 400-1000, Univ Mich Press, 00; auth, "The Construction and Uses of Sacred Space in the Early Middle Ages: From the Salvation of the Soul to the Healing of the Body," in Creating and Representing Sacred Spaces, forthcoming. **CONTACT ADDRESS** Dept Hist, Univ of Colorado, Boulder, 234 UCB, Boulder, CO 80309. **EMAIL** lozovsky@colorado.edu

LU, SUPING
DISCIPLINE LIBRARY SCIENCE, INTERNATIONAL RELATIONS **EDUCATION** Ohio Univ, MA, 92; Univ SC, MLIS, 94. **CAREER** ASST PROF, UNIV NEB, 94-. **CONTACT ADDRESS** Lincoln Love Libr, Univ of Nebraska, Lincoln, 319 Love, City Campus 0410, Lincoln, NE 68588-0410. **EMAIL** slu1@unl.edu

LUBBERS, JEFFREY S.
PERSONAL Born 01/26/1949, Madison, WI **DISCIPLINE** HISTORY AND GOVERNMENT **EDUCATION** Cornell Univ, BA, 71; Univ Chicago Law Sch, JD, 74. **CAREER** Instr, Univ Miami Sch of Law, 74-75; atty, 75-82; res dir, Admin Conf of US, 82-95; fel in Admin Law, Amer Univ Wash Col of Law, 95-. **HONORS AND AWARDS** Pres rank of meritorious exec, 91; Outstanding govt svc award, Amer Bar Asn, 94; Walter Gellhorn award for admin law, Fed Bar Asn, 97. **MEMBERSHIPS** Amer Bar Asn; DC Bar. **RESEARCH** Administrative law; Regulation; Alternative dispute resolution. **SELECTED PUBLICATIONS** Auth, A Guide to Federal Agency Rulemaking, 3rd ed, Amer Bar Asn Book Publ, 98; If It Didn't Exit, it Would Have to Be Invented--Reviving the Administrative Conference, 30, Ariz State Law Jour, 147, 98; The ABA Section of the Administrative Law and Regulatory Practice--From Objector to Protector of the APA, 50, Admin Law Rev, 157, 98; The Administrative Law Agenda for the Next Decade, 49, Admin Law Rev, 159, 97; Testimony on H.R. 2592, The Private Trustee Reform Act of 1997, before the Subcomt of Com and Admin Law, Comt on the Judiciary, US House of Rep, 9 Oct, 97; Ombudsman Offices in the Federal Government--An Emerging Trend?, 22, Admin & Regulatory Law News, 6, summer, 97; Paperwork Redux: The Stronger Paperwork Reduction Act of 1995, 49, Admin Law Rev, 111, 97; APA Adjudication: Is the Quest for Uniformity Faltering?, 10, The Admin Law Jour of the Amer Univ, 65, 96; The Regulatory Reform Recommendations of the National Performance Review, 6, RISK: Health Safety and Environ, 145, Franklin Pierce Law Ctr, spring, 95; Justice Stephen Breyer: Purveyor of Common Sense in Many Forums, part of Symposium: Justice Stephen Breyer's Contribution to Administrative Law, 8, The Admin Law Jour of the Amer Univ, 775, 95; Reinventing Chinese Administrative Law, 19, Admin Law News, 1, spring, 94; Better Regulations: The National Performance Review's Regulatory Reform Recommendations, paper presented to the Duke Law Jour Twenty-Fifth Annual Admin Law Conf, Durham, NC, 20 Jan, 94, publ, 43, Duke Law Jour, 94; Anatomy of a Regulatory Program: Comments on Strategic Regulators and the Choice of Rulemaking Procedures, Hamilton and Schroeder, 56, Law and Contemporary Problems, 161, 94;ed, Developments in Administrative Law and Regulatory Practice, 98-99; ed, Developments in Administrative Law and Regulatory Practice, 99-00; coauth, Federal Administrative Procedure Sourcebook, 3rd ed, with William Funk and Charles Pou, Jr., Amer Bar Asn Book Publ, 00; ed, Developments in Administrative Law and Regulatory Practive, 98-99, Am Bar Asn Book Publ, 00. **CONTACT ADDRESS** 4801 Massachusetts Av. NW, Washington, DC 20016. **EMAIL** jsl26@aol.com

LUBENOW, WILLIAM CORNELIUS
PERSONAL Born 07/28/1939, Freeport, IL, 1 child **DISCIPLINE** MODERN EUROPEAN HISTORY **EDUCATION** Cent Col, Iowa, BA, 61; Univ Iowa, MA, 62, PhD(hist), 68. **CAREER** Instr hist, Cent Col, Iowa, 62-64, from asst prof to assoc prof, 65-71; prof hist, Stockton State Col, 71-, Huntington Libr & Art Gallery fel hist, 74; visiting fell, Wolfson College, Cambridge, 90-. **MEMBERSHIPS** AHA; Conf Brit Studies, Comn Study Parliamentary & Rep Insts; fel, Royal Historical Soc. **RESEARCH** British politics; voting behavior; parliamentary behavior. **SELECTED PUBLICATIONS** Auth, Politics of Government Growth, David & Charles, 71; Social recruitment and social attitudes, Huntington Libr Quart, 77; Ireland, the Great Depression and the railway rates, Proc Am Philos Soc, 78; auth, Parliamentary Politics and the Home Rule Crisis, Oxford UP, 87; The Cambridge Apostles, 1820-1914: Liberalism Imagination and Friendship in British Lateral and Professional Life, Cambridge University Press, 98. **CONTACT ADDRESS** Richard Stockton Col, Pomona, NJ 08240-9999. **EMAIL** william.lubenow@stockton.edu

LUBICK, GEORGE MICHAEL
PERSONAL Born 01/08/1943, Butte, MT, m, 1971, 1 child **DISCIPLINE** AMERICAN HISTORY **EDUCATION** Univ Mont, BA, 66, MA, 68; Univ Toledo, PhD, 74. **CAREER** Asst prof, Mont Col Mineral Sci and Technol, 71-77; Asst prof, 77-84; Assoc prof, Northern Arizona Univ, 84-97; Prof, 97-. **HONORS AND AWARDS** Nat Endowment Humanities fel, 76; Northern Arizona Univ; Univ Organized Res Grants, 85, 86. **MEMBERSHIPS** Phi Alpha Theta, Am Soc for Environmental Hist, Arizona Historical Soc, Western Hist Asn. **RESEARCH** Conservation-environmental history; progressive movement in the Rocky Mountains. **SELECTED PUBLICATIONS** Auth, "The Jeffersonian Tradition in the South," Encyclopedia of Southern Culture, Univ of North Carolina Press, (89): 631-33; auth, "Preserving our Forests of Stone," Plateau 61 (90): 24-31; auth, The Japanese-American Experience, J West, Vol 0032, 93; From Coastal Wilderness to Fruited Plain--A History of Environmental Change in Temperate North America, 1500 to the Present, Amer Hist Rev, Vol 0101, 96; Petrified Forest National Park: A Wilderness Bound in Time, Univ of Arizona Press, 96. **CONTACT ADDRESS** Dept of Hist, No Arizona Univ, Liberal Arts, PO Box 6023, Flagstaff, AZ 86011-0001. **EMAIL** george.lubick@nau.edu

LUBRANO, LINDA L.
DISCIPLINE RUSSIAN POLITICS AND SOCIETY **EDUCATION** Hunter Col, BA; Indiana Univ, MA, PhD. **CAREER** Prof, Am Univ. **HONORS AND AWARDS** Grants, Nat Sci Found; Am Coun Learned Socs; Ford Found; Smithsonian Inst; dir, div comp reg studies, sch int ser. **RESEARCH** Comparative science studies with a focus on gender and the ethics of technique. **SELECTED PUBLICATIONS** Auth, Soviet Sociology of Science and The Social Context of Soviet Science. **CONTACT ADDRESS** American Univ, 4400 Massachusetts Ave, Washington, DC 20016.

LUCAS, MARION BRUNSON
PERSONAL Born 09/09/1935, m, 1957, 3 children **DISCIPLINE** UNITED STATES HISTORY **EDUCATION** Univ SC, BA, 59, MA, 62, PhD, 65. **CAREER** Asst prof hist, Morehead State Univ, 64-66; prof hist, Western KY Univ, 66-99, univ distinguished prof, 99-. **HONORS AND AWARDS** Phi Kappa Phi; Phi Alpha Theta. **MEMBERSHIPS** Southern Hist Asn; KY Hist Soc; Filson Club; KY Asn Tchr(s) Hist. **RESEARCH** Civil War Reconstruction hist; the Old South. **SELECTED PUBLICATIONS** Auth, Sherman and the Burning of Columbia, TX A&M Univ, 76; A History of Blacks in Kentucky, From Slavery to Segregation, 1760-1891, KY Hist Soc, 92. **CONTACT ADDRESS** Dept of Hist, Western Kentucky Univ, Bowling Green, KY 42101-3576. **EMAIL** marion.lucas@wku.edu

LUCAS, PAUL
PERSONAL Born 09/22/1934, New York, NY, d, 2 children **DISCIPLINE** EARLY MODERN AND MODERN EUROPEAN HISTORY **EDUCATION** Brandeis Univ, BA, 55; Princeton Univ, MA, 57, PhD, 63. **CAREER** From instr to assoc prof Europ hist, Wash Univ, 59-69; Assoc Prof Europ Hist, Clark Univ, 69-, Vis asst prof, Princeton Univ, 66-67; Am Coun Learned Soc fel, 67-68; vis lectr, Boston Univ, 73; mem, Inst Advan Studies, Princeton, NJ, 75-76. **RESEARCH** Quantitative analyses of French revolutionary assemblies, 1789-1799; French and English social and legal history, 1600-1850; European intellectual history, 1600-1850. **SELECTED PUBLICATIONS** Auth, Blackstone and the reform of the legal profession, English Hist Rev, 62; Blackstone and the natural law, Am J Legal Hist, 63; Edmund Burke's doctrine of prescription, Hist J, 68; Structure of politice in mid-eighteenth century Britain and its American colonies, William and Mary Quart, 71; Collective Biog of Lincoln's Inn, 1680-1804, J Mod Hist, 74. **CONTACT ADDRESS** Dept of Hist, Clark Univ, 950 Main St, Worcester, MA 01610-1477.

LUCAS, ROBERT HAROLD
PERSONAL Born 08/22/1933, Portland, OR **DISCIPLINE** MEDIEVAL HISTORY **EDUCATION** Univ Ore, BA, 54; Columbia Univ, MA, 58, PhD, 66. **CAREER** Instr medieval hist, Smith Col, 65-66; asst prof, Univ Calif, Irvine, 66-73; assoc prof, 73-80, prof hist, Williamette Univ, 80-, chmn dept, 81-. **HONORS AND AWARDS** Fulbright Scholarship, 59-60; res grant, Am Philos Soc, 70. **MEMBERSHIPS** Mediaeval Acad Am. **RESEARCH** Late medieval France and England. **SELECTED PUBLICATIONS** Auth, Two Notes on Jacques Legrand, Augustiniana, 62; ed, Le Livre du Corps de Policie par Christine de Pisan, Edition Critique, Droz, Geneva, 67; auth, Medieval French Translations of the Latin Classics, Speculum, 70; Ennoblement in Late Medieval France, Medieval Studies, 77. **CONTACT ADDRESS** Dept of History, Willamette Univ, 900 State St, Salem, OR 97301-3931.

LUCKERT, KARL WILHELM
PERSONAL Born 11/18/1934, Winnenden-Hoefen, Germany, m, 1957, 3 children **DISCIPLINE** HISTORY OF RELIGIONS **EDUCATION** Univ Kans, BA, 63; Univ Chicago, MA, 67, PhD, 69. **CAREER** Vis lectr, rel, NCent Col, 68-69; asst prof humanities, Northern Ariz Univ, 69-79; assoc prof, 79-82, prof relig studies, Southwest Mo State Univ, 82-; gen ed, Am Tribal Relig series, Univ Nebr Press, 77-. **HONORS AND AWARDS** NEH res fel anthrop, Okla Univ, 72-73; Rockefeller Found Humanities res fel, 77-78; res assoc, Mus Northern Ariz, 77-; Burlington Northern Found Fac Achievement Awd for Schol, 88; named hon prof, Univ Ningxia, China, 90; Excellence in Res Awd, SMSU Found, 95. **MEMBERSHIPS** Am Acad Relig. **RESEARCH** American Indian religions; religion in evolution. **SELECTED PUBLICATIONS** Auth, The Navajo Hunter Tradition, Univ Ariz, 75; Olmec Religion: A Key to Middle America and Beyond, Okla Univ, 76; Navajo Mountain and Rainbow Bridge Religion, Mus Northern Ariz Press, 77; A Navajo Bringing-Home Ceremony, Mus Northern Ariz Univ, 78; Coyoteway, A Navajo Holyway Healing Ceremonial, Univ Ariz, 79; Egyptian Light and Hebrew Fire: Theological and Philosophical Roots of Christendom in Evolutionary Perspective, State Univ NY Press, 91; coauth, Myths and Legends of the Hui, a Muslim Chinese People, State Univ NY Press, 94; Kazakh Traditions in China, Univ Press Am, 98; Uighur Stories from Along the Silk Road, Univ Press Am, 98; author numerous journal articles. **CONTACT ADDRESS** Dept Relig Studies, Southwest Missouri State Univ, Springfield, 901 S National, Springfield, MO 65804-0088. **EMAIL** luckert@dialnet.net

LUCKINGHAM, BRADFORD FRANKLIN
PERSONAL Born 05/15/1934, Fitchburg, MA, m, 1963, 1 child **DISCIPLINE** AMERICAN HISTORY **EDUCATION** Northern Ariz Univ, BS, 61; Univ Mo, Columbia, MA, 62; Univ Calif, Davis, PhD(hist), 68. **CAREER** Asst prof hist, Ind Univ, Kokomo Campus, 68-70; asst prof, 70-74, Assoc Prof Hist, Ariz State Univ, 74-. **RESEARCH** American urban history. **SELECTED PUBLICATIONS** Auth, Benevolence in the urban far west: The early San Francisco experience, Southern Calif Quart, 1/74; The city in the westware movement, Western Hist Quart, 4/74; Immigrant life in emergent San Francisco, J West, 10/74; auth, The Urban Southwest: A Profile History of Albuquerque, El Paso, Phoenix and Tucson, 82; auth, The American Southwest: An Urban View, Western Historical Quart, 7/84; auth, Phoenix: The History of A Southwestern Metropolis, 89; auth, Minorities in Phoenix: A Profile of Mexican American, Chinese American, ed. African American Communities, 1860-1992, 94. **CONTACT ADDRESS** Dept of Hist, Arizona State Univ, PO Box 872501, Tempe, AZ 85287-2501.

LUDLOW, JEANNIE
PERSONAL Born 06/02/1961, Fountain County, IN, p, 1995, 1 child **DISCIPLINE** AMERICAN CULTURE STUDIES **EDUCATION** Bowling Green State Univ, PhD, 92. **CAREER** Instr, 90-98; prof, 98-, Bowling Green State Univ. **HONORS AND AWARDS** Diss Res Fel; Shankin Awd, Res Excel. **MEMBERSHIPS** NWSA; ASA; MMLA. **RESEARCH** Cultural studies approaches to various aspects of American Women's lived experiences and cultural expressions. **SELECTED PUBLICATIONS** Auth, "Working (In) the In-Between: Poetry, Criticism, Interrogation and Interruption," SML: Studies in American Indian Literatures (94); auth, "Priorities and Power: Adjuncts in the Academy," Thought & Action (98); auth, "Seaming Meanings: Wendy Rose, Diane Glancy and Carol Sanchez Writing In Between," forthcoming. **CONTACT ADDRESS** American Culture Studies, Bowling Green State Univ, 910 N Main St, Bowling Green, OH 43402-1819. **EMAIL** jludlow@bgnet.bgsu.edu

LUDWIG, THEODORE MARK
PERSONAL Born 09/28/1936, Oxford, NE, m, 1960, 4 children **DISCIPLINE** HISTORY OF RELIGIONS, ASIAN RELIGIONS **EDUCATION** Concordia Sem St Louis, BA, 58, MDiv, 61, STM, 62, ThD, 63; Univ Chicago, PhD(Hist Relig), 75. **CAREER** Asst prof, 68-73, assoc prof 74-83, prof, Theol, Valparaiso Univ, 83-; Surjit Patheja prof of Wold Religions and Ethics, 98- **HONORS AND AWARDS** Research professorship, 79-80; Nat. Endow. For Humanities fel, 81-82; Distinguished teaching award, Valparaiso Univ, 79-80. **MEMBERSHIPS** Soc Bibl Lit; Am Acad Relig; Asn Asian Studies; Soc for Study of Japanese Regions. **RESEARCH** Buddhist Studies; Japanese religions; Comparative Religious Studies. **SELECTED PUBLICATIONS** Auth, The way of tea: a religioaesthetic mode of life, Hist Relig, 74; co-ed (with Frank Reynolds), Transitions and Transformations in the History of Religions: Essays in Honor of Joseph M Kitagawa, 80 & auth, Remember not the former things: Disjunction and transformation in Ancient Israel, In: Transitions and Transformations in the History of Religions: Essays in Honor of Joseph M Kitagawa, 80, E J Brill, Leiden; Christian self-understanding and other religions, Currents in Theol & Mission, 80; Before Rikyu: Religious and aesthetic influences in the early history of the tea ceremony, Monumenta Nipponica, 81; auth, Chanoyu and Momoyama, in Tea in Japan, 89, U of Hawaii Press; The Sacred Paths: Understanding the Religions of the World, 01; auth, Sacred Paths of the East, 01. **CONTACT ADDRESS** Dept of Theology, Valparaiso Univ, Valparaiso, IN 46383-6493. **EMAIL** Ted.Ludwig@valpo.edu.

LUEBKE, FREDERICK CARL
PERSONAL Born 01/26/1927, Reedsburg, WI, m, 1951, 4 children **DISCIPLINE** AMERICAN HISTORY **EDUCATION** Concordia Univ, Ill, BS, 50; Claremont Grad Univ, MA, 58; Univ Nebr, PhD(hist), 66. **CAREER** Ffrom asst prof to assoc prof hist, Concordia Univ, Nebr, 61-68; assoc prof, 68-72, prof hist, Univ Nebr, Lincoln, 72-87; to Charles J. Mach Distinguished Prof of Hist, 87-94; to Mach Prof Emeritus, 94- **HONORS AND AWARDS** Danforth assoc, Danforth Found, 70-; sr Fulbright res fel, Univ Stuttgart, West Germany, 74-75; fel state and local hist, Newberry Libr, Chicago, 77 and 78; scholar-in-residence, Rockefeller Found Study Ctr, Bellagio, Italy, 82; Outstanding Teacher Awd, UNL, 83; Outstanding Res and Creativity Awd, UNL, 85; Pound-Howard Distinguished Career Awd, UNL, 94. **MEMBERSHIPS** Orgn Am Historians; Western Hist Asn; Immigration Hist Soc. **RESEARCH** American immigration history; Western frontier history; Nebraska history. **SELECTED PUBLICATIONS** Auth, Bonds of Loyalty: German Americans and World War I, Northern Ill Univ Press, 74; co-ed, The Great Plains: Environment and Culture, Univ Nebr Press, 79; ed, Ethnicity on the Great Plains, Univ Nebr Press, 80; co-ed, Vision and Refuge: Essays on the Lit of the Great Plains, Univ Nebr Press, 82; ed, Mapping the North Am Plains, Univ Okla Press, 87; auth, Germans in Brazil: A Comparative Hist of Cultural Conflict during World War I, La State Univ Press, 87; auth, Germans in the New World, Univ Ill Press, 90; ed, A Harmony of the Arts: The Nebr State Capitol, Univ Nebr Press, 90; auth, Nebr: An Illustrated Hist, Univ Nebr Press, 95; ed, European Immigrants in the Am West, Univ New Mexico Prss, 98. **CONTACT ADDRESS** Dept Hist, Univ of Nebraska, Lincoln, 611 Oldfather Hall, Lincoln, NE 68588-0327. **EMAIL** fcluebke@alltel.net

LUEHRS, ROBERT BOICE
PERSONAL Born 10/05/1939, Portland, OR, m, 1965, 1 child **DISCIPLINE** EUROPEAN HISTORY **EDUCATION** Columbia Univ, AB, 61; Wash Univ, AM, 63; Stanford Univ, PhD, 69. **CAREER** Instr Ger & mod Europ hist, Univ OR, 66-67; asst prof hist, 68-71, dir honors prog, 72-74, assoc prof, 71-80, prof hist, Ft Hays State Univ, 80, Ch of Hist Dept, 94-96. **MEMBERSHIPS** AAUP; Phi Kappa Phi. **RESEARCH** Am and Brit deism; the Scottish Enlightenment; Myth and magic in hist; Early twentieth-century children's lit. **SELECTED PUBLICATIONS** Auth, Franz Overbeck and the theologian as antichrist, Katallagete, summer 73; Christianity against history: Franz Overbeck's concept of the Finis Christianismi, Katallagete, summer 75; The problematic compromise: The early deism of Anthony Collins, In: Studies in Eighteenth Century Culture, Vol VI, Univ Wis, 77; L. Frank Baum and the Land of Oz: A children's author as social critic, Nineteenth Century, autumn 80; Reginald Scot and the witchcraft controversy of the Sixteenth Century, Fort Hays Studies, 85; Population and utopia in the thought of Robert Wallace, Eighteenth Century Studies; John Locke and Jean-Jacques Roussseau, In: Research Guide to European Historical Biography, 1500 to the Present, Beacham Publ, 92-93. **CONTACT ADDRESS** Dept of Hist, Fort Hays State Univ, 600 Park St, Hays, KS 67601-4099. **EMAIL** rluehrs@fhsu.edu

LUFRANO, RICHARD
DISCIPLINE MODERN CHINESE HISTORY **EDUCATION** SUNY, BA, 74; Columbia, PhD, 87. **CAREER** Hist, Columbia Univ **SELECTED PUBLICATIONS** Auth, Jolting the Age: Xu Zi and the Evolution of Qing Statecraft Thinking, 97, Honorable Merchants: Self Cultivation and Commerce in Late Imperial China, 97. **CONTACT ADDRESS** Columbia Univ, 2960 Broadway, New York, NY 10027-6902.

LUFT, DAVID SHEERS
PERSONAL Born 05/06/1944, Youngstown, OH, m, 1967, 1 child **DISCIPLINE** MODERN EUROPEAN INTELLECTUAL HISTORY **EDUCATION** Wesleyan Univ, BA, 66; Harvard Univ, MA, 67, PhD(mod Europ hist), 72. **CAREER** Asst Prof Mod Europ Hist, Univ Calif, San Diego, 72-. **HONORS AND AWARDS** Excellence in Teaching, Revelle Col, Univ Calif, San Diego, 75. **RESEARCH** German and Austrian intellectual and social history since the 18th century. **SELECTED PUBLICATIONS** Auth, Robert Musil: An Intellectual Biography, 1880-1924, Harvard Univ, 72. **CONTACT ADDRESS** Dept of Hist and Soc Sci, Univ of California, San Diego, La Jolla, CA 92093.

LUFT, HERBERT
PERSONAL Born 08/17/1942, Frankfurt, Germany, m, 1991, 2 children **DISCIPLINE** HISTORY **EDUCATION** Pepperdine Univ, BA, 65; MA, 66; Univ S Calif, PhD, 76. **CAREER** From asst prof to prof, Pepperdine Univ, 67-. **HONORS AND AWARDS** German-American Medal of Friendship, Who's Who in Am **MEMBERSHIPS** Phi Alpha Theta Hist Honor Soc, Ger Studies Asn, AHA. **RESEARCH** 19th & 20th century intellectual history, 20th century Third Reich, Germany. **SELECTED PUBLICATIONS** Rev, of "The Russians in Germany. The History of the Soviet Occupation," by Norman M. Naimark, Harvard Univ Press, 96; rev, of "The Unmaking of Adolf Hitler," by Eugene Davidson, Univ of Mo Press, 97; rev, of "On the Road to the Wolf's Lair. German Resistance to Hitler," by Theodore S. Hamerow, Harvard Univ Press, 98; auth, ""A New-Age" School System: Rudolf Steiner and the Waldorf School Movement," Interdisciplinary Studies V (98); rev, of "Why Hitler? The Genesis of the Nazi Reich," by Samuel W. Micham Jr (London & Westport, CT: Preaeger, 99); rev, of "Hitler: The Pathology of Evil," by Victor George (Washington & London: Brassey's, 99); auth, Geschichte der Gemeinde Christi Mannheim, Eigenverlag (Mannheim), 99. **CONTACT ADDRESS** Dept Humanities, Pepperdine Univ, 24255 Pacific Coast Hwy, Malibu, CA 90263-4225. **EMAIL** hluft@pepperdine.edu

LUFT, SANDRA
PERSONAL Born 07/22/1934, Los Angeles, CA, m, 2 children **DISCIPLINE** HISTORY OF IDEAS **EDUCATION** Brandeis Univ, PhD, 63. **CAREER** Prof, Humanities, San Francisco State Univ. **RESEARCH** Giambattista Vico; F. Nietzsche; Post modern theory. **SELECTED PUBLICATIONS** Auth, Embodying the Eye of Humanism: Giambattista Vico and the Eye of Ingenium, Sites of Vision: The Discursive Construction of Vision in the History of Philosophy, MIT Press, 97; auth, The Postmodern: Raising the Questions Philosophy Doesn't Ask, Mag, 96; auth, Philosophy as Poiesis in Vico and Nietzsche, Proceedings of the Intl Soc for the Study of Europ Ideas Conf, 96; auth, Situating Vico Between Modern and Postmodern, Hist Reflections/Reflexions Historiques, 96; auth, The Secularization of Origins in Vico and Nietzsche, Personalist Forum, 94; auth, Derrida, Vico, Genesis, and the Originary Power of Language, The Eighteenth Century: Theory and Interpretation, 93; rev, Golden Doves with Silver Dots: Semiology and Textuality in the Rabbinic Tradition, New Vico Studies, 92. **CONTACT ADDRESS** San Francisco State Univ, 1600 Holloway Ave., San Francisco, CA 94132. **EMAIL** srluft@sfsu.edu

LUIS, WILLIAM
PERSONAL Born 07/12/1948, New York, NY, m, 3 children **DISCIPLINE** LATIN AMERICAN STUDIES **EDUCATION** SUNY at Binghamton, BA 1971; Univ of Wis Madison, MA 1973; Cornell Univ, MA 1979, PhD 1980. **CAREER** Bd of Educ NYC, tchr 1971-72, tchr 1973-74; Handbook of Latin Amer Studies; Latin Amer Literary Review, Natl Endowment for the Humanities, reader 1985; Natl Research Cncl/Ford Fndtn Fellowship Panel, 86; Dartmouth Coll, asst prof of Latin Amer & Caribbean, assoc prof 1985-88; visiting assoc, Washington Univ, 88; assoc prof, dir, Latin Amer and Caribbean Area Studies Prog, 88-91; Vanderbilt Univ, assoc prof, 91-96, prof, 96-; Yale Univ, visting prof, 98; Afro-Hispanic Review, Cuban Studies, Revista de Estudroa Hispanicos, Hispanic Journal, Caribe, Mundo AFRO. **HONORS AND AWARDS** Deans List SUNY at Binghamton 1968-71; Vilas Fellowship UW 1972; Grad Sch Fellowship UW 1973; Grad Sch Fellowship CU 1974-76; Berkowitz Travel & Rsch Fellowship CU 1974-76; Sigma Delta Pi 1975; Latin Amer Studies Prog Travel Grant CU 1977; Edwin Gould Awd Aspira 1974-76-78; Tchng Asst CU 1976-78; Summer Rsch Fellowships CU 1975-79; Special Grad School Fellowships CU 1975-79; Amer Coun of Learned Society's, Fellowship, 1994; Directory of Amer Scholars 1982; ed Voices from Under, Black Narrative inLatin Amer & the Caribbean 1984; Literary Bondage and Slavery in Cuban Narratives, 1990; Modern Latin Amer Fiction Writers, Vols 1&2, 1992, 1994; Dance Between Two Cultures: Latino-Caribbean Literature Written in the US, 1997 auth, The Culture and Customs of Cuba, 00; and numerous lectures, publications. articles auth, **MEMBERSHIPS** Mem Modern Lang Assn; Assn of Caribbean Studies; Am Assn of Tchrs of Spanish & Portuguese; mem adv bd Comm on Spec Educ Projects; mem Ad Hoc Comm to Study Hispanic Admissions & Recruitment; mem Minority Educ Council; mem Black Caucus; mem African Afro-Amer Studies Steering Comm; mem Literary Criticism Seminar; mem Latin Amer Literary Seminar; co-dir Latin Amer Literary Seminar; faculty advisor Phi Sigma Psi; mem African & Afro-Amer Studies Seminar; mem exec comm Assn of Caribbean Studies; mem Screening Comm for the Dir & Adjunct Curator of Film DC; mem Native Amer Studies Steering Comm; mem exec comm of the Faculty of DC; mem Agenda Subcomm of the Exec Comm of the Faculty of DC; mem Library Search Comm for the Humanities Bibliographer. **SELECTED PUBLICATIONS** Auth, The Culture and Customs of Cuba, 00. **CONTACT ADDRESS** Latin American Literature, Vanderbilt Univ, Nashville, TN 37235. **EMAIL** william.luis@vanderbilt.edu

LUKACS, JOHN ADALBERT
PERSONAL Born 01/31/1924, Budapest, Hungary, 2 children **DISCIPLINE** HISTORY **EDUCATION** Univ Budapest, PhD, 46. **CAREER** Lectr, Hungarian Inst Int Affairs, 45-46 & Columbia Univ, 46-47; from lectr to assoc prof, 47-65, prof hist, Chestnut Hill Col, Penn, 65-93, vis lectr, La Salle Col, 49-83; vis assoc prof, Columbia Univ, 54-55; vis prof, Univ Pa, 64, 67 & 68, 94-96; Johns Hopkins Sch Advan Int Studies, 70-71, vis prof Fletcher Sch Law, 72 & 73; vis prof Princeton Univ, 88; vis prof, Kozgazdasagi Univ, and Eotvos Univ, Budapest, 91. **HONORS AND AWARDS** Elected pres Am Cath hist Asn, 77; fel Soc of Am Hist, 82; hon doctorate, la Salle Univ, 89; Ingersoll Prize, 91; Cross of Merit of the Republic of Hungary, 94. **MEMBERSHIPS** Am Cath Hist Asn (pres, 77). **RESEARCH** Modern European history; diplomatic history; historiography; American history. **SELECTED PUBLICATIONS** Auth, Outgrowing Democracy: A History of the United States in the Twentieth Century, Doubleday, 84; auth, Budapest 1900: A Historical Portrait of a City and Its Cultures, Weidenfeld & Nicolson, 89; auth, Confessions of An Original Sinner, Ticknor & Fields, 90; auth, The Duel: The Eighty-Day Struggle Between Churchill and Hitler, Ticknor & Fields, 91; auth, The End of the Twentieth Century (And the End of the Modern Age) Ticknor & Fields, 93; auth, Destinations Past, Missouri, 94; auth, George F. Kennan and the Origins of Containment, 1944-1946: The Kennan-Lukacs Correspondence, Missouri, 97; auth, The Hitler of History, Knopf, 97; auth, A Thread of Years, Yale, 98; auth, Five Days in London, May 1940, Yale, 99. **CONTACT ADDRESS** 129 Valley Park Rd, Phoenixville, PA 19460.

LUMSDEN, IAN G.
PERSONAL Born 06/08/1945, Montreal, PQ, Canada **DISCIPLINE** ART HISTORY **EDUCATION** McGill Univ, BA, 68; Mus Mgt Inst, Univ Calif Berkeley, 91. **CAREER** Cur art dept, NB Mus St John, 69; cur, 69-83, DIR, BEAVERBROOK ART GALLERY, 83-; dir, Artsatlantic, 94-. **MEMBERSHIPS** Art Mus Dirs Org; Material Hist Steering Comt Univ NB; adv comt, Atlantic Conserv Ctr, Can Conserv Inst; Can Mus Asn; Atlantic Prov Art Gallery Asn; Am Asn Mus. **SELECTED PUBLICATIONS** Auth, New Brunswick Landscape Artists of the 19th Century, 69; auth, From Sickert to Dali: International Portraits, 76; auth, Bloomsbury Painters and Their Circle, 76; auth, The Murray and Marguerite Vaughan Inuit Print Collection, 81; auth, Drawings by Carol Fraser 1948-1986, 87; auth, Gainsborough in Canada, 91; auth, Early Views of British North America, 94. **CONTACT ADDRESS** Beaverbrook Art Gallery, PO Box 605, Fredericton, NB, Canada E3B 5A6.

LUNA, EILEEN
DISCIPLINE AMERICAN INDIAN STUDIES **EDUCATION** San Diego State Univ, AB, 68; Peoples Col Law, JD, 78; Harvard Univ, MPA, 96. **CAREER** Staff Atty, Serv Employees Int Union, 75-80; Campaign Dir, Commun Workers of Am, 80-81; Chief Investr, Police Rev Comn, 81-89; Sen Management Analyst, Berkeley City Manager's Off, 89-90; Chief Investr, San Franciso Off Citizens' Complaints, 90-92; Exec Off, San Diego Citizens' Law Enforcement Rev Board, 92-95; Asst Prof, Univ Ariz, 96-. **HONORS AND AWARDS** John B. Pickett Fel in Criminal Justice, Harvard Univ; Christian A Johnson Endeavor Found Native Am Fel, 95-96; Fel, Univ New S Wales, 98; **MEMBERSHIPS** Calif Bar Asn, Native Am Bar Asn, Western Soc Sci Asn, Am Soc Criminology. **RESEARCH** Tribal policing, violence against Indian women, Indian tribal government public policy. **SELECTED PUBLICATIONS** Auth, "Community Policing in Indian Country," in Church & Soc, vol 87, no 4 (97):; auth, "The Growth and Development of Tribal Police in Indian Country: Challenges and Issues for Tribal Sovereignty," in J of Contemp Criminal Justice, vol 14, no 1 (98): 75-86; auth, "The Impact of the Unfunded Mandates Reform Act of 1995 on Tribal Governments," Am Indian Law Rev, vol 22, issue 2 (98): 1-33; auth, "Indigenous Women, Domestic Violence and Self Determination," Indigenous Law Bulletin, Univ New S Wales Pr (99); auth, "Police Accountability in the American Indian Community," Georgetown Public Policy Rev, vol 4 no 2 (99); auth, "Special Issues for Evaluating Projects on Indian Tribal Lands," in Evaluation Guidebook (Urban Inst Pr, 97), 233-245; coauth, Pathological Gambling: A Critical Review, Nat Acad Pr, 99; **CONTACT ADDRESS** Dept Am Indian Studies, Univ of Arizona, PO Box 210076, Tucson, AR 85721-0076. **EMAIL** eluna@u.arizona.edu

LUND, ERIC
PERSONAL Born 09/06/1948, New Haven, CT, m, 1974, 2 children **DISCIPLINE** HISTORY OF CHRISTIANITY **EDUCATION** Brown Univ, AB, 70; Yale Divinity School, MDiv, 74; Yale Univ, MA, 76; PhD, 79. **CAREER** Dept relig, St Olaf Col, 79- . **HONORS AND AWARDS** Phi Beta Kappa, 69. **MEMBERSHIPS** Am Acad Relig; Am Soc Church Hist; Sixteenth Cent Student; Soc Student Christian Spirituality. **RESEARCH** Religion in 16th & 17th Century Europe, Religious conflict in the Middle East. **SELECTED PUBLICATIONS** Co-ed, Word, Church and State-Tyndale Quincentenary Essays, Wash, DC: Cath Univ Press. **CONTACT ADDRESS** Dept Relig, St. Olaf Col, 1520 Saint Olaf Ave, Northfield, MN 55057-1574. **EMAIL** lund@stolaf.edu

LUNDE, ERIK SHELDON
PERSONAL Born 10/16/1940, Hanover, NH, m, 1963, 2 children **DISCIPLINE** AMERICAN HISTORY, FILM HISTORY, FILM STUDIES **EDUCATION** Harvard Univ, AB, 63; Univ Md, MA, 66, PhD(Am Hist), 70. **CAREER** Asst prof Am Hist, Marquette Univ, 69-70; asst prof, 70-74, assoc prof, 74-79, prof Am Thought & Lang, Mich State Univ, 79-. **HONORS AND AWARDS** Outstanding Teacher Awd, Mich State Univ Chapter, Golden Key National Honor Society, 94. **MEMBERSHIPS** Am Film Institute. **RESEARCH** William Wyler; Alfred Hitchcock; D.W. Griffith; silent film. **SELECTED PUBLICATIONS** Auth, Horace Greeley, G K Hall, 81; co-ed with Douglas Noverr, Film Studies and Film History, Markus Wiener, 89; **CONTACT ADDRESS** Dept of American Thought & Lang, Michigan State Univ, 289 Bessey Hall, East Lansing, MI 48824-1033. **EMAIL** lundee@pilot.msu.edu

LUNENFELD, MARVIN
PERSONAL Born 09/10/1934, New York, NY, m, 1960, 1 child **DISCIPLINE** EARLY MODERN EUROPEAN & SPANISH HISTORY **EDUCATION** City Col NYork, BBA, 57 NYork Univ, MA, 63, PhD, 68. **CAREER** Lectr hist, Overseas Prog, Univ Md, 64; instr, City Col NY, 67-68; instr, Rutgers Univ, 68-70; Assoc Prof History, Distinguished Teaching Prof Emer, Dept of History, State Univ NY Col Fredonia, 70-97. Lectr hist, New Sch Social Res, 68-; Rockeller fel, Villa Serbelloni Residence, 94; fel, Aston Magna Acad on Baroque Spain & Latin Am, 95; Malone fel, Nat Counc US-Arab Rel, 96; NEH fel, 96-97. **HONORS AND AWARDS** Acad World Star Int Acad Auth Educ Moscow, 98. **MEMBERSHIPS** Soc Span & Port Hist Studies; AHA. **RESEARCH** Urban history; police and the military; Spanish Inquisition. **SELECTED PUBLICATIONS** Auth, The Council of the Santa Hermandad: A Study of Ferdinand and Isabella's Pacification Forces, Univ Miami, 70; Keepers of the City: The Corregidores of Isabella I of Castile (1474-1504), Cambridge Univ Press, 87; Los Corregidores de Isabel La Catolica, Ed Labor, 89; The 1492 Reader, Newberry Library, 89; 1492: Discovery, Invasion, Encounter, McMillan, 91; The Real World: How to Use College to Get Your Career Started, Semester Press, 89; College Basics: How to Start Right and Finish Strong, Semester Press, 92. **CONTACT ADDRESS** 231 Norwood Ave, Buffalo, NY 14222. **EMAIL** gailmarvin@webtv.net

LUPIA, JOHN N.
PERSONAL Born 05/18/1952, Orange, NJ, d, 6 children **DISCIPLINE** ART HISTORY **EDUCATION** City Coll CUNY, MA, 82; Rutgers Univ, PhD candidate, 82-87, MLS, 93. **CAREER** Prof, 83-87, Kean Univ; Prof, 87-90, Seton Hall Univ; Prof, 91-96, Brookdale Comm Coll; Prof in library, 96-98, Kean Univ. **HONORS AND AWARDS** Rutgers Univ Fel, Headstart Sev Awd. **MEMBERSHIPS** CBAA, ASP. **RE-**

SEARCH Biblical archaeology, Biblical textual criticism, philosophy, New Testament Studies, papyrology, information science, medieval & renaissance studies. **SELECTED PUBLICATIONS** Contrib auth, 21 articles for The Dictionary of Art, London Macmillan Pub Ltd, 95, Who's Minding the Church? A Brief Review of the Papacy 1100-1520, in: The Medieval & Renaissance Times, 94; auth, " The Seamless Garment of Christ," Worldwide Congress Sindone, Orvieto, Italy, 00. **CONTACT ADDRESS** 501 North Ave, Apt B1, Elizabeth, NJ 07208-1731.

LUPININ, NICKOLAS
PERSONAL Born 11/19/1941, Latvia, s **DISCIPLINE** RUSSIAN RELIGION AND HISTORY **EDUCATION** Syracuse Univ, BA, 64; New York Univ, MA, 66; PhD, 73. **CAREER** Assoc, Harvard Univ, 99-02; sr lectr, prof, Franklin Pierce Coll. **HONORS AND AWARDS** Hon Soc; Grad Fel, NYU; NDEA Fel; NYU Grad Excell Awd; Who's Who in World, 00. **MEMBERSHIPS** AHA; ARAS; AAASS; TSA; AAM; HS. **RESEARCH** Russian religion and culture; 20th century memoir record (Soviet Union). **SELECTED PUBLICATIONS** Auth, Religious Revolt in the XVIIth Century: The Schism of the Russian Church, Kingston Press (Princeton, NJ), 84; auth, "Novoierusalimskii Monastery," in Modern Encyclopedia of Russian & Soviet History (MERSH); auth, "Optina Pustyn" in Modern Encyclopedia of Russian & Soviet History (MERSH): 56-59; auth, "Patriarchate in Russia," in Modern Encyclopedia of Russian & Soviet History (MERSH): 56-60; auth, "Arsenius the Greek" in Modern Encyclopedia of Religion in Russia and the Soviet Union (MERRSU,91): 74-75; auth, "Alexander Nevski." in TIME: The International Military Encyclopedia, 99; auth, "Russia's Fears Are Valid," Provid J Bul (97); auth, "Flame of Democracy Warms up Bitter Cold of Russian Winter," Boston Herald (97); auth, "General Lebed Holds Out Hope for Russia After Boris Yeltsin," Provid J Bul (98). **CONTACT ADDRESS** Dept Humanities, Franklin Pierce Col, PO Box 60, Rindge, NH 03461-0060. **EMAIL** lupinin@fpc.edu

LUSIGNAN, SERGE
PERSONAL Born 10/22/1943, Montreal, PQ, Canada, m, 1967 **DISCIPLINE** MEDIEVAL INTELLECTUAL HISTORY **EDUCATION** Col Andre Grasset, BA, 64; Univ Montreal, MA, 67 and 68, PhD(medieval studies), 71. **CAREER** Res asst, 71-72, asst prof, 72-77, Assoc Prof Medieval Studies, Univ Montreal, 77-, Chmn Dept, 77-. **MEMBERSHIPS** Medieval Acad Am; Int Soc Study Medieval Philos. **RESEARCH** Medieval encyclopedia; 13th century logic; text processing by computer. **SELECTED PUBLICATIONS** Coed, Computing in the Humanities, Univ of Waterloo Pr, Waterloo, ON, 77; coauth, "Disambiguation by Short Contexts," Computers and the Humanities 19, (85): 147-57. **CONTACT ADDRESS** Dept of Hist, Univ of Montreal, PO Box 6128, Downtown, QC, Canada H3C 3J7. **EMAIL** lusignas@hst.umontreal.ca

LUTZ, JESSIE GREGORY
PERSONAL Born 08/06/1925, Halifax, NC, m, 1948 **DISCIPLINE** HISTORY **EDUCATION** Univ NC, BA, 46; Univ Chicago, MA, 48; Cornell Univ, PhD(Chinese hist), 55. **CAREER** From instr to assoc prof, 56-70, chmn dept, 72-75, Prof Hist, Rutgers Univ, 70-, Actg Dir Int Prog, 75-, Am Asn Univ Women fel, 63-64; Soc Sci Res Coun and Am Coun Learned Socs fels, 70-71. **HONORS AND AWARDS** Lindback Found Awd, 68; Bk Prize, Berkshire Conf Women Historians, 73. **MEMBERSHIPS** AHA; Asn Asian Studies; Berkshire Conf Women Historians. **RESEARCH** Modern Chinese nationalism, education, student movements, missions. **SELECTED PUBLICATIONS** Auth, A Phoenix Transformed--the Reconstruction of Education in Postwar Hong Kong, Amer Hist Rev, Vol 0100, 95. **CONTACT ADDRESS** Rutgers, The State Univ of New Jersey, New Brunswick, New Brunswick, NJ 08903.

LYDOLPH, PAUL E.
PERSONAL Born 01/04/1924, Bonaparte, IA, m, 1966, 5 children **DISCIPLINE** GEOGRAPHY **EDUCATION** Univ Wis, PhD, 55. **CAREER** Assoc prof, 52-59, Los Angeles St Col; prof, 59-96, geo dept, Univ WI, Milwaukee. **HONORS AND AWARDS** Ford Found Fel; Festschrift pub in his honor. **MEMBERSHIPS** Asn of Amer Geographers, Amer Asn for the Advancement of Slavic Stud. **RESEARCH** Geography of the USSR; climatology **SELECTED PUBLICATIONS** Auth, Geography of the USSR: Topical Analysis, Misty Valley Pub, 64, 70, 79, 90; auth, The Climate of the Earth, Rowman & Allenheld, 85; auth, Climates of the Soviet Union, Vol 7, World Survey of Climatology, Elsevier, 77. **CONTACT ADDRESS** No 8328 Snake Rd, Elkhart Lake, WI 53020-2011.

LYDON, GHISLAINE
PERSONAL Born Flushing, NY, m, 1996 **DISCIPLINE** HISTORY **EDUCATION** McGill Univ, BA, 92; Mich State Univ, MA, 94; PhD, 00. **CAREER** Asst prof, UCLA, 00-. **HONORS AND AWARDS** For Lang Areas Studies Fel, 92-96; Soc Sci Res Coun Summer Fel; Fulbright Fel, 96-97; Coun for Am Overseas Res Ctrs Res Fel, 98. **MEMBERSHIPS** African Studies Asn; Am Hist Asn; Asn of Concerned Africa Scholars. **RESEARCH** Western African History (social and economic). **SELECTED PUBLICATIONS** Auth, "Les peripeties d'une institution financiere: La Banque du Senegal 1844-1901," in AOF: Realites et Heritages. Societes Ouest-Africaines et Order Colonial, 1895-1960, (Dakar, 97), 475-491; auth, "The Unraveling of a Neglected Source: A Report on Women in Francophone West Africa in the 1930s," in Cahiers D'Etudes Africaines, (97): 555-584; auth, "Women, Children, and the Popular Front Missions of Inquiry in French West Africa," in French Colonial Empire and the Popular Front, St Martin's Press, 99. **CONTACT ADDRESS** Dept Hist, Univ of California, Los Angeles, 6265 Bunche, Box 951473, Los Angeles, CA 90095-1473. **EMAIL** lydon@ucla.edu

LYMAN, J. REBECCA
PERSONAL Born 10/21/1954 **DISCIPLINE** CHURCH HISTORY **EDUCATION** W Mich Univ, BA; Cath Univ Am, MA; Univ Oxford, DPhil. **CAREER** Samuel M. Garrett prof, Church Divinity Sch Pacific **HONORS AND AWARDS** Henry Luce Fel, 96. **SELECTED PUBLICATIONS** Auth, Christian Traditions, Cowley, 99; auth, The Making of a Heretic: The Life of Origen in Epiphanius' Panarion 64, Studia Patristica, 97; A Topography of Heresy: Mapping the Rhetorical Creation of Arianism, Arianism after Arius, Edinburgh, 93; Lex Orandi: Heresy, Orthodoxy, and Popular Religion, The Making and Remaking of Christian Doctrine, Oxford, 93; Christology and Cosmology: Models of Divine Action in Origen, Eusebius, and Athanasius, Oxford UP, 93. **CONTACT ADDRESS** Church Divinity Sch of the Pacific, 2451 Ridge Rd, Berkeley, CA 94709-1217.

LYMAN, RICHARD B.
PERSONAL Born 02/05/1936, New York, NY, m, 1971, 2 children **DISCIPLINE** HISTORY **EDUCATION** Bowdoin Coll, BA, 57; Harvard Univ, MA, 60, PhD, 74. **CAREER** Prof, Hist, Emer, Simmons Coll and Lecturer in Asian Studies, Brandeis Univ. **MEMBERSHIPS** Am Antiquarian Soc **RESEARCH** Japan, 20th Century World Hist. **CONTACT ADDRESS** 124 Chestnut Cir, Lincoln, MA 01773. **EMAIL** lyman@simmons.edu

LYNCH, CATHERINE
PERSONAL Born 11/07/1949, Cambridge, MA, s **DISCIPLINE** HISTORY **EDUCATION** Univ Chicago, BA, 71; Univ Wisc-Madison, MA, 73, PhD, 89. **CAREER** Instr, Colby Col, 83-84; instr to asst prof, Case Western Reserve Univ, 86-95; vis asst prof, Univ Wisc-Madison, fall 90; asst prof, Eastern Conn State Univ, 95-; vis res, Nanjing Univ, China, summer 91. **HONORS AND AWARDS** Phi Beta Kappa, 71; NDFL Fels, 72-73, 73-74; Fulbright-Hays Dis Res Abroad Awd, 75-77; student , Taipei, Taiwan, and Tokyo, Japan, 75-77; Soc Sci Res Coun Fel, 75-77, 78; exchange student, Nanjing Univ, China, 79-81; Certificate of Advan Study in Hist, 81; Newcombe Fel, 81-82; Soc for Values in Higher Ed, 83; Res fac, Hobart & Wm Smith-Colby-Bates Prog, Beijing Normal Col of Foreign Langs, 84-85; hon fel, Ctr for East Asian Studies, Univ Wisc-Madison, 90-91; Comt on Schol Commun with China, China Conf Travel Grant, 93; Chiang Chung-Kuo Found, Travel Grant, 96. **MEMBERSHIPS** AAUP, Asn Asian Studies, Int Soc Intellectual Hist, Phi Alpha Theta, Phi Beta Kappa, Soc for Values in Higher Ed,. **RESEARCH** Modern Chinese intellectual history. **SELECTED PUBLICATIONS** Auth, forty three entries, in The Encyclopedia of Japan, ed Gen Itasaka, 9 vol, Tokyo: Kodansha (83); transl, Li Zehou, "The Philosophy of Kant and a Theory of Subjectivity," Analecta Husserliana, 21: 135-49 (86); auth, "Renxin yu tuanti," (psyche and group), Chinese transl, Zhongguo wenhua shuyuan xuebao, J of the Acad of Chinese Culture, 5 (spring 88); twenty-four entries in Worldmark Encyclopedia of the Nations, ed Tomothy L. Gall, 8th ed, 5 vols, Detroit: Gale Res (95); transl, in "Reopening the Debate on Chinese Culture," Sources of Chinese Tradition, ed Wm Theodore de Barry, 2nd ed, vol II, 382-386, NY: Columbia Univ Press (99); auth, Liang Shuming and the Populist Alternative in China,Stanford Univ Press (forthcoming 2000); book revs in History: Rev of New Books, J of Asian Studies, Phenomenol Infor Bull, Mei yu (Aesthetic ed). **CONTACT ADDRESS** Dept Hist, Philos & Political Sci, Eastern Connecticut State Univ, 83 Windham St, Willimantic, CT 06226-2211.

LYNCH, HOLLIS R.
PERSONAL Born 04/21/1935, Port-of-Spain, Trinidad and Tobago, d **DISCIPLINE** AFRICAN STUDIES **EDUCATION** British Columbia, BA 1960; Univ of London, PhD 1964. **CAREER** Univ of IFE Nigeria, lecturer 1964-66; Roosevelt Univ Chicago, assoc prof 1966-68; State Univ of NY at Buffalo, assoc prof 1968-69; Columbia Univ, prof 1969-; Inst of African Studies Columbia Univ, dir 1971-74, 85-90. **HONORS AND AWARDS** Recipient Commonwealth Fellow London Univ 1961-64; Hoover Nat Fellow Stanford Univ 1973-74; fellow Woodrow Wilson Intl Ctr for Scholars 1976; ACLS (Am Council of Learned Soc) Fellowship 1978-79. **MEMBERSHIPS** Fmem African Studies Assn; Assn for Study of Afro-Am Life & History; Am Historical Assn. **SELECTED PUBLICATIONS** Apartheid in Historical Perspective: A Case For Divestment, Columbia College Today, 1985; The Foundation of American-Nigerian Ties: Nigerian Students in the United States, 1939-48, Black Ivory, The Pan-African Magazine, 1989; author Edward Wilmot Blyden Pan Negro Patriot 1967 & The Black Urban Condition 1973; Black Africa 1973; "Black Am Radicals & Liberaton of Africa" 1978; "Black Spokesman" 1970; "Selected Letters of Edward W Blyden" (with a foreword by Pres Leopold Sedar Senghor) 1978. **CONTACT ADDRESS** Inst of African Studies, Columbia Univ, New York, NY 10027.

LYNCH, JOHN EDWARD
PERSONAL Born 10/21/1924, New York, NY **DISCIPLINE** MEDIEVAL HISTORY **EDUCATION** St Paul's Col, AB, 47; Univ Toronto, MA, 56, PhD(philos), 65; Pontifical Inst Medieval Studies, Toronto, MSL, 59. **CAREER** Prof ecclesiastical hist, St Paul's Col, 59-73; prof hist, Catholic Univ Am, 66-, prof hist Canon Law, 68-, chmn dept hist Canon Law, 74-86, vice-provost for grad studies, 91-98. **HONORS AND AWARDS** Role of Law Awd, Canon Law Soc Am, 84. **MEMBERSHIPS** AHA; Am Soc Church Hist; Am Cath Hist Asn; Canon Law Soc Am; AAUP. **RESEARCH** Early CHURCH HIST; Medieval Canon Law. **SELECTED PUBLICATIONS** Auth, "Clement XI, Pope," Historical Dictionary of the Treatise of the War of the Spanish Succession, ed. I. Frey (Westport, Conn: Greenwood Pub., 95) 110-112; auth, "Kuttner, Stephan George," New Catholic Encyclopedia, 19 (96):234-236; auth, "A Conflict of Values: A Confusion of Laws," The Jurist, 56 (96): 182-199; auth, "The Office of Bishop in Mainline Protestant Churches," Cannon Law Soc of Am Proceedings, 60 (98): 103-123; auth, "The Canonical Contribution to English Law," Studia Canonica, 33 (99): 505-525; auth, "Cannons 273-289: The Obligations and Rights of Clerics," The Code of Cannon Law: A Text and Commentary, ref.ed. Canon Law Soc of Am, (NYork: Paulist Press), 00. **CONTACT ADDRESS** Catholic Univ of America, 3015 Fourth St NE, Washington, DC 20064. **EMAIL** lynch@cua.edu

LYNCH, JOSEPH HOWARD
PERSONAL Born 11/21/1943, Springfield, MA, m, 1965, 3 children **DISCIPLINE** MEDIEVAL & CHURCH HISTORY **EDUCATION** Boston Col, BA, 65; Harvard Univ, MA, 66, PhD, 71. **CAREER** Vis asst prof hist, Univ Ill, Urbana, 70-71; asst prof & asst dir Ctr Medieval & Renaissance Studies, 71-77, assoc prof hist, 77-85, dir ctr Medieval & Renaissance Studies, 78-83, prof hist, Ohio State Univ, 85; Joe R. Engle Prof of the Hist of Christianity, 00; Ohio State Distinguished Univ Prof, 00. **HONORS AND AWARDS** Am Coun Learned Soc fel, 75, Inst Advanced Study, 88, NEH Fel, 87-88; ACLS Fel, 99-00; Guggenheim Fel, 00-01. **MEMBERSHIPS** Mediaeval Acad Am; Soc Relig Higher Educ; AHA; Am Cath Hist Assoc; Int Sermon Studies; Am Soc of Church Hist. **RESEARCH** History of monasticism; Medieval church history. **SELECTED PUBLICATIONS** Auth, Simoniacal Entry into Religious Life, 76; auth, Godparents and Kinship in Early Medieval Europe, 86; auth, Spiritale Vinculum: the Vocabulary of Spiritual Kinship in Early Medieval Europe, 87; The Medieval Church: A Brief History, 92; auth, Christianizing Kinship: Ritual Sponsorship in Anglo-Saxon England, 98. **CONTACT ADDRESS** Dept of History, Ohio State Univ, Columbus, 230 W 17th Ave, Columbus, OH 43210-1361. **EMAIL** lynch.1@osu.edu

LYNN, JOHN A.
PERSONAL Born 03/18/1943, Glenview, IL, m, 1965, 2 children **DISCIPLINE** EARLY MODERN EUROPEAN HISTORY, MILITARY HISTORY **EDUCATION** Univ Ill Urbana Champaign, BA, 64; Univ Cal Davis, MA, 67; Univ Cal Los Angeles, PhD, 73. **CAREER** Vis Asst Prof, Ind Univ, 72-73; Asst Prof, Univ Maine, 73- 77; Asst Prof, Assoc Prof, PROF, UNIV ILL URBANA CHAMPAIGN, 78-. **HONORS AND AWARDS** Oppenheimer Prof of Marine Corps Warfighting Strategy, Univ Quantico, VA **MEMBERSHIPS** Soc Military Hist, Soc Fr Hist Studies, Am Hist Asn **RESEARCH** Early modern military hist. **SELECTED PUBLICATIONS** Auth, The Wars of Louis XIV, 1667-1714, 99, Longman, Ltd; auth, Giant of the Grand Siecle: the French Army, 1610-1715, 87, Cambridge Univ Press; auth, The Bayonets of the Republic: Motivation and Tactics in the Army of Revolutionary France, 1791- 94, rev ed 96, Westview Press; ed, Feeding Mars: Logistics in Western Warfare from the Middle Ages to the Present, 93, Westview Press; auth, "The Embattled Future of Academic Military History," Jour Military Hist, Oct 97; auth, The Evolution of Army Style in the Modern West, 800-2000," Int Hist Rev, Aug 96; auth, "War of Annihilation, War of Attrition, and War of Legitimacy: A New- Clausewitzian Approach to Twentieth-Century Conflicts," Marine Corps Gazette, Oct 96; auth, "Recalculating French Army Growth During the Gran Siecle, 1610-1715," Fr Hist Studies, Fall 94; auth, "How War Fed War: The Tax of Violence and Contributions During the Gran Siecle," Jour Modern Hist, June 93. **CONTACT ADDRESS** Univ of Illinois, Urbana-Champaign, 810 S Wright, Urbana, IL 61801. **EMAIL** j-lynn@uiuc.edu

LYNN, KENNETH SCHUYLER
PERSONAL Born 06/17/1923, Cleveland, OH, m, 1948, 3 children **DISCIPLINE** HISTORY **EDUCATION** Harvard Univ, AB, 47, MA, 50, PhD, 54. **CAREER** Instr, 54-55, Harvard Univ; from asst prof to prof Eng, 55-68, prof, 68-69, Am studies, Fed City Col; prof, 69-88, Johns Hopkins Univ, vis prof, 58, Copenhagen Univ & Univ Madrid, 63-64; assoc ed, 62-, Daedalus & New Eng Quart. **MEMBERSHIPS** AHA; Am Studies Assn; MLA. **SELECTED PUBLICATIONS** Auth, Hemingway, 87; auth, Charlie Chaplin and His Times, 97. **CONTACT ADDRESS** 1709 Hoban Rd NW, Washington, DC 20007.

LYNN, MARY CONSTANCE
PERSONAL Born 12/16/1943, Schnectady, NY, m, 1973, 2 children **DISCIPLINE** AMERICAN STUDIES **EDUCATION** Elmira Col, BA, 64; Univ Rochester, PhD(hist), 75. **CAREER** Lectr hist, Univ Col, Univ Rochester, 68-69; instr, 69-70, from instr to Assoc Prof, 70-92, Prof Am Studies, Skidmore Col, 92-, Chmn Dept, 77-87; Adv, Univ Without Walls, Skidmore Col, 71-74; consult, NY State Historian Residence Prog, 79-80; gov fac, Regents' External Degree, Univ State NY, 79-84. **HONORS AND AWARDS** Phi Beta Kappa. **MEMBERSHIPS** Am Studies Asn; Orgn Am Historians. **RESEARCH** History of women in America; popular culture and literature; 20th century United States. **SELECTED PUBLICATIONS** Auth, Women in 17th century New England, Empire State Col, 73; ed, Women's Liberation in the 20th Century, John Wiley & Sons, 75; co-ed, The Black Middle Class, Skidmore Col, 80; ed, An Eyewitness Account of the American Revolution and New England Life: The Journal of J.F. Wasmus, Greenwood Press, 90; auth, The American Revolution, Garrison Life in French Canada and New York: Journal of an Officer in the Prinz Friedrich Regiment, 1776-1783, Greenwood Press, 93; The Specht Journal: A Military Journal of the Burgoyne Campaign, Greenwood Press, 95. **CONTACT ADDRESS** Dept of Am Studies, Skidmore Col, 815 N Broadway, Saratoga Springs, NY 12866-1698. **EMAIL** mcl@skidmore.edu

LYONS, CLARE A.
DISCIPLINE HISTORY **EDUCATION** Lewis & Clark Col, BS, 80; Univ Calif at Santa Barbara, MA, 89; Yale Univ, PhD, 96. **CAREER** ASST PROF, HIST, UNIV MARYLAND AT COLLEGE PARK **HONORS AND AWARDS** Eggleston Prize, Yale Univ, 97. **MEMBERSHIPS** Am Antiquarian Soc **SELECTED PUBLICATIONS** Auth, "Sex Among the 'Rabble': Gender Transitions in the Age of Revolution, Philadelphia 1750-1830," Yale, 96. **CONTACT ADDRESS** Hist Dept, Univ of Maryland, Col Park, 2115 Francis Scott Key Blvd, College Park, MD 20742. **EMAIL** cl130@umail.umd.edu

LYONS, ROBIN
PERSONAL Born 06/27/1941, Brooks, Alberta, Canada, m, 1967, 4 children **DISCIPLINE** GEOGRAPHY **EDUCATION** Univ Brit Columbia, BA, 63; Brigham Young Univ, MS, 68; Univ Hawaii, PhD, 80. **CAREER** Instr, Ohio Univ, 67-68; Prof, Leeward Community Col, 71-96; Prof, San Joaquin Delta Col, 96-. **HONORS AND AWARDS** NSF Grant. **MEMBERSHIPS** AAG, NCAE, CGS. **RESEARCH** Geography. **SELECTED PUBLICATIONS** Auth, "Mystery of the Polynesians" (89); auth, "Popular Movies: Another Resource for Teaching Geography" (89); auth, "The Community Service-Minded Geographer: Geography and the Boy Scouts of America Merit Badge Program," J of Geog, vol a1, no 1 (92): 24-27; auth, Introduction to Physical Geography: Work Book and Lab Manual, Kendall-Hunt Publ, forthcoming. **CONTACT ADDRESS** Dept Sci, San Joaquin Delta Col, 5151 Pacific Ave, Stockton, CA 95207. **EMAIL** rlyons@sjdccd.cc.ca.us

LYONS, ROBIN R.
PERSONAL Born 12/09/1956, Salem, IL, m, 1992, 2 children **DISCIPLINE** RELIGIOUS STUDIES; PASTORAL THEOLOGY **EDUCATION** W Ky Univ, BA, 79; Drew Univ, M.Div, 82. **CAREER** Pastor, Murphysboro United Meth Church, 95-. **HONORS AND AWARDS** Various Seminary Awds; various Community Service Awds. **MEMBERSHIPS** AAR/SBL; Conf Board of Ordained Ministry **RESEARCH** Bonhoeffer Studies; Historical Jesus; Pastoral Theology; Church Growth Studies. **CONTACT ADDRESS** 1514 Pine St, Murphysboro, IL 62966. **EMAIL** faith1@globaleyes.net

LYONS, TIMOTHY JAMES
PERSONAL Born 07/06/1944, Framingham, MA, m, 1967, 2 children **DISCIPLINE** FILM HISTORY AND HISTORIOGRAPHY **EDUCATION** Univ Calif, Santa Barbara, BA, 66, MA, 68; Univ Iowa, PhD(speech and dramatic art), 72. **CAREER** From instr to asst prof radio, TV and film, Temple Univ, 72-76, chmn dept, 76-78, assoc prof, 76-80. Ed, J Univ Film Asn 76-. **MEMBERSHIPS** Soc Cinema Studies (secy, 75-77, pres, 77-79); Univ Film Asn. **RESEARCH** American silent film; Charles Chaplin. **SELECTED PUBLICATIONS** Auth, The Complete Guide to American Film Schools and Cinema and Television Programs, J Film and Video, Vol 0047, 95. **CONTACT ADDRESS** 2534 Poplar, Philadelphia, PA 19130.

LYTLE, MARK HAMILTON
PERSONAL Born 01/05/1945, Buffalo, NY, m, 1968, 1 child **DISCIPLINE** AMERICAN HISTORY, AMERICAN STUDIES **EDUCATION** Cornell Univ, BA, 66; Yale Univ, MPhil, 71, PhD(hist), 73. **CAREER** Instr hist, Yale Univ, 72-74, asst prof, 74-80, Assoc Prof Hist, Bard Col, 80-, Chmn Am Studies Prog, 80-, Co-chmn, Yale Univ, New Haven Hist Educ Proj, 71-74; consult social studies, Encycl Britannica Educ Corp, 72- and McGraw-Hill, 75-. **MEMBERSHIPS** AHA; Orgn Am Historians; Am Studies Asn. **RESEARCH** United States diplomatic history--Cold War Era; history of conservation in America. **SELECTED PUBLICATIONS** Coauth, The American city, 76, The American consumer, 76 & The American Presidency, 76, Encycl Britannica Educ Corp; auth, The US, the Middle East and the Cold War 1945-49, Proc AHA, 12/76; Film and history, New Lights, 78; The United States, Iran and the Cold War, Oxford Univ, (in press). **CONTACT ADDRESS** Bard Col, P O Box 5000, Annandale, NY 12504-5000.

M

MABRY, DONALD JOSEPH
PERSONAL Born 04/21/1941, Atlanta, GA, m, 2 children **DISCIPLINE** LATIN AMERICAN HISTORY **EDUCATION** Kenyon Col, AB, 63; Bowling Green State Univ, MEd, 64; Syracuse Univ, PhD (Latin Am hist), 70. **CAREER** Asst testing, Bowling Green State Univ, 63-64; mem fac hist, St Johns River Jr Col, 64-67; asst financial aids, Syracuse Univ, 67-68, US social hist, 68-69; from asst prof to assoc prof, 70-80, Prof Hist, Miss State Univ, 80-, Assoc Dean, Arts & Sci, 91-, Creator and Archivist, The Hist Text Arch; Sr Fel, Ctr for Int Security, 81-. **HONORS AND AWARDS** Fel, Newberry Libr, 75. **RESEARCH** Higher education and politics; United States-Latin American relations; Contemporary Mexico. **SELECTED PUBLICATIONS** Auth, Mexico's Accion Nacional: A Catholic Alternative to Revolution, Syracuse Univ, 73; Manuel Gomez Morin, In: Revolutionaries, Traditionalists, and Dictators in Latin America, Cooper, 73; Mexico, Am Ann, In: Encycl Am, Grolier, 73-92; Mexico's Party Deputy System, J Inter Am Studies & World Affairs, 74; Changing Models of Mexican Politics, New Scholar, 76; Mexican Anticlerics, Bishops, Cristeros and the Devout in the 1920's, J Church & State, 78; coauth, Neighbors-Mexico and the United States, Wetback and Oil, Nelson-Hall, 81; auth, The Mexican University and the State: Student Conflicts, 1910-1971, Tex A&M Univ, 82; ed, The Latin American Narcotics Trade and the United States National Security. **CONTACT ADDRESS** Drawer AS, Mississippi State, MS 39762-5508. **EMAIL** djm1@ra.msstate.edu

MACCAFFREY, WALLACE T.
PERSONAL Born 04/20/1920, LaGrande, OR, m, 1956 **DISCIPLINE** MODERN BRITISH HISTORY **EDUCATION** Reed Col, AB, 42; Harvard Univ, PhD, 50. **CAREER** From instr to asst prof hist, Univ Calif, Los Angeles, 50-53; from assoc prof to prof, Haverford Col, 53-68; prof hist, 68-80, Francis Lee Higginson Prof Hist, Harvard Univ, 80-, Guggenheim fel, 56-57; overseas res fel, Churchill Col, Cambridge, 68-69. **MEMBERSHIPS** AHA; Econ Hist Soc; fel Royal Hist Soc. **RESEARCH** Sixteenth and 17th century English history. **SELECTED PUBLICATIONS** Auth, Shaping of the Elizabethan Regime; auth, Queen Elizabeth; auth, Elizabeth and the Making of policy 1572-88; auth, Locality and Polity--a Study of Warwickshire Landed Society, 1401-1499, Amer Hist Rev, Vol 0098, 93; The European Dynastic State, 1494-1660, Renaissance Quart, Vol 0047, 94; The Newhaven Expedition, 1562-1563, Hist J, Vol 0040, 97. **CONTACT ADDRESS** Dept of Hist, Harvard Univ, Cambridge, MA 02138.

MACDONALD, J. FRED
PERSONAL Born 03/14/1941, New Waterford, NS, Canada, m, 1971 **DISCIPLINE** MODERN UNITED STATES HISTORY **EDUCATION** Univ Calif, Berkeley, BA, 63, MA, 64; Univ Calif, Los Angeles, PhD(hist), 69. **CAREER** Assoc prof, 69-78, prof hist, Northeastern Ill Univ, 78-, Chmn Inst Popular Cult Studies, 69-. **MEMBERSHIPS** Popular Cult Asn (pres, 80-82); Midwest Popular Cult Asn (vpres, pres, exec secy); Acad TV Arts & Sci; AHA. **RESEARCH** Social history of television and radio programming; film and popular music. **SELECTED PUBLICATIONS** Auth, The Foreigner in Juvenile Series Fiction, 1900-1945, J Popular Cult, winter 74; Radio's Black Heritage: Destination Freedom, 1948-1950, Phylon, 3/78; The Cold War as Entertainment in Fifties Television, J Popular Film & TV, 78; Government Propaganda in Commercial Radio: The Case of Tresury Star Parade, 1942-1943, J Popular Cult, 78; Don't Touch That Dial! Radio Programming in American Life, 1920-1960, Nelson-Hall, 79; Black perimeters-Paul Robeson, Nat King Cole and the role of Blacks in American TV, J Popular Film & TV, 79; Radio and Television Studies and American Culture, Am Quart, 80; Blacks and White TV: Afro-Americans in Television Since 1948, Nelson-Hall (in prep); ed, An Interview with Bud Freeman, Popular Music & Soc, summer 74; auth, The Foreigner in Juvenile Series Fiction, 1900-1945, J Popular Cult, winter 74; Radio's Black Heritage: Destination Freedom, 1948-1950, Phylon, 3/78; Don't Touch That Dial! Radio Programming in American Life, 1920-1960, Nelson-Hall, 78. **CONTACT ADDRESS** Dept of Hist, Northeastern Illinois Univ, 5500 N St Louis Ave, Chicago, IL 60625-4625.

MACDONALD, MARY N.
PERSONAL Born 12/29/1946, Maleny, Australia, s **DISCIPLINE** HISTORY OF RELIGION **EDUCATION** Univ Chicago, PhD, 88 **CAREER** Lctr, Melanesian Inst, New Guinea, 80-83; prof Hist Relig, LeMoyne Col, 88-98 **HONORS AND AWARDS** Newcombe Dissertation Fel, 87-88 **MEMBERSHIPS** Amer Acad Relig; Assoc Social Anthropology in Oceania **RESEARCH** Religions of Oceania; Religious Movements; Ecology and Religion **SELECTED PUBLICATIONS** "Magic and the Study of Religion in Melanesia," Religiologiques, 95; "Youth and Religion in Papua New Guinea," Catalyst, 96; "Religion and Human Experience," Introduction to the Study of Religion, Orbis, 98 **CONTACT ADDRESS** Relig Studies Dept, Le Moyne Col, Syracuse, NY 13214-1399. **EMAIL** macdonald@maple.lemoyne.edu

MACDONALD, RODERICK JAMES
PERSONAL Born 06/08/1933, Waltham, MA, m, 1964, 1 child **DISCIPLINE** HISTORY **EDUCATION** Univ Edinburgh, MA, 60, PhD, 69. **CAREER** Press officer, Ghana Info Serv, New York, 61; sr researcher Africa, Libr Cong, 63-64; lectr hist, Univ Malawi, 65-67; vis lectr, 67-69, asst prof, 69-74, Assoc Prof Hist--prof emeritus, Syracuse Univ, 74-. **HONORS AND AWARDS** Am Coun Learned Socs study fel hist, 71-72. **MEMBERSHIPS** African Studies Asn. **RESEARCH** Blacks in London, 1919-1948; Central Africa in the 20th century; 20th century linkages within the African Diaspora. **SELECTED PUBLICATIONS** Auth, The Quanah Route--a History of the Quanah Acme and Pacific Railway, Southwestern Hist Quart, Vol 0097, 93. **CONTACT ADDRESS** Syracuse Univ, 249 Jersey St., Caledonia, NY 14423.

MACDONALD, WILLIAM L.
PERSONAL Born 07/12/1921, Putnam, CT, 3 children **DISCIPLINE** FINE ARTS, HISTORY OF ARCHITECTURE **EDUCATION** Harvard Univ, AB (history, high honors), 49, AM (fine arts), 53, PhD (fine arts, history of architecture), 56. **CAREER** Boston Architectural Center, 50-54; Wheaton Col, 53-54; Yale Univ, 56-65; A P Brown Prof, Smith Col, 65-80; vis prof at: Berkeley, Emory, Georgetown, Harvard, MIT, Minnesota, Penn, Williams, etc. **HONORS AND AWARDS** Veterans Nat Scholar; Emerton, Shaw awards; Rome Prize, Am Acad in Rome, 54-56; Morse fel (Yale, Am Acad in Rome), 62-63; Getty Scholar, The Getty Ctr for the Fine Arts and the Humanities, 85-86; Hitchcock Prize, 87, 96; AIA Int Book Awd, 97; fel, Am Acad in Rome; fel, Am Acad of the Arts and Sciences. **MEMBERSHIPS** Soc for the Promotion of Roman Studies **RESEARCH** Classical architecture in its various manifestations; the Roman Empire; fireworks as art; flying boats. **SELECTED PUBLICATIONS** Auth, Early Christian and Byzantine Architecture, 62; The Architecture of the Roman Empire: I: An Introductory Study, 65, rev ed, 82, II: An Urban Appraisal, 86 (Hitchcock Prize, Soc of Architectural Historians; Kevin Lynch Award, MIT Dept of Urban Studies, III: An Historical Reconnaissance, in prep; Northampton Massachusetts Architecture & Buildings, 75; The Pantheon-Design, Meaning, and Progency, 76; assoc ed and contrib, The Princeton Encyclopedia of Classical Sites, 76; Piranesi's Carceri: Sources of Invention, 79; Hadrian's Villa and Its Legacy, co-auth with John A Pinto of Princeton, 95 (Hitchcock Prize, Soc of Architectural Historians; George Wittenborn Memorial Award; Book of the Year Award, Am Inst of Architects); Villa Adriana, La costruzione e il mito da Adriano a Louis Kahn, 97; Hadrian's World, in preparation; about 180 articles, reviews, chapters, and introductions in books, exhibitions catalogue essays, entries in reference works, etc. **CONTACT ADDRESS** 3811 39th St NW, Washington, DC 20016-2835.

MACDOUGALL, ELISABETH BLAIR
PERSONAL Born 01/01/1925, Chicago, IL, m, 1949, 1 child **DISCIPLINE** HISTORY OF ART **EDUCATION** Vassar Col, BA, 46; NYork Univ, MA, 54; Harvard Univ, PhD(art hist), 70. **CAREER** Instr art hist, Colo Col, 48-51; instr hist of archit, Boston Archit Ctr, 54-57; assoc surv dir, Cambridge Hist Dist Comn, 64-66; asst prof art hist, Boston Univ, 66-72; assoc prof, 72-76, Prof Hist Landscape Archit, Dumbarton Oaks, Harvard Univ, 76-, Dir Studies, 72-, Mem hist garden comt, Int Comn Monuments and Sites, 73-, exec comt mem, US Nat Comt, 75-. **MEMBERSHIPS** Soc Archit Historians (secy, 65-78). **RESEARCH** Italian Renaissance architecture; Italian Renaissance gardens; preservation of historic gardens. **SELECTED PUBLICATIONS** Coauth, Survey of architectural history in Cambridge, Report II: Mid Cambridge, 67; auth, Arts Hortulorum, Renaissance garden iconography, Italian Gardens 73, ed, The picturesque garden and its influence outside the British Isles, 74 & The French formal garden, 74, Dumbarton Oaks Series; auth, The sleeping nymph: Origins of a humanist fountain type, Art Bull, 75; ed, The Islamic garden, Dumbarton Oaks Series, 76; coauth, Fons Sapientiae: Garden fountains in illustrated books, sixteenth-eighteenth centuries, 77; auth, L'Ingegnoso Artifizio: Sixteenth century garden fountains in Rome, Renaissance Garden Fountains, 78. **CONTACT ADDRESS** Dumbarton Oaks, Harvard Univ, Cambridge, MA 02138.

MACEY, DAVID A. J.
PERSONAL Born 09/11/1942, United Kingdom, m, 1965, 2 children **DISCIPLINE** HISTORY **EDUCATION** Brooklyn Col, BA,68; Columbia Univ, Certificate of the Russian Inst, 70, MA, 71, M.Phil, 74, Ph.D, 76. **CAREER** Preceptor and Mellon Teaching Fel, Columbia Univ, 74-78; Vis Prof, Univ of Vermont, 79, 84, 88; Ful Prof, Middlebury Col, 78-. **HONORS AND AWARDS** ACLS travel grant, 86; Am Philos Soc grant, 88; IREX grant for short-term advanced research, 92: Nat Coun for Soviet and East European Res grant, 92. **MEMBERSHIPS** Soc of Fels in Humanities, Columbia Univ, Am Histol Asn (AHA), Am Asn for the Advancement of Slavic Studies (AAASS), NAFSA: Asn of International Educators, New England Study Abroad Advisors' Group (SAAG), 95-, Advisory

Bd, Inst for Study Abroad, Butler Univ, 95-, Advisory Bd, Ctr for Educ Abroad, 97-, Voting Representative, Coun on Int Educational Exchange, 97-, Member Coun, Williams-Mystic Program, 99-. **RESEARCH** Agrarian reform in pre-Revolutionary Russia between 1857 and 1916, with particular interest in the Stolypin reforms, 1906-1916. **SELECTED PUBLICATIONS** Auth, Government and Peasant in Russia, 1861-1906: The Prehistory of the Stolypin Reforms. Studies of the Harriman Inst, Columbia Univ, Dekalb: Northern Illinois Univ Pr, 87; auth, Modern Russian History, ed. By R.B. McKean, NY: St. Martins (92); 133-73; auth, " Stolypin is Risen! The Ideology of Land Reform in Contemporary Russia," in the "Farmer Threat": The Political Economy of Agrarian Reform in Russian, ed. By D. Van Atta., Boulder, CO: Westview Pr (93): 97-120; auth, "Is Agrarian Privatization the Right Path? A Discussion of Historical Models," in Socient and Post-Soviet Review, ed. Stephen K. Wegren, 94; auth, "Agricultural Reform and Political Change: The Case of Stolypin," in Reform in Modern Russian History: Progress or Cycle?, ed. T. Taranovski, New York: Cambridge, UP (95): 163-89; auth, "Reforming Agriculture in Russia: The 'Cursed Question' from Stolypin to Yeltsin," in Russia and Eastern Europe after Communism: The Search for New Political, Economic and Security Systems, ed. By Michael Kraus and Ronald D. Liebowitz, Westview Pr, 96; auth, "A Wagner on History: The Stolypin Agrarian Reforms as Process," in Transforming Peasants: Society, State and the Peasantry, 1861-1930. Proceedings of the Fifth World Congress on Slavic and East European Studies, Warsaw, August 1995, ed. Judith Pallot, Macmillan, 98; coauth, with Neil Waters, "Beyond the Area Studies Wars," in International Studies in the Next Millenium: Meeting the Challenge of Globalization, ed. By Julia A, Kushigian, Greenwood Pr, 98; auth, "The Role of the Peasant Land Bank in Imperial Russia's Agrarian Reforms, 1882-1917," Ukraine Report Series, Ctr for Agricultural and Rural Development, 98; auth, "Rural Reform in Russian Historical Context," in Adaptation and Change in Rural Russia, ed. By David J. O' Brien and Stephen Wegren, Woodrow Wilson Pr. **CONTACT ADDRESS** Middlebury Col, Freeman Int Ctr, Middlebury, VT 05753-6137. **EMAIL** macey@middlebury.edu

MACGILLIVRAY, ROYCE C.

PERSONAL Born 05/13/1936, Alexandria, ON, Canada **DISCIPLINE** HISTORY **EDUCATION** Queen's Univ, BA, 59; Harvard Univ, AM, 60, PhD, 65. **CAREER** Prof History, Univ Waterloo, 62-. **SELECTED PUBLICATIONS** Auth, Restoration Historians, 74; auth, The House of Ontario, 83; auth, The New Querist, 83; auth, The Mind of Ontario, 85; auth, The Slopes of the Andes, 90; auth, Bibliography of Glengarry County, 96; coauth, History of Glengarry County, 79; ed, Ontario History, 79-. **CONTACT ADDRESS** Dept of Hist, Univ of Waterloo, 200 Univ Ave W, Waterloo, ON, Canada N2L 3G1. **EMAIL** rcmacgil@watarts.uwaterloo.ca

MACH, THOMAS S.

PERSONAL Born Cleveland, OH, m **DISCIPLINE** HISTORY **EDUCATION** Cedarville Col, BA, 88; Cleveland State Univ, MA, 89; Univ Akron, PhD, 96. **CAREER** Tchg asst, Cedarville Col, 86-87; res asst, 89, grad asst, 88-89, Cleveland State Univ; res asst, 92, grad asst, 89-94, lectr, 92-93, Univ Akron; asst prof hist, 94-98, dir honors prog, 96- , assoc prof hist, 98-00 , Mount Vernon Nazarene Col, prof of history, Cedarville Univ. **HONORS AND AWARDS** Phi Alpha Theta; William and Dora Martin Hist Endowment Scholar, 91-94; President's Awd for Excellence in Tchg, 97-98. **MEMBERSHIPS** Conf on Faith and Hist; Nat Collegiate Honors Coun; Ohio Acad of Hist; Orgn of Am Hist. **RESEARCH** United States history; nineteench century United States history. **SELECTED PUBLICATIONS** Author, Calvin Stewart Brice, in American National Biography, Oxford, 99; auth, "George Hunt Pendleton: The Ohio Idea and Political Continuity in Reconstruction America," Ohio Hist, 108, 99: 125-44. **CONTACT ADDRESS** Dept of Social Science and History, Cedarville Col, P O Box 601, Cedarville, OH 45314. **EMAIL** tmach@mvnc.edu

MACHADO, DAISY L.

PERSONAL Born, Cuba, m, 1984 **DISCIPLINE** CHRISTIAN HISTORY **EDUCATION** Brooklyn Coll, BA, 74; Hunter Coll School of Social Work, MSW, 78; Union Theo Sem, MDiv, 81; Univ Chi Div School, PhD, 96. **CAREER** Ordained minister, 79-92, Disciples of Christ; Asst Prof Hispanic stud & church hist, 92-96, Texas Christian Univ, Brite Div School; Prog Dir Hispanic Theo Initiative, 96-, Emory Univ, Atlanta. **HONORS AND AWARDS** O E Scott Scholarship, TE Fund Doc Scholarship, E S Ames Scholarship, TE Fund Diss Fel. **MEMBERSHIPS** AAR **RESEARCH** History of latin Protestant church in USA, history Protestant Missions to Mexico, Caribbean, & Central Latin America. **SELECTED PUBLICATIONS** Auth, Jesus loves me..more than you? The Bible and Racism, in: J of the Christian Church, 97; From Anglo-American Traditions to a Multicultural World, in: Discipliana Hist J Disciples of Christ Hist Soc, 97; El Cantico de Maria, in: J for Preachers, 97; Kingdom Building in the Borderlands, The Church and Manifest Destiny, in: Hispanic/Latino Theology, Challenge and Promise, eds, A M Isasi-Diaz & F Segovia, Minneapolis Fortress Press, 96; Latinos in the Protestant Establishment, Is There a Place for Us at the Feast Table?, in: Protestantes/Protestants, eds, J L Gonzalez & D Maldonado, Nashville Abingdon forthcoming. **CONTACT ADDRESS** Brite Divinity Sch, Texas Christian Univ, 2800 S University Dr, Fort Worth, TX 76129. **EMAIL** d.machado@tcu.edu

MACHAFFIE, BARBARA J.

PERSONAL Born 11/29/1949, Philadelphia, PA, m, 1972 **DISCIPLINE** RELIGIOUS STUDIES; ECCLESIASTICAL HISTORY **EDUCATION** Col of Wooster, BA, 71; Univ of Edinburgh, Scotland, BD, 74, PhD, 77. **CAREER** Ref Libr, Princeton Theol Sem, 77-80; vis asst prof, Cleveland State Univ, 81-83; instr, Marietta Col, 83-87; assoc prof, Hist and Relig, Marietta Col, 92- . **HONORS AND AWARDS** Molly C. Putnam and Israel Ward Andrews Assoc prof Relig. **MEMBERSHIPS** Phi Beta Kappa; Scottish Ecclesiastical Hist Soc; Amer Acad Rel. **RESEARCH** 19th Century British Ecclesiastical History; Women and Religion. **SELECTED PUBLICATIONS** Auth, Her Story: Women in Christian Tradition, Fortress, 86; Readings in Her Story: Women in Christian Tradition, Fortress, 92. **CONTACT ADDRESS** Dept of History and Religion, Marietta Col, Marietta, OH 45750. **EMAIL** machaffb@marietta.edu

MACIAS, ANNA

PERSONAL Born 05/20/1930, Sewaren, NJ **DISCIPLINE** LATIN AMERICAN HISTORY **EDUCATION** Hunter Col, BA, 52; Smith Col, MA, 54; Columbia Univ, PhD(hist), 65. **CAREER** Instr Am hist, Dana Hall Sch, Mass, 54-56; asst Am studies, Amherst Col, 57-59; instr Latin Am hist, Smith Col, 62-63; from instr to assoc prof, 63-75, Prof Latin Am Hist, Ohio Wesleyan Univ, 75-, Foreign area fel individual res on Mex women, Am Coun Learned Soc-Soc Sci Res Coun grant, 73-74. **MEMBERSHIPS** AHA; Conf Latin Am Hist; Latin Am Studies Asn. **RESEARCH** Mexican women in the social revolution, 1900-1953; political developments in Mexico during the independence movement. **SELECTED PUBLICATIONS** Auth, Gathering Rage--the Failure of 20th-Century Revolutions to Develop a Feminist Agenda, Hisp Amer Hist Rev, Vol 0074, 94; Women of the Mexican Countryside, 1850-1990, Historian, Vol 0058, 96; The Secret History of Gender--Women, Men, and Power in Late Colonial Mexico, Historian, Vol 0059, 97; The Island of the Anishnaabeg--Thunderers and Water Monsters in the Traditional Ojibwe Life World, J West, Vol 0036, 97. **CONTACT ADDRESS** Dept of Hist, Ohio Wesleyan Univ, Delaware, OH 43015.

MACIEROWSKI, E. M.

PERSONAL Born 11/01/1948, Springfield, MA, m, 1994, 10 children **DISCIPLINE** PHILOSOPHY; MEDIEVAL STUDIES **EDUCATION** St. John's Col, BA, 70; Pontifical Inst of Mediaeval Studies, MSL, 76; Univ Toronto, MA, 73, PhD, 79. **CAREER** Tutor, Latin prog, St. Michael's Col & Univ Toronto, 78-79; lectr & asst prof, philos, Univ St. Thomas, 79-83; visiting asst prof, philos, Cath Univ of Amer, 83-86; res grant transl, Nat Endow for the Humanities, 86-87; assoc prof and chair, philos, Christendom Col, 87-93; lectr II, logic, Lord Fairfax Community Col, spring, 93; Benedictine Col, 93-. **HONORS AND AWARDS** Woodrow Wilson fel, 70-71; Can Coun Doctoral fel, 75-76; NEH Seminar in Arabic Paleography, Univ Penn, 76; Imperial Iranian Acad of Philos, Tehran, 76-77; NEH Transl grant, 86-87; guest cur, Smithsonian Inst, 87; NEH summer seminar, Columbia Univ, 93; Second Summer Thomistic Inst, Univ Notre Dame, 94; NEH Study grant, 95; pres, Kans City Area Philos Soc, mar, 97-98; World Congress of Mulla Sadra, 99. **MEMBERSHIPS** Amer Cath Philos Asn; Amer Philos Asn; Fel of Cath Scholars; Kans City Area Philos Asn. **RESEARCH** History of Philosophy; Logic; Greek Mathematics; Philosophy of Nature; Moral Philosophy; Metaphysics; Mnemonics; History of Cryptology; Hermeneutics. **SELECTED PUBLICATIONS** Auth, Thomas Aquina's Earliest Treatment of the Divine Essence, Ctr for Medieval and Renaissance Studies & Inst of Global Cultural Studies at Binghamton Univ; auth, On Cutting Off A Ratio, Apollonius of Perga, Critical Translation of the Treatise From the Two Extant MSS of the Arabic Version of the Lost Greek Original, The Golden Hind Press, 87; article, Latin Averroes on the Motion of the Elements, Archiv fur Geschichte der Philosophie, Band 74, Heft 2, 127-157, 92; article, John Philoponus on Aristotle's Definition of Nature: A Translation from the Greek with Notes, Ancient Philos, VIII, 73-100, Spring, 88; transl, Aquinas's Exposition of Aristotle's De Memoria et reminiscentia, Catholic Univ Press, forthcoming. **CONTACT ADDRESS** Dept. of Philosophy, Benedictine Col, 1020 N 2nd St, Atchison, KS 66002. **EMAIL** edwardm@benedictine.edu

MACISAAC, DAVID

PERSONAL Born 06/22/1935, Boston, MA, m, 1959, 4 children **DISCIPLINE** EUROPEAN AND MILITARY HISTORY **EDUCATION** Trinity Col, Conn, AB, 57; Yale Univ, AM, 58; Duke Univ, PhD(hist), 70. **CAREER** Instr hist, 64-66, asst prof, 68-70, assoc prof, 72-75, Prof Hist, US Air Force Acad, 76-, Vis prof strategy, US Naval War Col, 75-76; fel nat security affairs, Woodrow Wilson Int Ctr Scholars, 78-79. **MEMBERSHIPS** Inter-Univ Sem Armed Forces and Soc; Am Comt Hist Second World War. **RESEARCH** Air warfare, World War II to the present; history of military theory and strategy; European military affairs, ancient, medieval, modern. **SELECTED PUBLICATIONS** Auth, The Crucible of War, 1939-1945--the Official History of the Royal Canadian Air Force, Vol 3, J Mil Hist, Vol 0060, 96. **CONTACT ADDRESS** Dept of Hist, United States Air Force Academy, CO 80840.

MACIUIKA, BENEDICT VYTENIS

PERSONAL Born 11/16/1927, Kaunas, Lithuania, m, 1955, 3 children **DISCIPLINE** MODERN EUROPEAN AND SOVIET HISTORY **EDUCATION** Univ Chicago, MA, 54, PhD(int rels), 63. **CAREER** Res assoc, Soc Sci Div, Univ Chicago, 54-56, admin and res asst, Ctr Studies Am Foreign and Mil Policy, 56-58; from instr to assoc prof, 58-72, Prof Hist, Univ Conn, 72-, Univ Conn Res Found res grant, 72. **MEMBERSHIPS** AHA; Am Polit Sci Asn; Am Asn Advan Slavic Studies; Asn Advan Baltic Studies; Inst Lithuanian Studies. **RESEARCH** History and institutions of Lithuania since 1940; Russian and Soviet history. **SELECTED PUBLICATIONS** Auth, Russia as a Multi-National Empire--Emergence, History, Collapse, J Baltic Stud, Vol 0024, 93; The Nordic Way--a Path to Baltic Equilibrium, J Baltic Stud, Vol 0026, 95; The Sorcerer as Apprentice--Stalin as Commissar of Nationalities, 1917-1924, J Baltic Stud Vol 0026, 95. **CONTACT ADDRESS** Univ of Connecticut, Hartford, Hartford, CT 06112.

MACKENZIE, DAVID

PERSONAL Born 06/10/1927, Rochester, NY, m, 1953, 3 children **DISCIPLINE** MODERN HISTORY **EDUCATION** Univ Rochester, AB, 51; Columbia Univ, AM, 53, PhD, 62. **CAREER** Asst prof Russ lang & Europ hist, US Merchant Marine Acad, 53-58; lectr Russ & Europ hist, Princeton Univ, 59-61; from asst prof to assoc prof hist, Wells Col, 61-69; Prof Hist, Univ NC, Greensboro, 69-, Ford Found fel, Austria & Yugoslavia, 55-56; Inter-Univ Comt Travel Grants grant, USSR, 58-59; vis asst prof, Cornell Univ, 62; grants, Am Coun Learned Soc, 65-66, Am Philos Soc, 69, 74, 78 & 79 & Fulbright, 78 & 82. **MEMBERSHIPS** Am Asn Advan Slavic Studies; NAm Soc Serbian Studies; Southern Coun Slavic Studies. **RESEARCH** Russ hist, 19th century; Serbian and Yugoslav hist, 19th century; Russ for rel. **SELECTED PUBLICATIONS** Auth, The Serbs and Russian Pan-Slavism, 1875-1878, Cornell Univ, 67; Tashkent: Past and present, Russ Rev, 4/69; Expansion in Central Asia.. 1863-1866, Can Slavic Studies, summer 69; Lion of Tashkent: The Career of General M G Cherniaev, Univ Ga, 74; A History of Russia and the Soviet Union, Dorsey, 77, rev ed, 82; contribr, Modern Encycl of Russian and Soviet Hist, Int Asn Scholarly Publ, 77-; Ilija Garasanin: Balkan Bismarck, 85; Apis: The Congenial Conspirator, 89, Serbian ed, 89, 96; Imperial Dreams, Harsh Realities: Tsarist Foreign Policy, 93; From Messianism to Collapse: Soviet Foreign Policy, 94; The Black Hand on Trial: Salonika 1917, 95; Serbs and Russians, 96; Violent Solutions, 96; coauth, Russia and the USSR in the Twentieth Century, 3rd ed, 97; auth, The Exoneration of the 'Black Hand' 1917-1953, 98; coauth, A Hist of Russia, the Soviet Union and Beyond, 5th ed, 99. **CONTACT ADDRESS** Dept of Hist, Univ of No Carolina, Greensboro, 1000 Spring Garden, Greensboro, NC 27412-0001.

MACKEY, THOMAS C.

PERSONAL Born 08/17/1956, Radford, VA, m, 1999 **DISCIPLINE** HISTORY **EDUCATION** Beloit Col, BA, 78; Rice Univ, PhD, 84. **CAREER** Grad fel, Rice Univ, 81-84; Samuel I. Golieb Postdoctoral Fel, NYork Univ Sch of Law, 84-85; vis asst prof, Mich State Univ, 85-86; asst prof, Univ Nebr, 86-88; asst prof, Eastern Mont Col, 88-89; from vis asst prof to asst prof, Kans State Univ, 89-91; from asst prof to assoc prof, Univ Louisville Law Sch, 91-; chair of dept of Hist, Univ of Louisville, 99-04. **HONORS AND AWARDS** Longcope Awd for Best Dissertation, 84; Samuel I. Golieb Postdoctoral Fel, NY Univ Sch of Law, 84-85. **MEMBERSHIPS** Orgn of Am Historians, Am Soc for Legal Hist, Filsan Club Hist Soc. **RESEARCH** American Legal/Constitutional History, Nineteenth- and Twentieth-Century U.S., Civil War and Reconstruction, Gilded Age/Progressive Era. **SELECTED PUBLICATIONS** Auth, Red Lights Out: A Legal History of Prostitution, Disorderly Houses, and Vice Districts, 1870-1917, Garland Pub Co., 87; auth, "Anti-Vice Funding and the Apple: The Business of Anti-Vice Reform and the Committee of Fourteen in New York City, 1905-1932," Essays in Economic and Business Hist 12 (94): 287-306; auth, "'They Are Positively Dangerous Men': The Lost court Documents of Benjamin Gitlow and James Larkin Before the New York City Magistrates' Court, 1919," NY Univ Law Rev 69 (94): 421-436; auth, "'Learning, Deducting, and Reporting': Louisville, Kentucky's Vice Report of 1915--Part One: Methods and Recommendations," The Filson Club Hist Quart 74 (00): 13-29; auth, "Vice Report of 1915--Part Two: Local Conditions," The Filson Club Hist Quart (forthcoming). **CONTACT ADDRESS** Dept Hist, Univ of Louisville, 2301 S 3rd St, Louisville, KY 40292-0001. **EMAIL** thomasmackey@louisville.edu

MACKILLOP, JAMES J.

PERSONAL Born 05/31/1939, Pontiac, MI, m, 1964, 2 children **DISCIPLINE** IRISH STUDIES **EDUCATION** Wayne State Univ, BA, 62; MA, 68; Syracuse Univ, PhD, 75. **CAREER** Instr, Onondaga Community Col, 67-99; Prof, Syracuse Univ, 78-99; Lect, Syracuse Univ, 99-. **HONORS AND AWARDS** Nat Endowment for the Humanities Awd; Fel, 83-84; SUNY Sabbatical Fel, 89. **MEMBERSHIPS** Am Conf for

Irish Studies, Celtic Studies Assoc of N Am, Can Assoc for Irish Studies. **RESEARCH** Celtic mythology, Irish drama and cinema, twentieth-century theater. **SELECTED PUBLICATIONS** Ed, Irish Lit: A Reader, Syracuse Univ Pr, 87; auth, Dict of Celtic Mythology, Oxford Univ Pr, 98; auth, Contemp Irish Cinema, Syracuse Univ Pr, 99; auth, Fionn Mac Cumhaill, Syracuse Univ Pr, 86, 00. **CONTACT ADDRESS** Dept English, Syracuse Univ, 108 Limestone Ln, Syracuse, NY 13219-2144. **EMAIL** mackillj@yahoo.com

MACKINNON, ARAN S.
PERSONAL Born 12/16/1965, Edinburgh, Scotland, s **DISCIPLINE** HISTORY **EDUCATION** Queen's Univ, BA with honors, 88; Univ of Natal, MA, 91; Univ of London, PhD, 96. **CAREER** Vis asst prof, Univ of NC at Charlotte, 96-97; Asst Prof of Hist, State Univ of West GA, 97-. **HONORS AND AWARDS** Irwin Travelling Scholar Grant, 93; Univ of London Fees Scholar, 93, 94, & 95. **MEMBERSHIPS** African Studies Asn; Southeastern Regional Asn of African Studies; Royal African Soc. **RESEARCH** South Africa, Rural Africa, Aging. **SELECTED PUBLICATIONS** Auth, The Persistence of the Cattle Economy in Zululand, Canadian J of Africa Studies, 99. **CONTACT ADDRESS** Dept of History, 6523 English Hills Drive, Charlotte, NC 28223. **EMAIL** amackinn@westga.edu

MACKINNON, MICHAEL
PERSONAL Born 08/17/1966, Cambridge, ON, Canada **DISCIPLINE** ARCHAEOLOGY **EDUCATION** Univ Toronto, BSc, 89; BA, 91; Univ Alta, MA, 93; PhD, 99. **CAREER** Res Fel, Boston Univ, 99-. **HONORS AND AWARDS** Fel, Res Counc of Can; Izaak Walton Killam Mem Scholar, Univ of Alta; Andrew Stewart Mem Grad Prize, Univ of Alta; Silver Medal, Univ of St. Michael's Col. **MEMBERSHIPS** ICAZ; AIA. **RESEARCH** Zooarchaeology, roman Archaeology, Ancient Society and Culture. **SELECTED PUBLICATIONS** Coauth, "Excavations at San Giovanni di Ruoti, 1994", Echos du Monde Classique/Classical Views 39 (95): 61-73; auth, "Gourmets, Glamor, Gambling, and Gluttony: The Faunal Remains from a Pit at Gravina di Puglia", Am J of Archaeol 99.2 (95): 321; auth, "Land Snail Analysis in Classical Archaeology", Am J of Archaeol 101.2 (97): 366; auth, "Archaeological Field Survey in the Vicinity of Monte Irsi (Matera, Italy), 1996-1997", Am J of Archaeol 102.2 (98): 416-417; coauth, "Field Survey in the Basentello Valley on the Basilicata-Puglia Border", Echos du Monde Classique'Classical Views 42, (98): 337-371; auth, "The Faunal Remains", in A Roman Villa and a Late Roman Infant Cementary, Excavation at Poggio Gramignano (Lugnano in Teverina), eds D.S. Soren and N. Soren, L'Erma di Bretschneider (Rome, 99): 533-594; auth, "Husbandry, Hides and Hunting: Zooarchaeological Examination at Torre de Palma, Portugal", Am J of Archaeol 104.2 (forthcoming); auth, Animal Slaughter, Butchery and Meat Preservation in Roman Italy", in Eureka! The Archaeology of Innovation and Science: Proceeedings of the 29th Annual Chacmool Conf, Archaeol Assoc of the Univ of Calgary Pr, (forthcoming); auth, "The Terrestrial Molluscs", "The Mammalian Remains", in The Excavations of San Giovanni Di Ruoti, Vol III: The Fauna and Plant Remains (forthcoming). **CONTACT ADDRESS** Dept Archaeol, Boston Univ, 675 Commonwealth Ave, Boston, MA 02215. **EMAIL** michmack@bu.edu

MACKINNON, STEPHEN ROBERT
PERSONAL Born 12/02/1940, Columbus, NE, d, 2 children **DISCIPLINE** EAST ASIAN & MODERN CHINESE HISTORY **EDUCATION** Yale Univ, AB, 63, MA, 64; Univ Calif, Davis, PhD(hist), 71. **CAREER** Vis instr hist, New Asia Col, Chinese Univ Hong Kong, 68-69; prof hist, Ariz State Univ, 71-, Dir of Asian Stud, 88-95; Fulbright scholar India, 77-78; vis scholar, Acad Soc Sci, Peoples Rep China, 79-81, 85. **HONORS AND AWARDS** Res Fellow Am Council of Learned Socs, 78; Fulbright Found, India, 77-78; Res Sr Comnr on Scholarly Comn, Peoples' Repub of China, 92. **MEMBERSHIPS** Asn Asian Studies (bd dirs 90-91); Soc Ch'ing Studies; Am Coun Learned Soc. **RESEARCH** Modern Chinese social and political history; impact of war on twentieth century China; Chinese journalism during 1930's and 1940's. **SELECTED PUBLICATIONS** Auth, Power and Politics in Late Imperial China, 80; Co-auth, China Reporting, 87; auth, Agnes Smedley, 88; co-ed, Portrait of chinese Women in Revolution, 76; Tragedy of Wuhan, 1938, Modern Asian Studies, 8/96; Toward a History of the Chinese Press in the Republican Period, Modern China, 1/97; auth, Covering China, Media Studies, 99; Wuhan's Search for Identity, 00; co-ed, Scars of War, 01. **CONTACT ADDRESS** Dept of History, Arizona State Univ, PO Box 872501, Tempe, AZ 85287-2501. **EMAIL** stephen.mackinnon@asu.edu

MACLEAN, ELIZABETH
PERSONAL Born 05/17/1942, Cleveland, OH, m, 1964, 2 children **DISCIPLINE** HISTORY **EDUCATION** Conn Col, BA, 64; Univ Md, Col Pk, MA, 77, PhD, 86. **CAREER** Asst Prof, 86-91; Assoc Prof and Department Chair, Dept of Hist/Pol Sci, Otterbein Col, 91-97, PROF, Dept of History.Political Science, Otterbein College, 97-. **HONORS AND AWARDS** Phi Kappa Phi Honor Society. **MEMBERSHIPS** OAH; AHA; Ohio Academy of History; Society for Historians of American Foreign Relations. **RESEARCH** Soviet-American Relations; 20th Century American Political History. **SELECTED PUBLICATIONS** Rev, "David Mayers' The Ambassadors and America's Soviet Policy," American Historical Review, February 97; auth, "Joseph E. Davies, Envoy to the Soviets," Praeger, 92; auth, "Joseph E. Davies and Soviet-American Relations, 1941-43," Diplomatic History 4, Winter 80. **CONTACT ADDRESS** Dept of Hist/Pol Sci, Otterbein Col, 1 Otterbein, Westerville, OH 43081. **EMAIL** emaclean@otterbein.edu

MACLENNAN, ROBERT S.
PERSONAL Born 05/20/1941, Los Angeles, CA, m, 1966, 2 children **DISCIPLINE** HISTORY; ANCIENT STUDIES - 2ND TEMPLE JUDAISM **EDUCATION** Occidental Col, BA, 63; Princeton Theol Seminary, BD, 66; Univ Minn, PhD, 88. **CAREER** Presbyterian Minister, Presbyterian Congregation Churches, 66-98; Adjunct Prof Classics, Macalester Col, 94-98, Exec Dir Black Sea Archaeological Project, 94-98; archaeological excavations, City of David (Jerusalem), 78; Dir, Black Sea Ventures Group, 96-00; Mem, Bd of Moral Re-Armament, 98-. **SELECTED PUBLICATIONS** Auth, Early Christian Texts on Jew and Judaism, Schol Press, 90; coauth, Diaspora Jews and Judaism, Schol Press, 92; auth, In Search of the Jewish Diaspora: A First Century Synagogue in the Crimea?, Bibl Archaeol Rev, 96; coauth, To the Study of Jewish Antiquities From Chersonesus Tavrichesky, Archaeol, 97; auth, Diaspora Jews, Romans, Pagans, and Others in Sardis, Aphrodisias and the Crimea in the Greco-Roman Period, The Jewish Population in South Ukraine, Yearbook, Research, Memories and Documents, Jewish World, 98; author of several other articles and archaeological reports. **CONTACT ADDRESS** 6 Edgehill St., Princeton, NJ 08540. **EMAIL** RSMacL@aol.com

MACLEOD, DAVID
PERSONAL Born 06/08/1943, Chatham, Canada, m, 1970, 2 children **DISCIPLINE** HISTORY **EDUCATION** Univ of Toronto, BA, 65; Univ of Wis Madison, MA, 67; PhD, 73. **CAREER** Instr to prof, Central Mich Univ, 70-; vis asst prof, Univ of Toronto, 74-75. **MEMBERSHIPS** HES; OAH; SSHA. **RESEARCH** Childhood and youth, voluntary associations, progressive era U.S. **SELECTED PUBLICATIONS** Auth, Carnegie Libraries in Wisconsin, Univ of Wis (Madison), 68; auth, Building Character in the American Boy: The Boy Scouts, YMCA, and Their Forerunners, 1870-1920, Univ of Wis Pr, (Madison), 83; auth, The Age of the Child: Children in America, 1890-1920, Twayne Publ, (NY), 98; auth, "Socializing American Youth to be Citizen-Soldiers", in Anticipating Total War: The German and American Experiences, 1871-1914. Eds Manfred F. Boemeke, Roger Chickering and Stig Forster, Cambridge Univ Pr, (NY), 99. **CONTACT ADDRESS** Dept Hist, Central Michigan Univ, 100 W Preston Rd, Mount Pleasant, MI 48859-0001. **EMAIL** David.Macleod@cmich.edu

MACLEOD, RODERICK CHARLES
PERSONAL Born 05/11/1940, Calgary, AB, Canada, m, 1962, 2 children **DISCIPLINE** HISTORY **EDUCATION** Univ Alta, BA, 61; Queen's Univ, MA, 67; Duke Univ, PhD(hist), 71. **CAREER** Asst prof, 69-75, assoc prof, 75-81, PROF HIST, UNIV ALTA, 81-. Can Coun leave fel, 76; gen ed, Alta Rec Publ Bd, 78-; chmn hist dept, 80-83. **MEMBERSHIPS** Can Hist Asn; Am Soc Legal Hist. **RESEARCH** Canadian legal history; Canadian social history; history of western Canada. **SELECTED PUBLICATIONS** Auth, The Mounties; coed, From Rupert's Land to Canada: Essays in Honour of John E. Foster, Univ of Alberta Pr, Edmonton, AB, 01. **CONTACT ADDRESS** Dept of Hist & Classics, Univ of Alberta, 2-28 Henry Marshall Tony Bldg, Edmonton, AB, Canada T6G 2H4. **EMAIL** rmacleod@gpu.srv.ualberta.ca

MACMULLEN, RAMSAY
PERSONAL Born 03/03/1928, New York, NY, m, 1954, 4 children **DISCIPLINE** ANCIENT HISTORY **EDUCATION** Harvard Univ, AB, 50, AM, 53, PhD, 57. **CAREER** From instr to asst prof hist, Univ Ore, 56-61; from asst prof to assoc prof, Brandeis Univ, 61-65, 67-77, chmn dept classics, 67-67; chmn dept hist, 70-72, prof 67-79, DUNHAM PROF HIST AND CLASSICS, YALE UNIV, 79-, Fulbright res grant, Italy, 60-61; fel, Inst Advan Studies, 64-65; Guggenheim fel, 65; Nat Endowment for Humanities sr fel, 74-75; fel, Wolfson Col, Oxford Univ, 74-75. **MEMBERSHIPS** Soc Prom Roman Studies; AAUP; Asn Ancient Historians (pres, 78-81); Friends of Ancient Hist. **RESEARCH** Roman history. **SELECTED PUBLICATIONS** Auth, Religion and Society During the Roman Empire--a Colloquium in Honor of Vittinghoff, Friedrich, Gnomon Kritische Zeitschrift fur die Gesamte Klassische Altertumswissenschaft, Vol 0065, 93. **CONTACT ADDRESS** Dept of History, Yale Univ, New Haven, CT 06520. **EMAIL** rammac@pantheon.yale.edu

MACRO, ANTHONY DAVID
PERSONAL Born 07/10/1938, London, England, m, 1967, 2 children **DISCIPLINE** CLASSICAL PHILOLOGY, ANCIENT HISTORY **EDUCATION** Oxford Univ, BA, 61, MA, 64; Johns Hopkins Univ, PhD, 69. **CAREER** Teaching assoc classics, Ind Univ, Bloomington, 61-62; instr, Univ Md, College Park, 65-67; jr instr, Johns Hopkins Univ, 67-69; asst prof classics, 69-75, assoc prof, 75-85, prof, 85-, Hobart Prof Class Lang, 92-, Trinity Col. **HONORS AND AWARDS** Leverhulme Commonwealth fel, Univ Wales, 75-76. **MEMBERSHIPS** Am Philol Asn; Soc Prom Hellenic Studies; Soc Prom Roman Studies. **RESEARCH** Greek epigraphy; Roman imperial history; comparative linguistics. **SELECTED PUBLICATIONS** Auth, Sophocles, Trachiniai, 112-21, American Journal of Philology, 73; Imperial provisions for Pergamum: OGIS 484, Greek, Roman & Byzantine Studies, 76; "A Confirmed Asiarch," American Journal of Philology, 79; The Cities of Asia Minor under the Roman imperium, Aufstieg und Niedergang der romischen Welt, Vol 2, No 7, Berlin, 80; Applied classics: Using Latin and Greek in the modern world, Class Outlook, 81; auth, "Asiarch Reconfirmed," American Journal of Philology, 85; auth, Prolegemena to the Study of Galatian-Celtic Name Formations, Celtic Connections, ACTA, 94. **CONTACT ADDRESS** Dept of Classics, Trinity Col, Connecticut, 300 Summit St, Hartford, CT 06106-3186. **EMAIL** ad.macro@mail.trincoll.edu

MACY, GARY A.
DISCIPLINE RELIGIOUS HISTORY **EDUCATION** Univ Cambridge, PhD. **CAREER** Dept Theo, Univ San Diego **SELECTED PUBLICATIONS** Publ on, medieval theol and rel, espec the theol of the Eucharist. **CONTACT ADDRESS** Dept of Theological and Relig Studies, Univ of San Diego, 5998 Alcal Park, Maher 282, San Diego, CA 92110-2492. **EMAIL** macy@acusd.edu

MADDEN, PAUL
PERSONAL Born 12/08/1940, Morris, OK, m, 1961, 3 children **DISCIPLINE** HISTORY **EDUCATION** Oral Roberts Univ, BA, 71; Univ Okla, MA, 73; PhD, 76. **CAREER** Asst prof, 78-81; assoc prof, 81-87; prof, 87-; dept hd, 91-, Hardin-Simmons Univ. **HONORS AND AWARDS** Mellon Fel, 84; Best Paper, SSSC, 76, 81. **MEMBERSHIPS** SSSA. **RESEARCH** Nazi era Germany. **SELECTED PUBLICATIONS** Auth, Adolph Hitler and the Nazi Epoch, Scarecrow Press, 98; auth, Fidel Castro, Rourke, 93. **CONTACT ADDRESS** Dept History, Hardin-Simmons Univ, Abilene, TX 79698. **EMAIL** pmadden@hsutx.edu

MADDEN, THOMAS
PERSONAL Born 06/10/1960, Phoenix, AZ, m, 1994, 2 children **DISCIPLINE** MEDIEVAL HISTORY **EDUCATION** Univ NMex, BA, 86; Univ Ill, MA, 90; PhD, 93. **CAREER** From asst prof to assoc prof, St Louis Univ, 92-; hist dept chemn, St Louis Univ, 96-98. **HONORS AND AWARDS** Gladys Kneble Delmas Found Awd. **MEMBERSHIPS** Medieval Acad of Am, Catholic Hist Asn, The Hist Soc, Soc for the Study of the Crusades and the Latin East. **RESEARCH** Crusades, Medieval Venice. **SELECTED PUBLICATIONS** Auth, The Fourth Crusade: The Conquest of Constantinople, 97; auth, A Concise History of the Crusades, 99; auth, Medieval and Renaissance Venice, 99. **CONTACT ADDRESS** Dept Hist, Saint Louis Univ, 221 N Grand Blvd, Saint Louis, MO 63103-2006. **EMAIL** maddentf@slu.edu

MADDOX, ROBERT JAMES
PERSONAL Born 12/07/1931, Monroe, NY, m, 1958, 3 children **DISCIPLINE** AMERICAN DIPLOMATIC HISTORY **EDUCATION** Fairleigh Dickenson Univ, BS, 57; Univ Wis, MS, 58; Rutgers Univ, PhD(hist), 64. **CAREER** Instr hist, Paterson State Col, 62-64; asst prof, Mich State Univ, 64-66; from asst prof to assoc prof, 66-73, PROF HIST, PA STATE UNIV, 73-. **MEMBERSHIPS** AHA; Orgn Am Historians; Soc Hist Am Foreign Rels. **RESEARCH** American foreign policy, 1900-1940. **SELECTED PUBLICATIONS** Auth, William E Borah and the crusade to outlaw war, Historian, 1/67; Keeping cool with Coolidge, J Am Hist, 3/67; Woodrow Wilson, the Russian Embassy and Siberian intervention, Pac Hist Rev, 11/67; William E Borah and American Foreign Policy, La State Univ, 69; The New Left and the Origins of the Cold War, Princeton Univ, 73; The Unknown War with Russia: Wilson's Siberian Intervention, Presidio, 77. **CONTACT ADDRESS** Dept of Hist, Pennsylvania State Univ, Univ Park, 108 Weaver Bldg, University Park, PA 16802-5500.

MADISON, JAMES H.
PERSONAL Born 10/05/1944, York, PA, m, 1967, 2 children **DISCIPLINE** UNITED STATES HISTORY **EDUCATION** Gettysburg Col, BA, 66; Ind Univ, MA, 68, PhD(hist), 72. **CAREER** Fel bus hist, Harvard Univ, 72-73; vis asst prof, 73-76, asst prof, 76-81, ASSOC PROF HIST, IND UNIV, 81-89, Prof 89-00; Thomas and Kathryn Miller, Prof of Hist, IND UNIV, 00; Assoc ed, J Am Hist, 73-76; ed, Ind Mag Hist, 76-; Newberry Libr fel, 78; Rockefeller Arch Ctr grant-in-aid, 81. **HONORS AND AWARDS** Sylvia Bowman Outstanding Teacher Award, 94; Fulbright Prof, 97-98. **MEMBERSHIPS** Orgn Am Historians; AHA. **RESEARCH** Indiana, community and state history; World War II. **SELECTED PUBLICATIONS** Auth, Huntington, Henry, Edwards--a Biog, J Amer Hist, Vol 0082, 95; The War in American Culture--Society and Consciousness During World War II, Amer Hist Rev, Vol 0102, 97. **CONTACT ADDRESS** Dept of Hist, Indiana Univ, Bloomington, Ballantine Hall, Bloomington, IN 47405. **EMAIL** madison@indiana.edu

MADISON, KENNETH GLENN
PERSONAL Born 01/11/1942, Washington, DC **DISCIPLINE** MEDIEVAL HISTORY **EDUCATION** Univ Ill, Urbana, AB, 62, AM, 63, PhD, 68. **CAREER** Asst Prof Hist, IA State Univ, 67-. **MEMBERSHIPS** Mediaeval Acad Am, Richard III Soc. **RESEARCH** 14th and 15th century England and France **CONTACT ADDRESS** Dept of Hist, Iowa State Univ of Science and Tech, Ames, IA 50011-1202.

MADSEN, BRIGHAM DWAINE
PERSONAL Born 10/21/1914, Magna, UT, m, 1939, 4 children **DISCIPLINE** AMERICAN WESTERN HISTORY **EDUCATION** Univ Utah, BA, 38; Univ Calif, Berkeley, MA, 40, PhD(hist), 48. **CAREER** Assoc prof hist, Brigham Young Univ, 48-54 and Utah State Univ, 61-64; dean, Div Continuing Educ, Univ Utah, 66, deputy acad vpres admin, 67, admin vpres, 68-71, dir librs, 72-73, chmn dept hist, 74-75, PROF HIST, UNIV UTAH, 65-, Asst dir training, Peace Corps, Washington DC, 64; dir training, Vista, Washington DC, 65; dir Utah progs, Nat Endowment for humanities, 74-75. **MEMBERSHIPS** Western Hist Asn; Western Writers Am. **RESEARCH** Transportation in American West; American Indian history--PACIFIC Northwest and Utah; Utah history. **SELECTED PUBLICATIONS** Auth, The Bannock of Idaho, Caxton Printers Ltd, 58; ed, The Now Generation, Univ Utah Press, 71; Letters of Long Ago, Univ Utah Northland Press, 73; coauth, North to Montana, Univ Utah Press, 80; auth, The Lemhi: Sacajawea's People & The Northern Shoshoni, Caxton Printers, Ltd, 80; Corinne: The Gentile Capital of Utah, Utah State Hist Soc, 80; ed, A Utah Forty-Niner with Stansbury, Univ Utah Press, 82. **CONTACT ADDRESS** 2181 Lincoln Lane, Salt Lake City, UT 84117.

MADSEN, CAROL CORNWALL
PERSONAL Born Salt Lake City, UT **DISCIPLINE** AMERICAN AND WOMEN'S HISTORY **EDUCATION** Univ Utah, BA, 51; PhD, 86. **CAREER** Prof of Hist; Res Historian, Joseph Fielding Smith Inst for LDS Hist, Brigham Young Univ, 80-. **RESEARCH** Women in American history; women in Western American history; women in Mormon history. **SELECTED PUBLICATIONS** Auth, Sisters and Little Saints, A History of the Primary, 78; auth, In Their Own Words, Women and the Story of Nauvoo, 92; auth, Battle for the Ballot, Women Suffrage in Utah, 97; auth, Journey to Zion, Voices from the Mormon Trail, 97. **CONTACT ADDRESS** Smith Inst for Latter Day Saints Hist, Brigham Young Univ, 123 KMB, Provo, UT 84602. **EMAIL** carol_madsen@byu.edu

MAGNAGHI, RUSSELL MARIO
PERSONAL Born 10/12/1943, San Francisco, CA, m, 1993, 1 child **DISCIPLINE** AMERICAN HISTORY **EDUCATION** Univ San Francisco, BA, 65; St Louis Univ, MA, 67, PhD(hist), 70. **CAREER** Instr Am hist, Florissant Valley Community Col, 67-68; instr, St Louis Univ, 68-69; from instr to asst prof, 69-74, assoc prof, 74-80, PROF AM HIST, NORTHERN MICH UNIV, 80-; Mich Council for Humanities, 83. **HONORS AND AWARDS** Res grants, Northern Mich Univ, 76, 78, 92, 00; **MEMBERSHIPS** Western Hist Asn; Hist Soc of Mich; Am Hist Asn. **RESEARCH** Americas Native Americans, Regional; Am Indians. **SELECTED PUBLICATIONS** Auth, Miners, Merchants & Midwives, 87; ed, The Hasinai, 87; auth, Indian Slavery, 98; auth, Hebolton & The Historiography of the Americas, 98; auth, A Sense of Place, 97; auth, A Sense of Time, 99. **CONTACT ADDRESS** Dept of Hist, No Michigan Univ, 1401 Presque Isle Ave, Marquette, MI 49855-5301.

MAGNER, LOIS
PERSONAL Born 06/08/1943, Brooklyn, NY, m, 1972, 1 child **DISCIPLINE** HISTORY OF MEDICINE, LIFE SCIENCES **EDUCATION** Brooklyn Col, BS, 63; Univ Wis, PhD, 68. **CAREER** Res assoc to prof, Purdue Univ, 68-99; asst Dean, 78-80. **HONORS AND AWARDS** Fel, NIH; Fel in Human Values and Med. **MEMBERSHIPS** Am Assoc Hist Med; AHA; Hist of Sci Soc. **RESEARCH** History of Medicine, History of Life Sciences, Women's Studies. **SELECTED PUBLICATIONS** Auth, A History of Medicine, Dekker (NY), 92; auth, A History of Life Sciences, Dekker (NY), 94; auth, Doctors, Nurses, and Medical Practitioners: A Bio-Bibliographical Sourcebook, Greenwood Pub, 98. **CONTACT ADDRESS** Prof Emerita, Purdue Univ, 1521 SW 58th St, Cape Coral, FL 33914. **EMAIL** writing123@aol.com

MAGUIRE, JAMES HENRY
PERSONAL Born 04/02/1944, Denver, CO, m, 1967, 2 children **DISCIPLINE** AMERICAN LITERATURE AND STUDIES **EDUCATION** Univ Colo, Boulder, BA, 66; Ind Univ, Bloomington, MA, 69, PhD(English and Am studies), 70. **CAREER** Asst prof, 70-75, ASSOC PROF, 75-87, Prof, English and Am Lit, Boise State Univ, 87-, Co-Ed, Boise State Univ Western Writers Ser, 72-98; Co-Ed, Lit Hist Am West, 87-. **HONORS AND AWARDS** Distinguished Achievement Awd; Western Literature Assoc, 94. **MEMBERSHIPS** MLA; Am Studies Asn; Western Lit Asn. **RESEARCH** American realism; Western American literature; the novel. **SELECTED PUBLICATIONS** Auth, Mary Hallock Foote, 72; ed, The Literature of Idaho: an Anthology, 86; co-ed, Into the Wilderness and Dream, 94; coed, A Rendezvous Reader, 97. **CONTACT ADDRESS** Dept of English, Boise State Univ, Boise, ID 83725. **EMAIL** jmaguire@boisestate.edu

MAHAN, HOWARD F.
PERSONAL Born 10/14/1923, New York, NY, m, 1946, 3 children **DISCIPLINE** HISTORY, POLITICAL SCIENCE **EDUCATION** Drew Univ, BA, 48; Columbia Univ, MA, 51, PhD(hist and govt), 58. **CAREER** Assoc prof hist, Univ Ala, 54-64; PROF HIST AND CHMN DEPT, UNIV S ALA, 64-. **MEMBERSHIPS** AHA; Orgn Am Historians; Am Studies Asn; Southern Hist Asn. **RESEARCH** Origins of United States declarations of war; early republic, intellectual history. **SELECTED PUBLICATIONS CONTACT ADDRESS** 4158 Holly Springs Dr, Mobile, AL 36688.

MAHAN, SUSAN
PERSONAL Born 04/13/1949, San Jose, CA, m, 1997, 3 children **DISCIPLINE** HISTORIC THEOLOGY **EDUCATION** Univ South FL, BA, 71, MA, 77; Marquette Univ, PhD, 88. **CAREER** Adjunct prof: San Jose State Univ, 88-97, Santa Clara Univ, 92-97, Univ of San Francisco, 92-98; Adjunct Prof, Loyola-Marymount, 98-. **MEMBERSHIPS** AAR; CTSA; CTS. **RESEARCH** Amer spirituality; women mystics; Asceticism; spirituality and work; spirituality and marriage. **CONTACT ADDRESS** 181 Rainbow Lane, Watsonville, CA 95076. **EMAIL** smahan@got.net

MAHONEY, JOSEPH F.
PERSONAL Born 07/04/1927, Jersey City, NJ, m, 1953, 4 children **DISCIPLINE** AMERICAN HISTORY **EDUCATION** Duns Scotus Col, AB, 49; Seton Hall Univ, AM, 58; Columbia Univ, PhD(hist), 64. **CAREER** From asst prof to assoc prof, 59-69, prof hist, Seton Hall Univ, 69-97, prof emeritus, 98-, ed, NJ Hist, 69-80; dir, NJ Cath Hist Rec Comn, 76-. **MEMBERSHIPS** AHA; Am Cath Hist; Orgn Am Historians. **RESEARCH** New Jersey history; 20th century United States; late 19th century American history. **SELECTED PUBLICATIONS** Auth, Backsliding convert: Woodrow Wilson and the seven sisters, Am Quart, spring 66; Woman suffrage and the urban masses, NJ Hist, fall 69; Impact of industrialization on the New Jersey Legislature, 1870-1900, In: New Jersey Since 1860; New Findings and Interpretations, 72. **CONTACT ADDRESS** Dept of Hist, Seton Hall Univ, So Orange, 400 S Orange Ave, South Orange, NJ 07079-2697. **EMAIL** mahonejo@shu.edu

MAHONEY, MICHAEL SEAN
PERSONAL Born 06/30/1939, New York, NY, m, 1960, 2 children **DISCIPLINE** HISTORY OF SCIENCE AND TECHNOLOGY **EDUCATION** Harvard Univ, BA, 60; Princeton Univ, MA, 64, PhD(hist sci), 67. **CAREER** Instr hist, 65-67, asst prof, 67-72, assoc prof, 72-80, PROF HIST AND HIST OF SCI, PRINCETON UNIV, 80-, NSF-NATO fel, 69-70; Nat Humanities fac, 75-. **MEMBERSHIPS** Hist Sci Soc; Renaissance Soc Am; Soc Hist Tech. **RESEARCH** History of mathematics; scientific revolution. **SELECTED PUBLICATIONS** Auth, Another look at Greek geometrical analysis, Archive Hist Exact Sci, 68; Die anfaenge der algebraischen denkweise im 17 jahrhundert, Rete, 71; The Mathematical Career of Pierre de Fermat, Princeton Univ, 73; transl, introd & notes, Descartes's The World, Abaris Bks, 78; contribr, Mathematics, In: Science in the Middle Ages, Univ Chicago, 78; The determination of time and longitude at sea, In: Studies on Christian Huygens, Swets er Zeitinger, 80. **CONTACT ADDRESS** Dept of Hist, Princeton Univ, Princeton, NJ 08544.

MAHONEY, TIMOTHY
PERSONAL Born 02/07/1953, Milwaukee, WI, s **DISCIPLINE** 19TH CENTURY AMERICAN URBAN AND SOCIAL HISTORY **EDUCATION** Univ Chicago, PhD, 82. **CAREER** Prof, Univ Nebr, Lincoln. **HONORS AND AWARDS** NEH fel, Newberry Libr, Chicago, 91-92, 00; Mayers fel, Huntington Libr, 96; Kono Fel, Huntington Libr, 99. **MEMBERSHIPS** Exec sec, Urban Hist Assoc; OAH; AHA. **RESEARCH** Urban, regional, middle class; nineteenth century. **SELECTED PUBLICATIONS** Auth, River Towns in the Great West: The Structure of Provincial Urbanization in the American Middle West, 1820-1870, Cambridge UP, 90; auth, Provincial Lives Middle Class Experience in Antebellum Middlewest, Cambridge UP, 99. **CONTACT ADDRESS** Univ of Nebraska, Lincoln, 636 Oldfather, Lincoln, NE 68588-0417. **EMAIL** tmahoney@unl.edu

MAHONY, ROBERT E. P.
PERSONAL Born 09/08/1946, Bronxville, NY, m, 1973, 1 child **DISCIPLINE** ENGLISH LITERATURE & IRISH STUDIES **EDUCATION** Georgetown Univ, AB, 68; Trinity Col, Dublin, PhD, 74. **CAREER** Asst prof, Univ IL, Chicago Circle, 74-79; asst prof, 79-82, Assoc Prof Eng, Cath Univ Am, 82. **MEMBERSHIPS** Am Center for Irish Studies; Int Soc for Study of Irist Lit; Am Soc 18th Century Studies. **RESEARCH** Eighteenth century poetry and poetics; Anglo-Irish lit; bibl; Swift. **SELECTED PUBLICATIONS** Auth, Ed, Different Styles of Poetry, Cadenus, Dublin, 78; coauth (with Betty Rizzo), Christopher Smart: An Annotated Bibliograhy, Garland, 84; The Annotated Letters of Christopher Smart, Southern Ill Univ Press, 91; Jonathan Swift: The Irish Identity, Yale, 95. **CONTACT ADDRESS** Dept of Eng, Catholic Univ of America, 620 Michigan Ave N E, Washington, DC 20064-0002. **EMAIL** mahony@cua.edu

MAI, JAMES L.
PERSONAL Born 03/08/1957, Cheyenne, WY, m, 1980 **DISCIPLINE** PAINTING, DRAWING, DESIGN THEORY **EDUCATION** Univ Wyo, BFA, 82; MFA, 85. **CAREER** Asst prof, Wenatchee Valley Col, 87-96; assoc prof, Graceland Col, 96-00; asst prof, Ill State Univ, 00-. **HONORS AND AWARDS** Alumni Teaching Awd of Merit, Graceland Col, 00. **MEMBERSHIPS** Col Art Asn, Foundations in Art: Theory and Educ, Am Soc for Aesthetics. **RESEARCH** Color Theory, Composition Theory, Critical Theory, Semiotics, Philosophical Mathematics. **CONTACT ADDRESS** Dept Art, Illinois State Univ, Campus Box 5620, Normal, IL 61790-5620.

MAIDMAN, MAYNARD PAUL
PERSONAL Born 08/07/1944, Philadelphia, PA, m, 1971, 2 children **DISCIPLINE** ANCIENT HISTORY, BIBLICAL STUDIES **EDUCATION** Columbia Univ, AB, 66; Univ Pa, PhD(Oriental studies), 76. **CAREER** Lectr, 72-76, asst prof, 76-78, ASSOC PROF HIST AND HEBREW, YORK UNIV, 78-. **MEMBERSHIPS** Am Oriental Soc; Soc Bibl Lit. **RESEARCH** Private economic records from Late Bronze Age Iraq and their significance; the dynamics of ancient archive keeping; ancient Israelite political history. **SELECTED PUBLICATIONS** Auth, Reallexikon of Assyriology and Near Eastern Archaeology, Vol 8, Fascicles 1-2, Meek Miete, Fascicles 3-4, Miete Moab, J Amer Oriental Soc, Vol 0116, 96; Uncovering Ancient Stones--Essays in Memory of Richardson, H. Neil, J Amer Oriental Soc, Vol 0116, 96. **CONTACT ADDRESS** York Univ, North York, ON, Canada M3J 1P3. **EMAIL** mmaidman@yorku.ca

MAIER, DONNA J. E.
PERSONAL Born 02/20/1948, St. Louis, MO, 2 children **DISCIPLINE** HISTORY, AFRICA **EDUCATION** Col Wooster, BA, 69; Northwestern Univ, MA, 72, PhD(hist), 75. **CAREER** Asst prof, Univ TX, Dallas, 75-78; asst prof, 78-81, assoc prof, 81-86, prof hist, Univ Northern IA, 86-; consult, Scott, Foresman, 75-82, co-ed, Africa Economic Hist, 92-. **HONORS AND AWARDS** IA Board of Regents Faculty Excellence Awd, 96; Fulbright Hayes fel, 87. **MEMBERSHIPS** African Studies Asn; Ghana Studies Coun. **RESEARCH** Nineteenth century Asante (Ghana) history; African Islam; traditional African medicine. **SELECTED PUBLICATIONS** Auth, Priests and Power: The Case of the Dente Shrine in Nineteenth-Century Ghana, IN Univ Press, 83; Colonial Distortion of the Volta River Salt Trade, in African Economic Hist, 86; Slave Labor/ Wage Labor in German Togoland, in Arthur Knoll and Lewis Gann, eds, Germans in the Tropics: Essays in German Colonial History, Greenwood Press, 87; Asante War Aims in the 1869 Invasion of Ewe, in Enid Schildkrout, ed, The Golden Stool: Studies of the Asante Center and Periphery, Am Museum of Nat Hist Press, 87; The Military Aquisition of Slaves in Asante, in D. Henige and T C McCaskie, eds, West African Economic and Social History, African Studies, Madison, 90; coauth, History and Life, Scott, Foresman & Co, 77, 4nd ed, 90;Treasures of the World: Literature and Source Readings for World History, with H Roupp, Scott Foresman, 91; Persistance of Precolonial Patterns of Production: Cotton in German Togoland 1800-1914, in A Issacman and R Roberts, eds, Cotton, Colonialism, and Social History in Sud-Sahara Africa, Heinemann, 95; Islam and the Idea of Asylum in Asanta, in J Humwick and N Lawlor, eds, The Cloths of Many-Colored Silks, Northwestern Univ Press, 96. **CONTACT ADDRESS** Dept Hist, Univ of No Iowa, Cedar Falls, IA 50614-0001. **EMAIL** donna.maier@uni.edu

MAIER, PAUL LUTHER
PERSONAL Born 05/31/1930, St. Louis, MO, m, 1967, 4 children **DISCIPLINE** ANCIENT HISTORY **EDUCATION** Concordia Sem, AB, 52, BD, 55; Harvard Univ, MA, 54; Univ Basel, PhD, 57. **CAREER** From asst prof to assoc prof, 59-68, prof hist, Western Mich Univ, 68-, Lutheran Campus Chaplain, Western Mich Univ, 58-99. **HONORS AND AWARDS** Detur Awd, 50;Alumni Awd for Teaching Excellence, Western MI Univ, 74; Distinguished Fac Scholar Awd, Western Mich Univ, 81; Prof of the Year Citation, Council for the Advancement and Support of Education, 84; The Academy Citation, Michigan Academy of Science, Arts and Letters, 85; The Gold Medallion Book Awd for Josephus -- The Essential Writings, Evan Christian Publishers Assoc, 89; Doctor of Letters Degree award honoris causa by Concordia Seminary, St Louis, 95; Doctor of Laws degree awarded honoris cause by Concordia College, 00. **MEMBERSHIPS** AHA **RESEARCH** Ancient history; Palestine and Rome in first century AD. **SELECTED PUBLICATIONS** Auth, Caspar Schwenckfeld on the Person and Work of Christ, VanGorcum, Neth, 59; A Man Spoke, A World Listened, McGraw, 63; Pontius Pilate, Doubleday, 68; First Christmas--The True and Unfamiliar Story, 71, First Easter--The True and Unfamiliar Story, 73 & First Christians--Pentecost and the Spread of Christianity, 76, Harper; ed, The Best of Walter A Maier, Concordia, 80; auth, The Flames of Rome, Doubleday, 81; A Skeleton in God's Closet, Thomas Nelson, 94; ed, trans, Josephus, The Essential Works, Kregel, 95; auth, In Fullness of Time, Kregel, 97; Eusebius, The Church History, Kregel, 99. **CONTACT ADDRESS** Dept of History, Western Michigan Univ, 1903 W Michigan, Kalamazoo, MI 49008-3805. **EMAIL** paul.maier@wmich.edu

MAIER, PAULINE RUBBELKE
PERSONAL Born 04/27/1938, St. Paul, MN, m, 1961, 3 children **DISCIPLINE** AMERICAN HISTORY **EDUCATION** Radcliff Col, AB, 60; Harvard Univ, PhD(hist), 68. **CAREER** From asst prof to assoc prof hist, Univ MA, Boston, 68-77; Robinson-Edwards prof, Univ WI-Madison, 77-78; prof Hist, 78-89, Wm Rand prof Am Hist, MA Inst Technol, 90-; Chas Warren Ctr Study Am Hist fel, Harvard Univ, 74-75; Nat Endowment Humanities Younger Humanist fel, 74-75, 88-89; Guggenheim fel, 90. **HONORS AND AWARDS** Douglass G Adair Award, Inst Early Am Hist, 76; LLD (hon), Regis Col, 87; DHL (hon), Williams Col, 93. **MEMBERSHIPS** Soc Am Historians; Am Antiq Soc; Orgn Am Historians; AHA; SHEAR; Col Soc of MA; MA Hist Soc; Am Academy of Arts and Sciences. **RESEARCH** The Colonial, Revolutionary, and Early National Periods of American history. **SELECTED PUBLICATIONS** Auth, Popular Uprisings and Civil Authority in 18th Century America, William & Mary Quart, 70; The Charleston Mob and the Development of Popular Politics in Revolutionary South Carolina, 1765-1784, Perspectives Am Hist, 70; From Resistance to Revolution: Colonial Radicals and the Development of American Opposition to Britain, 1765-1776, Knopf, 72; Coming to Terms with Samuel Adams, Am Hist Rev, 76; co-ed, Interdisciplinary Studies of the American Revolution, Sage, 76; The Old Revolutionaries: Political Lives in the Age of Samuel Adams, Knopf, 80; The Road Not Taken: Nullification John C Calhoun, and the Revolutionary Tradition in South Carolina, SC Hist Mag, 81; Boston and New York in the 18th Century, Proc Am Antiq Soc, 82; The American People: A History, DC Heath, 86; Revolutionary Origins of the American Corporation, William and Mary Quart, 93; American Scripture: Making the Declaration of Independence, Knopf, 97; intro, The Constitution, the Bill of Rights, and the Declaration of Independence, Bantam, 98. **CONTACT ADDRESS** History Faculty, Massachusetts Inst of Tech, 77 Massachusetts Ave, Cambridge, MA 02139-4307. **EMAIL** pmaier@mit.edu

MAILLET, MARGUERITE
PERSONAL Born 03/17/1924, St. Norbert, NB, Canada **DISCIPLINE** CANADIAN, ACADIAN STUDIES **EDUCATION** Laval Univ, BPh, 57; Regina Mundi (Rome) & St Mary's Univ (Ind), MA (Sacred Stud), 66; Laval & Moncton Univ, MA (Fr), 71; Univ Ottawa, PhD, 82. **CAREER** Tchr, NB sch; prof, Ecole normale de Moncton, 68; prof, Univ Moncton, 73, dir Fr stud, 79-81, vice dean arts, 85, ch, d'etudes acadiennes, 87-90, PROF EMER, UNIV MONCTON, 94-. **RESEARCH** Acadian studies. **SELECTED PUBLICATIONS** Auth, Histoire de la litterature acadienne: de reve en reve, 83; auth, Bibliographie des publications d'Acadie 1609-1990: Sources premieres et sources secondes, 92; auth, Bibliographie des publications de l'Acadie des provinces Maritimes: livres et brochures 1609-1995, 97; coauth, Anthologie de textes litteraires acadiens, 79; coauth, The Bicentennial Lectures on New Brunswick Literature, 85; coauth, La Reception des oeuvres d'Antonine Maillet. **CONTACT ADDRESS** 101 Archibald St, Apt 3003, Moncton, NB, Canada E1C 9J7.

MAIN, GLORIA L.
PERSONAL Born 06/01/1933, San Francisco, CA, m, 1956, 3 children **DISCIPLINE** AMERICAN HISTORY **EDUCATION** Columbia Univ, PhD 72. **CAREER** Univ Colorado, assoc prof, 83-. **MEMBERSHIPS** AHA; AHEHA; SSHA; AOI; EAHC; AAS; NEHGS. **RESEARCH** Early American History; Native Amer History; Hist of Slavery in the Americas; Family History. **SELECTED PUBLICATIONS** Auth, Naming Children in Early New England, The Jour of Interdisciplinary Hist, 96; Auth, Gender Work and Wages in Colonial New England, WM and Mary Quart, 94; Family Structures: The British Colonies, Encycl of the N Amer Colonies, 93; auth, The English Family in America: A Comparison of Chesapeake New England and Pennsylvania Quaker Families in the Colonial Period, Lois Green Carr, The Chesapeake and Beyond: A Celebration, Crownsville MD, 92. **CONTACT ADDRESS** Dept of History, Univ of Colorado, Boulder, 2305 Dartmouth Ave, Boulder, CO 80303. **EMAIL** maing@spot.colorado.edu

MAIN, JACKSON T.
PERSONAL m, 3 children **DISCIPLINE** HISTORY **EDUCATION** Univ Wis, BA, 39, MA, 40, PhD, 48. **CAREER** Adj prof emer, Univ of Colo. **MEMBERSHIPS** AM Antiquarian Soc **SELECTED PUBLICATIONS** Auth, "Summary: The Hereafter," Forum; auth, Toward a History the Standard of Living in British America, Wm & Mary Quart 45, 88; auth, The Social Origins of Leaders, 2000 BC to 1845 AD, Brandywine Press. **CONTACT ADDRESS** 2305 Dartmouth Ave, Boulder, CO 80303.

MAISCH, CHRISTIAN
DISCIPLINE LATIN AMERICA **EDUCATION** Am Univ, PhD. **CAREER** Prof, Am Univ. **MEMBERSHIPS** Inter-American Develop Bank. **RESEARCH** International relations theory and international law and organization. **SELECTED PUBLICATIONS** Auth, A Legal and Historical Analysis of the Conflicting Anglo-Argentine Claims to the Falkland/Malvinas Islands,Universidad Inca Garcilaso, 95. **CONTACT ADDRESS** American Univ, 4400 Massachusetts Ave, Washington, DC 20016.

MAIZLISH, STEPHEN E.
PERSONAL Born 12/13/1945, Los Angeles, CA **DISCIPLINE** AMERICAN HISTORY **EDUCATION** Univ Calif, Berkeley, BA, 67; Univ Mich, MA, 68; Univ Calif, Berkeley, PhD(hist), 78. **CAREER** Actg instr, Univ Calif, Berkeley, 76; ASST PROF HIST, UNIV TEX, ARLINGTON, 78-84, Assoc prof, 84-. **MEMBERSHIPS** AHA; Orgn Am Historians; SHA. **RESEARCH** United States Civil War and reconstruction; United States political history; United States 19th century. **SELECTED PUBLICATIONS** Auth, Triumph of Sectonalism, 83. **CONTACT ADDRESS** Dept Hist, Univ of Texas, Arlington, Arlington, TX 76019. **EMAIL** maizlish@uta.edu

MAJOR, JOHN STEPHEN
PERSONAL Born 10/05/1942, Englewood, NJ **DISCIPLINE** CHINESE INTELLECTUAL HISTORY, HISTORY OF SCIENCE **EDUCATION** Haverford Col, BA, 64; Harvard Univ, MA, 65, PhD(hist and EAsian lang), 73. **CAREER** Instr, 71-73, asst prof, 73-79, ASSOC PROF HIST, DARTMOUTH COL, 79-, Am Coun Learned Soc res grant Chinese hist, 74; vis fel, Cambridge Univ, 81-82. **MEMBERSHIPS** Asn Asian Studies; Soc Study Early China; Soc Study Chinese Relig; Am Orient Soc. **RESEARCH** Early Chinese religion and cosmology; theoretical foundations of Chinese science. **SELECTED PUBLICATIONS** Auth, The Rise of Early Modern Science--Islam, China, and the West, Isis, Vol 0085, 94. **CONTACT ADDRESS** Dept of Hist, Dartmouth Col, Hanover, NH 03755.

MAKINO, YASUKO
PERSONAL Born 04/08/1937, Tokyo, Japan, m, 1963, 1 child **DISCIPLINE** LIBRARY SCIENCE; JAPANESE STUDIES **EDUCATION** Tokyo Women's Christian Univ, BA; Univ IL, MA, 70, MLS, 72. **CAREER** Univ IL, Urbana-Champaign, 72-91; Columbia Univ, 91-98; Princeton Univ Library, 98-. **MEMBERSHIPS** Asn for Asian Studies. **RESEARCH** Japanese bibliography and reference works. **SELECTED PUBLICATIONS** Auth, Japan Through Children's Literature, Greenwood Press, 85; Student Guide to Japanese Sources in the Humanities, Center for Japanese Studies, Univ MI, 94; Japan and the Japanese: A Bibliographical Guide to Reference Sources, Greenwood Press, 96. **CONTACT ADDRESS** Princeton Univ, Gest Libr, Princeton, NJ 08544. **EMAIL** ymakino@princeton.edu

MAKOWSKI, ELIZABETH
PERSONAL Born 03/13/1951, Milwaukee, WI **DISCIPLINE** HISTORY OF MEDIEVAL EUROPE **EDUCATION** Univ Wis-Milwaukee, BA, 73; MA, 76; Harvard Univ, AM, 77; Columbia Univ, PhD, 93. **CAREER** Asst prof, SW Tex State Univ, 93-98; assoc prof, 98- . **HONORS AND AWARDS** Columbia Univ President's Fel, 89-93; SWT Res Grants, 94, 96, 97; Sch of Lib Arts Awd for Scholarly Activ, 97; SWT research grant, 00. **MEMBERSHIPS** Am Cath Hist Asoc; Tex Cath Hist Asoc; Tex Medieval Asoc, Medieval Acad of Am. **RESEARCH** Canon law; Medieval religious women. **SELECTED PUBLICATIONS** Co-auth, Wykked Wyves and the Woes of Marriage, 90; auth, The Conjugal Debt and Medieval Canon Law, Equally in God's Image, Women in the Middle Ages, 90; auth, with James A. Brundage, Enclosure of Nuns: The Decretal Periculoso and Its Commentators, J Medieval Hist, 94; auth, Tomas Sanchez on the Cloistering of Nuns: Canonical Theory and Spanich Cololnial Practice, Cath Sothwest, 96; auth, Canon Law and Cloistered Women: Periculoso and Its Commentators 1298-1545, 97; "Mulieres Religiosae, Strictly Speaking: Some Fourteenth-Century Canonical Opinions," The Cath Hist Rev 99. **CONTACT ADDRESS** Dept of History, Southwest Texas State Univ, San Marcos, TX 78666. **EMAIL** em13@swt.edu

MALAMUD, MARGARET
DISCIPLINE HISTORY **EDUCATION** Boston Univ, BA, 80; Univ Calif Berk, MA, 83; PhD, 90. **CAREER** Lectr, postdoc fel, Stanford Univ, 90-92; asst prof, assoc prof, New Mex State Univ, 98-. **HONORS AND AWARDS** NEH, 99. **MEMBERSHIPS** APA; MESA. **RESEARCH** Classical tradition in modern popular culture. **SELECTED PUBLICATIONS** Auth, "The Politics of Heresy in Medieval Iran," J Iran Stud 27 (94): 37-51; auth, "Sufi Structures of Authority in Medieval Nishapur," Intl J Mid East Stud 26 (94): 427-442; auth, "Gender and Spiritual Self-Fashioning: The Master-Disciple Relationship in Medieval Islam," J Am Acad Relig LXIV/1 (96), 89-117; auth, "As the Romans Did? The Ancient Rome in Contemporary Las Vegas," Arion 6 (98): 11-39; auth, "The Imperial Metropolis: Ancient Rome in Turn-of-the-Century New York," Arion 7 (00): 64-108; co-ed, Imperial Projections: Ancient Rome in Modern Popular Culture, John Hopkins UP, 01; auth, "A Funny Thing Happened on the Way to Brooklyn: Roman Comedy on Broadway and in Film," Arion 8.3 001): 33-51. **CONTACT ADDRESS** Dept of Hist, New Mexico State Univ, MSC3H, Las Cruces, NM 88003.

MALAND, CHARLES J.
PERSONAL Born 09/21/1949, Albert Lea, MN, m, 1973, 1 child **DISCIPLINE** AMERICAN CULTURE **EDUCATION** Augsburg Col, BA, 71; Univ Mich, MA, 72; PhD, 75. **CAREER** Lake Forest Col, 76-78; asst prof, 78-83; assoc prof, 83-90; prof, 90-, Univ Tenn. **HONORS AND AWARDS** AFI, Rockefeller Found Sem; Lilly Found Fel; Fulbright Fel; Hodges Teach Awd; AA Outstand Teach Awd. **MEMBERSHIPS** ASA; SCS; IAMHIST. **RESEARCH** American film and its relationship to American culture. **SELECTED PUBLICATIONS** Auth, American Visions: The films of Chaplin, Ford, Capra and Welles, 1936-1941, 71; rev, ed, Frank Capra, 95; auth, Chaplin and American Culture: The Evolution of a Star Image, 89. **CONTACT ADDRESS** Dept English, Univ of Tennessee, Knoxville, 1345 Circle Park, Knoxville, TN 37996-0001.

MALANDRA, WILLIAM
DISCIPLINE CLASSICAL AND NEAR EASTERN STUDIES **EDUCATION** Haverford Col, BA, 64; Brown Univ, BA, 66; Univ Pa, PhD, 71. **CAREER** Assoc prof, Univ Minn, Twin Cities. **RESEARCH** Indo-Iranian philological studies. **SELECTED PUBLICATIONS** Auth, Avestan zanu-drajah: an Obscene Gesture, Indo-Iranian J 22, 80; An Introduction to Old Iranian Religion, Univ Minn Press, 83; Rasnu and the Office of Divine Judge: Comparative Reconstructions and the Varuna Problem, Festschrift for Ludo Rocher, Madras: Adyar Libr, 87. **CONTACT ADDRESS** Univ of Minnesota, Twin Cities, 9 Pleasant St. SE, 330 Folwell Hall, Minneapolis, MN 55455.

MALEFAKIS, EDWARD EMANUEL
PERSONAL Born 01/02/1932, Springfield, MA, m, 2 children **DISCIPLINE** EUROPEAN HISTORY **EDUCATION** Bates Col, AB, 53; Johns Hopkins Sch Advan Int Studies, DC, MA, 55; Columbia Univ, PhD(hist), 65. **CAREER** Vis instr hist, Northwestern Univ, Evanston, 62-63; asst prof, Wayne State Univ, 63-64; asst prof, Columbia Univ, 64-68; assoc prof, Northwestern Univ, Evanston, 68-71; prof, Univ Mich, Ann Arbor, 71-74; PROF HIST, COLUMBIA UNIV, 74-, Soc Sci Res Coun fac res grant, 67-68; dir, Prog Comp Studies in Hist, Univ Mich, 72-74; John Simon Guggenheim Mem Found fel, 74-75; Nat Endowment for Humanities res grant, 77-78. **HONORS AND AWARDS** Herbert Baxter Adams Prize, AHA, 71; Orden de Merito Civil, Spain, 81. **MEMBERSHIPS** AHA, Soc Span & Port Hist Studies, Soc Ital Hist Studies, Mod Greek Studies Asn, Mebrija Prize, 00. **RESEARCH** Spanish and Southern European history since 1750; social and quantitative history. **SELECTED PUBLICATIONS** Auth, Agrarian Reform and Peasant Revolution in Spain: Origins of the Civil War, Yale Univ, 70; contribr, The Republic and the Civil War in Spain, Macmillan, 71; Modern European Social History, Heath, 72; Civil Wars in the Twentieth Century, Univ Ky, 72; ed, Indalecio Prieto: Discursos Fundamentales, Turner, Madrid, 75; ed, La Guerra de Espana, 1936-1939, Taurus, 86; auth, Southern Europe in the 19th and 20th Centuries: An Historical Overview, Juan March, 92. **CONTACT ADDRESS** Dept of Hist, Columbia Univ, 2960 Broadway, New York, NY 10027-6900. **EMAIL** eem1@columbia.edu

MALIK, SALAHUDDIN
DISCIPLINE HISTORY **EDUCATION** Punjab Univ, BA, MA; McGill Univ, PhD. **CAREER** Prof. **RESEARCH** British imperialism in India; Nineteenth Century Muslims; Middle East history. **SELECTED PUBLICATIONS** Auth, Changing Emphasis on American Muslims with Emphasis on Pakistani Americans; God, England and the Indian Mutiny: Victorian Perspectives, Jour Islam, 83; Nineteenth Century Approaches to the Indian Mutiny, Jour Asian Hist, 80; Pakistanis in the American Melting Pot: History of Rochester NY, Islamic Studies, 93. **CONTACT ADDRESS** Dept of History, SUNY, Col at Brockport, Brockport, NY 14420. **EMAIL** smalik@acspr1.acs.brockport.edu

MALINO, FRANCES
PERSONAL Born 03/06/1940, Danbury, CT, d, 2 children **DISCIPLINE** EARLY MODERN FRENCH & JEWISH HISTORY **EDUCATION** Skidmore Col, BA, 61; Brandeis Univ, MA, 63, PhD(Judaic studies), 71. **CAREER** From asst prof to prof hist, Univ Mass, Boston, 70 89; assoc prof hist, Harbor Camput, Univ Mass, 70; Vis prof, Brandeis Univ, 71 & Yale Univ, 74; mem, Commission Francaise des Archives Juives, 77-; fel, Mary Ingraham Bunting Inst, Radcliff Col, 79-80, scholar-in-residence, Tauber Inst, Brandeis Univ, spring 83; vis prof Jewish Studies, Mount Holyoke Col, 86-87; Ecole des Haute Etudes en Sciences Sociales, Paris, 89; SOPHIA MOSES ROBINSON PROF JEWISH STUDIES AND HIST, WELLSLEY COL, 89-. **HONORS AND AWARDS** ACLS res grant, 79-80; ACLS travel grant, 87; Healey res grant, 88; guest fel, Wolfson Col, Oxford, 88; Wellsley Col res grant, 91, 96; Littauer Fdn res grant, 93, 96; Alumni Periclean schol award, Skidmore Col, 97; Barnett Miller Fac Dev grant for Int Studies, 98. **MEMBERSHIPS** AHA; Asn Jewish Studies; Soc French Hist Studies; Edit Bd, Jewish Soc Studies; Acad Adv Bd, Int Res Inst on Jewish Women. **RESEARCH** Jewish autonomy and citizenship in 18th century France; nationalism and modern national movements; contemporary Middle East; Jewish women teachers of the Alliance Israelite Universelle. **SELECTED PUBLICATIONS** Auth, Memoires d'un Patriole Proscrit, In: Michael IV, Diaspora Res Inst, Tel Aviv, 76; The Sephardic Jews of Bordeaux: Assimilation and Emancipation in Revolutionary and Napoleonic France, Univ Ala Press, 78; Furtado et les Portugais, Annales Hist Revolution Francaise, 1-3/79; Zalkind Hourwitz-Juif Polonais, Dix-Huitieme Siecle, 81; From patriot to Israelite: Abrahkam Furtado in revolutionary France, In: Es-

says in Jewish Intellectual History in Honor of Alexander Altmann, Duke Univ Press, 82; Attitudes toward Jewish communal autonomy in pre-revolutionary France, In: Essays in Modern Jewish History: A Tribute to Ben Halpern, Fairleigh Dickinson Univ Press, 82 & ed, Essays in Modern Jewish History; co-ed, The Jews in Modern France, Univ Press New England, 85; co-ed, From East and West: Jews in a changing Europe, Basil Blackwell, 90; ed, Profiles in Diversity: Jews in a Changing Europe, Wayne State Univ Press, 98; auth, A Jew in the French Revolution: The Life of Zalkind Hourwitz, Basil Blackwell, 96; auth, "Women teachers of the Alliance Israelite Universelle," in Jewish Women in Historical Perspective, Wayne State Univ Press, 98; auth, "Jewish Emancipation in France," in Religious Minorities, State and Society in Nineteenth-Century Europe, Manchester Univ Press, 98; auth, "Resistance and Rebellion: The Jews in Eighteenth Century France," in Jewish Historical Studies, No. 30, 89; auth, "Jewish Women in Early Modern Europe," in Women's Studies Encyclopedia, Greenwood Press, 91; auth, Un Juif rebelle dans la Revolution et sous l'Empire Zalkind Hourwitz (1751-1812), Berg Intl, 00. **CONTACT ADDRESS** Dept Hist, Wellesley Col, Wellesley, MA 02481. **EMAIL** fmalino@wellesley.edu

MALLARD, WILLIAM
PERSONAL Born 05/28/1927, New York, NY, m, 1961, 3 children **DISCIPLINE** RELIGION; CHURCH HISTORY **EDUCATION** Randolph-Macon, BA, 49; Duke Div School, Duke Univ, BD, 52; Duke Grad School, Duke Univ, PhD, 56. **CAREER** Instr Relig, Sweet Briar Col, 55-57; asst to full prof church hist, Candler School Theol, Emory Univ, 57- . **HONORS AND AWARDS** Dempster Grad fel, 54-55; Am Asn Theol Schools Fel, 62-63; Cross Disciplinary Fel Soc Relig, 69-70; Emory Wms Distinguished Teaching Awd, Emory Univ, 81; Thomas Jefferson Awd for Service, Emory Univ, 89; Chandler School Theol Serv Awd, 97 & 98. **RESEARCH** St. Augustine of Hippo, Theology and literary criticism. **SELECTED PUBLICATIONS** Auth, The Reflection of Theology in Literature, Trinity Univ Press, 77; auth, "The Incarnation in Augustine's Conversion," Recherches Augustiniennes XV, Paris, (80); auth, Language and Love: Introducing Augustine's Religious Thought through the Confessions Story, Penn State, 94; auth, "Jesus Christ," St Augustine through the Ages: an Encyclopedia, Erdman, (99). **CONTACT ADDRESS** School Theol, Emory Univ, 1364 Clifton Rd NE, Atlanta, GA 30322-1061. **EMAIL** wmallar@emory.edu

MALLORY, MICHAEL
PERSONAL Born 11/01/1936, Buffalo, NY, m, 2 children **DISCIPLINE** ART **EDUCATION** Yale Univ, BA, 59; Columbia Univ, MA, 62, PhD, 65. **CAREER** Prof, Brooklyn Col, CUNY, 65- **HONORS AND AWARDS** Fulbright Fel, 63-64; NEH, 67; CUNY Res Found Grants, 82-92. **SELECTED PUBLICATIONS** Coauth, Guido Riccio and the Resistance to Critical Thinking, Syracuse Scholar, 91; Sano di Pietro's Bernardino Triptych for the compagnia della Uergine, Burlington Mag, 91; Did Siena Get its Carta Before its Horse? J of Art, 91; auth, The Guido Riccio Controversy in Art History, in Confronting the Experts, St Univ NY Press, 96. **CONTACT ADDRESS** Art Dept, Brooklyn Col, CUNY, Brooklyn, NY 11210-2889.

MALONE, BARBARA S. (BOBBIE)
PERSONAL Born 01/02/1944, San Antonio, TX, m, 1977, 2 children **DISCIPLINE** AMERICAN HISTORY **EDUCATION** Newcomb College, BA 75; Tulane Univ, MS 79, MA 90, PhD 94. **CAREER** State Hist Soc of Wisconsin, dir off sch ser, 95. **MEMBERSHIPS** ASLH; NCSS; SJHS; WCSS **RESEARCH** Amer southern and other regional Jewish histories; WI hist; regional hist; materials related to hist for edu purposes; late 19th-20th century social and cultural hist **SELECTED PUBLICATIONS** Auth, Rabbi Max Heller: Reformer Zionist Southerner 1860-1929, Univ Alabama Press, 97; Rabbi Max Heller and the Negro Question New Orleans 1891-1911, in: The Quiet Voices: Southern Rabbis and Black Civil Rights, eds, Mark Bauman, Berkley Kalin, Univ Ala Press, 97; Jews in Christian America, by Naomi W. Cohen for Amer Jour of Legal Hist, 94; Back to Beginnings: The Early Days of Dane County, Dane Cty Cultural Affs Comm, 98; Learning for the Land: Wisconsin Land Use for 4th graders, coauth, accompanying teachers guide, 98; Wisconsin's Built Environment, coauth, classroom resource kit, 98. **CONTACT ADDRESS** Office of School Services, State Historical Soc of Wisconsin, 816 State St, Madison, WI 53706-1488. **EMAIL** bobbis.s.malone@ccmail.adp.wisc.edu

MALONE, BILL CHARLES
PERSONAL Born 08/25/1934, Smith County, TX, m, 1971, 3 children **DISCIPLINE** UNITED STATES CULTURAL HISTORY **EDUCATION** Univ Tex, Austin, BA, 56, MA 58, PhD(US hist), 65. **CAREER** Instr US hist, Southwest Tex State Col, 62-64, asst prof Southern hist, 64-67; assoc prof Southern and Black hist, Murray State Univ, 67-69; assoc prof Black hist, Univ Wis-Whitewater, 69-71; assoc prof, 71-80, PROF SOCIAL AND CULT HIST, TULANE UNIV, 80-. **MEMBERSHIPS** Orgn Am Historians; Southern Hist Asn. **RESEARCH** United States social and cultural history; Southern United States history; rural history. **SELECTED PUBLICATIONS** Auth, Country Music, USA: A Fifty Year History, Am Folklore Soc, 69. **CONTACT ADDRESS** Div of Arts and Sci Dept of Hist, Tulane Univ, New Orleans, LA 70118.

MALONE, CAROLYN
DISCIPLINE MEDIEVAL ART AND ARCHAEOLOGY **EDUCATION** Univ Calif ,Berkeley, PhD, 73. **CAREER** Assoc prof; Univ Southern Calif; lect, Kalamozoo, 96. **HONORS AND AWARDS** NEH grants, late 70s; Courtland-Elliot prize, Medieval Acad Am, 95; **RESEARCH** French Romanesque and English Gothic architecture and sculpture. **SELECTED PUBLICATIONS** Auth, Les Fouilles de Saint-Benigne de Dijon 1976-1978 et le probleme de l'eglise de l'an mil in the Bulletin Monumental; **CONTACT ADDRESS** Col Letters, Arts & Sciences, Univ of So California, University Park Campus, Los Angeles, CA 90089.

MALONE, DUMAS
PERSONAL Born 01/10/1902, Coldwater, MS, m, 1925, 2 children **DISCIPLINE** HISTORY, BIOGRAPHY **EDUCATION** Emory Univ, BA, 10; Yale Univ, BA, 16, MA, 21, PhD, 23. **CAREER** Instr hist, Yale Univ, -23, asst prof, 23; from assoc prof to prof, Univ Va, 23-29; ed, Dict Am Biog, 29-31, ed-in-chief, 31-36; dir and chmn bd Syndics, Harvard Univ Press, 36-43; prof hist, Columbia Univ, 45-59; Jefferson Found prof hist, 59-62, BIOGRAPHER IN RESIDENCE, UNIV VA, 62-, Vis prof, Yale Univ, 27, Sterling sr fel, 27-28; ed, Hist Bk Club, 48-; Guggenheim fels, 51-52 and 58-59; managing ed, Polit Sci Quart, 53-58; hon consult, Am hist, Libr Congr, 68. **HONORS AND AWARDS** Porter Prize, Yale Univ, 23, Wilbur L Cross Medal, 72; Thomas Jefferson Awd, Univ Va, 64; John F Kennedy Medal, Mass Hist Soc, 72; Pulitzer Prize in Hist, 75; dlitt, emory univ and rochester univ, 36, dartmouth col, 37 and col william and mary, 77; lld, northwestern univ, 35 and univ chattanooga, 62. **MEMBERSHIPS** AHA; Southern Hist Asn(pres, 67-68); Am Antiq Soc; Am Acad Arts and Sci; Soc Am Hist. **RESEARCH** Early American history. **SELECTED PUBLICATIONS** Auth, A Linguistic Approach to the Bakhtinian Hero in Martin, Steve 'Roxanne', Lit-Film Quart, Vol 0024, 96. **CONTACT ADDRESS** Alderman Libr, Univ of Virginia, Charlottesville, VA 22901.

MALSBERGER, JOHN WILLIAM
PERSONAL Born 01/18/1951, Allentown, PA, m, 1978, 1 child **DISCIPLINE** AMERICAN HISTORY **EDUCATION** Temple Univ, AB, 72, PhD, 80. **CAREER** Tchg asst US hist, Temple Univ, 74-76, res asst, 76-78; from Instr to Assoc Prof, 78-96, prof US hist, Muhlenberg Col, 96. **MEMBERSHIPS** AHA; Orgn Am Historians; Social Sci Hist Asn. **RESEARCH** US Congress in 20th Century; polit theory; Am conservatism. **SELECTED PUBLICATIONS** Auth, The political thought of Fisher Ames, J Early Repub, spring 82; The Transformation of Republican Conservatism: The US Senate, 1938-1952, Congress & the Presidency, Spring 87; From Obstruction to Moderation: The Transformation of Senate Conservatism, 1938-1952, Susquehanna Univ Press. **CONTACT ADDRESS** Dept of Hist, Muhlenberg Col, 2400 W Chew St, Allentown, PA 18104-5586. **EMAIL** malsberg@muhlenberg.edu

MALTBY, WILLIAM SAUNDERS
PERSONAL Born 10/23/1940, Cleveland, OH **DISCIPLINE** EARLY MODERN HISTORY **EDUCATION** Hiram Col, BA, 62; Duke Univ, MA, 65, PhD(hist), 67. **CAREER** Asst prof hist, Ohio Univ, 66-68; asst prof, 68-70, assoc prof, 70-82, PROF HIST, UNIV MO ST LOUIS, 82-, Exec dir, Ctr Reformation Res, 77-. **MEMBERSHIPS** AHA; Soc Relig Higher Educ; Renaissance Soc Am; Am Soc Reformation Res. **RESEARCH** Sixteenth century Spain; the revolt of the Netherlands; 16th century Anglo-Spanish relations. **SELECTED PUBLICATIONS** Auth, The Black Legend in England: The Development of Anti-Spanish Sentiment, 1558-1660, Duke Univ, 71; Alba: A Biography of Fernando Alvarez de Toledo, Third Duke of Alba, 1507-1582, Univ Calif (in prep). **CONTACT ADDRESS** Dept of Hist, Univ of Missouri, St. Louis, Saint Louis, MO 63121.

MANCA, FRANCO
PERSONAL Born Sardinia, Italy **DISCIPLINE** ITALIAN STUDIES **EDUCATION** Univ Calif, Berkeley, PhD. **CAREER** Assoc prof Ital, Univ Nev, Reno. **RESEARCH** Dante; the Italian renaissance. **SELECTED PUBLICATIONS** Published a number of articles on Dante and the Italian Renaissance; he has also published on contemporary Italian literature. **CONTACT ADDRESS** Univ of Nevada, Reno, Reno, NV 89557.

MANCKE, ELIZABETH
DISCIPLINE HISTORY **EDUCATION** Johns Hopkins Univ, PhD, 90. **CAREER** Assoc prof, Dept Hist, Univ Akron. **RESEARCH** Early modern British America. **CONTACT ADDRESS** Univ of Akron, Dept of History, Akron, OH 44325-1902. **EMAIL** emancke@uakron.edu

MANDAVILLE, JON ELLIOTT
PERSONAL Born 10/09/1937, Inglewood, CA, m, 1997, 3 children **DISCIPLINE** MIDDLE EAST HISTORY, ISLAMIC STUDIES **EDUCATION** Dartmouth Col, BA, 59; Univ Edinburgh, dipl Islamic studies, 61; Princeton Univ, MA, 64, PhD(Orient studies), 69. **CAREER** Asst prof, 65-69, assoc prof, 69-79, co-dir, Pub Hist Prog, 77-78, Prof Hist, Portland State Univ, 79-, Dir, Middle East Studies Ctr, 95-; dir, Am Inst Yemeni Studies, Yemen, 78-80. **HONORS AND AWARDS** Fulbright-Hays fac res fel, 70-71; fel, Am Res Inst, Turkey, 71; Soc Sci Res Coun res fel in Yemen, 76-. **MEMBERSHIPS** Am Orient Soc; fel Mid East Studies Asn NAm; Turkish Studies Asn. **RESEARCH** Ottoman Arab lands; Arabian Peninsula; Islamic law. **SELECTED PUBLICATIONS** Auth, Ottoman court records of Syria and Jordan, 66 & Ottoman province of al-Hasa, 70, J Am Orient Soc; Usurious piety: Cash trusts law in Ottoman Empire, Int J Mid Eastern Studies, 78; The New Historians, 80 & Yemen, 81, Aramco World. **CONTACT ADDRESS** Dept of Hist, Portland State Univ, PO Box 751, Portland, OR 97207-0751. **EMAIL** mandavillej@pdx.edu

MANESS, LONNIE E.
PERSONAL Born 07/30/1929, Henderson Co, TN, m, 1951, 2 children **DISCIPLINE** HISTORY, GOVERNMENT **EDUCATION** Univ Wis, BS, 61; Univ Wis, MS, 64; Memphis State Univ, PhD, 80. **CAREER** From Asst Prof to Prof, Univ Tenn, 68-. **HONORS AND AWARDS** Phi Kappa Phi, Phi Alpha Theta, Outstanding Teacher Awd, Univ Tenn, 84. **MEMBERSHIPS** THS, WTHS, Jackson Purchase Hist Soc, Southeastern Coun on Latin Am Studies. **RESEARCH** Nathan Bedford Forrest, Henry Emerson Etheridge. **SELECTED PUBLICATIONS** Auth, "Jefferson Davis as War Leader: The case of Fort Donelson Through the Kentucky Invasion of 1862," in The W Tenn Hist Soc Papers, vol XLIX (95); auth, "The Most Important Campaign of the American Revolution," in the Colonel Courier, vol XLII, no 3 (97); auth, "Congressman Henry Emerson Etheridge on the Slavery Question and the Kansas-Nebraska Act," in The W Tenn Hist Soc Papers (98); auth, "Alexander P Stewart," in Tenn Encycl of Hist and Cult (98); auth, "Henry Emerson Etheridge," in Tenn Encycl of Hist and Cult (98); rev, "Secessionists and Other Scoundrels: Selections from Parson Brownlow's Book," in NC Hist Rev (99); auth, "Nathan Bedford Forrest: Controversial Aspects of His Career," in J of the Jackson Purchase Hist Soc (99). **CONTACT ADDRESS** Dept Hist & Govt, Univ of Tennessee, Martin, 554 University St, Martin, TN 38238-0001. **EMAIL** lmaness@utm.edu

MANEY, PATRICK J.
PERSONAL Born 12/09/1946, Wausau, WI, m, 1970, 3 children **DISCIPLINE** HISTORY **EDUCATION** Univ of Wis, Stevens Point, BS, 69; Univ of MD, PhD, 76 **CAREER** Asst Prof, Prof, 80-98, Tulane Univ **RESEARCH** US Political Hist **SELECTED PUBLICATIONS** Auth, Young Bob La Follette: A biography of Robert M. La Follette, Jr. 1895-1953; The Roosevelt Presence: The Life and Legacy of FDR, Univ of CA Press, 98 **CONTACT ADDRESS** Dept of History, Univ of So Carolina, Columbia, Columbia, SC 29208. **EMAIL** maney@sc.edu

MANFRA, JO ANN
PERSONAL Born Schenectady, NY, m, 1980 **DISCIPLINE** AMERICAN HISTORY, LAW **EDUCATION** State Univ NYork at Cortland, BS, 63, MS, 67; Univ Iowa, PhD(hist), 75; Suffolk Univ Law Sch, JD, 77; Harvard Law Sch, LLM, 79. **CAREER** Teacher hist, Kingston High Sch, 64-66; instr Am hist, Ball State Univ, 66-67; asst prof, 72-75; Assoc Prof, 76-82; Full Prof Am Hist; Worcester Polytechnk Inst., 83-; Res fel, Nat Endowment for Humanities, summer 76, Mary Ingraham Bunting Inst, 77-79. **HONORS AND AWARDS** NAT Endowment for humanities Interpretive Research/Projects Grant, 88-90; Brinkley-Stephenson Awd, OAH, 86. **MEMBERSHIPS** Am Soc Legal Hist; Orgn Early Am Historians; Orgn Am Historians; Am Cath Studies Asn. **RESEARCH** American religious history; American social history; American legal history. **SELECTED PUBLICATIONS** Coed, "Law and Bioethics: Text with Commentary on Major U.S. Court Decisions," New York: Paulist Press, 82; auth, "The Politics of Ultimate Ends," in An American Church," ed. David J. Alvarez Moraga, California: St. Mary's College Press, 79, pp. 43-52; auth, "Serial Marriage and the Origins of the Black Stepfamily: The Rowanty Evidence, " Journal of American History, 72, June 85: 18-44; auth, "An Emendation on the Church-State Problematic: The French Connection, in The Lively Experiment Continued," ed. Jerald C. Brauer, Macon, Georgia: Mercer University Press, 87, pp. 185-202; auth, "The Selection of the American Catholic Hierarchy, 1789-1851," Mid-America, 76, Winter 94: 27-52; auth, "Hometown Politics and the American Protective Association, 1887-1890," Annals of Iowa 55, Spring 96: 138-66. **CONTACT ADDRESS** Worcester Polytech Inst, 39 Waterford Dr, Worcester, MA 01602. **EMAIL** jmanfra@wpi.edu

MANGRUM, ROBERT G.
PERSONAL Born 05/06/1948, Abilene, TX, m, 1980 **DISCIPLINE** HISTORY **EDUCATION** Hardin-Simmons Univ, BA, 70; Univ N Tex, MA, 75, PhD, 78. **CAREER** Commissioned off, Lt. Col, 70-98, US Army; chem, asst prof 78-80, Clarke Col; chemn, assoc prof, asst dir, dir, Robert D. Coley Distinguished prof, Univ hist, 80-, Howard Payne Univ. **HONORS AND AWARDS** Who's Who South Southwest, 80-98; Outstand Young Men Am, 81; Who's Who Tex, 85-86; pres, 86-87, treas, 90-92, Kiwanis Club Brownwood; Who's Who Among Am Tchrs, 94-95, 98-99; Who's Who World, 95-96, Who's Who Am Educ, 96-97; Council Member, Early City Council, 98-; grad, us army command, general staff col, 81; grad, nat de-

fense univ, 87; grad fac, ma prog, us army command, general staff col, 89-98; us military acad, post grad, workshop military history for rotc, 89. **MEMBERSHIPS** Am Hist Asn, Southern Hist Asn; Org Am Hist; Soc Military Hist; Tex State Hist Asn; Tex Oral Hist Asn; Nat Soc, Sons Am Revolution; Sons Confederate Veterans; Asn US Army; Nat Railway Hist Soc. **RESEARCH** US history; civil war; military; institutional history of Howard Payne University. **SELECTED PUBLICATIONS** Rev, Civil War History, 83-85; rev, Journal of Southern History, 85, 89, 91, 93; rev, Military Affair, 85; rev, Locus, 89; rev, American Historical Review, 94, 97. **CONTACT ADDRESS** Dept of Hist, Howard Payne Univ, 1000 Fisk Ave., HPU Station Box 831, Brownwood, TX 76801-2794. **EMAIL** rmangrum@hputx.edu

MANGUSSO, MARY C.
DISCIPLINE HISTORY **EDUCATION** TX Tech Univ, PhD, 78. **CAREER** Asst prof, Univ Alaska, Fairbanks. **RESEARCH** Alaska, recent U.S. diplomatic history. **SELECTED PUBLICATIONS** Coed, Alaskan Anthology: Interpreting the Past, Univ Wash Press, 96. **CONTACT ADDRESS** Dept of Hist, Univ of Alaska, Fairbanks, 606C Gruening, Fairbanks, AK 99775-7480. **EMAIL** ffmcm@uaf.edu

MANIKAS, WILLIAM T.
PERSONAL Born 09/24/1938, Herkimer, NY, m, 1991, 2 children **DISCIPLINE** US HISTORY, POLITICAL SCIENCE **EDUCATION** Boston Univ, BA, 63; Colgate Univ, MA, 64; Fla Atlantic Univ, EdS, 70; EdD, 74. **CAREER** Instr, Marymount Jr Col, 68-74; instr, Gaston Col, 74-. **HONORS AND AWARDS** Liberal Arts and Sci Instr of the Year, 91; Fulbright Scholar, China, 95. **MEMBERSHIPS** Blue and Gray Educ Soc; NEA; NC Assoc of Educ. **RESEARCH** Life in textile mill villages in the early 20th century. **SELECTED PUBLICATIONS** Auth, "Isolationism", Ready Ref: Ethics, Salem Pr, 93; auth, "Joyce Diane Brothers", Great Lives from History: Am Women, Salem Pr, 94; auth, "Brown v Board of Education, 1954", Latino Encycl, Salem Pr, 94; auth, "Everson v Board of Education", Ready Ref: Am Justice, Salem Pr, 95; auth, "Jewish Women", Ready Ref: Women's Issues, Salem Pr, 95; auth, "Lobbying and Lobbyists", Encycl of Contemp Soc Issues, Salem Pr, 95; auth, "Raleigh's Attempts at Colonization in the New World, 1584-1591", Great Events from Hist: N Am, Salem Pr, 95; auth, "Swann v Charlotte-Mecklenburg Board of Educ, 1971", Encycl of Mod Soc Issues, Salem Pr, 95; auth, "Nullification Controversy, 1832-1833", Great Events from Hist: N Am, Salem Pr, 95; auth, "Garibaldi's Thousand Read Shirts Land in Italy, 1860-1865", Great Events from Hist: Europ Series, Salem Pr, 96. **CONTACT ADDRESS** Dept Soc Sci, Gaston Col, 201 Highway 321 S, Dallas, NC 28034-1402. **EMAIL** manikas.bill@gaston.cc.nc.us

MANLEY, JAMES
PERSONAL Born 07/19/1967, Naperville, IL, m, 2000, 1 child **DISCIPLINE** HISTORY **EDUCATION** Univ W Fla, BA, 89; MA, 91; Univ Fla, PhD, 99. **CAREER** Adj Instructor, Central Fla Community Col, 95-; Adj Asst Prof, Santa Fe Cmty Col, 95-. **MEMBERSHIPS** Conf on Faith and Hist. **RESEARCH** Religion in the American South. **CONTACT ADDRESS** Dept Soc Sci & Humanities, Central Florida Comm Col, 3001 SW Col Rd, Ocala, FL 34474-4415. **EMAIL** afn22345@afn.org

MANN, ARTHUR
PERSONAL Born 01/03/1922, New York, NY, m, 1943, 2 children **DISCIPLINE** HISTORY **EDUCATION** Brooklyn Col, BA, 44; Harvard Univ, MA, 47, PhD, 52. **CAREER** Instr Fr, US Army Port of Embarkation Sch, Le Havre, 45; tutor hist, Brooklyn Col, 46; from instr to asst prof, Mass Inst Technol, 48-55; from asst prof to prof, Smith Col, 55-66; prof, 66-70, PRESTON AND STERLING MORTON PROF AM HIST, UNIV CHICAGO, 70-, Lectr, Columbia Univ, 56, Salzburg Sem Am Studies, 58, Univ Mich, 61, Univ Wyo, 62, Williams Col, 63, Harvard Univ, 65 and US State Dept, Venezuela, 70; Soc Sci Res Coun grant-in-aid, 59; Am Coun Learned Soc fel, 63; adv, Am Hist Ser, McGraw-Hill Films, 67-73; educ collab, Minorities Ser, Coronet Instruct Films, 69-73; adv-ed Am hist, Univ Chicago Press, 69-; panelist, Nat Endowment for Humanities, 72; Fulbright-Hays sr scholar, Univ Sydney, 74; co-adv, Oral Hist Proj of Holocaust Survivors, Am Jewish Comt's William E Wiener Oral Hist Libr, 74-76; lectr, USIA, Fiji, Indonesia, Malaysia, NZ, and Singapore, 74, Portugal, Ger, Yugoslavia and Rumania, 76, Hong Kong and Japan, 79. **MEMBERSHIPS** AHA; Orgn Am Historians; fel Soc Am Hist. **RESEARCH** American history. **SELECTED PUBLICATIONS** Auth, an Unknown Detail of Handel Biog, Bach, Vol 0025, 94; The 'Lions of Change', Stand Mag, Vol 0038, 97. **CONTACT ADDRESS** 4919 S. Woodlawn Ave., Chicago, IL 60615.

MANN, KRISTIN
DISCIPLINE HISTORY **EDUCATION** Stanford Univ, BA, 68, MA, 70, PhD, 77. **CAREER** Assoc prof **RESEARCH** 18th through 20th-century African social and economic history; history of marriage and the family; history of slavery, emancipation, and the slave trade; history of colonial political and legal changes; history of West African commercial and agricultural transformations. **SELECTED PUBLICATIONS** Auth, Marrying Well: Marriage, Status and Social Change among the Educated Elite in Colonial Lagos; co-ed, Law in Colonial Africa. **CONTACT ADDRESS** Dept History, Emory Univ, 221 Bowden Hall, 561 Kilgo Cir, Atlanta, GA 30322-1950. **EMAIL** kmann@socsci.ss.emory.edu

MANN, RALPH
DISCIPLINE HISTORY **EDUCATION** Duke Univ, BA, 65; Stanford Univ, MA, 66; PhD, 70. **CAREER** Prof, Univ Colo, 92-. **SELECTED PUBLICATIONS** Auth, After the Gold Rush: Society in Grass Valley and Nevada City, California, 1849-1870, Stanford, 82; Mountain Settlement: Appalachian and National Modes of Migration, J Appalachian Studies, 96; Diversity in the Antebellum Appalachian South: Four Farm Communities in Tazewell County, Virginia, Univ NC, 95. **CONTACT ADDRESS** History Dept, Univ of Colorado, Boulder, Boulder, CO 80309. **EMAIL** ralph.mann@colorado.edu

MANN, WILLIAM EDWARD
PERSONAL Born 05/06/1940, Los Angeles, CA, m, 1966, 2 children **DISCIPLINE** HISTORY OF PHILOSOPHY, PHILOSOPHY OF RELIGION **EDUCATION** Stanford Univ, BA, 62; MA, 64; Univ Minn, Minneapolis, PhD(Philos), 71. **CAREER** From instr to asst prof Philos, St Olaf Col, 67-72; asst prof, Ill State Univ, 72-74; assoc prof, 74-80, prof Philos, Univ VT, 80-; chmn dept, 80-91. **HONORS AND AWARDS** 1971 Dissertation Essay Competition, The Rev of Metaphys, 72. **MEMBERSHIPS** Am Philos Asn, div sec-treas, 94-; Soc Medieval Renaissance Philos. **RESEARCH** Philosophical theology; medieval philosophy, ancient philosophy. **SELECTED PUBLICATIONS** Auth, "The Best of All Possible Worlds," in Being and Goodness: The Concept of the Good in Metaphysics and Philosophical Theology, ed. Scott MacDonald (Ithaca, NY, Cornell Univ Press, 91), 250-277; auth, "Jephthah's Plight: Moral Dilemmas and Theism," Philosophical Perspectives 5 (91): 617-647; auth, "Duns Scotus, Demonstration, and Doctrine," Faith and Philosophy 9 (92): 436-462; auth, "Hope," in Reasoned Faith: Essays in Philosophical Theology in Honor of Norman Kretzmann, ed. Eleonore Stump (Ithaca, NY, Cornell University Press, 93), 251-280; auth, "Piety: Lending a Hand to Euthyphro," Philosophy and Phenomenological Research 58 (98): 123-142; auth, "Perplexity and Mystery," Metaphilosophy 29 (98): 209-222; auth, "Inner-Life Ethics," in The Augustinian Tradition, ed. Gareth B. Matthews (Berkeley, Univ of Calif Press, 99), 140-165; auth, "Believing Where We Cannot Prove: Duns Scotus on the Necessity of Supernatural Belief," in The Proceedings of the Twentieth World Congress of Philosophy: Volume 4: Philosophies of Religion, Art, and Creativity, ed. Kevin L. Stoehr (Bowling Green State Univ, Philosphy Documentation Center, 99), 58-68; auth, "Augustine on Evil and Original Sin," in The Cambridge Companion to Augustine, ed. Norman Kretzmann and Eleonore Stump (Cambridge, Cambridge Univ Press, forthcoming); auth, "Duns Scotus on Natural and Supernatural Knowledge of God," in The Cambridge Companion to Duns Scotus (Cambridge, Cambridge Univ Press, forthcoming). **CONTACT ADDRESS** Dept of Philosophy, Univ of Vermont, 70 S Williams St, Burlington, VT 05401-3404. **EMAIL** wmann@zoo.uvm.edu

MANNING, PATRICK
PERSONAL Born 06/10/1941, Orange, CA, m, 2 children **DISCIPLINE** HISTORY **EDUCATION** Cal Inst Tech, BS, 63; Univ Wis, Madison, MS, 66; MS, 67; PhD, 69. **CAREER** Vis asst prof, Stanford Univ; instr, Canada Col, 68-82; lectr, Bryn Mawr, 82-84; asst prof, 84-87; assoc prof, 87-89; prof, 89-99; prof, AASE, 99-, Northeastern Univ. **HONORS AND AWARDS** Guggenheim Fel; Dist Prof, CAS. **MEMBERSHIPS** ASA; AHA; WHA. **RESEARCH** Africa (economic, social, and demographic history); world history; global historiography. **SELECTED PUBLICATIONS** Auth, "Migrations from Africa to the Americas: Impact on Africans and on the Americas," Hist Teacher 26 (93): 279-96; auth, "History in the Era of Theory, Methodology, and Multiculturalism: New Configurations for the Discipline," in Gateways to Knowledge: The Role of Academic Libraries in Teaching Learning and Research, ed. Lawrence Dowler (Cambridge: MIT Press, 96), 19-34; auth, "The Problem of Interactions in World History," American Hist Rev 101 (96), 771-82; auth, "The Advantages and Limitations of Simulation in Analyzing the Slave Trade," in Source Material for Studying the Slave Trade and the African Diaspora, ed. Robin Law (Centre of Commonwealth Studies, Univ of Stirling, 97), 69-78; auth, "La traite negnere et l'evolution demographique de l'Afrique," in La chaine et le lien: Une vision de la traite negnere, ed. Doudou Diene (Paris: UNESCO, 98), 153-73; auth, "Pedagogy and Historiography in the Migration CD-ROM," Hist Teacher 32 (99), 329-43; auth, Migration in Modern World History CD-ROM, Wadsworth, 00; auth, Francophone Sub-Saharan Africa 1880-1995, 2nd ed, Cambridge U Press, 98; auth, Slave Trades. 1500-1800: Globalization of Forced Labor, Variorum, 96. **CONTACT ADDRESS** World History Center, Northeastern Univ, 270 Holmes Hall, Boston, MA 02115.

MANNING, ROBERTA THOMPSON
PERSONAL Born 01/24/1940, Austin, TX, m, 1964, 2 children **DISCIPLINE** RUSSIAN-SOVIET HISTORY **EDUCATION** Rice Univ, BA, 62; Columbia Univ, MA, 67, PhD(hist), 75. **CAREER** Asst prof, 75-81, assoc prof hist, Boston Col, 83-; actg asst prof hist, Univ Calif, San Diego, 75; mem, Nat Seminar in the Hist of Russian Soc in the Twentieth Century, 81-. **HONORS AND AWARDS** Herbert Baxter Adams Prize of the Am Historical Asn, 83; NEH Collaborative Projects Grant, 97; Guggenheim fel, 89. **MEMBERSHIPS** Nat Hist Soc; Am Asn Advan Slavid Studies. **RESEARCH** Russian-Soviet history, 1861 to the present; Stalin's Terror; Soviet politics and society, 1920s and 1930s; agrarian history. **SELECTED PUBLICATIONS** Auth, The Crisis of the Old Order in Russia: Gentry and Government, Princeton Univ Press, 82; auth, "Women in the Soviet Countryside on the Eve of World War II, 1835-1940," in Russian Peasant Women, ed. Beatrice Farnsworth and Lynne Viola (NYork, Oxford Univ Press, 92), 206-235; auth, Stalinist Terror: New Perspectives, Cambridge Univ Press, 93; coauth, How the Enclosed Farmers were Resettled," Byloe 5 (70) (97); coauth, "Kak sovetskaia vlast likvidirovala khutorskie khoiaistvo," Nauka I zhizn 4 (97): 48-53; auth, Belyi County, 1937, Smolensk State Pedagogical Univ Press (Smolensk, Russia), 98; auth, "Sel'skokhoziaistvennyi krizis 1931-1933 v svete zernovykh krizisov," Otvet R. W. Davies I S.G. Wheatcroft (98): 109-112; coed, The Tragedy of the Soviet Village: Collectivization and Dekulakization: Documents and Materials in Five Volumes, 1927-1939, 99-01; auth, "Maasovaia operatsii NKVD protiv 'kulakov' I prestupnikh elementakh: apogei Velikoi Chistki v Smolenshchine," Stalinism v rossiiskoi provintsii: smolenskie dokumenty v prochetenii zaruzhvnykh I rossiiskikh istorikov (99): 230-254; auth, "The Rise and Fall of the Extraordinary Measures, January-June, 1928: Towards a Reassessment of Onset of the Stalin Revolution," The Carl Beck Papers in Russian and East European Studies 1503 (00). **CONTACT ADDRESS** Boston Col, Chestnut Hill, Chesnut Hill, MA 02167. **EMAIL** manning@bc.edu

MANNING, ROGER B.
PERSONAL Born 01/23/1932, Washington, DC, m, 1961, 2 children **DISCIPLINE** MODERN BRITISH AND IRISH HISTORY **EDUCATION** Georgetown Univ, BS, 54, MA, 59, PhD, 61. **CAREER** From instr to asst prof hist, Ohio State Univ, 60-66; from asst prof to assoc prof, 66-73, chmn dept, 74-79, Prof Hist, Cleveland State Univ, 73-; Vis lectr, Case Western Reserve Univ, 65 and 67, vis prof, 74. **HONORS AND AWARDS** Harlaxton Prize, Albion and Univ Evansville, Ind, 74. **MEMBERSHIPS** Conf Brit Studies; Conf 16th Century Studies; fel Royal Hist Soc; AHA. **RESEARCH** Early-Modern Britain; Reformation Europe; 20th-century Great Britain. **SELECTED PUBLICATIONS** Auth, Religion and Society in Elizabethan Sussex, Leiciester Univ Press, 69; auth, "The Spread of the Popular Reformation in England," Sixteenth-Century Essays and Studies 1 (70); auth, "The Crisis of Episcopal Authority during the Reign of Elizabeth I," J of Brit Studies 11 (71); auth, "The Making of a Protestant Aristocracy: The Ecclesiastical Commissioners of the diocese of Chester," Bulletin of the Inst of Hist Res 49 (76); auth, "Violence and Social Conflict in Mid-Tudor Rebellious," J of Brit Studies 16 (77); auth, "The Origins of the Doctrine of Sedition," Albion 12 (80); auth, The Prosecution of Sui Michael Blount Lieutenant of the Tower of London, 1595," Bulletin of the Inst of Hist Res 62 (84); auth, Village Revolts: Social Protest and Popular Disturbances in England 1509-1640, Oxford Univ Press, 88; auth, "Antiquarianism over the Seignewrial Reaction: Sir Robert and Sir Thomas Cotton and their Tenants," Hist Res 63 (90); auth, Hunters and Poachers: A Cultural and Social History of Unlawful Hunting in England, 1485-1640, Oxford Univ Pr, 93; coauth, The English Heritage, 2 vols (Arlington Hts, IL), 99; auth, "Poaching as a Symbolic Substitute for War in Tudor and Early Stuart England," J of Medieval and Renaissance Studies 22.2 (92). **CONTACT ADDRESS** Dept of History, Cleveland State Univ, Cleveland, OH 44115.

MARABLE, MANNING
DISCIPLINE UNITED STATES HISTORY **EDUCATION** Earlham Univ, BA, 71; Md Univ, PhD, 76. **CAREER** Prof. **RESEARCH** African American history. **SELECTED PUBLICATIONS** Auth, Black Liberation in Conservative America, 97; Speaking Truth to Power: Essays on Race, Radicalism and Resistance, 96; Beyond Black and White, 95; The Crisis of Color and Democracy, 92; Race, Reform, and Rebellion: The Second Reconstruction in Black America 1945-1990, 91. **CONTACT ADDRESS** Dept of History, Columbia Col, New York, 2960 Broadway, New York, NY 10027-6902.

MARCELLO, RONALD E.
PERSONAL Born 12/31/1939, Wrightsville, PA **DISCIPLINE** HISTORY **EDUCATION** Millersville State Col, BS, 61; Duke Univ, MA, 65, PhD, 69. **CAREER** From asst prof to prof, 67- , coordr, Oral Hist Prog, 67-, North Tex State Univ. **HONORS AND AWARDS** H. Bailey Carroll Awd, 92, Tex State Hist Asn; univ scholar, 64-65, 66-67, southern res fel, 65-66, duke univ. **MEMBERSHIPS** Oral Hist Asn; Tex Oral Hist Asn; Tex State Hist Asn. **RESEARCH** New Deal; WW II. **SELECTED PUBLICATIONS** Coauth, With Only the Will to Live: Accounts of Americans in Japanese Prison Camps, 94; coauth, Building The Death Railway: The Ordeal of American Prisoners in Burma, 92; coauth, Remembing Pearl Harbor Eyewitnes Accounts by US Military Men and Women, 91; auth, art, Lone Star POWs: Texas National Guardsmen and the Building of the Burma-Thailand Railroad, 1942-1945, 92; auth, art,

Reluctance Versus Reality: The Desegregation of North Texas State College, 1954-1956, 96. **CONTACT ADDRESS** Univ of No Texas, Box 311214, Denton, TX 76203. **EMAIL** marcello@unt.edu

MARCHIONE, MARGHERITA FRANCES

PERSONAL Born 02/19/1922, Little Ferry, NJ **DISCIPLINE** ITALIAN, AMERICAN HISTORY **EDUCATION** Georgian Court Col, AB, 43; Columbia Univ, AM, 49, PhD(Ital), 60. **CAREER** Teacher parochial & private high schs, 43-54; instr lang, Villa Walsh Col, 54-67; assoc prof, 67-77, chmn dept lang, 67-68, Prof Ital, Fairleigh Dickinson Univ, Florham-Madison Campus, 77-, Res grants, Fairleigh Dickinson Univ, 68-69, 71-82; NDEA grant Ital inst undergrad, US Off Educ, 68; consult & rep, Gallery Mod Art, 68, 69; dir Ital Inst, Univ Salerno, 72, Tivoli, 73, Rome, 74; mem exec coun, Am Ital Hist Asn, 77-79; mem adv bd, NJ Cath Hist Rec Comn, 77-; NJ Hist Comn, 78-; Nat Hist Publ & Records Comn, 78, 79, 80 & 81; Nat Endowment for Humanities grant, 80-83. **HONORS AND AWARDS** Am-Ital Achievement Award in Educ, 71; UNICO Nat Rizzuto Award, 77; Star of Solidarity of Ital Repub, Pres Italy, 77. **MEMBERSHIPS** Am Asn Teachers Ital; MLA; Am Coun Teaching Foreign Lang; Am Inst Ital Studies (pres, 77-80); Am Ital Hist Asn. **RESEARCH** Contemporary Italian Culture and lit; Dante; the papers of Philip Mazzei. **SELECTED PUBLICATIONS** Auth, A Pitcorial History of St. Lucy Filippini Chapel, Edizioni del Palazzo, Prato, (92): 130; auth, Legacy and Misison: Religious Teachers Filippini, Villa Walsh, Morristown, NJ, (92): 50; auth, Philip Mazzei: World Citizen (Jefferson's "Zealous Whig"), Univ Press of Am, Lanham, MD, (94): 158; auth, Yours is a Presicous Witness (Memoirs of Jews and Catholics in Wartime Italy), Paulist Press, Mahwah, NJ, (96): 300; auth, Yours Is a Precious Witness: Memoirs of Jews and Catholics in Wartime Italy, 97; auth, Pio XII e gli ebrei, Editoriale Pantheon, Rome, (99): 288; auth, Pope Pius XII: Architect for Peace, 00; auth, Pope Pius XII: Architect for Peace, Paulist Pres, Mahwah, NJ, (00): 350; auth, Pio XII: Architetto di pace, Editoriale Pantheon, Rome, (00): 413; auth, Carteggio Giovanni Abbo-Giuseppe Prezzolini, Edizioni di Storia e Letteratura, Rome, (00): 233. **CONTACT ADDRESS** Col of Arts & Sci Fairleigh, Fairleigh Dickinson Univ, Florham-Madison, Madison, NJ 07940.

MARCOPOULOS, GEORGE JOHN

PERSONAL Born 06/30/1931, Salem, MA **DISCIPLINE** BALKAN & BYZANTINE HISTORY **EDUCATION** Bowdoin Col, AB, 53; Harvard Univ, AM, 55, PhD, 66. **CAREER** From instr to asst prof, 61-71, Assoc Prof Hist, Tufts Univ, 71-92; prof hist, Tufts Univ, 92. **HONORS AND AWARDS** Seymour O. Simcues Awd for Distinguished Tchg Advising, 97. **MEMBERSHIPS** AHA; New Eng Hist Asn. **RESEARCH** The reign of Greece's King George I, 1863-1913; 19th and 20th century Europ royalty and monarchic institutions. **SELECTED PUBLICATIONS** Auth, King George I and the expansion of Greece, 1875-1881, 6/68 & The selection of Prince George of Greece as High Commissioner in Crete, 69, Balkan Studies; Cyprus and Greece, In: Americana Annual, Grolier, 00; Capodistrias, Ioannes Antoniou, Vol V, 606-607, Chios, Vol VI, 601-602, Constantine I, King of the Hellenes, Vol VII, 651 & Iraklion, Vol XV, 367, Marco Dozzaris, Vol IV, p394, Cephalonia, vol VI, p192, Constantine II King of the Hellenes, vol VIII, p651, Corfu, vol VII, p791, The Encyclopedia Americana. **CONTACT ADDRESS** Dept of Hist, Tufts Univ, Medford, East Hall, Medford, MA 02155-5555. **EMAIL** gmarcopo@emerald.tufts.edu

MARCUS, ALAN I.

PERSONAL Born 08/15/1949, Red Bank, NJ, m, 1971, 2 children **DISCIPLINE** HISTORY **EDUCATION** Univ Wis, BA, 72; Univ Cincinnati, MA, 75; PhD, 79. **CAREER** Adj Asst Prof, Univ Cincinnati, 79-80; From Asst Prof to Prof, Iowa St Univ, 80-. **HONORS AND AWARDS** GTE Found Lectureship Prog Grant, 85-86; USDA Publ Grant, 88-90; Outstanding Acad Book of the Year Awd, 90; Nat Sci Found Res Grant, 91; NEH Sr Fel, 92; NEH Grant, 94. **MEMBERSHIPS** AHS, AAHM, HSS, OAH, SHT. **RESEARCH** Historical studies of technology and science, environmental considerations, health care, agriculture in historical perspective. **SELECTED PUBLICATIONS** Auth, "From Individual Practitioner to Regular Physician: Cincinnati Medical Societies and the Problem of Definition Among Mid-Nineteenth Century Americans," in Tech Knowledge in Am Cult: Sci, Tech and Med in Am Since the Early 1800s (Birmingham: Univ Ala Pr, 96), 55-70; auth, "Sweets for the Sweet: Saccharin, Knowledge and the Contemporary Regulatory Nexus," J of Policy Hist (96): 33-47; co-ed, Technical Knowledge in American Culture: Science, Technology and Medicine in America Since the Early 1800s, Univ Ala Pr (Birmingham, AL), 96; co-ed, Health Care Policy in Contemporary America, Pa St UP (College Park), 97; auth, Building Western Civilization from the Advent of Writing to the Age of Steam, Harcourt Brace and Co, 98; auth, Technology in America: A Brief History, 2nd Ed rev and expanded, Harcourt Brace and Co, 99; auth, "Nineteenth Century American Technology and Science: Studying Premodern Subjects in a Postmodern World," in Blackwell's Companion to Nineteenth Century Am (Blackwell Publ, 99); auth, "The Medieval Image in the Modern Mind: History and Turn-of-the-Century American Municipal Government," in Making Sense Out of the Urban Environ: Local Govt, Civic Cult and Community Life in Am Cities (Columbus: Ohio St UP, 00). **CONTACT ADDRESS** Dept Hist, Iowa St Univ, 1 Iowa State University, 635 Ross Hall, Ames, IA 50011-2010. **EMAIL** aimarcus@iastate.edu

MARCUS, HAROLD G.

PERSONAL Born 04/08/1936, Worcester, MA, 1 child **DISCIPLINE** AFRICAN HISTORY **EDUCATION** Clark Univ, BA, 58; Boston Univ, MA, 59, PhD, 64. **CAREER** Asst prof history, Addis Ababa Univ, 61-63; asst prof African hist, Howard Univ, 63-68; assoc prof, 68-75, prof history and African studies, 74-, assoc ch dir grad studies, dept history, 88-92; dist prof hist & African studies, 94-, Mich State Univ, 75-, vis asst prof hist, Johns Hopkins Univ, 68; Hoover Inst res award bibliog, 66-67; Smithsonian Inst res award bibliog, 67-68; Soc Sci Res Coun res grant, Ethiopia, 68-69; NDEA Area Ctr fac res grant, Ethiopia, 69-70; Soc Sci Res Coun fel, 76; vis prof African history, Univ Khartoum. 81; Fulbright-Hays, 81-82; NEH Fel Univ Tchr, 92-93; vis distinguished prof comp history, Osaka Gaidai Univ, 97; Fulbright-Hays grant, 98. **HONORS AND AWARDS** Mich State Univ Completion Grant, 82; Soc Sci Res Coun, 82 & 85; Am Philos Soc, 85; Nat Hum Ctr, 85-86; USIS Travel Grant, 87; CICALS Travel Grant, 90; USIA grants for 12th Int Conf Ethiopian Stud, 94; Rockafeller Grant res Ethiopia, 96. **MEMBERSHIPS** African Studies Asn; AHA. **RESEARCH** Ethiopian history from 1850 to present, particularly the reigns of Menilek II, 1889-1913, and Haile Sellassie I, regent, 1916-1928, king, 1928-30, emperor, 1930-1974, died, 1975; Africa, Sudan, Somaliland; colonial & national records. **SELECTED PUBLICATIONS** Auth, A History of Ethiopia, Univ Calif Press, 94; ed, Haile Sellassie, My Life and Ethiopia's Progress, Mich State Univ Press, 94; General Mohammed Farah Aidid and Ethiopia, Ethiopia Rev, 94; Haile Sellassie's Development Policies and Views 1916-1960, Etudes ethiopiennes, 94; Haile Selassie's Leadership, New Trends in Ethiopian Studies, 94; Papers of the 12th International Conference of Ethiopian Studies, Red Sea Press, 94; The Loss of Erutrea as a Consequence of Ethiopia's Victory at Adwa, Ethiopian Regist, 96. **CONTACT ADDRESS** Dept of History, Michigan State Univ, 319 Morrill Hall, East Lansing, MI 48824-1036. **EMAIL** ethiopia@hs1.hst.msu.edu

MARCUS, IRWIN MURRAY

PERSONAL Born 11/19/1935, New York, NY **DISCIPLINE** MODERN UNITED STATES HISTORY **EDUCATION** Pa State Univ, BS, 58; Lehigh Univ, MA, 59, PhD(hist), 65. **CAREER** Asst prof hist, Harrisburg Area Community Col, 64-65; assoc prof, 65-68, PROF HIST, INDIANA UNIV PA, 68-. **MEMBERSHIPS** Middle Atlantic Racial Historians Asn. **RESEARCH** History of the American labor movement; history of Black America; history of American radicalism. **SELECTED PUBLICATIONS** Auth, Hubert Harrison: Negro advocate, 1/71 & Benjamin Fletcher: Black labor leader, 10/72, Negro Hist Bull; Labor discontent in Tioga County, Pennsylvania, 1865-1905: the Gutman thesis, a test case, Labor Hist, summer 73. **CONTACT ADDRESS** Dept of Hist, Indiana Univ of Pennsylvania, Indiana, PA 15701.

MARCUS, MILICENT

DISCIPLINE ITALIAN STUDIES **EDUCATION** Cornell, BA, 68; Yale Univ, PhD, 74. **CAREER** Asst prof to prof, Univ Tx, 73-98; PROF, UNIV PA, 98-. **HONORS AND AWARDS** Phi Beta Kappa; Guggenheim fel; Getty grant; Fulbright fel; Marcus DiVito chair, Italian stud. **MEMBERSHIPS** MLA; AATI; AAIS; Am Boccaccio Asn. **RESEARCH** Medieval and mod Italian lit, Italian cinema. **SELECTED PUBLICATIONS** Auth, Filmmaking by the Book: Italian Cinema and Literary Adaptation, Johns Hopkins Univ Press, 93; auth, Italian Film in the Light of Neorealism, Princeton Univ Press, 86; auth, An Allegory of Form: Literary Self-Consciousness in the Decameron, in Stanford French and Italian Studies, 18, 79; auth, Liberating the Garden: Eden and the Fall from Paisa to Mediterraneo, in Italy and America, 1943-44, La Citta del Sole, 97; auth, I misteriosi fegatelli di Ginger e Fred Mystfest 1997, Mondadori, 97. **CONTACT ADDRESS** Dept of Romance Langs, Univ of Pennsylvania, Philadelphia, PA 19104. **EMAIL** mjmarcus@sas.upenn.edu

MARDER, TOD A.

DISCIPLINE RENAISSANCE-MODERN ARCHITECTURE **EDUCATION** Columbia Univ, PhD. **CAREER** Prof, Rutgers, The State Univ NJ, Univ Col-Camden. **RESEARCH** Bernini's architecture; urban planning in Rome;classical traditions in architecture. **SELECTED PUBLICATIONS** Auth, Alexander VII, Bernini and the Urban Setting of the Pantheon, J of the Soc of Architectural Historians, Sept 91; Bernini's Commission for the Equestian Statue of Constantine in St. Peter's, in An Architectural Progress in the Renaissance and Baroque, eds Henry A. Millon and Susan S. Munshowe, Papers in Art Hist from the Pa State Univ, VIII, 92; Sisto V e la fontana del Mose (Sixtus V and the Fountain of Moses), in Sisto V. Roma e Lazio, eds Marcello Fagiolo and Maria Luisa Madonna, 92; Review of Manfredo Tafuri, Ricerca del rinascimento: Principi, citta, archtetti, Art Bull, Mar 95; Gianlorenzo Bernini's Scala Regia and the Equestrian Statue of Constantine, Cambridge UP, 97. **CONTACT ADDRESS** Dept of Art Hist, Rutgers, The State Univ of New Jersey, New Brunswick, Voorhees Hall, 71 Hamilton St, New Brunswick, NJ 08903. **EMAIL** marder@rci.rutgers.edu

MARDIN, SERIF

DISCIPLINE INTERNATIONAL STUDIES **EDUCATION** Stanford Univ, BA, Johns Hopkins Sch Adv Int Studies, MA; Stanford Univ, PhD. **CAREER** Prof, Am Univ; Vis Prof, Columbia; Vis Prof, Princeton; Vis Prof, UCLA. **HONORS AND AWARDS** Islamic Chair, Am Univ. **RESEARCH** Middle East. **SELECTED PUBLICATIONS** Auth, Religion and Social Change in Modern Turkey, State Univ NY Press, 89. **CONTACT ADDRESS** American Univ, 4400 Massachusetts Ave, Washington, DC 20016.

MARGERISON, KENNETH

PERSONAL Born 03/22/1946, Philadelphia, PA, m, 1967, 1 child **DISCIPLINE** HISTORY **EDUCATION** Univ of NC, BA, 67; Duke Univ, MA, 69, PhD, 73 **CAREER** Inst, 69-72, Sacred Heart Col; Inst, 72-73, Asst Prof, 73-83, Assoc Prof, 83-87, Prof, 87-, SW TX St Univ **MEMBERSHIPS** Am Hist Asn; French Historical Studies. **RESEARCH** Political pamphlets and public opinion during French Revolution **SELECTED PUBLICATIONS** Auth, P.-L. Roederer: Political Thought and Practice During the French Revolution, The American Philosophical Society, 83; Pamphlets and Public Opinion: The Campaign for a Union of Orders in the Early French Revolution, Purdue Univ Press, 98 **CONTACT ADDRESS** Dept of History, Southwest Texas State Univ, San Marcos, TX 78666. **EMAIL** km04@swt.edu

MARGOLIN, VICTOR

PERSONAL Born 06/03/1941, New York, NY, m, 1975, 1 child **DISCIPLINE** ART HISTORY **EDUCATION** Union Inst, PhD. **CAREER** Assoc prof, Univ IL at Chicago. **HONORS AND AWARDS** Fulbright Fellowship, 63-64. **RESEARCH** Design hist; theories of mod and contemp art and soc. **SELECTED PUBLICATIONS** Ed, Design Discourse: History, Thought, Criticism; co-ed, Discovering Design: Explorations in Design Studies. **CONTACT ADDRESS** Art Hist Dept, Univ of Illinois, Chicago, 935 W Harrison St., Chicago, IL 60607-7039. **EMAIL** victor@uic.edu

MARINA, WILLIAM F.

DISCIPLINE HISTORY **EDUCATION** Univ Denver, PhD. **CAREER** Prof. **RESEARCH** Modern American history; business history; Florida history; evolution of civilizations; international relations; Southeast Asia history. **SELECTED PUBLICATIONS** Co-auth, American Statesman on Slavery and the Negro; A History of Florida; ed, News of the Nation. **CONTACT ADDRESS** History Dept, Florida Atlantic Univ, 777 Glades Rd, Boca Raton, FL 33431.

MARINO, JOHN ANTHONY

PERSONAL Born 05/18/1946, Chicago, IL, m, 2 children **DISCIPLINE** EARLY MODERN EUROPEAN HISTORY **EDUCATION** Univ Chicago, BA, 68, MA, 70, PhD(hist), 77. **CAREER** Instr humanities, Kennedy-King Col, 73-74; vis asst prof hist, Fla Int Univ, 76-77; asst prof hist, Univ Calif, San Diego, 78-86; assc prof, 86-; Fulbright, 74-75; Fel, Fondazione Luigi Einaudi, 77-79; Newberry Library Exxon fel, 85-86; Newberry Lib/NEH, 92-93. **MEMBERSHIPS** Am Hist Asn; Econ Hist Asn; Renaissance Soc Am; Sixteenth Century Studies Conference. **RESEARCH** Italian history; economic history. **SELECTED PUBLICATIONS** Auth, La Crisi di Venezia e la New Economic History, Studi Storici, 78; Professazione Voluntaria e Pecore in Aerea: Ragione Economica e Meccanismi de Mercato Nella Dogana de Foggia del Secolo Sedicesimo, Rivista Storica Italiana, 82; Economic Idylls and Pastoral Realities: The Trickster Economy in the Kingdom of Naples, Comparative Studies in Soc & Hist, 82; Pastoral Economics in the Kingdom of Naples, John Hopkins, 88. **CONTACT ADDRESS** Dept of Hist, 0104, Univ of California, San Diego, 9500 Gilman Dr, La Jolla, CA 92093-0104. **EMAIL** jmarino@ucsd.edu

MARKEL, STEPHEN

PERSONAL Born 04/30/1954, Pittsburgh, PA, s **DISCIPLINE** ASIAN ART HISTORY AND MUSEUM PRACTICE **EDUCATION** Univ Fla, BA, 76; Univ Mich, MA, 80, PhD, 89. **CAREER** Cur asst grad intern, asst cur, assoc cur, Los Angeles County Mus Art, 83-98; cur and dept head, South and Southeast Asian Art, 98- . **MEMBERSHIPS** Am Coun for Southern Asian Art; Asoc for Asian Studies. **RESEARCH** Art of India, especially Hindu Sculpture and Mughal Decorative Arts. **SELECTED PUBLICATIONS** Auth, Origins of the Indian Planetary Deities, Studies in Asian Thought and Religion, 95; auth, A Jaipur Ragamala in the [University of Michigan] Museum of Art, Bull of The Univ of Mich Mus of Art and Archael, 95; auth, Unpublished Ragmala in the Michigan Museum of Art, Roopankan: Recent Studies in Indian Pictorial Heritage, 95; auth, The Use of Flora and Fauna Imagery in Mughal Decorative Arts, Flora and Fauna in Mughal Art, forthcoming; ed, Chachati: Professor Walter M. Spink Felicitation Volume, Ars Orientalis, Univ of Mich, Supplement 1, 00; A New Masterwork by Mir Kalan Khan, New Discoveries in Indian Art: Essays in Honor of Anand Krishna, forthcoming. **CONTACT ADDRESS** South and Southeast Asian Art, Los Angeles County Museum of Art, 5905 Wilshire Blvd, Los Angeles, CA 90036. **EMAIL** smarkel@lacma.org

MARKS, ARTHUR S.
DISCIPLINE ART HISTORY **EDUCATION** Univ London, PhD. **CAREER** Prof, Univ NC, Chapel Hill. **RESEARCH** Am and Brit art and archit; mod archit. **SELECTED PUBLICATIONS** Articles and essays in var jour, including Am Art J, Apollo, Burlington Mag, Art Quart, J of the Warburg and Courtauld Inst, and exhibition catalogs. **CONTACT ADDRESS** Dept of Art Hist, Univ of No Carolina, Chapel Hill, Chapel Hill, NC 27599. **EMAIL** amarks@email.unc.edu

MARKS, ELAINE
PERSONAL Born 11/13/1930, New York, NY, d **DISCIPLINE** FRENCH STUDIES **EDUCATION** Bryn Mawr Col, AB(magna cum laude with Honors in French), 52; Univ PA, MA, 53; New York Univ, PhD, 58. **CAREER** Graduate asst, NY Univ, 54-56, instr, 57-60, asst prof, 60-62; assoc prof, Univ WI-Milwaukee, 63-65; prof, Univ MA-Amherst, 65-66; prof, Univ WI-Madison, 66-68; vis prof, Univ MA-Amherst, 71, prof, 71-73; lect, Univ WI-Madison, 77, prof to Germaine Bree prof, Dept of French and Italian and Women's Studies Prog, Univ WI-Madison, 80-. **HONORS AND AWARDS** Fulbright fel to Paris, 56-57; NY Univ Alumnae Pin for Scholarship, 58; Johnson fel, Inst for Res in the Humanities of the Univ WI, 62-63; grants from the Ford Found, the Johnson Found, the Stackner Family, 79-84; YWCA Women of Distinction Awd, 82; grad school res support (summer), 86, 88; WARF/Univ Houses professorship, 88; Vilas Assoc awarded and declined, 88; Univ WI Fac Development grant, 90; elected second vice pres, MLA, 91; John Simon Guggenheim Memorial Fund fel, 92; Chancellor's Awd for Excellence in Teaching, 93; pres, MLA, 93; NYU, Distinguished Alumni Awd, 94; Officier dans l'Ordre des Palmes Academiques, 94; Hilldale Awd in the Humanities, 95-96. **MEMBERSHIPS** MLA; MMLA; AATF; Nat Women's Studies Asn; Societe des Amis de Colette; Simone de Beauvoir Soc; Women in French. **RESEARCH** 19th and 20th Century French Lit; women writers. **SELECTED PUBLICATIONS** Auth, Marrano as Metaphor: the Jewish Presence in French Writing, Columbia Univ Press, 96. **CONTACT ADDRESS** Dept of French and Italian, Univ of Wisconsin, Madison, 1220 Linden Dr, 618 Van Hise Hall, Madison, WI 53706. **EMAIL** emarks@faestaff.wisc.edu

MARKS, ROBERT B.
PERSONAL Born 06/08/1949, Rhinelander, WI, m **DISCIPLINE** HISTORY **EDUCATION** Univ Wis Madison, BA, 71; MA, 73; PhD, 78. **CAREER** Asst to prof, Whittier Coll, 78-86; vice pres, AA, 86-92; prof, 92-. **HONORS AND AWARDS** NEH Fel, 92, 93, 00, ; CSCC Fel; Graves Awd; Fulbright Fel. **MEMBERSHIPS** AAS; Phi Alpha Theta; ASEH. **RESEARCH** Environmental history of China. **SELECTED PUBLICATIONS** Auth, The Making of the Modern World: Connected Histories, Divergent Paths, 1500 to the Present (NY: St. Martin's Press, sec rev ed, 94); coauth, "Price Inflation and Its Social, Economic, and Climatic Context in Guangdong Province, 1707-1800," T'oung Pao, 95; auth, "Are We Concerned Yet?: Environmental Crisis and Economic Development in China," Bulletin of Concerned Asian Scholars, 28 (96); auth, Tigers, Rice, Silk, and Silt: Environment and Economy in Late Imperial South China (Cambridge and New York: Cambridge Univ Press, 98); auth, "The Making of the Pearl River Delta." Chinese Environmental History (96); "Maritime Trade and the Agro-Ecology of South China, 1685-1850," in Dennis 0. Flynn, Pacific Centuries (London: Routledge, 99); auth, " 'It Never Used to Snow': Climate Change and Agricultural Productivity in South China, 1650-1850," in Sediments of Time: Environment and Society in China, eds. Mark Elvin, Liu Ts'ui-jung (Cambridge and New York: Cambridge Univ Press, forthcoming). **CONTACT ADDRESS** Dept History, Whittier Col, 13406 Philadelphia St, Whittier, CA 90601-4446. **EMAIL** rmarks@whittier.edu

MARKS, SALLY JEAN
PERSONAL Born 01/18/1931, New Haven, CT **DISCIPLINE** MODERN INTERNATIONAL & EUROPEAN HISTORY **EDUCATION** Wellesley Col, AB, 52; Univ NC Chapel Hill, MA, 61; Univ London, PhD, 68. **CAREER** Instr, Woman's Col, Univ NC, 60-62; from instr to prof hist, Rhode Island Col, 62-88. **HONORS AND AWARDS** Am Coun Learned Soc res fel, 77-78; G L Beer Prize, AHA, 81; Phi Alpha Theta Book Awd, 83; Bernadotte E. Schmitt Awd of AHA, 88. **MEMBERSHIPS** AHA; Am Coun Learned Soc; Institut Royal des Relations Internationales, Brussels; Conf Group Cent Europ Hist; Soc for French Hist Stud. **RESEARCH** Interwar Europe; Belgian history; diplomatic and financial history of the post World War I era. **SELECTED PUBLICATIONS** Auth, The Illusion of Peace: International Relations in Europe, 1918-1933, (London, Macmillan, NY, St Martins, 76); auth, Innicent Abroad: Belgium at the Paris Peace Conferene of 1919, (Chapel Hill, Univ of North Carolina Press, 81); auth, My Name is Ozymandias: The Kaiser in Exile, Cent Europ Hist, 83; art, Black Watch on the Rhine: A Study in Propaganda, Prejudice, and Prurience, Europ Stud Rev, 83; art, Diplomacy, Ency Britannica, 15th ed, Macropaedia, 91; art, Smoke and Mirrors in Smoke-Filled Rooms and the Galerie des Glaces in, The Versailles Treaty: A Reassessment after Seventy-Five years, Cambridge, 98. **CONTACT ADDRESS** 603 Hope St, Providence, RI 02906. **EMAIL** smarks@grog.ric.edu

MARME, MICHAEL
PERSONAL Born 05/03/1949, St. Paul, MN, m, 1973 **DISCIPLINE** ASIAN HISTORY AND MODERN EUROPEAN HISTORY **EDUCATION** Univ, CA-Berkeley, PhD. **CAREER** Ch, Columbia Univ sem on traditional China; asst prof. **MEMBERSHIPS** Asn for Asian Studies **RESEARCH** Ming-Qing social and economic history. **SELECTED PUBLICATIONS** Auth, Population and Possibility in Ming Suzhou: A Quantified Model, Ming Studies 12, 81; Heaven on Earth: The Rise of Suzhou, 1127-1550, Cities of Jiangnan in Late Imperial China, SUNY, 93; auth, Suzhou: State, Local Elites & The Making of Ming China's World System, Stanford UP, 01. **CONTACT ADDRESS** Dept of Hist, Fordham Univ, 113 W 60th St, New York, NY 10023. **EMAIL** mmarme@aol.com

MARONEY, JAMES C.
PERSONAL Born 10/06/1936, Houston, TX, m, 1957, 3 children **DISCIPLINE** UNITED STATES HISTORY **EDUCATION** Sam Houston State Univ, BA, 61, MA, 63; Univ Houston, PhD, 75. **CAREER** Instr hist, Sam Houston State Univ, 62-63 & Amarillo Col, 63-64; Mem Fac Hist, Lee Col, 64-, chmn dept Soc Sci, 78-92, 00-; vis scholar, New Handbook of Texas project, TX State Hist Asn, spring 94; co-managing ed, Touchstone (student journal), Walter Prescott Webb Soc, TX State Hist Asn, 95-. **MEMBERSHIPS** Orgn Am Historians; Southern Hist Asn; Labor Hist Asn. **RESEARCH** Early 20th century United States history; American labor history; Texas History. **SELECTED PUBLICATIONS** Auth, The Negro and Organized Labor: Selected Views, 1880-1920, Community Col Social Sci Quart, spring 76; coauth, Teaching College History: A Critique and Historiographical Analysis, Teaching Hist, spring 77; Survey United States history courses: Two and four-year institutions in Texas as a case study, Community Col Social Sci J, 8/77; auth, The Texas-Louisiana oil field strike of 1917, In: Essays in Southern Labor History, Greenwood, 77; The International Longshoremen's Association in the Gulf States during the Progressive Era, Southern Studies, summer 77; The Galveston Longshoremen's Strike of 1920, ETex Hist J, spring 78; The Unionization of Thurber, 1903, Red River Valley Hist Rev, spring 79; co-auth, The Heritage of Texas Labor, 1838-1980, TX AFL-CIO, 82; Labor's Struggle for Acceptance: The Houston Worker in a Changing Society, 1900-1929, Houston Rev 6, no 1, 84; co-ed, From Humble Beginnings, Exxon USA, 95. **CONTACT ADDRESS** Dept of Soc Sci, Lee Col, Texas, PO Box 818, Baytown, TX 77522-0818. **EMAIL** jmaroney@lee.edu

MARQUARDT-CHERRY, JANET TERESA
PERSONAL Born 10/20/1953, Los Angeles, CA, m, 1981, 2 children **DISCIPLINE** ART HISTORY **EDUCATION** UCLA, BA, MA, PhD. **CAREER** Art Dept, Eastern Ill Univ; Art Dept, USF, Tampa Fl. **HONORS AND AWARDS** Res Assistantship, UCLA; Tchg Assistantship, UCLA; Edward A. Dickson Hist Art fel, UCLA; Grad div grant, UCLA; Edward A. Dickson, Special Opportunity Grant, UCLA; Edward A. Dickson res grant, UCLA; Fac res grant, Eastern IL Univ; Tenure, Eastern IL Univ, Univ So Florida. **SELECTED PUBLICATIONS** Auth, Ottonian Imperial Saints in the Pruem Troper Manuscripta, 89; Ascension Sunday in Tropers: Innovative Scenes in the Pruem and Canterbury Tropers and Their Relationship to the Accompanying Texts, Proceedings Ill Medieval Asn, 89; King David In Germany: Royal Traditions at Pruem, Proceedings Ill Medieval Asn, 92; Rethinking the Cultural Context of Foundations, FATE Jour, 93-94; Katja Oxman: Working in the Tradition of the Woman Artist, Woman's Art Jour, 94; auth, Exhibition and catalog (nat'l), Objects of personal significance, 96-98; auth, B(l)ack Talk: Confrontational Art of Black Women Photographers, exposurers, Fall 00 . **CONTACT ADDRESS** Eastern Illinois Univ, 600 Lincoln Ave, Charleston, IL 61920-3099. **EMAIL** cfjtm@eiu.edu

MARQUIS, ALICE GOLDFARB
PERSONAL Born 03/30/1930, Munich, Germany, 1 child **DISCIPLINE** MODERN EUROPEAN AND CULTURAL HISTORY **EDUCATION** San Diego State Univ, BA, 66, MA, 69; Univ Calif, San Diego, PhD(hist), 78. **CAREER** Co-publ, PACIFIC Calif Tribune, 54-59 and Star-News Publ, San Diego, Calif, 61-72; instr hist, Univ Calif, San Diego, 78-81; RES AND WRITING, 81-, Instr art hist, San Diego Evening Col, 70-74; planning commr, San Diego County, 72-76. **HONORS AND AWARDS** Suburban Journalist of the Year, Suburban Newpapers of Am, 72. **MEMBERSHIPS** AHA **RESEARCH** Western culture between the two world wars; history of media and propaganda; Biog of 20th century cultural figures. **SELECTED PUBLICATIONS** Auth, Patron Saints--5 Rebels Who Opened America to a New Art, 1928-1943, Amer Hist Rev, Vol 0098, 93; The Private Worlds of Duchamp, Marcel--Desire, Liberation, and the Self in Modern Culture, Amer Hist Rev, Vol 0102, 97. **CONTACT ADDRESS** Univ of California, San Diego, San Diego, CA 92103.

MARRIN, ALBERT
DISCIPLINE HISTORY **EDUCATION** CUNY, BA, 58; Yeshiva Univ, MS, 59; Columbia Univ, MA, 61, PhD, 68. **CAREER** Lectr, 67, asst 68, assoc, 74, PROF, 79-, CHAIR HISTORY, 79- , YESHIVA UNIV. **CONTACT ADDRESS** 750 Kappock St, New York, NY 10463.

MARRONE, STEVE P.
PERSONAL Born 08/16/1947, Frederick, MD, m, 1983, 2 children **DISCIPLINE** HISTORY **EDUCATION** Harvard Col, BA, 69; Harvard Univ, PhD, 78. **CAREER** Asst prof to prof, Tufts Univ, 78-. **MEMBERSHIPS** Am Hist Asn, Soc Int pour l'Etude de la Philos Medievale, Soc for Medieval and renaissance Philos. **RESEARCH** Medieval philosophy, history of science, medieval cultural history. **SELECTED PUBLICATIONS** Auth, William of Auvergne and Robert Grosseteste. New Ideas of Truth in the Early Thirteenth Century, Princeton (83); auth, Truth and Scientific Knowledge in the Thought of Henry of Ghent, Cambridge, MA (85); auth, "Metaphysics and Science in the Thirteenth Century: William of Auvergne, Robert Grosseteste and Roger Bacon," in Routledge History of Philosophy, vol 3:Medieval Philosophy, ed John Marenbon, London (98); auth, "Duns Scotus on Metaphysical Potency and Possibility," in Essays in Honor of Dr. Girard Etzkorn, eds Gordon A. Wilson and Timothy B. Noone, Franciscan Studies, 56: 265-89 (98); auth, "Literacy, Theology and the Constitution of the Church: Scholastic Perspectives on Learning and Ecclesiastical Structure in the Late Thirteenth Century," in Geistesleben im 13. Jahrhundert, eds Jan A. Aertsen and Andreas Speer, 297-307, Miscellanea Mediaevalia, 27, Berlin (2000); auth, The Light of Thy Countenance. Science and Knowledge of God in the Thirteenth Century, Leiden (forthcoming). **CONTACT ADDRESS** Dept Hist, Tufts Univ, Medford, Medford, MA 02155. **EMAIL** smarrone@emerald.tufts.edu

MARSCHALL, JOHN PETER
PERSONAL Born 12/11/1933, Chicago, IL **DISCIPLINE** AMERICAN RELIGIOUS HISTORY **EDUCATION** Loyola Univ, Ill, AB, 56; St Louis Univ, MA, 61; Cath Univ Am, PhD(hist), 65. **CAREER** Lectr relig hist, Cath Univ Am, 65; asst prof, Viatorian Sem, Washington, DC, 61-65; asst prof Am relig hist, Loyola College, Ill, 66-69, mem grad fac, 68; dir, Ctr Relig and Life, 69-72, prog coordr, Ctr Relig and Life, 73-76; lectr, 69-80, ASSOC PROF AM HIST, UNIV NEV, RENO, 80-, Schmitt Found travel grant, Europe, 63-64; dir, Self-Studies Sisters of Charity, BVM, 66-68; co-dir, Self-Studies New Melleray Trappist Abbey, 68-69; mem subcomt hist, life and ministry priests, Nat Coun Bishops, 68-72; Western dir, Nat Inst for Campus Ministries, 75-79; ed consult, NICM J for Christian and Jews in Higher Educ, 75-79; asst to pres, Univ Nev, Reno, 80-. **MEMBERSHIPS** Cath Campus Ministry Asn (pres, 75-76); Am Acad Relig; Orgn Am Historians; Am Cath Hist Asn; Am Acad Polit and Soc Sci. **RESEARCH** Nineteenth century American Catholic history; history of religion in Nevada. **SELECTED PUBLICATIONS** Auth, The Premier See--a History of the Archdiocese-of-Baltimore, Church Hist, Vol 0065, 96. **CONTACT ADDRESS** Dept of Hist, Univ of Nevada, Reno, Reno, NV 89557-0001.

MARSDEN, G. M.
PERSONAL Born 02/25/1939, m, 1969, 2 children **DISCIPLINE** HISTORY OF CHRISTIANITY **EDUCATION** Haverford College, BA, honors, 59; Westminster Theol Sem, BD, 63; Yale Univ MA, 61, PhD, 65. **CAREER** Francis A McAnaney Prof of Hist, 92-, Univ Notre Dame; Prof 86-92, Duke Univ; vis Prof 86, 90, Univ Cal Berkeley; vis Prof 76-77, Trinity Evang Div Schl; Dir 80-83, Calvin College; Instr, Asst Prof, Assoc Prof, Prof, 65-86, Calvin College; Asst Instr, 64-65, Yale Univ. **HONORS AND AWARDS** Lippincott Prize; YHF for NEH; Calvin Cen Christ Schl fel; Eternity Book of the Year; Calvin Res Fel; J Howard Pew Freedom Gnt; Guggenheim Fel. **MEMBERSHIPS** ASCH. **SELECTED PUBLICATIONS** Auth, Fundamentalism and American Culture, NY: Oxford, 80; coed, The Secularization of the Academy, NY, Oxford Univ Press, 92; The Soul of the American University: From Protestant Establishment to Established Nonbelief, NY, Oxford Univ Press, 94; Understanding Fundamentalism and Evangelicalism, Grand Rapids, W B Eerdmans, 91, collection of previously pub essays; Reforming Fundamentalism: Fuller Seminary and the New Evangelicalism, Grand Rapids, W b Eerdmans, 87, reissued pbk, 95; Auth, The Outrageous Idea of Christian Scholarship, NY, Oxford Univ Press, 97; auth, American Culture, 1st ed, 1990, rev, (00), second ed. **CONTACT ADDRESS** Dept of History, Univ of Notre Dame, Notre Dame, IN 46556. **EMAIL** marsden.1@nd.edu

MARSH, CLIFTON
PERSONAL Born 07/10/1946, Los Angeles, CA, d, 1 child **DISCIPLINE** SOCIOLOGY, AFRICAN AMERICAN STUDIES **EDUCATION** Calif State Univ, Long Beach, BA; MA; Syracuse Univ NY, PhD. **CAREER** Prof, Calif State Univ Long Beach, Univ of Va, Va Commonwealth Univ, Va Union Col, Col of NJ, SUNY, Univ of the Virgin Islands, Morris Brown Univ. **HONORS AND AWARDS** Dean's Awd for Outstanding Scholar and Res; Res Awd, Bureau of Libr, Museums and Archeol Serv; NEH. **MEMBERSHIPS** Am Sociol Assoc; Nat Counc of Black Studies; Southern Sociol Assoc. **RESEARCH** The Nation of Islam, Social Movements, Homelessness, Domestic Violence, Sexual Assault, Caribbean Studies. **SELECTED PUBLICATIONS** Auth, Hartford County Homeless and Shelter Survey, Housing and Shelter in a Community in Transition, Univ Pr of Am, 66; auth, The Danish Virgin Islands: A Socio-Historical Analysis of the Emancipation of 1848 and the Labor Revolt of 1878; Wyndham Hall Pr, 84; auth, From Black Muslims to Muslims: The Transition from Separat-

ism to Islam. 1930-1980, Scarecrow Pr, 85. **CONTACT ADDRESS** Dept Soc Sci, Morris Brown Col, 643 Martin Luther King Dr NW, Atlanta, GA 30314-4140.

MARSH, PETER T.
PERSONAL Born 12/08/1935, Toronto, ON, Canada, m, 1962, 3 children **DISCIPLINE** MODERN BRITISH HISTORY **EDUCATION** Univ Toronto, BA, 58; Cambridge Univ, PhD(19th century Brit hist), 62. **CAREER** From inst to asst prof hist, Univ Sask, 62-67; chmn dept, 68-70, assoc prof, 67-78, PROF HIST, SYRACUSE UNIV, 78-, DIR, UNIV HONORS PROG, 78-, Can Coun res grant, 65 and res fel, 66-67; vis fel, All Souls Col, Oxford Univ, 66-67; vis prof, Victorian Studies Ctr, Univ Leicester, 70; vis fel, Emmanuel Col, Cambridge Univ, 73-74; Nat Prog Chmn, Conf Brit Studies, 75-77; Guggenheim fel, 80-81; hon res fel, Univ Birmingham, 80-81. **MEMBERSHIPS** Can Hist Asn; Anglo-Am Hist Conf; AHA; fel Royal Hist Soc. **RESEARCH** Modern British history. **SELECTED PUBLICATIONS CONTACT ADDRESS** Dept of Hist, Syracuse Univ, Syracuse, NY 13244.

MARSH, VINCENT
DISCIPLINE HISTORIC PRESERVATION; CITY AND REGIONAL PLANNING **EDUCATION** SUNY Buffalo, BS 70; Univ Connecticut, MSW 74; MIT Cambridge, MA 79-81; Cornell Univ, MRP 81. **CAREER** Planning Dept, CCSF, pres plan, 97-, sec plan 89-96, plan 86-89; United Way Sf, assoc 85; Democ Nat Conv, trans sch mgr 84; Earth Metrics Inc/ Revoir Devel Co, plan consul 82-83; Nat Trust Hist Pres, field rep/plan 81-82; Cornell Univ, tchg asst 80-81; Lane Frenchman MA, planner 80; Boston Landmarks Ex Off MA, res adv/consul 80; North End Union Inc MA, exec dir 74-79; Children's Museum MA, consul 77; Metro Plan Proj MA, consul 77; Greater Hartford Process Inc MA, planner 73-74; Office of Hist Preservation, Sacramento. **HONORS AND AWARDS** Calif Pres Foun Awd; Mast Thesis Support Awd; NEH Fel. **MEMBERSHIPS** BAHA; CHS; NTHP; APA; OHA; AIA; SAH; AANC; HPPA; SPURA; San Francisco Tomorrow; FSFAH; United Way SF; VAF; Vict Alliance SF. **RESEARCH** American Architecture 19th and 20th centuries; California and San Francisco history and architecture. **SELECTED PUBLICATIONS** Auth, San Francisco Planning Dept, Neighborhood Commercial Issues Paper, coauth, The Planning Dept, 98; Preservation, An Element of the General Plan of the City and County of San Francisco, Proposal for Adoption, Implementation Program Document and Appendices, coauth, The Planning Dept, 98; Revisions to Article 10, Landmarks Preservation, amending Part II Ch II of the San Francisco Municipal Code by repealing Article 10 thereof and adding a new Article 10, secs 1001-1024. Thereto creating a Landmarks Board, describing the power and the duties of the Landmarks Bd, re-designing previously designated Landmarks and Historic Districts, requiring Certificates of Appropriateness for alterations of Landmarks and Hist Districts, est guidelines doe decisions and imposing penalties for violations of Article 10, coauth, Text Amend for Adoption, 96; Thirty City Landmark Case Report Nominations, Appen to Article 10, coauth, ed, List of Designated Landmarks, 88-; Pocket Guide to the Historic Districts of San Francisco, coauth, SF Visitors Bureau and Vict Alliance, 93. **CONTACT ADDRESS** Office of Hist Preservation, 1231 I St, Ste 300, Sacramento, CA 95814. **EMAIL** vmarsh@cityofsacramento.org

MARSHALL, BYRON K.
DISCIPLINE HISTORY **EDUCATION** Stanford Univ, PhD, 66. **CAREER** Prof emer. **HONORS AND AWARDS** Ed, J Asian Studies. **RESEARCH** Japanese history; ideology and social change in late nineteenth- and early twentieth-century Japan. **SELECTED PUBLICATIONS** Auth, Capitalism and Nationalism in Prewar Japan: The Ideology of the Business Elite 1868-1941, Stanford, 97; Learning To the Modern: Education in Japanese Political Discourse, 94; Academic Freedom and the Japanese Imperial University 1868-1939, Univ Calif, 92; co-auth, A Comparative History of Civilizations in Asia, Westview, 86. **CONTACT ADDRESS** History Dept, Univ of Minnesota, Twin Cities, 614 Social Sciences Tower, 267 19th Ave S, Minneapolis, MN 55455. **EMAIL** marsh004@tc.umn.edu

MARSHALL, DOMINIQUE
DISCIPLINE HISTORY **EDUCATION** Univ de Montreal, BA, 83, MA, 85, PhD, 89. **CAREER** Assoc prof, Carleton Univ. **RESEARCH** Quebec and Canadian families and social politicies in the twentieth century. **SELECTED PUBLICATIONS** Auth, Family Allowances and Family Autonomy: Quebec 1945-1955, Can Family Hist: Selected Readings, Toronto, Copp Clark, 92; "The Language of Children's Rights, the Formation of the Welfare State and the Democratic Experience of poor Families, Quebec, 1940-1955," Can Hist Rev Vol 78, 97; Le recul du travail des enfants au Quebec entre 1940 et 1960: une explication des conflits entre les familles pauvres et l'Etat providence, Labour/Le Travail, 89; reprinted and as The Decline of Child Labour in Quebec, 1940-1960: Conflict Between Poor Families and the State, Hist Perspectives on Law and Soc in Caonada, Copp Clark, 94; "Nationalisme et politques sociales au Quebec depuis 1867: Un siecle de rendex-vous manques entre l'Etat, l'Eglise et les familes," Brit Jour of Can Stud, 94; auth, "The Language of Children's Rights, the Formation of the Welfare State and the Democratic Experience of poor Families, Quebec, 1940-1955," Canadian Historical Review, vol. 78, 97; ed, "Canada and Children's Rights at the United Nations, 1945-1959," in Greg Donaghy, ed., Canada and the Early Cold War, 1943-1957, (Ottawa, Dept of Foreign Affairs and International Trade, 98). **CONTACT ADDRESS** Dept of Hist, Carleton Univ, 1125 Colonel By Dr, Ottawa, ON, Canada K1S 5B6. **EMAIL** dmarsha2@ccs.carleton.ca

MARSHALL, HOWARD WIGHT
DISCIPLINE AMERICAN ARCHITECTURE **EDUCATION** Univ Mo, BA; Ind Univ, MA, PhD, 76. **CAREER** Prof; vis fel, Europ Ethnol Res Cte, Edinburgh; chair & prof emer, Univ of Mo. **HONORS AND AWARDS** Cofinalist for 2 Grammy awd(s). **RESEARCH** Vernacular architecture and cultural/historical monuments in Missouri; historic farm buildings in the central lowlands of Scotland. **SELECTED PUBLICATIONS** Auth, Little Dixie; British Isles Subregion Upper Avon River Valley, Central Scotland; Estate Worker's Housing, Scotland; & other chap in Encycl Vernacular Archit of the World, Cambridge UP, 98; Paradise Valley, Nevada: The People and Buildings of an American Place, Tucson: Univ Ariz Press, 95; Vernacular Architecture in Rural and Small Town Missouri: An Introduction, Columbia: Univ Mo Exten Div, 94; Architecture, Folk, chap in Folklore: An Encyclopedia of Forms, Methods, and History, NY, Garland, 97; Vernacular Architecture, chap in Amer Folklore: An Encycl, NY and London, Garland Publ, Inc, 95; Vernacular Housing and American Culture, lead chap in Amer Popular Housing, NY, Greenwood, 95 & Milestones and Stumbling Blocks, Continued, J Cult Geog 15 1, 94; coauth, Now That's a Good Tune: Masters of Traditional Missouri Fiddling, Columbia, Publ Univ Mo Cult Heritage Ctr, 89; co-ed, The German-American Experience in Missouri: Essays in Celebration of the Tricentennial of German Immigration to Ameria, 1683-1983, Columbia, Publ Univ Mo Cult l Heritage Ctr, 86. **CONTACT ADDRESS** Dept of Art History and Archaeology, Univ of Missouri, Columbia, 109 Pickard Hall, Columbia, MO 65211. **EMAIL** marshallh@missouri.edu

MARSHMAN, MICHELLE
PERSONAL Born 03/31/1968, Seattle, WA, m, 1989 **DISCIPLINE** HISTORY **EDUCATION** Univ CA, Riverside, PhD, 97. **CAREER** Asst prof, 97-, European And Women's Hist, Northwest Nazarene Univ. **MEMBERSHIPS** French Hist Soc; AAR; Soc for Sixteenth Cent Stud. **RESEARCH** Catholic women in 17th century France. **SELECTED PUBLICATIONS** Auth, "Exorcism as Empowerment: A New Idiom," Jrnl of Rel Hist 23,3 (99). **CONTACT ADDRESS** Northwest Nazarene Col, 623 Holly St, Nampa, ID 83686. **EMAIL** mlmarshman@nnu.edu

MARSZALEK, JOHN FRANCIS
PERSONAL Born 07/05/1939, Buffalo, NY, m, 1965, 3 children **DISCIPLINE** UNITED STATES HISTORY **EDUCATION** Canisius Col, BA, 61; Univ Notre Dame, MA, 63, PhD, 68. **CAREER** Teaching asst hist, Univ Notre Dame, 62-64; Capt, U.S. Army, 65-67; instr, Canisius Col, 67-68; from asst prof to assoc prof, Gannon Col, 68-73; from Assoc Prof to Prof Hist, 73-94, William L. Giles Distinguished Prof, Miss State Univ, 94. **HONORS AND AWARDS** NEH res grant, 71; Am Coun Learned Soc grant-in-aid, 73-74; travel grants, Cushwa Ctr, Univ Notre Dame, 84, Am Philos Soc, 88; Miss State Univ Alum Asn Grad Level Teaching Awd, 90; Ohioana Libr Non-Fiction Awd, 93; Non-Fiction Awd, Miss Libr Asn, 94; res grant, Criss Found, Miss State Univ, 96; Miss Legislature Outstanding Teacher Awd, 97; Southeastern Library Assoc Non-/fiction Awd, 98. **MEMBERSHIPS** Orgn Am Historians; Southern Hist Asn; Miss Hist Soc; Soc Civil War Hist; Lincoln Forum; Hist Civil War Western Theatre; Golden Triangle Civil War Roundtable. **RESEARCH** Civil War and Reconstruction; U.S. Middle Period; U.S. race relations. **SELECTED PUBLICATIONS** Auth, Court-Martial: A Black Man in America, Scribner, 72, paperback ed titled: Assault at West Point, 94; coauth, A Black Businessman in White Mississippi 1886-1974, Univ Miss, 77; ed, The Diary of Miss Emma Holmes, 1861-1866, La State Univ Press, 79; Shermans Other War: The General and the Civil War Press, Memphis State Univ Press, 81; coauth, A Black Physician's Story, Bringing Hope in Mississippi, 85; co-ed, Grover Cleveland, A Bibliography, 88; Encyclopedia of African-American Civil Rights, From Emancipation to the Present, 92; auth, Sherman, A Soldier's Passion for Order, 93; co-ed, American Political History, The State of the Discipline, 97; auth, The Petticoat Affair: Manners, Mutiny, and Sex in Andrew Jackson's White House, 98; author of numerous journal articles and book reviews. **CONTACT ADDRESS** Dept of Hist, Mississippi State Univ, Drawer H, Mississippi State, MS 39762-5508. **EMAIL** jfm1@ra.msstate.edu

MARTEN, JAMES
PERSONAL Born 09/10/1956, Madison, SD, m, 1977, 2 children **DISCIPLINE** AMERICAN HISTORY **EDUCATION** S Dakota St Univ, BA, 78; Univ S Dakota, MA, 81; Univ Texas, Austin, PhD, 86. **CAREER** Tchr, Eng, 78-80, Woodbine High Schl, IA; asst prof, 86-92, assoc prof, 92-00, Marquette Univ; Prof, 00-. **HONORS AND AWARDS** Fulbright Lect People's Rep of China, 99, NEH Grant, for childern in Urban America Project, 00-03. **MEMBERSHIPS** Org of Amer Hist; So Hist Assn, Soc of Civil War Hist. **RESEARCH** Civil war era; children; soc hist; African Amer. **SELECTED PUBLICATIONS** Auth, Texas Divided: Loyalty and Dissent in the Lone Star State, 1856-1874, Univ Press KY, 90; auth, Texas, World Bibliog Ser, Oxford Clio Bks, 92; art, For the Army, the People, and Abraham Lincoln: A Yankee Newspaper in Occupied Texas; Civil War Hist 39, 93; art, In the Best Interests of the Parent: Children, Material Culture, and the Law, Rev in Amer Hist 23, 95; art, Stern Realities: The Children of Chancellorsville and Beyond, Chancellorsville: The Battle & Its Aftermath, Univ NC Press, 96; art, Fatherhood in the Confederacy: Southern Soldiers and Their Children, J of S Hist 63, 97; auth, The Children's Civil War, Univ NC Press, 98; auth, Lessons of War: The Civil War in Children's Magazines, SR Bks, 98. **CONTACT ADDRESS** History Dept, Marquette Univ, PO Box 1881, Milwaukee, WI 53201-1881. **EMAIL** james.marten@marquette.edu

MARTER, JOAN
PERSONAL Born 08/13/1946, Philadelphia, PA, 1 child **DISCIPLINE** TWENTIETH CENTURY ART **EDUCATION** Univ Delaware, PhD. **CAREER** Prof, Rutgers, The State Univ NJ, Univ Col-Camden. **HONORS AND AWARDS** George Wittenborn Awd; Art Libraries Society of North America, 85; International Critics Assoc Awd, 99. **RESEARCH** Twentieth-century painting and sculpture in Europe and America; American sculpture from 1930 to the present. **SELECTED PUBLICATIONS** Auth, Alexander Calder, Cambridge UP, 91; Theodore Roszak: The Drawings, Univ Wash Press, 92; Dorothy Dehner: Sixty Years of Art, Univ Wash Press, 93; Sculpture in Postwar Europe and America, in Art J 53, 94; The Ascendancy of Abstraction for Public Art: The Monument to the Unknown Political Prisoner Competition; auth, "Off Limits: Rutgers University and the Avant-Garde, 1957-63," Rutgers University Press, 99. **CONTACT ADDRESS** Dept of Art Hist, Rutgers, The State Univ of New Jersey, New Brunswick, Voorhees Hall, 71 Hamilton St, New Brunswick, NJ 08901. **EMAIL** joanmarter@aol.com

MARTI, DONALD B.
DISCIPLINE HISTORY **EDUCATION** Univ Minn, BA, 61; Univ Wis, MS, 63, PhD, 66. **CAREER** ASSOC PROF, HISTORY, UNIV INDIANA SOUTH BEND **MEMBERSHIPS** AM Antiquarian Soc **SELECTED PUBLICATIONS** Auth, "The Rev Henry Colman's Agricultural Ministry," Agr Hist 51, 77; auth, "Agricultural Journalism and the Diffusion of Knowledge: The First Half-Century in America," Agr Hist 54, 80; auth, "Woman's Work in the Grange: Mary Ann Mayo of Michigan, 1882-1903," Agr Hist 56, 82; auth, "Francis William Bird: A Radical's Progress through the Republican Party," Hist Jour of Mass 11, 83; ed, Historical Directory of American Agricultural Fairs, Greenwood Press, 86; auth, Women of the Grange: Mutuality and Sisterhood in Rural America, 1866-1920, Greenwood Press, 91; auth, "Answering the Agrarian Question: Socialists, Farmers, and Algie Martin Simons, Agr Hist 65; auth, Rich Methodists: The Rise and Consequences of Lay Philanthropy in the Mid Nineteenth-Century, in Perspectives on American Methodism, Kingswood Books, 93. **CONTACT ADDRESS** 1322 E. South St, South Bend, IN 46615.

MARTIN, BENJAMIN F.
PERSONAL Born 05/03/1947, Winston-Salem, NC **DISCIPLINE** HISTORY, MODERN EUROPEAN HISTORY **EDUCATION** Davidson Col, AB, 69; Univ NC, Chapel Hill, PhD, 74. **CAREER** Instr, Univ NC, Chapel Hill, 74-75; asst prof, 75-78, assoc prof, WVa Wesleyan Col, 79-83; assoc prof, La State Univ, 83-86, prof, 86-. **HONORS AND AWARDS** Woodrow Wilson Fel, 69; AB cum laude, Davidson Col, 69; John Motley Morehead Fel, 69-74; Georges Lurcy Fel, 72-73; Outstanding Prof of 1988, LSU Col of Arts and Scis. **MEMBERSHIPS** Am Hist Asn, Soc for French Hist Studies, Soc Int d'Historie de l"Affaire Dreyfus. **RESEARCH** Third Republic France, criminality and justice. **SELECTED PUBLICATIONS** Auth, Count Albert de Mun: Paladin of the Third Republic; auth, The Hypocrisy of Justice in the Belle Epoque (84); auth, Crime and Justice Under the Third Republic: The Shame of Marianne (90); auth, France and the Apres Guerre: Illusions and Disillusionment (99). **CONTACT ADDRESS** Dept Hist, La State Univ Baton Rouge, Baton Rouge, LA 70803-0104.

MARTIN, JAMES I.
PERSONAL Born 10/12/1954, Homestead, PA, m, 1980, 1 child **DISCIPLINE** HISTORY **EDUCATION** Duke Univ, BA, 76; E Carolina Univ, MA, 81; Emory Univ, PhD, 90. **CAREER** Teacher, James Kenan High School, 86-91; asst prof to assoc prof, Campbell Univ, 91-. **HONORS AND AWARDS** Who's who Among Am Teachers, 96, 00. **MEMBERSHIPS** Phi Alpha Theta; Kappa Delta Pi; Pi Gamma Mu; Phi Kappa Phi; NC Assoc of Hist; NC Coun for the Soc Studies. **RESEARCH** Ethnohistory, Social Studies Education. **SELECTED PUBLICATIONS** Auth, Teaching About North Carolina's Varied Ethnic Heritage, NC Coun for the Soc Studies; auth, Preparing High School Students for College Level Courses, NC Coun for the Soc Studies. **CONTACT ADDRESS** Dept Govt and Hist, Campbell Univ, PO Box 356, Buies Creek, NC 27506-0356. **EMAIL** martin@mailcenter.campbell.edu

MARTIN, JAMES KIRBY
PERSONAL Born 05/26/1943, Akron, OH, m, 1965, 3 children **DISCIPLINE** HISTORY **EDUCATION** Hiram Col, BA, 65; Univ Wis, Madison, MA, 67, PhD, 69. **CAREER** From asst prof to prof, hist, 69-80, Rutgers Univ; prof, hist, 80-97, dept chemn, 80-83, acting dept chemn 90, Distinguished Univ Prof of Hist, 97-, Univ of Houston , Scholar-In Residence and Res Fel, David Lib of the Am Revolution, and Res Fel, Philadelphia Ctr for Early Am Stud, Univ Penn, 88; adj and vis assoc prof and Prof of Alcohol Stud, Rutgers Univ, 78-88; vis prof hist, Rice Univ, 92. **HONORS AND AWARDS** R.P. McCormick Prize, NJ Hist Comn, 84; NJ Soc of the Cincinnati Prize, 95; Homer D. Babbidge, Jr. Awd, Soc for the Stud of Conn Hist, 98. **MEMBERSHIPS** Phi Beta Kappa; Phi Kappa Phi; Phi Alpha Theta; Pi Gamma Mu; Omicron Delta Kappa; AHA; Org of Am Hist; So Hist Asn; Soc for Military Hist; Soc for Hist of the Early Am Republic; Inst of Early Am Hist and Culture; Eastern Natl Park and Monument Asn; Texas State Hist Asn; NJ Hist Soc. **RESEARCH** United States history: social, military, and early American. **SELECTED PUBLICATIONS** Auth, Men In Rebellion: Higher Governmental Leaders and The Coming of the American Revolution, New Brunswick, NJ.: Rutgers Univ Press, 73, Paperback edition, The Free Press, a division of the Macmillan Company, 76; ed., The Human Dimensions of Nation Making: Essays on Colonial and Revolutionary America, Madison: State Historical Society of Wisconsin Press, 76; ed., Interpreting Colonial America: Selected Readings (2nd ed., New York: HarperCollins, Publishers, 78, First edition published in 1973 by Dodd, Mead and Company, Inc., New York; auth, In The Course of Human Events: An Interpretive Exploration of the American Revolution, Arlington Heights, Ill,: Harlan Davidson, Inc., 79; ed., The American Revolution: Whose Revolution? Huntington, N.Y.: Robert E. Krieger Publishing Company, 77, With K.R. Stubaus, Revision, 81; ed, Citizen-Soldier: The Revolutionary War Journal of Joseph Bloomfield, (Collections of the New Jersey Historical Society, 82, With M. E. Lender, Awarded the 1984 R. P. McCormick Prize as the Outstanding Contribution to New Jersey History in book form, 82-84; Coauth, A Respectable Army: The Military Origins of the Republic, 1763-1789, Harlan Davidson, 82; coauth, Drinking in America: A History, 1620-1980, Free Press, 82; ed, Ordinary Courage: The Revolutionary War Adventures of Joseph Plumb Martin, Brandywine Press, 93; coauth, America and Its Peoples: A Mosaic in the Making, 4th ed, Longman, 00; auth, Benedict Arnold, Revolutionary Hero: An American Warrior Reconsidered, NY Univ, 97. **CONTACT ADDRESS** History Dept, Univ of Houston, Houston, TX 77204-3785. **EMAIL** jmartin@uh.edu

MARTIN, JOHN J.
PERSONAL Born 08/01/1951, Boston, MA, m, 1987, 2 children **DISCIPLINE** HISTORY **EDUCATION** Harvard Col, AB, 75; Harvard Univ, PhD, 82. **CAREER** Prof, Trinity Univ, 82-. **HONORS AND AWARDS** DAAD, 74; Danforth Fel, 75-81; Fulbright Hays Fel, 79-80; Krupp found, 80-81; NEH, 85-86, 95; Guggenheim Found, 96; Am Philos Soc, 99; Herbert Baxter Adams Prize. **MEMBERSHIPS** AHA, MLA, Renaissance Soc of Am, Sixteenth Century Studies. **SELECTED PUBLICATIONS** Auth, "L'inquisizione Romana e la criminalizazzione del dissenso religioso a Venezia," Quaderni storici, (87); auth, "A Journeymen's Feast of Fools," Jour of Medieval and Renaissance Hist, (87); auth, "Salvation and Society in Sixteenth-Century Venice," Jour of Mod Hist, (88); auth, "Spiritual Journeys," Renaissance Studies, (96); auth, Venice's Hidden Enemies, Univ of Calif, 93; auth, "Inventing Sincerity," Am Hist Rev, (97); coed, Venice Reconsidered, Johns Hopkins. 00; auth, "Myth of Renaissance Individualism," Blackwell Companion to the Renaissance, (01). **CONTACT ADDRESS** Dept Hist, Trinity Univ, San Antonio, TX 78209. **EMAIL** jmartin@trinity.edu

MARTIN, KENNETH R.
PERSONAL Born 02/12/1938, Upper Darby, PA **DISCIPLINE** AMERICAN HISTORY, MARITIME HISTORY, FOLK ART **EDUCATION** Dickinson Col, AB, 59; Univ Pa, MA, 51, PhD, 65. **CAREER** Readership, 64, Univ Pa; from instr to asst prof hist, 65-68, Gettysburg Col; assoc prof, 68-74, Slippery Rock State Col; Dir, 74-80, Kendall Whaling Mus; assoc, Hist Assoc Inc, 81-84; ed, 70-71, Mercer County Hist; Eleutherian Mills/Hagley Found grant-in-aid, 72; instr, 76-78, Univ Calif, Berkeley; self employed, author, hist, 85-. **MEMBERSHIPS** Kentucky Rifle Assn. **RESEARCH** American maritime history; 19th century whaling; business history; American and Canadian folk art. **SELECTED PUBLICATIONS** Auth, Phase One: A History of Thomas Group, Inc, TGI, 92; coauth, Time Warrior, Mcgraw-Hill, 92; coauth, Quality Alone is Not Enough, Am Mng Assn, 92; coauth, Survival at Nodulex, TGI/Heritage, 94; coauth, The Pattens of Bath: A Seagoing Dynasty, Maine Maritime Mus, 96; auth, A Life of Its Own..Nova Scotia Folk Art, 1975-1995, Art Gal of Nova Scotia, 97; auth, Heavy Weather and Hard Luck: Portsmouth Goes Whaling, Portsmouth Marine Soc, 98. **CONTACT ADDRESS** PO Box 284, Woolwich, ME 04579. **EMAIL** martink@gwi.net

MARTIN, MARTY
PERSONAL Born 02/05/1928, West Point, NE, m, 1982, 7 children **DISCIPLINE** RELIGIOUS HISTORY **EDUCATION** Lutheran School of Theol, Chicago, STM, 54; Univ of Chicago, PhD, 56. **CAREER** Lutheran Pastor, 49-63; prof, Univ Chicago, 63-98; sr, ed, Christian Century, 56-98; George B. Caldwell Sr Scholar in Residence, Park Ridge Center for Health, Faith and Ethics, 81-. **HONORS AND AWARDS** Natl Medal of Hum; Natl Book Awd; Medal of the Amer Acad of Arts and Sci; 64 honorary degrees. **MEMBERSHIPS** Past Pres Amer Acad of Rel; Amer Soc of Church Hist; Amer Catholic Hist Assoc. **RESEARCH** American Religious History, 18th and 20th centuries; comparative international studies of movements such as fundamentalism and ethnonationalism. **SELECTED PUBLICATIONS** Auth, Righteous Empire: The Protestant Experience in America, Dial, 70; Pilgrims in Their Own Land: 500 Years of Religion in America, Little Brown, 84; Religion and Republic: The American Circumstance, Beacon, 87; The One and the Many: America's Struggle for the Common Good, Harvard, 97; 3 volume Modern American Religion: The Irony of It All: 1893-1919, Univ of Chicago, 86; The Noise of Conflict, 1919-1941, Univ of Chicago, 91; Under God, Indivisible, 1941-1960, Univ of Chicago, 96. **CONTACT ADDRESS** 239 Scottswood Rd, Riverside, IL 60546.

MARTIN, RICHARD C.
PERSONAL Born 07/24/1938, Des Moines, IA, m, 1980, 1 child **DISCIPLINE** HISTORY OF RELIGIONS **EDUCATION** Princeton Theol Sem, ThM, 66; NYork Univ, PhD, 75. **CAREER** Chmn 83-89, Dept of Religious Stud, 75-95, Ariz State Univ; Chmn Relig Stud Prog, 95-96 Iowa State Univ; Prof, Chmn dept of Relig, 96-99; Emory Univ, 96-. **MEMBERSHIPS** ASSR **RESEARCH** Islamic religious thought, comparative religions. **SELECTED PUBLICATIONS** Co-auth, Defenders of Reason in Islam, Mu'tazilism from Medieval School to Modern Symbol, London, Oneworld, 97; auth, Islamic Studies, A History of Religious Approach, Englewood Cliffs NJ, Prentice Hall, 95; Public Aspects of Theology in Medieval Islam, The Role of Kalam in Conflict Definition and Resolution, in: J for Islamic Studies, 93. **CONTACT ADDRESS** Dept of Religion, Emory Univ, Atlanta, GA 30322. **EMAIL** rcmartin@emory.edu

MARTIN, RONALD EDWARD
PERSONAL Born 06/30/1933, Chicago, IL, m, 1956, 3 children **DISCIPLINE** ENGLISH; AMERICAN STUDIES **EDUCATION** Carroll Col, Wis, BA, 55; Boston Univ, AM, 57, PhD(Am lit), 63. **CAREER** Instr English, Boston Univ, 61-62; from instr to asst prof, 62-68, assoc prof, 68-81, Prof English, Univ Del, 81-99; Am Coun Learned Soc grant-in-aid, 67-68; dir, Ctr Sci & Cult, 81-85; Fulbright Distinguished Chr, Am Stud, Odense Univ, Denmark, 93-94; emeritus prof English, Univ Del, 99-. **MEMBERSHIPS** AAUP; AAAS. **RESEARCH** American literature since 1880; relationships of science, philosophy, and literature; American literature and anthropology, 1870-1940. **SELECTED PUBLICATIONS** Auth, The Fiction of Joseph Hergesheimer, Univ Pa, 65; American Literature and the Universe of Force, Duke Univ, 81; American Literature and the Destruction of Knowledge, Duke Univ, 91. **CONTACT ADDRESS** 234 W Main, Newark, DE 19711. **EMAIL** rmartin@udel.edu

MARTIN, RUSSELL
PERSONAL Born 04/25/1963, McKees Rocks, PA, m, 1987, 2 children **DISCIPLINE** HISTORY **EDUCATION** Univ of Pittsburgh, BA, 86; Harvard Univ, AM, 89; PhD, 99. **CAREER** Asst Prof, Westminster Col, 96-. **HONORS AND AWARDS** David L. Lawrence Nationalities Room Fel for study at Leningrad State Univ, 86; Cert in Russian and Europ Studies, Center for Russian and E Europe Studies, Univ of Pittsburgh, 86; Foreign Lang and Area Studies Fel, 87; Soc Sci Res Coun Res Initiative Grant, 92; Int res and Exchanges Bd fel, 92-93; Distinction in Teaching Awd, Derek Bok Center for Teaching, Harvard Univ, 93-95; Dissertation Finishing Grant, Soc Sci Res Coun, 95-96. **MEMBERSHIPS** Am Asn for the Advan of Slavic Studies, AHA , Early Slavic Studies Asn. **RESEARCH** Early Modern Russian/Muscovy, Succession to Imperial Russian Throne. **SELECTED PUBLICATIONS** Auth, "Royal Weddings and Crimean Diplomacy: New Sources on Muscovite Chancellery Practice during the Reign of Vasilii III," in Rhetoric of the Medieval Slavic World, Harvard Ukrainian Studies 19 (95): 389-427; auth, "Gifts for the Dead: Death, Kinship and Commemoration in Muscovy (The Case of the Mstislavskii Princely Clan)," in Russian History/Histoire Rusee (in press); auth, Dynastic Marriage in Muscovy, 1500-1729: A Study of the Politics and Rituals of Royal Marriage in Early Modern Russia, forthcoming. **CONTACT ADDRESS** Dept of Relig, Hist, Philos and Classics, Westminster Col, Pennsylvania, 319 S Market St., New Wilmington, PA 16172-0002. **EMAIL** martinre@westminster.edu

MARTIN, TONY
PERSONAL Born 02/21/1942, Trinidad and Tobago **DISCIPLINE** HISTORY **EDUCATION** Hon Soc of Gray's Inn, London, England, Barrister-at-Law, 65; Univ Hull, England, BS, 68; Mich State Univ, PhD, 73. **CAREER** Asst prof, Univ Mich-Flint, 71-73; from assoc prof to prof, Wellesly Col, 73-. **HONORS AND AWARDS** Am Phiolos Soc, res grant, 90. **MEMBERSHIPS** Asoc of Caribbean Historians; Asoc for the Study of Classical African Civilizations. **RESEARCH** Marcus Garvey; Pan-Africanism; Black intellectual history. **SELECTED PUBLICATIONS** Auth, Race First: The Ideological and Organizational Struggles of Marcus Garvey and the UNIA, Greenwood Press, 76; coauth, Rare Afro-Americana: A Reconstruction of the Adger Library, G.K. Hall, 81; auth, Literary Garveyism: Garvey, Black Arts and the Harlem Renaissance, Majority Press, 83; The Pan-African Connection, Majority Press, 84; auth, "A Pan-Africanist in Dominica," J of Caribbean Hist 21 (87); auth, "African and Indian Nationalism in the 20th Century," in General History of the Caribbean, vol 9 (UNESCO, 00); auth, "The Banneker Literary Institute of Philadelphia: African American Intellectual Activism before the War of the Slaveholders' Rebellion," Contours 1 (00). **CONTACT ADDRESS** Dept of Africana Studies, Wellesley Col, Wellesley, MA 02481. **EMAIL** amartin@wellesley.edu

MARTIN, VIRGINIA
PERSONAL Born 05/04/1962, Milwaukee, WI, m, 1989, 1 child **DISCIPLINE** HISTORY **EDUCATION** Vassar Col, BA, 84; Univ Wis, MA, 87; Univ S Calif, PhD, 96. **CAREER** Asst prof, Hist, Univ Ala, Huntsville, 96-. **HONORS AND AWARDS** IREX res fel, Kazakhstan, Rus, 93-94; Soc Sci Res Counc fel, 92-93; IREX fel, 92-93. **MEMBERSHIPS** AHA, AAASS, World Hist Asn, S Slavic Conf. **RESEARCH** Hist, soc, cult; anthrop; Kazakhstan; Rus Empire. **SELECTED PUBLICATIONS** Auth, Law and Custom in the Steppe: The Kazakhs of the Middle Horde and Russian Colonialism in the Nineteenth Century (London: Cruzon Press, 00); auth, Akhmet Baitursin, in The Supplement to the Modern Encylopedia of Russian, Soviet, and Eurasian History, Acad Int Press, forthcoming; auth, Barimta, in The Supplement to the Modern Encyclopedia of Russian, Soviet, and Eurasian History, Acad Int Press, forthcoming; auth, Barymta: Nomadic Custom, Imperial Crime, in Russia's Orient: Imperial Borderlands and Peoples, 1700-1917, Ind Univ Press, 97; auth, Nomads, Borders and the Resolution of Land Disputes in the Kazakh Steppe, Bull Am Asn Central Asian Res, IX, no 1, Spring 96. **CONTACT ADDRESS** Dept of History, Univ of Alabama, Huntsville, 402 Roberts Hall, Huntsville, AL 35801. **EMAIL** martinvi@email.uah.edu

MARTIN, WAYNE M.
DISCIPLINE HISTORY OF PHILOSOPHY **EDUCATION** Univ Calif-Berkeley, PhD, 93. **CAREER** Undergrad Adv, Univ Calif, San Diego. **RESEARCH** Post-Kantian idealists; Phenomenology. **SELECTED PUBLICATIONS** Auth, "Without a Striving, No Object is Possible:Fichte's Striving Doctrine and the Primacy of Practice," New Perspectives on Fichte, Hum Press, 96; Fichte's Anti-Dogmatism, Ratio V:2,92. **CONTACT ADDRESS** Dept of Philos, Univ of California, San Diego, 9500 Gilman Dr, La Jolla, CA 92093.

MARTINES, LAURO
PERSONAL Born 11/22/1927, Chicago, IL, m, 1957, 1 child **DISCIPLINE** RENAISSANCE HISTORY, ITALIAN LITERATURE **EDUCATION** Drake Univ, AB, 50; Harvard Univ, PhD(hist), 60. **CAREER** From instr to asst prof hist, Reed Col, 58-62; Prof Hist, Univ Calif, Los Angeles, 66-, Am Philos Soc grants, 60, 61, 66; Am Counc Learned Soc fel, 62-63; Harvard Ctr Ital Renaissance Studies fel, Villa I Tatti, Florence, Italy, 62-65; John Simon Guggenheim Mem Found fel, 64-65; Ford Found grant, 68-69; Nat Endowment for Humanities sr fel, 71, fel, 78-79; Rockefeller Fel, Villa Serbeloni, 90. **HONORS AND AWARDS** Harvard, Bayard-Cutting fel, 55-56; Sheldon Travelling fel, 57-58. **MEMBERSHIPS** AHA; Renaissance Soc Am; fel Mediaeval Acad Am. **RESEARCH** Seventeenth century Europe; the Italian Renaissance; the social analysis of English Renaissance verse. **SELECTED PUBLICATIONS** Auth, The Social World of the Florentine Humanists: 1390-1460, 63 & Lawyers and Statecraft in Renaissance Florence, 68, Princeton Univ; ed, Violence and Civil Disorder in Italian Cities, 1200-1500, Univ Calif, 72; coauth, Not in God's Image: A History of Women from the Greeks to the Nineteenth Century, Harper, 73; auth, Power and Imagination: City-States in Renaissance Italy, Knopf, 79; auth, Society and History in English Renaissance Verse, 85; auth, An Italian Renaissance Sextet, 94; auth, Strong Words: Writing and Social Strain in the Italian Renaissance, 01. **CONTACT ADDRESS** 8 Gloucester Crescent, London, England NW1 7DS. **EMAIL** louromartines@talk21.com

MARTINEZ, JOSE-LUIS
DISCIPLINE LATIN AMERICAN AND SPANISH CIVILIZATION **EDUCATION** Univ Puerto Rico, BA, 84; Univ Tex, MA, 87, PhD, 93. **CAREER** Tchg asst, asst instr, Univ Tex; Instr, Austin Comm Coll; Asst prof, Univ Central Ark, 92- . **RESEARCH** Spanish American literature and culture; Hispanic Caribbean literature and culture. **SELECTED PUBLICATIONS** Auth, El bolero y la guaracha en las novelas de Luis Rafael Sanchez, Revista Metafora; auth, Musica y literature: testimonio cultural de deferentes grupos raciales llegdos de Africa a las Antillas del Caribe hispano, Jour Afro-Latin Am Studies & Lit. **CONTACT ADDRESS** Univ of Central Arkansas, 201 Donaghey Ave, Conway, AR 72035-0001.

MARTINEZ, OSCAR J.
DISCIPLINE HISTORY **EDUCATION** Calif State Univ, Los Angeles, BA, 69; Stanford Univ, MA, 70; Univ Calif, Los An-

geles, PhD, 75. **CAREER** Instr, Foothill Comm Col, Calif, 70-71; lectr, Calif State Univ, Hayward, 70; from asst prof to prof, Hist Dept, 75-88, dir, Inst of Oral Hist, 75-82, dir, Ctr for Inter-Am and Border Stud, 82-87, Univ Texas, El Paso; prof, Hist Dept, 88- , dir Grad Stud, Hist Dept, 90-92, interim dir, Latin Am Area Ctr, 94-95, Univ Arizona; vis prof, Yale Univ, 95. **HONORS AND AWARDS** Fel, Ctr for Advanc Stud in Behavioral Sci, Stanford, 81-82; Fulbright Study Fel, S Am, 85; Border Regional Lib Asn, Southwest Book Awds, 78, 83, 88, 95; pres, Asn for Borderlands Scholars, 85-87; award for Outstanding Scholarship and Service, Asn of Borderlands Scholars, 92; book award, Fac of Soc and Behavioral Sci, Univ Arizona, 95; nom for Five-Star Tchg Awd, Univ Arizona, 96; inducted El Paso Writers Hall of Fame, 97; named Regents Prof, Univ of Ariz, 00. **MEMBERSHIPS** Asn for Borderlands Scholars; Latin Am Stud Asn; Natl Asn for Chicano Stud. **SELECTED PUBLICATIONS** Auth, Border Boom Town: Ciudad Juarez Since 1848, Texas, 78; auth, ed, Fragments of the Mexican Revolution: Personal Accounts from the Border, New Mexico, 83; auth, Across Boundaries: Transborder Interaction in Comparative Perspective, Texas Western, 86; auth, Troublesome Border, Arizona, 88; auth, Border People: Life and Society in the U.S.-Mexico Borderlands, Arizona, 94; ed, The U.S.-Mexico Borderlands: Historical and Contemporary Perspectives, Scholarly Resources, 95; auth, Mexican-Origin People in the United States, 01. **CONTACT ADDRESS** History Dept, Univ of Arizona, Tucson, AZ 85721. **EMAIL** oscar-martinez@ns.arizona.edu

MARTINEZ-FERNANDEZ, LUIS
PERSONAL Born 01/14/1960, Havana, Cuba, m, 1984, 2 children **DISCIPLINE** PUERTO RICAN AND HISPANIC CARIBBEAN STUDIES **EDUCATION** Univ Puerto Rico, BA, 82; MA, 84; Duke Univ, PhD, 90. **CAREER** Asst Prof, Augusta State Univ, 90-92; Asst Prof, Colgate Univ, 92-94; Asst Prof, Rutgers Univ 94-97; Assoc Prof and Chair, 97-. **HONORS AND AWARDS** Pew Evangelical Scholars Program Fel, 94-95, Board of Trustees Fellowship for Scholarly Excellence, Rutgers Univ, 97-98. **MEMBERSHIPS** Am Historical Asn, Latin American Studies Asn, Asn of Caribbean Historians. **RESEARCH** Cuban, Pureto Rican and Dominican History. **SELECTED PUBLICATIONS** Auth, "Caudillos, Annexationism, and the Rivalry between Empires in the Dominican Republic, 1844-1874," Diplomatic History 17 (93): 571-597; auth, "Torn Between Empires: Economy, Society, and Patterns of Political Thought in the Hispanic Caribbean, 1840-1878, Athens: Univ of George Press, 94; auth, "The Sword and the Crucifix: Church-State Relations and Nationality in the Nineteenth-Century Dominican Republic," Latin American Research Review 30 (95): 69-93; auth, "The Havana Anglo-Spanish Mixed Commission for the Suppression of the Slave Trade and Cuba's Emancipados," Slavery and Abolition 16:2 (95): 205-225; auth, "Life in a 'male city': Native and Foreign Elite Women in Nineteenth-Century Havana," Cuban Studies 25 (95): 27-49; auth, "Dominican Republic," Article-length entry in The Encyclopedia of U.S. Foreign Relations, 4 (New York; Oxford Univ Press, 97, II), 27-32; auth, "Puerto Rico in the Whirlwind of 1898: Conflict, Continuity, and Change," Magazine of History 12:3 (98): 24-29; auth, "Fighting Slavery in the Caribbean: The Life and Times of a British Family in Nineteenth-Century Havana, Armonk, NY:M.E, Sharpe Publishers, 98; auth, "Crypto-Protestants and Pseudo-Catholics in the Nineteenth-Century Hispanic Caribbean," forthcoming in The Journal of Ecclesiastical History 51:1 (00). **CONTACT ADDRESS** Dept Puerto Rican and Hispanic Caribbean Studies, Rutgers Univ, Tillett Hall, Rm 235, Livingston Campus, 53 Ave E, Piscataway, NJ 08854-8040. **EMAIL** lumartin@rci.rutgers.edu

MARTINOT, STEVE
PERSONAL Born 09/25/1939, New York, NY, s **DISCIPLINE** AMERICAN STUDIES **EDUCATION** Antioch Univ, BA, 62; Univ Colo, MA, 85; Univ Calif Santa Cruz, PhD, 94. **CAREER** Lectr, San Francisco State Univ. **MEMBERSHIPS** MLA; IAPL. **RESEARCH** Semiotics; structures of racialization. **SELECTED PUBLICATIONS** Transl, Albert Memnic, Racism (U Minn Pr); ed, Maps and Mirrors, Northwestern Univ Pr; auth, The Rule of Racialization, Temple Univ Pr, (forthcoming). **CONTACT ADDRESS** Humanities Dept Am Studies, San Francisco State Univ, 1600 Holloway Ave, Berkeley, CA 94132. **EMAIL** marto@ocf.berkeley.edu

MARTINSON, FRED
DISCIPLINE ART HISTORY **EDUCATION** Univ Chicago, PhD, 68. **CAREER** From prof to prof emer, Art Hist, Univ Tenn. **SELECTED PUBLICATIONS** Auth, "The Great Buddha Bend in Eastern Sichuan: The Ancient Stone Carvings at Dazu"; auth, "Instructional and Research Uses of Multimedia as Learning Empowerment for Faculty and Students: Teaching Chinese Art History with AVC," Charlottesville, 93; auth, "Stone Sculptures of Dazu," 91. **CONTACT ADDRESS** School of Art, Univ of Tennessee, Knoxville, Knoxville, TN 37996. **EMAIL** fmart@utk.edu

MARTY, MARTIN EMIL
PERSONAL Born 02/05/1928, West Point, NE, m, 1952, 5 children **DISCIPLINE** MODERN RELIGIOUS HISTORY **EDUCATION** Concordia Sem, BA, 49, MDiv, 52; Lutheran Sch Theol, Chicago, STM, 54; Univ Chicago, PhD(church hist), 56. **CAREER** From assoc prof to prof relig hist, 63-78, assoc dean divinity sch, 70-75, F M CONE DISTINGUISHED SERV PROF, UNIV CHICAGO, 78-, Vis assoc prof, Lutheran Sch Theol, Chicago, 61 & Union Theol Sem, New York, 65; bd mem, Nat Humanities Ctr, 76-; assoc ed, Christian Century, ed newslet, Context & coed, Church Hist. **HONORS AND AWARDS** Nat Humanities Medal; Nat Bk Awd; Medal of the Am Acad of Arts and Sciences, the Univ of Chicago Alumni Medal; Distinguished Serv Medal of the Asn of Theological Schools; nineteen from us cols & univs. **MEMBERSHIPS** Fel Am Acad Arts & Sci; Soc Am Historians; Soc Values Higher Educ. **RESEARCH** Nineteenth century religious history of United States, Great Britain and Western Europe; effects of political-industrial revolutions on religion; history of religious behavior in America. **SELECTED PUBLICATIONS** Auth, American Religious History in the 80s, Church Hist, vol 0062, 93; Dictionary of American Religious Biography, 2nd ed, Cath Hist Rev, vol 0079, 93; From the Centripetal to the Centrifugal in Culture and Religion, Theol Today, vol 0051, 94; Religion and Radical Politics, J Relig, vol 0074, 94; Defending the Faith, J Amer Hist, vol 0082, 95; Evangelicalism, J Southern Hist, vol 0061, 95; God in the Wasteland, J Relig, vol 0076, 96; Neale, J.M. and the Quest for Sobornost, J Relig, vol 0076, 96; Religion, Public Life, and the American Polity, J Relig, vol 0077, 97. **CONTACT ADDRESS** Divinity Sch Swift Hall, Univ of Chicago, 239 Scottswood Rd., Riverside, IL 60546. **EMAIL** memarty@aol.com

MARTY, MYRON AUGUST
PERSONAL Born 04/10/1932, West Point, NE, m, 1954, 4 children **DISCIPLINE** AMERICAN HISTORY **EDUCATION** Concordia Teachers Col, Ill, BS, 54; Wash Univ, MEd, 60; St Louis Univ, MA, 65, PhD(hist), 67. **CAREER** Teacher, Lutheran High Sch, St Louis, Mo, 57-65; from asst prof to assoc prof hist, Florissant Valley Community Col, 67-72, chmn div soc sci, 66-75, prof, 72-80; DEP DIR, EDUC PROG, NAT ENDOWMENT FOR HUMANITIES, 80-, Mem Comt exam soc sci-hist, Col Level Exam Prog, Educ Testing Serv, 67-76, consult-examr, NCent Asn Cols & Schs, 69-80; Nat Endowment for Humanities fel, 72-73; vis lectr, Univ Md, 72-73; bk reviewer, St Louis Post-Dispatch, 72-; mem exec bd, NCent Asn Cols & Schs, Comn Inst Higher Educ, 77-80: mem, Nat Bd Consults Nat Endowment for Humanities, 78-80. **MEMBERSHIPS** AHA; Orgn Am Historians; Am Soc Church Hist; Am Studies Asn; Am Asn State & Local Hist. **RESEARCH** Recent America; American nationality and ethnicity; family and community history. **SELECTED PUBLICATIONS** Auth, Lutherans and Roman Catholicism: The Changing Conflict, 1917-1963, Univ Notre Dame, 68; coauth, Retracing Our Steps: Studies in Documents from the American Past (2 vols), Harper, 72; Your Family History: A Handbook for Research and Writing, AHM, 78; auth, Nearby history: Exploring the past around you, Am Asn State & Local Hist, 82. **CONTACT ADDRESS** Educ Prog, National Endowment for the Humanities, Washington, DC 20506.

MARZIK, THOMAS DAVID
PERSONAL Born 12/15/1941, Bridgeport, CT **DISCIPLINE** HISTORY **EDUCATION** Col Holy Cross, AB, 63; Columbia Univ, MA & Cert, (Ecent Europe), 66, PhD, 76. **CAREER** Instr, 70-75, asst prof, 75-81, assoc prof, 81-97, Prof hist, St Joseph's Univ, PA, 97-; Book review ed, Slovakia, East Central Europe, 81-91. **HONORS AND AWARDS** Gold Medal of Pres of Slovak Repub, 98. **MEMBERSHIPS** AHA; Am Asn Advan Slavic Studies; Czechoslovak Hist Conf; Czechoslovak Soc Arts & Sci; Slovak Studies Asn; Immigration & Ethnic Hist Soc. **RESEARCH** Modern Slovak and Czech history. **SELECTED PUBLICATIONS** Auth, T G Masaryk and the Slovaks, 1882-1914, In: Columbia Essays in International Affairs: The Dean's Papers, 1965, Columbia Univ, 66; Masaryk's National Background, In: The Czech National Renascence of the Nineteenth Century: Essays Presented to Otakar Odlozilik in Honour of His Seventieth Birthday, Univ Toronto, 70; co-ed, Immigrants and Religion in Urban America, Temple Univ, 77; The Slovakophile Relationship of T G Masaryk and Karel Kalal prior to 1914, in T G Masaryk (1850-1937), vol 1, Thinker and Politician, St Martin Press, 90; co-ed R W Seton-Watson and His Relations with the Czechs and Slovaks: Documents 1906-1951, 95-96. **CONTACT ADDRESS** Dept of Hist, Saint Joseph's Univ, 5600 City Ave, Philadelphia, PA 19131-1395. **EMAIL** tmarzik@sju.edu

MARZOLF, MARION TUTTLE
PERSONAL Born 07/06/1930, Greenville, MI, m, 1953 **DISCIPLINE** AMERICAN JOURNALISM HISTORY **EDUCATION** Mich State Univ, BA, 52; Univ Mich, MA, 63, PhD(Am cult), 72. **CAREER** Copywriter, Wallace-Lindeman, 52-53; reporter & asst, Washington Post, 55-57; ed asst, Nat Geog Mag, 57-63; lectr English jour, Eastern Mich Univ, 64-68; asst prof, 68-73, assoc prof, 73-90, prof, 90-95, prof emer, Jour, Univ Mich, 95- . **HONORS AND AWARDS** Outstanding Ach Awd, Asn for Educ in jour Educ, 82. **MEMBERSHIPS** Asn for Educ Jour; Women in Communications, Inc; Immigration Hist Soc; Danish Am Heritage Soc; Soc Advan Scandinavian Studies. **RESEARCH** History of women in Jism; development of professional Jist in America, 1890-1920 era; immigrant press, especially Scandinavian. **SELECTED PUBLICATIONS** Auth, Up From the Footnote: A History of Women Journalists, Hastings House, 77; coauth (with Melba Tolliver), Kerner Plus 10: Minorities and the Media, Univ Mich, 77; auth, American studies--an example for journalism historians?, Jour Hist, spring 78; auth, The Danish-Language Press in America, Arno Press, 79; auth, The new journalism--a press revolution, Annales du CRAA Sem, France, 81; auth, Civilizing Voices, Longman, 90. **CONTACT ADDRESS** 1420 Granger, Ann Arbor, MI 48109. **EMAIL** mtmm@umich.edu

MASLOWSKI, PETER
DISCIPLINE HISTORY **EDUCATION** Miami Univ, BA, 66; Ohio State Univ, MA, 68; PhD, 72. **CAREER** Asst prof to prof, Univ of Nebr Lincoln, 74-. **HONORS AND AWARDS** Amoco Found Awd for Distinguished Undergrad Teaching; Col of Arts and Sci Awd for Outstanding Teaching. **MEMBERSHIPS** Soc for Milit Hist. **RESEARCH** U.S. Military History. **SELECTED PUBLICATIONS** Coauth, For the Common Defense: A Military History of the United States of America; auth, Armed With Cameras: The American Military Photographers of World War II. **CONTACT ADDRESS** Dept History, Univ of Nebraska, Lincoln, PO Box 88037, Lincoln, NE 68588-0327. **EMAIL** pmaslowski1@unl.edu

MASON, FRANCIS M.
DISCIPLINE HISTORY **EDUCATION** Univ CA Riverside, AB, 57; Wake Forest Univ, MA, 66; Univ CT, PhD, 74. **CAREER** Prof, 67-, St Anselm Col. **RESEARCH** Edwardian women's suffrage; the life of Sylvia Pankhurst; Manchester, NH hist. **SELECTED PUBLICATIONS** Auth, Charles Masterman and National Health Insurance, Albion, 78; The Newer Eve: The Catholic Women's Suffage Society in England 1911-1923, Cath Hist Rev, 86; bk revs in Albion, Hist NH, Historian, and Studies in Soviet Thought; ed, Childish Things: Reminiscences of Susan B. Blount, Thompson and Rutter, 88. **CONTACT ADDRESS** Dept of Hist, Saint Anselm Col, 100 Saint Anselm Dr, Manchester, NH 03102-1310. **EMAIL** frmason@anselm.edu

MASON, HERBERT W.
PERSONAL Born 04/20/1932, Wilmington, DE, m, 1982, 3 children **DISCIPLINE** ARABIC AND ISLAMIC HISTORY **EDUCATION** Harvard Col, AB, 55; AM, 65; PhD, 69. **CAREER** Teacher, Am School of Paris, 59-60; instr, St. Joseph's Col, 60-62; teaching fel, Harvard, 62-66; transl, Bollingen Found, 68-72; prof, Boston Univ, 72- **HONORS AND AWARDS** Kittredge Lit Awd; United Methodist Teacher of the Year Awd. **MEMBERSHIPS** PEN, Mark Twain Soc, Am Oriental Soc, Mediaeval Acad of Am, AHA, Am Acad of Poets. **RESEARCH** Sufism, Islamic History, Arabic translation, Celtic and Irish Histories, Ancient Near East Language and Literatures. **SELECTED PUBLICATIONS** Auth, Gilgamesh, a Verse Narrative; auth, The Death of al-hallaj, A Dramatic Narrative; auth, Al-Hallaj, a study; auth, Two Statesmen of Mediaeval Islam, a study; auth, A Legend of Alexander and the Merchant and Parrot, Dramatic Poems; auth, Summer Light, auth, Memoir of a Friend: Louis Massignon; auth, Testimonies and Reflections; auth, Disappearances, poems. **CONTACT ADDRESS** Dept Hist and Relig, Boston Univ, 745 Commonwealth Ave, Boston, MA 02215. **EMAIL** masonh@bu.edu

MASON, PHILIP P.
PERSONAL Born 04/28/1927, Salem, MA, m, 1951, 5 children **DISCIPLINE** AMERICAN HISTORY **EDUCATION** Boston Univ, BA, 50; Univ Mich, MA, 51, PhD, 56. **CAREER** Res assoc hist collections, Univ Mich, 51-53; dir, State Arch MI, 53-58; assoc prof, 58-65, prof hist, Wayne State Univ, 65, Univ Archivist, 58, dir, labor hist arch, 59; Distinguished Prof Hist, 90; Distinguished Graduate Faculty Award, 85. **HONORS AND AWARDS** Fellow, Soc Am Archivists. **MEMBERSHIPS** Orgn Am Historians; fel Soc Am Archivists (exec secy, 63-70, pres, 70-71); Oral Hist Assoc; Detroit Historical Commision; William L Clements Library Board Of Governors. **RESEARCH** Am Indian; labor hist; Am archival administration. **SELECTED PUBLICATIONS** Auth, Schoolcraft's Expedition to Lake Itasca: The Discovery of the Source of the Mississippi, Mich State Univ, 58; School craft, The Literary Voyager or Muzzeniegun, Mich State Univ, 62; coauth, Harper of Detroit, The Origin and Growth of a Great Metropolitan Hospital, 64 & auth, Detroit, Fort Lernoult, and the American Revolution, 64, Wayne State Univ; A History of American Roads, Rand McNally, 67; auth, Working in America, Am Asn State & Local Hist, 75;Copper Country Journal, Wayne State univ Press, MI Bureau of Hist, 90; Rum Running and the Roaring Twenties: Prohibition on the Michigan/Ontario Waterways, WSU Press, 95; Schoolcrafts Ojibwa Lodge Stories: Life on the Lake Superior Fronteer, MI State Univ Press, 97; co auth, The Ambassador Bridge: A Monument to Progress, Wayne State univ Press, 92. **CONTACT ADDRESS** Fac Admin Bldg, Rm 3109, Wayne State Univ, 838 Mackenzie, Detroit, MI 48202-3919.

MASON, ROBERT
PERSONAL Born 10/27/1955, Schenectady, NY, s **DISCIPLINE** GEOGRAPHY **EDUCATION** Univ Buffalo, BA, 77; Univ Toronto, MA, 79; Rutgers Univ, PhD, 86. **CAREER** Adj

assoc, Columbia Univ, 85; lectr, Ohio State Univ, 86; from asst to assoc prof, Temple Univ, 86-; dir of Environmental Studies Prog, Temple Univ, 98-. **HONORS AND AWARDS** Dartmouth Awd for Outstanding Reference Work, 92. **MEMBERSHIPS** Asn of Am Geographers, Am Geog Soc. **SELECTED PUBLICATIONS** Auth, "Sustainability, Regional Planning and the Future of New York's Adirondack Park," Progress in Rural Policy & Planning 5 (95): 15-28; auth, "Saving Place: Land Trusts as Conservators of Local and Regional Landscapes," Small Town 26.2 (95): 14-19; auth, "Transplanted Landscapes: The American Scene in Tokyo," Soc for Commercial Archeol J 14.2 (97): 10-14; coauth, "Motivations for Ecostewardship Partnerships: Examples from the Adirondack Park," Land Use Policy 16 (99): 1-9; coauth, "Comment: The Importance of Place in Partnerships for Regional Environmental Management," Environ Conservation 26.3 (99): 159-162; auth, "Whither Japan's Environmental Movement? An Assessment of Problems and prospects at the National Level," Pacific Affairs 72.2 (99): 187-207. **CONTACT ADDRESS** Dept Geog, Temple Univ, 309 Gladfelter Hall, Philadelphia, PA 19122.

MASON, STEVE
PERSONAL Born 09/14/1957, Toronto, ON, Canada **DISCIPLINE** EARLY JUDAISM AND CHRISTIAN ORIGINS **EDUCATION** McMaster Univ, BA, 80, MA, 81; Univ St Michaels Col, PhD, 86. **CAREER** Vis asst prof, Mem Univ NF, 87-89; prof and head, Dept Classics & Ancient Mediter Stud, Penn State Univ, 96-96; asst prof, 89-92, assoc prof, 92-98, prof, 98-, York Univ-Toronto. **MEMBERSHIPS** Soc Bibl Lit; Am Philol Asn; Studiorum Novi Testamenti Soc; Can Soc Bibl Stud. **RESEARCH** Philosophy and religion in the Greco-Roman world, especially Judaism (specialization: Flavius Josephus) and early Christianity. **SELECTED PUBLICATIONS** Coed An Early Christian Reader, Can Scholars Press, 90; auth Flavius Josephus on the Pharisees, E J Brill, 91; Josephus and the New Testament, Hendrickson, 92; ed Understanding Josephus: Seven Perspectives, Sheffield Acad Press, 98. **CONTACT ADDRESS** York Univ, 219 Vanier Col, Toronto, ON, Canada M3J 1P3. **EMAIL** smason@yorku.ca

MASS, JEFFREY PAUL
PERSONAL Born 06/29/1940, New York, NY, m, 1963, 2 children **DISCIPLINE** JAPANESE HISTORY **EDUCATION** Hamilton Col, BA, 62; New York Univ, MA, 65; Yale Univ, MPhil, 69, PhD(Japanese hist), 71. **CAREER** Lectr hist, Yale Univ, 72-73; asst prof, 73-76, ASSOC PROF HIST, STANFORD UNIV, 76-, Stanford Mellen fel, Stanford Univ, 75-76; Social Sci Res Coun fel, 76-76; Guggenheim Found fel, 78-79. **MEMBERSHIPS** Asn Asian Studies. **RESEARCH** Japanese medieval history. **SELECTED PUBLICATIONS** Co-ed, Medieval Japan: Essays in Institutional History, 74 & auth, Warrior Government in Early Medieval Japan, Yale Univ, 74; The Kamakura Bakufu: A Study in Documents, 76 & The Development of Kamakura Rule: A History with Documents, Stanford Univ, 78. **CONTACT ADDRESS** Dept of Hist, Stanford Univ, Stanford, CA 94305-1926.

MASSANARI, RONALD LEE
PERSONAL Born 06/04/1941, Champaign, IL, m, 1963, 2 children **DISCIPLINE** HISTORY OF CHRISTIAN THOUGHT **EDUCATION** Goshen Col, BA, 63; Univ Wis-Madison, MA, 65; Garrett Theol Sem, BD, 66; Duke Univ, PhD(relig), 69. **CAREER** Vis asst prof church hist, Divinity Sch, Duke Univ, 69-70; from asst prof to assoc prof, 70-80, Prof Relig, Alma Col, 80-, Adj prof, San Francisco Theol Sem, 77-. **MEMBERSHIPS** Am Soc Church Hist; Am Acad Relig **RESEARCH** Religion and imagination; myth and ritual; political theology. **SELECTED PUBLICATIONS** Auth, " Sexual Imagery and Religion: An Intercultural Exploration," Gender in World Religions, Vol II, (91); auth, "Dualism, Nondualism, and the Human Problem: An Exploration into Worldview Contexts of Western and Eastern Religions," Journal of Religious Studies, Vol 18, (92): 1-2; auth, "Nondualism Not Monism: A Response to Mark Wigierski," This World, 28, 93; auth, "Re-Imagining God: In the Very Presence Therof" Journal of the Interdenominational Theological Center, Vol. XXIII, 2, 96; auth, "Carnal Spirituality: A Nondual Response to Traditional Dualism: Journal of Religious Taditions, Vol 20, 97; auth, "When Mountains are Mountains and Gardens are Gardens: Explorations into Sacred Space, Worldviews, and Ethics," Journal of Developing Societies, Vol XIII, (97): 3-4; auth, "The Pluralisms of American 'Religious Pluralism: Journal of Church and State, Vol. 40, 3, 98; auth, "For Questioning is the Piety of Thought,' But, Not Without Consequences in Technocratic Society," Teaching Ttheology and Religion, Vol 1, 3, 98; auth, "A Problem in Environmental Ethics: Western and Eastern Styles," Journal of Christian-Buddhist Studies, Vol. 18, 98; auth, "The Net of Tantra On-line," Nova Religio, Vol 2, No 4, 99. **CONTACT ADDRESS** Dept of Relig, Alma Col, 614 W Superior St, Alma, MI 48801-1511. **EMAIL** massanari@alma.edu

MASTERS, DONALD C.
PERSONAL Born 02/08/1908, Shelburne, ON, Canada **DISCIPLINE** HISTORY **EDUCATION** Univ Toronto, BA, 30, MA, 31; Oxford Univ, PhD, 45; Bishop's Univ, DCI, 75. **CAREER** Lectr hist, Queen's Univ, 38-39; asst prof, 41-44, prof hist, Bishop's Univ, 44-66; prof Can hist, 66-74, Prof Emer, Univ Guelph, 77-. **MEMBERSHIPS** Can Hist Asn; Can Inst Int Affairs. **SELECTED PUBLICATIONS** Auth, The Reciprocity Treaty of 1854, 37; auth, The Rise of Toronto, 47; auth, The Winnipeg General Strike, 50; auth, A Short History of Canada, 58; auth, Protestant Church Colleges in Canada, 66; coauth, Ten Rings on the Oak: Mountain-Nicolls Family Story, 87; coauth, Henry John Cody: An Outstanding Life, 95. **CONTACT ADDRESS** 19 Monticello Cres, Guelph, ON, Canada N1G 2M1.

MATE, MAVIS
PERSONAL Born 11/12/1933, London, England, m, 1956, 2 children **DISCIPLINE** MEDIEVAL HISTORY **EDUCATION** Oxford Univ, BA, 56, MA, 61; Ohio State Univ, PhD, 67. **CAREER** Am Asn Univ Women fel, 67-68; Nat Endowment for Hum tchg resident, Denison Univ, 68-69; instr hist, OH State Univ, 69-72, lectr, 72-74; asst prof, 74-77, assoc prof hist, Univ OR, 77-84, Prof, 84-98, Am Coun Learned Soc fel, 81-82. **MEMBERSHIPS** Mediaeval Acad Am; AHA; Econ Hist Soc; Fellow of the Royal Hist soc. **RESEARCH** Monetary problems of 13th and 14th century Europe; the soc and economic position of Canterbury Cathedral priory; souteast Engl in late mid ages, Soc and Economic position of women in Engl. **SELECTED PUBLICATIONS** Auth, A mint of trouble, 1279-1307, Speculum, 69; Monetary policies of Edward I, 1272-1307, Brit Numis J, 72; The indebtedness of Canterbury Cathedral Priory, 1215-1290, 2nd ser, 73 & High prices in early fourteenth England: causes and consequences, 2nd ser, 75, Econ Hist Rev; Coping with inflation: a fourteenth century English example, J Medieval Hist, 78; The role of gold coinage in the English economy, 1338-1400, Numis Chronicle, 78; Profit and productivity on the estates of Isabella de Forz, 1260-92, Econ Hist Rev, 80; The impact of war on the economy of Canterbury Cathedral Priory, 1294-1340, Speculum, 82; 2 sections on Kent and Sussex in The Agarian History of England and Wales, v III (1350-1500), Cambridge, 91; ed, Daughters Wives and Widows after the Black Death (1350-1535), Boydell and Brewer, 98; auth, "Women in Medieval English Society," New Studies in Economic and Social Hist, Cambridge, 99. **CONTACT ADDRESS** Dept of Hist, Univ of Oregon, Eugene, OR 97403-1205. **EMAIL** memate@oregon.uoregon.edu

MATHENY, WILLIAM EDWARD
PERSONAL Born 12/23/1932, Sterling, IL, m, 1960, 4 children **DISCIPLINE** EUROPEAN HISTORY, LATIN AMERICAN STUDIES **EDUCATION** Univ IL, Urbana, BS, 56; Southwestern Baptist Sem, MDiv, 61; TX Christian Univ, MA, PhD(hist), 72. **CAREER** Prof, Baptist Theol Sem of Peru, 72-78; prof hist, Liberty Univ & Sem, 78-, chm, dept cross cultural studies, 82-. **MEMBERSHIPS** Am Soc Church Hist. **RESEARCH** The major themes and fate of dissenters in 16th century Spain; The origins and spread of Protestant Christianity in Latin America; Possible pre-Columbian arrival of Europeans in the Americas. **SELECTED PUBLICATIONS** Auth, La Multiplicacion de Iglesias en America Latina, Baptist Sem of Peru, 73; La Capacitacion de Obreros Cristianos en America Latina, Casa Bautista de Publ, El Paso, 75; Job, in Liberty Old Testament Commentary, Nelson, 82. **CONTACT ADDRESS** Dept Hist, Liberty Univ, 1971 University Blvd., Lynchburg, VA 24502-2269. **EMAIL** wmatheny@liberty.edu

MATHEWS, DONALD G.
PERSONAL Born 04/15/1932, Caldwell, ID, m, 1959 **DISCIPLINE** AMERICAN HISTORY **EDUCATION** Col Idaho, BA, 54; Yale Univ, BD, 57; Duke Univ, PhD(Am hist), 62. **CAREER** Instr hist, Duke Univ, 61-62; instr, Princeton Univ, 62-65, asst prof Am social hist, 65-68; assoc prof, 68-73, PROF AM SOCIAL HIST, UNIV NC, CHAPEL HILL, 73-, Soc Sci Res Coun fac res grant, 67-68; Nat Endowment for Humanities grant, 75-76. **HONORS AND AWARDS** Fel, Nat Endowment Humanities, 79-80; Bicentennial Chair Am Studies, Univ Helsinki, 81-82. **MEMBERSHIPS** AHA; Orgn Am Historians. **RESEARCH** American religious history; United States history, 1780-1850; American social history. **SELECTED PUBLICATIONS** Auth, Slavery and Methodism: A Chapter in American Morality, 1780-1845, Princeton Univ, 65; The abolitionists on slavery: the critique behind the social movement, J Southern Hist, 5/67; The second great awakening as an organizing process, Am Quart, winter 69; ed, Agitation for Freedom, Wiley, 71; auth, Religion in the Old South: speculation on methodology, SAtlantic Quart, winter 74; Religion in the Old South, Univ Chicago, 77. **CONTACT ADDRESS** Dept of Hist, Univ of No Carolina, Chapel Hill, Hamilton Hall 070-A, Chapel Hill, NC 27514.

MATHISEN, RALPH WHITNEY
PERSONAL Born 02/17/1947, Ashland, WI, m, 1979 **DISCIPLINE** ANCIENT HISTORY, CLASSICS **EDUCATION** Univ Wis, BS, 69, MA, 73, PhD(hist), 79; Rensselaer Polytech Inst, MS, 72. **CAREER** Vis asst prof Roman hist, Univ Ill, Chicago Circle, 79-80; ASST PROF ANCIENT & BYZANTINE HIST, UNIV SC, 80-. **MEMBERSHIPS** Asn Ancient Historians; Am Philol Asn; Am Hist Asn; Soc Ancient Numis. **RESEARCH** Late Roman society and religion; late Roman prosopography; Greek and Roman numismatics. **SELECTED PUBLICATIONS** Auth, Hilarius, Germanus and Lupus: The aristocratic background of the Chelidonius affair, Phoenix, 79; Resistance and reconciliation: Majorian and the Gallic aristocracy, Francia, 79; Sidonius on the reign of Avitus: A study in political prudence, 79 & Epistolography, literary circles and family ties in late Roman Gaul, 81, Trans Am Philol Asn; Antigonus Gonatas and the silver coinages of Macedonia circa 280-270 BC, Am Numis Soc Mus Notes, 81; Avitus, Italy and the East in AD 455-456, Byzantion, 81; The last year of Saint Germanus of Auxerre, Analecta Bollandiana, 81; Petronius, Hilarius and Valerianus: Prosopographical notes on the conversion of the Roman aristocracy, Hist, 81. **CONTACT ADDRESS** Dept of Hist, Univ of So Carolina, Columbia, Columbia, SC 29208.

MATILSKY, BARBARA C.
DISCIPLINE ART HISTORY **EDUCATION** NYork Univ, PhD. **CAREER** Adj assoc prof, Univ NC, Chapel Hill. **RESEARCH** Asian contemporary art & 19th century French painting. **SELECTED PUBLICATIONS** Auth, Francois-August Biard: Artist, Naturalist, Explorer, Gazette de Beaux Arts, 85; Classical Myth and Imagery in Contemporary Art, Exhib Cat, Queens Mus, 88; Fragile Ecologies: Artists' Interpretations and Solutions, Rizzoli Int, 92; The Survival of Culture and Nature: Perspectives on the History of Environmental Art, Art and Design, 94; auth, Art and Ritual from Nepal and Tibet, Exh. Cat Ackland Art Museum, 01. **CONTACT ADDRESS** Univ of No Carolina, Chapel Hill, Chapel Hill, NC 27599.

MATOSSIAN, MARY KILBOURNE
PERSONAL Born 07/09/1930, Los Angeles, CA, m, 1954, 4 children **DISCIPLINE** MODERN HISTORY **EDUCATION** Stanford Univ, BA, 51, PhD(hist), 55; Univ Beirut, MA, 52. **CAREER** Res assoc USSR hist, Columbia Univ, 55-56; res fel Kemalism, Ctr Mid Eastern Studies, Harvard Univ, 57-58; asst prof hist, State Univ NY Col Buffalo, 60-62; lectr, 63-67, asst prof, 67-72, ASSOC PROF HIST, UNIV MD, COLLEGE PARK, 72-. **MEMBERSHIPS** AHA: Am Asn Advan Slavic Studies. **RESEARCH** History of the family; European health history. **SELECTED PUBLICATIONS** Auth, Fevered Lives--Tuberculosis in American Culture Since 1870, J Amer Hist, vol 0084, 97. **CONTACT ADDRESS** Dept of Hist, Univ of Maryland, Col Park, College Park, MD 20742. **EMAIL** mm24@umail.umd.edu

MATRAY, JAMES IRVING
PERSONAL Born 12/06/1948, Evergreen Park, IL, m, 1971, 2 children **DISCIPLINE** AMERICAN HISTORY **EDUCATION** Lake Forest Col, BA, 70; Univ VA, MA, 73, PhD, 77. **CAREER** One year replacement appointments: Univ TX, Arlington, CA State Col, Bakersfield, Glenville State Col, WV, one semester at DE State Col, 75-80; vis assoc prof hist, Univ Southen CA, 88-89; Distinguished vis scholar, Grad Inst of Peace Studies, Kyung Hee Univ, Seoul, Korea, 90; vis asst prof, 80-81, asst prof, 82-86, assoc prof, 87-91, prof Hist, NM State Univ, 92-. **HONORS AND AWARDS** IL State scholarship recipient, 66-70; nominated for a Woodrow Wilson fel, 69; Phi Beta Kappa, 70; Harry S Truman Lib Found res grant, 75, 82; MacArthur Memorial Lib res grant, 84; nominee, Burlington Northern Outstanding Teacher Awd, 85; Donald C Roush Awd for Teaching Excellence, NMSU, 88; Fulbright Lecture Awd recipient, Univ Warsaw, 88-89 (declined); Gold Key Student Soc honorary membership for outstanding teaching, 90; NEH grant, 90; Outstanding Teacher, Academic-Athletics Awds Banquet, 94; finalist, El Paso Natural Gas Fac Achievement Awd, 96; numerous grants from the NM State Univ. **MEMBERSHIPS** Am Hist Asn; Soc for Historians of Am Foreign Relations. **SELECTED PUBLICATIONS** Auth, Hodge Podge: US Occupation Policy in Korea, 1945-1948, Korean Studies, XIX, 95; Civil is a Dumb Name for War, SHAFR Newsletter, XXXVII, 4, Dec 95; Foreward in We Will Not Be Strangers: Korean War Letters Between a MASH Surgeon and His Wife, ed Dorothy Horwitz, Univ Il Press, 97; Civil War of a Sort: the International Origins of the Korean War, In The Korean War in Retrospect, ed Daniel Meador, Univ Press Am, 98; Korea's Partition: Soviet-American Pursuit of Reunification, 1945-1948, Parameters, 98; Japan's Emergence as a Global Power, Greenwood Press, 00; Historical Dictionary of US-East Asian Relations, Greenwood Press, forthcoming 01; The Uncivil War: Korea, 1945-1953, M E Sharpe Inc, forthcoming 02; The Price of Intervention: American Foreign Policy in Korea, 1950-1953, in progress; numerous reviews and review essays, articles, books, book chapters, and dictionary entries. **CONTACT ADDRESS** Dept of History, New Mexico State Univ, Las Cruces, NM 88003. **EMAIL** jmatray@nmsu.edu

MATRICIAN, MARIAN
DISCIPLINE HISTORY **EDUCATION** Johns Hopkins Univ, BA, 85; Rutgers Univ, PhD, 97. **CAREER** Instructor; Rutgers Univ, 93-97; Asst Prof, Univ Ark, 97-. **HONORS AND AWARDS** Johns Hopkins Fel; NJ Scholars; Walter C Russell Scholarship; Res Fel, Deutsche Akademische Austauschdienst; Univ AR Grant. **MEMBERSHIPS** Am Hist Asn; Sixteenth Century Soc; Soc for Early Modern Women. **RESEARCH** Early Modern Legal Change; Northern Germany; Women. **CONTACT ADDRESS** Dept Hist, Univ of Arkansas, Little Rock, 2801 S Univ Ave, Little Rock, AR 72204-1000. **EMAIL** mfmatrician@ualr.edu

MATTER, EDITH ANN
PERSONAL Born 12/29/1949, Ft Smith, AR **DISCIPLINE** HISTORY OF CHRISTIANITY **EDUCATION** Oberline Col, AB, 71; Yale Univ, MA, 75, Mphil, 75, PhD(relig studies), 76. **CAREER** Vis prof, Universita degli Studi di Trento, 93; vis assoc prof, Haverford Col, 83-86, 87-90; vis scholar, Weston Sschool of Theology, 79; asst prof, Univ of Pa, 76-82; assoc prof, Univ of Pa, 82-90. **HONORS AND AWARDS** Whiting Fel for the Humanities, Yale Univ, 75-76; Am Philos Soc Grants, 77, 80, 84; Am Council of Learned Societies, Summer Grant, 78; auth, Univ of Pennsylvania Res Coun Grants, 78, 886, 89, 90, 92; NEH fel, 79, 88; Annenberg Res Institute Fel, 92; John Simon Guggenheim Fel, 96; Lindback Awd for Distinguished Teaching, Univ of Pa, 81; Outstanding Teaching Awd, Col Alumni Soc, Upenn, 95; . Jean Brownlee Term Prof of Religious Studies, 96. **MEMBERSHIPS** Am Acad Relig, Women's Caucus; Mediaeval Acad Am; Del Valley Medieval Asn; Am Asn of Univ Profs; Am Asn of Univ Women. **RESEARCH** History of Christian culture, from the middle ages to the 17th century; history of interpretation of the Bible; spirituality nd mysticism in the Christian tradition from the middle ages to the present; women in Christian history; sexuality in Christian history; medieval textual studies; music in the history of Christianity. **SELECTED PUBLICATIONS** Auth, The Voice of My Beloved: The Song of Songs in Western Medieval Christianity, Philadelphia: Univ of Pennsylvania Press, 90; co-ed, Creative Women in Medieval and Early Modern Italy: A Religious and Artistic Renaissance, Philadelphia: Univ of Pennsylvania Press, 94; auth, "Il matrimonio mistico," in Dome e Fede: santita e vita relitiosa, eds. L. Scaraffia and G. Zarri, (Bari and Rome: Laterza Editore, 94): 43-60; auth, "Political Prophecy as Reperssion: Lucia Brocadeli da Narni and Ercole d'Este," in Christendom and its Discontents, ed. S. Waugh, (Cambridge: Cambridge Univ Press, 95): 168-76; auth, "The Academic Culture of Disbelief: Religious Studies at the University of Pennsylvania," in Method and Theory in The Study of Relig 7, (95): 389-98. **CONTACT ADDRESS** Dept of Relig Studies, Univ of Pennsylvania, Col Hall, PO Box 36, Philadelphia, PA 19104-6303. **EMAIL** amatter@ccat.sas.upenn.edu

MATTESON, LYNN ROBERT
DISCIPLINE ART HISTORY **EDUCATION** Univ Calif, Berkeley, PhD, 75. **CAREER** Assoc prof, Univ Southern Calif; correspondent for Pantheon; dean, Sch Fine Arts, 88-93. **RESEARCH** 18th & 19th Century European art. **SELECTED PUBLICATIONS** Auth, The Sense of an Ending: Apocalyptic Imagery in British Romantic Painting, Proceedings Conf on the Apocalypse, Missiac, France, 97; contribur, International Dictionary of Art, 92. **CONTACT ADDRESS** Col Letters, Arts & Sciences, Univ of So California, University Park Campus, Los Angeles, CA 90089.

MATTHEWS, J. ROSSER
PERSONAL Born 09/27/1964, Williamsburg, VA, s **DISCIPLINE** HISTORY **EDUCATION** Col of William and Mary, BA 85; Duke Univ, MA 88, PhD 92; Col Wm And Mary, MPP 97. **CAREER** N Carolina State Univ, vis lectr, 92,93; Duke Univ, asst prof 93; Univ Oklahoma, asst prof 94; College William and Mary, adj prof 97, 99, 00. **MEMBERSHIPS** HSS; AAHM. **RESEARCH** Historical and philosophical issues raised by appeals to quantitative evidence in medicine including ethical aspects. **SELECTED PUBLICATIONS** Auth, Qualification and the Quest for Medical Certainty, Princeton, Princeton U Press, 95; auth, Practice Guidelines and Tort Reform: The Legal System Confronts the Technocratic Wish, Jour of Health Politics Policy and Law, 99; Why Should the Stroke Prevention Policy Model be Used?, coauth, in: The Stroke Prevention Policy Model: Linking Evidence and Clinical Decisions, coauth, Annals of Internal Medicine, 97; auth, History of Biostatistics, entries on J. Gavarret, PCA Louis, P Pinel, A Quetelet, in: Encyc of Biostatistics, Chichester UK, John Wiley & Sons, 98; auth, Alfred W Crosby, The Measure of Reality: Quantification and Western Society, 1250-1600. In: The Amer Hist Rev, 98; Marc Berg, Rationalizing Medical Work: Decision-Support Techniques and Medical Practices, in: Isis: An International Rev Devoted to the Hist of Science and it Cultural Influences, 97. **CONTACT ADDRESS** Col of William and Mary, 200 Captain Newport Circle, Williamsburg, VA 23185. **EMAIL** rmatthews@widomaker.com

MATTHEWS, JOHN F.
PERSONAL Born 02/15/1940, Leicester, England, m, 1965, 2 children **DISCIPLINE** CLASSICS, ANCIENT HISTORY **EDUCATION** Oxford Univ, BA, 63; MA, 67; PhD, 70. **CAREER** Res Fel, Balliol Coll, Oxford, 65-69; Univ Lecturer, Univ of Oxford, 69-90; reader, 90-92: prof, 92-96. **HONORS AND AWARDS** Fel of Brit Acad; Fel of Royal Hist soc; Fel of Soc of Antiquaries of London. **MEMBERSHIPS** Soc for the Promotion of Roman Studies London; Am Philol Asn, Byantine Studies Asn. **RESEARCH** Late Roman History. **SELECTED PUBLICATIONS** Auth, Western Aristocracitsand Imperial Court, 75,90; Political Life and Culture in Late Roman Society, 85; The Roman Empire of America, 89; Laying down the Law: a Study of the Theodosian Code, 00; coauth, Atlas of Roman World, 82; The Goths in the Fourth Century, 91. **CONTACT ADDRESS** 160 McKinley Ave, New Haven, CT 06515. **EMAIL** john.matthews@yale.edu

MATTHEWS, REBECCA
PERSONAL Born 12/23/1953, Salem, MO, m, 1991, 5 children **DISCIPLINE** ENGLISH, HISTORY **EDUCATION** SW Tex State Univ, BA, 86; Tex Tech Univ, MA, 89. **CAREER** From TA to lectr, Tex Tech Univ, 86-92; instr, New Mex State Univ, 92-98; adj fac, San Antonio Col, 98-. **MEMBERSHIPS** W Tex Hist Asn, Western Lit Asn, Tex Kolflore Soc, Tex/SW Popular Culture Asn. **RESEARCH** Southwestern literature, folklore **SELECTED PUBLICATIONS** Auth, "When Fact Becomes Legend: West Texas Folk Heroes," W Tex Hist Asn Year Book LXVII (91): 84-93; auth, "Roping Yarns," The Permian Hist Annual (91): 13-22; auth, "The West Texas Ribbon Wars," True West (93): 34-43; auth, "The Town That Cereal Built," True West (94): 38-43; auth, "Elmer Kelton's Women: Hummingbirds with Hard-Steel Strength," J of the West 37.1 (98): 19-24; auth, "Pearl Nance, a Remarkable Ranchwomen," W Tex Hist Asn Year Book LXXIV (98): 122-127; auth, "Jane Gilmore Rushing: A West Texas Romanticist," RE:AL, The J of Lib Arts XXIII.I (98): 108-115; auth, "The Dialect Joke Rides the Range: The Emergence of Dialect Humor in Cowboy Poetry," Southwestern Am Lit 24.2 (99): 25-33; auth, "Elmer Kelton's Most Unusual Villians," in Elmer Kelton: A Half Century in Print, ed. Preston Lewis (Lubbolk, TX: Tex Tech Press, 00); auth, "Writing the Un-Western: Jane Gilmore Rushing and Mary Dove," Concho River Review (00). **CONTACT ADDRESS** Dept English, San Antonio Col, 1300 San Pedro Ave, San Antonio, TX 78212-4201. **EMAIL** jbmatthews2@juno.com

MATTHEWS, ROY T.
PERSONAL Born 02/14/1932, Franklin, VA, m, 1959, 2 children **DISCIPLINE** MODERN EUROPEAN AND DIPLOMATIC HISTORY **EDUCATION** Wash & Lee Univ, BA, 54; Duke Univ, MA, 56; Univ NC, Chapel Hill, PhD(Europ hist), 66. **CAREER** Instr soc studies, Womans' Col Ga, 58-60; mod civilization, Univ NC, 61-64; instr Europ hist, Univ Houston, 64-65; from instr to asst prof humanities, 65-71, staff, Justin Morrill Col, 69-71, dept hist, 69-73, 76 & 81-82; assoc prof, 71-76, PROF HUMANITIES, MICH STATE UNIV, 76- **MEMBERSHIPS** AAUP; North Am Conf Brit Studies; Victorian Soc Am. **RESEARCH** History of caricature and cartooning; 19th century English social and cultural history; influence of caricaturists. **SELECTED PUBLICATIONS** Auth, F.C.G. + Gould, Francis, Carruthers, 19th Century Prose, vol 0019, 92; Rank, Arthur, J. and the British Film Industry, Albion, vol 0026, 94; The Victorians Biography of Bull, John, 19th Century Prose, vol 0022, 95; Dictionary of British Cartoonists and Caricaturists, 1730-1980, Albion, vol 0027, 95. **CONTACT ADDRESS** Michigan State Univ, East Lansing, MI 48824.

MATTINGLY, PAUL HAVEY
PERSONAL Born 02/04/1941, Washington, DC, m, 1964, 2 children **DISCIPLINE** AMERICAN HISTORY **EDUCATION** Georgetown Univ, AB, 62; Univ Wis, MA, 64, PhD, 68. **CAREER** Instr, Dept of Hist, Univ Wis, 67-68; asst to assoc prof, 68-76, prof, 76-81, Dept Of Cultural Foundations, Chemn,74-81, Ed, Hist of Education Quart, 71-85; Prof of Hist, Dir, Progra, in Public Hist, NYU 81-. **HONORS AND AWARDS** NEH, summer 85; Nat Res Coun Grant, 70-71; Spencer Fel, 74-79. **MEMBERSHIPS** Am Hist Asn; Org of Am Historians; Nat Coun on Public Hist; Social Sci Hist Asn; Hist of Ed Soc. **RESEARCH** American higher education; suburbanization & community formation; philanthropy & professionalization. **SELECTED PUBLICATIONS** Auth, Suburban Landscapes: Culture and Politics in a Metropolitan Community, forthcoming; Old Suburbia, Invisible Am, Henry Holt and Co, 95; Politics and Ideology in a Metropolitan Suburb, Contested Terrain: Power, Politics and Participation in Suburbia, Greenwood Press, 95; The Suburban Canon Over Time, Suburban Discipline, Princeton Architectural Press, 97; The Political Culture of Antebellum American Colleges, Hist of Higher Ed Annual, 97; coauth, The Pedagogy of Public History, J of Am Ethnic Hist, 98. **CONTACT ADDRESS** 53 Washington Square, South, #508, New York, NY 10003. **EMAIL** phma@is2.nyu.edu

MATTISON, ROBERT S.
DISCIPLINE HISTORY OF ART **EDUCATION** Middlebury Col, BA, 74; Williams Col, MA, 77; Princeton Univ, MFA, 79, PhD, 85. **CAREER** Asst prof, 81-86, assoc prof, 87-94, PROF, 95-, LAFAYETTE COL. **CONTACT ADDRESS** Art Dept, Lafayette Col, Easton, PA 18042. **EMAIL** mattisor@lafayette.edu

MATTISON, WILLIAM H.
PERSONAL Born 01/16/1937, Aberdeen, MS, m, 1959, 2 children **DISCIPLINE** HISTORY, PSYCHOLOGY **EDUCATION** Itawamba Jr Col, AA, 56; Miss State Univ, BS, 58; M Ed, 61; MSS, 65; EDS, 67; Uniiv Sarasota, PhD, 71. **CAREER** Instr, Zama High School, 58-59; instr, Jane-Macon Jr High School, 59-63; instr, Amory Middle School; 63-64; dir, Amory city School; 64-71; dir, Itawamba Community Col, 71-79; instr, Itawamba Community Col, 79-. **HONORS AND AWARDS** DAR Hist Nat Awd. **MEMBERSHIPS** Miss Hist Soc; MAE; NEA; Monroe County Hist Soc; Patriotic Order Sons of Am; Sons of Confederate Veterans; Sons of Am Revolution; Bonnie Blue Soc; Mil Order of Stars and Bars, Amory Fine Arts Coun. **RESEARCH** Regional/local history in the areas of Civil War, Revolutionary War, Railroad History, Native-American History. **CONTACT ADDRESS** Dept Soc Sci, Itawamba Comm Col, 602 W Hill St, Fulton, MS 38843-1022.

MATTSON, VERNON E.
DISCIPLINE HISTORY **EDUCATION** Univ Kans, PhD, 71. **CAREER** Assoc prof, Univ Nev Las Vegas. **RESEARCH** American intellectual history; American religious history; Holocaust studies. **SELECTED PUBLICATIONS** Auth, Frederick Jackson Turner: A Reference Guide, Boston, 85. **CONTACT ADDRESS** History Dept, Univ of Nevada, Las Vegas, 4505 Md Pky, Las Vegas, NV 89154.

MATUSOW, ALLEN JOSEPH
PERSONAL Born 05/18/1937, Philadelphia, PA **DISCIPLINE** AMERICAN HISTORY **EDUCATION** Ursinus Col, BA, 58; Harvard Univ, MA, 59, PhD(hist), 63. **CAREER** From asst prof to assoc prof, 63-70, PROF HIST, RICE UNIV, 70-, DEAN SCH HUMANITIES, 80-, Vis asst prof, Stanford Univ, 67-68. **MEMBERSHIPS** AHA; Orgn Am Historians. **SELECTED PUBLICATIONS** Auth, The mind of B O Flower, New Eng Quart, 12/61; coauth, Truman Administration: A Documentary History, Harper, 67; co-ed, Twentieth Century America: Recent Interpretations, 69; ed, Senator Joe McCarthy, 70. **CONTACT ADDRESS** Dept of Hist, Rice Univ, Houston, TX 77251.

MATYNIA, ELZBIETA
DISCIPLINE LIBERAL STUDIES, ART **EDUCATION** Univ Warsaw, PhD, 79. **CAREER** Sr Lctr Liberal Studies and dir New Schl Transregional Ctr for Democratic Studies. **RESEARCH** The hist of soc thought and the soc of art; origins of nationalism and the emergence of gender issues in the new Europ democracies. **SELECTED PUBLICATIONS** Auth, Poetics of the Revolution, Perf Arts Jour; Hitler and the Artists, Am Jour Soc; auth, A Michnik Reader, Sociological Forum, 88; auth, Grappling With Democracy: Deliberations on Post-Communist Societies, 1990-1995, ed. Prague, 95; auth, Finding a Voice: Women in Postcommunist Central Europe in The Challenges of Local Feminism's: Women's Movement in Global Perspective, Amrita Baus, ed. Westview Press, 95; auth, Furnishing Democracy at the end of the Century: Negotiating Transition at the Polish Round Table & Others, Social Res, 00. **CONTACT ADDRESS** Graduate Faculty, 65 Fifth Ave, New York, NY 10003.

MATZKO, JOHN A.
PERSONAL Born 09/18/1946, Audubon, NJ, m, 1976, 1 child **DISCIPLINE** HISTORY **EDUCATION** Bob Jones Univ, BA, 68; Univ of Cincinnati, MA, 72; Univ of Va, PhD, 84. **CAREER** Member of History Faculty, Bob Jones Univ, 71-74; 78-; Chair, Division of Social Science, 98-. **MEMBERSHIPS** OAH; Amer Society for Legal History. **RESEARCH** Public History. **SELECTED PUBLICATIONS** Auth, "President Theodore Roosevelt and Army Reform," Proceedings of the South Carolina Historical Association, 73: 30-40; rev, "Ideological Chaff," (review of Jerold Auerbach, Unequal Justice), National Review, 29, January 7, 1977: 40-42; auth, "The Best Men of the Bar: The Founding of the American Bar Association," in Gerard Gawalt, ed, The New High Priests, Greenwood Press, 84; rev, "From Patrician to Professional Elite: The Transformation of the New York City Bar Association," in American Journal of Legal History 34, October, 90: 435-36, rev, "Logic and Experience: The Origin of Modern American Legal Education," New York: Oxford University Press, 1994, in American Journal of Legal History 39, April, 95: 271-72; auth, "Ralph Budd and Early Attempts to Reconstruct Fort Union, 1925-1941," North Dakota History, 64, Summer 97: 2-19; auth, "A Global Encyclopedia of Historical Writing," contributor of three entries to D.R. Woolf, New York: Garland Press, 98; auth, "Reconstructing Fort Union," forthcoming, Univ of Nebraska Press, 01. **CONTACT ADDRESS** Dept Social Science, Bob Jones Univ, 1700 Wade Hampton Boulevard, Greenville, SC 29614-1000. **EMAIL** jmatzko@bju.edu

MAUGHAN, STEVEN
PERSONAL Born 10/09/1962 **DISCIPLINE** MODERN EUROPEAN AND NON-WESTERN HISTORY **EDUCATION** Col ID, BA, summa cum laude; Harvard Univ, MA, PhD. **CAREER** Prof, Albertson Col, 92. **HONORS AND AWARDS** Mellon fel, Harvard Univ; Fulbright grant, King's Col, London. **MEMBERSHIPS** Am Hist Asn, North Am Conf on Brit Studies. **RESEARCH** Victorian and Edwardian British foreign missions, the british churches, and the culture of imperialism. **SELECTED PUBLICATIONS** Auth, "'Mighty England Do Good': the Major English Denominations and Support of Foreign Missions in the Nineteenth Century." in Robert A Bickers and Rosemary Seton, eds, Missionary Encounters: Sources and Issues, (London: Curzon Pr (95); Civic Culture, Women's Foreign Missions, and the British Imperial Imagination,1860-1914," in Frank Trentmann, ed, Paradoxes of Civil Society: New Perspectives on Modern German and British History (Providence and Oxford: Berghahn, (00); auth, Explorers, Missionaries, Traders, in Stephen Wagley ed, Encycl of Europ Soc Hist (NY: Scribners, (00); auth, An Archbishop for Greater Britain: Bishop Montgomery, Missionary Imperialism, and the

Society for the Propagation of the Gospel, 1897-1915 in Daniel O'Connor, ed, Three Centuries of Mission: The United Society for the Propagation of the Gospel, 1701-2000 (London: Continuum, (00). **CONTACT ADDRESS** Albertson Col of Idaho, Caldwell, ID 83605. **EMAIL** smaughan@albertson.edu

MAUSKOPF, SEYMOUR HAROLD
PERSONAL Born 11/11/1938, Cleveland, OH, m, 1961, 3 children **DISCIPLINE** HISTORY OF CHEMISTRY **EDUCATION** Cornell Univ, BA, 60; Princeton Univ, PhD, 66. **CAREER** Instr to asst prof to assoc to Prof, Duke Univ, 64- **HONORS AND AWARDS** Dexter Awd, Am Chem Soc, 98. **MEMBERSHIPS** Hist of Science Soc **RESEARCH** Hist 18th-19th century science, hist chem. **SELECTED PUBLICATIONS** Auth, Crystals and Compounds, 76; The Elusive Science, 80; ed, Chemical Sciences in the Modern World, 93. **CONTACT ADDRESS** Dept History, Duke Univ, Box 90719, Durham, NC 27708-0719. **EMAIL** shmaus@acpub.duke.edu

MAUSS, ARMAND
PERSONAL Born 06/05/1928, Salt Lake City, UT, m, 1951, 8 children **DISCIPLINE** HISTORY; SOCIOLOGY **EDUCATION** Sophia Univ, Tokyo, BA, 54; Univ CA Berkeley, MA, 57, PhD, 70. **CAREER** Inst, 63-67, Diablo Valley coll; assoc prof, 67-69, Utah State Univ; prof, 69-99, Washington State Univ. **HONORS AND AWARDS** Ed, Journal for the Scientific Study of Religion, 89-92; pres, Mormon History Assn, 97-98; Chipman Awd for best book (MHA), 94; Arrington Career Awd, (MHA), 94. **MEMBERSHIPS** Soc for the Scientific Study of Religion; Assn for the Sociology of Religion; Religion Research Assn; Mormon History Assn; Mormon Social Science Assn. **RESEARCH** Sociology of Religion; deviant behavior and social problems **SELECTED PUBLICATIONS** Auth, Neither White nor Black: Mormon Scholars Confront the Race Issue in a Universal Church, Signature Books, Salt Lk City, 84; The Angel and the Beehive: The Mormon Struggle with Assimilation, Univ of Ill Press, 94; Marketing for Miracles: Mormonism in the Twenty-First Century, Dialogue: A Journal of Mormon Thought, Spring 96; The Impact Of Feminism and Religious Involvement on Sentiment toward God, Review of Religious Research, March 96; In Search of Ephraim: Tradition Mormon Conceptions of Lineage and Race, Journal of Mormon History, Spring 99. **CONTACT ADDRESS** 7 Springwater, Irvine, CA 92604-4660. **EMAIL** almauss@home.com

MAVOR, CAROL
DISCIPLINE ART HISTORY **EDUCATION** Univ CA, Santa Cruz, PhD. **CAREER** From Asst prof to assoc prof, Univ NC, Chapel Hill. **RESEARCH** Critical theory; Victorian cult. **SELECTED PUBLICATIONS** Auth, Pleasures Taken: Performances of Sexuality and Loss in Victorian Culture, Duke UP, 95; Becoming: The Photographs of Clementina Hawarden, Genre, 96; Collecting Loss, Cult Stud, 97. **CONTACT ADDRESS** Dept of Art Hist, Univ of No Carolina, Chapel Hill, Chapel Hill, NC 27599. **EMAIL** olive@email.unc.edu

MAXON, ROBERT MEAD
PERSONAL Born 12/10/1939, Oneonta, NY, m, 1968, 2 children **DISCIPLINE** HISTORY **EDUCATION** Duke Univ, BA, 61; Syracuse Univ, PhD(hist), 72. **CAREER** Asst prof, 69-74, ASSOC PROF HIST, W VA UNIV, 74-82; Prof Hist W VA Univ, 82-. **HONORS AND AWARDS** Benedum Distinguished Scholar, W Va Univ, 94. **MEMBERSHIPS** African Studies Asn; Hist Asn of Kenya; Asn of Third World Studies. **RESEARCH** Colonial history of Kenya; the traditional history of the Bunyore of Western Kenya; decolonization and Kenya. **SELECTED PUBLICATIONS** Co-auth, Historical Dictionary of Kenya, Scarecrow Press, 00. **CONTACT ADDRESS** Dept of Hist, West Virginia Univ, Morgantown, P O Box 6303, Morgantown, WV 26506-6303. **EMAIL** rmaxon@wvu.edu

MAXWELL, KENNETH R.
PERSONAL Born 03/02/1941, Wellington, United Kingdom, s **DISCIPLINE** HISTORY **EDUCATION** Cambridge Univ St John's, BA 63, MA 67; Princeton Univ, MA 67, PhD 70. **CAREER** Coun on For Rels, Rockefeller Sr Fel, 95-, vpres, dir of studies, 96; Tirke Found Inc, prog dir, 79-85; Columbia Univ, assoc prof, 76-84; Institute for adv stud, Princeton, 71-75. **HONORS AND AWARDS** Order of Rio Branco; Order of Sci Merit; Guggenheim Fel. **MEMBERSHIPS** AHA, LASA, IHGB. **RESEARCH** Latin America and Southern Europe; Spain and Portugal. **SELECTED PUBLICATIONS** Auth, Pombal, Paradox of the Enlightenment, Cambridge, 95; auth, The Making of Portuguese Democracy, Cambridge, 95; auth, The New Spain, coauth, Council On Foreign Relations, 94; auth, Conflicts and Conspiracies, Brazil and Portugal, 1750-1808, Cambridge, 73. **CONTACT ADDRESS** Council on Foreign Relations, 58 East 68th St, New York, NY 10021. **EMAIL** kmaxwell@cfr.org

MAY, ELAINE TYLER
PERSONAL Born 09/17/1947, Los Angeles, CA, m, 1970, 3 children **DISCIPLINE** AMERICAN HISTORY **EDUCATION** Univ Calif, Los Angeles, AB, 69, MA, 70, PhD(US hist), 75. **CAREER** Asst prof hist, Princeton Univ, 74-78; asst prof Am studies, 78-81, assoc prof, Am studies, Univ Minn, 81-88; to prof, 89-. **HONORS AND AWARDS** Res fel, Am Coun of Learned Soc, 83-84, 93-94; Rockefeller Found Res Grant, 85-87; William J. Goode Book Awd, runner-up for Barren in the Promised Land, Am Soc Asn Family Section, 96; Fulbright Distinguished Chair in Ireland, 96-97; Mary Ball Washington Prof of Am Hist, Univ Col Dublin, 96-97; Am Philos Soc Sabbatical Fel, 00-01. **MEMBERSHIPS** AHA; Orgn Am Historians; Women Hist Midwest; Am Studies Asn **RESEARCH** American social history; United States women's history; history of marriage and the family; politics of reproduction and sexuality. **SELECTED PUBLICATIONS** Auth, Great Expectations: Marriage and Divorce in Post-Victorian Am, Univ Chicago Press, 80; auth, Homeward bound: Am Families in the Cold War Era, Basic Books, 88; auth, Rosie the Riveter Gets Married + American Women and World War II, Mid America-Hist Rev, vol 0075, 93; auth, Pushing the Limits: American Women, 1940-1961, Oxford Univ Press, 94; auth, Barren in the Promised Land: Childless Am and the Pursuit of Happiness, Basic Books, 95; auth, Ideology and Foreign Policy, Diplomatic Hist, vol 0018, 94; The Radical Roots of American Studies, Amer Quart, vol 0048, 96; co-ed, Here, There, and Everywhere: The For Polit of Am Popular Culture, Univ Press of New England, 00. **CONTACT ADDRESS** Univ of Minnesota, Twin Cities, 88 Arthur Ave SE, Minneapolis, MN 55455. **EMAIL** mayxx002@umn.edu

MAY, GARY
PERSONAL Born 12/24/1944, Los Angeles, CA, m, 1973, 2 children **DISCIPLINE** HISTORY **EDUCATION** Univ Calif at Los Angeles, BA, 66, MA, 69, PhD, 74. **CAREER** Instr, Colgate Univ, 74-75; asst prof, Univ Del, 75-79, assoc prof, 79-94, prof, 94-. **HONORS AND AWARDS** Allan Nevins prize, Soc of Am Hists, 75. **MEMBERSHIPS** AHA, OAH, SHAFR. **RESEARCH** America since 1945. **SELECTED PUBLICATIONS** Auth, China Scapegoat: The Diplomatic Ordeal of John Carter Vincent, New Republic Books (79); auth, "Passing the Torch and Lighting Fires: The Peace Corps," in Thomas Paterson, ed, Kennedy's Quest for Victory: American Foreign Policy, 1961-1963; auth, Un-American Activities: The Trials of William Remington, Oxford Univ Press (94). **CONTACT ADDRESS** Dept Hist, Univ of Delaware, 15 Orchard Ave, Newark, DE 19716-2555. **EMAIL** garymay@udel.edu

MAY, HENRY FARNHAM
PERSONAL Born 03/27/1915, Denver, CO **DISCIPLINE** AMERICAN HISTORY **EDUCATION** Univ Calif, AB, 37; Harvard Univ, AM, 38, PhD, 47. **CAREER** From asst prof to assoc prof hist, Scripps Col, 47-52; from assoc prof to prof, 52-63, Margaret Byrne prof, 63-80, Emer Margaret Byrne Prof Hist, Univ Calif, Berkeley, 80-, Vis assoc prof, Bowdoin Col, 50-51; Pitt prof Am hist & inst, Cambridge Univ, 71-72; vis prof, Univ Leuvon, Belgium, 81; Berkeley Citatin, 80. **HONORS AND AWARDS** Merle Curti Awd, Orgn Am Historians & Beveridge Prize, Am Hist Asn, 77. **MEMBERSHIPS** AHA; Am Acad Arts & Sci. **RESEARCH** American intellectual and religious history. **SELECTED PUBLICATIONS** Auth, Protestant Churches and Industrial America, Harper, 49; The End of American Innocence, Knopf, 59; coauth, A Synopsis of American History, Rand McNally, 63; The Enlightenment in America, Oxford Univ, 76; auth, Ideas, Faiths, and Feelings, Oxford Univ Press, 83; auth, The Divided Heart, Oxford Univ Press, 91; auth, Coming to Terms, California, 93; auth, Three Faces of Berkeley, California, 93. **CONTACT ADDRESS** Dept of Hist, Univ of California, Berkeley, Berkeley, CA 94720. **EMAIL** henrymay@uclink.berkeley.edu

MAY, JUDE THOMAS
PERSONAL Born 06/07/1936, Grand Forks, ND, m, 1964, 2 children **DISCIPLINE** HISTORY OF MEDICINE **EDUCATION** St Mary's Univ, Tex, BS & BA, 58, Univ Pittsburgh, MA, 62; Tulane Univ, PhD(hist), 70. **CAREER** Res asst, Univ Pittsburgh, 61-62; asst prof, 68-76, assoc prof Hist of Med & Human Ecol, Univ OK, 76-; consult, Nat Study Consumer Participation Neighborhood Health Ctrs, Health Servs & Ment Health Admin, USPHS, 69-71 & Nat Ctr Health Servs Res & Develop, 71-; Am Philos Soc grant-in-aid, 71; consult, State-based Humanities Prog, Nat Endowment for Humanities, 73-. **HONORS AND AWARDS** David Ross Boyd Prof, Univ of OK, 95; Assoc Dean, Col of Public Health, Univ of OK, 90-93. **MEMBERSHIPS** AHA; Orgn Am Historians; Am Asn Hist Med; Southern Hist Asn; Am Pub Health Asn. **RESEARCH** History of health care delivery; sociology of health and medicine; social implications of patterns of the distribution of health services. **SELECTED PUBLICATIONS** Auth, Continuity and Change in the Labor Policies of the Union Army and the Freedmen's Bureau, Civil War Hist, 9/71; Conflict and Resolution in a Health Care Program: The Function of Historical Analysis, Anthrop Quart, 7/73; coauth, The Neighborhood Health Center Program, Washington, DC, 76; Professional Control and Innovation, In: New Research in the Sociology of Health Care, JAI Press, 80; Conflict, Consensus, and Exchange, Social Problems, 2/80; auth, The Professionalization of Neighborhood Health Centers, Health/PAC Bull, Vol 12, No 2. **CONTACT ADDRESS** Col of Public Health, Univ of Oklahoma, Box 26901, Oklahoma City, OK 73190.

MAY, LARY L.
DISCIPLINE HISTORY **EDUCATION** Univ Calif Los Angeles, PhD, 76. **CAREER** Assoc prof **RESEARCH** Am cultural hist. **SELECTED PUBLICATIONS** Auth, Screening Out the Past: The Birth of Mass Culture and the Motion Picture Industry, Oxford, 80; pubs on popular culture and modern society; ed, Recasting America: Culture and Politics in the Age of Cold War, Chicago, 89; auth, The Big Tommorow, Hollywood and the Politics of the American Way, Chicago, 00. **CONTACT ADDRESS** History Dept, Univ of Minnesota, Twin Cities, 614 Social Sciences Tower, 267 19th Ave S, Minneapolis, MN 55455. **EMAIL** mayxx001@tc.umn.edu

MAY, ROBERT EVAN
PERSONAL Born 07/06/1943, Brooklyn, NY, m, 1967, 2 children **DISCIPLINE** AMERICAN HISTORY **EDUCATION** Union Col, NYork, BA, 65; Univ Wis-Madison, MA, 66, PhD(hist), 69. **CAREER** Asst prof, 69-75, from assoc prof Hist, 75-86; to Prof Hist, 86-, Purdue Univ, West Lafayettte. **HONORS AND AWARDS** Grant-in-Aid, Am Coun Learned Soc, 80; McLemore Prize, Miss Hist Soc, 86; Willie D. Halsell Prize, Miss Hist Soc, 89; Frederick W. Beinecke Fel in Western Americana, Beinecke Rare Book and Manuscript Library, Yale Univ, 97-98. **MEMBERSHIPS** Orgn Am Historians; Southern Hist Asn; Soc for Hist of the Early Republic; Miss Hist Soc. **RESEARCH** Southern history; American expansionism. **SELECTED PUBLICATIONS** Auth, The Southern Dream of a Caribbean Empire, 1854-1861, La State Univ, 73; Dixie's Martial Image: A Continuing Historiographical Enigma, Historian, 2/78; Lobbyists for commercial empire: Jane Cazneau, William Cazneau and US Caribbean Policy, 1846-1878, Pac Hist Rev, 8/79; John A. Quitman: Old South Crusader, LSU Press, 85; ed, The Union, the Confederacy, and the Atlantic Rim, Purdue Univ Press, 95; auth, The Slave Power Conspiracy Revisited: United States Presidents and Filibustering, 1848-1861, In: Union & Emancipation: Essays on Politics and Race in the Civil War Era, Kent State Univ Press, 97; auth, Manifest Destiny's Filibusters, In: Manifest Destiny and Empire: American Antebellum Expansionism, College Station, 97; author of several other journal articles. **CONTACT ADDRESS** Dept of Hist, Purdue Univ, West Lafayette, West Lafayette, IN 47907-1358. **EMAIL** rmay@sla.purdue.edi

MAYER, ARNO JOSEPH
PERSONAL Born 06/19/1926, Luxembourg, 2 children **DISCIPLINE** MODERN EUROPEAN HISTORY **EDUCATION** City Col New York, BBA, 49; Yale Univ, MA, 50, PhD, 54. **CAREER** Teaching fel, Wesleyan Univ, 52-53; res consult, Found World Govt, 53-54; from instr to asst prof polit, Brandeis Univ, 54-58; asst prof hist, Harvard Univ, 58-61; prof, Hist, Princeton Univ, 61-, Am Coun Learned Soc fel, 60-61; Soc Sci Res Coun auxiliary res award, 62; Rockefeller Found res grant, 63-64; vis Prof, Columbia Univ, 66-70; Guggenheim fel, 67-68; res assoc, Inst War & Peace, Columbia Univ, 71-72; res fel, Lehrman Inst, 76-77. **HONORS AND AWARDS** Am Acad of Arts & Scis, Fel; Isaac Deutwcher Mem Pr, 90; Premi o Acqui Storia, 90; Awd for Schol Distinc, 01. **MEMBERSHIPS** AHA. **RESEARCH** Modern European politics. **SELECTED PUBLICATIONS** Auth, Political Origins of the New Diplomacy, 1917-1918, Yale Univ Pr, 59; auth, Politics and Diplomacy of Peacemaking: Containment and Counterrevolution at Versailles, 1918-1919, Knopf, 67; auth, Dynamics of Counterrevolution in Europe, 1870-1956, Harper & Row, 71; ed, History: Choice and Commitment, Harvard Univ Pr, 77; auth, The Persistence of the Old Regime: Europe to the Great War, Pantheon, 81; auth, Why Did the Heavens Not Darken?: The 'Final Solution' in History, Pantheon, 88; transl, The Furies : Violence and Terror in the French and Russian Revolutions, Princeton Univ Pr, 00. **CONTACT ADDRESS** Dept of Hist, Princeton Univ, Princeton, NJ 08544.

MAYER, FRANK A.
PERSONAL Born 09/22/1952, Santa Cruz, CA, m, 1983, 1 child **DISCIPLINE** HISTORY **EDUCATION** Univ Southern Calif, PhD, 88. **CAREER** Adj Prof, Calif State Univ Los Angeles, 91-. **HONORS AND AWARDS** John F Kennedy Presidential Library Found grant, 89; Usia Lecture Tour-Germ 94. **MEMBERSHIPS** Ger Studies Asn; US Comm on Civil Rights. **RESEARCH** Globalization and economic power. **SELECTED PUBLICATIONS** Auth, The Opposition Years, Winston S Churchill and the Conservative Party, 1945-1951, 92; Adenauer and Kennedy: A Study in German-American Relations 1961-1963, 96. **CONTACT ADDRESS** History Dept, California State Univ, Los Angeles, Los Angeles, CA 90032. **EMAIL** frama@earthlink.net

MAYER, HENRI ANDRE VAN HUYSEN
DISCIPLINE HISTORY **EDUCATION** Harvard Univ, BA, 70; Univ Calif, Berkeley, MA, 71, PhD, 73. **CAREER** MEMBER, BD REGENTS, COMM MASS **MEMBERSHIPS** Am Antiquarian Soc **SELECTED PUBLICATIONS** Auth, "Agriculture: The Island Empire," Daedalus, 74; auth, King's Chapel: The First Century, 76; auth, The Crocodile Man: A Case of Brain Chemistry and Criminal Violence, 76. **CONTACT ADDRESS** McCormack Bldg, Rm 619, Boston, MA 02108.

MAYER, THOMAS F.
PERSONAL Born 09/10/1951, McLeansboro, IL, m, 1983, 1 child **DISCIPLINE** HISTORY **EDUCATION** Mich State Univ, BA, 73; MA, 77; Univ Minn, PhD, 83. **CAREER** Asst prof, southwest Mo State Univ, 83-85; asst prof to assoc prof, Augustana Col, 85-. **HONORS AND AWARDS** Fel Royal Hist Soc, 89; Carl S. Moyer Prize, 78; NEH Fel, 92; Gladys Krieble Delmes foundation grant, 93; Fulbright Fel, Univ Rome, 89-90, Mellon Fel, Harvard Univ, 89-90; Am Philos Soc Grant, 97. **MEMBERSHIPS** Sixteenth Century Studies Conf, Renaissance Soc of Am, North Am Conf on British Studies, Am Hist Asn. **RESEARCH** Catholicism in the 16th century, political thought. **SELECTED PUBLICATIONS** Auth, Thomas Starkey and the Commonweal: Humanist Politics and Religion in the Reign of Henry VIII, Cambridge, 89; auth, "A Reluctant Author: Cardinal Pole and his Manuscripts, Transactions of the American Philosophical Society, 99; auth, Reginal Pole, Prince and Prophet, Cambridge, 00; ed, A Dialogue between Pole and Lupset, 89; auth, "Sixteenth Century Journal 'When Maecenas was Broke: Cardinal Pole's Spiritual Patronage, (96): 419-135. **CONTACT ADDRESS** Dept History, Augustana Col, Illinois, 639 38th St, Rock Island, IL 61201-2210. **EMAIL** himayer@augustana.edu

MAYFIELD, JOHN R.
PERSONAL Born 11/06/1945, Lubbock, TX, m, 1 child **DISCIPLINE** HISTORY, LITERATURE **EDUCATION** Columbia Univ, BA, 68; Johns Hopkins Univ, PhD, 73. **CAREER** Asst prof, Unif of Ky, 72-82; assoc prof, Univ of Baltimore, 85-95; prof, Samford Univ, 95-. **HONORS AND AWARDS** Distinguished Prof in Teaching, Univ of Baltimore, 91; Ford Fel, 72. **MEMBERSHIPS** Southern Hist Asn, Soc for Historians of the Early Am Republic. **RESEARCH** Southern U.S. literature and humor, Southern intellectual history. **SELECTED PUBLICATIONS** Auth, The New Nation: 1800-1845; auth, Rehearsal for Republicanism. **CONTACT ADDRESS** Dept Hist & Polit Sci, Samford Univ, 800 Lakeshore Dr, Birmingham, AL 35229-0001. **EMAIL** jrmayfie@samford.edu

MAYNES, MARY JO
DISCIPLINE HISTORY **EDUCATION** Univ Pa, BA, 71; Univ Mich, PhD, 77. **RESEARCH** German hist; European social/women's hist. **SELECTED PUBLICATIONS** Auth, Schooling For the People, Comparative Local Studies of Schooling History in France and Germany, 1750-1850, Holmes and Meier, 851 Schooling in Western Europe: A Social History, SUNY, 85; Taking the Hard Road: Lifecourse in French and German Workers' Autobiographies of the Industrial Era, Univ NC, 95; co-auth, Interpreting Women's Lives, Feminist Theory and Personal Narratives; The European Experience of Declining Fertility, Blackwell, 92; co-ed, German Women in the Eighteenth and Nineteenth Centuries, A Social and Literary History, Univ Ind, 86; Fraun im Osterreich; Gender, Kinship and Power: A Comparative and Interdisciplinary History; co-ed, History and theory: feminist research, debates, contestations, Univ of Chicago Press, 97; ed, Encyclopedia of European Social History, Scribner's 01. **CONTACT ADDRESS** History Dept, Univ of Minnesota, Twin Cities, 614 Social Sciences Tower, 267 19th Ave. S, Minneapolis, MN 55455. **EMAIL** mayne001@tc.umn.edu

MAZA, SARAH C.
PERSONAL Born 04/12/1953, New York, NY, m, 1999, 1 child **DISCIPLINE** FRENCH HISTORY **EDUCATION** Univ Porvence, BA, 73; Princeton Univ, PhD, 78. **CAREER** Asst prof, prof, 78-, Northwestern Univ. **HONORS AND AWARDS** NEH Fel; Nat Hum Cen Fel; Woodrow Wilson Fel; Guggenheim Fel. **MEMBERSHIPS** AHA; SFHS; ASECS. **RESEARCH** 18th and 19th C French social and cultural history. **SELECTED PUBLICATIONS** Auth, Servants and Master in 18th Century France (Princeton Univ Press, 83); auth, Private Lives and Public Affairs: The Causes Celebres d Pre-Revolutionary France (Univ Cal Press, 93). **CONTACT ADDRESS** Dept History, Northwestern Univ, 202 Harris, Evanston, IL 60208.

MAZLISH, BRUCE
PERSONAL Born 09/15/1923, New York, NY, m, 1960, 4 children **DISCIPLINE** HISTORY, POLITICAL SCIENCE **EDUCATION** Columbia Univ, BA, 44, MA, 47, PhD, 55. **CAREER** Instr hist, Univ Maine, 46-48; lectr, Columbia Univ, 49-50; instr, 50-53, 55-56, from asst prof to assoc prof, 56-65, chmn sect, 65-70, head dept humanities, 74-79, Prof ist, Mass Inst Technol, 65-. **HONORS AND AWARDS** Soc Sci Rs Coun Fel, 67-68; Toynbee Prize, 86. **MEMBERSHIPS** Fel Am Acad Arts & Sci, AHA. **RESEARCH** Modern intellectual and social history, personality and politics, psychoanalysis and history. **SELECTED PUBLICATIONS** Auth, In Search of Nixon : A Psychohistorical Study, Basic Books (New York City), 72; auth, Kissinger: The European Mind in American Policy, Basic Books, 76; coauth, Jimmy Carter: An Interpretive Biography, Simon & Schuster (New York City), 79; auth, The Meaning of Karl Marx, Oxford Univ Pr (New York City), 84; auth, A New Science: The Breakdown of Connections and the Birth of Sociology, Oxford Univ Pr, 89; auth, The Leader, the Led, and the Psyche: Essays in psychohistory, Univ Pr New England (Hanover, NH), 90; auth, The Fourth Discontinuity: The Co-Evolution of Humans and Machines, Yale Univ Pr (New Haven, CT), 93; coauth, The Global Imperative: The Spread of Humans Across the Earth, Westview (Boulder, CO), 97; coauth, Progress: Fact or Illusion?, Univ of Mich Pr (Ann Arbor), 98; auth, The Uncertain Sciences, Yale Univ Pr, 98. **CONTACT ADDRESS** Massachusetts Inst of Tech, 77 Massachusetts Ave, Cambridge, MA 02139.

MAZON, MAURICIO
DISCIPLINE HISTORY **EDUCATION** UCLA, PhD, 76; Southern California Psychoanalytic Inst, PhD. **CAREER** Assoc prof & ch; dir, Amer Stud and Ethnicity Prog, Univ Southern Calif. **RESEARCH** Chicano/a History; Psychohistory; American political biography. **SELECTED PUBLICATIONS** Auth, The Zoot-Suit Riots: The Psychology of Symbolic Annihilation, Univ Tex, 84. **CONTACT ADDRESS** Dept of History, Univ of So California, University Park Campus, Los Angeles, CA 90089. **EMAIL** mazon@bcf.usc.edu

MAZOR, LESTER JAY
PERSONAL Born 12/12/1936, Chicago, IL, m, 1992, 3 children **DISCIPLINE** PHILOSOPHY OF LAW, LEGAL HISTORY **EDUCATION** Stanford Univ, AB, 57, JD, 60. **CAREER** Instr law, Univ Va, 61-62; from asst prof to prof, Univ Utah, 62-70; Henry R Luce prof, 70-75, Prof Law, Hampshire Col, 75-, Reporter, Am Bar Asn Proj Standards Criminal Justice, 65-69; vis assoc prof law, Stanford Univ, 67-68; vis prof, State Univ NY Buffalo, 73-74; proj dir mat study, Am Bar Found Study Legal Educ, 74-. **MEMBERSHIPS** Law & Soc Asn; Int Soc Asn; Am Legal Studies Asn; Int Asn Philos Law & Soc Philos. **RESEARCH** Legal hist; legal and polit theory; future studies. **SELECTED PUBLICATIONS** Ed, Prosecution and Defense Functions, 67 & Providing Defense Services, 70, American Bar Asn; coauth, Introduction to the Study of Law, Found Press, 70; auth, Power and responsibility in the attorney-client relation, Stanford Law Rev, 68; The crisis of liberal legalism, Yale Law J, 72; Disrespect for law, In: Anarchism, NY Univ, 78. **CONTACT ADDRESS** Sch of Soc Sci, Hampshire Col, 893 West St, Amherst, MA 01002-3359. **EMAIL** lmazor@hampshire.edu

MAZRUI, ALI AL'AMIN
PERSONAL Born 02/24/1933, Mombasa, Kenya, 5 children **DISCIPLINE** POLITICAL SCIENCE; COMPARATIVE POLITICS; AFRICAN POLITICS; ISLAMIC POLITICS; POLITICS & CULTURE **EDUCATION** Univ Manchester, BA, 60; Columbia Univ, MA, 61; Oxford Univ, DPhil, 66. **CAREER** Dir inst Global Cult Studies, Albert Sshweitzer Prof Hum, Prof Polit Sci & Afrincan stud, SUNY-Binghamton; Albert Luthuli Prof-at-large, Univ Jos, Nigeria; Sr scholar Afrocana stud, & Andrew D White Prof-at-latge Emer, Cornell Univ; Ibn Khaldun Ptof-at-large, School of Islamic & soc sci, VA; Walter Rodney prof hist & Governance, Univ Guyana. **HONORS AND AWARDS** Distinguished Africanist Awd, 95; 50th Anniversary Distinguished Awd, Nat Univ Lesotho, S Af, 95; Distinguished Global Cult Hum Awd, 97; DuBois-Garvey Awd for Pan-African Unity, Morgan State Univ, 98; Icon of Twentieth Century Awd, Lincoln Univ, 98. **RESEARCH** The role of culture, particularly religion and language, in the formation and operation of politics. **SELECTED PUBLICATIONS** Coauth, Swahili, State and Society: The Political Economy of an African Language, E African Educ Publ, 95; Islam and Western Values, Foreign Affairs, 97; Three Stages of Globalization: Mombasa, Cities Fit for People UNDP, 97; The African Diaspora: African Origins and New World Identities, Ind Univ Press, 98; The Power of Babel: Language and Goverance in the African Experience, Iniv Chicago Press, 98; The Scottish Factor in the African Experience: Between Negritude and Scottitude, Jour African Stud, 98; The Failed State and Political Collapse in Africa, Peacemaking and Peacekeeping for the New Century, Rowman & Littlefield Publ, 98; Islam and Afrocentricity: The Triple Heritage School, The Postcolonial Crescent, Peter Lang Publ, 98. **CONTACT ADDRESS** Inst of Global Cult Stud, SUNY, Binghamton, PO Box 6000, Binghamton, NY 13902-6000. **EMAIL** amazrui@binghamton.edu

MAZZAOUI, MAUREEN FENNELL
PERSONAL Born 08/06/1938, New York, NY **DISCIPLINE** MEDIEVAL AND RENAISSANCE ITALIAN ECONOMIC HISTORY **EDUCATION** Hunter Col, BA, 58; Bryn Mawr Col, MA, 60, PhD(hist), 66. **CAREER** Asst prof hist, Ind Univ, Bloomington, 70-73; asst prof, 73-77, assoc, 77-84, PROF HIST, UNIV WIS-MADISON, 84-. **HONORS AND AWARDS** Fulbright-Hays fel, 67-69; Inst Res Hum fel, 72-73; Villa I tatti fel, 80-81; Div Hist & Philos Sci, NSF, summer fel, 81; ACLS fel, 83-84; mem, Sch Hist Stud, Inst Adv Stud, 83-84. **MEMBERSHIPS** Medieval Acad Am; Soc Ital Hist Studies. **RESEARCH** Medieval, Renaissance Italy; hist textile industry. **SELECTED PUBLICATIONS** Auth, The Weavers Art Revealed--Facsimile, Translation, and Study of the 1st 2 Published Books on Weaving, vol 1, Ziegler, Marx Weber Kunst und Bild Buch, Isis, vol 0084, 93; The Weavers Art Revealed--Facsimile, Translation, and Study of the 1st 2 Published Books on Weaving, vol 2, Lumscher, Nathaniel Neu Eingerichtetes Weber Kunst und Bild Buch, Isis, vol 0084, 93; co- auth, Prospettive nella Storia dell'Industria Tessile Veneta, Trieste, 72; auth, The Italian Cotton Industry in the Later Middle Ages, 1100-1600, Cambridge Univ Press, 81; co-ed, The Other Tuscany: Essays in the History of Lucca, Pisa and Siena during the Thirteenth, Fourteenth and Fifteenth Centuries, The Medieval Inst (Kalamazoo), 94; ed, An Expanding World: Textiles, Production, Trade and Demand, 1450-1800, Ashgate VAriorum, 98. **CONTACT ADDRESS** Dept of Hist, Univ of Wisconsin, Madison, 455 North Park St, Madison, WI 53706-1483. **EMAIL** mazzaoui@facstaff.wis.Edu

MBODJ, MOHAMED
DISCIPLINE AFRICAN HISTORY **EDUCATION** Univ Dakar, BA, 73; Univ Paris, PhD, 78. **CAREER** Assoc prof. **SELECTED PUBLICATIONS** Auth, The Abolition of Slavery in Senegal, 1820-1890: Crisis or the Rise of a New Entrepreneurial Class?, Slavery, Bondage, and Emancipation in Modern Africa and Asia, 93; Perspectives Historiques, and Dynamiques Regionales, La Population du Senegal, 94; La terre ne ment pas. Exploitation de donnes imparfaites sur l'agriculture ouest-africaine durant la priode coloniale, Conf on the 100th Anniversary Establishment of Fr W Africa, 95. **CONTACT ADDRESS** Dept of Hist, Columbia Col, New York, 2960 Broadway, New York, NY 10027-6902.

MC FARLAND, KEITH D.
PERSONAL Born 06/25/1940, Dover, OH, m, 1962, 3 children **DISCIPLINE** HISTORY **EDUCATION** Kent State Univ, BS, 62; Ohio State Univ, MA, 63; PhD, 69. **CAREER** Asst Dean, Col of Lib and Fine Arts/ Assoc Prof, Tex A&M Univ Commerce, 73-76; Prof, Head of Hist Dept, Tex A&M Univ Commerce, 76-83; Dean for Grad Studies and Res/Prof, Tex A&M Univ Commerce, 83-97; Interim Pres, Tex A&M Univ Commerce, 98; Pres, CEO, Prof, Tex A&M Univ Commerce, 98-. **HONORS AND AWARDS** Fac Senate Awd for Distinguished Achievement, E Tex State Univ, 76; Civilian of the Year, Northeast Tex Chap, Air Force Asn, 78, 79; Serv Above Self Awd, Commerce Rotary Club, 81; Governor's Outstanding Rotarian Awd, Rotary Dist 5810, 94; Asn of Tex Grad Sch Presidential Awd, 94. **MEMBERSHIPS** Asn for Bibliog of Hist, 75-94; Am Mil Inst, 70-; Conc of Grad Sch, 83-; Dover Hist Soc, 75-; Inter-Univ Sem on Armed Forces and Soc, 69-. **RESEARCH** Military History, War. **SELECTED PUBLICATIONS** Auth, Harry H. Woodring: A Political Biography of FDR's Controversial Secretary of War, Univ Press of Kans (Lawrence), 75; auth, The Korean War: An Annotated Bibliography, Garland Publ Co (NY), 86. **CONTACT ADDRESS** Dept Hist, Texas A&M Univ, Commerce, PO Box 3011, Commerce, TX 75429. **EMAIL** Keith_McFarland@tamu-commerce.edu

MC LEOD, ANN M.
PERSONAL Born 03/03/1939, New York, NY, w, 1990 **DISCIPLINE** PSYCHOLOGY, ARCHAEOLOGY **EDUCATION** Bennett Jr Col, AA, 59; Lindenwood Col, BA, 61; Wash Univ, MA, 64; NY State Univ, MS, 65. **CAREER** Asst to Dir, Villa Mercede, Bellosqurda, Florence, Ital, 65-67; Dir of Admis, Psychometrists, Learning Disabilities Specialist, Allen Stevenson New York City, 67-70; Sch Psychol, Polk Community Col, 70-71; Prof, Polk Community Col, 71-00. **HONORS AND AWARDS** Teacher of the Year, Polk Community Col, 73; Awd for salvaging documents, books, T.U. documentary "Angels in the Mud", Florence, Ital, Psi Beta. **MEMBERSHIPS** Archaeol Club, Psi Beta Nat Honors Soc, AM Univ Professors, Am Psychol Asn, Portrait Painters of Am. **RESEARCH** Archaeology: NAG Hammadi, Dead Sea Scrolls, Jewish revolt 66 AD, Abnormal Psychology: Bi Polar, Paranoia, Minoan, Mycenean, Troy. **SELECTED PUBLICATIONS** Auth, Excavations: Graves A and B Myceneacn Culture (Mycenae Greece), 63, 64; Salvaging documents, Libr in Florence, Ital, 66, 67. **CONTACT ADDRESS** Dept Arts, Letters and Soc Sci, Polk Comm Col, 3425 Winter Lake Rd, Lakeland, FL 33803.

MCAFEE, WARD MERNER
PERSONAL Born 09/20/1939, Salem, OR, m, 1962, 3 children **DISCIPLINE** AMERICAN HISTORY **EDUCATION** Stanford Univ, BA, 61, MA, 62, PhD, 66. **CAREER** From asst prof to assoc prof, 65-73, prof hist, 76-, Dean Soc & Behav Sci 71-74, 75-84; act vice pres, 84-85, Calif State Col, San Bernardino. **HONORS AND AWARDS** CSUSB outstanding prof, 93; **MEMBERSHIPS** California Fac Assoc; Phi Kappa Phi, **RESEARCH** California history; Civil War and Reconstruction, World Religions. **SELECTED PUBLICATIONS** Auth, Religion, Race and Reconstruction: The Public School in the Politics of the 1870's, SUNY Press, 98. **CONTACT ADDRESS** Dept of History, California State Univ, San Bernardino, 5500 University Pky, San Bernardino, CA 92407-7500. **EMAIL** wmcafee@wiley.csusb.edu

MCALEER, J. PHILIP
PERSONAL Born 06/16/1935, New York, NY **DISCIPLINE** ARCHITECTURAL HISTORIAN **EDUCATION** Columbia Univ, AB, 56; Princeton Unif, MFA, 59; Univ London, PhD, 63. **CAREER** Tchr, 61-; prof, Dalhousie Univ. **HONORS AND AWARDS** Fel, Soc of Antiq of London. **MEMBERSHIPS** CAA; ICMA; SAH; SAH-GB; RAI; BAA; Avista. **RESEARCH** Medieval architecture. **SELECTED PUBLICATIONS** Auth, A Pictorial History of St. Paul's Anglican

Church, Halifax, Nova Scotia, Technical Univ of Nova Scotia, 93; "The Former Benedictine Abbey Church of St. Mary and St. Modwen (Modwenna) at Burton-on Trent and the Problem of a West Transept There," Staffordshire Stud, 93; "The Facade of Norwich Cathedral," Norfolk Arch, 93; "Rochester Cathedral: The North Choir Aisle and the Space between it and 'Gundulf's' Tower," Archaeologia Cantiana, 93; "The Romanesque Facade of Winchester Cathedral," Proc of the Hampshire Field Club and Archaeol Soc, 96; "Some Observations about the Romanesque Choir of Ely Cathedral," Jrnl of the Soc of Archit Historians, 94; "Encore Lindisfarne Priory and the Problems of Its Nave Vault," The Antiq Jrnl, 94; "Towards an Architectural History of Kilwinning Abbey," Proc of the Soc of Antiq of Scotland, 95; "The Facade of Norwich Cathedral as It Might Have Been," Norfolk Archaeol, 97; "L.N. Cottingham's Central Tower for Rochester Cathedral: A Question of Style," Archaeol Jrnl, 97; "The So-called Gundulf's Tower at Rochester Cathedral. A Reconsideration of its History," Antiq Jrnl, 98. **CONTACT ADDRESS** 98 Bedford Hills Rd, Bedford, NS, Canada B4A 1J9.

MCBETH, HARRY LEON

PERSONAL m **DISCIPLINE** CHURCH HISTORY **EDUCATION** Wayland Baptist Univ, BA, 54; Southwestern Baptist Theol Sem, MDiv, 57, ThD, 61. **CAREER** Distinguished prof, Southwestern Baptist Theol sem, 60-. **HONORS AND AWARDS** Outstanding Young Men Am, 66; pastor, first baptist church, 55-60. **MEMBERSHIPS** S Baptist Hist Soc; Amer Soc Church Hist. **SELECTED PUBLICATIONS** Auth, The Baptist Heritage: Four Centuries of Baptist Witness, Broadman Press, 87; A Sourcebook for Baptist Heritage, Broadman Press, 90; Texas Baptists: A Sesquicentennial History, Baptist Way Press, 98. **CONTACT ADDRESS** Sch Theol, Southwestern Baptist Theol Sem, PO Box 22000, Fort Worth, TX 76122-0418. **EMAIL** hlm@swbts.swbts.edu

MCBRIDE, PAUL WILBERT

PERSONAL Born 05/23/1940, Youngstown, OH, m, 1962, 3 children **DISCIPLINE** UNITED STATES HISTORY, ETHNIC STUDIES **EDUCATION** Youngstown State Univ, BA, 63; Kans State Univ, MA, 65; Univ Ga, PhD(hist), 72. **CAREER** Instr hist, Augusta Col, 67; asst prof, 70-74, assoc prof Hist, Ithaca Col, 74-, Dana Teaching fel, 82. **MEMBERSHIPS** Orgn Am Historians; Immigration Hist Asn; Hist Educ Asn. **RESEARCH** Twentieth-century United States history; United States ethnic history; Italian American studies. **SELECTED PUBLICATIONS** Auth, The co-op industrial education experiment, Hist Educ Quart, summer 74; Culture Clash: Immigrants and Reformers 1880-1920, R & E Res Assocs, 75; Peter Roberts and the YMCA Americanization Program, Pa Hist, 4/77; Daniel Bell and the permissive society, summer 77, Occas Rev; Manipulated schools, manipulated history, Hist Educ Quart, spring 79; Masters of their fate, J Ethnic Studies, 11/79; The solitary Christians: Italian Americans and their church, 12/81 & Reflections on dreams and memories, summer 82, Ethnic Groups. **CONTACT ADDRESS** Dept of History, Ithaca Col, Ithaca, NY 14850-7002. **EMAIL** McBride@Ithaca.edu

MCBRIDE, THERESA MARIE

PERSONAL Born 11/07/1947, Seattle, WA **DISCIPLINE** EUROPEAN SOCIAL AND MODERN FRENCH HISTORY **EDUCATION** Seattle Univ, BA, 69; Rutgers Univ, New Brunswick, MA, 70, PhD(hist), 73. **CAREER** Asst prof, 73-79, Assoc Prof Hist, Col of the Holy Cross, 79-, Fel, Nat Endowment Humanities, 81-82. **MEMBERSHIPS** AHA; Europ Labor & Working Class Hist; Marxist Historians Asn; Fr Hist Studies Asn. **RESEARCH** French history, 19th and 20th centuries; comparative social history. **SELECTED PUBLICATIONS** Auth, Social Mobility for the Lower Classes: Domestic Servants, J Social Hist, 9/74; The Domestic Revolution, 76 & Child and Servant in Victorian England, In: The Victorian Family, 77, Croom Helm; The Long Road Home, In: Becoming Visible: Women in European History, Houghton, 77; Women's Work, J Mod Hist, 6/77; Women's Work and Department Stores, Fr Hist Studies, fall 79. **CONTACT ADDRESS** Dept of Hist, Col of the Holy Cross, 1 College St, Worcester, MA 01610-2322.

MCCAA, ROBERT

DISCIPLINE HISTORY **EDUCATION** Univ Calif Los Angeles, PhD, 78. **CAREER** Prof **RESEARCH** Latin American history; sexual violence; changing status of Mexican women; quantitative history and demography. **SELECTED PUBLICATIONS** Auth, Marriage and Fertility in Chile: Demographic Turning Points in the Petorca Valley, 1840-1976, 83; ed, Latin American Population History Bulletin. **CONTACT ADDRESS** History Dept, Univ of Minnesota, Twin Cities, 614 Social Sciences Tower, 267 19th Ave. S, Minneapolis, MN 55455. **EMAIL** rmccaa@tc.umn.edu

MCCAFFREY, JAMES M.

PERSONAL Born 05/10/1946, Springfield, IL, m **DISCIPLINE** CIVIL ENGINEERING, HISTORY **EDUCATION** Univ of Mo at Rolla, BS, 70; Univ of Houston, ME, 74, MA, 87, PhD, 90. **CAREER** Lectr, 89-91, asst prof, 91-95, assoc prof, Univ Houston -- Downtown, 95-. **HONORS AND AWARDS** USMA/ROTC Fel IN Military Hist, 91; Univ of Houston -- Downtown'a Awd for Excellence in Scholarly and Professional Activity, 00. **MEMBERSHIPS** Soc for Military Hist. **RESEARCH** American military history. **SELECTED PUBLICATIONS** Auth, This Band of Heroes: Granbury's Texas Brigade, C.S.A., Eakin Press, 85, Tx A&M Univ Press, 96; Army of Manifest Destiny: The American Soldier in the Mexican War, 1846-1848, NY Univ Press, 92; Surrounded by Dangers of All Kinds: The Mexican War Letters of Lieutenant Theodore Laidley, Univ of N Tex Press, 97; coauth, Wake Island Pilot: A World War II Memoir, Brassey's, 95. **CONTACT ADDRESS** Social Sciences Dept, Univ of Houston, Downtown, 1 Main St, Houston, TX 77002. **EMAIL** mccaffrey@dt.uh.edu

MCCAFFREY, LAWRENCE JOHN

PERSONAL Born 08/10/1925, Riverdale, IL, m, 1949, 3 children **DISCIPLINE** HISTORY **EDUCATION** St Ambrose Col, BA, 49; Ind Univ, MA, 50; Univ Iowa, PhD(hist), 54. **CAREER** Instr hist, Univ Iowa, 50-54, vis lectr, 58-59; instr humanities, Mich State Univ, 54-55; assoc prof hist, Col St Catherine, 55-58; from asst prof to assoc prof, Univ Ill, 59-64; prof, Marquette Univ, 64-69; prof, Univ Maine, Orono, 69-70; chmn dept, 70-73, Prof Hist, Loyola Univ Chicago 70-91. **HONORS AND AWARDS** Honorary Doctor of Humanities, St. Ambrose Univ, 83, Honorary Doctor of Lit, Nat Univ of Ireland, 87. **MEMBERSHIPS** AHA; Am Cath Hist Asn, Am Comt Irish Studies (secy, 58-68, vpres, 72-75, pres, 75-78), Histol Soc. **RESEARCH** Irish nationalism and Irish literature, 1800 to the present; politics and culture of Irish Catholicism; the Irish-American experience. **SELECTED PUBLICATIONS** Auth, Irish Federalism in the 1870s: A Study of Conservative Nationalsim, American Philosophical Soc, 62; auth, Daniel O'Connell and the Repeal Year, Univ Ky; ed and contrib, Irish nationalism and the American Contribution, 76 and ed. The Irish American Reprint Series, Arno, 76; auth, Ireland from Colony to Nation State, Prince Hall, 79; coauth, The Irish in Chicago, Univ Il, 87; coed and contrib, Perspectives on Irish Nationalism, Univ Press, Ky, 89; auth, Textures of Irish America, Syracuse Univ, 92; auth, The Irish Question: Two Centuries of Conflict, Univ Pr Ky, 95; auth, Ideology and the Irish Question--Ulster Unionism and Irish Nationalism, Albion, vol 0027, 95; Piety and Nationalism--Lay Voluntary Associations and the Creation of an Irish Catholic Community in Toronto, 1850-1895, J Ecclesiastical Hist, vol 0046, 95; The Orange Riots--Irish Political Violence in New York City, 1870 and 1871, Cath Hist Rev, vol 0081, 95; auth, The Irish Catholic Diaspora in America, Catholic Univ, 97. **CONTACT ADDRESS** Dept of Hist, Loyola Univ, Chicago, Chicago, IL 60611. **EMAIL** ljpmcc@aol.com

MCCANN, FRANCIS D., JR.

PERSONAL Born 12/15/1938, Lackawanna, NY, 2 children **DISCIPLINE** HISTORY **EDUCATION** Ind Univ, PhD. **CAREER** Prof, Univ NH, 71-. **HONORS AND AWARDS** Fulbright-Hays fel; Nat Hist Publ Comn fel; Am Philos Soc grants; Joint Soc Sci Res Coun and Am Coun of Learned Soc fel; vis scholar, Woodrow Wilson Int Ctr for Scholars; Heinz Endowment Grant; Herbert E. Bolton Mem Honorable Mention Awd, Conf on Latin Am Hist; Stuart L Bernath Prize, Soc for Hist of Am For Rel; New Eng Coun on Latin Am Stud Prize; Nat Univ Cont Educ Asn Prize; Pacificador Medal, Brazil. **MEMBERSHIPS** Corresp mem, Inst de Geografia e Hist Militar do Brasil and Inst do Ceara Comendador Order of Rio Branco, Brazil. **RESEARCH** Brazil and the United States; the Brazilian Army; Goes Moneiro; Roraima: Northern Amazon frontier. **SELECTED PUBLICATIONS** Auth, The Brazilian-American Alliance, 1937-1945, 73; auth, A Nacao Armada: Ensaios Sobre a Historia do Exercito Brasileiro, 82; ed and contribur, Modern Brazil: Elites and Masses in Historical Perspective, 89-91; auth, "Historical Setting" and "National Security," in Brazil: A Country Study, ed. Rex Hudson (Washington, Library of Congress, Federal Res Division, 98); auth, Le Bresil et les Etats-Unis: des relations complexes a Pepreuve du long terme, XIX e-Xxe siecles," in Le Bresil et le Monde, ed. Denis Rolland (Paris, L'Harmatan, 98). **CONTACT ADDRESS** Univ of New Hampshire, Durham, Durham, NH 03824. **EMAIL** fdm@christa.unh.edu

MCCARL, MARY RHINELANDER

PERSONAL Born 05/03/1940, m, 1987, 1 child **DISCIPLINE** HISTORY **EDUCATION** Radcliffe, BA, 61; Harvard Univ, MA, 66; Simmons, MLS, 79; Univ Mass Boston, MA, 82. **CAREER** IND SCHOLAR **MEMBERSHIPS** Am Antiquarian Soc **RESEARCH** Thomas Shepard **SELECTED PUBLICATIONS** Auth, "Thomas Shepard's Record of Religious Experiences, 1648-1649," Wm and Mary Q, 91; auth, "Spreading the News of Satan's Malignity in Salem: Benjamin Harris, Printer and Publisher of the Witchcraft Narratives," Essex Inst Hist Colls 129, 93; auth, The Plowman's Tale: The circa 1532 and 1606 editions of a spurious Canterbury Tale, Garland, 97; auth, "Publishing the Works of Nicholas Culpeper in Seventeenth Century London," Canad Bulletin Med Hist. **CONTACT ADDRESS** 1828 Mission Rd., Vestavia Hills, AL 35216-2229. **EMAIL** mrmccarl@post.harvard.edu

MCCARTHY, DENNIS MICHAEL PATRICK

PERSONAL Born 01/02/1944, East Cleveland, OH **DISCIPLINE** ECONOMIC HISTORY, BUSINESS HISTORY **EDUCATION** Boston Col, BA, 66; Yale Univ, MA, 70, PhD(econ hist prog), 72. **CAREER** Asst prof, 72-79, Assoc Prof Hist, Iowa State Univ, 79-. **MEMBERSHIPS** Econ Hist Asn; Econ Hist Soc; African Studies Asn; AHA. **RESEARCH** Comparative African colonial bureaucracies; implications for economic change past and present; history of under development. **SELECTED PUBLICATIONS** Auth, Media as ends: money and the under-development of Tanganyika to 1940, J Econ Hist, 9/76; Organizing Under-Development from the inside: The Bureaucratic Economy in Tanganyika, 1919-40, Int J African Hist Studies, 10/77; Language Manipulation in Colonial Tanganyika, 1919-40, J African Studies, 6/79; Colonial Bureaucracy and Creating Underdevelopment: Tanganyika, 1919-1940, Iowa State Univ Press, 82. **CONTACT ADDRESS** Dept of Hist, Iowa State Univ of Science and Tech, Ames, IA 50011-0002.

MCCARTHY, JOHN P.

DISCIPLINE ENGLISH HISTORY **EDUCATION** Columbia Univ, PhD. **CAREER** Prof, Fordham Univ. **HONORS AND AWARDS** Organizer, ch, G K Chesterton Conf; exec coun, Am Irish Hist Soc. **SELECTED PUBLICATIONS** Auth, Hilaire Belloc: Edwardian Radical, 78; Dissent from Irish America 93; ed, volume of the Collected Works of G. K. Chesterton; pub(s), articles and reviews in Am, Cath Hist Rev, the Irish Times, Nat Rev, The Recorder. **CONTACT ADDRESS** Dept of Hist, Fordham Univ, 113 W 60th St, New York, NY 10023.

MCCARTHY, JUSTIN

DISCIPLINE HISTORY **EDUCATION** John Carroll Univ, AB, 67; Univ Calif, PhD, 78; Princeton Univ, Cert Demog, 80. **CAREER** US Peace Corp, Turkey, 67-69; Instr, City Chicago, 69-70; Vis Fel, Univ London, 84-85; Vis Prof, Bogazici Univ, 85; Prof, Univ Louisville, 78-. **HONORS AND AWARDS** Order of Merit, Turkish Republic; Chairman's Educ Awd, Turkish Am Friendship Coun; Fulbright-Hays Fel; Sen Independent Study and Res Fel, Nat Endowment for the Humanities; Nat Sci Found Postdoctoral Fel; Distinguished Prof, Univ Louisville. **MEMBERSHIPS** Middle East Studies Asn, Middle East Inst, Assembly of Turkish Am Asns. **RESEARCH** Middle Eastern and Balkan history and demography. **SELECTED PUBLICATIONS** Coauth, Focus on Turkey, The World Project (New York, NY), 92; auth, Death and Exile, Darwin Pr, 95; auth, The Ottoman Turks, Longman (London, UK), 97; auth, The End of the Ottoman Empire, Arnold (London, UK), 00. **CONTACT ADDRESS** Dept Hist, Univ of Louisville, 2301 S 3rd St, Louisville, KY 40292-0001. **EMAIL** jmc@louisville.edu

MCCARTIN, JOSEPH A.

PERSONAL Born 05/12/1959, Chelsea, MA, m, 1996, 2 children **DISCIPLINE** HISTORY **EDUCATION** Col of the Holy Cross, BA, 81; SUNY Binghamton, MA, 85; PhD, 90. **CAREER** Lecturer, Univ RI, 90-92; Asst Prof to Assoc Prof, SUNY Geneseo, 92-99; Assoc Prof, Georgetown Univ, 99-. **HONORS AND AWARDS** Philip Taft Labor Hist Prize, 99. **MEMBERSHIPS** AHA; OAH; Labor and Working Class Asn; Scholars, Artists and Writers for Soc Justice. **RESEARCH** 20th Century US Labor, politics and society. **SELECTED PUBLICATIONS** Auth, Labor's Great War: The Struggle for Industrial Democracy and the Origins of Modern American Labor Relations, Univ NC Press, 97. **CONTACT ADDRESS** Dept Hist, Georgetown Univ, PO Box 571035, Washington, DC 20057-1035. **EMAIL** jam6@georgetown.edu

MCCASLIN, RICHARD

PERSONAL Born 02/21/1961, Atlanta, GA, m, 1979, 1 child **DISCIPLINE** HISTORY **EDUCATION** Delta State Univ, BA, 82; La State Univ, MA, 83; Univ Tex at Austin, PhD, 88. **CAREER** Res asst prof, Univ of Tenn, 88-90; asst prof to assoc prof, High Point Univ, 90-. **HONORS AND AWARDS** Listed in Contemporary Authors vol 144, 94; listed in The Writer's Directory, 96-98; listed in International Authors and Writers Who's Who, 97; listed in Who's Who in America, 97, 98, 99, & 00; listed in Who's Who Among Am Teachers, 98. **MEMBERSHIPS** Soc of Civil War Historians, Hist Soc of NC. **RESEARCH** Civil War, Texas, Frontier. **SELECTED PUBLICATIONS** Asst/assoc ed, The Papers of Andrew Johnson vol 8 and 9, Univ of Tenn, 89 & 91; auth, Andrew Johnson: A Bibliography, Greenwood Press, 92; auth, Tainted Breeze: The Great Hanging at Gainesville, Tex, October 1862, La State Univ, 94 & 97; auth, Portraits of Conflict: A Photographic History of North Carolina in the Civil War, Univ of Ark, 97; auth, Gibraltar of the South: The Fort Fisher Campaign, Grady McWhiney Res Found, forthcoming; coauth, Portraits of Conflict: A Photographic History of Tennessee in the Civil War, Univ of Ark, forthcoming; auth, A Distant Thunder: The Civil War in the Trans-Mississippi, Univ of Nebr, forthcoming; auth, In the Shadow of Washington: Robert E. Lee and the Southern Confederacy, La State Univ, forthcoming. **CONTACT ADDRESS** Dept Hist and Govt, High Point Univ, 933 Montlieu Ave, High Point, NC 27262-3555. **EMAIL** rmccas@acme.highpoint.edu

MCCAUGHEY, ROBERT ANTHONY

PERSONAL Born 04/13/1939, Pawtucket, RI, m, 1965, 2 children **DISCIPLINE** AMERICAN HISTORY **EDUCATION** Univ Rochester, AB, 61; Univ NC, MA, 65; Harvard Univ, PhD, 69. **CAREER** Asst prof, 69-74, assoc prof, 74-80, Prof

Hist, 80-97, Anne Whitney Olin Prof Hist, 97-, Dean of Faculty, 87-93, Barnard Col, Columbia Univ. **HONORS AND AWARDS** Fel, Charles Warren Ctr Studies Am Hist, 72-73; Guggenheim fel, 74-75. **MEMBERSHIPS** AHA **RESEARCH** History of American higher education; intellectual history. **SELECTED PUBLICATIONS** Auth, From Town to City: Boston in the 1820's, Polit Sci Quart, 73; Josiah Quincy: The Last Federalist, Harvard Univ, 74; The Transformation of American Academic life: Harvard University, 1821-1892, Perspectives Am Hist, 74; American University Teachers and Opposition to the Vietnam War: A Reconsideration, Minerva, 76; Four Academic Ambassadors: International Studies and the American University Before the Second World War, Perspectives in Am Hist, 79; In the Land of the Blind: American International Studies in the 1930s, The Annals of the Am Acad Polit & Soc Sci, 80; The Current Stake of International Studies: Special Consideration Reconsidered, J Higher Educ, 80; Am International Studies: The History of an Intellectual Enterprise, Columbia Univ, 84; auth, Scholars and Teachers: The Faculties of Select Liberal Arts Colleges and Their Place in American Higher Learning, Mellon Found, 95. **CONTACT ADDRESS** 375 Riverside Dr, New York, NY 10025. **EMAIL** ram31@columbia.edu

MCCLAIN, MOLLY A.
PERSONAL Born 10/19/1966, San Diego, CA **DISCIPLINE** HISTORY **EDUCATION** Univ Chicago, BA, 87; Yale, PhD, 94. **CAREER** Asst prof, Univ San Diego, 95-. **HONORS AND AWARDS** Andrew W. Mellon Dissertation Fel; Mellon Found Res Fel; Jacob K. Javits Grad Fel. **MEMBERSHIPS** AHA; ASECS; NACBS; Phi Alpha Theta **RESEARCH** Britain and colonial American; history of science. **SELECTED PUBLICATIONS** Auth, Beaufort: The Duke and His Duchess, 1657-1715, Yale Univ Press, 01; auth, art, The Wentwood Forest Riot: Property Rights and Political Culture in Restoration England, 95; auth, art, The Duke of Beaufort's Tory Progress Through Wales, 1684, 97; co-auth, Schaum's Quick Guide to Writing Great Essays, 98. **CONTACT ADDRESS** Dept of History, Univ of San Diego, 5998 Alcala Pk, San Diego, CA 92110. **EMAIL** mmcclain@acusd.edu

MCCLAY, WILFRED M.
PERSONAL Born 12/07/1951, Champaign, IL, m, 1983, 2 children **DISCIPLINE** UNITED STATES HISTORY **EDUCATION** St John's Col, BA, 74; Johns Hopkins Univ, PhD, 87. **CAREER** Vis instr, Towson State Univ, 85-86; asst prof, Univ of Dallas, 86-87; from asst prof to assoc prof, Tulane Univ, 87-; vis prof, Georgetown Univ, 98-9; SunTrust Chair of Excellence in Human and Prof of Hist, Univ of Tenn at Chattanooga, 99-. **HONORS AND AWARDS** Danforth Grad fel, 80-84; Nat Acad of Educ, Spencer Postdoctoral fel, 93-94; Merle Curti Awd in Intellectual Hist, Org of Am Hists, 95; Fac Res Awd, Tulane Univ, 96; Univ Profs fel, Nat Endowment for the Hums, 97-98; fel, Woodrow Wilson Int Ctr for Scholars, 97-98; Templeton Honor Rolls, J.Templeton Found, 97-98; app to Royden B. Davis Ch in Interdisciplinary Studies, Georgetown Univ, 98; Public Policy Fellow, Woodrow Wilson Int Cntr for Scholars, 00. **MEMBERSHIPS** Am Hist Asn; Org of Am Hists; The Hist Soc. **RESEARCH** The intellectual and cultural history of the United States. **SELECTED PUBLICATIONS** Where Have We Come Since the 1950s? Thoughts on Materialism and American Social Character, Rethinking Materialism: Perspectives on the Spiritual Dimension of Economic Behavior, ed R. Wuthnow, 95; The Soul of Man Under Federalism, First Things, no 64, 96; Filling the Hollow Core: Religious Faith and the Postmodern University, The New Religious Humanists: A Reader, ed G. Wolfe, 97; Mr Emerson's Tombstone, First Things, no 83, 98; The Lonely Crowd at Fifty, Wilson Quart, vol 22, no 3, 98; Is America an Experiment, The Public Interest, no 133, 98; auth, "Two Concepts of Secularism," Wilson Quart 24 (00); auth, A Student's Guide to U.S. History, 00; auth, "Clio's Makeshift Laboratory," in First Things (01); ed, Refurnishing the Public Square: Religion and Public Policy in Twentieth Century America, 01. **CONTACT ADDRESS** SunTrust Chair of Excellence in Humanities, Univ of Tennessee, Chattanooga, Dept. 6256, Fletcher 412C, 615 McCallie Ave., Chattanooga, TN 37403 37403. **EMAIL** mcclay@mindspring.com

MCCLEARY, ANN
PERSONAL Born 08/15/1954, Indianapolis, IN, m, 1983, 3 children **DISCIPLINE** AMERICAN CIVILIZATION **EDUCATION** Brown Univ, PhD, 96. **CAREER** Asst prof. **MEMBERSHIPS** Vernacular Architecture Forum; Am Studies Asn; Nat Council on Pub Hist; Ag Hist Soc; Am Asn of State and Local Hist; Am Asn of Museums; Am Folklore Soc. **RESEARCH** American women history; early American history; American architecture; American material culture. **SELECTED PUBLICATIONS** Auth, "Domesticity and the Farm Woman: A Case Study of Women in Augusta County, Virginia 1850-1940," in Camille Wells, ed, Perspectives in Vernacular Architecture I, Annapolis, MD: Vernacular Architecture Forum, 82. **CONTACT ADDRESS** History Dept, State Univ of West Georgia, Carrollton, GA 30118. **EMAIL** amcclear@westga.edu

MCCLELLAN, CHARLES W.
PERSONAL Born 06/16/1945, Brooklyn, NY **DISCIPLINE** AFRICAN & THIRD WORLD HISTORY **EDUCATION** Emporia State Univ, BSE, 67; Michigan State Univ, MA, 71, PhD(hist), 78. **CAREER** Asst prof hist, Murray State Univ, Ky, 79; asst prof, State Univ NY, Plattsburgh, 79-80; prof hist, Radford Univ, 80-98; Africa bk rev ed, Int J Oral Hist, 82. **HONORS AND AWARDS** Am Council of Learned Societies grant in Aid, 89; Fulbright-Hays Research Awd, 90; 2nd Vpres and member of Board of Trustees, Pi Gamma Mu, 90; Int observer for Ethiopian elections, 92. **MEMBERSHIPS** African Studies Asn; Am Assoc Univ Profs; National Council of Returned Peace Corps Volunteers. **RESEARCH** History 19th and 20th century Ethiopia, with special interest in the south; history and social anthropology of East Africa; nation-buiding as related to Africa. **SELECTED PUBLICATIONS** Coauth, "State Transformation and National Integration: gedeo and the Ethiopian Empire, 1895-1935," 88; auth, Perspective on the Neftenya-Gabbar system--the example of Darasa, Africa, Rome, Vol XXXIII, 78; The Ethiopian occupation of northern Sidamo--recruitment and motivation, Proc 5th Int Conf Ethiopian Studies, 79; Land, labor and coffee--the South's role in Ethiopian self-reliance, 1889-1935, African Econ Hist, Vol IX, 80; Observations on the Ethiopian Nation, Its Nationalism, and the Italo-Ethiopian War, Northeast African Studies, New Series, 96; The Tales of Yoseph & Woransa: Gedeo Experiences in the Era of the Italo-Ethopian War, in Personality and Political Culture in Modern Africa, 98. **CONTACT ADDRESS** Dept of History, Radford Univ, PO Box 6941, Radford, VA 24142-6941. **EMAIL** cmcclell@runet.edu

MCCLELLAN, WOODFORD
PERSONAL Born 03/20/1934, Martinsville, IL, d, 3 children **DISCIPLINE** MODERN RUSSIAN & EASTERN EUROPEAN HISTORY **EDUCATION** Stanford Univ, AB, 57, MA, 58; Univ Calif, Berkeley, PhD, 63. **CAREER** From instr to asst prof hist, US Mil Acad, 61-65; assoc prof, 65-72, fel, Ctr Advan Studies, 71-72, Prof Hist, Univ VA, 72-, Am Coun Learned Soc grant, 67-68; Nat Endowment for Humanities fel, 67-68; Am Coun Learned Soc & Acad Sci USSR exchange scholar humanities & soc sci, 73-74. **MEMBERSHIPS** AHA; Am Asn Advan Slavic Studies. **RESEARCH** History of Russia; history of socialist thought and movements. **SELECTED PUBLICATIONS** Auth, Svetozar Markovic, Princeton Univ, 64; Serbia and social democracy, Int Rev Social Hist, 66; Postwar political evolution of Yugoslavia, Contemporary Yugoslavia, Univ Calif, 69; Nechaevshchina: An unknown chapter, Slavic Rev, 9/73; Revolutionary Exiles: The Russians in the First International and the Paris Commune, Frank Cass, London, 78; Russia: The Soviet Period and After, 4th Ed, Prentice Hall, 98. **CONTACT ADDRESS** Dept Hist, Univ of Virginia, 1 Randall Hall, Charlottesville, VA 22903-3244. **EMAIL** wdm@virginia.edu

MCCLELLAND, CHARLES E.
DISCIPLINE GERMAN HISTORY **EDUCATION** Princeton Univ, AB, 62; Yale Univ, MA, 63, PhD, 67. **CAREER** Instr, Princeton Univ, 66-68; asst prof, Univ Pa, 68-74; assoc to full, 74-97, PROF EMER, 98-, UNIV NMEX. **CONTACT ADDRESS** 1002 Richmond Dr NE, Albuquerque, NM 87106. **EMAIL** cemcc@unm.edu

MCCLELLAND, JAMES
PERSONAL Born 04/29/1938, Berea, OH, m, 1985, 2 children **DISCIPLINE** HISTORY OF MODERN RUSSIA **EDUCATION** Princeton Univ, PhD, 70. **CAREER** Assoc prof, Univ Nebr, Lincoln. **HONORS AND AWARDS** Fulbright-Hays Fel; ACLS/SSRC Fel; IREX Fel. **RESEARCH** The relationship between the Russian revolution and education. **SELECTED PUBLICATIONS** Auth, "Proletarianizing the Student Body," Past & Present 80 (Aug 78); auth, Autocrats and Academics: Education, Culture and Society in Tsarist Russia, Univ Chicago Press, 79; auth, "Utopianism versus Revolutionary Heroism in Bolshevik Policy," Slavic Rev (Sept 80). **CONTACT ADDRESS** Dept of Hist, Univ of Nebraska, Lincoln, 612 OldH, Lincoln, NE 68588-0327. **EMAIL** jcm@unlserve.unl.edu

MCCLELLAND, WILLIAM LESTER
PERSONAL Born 08/25/1924 **DISCIPLINE** HISTORY OF CHRISTIANITY **EDUCATION** Westminster Col, BA, 48; Pittsburgh Theol Sem, BD, 51, ThM, 56; Princeton Theol Sem, PhD(hist theol), 67. **CAREER** Pastor, Knox United Presby Church, Des Moines, 51-53; pastor, Avalon United Presby Church, Pittsburgh, 53-56; from asst prof to assoc prof, 56-71, dir honors, 67-72, trustee, Bd Trustees, 76-77, chmn dept, 68-74, Prof Relig, Muskingum Col, 71, Chmn Dept Relig & Philos, 77, Coordr, Div Arts & Humanities, 81-, Vis lectr, Westminster Col, Eng, 67; Am Col Switz, 69. **MEMBERSHIPS** Am Soc Church Hist; Am Acad Relig; Soc Liturgica; AAUP. **RESEARCH** American religious experience as compared with European religious experience; Reformation history; liturgical history. **SELECTED PUBLICATIONS** Auth, Underhill, Evelyn--Artist of the Infinite Life, Church Hist, vol 0063, 94. **CONTACT ADDRESS** Dept of Relig & Philos, Muskingum Col, New Concord, OH 43762.

MCCLENDON, THOMAS
PERSONAL Born 07/27/1954, Berkeley, CA, m, 1991 **DISCIPLINE** HISTORY **EDUCATION** Pomona Col, BA, 76; Univ Calif, JD, 80; Stanford Univ, MA, 90; Stanford Univ, PhD, 95. **CAREER** Vis Asst Prof, Univ Calif, 95-96; Lectr, Univ Calif, 97-98; Asst Prof, Southwestern Univ, 98-. **HONORS AND AWARDS** Fulbright & SSRC Fels, 91-92; FLAS (Title 6) Awds for Zulu Study, 88-94; Summer NEH Fel, 97. **MEMBERSHIPS** ASA, AHA, St Bar Asn of Calif. **RESEARCH** South Africa, customary law generation conflict, gender and labor tenancy. **SELECTED PUBLICATIONS** Auth, "Tradition and Domestic Struggle in the Courtroom: Customary Law and the Control of Women in Segregation-Era Natal," The Int J of African Hist Studies, 28, no 3 (95): 527-561; auth, "'Hiding Cattle on the White Man's Farm': Cattle Loans and Commercial Farms in Natal 1930-1950," African Econ Hist, 25 (97): 43-58; auth, "'A Dangerous Doctrine': Twins, Ethnography and Inheritance in Colonial Africa," J of Legal Pluralism, 39 (97): 121-140. **CONTACT ADDRESS** Dept Hist, Southwestern Univ, Georgetown, TX 78626-6100.

MCCLESKEY, TURK
DISCIPLINE HISTORY **EDUCATION** Univ Texas Austin, 75; Col of William and Mary, PhD 90. **CAREER** Oakland Univ, asst prof 90-93; Virginia Military Inst, asst prof, assoc prof, 94-01. **CONTACT ADDRESS** Dept of History, Virginia Military Inst, Lexington, VA 24450.

MCCLINTOCK, THOMAS COSHOW
PERSONAL Born 10/06/1923, Lebanon, OR, m, 1954, 3 children **DISCIPLINE** UNITED STATES HISTORY **EDUCATION** Stanford Univ, AB, 49; Columbia Univ, MA, 50; Univ Wash, PhD(US intellectual hist), 59. **CAREER** From instr to assoc prof US Hist, 59-70, actg chmn dept hist, 67-68 & 71-72, Prof US Hist, Ore State Univ, 70-, Chmn Dept Hist, 72-, Danforth assoc, 69-; vis prof, Univ Manchester, 70 & Univ Stirling, 71; mem, Ore Comt for Humanities, 75-81. **MEMBERSHIPS** Orgn Am Historians; Western Hist Asn. **RESEARCH** The American frontier; the progressive movement; Oregon history. **SELECTED PUBLICATIONS** Auth, J Allen Smith, a Pacific Northwest progressive, Pac Northwest Quart, 4/62; Henderson Luelling, Seth Lewelling and the birth of the Pacific coast fruit industry, 6/67 & Seth Lewelling, William S U'Ren and the birth of the Oregon progressive movement, 9/67, Ore Hist Quart; Bandon-by-the-sea revisited, Ore Hist Quart, 12/74. **CONTACT ADDRESS** Dept of Hist, Oregon State Univ, Corvallis, OR 97331.

MCCLUSKEY, STEPHEN C.
PERSONAL Born Chicago, IL, m, 1969, 2 children **DISCIPLINE** HISTORY OF SCIENCE, MEDEIVAL HISTORY **EDUCATION** IL Inst Technol, BS, 61; Univ Wis-Madison, PhD, 74. **CAREER** Vis asst prof hist, KS Univ, 74-75; vis asst prof hist of sci, Univ Notre Dame, 75-76; vis asst prof, 76-80, prof hist, WVA Univ, 80. **HONORS AND AWARDS** NSF res grant, 78-80. **MEMBERSHIPS** Hist Sci Soc; Mediaeval Acad Am; Sigma Xi; Am astronomy soc. **RESEARCH** Medieval sci; hist of the physical sci(s). **SELECTED PUBLICATIONS** Auth, Astronomy of the Hopi Indians, J Hist Astron, 8/77; Astronomies and Cultures in Early Medieval Europe, Cambridge Univ Press, 98. **CONTACT ADDRESS** Dept of Hist, West Virginia Univ, Morgantown, PO Box 6303, Morgantown, WV 26506-6303. **EMAIL** scmcc@wvnvm.wvnet.edu

MCCLYMER, JOHN FRANCIS
PERSONAL Born 03/04/1945, Brooklyn, NY, m, 1969, 1 child **DISCIPLINE** AMERICAN HISTORY **EDUCATION** Fordham Col, AB, 66; State Univ NYork Stony Brook, MA, 67, PhD(Am hist), 73. **CAREER** Instr, 70-73, asst prof, 73-77, Assoc Prof Hist, Assumption Col, 77-, Fel, Nat Endowment for the Humanities summer sem, Vanderbilt Univ, 75 & Immigration Hist Res Ctr, Univ Minn, summer 77; Nat Endowment for the Humanities res fel, Washington, summer 76 & 79-80; reviewer & referee, J Urban Hist & J Am Ethnic Hist, 76-; teaching res fel, Newberry Libr, Chicago, summer 78. **MEMBERSHIPS** Am Hist Asn; Orgn Am Historians; Soc Hist Educ. **RESEARCH** Ethnic studies; community studies; women's studies. **SELECTED PUBLICATIONS** Auth, The Pittsburgh survey, 1907-1914: Forging an ideology in the steel district, Pa Hist, 74; coauth, The essay assignment as a teaching device, Hist Teacher, 77; Instructor's Manual for Irwin Ungar These United States, Little, Brown & Co, 78; auth, the Federal Government and the Americanization movement, Prologue: J Nat Archives, 78; coauth, An interdisciplinary approach to community studies, Hist Teacher, 79; auth, War and Welfare: Social Engineering in America, 1890-1925, Greenwood Press, 80; The study of community and the new social history, J Urban Hist, 80; Federal Americanization: The bureau of naturalization and the education of the foreign born adult, 1914-1925, In: Immigrants and Education, Univ Ill Press, 81. **CONTACT ADDRESS** Dept of Hist, Assumption Col, Worcester, MA 01609.

MCCOLLEY, ROBERT
DISCIPLINE HISTORY **EDUCATION** Univ Calif Berkeley, PhD, 60. **CAREER** Prof, Univ Ill Urbana Champaign. **RESEARCH** Early American history to 1830; high culture in the United States. **SELECTED PUBLICATIONS** Auth, Slavery

and Jeffersonian Virginia, Univ Ill, 73; Classical Music in Chicago and the Founding of the Symphony, 1850-1905, Ill Hist J, 85. **CONTACT ADDRESS** History Dept, Univ of Illinois, Urbana-Champaign, 52 E Gregory Dr, Champaign, IL 61820. **EMAIL** rmcolle@uiuc.edu

MCCOMB, DAVID GLENDINNING

PERSONAL Born 10/26/1934, Kokomo, IN, m, 1957, 3 children **DISCIPLINE** URBAN HISTORY, SPORTS HISTORY **EDUCATION** Southern Methodist Univ, BA, 56; Stanford Univ, MBA, 58; Rice Univ, MA, 62; Univ Tex, PhD(hist), 68. **CAREER** Instr hist, STex Jr Col, 62; asst prof, San Antonio Col, 62-66; instr, Univ Houston, 66-68; spec res assoc oral hist proj, Univ Tex, Austin, 68-69, consult, 69-72; from asst prof to assoc prof, 69-77, chmn dept, 75-80, Prof Hist, Colo State Univ, 77-, Nat Endowment Humanities younger humanist fel, 70-71; vis instr, Univ Pittsburgh, 82, 85. **MEMBERSHIPS** Am Hist Asn, TX State Hist Asn, World Hist Asn. **RESEARCH** United States urban history; world urban history; history of technology, Sports Hist. **SELECTED PUBLICATIONS** Auth, Houston, A History (Austin: TX), 81; auth, Galveston, A History (Austin, TX,), 86; auth, World History, Annuel Editions Guilford, CT; Dushkin, 88, 90, 92, 94, 97, 99; auth, Texas, A Modern History (Austin, TX), 89; auth, Colorado, History of the Centennial State, Colorado PR, 94; auth, In Memory of Frantz, Joe, B., Southwestern Hist Quart, vol 0097, 94; Galveston as a Tourist City, Southwestern Hist Quart, vol 0100, 97; auth, Sports, An Illustrated History (NY: Oxford), 98; auth, The Historic Seacoast of Texas (Austin, TX), 99. **CONTACT ADDRESS** Dept of Hist, Colorado State Univ, Fort Collins, CO 80523. **EMAIL** david.mccomb@colostate.edu

MCCONNELL, ROLAND CALHOUN

PERSONAL Born 03/27/1910, Amherst, NS, Canada, m, 1996 **DISCIPLINE** HISTORY **EDUCATION** Howard Univ, AB, 31, AM, 33; NYork Univ, PhD, 45. **CAREER** Instr soc sci, Elizabeth City State Teachers Col, NC, 38-39 & 41-42; archivist, Nat Arch, 43-47; assoc prof hist, 47-48, prof hist, 48-79, chmn div soc sci, 53-55, chmn dept hist, polit sci & geog, 68-79, prof emeritus, Morgan State cuniv; Consult, Afro-Am Bicentennial Corp, Washington, DC, 72-76; chmn, Md State Comn Afro-Am Hist & Cult, 77- . **HONORS AND AWARDS** MSU Heritage Awd, 99. **MEMBERSHIPS** AHA; Soc Am Archivists; Asn Study African-Am Life & Hist. **RESEARCH** Archives. **SELECTED PUBLICATIONS** Auth, Negro Troops of Antebellum Louisiana, A History of the Battalion of Free Men of Color, La State Univ, 68; Records in the National Archives Pertaining to the History of North Carolina, 1775-1943, NC Hist Rev; Importance of records in the National Archives on the history of the Negro & Isaiah Dorman and the Custer Expedition, J Negro Hist; The Black experience in Maryland, 1634-1900, In: The Old Line State, A History of Maryland, Annapolis, 71; Biographical sketches on Robert Purvis, Archibald Grimke, Thurgood Marshall, Louis Stokes and Roy Wilkins, In: Encycl of World Biography, Vols 1-12, McGraw-Hill, 73; Black life and activities in West Florida, 1762-1763, In: Eighteenth Century Florida, Life on the Frontier, Univ Fla, 76; coed, J of the Afro-Am Hist and Geneal Soc, special issue, African Americans in the Military, 91. **CONTACT ADDRESS** 2406 College Ave, Baltimore, MD 21214.

MCCORISON, MARCUS ALLEN

PERSONAL Born 07/17/1926, Lancaster, WI, m, 1950, 6 children **DISCIPLINE** AMERICAN HISTORY **EDUCATION** Ripon Col, AB, 50; Univ Vt, MA, 51; Columbia Univ, MS, 54. **CAREER** Librn, Kellogg-Hubbard Libr, Montpelier, Vt, 54-55; chief, Rare Bks Dept, Dartmouth Col Libr, 55-59; head spec collections, State Univ Iowa, 59-60; librn, 60-67, dir & librn, 67-89, pres & librn, 89-91, pres, 91-92, pres emer, 93-, Am Antiq Soc. **HONORS AND AWARDS** Pepys Medal, Ephemera Soc, 80; Laureate Awd, Am Printing Hist Asn, 98; Maurice Rickard Medal, Ephemera Soc Am, 00. **MEMBERSHIPS** Orgn Am Historians; Asn Col & Res Libr; Am Antiq Soc; Bibliog Soc Am. **RESEARCH** American bibliography; American printing history. **SELECTED PUBLICATIONS** Auth, "Ray Nash and the Pine Tree Press," Dartmouth Col Libr Bull 1 (87): 29-32; auth, "Personal Recollections of Harold Goddard Rugg," Vt Hist News 6 (90): 110-114; auth, "The Routine Handling of Forgeries in Research Libraries: or, Can Dishonesty Ever Be Routine?," in Forged Documents, Proceedings of the 1989 Houston Conference, ed. Pat Bozeman (DE: Oak Knoll Books, 90), 49-53; auth, "Humanists and Byte-Sized Bibliography, or, how to digest expanding sources of information," Proc of the Am Philos Soc 1 (91): 61-72; auth, "The Annals of American Bibliography, or Book History, Plain and Fancy," Libr and Cult 1 (91): 14-23; auth, "The Idylls of the Triune Idol, or the Joys of Publishing in 1820," in Prints of New England, ed. Georgia B. Barnhill (MA: Am Antiq Soc, 91), 69-81; auth, "Found at Last? The 'Oath of a Freeman,' the End of Innocence, and the American Antiquarian Society," in Judgment of Experts, Essays and Documents about the Investigation of the Forging of the Oath of a Freeman, ed. James Gilreath (MA: Am Antiq Soc, 91), 62-69; auth, "M.D. Gilman, The Bibliography of Vermont, 1897," in A Vermont 14 commemorative of the two-hundredth anniversary of Vermont's admission to the Union as the nation's fourteenth state, 1791-1991, ed. Edward Connery Lathem and Virginia L. Close (VT: Univ Vt Libr, 92); auth, "Some Eighteenth-Century American Book Collectors, Their Collections, and Their Legacies," in Publishing and Readership in Revolutionary France and America (CT: Greenwood Press, 93), 191-204; auth, The Humble Petition of George Faulkner and George Grierson, Printers and Booksellers, Fulcrum Publ (Golden, CO), 93. **CONTACT ADDRESS** Salisbury Green, 3601 Knightsbridge Close, Worcester, MA 01609-1161. **EMAIL** mamcc@worldnet.att.net

MCCORMICK, RICHARD P.

PERSONAL Born 12/24/1916, New York, NY **DISCIPLINE** AMERICAN HISTORY **EDUCATION** Rutgers Univ, AB, 38, AM, 40; Univ Pa, PhD, 48. **CAREER** Historian, Philadelphia Qm Dept, 42-44; instr, Univ Del, 44-45; from instr to prof hist, 45-74, univ historian, 48-82, chmn dept, 66-69, dean col, 74-77, univ prof, 74-82, Emer Univ Prof Hist, Rutgers Univ, 82-, Soc Sci Res Coun fel, 57-58; lectr Am hist, Cambridge Univ, 61; Commonwealth lectr, Univ London, 71. **HONORS AND AWARDS** LittD, Rutgers Univ, 82. **MEMBERSHIPS** AHA; Am Asn State & Local Hist; Orgn Am Historians. **RESEARCH** History of American politics; New Jersey history. **SELECTED PUBLICATIONS** Auth, The Ordinance of 1784, William and Mary Quart, vol 0050, 93. **CONTACT ADDRESS** Rutgers, The State Univ of New Jersey, New Brunswick, 111 Grad Sch Libr Serv, New Brunswick, NJ 08903.

MCCORMICK, ROBERT B.

PERSONAL Born, NC **DISCIPLINE** HISTORY **EDUCATION** Wake Univ, BA, 86; Univ SC, MA, 92; PhD, 96. **CAREER** Asst prof, chair, Newman Univ, 96- **MEMBERSHIPS** AAASS; NACBS. **RESEARCH** Ante Pavelic; Croatia during World War II. **CONTACT ADDRESS** Newman Univ, 3100 McCormick Ave, Wichita, KS 67213.

MCCOUBREY, JOHN W.

PERSONAL Born 11/04/1923, Boston, MA, m, 1948, 6 children **DISCIPLINE** HISTORY OF ART **EDUCATION** Harvard Univ, BA, 47; Ecole du Louvre, 52-53; Inst Fine Arts, NYork Univ, PhD, 58. **CAREER** From instr to asst prof hist of art, Yale Univ, 53-60, Univ Pa, 60-96; Farquhar Prof Emer Hist Art. **HONORS AND AWARDS** Fulbright fel, Paris, 52-53 & London, 64-65; Guggenheim fel, 64-65. **MEMBERSHIPS** Adv bd, Pa Acad Fine Arts; mem various comts, Philadelphia Mus Art; Col Art Asn Am. **RESEARCH** Nineteenth and twentieth century painting; J M W Turner; Cezanne. **SELECTED PUBLICATIONS** Auth, Baron Gros' battle of Eylau and Roman Imperial art, Art Bull, 6/61; American Tradition in Painting, Braziller, 63, new revised ed. UPENN Press, 99; The revival of Chardin in French still life, Art Bull, 3/64; ed, American Art 1700-1960, Prentice-Hall, 65; coauth, The Colonial Arts, Scribner, 67; Parliament on Fire, Turner's Burnings, Art in Am, 94; War and Peace in 1842: Turner Haydon and Wilkie, Turner Studies, 84; Time's Railway, Turner and teh Great Western, Turner Studies, 86; The Hero of a Hundred Fights, Turner Studies, 91; Turner's Slaveship, Abolition, Ruskin and Reception, Word & Image, 98. **CONTACT ADDRESS** Dept of Hist of Art, Univ of Pennsylvania, 3405 Woodland Walk, Philadelphia, PA 19104. **EMAIL** mccoubre@sas.upenn.edu

MCCREADY, WILLIAM DAVID

PERSONAL Born 07/29/1943, Guelph, ON, Canada, m, 1976 **DISCIPLINE** MEDIEVAL AND INTELLECTUAL HISTORY **EDUCATION** Univ Waterloo, BA, 66, MA, 67; Univ Toronto, PhD(medieval studies), 71. **CAREER** Lectr, 69-71, asst prof, 71-75, Assoc Prof Hist, Queen's Univ, Ont, 75-. **MEMBERSHIPS** Mediaeval Acad Am. **RESEARCH** Late medieval political theory and ecclesiology. **SELECTED PUBLICATIONS** Auth, The Theory of Papal Monarchy in the 14th Century (Studies and Texts 56), William D. McCready, Paperback, 82; auth, Signs of Sanctity: Miracles in the Thought of Gregory the Great, William D. McCready, (Studies and Texts 91), 89; auth, Miracles in the Venerable Bede, William D. McCready, (Studies and Texts, No 118), 94. **CONTACT ADDRESS** Dept of Hist, Queen's Univ at Kingston, Kingston, ON, Canada K7L 3N6. **EMAIL** mccready@post.queensu.ca

MCCRONE, KATHLEEN E.

PERSONAL Born Regina, Canada **DISCIPLINE** HISTORY **EDUCATION** Univ Sask, BA, 63; New York Univ, MA, 67, PhD, 71. **CAREER** Lectr, 68-72, asst prof, 72-76, head dept, 78-81, Prof Hist, Univ Windsor, 84-, Dean Social Sciences 90-. **MEMBERSHIPS** Can Conf Deans Arts Hum Soc Sci; Soc Sci Fedn Can; Can Hist Asn. **SELECTED PUBLICATIONS** Auth, Sport And The Physical Emancipation Of Women, 1870-1914, 88; auth, Class, Gender and English Women's Sport, 1890-1914, in J Sport Hist, 91. **CONTACT ADDRESS** Dept of History, Univ of Windsor, 101 Chrysler Hall Tower, Windsor, ON, Canada N9B 3P4. **EMAIL** kem@uwindsor.ca

MCCUE, ROBERT J.

PERSONAL Born 02/17/1932, Cardston, AB, Canada, m, 1956, 7 children **DISCIPLINE** SIXTEENTH CENTURY EUROPE **EDUCATION** Univ Alta, BA, 57, BEd, 60; Brigham Young Univ, MA, 59, PhD(hist), 70. **CAREER** Instr hist, Brigham Young Univ, 64-65; lectr, 68-70, Asst Prof Hist, Univ Victoria, BC, 70-. **MEMBERSHIPS** Can Asn Univ Teachers, Historians of Early Mod Europe. **RESEARCH** Religious history, particularly on the 16th and 19th centuries. **SELECTED PUBLICATIONS** Auth, Crossing the Boundaries--Christian Piety and the Arts in Medieval and Renaissance Confraternities, Quaderni d Italianistica, vol 0013, 92. **CONTACT ADDRESS** Dept of Hist, Univ of Victoria, Victoria, BC, Canada V8W 2Y2.

MCCULLAGH, SUZANNE FOLDS

PERSONAL Born 01/30/1951, Evanston, IL, m, 1975, 2 children **DISCIPLINE** ART HISTORY **EDUCATION** Williams Col, 71-72; Smith Col, BA (cum laude), 73; Harvard Univ, MA, 74, PhD (fine arts), 81. **CAREER** Intern, Metropolitan Museum Art, 72; curatorial asst in charge, print dept, Harvard Univ, Fogg Art Museum, 74-75; curatorial asst, 75-79, asst curator, 79-84, co-coor, self-study & long range plan, 80-82, assoc curator, 85-87, curator of Earlier Prints and Drawings, Dept of Prints and Drawings, The Art Institute of Chicago, 87-; adjunct prof, Northwestern Univ, 83-; Connoisseurship seminars, The Art Institute of Chicago, 85, 87, 94; vis prof, Univ Chicago, Dept Art, 94. **HONORS AND AWARDS** Phi Beta Kappa; Agnes Mongan Traveling fel, 77; Kemper Educational and Charitable Trust grant, 87-89, 90-; NEH Arts Documentation grant, 87-90; Getty Grant for Vis Scholars, 89-91; Art Hist Information prog, Getty Trust, 93-94; NEH Humanities grant reviewer, 94. **MEMBERSHIPS** Snite Art Museum, Notre Dame Univ (vis comm, 85-); Print Coun of Am (bd, 82-85); The North Shore Country Day School, Winnetka (trustee, 88-, chmn, art comm, 87-); Landmarks Preservation Coun of IL (dir, 95-); Harvard Club of Chicago (dir, 95-). **RESEARCH** French and Italian drawings. **SELECTED PUBLICATIONS** Auth, Nicholas Lancret 1690-1743, book rev with Margaret Morgan Grasselli, Master Drawings 32, no 2, summer 94; The Golden Age of Florentine Drawing: Two Centuries of Disegno from Leonardo to Volterrano, exhibition coord, AIC 5/26-7/17/94; The Extraordinary Eye, Erudition, Energy, and Example of Agnes Mongan, Drawing 16, July-Aug 94, Harvard Univ Art Museums Rev 3, no 2, spring 94; European Master Drawings from the Collection of Peter Jay Sharp, exhibition catalogue, Nat Academy of Design, 5/24-8/28/94, entry on Federico Barocci; preparing the Drawing Collection Catalogues, Print Coun of Am Newsletter, no 17, spring 95; The Touch of the Artist: Drawings in the Woodner Collection, exhibition catalogue, Nat Gallery of Art, Washington, entries on V Carpaccio and G de Saint-Aubin, 95; Gabriel de Saint-Aubin's Debt to Antoine Watteau and Francois Boucher, in Correspondances: Festschrift fur Margret Stuffmann zum 24, November 1996, Mainz, 96; Recent Acquisitions of Florentine Drawings in the Art Institute of Chicago, in L'Arte del Disegno: Festschrift fur Christel Thiem, Stuttgart, 97; Michelangelo and His Influence: Drawings from Windsor Castle, exhibition organizer, AIC 4/12-6/22/97; Italian Drawings before 1600 in The Art Institute of Chicago, proj dir and co-auth with Laura M Giles, AIC 4/12-6/22/97. **CONTACT ADDRESS** Curator of Earlier Prints and Drawings., Art Inst of Chicago, 111 S Michigan Ave, Chicago, IL 60603. **EMAIL** smcculla@artic.edu

MCCULLOCH, SAMUEL CLYDE

PERSONAL Born 09/03/1916, Aarat, Australia, m, 1944, 3 children **DISCIPLINE** HISTORY **EDUCATION** Univ Calif, AB, 40 MA, 42, PhD, 44. **CAREER** Teaching asst hist, Univ Calif, Los Angeles, 43-44; instr, Oberlin Col, 44-45; asst prof, Amherst Col, 45-46; vis asst prof, Univ Mich, 46-47; from asst prof to assoc prof, Rutgers Univ, 47-60; prof hist & assoc dean, Col Arts & Sci, 58-60, asst dean, 50-58; prof hist & dean, San Francisco State Col, 60-63; dean sch humanities, 63-70, actg chmn dept hist, 72-73, coordr, Educ abroad Prog, 75-, prof Hist, Univ Calif, Irvine, 64-87, Fulbright res fel, Univ Sydney, 54-55; assoc ed, J Brit Studies, 62-68; Fulbright res prof, Univ Melbourne & Monash Univ, Australia, 70; prof emer, 87-. **HONORS AND AWARDS** Grantee Am Philso Soc; Social Sci Res Coun and Rutgers Univ res Counc to Australia, 51; Fulbright res fel, Univ Sydney, Australia, 54-55; grantee Social Sci res Coun to Eng, 55; Fel, Royal Hist Soc; member Am Hist. **MEMBERSHIPS** AHA; Royal Australian Hist Soc; Conf Brit Studies (exec secy, 68-73, pres, 75-77); Am Soc Church Hist; fel Royal Hist Soc. **RESEARCH** English hist and the British Empire; British humanitarian movement of the 18th and 19th centuries; Australian political and economic hist of 19th century. **CONTACT ADDRESS** Dept of Hist, Univ of California, Irvine, Irvine, CA 92717.

MCCULLOH, JOHN MARSHALL

PERSONAL Born 09/13/1943, Abilene, KS, m, 1965 **DISCIPLINE** MEDIEVAL HISTORY **EDUCATION** Univ Kans, BA, 65; Univ Calif, Berkeley, MA, 66, PhD(hist), 71. **CAREER** Actg asst prof hist, Univ Calif, San Diego, 71-72 & Univ Calif, Los Angeles, 72-73; asst prof, 73-76, ASSOC PROF HIST, KANS STATE UNIV, 76-, Alexander von Humboldt Found fel, 77, 80; Fulbright fel, Ger, 80-81. **MEMBERSHIPS** AHA; Mediaeval Acad Am. **RESEARCH** Church history; hagiography; monasticism. **SELECTED PUBLICATIONS** Auth, The Passio Mauri Afri and Hrabanus Maurus' Martyrology, Analecta Bollandiana, 73; Cult of relics in the letters and dialogues of Gregory the Great, Traditio, 76; Rabani Mauri Martyrologium, Corpus Christianorum, Continuatio Mediaevalis, 78; Martyrologium Hieronymianum Cambrense: A new textual witness, Analecta Bollandiana, 78; Hrabanus Maurus' martyrology: The method of composition, Sacris Erudiri, 78-79; Martyrologium Excarpsatum: A New Text from the Early Middle Ages, In: Saints, Scholars and Heroes: Studies in Medieval Culture in Honour of Charles W Jones, St John's Univ, 79; From Antiquity to the Middle Ages: Continuity and Change in Papal Relic Policy from the 6th to the 8th Century, In: Pietas: Festschrift fuer Bernhard Koetting, Aschendorff, 80. **CONTACT ADDRESS** Dept of Hist, Kansas State Univ, 208 Eisenhower Hall, Manhattan, KS 66506-1000.

MCCURDY, CHARLES WILLIAM
PERSONAL Born 09/28/1948, Pasadena, CA, m, 1973, 2 children **DISCIPLINE** AMERICAN LEGAL HISTORY **EDUCATION** Univ Calif, San Diego, BA, 70, PhD, 76. **CAREER** Asst prof hist, 75-79; assoc prof hist & law, Univ Va, 79-99; prof Hist and Law, Univ of Va, 00-. **HONORS AND AWARDS** Louis Pelzer Awd, Orgn Am Historians, 73; Arthur Cole Awd, Econ Hist Asn, 79. **MEMBERSHIPS** Orgn Am Historians; Am Soc Legal Hist; Econ Hist Asn. **SELECTED PUBLICATIONS** Auth, "Justice Field and the Jurisprudence of Government-Business Relations," Journal of American History, 75; "Stephen J. Field and Public Land Law Development in California, 1850-1866," Law & Society Review, 76; "American Law and the Marketing Structure of the Large Corporation," Journal of Economic History, 78; "The Knight Sugar Decision of 1895 and the Modernization of American Corporation Law," Business History Review, 79. **CONTACT ADDRESS** Dept of History, Univ of Virginia, 1 Randall Hall, Charlottesville, VA 22903-3244. **EMAIL** cwm@virginia.edu

MCCUTCHEON, JAMES MILLER
PERSONAL Born 10/31/1932, New York, NY, m, 1959, 2 children **DISCIPLINE** AMERICAN HISTORY & STUDIES **EDUCATION** Hobart Col, BA, 54; Univ Wis-Madison, MS, 55, PhD, 59. **CAREER** Asst prof hist, Simpson Col, 61-62; from asst prof to assoc prof, 62-73, Prof Hist & Am Studies, Univ Hawaii, Manoa, 73-, spec asst pres, 79, Chair Am Studies Dept, 84-88; Fulbright fel, Univ London, 59-60; deleg, Cong Orient, Canberra, Australia, 71; Fulbright lectr, Beijing Inst Foreign Lang, 81-82; Prof Emer, 99-. **HONORS AND AWARDS** Robert W Clopton Award Distinguished Community Service, 78. **MEMBERSHIPS** AHA; Orgn Am Historians; Am Studies Asn; Urban Studies Asn. **RESEARCH** City in American history; Asian influences in American life; China and America. **SELECTED PUBLICATIONS** Auth, Missionary archives in England for East and Southeast Asia, J Asian Studies, 5/69; Tremblingly obey: British and other western responses to China, Historian, 8/71; China and America: A Bibliography of Interactions Foreign and Domestic, Univ Hawaii, 73; The Asian dimension in the American revolutionary period, In: The American Revolution: Its Meaning to Asians and Americans, 77; The Idea of Community in America, In: Educational Perspectives, 78; Sino-American Political Relations Since 1911, In: Proc of Int Am Studies Conf, 81; The Chinese People's Cultural Adjustment to the United States, Proceedings of the Conference on Sino-American Cultural and Educational Relations, Taipei, 88; The American City,Univ of the Air, Tokyo, 89; Making China Christian, Cousins, More's Utopia and the Utopian Inheritance, 95. **CONTACT ADDRESS** Dept of Am Studies, Univ of Hawaii, Manoa, 1890 E West Rd, Honolulu, HI 96822-2318. **EMAIL** jmcc@hawaii.edu

MCDANIEL, GEORGE WILLIAM
PERSONAL Born 05/04/1942, Washington, IA, s **DISCIPLINE** HISTORY **EDUCATION** St. Ambrose Univ, BA, 66; Mt. St. Bernard Sem & Aquinas Inst of Theol, 66-69; Cath Univ Am, 69-70; Aquinas Inst of Theol, MA, 74; Univ Iowa, MA, 77; PhD, 85. **CAREER** Ordained, Roman Catholic Priest, 70; assoc pastor, St. Peter's Parish & fac, Cardinal Stritch Jr-Sr High Sch, 70-73; assoc pastor, St. Patrick's Parish, Ottumwa, 73-74; Dean of Students, St. Ambrose Univ, 74-76; assoc dir dev, 76-77; Prof Hist, 77-. **HONORS AND AWARDS** Throne/Aldrich Awd Outstanding Article, Annals of Iowa, 97; Benjamin F. Chambaugh Awd, Outstanding Book in Iowa Hist, 96; Throne/Aldrich Awd, Hon Men, 95; Baecke Chair of Hum, St. Ambrose Univ, 93; Hoover Scholar, 82, 85, Herbert Hoover Libr. **MEMBERSHIPS** Org Am Historians; US Capitol Hist Asn; The Natl Trust for Hist Pres; The Hoover Pres Library Asn; St Hist Soc Iowa; Phi Alpha Theta; Soc Midland Authors. **RESEARCH** Iowa hist; populism; progressivism; Cath social action, local civil rights. **SELECTED PUBLICATIONS** Auth, Smith Wildman Brookhart: Iowa's Renegade Republican, 95; "Catholic Action in Davenport: St. Ambrose College and The League for Social Justice," The Annals of Iowa, 96. **CONTACT ADDRESS** St. Ambrose Univ, 518 W. Locust St., Davenport, IA 52803. **EMAIL** gmcdanil@saunix.sau.edu

MCDONALD, ARCHIE PHILIP
PERSONAL Born 11/29/1935, Beaumont, TX, m, 1957, 2 children **DISCIPLINE** AMERICAN HISTORY **EDUCATION** Lamar State Col, BS, 58; Rice Univ, MA, 60; La State Univ, PhD(Hist), 65. **CAREER** Asst prof, Murray State Col, 63-64; from asst prof to assoc prof, 64-72, prof Hist, Stephen F Austin State Univ, 72-, executive bd, Tex County Records Inventory Proj, 78-; Tex Comt for Humanities, 79-85; Tex Sesquicentennial Comn, 81-86; Texas Historical Comn, 91-97, vice chmn, 95-97. **HONORS AND AWARDS** Distinguished Prof Awd, Stephen F Austin Alumni Asn, 76; Regents Prof, 86. **MEMBERSHIPS** Southern Hist Assn; Texas State Hist Assn. **RESEARCH** Civil War, Texas and Southern history. **SELECTED PUBLICATIONS** Auth, Recollections of a Long Life, Blue & Gray, 73; Make Me a Map of the Valley: The Journal of Jedidiah Hotchkiss, Southern Methodist Univ, 73; The War with Mexico, Health; Travis, 77 & Eastern Texas History, 78, Pemberton; On This Day of New Beginnings, Tex State Libr, 79; The Texas Heritage, Forum, 80-; Texas, A Sesquicentennial Presentation, Dallas Times-Herald, 82; Nacogdoches with James G Partin, and Joe and Carolyn Ericson, Best of East Texas Publishers, Lufkin, TX, 95; Nacogdoches, Texas--A Pictorial History, with R G and Ouida Whitaker Dean, The Donning Company Publishers, Virginia Beach, VA, 96; Historic Texas: An Illustrated Chronicle of Texas' Past, Published for Preservation Texas, Inc, Lammert Publications, Inc, San Antonio Tx, 96. **CONTACT ADDRESS** Stephen F. Austin State Univ, 1936 North St, Box 6223, Nacogdoches, TX 75961-3940. **EMAIL** amcdonald@sfasu.edu

MCDONALD, FORREST
PERSONAL Born 01/07/1927, Orange, TX, m, 1963, 5 children **DISCIPLINE** HISTORY **EDUCATION** Univ of Tex Austin, BA, 49; MA, 49; PhD, 55. **CAREER** Assoc prof to prof, Brown Univ, 59-63; prof, Wayne State Univ, 67-76; prof to distinguished univ res prof, Univ of Ala, 76- **HONORS AND AWARDS** Fel, Soc Sci Res Coun, 51-53; Guggenheim Fel, 62-63; ACLS Grant, 75; Distinguished Grad Fac Awd, Wayne State Unive, 75; Pulitzer Prize finalist, 86; NEH 16th Jefferson Lectr, 87; James Pinckney Harrison Prof, William and Mary Col, 86-87; Ingersoll Prize, 90; Henry J. Salvatori Awd, 94; Blackmon-Moody Outstanding Prof Awd, Univ of Ala, 95. **RESEARCH** Early national United States, constitutional history, economic history, the presidency. **SELECTED PUBLICATIONS** Auth, We the People: The Economic Origins of the Constitution, 58; auth, Insull, 62; E Pluribus Unum: The Formation of the American Republic, 79; auth, The Presidency of George Washington, 74; auth, The Presidency of Thomas Jefferson, 87; auth, Alexander Hamilton, 79; auth, Novus Ordo Seclorum: The Intellectual Origins of the Constitution, 85; auth, The American Presidency: An Intellectual History, 94; auth, States' Rights and the Union 1776-1876, 00. **CONTACT ADDRESS** Dept Hist, Univ of Alabama, Tuscaloosa, PO Box 870212, Tuscaloosa, AL 35487-0154.

MCDONALD, ROBERT M. S.
PERSONAL Born 07/18/1970, Stratford, CT, s **DISCIPLINE** HISTORY **EDUCATION** Univ Virginia, BA, 92; Univ N Carolina, Chapel Hill, MA, 94, PhD, 98; Oxford Univ, MSt, 97. **CAREER** Asst prof, 98-, US Mil Acad. **RESEARCH** Colonial Anglo-Amer, revolutionary & early republican US, Thomas Jefferson. **CONTACT ADDRESS** Dept of History, United States Military Acad, West Point, NY 10996. **EMAIL** kr6691@usma.edu.

MCDONALD, WILLIAM
PERSONAL Born 09/07/1967, Daytona Beach, FL, m, 1992, 3 children **DISCIPLINE** HISTORICAL THEOLOGY **EDUCATION** Lenoir-Rhyne Col, AB, 85; Duke Univ, MTS, 91; Vanderbilt Univ, MA, 96; PhD, 98. **CAREER** Asst prof, chaplin, Tenn Wesleyan Col, 97-. **MEMBERSHIPS** AAR; AMPS; ASCH. **RESEARCH** Historical theology; liturgy; ecumenism. **SELECTED PUBLICATIONS** Ed, Gracious Voices: Shouts and Whispers for God Seekers, Discipleship Resources, 97. **CONTACT ADDRESS** Dept Religious Studies, Tennessee Wesleyan Col, Box 40, Athens, TN 37371-0040. **EMAIL** mcdonald@usit.net

MCDOUGALL, IAIN
DISCIPLINE ANCIENT GREEK HISTORY **EDUCATION** St. Andrews Univ, Scotland, MA, 64;, PhD, 81. **CAREER** Prof; dept ch. **RESEARCH** An Hist Commentary on Cssius Dio's Roman Hist Bks. 21-40; A Source-Book on Ancient Education; A Biography of C. Cassius Longinus; A Translation of Valerius Maximus; A Source-Book on and Discussion of Electoral Corruption in Rome. **SELECTED PUBLICATIONS** Auth, A Lexicon to Diodorus Siculus, Hildesheim, 83. **CONTACT ADDRESS** Dept of Classics, Univ of Winnipeg, 515 Portage Ave, Winnipeg, MB, Canada R3B 2E9. **EMAIL** iain.mcdougall@uwinnipeg.ca

MCDOWALL, DUNCAN L.
DISCIPLINE MODERN CANADIAN BUSINESS AND POLITICAL HISTORY **EDUCATION** Queen's Univ, BA, 72, MA, 73; Carleton Univ, PhD, 78. **CAREER** Prof, Carleton Univ. **RESEARCH** History of Bermuda and modern hist; modern Canadian business and political hist. **SELECTED PUBLICATIONS** Auth, Quick to the Frontier: Canada's Royal Bank, McClelland & Stewart, Toronto, 93; Trading Places: The Trade Policies of Canada's Grits and Tories, 1840-1988, The NAFTA Puzzle: Politics, Parties, and Trade in North America, Westview Press, 94; Business as Usual: Some Recent Business History, Acadiensis, 94; "From Pesthole to 'Nature's Fairyland': The Aesthetic and Practical Origins of Bermuda Tourism, 1800-1914," Bermuda Jour Archaeol and Maritime Hist, 96; auth, Another World: Bermuda and the Rise of Modern Tourism, London: Macmillan, (99): 244. **CONTACT ADDRESS** Dept of Hist, Carleton Univ, 1125 Colonel By Dr, Ottawa, ON, Canada K1S 5B6. **EMAIL** grad_history@carleton.ca

MCDOWELL, JOHN H.
PERSONAL Born 05/25/1903, Tiffin, OH, m, 1935, 3 children **DISCIPLINE** THEATRE HISTORY AND CRITICISM **EDUCATION** Boston Univ, BS, 29; Univ Wash, MA, 33; Yale Univ, PhD(theatre), 37. **CAREER** Instr theatre speech, Cornish Sch Theatre, Seattle, 30-34; asst prof, Wellesley Col, 36; asst prof hist theatre, Smith Col, 37-44; asst prof theatre speech, Manhattanville Col, 44-45; from asst prof to prof, 45-73, Emer Prof Hist Theatre, Ohio State Univ, 73-, Nat Theatre Conf fel, 50; Ohio State Univ res found grants-in-aid, 50-68; Ohio State Univ develop fund grant, 55-65; mem, Int Cong Libr Performing Arts, 61-; US mem, Comn Bibliog Iconographique Opera, 65- **HONORS AND AWARDS** Awd of Excellence, Am Col Theatre Festival, 74. **MEMBERSHIPS** Int Soc Theatre Res. **RESEARCH** The early history of the box set; Filippo Juvarra's theatre in the Palazzo della Cancelleria in Rome; Pierre Dumont's theatre in a Jesuit seminary in Rome. **SELECTED PUBLICATIONS** Auth, The Renaissance Stage: Documents of Serlio, Sabbattini, and Furttenbach, Univ Miami, 58; Original scenery and documents for productions of Uncle Tom's Cabin, Rev Hist Theatre, Paris, 63; The Ottoboni Theatre: A Research Adventure, Ohio State Univ Theatre Collection Bull, 64: The Ohio State University Theatre Collection: A Working and Teaching Collection, Acts VIIIe Congres Int Bibliot Muses Arts Spectacle, Amsterdam, 65; I'm Going There, Uncle Tom: A promptbook production, Theatre Studies, Ohio State Univ, 79. **CONTACT ADDRESS** 1977 Gulf Shore Blvd, Naples, FL 33940.

MCELVAINE, ROBERT S.
DISCIPLINE HISTORY **EDUCATION** Rutgers Univ, BA, 86; SUNY at Binghamton, MA, PhD, 74. **CAREER** Elizabeth Chisholm prof Arts and Letters & dept ch. **HONORS AND AWARDS** Millsaps' Distinguished prof, 83. **SELECTED PUBLICATIONS** Auth, Down and Out in the Great Depression: Letters from the Forgetten Man, NC, 83; The Great Depression: America, 1929-1941. Times Books 84, 93; The End of the Conservative Era: Liberalism After Reagan, Arbor House, 87; Mario Cuomo: A Biography, Scribners, 88; What's Left; A New Democratic Vision for America, Adams, 96; Sex: Women, Men, and History, 98 or 99. **CONTACT ADDRESS** Dept of History, Millsaps Col, 1701 N State St, Jackson, MS 39210. **EMAIL** mcelvrs@okra.millsaps.edu

MCFARLAND, GERALD W.
PERSONAL Born 11/07/1938, Oakland, CA, m, 1964 **DISCIPLINE** AMERICAN HISTORY **EDUCATION** Univ CA, Berkeley, AB, 60; Columbia Univ, MA, 62, PhD, 65. **CAREER** Instr Am hist, 64-65, from asst prof to assoc prof hist, 65-75, chmn dept, 75-78, prof hist Univ MA, Amherst, 75. **HONORS AND AWARDS** Am Coun Learned Soc grant-in-aid, 71-72; John Simon Guggenheim Mem found fel, 78-79, Conti Research Fellow, 92-93; Am Philos Soc Research Grant, 95. **MEMBERSHIPS** AHA; Orgn Am Historians. **RESEARCH** Late 19th century Am polit and cult. **SELECTED PUBLICATIONS** Ed, Mugwumps, Morals and Politics, 1884-1920, Univ Mass, 75; A Scattered People: An American Family Moves West, Pantheon, 85; "The Counterfeit Man": The True Story of the Boorn-Colvin Murder Case, Pantheon, 91; auth, Inside Greenwich Village: A New York City Neighborhood, 1898-1918, Univ Mass, forthcoming, 01. **CONTACT ADDRESS** Dept of Hist, Univ of Massachusetts, Amherst, Amherst, MA 01003-3930. **EMAIL** geraldm@history.umass.edu

MCFARLANE, LARRY ALLAN
PERSONAL Born 04/02/1934, Independence, MO, m, 1958 **DISCIPLINE** AMERICAN HISTORY **EDUCATION** Univ Mo, BA, 56, MA, 59, PhD, 63. **CAREER** From asst prof to assoc prof hist, Northern Ariz Univ, 62-70; assoc prof Am hist, Purdue Univ, Lafayette, 70-71; assoc prof, 71-73, Prof Am Hist, Northern Ariz Univ, 73-. **HONORS AND AWARDS** Am Philos Soc res grant, 72. **MEMBERSHIPS** AHA; Orgn Am Historians; Econ Hist Asn; Agr Hist Soc; Bus Hist Conf. **RESEARCH** American economic, business and agricultural history. **SELECTED PUBLICATIONS** Auth, The Finishing Touch, NMex Hist Rev, 94; auth, Prince Charming Goes West, Great Plains Quart, 94. **CONTACT ADDRESS** Dept of Hist, No Arizona Univ, Box 5810, Flagstaff, AZ 86011-0001.

MCFEELY, ELIZA
PERSONAL Born 05/24/1956, Port Chester, NY, m, 1990, 2 children **DISCIPLINE** HISTORY **EDUCATION** Kirkland Col, BA, 77; Brown Univ, MAT, 80, NYU, PhD, 96. **CAREER** Lectr, Princeton univ 96-99; adj fac, Col of NJ, 99-. **MEMBERSHIPS** OAH; ASA. **RESEARCH** Late 19th/20th Century American cultural history. **SELECTED PUBLICATIONS** Auth, Zuni and the American Imagination, Hilld Wang, (forthcoming). **CONTACT ADDRESS** Dept Hist, The Col of New Jersey, PO Box 7718, Trenton, NJ 08628-0718. **EMAIL** mcfeely@tcnj.edu

MCGEE, JAMES SEARS
PERSONAL Born 07/12/1942, Houston, TX, m, 1966, 2 children **DISCIPLINE** TUDOR-STUART ENGLAND **EDUCATION** Rice Univ, BA, 64; Yale Univ, MA, 66, MPhil, 68, PhD(hist), 71. **CAREER** Asst prof hist, Ga Southern Col, 69-71; asst prof, 71-78, Prof Hist, Univ Calif, Santa Barbara, 78-.

HONORS AND AWARDS UCSB Outstanding Teacher in the Social Sciences, 89. MEMBERSHIPS AHA; Conf Brit Studies; Fel, Royal Hist Soc, Eng; Am Soc Church Hist. RESEARCH Tudor-Stuart England; early modern European history. SELECTED PUBLICATIONS Auth, The Godly Man in Stuart England, 76; ed, The Miscellaneous Works of John Bunyan, 87; coauth, The West Transformed, 00. CONTACT ADDRESS Dept of Hist, Univ of California, Santa Barbara, Santa Barbara, CA 93106-9410. EMAIL jsmcgee@humanitas.ucsb.edu

MCGEHEE, R. V.
PERSONAL Born 08/01/1934, Tyler, TX, s, 2 children **DISCIPLINE** SPORT HISTORY **EDUCATION** Univ Texas, BA, 55; Yale Univ, MA, 56; Texas A&M Univ, MA, 78; Univ Texas Austin, PhD, 63. **CAREER** Span lang ed transl, Journ ICHPER-SD, 91-; sport hist res in Guatemala Mex Nicaragua Costa Rica La, 90-; Fulbright prof, Phys Educ and Geology, Univ Liberia Monrovia, 82-83; Fulbright prof, phys educ, Nat Teachers Col Honduras, 88; Vis prof of phys educ, Natl Univ of Honduras Tegucigalpa, 88; prof, SE Ls Univ, 78-; tchr, Tx A&M Univ, Univ Tx San Antonio, Nat Autonomous Univ Mex, W Mich Univ, SDak Sch Mines & Tech, Univ Ks, Univ Tx Austin, Yale Univ. **HONORS AND AWARDS** Fulbright scholar, Univ Liberia Monrovia, 82-83; scholar, Escuela Superior del Prof Francisco Morazan Tegucigalpa Honduras, 88; La Asn Health Phys Educ Rec Dance, 95-96; Sturgis Leavitt Prize, SE Coun Latin Amer Studies, 96; fel, AAHPERD Res Consortium, 97; ICHPER-SD Outstanding Contrib Serv Awd, 97. **MEMBERSHIPS** AAHPERD, 78-; hist acad chair, NASPE, 96-97; chair, S Dist Intl Rel Coun, 93-94; La AHPERD, 78-; chair, arch comt, 94-; Tx AHPERD, 78-; N Amer Soc Sport Hist, 89-; Sport Lit Asn, 89-; exec bd, Listserv, 96-; Intl Coun HPER-SD, 91-; hist phys educ and sport comn, 94-; Intl Soc Comparative Phys Educ and Sport, 91-; SE Coun on Latin Amer Studies, 93-; N Amer Soc Sociol of Sport, 95-. **SELECTED PUBLICATIONS** El papel del deporte en la cultura popular nicaraguense, 1889-1926, Revista de Historia de Nicaragua; The Impact of Imported Sports on the Popular Culture of Nineteenth and Twentieth Century Latin America, Karen Racine and Ingrid Fey eds, Strange Pilgrimages: Travel, Exile, and Foreign Residency in the Creation of Identity in Latin America, 1800-1990; Carreras, Patrias y Caudillos: Sport/Spectacle in Mexico and Guatemala, 1926-1943, S Eastern Latin Americanist, vol 41, pp 19-32, 98; The Virtual Wall: A Key to Learning the Basic Tennis Serve, Journ Phys Educ, Rec and Dance, vol 68, 7, pp 10-12, 97; Vollyball - The Latin American Connection, ICHPER-SD Journ, vol 33, n 4, pp 31-35, 97; El lugar del nino en el desarrollo inicial del deporte moderno en Centro America y Mexico, principios del siglo veinte, Memoria del XVI Congreso Panamericano de Educacion Fisica, vol 2, 97; Sergio Ramirez's Jeugo Perfecto and Tarde de Sol, Aethlon, v 13, 2, pp 121-123, 96; Pan American Games, David Levinson and Karen Christensen eds, Encycl World Sport, Santa Barbara, CA, ABC-CLIO, vol 2, pp 715-719, 96; Gymnastics, David Levinson and Karen Christensen eds, Encycl World Sport, Santa Barbara, CA, ABC-CLIO, vol 1, pp 388-397, 96; Baseball, Latin America, David Levinson and Karen Christensen eds, Encycl World Sport, Santa Barbara, CA, ABC-CLIO, v1, pp 84-91, 96 **CONTACT ADDRESS** SLU 677, Hammond, LA 70402. **EMAIL** rmcgehee@selu.edu

MCGEOCH, LYLE ARCHIBALD
PERSONAL Born 03/25/1931, Tanta, Egypt, m, 1958, 3 children **DISCIPLINE** MODERN EUROPEAN HISTORY **EDUCATION** Westminster Col, Pa, AB, 53; Univ Pa, MA, 56, PhD(hist), 64. **CAREER** Instr hist, Kent State Univ, 59-63; asst prof, Univ Dubuque, 63-66; asst prof, 66-70, Assoc Prof Hist, Ohio Univ, 70-, Grants, Am Philos Soc, 68 & 78, Baker Fund, Ohio Univ, 69-70. **MEMBERSHIPS** AHA; NAEBS; Brit Polit Group. **RESEARCH** Nineteenth century European diplomatic history; British foreign policy; British political biography. **SELECTED PUBLICATIONS** Auth, British Foreign Policy and The Spanish Corollary to the Anglo-French Agreement of 1904, in Diplomacy in an Age of Nationalism, ed. By N.N. Barker and M.L. Brown, Jr. The Hague, 71; auth, Implementing The Anglo-French Entente: The Uncertainty of Ratification, 1905-1906, Research Studies, 73; auth, Lord Lansdowne and the American Impact on British Diplomacy, 1900-1905, Theodore Roosevelt Assn Journal, 81; auth, The Old Diplomacy Revisited: Ambassador Monson in Paris, 1896-1904, European Studies Journal, 85; auth, The Limits of British Influence--South Asia and the Anglo American Relationship, 1947-56, Historian, vol 0057, 94; Channel Tunnel Visions, 1850-1945--Dreams and Nightmares, American Hist Review, vol 0101, 96; After Liberalism, Historian, vol 0059, 97. **CONTACT ADDRESS** Dept of Hist, Ohio Univ, Athens, OH 45701. **EMAIL** mcgeoch@ohio.edu

MCGERR, M.
PERSONAL Born 01/15/1955, New Rochelle, NY, m, 1978, 2 children **DISCIPLINE** HISTORY **EDUCATION** Yale, BA, 76, MA, 78, MPhil, 79, PhD, 84. **CAREER** Asst Prof, 84-89, Mass Inst of Tech; assoc prof, 89-, Indiana Univ. **HONORS AND AWARDS** NEH Fel for College Tchrs, 86. **MEMBERSHIPS** AHA; Org of Amer Historians. **RESEARCH** US since the Civil War. **SELECTED PUBLICATIONS** Auth, The Decline of Popular Politics The American North, 1865-1928, Oxford Univ Press, 86. **CONTACT ADDRESS** Dept of History, Indiana Univ, Bloomington, Ballantine 742, Bloomington, IN 47405. **EMAIL** mmcgerr@indiana.edu

MCGHEE, ROBERT J.
PERSONAL Born 02/27/1941, Wiarton, ON, Canada **DISCIPLINE** HISTORY, ARCHAEOLOGY **EDUCATION** Univ Toronto, BA, 64, MA, 66; Univ Calgary, PhD, 68. **CAREER** Arctic archaeol, Nat Mus Can, 68-72; assoc prof, Memorial Univ Nfld, 72-76; Curator Arctic Archaeology, Archaeological Survey of Canada, Canadian Museum of Civilization, 76-. **HONORS AND AWARDS** Fel, Royal Soc Can. **MEMBERSHIPS** Arctic Inst N Am; pres, Can Archaeol Asn, 87-90. **RESEARCH** Canadian prehistory; arctic prehistory. **SELECTED PUBLICATIONS** Auth, Canadian Arctic Prehistory, 78; auth, Ancient Canada, 89; auth, Canada Rediscovered, 91; auth, Ancient People of the Arctic, 96. **CONTACT ADDRESS** Canadian Mus of Civilization, Hull, QC, Canada J8X 4H2.

MCGIFFERT, MICHAEL
PERSONAL Born 10/05/1928, Chicago, IL, m, 1960 **DISCIPLINE** AMERICAN HISTORY **EDUCATION** Harvard Univ, BA, 49; Yale Univ, BD, 52, PhD(Am studies), 58. **CAREER** Instr hist, Colgate Univ, 54-55, Univ MD, 55-56 & Colgate Univ, 56-60; from asst prof to prof, Univ Denver, 60-72; Prof hist, Nat Endowment for Hum fel, 77-78; Col William & Mary fac res grant, 81,89; prof, The Institute of Early American History and Culture 72-97. **HONORS AND AWARDS** Fac Res Grants, Col of William and Mary, 81,89; Fel, Nat Endowment for the Hum, 77-78; Fac res grant, Univ of Denver, 1970. **MEMBERSHIPS** AHA; Orgn Am Historians; Am Studies Asn; AAUP. **RESEARCH** Early Am hist; Puritanism; Am intellectual hist. **SELECTED PUBLICATIONS** Auth, The Higher Learning in Colorado: An Historical Study, 1860-1940, Sage, 64; ed, The Character of Americans, Dorsey, 64, rev ed, 69; Puritanism and the American Experience, 69 & co-ed, American Social Thought: Sources and Interpretations (2 vols), 72, Addison-Wesley; ed, God's Plot: The Paradoxes of Puritan Piety: Being the Autobiography and Journal of Thomas Shepard, Univ Mass, 72; God's Plot: Puritan Spirituality in Thomas Shepard's Cambridge, Univ Mass, 94; ed, William and Mary Quarterly, 72-97. **CONTACT ADDRESS** 102 Old Glory Ct, Williamsburg, VA 23185-4914. **EMAIL** mcgiff@widomaker.com

MCGINN, BERNARD JOHN
PERSONAL Born 08/19/1937, Yonkers, NY, m, 1971, 2 children **DISCIPLINE** HISTORY OF CHRISTIANITY **EDUCATION** St Joseph's Sem, BA, 59; Pontif Gregorian Univ, STL, 63; Brandeis Univ, PhD, 70. **CAREER** Instr theol, Cath Univ Am, 68-69; instr theol & hist Christiantiy, 69-70, asst prof hist Christianity, 70-75, assoc prof, 75-78, Prof Hist Theol & Christianity, Univ Chicago, 78-, Am Asn Theol Schs res fel, 71. **MEMBERSHIPS** AHA; Medieval Acad Am; Am Cath Hist Asn; Am Acad Relig; Am Soc Church Hist. **RESEARCH** Hist of theol; intellectual and cult hist of the Middle Ages. **SELECTED PUBLICATIONS** Auth, The abbot and the doctors, Church Hist, 71; The Golden Chain, Cistercian Publ, 72; The Crusades, Gen Learning Press, 73; Apocalypticism in the Middle Ages, Mediaeval Studies, 75; ed, Three Treatises on Man, Cistercian Publ, 77; auth, Visions of the End, Columbia, 79; transl, Apocalyptic Spirituality, 79 & coauth (with E Colledge), Meister Eckhart, 81, Paulist; Foundations of Mysticism, Crossroad, 91; Growth of Mysticism, Crossroad, 94; Flowering of Mysticism, Crossroad, 98. **CONTACT ADDRESS** Divinity Sch, Univ of Chicago, 1025-35 E 58th St, Chicago, IL 60637-1577. **EMAIL** bmcginn@midway.uchicago.edu

MCGOLDRICK, JAMES EDWARD
PERSONAL Born 01/05/1936, Philadelphia, PA **DISCIPLINE** RENAISSANCE & REFORMATION HISTORY **EDUCATION** Temple Univ, BS, 61, MA, 64; WVa Univ, PhD(hist), 74. **CAREER** From instr to asst prof hist, John Brown Univ, 66-70; instr, WVa Univ, 70-73; from asst prof to assoc prof, Cedarvill Col, 73-75, prof hist, Cedarville Col, 75-. **HONORS AND AWARDS** Faculty Scholar of the Year, 94, Cedarville Col; elected a Fellow of Early Modern Studies by the Sixteenth Century Studies Conference, 98. **MEMBERSHIPS** Am Soc Church Hist; Am Soc Reformation Res; Sixteenth Century Studies Conf. **RESEARCH** Lutheran reformation; Tudor England, ecclesiastical biography. **SELECTED PUBLICATIONS** Auth, Edmund Burke; Christian activist, Mod Age, summer 73; Mussolini and the Vatican, Univ Dayton Rev, summer 76; 1776: a Christian Loyalist view, Fides et Historia, 11/77; Luther's English Connection, Northwestern Publ House, 79; Was William Tyndale a Synergist?, Westminster Theological Journal, 44 (58-70), 82; Baptists and the Reformation, Reformation Today, 68 (14-20), 82; Three Principles of Protestantism, Banner of Truth, 232 (1-12), 83; Luther on Life Without Dichotomy, Grace Theol J, 5 (3-11), 84; Patrick Hamilton, Luther's Scottish Disciple, Sixteenth Century J, 18 (81-88), 87; E.B. Pursey, Great Lives From History, British and Commonwealth Series, Pasadena, Ca: Salem Press, 88; St. Benedict of Nursia, Great Lives From History, Ancient and Medieval Series, Pasadena, Ca: Salem Press, 88; The Trail of Blood, Reformation Today, 75 (2-9), 88; Luther's Scottish Connection, Madison, NJ: Fairleigh Dickinson Univ Press, 89; Frederick the great, Great Lives From History, Renaissance to 1900 Series, Pasadena, Ca: Salem Press, 89; King Henry IV of France, Great Lives From History, Renaissance to 1900 Series, Pasadena, Ca: Salem Press, 89; Robert Barnes, Historical Dictionary of Tudor England, Westport, Ct: Greenwood Press, 91; Lollardy, Hist Dict of Tudor England, Westport, Ct: Greenwood Press, 91; Lutheranism in England, Hist Dict of Tudor England, Westport, Ct: Greenwood Press, 91; Lenin and the Communists Impose the 'Red Terror, Great Events from History, Human Rights Series II (218-24), Pasadena, Ca: Salem Press, 92; Stepping Beyond the Law, The Standard, 83 (10-11), May 93; Czar Nicholas Executed and Red Terror Begins, Great Events From Hist, Human Rights Series, Pasadena, Ca: Salem Press, 93; Lutheranism in Scotland, Dict of Scottish Church Hist and Theology, London: Hodder and Stoughton, 93; Baptist Successionism: A Crucial Question in Baptist History, Metuchen, NJ: Scarecrow Press, 94; Ellen Gould Harmon White, Great Lives From Hist, American Women Series, Pasadena, Ca: Salem Press, 94; Every Inch for Christ: Abraham Kuyper on the Reform of the Church, Reformation and Revival 3, 94; Robert Barnes, Encyclopedia of the Reformation, New York: Oxford Univ Press, 96; Henry Balnaves, Encyclopedia of the Reformation, New York: Oxford Univ Press, 96; Auth, God's Renaissance Man: The Life and Work of Abraham Kuyper, Darlington, Oklahoma, Evangelical Press, 00; many publications forthcoming;. **CONTACT ADDRESS** Cedarville Col, PO Box 601, Cedarville, OH 45314-0601. **EMAIL** McGold@Cedarville.edu

MCGOVERN, PATRICK E.
PERSONAL Born 12/09/1944 **DISCIPLINE** NEAR EASTERN ARCHAEOLOGY AND LITERATURE. **EDUCATION** Univ Penn, PhD, 80. **CAREER** Sr res sci & res assoc Near Eeast Sect, Adj assoc prof anthrop, Univ Penn, 79-. **HONORS AND AWARDS** Fullbright fel, Sweden, 93-94. **MEMBERSHIPS** Am Schools Oriental Res; Archaeol Inst Am. **RESEARCH** Archaeological chemistry. **SELECTED PUBLICATIONS** Coauth, The Late Bronze Egyptian Garrison at Beth Shan: A Study of Levels VII and VIII, Univ Penn Mus, 93; The Origins and Ancient History of Wine, Gordon & Breach, 95; auth Science in Archaeology: A Review, Am Jour Archaeol, 95; Technological Innovation and Artistic Achievement in the Late Bronze and Iron Ages of Central Transjordan, Studies in the History and Archaeology of Jordan V, 95; Neolithic Resinated Wine, Nature, 96; Vin Extraordinaire, The Sciences, 96; The Beginnings of Winemaking and Viniculture in the Ancient Near East and Egypt, Expedition, 97; Wine of Egypts Golden Age: An Archaeochemical Perspective, Jour of Egyptian Archaeol, 97; Wine for Eternity, Archaeol, 98. **CONTACT ADDRESS** Univ of Pennsylvania, 33rd and Spruce Sts, Philadelphia, PA 19104. **EMAIL** mcgovern@sas.upenn.edu

MCGRATH, ROBERT
DISCIPLINE ART HISTORY **EDUCATION** Middlebury Col, AB; Princeton Univ, MFA, PhD. **CAREER** Prof, Dartmouth Col. **RESEARCH** Art of the Adirondacks and White Mountains; Western Am art. **SELECTED PUBLICATIONS** Auth, Facing North and East: The Ideology of the Gaze in Scenes of Placid Lake (exh cat), 93; Sacred Spaces: The Adirondack Vision of Nathan Farb, (exh cat), 93; 'Everlasting and Unfallen': New Hampshire and the State of Redemption, (exh cat), 92; A Wild Sort of Beauty: Public Places and Private Visions (exh cat), 92; The Space of Morality: Death and Transfiguration in the Adirondacs, (exh cat), 91; auth, Gods in Granite: the art of the White Mountains of New Hampshire, Syracuse Univ Press, 98. **CONTACT ADDRESS** Art Hist Dept, Dartmouth Col, 6033 Carpenter Hall, Hanover, NH 03755. **EMAIL** robert.l.mcgrath@dartmouth.edu

MCGRATH, SYLVIA WALLACE
PERSONAL Born 02/27/1937, Montpelier, VT, m, 1966, 2 children **DISCIPLINE** AMERICAN HISTORY, HISTORY OF SCIENCE; HISTORY OF WOMEN **EDUCATION** Mich State Univ, BA, 59; Radcliffe Col, MA, 60; Univ Wis-Madison, PhD(Am hist & hist of sci), 66. **CAREER** Teacher pub schs, 60-62; res, proj & teaching asst hist, Univ Wis, 62-66, proj assoc, 66-67; asst prof, 68-73, Assoc Prof Hist, Stephen F Austin State Univ, 73-87; prof 87-, regents prof, 94-, Dept chair, 00-. **HONORS AND AWARDS** Regents prof, Stephen F. Austin State Univ. **MEMBERSHIPS** Orgn Am Historians; Southern Hist Asn; Hist Sci Soc; Forum for the Hist of Sci in Am; Am Soc for Environ Hist; Forest Hist Soc; Soc for the Hist of Technol; E Tex Hist Asn; Council for Women in Hist. **RESEARCH** History of American science; history of women. **SELECTED PUBLICATIONS** Auth, Charles Kenneth Leith, Scientific Advisor, Univ of Wis Press, 71; auth, Scientific Foundations, Societies, and Museums, in 100 Years of Science and Technology in Texas, Rice Univ Press, 86; auth, "Usually Close Companion: Frieda Cobb Blanchard and Frank Nelson Blanchard," in Creative Couples in the Sciences, ed. Helena M. Pycior et al (Rutgers Univ Press, 96). **CONTACT ADDRESS** Dept of Hist, Stephen F. Austin State Univ, Box 13013, Nacogdoches, TX 75962. **EMAIL** smcgrath@sfasu.edu

MCGREW, RODERICK ERLE
PERSONAL Born 09/06/1928, Mankato, MN, m, 1948, 2 children **DISCIPLINE** MODERN RUSSIAN HISTORY **EDUCATION** Ripon Col, BA, 50; Univ Minn, MA, 51, PhD(hist),

55. **CAREER** Asst, Univ Minn, 51-54; instr hist, Mass Inst Technol, 54-55; instr, Univ Mo, Columbia, 55, from asst prof to prof, 55-67, chmn dept, 62-65; Prof Hist, Temple Univ, 67-, Am Coun Learned Soc sr res fel, 61-62; vis prof hist, Univ Rochester, 69-70; Am Philos Soc grant-in-aid, 71-72; Am ed, Jahrbucher fur Geschichte Osteuropas, 76- **MEMBERSHIPS** AHA; Am Asn Advan Slavic Studies; Midwest Conf Asian Affairs(vpres, 59); AAUP; Study Group 18th Century Russia, Britain. **RESEARCH** Russian social and intellectual history, 18th and 19th centuries; history of development and modernization; medical history. **SELECTED PUBLICATIONS** Auth, Catherine the Great, the Autocrat of All the Russians, Jahrbucher fur Geschichte Osteuropas, vol 0040, 92; Rhubarb--The Wondrous Drug, Amer Hist Rev, vol 0098, 93; Catherine-II Charters of 1785 to the Nobility and the Towns, Jahrbucher fur Geschichte Osteuropas, vol 0041, 93; A Man of Honor--Czartoryski, Adam as a Statesman of Russia and Poland 1795-1831, Amer Hist Rev, vol 0099, 94; Imperial Russian Foreign Policy, Slavonic and East Europ Rev, vol 0073, 95; Alexander-I, Amer Hist Rev, vol 0101, 96; The Year 1812 as Remembered by Contemporaries, Jahrbucher fur Geschichte Osteuropas, vol 0045, 97. **CONTACT ADDRESS** Dept of Hist, Temple Univ, Philadelphia, PA 19122.

MCGUCKIN, JOHN A.
PERSONAL Born 06/21/1952, England, m, 1990, 3 children **DISCIPLINE** CHURCH HISTORY **EDUCATION** London Univ, BD, 75; Univ Durham, PhD, 80; MA, 86. **CAREER** Lect, LSU Col, 87-89; Lect, Univ Leeds, 89-94; Reader, Univ Leeds, 94-96; Prof, Union Theolog Sem, 96-. **HONORS AND AWARDS** Fel, London Royal Hist Soc. **MEMBERSHIPS** Soc for the Prom of Byzantine Studies, Church Hist Soc. **RESEARCH** Christian thought in Lake Antiquity. **SELECTED PUBLICATIONS** auth, "The Non-Cyprianic Scripture Texts in Lactantius' Divine Institutes," Vigiliae Christianae 36 (82): 145-163; auth, Symeon the New Theologian, Chapters and Discourses, Cistercian Publ (Kalamazoo), 82; auth, "The Theopaschite Confession: A Study in the Cyrilline Reinterpretation of Chalcedon," J of Ecclesiastical Hist 35,2 (84): 239-255; auth, St Gregory Nazianzen: Selected Poems, SLG Pr (Oxford, UK), 86; auth, The Transfiguration of Christ in Scripture and Tradition, Mellen Pr (Lewiston, NY), 87; auth, St Cyril of Alexandria and the Chistological Controversy, Brill (Leiden), 94; auth, St Cyril of Alexandria: On The Unity of Christ, SVS Pr (New York, NY), 95; auth, At the Lighting of the Lamps: Hymns From the Ancient Church, SLG Pr (Oxford, UK), 95. **CONTACT ADDRESS** Dept Church Hist, Union Theol Sem, New York, 3041 Broadway, New York, NY 10027-5710. **EMAIL** jmcguckn@uts.columbia.edu

MCHAM, SARAH BLAKE
DISCIPLINE ITALIAN RENAISSANCE ART **EDUCATION** New York Univ, PhD. **CAREER** Prof, chmn, dept Art Hist, Rutgers, The State Univ NJ, Univ Col-Camden. **HONORS AND AWARDS** Am Coun of Learned Soc Fe, 84; Am Philosophical Soc Grant-in-Aid, 86; St Anthony at the Santo and the Development of Venetian Reanissance Sculpture, 93; Res Fel, Int for Advanced Study, Princeton, 00; Gladys K. Delmas Found Fel, 00; Am Philosophical soc Fel, 00-01. **MEMBERSHIPS** Col Art Assoc; Renaissance Soc of Am; Italian Art Soc. **RESEARCH** Social and political context of painting and sculpture of the Venetian Empire and of Florence, especially patronage and religious practices, influence of Pliny's Natural Hist on Italian Renaissance Art. **SELECTED PUBLICATIONS** Auth, Donatello's Tomb of Pope John XXII, in Life and Death in Fifteenth-Century Florence, eds Rona Goffen, Marcel Tetel, and Ronald Witt, Duke UP, 89; Donatello's High Altar in the Santo, Padua, in Verrocchio and Late Quattrocento Sculpture, ed Steven Bule, et al, Casa Editrice Le Lettere, 92; The Cult of St. Anthony of Padua, in Sancta, Sanctus, Studies in Hagiography, Ctr for Medieval and Early Renaissance Stud, 94; The Chapel of St. Anthony at the Santo and the Development of Venetian Renaissance Sculpture, Cambridge UP, 94; Florentine Public Sculpture, in Looking at Italian Renaissance Sculpture, Cambridge UP, 98; ed, Looking at Italian Renaissance Sculpture, Cambridge UP, 98; ed, "Introduction to the Issues, Critical Methods, and Historiography Concerning Italian Renaissance Sculpture," Looking at Italian Renaissance Sculpture, Cambridge Univ Press, (98), 1-17; auth, The Exterior Sculptural Decoration of S. Maria Dei Miracoli," the Church of S. Mria dei Miracoli in Venice Post-Restoration; auth, The Role of Pliny's Naturla History in the Sixteenth-Century Redecoration of the Piazza of San Marco, Venice, Divese Approaches to the Representation of Classical Mythology in Art; auth, Istituto Veneto di Scienze, Lettere, forthcoming, 2001. **CONTACT ADDRESS** Dept of Art Hist, Rutgers, The State Univ of New Jersey, New Brunswick, Voorhees Hall, 71 Hamilton St, New Brunswick, NJ 08903. **EMAIL** mcham@rci.rutgers.edu

MCINERNEY, DANIEL J.
DISCIPLINE HISTORY **EDUCATION** Manhattan Col, BA, 72; Purdue Univ, MA, 75, PhD, 84. **CAREER** Vis instr, Purdue Univ, 84-86; asst prof, Utah State Univ, 86-93; ASSOC PROF, UTAH STATE UNIV, 93-. **CONTACT ADDRESS** History Dept, Utah State Univ, 0710 Old Main Hill, Logan, UT 84322-0710. **EMAIL** danielj@hass.usu.edu

MCINTIRE, CARL THOMAS
PERSONAL Born 10/04/1939, Philadelphia, PA, 2 children **DISCIPLINE** MODERN HISTORY, PHILOSOPHY OF HISTORY **EDUCATION** Univ Pa, MA, 62, PhD(hist), 76; Faith Theol Sem, MDiv, 66. **CAREER** Instr hist, Shelton Col, 65-67; asst prof hist, Trinity Christian Col, 67-71; vis scholar, Cambridge Univ, 71-73; Sr Mem Hist, Inst Christian Studies, Toronto, 73-, Am Philos Soc res grant, 81; Soc Sci & Humanities Res Coun Can res grant, 81-82; lectr, Trinity Col, Univ Toronto, 82- **MEMBERSHIPS** AHA; Conf Faith & Hist; Am Cath Hist Asn; Am Soc Church Hist. **RESEARCH** Secularization of modern thought and society; comparative views of history: Christian, Hindu, Jewish, Marxist, Liberal and African Tribal; English politics in relation to the papacy, especially 19th century. **SELECTED PUBLICATIONS** Auth, England against the Paapacy, 1858-1861, 83; auth, History and Historical Understanding, 84; auth, The Legacy of Herman Dooyeweerd, 85; auth, Toynbee: Reappraisal, 89; auth, Butterfield as Historian, forthcoming; auth, "Changing Religious Establishments and Religious Liberty in France, Part I: 1787-1879", 97; auth, "Changing Religious Establishments and Religious Liberty in France, Part II: 1879-1908"; coauth, The Parish and Cathedral of St. James, Toronto, 1797-1997, 98; auth, Women in the Life of St. James' Cathedral , Toronto, 1935-1998, 98; auth, "Secularization, Secular Religions, and Religious Pluralism in European and North American Societies," 99. **CONTACT ADDRESS** Dept of History, Univ of Toronto, 100 St George St, Room 2074, Toronto, ON, Canada M5S 3G3.

MCINTOSH, MARJORIE KENISTON
PERSONAL Born 11/15/1940, Ann Arbor, MI, m, 1961, 3 children **DISCIPLINE** ENGLISH HISTORY **EDUCATION** Radcliffe Col, AB, 62; Harvard Univ, MA, 63, PhD, 67. **CAREER** Res assoc, Radcliffe Inst, 67-68; lectr Europ hist, Simmons Col, 68-70; lectr, Univ Colo, Denver, 71-72; vis lectr English hist, 77-79; asst to assoc prof, English hist, 79-92, prof, 92-00; distinguished prof, 00-; exec dir, Ctr for British Stud, 88-90, Univ Colorado, Boulder. **HONORS AND AWARDS** Magna cum laude, 62; Phi Beta Kappa; President's Awd for Outstanding Service, 90; Essex Book Awd, 91; Excellence in Tchg Awd, 95; elected fel, British Royal Hist Soc, 96. **MEMBERSHIPS** AHA; Conf Brit Studies; Medieval Acad Am; Soc Sci Hist Asn; Am Soc Legal Hist. **RESEARCH** Local and social history of late medieval and early modern England; poverty in England, 1480-1660. **SELECTED PUBLICATIONS** Auth, Autonomy and Community: The Royal Manor of Havering, 1200-1500, Cambridge, 86; auth, A Community Transformed: The Manor and Liberty of Havering, 1500-1620, Cambridge, 91; auth, Controlling Misbehavior in England, 1370-1600, Cambridge, 98. **CONTACT ADDRESS** Dept of History, Univ of Colorado, Boulder, Box 234, Boulder, CO 80309-0234.

MCINTOSH, MARJORIE KENISTON
DISCIPLINE HISTORY **EDUCATION** Radcliffe Col, BA, 62; Harvard Univ, MA, 63; PhD, 66. **CAREER** Asst prof, 79-86; assoc prof, 86-92; prof, 92-00; dist prof, Univ Colo, 00-. **RESEARCH** Soc and econ hist of England, 1300-1600; compartive study ofr women in England and Africa. **SELECTED PUBLICATIONS** Auth, A Community Transformed: The Manor and Liberty of Havering, l500-l620, Cambridge, 91; Autonomy and Community: The Royal Manor of Havering, l200-1500, Cambridge, 86; auth, Controlling Misbehavior in England, 1370-1600, Cambridge, 98. **CONTACT ADDRESS** History Dept, Univ of Colorado, Boulder, Boulder, CO 80309-0234. **EMAIL** McIntosh@spot.colorado.edu

MCINTYRE, JERILYN S.
DISCIPLINE COMMUNICATION HISTORY **EDUCATION** Univ Wash, PhD, 73; Stanford Univ, AB, 64; MA, 65; Univ of Wash, PhD, 73. **CAREER** Prof. **MEMBERSHIPS** Asn Edu in Jour and Mass Commun; Am Hist Asn; Org Am Hist. **RESEARCH** Communication History, Higher Education Administration. **SELECTED PUBLICATIONS** Auth, Transportation Developments in a Mid-Nineteenth Century Frontier Community, Jour W, 95; Rituals of Disorder: A Dramatistic Interpretation of Radical Dissent, 89; The Avvisi of Venice: Toward an Archaeology of Media Forms, Jour Hist, 87; Repositioning a Landmark: The Hutchins Commission and Freedom of the Press, 87. **CONTACT ADDRESS** Off of Pres, Central Washington Univ, 400 E 8th Ave, Ellenberg, WA 98926. **EMAIL** mcintyrej@cwu.edu

MCJIMSEY, GEORGE TILDEN
PERSONAL Born 03/09/1936, Dallas, TX, m, 1970, 1 child **DISCIPLINE** UNITED STATES HISTORY **EDUCATION** Grinnell Col, BA, 58; Columbia Univ, MA, 59; Univ Wis, PhD, 68. **CAREER** Instr hist, Portland State Col, 64-65; from instr to prof hist, Iowa State Univ, 65-; chemn dept, Iowa State Univ, 92-. **HONORS AND AWARDS** Doctor of Humane Letters, Grinnell Col, 98. **RESEARCH** Political history of the United States, 1850-1900. **SELECTED PUBLICATIONS** Auth, Genteel Partisan: Manton Marble, 1834-1917, IA State Univ, 71; Dividing and Reuniting of America, 1848-1877; Harry Hopkins, Ally of the Poor and Defender of Democracy; The Presidency of Franklin Delano Roosevelt. **CONTACT ADDRESS** Dept of Hist, Iowa State Univ of Science and Tech, Ames, IA 50011-0002. **EMAIL** gmcjimse@iastate.edu

MCJIMSEY, ROBERT
PERSONAL Born 03/09/1936, Dallas, TX, m, 1961, 3 children **DISCIPLINE** MODERN HISTORY **EDUCATION** Grinnell Col, AB, 58; Univ Wis, AM, 61, PhD, 68. **CAREER** Instr hist, Oberlin Col, 65-66; instr, Ohio Wesleyan Univ, 66-68; asst prof, 68-75, assoc prof hist, CO Col, 75-83, prof 83. **MEMBERSHIPS** NACBS **RESEARCH** Seventeenth century Engl; Eng opinion and for policy during the reign of William III. **CONTACT ADDRESS** Dept of Hist, Colorado Col, 14 E Cache La Poudre, Colorado Springs, CO 80903-3294.

MCKALE, DONALD MARSHALL
PERSONAL Born 10/24/1943, Clay Center, KS, m, 1966, 3 children **DISCIPLINE** MODERN EUROPEAN HISTORY **EDUCATION** Iowa State Univ, BS, 66; Univ MoColumbia, MA, 67; Kent State Univ, PhD(hist), 70. **CAREER** Asst prof mod Europ hist, Ga Col, 70-74, assoc prof, 74-78, prof, 78-79; Prof Mod Europ Hist, Clemson Univ, 79-, Study visit to West Ger, Ger Acad Exchange Serv, 75; vis assoc prof mod Europ hist, Univ Nebr-Lincoln, 75-76. **MEMBERSHIPS** AHA; Conf Group Cent Europ Hist. **RESEARCH** Nazi Germany. **SELECTED PUBLICATIONS** Auth, A Case of Nazi Justice: The Punishment of Party Members Involved in the Kristallnacht, 1938, Jewish Social Studies, 7-10/73; The Nazi Seaman: Propagandist of the New Germany, New Ver Voor Zeegeschiedenis, 10/73; The Nazi Party Courts, Univ Kans, 74; Hitlerism for Export! The Nazi Attempt to Control Schools and Youth Clubs Outside Germany, J Europ Studies, 75; The Nazi Party in the Far East, 1931-1945, J Contemp Hist, 77; The Swastika Outside Germany, Kent State Univ, 77; Hitler's Children: A Study in Postwar Mythology, J Popular Cult, 81; Hitler: The Survival Myth, Stein & Day, 81. **CONTACT ADDRESS** Dept of Hist, Clemson Univ, Clemson, SC 29631.

MCKATE, DONALD M.
PERSONAL Born 10/24/1943, Clay Center, KS, m, 1966, 3 children **DISCIPLINE** HISTORY **EDUCATION** Iowa State Univ, BS, 66; Univ Mo, MA, 67; Kent State Univ, PhD, 70. **CAREER** Asst Prof, Ga Col, 70-74; Visiting Assoc Prof, Univ Neb, 75-76; Assoc Prof to Prof, Ga Col, 74-79; Prof to Memorial Prof, Clemson Univ, 79-. **MEMBERSHIPS** German Studies Asn, S Hist Asn. **RESEARCH** Nazi Germany; Holocaust; World War II. **SELECTED PUBLICATIONS** Auth, War by Revolution: Germany and Great Britain in the Middle East in the Era of World War I, Kent State Univ Press, 98; ed, Rewriting History: The Original and Revised World War II Diaries of Curt Prufer, Nazi Diplomat, Kent State Univ Press, 88; auth, Curt Prufer: German Diplomat from the Kaiser to Hitler, Kent State Univ Press, 87; auth, Hitler: The Survival Myth, Stein & Day, 81; auth, The Swastika Outside Germany, Kent State Univ Press, 77; auth, The Nazi Party Courts: Hitler's Management of Conflict in His Movement, 1921-1945, Univ Press of Kans, 74. **CONTACT ADDRESS** Dept Hist, Clemson Univ, 1 Clemson Univ, Clemson, SC 29634-0527. **EMAIL** mckaled@clemson.edu

MCKAY, JOHN PATRICK
PERSONAL Born 08/28/1938, St. Louis, MO, m, 1961, 2 children **DISCIPLINE** EUROPEAN ECONOMIC, SOCIAL HISTORY **EDUCATION** Wesleyan Univ, BA, 61; Fletcher Sch Law, MA, 62; Univ Calif, Berkeley, PhD, 68. **CAREER** From instr to assoc prof, 66-76, prof hist, 76-, Univ Ill; Guggenheim Found fel, 70-71; Fulbright-Hays fel, Soviet Union, 74. **HONORS AND AWARDS** Herbert Baxter Adams Award, AHA, 70. **MEMBERSHIPS** AHA; Econ Hist Asn; Bus Hist Conf; Am Asn Advan Slavic Studies; Fr Hist Asn. **RESEARCH** Russian economic hist; West European economic and social hist; hist of urban transportation, world hist. **SELECTED PUBLICATIONS** Auth, John Cockerill in Southern Russia, 1885-1905: A Study of Aggressive Foreign Entrepreneurship, Bus Hist Rev, 67; auth, Pioneers for Profit: Foreign Entrepreneurship and Russian Industrialization, 1885-1913, Univ Chicago, 70; ed & transl, Jules Michelet's The People, Univ Ill, 73; auth, Foreign Enterprise in Russian and Soviet Industry: A Long Term Perspective, Bus Hist Rev, 74; contrib, The Rich, The Well Born and The Powerful: Elites and Upper Classes in History, Univ Ill, 74; auth, Tramways and Trolleys: The Rise of Urban Mass Transport in Europe, Princeton Univ, 76; auth, A History of Western Society, Vol II, Houghton Mifflin, 99; auth, A History of World Societies, 96. **CONTACT ADDRESS** Dept of History, Univ of Illinois, Urbana-Champaign, 810 S Wright St, Urbana, IL 61801-3611. **EMAIL** j-mckay2@uiuc.edu

MCKEE, SALLY
PERSONAL Born 09/21/1955, New York, NY **DISCIPLINE** MEDIEVAL STUDIES **EDUCATION** San Francisco State Univ, BA, 83; Univ Toronto, MA, 86, PhD, 93. **CAREER** Asst prof, Univ Wisc, Oshkosk, 93-95; asst prof, Ariz State Univ, 95-2000; assoc prof, Univ Calif, Davis, 2000. **HONORS AND AWARDS** Dumbarton Oaks Fel; Gladys Krieble Delmas Fels. **MEMBERSHIPS** Medieval Acad of Am, Renaissance Soc of Am. **RESEARCH** Ethnicity, Venice, Venetian Crete, medieval colonization. **SELECTED PUBLICATIONS** Auth, "Greek Women in Latin Households of Fourteenth-Century Venetian Crete," J of Medieval Hist, 19 (93): 229-249; auth, "Households in Fourteenth-Century Venetian Crete," Speculum: A J of the

Medieval Acad of Am, 70 (Jan 95): 27-67; auth, "The Revolt of St Tito in Fourteenth-Century Venetian Crete: A Reassessment," Mediterranean Hist Rev, 9/2 (95): 173-204; ed, Wills from Late Medieval Venetian Crete (1312-1420), 3 vols, Washington, DC: Dumbarton Oaks (97); auth, "Women Under Venetian Colonial Rule: Some Observations on Their Economic Activities," Renaissance Quart, 51/1 (98): 34-67; ed, Crossing Boundaries: Issues of Cultural and Individual Identity in the Middle Ages and the Renaissance, Leiden: Brepols (99); auth, Uncommon Dominion: Venetian Crete and the Myth of Ethnic Purity, Univ of Pa Press (2000). **CONTACT ADDRESS** Dept Hist, Univ of California, Davis, One Shields Ave, Davis, CA 94616.

MCKEEN, WILLIAM
PERSONAL Born 09/16/1954, Indianapolis, IN, d, 3 children **DISCIPLINE** HISTORY; MASS COMMUNICATION; EDUCATION **EDUCATION** Indiana Univ, BA, 74, MA, 77; Univ OK, PhD, 86. **CAREER** Educator, 77-; Prof and ch, jour dept, Univ Florida. **HONORS AND AWARDS** Various teaching Awds **MEMBERSHIPS** Pop culture asn; SO book critics cir; AJHA; asn for edu in journ and mass comm. **RESEARCH** Pop cult; journ hist; music. **SELECTED PUBLICATIONS** Rock and Roll is Here to Stay, 00; Literary Journalism, 00; Tom Wolfe, 95; Bob Dylan: A Bio-Bibliography, 93; Hunter S Thompson, 91; The Beatles: A Bio-Bibliography, 90. **CONTACT ADDRESS** Univ of Florida, 2089 Weimer Hall, Gainesville, FL 32611. **EMAIL** wmckeen@jou.ufl.edu

MCKENNA, JOHN WILLIAM
PERSONAL Born 07/23/1938, West Warwick, RI, m, 1961, 2 children **DISCIPLINE** MEDIEVAL AND ENGLISH CONSTITUTIONAL HISTORY **EDUCATION** Amherst Col, AB, 60; Columbia Univ, MA, 62; Cambridge Univ, PhD(medieval hist), 65. **CAREER** Instr hist, Brooklyn Col, 65-66; asst prof, Univ Calif, Riverside, 66-69; Walter D & Edith M L Scull Assoc Prof English Constitutional Hist, Haverford Col, 69-. **MEMBERSHIPS** Mediaeval Acad Am; AHA; Conf Brit Studies; fel Royal Hist Soc. **RESEARCH** Royal political propaganda in Northern Europe; late medieval and early modern government and politics; medieval kingship and sovereignty. **SELECTED PUBLICATIONS** Auth, Holocaust Memorial Museum, Smithsonian, vol 0024, 93. **CONTACT ADDRESS** Dept of Hist, Haverford Col, Haverford, PA 19041.

MCKENNA, MARIAN CECILIA
PERSONAL Born 07/03/1926, Scarsdale, NY **DISCIPLINE** AMERICAN HISTORY **EDUCATION** Columbia Univ, BS, 49, MA, 50, PhD, 53. **CAREER** Instr hist, Hunter Col, 53-59; asst prof, Manhattanville Col, 59-66; assoc prof, 66-68, Prof Hist, Univ Calgary, 68-, Danforth fel, 64-65; Can Coun awards, 67, 68, 69, res fel, 72-73. **HONORS AND AWARDS** Penrose Awd, Am Philos Soc, 56. **MEMBERSHIPS** Orgn Am Historians; Immigration Hist Soc; Can Asn Am Studies; Can Hist Asn; Can Ethnic Studies Asn. **RESEARCH** Canadian-American immigration; American Civil War and Reconstruction; American political history post 1850. **SELECTED PUBLICATIONS** Ed, The Canadian and American Constitutions in Comparative Perspective, Univ Calgary Press, 93. **CONTACT ADDRESS** Dept of Hist, Univ of Calgary, 2500 Univ Dr NW, Calgary, AB, Canada T2N 1N4. **EMAIL** mmckenna@ucalgary.ca

MCKEVITT, GERALD
PERSONAL Born 07/03/1939, Longview, WA, s **DISCIPLINE** AMERICAN HISTORY, THEOLOGY **EDUCATION** Univ San Fancisco, AB, 61; Univ Southern CA, MA, 64; Univ CA, Los Angeles, PhD(hist), 72; Pontif Gregorian Univ, Rome, STB, 75. **CAREER** Res asst prof hist, 75-77, asst prof, 77-92, prof hist, Univ Santa Clara, 93-, dir Univ Arch, 75-85; Historian, 85-. **HONORS AND AWARDS** Oscar O Wither Awd, 91. **MEMBERSHIPS** Calif Hist Society; Cath Hist Society; Western Hist Society. **RESEARCH** California history; Jesuit education in California; Italian Jesuit history. **SELECTED PUBLICATIONS** Auth, Gold Lake myth, J West, 10/64; The Jesuit Arrival in California and the Founding of Santa Clara College, Records Am Cath Hist Soc, 9-12/74; From Franciscan Mission to Jesuit College: a Troubled Transition at Mission Santa Clara, Southern CA Quart, summer 76; Progress Amid Poverty, Santa Clara College in the 1870s, Pac Hist, winter 76; The Beginning of Santa Clara University, San Jose Studies, 2/77; The University of Santa Clara, A History, 1851-1977, Stanford Univ, 79; Jump That Saved Rocky Mountain Mission, Pacific Hist Rev, 86; Jesuit Missionary Linguistics, Western Hist Quart, 90; Hispanic Californians and Catholic Higher education, CA Hist, 90-91; Jesuit Higher Education in US, Mis-America, 91; Italian Jesuits in New Mexico, NM Hist Rev, 92; Christopher Columbus as Civic Saint, CA Hist, winter 92-93; Art of Conversion: Jesuits and Flatheads, US Cath Hist, 94. **CONTACT ADDRESS** Dept Hist, Santa Clara Univ, 500 El Camino Real, Santa Clara, CA 95053-0001. **EMAIL** gmckevit@scu.edu

MCKILLOP, A. B.
DISCIPLINE HISTORY **EDUCATION** Univ Manitoba, BA, 68, MA, 70; Queen's Univ, PhD, 77. **CAREER** Prof, Carleton Univ. **RESEARCH** Historiography of Canada; Cultural and intellectual hist in post-1920 English speaking Canada. **SELECTED PUBLICATIONS** Auth, Contours of Canadian Thought, Univ Toronto Press, 87; Marching as to war: Elements of Ontario Undergraduate Culture, 1880-1914, Univ, Youth and Soc, McGill-Queen's UP, 89; "Culture, Intellect and Context," Jour Can Stud 24, 89; Matters of Mind: the University in Ontario 1791-1951, Univ Toronto Press, 94; co-ed, God's Peculiar Peoples, Essay on Polit Cult in Nineteenth-Century Can, Carleton UP, 93; auth, "Who Killed Canadian History? A View form the Tenches," Canadian Historical Review 80, (99): 269-299. **CONTACT ADDRESS** Dept of Hist, Carleton Univ, 1125 Colonel By Dr, Ottawa, ON, Canada K1S 5B6. **EMAIL** brian_mckillop@carleton.ca

MCKINION, STEVEN A.
PERSONAL Born 09/23/1970, Mobile, AL, m, 1995, 2 children **DISCIPLINE** CHURCH HISTORY, THEOLOGY **EDUCATION** Miss Col, BA, 92; Univ Mobile, MA, 97; Univ Aberdeen, PhD, 98. **CAREER** Asst prof, Southeastern Baptist Theol Sem, 98-. **MEMBERSHIPS** Evangel Theol Soc; Am Acad of Relig; N Am Patristics Soc. **RESEARCH** Patristics, Antiquity, Theology. **SELECTED PUBLICATIONS** Auth, Words, Pictures and Christology in Cyril of Alexandria, E.J. Brill, (forthcoming); auth, Life and Practice in the Early Church, NY Univ Pr, (forthcoming); auth, Ancient Christian Commentary on Scripture: Isaiah 1-39, Inter Varsity Pr, (forthcoming). **CONTACT ADDRESS** Dept Church Hist, Southeastern Baptist Theol Sem, PO Box 1899, Wake Forest, NC 27588-1889.

MCKITRICK, ERIC LOUIS
PERSONAL Born 07/05/1919, Battle Creek, MI, m, 1946, 4 children **DISCIPLINE** AMERICAN HISTORY **EDUCATION** Columbia Univ, BS, 49, MA, 51, PhD, 59. **CAREER** Lectr hist, Sch Gen Studies, Columbia Univ, 52-54; asst prof, Univ Chicago, 55-59; asst prof, Douglass Col, Rutgers Univ, 59-60; assoc prof, 60-65, Prof Hist, Columbia Univ, 65-, Fel, Rockefeller Found, 54-55; Soc Sci Res Coun fel, 54; Ford Found grant, 56; Rockefeller Found grant, 62-63; Nat Endowment for Humanities grant, 67-68; fel, Inst Advan Studies, 70-71 & 76-77; Guggenheim fel, 70-71 & 76-77; Pitt prof Am hist & instr, Cambridge Univ, 73-74; Harmsworth prof, Am Hist Inst, Oxford Univ, 79-80. **HONORS AND AWARDS** Dunning Prize, AHA, 60. **MEMBERSHIPS** Am Studies Asn; AHA; Orgn Am Historians; Acad Polit Sci. **RESEARCH** Late 18th and 19th century political, social and intellectual American history. **SELECTED PUBLICATIONS** Auth, Andrew Johnson and Reconstruction, Univ Chicago, 60; Slavery Defended, Prentice-Hall, 63; Andrew Johnson: A Profile, Hill & Wang, 69; coauth, The Hofstadter Aegis: A Memorial, Knopf, 74. **CONTACT ADDRESS** Dept of Hist Grad Sch of Arts & Sci, Columbia Univ, New York, NY 10027.

MCKIVEN, HENRY M., JR.
DISCIPLINE HISTORY **EDUCATION** Auburn Univ at Montgomery, BA; Va Polytech Inst, MA; Vanderbilt Univ, PhD. **CAREER** Assoc prof; Univ W Al, 90-91; prof, Univ South Al, 89-90 & 91-. **RESEARCH** U.S. South, Civil War and reconstruction, labor **SELECTED PUBLICATIONS** Auth, Iron and Steel: Class, Race, and Community in Birmingham, Alabama 1870-1920, Chapel Hill, Univ NC Press, 95 & White Workers, White Capital, and the Struggle for Shop Floor Control in Birmingham, Alabama, 1880-1895, Locus 6 1, 93, Southern Hist. **CONTACT ADDRESS** Dept of History, Univ of So Alabama, 370 Humanities, Mobile, AL 36688-0002. **EMAIL** hmckiven@jaguar1.usouthal.edu

MCKNIGHT, JOSEPH WEBB
PERSONAL Born 02/17/1925, San Angelo, TX, m, 1975, 2 children **DISCIPLINE** LEGAL HISTORY, FAMILY LAW **EDUCATION** Univ Tex, Austin, BA, 47; Oxford Univ, BA, 49, BCL, 50, MA, 54; Columbia Univ, LLM, 59. **CAREER** Legal pract, Cravath, Swaine & Moore, New York, 51-55; from asst prof to prof, 55-63, assoc dean, 77-80, Prof Law, Sch Law, Southern Methodist Univ, 63-, Consult, Hemisfair, 67-69; dir, Family Code Proj, State Bar Tex, 66-75. **HONORS AND AWARDS** Phi Beta Kappa; Rhodes Scholar; Kent fel, 58-59; Academia Mexicana de Derecho Int, 88; State Bar of Texas Family Law Section Hall of Legends, 97. **MEMBERSHIPS** Am Soc Legal Hist (vpres, 67-69); Am Soc Int Law; Nat Legal Aid & Defenders Asn. **SELECTED PUBLICATIONS** Auth, Family Law: Husband and Wife, Annual Survey of Texas Law, SMU L Rev, 67-00; auth, Texas Community Property Law: Conservative Attitudes, reluctant Change, Law & Contemp Prob, 93; auth, The Mysteries of Spanish Surnames, El Campanario, 94; auth, Spanish Legitim in the United States: Its Survival and Decline, Am J Comp L, 96; auth, Survival and Decline of the Spanish Law of Descendent Succession on the Anglo-Hispanic Frontier of North America: Homenaje al Professor Alfonso Garcia-Gallo, 96; contribur, Tyler, ed, The New Handbook of Texas, 96; auth, Eugene L. Smith, 1933-1997, An Appreciation of His Achievements, Family Law Section Rept, 97; coauth, Texas Matrimonial Property Law, 2d ed, Lupus, 98. **CONTACT ADDRESS** Sch of Law, So Methodist Univ, Dallas, TX 75275. **EMAIL** mpmcknight@home.com

MCLACHLAN, ELIZABETH PARKER
DISCIPLINE MEDIEVAL ART **EDUCATION** Courtauld Inst of Art, PhD. **CAREER** Assoc prof, Rutgers, The State Univ NJ, Univ Col-Camden. **RESEARCH** Medieval manuscripts and iconography, especially English, 12th-century and earlier; influence of the liturgy and liturgical drama on medieval art; pictorial cycles in medieval psalters. **SELECTED PUBLICATIONS** Auth, The Scriptorium of Bury St. Edmunds in the Twelfth Century, Garland Publ, 86; coauth, Romanesque Reassembled in England: A Review, in Gesta 2 4;1, 85; coed, The Carver's Art: Medieval Sculpture in Ivory, Bone, and Horn, exh cat, The Jane Voorhees Zimmerli Art Mus, Rutgers Univ, 89. **CONTACT ADDRESS** Dept of Art Hist, Rutgers, The State Univ of New Jersey, New Brunswick, Voorhees Hall, 71 Hamilton St, New Brunswick, NJ 08903. **EMAIL** epmcl@rci.rutgers.edu

MCLAUGHLIN, KEN
DISCIPLINE HISTORY **EDUCATION** Univ Waterloo, BA, 65; Dalhousie Univ, MA, 67; Univ Toronto, PhD, 74. **CAREER** Prof, St. Jerome's Univ. **HONORS AND AWARDS** Arts Awd, 94; Outstanding Achievement Awd, 84; Awd Honour, 82. **SELECTED PUBLICATIONS** Cambridge: The making of a Canadian City; Doon Pioneer Village: Master Plan; Kitchener: An Illustrated History; Les Allemands au Canada; Made-in-Berlin; The Germans in Canada; Vital Signs: The First 100 Years, Kitchener-Waterloo Hospital; Waterloo: An Illustrated History. **CONTACT ADDRESS** Dept of History, St. Jerome's Univ, Waterloo, ON, Canada N2L 3G3. **EMAIL** kmclaugh@watarts.uwaterloo.ca

MCLAUGHLIN, MARY MARTIN
PERSONAL Born 04/15/1919, Grand Island, NE **DISCIPLINE** MEDIEVAL HISTORY **EDUCATION** Univ Nebr, AB, 40; MA, 41; Columbia Univ, PhD, 52. **CAREER** Instr hist, Wellesley Col, 43-46; instr, Vassar Col, 46-48; vis asst prof, Univ Nebr, 52-52, 54-55; asst prof, Vassar Col, 59-67; Ingram Merrill Found fel, 65-66; res & writing, 66-, Am Philos Soc travel grant, Europe, 55. **HONORS AND AWARDS** Berkshire Conference of Women historians, best article prize, 75; Columbia Univ-Barnard Col, "Medieval Religious Women," conference given in honor of, 91. **MEMBERSHIPS** AHA; Medieval Acad Am; Renaissance Soc Am; Am Cath Hist Asn. **RESEARCH** Medieval social and intellectual history, 10th-15th centuries, especially Abelard; history of women, especially religious life. **SELECTED PUBLICATIONS** Auth, "Looking for Medieval Women: An Interim Report on the Project, Women's Religious Life and Communities, 500-1500," Medieval Prosopography 8 (87): 61-91; auth, "Creating and Recreating Communities of Women: The Case of Corpus Domini, Ferrara, 1406-1452," Signs 14 (89): 293-320; auth, "The Oldest Vocation--Christian Motherhood in the Middle Ages," Cath Hist Rev (95); auth, "Male Authors, Female Readers--Representation and Subjectivity in Middle English Devotional Literature," Amer Hist Rev (97); auth, "Women in Christian History--A Bibliography," Church Hist (97); auth, "Heloise the Abbess: The Expansion of the Paraclete," in Listening to Heloise, ed. Bonnie Wheeler (St. Martin's Press, NYork, 00); auth, The Collected Correspondence of Abelard and Heloise and Related Writings, St. Martin's Press, forthcoming; auth, Heloise and the Paraclete: A Twelfth-Century Quest, St. Martin's Press, forthcoming. **CONTACT ADDRESS** 331 Valley Farm Rd, Millbrook, NY 12545.

MCLAUGHLIN, MEGAN
DISCIPLINE HISTORY **EDUCATION** Vassar Col, AB, 75; Stanford Univ, MA, 77; PhD, 85. **CAREER** Asst prof of Hist, Univ of Ill, 85-92; assoc prof, Univ of Ill, 92-. **HONORS AND AWARDS** Phi Beta Kappa; Stanford Fel, 75-78; Margaret Whiting Fel, 79-80. **RESEARCH** European religion and society to 1200; history of women and gender; sexuality, gender and politics in eleventh-century Europe. **SELECTED PUBLICATIONS** Auth, "Gender Paradox and the Otherness of God," Gender & History 3, (91): 147-59; auth, "On with Death," Journal of Medieval History 17, (91): 23-34; auth, "Familiarity and Love: Noble Friendship and Liturgical Commemoration in the Twelfth and Thirteenth Centuries," Proceedings of the Annual Meeting of the Western Society for French Hist 18, (91): 60-69; auth, Consorting with Saints: Prayer for the Dead in Early Medieval France, Ithaca, NY: Cornell Univ Press, 94; auth, The Twelfth-Century Ritual of Death and Burial at Saint-Jean-en-Vallee in the Diocese of Chartres," Revue Benedictine 105, (95): 155-66; auth, On Feminism and Medievalism: Musings from a Prone Position," Medieval Feminist Newsletter 19, (95): 21-23; auth, Abominable Mingling: Father-Daughter Incest and the Law, Medieval Feminist Newsletter 24, (97): 26-30; auth, "The Bishop as Bridegroom: Marital Imagery and Clerical Celibacy in the Eleventh and Twelfth Centuries," in Medieval Purity and Piety: Essays on Medieval Clerical Celibacy and Religious Reform, ed. Michael Frasetto, (New York: Garland Press, 98). **CONTACT ADDRESS** History Dept, Univ of Illinois, Urbana-Champaign, 52 E Gregory Dr, Champaign, IL 61820. **EMAIL** megmclau@uiuc.edu

MCLAURIN, MELTON ALONZA
PERSONAL Born 07/11/1941, Fayetteville, NC, m, 1961, 3 children **DISCIPLINE** UNITED STATES & LABOR HISTORY **EDUCATION** E Carolina Univ, BS, 62, MA, 64; Univ SC, PhD, 67. **CAREER** Prof hist, Univ S Ala, 67-77; prof hist, Univ NC, Wilmington, 77- ; assoc vice chancellor, academic affairs, 96- . **HONORS AND AWARDS** Lillian Smith Awd for Non-

fiction, 88. **MEMBERSHIPS** Southern Hist Asn; Orgn Am Historians. **RESEARCH** The American South; race relations. **SELECTED PUBLICATIONS** Auth, Paternalism and Protest, Southern Cotton Mill Workers and Organized Labor, 1875-1905, Greenwood, 71; auth, The Knights of Labor in the South, 78, Greenwood; coauth, The Image of Progress, Alabama Photographs, 1872-1917, Univ AL, 80; Separate Pasts, Growing Up White in the Segregated South, Univ GA, 87; Celia, A Slave, Univ GA, 91; co-ed, You Wrote My Life, Lyrical Themes in Country Music, Gordon & Breach, 92. **CONTACT ADDRESS** Provost Office, Univ of No Carolina, Wilmington, 601 S College Rd, Wilmington, NC 28403-3201. **EMAIL** mclaurinm@uncwil.edu

MCLEAN, ANDREW MILLER
PERSONAL Born 05/25/1941, Brooklyn, NY, 1 child **DISCIPLINE** ENGLISH RENAISSANCE LITERATURE & HISTORY **EDUCATION** St Olaf Col, BA, 63; Brooklyn Col, MA, 67; Univ NC, Chapel Hill, PhD(English), 71. **CAREER** Asst prof, 71-76, Assoc Prof English, 77-82, prof, 82- ,Univ Wis-Parkside; Rev ed, Clio: An Interdisciplinary Jour of Lit, Hist, and Philos of Hist, 71-93; res prof, Catholic Univ Louvain, 75-76. **MEMBERSHIPS** MLA; Soc Studies Midwestern Lit; Renaissance Soc Am; Shakespeare Asn Am. **RESEARCH** Sixteenth century English literature; Irish literature; interdisciplinary studies; film-Shakespeare. **SELECTED PUBLICATIONS** Auth, Emerson's Brahma, New England Quart, 3/69; James Joyce & A Doblin, Comp Lit, spring 73; English translation of Erasmus, Moreana, 11/74; Castiglione, Cicero & English dialogues, Romance Notes, 75; Barlow, More & the Anglican episcopacy, Moreana, 2/76; contribr, Bibliography on teaching Shakespeare, In: Teaching Shakespeare, Princeton Univ, 77; Barlow & the Lutheran Factions, Renaissance Quart, summer 78; auth, Shakespeare: Annotated Bibliographies and Media Guide for Teachers, MCTE, 80; ed, Work of William Barlowe, Sutton Courtenay press, 81; co-ed, Redefining Shakespeare: Literary Theory and Theater Practice in the German Democratic Republic. Univ Delaware, 98. **CONTACT ADDRESS** Dept of English, Univ of Wisconsin, Parkside, Box 2000, Kenosha, WI 53141-2000. **EMAIL** andrew.mclean@uwp.edu

MCLEOD, JANE
DISCIPLINE EVENTEENTH AND EIGHTEENTH-CENTURY EUROPEAN HISTORY **EDUCATION** Brock Col; Univ York, BA, MA, PhD. **CAREER** Assoc prof. **RESEARCH** Social and political history in seventeenth and eighteenth-century France. **SELECTED PUBLICATIONS** Co-auth, Amiraute de Guyenne: Source de l'histoire de la Nouvelle France, Ottawa: Nat Archv Can. **CONTACT ADDRESS** Dept of Hist, Brock Univ, 500 Glenridge Ave, Saint Catharines, ON, Canada L2S 3A1. **EMAIL** jmcleod@spartan.ac.BrockU.CA

MCLEOD, JOHN
PERSONAL Born 03/05/1963, Toronto, ON, Canada, m, 1991 **DISCIPLINE** HISTORY **EDUCATION** Univ Toronto, BA, 85; MA, 86; PhD, 93. **CAREER** Lecturer, Univ Toronto, 94-95; asst prof, Univ Louisville, 95-. **HONORS AND AWARDS** Postdoctoral Fel; Shastri Indo-Canadian Inst, New Delhi, 93-94. **MEMBERSHIPS** Asn for Asian Studies. **SELECTED PUBLICATIONS** Auth, Sovereignty, Power, Control: Politics in the States of Western India, 1916-1947, (Leiden: Brill, 99). **CONTACT ADDRESS** Dept Hist, Univ of Louisville, 2301 South 3rd St, Louisville, KY 40292-0001. **EMAIL** john.mcleod@louisville.edu

MCLEOD, JOHNATHAN
PERSONAL Born 10/02/1950, Berkeley, CA **DISCIPLINE** HISTORY **EDUCATION** Univ Calif, BA, 72; MA, 74; PhD, 87. **CAREER** From Asst Prof to Prof, San Diego Mesa Col, 89-. **MEMBERSHIPS** Fac Coalition for Public Higher Educ, Am Asn of Univ Profs, Am Fedn of Teachers, AHA, Fac Asn of Calif Community Cols, OAH, San Diego Hist Soc. **RESEARCH** U S History, labor and race/ethnicity, current higher education, policy and politics. **SELECTED PUBLICATIONS** Auth, Workers and Workplace Dynamics in Reconstruction-Era Atlanta, 89. **CONTACT ADDRESS** Dept Hist, San Diego Mesa Col, 7250 Mesa College Dr, San Diego, CA 92111-4902. **EMAIL** jmcleod@sdccd.net

MCLEOD, MARSHALL W.
PERSONAL Born 06/15/1941, Albemarle, NC, m, 1970, 3 children **DISCIPLINE** HISTORY **EDUCATION** Pfeiffer Col, AB, 65; Appalachian State Univ, MS, 66; Univ Fla, EdS, 67; EdD, 69. **CAREER** Instructor, Appalachian State Univ, 65-66; Asst to the Pres, Santa Fe JR Col, 68-69; Asst Prof, Appalachian State Univ, 71-73; Asst Dean and Co-ordinator, Univ Ill, 73-81; Provost and Dean, Rappahannock Cmty Col, 81-86; Dean and Provost, Pensacola JR Col, 86-. **HONORS AND AWARDS** Nat Fac Dir, 75; Who's Who in Health Care, 78; Who's Who in Education, the 70's, 79; Who's Who in the Midwest, 80; Who's Who in the South, 83; Who's Who in the Southeast, 89; Who's Who in Am Educ, 92-93; Peterson's Register of Higher Educ, 93; W.K. Kellogg Fel, SE Jr Col, 66-68; Appreciation Awd, Rappahannock Cmty Col Stud Govt Asn, 85. **MEMBERSHIPS** VA Cmty Col Asn; Nat AND Adv Group; FL Asn of Cmty Col; Escambia Vocational Asn; Nat Coun of Instructional Admin. **SELECTED PUBLICATIONS** Auth, "So What's New About the Current Nursing Shortage? A 1968 Florida Nurse Study Anticipated National Conditions," Florida Nurse, (87): 26-27; co-auth, "Community Colleges and the HIV Virus: Moral Imperatives," Community/Junior College, Quarterly of Research and Practice; co-auth, "Opinion: Registered Care Technicians: Progress or Problems?," The Community Junior College Times, (90): 2, 11); auth, "Dimensions of Ethical Conduct in Higher Education Decision Making," in Proceedings, 92; co-auth, "A Mini-Dictionary on Institutional Effectiveness Terms," Community Col Review, (92): 30-37; auth, "Some Basic Elements of Program Feasibility," in Occasional Papers of the Southern Association of Community, Junior and Technical Colleges, 94; co-auth, "Rescission and Reduction Lessons from the edge," Community College Review, 95; co-auth, "A Short Taxonomy of Rescissory Fiscal Measures; Cost Containment Options for Mid-Year Budget Reductions and Appropriations Cuts," Journal of Applied Research in the Community Col, 95; auth, "Leadership Principles for America's Future and for America's Community Colleges," Visions, 96; co-auth, "Essential Decisions in Institutional Effectiveness Assessment," Visions, 98. **CONTACT ADDRESS** Dept Hist, Lang & Lit, Pensacola Junior Col, 1000 Col Blvd, Pensacola, FL 32504-8910. **EMAIL** mmcleod@pjc.cc.fl.us

MCLOUD, MELISSA
PERSONAL Born 03/27/1954, Okinawa, Japan, m, 1982 **DISCIPLINE** HISTORY **EDUCATION** George Washington Univ, PhD 88; Brown Univ, BA 76. **CAREER** Chesapeake Bay Maritime Museum, dir , 96-; NEH Museums prog officer, 94-96; Natl Building Museum, curator, 88-94; Smithsonian Inst NMAH, edu consul, 85-86, admin asst, res fel, 81-83. **HONORS AND AWARDS** Smthsn Inst NMAH, pre-doc fel; Preservation Tst, fel; NMAH AACP, res fel; CO Women's fel; Phi Delta Beta sch; Myron Loe fel; exhibits: visions of home 94; making it work: pittsburgh defines a city 93; visions, revisions 92; washington: symbol and city 92; ideal place: rockefeller visions for america 92. **SELECTED PUBLICATIONS** Auth, Craftsmen and Entrepreneurs: Washington DC Builders, in progress; Urban Water Technology: An Alexandria Cistern and Filter System, 95; Washington: Symbol and the City, An Educator's Guide, coauth, 94; In a Workmanlike Manner, The Building of Residential Washington, coauth, 84. **CONTACT ADDRESS** Center for Chesapeake Studies, Chesapeake Bay Maritime Mus, PO Box 636, Saint Michaels, MD 21663-0636. **EMAIL** mmcloud@cbmm.org

MCMAHON, GREGORY
DISCIPLINE HISTORY **EDUCATION** Univ Chicago, PhD. **CAREER** Assoc prof, Univ NH, 88; assoc dir, Alisar Hoyuk Excavations, Turkey. **HONORS AND AWARDS** Fulbright-Hays fel. **RESEARCH** Hittite magical ritual. **SELECTED PUBLICATIONS** Auth, The Hittite State Cult of the Tutelary Deities, 91. **CONTACT ADDRESS** Univ of New Hampshire, Durham, Durham, NH 03824. **EMAIL** gmcmahon@christa.unh.edu

MCMAHON, ROBERT J.
PERSONAL Born 05/13/1949, Bayside, NY, m, 1976, 2 children **DISCIPLINE** HISTORY **EDUCATION** Fairfield Univ, BA, 71; Univ of Conn, PhD, 77. **CAREER** Historian, U.S. Dept of State, 78-82; prof of Hist, Univ of Fla, 82-; prof, Univ Col, Dublin, 99-00. **HONORS AND AWARDS** Teaching Excellence Award, Univ of FL, 95; Stuart L. Bernath Article Prize, 89, Bernath Lecture Award, 91, Pres, Soc for Historians of Am Foreign Relations, 01. **MEMBERSHIPS** Am Hist Asn; Org of Am Historians; Soc for Historians of Am Foreign Relations. **RESEARCH** U.S. history; U.S. foreign relations, especially during the 20th century. **SELECTED PUBLICATIONS** Auth, The Limits of Empire: The United States and Southeast Asia Since World War II, Columbia Univ Press, 99; auth, The Cold War on the Periphery: The United States, India, and Pakistan, Columbia Univ Press, 94; auth, Colonialism and Cold War: The United States and the Struggle for Indonesian Independence 1945-49, Cornell Univ Press, 81; co-ed, The Origins of the Cold War, Houghton-Mifflin, 99; ed, Major Problems in the History of the Vietnam War, Houghton-Mifflin, 92; auth, numerous articles in J of Am Hist, Political Sci Quarterly, Int Hist Rev, Pacific His Rev, and Diplomatic Hist. **CONTACT ADDRESS** Dept of History, Univ of Florida, 4131 Turlington Hall, Gainesville, FL 32611. **EMAIL** rmcmahon@history.ufl.edu

MCMANAMON, JOHN
DISCIPLINE HISTORY **EDUCATION** NC Chapel Hill, PhD, 84. **CAREER** Hist, Loyola Univ. **RESEARCH** Late Medieval-Renaissance European history. **SELECTED PUBLICATIONS** Auth, Continuity and Change in the Ideals fo Humanism: The Evidence from Florentine Funeral Oratory, In Life and Death in Fifteenth-Century Florence, Durham: Duke UP, 89; The Sinking fo the Wells Burt, Inland Seas 46, 90; Marketing a Medici Regime: The Funeral Oration of Marcello Virgilio Adriani for Giuliano de' Medici 1516, Renaissance Quart 44, 91. **CONTACT ADDRESS** Fine Arts Dept, Loyola Univ, Chicago, 6525 N. Sheridan Rd., Chicago, IL 60626. **EMAIL** jmcmana@wpo.it.luc.edu

MCMANUS, EDGAR J.
PERSONAL Born 03/04/1924, New York, NY, w **DISCIPLINE** AMERICAN COLONIAL, LEGAL & CONSTITUTIONAL HISTORY **EDUCATION** Columbia Univ, BS, 52, MA, 53, PhD, 59; NY Univ, JP, 59. **CAREER** Lectr hist, Columbia Univ, 53-56; from lectr to assoc prof, 57-73, prof hist, Queens Col, NY, 73, Adj prof law, NY Law Sch, 62-66; Am Coun Learned Soc fel, 68-69. **HONORS AND AWARDS** Fulbright lectr, New Zealand, 82; Norway, 89; jd, ny univ, 59. **MEMBERSHIPS** AHA; NY State Bar. **RESEARCH** Am Negro slavery; legal origins of American Negro slavery; American Legal and constitutional history. **SELECTED PUBLICATIONS** Auth, The status of res ipsa loquitor in New York, NY Univ Intramural Law Rev, 11/47; Antislavery legislation in New York, J Negro Hist, 10/61; The enforcement of acceleration clauses in New York, NY Law Forum, 12/62; A History of Negro Slavery in New York, 66, Black Bondage in the North, 73, Syracuse Univ; Law and Libery in Early New England, Univ of MA, 93. **CONTACT ADDRESS** Dept of Hist, Queens Col, CUNY, 6530 Kissena Blvd, Flushing, NY 11367-1597.

MCMILLAN, DANIEL
PERSONAL Born 05/16/1960, CA, m, 2001 **DISCIPLINE** HISTORY **EDUCATION** Stan Univ, BA, 82; Columb, PhD, 97. **CAREER** Adj prof, Drew Univ, 96-97; asst prof, East Ill Univ, 98-. **MEMBERSHIPS** AHA; GSA. **RESEARCH** 19th century German social, culture, political history; history of sports. **SELECTED PUBLICATIONS** Transl of, " '.die hochste und heiligste Pflicht.' : Das Mannlichkeitsideal der deutschen Turnbewegung, 1811 - 1871," in Mannergeschichte Geschlechtergeschichte, Mannlichkeit im Wandel der Moderne, ed. Thomas Kuhne pp. 88-100 (Franfurt a.M.: Campus-Verlag, 96): 88-100; auth, "Small Groups and the Chimera of Consensus: Local Politics and National Politics in Modern Germany," Res Rev (00); auth, "Energy, Willpower, and Harmony: On the Problematic Relationship between State and Civil Society in 19th-Century Germany," in The Making of Civil Society in Modern Germany and Britain: New Cultural, Political, and Theoretical Perspectives (Berghahn Books, 00). Berghahn Books, ~ **CONTACT ADDRESS** Dept History, Eastern Illinois Univ, 600 Lincoln Ave, Charleston, IL 61920.

MCMILLEN, NEIL RAYMOND
PERSONAL Born 01/02/1939, m, 1960, 2 children **DISCIPLINE** RECENT UNITED STATES HISTORY **EDUCATION** Univ Southern Miss, BA, 61, MA, 63; Vanderbilt Univ, PhD(hist), 69. **CAREER** Asst prof hist, Ball State Univ, 67-69; dean Basic Col, 70-71; from asst prof to assoc prof, 69-78, PROF HIST, UNIV SOUTHERN MISS, 78-, Danforth assoc, 73; vis assoc prof hist, Univ Mo-Columbia, 74-75; Moorman Distinguished Prof, 93-95. **HONORS AND AWARDS** Grant, Nat Endowment for Humanities, 75 & 81; Bancroft Prize, 90; McLemore Prize, 90; Gustavus Myers Outstanding Book award, 90. **MEMBERSHIPS** Southern Hist Asn; Orgn Am Historians. **RESEARCH** Recent South; black history. **SELECTED PUBLICATIONS** Auth, The Citizens' Council, Univ Ill, 71; coauth, Synopsis of American History, Rand McNally, 3d-8th ed, 77-98; auth, Dark Journey, Univ Ill, 89. **CONTACT ADDRESS** Dept of History, Univ of So Mississippi, Hattiesburg, MS 39401. **EMAIL** mcmillen@usm.edu

MCMORDIE, MICHAEL J.
PERSONAL Born 04/23/1935, Toronto, ON, Canada **DISCIPLINE** ARCHITECTURE, HISTORY **EDUCATION** Univ Toronto, BArch, 62; Univ Edinburgh, PhD, 72. **CAREER** Staff mem, Gordon S. Adamson & Assoc, 62-65; lectr, Univ Edinburgh; assoc prof to prof, Univ Calgary, 74-, prog dir archit, 79-82, dean gen stud, 90-98; vis assoc, 74-75, life mem, Clare Hall, Cambridge Univ, 76-. **MEMBERSHIPS** Soc Stud Archit Can; Asn Can Stud; Soc Archit Hist. **RESEARCH** History and theory of architecture. **SELECTED PUBLICATIONS** Coauth, Twelve Houses, 95; contribur, The Canadian Encyclopedia; ed bd, TRACE, 79-82; ed bd, Urban Hist Rev, 83-; ed bd, Interchange, 95-. **CONTACT ADDRESS** Fac of Environmental Design, Univ of Calgary, Calgary, AB, Canada T2N 1N4. **EMAIL** mcmordie@ucalgary.ca

MCMULLIN, STAN
DISCIPLINE HISTORY **EDUCATION** Univ Dalhousie, PhD. **CAREER** Assoc prof, Carleton Univ. **HONORS AND AWARDS** Coord, Cult and Cult Policy Prog Area. **RESEARCH** Canadian regionalism; history of spiritualism and psychic research in Canada; popular culture; provinvial parks; and public policy. **SELECTED PUBLICATIONS** Auth, A Matter of Attitude: The Subversive Margin in Canada, Post-Colonial Formations a special number of Cultural Policy (Australia), Vol 6, 94; The Canadian Perspective on Mexico, Mexico: Ante el bloque Norteamericano, Memorias, Univ Monterrey, 92. **CONTACT ADDRESS** Dept of Canadian Studies, Carleton Univ, 1125 Colonel By Dr, 1203 Dunton Tower, Ottawa, ON, Canada K1S 5B6. **EMAIL** stan_mcmullin@carleton.ca

MCMULLIN, THOMAS AUSTIN
PERSONAL Born 08/12/1942, Boston, MA, m, 1968, 2 children **DISCIPLINE** HISTORY **EDUCATION** Univ Mass, Amherst, BA, 64; Univ Wis, Madison, MA, 66, PhD Hist, 76.

CAREER Instr hist, Boston State Col, 65-73, asst prof, 73-78, assoc prof, 78-82; assoc prof hist, Univ Mass-Boston, 82-, grad sch lectr, Northeastern Univ, 80. **MEMBERSHIPS** Orgn Am Historians; Urban Hist Assoc. **RESEARCH** American urban and political history. **SELECTED PUBLICATIONS** Coauth, Biographical Directory of American Territorial Governors, with David Walker, Meckler/Greenwood, 84; auth, The Immigrant Response to Industrialism in New Bedford, 1865-1900, in Massachusetts in the Gilded Age: Selected Essays, University of Massachusetts Press, 85; auth, Industrialization and the Transformation of Public Education in New Bedford, 1865-1900, Historical Journal of Massachusetts, 87; auth, Overseeing the Poor: Industrialization and Public Relief in New Bedford, 1865-1900, Social Service Review, 91; auth, Lost Alternative: The Urban Industrial Utopia of William D Howland, New England Quart, 3/82; Part I: The Struggle For Power In Massachusetts, Introduction in Massachusetts Politics: Selected Historical Essays, Institute For Massachusetts Studies, 98. **CONTACT ADDRESS** Dept of History, Univ of Massachusetts, Boston, 100 Morrissey Blvd, Boston, MA 02125-3300. **EMAIL** thomas.mcmullin@umb.edu

MCMURRY, RICHARD MANNING
PERSONAL Born 09/13/1939, DeKalb Co, GA, m, 3 children **DISCIPLINE** UNITED STATES HISTORY **EDUCATION** Va Mil Inst, BA, 61; Emory Univ, MA, 64, PhD, 67. **CAREER** Lectr hist, Emory Univ, 66-67; from asst prof to prof hist, Valdosta State Col, 67-81; MEM FAC, NC STATE UNIV, 81-. **MEMBERSHIPS** Orgn Am Historians; Southern Hist Asn. **RESEARCH** Civil War and Reconstruction; Old South; American military history. **SELECTED PUBLICATIONS** Auth, The Atlanta campaign of 1864: A new look, Civil War Hist, 3/76; co-ed, Rank and File: Essays in Civil War History in Honor of Bell Irvin Wiley, Presidio, 76; auth, John Bell Hood and the War for Southern Independence, Ky, 82. **CONTACT ADDRESS** 3212 Caldwell Dr, Raleigh, NC 27607.

MCMURRY-EDWARDS, LINDA O.
PERSONAL Born 10/24/1945, Montgomery, AL, m, 1997, 1 child **DISCIPLINE** HISTORY **EDUCATION** Oxford Col of Emory Univ, AA, 64; Auburn Univ, BA, 68, MA, 72, PhD, 76. **CAREER** Asst prof, 76-79, assoc prof, Valdosta State Col, 79-81; ASSOC PROF, 81-87, PROF, 87-, NC STATE UNIV. **HONORS AND AWARDS** Rockefeller Fund Humanities Fel, 85-86; Ala Authors Awd for Nonfiction, 84; Auburn Univ Humanities Alumni Awd, 96; NC State Univ, Col of Humanities and Soc Sci Res Awd, 99; NC State Univ, CHASS nominee for the Board of Governor's Outstanding Teaching Awd, 99. **MEMBERSHIPS** Org of Am Historians; Southern Hist Asn; Asn for the Study of Afro-American Life & Hist. **RESEARCH** African American history, 1865-1940. **SELECTED PUBLICATIONS** Auth, To Keep the Waters Troubled: The Life of Ida B. Wells, 99, Oxford Univ Press; auth, Recorder of the Black Experience: A Biography of Monroe Nathan Work, La State Univ Press, 85; auth, George Washington Carver: Scientist and Symbol, Oxford Univ Press, 81; coauth, American and Its Peoples, Longman Green, 97. **CONTACT ADDRESS** 3503 Barron Berkeley Way, Raleigh, NC 27612. **EMAIL** linedwards@aol.com

MCNABB, DEBRA
PERSONAL Born Glace Bay, NS, Canada **DISCIPLINE** MUSEUM STUDIES **EDUCATION** Mt Allison Univ, BA, 79; Univ BC, MA, 86. **CAREER** Registrar, Nova Scotia Museum Indust. **HONORS AND AWARDS** MA fel, Soc Sci & Humanities, Res Coun Can. **SELECTED PUBLICATIONS** Auth, Working Worlds, plate 37, in Historical Atlas of Canada; auth, Old Sydney Town: Historic Buildings in Sydney's North End, 86. **CONTACT ADDRESS** Nova Scotia Mus of Industry, 147 N Foord St, Box 2590, Stellarton, NS, Canada BOK 1SO. **EMAIL** dmcnabb@fox.nstn.ca

MCNALLY, MICHAEL
DISCIPLINE HISTORY **EDUCATION** Harvard Univ, PhD. **CAREER** Asst prof, Eastern Michigan Univ. **RESEARCH** History of Native American religious traditions. **SELECTED PUBLICATIONS** Auth, A History of Russia, 2 vol, McGraw-Hill, 97; coauth, The Twentieth Century: A Brief Global History, 4th ed, McGraw-Hill, 94, 5th ed, 97; The Uses of Hymn Singing at White Earth: Toward a History of Practice, in Lived Religion in America, Princeton UP, 97. **CONTACT ADDRESS** Dept of History and Philosophy, Eastern Michigan Univ, 701 Pray-Harrold, Ypsilanti, MI 48197.

MCNALLY, RAYMOND T.
PERSONAL Born 04/15/1931, Cleveland, OH, m, 1957, 3 children **DISCIPLINE** RUSSIAN HISTORY **EDUCATION** Fordham Univ, AB, 53; Free Univ Berlin, PhD(Russian hist), 56. **CAREER** Instr Europ & Russ hist, John Carroll Univ, 56-58; from asst prof to assoc prof Russ hist, 58-71, PROF RUSS HIST, BOSTON COL, 71-, DIR SLAVIC & E EUROP CTR, 64-, InterUniv Comt travel grant, Leningrad State Univ, 61; Fulbright res exchange prof hist, Univ Bucharest, 69-70. **MEMBERSHIPS** AHA; Am Asn Advan Slavic Studies. **RESEARCH** Russian intellectual history in the first half of the nineteenth century. **SELECTED PUBLICATIONS** **CONTACT ADDRESS** Dept of Hist, Boston Col, Chestnut Hill, 140 Commonwealth Ave, Chestnut Hill, MA 02167.

MCNALLY, SHEILA
DISCIPLINE ART AND ARCHAEOLOGY OF LATE ANTIQUITY **EDUCATION** Vassar Col, AB, 53; Harvard Univ,PhD, 65. **CAREER** Prof, Univ Minn, Twin Cities. **RESEARCH** Architectural decoration in the time of Diocletian. **SELECTED PUBLICATIONS** Auth, The Architectural Decoration of Diocletian's Palace: Ornament in Context, BAR Int Ser, 96; coauth, Excavations in Akhmim, Egypt: Continuity and change in city life from late antiquity to the present, BAR Int Ser 590, 93; coauth & ed, Diocletian's Palace: Report on the Joint Excavations, Southeast Quart 1-6, 72-96. **CONTACT ADDRESS** Univ of Minnesota, Twin Cities, 9 Pleasant St. SE, 330 Folwell Hall, Minneapolis, MN 55455. **EMAIL** mcnal001@tc.umn.edu

MCNALLY, VINCENT J.
PERSONAL Born 02/06/1943, Philadelphia, PA, s **DISCIPLINE** CHURCH HISTORY **EDUCATION** St Charles Borromeo Col, BA, 65; Villanova Univ, MA, 71; Univ Dublib, trinity Col, PhD, 77; MSLS, 80; Catholic Univ, M Div, 82. **CAREER** Instr, Prince George Comm Col, 80-82; lectr, Seattle Univ, 82-83; adj prof, Simon Fraser Univ, CAN, 83-92; prof, Sacred Sch Theology, 92-. **HONORS AND AWARDS** Pew Charit Tr Res Awd; Lilly Found Res Awd; Lilly-Wabash Cen Teach Theol Awd; Western Canadian Pub Res Pub Awd; Soc Sci Hum Res Coun Awd, Canada. **MEMBERSHIPS** ACHA; CCHA; IAHA. **RESEARCH** Irish Cathoilc Church history; Canadian Catholic Church history. **SELECTED PUBLICATIONS** Auth, "Fighting for a Foundation: Oblate Beginnings in Far Western Canada, 1847-1864," in Western Oblate Studies 4/Etudes Oblate de L 'Ouest 4, Edmonton: Western Can Pub 96; auth, "Who is Leading? Archbishop John Thomas Troy and the Priests and People in the Archdiocese of Dublin 1787-1823," The Can Cath Hist Asn, Hist Studies, 61(95); auth, "Fighting City Hall: The Church Tax Exemption Baffle Between the City and the Roman Catholic Diocese of Victoria," J Can Church Hist Soc 34, (92); auth, "A Defence of the 'Durieu System,"' Bulletin, Western Canadian Pub 28 (98); auth, "A Question of Class? Relations between Bishops and Lay Leaders in Ireland and Newfoundland 1783-1807," The Canadian Catholic Hist Asn, Historical Studies, 64(98); auth, "Challenging the Status Quo: An Examination of the History of Catholic Education in British Columbia," The Canadian Cath Hist Asn, Historical Studies, 65 (99); auth, "Hope for the Future: Facing the Church's Challenges of the New Millennium," Centre de Patrimoine, Colloquium 99, Winnipeg: University of Manitoba, 00; auth, "The Lord's Distant Vineyard: A History of the Oblates and the Catholic Community in British Columbia," Univ Alberta Press, 00. **CONTACT ADDRESS** Dept Religion, Sacred Heart Sch of Theol, PO Box 429, Hales Corners, WI 53130-0429. **EMAIL** vmcnally@execpc.com

MCNAUGHTON, PATRICK
DISCIPLINE AFRICAN, OCEANIC, AND PRE COLUMBIAN ART **EDUCATION** Yale Univ, PhD. **CAREER** Prof. **RESEARCH** Aesthetics; technology and expertise; social roles of art; historical problems in African art; critical issues of theory and methodology. **SELECTED PUBLICATIONS** Auth, The Mande Blacksmiths: Knowledge, Power, and Art in West Africa. **CONTACT ADDRESS** Hist of Art Dep, Indiana Univ, Bloomington, 1201 E 7th St, Fine Arts 132, Bloomington, IN 47405. **EMAIL** mcnaughton@indiana.edu

MCNEIL, DAVID O.
PERSONAL Born 10/18/1942, OH, 3 children **DISCIPLINE** EARLY MODERN EUROPE **EDUCATION** Antioch Col, BA, 65; Stanford Univ, MA, 66, PhD(hist), 72. **CAREER** From asst prof to prof hist, San Jose State Univ, 70-. **MEMBERSHIPS** AHA; World History Assoc. Renaissance Society of America. **RESEARCH** Early modern French and Italian social and intellectual history. **SELECTED PUBLICATIONS** Guillaume Bude and Humanism in the Reign of Francis I, Droz, Geneva, 75. **CONTACT ADDRESS** Dept of Hist, San Jose State Univ, 1 Washington Sq, San Jose, CA 95192-0117. **EMAIL** dmcneil@sjsu.euj

MCNEIL, WILLIAM KINNETH
PERSONAL Born 08/13/1940, Canton, NC **DISCIPLINE** AMERICAN FOLKLORE AND HISTORY **EDUCATION** Carson-Newman Col, BA, 62; Okla State Univ, MA, 63; State Univ NYork, Oneonta, MA, 67; Ind Univ, PhD(Am folklore), 80. **CAREER** Historian, Off State Hist, Albany, NY, 67-70; adminr & folklorist, Smithsonian Inst, 75-76; FOLKLORIST, OZARK FOLK CTR, 76-, Adv & consult, Fr Cult Proj, Old Mines, Mo, 78-80; bd mem, Nat Coun Traditional Arts, 79-; chief consult, Echoes of Ozarks, 82. **MEMBERSHIPS** Am Folklore Soc; Am Asn State & Local Hist; Ozark States Folklore Soc; Southern Folklore Soc. **RESEARCH** American music, particularly 19th century popular and 20th century country; American theater; American folklore, particulary folklore of the Southern mountains. **SELECTED PUBLICATIONS** Auth, The autograph album custom: A tradition and its scholarly treatment, Keystone Folklore, spring 68; A Schoharie County songster, NY Folklore Quart, 3/69; We'll make the Spanish grunt: Popular songs about the sinking of the Maine, J Popular Cult, summer 69; Mrs F-Little Joe: The multiple personality experience and the folklorist, Ind Folklore, 71; coauth, American proverb literature, Folklore Forum, 71; auth, Syncopated slander: The Coon Song 1890-1900, Keystone Folklore, spring 72; Appalachian folklore scholarship, Appalachian J, spring 77; James Athearn Jones: Pioneer American folklorist, In: Folklore on Two Continents: A Festschrift for Linda Degh, 81. **CONTACT ADDRESS** PO Box 500, Nature View, AR 72560.

MCNEILL, JOHN R.
PERSONAL Born 10/06/1954, Chicago, IL, m, 1985, 4 children **DISCIPLINE** HISTORY **EDUCATION** Duke Univ, PhD, 81. **CAREER** Asst prof, 83-85, Goucher Col; asst prof to prof, 85-, Georgetown Univ. **HONORS AND AWARDS** Fulbright Fel, 87-88, 92-93; Woodrow Wilson Center Fel, 96-97; Guggenheim Fel, 97-98. **MEMBERSHIPS** Amer Hist Assoc; Amer Soc for Environmental Hist; World Hist Assoc. **RESEARCH** Environmental hist **SELECTED PUBLICATIONS** Auth, The Atlantic Empires of France and Spain, UNC Press, 85; auth, The Mountains of the Mediterranean World: An Environmental History, Cambridge Univ Press, 93; art, Of Rats and Men: A Synoptic Environmental History of the Island Pacific, J of World Hist; coed, Atlantic American Societies from Columbus through Abolition, 1492-1800, Routledge, 92. **CONTACT ADDRESS** History Dept, Georgetown Univ, Washington, DC 20007. **EMAIL** mcneillj@georgetown.edu

MCNEILL, PAULA L.
PERSONAL Born Fort Lauderdale, FL, 1 child **DISCIPLINE** ART **EDUCATION** Ariz State Univ, BA; Univ of NMex, MA; Univ Mo-Columbia, PhD. **CAREER** Prof, Valdosta State Univ Instr, Navajo Reservation in Ganado; instr, archv, Univ Mo-Columbia. **RESEARCH** The history of art education, the history of technology in art education, community-based art education. **SELECTED PUBLICATIONS** Published works in the area of the history of art education. **CONTACT ADDRESS** Dept of Art, Valdosta State Univ, 1500 N. Patterson St, Valdosta, GA 31698. **EMAIL** pmcneill@valdosta.edu

MCNEILL, WILLIAM HARDY
PERSONAL Born 10/31/1917, Vancouver, BC, Canada, m, 1946, 4 children **DISCIPLINE** HISTORY **EDUCATION** Univ Chicago, BA, 38, MA, 39; Cornell Univ, PhD(hist), 47. **CAREER** From instr to prof hist, 47-69, chmn dept, 61-67, ROBERT A MILLIKEN DISTINGUISHED SERV PROF HIST, UNIV CHICAGO, 69-, Vis prof, Univ Hawaii, winter, 80; George Eastman vis prof, Oxford Univ, 80-81. **HONORS AND AWARDS** Nat Bk Awd 63; dhl, washington col, md, 75, lawrence univ, 77, ri col, 78 & swarthmore col, 79; dsc, chicago med col, 77; dl, franklin col, 80. **MEMBERSHIPS** AHA; Am Acad Arts & Sci; Am Philos Soc; Asn Comp Hist & Law. **RESEARCH** Universal history; contemporary history; modern Greek and Balkan history. **SELECTED PUBLICATIONS** Auth, Venice, The Einge of Europe, 1081-1797, Univ Chicago Press, 74; The Shape of European History, Oxford Univ Press, 74; The Contemporary World, 1914-present, World Civilization Series, rev ed, 1/75; Plagues and Peoples, Doubleday & Basil Blackwell, England, 76; ed, Human Migration, Patterns and Policies, Ind Univ Press, 78; auth, Metamorphosis of Greece Since World War II, Univ Chicago Press, 78; A World History, Oxford Univ Press, 79; The Human Condition, Princeton Univ Press, 80. **CONTACT ADDRESS** Dept of Hist, Univ of Chicago, 1126 E 59th St, Chicago, IL 60637.

MCNUTT, JAMES CHARLES
PERSONAL Born 08/10/1950, Denison, TX, m, 1971, 2 children **DISCIPLINE** AMERICAN STUDIES, FOLKLORE **EDUCATION** Harvard Univ, BA, 72; Univ Tex, Austin, MA, 77, PhD(Am civilization), 82. **CAREER** Asst instr Am studies, Univ Tex, Austin, 80-82; res assoc, Univ Tex, San Antonio; asst prof, Thomas More Col. **MEMBERSHIPS** Am Studies Asn; Am Folklore Soc. **RESEARCH** Regionalism. **SELECTED PUBLICATIONS** Auth, Mark Twain and the American Indian: Earthly realism & heavenly idealism, Am Indian Quart, 8/78; John Comfort Fillmore: A student of Indian music reconsidered, Am Music. **CONTACT ADDRESS** Dept of Hist, Thomas More Col, 333 Thomas More Pkwy, Crestview Hills, KY 41017. **EMAIL** james.mcnutt@thomasmore.edu

MCNUTT, PAULA M.
PERSONAL Born 03/12/1955, Denver, CO, s **DISCIPLINE** HEBREW BIBLE, ANTHROPOLOGY AND ARCHAEOLOGY **EDUCATION** Univ Colorado, BA, 78; Univ Montana, MA, 83; Vanderbilt Univ, PhD, 89. **CAREER** Prof, Canisius Col, 87-. **HONORS AND AWARDS** NEH Fel for Col Tchr, 94-95. **MEMBERSHIPS** Amer Acad Relig; Soc Bibl Lit, Cath Bibl Asn, Amer Sch Oriental Res, Archaeol Inst Amer **RESEARCH** Social world of ancient Israel; social roles and statuses of artisans; religion and technology. **SELECTED PUBLICATIONS** Reconstructing the Society of Ancient Israel, Libr of Ancient Israel Series, Louisville, Westminster John Knox Press, 99; The Kenites, the Midianites, and the Rechabites as Marginal Mediators in Ancient Israelite Tradition, Semeia 67, p 109-132, 94; coauth with James W. Flanagan, David W. McCreery and Khair Yassin, Preliminary Report of the 1993 Excavations at Tell Nimrin, Jordan, Ann of the Dept of Antiquities of Jordan, XXXVIII, pp 205-244, 94; Kenites, P. 407 in The Oxford Companion to the Bible, Bruce M. Metzger and Michael D. Coogan eds, Oxford Univ Press, 93; The Development

and Adoption of Iron Technology in the Ancient Near East, Proceedings: The Eastern Great Lakes Biblical Society, 12, pp 47-66, 92; The African Ironsmith as Marginal Mediator: A Symbolic Analysis, Journ of Ritual Studies, 5/2, pp 75-98, 91; The Forging of Israel: Iron Technology, Symbolism, and Tradition in Ancient Society, The Social World of Biblical Antiquity Series, 8, Sheffield, Almond Press, 90; Sociology of the Old Testament, pp 835-839, Mercer Dict of the Bible, Macon, GA, Mercer Univ Press, 90; Egypt as an Iron Furnace: A Metaphor of Transformation, pp 293-301, Society of Biblical Literature 1988 Seminar Papers, David J. Lull ed, Atlanta, Schol Press, 88; Interpreting Ancient Israel's Fold Traditions, Journ for the Study of the Old Testament, 39, pp 44-52, 87. **CONTACT ADDRESS** Canisius Col, 2001 Main St., Buffalo, NY 14208. **EMAIL** mcnutt@canisius.edu

MCPHEE, SARAH
DISCIPLINE 17TH AND 18TH CENTURY ITALIAN ARCHITECTURE AND URBANISM **EDUCATION** Columbia Univ, PhD, 96. **CAREER** Archit, Emory Univ. **RESEARCH** Seventeenth and eighteenth century European archit, urbanism and drawings; hist of the book; artistic biog. **SELECTED PUBLICATIONS** Auth, Bernini's Bell Towers for St. Peter's: Architectural Competition at the Vatican; auth, "A new sketchbook by Filippo Juvarra," The Burlington Magazine, 93; auth, Drawings from the Drawings from the Roman Period 1704-1714, Part II, Edizioni dell'Elefante, Rome, 99. **CONTACT ADDRESS** Emory Univ, Atlanta, GA 30322-1950. **EMAIL** smcphee@emory.edu

MCPHERSON, JAMES ALAN
PERSONAL Born 09/16/1943, Savannah, GA, d, 1 child **DISCIPLINE** LITERATURE, HISTORY, LAW **EDUCATION** Morris Brown Col, BA, 65; Harvard Law School, LLB, 68; Writers Workshop, Univ IA, MFA, 71. **CAREER** Lect, Univ CA at Santa Cruz, 69-71; asst prof, Morgan State Univ, 75-76; assoc prof, Univ VA, 76-81; prof, Univ IA, 81-. **HONORS AND AWARDS** Pulitzer Prize, 78; MacArthur Prize Fellows Award, 81. **MEMBERSHIPS** ACLU; NAACP; Authors Guild; Am Acad of Arts and Scis; fel, Ctr for Advanced Studies, Stanford Univ, 97-98. **RESEARCH** Law. **SELECTED PUBLICATIONS** Auth, Hue and Cry, 69; auth, Railroad, 73; auth, Elbow Room, 77; auth, Crabcakes, 98; Fatherly Daughter, 98. **CONTACT ADDRESS** Dept of English, The Univ of Iowa, Iowa City, IA 52242.

MCPHERSON, JAMES MUNRO
PERSONAL Born 10/11/1936, Valley City, ND, m, 1957, 1 child **DISCIPLINE** AMERICAN HISTORY **EDUCATION** Gustavus Adolphus Col, BA, 58; Johns Hopkins Univ, PhD(hist), 63. **CAREER** From instr to assoc prof, 62-72, prof hist, 72-82, Edwards prof Am hist, 82-91, DAVIS PROF AM HIST, PRINCETON UNIV, 91-; Commonwealth Fund Lectr Am Hist, Univ Col London, 82; Fel Proctor & Gamble Fdn, 64-65; NEH 67-68; Guggenheim Fdn, 67-68; Huntington Libr, 77-78, 87-88, 95-96; Stanford Ctr Advan Study Behav Sci, 82-83; Rollins Fdn, 91-92. **HONORS AND AWARDS** Anisfield-Wolf Awd, 65, Pulitzer Prize, 89; Lincoln Prize, 98; six honorary degrees; Jefferson lectr, 00. **MEMBERSHIPS** AHA; Orgn Am Historians; Southern Hist Asn; Soc Am Historians; Am Phil Soc. **RESEARCH** Civil War and Reconstruction; slavery and antislavery; United States Reconstruction to World War I. **SELECTED PUBLICATIONS** auth, The Struggle for Equality, 64; auth, The Negro's Civil War, 65; auth, The Abolitionist Legacy from Reconstruction to the NAACP, Princeton Univ, 75; auth, Ordeal by Fire: The Civil War and Reconstruction, Knopf, 82, 92, 01; Batle Cry of Freedom: The Civil War Era, 88; auth, Abraham Lincoln and the Second American Revolution, 91; auth, Drawn with the Sword: Reflections on the American Civil War, 96; auth, For Cause and Comrades: Why Men Fought in the Civil War, 97; ed, Lamson of the Gettysburg: The Civil War Letters of Roswell H. Lamson, U.S. Navy, 97; ed, Writing the Civil War: The Quest to Understand, 98; auth, Is Blood Thicker Than Water? Crises of Nationalism in the Modern World, 98. **CONTACT ADDRESS** Dept Hist, Princeton Univ, Princeton, NJ 08544.

MCQUAID, KIM
PERSONAL Born 11/02/1947, Boothbay, ME **DISCIPLINE** AMERICAN HISTORY, ECONOMIC HISTORY **EDUCATION** Antioch Col, BA, 70; Northwestern Univ, MA, 73, PhD, 75. **CAREER** Asst prof hist, Lake Erie Col, 77- **HONORS AND AWARDS** Woodrow Wilson Fel, 70; Marv Ball Wash Prof Am Hist, Univ Col Dublin, 85-86; Fulbright Overseas Teaching Awd, Malaysia, 95-96. **MEMBERSHIPS** Econ Hist Asn; Bus Hist Conf; Soc Hist Technol; Am Hist Asn. **RESEARCH** American economic history; 20th century American business; evolution of United States welfare policies; science, technology, and society. **SELECTED PUBLICATIONS** Coauth, Creating the Welfare State: The Political Economy of Twentieth Century Reform, Praeger Spec Studies, 80, rev ed, Univ Press Kans, 92; auth, The Roundtable: Getting Results in Washington, Harvard Bus Rev, 5-6/81; Big Business and Presidential Power: from Roosevelt to Reagan, William Morrow & Co, autumn 82; coauth, Bureaucrats as Social Engineers: Federal Welfare Programs in Herbert Hoover's America, Am J Econ & Sociol, 10/80; Welfare Reform in the 1950's, The Social Serv Rev, 3/80; auth, Big Business and Government Policy in Post-New Deal America: From Depression to Detente, Antitrust Law & Econ Rev, 79; Big Business and Public Policy in the Contemporary United States, Quart Rev Econ & Bus, summer 80; auth, The Anxious Years: America in the Vietnam-Watergate Era, Basic Books, 89; Uneasy Partners: Big Business in American Politics, 1945-1990, Johns Hopkins Univ Press, 94. **CONTACT ADDRESS** Lake Erie Col, 391 W Washington St, Painesville, OH 44077-3389.

MCSEVENEY, SAMUEL THOMPSON
PERSONAL Born 10/03/1930, New York, NY, m, 1958, 1 child **DISCIPLINE** RECENT AMERICAN HISTORY **EDUCATION** Brooklyn Col, BA, 51; Univ Conn, MA, 53; Univ Iowa, PhD(hist), 65. **CAREER** From instr to asst prof hist, Calif State Col Los Angeles, 60-66; from asst prof to assoc prof, Brooklyn Col, 66-72; ASSOC PROF HIST, VANDERBILT UNIV, 72-, Res grants, Nat Endowment for Humanities, 70-71. **HONORS AND AWARDS** Outstanding Prof Awd, Calif State Col Los Angeles, 66. **MEMBERSHIPS** AHA; Orgn Am Historians. **RESEARCH** American politics, 1850-1900. **SELECTED PUBLICATIONS** Auth, The Michigan gubernatorial campaign of 1938, Mich Hist, 6/61; The Politics of Depression: Political Behavior in the Northeast, 1892-1896, Oxford Univ, 72; co-ed, Voters, Elections, and Parties: Quantitative Essays in the History of American Popular Voting Behavior, 72 & auth, Voting in the Northeastern states during the late nineteenth century, In: Voters, Elections, and Parties, 72, Xerox Col; Ethnic groups, ethnic conflicts, and recent quantitative research in American political history, Int Migration Rev, spring 73. **CONTACT ADDRESS** Dept of Hist, Vanderbilt Univ, Nashville, TN 37240.

MCSHEA, WILLIAM PATRICK
PERSONAL Born 08/16/1930, Pittsburgh, PA, m, 1955, 3 children **DISCIPLINE** HISTORY, LATIN CLASSICS **EDUCATION** St Vincent Col, BA, 52; Duquesne Univ, MA, 54. **CAREER** From instr to assoc prof hist, Mt Mercy Col, 53-70; PROF & CHMN, DEPT HIST, CARLOW COL, 70-, DIR, PEACE STUDIES PROG, 76-, Prof, Comp Communism Consortia, var univs in Pa, 73-; mem adv coun, Int Poetry Forum, 77-. **MEMBERSHIPS** Int Soc Psycho Historians. **RESEARCH** Reformation; psycho history; recent American history. **SELECTED PUBLICATIONS** Coauth, Community of Learners, Pittsburgh Pa Com Press, 70. **CONTACT ADDRESS** Carlow Col, 3333 Fifth Ave, Pittsburgh, PA 15213.

MCSHEFFREY, SHANNON
DISCIPLINE HISTORY **EDUCATION** Carleton Univ, BA; Univ Toronto, MA, PhD. **CAREER** Assoc prof. **RESEARCH** Gender, marriage, literacy, heresy, and popular religion in late medieval England. **SELECTED PUBLICATIONS** Auth, Gender and Heresy: Women and Men in Lollard Communities, 1420-1530, Univ Pa Press, 95; Love and Marriage in Late Medieval London, Medieval Inst Publ, 95. **CONTACT ADDRESS** Dept of Hist, Concordia Univ, Montreal, 1455 de Maisonneuve W, Montreal, QC, Canada H3G 1M8. **EMAIL** mcsheff@vax2.concordia.ca

MCTAGUE, ROBERT
PERSONAL Born 01/10/1968, Charleston, SC, m, 1995 **DISCIPLINE** HISTORY **EDUCATION** Loyola Univ, BA, 90; Drew Univ, MA, 93, MPhil, 96, PhD, 99. **CAREER** Hist adj, Essex Commun Col, 93; tchg asst, Drew Univ, 94-95; hist adj, Kean Univ, 94; hist adj, William Paterson Univ, 97; hist adj, 95-97, hist lectr, 98- , Fairleigh Dickinson Univ. **MEMBERSHIPS** Am Hist Asn. **RESEARCH** European intellectual history; Europe 1789-present; American political history; American intellectual history. **SELECTED PUBLICATIONS** Auth, Modern Physics, Kandinsky, and Klee, The European Legacy, 97; rev, The Land Arms Race and World War II, J of Conflict Stud, 98; rev of Ron Arnold's Ecoterror: The Violent Agenda to Save Nature: The World of the Unabomber, J of Conflict Studies, 99. **CONTACT ADDRESS** Dept of Social Sciences & History, Fairleigh Dickinson Univ, Florham-Madison, 285 Madison Ave, Madison, NJ 07940.

MCVAUGH, MICHAEL ROGERS
PERSONAL Born 12/09/1938, Washington, DC, m, 1961 **DISCIPLINE** HISTORY OF MEDICINE, MEDIEVAL HISTORY **EDUCATION** Harvard Univ, AB, 60; Princeton Univ, MA, 62; PhD, 65. **CAREER** From asst prof to prof, 64-96; Nat Sci Found fel & Mem, Sch Hist Studies, Inst Advan Study, 68-69; Guggenheim Fel 81-82; Wells Prof of Hist, Univ NC-Chapel Hill, 96-. **HONORS AND AWARDS** Welch Medal, Am Assoc Hist Med, 94; Garrison Lect, Am Assoc Hist Med, 96; corresp memb Acad Internat Hist Sci, 97. **MEMBERSHIPS** Am Assoc Hist Med, Hist Sci Society, Medieval Acad Am. **RESEARCH** Medieval and early modern medicine and surgery; Arabic-Latin scientific translations. **SELECTED PUBLICATIONS** Co-ed, Arnaldi de Villanova Opera Medica Omnia (11 vols.), 75-; auth, Medicine before the Plague: Practitioners and their Patients in the Crown of Aragon, 1285-1345, Cambridge Univ Pr, 93; Inventarium sive Chirurgia magna Guigonis de Caulhiaco, 97. **CONTACT ADDRESS** Dept of Hist, Univ of No Carolina, Chapel Hill, CB 3195, Chapel Hill, NC 27599-3195. **EMAIL** mcvaugh@email.unc.edu

MCWILLIAMS, TENNANT S.
PERSONAL Born 09/12/1943, Birmingham, AL, m, 1975, 1 child **DISCIPLINE** AMERICAN HISTORY **EDUCATION** Birmingham-Southern Col, AB, 65; Univ Ala, MA, 67; Univ Ga, PhD(hist), 73. **CAREER** Instr Am lit, Walker Col, 67-68, instr Am hist, 68-69; teaching fel, Univ Ga, 69-73; asst prof, Tidewater Col, 73-74; asst prof, 74-78, ASSOC PROF HIST, UNIV ALA, BIRMINGHAM, 78-, CHMN DEPT, 81-. **MEMBERSHIPS** Southern Hist Asn; Am Hist Asn. **RESEARCH** Recent America; American diplomatic history; Southern history. **SELECTED PUBLICATIONS CONTACT ADDRESS** Dept of Hist, Univ of Alabama, Birmingham, 1530 3rd Ave S, Birmingham, AL 35294-0001.

MEACHAM, STANDISH
PERSONAL Born 03/12/1932, Cincinnati, OH, d, 3 children **DISCIPLINE** MODERN ENGLISH HISTORY **EDUCATION** Yale Univ, BA, 54; Harvard Univ, PhD(hist), 61- **CAREER** From instr to asst prof hist, Harvard Univ, 61-67; assoc prof, 67-70, chmn dept, 69-72, 84-88, PROF HIST, UNIV TEX, AUSTIN, 70-98, Am Coun Learned Soc fel, 65-66, 79-80; Guggenheim fel, 72-73; Dean, Col of Liberal Arts, Univ of TX, 89-91. **HONORS AND AWARDS** Sheffield Centennial Prof of History, 89-98. **RESEARCH** Nineteenth century English church history; modern English labor history. **SELECTED PUBLICATIONS** Auth, Henry Thornton of Clapham, 1760-1815, 64; auth, Lord and Bishop: The Life of Samuel Wilberforce, 70; auth, A Life Apart: The English Working Class, 1890-1914, 77; auth, Western Civilizations, with Robert Lerner, Norton, 80; auth, Toynbee Hall and Social Reform, 1880-1914, 87; auth, Regaining Paradise: Englishness and The Early Garden City Movement, 99. **CONTACT ADDRESS** Dept of Hist, Univ of Texas, Austin, 0 Univ of Texas, Austin, TX 78712.

MEAD, CHRISTOPHER CURTIS
PERSONAL Born 04/30/1953, New Haven, CT, m, 1990 **DISCIPLINE** HISTORY OF ART & ARCHITECTURE **EDUCATION** Univ CA, Riverside, BA (summa cum laude), 75; Univ PA, MA, 78, PhD, 86. **CAREER** To full prof with joint appointment in Dept of Art & Art History and School of Architecture & Planning, Univ NM, 80-. **HONORS AND AWARDS** Phi Beta Kappa, 75; Penfield Res Scholarship, 78-79; Samuel H Kress Advanced Res fel, 88; Burlington Resources Found Fac Achievement Awd, 92. **MEMBERSHIPS** Pres., Soc of Architectural Historians, 00-02. **RESEARCH** History of architecture and urbanism in Europe and North America 1750-present. **SELECTED PUBLICATIONS** Auth, Space for the Continuous Present in the Residential Architecture of Bart Prince, Univ NM Art Museum, 89; ed, with an intro to, The Architecture of Robert Venturi, Univ NM Press, 89; Houses by Bart Prince, An American Architecture for the Continuous Present, Univ NM Pres, 91; Charles Garnier's Paris Opera: Architectural Empathy and the Renaissance of French Classicism, The Architectural Hist Found/ MIT press, 91; Shinen'kan, A Collaboration in L A, Cite, fall 92-winter 93; Urban Contingency and the Problem of Representation in Second Empire Paris, J of the Soc of Architectural Historians, LIV, no 2, June 95; The Architecture of Bart Prince: A Pragmatics of Place, W W Norton, 99. **CONTACT ADDRESS** Dept of Art & Art Hist, Univ of New Mexico, Albuquerque, Albuquerque, NM 98131. **EMAIL** ccmead@unm.edu

MEADE, CATHERINE M.
PERSONAL Born Boston, MA **DISCIPLINE** AMERICAN HISTORY **EDUCATION** Regis Col, AB, 54; Boston Col, PhD(hist), 72. **CAREER** Instr, 67-72, asst prof, 72-74, dean freshmen, 76-80, ASSOC PROF HIST, REGIS COL, 74-, CHMN, HIST DEPT, 81- **MEMBERSHIPS** AHA; Orgn Am Historians; Nat Women's Studies Asn. **RESEARCH** Social and intellectual history; woman's history; American culture and architecture; medieval history; medieval women. **SELECTED PUBLICATIONS** Auth, My Nature is Fire: Catherine of Siena, Alba House, 91. **CONTACT ADDRESS** Dept of History, Regis Col, Massachusetts, 235 Wellesley St, Weston, MA 02193-1505. **EMAIL** catherine.meade@regiscollege.edu

MEADE, DENIS
PERSONAL Born 10/16/1930, Des Moines, IA **DISCIPLINE** THEOLOGY, CHURCH HISTORY **EDUCATION** St Benedict's Col, Kans, AB, 52; Pontif Univ St Anselmo, Rome, STL, 56; Pontif Lateran Univ, JCD, 60. **CAREER** From instr to asst prof theol, 60-71, assoc prof, 71-80, prof relig Studies, Benedictine Col, 80-. **MEMBERSHIPS** Canon Law Soc Am; Federation Catholic Schs. **RESEARCH** Medieval monastic history: moral theology. **SELECTED PUBLICATIONS** Auth, From Turmoil to Solidarity: The Emergence of the Vallumbrosan Monastic Congregation, Am Benedictine Rev, 68. **CONTACT ADDRESS** Dept of Religious Studies, Benedictine Col, 1020 N 2nd St, Atchison, KS 66002-1499. **EMAIL** dmeade@benedictine.edu

MEADE, WADE C.
DISCIPLINE HISTORY **EDUCATION** La Tech Univ, BS, 59, MS, 61; Univ TX at Austin, 69. **CAREER** Asst and instr geol, 60-61, asst prof hist,67-70, assoc prof hist and archaeol, 70-76, prof hist and archaeol, La Tech Univ, 76-; hist asst, Univ TX at Austin, 64-66; geog instr, 65-66, hist and anthrop instr,

SW TX state Univ, 66. **HONORS AND AWARDS** Outstanding Research Awd for Col of Arts & Sci(s), La Tech Univ, 80-81. **MEMBERSHIPS** Am Asn Univ Prof; Am Hist Asn; Archaeol Inst Am; Class Asn Midwest & South; Class Soc Am Acad Rome; Int Asn Class Archaeol; Soc Prom Roman Studies; Soc Pressional Archeol; Soc Vertebrate Paleontol; SW Soc Sci Asn; Vergilian Soc. **RESEARCH** Rome hist; Near East hist; Greece; and Roman hist; Etruscan, Greek, Egyptian, and Indian Archeol. **SELECTED PUBLICATIONS** Auth, Road to Babylon, 74; auth, Handbook of Egyptian Archaeology, 75; auth, Ruins of Rome, 80; auth, Rome and Egyptology, 87. **CONTACT ADDRESS** Dept of Hist, Louisiana Tech Univ, PO Box 3178, Ruston, LA 71272. **EMAIL** caesar@latech.edu

MEADERS, DANIEL
DISCIPLINE HISTORY **EDUCATION** CUNY, Staten island, BA, 74; Yale Univ, MA, 79; PhD, 90. **CAREER** Asst prof, William Paterson State Col, 91- & adj prof, 91; adj prof, Manhattan Community Cole, NY City, 91; assoc ed, Frederick Douglass Papers, Yale Univ, 89-90 & res asst, 86-89. **HONORS AND AWARDS** Woodrow Wilson-Martin Luther King, fel, 74. **SELECTED PUBLICATIONS** Auth, South Carolina Fugitives as Viewed Through Local Colonial Newspapers with Emphasis on Runaway Notices, 1732-1801, J Negro Hist, 76; Dead or Alive: Fugitive Slaves and White Indentured Servants before 1830, Garland, 93. **CONTACT ADDRESS** Dept of History, William Paterson Col of New Jersey, 300 Pompton Rd., Wayne, NJ 07470. **EMAIL** meaders@frontier.wilpaterson.edu

MEARS, JOHN A.
PERSONAL Born 01/26/1938, St. Paul, MN, m, 1960, 2 children **DISCIPLINE** EARLY MODERN EUROPEAN HISTORY **EDUCATION** Univ Minn, BA, 60; Univ Chicago, MA, 62, PhD(hist), 64. **CAREER** Asst prof hist, NMex State Univ, 64-67; asst prof, 67-70, Assoc Prof Hist, Southern Methodist Univ, 70-. **HONORS AND AWARDS** Pres, World History Assoc, 94-95. **MEMBERSHIPS** AHA; Conf Group Cent Europ Hist; World History Assoc. **RESEARCH** Seventeenth century Germany, especially the Habsburg monarchy; seventeenth-century European military history; comparative revolutions. **SELECTED PUBLICATIONS** Auth, Teaching World History, Armonk, NY: M.E. Sharpe, Inc., 96, 81-84; auth, The Thirty Years War, the General Crisis, and the Origins of a Standing Professional Army in the Habsburg Monarchy, Central European History, Vol. 21, No. 2 , (88), 122-141; auth, Politics and War, Amer Hist Rev, vol 0099, 94; World Historians and Their Goals, J World Hist, vol 0005, 94; European Warfare 1660-1815, Amer Hist Rev, vol 0101, 96; Holland and the Dutch Republic in the 17th-Century, Historian, vol 0058, 96; ed., Integrating Prehistory into Humanity's Common Past, in Heidi Roupp; auth, Methodolical Considerations for the Comparative Study of Civilizations, Comparative Civilizations Review, No 34, (96), 1-10. **CONTACT ADDRESS** Dept of Hist, So Methodist Univ, P O Box 750001, Dallas, TX 75275-0001. **EMAIL** jmears@mail.smu.edu

MECKLER, MICHAEL LOUIS
PERSONAL Born 03/31/1965, Columbus, OH **DISCIPLINE** HISTORY **EDUCATION** Princeton, BA, 87; Chicago, AM, 88; Mich, PhD, 94. **CAREER** Asst Ed, J of Roman Achaeol, 92-93; Vis Asst Prof, Univ of Mich, 95; Lectr/Vis Fel, Yale Univ, 95-97; Lectr, Univ of Conn, 97; Vis Asst Prof, Union Col, 97-98; Vis Asst Prof, Ohio State Univ, 98-. **MEMBERSHIPS** Am Philol Asn, Am Hist Asn, Celtic Studies Asn of N Am, Asn of Ancient Historians, Soc for Promotion of Roman Studies, Medieval Latin Studies Group. **RESEARCH** Classic and medieval Latin, Roman imperial, Late antique and early medieval history, Celtic studies. **CONTACT ADDRESS** Dept of Greek and Latin, Ohio State Univ, Columbus, 230 N Oval Mall, Columbus, OH 43210-1319. **EMAIL** meckler.12@osu.edu

MEERBOTE, RALF
PERSONAL Born 05/08/1942, Merseburg, Germany **DISCIPLINE** HISTORY OF MODERN PHILOSOPHY **EDUCATION** Univ Chicago, BS, 64; Harvard Univ, MA, 67, PhD(philos), 70. **CAREER** Asst prof philos, Univ Ill, Chicago Circle, 69-73, assoc prof, 73-80; Assoc Prof Philos, Univ Rochester, 80-, Fulbright sr res fel, 76-77; Prof philos, Univ of Rochester, 93-. **MEMBERSHIPS** Am Philos Asn; Kantgesellschaft, North Am Kent Soc. **RESEARCH** Kant's metaphysics and theory of knowledge; theory of knowledge; aesthetics. **SELECTED PUBLICATIONS** Auth, The unknowability of things in themselves, Proc Int Kant Cong, Holland, 72; Kant's use of the notions of objective validity and objective reality, Kant Studien, 72; The distinction between derivative and non-derivative knowledge, Philos Studies, 73; Erkenntnisvorschriften, Akten des 4 Int Kant Kongresses, de Gruyter, Berlin, 74; Fallibilism and the possibility of being mistaken, Philos Studies, 77; Radical Failure, Grazer Philos Studien, 78; Kant on Intuitivity, Synthese, 81; auth, Kant's Funchionalism, in Historical Foundations of Cognitive Science Reidel Dondrecht, 89; auth, The Singularity of Pure Judgments of Fasle, in Kant's Aesthetics, deGrytec, Berlin, 98; auth, Kant, in a Companion to the Philosophers, Blackwell, Oxford, 99. **CONTACT ADDRESS** Dept of Philosophy, Univ of Rochester, Rochester, NY 14627.

MEHLER, BARRY ALAN
PERSONAL Born 03/18/1947, Brooklyn, NY, m, 1979, 1 child **DISCIPLINE** AMERICAN HISTORY **EDUCATION** Yeshiva Univ, BA, 70; City Col, MA, 72; Univ Ill, PhD, 88. **CAREER** Instr, Wash Univ, 77; res assoc, Nat Hist Found, 80; Instr, Univ Ill, 81-88; instr, 88-90; asst prof, 90-93; assoc prof, 94-. **HONORS AND AWARDS** Grant-in-Aid, Rockefeller found, 77; Joseph Ward Swain prize, Univ Ill, 84; Babcock fel, Univ Ill, 85-86; fac devel grant, 88; instructional develop grant, 88; Ferris State Bd Ctrl Cert of Recognition, 94; founder, exec dir, isar. **RESEARCH** History of science, behavior-genetic analysis, history of racism. **SELECTED PUBLICATIONS** Auth, In Genes We Trust: When Science Bows to Racism, Reform Judaism, 94; rev, republ, The Pub Eye, 95, RaceFile, 95; Networking: A Publication of the Fight The Right Network, 95; Israel Diary, 1996, Israel Horizons, 96; Heredity and Hereditarianism, Philos Education: An Encyclopedia, Garland Publ, 96; Beyondism: Raymond B. Cattell and the New Eugenics, Genetica, 97. **CONTACT ADDRESS** Dept of Hum, Ferris State Univ, 901 S State St, Big Rapids, MI 49307. **EMAIL** bmehler@netonecom.net

MEHLINGER, HOWARD DEAN
PERSONAL Born 08/22/1931, Hillsboro, KS, m, 1952, 3 children **DISCIPLINE** MODERN RUSSIAN HISTORY **EDUCATION** McPherson Col, AB, 53; Univ Kans, MS, 59, PhD(hist), 64. **CAREER** High sch teacher, Kans, 53-63; co-dir social studies curric develop ctr, Pittsburgh Pub Schs, 63-64; asst dir, NCent Asn Schs and Cols Foreign Rels Proj, 64-65; asst prof hist, 65-70, assoc prof hist and educ, 70-74, dep chmn inter-univ comt on travel grants, 65-66, dir high sch curric ctr govt, 66-71, PROF HIST and EDUC, IND UNIV, BLOOMINGTON, 74-, DIR SOCIAL STUDIES DEVELOP CTR, 68-, DEAN, SCH EDUC, 81-, Consult social studies curric ctr, Northwestern Univ, 64-65; dir, Educ Prof Develop Assistance Civics Dissemination Inst, 69-70; co-dir, Social Studies Field Agt Training Proj, 70-73; Am Polit Sci Asn polit sci course mem, 72-77; pres, Nat Coun Social Studies, 77. **MEMBERSHIPS** Am Educ Res Asn; Am Polit Sci Asn; Am Asn Advan Slavic Studies; Asn Supv and Curric Develop; Nat Coun Social Studies. **RESEARCH** Russian revolution of 1905; instructional development. **SELECTED PUBLICATIONS** Auth, Soviet Education Under Perestroika, Slavic Rev, Vol 53, 94. **CONTACT ADDRESS** 3606 Park Lane, Bloomington, IN 47401. **EMAIL** mehlinge@indiana.edu

MEIER, AUGUST
PERSONAL Born 04/20/1923, New York, NY **DISCIPLINE** AMERICAN NEGRO STUDIES **EDUCATION** Oberlin Col, AB, 45; Columbia Univ, AM, 48, PhD, 57. **CAREER** Asst prof hist, Tougaloo Col, 45-49; asst prof, Fisk Univ, 53-56, asst to pres, 53-54; from asst prof to assoc prof hist, Morgan State Col, 57-64; prof, Roosevelt Univ, 64-67; UNIV PROF HIST, KENT STATE UNIV, 67-, Ed, Negro in Am Life Ser, Atheneum, 66-74; Guggenheim fel, 71-72; GEN ED, SER ON BLACKS IN NEW WORLD, UNIV ILL PRESS, 72-; Nat Endowment for Humanities fel, 75-76; Ctr for Advan Studies Behav Sci fel, 76-77. **MEMBERSHIPS** Am Anthrop Asn; Am Studies Asn; Southern Hist Asn; Asn Study Negro Life and Hist; Orgn Am Historians. **SELECTED PUBLICATIONS** Co-ed, Negro Protest Thought in the Twentieth Century, 66, rev ed, Black Protest Thought in the Twentieth Century, 71 & Black Nationalism in America, 70, Bobbs; coauth, From Plantation to Ghetto, Hill & Wang, 66 & 76; co-ed, The Making of Black America, Atheneum, 69; The Transformation of Activism, Aldine, 70, rev ed, 73; coauth, CORE; a Study in the Civil Rights Movement, 1942-1968, Oxford Univ, 73; Along the Color Line, Univ Ill, 76; Black Detroit and the Rise of the UAW, Oxford Univ Press, 79. **CONTACT ADDRESS** Dept of Hist, Kent State Univ, Kent, OH 44242.

MEIKLE, JEFFREY L.
PERSONAL Born 07/02/1949, Columbus, OH, m, 2 children **DISCIPLINE** HISTORY **EDUCATION** Brown Univ, AB, 71; AM, 71; Univ of Tex at Austin, PhD, 77. **CAREER** Instr, Colby-Sawyer Col, 77-78; from asst prof to prof & chair, 79-. **HONORS AND AWARDS** NHPRC Fel, Peale Family Papers, Nat Portrait Gallery, 78-79; Sr Getty Res Grant, 89-90; Sr Fulbright Prof, Univ of London, 92-93; ACLS Fel, 95-96; Dexter Prize, Soc for the Hist of Technol, 96. **MEMBERSHIPS** Am Studies Asn, Orgn of Am Historians, Soc for the Hist of Technol, Design Hist Soc. **RESEARCH** 19th & 20th-century US cultural history, history of technology, history of design. **SELECTED PUBLICATIONS** Auth, Twentieth Century Limited: Industrial Design in America, 1925-1939, Temple Univ Press, 79; auth, American Plastic: A Cultural History, Rutgers Univ Press, 95. **CONTACT ADDRESS** Dept of Am Studies, Univ of Texas, Austin, 303 Garrison Hall, Austin, TX 78712-1013. **EMAIL** meikle@mail.utexas.edu

MEISEL, JANET ANNE
PERSONAL Born 01/30/1944, Dallas, TX **DISCIPLINE** MEDIEVAL ENGLISH & FRENCH HISTORY **EDUCATION** Oberlin Col, AB, 67; Univ Calif, Berkeley, MA, 71; PhD(Hist) 74. **CAREER** Asst prof, 74-81, assoc prof Hist, Univ Tex, Austin, 81-, Am Coun Learned Soc fel Hist, 77. **MEMBERSHIPS** AHA; Mediaeval Acad Am. **RESEARCH** Medieval frontier societies; medieval law; medieval nobilities. **SELECTED PUBLICATIONS** Auth, Barons of the Welsh Frontier: The Corbet, Pantulf, and Fitzwarin Families, 1066-1272, Univ Nebr Press, 80. **CONTACT ADDRESS** Dept of History, Univ of Texas, Austin, Austin, TX 78712-1026. **EMAIL** jmeisel@mail.utexas.edu

MEISSE, TOM
DISCIPLINE GEOGRAPHY, SOCIOLOGY **EDUCATION** Wayne State Univ, PhD. **CAREER** Adj Prof, Eastern Mich Univ; Adj Prof, Univ of Detroit; Dir of Res, US Dept of Housing Urban Develop, Mich. **HONORS AND AWARDS** Smithsonian Fel; Departmental Secretarial Citation. **RESEARCH** Urban studies, Entrepreneurship, Economic development, US, Middle East, Caribbean. **CONTACT ADDRESS** Dept Sociol, Univ of Detroit Mercy, PO Box 19900, Detroit, MI 48219.

MEISTER, MAUREEN
PERSONAL Born 08/25/1953, Spokane, WA, m, 1979, 2 children **DISCIPLINE** ART AND ARCHITECTURAL HISTORIAN **EDUCATION** Mt. Holyoke, AB, 75; Univ Pittsburgh, BA, 80; Brown Univ, AM, 83; Ph.D., 00. **CAREER** Visiting lectr, fall 85, Sch of the Museum of Fine Arts; lectr, fall 89, Northeastern Univ; visiting lectr, spring 98, Tufts Univ; instr, 82-86, adjunct asst prof, 86-91, assoc prof, 91-present, Art Inst of Boston. **HONORS AND AWARDS** Newspaper Fund award, 74; Univ Fel, Brown Univ, 80-81; Graham Found grant to edit symposium papers on HH Richardson for publication. **MEMBERSHIPS** Soc of Architectural Historians; Coll Art Assn; Soc of Architectural Historians-New England chapter, Victorian Soc in Amer; Gibson House Museum (past president), Winchester Historical Soc (dir and ed of architects series). **RESEARCH** 19th and early 20th century art and architecture. **SELECTED PUBLICATIONS** Auth, weekly exhibition reviews and interviews with artists, 77-79; Sulpturescape, Art News, Feb 78; Coauth, All the Banners Wave: Art and War in the Romantic Era, 82; Ed, The Architects of Winchester, Massachusetts, Winchester Historical Society, Winchester, MA, 94; Auth, Rand & Taylor, A Biographical Dictionary of Architects in Maine, Architects in Maine, 95; The Selling of Winslow Homer, Visual Resources: An International Journal of Documentation, 97; Rangeley: A Romantic Residential Park in Winchester, Massachusetts, Antiques, 97; **CONTACT ADDRESS** 38 Rangeley Rd., Winchester, MA 01890. **EMAIL** meisterm@interserv.com

MEISTER, MICHAEL WILLIAM
PERSONAL Born 08/20/1942, West Palm Beach, FL, m, 1970 **DISCIPLINE** HISTORY OF ART **EDUCATION** Harvard Univ, BA, 64, MA, 72, PhD, 74; Univ Pa, MA, 79. **CAREER** Asst prof hist art, Univ Tex, Austin, 74-76; asst prof hist art and SAsia studies, 76-79, assoc prof, Univ Pa, 79-; Ed, Encycl Indian Temple Archit. **MEMBERSHIPS** Asn Asian Studies; Am Comt SAsian Art; SAsian Relig Art Studies; Col Art Asn; Univ Res Club. **RESEARCH** South Asian architecture, particularly the Hindu temple; Indian sculpture, questions of style and idiom; icons and narrative in Indian imagery. **CONTACT ADDRESS** Hist of Art Dept, Univ of Pennsylvania, Philadelphia, PA 19104. **EMAIL** mmeister@sas.upenn.edu

MELANCON, MICHAEL S.
PERSONAL Born 09/06/1940, New Orleans, LA, s **DISCIPLINE** HISTORY **EDUCATION** Loyola Univ, BA, 71; Indiana Univ, MA, 75, PhD, 85. **CAREER** Vis asst prof, NMex State Univ, 81-83; vis asst prof, Univ Haw, 83-84; asst prof, Auburn Univ, 84-90, assoc prof, 90-2000. **HONORS AND AWARDS** IREX Res Fels, 77-78, 90-91; Fulbright Fel, 77-78. **MEMBERSHIPS** Am Hist Asn, Am Asn for the Advancement of Slavic Studies, Southern Slavic Asn. **RESEARCH** 19th and 20th century Russian and European history. **SELECTED PUBLICATIONS** Auth, The Socialist Revolutionaries and the Russian Anti-War Movement, 1914-1917, Columbus, Ohio: Ohio State Univ Press (90); author of numerous articles and reviews. **CONTACT ADDRESS** Dept Hist, Auburn Univ, Auburn, AL 36849-2900. **EMAIL** melanms@mail.auburn.edu

MELENDEZ, GABRIEL
DISCIPLINE AMERICAN STUDIES **EDUCATION** Univ NMex, PhD, 84. **CAREER** Assoc Prof, Res Assoc, Ctr for Reg Stud, Univ NMex; BD, Acad/El Norte Publ; Res Assoc, Southwest Hisp Res Inst. **HONORS AND AWARDS** Rockefeller Hum Fel, 91; Ctr for Reg Stud Grant, 92; Sr Res Fel, NMex Endowment for Hum, 93. **MEMBERSHIPS** Nat Asn for Chicano Stud; Am Stud Asn. **RESEARCH** Chicano/Latino culture, Film, Biography, Ethnopoetics, Literary Discourse, the Politics of Identity and all aspects of Hispanic Southwest culture **SELECTED PUBLICATIONS** Auth, So All is Not Lost: The Poetics of Print in Nuevomexicano Communities, 1834-1950, UNM Press, 97; coauth, Reflexiones del Corazon, 93. **CONTACT ADDRESS** Univ of New Mexico, Albuquerque, Albuquerque, NM 87131. **EMAIL** gabriel@unm.edu

MELENDY, HOWARD BRETT
PERSONAL Born 05/03/1924, Eureka, CA, m, 1952 **DISCIPLINE** HISTORY **EDUCATION** Stanford Univ, AB, 46, MA, 48, PhD(hist), 52. **CAREER** High sch teacher, Calif, 50-54;

instr hist, Fresno Jr Col, 54-55; from instr to prof, San Jose State Col, 55-70, head dept, 58-69, asst acad vpres, 68-70, actg acad vpres, 70; prof hist, Univ Hawaii, Manoa, 70-79; dean undergraduate studies, 79-81, PROF HIST, SAN JOSE STATE UNIV, 79-, ASSOC ACAD VPRES UNDERGRAD STUDIES, 81-, Reader Am hist, Educ Testing Serv, Princeton, NJ, 61-74; Am Philos Soc grants, 62 and 74; vis rep, Col Entrance Exam Bd, 65-66; fel, Am Coun Educ Acad Admin Internship Prog, 67-68; vpres, Community Cols, Univ Hawaii, 70-73; fel, Danforth Assoc, 74; Nat Endowment Humanities grant, 80-83. **MEMBERSHIPS** AHA; NEA; Am Asn Higher Educ. **RESEARCH** Asian immigration; West in twentieth century. **SELECTED PUBLICATIONS** Coauth, Governors of California, Talisman, 65; California's Discrimination against Filipinos, 1927-1935, Inst Asian Studies Proc, 68; Oriental Americans, Twayne, 72; auth, Filipinos in the United States, Pac Hist Rev, 74; Filipinos in the United States, In: The Asian American, Clio, 76; California's Discrimination Against Filipinos 1927-1935, In: Letters in Exile, USLA Asian Am Studies Ctr, 76; Asians in America, Twayne, 77; Filipinos, In: Harvard Encycl of American Ethnic Groups, Harvard Univ Press, 80; Filipino, Korean and Vietnamese Immigration to the United States, In: Contemporary American Immigration, Twayne, 81. **CONTACT ADDRESS** Dept of Hist, San Jose State Univ, San Jose, CA 95114.

MELI, DOMENICO BERTOLONI
DISCIPLINE HISTORY OF SCIENCE **EDUCATION** Pavia Univ, BA, 83; Cambridge Univ, PhD, 88. **CAREER** Assoc prof, Ind Univ. **HONORS AND AWARDS** Fel, Dibner Inst; res fel, Jesus Col, Cambridge; fel, Wellcome Trust. **RESEARCH** 16th to18th century mathematics and mechanics, medicine in the Scientific Revolution, Leibniz, Newton. **SELECTED PUBLICATIONS** Auth, Equivalence and Priority: Newton Versus Leibniz, Including Leibniz's Unpublished Manuscripts on the "Principia", Oxford, 93; The Relativization of Centrifugal Force, Isis, 90; Public Claims, Private Worries: Newton's Principia and Leibniz's Theory of Planetary Motion, 91; Guidobaldo dal Monte and the Archimedean Revival, Nuncius, 92; The Emergence of Reference Frames and the Transformation of Mechanics in the Enlightenment, 93; co-auth, Sphaera Mundi, 94; ed, Marcello Malpighi, Anatomist And Physician, Olschki, 97. **CONTACT ADDRESS** Dept of Hist and Philos of Sci, Indiana Univ, Bloomington, 1011 E Third St, 130 Goodbody Hall, Bloomington, IN 47405. **EMAIL** dbmeli@indiana.edu

MELLINI, PETER JOHN DREYFUS
PERSONAL Born 08/16/1935, Hermosa Beach, CA, m, 1977 **DISCIPLINE** MODERN EUROPEAN HISTORY **EDUCATION** Stanford Univ, BA, 62, MA, 65, PhD, 71. **CAREER** Tutor hist & polit, Stanford Univ; 66, instr hist, 68-70; asst prof, 70-73, assoc prof, 73-80, dir hist preserv prog, 75-80, prof hist, Sonoma State Univ, 80-; vis prof, San Francisco State Univ, 81; dir, Inst Hist Study, Victorian Soc, 80-82; lect Hist Jour, San Fran State Univ, 85-90. **HONORS AND AWARDS** NEH Fel, 83, 99-00; Fel Royal Hist Soc; Preserv Awd, Calif Coun Hist Soc, 80; NEH Jr Fel, 83; Sr Fel, 99-00. **MEMBERSHIPS** Conf Brit Studies; Nat Trust for Hist Preserv; Victorian Soc. **RESEARCH** Nineteenth and 20th century caricature and cartoons; British social history; National symbols; A biography of Punch. **SELECTED PUBLICATIONS** Auth, Sir Eldon Gorst: The Overshadowed Proconsul, Hoover, 77; coauth, (with K L Seavey), The rural field school: Jolon, California, Monterey Dept Parks, 79; auth 21 articles on Brit & Eur Hist coauth (with R T Matthews), In Vanity Fair, Scholar Press London & Univ Calif Berkeley, 82, 00. **CONTACT ADDRESS** Dept Hist, Sonoma State Univ, Rohnert Park, CA 94928-3609. **EMAIL** peter.mellini@sonoma.edu

MELLINK, MACHTELD JOHANNA
PERSONAL Born 10/26/1917, Amsterdam, Netherlands **DISCIPLINE** CLASSICAL AND NEAR EASTERN ARCHEOLOGY **EDUCATION** Univ Amsterdam, BA, 38, MA, 41; Univ Utrecht, PhD, 43. **CAREER** Field asst Tarsus excavations, Inst Advan Study, 47-49; from asst prof to assoc prof, 49-62, PROF CLASS ARCHAEOL, BRYN MAWR COL, 62-, FIELD DIR, COL EXCAVATIONS, KARATAS, TURKEY, 63-, MEM STAFF, UNIV MUS EXCAVATIONS, GORDION; VPRES, AM RES INST IN TURKEY, 80-; PRES, ARCHAEOL INST AM, 81- **MEMBERSHIPS** Sch Orient Res; Am Orient Soc; corp mem Royal Neth Acad Sci; fel Am Acad Arts and Sci; Am Philos Soc. **RESEARCH** Anatolian and Aegean archaeology. **SELECTED PUBLICATIONS** Auth Archaeology in Anatolia, Am J Archaeol, Vol 97, 93. **CONTACT ADDRESS** Dept of Class and Near Eastern Archaeol, Bryn Mawr Col, Bryn Mawr, PA 19010.

MELLON, STANLEY
PERSONAL Born 01/16/1927, Brooklyn, NY **DISCIPLINE** MODERN EUROPEAN AND FRENCH HISTORY **EDUCATION** Columbia Col, AB, 50; Princeton Univ, MA, 52, PhD, 54. **CAREER** Instr hist, Univ Mich, 54-58; asst prof, Univ Calif, Berkeley, 58-60; from asst prof to assoc prof, Yale Univ, 60-69; PROF HIST, UNIV ILL, CHICAGO CIRCLE, 69-, Vis assoc prof hist, Columbia Univ, 68-69. **MEMBERSHIPS** AHA; Soc Fr Hist Studies. **RESEARCH** Nineteenth century French history; intellectual history. **CONTACT ADDRESS** Dept of Hist, Univ of Illinois, Chicago, 601 S Morgan St, 913 University Hall, Chicago, IL 60607-7109.

MELOSI, MARTIN V.
PERSONAL Born 04/27/1947, San Jose, CA, m, 1971, 2 children **DISCIPLINE** HISTORY **EDUCATION** Univ Montana, BA, 69, MA, 71; Univ Texas, PhD, 75. **CAREER** From instr to prof, Texas A&M Univ, 75-84; from prof Hist to Distinguished Univ Prof, dir, Inst for Public Hist, 84- , Univ Houston; vis prof, Univ Paris VIII, 93; vis scholar, The Sea and the Cities Program, Univ Helsinki, 97, 98; Odense (Fulbright) Chair in Am Studies, Univ Southern Denmark, 00-01. **HONORS AND AWARDS** Ford Found fel, 74; Rockefeller Found fel, 76-77; Nat Hum Ctr, 82-83; NEH fel, 88-92; vis scholar, Smithsonian Inst, 91. **MEMBERSHIPS** Orgn of Am Hist; Am Soc for Environ Hist; Nat Coun on Public Hist; Public Works Hist Soc. **RESEARCH** Urban history; environmental history; public history; history of energy and technology. **SELECTED PUBLICATIONS** Auth, Thomas A. Edison and the Modernization of America, Addison, Wesley, Longman, 90; ed and contribur, Urban Public Policy: Historical Modes and Methods, Penn State, 93; auth, The Sanitary City: Urban Infrastructure in America from Colonial Times to the Present, Johns Hopkins, 00. **CONTACT ADDRESS** Dept of History, Univ of Houston, Houston, TX 77204-3785. **EMAIL** mmelosi@uh.edu

MELTON, JAMES V. H.
DISCIPLINE HISTORY **EDUCATION** Vanderbilt Univ, BA, 74; Univ Chicago, MA, 75, PhD, 82. **CAREER** Assoc prof **HONORS AND AWARDS** Biennial Bk Prize, Conf Group Cent Europ Hist. **RESEARCH** Enlightenment Europe; early modern German and Habsburg History; politics, culture, and the public sphere in Enlightenment Europe. **SELECTED PUBLICATIONS** Auth, Absolutism and the Eighteenth-Century Origins of Compulsory Schooling in Prussia and Austria; co-ed/trans, Land and Lordship: Structures of Governance in Medieval Austria; co-ed, Paths of Continuity: Historical Scholarship in Central Europe, 1933-1960. **CONTACT ADDRESS** Dept History, Emory Univ, 221 Bowden Hall, 561 Kilgo Cir, Atlanta, GA 30322-1950. **EMAIL** jmelt01@emory.edu

MELUSKY, JOSEPH
PERSONAL Born 06/02/1952, Pottsville, PA, m, 1976, 2 children **DISCIPLINE** HISTORY, POLITICAL SCIENCE **EDUCATION** W Chester State Col, BA, 74; Univ Del, MA, 78; Univ Del, PhD, 83. **CAREER** Lect, Univ Del, 79-80; Prof, St Francis Col, 80-. **HONORS AND AWARDS** Outstanding Fac Citation, Hon Soc, 83; Swatsworth Fac Merit Awd, 90; Distinguished Fac Awd, St Francis Nat Alumni Asn, 95; Who's Who in the East, 96; Who's Who in the World, 97; Who's Who Among Am Teachers, 96, 00. **MEMBERSHIPS** Pa Polit Sci Asn, Northeastern Polit Sci Asn, Am Polit Sci Asn, Pa Humanities Coun, Inst for Exp Learning. **RESEARCH** Presidential elections, American presidency, constitutional law. **SELECTED PUBLICATIONS** Auth, The Constitution: Our Written Legacy, Krieger Publ Co, 91; coauth, "To Preserve These Rights: The Bill of Rights 1791-1991," Pa Humanities Coun, 91; coauth, The Bill of Rights: Our Written Legacy, Krieger Publ Co, 93; auth, The American Political System: An Owner's Manual, McGraw-Hill, 00. **CONTACT ADDRESS** Dept Hist and Polit Sci, Saint Francis Col, Pennsylvania, Loretto, PA 15940-0600. **EMAIL** jmelusky@sfcpa.edu

MENARD, RUSSELL R.
DISCIPLINE HISTORY **EDUCATION** Univ Iowa, MA, PhD. **CAREER** Prof **RESEARCH** Economic, demographic, and social history of the Chesapeake region during early Colonial period; plantation slavery in British America; economic development of lower South in the eighteenth century; late nineteenth-century U.S. social history. **SELECTED PUBLICATIONS** Auth, Economy and Society in Early Colonial Maryland, Garland, 85; co-auth, The Economy of British America, 1607-1789, Univ NC, 91; Robert Cole's World: Agriculture and Society in Early Maryland, Univ NC, 91; co-ed The Economy of Early America: The Revolution Period, 1763-7190, Univ Va, 88. **CONTACT ADDRESS** History Dept, Univ of Minnesota, Twin Cities, 614 Social Sciences Tower, 267 19th Ave. S, Minneapolis, MN 55455. **EMAIL** menar001@tc.umn.edu

MENASHE, LOUIS
PERSONAL Born 12/10/1935, Brooklyn, NY, m, 1958, 2 children **DISCIPLINE** RUSSIAN AND SOVIET HISTORY; RUSSIAN CINEMA STUDIES **EDUCATION** City Col New York, BA, 59; NYork Univ, MA, 63, PhD(hist), 66. **CAREER** Asst prof, 65-68, ASSOC PROF HIST, POLYTECH INST NY, 68-, Adj prof hist, NY Univ, 70-73; Prof of hist, Polytechnic Univ, 84-; Charles S. Baylis Chair in hist, Polytechnic Univ, 95-00. **MEMBERSHIPS** Am Asn Advan Slavic Studies; AHA. **RESEARCH** Social and political history of the Russian Revolution; Soviet politics and society; Russian and Soviet Cinema. **SELECTED PUBLICATIONS** Co-ed, Teach-Ins: USA, Praeger, 67; contribr, Isaac Deutscher: The Man and His Work, MacDonald, London, 71; auth, Vladimir Iiyich Bakunin: An essay on Lenin, 11-12/73 & Solzhenitsyn and the Soviet experience, 4-6/76, Socialist Revolution; Demystifying the Russian Revolution, Radical Hist Rev, fall 78; contribr, The Politics of Eurocommunism, Southend Press, 80; co-ed, El Salvador: Central America in the New Cold War, Grove Press, 82; auth, New Wave from Russia, NY Times Magazine, 85; Revising the Revisionists: Sovietology in a New Key? Int Labor & Working-Class Hist, No. 50, fall 96. **CONTACT ADDRESS** Dept of Humanities and Soc Sciences, Polytech Univ, Brooklyn, 6 Metro Tech Ctr, Brooklyn, NY 11201-3840. **EMAIL** lmenashe@duke.poly.edu

MENDELSOHN, EVERETT IRWIN
PERSONAL Born 10/28/1931, Yonkers, NY, m, 1974, 4 children **DISCIPLINE** HISTORY OF SCIENCE **EDUCATION** Antioch Col, AB, 53; Harvard Univ, PhD, 60. **CAREER** From instr to assoc prof, 60-69; prof, hist sci, Harvard Univ, 69-; chmn dept, 71-; 96-00 Dir prog, Technol & Soc, Harvard Univ, 66-68; Macy sr fac fel, 68-69; overseas fel, Churchill Col, Cambridge Univ, 68-69; mem comt life sci & soc policy, Nat Acad Sci, 68-73; ed, J Hist Biol; fel, Zentrum fur Interdiszplinare Forschung, Bielefeld, 78-79; fel, Wissenschaftskolleg zu Berlin, 83-84; Prof Invitee, Conservatoire Nat Des Arts et Metiers, 89-90; Olaf Palme Prof, Sweden SCASSS, 94; co-ed, Sociol of Sci Yearbk; Ed Jour of Hist Of Biol. **HONORS AND AWARDS** Gregor Mendel Medal, Czech Acad Sci; DHL (hon); dhl, ri col, 77. **MEMBERSHIPS** Hist Sci Soc; fel AAAS (vpres, 73-74); Int Acad Hist Sci; fel, Am Acad Arts & Sci; Int Acad hist Med.; Int Coun for Sci Policy Studies, pres. **RESEARCH** Development of modern biological sciences; aspects of the social relations of science; social assessment of science. **SELECTED PUBLICATIONS** Auth, Heat and Life, Harvard Univ, 64; auth, Physical Models and Physiological Concepts: Explanation in Nineteenth Century Biology, Brit J Hist Sci, 66; ed, Human Aspects of Biomedical Innovation, Harvard Univ, 71; auth, Should Science Survive its Success?, Boston Study Philos Sci, 74; co-ed, Science and Values, Humanities, 74; auth, Revolution and Rejunction, Relations Between Science & Philosophy, Humanities, 76; coed, contribr, Topics in the Philosophy of Biology, 76; coed, contribr, Social Production of Scientific Knowledge, 77, Reidel; coed Technology, Pessimism, and Postmodernism, Soc of Sci Yearbk, Kluwer Acad Publ, 95; auth, Biology as Society, Society as Biology: Metaphors, Soc of Sci Yearbk, Kluwer Acad Publ, 95; coauth, The Practices of Human Genetics, 99; ed, Life Sciences in the Twentieth Century, Biographical Portraits, 01. **CONTACT ADDRESS** Dept of Hist of Sci, Harvard Univ, Science Ctr 235, Cambridge, MA 02138-3800. **EMAIL** emendels@FAS.Harvard.edu

MENDEZ, JESUS
PERSONAL Born 10/03/1951, Havana, Cuba **DISCIPLINE** LATIN AMERICAN HISTORY **EDUCATION** Univ Miami, BS, 72, MA, 74; Univ Tex, Austin, PhD(hist), 80. **CAREER** Instr hist, State Univ NY Binghamton, 81; ASST PROF HIST, BARRY UNIV, 81-, Jr fel, Fulbright Comn, 83. **MEMBERSHIPS** AHA; Am Cath Hist Asn; Latin Am Studies Asn; Conf Latin Am Historians. **RESEARCH** Argentine intellectual history; Spanish intellectual history. **SELECTED PUBLICATIONS** Auth, The orgins of Sur, Agrentina's elite cultural review, Inter-Am Rev Bibliog, 81. **CONTACT ADDRESS** Dept of Hist, Barry Univ, 11300 N E 2nd Ave, Miami, FL 33161-6695.

MENDLE, MICHAEL J.
PERSONAL Born 05/01/1945, d, 3 children **DISCIPLINE** HISTORY OF BRITISH POLITICAL THOUGHT **EDUCATION** WA Univ, PhD. **CAREER** History Dept, Univ Ala **MEMBERSHIPS** Ren Soc of America; NACBS. **RESEARCH** Early modern British Political Thought; Pamphlet Culture; Construction of historical memory. **SELECTED PUBLICATIONS** Auth, Dangerous Positions: Mixed Government, the Estates of the Realm, and the Making of the Answer to the XIX Propositions, 85; Henry Parker and the English Civil War: The Political Thought of the Public's Privado, 95. **CONTACT ADDRESS** Univ of Alabama, Tuscaloosa, Box 870212, Tuscaloosa, AL 35487. **EMAIL** mmendle@tenhoor.as.ua.edu

MENK, PATRICIA HOLBERT
PERSONAL Born 06/04/1921, Rutherford, NJ, m, 1943, 3 children **DISCIPLINE** MODERN HISTORY OF WESTERN CIVILIZATION **EDUCATION** Fla State Univ, AB, 41; Univ Va, MA, 42, PhD(hist), 45. **CAREER** Instr hist, Univ Va Exten, 44-50; from instr to assoc prof, 52-66, actg pres, 75-76, prof and chmn dept, 66-81, EMER PROF HIST, MARY BALDWIN COL, 81-, Researcher, Va Hist Comn World War II, 46-47; mem city coun, Staunton, Va, 62-66 and 69, mayor, 64-66; vis prof, Univ Va, 69. **MEMBERSHIPS** Southern Hist Asn; Orgn Am Historians. **RESEARCH** Twentieth century United States urban history; 19th century Valley of Virginia history; United States history. **SELECTED PUBLICATIONS CONTACT ADDRESS** Dept of Hist, Mary Baldwin Col, Staunton, VA 24401.

MENNEL, ROBERT MCKISSON
PERSONAL Born 10/18/1938, Toledo, OH **DISCIPLINE** AMERICAN HISTORY **EDUCATION** Denison Univ, BA, 60; Ohio State Univ, MA, 65, PhD(Am hist), 69. **CAREER** Instr hist, Denison Univ, 66-67; asst prof, 69-73, chmn dept, 74-77, assoc prof, 73-79, Prof Am Hist, Univ NH, 79-, Dir, Honors

Prog, 85-. **HONORS AND AWARDS** Am Philos Soc grant, 75; Charles Warren fel, 77-78. **MEMBERSHIPS** Orgn Am Historians. **RESEARCH** History of children and youth; social welfare history; comparative social history. **SELECTED PUBLICATIONS** Co-ed, Children and Youth in America, Harvard Univ, Vols I, II & III, 70, 71 & 74; auth, Origins of the Juvenile Court-Changing Perspectives on the Legal Rights of Juvenile Delinquents, Crime & Delinq, 1/72; Juvenile Delinquency in Perspective, Hist Educ Quart, fall 73; Thorns and Thistles: Juvenile Delinquents in the United States, 1825-1940, Univ New Eng, 73; Family System of Common Farmers: The Ohio Reform School for Boys, 1858-1880, Ohio Hist, spring & summer 80; Attitudes and Policies Toward Juvenile Delinquency in the United States: A Historiographical Review, In: Crime and Justice: An Annual Review of Research, Univ Chicago Press, 82; co-ed, Holmes and Frankfurter: Their Correspondence, 1912-34, Univ New Eng, 96. **CONTACT ADDRESS** Honors Prog, Univ of New Hampshire, Durham, Hood House, Durham, NH 03824-4724. **EMAIL** rmmennel@eisunix.unh.edu

MENTZER, RAYMOND A.

PERSONAL Born 09/20/1945, Pittsburgh, PA, m, 1968, 2 children **DISCIPLINE** HISTORY **EDUCATION** Fordham Univ, AB, 67, MA, 70; Univ Wisc, 73. **CAREER** From asst prof to assoc prof 73-83, prof, 83- , Montana St Univ. **HONORS AND AWARDS** Phi Beta Kappa, 67; Phi Kappa Phi, 71; Harold J. Grimm Prize, 87; Natl Huguenot Soc Book Prize, 95. **MEMBERSHIPS** AHA; Am Soc of Church Hist; Am Catholic Hist Asn; French Hist Stud; Renaissance Soc of Am; Sixteenth Century Stud Soc; Soc for Reformation Res. **RESEARCH** Early modern European history. **SELECTED PUBLICATIONS** Auth, Heresy Proceedings in Languedoc, 1500-1560, Am Philos Soc, 84; auth, Sin and the Calvinists: Morals Control and the Consistory in the Reformed Tradition, Sixteenth Century J Pub, 94; auth, Blood and Belief: Family Survival and confessional Identity among the Provincial Huguenot Nobility, Purdue Univ, 94; auth, The Persistence of Superstition and Idolatry among Rural French Calvinists, Church Hist, 96; auth, The Reformed Churches of France and the Visual Arts, Calvinism and the Visual Arts, Eerdmans, 98; ed, Sixteenth Century Essays and Studies. **CONTACT ADDRESS** Dept of History, Montana State Univ, Bozeman, Bozeman, MT 59717. **EMAIL** uhirm@montana.edu

MEO, SUSAN RIMBY

DISCIPLINE HISTORY **EDUCATION** Univ of Pittsburgh, PhD, 92; Kutztown St Col, MA, 81; Bloomsburg St Col, BS Ed, 76 **CAREER** Assoc/Asst Prof, 92-, Shippensburg Univ; Inst, 88-91, Millersville Univ; Tch Fel, 83-87, Univ of Pittsburgh; Soc Stud Tchr, 77-81, Gov Mifflin Sch Dist **HONORS AND AWARDS** Acad Achievmt Awd, 76; magna cum laude, bloomsburg **MEMBERSHIPS** Am Hist Asn; Orgn of Am Hist **RESEARCH** Women and Progressive Reform, 1920s Feminism **SELECTED PUBLICATIONS** Auth, "An Obligation to Participate: Married Nurses Labor Force Participation in the 1950s," in Not June Cleaver: Women and Gender in Postwar America, 1945-1960, ed. Joanne Meyerowitz (PA: Temple Univ Press, 94); auth, Nurses Questions/Women's Questions: The Impact of the Demographic Revolution and Feminism on United States Working Women, 1946-86, Peter Lang Publ Inc (New York), 96; auth, Lavina Lloyd Dock, Greenwood Press, 97; Coauth, The Antebellum Women's Movement: A Curriculum Unit for Grades 5-8, National Center for History in the Schools, 98; auth, "In Their Own Eyes: Using Journals with Primary Sources with College Students," The Hist Teacher 33 (May, 00): 335-341. **CONTACT ADDRESS** Dept of History, Shippensburg Univ of Pennsylvania, Shippensburg, PA 17257. **EMAIL** susanmeo@ship.edu

MERCHANT, CAROLYN

PERSONAL Born 07/12/1936, Rochester, NY, 2 children **DISCIPLINE** ENVIRONMENTAL HISTORY, PHILOSOPHY & ETHICS **EDUCATION** Vassar Col, AB, 58; Univ Wis, MA, 62, PhD, 67. **CAREER** Lectr hist of sci, Univ San Francisco, 69-74, asst prof, 74-78; asst prof environ hist, 79-80, assoc prof 80-86, Prof, 86-, Chancellor Prof Environ Hist, Philos & Ethics, Univ Calif, Berkeley, former chmn, Dept Conserv & Resource Studies; Vis prof, Ecole Normale Superieure, Paris, 6/86. **HONORS AND AWARDS** NSF, 76-78; NEH grant, 77, 81-83; Am Counc Learned Soc fel, 78; Center Advan Studies, Behavioral Sci, 78; Fulbright sr scholar, Umea Univ, Sweden, 84; Agr Exp Station, Univ Calif, Berkeley, 80-86, 86-92, 92-; Nathan Cummings Found, 92; Am Cultures fel, Univ Calif, Berkeley, 6/90; Vis fel, School Soc Sci, Murdoch Univ, Perth, Australia, 91; John Simon Guggenheim fel, 95; Doctor Honoris Causa, Umea Univ, Sweden, 95; National Humanities Center Fellow, 01. **MEMBERSHIPS** Hist Sci Soc; West Coast Hist Sci Soc; British Soc Hist Sci; Soc Hist Technol; Am Soc Environ Hist. **RESEARCH** Scientific revolution; American environmental history; women and nature. **SELECTED PUBLICATIONS** Auth, D'Alembert and the vis viva controversy, Studies in Hist and Philos of Sci, 8/70; Leibniz and the vis viva controversy, Isis, spring 71; The Leibnizian-Newtonian debates: Natural philosophy and social psychology, British J for the Hist of Sci, 12/73; Madame du Chatelet's metaphysics and mechanics, Studies in Hist and Philos of Sci, 5/77; The Death of Nature: Women, Ecology, and the Scientific Revolution, Harper and Row, San Francisco, 80, 2nd ed, 90; Earthcare: Women and the environmental movement, Environment, 6/81; Isis' consciousness raised, Isis, fall 82; Ecological Revolutions: Nature, Gender, and Science in New England, Univ NC Press, 89; Radical Ecology: The Search for a Liveable World, Routledge, 92; ed, Major Problems in American Environmental History: ed, Ecology, Humanities Press, 94; Earthcare: Women and the Environment, Routledge, 96; ed, Green Versus Gold: Sources in California's Environmental History, Island Press, 98; Reinventing Eden, in progress. **CONTACT ADDRESS** Dept of Environ Sci, Policy & Mgt, Univ of California, Berkeley, Berkeley, CA 94720-3310. **EMAIL** merchant@nature.berkeley.edu

MEREDITH, HOWARD

PERSONAL Born 05/25/1938, Galveston, TX, m, 1967, 2 children **DISCIPLINE** AMERICAN INDIAN STUDIES **EDUCATION** Univ Oklahoma at Norman, PhD, 70; S. F. Austin State Univ, MA, 63; Univ Tex at Austing, BS, 61. **CAREER** Univ of Science and Arts of Oklahoma 85-; Cookson Institute and Bacone Col, 79-85; Oklahoma Historical Society, 75-79. **HONORS AND AWARDS** Coke Wood Awd for Best Mongraph, 99; Superior Teaching Awd, USAO, 96 and 98; Nat'l Endowment for the Humanities Fel, 96. **MEMBERSHIPS** Native Circle of Writers; Western Writers of America. **RESEARCH** Cherokee and Caddo Thought. **SELECTED PUBLICATIONS** Auth, "The Native American Factor," (New York: Seabury Press, 73); auth, "Bacone Indian University: A History," Oklahoma City: Oklahoma Heritage Association, 80), edited with M.E. Meredith; auth, "The Life of George H. Shirk," (Oklahoma City: Oklahoma Heritage Association, 82), with M.E. Meredith; auth, "The Biography of B. D. Eddie," (Oklahoma City: Oklahoma Heritage Association, 82), with M.E. Meridith; auth, "Barley Milam: Principal Chief of the Cherokee Nation, (Muskogee: Indian Univ Press, 85); auth, "Modern American Indian Government and Politics and Study Guide," (Tsaile: Navajo Community College Press, 93-94; auth, "Caddo Federations," American Indians, (Pasadena: Salem Press, 95); auth, "Dancing on Common Ground: Tribal Cultures and Alliances on the Southern Plains," (Lawrence: University Press of Kansas, 95); auth, "Metaphor and Meaning in Anna Lee Walters, The Sun is Not Merciful," Southwestern American Literature, v. 22, (Spring, 97): 63-67; auth, "A Cherokee Vision of Elohi," (Oklahoma City: Noksi Press, 98), with B. Sobral, translation by W. Proctor. **CONTACT ADDRESS** Dept Social Science, Univ of Sciences & Arts of Oklahoma, PO Box 82345, Chickasha, OK 73018. **EMAIL** meredith623@aol.com

MERGEN, BERNARD M.

PERSONAL Born 03/30/1937, Reno, NV, m, 1991, 2 children **DISCIPLINE** AMERICAN STUDIES **EDUCATION** Univ Nev, BA, 59; Univ Pa, MA, 60; Univ Pa, PhD, 68. **CAREER** Asst Prof, George Wash Univ, 70-74; Assoc Prof, George Wash Univ, 75-80; Prof, George Wash Univ, 80-. **HONORS AND AWARDS** Fulbright Fel, Nat Univ of Mongolia, 96. **MEMBERSHIPS** Am Studies Assoc, Am Soc for Environmental Hist, Assoc for the Study of Play. **RESEARCH** Cultural and environmental history of the United States. **SELECTED PUBLICATIONS** Auth, "Made, Bought and Stolen: Toys and Adolescents in America," Small Worlds: Children and Adolescents in America, (92): 334-339; auth, Snow in America, Smithsonian Inst Pr, 97; auth, "Children's Lore in School and Playgrounds," Children's Folklore: A Sourcebook, Utah State Univ Pr (99): 229-250; auth, "Lake Tahoe: Microcosm of Environmental History," Proceedings of the Western Snow Conf (99). **CONTACT ADDRESS** Dept Am Studies, The George Washington Univ, 2035 H St Northwest, Washington, DC 20052-0001. **EMAIL** mergen@gwu.edu

MERKEN, KATHLEEN

DISCIPLINE EAST ASIAN STUDIES **EDUCATION** Univ British Columbia, PhD. **CAREER** Fac lectr. **RESEARCH** Modern novels, literary translation. **SELECTED PUBLICATIONS** Trans, Night Fragrance, The Literary Rev, Japanese Writing, 87; trans, Picture Brides: Japanes Women in Canada, Toronto: Multicultural Hist Soc of Ontario, 95. **CONTACT ADDRESS** East Asian Studies Dept, McGill Univ, 3434 McTavish St, Montreal, QC, Canada H3A 1X9. **EMAIL** kmerken@leacock.lan.mcgill.ca

MERKLEY, PAUL C.

DISCIPLINE HISTORY **EDUCATION** Univ Toronto, BA, 56, MA, 57, PhD, 65. **CAREER** Prof. **RESEARCH** Religion in the history of the United States. **SELECTED PUBLICATIONS** Auth, The Greek and Hebrew Origins of Our Idea of History, Lewiston: Mellen Press, 88; "Religion and Political Prosperity: Recent Historiography in American Religious Studies," Can Jour Hist, 91; Theodore Roosevelt Was Right!, The New Federation, 95. **CONTACT ADDRESS** Dept of Hist, Carleton Univ, 1125 Colonel By Dr, Ottawa, ON, Canada K1S 5B6. **EMAIL** pmerkley@ccs.carleton.ca

MERLING, DAVID

PERSONAL Born 06/14/1948, Pittsburg, PA, m, 1969, 2 children **DISCIPLINE** OLD TESTAMENT STUDIES, ARCHAEOLOGY, HISTORY OF ANTIQUITY **EDUCATION** Andrews Univ, PhD, 96. **CAREER** Assoc prof of Archaeol and Hist of Antiquities, Andrews Univ, 86-; Curator, Siegfried H. Horn Archaeol Museum, 91- . **HONORS AND AWARDS** Andrews Univ Fac Res Grant, 91-92, 94; Who's Who in Bibl Stud and Archaeol, 93; Zion Res found travel grant, 84, Tell e-Umeyri, Jordan. **MEMBERSHIPS** Adventist Theol Soc; Amer Sch Oriental Res; Bibl Archaeol Soc; Evangelical Theol Soc; Inst Bibl Res; Israel Exploration Soc; Near Eastern Archaeol Soc; Soc Bibl Lit. **RESEARCH** Archaeology and the Book of Joshua. **CONTACT ADDRESS** Dept of Archaeology, Andrews Univ, Berrien Springs, MI 49104-0990. **EMAIL** merling@andrews.edu

MERRELL, F.

PERSONAL Born 11/16/1937, Virden, NM, m, 1964, 3 children **DISCIPLINE** LATIN AMERICAN STUDIES **EDUCATION** Univ of NMex, PhD. **CAREER** PROF, PURDUE UNIV, 73-. **MEMBERSHIPS** Semiotic Soc of Am; MLA. **RESEARCH** Latin American studies; theory; Spanish American prose. **SELECTED PUBLICATIONS** Auth, Semiosis in the Postmodern Age, Purdue Univ Press, 95; auth, Peirce's Semiotics Now: A Primer, Canadian Scholars' Press, 95; auth, Signs Grow: Semiosis and Life Processes, Univ of Toronto Press, 96; auth, Peirce, Signs, and Meaning, Univ of Torontop Press, 97; auth, Simplicity and Complexity: Pondering Literature, Science and Painting, Univ of Mich Press, 98; auth, Sensing Semiosis: Toward the Possibility of Completmentary Cultural Longics, St Martin's Press, 98; auth, Semiosis, Science, Silver Linings: And Finally Literature, Semiotica, 96; auth, The Writing of Forking Paths: Borges, Calvino and Postmodern Models of Writing, Variaciones Borges, 97; auth, Just Waiting (Or Looking Back on the Lines of His Face), Variaciones Borges, 97; auth, Does the Life of Signs Yield a Meaningful Universe?, Semiotica, 98. **CONTACT ADDRESS** Dept of Foreign Lang & Lit, Purdue Univ, West Lafayette, West Lafayette, IN 47907. **EMAIL** fmerrell@purdue.edu

MERRETT, CHRISTOPHER D.

PERSONAL Born 03/02/1961, Sault Ste Marie, ON, Canada, m, 1989, 2 children **DISCIPLINE** GEOGRAPHY **EDUCATION** Univ Western Ont, BA, 83; Lake Superior State Univ, BS, 86; Univ Vt, MA, 88; Univ Iowa, PhD, 94. **CAREER** Adj asst prof, Univ of Northern Iowa, 93-94; vis asst prof, Univ of Iowa, 94-95; asst to assoc prof, Western IL Univ, 95-. **HONORS AND AWARDS** Award for Teaching Excellence, Univ of Vt, 87; Recognition for Contrib in Teaching, Univ of Northern Iowa, 94; Honors Fac Teaching Awd, Western IL Univ, 97; Phi Kappa Phi, 98. **MEMBERSHIPS** Am Geog Soc; Assoc of Am Geog; Assoc for Can Studies in the US; Can Assoc of Geog; Can Center for Policy Alternatives; Inst of British Geog; Nat Coun for Geog Educ. **RESEARCH** Political and Economic Geography, Community and Economic Development, Regional Planning, Geographic Education. **SELECTED PUBLICATIONS** Auth, Crossing the Border: The Canada-United States Boundary, Univ of Maine Pr, (Orono), 91; auth, Free Trade: Neither Free nor About Trade, Black Rose Books, (Montreal), 96; auth, "Culture wars and national education standards: Scale and the struggle over social reproduction", Prof Geogr 51.4 (99): 598-609; coed, A Cooperative Approach to Local Economic Development, Quorum Books, (Westport, CT), 00; coauth, "Putting Cooperative Theory into Practice: the 21st Century Alliance", "Rural Communities in Transition", and "Characteristics of New Generation Cooperatives", A Cooperative Approach to Local Economic Development, eds, C.D. Merrett and N. Walzer, Quorum Books, (Westport, CT, 00); auth, "Welfare to work in the urban and rural counties of Illinois: The role of nonprofit social service providers", Urban Geog 21, (00); auth, "The production of geographical scale and political identity: A review essay, Nat Identities 2.1 (forthcoming); coauth, "The study of Canadian Geography in the United States", Geography in America, eds G. Gaile and C. Wilmott Oxford Univ Pr, (NY, forthcoming). **CONTACT ADDRESS** Dept Geog, Western Illinois Univ, 1 University Circle, Macomb, IL 61455. **EMAIL** cd-merrett@wiu.edu

MERRIMAN, JOHN M.

PERSONAL Born 06/15/1947, Battle Creek, MI, m, 1980, 2 children **DISCIPLINE** FRENCH, EUROPEAN & URBAN HISTORY **EDUCATION** Univ MI, BA, 68, MA, 69, PhD, 72. **CAREER** Lectr soc & hist, Univ MI, 72-73; asst prof, 73-78, Assoc Prof Hist, 78-82, Prof, 83-95, Charles Seymour prof hist, Yale Univ, 96-, Guggenheim fel, 79-80. **MEMBERSHIPS** AHA; Fr Hist Studies. **RESEARCH** French soc hist, 19th century; French urban hist, 19th century; French labor hist, 19th to 20th century. **SELECTED PUBLICATIONS** Ed, 1830 in France & auth, Intro & The Demoiselles of the Ariege, 1829-31, In: 1830 in France, Franklin Watts, 75; auth, The Norman fires of 1830: Incendiaries and fear in rural France, Fr Hist Studies, spring 76; Agony of the Republic: The Repression of the Left in Revolutionary France, 1848-51, Yale Univ Press, 78; ed, Consciousness and Class Experience in Nineteenth Century Europe & auth, Intro & Incident at the statue of the Virgin Mary: The conflict of old and new in nineteenth century Limoges, In: Consciousness and Class Experience in Nineteenth Century Europe, Holmes & Meier, 79; ed, French Cities in the Nineteenth Century & auth, The changing image of the nineteenth century French city & Restoration town, bourgeois city, In: French Cities in the Nineteenth Century, Hutchison, London, 82; Ed, For Want of a Horse: Chance & Humor in History, Stephen Green Press, 85; The Red City: Limoges and the French Nineteenth

City, Oxford Univ Press, 85 and French trans: Limoges, la ville rouge, Belini, 90; The Margins of City Life, Oxford Univ Press; 91, and French trans: Aux marges de la ville, Editions du Sevil, 94; Co-ed, Edo and Paris: Urban Life and the State in the Early Modern Period, Cornell Univ Press, 94; A History of Modern Europe, 2 vol, W W Norton & Co, 96. **CONTACT ADDRESS** Dept of Hist, Yale Univ, PO Box 208324, New Haven, CT 06520-8324. **EMAIL** john.merriman@yale.edu

MERRIMAN, MIRA P.
DISCIPLINE ITALIAN RENAISSANCE AND BAROQUE ART **EDUCATION** Columbia Univ, PhD. **CAREER** Prof emer **SELECTED PUBLICATIONS** Auth, monograph and catalogue raisonne on Giuseppe Maria Crespi (1665-1747), Rizzoli; publ, The Burlington Mag, Paragone, Source; cat of exhib(s), London, Washington Nat Gallery, Bologna Pinacoteca, Kimbell Mus. **CONTACT ADDRESS** Dept of Art, Wichita State Univ, 1845 Fairmont, Wichita, KS 67260-0062.

MERRITT, RAYMOND HARLAND
PERSONAL Born 03/29/1936, Sioux Falls, SD, m, 1956, 3 children **DISCIPLINE** AMERICAN URBAN AND TECHNOLOGICAL HISTORY **EDUCATION** St Olaf Col, BA, 58; Luther Theol Sem, BD, 62; Univ Minn, MA, 63, PhD(hist), 68. **CAREER** Instr soc sci, SDak Sch Mines and Technol, 63-64 and Wis State Univ, River Falls, 64-66; from instr to asst prof Am hist, NDak State Univ, 66-69; asst prof hist, Univ Wis-Milwaukee, 69-70, assoc prof hist and systs design, 70-80, dir, Cult and Technol Studies Prog, 73-80; Caroline Werner Gannett prof, Rochester Inst Technol, 80-81; PROF and CHMN, MINNEAPOLIS COL ART and DESIGN, 81- **MEMBERSHIPS** Orgn Am Historians; AHA; Soc Hist Technol; Am Studies Asn; Pub Works Hist Soc (vpres, 77-78, pres, 78-79). **RESEARCH** History of American technology and engineering. **SELECTED PUBLICATIONS** Auth, Structures in The Stream--Water, Science, and The Rise of the US Army Corps of Engineers, Tech Cult, Vol 37, 96; Reshaping National Water Politics--The Emergence of the Water Resources Development Act of 1986, Public Hist, Vol 15, 93; Building Air Bases in the Negev--The US Army Corps of Engineers in Israel, 1979-1982, Tech Cult, Vol 36, 95. **CONTACT ADDRESS** Minneapolis, MN 55403.

MERTINS, DETLEF
DISCIPLINE ARCHITECTURE; HISTORY AND THEORY **EDUCATION** Univ Toronto, BArch 80; Princeton Univ, MA, 91, PhD, 96. **CAREER** Architect, Private Pract, Toronto, 80-89; lectr to Assoc Prof, Univ Toronto, 91-. **HONORS AND AWARDS** Vis scholar Can Ctr Archit, 98, Medal of Serv City of Toronto, 82. **MEMBERSHIPS** On Asn Archit; Royal Archit Inst Can; Soc Archit Hist; Soc Study Archit Can. **RESEARCH** Architectural history, theory and criticism; 20th Century; German, American, Canadian. **SELECTED PUBLICATIONS** Ed, Metropolitan Mutations: The Architecture of Emerging Public Spaces, Little, Brown, & Co, 88; The Presence of Mies, Princeton Archit Press, 94; auth, System and Freedom, Autonomy and Ideology, Monicelli, 97; Anything But Literal, Architecture and Cubism, MIT Press, 97. **CONTACT ADDRESS** Fac of Archit, Landscape, & Design, Univ of Toronto, 230 College St., Toronto, ON, Canada M5T 1R2. **EMAIL** detlef.mertins@utoronto.ca

MERTZ, PAUL ERIC
PERSONAL Born 02/27/1943, Bartlesville, OK, m, 1966, 2 children **DISCIPLINE** AMERICAN HISTORY **EDUCATION** Phillips Univ, BA, 65; Univ Okla, MA, 67, PhD, 71. **CAREER** Instr, 69-72, asst prof, 72-77, assoc prof, 77-82, Prof Hist, Univ Wis-Stevens Point, 82-, chmn, Hist Dept, 92-98. **HONORS AND AWARDS** Woodrow Wilson Nat fel, Univ Okla, 65-66. **MEMBERSHIPS** Orgn Am Historians; Southern Hist Asn. **RESEARCH** Recent south; New Deal era; civil rights movement. **SELECTED PUBLICATIONS** Auth, New Deal Policy and Southern Rural Poverty, La State Univ Press, 78. **CONTACT ADDRESS** 2100 Main St, Stevens Point, WI 54481-3897. **EMAIL** pmertz@uwsp.edu

MESCH, CLAUDIA
DISCIPLINE ART **EDUCATION** Yale Univ, BA, 82; Univ CA, MA, 89; Univ Chicago, PhD, 97. **CAREER** Asst Prof, Art Hist, Cleveland St Univ, 97-. **RESEARCH** Modern and contemp visual cult. **SELECTED PUBLICATIONS** Publ, Art History; The New Art Examiner; Checkpoint, Ger. **CONTACT ADDRESS** Dept of Art, Cleveland State Univ, 2307 Chester, Cleveland, OH 44115. **EMAIL** u.mesch@csuohio.edu

MESSER, ROBERT LOUIS
PERSONAL Born 07/11/1944, Indianapolis, IN, m, 1967, 2 children **DISCIPLINE** UNITED STATES DIPLOMATIC HISTORY **EDUCATION** Ind Univ, BA, 66, MA, 68; Univ Calif, Berkeley, PhD(hist), 75. **CAREER** Asst prof, 75-81, ASSOC PROF, UNIV ILL, CHICAGO, 81-, CONSULT HUMAN RIGHTS, WORLD WITHOUT WAR COUN, MIDWEST, 77-, BD DIR PEACE ISSUES CTR, 78- **MEMBERSHIPS** Am Hist Asn; Orgn Am Historians; Soc Historians Am Foreign Rels. **RESEARCH** Twentieth century American foreign policy; origins of Cold War; human rights. **SELECTED PUBLICATIONS** Auth, Paths not taken: The United States Department of State and alternatives to containment, 1945-1946, Diplomatic Hist, fall 77; End of an alliance: James F Byrnes, Roosevelt, Truman and the origins of the Cold War, Univ NC Press, 82. **CONTACT ADDRESS** Dept of Hist, Univ of Illinois, Chicago, Chicago Circle, Box 4348, Chicago, IL 60680.

MESSER-KRUSE, TIMOTHY
PERSONAL Born 03/13/1963, Tecumseh, NE, m, 1990, 3 children **DISCIPLINE** HISTORY **EDUCATION** Univ Wis-Madison, PhD, 94. **CAREER** Assoc Prof Labor Hist, Univ Toledo, 95-. **HONORS AND AWARDS** William Hesseltine Awd, 94. **RESEARCH** Hist Am Left; Knights of Labor; UAW; Great Depression. **SELECTED PUBLICATIONS** The Yankee International: Marxism and the American Reform Tradition, 1848-1876, Univ NC Press, 98; The Campus Klans of the Univ of Wisconsin: Tacit and Active Support for the Ku Klux Klan in a Culture of Intolerance, Wis Mag of Hist, 77, Autumn 93; The Best Dressed Workers in New York: Liveried Teamsters in the Gilded Age, Labor Hist, 95-96; The First International in America, The Greenback Labor Party, The Chinese Question, Richard Hinton, in the Encyclopedia of the American Left, Paul Buhle, ed, rev ed, 98; Socialism, The American Federation of Labor, The Knights of Labor, Eight Hour Day, Pullman Strike, in the Am Heritage Encyclopedia of Am Hist, forthcoming; The Bulldozing of Labor Hist: The Destruction of the Toledo's Historic Elm St Bridge, Northwest Ohio Quarterly, 96; Collaborative Publishing on the Net: Notes From Recent Experience, in Dennis Trinkle, ed, Writing, Teaching and Researching History in the Electronic Age, M E Sharpe, 98; auth, Webmaster, Toledo's Attic Virtual Museum. **CONTACT ADDRESS** Dept of History, Univ of Toledo, Toledo, OH 43606-3390. **EMAIL** tmesser@uoft02.utoledo.edu

MESTELLER, JEAN C.
DISCIPLINE AMERICAN LITERATURE, AMERICAN STUDIES, WOMEN WRITERS **EDUCATION** Lynchburg Col, BA; Univ Va, MA; Univ Minn, PhD 78. **CAREER** Instr, Univ Minn; Ill State Univ; prof, 78-. **HONORS AND AWARDS** Sally Ann Abshire Awds (3). **RESEARCH** Nineteenth-century popular fiction and the working girl. **SELECTED PUBLICATIONS** Auth, Romancing the Reader: From Laura Jean Libbey to Harlequin Romance and Beyond. **CONTACT ADDRESS** Dept of Eng, Whitman Col, 345 Boyer Ave, Walla Walla, WA 99362-2038. **EMAIL** mastellerj@whitman.edu

METCALF, ALIDA C.
PERSONAL Born 04/05/1954, Albany, NY, m, 1986, 2 children **DISCIPLINE** HISTORY **EDUCATION** Smith Col, BA, 76; Univ Tex, MA, 78, PhD, 83. **CAREER** Vist asst prof, Ind Univ, 83-84; asst prof, Univ Tex, 84-86; from asst prof to assoc prof to prof, 86-, Trinity Univ. **HONORS AND AWARDS** Honorale Mention Bolton Prize, 94; Harvey Johnson Book Awd, 93; Fulbright Lecturing Awd, 86; Fulbright-Hayes Doctoral Dissertation Awd, 79-81. **MEMBERSHIPS** Am Hist Asn; Latin Am Std Asn. **RESEARCH** Colonial Latin America **SELECTED PUBLICATIONS** Auth, article, Women of Means: Women and Family Property in Colonial Brazil, 90; auth, Family and Frontier in Colonial Brazil: Santana de Parnaiba, 1580-1822, 92; auth, Millenarian Slaves? The Santidde de Jaguaripe and Slave Resistance in the Americas, 99. **CONTACT ADDRESS** Dept of History, Trinity Univ, San Antonio, TX 78212-7200. **EMAIL** ametcalf@trinity.edu

METCALF, MICHAEL F.
PERSONAL Born 02/08/1944, Buffalo, NY, m, 1969, 2 children **DISCIPLINE** HISTORY **EDUCATION** Univ Stockholm, MA, PhD. **CAREER** Prof and Exec Dir. **MEMBERSHIPS** Am Hist Asn, Society for the Advancement of Scandinavian Study. **RESEARCH** Development of Danish and Swedish absolutism during the seventeenth century; eighteenth-century Swedish party politics. **SELECTED PUBLICATIONS** Auth, Russia, England, and Swedish Party Politics, 1762-1766: The Interplay Between Great Power Diplomacy and Domestic Politics During Sweden's Age of Liberty, 77; ed, The Riksdag: A History of the Swedish Parliament, 87. **CONTACT ADDRESS** History Dept, Univ of Mississippi, Croft Inst for Int Studies, P O Box 158, University, MS 38677-0158. **EMAIL** mmetcalf@olemiss.edu

METCALF, THOMAS R.
PERSONAL Born 05/31/1934, Schenectady, NY, 2 children **DISCIPLINE** MODERN HISTORY **EDUCATION** Amherst Col, BA, 55; Cambridge Univ, BA, 57, MA, 61; Harvard Univ, PhD, 60. **CAREER** Instr hist, Univ WI, 59-60; asst prof Univ CA, Santa Barbara, 61-62; from asst prof to assoc prof, 62-73, Prof Hist, Univ CA, Berkeley, 73-, Ford Found Foreign Area Training fel, IND, 60-61; Am Inst Indian Studies fac res fel, 64-65; Fulbright-Hays res fel, India, 69-70 & Pakistan, 73-74; trustee, Am Inst Indian Studies, 71-83. **HONORS AND AWARDS** Watumull Prize, AHA, 66. **MEMBERSHIPS** AHA; Asn Asian Studies. **RESEARCH** Nineteenth century India; the British Empire; history of modern India; the British Empire; imperialism and colonialism generally. **SELECTED PUBLICATIONS** Auth, The Aftermath of Revolt: India 1857-1870, Princeton Univ, 64; contribr, Social Structure and Land Control in Indian History, Univ WI, 69; A History of World Civilizations, Wiley, 72; Land, Landlords and British Raj, Univ CA, 78; An Imperial Vision, Univ Ca, 89; Ideologies of the Raj, Univ Cambridge, 95. **CONTACT ADDRESS** Dept of Hist, Univ of California, Berkeley, 3229 Dwinelle Hall, Berkeley, CA 94720. **EMAIL** tmetcalf@socrates.berkeley.edu

METCALFE, WILLIAM CRAIG
PERSONAL Born 07/17/1935, Toronto, ON, Canada, m, 1958, 2 children **DISCIPLINE** EUROPEAN HISTORY & CANADIAN STUDIES **EDUCATION** Univ Toronto, BA, 58; Univ MN, MA, 59, PhD, 67. **CAREER** Asst hist, Univ MN, 59-61, instr, 62-63; from instr to prof emeritus, Univ VT, 63-; assoc dir can studies, Univ Vt, 63; dir, Baroque Ensemble, 65-89; lectr, Inst Elizabethan Arts & Lett, 65-68; mem rev staff, Am Recorder, 69-; mem joint comt, Can Am Studies, AHA-Can Hist Asn, 72-74; ed, Am Rev Can Studies, 73-89; chmn dept music, Univ VT, 73-78; co-founder, Vt Mozart Fest, 74; Albert Corey Prize judge, AHA, 75-76; chmn dept hist, Univ Vt, 80-87; dir, Canadian Studies, Univ Vt, 87-97; conductor, Oriana Singers of Vt. **HONORS AND AWARDS** Douner Medal in Canadian Studies, 93. **MEMBERSHIPS** Can Hist Asn; Am Musicol Soc; Conf Brit Studies; Asn Can Studies US. **RESEARCH** Tudor-Stuart England; Can hist; music hist. **SELECTED PUBLICATIONS** Auth, Dolce or traverso? the flauto problem in Vivaldi's instrumental music, 8/65 & The recorder contatas of Telemann's Harmonischer Gottesdienst, 11/67, Am Recorder; Some aspects of the parliament of 1610, Historian, 11/72; contribr, Voices of Canada, Asn Can Studies in US, 78; ed, Understanding Canada: An Interdisciplinary Intro to Canadian Studies, New York Univ Press, 82; co-ed, Northern Approaches: Scholarship on Canada in the U S, Asn for Canadian Studies in the U S, 93; co-auth, Canadian Culture in the Late 1990's, In: Introducing Canada, Nat Coun Soc Studies, 97. **CONTACT ADDRESS** 39 Brookes Ave, Burlington, VT 05401-3327. **EMAIL** wmetcalf@zoo.uvm.edu

METZ, LEON CLAIRE
PERSONAL Born 11/06/1930, Parkersburg, WV, m, 1970, 4 children **DISCIPLINE** AMERICAN HISTORY **CAREER** Exec asst to Mayor of El Paso, 79-81; ASST TO PRES, UNIV TEX, EL PASO, 81-, LECTR WESTERN HIST, 68-; bk ed, El Paso Times, 71-79. **MEMBERSHIPS** Western Writers Am; Western Hist Asn; Coun Am Mil Past. **RESEARCH** Frontier military; frontier biography; Mexican history. **SELECTED PUBLICATIONS** Auth The Life of Horn, Tom Revisited, W Am Quart, Vol 24, 93; Desert Lawmen--The High Sheriffs of New Mexico and Arizona, 1846-1912, Montana Mag W Hist, Vol 44, 94; Judge Bean, Roy Country, Southw Am Quart, Vol 0100, 97; Border Cuates--A History of the United States Mexican Twin Cities, Southw Am Quart, Vol 99, 96; Billy The Kid--His Life and Legend, Montana Mag We Hist, Vol 45, 95. **CONTACT ADDRESS** Pres Off, Univ of Texas, El Paso, El Paso, TX 79968.

METZGER, THOMAS ALBERT
PERSONAL Born 07/02/1933, Berlin, Germany, m, 1995, 2 children **DISCIPLINE** CHINESE HISTORY **EDUCATION** Harvard Univ, PhD(Hist, Far Eastern Lang), 67. **CAREER** Prof Emer, Univ of Calif, San Diego, 90-; sr fel, Hoover Inst, Stanford Univ, 90-. **HONORS AND AWARDS** UCSD Award for Excellence in Res, 80; Ch'ien Mu Lect in Hist and Cult, 94. **RESEARCH** Contemporary Chinese political thought **SELECTED PUBLICATIONS** Auth, The Internal Organization of Ch'ing Bureacracy, 73, Harvard Univ Pr; auth, Escape from Predicament, 77, Columbia Univ Pr. **CONTACT ADDRESS** Hoover Inst, Stanford Univ, Stanford, CA 94305-6010.

MEVERS, FRANK CLEMENT
PERSONAL Born 10/10/1942, New Orleans, LA, m, 1967, 2 children **DISCIPLINE** UNITED STATES HISTORY **EDUCATION** La State Univ, Baton Rouge, BA, 65, MA, 67; Univ NC, Chapel HIll, PhD(Am hist), 72. **CAREER** Asst ed, Papers of James Madison, NH Hist Soc, 72-73, assoc ed, 73-74; ed, Papers of Josiah Bartlett, 74-77, ed, Papers of William Plumer, 77-79; DIR and STATE ARCHIVIST, NH DIV REC MGT and ARCH, 79- **HONORS AND AWARDS** Great Am Achievement, Bicentennial Coun of Thirteen Original States, 77. **MEMBERSHIPS** Orgn Am Historians; Soc Am Archivists; New Eng Archivists. **RESEARCH** American medical history; American Revolution and early national periods; military history. **SELECTED PUBLICATIONS** Auth, Celebrating the 4th-Independence Day and the Rites of Nationalism in the Early Republic, New England Quart Hist Rev New England Life Letters, Vol 70, 97; Wentworth, John and the American Revolution--The English Connection, New England Quart Hist Rev New England Life Letters, Vol 67, 94. **CONTACT ADDRESS** NH Hist Soc, 30 Park St, Concord, NH 03301. **EMAIL** fmevers@sos.state.nh.us

MEYER, DONALD
PERSONAL Born 10/29/1923, Lincoln, NE, m, 1965 **DISCIPLINE** HISTORY **EDUCATION** Univ Chicago, BA, 47; Harvard Univ, MA, 48, PhD, 53. **CAREER** Instr Am constitutional hist, Harvard Univ, 53-55; from asst prof to assoc prof Am intellectual and social hist, Univ Calif, Los Angeles, 55-65, prof US social hist, 65-67; PROF US SOCIAL HIST AND DIR AM

STUDIES, WESLEYAN UNIV, 67-, Soc Sci Res Coun fac res grants, 58 and 62; Guggenheim fel, 66; Am Philos Soc grant, 70-71. **MEMBERSHIPS** AHA; Orgn Am Historians. **RESEARCH** American cultural and social history. **SELECTED PUBLICATIONS** Auth, The Protestant Search for Political Realism, Univ Calif, 60 rev ed Wes Univ Pr, 88; auth, The Positive Thinkers, Doubleday, 65, rev ed, Pantheon, 80, rev 3rd ed, Wes Univ Pr, 88; auth, Sex and Power The Rise of Women I American, Russia, Sweden and Italy, Wes Univ Pr, 87 2nd ed, 89; auth, Beyond Politics, J Am Hist, Vol 83, 96; To the Ends of the Earth--Womens Search for Education in Medicine, Am Hist Rev, Vol 98, 93; Saskatchewan River Rendezvous Centers and Trading Posts--Continuity in a Cree Social Geography, Ethnohistory, Vol 42, 95; Return to Essentials--Some Reflections on the Present State of Historical Study, Hist Theory, Vol 32, 93; A Chains Reaction, Preservation, Vol 49, 97; The Powers of the Past--Reflections on the Crisis and the Promise of History, Hist Theory, Vol 32, 93. **CONTACT ADDRESS** Dept of Hist, Wesleyan Univ, Middletown, CT 06457.

MEYER, DONALD HARVEY
PERSONAL Born 06/28/1935, Rochester, NY, m, 1958 **DISCIPLINE** AMERICAN INTELLECTUAL HISTORY **EDUCATION** Univ Rochester, BA, 57; Univ Chicago, BD, 61; Univ Calif, Berkeley, PhD(Am hist), 67. **CAREER** Asst prof, 67-72, assoc prof, 72-80, PROF HIST, UNIV DEL, 80- **MEMBERSHIPS** AHA; Orgn Am Historians. **RESEARCH** American intellectual history, especially 19th century religious history. **SELECTED PUBLICATIONS** Auth, Paul Carus and the religion of science, Am Quart, spring 62; The scientific humanism of G Stanley Hall, J Humanistic Psychol, 71; The Instructed Conscience: The Shaping of the American National Ethic, Univ Pa, 72; The saint as hero: William Ellery Channing and the 19th-century mind, Winterthur Portfolio 8, 73; American intellectuals & the Victorian crisis of faith, 12/75 & The uniqueness of the American Enlightenment, summer 76, Am Quart; The Democratic Enlightenment, Putnam, 76. **CONTACT ADDRESS** Dept of Hist, Univ of Delaware, Newark, DE 19711.

MEYER, JAMES S.
DISCIPLINE AMERICAN AND EUROPEAN ART **EDUCATION** Yale Univ, BA in the History of Art, 84; Institute of Fine Arts, New York Univ, MA, 86; Johns Hopkins Univ, PhD, 95; auth, "AIDS and Postmodernism," Arts Magazine 66:8, Apr., 92: 62-68; auth, "Die Bedingung von Boheme" "The Condition of Bohemia" Texte zur Kunst 5:18, May 95: 77-81; auth, "The Macabre Museum" on Mark Dion, Frieze 32 January/February 97: 56-61; auth, "Normads," Parkett 49, May 97: 205-209; auth, "Der Gerbrauch von Merleau-Ponty" "The Uses of Merleau-Ponty," In minimalisms, Stuttgart: Cantz Verlag, 98, 178-189; auth, "Impure Thoughts: The Art of Sam Durant," Artforum 38:8 April 00: 112-117; auth, Refracting Vision: A Critical Anthology on the Writings of Michael Fried, Power Institute of Fine Arts, University of Sydney, 00; ed., Minimalism, Phaidon, 00; auth, Minimalism: Art and Polemics in the Sixties, Yale University Press, 01. **CAREER** Asst Prof, Art, Emory Univ, 94- **HONORS AND AWARDS** Scholar in Residence, Obermann Center for Advanced Study, Univ of Iowa, 01; Getty Res Institute Res Support Grant, 99; Fellowship, Institute of Fine Arts, 85-86; Cum Laude, Yale Univ **RESEARCH** Am and European art since 45, especiallu Minimalism, Conceptualism, Institutional Critique nd site-oriented installation, abstract painting and activist art. **SELECTED PUBLICATIONS** Auth, "AIDS and Postmodernism," Arts Mag 66:8 (Apr., 92), 62-68, Auth, "Die Bedingung von Boheme," ("The Condition of Bohemia"), 95, 77-81, Auth, "The Macabre Museum,"(On Mark Dion), 97, 56-61, Auth, "Nomads," Parket 49, 97, 205-209, Auth, "der gebrauchvo Merleau-ponty," stuttgart, 98, 178-189, Auth, "Impure thoughts: The Art of Sam Durant," 00, 112-117, Auth, Refactuing Vision: Critical Anthology on the Writings of Meichael Fried, 00, Ed, Minimalism, 00, Auth, Minimalism: Art and Polemics in the Sixties,01. **CONTACT ADDRESS** Emory Univ, Atlanta, GA 30322-1950. **EMAIL** jmeye03@emory.edu

MEYER, JERRY D.
PERSONAL Born 11/19/1939, Carbondale, IL, m, 1963, 2 children **DISCIPLINE** ART HISTORY **EDUCATION** SIU, BA, 62, NYork Univ, PHD, 73 **CAREER** Col Sci Tech, 66-68, Brooklyn Col; Art Historian, 68-pres, N IL Univ **MEMBERSHIPS** Col Art Assoc; Midwst Art Hist Soc; Am Acad of Relig **RESEARCH** Late 18th-20th Century American, British, European Art; Religious Imagery; References; Contemporary Art **SELECTED PUBLICATIONS** Auth, "Profane and Sacred Religious Imagery and Prophetic Expression in Postmodern Art," Journ of the Am Acad of Relig, 97, 19-46; Auth, "The Woman Clothed with the Sun," Stud in Inconography, 88, 148-60 **CONTACT ADDRESS** 3030 N First St, De Kalb, IL 60115. **EMAIL** jmeyer@niu.edu

MEYER, JUDITH
PERSONAL Born 10/22/1948, Detroit, MI, m, 1974, 2 children **DISCIPLINE** HISTORY **EDUCATION** Lawrence Univ, BA, 70; Univ Iowa, MA, 72; PhD, 77. **CAREER** Instr, Ind Central Univ, 77-78; asst prof, Smith Col, 78-79; lectr, Univ Conn at Stamford, 81-89; lectr, Fairfield Univ, 85, 87, & 89; from asst prof to assoc prof, Univ Conn at Waterbury, 89-. **HONORS AND AWARDS** Phi Beta Kappa, Lawrence Univ, 69; Raney Prize in Hist, Lawrence Univ, 70; NDEA Fel, Univ Iowa, 70-73; Fulbright Fel, 73-74; vis res fel, Univ Iowa, 79-80; jr fac summer fel & res grant, Res Found of Univ Conn, 91-92. **MEMBERSHIPS** AHA, Sixteenth-Century Studies Confr, New England Hist Asn. **RESEARCH** Protestant & Catholic Marriages in Early Modern France, Urban Reformation. **SELECTED PUBLICATIONS** Auth, "La Rochelle and the Failure of the French Reformation," The Sixteenth Century J 15.2 (84): 169-183; rev, of "History of a Voyage to the Land of Brazil," by Jean de Lery & transl by Janet Whatley, The Sixteenth Century J 22.4 (Winter, 91): 880-881; auth, "The Success of the French Reformation: the Case of La Rochelle," Archiv fur Reformationsgeschichte 84 (93): 242-275; auth, Reformation in La Rochell: Tradition and Change in Early Modern Europe, 1500-1568, Librairie Droz, 96; auth, "La Rochell," in Encyclopedia of the Reformation Vol 2," ed. Hans J. Hillerbrand (NY: Oxford Univ Press, 96): 392-394; rev, of "Nouvelles histoires tragiques," ed. Jean-Claude Arnould and Richard A. Carr, The Sixteenth Century J 28.4 (Winter, 97): 1357-1359. **CONTACT ADDRESS** Dept Soc Sci, Univ of Connecticut, 32 Hillside Ave, Waterbury, CT 06710-2217. **EMAIL** jpmeyer@uconnvm.uconn.edu

MEYER, KATHRYN E.
PERSONAL Born 09/15/1952, Dayton, WA, m, 1972, 4 children **DISCIPLINE** ANCIENT HISTORY, MODERN EUROPE, AND WOMEN'S HISTORY **EDUCATION** Wash State Univ, PhD, 92. **CAREER** Asst prof, Washington State Univ. **HONORS AND AWARDS** WSU Mortar Bd Distinguished Prof, 96; WSU Honors Fac Awd, 97; Women's Classical Caucus, 99. **MEMBERSHIPS** Classical Asn of the Pacific Northwest, Women's Classical Caucus. **RESEARCH** Currently workin gon the Femina Habiis Project with Mary Jane Engh (independent scholar), and C.A.E. Luschnig, Univ of Idaho; Femina Habilis will be a multi-volume biographical dictionary of active women in the Roman world from earliest times to 500 CE. **SELECTED PUBLICATIONS** Auth, The Political Influence of Livia Drusilla during the Reign of Augustus, Selecta II, 90 & The Chinese Must Go! Anti-Chinese Sentiment in Columbia County, 1870-1910, Pacific Northwest Forum, 84. **CONTACT ADDRESS** Dept of History, Washington State Univ, 341 Wilson Hall, PO Box 644030, Pullman, WA 99164-4030. **EMAIL** kemeyer@wsu.edu

MEYER, KENNETH JOHN
PERSONAL Born 08/24/1930, Manitowoc, WI, m, 1953, 4 children **DISCIPLINE** ENGLISH, AMERICAN STUDIES **EDUCATION** Lawrence Col, BA, 53; Univ Minn, MA, 56, PhD (Am studies), 65. **CAREER** Instr English, Monmouth Col, Ill, 57-61; assoc prof English, 64-67, coordr, Res and Planning Develop Proj, 67-71, Prof English, Huron Col, Sdak, 67-, Chmn Dept, 64- **MEMBERSHIPS** Am Studies Asn; NCTE; Conf Col Compos and Commun; Aaup. **RESEARCH** American literature and cultures, 1800-1900; curriculum in the small liberal arts college; the teaching of composition. **SELECTED PUBLICATIONS** **CONTACT ADDRESS** 1941 McClellan Dr, Huron, SD 57350.

MEYER, MICHAEL
PERSONAL Born 04/07/1940, Magdeburg, Germany, m, 1966, 2 children **DISCIPLINE** MODERN EUROPEAN & INTELLECTUAL & CULTURAL HISTORY **EDUCATION** Univ Calif, Los Angeles, BA, 61, MA, 64, PhD(hist), 71. **CAREER** Assoc prof, 70-80, prof hist, Calif State, Northridge, 80-, chmn dept, 75-87. **HONORS AND AWARDS** Res grant, Univ Calif, Los Angeles, Calif State Univ, Northridge, 75, 78, 90, 93, 95, 97, 98, & Am Philol Soc, 78; DAAD Grant 96-97; Fulbright, 99; Univ Pub Awd: The Politics of Music in the Third Reich, 91. **MEMBERSHIPS** AHA; Conf Group Cent Europ Studies; Coun European Studies; Ger Studies Asn. **RESEARCH** Anti-Semitism; music in the Third Reich; Ger Emisies in South Cal; modern ideologies and the arts. **SELECTED PUBLICATIONS** Auth, The Nazi Musicologist as Myth Maker in the Third Reich, J Contemp Hist, 10/75; Prospects of a New Music Culture in the Third Reich in Light of the Relationship between High and Popular Culture in European Musical Life, Hist Reflections, summer 77; The SA Song Literature: A Singing Ideological Posture, J Popular Cult, winter 77; Musicology in the Third Reich: A Gap in Historical Research, Europ Studies Rev, 78; A Reference in the Music Commentary of Theodor W Adorno: The Musicology of Volk and Race, Humanities in Soc, fall 79; Music on the Eve of the Third Reich, In: Towards the Holocaust: Fascism and Anti-Semitism in Weimar Germany, Greenwood Press, 83; The Politics of Music in the Third Reich, Peter Lang, 91; A Musical Facade for the Third Reich: 1933-1938, In: 1937: Modern Art and Politics in Prewar Germany, 91; Herr Linse Berichtet: Fotografien aus dem Magdeburger Umland 1933-1935 von Karl Meyer, Ziethan Verla Oschersleben, 96; National Socialist Germany: Art, In: Encyclopedic History of Modern Germany, Garland Publ, 98. **CONTACT ADDRESS** Dept of Hist, California State Univ, Northridge, 18111 Nordhoff St, Northridge, CA 91330-8200. **EMAIL** michael.meyer@csun.edu

MEYER, MICHAEL ALBERT
PERSONAL Born 11/15/1937, Berlin, Germany, m, 1961, 3 children **DISCIPLINE** JEWISH HISTORY **EDUCATION** Univ Calif, Los Angeles, BA, 59; Hebrew Union Col, Ohio, PhD, 64. **CAREER** Asst prof Jewish hist, Hebrew Union Col, Calif, 64-67; from asst prof to assoc prof, 67-72, Prof Jewish Hist, Hebrew Union Col, Ohio, 72-, Vis asst prof, Univ Calif, Los Angeles, 65-67; vis lectr, Antioch Col, 68; Fel, Leo Baeck Inst, 69-; vis sr lectr, Haifa Univ, 70-71 and Univ Negev, Israel, 71-72; vis prof, Hebrew Univ, Jerusalem, 77-78; **HONORS AND AWARDS** Frank and Ethel Cohen Awd, Jewish Bk Coun Am, 68; Am Coun Learned Soc fel, 82. **MEMBERSHIPS** AHA; Asn Jewish Studies. **RESEARCH** Jewish intellectual history of modern Europe; history of Reform Judaism. **SELECTED PUBLICATIONS** Auth, The Origins of the Modern Jew: Jewish Identity and European Culture in Germany, 1749-1824, Wayne State Univ Press (Detroit, MI), 67; ed, Ideas of Jewish History, Behrman House, 74; auth, Response to Modernity: A History of the Reform Movement in Judaism, Oxford Univ Press (New York, NY), 88; auth, Jewish Identity in the Modern World, Univ Wash Press (Seattle, WA), 90; ed & contribur, German-Jewish History in Modern Times, 4 vols, Columbia Univ Press (New York, NY), 96-98. **CONTACT ADDRESS** Dept of Hist, Hebrew Union Col-Jewish Inst of Religion, Ohio, Cincinnati, OH 45220. **EMAIL** mameyer@cn.huc.edu

MEYER, RICHARD
DISCIPLINE MODERN AND CONTEMPORARY ART **EDUCATION** Univ Calif, Berkeley, PhD. **CAREER** Asst prof, Univ Southern Calif; curated exhib on the early career of the realist painter Paul Cadmus for, Whitney Mus Amer Art. **RESEARCH** 20th-century art and cultural studies. **SELECTED PUBLICATIONS** Auth, Rock Hudson's Body, in Inside/Out: Lesbian Theories, Gay Theories, NY: 91; Robert Mapplethorpe and the Discipline of Photography, in The Lesbian and Gay Studies Reader, NY: 93; Warhol's Clones, in the Yale Journal of Criticism, 94; This Is To Enrage You: Gran Fury and the Graphics of AIDS Activism, in But Is It Art?: The Spirit of Art As Activism, Seattle: 95. **CONTACT ADDRESS** Col Letters, Arts & Sciences, Univ of So California, University Park Campus, Los Angeles, CA 90089. **EMAIL** rmeyers@usc.edu

MEYER, STEPHEN
PERSONAL Born 05/24/1942, Brooklyn, NY, m, 4 children **DISCIPLINE** HISTORY **EDUCATION** State Univ NYork, Stony Brook, BA, 67; Rutgers Univ, MA, 73; PhD, 77. **CAREER** Asst prof to assoc prof, IL Inst of Tech, 81-84; assoc prof to prof, Univ of Wis, 86-. **HONORS AND AWARDS** Rockefeller Found Fel, 85-86; NEH Fel, 00-01. **MEMBERSHIPS** AHA; Org of Am Hist; Soc Sci Hist Assoc; Soc for the Hist of Tech; Labor and Working Class Hist Assoc. **RESEARCH** American Social and Labor History, History of Technology, Gender-Masculinity. **SELECTED PUBLICATIONS** Auth, The Five Dollar Day: Labor Management and Social Control in the Ford Motor Company, 1908-1921, SUNY Pr, (Albany), 81; coed, On the Line: Essays in the History of Auto Work, Univ of IL Pr, (Urbana), 88; auth, Stalin Over Wisconsin: The Making and Unmaking of Militant Unionism, 1920-1950, Rutgers Univ Pr, (New Brunswick), 92. **CONTACT ADDRESS** Dept Hist, Univ of Wisconsin, Parkside, PO Box 2000, Kenosha, WI 53141-2000. **EMAIL** meyer@uwp.edu

MEYEROWITZ, JOANNE
PERSONAL Born 04/08/1954, Washington, DC **DISCIPLINE** HISTORY **EDUCATION** Univ Chicago, BA, 76; Stanford Univ, MA, 78; Stanford Univ, PhD, 83. **CAREER** Assoc prof Hist, Univ Cincinnati, 90- ; Asst prof, Univ Cincinnati, 85-90; Vis asst professor Hist, Claremont McKenna Col, 83-84; Prof, Indiana Univ, 99-; Editor, Journal of American Histiory, 99-. **HONORS AND AWARDS** Social Sci Res Coun, Sexuality Res Fellow, 96-97, McMicken Dean's Awd for Disting Tchg, Univ Cincinnati, 94; Ohio State Univ, Univ Postdoc Fellow, 84-85; Am Hist Asn, Beveridge Grant, 84; Nat Endow Human, Summer Stipend, 84; Newberry Libr, Exxon Ed Found Fellow, 83; National Humanities Center Fel, 99-00. **RESEARCH** 20th-Century US Social/Cultural History; US Women's/Gender History; History of Sexuality; **SELECTED PUBLICATIONS** Women and Migration: Autonomous Female Migrants to Chicago, 1880-1930, Jour Urban Hist, 13:2, Feb, 87, 147-168; Women Adrift: Independent Wage Earners in Chicago, 1880-1930, Univ Chicago Press, 88; Sexual Geography and Gender Economy: The Furnished Room Districts of Chicago, 1890-1930, Gender and History, 2:3, Autumn, 90; American Women's History: The Fall of Women's Culture, Canadian Rev Am Stud, 92; Beyond the Feminine Mystique: A Reassessment of Postwar Mass Culture, 1946-1958, Jour Am Hist, 79:4, Mar 93; Not June Cleaver: Women and Gender in Postwar America, 1945-1960, Temple Univ Press, 94; 'Sex Change' and the Popular Press: Historical Notes on Transsexuality in the United States, 1930-1955, GLQ: A Journal of Lesbian and Gay Studies, 4:2, 98; Women, Cheesecake, and Borderline Material: Responses to Girlie Pictures in the Mid-Twentieth-Century US, Jour Women's Hist, 8:3, Fall, 96; **CONTACT ADDRESS** Indiana Univ, Bloomington, Dept of History, Ballantine Hall, Bloomington, IN 47405. **EMAIL** jmeyerow@indiana.edu

MEYERS, DEBRA A.
DISCIPLINE HISTORY **EDUCATION** Univ Rochester, PhD, 97. **CAREER** Asst prof, Long Island Univ, 97-. **HONORS AND AWARDS** Instr Dev Gnt. **MEMBERSHIPS** OAH; AHA; OIEAHC; SSHA; Forum Euro Expan Global Interaction. **RESEARCH** Early modern women and religion. **SELECTED PUBLICATIONS** Auth, "Frank Lloyd Wright: The Architect as Preacher," J Interdisc Stud 6 (94): 24-40; auth, "Civil Lives of White Women in Seventeenth-Century Maryland," Maryland Hist Mag 94 (99): 309-328. **CONTACT ADDRESS** Dept History, Long Island Univ, C.W. Post, 720 Northern Blvd, Greenvale, NY 11548-1319. **EMAIL** dmeyers@liu.edu

MEZA, ALBERTO
PERSONAL Born 12/08/1941, Chile, m, 1982, 6 children **DISCIPLINE** ART **EDUCATION** Univ Chile, BA, 61; Syracuse Univ, BA, 68; MA, 70; Northern Ill Univ, PhD, 84. **CAREER** Instr, Waubonsee Cmty Col, 71-84; Assoc Prof, Miami Dade Cmty Col, 91-. **HONORS AND AWARDS** Nat Inst for Staff and Org Development, Univ Tex, 99; The Citibank of Fla Endowed Teaching Chair, 98; Fla Artists' Book Prize Awd, Broward Cty, 97. **MEMBERSHIPS** Asn of Fla Cmty Col, Asn of Fla Printmakers. **RESEARCH** Latin Am Folk Art; Cmty Folk Art in Miami; Commercial and non-commercial public imagery. **SELECTED PUBLICATIONS** Auth, Leonardo's Phobias, Artist Book, 97; auth, Bocccaccio's Plague, Artist Book, 98; auth, Cantos de Caminantes, Poetry, Santiago, Chile, 92. **CONTACT ADDRESS** Dept Visual Arts, Miami-Dade Comm Col, 11011 SW 104th St, Miami, FL 33176-3330. **EMAIL** ameza@mdcc.edu

MEZA, PEDRO THOMAS
PERSONAL Born 09/02/1941, New York, NY, m, 1973, 2 children **DISCIPLINE** ENGLISH & EARLY MODERN HISTORY **EDUCATION** NYork Univ, AB, 62, MA, 63, PhD(hist), 67. **CAREER** Lectr hist, Bronx Community Col, 66-67; asst prof, 67-74, assoc prof hist, 74-84, prof, 84-, chair, hist dept, Queensborough Community Col. **MEMBERSHIPS** Conf Brit Studies; AAUP; Soc Hist Technol. **RESEARCH** Early 18th century England--the Church of England. **SELECTED PUBLICATIONS** Co-ed, Readings in Western Civilization: The Early Modern Period, McCutchan, 70; The Question of Authority in the Church of England 1689-1717, 3/73 & Gilbert Burnet's Concept of Religious Tolerations, Hist Mag Protestant Episcopal Church, 9/81. **CONTACT ADDRESS** Queensborough Comm Col, CUNY, 22205 56th Ave, Flushing, NY 11364-1432.

MEZNAR, JOAN E.
DISCIPLINE HISTORY **EDUCATION** Univ Tex, Austin, 86. **CAREER** Asst prof, Mount Holyoke Col, 86-89; asst prof, Univ SC, 89-95; assoc prof, Westmont Col, 95-. **HONORS AND AWARDS** Fulbright-Hays grant, 83-84; NEH, 87; Fulbright sr scolar lectr/res award, 93; contrib ed, handbook of latin amer stud. **RESEARCH** Latin Am; Brazilian. **SELECTED PUBLICATIONS** Auth, Bound By Freedom: Peasants and the End of Slavery in Northeast Brazil, 1831-1888, Positivism, Survey of Social Science: Government and Politics, Salem Press, 95; Radioactive Powder Kills Four and Injures Hundreds in Goiania, Brazil, Brazilian President Announces Plans to Protect Rain Forest, Earth Summit Covenes in Rio de Janeiro, Brazil, Great Events from History II: Ecology and the Environment, Salem Press, 95. **CONTACT ADDRESS** Dept of Hist, Westmont Col, 955 La Paz Rd, Santa Barbara, CA 93108-1099.

MEZZATESTA, MICHAEL P.
DISCIPLINE ART HISTORY **EDUCATION** The Inst of Fine Arts, PhD. **CAREER** Adj prof, Duke Univ; Dir, Duke Univ, Museum of Art. **HONORS AND AWARDS** Fell, American Academy in Rome: Institute for Advanced Study. **RESEARCH** Renaissance and Baroque Italy **SELECTED PUBLICATIONS** Auth, The Art of Gianlorenzo Bernini: Selected Sculpture; auth, Russian and Latin American Art. **CONTACT ADDRESS** Duke Univ, Duke Univ Mus of Art, Box 98732, Durham, NC 27708. **EMAIL** mmezz@duke.edu

MICAL, THOMAS
PERSONAL Born 07/02/1965, Chicago, IL, m, 1996, 2 children **DISCIPLINE** ARCHITECTURE **EDUCATION** Univ Fla, B Design, 87; Harvard Univ, M Arch, 90; Ga Inst Tech, MS, 92; PhD, 98. **CAREER** Asst prof, Univ of Okla, 90-; vis prof, Univ of Fla, 91; archit designer, SOM - Chicago, 96-97; archit designer, Murphy/Jahn, 97-98; vis prof, IL Inst of Tech, 98-99. **HONORS AND AWARDS** Vis Scholar, getty Ctr for the Arts and Humanities, 94; Fel, Ga Inst of Tech, 90-95, Res Grant, Univ of Okla. **MEMBERSHIPS** Am Col Schools of Archit; Soc of Archit Hist; Am Soc for Aesthetics. **RESEARCH** Philosophy in Architecture, Aesthetics, Surrealism, Russian Avant-Garde. **SELECTED PUBLICATIONS** Auth, "The Stealth Landscape", Perforations 4, Atlanta, Ga, 93; auth, "The Eternal Recurrence of 'l'effroyablement ancien'", Perforations 20, Atlanta, Ga, 99. **CONTACT ADDRESS** Col Archit, Univ of Oklahoma, 162 Gould Hall, 830 Van Vleet Oval, Norman, OK 73019. **EMAIL** tmical@ou.edu

MICHAELS, PAULA A.
DISCIPLINE HISTORY **EDUCATION** Northwestern Univ, BA, 87; Univ NC Chapel Hill, MA, 91, PhD, 97. **CAREER** Asst prof, Univ Iowa, 97- . **HONORS AND AWARDS** IREX on-site lang training grant, 91-92; IREX advan res fel, 94-95; SSRC dissertation fel, 96-97. **MEMBERSHIPS** AAASS; AHA. **RESEARCH** Russia/USSR; Central Asia **SELECTED PUBLICATIONS** Auth, Ninety Winds of Change: The 1985 Alma-Ata Riots and the Mobilization of Kazak Ethnic Identity, Mich Discussions in Anthrop, 96; Kazak Women: Living the Heritage of a Unique Past, in Women in Muslim Societies: Diversity within Unity, Lynne Rienner Publ, 98; Medical Traditions, Kazak Women, and Soviet Medical Politics to 1941, Nationalities Papers, 98; Shamans and Surgeons: Medicine as Politics In Soviet Kazakstan, 1917-53, forthcoming 2002. **CONTACT ADDRESS** Dept of History, Univ of Iowa, Schaeffer Hall 280, Iowa City, IA 52242.

MICHAUX, HENRY G.
PERSONAL Born 01/19/1934, Morganton, NC, s **DISCIPLINE** ART HISTORY **EDUCATION** TX So Univ, BFA (magna cum laude) 1959; PA State Univ, MEd 1960, DEd 1971, grad grant-in-aid 1959-60, grad asst 1966-67. **CAREER** VA State Univ, tchr fine arts & art educ 1960-62; So Univ in New Orleans, 62-67; Cntrl State Univ, 67-68; TX So Univ, 68-70; Coll of the VI, 70; Appalachian State Univ, assoc prof art educ 1972-76; NC Central Univ, assoc prof art educ 1977-78; SC State University, Assoc Prof Art Educ 1978-. **HONORS AND AWARDS** Honorary mem Alpha Kappa Mu 1956-59; Jesse Jones Fine Arts Scholarship TX So Univ 1956-59; Selected Participant Japanese Seminar on Preserv of Cultural Continuity by SC Consortium for Intl Studies 1980; numerous exhibits; natl winner of competition for one-man shows; Madison Galleries, NY; work in Look Magazine; drawings owned by NC Arts Museum; "African American Artists, NC USA" NC Museum of Art 1980; interview and feature on "Carolina Camera" WBTV Charlotte 1981; apptd SC Acquisitions Comm a part of the SC Museum Commn 1982-84; NC Artist International, Hickory Museum of Art, 1987; Natl Invitationals "Dimensions and Directions, Black Artists of the South" Jackson MS 1983; "Changing Images,": Hickory Museum of Art, 1993 . **MEMBERSHIPS** National Association of Schools of Art and Design; National Sculpture Center; NC Coalition of Arts; mem Amer Craftsmen Council 1964-; National Council on Education for the Ceramic Arts; Seminar for Research in Art Education; Amer Assn of Univ Profs 1962-71; natl Art Educ Assn 1974-87; Black Art Festivals; first pres Caldwell Arts Council Lenoir, NC 1976; designed and coord first indoor/outdoor regional (NC, GA, SC, TN, VA) Sculptors Competition Lenoir NC 1986 through Lenoir Parks & Recreational Dept & the Caldwell Arts Cncl; developed Black Studies (African-Amer Studies for Caldwell Comm Coll Lenoir NC) Project proposal; ETV (WXEX-TV) participant VA State Coll. **CONTACT ADDRESS** So Carolina State Univ, 300 College St, NE, Orangeburg, SC 29117-0001.

MICHEL, SONYA
DISCIPLINE HISTORY **EDUCATION** Brown Univ, PhD, 86. **CAREER** Assoc prof, Univ Ill Urbana Champaign. **RESEARCH** Women and gender in the United States; comparative perspective, gender and social welfare; popular culture. **SELECTED PUBLICATIONS** Co-ed, Mothers of a New World: Maternalist Politics and the Origins of Welfare States, Routledge, 93. **CONTACT ADDRESS** History Dept, Univ of Illinois, Urbana-Champaign, 52 E Gregory Dr, Champaign, IL 61820. **EMAIL** s-michel@staff.uiuc.edu

MICHELS, ANTHONY
PERSONAL Born 11/17/1967, Kingston, NY, s **DISCIPLINE** HISTORY **EDUCATION** Santa Cruz Univ, BA; Stanford Univ, PhD. **CAREER** Asst Prof, Univ of Wisconsin. **MEMBERSHIPS** Assoc for Jewish Stud; Amer Hist Assoc **RESEARCH** Amer Jewish history; European Jewish history; socialism; nationalism; Yiddish culture; popular culture. **CONTACT ADDRESS** Dept of Hist, Univ of Wisconsin, Madison, 1401 Observatory Drive, Madison, WI 53706. **EMAIL** aemichels@facstaff.wisc.edu

MICHELS, EILEEN M.
PERSONAL Born 03/27/1926, Fargo, ND, m, 1955, 1 child **DISCIPLINE** ART HISTORY **EDUCATION** Univ Minn, BA, 47, MA, 53, MLS, 59, PhD, 71. **CAREER** Part time instr, lectr, art hist, Univ Minn, 63-71; asst prof, Univ Wisc, River Falls, 66-71; vis asst prof, Stanford Univ, 72-73; asst prof, art, Col of St Catherine, 74-78; vis prof, Univ Wisc, Milwaukee, 76; assoc prof and chemn 78-88, prof, 89-92, adj prof, 92-96, prof emerita, 92- , Dept of Art Hist, Univ St. Thomas. **HONORS AND AWARDS** Magna cum Laude, 47; Phi Beta Kappa, 47; Fulbright Awd, 56-57; NEH Summer Sem, 80; Vincent Scully Jr res grant from Archit Hist Found, 94. **MEMBERSHIPS** Soc Archit Hist; Col Art Asn; Frank Lloyd Wright Home and Studio Found; Frank Lloyd Wright Found; Minn Hist Soc; Minn Preservation Alliance. **RESEARCH** American architecture, painting and sculpture, seventeenth century to present; European nineteenth and twentieth century architecture, painting and sculpture; decorative arts; prehistoric art; ancient art; medieval art. **SELECTED PUBLICATIONS** Auth, Edwin Lundie, in Mulfinger, ed, The Architecture of Edwin Lundie, Minn Hist Soc, 95; contribur, Dictionary of Art, Grove's Dictionaries, Macmillan, 97; auth, The Buildings of Minnesota, Oxford, forthcoming. **CONTACT ADDRESS** 2183 Hendon Ave, Saint Paul, MN 55108. **EMAIL** epmichels@stthomas.edu

MICHELSON, BRUCE
PERSONAL Born 10/19/1948, Baltimore, MD, m, 1973, 2 children **DISCIPLINE** AMERICAN LITERATURE AND STUDIES, LITERARY THEORY **EDUCATION** Williams Col, AB, 70; Univ of Wash, MA, 74; PhD, 76. **CAREER** Asst prof to prof, Univ of IL, 76-, Dir, Campus Honors Prof, 96-. **HONORS AND AWARDS** Fulbright, Belgium, 83-84; Prokasy Awd for Dist Teaching, 92. **MEMBERSHIPS** MLA; Am Lit Assoc; Mark Twain Circle; Am Homor Studies Assoc; Am Studies Assoc; Richard Wilbury Soc. **RESEARCH** Mark Twain, literary wit, 20th century poetry, literature and technology. **SELECTED PUBLICATIONS** Auth, Wilbur's Poetry, 91; auth, Mark Twain on the Loose, 95; auth, Literary Wit, 00. **CONTACT ADDRESS** Dept English, Univ of Illinois, Urbana-Champaign, 608 s. Wright St., Urbana, IL 61801-3613. **EMAIL** brucem@uiuc.edu

MICKLER, MICHAEL L.
PERSONAL Born 10/21/1949, Providence, RI, m, 1982, 4 children **DISCIPLINE** HISTORICAL STUDIES **EDUCATION** Graduate Theological Union, PhD, 89 **CAREER** Asst Prof, Church History, 89-94, Assoc Prof, 95-, Academic Dean, 95-, Unification Theological Sem. **RESEARCH** Unification Church and tradition **SELECTED PUBLICATIONS** Auth, The Unification Church in America: A Bibliography and Research Guide, 87; auth, A History of the Unification Church in America, 59-74, 93; auth, Forty Years in America: An Intimate History of the Unification Movement, 1959-99, 00. **CONTACT ADDRESS** 30 Seminary Dr., Barrytown, NY 12507. **EMAIL** utsed@ulstn.net

MIDDLEKAUFF, ROBERT LAWRENCE
PERSONAL Born 07/05/1929, Yakima, WA, m, 1952, 2 children **DISCIPLINE** AMERICAN COLONIAL HISTORY **EDUCATION** Univ Wash, AB, 52, MA, 56; Yale Univ, PhD, 61. **CAREER** Instr hist, Yale Univ, 59-62; from Asst Prof to Prof, 62-81, Margaret Byrne Prof Hist, 81-88, Prof Hist, 88-91, Hotchkis Prof, Univ Calif, Berkeley, 91-, Provost & Dean, Col Lett & Sci, 81-83; Dir, Henry E. Huntington Libr and Art Gallery, 83-88. **HONORS AND AWARDS** Am Coun Learned Soc fel, 65-66; Bancroft Prize Am Hist, Columbia Univ, 72. **MEMBERSHIPS** AHA; Orgn Am Historians; Soc Am Hist; Am Acad Arts & Sci; Am Philos Soc. **RESEARCH** American Revolution; Puritanism in New England; early American history. **SELECTED PUBLICATIONS** Auth, A Persistent Tradition: The Classical Curriculum in 18th Century New England, William & Mary Quart, 1/61; Ancients and Axioms, Yale Univ, 63; Pity and Intellect in Puritanism, William & Mary Quart, 7/65; The Mathers: Three Generations of Puritan Intellectuals, Oxford Univ, 71; Why Men Fought in the American Revolution, Huntington Libr Quart, spring 80; The Glorious Cause: The American Revolution, 1763-1789, Oxford Univ Press, 1982; Benjamin Franklin and his Enemies, Calif, 96. **CONTACT ADDRESS** Dept of Hist, Univ of California, Berkeley, 3229 Dwinelle Hall, Berkeley, CA 94720-2551. **EMAIL** rlmiddlek@juno.com

MIDDLETON, CHARLES
PERSONAL Born 09/16/1944, Hays, 3 children **DISCIPLINE** HISTORY **EDUCATION** Florida State Univ, AB, 65; Duke Univ, MA, PhD, 69. **CAREER** Asst to Prof Hist Univ Col, Boulder, 69-96, Assoc Dean, Col Arts & Sciences, 80-88; Dean, 88-96; Prof Hist, Bowling Green State Univ 96-, Prov, vpres Acad Affairs, BGSU, 96-. **HONORS AND AWARDS** Phi Eta Sigma; Phi Alpha Theta; Phi Beta Kappa; Teaching Recognition Awd Univ Col; Fel Royal Hist Soc; Robert L Stearns Awd Univ Col; Univ Col Medal; Golden Key Nat Honor Soc; Phi Kappa Phi; numerous editions of Who's Who in West and Who's Who. **MEMBERSHIPS** Am Hist Asn; N Am Conf Brit Studies (life); Western Conf on Brit Studies; Southern Conf Brit Studies; Comt on Gay & Lesbian Hist AHA (life); Am Conf Irish Studies. **RESEARCH** Mod Brit soc hist; gay and lesbian hist. **SELECTED PUBLICATIONS** Administration of British Foreign Policy, 1782-1846, Duke Press, 77; Numerous Articles. **CONTACT ADDRESS** Bowling Green State Univ, McFall Center 230, Bowling Green, OH 43403. **EMAIL** charlrm@bgnet.bgsu.edu

MIDDLETON, STEPHEN
PERSONAL Born 01/16/1954, Cross, SC, m, 1979, 3 children **DISCIPLINE** CONSTITUTIONAL HISTORY **EDUCATION** Ohio State Univ, MA, 77; Miami Univ (OH), PhD, 87. **CAREER** ASSOC PROF, HIST, NC STATE UNIV **HONORS AND AWARDS** Goleb Fel in Legal Hist, NYU Law Sch, 99-00. **SELECTED PUBLICATIONS** Auth, Ohio and the Antislavery Activities of Attorney S.P. Chase, Garland, 90; auth, "We Must Not Fail: Horace Sudduth," Queen City Heritage 49; auth, The Black Laws in the Old Northwest, Greenwood, 93; "Law and Ideology in Ohio and Kentucky," Filson Club Hist Quart 67, 93. **CONTACT ADDRESS** Dept of Hist, No Carolina State Univ, Box 8108, Raleigh, NC 27695. **EMAIL** stephen_middleton@ncsu.edu

MIDELFORT, H. C. ERIK
PERSONAL Born 04/17/1942, Eau Claire, WI, 3 children **DISCIPLINE** REFORMATION & EARLY MODERN GERMAN HISTORY **EDUCATION** Yale Univ, BA, 64, MPhil, 67, PhD, 70. **CAREER** Instr Western civilization, Stanford Univ, 68-70; from Asst Prof to Assoc Prof. 70-87, Prof Hist, 87-, C. Julian Bishko Prof, Univ Va, 96-, Principal, Brown Col at Univ Va, 96-. **HONORS AND AWARDS** Gustave O Arlt Awd, Coun Grad Sch of US, 73; Guggenheim Mem Found fel, 75-76; NEH Fel, 87-88; Roland H. Bainton Awd, 16th Century Studies Conf, 95; Ralph Waldo Emerson Awd of Phi Beta Kappa. **MEMBERSHIPS** Am Soc Reformation Res. **RESEARCH** History of insanity; the vulgar Renaissance in Germany; Johann Joseph Gassner: Exorcism and the Enlightenment. **SELECTED PUBLICATIONS** Auth, Witch Hunting in Southwestern Germany, 1562-1684, Stanford Univ, 72; co-ed & transl, Bernd Moeller, Imperial Cities and the Reformation, Fortress, 72; auth, The revolution of 1525?, Cent Europ Hist, 78; co-ed & transl, Peter Blickle, The Revolution of 1525, Johns Hopkins Univ Press, 81; Madness and Civilization in Early Modern Europe, A Reappraisal of Michel Foucault, In: After the Reformation, Univ Pa, 80; auth, Mad Princes of Renaissance Germany, Univ Press Va, 94; transl, Wolfgang Behringer, Shaman of Oberstdorf. Conrad Stoeckhlim and the Phantoms of the Night, Univ Press Va, 98; transl and co-ed, Johann Weyer, On Witchcraft, Pegasus Press, 98; A History of Madness in 16th Century Germany, Stanford Univ Press, 99. **CONTACT ADDRESS** Dept of Hist, Univ of Virginia, Randall Hall, Charlottesville, VA 22903-3284. **EMAIL** hem7e@virginia.edu

MIGLIAZZO, ARLIN C.
PERSONAL Born 09/20/1951, South Gate, CA, m, 1977, 2 children **DISCIPLINE** HISTORY **EDUCATION** Biola Col, BA, 74; Northern Az Univ, MA, 75; Washington St Univ, PhD, 82. **CAREER** Instr, 77-78, Biola Col; lectr, 79-81, Washington St Univ; instr, 81, Pac Lutheran Univ; asst prof, 82-83, Judson Baptist Col; lectr, 86, Univ Pittsburgh; adj prof, 88, Spokane Comm Col; Fulbright/Hays prof, 90, Keimyung Univ Daegu, Rep of Korea; asst to full prof, 83-, Whitworth Col. **HONORS AND AWARDS** Lily Fellows Grant, 96, 96, 97; Who's Who Among Amer Teachers, 96; Whitworth Col Teaching Excellence Awd, 97; who's who among amer univ & col, 74; cum laude grad, biola col, 74; phi kappa phi; phi alpha theta. **MEMBERSHIPS** E Wa St Hist Soc; Conf on Faith & Hist. **RESEARCH** Race & ethnicity in Amer life; twentieth century Amer intellectual cult; hist of higher educ. **SELECTED PUBLICATIONS** Art, A Tarnished Legacy Revisited: Jean Pierre Purry and the Settlement of the Southern Frontier, 1718-1736, SC Hist Mag, 91; art, The Challenge of Educational Wholeness: Linking Beliefs, Values and Academics, Faculty Dialogue, 93; art, Korean Leadership in the Twenty-First Century: A Profile of the Corning Generation, Korea J, 93; art, Cultural Mimesis and Christian Higher Education: A personal Reconnaissance, Fides et Historia, 93; co-auth, Whitworth College: Evangelical in the Reformed Tradition, Models for Christian Higher Education: Strategies for Survival and Success in the Twenty-First Century, William B Eerdmans Press, 97. **CONTACT ADDRESS** Dept Hist/Polit & Int Stud, Whitworth Col, 300 W Hawthorne Rd, Spokane, WA 99218. **EMAIL** amigliazzo@whitworth.edu

MIHELICH, DENNIS
PERSONAL Born Cleveland, OH **DISCIPLINE** UNITED STATES HISTORY **EDUCATION** Kent State Univ, BA, 66; Case Western Reserve Univ, MA, PhD, 72. **CAREER** Adv, career plan and public hist internships; assoc prof Creighton Univ. **MEMBERSHIPS** Past pres, Hist Soc Douglas Co, Nebr State Hist Soc; mem, Nebr State Hist Records bd. **RESEARCH** African American history. **SELECTED PUBLICATIONS** Publ on res interest. **CONTACT ADDRESS** Dept of History, Creighton Univ, 2500 California Plaza, Omaha, NE 68178. **EMAIL** dnm@creighton.edu

MIHESUAH, DEVON ABBOTT
PERSONAL Born 06/02/1957, Wichita Falls, TX, m, 1990, 2 children **DISCIPLINE** AMERICAN HISTORY **EDUCATION** Tx Christian Univ, BS, 81; MED, 82; MA, 86; PhD, 89. **CAREER** Assoc prof, N Ariz Univ, 95-; asst prof, N Ariz Univ, 89-95; Ed, Amer Indian Quart, 98-; Women of the West Museum Proj, Boulder, CO, 92-; Consultant, Exhibit Content Develop Proj at Women of West Museum 94-96; Consultant, Edge of the Rez, Arizona Daily Sun & KNAU Radio Series on Bordertown Race Relations, 96; Consultant, Texas Indian Commission's and Texas Historical Commission's Committee on the Acquisition & Disposition of Humanities Remains & Sacred Objects, 84-89; Consultant, Northeastern State Univ Archives & Special Collections, 88-89; Prof, Applied Indigenous Studies NAU, 00; Prof, Hist, NAU, 98-. **HONORS AND AWARDS** Ford Found Postdoctoral Fel; Critics' Choice Awd of Amer Educ Studies Assoc for Cultivating the Rosebuds: The Education of Women at the Cherokee Female Seminary, 1851-1909; Native Amer Students United Awd for Outstanding Fac, 94; NAU Pres Awd for Outstanding Fac; NAU Organized Res Grant, 93; Ariz Humanities Council Studies Grant, 93; Amer Council of Learned Soc Fel; Amer Historical Assoc Albert Beveridge Res Grant, 92; Ntl Endowment Humanities Travel to Collections Grant, 92; NAU Outstanding Fac Woman of Year Awd, 92; NAU Organized Res Grant, 92; Critics Choice Awd of Am Ed Stud Assoc for Natives and Academics. **MEMBERSHIPS** Amer Historical Assoc; Amer Indian Historians' Assoc; Amer Soc for Ethnohistory; Okla Historical Soc; Phi Alpha Theta; Western History Assoc. **RESEARCH** American Indian History; Reparation Issues; Identity; Women **SELECTED PUBLICATIONS** Auth, Roads of My Relations, U of AZ Press, 00; auth, Who Owns Indian Remains?, U of NE Press, 00; Medicine Woman, Red Ink 5, 98, Univ AZ Pr; ed, Natives and Academics: Discussions on Researching and Writing About American Indians, Univ Nebr Pr, 98; American Indians: Stereotypes and Realities, Clarity Intl, 98; Cultivating the Rosebuds: The Education of Women at the Cherokee Female Seminary, 1851-1909, Univ Ill, 93. **CONTACT ADDRESS** Dept Applied Indigenous Studies, Devon Abbott Mihesuah, Northern AZ Univ, PO Box 15016, Flagstaff, AZ 86011-5016. **EMAIL** devon.mihesuah@nau.edu

MILAC, METOD M.
PERSONAL Born 10/02/1924, Prevalje, Slovenia, m, 1951, 3 children **DISCIPLINE** LIBRARIANSHIP; MUSICOLOGY; EMIGRATION STUDIES **EDUCATION** Cleveland Inst Mus, BM, 57; Cleveland Inst Mus, MM, 60; Western Reserve Univ, MSLS, 62; Syracuse Univ, MPh, 87; Syracuse Univ, PhD, 91. **CAREER** Mus Libr, Syracuse Univ Lib, 62-65; Head, Ref Dept, SUL, 65-68; Asst Dir, SUL, 68-73; Actg Dir, SUL, 73-74; Assoc Dir, SUL, 74-92. **HONORS AND AWARDS** Post Std Awd for Excel in Lib Serv, 82; Disting Serv Awd, Syracuse Univ Lib, 89. **MEMBERSHIPS** Am Musicol Soc; Am Assoc Advance of Slavic Stud; Soc Slovene Stud. **RESEARCH** Late 16th century music, composer Jacobus Gallus Carniolus (1550-1591); World War II, Central Europe. **SELECTED PUBLICATIONS** Anno Domini 1574: The Question of Jacobus Gallus and the Imperial Court Chapel, in Gallus Carniolus in Evropska Renesansa (Ljubljana: Slovene Acad of Sci and Arts, 91, 21-48; The War Years, 1941-1945: From My Experiences, Slovene Studies, v16, n2, 94, 31-47; Petje Druzi Nove Priseljence: Ustanovitev in Prva Leta Pevskega Zbora Korotan / Choral Singing Unifies New Immigrants: Founding and First Years of Singing Society Korotan, Dve Domovini/Two Homelands, Migration Studies 8, Ljubljana, Ctr Sci Res of the Slovene Acad Sci and Arts, The Inst for Slovene Emigration Res, 97, 49-70; Porocilo Avstrijskega Centra Za Etnicne Manjsine 1996, Volksgruppen Report/Ethnic Group Report, Zapiski, Chron Am Slovene Congress, Issue III, Autumn 97, 8-13. **CONTACT ADDRESS** 259 Kensington Pl, Syracuse, NY 13210-3307. **EMAIL** mmilac@syr.edu

MILES, EDWIN ARTHUR
PERSONAL Born 02/02/1926, Birmingham, AL **DISCIPLINE** AMERICAN HISTORY **EDUCATION** Birmingham-Southern Col, AB, 48; Univ NC, MA, 49, PhD(hist), 54. **CAREER** Instr soc sci, Univ NC, 49-50; researcher, State Dept Arch and Hist, NC, 52-54; from asst prof to assoc prof, 54-62, chmn dept, 69-73, PROF HIST, UNIV HOUSTON, 62- **MEMBERSHIPS** AHA; Orgn Am Historians; Southern Hist Asn. **RESEARCH** Southern history; early national period; Jacksonian period. **SELECTED PUBLICATIONS** Auth, Jacksonian Democracy in Mississippi, Univ NC, 60; The old South and the classical world, NC Hist Rev, summer 71; President Adams' billiard table, New England Quart, 3/72; After John Marshall's decision: Worcester v Georgia and the nullification crisis, J Southern Hist, 11/73; The young American nation and the classical world, J Hist Ideas, 4-6/74; The first people's inaugural--1829, Tenn Hist Quart, fall 78; cocompiler, The Era of Good Feelings and the Age of Jackson, AHM Publ, 79. **CONTACT ADDRESS** Dept of Hist, Univ of Houston, Houston, TX 77004.

MILES, MARGARET M.
PERSONAL Born 09/16/1952, Detroit, MI **DISCIPLINE** CLASSICAL ARCHAEOLOGY **EDUCATION** Wayne State Univ, 69-71; Univ Mich, AB, 73; MA, 76, PhD, 80, Princeton Univ. **CAREER** Visiting Asst Prof, 82-87, Univ California-Berkeley; Visiting Asst Prof, 88-90, Intercollegiate Center, Rome, Italy; Visiting Asst Prof, 91-92, Smith Col; Asst Prof, 92-94, Assoc Prof, 94-, Univ California-Irvine. **HONORS AND AWARDS** John Williams White Fellow 76-77; Olivia James Fellow, 89-90; Rome Prize Fellow, AAR, 87-88; Mellon Fellow, IAS, 90-91; NEH Fellow, 96-97. **MEMBERSHIPS** AIA; CAA; APA **RESEARCH** Greek and Roman art and architecture; ancient religion **SELECTED PUBLICATIONS** Auth, "The Propylon to the Sanctuary of Demeter Malophoros at Selinous," AJA, 98; auth, The Athenian Agora XXXI: The City Eleusinion, 98. **CONTACT ADDRESS** Dept of Art History, Univ of California, Irvine, Irvine, CA 92697-2785. **EMAIL** mmmiles@uci.edu

MILLAR, GILBERT J.
PERSONAL Born 04/07/1939, Kilwinning, AYE, Scotland, m, 1989, 5 children **DISCIPLINE** HISTORY **EDUCATION** Southeastern La Col, BA, 61; La State Univ, MA, 64; PhD, 74. **CAREER** Instr, Ark State Col, 65-67; asst prof, Longwood Col, 70-76; assoc prof, dept ch; prof, 96-. **HONORS AND AWARDS** Maude Glen Raiford Awd; Dir Am Shl; Contemp Auth. **MEMBERSHIPS** AMI; SBAHR; ESSHA. **RESEARCH** Medieval religious and Military history; Military history; early modern Europe. **SELECTED PUBLICATIONS** Auth, Tudor Mercenaries and Auxiliaries, Univ Press VA (Charlottesville, VA), 80; auth, "The Landknecht: His Origins and Recruitment, with Some Reference to the Reign of Henry VIII," Milit Aff (71); auth, "The Albanians: Sixteen Century Mercenaries," Hist Today (76); auth, "Mercenaries Under Henry VIII," Hist Today (77); auth, "The Lollards of Scotland," J Vir Soc Sci Asn (78); auth, "Henry VIII's Colonel's," J Soc Army Hist Res (79); auth, "Henry VII's Preliminary Letter of Retainer to Colonel Frederick von Rieffenberg for the Raising of 1500 Men-at-Arms," J Soc Army Hist Res (89). **CONTACT ADDRESS** Dept History, Political Science, Longwood Col, 201 High St, Farmville, VA 23909-1800.

MILLAR, JOHN F.
PERSONAL Born 01/19/1945, New York, NY, m, 1972, 1 child **DISCIPLINE** HISTORY **EDUCATION** Harvard Col, AB 66; Col of WM and Mary, MA 81. **CAREER** Lecturer in History, 72 to present. **RESEARCH** Eighteenth Century American. **SELECTED PUBLICATIONS** Auth, The Architects of the American Colonies, 68; auth, A Complete Life of Christ, 86; auth, Elizabethan County Dances, 86; auth, Early American Ships, 86; auth, Classical Architecture in Renaissance Europe 1419-1585, 87; auth, Building Early American Workshops, 88; auth, A Handbook on the Founding of Australia 1788, 88; auth, County Dances of Colonial America, 89. **CONTACT ADDRESS** 710 South Henry St, Williamsburg, VA 23185-4113.

MILLAR, STEVEN
DISCIPLINE ART **EDUCATION** Yale Univ, BA, 91; Washington Univ (St. Louis, MO), MFA, 95. **CAREER** Instr, St. Louis Comm Col, 96; Instr, Maryville Univ, 96; Lectr, Washington Univ, 96-97; Asst Prof, 97-, Fairfield Univ. **CONTACT ADDRESS** 48 Rayfield Rd, Westport, CT 06880.

MILLE, DIANE
DISCIPLINE ART HISTORY **EDUCATION** Rutgers Univ, BA, 79; Hunter Col, MA, 82; Cuny Grad Ctr, PhD, 93. **CAREER** Dir, Thomas J. Walsh Art Gallery, Fairfield Univ, 87-89; Adj Prof, Fairfield Univ, 96-; Adj Prof, 93-, Sacred Heart Univ. **HONORS AND AWARDS** Honorary Member of Samagundi Club, NYC, 98-. **CONTACT ADDRESS** Thomas J. Walsh Art Gallery, Fairfield Univ, Fairfield, CT 06430.

MILLEN, SHIRLEY A.
DISCIPLINE HISTORY **EDUCATION** Univ Minn, PhD, 85. **CAREER** Instr, Bethel Col, 79, 82-83; prof, Westmont Col, 84-. **RESEARCH** Philos of hist; ethics of David Hume; anti-semitism; Europ nationalism and liberalism; w civilization. **SELECTED PUBLICATIONS** Auth, Organized Freethought: the Religion of Unbelief in Victorian England, Garland, 87; Keeping the Faith: The Struggle for a Militant Atheist Press, 1839-62, Victorian Periodicals Rev, 92; Individualism in the Liberal Arts: Thoughts on Habits of the Heart, Fac Dialogue, 87; Women in History and Hannah More, Fides et Historia, 87. **CONTACT ADDRESS** Dept of Hist, Westmont Col, 955 La Paz Rd, Santa Barbara, CA 93108-1099.

MILLER, ANGELA L.
PERSONAL 2 children **DISCIPLINE** CULTURAL HISTORY 19TH- AND 20TH-C AM ART **EDUCATION** Yale Univ, PhD, 85. **CAREER** Assoc prof, art hist, Washington Univ. **HONORS AND AWARDS** John Hope Franklin Prize; Charles Eldredge Prize. **SELECTED PUBLICATIONS** Auth, Empire the Eye: Landscape Reprofesentation and Am Cultural Politics, 1825-1875, Cornell Univ Profess, 93; Breaking Down the Preserves Visual Production, Am Art, 97; The Moving Panorama, in Wide Angle: A Film Quarterly, 96. **CONTACT ADDRESS** Washington Univ, Box 1189, Saint Louis, MO 63130. **EMAIL** almiller@artsci.wustl.edu

MILLER, CARMAN I.
PERSONAL Born 05/31/1940, Moser's River, NS, Canada **DISCIPLINE** HISTORY **EDUCATION** Acadia Univ, BA, 60, BEd 61; Dalhousie Univ, MA, 64; Univ London, PhD, 70. **CAREER** Lectr, 67-70, asst prof, 70-76, assoc prof, 76-93, chmn, 78-81 & 90-93, prof history, McGill Univ, 94-, dean arts 95-; dir, Can Inst Hist Microreproduction, 86-89; ed bd, Can Rev Stud Nationalism, 73-78; Stud Hist Politics, 79-80; Int J, 92-; adv comt, Dict Can Biog, 93-. **HONORS AND AWARDS** Fels, Dalhousie Univ grad; Univ W Ont tchg; Can Coun doctoral; Can Coun leave; SSHRCC leave; schools, Ont govt, IODE over-seas postgrad; Can Coun res grant; SSHRCC aid to publ grant, res award, int conf award **MEMBERSHIPS** Can Hist Asn (coun, 71-73, chmn prog comt, 77) **SELECTED PUBLICATIONS** Auth, The Canadian Career of the Fourth Earl of Minto, 80; auth, Painting the Map Red, 94. **CONTACT ADDRESS** Dept of History, McGill Univ, 853 Sherbrooke St W, Montreal, QC, Canada H3A 2T6. **EMAIL** carman@artsci.lan.mcgill.ca

MILLER, CAROL
DISCIPLINE AMERICAN STUDIES AND AMERICAN INDIAN STUDIES **EDUCATION** Univ Okla, PhD, 80. **CAREER** Assoc prof, Morse Alumni Distinguished Prof Am Stud and Am Indian Stud, Univ Minn, Twin Cities. **MEMBER-**

SHIPS Cherokee Nat of Okla. **RESEARCH** Contemporary American Indian literatures. **SELECTED PUBLICATIONS** Published on the performance of students of color in composition and multicultural pedagogy; recently published articles or chapters in the field of American Studies and American Indian Studies have concerned the representation of urban Indian experience in Native fiction, how treatments of World War II by Native writers address the myth of assimilation, and issues of mediation in the writing of Mourning Dove and Ella Deloria. **CONTACT ADDRESS** Univ of Minnesota, Twin Cities, 206 Scott, Minneapolis, MN 55455. **EMAIL** mille004@maroon.tc.umn.edu

MILLER, CHAR
PERSONAL Born 11/23/1951, St Louis, MO, m, 1977, 2 children **DISCIPLINE** HISTORY **EDUCATION** Pitzer Col, Ba, 75; Johns Hopkins Univ, MA, 77; PhD, 81. **CAREER** Vis asst prof, Univ of Miami, 80-81; from asst prof to prof, Trinity Univ, 81-; Chair of Hist Dept, Trinity Univ, 98-. **HONORS AND AWARDS** Honorary Gilman Fel, Johns Hopkins Univ, 78-79; Outstanding Prof, Trinity Univ, 86; Bell Fel, Forest Hist Soc, 92; Archie K. Davis Fel, NC Soc, 93; Hoffman Fac Advisor Res Awd, Phi Alpha Theta, 93; Outstanding Prof, Trinity Univ, 96-97; The Dr. and Mrs. Z. T. Scott Fac Fel, Trinity Univ, 97. **MEMBERSHIPS** Am Hist Asn, Am Soc for Environmental Hist, Forest Hist Soc, Orgn of Am Historians, Tex State Historical Asn. **RESEARCH** Cultural, environmental, intellectual, and social histories. **SELECTED PUBLICATIONS** Auth, Gifford Pinchot: The Evolution of An American Conservationist, The Pinchot Lecture Series, Grey Towers Press (Milford, PA), 93; coed, Out of the Woods: Essays in Environmental History, Univ of Pittsburgh Press (Pittsburgh, PA), 97; ed, American Forests: Nature, Culture, and Politics, Univ Press of Kans (Lawrence, KS), 97; coauth, The Greatest Good: 100 Years of Forestry in America, The Soc of Am Foresters (Washington, DC), 99; ed, Western Water: A High Country News Reader, Ore State Univ Press (Corvallis, OR), 00. **CONTACT ADDRESS** Dept Hist, Trinity Univ, San Antonio, TX 78212-7200. **EMAIL** fmiller@trinity.edu

MILLER, DAVID
PERSONAL Born 09/18/1951, East Chicago, IL, m, 1989, 2 children **DISCIPLINE** AMERICAN STUDIES **EDUCATION** Stanford Univ, BA, 74; MA 75, PhD, 82, Brown Univ **CAREER** Visiting prof, Binnington Coll, 81-82; tutor, 82-84, Harvard Univ; visiting asst prof, 84-85, Reed Coll; Mellen Fel, 86-88, Stanford Univ; assoc prof, Allegheny Coll, 85-98 **MEMBERSHIPS** Amer Studies Assn **RESEARCH** Amer Art and Lit, 19th century, landscape **SELECTED PUBLICATIONS** Auth, "Infection and Imagination: Atmospheric Agency and the Problem of Romanticism in America," Prospects: An Annual of Americna Cultural Stud, 13, (88): 37-60; auth, Dark Eden: The Swamp in 19th-Century American Culture, Cambridge U Press, 89; ed, American Iconology: New Approaches to 19th-Century Art and Literature, Yale U Press, 93; auth, Review of Nathalia Wright, ed, The Correspondence of Washington Allston, New England Quarterly, June 94; Review of The Correspondence of Washington Allston, New England Quarterly, June 94; Washington Allston and the Sister Arts Tradition in America, European Romantic Review, Summer 94; Review of Robert K. Wallace, Melville & Turner: Spheres of Love and Fright, Journal of the Early Republic, Fall 94, Review of David M. Lubin, Picturing Nation: Art and Social Change in 19th-Century America, New England Quarterly, June 95; auth, "Swamp and Jungle Images and the Modernizing of American Culture," in The Swamp: On the Edge of Eden, Exhibition Catalogue, Samuel P. Harn Museum of Art, 00. **CONTACT ADDRESS** Dept of English, Allegheny Col, Meadville, PA 16335. **EMAIL** dmiller@alleg.edu

MILLER, DAVID B.
PERSONAL Born 01/01/1933, Ottumwa, IA, m, 1956, 3 children **DISCIPLINE** RUSSIAN HISTORY **EDUCATION** Univ Wis, BA, 54; Columbia Univ, MA, 59, PhD(hist), 67; cert, Russ Inst, 59. **CAREER** From Asst Prof to Prof, 61-98, PROF EMERITUS RUSS HIST, ROOSEVELT UNIV, 98-, CHMN DEPT HIST, 68-; vis lectr Russ hist, Univ Chicago, 65-66. **HONORS AND AWARDS** Inter-Univ Comt Travel Grants, US/USSR exchange fel, 63-64; Am Coun Learned Soc fel, Inst Hist, Acad Sci, USSR, 69-70. **MEMBERSHIPS** AHA; Am Asn Advan Slavic Studies. **RESEARCH** History and culture of medieval Russia. **SELECTED PUBLICATIONS** Auth, The coronation of Ivan IV as tsar, Jahrbucher Geschichte Osteuropas, 12/67; Legends of the icon of Our Lady of Vladimir, Speculum, 10/68; The Lubeckers Bartholomaus Ghotan and Nicolas Bulow in Novgorod and Moscow and the Problem of Early Western Influences on Russian Culture, Viator, 9/77; The Velikie Minei Chetii and the Stepennaia Kniga of Metropolitan Makarii and the Origins of Russian Nationa Consciousness, Forschungen zur osteuropaischen Geschichte, 26/79. **CONTACT ADDRESS** Dept of History, Roosevelt Univ, 430 S Michigan Ave, Chicago, IL 60605-1394.

MILLER, DAVID H.
PERSONAL Born 08/26/1938, Spangler, PA, m, 1963 **DISCIPLINE** MEDIEVAL HISTORY **EDUCATION** Baldwin-Wallace Col, BA, 63; Mich State Univ, MA, 65, PhD(hist), 67. **CAREER** Asst prof, 67-72, asst chmn dept, 76-78, ASSOC PROF HIST, UNIV OKLA, 72-, DIR CTR COMP FRONTIER STUDIES, 82-, Nat Endowment for Humanities younger scholar res fel, Belg, 68-69. **MEMBERSHIPS** AHA; Mediaeval Acad Am; Am Cath Hist Asn; Soc Comp Study Civilizations; Mid-Am Medieval Asn (pres, 78). **RESEARCH** historical theory; comparative history of complex pre-industrial societies; medieval European history. **SELECTED PUBLICATIONS** Auth, Before the Normans--Southern Italy in the 9th and-10th Centuries, Speculum J Medieval Stud, Vol 69, 94; War in the Tribal Zone--Expanding States and Indigenous Warfare, J World Hist, Vol 4, 93; The Early State and the Towns--Forms of Integration in Lombard Italy, Ad568 774, Speculum J Medieval Stud, Vol 69, 94; Frontiers of the Roman Empire--A Social and Economic Study, Am Hist Rev, Vol 0100, 95; The Early State and the Towns--Forms of Integration in Lombard Italy, Ad568-774, Speculum J Medieval Stud, Vol 69, 94; Before the Normans--Southern Italy in the 9th and 10th Centuries, Speculum J Medieval Stud, Vol 69, 94; Ethnogenesis and Religious Revitalization Beyond the Roman Frontier,The Case of Frankish Origins, J World Hist, Vol 4, 93. **CONTACT ADDRESS** Dept of Hist, Univ of Oklahoma, 455 W Lindsay, Norman, OK 73069.

MILLER, DAVID WILLIAM
PERSONAL Born 07/09/1940, Coudersport, PA, m, 1964 **DISCIPLINE** MODERN HISTORY **EDUCATION** Rice Univ, BA, 62; Univ Wis-Madison, MA, 63; Univ Chicago, PhD(hist of cult), 68. **CAREER** From instr to asst prof, 67-73, assoc prof, 73-80, PROF HIST, CARNEGIE-MELLON UNIV, 80-, Sr res fel, Inst Irish Studies, Queen's Univ, Belfast, 75-76. **MEMBERSHIPS** AHA; Am Comt Irish Studies. **RESEARCH** Irish history, religion, computer applications in history. **SELECTED PUBLICATIONS** Auth, Church, State and Nation in Ireland, 1898-1921, Gill & MacMillan Ltd & Univ Pittsburgh, 73: Irish Catholicism and the Great Famine, J Social Hist, fall 75; Queen's Rebels: Ulster Loyalism in Historical Perspective, 78 & Presbyterianism and Modernization in Ulster, Past and Present, 78, Gill & MacMillan Ltd & Barnes & Noble; auth, the Armaugh Troubles, 1784-95, in Irish Peasants, Univ Wis Press, 83; ed, Peep o'Day Boys and Defenders, Public Record Office Northern Ireland, 90; princ developer, The Great American History Machine, The ePress Project, Univ Md, 94; auth, Non-professional Soldiery, c 1600- 1800, in A Military History of Ireland, Cambridge Univ Press, 96; auth, Irish presbyterians and the grreat Famine," Luzury and Austerity, Papers read before the 23rd Irish Conf of Hist held at St Patricks's Col, Dublin: Univ Col Dublin Press, (99), 165-181; auth, Irish Christianity and Revolution," Jim Smyth, Revolution, Counter-Revolution and uinion, Inreland in the 1790's, Cambridge: Cambridge Univ Press, (00), 195-210; coed, Piety and Power in Ireland 1760-1960: Essays in Honour of Emmet Larkin, Belfast: Institue of Irish studies and Notre Dame, Notre Dame Press, 00. **CONTACT ADDRESS** Dept of Hist, Carnegie Mellon Univ, 5000 Forbes Ave, Pittsburgh, PA 15213-3890. **EMAIL** dwmiller@cmu.edu

MILLER, DOUGLAS T.
PERSONAL Born 05/27/1938, Orange, NJ, 2 children **DISCIPLINE** AMERICAN INTELLECTUAL HISTORY **EDUCATION** Colby Col, BA, 58; Columbia Univ, MA, 59; Mich State Univ, PhD(hist), 65. **CAREER** From instr to asst prof Am intellectual hist, Univ Maine, 63-66; from asst prof to assoc prof, 66-75, PROF HIST, MICH STATE UNIV, 75-, Coe res grant, Univ Maine, 64-65; all univ res grant, Mich State Univ, 67-82, res term, 68-69; Danforth Found assoc, 70-72; Am Philos Soc grant, 72-73; Fulbright Hays fel, Denmark, 79-80. **MEMBERSHIPS** AHA; Orgn Am Historians; Am Studies Asn; Popular Cult Asn. **RESEARCH** American history, 1815-1860 and 1945-1975; American utopianism. **SELECTED PUBLICATIONS** Auth, Picturing an Exhibition--The Family of Man and 1950s America, Am Hist Rev, Vol 0102, 97. **CONTACT ADDRESS** Dept of Hist, Michigan State Univ, East Lansing, MI 48824.

MILLER, E. WILLARD
PERSONAL Born 05/17/1915, Turkey City, PA, m, 1941 **DISCIPLINE** GEOGRAPHY **EDUCATION** Clarion Univ, BS, 37; Univ Neb, AM, 39; Ohio State Univ, PhD, 42. **CAREER** Instr, Ohio State Univ, 41-43; asst prof, Western Reserve Univ, 43-44; geog, DC, 44-45; assoc prof, 45-49; prof, 49-80; prof emer, 80-; Pa State Univ, assoc dean emeritus, 80-. **HONORS AND AWARDS** Pi Gamma Mu; Sigma Xi; Beta Gamma Sigma; OSS, Cet Merit; Ray Hughes Whitbeck Awd; AAAS Fel; AGS Fel; Explorers Clb Fel; NCGE Fel; Pres AAUP of PSU; PGS Merit Ser Awd; Dept Comm Merit Awd; Gov Cit; Dist Ser Awd; Dist Alum Awd; Hon DSc, OSU, Clarion Univ; Who's Who - World, Am, East, Am Men Women, Intl YB Statesmen. **MEMBERSHIPS** AAG; ASPG; NCGE; AIMMPE; AGS; EC; AAAS; PAS; PCGE; RCGS; GA; CCHS; MNS; Obelisk Soc; Boalsburg Vill Conserv. **SELECTED PUBLICATIONS** Coauth, Environmental Hazards: Radioactive Materials and Waste, ABC/CLIO (90); coauth, Energy and American Society, ABC/CLIO (93); co-ed, Water Resources of Pennsylvania, Penn Acad Sci (96); co-ed, Forests: A global Perspective, Penn Acad Sci (96); coauth, Environmental Hazards: Toxic Waste and Hazardous Materials, ABC/CLIO (97); co-ed, "The Era of Materials," Penn Acad Sci (98); coauth, Indoor Pollution, ABC/CLIO (99); co-ed, "Ecology Wetlands and Associated Systems," Penn Acad Sci (98); coauth, co-ed, "Academic Ethics," Penn Acad Sci (00); co-ed, "Renewable Energy," Penn Acad Sci (in press). **CONTACT ADDRESS** Dept Geography, Penn State Univ, 845 Outer Dr, State College, PA 16802. **EMAIL** kqs2@psu.edu

MILLER, GENEVIEVE
PERSONAL Born 10/15/1914, Butler, PA **DISCIPLINE** HISTORY OF MEDICINE **EDUCATION** Groucher College, BA, 35; Johns Hopkins Univ, MA, 39; Cornell Univ, PhD, 55. **CAREER** Research Sec to Dr. Henry E Sigerist Dir of JHIHM 37-42, Asst, 43-44, Instr, 45-48, research Assoc, Hist Med, 80-94, Johns Hopkins Inst Hist of Med; Curator, 62-67, Dir, 67-79, Howard Dittrick Museum Hist Med; Asst Prof 53-67, Assoc Prof 67-79, Emeritus, 79-, Case West Res Sch Med. **HONORS AND AWARDS** Phi Beta Kappa; Dean Van Meter Fel; Kate Campbell Hurd Mead Lectr, ; Wm H Welch Medal; Fielding H Garrison Lectr, ; Clendening Lectr, ; CMLA Hon Fel; Lifetime Achievement Awd AAHM; Who's Who In: the Midwest, the East, the World, America, Among Amer Women. **MEMBERSHIPS** AAHM; OAMH; AHA; ISHM; SAH; GSHM. **SELECTED PUBLICATIONS** Auth, Wm Beaumont's Formative Years, Two Early Notebooks 1811-1821: With Annotations and an Introductory Essay, NY, Henry Schuman, 46; The Adoption of Inoculation for Smallpox in England and France, Philadelphia, Univ of Penn Press, 57; Bulletin of the History of Medicine, Index to vols I-XX, 1933-1950, Baltimore, Johns Hopkins Press, 64; ed, Yankee in Grey: The Civil War Memoirs of Henry E Handerson, with a selection of his war-time letters, Cleveland, Press of West Res Univ, 62; Bibliography of the Writings of Henry E Sigerist, Montreal, McGill Univ Press, 66; Letters of Edward Jenner and Other Documents concerning the Early History of Vaccination, Baltimore and London, Johns Hopkins Press, 83. **CONTACT ADDRESS** 1890 E 107th St, Apt 816, Cleveland, OH 44106.

MILLER, GEORGE HALL
PERSONAL Born 08/05/1919, Evanston, IL **DISCIPLINE** AMERICAN HISTORY **EDUCATION** Univ Mich, AB, 41, PhD(hist), 51; Harvard Univ, MA, 49. **CAREER** Instr hist, Univ Mich, 51-54; from asst prof to assoc prof, 54-64, prof, 64-81, EMER PROF HIST, RIPON COL, 81-, Ford Found fel, 51-52. **MEMBERSHIPS** AHA; AAUP; Orgn Am Historians; Econ Hist Asn. **RESEARCH** American economic History; local history. **SELECTED PUBLICATIONS** Coauth, History of Ripon, Wisconsin, Ripon Hist Soc, 64; auth, Railroads and the granger laws, Univ Wis, 71. **CONTACT ADDRESS** Dept of Hist, Ripon Col, Ripon, WI 54971.

MILLER, HOWARD SMITH
PERSONAL Born 02/28/1936, Pontiac, IL, m, 1958, 3 children **DISCIPLINE** AMERICAN SOCIAL HISTORY, HISTORY OF SCIENCE **EDUCATION** Bradley Univ, AB, 58; Univ Wis, MS, 60, PhD(hist), 64. **CAREER** Asst prof hist, Univ Southern Calif, 64-71; ASSOC PROF HIST, UNIV MO-ST LOUIS, 71-, Graves Award fel humanities, 70-71; vis scholar, Piedmont Cols Vis Scholar Prog, Winston-Salem, NC, 71. **HONORS AND AWARDS** Univ Southern Calif Assocs Awd, 70. **MEMBERSHIPS** Orgn Am Historians; Hist Sci Soc; Soc Hist Technol. **RESEARCH** American social history; history of science; history of technology. **SELECTED PUBLICATIONS** Auth, Legal foundations of American philanthropy, 1776-1844, State Hist Soc Wis, 61; Dollars for research: Science and its patrons in nineteenth century America, Univ Wash, 70; The political economy of science, In: Science in Nineteenth Century America: A Reappraisal, Northwestern Univ, 72. **CONTACT ADDRESS** Dept of Hist, Univ of Missouri, St. Louis, Saint Louis, MO 63121.

MILLER, HUBERT J.
PERSONAL Born 12/09/1927, Hays, KS, m, 1957, 7 children **DISCIPLINE** LATIN AMERICAN HISTORY **EDUCATION** Univ Dayton, BA, 51; St Louis Univ, MA, 54; Loyola Univ, Ill, PhD(Hist), 65. **CAREER** Teacher, Acad Sacred Heart, Mo, 51-53 & St John's High Sch, 53-54; teacher, Am Sch & dir Night Sch, English inst, El Salvador, 55-56; fel lectr Hist, Loyola Univ, Ill, 56-59; from asst prof to assoc prof Latin Am Hist, St Mary's Univ, Tex, 60-71, chmn dept Hist, 63-69; assoc prof Mex Hist, Univ Tex-Pan American, 71-; prof, 82-93; prof Emeritus, 94; Tinker Found grant, 67. **HONORS AND AWARDS** Smith-Mundt Grant to Guatemala, 59-60; NEH Grants, 79, 86, 84. **MEMBERSHIPS** AHA; Latin Am Studies Asn; AAUP; Am Oral Hist Asn. **RESEARCH** Educational ideas of Thomas Jefferson; the church and the state in Latin America, especially in Guatemala; teaching methodology of Mexican-American heritage. **SELECTED PUBLICATIONS** Auth, Hernan Cortes, 72, Bartolome de las Casas, 72, Antonio de Mendoza, 73 & Juan de Zumarraga, 73, New Santander; El Estado y la Iglesia en Guatemala, 1871-1885, La Editorial de la Universidad de San Carlos, 76; ed, chap, In: The Texas Samplar, Tex Gov Comt Aging, 76; Jose Vasconcelos, 77 & Jose de Escandon, 80, New Santander; Three chapters in Historia General de Guatemala, 97-98, chapter in Central America, Historical Perspecitves on the Contemporary Crisis, ed, Ralph Lee Woodword, Greenwood Press, 88; chapter in Liberals, the Church and Indian Peasants, ed, Robert H Jackson, New Mexi-

co Univ Press, 97. **CONTACT ADDRESS** Dept of Philosophy, Univ of Texas, Pan American, 1201 W University Dr, Edinburg, TX 78539-2970.

MILLER, JACQUELYN C.
DISCIPLINE AMERICAN HISTORY, EARLY MODERN EUROPEAN HISTORY **EDUCATION** Milligan Col, BA, 77; Rutgers Univ, MLS, 84, MA, 88; Doctorate, 95. **CAREER** Instr, fac adv, Stud Res Asn, Phi Alfpa Theta Nat Hist Honor Soc, mem, Sullivan Leadership Award comt; Women's Stud Bd, Seattle Univ. **MEMBERSHIPS** Am Asn of Univ Women; AHA; Am Stud Asn; Inst of Early Am Hist and Cult; Orgn of Am Hist; Soc for the Hist of the Early Am Repub. **RESEARCH** Emotional self-control and the problem of domestic violence in 18th-century middle-class households. **SELECTED PUBLICATIONS** Auth, Franklin and Friends: Benjamin Fraklin's Ties to Quakers and Quakerism, Pa Hist, 57, 90; Beach Over Troubled Waters: Special Interest Groups and Public Policy Formation--The Morris Canal Abandonment Controversy, NJ Hist 109, 91; 'A Most Melancholy Scene of Devastation': The Public Response to the 1793 Philadelphia Yellow Fever Epidemic, The Pub Hist 16, 94; An 'Uncommon Tranquility of Mind': Emotional Self-Control and the Construction of a Middle-Class Identity in Eighteenth-Century Philadelphia, J of Soc Hist 30, 96; Passions and Politics: The Multiple Meanings of Bejamin Rush's Treatment for Yellow Fever, in A Melancholy Scene of Devastaton, eds, Billy G. Smith and J. Worth Estes, Watson, 97; coauth, Benjamin Rush, M.D.: A Bibliographic Guide, Greenwood, 96. **CONTACT ADDRESS** Seattle Univ, Seattle, WA 98122-4460. **EMAIL** jcmiller@seattleu.edu

MILLER, JAMES R.
PERSONAL Born 04/28/1943, Cornwall, ON, Canada **DISCIPLINE** HISTORY **EDUCATION** Univ Toronto, BA, 66, MA, 67, PhD, 72. **CAREER** Asst prof, 70-74, assoc prof, 75-79, prof Hist, Univ Saskatchewan, 79. **HONORS AND AWARDS** Can Hist Asn (pres, 96-97) **RESEARCH** Post-Confederation Canadian hist, particularly political and intellectual hist (1860-1920), French-English relations (1840-1920), and Indian-white relations. **SELECTED PUBLICATIONS** Auth, Equal Rights: The Jesuits' Estates Act Controversy, 79; auth, Skyscrapers Hide the Heavens: A History of Indian-White Relations in Canada, 89; auth, Mistahimusqua (Big Bear), 96; auth, Shingwauk's Vision: A History of Native Residential Schools, 96; ed, Sweet Promises: A Reader on Indian-White Relations in Canada, 91. **CONTACT ADDRESS** Dept of History, Univ of Saskatchewan, 9 Campus Dr, Saskatoon, SK, Canada S7N 5A5. **EMAIL** miller@sask.usask.ca

MILLER, JOHN E.
PERSONAL Born 03/28/1945, Beloit, KS, m, 1972, 2 children **DISCIPLINE** AMERICAN HISTORY **EDUCATION** Univ Mo, Columbia, BA, 66; Univ Wis, Madison, MA, 68, PhD, 73. **CAREER** Vis asst prof, Univ Tulsa, 73-74; asst prof, South Dakota State Univ, 74-78, assoc prof, 78-83, prof, 83-. **HONORS AND AWARDS** Mountain Plains Library Asn, Literary Contrib Awd, 93; Women Writing the West, WILLA Literary Awd, 99. **MEMBERSHIPS** Org Am Hists, Mid-America Am Studies Asn, South Dakota Hist Soc, The Hist Soc. **RESEARCH** Recent American history, midwestern history, small town histoy, social epistemology. **SELECTED PUBLICATIONS** Auth, Governor Philip F. La Follette, the Wisconsin Progressives, and the New Deal, Columbia: Univ Mo Press (982); auth, Looking for History on Highway 14, Ames: Iowa State Univ Press (93); auth, Laura Ingalls Wilder's Little Town: Where History and Literature Meet, Lawrence: Univ Press Kans (94); auth, Becoming Laura Ingalls Wilder: The Woman behind the Legend, Columbia: Univ Mo Press (98). **CONTACT ADDRESS** Dept Hist, So Dakota State Univ, PO Box 504, Brookings, SD 57007-0393. **EMAIL** John_Miller@sdstate.edu

MILLER, JOSEPH CALDER
PERSONAL Born 04/30/1939, Cedar Rapids, IA, m, 3 children **DISCIPLINE** AFRICAN HISTORY **EDUCATION** Wesleyan Univ, BA, 61; Northwestern Univ, MBA, 63; Univ Wis-Madison, MA, 67, PhD(hist), 72. **CAREER** Ad hoc instr hist, Exten Div, Univ Wis-Madison, 71-72, vis asst prof, 71-72; asst prof, 72-75, assoc prof hist, Univ VA, 75-82, prof 82-89, Commonwealth prof, 89-96, T. Cary Johnson Jr. prof, 96-; dean, Col of Arts and Sciences, 90-95; Am Coun Learned Socs study fel, 74-75; Am Coun Learned Socs & Soc Sci Res Coun res grant, Africa, 77; Nat Endowment for Humanities fel, 78-79, 85; Co-ed, Journal of African History, Cambridge Univ Press, 90-97. **HONORS AND AWARDS** Member, Center for Advanced Studies, Univ of Va, 89; Melville J. Herskovits Awd (African Studies Asn), 89; Special citation, Bolton Prize (Conference on Latin Am Hist), 89; Distinguished Vis Lect, Foreign Service Institute, 93; Research div, Am Hist Asn, 87-89; Catherine Gould Chism Visiting Lecturer, Univ of Puget Sound, 95; President-elect, AHA, 97-President, 98. **MEMBERSHIPS** Soc Sci Hist Asn; Int Conf Group Mod Portugal; African Studies Asn; AHA; Int African Inst. **RESEARCH** History of African verbal societies; Central African history, especially Portuguese Africa; history of slavery and the slave trade. **SELECTED PUBLICATIONS** Auth, The Imbangla and the Chronology of Early Central African History, Journal of African History 13: 549-74, 72; Requiem for the 'Jaga,' Cahiers d'etudes africaines 13:121-49, 73; Nzinga of Matamba in a New Perspective, Journal of African Hist 16: 201-16, 75; Kings and Kinsmen: Early Angola, in Martin L. Kilson and Robert I. Rotberg, eds, The African Diaspora: Interpretive Essays, Harvard Univ Press, pp 75-113, 76; Some aspects of the Commercial Organization of Slaving at Luanda, Angola-1760-1830, in H. Gemery and J. Hogendorn, eds, The Uncommon Market: Essays in the Economic History of the Atlantic Slave Trade, Academic Press, pp 77-106, 79; Mortality in the Atlantic Slave Trade: Statistical Evidence on Causality, Journal of Interdisciplinary Hist 11: 385-434, 80; ed, The African Past Speaks: Essays on Oral Tradition and History, Wm. Dawson and Sons and Archon Books, 80; auth, Lineages, Ideology, and the History of Slavery in Western Central Africa, in Paul E. Lovejoy, ed, The Ideology of Slavery in Africa, Sage Pubs, pp 40-71, 81; The Significance of Drought, Disease, and Famine in the Agriculturally Marginal Zones of West-Central Africa, Journal of African Hist 23: 17-61, 82; The Paradoxes of Impoverishment in the Atlantic Zone, in David Birmingham and Phyllis Martin, eds, History of Central Africa (Longmans), vol 1, pp118-59, 83; comp, Slavery: A Worldwide Bibliography, 1900-1982, Kraus Int, 85; auth, with John K. Thornton, The Chronicle as Source, History, and Hagiography: The 'Catalogo dos Governadores de angola,' Paideuma 33: 359-89, 87; with Dauril Alden, Unwanted Cargos: The Origins and Dissemination of Smallpox via the Slave Trade from Africa to Brazil, c. 1560-1830, in Kenneth F. Kiple, ed, The African Exchange, Duke Univ Press, pp 35-109, 88; Overcrowded and Undernourished: Techniques and Consequences of Tight-Packing in the Portuguese Southern Atlantic Slave Trade, in Serge Daget, ed, De la traite a l'esclavage (Societe Francaise d'Histoire du Monde Atlantique), vol 2, pp 395-424, 88; Way of Death: Merchant Capitalism and the Angolan Slave Trade, 1730-1830, Univ of Wisc Press, 88 (Winner, Melville J. Herskovits Prize, African Studies Asn, 89; Special Citation, Conference on Latin American History Bolton Prize Committee, 89); A Marginal Institution on the Margin of the Atlantic System: The Portuguese Southern Atlantic Slave Trade in the Eighteenth Century, in Barbara Solow, ed, Slavery and the Rise of the Atlantic System, Cambridge Univ Press, pp 120-50, 91; The Slave Trade, in Encyclopedia of the North American Colonies (Jacob Ernest Cooke, ed in chief), Charles Schribners' Sons, vol 2, pp 45-66, 93; Co-ed, with R. W. Harms, D. S. Newbury, and M. D. Wagner, Paths to the African Past: African Historical Essays in Honor of Jan Vansina, ASA Press, 94; auth, The Slave Trade, in Encyclopedia of Latin American History (Barbara Tenenbaum, ed), Charles Scribner's Sons, vol 5, pp 122-27, 95; History ed, Encyclopedia of Africa South of the Sahara, gen ed, John Middleton, Simon & Schuster, 4 vols, 97; Co-ed, with Paul Finkelman, Macmillan Encyclopedia of World Slavery, Macmillan, contrib, 10 articles, 98; Comp, Slavery and Slaving in World History, A Bibliography, 1900-1991, vol 1, Slavery and Slaving in World History: A Bibliography, 1902-1996, vol 2. M. E. Sharpe, 98. **CONTACT ADDRESS** Dept of Hist, Univ of Virginia, 1 Randall Hall, Charlottesville, VA 22903-3244.

MILLER, JUDITH A.
DISCIPLINE HISTORY **EDUCATION** Coll Wooster, BA, 78; Duke Univ, PhD, 87. **CAREER** Assoc prof **HONORS AND AWARDS** Gershenkron Prize, Econ Hist Assn; Koren Prize, Soc Fr Histl Studies. **RESEARCH** 18th and 19th-century French history; opera and theater from 1789 to 1830; modern European economic history. **SELECTED PUBLICATIONS** Auth, Politics and Urban Provisioning Crises: Bakers, Police, and Parlements in France, 1750-1793; auth, Mastering the Market: The State and the Grain Trade in Northern France, 1700-1860, Cambridge Univ Press, 98. **CONTACT ADDRESS** Dept History, Emory Univ, 221 Bowden Hall, 561 Kilgo Cir, Atlanta, GA 30322-1950. **EMAIL** histjam@emory.edu

MILLER, KERBY A.
PERSONAL Born 12/30/1944, Phoenix, AZ, m, 1979, 3 children **DISCIPLINE** AMERICAN & MODERN IRISH HISTORY **EDUCATION** Pomona Col, BA, 66; Univ Calif, Berkeley, MA, 67, PhD(Hist), 76. **CAREER** Lectr Hist, Univ Calif, Berkeley, 76-77; sr fel, Inst Irish Studies, Queen's Univ Belfast, 77-78; asst prof Hist, Univ Mo-Columbia, 78-; prof of Hist, Univ of Missouri-Columbia, 88-; Middlebush prof of Hist, Univ of Missouri-Columbia, 00-. **HONORS AND AWARDS** Gamma Sigma Delta Superior Teaching Award, 83; Merle Curti Award, 84-85; Organization of Am Historians, 86; Theodore Soloutos Award, Immigration Hist Soc, 86; Finalist, Pulitzer Prize in Hist, 86; Chancellor's Award for Outstanding Fac Res, 87; Outstanding Fac Member of the Year Award, 88; Sigma Kppa Outstanding Teacher Award, 95; William T. Kemper Fel for Teaching Excellence, 97; Greek Councils Outstanding Fac Award, 97, 98. **MEMBERSHIPS** AHA; Orgn Am Historians; Immigration Hist Soc; Irish Hist Soc; Am Comt Irish Studies. **RESEARCH** Irish immigration to North Am; Am social & urban hist; modern Irish socio-economic and cultural hist. **SELECTED PUBLICATIONS** Auth, Emigrants and exiles: Irish cultures and Irish emigration to North America, 1790-1922, Irish Hist Studies, 9/80; auth, "Assimilation and Alienation; Irish Emigrants Responses to Industrial America, 1871-1921," In P.J. Drudy, ed, Irish Studies 4: The Irish in America, Cambridge: Cambridge Univ Press, (85): 87-112; auth, "No Middle Ground: The Erosion of the Protestant Middle Class in Southern Ireland during the Pre-Famine Era," Huntington Library Quarterly, vol. 49, No. 4, (86): 295-306; auth, Emigrants and Exiles: Ireland and the Ireland and the Irish Exodus to North America, New York: Oxford Univ Press, 85; auth, "Emigration, Ideology, and Capitalism in Post-Famine Ireland," Migrations: The Irish at Home and Abroad, Dublin: Wolfhound Press, (90): 90-108; auth, Out of Ireland: The Story of Irish Emigration to America, Washington D.C., Elliot & Clark, 94; auth, "Ulster Migrants in an Age of Rebellion: The Crocketts of Raphoe," Irish Economic and Social Hist, 22, (95): 77-87; co-ed, Irish Popular Culture, 1650-1850, Dublin: Irish Academic Press, 98; auth, "'Scotch-Irish', 'Black Irish' and 'Real Irish': Immigrants and Identities in the Old South," in Andrew Bielenberg, ed., The Irish Diaspora, London: Addison, Wesley, Longman Press, (00): 139-57; auth, "' Scotch-Irish Myths' and 'Irish' Identities in Eighteenth and Nineteenth-Century America," in Charles Fanning, ed., New Perspectives on the Irish Diaspora, Carbondale, Il, Southern Illinois Univ Press, (00): 75-92. **CONTACT ADDRESS** Univ of Missouri, Columbia, 101 Read Hall, Columbia, MO 65211-0001. **EMAIL** milerk@missouri.edu

MILLER, M. SAMMYE
PERSONAL Born 02/23/1947, Philadelphia, PA, m, 1991, 2 children **DISCIPLINE** HISTORY **EDUCATION** Del State Univ, BA, 68; Trinity Col, MAT, 70; Catholic Univ of Am, PhD, 77. **CAREER** Prof, Bowie State Univ. **HONORS AND AWARDS** NAFEO Res Achievement Awd, 84; Brd of Trustees Scholar, Catholic Univ of Am; Penfield Fel. **MEMBERSHIPS** ASALH; Asn for the Study of African Am Life & Hist; NCSS; Nat Coun for the Soc Studies; OAH. **RESEARCH** Southern History; African American/Us Constitution. **SELECTED PUBLICATIONS** Auth, "Historiography of Charles H. Wesley," Journal of Negro History, 98. **CONTACT ADDRESS** Dept Hist & Govt, Bowie State Univ, 14000 Jericho Park Rd, Bowie, MD 20715-3319. **EMAIL** smiller@bowiestate.edu

MILLER, MARA
DISCIPLINE WOMEN'S VOICES AND IMAGES OF WOMEN IN JAPANESE ART **EDUCATION** Yale Univ, PhD, 87. **CAREER** Emory Univ. **SELECTED PUBLICATIONS** Auth, The Garden as an Art. **CONTACT ADDRESS** Dept of Art, William Jewell Col, 500 College Hill, Liberty, MO 64068-1896.

MILLER, MARION S.
PERSONAL Born 08/29/1927, E Orange, NJ, m, 1959 **DISCIPLINE** HISTORY **EDUCATION** Acadia Univ, BA, 48; Univ Pa, MA, 53; Univ Pa, PhD, 65. **CAREER** Asst Prof, Univ Ill, 67-84; Assoc Prof, Univ Ill, 84-. **HONORS AND AWARDS** Fulbright Fel, Italy, 54-56. **MEMBERSHIPS** Soc for Ital Hist Studies, Inst for Verdi Studies, Coun for European Studies. **RESEARCH** Modern Europe, modern Italy. **SELECTED PUBLICATIONS** Auth, "Perspectives on Counter-Revolutions in Central Italy 1799-1841," Tijdschrift voor Geschiedenis, 102 (89): 401-412; auth, "A 'Liberal International'? Perspectives on Comparative Approaches to the Revolutions in Spain, Italy and Greece in the 1820s," Greece and the Mediterranean (Kirksville: Thomas Jefferson Univ Pr, 90), 61-69; auth, "Who Owns Columbus?: Church, State and the Mediterranean in Italy in 1892," Mediterranean studies, V (95): 75-84; auth, "The Approaches to European Institution Building of Carlo Sforza, Italian Foreign Minister, 1947-1951," in European Construction: National Perspectives on Postwar Institution Building (London: Macmillan, 95), 55-69. **CONTACT ADDRESS** Dept Hist, Univ of Illinois, Chicago, Chicago, IL 60612. **EMAIL** msm@uic.edu

MILLER, MARLA R.
DISCIPLINE HISTORY **EDUCATION** Univ Wis - Madison, BA, 88; Univ N Carol at Chapel Hill, PhD, 97. **CAREER** HIST, UNIV NC CHAPEL HILL **MEMBERSHIPS** Am Antiquarian Soc **SELECTED PUBLICATIONS** Auth, My Daily Bread Depends Upon My Labor: Craftswomen, Community and the Marketplace in Rural Massachusetts, 1740-1820; coauth, "Common Parlors: Women and the Reservation Community Identity in Pittsfield, MA, 1870-1920," Gender & Hist 6, 94. **CONTACT ADDRESS** Dept of Hist, Univ of No Carolina, Chapel Hill, CB No. 3195, Chapel Hill, NC 27599. **EMAIL** mrm@email.unc.edu

MILLER, MARTIN ALAN
PERSONAL Born 05/23/1938, Baltimore, MD, m, 1964, 2 children **DISCIPLINE** RUSSIAN & EUROPEAN HISTORY **EDUCATION** Univ Md, AB, 60; Univ Chicago, MA, 62, PhD(Russ hist), 67. **CAREER** Instr western civilization, Stanford Univ, 67-70; prof Russ hist, Duke Univ, 70-, vis prof, New Sch Soc Res, 79-80; Ecole des Hautes Etudes en Science Sociales, 96; Venice Int Univ, 00; US-USSR cult exchange, 65 & 76; Nat Inst Ment Health fel, 78-79; Nat Coun for Soviet Res fel, 82; sr fel, Russ Inst, Columbia Univ, 82. **HONORS AND AWARDS** Ford Found 88-89; Int Research & Exchanges Board, 90; Nat Endowment for the Humanities, 90-91. **MEMBERSHIPS** AHA; Am Asn Advan Slavic Studies; Triange Prog in Intellectual Hist. **RESEARCH** Nineteenth century Russian intelligentsia, revolutionary movement, emigration; psychoanalysis; terrorism. **SELECTED PUBLICATIONS** Auth, Kropotkin, Univ Chicago Press, 76 & 79; The Russian Revolu-

tionary Emigres, 1825-1870, Hopkins, 86; Freud and the Bolsheviks: Psychoanalysis in Russia and the Soviet Union, Yale, 98. **CONTACT ADDRESS** Dept of History, Duke Univ, PO Box 90719, Durham, NC 27708-0719. **EMAIL** mmiller@duke.edu

MILLER, NAOMI
PERSONAL Born 02/28/1928, New York, NY, s **DISCIPLINE** ART HISTORY **EDUCATION** City Col, NYork, BS, 48; Columbia Univ, MA, 50; NYork Univ, Inst of Fine Arts, MA, 60; PhD, 66. **CAREER** Vis prof, RI Sch of Design, Providence, RI, 63-64; Univ BC, Vancouver, 67; Hebrew Univ of Jerusalem, 80; Univ Calif Berkeley, 69-70; from asst prof to prof, art hist, Boston Univ, 64- . **HONORS AND AWARDS** Fel, Nat Endow for the Humanities, 72-73; Dumbarton Oaks, Wash, DC, Harvard Univ Ctr for Landscape Studies, 76-77, 83-89; Villa I Tatti, Florence, 84-85; Ctr for Advan Studies in Visual Arts, Nat Gallery of Art, Wash, DC, Winter, 88, 95; Padua Facul Exchange Prog, Padua, Summer, 90. **MEMBERSHIPS** Col Art Asn; Soc of Archit Hist. **RESEARCH** Renaissance to modern: art, architecture and urbanism; Landscape studies. **SELECTED PUBLICATIONS** Coauth, Architecture in Boston, 1975-90, Munich, Prestel, 90; auth, Renaissance Bologna: A Study in Architectural Form and Content, Peter Lang, Univ Ks Humanistic Studies, 56, 89; Heavenly Caves: Reflections on the Garden Grotto, NY, Braziller, 82; coauth, Fons Sapientiae: Garden Fountains in Illustrated Books, Sixteenth-Eighteeth Centuries, Wash, DC, Dum Dumbarton Oaks, 77; auth, French Renaissance Fountains, NY, Garland, 77; book rev ed, Journal of the Society of Architectural Historians, 74-80; ed, JSAH, 80-84; auth, Mapping Cities, Univ of Wash Pr, 00. **CONTACT ADDRESS** Art History Dept., Boston Univ, 725 Commonwealth Av., Boston, MA 02215. **EMAIL** nmiller@bu.edu

MILLER, PATRICIA COX
PERSONAL Born 01/19/1947, Washington, DC, m **DISCIPLINE** RELIGION IN LATE ANTIQUITY **EDUCATION** Mary Washington Col of U Va, BA, 69; Univ Chicago, MA, 72; PhD, 79. **CAREER** Asst prof, Univ Wash, 75-76; asst prof, Syracuse Univ, 77-83; assoc prof, Syracuse Univ, 83-95; prof, Syracuse Univ, 95-; dir grad studies, dept relig, Syracuse Univ, 92-99. **HONORS AND AWARDS** Chair, Council of Grad Stud in Religion, 99-; pres, Namer Patristics Soc, 96-97; fel, NEH, 83; Kent fel, Univ Chicago, 72-75. **MEMBERSHIPS** Amer Acad Relig; Namer Patristics Soc. **RESEARCH** Religion and Aesthetics in Late Antiquity; Early Christian asceticism; Early Christian and Pagan hagiography. **SELECTED PUBLICATIONS** Auth, Dreams in Late Antiquity: Studies in the Imagination of a Culture, Princeton, Princeton Univ Press, 94; Biography in Late Antiquity: A Quest for the Holy Man, Berkeley, Univ Calif Press, 83; Articles, Differential Networks: Relics and Other Fragments in Late Antiquity, Jour of Early Christ Studies, 6, 113-38, 98; Strategies of Representation in Collective Biography: Constructing the Subject as Holy, Greek Biography and Panegyrics in Late Antiquity, ed Tomas Hagg and Philip Rousseau, Berkeley, Univ Calif Press, 98; Jerome's Centaur: A Hyper-Icon of the Desert, Jour of Early Christ Studies, 4, 209-33, 96; Dreaming the Body: An Aesthetics of Asceticism, Asceticism, ed Vincent Wimbush and Richard Valantasis, New York, Oxford Univ Press, 281-300, 95; Desert Asceticism and The Body from Nowhere, Jour of Early Christ Studies, 2, 137-53, 1994; The Blazing Body: Ascetic Desire in Jerome's Letter to Eustochium, Jour of Early Christian Studies, 1, 21-45, 93; The Devil's Gateway: An Eros of Difference in the Dreams of Perpetua, Dreaming, 2, 45-63, 92; Plenty Sleeps There: The Myth of Eros and Psyche in Plotinus and Gnosticism, Neoplatonism and Gnosticism, ed R. Wallis and J. Bregman, Stony Brook, State Univ of NY Press, 223-38, 92. **CONTACT ADDRESS** Dept of Religion, Syracuse Univ, 501 Hall of Languages, Syracuse, NY 13244-1170. **EMAIL** plmiller@syr.edu

MILLER, RANDALL MARTIN
PERSONAL Born 04/16/1945, Chicago, IL, m, 1968, 1 child **DISCIPLINE** AMERICAN HISTORY **EDUCATION** Hope Col, AB, 67; OH State Univ, MA, 68, PhD(Am hist), 71. **CAREER** Asst prof hist, Wesley Col, DE, 71-72; asst prof Am hist, 72-78, assoc prof hist, 78-82, prof hist, St Joseph's Univ, PA, 82-; Inst Ed Hist Doc fel, 73; Robert S Starobin Mem Libr fel, 75; Am Coun of Learned Soc fel, 75-76 & 80-81; Danforth assoc, 81-; ed, PA Magazine of Hist and Biography, 86-91. **HONORS AND AWARDS** Lindback Awd, 79; Tengelman Awd, 97. **MEMBERSHIPS** AHA; Orgn Am Historians; Southern Hist Asn. **RESEARCH** Ethnic studies; South and slavery; religion and politics. **SELECTED PUBLICATIONS** Auth, The Cotton Mill Movement in Alabama, Arno, 78; Kaleidoscopic Lens, Ozer, 80; auth, Afro-American Slaves, Krieger, 81; The Fabric of Control: Slavery in Antebellum Southern Textile Mills, Bus Hist Rev, 12/81; A Warm and Zealous Spirit: John J Zubly, Mercer Univ, 82; Dear Master: Letters of a Slavery Family, Cornell, 78, rev ed, GA, 90; Catholics in the Old South, Mercer, 83; Ethnic and Racial Images in American Film and Television, Garland, 87; co-ed, Dictionary of Afro-American Slavery, Greenwood, 88, rev ed, Praeger, 97; Book of American Diaries, AVon, 95; American Reform and Reformers, Greenwood, 97; Religion and the Civil War, Oxford, 98; and others. **CONTACT ADDRESS** Dept of Hist, Saint Joseph's Univ, 5600 City Ave, Philadelphia, PA 19131-1376. **EMAIL** miller@sju.edu

MILLER, RICHARD
PERSONAL Born 01/07/1946, Arkansas City, KS, s, 4 children **DISCIPLINE** GEOGRAPHY **EDUCATION** Univ Tulsa, BS, 71; SD School Mines, MS, 72; Univ Wisconsin, PhD, 86. **CAREER** Lect, Univ of Wisconsin, 78-79; dept chair, Milwaukee Area Tech Col, 81-82; inst chair, Milwaukee Area Tech Col, 84-86; ten instr, Milwaukee Area Tech Col, 72-; vis prof, Fla State Univ, 99-00. **HONORS AND AWARDS** Pi Lambda Theta; Outstanding MATC Fac Awd, 87; Outstanding Teach Awd, Coop Urban Teach Prog, 89; Elected 1st VP, MAT C's CQI com, 92-96; App Found co-chair AAC, 94-98; Fac Appreciation Awd, 96; 25-year Dist Ser Awd, Milwaukee Area Tech Coll, 97; Outstanding Contrib Awd, Milwaukee Area Tech Coll, 97; MATC Outstanding Fac Awd, 99. **MEMBERSHIPS** GSA; NSTA. **RESEARCH** Geographic information systems. **SELECTED PUBLICATIONS** Auth, Uncertainty. Science column in the MATC Times newspaper. Milwaukee: MATC Press (95-); auth, H.O.G. Mile and a Half Tour: Road Log. Milwaukee: MATC Press (98); auth, Discovery Science, Milwaukee: Personal Publication (96), 5th ed; auth, "Teach teachers," Geotimes 21 (86); coauth, "Recharge to the Dakota sandstone from outcrops in the Black Hills, South Dakota," Bulletin of the Association of Engineering Geologists (74): 221-234. **CONTACT ADDRESS** Dept Geography, Florida State Univ, PO Box 3062190, Tallahassee, FL 32306. **EMAIL** rmiller@mailer.fsu.edu

MILLER, RICHARD G.
DISCIPLINE HISTORY **EDUCATION** Univ Nebr, PhD, 70. **CAREER** Prof. **RESEARCH** Urbanization as an agent of social change. **SELECTED PUBLICATIONS** Auth, pubs on city and social classes in 19th century America. **CONTACT ADDRESS** History Dept, State Univ of West Georgia, Carrollton, GA 30118. **EMAIL** dmiller@westga.edu

MILLER, SALLY M.
PERSONAL Born 04/13/1937, Chicago, IL **DISCIPLINE** AMERICAN HISTORY **EDUCATION** Univ Ill, BA, 58; Univ Chicago, AM, 63; Univ Toronto, PhD, 66. **CAREER** From instr to asst prof Am thought & lang, Mich State Univ, 65-67; asst prof, 67-70, assoc prof, 70-75, Prof Hist, Univ of The PAC, 75-, Res awards, Univ of the Pac, 70, 71, 72, 76, 78 & 81; Am Philos Soc travel grants, 71 & 76; vis sr lectr hist, Univ Warwick, 78-79; Am Coun Learned Soc travel grant, 79; Calif Coun Humanities grant, 81. **HONORS AND AWARDS** Distinguished Fac Awd, Univ of the Pac, 76; Fulbright lectr, Univ Otago, NZ, 86; Fulbright lectr, Turku Univ, Finland, 96; newberry Lib Fel, 92; Missouri Hist Book Awd, 94. **MEMBERSHIPS** AHA; Orgn Am Hist; Immigration Hist Soc; Europ Labor & Working Class Hist Study Group. **RESEARCH** American intellectual history; progressive era; labor, immigration and women's history. **SELECTED PUBLICATIONS** Auth, Socialist Party Decline and World War I, Sci & Soc, winter 70; "The Socialist Party and the Negro, 1901-1920," Journal of Negro History, 7/71; Victor Berger and the Promise of Constructive Socialism, Greenwood, 73; The Radical Immigrant, 1820-1920, Twayne, 74; contribr, Milwaukee: Of Ethnicity and Labor, In: Socialism and the Cities, Kennikat, 75; auth, Americans and the Second International, Proc Am Philos Soc, 76; "From Sweatshop Worker to Labor Leader: Theresa Malkiel," American Jewish History Quarterly, 79; ed, Flawed Liberation: Socialism & Feminism, Greenwood, 81; The Writings and Speeches of Kate Richards O'Hare, La State Univ Press, 82; ed, The Ethnic Press in the United States; Historical Analysis and Sourcebook, Greenwood, 87; auth, From Prairie to Prison: The Life of Social Activist Kate Richards O'Hare, Missouri, 93; co-ed, American Labor in the Era of World War II, Greenwood, 93; auth, Race, Ethnicity and Gender in Early 20th Century American Socialism, Garland, 96. **CONTACT ADDRESS** Dept of History, Univ of the Pacific, Stockton, 3601 Pacific Ave, Stockton, CA 95211-0197. **EMAIL** pupshse@aol.com

MILLER, STEPHEN G.
PERSONAL Born 06/22/1942, Goshen, IN, M, 1999 **DISCIPLINE** CLASSICAL ARCHAEOLOGY **EDUCATION** Wabash Col, BA (Greek), 64; Princeton Univ, MA, 67, PhD, 70. **CAREER** Res asst, Inst Advanced Study, Princeton, 72-73; Dir, Nemea Excavations, 73-; asst prof, 73-75, assoc prof, 75-81, Prof, Dept of Classics, Univ CA, Berkeley, 81-; Dir, Am School of Classical Studies, Athens, 82-87; brd of dirs, Fulbright Found in Greece, 82-87; brd advisors to Minister of Culture, Greece, 95-. **HONORS AND AWARDS** Various fels, Dept Art and Archaeology, Princeton Univ, 64-68; Fulbright fel to Greece, 68-69; Agora Excavating fel, 69-72; Am Coucil Learned Socs, summer grant-in-aid, 72; principal investigator, NEH, 75-77, 77-79, 79-81; Humanities res fel, Univ CA, 76-77, 80-81; corresponding mem, Deutsches Archaologisches Institut, 79; Honorary citizen, Archaia Nemea, Greece, 81; Order of the Golden Bear, Univ CA, 91; Governor's Medal for Distinguished Service to the Korinthia, 91; active mem, Academia Scientarum et Artium Europaeae, 92; Phi Beta Kappa vis scholar, 92-93; President's res fel, Univ CA, 94-95; Honorary Citizen, Leontion, Greece, 95; Honorary President, Soc for the revival of the Nemean Games, 95; Honorary Doctorate, Univ Athens, 96; decorated by President K. Stephanopoulos of the Hellenic Republic, 96; other honorary awards, 97-98. **MEMBERSHIPS** Archaeological Institute of Am; American Philological Assoc; Assoc of Ancient Historians. **RESEARCH** Ancient Athletics, Greek Architecture, Topography. **SELECTED PUBLICATIONS** Architecture as Evidence for the Identity of a Polis, Acts of the Copenhagen Polis Centre II, 95; Nemea, Encyclopedia dell'Arte Antica, supp II, Rome, 95; A Day at the Races: Living the Olympic Idea, CA Monthly 107, 96; Nemea, An Encyclopedia of the History of Classical Archaeology, Westport, 96; Stadiums, The Oxford Encyclopedia of Archaeology in the Near East 5, Oxford, 97; There's No Place Like Home for Our Heritage, Mycenaean Treasures of the Aegean Bronze Age Repatriated, ed R. Howland, Washington, 97; "The Athenian Century," The Destiny of Parthenon Marbles, ed. R. Howland, (Washington, 00), 81-104; "Naked Democracy," Polis and Politics Festschrift M.H. Hansen, edd. P. Flensted-Jensen, T.H. Nielsen, L. Rubinstein, (Copenhagen: 00), 277-296; auth, Numea II: The Early Hellenistic Stadium, Berkeley (Los Angeles), 01. **CONTACT ADDRESS** Dept of Classics, Univ of California, Berkeley, MC #2520, Berkeley, CA 94720-2520. **EMAIL** sgmnemea@socrates.berkeley.edu

MILLER, SUSAN
DISCIPLINE NATIVE AMERICAN HISTORY **EDUCATION** Univ Nebr, Lincoln, PhD, 97. **CAREER** Asst prof Hist & Ethnic Stud, Univ Nebr, Lincoln. **HONORS AND AWARDS** Outstanding Dissertation on Okla Hist, Okla Hist Soc, 97; Distinguished Doctoral Dissertation, Univ Nebr, Lincoln, 98. **SELECTED PUBLICATIONS** Published several articles in the ethnohistory of native Americans and the American West. **CONTACT ADDRESS** Univ of Nebraska, Lincoln, 639 Oldfat, Lincoln, NE 68588-0417. **EMAIL** smiller@unlinfo.unl.edu

MILLER, TICE LEWIS
PERSONAL Born 08/11/1938, Lexington, NE, m, 1963, 2 children **DISCIPLINE** THEATRE HISTORY **EDUCATION** Kearney State Col, BA, 60; Univ Nebr, Lincoln, MA, 61; Univ Ill, Urbana, PhD(Theatre), 68. **CAREER** Instr speech & theatre, Kansas City Jr Col, 61-62; asst prof theatre, Univ WFla, 68-72; assoc prof, 72-79, prof Theatre & Drama, Univ Nebr, Lincoln, 79-, fel, Ctr Great Plains Studies, 78. **HONORS AND AWARDS** Fellow, College of Fellows of American Theatre, JFK Center, Washington, D.C., 92; Sam Davidson Theatre Awd, Lincoln Arts Council, 98. **MEMBERSHIPS** Am Soc Theatre Res; Am Theatre Asn; Univ & Col Theatre Asn; Mid-Am Theatre Conf. **RESEARCH** American theatre; 19th century American theatre; American theatre critics. **SELECTED PUBLICATIONS** Auth, John Ranken Towse: Last of the Victorian critics, Educ Theatre J, 5/70; Towse on Reform in the American Theatre, Cent States Speech Commun J, winter 72; Early Cultural History of Nebraska: The Role of the Opera House, Nebr Speech Commun J, 74; Alan Dale: The Hearst critic, Educ Theatre J, 3/74; From Winter to Nathan: The Critics Influence on the American Theatre, Southern Speech Commun J, winter 76; Identifying the Dramatic Writers for Wilkes's Spirit of the Times, 1859-1902, Theatre Survey, 5/79; Bohemians and Critics: Nineteenth Century Theatre Criticism, Scarecrow Press Inc, 81; Fitz-James O'Brien: Irish Playwright & Critic in New York, 1851-1862, Nineteenth Century Theatre Res, fall 82; co-ed, Cambridge Guide to American Theatre, 93; co-ed, The American Stage, Cambridge, 93; editorial advisory board & major contributor, Cambridge Guide to Theatre, 88, 92, 95; auth, "Plays and Playwrights: Civil War to 1896," The Cambridge History of American Theatre, Vol II, 99. **CONTACT ADDRESS** Dept of Theatre Arts, Univ of Nebraska, Lincoln, PO Box 880201, Lincoln, NE 68588-0201. **EMAIL** tmiller@unlinfo.unl.edu

MILLER, TIMOTHY
PERSONAL Born 08/23/1944, Wichita, KS, m, 1982, 2 children **DISCIPLINE** AMERICAN AND RELIGIOUS STUDIES **EDUCATION** Univ of Kans, AB, 66; MA, 69; PhD, 73; Crozer Theol Sem, MDiv, 68. **CAREER** Lectr to prof, Univ of Kans, 73-. **HONORS AND AWARDS** Outstanding Acad Book, Choice, 91; Distinguished Scholar Awd, Communal Studies Assoc, 99. **MEMBERSHIPS** Am Acad of Relig; Communal Studies Assoc; Int Communal Studies Assoc; Mid-Am Am Studies Assoc; Soc for Utopian Studies. **RESEARCH** American religious history, new/alternative religious movements in the United States, history of communitarianism. **SELECTED PUBLICATIONS** Auth, Following in His Steps: A Biography of Charles M Sheldon, Univ of Tenn Pr, 87; auth, American Communes, 1860-1960: A Bibliography, Garland, 90; auth, "Introduction", America's Alternative Religions, SUNY, Pr, (95): 1-10; auth, "Black Jews and Black Muslims", America's Alternative Religions, SUNY Pr, (95): 277-283; auth, The Hippies and American Values, Univ of Tenn Pr, 91; auth, The Quest for Utopia in Twentieth-Century America, Syracuse Univ Pr, 98; auth, "Our Beliefs, Our Lives: Communitarian Activists in the Early Twentieth Century", Communities: J of Cooperative Living 100, (98): 54-47; auth, "Academic Integrity and the Study of New Religious Movements: Introduction", Nova Religio 2.1 (98): 8-15; auth, The 60s Communes: Hippies and Beyond, Syracuse Univ Pr, 99; auth, "Communities in the 20th Century", Communities: J of Cooperative Living 105 (99); auth, "Cult's and Intentional Communities: Working Through Some Complicated Issues", Communities Directory: A Guide to Cooperative Living, 00. **CONTACT ADDRESS** Dept Relig, Univ of Kansas, Lawrence, Univ of Kansas, 103 Smith Hall, Lawrence, KS 66045-0001. **EMAIL** tkansas@ukans.edu

MILLER, VIRGINIA E.
PERSONAL Born 04/24/1948, London, Canada **DISCIPLINE** ART HISTORY **EDUCATION** Univ TX Austin, PhD. **CAREER** Assoc prof, Univ IL at Chicago. **HONORS AND AWARDS** National Endowment for the Humanities Fellowship; Fulbright (Guatemala); Fulbright (Mexico); Dumbarton Oaks Fellowship. **MEMBERSHIPS** College Art Association; Association for Latin American Art; Society for American Archaeology. **RESEARCH** Pre-Columbian and native Am art. **SELECTED PUBLICATIONS** Ed, The Role of Gender in Precolumbian Art and Architecture; auth, The Frieze of the Palace of the Stuccoes, Acanceh, Yucatan. **CONTACT ADDRESS** Art Hist Dept, Univ of Illinois, Chicago, Mail Code 201, 935 W. Harrison, PO Box 705, Chicago, IL 60607. **EMAIL** vem@cuic.edu

MILLER, WILBUR R.
PERSONAL Born 04/21/1944, Iowa City, IA, m, 1965 **DISCIPLINE** HISTORY **EDUCATION** Univ Calif, BA, 66; Columbia Univ, MA, 67; PhD, 73. **CAREER** From Instr to Asst Prof, Princeton Univ, 71-75; From Asst Prof to Prof, State Univ NYork (SUNY), 75- **HONORS AND AWARDS** Fel, Ford Found, 84; **MEMBERSHIPS** Orgn of Am Historians, Am Hist Asn, Soc Sci Hist Asn, Int Asn for the Hist of Crime and Criminal Justice. **RESEARCH** Police history, National Geographic Magazine. **SELECTED PUBLICATIONS** Auth, Cops and Bobbies: Police Authority in New York and London 1830-1870, Univ Chicago Pr, 77; auth, Revenuers and Moonshiners: Enforcing Federal Liquor Law in the Mountain South 1865-1900, Univ NC Pr, 91. **CONTACT ADDRESS** Dept Hist, SUNY, Stony Brook, 100 Nicolls Rd, Stony Brook, NY 11794-0001.

MILLER, WORTH ROBERT
PERSONAL Born 09/19/1943, Tucson, AZ **DISCIPLINE** HISTORY **CAREER** Instr, Univ Okla, 84-85; vis asst prof, E Texas State Univ, 85-86; vis asst prof, Texas A&M Univ, 86-87; ASST PROF TO PROF, SW MO STATE UNIV, 87-. **HONORS AND AWARDS** SMSU Found Fac Achievement Awd for Excellence in Research, 91-92. **MEMBERSHIPS** Southern Hist Asn, Soc for the Hist of the Gilded Age and Progressive Era. **RESEARCH** Populism, progressivism, Okla, Texas. **SELECTED PUBLICATIONS** Auth, Oklahoma Populism: A History of the People's Part in the Oklahoma Territory, 87, Univ Okla Press; auth, "Farmers and Third-Party Politics in Late Nineteenth Century America," in The Gilded Age: Essays on the Origins of Modern America, 96, Scholarly Resources; auth, "The Republican Tradition," in American Populism, 94, D.C. Heath; coauth, "Ethnic Conflict and Machine Politics in San Antonio," Journal of Urban History, Aug 93; auth, "A Centennial Historiography of American Populism," Kansas History: A Journal of the Central Plains, Spring 93. **CONTACT ADDRESS** Dept of History, Southwest Missouri State Univ, Springfield, Springfield, MO 65804. **EMAIL** bobmiller@mail.smsu.edu

MILLER, ZANE L.
PERSONAL Born 05/19/1934, Lima, OH, m, 1955 **DISCIPLINE** AMERICAN URBAN HISTORY **EDUCATION** Miami Univ, BS, 56, MA, 59; Univ Chicago, PhD(hist), 66. **CAREER** Instr hist, Northwestern Univ, 64-65; from instr to assoc prof, 65-74, prof hist, Univ Cincinnati, 74-; Nat Coun for Humanities younger scholar fel, 68; NSF res grant, 68-70; res assoc, Ctr Urban Studies, Univ Chicago, 70-71; fel, Newberry Libr, Chicago, winter 76; vis scholar, Afro Am Curric, Univ NC, spring 81; co-dir, Ctr Neighborhood Community Studies, Univ Cincinnati, 81-; Charles Phelps Taft prof emer, Univ Cincinnati. **MEMBERSHIPS** AHA; Southern Hist Asn; Orgn Am Historians. **RESEARCH** American urban and social history; American political history, 1865 to the present. **SELECTED PUBLICATIONS** Auth, Boss Cox's Cincinnati, J Am Hist, spring 68; Boss Cox's Cincinnati, Oxford Univ, 68; co-ed, Physician to the West, Univ Ky, 70; auth, Urbanization of Modern America: a Brief History, Harcourt, 73; contrib, The New Urban History, Princeton Univ, 75; The Urban History Yearbook, Leicester Univ, 77; auth, Scarcity, abundance and American urban history, J Urban Hist, 2/78; Suburb, Univ Tenn, 81; Changing Plans for America's Inner Cities: Cincinnatti's Over-the-Rhine and Twentieth Century Urbanism, Columbus: The Ohio State University Press, 98. **CONTACT ADDRESS** Dept of History, Univ of Cincinnati, PO Box 210373, Cincinnati, OH 45221-0373. **EMAIL** zane.miller@uc.edu

MILLETT, ALLAN REED
PERSONAL Born 10/22/1937, New York, NY, m, 1980, 3 children **DISCIPLINE** UNITED STATES MILITARY HISTORY **EDUCATION** DePauw Univ, BA, 59; OH State Univ, MA, 63, PhD(hist), 66. **CAREER** Asst prof hist, Univ MO-Columbia, 66-69; assoc prof & mem res fac, Mershon Ctr, 69-74, Prof hist & dir prog inter security & Mil affairs, Mershon Ctr, OH State Univ, 74-91, Univ MO Res Coun fel, 68; Nat Endowment for Hum fel, 69; Am Philos Soc fel, 69, Lec, Korea, 91; Korea Foundation, 96; General Raymond E. Mason, Jr. Prof of Mil Hist, OH State Univ, 91-. **HONORS AND AWARDS** Distinguished Fulbright **MEMBERSHIPS** Am Mil Inst; AHA; Orgn Am Historians; Inter-Univ Sem Armed Forces & Soc; US Commission of Mil Hist; SMH. **RESEARCH** US mil hist; Korean War; hist of the Marine Corps. **SELECTED PUBLICATIONS** Auth, 70; The United States and Cuba: The uncomfortable abrazo, 1898-1968, In: Twentieth Century American Foreign Policy, OH State Univ, 71; The politics of intervention: The military occupation of Cuba, 1906-1909, OH State Univ, 69; auth, The General: Robert L Bullard and Officership in the US Army, Greenwood, 75; Military Professionalism and Officership in America & Academic Education in National Security Policy, OH State Univ, 77; Semper Fidelis: History of the US Marine Corps, Macmillan, 80; In Many a Strife: Gerald C. Thomas and the US Marine Corps, Naval Inst Press, 93; coauth, For the Common Defense: The Military History of the United States of America, Free Press, 94, rev ed, 94; coauth, A War to Be Won, 00. **CONTACT ADDRESS** Dept of History, Ohio State Univ, Columbus, 230 W 17th Ave, Columbus, OH 43210-1361. **EMAIL** millett.2@osu.edu

MILLS, ERIC L.
PERSONAL Born 07/07/1936, Toronto, ON, Canada **DISCIPLINE** HISTORY OF SCIENCE **EDUCATION** Carleton Univ, BS, 59; Yale Univ, MS, 62; PhD, 64. **CAREER** Asst prof, Queen's Univ, 63-67; assoc prof, 67-71, PROF OCEANOGRAPHY & BIOL, 71-, PROF HIST SCIENCE, DALHOUSIE UNIV, 94-; vis fel, Cambridge Univ, 74-75; Nuffield fel, Univ Edinburgh, 81-82; guest prof, Univ Kiel, 84, 88; H Burr Steinbach Vis Scholar, Woods Hole Oceanographic Inst, 88; Ritter Mem Fel, Scripps Inst Oceanography, 90; Jack Ludwick Lectr, Old Dominion Univ, 91; vis scholar, Scripps Inst Oceanography, 95-96. **MEMBERSHIPS** NS Bird Soc; Hist Sci Soc; Soc Hist Natural Hist. **SELECTED PUBLICATIONS** Auth & ed, One Hundred Years of Oceanography, 75; Biological Oceanography: An Early History, 89. **CONTACT ADDRESS** Dalhousie Univ, Halifax, NS, Canada B3H 4J1. **EMAIL** e.mills@dal.ca

MILLS, KENNETH R.
PERSONAL Born 09/22/1964, Saskaton, Canada, m, 3 children **DISCIPLINE** HISTORY **EDUCATION** Oxford, PhD, 92. **CAREER** Princeton Univ, 93-. **HONORS AND AWARDS** Arthur H. Scribner Bicential Preceptor. **RESEARCH** Colonial Latin America, Early Modern Spanish World. **SELECTED PUBLICATIONS** Auth, An Evil Lost to View? An Investigation of Post-Evangelization Andean Religion in Mid-Colonial Peru, The Univ of Liverpool Monograph 18, Inst of Latin Am Studies (Liverpool), 94; auth, Idolatry and Its Enemies: Colonial Andean Religion and Extirpation, 1640-1750, Princeton Univ Press (Princeton), 97; coauth, Colonial Spanish America: A Documentary History, Scholarly Resources (Wilmington), 98. **CONTACT ADDRESS** Dept Hist, Princeton Univ, 130 Dickinson Hall, Princeton, NJ 08544-0001.

MILNER, CLYDE A., II
PERSONAL Born 10/19/1948, Durham, NC, m, 1977, 2 children **DISCIPLINE** HISTORY **EDUCATION** Univ NC, AB, 71; Yale Univ, MA, 73; MPhil, 74; PhD, 79. **CAREER** Instr, Yale, Univ, 74-75; Instr to Prof, Ut State Univ, 76-. **HONORS AND AWARDS** Charles Redd Prize, Ut Acad of Sci, Arts and Letters, 96; Frederick W. Beinecke Fel, Yale Univ, 97; Fac Res Fel, Brigham Young Univ, 96-97; Caughey Western Hist Asn Awd, 95; Western Heritage Awd, Nat Cowboy Hall of Fame, 94; Vivian A. Paladin Writing Awd, Mont, 87; Fac Serv Awd, Ut State Univ, 87; Outstanding Res of the Year, Ut State Univ, 83; Theron Rockwell Field Prize, Yale Univ, 79; Danforth Fel; Phi Beta Kappa. **MEMBERSHIPS** W Hist Asn; W Lit Asn; Org of Am Hist; AHA; Am Studies Asn; Am Soc for Environ Hist; Mont Hist Soc; Tex State Hist Asn; Phi Alpha Theta. **RESEARCH** Nineteenth-century North American West; Violence in the North American West; Biography and Life Writing in the North American West. **SELECTED PUBLICATIONS** Co-ed, Trails: Toward a New Western History, Univ Press of Kans, 91; auth, "National Initiatives," in The Oxford History of the American West, Oxford Univ Press, 94; co-ed, The Oxford History of the American West, Oxford Univ Press, 94; ed, A New Significance: Re-envisioning the History of the American West, Oxford Univ Press, 96; co-ed, Major Problems in the History of the American West, second edition, Hoghton Mifflin, 97. **CONTACT ADDRESS** Dept Hist, Utah State Univ, 0740 Old Main Hill, Logan, UT 84322-0740. **EMAIL** cmilner@hass.usu.edu

MINAULT, GAIL
PERSONAL Born 03/25/1939, Minneapolis, MN, m, 1992, 1 child **DISCIPLINE** HISTORY **EDUCATION** Smith Col, BA, 61; Univ Pa, MA, 66, PhD, 72. **CAREER** Asst prof to PROF, HIST, UNIV TEX, 72-. **HONORS AND AWARDS** NDFL For Lang Fel, 64-65, 65-66, 66-67; Fulbright-Hays fel, res India, 67-68; Nat Hum Ctr fel, 87-88; NEH fel, 94-95; SSRC, Am Inst Indian Studies fels. **MEMBERSHIPS** Asn Asian Stud; AHA; Berkshire Conf Women Historians. **RESEARCH** 19th, 20th cent India; women in S Asia; Islam in S Asia. **SELECTED PUBLICATIONS** Auth, Secluded Scholars: Women's Education and Muslim Social Reform in Colonial India, Oxford Univ Press, 98; auth, Sayyid Karamat Husain and Muslim Women's Education, in Lucknow:Memories of a City, Oxford Univ Press, 97; auth, Other Voices, Other Rooms: The View from the Zenana, in Women as Subjects, Stree (Calcutta) and Univ Press Va, 94. **CONTACT ADDRESS** History Dept, Univ of Texas, Austin, Garrison Hall 101, Campus Mail Code B7000, Austin, TX 78712. **EMAIL** gminault@utxvms.utexas.edu

MINEAR, RICHARD H.
DISCIPLINE HISTORY **EDUCATION** Harvard Univ, PhD, 68. **CAREER** Prof, Univ MA Amherst . **RESEARCH** Japan hist **SELECTED PUBLICATIONS** Auth, Japanese Tradition and Western Law, 70; Victors' Justice: The Tokyo War Crimes Trial, 71; ed, Through Japanese Eyes, 94; ed & transl, Requiem for Battleship Yamato, by Yoshida Mitsuru (85); ed & transl, Hiroshoma: Three Witnesses (90); ed & transl, Blackeggs, by Kurihara Sadako (94); ed & transl, Dr. Seuss Goes to War (99); ed & transl, Japan's Past, Japan's Future, by Ienaga Saburo (01). **CONTACT ADDRESS** Dept of Hist, Univ of Massachusetts, Amherst, Mass Ave, Amherst, MA 01003. **EMAIL** rhminear@history.umass.edu

MINER, CRAIG
PERSONAL m, 2 children **DISCIPLINE** REGIONAL AND BUSINESS HISTORY **CAREER** Prof, 69-. **HONORS AND AWARDS** Willard W Garvey distinguished prof hist, 88; Public Hum award, Kans Comm Hum, 87; Choice mag award for best acad bk(s), 87; Lyon award, Kans Author's Club, 88; Kans Preservation Alliance award, 93; Governor's Aviation Hon(s) award, 95; certificate of commendation, amer assn for state and local hist, 86. **RESEARCH** Regional and business history, **SELECTED PUBLICATIONS** Publ, eleven bk(s), Univ presses; seventeen bk(s), non-acad presses; forty two jour articles, numerous book rev(s); Auth, West Wichita: Settling the High Plains of Kansas, 1865-1890, 86; Uncloistered Halls, history of Wichita State Univ; Harvesting the High Plains: John Kriss and the Business of Farming, 20-50, 98. **CONTACT ADDRESS** Dept of Hist, Wichita State Univ, 1845 Fairmont, Wichita, KS 67260-0062.

MINER, MADONNE
DISCIPLINE AMERICAN LITERATURE AND WOMEN'S STUDIES **EDUCATION** SUNY, Buffalo, PhD, 82. **CAREER** Prof, ch, dept Eng, TX Tech Univ, 97-. **SELECTED PUBLICATIONS** Auth, Insatiable Appetites: Twentieth-Century American Women's Bestsellers, 84. **CONTACT ADDRESS** Texas Tech Univ, Lubbock, TX 79409-5015. **EMAIL** M.Miner@ttu.edu

MINGHI, JULIAN M.
PERSONAL Born 07/26/1933, London, England, m, 1960, 1 child **DISCIPLINE** GEOGRAPHY **EDUCATION** Durham Univ, BA, 57; Univ Wash, MA, 59; PhD, 62. **CAREER** Asst Prof, Univ of Conn, 61-64; from Asst Prof to Assoc Prof, Univ of Brit Columbia, 64-73; Geog Dept Chemn, Univ of SC, 73-90; Prof, Univ of SC, 73-. **HONORS AND AWARDS** Can Coun Res Fel, 69-70; Awd for Best Article, J of Geog, 66, 95; Fulbright Res Awd, 93-94. **MEMBERSHIPS** Asn for Am Geographers, Am Geog Soc, Nat Coun for Geog Educ, Cosmos Club Washington DC. **RESEARCH** Political Geography and the Region of Europe. **SELECTED PUBLICATIONS** Ed, "Introduction," in Peoples of the Living Land: Geography of Cultural Diversity in British Columbia (Vancouver: Tantalus, 72): 7-12; co-ed, "Introduction" and "Conclusion," in The Geography of Border Landscapes (London: Routledge, 91): 1-14, 195-198; coauth, "Powerscene: Application of New Geographic Technology to Revolutionize Boundary Making?," Boundary and Security Bull 4-2 (summer 96): 102-105; coauth, "The Political Geography of the Dayton Accords," Geopolitics and Int Boundaries 1-1 (summer 96): 77-92; auth, "Border Disputes: From Argentina to Somalia," in Tension Areas of the World, ed. Gordon Bennett (Dubuque, IO: Kendall/Hunt, 97), 71-87; auth, "Voting and Borderland Minorities: Recent Italian Elections in Eastern Friuli-Venezia Giulia," GeoJournal 43-3 (Nov 97): 263-271; coauth, "The Dayton Accords: Prediction and Reality in Bosnia," Geopolitics and Int Boundaries 2-3 (winter 97): 14-27; coauth, "Political Processes and Global Environmental Change in the Next Millennium," in Landscape and Sustainability, Global Change, Mediterranean Historic Centers: From Rediscovery to Exploitation, ed. Elio Manzi and Marcella Schmidt di Frieberg (Milano: Angelo Guerini, 99): 301-313; auth, "Borderland 'Day Tourists' from the East: Trieste's Transitory Shopping Fair," Visions in Leisure and Bus 17-4 (winter 99): 32-49; auth, "Common Cause for Borderland Minorities? Shared Status among Italy's Ethnic Communities," Geopolitics 4-2 (in press). **CONTACT ADDRESS** Dept Geog, Univ of So Carolina, Columbia, Columbia, SC 29225-0001. **EMAIL** minghi@sc.edu

MINKEMA, KENNETH P.
PERSONAL Born 10/30/1958, Ridgewood, NJ, m, 1984, 2 children **DISCIPLINE** HISTORY **EDUCATION** Univ CT, Storrs, PhD, 88. **CAREER** Exec Ed, Works of Jonathan Edwards, Yale Univ, 89-; Lect, Church Hist, Yale Divinity School, 96-. **MEMBERSHIPS** AHA; OAH; ASCH. **RESEARCH** US relig hist; colonial. **SELECTED PUBLICATIONS** Ed, with James F. Cooper, The Sermon Notebook of Samuel Parris, 1689-1694, Colonial Soc MA, 94; ed, with John E. Smith and Harry S. Stout, A Jonathan Edwards Reader, Yale Univ Press, 95; auth, The Lynn End 'Earthquake' Narratives of 1727, New England Quart LXIX, Sept 96; Jonathan Edwards, Messianic Prophecy, and the Other Unfinished 'Great Work': 'The Harmony of the Old and New Testaments,' in Jonathan Edward's Writings: Text, Context, Interpretation, ed, Stephen J. Stein, IN Univ Press, 96; Jonathan Edwards on Slavery and the Slave

Trade, William and Mary Quart LIV, Oct 97; ed, The Works of Jonathan Edwards, 14, Sermons and Discourses, 1723-1729, Yale Univ Press, 97; auth, 'The Devil Will Roar in Me Anon': The Possession of Martha Roberson, Boston, 1741, in Spellbound: Women and Witchcraft in America, ed, Elizabeth S. Reis, Scholarly Resources, 98; ed, with Wilson H. Kimnach and Douglas A. Sweeney, The Jonathan Edwards Sermons Reader, Yale Univ Press, 99. **CONTACT ADDRESS** Works of Jonathan Edwards, Yale Univ, 409 Prospect St., Box 250, New Haven, CT 06511. **EMAIL** Ken.Minkema@yale.edu

MINNICH, NELSON H.
DISCIPLINE HISTORY **EDUCATION** Boston Col, AB, 65; MA, 66; Gregorian Univ, STB, 70; Harvard Univ, PhD, 77. **CAREER** Instr, Loyola Acad, 66-68; Teaching Asst, Harvard Univ, 72-77; Asst Prof to Prof and Chair, Catholic Univ, 77-. **HONORS AND AWARDS** Fulbright Grant, Inst of Intl Educ, 72-73; Fel, Harvard Univ, 72-73, 73-74; NEH Summer Stipend; Fel, Am Acad, Rome, 80; Res Grant, Am Philos Soc, 84; NEH Grant, 85. **MEMBERSHIPS** Am Catholic Hist Asn, gesellschaft zur Herausgabe des Corpus Catholicorum, Sixteenth Century Studies Conf, Erasmus of Rotterdam Soc, Renaissance Soc of Am, Soc for Italian Hist Studies. **SELECTED PUBLICATIONS** Co-ed, Studies in Catholic History in Honor of John Tracy Eillis, Michael Glazier, 85; auth, The fifth Lateran Council (1512-1517): Studies on Its Membership, Diplomacy, and Proposals for Reform, London, 93; Assoc ed, The Encyclopedia of the Renaissance, Charles Scribner's Sons, 99; ed, The Controversies with Alberto Pio, Univ of Toronto Press, 00; auth, "Some Underlying Factors I the Erasmus-Pio Debate," The Erasmus of Rotterdam Society Yearbook, (93): 1-43; auth, "The Reform Proposals, (1513) of Stefano Taleazzi for the Fifth Lateran Council (1512-17)," Annuarium Historiae Concilorum, (96): 543-570; auth, "The Voice of Theologians in General Councils from Pisa to Trent," Theological Studies, (98): 420-441. **CONTACT ADDRESS** Dept Church Hist, Catholic Univ of America, 620 Mich Ave NE, Washington, DC 200064-0001. **EMAIL** minnich@cua.edu

MINOR, CLIFFORD EDWARD
PERSONAL Born 01/11/1946, Bronxville, NY, m, 1966 **DISCIPLINE** GREEK & ROMAN HISTORY **EDUCATION** Univ Wash, BA, 67, MA, 68, PhD, 72. **CAREER** Asst prof ancient hist, 71-75, assoc prof, 75-80, prof hist, CA State Univ, Chico 80. **MEMBERSHIPS** Asn Ancient Historians **RESEARCH** Graeco-Roman world of the third century CE; soc, relig and polit hist of the Later Roman Empire; Hellenistic hist. **SELECTED PUBLICATIONS** Auth, Bagaudae or Bacaudae?, Traditio, 75; The Robber Tribes of Isauria, Ancient World, 79; Lest We Forget: The Parthenon and an Overlooked Tricentennial, Ancient World, 89; Bacaudae: A Reconsideration, Traditio, 96; "Reclassifying the Bacaudae: Some Reasons for Caution. Part I: Who were the Third Century Bacaudae?," Ancient World, 97; auth, "Reclassifying the Bacaudae: Some Reasons for Caution, Part II, The Fourth Century Interim (286-407)," Ancient World, 99; auth, "Reclassifying the Bacaudae. Some Reasons for Caution, Part III, Ghost Bacaudae: The Britannian and Armorican Rellions, (ca. 408-17)," Ancient World, 00. **CONTACT ADDRESS** Dept of Hist (735), California State Univ, Chico, 101 Orange St, Chico, CA 95929-0753. **EMAIL** cminor@csuchico.edu

MINOR, VERNON H.
PERSONAL Born 02/24/1945, Steubenville, OH, m, 1994, 2 children **DISCIPLINE** ART **EDUCATION** Kent State Univ, BA, 68; Univ Kans, PhD, 76. **CAREER** Asst Prof to Prof, Univ Colo, 76-. **HONORS AND AWARDS** NEH Sen Fel, Rome, 99-00. **MEMBERSHIPS** Col Art Asn. **RESEARCH** Critical theory of Art history; Roman Art of the 17th and 18th Centuries. **SELECTED PUBLICATIONS** auth, Baroque and Rococo: Art and Culture, Calmann & King, 99; auth, Passive Tranquility: The Sculpture of Filippo della Valle, Am Philosophical Soc, 97; auth, Art History's History, Prentice Hall, 00. **CONTACT ADDRESS** Dept Fine Arts, Univ of Colorado, Boulder, PO Box 318, Boulder, CO 80309-0318. **EMAIL** vernon.minor@colorado.edu

MINTZ, LAWRENCE E.
DISCIPLINE AMERICAN STUDIES, ENGLISH **EDUCATION** Univ SC, BA, 66; MI State Univ, MA, 67, PhD, 69. **CAREER** Am Stud Dept, Univ Md. **RESEARCH** Ethnicity in popular culture and humor; performance comedy (standup comedy, variety theater humor, performance art, humor in magic, juggling, circus, and other performance entertainments). **SELECTED PUBLICATIONS** Auth, "The Standup Comedian as Social and Cultural Mediator," Am Humor, Oxford, 87; ed, Humor in America: A Research Guide to Genres and Topics, Greenwood Press, 88; auth, "Devil and Angel; Philip Roth's Humor" Studies in American Lit 8:2, 89; auth, "Ethos and Pathos in Chaplin's City Lights," in Charles Chaplin: Approaches to Semiotics, (Mouton deGryter, 91); auth, "Humor and Ethic Stereotypes in Vaudeville and Burlesque," MELUS, 96. **CONTACT ADDRESS** Am Stud Dept, Univ of Maryland, Col Park, 10632 Old Barn Rd, New Market, MD 21774. **EMAIL** lm36@umail.umd.edu

MINTZ, STEVEN
PERSONAL Born 02/16/1953, Detroit, MI, m, 1982, 2 children **DISCIPLINE** HISTORY **EDUCATION** Oberlin Col, BA, 73; Yale Univ, PhD, 79. **CAREER** Assoc Dean, Grad Stud, Col Hum Fine Arts, Communic, 98-, John and Rebecca Moores Prof Hist, 99-. **HONORS AND AWARDS** Phi beta Kappa, 73. **RESEARCH** History of Family, children, slavery, Reform, film **SELECTED PUBLICATIONS** Auth, African American Voices; auth, America and its Peoples, Auth, Boisterous Sea of Liberty; auth, Domestic Revolutions; auth, Hollywood's America; auth, Mexican American Voices; auth, Moralists Modernizers; auth, Native American Voices; auth, A Prison of Expectations. **CONTACT ADDRESS** History Dept, Univ of Houston, Houston, TX 77204-3785. **EMAIL** smintz@uh.edu

MIQUELON, DALE B.
PERSONAL Born 09/27/1940, Wetaskiwin, AB, Canada **DISCIPLINE** HISTORY **EDUCATION** Univ Alta, BA, 63; Carleton Univ, MA, 66; Univ Toronto, PhD, 73. **CAREER** Hist res, Nat Hist Sites Div NA & NR, Ottawa, 63-64; asst prof, 70-75, assoc prof 75-79, prof Hist, Univ Saskatchewar, 79-, assoc dean hum & fine art, 84-89, dept head 90-95. **HONORS AND AWARDS** Can Coun pre-doctoral fel, 66-70, doctoral thesis prize, 75, fel, 76-77; SSHRCC released time fel, 82-83. **RESEARCH** Eighteenth century diplomatic hist in North Am (French-Indian relations) and eighteenth century French business hist (textiles and dyeworks). **SELECTED PUBLICATIONS** Auth, Dugard of Rouen: French Trade to Canada and the West Indies 1729-1770, 78; auth, New France 1701-1744: 'A Supplement to Europe,' 87; auth, The First Canada: to 1791, 94; ed, Society and Conquest: The Debate on the Bourgeoisie and Social Change in French Canada 1799-1850, 77. **CONTACT ADDRESS** Dept of History, Univ of Saskatchewan, 9 Campus Dr, Saskatoon, SK, Canada S7N 5A5. **EMAIL** miquelon@sask.usask.ca

MISA, THOMAS J.
PERSONAL Born 05/31/1959, Port Angeles, WA, m, 1983, 2 children **DISCIPLINE** HISTORY **EDUCATION** Mass Inst Technol, SB, 81; Univ Pa, PhD, 87. **CAREER** From asst prof to assoc prof, Ill Inst of Technol, 87-. **HONORS AND AWARDS** IEEE Life Members Prize in Electrical Hist, Soc for the Hist of Technol, 87; Baner Family Excellence in Undergraduate Teaching Awd, Ill Inst of Technol, 93; Dexter Prize, Soc for the Hist of Technol, 97. **MEMBERSHIPS** Soc for the Hist of Technol, Hist of Sci Soc, Business Hist Confr, Am Hist Asn. **RESEARCH** Technology and Social Change: Leonardo to the Internet. **SELECTED PUBLICATIONS** Auth, A Nation of Steel: The Making of Modern America, 95; auth, Managing Technology in Society, 95. **CONTACT ADDRESS** Dept Humanities, Illinois Inst of Tech, 3300 S Federal St, Chicago, IL 60616-3795. **EMAIL** misa@iit.edu

MITCHELL, ARTHUR
PERSONAL Born 06/23/1936, Boston, MA, m, 1966, 2 children **DISCIPLINE** HISTORY **EDUCATION** Boston Univ, BA, 61; Trinity Col, PhD, 67. **CAREER** Curry Col, 67-70, 73-75; IL State Univ, 70-72; Univ of SC Salkehatchie, 76-. **HONORS AND AWARDS** NEH Fel, 80-81. **MEMBERSHIPS** Am Conf on Irish Studies. **RESEARCH** Ireland, 1900-1940, Irish-American history, 1860-1900, German and U.S. Occupation, 1945-1995. **SELECTED PUBLICATIONS** Auth, Labour in Irish Politics: 1890-1930; the Irish Labour Movement in an Age of Revolution, Barnes and Noble, 74; ed, Ireland and Irishmen in the American War of Independence: Some Documents, Dublin, 76; auth, The History of the Hibernian Society of Charleston, SC, 1799-1978, Charleston, 82; coed, Irish Political Documents, 1916-1949, Irish Acad Pr, 85; auth, Irish Political Documents, 1870-1916, Irish Acad Pr, 89; auth, JFK and His Irish Heritage, Moytura Pr, (Dublin), 94; auth, Revolutionary Government in Ireland: Dail Eireann, 1919-1921, Gill and Macmillan, (Dublin), 95. **CONTACT ADDRESS** Dept Humanities and Soc Sci, Univ of So Carolina, Salkehatchie Regional, PO Box 617, Allendale, SC 29810-0617. **EMAIL** mitchellarthur@hotmail.com

MITCHELL, BETTY L.
DISCIPLINE HISTORY **EDUCATION** Douglass, AB, 69; Univ Mass at Amherst, MA, 72, PhD, 79. **CAREER** Assoc, prof, hist, Univ SE Mass; PROF, HIST, UNIV MASS DARTMOUTH. **MEMBERSHIPS** AM Antiquarian Soc **SELECTED PUBLICATIONS** Auth, "Massachusetts Reacts to John Brown's Raid," Civil War Hist 19, 73; auth, "Realities Not Shadows," Civil War Hist 20, 74; auth, Edmund Ruffin: A Biography, 81; "Out of the Glass House: Robert Todd Lincoln's Crucial Decade, 1865-75," Timeline Mag, 88. **CONTACT ADDRESS** 56 Revell St, Northampton, MA 01060. **EMAIL** bmitchell@umassd.edu

MITCHELL, HELEN BUSS
PERSONAL Born 07/17/1941, New York, NY, m, 1964, 1 child **DISCIPLINE** HISTORY **EDUCATION** Hood Col, BA, 63; Loyola Col, MEd, 74; MMS, 79; Univ Md, PhD, 90. **CAREER** English Teacher, Howard Co Schs, 63-68; Freelance Feature Writer and Columnist, 72-77; From Dir to Assoc Dean, Howard Community Col, 77-93; Prof, Howard Community Col, 93-. **HONORS AND AWARDS** NISOD Excellence Awd, 97-98; Outstanding Fac Mem, Howard Community Col, 98; Inducted, Howard Community Col Women's Hall of Fame, 99; Distance Educr of the Year, PBS, 99. **MEMBERSHIPS** APA, Nat Women's Studies Assoc. **RESEARCH** Feminism, Asian and African philosophies. **SELECTED PUBLICATIONS** Auth, Roots of Wisdom, Wadsworth Publ Co, 96, 98; auth, Raices de la Sabiduria, Int Thomson Editors, 98; auth, Taking Sides: Clashing Views on Controversial Issues in World Civilizations, Dushkin/McGraw-Hill, 98, 00. **CONTACT ADDRESS** Arts and Humanities, Howard Community Col, 10901 Little Patuxent Pkwy, Columbia, MD 21044-3110. **EMAIL** hmitchell@howard.cc.edu

MITCHELL, REID
DISCIPLINE HISTORY **EDUCATION** Univ CA, PhD. **CAREER** Assoc prof, Univ MD Baltimore County . **RESEARCH** Civil War; Southern hist. **SELECTED PUBLICATIONS** Auth, Civil War Soldiers; The Vacant Chair: The Northern Soldier Leaves Home. **CONTACT ADDRESS** Dept of Hist, Univ of Maryland, Baltimore, Hilltop Circle, PO Box 1000, Baltimore, MD 21250. **EMAIL** mitchell@gl.umbc.edu

MITCHELL, RICHARD E.
PERSONAL Born 06/02/1934, Rainelle, WV, m, 1958, 1 child **DISCIPLINE** ANCIENT HISTORY **EDUCATION** Olivet Col, BA, 57, Univ MI, MA, 58; Univ Cincinnati, PhD, 65. **CAREER** Instr hist, Olivet Col, 58-61; From Asst Prof to Prof Hist, Univ Ill, Urbana-Champaign, 65. **HONORS AND AWARDS** Am Coun Learned Soc fel, 70-71. **MEMBERSHIPS** AHA; Am Philol Asn; Archaeol Inst Am; Am Numis Soc; Royal Numis Soc. **RESEARCH** Hist of the Roman Republic; Roman numismatics. **SELECTED PUBLICATIONS** Auth, The fourth century origin of Roman didrachms, Mus Notes, 69; Roman Carthaginian treaties: 306 & 279/8 BC, Historia, 71; The aristocracy of the Roman Republic, In: The Rich, the Wellborn, and the Powerful: Elites and Upper Classes in History, Univ Ill, 73; Patricians and Plebeians: The Origin of the Roman State, Cornell Univ Press, 90. **CONTACT ADDRESS** Dept of Hist, Univ of Illinois, Urbana-Champaign, 810 S Wright St, Urbana, IL 61801-3611. **EMAIL** rmitchell@staff.uiuc.edu

MITCHELL, RICHARD HANKS
PERSONAL Born 04/16/1931, Jacksonville, IL, m, 1960 **DISCIPLINE** MODERN JAPANESE HISTORY **EDUCATION** Univ Wis, BS, 57, MS, 58, PhD(EAsian hist), 63. **CAREER** Lectr hist, Far East Div, Univ Md, 63-66 & 67-68; assoc prof EAsian hist, Col New Paltz, State Univ NY, 66-67; vis assoc, Univ Nebr, Lincoln, 68-69; vis assoc prof Japanese hist, Univ Rochester, 69-70; assoc prof, 70-76, prof Japanese Hist, Univ MO St Louis, 76-, Sem assoc, Columbia Univ Sem EAsia, Japan, 70-82; Univ Mo-St Louis fac res grants, Japan, 72, 74, 76; Nat Endowment for Humanities fel, summer, 78. **HONORS AND AWARDS** Res & Publ Awd, Univ Md, Far East Div, 68; Chancellors Awd for Research, 92. **MEMBERSHIPS** Asn Asian Studies. **RESEARCH** Japanese justice system. **SELECTED PUBLICATIONS** Auth, The Korean minority in Japan, Univ Calif, 67; Japan's peace preservation law of 1925: Its origins and significance, Monumenta Nipponica, fall 73; Thought Control in Prewar Japan, Cornell Univ, 76; Political Bribery in Japan, U Hawaii, 96; Censorship in Imperial Japan; Princeton u.P., 83; Janus-Faced Justice: Political: Criminals in Imperial Japan, **CONTACT ADDRESS** Dept of History, Univ of Missouri, St. Louis, 8001 Natural Bridge, Saint Louis, MO 63121-4499.

MITCHINSON, WENDY
PERSONAL Born 12/28/1947, Hamliton, ON, Canada **DISCIPLINE** HISTORY **EDUCATION** York Univ, BA, 70, MA, 71, PhD, 77. **CAREER** Lectr & asst prof, Mt St Vincent Univ, 75-77; asst prof, 77-81, assoc prof, 81-85, Univ Windsor; assoc prof, 85-91, prof Hist, Univ Waterloo, 91-; vis prof, McMaster Univ, Hannah Inst Hist Med, 88-89; scholar-in-residence, Rockefeller Stud Ctr, Bellagio, Italy, 94; Fudacion, Valparaiso, Spain, 97. **MEMBERSHIPS** Can Hist Asn; Ont Hist Asn; Ont Women's Hist Network; Can Soc Hist Med; Can Stud Asn. **RESEARCH** Hist of childbirth in Canada, mothering, prenatal care, obstetrical intervention, and postnatal care; the way in which a childbirth has become medicalized and taken away from women. **SELECTED PUBLICATIONS** Auth, The Nature of Their Bodies: Women and Their Doctors in Victorian Canada, Toronto: UTP, 91; auth, "Women's History," in D. Owram, ed., Canadian History: A Reader's Guide Confederation to the Present, Toronto: UTP, (94): 202-227; coauth, Canadian Women: A History, Toronto: Harcourt, Brace, 96; co-ed, Canadian Women: A Reader, Toronto: Hartcourt Brace, 96; co-ed, "Marion Hilliard," in E. Cameron and J. Dickin, eds., Great Dames, (Toronto: UTP, 97); auth, "It's Not Society That's the Problem, It's Women's Bodies": A Historical View of Medical Treatment of Women, in Kerry Petersen ed., Intersections: Women on Lw, Medicine and Technology, (Aldershot: Dartmouth Pubishing, 97): 25-48; co-ed, "On the Case: Expolorations in Social History" Toronto: UTP, 98; auth, "Agency, Diversity, Constraints: Women and Their Physicians, Canaada 1850-1950," I nSue Sherwin, ed., The Politics of Women's Health: Exploring Agency and Autonomy, (Philadelphia: Tem-

ple Univ Press, 98): 122-49. **CONTACT ADDRESS** Dept of History, Univ of Waterloo, Waterloo, ON, Canada N2L 3G1. **EMAIL** wlmitchi@watarts.uwaterloo.ca

MITTAL, SUSHIL
PERSONAL Born 03/04/1967, ON, Canada, m, 1996, 2 children **DISCIPLINE** RELIGION, ANTHROPOLOGY, SOUTH ASIAN STUDIES **EDUCATION** McGill Univ, BA, 90; Carleton Univ, MA, 93; Univ Montreal, PhD, 98. **CAREER** Vis asst prof, Univ Fla, 98-99; asst prof, Millikin Univ, 99-. **HONORS AND AWARDS** Millikin Univ Fac Summer Res Grant, 00; Millikin Univ Merit Awd, 00; Am Acad of Relig Individual res grant, 99-00; Soc sci and Humanities res coun of Canada Doctoral Fel, 93-97; Nominated for fac teaching Awd, Univ Fla, 98-99. **MEMBERSHIPS** Am Acad of Relig. **RESEARCH** Comparative history of religions, Hindu civilization, Hindu theories of social and human sciences, Mahatma Gandhi, Occidentalism, Structure, logic and meaning of Hindu worldviews. **SELECTED PUBLICATIONS** Ed, International Journal of Hindu Studies, Quebec: World Heritage Press, 97-. **CONTACT ADDRESS** Dept Relig, Millikin Univ, 1124 W Main St, Decatur, IL 62522-2084. **EMAIL** smittal@mail.millikin.edu

MIXON, WAYNE
PERSONAL Born 08/19/1945, Winnsboro, SC, m, 1967, 2 children **DISCIPLINE** HISTORY **EDUCATION** Univ SC, BA, 67, MA, 70; Univ NC, Chapel Hill, PhD, 74. **CAREER** Asst prof, Univ Southern MS, Natchez, 75-77; from asst prof to assoc prof to prof, 77-96, Mercer Univ; prof, Augusta State Univ, 96-. **HONORS AND AWARDS** NEH Summer Fel, 86. **MEMBERSHIPS** Am Hist Asn; Southern Hist Asn; South Atlantic Modern Language Asn. **RESEARCH** The American South; US social and intellectual history. **SELECTED PUBLICATIONS** Auth, Southern Writers and the New South Movement, 1865-1913, 80; ed, My Young Master: A Novel by Opie Read, 87; auth, art, The Ultimate Irrelevance of Race: Joel Chandler Harris and Uncle Remus in Their Time, 90; auth, The Adaptable South: Essays in Honor of Goerge Brown Tindall, 91; auth, The People's Writer: Erskine Caldwell and the South, 95. **CONTACT ADDRESS** Dept of History and Anthropology, Augusta State Univ, Augusta, GA 30904. **EMAIL** wmixon@aug.edu

MODARRESSI, HOSSEIN
PERSONAL Born 04/25/1942, Iran **DISCIPLINE** NEAR EASTERN STUDIES **EDUCATION** Oxford Univ, PhD, 82. **CAREER** Prof, Princeton Univ, 84-; Res Schol, Columbia Univ, 91-. **HONORS AND AWARDS** Fel, St Antony's Col, Oxford Univ, 83-84, 89-. **RESEARCH** Near Eastern Studies. **SELECTED PUBLICATIONS** Auth, Kharaj in Islamic Law, 83; Auth, An Introduction to Shi'i Law, 84; Auth, Land in Islamic Law, vol 1&2, 83-84; Auth, Crisis and Consolidation in the Formative Period of Shi'ite Islam. **CONTACT ADDRESS** Dept N Eastern Studies, Princeton Univ, 110 Jones Hall, Princeton, NJ 08544-0001.

MOEHRING, EUGENE P.
PERSONAL Born 03/08/1947, s **DISCIPLINE** HISTORY **EDUCATION** City Univ NYork PhD, 76. **CAREER** Prof, Univ Nev Las Vegas. **RESEARCH** Modern American history; urban history; business history. **SELECTED PUBLICATIONS** Auth, Public Works and the Patterns of Urban Real Estate Growth in Manhattan, 1835-1894, 81; Resort City in the Sunbelt: Las Vegas, 1930-2000, 00. **CONTACT ADDRESS** History Dept, Univ of Nevada, Las Vegas, 4505 Md Pky, Las Vegas, NV 89154-5020. **EMAIL** emoehring@ccmail.nevada.edu

MOFFAT, FREDERICK
DISCIPLINE ART HISTORY **EDUCATION** Univ Chicago, PhD, 72. **CAREER** Assoc prof, Art Hist, Univ Tenn. **HONORS AND AWARDS** Vis schlr, Smithsonian Inst, 88; Sr Post-Doctoral Fel, Nat Mus of Am Art, 89-90. **SELECTED PUBLICATIONS** Auth, "Intemperate Patronage of Henry D. Cogswell," Winterthur Portfolio XXVII (92), 123-143; auth, "Arthur Dow Pont Aven," Rennes Univ, 86; auth, "Carl Sublett, The Painter," 84; auth, "Clark Stewart," 82; auth, "Sandra Blain," 82; auth, "Philip Livingston," 82. **CONTACT ADDRESS** Dept of Art, Univ of Tennessee, Knoxville, 1715 Volunteer Blvd, Knoxville, TN 37996. **EMAIL** fmoffatt@utkux.utcc.utk.edu

MOFFETT, SAMUEL HUGH
PERSONAL Born 04/07/1916, Pyongyang, Korea, m, 1942 **DISCIPLINE** HISTORY OF MISSIONS, ASIAN CHURCH HISTORY **EDUCATION** Wheaton Col, Ill, AB, 38; Princeton Theol Sem, ThB, 42; Yale Univ, PhD, 45. **CAREER** Lectr English & church hist, Yenching Univ, Peking, 48-49; asst prof church hist, Nanking Theol Sem, 49-50; vis lectr ecumenics, Princeton Theol Sem, 53-55; prof church hist, 60-81, dean Grad Sch, 66-70, assoc pres, 70-81, Presby Theol Sem, Seoul, Korea; pres, Asian Ctr Theol Studies & Mission, 74-81; prof missions & ecumenics, 81-87, Henry Winters Luce Prof of Ecumenics and Mission, emeritus, Princeton Theol Sem; bd dir, Yonsei Univ, Seoul, 57-81, Soongjun Univ, Seoul, 69-81 & Whitworth Col, Spokane, Wash, 73-79; mem, US Educ Comn, Korea, 66-67. **HONORS AND AWARDS** Order Civil Merit, Repub Korea, 81; DD, King Col, TN, 85; DD, Gordon Conwell Theol Sem, 95; DD, Presbyterian Col and Theol Sem, 96; hon PhD Soongsil Univ, SEoul, 97; littd, yonsei univ, seoul, korea, 81. **MEMBERSHIPS** Am Soc Missiology; Int Asn Missiological Studies; Korean Church History Soc; Royal Asiatic Soc (pres, Korean Br, 68-69). **RESEARCH** Asian church history; history of missions; Korean studies. **SELECTED PUBLICATIONS** Coauth, First Encounters: Korea 1880-1910, Dragon's Eye Press, Seoul, 82; auth, History of Christianity in Asia, Beginnings to 1500, Harper Collins, 92. **CONTACT ADDRESS** 150 Leabrook Ln, Princeton, NJ 08540.

MOHR, CLARENCE L.
PERSONAL Born 10/03/1946, Almont, MI, m, 2 children **DISCIPLINE** HISTORY **EDUCATION** Birmingham Southern Col, AB, 68; Univ Ga, MA, 70, PhD, 75. **CAREER** Prof & ch, Univ S Al, 98-; asst prof, 81-86, assoc chem, 84-86 & 89-90, assoc prof, 86-98; prof, 98-, Tulane Univ. **HONORS AND AWARDS** Avery O. Craven awd, Orgn Amer Historians, 87; listed in, Who's Who in the South and Southwest, 95-96; Contemp Authors; Directory Amer Scholars; Summer stipend, Nat Endowment for the Humanities, 87; grant-in-aid, Rockefeller Arch Ctr, Tarrytown, NY, 86; fel, Amer Coun Learned Soci, 79-80; grant-in-aid, Amer Philos Soc,78; fel in Advan Ed, Nat Hist Publ Comn, 75-76. **RESEARCH** Southern history,19th and 20th century; economic and social reform, higher education, Civil War,slavery and race relations. **SELECTED PUBLICATIONS** Auth, On the Threshold of Freedom: Masters and Slaves in Civil War Georgia, Athens and London: Univ Ga Press, 86; Schooling, Modernization, and Race: The Continuing Dilemma of The American South, Amer J Educ 106, 98 & Before Sherman: Georgia Blacks and the Union War Effort, 1861-1864, J Southern His XLV, 79, rep in, Major Problems in the History of the Civil War and Reconstruction, Lexington, Mass: D C Heath, 91 and The Day of Jubilee: The Civil War Experience of Black Southerners, NY: Garland Publ Inc, 94; contrib, The Impact of World War II on the American South, Jackson: UP Miss, 96; Dictionary of Afro-American Slavery, Westport: Greenwood Press, 88, paperback ed, 97; Dictionary of Georgia Biography, 2 vols, Athens: Univ Ga Press, 83 & Encyclopedia of the Confederacy, 93; auth, The Emergence of a Modern University, 1945-1980, LSU Press, 00. **CONTACT ADDRESS** Dept of History, Univ of So Alabama, 344 Humanities, Mobile, AL 36688-0002. **EMAIL** cmohr@jaguar1.usouthal.edu

MOHR, JAMES C.
PERSONAL Born 01/28/1943, Edgewood, MD, m, 1967, 2 children **DISCIPLINE** HISTORY **EDUCATION** Yale Univ, BA, 65; Stanford Univ, MA, 66; PhD, 69. **CAREER** CAS Distinguished Prof, Oregon, 98-; Prof, Oregon, 92-98; Prof, 77-92, UMBC; Vis Assoc Prof, Virginia, 77; Vis Assoc Prof, Stanford, 73-74; Asst & Assoc Prof, UMBC, 69-77. **HONORS AND AWARDS** Editorial Board, Journal of Negro History, 72-74; Danforth Fellow, 75-; Dean's Special List of Outstanding Teachers at the University of Virginia, 77; Editorial Board, Journal of American History, 82-85; Throne-Aldrich Awd, 90, State Historical Society of Iowa; Commonwealth Lecturer, William and Mary College, 93; Begando Lecturer, Illinois Medical School, 94; Fishbein Lecturer, Chicago Medical History Association, 94; Norman Brown Endowed Faculty Fellow, UO, 96-97; CAS Distinguished Prof, UO, 98; OSSHE Grant, 95-98; Center for the Study of the Recent History of the United States, 87; Guggenheim Fellow, 83-84; National Endowment for the Humanities, Editorial Research Grant, 79-80; Rockefeller and Ford Foundation, Policy Grant, 75-76. **SELECTED PUBLICATIONS** Auth, "Academic Turmoil and Public Opinion: The Ross Case at Stanford," Pacific Historical Review, XXXIX, No. 1, Feb 70, 39-61; auth, "The Cormany Diaries: A Northern Family in the Civil War, Univ of Pittsburgh Press, 82, Reissud 90; auth, "The Origins of Medical Malpractice in the United States," Transactions & Studies of the college of Physicians of Philadelphia: Medicine & History, Series 5, Vol 14, No. 1, March 92, 1-21; auth, "Doctors and the Law: Medical Jurisprudence in Nineteenth-Century America, Oxford University Press, 93, paperback, 96, Johns Hopkins University Press," auth, "Sexuality, Reproduction, Contraception, and Abortion: A Review of Recent Literature," Journal of Women's History, Vol. 8, No. 1 Spring 96, 172-184; coauth, OSSHE historical atlas and CD (1996-98); auth, "The Origins of Forensic Psychiatry in the United State and the Great Nineteenth-Century Crisis Over the Adjudication of Wills," Journal of the American Academy of Psychiatry and the Law, Vol. 25, No. 3, 97, 273-284; auth, "The Paradoxical Advance and Embattled Retreat of the 'Unsound Mind': Evidence of Insanity and the Adjudication of Wills in Nineteenth-Century America," Historical Reflections/Reflexions Historiues, Vol. 24, No. 3 Fall 98, 415-435; coauth, "Interative Historical Atlas of US History; "The History Place," Peregrine, subsidiary of Addison Weley Longman, 99-; auth, "American Medical Malpractice Litigation in Historical Perspective," JAMA: The Journal of the American Medical Association, Vol. 283, No. 13 April 5, 00, 1731-1737; **CONTACT ADDRESS** Dept History, Univ of Oregon, 1288 Univ of Or, Eugene, OR 97403. **EMAIL** jmohr@oregon.uoregon.edu

MONET, JACQUES
PERSONAL Born 01/26/1930, Saint-Jean, PQ, Canada **DISCIPLINE** HISTORY **EDUCATION** Univ Montreal, BA, 55; Immaculee-Conception, PhL, 56, ThL, 67; Univ Toronto, MA, 61, PhD, 64. **CAREER** Asst prof, Univ Toronto, 68; prof agrege, 69-80, prof titul, hist, 80-82, Univ d'Ottawa; pres, Regis Col, Toronto, 82-88; dir, Can Inst Jesuit Stud, 88-; RECTEUR, UNIV SUDBURY, 92-; prof emer, Regis Col, 00-. **HONORS AND AWARDS** Chev l'ordre des Palmes acad, 74; o. pretre, montreal, 66; derniers voeux dans la cie de jesus (jesuites) montmartre, 71. **MEMBERSHIPS** Soc Royale Can; Soc Hist Can (pres, 75-76); conseil Nat pour l'evaluation des Archives, 79-83; Commission des lieux et monuments historiques du Canada, 95-. **SELECTED PUBLICATIONS** Auth, The Last Cannon Shot: A Study of French Canadian Nationalism, 69; auth, The Canadian Crown, 79; auth, La Monarchie au Canada, 79; auth, La Premiere Revolution Tranquille, 81. **CONTACT ADDRESS** Univ of Toronto, 15 St Mary St, Toronto, ON, Canada M4Y 2R5.

MONEYHON, CARL HOFMANN
PERSONAL Born 06/07/1944, Brownwood, TX, m, 1978, 2 children **DISCIPLINE** CIVIL WAR & RECONSTRUCTION **EDUCATION** Univ TX, Austin, BA, 67, MA, 68; Univ Chicago, PhD(hist), 73. **CAREER** Asst prof, 74-78, assoc prof Hist, 78-82, prof hist, Univ AR, Little Rock, 83-. **MEMBERSHIPS** Southern Hist Asn; TX Hist Asn; AR Hist Asn. **RESEARCH** American Reconstruction politics; social history of the American South in the 19th century. **SELECTED PUBLICATIONS** Auth, Republicanism in Reconstruction Texas, Univ TX Press, 80; coauth, Portraits of Conflict: A Photographic History of Arkansas in the Civil War, Univ AR Press, 87; Historical Atlas of Arkansas, Univ OK Press, 89; Portraits of Conflict: A Photographic History of Louisiana in the Civil War, Univ AR Press, 90; Portraits of Conflict: A Photographic History of Mississippi in the Civil War, Univ AR Press, 93; auth, The Impact of the Civil War and Reconstruction in Arkansas, LA State Univ Press, 94; Arkansas and the New South, Univ AR Press, 97. **CONTACT ADDRESS** Dept Hist, Univ of Arkansas, Little Rock, 2801 S University Av, Little Rock, AR 72204-1000. **EMAIL** CHMoneyhon@UALR.edu

MONHEIT, MICHAEL L.
PERSONAL Born 10/04/1946, Brooklyn, NY, m, 1985, 1 child **DISCIPLINE** RENAISSANCE, REFORMATION, EARLY MODERN EUROPE **EDUCATION** Univ Calif Berkeley, BA, 76; Princeton Univ, PhD, 88. **CAREER** Assoc prof, Univ South Al. **HONORS AND AWARDS** Article "Renaissance Interpreters of Roman Law" won the Selma V. Forkosch Prize for best article in the Jour of the History of Ideas in 97. **MEMBERSHIPS** Sixteenth Century Studies Soc; Renaissance Soc of Am; Soc for Reformation Res. **RESEARCH** The Formative Years of the Protestant Reformer Jean Calvin; varieties of individual identity in Early Modern Europe **SELECTED PUBLICATIONS** Auth, Young Calvin, Textual Interpretation and Roman Law, Bibliotheque d'Humanisme et Renaissance, Tome LIX, 97; The Origins of the edictalis-decretalis bonorum possessio Distinction in a Renaissance Defense of Scholastic Hermeneutics, Quaderni fiorentini per la storia del pensiero giuridico moderno, 96; Guillaume Bude, Andrea Alciato, and Pierre de l'Estoile: Renaissance Interpreters of Roman Law, J Hist Ideas, vol 58, 97 & The Ambition for an Illustrious Name: Humanism, Patronage, and Calvin's Doctrine of the Calling, Sixteenth Century J, Vol XXIII, 92. **CONTACT ADDRESS** Dept of History, Univ of So Alabama, 376 Humanities, Mobile, AL 36688-0002. **EMAIL** mmonheit@jaguar1.usouthal.edu

MONKKONEN, ERIC H.
PERSONAL Born 08/17/1942, Kansas City, KS, m, 1964, 2 children **DISCIPLINE** HISTORY **EDUCATION** Univ Minnesota, BA, 64; MA, 68; PhD, 73. **CAREER** Prof, Univ Calif, Los Angeles **MEMBERSHIPS** FASL; SSHA; NCVR. **SELECTED PUBLICATIONS** Auth, The Dangerous Class: Crime and Poverty in Columbus, Ohio, 1860-1920, Harvard Univ Press (75); auth, Police in Urban America, 1860 to 1920, Cambridge Univ Press (81); ed, Walking to Work: American Tramps, 1800 To 1930, Nebraska Univ Press (84); auth, America Becomes Urban: The Development of US. Cities and Towns, 1790-1980, Univ California Press (88); ed, Engaging the Past: The Uses of History Across the Social Sciences, Duke Univ Press ((auth, The Local State: The Political Economy of the City, Stanf Univ Press (95); co-ed, The Civilization of Crime: Violence in Town and Country since the Middle Ages, Ill Univ Press (96).; auth, Murder in New York City, Univ California Press (00). **CONTACT ADDRESS** Dept Policy Studies, History, Univ of California, Los Angeles, PO Box 951473, Los Angeles, CA 90095-1473. **EMAIL** emonkkon@ucla.edu

MONMONIER, MARK
PERSONAL Born 02/02/1943, Baltimore, MD, m, 1965, 1 child **DISCIPLINE** GEOGRAPHY **EDUCATION** Johns Hopkins Univ, BA, 64; Pa State Univ, MS, 67, PhD, 69. **CAREER** Asst prof, Univ RI, 69-70; asst prof, State Univ of NY at Albany, 70-73; assoc prof, Syracuse Univ, 73-79, prof, 79-98, Distinguished Prof of Geography, 98-. **HONORS AND AWARDS** Guggenheim Fel, 84; Chancellor's Citation for Exceptional Academic Achievement, Syracuse Univ, 93; Media Achievement Awd, Asn of Am Geographers, 2000; three multi-tear Nat Sci Found Grants; ed, The Am Cartographer; President, Am Cartographic Asn. **MEMBERSHIPS** Asn Am Geogs, Am

Congress on Surveying and Mapping, Authors Guild, North Am Cartography Info Soc, Soc for the Hist of Technol. **RESEARCH** History of cartography in the twentieth century; map use and mapping policy; visual analysis of environmental information. **SELECTED PUBLICATIONS** Auth, How to Lie With Maps, 2nd ed, Chicago: Univ Chicago Press (96); auth, Cartographies of Danger: Mapping Hazards in America, Chicago: Univ Chicago Press (97); auth, "The earth made flat [a remembrance of John P. Snyder]," New York Times Mag (Jan 4, 98): 33; auth, Air Apparent: How Meteorologists Learned to Map, Predict, and Dramatize Weather, Chicago: Univ Chicago Press (99); auth, "Gathering the storm: H. W. Brandes and the first weather chart," Mercator's World, Vol 4, no 1 (99): 50-55; auth, "Coping with qualitative-quantitative data in meteorological cartography: standardization, ergonomics, and facilitated viewing," Proceedings, 19th International Cartographic Conference, Ottawa, Vol 1 (99): 947-954; auth of eighteen entries in Ron Johnston and others, eds, Dictionary of Human Cartography, 4th ed, London: Blackwell (2000). **CONTACT ADDRESS** Dept Geography, Syracuse Univ, 144 Eggers, Syracuse, NY 13244-1020. **EMAIL** mon2ier@syr.edu

MONOD, PAUL
PERSONAL Born 06/25/1957, Montreal, Canada, m, 1984, 1 child **DISCIPLINE** HISTORY **EDUCATION** Princeton Univ, AB; Yale Univ, MA, MPhil, PhD. **CAREER** Prof, 84-; Chair, History Dept, 99-01. **HONORS AND AWARDS** John Ben Snow Prize, 90; Leverhulme Fellowship, 90-91. **RESEARCH** Early modern Britain; early modern Europe; modern Britain & political, social and cultural history. **SELECTED PUBLICATIONS** Auth, Jacobitism and the English People, 1688-1788, Cambridge, 89; auth, The Power of Kings: Monarchy and Religion in Europe, 1589-1715, Yale, 99. **CONTACT ADDRESS** Dept of History, Middlebury Col, Middlebury, VT 05753. **EMAIL** monod@middlebury.edu

MONROE, BETTY I.
PERSONAL m **DISCIPLINE** ART HISTORY **EDUCATION** Mich Univ, PhD. **CAREER** Prof emerita, Northwestern Univ. **RESEARCH** Indian sculpture and painting; Chinese painting; Chinese ceramics. **SELECTED PUBLICATIONS** Auth, Chinese Ceramics in Chicago Collections; transl, ed & adapted, Japanese Painting in the Literati Style. **CONTACT ADDRESS** 325 College Court, Iowa City, IW 52245.

MONROE, WILLIAM S.
PERSONAL Born 03/15/1952, Pottstown, PA, m, 1978, 2 children **DISCIPLINE** HISTORY **EDUCATION** Temple Univ, BA, 79; Drexel Univ, MS, 84; MA, 88, Mphil, 91, Columbia Univ. **CAREER** Cataloger, Teachers Col, Columbia Univ, 84-86; Ref Libr, Humanities Bibliographer, NY Univ, 86-91; Head of Collection Devel, Brown Univ, 93-. **MEMBERSHIPS** ALA; Amer Historical Assoc; Medieval Acad of Amer; Amer Theological Library Assoc. **RESEARCH** Cultural and legal history; early middle ages **SELECTED PUBLICATIONS** Auth, Redefining the Library: The Year's Work in Collection Development 1991, Library Resources & Technical Services 36, 92; coauth, Western European Political Science: An Acquisition Study, College & Research Libraries, 94; coauth, A New Kind of Space for a New Kind of Collection, BiblioFile: Newsletter of Brown Univ Library, 96; auth, The Role of Selection in Collection Development: Past, Present, and Future, Collection Management for the 21st Century: A Handbook for Librarians, 97; auth, Via iustitiae: The Biblical Sources of Justice in Gregory of Tours, Gregory of Tours and His World, 00. **CONTACT ADDRESS** Library, Brown Univ, Box A, Providence, RI 02912. **EMAIL** william_monroe@brown.edu

MOODY, J. CARROLL
PERSONAL Born 01/03/1934, Abilene, TX, m, 1953, 5 children **DISCIPLINE** UNITED STATES ECONOMIC & LABOR HISTORY **EDUCATION** Univ Corpus Christi, BS, 56; Tex A&I Univ, MS, 60; Univ Okla, PhD, 65. **CAREER** High sch teacher, Tex, 56-61; from instr to asst prof hist, 64-68, asst dean, Col Arts & Sci, Univ Toledo, 66-68; prof hist, Northern Ill Univ, 68-, chmn dept, 74-. **RESEARCH** Steel industry and the National Industrial Recovery Act; labor relations in the steel industry; history of the credit union in the United States. **SELECTED PUBLICATIONS** Coauth, The credit union movement: Origins and development, 1850-1970, Univ Nebr, 71;art, The transformation of the American economy, 1877-1900, The Reinterpretation of American History and Culture, Nat Coun Social Studies, 73. **CONTACT ADDRESS** Provost's Office, No Illinois Univ, De Kalb, IL 60115-2825. **EMAIL** cmoody@niu.edu

MOOGK, PETER N.
PERSONAL Born 10/05/1943, Chiltington, England **DISCIPLINE** HISTORY **EDUCATION** Univ Toronto, BA, 65, MA, 66, PhD, 73. **CAREER** Asst prof Univ BC, 70-77; vis scholar, Darwin Col, Cambridge Univ, 82-83; Assoc Prof History, Univ BC, 77-. **HONORS AND AWARDS** Ste-Marie Prize Hist, 75; Can Asn Res Awds, 76, 87, 89; Daughters Colonial Wars Prize Early Am hist, 80. **MEMBERSHIPS** Fel, Can Numismatic Res Soc; Can Hist Asn; Fr Colonial Hist Soc; Vancouver Numismatic Soc. **RESEARCH** Social history of early French Canada; Eighteenth century French; Canadian military history. **SELECTED PUBLICATIONS** Auth, "Building a House in New France: An Account of the Perplexities of Client and Craftsmen in Early Canada," Toronto, McClelland & Stewat, (77), 144; auth, "Vancouver Defended: A History of the Men and Guns of the Lower Mainland Defences," New Westminster, Antonson Publishing Ltd., (78), 128; auth, "Les Petis Sauvages: The Children of Eighteenth Century New France," in Joy Parr, ed.; Childhood and Family in Canadian History, Toronto, (82), 14-43; auth, "Relucant Exiles: Emigrants from Fance in Canada Before 1760," in the William and Mary Quarterly, (89), 463-505; coauth, "Berczy," Ottawa: National Gallery of Canada, (92), 21-126; auth, La Nouvelle Fance: The Making of French Canada, East Lansing: Michigan State Univesity Press, 00. **CONTACT ADDRESS** Dept of History, Univ of British Columbia, Vancouver, BC, Canada V6T 1Z1. **EMAIL** moogk@interchange.ubc.ca

MOON, CYRIS HEE SUK
PERSONAL Born 09/04/1933, Korea, m, 1959, 3 children **DISCIPLINE** HISTORY **EDUCATION** Emory Univ, PhD, 71. **CAREER** Prof, San Franciso Theol Sem. **MEMBERSHIPS** AAP; SBL. **SELECTED PUBLICATIONS** Auth, A Cultural History of Korea, Seoul: Voice, 96. **CONTACT ADDRESS** 2915 Ballesteros Ln, Tustin, CA 92782. **EMAIL** cyrismoon@aol.com

MOONEY, L. R.
DISCIPLINE MEDIEVAL STUDIES **EDUCATION** Univ Toronto, PhD, 81. **CAREER** Asst Prof, Assoc Prof, 86-99, Prof, Univ Maine, 99-. **MEMBERSHIPS** MAA; EBS; AMARC; EETS; New Chaucer Soc, FSA. **RESEARCH** Medieval English Manuscripts, Literature and History. **SELECTED PUBLICATIONS** Auth, Index of Middle English Prose, vol XI, Trinity College, Cambridge, 95; coauth, The Chronicle of John Somer, OFM, Camden Soc Miscellany 98. **CONTACT ADDRESS** Dept of English, Univ of Maine, Orono, ME 04469.

MOONEY-MELVIN, PATRICIA
DISCIPLINE HISTORY **EDUCATION** Cincinnati, PhD. **CAREER** College of Wooster, vis asst prof, history, 79-81; Univ Arkansas Little Rock, asst to assoc prof, 81-89; consult, Civilian Conserv Corps Oral Hist Proj, Nat Asn of Civilian Conserv Corps Alumni, Little Rock, 81-86; actg dir, UALR Archives and Special Collections, Univ Ark at Little Rock, 83-84; Loyola Univ, asst to assoc prof and dir Public History Program, 89-; co-dir, Kingsley Hist Proj, Kingsley elem sch, Evanston, 95-96. **MEMBERSHIPS** Nat Coun on Public Hist; Organization of Am Historians; Am Asn of State and Local Hist; Am Asn of Museums. **RESEARCH** Urban hist, public hist, local hist, the built environment. **SELECTED PUBLICATIONS** Auth, The Organic City: Urban Definition and Neighborhood Organization 1880-1920, Lexington: UP Ky, 87; auth, The Path From Our Founding to Our Future: A City Tour of Loyola University Chicago's Historic Downtown Sites, Walking Tour Brochure, 95; auth, Reading Your Neighborhood: A History of East Rogers Park, Loyola Univ (Chicago), 93; coauth, The Urbanization of Modern America, 2nd ed, San Diego: Harcourt Brace Jovanovich, 87; ed & prin auth, American Community Organizations: A Historical Dictionary, Westport: Greenwood Press, 86; auth, "Beyond the Book: Historians and the Interpretive Challenge," Public Historian 17, 95; auth, "Professional Historians and Destiny's Gate," Public Historian 17, 95; auth, "Harnessing the Romance of the Past: Preserv, Tourism, and History", Public Historian 13, 91; auth, "Professional Historians and the Challenge of Redefinition," in Public History: Essays from the Field, ed., by James B. Gardner and Peter Lapalia, (Krieger Press, 99); co-ed, Making Sense of the City: Local Government, Civic Culture, and Community Life in American Cities, Ohio State Univ Press (forthcoming). **CONTACT ADDRESS** Hist Dept, Loyola Univ, Chicago, 6525 N. Sheridan Rd., Chicago, IL 60626. **EMAIL** pmooney@luc.edu

MOORE, A. LLOYD
PERSONAL Born 03/22/1931, Hamilton, ON, Canada, m, 1956, 4 children **DISCIPLINE** MODERN HISTORY **EDUCATION** Univ Toronto, BA, 54; Univ Minn, MA, 56; PhD(hist), 58. **CAREER** Res asst, Univ Minn, 57-58; lectr hist, Univ Toronto, 58- 61; asst prof, Univ Cincinnati, 61-62; from asst prof to assoc prof, 62-71, Prof Hist, Univ Southern Calif, 71-, Vis assoc prof, Queen's Univ, Ont, 65-66; Nat Endowment for Humanities Younger Scholar fel, 69-70; Guggenheim fel, 77. **HONORS AND AWARDS** Koren Prize, Soc French Hist Studies, 62. **MEMBERSHIPS** AHA; Soc Fr Hist Studies; Past & Present Soc, England. **RESEARCH** Seventeenth century France. **SELECTED PUBLICATIONS CONTACT ADDRESS** Dept of Hist, Univ of So California, Los Angeles, CA 90007.

MOORE, CHRISTOPHER H.
PERSONAL Born 06/09/1950, Stoke-on-Trent, England **DISCIPLINE** HISTORY **EDUCATION** Univ BC, BA, 71; Univ Ottawa, MA, 77. **CAREER** Staff Hist, Parks Can, 72-75; sec bd gov, Heritage Can Found, 77-78; hist columnist, The Beaver, 91-; lectr, Univ Guelph, 85; lectr, Univ Toronto, 89-91; vis scholar, Univ Guelph, 90. **HONORS AND AWARDS** Gov Gen Lit Awd, 82; Riddell Awd, Ont Hist, 84; Sec State, Prize Exellence Can Stud, 85; IODE Toronto Bk Awd, 93. **MEMBERSHIPS** Writers' Union of Can **SELECTED PUBLICATIONS** Auth, Louisbourg Portraits, 82; auth, The Loyalists, 84; auth, The Law Society of Upper Canada and Ontario's Lawyers, 97; auth, 1867: How the Fathers Made a Deal, 97; coauth, The Illustrated History of Canada, 87; coauth, The Story of Canada, 92. **CONTACT ADDRESS** 396 Pacific, No 202, Toronto, ON, Canada M6P 2R1.

MOORE, EDGAR BENJAMIN
PERSONAL Born 07/17/1928, Spring Lake, NJ, m, 1952, 3 children **DISCIPLINE** EUROPEAN HISTORY **EDUCATION** Wesleyan Univ, BA, 50; Drew Univ, BD, 54, MSacred Theol, 58; Univ St Andrews, PhD, 65. **CAREER** Chaplain & asst prof relig, 62-64, from asst prof to assoc prof hist, 64-70, chmn dept 64-73, prof hist, Baldwin-Wallace Col, 70-. **MEMBERSHIPS** AAUP; African Studies Assn; Am Soc Church Hist; AHA. **RESEARCH** Reformation history; African studies. **CONTACT ADDRESS** Dept of History, Baldwin-Wallace Col, 275 Eastland Rd, Berea, OH 44017-2088.

MOORE, GEORGE EAGLETON
PERSONAL Born 03/25/1927, Osaka, Japan, m, 1953, 3 children **DISCIPLINE** EASTERN ASIAN HISTORY **EDUCATION** Univ Calif, Berkeley, BA, 51, MA, 59, PhD(hist), 66. **CAREER** From instr to prof, 64-73 San Jose State Univ, 64-. **HONORS AND AWARDS** Ford Found Fel 62-63; NEH Summer Fel, 79; Meritorious Serv Awd, Col of Soc Scis, San Jose State Univ, 98. **MEMBERSHIPS** Assn Asian Studies. **RESEARCH** Modernization of Japan; modernization of Asia; world history. **SELECTED PUBLICATIONS** Auth, Samurai conversion: The case of Kumamoto, Asian Studies, 4/66; coauth, Changing Japanese attitudes toward the military: Mitsuya Kenkyu and the Japanese self defense force, Asian Surv, 9/67. **CONTACT ADDRESS** Dept of Hist, San Jose State Univ, 1 Washington Sq, San Jose, CA 95192-0117.

MOORE, JAMES TALMADGE
PERSONAL Born 10/23/1936, Houston, TX, m, 1974, 4 children **DISCIPLINE** AMERICAN HISTORY **EDUCATION** Univ Houston, BS, 58; Episcopal Theol Sem Southwest, MDiv, 61; Tex A&M Univ, MA, 73, PhD, 80. **CAREER** Asst prof, Tex A&M Univ, 80-81; Prof, Hist, North Harris Col, 81-98; pastor, Our Lady of Walsingham Church, 96-. **HONORS AND AWARDS** Paul J Foik C S C Awd, Hist res & writing, 94; Fellow of Texas Catholic Historical Soc, 01. **MEMBERSHIPS** Cath Hist Asn; Tex Cath Hist Soc (pres, 98-00. **RESEARCH** Colonial American history; American Indian history; Indian and missionary relations, American Church History. **SELECTED PUBLICATIONS** Auth, Indians and Jesuits: A Seventeenth Century Encounter, Loyola Univ Press, Chicago, 82; Through Fire and Flood, the Catholic Church in Frontier Texas, 1836-1900, Tex A & M Press, 92; Act of Faith, The Catholic Church in Texas, 1900-1950, Texas A&M Press, in press. **CONTACT ADDRESS** Our Lady of Walsingham Church, 21806 Galewood Ln, Houston, TX 77073.

MOORE, JAMES TICE
PERSONAL Born 08/08/1945, Greenville, SC, m, 1965, 3 children **DISCIPLINE** AMERICAN HISTORY **EDUCATION** Univ SC, BA, 66; Univ VA, MA, 68, PhD(hist), 72. **CAREER** Instr, 70-72, asst prof, 72-78, actg chmn, 81-82, ASSOC PROF HIST, VA COMMONWEALTH UNIV, 78-, chmn dept, 82-86. **HONORS AND AWARDS** Lecturer's Awd, Col Humanities & Sci, VA Commonwealth Univ, 82; Distinguished Teaching Awd, Col Humanities and Sci, VA Commonwealth Univ, 95. **MEMBERSHIPS** Orgn Am Historians; Southern Hist Asn; VA Hist Soc. **RESEARCH** New South 1865-1920, political history; conservation history, especially in relation to the South; Southern intellectual history. **SELECTED PUBLICATIONS** Auth, The University of Virginia and the Readjusters, VA Mag Hist & Biog, 1/70; Two Paths to the New South: The Virginia Debt Controversy, 1870-1883, Univ Press KY, 74; Black Militancy in Readjuster Virginia, 1879-1883, J of Southern Hist, 5/75; The Death of the Duel: The Code Duello in Readjuster Virginia, 1879-1883, VA Mag of Hist & Biog, 7/75; Majority and Morality: John Taylor's Agrarianism, Agr Hist, 4/76; Redeemers Reconsidered: Change and Continuity in the Democratic South, 1870-1900, J of Southern Hist, 8/78; Gunfire on the Chesapeake: Governor Cameron and the Oyster Pirates, 1882-1885, VA Mag of Hist & Biog, 7/82; co-ed, The Governors of Virginia, 1860-1978, Univ Press of VA , 82; Secession and the States: A Review Essay, VA Mag of Hist and Biog, 1/86; Of Cavaliers and Yankees: Frederic W.M. Holliday and the Sectional Crisis, 1845-1861, VA Mag of Hist and Biog, 7/91; From Dynasty to Disenfranchisement: Some Reflections About Virginia History, 1820-1902, VA Mag of Hist and Biog, winter 96. **CONTACT ADDRESS** Dept of Hist, Virginia Commonwealth Univ, Box 2001, Richmond, VA 23284-2001. **EMAIL** jtmoore@atlas.vcu.edu

MOORE, JOHN CLARE
PERSONAL Born 05/17/1933, Wichita, KS, m, 1956, 4 children **DISCIPLINE** MEDIEVAL EUROPEAN HISTORY **EDUCATION** Rockhurst Col, AB, 55; Johns Hopkins Univ, PhD(Hist), 60. **CAREER** Instr Hist, Hofstra Col, 59-62; asst prof, Parsons Col, 62-63; from asst prof to assoc prof, 63-72, assoc dean, 71-74, prof Hist, Hofstra Univ, 72-98, chmn dept, 76-82,

87-93, emer, 98. **MEMBERSHIPS** AAUP; AHA; Medieval Acad Am. **RESEARCH** Medieval church; papacy; medieval love. **SELECTED PUBLICATIONS** Auth, Count Baldwin IX of Flanders, Philip Augustus, and the Papal power, Speculum, 1/62; Papal justice in France around the time of Pope Innocent III, Church Hist, 72; Love in Twelfth-Century France, Univ Pa, 72; Courtly love: A problem of terminology, J Hist of Ideas, 79; Innocent III's de miseria humanae conditionis: A speculum curiae?, Cath Hist Rev, 81; auth, "Peter of Lucedio Cistercian Patriarch of Antioch, and Pope Innocent III," Romisihe Historische Mitteilungen 29 (87): 221-249; The Sermons of Pope Innocent II, Romische Historische Mitteilunger, 36, 94; Die Register Innocenz II, 6 Band, 6 Pontifikatsjahr (12-3-1204), one of three eds, Vienna: Verlag der Osterreichischen Akademie der Wissenschaften, 95; ed, Pope Innocent III and His World, Ashgate, 99. **CONTACT ADDRESS** Dept of History, 4324 Whitley Dr, Bloomington, IN 47401. **EMAIL** jclaremoore@yahoo.com

MOORE, MARIAN J.
PERSONAL Born Saginaw, MI **DISCIPLINE** AFRICAN HISTORY, CURATOR **CAREER** National Afro-American Museum and Cultural Center, former director; Museum of African American History, Detroit, MI, director, 88-93. **CONTACT ADDRESS** Museum of African American History, 301 Frederick Douglass, Detroit, MI 48202.

MOORE, MICHAEL J.
PERSONAL Born 09/16/1940, Seattle, WA, m, 1963, 2 children **DISCIPLINE** HISTORY **EDUCATION** Univ of Wash, BA, 63, MA, 66, PhD, 71. **CAREER** Instr, Western Wash Univ, 65-70; instr, Skagit Valley col, 70-71; asst prof, 71-79, prof, Appalachian State Univ, 80- . **HONORS AND AWARDS** Fel, Royal Hist Soc; ed & pub of albion. **MEMBERSHIPS** Am Hist Asn; North Am Confr on British Studies. **RESEARCH** Modern Britain: social & economic. **CONTACT ADDRESS** Dept of Hist, Appalachian State Univ, Box 32072, Boone, NC 28608. **EMAIL** mooremj@conrad.appstate.edu

MOORE, RAY A.
PERSONAL Born 11/14/1933, Waco, TX, m, 1957, 2 children **DISCIPLINE** JAPANESE & EAST ASIAN HISTORY **EDUCATION** Univ Mich, AB, 58, MA, 60, PhD(hist), 67. **CAREER** From asst prof to prof, 65-76, dir, Ctr for East Asian Studies, 75-80, chmn dept, 79-80, Prof Hist, Amherst Col, 76-, Trustee-fac fel, Amherst Col, 68-69; Nat Endowment for Humanities fel, 72-73; Fulbright res fel, Japan, 80-81. **HONORS AND AWARDS** MA, Amherst Col, 76. **MEMBERSHIPS** AHA; Asn Asian Studies. **RESEARCH** Early modern social history of Japan; postwar Japanese intellectual history; American-Japanese relations, 1945-55. **SELECTED PUBLICATIONS** Auth, Reflections on the Occupation of Japan, J Asian Studies, 8/79; The Occupation of Japan as history, Monumenta Nipponica, autumn 81; ed, Religion and Culture in Japanese-American Relations: Essays on Uchimura Kanzo, Univ Mich Ctr for Japanese Studies, 81; The Emperor and the Bible, Kodansha, 82; transl, The Birth of Japan's Postwar Constitution, Westview, 97; co-ed, The Japanese Constitution: A Documentary History of it's Framing and Adoption, 1945-1947, Princeton Univ, 98. **CONTACT ADDRESS** Dept of Hist, Amherst Col, Amherst, MA 01002-5003.

MOORE, ROBERT HENRY
PERSONAL Born 09/16/1940, Madisonville, KY, m, 1964, 2 children **DISCIPLINE** AMERICAN LITERATURE & HISTORY **EDUCATION** Davidson Col, AB, 62; Univ NC, Chapel Hill, MA, 64; Univ Wis-Madison, PhD(English), 70. **CAREER** Instr English, US Mil Acad, 68-70; asst prof, Univ Md, College Park, 70-76, assoc prof, 76-80. Contrib-reader, Dict Am Regional English, 68-; exec secy, Faulkner Concordance Proj, 70- , ed, Faulkner Concordance Newslett, 72-; reviewer, Nat Endowment for Humanities, 72; fel, Inter-Univ Sem Armed Forces & Soc, 73-. **MEMBERSHIPS** MLA; Am Studies Asn; Am Civil Liberties Union. **RESEARCH** twentieth century American language and literature, American studies; armed forces and society. **SELECTED PUBLICATIONS** Coauth, Black puritan, William & Mary Quart, 467; ed, Ellison at West Point, Contempt Lit, spring 74; coauth, School for Soldiers, Oxford Univ, 74; Cameras in state courts, An historical-perspective, judicature, vol 0078, 1994. **CONTACT ADDRESS** 9202 Saybrook Ave Branwell Park, Silver Spring, MD 20901.

MOORE, ROBERT JOSEPH
PERSONAL Born 04/29/1934, Medina, TN, m, 1980, 4 children **DISCIPLINE** AMERICAN HISTORY **EDUCATION** Lambuth Col, BA, 55; Boston Univ, MA, 57, PhD, 61. **CAREER** From asst prof to assoc prof, 60-67, prof hist, Columbia Col, SC, 67-, Chmn Dept, 60-83; Duke Univ-Univ NC Coop Prog fac fel int studies, 68-69. **MEMBERSHIPS** AHA; AAUP; Southern Hist Asn. **RESEARCH** Reconstruction period in American history; 20th century America; civil rights movement. **SELECTED PUBLICATIONS** Auth, Robert C Winthrop: Conservative opponent of Lincoln, Proc SC Hist Asn, 61; Interpretations of Reconstruction, The Search, 4/62; Andrew Johnson: The second swing 'round the circle, Proc SC Hist Asn, 66; Governor Chamberlain and the end of reconstruction, Proc SC Hist Asn, 77. **CONTACT ADDRESS** Dept of Hist, Columbia Col, So Carolina, 1301 Columbia Col, Columbia, SC 29203-5998. **EMAIL** bmoore@colucoll.edu

MOORE, ROBERT LAURENCE
PERSONAL Born 04/03/1940, Houston, TX, m, 1988, 3 children **DISCIPLINE** AMERICAN INTELLECTUAL & CULTURAL HISTORY **EDUCATION** Rice Univ, BA, 62; Yale Univ, MA, 64, PhD(hist), 68. **CAREER** Actg instr hist & Am studies, Yale Univ, 67-68, asst prof, 68-72; assoc prof, 72-78, Prof Hist, Cornell Univ, 78-, Chmn Dept, 80-; Howard A Newman Prof Am Stud, Cornell Univ, 98-, chmn dept hist, 80-83, dir, Am Stud Prog, 98-. **HONORS AND AWARDS** Yale Univ Morse fel, 70-71; Nat Endowment for Humanities fel, 75-76; Rockefeller Found fel, 79-80; fel, Woodrow Wilson Ctr Intl-Scholars, 87-88; Fulbright lectr, India, 97. **MEMBERSHIPS** AHA; Orgn Am Historians; Am Studies Asn. **RESEARCH** Am radicalism; Am relig hist; 20th cent Am thought. **SELECTED PUBLICATIONS** Auth, European Socialists and the American Promised Land, Oxford Univ, 70; ed, The Emergence of an American Left: Civil War to World War I, Wiley, 73; auth, In Search of White Crows, Spiritualism, Parapsychology and American Culture, Oxford Univ, 77; auth, Religious Outsider and the Making of Americans, Oxford Univ Press, 86; auth, Selling God: American Religion in the Marketplace of Culture, Oxford Univ Press, 94; co-auth, The Godless Constitution, The Case Against Religious Correctness, Norton, 96. **CONTACT ADDRESS** Dept of Hist, Cornell Univ, McGraw Hal, Ithaca, NY 14853-0001.

MOORE, WILLIAM HOWARD
PERSONAL Born 06/26/1942, Harriman, TN, m, 1986, 1 child **DISCIPLINE** AMERICAN HISTORY **EDUCATION** Univ Tenn, Knoxville, BS, 64, MA, 65; Univ Tex, Austin, PhD, 71. **CAREER** Instr hist, Southwest Tex State Univ, 71-72; asst prof, Ohio Univ, 72-73; asst prof, 73-78, assoc prof hist, 78-, prof, 89, chmn hist dept, 92, Univ Wyo. **HONORS AND AWARDS** NEH grant, 77, 90; travel grant, Herbert C Hoover Pres Lib Assoc; travel grant, Eisenhower World Affairs Inst, 90; Wyoming Coun for Hum Grants, 81; **MEMBERSHIPS** AHA; Orgn Am Historians; Ctr for Study of Presidency. **RESEARCH** Twentieth century United States; American social history; American labor history. **SELECTED PUBLICATIONS** Auth, Do We Like Ike?: Historians and the Eisenhower Presidency, Kansas History, 90; art, Crime and Justice, Encyclopedia of United States Congress, 95. **CONTACT ADDRESS** Dept of History, Univ of Wyoming, PO Box 3198, Laramie, WY 82071-3198. **EMAIL** budmoore@uwyo.edu

MOORE, WINFRED B., JR.
PERSONAL Born 11/24/1949, Cowpens, SC, m, 1981 **DISCIPLINE** HISTORY **EDUCATION** Furman Univ, BA, 71; Duke Univ, MA, 72, PhD, 75. **CAREER** Asst prof, 76-81, assoc prof, 81-89, Prof, The Citadel, 90-; Dir, The Citadel Conf on the South. **MEMBERSHIPS** AHA; Southern Hist Asn; SCar Hist Asn. **RESEARCH** Modern Southern History, Race Relations. **SELECTED PUBLICATIONS** Coed, From the Old South to the New, 81; auth, "James F. Byrnes: The Road to Politics, 1882-1910," SCar Hist Rev (83); coed, The Southern Enigma, 83; coed, Developing Dixie, 88; coed, Looking South, 89; auth, "The Unrewarding Stone: James F. Byrnes and the Burden of Race," in The South is Another Land, ed. Bruce Clayton and John Salmond (90); auth, "James F. Byrnes" in The Justices of the United States Supreme Court, ed. Clare Cushman (94). **CONTACT ADDRESS** Dept of History, The Citadel, The Military Col of So Carolina, Charleston, SC 29409. **EMAIL** bo.moore@citadel.edu

MOORHEAD, JAMES HOWELL
PERSONAL Born 01/16/1947, Harrisburg, PA, m, 1969, 2 children **DISCIPLINE** AMERICAN RELIGIOUS HISTORY **EDUCATION** Westminster Col, PA, BA, 68; Princeton Theol Sem, MDiv, 71; Yale Univ, MPhil, 73, PhD(relig studies), 75. **CAREER** Asst prof, 75-80, Assoc Prof Relig, NC State Univ, 80-, Fel independent study & res, Nat Endowment for Humanities, 81-82. **HONORS AND AWARDS** Brewer Prize, Am Soc Church Hist, 76. **MEMBERSHIPS** Am Soc Church Hist; Am Acad Relig; Am Hist Asn. **RESEARCH** Nineteenth century and early twentieth century American Protestantism; Millennialism; views of death and after life. **SELECTED PUBLICATIONS** Auth, Joseph Addison Alexander: Common sense, romanticism and Biblical criticism at Princeton, J Presbyterian Hist, spring 75; American Apocalypse: Yankee Protestants and the Civil War, 1860-1869, Yale Univ Press, 78; Social reform and the divided conscience of antebellum Protestantism, Church Hist, 79; Softly And Tenderly Jesus Is Calling - Heaven And Hell In American Revivalism, 1870-1920 - Butler,Jm, Church History, Vol 0062, 1993; Glorious Contentment - The Grand Army Of The Republic, 1865-1900 - Mcconnell,S, J Of American History, Vol 0080, 1993; A Field Of Divine Wonders - The New-Divinity And Village Revivals In Northwestern Connecticut, 1792-1822 - Kling,Dw, Theology Today, Vol 0051, 1994; A Friend To Gods Poor - Smith,Edward,Parmalee - Armstrong,Wh, J Of American History, Vol 0081, 1995; Church People In The Struggle - The National- Council-Of-Churches And The Black-Freedom Movement, 1950-1970 - Findlay,JF, J Of Interdisciplinary History, Vol 0026, 95; Peddler In Divinity - Whitefield, George And The Transatlantic-Revivals, 1737-1770 - Lambert,F, Theology Today, Vol 0051, 1995; Arguing The Apocalypse - A Theory Of Millennial Rhetoric - Oleary,Sd, Theology Today, Vol 0051, 1994; No Sorrow Like Our Sorrow Northern Protestant Ministers And The Assassination Of Lincoln - Chesebrough,Db, American Historical Review, Vol 0100, 1995; auth, Consumer Rites - The Buying And Selling Of American Holidays - Schmidt,LE, Theology Today, Vol 0053, 1996; The Myth Of American Individualism - The Protestant Origins Of American Political-Thought - Shain,BA, J Of Religion, Vol 0076, 1996; Our Southern Zion - A History Of Calvinism In The South-Carolina Low Country, 1690-1990 - Clarke,E, J Of Presbyterian History, Vol 0075, 1997; Law And Providence In Bellamy, Joseph New-England - Valeri,M, American Presbyterians-J Of Presbyterian History, Vol 0074, 1996; Spreading The Word - The Bible Business In 19th- Century America - Wosh,PJ, American Presbyterians, J Of Presbyterian History, Vol 0074, 1996. **CONTACT ADDRESS** Church Hist, Princeton Theol Sem, PO Box 821, Princeton, NJ 08542-0803.

MORAN, DIANE D.
DISCIPLINE ART HISTORY **EDUCATION** Univ ND, BS; Univ VA, PhD. **CAREER** Fac, 77-; prof, Sweet Briar Col. **RESEARCH** Feminist inquiry of 19th century mourning portraits in France and England and a new interpretation of a painting by Courbet. **SELECTED PUBLICATIONS** Auth, publ(s) which include articles and exhibition catalog essays on California artists Lorser Feitelson and Helen Lundeberg. **CONTACT ADDRESS** Sweet Briar Col, Sweet Briar, VA 24595.

MORBY, JOHN EDWIN
PERSONAL Born 03/19/1939, Berkeley, CA, d, 1 child **DISCIPLINE** EUROPEAN HISTORY **EDUCATION** Univ Calif, Berkeley, AB, 60, PhD(Europ hist), 71; Harvard Univ, MA, 61. **CAREER** Instr Europ hist, Univ Tex, Austin, 65-68; asst prof, Chico State Univ, 68-69; from asst prof to assoc prof, 69-80, prof Europ Hist, Calif State Univ, Hayward, 80-99. **RESEARCH** Musical institutions of 17th and 18th century France. **SELECTED PUBLICATIONS** Auth, The Great Chapel-Chamber Controversy, Musical Quart, 7/72; Biography of a Grand Motet: The Jean Gilles Requiem in Eighteenth Century Paris and Versailles, Proc Western Soc French Hist, 75; The French Classical Repertory in the 18th Century, Proc Western Soc Fr Hist, 78; The Sobriquets of Medieval European Princes, Can J Hist, 78; Dynasties of the World: A Chronological and Geneological Handbook, Oxford Univ Press, 89; Expanded versions in German, Hungarian, Polish, Japanese. **CONTACT ADDRESS** Dept of Hist, California State Univ, Hayward, 25800 Carlos Bee Bvd, Hayward, CA 94542-3001.

MORE, ELLEN SINGER
PERSONAL Born New York, NY **DISCIPLINE** BRITISH HISTORY, AMERICAN MEDICAL HISTORY **EDUCATION** State Univ NYork New Paltz, BA, 68; Univ Rochester, MA, 70, PhD(hist), 80. **CAREER** Instr hist, Harley Sch, 78-79; Asst Prof Hist, Univ Rochester, 80-, Vis Asst Prof Preventive Med, Sch Of Med, 82-, Consult, Sch of Nursing, Univ Rochester, 80-83; lectr, Nursing Asn of the Am Col of Obstet & Gynecol, 82. **MEMBERSHIPS** AHA; Conf British Studies. **RESEARCH** The new Arminians in Mid-Seventeenth Century England; women and the radical sects in seventeenth century England; women and the history of American health care. **SELECTED PUBLICATIONS CONTACT ADDRESS** Dept of Hist, Univ of Rochester, Rochester, NY 14627.

MORELLO, JOHN
PERSONAL Born 10/08/1951, Chicago, IL, m, 1986, 3 children **DISCIPLINE** HISTORY **EDUCATION** George Washington Univ, BA, 73, MA, 77; Univ Ill, PhD, 98-. **CAREER** Prof, Devry Inst Tech. **HONORS AND AWARDS** Best Prof Series; West Suburban Post Secondary Consortium. **MEMBERSHIPS** AHA; ISHS; Business History Conf Popular Culture Assn. **RESEARCH** Advertising history. **SELECTED PUBLICATIONS** Auth, Selling The Available Man, Praeger, (forthcoming). **CONTACT ADDRESS** 1221 N Swift Rd, Addison, IL 60101. **EMAIL** morello@dpg.devry.edu

MORGAN, ANN LEE
PERSONAL Born 01/12/1941, Minneapolis, MN, m, 1976, 2 children **DISCIPLINE** ART HISTORY **EDUCATION** Knox Col, BA, 62; Fla State Univ, MA, 63; Univ of Iowa, PhD, 73. **CAREER** Instr,Univ of Ill at Urbana, 68-73, asst prof, Dept of Art and Design, 73-78; ed, New Art Examiner, 79-82; ed, St James Pr, 82-85; vis asst prof, Univ of Ill at Chicago, Hist of Archit and Art Dept, 85-86; ed Twenty One/Art and Culture, Univ of Ill at Chicago, 87-90. **HONORS AND AWARDS** Phi Beta Kappa, 62; Yale Univ grant, 76; Who's Who in the East, 98. **MEMBERSHIPS** Coll Art Asn; Soc of Archit Hist; Am Stud Asn; Natl Coalition of Independent Scholars. **RESEARCH** American art. **SELECTED PUBLICATIONS** Auth, Arthur Dove: Life and Work, with a Catalogue Raisonne, Delaware, 84; ed, auth, Contemporary designers, Gale, 84; ed, International Contemporary Arts Directory, St. James, 85; coed, Contemporary Architects, 2d ed., St. James, 87; ed, Dear Stieglitz, Dear Dove, Delaware, 88; auth, Dictionary of American Art and Artists, Oxford, forthcoming; auth of numerous articles. **CONTACT ADDRESS** 17 Honey Brook Dr, Princeton, NJ 08540-7408. **EMAIL** alm@research.nj.nec.com

MORGAN, DAVID
PERSONAL Born 12/21/1957, m, 1980, 3 children **DISCIPLINE** HISTORY **EDUCATION** Concordia Col, BA, 80; Univ AR, MA, 84; Univ Chicago, PhD, 90. **CAREER** Assoc prof, Valparaiso Univ, 90-. **HONORS AND AWARDS** Fel, Yale Univ; Fel, Getty Program; Fel, Am Antiquarian Society; PSP Awd, Asn Am Publishers, 99; alpha lambda delta nat honors society; award for tchg excellence, valparaiso univ, 92. **MEMBERSHIPS** Col Art Asn; Am Acad of Religion; Org of Am Hist. **RESEARCH** Popular Religious Art **SELECTED PUBLICATIONS** Auth, Icons of American Protestantism: The Art of Warner Sallman, 96; auth,article, Ambiguous Icons: The Art of Ed Paschke, 97; auth,article, Domestic Devotion and Ritual: Visual Piety in the Modern American Home, 98; auth, Visual Piety A History and Theory of Popular Religious Images, 98; auth, Protestants and Pictures: Religion, Visual Culture, and the Age of American Mass Production, 99; co-ed, The Visual Culture of Am Religions, 01. **CONTACT ADDRESS** Art Dept, Valparaiso Univ, Valparaiso, IN 46383. **EMAIL** dmorgan@valpo.edu

MORGAN, DAVID TAFT
PERSONAL Born 01/05/1937, Fayetteville, NC, m, 1958, 2 children **DISCIPLINE** AMERICAN HISTORY **EDUCATION** BA Baylor Univ, 59; CH, MA 64, PhD 68, Univ NC. **CAREER** Asst Prof, Patrick Henry Col, 64-68; Asst Prof, TX A&M Univ, 68-73; Vis Assoc Prof Rhode Island Col, 70-71; Prof Univ Montevallo, 73-97. **HONORS AND AWARDS** Natl Pres, Phi Alpha Theta, 98-99. **MEMBERSHIPS** Southern Historical Assoc, Phi Alpha Theta. **RESEARCH** Colonial & Revolutionary Am; 2nd Hist of Am Rel. **SELECTED PUBLICATIONS** The New Crusade, the New Holy Land: Conflict in the Southern Baptist Convention, 69-91, Univ Alabama Press, 96; The Devious Dr Franklin, Colonail Agent: Benjamin Franklin's Years in London. **CONTACT ADDRESS** Dept of Soc Sci, Univ of Montevallo, Montevallo, AL 35115. **EMAIL** morgan2@ix.netcom.com

MORGAN, EILEEN M.
DISCIPLINE ENGLISH AND IRISH STUDIES **EDUCATION** Colgate Univ, BA, 89; Ind Univ, MA, 92; PhD, 98. **CAREER** Lectr, Univ Mich, 98-00; asst prof, SUNY Onconta, 00-. **HONORS AND AWARDS** James A Work Grad Studies Award, 96; Seed Grant, Univ Mich, 00; Fac Develop Grant, 00; Individual Develop Award, SUNY Onconta, 01. **MEMBERSHIPS** MLA; ACIS. **RESEARCH** Irish radio broadcasting; Edna O'Brien; 20th Century British literature; Irish-American literature (ethnicity studies). **SELECTED PUBLICATIONS** Auth, "Ireland's Lost Action Hero, or, Michael Collins, A Secret History of Irish masculinity," New Hibernia Rev, (98): 26-42; auth, "Mapping Out a Landscape of Female Suffering: Edna O'Brien's Demythologizing Novels," Women's Studies; An Interdisciplinary J, (00): 449-476; auth, "Rethinking the Abbey and the Concept of a National Theatre," in A Century of Irish Drama: Widening the Stage, (Bloomington, 01), xi-xxvii; auth, "Question Time: Radio and the Liberalization of Public Discourse in Ireland after WW2," History Ireland, (forthcoming). **CONTACT ADDRESS** Dept English, SUNY, Col at Oneonta, 85 Spruce St, Oneonta, NY 13820-1549. **EMAIL** morgane@onconta.edu

MORGAN, H. WAYNE
PERSONAL Born 05/16/1934, Ashland, OK **DISCIPLINE** UNITED STATES HISTORY **EDUCATION** Ariz State Univ, BA, 55; Claremont Grad Sch, MA, 56; Univ Calif, Los Angeles, PhD, 60. **CAREER** Instr hist, San Jose State Col, 60-61; from asst prof to prof, Univ Tex, Austin, 61-72; prof, 72-76, George Lynn Cross Res Prof, Univ Okla, 76-. **HONORS AND AWARDS** Am Philos Soc fel, 63. **MEMBERSHIPS** Orgn Am Historians. **RESEARCH** United States history, 1877-1914; American literary criticism, 1877-1932; art history. **SELECTED PUBLICATIONS** Auth, Eugene V Debs: Socialist for President, 62 & William McKinley and his America, 63, Syracuse Univ; coauth, The Gilded Age: A reappraisal, Syracuse Univ, 63, 70; ed, American Socialism, 1900-1964, Prentice-Hall, 64; auth, America's Road to Empire, Wiley, 65; From Hayes to McKinley: National Party Politics 1877-1896, Syracuse Univ, 69; Yesterday's Addicts: American Society and Drug Abuse, 1865-1920, Univ Okla, 74; coauth, Oklahoma: A Bicentennial History, Norton, 77; auth, New Muses: Art and American Society, 1865-1920, Univ Okla, 78. **CONTACT ADDRESS** Dept of Hist, Univ of Oklahoma, Norman, OK 73019. **EMAIL** h.w.morgan-1@ou.edu

MORGAN, JOSEPH
PERSONAL Born 07/09/1953, Chicago, IL, s **DISCIPLINE** HISTORY, GOVERNMENT **EDUCATION** Iona Col, BA, 75; Manhattan Col, MA, 81; Georgetown Univ, PhD, 93. **CAREER** Instr, Iona Col, 89-94; Asst Prof, Iona Col, 94-. **MEMBERSHIPS** Am Hist Asn, Asn of Asian Studies, Soc of Historians of Am For Rels. **RESEARCH** Vietnam War, American diplomacy, Chinese history. **SELECTED PUBLICATIONS** Auth, The Vietnam Lobby: The American Friends of Vietnam, 1955-1975, Univ of N Carolina Pr, 97. **CONTACT ADDRESS** Dept Hist and Govt, Iona Col, 715 North Ave, New Rochelle, NY 10801-1830. **EMAIL** jmorgan@iona.edu

MORGAN, KATHRYN L.
PERSONAL Born Philadelphia, PA, 1 child **DISCIPLINE** HISTORY, FOLKLORE **EDUCATION** VA State Col, BA, 46; Howard Univ, MA, 52; Univ Pa, MA, 68, PhD, 70. **CAREER** Asst prof folklore, Univ Del, 71-72; Assoc Prof to prof emer Hist & Folklore, Swarthmore Col, 72-, Guest lectr, Bryn Mawr Col, 71-73 & Haverford Col, 71-73; consult, Smithsonian Inst, 73-; assoc, Danforth Found. **HONORS AND AWARDS** Swarthmore's First African-American Prof. **MEMBERSHIPS** Am Folklife Soc, Am Soc Ethnohist, Oral Hist Asn, National Council of Black Studies, African American Folklore Association, National Afrocentric Inst, Philadelphia Folklore Project . **RESEARCH** Folklife history; Black studies. **SELECTED PUBLICATIONS** Contribr, Mother Wit from the Laughing Barrel Caddy Buffers: Legends of a Middle Class Negro Family in Philadelphia, Prentice-Hall, 73; In Search of the Miraculous, Bryn Mawr Col, 73; auth, Jokes among urban Blacks, In: Black Folk, 73; auth, Social Distance From Jews In Russia And Ukraine, Slavic Review, Vol 0053, 1994. **CONTACT ADDRESS** Swarthmore Col, 500 College Ave, Swarthmore, PA 19081-1390. **EMAIL** kmorgan1@swarthmore.edu

MORGAN, KEITH N.
PERSONAL Born 02/18/1949, Oberlin, OH, m, 1974, 3 children **DISCIPLINE** ART HISTORY **EDUCATION** Col Wooster, BA, 71; Univ Del, MA, 73; Brown Univ, PhD, 78. **CAREER** Prof, Boston Univ, 80-. **HONORS AND AWARDS** Sen Fel, Boston Univ, 91-92, 93-94, 99-00; Fel, Graham Found for Adv Studies in the Fine Arts, 96; Res Grant, NEH, 94-95, 8083; Jr Fel, Boston Univ Humanities Found, 88-89; Andrew Mellon Fac Fel, Harvard Univ, 83-84; Jr Fel, Harvard Univ, 76-78; Nominee, Metcalf Prize for Excellence in Teaching, Boston Univ, 88, 93, 99; Teaching Awd, Boston Univ, 99. **MEMBERSHIPS** Soc of Archit Hist; Vernacular Archit Forum. **RESEARCH** American and European architectural and landscape history from the eighteenth to the twentieth centuries. **SELECTED PUBLICATIONS** Co-auth, "Boston Architecture, 1975-1990," Prestel Verlag, 90; auth, Keeping Eden: A History of American Landscape Architecture, Bulfinch Press, 92; auth, Italian Gardens, Sagapress, 93; ed, Charles A. Platt: Shaping an American Landscape, Univ Press of N Eng, 95; auth, Charles Eliot, Landscape Architect, Univ Mass Press, 99. **CONTACT ADDRESS** Dept Art Hist, Boston Univ, 725 Commonwealth Ave, Boston, MA 02215. **EMAIL** knmorgan@bu.edu

MORGAN, MARJORIE
PERSONAL Born 04/18/1954, Detroit, MI, s **DISCIPLINE** HISTORY **EDUCATION** Rice Univ, BA, 75; Tulane Univ, MA, 82; PhD, 88. **CAREER** Asst prof to assoc prof and dept chair, S Il Univ Carbondale, 88-. **HONORS AND AWARDS** SIUC Outstanding Teacher of the Year, 97-98; SIUC Col of Liberal Arts Outstanding Teacher, 97-98; George S. And Gladys W. Queen Awd for Excellence in Hist Teaching, 93; Tulane's William R. Hogan Fel Awd for Outstanding Teaching, 84. **MEMBERSHIPS** Am Hist Asn; N Am Conf on Brit Studies; Midwest Conf on Brit Studies; Nineteenth Century Studies Asn. **RESEARCH** 18th and 19th Century British social/cultural history; Identity formation - national, regional, class; History of travel and tourism. **SELECTED PUBLICATIONS** Auth, Manners, Morals, and Class in England, 1774-1858, Macmillan, 94; auth, National Identities and Travel in Victorian Britain, Palgrave, 01. **CONTACT ADDRESS** Dept Hist, So Illinois Univ, Carbondale, MC 4519, Carbondale, IL 62901. **EMAIL** marjimor@siu.edu

MORGAN, PHILLIP D.
DISCIPLINE HISTORY **EDUCATION** Cambridge, BA, MA, 81; Univ Col London, PhD, 78. **CAREER** Prof hist, Fla State Univ; ED, WM & MARY QUARTERLY AND PROF, HIST, COLL OF WM & MARY. **MEMBERSHIPS** AM Antiquarian Soc **CONTACT ADDRESS** OIEAHC, PO Box 8781, Williamsburg, VA 23187-8781.

MORGAN, THOMAS SELLERS
PERSONAL Born 12/13/1934, Jackson, MS, m, 1960, 3 children **DISCIPLINE** UNITED STATES HISTORY **EDUCATION** Davidson Col, AB, 57; Duke Univ, MA, 62; Univ NC, Chapel Hill, PhD(hist), 69. **CAREER** Teacher social studies, Edmondson High Sch, Md, 59-62; instr hist, Wake Forest Univ, 64-65; instr hist & mod civilization, Univ NC, Chapel Hill, 66-67; from asst prof to assoc prof, 67-75, asst dean, Col Arts & Sci, 74-76, assoc dean, 76-80, Prof Hist, Winthrop Col, 75-, Dean, Col Arts & Sci, 80-, Danforth assoc, 72-. **MEMBERSHIPS** AHA; Southern Hist Asn; Orgn Am Historians; Social Welfare Hist Group; Am Asn Higher Educ. **RESEARCH** Recent United States; social welfare in the New Deal; post Civil War North Carolina. **SELECTED PUBLICATIONS** Auth, A folly .. manifest to everyone: The movement to enact unemployment insurance legislation in North Carolina, 1935-1936, NC Hist Rev, 7/75; contrib several biographies in Dict NC Biog, 78. **CONTACT ADDRESS** Col of Arts & Sci, Winthrop Univ, Rock Hill, SC 29733.

MORGAN, WILLIAM
PERSONAL Born 06/13/1944, Princeton, NJ, m, 1978, 4 children **DISCIPLINE** ARCHITECTURAL HISTORY **EDUCATION** Dartmouth, AB, 66; Columbia Univ, MA, certif. in archit, 68; Univ Delaware, PhD, 71 **CAREER** Lect, Princeton Univ, 71-74; Archit Critic, The Courier-Journal, 75-80; Chmn, Kentucky Historic Preservation Rev Bd, 75-90; Book Rev Ed, Landscape Archit, 76-78; Nat Endowment for the Humanities Sr Res Fel, 84-85; Ed Board, Competitions, 90-; Distinguished Teaching Prof, Univ Louisville, 74-. **HONORS AND AWARDS** Nomination for Pulitzer Prize in Criticism; President's Awd for Outstanding Scholar, Res, & Creative Activity. **MEMBERSHIPS** Soc of Archit Historians. **RESEARCH** Amer Archit, Scandinavian Archit, Amer Arts, Cities. **SELECTED PUBLICATIONS** Coauth, Bucks County, Horizon, 74; coauth, Old Louisville: The Victorian Ear, Courier-Journal, 75; auth, Louisville: Architecture and the Urban Environment, WL Bauhan, 79; auth, Collegiate Gothic: The Architecture of Rhodes College, Missouri, 89; auth, The Almighty Wall: The Architecture of Henry Vaughan, MIT, 93; auth, Heikkinen & Komonen Architects, Monacelli, 98. **CONTACT ADDRESS** Allen R. Hite Art Inst, Univ of Louisville, Louisville, KY 40292. **EMAIL** w0morg01@ulkyvm.louisville.edu

MORGANSTERN, ANNE MCGEE
PERSONAL Born 02/05/1936, Morgan, GA, m, 1966 **DISCIPLINE** HISTORY OF ART **EDUCATION** Wesleyan Col, Ga, BFA, 58; NYork Univ, MA, 61, PhD(Hist of Art), 70. **CAREER** Instr Hist of Art, Manhattanville Col Sacred Heart, 61 & Vassar Col, 65-66; lectr, Univ Wis-Milwaukee, 70-73; asst prof, 73-79, assoc prof History of Art, Ohio State Univ, 79-. **MEMBERSHIPS** Col Art Asn Am; Medieval Acad Am; Int Ctr Medieval Art; Historians of Neth Art. **RESEARCH** Late Gothic sculpture in France; Northern Renaissance painting; relation of the arts to social and political history. **SELECTED PUBLICATIONS** Auth, Quelques observations a propos de l'architecture du tombeau du Cardinal Jean de la Grange, Bull Monumental, 70; The La Grange Tomb and Choir, Speculum, 1/73; Pierre Morel, Master of Works in Avignon, Art Bull, 76; auth, The Pawns in Bosch's Death and the Miser, Nat Gal Art Studies in the Hist of Art, 82; The Bishop, the Lion and the Two-headed Dragon: The Burghersh Memorial in Lincoln Cathedral, Acts of the XXIVth Intern Congress of the History of Art, 96; Gothic Tombs of Kinship, Univ Park, PA, 00. **CONTACT ADDRESS** Dept of Hist of Art, Ohio State Univ, Columbus, 100 Hayes Hall, Columbus, OH 43210-1318. **EMAIL** morganstern.z@osu.edu

MORGANSTERN, JAMES
PERSONAL Born 10/16/1936, Pittsburgh, PA, m, 1966 **DISCIPLINE** HISTORY ART; ARCHITECTURE **EDUCATION** Williams College, BA 58; Yale Univ, Sch Archit 58-60; Univ Cal Berk, 61-62; NYork Univ Inst Fine Arts, MA 64, PhD 73. **CAREER** Univ Wisconsin, asst prof, 70-73; Ohio State Univ, asst prof, assoc prof, prof, 73 to 90-; Univ VA, vis lect, 87. **HONORS AND AWARDS** Dumbarton Oaks Cen Byzantine Stud Fel; ARI Turkey Fel; NEH; Outstanding Tchr OSU; Samuel Kress Foun Gnt; APS Gnt; Fulbright Fel; NEH; Florence Gould Foun Gnt **MEMBERSHIPS** AIA; BSC; CAA; ICMA; MAA; SAH; US Ntl Comm Byzan Stud; Soc Antiquaires Normandy; Soc Fran d'Archeologie **RESEARCH** Early Christian and Byzantine Art and Architecture; Western Medieval Art and Architecture. **SELECTED PUBLICATIONS** Auth, Reading Medieval Buildings: The Question of Diaphragm Arches at Notre-Dame de Jumieges, ed C. L. Striker, Archit Stud in Memory of Richard Krautheimer, Mainz, 96; The Fort at Dereagzi and Other Material Remains in Its Vicinity: From Antiquity to the Middle Ages, coauth, Istanbuler Forschungen, Tubingen, 93; et al. **CONTACT ADDRESS** Dept History of Art, Ohio State Univ, Columbus, 108 North Oval Mall, Columbus, OH 43210-1318.

MORGENTHALER, HANS RUDOLF
PERSONAL Born 06/07/1952, Switzerland, m **DISCIPLINE** ART HISTORY **EDUCATION** Univ Zurich, 80; Stanford Univ, MA, 84; PhD, 88. **CAREER** Asst prof, Conn Col, New London, 86; asst prof, Univ Ore, Eugene, 87-89; assoc prof, Univ Colo Denver, 89-. **MEMBERSHIPS** JSAH; CAA; GSA; ACSA. **RESEARCH** Architectural History of the 20th Century; Architectural Theory. **SELECTED PUBLICATIONS** Auth, Chronology versus System: Unleashing the Creative Potential of Architectural History, Journ Archit Educ, 48, May, 218-226, 95; The Early Sketches of German Architect Erich Mendelsohn: No Compromise with Reality, Edwin Mellen Press, 92; Erich Mendelsohn in the USA: Nuclear Physics and Urban Design, Selected Works: Coun of Educ in Landscape Archit, 1990 Conf, Washington, pp 59-65, 91; Pittsburgh's Golden Triangle: Opportunity Lost and Found?, Avant Garde, 4, Summer, 58-71, 90; coauth, Hansruedi Morgenthaler, Univ Zurich, Basel: Gesellschaft fur Schweizerische Kunstgeschichte, 80. **CONTACT ADDRESS** Univ of Colorado, Denver, Campus Box 126, PO Box 173364, Denver, CO 80217-3364. **EMAIL** hmorgent@carbon.cudenver.edu

MORI, BARBARA L.
PERSONAL Born 12/19/1946, Brooklyn, NY **DISCIPLINE** HISTORY, SOCIOLOGY **EDUCATION** Hofstra Univ, BA, 67; Univ HI, MA, 79; MA, 83; PhD, 88. **HONORS AND AWARDS** James Shigeta Awd, 79; FLAS, 80; Chado Scholar, Urasenke Found, 83-85; Res Scholar, Japan Found, 85-86; Pacific and Asian Scholar, 85-86; Affirmative Action Fac Dev, 88,

90, 91, 93, 94; Field Res Fel, 91; Grant, Calif Fac State, 94; Grant, Calif Poly Plan Fac Develop Prog, 96. **MEMBERSHIPS** Am Sociol Assoc; Assoc for Asian Studies; Calif Sociol Assoc; HI sociol Assoc; Int House of Japan; Soc for Women in Soc; Nat Women's Studies Assoc; Nat Orgn of Women; ASPAC; Phi Beta Delta; Int Center for Asian Studies; Can Asian Studies Assoc; Soc for the Sci Study of Relig. **RESEARCH** Traditional arts in Asian Societies, women's higher education in China, Korea and Japan, Buddhist studies, Asian immigration to the United States. **SELECTED PUBLICATIONS** Auth, "Japanese Women in Chado: Accommodations in a Male Dominated Profession", Midwest Feminist Papers 6, (Apr 86): 50-52; auth, "The Tea Ceremony: A Ritual in Transition", Gender & Soc 5.1, (91): 86-97; auth, Americans Studying the Traditional Japanese Art of the Tea Ceremony: The Internationalizing of a Traditional Art, Mellen Res Univ Pr, (San Francisco), 92; rev, of "The Japanese Woman" by Sumiko Iwao, Jof Asian Studies, 53.1 (Feb 94): 206-208; auth, "Traditional Arts as Leisure Activities for Contemporary Japanese Women", in Re-Imaging Japanese Women, ed Anne Imamura, Univ of Calif Pr, (Berkeley), 96; rev, of "Empire of Schools: Japan's Universities and the Molding of a National Power Elite", by Robert Cutts, Educ About Asia, Asian Studies Found J3.2 (Fall 98): 67-68, 70; rev, of "May Fourth women Writers: Memoirs", by Janet Ng and Janice Wickeri, Educ About Asia, Asian Studies Assoc J3.1 (spr 98): 66; rev, of "Sweet and Sour: One Woman's Chinese Adventure, One Man's chinese torture", by Brooks Robards and Jim Kaplan, Educ in Asia, Asian Studies Assoc J,4.2 (Fall 98): 50-52; auth, "On the Japanese Tea Culture", Jof Hanzhong Teachers Col, (98): 62-66; auth, Stand! Race and Ethic Relations, Coursewise Publishers, 99. **CONTACT ADDRESS** Dept Soc Sci, California Polytech State Univ, San Luis Obispo, 1 Grand Ave, San Luis Obispo, CA 93407-9000. **EMAIL** bmori@calpoly.edu

MORIARTY, THOMAS FRANCIS
PERSONAL Born 07/21/1934, Holyoke, MA, m, 1975, 1 child **DISCIPLINE** MODERN IRELAND **EDUCATION** Holy Cross Col, BA, 56; Univ Notre Dame, MA, 58, PhD(hist), 64. **CAREER** Instr & asst prof hist, Fordham Univ, 61-68; vis prof, Talladega Col, 68-69; Assoc Prof Hist, Col of Our Lady of the Elms, 69- **MEMBERSHIPS** Am Cath Hist Soc; Am Conf for Irish Studies. **RESEARCH** Eighteenth and 19th century Ireland; Irish American history. **SELECTED PUBLICATIONS** Auth, The Truth-Teller and Irish Americana of the 1820's, Rec Am Cath Hist Soc Philos, 3/69; The Irish absentee tax controversy of 1773: A study in Anglo-Irish politics on the eve of the American Revolution, Proc Am Philos Soc, 74; The Irish American response to the struggle for Catholic Emancipation, Cath Hist Rev, 7/80. **CONTACT ADDRESS** Dept of Hist, Col of Our Lady of the Elms, 291 Springfield St, Chicopee, MA 01013-2839. **EMAIL** moriartyt@elms.edu

MORISON, WILLIAM S.
PERSONAL Born 05/15/1965, Fresno, CA, m, 1997, 1 child **DISCIPLINE** CLASSICS, HISTORY **EDUCATION** Calif State Univ Fresno, BA, 87; MA, 90; BA, 91; Univ Calif Santa Barb, MA, 93; PhD, 98. **CAREER** Vis asst prof, Univ Calif, 98-99; vis asst prof, Utah State Univ, 99-00; vis asst prof, Temple Univ, 00-01; vis asst prof, Grand Val State Univ, 01. **HONORS AND AWARDS** Univ Calif Reg Fel, 91-92, 96-97; John Patrick Sullivan Trav Fel, 93-94; ASCS Fel, 93-94. **MEMBERSHIPS** APA; AAH. **RESEARCH** Classical Athens; critias; epigraphy; philosophy. **SELECTED PUBLICATIONS** Auth, "An Honorary Deme Decree and the Administration of a Palaistra in Kephissia," Zeits fur Papyr Epigr 131 (00); auth, "Attic Gymnasia and Palaistrai: Public or Private?," Ancient World 31 (00); co-auth, "An Encomium on the Life of Saint Theognius, Bishop of Bethelia by Paul of Elusa," Cist Stud Qtly 30 (95); rev, Plutarch: Greek Lives (Oxford, 98) and Plutarch: Roman Lives, trans by R. Waterfield (Oxford, 99) Ploutarchos 17 (00); auth, "Critias," Internet Encycl Philo (00); auth, "Lyceum," Internet Encycl Philo (00). **CONTACT ADDRESS** Dept Hist, Grand Valley State Univ, 1121 Au Sable Hall, Allendale, MI 49010. **EMAIL** wmorison@gvsu.edu

MORK, GORDON ROBERT
PERSONAL Born 05/06/1938, St. Cloud, MN, m, 1963, 3 children **DISCIPLINE** MODERN HISTORY, GERMAN HISTORY **EDUCATION** Yale Univ, BA, 60; Univ Minn, MA, 63, PhD, 66. **CAREER** Lectr Hist, Univ Calif, Davis, 66-68, asst prof, 68-70; fel, inst res in Humanities, Univ Wis-Madison, 69-70; asst prof, 70-73, from assoc prof to prof; 73-94, Hist, Purdue Univ, West Lafayette, 73-; Dep Head, 98-. **MEMBERSHIPS** AHA; Conf Group Cent Europ Hist; Conf Group Ger Polit; Intl Soc for Hist Didactics, Vice Pres, 95-. **RESEARCH** Nineteenth and twentieth century Germany; Western civilization. **SELECTED PUBLICATIONS** Auth, Flint and Steel..Military Technology and Tactics in 17th Century Europe, Smithsonian J Hist, 67; The Archives of the German Democratic Republic, Cent Europ Hist, 69; Bismarck and the Capitulation of German Liberalism, J Mod Hist, 71; Modern Western Civilization, Dorsey, 76, rev ed, Univ Press Am, 81, USMC edition, 94; German Nationalism and Jewish Assimilation, Leo Baeck Inst, 77; Teaching the Hitler Period: History and Morality, History Teacher, 80; Schindler's List: The Book and the Film, Informations/Mitteilungen/Communications, 16/2, 95; ed, The Homes of Oberammergau, Purdue U P, 00. **CONTACT ADDRESS** Dept of History, Purdue Univ, West Lafayette, West Lafayette, IN 47907-1968. **EMAIL** gmork@purdue.edu

MORRIS, BONNIE J.
PERSONAL Born 05/14/1961, Los Angeles, CA, s **DISCIPLINE** HISTORY, WOMEN'S STUDIES **EDUCATION** Am Univ, BA, 83; SUNY Binghamton, MA, 85, PhD, 90. **CAREER** Adjunct lectr, Binghamton Univ, 87-89; asst prof, Calif state Univ, Chico, 89-90; res assoc and vis scholar, Harvard Divinity Sch, 90-91; vis lectr, Northeastern Univ, 91-92; asst prof, Semester at Sea, Univ Pittsburgh, fall 93; asst prof, St Lawrence Univ, 92-94; asst prof, Northern Ky Univ, fall 95; vis asst prof, George Washington Univ, 94-99. **HONORS AND AWARDS** Rosa M. Colecchio Awd, SUNY Binghamton, 87; vis fel, Dartmouth Col, 89; winner, Millennium Inst int think-tank competition, 97; Who's Who in Am Women, 99-2000; George Washington Univ's Trachtenberg Teaching Prize, 97-99; nominated for a 1999 Lambda Literary Awd. **MEMBERSHIPS** Am Hist Asn, Mensa, Women's Sports Found. **RESEARCH** U.S. women's history, colonial era to present: work, wartime, ethnic identity, politics; feminist movements--Western and global--from radical subcultures to anti-feminist backlash; women's music; lesbian history; Jewish women; women's sports. **SELECTED PUBLICATIONS** Auth, The High School Scene in the Fifties: Voices From West L.A., Greenwood (97); auth, Lubavitcher Women in America: Identity and Activism, SUNY Press (98); auth, Eden Built by Eves: The Culture of Women's Music Festivals, Alyson (99); auth, "Teaching the Virtue of Women's Sports," Washington Times (March 15, 99); auth, Girl Reel: Growing Up at the Movies, Coffee House Press (spring 2000); coauth, Radical Harmonies: The Story of the Women's Music Movement, Univ Ill Press (2002). **CONTACT ADDRESS** Women's Studies Prog, The George Washington Univ, Funger Hall 506, Washington, DC 20052. **EMAIL** drbon@gwu.edu

MORRIS, CHRISTOPHER
PERSONAL Born 04/28/1958, Edmonton, Canada, m, 1990, 1 child **DISCIPLINE** HISTORY **EDUCATION** Univ Western Ontario, BA, 81; MA, 85; Univ Fla, PhD, 91. **CAREER** Vis asst prof, Simon Fraser Univ, 91-92; from asst prof to assoc prof, Univ of Tex, 92-96. **HONORS AND AWARDS** Doctoral Fel, Soc Sci and Humanities Res Coun of Canada; Milbaur Res Fel, Univ of Fla. **MEMBERSHIPS** Southern Hist Asn, Org of Am Historians, Miss Hist Soc. **RESEARCH** Southern U.S. History, U.S. Environmental History, Slavery in the Americas. **SELECTED PUBLICATIONS** Auth, Becoming Southern: The Evolution of a Way of Life, Vicksburg and Warren County, Mississippi 1770-1860, Oxford Univ Press, 95 & 99; co-ed, Manifest Destiny and Empire: American Antebellum Expansion, Tex A & M Press (College Station, TX), 97; auth, "The Articulation of Two Worlds: The Master-Slave Relationship Reconsidered," J of Am Hist 85 (98): 982-1007; auth, "What's So Funny?: Southern Humorists and the Market Revolution," in Southern Writers and Their Worlds, eds. Christopher Morris and Steven G. Reinhardt (TX: Tex A & M Press, 96) & (LA: La State Univ Press, 98): 9-26; co-ed, Southern Writers and Their Worlds, Tex A & M Univ (College Station, TX), 96 & La State Univ Press, 98; auth, "Within Slave Households: Domestic Violence Among Mississippi Slaves," in Over the Threshold: Intimate Violence in Early America 1640-1865, ed. Christine Daniels (NY: Routledge, 99); auth, "Impenetrable but Easy: The French Transformation of the Lower Mississippi Valley and the Founding of New Orleans," in Centuries of Change: Human Transformation of the Lower Mississippi, ed. Craig E. Colton (PA: Univ of Pittsburgh Press, 00). **CONTACT ADDRESS** Dept Hist, Univ of Texas, Arlington, PO Box 19529, Arlington, TX 76019. **EMAIL** morris@uta.edu

MORRIS, JAMES M.
PERSONAL Born 07/13/1935, Reed City, MI, m, 1958, 6 children **DISCIPLINE** HISTORY **EDUCATION** Aquinas Col, AB, 57; Central Mich Univ, MA, 62; Univ of Cincinnati, PhD, 69. **CAREER** Instr, Col of Steubenville, 62-64; Asst Prof, Providence Col, 67-71; From Asst to Full Prof, Christopher Newport Univ, 71-. **HONORS AND AWARDS** US Dept of Educ Awd, 85; Alpha Chi Distinguished Prof Awd, 85; Inductee, Hon Order of St. Barbara, 93. **MEMBERSHIPS** US Naval Inst, N Am Asn for Ocesive Hist, Soc for Mil Hist. **RESEARCH** U.S. Military History, U.S. utopian history. **SELECTED PUBLICATIONS** Auth, Our Maritime Heritage: Maritime Developments and Their Impact on American Life, Univ Press of Am, 79; sr res ed, America's Maritime Legacy: A History of United States Shipping and Shipbuilding Industries from Colonial Times to the Present, Westview, 79; auth, History of U.S. Navy, Bison Books, 84, 93, 97, and Brompton Books, 86, 92, 97; auth, America's Armed Forces: A History, Prentice Hall, 91, 96; coauth, Historical Dictionary of the U.S. Navy, Scarecrow, 98. **CONTACT ADDRESS** Dept Hist, Christopher Newport Univ, 1 University Place, Newport News, VA 23606-2988. **EMAIL** cnewton@cnu.edu

MORRIS, RICHARD J.
PERSONAL Born 01/13/1947, Boston, MA, m, 1970, 3 children **DISCIPLINE** AMERICAN HISTORY **EDUCATION** Boston State Col, BA, 68; Ohio Univ, MA, 70; NYork Univ, PhD, 75. **CAREER** Nat Hist Publ & Rec Comn fel, The Papers of Alexander Hamilton, 75-76; asst prof, 76-85, Assoc Prof Hist, Lycoming Col, 86-. **MEMBERSHIPS** Essex Inst; AHA. **RESEARCH** Colonial; revolutionary and early national American history. **SELECTED PUBLICATIONS** Auth, Wealth distribution in Salem, MA 1759-99, Essex Inst Hist Col, 78; assoc-ed, The Papers of Alexander Hamilton XXVI, Columbia Univ Press, 79; Urban migration in Revolutionary America: The case of Salem, Mass, J Urban Hist, 82; co-auth, Williamsport: Frontier Village to Regional Center, 84; Social change, Republican rhetoric and the American Revolution: The case of Salem, Mass, J Soc Hist, 97. **CONTACT ADDRESS** Lycoming Col, 700 College Pl, Box 19, Williamsport, PA 17701-5192. **EMAIL** morris@lycoming.edu

MORRIS, THOMAS DEAN
PERSONAL Born 11/01/1938, Eugene, OR, m, 1977, 3 children **DISCIPLINE** AMERICAN CONSTITUTIONAL HISTORY **EDUCATION** Univ Wash, BA, 60, MA, 66, PhD(hist), 69. **CAREER** Vis asst prof hist, Univ Wash, 73; from instr to asst prof, 67-74, Assoc Prof Hist, 74-80, Prof, 80-97, Emer Prof, 97-, Portland State Univ. **MEMBERSHIPS** Am Soc Legal Hist; Orgn Am Historians. **RESEARCH** Nineteenth century American constitutional and legal history. **SELECTED PUBLICATIONS** Auth, Free Men All: The Personal Liberty Laws of the North, 1780-1861, Johns Hopkins Univ, 74; auth, Southern Salvery and the Law, 1619-1860, Univ NCar, 96. **CONTACT ADDRESS** Dept of Hist, Portland State Univ, Portland, OR 97207.

MORRIS-HALE, WALTER
PERSONAL Born 01/30/1933, Chicago, IL **DISCIPLINE** BRITISH HISTORY **EDUCATION** Univ of CA Berkeley, 1957; Univ of Stockholm Sweden, MA 1962; Univ of Geneva Switzerland, PhD 1969. **CAREER** Smith Coll, asst prof 1969-75, assoc prof, full prof, currently. **SELECTED PUBLICATIONS** Publs "British Admin in Tanganyika from 1920-45, with Spec Reference to the Preparation of Africans for Admin Positions" 1969, "From Empire to Nation, the African Experience" in Aftermath of Empire Smith Coll Studies in History XIVII 1973; Conflict & Harmony in Multi-Ethnic Societies: An International Perspective, 1996. **CONTACT ADDRESS** Full Professor, Smith Col, Northampton, MA 01063.

MORRISON, DENNIS L.
PERSONAL Born 10/29/1949, Miami, FL, d **DISCIPLINE** HISTORY, GEOGRAPHY **EDUCATION** Queen's Col, BA, 75; Univ of Houston, MA, 89; EdD, 93. **CAREER** From instr to prof, San Jacinto Col S, 90-. **HONORS AND AWARDS** Teaching Fel, Univ of Houston, 89; Teacher of the Year, San Jacinto Col, 98; Monument Awd, San Jacinto Col, 99. **MEMBERSHIPS** ADCG, AAG, Phi Alpha Theta, Phi Kappa Phi, Phi Kappa Delta. **RESEARCH** Women's studies, post war and cultural studies. **SELECTED PUBLICATIONS** Auth, Woman of Conscience: Senator Margaret Chase Smith of Maine, 95; auth, Up, Down, & Out: Henry A. Wallace and Democrat Party Politics, 1940-1946, 96; auth, Silent No More, 96; auth, World Geography, 97; auth, Our Moral Duty: Educating Minority Students in the United States, 97. **CONTACT ADDRESS** Dept Soc & Behav Sci, San Jacinto Col, South, 2016 Main #2507, Houston, TX 77002. **EMAIL** surveypub@hotmail.com

MORRISON, G. GRANT
PERSONAL Born 09/12/1936, Live Oak, FL, m, 1961, 2 children **DISCIPLINE** AMERICAN HISTORY **EDUCATION** Univ FL, AB, 60; City Univ New York, PhD, 74. **CAREER** Lectr hist, Queens Col, City Univ NY, 68-73; asst prof hist, 73-79, assoc prof hist, C W Post Col, Long Island Univ, 79-86, prof hist, Long Island Univ, 86. **MEMBERSHIPS** Orgn Am Historians; Am Studies Asn. **RESEARCH** US Early Nat Period; US soc hist. **SELECTED PUBLICATIONS** Auth, Isaac Bronson and the Search for System in American Capitalism, 1789-1838, Arno, 78; A New York City Creditor and His Upstate Debtors, New York Hist, 7/80; Interregional Entrepreneurship in the 1830's: The Role of New Yorkers in the Founding of an Ohio Corporation, Old Northwest, spring 81; Boundlessness and Limits in America's Self-Images, Ventures in Research, fall 85; James Fenimore Cooper and American Republicanism, Modern Age, spring 92. **CONTACT ADDRESS** Dept of Hist, Long Island Univ, C.W. Post, 720 Northern Blvd, Greenvale, NY 11548-1300.

MORRISON, KARL F.
PERSONAL Born 11/03/1936, Birmingham, AL, m, 1964, 2 children **DISCIPLINE** HISTORY **EDUCATION** Univ Miss, BA, 56; Cornell Univ, MA, 57; PhD, 61. **CAREER** Acting instr, Stanford Univ, 60-61; from instr to asst prof, Univ Minn, 61-64; asst prof, Harvard Univ, 64-65; from assoc prof to prof, Univ Chicago, 65-84; Ahmanson-Murphy Distinguished Prof of Medieval and Renaissance Hist, Univ Kans, 84-88; Gotthold Ephraim Lessing Prof of Hist and Poetics, Rutgers Univ, 88-. **HONORS AND AWARDS** fel, Medieval Acad of Am, 86-; Fel, John Simon Guggenheim Memorial Found, 86-87; Page-Barbour Lectr, Univ of Va; Haskins Medal, Medieval Acad of Am, 94. **MEMBERSHIPS** Medieval Acad of Am, Am Hist Asn. **RESEARCH** Medieval History, Intellectual History, History of Christianity. **SELECTED PUBLICATIONS** Coauth,

Imperial Lives and Letters of the Eleventh Century, Columbia Univ Press, 64; auth, Carolingian Coinage, Am Numismatic Soc, 67; auth, Tradition and Authority in the Western Church: ca. 300-1140, Princeton Univ Press, 69; auth, The Mimetic Tradition of Reform in the West, Princeton Univ Press, 82; auth, "I am You": The Hermeneutics of Empathy in Western Literature, Theology, and Art, Princeton Univ Press, 88; auth, History as a Visual Art in the Twelfth-Century Renaissance, Princeton Univ Press, 90; auth, Understanding Conversion, Univ Press of Va, 92; auth, Conversion and Text: The Cases of Augustine of Hippo, Herman-Judah, and Constantine Tsatsos, with a Translation of Herman-Jundah's "A Short Account of His Conversion," Univ Press of Va, 92. **CONTACT ADDRESS** Dept Hist, Rutgers, The State Univ of New Jersey, New Brunswick, PO Box 5059, New Brunswick, NJ 08903-5059.

MORRISON, WILLIAM R.
PERSONAL Born 01/26/1942, Hamilton, ON, Canada **DISCIPLINE** HISTORY **EDUCATION** McMaster Univ, BA, 63, MA, 64; Univ Western Ont, PhD, 73. **CAREER** Fac mem, 69-85, prof history, Brandon Univ, 85-89; fac mem, 89-92, dir, Ctr Northern Stud, Lakehead Univ, 90-92; dean, res & grad stud, 92-97, prof Hist, Univ Northern British Columbia, 92-. **SELECTED PUBLICATIONS** Auth, The Sinking of the Princess Sophia: Taking the North Down With Her, Toronto: Oxford Univ Press, 90; Fairbanks: Univ of Alaska Press, 91; auth, My Dear Mggie: Letters from a Western Manitoba Pioneer, Regina: Canadian Plains Res Centre, 91; auth, The Alaska Highway in world War II: The U.S. Army of Occupation in Canada's Northwest, Norman, OK: Univ of Okla Press, Toronto: Univ of Toronto Press, 92; auth, The Forgotten North: Labor and the Northwest Defense Projects, 1942-1945, Fairbanks: Univ of Alaska Press, 94; auth, The Historiograpy of the Provincial Norths, Thunder Bay: Lakehead Univ Centre for Northern Studies, 96; auth, True North: The Yukon and Northwest Territories, Toronto: Oxford Univ Press, 98. **CONTACT ADDRESS** Dept of History, Univ of British Columbia, 3333 University Way, Prince George, BC, Canada V2N 4Z9. **EMAIL** morrison@unbc.ca

MORROW, JOHN HOWARD, JR.
PERSONAL Born 05/27/1944, Trenton, NJ, m **DISCIPLINE** HISTORY **EDUCATION** Swarthmore Coll, BA, (with honors), 1966; Univ of PA Philadelphia, PhD history 1971. **CAREER** Univ of TN Knoxville, asst prof to full prof & dept head 1971-; Natl Aerospace Museum Washington DC, Lindbergh prof of history 1989-90; University of Georgia Athens, GA Franklin prof of history 1989-, department chr, 91-93, assoc dean of arts & science's, 93-95 **HONORS AND AWARDS** Hon Soc Phi Kappa Phi 1980; Lindsay Young Professorship 1982-83; Outstanding Teacher UT Natl Alumni Assn 1983; UT Macebearer 1983-84; Univ Distinguished Serv Professorship 1985-88. **MEMBERSHIPS** Mem Amer Historical Assn 1971-; consult Coll Bd & Ed Testing Serv 1980-84, 1990-; chr, Coll Board Natl Academic ASN, 1993-95, mem Coll Board, bod of trustees, 1993-; mem AHA Comm on Committees 1982-85, AHA Prog Comm for 1984 Meeting 1983-84; mem edit adv bds Aerospace Historian 1984-87; and Military Affairs 1987-90; Smithsonian Inst Pr, 1987-93; chairman History Advisory Committee to the Secretary of the Air Force 1988-92. **SELECTED PUBLICATIONS** Author: Building German Airpower 1909-1914, 1976, German Airpower in World War I, 1982; The Great War in the Air, 1993; A Yankee Ace in the RAF, co-ed, 1996. **CONTACT ADDRESS** Department of History, Univ of Georgia, Athens, GA 30602. **EMAIL** jmorrow@arches.uga.edu

MORSTEIN-MARX, ROBERT
DISCIPLINE ROMAN HISTORY **EDUCATION** Univ Calif, Berkeley, PhD, 87. **CAREER** Assoc Prof, Univ Calif, Santa Barbara. **RESEARCH** Roman history; Cocero; Roman oratory and rhetoric; Hellensitic epigraphy. **SELECTED PUBLICATIONS** Auth, "Athens, Thebes, and the Foundation of the Second Athenian League," Classical Antiquity 4, 85; "Asconius 14-15 C and the Date of Q. Mucius Scaevola's Command in Asia," Class Philol 84; "The Trial of Rutilius Rufus," Phoenix 44, 90; Hegemony to Empire, The Development of the Roman Imperium in the East, UC Press, 95; "Quintus Fabius Maximus and the Dyme Affair," CQ 45, 95; "Two Athenian Decrees Concerning Lemnos of the Late First Century B.C.," Chiron 27, 97; Publicity, Popularity and Patronage in the Commentariolum Petitionis, Class Antiquity, 98. **CONTACT ADDRESS** Dept of Classics, Univ of California, Santa Barbara, Santa Barbara, CA 93106-7150. **EMAIL** morstein@humanitas.ucsb.edu

MORTON, DESMOND D. P.
PERSONAL Born 09/10/1937, Calgary, AB, Canada **DISCIPLINE** CANADIAN HISTORY **EDUCATION** Royal Mil Col Can, BA, 59; Oxford Univ, BA, 61, MA, 66; London Sch Econ, Univ London, PhD, 68. **CAREER** Asst prof, Univ Ottawa, 68-69; Asst prof, 69-70, assoc prof, 71-75, prof hist, Univ Toronto, 75-; vis asst prof, Univ Western Ont, 70-71; vis assoc prof, Mich State Univ, 75; assoc dean, 75-59, vice prin (acad), 76-79, prin, Erindale Col, 86-94; dir, McGill Institute for the Study of Canada. **HONORS AND AWARDS** City Toronto Book Prize, 71; Univ Toronto Alumni Awd, 83; Off, Order Can, 96. **MEMBERSHIPS** Can Hist Asn; Can Comn Mil Hist; Mem bd, Can Nat Hist Soc; mem bd, Inst Res Public Policy; ed bd, The Beaver. **SELECTED PUBLICATIONS** Auth, Working People: An Illustrated History of the Canadian Labour Movement, 90; auth, When Your Number's Up: The Canadian Soldier in the First World War, 93; auth, Victory 1945 Canadians From War to Peace, 95; coauth, A Military History of Canada, 85, 2nd ed, 90, 3rd ed A Military History of Canada: From Champlain to the Gulf War, 92; coauth, Winning the Second Battle: Canadian Veterans and the Return to Civilian Life, 87; coauth, Marching to Armageddon: Canada in the First World War, 89; coauth, Silent Battle: Canadian Prisoners of War in Germany, 1914-19, 92; coauth, A Short History of Canada, 95, rev ed 97. **CONTACT ADDRESS** McGill Inst for the Study of Canada, 3463 Peel St, Montreal, QC, Canada H3A 1W7. **EMAIL** dmorton@leacock.lan.mcgill.ca

MORTON, MARIAN JOHNSON
PERSONAL Born 05/19/1937, Cambridge, MA, m, 1959, 4 children **DISCIPLINE** AMERICAN STUDIES & HISTORY **EDUCATION** Smith Col, BA, 59; Case Western Reserve Univ, MA, 63, PhD(Am studies), 70. **CAREER** Vis lectr, 70-72, asst prof, 72-77, assoc prof, 77-81, FULL PROF HIST, JOHN CARROLL UNIV, 82-. **MEMBERSHIPS** Am Studies Asn; Orgn Am Historians; Western Reserve Historical Soc. **RESEARCH** American historiography; women's history. **SELECTED PUBLICATIONS** Auth, The Terrors of Ideological Politics: Liberal Historians in a Conservative Mood, Case Western Reserve Univ, 72; coauth, Cowboy Without a Cause: His Image in Today's Popular Music, Antioch Rev, 6-7/77; As Mothers, as Sisters, as Daughters: Women Reformers in the Western Reserve, Western Reserve Mag, 3-4/81; My dear, I don't give a damn: Scarlett O'Hara and the Great Depression, Frontiers: J Women's Studies, fall 80; Fallen Women, Federated Charities, and Maternity Homes, 1913-1973, Social Service Rev, March 88; From Saving Souls to Saving Cities: Women and Reform in Cleveland, in Bitrh of Modern Cleveland, 1865-1930, ed by Thomas F. Campbell and Edward M. Miggins, London and Ontario: Assoc Univ Presses, 88; Homes for Poverty's Children: Cleveland Orphanages, 1851-1933, OH Hist, winter/spring 89; Emma Goldman and the American Left: Nowhere at Home, NY: Twayne, 92; Maternity Homes in Encyclopedia of Childbearing: Critical Perspectives,ed by Barbara Katz Rothman, Phoenix: Oryx Press, 93; And Sin No More: Social Policy and Unwed Mothers in Cleveland, 1855-1990, Columbus: The OH State Univ Press, 93; First Person Past: American Autobiographies, co-ed with Russell Duncan, two volumes, St James, NY: Brandywine Press, 94; Women in Cleveland: An Illustrated History, Bloomington: IN Univ Press, 95; Cleveland's Child Welfare System and the American Dilema, 1941-1965, Social Service Rev, March 98; auth, "Surviving the Great Depression: Orphanages and Orphans in the Great Depression," Journal of Urban History, (00): 438-455. **CONTACT ADDRESS** Dept of Hist, John Carroll Univ, 20700 N Park Blvd, Cleveland, OH 44118-4581. **EMAIL** mmorton@aol.com

MORTON, PATRICIA A.
DISCIPLINE ARCHITECTURAL HISTORY **EDUCATION** Princeton Univ, PhD, 94. **CAREER** Asst prof, Art History, Univ Calif, Riverside, 93- . **HONORS AND AWARDS** DAAD scholar, Geothe Inst, Berlin, 88; Mellon Found grant, Princeton Univ, 88-90; Graham Found grant, 91-92; Predoctoral fel, The Getty Center for Hist of Art and Hum, Santa Monica CA, 92-93; Graham Found grant for WomEnhouse, WWW collaborative feminist proj, 95; res fel, Univ Calif Hum Res Inst, Irvine, 96; Fulbright Sr Scholar Prog, Umea Univ, Sweden, 99; Nat Endow for the Arts, (Los Angeles forum for Arch and Urban Des), Proj Dir, Redressing the Mall: Eagle Rock Plaza Comp, 01. **MEMBERSHIPS** AAUP; Col Art Assoc; Soc of Archit Hist. **RESEARCH** Twentieth century architecture and urbanism; contemporary architecture; theory of architecture; post-Colonial theory. **SELECTED PUBLICATIONS** Auth, The Building That Looks Back, in Angles of Incidence, Princeton Architec Pr, 92; auth, Arata Isozaki: A Report on the Postmodern Condition, in Casabella, 94; auth, Compare and Contrast: Mark Robbins' Borrowed Landscape, in Oz, 95; auth, The Apprehension of the City: Flanerie on the Margins of the Metropolis, in SURFACE: J of UCLA School of the Arts and Archit, 96; auth, Indochina at the 1931 Colonial Exposition in Paris, in Dialogue: An Internatl Forum for Archit Design and Culture, 97; auth, The Death of the Architect, in 1100 Architect: Work in Progress, Monacelli, 97; auth, A Visit to WomEnhouse, in Toward an Architecture of the Everyday: A Collection of Essays and Projects, Princeton Archit Pr, 97; auth, Notes on the Inside and Outside of Architecture, in From the Center: Design process at SCI-Arc, Monacelli, 98; auth, The Two Halves of the Orange, in Fabrications, San Francisco Museum of Modern Art, 98; auth, National and Colonial: The Musee des Colonies for the 1931 Colonial Exposition in Paris, in Art Bull, 98; auth, The Incommensurable and the Indissociable, in Practices, 98; auth, A Study in Hybridity: The Madagascar and Morocco Pavilions at the 1931 Colonial Exposition, in J of Archit Educ, 98; auth, Hybridity and Difference: The 1931 International Colonial Exposition in Paris, MIT, 99; auth, Hybrid Modernities: Architecture and Representation at the 1931 International Colonial Exposition in Paris, MIT Press (Cambridge, MA), 00; auth, "Feminist Theory" and "Primitivism," in Encycl of Twentieth Century Archit (Fitzroy Dearborn, forthcoming); auth, "Le Corbusier's Voyage d'Orient, 1911," in French Civilization and its Discontents: Nationalism, Colonialism, and Race, ed. Tyler Stovall and Georges van den Abbeele (Rowman and Littlefield, forthcoming); auth, "Consuming the Colonies," in Architecture and the Culinary Arts, ed. Paulette Singley and Jamie Horwitz (Princeton Archit Press,forthcoming). **CONTACT ADDRESS** Art History Dept, Univ of California, Riverside, Riverside, CA 92521-0319. **EMAIL** pamorton@ix.netcom.com

MORVAN, JENNIFER
PERSONAL Born 06/06/1973, Binghamton, NY, m, 1996 **DISCIPLINE** ARCHITECTURAL HISTORY **EDUCATION** Dartmouth Col, BA, 95; Univ Va, MA, 97. **CAREER** Architectural Historian, Heritage Consulting, private consul; PAL (Pawtucket, RI; a Cultural resources mgmt. Company) 98-99. **HONORS AND AWARDS** Fall 99' began PhD program at Yale in joint degree program bt/w departments of History of Art and Architecture and Renaissance Studies. **MEMBERSHIPS** SAH; VAF. **RESEARCH** 16th Century French and Italian Architecture; Franco-Italian Studies of the Renaissance. **CONTACT ADDRESS** 26 Howe St, Medway, MA 02053. **EMAIL** jennifer.morvan@yale.edu

MOSELEY, MICHAEL EDWARD
PERSONAL Born 03/29/1941, Dayton, OH, m, 1963, 1 child **DISCIPLINE** ANTHROPOLOGY, ARCHAEOLOGY **EDUCATION** Univ Calif, Berkeley, BA, 63; Harvard Univ, MA & PhD(anthrop), 68. **CAREER** From instr to assoc prof anthrop, Harvard Univ, 68-76, asst cur SAm archaeol, 70-76; Assoc Cur Mid & S AM Archaeol & Ethnol, Field Mus of Natural Hist, 76-. **MEMBERSHIPS** Soc Am Archaeol. **RESEARCH** The development of agriculture and the functioning of pre- industrial cities in the New World. **SELECTED PUBLICATIONS** Coauth, Twenty-Four Architectural Plans of Chan Chan, Peur, Peabody Mus, 74; auth, The Maritime Foundations of Andean Civilization, Cummings, 75; contribr, Social and technological management in dry lands, Westview, 78; coauth, Peru's Golden Treasures, Field Mus of Natural Hist, 78; Preagricultural coastal civilization in Peru, Carolina Biological, 78. **CONTACT ADDRESS** Field Mus of Natural History, Chicago, IL 60605.

MOSER, HAROLD DEAN
PERSONAL Born 10/31/1938, Kannapolis, NC, m, 1964, 2 children **DISCIPLINE** AMERICAN HISTORY, AMERICAN LITERATURE **EDUCATION** Wake Forest Univ, BA, 61, MA, 63; Univ Wis-Madison, PhD(hist), 77. **CAREER** Instr hist, Chowan Col, 63-65; teaching asst, Univ Wis- Madison, 67-69; res asst, State Hist Soc Wis, 68-71; from asst ed to co-ed, Papers of Daniel Webster, Dartmouth Col, 71-78, ed corresp ser, Papers of Daniel Webster, 78-79; Ed & Dir, Papers of Andrew Jackson, Univ Tenn, 79-, Nat Hist Pub Comn fel, Dartmouth Col, 71-72. **HONORS AND AWARDS** Philip M Hamer Awd, Soc Am Archivists, 75. **MEMBERSHIPS** Orgn Am Historians; Southern Hist Asn; AHA. **RESEARCH** Jacksonian America; the Old South; Daniel Webster. **SELECTED PUBLICATIONS** Auth, Reaction in North Carolina to the Emancipation Proclamation, NC Hist Rev, 67; New Hampshire and the ratification of the Twelfth Amendment, Dartmouth Libr Bull; co- ed, The Papers of Daniel Webster: Correspondence Series (Vols 1, 2 & 4), 75-78, ed, Vol 5, 82, Univ Press New Eng; The Papers of Andrew Jackson, Univ Tenn Press, Vol 2 (in prep); Liberty And Power - The Politics Of Jacksonian America - Watson,Hl, Virginia Magazine Of History And Biography, Vol 0101, 1993. **CONTACT ADDRESS** Papers of Andrew Jackson, Univ of Tennessee, Hermitage, Hermitage, TN 37066. **EMAIL** hmoser@utk.edu

MOSES, WILSON JEREMIAH
PERSONAL Born 03/05/1942, Detroit, MI, m, 1963, 2 children **DISCIPLINE** HISTORY **EDUCATION** Wayne State Univ, AB, 65; MA, 67; Brown Univ, PhD, 75. **CAREER** Instr to asst prof, Univ Iowa, 71-76; assoc prof, Southern Meth Univ, 76-80; assoc prof, to prof, Brown Univ, 80-88; prof, Boston Univ, 88-92; prof, PaState Univ, 92-00. **HONORS AND AWARDS** Cert Spec Tribute, Sen Jackie Vaughn III; Fac Schls Medal; PSU Class '33 Dist Awd. **MEMBERSHIPS** AHA; OAH; ASAALH; SHA. **RESEARCH** American literary and intellectual history; American social and political thought; Hamiltonian Tradition; African American history; 19th century Liberia. **SELECTED PUBLICATIONS** Auth, Classical Black Nationalism, NY Univ Press, 96; auth, Liberian Dreams, Penn St Univ Press, 98; auth, The Wings of Ethiopia: Studies in African American Life and Letters, Iowa State Univ Press (Ames), 90; auth, Afrotopia: Roots of African-American Popular History, Cambridge Univ Press 98; auth, Alexander Crummell: A Study in Civilization and Discontent, Oxford Univ Press (NY), 89; auth; Black Messiahs and Uncle Toms: Social and Literary Interpretations of a Religious Myth, Penn State Univ Press, 82, rev ed, 93; auth, The Golden Age of Black Nationalism, 1850-1925, Archon, 78, 2nd ed, Oxford Univ Press, 88; ed, Destiny and Race: Semons and Addresses, by Alexander Crummell Univ Massachusetts Press, 92; ed, Black Nationalism From the American Revolution to Marcus Garvey, NY Univ Press, 96; ed, Liberian Dreams: Records of an African Return 1853, Penn State Univ Press, 98. **CONTACT ADDRESS** Dept History, Pennsylvania State Univ, Univ Park, 108 Weaver Bldg, University Park, PA 16802-5500. **EMAIL** wjm12@psu.edu

MOSS, BERNARD HAYM
PERSONAL Born 04/17/1943, New York, NY, m, 1967 **DISCIPLINE** MODERN FRENCH & EUROPEAN LABOR HISTORY **EDUCATION** Univ Paris, dipl etudes francaises, 63; Cornell Univ, BA, 64; Columbia Univ, MA & cert Europ studies, 66, PhD(hist), 72. **CAREER** Instr hist, Univ Southern Calif, University Park, 69-71, asst prof, 72-80. Alternate Comn Relief in Belgium Am study fel, Belg, 71-72; Am Philos Soc grant, 73; actg ed, Newslett Europ Labor Hist, Study Group Europ Labor & Working Class Hist, 73-; Am Coun Learned Socs study fel, 76. **MEMBERSHIPS** AHA; Fr Hist Soc; Study Group Europ Labor & Working Class Hist. **RESEARCH** French labor and socialist history; Marxism; Euro- communism. **SELECTED PUBLICATIONS** Auth, Parisian workers and the origins of republican socialism, In: The Revolution of 1830, Thomas Watts, 74; Producers' associations and the origins of French socialism: Ideology from below, J Mod Hist, 75; The Origins of the French Labor Movement: The Socialism of Skilled Workers, 1830-1914, Univ Calif, 76. **CONTACT ADDRESS** 3835 W 59th, Los Angeles, CA 90043.

MOSS, ROGER W.
PERSONAL Born 01/31/1940, Zanesville, OH, m, 1981, 2 children **DISCIPLINE** CULTURAL HISTORY **EDUCATION** Univ Delaware, PhD 72; Ohio Univ, MA 66, BSed 63. **CAREER** Athenaeum of Philadelphia, exec dir 68-00; Univ Penn, adj prof 81-00; Univ Maryland, lectr 67-68; Univ Delaware, lectr 66-68. **HONORS AND AWARDS** NEH; NEA; Joel Polsky prize, ASID, 89. **MEMBERSHIPS** RSA; SAH; HSP. **RESEARCH** American architecture and hist preservation. **SELECTED PUBLICATIONS** Auth, Historic Houses of Philadelphia, Phil, UPP, 98; Philadelphia Victorian: The Building of the Athenaeum, Phil, The Athenaeum, 98; Paint in America, ed, NY, John Wiley & Son, 94; The American Country House, NY, Henry Holt & Co, 90; auth, Lighting for Historic Buildings, John Wiley & Son (New York), 88; auth, Victorian Exterior Decoration, henry Holt (New York), 87; auth, Victorian Interior Decoration, Henry Holt (New York), 86; auth, Biographical Dictionary of Philadelphia Architects, 1700-1930, G.K. Hall (Boston), 85; auth, Century of Color, Watkins Glen (New York), 81. **CONTACT ADDRESS** Athenaeum of Philadelphia, 219 S. Sixth St, Philadelphia, PA 19106. **EMAIL** rwmoss@pobox.upenn.edu

MOSS, WALTER GERALD
PERSONAL Born 04/20/1938, Cincinnati, OH, m, 1963, 3 children **DISCIPLINE** RUSSIAN HISTORY **EDUCATION** Xavier Univ, OH, BS, 60; Georgetown Univ, PhD, 68. **CAREER** From instr hist to asst prof, Wheeling Col, 67-70; asst prof, 70-74, assoc prof, 74-79, prof hist, Eastern MI Univ, 79-, Grant, NDEA Inst Methods Soc; Nat Endowment for Humanities grant, proj dir Southeastern MI Consortium Geront & Humanities, 73-75; consult, Choice; exec dir, Pres Comn on Future of Eastern MI Univ, 75-76; consult/panelist, Nat Endowment for Hum, 76-77 & 79-80. **MEMBERSHIPS** Am Asn Advan Slavic Studies; AAUP. **RESEARCH** Russ hist; 20th century world hist. **SELECTED PUBLICATIONS** Auth, Vladimir Soloviev and the Jews in Russia, Russ Rev, 4/70; co-ed, Growing Old, Pocket Bks, 75; ed, Humanistic Perspectives on Aging, Univ Mich/Wayne State Univ, 76; auth, Why the anxious fear?, Aging and death in the works of Turgenev, In: Aging and the Elderly, Humanities, 78; auth, A History of Russia, 2 vol, McGraw-Hill, 97; co-auth, The Twentieth Century: A Brief Global History, 5th ed, McGraw-Hill, 98; coauth, The Twentieth Century: Readings in Global Hist, McGraw-Hill, 99. **CONTACT ADDRESS** Dept of Hist & Philos, Eastern Michigan Univ, 701 Pray Harrold, Ypsilanti, MI 48197-2201. **EMAIL** his_moss@online.emich.edu

MOSSE, GEORGE L.
PERSONAL Born 09/20/1918, Berlin, Germany **DISCIPLINE** HISTORY **EDUCATION** Haverford Col, BS, 41; Harvard Univ, PhD, 46. **CAREER** Lectr hist, Univ Mich, 44; from instr to assoc prof, Univ Iowa, 44-55; from assoc prof to prof, 55-67, Bascom Prof Hist, Univ Wismadison, 65-, Huntington Libr grant, 49; vis expert, US High Comn, Ger, 51 & 54; Soc Sci Res Coun grant, 62; vis prof, Stanford Univ, 63-64; co-ed, J Contemp Hist, 66-; vis prof hist, Hebrew Univ Jerusalem, 69-70, 72, 74, 76 & 78 & Jewish Theol Sem Am, 77-; sr fel hist ideas, Australian Nat Univ, 72 & 79; bd gov, Wiener Libr, London, 73- & Leobaeck Inst, 74-; bd overseers, Tauber Inst, Brandeis Univ, 79-; Koebner prof hist, Hebrew Univ, Jerusalem, 79-; vis prof, Kaplan Ctr Jewish Studies, Univ Capetown, 80 & Univ Munich, 82. **HONORS AND AWARDS** Harbison Awd, Danforth Found, 70; Aqui Storia, Italy, 75; dlitt, carthage col, 73. **MEMBERSHIPS** Am Soc Church Hist; AHA; Am Soc Reformation Res (pres, 61- 62). **RESEARCH** European intellectual history. **SELECTED PUBLICATIONS CONTACT ADDRESS** Dept of Hist, Univ of Wisconsin, Madison, Madison, WI 53706.

MOSSHAMMER, ALDEN ADAMS
PERSONAL Born 03/22/1941, Greenwich, CT, m, 1971 **DISCIPLINE** ANCIENT HISTORY, CLASSICS **EDUCATION** Amherst Col, BA, 62; Brown Univ, PhD(classics), 71. **CAREER** Instr Latin, Laconia High Sch, NH, 62-63; instr classics, Mercersburg Acad, Pa, 63-67, registr, 65-67; instr, Kenyon Col, 70-71; asst prof, Swarthmore Col, 71-72; asst prof, 72-77, Assoc Prof Hist, Univ Calif, San Diego, 77-83; Prof Hist, 83-. **MEMBERSHIPS** Am Philol Asn, North Am Patristic Soc. **RESEARCH** Greek chronography; archaic Greek history; church history. **SELECTED PUBLICATIONS** Auth, The epoch of the seven sages, 76 & Phainias of eresos and chronology, 77, Calif Studies Class Antiq; The Chronicle of Eusebius and Greek Chronographic Tradition, Assoc Univ, 79; The Barberini manuscript of George Syncellus, Greek, Roman, Byzantine Studies, 80; Two fragments of Jerome's chronicle, Rheinisches Mus, 81; Thales' Eclipse, Am Philol Asn, 81; The date of the first pythiad-again, Greek, Roman, Byzantine Studies, 82; auth, "Non-Being and Evil in Gregory of Nyssa," Vigiliae Christianae 44 (90):136-67; ed, Ecolga Chronographiae Georgii Syncelli, Teubner ; Agatharchides Of Cnidos 'On The Erythraean Sea' - Burstein,Sm, J Of The American Oriental Society, Vol 0112, 1992; auth, "Gregory of Nyssa and Christian Hellenism," Studia Patristica 32 (97): 170-195; auth, "Gregory of Nyssa as Homilist," Studia Patristica, 01. **CONTACT ADDRESS** Dept of Hist B-007, Univ of California, San Diego, 9500 Gilman Dr, La Jolla, CA 92093-5003. **EMAIL** amosshammer@ucsd.edu

MOTT, MORRIS K.
DISCIPLINE HISTORY **EDUCATION** Univ Manitoba, BA, MA; Queen's Univ, PhD. **CAREER** Hist, Brandon Univ. **RESEARCH** Hist of sport. **SELECTED PUBLICATIONS** Coauth, Curling Capital: Winnipeg and the Roarin Game, 1876-1988, Winnipeg: Univ of Manitoba Press, 89; auth, Sports in Canada: Historical Readings, Mississauga: Copp Clark Pitman, 89; co-ed, "Tough to Make It: The History of Professional Team Sports in Manitoba," in J. Welsted, J. Everitt and C. Stadel, eds., The Geography of Manitoba: Its Land and Its People, Winnipeg: Univ of Manitoba Press, 96; auth, "Curling," and "Ice Hockey," in Encyclopedia of World Sport, Santa Barbara, CA: ABC-CLIO, 96; auth, "The Canadian National Team, 1963 to 1970," in Dan Diamond, Total Hockey, (Toronto: Don Diamond & Associates, 98). **CONTACT ADDRESS** History Dept, Brandon Univ, 270-18th St, Brandon, MB, Canada R7A 6A9. **EMAIL** mott@BrandonU.ca

MOULTON, EDWARD C.
DISCIPLINE HISTORY **EDUCATION** Memorial Univ, BA; MA; Univ London, PhD. **CAREER** Prof **RESEARCH** Asian history. **SELECTED PUBLICATIONS** Auth, Lord Northbrook's Indian Administration 1872-1876, 69; Indian Studies in Canada, 85; Problems of Municipal Self-Government and Urban Development in Nineteenth Century North India: Allan O. Hume and Municipal Beginnings in the Town of Etawah in the 1860s, 94. **CONTACT ADDRESS** Dept of History, Univ of Manitoba, Winnipeg, MB, Canada R3T 2N2. **EMAIL** emoultn@cc.umanitoba.ca

MOULTON, GARY EVAN
PERSONAL Born 02/21/1942, Tulsa, OK, m, 1969, 3 children **DISCIPLINE** AMERICAN HISTORY **EDUCATION** Northeastern OK State Univ, BA, 68; OK State Univ, MA, 70, PhD, 73. **CAREER** Instr hist, Southwestern OK State Univ, 73-74, asst prof, 74-79; assoc prof, 79-88, prof hist, Univ NE-Lincoln, 88-99, ed, papers Chief John Ross, Nat Hist Publ & Rec Comn, 75-79; ed, J Lewis & Clark Expedition, Univ NE-Lincoln, 79-99; Sorensen Prof Hist, Univ NE Lincoln, 99-. **HONORS AND AWARDS** Wrangler Awd, Best Western Non-fiction, Nat Cowboy Hall of Fame, Okla City, 84; Awd of Meritorius Achievement, Lewis & Clark Trail Heritage Found, 88; J Franklin Jameson Prize for Outstanding Ed Achievement, AHA, 90; Fulbright Scholar Awd, lectr, Universitat Hannover, Ger, 94; Distinguished Tchg Awd, Univ NE-Lincoln, 96. **MEMBERSHIPS** Asn Documentary Ed; Lewis & Clark Trail Heritage Found; NE State Hist Soc; Western Hist Asn. **RESEARCH** Lewis and Clark expedition; Am Indians; Am West. **SELECTED PUBLICATIONS** Auth, John Ross, Cherokee Chief, Univ GA Press, 78; The Specialized Journals of Lewis and Clark, Proc Am Philos Soc, 83; Papers of Chief John Ross, 2 vol, Univ OK Press, 85; On Reading Lewis and Clark: The Last Twenty Years, Montana, 88; Lewis and Clark: Meeting the Challenges of the Trail, In: Encounters with a Distant Land (Carlos A Schwantes, ed), Univ ID Press, 94; Journals of Lewis and Clard Expedition, 12 vol, Univ Nebr Press, 83; coauth, Prince Maximilian and new maps of the Missouri and Yellowstone rivers by William Clark, Western Historical Quart, 10/81. **CONTACT ADDRESS** Dept Hist, Univ of Nebraska, Lincoln, Lincoln, NE 68588-0327. **EMAIL** gmoulton@unl.edu

MOUNT, GRAEME S.
PERSONAL Born 07/26/1939, Montreal, PQ, Canada, m, 1964, 2 children **DISCIPLINE** HISTORY **EDUCATION** McGill Univ, BA, 61; Univ Toronto, MA, 67, PhD, 69. **CAREER** Asst prof, Laurentian Univ, 69-77, assoc prof, 77-85, prof, 85-. **RESEARCH** U.S.-Canadian relations during the Cold War; Chile and the Axis; Fort St. Joseph, 1796-1812. **SELECTED PUBLICATIONS** Auth, A History of St. Andrew's United Church, Sudbury, Sudbury: Journal Printing, 82; auth, Presbyterian Missions to Trinidad and Puerto Rico, Lancelot Press, 83; coauth, An Introduction to Canadian-American Relations, Toronto: Methuen, 84; auth, The Sudbury Region: An Illustrated History, Burlington: WindsorPublications, 86; auth, El Caribe, 92; auth, Canada's Enemies: Spies and Spying in the Peaceable Kingdom, Toronto: Dundurn Press, 93; coauth, The Border at Sault Ste. Marie, Toronto: Dundurn Press, 93; coauth, The Caribbean Basin: An International History, London and New York: Routledge, 98; coauth, "Review of Recent Literature on Canadian-Latin American Relations, Journal of Interamerican Studies and World Affairs, XXVII, (85): 127-151; auth, "Chile, the United States, and the Axis in 1942," Las RelacionesInternacionales en el Pacifico (Madrid: Bibliotecade Historia, 97), 453-474. **CONTACT ADDRESS** History Dept, Laurentian Univ, 935 Ramsey Lake Rd, Sudbury, ON, Canada P3E 2C6. **EMAIL** GMOUNT@NICKEL.LAURENTIAN.CA

MOWAT, FARLEY
PERSONAL Born 05/12/1921, Belleville, ON, Canada **DISCIPLINE** HISTORY **EDUCATION** Univ Toronto, BA, 49. **HONORS AND AWARDS** DLitt(hon), Laurentian Univ, 70; DLaws(hon), Univ Lethbridge, 73; DLaws(hon), Univ Toronto, 73; DLaws(hon), Univ PEI, 79; off, Order Can, 81; DLitt(hon), Univ Victoria, 82; DLitt(hon), Lakehead Univ, 86; Can Achievers Awd, Toshiba, Can, 90; Take Back Nat Awd, Coun Can, 91; Author's Awd, Can Found Advan Can Lett, 93; DLitt(-hon), McMaster Univ, 94; DLaws(hon), Queen's Univ, 95; DLitt(hon), Univ Col Cape Breton, 96 **SELECTED PUBLICATIONS** Auth, Sibir, 70; auth, A Whale for the Killing, 72; auth, Wake of the Great Sealers, 73; auth, Tundra, 73; auth, The Snow Walker, 75; auth, Canada North Now, 76; auth, And No Birds Sang, 79; auth, Sea of Slaughter, 84; auth, My Discovery of America, 85; auth, Virunga, 87; auth, The New Founde Land, 89; auth, Rescue the Earth, 90; auth, My Father's Son, 92; auth, Born Naked, 93; auth, Aftermath, 95. **CONTACT ADDRESS** Key Porter Books, 70 The Esplanade, 3rd Fl, Toronto, ON, Canada M5E 1R2.

MOYA, JOSE C.
PERSONAL Born 12/10/1952, Cuba, m, 1978, 2 children **DISCIPLINE** HISTORY **EDUCATION** Wean Univ, BA, 82; Rutgers Univ, PhD, 88. **CAREER** Asst prof, Univ Calif, Los Angeles, 89-94; assoc prof, 95-. **HONORS AND AWARDS** Fulbright Fel; NEH; Bolton Prize; Herring Bk Prize; Sharlin Memorial Awd. **MEMBERSHIPS** AHA; LASA; SSHA. **RESEARCH** Urbanist history; immigration; ethnicity; Argentina; Cuba. **SELECTED PUBLICATIONS** Auth, Cousins and Strangers: Spanish Immigrants in Buenos Aires, 1850-1930 (Berkeley: UC Press, 98); ed, La inmigracion espanola en la Argentina (Buenos Aires: Editorial Biblios, 99). **CONTACT ADDRESS** Dept History, Univ of California, Los Angeles, PO Box 951473, Los Angeles, CA 90095-1473. **EMAIL** moya@ucla.edu

MOYER, ANN E.
PERSONAL Born 06/14/1955, Monroe, MI, s **DISCIPLINE** HISTORY **EDUCATION** Univ Mich, AM, 80; PhD, 87. **CAREER** Asst prof, Rhodes Col, 87-88; Mellon instr, Univ Chicago, 88-91; vis asst prof, Univ Oregon, 91-92; asst prof, Univ Calif-Santa Barbara, 92-95; asst prof, Univ Pa, 95- . **HONORS AND AWARDS** Mich State Univ Bd Trustees Awd, 77; Phi Beta Kappa, 77; Gladys K. Delmas Found Fel, 83; Mellon Fel, 88-91; NEH Travel to Collections grant, 89; Helen & Howard R. Marraro Prize, 93. **MEMBERSHIPS** Am Hist Asn; Int Soc Intellectual Hist; Renaissance Soc Am; Sixteenth Century Studies; Soc Italian Hist Studies. **RESEARCH** Intellectual and cultural history of Renaissance Italy. **SELECTED PUBLICATIONS** Auth, Musica Scientia: Musical Scholarship in the Italian Renaissance. Cornell Univ Press, 92; auth, "Musical Scholarship in Italy at the End of the Renaissance, 1500-1650: From Veritas to Verisimilitude," in History and the Disciplines: The Reclassification of Knowledge in Early Modern Europe, ed, Donald R. Kelley, Rochester, NY: Rochester Univ Press, 97, 185-202; auth, "The Astronomers' Game: Astrology and University Culture in the Fifteenth and Sixteenth Centuries." Early Sci and Med 4, 99, 228-50; auth "Renaissance Representations of Islamic Science: Bernardino Baldi and his Lives of Mathematicians." Sci in Context 12, 99:469-84; auth, "Nostradamus." In Encycl of the Renaissance. NY: Scribner's, 99. **CONTACT ADDRESS** Dept Hist, Univ of Pennsylvania, 3401 Walnut St, 352 B, Philadelphia, PA 19104-6228. **EMAIL** moyer@sas.upenn.edu

MOYER, JAMES CARROLL
PERSONAL Born 11/30/1941, Norristown, PA, m, 1965, 3 children **DISCIPLINE** OLD TESTAMENT, ANCIENT HISTORY **EDUCATION** Wheaton Col, BA, 63; Gordon Divinity Sch, MDiv, 66; Brandeis Univ, MA, 68, PhD(Mediter studies), 69. **CAREER** Sachar Int fel, Brandeis Univ, 69-70; asst prof, 70-75, assoc prof hist, 75-78, assoc prof religious studies, 78-79, Prof Relig Studies, 79, Head of Relig Studies, 79--, Southwest MO State Univ; 85--Fel archaeol, Hebrew Union Col Bibl & Archaeol Sch, Jerusalem, 69-70. **MEMBERSHIPS** Soc Bibl Lit; Am Orient Soc; Am Schs Orient Res; Cath Bibl Asn; Nat Asn of Baptist Professors of Relig. **RESEARCH** Old Testament; Israelite historiography and chronology; Hittitology. **SELECTED PUBLICATIONS** Auth, Philistines and Samson, In: Zondervan Pictorial Encyclopedia of the Bible, 75; contribr 14 articles for the revision of Erdman's Int Standard Bible Encycl, Vol I, 79, Vol II, 82; co-ed, Hittite and Israelite cultic practices: A selected comparison, In: Scripture in Context II, 82; Ashke-

lon Discovered - From Canaanites And Philistines To Romans And Moslems - Stager,Le, J Of Biblical Literature, Vol 0112, 1993; contribr, The Anchor Bible Dictionary, 5 articles, 93; History And Technology Of Olive-Oil In The Holy-Land - Frankel,R, Avitsur,S, Ayalon,E, Jacobson,J, Biblical Archaeologist, Vol 0059, 1996; Through The Ages In Palestinian Archaeology - An Introductory Handbook - Rast,We, Biblical Archaeologist, Vol 0057, 1994; Scripture And Other Artifacts - Essays On The Bible And Archaeology In Honor Of King,Philip,J. - Coogan,Md, Exum,Jc, Stager,Le, Biblical Archaeologist, Vol 0058, 1995; coed, The Old Testament Text and Context, 97; contribr, Eerdmans Dictionary of the Bible, 5 articles, 00. **CONTACT ADDRESS** Dept of Religious Studies, Southwest Missouri State Univ, Springfield, Springfield, MO 65802. **EMAIL** jcmb25f@smsu.edu

MOYER, RONALD L.
PERSONAL Born 07/31/1944, Champaign, IL, m, 1988, 1 child **DISCIPLINE** THEATRE HISTORY, LITERATURE AND ACTING **EDUCATION** Univ IL, BA, 66, MA, 67; Univ Denver, PhD, 74. **CAREER** Prof & dir, Grad Stud; prof, Univ SD, 74-, dept ch, 78-83, 89-91, tenure, 80; dir, Black Hills Playhouse, 76- & assoc mng dir, 79 & 80; tchg fel, Univ Denver, 72-73; instr, Purdue Univ-Calumet, 67-71; grad asst, Univ IL, 66-67; local arrangements ch, SDHSAA One-Act Play Festival, 90 & 85; local arrangements supvr, Irene Ryan Competition, ACTF, Region V North, 89; hon mem, Bd Dir, The Black Hills Playhouse, 92-; second VP & mem, Bd Dir, The Black Hills Playhouse, 83-91; critic, Am Col Theatre Festival Region V N, 84; local arrangements ch, ACTF Region V North Festivention, 83; Univ/Col Theatre Asn Repr, Mid- Am Theatre Conf Coun, 81-83; treasurer, S Dakota Theatre Asn, 78-82, finance comt, 78-82 & nominating comt, 78; co-drafter, Const Rev, 78; local arrangements ch, SDHSAA One-Act Play Festival, 82; mem, Plan Comt, MATC Conv, 80-81; ch, Reg Theatre Auditions, MATC Conv, 81; critic & mem, Reg Screening Team, ACTF Region V North, 80-81; mem, Plan Comt, MATC Conv, 79-80; ch, Reg Theatre Auditions, MATC Conv, 80; local arrangements ch, SDHSAA One-Act Play Festival, 80; univ comt(s), Univ Graphics Rev Comt, 94-95; Grad Coun, 78-83,84-87, 89-; subcomt(s), Univ Senate, 77-78 & Rules and Nominating Comt, 87-89; Presidential-Alumni Scholar Selection Comt, 80, 81; Educ Media Comt, 76-77; Statewide Educ Serv Adv Comt, 75-77. **HONORS AND AWARDS** Sioux Falls Argus Leader, 95; USD Stud Theatre League Fac Appreciation Awd, 92; Courseware develop awd, IBM-Rochester, 91; The Divorce Colony, play won second prize, David Libr of the Am Revolution, 87; USD Stud Theatre League Fac Appreciation Awd, 86; first prize, 2 plays, David Libr Am Revolution nat contest, 76; NDEA Title IV fel, Univ Denver, 71-74; Bush Mini-Grant Prog, 95; USD fac develop prog, 93; vis prof, IBM-Rochester, 92 & 91; USD fac develop prog, 92; Bush Found grant, 89, 88 & 85; SD Arts Coun grant, 82-83. **RESEARCH** Use of the Internet for the study of theatre and drama; Shakespearean performance; methods of playscript analysis. **SELECTED PUBLICATIONS** Auth, American Actors, 1861-1910: An Annotated Bibliography of Books, Troy, NY, Whitston Publ Co, 79; coauth & ed advert brochure, IBM Ultimedia Video Delivery System/400, Rochester, MN, Int Bus Mach Corp, co 92. **CONTACT ADDRESS** Dept of Theatre, Univ of So Dakota, Vermillion, 414 E Clark St, Vermillion, SD 57069. **EMAIL** rmoyer@usd.edu

MOYLAN, PRUDENCE A.
DISCIPLINE HISTORY **EDUCATION** Univ Ill-Urbana, PhD, 75. **CAREER** Hist, Loyola Univ. **RESEARCH** Modern British history; gender & peace Stud. **SELECTED PUBLICATIONS** Auth, The Form and Reform of County Government: Kent, 1889-1914, Leicester UP, 78; Local Government, in Victorian Britain: an Encyclopedia, 86. **CONTACT ADDRESS** Fine Arts Dept, Loyola Univ, Chicago, 6525 N. Sheridan Rd., Chicago, IL 60626. **EMAIL** pmoylan@orion.it.luc.edu

MOYNIHAN, KENNETH J.
PERSONAL Born 07/27/1944, Newport, RI, m, 1990 **DISCIPLINE** HISTORY **EDUCATION** Holy Cross, AB, 66; Clark, MA, 69, PhD, 73. **CAREER** PROF, HIST, ASSUMPTION COLL **MEMBERSHIPS** Am Antiquarian Soc **RESEARCH** Hist of Worcester **SELECTED PUBLICATIONS** Auth, "Meetinghouse vs. Courthouse: The Struggle for Legitimacy in Worcester, 1783- 1788," in Shays' Rebellion: Selected Essays, 87; auth, "The Importance of Being Protestant: The Swedish Role in Worcester, Massachusetts, 1868-1930," in Swedes in America: New Perspectives, 93; auth, "Can the Scholars' History be the Public History?" Procs of the AAS 105, 95. **CONTACT ADDRESS** Hist Dept, Assumption Col, 500 Salisbury St, Worcester, MA 01615-0005. **EMAIL** kmoyniha@assumption.edu

MOYNIHAN, RUTH BARNES
PERSONAL Born 08/19/1933, Meriden, CT, m, 1953, 7 children **DISCIPLINE** AMERICAN HISTORY **EDUCATION** Smith College, ex, 55; Univ Conn, BA, 73; Yale Univ, PhD(hist), 79. **CAREER** Lectr hist, Univ Conn, 77 & 82, 85-97; vis asst prof, Univ Tex, Dallas, 79-80; vis lectr hist & women's studies, Yale Univ, 80- 81; Res & Writing, 81-, Am Coun Learned Soc grant, 80; vis asst prof, Lewis & Clark Col, Portland , OR, 83-84; guest curator, Ct Hist Soc, Ct women exhibition, 87-88; Historical Consultant, 91-; vis prof, St Joseph Col, Hartford, Ct, 91-92. **HONORS AND AWARDS** Beinecke Prize in Western Hist, Yale Univ, 79; Phi Betta Kappa, 73; Danforth Grad fel for Women, 73-79. **MEMBERSHIPS** AHA; Orgn Am Historians. **RESEARCH** American women's Colonial history to 1900. **SELECTED PUBLICATIONS** Auth, " Children and Young on the Overland Trail," Western Hist Quart, 75; auth, Rebel for Rights: Abigail Scott Duniway of Oregon, Yale Univ Press, 83; coed, So Much To Be Done: Women Settlers on the Mining & Ranching Frontier, U Nebraska Press, 89, 2nd edition 98; auth, Coming of Age: Four Centuries of CT Women; CT Hist Soc, 89,91; coed, Second to None: A Documentary History of American Women, 1540 to 1994, 2 vols., U Nebraska Press, 94; auth, " With Unshaken Heroism & Fortitude": Conn Women's Life & Work Two Hundred Years Ago; CT Acad of Arts & Sciences Transactions, Yale U Press, 00; auth, A New England Family, or How Did We Get Here Anyway?, forthcoming. **CONTACT ADDRESS** 37 Farrell Rd RR 1, Storrs, CT 06268. **EMAIL** ruthmoyn@snet.net

MOYSEY, ROBERT ALLEN
PERSONAL Born 06/27/1949, Richmond, IN **DISCIPLINE** CLASSICAL LANGUAGES, ANCIENT HISTORY **EDUCATION** Univ Cincinnati, BA, 71; Princeton Univ, MA, 73, PhD(class), 75. **CAREER** Teaching asst class, Princeton Univ, 73-75; vis asst prof, Hamilton Col, 77-78; vis asst prof hist, Univ Del, 79-80; asst prof class, 80-85, assoc prof class, 85-90, prof class, 90-, chair and prof class, Univ Miss, 93-. **HONORS AND AWARDS** Phi Beta Kappa; Charles McMicken Honors Prize. **MEMBERSHIPS** Archaeol Inst Am; Am Philol Asn; Asn Ancient Historians; Am Numis Soc. **RESEARCH** Greek & Persian history, 4th century BC; Greek epigraphy; Greek numismatics. **SELECTED PUBLICATIONS** Auth, The Date of the Strato of Sidon Decree, Am J of Ancient Hist, 76; The Thirty and the Pnyx, Am J of Archaeol, 81; Greek Funerary Monuments in Mississippi, Zeitschrift fur Papyrologie und Epigraphik, 88; Three Fragmentary Attic Inscriptions, Zeitschrift fur Papyrologie und Epigraphik, 89; Observations on the Numismatic Evidence relating to the Great Satrapal Refolt of 362/1 BC, Revue des Etudes Anciennes, 89; Thucydides, Kimon and the Peace of Kallias, Ancient His Bulletin, 91; Diodoros, the Satraps and the Decline of the Persian Empire: A Book Review of Michael Weiskopf's The So-Called Great Satrapal Revolt 366-360 BC, Ancient Hist Bulletin, 91; A Brief History of Olynthus, Olynthus: An Overview, Univ Miss, 92; Plutarch, Nepos and the Satrapal Revolt of 362/1 BC, Historia, 92. **CONTACT ADDRESS** Dept of Classics, Univ of Mississippi, University, MS 38677-9999. **EMAIL** clmoysey@olemiss.edu

MRUCK, ARMIN EINHARD
PERSONAL Born 06/06/1925, Osterode, Germany, m, 1952, 3 children **DISCIPLINE** MODERN HISTORY **EDUCATION** Univ Gottingen, DPhil, 51. **CAREER** Grant, Univ KY, 51-52; instr Ger, NY Univ, 53-55; from asst prof to assoc prof hist, Morgan State Col, 55-67, chmn div soc sci, 60-63; vp fac asn, 67-72, Prof Hist, Towson State Univ, 67- , Teacher, Gym & Lyceum, Ger, 61-62; sen, Fac Senate State Univs & Cols, 82-; Prof emeritus, 93-; Adjunct prof, 88-; Carl von Ossietjky U.- Germany; Coordinator/Consultant, Towson U, 88; U./Germany; 97-honors: Bunes-Verdienstkreuz by president Fed. Rep. Germany. **MEMBERSHIPS** AHA; AAUP **RESEARCH** Renaissance, reformation, national socialism and resistance against it. **SELECTED PUBLICATIONS** Auth, Deutschland im Europaeischen Spannungsfeld, 63; Der 29 Juli in amerikanischer Sicht, 65, Die amerikanische Ostpolitik, 66 & Deutsch-amerik Beziehungen im 20, Jahrhundert, 67, Europaeische Begegnung; coauth, An Austrian view of the US Navy, Am Neptune, 74; auth, Die Brucke zur Vergangenheit, Ostpreussenblat, 776; Neues aus der alten ostdtsch heimat, Washington J, 1076; Poland: An experiment in Eurocomms, Sun, 77; American Intelligence And The German Resistance To Hitler - A Documentary History - Heideking,J, Mauch,C, German Studies Review, Vol 0020, 1997; Frontsoldaten - The German Soldier In World-War-Ii - Fritz,Sg, International History Review, Vol 0019, 1997; auth, Chaper in Great Leaders; Great Tyrants; ed., Arnold Blumber, Greenwood Press, Westport, Connecticut, London, 95. **CONTACT ADDRESS** Dept of Hist, Towson State Univ, Baltimore, MD 21204.

MUCCIGROSSO, ROBERT HENRY
PERSONAL Born 07/13/1939, Elmira Heights, NY, m **DISCIPLINE** HISTORY **EDUCATION** Syracuse Univ, BA, 60; Columbia Univ, MA, 61, PhD, 66. **CAREER** From instr to asst prof, 66-75, assoc prof, 75-80, Prof Hist, Brooklyn Col, 81-98, prof emer, 98-; Fulbright jr lectr, Rome, 72-73. **MEMBERSHIPS** AHA; Orgn Am Historians; Soc Hist Educ. **RESEARCH** Late 19th and 20th century United States intellectual and cultural history. **SELECTED PUBLICATIONS** Auth, The city reform club: a study in late 19th century reform, NY Hist Soc Quart, 7/68; American gothic: Ralph Adams Cram, Thought, spring 72; Richard Ward Greene Welling, Dictionary of Am Biog, 74; Ambrose Bierce & Wallace Stevens, Encycl Am Biog, 74; Ralph Adams Cram: the architect as communitarian, Prospects, 75; Corruption and the Alienation of the Intellectuals, in Before Watergate, Brooklyn Col, 78; Television and the Urban Crisis, in The Impact of Television upon Aspects of Contemporary Civilization, Nelson-Hall, 79; American Gothic: The Mind and Art of Ralph Adams Cram, Univ Press Am, 80; co-auth, America in the Twentieth Century: Coming of Age, Harper & Row, 88; ed, Research Guide to American Historical Biography, 3 vol, Beacham Publ, 88; co-ed, Henry Adams and His World, Transactions of the Am Philos Soc, 93; Celebrating the New World: Chicago's Columbian Exposition of 1893, Ivan R Dee, 93; co-auth, Manufacturing in America: A Legacy of Excellence, Greenwich Publ Group, 95; coauth, Term Paper Resource Guide to Twentieth-Century United States History, Greenwood Press, 99. **CONTACT ADDRESS** 10704 Baylark Ave, Las Vegas, NV 89134.

MUELLER, HOWARD ERNEST
PERSONAL Born 08/04/1936, Danube, MN, m, 1959, 2 children **DISCIPLINE** HISTORY OF RELIGIONS **EDUCATION** NCent Col, BA, 58; Evangel Theol Sem, BD, 61; Yale Univ, Stm, 62; Northwestern Univ, PhD(relig), 73. **CAREER** Asst prof relig, Carleton Col, 73-76; asst prof Relig, 76-80, assoc prof, 81-85, Prof Relig, Ncent Col, 85-, Chmn Dept, 90-. **HONORS AND AWARDS** Toenniges Prof of Religious Studies, 92. **MEMBERSHIPS** Am Acad Relig. **RESEARCH** African traditional religions; death and dying; biblical studies. **CONTACT ADDRESS** Dept of Religious Studies, No Central Col, 30 N Brainard St, Naperville, IL 60566. **EMAIL** hem@noctrl.edu

MUELLER, ROLAND MARTIN
PERSONAL Born 06/16/1929, Athens, WI, m, 1951, 2 children **DISCIPLINE** AMERICAN & EUROPEAN HISTORY **EDUCATION** Concordia Teachers Col, Ill, BS, 51; Colo State Col, MA, 55; Univ Kans, PhD(US hist), 78. **CAREER** Asst prof hist, 56-64, assoc prof, 64-79, Prof Soc Sci, St John's Col, Kans, 79-. **MEMBERSHIPS** Orgn Am Historians; Nat Coun Geog Educ; Concordia Hist Inst. **RESEARCH** Clergy in the pre-Revolution period of Colonial history; the Chautauqua movement in Kansas. **SELECTED PUBLICATIONS** Auth, Reasons for seasons, 66 & Social studies and the local scene, + 72, Lutheran Educ; Teaching Beyond The Quincentennial + The 500th Anniversary Of Columbus Landfall In The America And The Dearth Of Reference Material Concerning It, Hispania-A J Devoted To The Teaching Of Spanish And Portuguese, Vol 0076, 1993. **CONTACT ADDRESS** 1714 E 11th, Winfield, KS 67156.

MUELLER, WOLFGANG
PERSONAL Born 09/25/1960, Braunschweig, Germany, s **DISCIPLINE** HISTORY **EDUCATION** Syracuse Univ, PhD, 91; Univ Augsburg, Dr. Phil Habil, 98. **CAREER** Res asst, Princeton Univ, 97-98; vis asst prof, Univ of Kansas, 98-00; assoc prof, Fordham Univ, 00-. **MEMBERSHIPS** AHA; Deutscher Hochschulverband. **RESEARCH** High/late medieval legal/social/institutional history. **SELECTED PUBLICATIONS** Auth, Huguccio. The Life, Works, and Thought of a Twelfth Century Jurist, CUA Pr (Washington), 94; auth, Die Abtreibung. Anfange der Krihwalisierung, 1140-1650, Bohlall, (Cologne, Weimar) 00. **CONTACT ADDRESS** Dept Hist, Fordham Univ, Bronx, NY 10458. **EMAIL** wpmueller@aol.com

MUHLBERGER, STEVEN
DISCIPLINE HISTORY **EDUCATION** Mich State Univ, BA, 72; Univ Toronto, MA, 74, PhD, 81. **CAREER** Asst prof, 89-93 to assoc prof, 93-, Nipissing Univ; asst prof, Trent Univ, Peterborough, Ont & Brock Univ, St Catharines, Ont, 88-89; asst prof, Univ Toronto, 82-84 and 85-88. **SELECTED PUBLICATIONS** Auth, The Fifth-Century Chroniclers: Prosper, Hydatius and the Chronicler of 452, Francis Cairns Publications, Ltd, 90; War, Warlords and Christian Historians from the Fifth to the Seventh Century, After Rome's Fall: Narratives and Sources of Early Medieval Hist, Univ Toronto Press, 98; Eugippius and the Life of St Severinus, Medieval Prosopography 17, 96; Looking back from from mid-century: The Gallic Chronicler of 452 and the crisis of Honorius' reign, Fifth-Century Gaul: A Crisis of Identity, Cambridge UP, 92; coauth, Democracy's Place in World History, J World Hist 4, 93. **CONTACT ADDRESS** Dept of History, Nipissing Univ, 100 College Dr, Box 5002, North Bay, ON, Canada P1B 8L7. **EMAIL** stevem@einstein.unipissing.ca

MUIR, EDWARD
PERSONAL Born 12/02/1946, Cambridge, MA, d **DISCIPLINE** HISTORY **EDUCATION** Univ Utah, BA, 64; Rutgers Univ, MA, 70, PhD, 75. **CAREER** Asst prof, Stockton State Col, 73-77; asst to assoc prof, Syracuse Univ, 77-86; assoc to prof, La State Univ, 86-93; Clarence L Ver Steng Prof Arts, Scis, Northwestern Univ, 93-. **HONORS AND AWARDS** Herbert Baxter Adams Prize, 82; Howard R Marraro Prize, 82, 93; Harold J Grimm Prize, 89. **MEMBERSHIPS** AHA; Renaissance Soc Am; Soc Italian Hist Stud. **RESEARCH** Italian Renaissance **SELECTED PUBLICATIONS** Auth, Mad Blood Stirring: Vendetta and Factions in Friuli during the Renaissance, Johns Hopkins Univ, 93; auth, The Italian Renaissance in America, Am Hist Rev 100, 95; auth, Ritual in Early Modern Europe, Cambridge Univ Press, 97. **CONTACT ADDRESS** Dept Hist, Northwestern Univ, 1881 Sheridan Rd, Evanston, IL 60208-2220. **EMAIL** e-muir@northwestern.edu

MUIR, MALCOLM, JR
PERSONAL Born 04/24/1943, Williamsport, PA, m, 1965, 2 children **DISCIPLINE** HISTORY, PHILOSOPHY **EDUCATION** Emory Univ, BA, 65; Fla St Univ, MA, 66; Ohio St Univ, PhD, 76. **CAREER** From asst prof to chemn, 77-; Austin Peay State Univ; SecNay Res Ch, Naval Hist Ctr, 87-88; vis prof, US Military Acad, 88-90; vis prof, Air War Col, 96-97. **HONORS AND AWARDS** Outstanding Civilian Serv Medal, U S Dept of the Army, 90; Richard M Hawkins Awd, 92; John Lyman Prize, N Am Soc for Oceanic Hist, 96; Larry Rowen Remele Awd, 99; Phi Alpha Theta; Phi Kappa Phi. **MEMBERSHIPS** Hist Soc, Nat Asn of Scholars. **SELECTED PUBLICATIONS** Auth, rev, 49 articles, entries and essays and 34 book rev; auth, The Iowa-Class Battleships: Iowa, New Jersey, Missouri and Wisconsin, Blandford Pr (Dorset, UK), 87; auth, Black Shoes and Blue Water: Surface Warfare in the United States Navy 1945-1975, Naval Hist Ctr (Washington, DC), 96. **CONTACT ADDRESS** Dept Hist & Philos, Austin Peay State Univ, 601 College St, Clarksville, TN 37044-0001. **EMAIL** muirm@apsu.edu

MUISE, D. A.
DISCIPLINE HISTORY **EDUCATION** Carleton Univ, MA, 64; Univ W Ontario, PhD, 70. **CAREER** Prof. **RESEARCH** Social and economic history of the Maritime Province; Hist of coal mining in Nova Scotia. **SELECTED PUBLICATIONS** Auth, "The Greatest Transformation: Changing the Urban Surface of Nova Scotia, 1871-1921," Nova Scotia Historical Review, 91; ed, "Iron Men? Yarmouth's Seamen in Tradition, 1871-1921," in Collin Howell, ed., Jack Tar At Wrok: Proceedings of the Jack Tar Conference, (Federiction: Acadiensis Univ Press, 91); ed, "The Industiral context of Inequality: Female Participation in Nova Scotia's Paid Workforce, 1871-1921," Acadiensis XX, 2, 91; ed, Urbanization in Atlantic Canada, 1867-1991: Demographic Change and Community Development, Canadian Museum of Civilization , Mercury Series, 93; ed, The Atlantic Provinces in Confederation, with E.R. Forbes, Toronto: Univ of Toronto Press and Acadiensis Press, 93; auth, Coal Mining in Canada: A Historical and Comparative Study, with Robert McIntosh, Ottawa: National Museum of Science and Technology, 96. **CONTACT ADDRESS** Dept of Hist, Carleton Univ, 1125 Colonel By Dr, Ottawa, ON, Canada K1S 5B6. **EMAIL** dmuise@ccs.carleton.ca

MULCAHEY, DONALD C.
DISCIPLINE HISTORY **EDUCATION** St. Paul Seminary, BA; Catholic Univ Am, MA, PhD; Univ Baltimore, JD. **CAREER** Assoc dir, Evening and Summer Prog, Towson State Univ, 71-74; Dean Col Continuing Educ, Univ Baltimore, 74-76; Assoc prof, dept hist & philos, 76-85; Dir Master of Arts in Legal Studies, 85-91, 95-; prof, Division of Legal, Ethical, Hist Studies, 86-; Dir, Jurisprudence Major, 83-85; 92-94. **MEMBERSHIPS** Baltimore County Bar Asn; Past & Present Univ Comt Mem; Provost's Task Force on Curriculum; Fac Mediation Commt; Provost's Commt Ethics Curriculum; Univ Acad Integrity Comt; Univ Fac Appeals Comt. **SELECTED PUBLICATIONS** Coauth, Advertising: Ethical Reflections, Md Hum, 96. **CONTACT ADDRESS** Univ of Baltimore, 1420 N. Charles Street, Baltimore, MD 21201.

MULCAHY, RICHARD P.
PERSONAL Born 03/18/1958, Greensburg, PA, m, 1987 **DISCIPLINE** HISTORY **EDUCATION** St Vincent Col, BA, 80; Duquesne Univ, MA, 82; Univ Pitt, MA, 85; West Virginia Univ, PhD, 88. **CAREER** Lectr, West Virginia, 88-89; asst' prof, UPT, 89-95; assoc prof, 95-; div dir, 97-, Univ Pitts Titusville. **HONORS AND AWARDS** Fac Appt, Chautauqua Inst, 95-99; Fel, CNAS; Grad, CSLA, Chautauqua Inst, 99; Who's Who Am, 01; Who's Who East, 98-99. **MEMBERSHIPS** ASA; AFT; AAUP. **RESEARCH** Labor relations; social policy and health care delivery; McCarthyism; Appalachia and the Bituminous coal industry. **SELECTED PUBLICATIONS** Auth, A Social Contract for the Coal Fields: The Rise and Fall of the UMWA Welfare & Retirement Fund, 1946 - 1978 (Knoxville: Univ of Tenn Press, 00); auth, "A New Deal for Coal Miners: The UMWA Welfare and Retirement Fund, and the Reorganization of Health Care Delivery in Appalachia," J Appalachian Stud 1 (96), 29-52; auth, "A Full Circle: Advocacy and Academic Freedom in Crisis," in Advocacy in the Classroom: Problems and Possibilities, ed. Patricia Meyer Spacks (NY, Saint Martin's Press, 96), 142-160; auth, "Replacing the Company Doctor: Pruden Valley, Tennessee and the Development of the Miners Clinics," Tennessee Medicine: J Tennessee Medical Asn 92 (99) 91-95; auth, "Law, Civil Liberties and Civil Rights on the World Wide Web," in History Highway Two-thousand: A Guide to History Sites on the Internet, ed. Dennis Trinkle (NY, ME, Sharp & Co., 99), 332-336; auth, "Imre Nagy: Father of the Soviet Collapse," in Hungary's Historical Legacies: Studies in Honor of Steven Bela Vardy, eds. Dennis Hupchick, R William Weisberg (Boulder: East European Monographs, Columbia Univ Press, 99), 187-9; auth, "Mining & Extraction in Nineteenth Century America," The Encyclopedia of Nineteenth Century American History (NY, Charles Scribner's Sons, Forthcoming). **CONTACT ADDRESS** Dept Social Sci, Univ of Pittsburgh, Titusville, Titusville, PA 16354.

MULDER, JOHN MARK
PERSONAL Born 03/20/1946, Chicago, IL, m, 1968, 2 children **DISCIPLINE** AMERICAN CHURCH HISTORY **EDUCATION** Hope Col, AB, 67; Princeton Theol Sem, MDiv, 70; Princeton Univ, PhD, 74. **CAREER** From ed asst to asst ed, Papers of Woodrow Wilson, 71-74; instr Am church hist, Princeton Theol Sem, 74-75, asst prof, 75-80, assoc prof, 80-81; Pres, Louisville Presby theol sem, 81-, Asst ed, Theology Today, 69-; fels hist, Asn Theol Schs in US & Can, 76 & Am Coun Learned Soc, 77. **HONORS AND AWARDS** D.Th, Institut de Portestant Theologie, Montpellier, 96; D D, Hanover College, 96; L H D, Bellarmine College, 90; D D, Rhodes College, 84; L H D, Centre College, 84. **MEMBERSHIPS** AHA; Orgn Am Historians; Am Soc Church Hist; Presby Hist Soc; Am Acad Relig. **RESEARCH** Woodrow Wilson; relig and polit in Am; relig in the Revolutionary and early national periods; 20th century Am relig. **SELECTED PUBLICATIONS** Coed, The Mainstream Protestand Decline: The Presbyterian Pattern, Louisville: Westminster/John Knox Press, 90; coed, The Presbyterian Predicament: Six Perspectives, Louisville: Westminster/John Knox Press, 90; coed, The Confessional Mosaic: Presbyterians in Twentieth-Century Theology, Lousiville: Westminster/John Knox Press, 91; coed, The Organizational Revolution: Presbyterians and American Denominationalism, Louisville: Westminster/John Knox Press, 91; coed, The Diversity of Discipleship: Presbyterians in Twentieth-Century Christian Witness, Louisville: Westminster/John Knox Press, 91; auth, Sealed in Christ: The Symbolism of th Seal of the Presbyterian Church U S A, Louisville: Presbyterian Publishing House, 91; coed, The Pluralistic Vision: Presbyterians in Mainstream Protestant Education and Leadership, Louisville: Westminster/John Knox Press, 92; coauth, the Re-forming Tradition: Presbyterians and Mainstream Protestantism, Louisville: Westminster/John Knox Press, 92; coauth, Vital Signs: The Promise of Mainstream Protestantism, Grand Rapides, Mich: Wm B Eerdmans, 95; coed, Woodrow Wilson: A Bibliography, Greenwood Press, 97. **CONTACT ADDRESS** Louisville Presbyterian Theol Sem, 1044 Alta Vista Rd, Louisville, KY 40205-1758. **EMAIL** jmmulder@lpts.edu

MULLANEY, MARIE
PERSONAL Born 09/21/1953, Newark, NJ, m, 1977, 3 children **DISCIPLINE** HISTORY **EDUCATION** Seton Hall Univ, BA, 75; Rutgers Univ, MA, 77, PhD, 80 **CAREER** Prof, 80-, dept chair, Caldwell Col **HONORS AND AWARDS** Danforth Fel, 75-80; steering com chair **MEMBERSHIPS** Am hist Asn; Nat Asn of Scholars **RESEARCH** Hist of Feminism **SELECTED PUBLICATIONS** Auth, Revolutionary Women: Gender and the Socialist Revolutionary Role, New York: Praeger, 83; Biographical Directory of the Governors of the United States, 1988-1994, Westport, Ct: Greenwood Press, 94 **CONTACT ADDRESS** Dept of Hist and Political Sci, Caldwell Col, 9 Ryerson Ave., Caldwell, NJ 07006. **EMAIL** mmullane@caldwell.edu

MULLEN, PIERCE C.
PERSONAL Born 03/04/1934, Hastings, NE, m, 1958, 2 children **DISCIPLINE** HISTORY OF SCIENCE **EDUCATION** Hastings Col, BA, 57; Univ Nebr, Lincoln, MA, 58; Univ Calif, Berkeley, PhD(hist), 64. **CAREER** Asst prof hist, San Francisco State Col, 63; from asst prof to assoc prof, 63-72, Prof hist, Mont State Univ, 72-96; prof emer, 96-. **MEMBERSHIPS** Hist Sci Soc. **RESEARCH** History of biology and medicine. **SELECTED PUBLICATIONS** Auth, The scientist as romantic: Lorenz Oken, Studies in Romanticism, 77; Educating In The American-West - 100 Years At Lewis-Clark-State-College, 1893-1993 - Petersen,K, Pacific Northwest Quarterly, Vol 0085, 1994; Commemoration - Burlingame,Merrill,G. 1901-1994, Montana-The Magazine Of Western History, Vol 0045, 1995; Roeder,Richard,B., 1930-1995 - In Commemoration, Montana-The Magazine Of Western History, Vol 0046, 1996; prof. Emeritus of Hist, 96-. **CONTACT ADDRESS** Dept of Hist, Montana State Univ, Bozeman, Bozeman, MT 59715. **EMAIL** pierce@montana.campuscwix.net

MULLER, EDWARD K.
PERSONAL Born 03/03/1943, Pittsburgh, PA **DISCIPLINE** AMERICAN HISTORY, HISTORICAL GEOGRAPHY **EDUCATION** Dartmouth Col, BA, 65; Univ Wis-Madison, MA, 68, PhD(geog), 72. **CAREER** Lectr geog, Univ Md, College Park, 70-72, asst prof, 72-77; Assoc Prof Hist, Univ Pittsburgh, 77-, Dir, Urban Studies, 78-. **MEMBERSHIPS** Asn Am Geogr; Social Sci Hist Asn. **RESEARCH** United States urban history; United States frontier settlement; United States settlement landscape. **SELECTED PUBLICATIONS** **CONTACT ADDRESS** Dept of Hist, Univ of Pittsburgh, 3p38 Forbes Quad, Pittsburgh, PA 15260-0001.

MULLER, JERRY Z.
PERSONAL Born 06/07/1954, Niagara Falls, ON, Canada, m, 1976, 3 children **DISCIPLINE** HISTORY **EDUCATION** Columbia Univ, PhD, 84. **CAREER** Asst prof to prof, Catholic Univ of Am, 84-. **HONORS AND AWARDS** Shepard Clough Diss Prize; ACLS Fel; Bradley Found Fel; Olin Found Fel. **MEMBERSHIPS** AHA; GSA; ISIH; Hist Soc. **RESEARCH** Modern European intellectual history. **SELECTED PUBLICATIONS** Auth, Conservatism: An Anthology of Social and Political Thought from David Hume to the Present, Princeton UP (97); co-ed, "The Politics of Cultural Despair Revisited," in Fritz Stern at Seventy: An Appreciation (Washington Ger Hist Inst, 97); auth, Adam Smith in His Time and Ours: Designing the Decent Society, Free Press, 93, softcover, Princeton UP, 95; auth, "Communism, Anti-Semitism, and the Jews," Commentary (88): 28-39. **CONTACT ADDRESS** Dept History, Catholic Univ of America, 620 Michigan Ave NE, Washington, DC 20064-0001. **EMAIL** mullerj@cua.edu

MULLER, PETER O.
PERSONAL Born 05/10/1942, England, m, 1966, 2 children **DISCIPLINE** GEOGRAPHY **EDUCATION** Rutgers Univ, PhD, 71. **CAREER** Asst prof, geog, Villanova Univ, 66-70; asst to assoc prof, Temple Univ, 70-80; Prpf/Chp, Geog, Univ Miami, 80-. **HONORS AND AWARDS** Phi Beta Kappa, 63; Urban Land Inst Fel, 88-94. **MEMBERSHIPS** Asn Am Geogs; Am Geog Soc. **RESEARCH** Urban geography; Economic geography **SELECTED PUBLICATIONS** coauth, "Beyond the Beltway: Suburban Downtowns in Northern Virginia," in the Capital Region, Rutgers Univ Pr, 92; coauth, "The Suburban Downtown and Urban Economic Development Today, in Sources of Metropolitan Growth, Rutgers Univ, 92; ed, "Transportation and Urban Form: Stages in the Spatial Evolution of the American Metropolis," in The Geog of Urban Transp, Guilford Press, 95; coauth, Physical Geography of the Global Environment, John Wiley & Sons, 96; auth, "The Suburban Transformation of the Globalizing American City," in Annals of the Am Acad of Polit Soc Sci, 97; coauth, Geography: Realms, Regions, and Concepts, John Wiley & Sons, 98; coauth, Economic Geography, John Wiley & Sons, 98. **CONTACT ADDRESS** Dept Geog, Univ of Miami, Po Box 8067, Coral Gables, FL 33124-2060. **EMAIL** pmuller@miami.edu

MULLER, PRISCILLA ELKOW
PERSONAL Born 02/15/1930, New York, NY, m **DISCIPLINE** ART HISTORY **EDUCATION** Brooklyn Col, BA, 51; NYork Univ, MA, 59, PhD(art hist), 63. **CAREER** Asst cur metalwork, 64-68, lectr, Brooklyn Col, 66; Cur Paintings & Metalwork, Hispanic Soc Am, 68-, Cur Mus, 70-, Cur Emer, 95. **HONORS AND AWARDS** Elected mem Real Acad de Ciencias, Bellas Letras y Nobles Artes de Cordoba; elected mem Real Acad de Bellas Artes de San Fernando; elected mem The Hispanic Soc of Am. **MEMBERSHIPS** Am Soc Hispanic Art Hist Studies; Int Found Art Res; Asn Latin Am Art. **RESEARCH** Spanish painting; graphic arts; metalwork. **SELECTED PUBLICATIONS** Auth, The Prophet David by Francisco Pacheco, Art Bull, 63; Francisco Pacheco as a Painter, Marsyas, 63; The Drawings of Antonio del Castillo, 64; Goya's The Family of Charles IV, Apollo, 70; coauth, Francisco Goya's Portraits, 72; auth, Jewels in Spain, 1500-1800, 72; Sorolla in America, Am Artist, 74; Francisco Bayeu, Tiepolo La Granja, Pantheon, 77; auth, Goya's Black Paintings: Truth and Reason in Light and Liberty, 84; auth, "Sorolla y Huntington," Sorolla y la Hisp Soc (98). **CONTACT ADDRESS** Hispanic Society of America, 613 W 155th St, New York, NY 10032. **EMAIL** muller@hispanicsociety.org

MULLIGAN, WILLIAM
PERSONAL Born 04/10/1948, Brooklyn, NY, d, 2 children **DISCIPLINE** HISTORY **EDUCATION** Assumption Col, AB, 70; Clark Univ, AM, 73; PhD, 82. **CAREER** Historian, Am Revolution Bicentennial Comm, 74-75; conf leader, Worcester Polytechnic Inst, 74-77; asst to dir, Mills-Hagley Foundation, 77-82; adj prof to asst prof, Cent Mich Univ, 82-90; asst to assoc prof, Murray State Univ, 93-. **HONORS AND AWARDS** NDEA Fel. **MEMBERSHIPS** Nat Coun of Pub Hist, KY Asn of Museums, KY Hist Soc, Hist Soc of Mich, George Wright Soc. **RESEARCH** Irish Immigration to the Us, Interpretation of historic sites, family during industrialization. **SELECTED PUBLICATIONS** Auth, The Family and Technological Change: The Shoemakers of Lynn Massachusetts during the Tansition from Hand to Machine Production, 1850-18880, New York, (forthcoming); auth, "Michigan in the Great Depression: The Dream Lost, The Dream Reclaimed" in Michigan Remembered: Photographs from the Farm Services Administration and the Office of War Information, (forthcoming); coed, "Sacred Ground: Preserving America's Civil War Heritage", 98; ed, "Preservation and Interpretation of Historic Sites, Landscapes, and Environments," 94;. **CONTACT ADDRESS** Dept History, Murray State Univ, 1 Murray St, Murray, KY 42071-3300. **EMAIL** bill.mulligan@murraystate.edu

MULLIN, ROBERT BRUCE
PERSONAL Born 10/24/1953, Plainfield, NJ, m, 1960, 1 child **DISCIPLINE** RELIGIOUS HISTORY **EDUCATION** Col of William & Mary, AB, 75; Yale Divinity School, MAR, 79; Yale Univ, PhD. **CAREER** Instr, Yale Univ, 84-85; asst prof to prof, North Carolina State Univ, 85-98; Sprl Prof of Hist & World Mission, General Theological Seminary, 98-. **MEMBERSHIPS** AAR; ASCH; Hist Soc of the Episcopal Church. **RESEARCH** American religious history; modern intellectual history; Anglicanism. **SELECTED PUBLICATIONS** Auth, Episcopal Vision/American Reality: High Church Theology and Social Thought in Evangelical America, Yale Univ Press, 86; The Scientific Theist: A Life of Francis Ellingwood Abbot, Mercer Univ Press, 87; Moneygripe's Apprentice: The Personal

Narrative of Samuel Seabury III, Yale Univ Press, 89; Reimaging Denominationalism: Interpretive Essays, Oxford Univ Press, 94; Miracles and the Modern Religious Imagination, Yale Univ Press, 96. **CONTACT ADDRESS** General Theol Sem, 175 Ninth Ave, New York, NY 10011-4977. **EMAIL** mullin@gts.edu

MULTHAUF, ROBERT PHILLIP
PERSONAL Born 06/08/1919, Sioux Falls, SD, m, 1948 **DISCIPLINE** HISTORY OF SCIENCE **EDUCATION** Iowa State Col, BS, 41; Univ Calif, MA, 50, PhD(hist), 53. **CAREER** Chem engr, Hercules Powder Co, 41-42, US Rubber Co, 42-43 & US Govt, Japan, 46-48; from cur div eng to head cur dept sci & technol, US Nat Mus, 54-67, dir mus hist & technol, 67-69, Sr Researcher Mus Hist & Techol, Smithsonian Inst, 70-, Fel, Inst Hist Med, Johns Hopkins Univ, 53-54; prof lectr, George Washington Univ, 64-; ed, Isis, Hist Sci Soc, 64-. **MEMBERSHIPS** AHA; Hist Sci Soc; Soc Hist Technol. **RESEARCH** History of chemistry and technology. **SELECTED PUBLICATIONS** Auth, Catalogue of instruments and models, Am Philos Soc; The origins of chemistry, Oldbourne, London, 67; Neptune's Gift: A History of Common Salt, Johns Hopkins Univ, 78; Science Has No National Borders - Kelly,Harry,C. And The Reconstruction Of Science And Technology In Postwar Japan - Yoshikawa,H, Kauffman,J, Technology And Culture, Vol 0036, 1995; Science And Civilization In China, Vol 5, Chemistry And Chemical-Technology .6. Military Technology - Missiles And Sieges - Needham,J, Yates,Rds, Technology And Culture, Vol 0037, 1996. **CONTACT ADDRESS** Mus of Hist & Technol, Smithsonian Inst, Washington, DC 20560.

MUMFORD, ERIC
PERSONAL Born 07/14/1958, Sandusky, OH, m, 1989, 1 child **DISCIPLINE** ARCHITECTURAL HISTORY & THEORY **EDUCATION** Princeton Univ, PhD, 96. **CAREER** Adjunct asst prof, Columbia Univ Sch of Archit, 90-93; visiting lectr, Harvard Grad Sch of Design, 95-96; asst prof of archit hist and theory, Wash Univ Sch of Archit, 94-. **HONORS AND AWARDS** Graham Found grant, 97; Butler prize, Princeton Univ, 92. **MEMBERSHIPS** ACSA; SAH. **RESEARCH** Architecture, 1880-present; Urban design. **SELECTED PUBLICATIONS** Auth, "CIAM Urbanism After the Athens Charter, Planning Perspectives, 7 (92): 391-417; auth, "The Tower in a Park in America: Theory and Practice 1920-1960", Planning Perspectives 10 (95); auth, Dictionnaire de l'architecture moderne et comtemporaine, Paris, 96, Encyclopedia of Twentieth Century Architecture (Chicago, forthcoming); 17-41; auth, "CIAM and Latin America/Els CIAM I America Llatina, Sert: Arquitecte a Nova York", Barcelona (97); auth, "CIAM Discourse on Urbanism", MIT Press, 00. **CONTACT ADDRESS** Sch of Archit, Washington Univ, 1 Brookings Dr., Campus Box 1079, Saint Louis, MO 63130. **EMAIL** epm@arch.wustl.edu

MUNDY, JOHN HINE
PERSONAL Born 12/29/1917, London, England, m, 1942, 2 children **DISCIPLINE** HISTORY **EDUCATION** Columbia Univ, BA, 40,MA, 41, PhD(hist), 50. **CAREER** Instr hist, Shrivenham Army Univ, Eng, 45 & NY Univ, 46; instr gen studies, 47-50, asst prof, 50-52, asst prof, Barnard Col, 52-56, assoc prof grad sch, 56-62, Prof Hist, Columbia Univ, 62-, Guggenheim Mem Found fel, 77-78; Am Acad Arts & Sci fel, 81. **MEMBERSHIPS** AHA; fel Mediaeval Acad Am. **RESEARCH** Medieval urban, military and ecclesiastical history. **SELECTED PUBLICATIONS** Auth, Liberty and Political Power in Toulouse, 1050-1230, Columbia Univ, 54; coauth, The Medieval Town, Van Nostrand, 58; The Council of Constance, Columbia Univ, 61; co-ed, Essays in Honor of Austin P Evans; auth, Charity and Social Work in Toulouse, 1100-1250, Traditio, 66; Europe in the High Middle Ages: 1150-1309, Longmans Canada & Basic Bks, 73. **CONTACT ADDRESS** Columbia Univ, 621 Fayerweather Hall, New York, NY 10027.

MUNGELLO, DAVID EMIL
PERSONAL Born 11/20/1943, Washington, PA, m, 1966, 2 children **DISCIPLINE** CHINESE & EUROPEAN HISTORY **EDUCATION** George Washington Univ, AB, 65; Univ Calif, Berkeley, MA, 69, PhD(hist), 73. **CAREER** Asst prof Chinese studies, Lingnan Col, 73-74; asst prof hist & relig, Briarcliff Col, 74-77; Humboldt res fel, Leibniz Arch, Niedersachsische Landesbibliot, Hannover, 78-80; Asst Prof Hist, Coe Col, 80-, Ed, China Mission Studies (1550-1800) Bull, 80- **MEMBERSHIPS** Leibniz Ges **RESEARCH** Confucianism; Western interpretations of Confucianism; Sin- Western cultural contacts. **SELECTED PUBLICATIONS** Auth, Neo-Confucianism and Wen-Jen aesthetic theory, 69 & On the significance of the question: Did China have science?, 72-73, Philos E & W; Reconciliation of neo-Confucianism with Christianity in writings of J Premare, Philos E & W, 76; Leibniz and Confucianism: The Search for Accord, Univ Press Hawaii, 77; Seventeenth century missionary interpretations of Confucianism, Philos E & W, 78; On understanding the confluence of Chinese & western intellectual history, J Hist Ideas, 79; auth, Malebranche and Chinese philosophy, J Hist Ideas, 80; Jesuits' use of Chang Chu-cheng (Zhang Juzheng's) commentary in their translation of the Confucian four Books (1687), China Mission Studies (1550-1800) Bull, 81. **CONTACT ADDRESS** Dept of Hist, Coe Col, Cedar Rapids, IA 52402.

MUNHOLLAND, JOHN KIM
DISCIPLINE HISTORY **EDUCATION** Princeton Univ, MA, 61; PhD, 64. **RESEARCH** Twentieth-century and modern French history; U.S.-French cultural conflicts during WWII. **SELECTED PUBLICATIONS** Auth, Origins of Contemporary Europe, 70; The Trials of the Free French in New Caledonia, 1940-1942, 86; The French Army and Intervention in Ukraine, 88; World War II and the End of Indentured Labor in New Caledonia, 91; L'image traditionnelle de la France et politique des Etats-Unis vers Charles de Gaulle, 1940-1944, 92; The United States and the Free French, 94; Wartime France: Remembering Vichy, 94; Michaud's Histoire des croisade and the French Crusade in Algeria, 94. **CONTACT ADDRESS** History Dept, Univ of Minnesota, Twin Cities, 614 Social Sciences Tower, 267 19th Ave. S, Minneapolis, MN 55455. **EMAIL** munho001@tc.umn.edu

MUNIR, FAREED Z.
DISCIPLINE ISLAMIC STUDIES **EDUCATION** Univ PA, BA 81; Temple Univ, MA, 88, PhD, 93. **CAREER** Tchg asst, Temple Univ, 88-92; instr, Rowan Col, 91-92; lectr, Thomas Jefferson, Univ Philadelphia, 91-92; instr, Commun Col, 90-92; Philadelphia Hea Counr, 80-92; Camden VCh & mem, City Plan Bd, 82-90; VChp, Human Rights Comt, 96-; mem, Human Rights Comt, 93-, Bd Instr, 94-96, Multicultural Comt, 95-, Search Comt app Dean of the Arts Div, 94-95 & Search Comt app Dir Multicultural Aff, 95-95; internal Rd, Self Stud Report Marketing and Managing Dept, 95; fac adv, Higher Educ Opportunity Prog, 93-, Black and Latino Stud Union, 93- & Freshman stud Arts Div. **MEMBERSHIPS** Am Acad Rel; Islam in Am Conf; Am Coun for the Study of Islamic Soc(s); Muslim Stud Asn of Can & Namerica; Nat Asn Self-Instral Lang Prog; Bonfils Sem. **SELECTED PUBLICATIONS** Auth, Malcolm Xes Religious Pilgrimage: An African American Muslim Transition from Black Separation to Universalism, Westminster John Knox Press, 96; rev, The Muslim Almanac: A Reference Work on the History,Faith, Culture, and Peoples of Islam, Multicultural Rev, 96; other, Martin and Malcolm: Two Sides of the Same Coin, The Times Union, 95. **CONTACT ADDRESS** Dept of Relig Studies, Siena Col, 515 Loudon Rd., Loudonville, NY 12211-1462.

MUNN, MARK H.
PERSONAL m, 2 children **DISCIPLINE** ANCIENT HISTORY (GREEK) **EDUCATION** Univ Calif, BA, 74; Univ Penn, PhD, 83. **CAREER** Asst prof, classics, Stanford Univ, 83-92; asst prof, history, Univ Calif-Santa Barbara, 94-95; asst prof, 95-98, ASSOC PROF, HISTORY AND CLASSICAL AND ANCIENT MEDITER STUDIES, PENN STATE UNIV, 98-. **SELECTED PUBLICATIONS** Auth, The Defense of Attica: The Dema Wall and Boiotian War 378-375 B.C., Univ Calif Press, 93; auth, The School of History: Athens in the Age of Socrates, Univ Calif Press, 00. **CONTACT ADDRESS** Department of History and CAMS, Pennsylvania State Univ, Univ Park, Weaver Bldg, University Park, PA 16802-5500. **EMAIL** mxm20@psu.edu

MUNROE, JOHN ANDREW
PERSONAL Born 03/15/1914, Wilmington, DE, m, 1945, 3 children **DISCIPLINE** AMERICAN HISTORY **EDUCATION** Univ Del, AB, 36, AM, 41; Univ Pa, PhD, 47. **CAREER** From instr to prof, 42-, alumni secy, 43-45, asst to dean arts & sci, 49-51, chm dept hist, 52-69, Sharp Prof Hist, Univ Del, 62-, **HONORS AND AWARDS** Phi Kappa Phi; Phi Beta Kappa; Fund Advan Educ fel, 51-52; vis prof, Univ Wis, 60; mem hist adv comt, Eleutherian Mills-Hagley Found, 62-64 & 65-68, trustee, 73-93. **MEMBERSHIPS** AHA; Org Am Historians; Soc Hist of Early Am Repub. **RESEARCH** Revolutionary and early national periods. **SELECTED PUBLICATIONS** Auth, Nonresident Representation in the Continental Congress, William & Mary Quart, 4/52; Federalist Delaware, 1775-1815, Rutgers Univ, 54; ed, Timoleon's Biographical History of Dionysius, Tyrant of Delaware, Univ Del, 58; auth, Delaware, a Student's Guide to Localized History, Columbia Univ, 65; Louis McLane, Federalist and Jacksonian, Rutgers Univ, 74; ed, Delaware History, Hist Soc Del, 69-95; auth, Colonial Delaware, KTO, 78; History of Delaware, Univ Del, 79, 3d ed, 93; coauth, Books, Bricks and Bibliophiles: The University of Delaware Library, Delaware, 84; auth, The University of Delaware: A History, Delaware, 86. **CONTACT ADDRESS** 215 Cheltenham Rd, Newark, DE 19711. **EMAIL** jmunroe@udel.edu

MUNSELL, FLOYD DARRELL
PERSONAL Born 12/30/1934, Gorham, KS, m, 1962, 1 child **DISCIPLINE** BRITISH AND MODERN EUROPEAN HISTORY **EDUCATION** Ft Hays Kans State Col, BA, 57, MA, 60; Univ Kans, PhD(hist), 67. **CAREER** Asst prof, 65-66, assoc prof, 66-78, prof hist, 78-97 West Texas A & M Univ. **HONORS AND AWARDS** Phi Alpha Theta; Pi Sigma Alpha; fac res award, 86. **MEMBERSHIPS** N Am Conf on British Stud; SW Conf on British Stud; SW Social Sci Asn; Consortium on Revolutionary Europe. **RESEARCH** Early and mid-Victorian England; Crimean War; Irish famine; Peelite Party (Gt Britain); Liberal Party (Gt Britain). **SELECTED PUBLICATIONS** Auth, The Unfortunate Duke: Henry Pelham, Fifth Duke of Newcastle, 1811-1864, Missouri, 85; contribur, Mitchell, ed, Victorian Britain: An Encyclopedia, Garland, 88; auth, The Victorian Controversy Surrounding the Wellington War Memorial: The Archduke of Hyde Park Corner, Edwin Mellen, 91. **CONTACT ADDRESS** PO Box 1485, Carbondale, CO 81623. **EMAIL** dmunsell@snowcap.net

MURDOCH, JAMES MURRAY
PERSONAL Born 07/08/1937, Belpre, OH, m, 1958, 2 children **DISCIPLINE** EARLY AMERICAN HISTORY **EDUCATION** Baptist Bible Col, BTh, 60; Northwestern Univ, Evanston, MA, 62, PhD, 71. **CAREER** Teaching asst Western civilization, Northwestern Univ, 63-64, lectr, 64-65; instr Am hist, Jewish Theol Sem Am, 64-65; assoc prof, 65-70; prof hist, Cedarville Col, 70-, coordr interdisplinary stud, 72-, chemn soc sci dept, 74-; lectr, Ohio Bicentennial Comn, 73-76. **MEMBERSHIPS** AHA; Orgn Am Historians; Conf Faith & Hist; Southern Hist Soc. **RESEARCH** Early 19th century history. **SELECTED PUBLICATIONS** Auth, Portrait of Obedience: A Biography of R T Ketcham, Regular Baptist Press, Chicago, 79; auth, A Century of Commitment, commissioned by Cedarville Col, Cedarville, 87. **CONTACT ADDRESS** Dept of History, Cedarville Col, PO Box 601, Cedarville, OH 45314-0601. **EMAIL** murdochm@cedarville.edu

MURDOCH, NORMAN H.
PERSONAL Born 05/15/1939, DuBois, PA, m, 1966, 3 children **DISCIPLINE** HISTORY **EDUCATION** Asbury Col, BA, 61; MDiv, 65; Univ Cincinnati, MEd, 68; MTh, 71; MA, 75; PhD, 85. **CAREER** Instr to prof, Univ of Cincinnati, 68-. **HONORS AND AWARDS** Phi Delta Kappa; Brodie Fel, 86; Ratcliff Awd, AAUP, 95; Fac Achievement Awd, Univ of Cincinnati, 96; Prof Scholarship Awd, Univ of Cincinnati, 99. **MEMBERSHIPS** AAUP; Am Soc of Church Hist; Oral Hist Assoc; Assoc of Third World Studies; Fides et Historia; Wesleyan Theol Soc; Ohio Acad of Hist. **RESEARCH** Salvation Army History, History of Southern Africa, the Historical Jesus, Oral History. **SELECTED PUBLICATIONS** Auth, "1787 US Constitution Ratification Debate: Federalist vs Anti-Federalist", OH Hist Comm, (88); auth, "William Booth's In Darkest England and the Way Out: A Reappraisal", Wesleyan Theol J 25.1 (90): 106-16; auth, "Anti-Saloon League", Political Parties and Elections in the United States: An Encyclopedia, ed Sandy Maisel, Garland, 91; auth, "Rose Culture and Social Reform: Edward Bellamy's Looking Backward (1888) and William Booth's Darkest England and the Way Out (1890)", Utopian Studies 3.2 (92): 91-101; auth, "From Militancy to Social Mission: The Salvation Army and Street Disturbances in Liverpool, 1879-1887", Popular Politics, Riot and Labour: Essays in Liverpool History, 1790-1940, ed John Belcham, Liverpool Univ Pr, (92): 160-72; auth, Origins of the Salvation Army, Univ of Tenn Pr, (Knowville), 94; auth, "Christian Heroes and Heroines - William Booth: The General and Catherine Booth: The Army Mother", Cross Point, (95): 32-39; auth, "Female Ministry in the Thought and Work of Catherine Booth", American Church History: A Reader, ed Henry Warner Bowden and PC Kemeny, Abingdon Pr, (Nashville, 98): 337-45; auth, History of the University College, University of Cincinnati, Part I, 1957-1970; Murdochistoria web site, 98; auth, "Colonialism, Conciliarism and Communism: Case Study of a Church-State Struggle in Zimbabwe", Rendering Unto Caesar: An Appraisal of the Theory and Practice of Mission-State Encounter, 1792-1992, ed Wilbert R Shenk, Mentor Univ Pr, (forthcoming). **CONTACT ADDRESS** Dept Hist, Univ of Cincinnati, PO Box 210373, Cincinnati, OH 45221-0373. **EMAIL** norman.murdoch@uc.edu

MURPHEY, MURRAY GRIFFIN
PERSONAL Born 02/22/1928, Colorado Springs, CO, 3 children **DISCIPLINE** AMERICAN CIVILIZATION **EDUCATION** Harvard Univ, AB, 49; Yale Univ, PhD, 54. **CAREER** Fel, 54-56, from asst prof to assoc prof, 56-67, Prof Am Civilization, Univ PA, 67-, Fulbright fel, Cambridge, 53-54; Rockefeller fel, 54-56. **MEMBERSHIPS** AHA; Am Studies Asn; Peirce Soc (pres, 68-69). **RESEARCH** History of philosophy; social history, philosophy of history. **SELECTED PUBLICATIONS** Auth, Development of Pierce's Philosophy, Harvard Univ, 61; coauth, Principals Tendencias de la Filosofia Norteamericana, Pan-Am Union, 63; auth, Our Knowledge of the Historical Past, Bobbs, 73; coauth, A History of Philosophy in America (2 vols), Putnam, 77; Philosophical Foundations of Historical Knowledge, SUNY, 94. **CONTACT ADDRESS** 200 Rhyl Lane, Bala-Cynwyd, PA 19004.

MURPHY, ALEXANDER B.
PERSONAL Born 07/10/1954, Washington, DC, m, 1981, 2 children **DISCIPLINE** GEOGRAPHY **EDUCATION** Yale Univ, BA, 77; Grad Prog, Universitat des Saarlandes, 78; Columbia Univ, JD, 81; Univ Chicago, PhD, 87. **CAREER** Lawyer, Katten, Muchin, Zavis, Pearl and Galler, 81-83; Asst Prof to Full Prof, Univ Ore, 87-. **HONORS AND AWARDS** Fulbright-Hays Res Grant, Belgium, 85-86; Fac Res Awd, Univ Ore, 89; Ersted Awd for Distinguished Teaching, Univ Ore, 91; NEH Summer Fel, 91; Humanities Ctr Fel, Univ Ore, 92; Richard A Bray Fac Fel, Univ Ore, 94-95, 96-97; Presidential Young Investigator's Awd, Nat Sci Foundation, 91-97. **MEMBERSHIPS** Acad Coun on the United Nations System, Am Geog Soc, Asn of Am Geog, Asn of Pacific Coast Geog, Coun for European Studies, European Community Studies Asn, Ill Bar, Intl

Geog Union, Nat Coun for Geog Educ, World Asn of Intl Studies. **RESEARCH** Political, Cultural, and Environmental Geography of Europe and the United States. **SELECTED PUBLICATIONS** Auth, Cultural Encounters with the Environment: Enduring and Evolving Geographic Themes, Rowman & Littlefield, forthcoming; auth, Human Geography: Culture, Society, and Space, 6th ed, John Wiley & Sons, 98; auth, The Regional Dynamics of Language Differentiation in Belgium: A Study in Cultural-Political Geography, Univ of Chicago, 88; auth, "Political Geography,: in International Encyclopedia of the Social and Behavioral Science, Pergamon, forthcoming; auth, "Measuring Potential Ethnic Conflict: The Case of Southeast Asia," Growth and Change, forthcoming; auth, "Regional Geography Revisited: The View From Oregon," Yearbook of the Association of Pacific Coast Geographers, (99): 160-174; auth, "The Use of National Names for International Bodies of Water: Critical Perspectives,: Journal of the Korean Geographical Society, (99): 507-516; auth, "Living Together Separately: Thoughts on the Relationship Between Political Science and Political Geography," Political Geography, (99): 887-894; auth, "Rethinking the Concept of European Identity," in Nested Identities: Nationalism, Territory, and Scale, Rowmand & Littlefield, 99; auth, "Advanced Placement Geography: Opportunities and Challenges for Geographers," Journal of Geography, (98: 132-136. **CONTACT ADDRESS** Dept Geog, Univ of Oregon, 1251 Univ of Ore, Eugene, OR 97403. **EMAIL** abmurphy@oregon.uoregon.edu

MURPHY, FRANCIS JOSEPH
PERSONAL Born 07/11/1935, Boston, MA **DISCIPLINE** MODERN EUROPEAN & CHURCH HISTORY **EDUCATION** Col of the Holy Cross, AB, 57; St Johns Sem, STB, 62; Cath Univ Am, MA, 70, PhD, 71. **CAREER** Assoc prof hist, Boston Col, 71-. **MEMBERSHIPS** AHA; Soc Fr Hist Studies; Am Cath Hist Asn. **RESEARCH** Twentieth century France; Christian-Marxist dialogue; Vatican diplomacy. **SELECTED PUBLICATIONS** Auth, La Main tendue: Prelude to Christian-Marxist dialogue in France, 1936-1939, Cath Hist Rev, 7/74; Milestones of Christian-Communist dialogue in France, J Ecumenical Studies, winter 78; Communists and Catholics in France, 1936-1939: The Politics of the Outstretched Hand, Univ Fla, 89; Pere Jacques: Resplendent in Victory, ICS Publ, 98. **CONTACT ADDRESS** Dept of History, Boston Col, Chestnut Hill, 140 Commonwealth Ave, Chestnut Hill, MA 02467.

MURPHY, JOHN C.
PERSONAL Born 11/16/1927, Buffalo, NY **DISCIPLINE** MEDIEVAL HISTORY **EDUCATION** St Bonaventure Univ, BA, 51; Univ Notre Dame, MSM, 61, DSM(mediaeval studies), 65. **CAREER** From Instr To Assoc Prof, 55-72, Prof Hist, Siena Col, Ny, 72-, Dean Col Of Arts, 77-, Prof Fine Arts & Vp Acad Affairs, 80-. **MEMBERSHIPS** Renaissance Soc Am. **RESEARCH** Franciscan College at the University of Paris in the 15th century. **SELECTED PUBLICATIONS** Auth, The early Franciscan Studium at the University of Paris, In: Studium Generale: Studies Offered to Astrik L Gabriel (Texts and Studies in the History of Mediaeval Education), Univ Notre Dame, 67; Pacific Sketchbook - From Training Camp To V-Jday, A Young Officers Crisp, Confident Drawings Of World-War-II Army Life, American Heritage, Vol 0044, 1993. **CONTACT ADDRESS** Dean Col of Arts Dept of Hist, Siena Col, Loudonville, NY 12211.

MURPHY, KEVIN D.
DISCIPLINE ARCHITECTURAL HISTORY **EDUCATION** Swarthmore Col, BA, 82; Boston Univ, MA, 85; Northwestern Univ, PhD, 92. **CAREER** From asst prof to prof, Univ Va; prof, CUNY. **RESEARCH** Modern European architecture. **SELECTED PUBLICATIONS** Auth, "Restoring Rouen: the Politics of Preservation in July Monarchy France," Word & Image 11 (April-June 95): 196-206; auth, "Cubism and the Gothic Tradition," in Architecture and Cubism, eds, Eve Blau & Nancy J. Troy, Can Ctr for Archit & MIT Pr, 97; auth, "'Of Gothic Extraction': Appleton's Preservation Campaign and the French Gothic Revival," Old-Time New England 76 (Fall 98): 46-66; co-ed, A Noble and Dignified Stream: The Piscataqua Region in the Colonial Revival, 1860-1930, Old York Hist Soc, Maine, 92; auth, Memory and Modernity: Viollet-le-Duc at Vezelay, Penn State Univ Pr, 00. **CONTACT ADDRESS** Art Hist Dept, Graduate Sch and Univ Ctr, CUNY, 365 Fifth Ave, New York, NY 10016. **EMAIL** kdm2g@virginia.edu

MURPHY, LARRY G.
PERSONAL Born 11/07/1946, Detroit, MI, m, 1967, 1 child **DISCIPLINE** AMERICAN AND AFRICAN AMERICAN RELIGIOUS HISTORY **CAREER** Lectr, African Amer studies, Univ Calif Berkeley, 72; lectr, hist dept, St. Mary's Col of Calif, 72-74; prof, hist of christ, Garrett-Evangelical Sem, 74-. **HONORS AND AWARDS** Henry McNeal Turner centennial lectr, Capetown, South Africa, 96. **MEMBERSHIPS** Soc for the Study of Black Relig; Oral Hist Asn; Amer Acad of Relig. **SELECTED PUBLICATIONS** Co-ed, Encyclopedia of African American Religions, Garland Press; ed, "Down by the Riverside": Readings in African Am Religion, NY Univ Press, 00. **CONTACT ADDRESS** 2121 Sheridan Rd., Evanston, IL 60201. **EMAIL** lmurphy1@nwu.edu

MURPHY, ORVILLE THEODORE
PERSONAL Born 10/09/1926, Louisville, KY, m, 1949, 2 children **DISCIPLINE** MODERN EUROPEAN HISTORY & DIPLOMACY **EDUCATION** Univ Louisville, BA, 50; Univ Minn, Minneapolis, MA, 51, PhD(hist), 57. **CAREER** Lectr hist, Univ Caen, 55-56; from instr to asst prof, Williams Col, 56-62; assoc prof, 62-70, asst to pres, 66-67, Prof Hist, State Univ NY Buffalo, 70-, Am Philos Soc grant, 61. **MEMBERSHIPS** AHA; Soc Fr Hist Studies; Soc Mod Hist, France. **RESEARCH** French diplomacy of the Old Regime; Charles Gravier de Vergennes, 1719-1787; the teaching of history. **SELECTED PUBLICATIONS** Auth, The Comte de Vergennes, the Newfoundland fisheries and the peace of 1783, Can Hist Rev, 365; DuPont de Nemours and the Anglo-French commercial treaty of 1786, Econ Hist Rev, 1266; Introducing the arts into a history course, Soc Sci Rec, 67; Spanish Observers And The American-Revolution, 1775-1783 - Cummins,Lt, J Of Southern History, Vol 0059, 1993; Preserving The Monarchy - The Comte-De-Vergennes, 1774-1787 - Price,M, American Historical Review, Vol 0102, 1997. **CONTACT ADDRESS** 63 Little Robin Rd, Getzville, NY 14068.

MURPHY, PAUL LLOYD
PERSONAL Born 09/05/1923, Caldwell, ID, m, 1946, 2 children **DISCIPLINE** HISTORY **EDUCATION** Col Idaho, BA, 47; Univ Calif, MA, 48, PhD(hist), 53. **CAREER** Asst prof US hist, Colo State Univ, 53; instr, Ohio State Univ, 53-57; asst prof hist, 57-60, assoc prof hist & Am studies, 60-70, Prof Hist & Am Studies, Univ Minn, Minneapolis, 70-, Vis prof, Northwestern Univ, 58-59; res fel, Ctr Studies Hist Liberty Am, Harvard Univ, 61-62; Guggenheim fel, 65-66; Fulbright sr lectr, Univ Lagos, 71-72; Danforth Found assoc, 73- ; Robert Lee Bailey prof hist,' Univ NC, Charlotte, 77; mem steering comt, Proj 87, AHAAm Polit Sci Asn, 77-80; chmn, comt bicentennial era, AHA, 79-81; Nat Endowment for Humanities fel, 81-82; Near vs Minnesota in The Context of Historical Developments, Minn Law Rev, 81. **HONORS AND AWARDS** LLD, Col Idaho, 76. **MEMBERSHIPS** AHA; Orgn Am Historians; Am Soc Legal Hist; Am Studies Asn; Southern Hist Asn. **RESEARCH** American constitutional and legal history; history of civil liberties and civil rights; United States political history. **SELECTED PUBLICATIONS** Co-ed, Liberty and Justice, Knopf, 58; auth, Sources and nature of intolerance in the 1920's, J Am Hist, 6/64; The Meaning of Freedom of Speech, Greenwood, 72; The Constitution in Crisis Times, 1918-1969, Harper, 72; ed, Political Parties in American History: 1890-present, Putnam, 74; co-ed, The Passaic Textile Strike of 1926, Wadsworth, 74; contribr, The Pulse of Freedom: American Liberties: 1920-1970's, 75 & auth, World War I and the Origin of Civil Liberties in the United States, 79, Norton. **CONTACT ADDRESS** 2159 Folwell St Flacon Heights, Saint Paul, MN 55108.

MURRAY, JACQUELINE
PERSONAL Born 10/01/1953, Trail, BC, Canada, s **DISCIPLINE** HISTORY **EDUCATION** Univ BC, BA, 77; Univ Toronto, MA, 78; PhD, 87. **CAREER** Curator, Center for Reformation and Renaissance Studies, 85-87; Asst Prof to Prof, Univ Windsor, 88-. **HONORS AND AWARDS** Can Res Fel, 88-91; Life Member, Cambridge Univ. **MEMBERSHIPS** Can Soc of Medievalists; Medieval Acad of Am; Am Hist Asn; Soc for Medieval Feminist Scholarship. **RESEARCH** Sexuality and gender in the Middle Ages; Ecclesiastical history; Social history. **SELECTED PUBLICATIONS** Co-trans, Agnolo Firenzuola, On the Beauty of Women, U Penn Press, 92; co-ed, Desire and Discipline. Sex and Sexuality in the Premodern West, Univ Toronto Press, 96; auth, Conflcted Identities and Multiple Masculinities. Men in the Medieval West, Garland Press, 99. **CONTACT ADDRESS** Dept Hist, Univ of Windsor, Windsor, ON, Canada N9B3P4. **EMAIL** jmurray@uwindsor.ca

MURRAY, JAMES
PERSONAL Born 03/27/1954, Baltimore, MD, m, 1977, 1 child **DISCIPLINE** MEDIEVAL EUROPEAN HISTORY **EDUCATION** Northwestern Univ, PhD, 83. **CAREER** Prof, Univ of Cincinnati, 99-, assoc prof, 90-99 asst prof, Univ of Cincinnati, 84-90, lectr dept of hist, Stanford Univ, 82-84. **HONORS AND AWARDS** Fulbright fel to Belgium; NEH Summer fel; Am Council of Learned Soc Fel; Belgian Am Educ Found Fel. **MEMBERSHIPS** Medieval Acad of Am. **RESEARCH** Economic and urban hist, Flanders and the Low Countries, Diplomatics and Palaeography. **SELECTED PUBLICATIONS** A History of Business in Medieval Europe, 1200-1500, with E.S. Hunt, Cambridge University Press, 99; Notarial Instruments in Flanders between 1280 and 1452, Commission royale d'histoire, Brussels, 1995; The Liturgy of the Count's Advent in Bruges, from Galbert to Van Eyck, in City and Spectacle in Medieval Europe, Univ of MN, 94 pp.137-152; The Profession of Notary Public in Medieval Flanders, Jour of Legal History, 61, 93:1-29. **CONTACT ADDRESS** Univ of Cincinnati, PO Box 210373, Cincinnati, OH 45221-0373. **EMAIL** murrayjm@uc.edu

MURRAY, JOAN
PERSONAL Born 08/12/1943 **DISCIPLINE** ART HISTORY **EDUCATION** Univ Toronto, BA, 65; Columbia Univ, MA, 66. **CAREER** Lectr, York Univ, 70-71, 73-75; cur, Can Art, Art Gall Ont, 70-73; cons, Ont Arts Counc, 72-75; coun, Can Mus Asn, 74-76; dir, Ont Heritage Found, 75-78; Dir, The Robert Mclaughlin Gallery 1974-. **HONORS AND AWARDS** Asn Cult Exec Awd, outstanding contrib in cult mgt, 93. **MEMBERSHIPS** Adv bd, Artmagazine, 74-78; fel, Royal Can Acad, 92. **SELECTED PUBLICATIONS** Auth, Letters Home: 1859-1906, The Letters of William Blair Bruce, 82; auth, The Beginning of Vision: The Drawings of Lauren Harris, 82; auth, Kurelek's Vision of Canada, 83; auth, Frederick Arthur Verner: The Last Buffalo, 84; auth, Daffodils in Winter: The Life and Letters of Pegi Nicol MacLeod, 84; auth, The Best of the Group of Seven, 84; auth, Northern Lights: Masterpieces of Tom Thomson and the Group of Seven, 94; auth, The Last Spring: Confessions of a Curator, 96. **CONTACT ADDRESS** 400 St. John St W, Whitby, ON, Canada L1N 1N7.

MURRAY, MICHAEL D.
PERSONAL Born 11/09/1947, St Louis, MO, m **DISCIPLINE** HISTORY, JOURNALISM **EDUCATION** St Louis Univ, BA, 70; MA, 71; Univ Mo, PhD, 74. **CAREER** Asst Proof, Va Tech Univ, 74-76; Assoc. Proof, Univ Louisville, 76-82; Proof, Univ Mo, 82-. **HONORS AND AWARDS** Goldsmith Roes Awd, Harvard Univ, 92; Feel, Stanford Univ, 93. **MEMBERSHIPS** Am Jour Historian's Assoc. **RESEARCH** Journalism and mass communication history. **SELECTED PUBLICATIONS** Auth, The Political Performers, Praeger Pr, 94; ed, Television in America, Iowa State Univ Pr, 98; ed, The Encyclopedia of TV News, Oryx Pr, 99. **CONTACT ADDRESS** Dept Hist, Univ of Missouri, St. Louis, 9870 Cupper Hill Rd, Saint Louis, MO 63124. **EMAIL** murraymd@umsl.edu

MURRAY, PETER
PERSONAL Born 10/20/1953, Orangeburg, SC, m, 1985, 2 children **DISCIPLINE** HISTORY **EDUCATION** Wofford Col, BA, 75; Ind Univ, MA, 77; PhD, 85. **CAREER** Instr, Ind Univ, 85-88; Prof, Methodist Col, 88-. **HONORS AND AWARDS** Rotary Int Fel, 96. **MEMBERSHIPS** OAH, AHA. **RESEARCH** United States civil rights movement, churches in 20th Century America. **SELECTED PUBLICATIONS** Auth, "The Racial Crisis in the Methodist Church," Methodist Hist 26 (87); auth, "The Origins of Racial Inclusiveness in the Methodist Church," in J of Relig Thought 45 (89). **CONTACT ADDRESS** Dept Hist, Methodist Col, 5400 Ramsey St, Fayetteville, NC 28311-1420. **EMAIL** pcmurray@methodist.edu

MURRAY, ROBERT KEITH
PERSONAL Born 04/09/1922, Union City, IN, m, 1943, 3 children **DISCIPLINE** HISTORY **EDUCATION** Ohio State Univ, BA & BS, 43, MA, 47, PhD(mod Am hist), 49. **CAREER** Res assoc, Nat Red Cross Hq, 48; instr Am hist, Ohio State Univ, 48-49; from instr to assoc prof hist, 49-59, head dept hist, 59-69, asst dean grad sch, 60-64, Prof Am Hist, PA State Univ, University Park, 59-, Mem comt expanding opportunities in educ, Am Coun Educ, 65-67; mem, Nat Arch Comn, US Govt, 71-74; mem, Nat Hist Adv Comt Bicentennial lectr, State of Pa, 75-76; CBS & PBS hist consult electrons, 76 & 80. **HONORS AND AWARDS** Nat Bk Awd, Phi Alpha Theta, 69; McKnight Distinguished Bk Awd, Univ Minn Regents, 69; Distinguished Res Serv Awd, State of Ohio, 69. **MEMBERSHIPS** AHA; Orgn Am Historians (treas, 76-); NEA; AAUP. **RESEARCH** Twentieth century history, especially social and political; the 1920's; presidential history and evaluation. **SELECTED PUBLICATIONS** Auth, Red Scare: A Study in National Hysteria, Minn Press, 55 & McGraw, 60; The Harding Era: Warren G Harding and his Administration, Univ Minn, 69; The twenties, In: Interpreting American History: Conversations with Historians, Macmillan, 70; The Politics of Normalcy: Governmental Theory and Practice in the Harding-Coolidge Era, Norton, 73; The 103rd Ballot: Democrats and the Disaster in Madison Square Garden, Harper, 76; Democrats vs frustration city, Smithsonian, 4/76; Trapped: The Saga of Floyd Collins, Putman's, 79; Hoover and the Harding Cabinet, Hoover as Secretary of Commerce, Univ Iowa, 81. **CONTACT ADDRESS** Pennsylvania State Univ, Univ Park, 816 Liberal Arts Tower, University Park, PA 16802.

MURRAY, SHOON
DISCIPLINE U.S. FOREIGN POLICY **EDUCATION** Oberlin Col, BA; Yale Univ, MA, MPhil, PhD. **CAREER** Prof, Am Univ. **RESEARCH** Public opinion, political psychology, andAmerican politics. **SELECTED PUBLICATIONS** Auth, Anchors Against Change: American Opinion Leaders' Beliefs After the Cold War, Univ Mich Press, 96. **CONTACT ADDRESS** American Univ, 4400 Massachusetts Ave, Washington, DC 20016.

MURRELL, GARY J.
PERSONAL Born 01/28/1947, Portland, OR, s **DISCIPLINE** HISTORY **EDUCATION** Southern Ore State Col, BS, 87; Univ Ore, MA, 92; Univ Ore, PhD, 95. **CAREER** Vis Instr, Southern Ore State Col, 93-94; Vis Instr, Grays Harbor Col, 94-. **HONORS AND AWARDS** Fac Excellence Awd, 96. **MEMBERSHIPS** AHA, OAH. **RESEARCH** Twentieth-Century radical and anti-radical movements, African-American. **SELECTED PUBLICATIONS** Auth, "Hunting Reds in Oregon," Ore Hist Quart (99); auth, Iron Pants: Ore-

gon's Anti-New Deal Governor, Charles Henry Martin, WSU Pr, 00; auth, "Herbert Apthelar and His Side of History: An Interview with Eric Foner," Radical Hist Rev (forthcoming). **CONTACT ADDRESS** Dept Hist, Grays Harbor Col, 1620 Edward P Smith Dr, Aberdeen, WA 98520-7500.

MURRIN, JOHN MATTHEW
PERSONAL Born 08/20/1935, Minneapolis, MN, m, 1967 **DISCIPLINE** AMERICAN HISTORY **EDUCATION** Col St Thomas, BA, 57; Univ Notre Dame, AM, 60; Yale Univ, PhD(hist), 66. **CAREER** From asst prof to assoc prof hist, Washington Univ, 63-73; assoc prof, 73-80, Prof Hist, Princeton Univ, 80-. **HONORS AND AWARDS** Nat Endowment for Humanities jr scholar fel, 69; NEH Fel, 86-87; Erasmus Inst Fel, 01; Am Antiquarian Soc Fel, 02. **MEMBERSHIPS** AHA; Orgn Am Historians; Southern Hist Asn. **RESEARCH** American colonial and revolutionary history; United States in the early national period, 1789-1861; 18th century Britain. **SELECTED PUBLICATIONS** Auth, "The Great Inversion on Court versus Country: The Revolution Settlements in England (1688-1721) and America (1776-1816)," Princeton V.P., 80; coed, Saints and Revolutionaries: Essays in Early American History, 84; auth, "English Rights as Ethnic Aggression: The English Conquest, the Charter of Liberties of 1683 and Leishler's Rebellion in NY," NYHS, 88; auth, "the Menacing Show of Louis XIV and the Rage of Jacob Leisler, NY St. Comm on Bicenten of Const, 90; auth, "Fundamental Values, the Founding Fathers, and the Constitution," U. Pr. Of Va, 92; auth, "The Making and Unmaking of an American Ruling Class," No Ill U.P., 93; auth, "Escaping Perfidious Albion: Federalism, Fear of Aristoeracy, and the Democratization of Corruption in Postrevolutionary America," Lehigh U.P, 94; auth, "Things Fearful to Name': Bestiality in Early America," Pa Hist, 98; auth, "The Jeffersonian Triumph and American Exceptionalism," Jour Early Rep, 00; auth, coauth, Liberty, Equality, Power: A History of the American People, 3rd ed, 01. **CONTACT ADDRESS** Dept of Hist, Princeton Univ, Princeton, NJ 08544-1098.

MURZAKU, INES A.
PERSONAL Born 06/02/1964, Tirana, Albania, m, 1987, 2 children **DISCIPLINE** ORIENTAL CHURCH HISTORY **EDUCATION** Ponitfical Oriental Institute, PhD, 95. **CAREER** Asst prof, Acad Arts, Tirana-Albania, 86-91; journalist, East Europe - Vatican Radio, 92-94; Adj Prof, St. John Fisher Col, 96-. **HONORS AND AWARDS** Prestigious Grant for Doctoral Studies, 91-95. **MEMBERSHIPS** AAUP, AAR, AHA, ACHA, AAASS, ASN. **RESEARCH** East Europe: religion, history and culture, Jesuit History, Albanian history, religious values and contemporary society, women in the church. **SELECTED PUBLICATIONS** Auth, Angazhimi yne Shoqeror, 94; auth, Religion in Post-Communist Albania, Missioni e Popoli, 94; auth, The Activity and the Role of the Jesuits in the Albanian History and Culture 1841-1946, 96; The Flying Mission (Missione Volante), Diakonia; The Beginning of the Jesuit Albanian Mission, Diakonia. **CONTACT ADDRESS** Religious Studies Dept, Seton Hall Univ, So Orange, 40 S Orange Ave, South Orange, NJ 07079. **EMAIL** murzakui@shu.edu

MUSCARELLA, OSCAR WHITE
PERSONAL Born 03/26/1931, New York, NY, m, 1957, 2 children **DISCIPLINE** ARCHAEOLOGY **EDUCATION** City Col New York, BA, 55; Univ Pa, MA, 58, PhD(class archaeol), 65. **CAREER** Lectr hist, City Col New York, 60-64; Assoc Cur, Dept Ancient Near Eastern Art, Metrop Mus Art, 64-, Sr Res Fel, 78-, Ed bds, Archaeol J Field Archaeol & Source. **MEMBERSHIPS** Archaeol Inst Am; Brit Inst Persian Studies; Asn Field Archaeol (secy, 74-). **RESEARCH** Greek-Near East relations; Iron Age Greece and Near East; Ancient Iran. **SELECTED PUBLICATIONS** Auth, Phrygian Fibulae from Gordion, B Quaritch, London, 67; The Tumuli at Se Girdan, Metrop Mus J, 69 & 71; Excavations at Agrab Tepe, Iran, 73 & The Iron Age at Dinkha Tepe, Iran, 974, Metrop Mus Art J; ed, Ancient Art, The Norbert Schimmel Collection, Mainz, 74; Ziwiye and Ziwiye the Forgery of a Provenience, J Field Archaeol, IV, 277; Un excavated Objects and Ancient Near Eastern Art, Bibliot Mesopotamica, VII, 77; The catalogue of ivories from Hasanlu, Iran, Phila, 80; Achaemenid History-iv - Center and Periphery - Sancisiweerdenburg,h, Kuhrt,a, American J of Archaeology, Vol 0097, 1993; Bronze and Iron, Met. Musm. Of Art, 1988. **CONTACT ADDRESS** Metropolitan Mus of Art, New York, NY 10028. **EMAIL** oscarbey@aol.com

MUSHKAT, JEROME
PERSONAL Born 05/05/1931, Livingston Manor, NY, m, 1961, 2 children **DISCIPLINE** AMERICAN & URBAN HISTORY **EDUCATION** Syracuse Univ, BA, 53, PhD, 64. **CAREER** From Instr to Assoc Prof, 62-76, prof hist, Univ Akron, 76. **HONORS AND AWARDS** Grant, Asn for Study State & Local Hist, 65. **MEMBERSHIPS** Am Asn Univ Professors; Orgn Am Historians; Am Studies Asn. **RESEARCH** Nineteenth century Am hist; NY hist; urban polit machines. **SELECTED PUBLICATIONS** Auth, The impeachment of Andrew Johnson: A contemporary view, NY Hist, 7/67; Epitaphs by Mordecai M Noah, NY Hist Soc Quart, 7/71; Tammany: The Evolution of a Political Machine: 1789-1865, Syracuse Univ Press, 71; Mineral and timber prospects in upper Michigan, Inland Seas, 74; Matthew Livingston Davis and the political legacy of Aaron Burr, NY Hist Soc Quart, 75; Ben Wood's Fort Lafayette as a peace democratic source, Civil War Hist, 75; The Reconstruction of the New York Democracy, 1861-1874, Fairleigh-Dickinson Press, 81; Fernando Wood and the Commercial Growth of New York City, Univ Va Press, 90; Fernando Wood: A Political Biography, Kent State Univ Press, 90; Martin Van Buren: Law, Politics, and the Shaping of Republican Ideology, Northern IL Univ Press, 98. **CONTACT ADDRESS** Dept of Hist, Univ of Akron, 302 Buchtel Mall, Akron, OH 44325-1902.

MUSTO, DAVID F.
PERSONAL Born 01/08/1936, Tacoma, WA, m, 1961, 4 children **DISCIPLINE** HISTORY, PSYCHOLOGY **EDUCATION** Univ Wash, BA, 56, MD, 63; Yale Univ, MA, 61. **CAREER** Spec asst to dir, Nat Inst Mental Health, 67-69; from asst prof to assoc prof hist & psychiat, 69-78, sr res scientist, Child Study Ctr, 78-80, Lectr Hist & Am Studies, Yale Univ, 78-, Prof Psychiat, Child Study Ctr & Prof Hist Med, 81-, Head, Sect Hist & Social Policy, Child Study Ctr & Bush Ctr, 81-, Residency psychiat, Yale Univ, 64-67; vis asst prof, Johns Hopkins Univ, 68-69; fel, Drug Abuse Coun, 72-73; consult, Nat Comn Marijuana & Drug Abuse, 72-73; prog dir, Nat Humanities Inst, 77-78; hist consult, President's Comn Ment Health, 77-78; mem US deleg, UN Comn Narcotic Drugs, 78 & 79; mem, White House Strategy Coun, Off Pres US, 77-81; mem, Nat Coun Smithsonian Inst, 81-; mem panel on alcohol policy, Nat Res Coun, 78-81. **HONORS AND AWARDS** William Osler Medal, Am Asn Hist Med, 60; Edward Kremers Awd, Am Inst Hist Pharmacy, 74. **MEMBERSHIPS** AHA; Am Psychiat Asn; Am Asn Hist Med. **RESEARCH** History of the family; application of psychology to history; history of drug control in America. **SELECTED PUBLICATIONS** Coauth, Strange encounter, Psychiatry, 868; auth, Youth of John Quincy Adams, Proc Am Philos Soc, 869; The American Disease: Origins of Narcotic Control, Yale Univ, 73; coauth, Historical perspectives on mental health and racism in the United States, In: Racism and Mental Health, Univ Pittsburgh, 73; Whatever happened to community mental health?, Pub Interest, spring 75; Continuity Across Generations, Smithsonian Inst Press, 79; Temperance and prohibition in America, In: Alcohol and Pubic Policy, Nat Acad Press, 81; Adams family, Proc Mass Hist Soc, 82; Drugs And Narcotics in History - Porter,r, Teich,m, J of Interdisciplinary History, Vol 0028, 1997. **CONTACT ADDRESS** Child Study Ctr, Box 90015. **EMAIL** david.musto@yale.edu

MUSTO, RONALD G.
PERSONAL Born 05/24/1948, New York, NY, m, 1970 **DISCIPLINE** HISTORY **EDUCATION** Fordham Univ, BA, Hist, 69; Columbia Univ, MA, Hist, 70, PhD, 77. **CAREER** Vis lectr, New York Univ, Hist, 76; fell, Am Acad Rome, 78-79; vis prof, Columbia Univ, 80; asst prof, Duke Univ, Hist, 80-81; writer & ed, New York City Hum Ref, 81-85; PUBL, ITALICA PRESS, dir, ACLS History E-Book Project, 99-. **HONORS AND AWARDS** New York State Teaching Fel, 69-74; Renaissance Soc of Am Paleography Fel, 74; Columbia Univ Dissertatim Distinction, 77; Am Academy in Rome Fel, 78; Andrew Mellon Fel, 80; Natural Catholic Book Awd, 87. **MEMBERSHIPS** Am Hist Asn; Am Catholic Hist Asn; Medieval Acad Am; Renaissance Soc Am; Am Acad Rome Soc Fellows **RESEARCH** Interaction of religious belief and civil life in the Middle Ages and modern period. **SELECTED PUBLICATIONS** Auth, Catholic Peace Tradition, Orbis Books, 86; auth, the Peach Tradition in the Catholic Church, Garland, 87; auth, Liberatim Theologies: A Research Guide, Garland, 91; auth, Catholic Peacemakers: A Documentary History, 2 vols, Garland, 93-96; ed, Petrarh, The Revolution y Cola d Rienzo, Italica Press, 96; auth, Marvels of Rome for the Macintosh, New York: Italica Press, 97; co-edr, The Holy Land on Disk, New York: Italica Press, 97; co-edr, The Road to Compostela, New York: Italica Press; Apocalypse in Rome: Cola di Rienzo and the Politics of the New Age, Univ Calif Press, forthcoming. **CONTACT ADDRESS** Italica Press, 595 Main St,, Ste 605, New York, NY 10044. **EMAIL** italica@idt.met

MUTHYALA, JOHN S.
PERSONAL Born Hyderabad, India **DISCIPLINE** AMERICAN, POSTCOLONIAL STUDIES **EDUCATION** Osmania Univ, MA, 88; MPhil, 91; Loyola Univ Chicago, PhD, 01. **CAREER** Vis asst prof, Luther Col, 00-01; asst prof, Univ Southern Maine, 01-. **HONORS AND AWARDS** Shakespeare Gold Medal, 88; Loyola Univ Fel, 99. **MEMBERSHIPS** MLA, MWMLA. **RESEARCH** Literatures of the Americas, Postcolonial Studies, Literary Theory and Cultural Criticism. **SELECTED PUBLICATIONS** Auth, "The Politics of Borrowing Theories in Postcolonial and Postmodern Discourse and Theory," Jour of Contemp Thought, (98); auth, "Migrancy, Narrative, and Identity in claude McKay's 'Banana Bottom,'" In Process: A Jour of African Am and African Diasporan Lit and Cult, (00); auth, "Border Crossings: Mestiza Feminism in the Borderlands," Can Rev of Am Studies, (00); auth, "Reworlding America: the Globalization of American Studies," Cultural Critique, (01). **CONTACT ADDRESS** Dept English, Univ of So Maine, Portland, MA 04103. **EMAIL** muthyalaj@yahoo.com

MUTSCHLER, BEN
DISCIPLINE HISTORY **EDUCATION** Harvard Univ, AB, 88; Columbia Univ, MA, 92; MPhil, 94. **CAREER** PHD CAND IN HIST, COLUMBIA UNIV **RESEARCH** Illness in New Eng, 1690-1820. **CONTACT ADDRESS** 20 Espie Ave, Maynard, MA 01754-1919. **EMAIL** bm35@columbia.edu

MUYUMBA, FRANCOIS N.
PERSONAL Born 12/29/1939, Luputa Kasai-orien, Zaire, m **DISCIPLINE** AFRICAN-AMERICAN STUDIES **EDUCATION** David & Elkins Coll Elkins WV, BA 1963-67; Portland State U, MS 1969-70; IN Univ Boomington, MA & PhD 1977. **CAREER** IN State Univ, asst prof 1977-; Univ Libre duCongo, asst prof/adminstrn asst 1968-69; Usaid-Kinshasa, asst training officer 1967-68; Youth Center (Carrefour deJeunes) Kinshasa Zaire, dir 1967. **HONORS AND AWARDS** Soccer Letters & Trophies Davis & Elkins Coll Elkins WV 1963-67; Travel Grant Intl Peace Research Assn 1975; Consult Grant Gilmore Sloane Presbyterian Center 1975. **MEMBERSHIPS** Mem Tchrs of Engl as Second Lang 1973-80; mem Intl Peace Research Assn 1975-80; consult Inst for World Order's Sch Progs 1975-78; mem World Council for Curriculum & Instr 1974-80; mem Peache Educ Council 1978-80; mem Nat Council for Black Studies 1976-80. **CONTACT ADDRESS** Afro-American Studies Dept, Indiana State Univ, Terre Haute, IN 47809.

MWAMBA, ZUBERI I.
PERSONAL Born 01/03/1937, Tanzania, 4 children **DISCIPLINE** AFRICAN STUDIES **EDUCATION** Univ Wis, BS 1968; Univ Pitts, MA 1968; Howard U, PhD 1972. **CAREER** Govt Tanzania, radio announcer, court clerk, interpreter, information asst 1957-62; Howard U, instr 1968-72; US State Dept 1969-70; African Studies TX So U, prof dir 1982-. **HONORS AND AWARDS** Fellows Fulbright 1965-68; WI Legislature 1965-67; Howard Univ Trust 1969-70; International Election Observer at the general elections in South Africa, 1994; TX Southern Univ, Distinguished Service of the Year Awd, 1997. **MEMBERSHIPS** Mem Am Political Sci Assn 1971-; Nat Council Black Political Scientists 1971-; Educator to Africa Assn 1972-; pres Pan African Students Orgn 1965-67; Tanzania Students Union 1968-70 1971-72; exec com East African Students Orgn 1968-70; adv TX So Univ Student Gov Assn 1974-75; faculty sponsor TSU YoungDemo 1974-75. **CONTACT ADDRESS** Texas So Univ, 3100 Cleburne Ave, Houston, TX 77004.

MYERS, DAVID
DISCIPLINE RELIGIOUS HISTORY **EDUCATION** Yale Univ, PhD. **CAREER** Assoc prof, Fordham Univ. **HONORS AND AWARDS** Herzog Aug Bibliothek Res Fel 99-00; Nat Endowment for the Humanities Fel, 01-02; reviewer, chicago tribune bk rev. **RESEARCH** History of sin and crime in early modern Europe. **SELECTED PUBLICATIONS** Auth, Poor, Sinning Folk: Confession and the Making of Consciences in Counter-Reformation Germany, Cornell UP, 96; Die Jesuiten die Beichte, und die katholische Reformation in Bayern, Beitge zur altbayerischen Kirchengeschichte 96; Ritual, Confession, and Religion in Early Sixteenth-Century Germany, Arch fur Reformationsgeschichte, 97. **CONTACT ADDRESS** Dept of Hist, Fordham Univ, Bronx, NY 10458. **EMAIL** dmyers@fordham.edu

MYERS, ELLEN H.
PERSONAL Born 02/16/1941, Bryan, TX, m, 1967, 1 child **DISCIPLINE** HISTORY **EDUCATION** Mount Vernon Col, Wash, DC, AA, 61; Tulone, BA, 63; Univ Va, MA, 65; PhD, 70. **CAREER** Adj, Univ of Houston, 66-67; Lectr, Okla State Univ, 67-70; From Asst Prof to Prof, San Antonio Col, 70-. **HONORS AND AWARDS** DuPont Fel, Univ of Va. **MEMBERSHIPS** Southwest Conf on Latin Am Studies, Tex Community Col Teachers Asn. **RESEARCH** Spain and Latin America. **SELECTED PUBLICATIONS** Auth, "A Comparison of Cabildos in Seville, Texerite, and Lima," The Americas (67); auth, Student Review Manuals and Instructors Manuals to accompany J. Garranty The American Nation, Harper and Row, 75-89; auth, Text to accompany Hollister et al, History of Western Civilization, Harcourt Brace, 99. **CONTACT ADDRESS** Dept Hist, San Antonio Col, 1300 San Pedro Ave, San Antonio, TX 78212-4201. **EMAIL** emyers@accd.edu

MYERS, JOHN L.
PERSONAL Born 06/13/1929, Findlay, OH, m, 1957, 3 children **DISCIPLINE** AMERICAN HISTORY **EDUCATION** Bowling Green State Univ, BS, 51; Univ Mich, MA, 54, PhD, 61. **CAREER** From asst prof to assoc prof hist, Southeast Mo State Col, 58-64; assoc prof, 64-68, Prof Hist, State Univ NY Col Plattsburgh, 68-; mem comt on status hist in schs, Orgn Am Historians, 74-80. **HONORS AND AWARDS** State Univ NY Res Found fel, 68 & 69. **MEMBERSHIPS** Orgn Am Historians; Soc Hist Early Am Rep. **RESEARCH** The antislavery movement; career of Henry Wilson. **SELECTED PUBLICATIONS** Auth, The beginning of antislavery agencies in New York State, NY Hist, 4/62; Antislavery activities of five Lane Seminary boys in 1835-1836, Hist & Philos Soc Ohio, 4/63; Organization of the seventy, Mid-Am, 1/66; American antislavery society agents and the free Negro, 1833-1838, J Negro Hist,

7/67; The major effect of antislavery agents in Neew Hampshire, 1835-1837, Hist NH, fall 71. **CONTACT ADDRESS** Dept of Hist, SUNY, Col at Plattsburgh, 95 Broad St, Plattsburgh, NY 12901.

MYERS, SAMUEL L., JR.
PERSONAL Born 03/09/1949, Boston, MA **DISCIPLINE** AFRICAN-AMERICAN STUDIES **EDUCATION** Morgan State Coll, BA 1971; MIT, PhD 1976. **CAREER** Univ of Minnesota, Roy Wilkins Chair prof, 92-; Univ of Maryland, prof; Univ of Texas at Austin, asst prof of economics; Prof, Univ of Pittsburgh, GSPIA, Federal Trade Commission. **HONORS AND AWARDS** Alpha Kappa Mu Merit Awd, 1970; Inst Fellow, MIT, 1971-73; Natl Fellowship Fund Fellow, 1973-75; Fulbright Lecturer in Economics, Cuttington Coll, Liberia, 1975-76; Fulbright Scholar, Univ of South Australia, Faculty of Aboriginal and Islander Studies, 1997. **MEMBERSHIPS** Amer Economics Assn; Natl Economics Assn; Amer Acad of Political & Social Science; Amer Assn for the Advancement of Science, Alpha Phi Alpha, co-coordinator, Black Grad Economics Assn 1973, Assn for Public Policy Analysis & Mgt, vp, 1997-99. **SELECTED PUBLICATIONS** Co-author: Bittersweet Success: Faculty of Color in Academe; Persistent Disparity: Race & Economic Inequality in the US 1998; The Black Underclass: Critical Essays on Race and Unwantedness, 1994; Editor: Civil Rights and Race Relations in the Post Reagan-Bush Era 1997; Co-editor: Economics of Race and Crime, Transaction Press, 1988; author, editor, and contributor of articles, chapters, and reviews to newspaper, periodicals, books, and journals. **CONTACT ADDRESS** H H Humphrey Institute of Public Affairs, Univ of Minnesota, Twin Cities, 301 19th Ave S, Minneapolis, MN 55455. **EMAIL** smyers@hhh.umn.edu

N

NADEL, STANLEY
PERSONAL Born 11/08/1944, New York, NY, 2 children **DISCIPLINE** HISTORY **EDUCATION** Univ Mich, BA, 66; Mich State Univ, Grad Stud, 66-67; Columbia Univ, MA, 74, PhD, 81. **CAREER** Col asst, Lehman Col, City Univ New York, 74-76; lectr, Marymount Manhattan Col, 77; vis asst prof, SUNY, 81-82, 83-84; vis asst prof, St Lawrence Univ, 82-83; vis asst prof, Univ Ill, Champaign-Urbana, 85-87; vis asst prof, Pa State Univ, 88; vis asst prof, Austin Peay State Univ, 88-91; vis asst prof, Central Conn State Univ, 91-92; adj assoc prof, St Marys Col, vis asst prof, Winona State Univ, 92-93; vist asst prof, SUNY, Plattsburgh, 93-94; asst prof, Mo State Univ, 94-95; assoc prof, dept chemn, Southwestern Okla State University, 95-. **HONORS AND AWARDS** Columbian Univ Readership Hist, 73-75; NEH Summer Stipend, Fac Res Fel, SUNY, 82; NEH Summer Sem, UCLA, 95. **RESEARCH** Am Social Hist; immigration and ethnicity; racial and ethnic minoritys; suicide and infanticide. **SELECTED PUBLICATIONS** Auth, Little Germany: Ethnicity, Religion and Class in New York City, 1845-1880, 90; auth, art, Those Who Would Be Free: the Eight-hour Day Strikes of 1872, 90; auth, art, German's in New York, 95; auth, art, Immigration Restrictionists: Historical Context and Critique, 95; auth, art, The German-American Left, 96. **CONTACT ADDRESS** Dept of Social Sciences, Southwestern Oklahoma State Univ, Weatherford, Weatherford, OK 73096. **EMAIL** nadels@swosu.edu

NADELL, PAMELA
PERSONAL Born 12/13/1951, Newark, NJ, m, 1976, 2 children **DISCIPLINE** HISTORY **EDUCATION** OH State Univ, PhD. **CAREER** Prof of History, dir, Jewish Studies Program, American Univ, 82-. **MEMBERSHIPS** Amer Jewish Hist Soc, Academic Council; Assoc for Jewish Studies, Board of Directors. **RESEARCH** American Jewish history. **SELECTED PUBLICATIONS** Auth, Women Who Would Be Rabbis: A History of Women's Ordination, 1889-1985, 98; Conservative Judaism in America: A Biographical Dictionary and Sourcebook. **CONTACT ADDRESS** Jewish Studies Program, American Univ, 4400 Massachusetts Ave NW, Washington, DC 20016. **EMAIL** pnadell@american.edu

NADER, HELEN
PERSONAL Born 04/29/1936, Miami, AZ **DISCIPLINE** RENAISSANCE & REFORMATION HISTORY **EDUCATION** Univ Ariz, BA, 58; Smith Col, MA, 59; Univ Calif, Berkeley, PhD(hist), 72. **CAREER** Actg instr hist, Univ Calif, Berkeley, 67-68; asst prof, Univ Hawaii, 71-75; asst prof, Stanford Univ, 75-76; asst prof, 76-79, Assoc Prof Hist, Ind Univ, 79-, Am Coun Learned Soc fel, 74-75, grant-in-aid, 76; Lilly Libr res fel, 76; consult, Nat Endowment for Humanities & ed, Bull Soc Span & Port Hist Studies, 77-79; Tinker Found Inc fel, 78; vis scholar, Stanford Univ Food Res Inst, 78-79; Nat Endowment for Humanities res fel, 82-83; assoc ed, Am Hist Rev, 82-. **MEMBERSHIPS** Soc Ital Hist Studies; Acad Am Res Historians Medieval Spain; AHA; Renaissance Soc Am; Soc Span & Port Hist Studies. **RESEARCH** Spain 1350-1700; humanism in southern Europe; the Mendoza Family. **SELECTED PUBLICATIONS** Auth, Josephus and Don Diego Hurtado de Mendoza, Romance Philol, 73; Noble income in sixteenth-century Castile: The case of the Marquises of Mondejar, Econ Hist Rev, 77; The Greek Commander Hernan Nunez de Toledo, Spanish humanist and civic leader, Renaissance Quart, 78; The Mendoza Family in the Spanish Renaissance, 1350-1550, Rutgers Univ, 79; Spanish Reaction to the Introduction of Habsburg Ceremonial, In: Arts, Letters and Ceremonial at the Court of the Spanish Habsburgs, Duke Univ (in prep). **CONTACT ADDRESS** Dept of Hist, Indiana Univ, Bloomington, Ballantine Hall, Bloomington, IN 47401.

NAESS, HARALD S.
PERSONAL Born 12/27/1925, Oddernes, Norway, m, 1950, 3 children **DISCIPLINE** SCANDINAVIAN STUDIES **EDUCATION** Univ Oslo, Cand Philol, 52. **CAREER** Lector Norweg, King's Col, Univ Durham, 53-58, lectr, 58- 59; vis lectr, 59-61, assoc prof, 61-67, Torger Thompson Prof Scand Studies, Univ Wis-Madison, 67-91, Fulbright scholar, 59-61; mem ed comt, Nordic Trans Serv, Univ Wis, 64-68; ed, Scand Studies, 73-77. **HONORS AND AWARDS** Knight, Order of Saint Olav, 85. **MEMBERSHIPS** Soc Advan Scand Studies; Norweg-Am Hist Soc. **RESEARCH** Norwegian eighteenth and nineteenth century literature, particularly the work of Knut Hamsun; American-Norwegian Immigration history. **SELECTED PUBLICATIONS** Auth, Knut Hamsun og Amerika, Gyldendal, 69; auth, Knut Hamsun, Twayne, 84; coauth, Knut Hamsun. Selected Letters I-II, Norvik Press, 90, 98; auth, Knut Hamsuns brev I-VII, Gyldendal, 94-01. **CONTACT ADDRESS** Dept of Scand Studies, Univ of Wisconsin, Madison, Madison, WI 53706. **EMAIL** Harnass@online.no

NAGAR, RICHA
PERSONAL Born 09/21/1968, Lucknow, India, m, 1993, 1 child **DISCIPLINE** WOMEN'S STUDIES, GEOGRAPHY **EDUCATION** Lucknow Univ, BA, 86; Punc Univ, MA, 89; Univ Minn, PhD, 95. **CAREER** Asst prof, Univ Colo, 95-97; asst prof, Univ Minn, 97-; adj asst prof, Univ Minn, 99-. **HONORS AND AWARDS** McKnight Land Grant; NSF Grant; Macarthur Fel. **MEMBERSHIPS** AAG; IGU. **RESEARCH** Gender; identity; communal politics; activism and development; politics. **SELECTED PUBLICATIONS** Auth, "I'd Rather be Rude than Ruled,Û Gender, Place, and Communal Politics among South Asian Communities in Dar es Salaam," Women's Stud Intl Forum 23 (00); auth, "Religion, Race and the Debate over Mut' a in Dar es Salaam," Feminist Studies, 26 (00); auth, "Communal Discourses, Marriage, and the Politics of Gendered Social Boundaries among South Asian Immigrants in Tanzania," Gender, Place and Culture 5 (98): 117-139, reprinted in Gender and Migration, eds. Katie Willis, Brenda Yeoh, The International Library Of Studies On Migration, series ed. Robin Cohen (Cheltenham: Edward Elgar Pub, 00); coauth, Contesting Social Relations in Communal Places: Identity Politics Among Asians in Dar es Salaam," in Cities of Difference, eds. Ruth Fincher, Jane Jacobs (NY: Guilford Press, 98): 226-251; auth, "The Making of Hindu Communal Organizations, Places and Identities in Postcolonial Dar es Salaam," Environment and Planning D: Society and Space 15 (98): 707-730; auth, "Communal Places and the Politics of Multiple Identities: The case of Tanzanian Asians," Ecumene: J Environ, Culture, Meaning 4 (98): 3-26; auth, "Exploring Methodological Borderlands Through Oral Narratives," in Thresholds in Feminist Geography, eds. John Paul Jones III, Heidi J Nast, Susan M Roberts (Lanham, Maryland: Rowman and Littlefield, 98): 203-224; auth, "The South Asian Diaspora in Tanzania: A History Retold," Comparative Studies of South Asia, Africa and the Middle East: J Polit Cult Econ 16 (96): 62-80. **CONTACT ADDRESS** Dept Women's Studies, Univ of Minnesota, Twin Cities, 224 Church St, Minneapolis, MN 55455.

NAGLE, D. BRENDAN
DISCIPLINE HISTORY **EDUCATION** Cath Univ Am, STB; USC, AM, PhD. **CAREER** National Endowment for the Humanities fel, Amer Acad in Rome, 70; dept chem, 76-83; prof, Univ Southern Calif. **HONORS AND AWARDS** CINE Golden Eagle. **RESEARCH** Social, cultural & political historian of the ancient world, with a special interest in Greece and Rome. **SELECTED PUBLICATIONS** Auth, The Ancient World: A Social and Cultural History, Prentice-Hall, 96, 3rd ed; coauth, The Ancient World: Readings in Social and Cultural History, Prentice-Hall, 95; **CONTACT ADDRESS** Dept of History, Univ of So California, University Park Campus, Los Angeles, CA 90089. **EMAIL** nagle@usc.edu

NAGY-ZEKMI, SILVIA
PERSONAL Born 05/15/1953, Budapest, Hungary, m, 1995 **DISCIPLINE** HISPANIC STUDIES, LATIN AMERICAN LITERATURE **EDUCATION** Rakoczi Ferenc Gimnasium, Budapest, BA, 71; Eotvos Lorand Univ, Budapest, 80, MA, PhD, 81. **CAREER** Asst prof, Loyola Univ, 87-90; asst prof, Catholic Univ, Washington, DC, 90-97; assoc prof, SUNY Albany, 98-. **HONORS AND AWARDS** PhD, Cum Laude, 81; Fac grants, Catholic Univ, 93, 95, SUNY, 98. **MEMBERSHIPS** MLA, LASA, CIEF. **RESEARCH** Post-colonial theory, literary theory, 20th century Latin American literature, women's writing, indigenous literature, cultural studies. **SELECTED PUBLICATIONS** Auth, Paralelismos transatlanticos: postcolonalismo y narrativa femenina en America Latina y Africa del Norte (Providence, RI: Ediciones INTI, 96); rev, of "Christine Achour," Anthologie de la lineraturе algerienne, Paris: Bordas, 90, Middle East Studies Asn Bulletin 30 (96): 233-234; auth, "Textualidad femenina en America Latina, " Letras Femeninas XXIII, 1-2: 41-58 (97); ed, Identidades en transformacion: El discurso neoindigenista de los paises andinos (Quito: Abya Yala, 97); auth, "Aquel Senor Muteczuma: Construccion literia del Otro en las cronicas mesoamericansas," Labertino II, 1-2 (98), http://www.utsa.edu/academics/cofah/laberinto/frameset1997.htm; auth, "Entierro en el Este: Orientalismo en la poesia de Neruda," MACLAS XI, 121-132 (98); ed, De texto a contexto: Practicas discurs vas en la literatura espanola e hispanoamericana (Barcelona: Puvill, 98); auth, "Ficcion y testimonio en la obra de Manlio Argueta," De texto a contaxto: practicas discursives en la literatura espanola e hispoamericana (Barcelona: Puvill, 55-62, 1998); auth, "La novela rosa como disfraz: ironia en Angeles Mastretta," in Reflecciones: esayos sobre escritoras hispanoamericanas, ed Priscilla Gac-Artigas, http://www.monmouth.edu/~pgacarti/M-Mastretto-Ensayo.htm, 99; auth, "Silencio y ambiguedad en Blanca Sol de Mercedes Cabello de Carbonera," in La voz de la majer en la literatura hispanoamericana, ed Luis A. Jimenez, 51-60 (San Jose: Univ de Costa Rica, 99). **CONTACT ADDRESS** Dept Hispanic Studies, SUNY Albany, 1400 Washington Ave, HV 215, Albany, NY 12222-0100. **EMAIL** sng@csc.albany.edu

NAIR, SUPRYIA M.
DISCIPLINE POSTCOLONIAL LITERATURE AND THEORY, AFRICAN AND DIASPORA STUDIES **EDUCATION** St Joseph's Col, Vizag, India, BA, 82; Univ Hyderabad, India, MA, 84; Baylor Univ, MA, 86; Univ TX at Austin, PhD, 92. **CAREER** Assoc prof, 92, Tulane Univ. **HONORS AND AWARDS** Tex Excellence Teaching Award, Univ of Tex, 91; Tulane Univ Excellence in Undergraduate Teaching Award, 98. **RESEARCH** Caribbean Literatures, cultural studies, feminist theory, postcolonial theory. **SELECTED PUBLICATIONS** Auth, Melancholic Women: The Intellectual Hysteric(s) in Nervous Conditions, Res African Lit 26.2, 95; auth, Caliban's Curse: George Lamming and the Revisioning of History, Univ of Michi Press, 96; auth, "Postmodern Utopias and Expressive Countercultures: A Caribbean Context," Res in African Lit 27.4, (96), 71-87; auth, "Homing Instincts: Immigrant Nostalgia and Genbder Politics in Representation, The Univ Press of Virgina, 99; auth, "Creolization, Orality and Nation Language in the Caribbean," A Companion to Postcolonial studies, (00), 236-251. **CONTACT ADDRESS** Dept of Eng, Tulane Univ, 6823 St Charles Ave, New Orleans, LA 70118. **EMAIL** supriya@tulane.edu

NAISON, MARK
DISCIPLINE AFRICAN-AMERICAN HISTORY **EDUCATION** Columbia Univ, PhD. **CAREER** Prof, Fordham Univ. **HONORS AND AWARDS** Founder, Bronx Youth Employ Proj. **SELECTED PUBLICATIONS** Auth, Communists in Harlem during the Depression, Univ Ill Press, 83; Outlaw Culture in Black Culture, Reconstruction, 94; African-Americans and the Rise of Buffalo's Post-Industrial City, Urban League's anthology, 90; co-auth, The Tenant Movement in New York City, 1940-1984, Rutgers UP, 86. **CONTACT ADDRESS** Dept of Hist, Fordham Univ, 113 W 60th St, New York, NY 10023.

NAJEMY, JOHN MICHAEL
PERSONAL Born 09/09/1943, Worcester, MA **DISCIPLINE** RENAISSANCE HISTORY **EDUCATION** Princeton Univ, BA, 65; Harvard Univ, PhD(hist), 72. **CAREER** From instr to asst prof hist, Harvard Univ, 71-75; from Asst Prof to Assoc Prof, 75-92, Prof Hist, Cornell Univ, 92-. **HONORS AND AWARDS** I Tatti Fel, 69-71; Fels hist, Villa I Tatti, Harvard Univ Ctr Ital Renaissance Studies & Leopold Schepp Found, 74-75; fac fel, Soc for Humanities, Cornell Univ, 82-83; Marraro Prize of the Am Hist Asn, for Corporatism and Consensus, 83; Marraro Prize of the Soc for Ital Hist Studies, for Between Friends, 95; Guggenheim fel, 85-86; NEH fel, 98-99. **MEMBERSHIPS** AHA; Renaissance Soc Am. **RESEARCH** Florence: politics, society, guilds, political thought, historiography, Machiavelli, Alberti; Medieval and Renaissance Italy. **SELECTED PUBLICATIONS** Auth, Corporatism and Consensus in Florentine Electoral Politics, 1280-1400, Univ of North Carolina Press, 82; contribr, The Dialogue of Power in Florentine Politics, In: City-States in Classical Antiquity and Medieval Italy, Franz Steiner Verlag, 91; Dante and Florence, In: The Cambridge Companion to Dante, Cambridge Univ Press, 93; Machiavelli and Geta: Men of Letters, In: Machiavelli and the Discourse of Literature, Cornell Univ Press, 93; auth, Between Friends: Discourses of Power and Desire in the Machiavelli-Vettori Letters of 1513-1515, Princeton Univ Press, 93; Brunetto Latini's "Politica", Dante Studies, 94; contribr, Language and The Prince, In: Niccolò Machiavelli's The Prince: New Interdisciplinary Essays, Manchester Univ Press, 95; The Republic's Two Bodies: Body Metaphors in Italian Renaissance Political Thought, In: Language and Images of Renaissance Italy, Clarendon Press, 95; Contribr, Giannozzo and His Elders: Alberti's Critique of Renaissance Patriarchy, In: Culture and Self in Renaissance Europe, Univ Calif Press (forthcoming); auth, Papirius and the Chickens, or Machiavelli on the Necessity of Interpreting Religion, Journal of the History of Ideas, 99; Contrib, Civic Humanism and Florentine Politics, In: Renaissance Civic

Humanism, Cambridge Univ Press, 00. **CONTACT ADDRESS** Dept of History, Cornell Univ, Mcgraw Hall, Ithaca, NY 14853-4601. **EMAIL** jmn4@cornell.edu

NAJITA, TETSUO
PERSONAL Born 03/30/1936, m **DISCIPLINE** HISTORY **EDUCATION** Grinell Col, BA, 58; Harvard Univ, MA, 60; PhD, 65. **CAREER** Carleton Col, 64-66; Wash Univ, 66-68; Univ Wisc, 68; distinguished service prof, Univ Chicago, 69-. **HONORS AND AWARDS** Woodrow Wilson Fel, Ford Foundation Fel, Fulbright Fel, Nat Endowment for the Humanities Res Fel, Guggenheim Fel, Japan Foundation Fel, Hon Doc of Law, Grinell Col, Fel of Am Acad of Arts and Sci. **MEMBERSHIPS** Am Hist Asn, Assn for Asian Studies. **RESEARCH** Intellectual history of Japan - early modern and modern. **SELECTED PUBLICATIONS** Auth, Japan, The Intellectual Foundations of Modern Japanese Politics; auth, Visions of Virtue in Tokugawa Japan: The Kaitokudo Merchangt Academy of Osaka. **CONTACT ADDRESS** Dept Hist, Univ of Chicago, 1126 E 59th St, Chicago, IL 60637-1580.

NAKHAI, BETH ALPERT
PERSONAL Born 07/05/1951, New York, NY, m, 1986, 1 child **DISCIPLINE** NEAR EASTERN ARCHAEOLOGY, BIBLICAL STUDIES **EDUCATION** Conn Col, BA, 72; Harvard Div Sch, MTS, 79; Univ Ariz, MA, 85, PhD, 93. **CAREER** Univ Ariz, 83-86, 88-89; adj instr, Prescott Col, 95; asst prof, Univ Ariz, 94- . **HONORS AND AWARDS** Robert H. Pfeiffer Found Trust, 78; Zion Res Found Travel Scholar, 79; Univ Ariz Grad Tuition Scholar, 82-83; Maurice Cohen Awd in Judaic Stud, 83; Bernard Ivan Amster Mem Awd, 83; tchg asst, Dept Oriental Stud, 1st yr Hebrew, 83-87; Samuel H. Kress found fel, 86-87; Univ Ariz Grad Acad Scholar, 87-89; Dorot Found doctoral fel, 88-89; Tchg asst, Dept Near East Stud, Ancient Civilizations Near East, 88-89; Res Asst, Dept Near East Stud, 90; Mem found Jewish Cult Doctoral Scholar, 86-91; Amer Sch Oriental Res Comm Archaeol Policy Endow Bibl Archaeol grant, 97; Amer Sch Oriental Res Comm Archaelo Policy Endow Bibl Archael grant, 97; Assoc Women fac travel grant, Univ Ariz, 97-98; American Assoc of Univ Women Summer Research grant, 00. **MEMBERSHIPS** Amer Sch Oriental Res; Soc Bibl Lit; Ctr Middle East Stud; Assn Women Fac, Univ Ariz. **RESEARCH** Canaanite and Israelite Religion; women in antiquity issues. **SELECTED PUBLICATIONS** Auth, Tell el-Wawiyat, Revue biblique, 95/2, 88, 247-251; Tell el-Wawiyat, 1987 Israel Exploration Jour, 39.1-2, 102 Tell el-Wawiyat, Encyclopedia of Archaelolgical Excavations in the Holy Land, 2nd ed, E. Stern, ed, Jerusalem, Israel Exploration Soc, 92; What's a Bamah? How Sacred Space Functioned in Ancient Israel, Bibl Archaeol Rev, 20, 18-19, 77-78; Wawiyat, Jell el-, Encyclopedia of Archaeology in the Bibl World, vol 5, 333-334, Eric M. Meyers, ed, New York, Oxford UP, 97; Syro-Palestinian Temples, Encyclopedia of Near Eastern Archaelology, vol 5, E.M. Meyers, ed, New York, Oxford UP, 169-174, 97; Locus, Encyclopedia of Near Eastern Archaeology, vol 3, E.M. Meyers, ed, NY, Oxford UP, 97, 383-384; Kitan, Tel., Encycolpedia of Near Eastern Archaeology, vol 3, E.M. Meyers, ed, New York, Oxford Univ Press, 97, 300; Furniture and Furnishings: Furnishings of the Bronze and Iron Ages, Encyclopedia of Near eastern Archaeology, vol 2, E.M. Meyers, ed, NY, Oxford UP, 97, 354-356; Beth Zur, Encyclopedia of near Eastern Archaeology vol 1, E.M. Meyers, ed, NY, Oxford UP, 97, 314; Featured in Written in Stones, People, Places and Society: A Publication for Alumni and Friends of the College of Social and Behavioral Sciences, Univ Ariz, Spring, 3, 98; Rev article, Jerusalem: An Archaeological Biography, Shofar, 16,3, 98, 174-176; auth, Iraelite Religion Beyond the Temple; The Archaeological Witness, The World of the Bible 1, (99): 38-43; auth, Archaelogy, Encyclopedia of Women and World Religions, vol 1, New York, Macmillan Reference, (99): 50-51; coauth, A Landscape Comes to Life: The Iron I Period, Near Eastern Archaelolgy 62/2, (99): 62-92, 101-127. **CONTACT ADDRESS** 905 N Tenth Ave, Tucson, AZ 85705-7623. **EMAIL** bnakhai@u.arizona.edu

NALL, GARRY LYNN
PERSONAL Born 08/12/1936, Loving, TX **DISCIPLINE** UNITED STATES HISTORY **EDUCATION** Univ Tex, Austin, BA, 58, MA, 59; Univ Okla, PhD(hist), 72. **CAREER** From instr to asst prof, 63-74, assoc prof, 74-81, Prof Hist, W TX State Univ, 81-. **MEMBERSHIPS** Orgn Am Historians; Agr Hist Soc; Western Hist Asn. **RESEARCH** United States agricultural history; the Great Plains; United States, 1876-1914. **SELECTED PUBLICATIONS** Auth, The farmers' frontier in the Texas Panhandle, 72, Panhandle farming in the golden era of American agriculture, 73, Specialization and expansion: Panhandle farming in the 1920's, 74 & Dust bowl days: Panhandle farming in the 1930's, 75, Panhandle-Plains Hist Rev; Rural Oklahoma, Okla Hist Soc, 77; The struggle to save the land, the soil conservation effort in the dust bowl, In: The Depression in the Southwest, Kennikat Press, 80. **CONTACT ADDRESS** Dept of Hist, West Texas A&M Univ, 2501 4th Ave, Canyon, TX 79016-0001.

NALLE, SARA TILGHMAN
DISCIPLINE HISTORY **EDUCATION** Bryn Mawr Col, BA, 75; Johns Hopkins Univ, MA, 78; PhD, 83. **CAREER** Assoc prof, William Paterson Col, 91-; vis assoc prof, Inst for Shipboard Educ, Univ Pittsburgh, 92; asst prof, William Paterson Col, 86-91; asst prof, Rhode Island Cole, Providence, 84-86; postdr tchg fel, Boston Col, Chestnut Hill, 82-84; asst prof, US Naval Acad, Annapolis, 81-82; tchg asst, Johns Hopkins Univ, Baltimore, 80-81 & 77-78. **HONORS AND AWARDS** Mem, Inst Advan Stud, 95; visitor, 96; Roland Bainton Bk Prize, 93; NJ Gov's fel in the Humanities, 89-90; Harold J Grimm Prize, 88; postdoctoral res grant, Treaty for Friendship, Defense, and Coop between the USA and the Kingdom of Spain, 85 & 86; grad fel, Johns Hopkins Univ, 79-80; Fulbright-Hays Dissertation Scholar, Spain, 78-79; finalist, Woodrow Wilson tchg fel, 75. **MEMBERSHIPS** Soc Span and Port Hist Stud; AHA; Int Inst Found in Spain; 16th century Stud Asn. **RESEARCH** Connections between religious radicalism, rebellion, and perceptions of sanity in 16th-century Spain. **SELECTED PUBLICATIONS** Auth, "Desde el olvido a la fama: el culto a San Julin en los siglos XVI y XVII," Almud, Revista de Estudios Manchegos 1 (81): 25-41; auth, "Inquisitors, Priests, and the People During the Catholic Reformation in Spain," The Sixteenth Century Journal 18 (87): 557-587; auth, "Popular Religion in Cuenca on the Eve of the Catholic Reformation," in Inquisition and Society in Early Modern Europe, ed. Stephen Haliczer (London, Croom-Helm, 87), 67-87; auth, "Literacy and Culture in Early Modern Castile," Past and Present (89): 65-96; auth, A Saint for All Seasons, in Culture and Control in Counter-Reformation Spain, Hisp Issues Ser, Minneapolis: Univ Minn Press, 91; auth, God in La Mancha: Religious Reform and the People of Cuenca, 1500-1650, Baltimore: Johns Hopkins Univ Press, 92; auth, Bones and Crosses: Recent Trends in Early Mod Spanish Historiography, Bul of the Soc for Span and Port Hist Stud, 94; auth, "Moya busca nuevo senor: aspectos de la rebelion comunera en el Marquesado de Moya," Diputacion Provincial de Cuenca (96); **CONTACT ADDRESS** Dept of History, William Paterson Col of New Jersey, 300 Pompton Rd., Atrium 20, Wayne, NJ 07470. **EMAIL** nalle@frontier.wpunj.edu

NANCE, BRIAN K.
DISCIPLINE HISTORY **EDUCATION** NMex State Univ, BA; Univ NC at Chapel Hill, MA, 86; PhD, 91. **CAREER** From asst prof to assoc prof, Coastal Carolina Univ, 91-00. **MEMBERSHIPS** Hist of Sci Soc, Am Asn for the Hist of Medicine, Renaissance Soc of Am. **RESEARCH** Medical History, Cultural and Intellectual History. **SELECTED PUBLICATIONS** Auth, The Art of Medical Portraiture: Turquet de mayzine as Baroque Physician, forthcoming. **CONTACT ADDRESS** Dept Hist, Coastal Carolina Univ, PO Box 261954, Conway, SC 29528-6054. **EMAIL** brian@coastal.edu

NANCE, JOSEPH MILTON
PERSONAL Born 09/18/1913, Kyle, TX, m, 1944, 3 children **DISCIPLINE** UNITED STATES & TEXAS HISTORY **EDUCATION** Univ Tex, BA, 35, MA, 36, PhD, 41. **CAREER** State supvr Am imprints, manuscripts & newspaper inventory, Hist Rec Surv, Works Prog Admin, 38-40; instr hist, Agr & Mech Col Tex, 41-42; instr radio code & typing, US Naval Training Sch, Tex, 42-43; head dept hist & govt, 58-68, head dept hist, 68-73, from instr to assoc prof, 46-57, Prof Hist, Tex A&m Univ, 57-, Fund Improvement Tex res grant, 57; mem Pub bd, Arizona & The West, 79-; mem Pub adv comt, Tex Hist Found, 79-. **HONORS AND AWARDS** Tex Inst Lett Awd, 63; Walter Prescott Awd, 66; Amoco Distinguish Awd in Res & Writing, 79; Col Law, Baylor Univ established Joseph Milton Nance Scholarships, 79; Dept Hist, Tex A&M Univ established J Milton Nance Lectures, 80-. **MEMBERSHIPS** AHA; Orgn Am Historians; Southern Hist Asn; Am Studies Asn; Western Hist Asn. **RESEARCH** Texas history; United States history before 1865; early Hawaiian history to 1860. **SELECTED PUBLICATIONS** Auth, Checklist of Texas Newspapers, 1813-1939, San Jacinto Mus of Hist, 41; Early history of Bryan and the surrounding area, Hood's Brigade-Bryan Centennial Comt, 62; After San Jacinto: Texas-Mexican Frontier Relations, 1836-1841, 63 & Attack and Counterattack: The Texas-Mexican Frontier, 1842, 64, Univ Tex; ed, Some Reflections Upon Modern America, Tex A&M Univ, 69; auth, Instructor's manual, 70 & Student's guide, 71, to accompany Graebner, Fite, White, A History of the American People, McGraw; The Gulf Coast and the Texas question during the presidential campaign of 1844, In: Americanization of the Gulf Coast, 1803-1850, Hist Peninsula Preserv Bd, 72; ed, Joseph D McCutchan's Narrative of the Texian Mier Expedition of 1842, Univ Tex, Austin, 78; Papers Concerning Robertson Colony in Texas, Vol 18, August 11, 1840 Through March 4, 1842, The End of an Era - Mclean,md, Western Historical Quarterly, Vol 0024, 1993. **CONTACT ADDRESS** 1403 Post Oak Circle, College Station, TX 77840. **EMAIL** j-nance10107@tamu.edu

NAPTON, DARRELL E.
PERSONAL Born 09/20/1951, Kansas City, KS, m, 1989 **DISCIPLINE** GEOGRAPHY **EDUCATION** Univ Miss, BS, 73; MA, 75; Univ Minn, PhD, 87. **CAREER** Asst prof, S W Tex State Univ, 87-92; assoc prof to prof, SDak State Univ, 92-. **MEMBERSHIPS** Assoc of Am Geog; Am Geog Soc; Sol and Water Conserv Soc. **RESEARCH** Land use and changing land use patterns in the United States. **SELECTED PUBLICATIONS** Auth, "Sources of Local Geographic Information", in Why Not Here: Teaching Geography to a New Standard, ed. Philip J. Gersmehl, Ind Univ of Pa, 96; auth, "Restructuring for rural Sustainability: Overcoming Scale Conflicts and Cultural Biases", in Agricultural Restructuring and Sustainability: A Geographical Perspective, eds Brian Ilbery, Quentin Chiotti, and Timothy Rickard, CAB Int, (Wallingford, UK, 97): 329-340; auth, "Achieving Excellence in Undergraduate Recruitment", Assoc of Am Geog, 97; coauth, "Continuity and Change in the Developed Countryside", in Reshaping the Countryside: Perceptions and Processes of Rural Change, eds Darrell E. Napton, Nigel Walford and John Everett, CAB Int, (Oxon, UK, 99): 1-12; coed, Reshaping the Countryside: Perceptions and Processes of Rural Change, CAB Int, (Wallingford Oxon:UK), 99. **CONTACT ADDRESS** Dept Geog, So Dakota State Univ, Brookings, SD 57007-0002. **EMAIL** Darrell_Napton@sdstate.edu

NAQUIN, SUSAN
PERSONAL Born 00/00/1944, Chicago, IL **DISCIPLINE** CHINESE HISTORY **EDUCATION** Stanford Univ, BA, 66; Yale Univ, MA, 69, PhD(hist), 74. **CAREER** Asst prof, 76-81, Assoc Prof Hist, Univ PA, 81-, Co-ed, Ching-shih wen-ti. **RESEARCH** Early modern hist of China, 16th through 19th centuries. **SELECTED PUBLICATIONS** Auth, Millenarian Rebellion in China: The Eight Trigrams Uprising of 1813, 76 & Shantung Rebellion: The Wang Lun Uprising of 1774, 81, Yale Univ Press; Chinese Local Elites And Patterns of Dominance - Esherick,j, Rankin,mb, American Historical Review, Vol 0098, 1993. **CONTACT ADDRESS** Dept of Hist, Princeton Univ, 124 Dickinson Hall, Princeton, NJ 08544. **EMAIL** snaquin@princeton.edu

NARDONE, RICHARD MORTON
PERSONAL Born 06/21/1929, Orange, NJ **DISCIPLINE** HISTORICAL THEOLOGY **EDUCATION** Seton Hall Univ, BA, 50; Cath Univ Am, STL, 54; Univ St Michael's Col, PhD(theol), 72. **CAREER** Assoc Prof Relig Studies, Seton Hall Univ, 68-, Judge, Matrimonial Tribunal-Archdiocese of Newark, NJ, 77-. **MEMBERSHIPS** Cath Theol Soc Am; Am Acad Relig. **RESEARCH** Patristics; liturgical studies; ecumenical studies. **SELECTED PUBLICATIONS** Auth, The Roman calender in ecumenical perspective, Worship, 5/76; coauth, The Church of Jerusalem and the Christian Calender, Standing Before God, KTAV Publ House, 81; auth, Liturgical change: A reappraisal, Homiletic & Pastoral Rev, 11/81; The Story of the Christian Year, Paulist Press, 91. **CONTACT ADDRESS** Dept of Relig Studies, Seton Hall Univ, So Orange, 400 S Orange Ave., South Orange, NJ 07079-2697.

NAREY, MARTHA
PERSONAL Born 08/06/1946, Little Rock, AR **DISCIPLINE** GEOGRAPHY **EDUCATION** Univ Colo, BA, 83; Univ Colo, MA, 88; Univ Denver, PhD, 99. **CAREER** Adj Instr, Univ Denver, 95-97; Asst Prof, Univ Nebr, 97-. **HONORS AND AWARDS** Sigma Xi, 95 **MEMBERSHIPS** Assoc of Am Geogrs, Am Indian Sci & Engineering Soc. **RESEARCH** Dendro climatology, climate history, historical climatology, American Indians. **SELECTED PUBLICATIONS** Auth, "Shifts Between Grassland and Cropland: Effects of Changing Valuation in Morgan County, Colorado," Great Plains/Rocky Mountain Geog J, vol 18, no 1 (90). **CONTACT ADDRESS** Dept Geog, Univ of Nebraska, Kearney, 905 W 25th St, Kearney, NE 68847. **EMAIL** nareym@unk.edu

NASGAARD, ROALD
PERSONAL Born 10/14/1941, Denmark **DISCIPLINE** ART HISTORY **EDUCATION** Univ BC, BA, 65, MA, 67; Inst Fine Art, NYork Univ, PhD, 73. **CAREER** Lectr, fine art, 71-74, asst prof, 74-75, Univ Guelph; cur contemp art, 75-78, dep dir & chief cur, 78-93, AGO; vis lectr, 83-92, adj prof, 92-95, Univ Toronto; prof & chair, dept art, Florida State Univ, 95-; co-dir prog, Inst Mod & Contemporary Art, Calgary, 95-. **MEMBERSHIPS** Trustee, Gershon Iskowitz Found, 91-; Toronto Pub Art Comn, 86-88; Col Art Asn; Univ Art Asn Can; Int Art Critics Asn. **SELECTED PUBLICATIONS** Auth, "Structures for Behaviour, new scuplture by Robert Morris, David Rabinowitch, Richard Serra and George Trakas," Art Gallery of Ontario, 78; auth, "Garry Kennedy: Painting Reinvented," Art Galery of Ontario, 79, 10 Canadian Artists in the 70s, Art Gallery of Ontario, 80; auth, "The Mystic North: Symbolist Landscape Painting in Northern Europe and North America, 1890-1940," University of Toronto Press, 84; auth, "Gerhard Richter: Paintings, London: Thames and Hudson, 88; auth, "The Book of Gestures: some thoughts on the early work," in Gary Dufour, Jochen Gerz: People Speak, Vancouver, 94, pp. 33-48; auth, "Guido Molinari et l'element destructeur en art," in Guido Molinari: Une Retrospective, Musee d'Art Contemporain de Montreal, 95, English language insert: "Guido Molinari and the destructive element in art," pp. 13-18; auth, "Strata and Stratagems, or Pretty in Pink," in Garry Neil Kennedy: Wall Paintings, Owens Art Gallery, Sackville, N.B. 96, pp 133-137; auth, "The Treachery of Gun Images," in Bang! The Gun as Image, Museum of Fine Arts, Florida State University, 97, pp. 6-13; auth, "Charles Burchfield and the Theme of North," in The Paintings of Carles Burchfield: North by Midwest, Columbus Museum of Art, Columbus, Ohio, 97, pp. 24-37; auth, "Chris Cran's States of Delicious Anxiety," in Chris Cran: Surveying the Damage 1977-1977, Kelowna Art Gallery, 98, pp. 28-45. **CONTACT ADDRESS** Dept of Art, Florida State Univ, Tallahassee, FL 32306-2037. **EMAIL** rnasgaar@rnailer.fsu.edu

NASH, ANEDITH
DISCIPLINE ART AND DESIGN **EDUCATION** Baylor Univ, BA, 64; Wash State Univ, MA, 70; Univ Minn, PhD, 83. **CAREER** Assoc acad dean, Minneapolis Col Art and Design, 97-; prof & ch, Liberal Arts Div, Minneapolis Col Art and Design, 92 & 96; coordr, Grad Prog, Minneapolis Col Art and Design, 93-; adj fac, Hamline Univ Grad Sch, 87-95; dean cont stud, Minneapolis Col Art and Design, 89-92; prog dir & primary fac, Metro Urban Stud Term and City Arts Prog, Higher Educ Consortium for Urban Aff, HECUA Hamline Univ, 82-89; lectr, Dept Soc, Macalester Col, 83-87. **SELECTED PUBLICATIONS** Coauth, The Skyway System and Urban Space: Vitality in Enclosed Public Places, The Community of the Streets, Greenwich, Conn, and London: JAI Press, Inc, 94. **CONTACT ADDRESS** Oregon Col of Art and Craft, 8245 SW Barnes Rd., Portland, OR 97225-6349. **EMAIL** anedith_nash@mn.mcad.edu

NASH, GARY B.
PERSONAL Born 07/27/1933, Philadelphia, PA, m, 1981, 4 children **DISCIPLINE** AMERICAN HISTORY **EDUCATION** Princeton Univ, BA, 55; PhD, 64. **CAREER** Assoc Prof, Univ Calif, Los Angeles, 66-68; prof, Univ Calif, Los Angeles, 74-; dir, Nat Center for Hist in the Schools, 94-. **HONORS AND AWARDS** Guggenheim Mem Fel; Am Coun of Learned Soc Fel. **MEMBERSHIPS** Am Antiq Soc; Soc of Am Historians; Am Acad of Arts and Sci. **RESEARCH** Colonial American history. **SELECTED PUBLICATIONS** Auth, Quakers and Politics: Pennsylvania, 1681-1726, 68; auth, "Poverty and Poor Relief in Pre-Revolutionary Philadelphia," William and Mary Quart (76); auth, The Urban Crucible: Social Change, Political Consciousness and the Origins of the American Revolution, 79; auth, Race, Class and Politics: Essays on American Colonial and Revolutionary Society, 86; auth, Forging Freedom: The Formation of Philadelphia's Black Community, 1720-1840, 89; auth, Race and Revolution: The Inaugural Merrill Jensen Lectures, 93; coauth, Freedom by Degrees: Emancipation and Its Aftermath in Pennsylvania, 1690-1840, 94; coauth, History on Trial: Culture Wars, and the Teaching of the Past, 98; coed, Empire, Society, and Labor: Essays in Honor of Richard S. Dunn, 98; auth, Forbidden Love: The Secret History of Mixed Race America, 99. **CONTACT ADDRESS** Dept of Hist, Univ of California, Los Angeles, Los Angeles, CA 90024. **EMAIL** gnash@ucla.edu

NASH, GERALD DAVID
PERSONAL Born 07/16/1928, Berlin, Germany, m, 1967, 1 child **DISCIPLINE** HISTORY **EDUCATION** NYork Univ, BA, 50; Columbia Univ, MA, 52; Univ Calif, Berkeley, PhD, 57. **CAREER** Instr, 57-58 asst prof, 59-60, Stanford Univ; asst prof, 58-59, Northern Ill Univ; post dr fel, 60-61, Harvard Univ; asst prof, 61-63, Univ N Mex; assoc prof, 63-68, prof, 68-, chmn, 74-80, dist prof, 85-94, prof emeritus, 94-, vis assoc prof, 65-66, New York Univ; George Bancroft Prof, 90-91, Goettingen Univ, Germany. **RESEARCH** US 20th century, West in 20th century, US economic policies. **SELECTED PUBLICATIONS** Auth, Issues in American Economic History, Heath, 63, ed, 2nd ed, 72 & 3rd ed, 80; Franklin Delano Roosevelt, Prentice- Hall, 67; Introduction to Administrative History, Univ Calif, 68; US Oil Policy, 1890-1964, Univ Pittsburgh, 68; The Great Transition, Allyn & Bacon, 71; The American West in the Twentieth Century, Prentice-Hall, 73; The Urban West, Sunflower, 79; The Great Depression and World War II, St Martin's, 79; The West Transformed, 1941-1945, Ind Univ, 85; with Richard W. Eterlain, ed. Twentieth Century West, Univ of NM Press, 88; with Noel Pugach ed., Social Security: The First Fifty Years Univ of N.M., Press, 88; World War II and the West Univ of Nebraska Press, 90; Creating the West, Univ of N.M. Press, 91; A.P Giannini and the Bank of America, Univ of Oklahoma Press, 92; with Richard W. Etulain ed. Researching Western History, Univ of N.M. Press, 97; The Federal Landscape, Univ of Arizona Press, 99; auth, A Brief History of the American Harcourt, 00. **CONTACT ADDRESS** 8809 New Hampton Rd, NE, Albuquerque, NM 87111. **EMAIL** gnash@unm.edu

NASH, LEE
PERSONAL Born 09/10/1927, North Bend, OR, m, 1951, 3 children **DISCIPLINE** HISTORY **EDUCATION** Cascade Col, AB, 50; Univ Wash, MA, 51; Univ Ore, PhD(hist), 61. **CAREER** Asst prof, 51-56, assoc prof, 59-60, prof & chmn Div Soc Sci, 60-67, Dean, 62-67, Cascade Col; res assoc, Univ Ore, 61-62; from assoc prof to prof, Northern Ariz Univ, 67-75; prof & chmn Div Soc Sci, 75-82, vice pres for acad aff, 84-92, Herbert Hoover prof, Hist, 92-96, prof, Hist, George Fox Col, 92-97, Dir biennial Herbert Hoover symposia, 77- . **HONORS AND AWARDS** Marion F McClain Award, 62; Joel Palmer Award, Ore Hist Q, 98. **MEMBERSHIPS** AHA; Orgn Am Historians; Western Hist Asn; Western Lit Asn; Conf Faith & Hist. **RESEARCH** 20th century United States; American thought and culture; Herbert Hoover. **SELECTED PUBLICATIONS** Auth, Portland's first history, Call Number, spring 60; auth, Kenneth Scott Latourette: 1888-1968, Fides et Historia, spring 69; auth, Scott of the Oregonian: The editor as historian, Ore Hist Quart, 69; auth, Liberalism in America, In: Westminster Dictionary of Church History, Westminster Press, 71; auth, Harvey Scott's cure for drones: An Oregon alternative to Pubic higher schools, Pac Northwest Quart, 473; auth, Scott of the Oregonian: Literary frontiersman, Pac Hist Rev, 8/76; auth, The Oregon Years, Mountain Pr, 85; auth, Understanding Herbert Hoover: Ten Perspectives, Hoover Inst Pr, 87; ed, F.F. Victor's River of the Westauth, Abigail versus Harvey: Sibling Rivalry in the Oregon Campaign for Woman Suffrage, Ore Hist Quart, Summer 97. **CONTACT ADDRESS** Dept of Hist, George Fox Univ, Newberg, OR 97132. **EMAIL** lnash@georgefox.edu

NASH, RODERICK W.
PERSONAL Born 01/07/1939, New York, NY, m, 1960, 2 children **DISCIPLINE** AMERICAN ENVIRONMENTAL HISTORY **EDUCATION** Harvard Univ, BA, 60; Univ Wis, MA, 61, PhD(hist), 64. **CAREER** Instr Am hist, Dartmouth Col, 64-66; asst prof Am intellectual hist, 66-71, assoc prof, 71-73, Prof Hist & Environ Studies, Univ Calif, Santa Barbara, 73-95, Chmn Dept Environ Studies, 71-76, Resources for Future fac grant, 67-70; consult, US Off Educ, 70-; mem bd dirs, Yosemite Inst, 71-; mem adv comt, US Nat Park Serv, 72-; consult, Rockefeller Found, 73- & State of Alaska, 80-; Lindbergh fel, 82. **MEMBERSHIPS** Am Studies Asn; Forest Hist Soc; Orgn Am Historians; AHA. **RESEARCH** American social and intellectual history; wilderness history and management; popular cultural history. **SELECTED PUBLICATIONS** Coauth, Philanthropy in the Shaping of American Higher Education, Rutgers Univ, 65; auth, Wilderness and the American Mind, Yale Univ, 67, rev ed, 73, 3rd ed, 82; The American Environment, Addison-Wesley, 68, rev ed, 76; ed, The American Culture: The Call of the Wild, Braziller, 70; Grand Canyon of the Living Colorado, Sierra Club, 70; Environment and Americans, Holt, 72; auth, From These Beginnings: A Biographical Approach to American History, Harper, 73; coauth, The Big Drops: Ten Legendary Rapids of the American West, Sierra Club, 78; The Sierra-club Centennial in Historical-perspective - Introduction to The Special Issue, California History, Vol 0071, 1992. **CONTACT ADDRESS** Dept of Hist, Univ of California, Santa Barbara, Santa Barbara, CA 93106.

NASKE, CLAUS M.
PERSONAL Born 12/18/1935, Stettin, Germany, m, 1960, 2 children **DISCIPLINE** HISTORY **EDUCATION** Univ of AK, BA, 61; Univ of MI, MA, 64; WA St Univ, PhD, 70 **CAREER** Inst, 65-67, Juneau-Douglas Community College of the Univ of Alaska, Teaching Asst, 67-69, WA St Univ; Asst Prof, 69-72, Univ of AK, Fairbanks; assoc prof, Univ of Alaska Fairbanks, 73-81, prof, 81-; dir, U A Press, 88-; Univ of AK; Exec Dir, 88-, UA Press. **HONORS AND AWARDS** Ten books **MEMBERSHIPS** Western Hist Asn **RESEARCH** Alaska; Circumpolar North; Canadian History; Native American. **SELECTED PUBLICATIONS** Auth, An Interpretative History of Alaska Statehood, 73; auth, Edward Lewis Bob Bartlett of Alaska©A Life in Politics, 79; auth, Anchorage: A Pictorial History, 81; auth, Fairbanks: A Pictorial History, 81, expaned edition, 95; auth, Alaska: A Pictorial History, 83; auth, A History of Alaska Statehood, 85; auth, Paving Alaska's Trails: The Work of the Alaska Road Commission, 86; auth, Alaska's Builders: 50 Years of Construction in the 49th State, 98. **CONTACT ADDRESS** Dept of Hist, Univ of Alaska, Fairbanks, PO Box 80721, Fairbanks, AK 99708. **EMAIL** ffcmn@aurora.alaska.edu

NASU, EISHO
PERSONAL Born 02/14/1961, Japan, m, 1996 **DISCIPLINE** CULTURAL AND HISTORICAL STUDY OF RELIGIONS; BUDDHIST STUDIES **EDUCATION** Kobe City Univ For Studies, BA, 83; Ryukoku Univ, MA, 86; Grad Theol Union, MA, 90, PhD, 96. **CAREER** Asst res, Jodo Shinshu Seiten Hensan Iinkaa, Jodo Shinshu Hongwanji, 85-88; adj prof, Inst of Buddhist Studies, Grad Theol union, 96-97; res fel, dept e asian lang, Univ Calif Berkeley, 96-98; acad ed, numata ctr buddhist transl res, 97-; asst prof, shin buddhism, inst buddhist studies, grad theol union; Henry Mayo Newhall Res Fel, 92-93. **HONORS AND AWARDS** Int Asn Buddhist Cult Scholar, 88-92; Horai Asn Scholar, 93-96. W E Friends Awd Outstanding Res Encounters W/E Cult, 90. **SELECTED PUBLICATIONS** Auth, A Critical Review of Joseph Kitagawa's Methodology of History of Religions in the Field of Japanese Religious Studies, Pacific World, 94; Popular Pure Land Teachings of the Zenkoji Nyorai and Shinran, The Pure Land, 95; Ocean of the One Vehicle: Shinran's View of the ekayana Ideal, Watanabe Takao kyoju kanreki kinen ronshu: Bukkyoshiso bunkashi ronso, Nagata bunshodo, 97; coed, Engaged Pure Land Buddhism: Challenges Facing Jodo Shinshu in the Contemporary World, Studies in Honor of Prof Alfred Bloom, WisdomOncean Publ, 98; auth, Ordination Ceremony of the Honganji Priests in Premodern Japanese Society, Engaged Pure Land Buddhism: Challenges Facing Jodo Shinshu in the Comtemporary World, 98. **CONTACT ADDRESS** 1821 Carleton St, Berkeley, CA 94703. **EMAIL** nasu_ibs@msn.com

NATAVAR, MEKHALA D.
PERSONAL Born 09/19/1955, Princeton, NJ, m, 1999, 2 children **DISCIPLINE** HINDI STUDIES **EDUCATION** Northwestern Univ, BS, 89; Univ Wis, MA, 91; PhD, 97. **CAREER** Prof, Univ Va, 97; Asst Prof, Duke Univ, 98-. **HONORS AND AWARDS** Res Grant, ASRC, 99; Jon B Higgins Mem Scholarship, Raga-Mala Performing Arts of Canada, 96; Fel, Foreign Lang and Area Studies, Univ Wisc, 92; Pell Grant, Northwestern Univ, 89. **MEMBERSHIPS** Triangle South Asia consortium, Rajasthan Studies Group, SALTA. **RESEARCH** Indian Dance and Hindu cosmology; Performance genres in south Asian Contexts; The Analysis and performance of Bhakti (devotional) Literature; Arts and Aesthetics in South Asia; Gender Categories within the South Asian context. **SELECTED PUBLICATIONS** Auth, "Performances at the Govindenji Temple in Jaipur," South Asian Folklore: An Encyclopedia, Garland Pub, in press; auth, "Hijra (transvestite/transsexual) Performances," in South Asian Folklore: An Encyclopedia, Garland Pub, in press; auth, "Kathak Dancers," in South Asian Folklore: An Encyclopedia, Garland Pub, in press; auth, "Music and Dance: Northern Area," in The Garland Encyclopedia of World Music Vol 5: South Asia, Garland Pub, (99): 492-506; auth, "Rajasthan," in The Garland Encyclopedia of World Music Vol 5: South Asia, Garland Pub, (99): 639-649; auth, "Music and Dance: Southern Area," in The Garland Encyclopedia of World Music Vol 5: South Asia, Garland Pub, (99): 507-523. **CONTACT ADDRESS** Dept Asian and African Lang & Lit, Duke Univ, 2101 Campus Dr, PO Box 90414, Durham, NC 27707. **EMAIL** mekhala@duke.edu

NATHAN, ANDREW J.
PERSONAL Born 04/03/1943, New York, NY **DISCIPLINE** ASIA **EDUCATION** Harvard Univ, BA, 63, MA, 65, PhD, 71. **CAREER** Teaching fel, Harvard Univ, 66; lectr hist, Univ Mich, 71; from asst prof to assoc prof, 71-82, prof polit sci, 82, dir grad studies, 97-, Columbia Univ. **HONORS AND AWARDS** Guggenheim Fel, 73-74; NEH Fel, 86-87, 92-93; Levenson Prize for best book on 20th century China, for Chinese Democracy, 87; recipient of numerous grants. **MEMBERSHIPS** Coun For Relations; Am Polit Sci Asn; Asn Asian Studies. **RESEARCH** Chinese politics and foreign policy; political participation; comparative politics. **SELECTED PUBLICATIONS** Auth, MFN and the Human Rights Issue, in Beyond MFN: Trade with China and American Interests, The AEI Press, 94; auth, The Mao Era and After, in Spotlight on China: Traditions Old and New, The Am Forum for Global Educ, 97; coauth, The Great Wall and the Empty Fortress: China's Search for Security, W.W. Norton, 97; auth, China's Transition, Columbia Univ Press, 97; auth, Modern China, 1840-1972: An Introduction to Sources and Research Aids; auth, Peking Politics, 1918-1923: Factionalism and the Failure of Constitutionalism Chinese Democracy, China's Crisis; co-ed and contribr, Popular Culture in Late Imperial China. **CONTACT ADDRESS** East Asian Inst, Columbia Univ, New York, NY 10027. **EMAIL** ajn1@columbia.edu

NAUENBERG, M.
PERSONAL Born 12/19/1934, Berlin, Germany **DISCIPLINE** PHYSICS, HISTORY OF SCIENCE **EDUCATION** Cornell Univ, PhD, 59. **CAREER** Prof, Univ Cal Santa Cruz, 66-94. **HONORS AND AWARDS** A.P. Sloan fel; Guggenheim fel; Alexandre von Humboldt fel. **MEMBERSHIPS** Am Phys Soc; Hist of Sci Soc. **RESEARCH** Theoretical physics; history of science. **SELECTED PUBLICATIONS** Auth, Newton's Principia and Inverse Square Orbits, The Col Math Jour, 94; auth, Huygens and Newton on Curvature and it's Applications to Dynamics, DE Zeventiende Eeeuw, 96; auth, On Hooke's 1685 Manuscript on Orbital Mechanics, Hist Math, 98; auth, Essay Review: The Mathemeatical Principles Underlying the Principia, Revisited, Jour for the Hist of Astron, 98; auth, Newton's Unpublished Perturbation Method for the Lunar Motion, Int Jour of Engineering Sci, 98; auth, Newton's Portsmouth Perturbation Method for the Three-Body Problem and its Application to Lunar Motion, 98. **CONTACT ADDRESS** Physics Dept, Univ of California, Santa Barbara, Santa Cruz, CA 95064.

NAUERT, CHARLES G.
PERSONAL Born 07/26/1928, Quincy, IL, m, 1964, 2 children **DISCIPLINE** HISTORY **EDUCATION** Quincy Col, AB, 50; Univ of Ill, AM, 51, PhD, 55. **CAREER** Instr, Bowdoin Col, 55-56, asst prof of hist, Williams Col, 56-61; from asst prof to prof emeritus hist, Univ Mo-Columbia, 61-; dept chemn, Univ Mo-Columbia, 65-68. **HONORS AND AWARDS** ACLS sr fel, 68-69; Thomas Jefferson Awd, Univ of Mo System. **MEMBERSHIPS** Phi Alpha Theta; Phi Kappa Phi; Am Hist Asn; Renaissance Soc of Am; Sixteenth Century Studies Confr; Am Soc for Reformation Res; Am Asn of Univ Prof. **RESEARCH** European intellectual and cultural history in the Renaissance-Reformation period; Humanism and Scholasticism. **SELECTED PUBLICATIONS** Auth, Introductions and annotations for Collected Works of Erasmus vol 11: Letters 1535 to 1657, January-December 1525, Univ of Toronto Press, 94; Humanism and the Culture of Renaissance Europe, Cambridge Univ Press, 95; The Humanist Challenge to Medieval German Culture, Daphnis: Zeitschrift fur mittlere deutsche Literatur, 86; Humanist Infiltration into the Academic World: Some Studies of Northern Humanism, Renaissance Quart, 90; Humanism as Method: Roots of Conflict with the Scholastics, Sixteenth Century J, 98. **CONTACT ADDRESS** Dept of Hist, Univ of Missouri, Columbia, 101 Read Hall, Columbia, MO 65211. **EMAIL** nauertc@missouri.edu

NAUGLE, RONALD C.
PERSONAL Born 09/18/1942, Mitchell, IN, m, 1963, 1 child **DISCIPLINE** HISTORY **EDUCATION** Purdue Univ, BA,

64; MA, 66; Univ Kansas, MPhil, 71; PhD, 76. **CAREER** Instr to prof, Nebr Wesleyan Univ, 66-; Chair, 80-; Huge-Kinne Prof, 85-. **HONORS AND AWARDS** Clarion Awd, 87; Roy G. Story Awd, Nebr Wesleyan Unv, 93; Frost Awd, Smithsonian Inst, 93; Addison E. Sheldon Awd, Nebr State Hist Soc, 98. **MEMBERSHIPS** Nebr State Hist Soc; Center for Great Plains Studies. **RESEARCH** Nebraska History, Great Plains History, Plains Indian History. **SELECTED PUBLICATIONS** Coauth, White Man's Way, Nebr Educ Television, 86; coauth, Nebraska Quilts and Quiltmakers, Univ of Nebr Pr, (Lincoln), 91; coauth, History of Nebraska, 3rd Ed, Univ of Nebr Pr, (Lincoln), 97; auth, "Indian Boarding Schools in the United States", Encyclopedia of the Great Plains, Center for Great Plains Studies (Lincoln), 00. **CONTACT ADDRESS** Dept Hist, Nebraska Wesleyan Univ, 5000 St Paul Ave, Lincoln, NE 68504-2760. **EMAIL** rcn@nebrwesleyan.edu

NAUMAN, ANN K.
PERSONAL Born 08/02/1931, Greensboro, NC, m, 1951, 2 children **DISCIPLINE** HISTORY **EDUCATION** La State Univ, BA, 61; BS, 66; MA, 65; MS, 69; PhD, 74. **CAREER** School librn, Baton Rouge, La, 65-75; asst prof to prof, S La Univ, 76- ; prof hist, St Joseph Sem Col, 80- . **HONORS AND AWARDS** OAS fel, 73; Mellon grant, 80. **MEMBERSHIPS** AAUP, AAUW, Am Libr Asn, Latin Am Asn, Phi Kappa Phi. **RESEARCH** Gender discrimination in education, Latin American history, Library science. **SELECTED PUBLICATIONS** Auth, An Introduction to Bibliographic Materials, Kendall-Hunt, (92); auth, Making Every Minute Count, NY Libr Learning Res, (94), auth, "La Integracion de la Mures en ola Fuerza de Trbajo Mexicana desde el TLC" in El Empleo Hou en Mexico y el Mundo, Univ Nac Autonoma Mex, (99); auth, Ines de Suarez, Conquitadors, NY Mellon Press, (00). **CONTACT ADDRESS** Soc & Behav Sci, Saint Joseph Sem Col, Saint Benedict, LA 70457-9999. **EMAIL** anauman@selu.edu

NAWROCKI, DENNIS ALAN
PERSONAL Born 12/29/1939, Grand Rapids, MI, s **DISCIPLINE** ART HISTORY **EDUCATION** Aquinas Col, BA, 62; Wayne State Univ, MA, 64; MA, 81. **CAREER** Intern to asst curator of Educ, Detroit Inst of Arts, Mich, 75-83; res assoc to Dir of Educ, Museum of Contemporary Art, Chicago, 83-88; assoc chair, lectr, and curator, Univ Mich Mus of Art, Ann Arbor, 88-90; adjunct fac, Wayne State Univ, 93-; adjunct fac, Sch of the Art Inst of Chicago, summers 90-; prof, Center for Creative Studies, Col of Art and Design, Detroit, Mich, 90-. **MEMBERSHIPS** Col Art Asn, Midwest Art Hist Soc. **RESEARCH** Modern and contemporary art, the artist as social critic, installation art. **SELECTED PUBLICATIONS** Auth, "Pendergast and Davies: Two Approaches to a Mural Project," Bull of the Detroit Inst of the Arts, 56, 4 (78); auth, "Artist' Biographies," in Kick Out the Jams: Detroit's Cass Corridor 1963-1977, (exh. Cat.) Detroit Inst of the Arts (80); auth, "Art Outside the Mainstream, Detroit-Style," J of Regional Cultures, 2, Bowling Green State Univ, (spring/summer 82); auth, Selections from the Permanent Collection, Vol 1 (selected entries), Mus of Contemporary Art, Chicago (84); auth, "Artist's Biographies, Selected Exhibitions, and Selected References," in A Quiet Revolution: British Sculpture Since 1965, Mus of Contemporary Art, Chicago, San Francisco Mus of Modern Art, & Thames and Hudson, Ltd, London (96); auth, "Gilbert and George: Parked in Nature," Bull of the Detroit Inst of the Arts, 8, 4 (89); auth, Paul Schwarz's Intuitive Geometry," Trait (Detroit), vol 1, #1 (spring 99); auth, Art in Detroit Public Places (revised ed), Wayne State Univ Press (99); auth, "Bill Viola: Intimations of Morality," Bull of the Detroit Inst of Arts, vol 74, #1/2 (2000). **CONTACT ADDRESS** Dept Liberal Arts, Center Creative Studies, 201 E Kirby St, Detroit, MI 48202-4048. **EMAIL** dnawro@ccscad.edu

NAYLOR, JOHN F.
PERSONAL Born 04/03/1937, Newburgh, NY, m, 1960, 2 children **DISCIPLINE** HISTORY **EDUCATION** Hamilton Col, BA, 59; Harvard Univ, MA, 60; PhD, 64. **CAREER** Lectr, Harvard Univ, 64-67; Asst prof to Prof, SUNY at Buffalo, 67-. **HONORS AND AWARDS** Phi Beta Kappa; Woodrow Wilson Fel, 59-60; John Ben Snow Book Prize, The N Am Conf on Brit Studies, 85. **MEMBERSHIPS** Am Conf on Brit Studies. **RESEARCH** 20th century British political and institutional history. **SELECTED PUBLICATIONS** Ed, The Peerage Bil of 1719 and the British Aristocracy, Oxford Univ Press (NY), 68; auth, Labour's International Policy: The Labour Party in the 1930s, Weidenfeld and Nicolson (London), and Houghton Mifflin Co (Boston), 69; ed, Britain, 1919-1970, Quadrangle Books (Chicago), 71; auth, A Man and an Institution: Sir Maurice Hankey, The Cabinet Secretariat, and the Custody of Cabinet Secrecy, Cambridge Univ Press, 84; auth, "British Memoirs and Official Secrecy: From Crossman to Thatcher," in Political Memoir: Essays on the Politics of Memory, ed. George Egerton (London: Frank Cass, 94); auth, "The Cabinet," in Twentieth Century Britain: An Encyclopedia, ed. Fred Leventhal (NY, London: Garland Press, 95). **CONTACT ADDRESS** Dept Hist, SUNY, Buffalo, Park Hall, PO Box 604130, Buffalo, NY 14260-0001. **EMAIL** jfnaylor@acsu.buffalo.edu

NAYLOR, NATALIE A.
PERSONAL Born 08/20/1937, Peekskill, NY, s **DISCIPLINE** AMERICAN HISTORY, WOMEN'S STUDIES, LONG ISLAND HISTORY **EDUCATION** Bryn Mawr Col AB, 59; Columbia Univ, MA, 62, EdD, 71. **CAREER** Res asst, Nat Bur Econ Res, 59-62; teacher social studies, Tuckahoe High Sch, 62-65; from instr hist & found educ to prof emerita, Hofstra Univ, 68-00; dir, Long Island Studies Inst, Hofstra Univ, 86-00. **HONORS AND AWARDS** Teaching Fel Am Hist, New College, Hofstra Univ, 76-. **MEMBERSHIPS** Am Educ Studies Asn; Orgn Am Historians; Am Studies Asn. **RESEARCH** History of education; women and education; Long Island history. **SELECTED PUBLICATIONS** Auth, The antebellum College movement: A reappraisal of Tewksbury's Founding of American Colleges and Universities, Hist Educ Quart, fall 73; Paul Monroe, In: Dict of American Biography, Supplement Four, Charles Scribner's Sons, 74; The theological seminary in the configuration of American higher education: The antebellum years, Hist Educ Quart, spring 77; Horace Mann, In: American Renaissance in New England Vol I, In: Dict of Literary Biography, Gale Res, 78; Hilda Taba In: Notable American Women: Modern Period, Belknap Press, 80; coauth, Teaching Today and Tomorrow, Charles E Merrill, 81; auth, "Mary Steichen Calderone" and "Emma Hart Willard," in Women Educators in the United States 1820-1993, ed. Maxine Schwartz Seller, (Westport: Greenwood Pr, 94) 86-94, 525-535; ed, Nassau County Historical Society Journal, 96-; auth, "The 'Encouragement of Seminaries of Learning': The Origins and Development of Early Long Island Academies," Long Island Historical Journal, 12 (fall 99): 11-30; co-ed, Nassau County: From Rural Hinterland to Suburban Metropolis, Empire State Books/Long Island Studies Inst (Interlaken, NYork), 00; **CONTACT ADDRESS** 496 Clarendon Road, Uniondale, NY 11553. **EMAIL** nucnzn@hofstra.edu

NEAMAN, ELLIOTT Y.
PERSONAL Born 01/28/1957, Vancouver, BC, Canada, d **DISCIPLINE** HISTORY **EDUCATION** Univ BC, BA, 79; Freie Universitat Berlin, MA 85; Univ Calif, Berkeley, PhD, 92. **CAREER** Assoc prof, Univ of San Francisco, 93-. **RESEARCH** 20th-Century German history - communism, fascism, conservation. **SELECTED PUBLICATIONS** Auth, "Mutiny on Board Modernity: Heidegger, Sorel and other Fascist Intellectuals", Critical Rev (Fall 95): 371-401; auth, "A New Conservative Revolution?: Xenophobia, Nationalism and the Ideology of the Young Right in Germany Today", Antisemitism and Xenophobia in Germany after Unification, eds Rainer Erb and Werner Bergmann, Oxford Univ Pr, (97): 190-210; auth, "The Holocaust: Nothing to Debate", Foghorn, Feb 26, 98; auth, "German Nazism was No Aberration", NY Times, Nov 15, 98; auth, "Ernst Junger's Millennium", Fascism's Return: Scandal, Revision and Ideology, ed Richard Golsan, Nebr Univ Pr, (Lincoln, 98): 218-243; auth, "Jacques Derrida, Wilhelm, Friedrich Heer, Kulturpessimismus, Wilhelm Levison, Erich Marcks", Daniel Woolf, The Encyclopedia of Historiography, Garland, (NY), 98; auth, "Ernst Junger's Legacy", S Central Rev (99): 54-67; auth, A Dubious Past: Ernst Junger and the Politics of Literature after Nazism, Univ of Calif Pr, (Berkley, Los Angeles), 99; auth, "In Austria, Shadows and Worries, NY Times, Feb 2, 00. **CONTACT ADDRESS** Dept Hist, Univ of San Francisco, 2130 Fulton St, San Francisco, CA 94117-1080.

NEARY, PETER F.
PERSONAL Born 08/15/1938, Bell Island, NF, Canada **DISCIPLINE** CANADIAN HISTORY **EDUCATION** Memorial Univ Nfld, BS, 59, MA, 62; London Sch Econ & Polit Sci, Univ London, PhD, 65. **CAREER** Asst prof, 65-71, assoc prof, 71-82, chmn, 78-81, prof Hist, 82-, dean, Fac of Social Sci, Univ Western Ont, 95-; Winthrop Pickard Bell Lectr, Mt Allison Univ, 89; WS MacNutt Lectr, Univ NB, 91. **HONORS AND AWARDS** Heritage Awd, Nfld Hist Soc, 95 **MEMBERSHIPS** Can Hist Asn (mem coun, 71-74, 87-90) **RESEARCH** Canadian political parties, Anglo-American-Canadian relations and the history of Newfoundland. **SELECTED PUBLICATIONS** Auth, The Political Economy of Newfoundland, 1929-1972, 73; auth, By Great Waters: A Newfoundland and Labrador Anthology, 74; auth, Newfoundland in the Nineteenth and Twentieth Centuries: Essays in Interpretation, 80; auth, Newfoundland in the North Atlantic World, 1929-1949, 88. **CONTACT ADDRESS** Faculty Soc Sci, Univ of Western Ontario, London, ON, Canada N6A 5C2. **EMAIL** neary@julian.uwo.ca

NEARY, TIMOTHY B.
PERSONAL Born 05/23/1970, Omaha, NE **DISCIPLINE** HISTORY **EDUCATION** Georgetown Univ, AB, 93; Loyola Univ, MA, 97. **CAREER** A.B.D to Instructor, Loyola Univ, 98-. **HONORS AND AWARDS** King V. Hostick Dessertation Awd, IL State Hist Soc, 99; Arthur . Schmitt Dissertation Fel, Loyola Univ, 00-01; Teaching Fel, Loyola Univ, 99-00. **MEMBERSHIPS** Am Hist Asn; Org of Am Hist; Urban Hist Asn. **RESEARCH** 20th Century U.S. Urban History; Neighborhoods; Race; Religion. **SELECTED PUBLICATIONS** Auth, "Crossing Parochial Boundaries: African Americans and Interracial Catholic Social Action in Chicago, 1914-1954." **CONTACT ADDRESS** Dept Hist, Loyola Univ, Chicago, 6525 N Sheridan Rd, Chicago, IL 60626-5344. **EMAIL** tneary@luc.edu

NEATBY, H. BLAIR
PERSONAL Born 12/11/1924, Renown, SK, Canada **DISCIPLINE** CANADIAN HISTORY **EDUCATION** Univ Sask, BA, 50; Oxford Univ, MA, 55; Univ Toronto, PhD, 56. **CAREER** Prof Emer History, Carleton Univ. **SELECTED PUBLICATIONS** Auth, W.L. MacKenzie King, vol I 1923-32, 63, vol II 1932-39, 76; auth, Laurier and a Liberal Quebec, 72; auth, The Politics of Chaos, 72. **CONTACT ADDRESS** Dept of Hist, Carleton Univ, 1125 Colonel By Dr, 400 Paterson Hall, Ottawa, ON, Canada K1S 5B6.

NECHELES-JANSYN, RUTH F.
PERSONAL Born 04/20/1936, Chicago, IL, m, 1978 **DISCIPLINE** MODERN HISTORY **EDUCATION** Univ Chicago, MA, 56, PhD(hist), 63. **CAREER** Asst prof hist, Mary Washington Col, Univ Va, 62-64; from asst prof to assoc prof, 64-73, dir Jewish studies prog, 72-76, chmn dept, 76-82, assoc dir, Univ Honors Prog, 88-92, co-dir, 92-94, prof hist, 73-94, Prof Emer, 94- , Ling Island Univ, Brooklyn Ctr. **HONORS AND AWARDS** Am Philos Soc grant, 66 **MEMBERSHIPS** AHA; Soc For Hist Studies; AAUP; Am Soc 18th Century Studies; Soc Hist Mod. **RESEARCH** French Revolution; emancipation era; church in a revolutionary era. **SELECTED PUBLICATIONS** Auth, The Abbe Gregoire's Work in Behalf of Jews, 1788-1791, Fr Hist Studies, 69; The Abbe Gregoire, 1787-1831, The Odyssey of an Egalitarian, Greenwood, 71; The Abbe Gregoire and the Jews, Jewish Social Studies, 71; The Abbe Gregoire and the Egalitarian Movement, Studies 18th Century Cult, 73; The Cures in the Estates General of 1789, J Mod Hist, 9/74; L'Emancipation des Juifs, 1787-1795-Aspects Intellectuels et Politiques, In: Les Juifs et la Revolution Francaise, 1976, Edouard Privat, 76; The Constitutional Church, 1794-1802: An Essay in Voluntarism, Proc of Consortium on Revolutionary Europe, Fla Univ Press, 76; Linguistic Nationalism or Ecclesiastical Universalism: The Controversy Over a French Sacramentary, Enlightenment Studies in Honour of Lester G Crocker, The Voltaire Found, 79; auth, French Dialect or Latin Mass? A Final Crisis Within the Revolutionary Church, in, Consortium on Revolutionary Europe: 1750-1850, Proceedings, 89; contrib, Horward, ed, Bicentennial of the French Revolution, Inst on Napoleon & the French Revolution, FSU, 90. **CONTACT ADDRESS** 70 Valentine St, Highland Park, NJ 08904. **EMAIL** jansynr@juno.com

NEEDELL, ALLAN A.
PERSONAL Born 07/02/1950, Paterson, NJ, m, 1987, 2 children **DISCIPLINE** HISTORY OF SCIENCE, TECHNOLOGY & PUBLIC POLICY **EDUCATION** Cornell Univ, BA, 72; Yale Univ, PhD, 80. **CAREER** Assoc hist, Ctr Hist of Physics, Am Inst Physics, 78-81; Curator, Space Sci & Exploration, Nat Air & Space Mus, Smithsonian Inst, 81-. **HONORS AND AWARDS** Am Phys Soc fel **MEMBERSHIPS** Am Phys Soc, Hist Sci Soc; Am Hist Asn. **RESEARCH** Am federal sci policy; gov/acad relations/ hist sci and tech. **SELECTED PUBLICATIONS** Auth, From Military Research to Big Science: Lloyd Berkner and Science-statesmanship in the Postwar Era, in Big Science: The Growth of Large-scale Research, Stanford Univ Press, 92; auth, Truth is Our Weapon: Project TROY, Political Warfare, and Government/Academic Relations in the National Security State, Diplomatic History, 17:3, 93; auth, Rabi, Berkner, and the Rehabilitation of Science in Europe: The Cold War Context of American Support for International Science 1945-1958, Chapter 13 of The United States and the Integration of Europe: Legacies of the Post War Era, St. Martin's Press, 96; co-auth, Science, Scientists and the CIA: Balancing International Ideals, National Needs, and Professional Opportunities, Intelligence and National Security, 12:1, 97; auth, Project Troy and the Cold War Annexation of the Social Sciences" in Universities and Empire: Money and Politics in the Social Sciences during the Cold War, The New Press, 98. **CONTACT ADDRESS** Space Hist Div, Nat Air & Space Mus, Smithsonian Inst, Washington, DC 20560-0311. **EMAIL** allan.needell@nasm.si.edu

NEEDELL, JEFFREY D.
PERSONAL Born 12/24/1951, New York, NY, m, 1980, 3 children **DISCIPLINE** HISTORY **EDUCATION** Univ Calif Berkeley, AB, 74; Yale Univ, MA, 78; Stanford Univ, PhD, 82. **CAREER** Asst prof, Univ of Ore, 82-87; Vis asst prof, Cath Univ of Am, 86-87; asst prof to assoc prof, Univ of Fla, 87-. **HONORS AND AWARDS** Phi Beta Kappa; Danforth Fel; Fulbright Fel, Brazil; Soc Sci Res Coun; NEH Fel; Woodrow Wilson Scholar. **MEMBERSHIPS** AHA; Conf for Latin Am Hist; Latin Am Studies Assoc; Brazilian Studies Assoc. **RESEARCH** 19th Century Brazilian Political and Intellectual History, Brazilian Urban and Cultural History, Amazonian History. **SELECTED PUBLICATIONS** Auth, A Tropical Belle Epoque: Elite Culture and Society in Turn-of-the-Century Rio de Janeiro, Cambridge Lat Am Studies 62, Cambridge Univ Pr, 87; auth, "A Liberal Embraces Monarchy: Jaoquim Nabuco and Conservative Historiography, The Americas 48.2 (91): 159-180; auth, "Brasilien, 1830-1889", in Hanbuch der Geschichte Lateinamerikas, ed Raymond Buve and John Fisher, (Stuttgart: Klett-Cotta, 92), 2: 441-497; auth, Belle Epoque Tropical: Sociedade e cultura de elite no Rio de Janeiro na virada do seculo, Companhia das Letras (Sao Paulo), 93; auth, "History, Race, and the State in the Thought of Oliveira Viana", Hispanic Am Hist Rev 48.2 (95): 1-30; auth, "Identity, Race, Gender, and Modernity in the Origins of Gilberto Freyre's Oeuvre" Am His

Rev 75.1 (95): 1-30; auth, "Rio de Janeiro and Buenos Aires: Public Space and Public Consciousness in Fin-de-Siecle Latin America", comp Studies in Soc and Hist 37.3, (95): 519-540; auth, "The Revolta Contra Vacina of 1904: The Revolt Against 'Modernization' in Belle-Epoque Rio de Janeiro" in Revolts in the Cities: Popular Politics and the Urban Poor in Latin America, 1765-1910, ed Sylvia Arrom and Servando Ortoll, Boulder: Sage, 96), 155-89; auth, "The Domestic Civilizing Mission: The Cultural Role of the State in Brazil, 1808-1930", Luso-Brazilian Rev 36.1 (99): 1-18; auth, "Optimism and Melancholy: Elite Response to the fin-depsiecle bonaerense", J of Latin Am Studies 31.3 (99): 551-88. **CONTACT ADDRESS** Dept Hist, Univ of Florida, PO Box 117320, Gainesville, FL 32611-7320. **EMAIL** jneedell@history.ufl.edu

NEEL, CAROL
DISCIPLINE HISTORY **EDUCATION** Bryn Mawr Col, BA; Cornell Univ, MA, 78, PhD, 81. **CAREER** Prof. **SELECTED PUBLICATIONS** Auth, A Philip of Harvengts Vita Augustini: The Medieval Premonstratensians and the Patristic Model, 95; Philip of Harvengt and Anselm of Havelberg: The Premonstratensian Vision of Time, 93. **CONTACT ADDRESS** Dept of History, Columbia Col, New York, 14 E Cache La Poudre St, Colorado Springs, CO 80903. **EMAIL** cneel@cc.colorado.edu

NEFF, AMY
DISCIPLINE ART HISTORY **EDUCATION** Univ Pa, PhD, 77. **CAREER** Assoc prof, Art Hist, Univ Tenn. **HONORS AND AWARDS** Rome Prize; Sr fellow, CASVA; NEH. **SELECTED PUBLICATIONS** A New Interpretation of the Supplicationes Variae Miniatures, 82; The Dialogus Beatae Mariae et Anselmi de Passione Domini: Toward an Attribution, 86; Wicked Children on Calvary and the Baldness of St. Francis, 90; auth, Manuscript Illuminators and the arte dei cristallari in Late Thirteenth-Century Venice, 92; auth, The Pain of Compessio: Mary's Labor at the Foot of the Cross, 98; auth, Byzantium Westernized, Byzantium Marginalized: Two Items in the Supplicationes Variae, 99. **CONTACT ADDRESS** Sch of Art, Univ of Tennessee, Knoxville, Knoxville, TN 37996.

NEIBERG, MICHAEL
PERSONAL Born 08/02/1969, Pittsburgh, PA, m, 1994 **DISCIPLINE** HISTORY **EDUCATION** Univ Mich, AB, 91; Carnegie Mella Univ, 92; Carnegie Mellon Univ, 96. **CAREER** Asst Prof of History, US Air Force Academy, 97; Assoc Prof of History, US Air Force Academy, 00. **HONORS AND AWARDS** Outstanding Academy Educator, US Air Force Academy, 99; Spencer Foundation Fellow, 97-98; Goldman Awd for teaching Excellence, 94. **MEMBERSHIPS** Society for Military History; Inter-University Seminar on Armed Forces and Society. **RESEARCH** Military and Society; Civil-Military Relations; Comparative History of Warfare. **SELECTED PUBLICATIONS** Auth, "Making Citizen-Soldiers: ROTC and the Ideology of American Military Service," Harvard Univ Press, 00. **CONTACT ADDRESS** Dept History, United States Air Force Acad, 2304 Cadet Dr, United States Air Force Academy, CO 80840-5099. **EMAIL** mike.neiberg@usafa.af.mil

NEILS, JENIFER
PERSONAL Born 10/16/1950, Minneapolis, MN, m, 1 child **DISCIPLINE** GREEK ART, ARCHAEOLOGY **EDUCATION** Bryn Mawr Col, AB, 72; Princeton Univ, MFA, 77; Sydney Univ, MA, 78; Princeton Univ PhD, 80; dept ch 86-98. **CAREER** Curatorial/teaching app, Cleveland Mus Art; Whitehead Vis prof Am Sch Classical Studies CWRU; Pres, American Academy in Rome. **HONORS AND AWARDS** Getty Fellow, AA Rome RCS, AIA, CAA; mus exhib comt archaeol inst am. **SELECTED PUBLICATIONS** Auth, The Youthful Deeds of Theseus, 87; Goddess and Polis: The Panathenaic Festival in Ancient Athens, 92; Worshipping Athena: Panathenaia and Parthenon, 96. **CONTACT ADDRESS** Case Western Reserve Univ, 10900 Euclid Ave, Cleveland, OH 44106. **EMAIL** jxn4@po.cwru.edu

NEILSON, JAMES WARREN
PERSONAL Born 06/19/1933, St. Louis, MO **DISCIPLINE** AMERICAN HISTORY **EDUCATION** Northeast MO State Tchr(s) Col, BS, 54, MA, 55; Univ IL, PhD, 58. **CAREER** Assoc prof, 58-59, chmn dept soc sci, 68-81, prof hist, Mayville State Col, 59-98; Prof Emeritus, May 98. **MEMBERSHIPS** AHA; Orgn Am Historians. **RESEARCH** Am hist, 1865-1930; railroad hist. **SELECTED PUBLICATIONS** Auth, Shelby M Cullom: Prairie State Republican, Univ IL, 62; From Protest to Preservation: What Republicans Have Believed, Christopher, 68; The School of Personal Service: A History of Mayville State College, private publ, 80. **CONTACT ADDRESS** Dept of Hist, Mayville State Univ, 330 3rd St NE, Mayville, ND 58257-1299.

NEIMAN, FRASER DUFF
DISCIPLINE ARCHITECTURAL HISTORY **EDUCATION** Yale Univ, BA, PhD. **CAREER** Lectr. **RESEARCH** Archaeological theory; quantitative methods; historical archaeology of the Chesapeake. **SELECTED PUBLICATIONS** Auth, pubs on collapse of Classic Maya civilization, and social relations in the 17th-century Chesapeake. **CONTACT ADDRESS** Dept of Architectural History., Univ of Virginia, Charlottesville, VA 22903. **EMAIL** fn9r@virginia.edu

NELLES, HENRY V.
PERSONAL Born 11/09/1942, Cambridge, ON, Canada **DISCIPLINE** HISTORY **EDUCATION** Univ Toronto, BA, 64, MA, 65; PhD, 70. **CAREER** Prof History, York Univ, 70-; vis prof Can stud, Tsukuba Univ, Keio Univ, Int Christian Univ 76-77; WLM King Prof Can stud, Harvard Univ, 81-82; chmn, Ont Coun Univ Affairs, 88-92; co-ed, Can Hist Rev, 88-92. **HONORS AND AWARDS** Newcomen Awd, 73; Toronto Bk Awd, 77; Fel, Royal Soc, 85; Sir John A. Macdonald Prize, 86. **MEMBERSHIPS** Can Hist Asn **RESEARCH** The Tercentenary of Quebec, 1908 Canadian Icons. **SELECTED PUBLICATIONS** Ed, The Philosophy of Railroads, 72; ed, Nationalism or Local Control, 72; auth, Politics of Development, 74; coauth, The Revenge of the Methodist Bicycle Company, 77;ed, But This Is Our War, 81; coauth, Monopoly's Moment, 86; gen ed, Social History of Canada, 78-88; coauth, Southern Exposure, 88; auth, "Borders in a Bordeless World," Trans of the Royal Soc of Can, vol 6, (95): 139-150; auth, "Historical Pageantry and the Fusion of the Races at the Tercentenary of Quebec, 1908," Hist Soc/Soc Hist, vol 29, (96), 391-415; auth, "American Exeptionalism: A Double Edged Sword," Am Hist Rev, vol 103, (97): 749-757; **CONTACT ADDRESS** History Dept, York Univ, 4700 Keele St, North York, ON, Canada M3J 1P3.

NELSON, ANNA K.
PERSONAL Born Ft Smith, AR, m, 2 children **DISCIPLINE** HISTORY **EDUCATION** Univ Okla, BA, 54; MA, 56; George Wash Univ, PhD, 72. **CAREER** Adj Lectr, George Wash Univ, 70-85; Adj Prof, Am Univ, 86-89; Adj Assoc Prof, Tulane Univ, 88-90; Adj Prof, Am Univ, 90-. **HONORS AND AWARDS** Roosevelt Prize, 88; James Madison Awd, 99. **MEMBERSHIPS** AHA, OAH, SFHFG, SHAFR. **RESEARCH** Nineteenth-Century U S diplomatic history, Twentieth-Century foreign policy. **SELECTED PUBLICATIONS** Auth, "The Importance of the Foreign Policy Process: Eisenhower and the National Security Council," in Eisenhower: A Centenary Assessment (95); auth, "The John F. Kennedy Assassination Records Review Board," A Culture of Secrecy: The Government Versus the People's Right to Know (98); rev, "History with Holes: The CIA Reveals Its Past," Diplomatic Hist (98); auth, "The Outsider as Insider: Reflections on the Kennedy Assassination Records Review Board," The Public Historian (99); auth, "Illuminating the Twilight Struggle: New Interpretations of the Cold War," Chronicle of Higher Educ (99). **CONTACT ADDRESS** Dept Hist, American Univ, 4400 Mass Ave NW, Washington, DC 20016. **EMAIL** anelson@american.edu

NELSON, DANIEL
PERSONAL Born 08/28/1941, Indianapolis, IN, m, 1963, 2 children **DISCIPLINE** HISTORY **EDUCATION** Ohio Wesleyan Univ, Ba, 63; Ohio State Univ, MA, 64; Univ Wis, PhD, 67. **CAREER** Prof to prof emeritus, Univ Akron, 97-. **HONORS AND AWARDS** Ph Beta Kappa, Outstanding res, Univ Akron, 81. **MEMBERSHIPS** EHA, IRRA, Am Soc for Environmental Hist, Bus Hist Conf. **RESEARCH** Scientific management, Midwestern economy, Alaska. **SELECTED PUBLICATIONS** Auth, Managers and Workers, rev, 95; auth, Farm and Factory, 95; auth, Shifting Fortunes, 97. **CONTACT ADDRESS** Dept Hist, Univ of Akron, 302 Buchtel Mall, Akron, OH 44325-0001. **EMAIL** nelson@uakron.edu

NELSON, GERSHAM
DISCIPLINE HISTORY **EDUCATION** Univ Ill, PhD. **CAREER** Prof & dept head, Eastern Michigan Univ. **HONORS AND AWARDS** Welcome Awd, 88, FSU Service, 94, FSU Teach Awd, 97. **MEMBERSHIPS** AHA **RESEARCH** Central America and the Caribbean. **SELECTED PUBLICATIONS** Auth, The Life and Works of Rudolph James: Founder of Black Adventism in Canada; co-ed, From Outside of Western Civilization; ed, Legacy of 1492. **CONTACT ADDRESS** Dept of History and Philosophy, Eastern Michigan Univ, 701 Pray-Harrold, Ypsilanti, MI 48197. **EMAIL** Gersham.Nelson@emich.edu

NELSON, J. DOUGLAS
PERSONAL Born 07/23/1941, Billings, MT, m, 1964, 2 children **DISCIPLINE** HISTORY OF AFRICA **EDUCATION** Linfield Col, BA, 63; Geo Wash Univ, AM 66, PhD, 74 **CAREER** Asst Prof, 66-68, KS St Univ; Assoc Dir, 70-72, Geo Wash Univ; Asst Prof, Dir, 72-75, Baldwin-Wallace col; Prof, 75-, Anderson Univ **HONORS AND AWARDS** Delegate, Internatl Human Rights conf, Capetown South Africa, 79; malone fel, 92 **MEMBERSHIPS** Midw Polit Sci Assn **RESEARCH** Eastern and Southern Africa **CONTACT ADDRESS** Anderson, IN 46011. **EMAIL** dnelson@anderson.edu

NELSON, JAMES DAVID
PERSONAL Born 02/13/1930, Luray, KS, m, 1957, 2 children **DISCIPLINE** HISTORY OF CHRISTIAN THOUGHT **EDUCATION** Westmar Col, AB, 52; United Theol Sem, BD, 59; Univ Chicago, MA, 61, PhD(church hist), 63. **CAREER** Asst prof & librn, 63-65, from asst prof to prof hist theol, 65-77, Prof Church Hist, United Theol Sem, 77-98, Mem comn arch & hist, United Methodist Church, 72-78; Dir, Ctr for Evangelical United Brethren Heritage, 96-. **HONORS AND AWARDS** Sr Scholar, Lily Found (ATS) 58-59; Rockefeller Doctoral Fel, 62-63. **MEMBERSHIPS** Am Acad Relig; Am Hist Asn; Am Soc Church Hist. **RESEARCH** German Lutheran Pietism; theological enlightenment in Germany; German romanticism; Moravians; Wesley. **SELECTED PUBLICATIONS** Auth, Piety and invention, In: The Impact of Christianity on its Environment, Univ Chicago, 68; Responsible Grace - Wesley.john Practical Theology - Maddox,rl, Theological Studies, Vol 0056, 1995. **CONTACT ADDRESS** 20 Greenmount Blvd, Dayton, OH 45419. **EMAIL** jnelson@united.edu

NELSON, KEITH LEBAHN
PERSONAL Born 05/24/1932, Omaha, NE, m, 1975, 1 child **DISCIPLINE** HISTORY **EDUCATION** Stanford Univ, BA, 53, MA, 54; Univ Calif, Berkeley, PhD(hist), 65; Dir Prog in Global Peace and Conflict Studies, Univ of CA, Irvine, 83-93; Asst Assoc, Full Prof History, 65-00; Dir for Sweden and Denmark Univ of CA Educ Abroad Prog, 99-01. **CAREER** Instr hist, Univ Tex, Austin, 63-65; Univ Calif, Irvine, Danforth assoc, Danforth Found, 68-72. **HONORS AND AWARDS** Phi Beta Kappa, Fulbright Res Prof, Lund Univ, 90-91. **MEMBERSHIPS** AHA; Soc Historians Am Foreign Rel; Conf Peace Res Hist. **RESEARCH** Twentieth century United States history; American relations with Europe; war and social change. **SELECTED PUBLICATIONS** Ed, C Hartley Grattan's Why We Fought, Bobbs Merrill, 69; ed, The Impact of War on American Life: The Twentieth Century Experience, Holt, Rinehart, & Winston, 71; auth, Victors Divided: America and the Allies in Germany, 1918-23, 75 & coauth, Why War?, Ideology, Theory, and History, 79, Univ Calif; auth, The Making of D¤tente: Soviet-American Relations in the Shadow of Vietnam, Johns Hopkins Univ Press, 95; coauth, Re-Viewing the Cold War: Domestic Factors and Foreign Policy in the East-West Confrontation, Greenwood, 00. **CONTACT ADDRESS** Dept of Hist, Univ of California, Irvine, Irvine, CA 92697. **EMAIL** klnelson@uci.edu

NELSON, LYNN HARRY
PERSONAL Born 09/21/1931, Harvey, IL, m, 1962, 1 child **DISCIPLINE** MEDIEVAL HISTORY **EDUCATION** Univ Chicago, BA, 48; Univ Tex, BA, 58, PhD(medieval hist), 63. **CAREER** From instr to assoc prof, 63-74, Prof Medieval Hist, Univ Kans, 74-, Fulbright Res Fel, Spain, 65-66. **HONORS AND AWARDS** H Bernard Fink Awd Outstanding Teaching, 68. **MEMBERSHIPS** Medieval Acad Am; Am Acad Res Historians of Medieval Spain; Soc Span & Port Hist Studies; Soc Comp Frontier Studies; Soc Sci Hist Asn. **RESEARCH** Twelfth century Britain; Aragon and Cataluna in the 11th and 12th centuries. **SELECTED PUBLICATIONS** Coauth, A lost fragment of the Defensio iuris domus Lancastriae, Speculum, 4/65; auth, The Normans in South Wales, 1070-1171, Univ Tex, 66; Rotrou of Perche and the Aragonese reconquest, Traditio, 70; Land use in early Aragon: the organization of a medieval society, Societas, 73; The Aragonese pardina: Its etymology and function, Bull Fac Arts & Lett, Univ Garyounis, 75; coauth, Orosius' commentary on the fall of Roman Spain, Classical Folia, 77; auth, The foundation of Jaca (1076): urban growth in early Aragon, Speculum 78; coauth, Occident 42 of the Notitia Dignitatum's Dating and Structure, Res Publ Literarum, 81. **CONTACT ADDRESS** Dept of Hist, Univ of Kansas, Lawrence, Lawrence, KS 66045-0001.

NELSON, OTTO MILLARD
PERSONAL Born 05/31/1935, Owatonna, MN, m, 1959, 4 children **DISCIPLINE** MODERN EUROPEAN HISTORY **EDUCATION** Univ Ore, BS, 56, MA, 61; Ohio State Univ, PhD(hist), 68. **CAREER** Instr hist, Ohio State Univ, 64-65; asst prof to assoc prof Hist, Tex Tech Univ, 65-, dir honors, 81-83, assoc dean, Col of Arts and Sci, 83-. **HONORS AND AWARDS** Distinguished Teaching Awd, AMOCO Foundation, 74. **MEMBERSHIPS** AHA; AAUP; Ger Studies Asn; Leo Baeck Inst; SW Soc Sci Asn. **RESEARCH** History of Caricature; modern Germany; European socialism. **SELECTED PUBLICATIONS** Auth, Thomas Theodor Heine: His Expatriate Correspondence, Libr Chronicle Univ Tex, Austin, fall 74; Simplicissimus and the Rise of National Socialism, Historian, 5/78; co-ed, War and Peace: Perspectives in the Nuclear Age, Lubbock, 88. **CONTACT ADDRESS** Dept of Hist, Texas Tech Univ, Lubbock, TX 79409-0001. **EMAIL** otto.nelson@ttu.edu

NELSON, PAUL D.
PERSONAL Born 05/15/1941 **DISCIPLINE** HISTORY **EDUCATION** Berea Col, AB, 65; Duke Univ, MA, 68; PhD, 70. **CAREER** Villanova Univ, 69-70; Berea Col, 70-. **HONORS AND AWARDS** Phi Kappa Phi, 65; Woodrow Wilson Fel, 65; NEH Awds, 75, 76, 89; Seabury Awd for Excellence in Teaching, 96. **MEMBERSHIPS** Hist Soc; Soc for Mil Hist; Scottish-Am Mil Soc; Nat Assoc of Scholars; Univ Fac for Life; Ky Hist Soc. **RESEARCH** American Revolution, War. **SELECTED PUBLICATIONS** Auth, General Horatio Gates, 76; auth, Anthony Wayne, 85; auth, William Alexander, Lord Stirling, 87; auth, William Tryon and the Course of Empire, 90; auth, General James Grant, 93; auth, Sir Charles Grey, First Early Grey, 96; auth, General Sir Guy Carleton, 00. **CONTACT ADDRESS** Dept Hist and Govt, Berea Col, 101 Chestnut St, Berea, KY 40404-0001. **EMAIL** david_nelson@berea.edu

NELSON, ROBERT S.
PERSONAL Born 10/27/1947, Temple, TX, 2 children **DISCIPLINE** ART HISTORY **EDUCATION** Rice Univ, BA, 69; New York Univ, MA, 73, PhD(art hist), 78. **CAREER** Asst prof art hist, Univ Chicago, 77-. **MEMBERSHIPS** US Nat Comt Byzantine Studies; Int Ctr Medieval Art; Medieval Acad. **RESEARCH** Byzantine art. **SELECTED PUBLICATIONS** Auth, The Iconography of Preface and Miniature in the Byzantine Gospel Book, New York Univ Press, 80; Theodore Hagiopetrites, A Late Byzantine Scribe and Illuminator, Vienna, 91; co-ed, Critical Terms for Art History, Chigago, 96. **CONTACT ADDRESS** 5540 Greenwood Ave, Chicago, IL 60637-1506. **EMAIL** olin@midway.uchicago.edu

NELSON, STEVEN D.
PERSONAL Born 09/02/1962, Boston, MA **DISCIPLINE** ART HISTORY **EDUCATION** Yale Univ, BA, 85; Harvard Univ, AM, 94; PhD, 98. **CAREER** Lectr to Asst Prof, Tufts Univ, 96-00; Asst Prof, UCLA, 00-. **HONORS AND AWARDS** Getty Postdoc Fel, 00-01. **MEMBERSHIPS** Col Art Asn; African Studies Asn; Arts Coun of the African Studies Asn. **RESEARCH** African, African American, Afro-Diasporal art and architectural history; Islamic art history; Contemporary art and architectural history; Current theory and practices in the humanities. **SELECTED PUBLICATIONS** Auth, "Wear Your Hat: Representational Resistance in Safer Sex Discours?" in Gay and Lesbian Studies in Art History, 94; co-ed, New Histories, Inst of Contemporary Art, 96; auth, "What is Black Art?" Art J, 98; auth, "Freeman Murray and the Beginnings of an African American History of Art," in Art History and Its Institutions, 01. **CONTACT ADDRESS** Dept Art Hist, Univ of California, Los Angeles, 100 Dodd Hall, 405 Hilgard Ave, Los Angeles, CA 90095-1417. **EMAIL** nelsons@humnet.ucla.edu

NELSON, SUSAN
DISCIPLINE EAST ASIAN ART **EDUCATION** Harvard Univ, PhD. **CAREER** Assoc prof. **RESEARCH** Chinese painting and literary culture. **SELECTED PUBLICATIONS** Auth, pubs on Chinese art theory and criticism. **CONTACT ADDRESS** Hist of Art Dept, Indiana Univ, Bloomington, 1201 E 7th St, Fine Arts 132, Bloomington, IN 47405. **EMAIL** senelson@indiana.edu

NELSON, WILLIAM B.
DISCIPLINE NEAR EASTERN LANGUAGES AND CIVILIZATIONS **EDUCATION** Harvard Univ, PhD, 91. **CAREER** Assoc prof, 86-; chaplain, US Air Force Reserves, 93-; asst pastor, First Baptist Church, 92. **HONORS AND AWARDS** Tchr yr, 90. **RESEARCH** Biblical lang; Old Testament hist; Old Testament theol. **SELECTED PUBLICATIONS** Auth, Revelation; Eschatology; Jebusites; Melchizedek; Promised Land; Rechabites, in Oxford Companion to the Bible, 93. **CONTACT ADDRESS** Dept of Rel, Westmont Col, 955 La Paz Rd, Santa Barbara, CA 93108-1099.

NENNER, HOWARD ALLEN
PERSONAL Born 09/18/1935, New York, NY, m, 1990, 2 children **DISCIPLINE** ENGLISH & LEGAL HISTORY **EDUCATION** Queens Col, BA, 56; Columbia Univ, LLB, 59; Univ Calif, Berkeley, PhD, 71. **CAREER** Pvt pract, 60-63; lectr hist, 68-71, asst prof, 71-75, assoc prof, 75-81, prof hist & Roe/Straut Prof, Smith Col, 81-, Am Bar Found fel legal hist, 78-79. **MEMBERSHIPS** AHA; Am Soc Legal Hist; Conf Brit Studies. **RESEARCH** Tudor and Stuart legal and constitutional history. **SELECTED PUBLICATIONS** Auth By Colour of Law, Univ Chicago, 77; The Right To Be King, MacMillan & Univ NC, 95; Ed, Politics and the Political Imagination in Later Stuart Britain, Univ Rochester, 97. **CONTACT ADDRESS** Dept Hist, Smith Col, 10 Prospect St, Northampton, MA 01063-0001. **EMAIL** hnenner@smith.edu

NESS, GARY CLIFFORD
PERSONAL Born 04/08/1940, Sioux City, IA, m, 1963, 2 children **DISCIPLINE** RECENT AMERICAN & SOUTHERN HISTORY **EDUCATION** Iowa State Univ, BS, 63; Duke Univ, AM, 69, PhD(hist, 72. **CAREER** Asst prof hist, Univ Cincinnati, 70-; consult, Am Tel & Tel Soc Sci Workshop, spring 71. **MEMBERSHIPS** AHA; Southern Hist Asn; Orgn Am Historians; AAUP. **RESEARCH** Recent United States politics; the South; historical methodology. **CONTACT ADDRESS** 700 Gatehouse Lane, Worthington, OH 43085.

NESS, LAWRENCE
PERSONAL Born 08/09/1946, Chicago, IL **DISCIPLINE** ART HISTORY **EDUCATION** Univ Chicago, BA, 66-70; Harvard Univ, MA, 74; PhD, 77. **CAREER** Vis sessional lectr, Univ Victoria (Canada), 76-77; lectr, Univ Mass, 77-78; vis asst prof, Harvard Univ, 80; vis prof, Bryn Mawr Col, 89, 00; adj prof, art conservation dept, 96-; asst prof, 78-82; assoc prof, 82-88; prof, 88-; assoc ch, 86-87. **HONORS AND AWARDS** Mellon Fellow, 81-82; grant-in-aid Amer Council of Learned Societies, 84; grant-in-aid for res, Amer Philos Soc, 93; summer stipend, NEH, 81, 95; grant, Samuel H Kress, 90, 91, 96; Guggenheim Fellow, 00-01. **SELECTED PUBLICATIONS** Auth, From Justinian to Charlemagne, European Art, A.D. 565-787, G K Hall Critical Bibliographies, Historical Art, G K Hall, 85; The Gundohinus Gospels, Medieval Acad Am Bk(s), 87; A Tainted Mantle:Hercules and the Classical Tradition at the Carolingian Court, Pa Univ Press, 91; ed, Approaches to Early-Medieval Art, 97; auth, Introduction, Approaches to Early-Medieval Art, ed. Lawrence Nees, Medieval Acad Am, 98; Art and Architecture, The New Cambridge Mediaeval Hist, Cambridge, 95; rev, Carolingian Art, Merovingian Art, Migrations Art, Medieval France: An Encyclopedia, NY and London, 95. **CONTACT ADDRESS** Dept of Art Hist, Univ of Delaware, 162 Ctr Mall, Newark, DE 19716. **EMAIL** nees@udel.edu

NESTINGEN, JAMES A.
DISCIPLINE CHURCH HISTORY **EDUCATION** Concordia Col, BA, 67; Luther Sem, MDiv, 71; MTh, 78; St. Michael's Col, Univ Toronto, ThD, 84. **CAREER** Instr, 76-78; asst prof, 80; prof, 92-. **HONORS AND AWARDS** Bruce prize in New Testament, 71; pastor, faith lutheran church, 71-74; curriculum ed, augsburg publ house, 74-76; asst to the pastor, st. ansgar lutheran church, can, 78-80. **SELECTED PUBLICATIONS** Auth, The Faith We Hold, 83; Martin Luther: His Life and His Writings, 82; Roots of Our Faith, 78; coauth, Free to Be, 75. **CONTACT ADDRESS** Dept of Church History, Luther Sem, 2481 Como Ave, Saint Paul, MN 55108. **EMAIL** jnesting@luthersem.edu

NEU, CHARLES ERIC
PERSONAL Born 04/10/1936, Carroll, IA, m, 1999, 2 children **DISCIPLINE** AMERICAN HISTORY **EDUCATION** Northwestern Univ, BA, 58; Harvard Univ, PhD, 64. **CAREER** From instr to assoc prof hist, Rice Univ, 63-70; assoc prof, 70-76, prof hist, Brown Univ, 76-, Chair, 95-; Comt Am Far Eastern Policy Studies res grant, Harvard Univ, 64-65; NEH Younger Scholar fel, 68-69; fel, Charles Warren Ctr Study Am Hist, 71-72; Am Coun Learned Socs fel, 75-76 & Howard Found fel, 76-77; dir, NEH summer sem, 79, 86, 87, 89, 92; Guggenheim fel, 81-82; guest schol, Woodrow Wilson Ctr, Summer 88. **MEMBERSHIPS** AHA; Orgn Am Historians; Soc Hist Am Foreign Rels. **RESEARCH** American foreign relations; Vietnam War. **SELECTED PUBLICATIONS** Auth, An Uncertain Friendship: Theodore Roosevelt and Japan, 1906-1909, Harvard Univ, 67; contrib, Twentieth-Century American Foreign Policy, Ohio State Univ, 71; American-East Asian Relations: A Survey, Harvard Univ, 72; auth, The Troubled Encounter: The United States and Japan, Wiley, 75; contribr, The New American State, 87; contribr and co-ed, The Wilson Era: Essays in Honor of Arthur S. Link, 91; contribr, Essays in Honor of Ernest R. May, 99; Ed, After Vietnam:Legacies of a Lost War, 00. **CONTACT ADDRESS** Dept of Hist, Brown Univ, 142 Angell St, Providence, RI 02912-9127. **EMAIL** Charles_Neu@brown.edu

NEUFELD, DIETMAR
PERSONAL Born 05/03/1949, m, 1977, 4 children **DISCIPLINE** CHRISTIAN ORGINS; RELIGIOUS STUDIES **EDUCATION** Univ Winnipeg, BA; Mennonite Biblical Seminary, MA; McGill Univ, PhD. **CAREER** Asst prof, Univ of British Columbia, 94- . **MEMBERSHIPS** CBA; CSBS; AAR/SBL; Context Group. **RESEARCH** Religious Rivalry - Pagans, Jews, Christians in Ancient Sardis and Smynna; States of Ecstasy in the Ancient Near East; The Social Sciences and the New Testament. **SELECTED PUBLICATIONS** Auth, Eating, Ecstasy and Exorcism, Biblical Theology Bulletin, 96; auth, Apocalypticsm: Context, Whose Historical Jesus, 97; auth, And When That One Comes: Aspects of Johannine Messianism, Eschatology, Messianism, and the Dead Sea Scrolls, 97. **CONTACT ADDRESS** Dept of Classical, Near East, and Religious Studie, Univ of British Columbia, 1866 Main Mall Buch C 270, Vancouver, BC, Canada V6T 1Z1. **EMAIL** dneufeld@interchange.ubc.ca

NEUHOUSER, FREDERICK
PERSONAL Born 05/26/1957 **DISCIPLINE** 19TH CENTURY GERMAN PHILOSOPHY **EDUCATION** Columbia Univ, PhD, 88. **CAREER** Harvard Univ; Univ Calif, San Diego; Assoc Prf, Cornell Univ. **HONORS AND AWARDS** Humboldt fel. **RESEARCH** Social and political phil, psychoanalysis. **SELECTED PUBLICATIONS** Auth, Fichte's Theory of Subjectivity, Cambridge Univ Press, 90; "Freedom, Dependence, and the General Will," The Philos Rev, 93; "Fichte and Foundatios of Hegel's Social Theory and the Relation between Right and Morality," Fichte: Historical Context/Contemporary Controverseries, Hum Press, 94; "The First Presentation of Fichte's Wissenschaftslehre (94/95)," The Cambridge Companion to Fichte, Cambridge Univ Press, 00. **CONTACT ADDRESS** Cornell University, Cornell Univ, 218 Goldwin Smith Hall, Ithaca, NY 14853. **EMAIL** fwn1@cornell.edu

NEVERDON-MORTON, CYNTHIA
PERSONAL Born 01/23/1944, Baltimore, MD, m **DISCIPLINE** AFRICAN-AMERICAN STUDIES **EDUCATION** Morgan State Univ, BA 1965, MS 1967; Howard Univ, PhD 1974. **CAREER** Baltimore Public School Syst, tchr of history 1965-68; Peale Museum, rschr/jr archivist 1965; Inst of Afro-Amer Studies, instructor curr develop 1968; MN Lutheran Synod Priority Prog, consultant 1969; Univ of MN, admissions assoc 1968-69, coordinator special programs 1969-71; Coppin State Coll, asst dean of students prof of hist 1971-72, assoc prof of history 1972-81, chairperson dept of history, geography, international studies 1978-81; prof of history, 81-; Historically Black Cols and Universities (HBCU) Fellow, EEO/Special Emphasis Programs, summer 1989-93, Dept of Defense, 50th Anniversary of WWII Commemoration Comm, 93-95; MI State Univ, Research for CD-ROM on Immigration and Migration in US 1900-1920, consultant, 96; MD Museum of African American History and Culture, head of academic team, 98-. **HONORS AND AWARDS** Publ "The Impact of Christianity Upon Traditional Family Values" 1978; "The Black Woman's Struggle for Equality in the South" 1978; NEH Fellowship for College Teachers 1981-82; publ "Self-Help Programs as Educative Activities of Black Women in the South 1895-1925, Focus on Four Key Areas" 1982; "Blacks in Baltimore 1950-1980, An Overview" with Bettye Gardner 1982; "Black Housing Patterns in Baltimore 1895-1925" publ MD Historian 1985; Annual Historical Review 1982-83, 1983-84; Ordnance Center & School Aberdeen Proving Ground 1986; mem consult ed bd Twentieth Century Black Amer Officials & Leaders publ Greenwood Press. **MEMBERSHIPS** Study grant to selected W African Nations 1974; participant Caribbean-Amer Scholars Exchange Program 1974; mem adv bd MD Commn of Afro-Amer Life 1977-; mem Assn of Black Female Historians 1979-; mem adv bd Multicultural Educ Coalition Com 1980-; mem Assn for the Study of Afro-Amer Life & History; reader & panelist Natl Endowment for the Humanities Smithsonian Inst Fellow 1986; Natl Forum for History Standards, 1992-94; reviewer, history dept, Howard Univ, 1995; mem MD State Dept of Educ Task Force on the Teacher of Social Studies, 1991, mem Accreditation Team; Nonstandard English and the School Environment Task Force, Baltimore County Public Schools, 1990. **SELECTED PUBLICATIONS** "Afro-American Women of the South and the Advancement of the Race 1895-1925" Univ of TN Press 1989; essay,"Through the Looking Glass: Reviewing the African American Female Exerience" in Feminist Studies 1988; wrote eight chapters, African American History in the Press, 1851-1899, Gale Press, 1996; "Securing the Double V: African-American and Japanese-american Women in the Military During World War II" in A Woman's War Too: US Women in the Military in World War II, 1996; "In Search of Equality: Maryland and the Civil Rights Movement, 1940-1970," Black Classic Press, 1997; guest editor, Negro History Bulletin, 1995-98; "Interracial Cooperation Movement," The Readers Companion to US Women's History, Houghton Mifflin, 1998; auth, "Janie Porter Barrett" in Am Nat Biography, Oxford Univ Press, (99); auth, "Mary Eliza Church Terrell" in Am Nat Biography, Oxford Univ Press, (99); auth, "Atlanta Neighborhood Union" in Organizing Black America: An Encyclopedia of African Am Associations, Garland Publishing (01); auth, "Baltimore: Civic, Literary, and Mutual Aid Associations," in Organizing Black America: An Encyclopedia of African Am Associations, Garland Publishing (01). **CONTACT ADDRESS** Coppin State Col, 2500 W North Ave, Baltimore, MD 21216. **EMAIL** cneverdon-morton@wye.coppin.edu

NEWBILL, JAMES
PERSONAL Born 09/30/1931, Yakima, WA, m, 1951, 3 children **DISCIPLINE** HISTORY **EDUCATION** Univ Wash, BA, 53; MA, 60. **CAREER** Teacher, Highland & Prosser High Schs, 53-60; instr & part-time adminr, Yakima Valley Community Col, 60-98; adj hist instr, Yakima Valley Community Col, 98-00. **HONORS AND AWARDS** Fulbright Fel, 58 & 64; William Robertson Coe Fel, 62; Exemplary Status, Wash Community col Humanities Asn, 86; Outstanding Teacher, Yakima Valley Community Col, 89. **MEMBERSHIPS** Am Hist Asn, Eastern District of Wash Hist Soc of the 9th Circuit Court. **RESEARCH** Industrial Workers of the World, Justice William O. Douglas, Reverend George Whitefield, Judge J. Stanley Webster, Yakima Valley History. **SELECTED PUBLICATIONS** Coauth, The American Spectrum, Wordsworth, 72; co-ed, Yakima: A Centennial Perspective, Franklin Press (Yakima, WA), 84; auth, "Farmers and Wobblies in the Yakima Valley 1933," The Pacific Northwest Quart (77); auth, "Yakima and the Wobblies, 1910-1936," in At the Point of Production, the Local History of the IWW, ed. Joseph Conlin (Greenwood Press, 81); auth, "William O. Douglas: Of a Man and Hist Mountains," Pacific Northwest Quart (88); auth, "My Brush with History," Am Hostage (98); auth, "Judge J. Stanley Webster," Western Legal Hist (forthcoming). **CONTACT ADDRESS** Dept Soc Sci, Yakima Valley Comm Col, PO Box 1647, Yakima, WA 98907-1647.

NEWBY, GORDON D.
PERSONAL Born 12/16/1939, Salt Lake City, UT, m, 1992, 4 children **DISCIPLINE** MIDDLE EASTERN STUDIES, HISTORY OF RELIGIONS **EDUCATION** Univ Utah, BA, 62; Brandeis Univ, MA, 64, PhD, 66. **CAREER** Affl prof hist dept/chemn dept Near Eastern Judaic Langs Lits. **HONORS AND AWARDS** Founding ed; Medieval Encounters, Fulbright Scholar (Malaysia); founding ed, medieval encounters. **MEMBERSHIPS** Am Soc for the Study of Religion, Am Oriental Soc, Am Academy of Religion, Middle East Studies Asn, Asn of Jewish Studies. **RESEARCH** Islamic history; medieval Jewish history; Muslim/non-Muslim relations; Comparative religions. **SELECTED PUBLICATIONS** Auth, A History of the Jews of Arabia; auth, The Making of the Last Prophet. **CONTACT ADDRESS** Middle Eastern Studies, Emory Univ, S-312 Callaway Ctr, 537 Kilgo Cir, Atlanta, GA 30322. **EMAIL** gdnewby@emory.edu

NEWBY, I. A.
PERSONAL Born 10/03/1931, Hawkinsville, GA **DISCIPLINE** UNITED STATES HISTORY **EDUCATION** GA Southern Col, BS, 51; Univ Sc, MA, 57; Univ Calif, Los Angeles, PhD(hist), 62. **CAREER** Asst prof hist, Western Wash State Col, 62-63 & Calif State Col, Fullerton, 63-66; assoc prof, Univ Hawaii, 66-67 & Calif State Col, Fullerton, 67-68; assoc prof, 68-70, Prof Hist, Univ Hawaii, 70-. **MEMBERSHIPS** AHA; Orgn Am Historians; Southern Hist Asn; Asn Study Negro Life & Hist. **RESEARCH** History of the South; Negro history; racism. **SELECTED PUBLICATIONS CONTACT ADDRESS** Dept of Hist, Univ of Hawaii, Manoa, Honolulu, HI 96822.

NEWCOMB, BENJAMIN H.
PERSONAL Born 07/01/1938, Philadelphia, PA, 2 children **DISCIPLINE** COLONIAL AMERICAN HISTORY **EDUCATION** Haverford Col, BA, 60; Univ PA, MA, 61, PhD, 64. **CAREER** Asst prof, 64-72, assoc prof hist, 72-93, Prof, TX Tech Univ 93-. **MEMBERSHIPS** AHA; Orgn Am Historians; AAUP. **RESEARCH** America in the 18th century; early American politics and religions. **SELECTED PUBLICATIONS** Auth, Effects of the Stamp Act on Colonial Pennsylvania politics, William & Mary Quart, 4/66; Franklin and Galloway: A Political Partnership, Yale Univ, 72; Political Partisanship in the Middle American Colonies, LSU, 95; English Puritan Clergy: Acceptence of Political Parties, J Religious Hist, 8/95. **CONTACT ADDRESS** Dept of Hist, Texas Tech Univ, Box 41013, Lubbock, TX 79409-0001. **EMAIL** fjbhn@ttacs.ttu.edu

NEWELL, MARGARET E.
DISCIPLINE HISTORY **EDUCATION** Brown Univ, AB, 84; Univ Va, MA, 86, PhD, 91. **CAREER** ASSOC PROF, HIST, OHIO STATE UNIV **MEMBERSHIPS** Am Antiquarian Soc **SELECTED PUBLICATIONS** Auth, "Robert Child and the Entrepreneurial Vision: Economic Ideology and Development in Early New England," NEQ 58; "Merchants and Miners: Economic Culture in Seventeenth Century Massachusetts and Peru," Revista de Indias 21, May-Sept 94; auth, "A Revolution in Economic Thought: From the Currency Act to the Imperial Crisis in Massachusetts," in Entrepreneurs: The Boston Business Community, 1750-1850, 97; auth, "Massachusetts Body of Liberties," and "John Leland," in Encyclopedia of Religion and the Law; auth, The Drove of Adam's Degenerate Seed: Indian Slavery in Colonial New England, Cornell Univ Press; auth, From Dependency to Independence: Economic Revolution in Colonial New England, Cornell Univ Press. **CONTACT ADDRESS** Dept of Hist, Ohio State Univ, Columbus, 230 W 17th Ave, Columbus, OH 43210. **EMAIL** newell.20@osu.edu

NEWHALL, DAVID SOWLE
PERSONAL Born 07/26/1929, Burlington, VT, m, 1952, 5 children **DISCIPLINE** MODERN HISTORY **EDUCATION** Univ Vt, BA, 51; Harvard Univ, MA, 56, PhD, 63. **CAREER** From instr to asst prof hist, Univ Vt, 59-66; from asst prof to assoc prof, 66-70, prof hist, 70-95, Pottinger Distinguished Prof of Hist Emer, 95- , Centre Col, 66- ; Phi Beta Kappa, 51; **HONORS AND AWARDS** Acorn Awd Ky Advocates for Higher Educ, 94. **MEMBERSHIPS** Soc Fr Hist Studies. **RESEARCH** Political history of the Third French Republic; Georges Clemenceau. **SELECTED PUBLICATIONS** Clemenceau: A Life at War, 91. **CONTACT ADDRESS** Dept of Hist, Centre Col, Danville, KY 40422.

NEWMAN, EDGAR LEON
PERSONAL Born 01/21/1939, New Orleans, LA, m, 1989, 2 children **DISCIPLINE** EUROPEAN HISTORY **EDUCATION** Ecole du Louvre, Paris, dipl, 59; Yale Univ, BA, 62; Univ Chicago, PhD, 69. **CAREER** Res asst hist, Univ Chicago, 63-64; teaching asst, Univ Ill, Chicago Circle, 66-67; asst prof, 69-75, Assoc Prof Hist, NM State Univ, 75-, NEH fels, Sem Hist Socialism, 74 & Sem High Cult & Popular Cult in 19th Century Europe, 77; NEH res grant, 75-76; res grant, NM State Univ, 78. **MEMBERSHIPS** AHA; Soc Fr Hist Studies; Southern Hist Asn; Western Soc Fr Hist (pres, 77-78); Dir, Soc Hist Revolution 1848. **RESEARCH** The intellectual and social aftermath of the French Revolutions of 1789 and 1830; the French worker-poets of the July Monarchy, 1830-50; workers and the liberal leadership of the July Revolution in France, 1830. **SELECTED PUBLICATIONS** Auth, What the Crowd Wanted in the French Revolution of 1830, In: 1830 and the Origins of the Social Question in France, Watts, 74; The Popular Idea of Liberty in the French Revolution of 1830, Proc Consortium Revolutionary Europe, 74; The Blouse and the Frock Coat: The Alliance Between the Common People and the Liberal Leadership During the Last Years of the Bourbon Restoration, 3/74; La blouse et la redingote, Ann Hist Revolution Francaise, 76; The French Women Worker Poets 1830-48, 19th Century Soc & Cult, 78; The Revolutionary Mentality of the French Worker-Poets, 1830-48, J Mod Hist; ed, Historical Dictionary of France From the Bourbon Restoration to the Second Empire, 1815-52, 2 vols, 87; auth, Franenstein, Les Lumineres et la Revolution comme monstre, Annales historiques de la Revolution francaise, 92; The Historian on Apostle: Romanticism, Religion, and the First Socialist History of the World, Jnal of the Hist of Ideas, 95; contrib to: Dictionaire de biographie francaise, Dictionaire biographique du mouvement ouvier francais, Am Hist Asn Giude to Hist Lit. **CONTACT ADDRESS** Dept of Hist, New Mexico State Univ, PO Box 30001, Las Cruces, NM 88003-8001. **EMAIL** enewman@nmsu.edu

NEWMAN, GERALD GORDON
PERSONAL Born 12/08/1938, Singapore, Malaya, m, 2 children **DISCIPLINE** MODERN BRITISH INTELLECTUAL AND SOCIAL HISTORY **EDUCATION** Univ Wash, BA, 60, MA, 64; Harvard Univ, PhD, 71. **CAREER** Instr hist, W Wash State Col, 65-66; asst prof, 70-78, Assoc prof hist to prof, Kent State Univ, 78-00. **HONORS AND AWARDS** Distinguished Teaching Awd, Kent State Univ Alum Asn, 76. **MEMBERSHIPS** AHA; Conf Brit Studies; World Hist Asn. **RESEARCH** Modern British intellectual and social history. **SELECTED PUBLICATIONS** Armchair History and the writings of Macaulay, Studies in Hist & Soc, spring 74; Anti-French propaganda and British liber nationalism in the early nineteenth century: Suggestions toward a general interpretation, Victorian Studies, 6/75; The vindication of Voltaire in the British periodical press, 1850-1900, J Popular Cult, spring 77; Voltaire in Victorian historiography, J Mod Hist, 12/77; Aspects of British Nationalism during the later eighteenth century, Consortium Revolutionary Europe: Proc 1981, 81; The Rise of English Nationalism, 87; Britain in the Hanoverian Age, 1714-1837: An Encycl, 97. **CONTACT ADDRESS** Dept Hist, Kent State Univ, 709 S. Adler St, Ellensburg, WA 98926. **EMAIL** barger@elltel.net

NEWMAN, J. R.
PERSONAL Born 03/26/1954, Chicago, IL, m, 1995, 1 child **DISCIPLINE** ANTHROPOLOGY, ARCHAEOLOGY **EDUCATION** Triton Col, AA, 74; Grinnell Col, BA, 76; Southern Methodist Univ, MA, 84, PhD, 97. **CAREER** Archaeologist, Southern Methodist Univ, 78-87; archaeologist, U.S. Army Corps of Engineers, 87-00. **HONORS AND AWARDS** Certificate of Appreciation, Office of the Secretary of Defense, 90; Achievement Medal for Civilian Service, 92; Design & Environmental Excellence Awd, 93, Commendations, 89, 90, 91, & 92, Certificate of Achievement, 90, 91, Dept of Army; Fort Burgwin Res Fel, 81 & 82; Grant, Inst for the Study of Earth and Man, 83 & 85; Weber Grant, 87, multiple small grants, 82-85, Southern Methodist Univ. **MEMBERSHIPS** Soc of Professional Archaeologists; Register of Professional Archaeologists; Tx Archeological Soc; Soc for Am Archaeology; Coun of Tx Archeologists. **RESEARCH** Lithic sourcing & analysis; Lithic economic procurement patterns & use; statistical analysis; cultural resources management. **SELECTED PUBLICATIONS** Contributing auth, Shoreline Survey of Lewisville Lake, Denton County, Texas, 1986, Univ of North Tx, 90; auth, A Cultural Resources Survey of the Proposed Central Distribution Center (CDC) Construction Site and Sanitary Landfill Area at the Red River Army Depot, Bowie County, Texas, U.S. Army Corps of Engineers, 88; coauth, An Archeological Inventory of a Proposed Incinerator Construction Site at the Louisiana Army Ammunition Plant, Webster Parish, Louisiana, U.S. Army Corps of Engineers, 88; auth, A Cultural Resources Survey of Proposed Actions Related to Test Area Expansions, Longhorn Army Ammunition Plant, Harrison County, Texas, U.S. Army Corps of Engineers, 88; auth, Initial Notes On the XRF Sourcing of Northern New Mexico Obsidians, Journal of Field Archaeol, Boston Univ, 85; auth, Initial Notes On the X-ray Flourescence Characterization of the Rhyodacite Sources of the Taos Plateau, New Mexico, Archaeometry, Oxford Univ, 87; auth, The Effects of Source Distance on Lithic Material Reduction Technology, J of Field Archaeology, 94; auth, Task Selection of Lithic Raw Materials in the Northern Rio Grande Valley, New Mexico, Bulletin of the Tx Archaeological Soc, 99. **CONTACT ADDRESS** CESWF-EV-EC, U.S. Army Corps of Engineers, PO Box 17300, Fort Worth, TX 76102-0300. **EMAIL** jay.r.newman@swf.usace.army.mil

NEWMAN, JUDITH H.
PERSONAL Born 02/01/1961, Alexandria, VA, m, 1987, 2 children **DISCIPLINE** NEAR EASTERN LANGUAGES AND CIVILIZATIONS **EDUCATION** Princeton, AB, 83; Yale Divinity School, MAR, 88; Harvard Univ, 96. **CAREER** Asst prof, General Theol Sem, 98-; Assoc Prof, 00. **HONORS AND AWARDS** Episcopal church Found fel, 92-95. **MEMBERSHIPS** SBL; CBA; AJS. **RESEARCH** History of Biblical interpretation; Second Temple Judaism; history of Jewish and Christian Liturgy. **SELECTED PUBLICATIONS** Auth, Praying By the Book: the Scripturalization of Prayer in Second Temple Judaism, EJL Series, Atlanta: Scholars, 99. **CONTACT ADDRESS** General Theol Sem, 175 Ninth Ave, New York, NY 10011-4977. **EMAIL** newman@gts.edu

NEWMAN, KATHY M.
PERSONAL Born 12/16/1966, Seattle, WA, s **DISCIPLINE** AMERICAN STUDIES **EDUCATION** Yale Univ, PhD. **CAREER** English, Literary and Cultural Theory. **RESEARCH** Media History; Marxist theory; Literary Studies. **SELECTED PUBLICATIONS** Auth, "Nice Work if We Can Keep it: Confessions of a Junior Professor," Academe (99); auth, "The Forgotten Fifteen Million: Black Radio, the 'Negro Market' and the Civil Rights Movement," Radical History Review 76 (00); auth, "'Poisons, Potions and Profits:' Radio Rebels and the Consumer Movement," in The Radio Reader, ed. Michele Hilmes and Jason Loviglio (Univ of Minnesota Press, forthcoming); auth, Radio-Active: Advertising and Consumer Activism in the Broadcast Age, Univ of Calif Press, forthcoming; auth, "True Lies: True Story Magazine and Working Class Consumption in Postwar America," Minnesota Review, forthcoming. **CONTACT ADDRESS** Carnegie Mellon Univ, 5000 Forbes Ave, Pittsburgh, PA 15213. **EMAIL** Kn4@andrew.cmu.edu

NEWMAN, LEX
DISCIPLINE THE HISTORY OF MODERN PHILOSOPHY **EDUCATION** Irvine, PhD, 94. **CAREER** Asst prof, Univ Nebr, Lincoln, 94-; vis asst prof, Univ Pittsburgh, 96. **SELECTED PUBLICATIONS** Auth, Descartes on Unknown Faculties and Our Knowledge of the External World, Philos Rev 103, 94; Descartes' epistemology, in The Stanford Encyclopedia of Philosophy, ed, Edward N Zalta, an online publication of Ctr for Stud of Lang and Infor, Stanford Univ, http://plato.stanford.edu/entries/descartes-epistemology, 97. **CONTACT ADDRESS** Univ of Utah, 260 Central Campus Dr., Room 341, Salt Lake City, UT 84112-9156.

NEWMAN, PETER C.
PERSONAL Born 05/10/1929, Vienna, Austria **DISCIPLINE** HISTORY, POLITICAL SCIENCE **EDUCATION** Univ Toronto, BA, 50, Inst Bus Admin, MCom, 54. **CAREER** Asst ed to prod ed, Financial Post, 51-55; asst ed to nat affairs ed, 56-63, ed, Maclean's mag, 71-83; ed to ed-in-chief, Toronto Star, 64-71; vis prof, polit sci, McMaster Univ, 69-71; vis prof, polit sci, York Univ, 79-80. **HONORS AND AWARDS** Nat Newspaper Awd Jour, 71; Achievement Life Awd, Encycl Britannia Publs, 77; off, 79, companion, Order Can, 90; Can Authors Asn Lit Awd Non-fiction, 86. **RESEARCH** Canadian economic and political history. **SELECTED PUBLICATIONS** Auth, Flame of Power, 59; auth, Renegade in Power: The Diefenbaker Years, 63; auth, The Distemper of Our Times, 68; auth, Home Country-People, Places and Power Politics, 73; auth, The Canadian Establishment-Vol I, The Great Business Dynasties, 75; auth, Bronfman Dynasty: The Rothschilds of the New World, 78; auth, The Acquisitors: The Canadian Establishment, Vol II, 81; auth, The Establishment Man: A Portrait of Power, 82; auth, True North: Not Strong and Free-Defending the Peaceable Kingdom in the Nuclear Age, 83; auth, Company of Adventurers: An Unauthorized History of the Hudson's Bay Company, 3 vols, 85-91; auth, Sometimes A Great Nation: Will Canada belong to the 21st Century?, 88; auth, Empire of Bay, 89; auth, Portrait of a Promised Land: The Canadian Revolution from Deference to Defiance, 95; auth, Defining Moments: Dispatches from an Unfinished Revolution, 97; gen ed, Debrett's Illustrated Guide to the Canadian Establishment, 83. **CONTACT ADDRESS** 2568 W 1st Ave, Vancouver, BC, Canada V6K 1G7.

NEWPORT, WILLIAM H. A.
PERSONAL Born 10/11/1965, Hartford, CT **DISCIPLINE** HISTORY **EDUCATION** Univ New York, AS, 90, BS, 91; Southern Conn, MLS, 98, MA, 98. **CAREER** Ref librn, 97, Avon Free Public Libr; grad asst, 96-98, Southern Conn State Univ; Librn, 98-, Mashantucket Pequot Museum and Res Ctr. **HONORS AND AWARDS** Grad Asst, 96-98, SCSU; CVC/SLA, 97, Conference Travel Stipend; Elma Jean and John Wiacek Jr Scholar, 97, SCSU. **MEMBERSHIPS** Asn Col Res Libr; Am Libr Asn; Am Aviation Hist Society; Conn Aeronautical Hist Asn; Army Air forces Roundtable Conn. **RESEARCH** Military history; aviation history. **SELECTED PUBLICATIONS** Auth, Evolution of American Fighter Aircraft Armament, 98. **CONTACT ADDRESS** Mashantucket Pequot Mus and Research Ctr, 110 Pequot Trl, PO Box 3180, Mashantucket, CT 06339-3180. **EMAIL** wnewport@mptn.org

NEWTON, JAMES E.
PERSONAL Born 07/03/1941, Bridgeton, NJ, m, 1967, 3 children **DISCIPLINE** AFRICAN-AMERICAN STUDIES **EDUCATION** NC Central Univ, BA 1966; Univ of NC, MFA 1968; IL State Univ, PhD 1972. **CAREER** Univ of NC, art instr 1967-68; W Chester State Coll PA, asst prof art 1968-69; IL State Univ Normal, asst prof art 1969-71; Western IL Univ Macomb, asst prof art 1971-72; Univ of DE Newark, asst prof ed 1972-73; Umiv of DE Neward, Prof, Dir Black Amer Studies 1973-. **HONORS AND AWARDS** Exhibitions, Natl Print & Drawing Show 11th Midwest Bienniel Exhib 1972; 1st prize Sculpture & Graphics 19th Annual Exhib of Afro-Amer Artists 1972; 23rd Annual Mid-States Art Exhibit 1972; Purchase Awd 13th Reg Art Exhibit Univ of DE 1974; DE Afro-Amer Art Exhib 1980; Exhibited Lincoln Univ, West Chester State Coll, FL A&M Univ, DE State Coll, Dover DE; Excellence in Teaching Awd Univ of Delaware 1988; EasternRegion Citation Awd Phi Deltappa National Sorority 1989; Wilmington News Journal, Hometown Hero Awd 1990; Jefferson Awd, Amer Inst for Public Service; Document Verifier for McDonald's, Little Known Facts of Black History. **MEMBERSHIPS** Mem edit bd, Natl Art Ed Assoc; Editorial board Education 1974-; mem exec counselor Assoc Study Afro-Amer Life & History 1976-77; bd mem Western Journal of Black Studies 1983-; bd mem past chairman Walnut St YMCA Delaware 1983-; State Dir Assn for the Study of Afro-American Life & History 1988-. **SELECTED PUBLICATIONS** Publ, College Student Jrnl, Jrnl of Negro Ed, Negro History Bulletin, Crisis, Education, Clearing House; books, A Curriculum Eval of Black Amer Studies in Relation to Student Knowledge of Afro-Amer History & Culture

R&E Assoc Inc 1976, Roots of Black Amer; aduio-tapes Slave Aritsans & Craftsmen, Contemporary Afro-Amer Art Miami-Dade Comm Coll 1976. **CONTACT ADDRESS** Col of Urban Affairs & Public Policy & Professor of Black American Studies, Univ of Delaware, 417 Ewing Bldg, Newark, DE 19711. **EMAIL** jnewton@udel.edu

NEWTON, MERLIN OWEN
PERSONAL Born 02/16/1935, Ashland, AL, m, 1958, 3 children **DISCIPLINE** POLITICAL HISTORY **EDUCATION** Tulane Univ, MA, Hist, 58; Univ Ala, PhD, 92. **CAREER** Retired, Huntingdon Coll, 95. **HONORS AND AWARDS** A.B. Moore (Albert Burton) Memorial Scholarship, 1989; Frank Lawrence Ouisley Memorial Scholarship, 1990; Outstanding Dissertation, U of Ala., 1991-1992, awarded 1993 . **MEMBERSHIPS** Ala Hist Soc; Souther Hist Soc **RESEARCH** Constitutional issues. **SELECTED PUBLICATIONS** Armed With the Constitution: Jehovah's Witnesses in Alabama and the U.S. Supreme Court, 1939-1946, Univ Ala Press, 95; "Roscoe Jones and Alabama Judiciary," Ala Rev, 96. **CONTACT ADDRESS** 4519 W Terict, Montgomery, AL 36106. **EMAIL** merlin.newton@gte.net

NEWTON, WESLEY PHILLIPS
PERSONAL Born 04/02/1925, Montgomery, AL, m, 1958, 3 children **DISCIPLINE** HISTORY **EDUCATION** Univ Mo, AB, 49; Univ Ala, MA, 53, PhD(hist), 64. **CAREER** Asst prof soc sci, Ala Col, 64; from asst prof to assoc prof, 64-74, Prof Hist, Auburn Univ, 74-. **MEMBERSHIPS** Latin Am Studies Asn; Southern Hist Asn; Southeastern Coun Latin Am Studies (pres, 80-81). **RESEARCH** United States-Latin American diplomatic history; history of aviation in Latin America and the United States; military history. **SELECTED PUBLICATIONS** Coauth, Air Force Combat Units of World War II, Watts, 64; auth, International aviation rivalry in Latin America, 1919- 1927, JInter-Am Studies, 65; The role of the Army air arm in Latin America, 1922-1931, Air Univ Rev, 967; Lindbergh comes to Alabama, Ala Rev, 73; The third flight: Charles A Lindbergh and aviation diplomacy in Latin America, J Am Aviation Hist Soc, summer 75; Bertram (Bert) Blanchard Acosta, In: Dictionary of American Biography, Supplement Five, 1951-1955, 77; The Perilous Sky: United States Aviation Diplomacy and Latin America, 1919- 1931, Univ Miami, 78; coauth (with W David Lewis), Delta: The History of an Airline, Univ Ga, 79; Storm Over Iraq - Air Power And The Gulf-war - Hallion,rp, Technology And Culture, Vol 0035, 1994. **CONTACT ADDRESS** Dept of Hist, Auburn Univ, Auburn, AL 36830.

NEYLAND, LEEDELL WALLACE
PERSONAL Born 08/04/1921, Gloster, MS, m **DISCIPLINE** HISTORY **EDUCATION** Virginia State College, AB, 1949; New York University, MA, 1950, PhD, 1959. **CAREER** Leland Coll Baker LA, professor of social science, dean of college, 50-52; Grambling Coll, associate professor of social sciences, 52-58; Elizabeth City Coll, dean, 58-59; Florida A&M University, professor of history, dean of humanities/social science, 59-84, College of Arts and Sciences, dean, 68-82, vice pres for academic affairs, 82-85; Consultant, Lecturer on Black History and Education, currently. **HONORS AND AWARDS** Carnegie Grant, 1965. **MEMBERSHIPS** Co-chairman, Governor's Dr Martin Luther King Jr Commemorative Celebration Commission, 1985-87; member, board of directors, Leon County/Tallahassee Chamber of Commerce, 1984-86; vice chairman, Tallahassee Preservation Board, 1984-88; member, Presbyterian National Committee on the Self-Development of People, currently; member, Florida Historical Records Advisory Board, currently; member, Phi Beta Sigma; member, Sigma Pi Phi; member, 32 Degree Mason, Modern Free and Accepted Masons of the World. **SELECTED PUBLICATIONS** Author, Unquenchable Black Fires, Leney Educational and Publishing Inc, 1994.Co-author: History of Florida A&M University, 1963; Twelve Black Floridians, 1970; History of the Florida State Teachers Assn, 1977; History of the Florida Interscholastic Assn, 1982; Florida A&M University: A Centennial History, 1887-1987, 1987; Historical Black Land-Grant Institutions and the Development of Agriculture and Home Economics, 1890-1990, 1990; author of numerous articles appearing in professional publications. **CONTACT ADDRESS** Florida A&M Univ, Tallahassee, FL 32307.

NG, FRANKLIN C.
PERSONAL Born 03/18/1947, Honolulu, HI, m, 2 children **DISCIPLINE** HISTORY **EDUCATION** John Hopkins Univ, BA, 68; Harvard Univ, MA, 70; Univ Chicago, MA, PhD, 75. **CAREER** Asst prof to assoc prof, Cal State Univ, 75-. **HONORS AND AWARDS** Ford Fel; Phi Kappa Phi; Scholar of the Year Awd; Choice Bk Awd. **MEMBERSHIPS** AHA; OAH; AAS; AAAS; SHAFR; CHS. **RESEARCH** Asian Americans; China-US relations; US Diplomatic Affairs; US History; East Asia. **SELECTED PUBLICATIONS** Co-ed, Racial and Ethnic Relations in America, 00; co-ed, Distinguished Asian Americans: A Biographical Dictionary, 99; coauth, Houghton Miffin Social Studies Texts: G Titles, Grade 3 to 8, 99; auth, The Taiwanese Americans, 98; ed, Asians in America: The Peoples of East, Southeast, and Southasian, 98; series ed, Asian Americans: Reconceptualizing Culture, History, Politics (Garland, 97); ed, The Asian American Encyclopedia, 95; co-ed, New Visions in Asian American Studies: Diversity, Community, Power, 94; auth, Chinese Americans Struggle for Equality, 92. **CONTACT ADDRESS** Dept Anthropology, California State Univ, Fresno, 5245 North Backer Ave, Fresno, CA 93740-8001.

NG, ON-CHO
PERSONAL Born 01/29/1953, Hong Kong, m, 1995 **DISCIPLINE** HISTORY, RELIGIOUS STUDIES **EDUCATION** Univ HI, PhD, 86. **CAREER** Vis asst prof, Univ CA, Riverside, 86-89; asst prof, 89-95, assoc prof, PA State Univ, 95-. **MEMBERSHIPS** Am Academy of Relig; Asn for Asian Studies; Soc for Comparative and Asian Philos; Soc of Chinese Religions. **RESEARCH** Intellectual hist of late Imperial China; 16th-18th centuries; Confucian tradition. **SELECTED PUBLICATIONS** Auth, Revisiting Kung Tzu-chen's (1792-1841) Chin-wen (New Text) Precepts: An Excursion in the History of Ideas, J of Oriental Studies, 31-2, fall 93; A Tension in Ch'ing Thought: Historicism in Seventeenth and Eighteenth Century Chinese Thought, J of the History of Ideas, 54-4, Oct 93; Hsing (Nature) as the Ontological Basis of Practicality in Early Ch'ing Ch'eng-Chu Confucianism: Li Kuang-ti's (1642-1718) Philosophy, Philos East and West 44-1, Jan 94; Mystical Oneness and Meditational Praxis: Religiousness in Li Yong's (1627-1703) Confucian Thought, J of Chinese Religions, no 22, fall 94; Mid-Ch'ing New Text (Chin-wen) Classical Learning and Its Han Provenance: The Dynamics of a Tradition of Ideas, East Asian History, no 8, Dec 94; Interpreting Qing Thought in China as a Period Concept: On the Construction of an Epochal System of Ideas, Semiotica: J of the Int Asn for Semiotic Studies, 107-3/4, 95; Is Emotion (Qing) the Source of a Confucian Antimony?, J of Chinese Philos, 98; Imagining Boundaries: Changing Confucian Doctrines, Texts, and Hermeneutics, co-ed with Kai-wing Chow and John Henderson, SUNY, March 99; and six book chapters. **CONTACT ADDRESS** History Dept, Pennsylvania State Univ, Univ Park, University Park, PA 16802. **EMAIL** oxn1@psu.edu

NI, TING
PERSONAL Born 05/15/1952, China, m, 1983, 1 child **DISCIPLINE** HISTORY **EDUCATION** Nankai Univ, China, BA, 82; MA, 84; Indiana Univ, MA, 97; PhD, 96. **CAREER** Instr, Nankai Univ, China, 85-87; asst prof, St Mary's Univ, 97-. **HONORS AND AWARDS** NEH Fel; Intl Fel; Starr Fel; Fulbright Gnt. **MEMBERSHIPS** OAH; AAS; MIC; CHUS. **RESEARCH** Asian Americans; US Foreign Policy; Modern China. **SELECTED PUBLICATIONS** Auth, "The Pullman Strike in 1894," Hist Teach 8 (83): 29-31; auth, "Historiography of Westward Movement." Worl Hist 6 (85): 33-36; auth, "Historiography of American Indian History," Hist Stud 1 (87): 54-62. **CONTACT ADDRESS** Dept History, Saint Mary's Univ of Minnesota, Winona, 700 Terrace Hts, Winona, MN 55987. **EMAIL** tni@smumn.edu

NICHOLLS, MICHAEL LEE
PERSONAL Born 09/10/1944, Des Moines, IA, m, 1966 **DISCIPLINE** AMERICAN HISTORY **EDUCATION** Cedarville Col, BA, 66; Univ Dayton, MA, 67; Col William & Mary, PhD(Am hist), 72. **CAREER** Asst prof, 70-80, Assoc Prof Am Hist, Utah State Univ, 80-. **MEMBERSHIPS** Orgn Am Historians; Southern Hist Asn. **RESEARCH** Early American history; American social history; American economic history. **SELECTED PUBLICATIONS** Co-auth, The Mormon Genealogical Society and Research Opportunities in Early American History, William & Mary Quart, 75; ed, News from Monrovia, VA Mag Hist & Biog, 77; co-ed, Legacies of the American Revolution, Utah State Univ, 78; auth, In the Light of Human Beings, VA Mag Hist & Biog, 81; coauth, Slaves in Piedmont Virginia, 1720-1790, William and Mary Quarterly, 89; auth, Competition, Credit and Crisis: Merchant-Planter Relations in Southside, Virginia," in Rosemary E. Ommer, ed. Academic Press, 90; auth, The Squint of Freedom: African American Freedom Suits in Post-Revolutionary Virginia, Slavery and Abolition, 99; auth, Strangers Setting Among Us: The Sources and Challence of the Urban Free Black Population of Early Virginia, Virginia Magazine of Hist Biog, 00. **CONTACT ADDRESS** Dept of Hist, Utah State Univ, Logan, UT 84321.

NICHOLS, C. HOWARD
PERSONAL Born 12/04/1935, St Louis, MO, m, 1975, 2 children **DISCIPLINE** HISTORY **EDUCATION** Shimer Col, AB, 54; Southeastern La Col, MA, 58. **CAREER** Prof, Southeastern La Univ, Prof Emeritus. **HONORS AND AWARDS** President's Awd for Teaching Excellence; Alumni Awd for Teaching Excellence; Prof of the Year; Fel, Johns Hopkins Univ, 67-68. **MEMBERSHIPS** Southern Hist Asn, La Hist Asn. **RESEARCH** State, local, regional history. **SELECTED PUBLICATIONS** Auth, Centennial Souvenir: A Hammond History Source Book, 89; auth, Mandeville on the Lake: A Sesquicentennial Album; auth, Gathered at the River: One Hundred Fifty Years of Christ Episcopal Church, Covington. **CONTACT ADDRESS** Dept Hist, Southeastern Louisiana Univ, 500 Western Ave, Hammond, LA 70402-0001. **EMAIL** hnichols@i-ss.com

NICHOLS, JALDEN
PERSONAL Born 02/28/1919, Westerly, RI, m, 1946, 3 children **DISCIPLINE** MODERN EUROPEAN HISTORY **EDUCATION** Wesleyan Univ, BA, 41; Columbia Univ, MA, 48, PhD(mod Europ hist), 51. **CAREER** From instr to asst prof hist, Wesleyan Univ, 48-61; asst prof, Skidmore Col, 50-51; Ford Found Fund Advan Educ fac fel, 51-52; ed soc sci & humanities, Col Dept, Ginn & Co, Boston, 52- 59; assoc prof, 61-67, Prof Hist, Univ IL, Urbanachampaign, 67-, Managing ed, Daedalus, 59-61. **MEMBERSHIPS** AHA **RESEARCH** German history, 1890-1914. **SELECTED PUBLICATIONS** Auth, Germany After Bismarck: The Caprivi Era, 1890-1894, Harvard Univ, 58; Bismarck, In: Vol II, Interpreting European History, Dorsey, 67; German Foreign-policy, 1890-1894 - From Bismarck Balance-of-power Policy to Caprivi Alliance Strategy - German - Lahme,r, J of Modern History, Vol 0066, 1994. **CONTACT ADDRESS** Dept of Hist, Univ of Illinois, Urbana-Champaign, Urbana, IL 61801.

NICHOLS, JOHN A.
PERSONAL Born 09/13/1939, New Kensington, PA, m, 1963, 1 child **DISCIPLINE** HISTORY **EDUCATION** Geneva Col, BA, 62; Fairleigh Dickinson Univ, MA, 66; Kent State Univ, PhD(medieval hist), 74. **CAREER** Teacher English, Franklin High Sch, NJ, 62-63; teacher hist, Mt Lakes High Sch, 63-66; from instr to assoc prof, 66-79, dean chemn soc sci & behav sci, 77-78, prof 79-, chemn hist, Slippery Rock Univ, 98-; vis prof, Mansfield Col, Oxford Univ, 84-85; pres, Conf Medieval & Renaissance cultures, 85-97, int summer prog dir, Florence, Italy, 89, Istanbul, Turkey, 93; fel Centre Europeen de Recherches sur les Congregations ed Ordres Religieux, 87. **HONORS AND AWARDS** Nat Endowment for Humanities grant, 76 & 80; SRU Learning Tech Award, 98; Fac Prof Development Coun Grant, 96, Honors Course, 94, Pa State System of Higher Ed; SRU Apple Polishing Award for Best Prof, 95; IBM Multimedia Teaching Award, 92; SRU Int Studies Prof Travel Award, 92, SRU Int Prof Developmental Award, 90. **MEMBERSHIPS** Am Catholic Hist Asn, 87-; Am Hist Asn, 83-; Asn of Cistercian Scholars, 73-; Medieval Acad of Am, 67-. **RESEARCH** Women's studies; medieval history. **SELECTED PUBLICATIONS** Auth, The architectural and physical features of an English Cistercian nunnery, Cistercian Ideals & Reality, 78; The internal organization of English Cistercian nunneries, Citeaux: Commentarii Cistercienses, 78; Why found a Cistercian Nunnery?, Mediaevalia, 79; Medieval English Cistercian Nunneries Their Art and Physical Remains, Melanges Dimier, 81; Distant Echoes: Medieval Religious Women, 84; Peaceweavers: Medieval Religious Women, 87; auth, Isabel D'Albigni, Countess of Arundel and Foundress of Marham Abbey, Medieval Prosopography, 91; Cistercian Monastic Women: Introduction to Hidden Springs, Cistercian Studies Quarterly, 93; Medieval Art of Sinningthwaite Nunnery, Studies in Cistercian Art & Archit; Cistercian nuns in Twelfth and Thirteenth Century England, Hidden Springs, 95; The cistercian Nunnery of Swine Priory: Its Church and Choir Stalls, Studiosorum Speculum, 93; co-ed, Hidden Springs: Cistercian Monastic Women, 95; auth, Women in Sport: Images from the Late Middle Ages, Scholars, 99. **CONTACT ADDRESS** History Dept, Slippery Rock Univ of Pennsylvania, 14 Maltby Dr, Slippery Rock, PA 16057-1326. **EMAIL** john.nichols@sru.edu

NICHOLS, ROGER L.
PERSONAL Born 06/13/1933, Racine, WI, m, 1959, 4 children **DISCIPLINE** UNITED STATES HISTORY **EDUCATION** Wis State Col, La Crosse, BS, 56; Univ Wis, MS, 59, PhD(US hist), 64. **CAREER** From instr to asst prof hist, Wis State Univ, Oshkosh, 63-65; assoc prof, Univ Ga, 65-69; assoc prof, 69-70, prof hist, Univ Az, 70-, res fel, Henry E. Huntington Libr & Art Gallery, 73; vis lectr hist, Univ Md, 75-76. **HONORS AND AWARDS** Senior Fulbright Lecturer, Martin Luther Univ, Halle, Germany, 97. **MEMBERSHIPS** AHA; Orgn Am Historians; Western Hist Asn; fel Am Philos Soc; Soc Hist Early Am Repub. **RESEARCH** American westward movement; 19th century United States frontier military history; American Indian history. **SELECTED PUBLICATIONS** Auth, General Henry Atkinson, 65 & Missouri Expedition, 1818-1820, 69, Univ Okla; co-ed, The American Indian: Past and Present, Xerox, 71; coauth, Stephen Long and American Scientific Exploration, Univ Del, 80; Natives and Strangers: Ethnic Groups and the Rise of Modern America, Oxford Univ, 79; ed, The American Indian: Past and Present, Wiley, 81; ed, The American Indian: Past and Present, Knopf, 86; McGraw-Hill, 92; ed, American Frontier and Western Issues: A Historigraphical Review, Greenwood, 86; co-auth, Natives and Strangers: Blacks, Indians, and Immigrants in America, Oxford Univ, 90; auth, Black Hawk and the Warrior's Path, Harlan Davidson, 92; co-auth, Natives and Strangers: A Multicultural History of Americans, Oxford Univ, 96; auth, Indians in the United States and Canada: A Comparative History, Univ Nebr, 98. **CONTACT ADDRESS** Dept of Hist, Univ of Arizona, Tucson, AZ 85721-0001. **EMAIL** nichols@u.arizona.edu

NICKELSBURG, GEORGE WILLIAM ELMER
PERSONAL Born 03/15/1934, San Jose, CA, m, 1965, 2 children **DISCIPLINE** NEW TESTAMENT & CHRISTIAN ORIGINS, EARLY JUDAISM **EDUCATION** Valparaiso Univ, BA, 55; Concordia Sem, St Louis, BD, 60, STM, 62; Harvard Div Sch, ThD, 68. **CAREER** From Asst Prof to Prof Relig, 69-98; Guest lectr, Concordia Sem, St Louis, 68, instr, 69; guest prof, Christ-Sem-Seminex, 79; vis scholar, Univ Munster, 74; assoc ed, Cath Bibl Quart, 79-87; Daniel J. Krumm Distin-

guished Prof New Testament and Reformation Studies, Univ Iowa, 98-00; Prof Emeritus, 00-. **HONORS AND AWARDS** Fel, John Simon Guggenheim Mem Found, 77-78; Fel, Netherlands Inst Advan Study, 80-81; Fel, Human Sci Res Coun of SAfrica, 93. **MEMBERSHIPS** Soc Bibl Lit; Studiorum Novi Testamenti Societas; Cath Bibl Asn. **RESEARCH** The synoptic gospels; New Testament christology; history and literature of early post-biblical Judaism. **SELECTED PUBLICATIONS** Auth, Resurrection, Immortality and Eternal Life in Intertestamental Judaism, Harvard/Oxford, 72; ed, Studies on the Testament of Abraham, Scholars Press, 76; auth, Apocalyptic and myth in 1 Enoch 6-11, J Bibl Lit, 77; collabr, A Complete Concordance to Flavius Josephus, Vol 3, Brill, 79; auth, The genre and function of the markan passion narrative, Harvard Theol Rev, 80; Jewish Literature between the Bible and the Mishnah, Fortress, 81; Enoch, Levi and Peter, recipients of revelation in Upper Galilee, J Bibl Lit, 81; coauth, Faith and Piety in Early Judaism, Fortress, 83. **CONTACT ADDRESS** 4691 Running Deer Woods, Iowa City, IA 52240. **EMAIL** george-nickelsburg@uiowa.edu

NICKLES, THOMAS
PERSONAL Born 02/14/1943, Charleston, IL, m, 3 children **DISCIPLINE** HISTORY AND PHILOSOPHY OF SCIENCE **EDUCATION** Princeton Univ, PhD, 69. **CAREER** Prof, Univ Nev, Reno. **MEMBERSHIPS** Philosophy of Science Assn; Am Assn for the Advancement of Science; History of Science Society; Society for Social Studies of Science **RESEARCH** History and philosophy of science and technology **SELECTED PUBLICATIONS** Edited SCIENTIFIC DISCOVERY, LOGIC, AND RATIONALITY and SCIENTIFIC DISCOVERY: CASE STUDIES (both Reidel, 1980) and THOMAS KUHN the Philosophy of Science, Philosophy of Science, Biology and Philosophy, Configurations, etc. **CONTACT ADDRESS** Philosophy (102), Univ of Nevada, Reno, Reno, NV 89557. **EMAIL** nickles@unr.edu

NIEMEYER, GLENN ALAN
PERSONAL Born 01/14/1934, Muskegon, MI, m, 1955, 3 children **DISCIPLINE** MODERN AMERICAN HISTORY **EDUCATION** Calvin Col, BA, 55; Mich State Univ, MA, 59, PhD, 62. **CAREER** Teacher, Grand Haven Christian Sch, 55-58, MSU; asst instr, 59-63, Grand Valley State Univ from asst prof to prof, 63-70, dean col arts & sci, 70-73, vpres cols, 73-76, vpres acad affairs, 76-, provost, 80-, Grand Valley State Univ. **MEMBERSHIPS** AHA; Orgn Am Historians; Am Assn Higher Educ. **RESEARCH** Twentieth century American political and economic history; biography. **SELECTED PUBLICATIONS** Auth, Automotive Career of Ransom E. Olds, Mich State Univ, 63; art, The Curved Dash Oldsmobile, Bus Topics, autumn 63; art, Oldsmar for Health, Wealth, Happiness, Fla Hist Quart, 7/76; coauth, The General of General Motors, Am Heritage, 8-73. **CONTACT ADDRESS** Grand Valley State Univ, 1 Campus Dr, Allendale, MI 49401-9401. **EMAIL** niemeyeg@gvsu.edu

NIESSEN, JAMES P.
PERSONAL Born 12/26/1952, Nutley, NJ, s **DISCIPLINE** HISTORY **EDUCATION** Notre Dame, BA, 75; Univ Indiana, MA, 79, PhD, 89; Univ Texas, M Lis, 94. **CAREER** Vis asst prof, 88-91, Univ S Miss; libr, history & foreign lang, 94-, Texas Tech Univ.; VP for Research & Publications, H-Net: Humanities & Social Sciences Online. **MEMBERSHIPS** Am Library Assoc; Am Historical Assoc. **RESEARCH** East European hist, libraries & archives. **CONTACT ADDRESS** Libr, Texas Tech Univ, Lubbock, TX 79409-0002. **EMAIL** lijpn@lib.ttu.edu

NIETO, JOSE CONSTANTINO
PERSONAL Born 04/07/1929, El Ferrol, Spain, m, 1959, 2 children **DISCIPLINE** HISTORY OF RELIGIOUS THOUGHT **EDUCATION** Univ Santiago, BS, 49; United Evangel Sem, Madrid, BD, 56; Princeton Theol Sem, ThM, 62, PhD(relig), 67. **CAREER** Pastor, Span Evangel Church, 58-61; from asst prof to assoc prof, 67-78, prof relig, 78-82, Mary S Geiger Prof Relig & Hist, Juniata Col, 82-. **MEMBERSHIPS** Am Soc Reformation Res; Sixteenth Century Studies Conf; Am Acad Relig; AAUP. **RESEARCH** Spanish 16th century religious thought, particularly reformation, humanism and mysticism. **SELECTED PUBLICATIONS** Auth, Juan de Valdes and the Origins of the Spanish and Italian Reformation, Librairie Droz, Geneva, 70 & transl, Madrid-Mexico, Fondo de Cultura Economica, 79; Mystic, Rebel, Saint: A study of St John of the Cross, Geneva, Droz, 79 & Spanish ed, Mistico, poeta, rebelde, Santo, En torno a San Juan de Cruz, Marid-Mexico, Fondo de Cultura Economica, 82; ed and auth introd notes, Valdes Two Catechisms, The Dialogue on Christian Doctrine and the Christian Instruction for Children, Coronado Press, 81, 2nd. Enlarged ed. 93; auth, San Juan de la Cruz, poeta del amor profano, Ed Swan, Madrid, 88; auth, Religious Experience and Mysticism. Otherness as Experience of Transcedence, Univ Press of America, Lanham, 97; auth, El Renacimiento y la Otra Espana. Vision Cultural Socioespiritual, Librairie Droz, Geneva, 97. **CONTACT ADDRESS** Dept History, Juniata Col, 1700 Moore St, Huntingdon, PA 16652-2196. **EMAIL** nieto@juniata.edu

NIEWYK, DONALD LEE
PERSONAL Born 12/21/1940, Grand Rapids, MI **DISCIPLINE** MODERN EUROPEAN HISTORY **EDUCATION** Western Mich Univ, BA, 62; Tulane Univ, MA 64, PhD(hist), 68. **CAREER** Asst prof hist, Ithaca Col 68-72; Assoc Prof Hist, Southern Methodist Univ, 72-, Res grants, Col Ctr Finger Lakes, 69 & Southern Methodist Univ, 73; Am Philos Soc res grant, 74-. **MEMBERSHIPS** AHA; Southern Hist Asn. **RESEARCH** German political and social history since 1871; 20th century Europe; Jewish history. **SELECTED PUBLICATIONS** Auth, Socialist, Anti-Semite, and Jew, La State Univ, 71; The Economic and Cultural Role of the Jews in the Weimar RePubic, Yearbk XVI, Leo Baeck Inst, 71; Jews and the courts in Weimar Germany, Jewish Social Studies, 75; transl & ed, History and Criticism of the Marcan Hypothesis, T&T Clark, 80; auth, The Jews in Weimar Germany, La State Univ, 80; The Impact of Inflation and Depression on the German Jews, Yearbk XXVII, Leo Baeck Inst, 82; Anti-semitism - The Longest Hatred - Wistrich,rs, Historian, Vol 0055, 1993; The Renaissance of Jewish Culture in Weimar Germany - Brenner,m, American Historical Review, Vol 0102, 1997; Anatomy of The Auschwitz Death Camp - Gutman,y, Berenbaum,m, Holocaust And Genocide Studies, Vol 0011, 1997. **CONTACT ADDRESS** Dept of Hist, So Methodist Univ, P O Box 750001, Dallas, TX 75275-0001.

NIGHTINGALE, CARL
PERSONAL Born, PA **DISCIPLINE** HISTORY **EDUCATION** Princeton Univ, PhD, 92. **CAREER** From asst to assoc prof, Univ Mass Amherst, 93- ; vis adj prof, York Univ, 00-01. **MEMBERSHIPS** AHA; OAH. **RESEARCH** Recent Am hist. **SELECTED PUBLICATIONS** Auth, On the Edge: A History of Poor Black Children and their American Dreams, 93; auth, "The Global Lunar City: Towards an Historical Analysis," 97. **CONTACT ADDRESS** Dept of Hist, Univ of Massachusetts, Amherst, Mass Ave, Amherst, MA 01003. **EMAIL** carl@history.umass.edu

NIGOSIAN, SOLOMON ALEXANDER
PERSONAL Born 04/23/1932, Alexandria, Egypt **DISCIPLINE** HISTORY OF RELIGION **EDUCATION** Univ Toronto, BA, 68; McMaster Univ, MA, 70, PhD(relig), 75. **CAREER** Teaching asst relig, McMaster Univ, 69-71; lectr, 72-75, Asst Prof Relig, Univ Toronto, 75-, Lectr relig, Ctr Christian Studies, Toronto, 71-74 & York Univ, 71-73; consult films relig, Ont Educ Commun Authority, Toronto, 72-73; assoc ed, Armenian Missionary Asn Am, Inc, Paramus, NJ, 72-76; asst prof, Ont Col Art, Toronto, 78-79. **MEMBERSHIPS** Int Asn Hist Relig; Can Soc Study Relig; Am Acad Relig. **RESEARCH** History of interreligious interactions with specialization in the Near East. **SELECTED PUBLICATIONS** Auth, World religions, S.A. Nigosian; auth, Judaism: The Way of Holiness, Solomon Nigosian; auth, Islam: The Way of Submission, Solomon Nigosian; auth, The Zoroastrian Faith: Tradition and Modern Research, S.A. Nigosian, Hardcover, 93; auth, World Faiths, S.A. Nigosian, 94; auth, The Zoroastrian Faith; Tradition and Modern Research, S.A. Nigosian, Paperback, 93; auth, World Religions: A Historical Approach, S.A. Nigosian, Paperback, 99. **CONTACT ADDRESS** Dept of Relig Studies, Univ of Toronto, 73 Queen's Park Crescent, Toronto, ON, Canada M5S 1K7. **EMAIL** nigosian@chass.utoronto.ca

NISCHAN, BODO
PERSONAL Born 05/03/1939, Berlin, Germany, m, 1968, 1 child **DISCIPLINE** RENAISSANCE AND REFORMATION HISTORY **EDUCATION** Yale Univ, BA, 61; Lutheran Theol Seminary, Philadelphia, M.Div, 65; Univ Pa, PhD(hist), 71. **CAREER** Asst prof, 69-77, Assoc Prof Hist, E Carolina Univ, 77-84, prof 84-; Am Philos Soc res grant hist, 76; Ger Acad Exchange Serv res grant, 77; grant, Herzog August Bibliothek, 78, 81 & 93; Dir Medieval and Renaissance Studies Prog, 94-. **HONORS AND AWARDS** Danforth Found Assoc, 74; Amos E. Simpson Prize, 87; Phi Kappa Phi, 88; Herzog August Bibliothek, Wolfenbuttel, Germany, 93; Elected secretary of the Soc for Reformation Res, 94-99, 99-; Stiftung Luftbruckendank, 96; NEH Fel, 01/02. **MEMBERSHIPS** AHA; Am Soc for Reformation Res; Am Soc Church Hist; Conf Group Cent Europ Hist; Sixteenth Century Studies Conf. **RESEARCH** History of the Reformation in Germany; Age of Confessionalization. **SELECTED PUBLICATIONS** Auth, Prince, People, and Confession: The Second Reformation in Brandenburg, University of Pennsylvania Press (Philadelphia), 94; auth, "Confessionalism and Absolutism: The Case of Brandenburg," in Calvinism in Europe 1540-1620, ed. Andrew Pettegree et al. (Cambridge: Cambridge University Press, 94), auth, "Ritual and Protestant Identity in Late-Reformation Germany," in Protestant History and Identity in Sixteenth-Century Europe, ed. Bruce Grodon (Aldershot, UK: Ashgate, 96): 142-158; auth, "Demarcating Boundaries: Lutheran Pericopic Sermons in the Age of Confessionalization," Archive for Reformation History 88 (97): 199-216; auth, Lutherans and Calvinists in the Age of Confessionalism, Variorum Collected Studies, Ashgate, Aldershot, UK, (99); auth, "Germany after 1550," in The Reformation World, ed. Andrew Pettegree (London: Routledge, 00): 387-409. **CONTACT ADDRESS** Dept of Hist, East Carolina Univ, Greenville, NC 27858. **EMAIL** nischanb@mail.ecu.edu

NISH, CAMERON
PERSONAL Born 07/05/1927, Montreal, PQ, Canada, m, 1948, 1 child **DISCIPLINE** CANADIAN HISTORY **EDUCATION** Sir George Williams Univ, BA, 57; Univ Montreal, MA, 59; Univ Laval, DHist, 66. **CAREER** Lectr hist, Sir George Williams Univ, 60-62; charge of hist course, Royal Mil Col, 62-65; from asst prof to assoc prof, 65- 72, Prof Hist, Concordia Univ, 72-, Res dir Ctr rech hist econ du Can francais, 66-; Can Coun grant, 67-68; dir, Ctr Etud Quebec, 67-. **MEMBERSHIPS** Can Hist Asn; AHA. **RESEARCH** Economic and social history of New France; social structures of New France; ideologies in French Canada. **SELECTED PUBLICATIONS** Ed, The French Regime, Prentice Hall, (Scarborough, ON), 65; auth, Les Bourgeois-gentilhommes de la Nouvelle-France, 1729-1748, Fides (Montreal, QC), 68. **CONTACT ADDRESS** Hist Dept, Concordia Univ, Montreal, Montreal, QC, Canada H3G 1M8.

NISSENBAUM, STEPHEN WILLNER
PERSONAL Born 01/13/1941, Jersey City, NJ, m, 1962, 4 children **DISCIPLINE** AMERICAN HISTORY **EDUCATION** Harvard Univ, AB, 61; Columbia Univ, MA, 63; Univ Wis-Madison, PhD, 68. **CAREER** Asst prof, 68-72, assoc prof, 72-79, prof hist, 79-, Univ Mass, Amherst; vis lectr, Smith Col, 73 & 76; vis lectr, Hampshire Col, 79, 94, 97; vis lectr, Mt Holyoke Col, 80, 98; NEH fel, 76-77, 91-92 & Charles Warren Ctr for Studies in Am Hist fel, Harvard Univ, 76-77, 94-95; Coun Am Studies Asn, 79-81, 97-00; New England Am Studies, vpres 78-81, pres 95-97; pres, Mass Found for the Hum, 87-89; Fulbright distinguished chair, Germany, 98-99. **HONORS AND AWARDS** John H Dunning Prize, Am Hist Asn, 74; finalist, Pulitzer Prize, history, 97. **MEMBERSHIPS** AHA; Orgn Am Historians; Am Studies Asn. **RESEARCH** American cultural history; American social history; history of the book. **SELECTED PUBLICATIONS** Ed, The Great Awakening at Yale College, 72; co-ed, Salem-Village Witchcraft: A Documentary Record of Local Conflict in Colonial New England, Wadsworth, 72; coauth, Salem Possessed: The Social Origins of Witchcraft, Harvard Univ, 74; co-ed, The Salem Witchcraft Papers, Da Cap Press, 77; auth, The Firing of Nathaniel Hawthorne, Essex Institute Historical Collections, 78; art, Sex, Diet, and Debility, Jacksonian America: Sylvester Graham and Health Reform, Greenwood Press, 80; coauth, All Over the Map: Rethinking American Region, Johns Hopkins, 95; auth, The Battle for Christmas, Knopf, 96. **CONTACT ADDRESS** Dept of History, Univ of Massachusetts, Amherst, Amherst, MA 01003. **EMAIL** snissenbaum@history.umass.edu

NITZOVA, PETYA
PERSONAL Born 08/18/1958, Troyan, Bulgaria, m, 1983, 2 children **DISCIPLINE** BALKAN EASTERN EUROPEAN STUDIES **EDUCATION** St Kliment Ohrid Univ, BA, 82; Bul Acad Sci, PhD, 88. **CAREER** Res assoc, Bul Acad Sci, 89-92; vis scholar, Hartford Sem, 92-93; adj prof, Univ Okla, 97-. **HONORS AND AWARDS** Fulbright Scholarshp. **MEMBERSHIPS** AAASS; ASN. **RESEARCH** Muslim minorities in South-Eastern Europe; religion and politics; Eastern Orthodox Christianity. **SELECTED PUBLICATIONS** Auth, "Bulgaria: Minorities, Democratization, and National Sentiments," Nationalities Papers 25 (97); auth, "Islam and Christianity in South Eastern Europe," in Religion in Contemporary Europe (Edwin Mellon Press, 94). **CONTACT ADDRESS** Dept History, Univ of Oklahoma, 455 West Lindsey St, Norman, OK 73019-200. **EMAIL** pnitzova@ou.edu

NOBLE, DAVID WATSON
PERSONAL Born 03/17/1925, Princeton, NJ, m, 1944, 4 children **DISCIPLINE** AMERICAN INTELLECTUAL HISTORY **EDUCATION** Princeton Univ, AB, 48; Univ Wis, MA, 49, PhD 52. **CAREER** From instr to assoc prof, 52-65, prof hist, Univ MN, Minneapolis, 65-, Lectr, Am Studies summer sem, Kyoto, Japan, 80. **HONORS AND AWARDS** Horace T Morse Awd, Standard Oil Co Ind, 68. **MEMBERSHIPS** Am Studies Asn. **RESEARCH** Am intellectual and cult hist. **SELECTED PUBLICATIONS** Auth, The Paradox of Progressive Thought, 58 & Historians Against History, 65, Univ Minn; Eternal Adam and New World Garden, Braziller, 68; The Progressive Mind, Rand McNally, 70 & Burgess, 81; coauth, The Restless Centuries, Burgess, 73, 2nd ed, 79; The Free and the Unfree, Penquin, 77; Twentieth Century Limited, Houghton Mifflin, 80; The End of American History, 85. **CONTACT ADDRESS** Am Studies Program, Univ of Minnesota, Twin Cities, 72 Pleasant St S E, Minneapolis, MN 55455-0270.

NOBLE, DOUGLAS
DISCIPLINE COMPUTERS IN ARCHITECTURE, DESIGN, DESIGN THEORIES AND METHODS **EDUCATION** CA State Polytech Univ, Pomona, BS, 81, BA, 82; Univ CA, Berkeley, MA, 83, PhD, 91. **CAREER** Asst prof, USC, 91-; lectr, Univ CA, Berkeley, 84-91; Kenneth S Wing & Assoc, Arch, 85-86; CHCG Arch, 78-84. **HONORS AND AWARDS** William Van Alen Memorial Prize, 94; ACSA AIAS New Fac Tchg Awd, 94; PhD Comt Prize, UC Berkeley, 89; Distinguished Tchg Asst Awd, 87; Pasadena/Foothill AIA Design Awd, 83; 1st Prize-AISC Stud Design Competition, 80. **MEMBERSHIPS** Asn for Comput Aided Design in Arch; Am Inst Arch; Asn Collegiate Schools Arch. **RESEARCH** Design theo-

ries and methods; site analysis through digital photography. **SELECTED PUBLICATIONS** Auth, Issues Regarding Architectural Records of the Future: Planning for Change in Libraries, 94; Mission, Method, Madness; Computer Supported Design in Architecture, ACADIA, 92; Software for Architects: A Guide to Software for the Architectural Profession, 92; Issues in the Design of Tall Buildings, 91; User's Guide to Berkeley Architecture, Daily Calif, 90; coauth, Computer Aided Architectural Design, Univ Calif, Berkeley, 90; Shading Mask: A Teaching Tool for Sun Shading Devices, 95-96; Student Initiated Explorations in the Design Studio, ACADIA, 94; Issues Regarding Architectural Records of the Future: Planning for Change in Libraries, Architronic: Elec J Arch, 94; The Sorcerers Apprentice, Computer Graphics World, 90. **CONTACT ADDRESS** School of Archit, Univ of So California, University Park Campus, Los Angeles, CA 90089. **EMAIL** dnoble@mizar.usc.edu

NOBLE, THOMAS FRANCIS XAVIER
PERSONAL Born 05/10/1947, Chicago, IL, m, 1967, 2 children **DISCIPLINE** MEDIEVAL HISTORY **EDUCATION** Ohio Univ, BA, 69; Mich State Univ, MA, 71, PhD(hist), 74. **CAREER** Instr hist, Albion Col, 75; instr humanities, Mich State Univ, 75-76; asst prof hist, Tex Tech Univ, 76-80; Asst Prof Hist, Univ VA, 80-; Asst Prof, Univ of Virginia, 80-85; Assoc Prof, Univ of Virginia, 85-95; Prof, Univ of Virginia, 95-00; Prof of History and Robert M. Conway Dir of the Medieval Inst, The Univ of Notre Dame, 00. **HONORS AND AWARDS** NEH Fellwoships, 1879-80, 1993-94; Am Philosophical Society Travel Grants, 79, 83; Visiting Fellow, Clare Hall; Member Inst for Advanced Study, 94; Fellow in Residence, Netherlands Inst for Advanced Study, 99-00. **MEMBERSHIPS** AHA; Medieval Acad Am; Am Cath Hist Asn; Archaeol Inst Am; Am Soc Church Hist. **RESEARCH** Carolingian history; early medieval Ecclesiastical history. **SELECTED PUBLICATIONS** Auth, The revolt of King Bernard of Italy in 817, Studi Medievali, 74; The Monastic Ideal as a model for empire, Rev Benedictine, 76; The place in Papal history of the Roman Synod of 826, Church Hist, 76; Louis the Pious and His Piety Re- reconsidered, Revue belge, 80; Papal Records in the Early- middleages - Diplomatic and Legal-historical Studies of the Letters of Gregory-the-great - German - Pitz,e, Speculum-a J of Medieval Studies, Vol 0068, 1993; The Formation of Europe, Ad840-1046 - German - Fried,j, Speculum-a J of Medieval Studies, Vol 0069, 1994; the Complete Works of Rather-of-verona - Reid,pld, Translator, Speculum-a J of Medieval Studies, Vol 0069, 1994; Emperor, Prefects and Kings - the Roman West, Ad395- 565 - Barnwell,ps, Speculum-a J of Medieval Studies, Vol 0069, 1994; The Peace of God - Social Violence and Religious Response in France Around the Year 1000 - Head,t, Landes,r, J of Interdisciplinary History, Vol 0025, 1995; The Ambiguity of the Book - Prince, Power, and People in Medieval Biblical Commentary - French - Buc,p, Church History, Vol 0064, 1995; The Germanization of Early-medieval Christianity - a Sociohistorical Approach to Religious Transformation - Russell,jc, American Historical Review, Vol 0100, 1995; History of Christianity from Apostolic Times to the Present, Vol 4 - Bishops, Monks, and Emperors Ad610-1054- French - Dagron,g, Riche,p, Vauchez,a, Editors, Speculum-a J of Medieval Studies, Vol 0071, 1996; Medieval France - an Encyclopedia - Kibler,ww, Zinn,g, Church History, Vol 0065, 1996; the Resurrection of the Body in Western Christianity, 240-1336 - Bynum,cw, American Historical Review, Vol 0101, 1996; The Church Triumphant - a History of Christianity up to Ad1300 - Hinson,eg, Church History, Vol 0066, 1997; Institutional Life in Medieval Europe - an Introduction - Italian - Ascheri,m, Speculum-a J of Medieval Studies, Vol 0072, 1997; Church Triumphant - a History of Christianity up to Ad1300 - Hinson,eg, Church History, Vol 0066, 1997; the 'Lives of the Ninth-century Popes' 'Liber Pontificalis' - the Ancient Biographies to 10 Popes from Ad817-891 - English, Latin - Davis,r, J of Ecclesiastical History, Vol 0048, 1997; The 'Lives of the Ninth-century Popes','Liber Pontificalis' - the Ancient Biographies to 10 Popes from Ad817-891 - English, Latin - Davis,r, J of Ecclesiastical History, Vol 0048, 1997; Institutional Life in Medieval Europe - an Introduction - Italian - Ascheri,m, Speculum-a J of Medieval Studies, Vol 0072, 1997; auth, The Republic of St. Peter: The Birth of The Papal State, 680-825 (Philadelphia: Univ of PA Press, 84; paper back ed. 86; Ital transl, 98; auth, Religion, Culture and Society in the Early Middle Ages: Studies in Honor of Richard E. Sullivan, co-ed. With John J. Contreni (Kalamazoo: Western MI Univ/The Medieval Inst, 87; auth, Western Cilivization: The Continuing Experiment, with five others (lead author and project originator), (Boston: Houghton-Mifflin Co., 93, 2nd ed, 98); auth, Soldiers of Chirst: Saints and Saints' Lives in Late Antiquity and the Early Middle Ages, with Thomas Head (Univ Park: PA State Univ Press, 94; auth, "Popes for All Season," First Things, 86 (98): 34-41; auth, "The Transformation of the Roman World: Reflections on Five Years of Work," in Evangelos Chrysos and Ian Wood eds., East and West: Modes of Communication, Transformation of the Roman World 5, Leiden (99): 256-77; auth, "Topography, Power, and Ritual in the Making of Papal Rome, 700-900," in Places of Power in the Early Middle Ages, ed. Mayke de Jong (Leiden: E.J. Brill, 00); auth, "The Changing Place of Biblical Testimonies in Carolingian Texts Concerning Images," in Esther Cohen ed., Medieval Transformations: Texts, Power, and Gifts (Leiden: E.J. Brill, 00); auth, "Gregory of Tours and the Roman Church," in The World of Gregory of Tours, eds. Ian Wood and Kathleen Mitchell (Leiden: E.J. Brill, 00); auth, "Paradoxes and Possibilities in the Sources for Roman Society in the Early Middle Ages," in Early Medieval Rome and the Christian West, ed. J.M.H. Smith and T.S. Brown, Leiden: Brill (00): 55-83. **CONTACT ADDRESS** Dept of Hist, Univ of Virginia, Randall Hall, Charlottesville, VA 22903-3248. **EMAIL** tfn@virginia.edu

NOBLE, WILLIAM P.
PERSONAL Born 01/25/1932, New York, NY, m, 1998, 2 children **DISCIPLINE** LAW & HISTORY **EDUCATION** Lehigh Univ, BA, 54; Univ Penn, JD, 61. **CAREER** Instr, 86- , writing assessment mentor, 94- , Commun Col of Vermont; Ver Hum Scholar, Ver Coun on Hum, 91- ; adj fac, external degree prog, Johnson State Col, 93- . **HONORS AND AWARDS** Nominated for Eli Oboler Awd, ALA Intellectual Freedom Roundtable, 92. **MEMBERSHIPS** Authors Guild; Freedom to Read Comt. **RESEARCH** Law; history; writing. **SELECTED PUBLICATIONS** Auth, Bookbanning in America, Eriksson, 90; auth, Show Don't Tell, Eriksson, 91; auth, Twenty-Eight Most Common Writing Blunders, Writer's Digest, 92; auth, Conflict, Action & Suspense, Writer's Digest, 94; auth, The Complete Guide to Writers' Conferences and Workshops, Eriksson, 95; auth, Three Rules for Writing a Novel, Eriksson, 97; auth, Writing Dramatic Nonfiction, Eriksson, 00. **CONTACT ADDRESS** PO Box 187, Island Heights, VT 05769. **EMAIL** bn777@voice.net

NOBLES, GREGORY H.
PERSONAL Born 01/19/1948, Dallas, TX, m, 1981, 2 children **DISCIPLINE** HISTORY **EDUCATION** Princeton Univ, BA, 70; Univ Mich, MA, 74, PhD, 79. **CAREER** Assoc prof, hist, tech & soc, and PROF & CHAIR, SCH HIST, TECH & SOC, GEORGIA TECH. **MEMBERSHIPS** Am Antiquarian Soc; AHA, OAH, SHEAR, OIEHC. **SELECTED PUBLICATIONS** Auth, Divisions Throughout the Whole: Politics and Society in Hampshire County, Massachusetts, 1740-1775, Cambridge Univ Press, 83; auth, "Breaking into the Backcountry: New Approaches to the Early American Frontier," Wm & Mary Quart 46, 89; auth, "Straight Lines and Stability: Mapping the Political Order of the Anglo-American Frontier," Jour of Am Hist 80, 93; auth, American Frontiers: Cultural Encounters and Continental Conquest, Hill & Wang, 97. **CONTACT ADDRESS** Hist, Tech, and Soc, Georgia Inst of Tech, Atlanta, GA 30332-0345. **EMAIL** gregory.nobles@hts.gatech.edu

NODES, DANIEL J.
PERSONAL Born 11/01/1951, Hoboken, NJ, m, 1972, 2 children **DISCIPLINE** MEDIEVAL STUDIES **EDUCATION** St. Peter's Col, BA, 74; Univ NH, MA, 76; Univ Toronto, PhD, 82. **CAREER** Asst prof, Sch Hum, Old Col, 82-87; assoc prof & ch, Dept Class & Hum, Conception Sem Col, 87-96; prof & dir, Col Liberal Arts, Hamline Univ, 96-. **HONORS AND AWARDS** Andrew Mellon Fel, 96; NEH Fel, 95; NEH Summer Stipend, Villanova Univ, 94; NEH Summer Seminar, Univ Penn, 93. **MEMBERSHIPS** Medieval Acad Am; N Am Patristic Soc; Renaissance Soc Am; Am Philol Asn; Class Asn Minn; Am Asn Univ Prof. **RESEARCH** Late Antiquity; Patristic theology; poetry based on biblical themes; Classical Tradition; Medieval scholasticism; Renaissance humanism. **SELECTED PUBLICATIONS** Auth, Doctrine and Exegesis in Biblical Latin Poetry, 93; auth, Origin of Alexandria Among the Renaissance Humanists and Their Twentieth-Century Historians, Vetus Doctrina: Studies in Early Christianity in Honor of Fredric W, Schlatter, SJ, 98; auth, Homeric Allegory in Egidio of Viterbo's Reflections on the Human Soul, Recherches de Theol et Philos Medievales, 98; auth, Rhetoric and Cultural Synthesis in the Hexaemeron of George of Pisidia, Virgiliae Christianae, 96; auth, Humanism in the Commentary ad mentem Platonis of Giles of Viterbo, Augustiniana, 95; auth, Salvation by Abduction in Giles of Viterbo's Commentary ad mentem Platonis, Studi Umanistici Piceni, 93. **CONTACT ADDRESS** Col Liberal Arts, Hamline Univ, 1536 Hewitt Ave., PO Box 178, Saint Paul, MN 55104. **EMAIL** djnodes@hamline.edu

NOE, KENNETH W.
PERSONAL Born 11/09/1957, Richmond, VA, m, 1985, 1 child **DISCIPLINE** HISTORY **EDUCATION** Emory & Henry Col, BA, 79; Virginia Tech, MA, 81; Univ Kentucky, MSLS, 83; Univ of Ill, PhD, 90. **CAREER** Librn, Blue Ridge Regional Librn Martinsville, VA, 83-85; instr, Berea Col, 87-88; arch, Ill Hist Survey, Urbana, IL, 88-90; asst prof History, 90-95, Assoc Prof History, 95-98, State Univ W GA, 90-00; assoc prof history, Auburn Univ, 00-; Beta Phi Mu; Phi Alpha Theta; Phi Kappa Phi. **HONORS AND AWARDS** Tenn Hist Book Awd, 96; Stud Govt Asn Fac Mem Yr, 96-97; J. David Griffin Tchg Awd, 93. **MEMBERSHIPS** Orgn Am Hist; S Hist Asn; Appalachian Stud Asn; Ga Hist Asn. **RESEARCH** American Civil War in the Upper South especially Appalachia. **SELECTED PUBLICATIONS** Southwest Virginia's Railroad: Modernization and the Sectional Crisis, Urbana, 92; A Southern Boy in Blue, 96; The Civil War in Appalachia, Knoxville, 97. **CONTACT ADDRESS** History Dept, Auburn Univ, 310 Thach Hall, Auburn, AL 36849.

NOEL, THOMAS J.
PERSONAL Born 05/06/1945, Cambridge, MA, m, 1973 **DISCIPLINE** HISTORY **EDUCATION** Univ Denver, BA, 67; MA, 69; Univ Colo, MA, 74; PhD, 78. **CAREER** Teacher, Hillel Acad, 69-71; teacher, E High, 71; itinerant hist instr, Colo Women's Col, 76-82; assoc prof, Colo Univ at Denver, 82-90; prof & dir public hist, Colo Univ at Denver, 90-; chemn, Colo Univ at Denver Hist Dept, 92-96. **HONORS AND AWARDS** Noel Park in Denver's Larimer Square; Thomas Hornsby Ferril Lifetime Lit Achievement Awd, Colo Ctr for the Book, 97; Who's Who Among Am Teachers, 98; Dana Crowford Prize for Excellence in Hist Preservation, Colo Preservation, Inc., 98; Who's Who in America, 00. **MEMBERSHIPS** Nat Register Rev Board, Denver Landmark Preservation Comn, Historic Denver, Inc., Colo Hist Soc, Denver Public Libr Friends Found Board, Soc of Architectural Historians, Denver Posse of Westerners, Smithsonian Inst Study, Railroading the Rockies. **RESEARCH** Denver, Colorado, Rocky Mountain West, Architecture, Social History, Transportation, Cemeteries, Churches, Saloons. **SELECTED PUBLICATIONS** Auth, The City and the Saloon, 84; coauth, Denver: The City Beautiful, 87 & 93; coauth, Colorado: The Highest State, 95; auth, Denver Landmarks, 96; coauth, Thomas Hornsby Fevril and the American West, 96; auth, Buildings of Colorado, 97; auth, Mile High City, 99; auth, Colorado: A Liquid History and Tavern Guide, 99. **CONTACT ADDRESS** Dept Hist, Univ of Colorado, Denver, PO Box 173364, Denver, CO 80217-3364. **EMAIL** tnoe@carbon.cudenver.edu

NOER, THOMAS JOHN
PERSONAL Born 11/29/1944, Emmetsburg, IA, m, 1968, 2 children **DISCIPLINE** AMERICAN HISTORY **EDUCATION** Gustavus Adolphus Col, BA, 66; Wash State Univ, MA, 68; Univ Minn, Phd(hist), 72. **CAREER** Asst prof hist, Univ Minn, Minneapolis, 72-73; asst prof, 73-77, Assoc Prof Hist, Carthage Col, 78-, Acad consult, Wis Humanities Comn, 77-; fel, Charles Warren Ctr Am Hist, Harvard Univ, 79-80; res grants, Am Philos Soc, 79 & Harry S Truman Inst, 79. **HONORS AND AWARDS** Res grant, Am Philos Soc, 79; res grant, Harry S. Truman found, 79; fel, Charles Warren Ctr Am Hist, Harvard Univ, 79-80; res grant, Nat Endowment for the Humanities, 82, 86; res grant, Gerald Ford Libr, 80; res grant, John F. Kennedy Found, 86; res grant, Spencer Found, 87; res grant, Phi Alpha Theta, 88. **MEMBERSHIPS** AHA; Orgn Am Historians; Soc Hist Am Foreign Rel. **RESEARCH** American foreign policy; comparative racial attitudes, United States and Africa. **SELECTED PUBLICATIONS** Auth, The American government and the Irish question during World War I, S Atlantic Quart, winter 73; auth, Commodore R W. Shufeldt and America's South African strategy, Am Neptune, fall 74; auth, Henry Kissinger's philos of hist, Mod Age, spring 75; auth, Briton, Boer, and Yankee: The US and Southern Africa, 1870-1914, Kent State Univ, 78; auth, "The United States and black Africa," in: Am For Rels, Greenwood Press, 81; auth, Truman, Eisenhower and South Africa, J of Ethnic Studies, spring 83; auth, The New Frontier and African Neutralism, diplomatic Hist, winter 84; auth, Cold war and Black liberation: the US and white Africa 1948-1968, Univ Mo, 85; auth, "New Frontiers and Old Priorities in Africa," in Kennedy's Quest for Victory, Oxford Univ, 89; auth, Martin Luther King and the Cold War, Peace and Change, spring 97; auth, Malcolm X's Philos of Hist and Int Politics, Proteus, spring 98; auth, "Segregationists and the World," in The American Civil Rights Movement and US For Policy, Univ NC, 00. **CONTACT ADDRESS** Dept of Hist, Carthage Col, 2001 Alford Dr, Kenosha, WI 53140-1994. **EMAIL** noertom@carthage.edu

NOLAN, CATHAL J.
PERSONAL Born 08/02/1956, Dublin, Ireland **DISCIPLINE** HISTORY **EDUCATION** Univ Alberta, BA, 78; Univ Toronto, MA, 82; PhD, 89. **CAREER** Asst Prof, St Francis Xavier Univ, 89-90; Asst Prof, Miami Univ, 90-91; Asst Prof, Univ BC, 91-95; Res Assoc, Univ BC, 93-94; Res Assoc Prof to Assoc prof, Boston Univ, 95-. **HONORS AND AWARDS** Robert R. McCormick Tribune Foundation, Boston Univ, 99-01; Grant, Carnegie Council on Ethics and International Affairs, 92, 93, 98; Grant, Cooperative Security Program Grant, Dept Foreign Affairs, Canada, 94-95; Barton Fel , Govt Canada, 93; Barton Post-Doc Fel, Dept Foreign Affairs, Canada, 94-95; Doctoral Fel, Univ Toronto, 83-86; Justice Harry Batshaw Fel, Canadian Human Rights Foundation, 84; Outstanding Academic Book of 1998, Asn Col and Research Libraries, 98; Nominated for Teaching Awd, Univ BC, 945; Outstanding Teaching Awd, Miami Univ, 91; Sigma Iota Rho, 91; Principal's Commendation, Nigeria, 80. **SELECTED PUBLICATIONS** Auth, Historical Encyclopedia of International Relations, Greenwood Press, forthcoming; auth, Ethics and Statecraft: The Moral Dimension of International Affairs, Praeger press, forthcoming; auth, "Theodore Roosevelt, Woodrow Wilson, and Armed Intervention," in Setting the 20th Century Stage, Greenwood Press, forthcoming; auth, Power and Responsibility in World affairs, Praeger press, 00; co-ed, Book series: International History, Praeger Pub, 99->; ed, Book series: Humanistic Perspectives on International Relations, Praeger Pub, 98->; auth, Maailma Poliitika Leksikon, Tallinn, Estonia, 99; ed, Notable US Ambassadors since 1775, Greenwood press, 97; ed, Ethics and Statecraft: The Moral Dimension of International affairs, Greenwood press, 95; auth, The Longman Guide to World Affairs, Longman, 95; auth, "The OSCE: Non-Military Dimensions of Cooperative Security in Europe," in Redefining European Security, Garland Pub, (99): 299-323; auth, "Bodyguard

of Lies': Franklin d. Roosevelt and Defensible Deceit in WWII," in Ethics and Statecraft, (95): 57-74. **CONTACT ADDRESS** Dept History, Boston Univ, 226 Bay State Rd, Boston, MA 02215-1403. **EMAIL** cnolan@bu.edu

NOLAN, JANET
DISCIPLINE HISTORY **EDUCATION** Conn Univ, PhD, 86. **CAREER** Hist, Loyola Univ. **HONORS AND AWARDS** Nat Endowment for the Humanities summer stipend, 97; Irish Am Cultural Inst res award, 99; Loyola Univ, Chicago, summer res Award, 99. **RESEARCH** Irish, Irish-American & oral history; women in the nineteenth and twentieth century. **SELECTED PUBLICATIONS** Auth, "The Great Famine and Women's Emigration from Ireland," in The Hungry Stream: Essays on Famine and Emigration (Belfast, Inst of Irish Stud/Queen's UP, 97); auth, "St. Patrick's Daughter: Amelia Dunne Hookway and Chicago's Public Schools," in At the Crossroads: Old St. Patrick's and the Chicago Irish (Chicago: Loyola UP, 97); auth, "The National Schools and Irish Women's Mobility in the Late Nineteenth and Early Twentieth Centuries," Irish Stud Review 18 (97); auth, "Education and Women's Mobility in Ireland and Irish America, 1880-1920: A Preliminary Look," The New Hibernia Review 2 (98); auth, "The Irish in America's Public Schools," The Encyclopedia of the Irish in America, ed. Michael Glazier (Notre Dame Univ Press, Notre Dame, 99); coed, "Northern Ireland: A Documentary History," in Cultures in Conflict (Greenwood Press, CT, 01). **CONTACT ADDRESS** Dept of Hist, Loyola Univ, Chicago, 6525 N. Sheridan Rd., Chicago, IL 60626. **EMAIL** jnolan@wpo.it.luc.edu

NOLAN, MARY
PERSONAL Born 01/17/1944, Chicago, IL, 2 children **DISCIPLINE** MODERN EUROPEAN & WOMEN'S HISTORY **EDUCATION** Smith Col, BA, 66; Columbia Univ, MA, 69, PhD, 75. **CAREER** Asst prof, Harvard Univ, 75-80; from Asst Prof to Assoc Prof, 80-92, prof hist, NY Univ, 92-. **RESEARCH** Modern German history; comparative working-class history. **SELECTED PUBLICATIONS** Auth, Social policy, economic mobilization and the working class in the Thrid Reich: A review of the literature, Radical Hist Rev, No 39, 77; Proletarischer anti-feminismus, Frauen und Wissenschaft Courage, Verlag, 77; coauth, The social democratic reform cycle in Germany, Polit Power & Social Theory, 81; auth, Social Democracy and Society: Working-class Radicalism in Dusseldorf, 1890-1920, Cambridge Univ Press, 82; The Historikenstreit & Social History, New Ger Critique 44, 88; Housework Made Easy: The Taylorized Housewife in Weimar Germany's Rationalized Economy, Feminist Studies, Fall 90; Vision of Modernity: American Business & The Modernization of Germany. Oxford, 94; Is Liberalism Really the Answer?, Int Labor & Working Class Hist 46, 94; Anti-Fascism Under Fascism: German Vision & Voices, New Ger Critique, 96. **CONTACT ADDRESS** Dept Hist, New York Univ, 53 Washington Square S, New York, NY 10003-4556. **EMAIL** mn4@is2.nyu.edu

NOLL, MARK ALLAN
PERSONAL Born 07/18/1946, Iowa City, IA, m, 1969, 3 children **DISCIPLINE** HISTORY OF CHRISTIANITY (NORTH AMERICAN) **EDUCATION** Wheaton Col, Ill, BA, 68; Univ Iowa, MA, 70, Trinity Evangel Divinity Sch, MA, 72; Vanderbilt Univ, PhD(church hist), 75. **CAREER** Asst prof hist, Trinity Col, Ill, 75-78; from assoc prof hist to McManis prof of Christian Thought, Wheaton Col, Ill, 78-, vis prof Regent Col, Vancouver, 90, 95, 97; vis prof Harvard Divinity School, spring 98. **HONORS AND AWARDS** Fels, Nat Endowment for Humanities 78-79, 87-88, Pew Charitable Trusts, 93-94. **MEMBERSHIPS** Am Cath Hist Asn; AHA; Am Soc Church Hist; Canadian Soc of Church Hist; Conf Faith & Hist; OAH. **RESEARCH** Theology, politics, society in America 1730-1860; Protestants in the North Atlantic region; cultural history of the Bible. **SELECTED PUBLICATIONS** Auth, Christians in the American Revolution, Eerdmans, 77; Between Faith and Criticism: Evangelicals, Scholarship, and the Bible in America, Harper & Row, 86; One Nation Under God? Christian Faith and Political Action in America, Harper & Row, 88; Princeton and the Republic, 1768-1822, Princeton Univ Press, 89; A History of Christianity in the United States and Canada, Eerdmans, 92; The Scandal of the Evangelical Mind, Eerdmans, 92; Turnung Points: Decisive Moments in the History of Christianity, Baker Books, 98. Co-ed and contrib, The Bible in America, Oxford Univ Press, 82; Religion and American Politics, Oxford Univ Press, 89; coauth, The Search for Christian America, 2nd ed, Helmers & Howard, 89; Evangelicalism: Comparative Studies of Popular Protestantism in North America, the British Isles, and Beyond, Oxford Univ Press, 93; Evangelicals and Science in Historical Perspective, Oxford Univ Press, 99. **CONTACT ADDRESS** Hist Dept, Wheaton Col, Illinois, Wheaton, IL 60187-5593. **EMAIL** Mark.Noll@wheaton.edu

NOONAN, THOMAS S.
DISCIPLINE HISTORY **EDUCATION** Univ Ind, PhD, 66. **CAREER** Prof **RESEARCH** Economic history of ancient and medieval Russia; Russian archaeology and numismatics. **SELECTED PUBLICATIONS** Auth, pubs on archaic Greek colonization in the northern Black Sea, medieval Russian-Estonian relations, impact of Mongol rule on Russian attitudes toward the West, Suzdalia's oriental trade in the pre-Mongol era, and relations between Arabs, Khazars, Rus', and Vikings in the nineteenth centuries. **CONTACT ADDRESS** History Dept, Univ of Minnesota, Twin Cities, 614 Social Sciences Tower, 267 19th Ave. S, Minneapolis, MN 55455. **EMAIL** noona001@tc.umn.edu

NOONE, TIMOTHY
PERSONAL Born 09/21/1957, Baltimore, MD, m, 1979, 3 children **DISCIPLINE** MEDIEVAL STUDIES **EDUCATION** Lock Haven State Univ, BA 79; Univ Toronto, MA 80; Pontifical Inst Medieval Studies Toronto ON CA, MSL 87; Univ Toronto, PhD 88. **CAREER** St. Bonaventure Univ, instr, 87; St. John's Univ, asst prof, 88-89; St Bonaventure Univ, asst prof, assoc prof, 89-94; Cath Univ Am Sch Philos, Cath Univ Am, asst prof, assoc prof, 94 to 96-;asst dean, 97-99; dir, Scotus Project, 99-01. **HONORS AND AWARDS** NEH; 3 SBU Fac Res Gnts; Bradley Foun Gnt; 3 CUA Res Awds. **MEMBERSHIPS** ACPA; APA; SMRP. **RESEARCH** Metaphysics in the high Middle Ages; History of Franciscan Philos; Albert the Great; Latin Commentaries on Aristotle's Metaphysics. **SELECTED PUBLICATIONS** Auth, Franciscan Studies: Essays in Honor of Dr Girard Etzkorn, co-ed, St Bonaventure NY, Franciscan Inst, 98; auth, Quastiones in libros Metaphysicorum Aristotelis Opera Philosophica III-IV, co-ed, St Bonaventure NY, Franciscan Inst, 97; auth, A Century of Medieval Scholarship, Philosophy in the Last One Hundred Years, ed, Rev Brian Shanley, Washington DC, Cath U Press of Am, forthcoming; Aquinas on Divine Ideas: Scotus's Evaluation, Franciscan Stud, 98; auth, The Originality of St. Thomas's Position on the Philosophers and Creation, The Thomist, 96; rev, William A. Frank, Allan B. Wolter, Duns Scotus, Metaphysician, Purdue, Purdue Univ Press, 96, Amer Cath Philos Quart; forthcoming; translation of, Thomas Celano's Vita prima Beati francisci, The New Omnibus of Franciscan Sources, NY, New City Press, 99. **CONTACT ADDRESS** 2899 Chalet Court, Woodbridge, VA 22192. **EMAIL** noonet@cua.edu

NORDLOH, DAVID JOSEPH
PERSONAL Born 05/03/1942, Cincinnati, OH, m, 1968, 2 children **DISCIPLINE** AMERICAN LITERATURE, AMERICAN STUDIES, BIBLIOGRAPHY **EDUCATION** Holy Cross Col, AB, 64; Ind Univ, PhD(English), 69. **CAREER** From instr to asst prof English, 68-75, assoc prof, 75-81, Prof English, Ind Univ, Bloomington, 81-, Textual ed, A selected edition of W D Howells, Ind Univ, 68-73, gen ed, 74-; textual expert, Ctr Eds Am Auth, MLA, 68-76; vis prof English, Univ Va, 78; ed, Twayne's United States Authors Series, 78-; chmn comt Scholarly Ed, MLA, 79-82; Fulbright Senior Prof, U of Heidelberg, Germany, 82-83; co-ed, American Literary Scholarship: An Annual, 91--. **MEMBERSHIPS** Soc Textual Scholar Am Lit Assoc. **RESEARCH** Nineteenth century American literature; bibliography and textual editing; W D Howells. **SELECTED PUBLICATIONS** W D Howells at Kittery Point, Harvard Lib Bull, 80; gen ed, Selected Howells Letters I-VI, 79-83; 19th Century American Literature, American Literary Scholarship, 85-87, 89-90; auth, American Literary Scholarship, 88-89, 93-94, 96, 98, 00; Setting Pages and Fixing Words - Bal and Critical Editing of American Literature, Papers of the Bibliographical Society of America, 92; co-ed, Selected Lit Crit, 3 vol., Selected ed. W.D. Howells, 93; Creating a Natl Agenda--and Abandoning It, Text, 94. **CONTACT ADDRESS** Dept of English, Indiana Univ, Bloomington, Bloomington, IN 47405. **EMAIL** nordloh@indiana.edu

NORDQUIST, BARBARA K.
PERSONAL Born 08/29/1940, Oxnard, CA, m, 1963, 3 children **DISCIPLINE** FASHION, HUMAN BEHAVIOR **EDUCATION** Ore State Univ, BS, 62; Cornell Univ, MS, 63; US Int Univ, San Diego, PhD, 69. **CAREER** Asst prof, San Diego State Univ, 63-70; Assoc Prof to Prof, Howard Univ, 70-. **HONORS AND AWARDS** Phi Kappa Phi; Alpha Omicron Nu; Alpha Lambda Delta. **MEMBERSHIPS** ITAA. **RESEARCH** Cultural textiles & dress. **SELECTED PUBLICATIONS** Auth, Creative West African Fashion, Textile Book Service, 72; auth, The Complete Guide to Pattern Making, Drake Publishers, 74; auth, Traditional Folk Textiles and Dress: Bibliography and Selected Readings, Kendall/Hunt, 86; auth, African Dress and Adornment: A Cultural Perspective, Kendall/Hunt, 90; auth, Punks, Dress, and Popular Culture, Bowling Green State Univ Press, 91; auth, Traditional African Textiles and Dress, Unbroken Threads from an African Past, Black Fashion Mus, 3/95; auth, Traditional Testiles and Dress, Core Publishers, 99. **CONTACT ADDRESS** Dept of Art, Howard Univ, 6th & Howard Place, Washington, DC 20059. **EMAIL** bnordquist@fac.howard.edu

NORDSTROM, BYRON JOHN
PERSONAL Born 08/30/1943, Minneapolis, MN, m, 1968, 2 children **DISCIPLINE** SCANDINAVIAN & EUROPEAN DIPLOMATIC HISTORY **EDUCATION** Lawrence Univ, Wis, BA, 65; Univ Minn, Minneapolis, MA, 68, PhD(hist), 72. **CAREER** Asst prof hist, Mankato State Univ, 71-73; res specialist, Minn Hist Soc, 73-74; asst prof area studies, Gustavus Adolphus Col, 74-76; asst prof Scand hist, Pac Lutheran Univ & Univ Wash, 76-77; asst prof to prof hist, Gustavus Adolphus Col, 77-. **MEMBERSHIPS** Upper Midwest Ethnic Studies Asn; Soc Advan Scand Study; Swed Pioneer Hist Soc. **RESEARCH** Swedish foreign policy and interest group influence in policy determination; Scandinavian immigration; Scandinavian immigrant communities in urban areas of the Midwest. **SELECTED PUBLICATIONS** Ed, The Swedes in Minnesota, Dennison, 76; auth, The Sixth Ward: A Minneapolis Swede Town in 1905, Proc Conf Swed Heritage, 78; auth, Swedish-American Bibliography, Swed Pioneer Hist Quart, 78-; Evelina Mansson and the Memoir of an Urban Labor Migrant, Swed Pioneer Hist Quart, 7/80; ed, Dict Scand Hist, Greenwood Press, 86; auth, Dict Scand Hist, 86; ed, Swed-Am Hist Quart, 97-; auth, A History of Modern Scandinavia, 00. **CONTACT ADDRESS** Gustavus Adolphus Col, 800 W College Ave, Saint Peter, MN 56082-1498. **EMAIL** byron@gac.edu

NORE, ELLEN
PERSONAL Born 01/15/1942, Loup City, NE, 2 children **DISCIPLINE** AMERICAN HISTORY **EDUCATION** Univ Nebr, Lincoln, BA, 63; Stanford Univ, MA, 64, PhD(hist), 80. **CAREER** Woodrow Wilson teaching intern hist, Lamar State Col Technol, 65-66; instr, San Jose State Col, 67-69; instr, 79-80, Asst Prof Hist, Southern Ill Univ, 80-. **MEMBERSHIPS** AHA; Orgn Am Historians; Concerned Asian Scholars; Soc Historians of the Early Am Repub. **RESEARCH** Intellectual history of the United States; biography; United States diplomatic history since 1945. **SELECTED PUBLICATIONS** Auth, Charles A Beard's Act of faith: Context and content, J Am Hist, 3/80; Charles A Beard: An Intellectual Biography, Southern Ill Univ Press (in prep). **CONTACT ADDRESS** Dept of Hist Studies, So Illinois Univ, Edwardsville, 6 Hairpin Dr, Edwardsville, IL 62026-0001.

NORLING, LISA A.
PERSONAL m, 2 children **DISCIPLINE** HISTORY **EDUCATION** Rutgers Univ, PhD, 92. **CAREER** Assoc prof. **RESEARCH** American women's history; early American social history; maritime history. **SELECTED PUBLICATIONS** Auth, How Frought With Sorrow and Heartpangs': Mariners' Wives and the Ideology of Domesticity in New England, New England Quarterly, 92; The Sentimentalization of American Seafaring, 1790-1870, Acadiensus, 91; auth,coed, Iron Men, Wooden Women, Johns Hopkins Univ Pr, 96; auth, Captain Ahab Had a Wife, Univ NC Pr, 00. **CONTACT ADDRESS** History Dept, Univ of Minnesota, Twin Cities, 614 Social Sciences Tower, 267 19th Ave. S, Minneapolis, MN 55455. **EMAIL** lnorling@tc.umn.edu

NORMORE, CALVIN GERARD
PERSONAL Born Corner Brook, NF, Canada **DISCIPLINE** PHILOSOPHY, MEDIEVAL STUDIES **EDUCATION** McGill Univ, BA, 68; Univ Toronto, MA, 69, PhD(philos), 76. **CAREER** Lectr philos, York Univ, 72-74; Killam fel, Univ Alta, 76- 77; Mellon Asst Prof Philos, Princeton Univ, 77-. **MEMBERSHIPS** Am Philos Asn; Can Medieval Acad Am; Soc Medieval & Renaissance Philos. **RESEARCH** Medieval philosophy; social and political philosophy; philosophy of time. **SELECTED PUBLICATIONS** Auth, Future contingents, In: Cambridge History of Later Medieval Philosophy, 82; Walter Burley on continuity, In: Infinity & Continuity in Ancient & Medieval Thought, 82; the Necessity in Deduction - Cartesian Inference and its Medieval Background, Synthese, Vol 0096, 1993. **CONTACT ADDRESS** Dept Philosophy, Univ of Toronto, Toronto, ON, Canada M5S 1A1. **EMAIL** normore@chass.utoronto.ca

NORRELL, ROBERT J.
DISCIPLINE HISTORY **EDUCATION** Univ Va, PhD, 83. **CAREER** Prof & Bernadotte Schmitt Ch of Excel, Hist, Univ Tenn. **RESEARCH** Modern South and American race relations. **SELECTED PUBLICATIONS** Auth, "Caste in Steel: Jim Crow Careers in Birmingham, Alabama," J of Am Hist (Dec 86); auth, A Promising Field: Engineering at Alabama, 1837-1987, Univ Ala Pr, 90; auth, James Bowron: The Autobiography of a New South Industrialist, UNC Pr, 91, auth, "Labor at the Ballot Box: Unions in Alabama Politics from the New Deal to the Dixiecrat Movement," J of So Hist (May 91). **CONTACT ADDRESS** Dept Hist, Univ of Tennessee, Knoxville, 915 Volunteer Blvd, 6th Fl, Dunford Hall, Knoxville, TN 37996-4065. **EMAIL** rnorrell@utk.edu

NORRIS, JAMES D.
PERSONAL Born 11/02/1930, Richmond, MO, m, 1957, 3 children **DISCIPLINE** AMERICAN FRONTIER & ECONOMIC HISTORY **EDUCATION** Univ Mo-Columbia, BS, 56, MA, 58, PhD, 61. **CAREER** Asst prof hist, Hiram Col, 61-65; vis assoc prof, Univ Wis, 65-66; assoc prof hist, Univ Mo-St Louis, 66-69, prof, 69-79; Dean, Col Lib Arts & Sci, 79-95, Prof Hist, Northern Ill Univ, 95-; Am lectr, Fulbright-Hays prog, Univ Ghana, 72-73. **MEMBERSHIPS** Orgn Am Historians; Bus Hist Asn. **RESEARCH** Business history; American frontier; American economic history. **SELECTED PUBLICATIONS** Auth, One price policy in antebellum country stores, Bus Hist Rev, 62; Frontier Iron: The Meramec Iron Works 1826-1876, 64; Business longevity and the frontier iron industry, Ann Bus Hist, 65; The Missouri and Kansas Zinc Miner's Association, Bus Hist, 66; History of American Zinc, 68, co-ed, Politics and Patronage in the Gilded Age, 70 & R G Dun & Co, 1841-1900: The Development of Credit Reporting in 19th Cen-

tury America, 78; coauth, Advertising & the Transformation of the American Economy, 1865-1920, Building a Tradition of Excellence, 91; The James Foundation in Missouri, 1941-1991, 96. **CONTACT ADDRESS** Col Lib Arts & Sci, No Illinois Univ, 1425 W Lincoln Hwy, De Kalb, IL 60115-2825.

NORTH, JAMES BROWNLEE
PERSONAL Born 01/21/1941, Hammond, IN, m, 1962, 2 children **DISCIPLINE** AMERICAN HISTORY **EDUCATION** Lincoln Christian Col, BA, 62; Lincoln Christian Sem, MA, 63; Univ Chicago Div Sch, MA, 67; Univ Il, PhD, 73. **CAREER** Prof, 72-77, San Jose Christian Col; prof to chair, interim dean, vice-pres, 77-, Cincinnati Bible Col & Sem; **HONORS AND AWARDS** Teacher of the Year, 88. **MEMBERSHIPS** Amer Soc of Church Hist; Conf on Faith & Hist; Disciples of Christ Hist Soc; Oh Acad of Hist. **RESEARCH** Amer relig hist; hist of Christian churches, churches of Christ. **SELECTED PUBLICATIONS** Auth, The Church of the New Testament; From Pentecost to the Present: A Short History of Christianity, Col Press Publ Co, 83; auth, Union in Truth: An Interpretive History of the Restoration Movement, Std Publ, 94; coauth, Coming Together in Christ: Pioneering a New Testament Way to Christian Unity, Col press Publ Co, 97. **CONTACT ADDRESS** Cincinnati Bible Col and Sem, 2700 Glenway Ave, Cincinnati, OH 45204. **EMAIL** Jim.North@cincybible.edu

NORTHRUP, DAVID ARTHUR
PERSONAL Born 05/01/1941, Rochester, NY, m, 3 children **DISCIPLINE** AFRICAN HISTORY **EDUCATION** Fordham Univ, BS, 63, MA, 65; Univ Calif, Los Angeles, MA, 69, PhD(hist), 74. **CAREER** Instr, Tuskegee Inst, 68-70 & 72; from Asst Prof to Assoc Prof, 74-89, Prof Hist, Boston Col, 89-. **HONORS AND AWARDS** Phi Beta Kappa, 63; NY State Teaching Fel, 63-64; Fulbright-Hays Doctoral Dissertation Res Abroad Grant, 72-73; Fulbright-Hays Fac Res Abroad Grant, African Studies Grant, Soc Sci Res Coun, Mellon Fund Grant, Boston Col, 80-81; Boston Col Fac Fel, 84; Development Grant, Boston Col Women's Studies Comt/Ford Found, 87; Travel Grant (London), Am Coun of Learned Soc, 88; Cult Diversity Core Grant, Ford Found/Xocomil, 92; Fac Teaching and Advising Grants, Boston Col, 91, 94; NEH Summer Stipends, 80, 95. **MEMBERSHIPS** African Studies Asn; Am Asn Univ Prof; Am Hist Asn; World Hist Asn. **RESEARCH** French indentured labor trade from Africa and India to the French Carribean; Africa's discovery of Europe 1450-1800: changing impressions and perceptions. **SELECTED PUBLICATIONS** Auth, The growth of trade among the Igbo before 1800, 72 & The compatibility of the slave and palm oil trades in the bight of Biafra, 76 J Africa Hist; African mortality in the suppression of the slave trade, J Interdisciplinary Hist, 78; Trade without rulers: Pre-colonial economic development in South-Eastern Nigeria, Clarendon Press, 78; Nineteenth-century patterns of slavery and economic growth in Southeastern Nigeria, Int J African Hist Studies, 79; The Ideological Context of Slavery in Southeastern Nigeria in the 19th Century, In: The Ideology of Slavery in Africa, Sage Publ, 81; A Church in Search of a State: Catholic Missions in Eastern Zaire, 1879-1930, J of Church and State, Spring 88; The Ending of Slavery in Eastern Zaire, 1888-1930, In: The End of Slavery in Africa, Univ Wis Press, 88; Beyond the Bend in the River: A Labor History of Eastern Zaire, 1870-1940, Ohio Univ Press, 88; ed and compiler, The Atlantic Slave Trade, D.C. Heath and Co, 94; auth, Indentured Labor in the Age of Imperialism, 1834-1922, Cambridge Univ Press, 95; coauth, The Earth and Its Peoples: A Global History, Houghton Mifflin Co, 97. **CONTACT ADDRESS** Dept of History, Boston Col, Chestnut Hill, 140 Commonwealth Ave, Chestnut Hill, MA 02167-3806. **EMAIL** northrup@bc.edu

NORTON, MARY BETH
PERSONAL Born 03/25/1943, s **DISCIPLINE** HISTORY **EDUCATION** Univ Mich, BA, 64; Harvard Univ, MA, 65, Phd, 69. **CAREER** Asst prof, Univ Conn, 69-71; asst to full prof, Cornell Univ, 71-87; Mary Donlon Alger prof, 87-. **HONORS AND AWARDS** Allan Nevins Prize, 70; Alice and Edith Hamilton Prize, 80; Douglass Adair Prize, 80; Berkshire Conf Prize, 81; Francis Parkman Prize, 92; Bancroft Prize, 98; finalist, Pulitzer Prize, 97; finalist, pulitzer prize, 97. **MEMBERSHIPS** Soc Am Hist; Am Antiquarian Soc; Mass Hist Soc; Am Hist Asn; Org Am Hist; Coordinating Coun Women Hist; Inst Early Am Hist Cult; Upstate NY Women's Hist Org; Am Academy of Arts & Sciences. **RESEARCH** Early American history; American women's and gender history. **SELECTED PUBLICATIONS** Auth, The British-Americans: The Loyalist Exiles in England 1774-1789, 72; auth, Liberty's Daughters: The Revolutionary Experience of American Women 1750-1800, 80, 96; auth, Rethinking American History Textbooks, 94; Founding Mothers & Fathers: Gendered Power and The Forming of American Society, 96; coauth, A People and a Nation, 6th ed 01; ed, The American Historical Association's Guide to Historical Literature, Oxford, 95; Major Problems in American Women's History, 95. **CONTACT ADDRESS** Dept of History, Cornell Univ, 450 McGraw Hall, Ithaca, NY 14852-4601. **EMAIL** mbn1@cornell.edu

NORTON, PAUL F.
PERSONAL Born 01/23/1917, Newton, MA, m, 1942, 3 children **DISCIPLINE** ART HISTORY **EDUCATION** Oberlin Coll, BA, 38; Princeton Univ, PhD, 52. **CAREER** Asst prof to assoc prof, 47-58, Penn State Univ; prof, 58-93, chairman, 58-71, Art Dept, Univ Mass Amherst; prof, emer. **HONORS AND AWARDS** Fulbright Res Awd to England, 53-54; grant, NEH; grant, Graham Found; fellowship, Brown Univ, Center for Amer Historical Soc, 93-96; fellowship, Rhode Island Historical Soc, 98-99. **MEMBERSHIPS** Soc Archit Historians (U.S.) ; Soc of Archit Hist (England); Pioneer Am Soc; Victorian Soc. **RESEARCH** American and European archit (19th and 20th c); American stained glass windows. **SELECTED PUBLICATIONS** "Oudinot's Windows for Trinity Church, Boston," Victorian Soc Journ, 93; "Life and Stained Glass Windows of Robert Barrie," Stained Glass Quarterly, summer, 97. **CONTACT ADDRESS** 57 Woodside Ave., Amherst, MA 01002-2524. **EMAIL** pnorton@arthist.umass.edu

NORWOOD, STEPHEN H.
PERSONAL Born 01/20/1951, Washington, DC, m, 1975 **DISCIPLINE** HISTORY **EDUCATION** Tufts Univ, BA, 72; Columbia Univ, MA, 75; MPhil, 78; PhD, 84. **CAREER** Instr, Memphis State Univ, 84-87; asst to assoc prof, Univ Okla, 87-. **HONORS AND AWARDS** Herbert G. Gutman Awd, 91. **MEMBERSHIPS** Am Hist Asn; Orgn Am Hist; S Hist Asn; Asn Jewish Student; N Am Soc Sport Hist. **RESEARCH** US social history, Labor and working-class history, Sport history, Jewish history. **SELECTED PUBLICATIONS** Auth, Labor's Flaming Youth: Telephone Operators and Worker Militancy, 1878-1923, Urbana:Univ Ill Press, (90); auth, "Men Doing Women's History: What's the Difference?", J Wom Hist, (96); auth "Ford's Brass Knuckles: Harry Bennett, The Cult of Muscularity, and Anti-Labor Terror, 1920-1945," Labor Hist, (96); auth, "Bogalusa Burning: The War Against Biracial Unionism in the Deep South, 1919," J S Hist, (97); auth, "Reclaiming Working-Class Activism: The Boston Women's Trade Union League, 1930-1950," Labor's Heritage, (98); auth, "Going to Bat for Jackie Robinson: The Jewish Role in Breaking Baseball's Color Line," J Sport Hist, (99); auth, "The Making of an Athlete: Interview with Joe Washington," J Sport Hist, (00). **CONTACT ADDRESS** Dept Hist, Univ of Oklahoma, 455 W Lindsey St, Norman, OK 73019-2000. **EMAIL** Stephen.h.norwood_1@ov.edu

NORWOOD, VERA
DISCIPLINE AMERICAN STUDIES **EDUCATION** Univ NMex, PhD, 74. **CAREER** Prof, ch, dept Am Stud, Univ NMex. **HONORS AND AWARDS** Grant, Rockefeller Found, Am Coun of Learned Soc, Nat Endowment for Arts, NMex Hum Coun. **RESEARCH** Women's responses to nature and the built environment. **SELECTED PUBLICATIONS** Auth, Made From This Earth: American Women and Nature, 93; ed, The Desert is No Lady: Women Writers and Artists of the Southwest, 87. **CONTACT ADDRESS** Univ of New Mexico, Albuquerque, Albuquerque, NM 87131. **EMAIL** norwood@law.unm.edu

NOSCO, PETER
PERSONAL Born New York, NY, m, 1976, 2 children **DISCIPLINE** HISTORY **EDUCATION** Cambridge Univ, BA/MA, 73/77; BA, 71, PhD, 78, Columbia Univ. **CAREER** Asst Prof, St. John's Univ, 79-85; Asst Prof, 86-89, Assoc Prof, 89-93, Prof, 93-, Univ Southern California. **HONORS AND AWARDS** DHEW Fulbright Fel, 75-76; Fulbright Senior Research Awd, 86, Historiographical Inst Tokyo Univ; Fulbright-Hays Group Projects Abroad Project Dir of Japan Field Study, 98. **MEMBERSHIPS** Assoc for Asian Studies; Amer Acad of Religion; Amer Soc for Eighteenth Century Studies **RESEARCH** Intellectual and social history of Japan; popular culture; confucianism; nativism; underground religious movements **SELECTED PUBLICATIONS** Auth, Remembering Paradise: Nativism and Nostalgia in 18th Century Japan, Harvard-Yenching Institute Monograph Series, 90; ed, Confucianism and Tokugawa Culture, 96 (revised ed); Japanese Identity: Cultural Analyses, 97; guest ed, Philosophy East and West, special issue on theme of Religious Dimension of Confucianism in Japan, 98. **CONTACT ADDRESS** Univ of So California, 226 Taper Hall, Los Angeles, CA 90089-0357. **EMAIL** nosco@usc.edu

NOTEHELFER, FRED G.
PERSONAL Born 04/13/1939, Tokyo, Japan, m, 1966 **DISCIPLINE** MODERN JAPANESE HISTORY **EDUCATION** Harvard Univ, AB, 62; Princeton Univ, PhD(hist), 68. **CAREER** Instr hist, Princeton Univ, 66-67, vis lectr, 67-68, lectr, 68-69; asst prof, 69-71, Assoc Prof Hist, Univ Calif, Los Angeles, 71-, Fulbright-Hays res grant, vis prof, Doshisha Univ & res fel, Inst Humanistic Studies, Kyoto Univ, Japan, 71-72; dir, Univ Calif, Educ Abroad Tokyo Study Ctr, 79-81; vis prof, Univ BC, 82. **MEMBERSHIPS** Asn Asian Studies. **RESEARCH** Meiji period socialist and Christian movements. **SELECTED PUBLICATIONS CONTACT ADDRESS** Dept of Hist, Univ of California, Los Angeles, Los Angeles, CA 90024.

NOVERR, DOUGLAS ARTHUR
PERSONAL Born 05/13/1942, Battle Creek, MI, m, 1968 **DISCIPLINE** AMERICAN LITERATURE & STUDIES **EDUCATION** Cent Mich Univ, BA, 65, MA, 66; Miami Univ, PhD(English), 72. **CAREER** Instr English, Cent Mich Univ, 66-67 & Miami Univ Ohio, 67- 69; from instr to asst prof, 70-78, Assoc Prof English, Mich State Univ, 78-, Nat Endowment Humanities fel English, Miami Univ Ohio, 68-69; sr Fulbright lectr Am lit, Marie Curie Sklodowska Univ, Poland, 76-77. **MEMBERSHIPS** MLA; Am Studies Asn; Popular Cult Asn; Thoreau Soc; Soc Am Baseball Res. **RESEARCH** Nineteenth century American literature; American painting and literature; American sports history. **SELECTED PUBLICATIONS** Auth, Emily Dickinson and the art of despair, Emily Dickinson Bull, 73; Bryant and Cole in the Catskills, Bull NY Pub Libr, 75; Midwestern travel literature in the nineteenth century: Romance and reality, MidAmerica, 77; coauth, The athletic revolution reconsidered, Sport Sociol Bull, fall 77; The Relationship of Painting and Literature: A Guide to Information Sources, Gale Res, 78; Midwestern Regionalist Painting and the Origins of Midwestern Popular Culture, Mid Am, 80; coauth, Violence in American sports, In: Sports in Modern America, River City Publ Ltd, 81; Sports in the twenties, In: The Evolution of Mass Culture in America, Forum Press, 82. **CONTACT ADDRESS** Dept of Lang, Michigan State Univ, 229 Bessey Hall, East Lansing, MI 48824-1033.

NOVICK, PETER
PERSONAL Born 07/26/1934, Jersey City, NJ, m, 1964, 1 child **DISCIPLINE** MODERN HISTORY **EDUCATION** Columbia Univ, BS, 57, PhD(hist), 65. **CAREER** Lectr hist, Rutgers Univ, 61-62; lectr, Columbia Univ, 61- 65; asst prof, Univ Calif, Santa Barbara, 65-66; asst prof, 66- 72, Assoc Prof Europ Hist & Soc Sci, 72-. **HONORS AND AWARDS** Clark M Ansley Awd, 65. **MEMBERSHIPS** AHA **RESEARCH** Twentieth Century United States and Europe. **SELECTED PUBLICATIONS** Auth, The Resistance vs Vichy, Columbia Univ, 68; That Noble Dream - Haskell,tl Vol 29, Pg 143, 1990, History And Theory, Vol 0032, 1993; Godforsaken Scholarship + Response to Wolfe,Alan Article on My Work on Ways of Knowing, Lingua Franca, Vol 0006, 1996. **CONTACT ADDRESS** Dept of Hist, Univ of Chicago, 1126 E 59th St, Chicago, IL 60637-1539.

NUGENT, DONALD CHRISTOPHER
PERSONAL Born 12/31/1930, Lousiville, KY, s **DISCIPLINE** HISTORY, THEOLOGY **EDUCATION** PhD Univ of IA, 65; MA Theol, Univ of San Francisco, 82. **CAREER** Asst Prof, Univ KY, 66-95; Vis Prof, Univ Col Dublin, 72-73; Univ Alberta, 61-62. **RESEARCH** Msyticism; Spirituality, esp St John of the Cross. **SELECTED PUBLICATIONS** Ecummenism in the Age of the Reformation, Harvard, 74; Masks of Satan: The Demonic in History, Sheed & Ward, 83; Mysticism, Deathe and Dying, Albany: SUNY, 94; Satori in St John of the Cross: The Eastern Buddhist, Kyoto, 95; Pax Sexuals: The Month, London, 98. **CONTACT ADDRESS** Dept Hist, Univ of Kentucky, Lexington, KY 40506.

NUGENT, WALTER
PERSONAL Born 01/11/1935, Watertown, NY, m **DISCIPLINE** HISTORY **EDUCATION** St Benedict's Col, AB, 54; Georgetown Univ, MA, 56; Univ Chicago, PhD, 61. **CAREER** Instr, Washburn Univ, 57-58; asst prof, Kans State Univ, 61-63; from asst prof to prof, Ind Univ, 63-84; vis prof, Columbia Univ, 66; vis prof, NYork Univ, 67; assoc dean of Col of Arts & Sci, Ind Univ, 67-76; dir, Univ Overseas Prog at Ind Univ, 67-76; chemn, dept of History, Ind Univ, 74-77; vis prof, Hebrew Univ of Jerusalem, 78-79; vis prof, Warsaw Univ, 82; Andrew V. Tackes Prof of Hist, Univ of Notre Dame, 84-00; vis prof, Univ Col Dublin, 91-92. **HONORS AND AWARDS** Guggenheim Fel, 64-65; NEH, Huntington Libr, 79-80; Fulbright, 78-79 & 91-92; Medal of Merit, Warsaw Univ, 92. **MEMBERSHIPS** Western Hist Asn, Soc for Historians of the Gilded Age & Progressive Era. **RESEARCH** American West, Migration, Demography. **SELECTED PUBLICATIONS** Auth, The Tolerant Populists, 63; auth, Creative History, 67; auth, Money Question during Reconstruction, 68; auth, Money and American Society 1865-1880, 68; Modern America, 73; auth, From Centennial to World War, 77; auth, Structures of American Social History, 81; auth, Crossings: The Great Transatlantic Migrations, 92; coauth, The American West: The Reader, 99; auth, Into the West: The Story of Its People, 99. **EMAIL** walter.nugent.1@nd.edu

NULL, ELISABETH M.
PERSONAL Born 12/01/1942, Worcester, MA, 2 children **DISCIPLINE** FOLKLORE, HISTORY, LIBRARY SCIENCE **EDUCATION** Sarah Lawrence Col, BA; MA; Yale Univ 85; MPhil, 89; Univ of Pa, MA, 86; Cath Univ of Am, MLIS, 95. **CAREER** Librarian, ed, digital content provider, Lib of Congress, 95-98; guest lectr, Georgetown Univ, 91-98; writer, cybrarian, Rural Sch Community Trust, 99-; co-chair, Washington Folk Festival, 99-00. **MEMBERSHIPS** Am Folklore Soc. **RESEARCH** American musical life and cultural history. **SELECTED PUBLICATIONS** Reviews in Journal of Am Folklore, New York Folklore Quarterly, New England Quarterly; produced ethnographic recordings, Green Linnet Records; edited digitized historical collections, Lib of Congress. **CONTACT ADDRESS** 706 Bonifant Street, Silver Spring, MD 20910-5534. **EMAIL** elisabeth.null@tcs.wap.org

NUMBERS, RONALD L.
PERSONAL Born 06/03/1942, Boulder, CO, m, 1999, 1 child **DISCIPLINE** HISTORY **EDUCATION** Southern Missionary Col, BA, 63; Fla State Univ, MA, 65; Univ of Calif, Berkeley, PhD, 69. **CAREER** Asst prof, Andrews Univ, 69-70; asst prof, Loma Linda Univ, 70-74; asst prof to prof, Univ Wisc, Madison, 74-91, William Coleman Prof of the Hist of Sci and Med, 91-, Hilldale Prof of the Hist of Sci and Med, 97-, chemn, Dept of the Hist of Med, 99-. **HONORS AND AWARDS** Josiah Macy, Jr Found Fel, 73-74; John Simon Guggenheim Found Fel, 83-84; Nat Sci Found Scholar's Awd, 84; Corresponding mem, Int Acad of the Hist of Sci, 93; Satrion Lectr, Am Asn for the Advancement of Sci, 95; Fel, Am Acad of Arts and Scis, 95; Garrison Lectr, Am Asn for the Hist of Med, 97; Grad of Distinction, Fla State Univ, 99; Pres, Am Soc of Church Hist, 99-2000; Pres, Hist of Sci Soc, 2000-2001; Benjamin Rush Awd, Am Psychiatric Asn, 2000. **MEMBERSHIPS** Am Asn for the Hist of Med, Am Hist Asn, Am Soc of Church Hist, Hist of Sci Soc, Org of Am Hists. **RESEARCH** The history of science and medicine in America; the historical relations of science, medicine, and religion. **SELECTED PUBLICATIONS** Auth, Prophetess of Health: A Study of Ellen G. White, NY: Harper and Row (76), reprinted under title of Prophetess of Health: Ellen G. White and the Origins of Seventh-Day Adventist Health Reform, Knoxville: Univ Tenn Press (92); auth, Creation by Natural Law: Laplace's Nebular Hypothesis in American Thought, Seattle and London: Univ of Washington Press (77); auth, Almost Persuaded: American Physicians and Compulsory Health Insurance, 1912-1920, Baltimore and London: Johns Hopkins Univ Press (89); auth, The Creationists, NY: Alfred A. Knopf (92), paperback, Berkeley and Los Angeles: Univ Calif Press (93); ed, Creationism in Twentieth-Century America: A Ten-Volume Anthology of Documents, 1903-1961, New York: Garland Pub (95); co-ed, The Scientific Enterprise in America: Readings from Isis, Chicago: Univ Chicago Press (96); auth, Darwinism Comes to America, Cambridge, Mass: Harvard Univ Press (98); co-ed, Disseminating Darwinism: The Role of Place, Race, Religion, and Gender, NY: Cambridge Univ Press (99). **CONTACT ADDRESS** Dept of Hist of Med, Univ of Wisconsin, Madison, 1300 Univ Ave, Madison, WI 53706-1320. **EMAIL** Rnumbers@med.wisc.edu

NUNIS, DOYCE BLACKMAN, JR.
PERSONAL Born 05/30/1924, Cedartown, GA **DISCIPLINE** HISTORY, EDUCATION **EDUCATION** BA, UCLA, 47; MS in Ed, USC,50; M Ed, USC, 52; PhD Hist, USC,58. **CAREER** Univ Southern Cal, Prof Emer, 89-, Hist Prof, 68-89, Assoc Prof, 65-68; UCLA, Assoc Prof, Edu, Assoc Research Hist, Office Oral Hist, 64-65, Asst Prof, Ed Hist, 61-64, Lectr, Hist Edu, 60-61; El Camino Col, Instr, 56-59; Los Angeles City Col, Instr, 52-57; Univ Southern Cal, Lectr, 53-56, Teaching Asst, Dept Am Civilizations Institutions, 51-53. **HONORS AND AWARDS** Huntington Library, Fel, 60; Guggenheim Found, Fel, 63-64; Fel Cal Hist Soc, 81; Am Philos Soc, Fel, 81; Benemerinti Medal, pontifical honor, 84; Henry R Wagner Mem Awd, CHS, 88; Fel Hist Soc of S Calif, 90; Knight Commander St Gregory, pontifical honor, 94; Distinguished Emer Awd, USC, 94; Order Isabel la Catholica, Spanish Govt., 95; Doyce B Nunis Jr Awd, est by the Historical Soc Southern Cal to honor 37 yrs as editor of its pub, Southern California Quarterly, 96; Oscar Lewis Awd, 98; five distinguished teaching awards, USC. **RESEARCH** Hist of Am West; California; Los Angeles; Hist of Medicine. **SELECTED PUBLICATIONS** Southern California Local Hist: A Gathering of the Writings of W W Robinson, ed, 93; From Mexican Days to the Gold Rush, ed, 93; Tales of Mexican California by Antonio Coronel, ed, 94; Land Policy and Land Use in Southern California, ed, 94; The St Francis Dam Disaster Revisited, ed, 95; Women in the Life of Southern California, ed, 96; Hispanic California Revisited: Essays by Francis F Guest, ed, 96; El Presidio de San Francisco: A History Under Spain and Mexico, 1776-1846, ed, 96; Mission San Fernando Rey de Espana: A Bicentennial Salute, 97. **CONTACT ADDRESS** 4426 Cromwell Ave, Los Angeles, CA 90089-0034.

NUNN, FREDERICK MCKINLEY
PERSONAL Born 10/29/1937, Portland, OR, m, 1960, 1 child **DISCIPLINE** LATIN AMERICAN HISTORY **EDUCATION** Univ Ore, BA, 59; Univ NMEX, MA & PhD, 63. **CAREER** Asst prof hist, Elbert Covell Col, Univ of the Pac, 63-65; from asst prof to assoc prof, 65-72, fac res grants, 65-68, asst dir Pac Rim Studies Ctr, 72-73; prof 72-80, Head Dept Hist, Portland State Univ 80-; Lectr & consult, Univ NMex Peace Corps Training Ctr, 65-66; Am Philos Soc fel, 69; Soc Sci Res Coun-Am Coun Learned Soc fel, 78; hon res fel, Inst Lat Amer Studies, Univ London 77-78. **HONORS AND AWARDS** Hubee & Herring Mem Awd, 80. **MEMBERSHIPS** AHA; Conf Latin Am Hist; Latin Am Studies Asn; Pac Coast Coun Latin Am Studies; Am Franciscan Hist. **RESEARCH** Modern Latin American history; historical role of the military in Latin America; Chilean political history. **SELECTED PUBLICATIONS** Auth, Military rule in Chile: The revolutions of September 5, 1924 and January 23, 1925, Hisp Am Hist Rev, 2/67; Chilean Politics, 1920-1931: The Honorable Mission of the Armed Forces, Univ NMex, 70; Emil Korner and the Prussianization of the Chilean army: Origins, process and consequences 1885-1920, Hisp Am Hist Rev, 70; Military professionalism and professional militarism in Brazil: Historical perspectives and political consequences 1870-1970, J Latin Am Studies, 72; The Military in Chilean History: Essays on Civil-Military Relations, 1810-1973, NMex Univ, 76; Latin American military lore: The introduction and a case study, The Americas, 4/79; Professional militarism in twentieth-century Peru: Historical and theoretical background to the Golpe de Esbedo of 1968, Hisp Am Hist Rev, 8/79. **CONTACT ADDRESS** Dept of Hist, Portland State Univ, PO Box 751, Portland, OR 97207-0751.

NUTT, R.
PERSONAL Born 07/31/1953, Kansas City, MO, m, 1978, 2 children **DISCIPLINE** US RELIGIOUS HISTORY **EDUCATION** Vanderbilt Univ, PhD, 86 **CAREER** Asst prof, 88-94, Assoc prof, 94-, Muskingum Coll. **HONORS AND AWARDS** Wm Rainey Harper Awd for Outstanding Scholarship, 94, 98 **MEMBERSHIPS** Amer Soc of Church Hist; Presbyterian Historical Soc; Amer Acad of Relig **RESEARCH** American Religious Hist; Church-State Issues; Presbyterian Hist **SELECTED PUBLICATIONS** Auth, Contending for the Faith: The First Two Centuries of the Presbyterian Church in Cincinnati Area, 91; Toward Peacemaking: Presbyterians in the South and National Security, 1945-1983, 94; Presbyterians and Nuclear Weapons: Fifty Years of a Life-and-Death Issue, American Presbyterians, Summer 95; The Whole Gospel for the Whole World: G Sherwood Eddy and American Protestant Social Mission, 97; G. Sherwood Eddy and Attitudes of the Protestants in the US toward Global Mission, Church History, 97. **CONTACT ADDRESS** Brown Chapel, Muskingum Col, New Concord, OH 43762. **EMAIL** rnutt@muskingum.edu

NUTTING, MAUREEN M.
PERSONAL Born 10/02/1946, New York, NY, m, 1975, 4 children **DISCIPLINE** HISTORY **EDUCATION** Forham Univ, BA; Univ Notre Dame, MA, 69, PhD, 75. **CAREER** Asst prof, Humboldt State Univ, asst prof, Chaminade Univ, Honolulu, 75-77; part-time lectr, Prince Georges Community Col, Largo, Md, 77; Special Asst to the Dir, Promotion of Minorities' and Women's Scholarly and Professional Interests, Am Hist Asn, Washington, DC, 79-81; vis asst prof, Univ Miami, Coral Gables, 87-90; vis asst prof, Seattle Univ, Wash, 90-91; history instr, Seattle Central Community Col, 92-96; history instr, North Seattle Community Col, 96-. **HONORS AND AWARDS** Hearst Fel in Am Hist, 69-70; NDEA Fel, Univ Notre Dame, 91-92; NEH Summer Insts, 94, 98; Asian Studies Develop Prog Travel grants for India, 95 and China, 96; Lifetime Learning Awd (teaching), Seattle Community Col District, 99; AHA/LOC Summer Res Sem, 99. **MEMBERSHIPS** Am Hist Asn, Org of Am Hists, Immigration and Ethnic Hist Soc, Coord Coun for Women in Hist, Community Col Humanities Asn, Western Asn of Women Hists. **RESEARCH** Transnational identity issues for Japanese Brazilians, 1930s to 1940s; U.S. immigration and ethnicity; pedagogical issues in history. **SELECTED PUBLICATIONS** Coauth with Shirley Yee, "Seattle: Where the Old and the New Meet," AHA Perspectives, Vol 36, No 8 (Nov 97); auth, "Teaching History in the Community Colleges: It's a Job for Historians," The Chronicle of Higher Educ (Oct 30, 98): A7-8; auth, "The Japanese Brazilians--Issues of Transnational Identity in the 1930s and 1940s," Community Col Humanities J (spring 2000); auth, "Linking the Past and Present in the Pacific Northwest," Teaching Anthropol (spring 2000). **CONTACT ADDRESS** Hist Dept, Div Soc Sci, No Seattle Comm Col, 9600 Col Way N, Seattle, WA 98103-3514. **EMAIL** mnutting@sccd.ctc.edu

NUZZO, ANGELICA
PERSONAL Born, Italy **DISCIPLINE** HISTORY OF PHILOSOPHY **EDUCATION** Liceo Classico, BA, 83; Univ Heidelberg, PhD, 91; Scuola Normale Superiore, PhD, 91. **CAREER** Vis asst prof, Univ Heidelberg, 93-94, 94-95; invest, Univ Studi dell'Aquila, 95-96; vis asst prof, DePaul Univ, 96-97; asst prof, 97-. **HONORS AND AWARDS** DAAD Fel; Postdoc Fel; TransCoop Res Grant; DU Res Grant. **MEMBERSHIPS** APA; HAS; NAKS; NAFS; NASS; SPEP; IPS; IHV; IHG. **RESEARCH** German idealism; political philosophy; ethics' logic; theory of translation. **SELECTED PUBLICATIONS** Auth, Rappresentazione a concetto nella 'logica' della Filosofia del diritto di Hegel, Guida (Napoli), 90; auth, Logica a sistema: Sull'idea hegeliana di filosofia, Pantograf (Genova), 92; auth, La logica a la metafisica di Hegel: Guida alla critica, a cura di A. Nuzzo, La Nuova Italia Scientifica (Roma), 93; auth, "Per una metodologia della storia della filosofia secondo Hegel: Le introduzioni berlinesi alle lezioni sulla storia della filosofia, 1819-1831, Il Cannocchiale 1 (97): 49-56; auth, "An Outline of Italian Hegelianism (1832-1998), Owl of Minerva 29 (98): 165-205; auth, "Nachklange der Fichte-Rezeption Jacobis in der Schrift, Von den gottlichen Dingen and ihrer Offenbarung," in Fichte and Jacobi, hrsg. V. K. Hammacher (Amsterdam, Rodophi: Fichte Studien, 98): 121-137; auth, "The Idea of 'Method' in Hegel's Science of Logic: A Method for Finite Thinking and Absolute Knowing," Hegel Soc Bull Gt Brit 39/40 (99): 1-18; rev of, Hegel's Idea of a Phenomenology of Spirit, European J Philo (99); auth, "Ding/Eigenschaft," "Idee," "Ganzes/Teil," "Gattung/Gattungswesen," "Spekulation," "Theorie," in Enzyklopadie Philosophie, ed. HJ Sandkuhler (Hamburg, Meiner, 00); auth, "Geschichte der Philosophie als Ubersetzungsproze," in Ubersetzung: Sprache and Interpretation, hrsg. W Buttemezer, HJ Sandkuhler, Peter Lang, 00; transl of, B. Bourgeois, Il destino francese dei Lineamenti di Filosofia del diritto di Hegel (Le destin francais des Principes de la Philosophie du Droit de Hegel), Giornale critico della filosofia italiana, 67 (88): 321-347. **CONTACT ADDRESS** Dept Philosophy, DePaul Univ, 2320 North Kenmore Ave, Chicago, IL 60614-3210.

NWADIKE, FELLINA
PERSONAL Born 07/24/1952, Nigeria, m, 1979, 1 child **DISCIPLINE** FINE ARTS **EDUCATION** Norfolk State Univ, BA, 78; Univ San Francisco, EdD, 90. **CAREER** Asst Prof, Coppin State Col, 92-. **MEMBERSHIPS** ASTD, ODN, MCA, NAWE. **RESEARCH** Sustainable education in Africa, group thinking process in decision-making, cultural conflict, role of women in intercultural diversity. **SELECTED PUBLICATIONS** Auth, Intercultural Communication - Global Village, 98. **CONTACT ADDRESS** Dept Fine Arts, Coppin State Col, PO Box 11387, Baltimore, MD 21239. **EMAIL** nwadike@netscape.net

NWAUBANI, CHIDIEBERE
PERSONAL Born, Nigeria **DISCIPLINE** HISTORY **EDUCATION** Univ Ilorin, BA, 79; Univ Ibadan, MA, 84; Univ Toronto, PhD, 95. **CAREER** Asst Lectr, Col of Educ, Sokoto Nigeria, 80-81; Asst Lectr, Alvan Ikoku Col of Educ, Nigeria, 81-85; Lectr I to Lectr II, Imo State Univ Nigeria, 86-88; Asst Prof, Univ Colo. **HONORS AND AWARDS** Fed Govt of Nigeria Scholar, 82-83; Jr Resident Fel, Univ Toronto, 90-93; Harry S. Truman Libr Inst Res Grant, 93; John F. Kennedy Libr Found Res Grant, 93; Abilene Travel Grant, Dwight D. Eisenhower World Affairs Inst, 93; Special Fel, Univ Toronto, 90-94; Predoc Fel, Frederick Douglass Inst for African and African-Am Studies, Univ Rochester, 93-95; Jr Fac Develop Awd, 96; Brit Acad Vis Fel, 97. **MEMBERSHIPS** African Studies Assoc; Hist Soc of Nigeria; Igbo Studies Assoc; Inst of Commonwealth Studies. **RESEARCH** Decolonization of British West Africa; Colonial Nigeria: constitutional and political history; Decolonization; Precolonial Igbo: history and culture. **SELECTED PUBLICATIONS** Auth, "The World Bank and Hunger in Africa: A Causal Analysis," J of Intl Studies, (92): 25-62; auth, "The British Labour Party, the 'Dual Mandate,' and Africa, 1945-1951," Trans-African Jl of Hist, (92): 93-110; auth, "Getting Behind a Myth: The British Labour Party and Decolonization in Africa, 1945-1951," The Australian J of Polit and Hist, (93): 197-217; auth, "Chieftaincy among the Igbo: A Guest on the Center-stage," Intl J of African Hist Studies, (94): 347-371; auth, "For Bread Alone: A PostScript on Nigeria's Wheat Entrapment," Scandinavian Journal of Develop Alternatives, (99): 47-57; auth, "The Political Economy of Aboh, 1830-1857," African Econ Hist, (99): 93-116; auth, "Kenneth Onwuka Dike, Trade and Politics and the Restoration of the African in History," in History in Africa, Vol 27, (00): 229-248; auth, "Acephalous Societies," in Africa, Vol 1: African History before 1885, (Carolina Acad Press, 00), 275-293; auth, The United States and Decolonization in West Africa, 1950-1960, Univ Rochester Press, 01. **CONTACT ADDRESS** Dept Hist, Univ of Colorado, Boulder, 234 UCB, Boulder, CO 80309-0234. **EMAIL** nwaubani@stripe.colorado.edu

NYANG, SULAYMAN
PERSONAL Born 08/12/1944, Banjul, Gambia, m, 1973, 2 children **DISCIPLINE** AFRICAN STUDIES **EDUCATION** Hampton Univ, BA, 69; Univ Va, MA, 71; PhD, 74. **CAREER** Chair, Howard Univ, 86-93. **HONORS AND AWARDS** Thomas Jefferson Fel, Univ of Va; Henry Luce Forum Fel, Univ of Hartford, 77. **MEMBERSHIPS** African Studies Assoc; Assoc of Muslim Soc Sci. **RESEARCH** Islam in Africa, Islam in North America, African thought and culture. **SELECTED PUBLICATIONS** Auth, Islam in the United States; coauth, Religious Plurality in Africa; auth, Islam, Christianity and African Identity; auth, A Line in the Sand; auth, Saudi Arabia's Role in the Gulf War. **CONTACT ADDRESS** Dept African Am Studies, Howard Univ, PO Box 590113, Washington, DC 20059.

NYBAKKEN, ELIZABETH I.
PERSONAL Born 11/26/1940, Iowa City, IA, m, 1977, 1 child **DISCIPLINE** HISTORY **EDUCATION** Carleton Col, BA, 62; Univ Del, MA, 70, PhD(Am Hist), 74. **CAREER** Teacher Hist, Montclair High Sch, 63-64 & H C Conrad High Sch, 64-67; instr, Univ Del, Wilmington, 72-74; asst prof, West Chester State Col, 74-76; asst prof, 76-81, assoc prof Hist, Miss State Univ, 81-. **HONORS AND AWARDS** Excellence in Teaching Awd; Outstanding Woman Professional Awd. **MEMBERSHIPS** Orgn Am Historians; Inst Early Am Hist & Culture; Southern Hist Asn; Am Soc for Eighteenth-Century Studies. **RESEARCH** Colonial & revolutionary America; women in American history; American Family History. **SELECTED PUBLICATIONS** Ed, The Centinel: Warnings of a Revolution, Univ Del Pres, 80; auth, New Light on the Old Side: Irish Influences on Colonial Presbyterianism, J Am Hist, 3/82; The Enlightenment and Calvinism: Mutual Support Systems for the Eighteenth-Century American Wilderness, Studies Voltaire & 18th Cent, 9/80; In the Irish Tradition: Pre-Revolutionary Academics in America, History of Education Quarterly, Summer, 97. **CONTACT ADDRESS** Dept of History, Mississippi State Univ, PO Box H, Mississippi State, MS 39762-5508. **EMAIL** ean1@ra.msstate.edu

NYE, MARY JO
PERSONAL Born 12/05/1944, Nashville, TN, m, 1968, 1 child **DISCIPLINE** HISTORY OF SCIENCE **EDUCATION** Univ Wisc, PhD, 70. **CAREER** Vis asst prof, to prof, hist of sci 70-91, G.L. Cross res prof hist of sci, 91-94, Univ Okla; Horning prof of hum and prof of hist, Oregon State Univ, 94-; vis prof of hist of sci, Harvard Univ, 88. **HONORS AND AWARDS** Phi Beta Kappa, 65; fel, Am Acad of Arts and Sci; pres, Hist of Sci Soc, 88-89; by-fel, Churchill Col, Cambridge, UK, 95. **MEMBERSHIPS** Am Hist Asn; Hist of Sci Soc; AAAS; Am Chem Soc. **RESEARCH** History of modern physical sciences; social and cultural history of science; science and politics. **SELECTED PUBLICATIONS** Auth, Molecular Reality: A Perspective on the Scientific Work on Jean Perrin, Elsevier, 72; ed, The Question of the Atom: From the Karlsruhe Congress to the First Solvay Conference, 1860-1911, A Selection of Primary Sources, Erwin Tomash, 84; auth, Science in the Provinces: Scientific Communities and Provincial Leadership in France, 1860-1930, California, 86; co-ed, The Invention of Physical Science: Intersections of Mathematics, Theology and Natural Philosophy Since the Seventeenth Century: Essays in Honor of Erwin N. Hiebert, Kluwer Academic, 92. auth, From Chemical Philosophy to Theoretical Chemistry: Dynamics of Matter and Dynamics of Disciplines, 1800-1950, California, 93; auth, Before Big Science: The Pursuit of Modern Chemistry and Physics, 1800-1940, Twayne, 96. **CONTACT ADDRESS** Dept of History, Oregon State Univ, Milam Hall 306, Corvallis, OR 97331. **EMAIL** nyem@ncs.orst.edu

NYE, ROBERT ALLEN
PERSONAL Born 06/15/1942, Concord, CA, m, 1968, 1 child **DISCIPLINE** MODERN EUROPEAN & FRENCH HISTORY **EDUCATION** San Jose State Col, BA, 64; Univ Wis, MA, 65, PhD, 69. **CAREER** Assoc prof, 69-79, Prof Hist, Univ Okla, 80-94; Thomas Hart and Mary Jones Horning Prof of Humanities, prof hist, Ore State Univ, 94-. **HONORS AND AWARDS** Nat Endowment of Humanities Jr Humanities fel, 72; Am Philos Soc fel, 70 & 77; Zeitlin-Verbrugge Prize, Hist of Sci Soc, 79. **MEMBERSHIPS** AHA; AAUP **RESEARCH** Modern French history since 1800; European intellectual history since 1700; the history of the social sciences since 1700. **SELECTED PUBLICATIONS** Auth, Two paths to a psychology of social action: Gustave LeBon and Georges Sorel, J Mod Hist, 973; The Origins of Crowd Psychology: Gustave LeBon and the Crisis of Mass Democracy in the Third RePubic, Sage, 75; Heredity or milieu: The foundations of Modern European criminological theory, Isis, 976; The Anti- Democratic Sources of Elite Theory: Pareto, Mosca, Michels, Sage, 77; Crime in Modern Societies: Some Research Strategies for Historians, JSocial Hist, 678; Gustave LeBon's Psychology of Revolution: History, Social Science and Politics in Nineteenth and Early Twentieth Century France, introduction to LeBon's La Revolution Francaise et la psychologie des revolutions, Clasics Social Sci, Transaction Bks, 80; Degeneration, Neurasthenia, and the Culture of Sport in Belle Epoque, JContemp Hist, 182; Degeneration and the Medical Model of Cultural Crisis in the French Belle Epoque, Political Symbolism in Modern Europe: Essays in Honor of George L Mosse, Transaction Press, 82; auth, Masculinity and Male Codes of Honor in Modern France, New York, 93. **CONTACT ADDRESS** Dept of Hist, Oregon State Univ, Milam Hall 305A, Corvallis, OR 97331. **EMAIL** nyer@ucs.orst.edu

NYSTROM, BRADLEY
DISCIPLINE HISTORY **EDUCATION** Univ Calif, Davis, BA, 74, MA, 77, PhD, 81. **CAREER** Assoc prof, Calif State Univ, Sacramento, 91-, coordr, Lib Arts Masters prog. **MEMBERSHIPS** Soc of Bibl Lit; Assoc of Ancient Hist. **RESEARCH** Classical Greece and Rome, Greek and Roman religions, New Testament, Christianity. **SELECTED PUBLICATIONS** Transl, ed, Ancient Greece, Kendall/Hunt, 90; The Song of Eros, Southern Ill, 91; auth, "Women, Priests and the Jewish Instriptions of Crete," Ariadne, 95. **CONTACT ADDRESS** Dept of Humanities and Religious Studies, California State Univ, Sacramento, 6000 J St, 2026 Medicino Hall, Sacramento, CA 95819-6083. **EMAIL** nystromb@csus.edu

NYSTROM, DAVID P.
PERSONAL Born 04/27/1959, San Mateo, CA, m, 1982, 1 child **DISCIPLINE** NEW TESTAMENT; ROMAN HISTORY **EDUCATION** UC Davis, BA, 81, PhD, 92; Fuller Theol Sem, MDiv, 86. **CAREER** Prof & chr bibli & theol student, N Park Univ. **HONORS AND AWARDS** Phi Beta Kappa; Outstanding Teaching Awd, UC Davis; Outstanding Teaching Awd, n Park Col. **MEMBERSHIPS** Soc for Prom Roman Studenties; Soc Bibl Lit; fel, Inst Bibl Res. **RESEARCH** New Testament, Gospel of John & James, Slavery, Women in the Roman Prov. **SELECTED PUBLICATIONS** Auth, James, (97); auth, "Josephus," NIDNTT, (97). **CONTACT ADDRESS** Bibl & Theol Stud, No Park Univ, 3225 W Foster Ave, Chicago, IL 60625-4823. **EMAIL** dnystrom@northpark.edu

NZEGWU, NKIRU
DISCIPLINE ART HISTORY **EDUCATION** Univ Ottowa, PhD, 88. **CAREER** Assoc prof, SUNY Binghamton. **RESEARCH** Philos of art; traditional African art and cult hist; colonialism and postcolonial influences in contemp African art; Black Canadian art. **SELECTED PUBLICATIONS** Auth, Questions of Identity and Inheritance: A Critical Review of Anthony Appiah's 'In My Father's House', Hypatia: Jour Feminist Philos, 96; Bypassing New York in Representing EKO: Production of Space in a Nigerian City in Re-Presenting the City: Ethnicity, Capital and Culture in the 21st Century Metropolis, Macmillan and NY UP, 96. **CONTACT ADDRESS** SUNY, Binghamton, PO Box 6000, Binghamton, NY 13902-6000. **EMAIL** panap@binghamton.edu

O

O'BOYLE, CORNELIUS
DISCIPLINE HISTORY **EDUCATION** Cambridge Univ, BA, 82, Mphil, 83, PhD, 87. **CAREER** Asst prof, Univ of Notre Dame, 90- . **RESEARCH** Medieval natural philosophy and medicine; early history of universities; historiography of science. **SELECTED PUBLICATIONS** Auth, Medieval Prognosis and Astrology, 91; Medicine, God and Aristotle in the Early Universities, 92; Surgical Texts and Social Contexts: Physicians and Surgeons in Paris 1270-1430, 94. **CONTACT ADDRESS** History and Philosophy of Science Dept, Univ of Notre Dame, Notre Dame, IN 46556. **EMAIL** Cornelius.O'Boyle.1@nd.edu

O'BRIEN, JEAN
PERSONAL Born Minnesota **DISCIPLINE** AMERICAN INDIAN HISTORY AND UNITED STATES COLONIAL HISTORY **EDUCATION** Univ Chicago, PhD, 90. **CAREER** Assoc prof Hist, Chmn, in Am Stud, Univ Minn, Twin Cities, 90-. **HONORS AND AWARDS** Res grant, Newberry Libr, Am Antiq Soc, and Mass Hist Soc; McKnight Land-Grant Professorship, 92; Recognition Awd for Emerging Scholars, Am Asn Univ Women. **RESEARCH** 19th century New Englanders' representations of local and regional Indian history. **SELECTED PUBLICATIONS** Auth, Divorced from the Land: Accomodation Strategies of Indian Women in 18th Century New England, in Gender, Kinship, and Power, Routledge, 96; Dispossession by Degrees: Indian Land and Identity in Natick, Massachusetts, 1650-1790, Cambridge UP, 97. **CONTACT ADDRESS** Univ of Minnesota, Twin Cities, 614 Soc Sci Bldg, Minneapolis, MN 55455. **EMAIL** obrie002@maroon.tc.umn.edu

O'BRIEN, MICHAEL
PERSONAL Born 04/13/1948, Plymouth, United Kingdom, m, 1969 **DISCIPLINE** HISTORY **EDUCATION** Univ Cambridge, BA, 69; MA, 73; PhD, 76; Vanderbilt Univ, MA, 73. **CAREER** Asst prof to prof, Univ of Ark, 80-87; Philip R Shriver Prof, Miami Univ, 87-. **HONORS AND AWARDS** Fel, Univ of Mich, 76-79; NEH Fel, 87-89, 95-96; Mellon Scholar, Cambridge, 93-. **MEMBERSHIPS** Org of Am Hist; Southern Hist Assoc; British Assoc of Am Studies. **RESEARCH** Modern Intellectual Culture, the American South. **SELECTED PUBLICATIONS** Auth, The Idea of the American South, 1920-1941, 79; ed, All Clever Men, Who Make Their Way: Critical Discourse in the Old South, 82; auth, A Character of Hugh Legare, 85; coed, Intellectual Life in Antebellum Charleston, 86; auth, Rethinking the South: Essays in Intellectual History, 88; ed, An Evening When Alone: Four Journals of Single Women in the South, 1827-67, 93. **CONTACT ADDRESS** Dept Hist, Miami Univ, 500 E High St, Oxford, OH 45056-1602. **EMAIL** obrienm@muohio.edu

O'BRIEN, THOMAS F.
PERSONAL Born 02/16/1947, Boston, MA, m, 1968, 3 children **DISCIPLINE** HISTORY **EDUCATION** Boston Col, BA, 68; Univ Conn, MA, 70, PhD, 76. **CAREER** From asst prof to assoc prof to prof to chemn, 77-99, Univ Houston. **HONORS AND AWARDS** Robertson Prize, 80, Honorable Mention Boltin Prize, 98, Conference on Latin American Hist. **MEMBERSHIPS** Conference on Latin Am Hist; Latin Am Stud Asn. **RESEARCH** US business in Latin America. **SELECTED PUBLICATIONS** Auth, art, The Antofagasta Co: A Case Study of Peripheral Capitalism, 80; auth, The Nitrate Industry and Chile's Crucial Transition, 82; auth, art, Rich Beyond the Dream of Avarice: The Guggenheim Brothers in Chile, 89; auth, art, The Revolutionary Mission: American Enterprise in Cuba, 93; auth, The Revolutionary Mission: American Enterprise in Latin America, 1900-1945, 96; auth, "The Century of U.S. Capitalism in Latin America," 99. **CONTACT ADDRESS** Dept of History, Univ of Houston, Houston, TX 77204-3785.

O'CONNOR, CAROL A.
PERSONAL Born 02/14/1946, Evanston, IL, m, 1977, 2 children **DISCIPLINE** HISTORY **EDUCATION** Manhattanville Col, BA, 67; Yale Univ, MPhil, 70; PhD, 76. **CAREER** Instr to asst prof, Knox Col, 74-77; asst prof to prof, Utah State Univ. **HONORS AND AWARDS** Bradley Senior Fel, Mont Hist Soc, 96. **MEMBERSHIPS** Org of Am Hist; Western Hist Assoc; Urban Hist Assoc. **RESEARCH** Cities and communities, 20th Century American West. **SELECTED PUBLICATIONS** Auth, A Sort of Utopia: Scarsdale, 1891-1981, 83; coed, The Oxford History of the American West, 94. **CONTACT ADDRESS** Dept Hist, Utah State Univ, 710 University Blvd, Logan, UT 84322-0710. **EMAIL** coconnor@hass.usu.edu

O'CONNOR, JOHN E.
PERSONAL Born 08/13/1943, New York, NY, m, 1965, 2 children **DISCIPLINE** AMERICAN HISTORY, CINEMA **EDUCATION** St Johns Univ, NYork, BA, 65; Queens Col, NYork, MA, 67; City Univ New York, PhD(early Am hist), 74. **CAREER** Lectr hist, Queens Col, NY, 66-69; asst prof, 69-79, assoc prof hist, 79-90, Prof, NJ Inst Technol, 79-00; coordr Man & Technol Prog, 77-89, assoc chmn, 70-76, chmn, 76- , Historians Film Comt, 70-76; co-ed, Film & Hist J, 71- . **HONORS AND AWARDS** AHA created John E. O'Connor Awd for Best Film or TV Production about History, 91. **MEMBERSHIPS** AHA; Orgn Am Historians; Am Studies Asn; Soc Cinema Studies. **RESEARCH** Early American history; history and technology; motion pictures and television. **SELECTED PUBLICATIONS** Coauth, Teaching History With Film, AHA, 74; ed, Film & the Humanities, Rockefeller Found, 77; auth, Legal reform in the Early Republic: The New Jersey Experience, Am J Legal Hist, 78; William Paterson: Lawyer and Statesman 1745-1806, Rutgers Univ Press, 79; ed, American History/American Film: Interpreting the Hollywood Image, Frederick Ungar Publ, 79; ed, I am a Fugitive From a Chain Gang, Univ Wis Press, 81; auth, Image as Artifact: The Historical Analysis of Film and Television, Kreiger, 91. **CONTACT ADDRESS** Dept of History, New Jersey Inst of Tech, 323 M L King Jr Blvd, Newark, NJ 07102-1824. **EMAIL** oconnor@admin.njit.edu

O'CONNOR, JOSEPH E.
PERSONAL Born 12/23/1937, Pittsburgh, PA, m, 1992, 2 children **DISCIPLINE** HISTORY **EDUCATION** Univ Notre Dame, BA; Univ Va, MA, PhD. **CAREER** Prof, 67-; Asso provost; former dept chair. **HONORS AND AWARDS** Alumni ass Dist Tchng Award; Archivist, interviewer, JFK Oral Hist Proj. **RESEARCH** Development op civilization, Russian-Soviet history; 20 Century Europe. **SELECTED PUBLICATIONS** Areas: Yugoslavian sculptor Ivan Mestrovic and on faculty development, instructional improvement programs, career planning and career change, and faculty re-direction; ed,Teaching in Higher Education. **CONTACT ADDRESS** Wittenberg Univ, Springfield, OH 45501-0720. **EMAIL** jeoconnor@wittenberg.edu

O'CONNOR, LEO F.
PERSONAL Born 07/24/1936, Jersey City, NJ, m, 1976, 6 children **DISCIPLINE** ENGLISH, AMERICAN STUDIES **EDUCATION** St Peter's Col, BS, 58; New York Univ, MA, 62, PhD, 72. **CAREER** Instr/asst prof, NYork Inst of Technol, 62-65; asst prof, Fairfield Univ, 65-75, assoc prof and dir of Am Studies, 76-86, prof and dir of Undergrad and Grad Am Studies progs, 86-. **HONORS AND AWARDS** Founders Day Awd, New York Univ, 72; Teacher of the Year, Fairfield Univ, 82; Distinguished Fac Awd, Fairfield Univ, 86; initiated and directed the Honors Prog at Fairfield Univ; initiated and directed the Am Studies prog which was the first interdisciplinary major in the Col of Arts and Scis; initiated and directed the first grad prog (MA in Am Studies). **MEMBERSHIPS** Am Studies Prog, Asn of Lit Scholars and Critics. **RESEARCH** Religion in American literature, film and literature. **SELECTED PUBLICATIONS** Auth, Religion in the American Novel: The Search for Belief (84); major contrib to The Dictionary of Contemporary Catholic Writers (88); auth, The Protestant Sensibility in the American Novel: A Critical Guide (91). **CONTACT ADDRESS** Dept English, Fairfield Univ, 1073 N Benson Rd, Fairfield, CT 06430-5171.

O'CONNOR, THOMAS H.
PERSONAL Born 12/09/1922, South Boston, MA, m, 1949, 3 children **DISCIPLINE** AMERICAN HISTORY **EDUCATION** Boston Col, AB, 49, MA, 50; Boston Univ, PhD, 58. **CAREER** From instr to assoc prof, 50-70, chmn dept, 62-70, fac asst to pres, 70-71, chmn coun libr educ, 71-75, prof hist, 70-93, emeritus, 93-, Boston Col; lectr, 67-, Harvard Univ. **HONORS AND AWARDS** Irish,Charitable Soc of Boston: Dist Irish-Amer Awd, 88; Shattuch Awd: tchng Excel, Harvard Univ, 90; Dr of Humane Lett, hon, Boston Col, 93; Dr of Humane Lett, hon, Merrimack Col, 95. **MEMBERSHIPS** AHA; AAUP; Am Cath Hist Assn; Orgn Am Historians; Bostonian Soc, res fel; Mass Archives Comm. **RESEARCH** Boston hist, New England hist, 1820-1860; the age of Jackson; the Civil War. **SELECTED PUBLICATIONS** Auth, Fitzpatrick's Boston: 1846-1866, Northeastern, 84; auth, South Boston: My Home Town, Northeastern, 94, Little Brown, 97; auth, Civil War Boston, Northeastern, 98; auth, Boston Catholics, Northeastern, 98. **CONTACT ADDRESS** Dept of History, Boston Col, Chestnut Hill, 140 Commonwealth Ave, Chestnut Hill, MA 02167-3800. **EMAIL** OCONNORT:thomas.oconnor.1@bc.edu

O'DONNELL, JAMES
PERSONAL Born 10/11/1937, Memphis, TN, m, 1972, 3 children **DISCIPLINE** HISTORY **EDUCATION** Lambuth Col, BA, 59; Duke Univ, MA, 61, PhD, 63. **CAREER** Prof, Radford

Col, 63-69; Thomas prof, Marietta Col, 69-. **HONORS AND AWARDS** Harness Fellow, McCoy Prof, 96-99. **MEMBERSHIPS** Ohio Acad Hist; Southern Hist Asn; Org Am Historians. **RESEARCH** Southern Indians before 1820; northern Indians before 1820; 19th century liberal arts Cols. **SELECTED PUBLICATIONS** Auth, Southern Indians in the American Revolution, 72; auth, Southeastern Frontiers, 83. **CONTACT ADDRESS** Marietta Col, 215 Fifth St, Marietta, OH 45750. **EMAIL** odonnelj@marietta.edu

O'DONNELL, KRISTA E.
DISCIPLINE HISTORY **EDUCATION** SUNY, Oneonta, BS, 88; SUNY, Binghamton, MA, 91; PhD, 96. **CAREER** Asst prof, William Paterson Univ, 97-; vis asst prof, Southwest State Univ, 96-97; asst, Workshop and Technical Support Staff, Humanities On Line H-Net, 94-95; tchg asst & lectr, Binghamton Univ, 90-95. **HONORS AND AWARDS** Distinguished Dissertation Soc Sci Awd, Binghamton Univ, 96; Alternate, Amer Asn Univ Women Dissertation fel, 94-95; Fulbright res fel, Universitat Bielefeld, Ger, 92-93; DAAD, Ger Acad Exchange Serv, res grant. **SELECTED PUBLICATIONS** Auth, Making War with Poison: Gendering Danger, Illicit Violence, and Domestic Work in German Southwest Africa, 96; **CONTACT ADDRESS** Dept of History, William Paterson Col of New Jersey, 300 Pompton Rd., Atrium 202, Wayne, NJ 07470. **EMAIL** mollyod@frontier.wilpaterson.edu

O'GORMAN, JAMES F.
PERSONAL Born 09/19/1933, St. Louis, MO, m, 1998, 3 children **DISCIPLINE** HISTORY OF ART **EDUCATION** Wash Univ, BA, 56; Univ IL, MArch 61; Harvard Univ, PhD, 66. **CAREER** Grace Slack McNeil Prof, 75-, Wellesley College. **HONORS AND AWARDS** Henry Russell Hitchcock Prize; SAH Awd. **SELECTED PUBLICATIONS** Auth, Accomplished in All Departments of Art: Hammatt Billings of Boston 1818-1874, Amherst MA, U of Mass Press, 98; ABC of Architecture, Philadelphia, U of Penn Press, 98; Living Architecture: A Biography of H H Richardson, NY, Simon & Schuster, 97; The Perspective of Anglo-American Architecture: Notes on some graphic attempts at three-dimensional representation in the colonies and early republic, Philadelphia, The Athenaeum, 95. **CONTACT ADDRESS** Dept of Art, Wellesley Col, 106 Central St, Wellesley, MA 02481-8203. **EMAIL** ogorman@wellesley.edu

O'KEEFE, J. PAUL
PERSONAL Born 11/30/1939, Boston, MA, s **DISCIPLINE** HISTORY **EDUCATION** Boston Col, BA, 61, MA, 63; Univ Wis, PhD, 79. **CAREER** Prof, Northland Col, 86-. **RESEARCH** Papacy; social-intellectual history. **CONTACT ADDRESS** 1650 Monroe St #G, Madison, WI 53711. **EMAIL** po'keefe@wheeler.northland.edu

O'MALLEY, JOHN WILLIAM
PERSONAL Born 06/11/1927, Tiltonsville, OH **DISCIPLINE** RENAISSANCE & REFORMATION HISTORY **EDUCATION** Loyola Univ, Ill, AB, 51, MA, 57, STL, 60; Harvard Univ, PhD, 66; DLitt, Loyola Univ, Ill, 82. **CAREER** From asst prof to prof hist, Univ Detroit, 65-79; prof hist, Weston Sch Theol, 79-; Harvard Ctr Ital Renaissance Studies fel, Italy, 66-68; vis assoc prof hist, Univ Mich, Ann Arbor, 72-73. **HONORS AND AWARDS** Guggenheim fel, 75-76; NEH fel, 83. **MEMBERSHIPS** Renaissance Soc Am; Am Cath Hist Assn; pres Am Cath Hist Assoc, 90; Fel Am Acad of Arts & Sci, 96; Mem Am Philos Soc, 97; pres, Renaissance Soc of Am, 98-2000. **RESEARCH** Religious culture of early modern Europe, especially Giles of Viterbo; Erasmus; Renaissance and reformation history; rhetoric and Renaissance oratory. **SELECTED PUBLICATIONS** Auth, Giles of Viterbo on Church and Reform, E J Brill, Leiden, 68; auth, Praise and Blame in Renaissance Rome, 79; auth, The First Jesuits, 93; auth, Trent and See That, 00. **CONTACT ADDRESS** 3 Phillips Pl, Cambridge, MA 02138-3495. **EMAIL** jomalley@wjst.edu

O'NEIL, PATRICK M.
PERSONAL Born 12/03/1947, Norwich, NY, s **DISCIPLINE** HISTORY; MODERN EUROPE; MODERN BRITAIN; BRITISH EMPIRE **EDUCATION** NYork State Univ, BA, 69;MA in English Lit, 73;MA in Philos, 79; MA History, 81; MA Soc Sci,89; PhD History, 93. **CAREER** Assoc prof, Broome Comm Col, 97-; asst prof, Broome Comm Col, 95-97; adjunct instr, Broome Comm Col, 85-95; adjunct lctr, SUNY, 91; instr Comm Educ Prog, Broome Comm Col, 86-; adjunct instr, St Univ NY at Morrisville, 85-91. **HONORS AND AWARDS** Notary Public, St of NY, 77-92; SUNY Tchg Assistanceship, 68-70; General Foods Scholar, 83-84; NY St Regents Scholar, 65-70. **MEMBERSHIPS** Amer Acad Polit Sci; Amer Intl Assoc for Philos of Law; Amer Assoc for Philos Study of Soc; Amer Historical Assoc; Amer Philos Assoc; Federalist Soc for Law & Pub Safety; Intercollegiate Studies Institute; NY St Assoc of European Historians; NY St Philos Assoc; Soc of Cath Social Scientists; Soc of Christian Philosophers; Intl Churchill Soc; Modern Lang Assoc. **RESEARCH** British Empire History; Winston S Churchill; American Constitutional Law; Ethical Philosophy; Philosophy of Law. **SELECTED PUBLICATIONS** Winston's S. Churchill's Philosophy of Empire: Mind of the Imperialist, Peter Lang, 99; A Reconciliation of the Humean Is/Ought Problem to an Objective Moral Order, Cath Social Sci Rev, Villanove Univ, 98; Encycl of Int Slavery, Macmillan, 98. **CONTACT ADDRESS** Depts of Humanities and Social Sciences, Broome Comm Col, 75 Colfax Ave, Binghamton, NY 13905. **EMAIL** oneil_p@sunybroome.edu

O'NEILL, JAMES E.
PERSONAL Born 02/02/1929, Renovo, PA, m, 1953, 5 children **DISCIPLINE** MODERN HISTORY **EDUCATION** Univ Detroit, AB, 52, MA, 54; Univ Chicago, PhD, 61. **CAREER** Ref librn, Univ Detroit, 56-57; from instr to asst prof hist, Univ Notre Dame, 57-63; Europ manuscript specialist, Libr Congr, 63-65; assoc prof hist, Loyola Univ, Ill, 65-69; dir, Franklin D Roosevelt Libr, 69-71; dep archivist of US, Nat Arch & Rec Serv, 72-80; ASST ARCHIVIST FOR PRESIDENTIAL LIBR, 80-, Am Coun Learned Soc res grant, 63; mem adv bd, US Army Mil Hist Res Collection, 73-78; mem bd dirs, Eleanor Roosevelt Inst, 73-; mem, Adv Comt, Senate Hist Off, 76, Exec Comt, Int Coun Arch, 80- & Dept Army Hist Adv Comn, 78-; ed, Int J Arch, 78-81. **HONORS AND AWARDS** LHD, St Edward's Univ, 75. **MEMBERSHIPS** AHA; fel Soc Am Archivists. **RESEARCH** Modern United States and British history; archives and historical manuscripts; social history. **SELECTED PUBLICATIONS** Auth, The Victorian background to the British welfare state, S Atlantic Quart, spring 67; Will success spoil the presidential libraries?, Am Archivist, summer 73; coauth, Episodes in American History, Ginn, 73; auth, The security classification of records in the United States, Indian Archivist, 74; co-ed, World War II: An Account of Its Documents, Howard Univ, 76; contribr, Access to the Papers of Recent Public Figures, Orgn Am Historians, 77; Replevin, Col & Res Libr, 79. **CONTACT ADDRESS** Nat Archives Bldg, Washington, DC 20408.

O'NEILL, W. PATRICK
PERSONAL Born 01/02/1953, Shevandoah, PA, m, 1984, 1 child **DISCIPLINE** MEDIEVAL STUDIES **EDUCATION** Blominsburgh Univ, MA Hist, 76; MEd, 76; MA Art Hist, 81; Pa State Univ, PhD. **CAREER** Instr, Susquehanna Univ, 84-90; Instr, Pa State Univ, 90-. **RESEARCH** Ancient, Medieval And Renaissance Religion and Art. **SELECTED PUBLICATIONS** Auth, Role of Mary as Mother Goddess Figure, Susquehanna Univ Press, 89. **CONTACT ADDRESS** Dept Lib Arts, Pennsylvania State Univ, Hazleton, Hazleton, PA 18201-1202.

O'NEILL, WILLIAM L.
PERSONAL Born 04/18/1935, Big Rapids, MI, m, 1960, 2 children **DISCIPLINE** HISTORY **EDUCATION** Univ Mich, AB, 57; Univ Calif, MA, 58; PhD, 63. **CAREER** Vis Asst Prof, Univ Pittsburgh, 63-64; Asst Prof, Univ Colo, 64-66; Asst Prof to Assoc Prof, Univ Wisc, 66-71; Vis Assoc Prof, Univ Pa, 69-70; Prof, Rutgers Univ, 71-. **HONORS AND AWARDS** Phi Beta Kappa, 58; Rutgers Fac Fel, 74; Sen Fel, Nat Endowment for the Humanities, 79; Excellence in Research, Rutgers Board of Trustees, 83; Who's Who in America. **MEMBERSHIPS** Am Historical Asn, The Historical Soc. **RESEARCH** 20th Century US. **SELECTED PUBLICATIONS** Auth, The Last romantic: a Life of Max Eastman, Oxford Univ Press, 78; auth, A Better World: The Great Schism: Stalinism and the American Intellectuals, Simon & Schuster, 82; auth, American High: The Years of Confidence, 1945-1960, The Free press, 86; auth, A Democracy at War: America's Fight at Home and Abroad in World War II, The Free Press, 93; auth, The Progressive Years: America Comes of Age, Dodd, Mead, 75; co-auth, Looking Backward: A Reintroduction to American History, McGraw-Hill, 74; co-auth, America Rediscovered, Houghton, 76; auth, World War II: A Student Companion, Oxford Univ Press, 99. **CONTACT ADDRESS** Dept History, Rutgers, The State Univ of New Jersey, New Brunswick, 16 Seminary Pl, New Brunswick, NJ 08901-1108. **EMAIL** wlohp@aol.com

O'SHAUGHNESSY, ANDREW J.
DISCIPLINE HISTORY **EDUCATION** Oxford Univ, BA, 82, MA, 87, DPhil, 88. **CAREER** Lect, Lincoln Coll, Oxford; ASST PROF, UNIV OF WIS-OSHKOSH. **MEMBERSHIPS** Am Antiquarian Soc **RESEARCH** British West Indies and the Am Revolution **SELECTED PUBLICATIONS** Coauth, "Accounting for Slaves in the British West Indies," Accounting Hist Rev; sub-ed, History Sixth. **CONTACT ADDRESS** 207 E Irving Ave., No. 203, Oshkosh, WI 54901.

OAKLEY, FRANCIS CHRISTOPHER
PERSONAL Born 10/06/1931, Liverpool, England, m, 1958, 4 children **DISCIPLINE** MEDIEVAL & RENAISSANCE HISTORY **EDUCATION** Oxford Univ, BA, 53; MA, 57; Yale Univ, MA, 58; PhD, 60. **CAREER** Instr, Yale Univ, 59-61; from lectr to prof, Williams Col, 61-; Edward Dorr Griffin Prof of the Hist of Ideas, Williams Col, 84-85, 94-; Sir Isaiah Berlin Vis Prof, Oxford Univ, 99; Dean Fac, Williams Col, 77-84; Pres, Williams Col, 85-94, pres emer, 94-. **HONORS AND AWARDS** Fel, Medieval Acad Am, 86; Hon Fel, Corpus Christi Col, Oxford, 91; Guest Scholar, Woodrow Wilson Int Center for Scholars, 94; Wilbur Lucius Cross Medal, Yale Univ Grad School Alumni Asn, 97; Fel, Am Acad Arts Sci, 98. **MEMBERSHIPS** Am Cath Hist Asn; Mediaeval Acad Am; Am Church Hist Soc; Am Hist Asn. **RESEARCH** Medieval political theory, conciliar studies, late medieval legal theory. **SELECTED PUBLICATIONS** Auth, The Political Thought of Pierre d' Ailly: The Voluntarist Tradition, Yale Univ Press, 64; coauth, Creation: The Impact of an Idea, Charles Scribner's Sons, 69; auth, Council over Pope? Towards a Provisional Ecclesiology, Herder and Herder, 69; auth, The Medieval Experience: Foundations of Western Cultural Singularity, Charles Scribner's Sons, 74; auth, The Western Church in the Later Middle Ages, Cornell Univ Press, 79; auth, Natural Law, Conciliarism, and Consent in the Late Middle Ages, Variorum, 84; auth, Omnipotence, Covenant, and Order: An Excursion in the History of Ideas from Abelard to Leibniz, Cornell Univ Press, 84; auth, Community of Learning: The American College and the Liberal Arts Tradition, Oxford Univ Press, 92; auth, Politics and Eternity: Studies in the History of Medieval and Early Modern Political Thought, E.J. Brill, 99. **CONTACT ADDRESS** Dept of Hist, Williams Col, 880 Main St, Williamstown, MA 01267-2600. **EMAIL** francis.c.oakley@williams.edu

OAKLEY, JOHN H.
PERSONAL m, 2 children **DISCIPLINE** CLASSICAL ART & ARCHAEOLOGY **EDUCATION** Rutgers Univ, BA, 72, MA, 76, PhD, 80. **CAREER** Asst prof, 80-86, assoc prof, 86-93, Col Wm & Mary; PROF, CHANCELLOR, COL WM & MARY, 93-; Forrest D. Murden , Jr. Prof, 00-; vis prof, Univ Canterbury, Christchurch, New Zealand, 97; Elizabeth G. WHitehead vis prof, Am Sch Class Stud, Athens, 97-98. **CONTACT ADDRESS** Dept of Class Stud, Col of William and Mary, Williamsburg, VA 23187. **EMAIL** jxoakl@wm.edu

OATES, JOHN FRANCIS
PERSONAL Born 08/07/1934, Holyoke, MA, m, 1957, 4 children **DISCIPLINE** ANCIENT HISTORY **EDUCATION** Yale Univ, BA, 56, MA, 58, PhD(Classics, Ancient Hist), 60. **CAREER** From instr to asst prof Classics, Yale Univ, 60-67; assoc prof Ancient Hist, 67-71, chmn Dept Class Studies, 71-80, prof Ancient Hist, Duke Univ, 71-, Morse fel, 65-66; hon res asst Greek, Univ Col, Univ London, 65-66; mem Managing Comt, Intercollegiate Ctr, Rome, 72-76 & Am Sch Class Studies, Athens, 73-; Am Coun Learned Socs fel, 73-74; mem Adv Coun, Sch Class Studies, Am Acad in Rome, 76-; member, NC Humanities Coun, 77-83; vpres & trustee, Triangle Univs Ctr for Advan Studies, Inc, 76-90; member, NC Humanities Counc, 77-83; trustee, Nat Humanities Ctr, 77-90; ch, 80-82; dir, Duke Data Bank of Documentary Papyri, 82-; dir, Nat Fedn State Humanities Coun, 80-83; dir Duke Papyrus Archive 92. **MEMBERSHIPS** Archaeol Inst Am; AHA; Class Asn MidW & South; Am Soc Papyrologists (pres, 75-); Am Philol Asn. **RESEARCH** Ancient hist; papyrology. **SELECTED PUBLICATIONS** Auth, The Status Designation, Yale Classical Studies 18, 63; auth, Yale Papyri in the Beinecke Library, Vol I, 67; auth, The Ptolemaic Basilikos Grammateus, 95; auth, Checklist of Greek, Latin, Demotic and Coptic Papyri, Ostraca and Tablets, 5th edition, 01. **CONTACT ADDRESS** Dept of Classical Studies, Duke Univ, Box 90103, Durham, NC 27708-0103. **EMAIL** joates@duke.edu

OBER, JOSIAH
PERSONAL Born 02/27/1953, Brunswick, ME, m, 1986 **DISCIPLINE** HISTORY **EDUCATION** Univ Minn, BA, 75; Univ Mich, PhD, 80. **CAREER** Asst Prof to full Prof Hist, 80-90, Montana State Univ; Prof of Classics 90-, dept Chmn Classics 93-, Princeton Univ. **HONORS AND AWARDS** APA Goodwin Awd of Merit, Guggenheim Fel, Martin Lect Oberlin Coll. **MEMBERSHIPS** APA **RESEARCH** Greek history, political theory, comparative democracy. **SELECTED PUBLICATIONS** Auth, Fortress Attica: Defense of the Athenian Land Frontier, E.J. Brill, 85; auth, Mass and Elite in Democratic Athens, Princeton Univ Press, 89; The Athenian Revolution, Essays on Ancient Greek Democracy and Political Theory, Princeton Univ Press, 96; Political Dissent in Democratic Athens, Intellectual Critics of Popular Rule, Princeton Univ Press, 98; Co-ed, The Craft of the Ancient Historian, Essays in Honor of Chester G Starr, Univ Press of Amer, Lanham MD, 85; co-ed, The Birth of Democracy, Amer School of Classical Stud, Princeton, 93; co-ed, Athenian Political Thought and the Reconstruction of American Democracy, Cornell Univ Press Ithaca, 94; co-ed, Demokratia, A Conversation on Democracies Ancient and Modern, Princeton Univ Press Princeton, 96. **CONTACT ADDRESS** Dept of Classics, Princeton Univ, 104 Pyne, Princeton, NJ 08544. **EMAIL** jober@princeton.edu

OBERDECK, KATHRYN J.
DISCIPLINE HISTORY **EDUCATION** Univ of Calif, BA, 81; Yale Univ, MA, 87; PhD, 91. **CAREER** Asst prof, Univ Ill Urbana Champaign, 93-; asst porf, Univ of Mich, 91-93, 94-95. **HONORS AND AWARDS** Phi Beta Kappa, 81; Whiting Fel in the Humanities, 88-89; NEH Fel, 97. **MEMBERSHIPS** Am Hist Asn; Am Studies Asn; Organization of Am Historians. **RESEARCH** American cultural and intellectual history popular culture; cultural criticism. **SELECTED PUBLICATIONS** Auth, 'Not Pink Teas': The Working-Class Women's Movement in Seattle, 1905-1918, Labor Hist, 91; Religion, Culture, and the Politics of Class: Alexander Irvine's Mission to Turn-of-the-Century New Haven, Am Quarterly, 95; auth, "Contested Cultures of American Refinement: Theatrical Manager Sylvester Poli, His Audiences, and the Vaudeville Industry, 1890-1920," Radical History Review 66, (96): 40-91; auth, Movie

Audience," "Atomic Age," "Suburbs," "TV," "Counterculture," Imagining the Twentieth Century, Univ of Illinois Press, 97; auth, "Popular Narrative and Working Class Identity: Alexander Irvine''s Early-Twentieth Century Literary Adventures," Univ of Illinois Press, 98. **CONTACT ADDRESS** History Dept, Univ of Illinois, Urbana-Champaign, 52 E Gregory Dr, Champaign, IL 61820. **EMAIL** k-oberd@uiuc.edu

OBERLY, JAMES W.
PERSONAL Born 03/05/1954, Chicago, IL, m, 1980, 3 children **DISCIPLINE** HISTORY **EDUCATION** columbia Univ, BA, 75; Univ Rochester, MA, 76; PhD, 83. **CAREER** Prof, Ulster County Cmty col, 79-81; prof, Col of William and Mary, 81-83; prof, Univ Wisc, 83-. **HONORS AND AWARDS** Univ Wisc system Excellence in Teaching Awd, 97. **MEMBERSHIPS** Ec Hist Asn, Am Hist Asn, Org of Am Historians, Soc Sci Hist Asn, M-NET, Agric Hist Soc, Ethrohistory Soc, State Hist Soc of Wisc, Minn Hist Soc. **RESEARCH** Great Lakes Region history, American Indian history, public lands and natural resources history, rural history. **SELECTED PUBLICATIONS** Auth, Sixty Million Acres: American Veterans and the Public Lands before the Civil War, 90; auth, United States History: A Critical bibliography, 97. **CONTACT ADDRESS** Dept History, Univ of Wisconsin, Eau Claire, PO Box 4004, Eau Claire, WI 54702-4004. **EMAIL** joberly@uwec.edu

OCHSNER, JEFFREY KARL
PERSONAL Born 08/25/1950, Milwaukee, WI, m, 1979 **DISCIPLINE** ARCHITECTURE **EDUCATION** Rice Univ, BA, 73, MArch, 76. **CAREER** Instr, part-time, School of Archit, Rice Univ, 80-86; owner, Ochsner Assoc, 84-87; from lectr, asst prof, assoc prof, Dept of Archit, Univ Washington, 88- , chemn dept, 96- . **HONORS AND AWARDS** Am Inst Archit fel, 96; Lionel Pries Tchg Awd, 90, 92. **MEMBERSHIPS** AIA; Soc of Archit Hist; Col Art Asn; Vernacular Archit Forum; Nat Trust for Hist Preservation; Congress for the New Urbanism. **RESEARCH** H.H. Richardson; nineteenth and twentieth century American architecture; Pacific Northwest architecture; urban design; preservation. **SELECTED PUBLICATIONS** Auth, H.H. Richardson: Complete Architectural Works, MIT, 82; ed and coauth, Shaping Seattle Architecture: A Historical Guide to the Architects, Univ Washington, 94; auth, Understanding the Holocaust through the United States Holocaust Memorial Museum, J of Archit Educ, 95; auth, In Search of Regional Expression: The Washington State Building at the World's Columbian Exposition, Chicago, 1893, Pacific NW Q, 95; auth, Willis A Ritchie and Public Architecture in Washington, 1889-1905, Pacific NW Q, 96; auth, Henry Hobson Richardson, in Dictionary of Art, Grove, 96; auth, A Space of Loss: The Vietnam Veterans Memorial, J of Archit Educ, 97. **CONTACT ADDRESS** Dept of Architecture, Univ of Washington, PO Box 355720, Seattle, WA 98195-5720. **EMAIL** jochsner@u.washington.edu

ODELL, GEORGE H.
PERSONAL Born 04/17/1942, Minneapolis, MN, m, 1975 **DISCIPLINE** ARCHEOLOGY **EDUCATION** Yale Univ, BA, 64; MA, 65; Harvard Univ, PhD, 77. **CAREER** Vis asst prof, Univ Br Columbia, 77-78; vis asst prof, Brown Univ, 78-79; director, Lithic Analysis Laboratory Center for Am Archeol, 79-84; prof, Univ Tulsa, 84-. **HONORS AND AWARDS** Citation of Merit for Preservation of Oklahoma's Heritage, 92; Robert E Bell Awd for distinguished service to OK archeology, 99. **RESEARCH** Archaeology, Midcontinental N Am, Lithic analysis, Lithic use-weat analysis. **SELECTED PUBLICATIONS** Ed, Stone Tools: Theoretical Insights into Human Prehistory, New York: Plenum Press, 96; auth, Stone Tools and Mobility in the Illinois valley: from Hunting-Gathering Camps to Agricultural Villages, Ann Arbor, 96; auth, "The Role of Stone Bladelets in Middle Woodland Society,: American Antiquity (94): 102-120; auth, "Prehistoric Hafting and Mobility in the North American Midcontinent: Examples from Illinois," Journal of Anthropological Archaeology, (94): 51-73; auth, "Atomic Absorption Spectrophotometry Analysis of Ceramic Artifacts from a Protohistoric Site in Oklahoma," Journal of Archaeological Science, (94): 343-358; auth, "Assessing Hunter-Gatherer Mobility in the Illinois Valley: Exploring Ambiguous Results," in The Organization of North American Prehistoric Chipped Stone Tool Technologies, (94): 70-86; auth, "Is Anybody Listening to the Russians," Lithic Technology, (95): 40-52; auth, "Economizing Behavior and the Concept of Curation," Stone Tools, (96): 51-80; auth, "Investigating Correlates of Sedentism and Domestication in Prehistoric North America," American Antiquity, (98): 553-571. **CONTACT ADDRESS** Dept Anthropol, Univ of Tulsa, 600 S Col, Tulsa, OK 74104. **EMAIL** george-odell@utulsa.edu

ODEM, MARY E.
DISCIPLINE HISTORY **EDUCATION** Wash Univ, BA, 80; Univ Calif Berkeley, MA, 84, PhD, 89. **CAREER** Assoc prof hist dept/Inst Women's Studies. **HONORS AND AWARDS** Pres Bk Awd, Soc Sci Hist Assn. **RESEARCH** US social history; women's history; history of sexuality; Progressive-era history; multi-cultural approaches to history and women's studies. **SELECTED PUBLICATIONS** Auth, Delinquent Daughters: Protecting and Policing Adolescent Female Sexuality in the United States, 1885-1920; ed, Confronting Rape and Sexual Assault. **CONTACT ADDRESS** Dept History, Emory Univ, 221 Bowden Hall, 561 Kilgo Cir, Atlanta, GA 30322-1950. **EMAIL** modem@emory.edu

ODOM, EDWIN DALE
PERSONAL Born 07/10/1929, Sanger, TX, m, 1949, 3 children **DISCIPLINE** UNITED STATES HISTORY **EDUCATION** NTex State Col, BA, 55, MA, 56; Tulane Univ, PhD(hist), 61. **CAREER** Instr hist, NTex State Col, 55-56; instr econ hist, Victoria Col, Tex, 56-57; instr hist, Tulane Univ, 57-59; from instr to asst prof, 59-64, Assoc Prof Hist, N Tex State Univ, 64-00. **MEMBERSHIPS** Southern Hist Asn; Econ Hist Asn; Agr Hist Soc. **RESEARCH** Local history; agricultural history since 1865; 20th century United States dairy industry. **SELECTED PUBLICATIONS** Auth, The Vicksburg, Shreveport and Texas: The Fortunes of a Scalawag Railroad, Southwestern Soc Sci Quart, 63; coauth, A Brief History of Denton County, Texas, Denton County Hist Comn, 75; auth, "Associated Milk Producers, Inc: Testing the Limits of Copper-Volsteal," Agricultural Hist, vol. 59, 85; Texas Through Time - Evolving Interpretations - Buenger,wl, Calvert,ra, Southwestern Historical Quarterly, Vol 0096, 1993; auth, An Illustrated Hist of Denton County From Peter Colony to Metroplex, 96. **CONTACT ADDRESS** 420 Headlee Lane, Denton, TX 76201. **EMAIL** dodom@unt.edu

OESTREICHER, RICHARD JULES
PERSONAL Born 08/09/1947, Morristown, NJ, m, 1972, 2 children **DISCIPLINE** AMERICAN HISTORY **EDUCATION** Mich State Univ, BA, 69, MA, 73, PhD, 79. **CAREER** Instr social sci, 76-77, asst prof, 79-80, Mich State Univ, 76-80; instr hist, Ariz State Univ, 77-79; asst prof history, 80-84, assoc prof history, Univ Pittsburgh, 84- ; Am Counc Learned Soc Fel, 81; **HONORS AND AWARDS** Arizona Hum Coun Grant, 78-79; Fac Arts Sci Summer Res Grant Univ Pittsburgh, 81, 84, & 89; Res Develop Grant, 87; Brinkley-Stephenson Awd, 89. **MEMBERSHIPS** Orgn Am Historians. **RESEARCH** United States working class history; comparative labor history; photographic history. **SELECTED PUBLICATIONS** Auth Labor: the Jacksonian Era through Reconstruction, Encycl Am Soc Hist, Charles Scribner's Sons, 93; The Counted and the Uncounted: The Occupational Structure of Early Am Cities, Jour Soc Hist, 94; The Two Souls of American Democracy, The Social Construction of Democracy, 1870-1990, NY Univ Press, 95; The Spirit of "92: Popular Opposition in Homestead's Politics and Culture, 1892-1937, Pittsburgh Surv Revisited, 96. **CONTACT ADDRESS** History Dept, Univ of Pittsburgh, 3p38 Forbes Quad, Pittsburgh, PA 15260-0001.

OGDEN, ESTRELLA V.
PERSONAL Born Havana, Cuba, m, 1 child **DISCIPLINE** SPANISH, LATIN AMERICAN STUDIES **EDUCATION** Univ Havana, Universidad de la Habana, Doctor in law, 61; Temple Univ, Philadelphia, PA, PhD, 80. **CAREER** Prof of Spanish, Latin American Studies. **HONORS AND AWARDS** Pennsylvania Humanities Council; Phi Kappa Phi National Honor Society 89-; International Honor Society; Latin Am Guild for Arts. **MEMBERSHIPS** Modern Language Assoc (MLA); Association International de Hispanistas (ILCH); Instituto Literario y cultural Hispanics (ILCH); Northeast modern Language (NEMLA). **RESEARCH** Latin Amer Poetry; Relationship between Literature & Art. **SELECTED PUBLICATIONS** Auth, "El creacionismo de Vicente Huidobro en sus relaciones con la estetica cubista, Madrid, Playor, 83; auth, "El juego en el teatro de Carlos Fuentes," Literatura Mexicana/ Mexican Literature, ed. Jose Miguel Oviedo, Philadelphia, University of Pennsylvania Press, 94; auth, "La Ruta del Tajo en El rio que nos lleva," Camineria Hispanica, Madrid, Ediciones AACHE, 96; auth, "Borges en la poesia de Gonzalo Rojas: Aleph, Aleph," Alba de America, 00; auth, "An interview with Gonzalo Rojas," Hispanic Literary Criticism Supplement, ed. Susan Sales, The Gale Group, 99. **CONTACT ADDRESS** Dept Modern Languages, Villanova Univ, 800 East Lancaster Ave, Villanova, PA 19085-1603. **EMAIL** estrella.ogden@villanova.edu

OGGINS, ROBIN S.
PERSONAL Born 10/30/1931, Paris, France, m, 1956, 3 children **DISCIPLINE** HISTORY **EDUCATION** Univ Chicago, BA; 52; MA, 59; PhD 67. **CAREER** Binghamton Univ, instr, 62-67; asst prof, 67-74; assoc prof, 74-. **HONORS AND AWARDS** Chancel Awd, Excel Teach, 75-76; Fel RHS, 90. **MEMBERSHIPS** RHS; MA; Haskins Soc; London Top Soc. **RESEARCH** Medieval English Falconry; medieval English social history; medieval bibliography. **SELECTED PUBLICATIONS** Auth, "Falconry and Medieval Social Status," Mediaevalia: A Special Volume in Honor of Aldo S. Bernardo 12 (89): 43-55; auth, "Richard of IlchesterÛs Inheritance: An Extended Family in Twelfth-Century England," Medieval Prosopography 12 (91): 57-122; auth, "Falconry and Medieval Views of Nature," in The Medieval World of Nature, ed. Joyce E Salisbury (NY, Garland Press, 93): 47-60; auth, Castles and Fortresses, Michael Friedman Pub Group (NY), 94; auth, Cathedrals, MetroBooks (NY), 96; auth, "A Select Bibliography of Bibliographies and Other Materials for Use in Medieval Studies," Mediaevalia (in press); Articles on "Falconry" and "Wardrobe" for Medieval England: An Encyclopedia, Garland Press (NY), 98. **CONTACT ADDRESS** Dept History, SUNY, Binghamton, PO Box 6000, Binghamton, NY 13902-6000. **EMAIL** roggins@binghamton.edu

OGILVIE, LEON PARKER
PERSONAL Born 10/28/1931, Kansas City, MO, 2 children **DISCIPLINE** AMERICAN HISTORY **EDUCATION** Cent Mo State Col, BS, 53; La State Univ, MA, 56; Univ Mo, Columbia, PhD(hist), 67. **CAREER** Instr hist, Metrop Jr Col, 62-67; asst prof, Cent Mo State Col, 67-69; assoc prof, Nicholls State Univ, 69-70; instr hist, Penn Valley Community Col, 70-81; chm, Soc Sci Dept, Maplewoods Community Col, 82-00, Chm, Comt V on Jr & Community Cols, AAUP, 79-82. **HONORS AND AWARDS** Governor's Awd for Excellence in Teaching, 98. **MEMBERSHIPS** AHA; Orgn Am Historians; Southern Hist Asn; AAUP. **RESEARCH** American South; Missouri history; recent American history. **SELECTED PUBLICATIONS** Auth, Governmental efforts of reclamation in the southeast Missouri lowlands, 1/70 & Populism and socialism in the southeast Missouri lowlands, 1/70 & Populism and socialism in the southeast Missouri lowlands, 1/70, Mo Hist Rev; contrib, biographical sketches, Dictionary of Missouri Biography, 99. **CONTACT ADDRESS** Soc Sci Dept, Maple Woods Comm Col, 2601 NE Barry Rd, Kansas City, MO 64156-1254.

OGLESBY, RICHARD E.
PERSONAL Born 03/27/1931, Waukegan, IL, m, 1957, 1 child **DISCIPLINE** AMERICAN HISTORY **EDUCATION** Northwestern Univ, BS, 53, MA, 57, PhD(hist), 62. **CAREER** Asst prof hist, Eastern Ill Univ, 61-65; chmn dept, 73-76, asst prof, 65-80, Prof Hist, Univ Calif, Santa Barbara, 80-. **MEMBERSHIPS** Western Hist Asn; Orgn Am Historians. **RESEARCH** American western history; California history. **SELECTED PUBLICATIONS CONTACT ADDRESS** Dept of Hist, Univ of California, Santa Barbara, Santa Barbara, CA 93106.

OGORZALY, MICHAEL
PERSONAL Born 07/30/1948, Chicago, IL, m, 1995 **DISCIPLINE** HISTORY **EDUCATION** Chicago State Univ, BA, 75; MA, 78; Notre Dame, MA, 80; PhD, 83. **CAREER** From instr to assoc prof, Chicago State Univ, 89-. **HONORS AND AWARDS** Fac Excellence Awd, Chicago State Univ, 95 & 97. **MEMBERSHIPS** Midwest Asn for Latin Am Studies **RESEARCH** The movement to end the so-called sport of bullfighting. **SELECTED PUBLICATIONS** Auth, Waldo Frank: Prophet of Hispanic Regeneration, Bucknell Univ Press (Lewisburg, PA), 94. **CONTACT ADDRESS** Dept Hist & Govt, Chicago State Univ, 9501 S King Dr, Chicago, IL 60628-1501.

OGREN, KATHY J.
PERSONAL Born 07/12/1955, Denver, CO, m, 1999 **DISCIPLINE** HISTORY **EDUCATION** Scripps Col, BA, 77; Johns Hopkins Univ, PhD, 86. **CAREER** Prof and Dir, Johnston Center for Integrative Studies, Redlands Univ. **HONORS AND AWARDS** Outstanding Tchg Awd, 96; Outstanding Res Awd, 90; Graves Foundation Res Awd, 92. **RESEARCH** Late 19th and 20th century social and cultural history of US. **SELECTED PUBLICATIONS** Auth, The Jazz Revolution: Twenties America and the Meaning of Jazz, Oxford, 89; Coming Full Circle in the Land of Northern Mysteries, Dry Crik Rev, 94; Debating With Beethoven: Understanding the Fear of Early Jazz, Greenwood, 92; What Is Africa To Me? African Strategies in the Harlem Renaissance, Verso, 94; Jazz Isn't Just Me: Jazz Autobiographies as Performance Personas, Wayne State Univ, 91. **CONTACT ADDRESS** Johnston Center, Univ of Redlands, 1200 E Colton Ave, Box 3090, Redlands, CA 92373-0999. **EMAIL** ogren@uor.edu

OHLINE, HOWARD ALBERT
PERSONAL Born 08/13/1936, St. Louis, MO, m, 1961, 3 children **DISCIPLINE** EARLY AMERICAN HISTORY **EDUCATION** Grinnell Col, AB, 58; Univ Mo, MA, 61, PhD(hist), 69. **CAREER** Instr hist, Kansas City Mo Jr Col, 61-63; asst prof, 66-80, Assoc Prof Hist, Temple Univ, 80-. **MEMBERSHIPS** Orgn Am Historians; Southern Hist Asn; assoc Inst Early Am Hist & Cult. **RESEARCH** Slavery in early American politics. **SELECTED PUBLICATIONS** Auth, Republicanism and slavery: Origins of the three-fifths clause in the US Constitution, William & Mary Quart, 10/71; Georgetown, SC: Racial anxieties and militant behavior, 1802, SC Hist Mag, 7/72; Jefferson and slavery, Forum Press Ser Am Hist, 75; Slavery, economics, and congressional politics, 1790, J Southern Hist, 8/80. **CONTACT ADDRESS** Dept of Hist Soc Sci, Temple Univ, 1114 W Berks St, Philadelphia, PA 19122-6029.

OHNUMA, REIKO
PERSONAL Born 04/10/1963, New Haven, CT, m, 1993, 1 child **DISCIPLINE** ASIAN STUDIES, BUDDHIST STUDIES **EDUCATION** Univ Calif, Berkeley, BA, 86; Univ of Michigan, Ann Arbor, MA, 93; PhD, 97. **CAREER** Vis lectr, 96-98, Univ of TX, Austin; Asst Prof, 98-99, Univ of AL, Tuscaloosa; asst prof, Dartmouth Col. **HONORS AND AWARDS** Charlotte Newcombe Doctoral Dissertation Fellowship. **MEMBERSHIPS** Intl Assoc of Buddhist Stud; Amer Acad of Rel. **RESEARCH** Indian Buddhist Literature, especially narrative literature; Women and Literature; Hagiography. **SELECTED**

PUBLICATIONS Auth, The Gift of the Body and the Gift of Dharma, History of Religions, 98. **CONTACT ADDRESS** Dept of Religion, Dartmouth Col, Hanover, NH 03755. **EMAIL** reiko.ohuma@dartmouth.edu

OJALA, CARL F.
PERSONAL Born 10/05/1941, Fitchburg, MA, m, 1967, 2 children **DISCIPLINE** GEOGRAPHY **EDUCATION** Kent State Univ, BA, 65; Univ Ga, MA, 67; PhD, 72. **CAREER** Instr, Univ of Ga, 67-70; asst prof, Eastern Mich Univ, 70-75, assoc prof, 75-81, prof, 81-. **HONORS AND AWARDS** Distinguished Fac Sr Teaching Awd, Eastern Mich Univ, 88; Mich Asn of Governing Boards Distinguished Fac Awd, 89; Outstanding Teacher-Scholars Recognition Awd, Asn of Am Geographers, 95. **MEMBERSHIPS** Asn of Am Geographers, Gamma Theta Upsilon, East Lakes Div of the Asn of Am Geographers, Mich Acad of Sci, Phi Kappa Phi, Am Meteorological Soc, Nat Lightening Safety Group, Nat Weather Asn, Eastern Mich Univ Collegium for Advanced Studies. **RESEARCH** Weather (esp. Severe and Unusual Phenomena), Climate (esp. Climate Change). **SELECTED PUBLICATIONS** Coauth with M. Gadwood, "The Geography of Major League Baseball Player Production, 1876-1988," in Cooperstown Symposium on Baseball and American Culture, Meckler Pub Co, Westport, Ct (91); auth, "The Heat/Humidity Imbroglio: A Case Study of Michigan," Mich Academician, Vol 28, no 2 (spring 96): 47-54; auth, "The Human Factor in Recent Climate Change Remains Unproven," The Geographical Bull, Vol 39, no 2 (Nov 97): 67-69; coauth with S. Loduca, "Earth History on the Gridiron," J of Geosci Educ, Vol 46 (98): 55-60; coauth with W. Babcock, "The Heat/Humidity Quandary: A Case Study of New England," The Geographical Bull, Vol 40, no 1 (spring 98): 46-52; coauth with K. Sherman, "Some Causes for Lightening Data Inaccuracies: The Case of Michigan," Bull of the Am Meteorological Soc, Vol 80, No 9 (Sept 99): 1883-1891. **CONTACT ADDRESS** Dept Geography & Geology, Eastern Michigan Univ, 203 Strong Hall, Ypsilanti, MI 48197. **EMAIL** geo_ojala@online.emich.edu

OKENFUSS, MAX JOSEPH
PERSONAL Born 09/14/1938, Ste. Genevieve, MO, m, 1 child **DISCIPLINE** RUSSIAN HIST **EDUCATION** Univ Mo, BA, 63, MA, 64; Harvard Univ, PhD, 71. **CAREER** Asst prof, 70-77, assoc prof hist, Wash Univ, 77-. **HONORS AND AWARDS** NEH fel, 74; Delmas Found, 83; Fulbright, 89; NEH, 94. **MEMBERSHIPS** AHA; Hist Early Mod Europe; Am Assn Advan Slavic Studies; Cent Slavic Conf. **RESEARCH** History of education and social change in 18th century Russia. **SELECTED PUBLICATIONS** Art, The Ages of Man on the Muscovite Frontiers of Early-Modern Europe, The Historian, 93; auth, The Rise and Fall of Latin Humanism in Early-Modern Russia: Pagan Authors, Ukrainians, and the Resiliency of Muscovy Brill's Series in Intellectual History, Leiden/New York/Koln, 95; co-auth & ed, Reemerging Russia: Search for Identity, Simon and Schuster, 95. **CONTACT ADDRESS** Dept of History, Washington Univ, 1 Brookings Dr, Saint Louis, MO 63130-4899. **EMAIL** okenfuss@artsci.wustl.edu

OKIHIRO, GARY Y.
PERSONAL Born 10/14/1945, Aiea, HI, m, 1971, 2 children **DISCIPLINE** HISTORY **EDUCATION** Univ Calif, Los Angeles, PhD, 76. **CAREER** Asst Prof, Humboldt State Univ, 76-80; Assoc Prof, Santa Clara Univ, 80-89; Prof, Cornell Univ, 89-. **MEMBERSHIPS** Am Hist Asn; Org of Am Hist; Am Stud Asn; Asn for Asian-Am Stud. **RESEARCH** Asian Am; S Africa. **SELECTED PUBLICATIONS** Auth, Margins and mainstreams: Asians in American History and Culture, 94; auth, Whispered Silences: Japanese Americans and World War II, 97. **CONTACT ADDRESS** Center for the Study of Ethnicity and Race, Columbia Univ, New York, NY 10027. **EMAIL** gyo3@columbia.edu

OKIN, LOUIS A.
PERSONAL Born 04/27/1940, Detroit, MI, m, 1966, 1 child **DISCIPLINE** HISTORY **EDUCATION** UCLA, BA, 62, MA, 65, PhD, 74. **CAREER** Lect, Univ of the Pacific, 68-69; Asst Prof, 69-75, Assoc Prof, 75-82, Prof, 82-, Chmn History Humboldt Univ. **HONORS AND AWARDS** NEH Sum Sem, Archaic Greece, Havard Univ, 81; NEH Sum Sem, Classical Greece, Stanford Univ, 76. **MEMBERSHIPS** APA, Archaeological Inst of Amer, Amer Hist Assoc, Amer Res Center in Egypt. **RESEARCH** Greek Historiography, Hellenistic Greek History, Classical Greek History. **SELECTED PUBLICATIONS** Coauth & Coed, Panhellenica: Essays in Ancient History and Historiography in Honor of Truesdell S. Brown, Coronado Press, 80; art, Herodotus and Panyassis Ethnics in Duris of Samos, Class View, Echos du Monde Classique, 82; art, Theognis of Megara and the sources for the History of Archaic Megara, in: Theognis of Megara, Poetry and the Polis; John Hopkins Univ Press, 85; coauth or coeditorm Panhellenica: Essays. **CONTACT ADDRESS** Humboldt State Univ, Dept of History, 1 Harpst S, Arcata, CA 95521-8299. **EMAIL** lao2@humboldt.edu

OKOYE, IKEM
DISCIPLINE HISTORY OF ART IN WEST AFRICA, CARABBEAN, AMERICAN SOUTH **EDUCATION** Mass Inst Tech, PhD. **CAREER** Prof, Northwestern Univ; Rockefeller fel, Inst for Advan Study and Res; fel, Advan Study Center, Univ Michigan. **MEMBERSHIPS** Inst for Advan Study, Princeton Univ. **RESEARCH** Historical interrogation of modernity; gender theory; race theory; contemporary art historiography. **SELECTED PUBLICATIONS** Auth, Shamanic Penumbra: Houston Conwill's Art of Color; History, Aesthetics, and the Political in Igbo Spatial Heterotopias; Tribe and Art History. **CONTACT ADDRESS** Dept of Art History, Northwestern Univ, 1801 Hinman, Evanston, IL 60208.

OKUNOR, SHIAME
PERSONAL Born 06/02/1937, Accra, Ghana, m, 1994, 1 child **DISCIPLINE** AFRICAN-AMERICAN STUDIES, RELIGION, COMMUNICATION, EDUCATION **EDUCATION** New York Univ, Certificate 1968; Grahm Jr College, AAS 1971; The Univ of NM, BA Speech Communications 1973, MPA 1975, PhD 1981; Yale Divinity School, MDiv, 1995. **CAREER** The University of NM, Afro-Amer studies 1981-82, dir academic affairs Afro-Amer studies 1982-, acting dean univ coll 1985-86, dean general coll 1986-87, asst prof educ found, Acting Assoc Dean Graduate Studies 1988-89. **HONORS AND AWARDS** Outstanding Sr Awd 1971; Outstanding Intl Awd 1971; Pres Recognition Awd Univ of NM 1981-85; AP Appreciation Awd Albuquerque Public Schools 1981; Comm Serv Awd NAACP 1982; WM Civitan Merit Awd 1984; Black Communication Serv Awd 1984; Presidency Awd Schomburg Ctr New York City 1985-86; NM Sec of State Cert of Apprec 1985; NM Assoc of Bilingual Teachers Awd 1986; US Military Airlift Command Cert of Recognition 1987; Cert of Apprec US Corps of Engrs 1987; Yvonne Ochillo, Southern Conference on African American Studies, 1990; MLK Awd, 96. **MEMBERSHIPS** Mem exec bd NAACP 1975-86; mem Affirmative Action Policy Comm; bd of dirs, pres NM Sickle Cell 1981-91; secretary, treasurer, New Mexico Endowment for the Humanities, 1987-92; member, New Mexico Jazz Workshop, 1991-92. **SELECTED PUBLICATIONS** Auth, Politics, Misunderstanding, Misconceptions, History of Colonial Universities. **CONTACT ADDRESS** Director, African-American Studies, Univ of New Mexico, Albuquerque, 4025 Mesa Vista Hall, Albuquerque, NM 87131. **EMAIL** shiame@unm.edu

OLASKY, MARVIN N.
PERSONAL Born 06/12/1950, Malden, MA, m, 1976, 4 children **DISCIPLINE** JOURNALISM, HISTORY **EDUCATION** Yale Univ, BA, 71; Univ Mich, MA, 74; Univ Mich, PhD, 76. **CAREER** From Asst Prof to Prof, Univ Tex, 83-. **HONORS AND AWARDS** Progress and Freedom Sen Fel, Acton Inst. **MEMBERSHIPS** NAS, Am United for Life. **RESEARCH** Poverty-fighting, religion, Christian journalism. **SELECTED PUBLICATIONS** Auth, Prodigal Press, 88; auth, Central Ideas in the Development of American Journalism, 90; auth, The Tragedy of American Compassion, 92; auth, Abortion Rites, 92; auth, Fighting for Liberty and Virtue, 95; auth, Renewing American Compassion, 96; auth, The American Leadership Tradition, 99; auth, Compassionate Conservatism, 00. **CONTACT ADDRESS** Dept Jour & Hist, Univ of Texas, Austin, Austin, TX 78712-1013. **EMAIL** molasky@aol.com

OLDAKOWSKI, RAYMOND K.
PERSONAL Born 10/13/1960, NJ, s **DISCIPLINE** GEOGRAPHY **EDUCATION** Stetson Univ, BA, 80; Univ Fla, MA; 82; Univ Ill, PhD, 87. **CAREER** Proj Co-Ord, Univ Ill, 84-90; Assoc Prof, Jacksonville Univ, 90-. **MEMBERSHIPS** Asn of Am Geog; Am Asn for Pub Opinion Res. **CONTACT ADDRESS** Dept Soc Sci, Jacksonville Univ, 2800 Univ Blvd N, Jacksonville, FL 32211. **EMAIL** roldako@mail.ju.edu

OLDSON, WILLIAM O.
PERSONAL Born 01/23/1940, Hampton, VA, m, 1967, 2 children **DISCIPLINE** EAST EUROPEAN HISTORY **EDUCATION** Spring Hall Col, BA, 65; Ind Univ, Bloomington, MA, 66, PhD (hist), 70. **CAREER** Asst prof, 69-74, assoc chemn of undergraduate affairs, 73-75, 83-84, assoc chemn of graduate affairs, 94, assoc prof, 74-79, prof hist, Fla State Univ, 79-, dir, hist admin and public hist prog, 87-00, hist computer progs and res, 93-, dir, Inst on WWII & The Human Experience, 97-, Int Res & Exchanges Bd res fel, Romania, 73; chief negotiator, United Fac Fla, 80-81. **HONORS AND AWARDS** Rus and East Europ Inst Fel, Indiana Univ, 65-66; Nat Defense Foreign Lang Fel, Indiana Univ, 66-67; Flubright-Hays Fel, 67-68; Romanian State Fel, 67-68; Rus and East Europ Inst Grantee, 67-68; Int Res & Exchanges Board Fel, 73; FLA State Univ Found Travel Grantee, 82; Phi Alpha Theta Prof of the Year, 88; Comt on Faculty Res Support Grantee, 72-73, 90; John Frederick Louis Awd, 91; Holocaust Project Microfilming Grant, 93; Teaching Incentive Program Awd, 94; Coun on Res & Creativity Planning Grant, 94-95; Univ Teaching Awd, 88, 95; Louis E & Patrice J Wolfson Found Grant, 95; Holocaust Educ Foundation Grant, 94, 96; Wolfson Family Found Grant, 96; Int Res and Exchanges Board Short-Term Travel Grant, 96. **RESEARCH** Cultural and intellectual history, especially the Balkans; ethnicity and nationalism; Anti-Semitism; The Holocaust. **SELECTED PUBLICATIONS** Auth, Faculty Relations Before and After Collective Bargaining, Ctr Employ Rels & Law Rev, 81; The Enlightenment and the Romanian National Revival (Moldvia, Wallachia, Transylvania), Can Rev Studies in Nationalism, 82; The Boyars Golesti: The Impact of French Revolutionary Thought in Romania, Proceedings of the Consortium on Revolutionary Europ, 1750-1850, Inst on Napolean and the French Revolution, 90; Rationalizing Anti-Semitism: The Romanian Gambit, Proceedings of the Am Philos Soc, 25-30, 94; Background to Catastrophe: Romanian Modernization to policies and the Environment, East Europ Quart, 517-27, 97. **CONTACT ADDRESS** Dept of History, Florida State Univ, 481 Bellamy, Tallahassee, FL 32306-2200. **EMAIL** woldson@garnet.acns.fsu.edu

OLENIK, JOHN KENNETH
PERSONAL Born 05/07/1941, Cleveland, OH, m **DISCIPLINE** MODERN CHINESE HISTORY AND LITERATURE **EDUCATION** John Carroll Univ, BSS, 63; Seton Hall Univ, MA, 66; Cornell Univ, MA, 70, PhD(hist China), 73. **CAREER** Asst prof, 71-78, Assoc Prof Hist E Asia, Montclair State Col, 78-, Am Coun Learned SocNat Endowment for Humanities lang & res fel, Japan, 76-77; vis scholar, Fac Law, Keio Univ, Japan, 76-77. **MEMBERSHIPS** AHA; Asn Asian Studies. **RESEARCH** China, Repubican Period; China, political parties and movements; China, poetry of the Six Dynasties Period. **SELECTED PUBLICATIONS CONTACT ADDRESS** 1 Normal Ave, Montclair, NJ 07043-1699.

OLESON, JOHN P.
PERSONAL Born 11/24/1946, Hackensack, NJ, m, 1970, 2 children **DISCIPLINE** CLASSICAL ARCHAEOLOGY **EDUCATION** Harvard Univ, BA, 67, MA, 71, PhD, 73. **CAREER** Asst prof, Florida State Univ, 73-76; assoc prof, prof, Univ of Victoria, 76-. **HONORS AND AWARDS** Fel of Royal Soc of Can. **MEMBERSHIPS** Archaeol Inst of Am; Am Sch of Oriental Res; Am Ctr of Oriental Res. **RESEARCH** Ancient technology; underwater archaeology; Roman Near East. **SELECTED PUBLICATIONS** Auth, The Humeima Excavation Project, Jordan: Preliminary Report of the 1992 Season, Echos du Monde Classique/Class Views, 93; auth, Humeima Hydraulic Survey, 1989, in, Chronique Archeologique Jordanie, Syria, 93; auth, An Ancient Lead Sounding-Weight in the National Maritime Museum, Sefunim: Bull of the Nat Maritime Mus, Haifa, 94; coauth, The Harbours of Caesarea Maritima, vol 2: The Finds and the Ship, British Archaeological Reports, 94; auth, The Origins and Design of Nabataean Water-Supply Systems, in Studies in the History and Archaeology of Jordan, Amman, Dept of Antiquities, 95; coauth, The Origins, Early History, And Applications of the Pyoulkos (Syringe), in Argoud, ed, Science et Vie Intellectuelle a Alexandrie (Ier-IIIe siecle apres JC), Saint-Etienne, 95; auth, Water-Lifting Devices at Herculaneum and Pompeii in the Context of Roman Technology, Bull Antieke Beschaving, 96; coauth, Artifactual Evidence for the History of the Harbors of Caesarea, in Raban, ed, Caesarea Maritima: A Retrospective after Two Millennia, Brill, 96; coauth, Baths of the Hisma Desert, Balnearia, 97; coauth, Greek and Roman Technology: A Sourcebook, Routledge, 97; auth, Humeima, in Bikai, ed, Archaeology in Jordan, Am Jour of Archaeol, 97. **CONTACT ADDRESS** Dept of Greek and Roman Studies, Univ of Victoria, PO Box 3045, Victoria, BC, Canada V8W 3P4. **EMAIL** jpoleson@uvic.ca

OLIEN, DIANA DAVIDS
PERSONAL Born 02/24/1943, Oceanside, NY, m, 1970, 1 child **DISCIPLINE** HISTORY **EDUCATION** Swarthmore Col, BA, 64; Yale Univ, MA, 66; M Phil, 67; PhD, 69. **CAREER** Asst prof, Southern Meth Univ, 69-73; Sr lectr, Univ Tex of the Permian Basin, 86- . **HONORS AND AWARDS** High Honors, Phi Beta Kappa, Swarthmore Col; Life fellow, Texas State Historical Asn. **MEMBERSHIPS** Bus Hist Conf; Tex State Hist Asoc; West Tex Hist Soc; Permian Basin Hist soc. **RESEARCH** U.S. petroleum industry, especially Texas; women's history; British history. **SELECTED PUBLICATIONS** Co-auth with Roger M. Olien, Oil Booms: Social Change in Five Texas Towns, 82; auth, Morpeth: A Victorian Public Career, 83; coauth, with Roger M. Olien, Wildcatters: Texas Independent Oilmen, 84; coauth, with Roger M. Olien, Life in the Oil Fields, 86; coauth, with Roger M. Olien, Easy Money: Promoters and Investors in the Jazz Age, 90; coauth, with Roger M. Olien, Oil and Ideology: The Cultural Construction of the American Petroleum Industry. **CONTACT ADDRESS** Univ of Texas of the Permian Basin, 4901 E. University, Odessa, TX 79762.

OLIN, JOHN C.
PERSONAL Born 10/07/1915, Buffalo, NY, m, 1942, 4 children **DISCIPLINE** HISTORY **EDUCATION** Canisius Col, BA, 37; Fordham Univ, MA, 41; Columbia Univ, PhD, 60. **CAREER** From asst prof to assoc prof medieval & mod Europ hist, 46- 69, Prof Hist, Fordham Univ, 69-. **MEMBERSHIPS** Renaissance Soc Am; Am Cath Hist Asn; Amici Thomae Mori. **RESEARCH** Renaissance and Reformation; Erasmus. **SELECTED PUBLICATIONS CONTACT ADDRESS** Van Houten Fields, West Nyack, NY 10994.

OLIN, MARGARET
PERSONAL Born 03/01/1948, Chicago, IL, m, 1982, 2 children **DISCIPLINE** ART HISTORY **EDUCATION** Univ Chicago, MA, 77, PhD, 82. **CAREER** Assoc prof, Sch of the Art Inst of Chicago, 92-. **HONORS AND AWARDS** Fulbright fel; Am Coun of Learned Soc; Res Grant; Nat Endow for the Humanities fel; Getty Res Inst for the Hist of Art and the Humanities; Vis Scholar. **RESEARCH** Art Theory; Hist of Art His; Film and Photog. **SELECTED PUBLICATIONS** Pub(s) Forms of Representation in Alois Riegl's Theory of Art; auth, "Forms of Representation in Alois Riegl's Theory of Art," (Penn State Press, 92); auth, "The Gaze" (Critical Terms For Art History, 96; auth, "Lanzmann's Shoah and the Topography of the Holocaust Film" (Representations, 97); auth, "The Nation withoutt Art: A Study of Modern Discourses on "Jewish Art" (University of Nebraska Press, 01); **CONTACT ADDRESS** Dept of Art Hist, Sch of the Art Inst of Chicago, 112 S Michigan Ave., Chicago, IL 60603. **EMAIL** molin@artic.edu

OLIVA, L. JAY
PERSONAL Born 09/23/1933, Walden, NY, m, 1961, 2 children **DISCIPLINE** MODERN EUROPEAN HISTORY **EDUCATION** Manhattan Col, BA, 55; Syracuse Univ, MA, 57, PhD, 60. **CAREER** Res assoc intel, Res Inst, Syracuse Univ, 57-58 & 59-60; from instr to assoc prof, 60-69, actg dean, Univ Col Arts & Sci, 72-73, vpres acad affairs, 77-80, prof Rus Hist, 69-, provost & exec vp acad aff, 80-83, chancel and exec vp acad aff, 83-91, pres, NY Univ, 91. **HONORS AND AWARDS** Chevalier of the French Leg of Hon; Medal of the Sorbonne, Univ of Paris; Man in Educ Awd, Ital Welfare; Premio Guido Dorso of Italy, 98; hon degrees from Tel Aviv Univ, Univ Col Dublin, Hebrew Union Col, Saint Thomas Aquinas Col, & Manhattan Col. **MEMBERSHIPS** AAU; Campus Compact; Royal Inst of Int Aff; CICU; Coun of For Rels; Coun for US and Italy; Nat Col Ath Assn; NY St New Compact for Learn; NY St Comm on Nat and Comm Svc; UNA NY; UAA; ABNY; Irish Am Cult Inst; Institute of International Education. **RESEARCH** Eighteenth century Russia; Franco-Russian relations; continuity in Russo-Soviet history. **SELECTED PUBLICATIONS** Auth, Misalliance: A Study of French Policy in Russia During the Seven Years' War, NYU, 64; cotransl, A Medical Journey in California, Zeithlin and ver Brugge, 67; auth, Russia in the Era of Peter the Great, Prentice Hall, 69, rev ed, Holmes and Meier, 92; ed, Peter the Great, Prentice Hall, 70; ed, Catherine the Great, Prentice Hall, 71; auth, Maxim Gorky Discovers America, NY Hist Soc Qrt, 66; auth, The Dorming of New York City, NY Times, 89; auth, Do the Right Thing About Athletucsm AGB Reports, 89; auth, What Trustees Should Know About Intercollegoate Athletics, AGB Spec Rpt, 89; auth, Academic Affairs at New York University, University, 89; auth, NYU's Networking: Historically Black Colleges Make A Difference, 90; auth, Showdown in Dallas, AGB, 90; auth, Presidents' Ten Commandments, The Charoltte Observ, 91; aut, Big Time or Not, Reform Starts at Home, The Washington Post, 91. **CONTACT ADDRESS** New York Univ, New York, NY 10003. **EMAIL** df7@is2.nyu.edu

OLIVER, JOHN E.
PERSONAL Born 10/21/1933, Dover, KY, United Kingdom, m, 1987, 5 children **DISCIPLINE** GEOGRAPHY **EDUCATION** London Univ, Bsc, 59; Columbia Univ, MA, 66; PhD, 69. **CAREER** Asst to assoc prof, Columbia Univ, 69-73; assoc prof, Ind State Univ, 73-. **HONORS AND AWARDS** Lifetime Achievement Awd, Asn of Am Geogr, Climate Group. **MEMBERSHIPS** Am Met Soc, Asn Am Geogr, NCGE. **RESEARCH** Climate, Physical Geography **SELECTED PUBLICATIONS** Auth, Climate and Man's Environment, Wiley, 73; auth, Perspectives on Applied Physical Geography, Duxbury, 73; auth, Physical Geography: Principles and Application, Duxbury, 77; auth, Climatology, Selected Application, Duxbury, 81; auth, Climatology: An Introduction, Merrill, 82; auth, The Encyclopedia of Climatology, Van Nostrand Reinhold, 86; auth, Climatology: An Atmospheric Science, Macmillan, 92. **CONTACT ADDRESS** Dept Geog & Geol-Sci Bldg, Indiana State Univ, 210 N 7th St, Terre Haute, IN 47809-0002. **EMAIL** geoliv@scifac.indstate.edu

OLM, LEE ELMER
PERSONAL Born 07/17/1928, Appleton, WI, m, 1954, 1 child **DISCIPLINE** COLONIAL-REVOLUTIONARY AMERICAN HISTORY **EDUCATION** Western Mich Univ, BA, 52; Cornell Univ, MA, 53; Univ Mich, PhD, 60. **CAREER** Instr high sch, Mich, 53-55; from asst prof to assoc prof, 59-64, Prof Hist, Sam Houston State Univ, 64-, Chmn Dept, 76-88, Prof Emer, 88-. **MEMBERSHIPS** AHA; Inst Early Am Hist & Cult; Orgn Am Historians. **RESEARCH** Revolutionary and Colonial America; 18th century England. **SELECTED PUBLICATIONS** Auth, The Mutiny Act for America: New York's Noncompliance, NY Hist Soc Quart, 7/74. **CONTACT ADDRESS** Dept of Hist, Sam Houston State Univ, P O Box 2239, Huntsville, TX 77341-2239.

OLSEN, GLENN WARREN
PERSONAL Born 11/27/1938, Minneapolis, MN, m, 1966, 4 children **DISCIPLINE** MEDIEVAL HISTORY **EDUCATION** North Park Col, BA, 60; Univ Wis, MA, 62, PhD, 65. **CAREER** Asst prof hist, Seattle Univ, 65-66 & Fordham Univ, 66-69; assoc prof medieval hist & dir hon prog, Seattle Univ, 69-72; Assoc Prof 2nd Prof Medieval Hist, Univ Utah, 72-, Seattle Univ fac res grant, 65-66; adv ed, Cath Hist Rev, 71-00; Univ Utah fac res grant, 73; mem bd regents, St Mary's Col, Ind, 73-79. **HONORS AND AWARDS** Fulbright Grant, 63-65; D P Gardner fel, Univ Utah, 77-78; Inst for Ecumenical & Cult Res fel, 78-79; Am Coun Learned Soc grant, 79; NEH Grant, 90. **MEMBERSHIPS** Medieval Asn of Pac; Soc Ital Hist Studies; Mediaeval Acad Am; AHA; Am Cath Hist Asn. **RESEARCH** Medieval intellectual history, canon law and philosophy; medieval church and cultural history. **SELECTED PUBLICATIONS** Auth, The definition of the ecclesiastical benefice in the twelfth century: The canonists' discussion of spiritualis, Studia Gratiana, Vol 11, 67; The idea of the ecclesia primitiva in the writings of the twelfth century canonists, Traditio 25, 69; Italian merchants and the performance of papal banking functions in the early thirteenth century, Explor Econ Hist, 69- 70; contribr, The investiture contest, In: Religion in the making of western man, St John's Univ, 74; auth, Allegory, typology and symbol: The sensus spiritalis, Communio 4, 77; Reference to the ecclesia primitiva in Eighth Century Irish Gospel Exegesis, Thought, Vol 54, 79; St Boniface and the vita apostolica, Am Benediction Rev, Vol 31, 80; Hans Urs Von Balthasar and the rehabilitation of St Anselm's doctrine of the atonement, Scottish J Theol, Vol 34, 81; auth, Christian Marriage: A Historical Study, (NY), 01. **CONTACT ADDRESS** Dept of Hist, Univ of Utah, 380 S 1400 E Rm 211, Salt Lake City, UT 84112-0311.

OLSEN, P.
PERSONAL Born 09/29/1958, Chicago, IL, s **DISCIPLINE** HISTORY **EDUCATION** Univ Illinois, AB, 80; Penn State Univ, MA, 91; PhD, 98. **CAREER** Ill State Univ, 00-. **HONORS AND AWARDS** Lewis Hanks Awd; Phi Beta Kappa; James Landing Diss Fel. **MEMBERSHIPS** LAH; LASA. **RESEARCH** US Foreign Intelligence; contemporary Mexico. **SELECTED PUBLICATIONS** Coauth, The Journey of Civilization, West/Wadsworth, CD ROM, (98). **CONTACT ADDRESS** Dept History, Stephen F. Austin State Univ, 1936 North St, Nacogdoches, TX 75961. **EMAIL** polsen@sfau.edu

OLSON, ALISON GILBERT
PERSONAL Born 10/10/1931, Oakland, CA, m, 1959 **DISCIPLINE** MODERN HISTORY **EDUCATION** Univ Calif, Berkeley, BA, 52, MA, 53; Oxford Univ, DPhil, 56. **CAREER** From instr to asst prof hist, Smith Col, 57-60; lectr, asst prof, 63-67, Douglass Col; lectr, asst prof, 63-67, Rutgers Univ; assoc prof, Am Univ, 67-73; prof hist, univ MD, College Park, 73-. **HONORS AND AWARDS** Am Philos Soc grants, 60 & 67-68; fels, Am Coun Learned Soc, 60-61, Am Assn Univ Women, 61-62 & Folger Libr, 67Guggen Hum Fel, 83-94; Outstanding Teacher, 88; Distinguished Scholastic Teacher, 87-88; Distinguished Fac Fel, 91-92. **MEMBERSHIPS** Conf Brit Studies. **RESEARCH** English and American history in the 17th and 18th centuries. **SELECTED PUBLICATIONS** Auth, The Radical Duke: Career and Correspondence of Charles Lennox, Third Duke of Richmond, Oxford Univ, 61; co-ed, Anglo-American Political Relations, 1675-1775, Rutgers Univ, 70; auth, Anglo-American Politics, Oxford Univ, 73. **CONTACT ADDRESS** Dept of History, Univ of Maryland, Col Park, College Park, MD 20742-0001. **EMAIL** ao5@umail.umd.edu

OLSON, GARY DUANE
PERSONAL Born 07/30/1939, Spring Grove, MN, m, 1960, 3 children **DISCIPLINE** AMERICAN HISTORY **EDUCATION** Luther Col, Iowa, BA, 61; Univ Nebr, Lincoln, MA, 65, PhD(hist), 68. **CAREER** Instr high sch, Minn, 61-63; asst prof, 68-74, assoc prof, 74-79, prof hist, Augustana Col, S Dak, 79-, dean acad serv, 81-87, dean of the Col and Vice Pres, 87-95, ex dir, ctr western studies, Augustana Col, 71-74. **MEMBERSHIPS** Orgn Am Historians; SD Hist Society. **RESEARCH** Retain original entry and Sioux Falls. **SELECTED PUBLICATIONS** Auth, Relief for Nebraska grasshopper victims: The official journal of Lt Theo E True, Nebr Hist, summer 67; Loyalists and the American Revolution: Thomas Brown and the South Carolina backcountry (2 parts), 1775-1776, SC Hist Mag, 10/67 & 1/68; The Soderstrom incident: A reflection upon Federal-State relations under the Articles of Cofederation, NY Hist Soc Quart, 4/71; coauth, Prelude to Glory: A Newspaper Accounting of Custer's 1874 Expedition to the Black Hills, Brevet, 74; auth, David Ramsay Thomas Brown: Patriot historian & loyalist critic, SC Hist Mag, 10/76; Thomas Brown and the East Florida rangers, Proc Fourth Ann Fla Bicentennial Symp, 78; ed, Microfilm edition of the Richard F Pettigrew papers, Augustana Col, 78; The historical background of land settlement in eastern South Dakota, In: Big Sioux Pioneers, Sioux Falls, 80; Dakota Resources: The Richard F. Pettigrew Papers, So Dak Hist, summer/fall, 82; co-auth, Sioux Falls, South Dakota, A Pictorial History, 85. **CONTACT ADDRESS** Dept of Hist, Augustana Col, So Dakota, 2001 S Summit Ave, Sioux Falls, SD 57197-0002. **EMAIL** olsm@wise.augie.edu

OLSON, JAMES S.
PERSONAL Born 07/15/1946, Downey, CA, m, 1965, 4 children **DISCIPLINE** HISTORY **EDUCATION** Brigham Young Univ, BA; State Univ NYork-Stony Brook, PhD. **CAREER** Distinguished prof; dept ch, Sam Houston State Univ, 88-. **HONORS AND AWARDS** Recipient, Excellence in Tchg, Excellence in Res awd(s); Nat Bk awd, Popular Culture Asn. **RESEARCH** Recent America, Vietnam war, American immigration. **SELECTED PUBLICATIONS** Coauth, Ethnic Dimension in American History; Saving Capitalism: The Reconstruction Finance Corporation and the New Deal, 1933-1940; Catholic Immigrants in America; Winning is the Only Thing: Sports in America since 1945; Where the Domino Fell: America and Vietnam, 1945 to 1990; John Wayne: American; My Lai: A Documentary History, Bedford Books, 98; A line in the Sand: The Alamo in Blood and Memory, Free Press, 01. **CONTACT ADDRESS** Dept of History, Sam Houston State Univ, Huntsville, TX 77341. **EMAIL** his_jso@shsu.edu

OLSON, JEANNINE
PERSONAL Born 11/01/1939, Caledonia, MN, d, 3 children **DISCIPLINE** HISTORY **EDUCATION** St Olaf Col, BA; Stanford Univ, MA; PhD, 80. **CAREER** Asst Prof, Univ Minn 72-76; Asst Prof, San Francisco Theol Sem, 79-86; Prof, Rhode Island Col, 86-. **HONORS AND AWARDS** Travel grant, Am Coun of Learned Soc, 95; Grant, Am Philos Soc, 94-95; Grant, Am Acad of Relig, 91-92, 94; grant, Univ Geneva, 94; NEH, Inst on Islam, 96; Woodrow Wilson Fel. **MEMBERSHIPS** Calvin Studies Soc, Am Soc of church Hist Inst Liaison committee, Humanities forum of RI steering committee, Am Hist Asn, Am Acad of Relig, Am Soc for Reformation Res, Danforth Asn of N England, Pacific Coast Theol Soc, Committee on Theol Educ of the Presbyterian Church. **RESEARCH** Reformation Europe, Social welfare, Geneva, Deacons and Deaconesses. **SELECTED PUBLICATIONS** Auth, Deacons and Deaconesses Through the Centuries, Concordia Pub House, 92; auth, Calvin and Social Welfare: Deacons and the Bourse Francaise, Susquehanna Univ Press, 89; auth, Histoire de l'Eglise, Vingt siecles et six continents, Cameroun France, 72; auth, "The Crisis of the Advent of Catholicism in a Protestant State: Changing Structures in Social Welfare," in The Identity of Geneva: The Christian Commonwealth, 1564-1864, forthcoming; auth, 'Friends of Jean (John) Calvin: The Family Bude,": in Calvin et ses contemorains, Geneva, 97; auth, "Jean Crespin, Humanist printer among the reformation martyrologists," in The Harvest of Humanism in Central Europe: Essays in Honor of Lewis W. Spitz, Concordia Pub House, 92; auth, "Calvin as person," Concordia Journal, (91): 393-403; auth, "Worship in the Early Reformed Tradition in Church, Home and Field," Liturgy: Journal of the Liturgical Conference, (88): 43-51. **CONTACT ADDRESS** Dept Hist, Rhode island Col, 600 Mount Pleasant Ave, Providence, RI 02908-1924. **EMAIL** jolson@ric.edu

OLSON, KEITH WALDEMAR
PERSONAL Born 08/04/1931, Poughkeepsie, NY, m, 1955, 2 children **DISCIPLINE** AMERICAN HISTORY **EDUCATION** SUNY, Albany, BA, 57; MA, 59; Univ Wis,Madison, PhD, 64. **CAREER** From instr to asst prof, Syracuse Univ, 63-66; from asst prof to prof, Univ Md, Col Park, 66-. **HONORS AND AWARDS** Fulbright Prof, Finland, 86-87, 93-94; Hon PhD, Univ of Tampere, Finland, 00. **MEMBERSHIPS** AHA; Org Am Hist; Soc for Hist in Am For Relations; Wis State Hist Soc; Finnish Hist Soc; Ctr for the Study of the Pres. **RESEARCH** 20th century United States presidential history. **SELECTED PUBLICATIONS** Auth, The G.I. Bill, The Veterans, and The College, Lexington, 74; auth, Biography of a Progressive: Franklin K. Lane, 1864-1921, Westport, 79; auth, "Finland: Between East and West," The Wilson Quart 10 (86); auth, "Franklin D. Roosevelt, the Ghost of Woodrow Wilson, and World War II," in The Road to War, ed. Silvo Hietanen et al (Tampere, Finland, 93); auth, "Foreign Policy in Post-Consensus Multicultural Post-Cold War United States," in After Consensus, ed. Hans Lofgren and Alan Shima (Gothenburg, Sweden, 98); auth, "American Historians and the History of Finland Since 1939," in Charting an Independent Course: Finland's Place in the Cold War and U.S. Foreign Policy, ed. T. Michael Ruddy (Claremont, 98). **CONTACT ADDRESS** Dept of History, Univ of Maryland, Col Park, 2115 Francis Scott Key Hall, College Park, MD 20742-0001. **EMAIL** ko6@umail.umd.edu

OLSON, ROBERT W.
PERSONAL Born 12/14/1940, Devils Lake, ND, m, 1970, 2 children **DISCIPLINE** HISTORY **EDUCATION** Bemrdi State Col, BS, 58; Indiana Univ, MA, 67; PhD, 73. **CAREER** Asst prof to prof, Univ Ky. 73-. **HONORS AND AWARDS** Fulbright Res Fel, 90-91; Hallem Teaching Awd, Univ of Ky, 99-00. **MEMBERSHIPS** Middle East Studies Assoc; Turkish Studies Assoc; Kurdish Studies Assoc. **RESEARCH** History of Ottoman Empire, Kurds, Turkey, Syria. **SELECTED PUBLICATIONS** Auth, The Siege of Mosul and Ottoman-Persian Relations, 1718-1743: A Study of Rebellion in the Capital and War in the Provinces of the Ottoman Empire, Ind Univ Pr, 75; auth, The Ba'th in Syria, 1947-1979 (An Interpretative Historical Essay)", the Middle East Inst, Rome, 80; coed, Iran: Essays on a Revolution in the Making, Mazda Pr, (Lexington, Ky), 81; auth, The Ba'th in Syria, 1947-1982: The Evolution of Ideology, Party and State from the French Withdrawal to the Era of Hafiz al-Asad, Kingston Pr, (Princeton, NJ), 83; coed, Orientalism, Islam and Islamists, Amana Books, (Brattleboro, VT), 84; ed, The Kurdish Nationalist Movement in the 1990s: Its Impact on Turkey and the Middle East, Univ Pr of Ky, (Lexington,

KY), 86; ed, Islamic and Middle Eastern Societies, Amana Books (Brattleboro, VT), 87; auth, The Emergence of Kurdish Nationalism and the Sheikh Said Rebellion: 1880-1925, Univ of Tex Pr, 89; auth, Imperial Meanderings and Republican By-Ways: Essays on Eighteenth Century Ottoman History and Twentieth Century History of Turkey, Isis Pr, (Istanbul), 97; auth, The Kurdish Question and Turkish-Iranian Relations: From World War to 1998, Mazda Pr, (Costa Mesa, CA), 98. **CONTACT ADDRESS** Dept Hist, Univ of Kentucky, 500 S Limestone St, Lexington, Ky 40506-0001. **EMAIL** hisposta@pop.uky.edu

OLSON, ROGER E.

PERSONAL Born 02/02/1952, Des Moines, IA, m, 1973, 2 children **DISCIPLINE** CHRISTIAN HISTORICAL THEOLOGY **EDUCATION** Open Bible Col, BA, 74; North Amer Baptist Sem, MA, 78; Rice Univ, MA, 82, PhD, 84; Stud Univ of Munich, Germany, 81-82. **CAREER** Asst Prof, Theol, 82-84, Oral Robert Univ; Prof Theol, 84-99, Bethel Col & Sem; Ed, Christian Scholar's Review, 94-; prof, Truett Theol Sem, 99- . **HONORS AND AWARDS** Bethel Col Fac Schlrshp Awd; Gold Medallion, Evangelical Christian Pub Asn, 99. **MEMBERSHIPS** ATS, AAR. **RESEARCH** History of Christian Theology and Contemporary Christian Thought. **SELECTED PUBLICATIONS** Co-auth, 20th Century Theology: God and the World in a Transitional Age, InterVarsity Press, 92; Who Needs Theology? An Invitation to the Study of God, InterVarsity Press, 96; auth, The Story of Christian Theology, Twenty Centuries of Tradition and Reform, forthcoming, 99. **CONTACT ADDRESS** Truett Theol Sem, PO Box 97126, Waco, TX 76798. **EMAIL** olsrog@aol.com; roger_olson@baylor.edu

OLUGEBEFOLA, ADEMOLA

PERSONAL Born 10/02/1941, Charlotte Amalie, St Thomas, Virgin Islands of the United States, 8 children **DISCIPLINE** ART HISTORY **CAREER** Artist lectr works include hundreds of vibrant cover designs & illustrations for leading authors pub by Doubleday, Broadside, William Morrow, Harper & Row, Am Museum of Natrl History and others; has been in numerous major exhibitions over 30 yr period; had over 50 one man exhibitions; work is in collections throughout US, S Am, Africa, Caribbean; Gumbs & Thomas Publishers, vp, currently. **HONORS AND AWARDS** Won critical acclaim for innovative set designs for Lew Lafayette Theatre, NY Shakespeare Fest, Nat Black Theatre; design comm, NY Urban Coalition, 1990; design comm, Literary Assistance Ctr, 1989; design comm, Chase Bank, 1997; Banco Popular de Puerto Rico, 1996. **MEMBERSHIPS** Vice Pres, International Communications Association; co-chair-arts & Culture Committee, Greater Harlem Chamber of Commerce; chmn Educ Dept of Weusi Acad of Arts & Studies; served as consultant to Mtro Museum of Art, NY Urban Coalition and is co-dir of Grinnell Fine Art Collection **RESEARCH** African and American Art & Culture influence on art of the 20th Century, The evolution of African American crative production and its effect on American politics and popular culture of the 1960's, post moedernict thought and its correlations to African diasporan traditional and conteemporary artistic expression. **CONTACT ADDRESS** 800 Riverside Dr, #5E, New York, NY 10032.

OMMER, ROSEMARY

PERSONAL Born Glasgow, Scotland **DISCIPLINE** HISTORY **EDUCATION** Glasgow Univ, MA, 64; Memorial Univ, MA, 74; McGill Univ, PhD, 79. **CAREER** High sch tchr, Scotland, 65-66; McConnell fel, McGill Univ, 74; asst prof, 78-83, econ hist, 83-85, Prof Hist, Memorial Univ 85-. **MEMBERSHIPS** SSHRCC; Vanier Inst Family; Can Hist Found. **SELECTED PUBLICATIONS** Auth, From Outpost to Outport, 91; co-ed, Volumes Not Values, 79; co-ed, Working Men Who Got Wet, 80. **CONTACT ADDRESS** Dept of History, Mem Univ of Newfoundland, Saint John's, NF, Canada A1C 5S7. **EMAIL** iser@morgan.ucs,mun.ca

ONORATO, MICHAEL P.

PERSONAL Born 08/03/1934, New York, NY, m, 1962, 1 child **DISCIPLINE** SOUTHEAST ASIAN HISTORY **EDUCATION** St Peter's Col, BS, 56; Georgetown Univ, MA, 59, PhD(hist), 60. **CAREER** From instr to asst prof, SE Asian hist, Canisius Col, 60- 65; from asst prof to assoc prof, 65-70, Prof Hist, Calif State Univ, Fullerton, 70-, Vis prof, Ateneo de Manila Univ, 63-64; Am Philos Soc grant-in-aid, 64-65, 68-69 & 71-72; exec secy, Philippine Studies Coun, 72-75. **MEMBERSHIPS** Asn Asian Studies; Asn Asian Studies Pac Coast (chairperson, 77-78). **RESEARCH** Philippines; comparative imperial institutions in Southeast Asia. **SELECTED PUBLICATIONS** Auth, Leonard Wood and the Philippine Cabinet Crisis of 1923, Univ Manila, 67; Independence rejected: The Philippines, 1924, Philippine Studies, 67; Leonard Wood as Governor General: A Calendar of Selected Correspondence, MCS Enterprises, 68; The United States and Philippine Independence, A Reappraisal, Solidarity, 70; A Brief Review of American Interest in Philippine Development and Other Essays (rev ed), MCS Enterprises, 72; Manuel Luis Quezon and His Modus Operandi, Asian Forum, 73; ed, Origins of the Philippine Republic: Extracts From the Diaries and Records of Francis Burton Harrison, Cornell Univ, 74; auth, Francis Burton Harrison: Liberal proconsul: The Filipinazation of the Philippine Islands, Bull Am Hist Collection, 76; Veracruz,philip - a Personal History of Filipino Immigrants And The Farmworkers Movement - Scharlin,c, Villanueva,lv, Pacific Historical Review, Vol 0062, 1993; Bound to Empire - The United-states And The Philippines - Brands,hw, American Historical Review, Vol 0098, 1993; Battle For Batangas - a Philippine Province at War - May,ga, Pacific Historical Review, Vol 0062, 1993. **CONTACT ADDRESS** 1202 Northwind Circle, Bellingham, WA 98226. **EMAIL** pacrimbks@aol.com

ONUF, PETER S.

DISCIPLINE HISTORY **EDUCATION** Johns Hopkins, AB, 67, PhD, 73. **CAREER** Asst prof, hist, Worcester Polytechnic Inst; THOMAS JEFFERSON MEM FDN PROF, HIST, UNIV VA. **MEMBERSHIPS** Am Antiquarian Soc **SELECTED PUBLICATIONS** Auth, "From Constitution to Higher Law: The Reinterpretation of the Northwest Ordinance, Ohio Hist 94, 85; auth, "Liberty, Development, and Union: Visions of the West in the 1780's," Wm & Mary Quart 43, 86; coauth, "Toward a Republican Empire: Interest and Ideology in Revolutionary America," Am Quart 37, 85; auth, Statehood and Union: A History of the Northwest Ordinance, 87; auth, essays on land policy, territorial policy, and federalism, The Origins of the Federal Republic: Juris Contros. in the United States, 1775-1787, 87; coauth, The Midwestern Nation, 90; coauth, A Union of Interests: Politics and Economics in Revolutionary America, 90; coauth, Federal Union, Modern World: The Law of Nations in an Age of Revolutions, 1776-1814, Madison House, 93; ed, Jefferson Legacies, Univ Press Va, 93. **CONTACT ADDRESS** Dept of Hist, Univ of Virginia, Randall Hall, Charlottesville, VA 22903. **EMAIL** dude@virginia.edu

OPPENHEIM, JANET

PERSONAL Born 05/05/1948, New York, NY, m, 1971, 1 child **DISCIPLINE** BRITISH HISTORY **EDUCATION** Bryn Mawr Col, BA, 70; Columbia Univ, MA, 71, PhD(hist), 75. **CAREER** Instr hist, Mary Washington Col, Fredericksburg, 74-75; asst prof, 75-80, Assoc Prof Hist, Am Univ, Washington, DC, 80-, Vis asst prof hist, Princeton Univ, 79. **MEMBERSHIPS** AHA; Conf Brit Studies; Northeast Victorian Studies Asn. **RESEARCH** Modern British cultural and intellectual history. **SELECTED PUBLICATIONS** Auth, The Nationalization of Culture: The Development of State Subsidies to the Arts in Great Britain, Hamish Hamilton & NY Univ, 77. **CONTACT ADDRESS** Dept of Hist, American Univ, Washington, DC 20016.

OPPENHEIM, SAMUEL

PERSONAL Born 11/11/1940, New York, NY, m, 1965, 4 children **DISCIPLINE** RUSSIAN & MODERN EUROPEAN HISTORY **EDUCATION** Univ Ariz, BA, 62; Harvard Univ, AM, 64; Ind Univ, PhD (Russ & mod Europ hist), 72. **CAREER** Instr Russ & hist, Bishop Col, 64-67; pt time Instr Russ lang & hist, Austin Col, 65-67; asst prof, 71-74, assoc prof, 74-79, Prof Hist, Calif State Col, Stanislaus, 79-; coord of Regional Distance Learning, 95-01. **MEMBERSHIPS** AAUP; Am Asn Advan Slavic Studies. **RESEARCH** Twentieth century Russian/Soviet history. **SELECTED PUBLICATIONS** Auth, Rehabilitation in the post-Stalinist Soviet Union, Western Polit Quart, 67; The Supreme Economic Council, 1917- 1921, Soviet Studies, 73; The making of a Right Communist--A I Rykov to 1917, Slavic Rev, 77; auth, A Bolshevik in Revolution: G Ya Sokolnikov, the Party and State, 1888-1921, Australian Slavonic and East European Studies, 90; auth, Between Left and Right--G.Ia. Sokolnikov and the Development of the Soviet State, 1921-29, Slavic Rev, 90; The Practical Bolshevik: A I Rykov and Russian Communism, 1881-1938, Hoover Inst Press, 79; auth, World History in Theory and Practice: An Essay, History Teacher, 96; auth, History and Instructional Television, History Teacher, 96. **CONTACT ADDRESS** 801 Monte Vista Ave, Turlock, CA 95382. **EMAIL** oppenhei@stan.csustan.edu

ORBACH, ALEXANDER

PERSONAL Born 02/16/1945, Dzalal Abad, USSR, m, 1967, 2 children **DISCIPLINE** MODERN JEWISH HISTORY **EDUCATION** Queens Col, New York, BA, 66; Univ Wis, MA, 69, PhD Hist, 75. **CAREER** Asst prof Relig, Oberlin Col, 73-76; asst prof Hist, Ind Univ, Bloomington, 76-77; assoc prof Relig Studies, Hist, Univ Pittsburgh, 77-. **MEMBERSHIPS** AHA; Am Asn Advan Slavic Studies; Asn Jewish Studies. **RESEARCH** Russian Jewry 19th century; modern Jewish thought. **SELECTED PUBLICATIONS** Auth, Jewish intellectuals in Odessa in the late 19th century: The nationalist theories of Ahad Ha'am and Simon Dubnov, Nationalities Papers, VI: 109-123; The Jewishness of Soviet-Jewish culture: Historical considerations, J Jewish Communal Serv, Vol L VII, No 2; New Voices of Russian Jewry: A Study of the Russian-Jewish Press in the Era of the Great Reforms, 1860-1871, Brill Press, Leiden, Holland, 80; The Saul M Ginsburg Archival Collection: A major source for the study of Russian-Jewish life and letters, Soviet Jewish Affairs, Vol XI, No 2. **CONTACT ADDRESS** Dept of Relig Studies, Univ of Pittsburgh, 2604 Cathedral/Learn, Pittsburgh, PA 15260-0001. **EMAIL** orbach@pitt.edu

OREL, SARA E.

PERSONAL Born 07/02/1962, Lawrence, KS **DISCIPLINE** ARCHAEOLOGY **EDUCATION** Bryn Mawr Col, BA; Univ Toronto, MA, PhD. **CAREER** Assoc prof of art, ch, Art Hist Fac Comm, Truman State Univ. **MEMBERSHIPS** Am Research in Egypt; Egypt Exploration Soc; College Art Assoc; Midwest Art His Soc. **RESEARCH** Egyptian Art and Archaeology. **SELECTED PUBLICATIONS** Co-auth, Murder in Ancient Egypt, in Death and Taxes in the Ancient Near East, 92; From Cave to Monastery: Changes at the Nome Frontier of Gebel el-Haridi in Upper Egypt, Shifting Frontiers in Late Antiquity: Proc of the First Intl Interdisciplinary Conf on Late Antiquity, 96; ed, Death and Taxes in the Ancient Near East, Edwin Mellen Press, 92; auth, Two Unpublished Stelae from Beni Hasan, Jour Egyptian Archaeol, 96; John Garstang/Excavations at Beni Hasan, KMT, 96. **CONTACT ADDRESS** Division of Fine Arts, Truman State Univ, 100 E Normal St, Kirksville, MO 63501-4221. **EMAIL** orel@atstruman.edu

ORIJI, JOHN

PERSONAL Born 03/03/1944, Nigeria, m, 1969, 5 children **DISCIPLINE** AFRICAN HISTORY **EDUCATION** Univ Nigeria, BA, 67; Johns Hopkins Univ, MA, 74; Rutgers Univ, MA, 75; PhD, 77. **CAREER** Sen Res Fel, Univ Nigeria, 77-80; Sen Lectr, Univ Nigeria, 80-87; Prof, Calif Polytechnic State Univ, 87-. **HONORS AND AWARDS** Univ Nigeria Found Scholar, 63; Gilman Fel, Johns Hopkins Univ, 72; Fac Support Grand, Calif State Univ, 94, 96. **MEMBERSHIPS** African Studies Asn, Hist Soc of Nigeria, Calif Fac Asn, NY African Studies Asn. **RESEARCH** African history and politics, trans-Atlantic slave trade, ethnicity in the United States and Africa, environmental history. **SELECTED PUBLICATIONS** Auth, "Sacred Authority in Igbo Society," Archives des Relig (89): 109-119; auth, "Ethical Ideals of Peace and the Concept of war in Igbo Society," Warfare, Diplomacy and Soc in Nigeria (Madison, WS: 92); auth, Traditions of Igbo Origin: A Study of Pre-Colonial Population Movements in Africa, Rev Ed, Peter Lang Publ (New York, NY), 94; auth, Ngwa History: A Study of Social and Economic Changes in Igbo Mini States in Time Perspective, Rev Ed, Peter Land Publ (New York, NY), 97; auth, "Igbo Women from 1929-1960," W African Rev (00). **CONTACT ADDRESS** Dept Hist, California Polytech State Univ, San Luis Obispo, 1 Grand Ave, San Luis Obispo, CA 93407-9000. **EMAIL** joriji@calpoly.edu

ORLIN, ERIC

PERSONAL Born 02/22/1964, Boston, MA, m **DISCIPLINE** MEDITERRANEAN ARCHAEOLOGY **EDUCATION** Yale Univ, BA 86; Univ Cal Berk, PhD 94. **CAREER** Cal State Univ Fresno, lect 94-96; Bard Col, asst prof 96-00; asst prof, Univ Pugent Sound, 00- . **MEMBERSHIPS** APA; AAH **RESEARCH** Social and cultural history of the Roman republic; Roman religion; early Judaism and Christianity; historiography; the Roman Near East. **SELECTED PUBLICATIONS** Auth, Temples, Religion and Politics in the Roman Republic, Brill, 96; auth, "Why a second temple for Venus Erycina?" Studies in Latin Lit & Roman Hist, v X (Brussels, 00), 70-90. **CONTACT ADDRESS** Classics Dept, Univ of Puget Sound, 1500 N Warner St, Tacoma, WA 98416. **EMAIL** eorlin@ups.edu

ORLOW, DIETRICH OTTO

PERSONAL Born 06/02/1937, Hamburg, Germany, m, 1959, 1 child **DISCIPLINE** MODERN EUROPEAN HISTORY **EDUCATION** Ohio Univ, AB, 58; Univ Mich, MA, 59, PhD, 62. **CAREER** From instr to asst prof, 62-67 Col William & Mary; assoc prof, 67-71, Syracuse Univ; prof hist, 71-, dept chmn, 79-84, Boston Univ; Duke Univ-Univ NC Coop Prog in Humanities fel, 66-67; Alexander von Humboldt Stiftung sr res fel, 74-75, fel, 78-79; vis prof, 75, Univ Hamburg, Ger; fel, Netherlands Inst for Advan Stud; Fulbright Europe, Reg Res Fel, 85, 86, 93. **MEMBERSHIPS** AHA; pres, 95-96, Conf Group Cent Europ Hist. **RESEARCH** History of National Socialist Germany; 20th century totalitarianism; history of the Weimar Republic. **SELECTED PUBLICATIONS** Auth, Weimar Prussia, 1925-1933: The Illusion of Strength, Univ Pitt Press, 91; auth, A History of Modern Germany, 1870 to the Present, Prentice-Hall, 98; auth, Common Destiny: A Comparative History of the Dutch, French, and German Social Democratic Parties 1945-1969, Berghahn Bks, 99. **CONTACT ADDRESS** Dept of History, Boston Univ, 226 Bay State Rd, Boston, MA 02215-1403. **EMAIL** dorlow@bu.edu

ORMSBY, MARGARET A.

PERSONAL Born Quesnel, BC, Canada **DISCIPLINE** HISTORY **EDUCATION** Univ BC, BA, 29, MA, 31; Bryn Mawr Col, PhD, 37. **CAREER** Lectr, McMaster Univ, 40-43; lectr, 43-46, asst prof, 46-49, assoc prof, 49-52, Prof Emer History, Univ BC, 65-. **HONORS AND AWARDS** DLitt, Univ BC, 74; LLD, Univ Manitoba, 60; LLD, Univ Notre Dame, Nelson BC; LLD, Simon Fraser Univ, 71; LLD, Univ Victoria, 76; BC LLD, Univ North BC, 95. **MEMBERSHIPS** Can Hist Asn; BC Hist Asn; Royal Soc Can; BC Heritage. **SELECTED PUBLICATIONS** Auth, British Columbia: A History, 58, 62, 64, 71; auth, A Pioneer Gentlewoman in British Columbia: the Recollections of Susan Allison, 76, 94; auth, Coldstream-Nulli Secundus, 90. **CONTACT ADDRESS** Dept of History, Univ of British Columbia, Vancouver, BC, Canada V6T 1Z1.

OROZCO, CYNTHIA E.
DISCIPLINE HISTORY, CHICANO STUDIES **EDUCATION** Univ Calif, Los Angeles, PhD, 92. **CAREER** Res assoc, Tex State Hist Assoc, 88-92; res assoc, Inst Texan Cultures, 92-93; vis prof, Univ Tex, San Antonia, 93-94; Instr, Eastern NMex State Univ, Ruidoso, 97-98; vis asst prof, 97-98, vis asst prof hist, Chicana/o Stud, Univ NMex, 98-. **RESEARCH** Chicana and Chicano Hist, the Southwest, the Am West, the Spanish Borderlands, women's hist, and politics. **SELECTED PUBLICATIONS** Auth, "Getting Started in Chiacna Studies," Women Studies Quarterly, (90): 46-69; auth, "Beyond Machismo, La Familia, and Ladies Auiliaries; A Historiography of Mexican-Origin Women's Participation in Voluntary Associtions and Politics in the United States, 1870-1990," Perspectives in Mexican Am Studies 5, (Tucson: Mexican Am Stud and Res Center, Univ of Arizona, 95): 1-34; auth, "Mexican-American Women" and "Selena Quintanilla Perez" in New Handbook of Texas, (Austin: Texas State Historical Asn, 96); co-ed, "Alice Dickerson Montemayor: Feminism and Mexican American Politics in the 1930s," Writing the Range: Race, Class, and Cultrue in the American Women's West, ed. Elizabeth Jameson and Susan Armitage, (Norman: Univ of Oklahoma Press, 97): 435-456; co-ed, "Chicano and Latino Arts and Culture Institutions in the Southwest: The Politics of Space, Race, and Money," in Latinos in Museums: A Heritage Reclaimed, ed. Antonio Rios Bustamente and Christine marin, (Malabar, Florida: Krieger Publishing Co., 98): 95-107; auth, "Regionalism, Poitics and Gender in Southwest History: The League of United American Citizens," Expansion into New Mexico from Texas, 1929-1945," Western Historical Quarterly, (98): 459-484. **CONTACT ADDRESS** Dept of Hist, Univ of New Mexico, Albuquerque, 1829 Sigma Chi Rd. NE, Albuquerque, NM 87131-1181. **EMAIL** corozco@unm.edu

ORR, LESLIE
PERSONAL Born 04/29/1948, Ann Arbor, MI **DISCIPLINE** HISTORY OF RELIGIONS, ASIAN RELIGIONS **EDUCATION** McGill Univ, BS, 70, MA, 81-82, PhD, 93. **CAREER** Full-time lectr, asst, assoc prof, 91-; full-time lect, McGill Univ, 89-91; part-time lectr, McGill Univ, 84-89; tchg asst, McGill Univ, 82-83; ch, dept of Relig, Concordia Univ, 99-. **HONORS AND AWARDS** Social Sciences and Humanities Res Council of Canada grant, 94-97; Am Academy of Relig grant, 98-99. **MEMBERSHIPS** Canadian Soc for the Study of Relig; Canadian Asian Stud Asn; Am Academy of Relig; Asn for Asian Stud; Am Oriental Soc. **RESEARCH** Women in the religions of India (Hinduism, Buddhism, and Jainism). **SELECTED PUBLICATIONS** Auth, "Women of Medieval South India in Hindu Temple Ritual: Text and Practice," Annual Rev of Women in World Religions, 3, (93): 107-141; ed, "The Concept of Time in ankara's Brahma-sutra-bhasya," In Hermeneutical Paths to the Sacred Worlds of India, eds. Katherine K. Young, Atlanta: Scholar's Press, 94; auth, "The Vaisnava Community at rirangam: The Testimony of the Early Medieval Inscriptions," The Journal of Vaisnava Stud, 3/3: (95): 109-136; auth, "Jain and Hindu Religious Women' in Early Medieval Tamilnadu," In Open Boundaries: Jain Communities and Cultures in Indian History, ed. John E. Cort, State Univ of New York Press, 98; ed, "Women's Wealth and Worship: Female Patronage of Hinduism, Jainism, and Buddhism in Medieval Tamilnadu," In the Captive Subject: A Social and Cultural Casebook for Indian Women, vol. 2: The Medieval Period, ed. Mandakranta Bose, New York: Oxford Univ Press, 99. **CONTACT ADDRESS** Dept of Rel, Concordia Univ, Montreal, 1455 de Maisonneuve W, Montreal, QC, Canada H3G 1M8. **EMAIL** orr@vax2.concordia.ca

ORTH, JOHN VICTOR
PERSONAL Born 02/07/1947, Lancaster, PA, m, 1972, 2 children **DISCIPLINE** HISTORY OF LAW, PROPERTY LAW **EDUCATION** Oberlin Col, AB, 69; Harvard Univ, JD, 74, PhD(hist), 77. **CAREER** Law clerk, US Ct Appeals, 77-78; asst prof, 78-81, Assoc Prof Law, Univ NC, 81-; assoc dean, UNC-Chapel Hill, 85-86. **MEMBERSHIPS** AAUP; Am Soc Legal Hist; Am Bar Asn; Selden Soc; Conf Brit Studies. **RESEARCH** American constitutional history; history of labor law. **SELECTED PUBLICATIONS** Auth, The Judicial Power of the United States: The Eleventh Amendment in Am History, 87; auth, Combination and Conspiracy: The Legal History of Trade Unionism, 1721-1906, 91; auth, The North Carolina State Constitution: A Reference Guide, 93. **CONTACT ADDRESS** Sch of Law, Univ of No Carolina, Chapel Hill, 5116 Van Hecke-Wettach Hall, Chapel Hill, NC 27514. **EMAIL** jvorth@email.unc.edu

ORTQUIST, RICHARD THEODORE
PERSONAL Born 12/22/1933, Muskegon, MI, m, 1958, 2 children **DISCIPLINE** RECENT UNITED STATES HISTORY **EDUCATION** Hope Col, BA, 56; Univ Mich, Ann Arbor, MA, 61, PhD(hist), 68. **CAREER** From instr to asst prof, 64-71, assoc prof, 71-80, Prof Hist, Wittenberg Univ, 80-, Chmn Dept, 80-; Prof Hist, 80-89; Chmn, 80-89, 94-97; Prof Emeritus Hist. 99-. **MEMBERSHIPS** AHA; Orgn Am Historians. **RESEARCH** Recent American political history; depression and New Deal period. **SELECTED PUBLICATIONS** Auth, Depression politics in Michigan: The election of 1932, Mich Acad, spring 70; Unemployment and relief: Michigan's response to the depression during the Hoover years, fall 73 & Tax crisis and politics early Depression Michigan, spring-summer 75, Mich Hist; Depression Politics in Michigan, 1929-1933, Garland Pub, Inc, 82; Exemplar of Americanism - The Philippine Career of Worcester,dean,c. - Sullivan,rj, Michigan Historical Review, Vol 0018, 1992. **CONTACT ADDRESS** Dept of Hist, Wittenberg Univ, Springfield, OH 45501.

ORVELL, MILES
PERSONAL Born 01/09/1944, New York, NY, m, 1987, 2 children **DISCIPLINE** AMERICAN LITERATURE, AMERICAN STUDIES **EDUCATION** Columbia Univ, BA, 64; Harvard Univ, MA, 65; PhD, 70. **CAREER** Prof, Temple Univ, 69-; dir of Am Studies, Temple Univ, 75-80; vis prof, Univ Pa, 86-87; Fulbright Prof in Am Studies, Univ Copenhagen, 88. **HONORS AND AWARDS** Woodrow Wilson Fac Development Grant, 82; Reva and David Logan Grant, 85; Fulbright Awd, Univ Coppenhagen, 88; John Hope Franklin Publication Prize, Am Studies Asn, 90; NEH Summer Sem Dir, 91, 93, 94, 95, & 99. **MEMBERSHIPS** Am Studies Asn. **RESEARCH** American Cultural Studies, American Literature, Photography, Visual Studies. **SELECTED PUBLICATIONS** Auth, Invisible Parade: The Fiction of Flannery O'Connor, Temple Univ Press, 72 (reprinted at Flannery O'Connor: An Introduction, Univ Press Miss, 91); auth, The Real Thing: Imitation and Authenticity in American Culture, 1880-1940, Univ NC Press, 89; auth, After the Machine: Visual Arts and the Erasing of Cultural Boundaries, Univ Press of Miss, 95; co-ed, Inventing America: Readings in Identity and Culture, St. Martin's Press, 95. **CONTACT ADDRESS** Dept English, Temple Univ, Philadelphia, PA 19122. **EMAIL** orvell@astro.ocis.temple.edu

OSBERG, RICHARD H.
PERSONAL Born 01/25/1947, Boston, MA, m, 1969, 1 child **DISCIPLINE** ENGLISH, MEDIEVAL STUDIES **EDUCATION** Dartmouth Col, BA, 69; Claremont Grad Sch, MA, 70; PhD, 74. **CAREER** Asst Prof, Barat Col, 75-78; Asst Prof, Hamilton Col, 78-82; From Asst Prof to Prof, Santa Clara Univ, 82-. **HONORS AND AWARDS** NEH Fel, 82. **MEMBERSHIPS** MLA, MAP, MAA. **RESEARCH** Chaucer, alliterative poetry, Medievalism. **SELECTED PUBLICATIONS** Auth, "Pages Torn From the Book: Narrative Disintegration in Terry Gilliam's 'The Fisher King'," Studies in Medievalism 8 (95): 194-224; auth, "A Voice for the Prioress: The Context of English Devotional Prose," Studies in the Age of Chaucer 18 (96): 25-54; auth, "The Prosody of Middle English 'Pearl' and the Alliterative Lyric Tradition," in English Hist Metrics (Cambridge: Cambridge Univ Pr, 96), 150-174; auth, "The Maimed King, the Wasteland, and the Vanished Grail in Iris Murdoch's 'The Green Knight'," in The Year's Work in Medievalism X (Holland, MI: 98), 21-32; auth, "Humanist Allusions and Medieval Themes: The 'Receyving' of Queen Anne, London 1533," in Medievalism in the Mod World: Essays in Hon of Leslie Workman (Brepols: Turnhout, 98), 27-41; auth, "Rewriting Romance: From 'Sir Gawain' to 'The Green Knight'," in The Future of the Middle Ages and the Renaissance: Problems, Trends and Opportunities for Research (Brepols: Turnhout, 98), 93-108; coauth, "Language Then and Language Now in Arthurian Film," in King Arthur on Film: New Essays on Arthurian Cinema (Jefferson, NC: McFarland & Co, 99), 39-66. **CONTACT ADDRESS** Dept English, Santa Clara Univ, 500 El Camino Real, St Joseph's 223, Santa Clara, CA 95053-0001. **EMAIL** rosberg@scu.edu

OSBORN, WAYNE S.
PERSONAL Born 06/11/1937, Cedar Rapids, IA, m, 1960, 4 children **DISCIPLINE** HISTORY **EDUCATION** Simpson, BA; Univ Iowa, MA, 63; PhD, 70. **CAREER** Asst prof, Univ of Wis at Eau Claire, 67-68; asst prof, Iowa State Univ, 68-. **MEMBERSHIPS** Latin Am Studies Asn, Confr on Latin Am Hist. **RESEARCH** Colonial Mexico, Peace. **SELECTED PUBLICATIONS** Auth, "Aprovechamiento de la tierra en metztitlan a fines del Siglo XVIII," Revista encuentro 17 (87): 67-85; auth, "Indian Land Retention in Colonial Metztitlan," in The Indian Community of Colonial Mexico, eds. Ariji Ouweneel and Simon Miller (Amsterdam, 90); auth, "United Nations University for Peace in Costa Rica: History and Prospects," Peace and Change (00): 309-338. **CONTACT ADDRESS** Dept Hist, Iowa State Univ, Ames, IA 50011-2010. **EMAIL** wsosborn@iastate.edu

OSBORNE, JOHN
DISCIPLINE ART HISTORY **EDUCATION** Univ Carleton, BA, 73; Univ Toronto, MA, 74; Univ London, PhD, 79. **CAREER** Asst prof, 79-85; assoc prof, 85-89; prof, 89; dir, Medieval Studies Programme, 93-96. **HONORS AND AWARDS** Visiting Fel, Corpus Christi Col, 85; Venice Fel, Istituto Ellenico di Studi Bizantini, 92; Summer Fel, Jumbarton Oaks Center for Byzantine Studies, 92. **MEMBERSHIPS** Universities Art Asn of Canada; Canadian Institute for Mediterranean Stud; Canadian Soc of Byzantinists; Canadian Soc of Medievalists; The Medieval Academy of Am. **RESEARCH** Material culture of medieval Europe and Byzantium; cities of Rome and Venice in the Middle Ages. **SELECTED PUBLICATIONS** Auth, Early Mediaeval Wall-Painting in the Lower Church of San Clemente, Rome, Garland Press, New York, 84; transl, Master Gregorius: The Marvels of Rome, Pontifical Institute of Mediaeval Studies, Toronto, 87; ed, Rome: Tradition, Innovation and Renewal, Univ of Victoria, with C. Brown, C. Kirwin, 91; auth, The Paper Museum of Cassiano dal Pozzo, Series A, Part II, Early Christian and Medieval Antiquities, Vol. I: Mosaics and Wallpaintings in Roman Churches, with Amanda Claridge, Harvey Miller, London, 96; auth, "A Tale of Two Cities: Sacred Geography in Christian Jerusalem," Queens Quarterly 103, (96): 741-749; auth, "The early medieval sculpture," in T.W. Potter and A.C. King, Excavations at the Mola di Monte Gelato: A Roman and medieval Settlement in South Etruria, (London, 97): 217-28; auth, "The Hagiographic programme of the mosaics in the south dome of San Marco at Venice," RACAR 22, (97): 19-28; auth, "The cross-under-arch motif in ninth-century Venetian sculpture: an imperial reading," Thesaurismata 27, (97): 7-18; auth, "Proclamations of Power and Presence: The Setting and Function of Two Eleventh-Century Mural Decorations in the Lower Church of San Clemente, Rome," Mediaeval Studies 59, (97): 155-172; auth, The Paper Museum Series A, Part II, Early Christian and Medieval Antiquities, Vol. 2: Other Mosaics, Paintings, Sarcophagi, and Small Objects, Harvey Miller, London, 98. **CONTACT ADDRESS** Dept of Hist in Art, Univ of Victoria, PO Box 1700, Victoria, BC, Canada V8W 2Y2. **EMAIL** josborne@finearts.uvic.ca

OSBORNE, JOHN WALTER
PERSONAL Born 08/19/1927, Brooklyn, NY, m, 1958, 1 child **DISCIPLINE** HISTORY **EDUCATION** Rutgers Univ, AB, 57, AM, 59, PhD(hist), 61. **CAREER** Asst hist, Rutgers Univ, 57-59; consult grad rec exam in hist, Educ Testing Serv, NJ, 59; asst prof hist, Newark State Col, 62-63; asst prof, Newark Col Eng, 63-64; from asst prof to assoc prof, 64-69, Prof Hist, Rutgers Univ, New Brunswick, 69-, Am Philos Soc grant, 66 & 75; consult ed, Irish Univ Press, 69- 71; ed, J Rutgers Univ Libr, 75-80. **MEMBERSHIPS** AHA; Conf Brit Studies. **RESEARCH** British history. **SELECTED PUBLICATIONS** Auth, Parliamentary career (1614-1621) of Sir Edwin Sandys, Bermuda Hist Quart, 62; William Cobbett and the Catholic emancipation crisis, 1823-1829, Cath Hist Rev, 63; William Cobbett: His Thought and His Times, Rutgers Univ, 66; The Silent Revolution: The Industrial Revolution in England as a Source of Cultural Change, Scribner, 70; John Cartwright, Cambridge, 72; The endurance of literary history in Great Britain: Charles Oman, G M Trevelyan and the genteel tradition, Clio, 1072; Henry Hunt's career in Parliament, Historian, 76; William Cobbett and Ireland, Studies, 81; Trevelyan,george,macaulay - a Life in History - Cannadine,d, Clio-a J of Literature History And The Philosophy of History, Vol 0022, 1993; Cobbett,william And Rural Popular-culture - Dyck,i, Albion, Vol 0025, 1993; Morison,samuel,eliot Historical World - Pfitzer,gm, Clio-a J of Literature History And The Philosophy of History, Vol 0023, 1993; Interests And Obsessions - Historical Essays - Skidelsky,r, Clio-a J of Literature History And The Philosophy of History, Vol 0024, 1995. **CONTACT ADDRESS** 24 Helen Ave, West Orange, NJ 07052.

OSBORNE, THOMAS
PERSONAL Born 05/17/1942, Long Beach, CA, m, 1975, 2 children **DISCIPLINE** HISTORY **EDUCATION** Cal State Univ, BA, 65; Claremont Grad Univ, MA, 68; PhD, 79. **CAREER** Prof, Santa Ana Col, 69-; asst vis prof, Chapman Univ World Campus Afloat, 70; asst vis prof, Univ of Haw, 81. **HONORS AND AWARDS** NDEA Title IV Fel, 68; Ford Found Diss Fel, 75; NEH Summer Seminar Fel, Yale, 80; Inaugural Distinguished Fac Lectr Awd, Santa Ana Coll, 88; Nat Teaching Excellence Awd, Univ of Tex, 88; Phi Alpha Theta, History Honor Soc. **MEMBERSHIPS** Orgn of Am Historians, AHA. **RESEARCH** Global and comparative history, history of American foreign relations. **SELECTED PUBLICATIONS** Auth, "Trade or War? America's Annexation of Hawaii Reconsidered," Pacific Hist Review L (81): 285-307; coauth, Paths to the Present: Thoughts on the Contemporary relevance of America's Past, John Wiley and Sons (New York, NY), 74; auth, Empire Can Wait: American Opposition to Hawaiian Annexation, Kent State Univ Press (Kent, OH), 81; contribur & auth, Readings in American Civilization, Univ of Silesia Press (Katowice, Poland), 85; contribur & auth, "Imperial Surge: The United States Abroad, The 1890s-Early 1900s," D.C. Heath and Co (Lexington, MA), 92; contribur & auth, "George Frisbie Hoar" and "Stephen Mallory White," in Am Nat Biog 24, ed. John Garraty (Oxford Univ Press, 99); auth, America's Past in Global Perspective, McGraw-Hill Publ (Boston), forthcoming. **CONTACT ADDRESS** Dept Hist, Santa Ana Col, 1530 W 17th St, Santa Ana, CA 92706-3398. **EMAIL** tomosborne@home.com

OSBORNE, THOMAS R.
PERSONAL Born 12/16/1943, Rochester, NY, m, 1963, 2 children **DISCIPLINE** HISTORY **EDUCATION** Univ Conn, BA, 64; MA, 68; PhD, 74. **CAREER** Asst prof, NYork Inst Technol, 75-78; Univ N Alabama, 78- . **HONORS AND AWARDS** Woodrow Wilson fel; Phi Beta Kappa; Phi Kappa Phi. **MEMBERSHIPS** Am Hist Asn; Soc Fr His Student; S His Asn. **RESEARCH** Modern European history. **SELECTED PUBLICATIONS** Auth, A Grand Ecole for the Grands Corps: The Recruitment and Training of the Frence Administrative Elite in the Nineteenth Century, Soc Sci Monogr, Boulder, 83. **CONTACT ADDRESS** Hist & Polit Sci Box 5190, Univ of No Alabama, Florence, AL 35632-0001. **EMAIL** Tosborne@unanov.una.edu

OSHEIM, DUANE JEFFREY
PERSONAL Born 05/28/1942, Story City, IA, m, 1968, 2 children **DISCIPLINE** HISTORY **EDUCATION** Luther Col, BA, 64; Univ Nebraska, MA, 67; Univ Calif, PhD, 73. **CAREER** Am Acad in Rome, Rome Prize fel hist, 74-76, Asst prof, 76-82, Assoc Prof Hist, Univ Va, 82-91, Prof, 91-. **HONORS AND AWARDS** Phi Beta Kappa; Diss Prize, Soc Ital Hist Studententententent, 74; Rome Prize fel, Am Acad Rome, 74-76. **MEMBERSHIPS** Medieval Acad Am; Renaissance Soc Am. **RESEARCH** Medieval & Renaissance Italy, Social and institutional history. **SELECTED PUBLICATIONS** Auth, An Italian Lordship: the Bishopric of Lucca in the Late Middle Ages, (77); auth, A Tuscan Monastery and Its Social World: San Michele of Guamo (1156-1348), (89); co-auth, Western Civilization: The Continuing Experiment, (98). **CONTACT ADDRESS** Dept Hist, Univ of Virginia, Randall Hall, Charlottesville, VA 22903. **EMAIL** djo@virginia.edu

OSTHAUS, CARL RICHARD
PERSONAL Born 06/02/1943, Sandusky, OH, m, 1992, 2 children **DISCIPLINE** HISTORY **EDUCATION** Kalamazoo Col, BA, 65; Univ Chicago, MA, 66, PhD(hist), 71. **CAREER** From instr to asst prof, 70-76, Assoc Prof Am Hist, Oakland Univ, 77-95; Prof, 96-. **HONORS AND AWARDS** Phi Beta Kappa, Oakland U Teaching Excellence Awd, 89. **MEMBERSHIPS** Southern Hist Asn. **RESEARCH** Civil War and Reconstruction; the American South. **SELECTED PUBLICATIONS** Auth, The rise and fall of Jesse Binga, Black Financier, J Negro Hist, 173; From the Old South to the New South: The editorial career of William Tappan Thompson of the Savannah Morning News, Southern Quart, 376; Freedmen, Philanthropy, and Fraud: A History of the Freedman's Savings Bank, Univ Ill, 76; Francis Warrington Dawson and South Carolina's spirit of 1876: A case study of the perils of Jistic heresy, Hayes Hist J, fall 77; An affair of honor--not an honorable affair: The Ritchie-Pleasants duel and the press, VA Cavalcade, winter 77; auth, Partisans of the Southern Press: Editorial Spokesmen of The Nineteenth Century, Univ Pr. Kentucky, 94; Inner World of Lincoln,abraham - Burlingame,m, Michigan Historical Review, Vol 0021, 1995; Pulling The Temple Down - The Fire- eaters And The Destruction of The Union - Heidler,ds, J of American History, Vol 0082, 1995. **CONTACT ADDRESS** Dept of Hist, Oakland Univ, Rochester, MI 48063. **EMAIL** osthaus@oakland.edu

OSTROW, STEVEN F.
PERSONAL Born 06/23/1954, Dallas, TX, m, 1994, 1 child **DISCIPLINE** ART HISTORY **EDUCATION** Princeton Univ, PhD, 87; MFA, 81; McGill Univ, BA, 76 **CAREER** Chair, 94-00, Assoc prof, 94-, Asst Prof, 92-94, Univ of CA, Riverside; Assoc prof with tenure, 92, Asst Prof, 87-92, Inst, 85-87, Vassar Col **HONORS AND AWARDS** Samuel H Kress Found Subvent Grant **MEMBERSHIPS** Art hist of Southrn CA, Col Art Asn; Sixteenth Century Studies Asn; Renaissance Soc of Am; Italian Art Soc. **RESEARCH** Italian art and culture **SELECTED PUBLICATIONS** Auth, Art and Sprituality in Counter-Reformation Rome, CUP, N.Y., 96; auth, Paolo Sanquirico: A Forgotten Virtuoso of Seicento Rome, Storia dell'arte, 98; ed, Dosso's Fate: Painting and Court Culture in Renaissance Italy, Getty Research Institute, LA, 98. **CONTACT ADDRESS** Dept of Hist of Art, Univ of California, Riverside, Riverside, CA 92521-0319. **EMAIL** steveo@mail.ucr.edu

OSTROWER, GARY BERT
PERSONAL Born 10/11/1939, New York, NY, m, 1979, 2 children **DISCIPLINE** DIPLOMATIC HISTORY **EDUCATION** Alfred Univ, BA, 61; Univ Rochester, MA, 62, PhD(hist), 70. **CAREER** Instr hist, Vassar Col, 67-68; asst prof, 69-75, Assoc Prof Hist, Alfred Univ, 75-98, Lyndon Baines Johnson Found Moody grant, 77; vis prof, Univ Pa, 79-80; Advan Placement reader, Educ Testing Serv, 77-00; Prof His, Alfred Univ, 79-. **MEMBERSHIPS** AHA; Soc Hist Am Foreign Rels; Orgn Am Historians. **RESEARCH** International organization; interwar diplomacy, 20th Century; modern political history. **SELECTED PUBLICATIONS** Auth, American ambassador to the League of Nations: A proposal postponed, 71 & Historical studies in American internationalism, 71, Int Orgn; Revising revisionist historians, Alfred News, 71; American decision to join the ILO, Labor Hist, 975; Collective Insecurity: The US and the League of Nations During the Early Thirties, Bucknell Univ Press, 79; Henry L Stimson and international organization, The Historian, 79; to End All Wars - Wilson,woodrow And The Quest For a New-world Order - Knock,tj, American Historical Review, Vol 0099, 1994; auth, The League of Nations: From 1919 to 1929, Avery, Penguin Putnam, 96; America Secret War Against Bolshevism - Us Intervention in The Russian Civil-war, 1917-1920 - Foglesong,ds, American Historical Review, Vol 0102, 1997; auth, The United Nations and the United States, Twayne, 98 **CONTACT ADDRESS** Div of Human Studies, Alfred Univ, Saxon Dr, Alfred, NY 14802-1205. **EMAIL** ostrower@alfred.edu

OSUMARE, HALIFU
PERSONAL Born 11/27/1946, Galveston, TX, m, 1978 **DISCIPLINE** AMERICAN STUDIES, DANCE **EDUCATION** Univ Without Walls, Berkeley, BA, 75; San Francisco State Univ, MA, 93; Univ Haw, PhD, 99. **CAREER** Lectr, Stanford Univ, 81-93; vis asst prof, Univ Calif Riverside, 99; vis lectr, Univ Calif Berkeley, 00; asst prof, Bowling Green State Univ, 00-. **HONORS AND AWARDS** HCH, Res Grant; Hon Men Gabriel Diss Prize; Brown-Denny Awd. **MEMBERSHIPS** DASA. **RESEARCH** My research focus encompasses the fields of Cultural Studies and African American Studies, with an emphasis on how African American performance has historically utilized resistance, complicity, and play in relation to social structures of power. **SELECTED PUBLICATIONS** Auth, "Aesthetic of the Cool Revisited: The Ancestral Dance Link in the African Diaspora," UCLA J Dan Ethnol 17 (93); auth, "Viewing African Women Through Dance," SAGE 2 (94); auth, "Phat Beats, Dope Rhymes, and Def Moves: Hip Hop's African Aesthetics as Signifying Intertext," in Cultural Patrimony: Africa, New World Connections, and Identities, ed. Niyi Afolabi (forthcoming); auth, "Beat Streets in the Global Hood: Connective Marginalities of the Hip Hop Globe," J Am Cult (forthcoming). **CONTACT ADDRESS** Sch Human Movement, Bowling Green State Univ, Bowling Green, OH 43403-0001. **EMAIL** hosuamre@aol.com

OSZUSCIK, PHILIPPE
PERSONAL Born 03/17/1941, Hattiesburg, MS, m, 1964 **DISCIPLINE** ART, ARCHITECTURAL HISTORY **EDUCATION** Univ Iowa, PhD , art and archit history, 79. **CAREER** Asst prof, Northwestern State Univ La, Natchitoches, 68-70; asst prof, Augustana Coll, 70-77; assoc prof, 77-, Univ South Ala; Ed. **HONORS AND AWARDS** Outstanding Scholars of the 20th Century, 00; Who's Who in the Humanities, 92; fellow, NEH summer seminar, Amer Folklife, 81; fellow, Amer Fed Art, Art Criticism, NYC, 68. **MEMBERSHIPS** Bd mem, 84-89, Pioneer Amer Soc; Vernacular Archit Forum; Soc Art Historians; pres, 89, newsletter ed, 88-95, Soc of Archit Historians, SE Chap, Soc of Archit Historians; SE Coll Art Conf; SE Amer Soc 18th-Century Studies; Art History Assn; Board of Dir, Archit Historians, SE Chap. **RESEARCH** Creole housing; ethnicities in vernacular archit; Southeastern archit; postmodern archit; African-American archit. **SELECTED PUBLICATIONS** Auth, "Passage of the Gallery and Other Caribbean Elements from the French and Spanish to the British in the United States," Pioneer America Transactions, vol. 14, 92; "French Creoles on the Gulf Coast," "African-Americans in the American South," in To Build a New Land, 92; "A Postmodern Public Public Monument: Design Elements Make Reference to Older Structures," in Renaissance by the River (special section), Mobile Register, 19 Sept 93; "Comparisons Between Rural and Urban French Creole Housing," Material Culture, fall 94; auth, "Sources to the City Plan and Structures of Old Mobile,"LeJournal, 00. **CONTACT ADDRESS** Dept of Art and Art History, Univ of So Alabama, UAB 152, Mobile, AL 36688-0002. **EMAIL** oszuscikp@cs.com

OTTAWAY, SUSANNAH R.
PERSONAL Born 03/26/1967, Poughkeepsie, NY, m, 1991, 2 children **DISCIPLINE** HISTORY **EDUCATION** Carleton Col, BA, 89; Brown Univ, MA, 92; PhD, 97. **CAREER** Asst prof, Carleton Col, 98-. **HONORS AND AWARDS** Fel, Brown Univ, 93, 94, 96; Travel Grant, Brown Univ, 93, 94; Emmison Fel, England, 94-95; Fel, Soc Sci Res Counc, 94-95; Fel, Brown Univ, 95, 96, 97; Res Inst for the Study of Man Landes Awd Grant, 96, 97-98. **SELECTED PUBLICATIONS** Auth, "Age and Want in Eighteenth-Century Essex", Essex J,Spring 96; auth, "Providing for the Elderly in Eighteenth-Century England", Continuity and Change 13.3, 98; coauth, "Reconstructing the Life-Cycle Experience of Poverty in the Time of the Old Poor Law", Archives, April 98; rev, of "Chronicling Poverty: the Voices and Strategies of the English Poor, 1640-1840", eds Tim Hitchcock, Peter King and Pamela Sharpe, Jof Interdisciplinary Hist, Summer 98; rev, of "New-born Child Murder: Women, Illegitimacy and the Courts in Eighteenth-Century England", by Mark Jackson, Population Studies 53.1, March 99; coed, Old Age in Pre-Industrial Society, Greenwood Pr, (forthcoming); auth, "The Old Woman's Home in Eighteenth-Century England", in women and Ageing in Brit Society Since 1500, ed L. Botelho and P. Thand, (London: Longman) (forthcoming). **CONTACT ADDRESS** Dept Hist, Carleton Col, 1 N College St, Northfield, MN 55057-4001. **EMAIL** sottaway@carleton.edu

OUELLET, FERNAND
PERSONAL Born 11/06/1926, Lac-Bouchette, PQ, Canada **DISCIPLINE** HISTORY **EDUCATION** Univ Laval, BA, 48, LL, 50, DL, 65. **CAREER** Asst archv, prov Que, 56-61; prof, Univ Laval, 61-65; prof, Carleton Univ, 65-75; prof, Univ Ottawa, 75-85; prof, 86-95, PROF EMER HISTOIRE, YORK UNIV, 95-. **HONORS AND AWARDS** Grand prix litteraire de la ville de Montreal, 67; Laureat des concours litteraires de la prov Que, 67; Prix David, 67; Medaille Tyrrell, soc royale Can; Prix gov gen Can, 77; Prix Sir John A. Macdonald, 77; off, ordre Can, 79; Medaille du centenaire Can, 67; Medaille du jubilee de la Reine, 77. **MEMBERSHIPS** Soc hist Can; soc royale Can. **SELECTED PUBLICATIONS** Auth, Histoire economique et sociale du Quebec (1760-1850), 66; auth, Le Bas-Canada 1771-1840, 76; dir, Histoire sociale/Social History, 71-88. **CONTACT ADDRESS** 92A Alcorn Ave, Toronto, ON, Canada M4V 1E4.

OURADA, PATRICIA K.
PERSONAL Born 04/20/1926, Menominee, MI **DISCIPLINE** AMERICAN INDIAN HISTORY **EDUCATION** Col St Catherine, BA, 47; Univ Colo, MA, 53; Univ Okla, PhD(Am Indian hist), 73. **CAREER** Teacher hist, Pub High Schs, NDak & Minn, 47-60; from instr to assoc prof US hist, 62-73, Prof Us & Indian Hist, Boise State Univ, 73-. **RESEARCH** American Indian history and history of sports in America. **SELECTED PUBLICATIONS CONTACT ADDRESS** Dept of Hist, Boise State Univ, Boise, ID 83725.

OVERACKER, INGRID
PERSONAL Born 01/08/1953, Gouveneur, NY, d **DISCIPLINE** HISTORY **EDUCATION** Univ Rochester, PhD, 95 **CAREER** Asst Prof, Jefferson Community Col, 96-; ch, Dept Soc Sci, Jefferson Cmty Col, 99-. **RESEARCH** American History, African American History. **SELECTED PUBLICATIONS** Auth, The History of the African American Church in Rochester, New York 1900-1940, Univ of Rochester Pr, 98; Auth, True to Our God: African American Christian Activists in Rochester, New York, (forthcoming). **CONTACT ADDRESS** Dept Soc Sci, Jefferson Comm Col, New York, 1220 Coffeen St, Watertown, NY 13601-1822.

OVERBECK, JAMES A.
PERSONAL Born 09/11/1940, Eau Claire, WI, m, 1966, 3 children **DISCIPLINE** ECCLESIASTICAL HISTORY **EDUCATION** Univ of Chicago, MA, PhD, Grad Library Sch, MALS. **CAREER** Librarian, professor. **MEMBERSHIPS** Amer Library Assn, Amer Acad of Religion. **RESEARCH** History of Religious Journalism **SELECTED PUBLICATIONS** Auth, The Rise and Fall of Presbyterian Official Journals 1925-1985, Diversity of Discipleship, Westminister Press, 91. **CONTACT ADDRESS** 517 Ridgecrest Rd, NE, Atlanta, GA 30307-1845. **EMAIL** Joverbec@ce1.af.public.lib.ga.us

OVERBECK, JOHN CLARENCE
PERSONAL Born 11/04/1933, Tulsa, OK, m, 1972, 1 child **DISCIPLINE** CLASSICAL ARCHEOLOGY, ANCIENT GREEK **EDUCATION** Univ Okla, AB, 55; Univ Cincinnati, PhD(classics), 63. **CAREER** Asst prof, 63-66, Assoc Prof Classics, State Univ NY Albany, 66-, Mem managing comt, Am Sch Class Studies, Athens, 66-75; dir archaeol surv, Dept of Antiquities, Repub of Cyprus, 70. **MEMBERSHIPS** Archaeol Inst Am; Soc Prom Hellenic Studies; Asn Field Archaeol; Mod Greek Studies Asn. **RESEARCH** Cycladic Bronze Age; early Greek literature. **SELECTED PUBLICATIONS** Auth, Tacitus and Dio on Boudicca's rebellion, Am J Philol, 4/69; Greek towns of the Early Bronze Age, Class J, 10/69; Some notes on the interior of the Erechtheum, Athens Ann Archaeol, 4/72; coauth, Two Cypriot Bronze Age Sites at Kafkallia, Paul Astrom, Goteborg, Sweden, 72; The date of the last palace at Knossos, Am J Archaeol, spring 76; auth, Pioneers of Attic Vase Painting, In: The Greek Vase, Hudson-Mohawk Asn Cols & Univs, 81; The hub of commerce: Keos and Middle Helladic Greece, In: Temple University Aegean Symposium, Betancourt, 82; coauth, Consistency and diversity in the Middle Cycladic Era, In: Papers in Cycladic Prehistory, Univ Calif, Los Angeles, 79. **CONTACT ADDRESS** Dept of Classics, SUNY, Albany, 1400 Washington Ave, Albany, NY 12222-1000.

OVERBY, OSMUND R.
PERSONAL Born 11/08/1931, Minneapolis, MN, m, 1954, 3 children **DISCIPLINE** ART HISTORY **EDUCATION** St Olaf Col, BA, 53; Univ Wash, BA, 58; Yale Univ, MA, 60; PhD, 63. **CAREER** Architect Hist Am Bldgs surv, US Nat Park Serv, 60-61; Lectr, Univ Toronto, 63-64; From Asst Prof to Emeritus Prof, Univ of Mo Columbia, 64-; Dir Mus Art and Archaeol, 77-83; Vis Prof, Univ of Calif Berkeley, 81; Univ of Louisville, 89; Wash Univ in St. Louis, 96. **MEMBERSHIPS** Col Art Asn, Nat Trust Hist Preserv, Soc Archit Hist. **RESEARCH** American architectural and art history, 17th through 19th century European architectural history, **SELECTED PUBLICATIONS** Auth, "Ammi B. Young," in Macmillan Encyclopedia of Architects (NY: The Free Press, 82), Vol 4, 463-464; coauth, "The First Tree-Ring Dating of a Building in Missouri," Mo Preservation news 7-2 (Fall 84): 1-2, 6-7; auth, "Architectural Treasures on Ste. Genevieve," Gone West, Jefferson Nat Expansion Hist Asn, 3-2 (Apr 95): 5-11; auth, "German Churches in the Pelster Housebarn Neighborhood," in The German-American Experience in Missouri, ed. Howard W. Marshall and James W. Goodrich (Columbia: The Univ of MoExtension Div, 86), 85-105; ed, Art and Religion: Faith, Form and Reform, 1984 Paine Lectures in Religion, The Univ of Mo (Columbia), 86; auth, "The Saint Louis Art Museum: An Architectural History," The Bul of the St Louis Art Museum, New Ser Vol XVIII, 3 (Fall 87); auth, "From 1947: The Society of Architectural Historians," J of the Soc of Archit Historians XLIX (Mar 90): 9-14, and Soc of Archit Historians Membership Dir, 50th Anniversary Ed (90); auth, "A Place Called Union Station: An Architectural History of St. Louis Union Station," in St. Louis Union Station, A Place for People, A Place for Trains, ed. H. Roger Grant, Don L. Hofsommer, and Osmund Overby (St. Louis: The Merchantile Libr, 94), 59-90; auth, "The Kress Study Collection Comes to MU," in Catalogue of the Samule H. Kress Study Collection, ed. Norman Land (Columbia: Univ of Mo Press, 99); auth, William Adair Bernoudy, Architect:

Bringing the Legacy of Frank Lloyd Wright to St. Louis, Univ of Mo Press (Columbia), 99. **CONTACT ADDRESS** 1118 W Rollins Rd, Columbia, MO 65201. **EMAIL** overbyo@missouri.edu

OVERHOLT, THOMAS WILLIAM
PERSONAL Born 08/09/1935, Bucyrus, OH, m, 1957, 2 children **DISCIPLINE** BIBLICAL STUDIES, HISTORY OF RELIGIONS **EDUCATION** Heidelberg Col, BA 57; Chicago Theol Sem, BD, 61; Univ Chicago, MA, 63, PhD, 67. **CAREER** Prof relig studies, Yankton Col, 64-75; assoc prof, 75-80, prof relig studies, Univ Wis-Stevens Point, 80-99. **HONORS AND AWARDS** Soc Values Higher Educ fel anthrop, Univ Ariz, 73-74. **MEMBERSHIPS** Am Acad Relig; Soc Bibl Lit; Soc Values Higher Educ. **RESEARCH** Old Testament; American Indian religions. **SELECTED PUBLICATIONS** Auth, Prophecy in Cross-Cultural Perspective: A Sourcebook for Biblical Researchers, Atlanta: Scholars Press, 86; auth, Jeremiah, Harper's Bible Commentary, San Francisco: Harper and Row, 88; auth, Channels of Prophecy: The Social Dynamics of Prophetic Activity, Minneapolis: Fortress Press, 89; auth, Cultural Anthropology and the Old Testament, Minneapolis: Fortress Press, 96. **CONTACT ADDRESS** Dept of Philosophy, Univ of Wisconsin, Stevens Point, 2100 Main St, Stevens Point, WI 54481-3897. **EMAIL** toverhol@uwsp.edu

OWEN, CHRISTOPHER H.
PERSONAL Born 06/22/1959, Bryan, TX, m, 4 children **DISCIPLINE** HISTORY **EDUCATION** Univ Ga, AB, 81; Baylor Univ, MA, 86; Emory Univ, PhD, 91. **CAREER** From asst prof to assoc prof, Northeastern State Univ, 92-. **RESEARCH** American south; American religion. **SELECTED PUBLICATIONS** Auth, art, To Refrain From Political Affairs: Southern Evangelical, Cherokee Missions, and the Spirituality of the Church, 94; auth, art, Heaven's Gate, American Religious History, and the Culture of Death, 97; auth, art, To Keep the Way Open for Methodism: Georgia Weseylan Neutrality Towards Slavery, 1844-1861, 98; auth, The Sacred Flame of Love: Methodism and Society in Nineteenth-Century Georgia, 98. **CONTACT ADDRESS** Dept of History, Northeastern State Univ, Tahlequah, OK 74464. **EMAIL** owen@cherokee.nsuok.edu

OWEN, DAVID I.
PERSONAL Born 10/28/1940, Boston, MA, m, 1964, 2 children **DISCIPLINE** ASSYRIOLOGY, ARCHEOLOGY **EDUCATION** Boston Univ, AB, 62; Brandeis Univ, MA, 63, PhD, 69. **CAREER** Res asst archaeol, Univ Mus, Univ PA, 64-65, asst cur archaeol, 69-71, res assoc Assyriol, 71-75; asst prof Ancient Near Eastern studies, Dropsie Univ, 71-74; asst prof, 74-77, assoc prof, 77-82, chmn dept, 75-79, prof ancient near eastern hist & archaeol, dept dept near eastern studies, Cornell Univ, 83, Fulbright scholar, Ankara Univ, 66-68; adj prof Ancient Near Eastern Studies, Inst Nautical Archaeol, TX A&M Univ. **HONORS AND AWARDS** NEH Sr Fel, Am Sch Oriental Res, Jerusalem, 88-89. **MEMBERSHIPS** Archaeol Inst Am; Am Orient Soc; Israel Exploration Soc; Fondation assyriologique George Dossin. **RESEARCH** Assyriology; hist and archaeol of the Ancient Near East. **SELECTED PUBLICATIONS** Auth, The John Frederick Lewis Collection: Texts from the Third Millennium in the Free Library of Philadelphia, Materiali per il Vocabolario Neosumerico, Multigrafica Editrice, Rome, 75; A Sumerian letter from an angry housewife(?), In: The Bible World, Studies in Honor of Cyrus H Gordon, KTAV, New York, 80; Widow's rights in Ur III Sumer, In: Zeitschrift for Assyriologie, Berlin, 80; An Akkadian letter from Ugarit at Tel Aphek, In: Tel Aviv, Tel Aviv, 81; Of birds, eggs and turtles, In: Zeitschrift for Assyriologie, Berlin, 81; co-ed (with M A Morrison), Studies on the Civilization and Culture of Nuzi and the Hurrians in Honor of Ernest R Lacheman, 81 &; Neo-Sumerian Archival Texts Primarily from Nippur in the University Museum, the Oriental Institute and the Iraq Museum, 82, Eisenbrauns; Selected Ur III Texts from the Harvard Semitic Museum, Materiali per il Vocabolario Neosumerico, Vol 11, Multigrafica Editrice, Rome, 82. **CONTACT ADDRESS** Dept of Near Eastern Studies, Cornell Univ, Rockefeller Hall, Ithaca, NY 14853-2502. **EMAIL** dio1@cornell.edu

OWEN, THOMAS C.
PERSONAL Born 04/23/1943, Milwaukee, WI, m, 1964 **DISCIPLINE** HISTORY, SOVIET STUDIES **EDUCATION** Univ Wis at Madison, BA, 64; Harvard Univ, AM, 69; PhD, 73. **CAREER** Asst prof to prof, La State Univ, 74-. **HONORS AND AWARDS** Phi Kappa Phi; Phi Beta Kappa. **MEMBERSHIPS** Am Asn for the Advancement of Slavic Studies, Southern Conference on Slavic Studies. **RESEARCH** Russian social and economic history, 1700-present. **SELECTED PUBLICATIONS** Auth, Capitalism and Politics in Russia: A Social History of the Moscow Merchants 1855-1905, Cambridge Univ Press (New York, NY), 81; auth, The Corporation under Russian Law 1800-1917: A Study in Tsarist Economic Policy, Cambridge Univ Press (New York, NY), 91; auth, Russian Corporate Capitalism from Peter the Great to Perestroika, Oxford Univ Press (New York, NY), 95. **CONTACT ADDRESS** Dept Hist, Louisiana State Univ, Baton Rouge, LA 70803-3601. **EMAIL** towen1@lsu.edu

OWENS, JOHN BINGNER
PERSONAL Born 02/26/1944, Baltimore, MD, m, 1966, 3 children **DISCIPLINE** SPANISH & RENAISSANCE HISTORY **EDUCATION** Oberlin Col, BA, 66; Univ Wis-Madison, MA, 68, PhD(hist), 72. **CAREER** From instr to asst prof hist, NY Univ, 71-73; asst prof, Lehigh Univ, 73-75; asst prof, 75-80, Assoc Prof Hist, Idaho State Univ, 80-, Consult Span hist, Libr Cong, 72-73; Joint US- Span Comt Educ & Cult Affairs fel, Spain, 78-79; head labor hist res group, Inst Murcian Studies, 78-80. **MEMBERSHIPS** Rocky Mountain Medieval & Renaissance Asn; Renaissance Soc Am; Soc Span & Port Hist Studies; Soc Reformation Res; Historians Early Mod Europe. **RESEARCH** Cultural and social history of Spain, 1450-1650. **SELECTED PUBLICATIONS** Auth, Diana at the Bar: Hunting, aristocrats and the law in Renaissance Castile, Sixteenth Century J, 77; The conception of absolute royal power in sixteenth century Castile, Il Pensiero politico, 77; A city for the King: The impact of a rural revolt on Talavera during the Communidades of Castile, Societas, 78; Spanish Euro communism and the communist party organization in Murcia, Iberian Studies, 79; Rebelion, monarquia y oligarquia murciana en la epoca de Carlos V, Univ de Murcia, Spain, 80; Los regidores y jurados de Murcia, 1500-1650: Una guia, Anales de Univ de Murcia, 81; Posicion social y poder politico en Murcia, 1490-1570, Vol 5, 81 & La oliguarquia en defensa de su posicion, 1570-1650, Vol 6, 82, Historia de Murcia. **CONTACT ADDRESS** Dept of Hist, Idaho State Univ, 921 S 8th Ave, Pocatello, ID 83209-0001.

OWENS, KENNETH NELSON
PERSONAL Born 06/06/1933, Tacoma, WA, m, 1954, 2 children **DISCIPLINE** AMERICAN HISTORY **EDUCATION** Lewis & Clark Col, BA, 55; Univ Minn, PhD, 59. **CAREER** From asst prof to assoc prof hist, Northern Ill Univ, 59- 68; assoc prof, 68-70, dir native Am studies, 69-70, Prof Hist & Ethnic Studies, Calif State Univ, Sacramento, 70. Consult, Sacramento Hist Ctr, 78-80, City of Sacramento, 79-81, Bur Land Mgt, 80-81 & Western Water Educ Found, 80-82. **MEMBERSHIPS** AHA; Orgn Am Historians; Western Hist Asn; Am Indian Hist Soc. **RESEARCH** American West; American Indian ethnohistory; Pubic history. **SELECTED PUBLICATIONS** Auth, Galena, Grant and the Fortunes of War, Northern Ill Univ, 63; Research opportunities in Western territorial history, Ariz & West, 66; Pattern and structure in Western Territorial politics, Western Hist Quart, 70; contribr, Reader's Encycl of American West, Crowell, 77; The California Mother Lode Region: Historical Overview, Folsom District, Bur Land Mgt, US Dept Interior, 79; The Sacramento Past: An Exhibition Document for the Sacramento History Center (2 vols), Sacramento Hist Ctr, 80; Government & Politics in the Nineteenth Century, In: Essays in Western Historiography, Nebr Univ Press, 82; ed, Wreck of the Sv Nikolai, Ore Hist Soc Press (in prep). **CONTACT ADDRESS** Dept of Hist, California State Univ, Sacramento, Sacramento, CA 95819.

OWENS, LARRY
DISCIPLINE HISTORY **EDUCATION** Princeton Univ, PhD, 87; Rutgers Univ, PhD, 72. **CAREER** Prof, Univ Mass Amherst. **RESEARCH** Hist of sci and tech. **SELECTED PUBLICATIONS** Auth, The Counterproductive Management of Science during WWII, Bus Hist, 94; Where are We Going, Phil Morse? Changing Agendas and the Rhetoric of Obviousness in the Transformation of Computing at MIT 1939-1957; Science in the U.S.-The Last Century, 97. **CONTACT ADDRESS** Dept of Hist, Univ of Massachusetts, Amherst, Mass Ave, Amherst, MA 01003.

OWENS, NORA ESTELLE
PERSONAL Born 09/16/1948, Buna, TX, s **DISCIPLINE** AMERICAN HISTORY **EDUCATION** Wayland Baptist Col, BA, 71; Baylor Univ, MA, 73; Auburn Univ, PhD, 83. **CAREER** Asst prof hist, Wayland Baptist Univ, 74-, Consult, Educ Serv Div, Tex State Hist Asn 79- , prof hist, chair, social sciences div , TSUA consultant, 79-93. **HONORS AND AWARDS** Tchr of the year,86, 87, 90; Sears Found Awd for Excellence in Tchg; Who's Who Among Am Tchr. **MEMBERSHIPS** Southern Hist Asn, Texas State Historical Assoc, Texas Oral History Assoc, Texas Baptist Historical Society. **RESEARCH** Civil War and reconstruction; Texas; Am women. **SELECTED PUBLICATIONS** Coauth, Colonial America: A Handbook for Teachers & Civil War and Reconstruction: A Handbook for Teachers, Wayland Press, 70; auth, Have tape recorder will travel: Organizing an oral history program, Tex Historian, 81; Preachers and politics: Texas Baptists and reconstruction, Tex Baptist Hist, 82, Holding Forth the Word of Life; A Hist Of the Panhandle Pastor's and Laymen's Conf 96. **CONTACT ADDRESS** Wayland Baptist Univ, 1900 West 7th St, 387, Plainview, TX 79072. **EMAIL** owensest@mail.wbu.edu

OWENS, PATRICIA
PERSONAL s **DISCIPLINE** HISTORY **EDUCATION** Ill State Univ, BA, 72; Southern Ill Univ, MA, 75; PhD, 86; Univ Wyo, MA, 91. **CAREER** Prof, Wabash Valley Col, 85-. **HONORS AND AWARDS** Teacher of the Year, Wabash Valley Col, 85, 90, 93, 97. **MEMBERSHIPS** NEA, IEA **RESEARCH** Nineteenth-Century American West, Abraham Lincoln, Civil War, environmental history, national park idea. **SELECTED PUBLICATIONS** Book reviewer for School Libr J, J of Ill Hist, Lincoln Herald, SDak Hist, Nebr Hist, Ut Hist Soc, Western Hist Quart, Mont Mag of Hist. **CONTACT ADDRESS** Dept Hist, Wabash Valley Col, 2200 College Dr, Mountt Carmel, IL 62863-2657. **EMAIL** owensp@iecc.cc.il.us

OWENS, RICHARD H.
PERSONAL Born 11/01/1947, Hudson, NY, m, 1973, 2 children **DISCIPLINE** HISTORY **EDUCATION** Manhattan Col, BA; Old Dominion Univ, MA; Univ Md, PhD. **CAREER** Instructor to Asst Prof, Univ Md, 74-81; Dir of Alumni, Catholic Univ, 81-83; Dir of Alumni, Univ NHamp, 83-86; Vice Pres, Rio Grande Col, 86-88; Vice Pres, Lewis Univ, 88-96; Pres, Heidelberg Col, 96-. **RESEARCH** U.S. civil war; U.S. diplomacy; Native American history; American presidency. **SELECTED PUBLICATIONS** Auth, Peaceful Warrior: A Biography of Horace Porter. **CONTACT ADDRESS** President, Heidelberg Col, 310 E Market St, Tiffin, OH 44883-2434. **EMAIL** rowens@heidelberg.edu

OWENS, SUZANNE
DISCIPLINE ENGLISH, AMERICAN STUDIES **EDUCATION** Miami Univ, BA, 76; Col Will Mary, MA, 77; Ohio State Univ, PhD, 82. **CAREER** Instr, Winthrop Univ, 79-80; instr, Univ Fla, 81-82; lectr, Ohio State Univ, 83-85; assoc prof, Ursuline Col, 85-88; prof, Lorain CC Col, 88-. **HONORS AND AWARDS** Post doc fel, 83; Who's Who Am Teachers, 96-00; Phi Beta Kappa. **MEMBERSHIPS** ASA; NCTE; CCCC; MMLA; CEA; WHGC. **RESEARCH** American studies: regional art, architectural and cultural history. **SELECTED PUBLICATIONS** Auth, "Home, House and Solitude: Journals and Diaries of May Sarton," in May Sarton: Woman and Poet, ed. Constance Hunting (Nat Poet Found, 82); auth, "Circles of Power: Domestic Authority in Novels of Marilynne Robinson and Joan Chase," Wom Study Rev (84); auth, "Charlotte Perkins Gilman and a Feminist Ghost Story," in Haunting the Houses of Fiction, eds. Lynette Carpenter, Wendy Kolmar (Univ Tenn Pr, 91). **CONTACT ADDRESS** Arts Humanities Div, Lorain County Comm Col, 1005 N Abbe Rd, Elyria, OH 44035. **EMAIL** sowens@loraincc.edu

OWRAM, DOUGLAS R.
PERSONAL Born 11/08/1947, Aurora, ON, Canada **DISCIPLINE** HISTORY **EDUCATION** Queen's Univ, BA, 70, MA, 72; Univ Toronto, PhD, 76. **CAREER** Asst prof, 76-80, assoc prof hist, 80-85, assoc dean Arts 88-90, assoc dean Grad Stud, 92-94, assoc vice pres Acad, 94-95, VICE PRES ACADEMIC, UNIV ALBERTA, 95-. **HONORS AND AWARDS** Fel, Royal Soc Can, 90; Kaplan Awd Res Excellence, Univ Alta, 94. **SELECTED PUBLICATIONS** Auth, Building for Canada, 79; Promise of Eden 80; Government Generation, 86; Born at the Right Time, 96; coauth, Imperial Dreams and Colonial Realities, 88; A History of the Canadian Economy, 91; 2nd ed 96. **CONTACT ADDRESS** Univ of Alberta, 3-4 University Hall, Edmonton, AB, Canada T6G 2E1. **EMAIL** dowram@gpu.srv.ualberta.ca

P

PACA, BARBARA
PERSONAL Born 11/21/1959, CA, m **DISCIPLINE** ARCHITECTURE **EDUCATION** Bachelor of Landscape Archit, Univ Ore, Eugene, 84; hist of archit, Princeton Univ, MFA, 92, PhD, 95. **CAREER** Private practice in landscape archit; res in the hist of landscape archit. **HONORS AND AWARDS** Postdoctoral Fulbright, Rep of Ireland, 95; visitor, Inst for Advan Study, Princeton Univ, 97. **MEMBERSHIPS** Soc of Archit Hist; Intl Coun on Monuments and Sites; Amer Soc of Landscape Archit; Intl Soc of Arboriculture; Royal Horticulture Soc; Garden Hist Soc; Royal Oak Soc. **RESEARCH** History of Landscape Architecture; Sculpture; Iconography. **SELECTED PUBLICATIONS** Auth, Miscellanea Structurea Curiosa: The Cross-Curvenives of Vitruvius Hibernicus, Jour of Garden Hist, 97; The Mathematics of an 18th century American Wilderness Garden, Jour of Garden Hist, 96. **CONTACT ADDRESS** 431 E. 12th St., Apt. 3B, New York, NY 10009-4049. **EMAIL** barbarapaca@atsnyc.rr.com

PACKARD, RANDALL M.
DISCIPLINE HISTORY **EDUCATION** Wesleyan Univ, BA, 67; Northwestern Univ, MA, 68; Univ Wis Madison, PhD, 76. **CAREER** Asa G. Candler Prof African Hist. **HONORS AND AWARDS** CHOICE Outstanding Bk Awd. **RESEARCH** African history; social history of health and disease. **SELECTED PUBLICATIONS** Auth, White Plague, Black Labour: the Political Economy of Health and Disease in South Africa; Chiefship and Cosmology: A Study of Political Competition; **CONTACT ADDRESS** Dept History, Emory Univ, 221 Bowden Hall, 561 Kilgo Cir, Atlanta, GA 30322-1950. **EMAIL** packard@fox.sph.emory.edu

PACKULL, WERNER O.
DISCIPLINE HISTORY **EDUCATION** University Guelph, BA, 69; Emmanuel Bible Col, BTh, 69; University Waterloo,

MA, 70; Queen's Univ, PhD, 74. **CAREER** Prof **RESEARCH** Radical Reformation; Magisterial Reformation; late medieval Renaissance and modern German history. **SELECTED PUBLICATIONS** Auth, Denck's Alleged Baptism by Hubmaier: Its Significance for the Origin of South German-Austrian Anabaptism, 73, Gottfried Seebass on Hans Hut: A Discussion, 75 & coauth, From Monogenesis to Polygenesis: The Historical Discussion of Anabaptist Origins, 75, Mennonite Quart Rev, 75; auth, Zur Entwicklung des Suddentschen Taufertums in: Umstrittenes. **CONTACT ADDRESS** Dept of History, Univ of Waterloo, Conrad Grebel Col, 200 Westmount Rd, Waterloo, ON, Canada N2L 3G6. **EMAIL** wopackul@uwaterloo.ca

PADOVANO, ANTHONY
PERSONAL Born 09/18/1934, Harrison, NJ, m, 1974, 4 children **DISCIPLINE** AMERICAN STUDIES **EDUCATION** St Thomas Intl Univ, Rome, MA, 62; Gregorian Univ, STD, 62; Fordham Univ, PhD, 80. **CAREER** Prof syst theol, Darlington Sem, 62-74; Prof AM Lit & Relig Studies, Ramapo Col, 71-, Consultor, Nat Cath Off Radio & TV, 67; vis prof, 25 American Universities, include Villanova Univ, 68, St. Mary's Col, Ind, 69, Univ St. Thomas, 69, Univ Wyo, 70, Barry Col, Fla, 71, Seattle Univ, 72, Fordham Univ, 73, Univ San Francisco, 73, Boston Col, 73, Assumption Col, Worcester, Mass 73, prof, Ramapo Col, NJ, 71-; rep US dialogue group, Lutheran-Roman Cath Theol Conversations, 70-72. **HONORS AND AWARDS** Nat Cath Bk Awd, 70; Angel Awd, 85; New Jersey Writers Conf Awd, 85; Golden, Silver Angel Awd, 86; 3 Plays, Hollywood; Silver Angel Awd, 88. **MEMBERSHIPS** Cath Theol Soc Am. **RESEARCH** Systematic theology; American literature; contemporary philosophy. **SELECTED PUBLICATIONS** Auth, Christmas to Calvary, Paulist Press (Ramsey, NJ), 87; auth, Love and Destiny, Paulist Press (Ramsey, NJ), 87; auth, Summer Lightening: A Play in Four Acts and Four Seasons, Paulist Press (Ramsey, NJ), 88; auth, Conscience and Conflict, Paulist Press (Mahwah, NJ), 89; auth, Reform and Renewal: Essays on Authority, Ministry and Social Justice Sheed & Ward (Kansas City, MO), 90; auth, A Celebration of Life, Resurrection Press (NY), 90; auth, The Church Today: Belonging and Believing, Franciscan Communications (Los Angeles, CA), 90; auth, Scripture in the Streets, Paulist Press (Mahwah, NJ), 92; auth, A Retreat with Thomas Merton: Biography as Spiritual Journey, St. Anthony Messenger Press, (Cincinnati, OH), 95; auth, Hope is a Dialogue, Caritas Communications (Mequon, WI), 98. **CONTACT ADDRESS** Dept American Studies, Ramapo Col of New Jersey, 505 Ramapo Valley Rd, Mahwah, NJ 07430-1623. **EMAIL** anthonypadovano@mail.com

PAGE, JAMES E.
PERSONAL Born 08/03/1942, Woodstock, ON, Canada **DISCIPLINE** CANADIAN STUDIES **EDUCATION** Queen's Univ, BA, 67, MA, 68. **CAREER** Dir, Can stud, Secy State Can, 84-89; dir gen, educ sup, 89-94, Exec Secy, National Literacy Secretariat, Human Resources Development Canada, 94-; adj res prof, Inst Can Stud, Carleton Univ, 91-. **MEMBERSHIPS** Can Asn Curric Stud; Champlain Soc; Australian & NZ Asn Can Stud; Brit Asn Can Stud; Gessellschaft fur Kanada-Studien; Asn francaise d'etudes canadiennes. **RESEARCH** Canadian studies; education. **SELECTED PUBLICATIONS** Auth, Canadian Studies in Community Colleges, 73; auth, Seeing Ourselves, 79; auth, A Canadian Context for Science Education, 80; auth, Reflections on the Symons' Report: The State of Canadian Studies in 1980, 81; coauth, Some Questions of Balance: Human Resources, Higher Education and Canadian Studies, 84; contribur, To Know Ourselves: The Report of the Commission on Canadian Studies, 76; ed bd, J Can Stud, 79-93. **CONTACT ADDRESS** National Literacy Secretariat, 15 Eddy St, Ottawa, ON, Canada K1A 1K5.

PAGE, STANLEY W.
PERSONAL Born 11/18/1913, Chicago, IL, m, 1966 **DISCIPLINE** MODERN RUSSIAN HISTORY **EDUCATION** City Col New York, BSS, 35; Harvard Univ, PhD(hist), 47. **CAREER** Instr hist, Simmons Col, 45-46; from instr to assoc prof, 47-65, Prof Hist, City Col New York, 65-, Instr, Harvard Univ, 47; prof hist, City Univ New York, 66-; Am Philos Soc grant, 68. **MEMBERSHIPS** AHA; Am Asn Advan Slavic Studies; Asn Advan Baltic Studies. **RESEARCH** Lenin; Russian revolution; Baltic states. **SELECTED PUBLICATIONS CONTACT ADDRESS** Dept of Hist, City Col, CUNY, New York, NY 10031.

PAGE, WILLIE F.
PERSONAL Born 01/02/1929, Dothan, AL, m **DISCIPLINE** AFRICAN-AMERICAN STUDIES **EDUCATION** Wayne State University, BSME, 1961; Adelphi University, MBA, 1970; NYork Univ, PhD, 1975. **CAREER** Brooklyn Coll, CUNY, asso prof, 79-; Dept of Africana Studies, Brooklyn Coll, chmn, asso prof, 74-79; Nassau-Suffolk CHES, exec dir, 72-74; Glen Cove Coop Coll Center, SUNY, dir, lectr, 71-72; Grumman Aerospace, asst to dir prodn, 67-70; The Boeing Co, engr, 61-63; New York City Head Start Regional Training Office, consult, 75-79; Natl Endowment for the Humanities, consult, 77-78; NY State Educ Dept, consult, 77-79. **HONORS AND AWARDS** EPDA Fellowship, USOE, NYU, 1973; Dissertation Year Fellowship Nat Fellowships Fund Atlanta, 1975; Henry Meissner Research Awd, Phi Delta Kappa, NYU, 1975; NEH, Fellowship Seminar on Slavery, Harvard Univ, 1978. **MEMBERSHIPS** African Heritage Studies Assn, 1974-80; Am Educ Research Assn, 1974-80; Weeksville Soc Brooklyn, board member, 1979-80. **CONTACT ADDRESS** Afro-American Studies, Brooklyn Col, CUNY, 2901 Bedford Ave, Brooklyn, NY 11210-2813.

PAINTER, NELL IRVINE
PERSONAL Born 08/02/1942, Houston, TX, m, 1989, 2 children **DISCIPLINE** HISTORY **EDUCATION** Univ Calif Berkeley, BA, 64; Univ Calif at Los Angeles, MA, 67; Harvard Univ, PhD, 74. **CAREER** Asst/Assoc Prof, Univ of Pa, 74-80; Prof, Univ of NC Chapel Hill, 80-88; Prof/Edwards Prof, Princeton Univ, 88-. **HONORS AND AWARDS** Guggenheim Fel, 82-83; Nat Endowment for Humanities, 91-92. **MEMBERSHIPS** AHA, Orgn of Am Historians, Am Studies Asn of Black Women Hist. **RESEARCH** Whiteness, Beauty. **SELECTED PUBLICATIONS** Auth, Exodusters: Black Migration to Kansas After Reconstruction, Alfred A. Knopf (NY), 77; auth, The Narrative of Hosea Hudson: His Life as a Negro Communist in the South, Harvard Univ Press (Cambridge, MA), 79; auth, Standing at Armageddon: The United States, 1877-1919, W.W. Norton (NY), 87; auth, Sojourner Truth, A Life, A Symbol, W.W. Norton (NY), 96; ed, Narrative of Sojourner Truth, Penguin Classic Ed, 98; ed, Incidents in the Life of a Slave Girl, Penguin Classic Ed, 00. **CONTACT ADDRESS** African Am Studies, Princeton Univ, 112 Dickinson Hall, Princeton, NJ 98544-0001. **EMAIL** painter@princeton.edu

PAJAKOWSKI, PHILIP E.
DISCIPLINE HISTORY **EDUCATION** PhD,History IN Univ, 89; MA, Hist IN Univ, 82; BA History Manchester Col 80. **CAREER** Assoc prof, 89, St Anselm Col. **RESEARCH** Polit thought and policies of Polish conservative landowners in the empire in the last half of the 19th century and their participation in the parliament in Vienna; soc order and perceptions of polit radicalism among Central Europ elite groups. **SELECTED PUBLICATIONS** Auth, The Polish, Club, Badeni, and the Austrian Parliamentary Crisis of 1897, Canadian Slavonic Papers, 93; Dynamics of Galician Polish Conservatism in the Late Nineteenth Century, Jahrbucher Geschichte Osteuropas, 95; Austrian Legislation against Social Radicalism 1886, Historian, 95. **CONTACT ADDRESS** Saint Anselm Col, 100 Saint Anselm Dr, Manchester, NH 03102-1310. **EMAIL** ppajakow@anselm.edu

PAL, PRATAPADITYA
PERSONAL Born 09/01/1935, Sylhet, Bangladesh, m, 1968, 2 children **DISCIPLINE** HISTORY OF ART **EDUCATION** Univ Delhi, BA, 56; Univ Calcutta, MA, 58, DPhil(archit of Nepal), 62; Cambridge Univ, PhD(sculpture & painting of Nepal), 65. **CAREER** Lectr Indian studies, Cambridge Univ, 63-64; res assoc, Am Acad Benares, India, 66-67; keeper Indian collections, Mus Fine Arts, 67-69; sr cur Indian & Islamic Art, Los Angeles County Mus of art, 70-95; Adj prof fine arts, Univ South Calif, 71-89, UCLA, 70; UCSB, 80; UC Irvine, 92-96; Vis cur of Indian, Himalayan & S.E. Asian Art, Art Inst of Chicago, 96-; fel for res, Norton Simon Mus, Pasadena, 96-; General ed, Marg Publications,Mumbai, 94-. **HONORS AND AWARDS** Distinguished Achievement Awd, Assoc Indians in N Am, 80; Univ Gold Medal, Calcutta Univ, 58; Sir. B.C., Law Memorial Gold Medal, Asiatic Soc, Calcutta, 79; Distinguished Achievement Awd, Asn Indians in North Am, 80; Getty Scholar, 96; hon fel, Asia Soc, Mumbai. **MEMBERSHIPS** Asia Soc; Asiatic Soc, Calcutta. **RESEARCH** History, religion, arts, and architecture of the Indian subcontinent, Himalayas, and S.E. Asia. **SELECTED PUBLICATIONS** Auth, Nepal Where the Gods are Young, Asia Soc, NY, 75; auth, The Sensuous Line, Los Angeles County Mus Art, 76; auth, The Sensuous Immortals, Los Angeles County Mus Art & Mass Inst Technol, 77; auth, The Ideal Image, Asia Soc, NY, 78; auth, In Her Image, Univ Calif, Santa Barbara, 80; auth, Hindu Religion and Iconology, Vichitra Press, 81; auth, Elephants and Ivories, 81; auth, Art of Tibet, 02; auth, Art of Nepal, 85; auth, Indian Sculptures, vol 1, 86; vol 2, 88; auth, Indian Painting, vol 1, 93, Los Angeles County Mus of Art; auth, Divine Images, Hujan Visions, 97, Nat Gallery of Canada, Ottowa; auth, Tibet: Traditions & Change, 98, Albuquerque Mus of Art. **CONTACT ADDRESS** Los Angeles County Mus of Art, 10582 Chevoit Dr, Los Angeles, CA 90064.

PALAIS, JAMES BERNARD
PERSONAL Born 03/08/1934, Cambridge, MA, m, 1959, 2 children **DISCIPLINE** HISTORY **EDUCATION** Harvard Univ, BA, 55, PhD(Far East lang), 68; Yale Univ, MA, 60. **CAREER** Asst prof hist, Norfolk State Col, 66-67; asst prof, Univ Maine, Portland-Gorham, 67-68; asst prof, 68-75, Assoc Prof Hist, Univ Wash, 75-, Assoc Prof E Asian Studies, 79-, Nat Defense Foreign Lang grant, Korean, 60-62; Foreign Area fel, 63-65; mem joint comt Korean studies, Soc Sci Res Coun-Am Coun Learned Soc, 71-; Nat Endowment for Humanities res fel, 75-76. **MEMBERSHIPS** Asn Asian Studies. **RESEARCH** Korean history, especially the 17th through the 20th centuries. **SELECTED PUBLICATIONS** Auth, Records and recordkeeping in nineteenth century Korea, J Asian Studies, 571; contribr, Stability in the Yi Dynasty (in Korean), Tradition & Change in Korea, Seoul, 73 & Democracy in South Korea, 1948-72, In: Without Parallel: Essay on Korea, Pantheon, 74; ed, Occasional Papers on Korea, Nos 1-5, 74-77; auth, Politics and Policy in Traditional Korea, 75; auth, Political leadership in the Yi Dynasty, In: Political Leadership in Korea, Univ Wash, 76; auth, "South Korea," in Asian Watch Committee, Human Rights in Korea, 86; a Search For Korean Uniqueness, Harvard J of Asiatic Studies, Vol 0055, 1995; Korea Since 1850 - Lone,s, Mccormack,g, American Historical Review, Vol 0100, 1995; auth, Confucian Statecraft and Korean Institutions: Yu Hyongwon and the Late Choson Dynasty, Univ Wash, 96. **CONTACT ADDRESS** Jackson Sch of Int Studies, Univ of Washington, PO Box 353650, Seattle, WA 98195. **EMAIL** palais@u.washington.edu

PALMEGIANO, EUGENIA M.
PERSONAL Born 03/09/1939, Lawrence, MA **DISCIPLINE** MODERN BRITISH HISTORY **EDUCATION** Georgian Court Col, AB, 60; Rutgers Univ, MA, 61, PhD(mod Brit hist), 66, JD, 79. **CAREER** Lectr mod Europ hist, Col Notre Dame, Md, 61-62; teaching asst, Rutgers Univ, 62-64; from instr to assoc prof, 66-77, dir honors prog, 70-77, Prof Mod Brit Hist, St Peter's Col, NJ, 77-, Fac fel, St Peter's Col, 72 & 82; mem, Fulbright-Hays Nat Selection Comt, UK, 77-81, chair, 78 & 79; consult, Nat Endowment for Humanities, 79- & NJ Comt Humanities, 80-; summer sem fel, Nat Endowment for Humanities, 81. **MEMBERSHIPS** AHA; Conf Brit Studies; Am Bar Asn. **RESEARCH** Victorian cultural history; history of Victorian periodical press. **SELECTED PUBLICATIONS CONTACT ADDRESS** Dept of Hist, Saint Peter's Col, 2641 Kennedy Blvd, Jersey City, NJ 07306-5997.

PALMER, PHYLLIS MARYNICK
PERSONAL Born 04/05/1944, Dallas, TX **DISCIPLINE** AMERICAN HISTORY **EDUCATION** Oberlin Col, AB, 66; Ohio State Univ, MA, 67, PhD(hist), 73. **CAREER** Asst prof hist, Mt Holyoke Col, 72-77; assoc prof Am studies, women's studies, George Washington Univ, 77-. **HONORS AND AWARDS** ACLS res fel 93. **MEMBERSHIPS** AHA; Orgn Am Historians; Am Studies Asn; Nat Women's Studies Asn. **RESEARCH** Women in United States; Race Studies and Postwar interracialism **SELECTED PUBLICATIONS** Auth, Domesticity and dirt: Domestic service in the nineteenth century, In: Quantification and Psychology; Toward a New History, Univ Press of Am, 80; White women/Black women: The dualism of female identity and experience, Feminist Studies 83. **CONTACT ADDRESS** American Studies Dept, The George Washington Univ, 2108G St NW, Washington, DC 20052-0001. **EMAIL** ppalmer@gwu.edu

PALMER, RUSS
PERSONAL Born 05/04/1936, Detroit, MI **DISCIPLINE** BIBLICAL STUDIES, THE HISTORY OF CHRISTIAN THOUGHT, AND CHRISTIAN ETHICS **EDUCATION** Wayne State Univ, BA; Dallas Theol Sem, MA; Univ Iowa, PhD. **CAREER** Instr, Univ Nebr, Omaha, 65-; ed, Karl Barth Soc Newsl. **MEMBERSHIPS** Exec bd, Karl Barth Soc of N Am; steering comt, Reformed Theol and Hist Consultation, Am Acad of Relig. **SELECTED PUBLICATIONS** Auth, Introduction to World Religions Study Guide, Kendall-Hunt Publ. **CONTACT ADDRESS** Univ of Nebraska, Omaha, Omaha, NE 68182.

PALMER, SCOTT W.
DISCIPLINE HISTORY **EDUCATION** Univ Kansas, BA, 89; Univ Ill, PhD, 97 **CAREER** Adjunct asst prof, Univ Ill, 97-98; asst prof, Western Ill Univ, 98- **HONORS AND AWARDS** Fulbright-Hays Res Fel; IREX Fel; Kennon Inst Grant; Center for Russian & East European Studies, Univ Kansas, 98- **MEMBERSHIPS** AAASS; Historical Soc **RESEARCH** Russian Intellectual & Cultural History; Technology; Culture & Process of Moderation **SELECTED PUBLICATIONS** Auth, "On Wings of Courage: Public Air-Mindedness and National Identity in Late Imperial Russia," Russian Rev, 95; auth, "O vliianii transatlanticheskogo pereleta Ch. Lindberga na amerikanskoe I evropeiskoe obshchestvo," Iz istorii aviatsii I kosmonavtiki, 95; auth, "A Crisis of Faith: Boris Savinkov and the Fighting Organization, 1903-1912," Scottish Slavonic Rev, 92 **CONTACT ADDRESS** Dept Hist, Western Illinois Univ, 438 Morgan Hall, Macomb, IL 61455. **EMAIL** SW-palmer@wiu.edu

PALMER, STANLEY HOWARD
PERSONAL Born 10/22/1944, Washington, DC, m, 1975, 4 children **DISCIPLINE** HISTORY **EDUCATION** Brown Univ, BA, 66; Harvard Univ, MA, 72, PhD(hist), 73. **CAREER** Asst prof, 73-78, Assoc Prof, 78-88, Prof 88-, Brit Hist, Univ Tex, Arlington, 80-, Fel, Woodrow Wilson Int Ctr for Scholars, 81. **HONORS AND AWARDS** Research Achievement Awd, 89; Academy of Distinguished Teachers, 96; Graduate Advisor Awd, Univ Tex, Arlington, 01; **MEMBERSHIPS** AHA; Conf Brit Studies; Am Comt Irish Studies; Irish Am Cult Inst. **RESEARCH** Eighteenth, nineteenth century; British and Irish history; police in England and Ireland; British empire; comparative frontiers. **SELECTED PUBLICATIONS** Auth, Economic Arithmetic: A Guide to the Statistical Source of English Commerce, Industry, and Finance, 1700-1850, Garland, 77; Essays in Frontiers in World History, Texas A&M, 83; Police and Protest in England and Ireland, 1780-1850, Cambridge, 88, repr,

90; co-ed, Essays on North American Discovery and Exploration, Texas A&M, 88. **CONTACT ADDRESS** Dept of Hist, Univ of Texas, Arlington, Box 19529, Arlington, TX 76019. **EMAIL** spalmer@uta.edu

PALMER, WILLIAM
PERSONAL Born 06/15/1951, Ames, IA, m, 1983, 2 children **DISCIPLINE** HISTORY **EDUCATION** Iowa State Univ, BS, 73; Univ Maine, PhD, 81. **CAREER** Asst prof his, Marshall Univ, 84-88; assoc prof his, Marshall Univ, 88-92; prof his, Marshall Univ, 92-. **HONORS AND AWARDS** Fel, Royal Historical Society; Reynolds Outstanding Teacher Awd; Who's Who in American Colleges and Universities. **MEMBERSHIPS** Am Hist Asn; North Am Conference on British Studies; Royal Hist Society. **RESEARCH** Early modern England and Ireland; historiography. **SELECTED PUBLICATIONS** Auth, The Political Career of Oliver St. John, 1637-1649, Univ of Delaware Press, 93; auth, "That 'Insolent Liberty': Honor, Rites of Power, and Persuasion in Sixteenth Century Ireland", in Renaissance Quart 44 2, 93; auth, The Problems of Ireland in Tudor Foreign Policy, 1485-1603, Boydell Press, 94; auth, "Borderlands and Colonies: Tudor Ireland in the Perspective of Colonial America", in Eire: Ireland 3, 94; auth, "Ireland and Tudor Foreign Policy in the 1570s", in The Historian 58 1, 95; auth, "Sir Richard Southern Looks Back: a Portrait of the Medievalist as a Young Man", Va Quart Review 74 1, 98; auth, "High Officeholding, Foreign Policy, and the British Dimension in the Tudor Far North, 1525-1563", in Albion 29 4, 97. **CONTACT ADDRESS** Department of History, Marshall Univ, Huntington, WV 25755. **EMAIL** Palmer@marshall.edu

PALUDAN, PHILLIP SHAW
PERSONAL Born 01/26/1938, St. Cloud, MN, m, 1990, 2 children **DISCIPLINE** UNITED STATES HISTORY **EDUCATION** Occidental Col, BA, 60, MA, 63; Univ Ill, Urbana-Champaign, PhD(hist), 68. **CAREER** Assoc prof, 68-80, Prof Hist, Univ Kans, 80-, Fel, Harvard Law Sch, 73-74; Am Coun Learned Soc study fel, 73-74 & res fel, 75; Guggenheim fel, 79-80. **HONORS AND AWARDS** Lincoln Prize, 95; Barondess-Lincoln Awd, 95. **MEMBERSHIPS** Orgn Am Historians. **RESEARCH** Civil War and Reconstruction; United States legal and constitutional history; 19th century social history. **SELECTED PUBLICATIONS** Auth, John Norton Pomeroy, State Right Nationalist, Am J Legal Hist, 68; Law and the Failure of Reconstruction: The Case of T M Cooley, J Hist Ideas, 72; American Civil War Considered as a Crisis in Law and Order, Am Hist Rev, 72; auth, American Civil War: Triumph Through Tragedy, Civil War Hist, 74; auth, A Covenant with Death, Univ Ill, 75; auth, Lincoln, the Rule of Law and the American Revolution, J Ill State Hist Soc, 77; ed, Issues Past and Present, Heath, 77; auth, Victims: A True Story of the Civil War, Univ Tenn; auth, Let Us Have Peace - Grant,Ulysses,S. and The Politics of War and Reconstruction, 1861-1868 - Simpson,bd, Pennsylvania Magazine of History and Biography, Vol 0117, 93; auth, Lincoln in American Memory - Peterson,md, Historian, Vol 0057, 95; auth, A People's Contest: The Union and Civil War, Harper-Collins, 88; auth, The Presidency of Abraham Lincoln, Univ Press of Kansas, 94. **CONTACT ADDRESS** Dept of Hist, Univ of Kansas, Lawrence, Lawrence, KS 66044. **EMAIL** ppaludan@eagle.cc.ukans.edu

PANAITESCU, ADRIAN
PERSONAL Born 03/07/1937, Bucharest, Romania, m, 1963, 1 child **DISCIPLINE** ARCHITECTURE **EDUCATION** Sch of Architecture, Romania, architect 63; PhD, 75. **CAREER** School of Arch, Romania, prof 64-78; sr designer, RBS & D, NYork. **HONORS AND AWARDS** 1st Prize Arch 75; 1st Prize Exequo Church Switzerland, 84 **MEMBERSHIPS** SAH **RESEARCH** Hist and theory of arch; painting. **CONTACT ADDRESS** 35 Scott Rd, Greenwich, CT 06831-2832.

PANELLA, ROBERT J.
DISCIPLINE ROMAN HISTORY AND HISTORIOGRAPHY **EDUCATION** Harvard, PhD. **CAREER** Prof, Fordham Univ. **SELECTED PUBLICATIONS** Auth, The Letters of Apollonius of Tyana: A Critical Text with Prolegomena, Translation, and Commentary, 79; Greek Philosophers and Sophists in the Fourth Century A.D.: Studies in Eunapius of Sardis, 90. **CONTACT ADDRESS** Dept of Class Lang and Lit, Fordham Univ, 113 W 60th St, New York, NY 10023.

PANKAKE, MARCIA J.
DISCIPLINE AMERICAN STUDIES **EDUCATION** Univ Minn, BA, 62, MA 67, MA, 71, PhD, 75. **CAREER** Prof and Bibliographer, Wilson Libr, Univ Minn. **MEMBERSHIPS** Am Antiquarian Soc; ALA; MLA. **RESEARCH** Am travel **SELECTED PUBLICATIONS** Coauth, "A Guide to Coordinated and Cooperative Collection Development," Lib Res & Tech Ser 27, 83; auth, "From Book Selection to Collection Management," Advan in Librnship 13, 83; coauth, "English and American Literature," in Selection of Library Materials in the Humanities, Social Sciences, and Sciences, Am Lib Asn, 85; co-ed, English and American Literature: Sources and Strategies for Collection Development, Am Lib Asn, 87; co-ed, The Prairie Home Companion Folk Song Book, Viking, 88; auth, A Prairie Home, Canonplace Book, 99. **CONTACT ADDRESS** Univ of Minnesota, Twin Cities, 309 19th Ave So, Minneapolis, MN 55455. **EMAIL** m-pank@tc.umn.edu

PAOLETTI, JO
DISCIPLINE AMERICAN CULTURE **EDUCATION** Syracuse Univ, BS, 71; Univ RI, MS, 76; Univ MD, PhD, 80. **CAREER** Am Stud Dept, Univ Md **RESEARCH** 1970s unisex trends, on-line exhibition and publ. **SELECTED PUBLICATIONS** Co-auth, Conclusion" in Men and Women: Dressing the Part, Smithsonian Inst Press, 89; The Children's Department,Men and Women: Dressing the Part, Smithsonian Inst Press, 89; auth, Little Lord Fauntleroy and His Dad, Hope and Glory, 91; The Value of Conversation in Teaching and Learning, Essays on Teaching, Univ Md IBM-TQ Project, 97; The Gendering of Infants' and Toddlers' Clothing in America, The Material Culture of Gender/The Gender of Material Culture, Winterthur Mus, 97. **CONTACT ADDRESS** Am Stud Dept, Univ of Maryland, Col Park, 4210 Underrwood St, University Park, MD 20782. **EMAIL** jp4@umail.umd.edu

PAPACOSMA, SOLON VICTOR
PERSONAL Born 07/11/1942, Freeport, NY, m, 1984, 1 child **DISCIPLINE** BALKAN & MODERN EUROPEAN HISTORY **EDUCATION** Bowdoin Col, AB, 64; Ind Univ, Bloomington, MA, 66, PhD(hist), 71. **CAREER** From asst prof to prof hist, Kent State Univ, 69-, Coordr Hellenic Studies, 76-; managing ed mat on Greece, Southeastern EuropeEurope du Sud-Est, 73-76; dir, Lennitzer Center for NATO and European Union Studies, 92-. **HONORS AND AWARDS** Am Coun Learned Soc grant res in Greece & Eng, 72-73; Fulbright-Hays fac res abroad grant, 78-79. **MEMBERSHIPS** AHA; Am Asn Advan Slavic Studies; Mod Greek Studies Asn; Am Asn Southeast Europ Studies. **RESEARCH** Politics in modern Greece; NATO; Balkans. **SELECTED PUBLICATIONS** Auth, The Military in Greek Politics: The 1909 Coup d'Etat, Kent State Univ, 77; Greek transl, Hestia, Athens, 81; co-ed, NATO after Forty Years, Scholarly Resources, Inc, 90; co-ed, NATO in the Post-Cold War Era: Does It Have a Future?, St. Martin's Pr, 95. **CONTACT ADDRESS** Dept of Hist, Kent State Univ, PO Box 5190, Kent, OH 44242-0001. **EMAIL** spapacos@kent.edu

PAPADAKIS, ARISTEIDES
PERSONAL Born 08/01/1936, Greece **DISCIPLINE** MEDIEVAL & BYZANTINE HISTORY **EDUCATION** Greek Archdiocese Holy Cross Orthodox Theol Sch, BA, 61; Fordham Univ, MA, 64; PhD, 68. **CAREER** Instr hist, Fordham Univ, 65-67; lectr, Col New Rochelle, 66-67; asst prof, 68-71, assoc prof, 71-84, prof, hist, 84-, Univ Md, Baltimore County . **MEMBERSHIPS** AHA; Mediaeval Acad Am; Am Cath Hist Asn; Mod Greek Studies Asn. **RESEARCH** Byzantine and medieval history; ecclesiastical history. **SELECTED PUBLICATIONS** Auth, The Unpublished Life of Euthymius of Sardis: Bodleianus Laudianus Graecus, 69; auth, Traditio, 70; auth, Grennadius II and Mehmet the Conqueror, Byzantion, 72; coauth, John X Camaterus Confronts Innocent III: an Unpublished Correspondence, Byzantino-slavica, 72; auth, Crisis in Byzantium: The Filoque Controversy in the Patriarchate of Gregory II, 1283-1289, Fordham Univ Press, 83; coauth, The Christian East and the Rise of the Papacy. The Church 1071-1453, St. Vladimir's Seminary Press, 94. **CONTACT ADDRESS** Dept of Hist, Univ of Maryland, Baltimore, Baltimore, MD 21250.

PAPADOPOULOS, JOHN K.
PERSONAL Born 08/29/1958, Sydney, Australia, m, 1991 **DISCIPLINE** ARCHAEOLOGY **EDUCATION** Univ Sydney, BA, 80; Univ Sydney, MA, 83; Univ Sydney, PhD, 88 **CAREER** Deputy dir, Australian Archaeol Inst Athens, 87-91; asst prof, Univ Sydney, 91-93; assoc curator, J Paul Getty Museum, 94- **HONORS AND AWARDS** Fel Athens Archaeol Soc **MEMBERSHIPS** Archaeol Inst Amer; Australian Archaeol Inst Athens **RESEARCH** Aegean Archaeology **SELECTED PUBLICATIONS** Auth, The Early Iron Age Cemetery at Torone, forthcoming; coauth, Torone I: The Excavations of 1975-1978, Athens Archaeol Soc, 98; auth, "Drawing Circles: Experimental Archaeology and the Pivoted Multiple Brush," Amer Jrnl Archaeol, 98 **CONTACT ADDRESS** J. Paul Getty Mus, 1200 Getty Center Dr, Suite 1000, Los Angeles, CA 90049-1687. **EMAIL** jpapadopoulos@getty.edu

PAPALAS, ANTHONY JOHN
PERSONAL Born 06/17/1939, Detroit, MI, m, 1974, 2 children **DISCIPLINE** HISTORY **EDUCATION** Wayne State Univ, BA, 61, MA, 63; Univ Chicago, PhD(hist), 69. **CAREER** Asst prof hist, Carthage Col, 69-70; Assoc Prof Hist, E Carolina Univ, 70-; full prof, 95. **MEMBERSHIPS** Am Philol Asn; Am Asn Ancient Historians; Classical Asn of the Middle West. **RESEARCH** Roman Athens; Greece under Roman rule; Naval history Greece and Rome, Panhellenic festivals. **SELECTED PUBLICATIONS** Auth, Lucius Verus and the Hospitality of Herodes Atticus, Athenaeum, 78; auth, Ancient Icaria, Chicago, 90; auth, "Box Athletes in Ancient Greece," Stadion 17, 2 (91): 165-193; auth, "Polycrates of Samos and the First Truemil Flut," Mariners Minor 85 (99): 3-4; auth, "The Pariam Expedition and the Development of the Athenian Navy," Ancient History Bulletin 14.3 (00): 107-119. **CONTACT ADDRESS** Dept of Hist, East Carolina Univ, Greenville, NC 27834. **EMAIL** papalasa@mail.ecu.edu

PAPAYANIS, NICHOLAS
PERSONAL Born 03/09/1940, New York, NY, m **DISCIPLINE** MODERN FRENCH SOCIAL AND URBAN HISTORY **EDUCATION** NYork Univ, BA, 61; Harvard Univ, MA, 63; Univ Wis, PhD, 69; Fulbright Fel, Univ Paris, 65-66. **CAREER** From lectr to asst prof, 68-78, prof hist, Brooklyn Col, 78-, Fac res grant, Res Found City Univ NY, 72-73. **HONORS AND AWARDS** Prof Staff Congess-City Univ NY Research Awd, 90, 93, 95, 97, 98, 00, 01; Dir, NEH Summer Seminar 94, 96; NEH Fel, 91-92, 98-99; Ethyle R Wolfe Inst for the Human Fel, 00-01. **MEMBERSHIPS** Phi Beta Kappa; Soc French Hist Studies; AHA; NY City Area Seminar French Hist; Western Soc French Hist. **RESEARCH** Urban planning in Paris; French transportation & labor hist. **SELECTED PUBLICATIONS** Auth, Alphonse Merrheim: The Emergence of Reformism in Revolutionary Syndicalism, 1871-1925, Martinus Nijhoff (Dordrecht/Boston/Lancaster), 85; auth, "La proletarisation des cochers de fiacres a Paris (1878-1889)," in Le Mouvement Social, no 132 (July-Spet 85): 59-82; auth, "The Coachment of Nineteenth-Century Paris: A Statistical Profile," The J of Contemp Hist 20 (April 85): 305-321; auth, "Un secteur des transports parisiens: le fiacre, de libre entreprise au monopole (1790-1855)," in Histoire, Economie, et Societe, no 4 (Jan 87): 559-572; auth, The Coachmen on Nineteenth-Century Paris: Service Workers and Class Consciousness, La State Univ Pr (Baton Rouge/London), 93; auth, Horse-Drawn Cabs and Omnibuses in Paris: The Idea of Circulation and the Business of Public Transit, La State Univ Pr (Baton Rouge/London), 96; auth, "Les Transports a Paris avant le metro," in Metro-Cite: Le Chemin de fer metropolitain a la conquete de Paris, 1871-1945, ed Francois Gasnault and Henri Zuber (Paris: paris Musees, 97), 15-30; auth, "Urbanisme de Paris souterrain: Premiers projects de chemin de fer urbain et naissance de l'urbanisme des cites modernes," in Histoire, Economie, et Societe, no 4 (Oct-Dec 98): 745-770; co-auth, "The Urban Infrastructure," in Encyclopedia of European Social History: From 1350-2000, ed Peter Stearns (NY: Charles Scribner's Sons, 01), 2:277-290; auth, "L'Emergence de l'urbanism moderne a Paris avant Haussmann," in La Modernite avant Haussmann: Formes de l'espace urbain a Paris, 1801-1853, ed Karen Bowie (Paris: Editions Recherches,01), 82-94 **CONTACT ADDRESS** Dept of Hist, Brooklyn Col, CUNY, 2900 Bedford Ave, Brooklyn, NY 11210-2899. **EMAIL** npapayan@brooklyn.cuny.edu

PAPAZIAN, DENNIS RICHARD
PERSONAL Born 12/15/1931, Augusta, GA, m, 1991, 2 children **DISCIPLINE** RUSSIAN & SOVIET HISTORY **EDUCATION** Wayne State Univ, BA, 54, MA, 56 Univ Mich, MA, 58, PhD(hist), 66. **CAREER** Lectr, 62-66,assoc prof, 66-71, Prof Hist, Univ Mich, Dearborn, 71-, chair, div LS & A, assoc dean acad affairs, 73-74, dir grad studies, 79-85, dir Armenian Res Center, 85-; mem bd dirs, Nat Asn Armenian Studies & Res, 69-79 & Armenian Assembly Am, Inc, 68-88; mem, exec counc, Soc Armenian Studies, 88-, pres, 88-93, 95-; ed, Jour Soc Armenian Studies, 95-. **MEMBERSHIPS** AHA; Am Asn Advan Slavic Studies; Nat Asn Armenian Studies & Res; AAUP; Soc Armenian Studies; Middle East Studies Asn **RESEARCH** Ukranian nationalism; 20th century Soviet and Russian history; Armenia and the Caucasus. **SELECTED PUBLICATIONS** Auth numerous articles & publications **CONTACT ADDRESS** Univ of Michigan, Dearborn, 4901 Evergreen Rd, Dearborn, MI 48128-1491. **EMAIL** papazian@umich.edu

PAPER, JORDAN
PERSONAL Born 12/03/1938, Baltimore, MD **DISCIPLINE** HISTORY OF RELIGIONS, EAST ASIA **EDUCATION** Univ Chicago, AB, 60; Univ Wis-Madison, MA, 65, PhD(Chinese), 71. **CAREER** Asst prof hist, Ind State Univ, 67-72; asst prof, 72-78, Assoc Prof Humanities, York Univ, 78-, Vis prof Am lit, Ching I Col, Taiwan, 73-74. **MEMBERSHIPS** Asn Asian Studies; Am Orient Soc; Soc Studies Pre-Han China; Soc Study Chinese Relig; Can Soc Study Relig. **RESEARCH** East Asian aesthetics; Chinese intellectual history; East Asian and Amerindian religion. **SELECTED PUBLICATIONS** Auth, The Spirits are Drunk: Comparative Approaches to Chinese Religion, Albany: State Univ of New York Press, 95; auth, "Chinese Religion," Harold Coward, ed, Population and the Environment: Population Pressures, Resource Consumption, Religions and Ethics, Albany: SUNY Press, (95): 173-91; auth, "Religions in Contact: The Effects of Domination from a Comparative Perspective," Iva Dolezalova, Bretislav Horyna, & Dalibor Papousek, eds, Religions-in Contact: Selected Proceedings of the Special IAHR Conference, Brno, 94, Brno: Czech Society for the Study of Religion: (96): 39-56; auth, "Communicating the Intangible: An Anishnabe Story," American Indian Ouarterly, Kenn Pitawanakwat, 20, (96): 451-67; auth, Through the Early Darkly: Female Spirtuality in Comparative Perspective, New York: Continuum, 97; auth, Chinese Way in Religion, 2nd ed, Belmont, Calif, Wadsworth, 98; auth, "Introduction -- Ascetic Culture: Renunciation and Wordly Engagement," "Eremitism in China," Journal of Asian and African Philosophy, 34, (99)1-3, 46-55; auth, "Chinese Religion, 'Daoism', and Deep Ecology," David Barnhill & Roger Gottlieb, eds, Deep Ecology and World Religions, Albany: State Univ of New York Press, (forthcoming). **CONTACT ADDRESS** Div of Humanities, York Univ, 4700 Keele St, Downsview, ON, Canada M3J 1P3. **EMAIL** jpaper@yorku.ca

PAPPAS, NICHOLAS C. J.
PERSONAL m **DISCIPLINE** HISTORY **EDUCATION** Stanford Univ, AB, AM, PhD. **CAREER** Assoc prof, Sam Houston State Univ, 90-. **RESEARCH** Ancient history, Eastern Europe, the Balkans, and Russia. **SELECTED PUBLICATIONS** Auth, Greeks in Russian Military Service in the Late Eighteenth and Early Nineteenth Centuries, Inst Balkan Stud, 91; Between Two Empires: Serbian Survival in the Years After Kosovo, Serbia's Hist Heritage, 94. **CONTACT ADDRESS** Dept of History, Sam Houston State Univ, Huntsville, TX 77341.

PAQUETTE, WILLIAM A.
PERSONAL Born 08/06/1947, Lawrence, MA, s **DISCIPLINE** HISTORY **EDUCATION** Grove City Col, AB, 69; Duquesne Univ, MA, 71; Emory Univ, PhD, 93. **CAREER** Chair of dept, Acad of the Holy Cross, 73-75; prof, Tidewater Cmty Col, 78-. **HONORS AND AWARDS** Who's Who Among Am Teachers, 00, 96, 94; Distinguished Service Awd, Cmty Col Humanities Asn, 97; Nat Endowment for the Humanities grants, 95-96; Summer Fel in Am Urban Hist, Columbus Univ, 85; Va Endowment for the Humanities Summer Grant, 88; Excellence in Teaching Awd, Tidewater Cmty col, 83. **MEMBERSHIPS** Am Hist Asn, Cmty Col Humanities Asn, Am Educ Res Asn, Am Coun for Quebec Studies, Comparative and Intl Educ Soc, Hist of Educ Soc, World Hist Asn. **RESEARCH** 20th Century Europe, China. **SELECTED PUBLICATIONS** Auth, "Faisal I of Iraq", "Hassan II of Morocco", "Hussein I of Jordan", "Bhumibol Adulyadej of Thailand", and "Faisal I of Saudi Arabia," in Encyclopedia of Twentieth Century World Leaders, Marshall Cavendish Corp: London, 00; auth, Dictionary of 20th Century World Biography, Marshall Cavendish Corp: London, 00; auth, "Instructor's Manual/Test Item File," in History of the Human Community, Prentice-Hall, 97; auth, "Canada's MultiCultural Act," in Encyclopedia of North America, Marshall Cavendish Corp, 98; auth, "Catherine of Aragon," in Dictionary of World Biography: Renaissance Series, Fitzroy Dearborn: London, 98; auth, "The Joshua Fuller family of Nunda,NY," The Mayflower Quareterly, 97; auth, "Adjunct Faculty at the Two-Year College," The Community College Humanist, 98; auth, "Sam Malone, Videos and the Research Paper," The Humanities Review, 96; auth, The Root Family of Bolivar, New York, Genealogical Press: Baltimore, 91; auth, Suffolk, A Pictorial History, Donning Pub: Norfolk, 87. **CONTACT ADDRESS** Dept Humanities & Soc Sci, Tidewater Comm Col, 7000 Col Dr, Portsmouth, VA 23703-6100. **EMAIL** tcpaquw@tc.cc.va.us

PARCHMENT, STEVEN
DISCIPLINE HISTORY OF MODERN PHILOSOPHY, SPINOZA, ANCIENT AND MEDIEVAL PHILOSOPHY **EDUCATION** Emory Univ, PhD, 96. **CAREER** Lectr, Ga State Univ. **SELECTED PUBLICATIONS** Published an article on Spinoza in Hist of Philos Quart. **CONTACT ADDRESS** Georgia State Univ, Atlanta, GA 30303. **EMAIL** phlsgp@panther.gsu.edu

PARET, PETER
PERSONAL Born 04/13/1924, Berlin, Germany, m, 1961, 2 children **DISCIPLINE** HISTORY **EDUCATION** Univ Calif - Berkeley, BA, 49; King's Col, Univ London, PhD, 60. **CAREER** Resident Tutor, Oxford Univ, 59-60; Res Assoc, Princeton Univ, 60-62, 63; Vis Asst Prof, 62-63, Assoc Prof Hist, Univ Calif - Davis, 63-66; Prof Hist, Univ Calif - Davis, 66-69; Vis Res Fe Fel, London Sch Econ & Polit Sci, 71-72; Prof Hist, 69-77, Raymond A. Spruance Prof Int Hist, Stanford Univ, 77-86; Andrew W. Mellon Prof Humanities, Sch Hist Studies, Inst Advanced Study, Princeton Univ, 86-97, emeritus, 97-. **HONORS AND AWARDS** Thomas Jefferson Medal, Am Philos Soc; Order of Merit, Ger Fed Repub; Samuel Eliot Morison Prize, Soc for Mil Hist; LittD, Univ London; DLitt, Univ SC; HHD, Col Wooster; Fel, Am Acad Arts & Letters; Honorary Fel, London Sch Econ & Polit Sci, Fel, Leo Baeck Inst, Hon Mem, Clausewitz Ges. **MEMBERSHIPS** Am Philos Soc. **RESEARCH** European cultural history, 18th-20th century; the history of war. **SELECTED PUBLICATIONS** Coauth, Guerrillas in the 1960s, Praeger, 61; auth, French Revolutionary Warfare, Praeger, 64; auth, Yorck and the Era of Prussian Reform, Princeton, 66; auth, Clausewitz and the State, Oxford, 76, rev ed, Princeton, 85; The Berlin Secession, Harvard, 80; ed, Makers of Modern Strategy from Machiavelli to the Nuclear Age, Princeton, 86; auth, Art as History, Princeton, 88, rev ed, 89; Understanding War, Princeton, 92; coauth, Persuasive Images, Princeton, 92; co-ed, Sammler, Stifter und Museen, Bohlau, 93; auth, Imagined Battles: Reflections of War in European Art, NC, 97; auth, German Encounters with Modernism, 1840-1945, Cambridge, 00. **CONTACT ADDRESS** Dept of History, Inst for Advanced Studies, Princeton, NJ 08540. **EMAIL** collinrf@cua.edu

PARINS, JAMES
DISCIPLINE NINETEENTH-CENTURY BRITISH STUDIES **EDUCATION** Univ Wisc, PhD. **CAREER** Prof, Univ Ark. **SELECTED PUBLICATIONS** Auth, John Rolling Ridge; William Barnes; The British Colonial Press of the Eighteenth and Nineteenth Centuries, Victorian Periodicals Rev; Coauth, American Native and Alaska Native Newspapers and Periodicals, 1826-1985. **CONTACT ADDRESS** Univ of Arkansas, Little Rock, 2801 S University Ave., Little Rock, AR 72204-1099. **EMAIL** jwparins@ualr.edu

PARK, DAVID ALLEN
PERSONAL Born 10/13/1919, New York, NY, m, 1945, 4 children **DISCIPLINE** THEORETICAL PHYSICS, HISTORY OF SCIENCE **EDUCATION** Harvard Univ, AB, 41; Univ Mich, Ann Arbor, PhD(physics), 50. **CAREER** From asst prof to assoc prof, 51-59, Prof Physics, Williams Col, 59-, Lloyd fel, Inst Advan Study, 50-51; vis lectr physics, Univ Sri Lanka, 55-56, 72 & Cambridge Univ, 62-63; vis prof, Univ NC, 64. **HONORS AND AWARDS** Bk Awd, Phi Beta Kappa, 80, 88. **MEMBERSHIPS** Fel Am Phys Soc; Int Soc Study Time (pres, 73-76). **RESEARCH** Quantum theory; natural philosophy of time; history of science. **SELECTED PUBLICATIONS** Auth, Introduction to the Quantum Theory, McGraw, 64, 74, 92; Contemporary Physics, Harcourt, 64; Introduction to Strong Interactions, Benjamin, 67; Classical Dynamics and Its Quantum Analogues, Springer, 79, 90; The Image of Eternity, Univ Mass, 80; The How and the Why, 88; The Fire Within the Eye, 97. **CONTACT ADDRESS** Dept of Physics, Williams Col, Williamstown, MA 01267. **EMAIL** dpark@williams.edu

PARK, HONG-KYU
PERSONAL Born 03/07/1938, Kyungbuk, Korea, m, 1968, 1 child **DISCIPLINE** HISTORY; POLITICAL SCIENCE **EDUCATION** Kent Wesleyan Col, BA, 62; Univ Tenn, MA, 64; Univ N Tex, PhD, 81. **CAREER** Instr to assoc prof, Wiley Col, 65-76; asst prof to prof, Jarvis Christian Col, 77-93; prof, Kilgore Col, 93- . **HONORS AND AWARDS** UNCF Distinguished Schol Awd, 85-86. **MEMBERSHIPS** Am Hist Asn; Asn Asian Student; Orgn Am Hist; Soc Hist Am For Relations; SW Sco Sci Asn. **RESEARCH** American-East Asian relations since 1945. **SELECTED PUBLICATIONS** Auth, The Korean War: An Annotated Bibliography, Demmer Co, (71); auth, "The Korean War Revisited: A Survey of Historical Writings," World Affairs 137, pp336-344, (75); auth "American-Sovient Rivalry in Korea, 1945-1948," Korea J 22, pp 4-15, (82); auth, "From Pearl Harbor to Cairo: America's Korean Diplomacy, 1941-43," Diplomatic Hist 13, pp 343-358, (89); auth, " America's Response to the Korean Problem, 1941-1945," Asian Profile 21, pp 23-30, (93). **CONTACT ADDRESS** Dept Soc & Behav Sci, Kilgore Col, 729 Pam Dr, Tyler, TX 75703-4852. **EMAIL** ProfHP@aol.com

PARKER, DAVID B.
PERSONAL Born 11/28/1956, NC, m, 1982, 2 children **DISCIPLINE** HISTORY **EDUCATION** Duke Univ, AB, 79; Univ NC, MA, 82; PhD, 88. **CAREER** Asst prof, Southwest Mo State Univ, 89-93; asst to assoc prof, Kennesaw State Univ, 93-. **MEMBERSHIPS** Southern Hist Asn. **RESEARCH** U.S. cultural history, American South. **SELECTED PUBLICATIONS** Auth, Alias Bill Arp: Charles Henry Smith and the South's 'Goodly Heritage,' Univ of Ga Press, 91; auth, Carpet Capital: The Rise of a New South Industry, Univ of Ga Press, 99. **CONTACT ADDRESS** Dept Hist, Kennesaw State Univ, 1000 Chastain Rd NW, Kennesaw, GA 30144-5588. **EMAIL** dparker@kennesaw.edu

PARKER, KEITH ALFRED
PERSONAL Born 06/01/1933, Hull, England, m, 1966, 1 child **DISCIPLINE** BRITISH & UNITED STATES RELATIONS **EDUCATION** Fairleigh Dickenson Univ, BA, 59; Univ Md, MA, 62, PhD(hist), 65. **CAREER** Instr hist, Univ Md, 62-63; asst prof, NY State Univ Col Oswego, 65-66; asst prof, 66-80, Assoc Prof Hist, Univ S Fla, 80-, Can studies proj dir, Univ SFla. **MEMBERSHIPS** Asn Can Studies US; AHA. **RESEARCH** North Atlantic community, Britain, United States and Canada; Canadian labor history. **SELECTED PUBLICATIONS** Coauth, Student in society, Littlefield, fall 68; Colonization roads and commercial policy, Ont Hist, 75; The making of a radical, Alta Hist, 78; British Evacuees in America During World-War-II, J of American Culture, Vol 0017, 1994. **CONTACT ADDRESS** Dept of Hist, Univ of So Florida, 4202 Fowler Ave, Tampa, FL 33620-9951.

PARKER, SIMON B.
PERSONAL Born 02/23/1940, Manchester, England, m, 1961, 2 children **DISCIPLINE** ANCIENT NEAR EASTERN STUDIES, SEMITIC LANGUAGES, HEBREW BIBLE **EDUCATION** Univ Manchester, BA, 60; Asbury Theol Sem, BD, 63; Johns Hopkins Univ, PhD, 67. **CAREER** Asst prof of Humanities and Relig, Reed Col, 67-75; asst to the Pres, Boston Univ, 77-78, asst provost, 78-81, assoc dean and assoc prof, Boston Univ School of Theol, 81-88, assoc prof of Hebrew Bible, 88-97, prof of Hebrew Bible, Boston Univ School of Theol, 97-. **HONORS AND AWARDS** Graves Awd, 72; Named First Harrell F Beck Scholar of Hebrew Scripture, Boston Univ. **MEMBERSHIPS** Am Oriental Soc; Am Schools of Oriental Res; Soc of Biblical Lit; Soc for Old Testament Study, UK. **RESEARCH** Continuities and discontinuities in the lit and relig of ancient Israel, Canaanite, Israelite culture and social hist. **SELECTED PUBLICATIONS** Auth, The Pre-Biblical Narrative Tradition: Essays on the Ugaritic Poems Keret and Aqhat, Resources for Biblical Study 24, Scholars Press, 89; Officials Attitudes Toward Prophecy at Mari and in Israel, Vetus Testamentum 45, 93; The Beginning of the Reign of God--Psalm 82 as Myth and Liturgy, Revue Biblique 102, 95; Stories in Scripture and Inscriptions, Oxford Univ Press, 97; ed and trans, Ugaritic Narrative Poetry, Writings From the Ancient World, Scholars Press, 97; gen ed since 1994 of Writings From the Ancient World, Scholars Press; numerous scholarly articles in books and journals. **CONTACT ADDRESS** School of Theology, Boston Univ, 745 Commonwealth Ave, Boston, MA 02215. **EMAIL** sbparker@bu.edu

PARMAN, DONALD LEE
PERSONAL Born 10/10/1932, New Point, MO, m, 1953, 2 children **DISCIPLINE** AMERICAN HISTORY **EDUCATION** Cent Mo State Col, BSEd, 58; Ohio Univ, MA, 62; Univ Okla, PhD (Am hist), 67. **CAREER** Instr soc studies, Cent Mo State Col, 61-62; Asst Prof, 66-75; Assoc Prof, 75-93, Prof Am Hist, Purdue Univ, West Lafayette, 93-; Consult, Proj Impact, Off Educ, 68; Consult, U.S. Dept Justice as expert witness in Navajo claims case, 84-87; Consult, Mudd Libr of Manuscripts, Princeton Univ, to evaluate the Asn Am Indians Affairs papers. **HONORS AND AWARDS** Nat Endowment for Humanities grant, 72-73; recipient of numerous grants, 73-96. **MEMBERSHIPS** Ind Hist Soc; Ind Asn Hist; Western Hist Asn. **RESEARCH** Twentieth century Indians of the United States. **SELECTED PUBLICATIONS** Auth, The Indian and the Civilian Conservation Corps, Pac Hist Rev, 2/71; J C Morgan: Navajo apostle of assimilation, Prologue, J Nat Arch, summer 72; coed, The American Search (2 vols), Forum, 73; auth, The Navajos and the New Deal, Yale Univ, 76; American Indians and the bicentennial, NMex Hist Rev, 7/76; auth, The Big Stick in Indian affairs, The Bai-a-lil-le incident in 1909, Ariz & the West, Vol 20, winter 78; Francis E Leupp, Commissioner of Indian Affairs, 1905-1909, In: The Commissioners of Indian Affairs, 1824-1977, Univ Nebraska Press, 79; A Whites Man's Fight: The Crow Scandal, 1906-1913, In: The American West: Essays in Honor of W Eugene Hollon, Univ Toledo, 80; Indians of the Modern West, In: Major Issues in Twentieth Century Western History, Univ New Mex Press, 89; Indians and the American West in the Twentieth Century, Ind Univ Press, 94; The Indian Reorganization Act of 1934, In: Classroom Activities on Wisconsin Indian History: Treaties and Tribal Sovereignty, Wis Dept Public Educ, 96; Window to a Changed World: The Personal Memoirs of William Graham, Ind Hist Soc, 98; author of numerous journal and encyclopedia articles. **CONTACT ADDRESS** Dept of History, Purdue Univ, West Lafayette, West Lafayette, IN 47907-1358. **EMAIL** history@sla.purdue.edu

PARMET, HERBERT S.
PERSONAL Born 09/28/1929, New York, NY, m, 1948, 1 child **DISCIPLINE** AMERICAN HISTORY **EDUCATION** State Univ NYork Col Oswego, BS, 51; Queens Col, NYork, MA, 57. **CAREER** Instr hist, Fairleigh Dickinson Univ, 58-64; from asst prof to assoc prof, 68-75, Prof Hist, Queensborough Community Col, City Univ, NY, 75-, Prof Grad Sch, 77-, Fac res fel, State Univ NY, 74; secy-treas bd dirs, Acad Humanities & Sci, City Univ NY. **MEMBERSHIPS** AHA; Orgn Am Historians. **RESEARCH** Recent American history. **SELECTED PUBLICATIONS** Coauth, Aaron Burr: Portrait of an Ambitious Man, 67, Never Again: A President Runs for a Third Term, 68, contribr, Our Presidents, 69 & auth, Eisenhower and the American Crusades, 72, Macmillan; contrib, Makers of American Diplomacy, 74 & Pinnacle of Power, 76, Scribners; auth, The Democrats: The Years After FDR, Macmillan, 76; Jack: The Struggles of John F Kennedy, Dial, 80; The Lafolletes of Wisconsin, Love And Politics in Progressive America - Weisberger,ba, Western Historical Quarterly, Vol 0026, 1995. **CONTACT ADDRESS** 18-40 211th St, Bayside, NY 11360.

PARMET, ROBERT DAVID
PERSONAL Born 12/11/1938, Bronx, NY, m, 1963, 1 child **DISCIPLINE** MODERN AMERICAN HISTORY **EDUCATION** City Col NYork, BA, 60; Columbia Univ, MA, 61, PhD, 66. **CAREER** Lectr hist, 62-65, City Col NY; asst prof, 65-67, Newark State Col; from asst prof to assoc prof, 67-77, chmn dept hist & philos, 72-75, prof hist, 78-, York Col, CUNY. **MEMBERSHIPS** AHA; Southern Hist Assn; Orgn Am Historians; Acad Polit Sci. **RESEARCH** US Labor and Immigration history. **SELECTED PUBLICATIONS** Auth, The Presidential Fever of Chauncey Depew, NY Hist Soc Quart, 70; art, Schools for the Freedmen, Negro Hist Bull, 71; coauth, American Nativism, 1830-1860, Van Nostrand Reinhold, 71; art, Competition for the World's Columbian Exposition: The New York Campaign, J Ill State Hist Soc, 72; auth, Labor and Immigration in Industrial America, Twayne Publ, 81. **CONTACT ADDRESS** One Highland Pl, Great Neck, NY 11020. **EMAIL** pdrmet@york.cuny.edu

PAROT, JOSEPH JOHN
PERSONAL Born 06/04/1940, Hammond, IN, m, 1962, 2 children **DISCIPLINE** AMERICAN RELIGIOUS & URBAN ETHNIC HISTORY **EDUCATION** Maryknoll College, 58; IN Univ, 59-60; St Joseph's Col, Ind, BA, 63; DePaul Univ, MA, 67; Northern IL Univ, PhD, 71. **CAREER** Instr hist, St Augustine High Sch, Chicago, 63-67; from instr to asst prof hist & bibliog, 67-74, assoc prof, 75-82, prof hist & head hist ctr,

Northern IL Univ, 82-, prof hist & head soc sci dept, 84; Instr soc sci, Chicago Comt Urban Opportunity Prog, 66-67; vis prof urban/ethnic studies, George Williams Col, 72-73; assoc ed, Polish-Am Studies, 73. **HONORS AND AWARDS** Ed Emer Awd, St Joseph's Col, 63; Lions Int, Outstanding Teacher Awd, Chicago rea, 66; Pi Gamma Mu, DePaul Univ, 67; Oscar Halecki Awd from Polish Am Hist Asn for outstanding book, 83; grants from Am Philos Soc, NEH; Honorariums from Multicultural Hist Soc of Ontario, 78; Pa Hist Comm, 76; Univ Notre Dame 82; Multicultural Curr Transformation Ins, 95. **MEMBERSHIPS** AHA; Polish-Am Hist Asn; Phi Gamma Mu (Natl Soc Sci Honor Soc); Friends of NIU Libraries, 90-. **RESEARCH** Immigration hist; urban hist; religious hist in Am. **SELECTED PUBLICATIONS** Auth, Ethnic versus Black metropolis: Origins of Polish Black housing tensions in Chicago, 71, Unthinkable thoughts on unmeltable ethnics, 74 & Racial dilemma in Chicago's Polish neighborhoods, 1920-1970, 75, Polish Am Studies; contribr, Bishop Francis Hodur, suppl five, In: Dict of American Biography, 77; Strangers in the city: Immigrant Catholics and the black community in Twentieth century Chicago, Black History Conference, Lincoln Univ, 4/78; Immigrant Labor and the Paradox of Pluralism in American Urban Society, 1860-1930: A Comparative Study and Census Analysis of Polish, German, Irish, Bohemian, Italian and Jewish Workers in Chicago, Polish Res Inst of the Jagiellonian Univ, Cracow, 79; Sources of community conflict in Chicago Polonia: A comparative analysis and historigraphical appraisal, Ethnicity, vol 7, winter 80; Polish Catholics in Chicago, 1850-1920: A Religious History, Northern Ill Univ Press, 81; The Serdeczna Matko of the sweatshops: Marital and family crises of immigrant working-class women in late nineteenth century Chicago, Poles in North America Conference, Multicult Hist Soc of Ont, 82; Steelmills, sweatshops, stockyards, and slums: The social fabric of the immigrant Catholic working class in Chicago, 1870-1930, Perspectives in American Catholicism, Univ Notre Dame, 11/82; Catholic manuscript and archival sources in the Greater Chicago area, Mdwest Archives Conf, Chicago 5/83; The urbanization and suburbanization of the ethnic working class in Chicago, 1870-1980, Celebrate Illinois: Its Cultural Heritage, Ill Humantities Counc, 4/85; Family and social history in the immigrant community, Polish Genealogical Soc, 11/88; auth, Praca Imigranta I Paradoks Pluralizmu w Amerykanskim Spoleczenstwie Miejskim w Latach, 1860-1930: Studium Porownaczne, Wroclaw: Ossolineum, 88; co-ed (with James Pula, et al), Polish History in America to 1908, vol 1-4; Catholic Univ of Am Press, 94-98, Kruszka Transl Proj; ed board of Ill Hist Jour, 95-98; The German immigrant in Illinois, 1840-1930, Elmhurst Hist Soc, 3/98; Reverend Vincent Barzynski, In: American National Biography, 99; Multicultural difficulties in the Polish Catholic community in Chicago, Ill Hist Teacher, 99; auth, "The Polish Roman Catholic Union," "The Polish National Alliance," and "Dziennik Zwiazkowy," in Enclyclopedia of Chicago History (00); numerous rev essays in Am Hist Rev, Cath Hist Rev, Ill Hist Jrnl, Ind Magazine of Hist, Intl Migration Rev, and Polish Am Studies. **CONTACT ADDRESS** Social Sci Dept; Dept of History, No Illinois Univ, Founders Libr, De Kalb, IL 60115-2825. **EMAIL** c60jjpl@wpo.cso.niu.edu

PARR, JAMES A.
PERSONAL Born 10/07/1936, Ritchie Co, WV, m, 1985, 1 child **DISCIPLINE** HISPANIC STUDIES **EDUCATION** Ohio Univ, BA, 59, MA, 61; Univ Pitts, PhD, 67. **CAREER** Instr, Univ Toledo, 63-64; prof, Murray State Univ, 64-70; assoc prof to prof, 70-90, Univ S Calif; prof, Univ Calif-Riverside, 90- . **HONORS AND AWARDS** Del-Amo, 85; Mellon, 61-63; Fulbright, 91. **MEMBERSHIPS** MAL; AATSP; AIH; ALSC; PAMLA; CSA. **RESEARCH** Cervantes, Golden Age literature. **SELECTED PUBLICATIONS** Auth, Don Quixote: An Anatomy of Subversive Discourse, 88; auth, After its Kind: Approaches to the Comedia, 93; auth, Confrontaciones calladas: el critico frente al clasico, 90; co-auth, El infenioso hidalgo don Quijote de la Mancha, 98. **CONTACT ADDRESS** Dept Hisp Stud, Univ of California, Riverside, 900 University Ave, Riverside, CA 92501-0001. **EMAIL** PATXIYYO@AOL.COM/JAMES.PARR@UCR.EDU

PARR, JOY
PERSONAL Born Toronto, ON, Canada **DISCIPLINE** HISTORY **EDUCATION** McGill Univ, BA, 71; Yale Univ, MPhil, 73, PhD, 77. **CAREER** Asst prof, Univ BC, 76-78; asst to assoc prof, Queen's Univ, 79-92; coordr, Women's Stud, 89-90, Farley prof Hist, Simon Fraser Univ, 92-. **HONORS AND AWARDS** Harold Innis Awd; Macdonald Prize; Berkshire Prize; Laura Jamieson Prize; Fred Landon Awd. **MEMBERSHIPS** Uppsala Univ; Radcliff Col; Royal Soc Can; All Souls Col, Oxford. **RESEARCH** History of gender and the family, industrialization and deindustrialization, the study of material culture and modern economic policy. **SELECTED PUBLICATIONS** Auth, The Gender of Breadwinners: Women, Men and Industrial Change in Two Ontario Towns, 1880-1950, Toronto, Univ Press, 90; ed, A Daunting Modenity: A Reader on Post-Confederation Canadian History, Toronto: McGraw-Hill, 92; co-ed, Public History Special Issue, Gender and History, 94; auth, "Womanly Militance, Neighbourly Wrath: New Scripts for Old Roles in a Small Town Textile Strike," in Women, Work and Place, eds. Audrey Kobayashi and John Bradbury, (Montreal: McGill-Queen's Univ Press, 94); auth, Labouring Children: British Immigrant Apprentices to Canada 1869-1924, second edition, Toronto: Univ of Toronto Press, 94; auth, "Gender, History and Historical Practice," Canadian Historical Review, 95; auth, A Diversity of Women: Ontario, 1945-1980, Toronto: Univ of Toronto Press, 95; co-ed, Gender and History in Canada, Toronto: Copp Clark, 96; auth, Domestic Goods: the Material, the Moral, and the Economic in the Postwar Years, Toronto: Univ of Toronto Press, 98. **CONTACT ADDRESS** Dept of History, Simon Fraser Univ, Burnaby, BC, Canada V5A 1S6. **EMAIL** joy-parr@sfu.ca

PARRISH, MICHAEL EMERSON
PERSONAL Born 03/04/1942, Huntington Park, CA, 2 children **DISCIPLINE** AMERICAN HISTORY **EDUCATION** Univ Calif, Riverside, BA, 64; Yale Univ, PhD(hist), 68. **CAREER** Asst prof, 68-73, assoc prof, 73-80, Prof Hist, Univ Calif, San Diego, 80-. **SELECTED PUBLICATIONS** Auth, Securities Regulation and the New Deal, Yale Univ Press, 70; Cold war justice: The Supreme Court and the Rosenbergs, Am Hist Rev, 77; The Hughes Court, the Great Depression, and the historians, The Historian, 78; Felix Frankfurter and His Times: The Reform Years, Free Press, 82. **CONTACT ADDRESS** Dept of Hist, Univ of California, San Diego, San Diego, CA 92039.

PARRISH, WILLIAM E.
PERSONAL Born 04/07/1931, Garden City, KS, m, 1972, 2 children **DISCIPLINE** AMERICAN HISTORY **EDUCATION** Kans State Univ, BS, 52; Univ Mo, MA, 53; PhD, 55. **CAREER** From asst prof to prof, Westminster Col, Mo, 55-71, dean col, 73-75, Truman prof Am hist, 71-78; prof & head, dept hist, Miss State Univ, 78-85, prof, 85-96, prof emer, 96- . **HONORS AND AWARDS** Ed, Sesquicentennial Hist Mo, 71; mem, Mo Adv Coun on Hist Preserv, 67-78; Awd of Merit, Am Asn State & Local Hist, 74; chm, Mo Am Rev Bicentennial Comt, 74-77. **MEMBERSHIPS** Org Am Historians; Southern Hist Asn; Nat Trust Hist Preserv; Western Hist Asn. **RESEARCH** Sectionalism, Civil War and Reconstruction; American West. **SELECTED PUBLICATIONS** Auth, David Rice Atchison of Missouri: Border Politican, 61, Turbulent Partnership: Missouri and the Union, 1861-1865, 63 & Missouri Under Radical Rule, 1865-1870, 65, Univ Mo; ed, The Union: State and Local Studies, In: Vol II, Civil War Books: A Critical Bibliography, La State Univ, 68; contrib, Radicalism, Racism and Party Realignment: The Border States During Reconstruction, Johns Hopkins Univ, 69; ed, The Civil War: A Second American Revolution?, Dryden, 70 & Kreiger, 77; auth, A History of Missouri, Vol 3, Univ Mo, 73; auth, Missouri: The Heart of the Nation, Forum, 80, 2d ed, Harlan Davidson, 92; auth, Frank Blair: Lincoln's Conservative, Missouri, 98. **CONTACT ADDRESS** Dept of Hist, Mississippi State Univ, Mississippi State, MS 39762. **EMAIL** whps@futuresouth.com

PARSONS, KEITH M.
PERSONAL Born 08/31/1952, Macon, GA, s **DISCIPLINE** HISTORY & PHILOSOPHY OF SCIENCE; PHILOSOPHY OF RELIGION **EDUCATION** Queens Univ, PhD, 86; Univ Pitts, PhD, 96. **CAREER** Asst Prof Univ Houston-Clear Lake; Ed, Philo, Jour Soc Humanist Phil **MEMBERSHIPS** Philos Sci Asn; Am Philos Asn. **RESEARCH** Rationality & theory change in science; history of the earth sciences; Darwinism; science and religion. **SELECTED PUBLICATIONS** Auth, God and the Burden of Proof, Prometheus Books, 89; Drawing Out Leviathan: Dinosaurs and the Science Wars, Ind Univ Press. **CONTACT ADDRESS** Univ of Houston, 2700 Bay Area Blvd., Houston, TX 77058-1098. **EMAIL** parsons@cl.uh.edu

PARSONS, LYNN
PERSONAL Born 04/09/1937, Lynn, MA, m, 1958, 2 children **DISCIPLINE** HISTORY **EDUCATION** Grinnell Col, BA, 58; Johns Hopkins Univ, MA, 64, PhD, 67. **CAREER** Prof. **HONORS AND AWARDS** Suny Chancellor's Awd for excellence in Teaching. **RESEARCH** American history **SELECTED PUBLICATIONS** Auth, John Quincy Adams: An American Profile, Madison, 98; European Offshoot or Unique Experiment: The United States in World History, St Martin, 95; co-ed, The Home Front, Greenwood, 95. **CONTACT ADDRESS** Dept of History, SUNY, Col at Brockport, Brockport, NY 14420. **EMAIL** lparsons@brockport.edu

PARSSINEN, TERRY
DISCIPLINE HISTORY OF NARCOTIC DRUGS AND THEIR IMPACT ON SOCIETY **EDUCATION** Grinnell Col, BA, 65; Brandeis Univ, MA, 63, PhD, 68. **CAREER** Prof; dean, clas, 92-95, Univ of Tampa. **SELECTED PUBLICATIONS** Auth, Secret Passions, Secret Remedies: Narcotic Drugs and British Society, 1820-1930, ISHI Publ & Manchester UP, 83. **CONTACT ADDRESS** Dept of Hist, Univ of Tampa, 401 W. Kennedy Blvd, Tampa, FL 33606-1490.

PASCOE, LOUIS B.
PERSONAL Born 05/26/1930, Carbondale, PA, s **DISCIPLINE** MEDIEVAL HISTORY **EDUCATION** Univ Scranton, BA, 52; Woodstock Col, Md, PhL, 58, STL, 65; Fordham Univ, MA, 60; Univ Calif, Los Angeles, PhD(hist), 70. **CAREER** Asst prof, Woodstock Col, 71-73; asst prof to prof hist, Fordham Univ, 73-; Fel, Woodstock Col, 70-71; Fordham Univ, 78-79; 84-85, 90-91, 97-98; Instr, Georgetown University, 58-61; prof hist, Fordham Univ, 73-00, Prof Emeritus, Fordham Univ, 00-. **MEMBERSHIPS** Mediaeval Acad Am; Cath Hist Asn; Cusanus Soc of Am. **RESEARCH** Medieval ecclesiastical and intellectual history. **SELECTED PUBLICATIONS** Auth, The Council of Trent and Bible study: Humanism and Scripture, Cath Hist Rev, 66; Jean Gerson: Principles of Church Reform, Brill, 73; Gerson and the Donation of Constantine, Viator, 74; Jean Gerson: The Ecclesia Primitiva and Reform, Traditio, 74; Jean Gerson: Mysticism, Conciliarism, and Reform, Annuarium Hist Conciliarum, 74; Nobility and Ecclesiastical Office in Fifteenth-Century Lyons, Mediaeval Studies, 76; Theological Dimensions of Pierre d'Ailly's Teaching on the Papal Plenitude of Power, Ann Hist Conciliorum, 789; Pierre d'Ailly: Histoire, Schisme et Antechrist, Genese et debuts du Grand Schisme d'Occident, 80; Jean Gerson, Dictionary of the Middle Ages, 85; Law and Evangelical Liberty in the Thought of Jean Gerson, 85; Religious Orders, Evangelical Liberty, and Reform in the Thought of Jean Gerson, 89; auth, Religious Order, Evangelical Liberty, and Reform in the Thought of Jean Gerson in Reformbemuhungen und Observanzbestrebungen in spatmittelalterlichen Ordenswesen, 89; auth, Modus Parisiensis: A Response, The Jesuit Ratio Studiorium of 1599: Four Hundredth Anniversary Perspectives, 00. **CONTACT ADDRESS** Dept of Hist, Fordham Univ, Loyola Hall, Bronx, NY 10458.

PASQUALETTI, MARTIN J.
PERSONAL Born 02/05/1945, San Francisco, CA, m, 1972, 1 child **DISCIPLINE** GEOGRAPHY **EDUCATION** Univ Calif, BA, 67; Louisiana State Univ, MA, 69; Univ Calif Riverside, PhD, 77. **CAREER** Prof, Ariz State Univ, 77-. **HONORS AND AWARDS** Hon Res Prof, 83; Environ Edu of Yr, 93. **MEMBERSHIPS** AAG; AGS; SHT; APCG. **RESEARCH** Energy issues at the Mexican border; energy landscapes; renewable energy; geography of energy; energy and environment; geography of North America; nuclear power plant decommissioning. **SELECTED PUBLICATIONS** Ed, The Evolving Landscape, John Hopkins UP, 97; ed, Wind Power in View, Acad Press (01); ed, Nuclear Decommissioning and Society, Routledge Press, 90; co-ed, Nuclear Power: Assessing and Managing Hazardous Technology, Westview Press, 84; auth, "Landscape Permanence and Nuclear Warnings: Geo rev (97); auth, "The Unsiting of Nuclear Power," Prof Geo (96); auth, "Wind energy landscapes: a convergence of society and natural resources," Soc Nat Resour (01); auth, "Nuclear oversight: a critical analysis of the public element in decommissioning policy," Pergamon (91); co-auth, "Who pays to close a nuke?," Pub Util Fort (93); auth, "Decommissioning nuclear power plants," Controlling the Atom in the 21st Cent (94). **CONTACT ADDRESS** Dept of Geog, Arizona State Univ, Tempe, AZ 85287-0104. **EMAIL** pasqualetti@asu.edu

PASTAN, ELIZABETH C.
PERSONAL Born 05/03/1955, Philadelphia, PA, m, 1980, 3 children **DISCIPLINE** ART HISTORY; MEDIEVAL FIELD **EDUCATION** Smith Col, BA, 77; Columbia Univ, MA, 79; Brown Univ, PhD, 86. **CAREER** Visit asst prof, Wellesley Col, 85-88; asst prof, Indiana Univ, Bloomington, 88-95; Assoc Prof, Emory Univ, 95-. **HONORS AND AWARDS** Kross Fnd Pub Subsidy, 97-98; Col Art Asn Millard Meiss Pub Subsidy, 95-96; NEH Summer Travel Stipend, 94; Indiana Univ Summer Fac Fel, 94. **MEMBERSHIPS** Societe academique de l'Aube; Int Ctr of Medieval Art; Medieval Acad of Am; Col Art Asn. **RESEARCH** Cult of relics; hagiography; stained glass representation of Jews and Heretics; Champagne (France); Medieval art and archit; Medievalism; Islam and the West. **SELECTED PUBLICATIONS** Auth, "Restoring the Stained Glass of Troyes Cathedral: The Ambiguous Legacy of Viollet-le-Duc," Gesta 29/2, (90): 155-166; coauth, Stained Glass Before 1700 in American Collections: Midwestern and Western States, Marie-Dominique Gauthier-Walter, Cahiers de Civilisation Medievale XXXVII, (94): 131-132; auth, "Process and Patronage in the Decorative Arts of the Early Campaigns of troyes Cathedral, c. 1200-1220s," Journal of the Society of Architectural Historians 53, (94): 215-231; auth, "Tam haereticos uam Judaeos: Shifting Symbols Themes in the Glazing of Troyes Cathedral," Word & Image 10, (94): 66-83; ed, The Dictionary of Art, Macmillan Publishers, London, 96; auth, "The Troture of the Saint George Medallion from Chartres Cathedral in Princeton," Record of The Art Museum, Princeton Univ 56, (97): 10-34; auth, "And he shall gather together the dispersed": The Tree of Jesse at Troyes Cathedral," Gesta 37, (98): 232-239; auth, "The Tree of Jesse at Troyes Cathedral," Krakow, (98): 55-65. **CONTACT ADDRESS** Dept of Art History, Emory Univ, Atlanta, GA 30322. **EMAIL** epastan@emory.edu

PASTERNACK, CAROL BRAUN
PERSONAL 1 child **DISCIPLINE** ENGLISH LITERATURE AND MEDIEVAL STUDIES **EDUCATION** UCLA, PhD, 83. **CAREER** Assoc Prof, Eng, Univ Calif, Santa Barbara. **RESEARCH** Hist of Eng lang; Gender in the middle ages information technology. **SELECTED PUBLICATIONS** Auth, Stylistic Disjunctions in The Dream of the Rood in Anglo-Saxon England, 84; Textuality in Old English Poetry, Cambridge Univ Press, 95; "Anonymous Polyphony and the Textuality of the Wanderer," Anglo-Saxon Eng, 91; co-ed, Vox intexta: Orality

and Textuality in the Middle Ages, Univ Wis Press, 91; auth, "Post-structuralist Theories: The Subject and the Text, Reading Old English Texts, ed, K. O'Brien O'Keeffe, Cambridge Univ Press, 97. **CONTACT ADDRESS** Dept of Eng, Univ of California, Santa Barbara, Santa Barbara, CA 93106-7150. **EMAIL** cpaster@humanitas.ucsb.edu

PASTOR, LESLIE P.

PERSONAL Born 05/08/1925, 2 children **DISCIPLINE** EUROPEAN HISTORY, GERMAN **EDUCATION** Educ: Seton Hall Univ, AB, 56; Columbia Univ, MA, 59, PhD, 67; Inst E Cent Europe, cert, 60. **CAREER** Instr Seton Hall Prep Sch, 56-60; from instr to asst prof, 60-68, Assoc Prof Ger, Seton Hall Univ, 68-. **MEMBERSHIPS** Am Asn Advan Slavic Studies; Am Asn Tchr(s) Ger; Am Asn for Study Hungarian Hist. **RESEARCH** Ger lang and lit; 18th and 19th century Hungarian hist; hist of East Central Europe; mod East Europ hist. **SELECTED PUBLICATIONS** Auth, Young Szechenyi; The Shaping of a Conservative Reformer, 1791-1832 (Ann Abor, MI), 70. **CONTACT ADDRESS** Dept of Mod Lang, Seton Hall Univ, So Orange, 400 S Orange Ave, South Orange, NJ 07079-2697. **EMAIL** pastorle@shu.edu

PASTOR, PETER

PERSONAL Born 03/04/1942, Budapest, Hungary, m, 1975, 1 child **DISCIPLINE** HISTORY **EDUCATION** City Col CUNY, BA, 64; NY Univ, MA, 65; NY Univ, PhD, 69. **CAREER** Prof, Montclair State Univ, 69- **HONORS AND AWARDS** IREX Res Grant to Hungary, 78; ACLS Travel Grant to Hungary, 85. **MEMBERSHIPS** AHA, AAASS, Am Asn for the Study of Hungarian Hist. **RESEARCH** Hungarian and Russian relations, the Hungarian revolutions of 1918-1919. **SELECTED PUBLICATIONS** Auth, Hungary Between Wilson and Lenin: The Hungarian Revolution of 1918-1919 (New York), 76; ed, Essays on World War I: A Case Study of Trianon (New York), 82; ed, Revolutions and Interventions in Hungary and its Neighbor States, 1918-1919 (New York); auth, "French War Aims Against Austria-Hungary and the Treaty of Trianon," in 20th Century Hungary and the Great Powers (NY: 95). **CONTACT ADDRESS** Dept Hist, Montclair State Univ, 1 Normal Ave, Montclair, NJ 07043-1624. **EMAIL** pastorp@mail.montclair.edu

PASZTOR, SUZANNE B.

DISCIPLINE HISTORY **EDUCATION** Adams State Col, BA, 86; TX Univ, MA, 88; NM Univ, PhD, 94. **CAREER** Asst prof, Univ Pacific. **SELECTED PUBLICATIONS** Auth, Modern Mexico, Libr Congress. **CONTACT ADDRESS** Hist Dept, Univ of the Pacific, Stockton, 3601 Pacific Ave, PO Box 3601, Stockton, CA 95211. **EMAIL** spasztor@uop.edu

PATE, J'NELL

PERSONAL Born 07/31/1938, Jacksboro, TX, m, 1960 **DISCIPLINE** HISTORY **EDUCATION** Tex Christian Univ, BS, 60; MA, 64; Univ N Tex, PhD, 82. **CAREER** Soc student teacher, Fort Worth Indep Sch Dist, 60-67; ed, Forth Worth ISD, 68-72; Azel News, 68-72; teacher, Tarrant Co Col, 68- . **HONORS AND AWARDS** Coral H. Tullis Awd, 88; Outstanding Centiennial Alumnus, UNT, 90; Outstanding Hist Alumna, 92; Outstanding Fac Awd, Tarrant County Col, 92; Fel, Tex State Hist Asn, 94. **MEMBERSHIPS** Tx State Hist Asn, W Tx Hist Asn, W Hist Asn, N Fort Worth Hist Soc. **RESEARCH** Western United States History, Texas history, Fort Worth history. **SELECTED PUBLICATIONS** Auth, Livestock Legacy, The Fort Worth Stockyards; auth, North of the River A Brief History of North Fort Worth; auth, Ranald Slidell Mackenzie Brave Calvary Colonel; auth, Hazel Vaughn and the Fort Worth Boys' Club, TCU Press, 00. **CONTACT ADDRESS** Dept Hist & Philos, Tarrant County Junior Col, 1104 Carpenter St, Azle, TX 76020. **EMAIL** jnell.pate@tccd.net

PATE, JAMES PAUL

PERSONAL Born 09/01/1942, Tremont, MS, m, 1963, 2 children **DISCIPLINE** EARLY AMERICAN HISTORY **EDUCATION** Delta State Univ, BSEd, 64; Miss State Univ, MA, 65, PhD (Am hist), 69. **CAREER** Teaching asst Am hist surv, Miss State Univ, 65-67; from asst prof to assoc prof, 67-76, chmn div hist & soc sci, 72-74, Prof Hist, Livingston Univ, 76-, Dean, Col Gen Studies, 74-. **MEMBERSHIPS** AHA; Orgn Am Historians; Southern Hist Asn. **RESEARCH** American Indians; Alabama History; Southern frontier. **SELECTED PUBLICATIONS** Colonial Alabama, Ala News Mag, 76; Women of the revolution & the road to revolution, Sumter County J, Bicentennial Spec, 76; John Sevier, Catawba Indians, Chickamauga Indians, & Battle of Mauvilla, In: Encycl of Southern History, La State Univ, 79; The Fort Tombecbe Historical Research & Documentation Project, Livingston Univ, 80; Deerskins And Duffels - The Creek Indian Trade With Anglo-america, 1685-1815 - Braund,keh, J of Southern History, Vol 0061, 1995. **CONTACT ADDRESS** Dean Col of Gen Studies, Univ of West Alabama, Livingston, AL 35470.

PATERSON, THOMAS GRAHAM

PERSONAL Born 03/04/1941, Oregon City, OR **DISCIPLINE** AMERICAN HISTORY **EDUCATION** Univ NH, BA, 63; Univ Calif, Berkeley, MA, 64, PhD (hist), 68. **CAREER** From asst prof to assoc prof, 67-73, Prof Hist, Univ Conn, 73-, Harry S Truman Inst grants-in-aid, 67-68, 72 & 75; Am Philos Soc res grant, 72; Eleanor Roosevelt Inst grant-in-aid, 75; NEH fel, 76-77; dir, NEH summer sem, 80. **MEMBERSHIPS** Soc Historians of Am Foreign Rels; Orgn Am Historians; AHA; AAUP. **RESEARCH** The Cold War; United States and the Cuban Revolution; Inter-American relations. **SELECTED PUBLICATIONS** Auth, Soviet-American Confrontation, Baltimore: The Johns Hopkins Univ Press, 73; auth, Meeting the Communist Threat: Truman to Reagan, New York: Oxford Univ Press, 88; auth, Kennedy's Quest for Victory: American Foreign Policy, 1961-1963, New York: Oxford Univ Press, 89; auth, Explaining the History of American Foreign Relations, with Michael J. Hogan, New York: Cambridge Univ Press, 91; auth, On Every Front: The Making and Unmaking of the Cold War, New York: W.W. Norton, 92; auth, Contesting Castro: The United States and the Triumph of the Cuban Revolution, New York: Oxford Univ Press, 94; auth, American Foreign Relations, Lexington, Mass, D.C. Heath, 95. **CONTACT ADDRESS** Dept of Hist, Univ of Connecticut, Storrs, Storrs, CT 06268. **EMAIL** paterson@neca.com

PATRIARCA, SILVANA

DISCIPLINE MODERN WESTERN EUROPE HISTORY **EDUCATION** Johns Hopkins Univ, PhD, 92. **CAREER** Assoc prof. **RESEARCH** Italy, history of quantification and the social sciences. **SELECTED PUBLICATIONS** Auth, Numbers and Nationhood: Writing and Statistics in 19th Century Italy, 96. **CONTACT ADDRESS** Dept of Hist, Columbia Col, New York, 2960 Broadway, New York, NY 10027-6902.

PATRIAS, CARMELA

DISCIPLINE CANADIAN LABOUR AND IMMIGRATION HISTORY **EDUCATION** Brit Columbia Univ, BA; Sussex Col, MA; Univ Toronto, PhD. **CAREER** Asst prof. **RESEARCH** Studies of immigrant labor in the Niagara Peninsula. **SELECTED PUBLICATIONS** Auth, Patriots and Proletarians; Politicizing Hungarian Immigrants in Interwar Canada, McGill-Queen's UP. **CONTACT ADDRESS** Dept of Hist, Brock Univ, 500 Glenridge Ave, Saint Catharines, ON, Canada L2S 3A1. **EMAIL** cpatrias@spartan.ac.BrockU.CA

PATRICK, DARRYL L.

PERSONAL Born 10/05/1936, Havre, MT, m, 1966, 2 children **DISCIPLINE** ART HISTORY **EDUCATION** Univ WA, MA, 70; N TX State Univ, PhD, 72. **CAREER** Tchg Asst, N TX State Univ, 75-. **SELECTED PUBLICATIONS** Auth, Venetian Palaces, Educl Filmstrips, 73; Times and Places Gone By Historic Photographic Exhib, Sam Houston Memorial Mus, 79; Pop Art, Popular Culture and Libraries, Shoe String Press, 84. **CONTACT ADDRESS** Dept of Art, Sam Houston State Univ, PO Box 2089, Huntsville, TX 77341-2089. **EMAIL** art_dlp@shsu.edu

PATRICK, KEVIN J.

PERSONAL Born 06/29/1961, Camden, NJ, m, 1985, 2 children **DISCIPLINE** GEOGRAPHY **EDUCATION** Glassboro State Col, BA, 83; Univ IL, MA, 85; Univ NC, PhD, 96. **CAREER** Asst prof, Ind Univ. **MEMBERSHIPS** Assoc of Am Geog; Pa Geog Soc; Soc for Com Archeol; Lincoln Highway Assoc. **RESEARCH** Cultural Landscapes, Transportation, Urban Geography. **SELECTED PUBLICATIONS** Auth, "GIS and Heritage Tourism: The Analysis and Management of Cultural Resources Along Pennsylvania's Lincoln Highway", Pa Geog Info System Res and Devlop Guide, ed, Robert Sechrist (PA: Center for Rural Pa, 96); auth, "Pennsylvania Parade: From 'P' to Shining 'P'", Lincoln Highway Forum 4.2, 97; auth, "Tourism in Marginalized Areas; Spinning Straw into Gold on Pennsylvania's Lincoln Highway", in Tech, Landscape and Arrested Develop: Essays on the Geog of Marginality, ed Vincent P. Miller, (Ind Univ of Pa, 97); auth, "Sidetracked by Scale While in Search of the Ten Best Lincoln Highway Landmarks", Lincoln Highway Forum 4.3, 97; auth "Until the Cows Come Home", Lincoln Highway Forum, 4.4, 97; auth, "Roadside Ephemera on the Eve of Destruction", Lincoln Highway Forum, 5.2, 98; auth, "Double-Headed Drive: The Third Annual Lincoln Highway Heritage Corridor Road Rally, Lincoln Highway Forum, 6.1, 98; coauth, "Illinois Lincoln Highway Adventure, Lincoln Highway Forum 6.3/4, 99; coauth, Diners of Pennsylvania, Stackpole Books (Mechanicsburg), 99; coed, A Geographic View of Pittsburgh and the Allegheníes, (WA: Assoc of Am Geog), 00. **CONTACT ADDRESS** Dept Geog, Indiana Univ of Pennsylvania, 747 Croyland Ave, Indiana, PA 15705-0001.

PATROUCH, JOSEPH F.

PERSONAL Born 07/12/1960, Cincinnati, OH, m, 1994, 1 child **DISCIPLINE** HISTORY **EDUCATION** Boston Univ, BA, 82; Univ Calif Berkeley, MA, 85; PhD, 91. **CAREER** Asst prof to assoc prof, Fla Int Univ, 91-. **HONORS AND AWARDS** Fulbright Fel, 88-89; NEH Sem, 92; FIU Grants, 91-93, 96; Teaching Incentive Prog Awd, State Univ System of Fla, 96; Fulbright Scholar, 99. **MEMBERSHIPS** AHA; Am Folklore Soc; Am Cath Hist Assoc; Czecho-Slovak Hist Conf; Am Assoc for the Advan of Slavic Studies; Sixteenth Century Studies Conf. Southern Hist Assoc. **SELECTED PUBLICATIONS** Auth, "The Investiture Controversy Revisited: Religious Reform, Emperor Maximilian II, and the Klosterrat", Austrian Hist Yearbook 25, (94); 59-77; auth, "Who Pays for Building the Rectory? Religious Conflicts in the Upper Austrian Parish of Dietach, 1540-1582", Sixteenth Century J 26, (95): 299-312; auth, "Macht als Handlung: Sierning, Das Land ob der Enns, 29 Mai, 1629", Fruhneuzeit-Info 7, (96): 18-24; auth, "Counter Reformation", "Holy Roman Empire", Encycl of Historians and Hisotrical Writing, ed Kelly Boyd, Fitzroy Dearborn, (London), 99; auth, "The Archduchess Elisabeth (1554-1592): Where Spain and Austria Met", The Lion and the Eagle: Interdisciplinary Essays on German-Spanish Relations Over the Centuries, eds CMK Hewitt, C Kent and T Wolber, Berghahn Books, (00); 77-90; auth, A Negotiated Settlement: The Counter-Reformation in Upper Austria Under the Habsburgs, Humanities Pr, (Boston), (forthcoming); auth, "Ysabell/Elizabeth/ Alzbeta: Erzherzogin. Konigin. Forschungsgegenwurff", Fruhneuzeit-Info, (forthcoming); auth, "Mary of Hungary", Thirty Years War, Women in", Biographical Dict of Military Women, ed Reina Pennington, Greenwood Pr, (forthcoming); auth, "Elisabeth of Habsburg", Women in world History: A Biographical Encycl, eds Anne Commire and Deborah Klezmer, Gale Group (Farmington Hills), (forthcoming). **CONTACT ADDRESS** Dept Hist, Florida Intl Univ, Miami, FL 33199. **EMAIL** patrouch@fiu.edu

PATSOURAS, LOUIS

PERSONAL Born 05/05/1931, Steubenville, OH, d, 1 child **DISCIPLINE** HISTORY **EDUCATION** Kent State Univ, BA, 53, MA, 59; Ohio State Univ, PhD, 66. **CAREER** Inst, Asst, Assoc, Prof, 63-88-, Kent State Univ. **MEMBERSHIPS** OAH **RESEARCH** French social History; Socialism. **SELECTED PUBLICATIONS** Auth, Atlantic Highlands, NJ, Humanities Press International; coed, Continuity and Change in Marxism," Humanities Press, NJ and Harvester Press, Sussex, UK, 82; ed, "The Crucible of Socialism," 87; auth, "Simone Weil and the Socialist Tradition," San Francisco, Mellen Res Univ Press, 91; ed, Debating Marx, San Francisco, Mellen Res Univ Press, 93; coed, Essays On Socialism, San Fran, Mellen Res Univ Press, 93; coed, Rebels Against the Old Order: Essays in Honor of Morris Salvin, Youngstown OH, YSU Press, 94; auth, Jean Grave and the Anarchist Tradition in France, Middletown NJ, Caslon Press, 95. **CONTACT ADDRESS** 494 Moore RD, Akron, OH 44319.

PATTERSON, CYNTHIA

DISCIPLINE HISTORY **EDUCATION** Stanford Univ, BA, 71; Univ Penn, PhD, 76. **CAREER** Assoc prof **RESEARCH** Greek history, particularly social and family history; Greek historians. **SELECTED PUBLICATIONS** Auth, articles on marriage law, family structures, and the relation of family and state in the Greek polis. **CONTACT ADDRESS** Dept History, Emory Univ, 221 Bowden Hall, 561 Kilgo Cir, Atlanta, GA 30322-1950. **EMAIL** cpatt01@emory.edu

PATTERSON, DAVID SANDS

PERSONAL Born 04/26/1937, Bridgeport, CT, m, 1968, 1 child **DISCIPLINE** AMERICAN DIPLOMATIC HISTORY, INTERNATIONAL RELATIONS **EDUCATION** Yale Univ, BA, 59; Univ Calif, Berkeley, MA, 63, PhD(hist), 68. **CAREER** Instr hist, Ohio State Univ, 65-69; asst prof, Univ Ill, Chicago Circle, 69-71; asst prof, Rice Univ, 71-76; vis assoc prof US hist, Colgate Univ, 76-78; Historian, Dept of State, 80-; John Hopkins-Nanjing Univ Ctr, 90-91; Dep Hist & Gen Ed Foreign Relations Series, 96-00; Acting Historian, 00-. **HONORS AND AWARDS** Mershon Soc Sci fel, 66; Nat Endowment for Humanities summer fel, 71-; Bernath lectr Am diplomatic hist, Soc Hist Am Foreign Rel, 78. **MEMBERSHIPS** Peace Hist Soc, pres 86-89; Soc Hist Am Foreign Rel, council 98-. **RESEARCH** American diplomatic history; national security affairs; arms control. **SELECTED PUBLICATIONS** Auth, "Woodrow Wilson and the mediation movement, 1914-17," Historian, 8/71; auth, Toward a Warless World: The Travail of the American Peace Movement, 1887-1914, Ind Univ, 76; auth, "The United States and the origins of the world court," Polit Sci Quart, summer 76; auth, "What's wrong (and right) with American diplomatic history: A diagnosis and prescription," Soc Hist Am Foreign Rel Newslett, 78; auth, "A historical view of American security," Peace & Change, Fall 81; auth, "President Eisenhower and Arms Control," Peace & Courage, No 3/4, 86; auth, "The Department of State: The Formative Years, 1775-1800," Prologue, winter 92; auth, The Legacy of President Eisenhower's Arms Control Policies, The Military-Industrial Complex: Eisenhower's Warning Three Decades Later, Peter Lang, 92; auth, Pacifism and Arms Limitation, Encyclopedia of the United States in the Twentieth Century, Scribner's, 96; auth,"Expanding the Horizons of the Foreign Relations Series", The Soc for Hist of Am Foreign Rel Newsletter, June 99. **CONTACT ADDRESS** 9011 Montgomery Ave, Chevy Chase, MD 20815. **EMAIL** pattersonds@state.gov

PATTERSON, JAMES A.

PERSONAL Born 12/01/1947, Camden, NJ, m, 1971, 2 children **DISCIPLINE** CHURCH HISTORY **EDUCATION** Rutgers Univ, BA, 70; Gordon-Conwell Theol Sem, MDiv, 73; Princeton Theol Sem, PhD, 80. **CAREER** From asst prof to prof, Toccoa Falls Col, 77-89; from assoc prof to prof, Mid-America Baptist Sem, 89-99; prof, Union Univ, 99-. **HONORS**

AND AWARDS Recipient of a dedication in Toccoa Falls Col Yearbook, 89. **MEMBERSHIPS** Am Soc of Church Hist, Confr on Faith and Hist, Evangelical Theol Soc, Southern Baptist Hist Soc. **RESEARCH** American Christianity, History of Missions, Religion and Politics. **SELECTED PUBLICATIONS** Auth, "The Loss of a Protestant Missionary Consensus: Foreign missions and the Fundamentalist-Modernist Conflict," in Earthen Vessels: American Evangelicals and Foreign Missions, 1880-1890, eds. Joel A. Carpenter and Wilbert S. Shenk, (Wm. B Eerdmans Pub Co., 97); contribur, The Dictionary of Christianity in America, ed. Daniel Reid, et al. (IL: InterVarsity Press, 90); auth, "The Kingdom and the Great Commission: Social Gospel Impulses and American Protestant Missionary Leaders, 1890-1920," Fides et Historia 25 (93): 48-61; auth, "Robert P. Wilder, 1863-1938: Recruiting Students for World Mission," in Mission Legacies, ed. Gerald H. Anderson (NY: Orbis Books, 94); auth, "The Theocratic Impulse in American Protestantism: The Persistence of the Puritan Tradition," in God and Caesar, eds. Michael Bauman and David Hall (PA: Christian Pub, 94); auth, To All the World: A History of Mid-America Baptist Theological Seminary, 1972-1997, Disciple Press (Memphis, TN), 97; contribur, Biographical Dictionary of Christian Missions, ed. Gerald H. Anderson (NY: Simon & Schuster Macmillan, 98). **CONTACT ADDRESS** Christian Studies, Union Univ, 1050 Union University Dr, Jackson, TN 38305. **EMAIL** jpatters@uu.edu

PATTERSON, JAMES TYLER
PERSONAL Born 02/12/1935, Bridgeport, CT, 2 children **DISCIPLINE** HISTORY **EDUCATION** Williams Col, AB, 57; Harvard Univ, AM, 61, PhD, 64. **CAREER** From asst prof to prof hist, 64-72 chmn dept, 76-79, Ind Univ, Bloomington; Guggenheim fel, 69-70; NEH jr fel, 69, consult, 75-77; Am Hist Assn rep, Adv Comt to Nat Arch, 75-77; consult/reviewer, 75-80, Hist Bk Club; NEH fel, 79-80; Harmsworth prof Am hist, Univ Oxford, 81-82; prof hist, 90-, Ford Found, Brown Univ; John Adams Prof, Am Hist, 88-89, Univ Amsterdam; Pitt Prof of Amer Inst, 99-00, Cambridge Univ. **HONORS AND AWARDS** Frederick Jackson Turner Award, Orgn Am Historians, 66; Ohioana Award, Martha Kinney Cooper Ohioana Libr Assn, 73; Dr of Let, LaTrobe Univ, Melbourne, Australia, 97; Bancroft Prize in History, 97; Amer Acad of Arts & Sci, 97. **MEMBERSHIPS** AHA; Orgn Am Historians; Soc Am Historians. **SELECTED PUBLICATIONS** Auth, The Welfare State in America, 1930-1980, Brit Assn Am Studies, Pamphlet No 7, 81; auth, The Dread Disease: Cancer and Modern American Culture, Harvard Univ Press, 87; auth, Grand Expectations: The Unites States, 1945-1974, Oxford Univ Press, 96. **CONTACT ADDRESS** Dept of History, Brown Univ, Providence, RI 02912. **EMAIL** james_patterson@brown.edu

PATTERSON, JOBY
PERSONAL Born 01/01/1942, Cheyenne, WY, m, 3 children **DISCIPLINE** ART HISTORY **EDUCATION** Univ CO, Boulder, BA (French & Psychol), 64, MA (Art Hist), 70; Babes-Bolyai Univ of Cluj, Romania, PhD (Art Hist), 98. **CAREER** Part-time, art history (adjunct fac), Eastern OR Univ, La Grande, OR, 80-95. **HONORS AND AWARDS** Smithsonian Res fel, Nat Museum of Am Art, Washington, DC, 90; Fulbright Res fel, Romania, 80-95. **MEMBERSHIPS** Soc of Architectural Hists; Nat and local (Marion D Ross) chapters, Soc for Romanian Studies. **RESEARCH** History of Am and European prints; Old Master prints; Mediaeval European Art/City Planning; history of Am and European architecture, esp vernacular and wooden architecture; Islamic architecture; Byzantine architecture and art. **SELECTED PUBLICATIONS** Auth, Hesychastic Thought as Revealed in Byzantine Greek and Romanian Frescoes: A Theory of Origin and Diffusion, Revue des Etudes Sud-Est Europeennnes, XVI:4 (Oct-Dec), 78; A Mediaeval Buddhist Bronze from Swat and Its Connections with Kashmir, Art and Archaeol Res Papers, vol 13, June 78; Romanian Folk Architecture: the Wood tradition, Festschrift (for Marion D Ross): A Collection of Essays on Architectural History, Northern Pacific Coast Chapter, Soc of Architectural Hists, 78; the Palace of the Lascarids at Nymphaeum, Abstracts of Papers, Fourth Annual Byzantine Studies Conference, 78; Contemporary Wooden Church Building in Maramures: Revision, Revival, or Renaissance?, Transylvanian Rev, V:1, spring 96; Bertha E Jacques and the Chicago Society of Etchers, Assoc Univ Presses, forthcoming 99; Romanian Wooden Churches from Mediaeval Maramures, East European Monographs, Columbia Univ Press, forthcoming 99; numerous other articles. **CONTACT ADDRESS** 402 Walnut St, La Grande, OR 97850. **EMAIL** patterj@eou.edu

PATTERSON, KARL DAVID
PERSONAL Born 04/06/1941, Newport News, VA, m, 1963, 3 children **DISCIPLINE** AFRICAN HISTORY, MEDICAL HISTORY **EDUCATION** Syracuse Univ, BS, 63, MA, 67; Stanford Univ, PhD(hist), 71; Univ NC, Chapel Hill, MSPH, 82. **CAREER** Asst prof, 71-76, assoc prof, 76-80, Prof Hist, Univ NC, Charlotte, 80-. **MEMBERSHIPS** Am Asn Hist Med; African Studies Asn. **RESEARCH** Nineteenth and twentieth century western Africa; medical and demographic history; modern Ghana. **SELECTED PUBLICATIONS** Auth, The Northern Gabon Coast to 1875, Oxford Univ, 75; The vanishing Mpongwe: European contact and demographic change in the Gabon River, J African Hist, Vol XVI, 75; The influenza epidemic of 1918-19 in the Gold Coast, Trans Hist Soc Ghana, Vol XVI, No 2; co-ed, History and Disease in Africa, 78 & auth, River blindness in the Northern Gold Coast, 1900-1950, In: History and Disease in Africa, 78, Duke Univ; Health in Urban Ghana: The case of Accra, 1900-1940, Soc Sci & Med, Vol 13; Veterinary dept and animal industry in the Gold Coast, 1909-1955, Int J African Hist Studies, Vol 13, 80; Health in Colonial Ghana: Disease, medicine and socio-economic change, 1900-1955, 81. **CONTACT ADDRESS** Dept of Hist, Univ of No Carolina, Charlotte, Charlotte, NC 28213.

PATTERSON, ROBERT BENJAMIN
PERSONAL Born 04/30/1934, West Hartford, CT, m, 1960, 2 children **DISCIPLINE** MEDIEVAL HISTORY **EDUCATION** St Bernard's Sem & Col, BA, 56; Trinity Col, Conn, MA, 58; Johns Hopkins Univ, PhD(medieval hist), 62. **CAREER** From asst prof to assoc prof, 62-71, Prof Hist, Univ SC, 71-, Vis assoc prof, Univ Conn, 65-66; consult, Nat Endowment for Humanities, 71-73 & 76-77; lectr hist, Merton Col, Oxford Univ, 75-76. **MEMBERSHIPS** Conf Brit Studies; Pipe Roll Soc; Southern Hist Asn; AHA; Mediaeval Acad Am. **RESEARCH** The medieval Mediterranean and the Crusades; Anglo-Norman history in the 11th and 12th centuries. **SELECTED PUBLICATIONS** Ed, The early existence of the Funda and Catena in the twelfth-century Latin Kingdom of Jerusalem, Speculum, 7/64; William of Malmesbury's Robert of Gloucester: A reevaluation of the Historia Novella, Am Hist Rev, 7/65; Stephen's Shaftsbury Charter: Another case against William of Malmesbury, Speculum, 7/68; auth, An un-edited charter of Henry Fitz Empress and Earl William of Gloucester's comital status, English Hist Rev, 10/72; ed, Earldom of Gloucester to AD 1717, Clarendon, 73; auth, Anarchy in England 1135-54: the theory of the constitution, Albion, fall 74; Vassals and the earldom of Gloucester's scriptorium, J Nat Libr Wales, winter 78. **CONTACT ADDRESS** Dept of Hist, Univ of So Carolina, Columbia, Columbia, SC 29208.

PATTERSON, ROBERT LEYBURNE
PERSONAL Born 06/01/1932, Camden, NJ, w, 1960 **DISCIPLINE** HISTORY **EDUCATION** Yale Univ, BA, 53; MA, 55; PhD, 60. **CAREER** From asst prof to assoc prof, 60-70, chmn dept soc sci, 63-69, coordr, 72-75; vis assoc prof hist, Dartmouth Col, 66-67; Nat Endowment for Humanities fel, 70-71; prof hist, 70-87, emeritus, 87-, Castleton State Col. **MEMBERSHIPS** Conf Brit Studies. **RESEARCH** Historiography and mythology of the Whig party; modern British intellectual class; social mobility. **CONTACT ADDRESS** 315 Audubon Ct., New Haven, CT 06510. **EMAIL** Robert.Patterson@castelton.edu

PATTERSON, WAYNE KIEF
PERSONAL Born 12/20/1946, Philadelphia, PA, m, 1977 **DISCIPLINE** HISTORY, INTERNATIONAL RELATIONS **EDUCATION** Swarthmore Col, BA, 68; Univ Pa, MA, 69 & 74, PhD(int rels), 77. **CAREER** Prof hist, St Norbert Col, 77-. **MEMBERSHIPS** Asn Asian Studies; Int Studies Asn; Immigration Hist Soc; AHA; Soc Historians of Am Foreign Relat. **RESEARCH** Korean immigration to, and Koreans in, America; Korean-American relations; modern Korean and East Asian history. **SELECTED PUBLICATIONS** Co-ed, The Koreans in America, 1882-1974: A Chronology and Fact Book, Oceana, 74; coauth, The Koreans in America, Lerner, 77. **CONTACT ADDRESS** Dept of Hist, St. Norbert Col, 100 Grant St, De Pere, WI 54115-2099. **EMAIL** pattwk@mail.snc.edu

PATTERSON, WILLIAM BROWN
PERSONAL Born 04/08/1930, Charlotte, NC, m, 1959, 4 children **DISCIPLINE** HISTORY **EDUCATION** Univ of the South, BA, 52; Harvard Univ, MA, 54, PhD, 66; Oxford Univ, BA, 55, MA, 59; Episcopal Divinity Sch, Cambridge, Mass, MDiv, 58. **CAREER** Asst prof, Davidson Col, NC, 63-66, assoc prof, 66-76, prof, 76-80; Dean of the Col of Arts and Scis and Prof of Hist, Univ of the South, 80-91, prof, 91-. **HONORS AND AWARDS** Phi Beta Kappa, 52; Am Coun of Learned Socs First-Year Grad Fel, 52-53; Rhodes Scholar, 53-55; Danforth Fel, 52-61; NEH Fel, Cambridge Univ, Newberry Library, 67; Folger Library Short-Term Fel, 75; Mellon Appalachian Fel, Univ Va, 92; Albert C. Outler Prize in Ecumenical Church Hist, 99. **MEMBERSHIPS** Am Hist Asn, Am Soc of Church Hist, Royal Hist Soc, Ecclesiastical Hist Soc, North Am Conf on British Studies. **RESEARCH** Tudor and Stuart England, especially the religious, political, and intellectual history of the early seventeenth century. **SELECTED PUBLICATIONS** Auth, "The Synod of Dort and the Early Stuart Church," in Donald S. Armentrout, ed, This Sacred History: Anglican Reflections for John Booty, Cambridge, MA: Cowley Pub (90): 199-221; auth, "Hooker on Ecumenical Relations: Conciliarism in the English Reformation," in A. S. McGrade, ed, Richard Hooker and the Construction of Christian Community, Tempe, Az: Medieval and Renaissance Texts and Studies (97): 283-303; auth, King James VI and I and the Reunion of Christiandom, Cambridge: Cambridge Univ Press (97). **CONTACT ADDRESS** Dept Hist, Univ of the South, 735 University Ave, Sewanee, TN 37383-0001. **EMAIL** bpatters@sewanee.edu

PAUL, GEORGE MACKAY
PERSONAL Born 07/16/1927, Glasgow, Scotland, m, 1956, 3 children **DISCIPLINE** CLASSICS, ANCIENT HISTORY **EDUCATION** Oxford Univ, BA & MA, 54; Univ London, PH-D(classics), 63. **CAREER** From asst lectr to lectr classics, Univ W Indies, 55-64; from asst prof to assoc prof, 64-70, chmn dept, 73-76, Prof Classics, McMaster Univ, 70, Mem, Comt Coord Acad Libr Serv Ont Univs, 66-67; Can Coun leave fel, 71-72. **MEMBERSHIPS** Class Asn Can (treas, 67-69); Am Philol Asn; Soc Prom Roman Studies; Asn Ancient Historians; Soc Prom Hellenic Studies. **RESEARCH** Greek and Roman historiography; Roman history. **SELECTED PUBLICATIONS** Ed, Roman Coins and Public Life under the Empire: E. Togo Salmon Papers II, Univ Mich Press, (Ann Arbor, Mi), 99. **CONTACT ADDRESS** Dept of Classics, McMaster Univ, 1280 Main St W, Hamilton, ON, Canada L8S 4M2. **EMAIL** gepaul@mcmaster.ca

PAUL, HARRY W.
PERSONAL Born 09/21/1933, NF, Canada **DISCIPLINE** MODERN EUROPEAN RELIGIOUS & INTELLECTUAL HISTORY **EDUCATION** Univ Nfld, BA, 54; Columbia Univ, MA, 58, PhD(hist), 62. **CAREER** Asst prof hist, Md State Col, 62-63 & Newark State Col, 63- 66; assoc prof, 66-73, Prof Hist, Univ FL, 73-, Nat Endowment for Humanities fel, 71-72; NSF grants soc sci, 77, 81-90. **MEMBERSHIPS** AAHM. **RESEARCH** History of medicine; history of science. **SELECTED PUBLICATIONS** Auth, The Second Ralliement: The Rapprochement Between Church and State in France in the 20th Century, Cath Univ Am, 67; The Sorcerer's Apprentice: The French Scientist's Image of German Science, 1840-1919, Univ Fla, 72; Religion and Darwinism, In: The Comparative Reception of Darwinism, Univ Tex, 74; The Edge of Contingency: French Catholic Reactions to Scientific Change from Darwin to Duhem, Univ Fla, 79; Apollo courts the Vulcans: The applied science institutes in nineteenth-century French science faculties, In: The Organization of Science and Technology in France, 1808-1914, Cambridge Univ Press, 80; The role and reception of monographs in nineteenth-century French science, In: Development of Science Pubishing in Europe, Elsevier, 80; coauth (with T W Shinn), The state and structure of science in France, Contemp Fr Civilization, fall 81-winter 82; auth, From Knowledge to Power, The Rise of the Science Empire in France 1860-1939, Cambridge Univ Press, 85; auth, Science, Vine, and Wine in Modern France, Cambridge Univ Press, 96. **CONTACT ADDRESS** Dept of Hist, Univ of Florida, Gainesville, FL 32611. **EMAIL** hpaul@history.ufl.edu

PAUL, JUSTUS F.
PERSONAL Born 05/27/1938, Boonville, MO, m, 1960, 3 children **DISCIPLINE** RECENT UNITED STATES HISTORY **EDUCATION** Doane Col, AB, 59; Univ Wis-Madison, MA, 60; Univ Nebr, PhD(hist), 66. **CAREER** Instr, High Sch, Wis, 60-62; instr hist, Univ Nebr, 63-64 & 65-66; from asst prof to assoc prof, 66-75, prof hist, Univ Wis-Stevens Point, 75-, dept, 69-86, dean Col Of Letters & Sci, 86-, Res grants, Univ Wis, 66-67, 68-69, 76 & 77 & 79-79; Am Asn State & Local Hist res grant, 68-69; Nat Endowment for Humanities, summer 78. **HONORS AND AWARDS** Univ Sci Awd, 84; Win Rothman Local Hist Awd, 96; Paul Kersenbrok Humanitarian Ward, 96. **MEMBERSHIPS** AHA; Orgn Am Historians; State Hist Soc Wis; Nebr State Hist Soc. **RESEARCH** Political history; Midwestern state and local history. **SELECTED PUBLICATIONS** Auth, Senator Hugh Butler and Nebraska Republicanism, Nebr State Hist Soc, 76; The World is Ours: A History of the University of Wisconsin-Stevens Point, 1894-1994, UWSP Foundation, 94; ed, Selected Writings of Rhys W Hays, Palmer Printers, 77; co-ed, The Badger State: A Documentary History of Wisconsin, Wm B Eerdmans, 79; co-ed, Wisconsin History: An Annotated Bibliography, Greenword Press, 99. **CONTACT ADDRESS** Dept of History, Univ of Wisconsin, Stevens Point, 130 CCC, Stevens Point, WI 54481-3897. **EMAIL** jpaul@wsp.edu

PAULEY, BRUCE F.
PERSONAL Born 11/04/1937, Lincoln, NE, m, 1963, 2 children **DISCIPLINE** CENTRAL EUROPEAN HISTORY **EDUCATION** Grinnell Col, BA, 59; Univ Nebr, MA, 61; Univ Rochester, PhD, 66. **CAREER** Instr hist, Col Wooster, 64-65 & Univ Nebr, 65-66; asst prof, Univ Wyo, 66-71; from assoc prof to prof hist, Univ Cent Fla, 71-; Vis instr hist, Col William & Mary, 75; Vis prof, Univ New Orleans, Austia, 91. **HONORS AND AWARDS** Fulbright-Hays Fel, 63-64; Charles Smith Awd for best bk, S Hist Asn, 91-92; Austrian Cult Inst Awd for best bk, 92-93. **MEMBERSHIPS** AHA; Ger Studies Asn; Austrian & Habsburg Historians. **RESEARCH** Hahnenschwanz and Swastika; The Styrian Heimatschutz and Austrian National Socialism, 1918-1934. **SELECTED PUBLICATIONS** Auth, Hahnenschwanz und Hakenkreuz: Steirische Heimatschutz und Osterreichischer Nationalsozialismus, 1918-1934, Europa, 72; auth, The Habsburg Legacy, 1867-1939, Holt, 72; auth, Hitler and the Forgotten Nazis: A History of Austrian National Socialism, Univ NC, Chapel Hill, 81; auth, Der Weg in den Nationalsozialismus: Ursprunge und Entwicklung in Osterreich, Osterreichischer Bundesverlag, 88; auth, From Prejudice to Persecution: A History of Austrian Anti-Semitism, Univ NC, Chapel Hill, 92; auth, Eine Geschichte des Osterreichischen Antisemitimus: Von der Ausgrenzung zur

Auschl¤schung, Kremayr & Scheriau, 93; auth, Hitler, Stalin, and Mussolini: Totalitarianism in the Twentieth Century, Harlan Davidson, 97. **CONTACT ADDRESS** Dept of Hist, Univ of Central Florida, P O Box 161350, Orlando, FL 32816-1350.

PAULI, LORI
PERSONAL Born Guelph, ON, Canada **DISCIPLINE** ARTS HISTORIAN **EDUCATION** Univ Waterloo, BA, 82; Queen's Univ, MA, 90. **CAREER** Cur, York Sunbury Hist Soc Mus; tchr, dept art, Queen's Univ; asst cur, Photographs, Nat Gallery Can. **SELECTED PUBLICATIONS** Auth, Disciple of the American Dream: Listte Model in The World and I 4 vol.7; auth, Silent Communion: Christel Gang and Edward Weston in History of Photography 2 vol.19; auth, A Few Hellers: Women at the Clarence H. White School of Photography in Margaret Watkins 1884-1969 Photographs, 94. **CONTACT ADDRESS** Photographs Collection, National Gallery of Canada, 380 Sussex Dr, Ottawa, ON, Canada K1N 9N4. **EMAIL** lpauli@ngc.cwn.gc.ca

PAULOVSKAYA, MARIANNA
PERSONAL Born Moscow, Russia **DISCIPLINE** GEOGRAPHY **EDUCATION** Moscow State Univ, MA, 87; Clark Univ, PhD, 98. **CAREER** Vis asst prof, FAU, 97-98; asst prof, Hunter Col, 98-. **HONORS AND AWARDS** Diploma with honors from Moscow State. **MEMBERSHIPS** Asn Am Geogs. **RESEARCH** Urban, GIS, gender and class, urban environment. **SELECTED PUBLICATIONS** Coauth with Susan Hanson, "Privatization of the Urban Fabric: Gender and Local Geographies of Transition in Downtown Moscow," (under review). **CONTACT ADDRESS** Dept Geog & Geol, Hunter Col, CUNY, 695 Park Ave, New York, NY 10021. **EMAIL** mpavlov@everest.hunter.cuny.edu

PAUWELS, HEIDI
PERSONAL Born, Belgium **DISCIPLINE** ASIAN STUDIES **EDUCATION** Univ Washington, PhD, 94. **CAREER** Lectr, School of Oriental and African Studies, 94-97; Asst Prof, Univ Washington, 97-. **HONORS AND AWARDS** Fulbright to study at Univ Wash; Grant from Belgian Embassy for 1 yr field work in India. **MEMBERSHIPS** AAR; AOS; AAS **RESEARCH** Hinduism (Bhakti/Hagiography/Reworking of Scripture); Gender issues; Hindi Lit. **SELECTED PUBLICATIONS** Auth, Krishna's Round Dance Reconsidered **CONTACT ADDRESS** Dept Asian Language & Literature, Univ of Washington, Seattle, WA 98195-3521.

PAVLAC, BRIAN A.
PERSONAL Born 07/11/1956, Berea, OH, m, 1981, 2 children **DISCIPLINE** HISTORY **EDUCATION** Bowling Green State Univ, BA, 78; MA, 80; Univ Notre Dame, MA, 82; PhD, 86. **CAREER** Asst Prof, Valparaiso Univ, 87-88; Asst prof & Dir, Univ Notre Dame, 88-92; Asst Prof, Univ New Orleans, 92, 93, 97; Asst Prof to Assoc Prof, Kings Col, 93-. **HONORS AND AWARDS** Fulbright-Hays Grad, Germany, 82-83; Delta Epsilon Sigma; Delta Phi Alpha; Phi Alpha Theta. **MEMBERSHIPS** Medieval Acad of Am; Am Hist Asn; German Hist Soc; Am Cusanus Soc. **RESEARCH** Medieval German History; Prince-Bishops. **SELECTED PUBLICATIONS** Auth, "Excommunication and Territorial Politics in High Medieval Trier," Church History (91): 20-36; auth, "Nicolaus Cusanus as Prince-Bishop of Brixen (1450-64): Historians and a Conflict of church and State," Historical Reflections, (95): 131-154; auth, "Die Verhangung des Kirchenbannes uber Graf Meinhard II von Tirol (1259-95)," Veroffentlichungen des Tiroler Landesmuseums Ferdinandeum, (95): 219-232; auth, "Emperor Henry VI (1191-97) and the papacy: Similarities with Innocent III's Temporal Policies," in Pope Innocent III and His World, (Ashgate, 99), 255-269. **CONTACT ADDRESS** Dept Hist, King's Col, 133 N River St, Wilkes-Barre, PA 18711-0851. **EMAIL** bapavlac@kings.edu

PAXTON, FREDERICK S.
PERSONAL Born 07/08/1951, Detroit, MI, m, 1975, 2 children **DISCIPLINE** HISTORY **EDUCATION** Michigan State Univ, BA; Univ Wash, MA; Univ Calif at Berkeley, PhD. **CAREER** Assoc prof; Conn Col, 85-; vis prof, Chalice of Repose Proj in Missoula, Mont; prof 96-. **MEMBERSHIPS** Amer Coun Learned Soc, Yale Univ, Mellon Found, Fulbright Comn & Camargo Found, grants and fel(s). **RESEARCH** Medieval European cultural history; Ritual, Medicine, and Religion; Historical context of Music-Thanatology. **SELECTED PUBLICATIONS** Auth, Christianizing Death: The Creation of a Ritual Process in Early Medieval Europe, 90; A Medieval Latin Death Ritual: The Monastic Customaries of Bernard and Ulrich of Cluny, 93; Liturgy and Anthropology, 93. **CONTACT ADDRESS** Dept of History, Connecticut Col, 270 Mohegan Ave, Box 5063, New London, CT 06320. **EMAIL** fspax@conncoll.edu

PAXTON, ROBERT OWEN
PERSONAL Born 06/15/1932, Lexington, VA, m **DISCIPLINE** EUROPEAN HISTORY **EDUCATION** Washington & Lee Univ, AB, 54; Oxford Univ, BA, 56, MA, 61; Harvard Univ, PhD, 63. **CAREER** From acting instr to asst prof hist, Univ Calif, Berkeley, 61-67; assoc prof, State Univ NY Stony Brook, 67-69; prof Hist, Columbia Univ, 69-, chmn dept, 80-82; Am Coun Learned Soc fel, 74-75; Rockefeller Found fel, 78-79; German Marshall Fund fel, 85; prof emer, 97. **HONORS AND AWARDS** Honorary Degrees WA and Lee, State Univ of New York, 74, Univ de Caen, 94; Elected member Am Philos Soc, 99; dlitt, washington & lee univ, 74. **MEMBERSHIPS** Fel Am Acad Arts & Lett. **RESEARCH** Modern France; Fascism. **SELECTED PUBLICATIONS** Auth, Parades and Politics at Vichy, Princeton Univ, 66; auth, The Spirit of the City, Laband Art Gallery, Loyola Marymount Univ, 86; Vichy France and the Jews, Stanford Univ Press, 95; DeGaulle and the United States, 95; French Peasant Fascism, Oxford, 96; Vichy France: Old Guard and New Order forthcoming in 2nd edition, Colunbia Univ Press, 01; auth, Europe in the Twetieth Century forthcomingg in 4th edition, Harcourt Col Publishers, 01. **CONTACT ADDRESS** Dept of Hist, Columbia Univ, 2960 Broadway, New York, NY 10027-6900. **EMAIL** rop1@columbia.edu

PAYNE, HARRY CHARLES
PERSONAL Born 03/25/1947, Worcester, MA **DISCIPLINE** MODERN EUROPEAN & EUROPEAN INTELLECTUAL HISTORY **EDUCATION** Yale Univ, BA & MA, 69, MPhil, 70, PhD, 73. **CAREER** From instr to asst prof, 73-78, assoc prof, 78-82, Prof Hist, Colgate Univ, 82-, Adv ed Europ hist, Eighteenth-Century Studies, 77; assoc ed, Eighteenth-Century Life, 77; overseas fel, Churchill Col, Cambridge Univ, 77. **HONORS AND AWARDS** Article Prize, Am Soc Eighteenth-Century Studies, 77. **MEMBERSHIPS** Am Soc Eighteenth-Century Studies. **RESEARCH** French enlightenment; European intellectual history, 1880- 1914; ritual in modernizing Europe, 1800-1945. **SELECTED PUBLICATIONS** Auth, Elite vs popular mentality in the eighteenth century, Hist Reflections, 75; Pauvrete, misere and the aims of enlightened economics, Studies on Voltaire & the 18th Century, 76; The Philosophes and the People, Yale Univ, 76; Modernizing the Ancients: The Reconstruction of Ritual Drama 1870-1920, Proc Am Philos Soc, 77; The novel as social history: A methodological reflection, Hist Teacher, 77; Rituals of balance and silence: The ideal Theater of Gordon Craig, Bull Res Humanities, 79; ed, Studies in Eighteenth-Century Culture, Vols 10-12, Univ Wis Press, 81-83; Malinowski's Style, Proc Am Philos Soc, 81. **CONTACT ADDRESS** Dept of Hist, Colgate Univ, Hamilton, NY 13346.

PAYNE, STANLEY GEORGE
PERSONAL Born 09/09/1934, Denton, TX, m, 1961, 1 child **DISCIPLINE** MODERN EUROPEAN HISTORY **EDUCATION** Pac Union Col, BA, 55; Claremont Grad Sch, MA, 57; Columbia Univ, PhD, 60. **CAREER** Instr mod Europ hist, Univ Minn, 60-62; from asst prof to prof, Univ Calif, Los Angeles, 62-68; Prof Mod Europ Hist, Univ Wis-Madison, 68-; Lectr, Columbia Col, 59-60; instr, Hunter Col, 60; Am Philos Soc grant, 61, 67; Soc Sci Res Coun grant, 61; Guggenheim fel, 62-63; mem exec comt, Coun Europ Studies, 76-78. **MEMBERSHIPS** Soc Span & Port Hist Studies; Ital Hist Soc; AHA. **RESEARCH** Modern west European history; Spanish history. **SELECTED PUBLICATIONS** Auth, Falange: A History of Spanish Fascism, Stanford Univ, 61; coauth, Modern Times: Europe since 1815, Heath, 64; auth, Politics and the Military in Modern Spain, Stanford Univ, 67; Franco's Spain, Crowell, 67; The Spanish Revolution, Norton, 70; A History of Spain and Portugal (2 vols), Univ Wis, 73; Basque Nationalism, Univ Nev, 75; Fascism: Comparison and Definition, Univ Wis, 80; The Franco Regime 1936-1975, Univ Wis, 87; A History of Facism, 1914-1945, Univ Wis, 95. **CONTACT ADDRESS** Dept of Hist, Univ of Wisconsin, Madison, 455 North Park St, Madison, WI 53706-1483. **EMAIL** sgpayne@facstaff.wisc.edu

PAZ, FRANCIS XAVIER
PERSONAL Born 11/05/1931, Chicago, IL, m, 1973, 1 child **DISCIPLINE** COMPARATIVE LITERATURE, ORIENTAL STUDIES **EDUCATION** Univ Chicago, BA, 52, MA, 57; Columbia Univ, PhD(Orient studies), 72. **CAREER** Lectr humanities, Bishop Col, 56-57; lectr Orient humanities, Columbia Univ, 63-65; Prof English & Comp Lit, State Univ NY, New Paltz, 66, Univ fel Arabic lit, Columbia Univ, 77-. **HONORS AND AWARDS** Fulbright Fels to Pakistan, 79 and Syna, 01. **MEMBERSHIPS** MLA; Am Orient Soc; Mideast Studies Asn. **RESEARCH** Modern American and Arabic fiction. **SELECTED PUBLICATIONS** Translr, The Assemblies of Al-Hamadhani, State Univ NY, (in press); The Monument - Art, Vulgarity And Responsibility in Iraq - Alkhalil,s, J of The American Oriental Society, Vol 0113, 1993. **CONTACT ADDRESS** Dept Lit, SUNY, New Paltz, New Paltz, NY 12562.

PEABODY, SUSAN
DISCIPLINE EARLY MODERN EUROPEAN **EDUCATION** Univ Iowa, PhD, 93. **CAREER** Asst prof, Washington State Univ. **RESEARCH** Comparative history of slavery, history and multimedia. **SELECTED PUBLICATIONS** Auth, There are No Slaves in France: The Political Culture of Race and Slavery in the Ancient Regime, Oxford UP, 96. **CONTACT ADDRESS** Dept of History, Washington State Univ, 301 Wilson Hall, PO Box 644030, Pullman, WA 99164-4030. **EMAIL** peabody@vancouver.wsu.edu

PEARSON, BIRGER ALBERT
PERSONAL Born 09/17/1934, Turlock, CA, m, 1966, 6 children **DISCIPLINE** HISTORY OF RELIGIONS **EDUCATION** Upsala Col, BA, 57; Univ Calif, Berkeley, MA, 59; Pac Lutheran Sem, BDiv, 62; Harvard Univ, PhD(Christian origins), 68. **CAREER** Instr Greek, Pac Lutheran Sem, 59-62; lectr New Testament, Episcopal Theol Sch, 65-66; from instr to asst prof relig, Duke Univ, 66-69; from asst prof to assoc prof relig studies, 69-75, assoc dir, Educ Abroad Prog, 74-76, Prof Relig Studies, Univ Calif, Santa Barbara, 75-, Fel, Humanities Inst, Univ Calif, 70-71, 72-73; Am Philos Asn grant, 72; chmn dept, 76-79, dir, Univ Calif Study Ctr, Lund, Sweden,79-81; emer, UCSB, 94-. **MEMBERSHIPS** Soc Bibl Lit; Am Acad Relig; Archaeol Inst Am; Soc New Testament Studies; Soc Coptic Archaeol. **RESEARCH** Gnosticism; Early Christianity; Hellenistic religions. **SELECTED PUBLICATIONS** Auth, The Pneumatikos-Psychikos Terminology in I Corinthians, Soc Bibl Lit, 73, Scholars, 76; ed & transl, The Gnostic Attitude, Univ Calif Inst Relig Studies, 73; ed & contribr, Religious Syncretism in Antiquity, Scholars, 75; contribr, The Nag Hammadi Library in English, BrillHarper, 77, 3rd ed 88; coed, & contribr, The Roots of Egyptian Christianity, Fortress, 86, 92; auth, Gnosticism, Judaism, and Egyptian Christianity, Fortress, 90; ed, Naghammad, Codex VII, Brill, 96; auth, The Emergence of the Christian Religion, Trinity Press International, 97. **CONTACT ADDRESS** Dept of Relig Studies, Univ of California, Santa Barbara, 27345 E Vine Ave, Escalm, CA 95320. **EMAIL** bpearson@thevision.net

PEARSON, EDWARD
DISCIPLINE HISTORY **EDUCATION** Birmingham, BA, 80; Bowling Green State, MA, 83; Univ Wis-Madison, PhD, 92. **CAREER** ASST PROF, HIST, FRANKLIN & MARSHALL **MEMBERSHIPS** Am Antiquarian Soc **CONTACT ADDRESS** 303 N West End Dr, Lancaster, PA 17603.

PEARSON, SAMUEL C.
PERSONAL Born 12/10/1931, Dallas, TX, m, 1955, 2 children **DISCIPLINE** HISTORY OF CHRISTIANITY **EDUCATION** TX Christian Univ, AB, 51; Univ Chicago, DB, 53, MA, 60, PhD, 64. **CAREER** Asst prof, 64-69, assoc prof, 69-74, prof, hist stud, 74-, dept chmn, 72-77 & 81-83, act dir, 86-87, Reg Res & Develop Serv, Dean, Sch of Soc Sci, 83-95, dean emeritus, 95-, Southern Ill Univ, 74-98; prof emeritus, 98. **HONORS AND AWARDS** Phi Eta Sigma; Phi Kappa Phi (Emeritus Lifetime Member); Phi Alpha Theta; Outstanding Foreign Expert Northeast Normal Univ, 95, appointed vis prof, 96; Nat Endowment for the Hum Sum Sem grants to Yale Univ, 76, and Univ Hawaii, 98; Fulbright Prof of Am Hist, Nanjing Univ, 00-01. **MEMBERSHIPS** Am Soc Church Hist; Am Hist Asn; Org of Am Hist; Am Academy of Relig. **RESEARCH** Religions in the modern world. **SELECTED PUBLICATIONS** Auth, From Church to Denomination: American Congregationalism in the Nineteenth Century, Church Hist, XXXVIII, 69; auth, Enlightenment Influence on Protestant Thought in Early National America, Encounter, XXXVII, 77; auth, The Great Awakening and Its Impact on American History, Forum Press, 78; auth, The Campbell Institute: Herald of the Transformation of an American Religious Tradition, The Scroll, LXII, 78; auth, Rationalism in an Age of Enthusiasm: The Anomalous Career of Robert Cave, The Bul of MO Hist Soc, XXXV, 79; auth, The Cave Affair: Protestant Thought in the Guilded Age, Encounter, XLI, 80; auth, The Religion of John Locke and the Character of His Thought, John Locke: Critical Assessments, 4 vols, Routledge, 91; Alexander Campbell, 1788-1866, Makers of Christian Theology in America, Abingdon Press, 97. **CONTACT ADDRESS** Dept of Historical Studies, So Illinois Univ, Edwardsville, Edwardsville, IL 62026-1454. **EMAIL** spearso@siue.edu

PEARSON, THOMAS SPENCER
PERSONAL Born 09/19/1949, Rockville Center, NY, m, 1971 **DISCIPLINE** RUSSIAN HISTORY, NINETEENTH CENTURY EUROPE **EDUCATION** Univ Santa Clara, BA, 71; Univ NC, MA, 73, PhD(Russ hist), 77. **CAREER** Asst prof Russ & world hist, Auburn Univ, 77-78; Asst Prof Russ & Europ Hist, Monmouth Col, 78-. **MEMBERSHIPS** AHA; Am Asn Advan Slavic Studies; Southern Conf Slavic Studies. **RESEARCH** Imperial Russian administrative and social history; Russian intellectual history. **SELECTED PUBLICATIONS** **CONTACT ADDRESS** Dept of Hist, Monmouth Univ, 400 Cedar Ave, West Long Branch, NJ 07764-1898.

PEASE, JANE HANNA
PERSONAL Born 11/26/1929, Waukegan, IL, m, 1950 **DISCIPLINE** AMERICAN HISTORY **EDUCATION** Smith Col, AB, Univ Rochester, MA, 57, PhD(hist), 69; Western Reserve Univ, MS, 58. **CAREER** Instr hist, Emma Willard Sch, 55-64, chmn dept, 63-64; lectr, Univ Calgary, 64-65, instr, 65-66; from instr to assoc prof, 66-79, Prof Hist, Univ Maine, Orono, 79-, Am Coun Learned Soc grant-in-aid, 65; Am Philos Soc grants-in-aid, 66 & 73; Nat Endowment for Humanities res grant, 80-82; Nat Sci Found res grant, 81-82. **MEMBERSHIPS** AHA; Orgn Am Historians; Southern Hist Asn; New Eng Hist Asn (pres, 75-76); Soc Historians Early Am Republic. **RESEARCH** Nineteenth century American social history; antebellum urban history. **SELECTED PUBLICATIONS** Coauth, Black Utopia: Negro communal experiments in America, Wis State Hist

Soc, 63; co-ed, Anti-Slavery Argument, Bobbs, 65; coauth, Bound With Them In Chains: A Biographical History of the Antislavery Movement, Greenwood, 72; They Who Would Be Free: Blacks' Search for Freedom, 1830-1861, Athenum, 74; The Fugitive Slave Law and Anthony Burns: A Problem in Law Enforcement, Lippincott, 75; Paternal Dilemmas: Education, property, and patrician persistence in Jacksonian Boston, New England Quart, 6/80; The economics and politics of Charleston's nullification crisis, J Southern Hist, 8/81; Social structure and the potential for urban change: Boston and Charleston in the 1830's, J Urban Hist, 2/82. **CONTACT ADDRESS** Dept of Hist, Univ of Maine, 205 E Annex, Orono, ME 04473.

PEASE, OTIS ARNOLD
PERSONAL Born 07/31/1925, Pittsfield, MA, m, 1949, 4 children **DISCIPLINE** HISTORY **EDUCATION** Yale Univ, BA, 49, PhD, 54. **CAREER** Instr hist, Univ Tex, 53-55; asst prof, Univ Wash, 55-56; from asst prof to assoc prof, Stanford Univ, 56-64, W R Coe prof hist & Am studies, 64-66; chmn dept hist, 67-72, Prof Am Hist, Univ Wash, 66-, Soc Sci Res Coun res fel, 62-63; Phi Beta Kappa scholar, 68-69, lectr, 76-; mem bd trustees, Stanford Univ, 69-; mem, Nat Advert Rev Bd, 71-75. **MEMBERSHIPS** AHA (vp prof div, 78-); Orgn Am Historians; Am Studies Asn. **RESEARCH** American political, social and intellectual history; American historiography. **SELECTED PUBLICATIONS** Auth, Parkman's History: The Historian as Literary Artist, 53 & Responsibilities of American Advertising, 1920-1940, 58, Yale Univ; ed, Progressive Years, Braziller, 62; The City, Univ Wash, 67; auth, Leland Stanford, Stanford Mag, No 2, 6/74; Teaching Americans to Consume, In: Advertising and the Public, Univ Ill, 79. **CONTACT ADDRESS** Dept of Hist DP-20, Univ of Washington, Seattle, WA 98195.

PECK, WILLIAM HENRY
PERSONAL Born 10/02/1932, Savannah, GA, m, 1967, 3 children **DISCIPLINE** ART HISTORY & ARCHAEOLOGY **EDUCATION** Wayne State Univ, BFA, 60, MA, 61. **CAREER** Jr cur, 60-62, from asst cur to assoc cur, 62-68, Cur Ancient Art, Detroit Inst Arts, 68-, Lectr art hist, Cranbrook Acad, Bloomfield Hills, Mich, 62-65; field archaeologist, Inst Fine Arts, NY Univ-Am Res Ctr Egypt, excavation at Mendes, Egypt, 64-66; adJprof art hist, Wayne State Univ, 66-; vis lectr, Univ Mich, 70; field archaeologist, Brooklyn Mus Theban Exped-Mut Temple Project, Egypt, 78-. **HONORS AND AWARDS** Ford Motor Co. of England travel grant, 62; Am Research Cntr in Egypt Fellow, 71; Smithsonian Institution travel grant, 75; Wayne St Univ Awd in the Arts, 85. **MEMBERSHIPS** Archaeol Inst Am; Am Asn Mus; Int Asn Egyptologists. **RESEARCH** Drawing and Painting in New Kingdom Egypt. **SELECTED PUBLICATIONS** Auth, Mummy Portraits from Roman Egypt, Detroit Inst Arts, 67; The present state of Egyptian art in Detroit, Connoisseur, 1270; A seated statue of Amun, J Egyptian Archaeol, 71; A ramesside ruler offers incense, J Near Eastern Studies, 172; Drawings from Ancient Egypt, Thames & Hudson, 78, Ger trans, 79 & Fr trans, 80, arabic trans, 85; Ancient art in Detroit, Archaeol, 578; ; The constant lure, In: Ancient Egypt: Discovering its Splendors, Nat Geog Soc, 78; contribr, Mummies of ancient Egypt, In: Mummies, Disease and Ancient Cultures, Cambridge Univ, 81; After Tutankhamun - Research And Excavation in The Royal Necropolis at Thebes - Reeves,cn, American J of Archaeology, Vol 0097, 1993; The Private Chapel in Ancient-egypt - a Study of The Chapels in The Workmens Village at El-amarna With Special Reference to Deir-el-medina And Other Sites - Bowman,ah, Classical World, Vol 0086, 1992; Reading Egyptian Art - a Hieroglyphic Guide to Ancient Egyptian Painting And Sculpture - Wilkinson,rh, American J of Archaeology, Vol 0097, 1993; Mesopotamia - Writing, Reasoning, And The Gods - Bottero,j, Classical World, Vol 0087, 1994; Carter,howard The Path to Tutankhamun - J Ames,tgh, American J of Archaeology, Vol 0097, 1993;The Offering Chapel of Kayemnofret in The Museum-of- fine-arts, Boston - Simpson,wk, J of Near Eastern Studies, Vol 0055, 1996; The Offering Chapel of Kayemnofret in The Museum-of- fine-arts, Boston - Simpson,wk, J of Near Eastern Studies, Vol 0055, 1996; Macmillan Dictionary of Art, 96; The Splendors of Ancient Egypt, 97; Encyclopedia of the Archaeology of Ancient Egypt, 99; Oxford Encyclopedia of Ancient Egypt, 00. **CONTACT ADDRESS** Dept of Ancient Art, Detroit Inst of Arts, 5200 Woodward Ave, Detroit, MI 48202. **EMAIL** ad9646@Wayne.edu

PEDERSEN, DIANA
DISCIPLINE HISTORY **EDUCATION** Univ Brit Columbia, BA; Carleton Univ, MA, PhD. **CAREER** Instr, Queen's Univ; Univ W Ontario; asst prof, 91-. **SELECTED PUBLICATIONS** Auth, articles on Can middle-class women's organizations and social reform movements, and on the uses of photographs as documents for women's history; bibliography on Can women's history. **CONTACT ADDRESS** Dept of Hist, Concordia Univ, Montreal, 1455 de Maisonneuve W, Montreal, QC, Canada H3G 1M8. **EMAIL** dpeders@vax2.concordia.ca

PEDERSON, WILLIAM DAVID
PERSONAL Born 03/17/1946, Eugene, OR **DISCIPLINE** AMERICAN HISTORY & GOVERNMENT **EDUCATION** Univ Ore, BS, 67, MA, 72, PhD(polit sci), 79. **CAREER** Teaching & res asst polit sci, Univ Ore, Eugene, 75-77; instr govt, Lamar Univ, Beaumont, Tex, 77-79; asst prof polit sci, Westminster Col, Fulton, Mo, 79-80; asst prof & head, dept polit sci, Yankton Col, Univ SDak, 80-81; prof, Am Studies Chmn, coordr polit sci, dir am studies, dept soc sci, La State Univ, Shreveport, 81-; Intern, Operations Ctr, Dept State, Washington, DC, summer 71; prog analyst, off of the dir, Nat Inst Health, Bethesda, Md, summer, 74; vis res prof, NY Univ, summer, 81; res assoc, Russian & East Europe Ctr, Univ Ill, Urbana, summer, 82-. **HONORS AND AWARDS** Westcoast Lumbermen's Assoc Scholar, 65; Eugene Educ Assoc Scholar, 65; Oregon State Scholar Comn Scholars, 65; Nat Inst of Health Training Awd, 74; Deutsche Sommerschule am Pazifik Scholar, 75; Coun for Eurpoean Studies/DAAD Grant, 75; Kosciuszko Found Grant, 79; Westminster Col Student Gov Assoc Outstanding Leadership and Service Awd, 80; NY Univ, 81, Harvard Univ, 85, Nat Endowment for the Humanities Fel; Fac Res Grant on Soviet and Russian Military Amnesties, 82; Kappa Alpha Fraternity Prof of the Month, 9/85; Fac Excellence Awd, 94-95, La State Univ in Shreveport; Essay Competition for Colum on the Bicentennial of the US Constitution, 87; Special Humanities Awd, 98, La Endowment for the Humanities; Annual Awd of Achievement, Abraham Lincoln Assoc, Springfield, IL, 2/94; Cultural Olympiad, Regional Designation Awd in the Humanities, 95-96; The Times Journal page Shreveport Rose Awd, 9/95; Phi Kappa Phi, 96. **MEMBERSHIPS** Am Asn Advan Slavic Studies; Am Polit Sci Asn; Int Soc Polit Psychol; Int Lincoln Assoc; La Hist Asn; North La Hist Asn; Acad of Criminal Justice Sci; Lincoln Fel of Wisconsin; Center for the Study of the Presidency; Presidency Res Group; Ger Studies Asn; Amnesty Int; Am Studies Prog; Am Soc Public Admin; Smithsonian Inst. **RESEARCH** American politics; presidental behavior; human rights. **SELECTED PUBLICATIONS** Co-ed, Abraham Lincoln: Sources and Style of Leadership, Greenwood Press, 94, 95; Ambraham Lincoln: Contemporary, Savas Woodbury, 95; FDR and the Modern Presidency. Leadership and Legacy, Praeger, 97; co-ed, International Abraham Lincoln Journal, 00-; Journal of Contemporary Thought, 97; The New Deal and Public Policy, St Martin's Press, 98; A Comparative Test of Jimmy Carter's Character, The Presidency and Domestic Policies of Jimmy Carter, Greenwood Press, 94; Preface to Lincoln and Leadership Summer Teachers Institute, The 1993 ILA Annals, International Lincoln Assoc, 94; Preface in Abraham Lincoln: Sources and Style of Leadership, Greenwood Press, 94; Congressman Thomas Hale Boggs, Encyclopedia of the US Congress Vol 3, Simon and Schuster, 95; guest ed, Quarterly Journal of Ideology, 6/94. **CONTACT ADDRESS** Dept of Soc Sci, Louisiana State Univ, Shreveport, 1 University Pl, Shreveport, LA 71115-2301. **EMAIL** wpederso@pilot.lsus.edu

PEDLEY, JOHN GRIFFITHS
PERSONAL Born 07/19/1931, Burnley, England, m, 1969 **DISCIPLINE** CLASSICAL ARCHEOLOGY **EDUCATION** Cambridge Univ, BA, 53, MA, 59; Harvard Univ, PhD(class archaeol), 65. **CAREER** From asst prof to prof, 65-74, actg chmn dept classical studies, 71-72 & 75-76, Dir Kelsey Mus Ancient & Medieval Archaeol, 73-86; Prof Class Archseol & Greek, Univ Mich, Ann Arbor, 74- . **HONORS AND AWARDS** Julia Lockwood Awd, 94; NES Fel, 86-87; Am Philos Soc grant, 79; NEH grants, 75, 77, 83, 84; Nat Endowment for Arts grants, 74, 75, 77, 79, 80; Am Coun Learned Socs Fel, 72-73; James Loeb Res Fel class Archaeol, Harvard Univ, 69-70; Nat Found Arts and Humanities grants, 67-68. **MEMBERSHIPS** Int Asn Class Archaeol; Soc Promotion Hellenic Studies; Archaeol Inst Am; Asn Field Archaeol; Soc Libyan Studies. **RESEARCH** Archaeology of Asia Minor and North Africa; Greek sculpture. **SELECTED PUBLICATIONS** Coauth, The statue of Meleager, Antike Plastik, 64; auth, Sardis in the Age of Croesus, Univ Okla, 68, reprint, 00; auth, The archaic Favissa at Cyrene, Am J Archaeol, 71; auth, Ancient Literary Sources on Sardis, Harvard Univ, 72; auth, Carians in Sardis, J Hellenic Studies, 74; auth, Greek Sculpture of the Archaic Period: The Island Workshops, Philipp von Zabern, Mainz, 76; coauth, Apollonia, the Port of Cyrene, suppl vol to Libya Antiqua IV, 77; ed, New Light on Ancient Carthage, Univ Mich Press, 80; auth, Paestum: Greeks & Romans in Southern Italy, 90; Greek Art & Archaeology, 92, 2nd ed, 98, 3rd ed forthcoming; coauth, Sanctuary of Santa Venera at Paestum, 93; coauth, Corpus des Mosaiques de Tunisie, III, Thysdrus, 96. **CONTACT ADDRESS** Dept of Classical Studies, Univ of Michigan, Ann Arbor, Ann Arbor, MI 48109-1003. **EMAIL** jpedley@umich.com

PEEK, MARVIN E.
PERSONAL Born 08/21/1940, Cleveland, OH, m **DISCIPLINE** HISTORY **EDUCATION** Allen Univ, BA History 1964-65; IN Univ, MA History 1965-67; Univ of TN, PhD History 1971. **CAREER** US Park Service, park ranger 1963-65; Lane Coll, chair social scis div 1970-71; Univ of TN Afro-Amer Studies, dir 1971-86, asst to the provost 1987-. **HONORS AND AWARDS** Alpha Phi Alpha Scholarship; Ford Found Educ Study Grant; Faculty Develop Grant. **MEMBERSHIPS** Sec Natl Cncl for Black Studies 1984-86; pres elect Assn of Social & Behavorial Scientists 1986; consul Memphis State Univ Wm Patterson Coll Comm for the Humanities; reader Natl Endowment for the Humanities; LSU Press; Univ TN Press. **CONTACT ADDRESS** Univ of Tennessee, Knoxville, 812 Volunteer Blvd, Knoxville, TN 37916.

PEGRAM, THOMAS R.
PERSONAL Born 11/29/1955, Hammond, IN, m, 1986, 2 children **DISCIPLINE** AMERICAN HISTORY **EDUCATION** Brandeis Univ, PhD, 88. **CAREER** Instr in History, 88-90, Ohio State Univ; from asst prof to assoc prof history, Loyola Col, 90-; chr, hist dept, 98-, Loyola Col, 90-. **HONORS AND AWARDS** Phi Beta Kappa, Santa Clara Univ, 78; Irving & Rose Crown fel, Brandeis Univ, 78-84; Choice Outstanding Acad Book, 94; Illinois State Historical Soc Awd of Superior Achievement. **MEMBERSHIPS** OAH; SHGAPE. **RESEARCH** 19th and 20th century American political and social history; Progressivism; Temperance reform and prohibition. **SELECTED PUBLICATIONS** auth "The Dry Machine: The Formation of the Anti-Saloon League of Illinois," IL Hist Jour, 90; "Public Health and Progressive Dairying in Illinois," Agric Hist, 91; Partisans and Progressives: Private Interest and Public Policy in Illinois, 1870-1922, Urbana: Univ IL Press; "Temperance Politics and Regional Political Culture: The Anti-Saloon League in Maryland and the South, 1907-1915," Jour S Hist, 97; Battling Demon Rum: The Struggle for a Dry America, 1800-1933, Chicago: Ivan Dee, 98. **CONTACT ADDRESS** Dept of History, Loyola Col, 4501 N Charles St, Baltimore, MD 21210-2699. **EMAIL** pegram@loyola.edu

PEGUES, FRANKLIN J.
PERSONAL Born 04/29/1924, Cheraw, SC, m, 1986, 4 children **DISCIPLINE** MEDIEVAL HISTORY **EDUCATION** Duke Univ, AB, 47; Cornell Univ, MA, 48, PhD, 51. **CAREER** Instr hist, Univ Colo, 52-54; from asst prof to assoc prof, 54-63, Prof Hist, Ohio State Univ, 63-, Fulbright grant, France, 51-52; mem nat selection comt France, Fulbright Found, 58-59; Guggenheim fel, 61-62; ed, J Higher Educ, 64-66. **MEMBERSHIPS** AHA; Mediaeval Acad Am; Conf Brit Studies; Soc Fr Hist Studies. **RESEARCH** Administrative and legal history of medieval England and France; history of philanthropy in medieval education; medieval French and English social and economic history. **SELECTED PUBLICATIONS** Auth, Lawyers of the Last Captains, Princeton Univ, 62; The Origins of The English Legal Profession - Brand,p, American Historical Review, Vol 0098, 1993; English Law in The Age of The Blackdeath, 1348-1381 - a Transformation of Governance And Law - Palmer,rc, American Historical Review, Vol 0100, 1995. **CONTACT ADDRESS** Dept of Hist, Ohio State Univ, Columbus, Columbus, OH 43210. **EMAIL** pegues.2@osu.edu

PEIRCE, SARAH
DISCIPLINE GREEK RELIGION, DRAMA, HISTORY **EDUCATION** Bryn Mawr Univ, PhD. **CAREER** Dir, summer session, Amer Sch Class Stud, Athens, 98; assoc prof, Fordham Univ. **HONORS AND AWARDS** Fel, Ctr Hellenic Stud Wash DC, 96-97. **SELECTED PUBLICATIONS** Auth, Death, Revelry, and Thysia, Class Antiquity, 93; Visual Language and Concepts of Cult on the 'Lenaia Vases, Class Antiquity, 97. **CONTACT ADDRESS** Dept of Classics, Fordham Univ, 113 W 60th St, New York, NY 10458. **EMAIL** peirce@fordham.edu

PEISS, KATHY
DISCIPLINE HISTORY **EDUCATION** Carleton Col, BA, 75; MA, 77, PhD, 82, Brown Univ. **CAREER** Asst Prof, Univ Maryland, 81-86; Assoc Prof, 86-91, Prof, 91-, Univ Massachusetts (Amherst). **HONORS AND AWARDS** Soc of Am Historians Fell; Finalist, Los Angeles times Bk Prize, 99. **SELECTED PUBLICATIONS** Auth, Cheap Amusements: Working Women and Leisure in Turn-of-the-Century New York, 86; Passion and Power: Sexuality in History, 89; Love Across the Color Line, 96; Hope in a Jar: The Making of America's Beauty Culture, 98; Major Problems in the History of American Sexuality, 01. **CONTACT ADDRESS** History Dept, Univ of Massachusetts, Amherst, Herter Hall, Box 33930, Amherst, MA 01003-3930. **EMAIL** peiss@history.umass.edu

PELIKAN, JAROSLAV J.
PERSONAL Born 12/17/1923, Akron, OH, m, 1946, 3 children **DISCIPLINE** HISTORY **EDUCATION** Concordia Sem, BD, 46; Univ Chicago, PhD, 46. **CAREER** Mem fac hist & philos, Valparaiso Univ, 46-49, Concordia Sem, 49-53, Univ Chicago, 53-62; Titus Street prof ecclesiastical hist, 62-72, actg dean grad sch, 73-74, chmn medieval studies, 74-75 & 78-80, Sterling Prof Relig Studies, Yale Univ, 72-, Relig ed, Encycl Britannica, 55-68; ed, Makers of Mod Theol, 66-68; Nat Endowment for Humanities sr fel, 67-68; pres, IV Int Congr Luther Res, 71. **HONORS AND AWARDS** Abingdon Awd, 59; Pax Christi Awd, St John's Univ, Minn, 66; John Gilmary Shea Prize, Am Cath Hist Asn, 71; Nat Awd, World Slovak Cong, 73; dd, concordia col, moorhead, minn, 60, concordia sem, 67; littd, wittenberg univ, 60, wheeling col, 66, pac lutheran univ, 67 & gettysburg col, 67; ma, yale univ, 61; lhd, valparaiso univ, 66, rockhurst col, 67 & albertus magnus col, 73; dh, providence co **MEMBERSHIPS** Am Soc Church Hist (pres, 65); AHA; Mediaeval Acad Am. **SELECTED PUBLICATIONS** Ed, Interpreters of Luther, Fortress, 68; auth, Development of Christian Doctrine, Yale Univ, 69; ed, Twentieth Century Theology in the Making, (3 vols), Harper & Collins, 69-71; auth, Historical Theology: Continuity and Change in Christian Doctrine, Westminster, 71; The emergency of the Catholic tradition (100-600), Vol I, 71, The spirit of Eastern Christendom (600-1700),

Vol II, 1974 & The growth of medieval theology (600-1300), Vol III, 78, In: The Christian Tradition: A History of the Development of Doctrine, Univ Chicago; ed, The Preaching of Augustine: Our Lord's Sermon the Mount, Fortress, 73; The Historian as Polyglot, Proceedings of The American Philosophical Society, Vol 0137, 1993; Giamatti,a.bartlett April 4,1938 September 1,1989, Proceedings of The American Philosophical Society, Vol 0139, 1995. **CONTACT ADDRESS** Dept of Hist, New Haven, CT 06520. **EMAIL** jaroslav.pelikan@yale.edu

PELLECCHIA, LINDA
DISCIPLINE ART HISTORY **EDUCATION** Harvard Univ, PhD 83. **CAREER** Univ Delaware, assoc prof. **HONORS AND AWARDS** Amer Acad Rome; Villa I Tatti Harv U Cen Ren Stud. **MEMBERSHIPS** CAA; SAH; IAS; RSA. **RESEARCH** Renaissance art and architecture. **SELECTED PUBLICATIONS** Auth, Property and Identity in Renaissance Florence: The Gondi Palace, in progress; articles in: Renaissance Quart, Jour of Soc Architectural Histories. **CONTACT ADDRESS** Dept of Art History, Univ of Delaware, Old College, Newark, DE 19711. **EMAIL** lpell@udel.edu

PELLS, RICHARD HENRY
PERSONAL Born 11/06/1941, Kansas City, MO, m, 1999, 2 children **DISCIPLINE** HISTORY **EDUCATION** Rutgers Univ, BA, 63; Harvard Univ, MA, 64, PhD, 69. **CAREER** Lectr hist, Harvard Univ, 68-71; asst prof, 71-74, assoc prof hist, Univ TX, Austin, 75, prof Hist, Univ of Tex, 85-; Fel, Charles Warren Ctr Studies Am Hist, Harvard Univ, 70-71; Rockefeller humanities fel, 76; Fulbright sr lectr, Univ Amsterdam, 79 & Univ Copenhagen, 82-83; fellow, Woodrow Wilson Intl Center for scholars, 86-87; Guggenheim Fel, 93-94; 50th anniv, fulbright ch, Amer Studies, Ger, 97-98; DAAD vis prof, Free Univ of Berlin and Univ of Coogne, 00. **RESEARCH** Twentieth century Am intellectual hist; Am lit period since 1920; popular cult, films, radio and television; the global impact of Am culture. **SELECTED PUBLICATIONS** Auth, Radical Visions and American Dreams; Culture and Social Thought in the Depression Years, Harper, 73; The Liberal Mind in a Conservative Age: American Intellectuals in the 1940s and 1950s, Harper, 85; Not Like Us: How Europeans Have Loved Hated and Transformed American Culture Since World War II, Basic Books, 97. **CONTACT ADDRESS** Dept of Hist, Univ of Texas, Austin, Austin, TX 78712-1026. **EMAIL** rpells@aol.com

PELOSO, VINCENT C.
PERSONAL Born 10/30/1938, Brooklyn, NY, m, 2 children **DISCIPLINE** HISTORY **EDUCATION** SUNY, BS, 61; Univ Ariz, MA, 65; PhD, 69. **CAREER** Instr, Central Mich Univ, 62-68; Instr to Full Prof, Howard Univ, 68-. **HONORS AND AWARDS** Fel, Univ Ariz., 66; Fulbright Res Fel; Am Philos Asn Awd. **MEMBERSHIPS** Am Hist Asn, Conf on Latin Am Hist, Latin Am Studies Asn. **RESEARCH** Andean Society; Nineteenth Century. **SELECTED PUBLICATIONS** Auth, "Cotton Planters, the State and Rural Labor Policy: The Origins of the Peruvian," Republica Aristocratica, 1895-1908," in The Americas. A Quarterly Review of Inter-American Cultural History, 83; auth, "Succulence and Sustenance: Region, Class and Diet in Nineteenth-Century Peru," in Food, Politics, and Society in Latin America, Univ Neb Press, 85; auth, "Liberals, Electoral Reform, and the Popular Vote in Mid-Nineteenth-Century Peru," in Liberals, Politics, and Power: State Formation in Nineteenth-Century Latin America, Univ Ga Press, 96; auth, "Juan Esquivel: Cotton Plantation Tenant," in The Human Tradition in Modern Latin America, Scholarly Resources, 97; auth, Peasants on Plantations: Subaltern Strategies of Labor and Resistance in the Pisco Valley, Peru, Duke Univ Press, 99. **CONTACT ADDRESS** Dept Hist, Howard Univ, 2400 6th St NW, Washington, DC 20059-0001. **EMAIL** vpeloso@howard.edu

PELZ, STEPHEN ERNEST
PERSONAL Born 12/01/1942, New Haven, CT, m, 1966, 2 children **DISCIPLINE** HISTORY **EDUCATION** Johns Hopkins Univ, BA, 64; Harvard Univ, MA, 66, PhD, 71. **CAREER** Asst prof, 71-76, assoc prof hist, Univ Mass, Amherst, 76-81, Nat fel, Hoover Inst War, Revolution & Peace, Stanford Univ, 73-74; Nat Security Studies fel, Woodrow Wilson Int Ctr Scholars, Washington, DC, 78-79; fel, East Asian Inst, Columbia Univ, 79-80. **HONORS AND AWARDS** Stuart L Bernath Prize, Soc Hist Am Foreign Rel, 75. **MEMBERSHIPS** AHA; Soc Hist Am Foreign Rels. **RESEARCH** American diplomatic history; American-East Asian relations; international relations. **SELECTED PUBLICATIONS** Auth, Race to Pearl Harbor: The failure of the Second London Naval Conference and the onset of World War II, In: Am East Asian Rel Ser, Harvard Univ, 74; contribr, Japanese Attitudes Toward the Outside World, Tokyo Univ, 74; auth, "A Taxonomy for American Diplomatic History," J of Interdisciplinary Hist, XIX:2 (Autumn 88): 259-276; auth, "The Case for Limiting NATO Enlargement," Nat Sec Studies Q III, 3 (Summer 97): 59-72. **CONTACT ADDRESS** Dept of History, Univ of Massachusetts, Amherst, Amherst, MA 01003-0002.

PEMBERTON, GAYLE R.
PERSONAL Born 06/29/1948, St. Paul, MN, s **DISCIPLINE** AFRICAN-AMERICAN STUDIES **EDUCATION** Lake Forest College, attended, 1966-68; University of Michigan, BA, 1969; Harvard University, MA, 1971, PhD, 1981. **CAREER** Columbia University, lecturer, 74-77; Middlebury College, inst, 77-80; Northwestern Univ, asst prof, 80-83; Reed College, vist assoc prof, 83-84; Bowdoin College, African-American Studies, vist assoc prof, actg dir, 86-88, Minority Affairs, dir, 88-90; Princeton Univ, African-American Studies, Assoc Dir, 90-. **HONORS AND AWARDS** W E B DuBois Foundation, 1975; Ford Foundation, Doctoral Fellowship, 1969-74; Southwest Review, Margaret Hartley Memorial Awd, 1992. **MEMBERSHIPS** Modern Language Assn. **SELECTED PUBLICATIONS** Author: "A Sentimental Journey," Race-ing Justice En-Gendering Power, 1992; The Hottest Water in Chicago, 1992; "It's The Thing That Counts," State of Black America, 1991; John Simon Guggenheim Fellow, 1993; New Jersey Committee for the Humanities, Book of the Year Award, for Hottest Water. **CONTACT ADDRESS** African-American Studies, Princeton Univ, 112 Dickinson Hall, Princeton, NJ 08544-1017.

PEMBERTON, WILLIAM ERWIN
PERSONAL Born 03/26/1940, Duncan, OK, m, 1967, 1 child **DISCIPLINE** RECENT UNITED STATES HISTORY **EDUCATION** Univ Okla, BA, 63; Univ Mo, MA, 65, PhD, 74. **CAREER** Prof US Hist, Univ WI-LaCrosse, 66-. **MEMBERSHIPS** Orgn Am Historians; Ctr Study Presidency; Am Soc Pub Admin. **RESEARCH** Recent United States political history; administrative history; United States economic history. **SELECTED PUBLICATIONS** Auth, The Politics of Bureaucracy: Executive Reorganization During the Truman Administration, Univ Mo, 78; Harry S Truman: Fair Dealer and Cold Warrior, Twayne, 89; Exit with Honor: The Life and Presidency of Ronald Reagan; M E Sharpe, 97. **CONTACT ADDRESS** Dept Hist, Univ of Wisconsin, La Crosse, 1725 State St, La Crosse, WI 54601-3788. **EMAIL** BillPember@aol.com

PENCAK, WILLIAM A.
PERSONAL Born 10/08/1951, Brooklyn, NY **DISCIPLINE** HISTORY **EDUCATION** Columbia Univ, BA, 72; MA, 73; PhD, 78. **CAREER** From Asst Prof to Prof, Pa St Univ, 83-. **HONORS AND AWARDS** Andrew Mellon Fel, Duke Univ, 78-79; NEH Fel, Princeton Univ, 82; Sr Fulbright Fel, Univ Monterrey, 89-90. **MEMBERSHIPS** CSM, MHS, AHA, OAH, IEAHC, SSA, PHA. **RESEARCH** Early American history, historiography, semiotics. **SELECTED PUBLICATIONS** Auth, War, Politics and Revolution in Provincial Massachusetts, Northwestern UP, 81; auth, America's Burke: The Mind of Thomas Hutchinson, UP of Am, 82; auth, For God and Country: The American Legion 1919-1941, Northwestern UP, 89; auth, History, Signing In: Essays in History and Semiotics, Peter Lang Publ, 93; ed, "Worldmaking," collection 17 essays, Critic of Inst Ser, Peter Lang Publ (96); auth, The Conflict of Law and Justice in the Icelandic Sagas, Rodopi, 96. **CONTACT ADDRESS** Dept Hist, Pennsylvania State Univ, Univ Park, 108 Weaver Bldg, University Park, PA 16802-5500. **EMAIL** wap1@psu.edu

PENHALL, MICHELE M.
PERSONAL Born 07/30/1953, CA, m, 1990 **DISCIPLINE** ART HISTORY **EDUCATION** Univ Hawaii, BFA, 80; CUNY Queens College, MA, 87; Univ New Mexico, PhD, 97. **CAREER** Independent Scholar. **HONORS AND AWARDS** Phi Kappa Phi; UNM Regents Fel; Samuel H Kress Fel; UNM Grad res Gnt; Mellon Res Gnt; Bainbridge Bunting Fel; UNM Res Gnt. **MEMBERSHIPS** SAH; Phi Beta Kappa. **RESEARCH** Latin American Photography; Vernacular Photography. **SELECTED PUBLICATIONS** Martin Chambi as Artist, Hist of Photography, guest ed, Hist Photog Latin Amer, Hist of Photog, 00; ed, Betty Hahn: Photography or Maybe Not, Albuquerque, UNM Press, 95; rev Stones in the Road: Photographs of Peru, by Nubar Alexanian, Hist of Photog, 93; contrib, Christopher Curtis Mead, The Architecture of Bart Prince: A Pragmatics of Place, preface by David Van Zanten, NY, London, WW Norton & Co, 99; Michael Webb, Architecture: Twist and Shout-A Dynamically Expressive House for the Coast of N Cal, Archit Digest, NY, Conde Nast, 97; Space Design Art and Architecture, Tokyo, Kajima, Pub 97; Philip Jodido, New Forms: Architecture in the 1990's, Koln, Taschen Verlag, 97; Christopher Mead, When Architects Serve Their Clients, Designer/Builder, Santa Fe, Fine Adds Inc, 97; Contemporary American Architects, vol II, Koln, Taschen Verlag, 96. **CONTACT ADDRESS** 4504 Sunningdale Ave NE, Albuquerque, NM 87110. **EMAIL** kapu@unm.edu

PENKOWER, MONTY NOAM
PERSONAL Born 07/15/1942, New York, NY, m, 1969, 4 children **DISCIPLINE** HISTORY, JEWISH STUDIES **EDUCATION** Yeshiva Univ, BA, 63; Columbia Univ, MA, 64; PhD, 70. **CAREER** Asst prof, Bard Col, NY, 70-74; vis assoc prof, 73-74, chmn dept, 76-79, assoc prof to prof and Victor J. Selmanowitz Ch, Modern Jewish Hist, Touro Col, NY, 74-. **HONORS AND AWARDS** Eleanor Roosevelt Inst grant hist, 71-73 & 78-79 & Harry S Truman Libr, 73-75; Mem Found Jewish Cult fel hist, 74-75 & 77-78; Nat Found Jewish Cult fel hist, 75-76; acad coun, World Jewish Cong. **MEMBERSHIPS** AHA; Am Jewish Hist Asn; Orgn Am Historians. **RESEARCH** American political history; diplomacy of the Holocaust; Palestine and the Anglo-American alliance. **SELECTED PUBLICATIONS** Auth, The Federal Writer's Project: A Study in Government Patronage of the Arts, Univ Ill, 77; The 1943 joint Anglo- American statement on Palestine, Herzl Yearbk, 78; Reluctant Ally - United States Foreign Policy Toward The Jews From Wilson to Roosevelt American Jewish History, 93. **CONTACT ADDRESS** Touro Col, New York, 75-31 150th St., Kew Gardens Hills, NY 11367.

PENNER, HANS HENRY
PERSONAL Born 01/29/1934, Sacramento, CA, m, 1959 **DISCIPLINE** HISTORY OF RELIGIONS **EDUCATION** Univ Chicago, DB, 58, MA, 62, PhD, 65. **CAREER** Instr hist of relig, Univ VT, 62-65; asst prof, 65-72, assoc prof relig, 72-74, John Phillips prof, & chmn dept, 74-79, Dean Fac, Dartmouth Col, 81-, Fulbright res scholar, India, 66; Soc Relig Higher Educ-Danforth Cross-disciplinary fel, 68-69; Dartmouth fac fel, 68-69. **MEMBERSHIPS** Asn Asian Studies; Soc Sci Studies Relig; Am Acad Relig; Int Asn Hist Relig. **RESEARCH** Methodological approaches to understanding relig; myth and ritual-phenomenology; relig traditions of India. **SELECTED PUBLICATIONS** Auth, Cosmogony as Myth in Vishnu Purana, Hist Relig, 66; The Study of Religion According to Jan de Vries, J Relig, 1/69; Myth and Ritual: Wasteland or Forest of Symbols, Hist & Theory, 69; The poverty of functionalism, Hist Relig, 71; Ritual, In: Encyl Britannica; Creating a Brahman & The problem of semantics in the study of religion, Method Issues Relig Studies, 75; Impasse & Resolution: A Critique of the Study of Religion, 89; Why Does Semantics Matter to the Study of Religion, Method and Theory in the Study of Religion, 7/95. **CONTACT ADDRESS** Dept Relig, Dartmouth Col, 6036 Thornton Hall, Hanover, NH 03755-3592. **EMAIL** Hans.Penner@Dartmouth.edu

PENTON, MARVIN J.
PERSONAL Born 04/27/1932, Clarkbridge, SK, Canada **DISCIPLINE** HISTORY **EDUCATION** Univ Arizona, BA, 56; Univ Iowa, MA, 58, PhD, 65. **CAREER** Asst prof, Univ Puerto Rico, 59-60; asst prof, Univ Wisconsin, 64-65; asst prof, Univ Calgary, 65-67; asst prof, 67-76, prof, 76-89, Prof Emer History, Univ Lethbridge, 89-. **MEMBERSHIPS** Mem, Christian Renewal Ministries; past pres, Can Soc Church Hist **RESEARCH** Religion; Jehovah's Witnesses **SELECTED PUBLICATIONS** Auth, Jehovah's Witnesses in Canada, 76; auth, The Story of Jehovah's Witnesses, 85, 97; ed, Eng edition The Gentile Times Reconsidered, 83; ed, The Bible Examiner, 82-84; ed, The Christian Quest, 86-91. **CONTACT ADDRESS** 58 Coachwood Point W, Lethbridge, AB, Canada T1K 6A9.

PENVENNE, JEANNE MARIE
PERSONAL Born 06/20/1947, Pittsfield, MA, m, 1976, 2 children **DISCIPLINE** HISTORY **EDUCATION** Berkshire Community Col, AA, 67; Northeastern Univ, BS, 72; Boston Univ, MA, 74, PhD, 82. **CAREER** Teaching asst, Harvard Univ, fall 85-86; lectr, Boston Univ Metropolitan Col, spring 87; vis asst prof, Tufts Univ, 86-87; vis asst prof, Boston Univ, spring 90; lectr, Brandeis Univ, 88-90; vis asst prof, Tufts Univ, 90-91; instr, Dept Hist, Boston Univ, 91-92, assoc prof, 93-; Volunteer Vis Fac, Univ Eduardo Mondlane, 92-93, res fel, 77; res fel, African Studies Center, Boston Univ, 83-. **HONORS AND AWARDS** Fulbright-Hays Scholar to Portugal, 76-77; Int Fel of Fundacao Calouste Gulbenkian, 77-78; NEH grant, 88-90, 89-90; Finalist, Herskovits Awd, 95, for African Workers and Colonial Racism; Tufts Fac Res Awd Comt, Int Res, 96; Am Coun of Learned Socs, Int Travel Grant, 96; nominated for the Berkshire Conf Article Prize, 97; U.S. Speaker and Specialist Awd, United States Information Agency, 98; Winner, 1999 Lerman-Neubauer Prize for Outstanding Teaching and Advising. **RESEARCH** African studies. **SELECTED PUBLICATIONS** Auth, " 'We are all Portuguese!': Challenging the Political Economy of Assimilation, Lourenco Marques, 1870-1933," in Leroy Vail, ed, The Creation of Tribalism in Southern Africa, Berkeley: Univ Calif (89): 255-288; auth, Trabalhadores de Lourenco Marques, 1870-1974, Maputo: Atquivo Historico de Mozambique (94); auth, African Workers and Colonial Racism: Mozambican Strategies for Survival in Lourenco Marques, Mozambique 1877-1962, Portsmouth: Heinemann, Soc Hist of Africa Series (95); auth, "Joao dos Santos Albasini (1876-1922); The Contraindications of Politics and Identity in Colonial Mozambique," J of African Hist, Vol 37, No 3 (96): 417-464; auth, "Seeking the Factory for Women, Mozambican Urbanization in the Late Colonial Era," J of Urban Hist, Vol 23, No 3 (March 97): 342-379; auth, "A Tapestry of Conflict: Mozambique 1960-1995," in David Birmingham and Phyllis Martin, eds, History of Central Africa: The Contemporary Years, London, Longman (98): 230-266; auth, "Poppie Nongena and South African History," in Jean Hay, ed, African Novels in the Classroom, Boulder, Co, Lynne Reinner (forthcoming). **CONTACT ADDRESS** Dept Hist, Tufts Univ, Medford, 520 Boston Ave, Medford, MA 02155-5500. **EMAIL** jpenvenn@emerald.tufts.edu

PERELMUTER, HAYIM GOREN
PERSONAL Born 06/02/1914, Montreal, PQ, Canada, m, 1940, 2 children **DISCIPLINE** JEWISH HISTORY **EDUCATION** McGill Univ, BA, 35; Jewish Inst Relig, MHL, 39; Hebrew Union Col Jewish Inst Relig, DHL, 79. **CAREER** Rabbi,

Beth Israel, Waltham MAss, 39-41; rabbi, Beth Zion Temple, Johnstown Penn, 41-57; rabbi, KAM Isaiah Israel, 57-79; prof Jewish Stud, Catholic Theol Union, 49- . **MEMBERSHIPS** Am Acad Relig; Conf of Am Rabbis; North Am Acad of Liturgy; Soc of Bibl Lit; Am Jewish Hist Soc. **SELECTED PUBLICATIONS** Trans, Song of the Steps and In Defense of Preachers, Hebrew Union Col, 84; auth, This Immortal People: A Short History of the Jews, Paulist, 85; coauth, Von Kanaah nach Israel, Deutsche Tascherbuch Verlag, 86; auth, Siblings: Rabbinic Judaism and Early Christianity at Their Beginnings, Paulist, 89; coauth, Paul the Jew: Jewish-Christian Dialogue, Center for Hermeneutical Stud, Grad Theol Union, 90; auth, Do Not Destroy in the Ecological Challenge, Liturgical, 94; coauth, Harvest of a Dialogue, Ktav, 97. **CONTACT ADDRESS** Catholic Theol Union at Chicago, 5401 S Cornell Ave, Chicago, IL 60615. **EMAIL** goodper@ctu.edu

PERERA, NIHAL
PERSONAL Born 12/14/1953, Sri Lanka, m, 1976, 3 children **DISCIPLINE** HISTORY AND THEORY OF URBANISM **EDUCATION** SUNY, Binghamton, PhD, 95. **CAREER** Regional and Physical Planner, Transmigration Project, Indonesia, 88; Chief Archit-Planner, Mahaweli Authority of Sri Lanka, 83-89; Adj Lectr, Binghamton Univ, 91-95; Asst Prof Urban Planning, Ball State Univ, 95-. **HONORS AND AWARDS** Univ Fel, SUNY, 89-91; Dissertation Year Fel, SUNY, 91-92; Grad Student Awd for Excellence in Teaching, SUNY, 95; Wings Int grant for the Virtual International Education project, 97; Graham Found Fel, 97. **MEMBERSHIPS** Am Planning Asn; Int Planning Hist Soc; Royal Inst British Archit; Inst Town Planners, Sri Lanka; Asn Asian Studies. **RESEARCH** Society and space: investigating the crucial correlation between transformations in urban and regional spatial structures and landscapes, and economic, political, and cultural developments. **SELECTED PUBLICATIONS** Auth, Critical Vernacularism: The Subversion of Universalizing Trends in Architecture, Proceedings of the 83rd ACSA Annual Meeting, 95; Exploring Columbo: The Relevance of a Knowledge of New York, Representing the City: Ethnicity, Capital, and Culture in the 21st Century Metropolis, Macmillan, 96; coauth, Winning on the Net: Virtual International Design Education, Proceedings of the Asn Collegiate Sch Archit Int Conf, 97; auth, Society and Space: Colonialism, Nationalism, and Postcolonial Identity in Sri Lanka, Westview Press, 98. **CONTACT ADDRESS** Dept Urban Planning, Ball State Univ, Muncie, IN 47306-0315. **EMAIL** nperera@bsu.edu

PERETTI, BURTON W.
PERSONAL Born 01/06/1961, San Francisco, CA, m, 1995, 1 child **DISCIPLINE** HISTORY **EDUCATION** Pomona Col, BA, 82; Univ CA, Berkeley, MA, 85, PhD, 89. **CAREER** Vis prof, Univ Kans, 89-92; vis prof, Colo Col, 93-94; asst prof, Pellissippi State Col, 95-98; assoc prof, Western Conn State Univ, 98-. **HONORS AND AWARDS** Nat Endowment for the Humanities Fel, 98. **MEMBERSHIPS** Org of Am Hist, Am Studies Asn. **RESEARCH** U.S. urban, cultural, music history; New York City nightlife. **SELECTED PUBLICATIONS** Auth, The Creation of Jazz: Music, Race, and Culture in Urban America, Urbana (92); auth, Jazz in American Culture, Chicago (97). **CONTACT ADDRESS** Dept Hist, Western Connecticut State Univ, 181 White St, Danbury, CT 06810-6826. **EMAIL** PerettiB@vax.wcsu.edu

PEREZ, LOUIS
PERSONAL Born 09/20/1946, Los Angeles, CA, m, 1971, 2 children **DISCIPLINE** HISTORY **EDUCATION** Calif State Univ, BA, 73; MA, 75; Univ Mich, PhD, 86. **CAREER** Instr, Charles S Mott Community Col, 84-86; asst prof to prof, IL State Univ, 87-. **SELECTED PUBLICATIONS** Auth, "Mutsu Munemitsu and the Diet Crisis of 1893", J of Asian Hist 25.1 (91): 29-59; auth, "The Accommodation of Buddhism into Japan: An Historiographical Approach", Asian Cult Quarterly 20.4 (92): 23-44; auth, "Japan Withdraws from League of Nations over Lytton Report", "Japan Protests Segregation of Japanese in California Schools", Great Evens from History II: Human Rights, ed AJ Sobczak, Salem Pr, (Pasadena, CA), 94; auth, "1974: Eisaku Sato", The Nobel Prize Winners: Peace or Economics, ed James A Magrill, Salem Pr, (Pasadena, 95): 249-255; auth, "Revision of the Unequal Treaties and Abolition of Extraterritoriality", New Directions in the Study of Meiji Japan, eds Helen Hardacre and Adam Kern, E.J. Brill (Leiden, 97): 320-334; auth, "Hoan Jorei", Modern Japan: An Encyclopedia of History, Culture and Nationalism, ed James Huffman, Garland Pr, (NY, 98); auth, The Dalai Lama, Rourke Pr, (Pasadena, CA), 93; auth, The History of Japan, Greenwood Pr, (Greenwich, CT), 98; auth, Japan Comes of Age: Mutsu Munemitsu and the Revision of the Unequal Treaties, Fairleigh Dickinson Univ Pr, (London), 99; auth, "The Establishment of the Tokugawa Shogunate, 1603", Events That Changed the World in the Seventeenth Century, eds Frank W Thackeray and John E Findling, Greenwood Pr, (Westport, 99): 21-40. **CONTACT ADDRESS** Dept Hist, Illinois State Univ, 1 Campus, Box 4420, Normal, IL 61790-0001. **EMAIL** lgperez@ilstu.edu

PEREZ-LOPEZ, RENE
PERSONAL Born 05/12/1945, Santa Clara, Cuba, m, 1971, 2 children **DISCIPLINE** LATIN AMERICAN STUDIES, INTERPRETATION **EDUCATION** SUNY, BA, 67, MLS, 71; Case Western Reserve Univ, MA, 69. **CAREER** Coordr, Norfolk Public Libr, 71-86; libr dir, 86-99, adj, 88-99, vp, 95-99, Va Wesleyan Col; branch manager, Norfolk Pub Libr; court interpreter, 86-. **HONORS AND AWARDS** Red Cross, 97; Pres, Club Hispano Americano de Tidewater, 97-; Founder, El Eco de Virginia bilingual newspaper, 91-92. **MEMBERSHIPS** ALA; Am Translators Asn; VLA. **RESEARCH** Cuban Stud **SELECTED PUBLICATIONS** Auth, An Index to the First 25 Years of Cuban Studies, 97; auth, Recent Work in Cuban Stud, 98. **CONTACT ADDRESS** 6429 Newport Ave, Norfolk, VA 23505. **EMAIL** rperlop@exis.net

PERKINS, BRADFORD
PERSONAL Born 03/06/1925, Rochester, NY, m, 1949, 4 children **DISCIPLINE** HISTORY **EDUCATION** Harvard Univ, AB, 47, PhD(hist), 52. **CAREER** From instr to assoc prof hist, Univ Calif, Los Angeles, 52- 62; Prof to prof emer Hist, Univ Mich, Ann Arbor, 62-, mem counc, Inst Early Am Hist & Cult, Williamsburg, Va, 68-71. **HONORS AND AWARDS** Bancroft Prize, 65; Albert Shaw lectr, Johns Hopkins Univ, 80; Soc Sci Res Coun fac res fel, 57-60; Guggenheim fel, 62-63; Commonwealth Fund lectr, Univ Col, Univ London, 64. **MEMBERSHIPS** AHA; Orgn Am Historians; Soc Historians of Am Foreign Rels. **RESEARCH** American diplomatic history; Anglo-American relations. **SELECTED PUBLICATIONS** Auth, First Rapprochement: England and the United States, 1795-1805, Univ Pa, 55; Youthful America, 60, Prologue to War: England and the United States, 1805-1812, 61 & Castlereagh and Adams: England and the United States, 1812-1823, 74, Univ Calif; The Great Rapprochement: England and the United States, 1895- 1914, Atheneum, 68; Adams,john,quincy And The Pubic Virtues of Diplomacy - Russell,g, William And Mary Quarterly, Vol 0053, 1996. **CONTACT ADDRESS** Dept of Hist, Univ of Michigan, Ann Arbor, 1029 Tisch Hall, 555 S. State St., Ann Arbor, MI 48109-1003. **EMAIL** bperkins@umich.edu

PERKINS, KENNETH J. AMES
PERSONAL Born 03/27/1946, Weehawken, NJ, m, 1971, 2 children **DISCIPLINE** HISTORY **EDUCATION** VA Mil Inst, BA, 68; Princeton Univ, MA, 71, PhD(Mid E studies), 73. **CAREER** Res assoc, Inst Islamic Studies, McGill Univ, 73-74; asst prof, 74-80, Assoc Prof Islamic Hist, Univ SC, 80-. **MEMBERSHIPS** Mid E Studies Asn N Am; Mid E Inst; French Colonial Hist Soc. **RESEARCH** Nineteenth and 20th century North Africa; colonial military administrative structures. **SELECTED PUBLICATIONS CONTACT ADDRESS** Dept of Hist, Univ of So Carolina, Columbia, Columbia, SC 29208.

PERKINS, LINDA MARIE
PERSONAL Born 11/22/1950, Mobile, AL, m **DISCIPLINE** AFRICAN-AMERICAN STUDIES **EDUCATION** Kentucky State University, BS, 1971; Univ of Illinois, C-U, MS, 1973, PhD, 1978. **CAREER** Univ of Ill-Champaign Urbana, Asst Dir of Minority Affrs, 73-75; William Paterson Coll Dir of Affirmative Action, 78-79; Radcliffe College, The Mary Bunting Institute, Research Fellow, Asst Dir, 79-83; The Claremont Coll, asst vice pres, 83-86; Center for Afro-Amer Studies, UCLA, visiting scholar, 86-. **HONORS AND AWARDS** Research Grant, Natl Inst of Educ, 1979-81; Natl Endowment for the Humanities, 1984; Spencer Foundation, 1986- . **MEMBERSHIPS** Big Sisters of Boston, 1981-83; Pomona Valley YWCA, Board Member, 1984-; Los Angeles United Way, Allocation Team, 1984-86. **CONTACT ADDRESS** Visiting Scholar, Univ of California, Los Angeles, 738 Santa Barbara Drive, Los Angeles, CA 90024.

PERLIS, VIVIAN
PERSONAL Born 04/26/1928, Brooklyn, NY, w, 1949, 3 children **DISCIPLINE** MUSIC LITERATURE, HISTORY **EDUCATION** Univ Mich, BA, 49, MA, 52; Columbia Univ, PhD, 65-67. **CAREER** Vis lectr, USC, Eastman, Duke, Smith, Cornell, Wesleyan; sr res assoc, lectr, Dir Oral History & Am Music, Yale School Music & Library, 73-. **HONORS AND AWARDS** Am Inst Acad Arts & Lectrs Ines Awd, 71; Kinkeldey Awds, 75; ASCAP Book Awd, 85; Sovneck Soc Book Awd, 89. **MEMBERSHIPS** Am Musicol Soc; Sovneck Soc; Oral Hist Asn. **RESEARCH** Contemporary composition; 20th Century music history. **SELECTED PUBLICATIONS** Auth Charles Ives, Remembered, 74; coed An Ives Celebration, 75; Copeland 1900-'942, 84; Copeland since 1943, 89. **CONTACT ADDRESS** School of Music and Library, Yale Univ, 425 College St, New Haven, CT 06520. **EMAIL** vivian.perlis@yale.edu

PERMAN, MICHAEL
PERSONAL Born 03/07/1942, London, England, d, 2 children **DISCIPLINE** HISTORY **EDUCATION** Hertford Col, BA, 63; Univ Ill at Urbana, MA, 65; Univ Chicago, PhD, 69. **CAREER** Lectr, Univ Manchester, 68-70; asst prof to prof, Univ Ill, 70-; res prof, Humanities, 90-. **HONORS AND AWARDS** Guggenheim Fel; Avery O Craven Awd; V O Key Prize; Comm Nom Pulitzer Prize Co-Winner, 74. **MEMBERSHIPS** SHA; OAH. **RESEARCH** Southern history; Civil War and reconstruction; political theory; history of race relations. **SELECTED PUBLICATIONS** Auth, The Road to Redemption: Southern Politics, 1869-1879, 84; auth, Emancipation and Reconstruction, 1862-1879, 87; auth, Major Problems in the Civil War and Reconstruction, 98, 2nd ed.; auth, Struggle for Mastery: Disfranchisement in the South, 1888-1908, Univ NC Press, forthcoming. **CONTACT ADDRESS** Dept History, Univ of Illinois, Chicago, 601 S Morgan St, 913 University Hall, Chicago, IL 60607-7109. **EMAIL** mperman@uic.edu

PERNAL, ANDREW B.
DISCIPLINE HISTORY **EDUCATION** Assumption Univ, BA; Windsor Univ, MA; Univ Ottawa, PhD. **CAREER** Hist, Brandon Univ. **RESEARCH** Hist of Poland, Russia and Ukraine; diplomatic relations; historiography; historical cartography. **SELECTED PUBLICATIONS** Coauth, La Description d'Ukrainie de Guillaume Le Vasseur de Beauplan, Ottawa: Les Presses de L'Universite d'Ottawa, 90; coauth, Beauplan's A Description of Ukraine, Cambridge, Mass, Harvard Univ Press for the Harvard Ukraainian Res Institute, 93; auth, "An Anaylsis of Disbursements for Diplomacy during the Ratification of the Hadiach Union Treaty at the Warsaw Diet of 1659," Harvard Ukrainian Studies, 17, 1-2, (93): 72-109; auth, "Diplomatic Contacts between Boguslaw Radziwill and Bohdan Khmel'nyts'kyi in 1656: Two Unpublished Documents," in Mappa Mundi, (L'viv-Kiev-New York, 96); coauth, "Giiom Le Vasser de Boplan-viis'kovyi in zhener, kartohraf, avtor,' in Boplan I Ukraina, Zbirnyk naukovykh prats, (L'viv, 98); coauth, "The 1651 Polish Subsidy to the Exiled Charles II," Oxford Slavonic Papers, New Series 32, 99. **CONTACT ADDRESS** History Dept, Brandon Univ, 270-18th St, Brandon, MB, Canada R7A 6A9. **EMAIL** pernal@brandonu.ca

PERNICK, MARTIN STEVEN
PERSONAL Born 06/02/1948, New York, NY, m, 1 child **DISCIPLINE** HISTORY OF MEDICINE, AMERICAN HISTORY **EDUCATION** Brandeis Univ, BA, 68; Columbia Univ, MA, 69, PhD(hist), 79. **CAREER** Instr hist of med, Pa State Univ, 72-79; vis lectr, Harvard Univ, 75-76; from Asst Prof to Assoc Prof, 79-92, Prof Hist, Univ Mich, Ann Arbor, 92-, Assoc Dir, Prog Soc & Med, 92-. **HONORS AND AWARDS** NEH Fel, 79-83; Fel, Spencer Found, 82-83; Nat Libr Med grant, 84-85, 98; NEH grant, 85-88; Excellence in Education Awd, Univ Mich, 94, 99; Rackham Fac Recognition Awd, Univ Mich, 97-2000; Burroughs Welcome Fund grant, 97-99. **MEMBERSHIPS** Am Asn Hist of Med; Orgn Am Historians; AHA; Hist Sci Soc. **RESEARCH** History of disease, health, and the body; film and the mediation of professional and popular culture; history of ethics and value issues in medicine; histories of eugenics, euthanasia, and suffering. **SELECTED PUBLICATIONS** Contribr, Medical professionalism, In: Encycl of Bioethics, Free Press, Macmillan, 78; auth, A Calculus of Suffering: Pain, Professionalism, and Anesthesia in Nineteenth Century America, Columbia Univ Press, 85; The Black Stork: Eugenics and the Death of "Defective" Babies in American Medicine and Motion Pictures since 1915, Oxford Univ Press, 96; Eugenic Euthanasia in Early-Twentieth-Century America and Medically-Assisted Suicide Today, In: Law at the End of Life, Univ Mich Press, 00; historical consultant on script and archival film project, Fit: Episodes in the History of the Body, Straight Ahead Films, 92, syndicated on PBS, 94; The People's Plague: Tuberculosis in America, Florentine Films, 95, PBS broadcast, 10/2/95; author of numerous articles and other publications. **CONTACT ADDRESS** Dept of Hist, Univ of Michigan, Ann Arbor, 435 S State St, Ann Arbor, MI 48109-1003. **EMAIL** mpernick@umich.edu

PERREIAH, ALAN RICHARD
PERSONAL Born 04/11/1937, Los Angeles, CA, m, 1958, 5 children **DISCIPLINE** LOGIC, HISTORY OF PHILOSOPHY **EDUCATION** Loyola Univ, Los Angeles, BA, 59; Marquette Univ, MA, 61; Ind Univ, Bloomington, PhD(philos), 67. **CAREER** Asst prof philos, Univ Wis-Whitewater, 66-67; asst prof, 67-69, Assoc Prof Philos, Univ Ky, 69-82, prof, 82-. **HONORS AND AWARDS** Fulbright Fel, 65-66; Am Coun of Learned Societies and Social Science Res Coun-Joint Grant, 68; int Res and Exchanges Bd grant, 70; Afro-Am Traineeship, 70; coun for Philol Studies-Inst in the Philos of Language, Univ of Calif, Carnegie Foundation, 71; fel, Inst Advan Studies, Princeton Univ, 73-74; Am Coun of Learned Societies Res Grant, 73-74; Nat Endowment for Humanities Award, 74; Nat Endowment for Humanities Awards, 74, 78, 79, 80-81; fel, Villa i Tatti, Harvard Univ Ctr Ital Renaissance Studies, 80-81. **MEMBERSHIPS** Am Philos Asn, Southeastern Medieval Asn, Soc Int Pour L'Etude Philos Medievale, Ky Philos Asn. **RESEARCH** History of logic, particularly 14th and 15th century; history of science; Paul of Venice. **SELECTED PUBLICATIONS** Auth, George Santayana and recent theories of man, Philos Today, 69; Approaches to supposition-theory, New Scholasticism, 71; ed, Treatise on Suppositions From the Logica Magna by Paul of Venice, Text Ser 15, Franciscan Inst, 71; auth, Buridan and the definite description, J Hist Philos, 72; transl, Paul of Venice: Logics Parva Philosophia Verlag, Munich, 82; Paul-of- venice, 'Logica Magna', Vol 2 Pt 4 - Capitula-de-conditionali- et-de-rationali - Latin And English - Hughes,ge, Editor And Translator, Speculum-a J of Medieval Studies, Vol 0068, 1993; Medieval Mereology - Henry,dp, History And Philosophy of Logic, Vol 0014, 1993; Aristotle Axiomatic Science, Peripatetic Notation or Pedagogical Plan, History And Philosophy of Logic, Vol 0014, 1993; Sophisms in

Medieval Logic And Grammar - Read,s, History And Philosophy of Logic, Vol 0015, 1994; Buridanus,iohannes Summulae in Praedicamenta - Latin - Bos,ep, History And Philosophy of Logic, Vol 0017, 1996; Semantics And Speculative Grammar in Scholarly Discourse - Paris, Bologna, And Erfurt, 1270-1330 - The Modist Semiotics - Italian - Marmo,c, Speculum-a J of Medieval Studies, Vol 0071, 1996; Buridanus,iohannes Questiones-elencorum - Latin - Vanderlecq,r, Braakhuis,hag, History And Philosophy of Logic, Vol 0017, 1996; Buridanus,iohannes Summulae-de-praedicabilibus - Latin - Derijk,lm, History And Philosophy of Logic, Vol 0017, 1996; Semantics And Speculative Grammar in Scholarly Discourse - Paris, Bologna, And Erfurt, 1270-1330 - The Modist Semiotics - Italian - Marmo,c, Speculum-a J of Medieval Studies, Vol 0071, 1996. **CONTACT ADDRESS** Dept of Philos, Univ of Kentucky, 1415 Patterson Office Tower, Lexington, KY 40506-0027. **EMAIL** peera@pop.uky.edu

PERRY, CHARLES R.
PERSONAL Born 09/29/1946, Atlanta, GA **DISCIPLINE** HISTORY **EDUCATION** Davidson Col, AB, 68; Harvard Univ, AM, 69; PhD, 76. **CAREER** Instr to Prof, Univ of the South, 74-. **HONORS AND AWARDS** Phi Beta Kappa; NEH Fel; Royal Hist Soc, Fel. **MEMBERSHIPS** Am Hist Asn, N Am Conf on British Studies. **RESEARCH** Modern British History. **SELECTED PUBLICATIONS** Auth, The Victorian Post Office: The Growth of a Bureaucracy, 92. **CONTACT ADDRESS** Dept Hist, Univ the South, 735 Univ Ave, Sewanee, TN 37383-0001. **EMAIL** cperry@sewanee.edu

PERRY, EDMUND
PERSONAL Born 05/18/1923, GA, m, 3 children **DISCIPLINE** HISTORY OF RELIGIONS **EDUCATION** Univ Ga, AB, 44; Emory Univ, BD, 46; Northwestern Univ, PhD(bibl theol, hist of relig), 50. **CAREER** Dir Wesley Found, GA State Col Women, 46-48; from instr to asst prof Bible & hist of relig, Duke Univ, 50-54; assoc prof, 54-62, Prof Hist Of Relig, Northwestern Univ, 62-, Chmn Dept, 54-, Mem univ senate, Methodist Church, 54-60; educ consult, Am Tel & Tel Co, 60-62; Fulbright prof, Vidyodaya Univ Ceylon, 67- 68. **HONORS AND AWARDS** DLitt, Vidyodaya Univ Ceylon, 68. **MEMBERSHIPS** Am Orient Soc; Am Theol Soc; Am Acad Relig; Soc Bibl Lit; Int Soc Buddhist-Christian Friends (exec secy, 68-). **RESEARCH** History and methods of studying religions; history and the history of religions; a Christian theology of religion. **SELECTED PUBLICATIONS** Coauth, Jews and Christians in North America, Westminster, 65; auth, The Study and Practice of Religion Today, Vidyodaya Univ Ceylon, 68; Buddhist Studies in Honour of Walpola Rahula, Fraser, London, 80; Theravada Buddhism - a Social-history From Ancient Benares to Modern Colombo - Gombrich,rf, J of The American Oriental Society, Vol 0117, 1997. **CONTACT ADDRESS** Dept of Hist & Relig, Northwestern Univ, Evanston, IL 60201.

PERRY, ELIZABETH ISRAELS
PERSONAL Born 03/29/1939, New York, NY, m, 1970, 2 children **DISCIPLINE** HISTORY **EDUCATION** Univ Calif at Los Angeles, BA, 60; PhD, 67. **CAREER** Lectr, Cal State Col, 66-67; asst prof, Univ Colorado, 67-69; vis asst prof, SUNY, 70-71, Univ Cincinnati, 81-82, Indiana Univ, 83, Univ Iowa, 84; asst prof, assoc prof, Vanderbilt Univ, 84-93; Dir NEH, 87, 90, 91, 95, 00; vis prof, CUNY, 91-92; prof, Sarah Lawrence Col, 93-97; vis prof, Univ Hartford, 95-96; res prof, Vanderbilt Univ, 98-99; prof, St Louis Univ, 99-. **HONORS AND AWARDS** Fulbright Fel; NEH Fel; MS Prize; Pres SHGAPE. **RESEARCH** US women's history; progressive era. **SELECTED PUBLICATIONS** Auth, Belle Moskowitz: Feminine Politics and the exercise of Power in the Age of Alfred E. Smith, Ox Univ Press (NY), 87; new ed, Northeastern Univ Press, 00; co-ed, The Challenge of Feminist Biography: Writing the Lives of Modern American Women, co-. Univ Ill Press (Champaign), 92; coauth, America: Pathways to the Present Prentice Hall (Englewood Cliffs, NJ), 94; co-ed, We Have Come to Stay: American Women and Political Parties, 1880-1960, Univ New Mex Press (Albuquerque, NM), 99. **CONTACT ADDRESS** Dept History, St. Louis Univ, PO Box 56907, Saint Louis, MO 63156. **EMAIL** perrye@slu.edu

PERRY, JOHN CURTIS
PERSONAL Born 07/18/1930, Orange, NJ, m, 1957, 5 children **DISCIPLINE** MODERN HISTORY **EDUCATION** Yale Univ, BA, 52, MA, 53; Harvard Univ, PhD(hist), 62. **CAREER** From instr to asst prof hist, Conn Col, 62-66; from asst prof to assoc prof hist, Carleton Col, 66-74, dir Asian studies prog, 66-73, chm dept hist, 71-74, acting dir of libr, 75-76, prof, 74-80; vis prof diplomacy, 80-81, Henry Willard Denison Prof Hist, Fletcher Sch Law & Diplomacy, Tufts Univ, 81-, Vis res assoc, Fairbank E Asia Res Ctr, Harvard Univ, 76-77 & Japan Inst, Harvard Univ, 77-80. **HONORS AND AWARDS** Japanese Imperial Decoration, Order of the Sacred Treasure, 91 **MEMBERSHIPS** AHA; Japan Soc. **RESEARCH** Oceanic history. **SELECTED PUBLICATIONS** Auth, Beneath the Eagle's Wings: Americans in Occupied Japan, 80; coauth, Sentimental Imperialists: The American Experience in East Asia, 81; Facing West: Americans and the Opening of the Pacific, 95; coauth, Flight of the Romanous: A Family Saga, 99. **CONTACT ADDRESS** Fletcher Sch of Law and Diplomacy, Tufts Univ, Medford, Packard Ave, Medford, MA 02155-5555. **EMAIL** johncurtis.perry@tufts.edu

PERRY, LEWIS C.
PERSONAL Born 11/21/1938, Somerville, MA, m, 1970, 3 children **DISCIPLINE** HISTORY **EDUCATION** Oberlin Col, BA, 60; Cornell Univ, MS, 64; PhD, 67. **CAREER** Lecture to Assoc Prof, State Univ of NY, 66-78; Prof, Ind Univ, 78-85; Ed, Journal of Am Hist, 78-84; Vis Prof, Univ of Leeds, 88-89; Prof, Vanderbilt Univ, 85-99; Prof, Saint Louis Univ, 99-. **HONORS AND AWARDS** Fel, ACLS, 72-73; Fel, Nat Humanities Inst, 75-76; John Simon Guggenheim, 82; NEH 87-88; Harry Frank Guggenheim, 91-92. **MEMBERSHIPS** Org of Am Hist, Am Hist Asn, Soc of Hist of the Early Am Repub, Am Studies Asn. **RESEARCH** US Intellectual life and culture; Antislavery and reform movements, Early republic. **SELECTED PUBLICATIONS** Auth, Radical Abolitionism: Anarchy and the Government in God in Antislavery Thought, Cornell Univ Press, 73; auth, childhood, Marriage and Reform: Henry Clarke Wright, 1797-1870, Univ Chicago Press, 80; auth, Intellectual Life in America: A History, Univ Chicago Press, 89; auth, Boats Against the current: American culture Between Revolution and Modernity, 1820-1860, Oxford Univ Press, 93; ed Patterns of Anarchy: A collection of Writings on the anarchist Tradition, Doubleday Anchor Books, 66; ed, Antislavery Reconsidered: New Perspectives on the Abolitionists, Louisiana State Univ Press, 79; ed, Moral problems in American Life: new Perspectives on Cultural History, Cornell Univ Press, 98; ed "United States-General," AHA Guide to Historical literature, Oxford Univ Press, (95): 1280-1323; auth, "Two Academic Careers and One Fulfilling Job," Chronicle of Higher education, (00): B7-8. **CONTACT ADDRESS** Dept Hist & Am Studies, Saint Louis Univ, 3800 Lindell Blvd, Saint Louis, MO 63156-0907. **EMAIL** perryl@slu.edu

PERRY, MARILYN
PERSONAL Born 04/03/1940, Glendale, CA **DISCIPLINE** HISTORY OF ART **EDUCATION** Stanford Univ, BA, 62, MA, 63; Univ NC, Chapel Hill, MA, 66; Univ London, MPhil, 68, PhD(hist Europ art), 75. **CAREER** Lectr hist of art, Am, Brit & Can univ & col progs abroad, Italy & England, 58-82; Exec VP to President, Samuel H. Kress Found, 82-. **HONORS AND AWARDS** Fel, Villa I Tatti, Harvard Univ Ctr for Ital Renaissance Studies, 76-77; fel, Gladys Krieble Delmas Found for res in Venice, 77- 78. **RESEARCH** Italian Renaissance art; collections of art and antiquities in Renaissance Venice; Stendhal in Rome. **SELECTED PUBLICATIONS** Auth, The pride of Venice, Aquileia nostra, 74-75; A Greek bronze in Renaissance Venice, 75 & Candor Illaesus: the impresa of Clement VII and other Medici devices in the Vatican Stanze, 77, Burlington Mag; Saint Mark's trophies: legend, superstition and archaeology in Renaissance Venice, 77 & Cardinal Domenico Grimani's legacy of ancient art to Venice, 78, J Warburg & Courtauld Inst; La pauvre Miss Bathurst: memorials to a tragedy in Stendhal's Rome, Connoisseur, 78; On Titian's borrowings from ancient art: A cautionary case, Tiziano e Venezia, 76; A Renaissance showplace of art: The Palazzo Grimani at Santa Maria Formosa, Venice, Apollo, 81. **CONTACT ADDRESS** Samuel H. Kress Foundation, 174 East 80th St, New York, NY 10021.

PERRY, ROBERT LEE
PERSONAL Born 12/06/1932, Toledo, OH, m **DISCIPLINE** ETHNOHISTORY **EDUCATION** Bowling Green St Univ, BA sociology 1959, MA sociology 1965; Wayne St Univ, PhD sociology 1978. **CAREER** Lucas Cnty Juv Ct Toledo, OH, probation counselor 1960-64, juvenile ct referee 1964-67; Detroit Inst Techn, asst prof 1967-70; Department of Ethnic Studies, Bowling Green State Univ Chmn, 70-; licensed professional counselor, 88; Ohio certified prevention consultant, 89-. **HONORS AND AWARDS** Sigma Delta Pi natl Spanish Hon Soc 1958; Alpha Kappa Delta Natl Soc Honor Soc 1976; $37,000 Grant, Dept HEW 1979; Post Doct Fellowship Amer Social Soc Inst for Soc Research UCLA 1980; Charles C Irby National Association of Ethnic Studies (NAES), Distinguished Service Awd, 1994. **MEMBERSHIPS** Consult Natl Inst of Law Enf and Crimin Just 1978-82; consult Div Soc Law and Econ Scis Natl Sci Found 1980; consult Children's Def Fund Task Force on Adoption Assist 1980; chair Status of Women & Minorities Comm N Cent Sociol Soc 1983-85; bd mem Citizens Review Bd Lucas Cnty Juv Ct Toledo, OH 1979-91; bd mem Inst for Child Advocacy Cleveland, OH 1981-85. **CONTACT ADDRESS** African American Studies Dept, Eastern Michigan Univ, 620 Pray Harrold, Ypsilanti, MI 48197.

PESELY, GEORGE E.
PERSONAL Born 01/24/1949, Quantico, VA **DISCIPLINE** ANCIENT HISTORY **EDUCATION** San Diego State Univ, AB, 70; Univ of IL, Urbana-Champaign, MA, 71; Univ of CA, Berkeley, PhD, 83. **CAREER** Lectr, Class, 83-84, State Univ NY at Buffalo; Asst Prof, Hist, 84-85, Arkansas Tech Univ; Asst Prof, Hist, 85-86, Univ of IL, Urbana-Champaign; Asst Prof, Class, 86-87, Memphis State Univ; Asst Prof, Hist, 87-88, Clarion Univ; Asst Prof, Hist, 88-90, Univ of Northern Iowa; Asst Prof to Assoc Prof, Hist, 90-, AustinPeay State Univ. **MEMBERSHIPS** Amer Philo Assoc; Archaeol Inst of Amer; Assoc of Ancient Hist; Class Assoc of the Middle West and South; Class Assoc of Canada; Amer Numismatic Soc; Amer Soc of Greek and Latin Epigraphy. **RESEARCH** Greek Political and Constitutional History; Greek History. **SELECTED PUBLICATIONS** Auth, Did Aristotle use Androtion's Atthis?, Klio 76, 94; Aristotle's Source for the Tyranny of Peisistratos, Athenaeum 83, 95; Andron and the Four Hundred, Illinois Classical Studies 20, 95; Franciscus Patricius's Ordering of the Platonic Dialogues, Zbornik O Frani Petricu, Zagreb, 99; Hagnon, Athenaeum, 89; The Speech of Endius in Diodorus Siculus, Classical Philology, 85. **CONTACT ADDRESS** Dept History, Austin Peay State Univ, Box 4486, Clarksville, TN 37044. **EMAIL** peselyg@apsu.edu

PESKIN, ALLAN
PERSONAL Born 03/16/1933, Cumberland, MD, m, 1963, 2 children **DISCIPLINE** AMERICAN HISTORY **EDUCATION** Univ Chicago, AB, 53; Western Reserve Univ, AB, 55, MA, 56, PhD(Hist), 65. **CAREER** Instr Hist & Govt, Fenn Col, 62-64; asst prof, 64-67, assoc prof, 67-81, prof Hist, Cleveland State Univ, 81-. **HONORS AND AWARDS** Outstanding Publication Awd, Ohio Acad Hist, 78; Ohioana Book Awd--Biography, Ohioana Libr Asn, 79. **MEMBERSHIPS** Orgn Am Historians; Southern Hist Asn. **RESEARCH** Nineteenth century America. **SELECTED PUBLICATIONS** Auth, North into Freedom: The Autobiography of John Malvin, Free Negro, 1795-1880, Western Reserve Univ, 66; contrib, For the Union: Ohio Leaders in the Civil War, Ohio State Univ, 68; auth, The put-up job: Wisconsin and the Republican National Convention of 1880, Wis Mag Hist, Summer 72; Was there a compromise of 1877?, J Am Hist, 6/73; Garfield, Kent State Univ, 78; The historiography of reconstruction, Encycl Southern Hist, La State Univ Press, 79; James A Garfield, Historian, The Historian, 8/81; Who Were the Stalwarts? Who Were Their Rivals? Poli Sci Q, Winter, 84-85; Volunteers, The Mexican War Journals of Private Richard Coulter & Sergeant Thomas Barelay, Kent State Univ, 91. **CONTACT ADDRESS** Dept of History, Cleveland State Univ, 1983 E 24th St, Cleveland, OH 44115-2440. **EMAIL** a.peskin@csuohio.edu

PESSEN, EDWARD
PERSONAL Born 12/31/1920, New York, NY, m, 1940, 5 children **DISCIPLINE** HISTORY **EDUCATION** Columbia Univ, BA, 47, MA, 48, PhD(hist), 54. **CAREER** Lectr hist, City Col NY, 48-54; assoc prof, Fisk Univ, 54- 56; prof hist & chmn dept hist & div lib arts & sci, Staten Island Community Col 56-70; Distinguished Prof Hist, Baruch Col & City Univ NY Grad Ctr, 70-, Vis prof, new Sch Soc Res, 65-66; State Univ NY Res Found fel grant, 65-66; mem adv bd, Martin Van Buren Papers Proj, 69-; Guggenheim fel, 77-78; Rockefeller Found fel, 78. **MEMBERSHIPS** AHA; Soc Am Historians; Orgn Am Historians; Soc Historians of Early Am Repub. **RESEARCH** American social and intellectual history; politics and political history; Jacksonian era. **SELECTED PUBLICATIONS** Auth, Most Uncommon Jacksonians, State Univ NY, 67; The egalitarian myth and the American social reality: Wealth, equality, and mobility in the era of the common man, Am Hist Rev, 10/71; Who governed the nation's cities in the era of the common man?, Polit Sci Quart, 12/72; Riches, Class and Power Before the Civil War, 73 & ed, Three Centuries of Social Mobility in America, 74, Heath; auth, Jacksonian Panorama, Bobbs, 76; Prologue to Who rules America? Power and politics in the Democratic Era, 1825-1975, J Nat Arch, spring 77; Jacksonian America: Society, Personality and Politics, Dorsey, rev ed, 78; How different from each other were the Antebellum North & South?, Am Hist Rev, 12/80. **CONTACT ADDRESS** Dept of Hist, Baruch Col, CUNY, New York, NY 10010.

PESTANA, CARLA GARDINA
PERSONAL Born 10/24/1958, Burbank, CA, m, 1981, 2 children **DISCIPLINE** HISTORY **EDUCATION** Loyola Marymount Univ, BA, 80, UCLA, MA, 83, PhD, 87. **CAREER** John Carter Brown Library, res assoc, 85-86; OH State, asst prof, 87-93, assoc prof, 93 -. **HONORS AND AWARDS** Walter Muir Whitehill Prize in Colonial Hist, 83; NEH Summer Stipend, 00; NEH-Huntington Senior Fel, 97-98 ; Am Philos Soc Research Grant, 94-95; Fletcher Jones Research Fel, Huntington Library, 94-95; Huntington Library-Brit Acad Exchange, 92-93, 87: Lilly Tchg Fel, OH State Univ, 91-93; Recent Recipients of the PhD Fel, Am Council of Learned Soc, 89-90; Kate B. and Hall J. Peterson Fel, Am Antiquarian Soc, 88-89; Graduate Woman of the Year Awd, UCLA Assoc of Acad Women 87; Charlotte W. Newcombe Doctoral Dissertation Fel, Woodrow Wilson National Fel Found 86-87; Huntington-Frank Hideo Kono Memorial Fel, Huntington Library 85-86; Distinguished Scholar Awd, UCLA Alumni Assoc 84; Research Fel, John Carter Brown Library 83. **MEMBERSHIPS** AHA; OAH; Assoc of the Omohundro Institute of Early Am Hist and Cult, Colonial Soc of MA, coord council for women in hist, North Am Conference on Brit Studies. **RESEARCH** Anglo-Atlantic in the 17th century; Quakers. **SELECTED PUBLICATIONS** Quakers and Baptists in Colonial Massachusetts, 91; Liberty of Conscience and the Growth of Religious Deversity in Early America, 1636-1786, 86; The Quaker Executions as Myth and hist, Jour of Amer Hist, 93; The City upon the Hill under siege: Puritan Perceptions of the Quaker threat to Massachusetts Bay, New England Quarterly 84, The Social World for Salem: William King's 1681 Blasphemy Trial, Amer Qrt 89. **CONTACT ADDRESS** Ohio State Univ, Columbus, 230 W 17th Ave, Columbus, OH 43210-1367. **EMAIL** Pestana.1@osu.edu

PETERS, EDWARD MURRAY
PERSONAL Born New Haven, CT, m, 1961, 3 children **DISCIPLINE** MEDIEVAL HISTORY **EDUCATION** Yale Univ, BA, 63, MA, 65, PhD(medieval studies), 67. **CAREER** Instr English, Quinnipiac Col, 64-66; asst prof hist, Univ Calif, San Diego, 67-68; Henry C Lea asst prof, 68-70, Henry C Lea assoc prof, 70-81, Henry C Lea Prof Medieval Hist, Univ PA, 81-; Cur, Henry C Lea Libr, 68-. **HONORS AND AWARDS** John Simon Guggenheim Fel 88-89; Am Coun Learned Soc fel, 81-82; ma, univ pa, 72. **MEMBERSHIPS** Mediaeval Acad Am; AHA; fel Royal Hist Soc, London; Dante Soc Am; ICMAC; Am Soc Legal Hist; Ren Soc Am. **RESEARCH** Medieval legal and political theory; medieval kingship and governance; medieval and Renaissance cultural history. **SELECTED PUBLICATIONS** Auth, The Shadow King: Rex Inutilis in Medieval Law and Literature, 751-1327, Yale Univ, 70; co-ed, Witchcraft in Europe, 1100-1700: A Documentary, 72 & The World of Piers Plowman, 75, Univ Pa; auth, Europe: The World of the Middle Ages, Prentice-Hall, 77; The Magician, the Witch and the Law, Univ Pa, 78; Heresy and Authority in Medieval Europe, Univ Pa, 80; Europe and the Middle Ages: A Short History, Prentice-Hall, 82; auth, Europe and the Middle Ages, 3rd ed, 96; auth, Torture, 85; auth, Inquisition, 89; auth, The First Crusade, 2nd ed 98. **CONTACT ADDRESS** Dept of Hist, Univ of Pennsylvania, 3401 Walnut St, Ste 352B, Philadelphia, PA 19104-6228. **EMAIL** empeters@sas.upenn.edu

PETERS, ISSA
PERSONAL Born 03/15/1935, Mishtaya, Syria, m, 1965, 1 child **DISCIPLINE** ARABIC, MIDDLE EAST HISTORY **EDUCATION** Univ Damascus, BA, 58; Mich State Univ, MA, 60; Columbia Univ, PhD(Arabic), 74. **CAREER** Teacher English, Midway Jr Col, 64-65; instr English, Northern Ill Univ, 65-68; assoc prof Arabic, Defense Lang Inst, 71-76; assoc prof, 76-80, Prof Arabic & Middle East Studies, Am Grad Sch Int Mgt, 80- **MEMBERSHIPS** Am Asn Teachers Arabic; Am Orient Soc; Middle E Studies Asn. **RESEARCH** Contemporary Arabic literature and thought; Middle East history. **CONTACT ADDRESS** Dept of Int Studies, American Graduate Sch of Intl Mgt, 15249 N 59th Ave, Glendale, AZ 85306-3236. **EMAIL** petersi@t-bird.edu

PETERS, JULIE
DISCIPLINE DRAMA AND THEATRE HISTORY **EDUCATION** Yale Univ, AB, 81; Princeton Univ, PhD, 87. **CAREER** Asoc prof. **HONORS AND AWARDS** Fel, Fulbright found; fel, Folger Library; fel, Amer Coun Learned Soc; fel, Humboldt found. **RESEARCH** Law and literature. **SELECTED PUBLICATIONS** Auth, Congreve, the Drama, and the Printed Word, Stanford, 90; co-ed, Women's Rights, Human Rights: International Feminist Perspectives, Routledge, 95. **CONTACT ADDRESS** Dept of Eng, Columbia Col, New York, 2960 Broadway, New York, NY 10027-6902.

PETERS, TOM F.
DISCIPLINE HISTORY OF ARCHITECTURAL AND CIVIL ENGINEERING TECHNOLOGY **EDUCATION** Dr. Sc. Techn., ETH Zurich **CAREER** Prof, Lehigh Univ **HONORS AND AWARDS** Dir, Inst Study Highrise Habitat. **RESEARCH** Current and historical topics in building. **SELECTED PUBLICATIONS** The Evolution of Long-span Bridge Building, Transitions In Engineering and Building the 19th Century. **CONTACT ADDRESS** Dept of Art and Archit, Lehigh Univ, Bethlehem, PA 18015. **EMAIL** tfp0@lehigh.edu

PETERSON, CHARLES S.
PERSONAL Born 01/30/1927, Snowflake, AZ, m, 1953, 5 children **DISCIPLINE** HISTORY OF AMERICAN WEST **EDUCATION** Brigham Young Univ, BA, 52, MA, 58; Univ Utah, PhD, 67. **CAREER** Instr hist, Col Eastern Utah, 58-66, dean instr, 66-68; asst prof hist, Univ Utah, 68-69; dir Utah State Hist Soc 69-71; assoc prof, 71-74, prof Hist & Geog to prof emeritus, Utah State Univ, 74-, Ed, Utah Hist Quart, 69-71; coed, Western Hist Quart, 71-; dir, Man & His Bread Mus, 71-. **HONORS AND AWARDS** Nat Endowment for Humanities fel, Huntington Libr, 78. **MEMBERSHIPS** Western Hist Asn; Orgn Am Historians; Am Asn State & Local Hist; Agr Hist Soc; Forest Hist Soc. **RESEARCH** Frontier history; agricultural and conservationist related topics; Mormon history with emphasis on the colonizing process of the church. **SELECTED PUBLICATIONS** Contribr, A Trail Guide to the Trail of the Mormon Battalion, Utah Hist Soc, 72; auth, Take Up Your Mission: Mormon Colonizing Along the Little Colorado 1870-1900, Univ Ariz, 73; auth, Small Holding Land Patterns in Utah and the Problem of Forest Watershed Management, Forest Hist, 773; ed, A Levi Mathers Savage: The Look of Utah in 1873, Utah Hist Quart, 73; auth, Look to the Mountains: Southeastern Utah and the La Sal National Forest, 75 & contribr, Utah's History: A College Text, 77, Brigham Young Univ; auth, Utah: A Bicentennial History, Norton, 77; auth, Quest For The Golden Circle - The Four-Corners and The Metropolitan West, 1945-1970, Western Historical Quarterly, 96. **CONTACT ADDRESS** Dept of Hist & Geog, Utah State Univ, Logan, UT 84322.

PETERSON, EDWARD NORMAN
PERSONAL Born 08/27/1925, St. Joseph, MO, m, 1946, 2 children **DISCIPLINE** HISTORY **EDUCATION** Univ Wis, PhD(hist), 53. **CAREER** Teaching asst, Univ Wis, 52-53; asst prof Eastern Ky State Col, 53-54; chmn dept soc sci, 63, Prof Hist, Univ Wis-river Falls, 54-, Chmn Dept, 62-90, Humboldt Found fel, 63-64; State Univ Regents grant, 66; fels, Nat Endowment for Humanities, 69- 70 & Soc Sci Res Coun, 69-71; consult, Nat Endowment for Humanities, 72-. **MEMBERSHIPS** AHA; Conf Ger Politics. **RESEARCH** Source and use of power; World War II; 20th century Germany. **SELECTED PUBLICATIONS** Auth, Hjalmar Schacht, Christopher, 54; Geographic dichotomy, Soc Studies, 62-; The bureaucracy and the Nazi party, Rev Polit, 66; Die Burokratie und die NSDAP, Der Staat, 67; The Limits of Hitler's Power, Princeton Univ, 69; Beurteilung der einwirkung Amerikas auf Deutschland 1945-52, In: Tradition und Neubeginn, Heymanns, Koln, 76; American Occupation of Germany, Wayne State Univ, 78; Die-spd-aber-aufgehort-hat-zu-existieren - Social-democrats Under Soviet Occupation - German - Bouvier,bw, Schulz,hp, German Studies Review, Vol 0017, 1994; Flight And Defection From The Sbzddr 1945, 1949, 1961, Refugee Policy of The Federal-repubic-of-germany Before The Berlin-wall - German - Heidemeyer,h, American Historical Review, Vol 0100, 1995; The Russians in Germany - a History of The Soviet-zone-of- occupation, 1945-1949 - Naimark,nm, German Studies Review, Vol 0019, 1996; a Blitzkrieg Legend - The Military Campaign in The West - German - Frieser,kh, German Studies Review, Vol 0020, 1997; The Soviet-union And The Origins of The Second-world-war - Russo-german Relations And The Road to War, 1933-1941 - Roberts,g, German Studies Review, Vol 0020, 1997; auth, "An Analytical History of World War II," 2 volumes The Many Faces of Defeat: German Experience in 1945, Russian Commands and German Resistance. **CONTACT ADDRESS** Dept of Hist, Univ of Wisconsin, River Falls, 410 S 3rd St, River Falls, WI 54022-5013.

PETERSON, FRANK ROSS
PERSONAL Born 09/07/1941, Montpelier, ID, m, 1963, 3 children **DISCIPLINE** CONTEMPORARY AMERICAN HISTORY **EDUCATION** Utah State Univ, BA, 65; Wash State Univ, PhD(Am studies), 68. **CAREER** Asst prof hist, Univ Tex, Arlington, 68-71; from asst prof to assoc prof, 71-78, Prof Hist, Utah State Univ, 78-, Chmn Dept Hist & Geog, 76-, Nat Endowment for Humanities Younger Humanist fel, 72-73; lectr, Fulbright-Hays Fel, New Zealand, 78. **MEMBERSHIPS** Orgn Am Historians; Western Hist Asn; Asn Studies Afro-Am Life & Hist. **RESEARCH** Contemporary political history; school integration; conservation history. **SELECTED PUBLICATIONS** Contribr, Essays on Radicalism in Contemporary America, Univ Tex, 72; auth, Prophet Without Honor, Univ Ky, 74; Idaho: A Bicentennial History, Norton, 76; contribr, Utah's History, Brigham Young Univ, 79. **CONTACT ADDRESS** Dept of Hist & Geog, Utah State Univ, 710 University Blvd, Logan, UT 84322-0710.

PETERSON, JACQUELINE
DISCIPLINE NATIVE AMERICAN, NORTH AMERICAN HISTORY **EDUCATION** Univ Ill, Chicago, PhD, 81. **CAREER** Prof, Washington State Univ. **SELECTED PUBLICATIONS** Auth, Sacred Encounters: Father De Smet and the Indians of the Rocky Mountain West, Univ Okla Press, 93; ed, The New Peoples: Being and Becoming Metis in North America, Univ Manitoba Press, 91. **CONTACT ADDRESS** Dept of History, Washington State Univ, 301 Wilson Hall, PO Box 644030, Pullman, WA 99164-4030. **EMAIL** peterson@vancouver.wsu.edu

PETERSON, JON ALVAH
PERSONAL Born 09/21/1935, Columbus, OH, m, 1963, 2 children **DISCIPLINE** AMERICAN HISTORY **EDUCATION** Swarthmore Col, BA, 57; Ohio State Univ, MA, 59; Harvard Univ, PhD(Am hist), 67. **CAREER** Lectr, 66-67, asst prof, 67-81, asst chmn dept hist, 74-76, Assoc Prof US Urban & Immigration Hist, Queens Col, NY, 81-, Adj asst prof, Fordham Univ, 68, 70; grants-in-aid, Am Coun Learned Soc, 76-77 & Am Philos Soc, 76-77; fel, Charles Warren Ctr Studies Am Hist, 76-77; Dept Chair, 90-94; Graduate Advisor, 00-. **MEMBERSHIPS** AHA; Orgn Am Historians; Soc Welfare Hist Group; Immigration Hist Group; Soc Archit Historians; Society for Am City and Regional Planning History. **RESEARCH** Urban history; history of city planning in the United States. **SELECTED PUBLICATIONS** Auth, From social settlement to social agency: settlement work in Columbus, Ohio, 1898-1958, Soc Serv Rev, 65; The city beautiful movement: forgotten origins and lost meanings, J Urban Hist, 76; The impact of sanitary reform upon American urban planning, 1840-1890, J Soc Hist, fall 79; auth, "The Nations's First Comprehensive City Plan: A Political Analysis of the McMillian Plan for Washington, DC, 1900-1902," Journal of the American Planning Association 51 (85): 134-150; Company Town - Architecture and Society in the Early Industrial-age - Garner,js, J of American History, Vol 0081, 1994; the Nation and its City - Politics, Corruption, and Progress in Washington, Dc, 1861-1902 - Lessoff,a, American Studies International, Vol 0032, 1994; auth, "Frederick Law Olmsted Sr. and Frederick Law Olmsted Jr.: The Visionary and the Professional, " in Mary Corbin Siesand Christopher Silver, Planning the Twentieth Century American City, (Baltimore, Johns Hopkins Univ Press, 96), 32-54; auth, City Planning in the United States, 1840-1917: The Birth of a Comprehensive Vision, Johns Hopkins Univ Press, 02. **CONTACT ADDRESS** 11 Baker Hill Rd, Great Neck, NY 11023. **EMAIL** japhist@qc.qc1

PETERSON, JOYCE SHAW
PERSONAL Born 06/18/1939, Greenport, NY, m, 1967, 2 children **DISCIPLINE** HISTORY **EDUCATION** Denison Univ, BA, 61; Boston Univ, MA, 63; Univ Wis- Madison, PhD(hist), 76. **CAREER** Asst Prof Hist, Fla Int Univ, 77-. **MEMBERSHIPS** AHA; Orgn Am Historians. **RESEARCH** Labor history; women's history; social history. **SELECTED PUBLICATIONS** Auth, Black automobile workers in Detroit, 1910-1930, J Negro Hist, summer 79; American automobile workers and their work, 1897-1933, Labor Hist, spring 81. 1995; The Gentle General - Pesotta,rose, Anarchist and Labor Organizer - Leeder,e, American Historical Review, Vol 0100, 1995. **CONTACT ADDRESS** Dept of Hist, Florida Intl Univ, Tamiami Trail, Miami, FL 33199.

PETERSON, LARRY R.
PERSONAL Born 05/25/1947, Denver, CO, w, 1968, 2 children **DISCIPLINE** HISTORY **EDUCATION** Moorhead State Univ, BA, 70; Univ Minn, MA, 75; PhD, 78. **CAREER** From vis asst prof to prof, NDak State Univ, 77-. **HONORS AND AWARDS** Fulbright Jr Lectureship, Univ Oldenburg, 82-83; Burlington Northern Fac Achievement Awd, 85; Outstanding Services Awd, Col of Humanities and Soc Sci, 92; NDSU Women's Week Honoree, 93; NDSU Tapestry of Diverse Talents, 94; Outstanding Acad Advisor, The Mortar Board Honor Soc, 97; Sarah Nelson Friend Awd, Fargo-Moorhead Chapter of Parents and Friends of Lesbians and Gays, 98; Leslie Hewes Awd for Best Soc Sci Article published in Great Plains Res, 99; listed in Who's Who in America, 01. **MEMBERSHIPS** Am Hist Asn, Am Studies Asn, The Radical Historians' Orgn, Nat Educ Asn, NDak Higher Educ Asn, NDak Multicultural Asn, 90; Orgn of Am Historians. **RESEARCH** Long-term Trends Among Families in the Northern Great Plains, Gays and Lesbians in the Northern Great Plains. **SELECTED PUBLICATIONS** Coauth, "The Aggie and the Ecstasy: A Descriptive Analysis of the Process of General Education Reform at a Land-Grant University," JGE: The J of General Educ 45.4 (96): 319-334; auth, "North Dakota," Dictionary of American History: Supplement, eds. Joan Hoff and Robert Ferrell (Charles Scribner's Sons Reference Books, 96); coauth, "Survey Data and General Education Reform: A Case of Alumni Responses," JGE: The J of General Educ 47.4 (98): 327-339; auth, "Is the Family Disappearing? Northern Great Plains vs. National Trends in Family Structure," Great Plains Res 9.1 (99): 145-163; coauth, "Differences in How Men and Women Experience General Education: Implications for Curricular Reform and Assessment," JGE: The J of General Educ 48.4 (99): 248-264. **CONTACT ADDRESS** Dept Hist, No Dakota State Univ, PO Box 5075, Fargo, ND 58105-5075. **EMAIL** lpeterso@plains.nodak.edu

PETERSON, LUTHER D.
DISCIPLINE HISTORY **EDUCATION** Univ Wis Madison, MS; PhD. **CAREER** Prof, SUNY Oswego. **HONORS AND AWARDS** Vollstipendium, Govt Niedersachsen and Volkswagenstiftung, 81. **RESEARCH** Renaissance and Reformation; hist of Judaism and Christianity. **SELECTED PUBLICATIONS** Auth, Melanchthon on Resisting the Emperor in Regnum, Religio et Ratio, 87; Justus Menius, Philipp Melanchthon and the Writing of the 1547 Treatise, Von der Notwehr Unterricht in Archiv fuerReformationsgeschichte 81, 90; Philippism, Justus Menius, and Synergistic Controversy, in The Encyclopedia of the Reformation, Oxford UP, 95. **CONTACT ADDRESS** Dept Hist, SUNY, Oswego, 101 Mahar Hall, Oswego, NY 13126.

PETERSON, M. JEANNE
PERSONAL Born 11/26/1937, Hibbing, MN **DISCIPLINE** MODERN BRITISH HISTORY **EDUCATION** Univ Calif, Berkeley, BA, 66, PhD, 72. **CAREER** Lectr, 71-72, asst prof, 72-78, Assoc Prof Hist, Ind Univ, Bloomington, 78-, Assoc Mem Dept Hist & Philos Sci, 76-, Woodrow Wilson fel, 66-67; Univ Calif-Berkeley grad career prize, 66-71; Am Asn Univ Women fel, 69-70; Am Coun Learned Soc grant-in-aid, 75; Nat Endowment for Humanities fel, 78-79. **MEMBERSHIPS** AHA; Conf British Studies; Soc Social Hist Med. **RESEARCH** Victorian social history; history of professions; family history. **SELECTED PUBLICATIONS CONTACT ADDRESS** Dept of Hist, Indiana Univ, Bloomington, 742 Ballantine Hall, Bloomington, IN 47401.

PETERSON, MERRILL DANIEL
PERSONAL Born 03/31/1921, Manhattan, KS, m, 1944, 2 children **DISCIPLINE** HISTORY **EDUCATION** Univ Kans, AB, 43; Harvard Univ, PhD(hist Am civilization), 50. **CAREER** From instr to asst prof Am civilization, Brandeis Univ, 49- 55, from assoc prof to prof, 58-63, dean students, 60-62; asst prof hist, Princeton Univ, 55-58; Jefferson Prof Hist, Univ VA, 63-, Dean Fac, 81-, Guggenheim fel, 62-63; fel, Ctr Advan Studies Behav Sci, 68-69; Nat Endowment for Humanities fel, 80- 81. **HONORS AND AWARDS** Bancroft Prize, 61; dhm,

washington col, 76. **MEMBERSHIPS** AHA; Orgn Am Historians; Southern Hist Asn; Soc Am Historians. **RESEARCH** Jefferson; middle period; American intellectual history. **SELECTED PUBLICATIONS** Auth, Jefferson Image in the American Mind, Oxford Univ, 60; coauth, Major Crises in American History (2 vols), Harcourt, 62; ed, Democracy, Liberty and Property, Bobbs, 66; Thomas Jefferson: A Profile, Hill & Wang, 67; auth, Thomas Jefferson and the New Nation: A Biography, Oxford Univ, 70; James Madison: A Biography in His Own Words, Harper, 74; ed, The Portable Jefferson, Viking, 75; auth, Adams and Jefferson: A Revolutionary Dialogue, Univ Ga, 76; Olive Branch and Sword: The Compromise of 1833, La State Univ Press, 82; Commemorations - the Politics of National Identity - Gillis,jr, J of American History, Vol 0082, 1995. **CONTACT ADDRESS** Dept of Hist, Univ of Virginia, Charlottesville, VA 22901.

PETERSON, MICHAEL
PERSONAL Born 04/26/1954, Richmond, KY, m, 1981, 2 children **DISCIPLINE** GEOGRAPHY **EDUCATION** Univ Wisc, BA, 76; Boston Univ, MA, 78; SUNY, PhD, 82. **CAREER** Post-doctoral Assistant, Univ Zurich, 82; Vis Prof, Univ Wash, 85; Fulbright Prof, Free Univ Berlin, 90-91; Vis Prof, Univ Hawaii, 95; Fulbright Prof, Technical Univ, Vienna, 99. **HONORS AND AWARDS** Best article, The Am Cartographer, 79,85. **MEMBERSHIPS** AAG, NACIS. **RESEARCH** Computer cartography. **SELECTED PUBLICATIONS** Auth, "The Web and Ethics in Cartography," Institute of Cartography and Reproduction Techniques; auth, "Trends in Internet Map Use: A Second Look," 19th Intl Cartographic Conference, 99; auth, "Active Legends for Interactive Cartographic animation," International Journal of Geographical Information Science, (99): 375-383; auth, Multimedia Cartography, Springer Verlag, 99; auth, "Elements of Multimedia Cartography," in Multimedia Cartography, Berlin: springer Verlag, 99; auth, Interactive and Animated Cartography, Englewood cliffs, 95. **CONTACT ADDRESS** Dept Geog & Geol., Univ of Nebraska, Omaha, 6001 Dodge St, Omaha, NE 68182-0002. **EMAIL** geolib@unomaha.edu

PETERSON, NORMA LOIS
PERSONAL Born 12/22/1922, Roseau, MN **DISCIPLINE** AMERICAN HISTORY **EDUCATION** Colo Col, BA, 49; Univ Mo, MA, 51; PhD, 53. **CAREER** From Asst prof to assoc prof, 53-57, chmn div soc studies, 57-71, chmn div hist, govt & philos, 71-79, Prof Hist, Adams State Col, 57-, Chmn Div Arts and Letters, 79-, Am Asn Univ Women Florence Sabin fel, 57-58; vis lectr, Univ Va, 67-68. **HONORS AND AWARDS** LLD, Colo Col, 78. **MEMBERSHIPS** Orgn Am Historians; Southern Hist Asn: AHA. **RESEARCH** American intellectual history, 1850-1940; early 19th century America. **SELECTED PUBLICATIONS** Auth, Freedom and Franchise, Univ Mo, 65; coauth, Letters of William S Stewart, Mo Hist Rev, 167, 467 & 767; auth, The Defence of Norfolk, Norfolk Co Hist Soc, 70; Littleton Waller Taxewell, VA Cavalcade, spring 73; Clay,henry - Statesman for the Union - Remini,rv, J of Southern History, Vol 0059, 1993. **CONTACT ADDRESS** Div of Hist Govt & Philos, Adams State Col, Alamosa, CO 81102.

PETERSON, RICHARD HERMANN
PERSONAL Born 01/16/1942, Berkeley, CA, m, 1970, 1 child **DISCIPLINE** AMERICAN & WESTERN AMERICAN HISTORY **EDUCATION** Univ Calif, Berkeley, AB, 63; Calif State Univ, San Francisco, MA, 66; Univ Calif, Davis, PhD(hist), 71. **CAREER** Asst prof US hist, Ind Univ, Kokomo, 71-76; Col Redwoods, 76-78; Assoc Prof Hist, San Diego State Univ, 78-, San Diego State Univ summer fac fel, 80. **MEMBERSHIPS** Orgn Am Historians; Western Hist Asn. **RESEARCH** Trans-Mississippi West; 19th century United States; entrepreneurial history. **SELECTED PUBLICATIONS** Auth, Conflict and consensus: Labor relations in Western mining, J West, 173; The failure to reclaim: California state swamp land policy and the Sacramento Valley, 1850-1866, Southern Calif Quart, spring 74; Manifest Destiny in the Mines: A Cultural Interpretation of Anti-Mexican Nativism in California, 1848-53, R&E Res Assoc, 75; The frontier thesis and social mobility on the mining frontier, Pac Hist Rev, 75; The Bonanza Kings: The Social Origins and Business Behavior of Western Mining Entrepreneurs, 1870-1900, Univ Nebr, 77; Simeon Gannett Reed and the Bunker Hill and Sullivan: The frustrations of a mining investor, fall 79 & Pacific northwest entrepreneur: The social and political behavior of Simeon Gannett Reed, fall 80, Idaho Yesterdays; Anti-Mexican nativism in California, 1848- 1853: A study of cultural conflict, Southern Calif Quart, winter 80; California History, Vol 0073, 1994; Giannini,a.p. and the Bank of America - Nash,gd, Western Historical Quarterly, Vol 0024, 1993; the United-states-sanitary-commission and King,thomas,starr in California, 1861-1864, California History, Vol 0072, 1993; The Life and Personality of Hearst,phoebe,apperson - Bonfils,wb, California History, Vol 0073, 1994; Gold Seeking - Victoria and California in the 1850s - Goodman,d, Western Historical Quarterly, Vol 0026, 1995; The Western Rides Again, J of the West, Vol 0035, 1996. **CONTACT ADDRESS** Dept of Hist, San Diego State Univ, San Diego, CA 92182.

PETERSON, WILLARD JAMES
PERSONAL Born 08/01/1938, Oak Park, IL, m **DISCIPLINE** CHINESE HISTORY **EDUCATION** Harvard Univ, PhD, 70 **CAREER** Asst Prof, Dartmouth Col, 70-71; Asst Prof to Prof, Princeton Univ, 71-. **MEMBERSHIPS** Asn Asian Studies **RESEARCH** Chinese intellectual history. **SELECTED PUBLICATIONS** Auth, Life of Yen-Wu (1613-1682), Harvard J Asiatic Studies 28 & 29, 68-69; auth, Bitter Gourd: Fang I-Chih and the Impetus for Intellectual Change, Yale Univ Press, 79; auth, Power of Culture, Chinese Univ Press, Hong Kong, 91. **CONTACT ADDRESS** Dept East Asian Studies, Princeton Univ, 211 Jones Hall, Princeton, NJ 08544.

PETILLO, CAROL MORRIS
PERSONAL Born 09/05/1940, Clarksburg, WV, 4 children **DISCIPLINE** AMERICAN HISTORY **EDUCATION** Montclair State Col, BA, 74; Rutgers Univ, MA, 76, PhD(Am hist), 79. **CAREER** Instr Am hist, Douglass Col, Rutgers Univ, 75-79; asst prof, 79-82, Assoc Prof Am Hist, Boston Col, 82-, consult, Round Hill Prod, Inc, 81. **MEMBERSHIPS** Orgn Am Historians; Am Mil Inst; Soc Historians Am Foreign Relations. **RESEARCH** United States relations with developing nations, particularly Southeast Asia; phychobiography of national and international leaders; the role of military in the third world. **SELECTED PUBLICATIONS** Auth, Douglas MacArthur and Manuel Quezon: A note on an imperial bond, Pac Hist Rev, 2/79; On the importance of a central archival repository, Prologue, summer 80; Douglas MacArthur: The Philippine Years, Ind Univ Press, 81. **CONTACT ADDRESS** Hist Dept, Boston Col, Chestnut Hill, 140 Commonwealth Ave, Chestnut Hill, MA 02167-3800.

PETRAGLIA, MICHAEL
PERSONAL Born 10/06/1960, New York, NY, m, 1994 **DISCIPLINE** ANTHROPOLOGY AND ARCHAEOLOGY **EDUCATION** Univ NYork, BA, anthrop, 82; Univ Nmex, anthrop, MA, 84, PhD, 87. **CAREER** Dir, Cultural Resources Dept, Parsons, 88-; res, Nat Mus of Natural Hist; Smithsonian Inst, 88-. **HONORS AND AWARDS** Postdoctoral fel, Smithsonian Inst. **MEMBERSHIPS** Soc for Amer Archaeol; Amer Anthrop Asn. **RESEARCH** Early human behavior; Hunter-gatherers; Lithic technology; Site formation. **SELECTED PUBLICATIONS** Co-ed, Early Human Behavior in Global Context: the Rise and Development of the Lower Paleolithic Record, London, Routledge Press, 98; coauth, The Old World Paleolithic Collections of the National Museum of Natural History, Smithsonian Inst, Smithsonian Press, 98; coauth, The Prehistory of Lums Pond: The Formation of a Woodland Site in Delaware, vols I and II, Del Dept of Transp Archaeol Series, 98; co-ed, The Lower Paleolithic of India and its Bearing on the Asian Record, in Early Human Behavior in Global Context: the Rise and Diversity of the Lower Paleolithic Record, London, Routledge Press, 98; coauth, Upper Paleolithic Collections from the Salat Valley of Pyrenean France, 98; coauth, Specialized Occupations on Kettle Creek, a Tributary of the West Branch of the Susquehanna, Archaeol of Eastern N Amer, 98; coauth, Assessing Prehistoric Chronology in Piedmont Contexts, N Amer Archaeol, 17, 37-59, 96; coauth, Immunological and Microwear Analysis of Chipped-stone Artifacts from Piedmont Contexts, Amer Antiquity, 61, 127-135, 96; coauth, Prehistoric Occupation at the Connoquenessing Site, an Upland Setting in the Upper Ohio River Valley, Archaeol of Eastern N Amer, 24, 29-57, 96; auth, Reassembling the Quarry: Quartzite Procurement and Reduction along the Potomac, N Amer, Archaeol, 15, 283-319, 94; coauth, Status, Technology, and Rural Traditions in Western Pennsylvania: Excavations at the Shaeffer Farm Site, Northeast Hist Archaeol, 23, 29-58, 94. **CONTACT ADDRESS** 4557 Sawgrass Ct., Alexandria, VA 22312. **EMAIL** petraglia.michael@nmnh.si.edu

PETRIK, PAULA E.
DISCIPLINE HISTORY **EDUCATION** Cornell Univ, BA, 69, Univ Mont, MFA, 73; SUNY-Binghampton, MA, 79, PhD, 82. **CAREER** Assoc prof, hist, Montana State Univ; PROF, HIST, UNIV MAINE. **MEMBERSHIPS** Am Antiquarian Soc **SELECTED PUBLICATIONS** Auth, No Step Backward: Women and Family on the Rocky Mountain Mining Frontier, Helena, Montana, 1865-1900; auth, "The House that Parcheese Built," Bus Hist Rev, 86; auth, If She Be Content: The Development of Montana Divorce Law, 1865-1907, Western Hist Quart, 87; auth, "Desk-Top Publishing: The Making of the American Dream," Hist Today 39, 89; auth, "The Youngest Fourth Estate: Race, Gender, and the Novelty Toy Printing Press," in Small Worlds: Children and Adolescents in America, Univ Kans Press, 92. **CONTACT ADDRESS** Dept of Hist, Univ of Maine, Orono, ME 04469.

PETRONE, KAREN
DISCIPLINE HISTORY **EDUCATION** Harvard Univ, BA, 87; Univ Mich, MA, 90, PhD, 94. **CAREER** Asst prof, 94-, Univ Ky. **HONORS AND AWARDS** Nat Endow for the Humanities Summer Stipend, 97; Chancellor's Awd for Outstanding Teaching-Univ Ky, 98; int res & exchanges bd-res fel, 91-92; fulbright-hays dissertation res fel, 91-92; soc sci res coun-dissertation fel, 92-93. **MEMBERSHIPS** AHA; AAASS. **RESEARCH** Soviet celebrations in the 1930s; Imperial & Soviet military heroes & patriotic cultures, 1900-1950. **SELECTED PUBLICATIONS** Auth, Soviet Celebrations Against a Backdrop of Terror: Holidays in 1937, Konets stoletiia: predvaritel'nye itogi Kul'turologicheskie zapiski, 93; art, Parading the Nation: Physical Culture Celebrations and the Construction of Soviet Identities, Michigan Discussions in Anthropology: Post Soviet Eurasia, 96; art, Family, Masculinity, and Heroism in Russian Posters of the First World War, Borderlines: Genders and Identities in War and Peace, 1880-1930, Routledge, 98; art, Gender and Heroes: The Exploits of Soviet Pilots and Arctic Explorers in the 1930s, Women and Political Change: Perspectives from East-Central Europe, St Martin's Press, 98. **CONTACT ADDRESS** Dept of History, Univ of Kentucky, Lexington, KY 40506-0027. **EMAIL** knpetro@ukcc.uky.edu

PETROVICH, ALISA
PERSONAL Born 03/18/1961, Midland, MI, s **DISCIPLINE** HISTORY **EDUCATION** Univ Tex, DDS, 89; Univ Houston, PhD, 96. **CAREER** Adjunct fac prof, Brazaport Col, 94-00; adjunct fac, Univ Houston, 96; adjunct fac, Univ of Houston, Clear Lake, 96-99; lectr, Univ of Houston, Clear Lake, 2000. **HONORS AND AWARDS** Phi Theta Alpha, 94; Murray Miller Scholar, 94, 95; C. W. Moore Fel, 96; Outstanding Hist Prof, Univ Houston at Clear Lake, 99; Phi Kappa Phi Fac, 2000. **MEMBERSHIPS** Am Hist Asn, Soc of Ethnohistorians, French Colonial Hist Soc, East Tex Hist Asn. **RESEARCH** Colonial history-Spanish, French, and English; Latin American ethnohistory. **SELECTED PUBLICATIONS** Auth, "Jean-Baptiste Cabert's Native American Policy," La Hist; auth,. "The Myth and Reality: The Jacksons of Texas," East Tex Hist, auth, "Perceptions and Reality: Count Frontenac and the Icoquas League," UCLA Hist; auth, "Jean-Charlesde Boas," Proceedings of the French Colonial Historical Society. **CONTACT ADDRESS** Dept Human Scis, Univ of Houston, Clear Lake, 2700 Bay Area Blvd, Houston, TX 77058-1025. **EMAIL** PetrovichA@cl.uh.edu

PETRUSEWITZ, MARTA
PERSONAL Born 04/25/1948, Warsaw, Poland **DISCIPLINE** HISTORY **EDUCATION** Univ Bologna, PhD, 75; Univ Warsaw, BA. **CAREER** Lecturer, Social Studies, Harvard Univ, 78-82; Asst Prof, Princeton Univ, 82-89; Prof of Modern European History, CUNY Hunter Col and the Graduate Ctr. **HONORS AND AWARDS** "Sila Prize" for the best scholarly work in Social Sciences for Latifondo, 89; "Salvatore Valititi Prize" for Come il Meridione; 98; Melloy Foundation, ACLS, Jean Mounet, Fulbright, Ford Foundation, National Humanities. **RESEARCH** European "peripheries" (Poland, Italy, Ireland); Haliau history; 19th century social and economic. **SELECTED PUBLICATIONS** Auth, Passaggi di frontiera: conversazione con Albert O. Hirschman, ed. With Carmine Donzelli and Claudia Rusconi (Rome: Donzelli, 94); auth, Latifundium: Moral Economy and Material Life in a 19th-Century Periphery (Ann Arbor: Univ of MI Press), 96; auth, Un sogno irlandese: la sortia die Constance Markiewicz comandante dell'IRA (Roma: ManifestoLIbri), 98; auth, Come il Meridione divenne una Questione. Rappresentazioni del Sud prima e dopo il Quarantotto (Soveria Manelli: Rubettino), 98; auth, "Letteratura e scienze sociali," in Letteratura e, ed. Lia de Finis, Associazione Culturale," (Antonio Rosmini, Trento), 98; auth, "Before the Southern Question" in Jane Scheneider, ed., Italy's Southern Question: 'Orientalism' in One Country (Oxford: Berg Publishers, 98); auth, "The Demise of Latifundism," in: The New History of the Italian South. Revisiting the Mezzogiorno, ed. By Robert Lumley and Jonathan Morris (Edinburg: Exeter Pr, 98); auth, Oltre il meridionalismo: Nuove prospettive sul Mezzogiorno d' Italia (Roma: Carocci, 99); auth, "A nazione mancata: The Construction of the Mezzogiorno after 1848", in: Memory and Myth in the Construction of Community, ed. By Bo Strath (Brussels: P.I.E.-Peter Lang, 00). **CONTACT ADDRESS** Dept History, Hunter Col, CUNY, 695 Park Ave, New York, NY 10021-5024. **EMAIL** mpetruse@shiva.hunter.cuny.edu

PETRY, CARL F.
PERSONAL Born 06/29/1943, Camden, NJ, s **DISCIPLINE** HISTORY **EDUCATION** Carleton Col, BA, 65; Univ Mich, MA, 66; PhD, 74. **CAREER** Asst prof, Northwestern Univ, Evanston, 74-80, assoc prof, 80-92, prof, 92-. **HONORS AND AWARDS** C. D. McCormick Prof of Teaching Excellence, NYU; Am Res Center in Egypt, 81; U.S. Information Agency, Cairo, 85; John Simon Guggenheim Fel, 87; Inst for Advanced Study, 96; ACLS, 200-2001; Nat Humanities Center, 2000-01. **MEMBERSHIPS** Middle East Studies Asn of North Am, Am Res Center in Egypt. **RESEARCH** Medieval and modern history of the Islamic Middle East. **SELECTED PUBLICATIONS** Auth, The Civilian Elite of Cairo in the Later Middle Ages: Social Autonomy and Political Adversity in Mamluk Egypt, Princeton Univ Press, Princeton Studies in the Near East (82); auth, Twilight of Majesty: The Reigns of the Mamluk Sultans al-Ashraf Qaytbay and Qansuh al-Ghawri in Egypt, Univ Washington Press(93); auth, Protectors of Praetorians? The Last Mamluk Sultans and Egypt's Waning as a Great Power, SUNY Press (Medieval Middle East Hist Series, 94); auth, "Conjugal Rights vs Class Perogatives: A Divorce Case in Mamluk Cairo," in Women in the Medieval Dar al-Islam: Power, Patronage and Piety, ed by Gavin Hambly, St Martin's Press (97): 227-40; auth, ""Disruptive 'Others' as Depicted in Chronicles of the Late Mamluk Period," Proceedings of the Conf on the Histori-

ography of Islamic Egypt, St Andrews Univ (Aug 97); auth, "A Geniza for Mamluk Studies? Charitable Trust (Waqf) Documents as a Source for Economic and Social History," Mamluk Studies Rev, 2 (98): 51-60; ed and contribur, The Cambridge History of Egypt, Vol, 1: Islamic Egypt, 6400-1517, Cambridge Univ Press (98); auth, " 'Quis Custodiet Custodes?' Revisited: The Prosecution of Crime in the Late Mamluk Sultanate," Mamluk Studies Rev 3 (99); auth, "Robing Ceremonials in Late Mamluk Egypt: Hallowed Traditions, Shifting Protocols," Robes and Honor: The Medieval World of Ihvestiture, ed by Stewart Gordon, The New Middle Age Series, ed by Bonnie Wheeler, St Martin's Press (2000); auth, "Egypt, Medieval," in The MacMillan Encyclopedia of Slavery, ed by T. McCarthy, MacMillan (forthcoming). **CONTACT ADDRESS** Dept Hist, Northwestern Univ, 2020 Harris, Evanston, IL 60208-2220. **EMAIL** c-petry@northwestern.edu

PFAFF, RICHARD W.
PERSONAL Born 08/06/1936, Oklahoma City, OK, m, 1962, 1 child **DISCIPLINE** HISTORY **EDUCATION** Harvard Univ, AB, 57; Oxford Univ, BA, 59; MA, 63; DPhil, 65; DD, 95. **CAREER** Asst prof, Univ North Car, 67; assoc prof, 70; prof, 75-. **HONORS AND AWARDS** Phi Beta Kappa; Rhodes Scholarshp; Hon Vpres Henry Bradshaw Soc; Fellow of RHS, SAL, NHC, MAA. **MEMBERSHIPS** ASCH; EHS; Hagiography Soc; ISAS; MAA; RHS; SAL; NHC. **RESEARCH** Medieval England; liturgy; manuscripts; architecture; monastic culture; Anglo-Saxon England; liturgy in general. **SELECTED PUBLICATIONS** Auth, New Liturgical Feasts in Later Medieval England, 70; auth, Montague Rhodes James, 80; auth, Medieval Latin Liturgy: A Select Bibliography, 82; coauth, The Eadwine Psalter, 92; ed, The Liturgical Books of Anglo-Saxon England, 97; ed, Liturgical Calendars, Saints and Services in Medieval England, 98. **CONTACT ADDRESS** Dept History, Univ of No Carolina, Chapel Hill, CB 3195, Chapel Hill, NC 27599-2319. **EMAIL** pfaffrw@email.unc.edu

PFEFFER, PAULA F.
PERSONAL Born Chicago, IL, m, 3 children **DISCIPLINE** HISTORY **EDUCATION** NEast Univ, BA, 70; MA, 74; PhD, 80. **CAREER** Grad asst, 71-73, instr, 74-76; NEast Univ; teach asst, 76-79; instr, 80, NWest Univ; instr, 74-79; asst prof, 79-87; assoc prof, 87-91; MunD Coll; assoc prof, 91-00; prof, 00-, Loy Univ. **HONORS AND AWARDS** Hum Rts Awd, GMC-SHR, 91; Loyola Univ Res Lve, 97-98; McCormick Fac Fel; Pulitzer Prize Consideree, 91. **MEMBERSHIPS** AAUW; CAWHC; AHA; CCW; AG; OAH; ILHS; SWHG. **RESEARCH** Social welfare history; women's history; labor history; US cultural history. **SELECTED PUBLICATIONS** Auth, A Philip Randolph, Pioneer of the Civil Rights Movement, Louisiana State Univ Press (Baton Rouge), 90; pb, (96); auth, "A Philip Randolph and Bayard Rustin After 1960," in Black Conservatism, ed. Peter Eisenstadt (NY: Garland Pub, 99); auth, "Eleanor Roosevelt, the National and World Women's Parties," Hist 59 (96): 39-57; auth, "The Women Behind the Union: Halena Wilson, Rosina Tucker, and the Ladies' Auxiliary to the Brotherhood of Sleeping Car Porters," Labor Hist 36 (95): 557-78; auth, "A Philip Randolph," in American National Biography, ed. John A. Garraty (Cary, NC: Oxford Univ Press, 99); auth, "Esther Loeb Kohn," in Jewish Women in America: An Historical Encyclopedia, eds. Paula Hyman, Beborah Dash Moore (NY: Routledge, 97); auth, "Brotherhood of Sleeping Car Porters," in Encyclopedia of African-American Culture and History (NY: Macmillan Pub, 95); auth, "Frank Crosswaith," in Encyclopedia of African-American Culture and History (NY: Macmillan Pub, 95); auth, "Halena Wilson," in African American Women: A Biographical Dictionary, ed. Dorothy C Salem (NY: Garland Pub, 93); auth, "Anna Arnold Hedgeman," in Black Women in the United States: An Historical Encyclopedia, ed. Darlene Clark Hine (Brooklyn, NY: Carlson Pub, 93). **CONTACT ADDRESS** Dept History, Loyola Univ, Chicago, 6525 North Sheridan Rd, Chicago, IL 60626-5344. **EMAIL** ppfeffe@orion.it.luc.edu

PFLUGFELDER, GREGORY
DISCIPLINE JAPANESE HISTORY **EDUCATION** Harvard Univ, BA, 81, Stanford Univ, PhD, 96. **CAREER** Asst prof. **SELECTED PUBLICATIONS** Auth, Seiji to daidokoro: Akita-ken joshi sanseiken undoshi (Politics and the kitchen: a history of the women's suffrage movement in Akita prefecture), 86; "Strange Fates: Sex, Gender, and Sexuality, in Torikaebaya Monogatari", Monumenta Nipponica 47, (92); auth, Cartographies of Desire: Male-Male Sexuality in Japanese Discourse, 1600-1950, 99. **CONTACT ADDRESS** Dept of Hist, Columbia Col, New York, 2960 Broadway, New York, NY 10027-6902.

PFUND, PETER H.
PERSONAL Born 10/06/1932, Bryn Mawr, PA, m, 1959, 2 children **DISCIPLINE** HISTORY, LAW **EDUCATION** Amherst Col, BA, 54; Univ of PA Law Sch, JD, 59. **CAREER** US Dept of St, Office of the Legal Adviser, full-time, 59-97; asst legal adviser for private int law, 79-97; special adviser for pvt int law, 97-. **HONORS AND AWARDS** Am Bar Asn, Sect for Int Law & Pract, Leonard J. Theberge Prize for Pvt Int Law, 87; Commendation, ABA Section of Intl Law Practice, 97; Awd of Appreciation, Joint Council on Intl Children's Services, 99; Special Achiev Awd, New York State Bar Assoc, 99; Hall of Fame Awd, Nat Council for Adoption, 00 . **MEMBERSHIPS** Am Law Inst; German-American Lawyers Asn, Bonn, Ger. **SELECTED PUBLICATIONS** Auth, Contributing to Professional Development of Private International Law: The International Process and the United States Approach, 249 Receuil des cours 9-144, 94-V; and other publications. **CONTACT ADDRESS** 10419 Pearl St, Fairfax, VA 22032-3824. **EMAIL** pfund.ph@gateway.net

PHILLIPS, ANN
DISCIPLINE EUROPEAN POLITICS **EDUCATION** Denison Univ, BA; John Hopkins Univ, MA; Georgetown Univ, PhD. **CAREER** Prof, Am Univ. **RESEARCH** Transferability of institutions from west to east in the democratization of Central-East Europe. **SELECTED PUBLICATIONS** Auth, Soviet Policy Toward East Germany Reconsidered: The Postwar Decade, Greenwood Press, 86; An Island of Stability? The German Political Party System and the Elections of 1994, W Europ Pol, 95. **CONTACT ADDRESS** American Univ, 4400 Massachusetts Ave, Washington, DC 20016.

PHILLIPS, C. ROBERT, III
DISCIPLINE ANCIENT HISTORY AND LITERATURE **EDUCATION** PhD, Brown Univ. **CAREER** Prof, Lehigh Univ **RESEARCH** Social history and Greco-Roman religion. **SELECTED PUBLICATIONS** Areas: Roman religion, early christianity, and magic. **CONTACT ADDRESS** Lehigh Univ, Bethlehem, PA 18015.

PHILLIPS, CARLA RAHN
PERSONAL Born 11/14/1943, Los Angeles, CA, m, 1970 **DISCIPLINE** HISTORY **EDUCATION** Pomona Col, BA, 65; NYork Univ, MA, 66, PhD, 72. **CAREER** Instr, 70, Rhode Island Col; instr, 70-72, San Diego City Col & San Diego Mesa Col; asst prof, 72-78, assoc prof, 78-86, prof, 86-, Univ Minn; vis prof, 87, Univ Calif San Diego. **HONORS AND AWARDS** Woodrow Wilson Dissertation Fellowship, 69-70; Leo Gershoy Prize, American Historical Association, 87 and 98; Spain in America Prize, Spain's Ministry of Culture, 87 and 92; Mcknight Foundation: Research Awd, 97-00; Busch Foundation: Sabbatical Supplement Grant, 91-92 and 00-01; Guggenheim foundation: Post-doctoral Fellowship, 87-88; Tinker Foundation: Post doctoral Fellowship, calendar year 83; Post-doctoral research fellowship: Program for Cultural Cooperation between Spain's Ministry of Culture and U.S. universities, 78. **RESEARCH** European hist, 1300-1800; Spain; economy & soc; exploration & discovery, maritime hist. **SELECTED PUBLICATIONS** Auth, Ciudad Real, 1500-1750: Growth, Crisis and Readjustment in the Spanish Economy, Harvard Univ, 79; coauth, "Spain's Golden Fleece: Wool Production and the Wool Trade from the Middle Ages to the Nineteenth Century," Johns Hopkins Univ, 97; coauth, "The Worlds of Christopher Columbus," Cambridge Univ 92; auth, "Six Galleons for the King of Spain: Imperial Defense in the Early Seventeenth Century, Johns Hopkins Univ, 86; auth, "Ciudad Real, 1500-1750: Growing Crisis and Readjustment in the Spanish Economy, Harvard Univ, 79. **CONTACT ADDRESS** Dept of History, Univ of Minnesota, Twin Cities, 614 Social Sciences, 267 19th Ave S., Minneapolis, MN 55455. **EMAIL** phill002@tc.umn.edu

PHILLIPS, GLENN OWEN
PERSONAL Born 09/26/1946, Bridgetown, Barbados, m, 1972, 1 child **DISCIPLINE** HISTORY **EDUCATION** Atlantic Union College, BA 1967; Andrews Univ, MA 1969; Howard Univ, PhD 1976. **CAREER** Caribbean Union Coll, lecturer 1969-71, Howard Univ, asst prof history 1981-82, Morgan State Univ, asst prof history 1978-, asst dir Univ Honors Program 1981-82, research assoc 1982-92, acting dir of Institute for Urban Research 1986-89, asst prof 1989-90; Morgan State Univ, Baltimore, MD, acting chair, dept of history, 89-90, 95-96, assoc prof, 90-. **HONORS AND AWARDS** HBCU Fac Fel United Negro Col Fund/US Dept of Lab, 80; Morgan State Univ Hon Member (Promethean Kappa Tau), 82; Cited Nat Dir Latin Am; Assoc ed Afro-Hispanic Rev, 82-84; Fulbright Summer Scholar, Cairo, Egypt, 94; Pride of Barbados Distinguished Awd, Nat Asn of Barbados Organization, 98. **MEMBERSHIPS** Asn of Caribbean Historians; Nat Historical Honors Soc; Am Asn of Univ Prof; Asn for the Study of African Am Life and Culture; Caribbean Studies Asn. **SELECTED PUBLICATIONS** Co-ed, The Caribbean Basin Initiative," 87; auth, The Makin gof Christian Col, 88; auth, Over a Century of Adventism; auth, The African Diaspora Experience, 98. **CONTACT ADDRESS** Department of History, Morgan State Univ, Cold Spring Ln & Hillen Rd, Baltimore, MD 21239. **EMAIL** gphillips@moac

PHILLIPS, IVORY
PERSONAL Born 08/14/1942, Rosedale, MS, m, 1986, 3 children **DISCIPLINE** HISTORY, SOCIAL STUDIES **EDUCATION** Jackson State Univ, BS, 63; Calif State Univ, MAT, 68; Univ Wash, PhD, 72. **CAREER** Social Studies Chemn, Immaculate Conception High Sch, 64-68; Soc Sci Chemn, Jackson State Univ, 71-84; Prof, Jackson State Univ, 68-; Fac Senate Pres, Jackson State Univ, 91-. **HONORS AND AWARDS** High Sch Valedictorian; Col Salutorian; STAR Teacher, Immaculate Conception; Teacher of the Year, Jackson State Univ; Who's Who Among Students; Who's Who Among Teachers; Alpha Kappa Mu; Sigma Rho Sigma; Alumnus of the Year, Rosedale High Sch. **MEMBERSHIPS** Asn of Soc and Behav Scientists, Nat Asn of African Am Studies, Asn for Study of African Am Life and Hist, Nat Coun for the Soc Studies. **RESEARCH** African American History and Culture. **SELECTED PUBLICATIONS** Auth, A Religion for Blacks in America; auth, Old Man Rivers Says Something; auth, The Black Bible; auth, White Racism and Black Powerlessness. **CONTACT ADDRESS** Dept Curriculum and Inst, Jackson State Univ, 1400 Lynch St, Jackson, MS 39217.

PHILLIPS, JOHN ALLEN
PERSONAL Born 09/22/1949, Dahlonega, GA, m, 1980, 1 child **DISCIPLINE** HANOVERIAN AND VICTORIAN ENGLAND **EDUCATION** Univ Ga, BA, 71; Univ Iowa, MA, 72, PhD(hist), 76. **CAREER** Asst prof, 76-82, Assoc Prof Hist, Univ Calif, Riverside, 82-, Regent's fac fel, Univ Calif, 77 & 80. **MEMBERSHIPS** Conf Brit Studies. **RESEARCH** Electoral behavior in unreformed and reformed Britain; English social history. **SELECTED PUBLICATIONS** Auth, Nominal Record Linkage, Univ Iowa, 76; Achieving a critical mass while avoiding an explosion: Letter-cluster sampling, J Interdisciplinary Hist, 79; The structure of the unreformed electorate, J Brit Studies, 79; Popular politics in unreformed England, J Mod Hist, 80; Electoral Behavior in Unreformed England, Princeton Univ Press, 82; Britons, Forging the Nation, 1707-1837 - Colley,L, Albion, Vol 0025, 1993; The Great-reform-act of 1832 and the Political Modernization of England, American Historical Review, Vol 0100, 1995; The Origins of Middle-class Culture - Halifax, Yorkshire, 1660-1780 - Smail,J, American Historical Review, Vol 0101, 1996; The Politics of the People in 18th-century Britain - Dickinson,T, J of Modern History, Vol 0069, 1997. **CONTACT ADDRESS** Dept of Hist, Univ of California, Riverside, Riverside, CA 92521.

PHILLIPS, RICHARD E.
PERSONAL Born 12/13/1950, Los Angeles, CA, d, 2 children **DISCIPLINE** ART HISTORY **EDUCATION** Univ Texas, PhD 93. **CAREER** Univ of Texas - Pan American, asst prof 00-; VA commonwealth Univ, asst prof 95-00, Savannah Col, prof 92-93. **HONORS AND AWARDS** Samuel H. Kress Gnt. **MEMBERSHIPS** CAA; SAH; ALAA; ASHAHS. **RESEARCH** Spanish colonial architecture and its decoration in Latin America. **SELECTED PUBLICATIONS** Auth, " LaParticipacion Indigena en las Procesiones Claustrales," Relaciones, Univ deMichoacan, 99; auth, " Prilidiano Pueyrredon: The Pampas Landscapes," Latin Amer Art Mag, 90. **CONTACT ADDRESS** Pan American, Univ of Texas, Edinburg, 1201 W Univ Dr, Edinburg, TX 78539. **EMAIL** rphillip@hibbs.vcu.edu

PHILLIPS, RODERICK
DISCIPLINE MODERN HISTORY **EDUCATION** Trent Univ, BA, 71; Univ Otago, New Zealand, post grad dipl with credit, 72; Univ Oxford, PhD, 76. **CAREER** Prof, Carleton Univ. **RESEARCH** French Revolution. **SELECTED PUBLICATIONS** Auth, Putting Asunder: A History of Divorce in Western Society, New York and Cambridge: Cambridge Univ Press, 88; ed, "Reforming the French Family: The Reception of Law nad Policy in the Provinces," in Steven Reinhardt and Elizabeth Cawdon, eds., The French revolution: Paris and the Provinces, (Col Station, Tex: Tex A & M Univ Press, 91): 64-89; ed, "Une Perspectiva sobre la historia de la paternidad," int La Figura del padre en las Familias de la Sociedades Desarrolladas, (Las Palmas de Gran Canaria: Gobierno de Canarias, (95): 113-35; auth, Untying the Knot: A Short History of Divorce, Cambridge and New York: Cambridge Univ Press, 91; auth, "Historical Perspectives on stepfamilies," Marriage and Family Review 28, (96), (forthcoming); auth, Society, State and Nation in Twentieth-Century Europe, Upper Sallde River, NJ: Prentice Hall, 96; ed, "Divorce, Remarriage, and Step-Families," in A History of the European Family, eds., Marzio Barbagli and David I. Kertzer, (Milan: Laterza and New Haven: Yale Univ Press, (forthcoming 00). **CONTACT ADDRESS** Dept of Hist, Carleton Univ, 1125 Colonel By Dr, Ottawa, ON, Canada K1S 5B6. **EMAIL** rodphill@ccs.carleton.ca

PHILLIPS, WILLIAM D., JR
PERSONAL Born 06/26/1943, Dallas, TX, m, 1970 **DISCIPLINE** HISTORY **EDUCATION** Univ Miss, BA, 64; Univ Tenn, MA, 66; NYork Univ, PhD, 71. **CAREER** Instr, Rhode Island Col, 69-70; asst prof, San Diego State Univ, 70-75, assoc prof, 75-78, prof, 78-88; prof, Univ Minn, 88-. **HONORS AND AWARDS** Nat Endowment for the Humanities, fel, 88-89; Spain in America Prize, second prize, 93; Leo Gershoy Awd, Am Hist Asn, 98. **MEMBERSHIPS** Am Hist Asn, Medieval Acad of Am, Soc for Spanish and Portuguese Hist Studies. **RESEARCH** History of Medieval Spain, European expansion, slavery. **SELECTED PUBLICATIONS** Auth, Enrique IV and the Crisis of Fifteenth-Century Castile, 1425-1480, Speculum Anniversary Monographs , 3, Cambridge, Mass: Medieval Acad of Am (78); auth, Slavery from Roman Times to the Early Transatlantic Trade, Minneapolis: Univ Minn Press (85), British ed, Manchester, England: Manchester Univ Press (85), Spanish transl, La esclavitud desde la epoca romana hasta los

inicios del comercio transatlantica, transl, Elena Perez Ruiz de Velasco, Madrid: Siglo XXI de Espana (89); auth, Historia de la esclavitud en Espana, transl, Leopoldo Fornes Bonavia, Madrid: Editorial Playor (90); coauth with Carla Rahn Phillips, The Worlds of Christopher Columbus, Cambridge and New York: Cambridge Univ Press (92), paperback (93), "Spain in America Prize," second prize from Spanish government, 1993, cited by the New York Times Book Rev as a notable book of 1992; coauth with Carla Rahn Phillips, Spain's Golden Fleece: Wool Production and the Wool Trade from the Middle Ages to the Nineteenth Century, Baltimore: Johns Hopkins Univ Press (97), "Leo Gershoy Award" of the Am Hist Asn for 1998. **CONTACT ADDRESS** Dept Hist, Univ of Minnesota, Twin Cities, 267 19th Ave S, Minneapolis, MN 55455. **EMAIL** phill004@umn.edu

PHILP, KENNETH
PERSONAL Born 12/06/1941, Pontiac, MI, m, 1968, 1 child **DISCIPLINE** RECENT AMERICAN HISTORY **EDUCATION** Mich State Univ, BA, 63, PhD, 68; Univ Mich, MA, 64. **CAREER** Asst prof, 68-73, assoc prof, 73-80, prof hist, Univ Tx, 80-, mem, Region 7 Nat Arch Adv Coun, 76-78. **MEMBERSHIPS** AHA; Orgn Am Historians; Western Hist Asn. **RESEARCH** American Indian history. **SELECTED PUBLICATIONS** Auth, Albert Fall and the protest from the Pueblos, 1921-1923, Ariz & the West, fall 70; Herbert Hoover's new era: A false dawn for the American Indian, 1929-1932, Rocky Mountain Soc Sci J, 4/72; John Collier's crusade to protect Indian religious freedom, J Ethnic Studies, spring 73; contribr, Indian-White Relations: A Persistent Paradox, Howard Univ, 76; auth, Turmoil at Big Cypress: Seminole deer and the Florida cattle tick controversy, Fla Hist Quart, 7/77; John Collier's Crusade For Indian Reform, 1920-1954, Univ Ariz, 77; John Collier and the Indians of the Americas: The dream and the reality, Prologue: The J Nat Arch, spring 79; New Deal for Alaska natives, Pac Hist Rev, 8/81; Termination: A Legacy of the Indian New Deal, W Hist Quart, 83; Stride Toward Freedom: The Relocation of Indians to Cities, 1952-1960, W Hist Quart, 85; Dillon S Myer and the Advent of Termination, West Hist Quart, 88; Ed, Indian Self-Rule: First-Hand Accounts of Indian-White Relations from Roosevelt to Reagan, Howe Bros, 86; Termination Revisited Native Americans on the Trail to Self-Determination, 1933-1953, Univ Ne, 99. **CONTACT ADDRESS** Dept Hist, Univ of Texas, Arlington, Arlington, TX 76019.

PHILYAW, SCOTT L.
DISCIPLINE HISTORY **EDUCATION** Univ NC, PhD. **CAREER** Hist, W Carolina Univ. **SELECTED PUBLICATIONS** Auth, After the Backcountry: Rural Life and Society, Nineteenth-Century Valley of VA, 98. **CONTACT ADDRESS** Dept of Hist, Western Carolina Univ, Cullowhee, NC 28723. **EMAIL** registrar@wcu.edu

PICCATO, PABLO
DISCIPLINE LATIN AMERICAN HISTORY **EDUCATION** La Universidad Nacional Autonoma de Mexico, BA, 90; Univ Tex, PhD, 97. **CAREER** Hist, Columbia Univ **SELECTED PUBLICATIONS** Auth, Understanding Society: Porfirian Discourse about Criminality and Alcolohism; Los intentos de establecer el parlamentarismo desde la Camara de Diputados, 1912-1921: Entre la opinion publica y los grupos de choque; La experiencia penal en la ciudad de Mexico: cambios y permanencias tras la revolucion. **CONTACT ADDRESS** Columbia Univ, 2960 Broadway, New York, NY 10027-6902.

PICKENS, DONALD KENNETH
PERSONAL Born 05/28/1934, FOSS, OK, m, 1957, 2 children **DISCIPLINE** UNITED STATES SOCIAL & INTELLECTUAL HISTORY **EDUCATION** Univ Okla, BA, 56, MA, 57; Univ Tex, PhD(hist), 64. **CAREER** Asst prof US hist, Tarleton State Col, 57-58; assoc prof, Southwestern State Col, 62-65; assoc prof, 65-76, Prof Us Hist, North Tex State Univ, 76-. **MEMBERSHIPS** Orgn Am Historians; Am Studies Asn. **RESEARCH** Women in United States history; United States historiography; history of ideas. **SELECTED PUBLICATIONS** Auth, The sterilization movement, Phylon, 67; Eugenics and the Progressives, Vanderbilt Univ, 68; coauth, America in Process, Winston, 73; auth, Infinite desires in a finite world, Soc Sci Quart, 9/76; Henry Adams's failures: A success story, Am Quart, fall 81; Westward expansion and the end of American exceptionalism: Sumner, Turner, and Webb, Western Hist Quart, 10/81; The historical images in Republican campaign songs, 1860- 1900, J Popular Cult, winter 81; Walter Prescott Webb's tomorrow, Red River Hist Rev, winter 81; the End of American Exceptionalism - Frontier Anxiety from the Old West to the New- deal - Wrobel,dm, J of the West, Vol 0034, 1995; Race and Labor in Western Copper - the Fight for Equality, 1896-1918 - Mellinger,pj, J of the West, Vol 0035, 1996. **CONTACT ADDRESS** Dept of Hist, Univ of No Texas, Denton, TX 76201. **EMAIL** dpickens@facstaff.cas.unt.edu

PICKETT, TERRY H.
PERSONAL Born 04/14/1941, Washington, GA, m, 1962, 2 children **DISCIPLINE** GERMAN STUDIES **EDUCATION** Univ of Ga, AB, 66; Univ of Ala, MA, 68; Vanderbilt Univ, PhD, 70. **CAREER** Prof Emeritus, Univ of Ala, 69-97; vis prof, N Ga Col and State Univ, 98-00. **HONORS AND AWARDS** Fulbright Scholar, 72-73, 80-81, & 89-90; IREX; NEH; DAAD; Univ Res Grants. **MEMBERSHIPS** SAMLA. **RESEARCH** 18th-19th Century. **SELECTED PUBLICATIONS** Auth, "The Unseasonable Democrat: K. A. Varnhagen von Ense 1785-1858," Modern Ger Studies vol 14, Bouvier Verlag Herbert Grundmann (Bonn), 85; coauth, The Letters of the American Socialist Albert Brisbane To K. A. Varnhagen von Ense, Carl Winter Univ Publ, 86; auth, "Bettina's englisches Wagnis in Light of the Correspondence between Sarah Austin and Bettina von Amim," Euphorion. Zeitschrift fuer Literaturgeschichte 84 (90): 397-407; auth, "Harriet Grote's Correspondence with K. A. Varnhagen von Ense 1845-1854," Cahiers Victoriens & Edouardiens 37 (93): 13-53; auth, "The Bruderkrieg and the Crisis of Constitutional Government: The Treatment of the American Civil War by Georg von Cotta's German War Correspondents 1861-65," Schatzkammer der deutschen Literatur und Geschichte XX (94): 13-15; auth, "Inventing Nations: Justifications of Authority in the Modern World," Contributions in Philos 56, Westport (London, Eng), 96. **CONTACT ADDRESS** Dept Lang and Lit, No Georgia Col, 100 College Cr, Dahlonega, GA 30597-0001. **EMAIL** tpic940967@aol.com

PICKLESIMER, DORMAN
DISCIPLINE COMMUNICATION, HISTORY **EDUCATION** Morehead State Univ, AB, 60; Bowling Green State Univ, MA, 65; Ind Univ, PhD, 69. **CAREER** Prof, Boston Col, 69-. **HONORS AND AWARDS** Phi Kappa Delta; Gold Key Honor Soc. **MEMBERSHIPS** Nat Communication Asn; Eastern Communication Asn; World Communication Asn. **RESEARCH** History of American public address; classical rhetoric. **CONTACT ADDRESS** Dept of Communcations, Boston Col, Chestnut Hill, Lyons Hall 215, Chestnut Hill, MA 02167. **EMAIL** picklesi@bC.edu

PIEHLER, G. KURT
DISCIPLINE AMERICAN MILITARY, SOCIAL HISTORY, PUBLIC HISTORY **EDUCATION** Drew Univ, BA, 82; Rut Univ, MA, 85; PhD, 90. **CAREER** Asst ed, CUNY, 90-93; dept dir, Rut Univ, 94-98; asst prof, dept dir, Univ Tenn, 99-. **HONORS AND AWARDS** RCHA Fel; NHPR Fel. **MEMBERSHIPS** AHA; OAH; SMH; OHA; NCPH; ADE. **RESEARCH** World War II; Veterans and American society; history and memory; oral history. **SELECTED PUBLICATIONS** Auth, Remembering the American Way, Smithson Inst Press (Washington), 95; coauth, Major Problems in American Military History, Houghton Mifflin (Boston), 99; consul ed, Oxford Companion to American Military History, Oxford Univ Press (NY), 99. **CONTACT ADDRESS** Dept History, Univ of Tennessee, Knoxville, 915 Volunteer Blvd, Knoxville, TN 37996-4065. **EMAIL** gpiehler@utk.edu

PIERARD, RICHARD VICTOR
PERSONAL Born 05/29/1934, Chicago, IL, m, 1957, 2 children **DISCIPLINE** MODERN EUROPEAN HISTORY, HISTORY OF CHRISTIANITY **EDUCATION** CA State Univ, Los Angeles, BA, 58, MA, 59; Univ IA, PhD, 64. **CAREER** Tchg asst Western civilization, Univ IA, 59-64; from asst prof to assoc prof, 64-72, prof hist, IN State Univ, Terre Haute, 72-00, emer, 00; Vis prof, Greenville Col, 72-73; vis prof, Fuller Theol Seminary, 88, 91; Fulbright prof, Univ Frankfurt, Ger, 84-85; Univ Halle-Wittenberg, Ger, 89-90; vis prof, Gordon Col, 00-01. **HONORS AND AWARDS** Research and Creativity award, In-State Univ, 94; Eternal Flame award, Scholars' conf on the Holocaust and the Churches, 00. **MEMBERSHIPS** AHA; Conf Faith & Hist (secy-treas, 67-); Am Soc Church Hist; Am Soc Missiology. **RESEARCH** Europ polit and relig expansion into Africa since 1800; mod Germany; conservative relig and polit ideas. **SELECTED PUBLICATIONS** Ed, The Revolution of the Candles, Mercer, 96; auth, Shaking the Foundations: World War I, The Western Allies, and German Protestant Missions, International Bulletin of Missionary Research, 98; auth, Informers or Resisters? The East German Secret Police and the Church, Christian Scholars Rev, 98; auth, Christianity Outside North American, In World War II in Asia and the Pacific and the War's Aftermath, Greenwood, 98; auth, Evangelical and Ecumenical: Missionary Leaders in Mainline Protestantism, In Re-forming the Center, Eerdmans, 98; auth, The Coming of the New Millennium, Evangelical Rev of Theology, 99; auth, The New Millenium Manual, Baker, 99; auth, The Globalization of Baptist History, American Baptist Quarterly, 00. **CONTACT ADDRESS** 633 Hollowbrook Ct, Terre Haute, IN 47803. **EMAIL** CharRichP@aol.com

PIERCE, RICHARD A.
DISCIPLINE RUSSIAN AMERICA **EDUCATION** Univ CA, PhD, 56. **CAREER** Univ Alaska **SELECTED PUBLICATIONS** Auth, Russian America: A Biographical Dictionary; Ed, G.H. van Langsdorff, Remarks and Observations on a Voyage Around the World, 1803-1807; K.T. Khlebnikov. Notes on Russian America. **CONTACT ADDRESS** Univ of Alaska, Fairbanks, PO Box 757480, Fairbanks, AK 99775-7480.

PIERPAOLI, PAUL G.
PERSONAL Born 04/17/1962, Ann Arbor, MI **DISCIPLINE** HISTORY **EDUCATION** Hampden Sydney Col, BA, 84; Ohio State Univ, MA, 90; PhD, 95. **CAREER** Vis asst prof, Hampden Sydney Col, 95-96; vis asst prof, Univ Ariz, 96-98; adj prof, asst to pres, Vir Mil Inst, 98-00. **HONORS AND AWARDS** Truman Fel; DuPont Sum Sem; Phi Kappa Phi; Pi Delta Phi; Pi Sigma Alpha; Phi Alpha Theta; Who's Who in Am, 00. **MEMBERSHIPS** AHA; OAH; SHAFR; SMH; EBHS. **RESEARCH** Contemporary US History; National Security; Social and Political History. **SELECTED PUBLICATIONS** Auth, Truman and Korea: The Political Culture of the Early Cold War, 99; assoc ed, The Encyclopedia of the Korean War, 00; Auth, "Truman's Other War: The Battle for the American Homefront, 1950-53," OAH Hist (00); auth, "From Fair Deal to No Deal: Truman's Domestic Agenda and the Korean War," The Encyclopedia of the Korean War, (00); auth, "Corporatist and Voluntarist Approaches to Cold War Rearmament: The Private Side of Industrial and Economic Mobilization, 1950-1953," Essays in Economic Bus Hist, (97); auth, "Mobilizing for the Cold War: The Korean Conflict and the Birth of the National Security State," Essays in Economic Bus Hist, (94). **CONTACT ADDRESS** Dept History, Virginia Military Inst, 210 Smith Hall, Lexington, VA 24450-0304. **EMAIL** pierpaolipg@vmi.edu

PIERSON, PETER O'MALLEY
PERSONAL Born 10/04/1932, Indianapolis, IN **DISCIPLINE** EARLY MODERN EUROPEAN HISTORY **EDUCATION** UCLA, BA, 54, MA, 63, PhD, 66. **CAREER** From instr to asst prof, 66-77, assoc prof 77-89, prof to prof emer hist, Univ Santa Clara, 89-, Dept Ch, 88-92. **HONORS AND AWARDS** Lee and Seymour Graff Prof, 93; Fac Senate Prof; Fulbright Fel, Spain, 64-66; Nat Endowment for Hum fel, 74. **MEMBERSHIPS** Soc Span & Port Hist Studies; Historians Early Mod Europe. **RESEARCH** Span government and nobility of the period of Philip II. **SELECTED PUBLICATIONS** Auth, A commander for the Armada, Mariner's Mirror, 11/69; Philip II of Spain, Thames & Hudson, 75; Commander of the Armada: The Seventh Duke of Medina Sidonia, Yale, 89; Brethren of the Coast, MHQ: Quart Jour Military Hist, autumn 94; Elizabeth's Pirate Admiral, MHQ, summer 96; Lepanto, MHQ, winter 97; History of Spain, Greenwood, 98. **CONTACT ADDRESS** Dept of Hist, Santa Clara Univ, 500 El Camino Real, Santa Clara, CA 95053-0285. **EMAIL** ppierson@mailer.scu.edu

PIERSON, RUTH
PERSONAL Born Seattle, WA **DISCIPLINE** HISTORY **EDUCATION** Univ Wash, BA, 60, MA, 63; Yale Univ, PhD, 70. **CAREER** Tchg asst, Univ Wash, 61-63; asst instr, Yale Univ, 66-67; lectr, Univ Maryland, Col Park, 68-69; asst prof, 70-76, assoc prof, 76-80, Memorial Univ Newfoundland; assoc prof, 80-90, prof, Ont Inst Stud Educ, Univ Toronto, 90-. **MEMBERSHIPS** Can Hist Asn; Can Comt Women's Hist; Can Women's Stud Asn; Int Fedn Res Women Hist. **RESEARCH** Race, class and gender in hist sociology; women and colonialism, imperialism, and nationalism; feminist studies in education. **SELECTED PUBLICATIONS** Auth, They're Still Women After All: the Second World War and Canadian Womanhood, 86; auth, Women and Peace: Theoretical, Historical and Practical Perspectives, 87; auth, No Easy Road: Women in Canada 1920s to 1960s, 90; coauth, Strong Voices, Vol 1 in Can Women's Issues, 93. **CONTACT ADDRESS** OISE, Univ of Toronto, 252 Bloor St W, Toronto, ON, Canada M5S 1V6. **EMAIL** rrpierson@oise.utoronto.ca

PIKE, FREDRICK B.
PERSONAL Born 12/23/1924, Los Angeles, CA, m, 1971, 3 children **DISCIPLINE** HISTORY **EDUCATION** Loyola Univ, Los Angeles, BA, 49; Univ Tex, MA, 51, PhD, 56. **CAREER** From asst prof to assoc prof, 53-69, Prof Hist, Univ Notre Dame, 69-88 (emeritus), Grants, Doherty Found, Chile, 59-60 & Soc Sci Res Coun, Peru, 63-. **HONORS AND AWARDS** Guggenheim Found, Spain, 68-69; Bolton Prize, (AHA), 63. **RESEARCH** Colonial Latin American institutions; United States-Latin American relations; Spain and Sp. Am. **SELECTED PUBLICATIONS** Auth, Chile and the United States, 1880-1962, 62 & ed, Freedom and Reform in Latin America, 59, Univ Notre Dame; auth, Hispanismo 1898-1936, US and Andean Republics, 77; auth, Politics of the Miraculous in Pera, 86; auth, US and Latin America, 92; Peru Apra, Parties, Politics, and the Elusive Quest for Democracy - Graham,c/, Hispanic American Historical Review, Vol 0073, 1993; auth, FOR's Good Neighbor Policy, 95. **CONTACT ADDRESS** 4548 Middleton Park Cir W, Jacksonville, FL 32224-6627.

PIKE, RUTH
PERSONAL Born 07/26/1931, New York, NY **DISCIPLINE** MODERN EUROPEAN HISTORY **EDUCATION** Columbia Univ, BS, 53, MA, 54, PhD(Span hist), 59. **CAREER** Lectr, Brooklyn Col, 55-56; instr, Douglass Col, Rutgers Univ, 55-57; lectr Europ hist, Hunter Col, 57-58 & 59-60; instr Europ & Latin Am hist, Rutgers Univ, 60-61; from asst prof to assoc prof, 61-71, Prof Europ & Span Hist, Hunter Col, 72-, Am Coun Learned Soc grant-in-aid, 63-64; mem PhD prog in hist, City Univ NY, 67-; vis assoc prof hist, Johns Hopkins Univ, 69-; City Univ NY Res Found fac res award, 70-71 & 79-80. **HONORS AND AWARDS** John A Krout Prize Hist, Columbia Univ, 53; Newcomen Awd Bus Hist, 65. **MEMBERSHIPS** AHA; Econ Hist Asn; Conf Latin Am Hist; Am Asn Teachers Span & Port; Soc Span & Port Hist Studies. **SELECTED PUB-**

LICATIONS Auth, Enterprise and Adventure: The Genoese in Seville and the Opening of the New World, Cornell Univ, 66; The Converso family of Baltasar del Alcazar, Ky Romance Quart, 69; Slavery in Seville at the time of Columbus, In: From Reconquest to Empire: The Iberian Background of Latin American History, Knopf, 70; An urban minority: The Moriscos of Seville, Int J Mid E Studies, 71; Aristocrats and Traders: Sevillian Society in the Sixteenth Century, Cornell Univ, 72; Penal labor in sixteenth-century Spain: The mines of Almaden, Societas-Rev Soc Hist, 73; Crime and punishment in sixteenth-century Spain, J Europ Econ Hist, 76; Penal servitude in the Spanish Empire: Presidio labor in the eighteenth century, Hisp Am Hist Rev, 78. **CONTACT ADDRESS** Dept of Hist, Hunter Col, CUNY, 695 Park Ave, New York, NY 10021.

PILANT, CRAIG WESLEY
PERSONAL Born 08/26/1952, San Francisco, CA **DISCIPLINE** THEOLOGY, AMERICAN RELIGIOUS STUDIES, HISTORICAL THEOLOGY **EDUCATION** Loyola Univ, Chicago, BA, 74; Univ Ill, Chicago, MA, 83; Fordham Univ, MSEd, 87, PhD, 97. **CAREER** Dir of admissions, GSAS, 90-97, asst dean, GSAS, 97-, Fordham Univ. **MEMBERSHIPS** AAR; CHS; NAGAP. **RESEARCH** American religious history; hagiography; music and theology; Social Gospel; Orestes A. Brownson. **SELECTED PUBLICATIONS** Auth, Inward Promptings: Orestes A. Brownson, Outsidership and Roman Catholicism in the United States, 96. **CONTACT ADDRESS** Fordham Univ, 216 Keating Hall, 441 E Fordham Rd, Bronx, NY 10458-5161. **EMAIL** cwphd@aol.com

PILE, JOHN F.
PERSONAL Born 12/03/1924, Philadelphia, PA, m, 1965, 2 children **DISCIPLINE** ARCHITECTURE **EDUCATION** Univ Penn, BA; Beaux Arts Inst of Design, cert; Friends Design School, Philadelphia. **CAREER** Prof of Design, Pratt Inst, 48-98 ; assoc, George Nelson and Co., 51-61; independent design consult, 61- . **MEMBERSHIPS** Soc of Archit Hist. **RESEARCH** Architecture; design. **SELECTED PUBLICATIONS** Auth, Interior Design, Abrams; auth, Dictionary of 20th Century Design, Facts on File; auth, Furniture, Modern and Post Modern, Wiley; auth, Color in Interior Design, McGraw-Hill; auth, Hist of Interior Design, Calmann & King, John Wiley; auth, Perspective for Interior Designers, Whitney Library; auth, Open Office Planning, Whitney Library; auth, Design: Purpose, Form and Meaning, Univ Mass Press; coauth, Sketching Interior Architecture, Whitney Library; coauth, Drawing Interior Architecture, Whitney Library; auth, Interiors Third Book of Offices, Whitney Library; auth, Interiors Second Book of Offices, Whitney Library. **CONTACT ADDRESS** 13 Grace Court Alley, Brooklyn, NY 11201.

PILLSBURY, JOANNE
DISCIPLINE ART HISTORY, ARCHAEOLOGY **EDUCATION** Univ CA, Berkeley, BA (anthropology), 82; Columbia Univ, MA (art hist/anthropoplgy), 86, M Phil (art hist/anthropol), 87, PhD (art hist/anthropol), 93. **CAREER** Asst Dean, Center for Advanced Study in the Visual Arts, Nat Gallery of Art; lect (asst prof), Sainsbury Research Unit for the Arts of Africa, Oceania and the Americas, Univ of East Anglia, 91-; vis prof, The Johns Hopkins Univ, spring, 98, spring, 99. **HONORS AND AWARDS** Am Asn of Univ Women Fel, 89-90; Dumbarton Oaks Jr Fel in Pre-Columbian Studies, Washington, DC, 89-90; Samuel H Kress Found Project grant, 90; Fulbright Scholarship, Peru, 90-91; Andrew W Mellon, The Metropolitan Museum of Art, New York, 94-95. **MEMBERSHIPS** Asn for Latin Am Art (officer); Col Art Asn; Acive member, Inst of Andrean Studies, Berkeley (elected); Fel, Royal Anthropol Inst, London (elected); Soc for Am Archaeology. **RESEARCH** Pre-Columbian Art Hist: Archaeology. **SELECTED PUBLICATIONS** Auth, Technical Evidence for Temporal Placement: Sculpted Adobe Friezes of Chan Chan, Peru, in Materials Issues in Art and Archaeology III, eds, Pamela Vandiver, James Druzik, George Wheeler and Ian Freestone, Materials Res Soc Symposium Proceedings vol 267, 92; Los Relieves de Chan Chan: Nuevos Datos para el Estudio de la Sequencia y Ocupacion de la Ciudad, Revista del Museo Arqueologico de la Universidad Nacional de Trujillo, 95; Pre-Columbian Shellwork of South America, in The Dictionary of Art, ed, Jane Shoaf Turner, Macmillan, 96; The Thorny Oyster and the Origins of Empire: Implications of Recently Uncovered Spondylus Imagery from Chan Chan, Peru, Latin Am Antiquity, 7 (4), 96; Inka and Chimu entries, in The Spirit of Ancient Peru: Treasures from the Mudeo Arqueologico Rafael Larco Herrera, ed, Kathleen Berrin, Fine Arts Museums of San Francisco, 97; The Arts of Ancient Mesoamerica, with T Leyenaar, in Catalogue of the Robert and Lisa Sainsbury Collection, eds Steven Hooper, Yale Univ Press, 97; ed, Moche: Art and Archaeology of Ancient Peru, 01; coed, Palaces of the Ancient New World, (forthcoming). **CONTACT ADDRESS** Univ of East Anglia, Sainsbury Centre for Visual Arts, Norwich NR4 7TJ. **EMAIL** j.pillsbury@uea.ca.uk

PINA, LESLIE
PERSONAL Born Cleveland, OH, m, 1 child **DISCIPLINE** HISTORIC PRESERVATION **EDUCATION** Case Western Reserve Univ, BA, MA, PhD. **CAREER** Assoc prof. **SELECTED PUBLICATIONS** Auth, 50+ books, pubs on 20th century decorative arts. **CONTACT ADDRESS** Dept of Interior Design, Ursuline Col, 2550 Lander Road, Pepper Pike, OH 44124. **EMAIL** lpina@ursuline.edu

PINCH, TREVOR J.
PERSONAL Born 01/01/1952, Lisnaskea, N. Ireland, m, 1992, 2 children **DISCIPLINE** SOCIOLOGY, SCIENCE AND TECHNOLOGY STUDIES **EDUCATION** Bath Univ, UK, PhD, 82. **CAREER** Lectr, Dept of Sociology, York Univ, UK, 83-90; prof, Dept of Sci and Technol Stud, Cornell Univ, 90- . **HONORS AND AWARDS** Merton Prize, Am Sociol Asn, 95. **MEMBERSHIPS** ASA; SHOT; HSS. **RESEARCH** Sociology of science and technology, sound technologies and the synthesizer. **SELECTED PUBLICATIONS** Coauth, The Golem: What Everyone Should Know about Science, Cambridge, 94, 2d ed,98; co-ed, The Handbook of Science and Technology Studies, Sage, 95; coauth, The Golem at Large: What You Should Know about Technology, Cambridge, 98; auth, The Hard Sell: The Language and Lessons of Street-Wise Marketing, HarperCollins, 96. **CONTACT ADDRESS** Dept of Science and Technology Studies, Cornell Univ, Clark Hall 622, Ithaca, NY 14853. **EMAIL** TJP2@cornell.edu

PINDER, KYMBERLY
PERSONAL Born Baltimore, MD, m, 1994 **DISCIPLINE** ART HISTORY **EDUCATION** Middlebury Col, BA; Yale Univ, PhD. **CAREER** Instr, Middlebury Col; Saint Michael's Col; asst prof, 96-. **HONORS AND AWARDS** Henry Luce foundation fel; Sumner, McKnight, Crosby res grant. **SELECTED PUBLICATIONS** Pub(s), numerous critical essays. **CONTACT ADDRESS** Dept of Art Hist, Sch of the Art Inst of Chicago, 37 S Wabash Ave, Chicago, IL 60603. **EMAIL** kpinder@artic.edu

PINE, MARTIN L.
PERSONAL Born 11/04/1932, Bronx, NY, m, 1963, 1 child **DISCIPLINE** HISTORY **EDUCATION** Columbia Univ, BA, 54; MA, 56; PhD, 65. **CAREER** Asst Prof to Prof, Queens Col, 68-. **HONORS AND AWARDS** President's Awd, 91. **MEMBERSHIPS** Renaissance Soc of Am; Soc for Medieval and Renaissance Philos. **RESEARCH** Medieval and Renaissance intellectual history. **SELECTED PUBLICATIONS** Auth, "Pietro Pomponazzi," in The Routlege Encyclopedia of Philosophy, 98; auth, "Pietro Pomponazzi's Battle Against Religion and the Problem of the Defato," 99. **CONTACT ADDRESS** Dept Hist, Queens Col, CUNY, 6530 Kissena Blvd, Flushing, NY 11367-1575.

PINEO, RONN
PERSONAL Born 04/15/1954, Seattle, WA, m, 1978, 1 child **DISCIPLINE** HISTORY, LATIN AMERICAN STUDIES **EDUCATION** Univ Calif, Irvine, PhD, 87. **CAREER** To assoc prof and coordr for Latin Am Studies, Towson Univ, 88-. **HONORS AND AWARDS** Sturgis Leavitt Prize for best article, Southeastern Coun of Latin Am Studies, 92; NEH Summer Stipend, 92; NEH Study Grant, 93; Fulbright Lecturing and Res Awd, Ecuador, 97-98; Univ System of Md Bd of Regent's Fac Awd for Excellence in Teaching, 2000-2001. **MEMBERSHIPS** Pacific Coast Coun for Latin Am Studies. **RESEARCH** Andean history, public health care history. **SELECTED PUBLICATIONS** Auth, "Reinterpreting :Labor Militancy: The Collapse of the Cacao Economy and the General Strike of Guayaquil, Ecuador, 1922," Hispanic Am Hist Rev, 68:4 (Nov 88): 707-736; auth, "Misery and Death in the Pearl of the Pacific: Public Health Care in Guayaquil, Equador 1870-1925," Hispanic Am Hist Rev, 70:4 (Nov 90): 609-637; auth, "Recent Contributions to Ecuadorian Political History," Latin Am Perspectives 24: 3 (May 97): 104-116; auth, Social and Economic Reform in Ecuador: Life and Work in Guayaquil, 1870-1925, Gainesville, Fla: Univ Press of Fla (96); contrib co-ed with James Baer, Cities of Hope: People, Protests, and Progress in Urbanizing Latin America, 1870-1930, Boulder: Westview Press (98). **CONTACT ADDRESS** Dept Hist, Towson State Univ, 8000 York Rd, Baltimore, MD 21252-0001. **EMAIL** pineo@towson.edu

PINKETT, HAROLD THOMAS
PERSONAL Born 04/07/1914, Salisbury, MD, m, 1943 **DISCIPLINE** ARCHIVES, HISTORY **EDUCATION** Morgan Col, AB, 35; Univ Pa, AM, 38; Am Univ, PhD, 53. **CAREER** Teacher, High Sch, Md, 36-38; prof hist, Livingstone Col, 38-39 & 41-42; archivist, Nat Archs, 42-79; consult archivist & historian, 80-, Coun Libr Resources fel, 72-73; lectr hist & archival admin, Howard Univ, 70-76; lectr, Am Univ, Washington, DC, 76-77. **HONORS AND AWARDS** Bancroft Hist Prize, 47 & 48; book award, agric hist soc, 68. **MEMBERSHIPS** Fel Soc Am Archivists; AHA; Orgn Am Historians; Forest Hist Soc (pres, 76-78); Agr Hist Soc (pres, 82-83); SAA established Harold T. Pinkett Minority Student Award, 88. **RESEARCH** Archival administration, history and use; American conservation history; progressive era. **SELECTED PUBLICATIONS** Art, American Archival Theory: The State of the Art, American Archivist, summer 81, and other articles on M. H. Review, J. of Am. Histroy, Agric. History, and J. of Forest History; auth, National Church of Zion Methodism, 89; auth, Conservationists at the Cosmos Club, 90. **CONTACT ADDRESS** 5741 27th Street NW, Washington, DC 20015.

PINNELL, RICHARD
PERSONAL Born 01/09/1942, Whittier, CA, m, 1966, 3 children **DISCIPLINE** MUSIC HISTORY, GUITAR **EDUCATION** Univ Utah, BA; BYU, MA; UCLA, PhD, 76. **CAREER** Dept Music, Wisc Univ **HONORS AND AWARDS** Senior Res Fulbright to Argentina and Uruguay, 88-89. **RESEARCH** Women's music; jazz; Latin American music. **SELECTED PUBLICATIONS** Auth, Francesco Corbetta and the Baroque Guitar, UMI Res, 80; The Rioplatense Guitar, Bold Strummer, 93. **CONTACT ADDRESS** Dept of Music, Univ of Wisconsin, La Crosse, 1725 State St, La Crosse, WI 54601. **EMAIL** pinnell.rich@uwlax.edu

PINNEY, GLORIA FERRARI
DISCIPLINE CLASSICAL ARCHAELOGY **EDUCATION** Univ Cincinnati, PhD, 76. **CAREER** Asst prof, Wilson Col, 76-77; Lectr, Bryn Mawr Col, 71-81; Asst prof, 81-87; Assoc prof, 87-90; Prof, 90-93; Prof, Univ Chicago, 93-. **HONORS AND AWARDS** Fulbright Fel; Pew memorial Trust; Ailsa Mellon Bruce Senior Fel; Guggenheim Found; NEH grant. **SELECTED PUBLICATIONS** Auth, Il commercio dei sarcofagi asiatici, Rome, 66; Co-ed, Aspects of Ancient Greece, Allentown, 79; auth, Materiali del Museo Archeologico Nazionale di Tarquinia XI: I vasi attici a figure rosse del periodo arcaico, Rome, 88. **CONTACT ADDRESS** Dept of Art, Univ of Chicago, 5540 S Greenwood Ave, Chicago, IL 60637.

PINO, JULIO CESAR
PERSONAL Born 12/30/1960, Havana, Cuba, m, 1992 **DISCIPLINE** HISTORY **EDUCATION** Univ Calif, Los Angeles, BA, 84, MA, 87, PhD, 91. **CAREER** Vis prof, Univ Calif, Los Angeles, 91; vis prof, Bowdoin Col, 91-92; ASSOC PROF, HISTORY, KENT STATE UNIV, 92-. **HONORS AND AWARDS** Fulbright-Hays fel, 89-90; Kent State Univ summer grants, 93, 97, 99. **MEMBERSHIPS** AHA; Lat Am Stud Asn; Third World Studies Asn. **RESEARCH** Brazil; Cuba; African diaspora. **SELECTED PUBLICATIONS** Auth, Family and Favela: Reproduction of Poverty in Rio de Janeiro, Greenwood Press, 97; auth, Labor in the Favelas of Rio de Janeiro, Latin American Research Review 32:3, Nov 97; auth, Urban Squatter Households in Rio de Janeiro, 1940-1969, Locus: Regional and Local History of the Americas 8:2, May 96; auth, Teaching the History of Race in Latin America, Perspectives: Newsletter of the AHA 35:7, Oct 97; auth, Bay of Pigs Invasion, in Great Events from History: North American Series, Salem Press, 97. **CONTACT ADDRESS** Dept of History, Kent State Univ, Kent, OH 44242-0001. **EMAIL** jpino@phoenix.kent.edu

PINTNER, WALTER MCKENZIE
PERSONAL Born 06/19/1931, Yonkers, NY, m, 1958, 2 children **DISCIPLINE** RUSSIAN HISTORY **EDUCATION** Univ Chicago, AB, 51, MA, 57; Harvard Univ, MA, 55, PhD, 62. **CAREER** Res specialist econ, US Dept State, 56-58; instr hist, Princeton Univ, 61-62; asst prof, 62-68, assoc prof, 68-79, prof hist, Cornell Univ, 79-; vis schol, USSR Acad Sci, Moscow, 81; vis prof, Univ London, 87-88; vis schol, Saitama Univ, Japan, 96. **HONORS AND AWARDS** Inter-Univ Comt Travel Grants fel, Leningrad State Univ, 66 & Int Res & Exchanges Bd travel fel, 70; res fel, Russ Res Ctr, Harvard Univ, 65-66; fel, Woodrow Wilson Ctr, Smithsonian Inst, 77-78. **MEMBERSHIPS** Am Asn Advan Slavic Studies; Study Group 18th Century Russia. **RESEARCH** Eighteenth and 19th century Russian economic, administrative and military history. **SELECTED PUBLICATIONS** Auth, Inflation in Russia During the Crimean War, in Am Slavic & East Europ Rev, 1/59; Russian Economic Policy Under Nicholas I, Ithaca Univ, 67; Social Characteristics of the Early 19th Century Russian Bureaucracy, in Slavic Rev, 3/70; The Russian Higher Civil Service on the Eve of the Great Reforms, in J Soc Hist, spring 75; ed (with D K Rowney), Russian Officialdom, Chapel Hill, 80. **CONTACT ADDRESS** Dept of Hist, Cornell Univ, McGraw Hall, Ithaca, NY 14853-8703. **EMAIL** wmp1@cornell.edu

PIOTROWSKI, THADDEUS M.
PERSONAL Born 02/10/1940, Poland, m, 1971, 3 children **DISCIPLINE** SOCIOLOGY, POLISH HISTORY **EDUCATION** St Francis Col, BA, 63; Univ Penn, MA, 71; PhD, 73. **CAREER** Prof, Univ NH, 72-. **HONORS AND AWARDS** Outstanding Assoc Prof Awd, Univ NHamp; Fac Scholar Awd, Univ NH; Carpenter Professorship Awd, Univ NH; Cultural Achievement Awd, Am Council for Polish Culture; Literary Awd, Polish Sociol-Cultural Ctr London; Perennial Wisdom Awd, Monuments Conservancy of New York. **MEMBERSHIPS** Am Sociol Asn, Polish Inst of Arts and Sci of Am. **RESEARCH** East Central Europe, Poland, Holocaust. **SELECTED PUBLICATIONS** Auth, Genocide and Rescue in Wolyn: Recollections of the Ukrainian Nationalist Ethnic Cleansing Campaign Against the Poles During World War II, McFarland, 00; auth, Poland's Holocaust: Ethnic Strife, Collaboration with Occupying Forces, and Genocide in the Second Republic, 1918-1947, McFarland, 98; auth, Vengeance of the Swallows: Memoir of a Polish Family's Ordeal Under Soviet Aggression, Ukrainian Ethnic Cleansing and Nazi Enslavement, and Their Emigration to America, McFarland, 95; auth, Ukrainian Integral Nationalism: Chronological Assessment and Bibliography, Toronto, 97; auth, Polish-Ukrainian Relations During World War II: Ethnic Cleansing in Volhynia and Eastern Galicia, To-

ronto, 95. **CONTACT ADDRESS** Dept Science, Univ of New Hampshire, Manchester, 220 Hackett Hill Rd, Manchester, NH 03102. **EMAIL** thaddeus@cisunix.unh.edu

PIOTT, STEVEN L.
DISCIPLINE HISTORY **EDUCATION** Univ Utah, BA, 70, MA, 72; Univ Mo, PhD, 78. **CAREER** Prof Hist, Clarion Univ, 85-. **HONORS AND AWARDS** Fulbright Teaching Fel, Massey Univ, New Zealand, 92. **MEMBERSHIPS** Pa Hist Asn, Soc for Hists of the Gilded Age & Progressive Era (SHGAPE), Fulbright Asn. **RESEARCH** American reform, U. S. 1870-1920. **SELECTED PUBLICATIONS** Auth, The Anti-Monopoly Persuasion: Popular Resistance to the Rise of Big Business in the Midwest, Greenwood Press (85); auth, Holy Joe: Joseph W. Folk and the Missouri Idea, Univ Mo Press (97); articles in Mo Hist Rev, Gateway Heritage, Great Plains Quart, Hayes Hist J, Pa Hist, J of Am Culture, and Labor Hist. **CONTACT ADDRESS** Dept Hist, Clarion Univ of Pennsylvania, 840 Wood St, Clarion, PA 16214-1240. **EMAIL** Piott@Mail.Clarion.edu

PIPER, LINDA JANE
PERSONAL Born 04/10/1935, Blairsville, PA **DISCIPLINE** ANCIENT HISTORY **EDUCATION** Univ Pittsburgh, AB, 57; Ohio State Univ, MA, 60, PhD(class hist), 66. **CAREER** Asst prof hist, Univ GA, 66-81. **MEMBERSHIPS** AHA; Am Philol Asn; Archaeol Inst Am; AAUP. **RESEARCH** Hellenistic Sparta. **SELECTED PUBLICATIONS** Auth, Livy's portray of early Roman women, Class J, 12/71; War, Women and Children in Ancient-rome - Evans,jk/, Histoire Sociale-social History, Vol 0026, 1993. **CONTACT ADDRESS** 310 S Church St, Athens, GA 30605.

PIPES, DANIEL
PERSONAL Born 09/09/1949, Boston, MA, d, 2 children **DISCIPLINE** HISTORY **EDUCATION** Harvard Univ, BA 71, PhD 78. **CAREER** Univ Chicago, tch 78-82; State Dept, 82-83; Harvard Univ, lectr 83-84; Naval War Col, prof 84-86; For Policy Research Inst, director 86-93; Middle East Forum, director 94. **HONORS AND AWARDS** Vice Chmn of J Fulbright Bd of Foreign Scholarships; Who's Who in the East; Who's Who in Entertainment; Who's Who in America; Who's Who in the World; has served twice on the bush for pres campaigns and recently helped bob dole, testified before five senate and house committees. **SELECTED PUBLICATIONS** Auth, Greater Syria, 70; Conspiracy: How the Paranoid Style Flourishes, and Where it Comes From, 97; The Rushdie Affair, 90; In the Path of God: Islam and Political Power, 83; Slave Soldiers and Islam, 81; Syria Beyond the Peace Process, 96; The Hidden hand: Middle East Fears of Conspiracy, 96; The Long Shadow: Culture and Politics in the Middle East, 89; Articles in major newspapers and other publ. **CONTACT ADDRESS** Middle East Forum, 1500 Walnut St., Ste 1050, Philadelphia, PA 19102. **EMAIL** mcgmef@aol.com

PISTON, WILLIAMS GARRETT
PERSONAL Born 02/14/1953, Johnson City, TN, m, 1982 **DISCIPLINE** HISTORY **EDUCATION** Vanderbilt Univ, BA, 75; MA, 77; Univ SC, PhD, 82. **CAREER** Prof, Louise S McGehee Sch, 82-85; Prof, Southwest Mo State Univ, 88-. **MEMBERSHIPS** Southern Hist Asn, Soc for Military Hist. **RESEARCH** American Civil War, military history. **SELECTED PUBLICATIONS** Auth, Lee's Tarnished Lieutenant: James Longstreet and His Place in Southern History, Univ Ga Pr, 87; auth, Wilson's Creek: The Second Battle of the Civil War and the Men Who Fought it, Univ NC Pr, 00. **CONTACT ADDRESS** Dept Hist, Southwest Missouri State Univ, Springfield, 901 S National Ave, Springfield, MO 65804-0027. **EMAIL** williampiston@mail.smsu.edu

PITRE, MERLINE
PERSONAL Born Opelousas, LA, s **DISCIPLINE** AFRICAN AMERICAN HISTORY, AFRO TEXAS POLITICAL HISTORY **EDUCATION** Southern Univ, BS, 66; Atlanta Univ, MA, 67; Temple Univ, PhD, 76. **CAREER** Instr French, St Augustine's Col, 67-70; teacher, St Landry Parish Sch, 71-72; asst prof hist, Tex Southern Univ, 76- **HONORS AND AWARDS** Book titled Through Many Danger, Toils and Snares was used for state-wide exhibit and Black Legislators of Texas. **MEMBERSHIPS** Asn Study Afro-Am Life & Hist; Orgn Am Historians. **RESEARCH** Afro-American political history; Frederick Douglass 1870-1895; The Black Press in Houston, Texas, 1920-1950; Reconstruction in Texas, Afro Texas Political History. **SELECTED PUBLICATIONS** Auth, Frederick Douglass and the Annexation of Santo Domingo, J Negro Hist, 10/77; Frederick Douglas: The Politician vs the Social Reformer, Phylon, 9/79; The Economic Philosophy of Martin Luther King, Jr., J Black Polit Econ, Winter 79; The Evolution of a Black University in Texas, Western J Black Studies, 79; The Partisan Politics of Frederick Douglass, J Soc and Behavioral Sci, Fall 80; Scholar's Reaction to Bakke, Western J Black Studies, Summer 81; Frederick Douglass and Republican Presidents, Girot, Summer 83; Black Houstonians and the Doctrine of Separate But Equal: Lulu White v Carter Wesley, Houston Rev, 7/90; Barbara Jordan, in Black Women in America: Historical, Carlson Publ Co, 93; author numerous other articles and book reviews; auth, "Through Many Dangers, toils and Snares: The Black Leadership of Texas," 97; auth, "In Struggle Against Jim Crow," Lulu B. White and the NAACP 1900-1957. **CONTACT ADDRESS** Dept of Hist, Texas So Univ, 3100 Cleburne St, Houston, TX 77004-4597. **EMAIL** pitre_mx@tsu.edu

PITTENGER, MARK A.
DISCIPLINE HISTORY **EDUCATION** Denison Univ, BA, 74; Univ Mich, MA, 77; PhD, 84. **CAREER** Prof. **HONORS AND AWARDS** Teaching Excellence Award, Boulder Fac Assembly, 94; Constance Rourke Prize, Am Studies Asn: best Am Quarterly article, 98. **SELECTED PUBLICATIONS** Auth, American Socialists and Evolutionary Thought, 1870-1920, Univ Wis, 93; A World of Difference: Constructing the 'Underclass' in Progressive America, Am Quarterly, 97; Imagining Genocide in the Progressive Era: The Socialist Science Fiction of George Allan England, Am Studies, 94. **CONTACT ADDRESS** History Dept, Univ of Colorado, Boulder, Boulder, CO 80309. **EMAIL** mark.pittenger@spot.colorado.edu

PITTS, BILL
PERSONAL Born 12/27/1937, Winfield, KS, m, 1961, 2 children **DISCIPLINE** RELIGION; CHURCH HISTORY **EDUCATION** Baylor Univ, BA, 60; Vanderbilt Divinity School, MD, 63; Vanderbilt, PhD, 69. **CAREER** Instr, Mercer Univ, 66-69; asst prof, Houston Baptist Univ, 69-70; assoc prof, Dallas Baptist Univ, 70-75; assoc prof & prof, Baylor Univ, 75- . **HONORS AND AWARDS** Luke Acts Prize & Hist Prize, Vanderbilt, 63; Lilly Scholar, 64-65; Piper Prof Nominee, 74; Mortar Bd Distinguished Prof, 93. **MEMBERSHIPS** Soc Study Christian Spirituality; Am Acad Relig; Am Soc Church Hist; Nat Asn Baptist Prof Relig; Conf Faith & Hist. **RESEARCH** New religious movements; historiography; spirituality; Baptist history. **SELECTED PUBLICATIONS** Auth, Millennial Spirituality of the Branch Davidians, Christian Spirituality Bull, 93; The Mount Carmel Davidians: Adventist Reformers, 1935-1959, Syzgy, 93; The Davidian Tradition, The Coun Soc for Study Relig Bull, 93; The Davidian Tradition, From the Ashes: Making Sense of Waco, Rowman & Littlefield Publ, 94; Davidians and Branch Dividians: 1929-1987, Armageddon in Waco, Univ Chicago Press, 95; Davidians and Branch Davidians, New Cath Encycl, Cath Univ Press, 95; The Persistence of the Millennium, Medieval Perspectives, 97. **CONTACT ADDRESS** Religion Dept, Baylor Univ, Waco, Waco, TX 76798. **EMAIL** william_pitts@baylor.edu

PITZER, DONALD ELDEN
PERSONAL Born 05/06/1936, Springfield, OH, m, 1960, 2 children **DISCIPLINE** AMERICAN SOCIAL & INTELLECTUAL HISTORY **EDUCATION** Wittenberg Univ, AB, 58; Ohio State Univ, MA, 62, PhD(hist), 66. **CAREER** Instr social studies, Messiah Col, 59-61; asst prof hist, Taylor Univ, 66-67; from asst prof to assoc prof, 67-74, Prof Hist, Ind State Univ Evansville, 74-, Mem & historian, Ind New Harmony Comn, 72-; ed, Nat Hist Communal Socs Asn Newsletter, 74-; dir, Ctr Communal Studies, Ind State Univ Evansville, 76-; exec dir, Nat Hist Communal Socs Asn, 77-. **MEMBERSHIPS** Orgn Am Historians; AHA; Conf Faith & Hist; Nat Hist Communal Socs Asn (pres, 74-77). **RESEARCH** Communal societies; effects of modern physics and existentialism on American thought; Mayan civilization. **SELECTED PUBLICATIONS** Ed, Robert Owen's American Legacy, Ind Hist Soc, 72; Organizing historic communes for preservation and scholarship, Communal Studies Newsletter, 7/76; coauth, New Harmony's Fourth of July Tradition, Raintree Bks, 76; auth, The Harmonist heritage of three towns, 10-12/77 & Harmonist folk art discovered, 10/12/77, Hist Preserv; Education in Utopia: The New Harmony experience, In: The History of Education in the Middle West, Ind Hist Soc, 78; New Harmony's First Utopians, Ind Mag Hist, 9/79. **CONTACT ADDRESS** Dept of Hist, Indiana State Univ, 8600 University Blvd, Evansville, IN 47712-3591.

PIVAR, DAVID J.
PERSONAL Born 06/06/1933, Philadelphia, PA, m, 1991, 4 children **DISCIPLINE** AMERICAN SOCIAL HISTORY **EDUCATION** Millersville State Col, MSEd, 57; Temple Univ, MA, 61; Univ Pa, PhD(hist), 65. **CAREER** Teaching asst hist, Univ Pa, 63-64; assoc prof Am Hist, 65- 71, Prof Hist & Am Studies, Calif State Univ, Fullerton, 71-. **MEMBERSHIPS** AHA; Am Studies Asn. **RESEARCH** American social history. **SELECTED PUBLICATIONS** Auth, The hosiery workers and the Philadelphia Third Party impulse, 1927-35, Labor Hist, winter 64; Theocratic businessmen and Philadelphia municipal reform, 1870-1900, PA Hist, 10/66; Purity Crusade: Sexual Morality and Social Control, 1868-1900, Greenwood, 73; Cleansing the Nation: The War on Prostitution, 1917-21, Prologue, spring 80; The Military Prostitution and Colonial Peoples: India and the Philippines, 1885-1917, J Sex Res, 8/81; City of Eros - New-york-city, Prostitution, and the Commercialization of Sex, 1790-1920 - Gilfoyle,tj, Reviews in American History, Vol 0021, 1993; Unsubmissive Women - Chinese Prostitutes in 19th-century San-francisco - Tong,b/, American Historical Review, Vol 0101, 1996; Sin and Censorship - the Catholic-church and the Motion-picture Industry - Walsh,f, American Historical Review, Vol 0102, 1997. **CONTACT ADDRESS** Dept of Hist, California State Univ, Fullerton, Fullerton, CA 92631.

PIXTON, PAUL BREWER
PERSONAL Born 06/22/1940, Salt Lake City, UT, m, 1965, 3 children **DISCIPLINE** MEDIEVAL HISTORY **EDUCATION** Univ Utah, BA, 65, MA, 67; Univ Iowa, PhD(hist), 72. **CAREER** Asst prof hist, Univ Wis-Superior, 71-74; asst prof, 74-78, Assoc Prof Hist, Brigham Young Univ, 78-. **MEMBERSHIPS** AHA; Medieval Acad Am. **RESEARCH** Medieval ecclesiastical reform in Germany; German cathedral schools; crusade recruitment. **SELECTED PUBLICATIONS** Auth, Dietrich von Wied: Geistlicher ehrgeiz und politischer opportunismus im fruhen dreizehnten jahrhundert, Archiv fur mittelrheinische Kirchengeschichte, 74; Auf Gottes Wachturm: Ein erzbischofliches Reformprogramm im Trier des fruher 13 Jahrhunderts, Trierisches Jahrbuch, 77; Das Anwerben des Heeres Christi: Prediger des funften Kreuzzuges in Deutschland, Deutsches Archiv, 78. **CONTACT ADDRESS** Dept of Hist, Brigham Young Univ, Provo, UT 84601.

PLAKANS, ANDREJS
PERSONAL Born 12/31/1940, Riga, Latvia, m, 1964, 2 children **DISCIPLINE** EUROPEAN SOCIAL HISTORY **EDUCATION** Franklin & Marshall Col, BA, 63; Harvard Univ, MA, 64, PhD(hist), 69. **CAREER** Asst prof, Boston Col, 69-74; assoc prof, 75-82, Prof Hist, Iowa State Univ, 82-, Res assoc, Dept Anthrop, Univ Mass, Amherst, 74-75. **MEMBERSHIPS** AHA; Social Sci Hist Asn; Am Asn Advan Slavic Studies; Asn Advan Baltic Studies; Int Union Sci Study Pop. **RESEARCH** Social structure of pre-industrial Eastern European peasantries; history of family and kinship; history of the Baltic area. **SELECTED PUBLICATIONS** Auth, Peasant, intellectuals and nationalism in Russian Baltic provinces, J Mod Hist, 74; Peasant farmsteads and households in Baltic littoral, Comp Studies Soc & Hist, 75; Seigneurial authority and peasant family life, J Interdisciplinary Hist, 75; contribr, Sozialgeschichte der Familie in der Neuzeit Europas, Klettverlag, 76; auth, Identifying kinfolk beyond the household, J Famly Hist, 77; contribr, Family In Imperial Russia, Univ Ill Press, 78; coauth, Russification in Baltic Provinces and Finland in 19th Century, Princeton Univ Press, 81; Kinship and kinship roles in East European peasant communities, J Family Hist, 82. **CONTACT ADDRESS** Dept Hist, Iowa State Univ of Science and Tech, Ames, IA 50011-0002.

PLANEAUX, CHRISTOPHER
PERSONAL Born 04/10/1967, Atlanta, GA, m, 1996 **DISCIPLINE** PHILOSOPHY; HISTORY; CLASSICS GREEK **EDUCATION** Ind Univ, AB, 93, AB, 94; Univ Cambridge, MPhil, 97. **CAREER** Dept For Lang, Ind Univ **HONORS AND AWARDS** Fac Develop Mentorship grant, Ind Univ, 94; Sur Grant, Ind Univ, 93; Univ Cambridge Res Grant, 94. Thelander Mem Awd, Ind Univ, 94. **MEMBERSHIPS** Amer Philol Asn; Class Asn Mid W & S; Asn Ancient Hist; Soc Greek Philos; Univ London Inst Class Studies; Cambridge Philol Soc; Darwin Col Soc. **RESEARCH** Dramatic settings of Platos Dialogues; Athens (ca.470-399 BCE); Peloponnesian War; Thirty Tyrants; Athenian calendar; Athenian Cultic societies; Philosophical schools; Alcibiades. **SELECTED PUBLICATIONS** Auth, Socrates, Alcibiades, and Plato's: Does the Charmides Have an Historical setting?, Mnemosyne, 99; coauth, "Who's Who in the Timaeus-Critias and Why," Review of Metaphysics, 98; auth, "The Date of Bendis' Entry into Attica," Classical Jrnl, 00. **CONTACT ADDRESS** Dept of Foreign Languages & Cultures, Indiana Univ-Purdue Univ, Indianapolis, 425 Univ Blvd, Indianapolis, IN 46202. **EMAIL** cplaneau@iupui.edu

PLANK, GEOFFREY
DISCIPLINE HISTORY **EDUCATION** Swarthmore, BA, 80; Univ Conn, JD, 84; Princeton Univ, PhD, 94. **CAREER** ASSOC PROF, HIST, UNIV CINCINNATI **MEMBERSHIPS** Am Antiquarian Soc **SELECTED PUBLICATIONS** Auth, "The Changing Country of Anthony Casteel: Language, Religion, Geography, Political Co and Nationalism in Mid-Eighteenth Century Nova Scotia," Studies in Eighteenth- Century Culture, vol 27, 97; auth, The Two Majors Cope: The Boundaries of Nationality in Mid-Eighteenth Century Nova Scotia, Acadiensis, 97. **CONTACT ADDRESS** Dept of Hist, Univ of Cincinnati, ML 373, Cincinnati, OH 45221. **EMAIL** geoffrey.plank@uc.edu

PLATT, FRANKLIN DEWITT
PERSONAL Born 11/15/1932, Marion, LA, m, 1956, 1 child **DISCIPLINE** BRITISH HISTORY **EDUCATION** La State Univ, BA, 55; Wash Univ, AM, 63, PhD(hist), 69. **CAREER** From instr to asst prof, 64-72, asst chmn dept humanities, Mich State Univ, 71-, assoc prof, 72-. **MEMBERSHIPS** AHA **RESEARCH** Contemporary humanities; 19th century England. **SELECTED PUBLICATIONS** Auth, Reflections on a new breed of student, Bull Res Humanities Educ, I:8-11. **CONTACT ADDRESS** Dept of Humanities, Michigan State Univ, East Lansing, MI 48824.

PLATT, HAROLD L.
DISCIPLINE HISTORY **EDUCATION** Rice, PhD. **CAREER** Hist, Loyola Univ. **RESEARCH** Urban history; Civil War & reconstruction. **SELECTED PUBLICATIONS** Auth, The Electric City: Energy and the Growth of the Chicago Area,

1880-1930, Univ Chicago Press, 91. **CONTACT ADDRESS** Fine Arts Dept, Loyola Univ, Chicago, 6525 N. Sheridan Rd., Chicago, IL 60626.

PLECK, ELIZABETH
DISCIPLINE HISTORY **EDUCATION** Brandeis Univ, BA, 67; Brandeis Univ, MA, 69; Brandeis Univ, PhD, 73 **CAREER** Asst prof, Univ of Mich, 73-78; Fel comt, 74-75, 76-77; Coun for Undergraduates, 74, 77; NEH Fac sem on women and cult, 77; vis assoc prof, Univ of Penn, Summer, 79; Summer, 80; vis assoc prof, Wellesley Col, 82; vis assoc prof, MIT, 82; vis res sch, ctr for res on women, Wellesley Col, 78-94; proj historian, legacies: family hist in Sound, 85-97; proj dir, Women in Am politics, 92-93; vis lect, Wheaton Col, 90; vis lect, Brown Univ, 91; vis prof, NY Coun for the humanities Summer instit, State Univ of NY at Albany, 94; Grad Res Sch, Univ of Ill, 94-96; vis assoc prof, Univ of Ill at Urbana-Champaign, 94-96; vis assoc prof, Univ of Ill at Urbana-Champaign, 94-96; assoc prof, Univ of Ill at Urbana-Champaign, 96-; search comt, HDFS, 96-97; assoc prof, dept of history, Univ of Ill at Urbana-Champaign, 96-. **HONORS AND AWARDS** Ford Found Dissertation Fel in ethnic studies, 72-73; Irving and Rose Crown fel, Brandeis Univ, 71-73; Nat Sci Found Doctoral Diss Grant, 72-73; Newberry libr family and community hist prog, summer, 74; Rackham fac res grant, Univ of Mich, 74-75; Ford found fac fel for the study of the role of women in soc, 75-76; Bunting Instit of Radcliffe Col, 79-80; Annenberg Grant for Legacies: Family hist in sound, 85-87; Nat Endow for the hum, women in Am Politics, Summer Instit for col Teachers, 92-93; Ill res bd grant, 95; Univ of Ill fel, Instit for the study of values and ethics, 97-98; Incomplete list of teachers deemed excellent, fall, 97, spring 99, fall, 99. **RESEARCH** American family history. **SELECTED PUBLICATIONS** Auth, "Black Migration and Poverty: Boston, 1870-1900, New York: Academic Press, 79; ed, "A Heritage of Her Own: Toward a New Social History of American Women, New York: Simon and Schuster, 79; auth, "The American Man," Englewood Cliffs, NJ: Prentice Hall, 80; auth, "The History of Criminal Approaches Toward Family Violence," in Lloyd Ohlin and Michael Tonry, Crime and Justice: Annual Review, Chicago: University of Chicago, 88, 19-57; auth, "Domestic Tyranny: The Making of Social Policy Against Family Violence," New York: Oxford University Press, 87; auth, "Rape and the Politics of Race, 1865-1900," Working Paper of the Center for Research on Women, Wellesley College, 90; auth, "Fatherhood Ideals in the United States: Historical Dimensions," in Michael Lamb, The Role of the Father in Child Development, 3rd ed, 97; auth, "The Making of a Domestic Occasion: The History of Thanksgiving," Journal of Social History, June, 99; auth, "White Weddings: Consumerism, Choice, and Cultural Debate," Univ of California Press, Celebrating the Family: Ritual, Consumer Culture and Ethnicity, Cambridge: Harvard University Press, 00; auth, "Christmas in the 1960s," in Richard Horsley and James Tracey, Christmas: The Religion of Consumer Capitalism, Boston: Trinity Press International, 00; **CONTACT ADDRESS** History Dept, Univ of Illinois, Urbana-Champaign, 314a Gregory Hall, 810 S. Wright, mc 466, Urbana, IL 61801. **EMAIL** e-pleck@staff.uiuc.edu

PLESCIA, JOSEPH
PERSONAL Born 08/23/1928, Italy, d, 2 children **DISCIPLINE** GREEK HISTORY & PHILOSOPHY, ROMAN HISTORY & LAW **EDUCATION** Gregorian Univ, Baccalaureatum in Philos, 50; Univ CA, Berkeley, BA, 58; Stanford Univ, MA, 60, PhD, 65. **CAREER** From instr to assoc prof, 62-78, prof hist, FL State Univ, 78-. **HONORS AND AWARDS** Richardson Latin Composition Prize, Univ Calif, Berkeley, 57-58; Woodrow Wilson Fel, 59; Summer Awd, Am Coun Learned Soc, Univ Calif, Berkeley, 72, 73; Vis Schol, Yale Law Sch, 76-77; mem Governor's Challenge Prog Fla 2000: Creative Crime Control, 82; mem Conf on Agreement Between Ital and Am Universities Related to Doctoral Programs, Study and Conf Ctr of the Rockefeller Found, Villa Serbelloni, Bellagio (Lago di Como), 83. **RESEARCH** Greek and Roman law. **SELECTED PUBLICATIONS** Auth, Oath and Perjury in Ancient Greece, Fla State Univ Press, 70, sold out, Cited in the Oxford Classical Dictionary, 3rd ed, 96; Roman Law on Water, Index 21, 93; Ius Pacis in Roman Law, RIDA 41, 94; The Bill of Rights and Roman Law, Austin & Winfield, 95, 2nd printing, 97, 2nd ed; The Doctrine of Liability in Roman Law, Studies in Roman Law (opuscula series), Frederic II Univ, Italy; International Law in Ancient Rome. **CONTACT ADDRESS** Dept of Hist, Florida State Univ, 205 Williams Bldg., Tallahassee, FL 32306-2200.

PLETCHER, DAVID MITCHELL
PERSONAL Born 06/14/1920, Faribault, MN **DISCIPLINE** HISTORY **EDUCATION** Univ Chicago, AB & AM, 41, PhD, 46. **CAREER** Instr hist, State Univ Iowa, 44-46; assoc prof, Knox Col, 45-56; from assoc prof to prof, Hamline Univ, 56-65; Prof Hist, Ind Univ, Bloomington, 65-, Lectr, Inst Int Affairs, Grinnell Col, 47; Fulbright sr res grant, London, 53-54; Soc Sci Res Coun grant 62-63; assoc ed, Hisp Am Hist Rev, 65-70. **HONORS AND AWARDS** Albert J Beveridge Mem Prize, AHA, 57; McKnight Found award in humanities, 62. **MEMBERSHIPS** AHA; Soc Historians of Am Foreign Rels (pres, 80). **RESEARCH** United States diplomatic history; United States-Latin American relations. **SELECTED PUBLICATIONS** Auth, The fall of silver in Mexico and its effect on American investments, J Econ Hist, 3/58; Rails, Mines and Progress: Seven American Promoters in Mexico, 1867-1911, Cornell Univ, 58; Mexico opens the door to American capital, 1877-1880, Americas, 7/59; The Awkward Years: American Foreign Relations Under Garfield and Arthur, 62 & The Diplomacy of Annexation: Texas, Oregon, and the Mexican War, 73, Univ Mo; Rhetoric and Results: A pragmatic view of American Expansionism, 1865-1898, Diplomatic Hist, spring 81; auth, The Diplomacy of Trade and Investment: American Economic Expansion in the Hemisphere, 1865-1900, 98, Univ Mo; auth, The Diplomacy of Involvement: American Economic Expansion across the Pacific, 1784-1900, 01, Univ Mo. **CONTACT ADDRESS** Dept of Hist, Indiana Univ, Bloomington, Bloomington, IN 47401.

PLUMMER, MARGUERITE R.
DISCIPLINE HISTORY **EDUCATION** LSU, MA; MBA; MA; Univ Tex, PhD. **CAREER** Director, Pioneer Heritage Center, 82; instr to asst prof, La State Univ - Shreveport, 92-. **MEMBERSHIPS** La Hist Asn, Am Hist Asn, Southern Asn of Women Hist, SE Museum Conf, Am Asn of State & Local Hist, La Asn of Museums. **RESEARCH** Public history, American history: colonial and new deal era, Political history. **SELECTED PUBLICATIONS** Auth, Historic Shreveport-Bossier, San Antonio: Historical Pub, (forthcoming); auth, "George Washington's founding Vision for America," George Washington In and As Culture, 00; auth, "Louis d. Brandeis: Pioneer Progressive," and "Benjamin Cardozo: Pathfinder for progress," in Great Justices of the Supreme Court, 93. **CONTACT ADDRESS** Dept Soc Sci, Louisiana State Univ, Shreveport, 1 Univ Place, Shreveport, LA 71115-2301. **EMAIL** mplummer@pilot.lsus.edu

PO-CHIA HSIA, RONNIE
PERSONAL Born 11/15/1955, Hong Kong, China, m, 1995, 1 child **DISCIPLINE** HISTORY **EDUCATION** Swarthmore, BA, 77; Harvard Univ, AM, 78; Yale, PhD, 82. **CAREER** Fel, Columbia Univ, 82-84; Asst Prof, Cornell Univ, 84-87; Assoc Prof to Prof, Univ Mass, 87-90; Prof, New York Univ, 90-. **HONORS AND AWARDS** ACLS; Guggenheim; Franz Vogt Prize, Univ Giessen; Humboldt Fel; Wilson Fel; NEH Fel. **MEMBERSHIPS** AHA. **RESEARCH** Early Mod Europe. **SELECTED PUBLICATIONS** Auth, Countess Maria Theresia von Fugger (1680-1752) and the Jesuit Mission in China: Documents and Interpretation, forthcoming; auth, Reformation Europe 1480-1580, London, forthcoming; auth, Gegenreformation. Die Welt der katholischen Erneuerung, 1540-1770, Frankfurt, 97; auth, The World of Catholic Renewal, 1540-1770, Cambridge Univ Press, 97; co-auth, The Challenge of the West. Peoples and Cultures from the Stone Age to the Global Age, D.C. Heath Pub, 94; ed, Historical Companion to the World of the Reformation, Blackwell Pub, forthcoming; ed, Religious Toleration and Calvinist Hegemony in the Dutch Golden Age, Amsterdam Univ Press, forthcoming; trans, The Fontana Economic History of Europe: The Middle Ages, Taipei, Yun-ch'en, 84; auth, "Reuchin und die Juden," in Reuchlin und die Renaissance, Thorbeck, forthcoming; auth, "The Reformation and the Counter-Reformation," in The Oxford encyclopedia of the Social Sciences, forthcoming; auth, "L'Edit de tolerance de Kangxi et la mission chretienne en Chnie," in La Tolerance: Colloue international de Nantes, mai 1998. Quatrieme centenaire de l'edit de Nantes, 99. **CONTACT ADDRESS** Dept Hist, New York Univ, 53 Washington Sq S, New York, NY 10012. **EMAIL** rph1@is6.nyu.edu

POBST, PHYLLIS E.
DISCIPLINE HISTORY **EDUCATION** Gonzaga Univ, BA, 75; Harvard Univ, MTS, 84; Univ Toronto, MA, 85; MSL, 89; PhD, 92. **CAREER** TA, Univ of Toronto, 87-91; instr to assoc prof, Ark State Univ, 91-01. **MEMBERSHIPS** AAUP, Am Cath Hist Assoc, AHA, Ark Assoc of Col Hist Teachers, Ecclesiastical Hist Soc, Medieval Acad of Am, Phi Kappa Phi Nat Honor Soc, S Hist Assoc. **RESEARCH** Medieval ecclesiastical records, especially English episcopal registers, the Black Death. **SELECTED PUBLICATIONS** Auth, The Register of William Bateman, Bishop of Norwich, A.D. 1344-1355, Vol I, Roydell Pr, 96; auth, The Register of William Bateman, Bishop of Norwich, A.D. 1344-1355, Vol II, Roydell Pr, 00. **CONTACT ADDRESS** Dept Hist, Arkansas State Univ, PO Box 1690, State University, AR 72647-1690. **EMAIL** ppobst@toltec.astate.edu

POCOCK, EMIL
PERSONAL Born New York City, NY, m, 1988 **DISCIPLINE** HISTORY AND AMERICAN STUDIES **EDUCATION** Univ MD, BA, 68; NYork Univ MA, 71; IN Univ, MA, PhD. **CAREER** Eng Dept, Eastern Conn State Univ **MEMBERSHIPS** Organization of Am Historians; Am Studies Assoc; DANE Fellow; Soc of Historians of the Early Am Republic. **RESEARCH** US Frontier; Early Republic; Cultural geography. **SELECTED PUBLICATIONS** Auth, Popular Roots of Jacksonian Democracy: The Case of Dayton, Ohio, 1815-1830, Jour, Early Republic, 89; 'I enjoy but little sunshine on my path': Reverend James Welsh on Three Frontiers, 1790-1825, IN Mag Hist, 90; 'A Candidate I'll Surely Be': Election Practices in Early Ohio, 1798-1825, Kent State Univ Press, 94. **CONTACT ADDRESS** Eastern Connecticut State Univ, 83 Windham Street, Willimantic, CT 06226. **EMAIL** pocock@mail.ecsu.ctstateu.edu

PODAIR, JERALD E.
PERSONAL Born 11/01/1953, New York, NY, m, 1985, 1 child **DISCIPLINE** HISTORY **EDUCATION** New York Univ, BA, 74; Columbia Univ, Law Sch, JD, 77; Princeton, MA, 91; PhD, 97. **CAREER** Lectr, Princeton Univ, 97-98; asst prof, Lawrence Univ, 98-. **HONORS AND AWARDS** Allen Nevins Prize, SAH, 98; Hon Men, Man Prize, NYSHA, 98. **MEMBERSHIPS** AHA; OAH. **RESEARCH** 20th century US history; Us racial and ethnic relations; US urban history. **SELECTED PUBLICATIONS** Auth, "The Failure to 'See': Jews, Blacks, and the Ocean Hill-Brownsville Controversy," (Temple Univ Cen Am Jewish Hist, 92); auth," 'White' Values, 'Black' Values: The Ocean Hill-Brownsville Controversy and New York City Culture, 1965-1975," Radical Hist Rev 59 (94): 36-59; auth, "Ocean Hill" and "Albert Shawnee,", in The Encyclopedia of New York State, ed. Peter Eisensyadt (Syracuse Univ Press, forthcoming); auth, "New York", in Civil Rights in the United States, eds. Waldo E Mortin, Patricia Sullivan (Macmillan Ref, forthcoming); auth, Like Strangers: Blacks, Whites, and New York City's Ocean Hill-Brownsville Crisis, 1945-1980 (Yale Univ Press, forthcoming). **CONTACT ADDRESS** Dept History, Lawrence Univ, Box 599, Appleton, WI 54912-0599.

PODANY, AMANDA H.
PERSONAL Born 06/24/1960, England, m, 1981, 2 children **DISCIPLINE** HISTORY **EDUCATION** Univ Calif at Los Angeles, BA, 80; Univ London, MA, 82; Univ Calif at Los Angeles, MA, 84, PhD, 88. **CAREER** Asst prof, Calif State Polytechnic Univ Pomona, 90-96, assoc prof, 96-; exec dir, Calif Hist-Soc Sci Project, 93-97. **MEMBERSHIPS** AHA, Am Oriental Soc, Am Schs of Oriental Res, Western Asn of Women Historians, World History Asn. **RESEARCH** Ancient Near East: Hana kingdom; Old Babylonian legal history; Late Bronze Age Syria. **SELECTED PUBLICATIONS** Auth, "A Middle Babylonian Date for the Hana Kingdom," J of Cuneiform Studies 43-45 (91-93): 53-62; coauth with Gary M. Beckman and Gudrun Colbow, "An Adoption and Inheritance Contract from the Reign of Iggid-Lim of Hana," J of Cuneiform Studies 43-45 (91-93): 39-51; auth, "Some Shared Traditions between Hana and the Kassites," in Crossing Boundaries and Linking Horizons: Studies in Honor of Michael C. Astour on His 80th Birthday, Gordon D. Young, Mark W. Chavalas and Richard E. Averbeck, eds, Bethesda, Md: CDL Press (97): 417-432; auth, Five Centuries of Hana Texts: Scibal Tradition in Syro-Mesopotamia in the Second Millennium BC, Bethesda, Md: CDL Press (forthcoming). **CONTACT ADDRESS** Dept Hist, California State Polytech Univ, Pomona, 3801 W Temple Ave, Pomona, CA 91768-2557. **EMAIL** AHPodany@csupomona.edu

PODET, ALLEN HOWARD
PERSONAL Born 12/18/1934, Cleveland, OH, m, 1981 **DISCIPLINE** MODERN JEWISH HISTORY **EDUCATION** Univ Ill, Urbana, BA, 56; Hebrew Union Col, BHL, 58, MA, HL, 62, DHL, 64; Univ Wash, PhD(hist), 79. **CAREER** Lectr, Dept Near Eastern Lang & Lit, Univ Wash, Seattle, 70-73; asst prof, 69-73, prof, Dept Philos & Relig Studies, State Univ NYork Col Buffalo, 80-, Consult, Jewish Collection, Folklore Archives, Buffalo, 80-; contrib ed, Am Books by Europ Judaism J, 77-; Univ lectr, Univ Vienna, Austria, 98. **HONORS AND AWARDS** Fulbright-Hays fel, Jerusalem, 95-96. **MEMBERSHIPS** Cent Conf Am Rabbis; Asn Jewish Studies. **RESEARCH** Rabbinics. **SELECTED PUBLICATIONS** Auth, The Sephardim of Seattle, Jewish Digest, 9/68; Secular studies and religious uniqueness: A view of Hanukkah, Relig Educ, Vol 71, No 6, 11-12/76; The Jew as witness to history, Europ Judaism, Vol II, No 1, winter 77; Ein historischer Zuzang zu einem Philsophen: Moses Maimonides in seiner Zeit, Emuna, Vol 4, No 77, winter 77; The unwilling midwife: Ernest Bevin and the birth of Israel, Europ Judaism, Vol II, No 2, winter 77; Anti-Zionism in a key United States Diplomat: Loy Henderson at the end of World War II, Am Jewish Archives, Vol 30, No 2, 11/78; The Al-Barazi Testimony: a Secret Syrian Peace Proposal Recognizing the State of Israel, Mid East Studies Anthology; The Soviet Jewish problem, J Assembly of Rabbis; auth, Success & Failure of the Anglo-American Comm of Inquiry, 1945-1946, Mellon Press, Lewiston NY, 87; auth, A Translation of the Magen Wa-Hereb of Leon Woodoner, 1571-1648, Union Press, Lewiston, NY, 00. **CONTACT ADDRESS** Dept of Philos & Relig Studies, SUNY, Buffalo, 1300 Elmwood Ave, Buffalo, NY 14222-1095. **EMAIL** podetah@buffalostate.edu

POEN, MONTE MAC
PERSONAL Born 11/25/1930, Lake City, IA, 3 children **DISCIPLINE** RECENT UNITED STATES HISTORY **EDUCATION** San Jose State Col, BA, 61; Univ Mo, MA, 64, PhD(recent US hist), 67. **CAREER** Instr US hist, Univ Mo, 64-66; asst prof, 66-70, assoc prof, 70-79, Prof Recent US Hist, Northern Ariz Univ, 79-; ed, Mary W Lasker Oral Hist Proj, Albert D Lasker Found, 67- **MEMBERSHIPS** Org Am Historians; Oral Hist Asn; Ctr Study Presidency's. **RESEARCH** Recent United States social and political development; medical politics, history of the national health insurance movement; Harry S Truman. **SELECTED PUBLICATIONS** Auth, Harry S Truman vs The Medical Lobby, Univ Mo, 79; ed, Strictly Personal and Confidential: The Letters Harry Truman Never Mailed, Little, Brown & Co, 82. **CONTACT ADDRESS** 3703 N Grandview Dr, Flagstaff, AZ 86001.

POHL, JAMES WILLIAM
PERSONAL Born 07/26/1931, Dubuque, IA, m, 1965, 2 children **DISCIPLINE** MILITARY HISTORY **EDUCATION** Univ N Tex, BA, 53, MA, 55; Univ Tex, PhD, 67. **CAREER** Instr hist, Univ Tex, 60-63; from instr to assoc prof, 64-74, prof, Hist, Southwest Tex State Univ, 74-; visit prof, Univ Tex, 85-86; Dir Tex State Hist Asn, 85-86; Dir, Ctr for Stu of Hist, Univ Tex, 85-86; Res Fel, Mosher Inst for Defense Stu, Tex A & M Univ 88-; Pres, Tex State Hist Asn, 87-88; Visit Sr Prof; Sch for Advanced Study, U.S. Army Command and Gen Staff Col, 98. **HONORS AND AWARDS** Dist Svc Awd, Tex State Hist Asn, 86, 88, 96; Gov's Letter of Commendation for Svc to the State of Tex, 86, 87; John Bell Hood Awd, H.B. Simpson Civil War Res Ctr, 90; Outstanding Centennial Alumnus Awd, Univ of N Tex, 90; Fel, Tex State Hist Asn, 94; Jefferson Davis Awd, UDC, 96; Fehrenbach Awd, Texas Histol Commission, 96-99; Prof of the Year, NTSO, SWT, 99. **MEMBERSHIPS** Am Mil Inst, Tex State Hist Asn, Nat, Assessment Board, Nat Archives and Presidential Libr, 95. **RESEARCH** Military history, particularly United States and European. **SELECTED PUBLICATIONS** Auth, The congress and the secretary of war, 1915: An instance of political pressure, NJ Hist, fall 71; coauth, People of America, Benson, 73; auth, The influence of Antoine Henri de Jomini on Winfield Scott's campaign in Mexico, Southwestern Hist Quart, 7/73; The American Revolution and the Vietnam War: Pertinent military analogies, Hist Teacher, 2/74; auth, The Military History of the Texas Revolution, Southwestern, Hist Qrt, 86; ed, Southwestern Historical Quarterly, 85-86; auth, Battle of San Jacinto, 89; coed-in-chief, The New Handbook of Texas, 6 vols, 96. **CONTACT ADDRESS** Dept of History, Southwest Texas State Univ, 601 University Dr, San Marcos, TX 78666-4685. **EMAIL** JP19@swt.edu

POINTER, RICHARD W.
PERSONAL Born 09/11/1955, Brooklyn, NY, m, 1978, 3 children **DISCIPLINE** HISTORY **EDUCATION** Johns Hopkins Univ, PhD, 82; post doc res, Univ Pa, 85-86. **CAREER** Vis asst, Wheaton Col, 82-83; assoc prof, Trinity Col, 83-84; Assoc Prof, Trinity College, 83-87; Assoc Prof, 87-94; Assoc Prof, Westmont College, 94-96; assoc prof, Westmont Col, 94-; Prof, Westmont College, 96-. **HONORS AND AWARDS** Kerr prize, NY State Hist Assn, 86; assoc ed, hist and polit sci, 95-. **RESEARCH** Colonial & revoluationary hist; native Am hist; relig in Am. **SELECTED PUBLICATIONS** Auth, Recycling Early American Religion: Some Historiographical Problems and Prospects, Fides et Historia 23, 91; auth, Poor Indians, Poor in Spirit: The Indian Impact on David Brainerd, New Englland Enceenters, Northwestern Univ Pr, 99; Kenneth S. Latourette, Handbook of Church Historians, Broadman Press, 95; The New York Review, The Conservative Pr in Eighteenth-and Nineteenth-Century America, Greenwood Press, 99. **CONTACT ADDRESS** Dept of Hist, Westmont Col, 955 La Paz Rd, Santa Barbara, CA 93108-1099. **EMAIL** pointer@westmont.edu

POINTER, STEVEN R.
DISCIPLINE AMERICAN AND BRITISH CHURCH HISTORY **EDUCATION** Duke Univ, BA, 72, PhD, 71; Trinity Evangelical Divinity Sch, MA, 76. **CAREER** History, Trinity Int Univ **SELECTED PUBLICATIONS** Auth, Joseph Cook, Boston Lecturer and Evangelical Apologist, 91. **CONTACT ADDRESS** Trinity Intl Univ, Col of Arts and Sciences, 2065 Half Day Road, Deerfield, IL 60015.

POIS, ROBERT
PERSONAL Born 04/24/1940, Washington, DC, m, 1972, 3 children **DISCIPLINE** HISTORY **EDUCATION** Grinnell Col, AB, 61; Univ Wisc, MA, 62; PhD, 65. **CAREER** Asst prof to prof, Univ Colo, 65-; vis prof, UCLA, 77-78. **HONORS AND AWARDS** Woodrow Wilson Fel, 61; Fac Teaching Award, 87; BFA Award; SOAR Award; Coun of Creative Res Book Award; Farrand Hall Teaching Award, 96; Intl Affairs Teaching Award, 96, 97. **MEMBERSHIPS** Am Hist Asn; German Studies Asn. **RESEARCH** Nazi Germany; Weimar Germany; German Expressionism in the plastic arts; Historiography, with particular emphases upon Historicism; Psychohistory, The Great War. **SELECTED PUBLICATIONS** Auth, The Role of clinical Training in Psychohistory, 90; auth, The National Socialist Volksgemeinschaft Fantasy and the Drama of National Rebirth, in Theatre in the Third Reich, the Prewar Years, 95; auth, "The Great War and the Holocaust," in German Studies in the Post-Holocaust Age. **CONTACT ADDRESS** Dept Hist, Univ of Colorado, Boulder, Hellems Bldg Room 204, 234 UCB, Boulder, CO 80309. **EMAIL** poisr@Colorado.edu

POLAK, EMIL J.
PERSONAL Born 08/16/1936, Bayshore, NY, m, 1968 **DISCIPLINE** HISTORY **EDUCATION** State Univ NYork, Albany, AB, 57; Columbia Univ, AM, 58; PhD, 70. **CAREER** Lectr, CUNY, Brooklyn, 61-65; lectr, St. John's Univ, 65-66; lectr, Staten Island Community Col, 66-67; instr, CUNY, 67-70; Queensborough Community Col, 70-. **HONORS AND AWARDS** Pi Gamma Mu, 56; Kappa Phi Kappa, 57; Rome Prize Fel, 63; Res Awds, PSC/CUNY, 77-99; ACLS/USSR Acad of Sci Grant, 81; Gladys Krieble Delmas Found Grant, 95; Distinguished Alumnus Awd, SUNY, Albany; NEH Summer Stipend, 97. **MEMBERSHIPS** Am Philog Assoc; AHA; Renaissance Soc of Am; Medieval Acad of Am; Int Soc for the Hist of Rhetoric; Am Soc for the Hist of Rhetoric; Int Assoc for Neo-Latin Studies; Medieval Latin Studies Group; Early Book Group. **RESEARCH** Medieval and Renaissance epistolography and secular oratory. **SELECTED PUBLICATIONS** Auth, "A Textual Study of Jacques de Dinant's Summa dictaminis", Etudes de philogie et d'histoire 28, (Geneva), 75; auth, Medieval and Renaissance Letter Treatise and Form Letters: A Census of Manuscripts Found in Eastern Europe and the Former U. S.S.R., Davis Medieval Texts and Studies, Koln, 93; auth, Medieval and Renaissance Letter Treatises and Form Letters: A Census of Manuscripts Found in Part of Western Europe, Japan, and the United States of America, Koln, 94. **CONTACT ADDRESS** Dept Hist, Queensborough Comm Col, CUNY, 22205 56th Ave, Bayside, NY 11364-1497.

POLAKOFF, KEITH IAN
PERSONAL Born 12/12/1941, New York, NY, m, 1964, 2 children **DISCIPLINE** AMERICAN HISTORY **EDUCATION** Clark Univ, BA, 63; Northwestern Univ, MA, 66, PhD, 68. **CAREER** Lectr US hist, Lehman Col, 67-69; from asst prof to assoc prof, 69-78, Prof US Hist, Calif State Univ, Long Beach, 78-, Ed, Hist Teacher, 72-77, prod mgr, 77-80; assoc dean, Sch Soc & Behav Sci, Cal State Univ, Long Beach, 80-84; Dean, School Fine Arts, 84-85; Dean School Soc Behav Sci, 85-86; Assoc VPres Acad Affairs, 86-, Calif State Univ. **MEMBERSHIPS** Orgn Am Historians. **RESEARCH** Reconstruction; post Civil War politics; history of American political parties. **SELECTED PUBLICATIONS** Auth, The Politics of Inertia, La State Univ, 73; coauth, Generations of Americans, St Martin's, 76; Political Parties in American History, John Wiley & Sons, 81. **CONTACT ADDRESS** Off of Acad Affairs, California State Univ, Long Beach, 1250 N Bellflower, Long Beach, CA 90840-0118. **EMAIL** kip@csulb.edu

POLASKY, JANET
DISCIPLINE COMPARATIVE EUROPEAN, EARLY MODERN AND MODERN FRENCH HISTORY **EDUCATION** Stanford Univ, PhD. **CAREER** Prof, Univ NH, 80-. **HONORS AND AWARDS** Prize in Arts and Lett, Belgian Royal Acad, 84; UNH Bk Prize, 85; Fulbright, 85-86, 96-97; NEH, 88; Pierlot Prize in Contemp Hist, 93; Lindberg Awd, 96; Gustavson fel, 97. **RESEARCH** Social Planning in Britain, France and Belgium, 1869-1914; Comparative History of Women in Revolution, 1787-1793. **SELECTED PUBLICATIONS** Auth, Revolution in Brussels, 1787-1793, 86; auth, Le Patron du Parti ourier belge, 94; auth, The Democratic Socialism of Emile Vandervelde, Between Reform and Revolution, 94. **CONTACT ADDRESS** Univ of New Hampshire, Durham, Durham, NH 03824. **EMAIL** jpolasky@christa.unh.edu

POLENBERG, RICHARD
PERSONAL Born 07/21/1937, New York, NY, m, 1988, 4 children **DISCIPLINE** AMERICAN HISTORY **EDUCATION** Brooklyn Col, BA, 58; Columbia Univ, MA, 59, PhD, 64. **CAREER** Lectr hist, Queens Col, 60-61; lectr, Brooklyn Col, 61-64, from instr to asst prof, 64-66; from asst prof to prof, 66-86, Goldwin Smith prof Am hist, Cornell Univ, 86-, Grants, Soc Sci Res Coun & Am Coun Learned Soc, 70-71. **HONORS AND AWARDS** Clark Distinguished Tchg Awd, 79; Am Bar Asn Silver Gavel Awd, 88. **RESEARCH** Twentieth century Am hist. **SELECTED PUBLICATIONS** Auth, Reorganizing Roosevelt's Government: 1936-1939, Harvard Univ, 66; ed, America at War: The Home Front, 1941-1945, Prentice-Hall, 68; Radicalism and Reform in the New Deal, Addison-Wesley, 72; auth, War and Society: The United States, 1941-1945, Lippincott, 72; coauth, The American Century, Wiley, 75; One Nation Divisible: Class, Race and Ethnicity in the United States Since 1938, Viking, 80; Fighting Faiths: The Abrams Case, The Supreme Court, and Free Speech, Viking, 87; The World of Benjamin Cardozo: Personal Values anda the Judicial Process, Harvard Univ, 97; auth, "The Era of Franklin D. Roosevelt A Brief History with Document," Bedford, 00. **CONTACT ADDRESS** Dept of Hist, Cornell Univ, Mcgraw Hall, Ithaca, NY 14853-0001. **EMAIL** rp19@cornell.edu

POLING, CLARK V.
PERSONAL 2 children **DISCIPLINE** ART HISTORY **EDUCATION** Yale Univ, BA, 62; Columbia Univ, MA, 66, PhD(art hist), 73 **CAREER** Asst prof, 73-79, assoc prof, 79-88, Prof Art Hist, Emory Univ, 88-; dir, Emory Univ Mus Fine Art and Archaeol, 1/82-12/86. **HONORS AND AWARDS** Ger Acad Exchange Serv grants, 77 & 81; NEH grant 78. **MEMBERSHIPS** Col Art Asn Am **RESEARCH** Bauhaus theories of art and design; Wassily Kandinsky; color theories of modern artists; surrealism; Andre Masson. **SELECTED PUBLICATIONS** Auth, Bauhaus Color, 76 & Contemporary Art in Atlanta Collections, 76, Atlanta High Mus Art; Contemporary Art in Southern California, 80; auth, Kandinsky au Bauhaus: Theories de la couleur et grammaire picturale, Change, Paris, spec issue, La Peinture, 2/76; auth, Kadinsky's Teaching at the Bauhaus: Color Theory and Analystical Drawing, Rizzoli, 87; Kadinsky: Russian and Bauhaus Years, 1815-1933, Solomon R Guggenheim Mus, 83; Henry Hornbostel/Michael Graves, Emory Univ Mus of Art & Archaeol, 85; Surrealist Vision and Technique: Drawings and Collages from the Pompidou Center and the Picasso Museum, Paris, Michel C Carlos Mus, Emory Univ, 96. **CONTACT ADDRESS** Art Hist Dept, Emory Univ, Carlos Hall, Atlanta, GA 30322. **EMAIL** cpoling@emory.edu

POLK, JIM
PERSONAL Born 07/26/1949, Spartanburg, SC, m, 1974, 2 children **DISCIPLINE** HISTORY **EDUCATION** Univ NC, AB, 71; Clemson Univ, MA, 81; Univ Sc, Eds, 86. **CAREER** Adj Prof, Univ SC at Aiken, 81-; Adj Prof, Col of Charleston, 98-. **RESEARCH** Local history. **SELECTED PUBLICATIONS** Auth, "Heros Among Us," column in Crosswalk News, Monchs Corner, SC; auth, "Doghouse Commentaries," column in The Monitor, Monchs Corner, SC; auth, "One Last Call to Colors," summer 99. **CONTACT ADDRESS** Hist, Polit Sci, Philos, Univ of So Carolina, Aiken, 471 Univ Pky, Aiken, SC 29801-6389. **EMAIL** jpolk@infoave.net

POLLACK, NORMAN
PERSONAL Born 05/29/1933, Bridgeport, CT, m, 1957, 1 child **DISCIPLINE** AMERICAN HISTORY **EDUCATION** Univ Fla, BA, 54; Harvard Univ, AM, 58, PhD(Am civilization), 61. **CAREER** From instr to asst prof hist, Yale Univ, 61-65; assoc prof, Wayne State Univ, 65-68; Prof Hist, Mich State Univ, 68-98, prof emeritus, 98-, Morse fac fel, Yale Univ, 64-65; Guggenheim fel, 68-69. **RESEARCH** American political and cultural history. **SELECTED PUBLICATIONS** Auth, Hofstadter on Populism: a critique of the age of reform, J Southern Hist, 60; The myth of Populist Anti-Semitism, Am Hist Rev, 62; The Populist Response to Industrial America, Harvard Univ, 62; coed, Builders of American Institutions, Rand McNally, 63; auth, Fear of man: Populism, authoritarianism and the historian, Agr Hist, 65; The Populist Mind, Bobbs, 67; coed, American Issues in the Twentieth Century, Rand McNally, 67; auth, The Just Polity, Illinois, 87; auth, The Humane Economy, Rutgers, 90. **CONTACT ADDRESS** 929 Roxburgh Ave, East Lansing, MI 48823.

POLLAK, MARTHA
PERSONAL Born 07/14/1951, Sighet, Romania **DISCIPLINE** ARCHITECTURE AND ARCHITECTURAL HISTORY **EDUCATION** Cornell Univ, BA, 75; MIT, PhD, 85. **CAREER** Assoc prof, Univ Ill, 91- . **HONORS AND AWARDS** Univ scholar, Unvi Ill; Visiting fel, CASUA, Nat Gallery of Art. **MEMBERSHIPS** SAH; CAA; Renaissance Soc of Am. **RESEARCH** Seventeenth century Italian architecture and urbanism. **SELECTED PUBLICATIONS** Auth, Turin, 1560-1680: Urban Design, Military Culture and the Creation of the Absolutist Capital, 91; ed, The Education of the Architect, 97. **CONTACT ADDRESS** Dept. of Art History, Univ of Illinois, Chicago, 935 W. Harrison, Mail Stop 201, Chicago, IL 60607-7039. **EMAIL** mpollak@uic.edu

POLLAK, OLIVER
PERSONAL Born 11/10/1943, London, England, m, 1966, 2 children **DISCIPLINE** HISTORY **EDUCATION** Calif State Univ, BA, 64; Univ Calif, Los Angeles, MA, 68; PhD, 73; Creighton Univ Law School, JD, 82. **CAREER** Univ Rhodesia; Univ Calif, Los Angeles; Univ Neb. **HONORS AND AWARDS** Mari Sandoz Spirit Awd, 96. **MEMBERSHIPS** Am Hist Asn, Neb State Bar Asn, Iowa State Bar Asn. **RESEARCH** History; British; Burma; Zimbabwe; Jewish; Bankruptcy; Debtor Creditor Relations. **SELECTED PUBLICATIONS** Auth, Theses and dissertations on southern Africa: An International Bibliography, G.K. Hall, 76; auth, Empires in Collision: Anglo-Burmese Relations in the Mid-Nineteenth Century, Greenwood Press, 79; auth, World Bibliography Series: Rhodesia/Zimbabwe, Clio Press, 79; auth, "Please, Sir I want some more, Loopholes, Austerity and the Cost of Living -Nebraska Exemption Policy Revisited," Nebraska Law Review, (94): 298-341; auth, "Workmen's Circle and the Labor Lyceum in Omaha, 1907-1977," Nebraska History, (95): 30-42; auth, "The Education of Henry Monsky, 1890-1938 - Omaha's American Jewish Hero," in Crisis & Reaction: The Hero in Jewish History, Creighton Univ Press, 95; auth, "Be Just Before You're Generous: tithing and charitable Contributions in Bankruptcy," Creighton Law Review, (96): 527-581; auth, "Gender and Bankruptcy: An Empirical Analysis of Evolving Trends in Chapter 7 and Chapter 13 Bankruptcy Filings, 1967-1997," Commercial Law Journal, (97): 333-338; auth, "A Medical Memoir of Terezin/Theresienstadt Concentration Camp by Felix Bachmann, MD," Kosmas: Czechoslovak and Central European Journal, (97): 127-155; auth, "Capitalism, Culture and Philanthropy - Charles N and Nettie Fowler Dietz of Omaha, 1881-1939," Nebraska History, (98): 34-43; auth, "Nathan S Yaffe and the Early Years of Yaffe Printing Co," Memories of the Jewish Midwest, (98): 29-40; auth, "The Yiddish Theater in Omaha, 1919-1969," in Yiddish Culture, Creighton Univ Press, 98; auth, "Robert Talbot Kelly and Picturesque Burma," Journal of Burma Studies, (98): 35-45; auth, "Fred Morrow fling - A One Hundred Year Retrospective on Historical Methodology," Nebraska History, (99): 166-168; auth, "Death of a Poet at a Young Age: George Inman Ellis," Platte Valley Review, (00): 89-96; auth, "Eric M Bonner, Africana Bookseller," African Research & Documentation, (99): 53-62. **CONTACT ADDRESS** Dept of Hist, Univ of Nebraska, Omaha, 6001 Dodge St, Omaha, NE 68182-0001. **EMAIL** opollak@unomaha.edu

POLLINI, JOHN
PERSONAL Born 10/15/1945, Boston, MA, m, 1967, 2 children **DISCIPLINE** ART AND ARCHAEOLOGY **EDUCATION** Univ Washington, BA, 68; Univ Calif, Berkeley, MA,

73, PhD, 78. **CAREER** Asst prof, Johns Hopkins, Dept of Classics, Curator of Archaeol Mus, 80-87; assoc prof, 87-91, prof, 91- , chr, 90-93, Dept of Art Hist, Univ Southern Calif, Dean, School of Fine Arts, 93-96. **HONORS AND AWARDS** Magna Cum Laude, 68; Fulbright Fel, 75-76; NEH Fel, 83-84, 95-96; ACLS Fel, 87-88. **MEMBERSHIPS** Archaeol Inst Am; Col Art Asn; Am Philol Asn; Soc for the Promotion of Roman Stud; Asn of Ancient Hist; German Archaeological Inst. **RESEARCH** Greek, Etruscan and Roman art and archaeology; ancient religion, mythology, narratology, rhetoric, propaganda and gender issues. **SELECTED PUBLICATIONS** Auth, The Portraiture of Gaius and Lucius Caesar, 87; auth, Roman Portraiture: Images of Character and Virtue, 90; auth, The Gemma Augustea: Ideology, Rhetorical Imagery, and the Construction of a Dynastic Narrative, in Narrative and Event in Ancient Art, Cambridge, 93; auth, The Acanthus of the Ara Pacis as an Apolline and Dionysiac Symbol of Anamorphosis, Anakyklosis and Numen Mixtum, in Von der Bauforschumg zur Denkmalpflege, 93; auth, The Augustus from Prima Porta and the Transformation of the Polykleitan Heroic Ideal, in Polykleitos, the Doryphoros, and Tradition, 95; auth, The Dart Aphrodite: A New Replica of the Arles Aphrodite Type, The Cult Image of Venus Victrix in Pompey's Theater at Rome, and Venusian Ideology and Politics in the Late Republic-Early Principate, in Latomus, 97; auth, The Warren Cup: Homoerotic Love and Sympotic Rhetoric in Silver, in Art Bull, 99; auth, Two Bronze Portrait Busts of Slave-Boys from a Shrine of Cobannus in Roman-Gaul, in Studia Varia: Occasional Papers on Antiquities of the J Paul Getty Museum, 01; auth, The Riace Bronzes: New Observations, in Acten des 14, Internationalen KongreBes fur Antiken Bronzen, 01; auth, Frieden-durch-Sieg-Ideologie und die Ara Pacis Augustae: Bildrhetorik und die Schopfung einer dynastischen Erzahlweise, in Interdisziplinares Kolloquium Historische Achitekturreliefs vom Alten Agypten bis zum Mittelalter, 02. **CONTACT ADDRESS** Dept of Art Hist, Von Kleinsmid Ctr 351, Univ of So California, Los Angeles, CA 90089-0047. **EMAIL** pollini@atsusc.edu

POLLITT, JEROME J.

PERSONAL Born 11/26/1934, Fair Lawn, NJ **DISCIPLINE** HISTORY OF ART, CLASSICAL PHILOLOGY **EDUCATION** Yale Univ, BA, 57; Columbia Univ, PhD(hist of art), 63. **CAREER** Instr classics, 62-65, from asst prof to assoc prof class art & archaeol, 65-73, chmn, Dept Classics, 75-77, Prof Class Archaeol & Hist of Art, Yale Univ, 73-98, prof emer, 98-, Chmn, Dept Hist of Art, 81-, Dean, 86-91; Morse fel, 67-68; ed, Am J Archaeol, 73-77. **MEMBERSHIPS** Archaeol Inst Am **RESEARCH** Greek art and archaeology; art criticism. **SELECTED PUBLICATIONS** Auth, The Art of Greece: 1400-31 BC, 65 & The Art of Rome: c 753 BC-337 AD, 66, Prentice-Hall; Art and Experience in Classical Greece, Cambridge Univ, 72; The Ancient View of Greek Art, Yale Univ, 74; The impact of Greek art on Rome, Trans Am Philol Asn, 78; Kernoi from the Athenian Agora, Hesperia, 79; Art in the Hellenistic Age, Cambridge Univ, 86; The Art of Greece, Sources and Documents, Cambridge Univ, 90; Personal Styles in Greek Sculpture, Cambridge Univ, 96. **CONTACT ADDRESS** Dept of Classics, Yale Univ, PO Box 208272, New Haven, CT 06520-8272. **EMAIL** jerome.pollitt@yale.edu

POMEROY, EARL

PERSONAL Born 12/27/1915, Capitola, CA, w, 1940, 4 children **DISCIPLINE** HISTORY **EDUCATION** San Jose State Col, AB, 36; Univ Calif, AM, 37, PhD, 40. **CAREER** Instr hist, Univ Wis, 40-42; asst prof hist, Univ NC, 42-45 & Ohio State Univ, 45-49; from assoc prof to prof hist, Univ Ore, 49-61, Beekman prof, 61-76; Prof Hist, Univ Calif, San Diego, 76-84, Ford fel, 53-54; Guggenheim fel, 56-57 & 72; Huntington Libr fel, 58; lectr, Bologna Ctr, Johns Hopkins Univ, 63-64; Coe vis prof, Stanford Univ, 67-68; Nat Endowment for Humanities fel, 68; fel, Ctr Advan Study Behav Sci, 74-75; vis prof hist, Univ Calif, San Diego, 75-76. **MEMBERSHIPS** AHA; Orgn Am Historians; Agr Hist Soc; Western Hist Asn. **RESEARCH** American Far West, especially in the 20th century. **SELECTED PUBLICATIONS** Auth, The Territories and the United States, 1861-1890, 47 & 69; Pacific Outpost, American Strategy in Guam and Micronesia, 51; In Search of the Golden West: The Tourist in Western America, Knopf, 57, 90; The Pacific Slope: A History of California, Oregon, Washington, Idaho, Utah and Nevada, Knopf, 65 & Univ Wash, 74-91; Computers in the Desert + Technology in Undeveloped Places - Transforming the Simple Life, Western Historical Quarterly, Vol 0025, 1994. **CONTACT ADDRESS** Dept of Hist, Univ of Oregon, Eugene, OR 97403-1288.

POMEROY, GEORGE

PERSONAL Born 08/14/1965, Bellingham, WA **DISCIPLINE** GEOGRAPHY **EDUCATION** W WA Univ, BA, 88; MS, 95; Univ Akron, PhD, 99. **CAREER** Instructor, Univ Akron, 95-99; Asst Prof, Shippensburg Univ, 99-. **MEMBERSHIPS** Asn of Am Geog; Am Planning Asn. **RESEARCH** Urban Geography; Urban and Regional Planning; Asia. **SELECTED PUBLICATIONS** Auth, "Perspectives on the Urban Fringe and Growth Boundary of a Small Metropolitan City," in Festschrift in Honor of Vladimir Milicic, W WA Univ Press, 95; co-auth, "Cultural Patterns of India," in New Frontiers in Indian Geography, (Allahabad Univ Press, 96), 58-84; co-auth, "Population Dynamics and Planning: China and India," in Regional Development and Planning for the 21st Century: New Priorities, New Philosophies, (Ashgate, 98), 81-100; co-auth, "Spatial Patterns of Crime in Indian Cities," in Urban Growth and Development in Asia, Vol II: Living in the Cities, Ashgate, 99; auth, "Urban Processes and Models of Urban Form in an Asian Context," in Geographical Research Perspectives for a New Millennium: Felicitations in Honor of Ashok K. Dutt, (Vikas Pub House, 00), 319-337; auth, "Chatham Village: The Enduring Legacy of Collaborative Genius," in A Geographic View of Pittsburgh and the Alleghenies: Precambrian to Post-Industrial, 00. **CONTACT ADDRESS** Dept Geog & Geol, Shippensburg Univ of Pennsylvania, 1871 Old Main Dr, Hippensburg, PA 17257. **EMAIL** gmpome@ship.edu

POMEROY, SARAH B.

PERSONAL Born 03/13/1938, New York, NY, m, 3 children **DISCIPLINE** CLASSICAL PHILOLOGY AND ANCIENT HISTORY **EDUCATION** Barnard Col, BA, 57; Columbia Univ, MA, 59, PhD, 61. **CAREER** Instr class lang, Univ Tex, 61-62; lectr classics, 63-68, asst prof, 68-75, Assoc Prof Classics, 75-97, distinguished prof, 97- , Hunter Col; Coordr, Women's Studies Prog, 75-, Lectr classics, Brooklyn Col, 66-67; Am Coun Learned Soc grant-in-aid, 73-74; Nat Endowment for Humanities summer stipend, 73; fel, 81-82; Ford Found fel, 74-75; res grant, Fac Res Award Prog, City Univ New York, 75-79 & 82-83; Danforth assoc, 76-. **HONORS AND AWARDS** ACLS grant, 73, 74; NEH summer stipend, 73; Hunter Col grant, 73-74; Ford Found fel, 74-75; fac res award CUNY 75-77, 82-83, 85-86; NEH fel 76; Danforth Assoc, 76-82; NEH grant, 79-81; NEH fel, 81-82; NEH, dir, Hum Inst on Women in Classical Antiquity, 83; fel, Hum Res Ctr, Australian Natl Univ, 86; NEH, dir, Summer Sem, 87, 89; NEH sr fel, 87-88; Scholars Incentive Awd, CUNY, 87; Pres Awd for Excellence in Scholarship, 95; Guggenheim fel, 99. **MEMBERSHIPS** Am Philol Asn; Archaeol Inst Am; Am Soc Papryologists; Friends Ancient Hist; Asn Ancient Historians; American Historical Assoc. **RESEARCH** Greek literature; women in classical antiquity; social history. **SELECTED PUBLICATIONS** Auth, Women in hellenistic Egypt from Alexander to Cleopatra, Wayne State Univ, reissue, 90; ed, Women's History and Ancient History, Univ North Carolina, 91; auth, Goddesses, Whores, Wives, and Slaves: Women in Classical Antiquity, Schocken, reissue 94; coauth, Women in the Classical World: Image and Text, Oxford, 94; auth, Xenophon Oeconomicus: A Social and Historical Commentary, Oxford, 94; coauth, Women's Realities, Women's Choices: An Introduction to Women's Studies, 2d ed, Oxford, 95; auth, Families in Classical and Hellenistic Greece: Representations and Realities, Oxford, 97; coauth, Ancient Greece, Oxford, 98; auth, Plutarch Advice to the Bride and Groom, Oxford, 99. **CONTACT ADDRESS** Dept of Classics, Hunter Col, CUNY, 695 Park Ave, New York, NY 10021-5085.

POMPER, PHILIP

PERSONAL Born 04/15/1936, Chicago, IL, m, 3 children **DISCIPLINE** HISTORY, RUSSIAN HISTORY AND PSYCHOHISTORY **EDUCATION** Univ Chicago, BA; MA; PhD; Wesleyan Univ, MAAE. **CAREER** Wesleyan Univ. **HONORS AND AWARDS** Assoc ed, History and Theory. **SELECTED PUBLICATIONS** Auth, Peter Lavroc and the Russian Revolutionary Movement, 72; auth, Sergei Nechaev, 79; auth, The Structure Of Mind In History, 85; ed, Trotsky's Notebooks, 1933-1935, 86; auth, Lenin, Trotsky, and Stalin: The Intelligentsia and Power, 90; auth, The Russian Revolutionary Intelligentsia, 2nd ed., 93; coed, History and Theory: Contemporary Readings, 98. coed, World History: Ideologies, Structures, and Identities, 98. **CONTACT ADDRESS** Wesleyan Univ, Middletown, CT 06459-0002. **EMAIL** ppomper@wesleyan.edu

PONG, DAVID

PERSONAL Born 09/28/1939, Hong Kong **DISCIPLINE** HISTORY **EDUCATION** Univ London, BA, 63; PhD, 69. **CAREER** Fel, Univ London, 66-69; asst prof, Univ Delaware, 69-73; assoc prof, 73-89; res fel, Australian Nat Univ, 78-81; vis prof, Princeton Univ, 88; prof, Univ Delaware, 89-; dir, EASP, 89-; ch, 92-98. **HONORS AND AWARDS** IHR Res Fel; ACLS Fel; Australian Nat Univ, Res Fel; Phi Kappa Phi. **MEMBERSHIPS** AAS; SQS. **SELECTED PUBLICATIONS** Auth, "Li Hung-chang and Shen Pao-chen: The Politics of Modernization," in Li Hung-chang and China's Early Modernization, eds. Samuel Chu, Kwan-ching Liu (ME Sharpe, 94): 79-107; auth, "China's Defense Modernization and the Revenue of the Maritime Customs Service, 1875-79," in Tradition and Metamorphosis in Modern Chinese History: Essays in Honor of Professor Kwan-ching Liu's Seventy-fifth Birthday, ed. Yenping Hao (Inst Mod Hist, Acad Sinica: Taipei, 98); auth, "China's Modern Navy and Changing Concepts of Naval Warfare up to the Time of the Sino-French War," in Coastal Defense and Maritime Economy of Modern China, Lee Kam-keung, eds. Lau Yee-cheung, Mak King-sang (Hong Kong: Mod Chinese Hist Soc: Hong Kong, 99): 341-66; auth, Shen Pao-chen and China's Modernization in the Nineteenth Century, Cambridge Univ Press (94), Chinese edition "Shen Baozhen yu Shijiushiji di Zhongguo xiandaihua, Guji Chubanshe (Shanghai), 00. **CONTACT ADDRESS** Dept History, Univ of Delaware, Newark, DE 19716-2555. **EMAIL** dpong@udel.edu

PONTIUS, ROBERT GILMORE, JR.

PERSONAL Born Pittsburgh, PA **DISCIPLINE** GEOGRAPHY **EDUCATION** Univ Pittsburgh, BS, 84; Ohio State Univ, MAS, 89; SUNY, PhD, 94. **CAREER** Teacher, US Peace Corp,s 85-87; TA to res asst, SUNY, 90-94; asst prof, Boston Univ, 94-95; assoc scientist, Tellus Inst & Stockholm Environ Inst, 95-97; president, Ecowise, 97-; vis asst prof, Clark Univ, 98-. **HONORS AND AWARDS** Phi Kappa Phi, 89; Fel, Syracuse Univ, 91-92; Fel, SUNY, 93-94; Grant, Oxfam Am, 95; grant, Nat Counc for the Soc Studies, 99; NSF Grant, 99. **MEMBERSHIPS** Int Soc for Ecol Econ; Assoc of Am Geogr; Phi Kappa Phi; Union of Concerned Sci; Coes & Patches Pond Watershed Assoc. **RESEARCH** Geographic Information Science, Statistics, International Development. **SELECTED PUBLICATIONS** Coauth, "Modeling spatial and temporal patterns of tropical land-use change", J of Biogeography 22, (95): 753-757; coauth, Polestar System Manual, Stockholm Environ Inst, 96; coauth, Energy Resources and Sustainability, Global Industrial and Soc Progress Inst, Tokyo), 96; coauth, "Water Futures: Assessment of Long-range Patterns and Problems", Comprehensive Assessment of the Freshwater Resources of the World, 96; coauth, "Identifying conservation priority areas in the tropics: a land-use change modeling approach, Conserv Biol, 00; coauth, Modeling land-use in the Ipswich watershed, Massachusetts, USA, Agr, Ecosystems & Environ, 00; coauth, Modeling the spatial pattern of land-use change with GEOMOD2: application and validation with Costa Rica, Agr, Ecosystems & Environ, 00; coauth, Land-use change model validation by a ROC method, Agr, Ecosysystem & Environ, 00; auth, Quantification error versus location error in comparison of categorical maps, Photogrammetic Eng & Remote Sensing, 00. **CONTACT ADDRESS** Dept Geog, Clark Univ, 950 Main St, Worcester, MA 01610.

POOS, L. R.

PERSONAL Born 02/08/1954, Richmond, IN, s **DISCIPLINE** HISTORY **EDUCATION** AB, Harvard Univ, 76; PhD, Cambridge Univ, UK, 84. **CAREER** Fel, Fitzwilliam Col, Cambridge Univ, UK, 80-83; asst prof, 83-89, assoc prof, 89-95, prof and chair, 95-, dept of hist, The Cath Univ of Amer. **HONORS AND AWARDS** Fel, Royal Hist Soc, UK. **MEMBERSHIPS** Social Sci Hist Asn; Selden Soc. **RESEARCH** English history 1300-1600; Social, economic, demographic, and legal history. **SELECTED PUBLICATIONS** Coauth, A Consistory court from the Diocese of Rochester 1363-4, The Eng Hist Rev, cvi, 652-65; 91; auth, A Rural Society after the Black Death: Essex, Cambridge Univ Press, (91), 1350-1525; auth, "The heavy-handed marriage counsellor: Regulating marriage in some later-medieval English local ecclesiastical-court jurisdictions," Amer Jour of Legal Hist, xxxix, (95), 291-309; Sec, lies and the church courts of pre-Reformation England, Jour of Interdisciplinary Hist, xxv, 585-607, 95; Coauth, with Lloyd Bonfield, Select cases in manorial courts 1250-1550: Property and family law, cxiv, Selden Soc, London, 98. **CONTACT ADDRESS** Dept. of History, Catholic Univ of America, Washington, DC 20064. **EMAIL** poos@cua.edu

POPE, DANIEL

PERSONAL Born 01/13/1946, Brooklyn, NY, m, 1970, 1 child **DISCIPLINE** AMERICAN HISTORY **EDUCATION** Columbia Univ, PhD, 73. **CAREER** Vis Asst Prof, 73-75, Carleton College; asst prof, 75-83; assoc prof, 83-, Univ Oregon; dept head, 00-. **HONORS AND AWARDS** Fulbright Sr Lectr, Phi Beta Kappa; Harvard Postdoc Fel; Burlington-Northern Dist Teaching Awd. **MEMBERSHIPS** AHA; OAH. **RESEARCH** Business and Economic History, history of nuclear power, advertising, marketing and consumer culture, radicalism and social movements. **SELECTED PUBLICATIONS** Auth, The Making of Modern Advertising, NY, Basic Books, 83, Japanese, Tokyo, Dentsu, 87; We Can Wait, We Should wait, Eugene's Nuclear Power Controversy 1968-70, Pacific Hist Rev, 90; Advertising as a Consumer Issue: An Historical View, J Social Issues, 91; Utilities and WPPSS Nuclear Plants 4 and 5: Seduced and Abandoned?, Columbia, 91; Antinuclear Activism in the Pacific Northwest: WPPSS and Its Enemies, in: John Findlay, ed, The Atomic West, Seattle, Univ WA Press, 98; ed, American Radicalism, Malden, MA: Basil Blackwell, 01. **CONTACT ADDRESS** Dept of History, Univ of Oregon, Eugene, OR 97403. **EMAIL** dapope@oregon.uoregon.edu

POPE, ROBERT G.

DISCIPLINE HISTORY **EDUCATION** Yale Univ, PhD. **CAREER** RETIRED, ASSOC PROF, HIST, STATE UNIV NY-BUFFALO **MEMBERSHIPS** Am Antiquarian Soc **SELECTED PUBLICATIONS** The Halfway Covenant, 69; The Notebook of the Reverend John Fiske, Colonial Soc, 74. **CONTACT ADDRESS** 1501 W Highway 160 #3, Pagosa Springs, CO 81147-9002.

POPKIN, JEREMY D.

PERSONAL Born 12/19/1948, Iowa City, IA, m, 1980, 2 children **DISCIPLINE** HISTORY **EDUCATION** Univ CA, Berkeley, BA 70, PhD 77; Harvard Univ, AM 71. **CAREER** Univ KY, asst prof to prof 78-; Univ Pitts, vis asst prof 77-78. **HONORS AND AWARDS** NEH-Newberry Library fel, 83; Max-Planck-Institut fur Geschichte, 85; Co-directory, NEH Summer Seminar for Col Teachers, 87; NEH res fel, 88-89; Fulbright Res Fel (France), 91-92; Vis scholar at Maison des Sciences de l'Home-Rhone-Alpes, 91-92; John Simon Guggenheim fel, 92-93; UK Arts and Sciences Distinguished Prof, 95-96. **MEMBERSHIPS** AHA; Soc French Hist Stud; ASECS. **RESEARCH** Europe, 1700-1870; French Revolution; history of the press; Jewish history. **SELECTED PUBLICATIONS** Auth, The Right-Wing Press in France, 1792-1800, 80; co-ed, Press and politics in Pre-Revolutionary France, 87; auth, News and Politics in the Age of Revolution: Jean Luzac's Gazette de Leyde, 89; auth, Revolutionary News: the Press in France, 1789-1799, 90; auth, History of Modern France, 93; ed, Media and Revolution, 95; auth, Short History of the French Revolution, 95; auth, The Memoires, secrets and the Culture of Publicity in 18th Century France, 98. **CONTACT ADDRESS** Dept of Hist, Univ of Kentucky, 1725 Patterson Office Tower 0027, Lexington, KY 40506. **EMAIL** popkin@pop.uky.edu

POPPINO, ROLLIE EDWARD
PERSONAL Born 10/04/1922, Portland, OR, m, 1950, 3 children **DISCIPLINE** LATIN AMERICAN HISTORY **EDUCATION** Stanford Univ, AB, 48, MA, 49, PhD(Brazilian hist), 53. **CAREER** Instr hist, Stanford Univ, 53-54; intel res spec Latin Am Off Res & Anal, US Dept State, 54-61; from asst prof to assoc prof, 61-67, Prof Hist, Univ Calif, Davis, 67-, Chmn Dept, 78-89, Lectr, Am Univ, 59-61; consult, US Dept State, 62-74; Soc Sci Res Coun res grant, Brazil, 63, travel grant, Brazil, 67-68; Nat Endowment for Humanities sr fel, Brazil, 67-68; Fulbright lectr, Brazil, 74. **HONORS AND AWARDS** Color D Pedro Awd, Sao Paulo Hist & Geog Inst. **MEMBERSHIPS** Am Hist Asn; Conf Latin Am Hist; Inst Hist Geografico Brasileiro. **RESEARCH** History of Brazil; Latin American international relations; Communism in Latin America. **SELECTED PUBLICATIONS** Auth, O processo politico no Brasil, 1929-45, Rev Brasileira Estud Polit, 64; International Communism in Latin America, Free Press, 64; coauth, A History of Modern Brazil, 1889-1964, Stanford Univ, 66; auth, Brazil: The Land and People, 68 & 73; Feira de Santana, Editora Itapua Salvador, 68; Las fuerzas armadas en la politica Brasilena, Estrategia, 71; contribr World Communism, A Handbook, 1918-1965, Hoover Inst, Stanford, 73; auth, Brazil after a decade of revolution, Current Hist, 74; Strategies of an Illusion - the World Revolution and Brazil 1922-1935 - Portuguese - Pinheiro,ps, American Historical Review, Vol 0097, 1992. **CONTACT ADDRESS** Dept of Hist, Univ of California, Davis, Davis, CA 95616.

PORRUA, ENRIQUE J.
PERSONAL Born 09/01/1967, Madrid, Spain, m, 2000, 2 children **DISCIPLINE** HISTORY **EDUCATION** Univsidad Complutense de Madric, Diplomatura, 90; BA, 93; Texas Tech Univ, MA, 99. **CAREER** President, Asociacion de Jovenes Antropologos, 93-95; TA to instr, Texas Tech Univ, 95-00. **HONORS AND AWARDS** Texas Tech Univ, Fel, 88, 95, 96, 98, 99. **MEMBERSHIPS** Phi Alpha Theta, Sigma Delta Pi, Soc for the Hist of Discoveries, Hakluyt soc, W Tex Hist Assoc, World Hist Assoc of Tex, MLA, Am Assoc of Teachers of Sp and Port. **RESEARCH** History of Exploration and Discoveries, History of the Pacific, Malaspina Expedition. **SELECTED PUBLICATIONS** Auth, "Noticias de Chiloe: Antonio de tova Arrendondo y su comision a la isla de Chiloe en 1791," Chiloeweb, Revista Online, (00); auth, "Malaspina in the Pacific," Main's Haul, (00); ed, The Diary of Antonio de tova on the Malaspina Expedition, 1789-1794, Edwin Mellen Pr, forthcoming. **CONTACT ADDRESS** 1661 Pepper Dr, El Centro, CA 92243. **EMAIL** enporrua@aol.com

PORSILD, CHARLENE
PERSONAL Born 02/14/1965, Yukon, Canada, m, 1995 **DISCIPLINE** HISTORY **EDUCATION** Univ Alberta, BA, 87; Univ Ottawa, MA, 98; Carleton Univ, PhD, 94. **CAREER** Vis Fulbright Fellow, Univ of Colorado-Boulder, 93-94; Asst Prof, Simon Fraser Univ, 95-97; Asst Prof, Univ Nebraska, 97-. **HONORS AND AWARDS** Fulbright Scholar, 93-94; W. Turrentine Jackson Prize & Clio Prize, 99. **MEMBERSHIPS** Canadian Historical Assoc; Western History Assoc. **RESEARCH** North Amer West; Women's History; Yukon & Alaska History. **SELECTED PUBLICATIONS** Auth, "Gamblers and Dreamers: Women, Men & Community in the Klondike," Vancouver, UBC Press, 98. **CONTACT ADDRESS** Dep History, Univ of Nebraska, Lincoln, 610 Oldfather, PO Box 880327, Lincoln, NE 68588-0327. **EMAIL** cporsild2@unl.edu

PORTER, DAVID L.
PERSONAL Born 02/18/1941, Holyoke, MA, m, 1970, 2 children **DISCIPLINE** HISTORY, POLITICAL SCIENCE **EDUCATION** Franklin Col, BA, 63; Ohio Univ, MA, 65; Pa State Univ, PhD (hist), 70. **CAREER** Asst prof hist, Rensselaer Polytech Inst, 70-75; educ admin asst, Troy Civil Ser Comn, NY, 75-76; from asst prof to prof, 76-86, Louis Tuttle Shangle Prof Hist, William Penn Univ, 86-, Dir Pre-Law Prog, 79-; Co-dir Am studies, Rennselaer Polytech Inst, 72-74; chmn hist, Troy Area Bicentennial Comt, 75-76; consult, Midwest Rev, 77-78; acting chair, Social and Behavioral Sciences Div, Wm Penn Univ, 00. **HONORS AND AWARDS** President's Schol, 59-63; Franklin's Schol, 62-63; Lancers; Blue Key; Alpha; Phi Alpha Theta, advisor, 77; Kappa Delta Pi; Nat Sci Found Grant, 67; Fac Travel Grants, 74, 77, 81, 86; NEH grant, 79; Eleanor Roosevelt Inst Grant, 81; Distinguished Service Awd, United Nations Asn, 81; Prof Development Grant, 86, 89, 92; Choice Outstanding Academic Book, 88, 89. **MEMBERSHIPS** AHA; Orgn Am Historians; Soc Hist Am Foreign Rels; North Am Soc Sport Hist; Soc Am Baseball Res; Ctr for the Study of the Presidency; State Hist Soc Iowa; Professional Football Res Asn; Col Football Res Asn. **RESEARCH** United States political history; United States diplomatic history; United States sport history. **SELECTED PUBLICATIONS** Auth, The Seventy-Sixth Congress and World War II, 1939-1940, Univ Mo Press, 79; Congress and the Waning of the New Deal, Kennikat Press, 80; Biographical Dictionary of American Sports: Baseball, Greenwood Press, 87; Biographical Dictionary of American Sports: Football, Greenwood Press, 87; Biographical Dictionary of American Sports: Outdoor Sports, Greenwood Press, 88; Biographical Dictionary of American Sports: Basketball and Other Indoor Sports, Greenwood Press, 89; Biographical Dictionary of American S ports: 1989-1992 Supplement for Baseball, Football, Basketball, and Other Sports, Greenwood Press, 92, (92-95 supplement, 95); compiler, A Cumulative Index to the Biographical Dictionary of American Sports, Greenwood Press, 93; auth, African-American Sports Greats, Greenwood Press, 95; author of numerous book and journal articles and book reviews; auth, Biographical Dictionary of Am Sports: Baseball, Revised and Expanded Edition, 3 vols. Greenwood Press, 00; co-auth, San Diego Padres Encyclopedia, Sports Publishing, 00 Assoc ed (with others) Am National Biography, 24 vols. Oxford Univ Press, 99. **CONTACT ADDRESS** Soc and Behav Sci Div, William Penn Univ, 201 Trueblood Ave, 110C Penn , Oskaloosa, IA 52577-1799. **EMAIL** porterd@wmpenn.edu

PORTER, ELLEN-JANE LORENZ
DISCIPLINE HISTORY OF MUSIC **EDUCATION** Wellesley, BA, 29; Wittenberg, MSM, 71; Union Grad Sch, PhD, 78. **CAREER** IND LECT, AUTHOR, COMPOSER. **MEMBERSHIPS** Am Antiquarian Soc **RESEARCH** Spirituals **SELECTED PUBLICATIONS** Auth, Folk Hymns for Handbells, 75; auth, Music Our Forefathers Sang, 78; auth, articles on Am mus; comp, for choruses, chamber groups; auth, Glory Hallelujah: The Story of the Campmeeting Spiritual, 80; comp, anthem arr of Am folk hymns, The Hymn 41; auth, "The Hymnody of the Evangelical United Brethren Church," Jour of Theol 91, 87. **CONTACT ADDRESS** 6369 Pebble Court, Dayton, OH 45459.

PORTER, GLENN
PERSONAL Born 04/02/1944, New Boston, TX, m, 1987 **DISCIPLINE** HISTORY **EDUCATION** Rice Univ , BA 66; John Hopkins Univ, MA 68, PhD 70. **CAREER** Harvard Grad Sch of Bus, asst prof 70-76; Hagley Museum and Lib, dir Reg Ec Hist Res Cen, 76-83, dir 84. **HONORS AND AWARDS** Pres, Bus Hist Con; Pres, Ind Res Lib Assn. **MEMBERSHIPS** BHC; SHT; SAH; AAM **RESEARCH** Hist of Am Business; the business use of design and archit. **SELECTED PUBLICATIONS** Cultural Forces and Commercial Constraints: Designing Packaging in the Twentieth Century United States, in: Journal of Design History, 98; Industrialization and the Rise in Big Business, in: Charles W Calhoun, ed, The Gilded Age, 96; Troubled Marriage: Raymond Loewy and the Pennsylvania Railroad, in Amer Herit of Invention and Technology, 96; The Rise of Big Business, 73, revised 92. **CONTACT ADDRESS** Hagley Mus and Libr, Wilmington, DE 19807.

PORTER, JEANNE CHENAULT
PERSONAL Born 03/18/1944, New York, NY, m, 1977, 2 children **DISCIPLINE** ART HISTORY **EDUCATION** Columbia Univ, BA, 65; Univ Mich, Ann Arbor, MA, 66, PhD, 71. **CAREER** Asst prof Baroque, Univ Tenn, Knoxville, 69-72; from asst prof to assoc prof Baroque & Renaissance, Finch Col, 72-74; assoc prof Baroque art, Pa State Univ, University Park, 74-, Adj asst prof surv, Hunter Col, 74. **HONORS AND AWARDS** Ford Foundation Grant, 67; Fulbright Grant to Rome, 68-9; Belgian Gov't Grant, 68. **MEMBERSHIPS** Col Art Asn Am. **RESEARCH** Italian, Spanish and French Baroque painting; Rococo painting; modern American painting. **SELECTED PUBLICATIONS** Contributing auth, Raffuello e l'Europa, Accademia Nazionale dei Lincei, Centro di Studi cultura e l'imagine a Roma, Rome, 92; co-ed, Parthenope's Splendor, Art of the Golden Age in Naples, Papers in Art Hist from the Penn State Univ, Vol VII, 94; A Documentary History of Naples, 1600-1800, Italica Press, Vol IV of a 5 vol anthology, 98-99; James Brooks, Am Nat Biog, 98. **CONTACT ADDRESS** Pennsylvania State Univ, Univ Park, 229 Arts Bldg, University Park, PA 16802-2901. **EMAIL** jcp1@psu.edu

PORTER, JOHN R.
PERSONAL Born 04/28/1949, Levis, PQ, Canada **DISCIPLINE** ART HISTORY **EDUCATION** Laval Univ, LL, 71, MA, 72; Univ Montreal, PhD, 82. **CAREER** Asst cur, Can art, Nat Gallery Can, 72-78; prof, art hist, Laval Univ; chief cur, Montreal Mus Fine Arts, 90-93; Dir, Musee Du Quebec, 93-. **SELECTED PUBLICATIONS** Auth, number of books on the history of early painting, sculpture and furniture production in Quebec. **CONTACT ADDRESS** Univ of Saskatchewan, 9 Campus Dr, Saskatoon, SK, Canada S7N 5AZ.

PORTER, JONATHAN
PERSONAL Born 06/20/1959, Boston, MA, m, 1959 **DISCIPLINE** HISTORY **EDUCATION** Harvard Univ, AB, 60; Univ Colo, MA, 63; Univ Calif, Berkeley, PhD, 71. **CAREER** Instr, Univ of Colo, 64-65; Instr, Univ N Mex, 69-71, Asst Prof, 71-74, Assoc Prof, 74-57, Prof, 57-. **HONORS AND AWARDS** Soc Sci Res Coun, Am Coun of Learned Socs. **MEMBERSHIPS** Asn for Asian Studies, Int Conf Group on Portugal. **RESEARCH** Early Modern Chinese History, History of European Expansion in Asia, Macau. **SELECTED PUBLICATIONS** Auth, Tseng Kuo-fan's Private Bureaucracy, Berkeley: Univ of Calif, Center for Chinese Studies, Monograph No 9, 72; auth, All Under Heaven: The Chinese World, (photographs by Eliot Porter, NY: Pantheon Books), 83; auth, Iceland, photographs by Eliot Porter, Boston: Little, Brown and co, 89; auth, "The Transformation of Macau," in Pacific Affairs, 66, 1, (93), 7-20; auth, Macau: The Imaginary City, Culture and Society, 1557 to the Present, (Boulder: Westview Press), 96; auth, "Macau 1999," in Current History, 96, 611 (97), 282-286; auth, "The Troublesome Feringhi: Late Chinese Perceptions of the Portuguese and Macau," in Portuguese Studies Rev, 7, 2, (99), 11-35. **CONTACT ADDRESS** Dept Hist, Univ of New Mexico, Albuquerque, Albuquerque, NM 87131-0001. **EMAIL** jporter@unm.edu

PORTER, MICHAEL LEROY
PERSONAL Born 11/23/1947, Newport News, VA, s **DISCIPLINE** LITERATURE, HISTORY **EDUCATION** VA State Univ, BA, (hon) sociology 1969; Atlanta Univ, MA, hist 1972; Leonardo DaVinci Acad, Rome, Italy, MCP Contem 1983-84; Emory Univ, PhD hist/Amer studies 1974; Sorbonne Univ, postdoct, hist, Paris France, 1979; Thomas Nelson Community Coll, cert crim justice 1981; US Armed Forces Staff Coll, Norfolk VA, US Pres Appt, 1987. **CAREER** WA State Univ, asst prof of history, black studies prog 1974-75; Mohegan Comm Coll, Dept History lectr 1975-76; Newport News VA, asst education coord, education comp, target proj prog 1977; Hampton Univ, asst prof history 1977-80; NC Mutual Ins Co, life ins underwriter 1980-81; Mullins Prot Serv VA Bch, private investigator, 81-83; Amer Biographical Inst Raleigh, media freelancer 1984-85, publications dir/deputy governor 1985-; Old Dominion Univ, Norfolk VA, consultant 1985; Michael Porter Enterprises International, president, founder, 85-88; INTL Biographical Ctr, Cambridge England, Deputy Dir Gen, 86-. **HONORS AND AWARDS** 1st Black Concert Pianist to play Carnegie Hall, 1963; Lyon Dissertation Prize, 1974; Ebony Magazine, Eligible Bachelor, 1975; Outstanding Black, 1992; Hero, 1992; International Honors Cup, 1992; Abira Genius Grant, 1992; World Greetings, 1992; Pioneer Awd, 1992; Great American, 1991; World Intellectual, 1993; Golden Academy Awd, 1991; One of 500 Leaders of Influence in the 20th Century; Intl Hall of Leaders, Amer Biographical Inst, 1988; participant (exhibit), DuSable Museum of Black History, 1988; honoree, Intl Exhibit, Singapore, Malaysia, 1988; Outstanding Man of the World, Ormiston Palace, Tasmania, Australia, 1989; Exhibit, Intl Music Museum, London, ENG, 1989; Poetry Reading, Royal Palace, Lisbon, Portugal, 1998; Michael Porter Poetry Exhibit, Internet Intl Poetry Hall of Fame, 1997-2002; Lecture, Oxford Univ, Oxford, ENG, 1997; Famous Quote, Leningrad, Russia, 1998; 20th Century Awd for Achievement, 1990; Black History Maker, 1992; International Man of the Year, 1992; Most Admired Person of the Decade, 1990-99; Recipient, Grant For Exceptionally Gifted Poets, 1998; US Congress, Certificate of Appreciation, 1991; Honorary US Congressman, 1993; Hampton History Center, Historical Marker, 1992; Appearances before US President's Council of Economic Advisors & Senate Finance Committee, 1992; Honorary Knighthood, 1997; US Presidential Medal of Freedom, 1993; Outstanding People of the 20th Century. **MEMBERSHIPS** Life patron World Inst of Achievement 1985; curator "Michael L Porter Historical & Literary Collection"; World Literary Acad 1984-85; World Biographical Hall of Fame 1985; Federal Braintrust, 1990; Intl Advisory Council, 1989-; African American Hall of Fame, 1994; Elite International, 1992; bd of governors, Amer Biog Inst, 1986; Phi Beta Kappa; Intl Academy of Intellectuals, 1993; Famous Poet's Society, 1996; chairman, US Selective Service Bd #32, 1986-92; chief delegate, Intl Congress on Arts & Communications, Nairobi, Kenya, 1990. **SELECTED PUBLICATIONS** Auth, "Black Atlanta: The Formation of a Black Community, 1905-1930," Journal of Ethnic Studies (78); auth, "Atlanta's Black Constructed Buildings: Expressions of the Black Experience," Journal of Ethnic Studies (78); Television Programs: Cited On World News Tonight; Hard Copy; 60 Minutes; Current Affairs; Entertainment Tonight; CBS Evening News; The Remarkable Journey; Journey of African American Athelete, 1995; Eve's Bayou, 1997; 4 Little Girls; NBC Nightly News; Film: The Making of Black Atlanta, 1974; 1st Black Elected to Intl Academy of Intellectuals, Paris, France, 1993; Radio: Empire State Bldg Broadcasting Ctr, WRIN, 1997; Publications: Ebony, Jet, Intl, Digest, Talent; Contemporary Authors, Outstanding Scholars of the 20th Century. **CONTACT ADDRESS** Archives Administrator, 3 Adrian Circle, Hampton, VA 23669-3814.

PORTER, THEODORE
PERSONAL Born 12/03/1953, Kelso, WA, m, 1979, 1 child **DISCIPLINE** HISTORY **EDUCATION** Stanford Univ, AB, 76; Princetion Univ, PhD, 81. **CAREER** Mellon Postdoctoral,

Calif Inst of Technol, 81-84; from asst prof to assoc prof, Univ Va, 84-91; from assoc prof to prof, Univ Calif at Los Angeles, 91-. **HONORS AND AWARDS** Ludwik Fleck Book Prize, Soc for Soc Studies of Sci; grants and fels from Nat Sci Found & Guggenheim Found. **MEMBERSHIPS** Hist of Sci Soc, Am Hist Asn, Soc for Soc Studies of Sci, Soc for Lit and Sci. **RESEARCH** Cultural History of Physical and Social Sciences in Modern Europe, History of Statistics, Measurement, and Quantification. **SELECTED PUBLICATIONS** Auth, The Rise of Statistical Thinking 1820-1900, Princeton Univ Press, 86; auth, Trust in Numbers: The Pursuit of Objectivity in Science and Public Life, Princeton Univ Press, 95. **CONTACT ADDRESS** Dept Hist, Univ of California, Los Angeles, PO Box 951473, Los Angeles, CA 90095-1473. **EMAIL** tporter@history.ucla.edu

PORTERFIELD, RICHARD MAURICE
PERSONAL Born 07/19/1933, Baltimore, MD, m, 1993, 2 children **DISCIPLINE** EUROPEAN EXPANSION **EDUCATION** Johns Hopkins Univ, BA, 55; Univ Pa, MA, 57; Temple Univ, PhD, 78. **CAREER** Asst prof, 61-71, assoc prof hist, 71-, Chrmn Dept, 79-92, Glassboro St. Col; Prof Emer, Rowan Univ NV, 98. **MEMBERSHIPS** AHA; Conf Brit Studies; Asn Can Studies US. **RESEARCH** Canada and British Empire; Imperialism; European expansion. **SELECTED PUBLICATIONS** Auth, British Imperial Policy and the Quebecois in the Nineteenth Century, Quebec Studies, Vol I 17-43, 83; auth, Cecil Rhodes, Historic World Leaders, 94; auth, H.H. Kitchener, Historic World Leaders, 94. **CONTACT ADDRESS** Dept of History, Rowan Univ, 201 Mullica Hill Rd, Glassboro, NJ 08028-1702. **EMAIL** richport@bellatlantic.net

PORTON, GARY GILBERT
PERSONAL Born 03/12/1945, Reedley, CA, m, 1968, 2 children **DISCIPLINE** HISTORY OF JUDAISM **EDUCATION** UCLA, BA, 67; Hebrew Union Col, MA, 69; Brown Univ, PhD, 73. **CAREER** Asst prof, 73-80, assoc prof Relig Studies, 80-84, prof relig studies, Univ IL, 84-, prof Dept Hist, 91, prof Prog Comp Lit, Guggenheim fel, 82-83; assoc, Ctr Advan Study, Univ Ill, 82-83. **MEMBERSHIPS** Soc Bibl Lit; Europ Asn Jewish Studies. **RESEARCH** Rabbinic lit; Jewish Bibl exegesis; hist of Rabbinic Judaism. **SELECTED PUBLICATIONS** Auth, The Traditions of Rabbi Ishmael I, 76, II, 77, III, 78 & IV, 82, E J Brill; The Grape Cluster in Jewish art and literature in late antiquity, J Jewish Studies, 76; Midrash: The Bible and the Palestinian Jews in the Greco-Roman period, Aufsteig Niedergang Romischen Welt, 78; Understanding Rabbaic Midrash, KTAU, 85; Goyim: Gentiles and Israelites in Moshrah-Csefla, Scholars Press, 88; The Stranger within Your Gates: Converts and Conversion in Rabbinic Literature, Chicago, 94. **CONTACT ADDRESS** Univ of Illinois, Urbana-Champaign, 707 S Mathews Ave, Urbana, IL 61801-3625. **EMAIL** g_porton@uiuc.edu

POSADAS, BARBARA MERCEDES
PERSONAL Born 10/02/1945, Chicago, IL, m, 1982 **DISCIPLINE** AMERICAN HISTORY **EDUCATION** DePaul Univ, BA, 67; Northwestern Univ, MA, 71, PhD(US hist), 76. **CAREER** Instr, 74-76, asst prof , 76-89, assoc prof Hist, 89-99, Prof, Northern Ill Univ, 99-. **HONORS AND AWARDS** Senior Fulbright Research Awd, 82-83, Phillipines; Postdoctoral Research Fellowship, Asian American Studies Center, Institute of American Cultures, U.C.L.A., 87-88; Harry E. Pratt Memorial Awd, Il State Historical Society, 92 (given annually for the best article in the Il Historical Journal; VIP Gold Awd, Filipino American National Historical Society, 94; Fil-Am Image Magazine 1996-97 Twenty Outstanding Filipino-Americans in the United States and Canada Awd; Summer research Grant, Northern Il Univ, 97; Summer Research Stipend, National Endowment for the Humanities, 97. **MEMBERSHIPS** Orgn Am Historians, Am Hist Asn, Urban Hist Asn, Immigration and Ethnic Hist Soc, Asn for Asian American Studies, Filipino Am National Hist Soc, Filipino Am Hist Soc of Chicago, Il State Hist Soc, Chicago Hist Soc. **RESEARCH** United States urban history; United States women's history; United States social history. **SELECTED PUBLICATIONS** Auth, A home in the country: Suburbanization in Jefferson Township, 1870-1889, Chicago Hist, fall 78; Crossed Boundaries in Interracial Chicago: Philipino American families since 1925, Amerasia J, fall/ winter 81; The Hierarchy of Color and Psychological Adjustment in an Industrial Environment: Filipinos, the Pullman Company and the Brotherhood of Sleeping Car Porters, Labor Hist, summer 82; Suburb into Neighborhood: The Transformation of Urban Identity on Chicago's Periphery--Irving Park as a Case Study, 1970-1910, J Il State Hist Soc, autumn 83; To Preserve the Home: Reform, Suffrage, and the Changing Role of Illinois Club Women, in Roger D. Bridges & Rodney O. Davis, eds, Illinois:Its History and Legacy, 84; Hancock County's Cambre House, A Rare Survivor of Icarian Community, Historic Ill, Feb 85, written with Wm. B. Coney; Will the Real Pinoy Please Stand Up? Filipino Immigration to America: A Review Article, Pilipinas: J of Philipine Studies, fall 85, written with Roland Guyotte; At a Crossroad: Filipino American History and the Old-Timer' Generation, Amerasia J, 86-87; Concrete in Illinois: Its History and Preservation, Ill Preservation Series Number 8, 87, written with William B. Coney; Mestiza Girlhood: Interracial Families in Chicago's Filipino American Community Since 1930, in Judy Yung, ed, Making Waves: Writings About Asian American Women (89); Ethnic Life and Labor in Chicago'sPre-World War II Filipino Community, in Robert Asher and Charles Stephenson, eds, Labor Divided: Race and Ethnicity in United States Labor Struggles, 1940-1960 , 90; Unintentional Immigrants: Chicago's Filipino Foreign Students Become Settlers, 1900-1941, J Amer Ethnic Hist, spring 90, written with Roland L. Guyotte; Jose Rizal and the Changing Nature of Filipino Identity in an American Setting: Filipinos in Twentieth Century Chicago, Revue Francais d'Etudes Americaines, Feb 92, written with Roland L. Guyotte; Aspiration and Reality: Occupational and Educational Choice among Filipino Migrants to Chicago, 1900-1935, Ill Hist J, summer 92, written with Roland L. Guyotte; Northern Illinois University, in Gary Y. Okihiro and Lee C. Lee, eds, East of California: New Perspectives in Asian American Studies, 92; Celebrating Rizal Day: The Emergence of a Filipino Tradition in Twentieth Century Chicago, in Genevieve Fabre and Ramon A. Gutierrez, eds, Feasts and Celebrations in North American Ethnic Communities, 95, written with Roland L. Guyotte; Teaching About Chicago's Filipino Americans, OAH Magazine of History, summer 96; Filipino Americans, in Cynthia Linton, ed, The Ethnic Handbook: A guide to the Cultures and Traditions of Chicago's Diverse Communities, 96; Crossing the Collar Line: Working Women at Desks, Switchboards, and Tables, J Urban Hist, Sept 97; Filipinas, in Wilma Mankiller, et al, eds, The Reader's Companion to U.S. Women's History, 98; America's History, Vol 1 to 1877: Student Guide, 93, written with Stephen J. Kneeshaw, Timothy R. Mahoney, Gerald J. Goodwin, and Linda Moore; Refracting America: Gender, Race, Ethnicity, and Environment in American History to 1877, 93, ed with Robert McColley; auth, The Filipino Americans, 99. **CONTACT ADDRESS** Dept of Hist, No Illinois Univ, 1425 W Lincoln Hwy, De Kalb, IL 60115-2825. **EMAIL** bposadas@niu.edu

POST, GAINES
PERSONAL Born 09/22/1937, Madison, WI, m, 1969, 2 children **DISCIPLINE** HISTORY **EDUCATION** Cornell Univ, BA, 59; Oxford Univ, BA, 63; Stanford Univ, PhD, 69. **CAREER** Asst prof, 69-73, assoc prof, 73-83, Univ Texas Austin; exec dir, Rockefeller Found Comn on the Humanities, 78-80; dean of faculty and sr vpres, 83-88, assoc prof hist, 83-88, prof hist, 88-, Claremont McKenna Col. **HONORS AND AWARDS** Rhodes scholar, 61-63. **MEMBERSHIPS** Amer Hist Asn, Inter-Univ Sem on Armed Forces and Soc. **RESEARCH** Twentieth century European diplomatic and military history; twentieth century Germany **SELECTED PUBLICATIONS** The Civil-Military Fabric of Weimar Foreign Policy, Princeton, Princeton Univ Press, 73; Co-ed, Essays in Honour of Gordon Craig, The Intl Hist Rev, v1, n4, Oct, 79; The Humanities in American Life: Report of the Commission on the Humanities, Berkeley, Univ Calif Press, 80; Ed, German Unification: Problems and Prospects, Claremont, Keck Ctr for Intl and Strat Studies, 92; Dilemmas of Appeasement: British Deterrence and Defense, 1934-1937, Ithaca, Cornell Univ Press, 93; auth, Memoirs of a Cold War Son, Univ of Iowa Press (Iowa City), 00. **CONTACT ADDRESS** Claremont McKenna Col, 850 Columbia Ave., Claremont, CA 91711. **EMAIL** gpost@mckenna.edu

POST, ROBERT C.
PERSONAL Born 03/24/1937, Pasadena, CA, m, 1971 **DISCIPLINE** U.S. HISTORY **EDUCATION** UCLA, PhD, 73. **CAREER** Historian, National Park Service, 72-73; historian, National Museum of History & Technology, 74-80; curator, National Museum of Am History, 80-95, emer, 95-; assoc dir, Lemelson Ctr for the Study of Invention and Innovation, 96; adjunct prof, Univ Maryland, 97-; ed board, Fitzroy Dearborn Publishers. **HONORS AND AWARDS** President, Soc for the History of Technology; Distinguished Retiring Ed Awd, Council of Editors of Learned Journals; Resident Fel, Dibner Inst for the History of Science and Technology; Awds in Recognition of Exceptional Services, Smithsonian Inst; Certificate of Merit, Art Directors Club of Metropolitan Washington; Res Fel, Smithsonian Res Foundation. **MEMBERSHIPS** Soc for the History of Technology; Am Historical Asn; Org of Am Historians; Soc for Industrial Archaeology; Railway and Locomotive Historical Soc. **RESEARCH** History and historiography of technology; technical museums; urban history; social construction of technological systems. **SELECTED PUBLICATIONS** Auth, Physics, Patents, and Politics, Science History Publications, 76; ed, 1876: A Centennial Exhibition, National Museum of History and Technology, 76; ed, Every Four Years: The American Presidency, Smithsonian Books, 84; auth, The Tancook Whalers: Origins, Rediscovery, Revival, Maine Maritime Museum, 86; ed, In Context: History and the History of Technology, Lehigh Univ Press, 89; auth, Street Railways and the Growth of Los Angeles, Golden West Books, 89; ed, Yankee Enterprise: The Rise of the American System of Manufacturers, Smithsonian Inst Press, 95; auth, High Performance: The Culture and Technology of Drag Racing, Johns Hopkins Univ Press, 96. **CONTACT ADDRESS** National Museum of American History, Smithsonian Inst, Washington, DC 20560. **EMAIL** 75762.2476@compuserve.com

POSTLE, MARTIN J.
DISCIPLINE BRITISH PAINTING **EDUCATION** Univ London, PhD. **CAREER** Adj asst prof; dir, London prog. **SELECTED PUBLICATIONS** Co-auth, The Artist's Model: Its Role, British Art from Lely to Etty, Nottingham, 91; auth, Sir Joshua Reynolds and the Great Style, Cambridge, 93. **CONTACT ADDRESS** Dept of Art Hist, Univ of Delaware, 18 E Main St, #318, Newark, DE 19716-2520.

POSTMA, JOHANNES
PERSONAL Born 01/14/1935, Netherlands, m, 1961, 2 children **DISCIPLINE** MODERN HISTORY **EDUCATION** Graceland Col, BA, 62; Univ Kans, MA, 64; Mich State Univ, PhD, 70. **CAREER** Instr hist, Western Mich Univ, 64-66; from asst prof to assoc prof, 68-76, Prof Hist, Minnesota State Univ, 76-01. **HONORS AND AWARDS** Am Coun Learned Soc fel, 72-73; NIAS (Netherlands Inst of Advanced Studies) fel, 95-96. **MEMBERSHIPS** AHA **RESEARCH** Atlantic slave trade; Dutch colonial empire. **SELECTED PUBLICATIONS** Auth, "The Dimension Of The Dutch Slave Trade From Western Africa," J African Hist (72); auth, "West African Exports And The Dutch West India Company, 1675-1731," Econ & Soc Hist J (73); auth, "The Origin Of African Slaves," in Race And Slavery In The Western Hemisphere, Princeton Univ (74); auth, The Dutch Slave Trade, Revue Francaise D'outre-Mer, 75; auth, "Mortality In The Dutch Slave Trade," in The Uncommon Market (Acad Press, 79); auth, The Dutch in the Atlantic Slave Trade, 1600-1815, Cambridge Univ Press (NYork), 90; auth, "The Dispersal of African Slaves in the West by Dutch Slave Traders,m 1630-1803," in The Atlantics Slave Trade: Effects on Economies, Societies, and Peoples in Africa, the Americas, and Europe, ed. Inikori and Engerman (Durham, Duke Univ Press, 92); auth, "The Merchant-Warrior Pacified--The Voc: The Dutch-East-India-Company And Its Changing Political-Economy In India," Am Hist Rev 99 (94); auth, "Slave Society In The Danish West-Indies--St-Thomas, St-John, And St-Croix-Nat Hall," J Of Am Hist 80 (94); coauth, "Brazil and Holland as Commercial Partners on the West African Coast During the Eighteenth Century," in Melanges offerts a Frederic Mauro, series Arquivos do Centro Cultural Calouste Gulbenkian 34 (95): 399-427; auth, "Blacks In The Dutch World--The Evolution Of Racial Imagery In A Modern Society," J Of Interdisciplinary Hist 26 (96); auth, "A Monopoly Relinguished: The West India Company and the Atlantic Slave Trade," De Halve Maen 70 (97): 81-88; auth, "Breaching the Mercantile Barriers of the Dutch Colonial Empire: North American Trade with Surinam during the Eighteenth Century," in Research in Maritime History, ed. Olaf Janzen (St. Johns, NF, Int Maritime Economic History Asn, 98), 107-131. **CONTACT ADDRESS** Dept of Hist, Minnesota State Univ, Mankato, Mankato, MN 56001. **EMAIL** Johannes@Postma.net

POTASH, ROBERT AARON
PERSONAL Born 01/02/1921, Boston, MA, m, 1946, 2 children **DISCIPLINE** HISTORY **EDUCATION** Harvard Univ, PhD, 53. **CAREER** Vis lectr regional studies, Boston Univ, 49; instr Latin Am hist, 50-55, from asst prof to assoc prof, 55-61, acting head dept, 66-67, head, 68-69, chmn Latin Am Studies Comt, 68-76, Prof Hist, Univ Mass, Amherst, 61-86, Foreign serv reserve officer, US Dept State, 55-57, consult, 62-; Am Coun Learned Soc-Soc Sci Res Coun Joint Comt Latin Am Studies fel, 61-62, 65, 69-70, 83-84; Orgn Am States fel, Arg, 61-62; mem, Latin Am Adv Comt Soc Sci, 66-68; chmn nat steering comt, Consortium Latin Am Studies Prog, 71-72; mem nat screening comt, Foreign Area Fel Prog, 72-75; mem, Five Col Latin Am Studies Coun, 80-82; Haring Prof Emeritus, 86-; Advisor on Graduate Hist Programs, San Andres Univ, Argentina, 98-; Argentine War Acad, 00-. **HONORS AND AWARDS** Elected Coor. Mem, Mexican Acad of Hit, 85; Chancellor's Medal, Univ Mass, 87; Hon Prof, Fac of Law, Nat Univ of La Plata, 89; Corr. Mem, Academia Sanmartiniana, 90; Corr. Mem, Argentine Acad of Hist, 92; Order of Distinguished Services, Argentine Army, 99. **MEMBERSHIPS** AHA; Conf Latin Am Hist; Latin Am Studies Asn; New Eng Coun Latin Am Studies (pres, 73-74). **RESEARCH** Mexican economic history; Mexican historiography; contemporary Argentina. **SELECTED PUBLICATIONS** Auth, El Banco De Avio De Mexico, Fondo Cult Econ, 59; auth, "Historiography Of Mexico Since 1821," Hisp Am Hist Rev (8/60); auth, The Army And Politics In Argentina, 1928-1945, Stanford Univ Press, 69, Transl, Editorial Sudamericana, 71; auth, The Impact Of Professionalism On The Twentieth Century Argentine Military, Prog Latin Am Studies, Occasional Papers Ser No 3, Univ Mass, 4/77; auth, The Army And Politics In Argentina, 1945-1962, Stanford Univ Press, 80, Transl, Editorial Sudamerica, 94; auth, Argentina Lost Patrol--Armed Struggle, 1969-1979, Hispanic Am Hist Rev, Vol 76, 96; auth, The Army and Politics in Argentina, 1962-1973, Stanford Univ Press, 96; auth, "El Ejercito, la autoridad civil y la sociedad en la Argentina. La busqueda de una nueva relacion (1983-1997)," in Revisto del Museo Mitre 10 (97). **CONTACT ADDRESS** 235 Spencer Dr., Amherst, MA 01002. **EMAIL** potash@history.umass.edu

POTTER, DOROTHY T.
PERSONAL Born 07/17/1942, Waynesboro, VA, m, 1966 **DISCIPLINE** HISTORY **EDUCATION** Lynchburg Col, BA, 64; Univ Vir, MA, 66; PhD, 00. **CAREER** Adj prof, 84, 98, Randolph Macon WC; asst prof, 84-, prog coord, 98-, Lynchburg Coll. **MEMBERSHIPS** CSBS; MSA; Phi Alpha Theta. **RESEARCH** Virginia history; Mozart's music in America (pre-Civil War); Napoleonic history. **SELECTED PUBLICATIONS** Auth, "1816: The Year Without a Summer," Lynch's

Ferry, J Local Hist, (98); auth, "Napoleon Rises to Power in France," and "Coronation of Napoleon as Emperor," Chronology of Euro History, 15,000 BC-1996, Salem Press (98); auth, "Jenny Lind," Salem Press Encyc Euro Biog (99); auth, "Nancy Astor," Biog Encyc of 20th C Leaders (99); auth, "The 'Year Without a Summer," Natural Disasters, Salem Press, 00; auth, "Friedland" [battle, 1807], "Jean Lannes, Duc de Montebello" [Napoleonic marshal), and "Saragossa" [Siege, 1808-1809), Mapill's Guide to Military Hist (00); auth, "Jamestown National Historic Site," Historic Places in the United States, Salem Press, 00. **CONTACT ADDRESS** Dept History, Lynchburg Col, PO Box 9331, Lynchburg, VA 24501. **EMAIL** potter1@aca.vax.lynchburg.edu

POTTS, CASSANDRA W.
DISCIPLINE HISTORY **EDUCATION** Pomona Col AB; Univ Cali at Santa Barbara, PhD. **CAREER** Assoc prof, 90-. **RESEARCH** Monasticism and hagiography. **SELECTED PUBLICATIONS** Auth, Monastic Revival and Regional Identity in Early Medieval Normandy, 97; Normandy or Brittany? A Conflict of Interests at Mont-Saint-Michel 996-1035, Anglo-Norman Stud, 89, 12, 90; Atque unum ex diversis gentibus populum effecit: Historical Tradition and the Norman Identity, Anglo-Norman Stud, 95, 18, 96. **CONTACT ADDRESS** Dept of History, Middlebury Col, Middlebury, VT 05753. **EMAIL** potts@panther.middlebury.edu

POTTS, DAVID B.
PERSONAL Born 03/24/1938, Bridgeport, CT, m, 1960, 3 children **DISCIPLINE** HISTORY **EDUCATION** Wesleyan Univ, BA, 60; Harvard Univ, PhD, 67. **CAREER** Asst Prof to Assoc Dean of faculty, Union Col, 67-79; Scholar in residence, Wesleyan Univ, 86-94; Prof and Academic VP, Univ Puget Sound, 94-99; Historical consultant, speaker and writer, 99-. **HONORS AND AWARDS** Homer D Babbidge Jr. Awd. **MEMBERSHIPS** Hist of Educ Soc. **RESEARCH** History of American higher education; 19th Century American history. **SELECTED PUBLICATIONS** Auth, "Curriculum and Enrollments: Thoughts on Assessing the Popularity of Antebellum Colleges," in the American College in the Nineteenth Century, Vanderbilt, 00. **CONTACT ADDRESS** Dept Hist, Univ of Puget Sound, 4118 N 38th St, Tacoma, WA 98407. **EMAIL** dpotts@ups.edu

POTTS, LOUIS WATSON
PERSONAL Born 05/23/1944, Waterbury, CT, m, 1966, 3 children **DISCIPLINE** EARLY AMERICAN HISTORY; HISTORY OF TECHNOLOGY **EDUCATION** Lafayette Col, BA, 66; Duke Univ MA, 68, PhD(hist), 70. **CAREER** Instr Am hist, Duke Univ, 70-71; from asst prof to prof Am hist, Univ Mo, Kansas City, 71-; assoc dean grad studies, 76-83. **HONORS AND AWARDS** USIA Lectr on Am Soc and Values, in Russia; Fulbright Distinguished Lectr, Moscow State Univ, 99. **MEMBERSHIPS** Soc for Hist of the Early Am Repub; Soc for Indust Archael; Russian Asn for Am Studies. **RESEARCH** Nature of American Revolution; U.S. Constitution. **SELECTED PUBLICATIONS** Auth, Arthur Lee: A Virtuos Revolutionary, LSU, 81; series co-ed, Russian American Dialogues on American History, Univ Mo, 95-. **CONTACT ADDRESS** Dept of Hist, Univ of Missouri, Kansas City, 5100 Rockhill Rd., Kansas City, MO 64110-2499. **EMAIL** pottsl@umkc.edu

POTVIN, GILLES E. J.
PERSONAL Born 10/23/1923, Montreal, PQ, Canada **DISCIPLINE** MUSIC, HISTORY **CAREER** Journalist, Le Canada, 46-48; librn, 48-50, public relations, 50-53, radio/TV producer 54-58, dir casting, CBC, 62-65; instr, McGill opera stud, 57; critic, Nouveau Journal, 61; critic, Le Devoir, 61-66; critic, La Presse, 66-70; instr, Can music, Ecole Normale de Musique, 70-71; critic, Le Devoir, 73-89. **HONORS AND AWARDS** Canada 125 Medal; mem, Royal Soc Can; Order Can. **MEMBERSHIPS** CMC Coun (bd mem), 68-77; Jeunesses Musicales (pres, 76-80); Asn des retraites de Radio-Can. **SELECTED PUBLICATIONS** Ed, Canada Music Book, 70-76; Fr ed, Encyclopedia of Music in Canada, 81. **CONTACT ADDRESS** 208 Bloomfield Rd, Outremont, QC, Canada H2V 3R4.

POWELL, JAMES MATTHEW
PERSONAL Born 06/09/1930, Cincinnati, OH, m, 1954, 5 children **DISCIPLINE** MEDIEVAL HISTORY **EDUCATION** Xavier Univ, Ohio, AB, 53, MA, 55; Ind Univ PhD, 60. **CAREER** Acting chmn dept, 72-73 & 80, prof Hist, Syracuse Univ, 72-, Vis lectr medieval hist, Univ Wis, Milwaukee, 63-64; res fel, Pontif Inst Mediaeval Studies, Toronto, 70; resident chmn, Syracuse Univ Semester in Italy, Florence, 70-71; Nat Endowment for Humanities res grant, 77-83; prof of Medieval Hist, Syracuse Univ, 72-97; prof, emer of Medieval Hist, Syracuse Univ, 97. **HONORS AND AWARDS** NEH Res Grant, 77-84; John Gilmary Shea Prize, Am Catholic Hist Asn, 87; Fritz Thyssen Found Grant, 88. **MEMBERSHIPS** AHA; Mediaeval Acad Am; Mid W Medieval Conf (pres, 65-66); Soc Ital Hist Studies; Am Cath Hist Asn. **RESEARCH** Medieval society and culture. **SELECTED PUBLICATIONS** Auth, Liber Augustalis or Constitutions of Melfi, Promulgated by Frederick II in 1231, Syracuse Univ Press, 71; auth, Medieval Studies: An Introduction, Syracuse Univ Press, 76; auth, Anatomy of a Crusade, 1213-1221, Philadelphia: Univ of Pennsylvania Press, 86; ed, Leopold von Ranke and the Shaping of the Historical Discipline, ed. with George G. Iggers, Syracuse: Syracuse Univ Press, 89; auth, Muslims under Latin Rule, 1100-1300, Princeton: Princeton Univ Press, 90; auth, Albertanus of Brescia: The Pursuit of Happiness in the Early Thirteenth Century, Philadelphia: Univ of Pennsylvania Press, 92; auth, Innocent III: Vicar of Christ or Lord of the World? 2nd ed., revised and enlarged, Washington: Catholic Univ of Am Press, 94; ed, "Economy and Society in the Kingdom of Sicily under Frederick II: Recent Perspectives," Intellectual Life at the Court of Frederick II Hohenstaufen, ed. William Tronzo, Washington, D.C.: Nat Gallery of Art, (94): 263-271; ed, "Frederick II, the Hohenstaufen, and the Teutonic Order in the Kingdom of Sicily," in The Military Orders, ed. Malcom Barbara, Aldershot, England: Ashgate Publishing Ltd., (94): 236-244; auth, "Frederick II and the Muslims: The Making of an Historiographical Tradition," Iberia and the Mediterranean World of the Middle Ages, Leiden: E.J. Brill, (95): 261-269. **CONTACT ADDRESS** Dept of Hist, Syracuse Univ, 145 Eggers Hall, Syracuse, NY 13210.

POWELL, THOMAS F.
PERSONAL Born 08/27/1933, Watertown, NY, m, 1957, 2 children **DISCIPLINE** AMERICAN STUDIES **EDUCATION** NYork State Col Potsdam, BS, 59; Syracuse Univ, MA, 61, PhD(soc -ci), 64. **CAREER** From instr to asst prof hist, Univ Akron, 62-65; asst prof soc sci, Syracuse Univ, 65-67; assoc prof, 67-68, dean arts & sci, 68-71, Prof Hist, State Univ NY Col Oswego, 71-, Regents col teaching fel, 59-62; dir, State Univ NY prog & guest prof, Univ Wuerzburg, WGer, 79-81. **HONORS AND AWARDS** Chancellor's Awd for Excellence in Teaching, State Univ NY Col Oswego, 76. **RESEARCH** American intellectual history; American biography. **SELECTED PUBLICATIONS CONTACT ADDRESS** Dept of Hist, SUNY, Oswego, 7060 State Route 104, Oswego, NY 13126-3599.

POWER, MARGARET
PERSONAL Born 08/15/1953, Nashville, TN, s **DISCIPLINE** PHILOSOPHY, FRENCH, HISTORY **EDUCATION** Georgetown Univ, BA, 75; San Francisco State Univ, MA, 79; Univ Ill Chicago, PhD, 97. **CAREER** Vis Asst Prof/Asst Prof, Ill Inst of Technology, 98-. **HONORS AND AWARDS** Orgn of Am States, Res, 93-94; Woodrow Wilson Women Studies, 95; Guggenheim, 96-97. **MEMBERSHIPS** AHA, Latin Am Studies Asn, Congress on Latin Am Hist. **RESEARCH** Women, gender, the Armed Forces, technology, the right in Chile and Latin America. **SELECTED PUBLICATIONS** Auth, Right-using Women in Chilean Politico, 1964-1973, Penn State Press, forthcoming; auth, Right-using Women Across the Ilahe, Routledge Press, forthcoming. **CONTACT ADDRESS** Dept Humanities, Illinois Inst of Tech, 3300 S Federal St, Chicago, IL 60616-3795. **EMAIL** Power@iit.edu

POWERS, DAVID STEPHEN
PERSONAL Born 07/23/1951, Cleveland, OH, m, 1984, 3 children **DISCIPLINE** ISLAMIC HISTORY, LAW **EDUCATION** Yale Univ, BA, 73; Princeton Univ, MA & PhD(Islamic hist), 79. **CAREER** Prof Arabic & Islamics, Cornell Univ, 79-. **MEMBERSHIPS** Am Oriental Soc; Mid Eastern Studies Asn. **RESEARCH** Islamic law; Islamic history; medieval social history. **SELECTED PUBLICATIONS** Auth, Studies in Quran and Hadith: The Formation of the Islamic Law of Inheritance, Berkeley, 86; Islamic Legal Interpretation: Muftis and Their Fatwas, Harvard, 86; The History of al-Tabari, volume XXIV The Empire in Transition, tras, David Stephen Powers, Suny Press, 89. **CONTACT ADDRESS** Cornell Univ, Rockefeller Hall, Ithaca, NY 14853-0001. **EMAIL** dsp4@cornell.edu

POWERS, JAMES FRANCIS
PERSONAL Born 06/16/1935, Washington, DC, m, 1988, 4 children **DISCIPLINE** MEDIEVAL & SPANISH HISTORY **EDUCATION** Univ Va, BA, 57, MA, 61, PhD(medieval hist), 66. **CAREER** Instr Europ hist, 63-66, from asst prof to assoc prof, 66-78, Prof Hist, Col Holy Cross, 78-, Mem bd corporators, Int Inst in Madrid. **HONORS AND AWARDS** Vis fel in the Fac of Arts, Harvard Univ, 76; Postdoctoral res grant to Spain for United States Citizens, United States-Spanish Joint Committee for Cultural and Educational Cooperation, 79, 88; NEH Travel to Collections grant, Getty Inst, 86; Best Bk Prize for the period of 88-90, Soc for Spanish and Portuguese Hist Studies, "A Society Organized for War: The Iberian Municipal Militias in the Central Middle Ages, 1000-1284," 92; NEH Travel to Collections grant, Cuenca, Spain, 93; Awarded a membership at the Inst for Advanced Study, Princeton, 98. **MEMBERSHIPS** AHA; Mediaeval Acad Am; Am Acad Res Historians on Medieval Spain (secy-treas, 73-75); Soc Span & Port Hist Studies. **RESEARCH** Medieval Spain; military history; urban history; art history; film studies. **SELECTED PUBLICATIONS** Auth, "The Creative Interaction Between Portuguese and Leonese Municipal Law, 1055-1279," Speculum 62 (87): 53-80; auth, "The Kingdom of Navarre in the Middle Ages," The Dictionary of the Middle Ages 9 (NYork, 87): 67-73; auth, A Society Organized for War: The Iberian Municipal Militias in the Central Middle Ages, 1000-1284, Univ of Calif Press (Berkeley), 88; auth, "Alcance y provision: Las Milicias municipales en campana por lo largo de las frontera de la Reconquista Iberica," in Historia economica y de las instituciones fiancieras en Europa, Trabajos en homenaje a Ferran Valls I Taberner, ed. Manuel J. Palaez (Malaga, 90), 3419-3433; coauth, "Manuscript Illustration: The Cantigas in the Context of Contemporary Art," in Emperor of Culture: Alfonso X the Learned of Castile and His Thirteenth-Century Renaissance, ed. Robert I. Burns (Philadelphia, Univ of Pennsylvania Press, 90): 46-58, 221-223; auth, "Claudio Sanchez-Albornoz y Menduina (1893-1984)," in Medieval Scholarship: Biographical Studies on the Formation of a Discipline, Vol 1, ed. Helen Damico and Joseph B. Zavadil (Garland Press, 95), 233-246; auth, "Life on the Cutting Edge: The Besieged Town on the Luso-Hispanic Frontier in the Twelfth Century," in The Medieval City Under Siege, ed. Ivy A. Corfis and Micahel Wolfe (Woodbridge, England, Boydell Press, 95), 17-34; auth, "Lessons in the Dark: Teaching the Middle Ages with Film," in Perspectives on Audiovisuals in the Teaching of History, ed. Susan W. Gillespie (Washington D.C., Am Hist Asn, 99), 59-68; auth, The Code of Cuenca: Municipal Law on the Twelfth-Century Frontier, Univ of Pennsylvania Press (Philadelphia), 00. **CONTACT ADDRESS** Dept of Hist, Col of the Holy Cross, 1 College St, Worcester, MA 01610-2322. **EMAIL** jpowers@holycross.edu

POWICKE, MICHAEL RHYS
PERSONAL Born 10/02/1920, Manchester, England, m, 1948, 3 children **DISCIPLINE** HISTORY **EDUCATION** Oxford Univ, MA, 43. **CAREER** Lectr, 46-52, from asst prof to assoc prof, 52-63, Prof Hist, Univ Toronto, 63- **MEMBERSHIPS** Mediaeval Acad Am; fel Royal Hist Soc. **RESEARCH** Medieval history; religion and history; Medieval war and politics. **SELECTED PUBLICATIONS** Auth, Military Obligation In Medieval England, Oxford Univ, 62; Coauth, The Hundred Year War, Macmillan, 69; Coauth & Coed, Essays In Medieval History Presented To Bertie Wilkinson, Univ Toronto, 71; auth, The Community Of The Realm, Random, 73. **CONTACT ADDRESS** 67 Lee Ave, Toronto, ON, Canada M4E 2P1.

POZZETTA, GEORGE ENRICO
PERSONAL Born 10/29/1942, Great Barrington, MA, m, 1966, 2 children **DISCIPLINE** AMERICAN HISTORY **EDUCATION** Providence Col, BA, 64, MA, 65; Univ NC, Chapel Hill, PhD(hist), 71. **CAREER** Instr hist, Providence Col, 65-66 & Far East Ext Div, Univ Md, 68; teaching asst, Univ NC, Chapel Hill, 69-71; asst prof, 71-76, Assoc Prof Hist & Soc Sci, Univ Fla, 76- **MEMBERSHIPS** Am Ital Hist Asn (pres, 78-80); Orgn Am Historians; Southern Hist Asn; AHA; Immigration Hist Soc. **RESEARCH** History of immigration; ethnicity in American Life; social problems in urban America. **SELECTED PUBLICATIONS** Such Hardworking People--Italian Immigrants In Postwar Toronto, Canadian Hist Rev, Vol 74, 93; Italian Am Material Culture--A Dictionary Of Collections, Sites, And Festivals In The United-States And Canada, J Of Am Hist, Vol 79, 93; A Trade For Leaving--Tradition, Migration, Work, And Community In An Alpine Valley, Revs In Am Hist, Vol 21, 93; Indifferent Socialism--Italian Immigrants And The Socialist-Party In The United-States During The Early-20th-Century, Revs In Am Hist, Vol 21, 93; Dictionary Of Am Immigration History, J Of Am Ethnic Hist, Vol 12, 93; The Immigration History Research-Center--A Guide To Collections, J Of Am Hist, Vol 79, 93. **CONTACT ADDRESS** Dept of Hist, Univ of Florida, Gainesville, FL 32611.

PRALL, STUART E.
PERSONAL Born 06/02/1929, Saginew, MI, m, 1958, 2 children **DISCIPLINE** HISTORY **EDUCATION** Mich State Univ, BA, 51; Univ RI, MA, 53; Columbia Univ, PhD, 60. **CAREER** Lectr, Queens Col CUNY, 55-58; Asst Prof, Kean Col, 58-60; from Instr to Prof, Queens Col CUNY, 60-; Prof, Grad Center, CUNY, 72-. **HONORS AND AWARDS** Phi Beta Kappa; Fulbright Scholar, Manchester Eng, 53-54; Fel, Royal Hist Soc, 78-. **MEMBERSHIPS** AHA, Royal Hist Soc, N Am Conf on Brit Studies. **RESEARCH** Tudor-Stuart England and Ireland. **SELECTED PUBLICATIONS** Auth, The Agitation for Law Reform During the Puritan Revolution, 1640-1660, Martinus Nijhoff (The Hague), 66; auth, The Puritan Revolution: A Documentary History, Doubleday Anchor (NY), 68, Routledge and Kegan Paul (London), 69, Peter Smith (Gloucester, MA), 73; auth, The Bloodless Revolution: England, 1688, Doubleday Anchor (NY), 72, Peter Smith (Gloucester, MA), 72, Univ of Wis Press (Madison), 85; coauth, A History of England, Holt Rinehart and Winston (NY), 84, 91; auth, Church and State in Tudor and Stuart England, Harlan Davidson (Arlington Heights, Ill), 93. **CONTACT ADDRESS** Dept Hist, Queens Col, CUNY, 6530 Kissena Blvd, Flushing, NY 11367-1575.

PRANG, MARGARET E.
PERSONAL Born 01/23/1921, Stratford, ON, Canada **DISCIPLINE** HISTORY **EDUCATION** Univ Man, BA, 45; Univ Toronto, MA, 53, PhD, 59; Univ Winnipeg, LLD, 78; Univ BC, DLitt, 90. **CAREER** Mem, dept hist, 58-86, head dept, 74-79, 82-83, Univ BC. **HONORS AND AWARDS** UBC Medal Biog, 75. **MEMBERSHIPS** Coun Trustees, Inst Res Pub Policy 1973-79; bd Gov, Vancouver Sch Theol, 84-87; pres, Can Hist Asn, 76-77. **SELECTED PUBLICATIONS** Auth, N.W. Rowell: Ontario Nationalist, 75; auth, A Heart at Leisure from Itself: Caroline Macdonald of Japan, 95. **CONTACT ADDRESS** 2409 W 43rd Ave, No 401, Vancouver, BC, Canada V6M 2E6.

PRATT, WILLIAM C.
PERSONAL Born 12/15/1941, Reading, PA, m, 1969 **DISCIPLINE** AMERICAN HISTORY **EDUCATION** Ursinus Col, BA, 63; Univ Md, College Park, MA, 65; Emory Univ, PhD(hist), 69. **CAREER** Instr hist & polit sci, Philadelphia Col Textiles & Sci, 65-66; instr hist, Hope Col, 68-69; asst prof, 69-72, chmn dept, 75-78, Assoc Prof Hist, Univ Nebr at Omaha, 72- **MEMBERSHIPS** AHA **RESEARCH** The American left. **SELECTED PUBLICATIONS** Auth, Glen H Taylor: Public Image And Reality, Pac Northwest Quart, 1/69; Contribr, Senator Glen H Taylor: Questioning American Unilateralism, In: Cold War Critics, Quadrangle, 71; Auth, Women And American Socialism: The Reading Experience, Pa Mag Hist & Biog, 1/75; Contribr, Jimmie Higgins' And The Reading Socialist Community: An Exploration Of The Socialist Rank And File, In: Socialism And The Cities, Kennikat, 75; Workers, Unions And Historians On The Northern Plains, Great Plains Quart, Vol 16, 96; The Farmers-Union, Mccarthyism And The Demise Of The Agrarian Left, Historian, Vol 58, 96; Women And The Farm Revolt Of The 1930s, Agricultural Hist, Vol 67, 93. **CONTACT ADDRESS** Dept of Hist, Univ of Nebraska, Omaha, 6001 Dodge St, Omaha, NE 68182-0002.

PREISSER, THOMAS
PERSONAL Born 04/12/1939, New Orleans, LA, m, 1964, 2 children **DISCIPLINE** HISTORY, POLITICAL SCIENCE **EDUCATION** Stanford Univ, BA, 64; Northwestern Univ, MA, 68; Col of William and Mary, PhD, 77. **CAREER** Instr, Oakland Community Col, 68-70; Prof and Chair, Sinclair Community Col, 73-. **HONORS AND AWARDS** NEH Fel, 84, 99. **MEMBERSHIPS** Am Hist Asn, Ohio Acad of Hist, Nat Coun for Hist Educ. **RESEARCH** European History especially Renaissance, Reformation and Early Modern Europe. **SELECTED PUBLICATIONS** Auth, "The Virginia Decision to Use Negro Soldiers in the Civil War, 1864-1965," Virginia Magazine of History and Biography, 75; auth, "The 'Precarious Trade' of a Virginia tobacco Merchant: Harry Piper of Alexandria, 1749-1776," Alexandria History, 78; auth, "Alexandria and the Evolution of the Northern Virginia Economy, 1749-1776," Virginia Magazine of History and biography, 81; auth, "White Servant labor in Colonial Alexandria, 1749-1776," Northern Virginia Heritage, 82; auth, "Working on the Hot Side of the Lights: Several Techniques for Effective Television Instruction," social Science Perspectives Journal, 89; auth, "Strengthening Our Community Ties: Corporate Training Programs," Journal of the Ohio Association of Two-Year Colleges, 94. **CONTACT ADDRESS** Dept Humanities, Sinclair Comm Col, 444 W 3rd St, Dayton, OH 45402-1421. **EMAIL** tpreisse@sinclair.edu

PRELL, RIV-ELLEN
PERSONAL Born 10/15/1947, Los Angeles, CA, m, 1970, 2 children **DISCIPLINE** AMERICAN STUDIES, JEWISH STUDIES, ANTHROPOLOGY **EDUCATION** Univ S Calif, BA; Univ Chicago, MA; PhD. **CAREER** From assoc prof to prof of Am Studies, Univ Minn, Twin Cities. **HONORS AND AWARDS** Phi Beta Kappa; Nat Jewish Bk Awd, 89. **MEMBERSHIPS** ASA; ASSJ; JSA. **RESEARCH** Ethnicity, 20th century American Jews, ritual, religion. **SELECTED PUBLICATIONS** Auth, Fighting to Become Americans: Jews, Gender and the Anxiety of Assimilation; auth, Prayer and Community: The Hauura in American Judaism; coed, Interpreting Women's Lives: Personal Narratives and Feminist Theory. **CONTACT ADDRESS** Dept Am Studies, Univ of Minnesota, Twin Cities, 72 Pleasant St SE, 203 Scott Hall, Minneapolis, MN 55455. **EMAIL** prell001@tc.umn.edu

PRESLEY, PAULA
PERSONAL Born 06/08/1938, Des Arc, AR, d, 1958, 3 children **DISCIPLINE** HISTORY **EDUCATION** Truman St Univ, BA, 85, MA, 87; Univ of IA, MLIS, 91 **CAREER** Prod ed, 82-, Sixteenth Cent Journ; Asst Ed, 86-91, Asoc Ed, 91-98, Dir, Ed in Chief, 98-, Truman St Univ Press. **HONORS AND AWARDS** Who's Who of American Women, 00-01. **MEMBERSHIPS** Am Lib Asn; Am Soc of Indexers; Soc for Schol Pub; Calvin Studies Soc; Sixteenth Century Studies Conf. **RESEARCH** Incunabula **SELECTED PUBLICATIONS** Ed, Books Have Their Own Destiny: Essays in Honor of Robert V. Schnucker, Thomas Jefferson Univ Press (Kirksville, MD), 98. **CONTACT ADDRESS** Truman State Univ, Kirksville, MO 63501-4221. **EMAIL** ppresley@truman.edu

PRESSLY, WILLIAM L.
PERSONAL Born, TN, m, 1970, 1 child **DISCIPLINE** ART HISTORY **EDUCATION** Princeton Univ, AB, 66; Inst Fine Arts, NYork Univ, PhD, 74. **CAREER** Asst prof, 73-79, assoc prof, 79-82, Yale Univ; sen lectr, Univ Tex, Austin, 82, 83; assoc prof, Duke Univ, 85-87; assoc prof, 87-93, PROF, 93, CHAIR, DEPT ART HIST, ARCHAEOLOGY, 96-99, UNIV MD. **HONORS AND AWARDS** Guggenheim Fellow, 83-84; grant, Inst for Adv Study, 99. **SELECTED PUBLICATIONS** Auth, The Life and Art of James Barry (New Have and London), Yale Univ Press, 81; auth, James Barry: The Artist as Hero (London), The Tate Gallery, 83; ed, Facts and Recollections of the XVIIIth Century in a Memoir of John Francis Rigaud, Esq, R.A., The Journal of the Walpole Society, 84; auth, A Catalogue of Paintings in the Folger Shakespeare Library: As Imagination Bodies Forth (New Haven & London), Yale Univ Press, 93; auth, The French Revolution as Blasphemy: Johan Zoffany's Paintings of the Massacre at Paris, on August 10, 1792, The UC Press, 99. **CONTACT ADDRESS** Dept of Art Hist & Archaeol, Univ of Maryland, Col Park, 1211B Art/ Sociology Bldg, College Park, MD 20742. **EMAIL** wp12@umail.umd.edu

PRESTON, CAROL
PERSONAL Born Brandon, MB, Canada **DISCIPLINE** HISTORY **EDUCATION** Univ Man, BA, 66; Univ Toronto, MLS, 75. **CAREER** Librn, Winnipeg, 66-73; librn, Hist Res Libr, Hudson's Bay Co, 75-77; asst ed, The Beaver, 77-85, mgr ed, 85-95, assoc ed, 95-. **MEMBERSHIPS** Can Club Winnipeg; Women & Hist Asn Manitoba; Can Mag Publs Asn. **SELECTED PUBLICATIONS** Contribur, Manitoba: 125, Vol 1, 93; ed, A Brief History of the Hudson's Bay Company, 89, 90, 94. **CONTACT ADDRESS** The Beaver: Exploring Canada's History, 167 Lombard Ave, Ste 478, Winnipeg, MB, Canada R3B 0T6.

PRESTON, GEORGE NELSON
PERSONAL Born 12/14/1938, New York, NY, s, 4 children **DISCIPLINE** ART HISTORY **EDUCATION** City College of New York, BA, 1962; Columbia University, MA, 1967, PhD, 1973. **CAREER** Dept of art, City Coll, City Univ, NY, prof, art & art hist, 80-86, prof art & art history, 71-73; dept of art, Livingston Col, Rutgers University, asst prof, art & art hist, 70-73; Independent curator: Bronx Museum of the Arts, Brooklyn Museum, of Agrican Art, Studio Museum in Harlem; Regular contributor to Review: The Critical State of Art in NY. **HONORS AND AWARDS** Foreign area fellow, Joint Comm of the American Council of Learned Soc & the Soc Science Rsch Council, 1968-70, 1972. **MEMBERSHIPS** Special consultant, New York State Commn on the Arts, 1967-68; special consultant, New World Cultures, Brooklyn Museum, 1968; associate, Columbia Univ Seminar on Primitive & Precolumbian Art, 1973-; bd of dir, Bd of Adult Educ, Museum of African Art, Washington, DC, 1972-80; Roger Morris-Jumel Hist Soc, 1973-80; bd of dir, Cinque Gallery, New York, NY, 1977-79. **RESEARCH** African art and leadership, visual art in relation to performance art in traditional Africa, video documentation of art/art making in Africa, Contemporary art in relation to critical theory. **SELECTED PUBLICATIONS** numerous publications, incl; Sets, Series and Ensembles in African Art, 85; Emanuel Aranjo: Afrominialista Brasileiro, 86; African art Masterpieces, 91. **CONTACT ADDRESS** Art Dept, City Col, CUNY, 160 Convent Ave, New York, NY 10031-9101.

PRESTON, KATHERINE K.
PERSONAL Born 12/07/1950, Hamilton, OH, m, 1 child **DISCIPLINE** HISTORY OF MUSIC **EDUCATION** Evergreen State Col, BA, 71; Univ Maryland, MM, 81; CUNY, PhD, 89. **CAREER** ASSOC PROF, MUS, COLL WM & MARY **HONORS AND AWARDS** Various Fellowships. **MEMBERSHIPS** Am Antiquarian Soc, Soc for Am Music, Am Musicological Soc, College Music Soc. **RESEARCH** History of Music in the United States Emp 19th century, Music & Theatre in U.S. **SELECTED PUBLICATIONS** Auth, articles for New Grove Dictionary of American Music; auth, "Popular Music in the Gilded Age," Popular Music: A Year Book, 85; auth, Music for Hire: The Working Journeyman Musicians in Washington, DC 1875-1900, Pendragon Press, 92; auth, Opera on the Road: Traveling Opera Troupes in the United States, 1820-1860, Univ Ill Press, 93; consult ed/auth on itinerant opera companies for New Grove Dictionary of Opera, Macmillan Press, 93; auth, "Antebellum Concert-Giving and Opera-Singing: The Triumphant 1838-1840 American Tour by Jane Shereff and John Umlson, British Vocal Stars," in American Musical Life in Context and Practice to 1865, Garland, 94; coauth, The Mulligan Guard Ball and Reilly and the 400, in Nineteenth- Century : American Musical Theater, Garland, 94; auth, bibliog entries, American National Biography, Oxford Univ Press; auth, "The Development of Art Music in the United States, 1800-1865," in The Cambridge History of American Music, Cambridge Univ Press. **CONTACT ADDRESS** Dept of Music, Col of William and Mary, Williamsburg, VA 23185. **EMAIL** kkpres@wm.edu

PRESTON, WILLIAM L.
PERSONAL Born 09/14/1949, Tulane, CA, m **DISCIPLINE** GEOGRAPHY **EDUCATION** Col Sequoias, AA, 69; Fresno State Col, BA, 71; MA, 73; Univ Ore, Eugene, PhD, 78. **CAREER** Prof, Calif Poly, SLO, 80- **HONORS AND AWARDS** Distinguished Teacher Awd, Calif Poly, 84. **MEMBERSHIPS** Asn of Am Geogr. **RESEARCH** Environmental management process of epidemiology of native Californians. **SELECTED PUBLICATIONS** Auth, Vanishing Landscapes: Land and Life in the Tulane Lake Basin, Univ of Calif Press (Berkeley), 81. **CONTACT ADDRESS** Dept Soc Sci, California Polytech State Univ, San Luis Obispo, 1 Grand Ave, San Luis Obispo, CA 93407. **EMAIL** wpreston@calpoly.edu

PRETE, ROY A.
DISCIPLINE HISTORY **EDUCATION** Saskatchewan, BA; Brigham Young Univ, MA; Alberta, PhD, 79. **CAREER** Assoc Prof, Royal Milit Col. **RESEARCH** Modern European and Canadian History; European diplomatic and military history. **SELECTED PUBLICATIONS** Auth, Strategy and Command: the Anglo-French Coalition on the Western Front, 1914-1918. **CONTACT ADDRESS** Dept of Hist, Royal Military Col, PO Box 17000, Kingston, ON, Canada K7K 7B4. **EMAIL** prete_r@rmc.ca

PRICE, DON C.
PERSONAL Born 02/28/1937, Washington, DC, m, 1970, 1 child **DISCIPLINE** HISTORY **EDUCATION** Amherst Col, BA, 58; Harvard Univ, MA, 62; PhD, 68. **CAREER** Asst prof, John Hopkins Univ, 67-68; asst prof, Yale Univ, 68-72; asst prof to prof, Univ Cal at Davis, 73-82-. **HONORS AND AWARDS** Woodrow Wilson Fel; Ford Found Fel; NDFL Fel; SSRC Fel; CSCPRC Fel; Wang Fel; Chiang Fel; Ching-Kuo Fel. **MEMBERSHIPS** AAS; SSHA. **RESEARCH** Modern China. **SELECTED PUBLICATIONS** Auth, Russia and the Roots of the Chinese Revolution 1896-1911, Harvard UP (Cambridge, MA), 74; auth, "The Late Ch'ing: Political History," Gilbert Rozman, ed., Soviet Studies of Premodern China (Cen Chinese Studies, Univ Mich, Ann Arbor,84): 133-148; auth, "Diary as Autobiography: Two Modern Chinese Cases," Carol Ramelb, ed., Biography East and West (Univ Hawaii, Honolulu, 89): 74-86; auth, "Constitutional Alternatives and Democracy in the Revolution of 1911," in Paul A. Cohen, Merle Goldman, ed., Ideas across Cultures: Essays on Chinese Thought in Honor of Benjamin I. Schwartz (Harvard Council on East Asian Studies: Cambridge, MA, 90): 223-260; auth, "Escape from Disillusionment: Personality and Value Change in the Case of Sung Chiao-jen," in Richard J. Smith, D W Y Kwok, ed., Cosmology, Ontology, and Human Efficacy (Univ Hawaii Press, 93): 217-236; auth, "From Civil Society to Party Government: Models of the Citizen's Role in the Late Qing," in Joshua A Fogel, Peter G Zarrow, eds., Imagining the People Chinese Intellectuals and the Concept of Citizenship, 1890-1920 (Sharpe Press: Armonk, NY, 97): 142-164. **CONTACT ADDRESS** Dept History, Univ of California, Davis, 1 Shields Ave, Davis, CA 95616-5270. **EMAIL** dcprice@ucdavis.edu

PRICE, GLENN WARREN
PERSONAL Born 10/16/1918, Libertyville, IA, m, 1940, 2 children **DISCIPLINE** UNITED STATES HISTORY **EDUCATION** LaVerne Col, AB, 40; Univ Southern Calif, AM, 50, PhD(hist), 66. **CAREER** Cur hist, Calif State Park Syst, 48-58; asst prof, Univ Pac, 58-66; assoc prof, 67-71, chmn dept, 71-74, chmn, Div Soc Sci, 77-80, prof hist, 71- , prof emeritus, Sonoma State Univ. **MEMBERSHIPS** AHA; Orgn Am Historians; Pac Hist Asn. **RESEARCH** United States foreign relations, midnineteenth century; cultural & intellectual history of American far West, 19th century; restoration of historic structures. **SELECTED PUBLICATIONS** Auth, Restoration of historic structures, Proc Conf Calif Hist Soc, 57; ed, From Hannibal to the gold fields in 1849, 11/60, 2-5/61 & auth, A golden age in Western history, 8/64, Pac Hist; Origins of the War with Mexico: The Polk-Stockton Intrigue, Univ Tex, 67. **CONTACT ADDRESS** 1320 Darby Rd, Sebastopol, CA 95472.

PRICE, RICHARD
PERSONAL Born 11/11/1944, Ashford, England, d, 1 child **DISCIPLINE** HISTORY **EDUCATION** Univ Sussex, BA, 65; Univ Sussex, PhD, 68 **CAREER** Asst Prof, N Illinois Univ, 68-82; Prof, Maryland Col Park, 82-; Chair, Dept Hist, Univ Maryland, 86-92 **HONORS AND AWARDS** AELS Fel, 74 **RESEARCH** Modern British history **SELECTED PUBLICATIONS** co-ed, History of Labour Law in Comparative Perspective, Lang, 99; Dynamism Bounded: Containment and Change in Britain 1680-1880, 99; "Postmodernism and History," Language and Labour, Ashgate, 97; "Languages of Revisionism," Jour Soc Hist, 96 **CONTACT ADDRESS** Dept of Hist, Univ of Maryland, Col Park, 2115 Francis Scott Key Hall, College Park, MD 20742. **EMAIL** rp36@umail.umd.edu

PRICE, ROBERT GEORGE
PERSONAL Born 06/01/1934, New York, NY, m, 1955, 2 children **DISCIPLINE** HISTORY OF LOGIC, ETHICS **EDUCATION** Yale Univ, BA, 55, MA, 57, PhD(philos), 63. **CAREER** From instr to asst prof, 59-66, Assoc Prof Philos, PA State Univ, University Park, 66- **MEMBERSHIPS** Am Philos Asn; Asn Symbolic Logic; Mind Asn. **RESEARCH** History of logic; moral and political philosophy; Greek philosophy. **SELECTED PUBLICATIONS** Auth, Some Antistrophes To The Rhetoric, Philos & Rhet, 68; Ockham And Supposito Personalis, Franciscan Studies, 71; A Refutative Demonstration In Metaphysics Gamma, Philos And Rhetoric, Vol 29, 96. **CONTACT ADDRESS** Dept Philos, Pennsylvania State Univ, Univ Park, 240 Sparks Bldg, University Park, PA 16802-5201.

PRICE, WILLIAM
PERSONAL Born 01/19/1941, Asheboro, NC, m, 1964, 2 children **DISCIPLINE** U.S. HISTORY **EDUCATION** Duke Univ, AB, 63; Univ NC, MA, 69; PhD, 73. **CAREER** Editor, NC Div of Archives and Hist, 71-75; asst dir, NCDAH, 75-81; dir, NCDAH, 81-95; prof, Meredith Col, 95-. **HONORS AND AWARDS** Cannon cup of Preservation NC, 95; Crittenden Awd, 95; Archie K. Davis Fel, 98. **MEMBERSHIPS** S Hist Assoc; Am Assoc for State and Local Hist. **RESEARCH** Early South, Public History. **SELECTED PUBLICATIONS** Auth, Not a Conquered People: Two Carolinians View Parliamentary

Taxation, Raleigh, 75; ed, North Carolina Higher court Minutes, 1709-1723, Raleigh, 77; coauth, Discovering North Carolina, Chapel Hill, 91. **CONTACT ADDRESS** Dept Hist and Govt, Meredith Col, 3800 Hillsborough St, Raleigh, NC 27607-5237. **EMAIL** pricew@meredith.edu

PRIMACK, MAXWELL
PERSONAL Born 06/04/1934, Brooklyn, NY, m, 1955, 4 children **DISCIPLINE** PHILOSOPHY; INTELLECTUAL HISTORY **EDUCATION** Brandeis Univ, BA, 56; John Hopkins Univ, PhD, 62. **CAREER** Erie Community Col, 26 years; Univ Buffalo (SUNYAB); Lincoln Univ in Pennsylvania; Illinois Inst Tech; Bloomsburg State College. **HONORS AND AWARDS** Cume Laude; Phi Betta Kappa **MEMBERSHIPS** Amer Phil Assoc. **RESEARCH** Marx; Lenin; The Bible Biomedical Ethics. **SELECTED PUBLICATIONS** Auth, A Reinterpretation of Francis Bacon's Philosophy, 68; The Last American Frontier: Education, 72. **CONTACT ADDRESS** 20 Marjann Ter., Buffalo, NY 14223. **EMAIL** mprinted@aol.com

PRIMM, JAMES NEAL
PERSONAL Born 02/05/1918, Edina, MO, m, 1946 **DISCIPLINE** HISTORY **EDUCATION** Northeast Mo State Teachers Col, BS, 41; Univ Mo, MA, 49, PhD(hist), 51. **CAREER** From asst dir to dir, Western Hist Manuscripts Collection, Univ Mo, 51-58, from asst prof to assoc prof hist, 54-58; dean, Hiram Col 58-64, pres, 64-65; chmn dept, 65-70, prof hist, Univ Mo St Louis, 65-. **HONORS AND AWARDS** Thomas Jefferson Awd, Univ Mo, 76. **MEMBERSHIPS** Econ Hist Asn; Orgn Am Historians; Southern Hist Asn. **RESEARCH** State economic policy; history of St Louis. **SELECTED PUBLICATIONS** Auth, The GAR in Missouri, 1866-1870, J Southern Hist; Economic Policy in the Development of a Western State--Missouri, 1820-1860, Harvard Univ, 54; The Haywood Case, Chandler Publ, 63; The American Experience, Forum, 72; Lion of the Valley: St Louis, 1764-1980, Pruett Publ, 81, 2nd ed, 91, 3rd ed, 98; A Foregone Conclusion: Founding of the Federal Reserve Bank of St. Louis, published by the Federal Reserve Bank, 91. **CONTACT ADDRESS** Dept of Hist, Univ of Missouri, St. Louis, 8001 Natural Bridge, Saint Louis, MO 63121-4499.

PRINCE, CARL E.
PERSONAL Born 12/08/1934, Newark, NJ, m, 1959, 2 children **DISCIPLINE** AMERICAN HISTORY **EDUCATION** Rutgers Univ, BA, 56, MA, 58, PhD(hist), 63. **CAREER** Instr hist, Fairleigh Dickinson Univ, 60-63; from asst prof to assoc prof, Seton Hall Univ, 63-68; assoc prof, 68-74, acting chmn dept, 76-77, Prof Hist, NY Univ, 74-, Chmn Dept, 78-, Nat Endowment for Humanities younger scholar fel, 68-69; Fulbright Scholar, Hebrew Univ, Jerusalem & Haifa Univ, 72-73. **HONORS AND AWARDS** Pres, SHEAR, 84-85. **MEMBERSHIPS** AHA; Orgn Am Historians; Inst Early Am Hist & Cult, SHEAR. **RESEARCH** Early American political behavior; early national American history, sports history. **SELECTED PUBLICATIONS** Auth, New Jersey's Jeffersonian Republicans, Inst Early Am Hist & Cult, Univ NC, 67; auth, Federalists and the Origins of the U.S. Civil Service, NY Univ, 78; ed, Papers of William Livingston, 5 vols, 79-88; auth, The U.S. Customs Service: A Bicentennial History, 89; auth, Brooklyn's Dodgers, 96,97. **CONTACT ADDRESS** Dept of Hist, New York Univ, 53 Washington Sq S, New York, NY 10012. **EMAIL** cp2@is7.nyu.edu

PRINDLE, TAMAE K.
PERSONAL Born 09/21/1944, Manchuria, m, 1968, 2 children **DISCIPLINE** EAST ASIAN STUDIES **EDUCATION** Gakushuin Univ, Tokyo, 63-65; State Univ NY, Binghamton, BA, 68; Washington State Univ, MA, 70; Cornell Univ, MA, 82, PhD, 85. **CAREER** Lectr, Pahlavai Univ, Shiraz, Iran, 76-77; English Tutor, Writing Center, State Univ of NY, Cortland, 80; teaching asst, Cornell Univ, 84-85; asst prof of Japanese Lang & Lit, Dept of Modern Foreign Langs, East Asian Studies Prog, Colby Col, 85-86, Dana Fac Fel and asst prof of East Asian Studies, 86-88, acting chair, 88-89, Dana Fac Fel and asst prof, 89-91, assoc prof, 91-93, East Asian Langs and Culture Dept Chair, 94-95; Japan Found Res Fel, Ochanomizu Women's Univ, Gender Studies Center, Foreign Researcher, Ochanomizu Univ, Tokyo, Japan, 95-96; East Asian Studies Dept Chair, Colby Col, 96-97; assoc Kyoto Prog Res Fel, Doshisha Univ, AKP Center, Kyoto, Japan, fall 97; prof of East Asian Studies, Colby Col, 98-2000; res assoc, Edwin O. Reishauer Inst of Japanese Studies, 91-. **HONORS AND AWARDS** Tokyo-to Ikuei-kai Scholar, Gakushuin Univ, 63-65; Tuition waiver, SUNY, Binghamton, 65-68; Asian Studies Tuition and Fees Fel, Cornell Univ, 82-84; Int Studies Travel grant, Cornell Univ, 84; Mellon Course Develop grant, summer 90; summer res fund, Colby Col, 91; Japan Found grant, 91; Northeast Asia Coun of the Asn for Asian Studies grant, 91; Japan Forum grant, 91; Colby Col "Instructional Development Grant," 91; Harvard-Yenching Library Res grant, 92; Hewlett Curriculum Develop grant, 93; Colby Col Humanities grant, 86, 94, 95; Japan Found Res Fel, 96; Mellon Computer Software Develop grant, 96; Assoc Kyoto Prog Fac Fel, 97; Mellon Found Student Assistant grant, 97-98; CBB Mellon Webpage Develop grant, 98; Fac Travel grant, Colby Col, two to five trips yearly. **MEMBERSHIPS** Asn of Teachers of Japanese, Asn for Asian Studies, New England Region Asn for Asian Studies, New York Region Asn for Asian Studies, New England Japan Sem, Maine Asian Studies Asn. **SELECTED PUBLICATIONS** Ed and transl, Made in Japan and Other Japanese "Business Novels," Armonk: M. E. Sharpe (89, 95); auth, Kinjo the Corporate Bouncer and Other Stories from Japanese Business, NY: Weatherhill (92); transl and intro to Kazuo Watanabe, auth, Labor Relations: Japanese Business Novel, Lanham, MD: Univ Press of Am (94); transl, intro, ed of The Dark Side of Japanese Business: Three "Industry Novels," by Ikko Shimizu, Armonk: M. E. Sharpe (95); auth, "Karayuki-san' eiga ni okeru 'otoko no jikan' to 'onna no jikan'," ["Man's Time" and "Woman's Time" in "Karayuki-san" Films], Nichibei Josei Janaru [U.S.-Japan Women's J], No 21 (97); auth, "A Cocooned Identity: Japanese Girl Films: Nobuhiko Oobayashi's Chizuko's Younger Sister and Jun Ichikawa's Tsugumi," Postscript, Vol 18, No 1 (fall 98): 24-37; rev, "Vera Mackie, Creating Socialist Women in Japan, Cambridge Univ Press (77)," J of Asian and African Studies, XXXIII.4 (98): 384-85; transl and intro, The Paradise: Beautiful Birds of Seychelles (photography book) by Shogo Asao, Tokyo: Lunatec Carrot, Ltd (99); auth, "Self-sacrificing Mothers or Frustrated Mothers?: A Paradigm Shift of Motherhood in Modern Japan," Japan Studies: Publication of the Center for Japan Studies at Teikyo Loretto Heights Univ, No 3 (99): 85-101; ed, Japan Studies: Publication of the Center for Japanese Studies at Teikyo Loretto Heights University, No 3: Japan in the 20th Century: Int Perspectives (99); **CONTACT ADDRESS** Dept Asian Lang & Lit, Colby Col, 150 Mayflower Dr, Waterville, ME 04901-4799.

PRISCO, SALVATORE
PERSONAL Born 10/01/1943, Jersey City, NJ, m, 1967, 1 child **DISCIPLINE** HISTORY **EDUCATION** St Peter's Col, BS, 64; Rutgers Univ, MA, 65; Rutgers Univ, PhD, 69. **CAREER** Assoc Prof, Univ Al, 69-74; Prof, Stevens Inst of Tech, 75-. **HONORS AND AWARDS** Hon Degree, Stevens Inst, 99; ch, Dept Humanities, 93-97; Woodrow Wilson Found Grant, 88-89; Freedoms Found Grant, 84; NEH Grant, 79; U.S. Steel Fel, 68-69. **MEMBERSHIPS** OAH, AHA. **RESEARCH** U.S. diplomatic history, international politics, psychohistory, economic history. **SELECTED PUBLICATIONS** Auth, Progressive ERA Diplomat: John Barrett, 73; Auth, An Introduction to Psychohistory: Theories and Case Studies, 80; Auth, Industrialism, Foreign Expansion and the Progressive ERA, 98. **CONTACT ADDRESS** Dept Humanities/Soc Sci, Stevens Inst of Tech, 1 Castle Point Terr, Hoboken, NJ 07030-5906. **EMAIL** sprisco@attila.stevens-tech.edu

PROCHASKA, DAVID
DISCIPLINE HISTORY **EDUCATION** Univ Calif Berkeley, PhD, 81. **CAREER** Assoc prof, Univ Ill Urbana Champaign. **RESEARCH** Comparative colonial history; postcolonial studies. **SELECTED PUBLICATIONS** Auth, Making Algeria French: Colonialism in Bone, 1870-1920, Cambridge, 90; Art of Colonialism, Colonialism of Art: the Description de l'Egypte (1809-1828), 94; History as Literature, Literature as History: Cagayous of Algiers, Am Hist Rev, 96. **CONTACT ADDRESS** History Dept, Univ of Illinois, Urbana-Champaign, 52 E Gregory Dr, Champaign, IL 61820. **EMAIL** dprochas@staff.uiuc.edu

PROCKO, BOHDAN P.
PERSONAL Born 07/18/1922, Poland, m, 1954, 5 children **DISCIPLINE** RUSSIAN HISTORY **EDUCATION** Albright Col, BS, 45; Columbia Univ, MA, 46; Univ Ottawa, PhD(hist), 64. **CAREER** From instr to assoc prof, 49-69, Prof Hist, Villanova Univ, 69- **MEMBERSHIPS** AHA; Am Asn Advan Slavic Studies. **RESEARCH** East European nationalism; Byzantine rite churches. **SELECTED PUBLICATIONS** Auth, American Ukrainian Catholic Church: Humanitarian And Patriotic Activities, World War I, Summer 67 & Ukraine, 1967: A Historian's Personal Impressions, Fall 68, Ukrainian Quart; Soter Ortynsky: First Ruthenian Bishop In The United States, 1907-1916, Cath Hist Rev, 1/73; Contribr, Chap, In: The Ethnic Experience In Pennsylvania, Bucknell Univ, 73; Auth, The Establishment Of The Ruthenian Church In The United States, 1884-1907, Pa Hist, 4/75; Chap, In: The Ukrainian Experience In The United States, Harvard Ukrainian Res Inst, 79; Auth, Ukrainian Catholics In America: A History, Univ Press Of Am, 82; Rev, Wedded To The Cause: Ukrainian-Canadian Women And Ethnic-Identity 1891-1991, American Hist Rev, Vol 99, 94. **CONTACT ADDRESS** 507 Hagey Pl, Collegeville, PA 19426.

PROCTER, BEN
PERSONAL Born 02/21/1927, Temple, TX, m, 1952, 1 child **DISCIPLINE** AMERICAN HISTORY **EDUCATION** Univ Tex, BA, 51, MA, 52; Harvard Univ, PhD, 61. **CAREER** From instr to assoc prof, 57-68, Piper prof, 73, Prof Hist, Tex Christian Univ, 68-, Consult, St Marks Sch, Dallas, 62. **HONORS AND AWARDS** Summerfield G. Roberts Awd; Minnie Piper Fel; Sons of the Rep of TX; Longhorn Hall of Fame, Univ of TX; Phi Alpha Theta. **MEMBERSHIPS** Phi Beta Kappa; Phi Alpha Theta; W Hist Asn; SW Social Sci Assn; Am Hist Assn; Am Assn of Univ Profs; S Hist Assn; TX St Hist Assn **RESEARCH** American history from 1877-1941; the American frontier; Texas history, 1835 to the present. **SELECTED PUBLICATIONS** Auth, Not Without Honor: The Life of John H Reagan, Univ Tex, 62; The modern day Texas Rangers, In: Reflections by Western Historians, Univ Ariz, 69 & In: The Mexican-Americans: An Awakening Minority, Glencoe, 69; Ben McCulloch, In: Rangers of Texas, 69 & Washington-on-the Brazos, In: Capitols of Texas, 70, Texian; coauth, The Land and its People, Hendrick-Long, 71; Texas Under a Cloud, Pemberton, 72; coauth, The Texas Heritage, Forum, 80; coauth, Texas Under a Cloud, Pemberton, 72; auth, Battle of the Alamo, Texas State Hist Asn, 86; auth, Just One Riot: Episodes of 20th Century Texas Rangers, Eakin, 91; ed, A Texas Ranger, R.R. Donnelley & Sons, 92; auth, The Texas Gubernatorial Election of 1990: Claytie vs. the Lady, Essays by Western Historians on the Twentieth Century West, Univ of Okla, 94; auth, coauth, The Texas Heritage, Harlan Davidson, 97; auth, William Randolph Hearst: The Early Years 1863-1910, Oxford Univ, 98. **CONTACT ADDRESS** Dept of Hist, Texas Christian Univ, TCU Box 297260, Fort Worth, TX 76129-0002. **EMAIL** b.procter@tco.edu

PROMEY, SALLY M.
DISCIPLINE AMERICAN ART **EDUCATION** Univ Chicago, PhD. **CAREER** Prof, Univ MD. **HONORS AND AWARDS** Charles C Eldredge prize, Nat Mus Amer Art, 93; Ailsa Mellon Bruce sr fel, Ctr for Advan Stud Visual Arts; fel, NEH; summer res fel(s), NEH; adv comm, archiv am art; ed bd, am art. **RESEARCH** Relationships between visual cult and relig experience. **SELECTED PUBLICATIONS** Auth, Spiritual Spectacles: Vision and Image in Mid-Nineteenth-Century Shakerism, Ind, 93; publ(s), articles in Art Bulletin, Am Art, and Am Art Jour. **CONTACT ADDRESS** Dept Of Art and Archeol, Univ of Maryland, Col Park, 4229 Art-Sociology Building, College Park, MD 20742-1335. **EMAIL** sp80@umail.umd.edu

PROROK, CAROLYN V.
PERSONAL Born 02/17/1956 **DISCIPLINE** GEOGRAPHY **EDUCATION** Slippery Rock Univ, BS, 78; Univ Pittsburgh, MA, 82; La State Univ, PhD, 88. **CAREER** Instructor, La State Univ, 87; Asst Prof to Prof, Slippery Rock Univ, 87-. **HONORS AND AWARDS** Robert West Grant, 84, 85; William Haag Awd, 85; SRU Intl Prof Dev Awd, 88; NEH Inst, 93; SRU Foundation, 93; Outstanding Advisor Awd, 99. **MEMBERSHIPS** Nat Coun for Geog Educ; PA Geog Soc; Conf of Latin Am Geog; Caribbean Studies Asn; Nat Asn of Geog. **RESEARCH** Geography of Religions **SELECTED PUBLICATIONS** Auth, "Creating the Sacred from the ordinary," Scholars, (93): 4-11; auth, "Hindu Temples in the Western World: A Study in Social Space and Ethnic Identity," Geographia Religionum, (94): 95-108; auth, "The Hindu Temple Gardens of Trinidad: cultural Continuity and Change in a Caribbean Landscape," Pennsylvania Geog, (97): 98-135; auth, "Women at Work: Incorporating Gender in a Geography Lesson," Social Education, (97): 385-389; auth, "Holding up More than Half the Sky: A Woman's Place in China," in Asian Women and Their Work: A Geography of Gender and Development, (NCGE, 98), 8-14; co-ed, Asian Women and Their Work: A Geography of Gender and Development, NCGE, 98; auth, "Dancing in the Fire: The Politics of Hindu Identity in a Malaysian Landscape," Journal of Cultural Geography, (98): 89-114; auth, "Boundaries are Made for Crossing: The Feminized spatiality of Puerto Rican Espiritismo in New York City," Gender, Place and Culture: A Journal of Feminist Geography, (00): 57-79. **CONTACT ADDRESS** Dept Geog & Anthropol, Slippery Rock Univ of Pennsylvania, PO Box 111, Slippery Rock, PA 16507-0111. **EMAIL** carolyn.prorok@sru.edu

PROSSER, PETER E.
PERSONAL Born 12/16/1946, Birmingham, England, m, 1970, 2 children **DISCIPLINE** CHURCH HISTORY; ETHICS **EDUCATION** Univ Montreal, MDiv, 75, MA, 78, PhD, 89. **CAREER** Lectr, Inst Biblique Beree, Montreal, 72-75; fel, Univ Montreal, 82-83; asst prof, Church Hist, Regent Univ, 83-90; Assoc prof, 91-97; prof, 98- . **HONORS AND AWARDS** Who's Who in Am, 79, 84, 90-92, 98; Int Men of Distinction, 79; Silver medal, Cambridge Biographical Institute, UK; International Scholar Awd 00, (Cambridge) Int. Order of Merit, UK, Fellowship, Westminister College, Oxford, 00; International Who's Who, 01 **MEMBERSHIPS** AAR/SBL; SPS; ETS. **RESEARCH** Millennialism; Reformation; apocalypticism; Methodist history. **SELECTED PUBLICATIONS** Auth, Prophecy: A Vital Gift to the Church, Including Yours, Acts 29 Mag, 92; Spirit-Filled Life Bible, Sections on 1 and 2 John, Thomas Nelson publ; auth, Dispenstional Eschatology, Mellen Press (486 pgs), The Papacy, Chi Hist, Magazine, 00. **CONTACT ADDRESS** School of Divinity, Regent Univ, 1000 Regent Dr, Virginia Beach, VA 23464-9800. **EMAIL** petepro@regent.edu

PROWE, DIETHELM MANFRED-HARTMUT
PERSONAL Born 01/04/1941, Bonn, Germany, m, 1968, 2 children **DISCIPLINE** MODERN & GERMAN HISTORY **EDUCATION** Kent State Univ, BA, 62; Stanford Univ, MA, 63, PhD(hist) 67. **CAREER** From instr to assoc prof, 66-78, prof hist, Carleton Col, 78-, Humboldt Found res fel, 75-76 & 79-80. **MEMBERSHIPS** AHA; Conf Group Cent Europ Hist; Ger Studies Asn. **RESEARCH** Germany; topics in foreign policy; post-World War II Germany. **SELECTED PUBLICA-**

TIONS Auth, Berlin--Weltstadt in Krisen, 1949-1958, Gruyter, 73; Die AnfÕnge der Brandtschen Ostpolitik in Berlin 1961-1963, Schriftenreihe der Vierteljahrshefte fur Zeitgeschichte, 76; The new Nachkriegsgeschichte, 1945-49: West Germans in search of their historical origins, Cent Europ Hist, 12/77; Wirtschaftsdemokratische AnsÕtze 1945-49, WSI-Mitteilungen, 7/81; The Evolution and New Research Agenda of Postwar German History: A Historian's View, Working Papers of theVolkswagen-Foundation Seminars in Post-War German History, Working Paper 1, Washington, DC: American Institute for Contemporary German Studies and German Historical Institute, 95; The Making of ein Berliner, Kennedy, Brandt, and the Origins of Detente Policy in Germany, David Wetzel, ed, From the Berlin Museum to the Berlin Wall: essays on the Cultural and Political History of Modern Germany, Festschrift for Gordon A. Craig, Vol 1, New York, Praeger, 96; Ordnungsmacht and Mitbestimmung: The Postwar Labor Unions and the Politics of Reconstruction, David E. Barclay and Eric D Weitz, eds, Between Reform and Revolution: German Socialism and Communicsm from 1840 to 1990, Providence, RI and Oxford, Berghahn Publishers, 98. **CONTACT ADDRESS** Dept of History, Carleton Col, 1 N College St, Northfield, MN 55057-4044. **EMAIL** dprowe@carleton.edu

PROWN, JULES D.
PERSONAL Born 03/14/1930, Freehold, NJ, m, 1956, 5 children **DISCIPLINE** HISTORY OF ART **EDUCATION** Lafayette Col, AB, 51; Harvard Univ, AM, 53, PhD(fine arts), 61; Univ Del, AM, 56. **CAREER** Asst to dir, Fogg Art Mus, Harvard Univ, 59-61; from instr to assoc prof, Yale Univ, 61-71; from cur designate to cur, Garvan Collection Am Art, 63-68; vis lectr, Smith Col, 66-67; dir, Yale Ctr Brit Art & Brit Studies, 68-76; from prof hist of art to Paul Mellon prof hist of art Emeritus, Yale Univ, 71-99; mem adv comt, Fulbright Scholars 67-68; mem adv comn, Nat Portrait Gallery, DC, 69-76; mem bd gov, Yale Univ Press, 69-76; chief exec off, Paul Mellon Ctr Studies in Brit Art, London, 70-76; mem adv comt, Yale Ed of Horace Walpole's Corresp, 71-76; mem adv coun, Inst Early Am Hist & Cult, Va, 72-75; Benjamin Franklin fel, Royal Soc Arts, 72-; mem bd trustees, Whitney Mus Art, 75-94; mem exec bd, Nat Humanities Inst, New Haven, Ct, 75-78; mem coun, Am Antiquarian Soc, 77-94, mem editing adv bd, Am Art, 86-. **HONORS AND AWARDS** Guggenheim Fel, 64-65; Robert C. Smith Awd, 83; Distinguished Teaching of Art Hist Awd, Col Art Asn Am, 95; Fel, Whitney Humanities Center, Yale Univ, 92-94; George Washington Kidd, Class of 1836, Awd, Lafayette Col Alumni Asn, 86; am, yale univ, 71; dfa, lafayette col, 79. **MEMBERSHIPS** Col Art Asn Am; Am Studies Asn; Am Soc 18th Century Studies. **RESEARCH** American and British painting. **SELECTED PUBLICATIONS** Auth, Text for John Singleton Copley Catalogue, October House, 65; John Singleton Copley, (2 vols), Harvard Univ, 66; co-auth, The Visual Arts in Higher Education, Yale Univ, 66; auth, American Painting from Its Beginnings to the Armory Show, Skira, 69; auth, Style as Evidence, 80 & Mind in Matter, Winterthur Portfolio, 82; auth, The Truth of Material Culture: History of Fiction?, History from Things: Essays on material Culture, Smithsonian Inst Press, 93; auth, "Benjamin West and The Use of Antiquity," Am Art Vol 10, no.2, 96; auth, 18th Century Studies, Vol 31, no. 1, 97; auth, A Course of Antiquities at Rome 1764, Reading Am Art, Yale Univer Press, 98; contribur, Thomas Eakins Winslow Homer, Encycl Britannica. **CONTACT ADDRESS** Yale Univ, PO Box 208280, New Haven, CT 06520-8280. **EMAIL** jules.prown@yale.edu

PRUCHA, FRANCIS PAUL
PERSONAL Born 01/04/1921, River Falls, WI, s **DISCIPLINE** AMERICAN HISTORY **EDUCATION** Wis State Col, River Falls, BS, 41; Univ Minn, MA, 47; Harvard Univ, PhD(hist), 50; St Louis Univ, philosophy and theology studies, 52-59. **CAREER** From asst prof to assoc prof, 60-66, chmn dept hist, 62-69, Prof Am Hist, Marquette Univ, 66-92, Soc Sci Res Coun fac res grant, 59; Guggenheim fel, 67-68; sr fel, Nat Endowment for Humanities, 70-71 & 81-82, Emeritus 92-. **MEMBERSHIPS** AHA; Orgn Am Historians; Western Hist Asn; Member of Society of Jesus, 50, Mass Hist Soc; Am Antiquarian Soc; Soc of American Historians. **RESEARCH** Western military frontier; federal Indian policy. **SELECTED PUBLICATIONS** Auth, Broadax And Bayonet, Wis State Hist Soc, 53; American Indian Policy In The Formative Years, Harvard Univ, 62; The Sword Of The Republic, Macmillan, 69; Indian Peace Medals In American History, Wis State Hist Soc, 71; Ed, Americanizing The American Indians, Harvard Univ, 73; Auth, American Indian Policy In Crisis, Univ Okla, 76; A Bibliographical Guide To The History Of Indian-White Relations In The United States, Univ Chicago, 77; The Churches And The Indian Schools, Univ Nebr, 79; ed, Documents of United States Indian Policy, Univ Nebraska, 75,88.00; auth, Cherokee Removal, Univ TN, 81; auth, Indian Policy in the United States, Univ Nebraska, 81; auth, The Great Father, Univ Nebraska, 84; auth, The Indians in American Society, Univ CA, 85; auth, Handbook of Research in Am Hist, Univ Nebraska, 87,94; Atlas of American Indian Affairs, Univ Nebraska, 90; American Indian Treaties, Univ CA, 94. **CONTACT ADDRESS** Dept of Hist, Marquette Univ, Milwaukee, WI 53233.

PRUDE, JONATHAN
DISCIPLINE HISTORY **EDUCATION** Amherst, BA, 68; Harvard Univ, PhD, 76. **CAREER** Asst prof to ASSOC PROF, HIST, EMORY UNIV **HONORS AND AWARDS** E. Harold Hugo Prize **MEMBERSHIPS** Am Antiquarian Soc **SELECTED PUBLICATIONS** Auth, "The Social System of Early New England Textile Mills," in Working-Class America, 83; auth, "Town-Factory Conflicts in Antebellum Rural Massachusetts," in The Countryside in the Age of Capitalist Transformation: Essays in the Social History of Rural America, 85; co-ed, The Countryside in the Age of Capitalist Transformation: Essays in the Social History of Rural America, 85; auth, "To Look Upon the Lower Sort: Runaway Ads and the Appearance of Unfree Laborers in America, 1750-1800," Jour of Am Hist, June 91; auth, "Capitalism, Industrialization, and the Factory in Post-Revolutionary America," in Jour of the Early Rep 16, 96, repr, in Wages of Independence: Capitalism in the Early American Republic, 97; auth, The Coming of Industrial Order: Town and Factory Life in Rural Massachusetts, 1810-1860, Univ Mass Pr, 99. **CONTACT ADDRESS** Dept of Hist, Emory Univ, Atlanta, GA 30322. **EMAIL** histjp@emory.edu

PRUETT, GORDON EARL
PERSONAL Born 10/16/1941, Raton, NM, m, 1966, 1 child **DISCIPLINE** HISTORY OF RELIGION **EDUCATION** Yale Univ, BA, 63; Oxford Univ, BA & MA, 65; Princeton Univ, PhD, 68. **CAREER** Asst prof relig, Lehigh Univ, 68-69; asst prof, 69-74; acting chmn dept eng, 76-80; assoc prof philos & relig, Northeastern Univ, 74- . **RESEARCH** History of Christianity; Sociology of religion; Mysticism and psychoanalysis. **SELECTED PUBLICATIONS** Auth, A note on Robert Bellah's theory of religious evolution: The early modern period, Sociol Analysis, 73; History, transcendence, and world community in the work of Wilfred Cantwell Smith, Jour Am Acad Relig, 73; Christianity, history and culture in Nagaland, Contribs to Indian Sociol, 74; A Protestant doctrine of the Eucharistic presence, Calvin Theol Jour, 75; Thomas Cranmer's progress in the doctrine of the Eucharist, 1535-1548, Hist Mag Protestant Episcopal Church, 76; Will and freedom: Psychoanalytic themes in the work of Jacob Boehme, Studies Relig & Sci Relig, 77; Religion in higher education, Int Encycl Higher Educ, 78; The escape from the Seraglio: Anti-orientalist trends in modern religious studies, Arab Studies Quart, 80; Preparatio Evangelii: Religious Studies and Secondary Education, Nat Asn of Episcopal Schools Jour 1:1, 84; Islam and Orientalism, Orientalism, Islamists and Islam, ed Asaf Hussain, Robert Olson, and Jamil Qureshi, Amana, 84; Through a Glass Darkly: Knowledge of the Self in Dreams in Ibn Khaldun's Mugaddima, The Muslim World LXXV:1, 85; The Meaning and End of Suffering for Freud and the Buddhist Tradition, 87; World Theology and World Community: The Vision of Wilfred Cantwell Smith, Studies in Religion 19:4, 1990; Theravadin Buddhist Commentary on the Current State of Western Epistemology, Buddhist-Christian Studies 10, 1990; As a Father Loves His Children: The Image of the Supreme Being as Loving Father in Judaism, Christianity and Islam, 94. **CONTACT ADDRESS** Dept of Philosophy and Religion, Northeastern Univ, 360 Huntington Ave, Boston, MA 02115-5000.

PRUETT, JOHN H.
PERSONAL Born 06/03/1947, Richmond, VA **DISCIPLINE** HISTORY **EDUCATION** Univ of Va, BA, 69; Princeton Univ, MA, 71; PhD, 73. **CAREER** Visiting asst prof, Univ of Illinois, 73-74; asst prof, Univ of Illinois, 74-79; assoc prof, Univ Ill Urbana Champaign, 79-. **HONORS AND AWARDS** Phi Beta Kappa, 68; Danforth Scholar, 69-73. **RESEARCH** Colonial and revolutionary America. **SELECTED PUBLICATIONS** Auth, Career Patterns among the Clergy of Lincoln Cathedral, 1660-1750, Church Hist, 75; The Parish Clergy under the Later Stuarts, Univ Ill, 78; A Late Stuart Leicestershire Parson (rev), J Relig Hist, 79. **CONTACT ADDRESS** History Dept, Univ of Illinois, Urbana-Champaign, 52 E Gregory Dr, Champaign, IL 61820. **EMAIL** j-pruett@uiuc.edu

PUCCI, FRANK J.
PERSONAL Born 01/24/1939, Boston, MA, d, 2 children **DISCIPLINE** GEOGRAPHY **EDUCATION** Univ Minn, BA, 85; MA, 87; PhD, 93. **CAREER** Instr, Millersville Univ, 90-91; Instr, Oh Univ, 91-92; Adj Fac, Millersville Univ, 93-94; Adj Prof, Univ Nmex, 94-95; Adj Prof, Millersville Univ, 95-. **MEMBERSHIPS** Asn of Am Geogrs, Pa Geog Soc, Popular Cult Assoc. **RESEARCH** United States/Mexico borderlands region, colonial Mexico. **SELECTED PUBLICATIONS** Auth, Handbook for Resource and Community Development, Col of Agr, Univ Minn, 87. **CONTACT ADDRESS** Dept Geog, Millersville Univ of Pennsylvania, PO Box 1002, Millersville, PA 17551. **EMAIL** fpucci@sha.state.md.us

PUDSELL, F. DAVID
PERSONAL Born 07/09/1934, Baltimore, MD, d, 3 children **DISCIPLINE** HISTORY, PHILOSOPHY **EDUCATION** Tuscuhum Col, BA; Ind Univ, MA; Pittsburgh Theol Sem, MTh. **CAREER** Assoc Prof, Fairmont State Col, 68-. **RESEARCH** Greek Philosophy; Medical Ethics; Cosmology; Russian History. **CONTACT ADDRESS** Dept Soc Sci, Fairmont State Col, 1201 Locust Ave, Fairmont, WV 26554-2451.

PUGACH, NOEL H.
PERSONAL Born 04/13/1939, Brooklyn, NY, m, 1965, 2 children **DISCIPLINE** HISTORY **EDUCATION** Brooklyn Col, BA, 60; Univ of Wisc Madison, MA, 62; PhD, 67. **CAREER** Instr, Kent State Univ, 65-68; asst prof to prof, Univ of NMex, 68-. **HONORS AND AWARDS** Phi Beta Kappa; Phi Alpha Theta; Wisc State Hist Soc Awd. **MEMBERSHIPS** Soc for Hist of Am For Rel; AHA; Org of Am Hist. **RESEARCH** U.S. - East Asian Relations, 20th Century. **SELECTED PUBLICATIONS** Auth, Paul S. Reinsch: Open Door Diplomat in Action, 79; auth, "The Sinicization of the Chinese American Bank of Commerce: Causes and Consequences", Sino-American Relations Since 1900, ed Priscilla Roberts, 91; auth, Same Bed, Different Dreams: A History of the Chinese American Bank of Commerce, 97. **CONTACT ADDRESS** Dept Hist, Univ of New Mexico, Albuquerque, 1 University Campus, Albuquerque, NM 87131-0001. **EMAIL** npugach@unm.edu

PUGLIESE, STANISLAO
PERSONAL Born 03/24/1965, New York, NY, m, 1992, 2 children **DISCIPLINE** HISTORY **EDUCATION** Hofstra Univ, BA, 87; CCNY, MA, 91; CUNY Grad Sch, PhD, 95. **CAREER** Asst prof, Hofstra Univ, 94-2000. **MEMBERSHIPS** Am Hist Asn, Soc for Italian Hist Studies, Am Italian Hist Asn. **RESEARCH** Modern Italy, fascism, antifascism, holocaust. **SELECTED PUBLICATIONS** Auth, Carlo Rossell: Socialist Heretic and Antifascist Exile, Harvard Univ Press (99). **CONTACT ADDRESS** Dept Hist, Hofstra Univ, 1000 Fulton Ave, Hempstead, NY 11550-1030.

PUGLISI, CATHERINE
PERSONAL Born 04/08/1953, New York City, NY, m, 1984, 2 children **DISCIPLINE** ART HISTORY **EDUCATION** NYork Univ, PhD. **CAREER** Assoc prof, grad dir, Rutgers Univ. **HONORS AND AWARDS** Rome Prize, 80. **MEMBERSHIPS** CAA; Ital Art Soc. **RESEARCH** Baroque art; Bolognese painting; painting and sculpture in 17th-century Rome; 18th-century Venice. **SELECTED PUBLICATIONS** Auth, Francesco Albani, Yale UP, 99; Guido Reni's "Pallione del Voto" and the Plague of 1630, Art Bulletin, 95; auth, Caravaggio, Phaidon Press, 98. **CONTACT ADDRESS** Dept of Art Hist, Rutgers, The State Univ of New Jersey, New Brunswick, Hamilton St., New Brunswick, NJ 08903. **EMAIL** cpuglisi@rci.ruters.edu

PULLEN, DANIEL J.
PERSONAL Born 05/19/1954, Pittsburg, KS **DISCIPLINE** CLASSICAL ARCHAEOLOGY; ANTHROPOLOGY **EDUCATION** Univ Kans, BA, 76; Indiana Univ, MA, 78,PhD, 85. **CAREER** Administrator, Sardis Expedition, Harvard Univ Art Museums; asst prof, classics dept, 88-93, assoc prof, 93- , FL State Univ. **HONORS AND AWARDS** Univ Teaching Awd, FL State Univ, 98. **MEMBERSHIPS** Archaeological Institute of Am; Soc for Amer Archaeology; **RESEARCH** Classic studies Aegean Prehistory; Classical Archaeology; Complex Societies **SELECTED PUBLICATIONS** Auth, Modelling Mortuary Behavior on a Regional Scale: A Case Study from Mainland Greece in the Early Bronze Age, Beyond The Site: Regional Studies in the Aegean Area, 94; auth, A lead seal from Tsoungiza Hill, Ancient Nemea, and Early Bronze Age Sealing Systems, American Journal of Archaeology, 94; auth, Artifact and Assemblage: The Finds from a Regional Survey of the Southern Argolid, Greece, vol I: The Prehistoric and Early Iron Age Pottery and the Lithic Artifacts, 95. **CONTACT ADDRESS** Dept of Classics, Florida State Univ, Tallahassee, FL 32306-1510.

PULLEYBLANK, EDWIN GEORGE
PERSONAL Born 08/07/1922, Calgary, AB, Canada, m, 3 children **DISCIPLINE** CHINESE LANGUAGE & HISTORY **EDUCATION** Univ Alta, BA, 42; Univ London, PhD(Chinese), 51; Cambridge Univ, MA, 53. **CAREER** Lectr, Univ of London, 48-53; Prof, Univ of Cambridge, 53-66; Prof, Univ of BC, 66-87; Prof Emer, Univ of BC, 88-. **HONORS AND AWARDS** Fel, Royal Soc of Canada, 80; Corresponding Fel, Istituto Italiana per il Medio ed Estramo Oriente, 93. **MEMBERSHIPS** Asn Asian Studies; Am Orient Soc; Ling Soc Am; Can Soc Asian Studies (pres, 71-74); fel Royal Soc Can. **RESEARCH** Chinese history; historical phonology and grammar of classical Chinese. **SELECTED PUBLICATIONS** Auth, The Background of the Rebellion of An Lu-shan, London: Oxford Univ Press, 55; auth, Chinese History and World History: An inaugural lecture, Cambridge, Cabridge Univ Press, 55; auth, Historians of China and Japan, ed with W.G. Beasley, London: Oxford Univ Press, 61; auth, Middle Chinese: A Study in Historical Phonology, Vancouver: UBC Press, 84; auth, Studies in Language Origins, Vol I, ed by Jan Wind, Edwin G. Pulleyblank, Eric de Grolier and Bernard H. Bichakjian, Amsterdam and Philadelphia: Benjamins, 89; auth, A Lexicon of Reconstructed Pronunciation in Early Middle Chinese, Late Middle Chinese and Early Madarin, Vancouver: UBC Press, 91; auth, A Chinese text in Central Asian Brahmi script: New evidence for the pronunciation of Late Middle Chinese and Khotanese, With R.E. Emmerick, Rome: Istituto Italiano per il Medio ed Estremo Oriente, 94; auth, Outline of Classical Chinese Grammar, Vancouver: UBC Press, 95; auth, 'Morphology in Old Chinese,' Journal of Chinese Linguistics 28, (00): 26-51.

CONTACT ADDRESS Dept of Asian Studies, Univ of British Columbia, 2708 W 3rd Ave, Vancouver, BC, Canada V6K 1M5. **EMAIL** edwin@interchange.ubc.ca

PURCELL, E. A.
PERSONAL Born 07/20/1941, Kansas City, MO, m, 1982, 2 children **DISCIPLINE** HISTORY, LAW **EDUCATION** Rockhurst Col, AB 62; Univ Kansas, MA 64; Univ Wisconsin, PhD 68; Harvard Law, JD 79. **CAREER** Univ Cal Berk, asst prof, 67-69; Univ Missouri Col, asst prof, assoc prof 69-77; New York Law Sch, prof law, 89-. **HONORS AND AWARDS** Louis Peltzer Awd; Frederick Jackson Turner Prize. **MEMBERSHIPS** OAH; ASLH; ABNY **RESEARCH** 19th, 20th Century Amer Social Intellectual and Legal Hist. **SELECTED PUBLICATIONS** Auth, The Crisis of Democratic Theory, 73; Litigation and Inequality, 92; auth, Brandeis and the Progressive Constitution, 00. **CONTACT ADDRESS** New York Law Sch, 57 Worth St, New York, NY 10013-2960.

PURCELL, SARAH
PERSONAL Born Iowa City, IA, s **DISCIPLINE** AMERICAN HISTORY **EDUCATION** Grinnell Col, BA, 92; Brown Univ, AM, 93; PhD, 97. **CAREER** Asst Prof, Cent Mich Univ, 97-. **HONORS AND AWARDS** Filson Club Hist Soc Fel; Mellon Sem Hist & Lit; John Nicholas Brown Ctr for the Study of Am Civilization. **MEMBERSHIPS** AHA, OAH, SHEAR, OIEAHC. **RESEARCH** America, 1775-1848, Political Culture, Travel, Military History, Women's History. **SELECTED PUBLICATIONS** Auth, The Encyclopedia of Battles in North America, 1517-1916, NY,00; auth, "'Spread This Martial Fire': The New England Patriot Clergy & Civil Military Inspiration," The Journal of Church and State38 (96): 621-638. **CONTACT ADDRESS** Dept Hist, Central Michigan Univ, 100 W Preston Rd, Mount Pleasant, MI 48859-0001. **EMAIL** sarah.purcell@cmich.edu

PUREFOY MORRIS, SARAH
DISCIPLINE CLASSICAL ARCHAEOLOGY **EDUCATION** Univ N Carolina, BA, 76; Amer Sch Class Stud, Athens, Greece, 78-80; Harvard Univ, MA, MPhil, PhD, 81. **CAREER** Asst prof, 81-86; assoc prof, 89-93; Prof, UCLA, 93-, Dept Ch, 97-. **HONORS AND AWARDS** Eben Alexander Greek Translation prize, Univ NC, 76; Sinclair Kennedy Travelling fel, Harvard Univ, 78-79; Arthur W Parsons fel, Amer Sch Class Stud, Greece, 79; Charles Eliot Norton fel, Harvard Univ, 80; Olivia James fel, Archaeol Inst Am, 80; A Whitney Griswold fac res grant, Yale univ, 82, 84; res grant, Kress Found, 83; Susan Hilles Morse jr fac fel, Yale Univ, 84-85; res grant, Grant-in-Aid, Amer Coun Learned Soc, 88; James R Wiseman bk award, Archaeol Inst Amer, 93. **SELECTED PUBLICATIONS** Auth, The Black and White Style: Athens and Aigina in the Orientalizing Period, Yale Class Monogr 6, Yale Univ Press, 84; Daidalos and the Origins of Greek Art, Princeton Univ Press, 92, 95; The Ages of Homer, A Tribute to Emily Townsend Vermeule, Austin, 95, 97; "Greek and Near Eastern Art in the Age of Homer," New Light on a Dark Age, Exploring the Culture of Geometric Greece, Columbia, Mo, 97; "Homer and the Near East," A New Companion to Homer, Leiden: Brill, 97; co-ed, "Ancient Towers on Leukas, Greece," Structures Rurales et Societes Anciennes, Besancon, 94; "The Sacrifice of Astyanax: Near Eastern Contributions to the Trojan War," The Ages of Homer, Austin, Texas, 95; "The Legacy of Black Athena," Black Athena Revisited, Chapel Hill, NC, 96; rev(s), "From Modernism to Manure: Perspectives on Classical Archaeology," review of Classical Greece: Ancient Histories & Modern Archaeologies, Antiquity 69, 95; Ex Oriente Books: Near Eastern Resources for Classicists, AJA 101, 97. **CONTACT ADDRESS** Dept of Classics, Univ of California, Los Angeles, PO Box 951436, Los Angeles, CA 90095-1436. **EMAIL** sarahm@humnet.ucla.edu

PURSELL, CARROLL W.
PERSONAL Born 09/04/1932, Visalia, CA, m, 1986, 2 children **DISCIPLINE** HISTORY **EDUCATION** City Col San Francisco, AA, 54; Univ Ca Berkeley, BA, 56; Univ Del, MA, 58; Univ Ca Berkeley, PhD, 62. **CAREER** Asst prof, Case Inst of Technology, 63-65; asst prof, Univ Ca Santa Barbara, 65-88; prof, Lehigh Univ, 74-76, prof, Case W Reserve Univ, 88-. **HONORS AND AWARDS** Leonardo da Vinci Medal, Soc for the Hist of Technology. **MEMBERSHIPS** AHA; Orgn of Am Hist; Soc for the Hist of Technology. **RESEARCH** History of American Technology. **SELECTED PUBLICATIONS** Auth, White Heat, Univ Ca Pr (Berkeley), 94; auth The Machine in America, Johns Hopkins Univ Pr (Baltimore), 95. **CONTACT ADDRESS** Dept Hist, Case Western Reserve Univ, 10900 Euclid Ave, Cleveland, OH 44106-1712. **EMAIL** cxp7@po.cwru.edu

PURTLE, CAROL JEAN
DISCIPLINE ART HISTORY **EDUCATION** Maryville Univ, St Louis, BA, 60; Manhattanville Col, NYork, MA, 66; Washington Univ, PhD, 76. **CAREER** Advan res fel, Belgian-Am Educ Found, 74-75; Danforth assoc, 75-79; fac develop award, Memphis State Univ, 80, 85, 95; prof and coord art hist, Univ Memphis, 79-; **HONORS AND AWARDS** Alum Awd Prof Achievement 87; Nat Endowment for Hum Fel, 82, 88. **MEMBERSHIPS** Hist of Netherlandish Art; Col Art Asoc **SELECTED PUBLICATIONS** Auth, The Marian Paintings of Jan van Eyck, Princeton Univ Press, 82; auth, St. Luke Drawing the Virgin: Selected Essays in Context, Brepols, 97; auth, Narrative Time and Metaphoric Tradition in the Development of Jan van Eyck's Washington Annunciation, Art Bulletin, 99; auth, Le Sacerdoce de la Vierge et l'enigme d'un Parti leonographique Exceptionnel, Revue de Louvre, 96; The Iconography of Campin's Madonnes in Interiors: A Search for Common Ground, New Directions in Scholarship, National Gallery of Art, 171-182, 96; auth, The Iconography of Prayer, Jean de Berry and the Origin of the Annunciation in a Church, Simiolus, 227-239, 90. **CONTACT ADDRESS** Dept of Art, Univ of Memphis, 3706 Alumni St, Memphis, TN 38152-0001. **EMAIL** cpurtle@memphis.edu

PURVIS, THOMAS L.
PERSONAL Born 02/02/1949, Newport, KY, m, 1997, 1 child **DISCIPLINE** HISTORY **EDUCATION** Wash Univ, AB, 71; Johns Hopkins Univ, MA, 77; PhD, 79. **CAREER** Asst prof, Stockton State Col, 79-80; asst prof, Oswego State Univ, 81-82; asst prof, Univ of Ga, 82-85; asst prof, Auburn Univ at Montgomery, 86-87; assoc prof, William and Mary & ed of publ, Inst for Early American Culture, 88-89; free-lance auth, 90-00. **HONORS AND AWARDS** Andrew Mellon Fels, 78-79, 85-86; Huntington Libr Res Fel, 85, 87-8; Am Antiquarian Soc Res Fel, 88; NEH Res Grants, 83, 89; Am Philos Soc Res Grant, 88. **RESEARCH** Colonial & Revolutionary U.S. **SELECTED PUBLICATIONS** Auth, Proprietors, Patronage and Paper Money: Legislative Politics in New Jersey, 1703- 1776, 86; coauth, The Enduring Vision: A History of the American People, Heath, 90; Historical Almanac of Revolutionary America, 1763-1800, Facts on File, 95; Dictionary of American History, Basil Blackwell, 95; auth, Newport, Kentucky: A Bicentennial History, Zimmerman Printers, 96; Historical Almanac of Colonial America, 1500-1763, Facts on File of New York, 98. **CONTACT ADDRESS** 812 York St., Newport, KY 41071-1823.

PUTNAM, JACKSON K.
PERSONAL Born 02/10/1929, Emmons Co, ND, D, 4 children **DISCIPLINE** AMERICAN HISTORY **EDUCATION** Univ NDak, BS, 52, MA, 55; Stanford Univ, PhD(hist), 64. **CAREER** From instr to asst prof hist, Ore State Univ, 58-65; from asst prof to assoc prof, 65-73, Prof Hist, Calif State Univ, Fullerton, 73-96, Emeritus 91- . **HONORS AND AWARDS** Oscar O Winter Awd, Western Hist Asn 77. **MEMBERSHIPS** Pacific Coast Branch, AHA; California Historical Society; Historical Society of Southern California. **RESEARCH** Westward movement in United States history; California history. **SELECTED PUBLICATIONS** Auth, The Role Of The Socialist Party In North Dakota History, Ndak Quart, Fall 56; The Presistence Of Progressivism In The 1920's: The Case Of California, Pac Hist Rev, 11/66; Old Age Politics In California, From Richardson To Reagan, Stanford Univ, 70; Down To Earth: A B Guthrie's Quest For Moral And Historical Truth, Ndak Quart, Summer 71; The Turner Thesis And The Westward Movement: A Reappraisal, Western Hist Quart, 10/76; Historical Fact And Literary Truth: The Problem Of Authenticity In Western American Literature, Western Am Lit, 5/80; auth, This Pattern of Modern California Politics, Pacific Historical Review, LXI, Feb. 92, 23-52; auth, The Progressivism Legacy in California: Fifty Years of Politics, 1917-1967, in California Progressivism Reviisited, eds. Wm Deverelt and Tom Sitton, Berkeley: Univ. of California press, 94, pp. 247-268; auth, A Half-Century of Conflict, The Rise and Fall of Liberalism in California Politics, in Politics in the Postwar American West, ed. Richard Lowitt, Norman University of Oklahoma Press, 95, pp 42-63; On Turners Trail--100 Years Of Writing; auth, Jesse and Pat: A Creative Conflict in California Political History, California Politics and Policy, 97 Special Issue, pp. 79-91. **CONTACT ADDRESS** Dept of Hist, California State Univ, Fullerton, Fullerton, CA 92834.

Q

QIAN, WEN-YUAN
PERSONAL Born 04/14/1936, Shanghai, China, d **DISCIPLINE** HISTORY **EDUCATION** Beijing Univ, BS, 59; Northwestern Univ, MA, 84; Univ Mich, PhD, 88. **CAREER** Asst prof, hist, Blackburn Col, 88-92; asst prof, hist, 92- 98, Assoc Prof, MacMurray Col, 98-. **HONORS AND AWARDS** Dist Dept Hist Scholarship, Univ Mich, 84-87; neh inst, 92, 94. **RESEARCH** History sci, tech; Chinese hist; world hist. **SELECTED PUBLICATIONS** Auth, The Great Inertia: Scientific Stagnation in Traditional China, 85; "A Definition of Science as an Antidote Against Either Mystifying or Demystifying Science, Organon, 22/23: 86, 87. **CONTACT ADDRESS** Dept of History, MacMurray Col, 447 E. College, Jacksonville, FL 62650. **EMAIL** wenqian@highlanders.mac.edu

QUATAERT, DONALD GEORGE
PERSONAL Born 09/10/1941, Rochester, NY, m, 1970, 2 children **DISCIPLINE** MIDDLE EAST HISTORY **EDUCATION** Boston Univ, AB, 66; Harvard Univ, AM, 68; Univ Calif, Los Angeles, PhD(hist), 73. **CAREER** Scholar hist, Near East Ctr, Univ Calif, Los Angeles, 73-74; asst prof, 74-79, asst to assoc prof, Univ Houston, 74-87; assoc to Prof, Binghamton Univ, 87; Mem, Am Coun Learned Soc Comt Teaching Mat Islamic Civilization, 76- **MEMBERSHIPS** AHA; Mideast Studies Asn; Turkish Studies Asn. **RESEARCH** Social, economic and labor history of the Ottoman Middle East, 1700-1922. **SELECTED PUBLICATIONS** Auth, Social Disintergration and Popular Resistance in the Ottoman Empire 1881-1908, 83; auth, Ottoman Manufacturing in the Age of the Idustrial Revolution, 93; auth, Technnology Transfer in the Ottoman Empire, 92; co-ed, An Economic and Social History of the Ottoman Empire, 1300-1914, 94; auth, The Ottoman Empire, 1700-1922, 00. **CONTACT ADDRESS** Dept of Hist, SUNY, Binghamton, Binghamton, NY 13902-6000. **EMAIL** dquataer@binghamton.edu

QUERE, RALPH WALTER
PERSONAL Born 09/26/1935, Cleveland, OH, m, 1957, 3 children **DISCIPLINE** HISTORY OF CHRISTIAN THOUGHT **EDUCATION** Princeton Univ, AB, 57; Trinity Sem, Columbus Ohio, BD, 64; Princeton Theol Sem,, 70. **CAREER** From instr to assoc prof, 69-84, Prof Hist & Theol, Wartburg Theol Sem, 84-. **MEMBERSHIPS** Am Soc Reformation Res; Am Soc Church Hist; Acad Evangel Theol Educ; Sixteenth Century Cong; Concordia Acad. **RESEARCH** Melanchthon's eucharistic thought; history of Christological thought; history of worship. **SELECTED PUBLICATIONS** Auth, Confrontation at Marburg, Harvard Case Study Inst, 73; Superstar and Godspell, Dialogue, summer 73; Evangelical Witness, Augsburg, 75; The spirit and the gifts are ours.., ordination rites, Lutheran Quart, 11/75; Melanchthonian motifs in the formula, in Dialogue, Discord and Concord, Fortress, 77; Melanchthon's Christum Cognoscere, DeGraaf, 77; Christ's efficacious presence in The Lord's Supper, Lutheran Quart, 2/77. **CONTACT ADDRESS** Wartburg Theol Sem, 333 Wartburg Pl, Dubuque, IA 52004-5004. **EMAIL** quere@mwci.com

QUINAN, JACK
PERSONAL Born 11/28/1939, Somerville, MA, m, 1991, 1 child **DISCIPLINE** ART HISTORY **EDUCATION** Brown Univ, PhD. **CAREER** Fac, SUNY Buffalo, present; adj prof archit, Frank Lloyd Wright Schl Archit, concurrent. **HONORS AND AWARDS** Fellow, NEH; curator of the darwin d. martin house. **MEMBERSHIPS** SAH; Frank Lloyd Wright Bldg Conservancy. **RESEARCH** 19th- and 20th-century archit hist, Am archit. **SELECTED PUBLICATIONS** Auth, Frank Lloyd Wright's Larkin Building: Myth and Fact, AHF/MIT, 87. **CONTACT ADDRESS** Dept of Art Hist, SUNY, Buffalo, 608 Clemens Hall, Amherst, NY 14260-6010. **EMAIL** guinan@acsu.buffalo.edu

QUINLIVAN, MARY E.
DISCIPLINE HISTORY **EDUCATION** St. Scholastica, BA, 54; Loyola, MA, 64; Univ Wis, PhD, 71. **CAREER** Assoc prof, hist, Univ Texas at Permian Basin; PROF, HIST, UNIV WIS WHITEWATER. **MEMBERSHIPS** Am Antiquarian Soc **SELECTED PUBLICATIONS** Auth, "Race Relations in the Antebellum Children's Literature of Jacob Abbott," Jour of Pop Cult, 82; auth, entries in American Writers Before 1800, Greenwood, 83. **CONTACT ADDRESS** PO Box 74, Whitewater, WI 53190.

QUIRIN, JAMES
PERSONAL Born 07/27/1943, Raleigh, NC, m, 2 children **DISCIPLINE** HISTORY **EDUCATION** Univ Ore, Ba, 65; MA, 71; Univ Minn, PhD, 77. **CAREER** Adj prof, Vanderbilt Univ, 95-96; from asst prof to prof, Fisk Univ, 81-. **HONORS AND AWARDS** Dissertation Fel, Soc Sci Res Coun, 74-76; Dissertation Write-Up Fel, Soc Sci Res Coun, 76; Grant-in-Aid, ACLS, 78; Int Travel Grant, ACLS, 82; NEH summer sem, Yale Univ, 82; NEH summer stipend, 84; res grant, Am Philos Soc, 85; NEH summer sem, CUNY, 85; res grant, United Negro Col Fund, 85; NEH travel grant, 89; NEH summer sem, Univ of Wis, 90; Joseph P. Malone Fel, Am Univ of Cairo, 91; Pew Fac Fel, Harvard, 93-94; NEH study grant, 94; res grant, Fisk Univ, 98; Carnegie Scholar, Carnegie Found for the Advancement of Teaching, 00-01. **MEMBERSHIPS** Am Hist Asn, African Studies Asn, Soc for the Study of Ethiopian Jewry, World Hist Asn, United Nations Asn. **RESEARCH** Ethiopia & the Horn of Africa, Africa's Relationship to World History. **SELECTED PUBLICATIONS** Auth, The Evolution of the Ethiopian Jews: A History of the Beta Israel (Falasha) to 1920, Pa Press (Philadelphia, PA), 92; auth, "Caste and Class in Historical Northwest Ethiopia: The Beta Israel (Falasha) and Kemant, 1300-1900," J of African Hist 39 (98): 195-220; auth, "Society and the State: Reflections from the Northwest, 1300-1900," Ethiopia in Broader Perspective: Papers of the XIIIth International Conference of Ethiopian Studies, Kyoto, 12-17 December 1997, Shokado Book Sellers (Kyoto, Japan), 97; auth, "Ayhud and Falasha: Oral and Written Traditions Concerning the Reign of King Yeshaq in Fifteenth-Century Ethiopia," Between Africa and Zion: Proceedings of the First International Congress of the Society for the Study of Ethiopian Jewry, Ben Zvi Inst, 95; auth, "Ethnic History in the Northwest: Who Were the Zallan?" New Trends in Ethiopian Studies: Papers of the 12th International Conference of Ethiopian Studies, Michigan State University, September 5-10, 1994, Red Sea Press (Lawrenceville, NJ), 94. **CONTACT ADDRESS** Dept Hist, Fisk Univ, 1000 17th Ave N, Nashville, TN 37208-3045. **EMAIL** jquirin@dubois.fisk.edu

QUIST, JOHN W.
PERSONAL Born 04/08/1960, Santa Monica, CA, m, 1982, 2 children **DISCIPLINE** HISTORY **EDUCATION** Univ Michigan, AM, 86; PhD, 92. **CAREER** Teach fel, Univ Michigan, 85-91; lect, E Michigan Univ, 92-95; asst prof, D'Youville Coll, 95-97; asst prof, Shippensburg Univ, 97-. **HONORS AND AWARDS** Ralph D Gray Article Prize, 95. **MEMBERSHIPS** SHEAR; SHA; OAH; AHA. **RESEARCH** Antebellum, United States, 1815-1877. **SELECTED PUBLICATIONS** Auth, "John E Page: An Apostle of Uncertainty," J Mormon Hist 12 (85): 53-68; auth, "Polygamy among James Strang and His Followers," The John Whitmer Hist Asn J 9 (89): 31-48; auth, "Slaveholding Operatives of the Benevolent Empire: Bible, Tract, and Sunday School Societies in Antebellum Tuscaloosa County, Alabama," J Southern Hist 62 (96): 481-526; auth, "The Great Majority of our Subscribers are Farmers': The Michigan Abolitionist Constituency of the 1840s," J Early Rep 14 (94): 325-358; auth, Restless Visionaries: The Social Roots of Antebellum Reform in Alabama and Michigan, LA State Univ Press (Baton Rouge, LA), 98. **CONTACT ADDRESS** Dept Hist, Shippensburg Univ of Pennsylvania, 1871 Old Main Dr, Shippensburg, PA 17257-2200. **EMAIL** jwquis@ship.edu

QUITT, MARTIN HERBERT
PERSONAL Born 11/22/1940, Boston, MA, m, 1971 **DISCIPLINE** AMERICAN COLONIAL HISTORY **EDUCATION** Brandeis Univ, BA, 62; Washington Univ, MA, 66, PhD, 70. **CAREER** Instr hist, Tex A&M Univ, 67-68; from instr to asst prof, 68-75, assoc prof, 74-80, Prof Hist, Boston State Col, 80-, Co-Dir, Ctr Family Studies, 74-, prof, Univ Mass Boston; Co-ed, Psychohistory, Bull Int Psychohist Asn, 76- **MEMBERSHIPS** Orgn Am Historians; Southern Hist Asn; Int Psychohist Asn; Assoc of Inst Early Am Hist & Cult. **RESEARCH** Psychohistory; institutional and demographic history of colonial Virginia; the family in the early modern era. **SELECTED PUBLICATIONS** Auth, Jackson, Indians And Psychohistory, Hist Of Childhood Quart, 76; Contemporary Crisis Of American Family, J Psychohistory, 76; Schism And Narcissism At Stockton, Psychohistory, 77; Adapting To A New-World - English Society In The 17th-Century Chesapeake, William And Mary Quarterly, Vol 52, 95; The Pleasure Gardens Of Virginia--From Jamestown To Jefferson, Va Magazine Of Hist And Biography, Vol 101, 93; Trade And Acculturation At Jamestown, 1607-1609--The Limits Of Understanding, William And Mary Quart, Vol 52, 95. **CONTACT ADDRESS** Dept of Hist, Univ of Massachusetts, Boston, 100 Morrissey Blvd., Boston, MA 02125-3393.

QUIVIK, FREDRIC L.
PERSONAL Born 08/10/1949, Northfield, MN, m, 1971 **DISCIPLINE** HISTORY, SOCIOLOGY OF SCIENCE **EDUCATION** Univ Pa, PhD, 98 **CAREER** Archit hist, 82-90; Consulting Hist Tech, 94-. **MEMBERSHIPS** Soc Ind Archeol; Soc Hist Tech; Soc Archit Historians. **RESEARCH** Hist tech; Am West, 19th, 20th cent especially hist of metallurgical engg. **SELECTED PUBLICATIONS** Auth, The Industrial Landscape of Butte and Anaconda, in Images of an American Land, Univ NM, 97. **CONTACT ADDRESS** 2830 Pearl Harbor, Alameda, CA 94501. **EMAIL** fquivik@lmi.net

R

RAACK, RICHARD C.
PERSONAL Born 07/10/1928, Los Angeles, CA, 1 child **DISCIPLINE** MODERN EUROPEAN HISTORY **EDUCATION** Univ Calif, Los Angeles, BA, 50, MA, 53; Harvard Univ, PhD, 57. **CAREER** Instr hist, RI Sch Design, 56-57; instr, Mass Inst Technol, 57-59; asst prof, Long Beach State Col, 61-65; from asst prof to assoc prof, 65-70, Prof Hist, Calif State Univ, Hayward, 70- **MEMBERSHIPS** AHA; Am Asn Advan Slavic Studies. **RESEARCH** History of East Central Europe; historiography; film as history. **SELECTED PUBLICATIONS** **CONTACT ADDRESS** Dept of Hist, California State Univ, Hayward, Hayward, CA 94542.

RAAT, WILLIAM D.
PERSONAL Born 07/01/1939, Ogden, UT, m, 1984, 2 children **DISCIPLINE** WORLD, LATIN AMERICAN & MEXICAN HISTORY **EDUCATION** Univ Utah, BS, 61, PhD, 67. **CAREER** Teaching assoc hist, Univ Utah, 65-66; from asst prof to assoc prof, Moorhead State Col, 66-70; assoc prof, 70-77, chmn dept, 73-74, prof hist State Univ NY Col Fredonia, 77-, Grant-in-aid, State Univ NY, 73, 75 & 79; Am Coun Learned Soc fel, 76-77; vis prof, Univ of Utah, 84-85. **HONORS AND AWARDS** James A Robertson Awd, Conf Latin Am Hist, 68; Edwin Lieuwen Mem Prize, RMCLAS for Excellence in Teaching, 88. **MEMBERSHIPS** AHA; Conf Latin Am Hist; Latin Am Studies Asn. **RESEARCH** World history; Mexican intellectual and social history; inter-American relations; American Southwest and Mexico's northern frontier. **SELECTED PUBLICATIONS** Auth, Leopoldo Zea and Mexican positivism, in Hisp Am Hist Rev, 2/68; Ideas & History in Mexico, Univ Tex & Nat Univ Mex, 71; Ideas & Society in Don Porfirio's Mexico, in Americas, 7/73; El positivismo durante el Porfiriato, Sep Setentas, 75; The Diplomacy of Suppression: Revoltosos, in Hisp Am Hist Rev, 11/76; Revoltosos, Mexico's Rebels in the US, 1903-1923, Tex A&M Univ Press, 81; Mexico: From Independence to Revolution, 1810-1910, Nebr, 82; The Mexican Revolution: Historiography and Bibliography, G K Hall, 82; Mexico and the United States: Ambivalent Vistas, Univ Ga, 92, 96; Mexico's Sierra Tarahumari: A Photo-History of the People of the Edge, Univ Okla, 96. **CONTACT ADDRESS** Dept of Hist, SUNY, Col at Fredonia, Suny at Fredonia, Fredonia, NY 14063-1143. **EMAIL** raat@fredonia.edu

RABB, THEODORE K.
PERSONAL m, 3 children **DISCIPLINE** HISTORY **EDUCATION** Que Coll, BA, 58; MA, 62; Princeton Univ, MA, 60; PhD, 61. **CAREER** Instr, Fordham Univ, 61-62; instr, Northwestern Univ, 62-63; asst prof, Harvard Univ, 63-67; vis assoc prof, John Hopkins Univ, 69; vis assoc prof, SUNY, 72-73; assoc prof, Princeton Univ, 67-76; prof, 76-; vis prof, European Univ Inst, 94. **HONORS AND AWARDS** Floger Awd; SSRC Awd; Guggenheim Fel; NEH Fel; ACLS Fel; APS Fel. **SELECTED PUBLICATIONS** Auth, "Artists on War: Andrea del Verrocchio[: Colleoni]," Mil Hist Ouart 1 (98): 72-75; "Artists on War: Titian: Allegory of the Battle of Lepanto," Mil Hist Ouart 2 (98): 84-87; auth, Jacobean Gentleman: Sir Edwin Sandys 1561-1629, Princeton Univ Press (Princeton), 98; auth, "The Uses of Film in the Teaching of History: Results of a National Workshop, "Perspectives on Audiovisuals in the Teaching of History, Am Hist Asn (99): 7-10; auth, "If Only It Had Not Been Such A Wet Summer: The Critical Decade of the 1520s, "in What If?,¤ ed. Robert Cowley (NY: Putnam, 99); auth, "Artists on War: The Sculptures of Nineveh, "Mil Hist Ouart 3 (99): 28-31; auth, "Artists on War: John Singer Sargent Visits the Front, "Mil Hist Ouart 4 (99): 56-59; auth, "Artists on War: Pieter Bruegel, The Massacre of the Innocents, "Mil Hist Ouart 1 (99): 98-101; auth, "Artists on War: The Painter of the Heiji Monogatari Emaki, "Mil Hist Ouart 2 (00): 50-53; auth, "History Amidst the Hype: Taking Advantage of the Millennium," History Matters 4 (99): 1-7. **CONTACT ADDRESS** Dept History, Princeton Univ, 130 Dickinson Hall, Princeton, NJ 08544-0001.

RABBAT, NASSER O.
PERSONAL Born 05/21/1956, Damascus, Syria, m **DISCIPLINE** HISTORY OF ARCHITECTURE **EDUCATION** MIT, PhD 91; UCLA, M Arch 84; Univ Damascus Syria, BArch 79. **CAREER** MIT, asst prof, 91-95; assoc prof, 91 to 95-; Aga Khan Prof, 99-. **HONORS AND AWARDS** Getty Postdoc Fel; Malcolm H. Kerr Diss Awd; Am Res Ctr in Egypt (ARCE) Fellowship; Getty Postdoc Fel; Malcolm H. Kerr Diss Awd. **MEMBERSHIPS** AHA; SAH; CAA; MESA; ARCE; HIA. **RESEARCH** History of medieval Islamic architecture; Ancient and medieval urban history; 19th century Orientalism. **SELECTED PUBLICATIONS** Auth, The Citadel of Cairo: A New Interpretation of Royal Mamluk Architecture, Leiden NY, EJ Brill, 95; auth, Architects and Artists in Mamluk Society: The Perspective of the Sources, Jour of Archi Edu, 98; auth, The Formation of Neo-Mamluk Style in Modern Egypt, The Education of the Architect: Historiography Urbanism and the Growth of Arch Knowledge, ed Martha Pollack, Cambridge MA, MIT Press, 97; auth, My Life With Salah-al-Din: The Memoirs of Imad al-Din al-Katib al-Isfahani, Edebiyat. 96; auth, Al-Azhar Mosque: An Architectural Chronicle of Cairo's History, Muqarnas, 96; auth, The Art and Architecture of Islam 1250-1800, Sheila S. Blair, Jonathan M. Bloom, rev, Design Bk Rev, 96; auth, A Guide to the Late Antique World, eds GW Bowersock, P. Brown, O. Graber, Harvard Univ Press, 97; auth, "The Interplay of History and Archaeology in Beirut," in Projecting Beirut: Episodes in the Construction and Reconstruction of the Modern City," Munich; London; New York: Prestel, 98, 19-22; auth, "The Mosaics of the Qubba al-Zahiriyya in Damascus: A Classical Syrian Medium Acquires a Mamluk Signature," Aram 9-10, 99, 1-13; auth, Encycl of the Qur'an, Leiden Nthlnds, EJ Brill Pub, 98 cont, article The City; auth, Representing the Mamluks in Mamluk Historical Writing," in The Historiography of Islamic Egypt, c. 950-1800, Hugh Kennedy," Leiden, E. J. Brill, 00, 59-75; auth, "The Changing Concept of Mamluk in the Mamluk Sultanate in Egypt and Syriaz," in Slave Elites in The Middle East and Africa: A Comparative Study, London and New York: Kegan Paul International, 00, 81-98; **CONTACT ADDRESS** Dept of Architecture, Massachusetts Inst of Tech, 77 Massachusetts Ave., Rm 10-303, Cambridge, MA 02139. **EMAIL** nasser@mit.edu

RABE, STEPHEN
PERSONAL Born 05/16/1948, Hartford, CT, m, 1 child **DISCIPLINE** HISTORY **EDUCATION** Univ Conn, PhD, 77. **CAREER** Prof. **RESEARCH** American foreign relations; American slavery. **SELECTED PUBLICATIONS** Auth, The Road to OPEC: United States Relations with Venezuela 1919-1976, Univ Tex, 82; Eisenhower and Latin America: The Foreign Policy of Anticommunism, Univ NC, 88; coauth, Imperial Surge: The United States Abroad, The 1890-Early 1900's, D.C. Heath, 92; Slavery in American Society, D.C. Heath, 93; auth, The Most Dangerous Area n the World: John F. Kennedy Confronts Communist Revolution in Latin America, Univ of NC Press, 99. **CONTACT ADDRESS** Dept of History, Univ of Texas, Dallas, Richardson, TX 75083-0688. **EMAIL** rabe@utdallas.edu

RABINOWITCH, ALEXANDER
PERSONAL Born 08/30/1934, London, England, m, 1962, 2 children **DISCIPLINE** EUROPEAN & MODERN RUSSIAN HISTORY **EDUCATION** Knox Col, BA, 56; Univ Chicago, MA, 61; Ind Univ, PhD(hist), 65. **CAREER** US-USSR exchange res scholar hist, Moscow State Univ, 63-64; asst prof, Univ Southern Calif, 65-67; from asst prof to assoc prof, 67-75, dir grad studies hist, 71-73, Prof Hist & Dir Russ & E Europ Inst, Ind Univ, Bloomington, 75-, Univ Southern Calif res grant, 65-66; Nat Endowment for Humanities fel, 67-68; Am Coun Learned Soc fel & US-USSR exchange sr scholar, Moscow State Univ, 70-71; mem, Inst Advan Study, Princeton Univ, 73-74; mem coun, Int Exchange of Scholars Adv Comt for EEurope & USSR, 77-; mem, Nat Coun Soviet & EEurop Res, 78. **MEMBERSHIPS** AHA; Midwest Slavic Conf; Am Asn Advan Slavic Studies. **RESEARCH** Nineteenth century Russian history; The Russian Revolution; Soviet history. **SELECTED PUBLICATIONS** Auth, Prelude To Revolution: The Petrograd Bolsheviks And The July 1917 Uprising, 68, Co-Ed, Revolution And Politics In Russia: Essays In Memory Of B I Nicolaevsky, 72 & Auth, The Petrograd Garrison And The Bolshevik Seizure Of Power, In: Revolution And Politics In Russia: Essays In Memory Of B I Nicolaevsky, 72, Ind Univ; Auth, The Bolsheviks Come To Power: The Revolution Of 1917 In Petrograd, Norton, 76; I Bolscevichi Al Potere: La Rivoluzione Del 1917 A Pietrogrado, Feltrinelli, 78.; Revolutionary Terrorist In Late Czarist Russia, Leader Of The Radical Agrarian Left-Socialist-Revolutionaries Party After The October 1917 Revolution, Russian Review, Vol 54, 95. **CONTACT ADDRESS** Dept of Hist, Indiana Univ, Bloomington, Bloomington, IN 47401.

RABINOWITZ, HOWARD
DISCIPLINE U.S. URBAN HISTORY, SOUTHERN HISTORY **EDUCATION** Univ Chicago, PhD, 73. **CAREER** Prof, Univ NMex. **HONORS AND AWARDS** Fel, Ctr for Adv Stud in Behav Sci, Stanford Univ; grant and fel, NEH. **RESEARCH** American urban history; Southern history. **SELECTED PUBLICATIONS** Auth, Race Relations in the Urban South, 1865-1890, 78, 80, 96; Southern Black Leaders of the Reconstruction Era, 82; The First New South, 1865-1920, 92; Race, Ethnicity, and Urbanization, 94. **CONTACT ADDRESS** Univ of New Mexico, Albuquerque, Albuquerque, NM 87131.

RABINOWITZ, PAULA
PERSONAL Born 12/25/1951, Brooklyn, NY, m, 1978, 2 children **DISCIPLINE** AMERICAN CULTURAL STUDIES **EDUCATION** Brandeis Univ, BA, 74; Univ Mich, MA, 80; PhD, 86. **CAREER** Lectr, Univ of Mich, 85-87; asst prof to prof, Univ of Minn, 87-. **HONORS AND AWARDS** Avery and Julie Hopwood Awd, 83; Ralph Henry Gabriel Diss Prize, 87; CLA/McMillan Grant, 88; Mellon Fel, 90-91; Bush Fac Fel, 93-94; Fulbright Scholar, 97; Rockefeller Residency, Italy, 00. **MEMBERSHIPS** ASA, AAUP. **RESEARCH** 20th century American cultural studies, feminism, proletarian culture, the 1930's. **SELECTED PUBLICATIONS** Coed, Writing Red: An Anthology of American Women Writers, 1930-1940, Feminist Pr, (NY), 87; auth, Labor and Desire: women's Revolutionary Fiction in Depression America, Univ of NC Pr, (Chapel Hill), 91; auth, They Must Be Represented: The Politics of Documentary, Verso, (London), 94; auth, "Margaret Bourke-White's Red Coat, or Slumming in the Thirties", Radical Revisions: Rethinking 1930s Culture, eds Sherry Linken and Bill Mullens, Univ of IL Pr, (96): 187-207; auth, "Sentimental Contracts: Dreams and Documents of American Labor", Media Int Australia 82, (96): 56-65; auth, "City Noir: Wri9gh)ting the Dark Streets of Post-War US", Citta: Reali e Immaginairie del Continente Americano, eds Cristina Giorcelli, Camilla Catarulla, Anna Scacchi, Edizione Associate Editrice Int, (98): 307-324; auth, "Pulp Theory: On Literary History", Poetics/Politics: Radical Aesthetics for the Classroom, ed Amitava Kumar, St Martin's (NY, 99): 83-100; auth, "Not Just the Facts, Ma'am: Social Workers, Detectives and Child Prostitutes in Caroline Slade's Novels", Legacy 16, (99): 106-119; auth, "Great Lady Painters, Inc: Feminism, Modernism, Nationalism and Painting", Modernism, Inc, eds Jani Scandura and Michael Thurston, NY Univ Pr, (forthcoming). **CONTACT ADDRESS** Dept English, Univ of Minnesota, Twin Cities, 207 Church St SE, 207 Lind Hall, Minneapolis, MN 55455-0134. **EMAIL** rabin001@tc.umn.edu

RABLE, GEORGE CALVIN
PERSONAL Born 06/08/1950, Lima, OH, m, 1972, 1 child **DISCIPLINE** AMERICAN HISTORY **EDUCATION** Bluffton Col, BA, 72; La State Univ, MA, 73, PhD(hist), 78. **CAREER** Asst prof hist, La State Univ, Alexandria, 79; Asst Prof Hist & Dir Am Studies, Anderson Col, 79-, Mem Nat Endowment for the Humanities summer sem, 82. **MEMBERSHIPS** Orgn Am Historians; Southern Hist Asn. **RESEARCH** Nineteenth century United States history; Civil War and Reconstruction; women's history. **SELECTED PUBLICATIONS** Auth, Anatomy of a unionist: Andrew Johnson in the secession crisis, Tenn Hist Quart, winter 73; Slavery, politics and the South: The gag rule as a case study, Capitol Studies, fall 75; Memphis: The first modern race riot, Geosci & Man, Vol XIX, 123-127; Forces of darkness, forces of light: The impeachment of Andrew Johnson and the paranoid style, Southern Studies, summer 78; Southern interests and the election of 1876: A re-appraisal,

Civil War Hist, 12/80; Patriotism, platitudes and politics: Baseball and the American Presidency, Am Heritage (in prep); Republican Albatross: The Louisiana question, national politics and the failure of reconstruction, La Hist (in prep). **CONTACT ADDRESS** Dept. of History, Univ of Alabama, Tuscaloosa, PO Box 870212, Tuscaloosa, AL 35487-0212.

RABSON, STEVE

PERSONAL Born 05/07/1943, Detroit, MI **DISCIPLINE** EAST ASIAN STUDIES **EDUCATION** Harvard Univ, PhD, 79. **CAREER** Brown Univ, 79-. **HONORS AND AWARDS** Fulbright Fel; Japan Found Fel. **MEMBERSHIPS** Asn Asian Studies. **RESEARCH** 20th Century Japanese Literature. **SELECTED PUBLICATIONS** Auth, Okinawa: Two Postwar Novellas, Inst East Asian Stud (Univ Cal, Berkeley), 89; auth, Righteous Cause or Tragic Folly: Changing Views of War in Modern Japanese Poetry, Cen Japanese Stud (Univ Mich), 98; co-ed, Southern Exposure: Modern Japanese Literature from Okinawa, Univ Hawaii Press, 00. **CONTACT ADDRESS** Dept East Asian Studies, Brown Univ, 341 Brook St, Providence, RI 02912.

RACHLEFF, PETER J.

PERSONAL Born 03/09/1951, New London, CT, m, 1997 **DISCIPLINE** HISTORY **EDUCATION** Univ Pitts, PhD 81, MA 76; Amherst Coll, BA 73. **CAREER** Macalester Col, prof hist 95-, assoc prof 87-95, asst prof 82-87. **HONORS AND AWARDS** Phi Beta Kappa **MEMBERSHIPS** OAH; Nat Writers Union; Workers Ed Loc 189. **RESEARCH** US labor, race immigration **SELECTED PUBLICATIONS** The Failure of Minnesota Farmer-Laborism, in: Kevin Boyle, ed, Organized Labor and Amer Politics, Albany State, Univ NY Press, forthcoming; The Dynamics of Americanization: The Croatian Fraternal Union in the 30's, in: Eric Arnesen, Julie Greene, Bruce Laurie, eds, Labor Histories: Class Politics and the Working Class Experience, Urbana IL, Univ IL Press, 98; Unbroken Mirror: One Hundred Years of the St Paul Union Advocate, with Barb Kucera, Labor's Heritage, 98; Organizing Wall to Wall: The Independent Union of All Workers 1933-37,in: Shelton Stromquist and Marvin Bergman, eds, Unionizing the Jungles: Labor and Community in the Twentieth Century Meatpacking Industry, IA City, Univ of IA Press, 97; numerous other pub. **CONTACT ADDRESS** Dept of Hist, Macalester Col, 1600 Grand Ave, Saint Paul, MN 55105. **EMAIL** rachleff@macalester.edu

RACINE, PHILIP N.

PERSONAL Born 12/25/1941, Brunswick, ME, m, 1968, 2 children **DISCIPLINE** AMERICAN HISTORY **EDUCATION** Bowdoin Col, AB, 64; MA, 65; Emory Univ, PhD, 69. **CAREER** Prof, Wofford Col, 69-. **HONORS AND AWARDS** Founders Awd, Mus of the Confederacy, 86; Phi Beta Kappa, 91. **MEMBERSHIPS** Am Hist Asn; Southern Hist Asn; Org of Am Historians. **RESEARCH** History of the American South; American Civil War. **SELECTED PUBLICATIONS** Auth, The Fiery Trail: A Union Officer's Account of Sherman's Last Campaigns, Univ Tenn Pr, 86; auth, Piedmont Farmer: The Journals of David Golightly Harris, 1855-1870, Univ Tenn Pr, 90; auth, 'Unspoiled Heart': The Journal of Charles Mattocks of the 17th Maine, Univ Tenn Pr, 94; auth, Seeing Spartanburg: A History in Images, Hub City Writers Proj, 99. **CONTACT ADDRESS** Wofford Col, 429 N. Church St., Spartanburg, SC 29303-3363. **EMAIL** racinepn@wofford.edu

RADAN, GEORGE T.

PERSONAL Born 12/31/1923, Budapest, Hungary, m, 1958, 2 children **DISCIPLINE** ARCHAEOLOGY; ART HISTORY **EDUCATION** Ecole du Louvre, Paris, AEM, 67; Univ Budapest, Hungary, MA PhD, 78-79. **CAREER** Haifa Maritime Museum, Haifa, Israel, assoc dir, 54-59; Institute of Mediterranean Archaeol, assoc pres, 70-79; Villanova Univ, prof, dept art, hist, 60-. **HONORS AND AWARDS** Fr Nat Schol; Post-Doctoral, Univ Penna; IREX ACLS; ACLS; Israel Nat Maritime Res. **MEMBERSHIPS** Renaissance Scholars; Ancient Historians **RESEARCH** Medieval Archaeology **SELECTED PUBLICATIONS** Augustine In Iconography: History and Legend, with others, Lang, 98; Archaeological Excavations at San Leonardo al Lag and Santa Lucia di Rosia, Analecta Augustiniana, LX, 97; Lecceto e gli eremi Agostiniani in terra di Siena, w/o, Milano, 93; and more. **CONTACT ADDRESS** Dept History, Villanova Univ, Villanova, PA 19085-1699. **EMAIL** tapiki@aol.com

RADDING, CYNTHIA

DISCIPLINE HISTORY **EDUCATION** Smith Col, BA, 68; Univ Calif San Diego, MA, 70; PhD, 90. **CAREER** Res Hist, 73-90; asst prof, Univ of Missouri-St. Louis, 90-95; asst prof of hist, Univ of Illinois, 95-. **HONORS AND AWARDS** Tinker Foundation Res Grant, 88; Fulbright-Hays Doctoral Dissertation Fel, 88-89; Assoc and member of Academic Board of International Center for Tropical Ecology, 93; Fel and Res Assoc, Center for International Studies, 90-93; Improved Res Quality Grant, 92-93; NEH Travel Grant, 92; Am Philosophical Soc Res Grant, 92; Am Council of Learned Societies Fel, 92-93; Fac Res Leave, 93-94; UIUC Res Board Grant for travel and res asst, 95-97. **RESEARCH** Hist of Latin Am, hist of Mexico, ethnohistory, peasant studies, comparative frontiers, ethnohistory of Northwest Mexico, environmental hist, ecology and cultural persistence in northwest Mexico and Eastern Bolivia. **SELECTED PUBLICATIONS** Ed, Sonora Moderno: 1880-1929, Vol IV, in Historia General de Sonora, Mexico, Gobierno del Estado de Sonoro, 85; coauth, Sonora, Una historia compartida, with Juan Jose Gracida romo, Mexico, Instituto Mora, 89; auth, Entre el desierto y la sierra, Las naciones o'odham y teguima de Sonora, 1530-1840, Mexico, CIESAS, INI, 95; auth, Wandering Peoples: Colonialism, Ethnic Spaces, and Ecological Frontiers in Northwestern Mexico, 1700-1850; Durham and London, Duke Univ Press, 97; auth, "Comentario," in Carmen Castaneda, ed, Elite, clases sociales y rebelion en Guadalajara y Jalisco, siglos XCIII y XIX, Guadalajara, El Colegio de Jalisco, (88); auth, "Ciclos demograficos, trabajo y comunidad en los pueblos serranos de la Provincia de Sonora, siglo XVIII," Historia e Populacao, Estudos sobre a America Latina, Sao Paullo, Asociacao Brasileiro de Estudos Populacionais (ABEP), International Union for the Scientific Study of Population (IUSSP), (90): 265-275; auth, "pueblos errantes: formacion y reproduccion de la familia en la sierra de Sonora durante el siglo XVIII," in Familias novohispanas, siglos XVI al XIX, Pilar Gonzalbo Aizpuru, coord, Mexico, El Colegio de Mexico, (91): 243-272; auth, "Los o'odham, los espanoles y los mexicanos en la frontera desertica de Sonora, 1768-1843," en La cuidad y el campo en la historia de Mexico, Memoria de la VII Reunion de Historiadores Mexicanos y Norteamericanos, Mexico, Universidad Nacional Autonoma de Mexico, 92; auth, "Sonora," Encyclopedia of Latin American History and Culture, Tenenbaum, General Ed, New York, Scribner's, (96): 147-8; auth, "Pimeria Alta," Encyclopedia of Latin American History and Culture, IV, Tenenbaum, General Ed, New York, Scribner's, (96): 404-5. **CONTACT ADDRESS** History Dept, Univ of Illinois, Urbana-Champaign, 421 gregory hall, mc 466, 810 s wright, Urbana, IL 61801. **EMAIL** radding@staff.uiuc.edu

RADER, BENJAMIN G.

PERSONAL Born 08/25/1935, Delaware, MO, m, 1961, 2 children **DISCIPLINE** AMERICAN HISTORY **EDUCATION** Southwest MO State Col, BA, 58; Okla State Univ, MA, 59; Univ MD, PhD, 64. **CAREER** Instr Hist, Okla State Univ, 61-62; instr to asst prof, Univ Mont, 62-67; assoc prof, 67-72, prof History, Univ Nebr, Lincoln, 72-, Nat Humanities Found jr fel, 69; James L Sellers prof, 97. **MEMBERSHIPS** Orgn Am Historians; AHA. **RESEARCH** American intellectual history; history of economic ideas; history of American sport. **SELECTED PUBLICATIONS** Auth, Academic Mind and Reform: The Influence of Richard T Ely in American Life, Univ KY, 66; Richard T Ely: Lay spokesman for the social gospel, J Am Hist, 4/66; Montana lumber strike of 1917, Pac Hist Rev, 5/67; Federal taxation in the 1920's, Historian, 5/71; Quest for subcommunities and the rise of American Sport, Am Quart, Fall 77; American Sports: From the Age of Folk Games to the Age of the Spectator, Prentice-Hall, 82, 00; Baseball: A History of America's Game, Univ Illinois, 95; auth, Am Ways: A Brief Hist of Am Cultures, Harcourt, forthcoming 01. **CONTACT ADDRESS** Dept of History, Univ of Nebraska, Lincoln, PO Box 880327, Lincoln, NE 68588-0327. **EMAIL** brader@unlserve.unl.edu

RADER, ROSEMARY

PERSONAL Born St Leo, MN, s **DISCIPLINE** HISTORY OF CHRISTIANITY **EDUCATION** Col St Catherine, BA; Univ Minn, MA; Stanford Univ, PhD. **CAREER** Religion, Carleton Univ. **HONORS AND AWARDS** Fulbright Schlr, Italy, 66-67; Whiting Fel, Italy, 76-77; Res Grant, Oxford, England, 92-94. **MEMBERSHIPS** AAR. **SELECTED PUBLICATIONS** Auth, Breaking Boundaries: Male/Female Friendship in Early Christian Communities; Coauth, Women Writers of the Early Church. **CONTACT ADDRESS** Carleton Col, 100 S College St., Northfield, MN 55057-4016. **EMAIL** rrader@carleton.edu

RADICE, MARK A.

PERSONAL Born 07/17/1951, Passail, NJ, m, 4 children **DISCIPLINE** MUSIC HISTORY; COMPOSER **EDUCATION** Boston Univ, BM; Univ Cincinnati, MM; Eastman Sch Music, PhD. **CAREER** Assoc prof. **SELECTED PUBLICATIONS** Auth, "History of Opera Staging, Music Research Techniques," Original Compositions, editions of music. **CONTACT ADDRESS** Dept of Music History, Theory and Composition, Ithaca Col, Center for Music/ 953 Dansy Rd., Ithaca, NY 14850. **EMAIL** mradice@ithaca.edu

RADISICH, PAULA

DISCIPLINE ART AND ART HISTORY **EDUCATION** Univ Calif, Santa Barbara, 65-67; Univ Calif, Los Angeles, BA, 69; MA, 72; PhD, 77. **CAREER** Tchg asst, Univ Calif, 70-72; pt time instr, La Fashion Inst, 73; Calif Univ, 78; instr, UCLA, 78; Claremont Grad Sch, 79, 80, 81; LA County Mus, 80, 81; adj asst prof, 78-82; asst prof, 82; assoc prof, 87; prof, 95-. **HONORS AND AWARDS** Borchard grant, 96; Irvine grant award, 93; grants, 86, 90, 95 NEH; fac res grant, 86, Whittier col; four-yr Chancellor's tchg fel, 69; ed, eighteenth-century stud, 89-92; 93-94; co-winner, asecs tchg competition award, 90. **RESEARCH** Women and the visual arts; visual arts of the eighteenth century, age of impressionism, age of DADA and Surrealism. **SELECTED PUBLICATIONS** Co-auth, Deconstructing Dissipation, Eighteenth-Century Stud, 95-96; auth, La Chose Publique: Hubert Robert's Decorations for the petit salon at Mereville, The Consumption of Culture: Word, Image, and Object in the 17th and 18th Centuries, Routledge, 95; Evolution and Salvation: The Iconic Origins of Druellet's Monstrious Combatants ofthe Night, Flights of Fancy, Univ of Ga Press, 93. **CONTACT ADDRESS** Dept of Art, Whittier Col, 13406 Philadelphia St, Whittier, CA 90608.

RADYCKI, DIANE

PERSONAL Born 12/04/1946, Chicago, IL, m, 1998 **DISCIPLINE** ART HISTORY **EDUCATION** Univ Ill, BA; Hunter Col/CUNY, MA; Harvard Univ, PhD, 93. **CAREER** Tchng fel, 87, Harvard Univ; dir, 99, Payne Gallery of Moravian Col; vis lectr, 97, Rutgers Univ; asst prof, 92-96, Univ Houston; asst prof, 98-, Moravian Col. **HONORS AND AWARDS** Fulbright Fel, Germany, 89-91; AAUW Fel, 91. **RESEARCH** paula Modersohn-Becker: translated journals. **CONTACT ADDRESS** Art Dept, Moravian Col, 1200 Main, Bethlehem, PA 18018. **EMAIL** medjr01@moravian.edu

RAEBURN, JOHN H.

PERSONAL Born 07/18/1941, IN, m, 1986, 2 children **DISCIPLINE** AMERICAN STUDIES, ENGLISH **EDUCATION** Ind Univ, BA, 63; Univ Pa, MA, 64; PhD, 69. **CAREER** Asst prof, Univ Mich, 67-74; vis lectr, Univ Iowa, 75; assoc prof, Univ Louisville, 75-76; from assoc prof to prof, Univ Iowa, 76-; chemn, Univ Iowa English Dept, 85-91; chemn, Univ Iowa American Studies Dept, 83-85 & 94-00. **MEMBERSHIPS** ASA, OAH. **RESEARCH** Photography as a cultural practice. **SELECTED PUBLICATIONS** Auth, Fame Because of Him: Hemingway as Public Writer, Ind Univ Pr, 84. **CONTACT ADDRESS** Dept Am Studies, The Univ of Iowa, 202 E Jefferson St, Iowa City, IA 52245-2135. **EMAIL** john-raeburn@uiowa.edu

RAEFF, MARC

PERSONAL Born 07/28/1923, Moscow, Russia **DISCIPLINE** HISTORY **EDUCATION** Harvard Univ, PhD, 50. **CAREER** From assoc prof to prof Russ hist, 61-73, Bakhmeteff Prof Russ Studies, Columbia Univ, 73- **MEMBERSHIPS** Modern and intellectual Russian history; eighteenth century European history. **SELECTED PUBLICATIONS CONTACT ADDRESS** Dept of Hist, Columbia Univ, New York, NY 10027.

RAGAN, BRYANT T., JR.

DISCIPLINE FRENCH HISTORY **EDUCATION** Univ, CA-Berkeley, PhD. **CAREER** Asst prof, Fordham Univ. **HONORS AND AWARDS** Grant, Florence Gould found. **MEMBERSHIPS** French Historical Studies; Social Sci Hist Asn. **RESEARCH** Hist of sexuality, gender history. **SELECTED PUBLICATIONS** Co-ed, Re-creating Authority in Revolutionary France, Rutgers UP, 92; Homosexuality in Modern France, Oxford UP, 96; co-ed, Homosexuality in Early Modern France: A Documentary Collection, Oxford, 00. **CONTACT ADDRESS** Dept of Hist, Fordham Univ, 113 W 60th St, New York, NY 10023. **EMAIL** ragan@murray.fordham.edu

RAINGER, RONALD

PERSONAL Born 06/28/1949, Salt Lake City, UT, m, 1983 **DISCIPLINE** HISTORY **EDUCATION** Willamette Univ, BA, 71; Univ Ut, MA, 76; Ind Univ, MA, 77; Ind Univ, PhD, 82. **CAREER** Teacher, Santa Fe Prep Sch, 80-82; Vis Asst Prof, Univ Ariz, 82-83; From Asst Prof to Prof, Tex Tech Univ, 84-. **HONORS AND AWARDS** Nat Sci Found Grants (4); Nat Endowment Humanities Grant; Mellon Postdoctoral Fel; 5 Teaching Awds. **MEMBERSHIPS** Hist of Sci Soc, AHA, Soc for Hist of Technol. **RESEARCH** History of 19th and 20th-Century science. **SELECTED PUBLICATIONS** Auth, The American Development of Biology, 88; auth, The Expansion of American Biology, 91; auth, An Agenda for Antiquity: Henry Fairfield Osborn and the American Museum of Natural History, 91. **CONTACT ADDRESS** Dept Hist, Texas Tech Univ, 1 Texas Tech University, Lubbock, TX 79409-0999. **EMAIL** j3ron@ttacs.ttu.edu

RAJAGOPAL, ARVIND

DISCIPLINE CULTURAL STUDIES, MASS MEDIA, POSTCOLONIAL STUDIES **EDUCATION** Madras, BF, 81; Univ of Ky, MA, 84; Univ of Calif, Berkeley, PhD, 92. **CAREER** Asst prof, Purdue Univ. **HONORS AND AWARDS** Eli Sagan Awd, Univ of Calif, 90; Univ of Calif, Berkeley, Departmental Fel, 90-91; Rockefeller Fel, Univ of Chicago, 93; Amer Inst of Indian Studs Sr Fel, 93-94, 96-97; Macarthur Found Fel for Res and Writing on Peace and Int Coop, 96-97; Sawyer Fel, Int Inst, Univ of Mich, 96-97; NYork Univ challenge Grant, 99-00. **RESEARCH** Political economy of culture, social theory, contemporary South Asia, globalization. **SELECTED PUBLICATIONS** Auth, "Communalism and the Consuming Subject," Econ & Polit Weekly Vol 31, No 6 (96): 341-348; auth, "Mediating Modernity: Theorizing Reception in a Non-Western society," Commun Rev Vol 1, no 4 (96): 441-469; auth, "Hindu Immigrants in the US: Imagining Different Communities?" Bulletin of Concerned Asian Scholars (97): 51-65; auth, "Advertising, Politics and the Sentimental Education of the Indian

Consumer," Visual Anthrop Rev Vol 14, No 2 (98/99): 14-31; auth, "Communities Imagined and Unimagined: Contemporary Indian Variations on the Public Sphere," Discourse: J for the Theoret Study of Media & Cult Vol 21, No 2 (99): 48-84; auth, "Thinking through emerging markets: brand logics and the cultural forms of political society in India," Social Text 60 (Fall 99): 131-149; auth, "Hindu Nationalism in the US: Changing Configurations of Political Practice," Ethnic & Racial Studies Vol 23, No 3 (00), 67-96. **CONTACT ADDRESS** Dept of Cult & Commun, New York Univ, Sch of Education, East Bldg 7th Fl, 239 Greene St, New York, NY 10003. **EMAIL** arvind.rajagopal@nyu.edu

RAKOVE, JACK NORMAN
PERSONAL Born 06/04/1947, Chicago, IL, m, 1969, 1 child **DISCIPLINE** AMERICAN HISTORY **EDUCATION** Haverford Col, AB, 68; Harvard Univ, PhD(hist), 75. **CAREER** Asst prof hist, Colgate Univ, 75-80; Assoc Prof Hist, Stanford Univ, 80-; prof, 90-; coe prof, 96-; prof of pol sci, 99-. **HONORS AND AWARDS** Delancey K Jay Prize, Harvard Univ, 76; Pulitzer Prize Hist, 97. **MEMBERSHIPS** Orgn Am Historians; AHA; APSA; SHEAR; Am Acad Arts and Sciences. **RESEARCH** American Revolution. **SELECTED PUBLICATIONS** Auth, The Beginnings of National Politics: An Interpretive History of the Continental Congress, Knopf, 79; auth, James Madison and the Creation of the American Republic, Addison, Wesley, 90; auth, Original Meanings: Politics and Ideas in the Making of the Constitution, Knopf, 96; auth, Delaring Rights, Bedford, 97; ed, James Madison: Writings, Library of America, 99. **CONTACT ADDRESS** Dept of Hist, Stanford Univ, Stanford, CA 94305-2024. **EMAIL** rakove@stanford.edu

RALPH, JAMES R.
PERSONAL Born 07/04/1960, Akron, OH, s **DISCIPLINE** HISTORY **EDUCATION** Middlebury Col, BA 82; Harvard Univ, MA 84, PhD 90. **CAREER** Middlebury Col, asst prof, assoc prof, 89 to 96-. **HONORS AND AWARDS** Fulbright Fel; Lectr DeMontFort Univ UK. **MEMBERSHIPS** OAH; AHA; VHS; SHA. **RESEARCH** Civil rights movement. **SELECTED PUBLICATIONS** Auth, Northern Protest: Martin Luther King Jr, Chicago, and the Civil Rights Movement, Cambridge MA, Harvard Univ Press, 93. **CONTACT ADDRESS** Dept of History, Middlebury Col, Middlebury, VT 05753. **EMAIL** ralph@middlebury.edu

RAMAGE, JAMES A.
PERSONAL Born 05/06/1940, Paducah, KY, m, 1964, 1 child **DISCIPLINE** HISTORY **EDUCATION** Murray State Univ, BS, 65, MA, 68; Univ Ky, PhD, 72. **CAREER** High sch hist teacher, Mehlville High Sch, St Louis County, Mo, 65-67; asst to the Pres, Northern Ky Univ, 72-76, full-time col teacher, 76-, Regents Prof of Hist, 94-. **HONORS AND AWARDS** Kentucky Governor's Volunteer Activist Award, 78; Outstanding Prof of the Year, 88; Douglas Southall Freeman Award, 86; Kentucky Governor's Award for Rebel Raider, 86; Regents Prof, 94; Alumni Asn Strongest Influence Award, 95. **MEMBERSHIPS** Southern Hist Asn; KY Hist Soc. **RESEARCH** U.S. Civil War; Gen John Hunt Morgan; Col John S. Mosby. **SELECTED PUBLICATIONS** Auth, John Wesley Hunt: Pioneer Merchant, Manufacturer and Financier, 74; auth, Rebel Raider: The Life of General John Hunt Morgan, 86; auth, "Introduction," in A History of Morgan's Cavalry by Basil W. Duke, 97; auth, "Introduction," in Kentucky Cavaliers in Dixie by George D. Mosgrove, 99. **CONTACT ADDRESS** Dept Hist & Geog, No Kentucky Univ, 1 Northern Ky Univ, Newport, KY 41099. **EMAIL** Ramage@nku.edu

RAMAGE, NANCY HIRSCHLAND
PERSONAL Born 03/29/1942, New York, NY, m, 1969, 2 children **DISCIPLINE** HISTORY OF ART, CLASSICAL ARCHAEOLOGY **EDUCATION** Wheaton Col, Mass, BA, 63; Harvard Univ, MA, 65, PhD, 69. **CAREER** Asst prof Greek & archaeol, Boston Univ, 70-71; asst prof art hist, State Univ NY Binghamton, 77; asst prof art hist, Cornell Univ, 78-; draftsman ancient pottery, Brit Sch at Rome, 66-68; res asst ancient sculpture, Harvard Univ/Cornell Univ Sardis Expedition, 66-71; prof art hist, Ithaca Col, 72-. **HONORS AND AWARDS** Phi Beta Kappa; NEH summer grant; NEH summer seminars; Charles A Dan Prof of the Humanities and Arts; Excellence in Teaching Awd; Getty Res Grant; Distinguish Prof, SUNY Potsdam, 01. **MEMBERSHIPS** Archaeol Inst Am; Col Art Asn; Int Asn Class Archaeol. **RESEARCH** Greek and Roman sculpture; Greek pottery; Etruscan pottery; 18th century Neoclassicism and the history of collecting. **SELECTED PUBLICATIONS** Auth, A Merrythought Cup from Sardis, American Journal of Archaeology, 83; auth, Two New Attic Cups and the Siege of Sardis, American Journal of Archawology, 86; auth, The Initial Letters in Sir William Hamilton's Collection of Antiquities, The Burlington Magazine, 87; auth, Sir William Hamilton as a Collector, Exporter and Dealer, American Journal of Archaeology, 90; auth, Goods, Graves, and Scholars: 18th Century Archaeologists in Britain and Italy, American Journal of Archaeology, 92; coauth, Bucking the Tide: The Cone Sisters of Baltimore, Journal of the History of Collections, 96; coauth, Corinthian, Attic, and Laconian Pottery from Sardis, 97; auth, The Pacetti Papers and Restoration of Ancient Sculpture in the 18th Century, in Von der Schoenheit Weissen Marmors, 99; coauth, Roman Art: Romulus to Constantine, 3rd ed, 00; auth, Restorer and Collector: Notes on 18th Century Recreations of Roman Statues, in the Ancient Art of Emulation, 01. **CONTACT ADDRESS** Dept of Art History, Ithaca Col, 953 Danby Rd, Ithaca, NY 14850. **EMAIL** ramage@ithaca.edu

RAMOS, DONALD
PERSONAL Born 07/12/1942, New Bedford, MA, m, 1964, 1 child **DISCIPLINE** LATIN AMERICAN HISTORY **EDUCATION** Univ Mass, BA, 64; Univ Fla, PhD(hist), 72. **CAREER** From instr to asst prof, 71-76, Assoc Prof Hist, Cleveland State Univ, 76-, Dir, First Col, 78- **MEMBERSHIPS** Latin Am Studies Asn. **RESEARCH** Demographic history; social history, particularly family history; race relations. **SELECTED PUBLICATIONS** **CONTACT ADDRESS** Dept of Hist, Cleveland State Univ, 1983 E 24th St, Cleveland, OH 44115-2440.

RAMSBOTTOM, MARY MACMANUS
DISCIPLINE HISTORY **EDUCATION** Mt Holyoke, BA, 75; Yale Univ, MA, 76; MPhil, 78; PhD, 87. **CAREER** ASSOF PROF, HIST, TRUMAN STATE UNIV **MEMBERSHIPS** Am Antiquarian Soc **RESEARCH** Rel Experience, 17th Century New Eng. **SELECTED PUBLICATIONS** Auth, "Religious Society and the Family in Charlestown, Massachusetts, 1630-1740." **CONTACT ADDRESS** 2314 York St, Kirksville, MO 63501. **EMAIL** mmacrams@truman.edu

RAMSEY, JEFF
DISCIPLINE HISTORY AND PHILOSOPHY OF SCIENCE **EDUCATION** Kans State Univ, BA; Univ Chicago, MS (chem), PhD (hist & plilos science). **CAREER** Asst prof, Ore State Univ, 94-. **RESEARCH** Three-dimensional molecular shape, interaction of science and policy. **SELECTED PUBLICATIONS** Area: how approximations and idealizations affect our notions of justification and reduction. **CONTACT ADDRESS** Dept Philos, Oregon State Univ, Hovland Hall 102E, Corvallis, OR 97331-3902. **EMAIL** jramsey@orst.edu

RAMUSACK, BARBARA N.
PERSONAL Born 11/05/1937, Gary, IN, s **DISCIPLINE** HISTORY **EDUCATION** Alverno Col, BA, 60; Univ Mich, MA, 62, PhD, 69. **CAREER** Asst prof to prof, Univ Cincinnati, 67-; Dir Graduate Studies Hist, 79-83, 89-94; head, 99-2003; Charles Phelps Taft Prof, 00. **HONORS AND AWARDS** Phi Beta Kappa, 63; Outstanding Alumnae Awd, Alverno Col, 75; McMicken Dean's Awd for Dist Service, 91. **MEMBERSHIPS** Am Coun Southern Asian Art; Am Hist Asn; Asn Asian Studies. **RESEARCH** Princes of India; Interaction among Brit & South Asian Women; Maternal & Infant Welfare in Colonial India. **SELECTED PUBLICATIONS** Auth, The Princes of India in the Twilight of Empire: Dissolution of a Patron-Client System, 1914-1939, Columbus, 78; auth, Embattled Advocates: The Debate over Birth Control in India, 1920-1940, J Women's Hist, 89; auth, Cultural Missionaries, Maternal Imperialists, Feminist Allies: Brit Women Activists in India, 1865-1945, Women's Studies Int Forum, 90; auth, Indian Princes as Fantasy: Palace Hotels, Palace Museums, Palace-on-Wheels, in Consuming Modernity: Public Culture in a South Asian World, 66-89, ed Carol A Breckenridge, Minneapolis, 95; coauth, Women in Asia: Restoring Women to History, Bloomington, 99. **CONTACT ADDRESS** Dept of History, Univ of Cincinnati, PO Box 210373, Cincinnati, OH 45221-0373. **EMAIL** barbara.ramusack@uc.edu

RAND, HARRY
PERSONAL Born 01/10/1947, New York, NY, m, 1988, 1 child **DISCIPLINE** HISTORY **EDUCATION** CUNY, BA, 69; Harvard Univ, AM, 71, PhD, 74. **CAREER** Assoc Curator, 77-79, chmn, 78-84, dept 20th century painting & sculpture, curator, 79-93, sr curator, 93-97, painting & sculpture, Natl Museum of Amer Art, curator, 97-, cultural hist, Smithsonian Institution. **RESEARCH** Methodology of art hist; human stud; relig/theol in modern life. **SELECTED PUBLICATIONS** Auth, Seymour Lipton: Aspects of Sculpture, 79; auth, Archile Gorky, 80; auth, Manet's Contemplation at the Gare St. Lazare, 87; auth, Paul Manship, 89; auth, Friedensreich Hundertwasser, 91. **CONTACT ADDRESS** NMAH, Smithsonian Inst, Washington, DC 20560-0616. **EMAIL** rand@nmah.si.edu

RANDALL, FRANCIS BALLARD
PERSONAL Born 12/17/1931, New York, NY, m, 1957, 2 children **DISCIPLINE** HISTORY **EDUCATION** Amherst Col, BA, 52, Columbia Univ, MA, 54, PhD, 60. **CAREER** Instr hist, Amherst Col, 56-59; from instr to asst prof, Columbia Univ, 59-61; trustee, 71-76, Mem hum fac, Sarah Lawrence Col, 61-, Fulbright fel, India, 65; vis prof, Columbia Univ, 67-68. **MEMBERSHIPS** AHA; Am Asn Advan Slavic Studies. **RESEARCH** Hist of Communism; hist of Russ; hist of Russ art. **SELECTED PUBLICATIONS** Coauth, Essays in Russian and Soviet history, Columbia Univ, 63; Stalin's Russia: An Historical Reconsideration, Free Press, 65; N G Chernyshevskii, Twayne, 67; Vissarion Belinskii, Oriental Research Partner, 87; Articles: Grandiosity and overdecoration in Russian art, summer 72 & History as icon: the Tret'iakov Gallery of Russian Art, 2/73, Art News; Maoism is dead, Nat Rev, 3/77, Ten days that shook China: the October revolution in Shanghai, Contemp China, 3/77. **CONTACT ADDRESS** 425 Riverside Dr, Apt 10-I, New York, NY 10025-7730.

RANDALL, WILLARD
PERSONAL Born 03/13/1942, Philadelphia, PA, m, 1985, 4 children **DISCIPLINE** HISTORY **EDUCATION** Thomas Edison State Col, BA, 82; Princeton Univ, MA, 84. **CAREER** Instructor, Newark Acad, 81-82; Grad Fel, Princeton Univ, 82-84; Lecturer to Visiting Asst Prof, Univ VT, 85-94; Visiting Prof, John Cabot Univ, 94-; Visiting Prof, Champlain Col, 98-. **HONORS AND AWARDS** Nat Magazine Awd for Public Service, Columbia Grad Sch, 72; John Hancock Awd for Excellence in financial Writing, 76; Gerald Loeb Awd, UCLA Grad Sch, 76; Sidney Hillman foundation Awd, 76; Colonial Dames Scholarship, Princeton Univ, 83; Davis Prize in British History, Princeton Univ, 83; Frank Luther Mott Awd, Univ MO Grad Sch, 85, Medallist, MY Soc of Colonial Wars, 86; Best Book of 2990, Am Revolution round Table, 90; Best Book, Colonial Dames of Am, 91; Fraunces Tavern Book Awd, Sons of the Am Revolution, 91; Nominated for the Pulitzer Prize, 90; Who's Who in Am; Who's Who in the East' Who's Who of emerging Leaders in the U.S.; Who's Who in Vermont; Contemporary Authors. **MEMBERSHIPS** NY Authors Guild; NY Acad of Sci; Princeton club of NY; Am Revolution Round Table; VT Hist Soc; Center for Res on VT. **RESEARCH** American, British, and Modern European History; Biography. **SELECTED PUBLICATIONS** Auth, Thomas Jefferson: A Life, Henry Holt, New York, 93; co-auth, American Lives 2 vols, Longmans, 96; auth, George Washington; A Life, Henry Holt, New York, 97; co-auth, Forgotten Americans, Addison Wesley, Perseus Paperback, 99; auth, "The Battle for Philadelphia," MHQ: The Quarterly Journal of Military History, 99; co-auth, History of the United States, Addison Wesley Longman, forthcoming; auth, Biography of John and Abigail Adams, Harper Collins, forthcoming; auth, Biography of Alexander Hamilton, Henry Holt, forthcoming. **CONTACT ADDRESS** Dept Arts & Sci, Champlain Col, 163 S Willard St, Burlington, VT 05401-3902. **EMAIL** willnn@aol.com

RANDOLPH, ADRIAN W. B.
DISCIPLINE ART HISTORY **EDUCATION** Princeton Univ, AB; Courtauld Inst Art, MA; Harvard Univ, MA, PhD. **CAREER** Asst prof, Dartmouth Col. **RESEARCH** Italian 15th-century cult; gender studies. **SELECTED PUBLICATIONS** Auth, Regarding Women in Sacred Space, Picturing Women in Renaissance and Baroque Italy, Cambridge UP, 97; Black Male Suspect? Auseinandersetzungen mit Stereotypen afro-amerikanischer Mannlichkeit in der zeitgenossischen US-Kunst, Kritische Berichte, 95; various other articles; coauth, The Bastides of Southwest France, Art Bulletin, 95. **CONTACT ADDRESS** Dartmouth Col, 3529 N Main St, #207, Hanover, NH 03755. **EMAIL** adrian.randolph@dartmouth.edu

RANSBY, BARBARA
PERSONAL Born 05/12/1957, Detroit, MI, m **DISCIPLINE** AFRICAN-AMERICAN HISTORY **EDUCATION** Columbia Univ, BA, 1984; Univ of MI, MA, 1987, PhD, 1996. **CAREER** Institute for African Affairs and Department of History, Columbia University, research asst, 82-84; Univ of MI, instructor, 86-87, 89, teaching asst, 87, research asst, 88; Museum of African American History, curator of Nineteenth and Twentieth Century special projects, 89-90; Chicago Clergy and Laity Concerned, group trainer, 92; Crossroads Foundation, group trainer, 92; DePaul Univ, instructor, 92-95, director, asst prof, 95-96; Ancona School, consultant, group facilitator, 93; Chicago Historical Society, consultant, panelist, 93; Mac Arthur Foundation, consultant, 94; American College Testing, consultant, 96; Univ of IL at Chicago, Asst Prof, 96-; Northwestern Univ, manuscript reviewer, 97. **HONORS AND AWARDS** Univ of MI, Student Recognition Awd for Leadership, 1987; Women's Action for Nuclear Disarmament, Annual Peace Awd, 1988; Columbia University, Herman Ausubel Student Awd for Achievement in History, 1983; Univ of MI, Women Studies Program fellow, 1986; Univ of MI, Student Essay Competition Awd, 1986; Woodrow Wilson Fellowships Foundation, National Mellon Fellowship, 1984-86; Univ of MI Rackham Graduate School Fellowships, Michigan Minority Merit Fellowship, 1986-90; Ford Foundation and Center for Afro-American and African Studies, Grad Student Research grant, 1990; DePaul Univ School of Liberal Arts and Sciences, Summer Faculty Research Awd, 1993; Univ of IL at Chicago, Office of Social Science Research Seed Fund Initiative, grant, 1996. **MEMBERSHIPS** Anti-Racism Institute, Clergy and Laity Concerned, bd mem; Chicago Coalition in Solidarity with Southern Africa, bd mem; Univ of MI, History Dept Search Committee, student mem; Editorial Board of the Journal Race and Class; Ella Baker-Nelson Mandela Center for Anti-Racist Education, Univ of MI, bd mem; Association for the Study of Afro-American Life and History; Association of Black Women Historians; Coordinating Committee for Women in the Historical Profession; Organization of American Historians; United Coalition Against Racism, co-founder; Free South Africa Coordinating Committee, co-founder, co-chair. **SELECTED PUBLICATIONS** Author, works include: "Ella Baker and the Black Radical Tradition," U of NC Press, 1999; "Black Women and the Black Freedom Movement: Following Ella Baker's Path", 1998; "US:

The Black Poor and the Politics of Expendability", Race and Class, 1996; numerous articles and essays. **CONTACT ADDRESS** African American Studies and History, Univ of Illinois, Chicago, 601 S Morgan, M/C 069, Chicago, IL 60607.

RANSEL, DAVID
PERSONAL Born 02/20/1939, Gary, IN, m, 1969, 2 children **DISCIPLINE** HISTORY **EDUCATION** Coe Col, BA, 61; Northwestern Univ, MA, 62; Yale Univ, PhD, 69. **CAREER** Instr, Tollare Folkhogskola, Sweden, 59-60; asst instr, Yale Univ, 66-67; instr to prof, Univ of IL at Urbana Champaign, 67-85; prof, Ind Univ, 85-. **HONORS AND AWARDS** Phi Beta Kappa, 60; Phi Kappa Phi, 60; Woodrow Wilson Fel, 61-62; Danforth Fel, 61-68; Soviet-Am Exchange UICTG Grant to USSR, 65-66; Lounsbury-Scott Yale Fe, 66-67; NEH Grants, 76-77, 98-99; IREX Grants, 79, 87, 90, 93, 94-96, 99; Fulbright Grant, USSR, 79, 90; Woodrow Wilson Int Fel, 89-90; Guggenheim Fel, 89-90; Mellon Grant, 93. **MEMBERSHIPS** AHA; Am Assoc for the Advanc of Slavic Studies. **SELECTED PUBLICATIONS** Auth, The Politics of Catherinian Russia: The Panin Party, Yale Univ Pr, (New Haven), 75; ed, The Family in Imperial Russia: New Lines of Historical Research, Univ of IL Pr, (Urbana), 78; auth, Mothers of Misery: Child Abandonment in Russia, Princeton Univ Pr, 88; ed, transl, Village Life in Late Tsarist Russian by Olga Semyonova, Ind Univ Pr, (Bloomington), 93; auth, "Baptism in Rural Russia: Village Women Speak of Their Children and Their Way of Life", Hist of the Family: An Int Quarterly 1.1 (Spring 96): 63-80; auth, "First Half of the Nineteenth Century", Russia: A History, Oxford Univ Pr, 97; coed, Imperial Russia: New Histories for the Empire, Ind Univ Pr, (Bloomington), 98; auth, "An Eighteenth-Century Russian Merchant Family in Prosperity and Decline", Imperial Russia: New Histories for the Empire, eds Jane Burbank and David L. Ransel, (Bloomington, 98): 256-280; auth, "Enlightenment and Tradition: The Aestheticized Life of an Eighteenth-Century Provincial Merchant", Self and Story in Russian History, eds Laura Engelstein and Stephanie Sandler, Cornell Univ Pr, (Ithaca), 00; auth, Village Mothers: Three Generations of Change in Russia and Tataria, Ind Univ Pr, (Bloomington), 00. **CONTACT ADDRESS** Dept Hist, Indiana Univ, Bloomington, 1020 E Kirkwood Ave, Bloomington, IN 47405-7103. **EMAIL** ransel@indiana.edu

RANUM, OREST
PERSONAL Born 02/18/1933, Lyle, MN, m, 1955, 2 children **DISCIPLINE** HISTORY **EDUCATION** Macalester Col, BA, 55; Univ Minn, MA, 57, PhD, 60. **CAREER** Instr hist, Univ Southern Calif, 60-61; from instr to assoc prof, Columbia Univ, 61-69; chmn dept, 72-76, Prof Hist, Johns Hopkins Univ, 69-, Guggenheim fel, 68-69; fel, Inst Advan Studies, 73-74; prof, Col de France, 94-95. **HONORS AND AWARDS** Corresponding Mem, Institut de France, 89. **MEMBERSHIPS** AHA; Soc Fr Hist Studies (vpres, 73-74). **RESEARCH** Early modern French history. **SELECTED PUBLICATIONS** Auth, Richelieu and the Councillors of Louis XIII, Clarendon, 63; Paris in the Age of Absolutism, Wiley, 68; auth, Artisans of Glory, 80; auth, The Fronde, a French Revolution, Norton, 93. **CONTACT ADDRESS** Dept of Hist, Johns Hopkins Univ, Baltimore, 3400 N Charles St, Baltimore, MD 21218-2680. **EMAIL** pranum@compuserve.com

RAPPAPORT, RHODA
PERSONAL Born 08/10/1935, New York, NY **DISCIPLINE** HISTORY OF SCIENCE **EDUCATION** Goucher Col, 55; Cornell Univ, MA, 58, PhD(hist sci), 64. **CAREER** From instr to assoc prof, 61-76, Prof Hist, Vassar Col, 76-00. **MEMBERSHIPS** Hist Sci Soc; Brit Soc Hist Sci; Soc Fr Hist Studies. **RESEARCH** History of geology in the 18th century; 18th century France. **SELECTED PUBLICATIONS** Auth, James Hutton And The Hist Of Geology, Isis, Vol 85, 94; James Hutton And The Hist Of Geology, Isis, Vol 85, 94, Questions Of Evidence--An Anonymous Tract Attributed To John Toland, J Of The Hist Of Ideas, Vol 58, 97; auth, When Geologists Were Historians, 1665-1750, Cornell Univ Pr, 97. **CONTACT ADDRESS** 141 Fulton Ave, Apt 810, Poughkeepsie, NY 12603.

RAPSON, RICHARD L.
PERSONAL Born 03/08/1937, New York, NY, m, 1982, 1 child **DISCIPLINE** HISTORY **EDUCATION** Amherst Col, BA, 58; Columbia Univ, PhD, 66. **CAREER** Asst prof, Univ of Calif, 65-66; asst prof to prof, Univ of Haw, 66-68. **HONORS AND AWARDS** Phi Beta Kappa; Bond Prize; Woodrow Wilson Fel, 58-59; Amherst-Columbia Fel, 59-60; Edward J Perkins Scholar 60-61; Danforth Grant, 64-65; SSRC Res Grant, 68; Outstanding Teacher Awd, 92; Headliner Awd, Hni Prof Chapter of women in Commun, 95. **SELECTED PUBLICATIONS** Auth, American Life and Thought Since 1880: A Guided Study Course, Univ of Haw, 76; auth, The Pursuit of Meaning: American 1600-2000, Univ Pr of Am, 77; auth, Denials of Doubt: An Interpretation of American History, Univ Pr of Am, 78; auth, Fairly Lucky You Life Hawaii! Cultural Pluralism in the Fiftieth State, Univ Pr of Am, 80; auth, American Yearnings: Love, Money, and Endless Possibility, UPA, (NY/London), 88; coauth, Love, Sex and Intimacy: Their Psychology, Biology, and History, Harpercollins, (NY), 93; coauth, Emotional Contagion, Cambridge Univ Pr, (Cambridge, England), 94; auth, Love and Sex: Cross-Cultural Perspectives, Allyn & Bacon, 96; auth, Rosie, SterlingHouse, (Pittsburgh, PA), 00. **CONTACT ADDRESS** Dept Am Studies, Univ of Hawaii, Honolulu Comm Col, 1890 E West Blvd, Honolulu, HI 96822-2318. **EMAIL** rapson@hawaii.edu

RASCH, WILLIAM
PERSONAL Born 10/25/1949, Waterbury, CT, m, 1977, 1 child **DISCIPLINE** GERMAN STUDIES **EDUCATION** Univ Wash, PhD. **CAREER** Lect, 87-90, Univ Mo; vis asst prof, 90-94, asst prof, Ind Univ, 00-. **MEMBERSHIPS** MLA; AATG; GSA; Int Brecht Soc. **RESEARCH** German philos tradition; social and political theory; Brecht and theater. **SELECTED PUBLICATIONS** Co-ed, Niklas Luhmann's Modernity: The Paradoxes of Differentation edited volume: Observing Complexity: Systems Theory and Postmodernity; ed, Niklas Luhmann: Theories of Sistinction: Re-Describing the Descriptions of Modernity, (forthcoming); Plus numerous articles on Carl Schmitt, Brecht, and the 18th century. **CONTACT ADDRESS** Dept of Germanic Studies, Indiana Univ, Bloomington, Ballantine Hall 644, 1020 E Kirkwood Ave, Bloomington, IN 47405-7103. **EMAIL** wrasch@indiana.edu

RASMUSSEN, CHRIS
DISCIPLINE HISTORY **EDUCATION** Rutgers Univ, PhD, 92. **CAREER** Asst prof, Univ Nev Las Vegas. **RESEARCH** Intellectual history; environmental history. **SELECTED PUBLICATIONS** Auth, pubs on American Culture History. **CONTACT ADDRESS** History Dept, Univ of Nevada, Las Vegas, 4505 Md Pky, Las Vegas, NV 89154.

RASPORICH, ANTHONY W.
PERSONAL Born 01/09/1940, Port Arthur, ON, Canada **DISCIPLINE** HISTORY **EDUCATION** Queen's Univ, BA, 62, MA, 65; Univ Manitoba, PhD, 70. **CAREER** Asst prof, 66-71, assoc prof, 71-76, head dept, 73-76, assoc dean, soc sci, 76-81, Prof History, Univ Calgary, 77-; CD Howe Postdoct Fel, 70-71; Killiam Res Fel, 79; SSHRC Leave Fel, 81-82; exec, Alta Hist Soc Pub Bd, 75-81; exec, Can Ethnic Stud Asn, 79-83. **SELECTED PUBLICATIONS** Auth, For a Better Life, 82; ed, adv bd, Encyclopedia of Canada's Peoples, 92-97; ed, William Lyon Mackenzie, 72; ed, Western Canada: Past and Present, 75; ed, The Making of the Modern West, 84; co-ed, Prairie Perspectives II, 73; co-ed, Can Ethnic Studies, 80-98; co-ed, Winter Sports in the West, 90. **CONTACT ADDRESS** Dept of History, Univ of Calgary, Calgary, AB, Canada T2N 1N4. **EMAIL** awraspor@ucalgary.ca

RAST, WALTER EMIL
PERSONAL Born 07/03/1930, San Antonio, TX, m, 1955, 4 children **DISCIPLINE** OLD TESTAMENT, ARCHEOLOGY **EDUCATION** St John's Col, BA, 52; Concordia Theol Sem, MDiv, 55, STM, 56; Univ Chicago, MA, 64, PhD(Old Testament), 66. **CAREER** From asst prof to assoc prof, 61-73; Prof Old Testament & Archaeol, Valparaiso Univ, 73-, James Alan Montgomery fel, Am Schs Orient Res, Jerusalem, 66-67; res prof, Albright Inst Archaeol Res, Jerusalem, 71-72; Danforth assoc, 73-; co-dir, Excavations at Bab edh-Dhra & Numeira, 75-; Nat Endowment for Humanities res grants, 75, 77, 79 & 81; Univ Chicago fel, 76; vis prof Old Testament, Univ Notre Dame, 77-78 & 82; pres, Am Ctr of Orental Res Amman, 78-82; prof, Albright Inst Archaeol Res, Jerusalem, 82-83; Am Coun Learned Soc fel, 71-72; Nat Endowment for Humanities fel, 82. **MEMBERSHIPS** Archaeol Inst Am; Am Schs Orient Res; Soc Bibl Lit; Israel Explor Soc. **RESEARCH** Old Testament; Syro-Palestinian archeology; Semitic languages. **SELECTED PUBLICATIONS** Auth, Tradition History and the Old Testament, Fortress, 72; coauth, Survey of the Southeastern plain of the Dead Sea, Ann Dept Antiq Jordan, 74; A preliminary report of excavations at Bab edh, Dhra, 1975, Ann Am Schs Orient Res, 76; auth, Tannach I: Studies in the Iron Age Pottery, Am Scholars Orient Res, 78; Joshua, Judges, Samuel and Kings, Fortress, 78; An Ostracon from Tell el-Ful, 78 &; co-ed, The Southeastern Dead Sea Plain Expedition: An Interim Report of the 1977 Season, 79, Annals Am Scholars Orient Res; coauth, Preliminary Report of the 1979 Expedition to the Dead Sea Plain, Jordan, Bull Am Scholars Orient Res, 240. **CONTACT ADDRESS** Dept of Theol, Valparaiso Univ, Valparaiso, IN 46383.

RATHER, SUSAN
DISCIPLINE ART AND ART HISTORY **EDUCATION** Univ DE, PhD. **CAREER** Assoc prof; adv, Art Hist Grad, Univ of TX at Austin. **HONORS AND AWARDS** Nat Endowment for the Hum, Winterthur Mus, Am Coun Learned Soc, Yale Ctr for Brit Art, Mass Hist Soc & Univ TX. **RESEARCH** 18th-century Brit and Am portraiture, specifically, the representation of the artist. **SELECTED PUBLICATIONS** Auth, Archaism, Modernism, and the Art of Paul Manship, early 20th-century sculpture, 93 & several exhibition catalogue essays; publ in, Archives Amer Art J, Art Bulletin, Art J, Arts Mag, 18th-century Stud, Metropolitan Mus J, Pa Mag Hist and Biog & Winterthur Portfolio. **CONTACT ADDRESS** Dept of Art and Art Hist, Univ of Texas, Austin, 2613 Wichita St, FAB 2.130, Austin, TX 78705.

RATNER, LORMAN A. (LARRY)
DISCIPLINE HISTORY **EDUCATION** Cornell Univ, PhD, 61. **CAREER** Prof emer, Hist, Univ Tenn; adj prof, Univ Ill-Urbana Champaign. **RESEARCH** Nineteenth-century US intellectual and cultural history. **SELECTED PUBLICATIONS** Auth, Pre Civil War Reform, Antimasonry, Powder Keg: Northern Opposition to Antislavery, 1831-1840; co-ed, The Development of An American Culture; Multi-Culturalism in the United States. **CONTACT ADDRESS** Dept Hist, Univ of Illinois, Urbana-Champaign, MC-466, Urbana, IL 61801. **EMAIL** l_ratner@hotmail.com

RAUCHER, ALAN R.
PERSONAL Born 01/27/1939, New York, NY, 1 child **DISCIPLINE** AMERICAN BUSINESS HISTORY, AMERICAN SOCIAL & INTELLECTUAL HISTORY **EDUCATION** Univ Calif, Los Angeles, BA, 60; MA, 61, PhD, 64. **CAREER** Vis asst prof hist, Univ Pittsburgh, 64-65; vis asst prof, Rice Univ, 65-66; vis asst prof, Univ Ariz, 66-67; asst prof, 67-68, asst prof, 68-74, assoc prof hist, 74-86, chmn hist, 86-95, act dean, coll lib arts, 96-97, act assoc dean, coll lib arts, 96-97, Wayne State Univ. **MEMBERSHIPS** Orgn Am Historians. **RESEARCH** Recent American history. **SELECTED PUBLICATIONS** Auth, Employee Relations at General Motors, Labor History, 87; art, Dime Store Chains, Business Hist Rev, 91; art, Sunday Business and the Decline of Sunday Closing Laws, Journal of Church and State, 94. **CONTACT ADDRESS** Dept of History, Wayne State Univ, 838 Mackenzie, Detroit, MI 48202-3919. **EMAIL** ad5919@wayne.edu

RAUSCH, JANE M.
PERSONAL Born 12/12/1940, Indianapolis, IN, m, 1983 **DISCIPLINE** LATIN AMERICAN HISTORY **EDUCATION** DePauw Univ, BA, 62; Univ Wis-Madison, MA, 64; PhD, 69. **CAREER** Lecturer, Mount St. Mary's Col, 68-69; lecturer, UCLA, 68-69; instr, Univ Mass-Amherst, 69-71; asst prof, 71-76; assoc prof, 76-84; Prof, 84- . **HONORS AND AWARDS** Alpha Lambda Delta, Phi Beta Kappa, Fulbright-Hays Sr Lectureship, 87; Conf on Latin Am Hist Robertson Prize, 81; Corresp Mem, Acad de Hist del Meta (Columbia), 87; Hon Mem, Centro de Hist de Casanare, 89. **MEMBERSHIPS** Am Hist Asoc; Latin Am Studies Asoc; Conf on Latin Am Hist; New England Coun of Latin Am Studies; Asoc de Colombianistas Norteamericanos. **RESEARCH** Columbian history; comparative frontier history; colonial Latin Am history; Latin Am hist, 19th and 20th centuries. **SELECTED PUBLICATIONS** Auth, People and Issues in Latin American History: The Colonial Experience, Rev. 2000; ed. with David J. Weber, Where Cultures Meet: Frontiers in Latin American History, 94; auth, Una Frontera de la sabana tropical: Los llanos de Colombia, 1531-1831, 94; auth, Fronteras en crisis: la desintegracion de las misiones en el extremo norte de Mexico y en la Nueva Granada: 1821-1849, Boletin Cultural y Bibiografico, 96; auth, La comuneros olvidados: La insurreccion de 1781 en los llanos del Casanare, Boletin Cultural y Bibliografico, 96; auth, "Colombia: Territorial Rule and the Llanos Frontier," Gainesville: University Press of Florida, 99; auth, "People and Issues in Latin American History: From Independence to the Present," rev. ed. Princeton: Markus Wiener, 99. **CONTACT ADDRESS** Dept of Hist, Univ of Massachusetts, Amherst, Amherst, MA 01003. **EMAIL** jrausch@history.umass.edu

RAUSCHENBERG, ROY A.
PERSONAL Born 10/07/1929, Chicago, IL, m, 1958, 4 children **DISCIPLINE** ENGLISH HISTORY **EDUCATION** Univ IL, BA, 51, MA, 56, PhD, 60. **CAREER** From instr to asst prof hist, E TX State Col, 59-61; asst prof, Chicago Teachers Col, 61-63; asst prof, Baldwin-Wallace Col, 63-64; asst prof, 64-68, assoc prof English Hist, OH Univ, 68-, retired. **MEMBERSHIPS** AHA; Hakluyt Soc; Conf Brit Studies; Asn Can Studies United States. **RESEARCH** Eighteenth century English science; 18th century English culture; John Ellis. **SELECTED PUBLICATIONS** Auth, Daniel Carl Solander, naturalist on the Endeavour voyage, Am Philos Soc Trans, Vol 58, No 8; A letter of Sir Joseph Banks describing the life of Daniel Solander, Vol 55, No 179 & Daniel Carl Solander, the naturalist on the Endeavour voyage, Vol 58, No 193, ISIS; ed, The journals of Joseph Bank's voyage up Great Britain's west coast to Iceland and to the Orkney Isles July to October 1772, Proc Am Philos Soc, Vol 117, No 3; John Ellis, FRS: Eighteenth century naturalist and royal agent to west Florida, Notes & Rec Royal Soc, London, 3/78. **CONTACT ADDRESS** Dept Hist, Ohio Univ, Athens, OH 45701-2979.

RAVERTY, DENNIS
DISCIPLINE TWENTIETH CENTURY EUROPEAN AND AMERICAN ART AND ARCHITECTURE **EDUCATION** Univ Minn, BA, 90; Univ Iowa; MA, 92; Rutgers Univ, PhD, 96. **CAREER** Instr, Boston Inst Contemp Art, 82-83; Boston Ctr Adult Edu, 86-87; tchg asst, Univ Iowa, 90-92; lectr, Univ Konstanz, 94; Rutgers Univ, 94-96; asst prof, Pittsburg State Univ, 96-99; asst prof, Iowa State Univ, 99-. **HONORS AND AWARDS** Grad scholar, Univ Iowa, 90-91; Russell scholar, Rutgers Univ, 93-94; grad asstship, Rutgers Univ, 95-96; Fac of the Year, Col of Design, IA State Univ, 01; Dean's Awd for Outstanding Performance IA State Univ, 01. **SELECTED PUBLICATIONS** Auth, A Split in the American Avant Garde,

Rutgers Art Rev 14, 96; Critical Perspectives on New Images of Man, Art Jour 53, 95; Rob Moore and the Limitations of Style, The Art of Rob Moore, exhib cat, Mass Col Art Gallery, 94; auth, The Self as Other: A Search for Indentity in the Painting of Archibald Motley, Jr, Intl Rev of African Am Art-in press; auth, The Needs of Postwar America and the Origins of the Jackson Pollock Myth, Midwest Quarterly-in press; auth, Visions From a Sinking World: Representatiobs of the Future in Japanese Anime, New Art Examiner-in press; auth, Stylistic Vacillation and Unresolved Autonomy Issues: Notes on the Relationship Between Michelangelo and Jacopo Pontormo, in European Studies Conference Proceedings: Selected Papers from 1990-1999, Vienna, Austria, 01-in press; auth, Siah Armajani and the Architectural Text, Art Papers-25, 01, 28-33; auth, Kaprow's Strategy, Art Criticism, 15, 00, 23-33; auth, A Cultural Worker and the Prophetic Imagination: The Artistic Vocation of Margaret Burroughs, A Lifetime in Art; A Retrospective Exhibition of the Work of Margaret Taylor Goss Burroughs, exhibition catalogue, DuSable Museum of African-Am Hist Chicago, 01, 12-15; auth, Art Theory and Psychological Thought in Mid-Nineteeth Century America: The Case of the Crayon, Prospects: An Annual of Am Cultural Studies 34, 99, 285-296; auth, The Controversy Over Ernst Barlach's Geistkampfer, Source: Notes in the Hist of Art 8, 99, 48-54. **CONTACT ADDRESS** Col of Design, Iowa State Univ, Ames, IA 50011. **EMAIL** raverty@iastate.edu

RAVINA, MARK
DISCIPLINE HISTORY **EDUCATION** Columbia Univ, AB 83; Stanford Univ, MA, 88, PhD, 91. **CAREER** Assoc prof **RESEARCH** Japanese history; political activism in the 1870s and 1880s--linking the jiyu minken undo with Tokugawa-era political thought. **SELECTED PUBLICATIONS** Auth, Wasan and the Physics that Wasn't; State-building and Political Economy in Early Modern Japan. **CONTACT ADDRESS** Dept History, Emory Univ, 221 Bowden Hall, 561 Kilgo Cir, Atlanta, GA 30322-1950. **EMAIL** histmr@emory.edu

RAWLEY, JAMES A.
PERSONAL Born 11/09/1916, Terre Haute, IN, m, 1945, 2 children **DISCIPLINE** HISTORY **EDUCATION** Univ Mich, AB, 38, AM, 39; Columbia Univ, PhD, 49. **CAREER** Instr hist, NY Univ, 46-51; instr, Hunter Col, 51-53; assoc prof, Sweet Briar Col, 53-58, chmn dept hist, 53-57, prof, 58-64, chmn div social studies, 61-64; chmn dept, 66-67, Prof Hist, Univ Nebr, Lincoln, 64-, Chmn Dept, 73-82, Scholar-in-residence, Rockefeller Found Study & Conf Ctr, Bellagio, Italy, 77; Huntington-Nat Endowment for Humanities fel, Huntington Libr, 79; Huntington Libr fel, 81; Actg dean, Univ Libraries. **HONORS AND AWARDS** Phi Beta Kappa; Outstanding Research and Creativity; Pound-Howard Awds, Univ of Nebraska. **MEMBERSHIPS** AHA; Orgn Am Historians: fel Royal Hist Soc; fel, Soc American Historian; Southern Hist Asn. **RESEARCH** American Civil War era; Atlantic slave trade; the Gilded Age; Abraham Lincoln. **SELECTED PUBLICATIONS** Auth, Edwin D. Morgan: Merchant in Politics, 1811-1883, 55; Turning Points of the Civil War, Univ Nebr, 66; auth, Race and Politics, 69; ed, Lincoln and Civil War Politics, Holt, 69; The Politics of Union, Dryden, 74; The Transatlantic Slave Trade, Norton, 81; auth, Secession: The Disruption of the American Republic, 1844-1861, 89; The Culture Of English Antislavery, 1780-1860, Am Hist Rev, Vol 97, 92; Gordon, Nathaniel The Only American Executed For Violating The Slave-Trade Laws, Civil War Hist, Vol 39, 93; auth, Abraham Lincoln and a Nation Worth Fighting For, 96. **CONTACT ADDRESS** Dept of Hist, Univ of Nebraska, Lincoln, Lincoln, NE 68588-0327.

RAWLS, JAMES J.
PERSONAL Born 11/10/1945, Washington, DC, m, 1967, 2 children **DISCIPLINE** HISTORY **EDUCATION** Stanford Univ, BA, 67; Univ Calif-Berkeley, MA, 69, PhD, 75. **CAREER** Instr, San Francisco State Univ, 71-75; Instr, Diablo Valley Col, 75-; Vis Lectr, 77-81, Vis As Assoc Prof, Univ Calif-Berkeley, 89. **HONORS AND AWARDS** Honors in Hist, Stanford Univ, 67; Schol-in-Residence, Calif State Univ, 87; Fac Lectr Awd, Diablo Valley Col, 88; Fel, Calif Hist Soc, 88; Nat Teaching Excellence Awd, Univ Tex, 89; Awd of Merit, League for Hist Preservation, 93. **MEMBERSHIPS** Am Hist Asn; Calif Hist Soc; Calif Coun Humanities. **RESEARCH** California history; Native American history. **SELECTED PUBLICATIONS** Co-auth, Land of Liberty: A United States History, Holt, Rinhart, and Winston, 85; auth, Indians of California: The Changing Image, Univ Okla Press, 86; ed, New Directions in California History, McGraw-Hill Bk Co, 88; auth, Never Turn Back: Father Sevva's Mission, Steck-Vaughn Co, 93; auth, Dame Shirley and the Gold Rush, Steck-Vaughn Co, 93; auth, Dr. History's Sampler: More Stories of California's Past, McGraw-Hill Bk Co, 94; California Dreaming: More Stories from Dr. History, McGraw-Hill Bk Co, 95; Chief Red Fox is Dead: A History of Native Americans Since 1945, Harcourt Brace Publ, 96; auth, California: An Interpretive History, McGraw-Hill Bk Co, 98; A Voyage through the Sea of Cortez, Special Expeditions, 97; co-ed, A Golden State: Mining and the Development of California, Univ Calif Press 99. **CONTACT ADDRESS** History Dept, Diablo Valley Col, Pleasant Hill, CA 94523. **EMAIL** rawls@netdex.com

RAWSKI, EVELYN S.
PERSONAL Born 02/02/1939, Honolulu, HI, m, 1967 **DISCIPLINE** HISTORY **EDUCATION** Cornell Univ, BA, 61; Radcliffe Col, MA, 62; Harvard Univ, PhD, 68. **CAREER** Asst prof to prof, Univ of Pittsburgh, 67-. **HONORS AND AWARDS** Guggenheim Fel, 90; Woodrow Wilson Center Fel, 92-93. **MEMBERSHIPS** AHA; Assoc for Asian Studies. **RESEARCH** Chinese social and cultural history. **SELECTED PUBLICATIONS** Auth, Agricultural Change and the Peasant Economy of South China, Harvard Univ Pr, 72; auth, Education and Popular Literacy in Ch'ing China, Univ of Mich Pr, 79; coed, Popular Culture in Late Imperial China, Univ of Calif Pr, 85; coauth, Chinese Society in the Eighteenth Century, Yale Univ Pr, 87; coed, Death Ritual in Late Imperial and Modern China, Univ of Calif Pr, 88; coed, Harmony and Counterpoint: Ritual Music in Chinese Context, Stanford Univ Pr, 96; auth, The Last Emperors: A Social History of Qing Imperial Institutions, Univ of Calif Pr, 98; coed, European Intruders and Changes in Behavior and Customs in Africa and Asia before 1800, Vol 30 in An Expanding World: the European Impact on World History 1450-1800, Ashgate, 98. **CONTACT ADDRESS** Dept Hist, Univ of Pittsburgh, 3P38 Forbes Quad, Pittsburgh, PA 15260. **EMAIL** esrxt@pitt.edu

REA, KENNETH W.
PERSONAL Born 07/20/1944, Ruston, LA, m, 1964, 2 children **DISCIPLINE** HISTORY **EDUCATION** La Tech Univ, BA, 66; Univ CO at Boulder, MA, 68; PhD, 70. **CAREER** Vice President for Academic Affairs and Hist, LA Tech, Univ. **HONORS AND AWARDS** Outstanding Research Awd, 79. **MEMBERSHIPS** Am Asn Chinese Studies; Asn Asian Studies. **RESEARCH** Mod China; Sino-Am rel; Pacific Rim; Am for policy. **SELECTED PUBLICATIONS** Ed, Canton in Revolution, 1925-1928,Westview, 77; Early Sino-American Relations, 1841-1912, Westview, 78; "Dr. John Leighton Stuart and United States Policy Toward China, 1946-1949," ME Sharpe, 90; co-ed, The Forgotten Ambassador: John Leighton Stuart, 1946-1949, Westview, 81;China: An Analytic Reader, Milburn: RF, 75. **CONTACT ADDRESS** Academic Affairs, Louisiana Tech Univ, PO Box 3188, Ruston, LA 71272. **EMAIL** rea@latech.edu

REAGAN, LESLIE J.
DISCIPLINE HISTORY **EDUCATION** Madison Am Women's Hist Progam, Univ of Wis; Univ of Wis, MA, 85; Univ Wis Madison, PhD, 91. **CAREER** Visiting res fel, The John Hopkins Univ Medical School, 91-2; visiting asst prof of hist, The John Hopkins Univ, 91-92; asst prof, Univ of Illinois, 92-98; assoc prof, Univ of Illinois, 98-. **HONORS AND AWARDS** Am Legal Hist Fel, 90-91; Louis Pelzer Memorial Awd from the Organization of Am Historians for the essay, 90; Lerner Scott Prize from the Organization of am Historians for the best dissertation in U.S Women's Hist, 92; Am Hist Asn Littleton-Griswold Res Grant, 92; Fel at the Center for Advanced Study, 93-94; President's Book Awd, 95; Radcliffe Col Schlesinger Library Res Support Grant, 95-96; "Outstanding Academic Book of the Year" awarded by Choice to When Abortion was a Crime, 97; UIUC Campus Res Board for "Breast Cancer, Bodily Integrity, and Am Culture," 97-98. **MEMBERSHIPS** Member, President's Book Prize Committee, Social Science Hist Asn, 96; Member, Illinois State Archives Advisory Board, 95-. **RESEARCH** History of medicine; American women's history; sexuality; twentieth century American social history; the hist of illegal abortion; the intersections between law and medicine; and breast cancer and public health. **SELECTED PUBLICATIONS** Auth, "About to Meet Her Maker': Women, Doctors, Dying Declarations, and the State's Investigation of Abortion, Chicago, 1867-1940; Journal of Am History 77:4, (91): 1240-1264; auth, "About to Meet Her Maker," in Women and Health in America, ed, Judith Walzer Leavitt, 2nd rev, ed, Madison: Univ of Wis Press, (in press); auth, "About to Meet Her Maker," CE-ROM, Abortion and Reproductive Rights: A Comprehensive Guide to Medicine, Ethics and the Law, ed, J. Douglas Butler, (forthcoming); ed, Excerpt from When Abortion Was a Crime reprinted in Major Problems in American History, 1920-1945, ed, by Colin Gordon, Houghton Mifflin Company, (in press); auth, "Creating a Feminist Health Agency: California Activists and Mexican Abortion Clinics in the 1960s,"; auth, "Linking Midwives and Abortion in the Progressive Era," Bulletin of the History of Medicine 69, (95): 569-598; auth, "Engendering the Dread Disease: Women, Men, and Cancer," American Journal of Public Health 87:11, (97): 1779-1787; auth, When Abortion Was a Crime: Women, Medicine, and Law in the United States, 1867-1973; Univ of California Press, 97; auth, "Barbie," Imagining the Twentieth Century, Peter Fritzche and Charles Stewart, eds., Urbana: Univ of Illinois Press, 97; "Roe v. Wade" entry, Oxford Companion to United States History, New York: Oxford Univ Press, (in press). **CONTACT ADDRESS** History Dept, Univ of Illinois, Urbana-Champaign, 309 Gregory Hall, MC 466, 810 S Wright, Urbana, IL 61801. **EMAIL** lreagan@staff.uiuc.edu

REAGAN, PATRICK
PERSONAL Born St Paul, MN, m, 1988 **DISCIPLINE** HISTORY **EDUCATION** Kenyon Col, AB; Ohio State Univ, MA, 76; PhD,82. **CAREER** Vis instr, Kenyon Col, 80-82; from asst prof to prof, Tenn Tech Univ, 82-. **HONORS AND AWARDS** NEH, 84; Most Outstanding Teacher in Honors Prog, Tenn Tech Univ, 93; Dean's Awd for Innovative Teaching, Tenn Tech Univ, 97. **MEMBERSHIPS** Am Hist Asn, Orgn of Am Historians, The Hist Soc, Business Hist Confr, Economic Hist Asn, Soc for Military Hist, Soc for Historians of the Gilded Age and Progress progressive Era, Am Asn of Univ Professors. **RESEARCH** History of Public Policy in Twentieth-Century America, Progressive Reform, New Deal, World War II. **SELECTED PUBLICATIONS** Auth, For the General Welfare, Peter Lang, 89; auth, Designing a New America: The Origins of New Deal Planning 1890-1943 Univ of Mass Press (Amherst, MA), 99; auth, American Journey: World War I and the Jazz Age, Gale Group/Primary Source Media (Farmington Hills, MI), 00. **CONTACT ADDRESS** Dept Hist, Tennessee Tech Univ, PO Box 5064, Cookeville, TN 38505-0001. **EMAIL** preagan@tntech.edu

REAGAN, RHONDA
PERSONAL Born 07/28/1962, Amherst, TX, m, 1988 **DISCIPLINE** GEOGRAPHY **EDUCATION** Tex Tech Univ, BA, 84; Tex A & M Univ, MS, 86, also postgrad. **CAREER** Geog instr, Blinn Col, 86-. **MEMBERSHIPS** GISTXED, GITA, TAGE. **RESEARCH** Chinese geography, GIS. **CONTACT ADDRESS** Dept Soc Sci, Blinn Col, PO Box 6030, Bryan, TX 77805. **EMAIL** rreagan@acmail.blinncol.edu

REAGON, BERNICE JOHNSON
PERSONAL Born 10/04/1942, Albany, GA **DISCIPLINE** AFRICAN HISTORY **EDUCATION** Albany State College, Albany, GA, BA, 1959-; Spelman College, Atlanta, GA, BA, 1970; Howard University, Washington, DC, PhD, 1975. **CAREER** Student Non-Violent Coordinating Comm, civil rights activist, 61-62, field sec & freedom singer, 62-64; African American Folklore, Field Researcher, 65-; Sweet Honey in the Rock, Washington, DC, Founder/Artistic Dir, 73-; Smithsonian Institution, Museum of American History, Program in Black American Culture, program director and cultural historian, 76-88; Smithsonian Institution, Museum of American History, Division of Community Life, Curator, 88-; Amer Univ, Distinguished Prof of History, 93-. **HONORS AND AWARDS** MacArthur Fellowship, 1989; Charles E. Frankel Prize, 1995. **SELECTED PUBLICATIONS** Publications: Voices of the Civil Rights Movement: Black American Freedom Songs, 1960-1966. **CONTACT ADDRESS** Dept of History, American Univ, 4400 Massachusetts Ave NW, Washington, DC 20016.

REARDON, JOHN J.
DISCIPLINE HISTORY **EDUCATION** Georgetown Univ, PhD. **CAREER** Hist, Loyola Univ. **RESEARCH** Thematic research into the cosmopolitan dimensions in American history. **SELECTED PUBLICATIONS** Auth, Edmund Randolph: A Biography, NY: Macmillan, 75; Payton Randolph: 1721-1775 One Who Presided, NC: Carolina Acad Press, 82; America and the Multinational Corporation: The History of a Troubled Partnership 1945-1990, Praeger, 92. **CONTACT ADDRESS** Loyola Univ, Chicago, 6525 N Sheridan Rd, Chicago, IL 60626-5385. **EMAIL** jreardo@wpo.it.luc.edu

REARICK, CHARLES
PERSONAL Born 08/02/1942, St. James, MO, 3 children **DISCIPLINE** MODERN EUROPEAN HISTORY **EDUCATION** Col Idaho, BA, 64; Harvard Univ, MA, 65, PhD, 68. **CAREER** Asst prof 68-74, assoc prof hist 74-83, prof hist 83-, Univ Ma, Amherst, 74- **MEMBERSHIPS** Soc Fr Hist Studies. **RESEARCH** Modern French history; modern European cultural history. **SELECTED PUBLICATIONS** Auth, Symbol, legend, and history: Michelet as folklorist-historian, Fr Hist Studies, spring 71; Henri Martin--from Druidic traditions to Republican politics, J Contemp Hist, 10/72; Beyond the Enlightenment: Historians and Folklore in Nineteenth Century France, Ind Univ, 74; Festivals and politics: The Michelet centennial of 1898, Historians in Politics, Sage, 74; Festivals in modern France: The experience of the Third Republic, J Contemp Hist, 7/77; Pleasures of the Belle Epoque: Entertainment and Festivity in Turn-of-the-Century France, 85; The French in Love and War: Popular Culture in the Era of the World Wars, 97. **CONTACT ADDRESS** Dept Hist, Univ of Massachusetts, Amherst, Amherst, MA 01003-0002.

REBER, VERA BLINN
PERSONAL Born 05/23/1941, Hong Kong, m, 1979, 1 child **DISCIPLINE** LATIN AMERICA AND AFRICAN HISTORY **EDUCATION** Univ Indianapolis, BA, 63 (History and Social Science); Univ Wis, Madison, MA, 67 (Comparative Tropical Hist); PhD, 72 (Latin America and African Hist). **CAREER** Asst prof, 70-72, assoc prof, 72-78, Prof, Shippensburg Univ, 78-. **HONORS AND AWARDS** Tinker Found, 79; NEH Summer Seminar, 76, 82, 93; Social Science Res grant, 86; Arthur P. Whitaker Prize, Honorable Mention, 88; NEH Institute, History of Medicine, 95; Tibesar Prize, Conference on Latin American History, 00. **MEMBERSHIPS** Am Hist Asn; Conference on Latin Am Hist; Latin Am Studies Asn; World Hist Asn. **RESEARCH** 19th Century Argentina and Paraguay-economic, medical and social history. **SELECTED PUBLICATIONS** Auth, The Demographics of Paraguay: A Reinterpretation of the Great War, 1864-1870, The Hispanic Am Hist Rev 68: 2, May 88; Teaching Undergraduates to Think Like Historians, in His-

tory Anew: Innovations in the Teaching of History Today, ed Robert Blackey, The Univ Press, CA State Univ, 93; A Nineteenth Century Development Model with Lessons for the 1990's: The Case of Paraguay 1810-1864, Latin American Essays, Vol VII, ed Alvin Cohen, Juan Espadas and Vera Reber, Middle Atlantic Council of Latin Am Studies, 94; El Comercio Exterior en la Economica del Paraguay (1810-1860), Investigationes y Ensayos, Vol 44, Buenos Aires, Argentina; Small Farmers in the Economy: The Paraguayan Example, 1810-1865, The Americas, April 95; Pocket Folders and Discussion Participation, The Teaching Professor, 12:2, May 98; Blood, Coughs, and Fever: Tuberculosis and the Working Class of Buenos Aires, Argentina, 1885-1915, in Social Hist of Medicine, 12, (99); "Misery, Pain and Death: Tuberculosis in Nineteenth Century Buenos Aires,"The Americas 56 (00); 497-528. **CONTACT ADDRESS** 314 E. King St., Shippensburg, PA 17257. **EMAIL** vbrebe@ark.ship.edu

RECTOR, JOHN L.
PERSONAL Born 08/08/1943, Walla Walla, WA, m, 1969, 5 children **DISCIPLINE** HISTORY **EDUCATION** Whitman Col, BA, 65; Ind Univ, MA, 70; PhD, 76. **CAREER** Instr, Lewis and Clark Col, 76; assoc prof, Catholic Univ Puerto Rico, 77-87; asst prof, Catholic Univ of Chile, 83-84; prof, Western Ore Univ, 87-. **HONORS AND AWARDS** Fulbright Dissertation Fel; Orgn of Am States Fel; Fulbright Teaching Fel. **MEMBERSHIPS** Latin Am Studies Asn, Phi Alpha Theta. **RESEARCH** Chilean History. **SELECTED PUBLICATIONS** Auth, "Pensamiento realidad economica durante la independencia de Chile," Quintas Jornalas de Historia de Chile (80); auth, "Arturo Alessandr" in Dictionary of Modern Peal Leaders (85); auth, "El impacto economico de la independencia de Chile," Historia 20 (86). **CONTACT ADDRESS** Dept Soc Sci, Western Ore Univ, 345 Monmouth Ave N, Monmouth, OR 97361-1314. **EMAIL** rectorj@wou.edu

REDIKER, MARCUS
PERSONAL Born 10/14/1951, Owensboro, KY, m, 1983, 2 children **DISCIPLINE** HISTORY **EDUCATION** Va Commonwealth Univ, BA, 76; Univ Pa, MA, 78; PhD, 82. **CAREER** Asst/Assoc Prof, Georgetown Univ, 82-94; Assoc Prof, Univ of Pittsburgh, 94-. **HONORS AND AWARDS** Nat Endowment for Humanities Fel; John Simon Guggenheim Memorial Found Fel; Andrew P. Mellon Found Fel; John Hope Franklin Prize, Am Studies Asn, 88; Merle Curti Soc Hist Awd, Orgn of Am Historians, 88. **MEMBERSHIPS** AHA, Orgn of Am Historians, Am Studies Asn. **RESEARCH** Early American History, Atlantic History, Working-Class History, Maritime History. **SELECTED PUBLICATIONS** Auth, Between the Devil and the Deep Blue Sea: Merchant Seamen, Pirates, and the Anglo-American Maritime World, 1700-1750, Cambridge Univ Press, 87; coauth, The Many-Headed Hydra: The Hidden History of the Revolutionary Atlantic, Beacon Press, 00. **CONTACT ADDRESS** Dept Hist, Univ of Pittsburgh, 3K25 Posvar Hall, Pittsburgh, PA 15260. **EMAIL** red1@imap.pitt.edu

REDMOUNT, CAROL A.
PERSONAL Born 09/15/1952, Indianapolis, IN, m **DISCIPLINE** ARCHAEOLOGY **EDUCATION** Oberlin Col, BA, 70; Harvard Div Sch, MTS, 74; Univ Chicago, PhD, 89. **CAREER** Lectr, asst and assoc prof, Near East Studies, Univ Calif, Berkeley, 90- . **HONORS AND AWARDS** Phi Beta Kappa; Hellman Family Fac Fund Awd. **MEMBERSHIPS** Am Sch of Oriental Res; Am Res Ctr in Egypt; Soc for Stud of Egyptian Antiquities; ICOMOS. **RESEARCH** Egyptian archaeology; Syro-Palestinian archaeology; interrelations among the Aegean, Egypt and The Levant; pottery studies. **SELECTED PUBLICATIONS** Coauth, The City of the Lions: New Explorations at Tell el-Muqdam, Bull of the Egyptian Exploration Soc, 93; coauth, The 1993 Field Season of the Berkeley Tell el-Muqdam Project: Preliminary Report, Newsl of the Am Res Ctr in Egypt, 94; auth, Ethnicity, Pottery and the Hyksos at Tell el-Maskhuta in the Egyptian Delta, Bibl Archaeol, 95; auth, The Wadi Tumilat and the Canal of the Pharaohs, J of Near Eastern Stud, 95; auth, Of Silts and Marls and Mixes: Analysis of Modern Egyptian Pottery, Gottinger Miszellen, 95; auth, Major and Trace Element Analysis of Modern Egyptian Pottery, J of Archaeol Sci, 96; coauth, Tales of a Delta Site: Preliminary Report on the 1995 Field Season at Tell el-Muqdam, J of the Am Res Ctr in Egypt, 97; auth, Bitter Lives: Israel In and Out of Egypt, in Coogan, ed, Oxford History of the Biblical World, Oxford, 98. **CONTACT ADDRESS** Near East Studies Dept, Univ of California, Berkeley, Berkeley, CA 94720-1940. **EMAIL** redmount@socrates.berkeley.edu

REED, BRADLEY W.
PERSONAL Born 09/14/1956, OR **DISCIPLINE** HISTORY **EDUCATION** Univ OR, BA, 80; Univ WA, MA, 89; Univ Calif at Los Angeles, PhD, 94. **CAREER** From asst prof to assoc prof, Univ of Virginia, 94-00. **MEMBERSHIPS** AHA; AAS. **RESEARCH** Local history; History of Imperial and modern China; Urban history. **SELECTED PUBLICATIONS** Auth, "The Chinese Passive: Language Function as an Item of Interlingual Transfer in Second Language Acquisition," Proc Chicago Ling Soc (86); coauth, "On Applying Psycholinguistic Methodology to the Investigation of Syntactic Change," in Synchronic and Diachronic Approaches to Linguistic Variation and Change, ed. Thomas J. Walsh, (Georgetown Univ Pr, 88); coauth, "Experimental evidence of the transfer of L1 implicature in L2 acquisition," Proc of the 16th Annual Meeting of the Berkeley Ling Soc (90); auth, "Money and Justice: Clerks, Runners, and the Magistrate's Court in Late Imperial Sichuan," Modern China 21-3 (July 95), 345-382; auth, "Administrative financing and tax collection in the 19th-century Sichuan, a report from Ba County," Assoc Stud Chinese Soc and Cult 13 (98); auth, "Three Fees Bureau, Gentry Activism in Late Imperial Sichuan," Late Imperial China (Forthcoming); auth, "Talons and Teeth, County Clerks and Runners in the Qing Dynasty," Stanford Univ Pr 00. **CONTACT ADDRESS** Dept of Hist, Univ of Virginia, Randall Hall, Charlottesville, VA 22903-3244.

REED, CHRISTOPHER A.
DISCIPLINE HISTORY **EDUCATION** McGill Univ, BA, 78; Univ Glasgow, MPhil, 84; Univ Calif at Berkeley, PhD, 96. **CAREER** Fac member, Univ Okla, 95-96; vis instr, Reed Col, 96-97; vis asst prof to asst prof, Ohio State Univ, 97-. **HONORS AND AWARDS** Two Fulbrights; Comt for Scholarly Correspondence with China; U.S. Govt For Lang & Area Studies Awds; McGill-Glasgow Exchange Fel; Fulbright Senior Scholar Res Awd, 99. **MEMBERSHIPS** Am Hist Asn, Asn of Asian Studies, Chinese Business Hist Res Group, Business Hist Confr. **RESEARCH** Modern Chinese Urban and Business History, History of Technology, History of the Media (particularly print culture). **SELECTED PUBLICATIONS** Auth, "Steam Whistles and Fire-Wheels: Lithographic Printing and the Origin of Shanghai's Printing Factory System, 1876-1898," Shanghai Acad of Soc Sci Publications (94); auth, "The Communist Party in Shanghai, 1927-49," Chinese Studies in Hist: A J of Translations 28.2 (Winter 94-95); auth, "'Sooty Sons of Vulcan': Shanghai's Printing Machine Manufacturers, 1895-1932," Republican China 20.2 (95); auth, "A Hundred Fathers to One: Success & Failure in Two Wuhan Mutinies, 1911 & 1967", 00. **CONTACT ADDRESS** Dept Hist, Ohio State Univ, Columbus, 230 W 17th Ave, Columbus, OH 43210-1361. **EMAIL** reed.434@osu.edu

REED, JAMES WESLEY
PERSONAL Born 10/17/1944, New Orleans, LA, m, 1962, 2 children **DISCIPLINE** SOCIAL HISTORY **EDUCATION** Univ New Orleans, BA, 67; Harvard Univ, AM, 68, PhD, 74. **CAREER** Res fel hist, Schlesinger Libr, 73-75; prof hist, Rugers Univ, 75-, Dean, Rutgers Col, 85-94. **RESEARCH** Soc hist; hist of med; hist of behavioral sci. **SELECTED PUBLICATIONS** Auth, From Private Vice to Public Virtue: The Birth Control Movement and American Society Since 1830, Basic Bks, 78. **CONTACT ADDRESS** Dept of Hist, Rutgers, The State Univ of New Jersey, New Brunswick, 16 Seminary Place, New Brunswick, NJ 08901-1108. **EMAIL** jwr@rci.rutgers.edu

REED, JOHN JULIUS
PERSONAL Born 01/16/1913, Rochester, NY, m, 1941, 2 children **DISCIPLINE** AMERICAN HISTORY **EDUCATION** Univ Rochester, BA, 34, MA, 40; Univ PA, PhD(US hist), 53. **CAREER** Teacher, High Sch, NY, 35-41; instr hist & math, Univ PA, 42-45; from instr to assoc prof hist, 48-63, prof hist, 63-78, chmn dept, 71-78, dir Am studies, 72-78, emer prof hist, Muhlenberg Col, 78-; lectr, Trenton Ctr, Rutgers Univ, 47-48; La State Univ New Orleans, 64; Lehigh Univ, 79; Moravian Col, 80 & 81; Temple Univ, 81. **HONORS AND AWARDS** Lindback Found Awd, 61. **MEMBERSHIPS** OAH; Orgn Am Historians; PA History Asn, AAUP, OAH. **RESEARCH** History of United States political parties; the origins, early development, and quantitative analysis of the Whig party; Thaddeus Stevens and early history of the Whig party. **CONTACT ADDRESS** 320 S 23rd St, Allentown, PA 18104. **EMAIL** dadhistory@aol.com

REED, LINDA
DISCIPLINE AMERICAN HISTORY, POST-1865 **EDUCATION** Ind Univ at Bloomington, PhD, 86. **CAREER** Assoc instr, Ind Univ, 80-81; asst prof of Hist, UNC-Chapel Hill, 88; Martin Luther King, Jr/Cesar Chavez/Rosa Parks visiting prof, Mich State Univ, 89; ed asst, J of Am Hist, Ind Univ, 81-83; ASST PROF OF HIST, 88-92, DIR, AFRICAN-AM STUDIES PROG, 92-, ASSOC PROF OF HIST, 92-, UNIV OF HOUSTON. **HONORS AND AWARDS** Greenwood Award, Univ of Houston/Houston City Coun, 93; Young Black Achievers of Houston Award, 92; Carter G. Woodson Inst for Afro-Am and African Studies Res Fel, Univ of Va, 83-85; Hist Dept Scholar, 82, Foundation Grant, 82, W.E.B. Du Bois Writing Contest Winner, 81, Black Hist Month Scholar Award, 83, Ind Univ; CIC Minorities Fel, 78-80; B.S. awarded with great honors, 77; Alpha Kappa Mu Honor Soc, 76-77; Acad achievement awards and acad scholar, 73-77; Ford Found Fel, Univ of Va, 91-92; Res Initiation Grant, Univ of Houston, 90. **MEMBERSHIPS** Asn for the Study of Afro-Am Life and Hist; Asn of Black Women Historians; Org of Am Historians; Southern Hist Asn; Southern Asn for Women Historians. **RESEARCH** Twentieth Century U.S.; Women's History; the Civil Rights Era. **SELECTED PUBLICATIONS** Auth, Montgomery Bus Boycott, Mississippi Freedom Democratic Party, & Mississippi Freedom Summer, The Reader's Companion to U.S. Women's Hist, Houghton Mifflin Co, 98; auth, The Brown Decision: Historical Context in a Historian's Refl'ctions, Extensions, 94; auth, Simple Decency and Common Sense: The Southern Conference Movement 1938-1963, Ind Univ Press, 91; auth, Fannie Lou Hamer: Civil Rights Leader, Black Women in Am: An Historical Encycl, 93; ed, We Spcialize in the Wholly Impossible: A Reader in Black Women's History, Carlson Pub Co, 95; America: Pathways to the Present, Prentice Hall, 00. **CONTACT ADDRESS** Dept of Hist, Univ of Houston, Houston, TX 77204-3785. **EMAIL** lreed@uh.edu

REED, MERL E.
PERSONAL Born 08/14/1925, Syracuse, NY, m, 1958 **DISCIPLINE** AMERICAN HISTORY **EDUCATION** Syracuse Univ, AB, 50, MA, 52; La State Univ, PhD, 57. **CAREER** Asst, La State Univ, 52-57; instr hist, Tex Woman's Univ, 57-58; instr, Del Mar Col, 58-60, assoc prof & chmn dept, 60-61; asst prof soc sci, Ball State Teachers Col, 61-65; assoc prof hist, 65-72, Prof Hist, GA State Univ, 72- **MEMBERSHIPS** Orgn Am Historians; Southern Hist Asn; Labor Hist Asn. **RESEARCH** United States economic history; labor history; Jackson period. **SELECTED PUBLICATIONS** **CONTACT ADDRESS** Dept of Hist, Georgia State Univ, 33 Gilmer St SE, Atlanta, GA 30303-3080.

REED, T. V.
DISCIPLINE CULTURAL THEORY, CONTEMPORARY AMERICAN FICTION, AND THE 1960S **EDUCATION** Univ Calif, Santa Cruz, PhD. **CAREER** Assoc prof & dir Amer Stud, Washington State Univ. **RESEARCH** Various art forms as they have helped to shape social movement cultures from the Civil Rights era to the 1990s. **SELECTED PUBLICATIONS** Auth, Fifteen Jugglers, Five Believers: Literary Politics and the Poetics of American Social Movements, 92. **CONTACT ADDRESS** Dept of English, Washington State Univ, 1 SE Stadium Way, PO Box 645020, Pullman, WA 99164-5020. **EMAIL** reedtv@wsu.edu

REEDY, CHANDRA L.
PERSONAL Born 12/11/1953, NM, m, 1975, 1 child **DISCIPLINE** ARCHAEOLOGY **EDUCATION** Univ Calif, BA, 75, MA, 82, PhD, 86. **CAREER** Vis lectr, 88, asst prof, art cons dept, 89-94, Univ Calif; fel, Inst Transforming Undergrad Ed, dir, PhD prog in art cons res, 89-, sr staff mem, Ctr for Hist Archit & Design, 98-, assoc prof, Museum Stud Prog, Art Cons Dept, 94-, Univ Del. **HONORS AND AWARDS** Fel, Amer Anthrop Assn; Fel, Inst for Transforming Undergrad Ed. **MEMBERSHIPS** Amer Anthrop Assn; Amer Inst for Conser of Hist & Artistic Works; Amer Com for South Asian Art; Col Art Assn of Amer; Intl Inst for Conser of Hist & Artistic Works; Soc for Amer Archaeol; Soc for Archaeol Sci. **RESEARCH** South Asian art; history of cultural materials & technology; art & architectural conservation research. **SELECTED PUBLICATIONS** Coauth, Statistical Analysis in Art Conservation Research, Res in Conser ser no 1, J Paul Getty Trust, 88; coauth, Principles of Experimental Design for Art Conservation Research, GCI Sci Prog Rep, J Paul Getty Trust, 92; auth, The Role of a PhD Degree in the Education of a Conservator, ICOM Com for Conser 10th Triennial Mtg Preprints, ICOMCC, 93; coauth, Relating Visual and Technological Styles in Tibetan Sculpture Analysis, World Archaeol vol 25, 94; art, Thin Section Petrography in Studies of Cultural materials, J of Amer Inst for Conser vol 33, 94; coauth, Statistical Analysis in Conservation Science, Archaeometry vol 36, 94; coauth, Interdisciplinary Research on Provenance of Eastern Indian Bronzes: Preliminary Findings, S Asian Stud, vol 10, 94; co-ed, Research Priorities in Art and Architectural Conservation, Amer Inst for Conser, Wash, 94; auth, Optical Mineralogy, in Excavations at Anshan (Tal-e Malyan): The Middle Elamite Period, Univ Penn Museum, Phil, 96; coauth, Application of PIXE to the Study of Renaissance Style Enamelled Gold Jewelry, Nuclear Instrumental Methods in Physics Res, B: Beam Interactions with Materials & Atoms, vol 109/10, 96; auth, Tibetan Bronzes: Technical Observations, Marg vol XLVII, 96; auth, Tibetan Sculpture, Dict of Art, MacMillan, 96; auth, "Introduction" to Thin-Layer Chromatography for Binding Media Analysis, Getty Conser Inst, LA, 96; auth, Himalayan Bronzes: Technology, Style, and Choices, Univ Del Press, 97; coauth, The Sacred Sculpture of Thailand, Walter Art Gallery Baltimore, 97; auth, Technical Studies of Gandharan Art, Gandharan Art in Context: East-West Exchanges at the Crossroads of Asia, Cambridge & New Delhi, 97; coauth, Electrochemical Tests as Alternatives to Current Methods for Assessing Effects of Exhibition Materials on Metal Artifacts, Stud in Conser, vol 43, 98. **CONTACT ADDRESS** Museum Studies Prog, Univ of Delaware, 301 Old College, Newark, DE 19716. **EMAIL** clreedy@udel.edu

REEDY, JAY
PERSONAL Born 12/21/1947, Long Beach, CA, m, 1978 **DISCIPLINE** HISTORY **EDUCATION** Univ Wis, Milwaukee, BA, 69; MA, 71; Univ Calif, Santa Barbara, PhD, 76. **CAREER** Asst to assoc prof, N Dak State Univ, 78-89; assoc to full prof, Bryant Col, 90-. **HONORS AND AWARDS** Phi Alpha Theta; Am Philos Soc Res Grant; NEH Summer Sem Awds. **MEMBERSHIPS** Am Hist Asn, Int Soc for Intellectual Hist, Western Soc for French Hist, New England Hist Asn. **SELECTED PUBLICATIONS** Auth, "The Traditionalist Critique of Individualism in Post-Revolutionary France: The Case

of Louis de Bonald," Hist of Political Thought, vol XVI (95): 49-75; auth, "The Relevance of Rousseau to Contemporary Communitarianism: The Example of Benjamin Barber," Philos and Soc Criticism, vol 21 (95): 51-84; auth, "Language, Counter-Revolution and the 'Two Cultures'," in Nancy Struever, ed, Language and the History of Thought, Rochester: Univ of Rochester Press (96): 185-203; auth," From Enlightenment to Counter-Enlightenment Semiotics," Historical Reflections/ Reflexions historiques (forthcoming 2000); auth, "Louis de Bonald," in Oxford Encyclopedia of the Enlightening (forthcoming). **CONTACT ADDRESS** Dept Soc Scis & Hist, Bryant Col, 1150 Douglas Pike, Smithfield, RI 02917-1291. **EMAIL** jreedy@bryant.edu

REEDY, WILLIAM T.
PERSONAL Born 08/19/1932, Reading, PA, s **DISCIPLINE** MEDIEVAL ENGLISH HISTORY **EDUCATION** Yale Univ, BA, 54; Johns Hopkins Univ, PhD(hist), 63. **CAREER** Instr hist, State Univ NY Col New Paltz, 63-64; asst prof, 64-72, assoc, 72-96, prof 96-99, Emer Prof Medieval Hist, State Univ NY Albany, 99- **HONORS AND AWARDS** Am Phil Soc,67;Am coun learned soc,76-77 **MEMBERSHIPS** Mediaeval Acad Am; Haskins Soc. **SELECTED PUBLICATIONS** Auth, 'The origins of the general eyre in the reign of Henry I', Speculum, 10/66; Auth,'The first two Bassets of Weldon--Novi Barones in the early and mid-twelfth century', Northamptonshire Past & Present, 69-70; Auth, 'Were Ralph and Richard Basset really Chief Justiciars of England in the Reign of Henry I?', Acta, Vol II, The Twelfth Century, 75; Auth, Basset Charters, c1120-1250, Pipe Roll Soc London, 95. **CONTACT ADDRESS** Dept of Hist, SUNY, Albany, 1400 Washington Ave, Albany, NY 12222-1000. **EMAIL** wreedy@csc.albany.edu

REES, ELLEN R.
PERSONAL Born 09/04/1967, Providence, RI **DISCIPLINE** SCANDINAVIAN STUDIES **EDUCATION** Evergreen State Col, BA, 89; Univ Wash, MA; PhD, 95. **CAREER** Asst Prof, Ariz State Univ, 96-. **MEMBERSHIPS** Soc for the Adv of Scandinavian Study; MLA; Ibsen Soc of Am. **CONTACT ADDRESS** Dept Lang and Lit, Arizona State Univ, Box 0202, Tempe, AZ 85287-0202. **EMAIL** Ellen.Rees@asu.edu

REESE, JAMES VERDO
PERSONAL Born 12/23/1934, Itasca, TX, m, 1958, 2 children **DISCIPLINE** UNITED STATES HISTORY **EDUCATION** Rice Univ, BA, 57; Univ Tex, Austin, MA, 61, PhD(hist), 64. **CAREER** From instr to assoc prof hist, Tex Tech Univ, 62-77, assoc dean grad sch, 73-76, dir mus, 76-77; Prof Hist & Dean Sch Lib Arts, Stephen F Austin State Univ, 77-, Vis assoc prof hist, Univ Tex, Austin, 72. **MEMBERSHIPS** AHA; Orgn Am Historians; Southern Hist Asn; AAUP. **RESEARCH** Jacksonian era of United States history; American labor history; Texas history. **SELECTED PUBLICATIONS** Coauth, Texas: Land of Contrast, Benson, 72, 2nd ed, 78; auth, Early history of labor organizations in Texas, 68 & The evolution of an early Texas union, 71, Southwestern Hist Quart. **CONTACT ADDRESS** Off of the Dean of Lib Arts, Stephen F. Austin State Univ, Nacogdoches, TX 75962.

REESE, ROGER R.
PERSONAL Born 05/18/1959 **DISCIPLINE** HISTORY **EDUCATION** Tex A & M Univ, BA, 81; Univ Tex at Austin, MA, 86; PhD, 90. **CAREER** From asst prof to assoc prof, Tex A & M Univ, 90-00. **MEMBERSHIPS** Am Asn for the Advancement of Slavic Studies, Military Hist Soc. **RESEARCH** Soviet Social History, Soviet Military History. **SELECTED PUBLICATIONS** Auth, Stalin's Reluctant Soldiers, Univ Press of Kans, 96; auth, The Soviet Military Experience, Routledge, 00. **CONTACT ADDRESS** Dept Hist, Texas A&M Univ, Col Station, College Station, TX 77843-0001. **EMAIL** rreese@tamu.edu

REEVES, ALBERT COMPTON
PERSONAL Born 11/04/1940, Kansas City, KS, m, 2000, 2 children **DISCIPLINE** MEDIEVAL HISTORY **EDUCATION** Univ Kans, BA, 62; MA, 64; Emory Univ, PhD(Hist), 67. **CAREER** Asst prof Medieval Hist, Univ Ga, 67-70; asst prof, 70-73, assoc prof, 73-81, prof Hist, Ohio Univ, 81-98, prof emeritus, 98-; adjunct prof, Arizona Ctr for Medieval and Renaissance Studies, 99-. **HONORS AND AWARDS** Chairman, Ohio Univ Judiciaries Hearing Board, 79-98; asst chairman, dept of hist, Ohio Univ, 80-83; chairman, dept of hist, Ohio Univ, 83-87; vis fel in Medieval Hist, Borthwick Inst of Hist Res/Dept of Hist, Univ of York, UK, 88, 96; Student Affairs Fac Contribution Award, 90; Chairman, Richard III Soc (Am Branch), 94-98; Dickon Award, Richard III Soc, 97; Moffat Lecturer, Marshall Univ, 98. **MEMBERSHIPS** AHA; Medieval Acad Am; fel, Royal Hist Soc; Canterbury & York Soc; Ecclesiastical Hist Soc; North Am Conference on British Studies; North Am Asn for the Study of Welsh Culture and Hist; Richard III Soc. **RESEARCH** Medieval Wales; later medieval England. **SELECTED PUBLICATIONS** Auth, Pleasures and Pastimes in Medieval England, Alan Sutton Publishing (Stroud), 95; auth, "The Crisis of 1450 in English Public Life," Medieval Life 7 (97): 26-31; coed, Estrangement, Enterprise, and Educaiton in Fifteenth-Century England, Sutton Publishing (Stroud), 98; auth, "Great Seal," "Privy Seal," and "Signet," in Medieval England: An Encyclopedia, ed. P.E. Szarmach, M.T. Tavormina, and J.T. Rosenthal (Hamden, Garland, 98), 326-327, 614-615, 699-700; auth, "Jan Hus," Medieval Life 9 (98): 21-24; auth, "Richard II: A Case of Narcissistic Personality Disorder?" Medieval Life 12 (99): 19-22; auth, "Creative Scholarship in the Cathedrals, 1300-1500," in The Church and Learning in Late Medieval Society: Essays in Honour of Barrie Dobson, ed. C. Barron and J. Stratford (Stamford, Paul Watkins, forthcoming). **CONTACT ADDRESS** Arizona Ctr for Medieval and Renaissance Studies, 1560 Southpark Circle, Prescott, AZ 86305. **EMAIL** ProfCR@kachina.net

REEVES, THOMAS C.
PERSONAL Born 08/25/1936, Tacoma, WA, m, 1958, 3 children **DISCIPLINE** RECENT AMERICAN HISTORY **EDUCATION** Pac Lutheran Univ, BA, 58; Univ Wash, MA, 61; Univ Calif, Santa Barbara, PhD, 66. **CAREER** Asst prof hist, Univ Colo, 66-70, assoc prof, 70-73, prof hist, Univ of Wis Parkside, 73-; hist consult, WHA-TV, Madison, 76-78; historiographer, Episcopal diocese of Milwaukee, 81-85; historical adviser, PBS series on the American Presidency, 98. **HONORS AND AWARDS** Numerous research grants; Eleanor Roosevelt Inst fel, 74; Nat Endowment for Humanities fel, 76; Excellence in Res Awd, Univ Wis-Parkside, 92. **MEMBERSHIPS** Nat Asn Schol; Fel Cath Schol. **RESEARCH** The U.S. from 1877; politics and religion. **SELECTED PUBLICATIONS** Auth, Freedom and the Foundation: The Fund for the Republic in the Era of McCarthyism, Knopf, 69; ed, Foundations under Fire, Cornell Univ, 70 & McCarthyism, Dryden, 73; auth, Gentleman Boss: The Life of Chester Alan Arthur, Knopf, 75; ed, James de Koven, Anglican Saint, 78; auth, The Life and Times of Joe McCarthy, Stein and Day, 82; A Question of Character: A Life of John F. Kennedy, 91; ed, James Lloyd Breck, Apostle of the Wilderness, 92; auth, The Empty Church: the Suicide of Liberal Christianity, 96. **CONTACT ADDRESS** Dept of Hist, Univ of Wisconsin, Parkside, Box 2000, Kenosha, WI 53141-2000. **EMAIL** tcreeves@execpc.com

REEVES, WILLIAM DALE
PERSONAL Born 08/16/1941, New Orleans, LA, m, 1980, 2 children **DISCIPLINE** US HISTORY **EDUCATION** Williams Col, BA, 63; Tulane Univ, MA, 65; PhD, 68. **CAREER** Director, New Orleans Bicentennial Commission, 74-76; Trustee Terra Firma, 74-94; Pres, Louisiana Life Insurance Company, 84-91; Instructor of Hist, Tulane Univ, 67-68; Instructor of Hist, Univ of New Orleans, 68; Asst prof of hist, Xavier Univ, 68-74, Chairman of Hist dept, 71-74; Independent scholar. **MEMBERSHIPS** LA Hist Soc; LA Hist Asn; Nat Coalition of Ind Scholars. **RESEARCH** Louisiana hist, plantations, towns. **SELECTED PUBLICATIONS** Auth, PWA and the Competitive Theory of Administration, J of Am Hist, 73; auth, De La Barre: Life of a French Creole Family in Louisiana, vol IV in Jefferson Parish Hist series, Polyanthos, 80; auth, Public Works Administration in Government Agencies, Greenwood Encyclopedia of American Institutions, 82; auth, Historic City Park: New Orleans, Friends of City Park, 82; auth, West we go: From Cheniere to Canal, vol XIV in Jefferson Parish Hist series, Dan Alario, 96; auth, Manresa on the Mississippi: for the Greater Glory of God, Manresa, 96; auth, A Transitional Plantation House in Louisiana Architecture, Arris, the J of the Southeast Chapter of the Soc of Architectural Hists, 98; auth, "The Founding of a City," New Orleans Magazine International Edition, 98/99. **CONTACT ADDRESS** 5801 St Charles, New Orleans, LA 70115. **EMAIL** wdr@acadiacom.net

REFAI, SHAHID
PERSONAL Born 12/17/1936, Baroda (Vadodra), India, m, 1998, 4 children **DISCIPLINE** HISTORY **EDUCATION** MS Univ, BA, 59; MA, 62; Univ of Cambridge, PhD, 68. **CAREER** Vis Lecturer, Univ of CA, 71; Asst Prof, Central Washington Univ, 71-77; Assoc Prof, College of St Rose, 84-88; Prof of History, College of St Rose, 88-. **HONORS AND AWARDS** Abul Kalam Azad Prize, SSC Examination, 55, Society Scholarship, Cambridge Univ, 64-66, Lady Mountbatton Awd, Cambridge Univ, 67, College of St Rose Achievement Awds, 89-98. **MEMBERSHIPS** New York Conference on Asian Studies, State Univ of New York, 99-01, New York Conference on Asian Studies, The College of St Rose, 00. **RESEARCH** History of India, Indian Women's History, and Economic History of India. **SELECTED PUBLICATIONS** Rev, "The Association for Asian Studies Abstract of Papers," Univ of MI (Ann Arbor, MI), 96; rev, "The Review of Religious Research, 97; rev, "The Review of Religious Research, 98. **CONTACT ADDRESS** Dept Humanities & Fine Arts, Col of Saint Rose, College of St Rose, Albany, NY 12203. **EMAIL** refais@mail.strose.edu

REFF, THEODORE FRANKLIN
PERSONAL Born 08/18/1930, New York, NY, m, 1990, 2 children **DISCIPLINE** HISTORY OF ART **EDUCATION** Columbia Col, AB, 52; Harvard Univ, AM, 53, PhD, 58. **CAREER** From instr to assoc prof art hist, 57-67, grants from coun on res hum, 59, 61 & 63, Prof of Art Hist, Columbia Univ, 67-, Mem, Inst Advan Studies, 63; Am Coun Learned Soc & Am Philos Soc grants, 63 & 64; chmn nominating comt, Porter Prize, 66-67, chmn selection comt, 71-72; Guggenheim fel, 67-68 & 74-75; consult, Libr Art Ser, Time-Life Bks, 68-70; vis prof art hist, Johns Hopkins Univ, 70, City Univ NY, 71-72, Princeton Univ, 73 & NY Univ, 74; Am Philos Soc grant, 72; guest cur, Metrop Mus Art, 76-77; dir Sem Col Tchrs, Nat Endowment for Hum, 77-78; Am Coun Learned Soc fel, 81-82; Nat Endow for Hum fel, 88-89; Chevalier, Ordre des Arts & des Lettres, 89. **MEMBERSHIPS** Col Art Asn Am. **RESEARCH** Mod Art; esp Manet, Degas, Cezanne, Picasso. **SELECTED PUBLICATIONS** Auth, Love and death in Picasso's early work, Artforum, 5/73 & In: Picasso: 1881-1973, London, 73; Matisse: Meditations on a statuette and goldfish, Arts Mag, 11/76; Manet: Olympia, Penguin Bks, London, 76 & Viking, 77; Degas: The Artist's Mind, Metrop Mus Art & Harper, 76 & Thames & Hudson, London, 76; The Notebooks of Edgar Degas (2 vols), Clarendon, 76; Duchamp and Leonardo: L H O O Q-alikes, Art in America, 1-2/ 77; Degas: A master among masters, Metrop Mus Art Bull, spring 77; Painting and theory in the final decade, In: Cezanne: The Late Work, 77; ed, Modern Art in Paris, 1850-1900, Garland,81; Manet & Modern Paris, Nat Gal Art, 83; Degas et Son Oeuvre: A Supplement, Garland, 84; Paul Cezanne: Two Sketchbooks, Phila Mus Art, 89; Jean Louis Forain: The Impressionist Years, Dixon Gal, Memphis, 95. **CONTACT ADDRESS** Dept of Art History, Columbia Univ, 2960 Broadway, New York, NY 10027-6900. **EMAIL** tfr2@columbia.edu

REGALADO, SAMUEL
PERSONAL Born 03/22/1953, Glendale, CA, s **DISCIPLINE** HISTORY **EDUCATION** Calif State Univ at Northridge, BA, 80; Calif State Univ, MA, 83; PhD, 87. **CAREER** From vis lectr to prof, Calif State Univ at Stanislaus, 87-. **HONORS AND AWARDS** Smithsonian Inst Fac Fel, 94; Louise M. Davies Fel, Univ of San Francisco, 98. **MEMBERSHIPS** Orgn of Am Hist, Am Hist Asn, N Am Soc for Sport Hist, Western Hist Asn, Phi Alpha Theta. **RESEARCH** Sport in American History, Ethnic and Immigration History. **SELECTED PUBLICATIONS** Auth, Viva Baseball!: Latin Major Leaguers and Their Special Hunger, Univ of Ill Press, 98. **CONTACT ADDRESS** Dept Hist, California State Univ, Stanislaus, 801 W Monte Vista Ave, Turlock, CA 95382-0256. **EMAIL** regalado@toto.csustan.edu

REGUER, SARA
PERSONAL Born Brooklyn, NY, 2 children **DISCIPLINE** MIDDLE EAST & JEWISH HISTORY **EDUCATION** City Col New York, BA, 66; Yeshiva Univ, BReligEduc, 66; Columbia Univ, MA, 69, PhD(MidE hist), 76. **CAREER** Instr, 74-77, asst prof to prof Judaic Studies, Brooklyn Col, 77-, chp, 87-; Consult, Fed Off Educ, 76-; vis asst prof Jewish hist, Yeshiva Univ, 77-78; vis distinguished prof, Univ Naples, 97. **HONORS AND AWARDS** Res fel, City Univ New York, 78-79. **MEMBERSHIPS** AHA; MidE Studies Asn; Asn for Jewish Studies; Coord Comt Women Hist Prof. **RESEARCH** Contemporary Middle East; Jews of the Middle East. **CONTACT ADDRESS** Dept of Judaic Studies, Brooklyn Col, CUNY, 2901 Bedford Ave, Brooklyn, NY 11210-2813.

REHER, MARGARET MARY
PERSONAL Born Reading, PA **DISCIPLINE** HISTORICAL THEOLOGY, CHURCH HISTORY **EDUCATION** Immaculata Col, BA, 60; Providence Col, MA, 64; Fordham Univ, PhD, 72. **CAREER** Asst prof theol, Immaculata Col, 60-64; asst prof, 73-76, assoc prof, 76-80, Prof Relig, Cabrini Col, 80-93, Prof Emerita, 93. **MEMBERSHIPS** Col Theol Soc Am; Cath Hist Soc; Am Cath Hist Asn. **RESEARCH** Domestic and for outreach of communities of women relig established in Philadelphia. **SELECTED PUBLICATIONS** Auth, Pope Leo XIII and Americanism, In: The Inculcation of American Catholicism 1820-1900, Garland Publ Inc, 88; Americanism and Modernism -- Continuity or Discontinuity?, In: Modern American Catholicism, 1900-1965, Garland Publ Inc 88; Catholic Intellectual Life in America: A History of Persons and Movements, Macmillan Co, 89; Den[n]is J Dougherty and Anna M Dengle: The Missionary Alliance, Records Am Cath Hist Soc of Philadelphia, spring 90; Bishop John Carroll and Women, Archbishop Gerety Lectures, 1988-89, Seton Hall Univ, 89; Get Thee to a [Peruvian] Nunnery: Cardinal Dougherty and the Philadelpha IHM's, Records Am Cath Hist Soc of Philadelphia, winter 92; Phantom Heresy: A Twice-Told Tale, U S Cath Hist, summer 93; Review Symposium on Begin Catholic: Commonweal from the Seventies to the Nineties, Loyola Univ Press, 93, Horizons, spring 94; co-auth, From St Edward's School to Providence Center: A Story of Commitment, Records Am Cath Hist Soc of Philadelphia, spring-summer, 96; Mission of America: John J Burke in Peru, U S Cath His, fall 97. **CONTACT ADDRESS** Dept of Relig, Cabrini Col, 610 King of Prussia, Radnor, PA 19087-3698. **EMAIL** margaret.mcguinness@cabrini.edu

REICHMAN, HENRY F.
PERSONAL Born 02/10/1947, New York, NY, m, 1976, 2 children **DISCIPLINE** HISTORY **EDUCATION** Columbia Univ, AB, 69; Berkeley, PhD, 77. **CAREER** Asst prof, Memphis State Univ, 83-89; from asst prof to prof & dept chair, CSU Hayward, 89-. **HONORS AND AWARDS** Outstanding Univ Prof, CSU, 98-99. **MEMBERSHIPS** AHA, Am Asn for the Advancement of Slavic Studies. **RESEARCH** Russia and Soviet Union. **SELECTED PUBLICATIONS** Auth, "The Rostov General Strike of 1902," Russian Hist 9(1) (82): 67-85; auth, "Tsarist Labor Policy and the Railroads, 1885-1914," Russian

Review 42(1) (83): 51-72; auth, Railwaymen and Revolution: Russia, 1905, Univ of Calif Press, 87; auth, "The 1905 Revolution on the Siberian Railroad," Russian Review 47(1) (88): 25-48; auth, Censorship and Selection: Issues and Answers for Schools, Am Asn of Sch Admin/Am Libr Asn, 88; auth, "Reconsidering 'Stalinism'," Theory and Soc 17(1) (88): 57-90; auth, "On Kanatchikov's Bolshevism: Workers and Intelligenty in Lenin's "What is to be Done?"" Russian Hist 23(1-4) (96). **CONTACT ADDRESS** Dept Hist, California State Univ, Hayward, 25800 Carlos Bee Blvd, Hayward, CA 94542-3001. **EMAIL** hreichma@csuhayward.edu

REID, DONALD MALCOLM
PERSONAL Born 12/24/1940, Manhattan, KS, m, 1964, 2 children **DISCIPLINE** MIDDLE EASTERN HISTORY **EDUCATION** Muskingum Col, BA, 62; Princeton Univ, PhD(Mid Eastern & Europ hist), 69. **CAREER** Asst prof hist, Ohio Univ, 68-69; asst prof, 69-76, assoc prof hist, Ga State Univ, 76-83, prof, 83-; Am Res Ctr in Egypt fel, 77-78. **HONORS AND AWARDS** NEH Fel, 71-72; Fulbright Islamic Civ Res Fel, 82-83; Fulbright-Hays Fac Res Abroad Fel, 87-88; Fulbright Res Fel, 98-99; Am Res Ctr in Egypt NEH Fel, 99. **MEMBERSHIPS** MidE Studies Asn; AHA; Am Res Ctr, Egypt. **RESEARCH** Modern Middle Eastern hist. **SELECTED PUBLICATIONS** Auth, The return of the Egyptian Wafd--1978, Int J African Hist Studies, Vol XII, 79; Fu'ad Siraj al-Din and the Egyptian Wafd, J Contemp Hist, Vol XV, 80; Lawyers and Politics in the Arab World, 1880-1960, Biblotheca Islamica, 81; Dawr Jamiat al-Qahira fi Bina Misr al-Haditha, Cairo: Markaz al-Mahrusa, 97; Cairo University and the Making of Modern Egypt, Cambridge Univ Press, 90, 91; Cromer and the Classics: Imperialism, Nationalism, and the Greek and Roman past in Modern Egypt, Middle Eastern Studies, 32, 1-29, 96; French Egyptology and the Architecture of Orientalism: Deciphering the Facade of Cairo's Egyptian museum, Franco-Arab Encounters: Studies in Memory of David C. Gordon, eds. Mathew Gordon and L. Carl Brown, Am Univ-Beirut, 35-69, 96; auth, "Whose Pharaohs? Museums, Archaeology and Egyptian National Identity form Napoleon to World War I, Univ of Calif Press, 01. **CONTACT ADDRESS** Dept of History, Georgia State Univ, Atlanta, GA 30303-3080. **EMAIL** dreid@gsu.edu

REIFF, DANIEL D.
PERSONAL Born 08/17/1941, Potsdam, NY, m, 1975, 2 children **DISCIPLINE** ART AND ARCHITECTURAL HISTORY **EDUCATION** Harvard Col, BA, 63; Harvard Univ, MA, 64, PhD, 70. **CAREER** Instr, Art Hist, Baylor Univ, 64-65, 66-67; acting asst sec, US Commission of Fine Arts, Washington, DC, 69-70; prof, Art Hist, State Univ of New York Col, 70-. **HONORS AND AWARDS** Kasling Memorial Lect, SUNY, Fredonia, 75; NEH fel for College Teachers, 84; Preservation League of NY State Architectural Heritage Honor Awd, 86; Graham Found for Advanced Studies in the Fine Arts fel grant, 91. **MEMBERSHIPS** Soc of Architectural Historians; Col Art Asn; Nat Trust for Historic Preservation; Soc for the Preservation of New England Antiquities; Victorian Soc in Am; Preservation League of NY State. **RESEARCH** Am architecture, 18th-20th centuries. **SELECTED PUBLICATIONS** Auth, Washington Architecture, 1791-1861: Problems in Development, US Commission of Fine Arts, 71, reprinted 77; Architecture in Fredonia, 1811-1972: Sources, Context, Development, Thorner-Sidney Press, 72; Small Georgian Houses in England and Virginia: Origins and Development through the 1750's, Univ of DE Press, 86; Historic Camps of Mt Arab and Eagle Crag Lakes, Mt Arab Preserve Asn, 95; Architecture in Fredonia, New York, 1811-1997: From Log Cabin to I M Pei, White Pine Press, 97; Houses from Books: Treatises, Pattern Books, and Catalogs in American Architecture, 1738-1950, A Hist and Guide, PA State Univ Press, forthcoming fall 2000. **CONTACT ADDRESS** Dept of Art, SUNY, Col at Fredonia, Fredonia, NY 14063-1198. **EMAIL** reiff@fredonia.edu

REIGSTAD, RUTH
PERSONAL Born 04/24/1923, Minneapolis, MN **DISCIPLINE** CLINICAL PHYSICAL THERAPY, HISTORY OF ENGLISH, SCIENCE **EDUCATION** St Olef Coll, BA, 45; Univ Minn, RTP, 47. **CAREER** Consultant, Wash State Health Dept, 41-73; clin phys therapist, 47-61; volunteer activities. **HONORS AND AWARDS** Stipends for Post Grad Study, UCLA, USC, NYU; Children's Bureau; US Public Health. **MEMBERSHIPS** Public Health Asn; Am Phys Therapy Asn; Am Acad of Rel; AF Asn. **RESEARCH** Correlations between studies of science and religion; Early childhood development. **CONTACT ADDRESS** Box 4237, Tacoma, WA 98438-0001.

REILL, PETER HANNS
PERSONAL Born 12/11/1938, New York, NY, m, 1968 **DISCIPLINE** GERMAN & INTELLECTUAL HISTORY **EDUCATION** NYork Univ, BA, 60; Northwestern Univ, Evanston, MA, 61, PhD(hist), 69. **CAREER** Lectr hist, Northwestern Univ, 65-66; asst prof, 66-73, Assoc Prof Hist, Univ Calif, Los Angeles, 73-, Consult ed, Jour Hist of Ideas, 77-80; Guggenheim grant, 78; Fulbright res grant, 79-80. **MEMBERSHIPS** AHA; Am Soc 18th Century Studies; Western Asn Ger Studies; Goethe Soc. **RESEARCH** Philosophy of history. **SELECTED PUBLICATIONS** Auth, History and hermeneutics in the Afklarung, J Mod Hist, 3/73; The German Enlightenment and the Rise of Historicism, Univ Calif, 74; Philology, culture and politics in early 19th century Germany, Romance Philol, suppl, 11/76; Johann Christoph Gatterer, Deutsche Historiker, 80; Barthold Georg Niebuhr and the enlightenment tradition, Ger Studies Rev, 2/80; Science And The Construction Of The Cultural Sciences In Late Enlightenment Germany - The Case Of Humboldt, Hist And Theory, Vol 33, 94. **CONTACT ADDRESS** Dept of Hist, Univ of California, Los Angeles, Los Angeles, CA 90290.

REILLY, BERNARD
PERSONAL Born 06/08/1925, Audubon, NJ, m, 1948, 10 children **DISCIPLINE** HISTORY **EDUCATION** Villanova Univ, BA, 50; Univ Pa, MA, 55; Bryn Mawr Col, PhD, 66. **CAREER** From Asst Prof to Prof, Villanova Univ, 66-. **HONORS AND AWARDS** John Nicholas Brown Prize, 82; Res Grant, 87; Premio del Rey Prize, Am Hist Asn, 90. **MEMBERSHIPS** AHA, Hisp Soc of Am, Am Cath Hist Asn, Medieval Acad of Am, Am Acad Res Historians of Medieval Spain. **RESEARCH** History, Medieval Spain. **SELECTED PUBLICATIONS** Auth, The Contest of Christian and Muslim Spain: 1031-1157, Basil Blackwell, 92; auth, The Medieval Spains, Cambridge Univ Pr, 93; auth, Cristaos e Muculmanos, Ed Teorema (Lisbon), 96; auth, Las Espanas medievales, Ediciones Peninsula (Barcelona, Spain), 96; auth, The Kingdom of Leon-Castilla under King Alfonso VII 1126-1157, Univ Pa Pr, 98. **CONTACT ADDRESS** Dept Hist, Villanova Univ, 800 E Lancaster Ave, Villanova, PA 19085-1603. **EMAIL** bernardreilly@villanova.edu

REILLY, LISA
DISCIPLINE ARCHITECTURAL HISTORY **EDUCATION** Vassar Col, BA, 78; York Univ, MA, 80; Univ NYork, PhD, 91. **CAREER** Asst prof. **RESEARCH** Medieval architecture. **SELECTED PUBLICATIONS** Auth, pubs on Peterborough Cathedral, Oxford. **CONTACT ADDRESS** Dept of Architectural History., Univ of Virginia, Charlottesville, VA 22903. **EMAIL** lar2f@virginia.edu

REILLY, TIMOTHY F.
PERSONAL Born 11/30/1940, Chicago, IL, m, 1990 **DISCIPLINE** HISTORY, GEOGRAPHY **EDUCATION** Univ Mo, MA, 67; PhD, 72. **CAREER** Teaching Asst, Univ Mo, 67-70; Asst Prof to Prof, Univ La, 70-. **HONORS AND AWARDS** J.W. Fulbright Group Projects Abroad, India, 74, China, 85, Brazil, 91. **MEMBERSHIPS** S Hist Asn, La Hist Asn, SW Soc Sci Asn, Am Asn of Univ Prof, Gulf S Hist Asn. **RESEARCH** Social, Religious and Intellectual History of the American South; Historical Geography of North America, Latin America, and Europe; Social History of Latin America, Africa. **SELECTED PUBLICATIONS** Auth, "The Conscience of a Colonizationist: Parson Clapps and the Slavery Dilemma," Louisiana History, 98; auth, "Updating the North-South Contrast: Anglo-Saxon and Latin Louisiana," Gulf Coast Historical Review, 98; auth, "Le Liberateur: New Orleans' Free Negro Newspaper," Gulf Coast Historical Review, 86. **CONTACT ADDRESS** Dept Hist & Geog, Univ of Louisiana, Lafayette, 200 Hebrand Blvd, PO Box 42531, Lafayette, LA 70504-2531.

REINER, ERICA
PERSONAL Born Budapest, Hungary **DISCIPLINE** ASSYRIOLOGY **EDUCATION** Sorbonne, Dipl Assyriol, 51; Univ Chicago, PhD(Assyriol), 55. **CAREER** From res asst to res assoc Assyriol, 52-56, from asst prof to prof, 56-73, John A. Wilson Prof Assyriol, Univ Chicago, 73-, Distinguished Serv Prof, 83-; Assoc ed, Assyrian Dictionary, Orient Inst, Univ Chicago, 57-62, ed, 62-, ed-in-charge, 73-96. **HONORS AND AWARDS** Guggenheim fel, 74. **MEMBERSHIPS** Am Orient Soc; Ling Soc Am; Am Philos Soc; fel Am Acad Arts & Sci. **RESEARCH** Linguistics; Babylonian literature. **SELECTED PUBLICATIONS** Auth, Surpu: A Collection of Sumerian and Akkadian Incantations, Weidner, Graz, 58; A Linguistic Analysis of Akkadian, Mouton, The Hague, 66; Elamite language, In: Handbuch der Orientalistik, Brill, Leiden, 69; Akkadian, In: Current Trends in Linguistics, Mouton, The Hague, 69; Babylonian Planetary Omens: Parts 1 & 2, Undena, 75 & 81, Part 3, Styx, 98; Astral Magic in Babylonia, Transactions Am Philos Soc, 85/4, 95. **CONTACT ADDRESS** Orient Inst, Univ of Chicago, 1155 E 58th St, Chicago, IL 60637-1540.

REINERMAN, ALAN JEROME
PERSONAL Born 03/22/1935, Cincinnati, OH, m, 1967, 1 child **DISCIPLINE** MODERN EUROPEAN HISTORY **EDUCATION** Xavier Univ, OH, BS, 57, MA, 58; Loyola Univ Chicago, PhD, 64. **CAREER** Instr hist, Loyola Univ Chicago, 62-63; from asst prof to assoc prof, Sacred Heart Univ, 63-70; prof, Appalachian State Univ, 70-73; prof hist, Boston Col, 73. **MEMBERSHIPS** AHA; Am Cath Hist Asn; Southern Hist Asn; Soc Ital Hist Studies (secytreas, 75-); Conf Group Cent Europ Hist. **RESEARCH** Metternich and the Papacy; Austria and the risorgimento; peasant unrest in Southern Italy. **SELECTED PUBLICATIONS** Auth, Austria and the papal election of 1823, Cent Europ Hist, 9/70; Metternich and reform: The case of the papal state, J Mod Hist, 12/70; Metternich, Italy, and the Congress of Verona, Hist J, 6/71; Metternich, Alexander I, and the Russian Challenge in Italy 1815-1820, J Mod Hist, 6/74; Metternich, the Powers and the 1831 Italian Crisis, Cent Europ Hist, 9/77; Metternich vs Chateaubriand, Austrian Hist Yearbk, 77; Austria and the Papacy in the Age of Metternich: Between Conflict and Cooperation, 1809-1830, Vol I, Cath Univ Am Press, 79; Austria and the Papacy in the Age of Metternich, In: Revolution and Reaction, 1830-1838, vol 2, 89. **CONTACT ADDRESS** Dept of Hist, Boston Col, Chestnut Hill, 140 Commonwealth Ave, Chestnut Hill, MA 02167-3800.

REINHARTZ, DENNIS PAUL
PERSONAL Born 04/29/1944, Irvington, NJ, m, 1966 **DISCIPLINE** RUSSIAN & EAST EUROPEAN HISTORY **EDUCATION** Rutgers Univ, AB, 66, AM, 67; NYork Univ, PhD, 70. **CAREER** Instr hist, Newark Col Eng, 68-70; from asst prof to assoc prof, Madison Col, 70-73; from asst prof to assoc prof, 73-98, asst dean lib arts, 76-79, prof hist & Russ, Univ Tex, Arlington, 98-; Reviewer, NEH, 74-; assoc ed, Red River Valley Hist J, 75-. **HONORS AND AWARDS** NY Univ Founders Day Awd for Acad Schol Achievement, 70; Col Lib Arts Constituency Coun Awd for Excellence in Teaching, 76; Notable NJ Author Citation for Milovan Djilas, 83; Presidio La Bahia Awd for The Mapping of the American Southwest, 87; The Adele Mellen Prize for The Cartographer and the Literati, Friends of the UTA Libr Fac Awd, 96; Fort Worth Country Day Sch Mack Family Schol; recipient of numerous grants and fellowships. **MEMBERSHIPS** Southwestern Asn Slavic Studies-(pres, 76-77); AHA; Am Asn Advan Slavic Studies; Southern Conf Slavic Studies; Rocky Mountain Assoc for Slavic Studies (pres. 84-85); Western Social Science Assoc, (pres. 90-91); Society for the History of Discoveries, (pres.) 93-95. **RESEARCH** Pre-Marxist 19th century Russian intellectual history; the Yugoslav Revolution; 20th century Balkan history; history of Cartography. **SELECTED PUBLICATIONS** Auth, Milovan Djilas: A Revolutionary as a Writer, Columbia Univ Press, 81; coauth, Teach-Practice-Apply: The TPA Instructional Model, Nat Educ Asn, 88; Geography Across the School Curriculum, Nat Educ Asn, 90; Tabula Terra Nova, The Somesuch Press, 92; auth, The Cartographer and the Literati: Herman Moll and his Intellectual Circle, The Edwin Mellen Press, 97; author of numerous journal articles, book essays, reviews, and other scholarly publications. **CONTACT ADDRESS** Dept of Hist, Univ of Texas, Arlington, PO Box 19529, Arlington, TX 76019-0529. **EMAIL** dprein@utarlg.uta.edu

REINHARZ, JEHUDA
PERSONAL Born 08/01/1944, Haifa, Israel, m, 1967, 2 children **DISCIPLINE** MODERN JEWISH & EUROPEAN HISTORY **EDUCATION** Jewish Theol Sem Am, BRE, 67; Columbia Univ, BS, 67; Harvard Univ, MA, 68; Brandeis Univ, PhD(Jewish hist), 72. **CAREER** Asst prof Jewish hist, Univ Mich, 72-76, assoc prof, 76-81, prof, 81-82; Richard Koret Prof Mod Jewish Hist, Brandeis Univ, 82-,Pres, Bradeis Univ, 94-. **HONORS AND AWARDS** Sr res fel, Nat Endowment for the Humanities, 79-80; Elected fel, of Leo Baeck Institute, 82; Shazar Prize in Hist (Israel-88); First recipient of the Pres of Israel Prize, 90; recipient of the Akiba Awd, presented by the Am Jewish comt, 96. **MEMBERSHIPS** AHA; Asn Jewish Studies; World Union Jewish Studies; Am Acad of Arts and Sci; Pres Advisory Commission on Holocaust Assets in the United States; Coun on Foreign Rel. **RESEARCH** German Jewish history; history of Zionism. **SELECTED PUBLICATIONS** Auth, Fatherland or Promised Land, The Dilemma of the German Jew 1893-1914, Univ Mich Press, 75; ed, The Letters and Papers of Chaim Weizmann 1918-1920, Rutgers Univ Press, 77; co-ed, The Jew in the Modern World, Oxford Univ Press, 80; ed, Dokumente zur Geschichte des Deutschen Zionismus, J C B Mohr, Tuebingen, 81; co-ed, Mystics, Philosophers & Politicians, Duke Univ Press, 82; auth, Chaim Weizmann: The Making of a Zionist Leader, Oxford University Press, 85; auth, Chaim Weizmann: The Making of a Statesman, Oxford University Press, 93; Israel in the Middle East, Oxford Univ Press; 2nd Chance--2 Centuries Of German-Speaking Jews In The United-Kingdom, J Of Modern Hist, Vol 65, 93; coauth, with Ben Halpern, Oxford Univ Press, 98. **CONTACT ADDRESS** President's Office, Brandeis Univ, 415 South St MS 100, Waltham, MA 02454-9110. **EMAIL** gould@brandeis.edu

REISCH, GEORGE
PERSONAL Born 12/25/1962, NJ **DISCIPLINE** HISTORY AND PHILOSOPHY OF SCIENCE **EDUCATION** Univ Chicago, MA, 90, PhD, 95. **CAREER** res fel, Northwestern Univ, 95-96; Vis asst prof, Il Inst Tech, 96-97; columnist, Stereophile, 96; technical writer, Shure Inc, 98-. **HONORS AND AWARDS** Phi Beta Kappa. **MEMBERSHIPS** Philos of Sci Assoc; Hist of Sci Soc; Hist of Philos of Sci Working Group. **RESEARCH** Philosophy of science; philosophy of history; history of physics and astronomy; history of philosophy; general history of science. **SELECTED PUBLICATIONS** Auth, "Did Kuhn Kill Logical Empiricism?" Philosophy of Science, 58 (91): 264-277; auth, "Planning Science: Otto Neurath and the International Encyclopedia of Unified Science," British Journal for the History of Science 27 (94): 153-175; auth, "Scientism Without Tears: A Reply to Roth and Ryckman," History and Theory 34 (95): 45-58; auth, "Terminology in Action," in Encyclopedia and Utopia, Kluwer, 96; "How Postmodern was Neurath's Idea of Unified Science," Stud in Hist and Philos of Sci, 97; "Epistemologist, Economist..and Censor: On Otto Neurath's Infamous Index Verborum Prohibitorum," Perspectives on Sci, 97; auth, "Pluralism, Logical Empiricism, and the Problem of Pseudoscience," Philosophy of Science 65 (98): 333-

348; coauth, "The Nature of Science: A Perspective from the Philosophy of Science," Journal of Research in Science Teaching 36 (99): 107-116; auth, "The Neurath-Carnap Disputes in the Context of World War Two," in proceedings of Analytical and Continental Aspects of Logical Empiricism: Historical and Contemporary Perspectives, (Univ of Pittsburgh Press, Paolo Parrini, ed), forthcoming; auth, "Logical Empiricism and the Unity of Science Movement," Cambridge Companion to Logical Empiricism, (Cambridge Univ Press), forthcoming. **CONTACT ADDRESS** 5246 N. Kenmore Ave., 1N, Chicago, IL 60640. **EMAIL** reischg@ripco.com

REISDORFER, KATHRYN
PERSONAL Born 04/10/1945, Slayton, MN **DISCIPLINE** HISTORY **EDUCATION** Univ Minn, BA, 68; St Cloud State Univ, MA, 87; Univ Minn, PhD, 93. **CAREER** Adj, St. Cloud State Univ, 87-93; TA andres asst, Univ of Minn, 87-93; instr, Yavapai Col, 93-98; vis prof, Embry Riddle Univ, 98-99; instr, Yavapai Col, 98-. **HONORS AND AWARDS** NEH Summer Sem, CUNY, 96; Harold Leonard Memorial Film Study Grant, Univ Minn, 90-91; Thomas F. Wallace Endowed Fel; Univ Minn, 89-90; **RESEARCH** Gender representations in literature and film, women in Arizona, dealing with inventorying and cataloguing archival material in Arizona. **SELECTED PUBLICATIONS** Auth, "The Last 100 Years: Arizona History Through Art", Am Art Rev, 00; auth, "Fatherhood - great expectations", Naming the Father: Legacies, Genealogies, and Explorations of Fatherhood in Modern and Contemporary Literature", Lexington, 00; auth, "The representation of women as mothers in Cather's My Antonia and Chopin's The Awakening", Literary Biography, Krieger, (forthcoming); auth, Yavapai Heritage Roundup: A Guide to Archival Repositories in Yavapai County, Yavapai County Lib Dist, (forthcoming). **CONTACT ADDRESS** Dept Lib Arts, Yavapai Col, 1100 E Sheldon St, PO Box 6121, Prescott, AZ 86301-3220. **EMAIL** Kathryn_Reisdorfer@yavapai.cc.az.us

REITZES, LISA B.
DISCIPLINE EIGHTEENTH TO TWENTIETH-CENTURY ARCHITECTURE AND AMERICAN ART **EDUCATION** Univ DE, PhD. **CAREER** Assoc prof, Truman State Univ. **SELECTED PUBLICATIONS** Pub(s), early twentieth-century Am pub arch, nineteenth-century Am sculpt, and women in arch. **CONTACT ADDRESS** Dept of Art Hist, Trinity Univ, 715 Stadium Dr, San Antonio, TX 78212. **EMAIL** lreitzes@trinity.edu

REMAK, HENRY HEYMANN HERMAN
PERSONAL Born 07/27/1916, Berlin, Germany, m, 1946, 4 children **DISCIPLINE** GERMAN, COMPARATIVE LITERATURE, WEST EUROPEAN STUDIES **EDUCATION** Univ Montpellier, lic es let, 36; Ind Univ, AM, 37; Univ Chicago, PhD, 47. **CAREER** Instr Ger & Span, Indianapolis Exten Ctr, Ind Univ, 39-43; from instr to prof Ger, 46-64, chmn W Europ studies, 66-69, vchancellor & dean fac, 69-74, Prof Ger & Comp Lit, Ind Univ, 64-, Dir Ger summer sch Middlebury College, Vermong, 67-71; assoc ed, Ger Quart, 58-62; ed, assoc ed, ed comm, 61-99, assoc ed, Yearbk Comp Lit, 61-66, ed, 66-78; Fulbright lectr comp & Ger lit, Univ Hamburg, 67; Guggenheim fel, 67-68; Nat Endowment for Humanities fel, 77-78; dir summer & yr-long seminars, Nat Endowmen for Humanities, 77 & 78-79; pres, Coordr Comt Comp Hist Lit in Europ Langs, Int Comp Lit Asn, 77-83 ; prof emer, 67-00. **HONORS AND AWARDS** Litt , Univ Lille, 73; Hon Prof, U of Sichuan, 99; litt d, univ lille, 73. **MEMBERSHIPS** Corresp mem Acad Sci, Arts & Lett, Marseilles. **RESEARCH** Franco-German literary relations; modern German literature; general comparative literature. **SELECTED PUBLICATIONS** Contribr, Comparative Literature: Method and Perspective, Southern Ill Univ, 71; auth, Der Rahmen in der deutschen Novelle, Delp, Munich, 72; Exoticism in Romanticism, Comp Lit Studies, 3/78; Der Weg zur Weltliteratur: Fontanes Bret Harteentwurf, 80; The Users of Comparative Literature, Value Judgment, 81; Die novelle in der Klassik uhd, Romanttik, 82; auth, Novellistische Struktur: Bassompierre, Goethe, Hofmannsthal, 83; Literary-History And Comparative Literary-History--The Odds For And Against It In Scholarship, Neohelicon, Vol 20, 93; auth, Structural Elements of the German Novelle from Goethe to Thomas Mann, 96. **CONTACT ADDRESS** Dept of Lit, Indiana Univ, Bloomington, Bloomington, IN 47401. **EMAIL** complit@indiana.edu

REMAK, JOACHIM
PERSONAL Born 12/04/1920, m, 1948, 2 children **DISCIPLINE** MODERN EUROPEAN HISTORY **EDUCATION** Univ Calif, Berkeley, BA, 42, MA, 46; Stanford Univ, PhD, 55. **CAREER** Instr hist, Stanford Univ, 54-58; from asst prof to assoc prof, Lewis & Clark Col, 58-65, chmn dept, 62-63; assoc prof, 65-67, Prof Hist Univ Calif, Santa Barbara, 67-, Chmn Dept, 77-, Danforth fac res grant, 60; vis assoc prof, Ind Univ, 63-64; Guggenheim fel, 66-67; Humanities Inst grant, 68; dir, Nat Endowment for Humanities Sem for Col Teachers, 75 & 77-78. **HONORS AND AWARDS** Borden award, Hoover Libr, Stanford Univ, 60; Higby Prize, J Mod Hist, 70. **MEMBERSHIPS** AHA **RESEARCH** German history; diplomatic history; Southeastern Europe. **SELECTED PUBLICATIONS** Auth, The Emperor's New Clothes, Yale Rev, 12/62; auth, The Gentle Critic, Theodor Fontane and German Politics, Syracuse Univ, 64; auth, The Origins of World War I, Holt, 67; rev ed, Harcourt Brace, 95; auth, Journey to Sarajevo, Commentary 7/68; auth, The Nazi Years, A Documentary History, Simon & Schuster, 69; ed, The First World War, Causes, Conduct, Consequences, Wiley NY, 71; ed, The Origins of the Second World War, Prentice-Hall, 76; co-ed, Another Germany, A Reconsideration of the Imperial Era, Westview, 88; auth, A Very Civil War, The Swiss Sonderbund War of 1847, Westview, 93; auth, Bruderzwist, nicht Brudermord: Der Schweizer Sonderbundskrieg von 1847, Orell Fussli Zurich, 97. **CONTACT ADDRESS** 22 Miramar Ave, Santa Barbara, CA 93108.

REMER, ROSALIND
DISCIPLINE HISTORY **EDUCATION** Univ Calif at Berkeley, BA, 84; UCLA, MA, 86, PhD, 91. **CAREER** ASST PROF, HIST, MORAVIAN COLL **MEMBERSHIPS** Am Antiquarian Soc **RESEARCH** Philadelphia Publishers, 1790-1830. **SELECTED PUBLICATIONS** Auth, "Old Lights and New Money: A Note on Religion, Economics, and the Social Order in Boston, 1740," Wm & Mary Quart 48, Oct 90; auth, "Preachers, Peddlers, and Publishers: Philadelphia's Backcountry Book Trades, 1800-1830," Jour of the Early Rep 14, Winter, 94; auth, "Building an American Book Trade: Philadelphia Publishing in the New Republic," Bus & Econ Hist 23, Fall, 94; auth, Printers and the Men of the Capital: The Philadelphia Book Trade in the New Republic, Univ Penn Press, 96; auth, "A Scottish Printer in Late Eighteenth-Century Philadelphia: Robert Simpson's Journey from Apprentice to Entrepeneur," Penn Mag of Hist & Biog, Jan/Apr 97; auth, "Capturing the Bard: An Episode in the American Publication of Shakespeare's Plays, 1822-1851," Papers of the Bibliog Soc of Am 91, June 97. **CONTACT ADDRESS** Dept of Hist, Moravian Col, 1200 Main St, Bethlehem, PA 18018. **EMAIL** mernr01@moravian.edu

REMINI, ROBERT VINCENT
PERSONAL Born 07/17/1921, New York, NY, m, 1948, 3 children **DISCIPLINE** AMERICAN HISTORY **EDUCATION** Fordham Univ, BS, 43; Columbia Univ, MA, 47, PhD(hist), 51. **CAREER** From instr to assoc prof hist, Fordham Univ, 47-65; chmn dept, 65-66, 67-71, Prof Hist, Univ Ill, Chicago Circle, 65-, Vis lectr, Columbia Univ, 59-60; Am Coun Learned Soc grant-in-aid, 60; Am Philos Soc grant-in-aid, 65-66 & 80; consult ed, Papers of Andrew Jackson, 72-; res prof humanities, Univ Ill, 77-; Guggenheim Mem Found fel, 78. **HONORS AND AWARDS** Encaenia award for Distinguished Tching, Fordham Univ, 63; Friends of American Writers award of Merit, 77; John Simon Guggenheim Fellow, 78-79; Huntington Library Fellow, 79; Rockefeller Found Fellow, 79 & 89; Silver Circle award for Tching Excellence, Univ of Ill at Chicago, 81; George Washington Medal of Honor, Freedom Found, 82; National Book award for Non-fiction, 84; Walter Lynwood Fleming Lectr, LA State Univ, 84; Chicago Found for Lit award for Non-fiction, 85; English-speaking Union of the US Ambassador of Honor Book award, 85; Phi Beta Kappa, Iota of Ill Chptr, 86; Univ Scholar award, Univ of Ill, 86, Carl Sandburg award for Non-Fiction, 89; Presidential Lecture, The White House, 91; Soc of Midland Authors award for Biography, 92; John Trotwood and Mary Daniel Moore Mem award for Best Article on TN hist, 96; D.B. Hardeman Prize, Lydon Baines Johnson Found award, 98. **MEMBERSHIPS** AHA; Orgn Am Historians; Southern Hist Asn. **RESEARCH** American history, 1789-1877; early national period; Jacksonian era. **SELECTED PUBLICATIONS** Auth, Martin Van Buren and the Making of the Democratic Party, Columbia Univ, 59; Election of Andrew Jackson, Lippincott, 63; Andrew Jackson, Twayne, 66; Andrew Jackson and the Bank War, Norton, 68; ed, The Age of Jackson, Harper, 72; auth, The Revolutionary Age of Andrew Jackson, 76, Andrew Jackson and the Course of American Empire, 1767-1821, 78 & Andrew Jackson and the Course of American Freedom, 1822-1832, Vol II, 81; auth, Andrew Jackson and the Course of American Freedom, 1822-1833, Harper & Row, Inc., New York, 81; auth, Andrew Jackson and the Course of American Democracy, 1833-1845, Harper & Row, Inc., New York, 84; auth, The Legacy of Andrew Jackson: Essays on Democracy Indian Removal and Slavery, LA St Univ Press, Baton Rouge, LA, 88; auth, The Life of Andrew Jackson, Harper & Row, Inc., New York, 88; auth, The Jacksonian Era, Harlan Davidson Pub Co, Arlington Heights, Ill, 89; co-auth, Andrew Jackson: A Bibliography, Bibliographies of Presidents of the United States, Meckler Corp, Westport, CT, 91; auth, Henry Clay: Statesman for the Union, W. W. Norton & Co, New York, 91; auth, The Battle of New Orleans, Viking Press, New York, 91; auth, Daniel Webster: The Man and His Time, W. W. Norton & Co, New York, 97; co-auth, The University of Illinois at Chicago: A Pictorial History, Arcadia Press, Charleston, S.C., 00. **CONTACT ADDRESS** Dept of Hist, Univ of Illinois, Chicago, Chicago, IL 60680.

REMPEL, RICHARD A.
DISCIPLINE HISTORY **EDUCATION** Saskatchewan Univ, BA; Oxford Univ, MA, PhD. **RESEARCH** Victorian and 20th century British political, social and intellectual hist. **SELECTED PUBLICATIONS** Auth, Unionists Divided: Joseph Chamberlain, Arthur Balfour and the Unionist Free Traders 1903-1914; auth, Prophecy and Dissent 1914-1916; auth, Pacifism and Revolution 1916-1918. **CONTACT ADDRESS** History Dept, McMaster Univ, 1280 Main St W, Hamilton, ON, Canada L8S 4L9. **EMAIL** rempelr@mcmaster.ca

RENDA, LEX
PERSONAL Born 03/16/1960, Plainfield, NJ, m, 1992, 1 child **DISCIPLINE** HISTORY **EDUCATION** Rut Univ, BA, 82; Univ Vir, MA, 84; PhD, 91. **CAREER** Instr, Caltech Univ, 91-92; asst prof, Univ Wis, 92-98; assoc prof, 98-. **HONORS AND AWARDS** Henry E Huntington Postdoc Fel; Grad Sch Res Comm Gnt. **MEMBERSHIPS** SSHA. **RESEARCH** US Political history. **SELECTED PUBLICATIONS** Auth, Running on the Record: Civil War Era Politics in New Hampshire, Univ Press Vir (Charlottsville), 97. **CONTACT ADDRESS** Dept History, Univ of Wisconsin, Milwaukee, PO Box 413, Milwaukee, WI 53201. **EMAIL** renlex@uwm.edu

RENDSBURG, GARY A.
PERSONAL Born 02/13/1954, Baltimore, MD, m, 1977, 3 children **DISCIPLINE** NEAR EASTERN STUDIES **EDUCATION** Univ NC, BA, 75; NY Univ, MA, 77; NY Univ, Phd, 80. **CAREER** Asst Prof, Canisius Col, 80-86; Prof, Cornell Univ, 86- **HONORS AND AWARDS** Nat Endowment for the Humanities Fel, 87. **MEMBERSHIPS** Am Orient Soc, Asn for Jewish Studies, Soc of Bibl Lit. **RESEARCH** The Bible, Hebrew language, Semitics **SELECTED PUBLICATIONS** Auth, The Redaction of Genesis, Eisenbrauns (Winona Lake, IN), 86; auth, Linguistic Evidence for the Northern Origin of Selected Psalms, Schol Pr, 90; auth, Diglossia in Ancient Hebrew, Am Orient Soc (New Haven, CT), 90; ed, Eblaitica: Essays on the Ebla Archives and Eblaite Language, 4 vol, Eisenbrauns (Winona Lake, IN), 87-00; coauth, The Bible and the Ancient Near East, W.W. Norton (New York), 97; **CONTACT ADDRESS** Dept Near Eastern Studies, Cornell Univ, Rockefeller Hall, Ithaca, NY 14853. **EMAIL** gar4@cornell.edu

RENGERT, GEORGE
PERSONAL Born 01/31/1940, Cardington, OH, m, 1967, 5 children **DISCIPLINE** GEOGRAPHY **EDUCATION** Ohio State Univ, BS, 64; MA, 67; Univ N C, PhD. **CAREER** Prof, Temple Univ, 70-. **MEMBERSHIPS** Am Soc Criminol, Asn of Am Geogr. **SELECTED PUBLICATIONS** Auth, Geography of Illegal Drugs, Westview Press; auth, Suburban Burglary, Charles Thomas Pub. **CONTACT ADDRESS** Dept Geog, Temple Univ, 1115 W Berks St, Philadelphia, PA 19122. **EMAIL** grengert@nimbus.temple.edu

RENNA, THOMAS JULIUS
PERSONAL Born 08/18/1937, Old Forge, PA, m, 1969, 3 children **DISCIPLINE** MEDIEVAL HISTORY **EDUCATION** Univ Scranton, BA, 65; Univ Nebr-Lincoln, MA, 67; Brown Univ, PhD(medieval hist), 70. **CAREER** Asst prof, 70-74, assoc prof, 74-79, prof hist, Saginaw Valley State Univ, 79-, Am Philos Soc res grant, 74. **MEMBERSHIPS** AHA; Mediaeval Acad Am; Am Soc Church Hist; Cath Hist Asn. **RESEARCH** Political thought; hagiography; Franciscan history; monasticism; France 800-1500. **SELECTED PUBLICATIONS** Auth, over 90 articles dealing with political theory, St. Augustine, monastic thought, and early Franciscan hist; Church and State in Medieval Europe 1050-1314, Kendall/Hunt, 74; The West in the Early Middle Ages, Univ Press Am, 77; The Idea of Jerusalem in Monastic Thought 400-1400, under review. **CONTACT ADDRESS** Dept of History, Saginaw Valley State Univ, 7400 Bay Rd, University Center, MI 48710-0001. **EMAIL** renna@svsu.edu

RESCH, JOHN P.
DISCIPLINE HISTORY **EDUCATION** Denison, BA, 62; Ohio State, MA, 65, PhD, 69. **CAREER** Assoc prof, Hist, Univ NHamp Manchester; prof of Hist, Univ of NHamp at Manchester. **HONORS AND AWARDS** NEH fel, 87-88; Sr Scholar, Fulbright Award, 01-02. **MEMBERSHIPS** Am Hist Soc; Am Hist Soc; Soc for Hist of the Early Republic. **SELECTED PUBLICATIONS** Auth, "Politics and Public Culture: The 1818 Revolutionary War Pension Act," Jour of the Early Rep, Summer 88; Auth, "Peterborough, New Hampshire: After the Revolution," in New Hampshire: The State that Made us a Nation, Peter Randall, 89; auth, "Peterborough, New Hampshire, 1750-1800: A Case Study of the Transformation of a Frontier Agricultural Community," in Themes on Rural History of the Western World, Iowa State Univ Press, 93; auth, Suffering Soldiers: Revoutionary War Veterans, Moral Sentiment and Political culture in the Early Republic, (Amherst: Univ of Mass Press, 99). **CONTACT ADDRESS** Univ of New Hampshire, Manchester, 400 Commercial St., Manchester, NH 03101-1113. **EMAIL** jpr@christa.unh.edu

RESIS, ALBERT
PERSONAL Born 12/16/1921, Joliet, IL **DISCIPLINE** RUSSIAN HISTORY **EDUCATION** Northwestern Univ, BS, 47, MA, 48; Russian Inst, Columbia Univ, cert, 50, PhD(hist), 64. **CAREER** Teacher hist, Joliet Twp High Sch & Jr Col, 50-53; field rep, Am Found Polit Educ, 53-54; lectr, univ col, Rutgers Univ, 56-58; asst prof hist, Paterson State Col, 58-64; asst prof, 64-67, Assoc Prof Hist, Northern Ill Univ, 67-; Prof, 73; Prof Emer, 92. **MEMBERSHIPS** AHA; Am Assoc Advan Slavic Studies. **RESEARCH** Communist policy toward world trade union movement; Lenin and the Russian revolutionary movement; Soviet foreign policy. **SELECTED PUBLICATIONS** Auth, The Profintern, In: Soviet Foreign Relations and World Communism, Princeton Univ, 63; Das Kapital comes to Russia,

Slavic Rev, 6/70; Lenin, Valdimir Ilich, In: Encycl Britannica, 74; Lenin on Freedom of the press, Russ Rev, 7/77; The Churchill-Stalin Secret Percentages Agreement on the Balkans: Moscow, October, 1944, Am Hist Rev, 4/78; Lenin, In: Enciclopedico Dizionario, 78; Collectivization of agriculture in the USSR, In: Mod Encycl Russ & Soviet Hist, 78; Spheres of influence in Soviet wartime diplomacy, J Mod Hist, 3/81; 1939, On The Eve Of World-War-II--The Unleashing Of World-War-I and the International System, Jahrbucher Fur Geschichte Osteuropas, Vol 40, 92; Cold-War And Revolution--Soviet-Amn Rivalry And The Origins Of The Chinese Civil-War, 1944-1946, Russian Hist-Histoire Russe, Vol 21, 94; auth, "Litvinov: Harbinger of the German-Soviet Non Aggression Pact," Europe-Asia Studies, 00. **CONTACT ADDRESS** Dept of Hist, No Illinois Univ, De Kalb, IL 60115. **EMAIL** resis@niu.edu

RESLER, MICHAEL
PERSONAL Born 07/07/1948, s **DISCIPLINE** GERMAN STUDIES **EDUCATION** William & Mary Col, AB, 70; Harvard Univ, AM, 73; Harvard Univ, PhD, 76. **CAREER** Teaching Fel, Harvard Univ, 72-76; Lectr, New England Conserv of Music, 74; From Asst Prof to Prof, Boston Col, 76-. **HONORS AND AWARDS** Phi Beta Kappa, William & Mary Col, 69; Woodrow Wilson Fel, 70; DAAD/Fulbright Fel, 70-71; Bernhard Blume Awd for Acad Excellence, Harvard Univ, 72-76; Grad Soc Prize, Harvard Univ, 75; Nat Endowment Humanities Fel, 80-81; Outstanding Acad Book Awd, Choice Mag, 88-89; Phi Beta Kappa Teaching Awd, Boston Col, 97. **MEMBERSHIPS** Goethe Soc of New England, MAA, AATG, Gesellschaft fur deutsche Sprache. **RESEARCH** Arthurian romance, Germanic philology, language pedagogy. **SELECTED PUBLICATIONS** Auth, "The Endings of the Definite Article as Primary Determinants in the Adjectival Phrase," Die Unterrichtspraxis 22 (89): 46-51; auth, "Daniel of the Blossoming Valley by der Stricker: Translation with Introduction and Notes," Garland Libr of Medieval Lit, vl 58 (94); auth, "Der Stricker," in Ger Writers and Works of the High Middle Ages: 1170-1280, Dict of Lit Biog, vol 138 (Detroit: Bruccoli Clark Layman, 94), 117-132; auth, "Thomasin von Zerclaere," in Ger Writers and Works of the High Middle Ages: 1170-1280, Dict of Lit Biog, vol 138 (Detroit: Bruccoli Clark Layman, 94), 133-140; auth, "Der Stricker, Daniel con dem Bluhenden Tal," Altdeutsche Textbibliothek, vol 92, 2nd rev Ed (95). **CONTACT ADDRESS** Dept Ger Studies, Boston Col, Chestnut Hill, 140 Commonwealth Ave, Lyons Hall 201c, Chestnut Hill, MA 02467-3800. **EMAIL** resler@bc.edu

REUTER, WILLIAM C.
PERSONAL Born 08/14/1933, Yosemite National Park, CA, m, 1954, 2 children **DISCIPLINE** UNITED STATES HISTORY **EDUCATION** Univ Calif, Berkeley, AB, 55, MA, 59, PhD(US hist), 66. **CAREER** Assoc prof, 65-74, Prof US Hist, Calif State Univ, Hayward, 74-95, Emeritus Prof Hist, 95-. **MEMBERSHIPS** AHA; Orgn Am Historians. **RESEARCH** United States political and social history, 1865-1920. **SELECTED PUBLICATIONS** Auth, The Anatomy of Political Anglophobia in the United States, 1865-1900, Mid-America, 61 & 5-7/79; Business Journals And Gilded Age Politics, Historian, Vol 56, 93. **CONTACT ADDRESS** Dept of Hist, California State Univ, Hayward, Hayward, CA 94542. **EMAIL** wreuter493@aol.com

REYERSON, KATHRYN L.
DISCIPLINE HISTORY **EDUCATION** Radcliffe Univ, PhD, 74. **CAREER** Prof **RESEARCH** Social and economic history of France in the twelfth through the fourteenth centuries. **SELECTED PUBLICATIONS** Auth, Business, Banking and Finance in Medieval Montpellier, 85; co-ed, The Medieval Castle: Romance and Reality, 84; The Medieval Mediterranean: Cross-Cultural Contacts, 89; City and Spectacle in Medieval Europe, 94. **CONTACT ADDRESS** History Dept, Univ of Minnesota, Twin Cities, 614 Social Sciences Tower, 267 19th Ave. S, Minneapolis, MN 55455. **EMAIL** reyer001@tc.umn.edu

REYNOLDS, ANN
DISCIPLINE ART AND ART HISTORY **EDUCATION** CUNY, PhD. **CAREER** Asst prof; taught at, Hunter Cole, Queens Cole, Ramapo Col & Fordham Univ. **HONORS AND AWARDS** Univ Tchg Excellence awd, Students' Asn. **RESEARCH** Post 1945 visual cult in the US and Europe; mod archit; museum exhibition practice; feminist theory. **SELECTED PUBLICATIONS** Publ in, Oct, Ctr & Art and Text. **CONTACT ADDRESS** Dept of Art and Art Hist, Univ of Texas, Austin, 2613 Wichita St, FAB 2.130, Austin, TX 78705.

REYNOLDS, CLARK G.
PERSONAL Born 12/11/1939, Pasadena, CA, m, 1963, 3 children **DISCIPLINE** HISTORY **EDUCATION** Univ Calif-Santa Barbara, BA, 61; Duke Univ, MA, 63; PhD, 64. **CAREER** Porf hist, US Naval Acad, 64-68, Univ Maine, 68-76, US Merchant Marine Acad, 76-78, Univ of Charleston, 88- ; cur & hist, Patriots Point Naval & Maritime Mus, Charleston, 78-87. **HONORS AND AWARDS** Distinguished Prof, Distinguished Teaching Awd, Distinguished Res Awd, Col of Charleston, 99. **RESEARCH** Maritime civilizations, Minoan civilization, Naval history. **SELECTED PUBLICATIONS** Auth, The Fast Carriers: The Forging of an Air Navy, (68); auth, Admiral John H. Towers: The Struggle for Naval Air Supremacy, (91); auth, Navies in History, (98). **CONTACT ADDRESS** Dept Hist, Col of Charleston, 66 George St, Charleston, SC 29424-1407.

REYNOLDS, DONALD E.
PERSONAL Born 07/20/1931, Munday, TX, m, 1960, 2 children **DISCIPLINE** AMERICAN HISTORY **EDUCATION** N Tex State Col, BA, 57, MA, 58; Tulane Univ, PhD(hist), 66. **CAREER** Instr hist & govt, Decatur Baptist Col, 58-61; assoc prof, 65-72, Prof Hist, E Tex State Univ, 72- **HONORS AND AWARDS** Tex Writer's Roundup Awd, 71. **MEMBERSHIPS** AHA; Southern Hist Asn; Orgn Am Historians. **RESEARCH** Southern history; Civil War and Reconstruction; military history. **SELECTED PUBLICATIONS CONTACT ADDRESS** Dept of Hist, East Texas State Univ, Texarkana, Commerce, TX 75428.

REYNOLDS, E. BRUCE
PERSONAL Born 05/29/1947, Kansas City, MO, m, 1982 **DISCIPLINE** HISTORY **EDUCATION** Cen Mo State Univ, BS, 69; MA, 77; Univ Hawaii, PhD, 88 **CAREER** Asst prof to prof & dept chair, San Jose State Univ, 88-. **HONORS AND AWARDS** Fulbright Grad Fel, Japan, 86-87; Thailand, 87-88; Crown Fpince Akihito Scholarship 75-86. **MEMBERSHIPS** Asn for Asian Studies, Am Hist Asn, The Hist Soc, Soc for Hist of Am For Rel, World War II Studies Asn, World Hist Asn. **RESEARCH** International relations in East and SE Asia, 1900-1950. **SELECTED PUBLICATIONS** Auth, Thailand and Japan's Southern Advance 1940-1945, St Martin's Press: New York, 94; auth, "From Anomaly to Model: Thailand's Role in Japan's Shifting Asian Strategy, 1941-1943," in The Japanese Wartime Empire, Princeton Univ Press, 96; auth, "The Opening Wedge: The OSS in Thailand," in The Secrets War, Washington, 92; auth, "Imperial Japan's Cultural Program in Thailand," in Japanese Cultural Policies in Southeast Asia During World War 2, New York, 91; auth, "International Orphans: The Chinese in Thailand During World War II," Journal of Southeast Asian Studies, (97); auth, "Aftermath of Alliance: The Wartime Legacy in Thai-Japanese Relations," Journal of Southeast Asian Studies, (90). **CONTACT ADDRESS** Dept Hist, San Jose State Univ, 1 Washington Sq, San Jose, CA 95192-0117. **EMAIL** ereynold@email.sjsul.edu

REYNOLDS, ELAINE A.
PERSONAL Born 11/30/1957, Ilion, NY, s **DISCIPLINE** HISTORY **EDUCATION** State Univ NYork at Buffalo, BA, 79; Cornell Univ, MA, 82; PhD, 91. **CAREER** Vis lectr, Hobart and William Smith Cols, 84-85; instr, Cornell Univ, 86; instr, William Jewell Col, 86-89; vis asst prof, Harlaxton Col, Grantham, England, 92; asst prof, William Jewell Col, 89-94, assoc prof, 94-99, prof, 99-. **HONORS AND AWARDS** Phi Beta Kappa, 79; Herbert H. Lehman Fel, 79-83; Cornell Univ Grad Fel, 79-82; Gertrude Gilmore Fel, fall 85; NEH Summer Stipend, 92; William Jewell Col Fac Lang Study Grant, 94; Parkway Baptist Church Distinguished Prof Awd, May 99. **MEMBERSHIPS** Am Hist Asn, North Am Conf on British Studies, Int Asn for the Hist of Crime and Criminal Justice, Coord Coun for Women in Hist. **RESEARCH** Women in English local government in late 18th and early 19th centuries; policing and local government in London in 18th and 19th centuries. **SELECTED PUBLICATIONS** Auth, "St Marylebone: Local Police Reform in London, 1755-1829," The Historian, LI, 3 (May 89): 446-466; coauth, "Politicians, Parishes and Police: The Failure of the 1812 Night Watch Bill," Soc Hist Soc Bull, 19 (spring 94): 25-26; auth, Before the Bobbies: The Night Watch and Police Reform in Metropolitan London, 1720-1830, Macmillan/Stanford Univ Press (98); auth, "Sir John Fielding, Sir Charles Whitworth, and the Westminster Night Watch Act, 1770-1775," Criminal Justice Hist, XVI (forthcoming). **CONTACT ADDRESS** Dept Hist, William Jewell Col, 500 College Hill, Liberty, MO 64068-1843. **EMAIL** reynoldse@william.jewell.edu

REYNOLDS, FRANK E.
PERSONAL Born 11/13/1930, Hartford, CT, m, 1997, 3 children **DISCIPLINE** HISTORY OF RELIGION, BUDDHIST STUDIES **EDUCATION** Princeton; Oberlin Col, BA, 52; Yale Univ, BD, 55; Univ Chicago, MA, 64, PhD, 71. **CAREER** Prog dir, Student Christian Ctr, Bangkok, 56-59; minister to foreign students, Univ Chicago, 62-65; from instr to asst prof, 67-71, assoc prof, 72-79, Prof Hist Relig & Buddhist Studies; Univ Chicago, 79-, chmn, Comt Asian Southern Asian Studies, 78-83, dir, Inst Advan Studies Relig, 92-00; Lectr hist, Chulalonkorn Univ, 57-59; vis prof, Stanford Univ, 70-71; ed, Hist Relig J, 76-; Asn Asian Studies Monograph Series, 77-83; assoc ed, J Relig Ethics, 90-, assoc ed, J Relig, 88-. **HONORS AND AWARDS** Jacob L. Fox fellow, 52; Danforth fellow, 60-64; Fullbright senior research fellowship, 73-74; NEH senior research fellowship, 78-79; NEH translation grant, 90-91. **MEMBERSHIPS** Am Soc Study Relig; Am Acad Relig; Asn Asian Studies; NAm Soc Buddhist Studies; Int Asn Buddhist Studies; Law & Soc. **RESEARCH** Therauada Buddhism; Thailand; comparative ethics. **SELECTED PUBLICATIONS** Coauth, Two Wheels of Dhamma, Am Acad Relig, 72; co-ed, Religious Encounters with Death, Pa State Univ, 77; co-ed & contribr, The Biographical Process, Mouton, 76; Transitions and Transformations in the History of Religion, E J Brill, 80; auth, Guide to Buddhist Religion, 80; co-ed & transl, Those Worlds according to King Buang: A Thai Buddhists Cosmology, Asian Humanities Press, 82; co-ed, Cosmogony and Ethical Order, Chicago, 85; co-ed, Myth and Philosophy, SUNY, 90; co-ed, Discourse and Practice, SUNY, 92; co-ed, Religion and Practical Reason, 94; co-ed, Life of Buddhism, 00. **CONTACT ADDRESS** Swift Hall, Univ of Chicago, 1025-35 E 58th St, Chicago, IL 60637-1577. **EMAIL** mgp2@midway.uchicago.edu

REYNOLDS, TERRY S.
PERSONAL Born 01/15/1946, Sioux FallS, SD, m, 1967, 4 children **DISCIPLINE** HISTORY **EDUCATION** Southern State Col, BS, 66; Univ Kans, MA, 68; PhD, 73. **CAREER** Asst Prof to Assoc Prof, Univ Wisc, 73-83; Assoc Prof to Prof and Dept Chair, Mich Technol Univ, 83-. **HONORS AND AWARDS** Norton Prize, Soc for Industrial Archeol, 85, 98. **MEMBERSHIPS** soc for the Hist of Technol, Soc for Industrial Archeol, The Newcomen Soc, Intl committee for the Hist of Technol. **RESEARCH** History of technology, especially history of engineering education, history of water power, history of mining. **SELECTED PUBLICATIONS** Auth, Sault Ste. Marie, Washington, 82; auth, Stronger Than a Hundred Men: A History of the Vertical Water Wheel, Johns Hopkins Univ Press, 83; auth, A History of the American Institute of Chemical Engineers, 1908-1983, New York, 83; ed, The Machine in the University: Sample Course Syllabi for the History of Technology and Technology Studies, Bethlehem, Penn, 87; ed, The Engineer in America, Univ Chicago Press, 91; co-ed, Technology and the West, Univ of Chicago Press, 97; co-ed, Technology and American History, Univ of Chicago Press, 97. **CONTACT ADDRESS** Dept Soc Sci, Michigan Tech Univ, 1400 Townsend Dr, Houghton, MI 49931-1200. **EMAIL** treynold@mtu.edu

RHIE, MARYLIN
DISCIPLINE ART HISTORY **EDUCATION** Univ Chicago, MA, PhD. **CAREER** Dir, Prog E Asian Stud; Jessie Wells Post Prof. **RESEARCH** Chinese Buddhist art. **SELECTED PUBLICATIONS** Collab as curator of a major exhibition of Tibetan art, Wisdom and Compassion, the Sacred Art of Tibet & coauth, bk of the exhibition, 91; auth, Early Buddhist Art of China and Central Asia, Leiden, Brill, Vol. I, 99. **CONTACT ADDRESS** Dept of Art, Smith Col, Hillyer Hall 111, Northampton, MA 01063. **EMAIL** mrhie@smith.edu

RHOADS, EDWARD J. M.
PERSONAL Born 01/07/1938, Canton, China **DISCIPLINE** HISTORY **EDUCATION** Yale Univ, BA, 60; Harvard Univ, MA, 61; PhD, 70. **CAREER** Asst Prof to Prof, Univ Tex, 67-; Res Assoc, Univ Pittsburgh, 98-99. **HONORS AND AWARDS** Fel, Woodrow Wilson Nat Found, 60-61; Fel, Nat Defense For Lang, 62-65; Grant, Am Coun of Learned Soc, 74-75. **MEMBERSHIPS** Asn for Asian Studies; Asn for Asian Am Studies. **RESEARCH** Modern Chinese history; History of the Chinese in the United States. **SELECTED PUBLICATIONS** Auth, "Asian Pioneers in the Eastern United States: Chinese Cutlery Workers in Beaver Falls, Pennsylvania, in the 1870s," Journal of Asian Am Studies, 99; auth, Manchus and Han: Ethnic Relations and Political Power in Late Qing and Early Republican China, 1861-1928, Univ Wash Press, 00. **CONTACT ADDRESS** Dept Hist, Univ of Texas, Austin, 1605 Pease Rd, Austin, TX 78703. **EMAIL** erhoads@mail.utexas.edu

RHOADS, LINDA S.
PERSONAL Born 02/22/1949, Harrisburg, PA, m, 1969, 2 children **DISCIPLINE** HISTORY OF THE BOOK, WOMEN'S HISTORY **EDUCATION** Simmons Col, BA, 71; Univ of Chicago, MA; ABD. **CAREER** Managing ed, Critical Inquiry, 74-77; asst ed to co-ed, New England Quart, 81-. **MEMBERSHIPS** Paul Revere Mem Asn, Mass Hist Soc, Col Soc of Mass, New England Women's Diaries Proj, Am Studies Asn, MLA. **RESEARCH** History of the Book, Women's History. **SELECTED PUBLICATIONS** Ed, Tradition and Innovation: Reflections on Northeastern University's First Century, Northeastern Univ, 98; auth, Amelia Peabody: A Biographical Study, 98; auth, Lt Col Ruby Winslow Linn: Doubling a Life of Service, 01. **CONTACT ADDRESS** Mass Hist Soc, 1154 Boylston St, Boston, MA 02215. **EMAIL** lrhoads@masshist.org

RHOADS, WILLIAM B.
PERSONAL Born 03/11/1944, Harrisburg, PA, m, 1966, 2 children **DISCIPLINE** ART HISTORY **EDUCATION** Princeton Univ, PhD, 75. **CAREER** SUNY New Paltz, currently Prof, Art Hist Dept, since 1970. **RESEARCH** Colonial Revival; FDR's sponsorship of art and architecture; art and architecture of the Hudson Valley; street and inter urban railways in America art and culture. **SELECTED PUBLICATIONS** Franklin D Roosevelt and Washington Architecture, Records of the Columbia Historical Soc, 89; Colonial Revival in American Craft, in: Revivals! Diverse Traditions, NY, Abrams, 94; auth, The Architecture of the Catskill Mountain Heritage Trail, Hudson Valley Reg Rev, 97; auth, "New York's White Wings and the Great Saga of Sanita," New York Hist 80, (99): 153-184; auth, "The Machine in the Garden: The Trolley Cottage as Ro-

mantic Artifact," Perspective in Vernacular Architecture 8, (00): 17-32. **CONTACT ADDRESS** 34 Plattekill Ave, New Paltz, NY 12561. **EMAIL** rhoadsw@matrix.newpaltz.edu

RHODES, RANDALL
PERSONAL Born 02/01/1959, Rochester, NY, s **DISCIPLINE** ART HISTORY **EDUCATION** Univ Chicago, BA, 79; Univ Chicago, MA, 81; Univ Chicago, PhD, 91. **CAREER** Buffalo State Col, 93-96; asst prof, Frostburg State Univ, 96-. **MEMBERSHIPS** CAA; AAH. **RESEARCH** Art hist; post-modernism; gender studies. **CONTACT ADDRESS** Frostburg State Univ, 101 Braddock Rd., Frostburg, MD 21532. **EMAIL** rrhodes@frostburg.edu

RIASANOVSKY, NICHOLAS
PERSONAL Born 12/21/1923, Harbin, China, m, 1955, 3 children **DISCIPLINE** MODERN HISTORY **EDUCATION** Univ OR, BA, 42; Harvard Univ, AM, 47; Oxford Univ, DPhil, 49. **CAREER** From Asst prof to assoc prof hist, Univ IA, 49-57; from assoc prof to prof, 57-69, Sidney Hellman Ehrman prof Europ hist, Univ CA, Berkeley, 69-, Fulbright grant, 54-55; Guggenheim fel, 69; sr fel, Nat Endowment for Hum, 75; Fulbright sr scholar, 79. **HONORS AND AWARDS** Am Asn Advan Slavic Studies Distinguished Contributor Awd, 93; AHA Awd for Scholarly Distinction, 95. **MEMBERSHIPS** AHA; Am Asn Advan Slavic Studies. **RESEARCH** Russ intellectual hist in the first half of the nineteenth century. **SELECTED PUBLICATIONS** Auth, Russia and the West in the Teaching of the Slavophiles, Harvard Univ, 52; Nicholas 1st and Official Nationality in Russia, 1825-1855, Univ Calif, 59; History of Russia, Oxford Univ, 63; The Teaching of Charles Fourier, Univ Calif, 69; A Parting of Ways: Government and the Educated Public in Russia, 1801-1855, Clarendon, 10/76; The Image of Peter the Great in Russian History and Thought, Oxford Univ, 85; The Emergence of Romanticism, Oxford Univ, 92; Collected Writings, Charles Schlacks, Jr. Publ, 93. **CONTACT ADDRESS** Dept of Hist, Univ of California, Berkeley, 3229 Dwinelle Hall, Berkeley, CA 94720-2550.

RICE, ARNOLD SANFORD
PERSONAL Born 05/09/1928, Albany, NY, m, 1954, 1 child **DISCIPLINE** AMERICAN HISTORY **EDUCATION** State Univ NYork Albany, BA, 50; Columbia Univ, MA, 51; Ind Univ, PhD, 59. **CAREER** From instr to assoc prof Am hist, 58-66, chmn dept hist, 71-77, Prof Am Hist, Kean Col NJ, 67-, Adj prof, Rutgers Univ, 59-63; Fulbright exchange prof, Netherlands, 64-65; Fulbright scholar, Dept Health, Educ & Welfare, 64-65; consult on minority hist & cult approx fifty sch districts in NJ, 67-73; res grantee, NJ Hist Comn, 71-72. **HONORS AND AWARDS** Distinguished alumnus award, SUNY Albany; distinguished tchg award, Kean Univ; Tchr of the Year, Kean Univ; Presidential Excellence Awd for Distinguished Scholarship, Kean Univ. **MEMBERSHIPS** Am Hist Asn; Pi Gamma Mu; Phi Alpha Theta; Alpha Sigma Lambda; Phi Kappa Phi. **RESEARCH** Ku Klux Klan in the 20th century; 20th century American social and cultural history. **SELECTED PUBLICATIONS** Auth, The Ku Klux Klan in American Politics, Pub Affairs, 62; The American Political Right Wing, Algemeen Dagblad, 4/65; Herbert Hoover, 1874-1964, 71 & Newark, 1666-1970, 77, Oceana; coauth, United States since 1865, Harper, 77; auth, American Civilization since 1900, Harper, 83; auth, The Warren Court, Assoc Faculty Press, 87; auth, United States History to 1977, HarperCollins, 91; auth, United States History from 1865, HarperCollins, 91. **CONTACT ADDRESS** Dept of History, Kean Col of New Jersey, Union, NJ 07083-7131.

RICE, EILEEN F.
PERSONAL Born 10/04/1914, Chicago, IL **DISCIPLINE** AMERICAN DIPLOMATIC HISTORY **EDUCATION** Siena Heights Col, BA, 39; Univ Detroit, MA, 46; St Xavier Col, Ill, cert theol, 51; Cath Univ AM, PhD, 59. **CAREER** Instr elem sch, MI & NM, 35-46; instr hist, Aquinas High Sch, Ill, 46-49; instr, St Ambrose High Sch, Mich, 49-50; instr, Cath Cent High Sch, 50-53; instr, Hoban Dominican High Sch, Ohio, 57-62; from asst prof to assoc prof, 62-69, chmn dept hist, 69-75, prof hist, Barry Univ, 69-, chmn soc sci, 75. **MEMBERSHIPS** AHA; Am Cath Hist Asn; Southern Hist Asn. **RESEARCH** US-Mex diplomacy. **SELECTED PUBLICATIONS** Auth, Diplomatic relations between the United States and Mexico as effected by the problem of religious liberty in Mexico 1925-1929, 59. **CONTACT ADDRESS** Dept of Hist, Barry Univ, 11300 N E 2nd Ave, Miami, FL 33161-6695.

RICE, LOUISE
DISCIPLINE ART HISTORY **EDUCATION** Harvard Univ, BA; Columbia Univ, PhD. **CAREER** Asst prof, Duke Univ. **RESEARCH** Renaissance and Baroque art and archit. **SELECTED PUBLICATIONS** Auth, The Altars and Altarpieces of New St. Peter's; pubs on seventeenth century Roman topics. **CONTACT ADDRESS** Dept of Art and Art Hist, Duke Univ, East Duke Building, Durham, NC 27706. **EMAIL** lrice@acpub.duke.edu

RICE, RICHARD
DISCIPLINE HISTORY **EDUCATION** Portland State Univ, BA, 66; Univ Ill, MA, 67; Harvard Univ, MA, 67, PhD, 74. **CAREER** Prof. **SELECTED PUBLICATIONS** Auth, The Role of Meiji Militarism in Japan's Technological Progress (rev), Jour Econ Hist, 77; Economic Mobilization in Wartime Japan: Business, Bureaucracy, and Military in Conflict, Jour Asian Studies, 79. **CONTACT ADDRESS** Dept of History, Univ of Tennessee, Chatanooga, 615 McCallie, Chattanooga, TN 37403. **EMAIL** Richard-Rice@utc.edu

RICE, STEPHEN P.
DISCIPLINE AMERICAN STUDIES, HISTORY **EDUCATION** Conzaga, BA, 86; Yale Univ, MA, 93, PhD, 96. **CAREER** ASST PROF, AM STUD & HIST, RAMOPO COLL **MEMBERSHIPS** Am Antiquarian Soc **SELECTED PUBLICATIONS** Auth, "Minding the Machine: Languages of Class in Early Industrial America, 1820-1860." **CONTACT ADDRESS** Am/Intl Stud, Ramapo Col of New Jersey, 505 Ramopo Valley Rd, Mahwah, NJ 10960. **EMAIL** srice@ramapo.edu

RICH, NORMAN
PERSONAL Born 04/19/1921, Cleveland, OH, m, 1952, 3 children **DISCIPLINE** MODERN HISTORY **EDUCATION** Oberlin Col, BA, 42; Univ CA, Berkeley, MA, 43, PhD, 49. **CAREER** Ed, Captured Ger For Ministry Archs, US Dept State, 49-54; res fel hist, Princeton Univ, 54-55; lectr, Bryn Mawr Col, 55-56; from asst prof to prof, Mich State Univ, 56-68; Prof hist, Brown Univ, 68-85, Emer Prof, 85- Res fel, St Antony's Col, Oxford Univ, 62-63; Guggenheim fel, 63-64. **HONORS AND AWARDS** Flbright fel, 80-81. **RESEARCH** Nineteenth and twentieth century Ger and Europ diplomatic hist, Baroque cult. **SELECTED PUBLICATIONS** Coauth, The Holstein Papers (4 vols), 56-63 & Friedrich von Holstein: Politics and Diplomacy in the era of Bismarck and Kaiser Wilhelm II, 64, Cambridge Univ; Age of Nationalism and Reform, 1850-1890, first ed, 70, sec ed, 77, & Ideology, the Nazi State, and the Course of Expansion, Vol I & The Establishment of the New Order, Vol II, In: Hitler's War Aims, 73-74, Norton; Why the Crimean War? A Cautionary Tale, New England Press, 90; Great Power Diplomacy, 1814-1914, McGraw Hill, 92. **CONTACT ADDRESS** 230 Arlington Ave, Providence, RI 02906.

RICHARD, CARL
PERSONAL Born 12/16/1962, Gueydan, LA, m, 1997, 2 children **DISCIPLINE** HISTORY **EDUCATION** Univ of Southwestern La, BA, 83; MA, 85; Vanderbilt, PhD, 88. **CAREER** Assoc Prof of History, Univ of Louisiana at Lafayette, 91-; Asst Prof of Hist, Univ of Southern Mississippi, 89-91; Vis Asst Prof of Hist, Univ of Texas at Arlington, 88-89. **HONORS AND AWARDS** Honorable Mention in History, Assoc of Amer Publishers, 94; Fraunces Tavern Museum Book Awd, 95; USL Foundation Distinguished Professor Awd, 97. **RESEARCH** US Intellectual History; Ancient Greece and Rome. **SELECTED PUBLICATIONS** Auth, "The Founders and the Classics: Greece, Rome, and the American Enlightenment, Harvard, 94; auth, "The Louisiana Purchase," Center for Louisiana Studies, 95. **CONTACT ADDRESS** Dept History & Geography, Univ of Louisiana, Lafayette, 200 Hebrard Boulevard, Lafayette, LA 70504-8400. **EMAIL** richard_carl@hotmail.com

RICHARDS, CONSTANCE S.
PERSONAL Born 09/18/1948, Columbus, OH, s **DISCIPLINE** ENGLISH, WOMEN'S STUDIES, BLACK STUDIES **EDUCATION** Ohio State Univ, BA, 90; MA, 92; PhD, 96. **CAREER** Lectr, Ohio State Univ, 96-; adj asst prof, Ohio Wesleyan Univ, 97-. **MEMBERSHIPS** Nat Womens Studies Assoc, Mod For Lang Assoc. **RESEARCH** Global/TransNational Women's Literature. **SELECTED PUBLICATIONS** Auth, On the Winds and Waves of Imagination: Transnational Feminism and Literature, (Garland, NY), 00. **CONTACT ADDRESS** Ohio Wesleyan Univ, 3550 Olentangy Blvd, Columbus, OH 43214-4023. **EMAIL** richards.5@osu.edu

RICHARDS, JOAN LIVINGSTON
PERSONAL Born Boston, MA, m, 2 children **DISCIPLINE** HISTORY OF SCIENCE **EDUCATION** Radcliffe Col, BA, 71; Harvard Col, MA, 79, PhD, 80. **CAREER** Tutor hist of sci, Harvard Univ, 75-78; lectr, Cornell Univ, fall, 79 & Harvard Univ, spring, 80; vis asst prof, Cornell Univ, 80-81, fel, 81-82; asst prof, 82-90, assoc prof hist of sci, Brown Univ, 90. **RESEARCH** Hist of mathematics; hist of Victorian sci; philos of mathematics. **SELECTED PUBLICATIONS** Auth, Evolution of empiricism: The non-euclidean geometry of Hermann von Helmholt, Brit J Philos Sci, 9/77; The reception of a mathematical theory non-euclidean geometry in England 1868-1883, In: Natural Order: Historical Studies of Scientific Culture, Sage Publ Inc, 79; The art and the science of British algebra: A study in the perception of mathematical truth, Hist Math, 80; Mathematical Visions, Academic Press, 89; auth, Angles of Reflection, W.H. Freeman, 00. **CONTACT ADDRESS** Hist Dept, Brown Univ, PO Box N, Providence, RI 02912-9127.

RICHARDS, JOHNETTA GLADYS
PERSONAL Born 07/18/1950, Bronx, NY, s **DISCIPLINE** AFRICAN-AMERICAN STUDIES **EDUCATION** Virginia State Coll, BA 1972; Univ of Cincinnati, MA 1974, PhD 1987. **CAREER** Trinity Coll, asst prof of history 1979-84; Univ of California Santa Barbara, lecturer Afro-Amer history 1977-78; Univ of Cincinatti, lecturer Amer history 1976-77; Northeastern Univ, adjunct instructor Afro-Am history 1971; Women's Studies California State Univ at Fresno, assoc prof 1984-88; San Francisco State Univ, assoc prof Black Studies 1988-. **HONORS AND AWARDS** Doctoral Fellowship, Natl Fellowship Fund, Atlanta GA 1978-79; Dissertation Fellowship, Center for Black Studies Univ of California 1977-78; Graduate Research Grant, Univ of Grad 1977; Danforth Fellowship, Univ of Cincinnati 1972-73; Mellon Research Grant 1981. **MEMBERSHIPS** Mem Assn for the Study of Afro-Am Life & History 1978-; mem Phi Alpha Theta Natl Honorary Frat of Historians 1974-; mem NAACP Hartford CT 1979-80;life mem Assn of Black Women Historians, 1983-; chair Far Western Region of the Assn of Black Women Historians 1986-88; Amer Historical Assoc, Pacific Coast Branch; national director, Assn of Black Women Historians, 1990-92; African American Museum and Library, Oakland, life member. **CONTACT ADDRESS** San Francisco State Univ, 1600 Holloway Ave, San Francisco, CA 94132.

RICHARDS, LEONARD
DISCIPLINE HISTORY **EDUCATION** Univ CA, PhD, 68. **CAREER** Prof, Univ Mass Amherst. **SELECTED PUBLICATIONS** Auth, Gentlemen of Property and Standing: Anti-Abolition Mobs in Jacksonian America, 70; The Advent of American Democracy, 77; The Life and Times of Congressman John Quincy Adams, 86; auth, The Slave Power: The Free North and Southern Domination 1780-1860, 00. **CONTACT ADDRESS** Dept of Hist, Univ of Massachusetts, Amherst, Mass Ave, Amherst, MA 01003. **EMAIL** llr@history.umass.edu

RICHARDS, MICHAEL DULANY
PERSONAL Born 11/03/1941, Great Bend, KS, m, 1961, 3 children **DISCIPLINE** HISTORY **EDUCATION** Univ Tulsa, BA, 62; Duke Univ, AM, 64, PhD, 69. **CAREER** From instr to asst prof hist, 66-74; assoc prof hist, Sweet Briar Col, 74-82,Prof Hist,82-; Nat Endowment for Hum fel hist, 75-76. **MEMBERSHIPS** Eur hist sec southern historical asn; Ger Stu Asn; Southeastern World Hist Asn; World Hist Asn. **RESEARCH** Popular cult in Europe; revolutions and revolutionary movements; 20th Century World. **SELECTED PUBLICATIONS** Auth, Rosa Luxemburg, heroine of the left, Hist Today, 2/72; Leiden relieved, Holland saved, Mankind, 12/74; Revolution in the twentieth century, Forum, 76; The lower classes and politics, 1800-1850, Int Labor & Working Class Hist, 11/77; Europe, 1900-1980: A Brief History, Forum, 82; Co ed, Makers of Modern Europe, 87, Twentieth Century Europe: A Brief History, Harland Davidson 98, Tamina As Alter Ego: Autobiography and History in: The Book of Laughter and Forgetting, 92, Ed. European History Newsletter, 97-02; auth, "How to succeed in revolution without really trying," J Soc History, Summer 95; auth, "Term Paper Resource Guide to Twentieth-Century World History," Greenwood. **CONTACT ADDRESS** Box AL, Sweet Briar, VA 24595-1056. **EMAIL** richards@sbc.edu

RICHARDSON, CHARLES O.
PERSONAL Born 03/13/1928, Reading, PA, m, 1969, 2 children **DISCIPLINE** MODERN HISTORY **EDUCATION** Lafayette Col, BA, 51; Univ Pa, MA, 55; Georgetown Univ, PhD, 63. **CAREER** Instr Hist, Otterbein Col, 61-62; instr, Albright Col, 62-64; asst prof, Rutgers Univ, 64-67; asst prof, 67-71, assoc prof Hist, Rider Col, 72-83; prof Hist, Rider Univ, 83-. **MEMBERSHIPS** AHA; Soc Fr Hist Studies; Am Acad Polit & Soc Sci. **RESEARCH** French diplomatic history, 1933-1940. **SELECTED PUBLICATIONS** Auth, French plans for allied attacks on the Caucasus oil fields, January-April, 1940, Fr Hist Studies, Spring 73; The Rome Accords of January 1935 and the coming of the Italian-Ethiopian War, The Historian, 11/78. **CONTACT ADDRESS** Rider Univ, 2083 Lawrenceville, Lawrenceville, NJ 08648-3099. **EMAIL** crichardson@rider.edu

RICHARDSON, JOE M.
PERSONAL Born 12/17/1934, Stella, MO, m, 1966 **DISCIPLINE** UNITED STATES HISTORY **EDUCATION** Southwest Mo State Col, BA, 58; Fla State Univ, MA, 59; PhD, 63. **CAREER** Asst prof hist, Univ Miss, 62-64; from asst prof to assoc prof, 64-71, Prof Hist, Fla State Univ, 71-, Sr fel, Inst Southern & Negro Hist, Johns Hopkins Univ, 68-69. **HONORS AND AWARDS** William R. Jones Most Valuable Mentor Awd, McKnight Found, 94. **MEMBERSHIPS** Asn Study Afro-Am Life & Hist; Southern Hist Asn. **RESEARCH** Black history; Post civil war; history of education. **SELECTED PUBLICATIONS** Auth, A Negro success story: James Dallas Burrus, J Negro Hist, 10/65; The Negro in the Reconstruction of Florida, Fla State Univ, 65; Christian Abolitionism: The American MIssionary Association and the Florida Negro, J Negro Educ, 71; Trial and Imprisonment of Jonathan Walker, Univ Fla, 74; To Help a Brother On: The first years of Talladega College, Ala Hist Rev, 75; Francis L Cardozo: a Black educator

during Reconstruction, J Negro Educ, 78; A History of Fisk University, 1865-1946, Univ Ala Press, 80; The failure of the American Missionary Association to expand congregationaliam among southern Blacks, Southern Studies XVIII, 79; auth, Christian Reconstruction: The American Missionary Association and Southern Blacks, 1861-1890, Univ Ga Pr, 85; coauth, Talladega College: The First Century, Univ Ala Pr, 90; "The Freedmen Bureau And Black Texans," Southwestern Hist Quart, 97 (93); "New-Orleans Dockworkers--Race, Labor And Unionism, 1892-1923," Labor Hist 34 (93). **CONTACT ADDRESS** Dept of Hist, Florida State Univ, 600 W College Ave, Tallahassee, FL 32306-1096.

RICHARDSON, LAWRENCE, JR.
PERSONAL Born 12/02/1920, Altoona, PA, w, 1952 **DISCIPLINE** LATIN ARCHAEOLOGY **EDUCATION** Yale Univ, BA, 42, PhD(classics), 52. **CAREER** Instr classics, Yale Univ, 46-47; field archaeologist, Am Acad Rome, 52-55; from instr to assoc prof, Yale Univ, 55-66; prof to James B Duke Prof, 66-91, Prof Emeritus Latin, Duke Univ, 91-; mem, Inst Advan Studies, 67-68; Mellon prof Am Acad Rome, 80-81. **HONORS AND AWARDS** Guggenheim fel, 58-59, Am Coun Learned Soc fels, 67-68 & 72-73; Nat Endowment for Humanities fel, 79-80; **MEMBERSHIPS** Corresp mem, Ger Archaeol Inst; Am Philol Asn; Archaeol Inst Am. **RESEARCH** Latin poetry; Roman archaeology. **SELECTED PUBLICATIONS** Auth, Pompeii: The House of the Dioscuri, Am Acad Rome, 55; Cosa and Rome: Comitium and curia, Archaeology, 57; coauth, Cosa: The Temples of the Arx, Am Acad Rome, 60; auth, Furi et Aureli, comites Catulli, Class Philol, 63; Catullus 67: Interpretation and form, Am J Philol, 68; The tribunals of the praetors of Rome, Roemische Mitteilungen 80, 73; ed, Propertius, Elegies I-IV, Univ Okla, 77; auth, Curia Julia and Janus Geminus, Roemische Mitteilungen 85, 78; Pompeii, an Architectural History, The Johns Hopkins Univ Press, 88; A New Topographical Dictionary of Ancient Rome, The Johns Hopkins Univ Press, 92; coauth, Cosa: The Buildings of the Forum, Am Acad Rome, 93; auth, A Catalog of Identifiable Figure Painters of Ancient Pompeii, Herculaneum, and Stabiae, The Johns Hopkins Univ Press, 00. **CONTACT ADDRESS** Dept of Class Studies, Duke Univ, PO Box 90103, Durham, NC 27708-0103.

RICHEY, RUSSELL EARLE
PERSONAL Born 10/19/1941, Asheville, NC, m, 1965, 2 children **DISCIPLINE** CHURCH HISTORY **EDUCATION** Wesleyan Univ, BA (high honors), 63; Union Theol Sem, BD (M Div), 66; Princeton Univ, MA, 68, PhD, 70. **CAREER** Instr, asst prof, assoc prof, prof of church history, Drew Univ Theol and Graduate Schools, 69-86; assoc dean for academic progs and res prof of church hist, The Divinity School, Duke Univ, 86-92, assoc dean for Academic Progs and prof Church Hist, 92-, prof Church Hist, Duke Univ, 97-00; dean, Candler Sch of Theol, Emory Univ, 00-. **HONORS AND AWARDS** Wesleyan: High Honors, Distinction in Hist, Phi Beta Kappa, Sophomore, Junior, and Senior Honor Societies, French Prize in Relig, Honorary Woodrow Wilson; Union Theol Sem: Int Fels Prog, Columbia, Prize in Church Hist, Senior Honor Society; Princeton: Rockefeller Doctoral Fel (withdrew to be Univ Teaching Fel, 68-69), Frelinghuysen Fel, dissertation received with distinction; Ecumenical fac assoc grant, Gen Comm on Christian Unity and Interreligious Concerns, for Bossey conf on Teaching Ecumenics and subsequent three-year service as liason from Commision to United Methodist seminaries, ended 92; Lilly Endowment grant, 91; planning and implementation grant from the Lilly Endowment for a major study of US United Methodism. **MEMBERSHIPS** Am Soc of Church Hist (member, Council 76-78, 95-97); Am Academy of Relig; Hist Soc of the United Methodist Church; adv bd: Quart Rev, Christian Hist, Church Hist, and J of Southern Relig. **SELECTED PUBLICATIONS** Co-ed with Donald Jones, American Civil Religion, Harper & Row, 74, Mellon Res Univ Press, 90; ed and coauth, Denominationalism, Abingdon Press, 77; co-ed with Kenneth E Rowe, Rethinking Methodist History, United Methodist Pub House, 85; auth, Early American Methodism, IN Univ Press, 91; co-auth and ed, Ecumenical and Interreligious Perspectives: Globalization in Theological Education, Quart Rev Imprint, 92; co-ed with Kenneth E Rowe and Jean Miller Schmidt, Perspectives on American Methodism, IN Univ Press, Kingswood/Abingdon, 93; co-ed and co-auth with R Bruce Mullin, Reimagining Denominationalism, Oxford Univ Press, 94; auth, The Methodist Conference in America: A History, Kingswood/Abingdon, 96; The Methodists, with James Kirby and Kenneth Rowe, Greenwood, 96; Connectionalism: Ecclesiology, Mission, and Identity, primary co-ed with Dennis M Campbell and William B Lawrence, UMAC, I, Abingdon, 97; The People(s) Called Methodist: Forms and Reforms of Their Life, co-ed with Dennis M Campbell and William B Lawrence, UMAC, II, Abingdon, 98; Doctrines and Discipline, co-ed with Dennis M Campbell and William B Lawrence, UMAC, III, Abingdon, forthcoming 99; Questions for the Twenty-First Century Church, co-auth and primary co-ed with Dennis M Campbell and William B Lawrence, UMAC, IV, forthcoming 99. **CONTACT ADDRESS** Candler School of Theology, Emory Univ, Atlanta, GA 30322. **EMAIL** rrichey@mail.duke.edu

RICHMOND, DOUGLAS WERTZ
PERSONAL Born 02/21/1946, Walla Walla, WA, m, 1979, 1 child **DISCIPLINE** HISTORY **EDUCATION** Univ Wash, BA, 68, MA, 71, PhD(hist), 76. **CAREER** Asst prof, 76-82, assoc prof hist, Univ Tex, Arlington, 82-92, prof, 92-, chemn, Latin Am studies comt, 76-89. **MEMBERSHIPS** AHA; Conf Latin Am Hist; Southwest Coun of Latin Am Stud. **RESEARCH** Nineteenth and twentieth century Mexico. **SELECTED PUBLICATIONS** Auth, The Venustiano Carranza Archive, Hispanic Am Hist Rev, 5/76; El nacionalismo de Carranza y los cambios socioeconomicos, 1915-1920, Historia Mexicana, 7-9/76; co-ed, Essays on the Mexican Revolution, Univ Tex, 79; auth, Mexican politics and society during the Carranza Epoch, 1913-1920, In: Essays on the Mexican Revolution, 79; Factional political strife in Coahuila, 1910-1920, Hispanic Am His Rev, 2/80; La guerra de Texas se renova: Mexican Insurrection and Carrancista Ambitions, 1900-1920, Aztlan, spring 80; Mexican immigration and border strategy during the revolution, 1920-1920, New Mex Hist Rev, 7/82; Venustiano Carranza's Nationalist Struggle, 1893-1920, Univ Nebr Press, 83; auth, Comparative Elite Systems in Latin Amica and the United States, 1876-1914, Revista de historia de Am, 114, 7/92-12/92; ed, Essays on the Mexican War, Texas A&M Press, 86; auth, Carlos Pellegrini and the Crisis of the Argentine Elites, 1880-1916, Praeger, 89; co-ed, Dueling Eagles: Reinterpreting the U.S. Mexican Conflict, 1846-1848, Texas Christian Univ Pr, 00. **CONTACT ADDRESS** Dept of History, Univ of Texas, Arlington, Box 19529, Arlington, TX 76019-0529. **EMAIL** richmond@uta.edu

RICHMOND, VELMA BOURGEOIS
PERSONAL Born 03/12/1931, New Orleans, LA, m, 1958, 2 children **DISCIPLINE** ENGLISH LITERATURE; MEDIEVAL STUDIES **EDUCATION** La State Univ, BA, 51, MA, 52; Oxford Univ, BLitt, 57; Univ NC, PhD, 59. **CAREER** Instr, La State Univ, 57-58; Instr to Prof, 58-96, Prof Emeritus English, Holy Names Col, 96-, Chmn English, 70-76, Dean Acad Affairs, 80-85. **HONORS AND AWARDS** Fulbright Schol, Oxford Univ, 55-57; ACLS Fel, 76; Project Dir, NEH Implementation Grant for Core Prog in Humanities Studies, 81-84; Conf on Christianity & Lit Bk Awd, 00. **MEMBERSHIPS** Medieval Acad; New Chaucer Soc; Medieval Asn Pac; Mod Lang Asn; Mod Humanities Res Asn; Christianity and Lit; Int Arthurian Soc. **RESEARCH** Chaucer; medieval romance; Shakespeare; children's literature; contemporary Catholic fiction. **SELECTED PUBLICATIONS** Auth, Laments for the Dead in Medieval Narrative, Duquesne Univ Press, 66; The Popularity of Middle English Romance, Bowling Green State Univ Press, 75; Muriel Spark, Frederick Ungar Publ Co, 84; Geoffrey Chaucer, Continuum, 92; The Legend of Guy of Warwick, Garland, 96; author of numerous articles and reviews; auth, Shakespeare, Catholicism, and Romance, Continuum, 00. **CONTACT ADDRESS** 1280 Grizzly Peak Blvd., Berkeley, CA 94708.

RICHTARIK, MARILYNN J.
PERSONAL Born 10/11/1965, Madison, WI, s **DISCIPLINE** IRISH STUDIES **EDUCATION** Harvard Univ, AB, 88; Oxford Univ, MPhil, 90; DPhil, 92. **CAREER** Instr, Northern Ariz Univ, 92-93; post-doctoral res fel, Univ of British Columbia, 93-95; asst prof, Ga State Univ, 95-. **HONORS AND AWARDS** Killim Post Doctoral Res Fel, Univ of British Columbia, 93-95; Res Fel, Nat Humanities Ctr, 98-99. **MEMBERSHIPS** MLA, Am Confr for Irish Studies, Int Asn for the Study of Irish Lit. **RESEARCH** Irish drama, Northern Irish literature and culture, theatre. **SELECTED PUBLICATIONS** Auth, Acting Between the Lines: The Field Day Theatre Company and Irish Cultural Politics 1980-1984, Oxford Univ Press, 95. **CONTACT ADDRESS** Dept English, Georgia State Univ, University Plaza, Atlanta, GA 30303-3083. **EMAIL** engmjr@panther.gsu.edu

RICHTER, DANIEL K.
DISCIPLINE HISTORY **EDUCATION** Thomas More, BA, 76; Columbia Univ, MA, 77, MPhil, 79; PhD, 84. **CAREER** PROF, HIST, DICKINSON COLL **MEMBERSHIPS** Am Antiquarian Soc **SELECTED PUBLICATIONS** Coauth, "Crossing the Cultural Divide: Indians and New Englanders, 1605-1763," Procs of the AAS 80, 80; auth, "Rediscovered Links in the Covenant Chain: Previously Unpublished Transcripts of New York Indian Treaty Minutes, 1677-1691," Procs of the AAS 92, 82; auth, "War and Culture: The Iroquois Experience," Wm & Mary Quart 40, 83; auth, "Iroquois versus Iroquois: Jesuit Missions and Christianity in Village Politics, 1642-1686," Ethnohist 32, 85; co-ed, Beyond the Covenant Chain: The Iroquois and Their Neighbors in Indian North America, 1600-1800, Syracuse Univ Press, 87; auth, "Cultural Brokers and Intercultural Politics: New York-Iroquois Relations, 1664-1701," Jour of Am Hist 75, 88; auth, "A Framework for Pennsylvania Indian History," Penn Hist 57, 90; auth, The Ordeal of the Longhouse: The Peoples of the Iroquois League in the Era of European Colonization, Univ NC Press, 92; auth, "Some of Them Would Always Have a Minister with Them: Mohawk Protestantism, 1683-1719," Am Indian Quart XVI, 92; auth, "Whose Indian History?" Wm & Mary Quart, 93; auth, "Native Peoples of North America and the British Empire," in The Oxford History of the British Empire, vol II: The Eighteenth Century. **CONTACT ADDRESS** Dept of Hist, Dickinson Col, PO Box 1773, Carlisle, PA 17013. **EMAIL** richter@dickinson.edu

RICHTER, DONALD CHARLES
PERSONAL Born 03/13/1934, New York, NY, m, 1962, 2 children **DISCIPLINE** ANCIENT HISTORY **EDUCATION** Atlantic Union Col, BA, 55; Andrews Univ, MA, 57; Univ Md, MA, 58, PhD(hist), 65. **CAREER** Asst prof hist, Chapman Col, World Campus Afloat, 65-66; asst prof, 64-71, Assoc Prof Hist, Ohio Univ, 71-. **MEMBERSHIPS** AHA; Archaeol Inst Am. **SELECTED PUBLICATIONS CONTACT ADDRESS** Dept of Hist, Ohio Univ, Athens, OH 45701-2979.

RIDDEL, FRANK STEPHEN
PERSONAL Born 10/25/1940, Sistersville, WV, m, 1964, 2 children **DISCIPLINE** SOCIAL STUDIES EUROPEAN HISTORY **EDUCATION** Marshall Univ, AB, 62, MA, 65; Ohio State Univ, PhD, 71. **CAREER** Instr, 62-63 Gallia Acad High Sch; instr, 63-68, Barboursville High Sch; instr, 68-69, Marshall Univ; res assoc, 69-71, Ohio St Univ; asst prof, 71-78, assoc prof, 78-84, prof, soc stud, 84-94, prof, hist, 94-, Marshall Univ. **MEMBERSHIPS** Soc Spanish & Portuguese Hist Studies; Nat Coun Social Studies; AHA; Am Studies Assn. **RESEARCH** Spanish politics during the Franco Regime; history and culture of Appalachia; methods of teaching social studies. **SELECTED PUBLICATIONS** Art, Improving the Teaching of History: How Can The Social Studies Methods Class Contribute?, J Teaching & Learning, 80; auth, Defining and Shaping the Good Citizen in an Authoritarian Society: Civic Education in Franco's Spain, Clearinghouse for Soc Sci Ed, 80; coauth, West Virginia Government, WV Hist Ed Found, 83; coauth, American Government: The USA and West Virginia, WV Hist Ed Found, 90; coauth, Undermining Authoritarianism: The Colegio Estudio and the Preservation of Liberal Education in Franco's Spain, J WV Hist Assn, 93. **CONTACT ADDRESS** Dept of History, Marshall Univ, Old Main 107, Huntington, WV 25755. **EMAIL** riddel@marshall.edu

RIDDELL, J. BARRY
PERSONAL Born 07/29/1940, Belleville, ON, Canada, m, 1963, 2 children **DISCIPLINE** GEOGRAPHY **EDUCATION** Univ Toronto, BA, 63; MA, 65; Penn State Univ, PhD, 69. **CAREER** Asst prof, assoc prof, prof, Queen's Univ, 69-. **HONORS AND AWARDS** Julian Szeicz Awd Excel in Teach, 00; Ed, Can J of African Stud, 89-00. **MEMBERSHIPS** CAG; AAG; CAAS; AAS. **RESEARCH** Third world development; tropical Africa; Trinidad and Tobago. **SELECTED PUBLICATIONS** Auth, The Spatial Dynamics of Modernization in Sierra Leone, N Western UP, 70; auth, "Structural Adjustment Programmes and the City in Tropical Africa," Urban Studies 34 (97): 1297-1307; auth, "Things Fall Apart Again: Structural adjustment programmes in Sub-Saharan Africa," J Mod Afro Stud 30 (92): 53-68; auth, "On Mobility in a Southern City's Suburbs," Appl Geog Stud 1 (97): 115-128; auth, "The Cruel Enigma: Development, International Finance, and Third World Poverty," Lab Cap Soc 28 (95): 215-222; auth, "The World Bank Speaks to Africa Yet Again," Can J Afro Stud 29 (95): 235-239; auth, "Let There Be Light: The voices of West African novels," J Mod Afro Stud 28 (90): 473-486; auth, "Beyond the Geography of Modernization: The state as a redistribution mechanism in independent Sierra Leone," Can J Afro Stud 19 (85): 529-545. **CONTACT ADDRESS** Dept Geog, Queen's Univ at Kingston, 99 University Ave, Kingston, ON, Canada K7L 3N6. **EMAIL** riddellb@qsilver.queensu.ca

RIDGWAY, BRUNILDE SISMONDO
PERSONAL Born 11/14/1929, Chieti, Italy, m, 1958, 4 children **DISCIPLINE** ARCHAEOLOGY **EDUCATION** Univ Messina, Dr Let, 53; Bryn Mawr Col, MA, 54, PhD, 58; Georgetown Univ, Dr of Humane Let, Honoris Causa, 92; Union Col, Dr of Let, Honoris Causa, 92. **CAREER** Instr archaeol, 58-60, Bryn Mawr Col; asst prof classics, 60-61, Hollins Col; asst prof class Near Eastern archaeol, 61-67, from assoc prof to prof archaeol, 67-77, Rhys Carpenter Prof Archaeol, 77-94, prof emer, Bryn Mawr Col; cor mem, Ger Archaeol Inst, 67-; dir summer session, Am Sch Class Studies, Athens, 67 & 71; consult & panelist, NEH, 72-; exec comt mem, Int Lexicon Classical Mythology, 74-84; Guggenheim fel, 74-75; ed-in-chief, Am J Archaeol, 77-85; lectr, 81-82, Thomas Spencer Jerome Lectures, Univ Mich & Amer Acad Rome; Sather Lectures, U of CA at Berkeley, 96. **HONORS AND AWARDS** Christian R & Mary F Lindback Found Awd Dist Tchng, 81; Gold Medal of Archaeol Inst of Am for Dist Archaeol Achievement; Natl Gold Medalist, prof of Year prog, 89, Coun for Advancement & Sup of Ed (CASE); Penn Prof Year, 89, CASE, **MEMBERSHIPS** Archaeol Inst Am; German Archaeol Inst; Alumni Assn Am Schl of Class Stud at Athens; Amer Phil Soc, elected 93; Soc for the Promotion of Hellenic Stud, elected 97. **RESEARCH** Greek sculpture; Greek architecture. **SELECTED PUBLICATIONS** Auth, The Severe Style in Greek Sculpture, Princeton, 70; auth, The Archaic Style in Greed Sculpture, 1st ed, Princeton, 77, 2nd expanded ed, Chicago, 93; auth, Fifth Century Styles in Greek Sculpture, Princeton Univ, 81; auth, Roman Copies of Greek Sculpture: The Problem of the Originals, Ann Arbor, 84; co-ed, Ancient Anatolia, Essays in Honor of Machteld J Mellink, Madison 86; coauth, The Porticello Shipwreck: A Mediterranean Merchant Vessel of 415-385 BC, Texas A&M Univ Press, 87; auth, Hellenistic Sculpture I: The Styles of ca 331-200 BC, Madison, 90; auth, Fourth-Century Styles in Greek Sculpture, Madison, 97; auth, Prayers in Home: Greek Architectural Sculpture ca. 600-

100 BCE, Univ of Calif Press, 99; auth, Hellenistic Sculpture II: The Styles of ca. 200-100 BC, Madison, 00. **CONTACT ADDRESS** Dept of Classics & Near Eastern Archaeol, Bryn Mawr Col, Bryn Mawr, PA 19010. **EMAIL** bridgeway@brynmawr.edu

RIDGWAY, WHITMAN HAWLEY
PERSONAL Born 11/13/1941, Schenectady, NY, 4 children **DISCIPLINE** UNITED STATES HISTORY, 1760-1860 **EDUCATION** Kenyon Col, AB, 63; San Francisco State Univ, MA, 67; Univ Pa, PhD, 73; Univ Md, JD, 85. **CAREER** From lectr to assoc prof, 69-78, assoc prof hist, Univ Md, College Park, 78-, assoc chair, 93-97. **HONORS AND AWARDS** Soc Sci Res Coun Awd, 79.Newberry Libr fels, 74 & 77; NEH summer grant, 76; hon fel, Dept Geog, Univ Wis-Madison, 79-80; Libr Congress fel, 88. **MEMBERSHIPS** Orgn Am Historians; DC Bar Asn; Am Asn for Legal Hist; Md Hist Asn; Pa Hist Soc. **RESEARCH** Early national to middle period political culture; Bill of Rights, constitutional. **SELECTED PUBLICATIONS** Auth, Community Leadership in Maryland, 1790-1840: A Comparative Analysis of Power in Society, Univ NC, Chapel Hill, 79; coauth, Maryland: A History of Its People, Johns Hopkins Press, 86; co-ed, The Bill of Rights: Our Written Legacy, Krieger Publ Co, 93; auth, Popular Sentiment and the Bill of Rights Controversy, in The Bill of Rights: Government Proscribed, Univ Press Va, 97. **CONTACT ADDRESS** Dept of Hist, Univ of Maryland, Col Park, College Park, MD 20742-7315. **EMAIL** wr9@umail.umd.edu

RIDLEY, JACK
PERSONAL Born 10/12/1940, Hobarr, OK, m, 1963, 2 children **DISCIPLINE** HISTORY **EDUCATION** Southwestern Okla State Univ, BA, 62; Univ of SDak, MA, 63; Univ Okla, PhD, 70. **CAREER** Instr, Murray State Col, Okla, 64-65; instr, Univ of New Orleans, 67-68; to prof, Univ Mo-Rolla, 86-89, Distinguished Teaching Prof of History, 90-2000. **HONORS AND AWARDS** Governor's Awd for Excellence in Teaching, Mo; Univ of Mo President's Awd of Outstanding Teaching, Burlington Northern Fac Achievement Awd, Twenty Outstanding Teaching Awds, Univ of Mo-Rolla; Finalist, Eugene Asher Awd for Distinguished Teaching, Am Hist Asn. **MEMBERSHIPS** The State Hist Soc of Mo, Western Soc for French Hist, Am Asn of Higher Ed. **RESEARCH** Modern France; history of engineering education; minerals industry history of Missouri. **SELECTED PUBLICATIONS** Coauth with L. O. Christensen, UM-Rolla: A History of MSM/UMR, Columbia, Mo (83); auth, "Stepchild of the University," Mo Hist Rev LXXIX, #4 (July 85); auth, "Mining and Manufacturing in a Frontier Environment: The Iron Industry in South Central Missouri in the 19th century," Locus, I (spring 89): 31-46. **CONTACT ADDRESS** Dept Hist & Govt, Univ of Missouri, Rolla, 1870 Miner Cir, Rolla, MO 65409-0001. **EMAIL** ridley@umr.edu

RIEDINGER, EDWARD
PERSONAL Born 03/26/1944, Cincinatti, OH, s **DISCIPLINE** BRAZILIAN HISTORY **EDUCATION** Univ of Chicago, MA, 69, PhD, 78; Univ of Calif, MLIS, 89. **CAREER** Pvt secy for English Correspondence, Juscelino Kubitschek, Rio de Janeiro, 72-76; asst prof, Pontifical Cath Univ, Rio de Janeiro, 76-77; asst prof, Univ of the Americas, Puebla, Mexico, 78; educ advising off, Fulbright Comn of Brazil, Am Consulate Gen, Rio de Janeiro, 79-88; vis lectr, San Francisco State Univ, 90; acting bibliogr, Univ of Calif, 90; prof, Ohio State Univ, 91-. **HONORS AND AWARDS** Res Travel Awd, NEH, 92; Res Travel Awd, Tinker Found/Ohio State Univ Latin Am Studies Prog, 92, 96; Commendation, US-Brazil Cult Inst, Rio de Janeiro, 96; Fulbright Scholar Awd, 96. **MEMBERSHIPS** Brazilian Studies Asn; Latin Am Studies Asn; Sem on the Acquisition of Latin Am Libr Materials. **RESEARCH** Modern Brazilian cultural history and politics. **SELECTED PUBLICATIONS** Como se faz um presidente: A campanha de JK, 88; Proceedings of the Brazilian Studies Association (BRASA): First Conference, Atlanta, Georgia, 10-12 March 1994, 94; Where in the World to Learn: A Guide to Library and Information Science for International Education Advisers, 95; Turned-on Advising: Computer and Video Resources for Educational Advising, 95; Proceedings of the Brazilian Studies Association (BRASA): Second Conference, Univ of Minn, Minneapolis, 11-13 May 1995, 95. **CONTACT ADDRESS** Latin American Studies Library, Ohio State Univ, Columbus, 1858 Neil Ave Mall, Rm 312, Columbus, OH 43210-1286. **EMAIL** riedinger.4@osu.edu

RIELY, JOHN CABELL
PERSONAL Born 08/27/1945, Philadelphia, PA, m, 1969, 2 children **DISCIPLINE** ENGLISH LITERATURE; ART HISTORY **EDUCATION** Harvard Col, AB, Cum laude, 67; Univ Pa, MA, 68, PhD, 71. **CAREER** Assoc res ed, Yale Edition Horace Walpole's Correspondence, 71-79; lectr, Yale Univ, 73-79; asst prof, Columbia Univ, 79-80; vis prof, Univ Minn, 80-81; from asst to assoc prof, Boston Univ, 81-. **HONORS AND AWARDS** Huntington Lib Fel, 73; ACLS Grant, 72; Vis Fel, 82-83, Yale Ctr for British Art; NEH Senior Fel, 88-89, Boston Public Libr Fel, 95-96; Fel Soc Antiquanes London and Royal Soc Arts. **MEMBERSHIPS** ASECS, NEASECS, Asn Lit Scholar Critics, Col Art Asn, Walpole Soc, The Johnsonians (USA), Johnson Club (UK). **RESEARCH** Late 17th thru early 19th early literature and art history; Johnson and his circle; Sir Joshua Reynolds; Horace Walpole; Alex Pope; Biography and Portraiture; caricature and comic art, esq Thomas Rowlandson; English country house and landscape garden, The history of taste and connoisseruship. **SELECTED PUBLICATIONS** Auth, Rowlandson Drawings from the Paul Mellon Collection, 77; auth, The Age of Horace Walpole in Caricature 73, 90; ed, Horace Walpole's Miscellaneous Correspondence, 80; coauth, "Gainsborough and Rowlandson, 90. **CONTACT ADDRESS** Dept of English, Boston Univ, 236 Bay State Rd, Boston, MA 02215. **EMAIL** johnriely@aol.com

RIES, NANCY
DISCIPLINE RUSSIAN CULTURE AND SOCIETY **EDUCATION** Cornell Univ, PhD, 93. **CAREER** Asst prof, Colgate Univ. **RESEARCH** Modes of discourse, and how they reproduce cult forms and soc value syst. **SELECTED PUBLICATIONS** Auth, Culture and Conversation during Perestroika, Cornell UP, 97. **CONTACT ADDRESS** Dept of Russ Stud, Colgate Univ, 13 Oak Drive, Hamilton, NY 13346.

RIESENBERG, PETER
PERSONAL Born 11/17/1925, New York, NY, m, 1951, 2 children **DISCIPLINE** MEDIEVAL HISTORY **EDUCATION** Rutgers Univ, AB, 47; Univ Wis, MA, 49; Columbia Univ, PhD(medieval hist), 54. **CAREER** Instr hist, Rutgers Univ, 53-54; from instr to asst prof, Swarthmore Col, 54-60; from asst prof to assoc prof, 60-66, Prof Hist, Wash Univ, 66-, Soc Sci Res Coun fel, Italy, 57-58; fel, I Tatti, Harvard Ctr Renaissance Studies, 64-65; Guggenheim fel, 64-65; mem, Col Entrance Exam Bd Examining Comt Europ Hist & World Cult, 67-70, chmn, 70-72; vis prof, Univ Calif, Berkeley, 68; fel, Nat Humanities Ctr, 78-79. **MEMBERSHIPS** Mediaeval Acad Am; Int Comn Hist Rep & Parliamentary Insts; Renaissance Soc Am. **RESEARCH** Medieval political thought and institutions; medieval urban history; medieval legal history. **SELECTED PUBLICATIONS** Auth, Inalienability of Sovereignty in Medieval Political Thought, Columbia Univ, 56; coauth, Medieval Town, Van Nostrand, 58; The Traditions of the Western World, Rand McNally, 67; auth, Civilism and Roman law in fourteenth century Italian society, Explor Econ Hist, fall 69; Citizenship and equality in late Medieval Italy, Studia Gratiana, 72; Citizenship at law in late Medieval Italy, Viator, 74; Violence, social control and community planning in medieval Italian city states, Washington Univ Law Quart, 75; The Jews in the structure of Western institutions, Judaism, 79. **CONTACT ADDRESS** Dept of Hist, Washington Univ, Saint Louis, MO 63130.

RIESS, STEVE ALLEN
PERSONAL Born 08/26/1947, New York, NY, 3 children **DISCIPLINE** AMERICAN HISTORY **EDUCATION** NYork Univ, BA, 68; Univ Chicago, MA, 69, PhD(Am hist), 74. **CAREER** Asst prof hist, State Univ NY, Brockport, 74-75; lectr social sci, Univ Mich, Dearborn, 75-76; asst prof, 76-80, assoc prof hist, 80-84, prof hist, Northeastern Ill Univ, 84-. **HONORS AND AWARDS** Presidential Merit Awd, Northeastern Ill Univ, 81, 85, 89-93, 95-98; Fel for Col Teachers, Nat Endowment for the Humanities, 83-84; Webb-Smith Essay Prize, Univ Tex, 89; Outstanding Acad Book, City Games, 90-91; Summer Stipend for Independent Res, Nat Endowment for the Humanities, 92; Honorary Fel, Prog on Sports Studies, DeMontfort Univ, 96; Outstanding Acad Book, Sports in Industrial America, 96; Outstanding Acad Book, Sports and the American Jew, 99. **MEMBERSHIPS** Orgn Am Historians; NAm Soc Sport Hist; Soc for Am Baseball Res; Chicago Seminar on Sport and Culture. **RESEARCH** United States social history; United States urban history; American sport history. **SELECTED PUBLICATIONS** Ed, The American Sporting Experience: Essays and Documents, Leisure Press, 84; Major Problems in American Sport History, Houghton mifflin, 97; Sports and the American Jew, Syracuse Univ Press, 98; Sports in North America: A Documentary History Vol 6: Sports in the Progressive Era, 1900-1920, Acad Int Press, 98; auth, Touching Base: Professional Baseball and American Culture in the Progressive Era, Greenwood Press, 80, 2nd ed, rev, Univ of Illinois Press, 99; City Games: The Evolution of American Society and the Rise of Sports, Univ Ill Press, 89, 91; Sports in the Industrial Age 1850-1920, Harlan Davidson, 95. **CONTACT ADDRESS** Dept of History, Northeastern Illinois Univ, 5500 N St Louis Ave, Chicago, IL 60625-4625. **EMAIL** s-riess@neiu.edu

RIGGS, CHERYL A.
PERSONAL Born 01/04/1950, m, 1968, 2 children **DISCIPLINE** HISTORY **EDUCATION** Oxnard Col, AA, 78; Univ Calif, Santa Barbara, BA, 80, MA, 82, PhD, 89. **CAREER** Asst prof, Calif State Univ, San Bernardino, 88-94, assoc prof, 94-98, prof, 99-, chair, Dept Hist, 97-. **HONORS AND AWARDS** Bruce Anderson Fel, Univ Calif, 85; Regents Fel, Univ Calif, Santa Barbara, 85-86; nominated, Outstanding Prof Awd, Calif State Univ, San Bernardino, 97-98; nominated, Golden Apple Teaching Awd, 99-2000. **MEMBERSHIPS** Medieval Academy, Medieval Asn of the Pacific, Am Soc of Church Hist. **RESEARCH** Medieval church history, history of Christianity, Christian cosmology, mysticism. **SELECTED PUBLICATIONS** Auth, "Julian of Norwich and the Ecstatic Experience," in Tradition and Ecstacy: The Agony of the Fourteenth Century, Nancy van Deusen, gen ed, The Inst of Medieval Music, Ottawa, Can, Musicological Studies, Vol LXII/3 (97); auth, "Prophesy and Orsder: Mysticism and Medieval Cosmologies in the Twelfth and Thirteenth Centuries," in The Devil Heresy and Witchcraft in the Middle Ages, Alberto Ferreiro, ed, Brill (98); coauth with Fields and Barber, The Global Past, Bedford of St Martin's Press (98). **CONTACT ADDRESS** Dept Hist, California State Univ, San Bernardino, 5500 University Pkwy, San Bernardino, CA 92407-2318. **EMAIL** criggs@csusb.edu

RIGGS, TIMOTHY A.
DISCIPLINE ART HISTORY **EDUCATION** Yale Univ, PhD. **CAREER** Asst dir, Ackland Art Mus; adj prof, UNC-Chapel Hill. **MEMBERSHIPS** Print Coun of Am, Historians of Netherlandish Art. **RESEARCH** Prints and photographs. **SELECTED PUBLICATIONS** Auth, Hieronymus Cock, Printmaker and Publisher, Garland Publ Co, 77; Visions of City and Country: Prints and Photographs of Nineteenth-Century France, Worcester Art Museum and American Federation of Arts, 82; The Rise of Professional Printmakers in Antwerp and Haarlem, 1540-1640, in The Print Council Index to Oeuvre-Catalogues of Prints by European and American Artists, Kraus Int Publ, 83. **CONTACT ADDRESS** Univ of No Carolina, Chapel Hill, Chapel Hill, NC 27599-3400. **EMAIL** trcpc@email.unc.edu

RIGSBY, KENT JEFFERSON
PERSONAL Born 02/25/1945, Tulsa, OK, m, 1969, 2 children **DISCIPLINE** CLASSICAL LANGUAGES, ANCIENT HISTORY **EDUCATION** Yale Univ, BA, 66; Univ Toronto, MA, 68. **CAREER** Asst prof, 71-77, Assoc Prof Classics, Duke Univ, 77-, Asst ed, Greek, Roman & Byzantine Studies, 72-77, assoc ed, 77-79, Roman ed, 79 & sr ed, 80- **MEMBERSHIPS** Am Philol Asn. **RESEARCH** Greek epigraphy; Hellenistic history; ancient religion. **SELECTED PUBLICATIONS** Auth, Cnossus and Capua, Trans Am Philol Asn, 76; Sacred Ephebie games at Oxyrhynchus, Chronique D'Egypte, 77; The era of the Province of Asia, Phoenix, 79; Seleucid Notes, Trans Am Philol Asn, 80. **CONTACT ADDRESS** Dept Class Studies, Duke Univ, Durham, NC 27706.

RIKARD, MARLENE HUNT
PERSONAL Born, TN, m, 1961, 2 children **DISCIPLINE** HISTORY **EDUCATION** Auburn Univ, BAA, 60; Samford Univ, MA, 71; Univ Ala, PhD, 83. **CAREER** From asst prof to prof, 79-, Samford Univ; Dir of London prog 89-00. **HONORS AND AWARDS** AAUW Fel, 80-81; John E. Rovensky Fel, Business, Economic Hist, 84, Ec Hy Asn; Sears Found Campus Leadership, Tchg, Res, 90, Samford Univ; Danforth Assoc; Phi Kappa Phi; ed, the newsletter of the ala hist asn, 84-89; chemn, ala baptist hist commission, 84-88; chemn, sou baptist hist commission; 92-93; pres, sou asn women historians, 90-91; pres, ala asn historians, 90-92. **MEMBERSHIPS** Southern Hist Asn; Southern Asn Women's Historians; OAH; Asn Ala Historians; Ala Hist Asn. **RESEARCH** Southern history; Southern labor history; women's history. **SELECTED PUBLICATIONS** Auth, art, Goerge Gordon Crawford: Man of the New South, 87; auth, art, Alabama Enterprise, 87; auth, art, Company Towns, 89; auth, art, The Influence of Laywomen on Baptist Life, 89; auth, art, Henry DeBardeleben, 98. **CONTACT ADDRESS** Dept of Hist & Pol Sci, Samford Univ, Birmingham, AL 35229. **EMAIL** mhrikard@samford.edu

RILEY, GLENDA
PERSONAL Born 09/06/1938, Cleveland, Ohio, 1 child **DISCIPLINE** AMERICAN HISTORY **EDUCATION** Western Reserve Univ, BA, 60; Miami Univ, MA, 63; Ohio State Univ, PhD(hist), 67. **CAREER** Instr hist, Denison Univ, 67-68; asst prof, Ohio State Univ, 68-69; from asst prof to assoc prof, 69-77, Prof Hist, Univ Northern Iowa, 77-, Coordr Women's Studies Prog, 81-, Mem, Nat Records Adv Bd, 76-79; Pres, Western History Asn, 96-97. **HONORS AND AWARDS** Outstanding Research Awd, Ball State Univ, 95; Fulbright Research Awd, 98. **MEMBERSHIPS** Nat Coun Pub Hist; Nat Women's Studies Asn; Women Historians of Midwest. **RESEARCH** History of women in the United States; early national period in the United States; history of the American Midwest. **SELECTED PUBLICATIONS** Auth, Integrating women's history into existing course structures, Hist Teacher, 8/79; Not Gainfully Employed: Women on the Iowa frontier, 1833-1870, Pac Hist Rev, 5/80; Women in the West, J Am Cult, summer 80; Frontierswomen: The Iowa Experience, Iowa State Univ Press, 81; Reaching undergraduates with the public history message, Pub Historian, fall 81; The frontier in process: Iowa's Trail Women as a paradigm, Ann of Iowa, winter 82; European views of white women in the American West, J of West, 4/82; History goes public (slides), Nat Coun Pub Hist, spring 82; auth, The Life and Legacy of Annie Oakley, Norman: Univ of Oklahoma Press, Western Biography Series, 94; auth, Inventing the American Woman: An Inclusive History, Wheeling, IL, Forum Press, Inc., 95 and 00; auth, Building and Breaking Families in the American West, Albuquerque: Univ of New Mexico Press, 96; auth, Prairie Voices: Iowa's Pioneer Women, Ames: Iowa State Univ Press, 96; auth, Eleven Women Who Shaped the American West, with Richard W. Etulain, eds. Grit and Grace, Golden, CO: Fulcrum Pub, 97; auth, Women and Nature: Saving the "Wild" West, Lincoln: Univ of Nebraska Press,

99; auth, With Badges and Bullets: Lawmen and Outlaws in the Old West, with Richard W. Eutlain, Golden, CO: Fulcrum Pub, 99; auth, The Hollywood West, with Richard W. Etulain, Golden, CO: Fulcrum Press, 00. **CONTACT ADDRESS** Dept of Hist, Ball State Univ, 2000 W University Ave, Muncie, IN 47306-1022. **EMAIL** griley@gw.bsu.edu

RILEY, JAMES
PERSONAL Born 09/02/1946 **DISCIPLINE** HISTORY **EDUCATION** Univ NC, BA, 65; MA, 67; PhD, 71. **CAREER** Asst Prof, Univ Houston, 70-75; Asst Prof, to Prof, Ind Univ, 75-. **HONORS AND AWARDS** James A Shannon Director's Awd, Nat Inst of Health, 94, 96-98, 99-01; Grant, IU Ctr on Philanthropy, 98-01; NEH Grant, 90-93; Visiting Fel, Australian Nat Univ, 89; Grant, Intl Res and Exchange Board, 89; Ernst Meyer Prize, Asn Intl pour l'Etude de l'Economie de l'Assurance, 88; Guggenheim Fel, 86-87; Fel, Netherlands Inst for Adv Study, 85-86; Summer Res Awd, W European Studies Prog, 83, 87, 88, 89. **MEMBERSHIPS** Economic Hist Asn, Intl Economic Hist Asn, Soc for French Hist studies, Am Asn for the History of Medicine, Population Asn of Am, Intl Union for the Sci Study of Population, World Hist Asn, REVES. **RESEARCH** Health; Mortality; Historical Demography; Old Regime Europe. **SELECTED PUBLICATIONS** Auth, Sick, Not Dead: The Health of British Workingmen During the Mortality Decline, Johns Hopkins Univ Press, 97; auth, Sickness, Recovery, and Death: A History and Forecast of Ill Health, Macmillan, 89; auth, "Mortality and Morbidity: Trends and Determinants," World Health Statistics Quarterly, forthcoming; auth, "Why Sickness and Death Rates do Not Move Parallel to One Another over Time," Social History of Medicine, (99): 101-124; auth, "A Widening Market in Consumer Goods," in Early Modern Europe: An Oxford History, (99)(: 233-264; auth, "Morbidity," The Social Science Encyclopedia, forthcoming; auth, "The Morbidity of Medical Practitioners," Social History of Medicine, (96): 467-471; auth, "The Sick and the Well: Adult Health in Britain during the Health Transition," Health Transition Review, (96): 19-44; auth, "Height, Nutrition, and Mortality risk reconsidered," Journal of Interdisciplinary History, (94): 465-492; auth, "Interest Rates in Antwerp, 1664-1787," in entrepreneurship and the Transformation of the Economy (10th - 20th Centuries): Essays in Honour of Herman Van der Wee, Leuven, (94): 497-505. **CONTACT ADDRESS** Dept Hist, Indiana Univ, Bloomington, 1020 E Kirkwood Ave, Bloomington, IN 47405-7103. **EMAIL** rileyj@indiana.edu

RILEY, JAMES DENSON
PERSONAL Born 10/11/1943, Oakland, CA, m, 1966, 3 children **DISCIPLINE** LATIN AMERICAN HISTORY **EDUCATION** St Mary's Col Calif, BA, 65; Tulane Univ, MA, 67, PhD(Latin Am hist), 72. **CAREER** Asst prof hist, Benedictine Col, 70-76; asst prof, 76-80, Assoc Prof Hist, Cath Univ Am, 81- **MEMBERSHIPS** AHA; Conf Latin Am Hist; Latin Am Studies Asn. **RESEARCH** Colonial rural history in Mexico. **SELECTED PUBLICATIONS** Auth, Hacendados Jesuitas En Mexico, SepSetentas, Mexico, 76; Jesuit wealth in Mexico, 1675-1767, The Americas, 10/76; Santa Lucia: Desarrollo y administracion de una hacienda jesuita en el siglo XVIII, Historica Mexicana, 10/73; Landlords, Laborers and Royal Government: The Administration of Labor in Tlaxcala, 1680-1750, In: El trabajo y lost trabajadores en la historia de Mexico, Univ Ariz Press, 79. **CONTACT ADDRESS** Dept of Hist, Catholic Univ of America, Washington, DC 20017.

RILEY, PHILIP FERDINAND
PERSONAL Born 08/21/1941, South Bend, IN, m, 1967, 4 children **DISCIPLINE** EARLY MODERN EUROPE, OLD REGIME FRANCE **EDUCATION** Univ Notre Dame, AB, 63, AM, 64, PhD, 71. **CAREER** From Assoc Prof to Prof Hist, James Madison Univ, 71-. **HONORS AND AWARDS** Distinguished Teaching Awd, James Madison Univ. **MEMBERSHIPS** Soc Fr Hist Studies; AHA; WHA. **RESEARCH** Louis XIV's Paris; world history. **SELECTED PUBLICATIONS** Auth, The Global Experience: Readings in World History, 2 vols, Prentice-Hall, 87, 3rd ed, 98; auth, "Michel Foucault, Lust, Women and Sin in Louis XIV's Paris," Church Hist 59 (90): 35-50; auth, Louis XIII 1601-1643, Research Guide to European Historical Biography 1450 to the Present, Beacham Publ Inc, 92; Louis XIV, 1638-1715, Research Guide to European Historical Biography 1450 to the Present, Beacham Publ Inc, 92; Madame de Maintenon Francoise d'Aubigne, 1635-1719, Research Guide to European Historical Biography 1450 to the Present, Beacham Publ Inc, 92; Mr. Madison's University, Va 18, Winter 95; coauth, Term Paper Resource Guide to Twentieth-Century World Hist, Greenwood Publ Group (Westport, Conn), 00; author of other articles. **CONTACT ADDRESS** Dept of Hist, James Madison Univ, Harrisonburg, VA 22807-0002. **EMAIL** rileypf@jmu.edu

RILEY, TERENCE
PERSONAL Born 11/06/1954, IL, s **DISCIPLINE** ARCHITECTURE, DESIGN **EDUCATION** Univ Notre Dame, BA, 78; Columbia Univ, MS, 82. **CAREER** Gen partner, 84-91, limited partner, 91-, Keenen/Riley Architects; curator, 91-92, chief curator, 92-, Dept of Architecture and Design. **SELECTED PUBLICATIONS** Auth, Between the Museum and the Marketplace: Selling Good Design, Stud in Modern Art 4: The Museum of Modern Art at Mid-Century at Home and Abroad, Museum of Modern Art, NY, 94; coed, Frank Lloyd Wright: Architect, Museum of Modern Art, NY, 94; auth, Light Construction, Museum of Modern Art, NY, 95; auth, The Architectural Competition, Studies in Modern Art 7: Imagining the Future of the Museum of Modern Art, Museum of Modern Art, NY 95; auth, The Charette, Studies in Modern Art 7: Imagining the Future of the Museum of Modern Art, Museum of Modern Art, NY, 98; auth, Portrait of the Curator as a Young Man, Studies in Modern Art 6: Philip Johnson and the Museum of Modern Art, Museum of Modern Art, NY, 98. **CONTACT ADDRESS** Dept of Architecture and Design, Mus of Modern Art, 11 W 53rd St, New York, NY 10019. **EMAIL** Terence_Riley@moma.org

RILLING, JOHN R.
PERSONAL Born 04/28/1932, Wausau, WI, m, 1953, 2 children **DISCIPLINE** HISTORY, EARLY MODERN ENGLAND **EDUCATION** Univ Mn, BA, 53; Harvard Univ, AM, 57, PhD, 59. **CAREER** Asst prof to assoc prof to prof, chair, 59-, Univ Richmond; chair, 77-83, Westhampton Col, Prof Emeritus, 99. **HONORS AND AWARDS** Grad, Summa Cum Laude 53; Phi Beta Kappa, 53 Woodrow Wilson Fel, 53; Archibald Coolidge Fel, 55-58; Harvard Traveling Fel, 58-59; Fel Folger Libr, 60; Omicron Delta Kappa, 72; Univ of Richmond Distinguished Educr Awd, 75-77, 80, 87; ODK Prof of the Year, 96; distinguished educ award, 75, 76, 77, 80, 87; finalist, prof of the year, 81. **MEMBERSHIPS** Amer Hist Assoc; N Amer Conf on British Hist; Carolinas Symp on British Stud. **RESEARCH** Tudor/Stuart: late Tudor & early Stuart; admin & soc hist. **SELECTED PUBLICATIONS** Art, Amer Hist Rev; art, Renaissance News; art, Historian; art, J of Church & State. **CONTACT ADDRESS** History Dept, Univ of Richmond, 1507 Wilmington Ave, Richmond, VA 23227. **EMAIL** jrilling@richmond.edu

RINDERLE, WALTER
PERSONAL Born 08/31/1940, Vincennes, IN, m, 1974, 2 children **DISCIPLINE** CHURCH HISTORY, THEOLOGY, EURO HISTORY **EDUCATION** St Meinrad Col, AB 62; State Univ Innsbruck, Austria, STL 66, MA 67; Univ Notre Dame, MA 73, PhD 76; Ind State , MS, 00. **CAREER** Vincennes Univ, asst prof 90-94; Univ Southern IN, asst prof 94-97; Univ St Francis, instr 98; Instr, Ind State Univ, 00. **HONORS AND AWARDS** 2 NEH awds. **MEMBERSHIPS** Indiana Hist Soc; Catholic Hist Soc. **RESEARCH** Role of the Lutheran Church in the collapse of East Germany; Medical hist; Nazi Germany. **SELECTED PUBLICATIONS** Nazi Impact on a German Village; 200 Years of Catholic Education; Permanent Pastors in Knox County. **CONTACT ADDRESS** 2814 N Church Rd, Vincennes, IN 47591. **EMAIL** rinderle@charter.net

RINEY-KEHRBERG, PAMELA
DISCIPLINE HISTORY **EDUCATION** Colo Col, BA, 85; Univ Wis, MA, 86; PhD, 91. **CAREER** Asst to assoc prof, IL State Univ, 91-00; assoc prof, Iowa State Univ, 00. **HONORS AND AWARDS** Fulbright Res Fel, New Zealand, 98; Wayne Aspinall Chair of Hist, Polit Sci and Pub Affairs, Mes State Col 99. **MEMBERSHIPS** Agri Hist Soc; W His Assoc; Soc Sci Hist Assoc. **RESEARCH** Rural and Agricultural History, History of the Family, Women's History, American West. **SELECTED PUBLICATIONS** Auth, Rooted in Dust: Surviving Drought and Depression in Southwestern Kansas, Univ Pr of Kans (Lawrence), 94; auth, "'Broke in Spirits': Death, Depression and Endurance Through Writing", Frontiers: A Jour of Women's Studies XVIII, (96):70-86; auth, "Feeding a Family of Five: Role Playing the Great Depression", Teaching Hist: A Jour of Methods 22 (97):59-63; auth, "The Limits of Community: Martha Friesen of Hamilton County, Kansas" in Midwestern Women: Work, Community, and Leadership at the Crossroads, ed. Wendy H. Venet and Lucy Eldersveld (Bloomington: Ind Univ Pr, 97), 76-91; auth, "The Radio Diary of Mary Dyck, 1936-1955: The Listening Habits of a Kansas Farm Woman", Jour of Radio Studies 5 (98):22-35; coauth, "'Readers' Theatre as a History Teaching Tool", The Hist Teacher 32 (99):525-545; auth, Waiting on the Bounty: The Dust Bowl Diary of Mary Knackstedt Dyck, Univ of Iowa Pr (Iowa City), 99. **CONTACT ADDRESS** Dept Hist, Iowa State Univ, 603 Ross Hall, Ames, IA 50011-1202.

RINGENBERG, WILLIAM C.
PERSONAL Born 08/18/1939, Fort Wayne, IN, m, 1962, 4 children **DISCIPLINE** HISTORY **EDUCATION** Taylor Univ, BS, 61; Ind Univ, MA, 64; Mich State Univ, PhD, 70. **CAREER** Asst Prof, 68-72; Assoc Prof, 72-77; Prof, 77-, Assoc Academic Dean, 74-79; Chair, Dept of History, 82-, Dir of Honors Program, Taylor Univ, 83-94 & 96-98; Vice Pres 87-88; Pres 89-90 biennium; Conference on Faith and History. **HONORS AND AWARDS** Chi Alpha Omega Scholastic Honor Society, Taylor Univ, 61; Lilly Fellow in American History, Indiana Univ, 62,63; Institute for Advanced Christian Study, Scholar, Spring, 81. **MEMBERSHIPS** Organization of American Historians; American Society of Church History; Conference on Faith and History. **RESEARCH** Amer Religion; Amer Higher Education. **SELECTED PUBLICATIONS** Auth, "Taylor Univ: The First 125 Year, Grand Rapids: Eerdmans Publishing Co, 73; auth, "The Christian Coll: A History of Protestant Higher Education in America, Grand Rapids: Eerdmans, 84; auth, Taylor Univ: The First 150 Years, Grand Rapids: Eerdman, 96. **CONTACT ADDRESS** Dept History, Taylor Univ, Upland, 500 W Reade Ave, Upland, IN 46989-1001. **EMAIL** wlringenb@tayloru.edu

RINGER, FRITZ K.
PERSONAL Born 09/25/1934, Ludwigshafen, Germany, m, 1957, 2 children **DISCIPLINE** HISTORY **EDUCATION** Amherst Col, BA, 1956; Harvard Univ, PhD, 1961 **CAREER** Harvard University, full-time instr 1960-62, asst. professor, 1962-66; Indiana University, associate professor, 1996-69; Boston University, full professor, 1970-84; University of Pittsburgh, Mellon Professor of History, 1984-2002; Fellow, Center for Philosophy of Science. **HONORS AND AWARDS** National Endowment for the Humanities Junior Fac Research Fel, 1969-70; NEH Senior Fac Research Fel, 1976-77; National Science Foundation and Netherlands Institute for Advance Study, Joint Research Fel, 1985-86; National Humanities Ctr Fellow, 1993-94; Guggenheim Fellow, July-December, 1994; Fel, Wissenschaftskolleg/Institute for Advance Study, Berlin, 2001-02. **MEMBERSHIPS** American Historical Association **RESEARCH** Modern European intellectual history; history and philosophy of the cultural and social sciences; Social and intellectual history of modern European higher education, scholarship, and social thought. **SELECTED PUBLICATIONS** Auth, The Decline of the German Mandarins ,Harvard University Press , 69; auth, Education and Society in Modern Europe, Indiana University Press (Bloomington), 79; auth, Fields of Knowledge: French Academic Culture in comparative Perspective, 1890-1920, Cambridge University Press, 92; auth, Max Weber's Methodology: The Unification of the Cultural and Social Sciences, Harvard University Press, 98; auth, Toward a Social History of Knowledge: Collected Essays, (New York: Berghahn), 00. **CONTACT ADDRESS** Dept History, Univ of Pittsburgh, 3P38 Forbes Quad, Pittsburgh, PA 15260. **EMAIL** fringer@pitt.edu

RINGROSE, DAVID R.
PERSONAL Born 06/01/1938, Minneapolis, MN, m, 1961, 1 child **DISCIPLINE** EUROPEAN ECONOMIC HISTORY, HISTORY OF SPAIN **EDUCATION** Carleton Col, BA, 60; Univ Wis, MA, 62, PhD(hist), 66. **CAREER** From asst prof to assoc prof hist, Rutgers Univ, New Brunswick, 65-74; assoc prof, 74-80, assoc dir, Ctr Iberian & Latin Am Studies, 77-80, Prof Hist, Univ Calif, San Diego, 80-, Chmn, 81-. Rutgers res coun fac fel, 68-69; Fulbright res fel, Spain, 68-69; Nat Endowment for Humanities fel, 73-74. **MEMBERSHIPS** Econ Hist Asn; AHA; Soc Span & Port Hist Studies (gen secy, 73-75); Social Sci Hist Asn; Assoc Hist Economica Espana. **RESEARCH** Spanish economic history of the 17th to the 19th centuries; preindustrial Europe; urban history. **SELECTED PUBLICATIONS CONTACT ADDRESS** Dept of Hist, Univ of California, San Diego, 9500 Gilman Dr, La Jolla, CA 92093-5003.

RINK, OLIVER A.
PERSONAL Born 12/12/1947, Monahans, TX, m, 1988, 3 children **DISCIPLINE** AMERICAN HISTORY **EDUCATION** Univ Southern Calif, AB, 70, AM, 73, PhD(hist), 76. **CAREER** Lectr, 75-76, asst prof, 76-79, Assoc Prof Hist, Calif State Univ, Bakersfield, 79-82, prof hist, Calif State Univ Bakersfield. **MEMBERSHIPS** AHA; Orgn Am Historians; Werkgroep voor Europaische Expansie. **RESEARCH** New Netherland (nee New York) 1609-1700; North Atlantic trade 1600-1800. **SELECTED PUBLICATIONS** Auth, Company management or private trade: The two patroonship plans for New Netherland, NY Hist, 1/78; The people of New Netherland: Notes on non-English immigration to New York in the seventeenth century, NY Hist, 1/81; auth, Holland On the Hudson: An Economic and Social History of Dutch New York, Cornell Univ, 86; Private Interest And Godly Gain--The West-India-Company And The Dutch-Reformed-Church In New-Netherland, 1624-1664/, New York Hist, Vol 75, 94; Inheritance And Family-Life In Colonial New-York-City, William And Mary Quart, Vol 52, 95; The Origins Of Amn Capitalism--Collected Essays, Am Hist Rev, Vol 98, 93. **CONTACT ADDRESS** California State Univ, Bakersfield, 9001 Stockdale Hwy, Bakersfield, CA 93309. **EMAIL** orink@csubak.edu

RIPPLEY, LA VERN J.
PERSONAL Born 03/02/1935, Waumandee, WI, m, 1960, 2 children **DISCIPLINE** GERMAN ROMANTICISM & IMMIGRATION HISTORY **EDUCATION** Col Holy Cross, BA, 56; Univ Wis, BS, 58; Kent State Univ, MA, 61; Ohio State Univ, PhD(Ger), 65. **CAREER** Teacher, River Falls Sr High Sch, 58-60; teaching asst, Ohio State Univ, 61-63; asst prof Ger, Ohio Wesleyan Univ, 64-67; assoc prof, 67-71, chmn dept, 67-74, Prof Ger, St Olaf Col, 71-, Ed, Newsletter Soc Ger-Am Studies; Fulbright fel, 63-64 & Deutscher Akademischer Austauschdienst Fulbright, 82. **MEMBERSHIPS** Cent States Mod Lang Asn; MLA; Am Asn Teachers Ger; Am Hist Soc Ger from Russia; Norweg Am Hist Asn. **RESEARCH** German-Americana; German Romanticism; German immigration hist. **SELECTED PUBLICATIONS** Transit, Excursion through America, R.R. Donnelley, 73; auth, The German-Americans, Twayne, 74; Germans from Russia, In: Harvard Encycl of American Ethnic Groups, Harvard Univ Press, 80; Immigrant Wisconsin,

Twayne, 85; German Place Names in Minnesota / Deutsche Ortsnamen in Minnesota, St. Olaf Col / Rainer Schmeissner, 89; co-transl, The German Colonies on the Lower Volga, Their Origin and Early Development, Am Hist Soc of Germans from Russia, 91; auth, The Whoopee John Wilfahrt Dance Band. His Bohemian-German Roots, Northfield, 92; coauth, The German-American Experience, Ind-Purdue Univ at Indianapolis, 93; auth, German-Bohemians: The Quiet Immigrants, Northfield, 93; co-ed, Emigration and Settlement Patterns of German Communities in North America, Ind-Purdue Univ at Indianapolis, 95; Noble Women, Restless Men. The Rippley (Rieple, Ripley, Ripli, Rippli) Family in Wisconsin, North Dakota, Minnesota and Montana, St. Olaf Col Press, 96; author of numerous articles. **CONTACT ADDRESS** 1520 St Olaf Ave, Northfield, MN 55057-1098. **EMAIL** rippleyl@stolaf.edu

RISCHIN, MOSES
PERSONAL Born 10/16/1925, New York, NY, m, 1959, 3 children **DISCIPLINE** AMERICAN HISTORY **EDUCATION** Brooklyn Col, AB, 47; Harvard Univ, AM, 48, PhD, 57. **CAREER** Lectr hist, Brooklyn Col, 49-53; instr Am civilization, Brandeis Univ, 53-54; res Am Hist, Am Jewish Comt, 56-58; asst prof, Long Island Univ, 58-59; asst ed, Notable American women, 1607-1950, Radvliffe Col, 59-60; lectr, Univ Calif, Los Angeles, 62-64; assoc prof hist, 64-67, Prof Hist, San Francisco State Univ, 67-, Tercentenary fel, Am Jewish hist, 54-55; Am Philos Soc Penrose Fund grant, 62-64; Am Coun Learned Soc grant, 64 & fel, 66-67; Guggenheim fel, 68; Fulbright Hays lectr, Univ Uppsala, 69; mem, Am Issues Forum, San Francisco Bicentennial Comn, 74-76; consult, Nat Endowment Humanities, 74-, fel 77-78; consult, Calif Coun Humanities, 77-, San Diego Found, 80- **MEMBERSHIPS** AHA; Am Jewish Hist Soc; Orgn Am Historians; Immigration Hist Soc (vpres, 73, pres, 76-79). **RESEARCH** American social history; American immigration history; American urban history. **SELECTED PUBLICATIONS** Sea-Changes--British Emigration And Am Literature, Am Hist Rev, Vol 99, 94; The Promised Land in 1925: America, Palestine, and Abraham Cahan, Yivo Annual, vol 22, 95; Crossings--The Great Transatlantic Migrations, 1870-1914, J Of Am Ethnic Hist, Vol 15, 96; United-States Jewry 1776-1985--Vol 1--The Sephardic Period, Am Jewish Hist, Vol 85, 97; The Warburgs--The 20th-Century Odyssey Of A Remarkable Jewish Family, J Of Am Hist, Vol 81, 94; Round-Trip To Am--The Immigrants Return To Europe, 1880-1930, J Of Am Ethnic Hist, Vol 15, 96; In The Shadow Of The Statue Of Liberty--Immigrants, Workers, And Citizens In The American Republic, 1880-1920, J Of Am Ethnic Hist, Vol 15, 96; This I Believe--Documents Of American Jewish Life, Am Jewish Hist, Vol 85, 97; The Jew In The American World--A Source-Book, Am Jewish Hist, Vol 85, 97; The Megashtetl/ Cosmopolis: New York Jewish History Comes of Age, Studies in Contemporary Jewry, vol 15, 99; Toward the Onomastics of the Great New York Ghetto: How the Lower East Side Got Its Name, Remembering the Lower East Side, Indiana U Pr, 00; **CONTACT ADDRESS** Dept of Hist, San Francisco State Univ, 1600 Holloway Ave, San Francisco, CA 94132-1740. **EMAIL** mrischin@sfsu.edu

RISJORD, NORMAN KURT
PERSONAL Born 11/25/1931, Manitowoc, WI, m, 1959, 2 children **DISCIPLINE** AMERICAN HISTORY **EDUCATION** Col William & Mary, AB, 53; Univ Va, MA, 57, PhD, 60. **CAREER** Asst prof hist, DePauw Univ, 60-64; from asst prof to assoc prof, 64-69, Prof Hist, Univ Wis-Madison, 69- **RESEARCH** American history, early national period; the Old South. **SELECTED PUBLICATIONS** Auth, The Old Republicans, Columbia Univ, 65; Chesapeake Politics, 1781-1800, Columbia Univ, 78; Representative Americans: Revolutionary Generation, 01; Representative Americans: The Colonists, 01; Madison House; auth, Jefferson's America, 1760-1815, 91; auth, Thomas Jefferson, 93. **CONTACT ADDRESS** Dept of Hist, Univ of Wisconsin, Madison, Madison, WI 53706.

RISSO, PATRICIA
DISCIPLINE MIDDLE EAST, ISLAM, SOUTH ASIA **EDUCATION** McGill Univ, PhD, 82. **CAREER** Assoc prof, Univ NMex. **RESEARCH** The construct of piracy in the Indian Ocean. **SELECTED PUBLICATIONS** Auth, Oman and Muscat: an early modern history, 86; Muslim Identity in Maritime Trade: General Observations and Some Evidence from the 18th-century Persian Gulf/Indian Ocean Region, Int J of Mid Eastern Stud, 89; Indian Muslim Legal Status, 1964-1986, J of S Asian and Mid Eastern Stud, 92; Merchants and Faith: Muslim Commerce and Culture in the Indian Ocean, 95. **CONTACT ADDRESS** Dept of Hist, Univ of New Mexico, Albuquerque, Albuquerque, NM 87131. **EMAIL** prisso@unm.edu

RITCHIE, DONALD ARTHUR
PERSONAL Born 12/23/1945, New York, NY, m, 1988, 2 children **DISCIPLINE** AMERICAN HISTORY **EDUCATION** City Col NYork, BA, 67; Univ Md, MA, 69, PhD, 75. **CAREER** Ed, Md Historian, 72-73; instr hist, 74-76 Univ Col, Univ Md; assoc historian, 76-, US Senate Hist Off; Eleanor Roosevelt Inst res grant, 74; investr bibliog surv, AHA, 75-76; adj fac, 90-, Cornell Wash; ed, Twayne's Oral Hist Ser, 88-98. **HONORS AND AWARDS** Richard W. Leopold Prize, Orgn Am Hist, 92; Henry Adams Prize, Soc Hist in Fed Govt, 92; Letitia Woods Brown Mem Lectr, Hist Soc of Wash DC, 90; Forrest C. Pogue Awd, Oral hist Mid-Atlantic Reg, 84 **MEMBERSHIPS** AHA; Orgn Am Historians; Oral Hist Assn; Soc Hist in Fed Govt. **RESEARCH** 20th century United States political and economic history; United States Senate history. **SELECTED PUBLICATIONS** Auth, Press Gallery: Congress and the Washington Correspondents, Harvard Univ Press, 91; auth, The Young Oxford Companion to the Congress and the Washington Correspondents, Harvard Univ Press, 91; auth, Doing Oral History, Twayne, 95; auth, American Journalists: Getting the Story, Oxford Univ Press, 97; auth, History of a Free Nation, Glencoe/ McGraw-Hill, 98. **CONTACT ADDRESS** US Senate, Hist Office, Washington, DC 20510. **EMAIL** Don_Ritchie@sec.senate.gov

RITSCHEL, DANIEL
DISCIPLINE HISTORY **EDUCATION** Oxford Univ, PhD. **CAREER** Assoc prof, Univ MD Baltimore County. **RESEARCH** Europ hist; econ and polit hist of mod Britain. **SELECTED PUBLICATIONS** Auth, The Politics of Planning: The Debate on Economic Planning in Britain in the 1930s. **CONTACT ADDRESS** Dept of Hist, Univ of Maryland, Baltimore, Hilltop Circle, PO Box 1000, Baltimore, MD 21250. **EMAIL** connect@umbc.edu

RITSON, G. JOY
PERSONAL Born 12/18/1945, Highworth, England **DISCIPLINE** HISTORICAL THEOLOGY **EDUCATION** Graduate Theo Union, PhD, 97. **CAREER** Seeking first position. **MEMBERSHIPS** AAR/SBL, APA, SSSR. **RESEARCH** History of Christian Spirituality; Early and Medieval Church; Linguistic Issues involving Latin and Greek Text. **SELECTED PUBLICATIONS** Auth, Eros, Allegory and Spirituality, in preparation, based on PhD Dissertation; Shame in the Developing Though of Augustine, in preparation. **CONTACT ADDRESS** 1277 Sun Cir E, Melbourne, FL 32935. **EMAIL** MINDOX@ix.NETCOM.COM

RITTER, HARRY R.
PERSONAL Born 02/19/1943, St. Louis, MO, m, 1972, 1 child **DISCIPLINE** MODERN EUROPEAN HISTORY **EDUCATION** Univ AZ, BA, 65; Univ VA, MA, 67, PhD, 69. **CAREER** From asst prof to assoc prof hist, 69-86, prof hist, Western WA Univ, 86, Woodrow Wilson fel, 65-66. **HONORS AND AWARDS** Am Philos Soc res grant, 85; Austrian Cult Inst Prize, 89. **MEMBERSHIPS** Ger Studies Asn. **RESEARCH** Nineteenth and 20th century central Europe. **SELECTED PUBLICATIONS** Auth, Hermann Neubacher and the Austrian Anschluss Movement, 1918-40, Cent Europ Hist, 12/75; Friedrich Engels and the East European nationality problem, East Europ Quart, 2/76; Science and the imagination in the thought of Schiller and Marx, In: The Quest for the New Science, Southern Ill Univ Press, 79; Progressive historians and the historical imagination in Austria: Heinrich Friedjung and Richard Charmatz, Austrian History Yearbook, 83-84; Austro-German liberalism and the modern liberal tradition, Ger Studies Rev, 5/84; Dictionary of Concepts in History, Greenwood, 86; German policy in occupied Greece and its economic impact, In: Germany and Europe in the Era of the Two World Wars (Frank X J Homer and Larry Wilcox, ed), 86; Austria and the struggle for German identity, Ger Studies Rev, winter 92; auth, "From Hasburg to Hitler Haider: The Peculiarities of Austrian History," Ger Studies Rv, 99. **CONTACT ADDRESS** Dept of Hist, Western Washington Univ, M/S 9056, Bellingham, WA 98225-5996. **EMAIL** harryr@cc.wwu.edu

RITVO, HARRIET
DISCIPLINE HISTORY; ENGLISH **EDUCATION** Harvard Univ, AB, 68, PhD, 75. **CAREER** Arthur J. Conner Prof of Hist, MIT. **HONORS AND AWARDS** Guggenheim Fel; Nat Endowment for the Humanities Fel; Whiting Writers Prize. **MEMBERSHIPS** AHA; SHNH; PEN; HSS. **RESEARCH** British cultural history; history of biology/natural history; human-animal relations. **SELECTED PUBLICATIONS** Auth, The Platypus and the Mermaid and Other Figments of Classifying Imagination, Harvard Univ Press, 97; The Animal Estate: The English and Other Creatures in the Victorian Age, Harvard Univ Press, 87, Penguin Books, 90; The Sincerest Form of Flattery, Dead or Alive: Animal Captives of Human Cultures, Princeton Univ Press, 99; The Roast Beef of Old England, Mad Cows and Modernity: Cross-disciplinary Reflections on the Crisis of Creutzfeldt-Jacob Disease, Humanities Res Centre, 98; Introduction, The Variation of Animals and Plants under Domestication, Johns Hopkins Univ Press, 98; Zoological Nomenclature and the Empire of Victorian Science, Contexts of Victorian Science, Univ of Chicago Press, 97; co-ed, The Macropolitics of Nineteenth-Century Literature: Nationalism, Imperialism, Exoticism, Univ of Pa Press, 91, Duke Univ Press, 95. **CONTACT ADDRESS** Massachusetts Inst of Tech, 77 Massachusetts Ave., E51-285, Cambridge, MA 02139. **EMAIL** hnritvo@mit.edu

RIVES, JAMES
DISCIPLINE ANCIENT HISTORY **EDUCATION** Univ Wash, BA, 83; Stanford Univ, PhD, 90. **CAREER** Assoc prof. **RESEARCH** Social and religious history of the Roman Empire. **SELECTED PUBLICATIONS** Auth, Religion and Authority in Roman Carthage: From Augustus to Constantine, 95. **CONTACT ADDRESS** Dept of Hist, Columbia Col, New York, 2960 Broadway, New York, NY 10027-6902.

RIX, BRENDA
PERSONAL Born Belleville, ON, Canada **DISCIPLINE** ART HISTORY **EDUCATION** Univ Toronto, BA, 78, MA, 80. **CAREER** Librn, 79-81, tchg asst, 79-81, Univ Toronto; res asst, educ off, 80-81, asst cur, 82-87, guest cur, 88-, Supervisor, Prints & Drawings Study Centre, Art Gallery Ontario, 93-. **MEMBERSHIPS** Print Coun Am; William Morris Soc Can; Friends Thomas Fisher Rare Book Libr. **SELECTED PUBLICATIONS** Auth, Pictures for the Parlour: The English Reproductive Print from 1775 to 1900, 83; auth, Our Old Friend Rolly: Watercolours, Prints, and Book Illustrations by Thomas Rowlandson in the Collection of the Art Gallery of Ontario, 87; auth, Prints in The Earthly Paradise: Arts and Crafts by William Morris and his Circle from Canadian Collections, 93. **CONTACT ADDRESS** Art Gallery of Ontario, 317 Dundas St W, Toronto, ON, Canada M5T 1G4.

ROARK, JAMES L.
DISCIPLINE HISTORY **EDUCATION** Univ Calif Davis, BA, 63, MA, 64; Stanford Univ, PhD, 73. **CAREER** Samuel Candler Dobbs Prof Am Hist. **RESEARCH** Southern history; 19th-century American history. **SELECTED PUBLICATIONS** Auth, Masters without Slaves; Southern Planters in the Civil War and Reconstruction; The American Promise: A History of the United States; coauth, Black Masters: A Free Family of Color in the Old South ; co-ed, No Chariot Let Down Charleston's Free People of Color on the Eve of the Civil War. **CONTACT ADDRESS** Dept History, Emory Univ, 221 Bowden Hall, 561 Kilgo Cir, Atlanta, GA 30322-1950. **EMAIL** jlroark@emory.edu

ROBB, GEORGE
DISCIPLINE EUROPEAN HISTORY **EDUCATION** Univ Tex at Austin, BA, 84; Northwestern Univ, PhD, 90. **CAREER** Dept Hist, William Paterson Univ **HONORS AND AWARDS** Mellon res fel at the Huntington Libr, 96; Amer Coun of Learned Soc, Summer Res Grant, 94; Fulbright, UK, 87-88. **RESEARCH** British Social and Cultural History during the 19th and 20th centuries; History of Crime; Women's History; British Eugenics Movement. **SELECTED PUBLICATIONS** Auth, White-Collar Crime in Mod England: Financial Fraud and Business Morality, 1845-1929, Cambridge Univ Press, 92; Out of the Doll's House: The Trial of Florence Maybrick and Anxiety Over the New Woman, Proteus, 96; The Way of All Flesh: Degeneration, Eugenics, and the Gospel of Free Love, J Hist Sexuality, 96; Popular Religion and the Christianization of the Scottish Highlands in the Eighteenth and Nineteenth Centuries, J Rel Hist, 90; rev(s), English Local Prisons 1860-1900, TLS, 95; The Hanging Tree, TLS, 94; Apprehending the Criminal: The Production of Deviance in Nineteenth-Century Discourse, Victorian Stud, 94; The Cambridge Social History of Britain, 1750-1950, 3 vols, J Econ Hist, 93. **CONTACT ADDRESS** Dept of History, William Paterson Col of New Jersey, 300 Pompton Rd, Atrium 210, Wayne, NJ 07470. **EMAIL** robb@frontier.wpunj.edu

ROBB, STEWART A.
PERSONAL Born 03/10/1943, Montreal, PQ, Canada **DISCIPLINE** HISTORY **EDUCATION** Univ BC, BA, 66; Simon Fraser Univ, MA, 69. **CAREER** Prof History, Univ PEI, 71-; dir, PEI Mus Heritage Found. **MEMBERSHIPS** Exec mem, Asn Can Stud, 74-80; ch, Coun Can Stud Prog Admins, 80-82. **RESEARCH** Canadian studies. **SELECTED PUBLICATIONS** Contribur, Dictionary of Canadian Biography; contribur, New Canadian Encyclopedia; bk rev ed, Can Rev Stud Nationalism. **CONTACT ADDRESS** History Dept, Univ of Prince Edward Island, 550 University Ave, Charlottetown, PE, Canada C1A 4P3. **EMAIL** robb@upei.ca

ROBBERT, LOUISE BUENGER
PERSONAL Born 08/18/1925, St. Paul, MN, m, 1960, 1 child **DISCIPLINE** MEDIEVAL STUDIES **EDUCATION** Carleton Col, BA, 47; Univ of Cincinnati, MA, 48, BEd, 49; Univ of Wis-Madison, 55, PhD. **CAREER** Instr, Smith Col, 54-55; instr in hist, Hunter Col of the City of NY, 57-60; asst prof, 62-63, assoc prof of hist, Tex Tech Univ, 64-75; Vis Assoc Prof, 78-79, Assoc Adjunct Prof, 79-91, Prof, Univ of MO, 91-. **HONORS AND AWARDS** Fulbright Scholar, 55-57; Grant in Aid, ACLS, 60; Gladys Krieble Delmas Grant in Aid, 83 & 87; Grant in Aid, Newberry Libr, 91 & 92. **MEMBERSHIPS** Am Hist Asn; Medieval Acad of Am; Soc for the Study of the Crusades and the Latin East; Midwest Medieval Hist Confr. **RESEARCH** Medieval Venice, especially money, business, colonies, and Crusades. **SELECTED PUBLICATIONS** Auth, Money and prices in thirteenth-century Venice, J of Medieval Hist, 94; Rialto businessmen and Constantinople 1204-61, Dumbarton Oaks Papers, 95; Il Sistema monetario, Storia di Venezia dalle origini alla caduta della serenissima, 95; Donald E. Queller, Memoirs of Fellows and Corresponding Fellows of the Medieval Academy of America, Speculum, 96; Venetian Participation in the Crusade of Damietta, Studi Veneziani, 95. **CONTACT ADDRESS** Dept of Hist, Univ of Missouri, St. Louis, 8001 Natural Bridge Rd, Saint Louis, MO 63121.

ROBBINS, EDWARD
PERSONAL Born 01/19/1944, Brooklyn, NY, s **DISCIPLINE** URBAN PLANNING **EDUCATION** Grinnell Col, BA, 64; Univ Mich, MA, 66; PhD, 74. **CAREER** Lectr, Harvard Grad Sch Design, 89-. **RESEARCH** Urban Society, Community, Design and Social/Cultural life. **SELECTED PUBLICATIONS** Auth, "Valdez", Social Indicators Study of Alaska Coastal Villages: IV, Post-Spill Key Informant Summary Schedule C: Communities, part I, (Cordova, Taitlek and Valdez), US Dept of Interior, (Anchorage, 93): 30-126; auth, Why Architects Draw, MIT Press, (Cambridge), 94; coauth, "Reuse Strategies for Military Base Conversions: Summary Report", US Dept of Commerce, (Washington, DC), 97; coauth, "Reuse Strategies for Military Base Conversions", US Dept of Commerce, (Washington, DC), 97; auth, "The New Urbanism and the Fallacy of Singularity", Urban Design Int 3.1 (98): 33-42; auth, "Thinking the City Multiple", Harvard Arch Rev, Princeton Archit Pr, (NY), 98; auth, "Rethinking Base Reuse: Community Responses to Closure", Econ Develop Commentary 22.3 (98): 22-28; ed, "Engaging the City Plural: Urban Design and Planning in the Contemporary Context", Urban Design Int, 3.1 (98); auth, "The Trouble with Trialectics, Space, Time and the City", Design Book Rev, (forthcoming); auth, "Can/Should Designers Foster Community", Builder/Designer, (forthcoming). **CONTACT ADDRESS** Dept Urban Planning and Design, Harvard Univ, 48 Quincy St, Cambridge, MA 02138.

ROBBINS, RICHARD G.
PERSONAL Born 03/06/1939, Buffalo, NY, m, 1966, 2 children **DISCIPLINE** HISTORY **EDUCATION** Williams Col, BA, 61; Columbia Univ, MA, 65; PhD, 70. **CAREER** Asst prof to prof, chair, Univ of NMex, 69-. **HONORS AND AWARDS** Fulbright-Hays Fel, USSR, 67-68, 81; IREX Grants, 67-68, 76, 81, 90. **MEMBERSHIPS** AHA; Am Assoc for Advanc of Slavic Studies; Hist Soc. **RESEARCH** Russian hist, Eastern Europ hist, Institutional hist. **SELECTED PUBLICATIONS** Auth, Famine in Russia 1891-1892: The Imperial Government Responds to a Crisis, 75; auth,"Russia's Famine Relief Law of June 12, 1900: A Reform Aborted, Canadian-American Slavic Studies, 76; auth, Choosing the Russian Governors: The Professionalization of the Gubernationrial Corps, Slavonic and East Europ Rev, 80; auth, The Tsar's Viceroyus: Russian Provincial Governoirs in the Last Years of the Empire, 87. **CONTACT ADDRESS** Dept Hist, Univ of New Mexico, Albuquerque, 1 University Campus, Albuquerque, NM 87131-0001. **EMAIL** rrobbins@unm.edu

ROBBINS, WILLIAM GROVER
PERSONAL Born 09/20/1935, Torrington, CT, 4 children **DISCIPLINE** AMERICAN HISTORY **EDUCATION** Western Conn State Col, BS, 62; Univ Ore, MA, 65, PhD(hist), 69. **CAREER** Asst prof hist, Ore Col Educ, 69-71; asst prof, 71-77, Assoc Prof Hist, Ore State Univ, 77- **MEMBERSHIPS** Orgn Am Historians; AHA; Forest Hist Soc. **RESEARCH** Indian-white relations; conservation history; forest history. **SELECTED PUBLICATIONS** Auth, The founding of the Massachusetts Bay Company: An analysis of motives, Historian, 69; Opportunity and persistence in the Pacific Northwest: A quantitative study of early Roseburg, Oregon, Pac Hist Rev, 70; Community conflict in western Oregon, 1870-1885, J of the West, 73; The conquest of the American West: History as eulogy, Indian Historian, 77; The political economy of water resource development: Oregon's Willamette Valley Project, Pac Hist Rev, 78; Herbert Hoover's Indian reformers under attack: The failures of administrative reform, Mid-Am, 82; Voluntary cooperation vs regulatory paternalism: The lumber trade in the 1920's, Bus Hist Rev, 82; Lumberjacks and Legislators: The Political Economy of the Lumber Industry, 1890-1941, Tex A&M Univ Press, 82. **CONTACT ADDRESS** Dept of Hist, Oregon State Univ, 306 Milam Hall, Corvallis, OR 97331-5104.

ROBERGE, RENE-MICHEL
PERSONAL Born 07/08/1944, Charny, PQ, Canada **DISCIPLINE** THEOLOGY, HISTORY **EDUCATION** Univ Laval, BA, 65, BTh, 67, LTh, 69, DTh, 71. **CAREER** PROF THEOLOGIE FONDAMENTALE ET D'HISTOIRE DE LA THEOLOGIE, UNIV LAVAL, 71-, prof titulaire, 83-, vice-doyen theol, 88-89, doyen, 89-97; dir de la revue Laval theologique et philosophique, 87-92. **MEMBERSHIPS** Int Asn Patristic Stud; Can Soc Patristic Stud; N Am Patristic Soc; Soc can de theologie. **SELECTED PUBLICATIONS** Auteur d'une cinquantaine de pubs et de nom communications en patristique, en theol fond et system, et en documentation spec. **CONTACT ADDRESS** Fac de Theologie, Univ of Laval, Laval, QC, Canada G1K 7P4. **EMAIL** Rene-Michel.Roberge@fes.ulaval.ca

ROBERT, JEAN-CLAUDE
PERSONAL Born 04/27/1943, Montreal, PQ, Canada **DISCIPLINE** HISTORY **EDUCATION** Univ Montreal, BA, 66, LL, 69, MA, 71; Univ Paris, doctorat en histoire, 77. **CAREER** Hist tchr, sec sch Mont-de-Lasalle, 67-69; socio cult serv, CEGEP de Joliette, 69-71; instr, Univ Que Chicoutimi, 74; PROF REGULIER HISTOIRE, UNIV QUEBEC MONTREAL, 75-, dir dept, 77-79, 97-. **MEMBERSHIPS** Inst hist Am francaise; Can Hist Asn (coun, 80-83, 88-92, vice pres, 88-89, pres, 89-90); Comite Int des Sci Historiques. **SELECTED PUBLICATIONS** Auth, Du Canada francais au Quebec libre, 75; auth, Atlas historique de Montreal, 94; coauth, Histoire du Quebec contemporain, 79; coauth, Quebec: A History 1867-1929, 83; coauth, Le Quebec depuis 1930, 86; coauth, Quebec Since 1930, 91; coauth, Atlas historique du Quebec: le pays Laurentian au XIX siecle, 95. **CONTACT ADDRESS** Dept of history, Univ of Quebec, Montreal, CP 8888, Montreal, QC, Canada H3C 3P8. **EMAIL** robert.jean-claude@uqam.ca

ROBERTS, BARBARA A.
PERSONAL Born Riverside, CA **DISCIPLINE** HISTORY, WOMEN'S STUDIES **EDUCATION** Simon Fraser Univ, BA, 72, MA, 76; Univ Ottawa, PhD, 80. **CAREER** Vis prof, 80-82, lectr, Univ Winnipeg, 82-83; asst prof, Univ Sask, 83-84; asst prof, Concordia Univ, 87-88; assoc prof, 89-92, Prof Women's Studies, Athabaska Univ 92-. **MEMBERSHIPS** Bd dir, Can Res Inst Advan Women; Voice of Women. **SELECTED PUBLICATIONS** Auth, Whence They Came: Deportation from Canada 1900-35, 88; auth, A Decent Living: Women in the Winnipeg Garment Industry, 91; auth, Strategies for the Year 2000: A Women's Handbook, 95; auth, A Reconstructed World: A Feminist Biography of Gertrude Richardson, 96. **CONTACT ADDRESS** Dept of Women's Studies, Athabasca Univ, Athabasca, AB, Canada TOG 2RO. **EMAIL** barbara@cs.athabaska.ca

ROBERTS, CHARLES EDWARD
PERSONAL Born 08/25/1941, Bennington, OK, m, 1971, 2 children **DISCIPLINE** AMERICAN INDIAN HISTORY **EDUCATION** Fresno State Col, BA, 62; Univ Ore, MA, 67, PhD(hist), 75. **CAREER** Asst prof, 70-76, assoc prof Hist, Califor State Univ, Sacremento, 82-. **MEMBERSHIPS** Am Indian Historians Asn; Orgn Am Historians; Western History Asn; Am Soc Ethnohist. **RESEARCH** Choctaw Indian hist; Northern California Indian history; American Indian literature. **SELECTED PUBLICATIONS** Coauth, The Choctaws: A Critical Bibliography, Ind Univ Press, 80; auth, The Second Choctaw Removal, 1903 in After Removal: the Choctaw in Mississippi, Univ Press of Mississippi, 86; the cushman Indian Trades School and World War I, American Indian Quarterly, 87; A Choctaw Odyssey: the Life of Lesa Phillip Roberts, American Indian Quarterly, 90. **CONTACT ADDRESS** Dept of History, California State Univ, Sacramento, 6000 J St, Sacramento, CA 95819-2694.

ROBERTS, MARION ELIZABETH
PERSONAL Born 05/26/1939, Berwyn, IL, m, 1973 **DISCIPLINE** ART HISTORY **EDUCATION** Duke Univ, BA, 60; Columbia Univ, MA, 62; Univ Chicago, PhD(art hist), 70. **CAREER** Asst prof art hist, Northern IL Univ, 66-68; from asst prof to assoc prof art hist, Univ Va, 68-; sesquicentennial assoc, Inst Advan Studies, 73. **MEMBERSHIPS** British Archaeol Asn; Medieval Acad Am; Col Art Asn; Int Center for Medieval Art. **RESEARCH** Salisbury Catherdral; illustrated pubs of Sir William Dugdale; English 13th Century architecture and sculpure; English medievalist antiquaries. **SELECTED PUBLICATIONS** Auth, Towards a Literary Source for the Scenes in the Passion in Queen Mary's Psalter, J Warburg & Courtauld Insts, 73; The Ark, Friends of Wells Cathedral Report, 73; The Tomb of Bishop Giles de Bridport in Salisbury Cathedral, Art Bull, LXV, 83; The Relic of the Holy Blood and the Iconography of the 13th-century North Transept Portal of Westminster Abbey, England in the 13th century, Proceedings of the 1984 Harlaxton Symposium, Grantham, 86; John Carter at St Stephen's Chapel, Westminster: a Romantic turns Archaeologist, England in the 14th century, Proceedings of the 1985 Harlaxton Symposium, Grantham, 86; The Dictionary of Art, London, John Carter; The Effigy of Bishop Hugh de Northwold in Ely Cathedral, The Burlington Magazine, vol CXXX, no 1019, Feb 88; The Emergence of Clarity, Images of English Cathedrals 1640-1840, Charlottesville, VA, 88; The Dictionary of Art, London, French Painting; Architectural History, London, Thomas Gray's Contribution to the Study of Medieval Architecture, vol 36, 93; The Seventeenth-century Restoration (catalogue of an exhibition of rare books in Alderman Library), with Prof Everett Crosby, Charlottesville, 93; auth, Dugdale and Hollar: Hist Illustrated, forthcoming. **CONTACT ADDRESS** McIntire Dept of Art, Univ of Virginia, 102 Fayerweather Hall, Charlottesville, VA 22903.

ROBERTS, WARREN ERROL
PERSONAL Born 05/08/1933, Los Angeles, CA, m, 1957, 4 children **DISCIPLINE** MODERN HISTORY **EDUCATION** Univ Southern Calif, BS, 55; Univ Calif, Berkeley, BA, 59, MA, 60, PhD, 66. **CAREER** Asst prof, 63-71, assoc prof, 71-80, Prof Hist, State Univ NY Albany, 80-; Distinguished, Teacher Prof, 84-. **RESEARCH** England, France, 1780-1830 literature and history; Jane Austen. **SELECTED PUBLICATIONS** Auth, Literature and Painting, Morality and Society in 18th-Century France, Univ Toronto, 74; Jane Austen and the French Revolution, Macmillan, Gt Brit, 79; auth, Revolutionary arts-art Politics and the French Revolution, Univ of NC, 89; auth, The Public, the Populace, and Images of the French Revolution, SUNY Press, 99. **CONTACT ADDRESS** Dept of Hist, SUNY, Albany, Albany, NY 12222.

ROBERTS, WESLEY A.
PERSONAL Born 01/03/1938, Jamaica, WI, m, 1962, 4 children **DISCIPLINE** HISTORY **EDUCATION** Waterloo Lutheran Univ, BA 1965; Toronto Baptist Seminary, MDiv 1965; Westminster Theological Seminary, ThM 1967; Univ of Guelph, MA 1968, PhD 1972 **CAREER** Gordon-Conwell Theological Seminary, asst prof of black studies 1972-73, asst prof of Christian Thought 1974-75, assoc prof of Church History, 77-84, asst dean for acad prog 1980-84, prof of Church History 1984-85; Peoples Baptist Church of Boston, MA, interim pastor, 80-82, pastor, 82-; Gordon College, Wenham, MA, adjunct professor of History, 74-. **MEMBERSHIPS** Mem Soc for the Study of Black Religion, Amer Soc of Church History, Conf of Faith & History; mem exec comm The Assoc of Theological Schools in the US & Canada 1980-84; pres, Black Ministerial Alliance of Greater Boston 1994-. **SELECTED PUBLICATIONS** Articles published in Eerdman's Handbook of Amer Christianity, Eerdman's Handbook of the History of Christianity, Fides et Historia; Ontario Grad Fellowship Government of Ontario 1968-70; Canada Council Doctoral Fellowship Government of Canada 1970-72; author, Chapter on Cornelius VanTil in Reformed Theology in America, Wm B Eerdman, 1985, in Dutch Reformed Theology, Baker Bookhouse, 1988; article, Martin Luther King Jr and the March on Washington, in Christian History Magazine, 1989; article, Rejecting the "Negro Pew," in Christian History Magazine, 1995. **CONTACT ADDRESS** Senior Pastor, Peoples Baptist Church of Boston, 134 Camden Street, Boston, MA 02118. **EMAIL** waroberts@mediaone.net

ROBERTS, WILLIAM
PERSONAL Born 07/24/1960, Weehawken, NJ, s **DISCIPLINE** HISTORY, GOVERNMENT **EDUCATION** Fairleigh Dickinson Univ, BA, 67; Fordham Univ, MA, 69; City Univ NY (CUNY), MPhil, 87; City Univ NY (CUNY), PhD, 88. **CAREER** Prof, Fairleigh Dickinson Univ, 88-. **HONORS AND AWARDS** EWC Outstanding Fac Awd, 92; Who's Who in the East, 93; FDU Outstanding Fac Awd, 94; FDU Distinguished Fac Awd for Serv, 99. **RESEARCH** Intellectual history, modern European history. **SELECTED PUBLICATIONS** Coauth, Mazzinianesimo nel Mondo, Pisa: Instituto Domus Mazziniana, 95; coauth, "Mazzini and Lamennais," Encycl of the Essay, Fitzroy Dearborn (97); auth, Controversial Concordats: The Church and the Dictators, CUA Pr (Washington, DC), 99. **CONTACT ADDRESS** Dept Hist & Govt, Fairleigh Dickinson Univ, Teaneck-Hackensack, 1000 River Rd, Teaneck, NJ 07666-1914.

ROBERTSON, JAMES I.
PERSONAL Born 07/18/1930, Danville, VA, m, 1952, 3 children **DISCIPLINE** HISTORY **EDUCATION** Randolphy-Macon Col, BA, 55; Emory Univ, MA, 56; PhD, 59. **CAREER** Assoc Prof, Univ Mo, 65-67; Prof, Va Polytech Inst, 67-. **RESEARCH** Southern Confederacy; Civil War biography. **SELECTED PUBLICATIONS** Auth, The Sonewall Brigade; auth, General A.P. Hill; auth, Civil War! America Becomes One Nation; auth, Soldiers Blue and Gray; auth, Stonewall Jackson: The Man, The Soldier, The Legend. **CONTACT ADDRESS** Dept Hist, Virginia Polytech Inst and State Univ, Blacksburg, VA 24061-0117.

ROBERTSON, JAMES IRVIN
PERSONAL Born 07/18/1930, Danville, VA, m, 1952, 3 children **DISCIPLINE** HISTORY **EDUCATION** Randolph-Macon Col, BA, 55; Emory Univ, MA, 56, PhD, 59; Randolph-Macon Col, Litt. D., 80. **CAREER** Ed, Civil War History, Univ of Iowa, 59-61; exec. dir U.S. Civil War Centennial Comn, Wash, D.C., 61-65; assoc prof, Univ Mont, 65-67; prof, Va Polytech Inst and State Univ, 67-. **HONORS AND AWARDS** Douglas Southall Freeman Awd; Fletcher Pratt Lit. Awd; Richard Barksdale Harwell Awd; Jefferson Davis Awd; Lit Achievement Awd; Special resolution of thanks from both houses of the Va Gen Assembly, 97-98; Va Press Assoc "Virginian of the Year 2000 Awd." **MEMBERSHIPS** Southern Hist Asn, Va Hist Soc, Museum of the Confederacy, Stonewall Jackson Found. **RESEARCH** Confed. States of Am; Confed. Va, Am Presidency. **SELECTED PUBLICATIONS** Coauth, Jackson & Lee: Legends in Gray, 95; ed, Four Years with General Lee, 96; auth, Stonewall Jackson: The Man, The Soldier, The Legend, 97; Soldiers Blue and Gray, 98. **CONTACT ADDRESS** Dept of History, Virginia Polytech Inst and State Univ, Blacksburg, VA 24061.

ROBINET, HARRIETTE GILLEM
PERSONAL Born 07/14/1931, Washington, DC, m, 1960, 6 children **DISCIPLINE** HISTORY OF SCIENCE **EDUCATION** Col New Rochelle, BS, 53; Catholic Univ Am, MS, 57; PhD, 63. **CAREER** Bacteriologist, Walter Reed Army Med Ctr, 53-63; writer, 63-. **HONORS AND AWARDS** Friends Am Writers; Carl Sandburg Awd; Midwest Writers Awd; Scott O'Dell Award for Children's Historical Fiction. **MEMBERSHIPS** Soc Children's Bk Writers & Illustrators; Soc of Midland Authors; Sisters in Crime; Mystery Writers of Am; Nat Writers Union. **SELECTED PUBLICATIONS** Auth, Children of the Fire, Atheneum, 91; auth, Mississippi Chariot, Atheneum, 94; auth, If You Please, President Lincoln, Atheneum, 95; auth, Washington City is Burning, Atheneum, 96; auth, The

Twins, The Pirates, and the Battle of New Orleans, Atheneum, 97; auth, Forty Acres and Maybe a Mule, Atheneum, 98; auth, Walking to the Bus-Rider Blues, Atheneum, 00; auth, The Stolen Key and the Haymarket Struggle, Atheneum, 01. **CONTACT ADDRESS** 214 S Elmwood Ave, Oak Park, IL 60302.

ROBINS, GAY
PERSONAL Born 06/28/1951, Fleet, England, m, 1980 **DISCIPLINE** EGYPTOLOGY **EDUCATION** Univ Durham, BA (honors), 75; Univ Oxford, DPhil, 81. **CAREER** Lady Wallis Budge Fellow in Egyptology, Christ's College, Cambridge, 79-83; honorary research fel, Univ Coll London, 84-88; asst prof, 88-94, assoc prof, 94-98, prof, 98-, Art History Dept, curator of Egyptian art, 88-94, faculty curator of ancient Egyptian art, 94-98, faculty consult for ancient Egyptian art, 98-, Michael C. Carlos Museum, Emory Univ. **HONORS AND AWARDS** Thomas Mulvey Fund grant, H.M. Chadwick Fund grant, Univ Cambridge, 85; Suzette Taylor Travelling Fellow, Lady Margaret Hall, Oxford, 85-86; Wainwright Near Eastern Archeol Fund grant, 87; Natl Endowment for the Humanities grant, 92; Univ Research Comm grant, Emory Univ, 95-96. **MEMBERSHIPS** Amer Res Center in Egypt; Coll Art Assn; Egyptian Exploration Soc; Egyptological Seminar of New York; Soc Study Egyptian Antiquities; Archaeological Institute of Am. **RESEARCH** The content and function of ancient Egyptian art; use of the squared grid and changes in the proportions of figures in ancient Egyptian art; the Amarna grid system; composition of whole scenes in ancient Egyptian art; hierarchies in ancient Egyptian art; status of women in ancient Egypt. **SELECTED PUBLICATIONS** Auth, Egyptian Painting and Relief, Shire Publications, 86; auth, The Rhind Mathematical Papyrus: an Ancient Egyptian Text with C.C.D. Shute; British Museum Publications and Dover Publications, 87; reprinted 90, 98; ed., and contri, Beyond the Pyramids: Egyptian Regional Art from the Museo Egizio, Turin, catalogue of exhibition at the Emory University Museum of Art and Archaeology editor and contributor; Atlanta, 90; auth, Women in Ancient Egypt British Museum Press and Harvard University Press, 93; reprinted 96; German translation 96; Spanish translation 96; taken by The History Bookclub, 97; auth, Proportion and Style in Ancient Egyptian Art University of Texas Press and Thames and Hudson, 94, auth, Reflections of Women in the New Kingdom: Ancient Egyptitan Art from The British Museum, catalogue of exhibition at the Michael C. Carlos Museum, Emory University, assisted by Sheramy D. Bundrick; San Antonio, Texas, 95; auth, The Art of Ancient Egypt, British Museum Press and Harvard University Press, 97; taken by The History Book Club 97. **CONTACT ADDRESS** Art History Dept, Emory Univ, Carlos Hall, Atlanta, GA 30322. **EMAIL** grobins@emory.edu

ROBINS, MARIANNE RUEL
DISCIPLINE EARLY MODERN EUROPE HISTORY **EDUCATION** Univ, Paris-Sorbonne, 97. **CAREER** Instr, Duke Univ, 91; instr, Calvin Col, 93-96; asst prof, Westmont Col, 96-. **RESEARCH** French civilization and culture **SELECTED PUBLICATIONS** Auth, Un prophete en son pays: la Lettre chretienne d'une dame de la noblesse d'Argula von Stauffen, Paroles d'Evangiles, Publ de la Sorbonne, 95; Les chretiens et la danse dans l'Europe du Nord-Ouest, Historiens et Geographes, 94. **CONTACT ADDRESS** Dept of Hist, Westmont Col, 955 La Paz Rd, Santa Barbara, CA 93108-1099.

ROBINSON, DAVID W.
PERSONAL Born 10/07/1938, Columbia, SC, m, 1972 **DISCIPLINE** HISTORY **EDUCATION** Davidson Col, BA, 60; Columbia Univ, PhD, 71. **CAREER** From Asst Prof to Assoc Prof, Yale Univ, 70-78; From Assoc Prof to Prof, Mich State Univ, 78-. **HONORS AND AWARDS** SSRC, NEH, Fulbright Fels; Distinguished Fac Awd, Mich State Univ, 91; Univ Distinguished Prof, Mich State Univ, 92. **MEMBERSHIPS** African Studies Asn. **RESEARCH** African and Islamic history, French imperial history. **SELECTED PUBLICATIONS** Coauth, After the Jihad: The Reign of Ahmad al-Kabir in the Western Sudan, Mich St Univ Press, 91; ed, Le Temps des marabouts: Itineraires et strategies islamiques en Afrique Occidentale Francaise, 1880-1960, Karthala Publ, 97; auth, Paths to Accommodation: Muslim Communities, Colonial Authorities and Civil Society in Senegal and Mauritania, Ohio UP, 00. **CONTACT ADDRESS** Dept Hist, Michigan State Univ, 301 Morrill Hall, East Lansing, MI 48824-1036. **EMAIL** robindav@mail.matrix.msu.edu

ROBINSON, ELLA S.
PERSONAL Born 04/16/1943, Wedowee, AL, d, 1980, 1 child **DISCIPLINE** ENGLISH, HISTORY **EDUCATION** Ala St Univ, BS, 65; Univ of Nebr, MA, 70; PhD, 76. **CAREER** Asst Prof, Univ of Nebraska, 81-91; Assoc Prof, Tuskegee Univ, 94-00; Asst Prof, Univ of Illinois, 75-77; Asst Prof, Atlanta Univ, 77-79. **HONORS AND AWARDS** Who's Who of American Women; Who's Who in the South and Southwest; Who's Who Among Black Americans. **MEMBERSHIPS** Modern Language Assoc (MLA); African Lit Assoc (ALA); Lincoln Nebraska Chaparral Poets (LCNP); National Council of Teachers of English (NCTE). **RESEARCH** African American; Women's Lit; Poetry and Crititcism. **SELECTED PUBLICATIONS** Auth, "The Tragic Life of Bessie Head: Lit in South Africa;" auth, "Myth as Regeneration in Aime Cesaire's Poetry." **CONTACT ADDRESS** Dept English and Reading, Tuskegee Univ, 1 Tuskegee Univ, Tuskegee Institute, AL 36088-1600. **EMAIL** e-robin@acd.tusk.edu

ROBINSON, GENEVIEVE
PERSONAL Born 04/20/1940, Kansas City, MO, s **DISCIPLINE** HISTORY **EDUCATION** Mt St Scholastica Coll, BA history 1968; New Mexico Highlands Univ, MA history 1974; The Catholic Univ of Amer, history 1978-79; Boston Coll, PhD history 1986. **CAREER** Lillis HS, history teacher 1969-73, 74-75, history dept chairperson 1970-73, admin/curriculum dir 1974-75; Donnelly Comm Coll, instructor 1976-78; Boston Coll, instructor 1983; Rockhurst Univ, instr 1985-86, asst prof 1986-91, dir, honors program, 90-, associate professor, 91-, chair of dept of history, 94-. **HONORS AND AWARDS** Gasson Fellowship Boston Coll 1984-85; Natl Endowment for the Humanities Coll Teachers Summer Seminar Grant 1987, Presidential Grant, Rockhurst Coll, 1988; Natl Endowment for the Humanities Summer Inst, NEH, 1990; Lilly Workshop on the Liberal Arts, Lilly Endowment, Inc, 1990; Rockhurst College, Presidential Grant, 1988, 1992; Vietnam: Distinguished Alumnus, New Mexico Highlands Univ, 00; International Faculty Development Seminar, 01; Rockhurst Title III Grant; Wills Travel Grant. **MEMBERSHIPS** Mem Phi Alpha Theta, Kappa Mu Epsilon, Organization of Amer Historians, Immigration History Soc, Pi Gamma Mu; mem Ethical Review Board 1988-; Notre Dame de Sion Schools, board of directors, 1990-95; National Assn of Women in Catholic Higher Education, St Monica School Bd, 00-. **RESEARCH** Immigration History. **CONTACT ADDRESS** Chair/History Dept, Assoc Prof, Rockhurst Col, 1100 Rockhurst Rd, Kansas City, MO 64110-2508. **EMAIL** genevieve.robinson@rockhurst.edu

ROBINSON, IRA
PERSONAL Born 05/02/1951, Boston, MA, m, 1976, 2 children **DISCIPLINE** NEAR EASTERN LANGUAGES AND CIVILIZATIONS **EDUCATION** Johns Hopkins Univ, BA, 73; Columbia Univ, MA, 75; Harvard Univ, PhD, 80. **CAREER** Lectr, Concordia Univ, 79-80; asst prof, Concordia Univ, 80-84; assoc prof, Concordia Univ, 84-93; prof, relig, Concordia Univ, 93-. **HONORS AND AWARDS** Toronto Jewish Book award, 97; Kenneth B. Smilen book prize, Jewish Mus, 86. **MEMBERSHIPS** Asn for Can Jewish Studies; Asn for Jewish Studies; Soc Quebecois pour lietude de la religion; Am Jewish Hist Soc; Am Academy of Relig; Israel Hist Soc; Canadian Ethnic Studies Asn. **RESEARCH** Canadian Jewry; Orthodox Judaism in North America. **SELECTED PUBLICATIONS** Ed, The Thought of Moses Maimonides: Philosophical and Legal Studies, (Lewiston, Queenston and Lampeter, Edwin Mellen Press, 90; transl, Menahem Kaufman, An Ambiguous Partnership: Non-Zionist and Zionist in America, 1939-1948, (Jerusalem, Magnes Press, 91); auth, Moses Cordovero's Introduction to Kabbala: An Annotated Traslation of His or Ne'Erav, (Ktav/Yeshiva Univ Press, 94); co-ed, The Interaction of Scientific and Jewish Cultures In Modern Times, (Lewiston, Queenston and Lampeter, Edwin Mellen Press, 94); ed, Renewing Our Days: Montreal Jews in the Twentieth Century, (Montreal, Vehicule Press, 95); auth, "The Zaddik as Hero in Hasidic Hagiography," in Crisis and Reaction: the Hero in Jewish History, ed. Menachem Mor, (Omaha, Nebraska, Creighton Univ Press, (95): 93-103; auth, "Foreword," in A Selected Bibliography of Research on Canadian Jewry, 1900-1980, ed. Susan Vadnay, 95; auth, "An Identification and a Correction," Am Jewish Archives 47, (95): 331-332; auth, "The Foundation Documents of the Jewish Community Council of Montreal," New York, Jewish Theological Sem of Am, vol. 1, (97): 103-159; auth, "Virtual Reality Comes to Canadian Jewry," Jerusalem Letter/ Viewpoints no. 389, (98): 1-5. **CONTACT ADDRESS** Dept. of Religion, Concordia Univ, Montreal, 1455 Maisonneuve Blvd. W, Montreal, QC, Canada H3G 1M8. **EMAIL** robinso@vax2.concordia.ca

ROBINSON, JIM C.
PERSONAL Born 02/09/1943, Ackerman, MS **DISCIPLINE** AFRICAN-AMERICAN STUDIES **EDUCATION** CA St, BA 1966; CA St, MA 1968; Stanford U, MA 1972; Stanford U, PhD 1973. **CAREER** CA St Univ Long Beach, assoc prof Black Studies; CA St, spec asst vice pres acad affrs; CA St, dean faculty & staff affairs; San Jose St Coll, teacher. **MEMBERSHIPS** Mem, Nat Alliance of Black Sch Educators; Am Assn of Univ & Prof; dir of Reg Programs in W for Am Assn for Higher Edn; chmn Assn of Black Faculty &Staff of So CA; mem Mayor's Task Force Fiscal Mgmt & Cntrl, Compton. **CONTACT ADDRESS** California State Univ, Long Beach, 1250 Bellflower Blvd, Long Beach, CA 90840.

ROBINSON, JONTYLE THERESA
PERSONAL Born 07/22/1947, Atlanta, GA, 1 child **DISCIPLINE** ART HISTORY **EDUCATION** Clark College, BA, Spanish, 1968; Univ of Georgia, MA, art history, 1971; Univ of Maryland, PhD, contemporary Caribbean and Latin American art history, 1983. **CAREER** University of Georgia, Study Abroad Program (Europe) Fellowship, research assistant, 70; Atlanta University, instructor, summer 1971, 72; Philander Smith College, acting chairperson, 71-72; University of Maryland, Eastern Shore, instructor, 72-75; Emory University, instructor, 78-83, assistant professor, joint appointment in African-American and African Studies Program/art history, 83-86, director, designer, African-American and African studies/art history, Summer Study Abroad Program, Haiti, Jamaica, 84, 86, Haiti, The Dominican Republic, Puerto Rico, 85; West Virginia State College, associate professor, 86-87; Smithsonian Institution/Archives of American Art, research for a retrospective exhibition, catalogue raisonne, American painter Archibald John Motley Jr, 86-88; Kenkeleba Gallery, research fellow, cocurator, Three Masters: Cortor, Lee-Smith, Motley, 87-88; Winthrop College, associate professor, 89; Spellman College, Department of Art, Associate Prof, 89-. **HONORS AND AWARDS** Spelman College, Coca-Cola Fund Grant for presentation/lecture for the African Americans in Europe Conference, Paris, France, 1992, Department of Art, Amoco Faculty Awd, nominee, 1992, Bush Faculty Development Grant, Research for African American Architects, City Planners, Artisans, and Designers 1619-1850, 1993; Bessie L Harper Estate, Grant for The Art of Archibald J Motley Jr, 1990-91; numerous others. **MEMBERSHIPS** Delta Sigma Theta; National Conference of Artists, national executive secretary, 1971-72; Phi Kappa Phi Natl Hon Society. **RESEARCH** African American women artists; images and ideas regarding the African American women. **SELECTED PUBLICATIONS** Auth, African Diaspora and the World (core currlculum course); Gomez, Michael, Robinson, Jontyle, et al. Readings for 111 and 112, Massachusetts Copley Publishing, 95, 96, 98; auth, Bearing Witness: Contemporary Works by African Am Women Artists, Atlanta, Spelman Col and Rizzoli International Publications, 96; auth, The Art of Ronald Burns; A Retrospective, Jontyle Theresa Robinson and Richard Powell, Atlanta, The Dept of Art, Spelman Col, 94; auth, BH3 Decades; The Art of Varnett P. Honeywood, Robinson, Jontyle Theresa Atlanta, The Dept of Art, Spelman Col, 92; auth, The Art of Archibald John Motley, Jr, Chicago, Chicago Historical Soc, 91; auth, Three Masters Eldzier Cortor, Huey Lee-Smith, Archibald John Motley, Jr., New York, The Kenkeleba Gallery, 88; auth, "Archibald John Motley, Jr." The Encyclopedia of Chicago History, Chicago, 98; auth, "Black Artists," Detroit, St. James Press, 97; auth, "James Adair Retrospective and Floyd Coleman Retrospective," Dept of Art, Spelman Col, Atlanta, Georgia, 95; auth, "Three African American Female Artists, Tina Allen, Synthia St. James, Beverly Buchanan," interview, Essence, 95; auth, "Ronald Burns, Artist," from Ronald Burns: A Retrospective," Dept of Art, Spelman Col, Atlanta, Georgia, 94. **CONTACT ADDRESS** Spelman Col, 350 Spelman Ln SW, Atlanta, GA 30314. **EMAIL** jayrobin@spelman.edu

ROBINSON, JOYCE H.
PERSONAL Born 06/04/1961, Norfolk, VA, m, 1992, 2 children **DISCIPLINE** AMERICAN AND AFRICAN AMERICAN ART **EDUCATION** Davidson Col, BA; Univ Va, MA, PhD. **CAREER** Affiliate asst prof, Pa State Univ, 96-; Palmer Museum of Art, assoc cur, 97-00; cur, 01-. **HONORS AND AWARDS** Kress Found Fel **MEMBERSHIPS** Col Art Asn; 19th Century Studies Asn. **RESEARCH** Modern American and Europe art. **SELECTED PUBLICATIONS** Auth, Musical Notes by Honore Danmier, PMA, 98; auth, Red Grooms and the Heroism of Modern Life, PMA, 98; auth, An Interlude in Giverny: The French Chevalier by Frederick MacMonries, PMA, 00; auth, An Artistic Friendship: Beauford Delaney and Lawrence Calcagro, Palmer Museum of Art, 01. **CONTACT ADDRESS** Palmer Museum of Art, Pennsylvania State Univ, Univ Park, University Park, PA 16802. **EMAIL** jhr11@psu.edu

ROBINSON, LILIEN F.
PERSONAL Born Liubljana, Yugoslavia, m **DISCIPLINE** FINE ARTS **EDUCATION** Johns Hopkins, PhD, 78; Geo Wash Univ, MA, 65, BA, 62 **CAREER** Prof, 79-, Chair, 77-91, 93-00; Assoc Prof, 76-79, Asst Prof, 65-76, Geo Wash Univ **HONORS AND AWARDS** Trachtenberg Svc Prize; Geo Wash Awd; Outstanding Teacher; Phi Beta Kappa; Grad Columbia College w/honors; fels, schols; phi beta kappa; grad w/ honors; fels, schols **MEMBERSHIPS** Col Art Asn; N Am Serbian Studies Asn **RESEARCH** Contemporary exhibit artists **SELECTED PUBLICATIONS** Auth, Clay Variance, Lyons Agency, 95; Anna Klumpke: In Context, AZ St Univ, 93; Antoine Louis Barye, 88. **CONTACT ADDRESS** Dept of Fine Arts & Art History, The George Washington Univ, Washington, DC 20052. **EMAIL** lfr@gwu.edu

ROBINSON, RAYMOND H.
PERSONAL Born 07/23/1927, Clearfield, PA, s **DISCIPLINE** HISTORY **EDUCATION** Penn State Univ, BA, 49; MA, 50; Harvard Univ, PhD, 58. **CAREER** Instr, Pa State Univ, 50-51; from instr to prof, Northeastern Univ, 52-. **HONORS AND AWARDS** Phi Beta Kappa, Phi Kappa Phi, Phi Alpha Theta, Pi Gamma Mu, Phi Mu Alpha. **MEMBERSHIPS** Am Hist Asn, Orgn of Am Historians, Mass Hist Soc, Wellesley Hist Soc. **RESEARCH** The Families of Commonwealth Avenue, Boston, since 1861, The First 222 Doctorates in History in the U.S., 1873-1900, The Iconography of George Washington. **SELECTED PUBLICATIONS** Auth, America's Testing Time 1848-1877, 73; auth, "The Families of Commonwealth Avenue," Mass Hist Soc Proceedings, 81; auth, The Boston Economy During the civil War, 88; auth, The Growing of America 1789-1848, 93; auth, "The Marketing of an Icon," in George Washington: American Symbol, 99. **CONTACT ADDRESS** Dept Hist, Northeastern Univ, 360 Huntington Ave, Boston, MA 02115-5005.

ROBINSON, SUSAN BARNES
DISCIPLINE ART HISTORY **EDUCATION** UCLA, BA, MA; Michigan Univ, PhD. **CAREER** Prof. **HONORS AND AWARDS** Fulbright fel, Italy. **MEMBERSHIPS** CAA; CRSLA. **RESEARCH** 20th century American and European Art. **SELECTED PUBLICATIONS** Auth, Francoise Gilot: A Retrospective, 1943-1978, Art Gallery, Loyola Marymount Univ, 79; auth, The spirit of the City, Laaband Art Gallery, Loyola Marymount Univ, 86; auth, Giacomo Balla: Divisionism and Futurism, UMI Res Press, 81; Mabel Dwight: a catalogue raisonne of the lithographs, Smithsonian, 96. **CONTACT ADDRESS** Dept of Art and Art History, Loyola Marymount Univ, 7900 Loyola Blvd, Los Angeles, CA 90045. **EMAIL** srobinso@popmail.lmu.edu

ROBINSON, TOM
DISCIPLINE HISTORY **EDUCATION** Univ New Brunswick, BA; McMaster Univ, PhD. **RESEARCH** Development of Christianity in the second and third century; development of computer programs for language training. **SELECTED PUBLICATIONS** Auth, pubs on Greek and early Christianity. **CONTACT ADDRESS** Dept of History, Univ of Lethbridge, 4401 University Dr W, Lethbridge, AB, Canada T1K 3M4. **EMAIL** robinson@uleth.ca

ROBSON, ANN W.
PERSONAL Born, England **DISCIPLINE** HISTORY **EDUCATION** Univ Toronto, BA, 53, MA, 54; Univ London, Eng, PhD, 58. **CAREER** Prof Hist to Prof Emer, Univ Toronto, 68-. **SELECTED PUBLICATIONS** Auth, A Moralist In and Out of Parliament; auth, Sexual Equality. **CONTACT ADDRESS** Dept of Hist, Univ of Toronto, 100 St George St, 2074 Sidney Smith Hall, Toronto, ON, Canada M5S 3G3. **EMAIL** arobson@epas.utoronto.ca

ROBSON, DAVID
PERSONAL Born 11/02/1946, Miami, FL, m, 1995 **DISCIPLINE** AMERICAN HISTORY **EDUCATION** Yale Univ, PhD, 74. **CAREER** Asst prof, Agnes Scott Coll, 71-74; vis asst prof, St Mary;s Univ, Nova Scotia, 74-75; asst prof, Emory Univ, 75-76; asst prof, Univ Wyo, 76-84; asst prof, John Carroll Univ, 85-93; PROF, DIR GRAD STUD, JOHN CARROLL UNIV, 93-. **MEMBERSHIPS** Am Hist Asn; Org Am Hist; Assoc Omihundro Inst Early Am Hist & Cult; Soc Hist of Early Am Repub; South Hist Asn **RESEARCH** American politics, intellectual, & higher educational history of 1750-1815. **SELECTED PUBLICATIONS** "Enlightening the Wilderness: Charles Nisbet's Failure at Higher Education in Post-Revolutionary Pennsylvania," History of Education Quarterly, 97; "Anticipating the Brethren: The Reverend Charles Nisbet Critiques the French Revolution," The Pennsylvania Magazine of History and Biography, 97. **CONTACT ADDRESS** John Carroll Univ, 20700 N Park Blvd, University Heights, OH 44118. **EMAIL** Robson@jcu.edu

ROCCA, AL M.
PERSONAL Born 05/08/1949, Brooklyn, NY, m, 1970, 2 children **DISCIPLINE** HISTORY, EDUCATION **EDUCATION** San Jose City Col, AA, 70; San Jose State Univ, BA, 72; San Jose State Univ, Elem Teach Cred, 73; San Jose State Univ, MA; Univ Calif at Davis, PhD. **CAREER** History Teacher, Sequoia Middle School, Redding, CA, 77-92; History Instr, Shasta Col, 80-; Assoc Prof of Education & History, Simpson Col, 92-. **HONORS AND AWARDS** Numerous local and state teaching Awds including outstanding history teacher by the Native Daughters of the Golden West. **MEMBERSHIPS** California Council for the Social Studies; National Council for the Social Studies; California Council on the Education of Teachers; Assoc for Supervision and Curriculum Development. **RESEARCH** Integration of geography into historical studies; building in the American West. **SELECTED PUBLICATIONS** Auth, "The Shasta Boomtowns: Community Building in the New Deal Era 93; "America's, Shasta, 1995. **CONTACT ADDRESS** Dept Arts & Sciences, Simpson Col, California, 2211 Coll View Dr, Redding, CA 96003-8601. **EMAIL** arocca@simpsmca.edu

ROCK, HOWARD BLAIR
PERSONAL Born 07/11/1944, Cleveland, OH, m, 1975, 2 children **DISCIPLINE** UNITED STATES HISTORY **EDUCATION** Brandeis Univ, BA, 66; NYork Univ, MA, 69, PhD(hist), 74. **CAREER** Asst prof, 73-79, assoc prof hist, FL Int Univ, 79-; NEH res fel, colonial value systs, Northwestern Univ, 78-79; Prof of History, Fl. Intl. Univ., 89-; Chair Faculty Senate, 99-. **MEMBERSHIPS** AHA; Orgn Am Historians; Soc Hist Early Am Repub. **SELECTED PUBLICATIONS** Auth, The Mechanics of New York City and the American Revolution: One Generation Later, NY Hist, 7/76; The Perils of Laissez-faire: The Aftermath of the New York Bakers Strike of 1801, Labor Hist, summer 76; Artisans of the New Republic: The Tradesmen of New York City in the Age of Jefferson, NY Univ, 79; A Delicate Balance: The Mechanics & the City in the Age of Jefferson, NY Hist Quart, 4/79; ed, The New York City Artisan, 1789-1825, 85; ed, Keepers of the Revolution, New Yorkers at Work in the New Republic, 93; auth, American Artisans: Explorations in Social Identity, John Hopkins Univ. Press, Paul Gilje and Robert Asher, coeditors; auth, Cityscapes: A History Of New York in Images, Columbia University Press, 01, Debra Dash Moore, coauthor **CONTACT ADDRESS** Dept of Hist, Florida Intl Univ, 1 F I U South Campus, Miami, FL 33199-0001. **EMAIL** rockh@fiu.edu

ROCK, KENNETH WILLETT
PERSONAL Born 12/12/1938, Abilene, KS, m, 1964, 2 children **DISCIPLINE** EAST CENTRAL EUROPEAN & EUROPEAN EMIGRATION HISTORY **EDUCATION** Univ Kans, BA, 60; Stanford Univ, MA, 62, PhD(hist), 69. **CAREER** From instr to asst prof, 65-72, assoc prof Hist, Colo State Univ, 72-83, prof hist, 83-; Danforth assoc, 78-84; Univ Honor's Prog, RECES Prog Russian, East & Central European Studies coord; Passim; pres, Colo Delta Phi Beta Kappa, 88-90, PBK Screening Officer, 94-; act dir, CSU Office of Int Ed, 84-85; vis scholar, Tech Univ of Budapest, Hungary, 93; Bradley Univ Berlin Seminar, 93, 96; vis lect, Univ of Economics, Prague, Czech Rep, 99. **HONORS AND AWARDS** Honors Prof, Colo State Univ, 78; Outstanding Hist Prof, 86; Eddy Teacher Awd, 96. **MEMBERSHIPS** Phi Beta Kappa; Phi Alpha Theta; AHA; Am Asn Advan Slavic Studies; Conf Group Cent Europ Hist; Rocky Mountain Asn Slavic Studies; Am Hist Soc Germans from Russia. **RESEARCH** Habsburg monarchy; European emigration history; East Central Europe. **SELECTED PUBLICATIONS** Auth, Schwarzenberg versus Nicholas I, round one: The negotiation of the Habsburg-Romanov alliance against Hungary in 1849, In: Austrian History Yearbook, 70-71; Felix Schwarzenberg, military diplomat, In: Austrian History Yearbook, Vol II, 75; The Colorado Germans from Russia study project, Soc Sci J, 4/76; Germans from Russia in America; the first hundred years, Colo State Univ, Germans from Russia in Am, Vol 1, 76; Unsere Leute: Colorado's Germans from Russia, Colo Mag, Spring 78; Loyalty & legality: Austria and the Western Balkans, In: Nation & Ideology: Essays in Honor of Wayne S Vucinich, East Europ Monographs, 81; A Time for Deeds and Courage: The Austrian State after 1848, Proceedings 1986, Consortium on Revolutionary Europe, 87; Rejuvenation by Edict: Schwarzenberg, Stadion, and Bach in 1848-1849, Selected Papers 1995, Consortium on Revolutionary Europe, 96; auth, "Schwarzenberg, the Ballplatz and the Balkans: The Danubian Principalities, 1848-1852," Essays in European History, 1988-1989, Vol II, Univ Press of Am, 96. **CONTACT ADDRESS** Dept of History, Colorado State Univ, Fort Collins, CO 80523-0001. **EMAIL** ken.rock@colostate.edu

ROCKE, ALAN J.
PERSONAL Born 09/20/1948, Chicago, IL, m, 1976 **DISCIPLINE** HISTORY OF SCIENCE **EDUCATION** Beloit Col, BA, 69; Univ Wis-Madison, MA, 73, PhD(hist of sci), 75. **CAREER** Lectr hist, Univ WI-Milwaukee, 76-77; lectr interdisciplinary studies, Univ WI-Madison, 76-78; from asst prof to Bourne Prof Hist, Case Western Reserve Univ, 78-, chair, dept of Hist, Case Western Reserve Univ, 95-98. **HONORS AND AWARDS** Wittke Awd, undergrad teaching, 88-; Dexter Awd, Am Chem Soc, 00. **MEMBERSHIPS** Hist Sci Soc; Soc Hist Technol; AAAS; corresp, Fedn Am Scientists; Sci Res Soc NAm. **RESEARCH** History of chemistry; history of nuclear weapons; history of atomic theories. **SELECTED PUBLICATIONS** Auth, Atoms and equivalents: The early development of the chemical atom and theory, Hist Studies in the Phys Sci, 78; Gay-Lussac and Dumas: Adherents of the Avogadro-Ampere hypothesis, 79 & The reception of chemical atomisn in Germany, 79, Isis; Salt II: A step forward, Cleveland Plain Dealer, 79; coauth, A badger chemist genealogy, J Chem Educ, 79; contribr, Geoge Barger & Walter Jacobs, In: Dict of Scientific Biography, 80; auth, Kekule, Butlerov and the historiography of the theory of chemical structure, Brit J for the Hist Sci, 81; Subatomoc Speculations and the Origin of Structure Theory, Ambix ; Chemical Atomism in the 19th Century, OH State Univ Press, 84; The Quiet Revolution, Univ CA Press, 93; auth, Nationalizing Science, MIT Pr, 00. **CONTACT ADDRESS** Dept Hist of Sci, Case Western Reserve Univ, 10900 Euclid Ave, Cleveland, OH 44106-4901. **EMAIL** ajr@po.cwru.edu

ROCKEFELLER, STEVEN C.
DISCIPLINE HISTORY OF RELIGION, PHILOSOPHY OF RELIGION, AND RELIGION, ETHICS **EDUCATION** Princeton Univ, AB; Union Theol Sem, MDiv; Columbia Univ, PhD. **CAREER** Prof; Middlebury Col, 71-. **SELECTED PUBLICATIONS** Auth, John Dewey: Religious Faith and Democratic Humanism; co-ed, Spirit and Nature: Why the Environment is a Religious Issue-An Interfaith Dialogue. **CONTACT ADDRESS** Dept of Religion, Middlebury Col, Middlebury, VT 05753.

ROCKLAND, MICHAEL AARON
PERSONAL Born 07/14/1935, New York, NY, m, 1978, 5 children **DISCIPLINE** AMERICAN & LATIN AMERICAN STUDIES **EDUCATION** Hunter Col, BA, 55; Univ Minn, MA, 60, PhD(Am studies), 68. **CAREER** Teaching asst Am studies, Univ Minn, 57-59, instr, 60-61, counsel, Col Arts & Sci, 59-61; asst cult attache, Am Embassy, Buenos Aires, 62-63, asst cult attache & dir, Casa Am Cult Ctr, Am Embassy, Madrid, 63-67; exec asst to chancellor, NJ State Dept Higher Educ, 68-69; asst prof, 69-71, asst dean col, 69-72, assoc prof, 72-81, Prof Am Studies, Douglass Col, Rutgers Univ, 81-, Chm Dept, 69-; Lectr, Univ Santa Fe, Arg, 63; guest lectr, Span Univ Syst, 64-67; publ subventions, Rutgers Univ & Arg Embassy, 70; fac chm contemporary Am sem returning foreign serv officers, US Info Agency, 72-73, mem bd, Int Inst Women Studies, 72-; contrib ed, NJ Monthly, 77-; contrib reporter, NJ Nightly News, 78-. **HONORS AND AWARDS** Alumni Hall of Fame, Hunter Col, 73; NJ Pres Assoc Award, 80; Pulitzer Prize nominee, 80; Fulbright Lectureships in Uruguay, 82, and Peru, 85; First Prize for Feature Journalism, Am Soc of Jour, 92; The Nat Am Studies Prize for Distinguished Teaching, 97; The Warren Susman Award for Distinguished Teaching, 97; Teacher of the Year Award, Rutgers Col, 98; Served as distinguished lectr in India, Pakistan, Israel, Canada, Italy, Norway, Spain, Argentina, Colombia, El Salvador, Peru, Portugal, Korea, and Japan. **MEMBERSHIPS** Am Studies Asn (pres, 71-72); Orgn Am Historians; hon mem Inst Sarmiento, Arg; member, Spanish Asn for Am Studies. **RESEARCH** Foreign commentators on the United States; ethnic affairs in the United States, especially the relationship between Jews and the other ethnic groups; mobility in America; Am Aesthetics. **SELECTED PUBLICATIONS** Auth, Sarmiento's Travels in the United States in 1847, Princeton Univ, 70; ed, America in the Fifties and Sixties: Julian Marias on the United States, Pa State Univ, 72; coauth, Three Days on Big City Waters (film), Nat Educ TV, 74; auth, The American Jewish Experience in Literature, Haifa Univ, 75; Homes on Wheels, Rutgers Univ Pres, 80; A Bliss Case, Coffee House Press, 89; coauth, Looking for America on the New Jersey Turnpike, Rutgers Univ Press, 80; auth, Snowshoeing Through Sewers, Rutgers Univ Press, 94; auth, "what's American About American things?, Univ of Salamanca, 96; coauth, "The Jews of New Jersey: A Pictorial History, Rutgers Univ Press, 01. **CONTACT ADDRESS** Dept of Am Studies, Rutgers, The State Univ of New Jersey, New Brunswick, PO Box 270, New Brunswick, NJ 08903-0270. **EMAIL** rockland@rci.rutgers.edu

RODER, WOLF
PERSONAL Born 10/09/1932, Sekenectady, NY, m, 1959, 2 children **DISCIPLINE** GEOGRAPHY **EDUCATION** Univ Chicago, PhD, 65. **CAREER** Prof, Univ of Cincinnati. **MEMBERSHIPS** Asn Am Geogr, African Studies Asn. **RESEARCH** Development in Africa. **SELECTED PUBLICATIONS** Auth, "Magic, Medicine and Metaphysics in Nigeria," Skeptical Inquirer 15 (Spring 91): 290-295; auth, Human Adjustment to Kainji Reservoir in Nigeria, Univ Press of Am (Lanham, MD), 94. **CONTACT ADDRESS** Dept Geog, Univ of Cincinnati, PO Box 210131, Cincinnati, OH 45221-0131. **EMAIL** Wolf.Roder@uc.edu

RODNEY, WILLIAM
PERSONAL Born 01/01/1923, Drumheller, AB, Canada **DISCIPLINE** HISTORY **EDUCATION** Univ Alta, BA, 50; Univ Cambridge, BA, 52, MA, 56; Univ London, PhD, 61. **CAREER** Nato Fel, 63-64; Can Coun Leave Fel, 68-69; Can Coun Sr Leave Fel, 78-79; dean arts, 79-88, Prof Emer, Royal Military College, 88-. **HONORS AND AWARDS** Awd Merit Distinction, Am Asn State Local Hist, 70; Univ BC Medal Popular Biog, 70. **MEMBERSHIPS** Life mem, Can Hist Asn; mem, Can Inst Int Affairs; Johnian Soc; Royal Commonwealth Soc; Fellow, Royal Geog Soc; Royal Hist Soc. **SELECTED PUBLICATIONS** Auth, Neutralism in the Northern Nato States, 65; auth, Soldiers of the International: A History of the Communist Party of Canada 1919-1929, 68; auth, Kootenai Brown His Life and Times, 69, 2nd ed, 95; auth, Joe Boyle King of the Klondike, 74. **CONTACT ADDRESS** 308 Denison Rd, Victoria, BC, Canada V8S 4K3.

RODNITZKY, JEROME L.
PERSONAL Born 08/01/1936, Chicago, IL, m, 1966, 2 children **DISCIPLINE** UNITED STATES SOCIAL CULTURAL & INTELLECTUAL HISTORY **EDUCATION** Univ Chicago, BA, 59, MAT, 62; Univ Ill, PhD(Hist), 67. **CAREER** From instr to assoc prof, 66-76, prof History, Univ Texas, Arlington, 76-. **MEMBERSHIPS** Am Studies Asn; Popular Cult Asn. **RESEARCH** History of American popular culture; history of 1960s counterculture; history of American feminism. **SELECTED PUBLICATIONS** Auth, David Kinley: A paternal university president in the roaring twenties, J Ill State Hist Soc, 73; Popular music and American studies, Hist Teacher, 74; The new revivalism: American protest songs, 1945-1968, In: American Vistas, Oxford Univ, 2nd ed, 75; Minstrels of the Dawn: The Folk-Protest Singer as a Cultural Hero, Nelson-Hall, 76; The Essentials of American History, instructor's manual, Knopf, 2nd ed, 80; Henry David Thoreau: Nearsighted native son, Modern Age, 81; Jazz Age Boomtown, Texas Arm, University Press, 97; auth, Feminist Phoenix: The Rise and Fall of a Feminist Counterculture, Praeger, 99; auth, "Amerika: The Miniseries: Television's Last Cold War Gasp," Studies in the Social Sciences 36, (99). **CONTACT ADDRESS** Dept of History, Univ of Texas, Arlington, Arlington, TX 76019. **EMAIL** Jerry.Rodnitzley@uth.edu

RODRIGUEZ, JUNIUS
PERSONAL Born 06/26/1957, Thibodaux, LA, m, 1994 **DISCIPLINE** HISTORY **EDUCATION** Nicholls State Univ, BS,79; LA State Univ, MA, 87; Auburn Univ, PhD, 92. **CAREER** High School Teacher, Central Lafourche High School, 79-88; assoc prof, Eureka Col, 92-. **HONORS AND AWARDS**

Helen Cleaver Distinguished Teaching Awd, 97. **MEMBERSHIPS** Southern Hist Asn, LA Hist Asn, Soc Sci Hist Asn. **RESEARCH** Slavery, resistance studies. **SELECTED PUBLICATIONS** Auth, The Historical Encyclopedia of World Slavery, two vols, Santa Barbara, 97; auth, Chronology of World Slavery, Santa Barbara, 99. **CONTACT ADDRESS** Dept Bus & Soc Sci, Eureka Col, 300 E Col Ave, Eureka, IL 61530-1562. **EMAIL** jrodrig@eureka.edu

RODRIGUEZ, RICHARD T.
PERSONAL Born 03/12/1971, Santa Ana, CA, s **DISCIPLINE** CHICANO STUDIES **EDUCATION** Univ Calif, BA, 93; PhD, 00. **CAREER** Lectr to asst prof, Calif State Univ, 98-. **HONORS AND AWARDS** Outstanding New Lectr, CSU, 97-98. **MEMBERSHIPS** MLA; Nat Assoc For Chicana and Chicano Studies; Soc for Cinema Studies; Am Studies Assoc. **RESEARCH** Chicano/a studies, media and cultural studies, race and representation. **SELECTED PUBLICATIONS** Rev, of "Urban Exile: The Collected Writings of Harry Gamboa Jr," Theatre Jour, (00); auth, "On the Subject of Gang Photography," Aztlan: A Jour of Chicano Studies, (00). **CONTACT ADDRESS** Dept of Chicano Studies, California State Univ, Los Angeles, 5151 State Univ Dr, Los Angeles, CA 90032. **EMAIL** rtrodrig71@yahoo.com

ROEBER, ANTHONY G.
DISCIPLINE HISTORY **EDUCATION** Univ Denver, BA, 71, MA, 72; Brown Univ, AM, 73, PhD, 77. **CAREER** Instr, hist, Princeton Univ; PROF, HIST, UNIV ILL CHICAGO and ADJ LECTR, LAW, KENT LAW COLL. **MEMBERSHIPS** Am Antiquarian Soc **SELECTED PUBLICATIONS** Auth, A New England Women's Perspective on Norfolk, Virginia, 1801-1802: Excerpts from the Diary of Ruth Henshaw Bascom," Procs of the AAS 89, 79; auth, "Authority, Law, and Custom: The Rituals of Court Day in Tidewater Virginia, 1720-1750," Wm & Mary Quart 37, 80, and in Material Life in America, 1600-1860, Northeastern Univ Press, 88; auth, Faithful Magistrates and Republican Lawyers: Creators of Virginia Legal Culture, 1680-1810, 81; auth, "The Scrutiny of the Ill-Natured Ignorant Vulgar: Lawyers and Print Culture in Virginia, 1716-1774," Virginia Mag Hist and Biog 91, 83; auth, "He Read it to me from a Book of English Law: Germans, Bench, and Bar in the Colonial South, 1715-1770," in Ambivalent Legacy: A Legal History of the South, Univ Press of Miss, 84; auth, "Germans, Property, and the First Great Awakening: Rehearsal for a Revolution?" in The Transit of Civilization from Europe to America: Essays in Honor of Galinsky, Gunter Narr Verlag, 86; auth, "Subjects or Citizens? German Lutherans and the Federal Constitution in Pennsylvania, 1789-1800," Am Stud, 89; auth, Palatines, Liberty, and Property: German Lutherans in Colonial British America, 92; auth, "Der Pietismus in Nordamerika," in Die Geschichte des Pietismus, 95. **CONTACT ADDRESS** 515 N 3rd Ave, Maywood, IL 60153.

ROEDER, GEORGE H., JR.
PERSONAL Born 01/22/1944, Balitmore, MD, m, 1989, 4 children **DISCIPLINE** HISTORY **EDUCATION** Univ MD, BA, 65, MA, 73; Univ Wis, PhD, 77. **CAREER** Instr, Univ MO; Northwestern Univ; undergrad div ch, 93-96 prof, 80-; Dir, Visual and Critical Studies. **HONORS AND AWARDS** Fel, NEH. **MEMBERSHIPS** OAH, AHA. **RESEARCH** History of Visual Experience. **SELECTED PUBLICATIONS** Auth, Forum of Uncertainty: Confrontations with Modern Painting in Twentieth-Century American Thought; The Censored War; American Visual Experience During World War II. **CONTACT ADDRESS** Dept of Lib Arts, Sch of the Art Inst of Chicago, 37 S Wabash Ave, Chicago, IL 60603. **EMAIL** groeder@artic.edu

ROEDIGER, DAVID
PERSONAL Born 07/13/1952, East St. Louis, IL, m, 1979, 2 children **DISCIPLINE** U.S. HISTORY **EDUCATION** Northern IL, BS, 75; Northwestern, PhD, 80 **CAREER** Asst prof of history, 80-84, Northwestern; asst prof, assoc prof, full prof of hist, 85-94, Univ of MO; prof of hist, 94- , Univ of MN; Chair of Amer studies program, 96- , Univ of MN. **HONORS AND AWARDS** Merle Curti Prize, 92; Gustavus Myers Awd, 92; Choice Outstanding Academic Book Awd, 92; Northern IL Distinguished Alumni Awd, 97. **MEMBERSHIPS** Organization of Amer Historians; Amer Studies Assn. **RESEARCH** Race in the U.S.; U.S. Working class hist. **SELECTED PUBLICATIONS** Auth, The Wages of Whiteness: Race and the Making of the American Working Class, Verso Books, 98; Black on White: Black Writers on What It Means to Be White, Schocken, 98; The North and Slavery, includes afterword, What Frederick Douglass Knew, Garland, 98. **CONTACT ADDRESS** 75 S. Victoria St., Saint Paul, MN 55105. **EMAIL** roedi001@tc.umn.edu

ROELL, CRAIG
PERSONAL Born 10/25/1954, Victoria, TX, m, 1998, 2 children **DISCIPLINE** HISTORY **EDUCATION** Victoria Col, AA, 74; Univ Houston, BA, 77; Univ Tex, MA, 80; PhD, 86. **CAREER** Vis scholar, Tex State Hist Asn, 86-88; vis prof, Ohio State Univ, 88-89; prof, Ga Southern Univ, 89-. **HONORS AND AWARDS** Ga Southern Univ Awd for Excellence in Research and Scholarly Activity, 96; Sons of the Republic of Tex La Bahia Awd, 95; Samuel Davis Fel in Bus Hist, Ohio State Univ, 88. **RESEARCH** American Business, economic and cultural history, American consumer culture/advertising, American piano culture and piano industry and trade, Texas history. **SELECTED PUBLICATIONS** Auth, Remember Goliad! A History of La Bahfa, Texas State Hist Asn: Austin, 94; auth, The Piano in America, 1890-1940; Univ NC Press: Chapel Hill, 89; auth, Lyndon B. Johnson: A Bibliography, Volume Two; The Career, Times and Family of the Thirty-Sixth President, Univ Tex Press: Austin, 88; auth, William McKinley: A Bibliography, Meckler Corporation: Westport, 88; auth, "The Piano in the American Home," in The Arts and the American Home, 1890-1930, (94): 85-110; auth, "The Development of Tin Pan Alley," in America's Musical Pulse: Popular Music in Twentieth-Century Society, Greenwood Press, (92): 113-121; auth, "Federal Music Project in Texas," in The New Handbook of Texas, Tex State Hist Asn: Austin, 96; auth, "The Piano Industry in the United States," in The Encyclopedia of Keyboard Instruments, Vol I The Piano, Garland Pub: New York, 94. **CONTACT ADDRESS** Dept Hist, Georgia So Univ, PO Box 8054, Statesboro, GA 30460-1000. **EMAIL** croell@gasou.edu

ROEMER, KENNETH M.
PERSONAL Born 06/06/1945, East Rockaway, NY, m, 1968, 2 children **DISCIPLINE** AMERICAN LITERATURE, AMERICAN STUDIES **EDUCATION** Harvard Univ, BA, 67; Univ Pa, MA, 68; PhD, 71. **CAREER** From asst prof to prof, Univ Tex at Arlington, 71-; vis prof, Shimane Univ, 82-83; vis prof, Int Christian Univ, 88. **HONORS AND AWARDS** Grant, Exxon Educ Found, 78; Grant, ACLS, 86; Chancellor's Outstanding Teaching Awd, 88; Sr Scientist Fel, Japan Soc for the Promotion of Sci, 88; Director Grants, NEH Summer Sem, 92, 94, 96, & 98; Acad of Distinguished Teachers Awd, 98; Writer of the Year, Wordcraft Circle of Native Am Writers & Storytellers, 98. **MEMBERSHIPS** MLA; Soc for Utopia Studies; Asn for the Study of Am Indian Lit; ASA; Melville Soc. **RESEARCH** American Indian Literatures, Utopian Literature. **SELECTED PUBLICATIONS** Auth, The Obsolete Necessity: American in Utopian Writings, 1888-1900, Kent State Univ Pr, 76; auth, "The Nightway Questions American Literature," Am Lit 66 (94): 817-829; auth, "Indian Lives: The Defining, the Telling," Am Quart 46 (94): 81-91; auth, "Contemporary American Indian Literature: The Centrality of Canons at the Margins," Am Lit Hist 6 (94): 583-599; ed, Native American Writers of the united States Volume 175, The Gale Group (Detroit, MI), 97; auth, "Silko's Arroyos as Mainstream," Modern Fiction Studies 45.1 (99): 10-37. **CONTACT ADDRESS** Dept English, Univ of Texas, Arlington, PO Box 19035, Arlington, TX 76019. **EMAIL** roemer@uta.edu

ROGERS, CLIFFORD J.
PERSONAL Born 10/17/1967, Nairobi, Kenya **DISCIPLINE** HISTORY **EDUCATION** Rice Univ, BA, 89; Ohio St Univ, MA, 90; PhD, 94. **CAREER** Olin Post dr fel, mil & strategic hist, 94-95,Yale Univ; asst prof, 95-, US Mil Acad. **HONORS AND AWARDS** Royal Hist Soc Alexander Prize Medal, for "Edward III and the Dialectics of Strategy, 1327-1360," 93; Soc for Military Hist Moncado Prize, for "The Military Revolutions of the Hundred Years War," 94; Excellence in Teaching Award, U.S. Military Acad, Dept of Hist, 97; Phi Kappa Phi Scholastic Achievement Award, 00; Fulbright Fel, United Kingdom, 91-92. **RESEARCH** Late Medieval England & France; medieval military; military revolutions. **SELECTED PUBLICATIONS** Auth, "The Efficacy of the Medieval Longbow: A Reply to Kelly DeVries," War in History 5.2 (98): 233-242; auth, "The Scottish Invasion of 1346," Northern History XXXIV (98): 51-69; coauth, "Three New Accounts of the Neville's Cross Campaign," Northern History XXXIV (98): 70-81; auth, "An Unknown News Bulletin from the Siege of Tournai in 1340," War in History 5.3 (98): 358-366; auth, "The Age of the Hundred Years War," in Medieval Warfare: A History, ed. Maurice Keen (Oxford, Oxford Univ Press, 99), 136-160; auth, "A Continuation of the Manuel d'histoire de Phillippe VI for the Years 1328-1339," English Historical Review CXIV (99): 1256-1266; ed, The Wars of Edward III: Sources and Interpretations, Boydell and Brewer (Woodbridge), Warfare in History series, 99; auth, "'Military Revolutions' and 'Revolutions in Military Affairs:' A Historian's Perspective," in Toward a Revolution in Military Affairs? Defense and Security at the Dawn of the 21st Century, ed. Thierry Gongora and Harald von Reikhoff (Greenwood Press, 00). **CONTACT ADDRESS** Dept of History, United States Military Acad, Thayer Hall, West Point, NY 10996. **EMAIL** kc1870@usma.edu

ROGERS, DANIEL E.
PERSONAL Born Birmingham, AL, m, 1997 **DISCIPLINE** MODERN EUROPEAN HISTORY **EDUCATION** Univ Ala, BA, 84; Univ N Car, MA, 86; PhD, 90. **CAREER** Vis asst prof, Univ Mryld, 90-91; asst prof, Univ S Ala, 91-97; assoc prof, 97-. **HONORS AND AWARDS** Phi Beta Kappa; Fulbright Sr Schl. **MEMBERSHIPS** AAH. **RESEARCH** Post-1945 Germany; political legacy of the Holocaust. **SELECTED PUBLICATIONS** Auth, Politics After Hitler: The Western Allies and the German Party System, Macmillan and NYU Press, 95. **CONTACT ADDRESS** Dept History, Univ of So Alabama, 307 Univ Blvd, Mobile, AL 36688-3053. **EMAIL** drogers@jaguar1.usouthal.edu

ROGERS, KIM L.
PERSONAL Born 02/26/1951, Plant City, FL, m **DISCIPLINE** AMERICAN STUDIES **EDUCATION** Fla State Univ, BA, 73; Univ Minn, MA, 76; PhD, 82. **CAREER** Vis asst prof, Univ Mo, 82-83; asst prof, Dickinson Col, 83-88; assoc prof, 89-97; cen dir, 97-99; prof, 97-. **HONORS AND AWARDS** NEH; NHC Fel; Gen J Kemper Williams Prize. **MEMBERSHIPS** OHA. **RESEARCH** Oral history; narrative; African American history; life-history research; family history; qualitive methods; community studies. **SELECTED PUBLICATIONS** Auth, Righteous Lives: Narratives of New Orleans Civil Rights Movement, NYU Press, 93; co-ed, Interactive Oral History Interviewing, LEA, 94; co-ed, Trauma and Life Stories: International Perspectives, Routledge Studies in Memory and Narrative, 99; auth, "Lynching Stories: Family and Community Memory in the Mississippi Delta," Trauma and Life Stories; auth, "The Movement and Mobility: Federal Intervention and Political Power in the Mississippi Delta," Rev de Sci Polit (98); coauth, "They Couldn't Scare Me, They Tried Their Best to Scare Me: An Interview with Mary Tyler Dotson," Acoma Rev Intl de Shedi Nord-American (97): 19-28. **CONTACT ADDRESS** Dept History, Dickinson Col, Carlisle, PA 17013-2846. **EMAIL** rogersk@dickinson.edu

ROHRBOUGH, MALCOLM J.
PERSONAL Born 08/03/1932, Cambridge, MA, m, 1986, 3 children **DISCIPLINE** HISTORY **EDUCATION** Harvard Univ, AB, 54; Univ Wis, MA, 58; PhD, 63. **CAREER** Instr, Princeton Univ, 62-64; asst prof, Univ Iowa, 64-68; assoc prof, 68-71; prof, 71; ch, 83-86. **HONORS AND AWARDS** Fulbright Fel; NEH Fel; Camargo Found Fel; Caughey Bk Prize; Billington Bk Prize; Caughey Prize, Western Hist Assn, 98; Billington Prize Org of Am Hists, 99 **MEMBERSHIPS** AHA; OAH; WHA. **RESEARCH** The American Frontier; American West; world impact of the California Gold Rush with particular reference to France. **SELECTED PUBLICATIONS** Auth, The Land Office Business: The Settlement and the Administration of American Public Lands, 1785-1837, 98; auth, The Trans-Appalachian Frontier: People, Societies, and Institutions, 1775-1850, 78; auth, Aspen: The History of a Silver Mining Town, 1879-1893, 86; auth, Days of Gold: The California Gold Rush and the American Nation, 97. **CONTACT ADDRESS** Dept History, Univ Iowa, 205 Schaeffer Hall, Iowa City, IA 52242-1409. **EMAIL** malcolm-rohrbough@uiowa.edu

ROHRER, JUDITH C.
DISCIPLINE EUROPEAN ARCHITECTURE **EDUCATION** Columbia Univ, PhD, 84. **CAREER** Archit, Emory Univ; assoc prof. **RESEARCH** European archit, modern and contemporary with emphasis upon the archit of Barcelon; space and gender theory. **SELECTED PUBLICATIONS** Auth, Josep Puig I Cadafalch: Architecture between the House and the City, Fundacio La Ciaxa, Barcelona, 89; Articles on contemporary feminist art, architecture and politics, public art and contemproary architecture. **CONTACT ADDRESS** Emory Univ, Atlanta, GA 30322-1950. **EMAIL** jcrohre@emory.edu

ROHRS, RICHARD CARLTON
PERSONAL Born 02/01/1948, Brooklyn, NY, m, 2000, 2 children **DISCIPLINE** AMERICAN HISTORY **EDUCATION** Bucknell Univ, BA, 69; Univ NE, MA, 73, PhD(hist), 76. **CAREER** Vis asst prof, 76-77, asst prof, 77-82, assoc prof, 82-98, Prof Hist, OK State Univ, 98-. **HONORS AND AWARDS** Phi Alpha Theta; Phi Kappa Phi. **MEMBERSHIPS** Orgn Am Historians; Soc Historians Early Am Repub. **RESEARCH** Nineteenth century American history. **SELECTED PUBLICATIONS** Auth, The Germans in Oklahoma, Univ OK Press, 80; Partisan Politics and the Attempted Assassination of Andrew Jackson, J Early Am Repub, summer 81; The Federalist Party and the Convention of 1800, Diplomatic History, summer 88; Antislavery Politics and the Pearl Incident of 1848, The Hist, summer 94; American Critics of the French Revolution of 1848, J of Early Am Repub, fall 94; A Guide to Quantitative History, Praeger, 95; auth, "The Attempt to Relocate the US Capital in 1814," The Hist, spring 00. **CONTACT ADDRESS** Dept of Hist, Oklahoma State Univ, Stillwater, Stillwater, OK 74078-0002. **EMAIL** ler4s@okstate.edu

ROINILA, MIKA
PERSONAL Born 01/27/1961, Helsinki, Finland, m, 1987, 4 children **DISCIPLINE** GEOGRAPHY **EDUCATION** Univ Winnipeg, BAH, 86; Univ Turku, MSc, 87; Univ Saskatchewan, PhD, 97. **CAREER** Visiting Asst Prof, James Madison Univ, 97-98; Visiting Asst Prof, WV Univ, 98-. **MEMBERSHIPS** AAG; AHA; Geog Soc of Finland; Inst of Migration; Swede-Finn Hist Soc. **RESEARCH** Migration and settlement; Cultural geography; Ethnic groups. **SELECTED PUBLICATIONS** Auth, "Finland-Swedish immigrants in the Scandinavia colony of Manitoba, Canada," Terra, (97): 226-231; auth, "The Finland-Swedes in Canada: Past and present," Melting into Great Waters: Papers from Finn forum V, Journal of Finnish Studies, (97): 90-99; auth, "A Finnish run-away sailor in New Brunswick: The experiences of George (Yrjo) Laakso," Acadiensis, (97): 105-108; auth, "Ethnic outcasts: The dilemma of not belonging for Canadian Finland-Swedes," Canadian Ethnic Studies, (98): 1-10; auth, "The loss of identity of Swedes-Swedes in Canada," Proceedings, 98; auth, "Scandinavia Gazet-

teer (Including Finland)," Encyclopedia of World Geography, 00; auth, "Scandinavia (Including Finland) as a Geographical Region," Encyclopedia of World Geography, 00; auth, "Gazetteer of Canada," Encyclopedia of World Geography, 00; auth, "Canada as a Geographical Region," Encyclopedia of World Geography, 00; auth, "Finland-Swedes of British Columbia," Journal of Finnish Studies, 00. **CONTACT ADDRESS** Dept Geog & Geol, West Virginia Univ, Morgantown, PO Box 6300, Morgantown, WV 26506. **EMAIL** mroinila@geo.wvu.edu

ROJAS, CARLOS
PERSONAL Born 08/12/1928, Barcelona, Spain, m, 1966, 2 children **DISCIPLINE** SPANISH LITERATURE, HISTORY **EDUCATION** Barcelona Univ, MA, 51; Univ Cent, Madrid, PhD(Span lit), 55. **CAREER** Asst prof Romance lang, Rollins Col, 57-60; from asst prof to assoc prof, 60-68, prof, 68-80, Charles Howard Candler Prof Romance Lang, 80-, emeritus, Emory Univ. **HONORS AND AWARDS** Nat Prize for Lit, Govt Spain, 68; Planeta Prize, Ed Planeta, 73; Ateneo de Sevilla Prize, 77; Nadal Prize, 80. **MEMBERSHIPS** MLA; SAtlantic Mod Lang Asn. **RESEARCH** Contemporary Spanish; art history. **SELECTED PUBLICATIONS** Auth, Dialogos Para Otra Espana, Ariel, 66; Auto de Fe, Guadarrama, 68; Diez Figuras Ante la Guerra Civil, Nauta, 73; Azana, 73, La Guerra Civil Vista por los Exiliados, 75, Retratos Antifranquistas, 77 & Memorias Ineditas, 78, Planeta; El Ingenioso Hidalgo y Poeta Federico Garcia Lorca Asciende a los Infiernos, 80, La Barcelonade Picasso, 81. **CONTACT ADDRESS** Dept of Romance Lang, Emory Univ, Atlanta, GA 30322.

ROLAND, ALEX
PERSONAL Born 04/07/1944, Providence, RI, m, 1979, 4 children **DISCIPLINE** HISTORY **EDUCATION** US Naval Acad, BS, 66; Univ Hawaii, MA, 70; Duke Univ, Phd, 74. **CAREER** Capt, US Marine Corps, 66-70; Historian, Nat Aeronautics & Space Admin, 73-81; Assoc prof to prof, Duke Univ, 87-. **HONORS AND AWARDS** Harold K Johnson vis prof of Military Hist, US Army War Col; Sr Fel, Dubner Inst for Hist of Sci and Tech, MIT, 94-95; Leo Shifrin Prof of Naval-Military Hist, US Naval Acad, 01-02. **MEMBERSHIPS** Soc for the Hist of Technol; Soc of Milit Hist; Hist of Sci Soc. **RESEARCH** Military hist; hist of technol. **SELECTED PUBLICATIONS** Auth, Underwater Warfare in the Age of Sail, Bloomington, Univ Press, 78; art, Model Research: The National Advisory Committee for Aeronautice, 1915-1958, Washington: NASA, 85; ed, A Spacefaring People: Perspectives on Early Spaceflight, Washington: NASA, 85; co-auth, Men in Arms: A History of Warfare and Its Interrelationships with Western Society, New York: Holt, Rinehart and Winston, 91; The Military-Industrial Complex, WA: Am Hist Asn, 01. **CONTACT ADDRESS** Dept of History, Duke Univ, Durham, NC 27708. **EMAIL** alex.roland@duke.edu

ROLAND, CHARLES G.
PERSONAL Born 01/25/1933, Winnipeg, MB, Canada **DISCIPLINE** HISTORY OF MEDICINE **EDUCATION** Univ Toronto, pre-med, 52-54; Univ Man, MD, BS(Med), 58. **CAREER** Pvt med pract, Tillsonburg, Ont, 59-60; Grimsby, Ont, 60-64; sr ed, J Am Med Asn, 64-69; lectr, Northwestern Univ, 68-69; chmn, Biomed Commun, Mayo Clinic & Mayo Found, 69-77; assoc prof, 69, prof, Mayo Med Sch, 73-77; Jason A. Hannah Prof Hist of Med, McMaster Univ, 77-99, Hannah Prof Emer, 99-, assoc mem dept hist, 78-95; cur, Osler Libr, McGill Univ, 82-99; Sid Richardson Vis Prof Med Hum, Univ Texas, 84. **HONORS AND AWARDS** Jason A. Hannah Medal, Royal Soc Can, 94 **MEMBERSHIPS** Am Osler Soc (pres, 86-87); Can Soc Hist Med (pres, 93-95); Int Soc Hist Med; Am Asn Hist Med; ed bd, Can Bull Hist Med; J Hist Med & Allied Sci; Scientia Can. **RESEARCH** Medical experiences of prisoners of war in Asia and Europe. **SELECTED PUBLICATIONS** Auth, Clarence Meredith Hincks: A Biography, 90; auth, Courage Under Siege: Disease, Starvation and Death in the Warsaw Ghetto, 92; auth, Harold N. Segall, Cardiologist and Historian, 96; coauth, An Annotated Checklist of Osleriana, 76; coauth, An Annotated Bibliography of Canadian Medical Periodicals 1826-1975, 79; ed, Health, Disease and Medicine: Essays in Canadian History, 83; co-ed, Secondary Sources in Canadian Medical History: A Bibliography, 84; co-ed, Sir William Osler: An Annotated Bibliography with Illustrations, 87. **CONTACT ADDRESS** Dept of Hist of Health and Med, McMaster Univ, 1280 Main St West, 3G51 Health Sciences Centre, Hamilton, ON, Canada L8S 4L8. **EMAIL** rolandc@mcmaster.ca

ROLAND, CHARLES P.
PERSONAL Born 04/08/1918, Maury City, TN, m, 1948, 3 children **DISCIPLINE** UNITED STATES HISTORY **EDUCATION** Vanderbilt Univ, BA, 38; La State Univ, PhD, 51. **CAREER** Teacher, High Sch, Tenn, 38-40; hist tech, Natl Park Serv, 40-42, 46-47; instr hist, La State Univ, 50-51; asst to chief historian, US Dept Army, 51-52; from instr to prof hist, Tulane Univ, 52-70, head arts & sci dept hist, 63-67, chmn dept hist, 67-70; Alumni prof Hist, 70-88, Prof Emer, 88- , Univ KY, 70-, Guggenheim Found fel, 60-61; Harold Keith Johnson vis prof mil hist, US Army Mil Hist Inst, 81-82; vis prof Mil Hist, US Mil Acad, 85-86 & 91-92. **HONORS AND AWARDS** La Lit Award, 57; Dept of Army: Outstanding Civilian Serv Medal; Comdr Award Public Serv; Declaration Distinguished Civilian Serv. **MEMBERSHIPS** Ky Hist Soc; Southern Hist Asn (pres, 80-81). **RESEARCH** Civil War; modern South; Old South. **SELECTED PUBLICATIONS** Auth, Louisiana Sugar Plantations During the American Civil War, E J Brill, 57; The Confederacy, Univ Chicago, 60; Albert Sidney Johnston: Soldier of Three Republics, Univ Tex, 64; coauth, A History of the South, Knopf, 72; The Improbable Era: The South Since World War II, Univ Press Ky, 75; ed, New Perspectives on the South, Univ Press Ky; An American Iliad: The Story of the Civil War, McGraw-Hill, 91; Reflections on Lee: A Historians Assessment, Stackpole Books, 95; auth, Jefferson Davis's Greatest General, Albert Sidney Johnston, McWhiney Found Press, 00. **CONTACT ADDRESS** 814 Sherwood Dr, Lexington, KY 40502.

ROLATER, FREDERICK STRICKLAND
PERSONAL Born 07/22/1938, McKinney, TX, m, 1960 **DISCIPLINE** AMERICAN HISTORY, CHURCH HISTORY **EDUCATION** Wake Forest Univ, BA, 60; Univ Southern Calif, MA, 63, PhD, 70 **CAREER** Assoc prof soc sci, Blue Mountain Col, 63-64; assoc prof hist & soc sci & chmn dept, Grand Canyon Col, 64-67; asst prof, 67-70, assoc prof, 70-80, dir grad studies, Dept Hist, 72-80, Prof Church Hist, Korea Bapt Theol Univ and Seminary, 00-. **HONORS AND AWARDS** Fulbright lectr, Japan, 87; Comnr, Southern Baptist Hist Comn, 84-92. **MEMBERSHIPS** Tenn Hist Soc; West Tenn Hist Soc; Southern Baptist Hist Soc; Tenn Baptist Hist Comt (chmn). **RESEARCH** History of the American Indian; Tennessee history; Public administration during the American Revolution. **SELECTED PUBLICATIONS** Auth, Charles Thomson, Prime Minister of the United States, Penn Mag Hist & Biogr, 7/77; The Doctor of Arts Degree and its Development at MTSU, in Proceedings of the Fifth Intl Conf on Improving Univ Teaching, 79; The Time They Cried (in Japanese), J Am Studies (Japan), 88; Japanese Americans, Rourke Press, 91; The American Indian and the Origin of the Second American Party System, Wis Mag Hist, spring 93; auth, Padlocking the Building; auth, Releasing the Spirit: Concord Baptist Association, 1930-50, Ten Bapt Hist, fall, 99. **CONTACT ADDRESS** 740-7 O Jung Dong, Daeduk-Gu, Taejon, Korea 306-817. **EMAIL** frolater@mtsu.edu

ROLLER, MATTHEW B.
PERSONAL Born 07/27/1966, Denver, CO **DISCIPLINE** CLASSICS, ROMAN STUDIES **EDUCATION** Stanford Univ, BA, 88; Univ Cal-Berkeley, MA, 90; PhD, 94. **CAREER** Asst prof of Classics, Johns Hopkins Univ, 94-00, assoc prof Classics, Johns Hopkins Univ, 00-; Mellon fel Hum, 88-90 and 93; Mellon Diss fel, 92 & 94. **HONORS AND AWARDS** Am Coun of Learned Societies Jun Fel, 00-01; Solmsen Fel, Inst for Res in the Humanities, Univ of Wisc-Madison, 00-01. **MEMBERSHIPS** Am Philol Asn; Archaeol Inst Am; Class Asn Atlantic Stud. **RESEARCH** Latin literature; Roman social and cultural history; Graeco-Roman philosophy. **SELECTED PUBLICATIONS** Auth Ethical Contradiction and the Fractured Community in Lucan's Bellum Civile, Class Antiquity, 96; Color-blindness: Cicero's death, declamation, and the production of history, Class Philol, 97; Pliny's Catullus: the politics of literary appropriation, Transactions of the Am Philol Asn; 98; auth, Constructing Autocracy: Aristocrats and Emperors in Julio-Claudian Rome, Princeton Univ Press, 01. **CONTACT ADDRESS** Dept of Classics, Johns Hopkins Univ, Baltimore, 3400 N Charles St, Baltimore, MD 21218-2690. **EMAIL** mroller@jhu.edu

ROLLINGS, WILLARD H.
DISCIPLINE HISTORY **EDUCATION** Tex Tech Univ, PhD, 83. **CAREER** Assoc prof, Univ Nev Las Vegas. **MEMBERSHIPS** Native American history; ethnohistory. **SELECTED PUBLICATIONS** Auth, An Ethnohistorical Study of Hegemony on the Prairie Plains, Columbia, 92; The Comanche, Univ NY, 89. **CONTACT ADDRESS** History Dept, Univ of Nevada, Las Vegas, 4505 Md Pky, Las Vegas, NV 89154.

ROLLINS, JUDITH
PERSONAL Born Boston, MA, s **DISCIPLINE** AFRICANA STUDIES, SOCIOLOGY **EDUCATION** Howard Univ, BA, 70; MA, 72; Brandeis Univ, PhD, 83. **CAREER** Asst prof, 84-89; assoc prof, 89-92, Simmons Coll; assoc prof, 92-95; prof, 95-; Wellesley Coll. **HONORS AND AWARDS** Jessie Barnard Awd, ASA, 87. **MEMBERSHIPS** ASA; SSSP. **RESEARCH** Social psychology of domination; women's studies. **SELECTED PUBLICATIONS** Auth, "Between Women: Domestics and Their Employers," Temple Univ Press (85); auth, "All is Never Said: The Narrative of Odette Harper Hines," Temple Univ Press (95); auth, "Part of a Whole: The Interdependence of the Civil Rights Movement With Other Social Movements," Phylon 1 (86); auth, "Ideology and Servitude" in At Work in Homes: Domestic Work in World Perspective, eds. Roger Sanjek, Shellee Colen, Am Ethno Soc Monograph 3 (90); auth, "Housing Civil Rights Workers," J Women's Hist 5 (93); auth, "Feminism and Parasitism," Abafazi 1 (91); auth, "Entre Femmes: Les Domestiques et Leurs Patronnes," Actes de la Recherche en Sci Soc 84 (90). **CONTACT ADDRESS** Dept Africana, Sociology, Wellesley Col, 106 Central St, Wellesley, MA 02481. **EMAIL** jrollins@wellesley.edu

ROMAN, ERIC
PERSONAL Born 03/26/1926, Bekescsaba, Hungary, m, 1953, 2 children **DISCIPLINE** MODERN HISTORY, WESTERN PHILOSOPHY **EDUCATION** Hunter Col, BA, 58; NYork Univ, MA, 59, PhD(Hist), 65. **CAREER** From instr to assoc prof, 65-77, prof Hist, Western Conn State Univ, 77-. **HONORS AND AWARDS** Americanism Medal, Nat Daughters Am Revolution, 70. **MEMBERSHIPS** AHA. **RESEARCH** Modern German history; immediate origins of World War II; diplomacy of interwar period. **SELECTED PUBLICATIONS** Auth, The Best Shall Die, Prentice-Hall, 61, Davies, London, 61 & Plaza & Janes, Madrid, 64; After the Trial, Citadel, 68 & Carl Scherz, Berne, 69; Munich and Hungary, Eastern Europ Quart, 74; Will, Hope and the Noumenon, J Philos, 2/75; A Year as a Lion, Stein & Day, 9/78; Hungary and the Victor Powers, New York, St Martin's Press, 96; auth, The Stalin Years in Hungary, The Edwin Mellen Press, 99. **CONTACT ADDRESS** 181 White St, Danbury, CT 06810-6826. **EMAIL** romane@wsu.ctstateu.edu

ROMANO, DAVID GILMAN
PERSONAL Born 11/29/1946, Rochester, NY, m, 1978, 3 children **DISCIPLINE** GREEK AND ROMAN ARCHAEOLOGY **EDUCATION** Washington Univ St Louis, AB, 69; Univ Oreg, MA, 72; Univ Pa, PhD, 81. **CAREER** Curatorial Cons, Glencairn Mus, 82-82; lectr, Univ Pa, 82-87; Keeper of the Collections, Univ Pa Mus, 85-99; adj assoc prof, Univ Pa, 91-94; 97- **HONORS AND AWARDS** Eugene Vanderpool Fel, Am Sch of Class Studies, Athens, 78-79; Olivia James Travelling Fel, Archaeol Inst Am 81; John Frederick Lewis Awd, Am Philos Assoc, 93; Markoe Fel, Univ of Pa Mus, 94=95. **MEMBERSHIPS** Archaeol Inst of Am, Col Art Assoc, AAAS, Class Assoc of Atlantic Studies, Pa Class Assoc, Am Philog Assoc, Philadelphia Class Assoc. **RESEARCH** Greek and Roman athletics, Greek and Roman city and land planning, Greek and Roman architecture, computer applications in archeology, Greek and Roman Corinth. **SELECTED PUBLICATIONS** Auth, "The Panathenaic Stadium and theater of Lykurgus: A Re-examination of the Facilities on the Pnyx Hill," am Jour of Archaeol 89, (85); auth, "Athletics and Mathematics in Archaic Corinth: The Originals of the Ancient Stadium," Am Philos Soc, (93): coauth, Catalogue of the Classical Collection of the Glencairn Museum, Glencairn Museum, 99; auth, "Tale of Two Cities: Roman Colonies at Corinth," Jour of Roman Archaeol, Supplement 18, (00). **CONTACT ADDRESS** Mus Archaeol and Anthrop, Univ of Pennsylvania, Thirty-third and Spruce Sts, Mediterranean Section, Philadelphia, PA 19104-6324. **EMAIL** dromano@sas.upenn.edu

ROMANOWSKI, WILLIAM D.
PERSONAL Born 08/02/1954, m, 1977, 2 children **DISCIPLINE** AMERICAN CULTURE STUDIES **EDUCATION** Ind Univ Pa, BA, 76; Youngstown State Univ, MA, 81; Bow Gr State Univ, PhD, 90. **CAREER** Min, CCO, 76-88; grad asst, Bowling Green State Univ, 86-88; vis fac fel, Calvin Col, 88-89; assoc prof, 92-96; prof, 96-. **HONORS AND AWARDS** Thomas F Staley Dist Schl, 91-; Peter J Steen Awd, 88; CCCS Res Fel, 88; Christ Today Crit Choic Awd; CC Alum Res Gnt; CC Res Fel, 93, 98, 00; Billy Graham Res Gnt; Who's Who in Midwest; CCA Res Gnt, 94, 95; CCC Schl Gnt, 00. **RESEARCH** American pop culture; film; religion. **SELECTED PUBLICATIONS** Auth, Pop Culture Wars: Religion and the Role of Entertainment in American Life, InterVar Press (Downers Grove, IL), 96; coauth, Dancing in the Dark: Youth, Popular Culture and the Electronic Media, Eerdmans Pub (Grand Rapids, Mich), 91; coauth, Risky Business: Rock in Film, Trans Bks (New Brunswick), 91; auth, Evan gelicals and Popular Music: The Contemporary Christian Music Industry," in Religion and Popular Culture in America, eds. Jeffrey H Mahan, Bruce Forbes (LA: Univ Cal Press, 00): 105-24; auth, "Boycotts, Baptists, and NYPD Blue," Theol News Notes (97): 14-17; " 'Take Your Girlie to the Movies': Dating and Entertainment in Twentieth-Century America," in Religion, Feminism and the Family, eds. Ann Cair, Mary Stewart Van Leeuwen (The Family, Religion, and Culture, eds. Don S Browning, Ian S Evison, Philadelphia: Westminster John Knox Press, 96); auth, "'You Talkin' to Me?': The Christian Liberal Arts Tradition and the Challenge of Popular Culture," in Keeping Faith: Embracing the Tensions in Christian Higher Education (Grand Rapids, MI: Eerdmans, 96); auth, "John Calvin Meets the Creature from the Black Lagoon: The Christian Reformed Church and the Movies 1928-1966," Christ Schol Rev 25 (95): 47-62; auth, "The Joys Are Simply Told: Calvin Seerveld's Contribution to the Study of Popular Culture," in Pledges of Jubilee: Essays on the Arts and Culture in Honor of Calvin G Seerveld, eds. Lainbert Zuidervarrt, Henry Luttikhuizen (Grand Rapids, Mich: Eerdmans, 95). **CONTACT ADDRESS** Dept Communication Arts Sciences, Calvin Col, 3201 Burton St S, Grand Rapids, MI 49546-4301. **EMAIL** romw@calvin.edu

ROMEY, WILLIAM DOWDEN
PERSONAL Born 10/26/1930, Richmond, IN, m, 1955, 3 children **DISCIPLINE** GEOLOGY AND GEOGRAPHY **EDUCATION** IN Univ, AB, 52; Univ CA, Berkeley, PhD, 62. **CAREER** Asst to assoc prof, geology and science ed, Syracuse Univ, 62-69; exec dir, Earth Science Educational Progs, Am Geological Inst, 69-72; prof geology, 71-83, dept chair, 71-76, prof geography and dept chair, St Lawrence Univ, 83-93, prof

Emeritus, 93-. **HONORS AND AWARDS** Phi Beta Kappa; Nat Science Found Science fac fel, Univ of Oslo, 67-68. **MEMBERSHIPS** Nat Asn Geoscience Teachers (pres, 73); Geological Soc Am (fel); Am Asn for Advancement of Science (fel); Geological Soc of Norway; Asn of Am Geographers; Can Geographers Asn; Nat Coun for Geog Ed; Am Geophysical Union; Int Asn for Volcanology and Chemistry of... **RESEARCH** Literature and geography; art and geography and geology; the geology of travel; volcanology; structural geology. **SELECTED PUBLICATIONS** Auth, Consciousness and Creativity: Transcending Science, Humanities, and the Arts, Ash Lad Press, 75; Confluent Education in Science, Ash Lad Press, 76; Teaching the Gifted and Talented in the Science Classroom, Nat Ed Asn, 80; The Effects of Volcanoes on the Landscapes and Peoples of the Americas, in T Martinson and S Brooker-Gross, eds, Revisiting the Americas: Teaching and Learning the Geography of the Western Hemisphere, Nat Coun for Geographic Ed, 92; Teaching Geology Through a Porthole-Opportunities on a World Cruise, J of Geological Ed, vol 42, 94; Teaching Geography Aboard Ship, proceedings, meeting of the New England-St Lawrence Valley Geographical Soc (Nesval), vol 23, 94; Plus Ca Change..: For the Love of France, Ash Lad Press, 96; Volcanoes in Kamchatka, GSA Today, vol 6, no 4, April 96; Stop-off at Tristan da Cunha: Focus, Am Geographical Soc, Aug 98. **CONTACT ADDRESS** PO Box 294, East Orleans, MA 02643. **EMAIL** wromey@capecod.net

ROMM, JAMES S.
DISCIPLINE GREEK HISTORIOGRAPHY, GREEK PROSE LITERATURE **EDUCATION** Princeton, PhD. **CAREER** Vis assoc prof, Fordham Univ. **SELECTED PUBLICATIONS** Auth, The Edges of the Earth in Ancient Thought: Geography, Exploration, and Fiction, Princeton, 92; Strabo, Greek Authors, Dictionary of Lit Biog, 97. **CONTACT ADDRESS** Dept of Class Lang and Lit, Fordham Univ, 113 W 60th St, New York, NY 10023.

ROMO, RICARDO
PERSONAL Born 06/23/1943, San Antonio, TX, m, 1967, 2 children **DISCIPLINE** UNITED STATES SOCIAL HISTORY **EDUCATION** Univ Tex, Austin, BS, 67; Loyola Univ, Los Angeles, MA, 70; Univ Calif, Los Angeles, PhD, 75. **CAREER** Teacher social studies, Franklin High Sch, Los Angeles, 67-70; asst prof hist, Calif State Univ, Northridge, 70-73; asst prof hist, Univ Calif, San Diego, 73-80; Assoc Prof Hist, Univ Tex, Austin, 80-, Vice-Provost Undergrad Studies, 93-. **HONORS AND AWARDS** Chancellor's Distinguished Lectureship, Univ Calif, Berkeley, Spring 85; Fel, Ctr for Advanced Studies in the Behavioral Studies, Stanford Univ, 89-90. **MEMBERSHIPS** Nat Asn Chicano Studies; AHA; Orgn Am Historians; Am Asn Higher Educ; Tex State Hist Asn; Inst Latin Am Studies. **RESEARCH** American southwest; 20th century social history of the United States. **SELECTED PUBLICATIONS** Coauth, New Directions in Chicano Scholarship, Monographs in Chicano Studies No. 1, Ctr for Chicano Studies, Univ Calif, Santa Barbara, 84; co-ed, The Mexican Origin Experience in the United States, Social Science Quart, Vol 65, No 2, 84; auth, East Los Angeles: History of a Barrio, Univ Tex Press, 83, 4th printing, 92; author of numerous articles and book chapters. **CONTACT ADDRESS** Office of the Pres, Univ of Texas, San Antonio, San Antonio, TX 78249-0601.

RONEY, JOHN B.
PERSONAL Born 02/26/1954, 1 child **DISCIPLINE** HISTORY **EDUCATION** Univ Toronto, PhD, 89. **CAREER** Assoc prof, Sacred Heart Univ . **RESEARCH** Early Mod and Mod France and the Low Countries (1500-1900); historiography: Reformation, Calvinism, Catholicism, Romanticism, French Revolutionary Europe; relig and soc. **SELECTED PUBLICATIONS** Auth, The Inside of History: Jean Henri Merle d'Aubigne and Romantic Historiography, Greenwood, 96; ed, The Identity of Geneva: The Christian Commonwealth, 1564-1864, Greenwood, 98. **CONTACT ADDRESS** Sacred Heart Univ, 5151 Park Ave, Fairfield, CT 06432. **EMAIL** roneyj2@sacredheart.edu

ROOP, EUGENE F.
PERSONAL Born 05/11/1942, South Bend, IN, m, 1963, 2 children **DISCIPLINE** HISTORY; BIBLE; OLD TESTAMENT; HEBREW BIBILE **EDUCATION** Manchester Col, BS, 64; Bethany Theological Seminary, MDiv 67; Claremont Graduate Univ, PhD, 72. **CAREER** Prof of Old Testament, 70-77, Earlham Sch of Relig; prof of Biblical Studies, 77-92, president, 72- , Bethany Theological Seminary. **HONORS AND AWARDS** Wieand professor of biblical studies, Bethany Theological Seminary; ordained minister, Church of the Brethren. **MEMBERSHIPS** Soc of Biblical Lit **RESEARCH** Narrative lit in the Hebrew bible. **SELECTED PUBLICATIONS** Coauth, A Declaration of Peace, 90; authm Master Dreamer, The Bible Today, January, 90; auth, Heard in Our Land, 91; auth, Let The Rivers Run, 91; auth, Esther, Covenant Bible Series, 97; auth, Commentary on Ruth, Jonah, and Esther, forthcoming. **CONTACT ADDRESS** Bethany Theol Sem, 615 National Rd W, Richmond, IN 47374-4019. **EMAIL** roopge@earlham.edu

ROPP, PAUL
PERSONAL Born 03/25/1944, Bloomington, IL, m, 1965, 3 children **DISCIPLINE** HISTORY **EDUCATION** Bluffton Col, BA, 66; Univ Mich, MA, 68; PhD, 74. **CAREER** Asst Prof, Memphis State Univ, 75-84; assoc prof, Clark Univ, 85-. **MEMBERSHIPS** Asn for Asian Studies, Am Hist Asn, Soc for Qing Studies. **RESEARCH** Chinese History. **SELECTED PUBLICATIONS** Auth, Dissent in Early Modern China: "Julin wai-shih" and Ch'ing Social Criticism, Univ of Calif Press (Ann Arbor, MI), 81; ed, Heritage of China: Contemporary Perspectives on Chinese Civilization, Univ of Calif Press (Berkeley, CA), 90; auth, "A Confucian View of Women in the Ch'ing Period--Literati Laments for Women in the Ch'ing shih tuo", Chinese Studies 10.2 (92): 399-435; auth, Love, Literacy, and Laments: Themes of Women Writers in Late Imperial China," Women's History Review 3.3 (93): 107-141; auth, Banished Immortal: Searching for Shuangqing, China's Peasant Woman Poet, Univ of Mich Press (Ann Arbor, MI), (forthcoming). **CONTACT ADDRESS** Dept History, Clark Univ, 950 Main St, Worcester, MA 01610-1477. **EMAIL** propp@clarku.edu

RORABAUGH, WILLIAM J.
PERSONAL Born 12/11/1945, Louisville, KY, s **DISCIPLINE** HISTORY **EDUCATION** Stanford Univ, AB, 68; Univ Calif, Berkeley, MA, 70, PhD, 76. **CAREER** Asst prof, Univ of Washington, 76-82, assoc prof, 82-87, prof, 87-. **HONORS AND AWARDS** Nat Endowment for the Humanities Fel; Nat Humanities Ctr Fel; Newberry Library Fel; Huntington Library Fel; Kennedy Library Fel. **MEMBERSHIPS** Am Hist Asn, Org of Am Hists, Soc for Hist of the Early Am Republic, Alcohol and Temperance Group. **RESEARCH** Early 19th century United States social history; 1960s; alcohol. **SELECTED PUBLICATIONS** Auth, The Alcoholic Republic (79); auth, The Craft Apprentice (86); auth, Berkeley at War (89). **CONTACT ADDRESS** Univ of Washington, History Box 353560, Seattle, WA 98195-3560. **EMAIL** rorabaug@u.washington.edu

RORLICH, AZADE-AYSE
DISCIPLINE HISTORY **EDUCATION** Univ Wisconsin, PhD, 76. **CAREER** Assoc prof, Univ Madison, Southern Calif. **HONORS AND AWARDS** IREX, ACLS, Haynes, American Philos Society Grants, USC Teaching Excellence Awd, Am Muslim Achievement Awd. **MEMBERSHIPS** Am Asn for the Advancement of Slavic Studies, European Society for Central Asian Studies, Asn for the Study of Nationalities. **RESEARCH** 19th to 21st Century Russia and Eurasia, Islam, Minorities, Natiionality Policy, Women, Identity Discourse. **SELECTED PUBLICATIONS** Auth, The Volga Tartars, Hoover Inst, 86. **CONTACT ADDRESS** Dept of History, Univ of So California, University Park Campus, SOS No 258, Los Angeles, CA 90089. **EMAIL** arorlich@usc.edu

ROSAND, DAVID
PERSONAL Born 09/06/1938, Brooklyn, NY, m, 1961, 2 children **DISCIPLINE** ART HISTORY **EDUCATION** Columbia Univ, BA, 59, PhD(art hist), 65. **CAREER** From instr to assoc prof, 64-73, prof art hist, 73-95, Meyer Schapiro Prof Art Hist, Columbia Univ, 95-; Nat Endowment for Humanities younger scholar fel, 71-72, fel for independent study, 85-86, 91-92; Am Coun Learned Socs grant-in-aid, 70 & 77; Fulbright travel grant, 71-72; John S Guggenheim Mem Found fel, 74-75; Rockefeller Found Bellagio Study Center fel, 92. **HONORS AND AWARDS** Premio Cultura, Citta di Bassano del Grappa, 92; Great Teacher Award, Soc of Columbia Graduates, 97. **MEMBERSHIPS** Col Art Asn Am; Renaissance Soc Am; Ateneo Veneto, Venice; Am Acedemy of Arts and Sciences. **RESEARCH** History of drawings and prints; Renaissance and baroque art; Venetian painting; theory and criticism. **SELECTED PUBLICATIONS** Coauth, Titian and the Venetian Woodcut, Int Exhibs Found, 76; auth, Titian, Abrams, 78; Painting in Cinquecento Venice: Titian, Veronese, Tintoretto, Yale, 82; The Meaning of the Mark: Leonardo and Titian, Spenser Museum, 88; coauth, Places of Delight: The Pastoral Landscape, Philips Collection and National Gallery of Art, 88; coauth, Robert Motherwell on Paper: Drawings, Prints, Collages, Abrams, 97; auth, Myths of Venice: The Figuration of a State, 01. **CONTACT ADDRESS** Dept of Art Hist & Archaeol, Columbia Univ, 826 Schermerhorn Hall-mail code 5517, New York, NY 10027. **EMAIL** dr17@columbia.edu

ROSE, BRIAN
DISCIPLINE ART HISTORY AND ARCHAEOLOGY **EDUCATION** Haverford Col, BA, 78; Columbia Univ, MA, 80, MPhil, 82, PhD, 87. **CAREER** Researcher, Municipal Art Soc, New York City, 79-81; asst prof, Univ Cincinnati, 87-94; assoc prof, Univ Cincinnati, 94-. **HONORS AND AWARDS** President's Fel, Columbia Univ, 79-82; Fel, Am Res Institute in Turkey, 85; Helen M. Woodruff Fel of the Archaeological Institute of Am, 91-92; Am Academy in Rome, 91-92; Fac Achievement Awd, Univ of Cincinnati, 94; Storer Found Grant, 94, 95, 98, 99; Max Planck Res Prize, 94; Awd for Distinguished Scholarship (McMicken Dean's Awds for Fac Excellence), 95; Samuel H. Kress Grant, 00; Institute for Aegean Prehistory, 00; Storer Found Grant, 00. **MEMBERSHIPS** Archaeol Inst Am; Am Res Inst in Turkey. **SELECTED PUBLICATIONS** Auth, The Theater of Ilion, Studia Troica 1, 91; auth, Greek and Roman Excavations at Troy, 1991, Studia Troica 2, 92; auth, Greek and Roman Excavations at Troy, 1992, Studia Troica 3, 93; auth, Greek and Roman Excavations at Troy 1993, Studia Troica 4, 94; auth, Greek and Roman Excavations at Troy 1994, Studia Troica 5, 95; auth, Greek and Roman Excavations at Troy 1995, Studia Troica 6, 96; auth, Dynastic Commemoration and Imperial Portraiture in the Julio-Claudian Period, Cambridge Univ Press, 97; "The 1997 Post-Bronze Age Excavations at Troy," Studia Troica 8, (98): 71-113; auth, "The 1998 Post-Bronze Age Excavations at Troy," Studia Troica 9, (99): 35-71; coauth, "A Child's Sarcophagus from the Salvage Excavations at Gumuscay," with Nurten Sevinc, Studia Troica 9, (99): 489-509. **CONTACT ADDRESS** Dept of Classics, Univ of Cincinnati, PO Box 210226, Cincinnati, OH 45210-0226. **EMAIL** brian.rose@uc.edu

ROSE, JONATHAN
PERSONAL Born 11/27/1952, New York, NY, m, 1995, 2 children **DISCIPLINE** HISTORY **EDUCATION** Princeton Univ, 74; Univ Pa, MA, 75; PhD, 81. **CAREER** Prof, Drew Univ, 84-; chair of grad prog in Mod Hist and Lit, Drew Univ, 94-97; Dir of grad prog in Book Hist, 98-. **HONORS AND AWARDS** Res Grant, English-Speaking Union, 78; Res Grant, Am Philos Soc, 86; Res Grant, Brit Inst of the US, 87; Res Grant, Nat Endowment for the Humanities, 93. **MEMBERSHIPS** AHA, Soc for the Hist of Authorship, Reading and Publ, NE Victorian Studies Asn. **RESEARCH** History of Reading and Publishing in Britain. **SELECTED PUBLICATIONS** Auth, The Edwardian Temperament 1895-1919, Ohio Univ Press (Ohio), 86; co-ed, contrib, British Literary Publishing Houses, 1820-1965, Gale Res (Detroit), 91; ed, contrib, The Revised Orwell, Mich State Univ Press (East Lansing), 92; auth, "Intellectuals Among the Masses; or, What Was Leonard Bast Really Like?," Biblion (Spring 94); auth, "Marx, Jane Eyre, Tarzan: Miners' Libraries in South Wales, 1923-1952," Leipziger Jahrbuch zur Buchgeschichte (94); auth, "How Historians Study Reading," in Literature in the Marketplace, ed. John O. Jordan and Robert Patten (Cambridge: Cambridge Univ Press, 95); auth, "A Conservative Canon: Cultural Lag in British Working-Class Reading Habits," Libr and Cult (Winter 98); auth, "The History of Books: Revised and Enlarged," Studies on Voltaire and the Eighteenth Century 359 (98); ed, The Holocaust and the Book: Destruction and Preservation, Univ of Mass Press, forthcoming; auth, The Intellectual Life of the British Working Classes 1750-1945, forthcoming. **CONTACT ADDRESS** Dept Hist, Drew Univ, 36 Madison Ave, Madison, NJ 07940-1434. **EMAIL** jerose@drew.edu

ROSE, MARK
PERSONAL Born 09/11/1942, Chicago, IL, m, 1967, 2 children **DISCIPLINE** HISTORY **EDUCATION** Ohio State Univ, PhD. **CAREER** Prof. **HONORS AND AWARDS** NSF, NEH, Woodrow Wilson Int Center for Scholars. **MEMBERSHIPS** AHA, OAH, SHOT, BHC, VHA, SACRPH, IEHS. **RESEARCH** American City and Technology since 1945. **SELECTED PUBLICATIONS** Auth, Cities of Light and Heat: Domesticating Gas and Electricity in Urban American, 95; pubs in Technology and Culture; Journal of Policy History; auth, Interstate: Express Highway Politics, 1939-1989, 90; auth, Journal of Urban History. **CONTACT ADDRESS** History Dept, Florida Atlantic Univ, 777 Glades Rd, Boca Raton, FL 33431. **EMAIL** mrose@fau.edu

ROSE, PAUL LAWRENCE
PERSONAL Born 02/26/1944, Glasgow, Scotland, m, 1969, 4 children **DISCIPLINE** HISTORY **EDUCATION** Oxford, BA, MA, 68; Paris-Sorbonne, PhD, 73. **CAREER** Lectr, UCLA, 68-69; res assoc, Univ Toronto, 69-70; instr, St. Johns, 70-71; asst prof, NYU, 71-74; aps fel, Cambridge Univ, 74-75; res prof, James Cook Univ, 74-84; prof, Univ Haifa, 83-92; prof, Pa State Univ, 92-. **HONORS AND AWARDS** Fel of the Royal Hist Soc; Inst Adv Stud, Princeton; Robarts prof, 90-92, York Univ. **RESEARCH** German history; intellectual history; Jewish studies. **SELECTED PUBLICATIONS** Auth, The Italian Renaissance of Mathematics. Studies on Humanists and Mathematicians from Petrarch to Galileo, 75; auth, Bodin and the Great God of Nature: The Moral and Religious Universe of a Judaiser, 80; auth, German Question/Jewish Question. Revolutionary Antisemitism in Germany from Kant to Wagner, 90; auth, Wagner: Race and Revolution, 96; auth, Heisenberg and the Nazi Atomic Bomb Project, 1939-1945: A Study in German Culture, 98. **CONTACT ADDRESS** Dept of History, Pennsylvania State Univ, Univ Park, Weaver 108, University Park, PA 16802. **EMAIL** plr2@psu.edu

ROSELL, GARTH M.
PERSONAL Born 05/27/1939, Rochester, MN, m, 1965, 2 children **DISCIPLINE** CHURCH HISTORY **EDUCATION** Wheaton Col, BA; Princeton Theol Sem, MDiv, 64, ThM, 66; Univ Minn, PhD, 71. **CAREER** Prof, Bethel Theol Sem 70-78; acad dean, Conwell Theol Sem; prof, Gordon-Conwell Theol Sem, 78-; dir, Ockenga Inst. **MEMBERSHIPS** Mem, AAR, ASCH, AHA ETS. **SELECTED PUBLICATIONS** Co-auth, The Memoirs of Charles G. Finney: The Complete Restored Text, Zondervan, 89; American Christianity, Eerdmans, 86; The Millionaire and The Scrublady and Other Parables by William E. Barton, Zondervan, 90; auth, Shoeleather Faith, Bruce, 62;

Cases in Theological Education, ATS, 86. **CONTACT ADDRESS** Gordon-Conwell Theol Sem, 130 Essex St, South Hamilton, MA 01982. **EMAIL** grosell@gcts.edu

ROSEN, RUTH E.
PERSONAL Born 07/25/1945, m, 1996, 2 children **DISCIPLINE** HISTORY **EDUCATION** Univ of Rochester, Ba, 67; Univ of Calif at Berkely, MA, 69, PhD, 76. **CAREER** FULL PROF, HIST DEPT, UNIV OF CALIF AT DAVIS, 74-. **HONORS AND AWARDS** Distinguished teaching award; Visiting Scholar, European Peace Univ;Rockefeller Humanities Fellowship, Fellow, Beatrice Baun Institute , UC Berkeley; Fellow, Institute on Conflict and Cooperation, Univ of CA; Rockefeller Gender Roles Fel; Fellow, Beatrice Bais Institute, UC Berkeley; Inducted Honorary Women at Cal; Fellow, Institute on Conflict & Cooperation, U of Cal. **MEMBERSHIPS** Am Hist Asn; Bershire Confr on Women's Hist; Org of Am Historians. **RESEARCH** U.S. History, post 1945; Cold War culture; public policy; media; gender & culture; immigration. **SELECTED PUBLICATIONS** Auth, The Maimie Papers, 78, 96; auth, The Lost Sisterhood, 82; auth, Through Their Own Eyes, forthcoming; auth, The World Split Open: How the Modern Women's Movement Changed America, 00. **CONTACT ADDRESS** Dept of Hist, Univ of California, Davis, Davis, CA 95616. **EMAIL** rerosen@ucdavis.edu

ROSENBERG, EMILY SCHLAHT
PERSONAL Born 07/21/1944, Sheridan, WY, m, 1966, 4 children **DISCIPLINE** AMERICAN HISTORY, INTERNATIONAL RELATIONS **EDUCATION** Univ NE, BA, 66; State Univ NYork Stony Brook, MA, 69, PhD, 73. **CAREER** Asst prof, Honors Prog, Cent Mich Univ, 73-74; asst prof, 74-80, assoc prof, Macalester Col, 80-85; prof hist, 86-93; Dewitt Wallace prof, 93-, Stanford prof hist, San Diego State Univ, 96-97. **HONORS AND AWARDS** Phi Beta Kappa, 66, AAUW Fel, 71-72; NEH Fel, 83-84; SSRC Fel, 91-92; Burlington-Northern Tchg Awd, 93; Thomas Jefferson Awd, 94. **MEMBERSHIPS** OHA; AHA; SHAFR. **RESEARCH** 20th century US for rel(s); US cult and economic rel(s). **SELECTED PUBLICATIONS** Auth, Dollar Diplomacy under Wilson: An Ecuadoran Case, Inter-American Econ Affairs, 71; Co-auth, America: A Portrait in History, Prentice-Hall, 73, rev ed, 78; World War I and Continental Solidarity, The Americas, 75; Economic Pressures in Anglo-American Diplomacy in Mexico, 1917-18, Jour of Inter-Am Studies and World Affairs, 75; Co-ed, Postwar America: Readings and Reminiscences, Prentice-Hall, 76; Anglo-American Economic Rivalry in Brazil during World War I, Diplomatic Hist, 78; Emergency Executive Controls over Foreign Comerce and United States Economic Pressure on Latin American during World War I, Inter-Am Econ Affairs, spring 78; Spreading the American Dream: American Economic and Cultural Expansion, 1890-1945, Hill and Wang, 82; Foundations of United States International Financial Power: Gold Standard Dipolmacy, 1900-1905, Bus Hist Rev, 85; The Invisible Protectorate: The United States, Liberia and the Evolution of Neocolonialism, 1909-1940, Diplomatic Hist, 85; World War I and the Growth of United States Predominance in Latin America, Garland, 86; Co-auth, From Colonialism to Professionalism: The Public-Private Dynamic in United States Foreign Financial Policy, 1898-1930, Jour Am Hist, 87; Gender in A Round Table: Explaining the History of American Foreign Relations, Jour Am Hist, 90; Walking the Borders, Diplomatic Hist, 90; Signifying the Vietnam Experience, Rev in Am Hist, 91; Walking the Borders, In: Explaining the History of American Foreign Relations, Cambridge Univ Press, 91; The Rocky Mountain West: Region in Transit, Mont Bus Quart, 92; NSC-68 and Cold War Culture, In: American Cold War Strategy: Interpreting NSC 68, St. Martin's Press, 93; The Cold War and the Discourse of National Security, Dplomatic Hist, 93; A Century of Exporting the American Dream, In: Exporting America: Essays on American Studies Abroad, Garland, 93; Economic Interest and US Foreign Policy, In: American Foreign Relations Reconsidered, Routledge, 94; Foreign Affairs after World War II: Connecting Sexual and International Politics, Diplomatic Hist, 94; Cultural Interactions, In: The Encyclopedia of the United States in the Twentieth Century, Scribners, 96; A Call to Revolution: A Roundtable on Early U.S. Foreign Relations, Diplomatic Hist, 98; Revisiting Dollar Diplomacy: Narratives on Money and Manliness, Diplomatic Hist, 98; Co-auth, In Our Times: America since 1945, Prentice-Hall, rev ed, 99; Co-auth, Liberty, Equality, Power: A History of the American People, Harcourt-Brace, rev ed, 99; auth, "Consuming Women: Images of Americanization in the 'American Century'," in Michael Hogan, ed., The Ambitious Legacy: U.S. Foreign Relations in the 'American Century,' (Cambridge University Press, 99) 437-62; auth, Financial Missionaries to the World: The Politics and Culture of Dollar Diplomacy, 1900-1930, Harvard Univ Press, 99; auth, "Turning to Culture," in Gilbert Joseph, et al, eds, Close Encounters of Empire (Duke University Press, 98). **CONTACT ADDRESS** 1600 Grand Ave, Saint Paul, MN 55105-1899. **EMAIL** rosenberg@macalester.edu

ROSENBERG, HARRY
PERSONAL Born 03/11/1923, Toledo, OH, w, 1947, 3 children **DISCIPLINE** HISTORY **EDUCATION** Univ Calif at Berkeley, BA, 49; PhD, 59. **CAREER** Fac, Stanford Univ, 56-59; fac, Univ Wash, 59; fac, Colo State Univ, 59-. **HONORS AND AWARDS** Distinguished Service Awd, Colo State Univ, 76; Honors Prof, Colo State Univ, 76; Charles A. Lory Awd, Colo State Univ Alumni Asn, 91; Distinguished Prof Awd, Colo State Univ Alumni Asn, 98; John Stern Distinguished Prof Awd, Colo State Univ Col of Liberal Arts, 98. **MEMBERSHIPS** AHA, Medieval Acad of Am, Am Soc of Church Hist. **RESEARCH** Church & State in Late Antiquity and Early Middle Ages, Historiography in Late Antiquity and Early Middle Ages. **CONTACT ADDRESS** Dept Hist, Colorado State Univ, Fort Collins, CO 80523-0001. **EMAIL** hrosenberg@vines.colostate.edu

ROSENBERG, JONATHAN
DISCIPLINE AMERICAN HISTORY **EDUCATION** Juilliard Sch, Dipl Music, 80; Harvard Univ, MA, 91; PhD, 97. **CAREER** Lectr, Harvard Univ, 97-98; asst prof, Fla Atlantic Univ, 98-99; res sch, Miller Ctr of Pub Affairs, Univ of Va, 99-00; Charles Warren Fel in Am Hiost, Harvard Univ, 00-01. **HONORS AND AWARDS** GSAS Fel, Harvard Univ, 92-96; Derek Bok Ctr Cert for Distinctin in Tchg, 94; Charles Warren Res Fel, 93, 95; Harvard hist Dept Traveling Fel, 94-95; Kittredge Fund Fel, 95; Mark DeWolfe Howe Fel, 96; Harold K. Gross Dissertation prize, 98; Fel, Du Bois Inst for Afro-Am Res, Harvard Univ, 98-99. **MEMBERSHIPS** Am Hist Asn. **RESEARCH** 20th century American history; political history; race relations. **SELECTED PUBLICATIONS** Auth, "The Making of a Dissertation," in Rethinking International Relations, ed, Akira Iriye (Imprint, 98); auth, "The Cold War and the U.S. Civil Rights Movement," in History in Dispute: American Social and Political movements, ed, Robert Allison (St James Pr, 99); auth, "Winston Churchill," in Cold War Statesman Confront the Bomb, eds, Gaddis, May, Rosenberg (Oxford Univ Pr, 99); auth, "For Democracy, Not Hypocrisy: World War and Race Relations in the United States, 1914-1919," Int Hist Rev (Sept 99); co-ed, Cold War Statesmen Confront the Bomb: HNuclear Diplomacy Sicne 1945, Oxford Univ Pr, 99; auth, "Fascists at Home and Abroad: The Struggle for Racial Justice in 1930s America," in The Cultural Turn: Essays on the History of U.S. Foreign Relations, eds, Fank Ninkovich & Liping Bu (Imprint Pubs, 00); auth, "The Global Editor: Du Bois, The Crisis, and the World," The Crisis (July/Aug 00); auth, "'From Deep in the Heart of Russa': Images of the Soviet Union and the American Civil Rights Movement in the 1920s," in African Americans in the Age of American Expansion, ed Cary Fraser (forthcoming); ed, Crises and Conscience: Kennedy, Johnson, and the Quest for Racial Justice, Norton, forthcoming; auth, "How Far the Promised Land?": World Affairs and the American Civil Rights Movement from the First World War to Vietnam (Princeton Univ Pr, forthcoming). **CONTACT ADDRESS** Charles Warren Ctr, Harvard Univ, Levine Hall, Cambridge, MA 02138. **EMAIL** jrosen8637@aol.com

ROSENBERG, MILLA
PERSONAL Born 07/06/1974, Harvey, IL, s **DISCIPLINE** HISTORY **EDUCATION** Univ Ill, BS, 96; Ohio State Univ, MA, 99. **CAREER** Instr, Franklin Univ, 99-01. **MEMBERSHIPS** MLA. **RESEARCH** Lesbian, Gay, Bisexual and Transgender studies, American Jewish History, Fin de Siecle Cultures. **SELECTED PUBLICATIONS** Auth, "Friendship," Reader's Guide to Lesbian and Gay Studies, ed Timothy Murphy, (Chicago: Fitzroy-Dearborn, 00); auth, "Feygele Girlchicks? Jewish Lesbian Identity and the Jewish Student Centres," Queer Jews, Changing Communities, ed Caryn Aviv and David Schneer, (NY: Routeledge, forthcoming). **CONTACT ADDRESS** 65 W Starr Ave, Apt B, Columbus, OH 43201-3447.

ROSENBERG, NORMAN LEWIS
PERSONAL Born 02/15/1942, Lincoln, NE, m, 1966, 4 children **DISCIPLINE** AMERICAN HISTORY **EDUCATION** Univ NE-Lincoln, BA, 64, MA, 67; State Univ NYork Stony Brook, PhD, 72. **CAREER** Asst prof, Cent MI Univ, 71-74; from asst prof to assoc prof, 74-85, prof hist, Macalester Col, 86-93, Dewitt Wallace Prof, 93-; Mem fac, Dept Jour, Univ Calif, Berkeley, 76; San Diego State, 96-97, Univ MN, 98. **HONORS AND AWARDS** Phi Beta Kappa, 64; SUNY fel, 67-70; Burlington-Northern Distinguished Teaching Awd, 93. **MEMBERSHIPS** Am Soc Legal Hist; Am Hist Assoc; Org Am Hist. **RESEARCH** US legal-constitutional hist; US 20th century; US popular cult and media. **SELECTED PUBLICATIONS** Auth, Protecting the Best Men: An Interpretive History of the Law of Libel, Univ NC Press, 90; Perry Mason: Above But Not Beyond the Law, In: Prime Time Law, 98; Law Noir, In: Legal Reelism, Univ Ill Press, 96; Professor Lightcap Goes to Washington: Re-reading Talk of the Town, Univ of San Francisco Law Rev, 96; The Popular First Amendment and Classical Hollywood, 1930-1960, In: Freeing the First Amendment, NYU Press, 95; Young Mr Lincoln: The Lawyer as Super-Hero, Legal Studies Forum, 91; Gideon's Trumpet: Sounding the Retreat from Legal Realism, In: Recasting America, Univ Chicago Press, 88; co-auth, In Our Times: America Since 1945, Prentice-Hall, 6th ed, 99; Liberty, Equality, Power: A History of the United States, 2nd ed, Harcourt Brace, 99; America Transformed, Harcourt Brace, 99; From Colonialism to Professionalism: The Public-Private Dynamic in U S Foreign Financial Advising, 1898-1929, Jour Am Hist, 87. **CONTACT ADDRESS** Dept of Hist, Macalester Col, 1600 Grand Ave, Saint Paul, MN 55105-1899. **EMAIL** rosenbergn@macalester.edu

ROSENBERG, ROSALIND NAVIN
PERSONAL Born 06/15/1946, Boston, MA, m, 1967, 2 children **DISCIPLINE** AMERICAN HISTORY **EDUCATION** Stanford Univ, BA, 68, PhD(hist), 74. **CAREER** Asst prof Am hist, Columbia Univ, 74-82; Asst prof AM Hist, Wesleyan Univ, 82-84; assoc prof, Barnard College, 84-92; prof, Barnard College, 92-. **MEMBERSHIPS** AHA; Orgn Am Historians. **RESEARCH** Women's hist; intellectual hist; legal hist. **SELECTED PUBLICATIONS** Auth, Beyond Separate Spheres: Intellectual Roots of Modern Feminism, Yale Univ Press, 82, Divided Lives: American Women in the Twentieth Century, 92; Pauli Murray and the Killing of Jane Crow, in Forgotton Heroes of the Past, 98. **CONTACT ADDRESS** Barnard College, Columbia Univ, New York, NY 10028. **EMAIL** rr91@columbia.edu

ROSENBLOOM, JOSEPH R.
PERSONAL Born 12/05/1928, Rochester, NY, m, 1952, 3 children **DISCIPLINE** MIDDLE EASTERN HISTORY **EDUCATION** Univ Cincinnati, BA, 50; Hebrew Union Col, OH, BHL, 52, MHL, 54, DHL(hist), 57; Eden Theol Sem, St Louis, MO, 73. **CAREER** Instr Mid Eastern hist, Univ KY, 57-61; adj prof classics, Washington Univ, 61-; Am Philos Soc grant, 65. **HONORS AND AWARDS** DD, Hebrew Union Col, 79. **MEMBERSHIPS** AHA; Am Orient Soc; Am Asn Mid E Studies. **RESEARCH** Hebrew language and culture. **SELECTED PUBLICATIONS** Auth, Biographical Dictionary of Early American Jewry, Univ, KY, 60; Notes on Chinese Jewry, Chicago Jewish Forum, fall 60; An Ancient Controversy and its Modern Effects, America, 4/64; A Literary Analysis of the Dead Sea Isaiah Scroll, Eerdmans, 68; Social Science Concepts and Biblical History, J Am Acad Relig, 12/72; Conversion to Judaism, Hebrew Union Col Press, 78. **CONTACT ADDRESS** Dept Asian Languages & Lit, Washington Univ, Box 1111, Saint Louis, MO 63130-4899.

ROSENBLUM, ROBERT
PERSONAL Born 07/24/1927, New York, NY, 2 children **DISCIPLINE** HISTORY OF ART **EDUCATION** Queens Col, BA, 48; Yale Univ, MA, 50; NYork Univ, PhD, 56; Oxford Univ, MA, 71. **CAREER** Instr hist art, Univ Mich, 55-56; from instr to asst prof, Princeton Univ, 56-66; prof fine arts, NY Univ, 66-, Vis asst prof, Columbia Univ, 60-63; Am Coun Learned Soc fel, 62-63; Slade Prof fine arts, Oxford Univ, 72; part time curator, Guggenheim Museum, 96-. **HONORS AND AWARDS** Frank Jewell Mather Awd, 81; Commandeur de l'Order des Arts et des Lettres, 99; nominated for PEN award, Writing on the Visual Arts, 00. **RESEARCH** Contemporary art; neoclassic and romantic art and architecture. **SELECTED PUBLICATIONS** Auth, Cubism and Twentieth Century Art, 60 & Ingres, 67, Abrams; Transformations in Late Eighteenth Century Art, Princeton Univ, 67; Frank Stella, Penguin, 71; Modern Painting and the Northern Romatic Tradition: Friedrich to Tothko, Harper, 75; 19th-Century Art, Abrams, 84; Paintings in the Musee d'Orsay, Stewart, Tabon, Chang, 89; The Jeff Koons Handbook, Thames and Hudson, 92; auth, The Paintings of August Strindberg, Blondal, 95; auth, On Modern American Art: Selected Essays, Abrams, 99; auth, 1900: Art at the Cross Roads, Royal Academy, 00. **CONTACT ADDRESS** Dept of Fine Arts, New York Univ, 100 Washington Sq E, Fine Arts, 303 Main, New York, NY 10003-6688.

ROSENHEIM, JAMES MORTON
PERSONAL Born 07/12/1951, Chicago, IL **DISCIPLINE** ENGLISH HISTORY **EDUCATION** Harvard Univ, BA, 72; Princeton Univ, MA, 78, PhD, 81. **CAREER** Instr, Westminster Choir Col, 78-81, asst prof, 81-82; Asst Prof, 82-89, assoc prof hist, TX A&M Univ, 89-99, Assoc Head Dept Hist, 96-99, Dir, Interdisciplinary Group for Hum Studies, 98-99; prof hist, 99-; dir, Center for Humanities Res, 99-. **MEMBERSHIPS** AHA; NAm Conf Brit Studies; ASECS. **RESEARCH** Early mod Eng soc hist; early mod Brit cult studies. **SELECTED PUBLICATIONS** Auth, The Townshends of Raynham: Nobility in Transition in Restoration and Early Hanoverian england, Wesleyan Univ Press, 89; co-ed, The First Modern Society: Essays in English History in Honour of Lawrence Stone, Cambridge Univ Press, 89; auth, The Notebook of Robert Doughty 1662-1665, Norfolk Record Soc, vol LIV, 91; Landownership, the Aristocracy, and the Country Gentry, In: The Reigns of Charles II and James VII and II, Macmillan Press Ltd, 97; The Emergence of a Ruling Order: English Landed Society 1650-1750, Addison Wesley Longman, 98; auth of other articles and publi. **CONTACT ADDRESS** Dept of Hist, Texas A&M Univ, Col Station, College Station, TX 77843-4236. **EMAIL** j-rosenheim1@tamu.edu

ROSENSTONE, ROBERT ALLAN
PERSONAL Born 05/12/1936, Montreal, PQ, Canada, m, 1997 **DISCIPLINE** HISTORY **EDUCATION** Univ Calif, Los Angeles, BA, 57, PhD(hist), 65. **CAREER** Vis asst prof Hist, Univ Ore, 65-66; from asst prof to assoc prof, 66-76, prof Hist, Calif Inst Technol, 76-, Am Philos Soc travel grant, 70; vis prof Am Studies, Kyushu Univ & Seinan Gakuin Univ, Fukuoka, Japan, 74-75; Fulbright-Hays sr lectr, Japan, 74-75; Nat Endowment Humanities sr fel, 81-82; res fel, East-West Ctr, Honolulu, fall 81; vis scholar, Doshisha Univ, Kyoto, Japan, spring 82; Humanities Center Vis Scholar, Univ of Georgia, 97; Distin-

guished Vis Fel, Univ of Manchester, 97; Vis Lecturer, European Humanities Research Center, Oxford Univ, 97; Fulbright chair, Europeon Univ Institute, Florence, 98. **HONORS AND AWARDS** Silver Medal Lit Awd, Commonwealth Club Calif, 76; Nat Endowment for the Humanities, Senior Fel, 89-90; Nat Endowment for the Humanities, Summer Fel, 94; Fulbright-Hays Senior Teaching/Res Fel, Univ of Barcelona, 94; Book of the Year, Film Historia, Univ of Barcelona, Visions of the Past: The Challenge of Film to Our Idea of History. **MEMBERSHIPS** AHA; Orgn Am Historians; **RESEARCH** History and the visual media, radical movements, biography. **SELECTED PUBLICATIONS** Auth, Protest from the Right, Glencoe, 68; Crusade of the Left: The Lincoln Battalion in the Spanish Civil War, Pegasus, 69; ed, Seasons of Rebellion: Protest and Radicalism in Recent America, Holt, 73; coauth, Los cantos de la conmocion: Veinte anos de rock, Tusquets, 74; auth, The counter culture in America, Am Studies Newslett, Tokyo, 5/75; Romantic Revolutionary: A Biography of John Reed, Knopf, 75, Ital transl, Riuniti, Rome, 76, Fr transl, Maspero, Paris, 77, Span transl, Ediciones Era, Mexico City, 79, Kossuth, Budapest, 80; Mabel Dodge: Evenings in New York, In: The Genius in the Drawing Room: The Salon in Europe and America from the 18th to the 20th Century, Widenfeld & Nicolson, London, 80; Learning from those imitative Japanese: Another side of the American experience in the Mikado's empire, Am Hist Rev, 6/80; auth, Mirror in the Shrine: American Encounters in Meiji Japan, Cambridge: Harvard, 88; Japanese transl: Han, Mosu, Gurifisu no Nihon, Tokyo: Heibonsha, 99; auth, Visions of the Past: The Challenge of Film to Our Idea of History, Cambridge: Harvard Univ Press, 95; Spanish transl, El Pasado en imagenes: El Desafio del cine a nuestra idea de la historia, Madrid, Ariel, 97; auth, Revisioning History: Filmmakers and the Construction of the Past, Princeton, N J, Princeton Univ Press, 95. **CONTACT ADDRESS** Div Humanities & Soc Sci, California Inst of Tech, 1201 E California, Pasadena, CA 91125-0002. **EMAIL** rr@hss.caltech.edu

ROSENTHAL, ANGELA H.
PERSONAL m, 1996 **DISCIPLINE** ART HISTORY **EDUCATION** Trier Univ, PhD. **CAREER** Asst prof, Dartmouth Col. **HONORS AND AWARDS** AAH ASECS, CAA, Frauen Kunst Wissenschaft; HECAA; Ulmer Verein fuer Kunstgeschichte. **RESEARCH** Eighteenth-century Eng art and cult, contemporary theory, feminism and gender studies. **SELECTED PUBLICATIONS** Auth, She's Got the Look!: Eighteenth-Century Female Portrait Painters and the Psychology of a Potentially 'Dangerous Employment' in Portraiture: Facing the Subject, Manchester UP, 97; Double-Writing in Painting in Strategien der Selbstdarstellung von Kunstlerinnen im 18. Jahrhundert, Kritische Berichte, 93; Kauffman and Portraiture in Angelika Kauffman: a Continental Artist in Georgian England, Reaktion Bks, 92; Angelica Kauffman Ma(s)king Claims, Art Hist, 92; Die Zeichnungen der Angelika Kauffmann im Vorarlberger Landesmuseum in Bregenz, Jahrbuch des Vorarlberger Landesmuseumsvereins, Bregenz, 90; var other articles; auth, Angelika Kauffman: Bildnismalerei im 18, Jahrhundert, Berlin: Reimers Verlag, 96; co-ed, The Other Hogarth: Aesthetics of Difference, Princeton Univ Pr, 01; co-ed, Frauen Kunst Wissenschaft, Marburg: Jonas Verlag, various other articles on contemporary art. **CONTACT ADDRESS** Dartmouth Col, 3529 N Main St, #207, Hanover, NH 03755. **EMAIL** angela.rosenthal@dartmouth.edu

ROSENTHAL, BERNICE GLATZER
PERSONAL Born 03/24/1938, New York, NY, d, 1 child **DISCIPLINE** HISTORY **EDUCATION** CCNY, BA, 59; Univ Chicago, MA, 60; Univ Cal, Berkeley, PhD, 70. **CAREER** Asst prof, Fordham Univ, 70; assoc prof, 75; prof, 80-. **HONORS AND AWARDS** Phi Beta Kappa; Magna cum Laude; NEH; NCREES; AAUW. **MEMBERSHIPS** AAASS. **RESEARCH** Russian Soviet history; intellectual history. **SELECTED PUBLICATIONS** Auth, "Wagner and Wagnerian Ideas in Russia," in Wagnerism in European Culture and Politics, ed. David Large, William Weber, Cornell University Press (84): 198-245; auth, "Lofty Ideals and Worldly Consequences: Visions of Sobornost' in Early Twentieth Century Russia," Festschrift for Nicholas Riasanovsky, Russian Hist 20 (93): 179-95; ed, The Occult in Modern Russian and Soviet Culture, auth of Introduction and chapter, "The Political Implications of the Early 20th Century Occult Revival," Cornell Univ Press (97); co-ed, East Europe Reads Nietzsche, author of chapter "Nietzsche, Nationality, Nationalism," East European Monographs, Columbia U. Press (98); co-ed, "Merezhkovskii i Nitsshe (K istorii zaimstvovanii), D. S. Merezhkovskii: Mysl' i slovo (Moscow, Nasledie, 99); auth, "The Nature and Function of Sophia in Sergei Bulgakov's Pre-Revolutionary Thought," in Russian Religious Thought: Contexts and New Perspectives, ed. Judith Deutsch Kornblatt, Richard Gustafson (Univ Wisconsin Press, Madison, 96); auth, "Nietzsche's Hidden Voice in Socialist Realism," in Cold Fusion, ed. Evgeny Barabtarlo (Berham Press, NY, forthcoming). **CONTACT ADDRESS** Dept History, Fordham Univ, 441 East Fordham Dr, Bronx, NY 10458-5149. **EMAIL** rosenthal@fordham.edu

ROSENTHAL, LISA
DISCIPLINE RENAISSANCE AND BAROQUE ART **EDUCATION** Univ Calif, Berkeley, PhD. **CAREER** Asst prof **HONORS AND AWARDS** J Paul Getty postdoc fel. **RESEARCH** Representation of family and gender and its relationship to philosophical and political discourse in the Early Modern period, especially Peter paul Rubens. **SELECTED PUBLICATIONS** Publ, articles in Amer and Brit sch jour(s) on seventeenth-century Dutch and Flemish art. **CONTACT ADDRESS** Dept Art Hist, Univ of Illinois, Urbana-Champaign, 408 East Peabody Dr, 143 Art & Design Bldg, Champaign, IL 61820.

ROSENTHAL, NAOMI
DISCIPLINE SOCIOLOGY, HISTORY **EDUCATION** Univ Chicago, BA, 63; London Sch Econ, MScEcon, 66; SUNY, PhD, 76. **CAREER** From Instr to Prof, State Univ NYork (SUNY), 75-. **HONORS AND AWARDS** Res Grant, Nat Sci Found, 81-84; Nat Endowment Humanities Fel, 95-96; Grants, United Univ PDQWL, 87, 89, 99. **MEMBERSHIPS** ASA, SWS, NSF. **RESEARCH** Gender, historical sociology, social movements. **SELECTED PUBLICATIONS** Auth, "Social History and 19th Century Women: A Review Essay," CHOICE (87): 67-77; auth, "Centrality Analysis for Historians," Hist Methods Quart, vol 20, no 2 (87): 53-62; coauth, "Spontaneity and Democracy in Social Movements," in Int Soc Movement Res: Organizing for Change, vol 2 (JAI Pr, 89), 1-17; coauth, "Social Movements and Network Analysis: A Case Study of 19th Century Women's Reform in New York State," Collective Behav and Soc Movements (93): 157-167; coauth, "Structural Tensions in the Nineteenth Century Women's Movement," Mobilization 2:1 (97): 21-46; auth, Spinsterhood and Womanly Possibilities in the Twentieth Century, SUNY Pr (Albany, NY), forthcoming. **CONTACT ADDRESS** 116 Jones Ave, Port Jefferson, NY 11777. **EMAIL** rosenthaln@soldvb.oldwestbury.edu

ROSENWEIN, BARBARA HERSTEIN
PERSONAL Born 03/01/1945, Chicago, IL, m, 1966, 2 children **DISCIPLINE** MEDIEVAL HISTORY **EDUCATION** Univ Chicago, BA, 66, MA, 68, PhD, 74. **CAREER** From instr to Assoc Prof, 71-88, Prof Hist, Loyola Univ of Chicago, 88-. **HONORS AND AWARDS** NEH Fel, 86-87, 97-98; Guggenheim Fel, 92. **MEMBERSHIPS** AHA; Mediaeval Acad Am. **RESEARCH** Medieval religion and society; medieval culture; monasticism. **SELECTED PUBLICATIONS** Auth, Association through Exemption: St. Denis, Salonnes and Metz, In: Vom Kloster zum Klosterverband: Das Werkzeug der Schriftlichkeit, Wilhelm Fink, 97; Cluny's Immunities in the Tenth and Eleventh Centuries: Images and Narratives, In: Die Cluniazenser in ihrem politisch-sozialen Umfeld, Monster, 98; ed, Anger's Past: The Social Uses of an Emotion in the Middle Ages, Cornall Univ Press, 98; auth, Negotiating Space: Power, Restraint, and Privileges of Immunity in Early Medieval Europe, Ithaca, NY, 99; co-ed, "L'an mil en 2000," Medievales, 37 (99); co-ed, Monks and Nuns, Saints and Outcasts: Religion in Medieval Society, Cornell Univ Press, 00; auth, "Property Transfers and the Church, Eighth to Eleventh Centuries: An Overview," in Les transferts partimoneaux en Europe occidentale VIIIe-Xe siecle (I), ed. Regine Le Jan, Francois Bougard, and Cristina La Rocca (Rome: Ecole francaise de Rome) 00; auth, "Francia and Polynesia: Rethinking Anthropological Approaches," in Negocier le don: Negotiating the Gift, ed. Gadi Alagazi, Valentin Groebner, and Bernhard Jussen, (Vandenhoeck and Ruprecht), 01; auth, "One Site, Many Meanings: Saint-Maurice d'Agaune as a Place of Power in the Early Middle Ages," in Topographies of Power in the Early Middle Age, ed. Mayke de Jong and Frans Theuws (Leiden: Brill), 01; auth, A Short History of the Middle Ages (Petersborough, ONT), 01. **CONTACT ADDRESS** Dept of History, Loyola Univ, Chicago, 6525 N Sheridan Rd, Chicago, IL 60626. **EMAIL** bhr55@enteract.com

ROSENZWEIG, ROY A.
PERSONAL Born 08/06/1950, New York, NY, m, 1981 **DISCIPLINE** HISTORY **EDUCATION** Columbia Col, BA, 71; Harvard Univ, PhD, 78. **CAREER** Asst Prof, Worcester Polytech Inst, 78-80; Fel, Wesleyan Univ, 80-81; Asst Prof to Distinguished Prof and Center Dir, George Mason Univ, 81-. **HONORS AND AWARDS** NEH Fel, Col Teachers, 84-85; Grant, Am Asn for State and Local Hist, 85; NEH Grant, 86-88; Forrest G. Pogue Awd, 87; Guggenheim Fel, 89-90; Best Book, Urban Hist Asn; Abel Wolman Prize; Abbott cumming Lowell Prize, 92; Hist Preservation Book Prize, Ctr for Hist Preservation; Best Manuscript, NY Hist Asn, 91; James Harvey Robinson Prize, Am Hist Asn; Best Book, Ctr for Hist Preservation, 98; Awd of Merit, Am Asn for State and Local Hist, 98; Outstanding Fac Awd, State of VA, 99. **SELECTED PUBLICATIONS** Co-auth, The Park and People: A History of Central Park, Cornell Univ Press, 92; co-auth, Who Built America? From the Centennial of 1876 to the Great War of 1914, Voyager, 93; co-auth, "Historians and the Web: a Guide," AHA Perspectives, (96): 11-16; co-auth, "Brave New World or Blind Alley? American History on the World Wide Web," Journal of American History, (97): 132-155; auth, "Wizards, Bureaucrats, Warriors, and Hackers: Writing the History of the Internet," American Historical Review, (98): 1530-1552; co-auth, The Presence of the Past: Popular Uses of History in American Life, Columbia Univ Press, 98; auth, "Live Free or Die? Death, Life, Survival, and Sobriety on the Information Superhighway," American Quarterly, (99): 160-174; auth, "Crashing the System: Hypertext and American Studies Scholarship," American Quarterly, 99; co-auth, Who Built America? From the Great War of 1914 to the Dawn of the Atomic Age in 1946, Worth Pub, 00; co-auth, Who Built America? Working People & the Nation's Economy, Politics, Culture & Society, Worth Pub, 00. **CONTACT ADDRESS** Dept Hist, George Mason Univ, Fairfax, 4400 University Dr, Fairfax, VA 22030-4422. **EMAIL** rrosenzw@gmu.edu

ROSIN, ROBERT L.
PERSONAL Born 02/12/1951, Lexington, MO, m, 1975 **DISCIPLINE** HISTORICAL THEOLOGY **EDUCATION** Concordia Tchrs Col, BA, 72; Concordia Sem, MDiv, 76; Stanford Univ, MA, 77, PhD, 86. **CAREER** From instr to assoc prof, 81-97, prof hist theol, 97- , chemn dept, 95- , Concordia Sem; guest instr, Martin Luther Sem, Papua New Guines, 83; actg dir lib services, 88-90, fac marshal, 89-97, ed, Concordia Sem Publ, 95- ; Exec dir Center for Reformation Res, 97- . **MEMBERSHIPS** Soc for Reformation Res; Sixteenth-Century Stud Conf; Renaissance Soc of Am; Luther-Gesellschaft; Am Soc of Church Hist; Lutheran Hist Conf; Am Friends of the Herzog August Biliothek. **RESEARCH** Reformation and education/ curriculum in the sixteenth century. **SELECTED PUBLICATIONS** Auth, Christians and Culture: Finding Place in Clio's Mansions, in, Christ and Culture: The Church in Post-Christian(?) America, Concordia Sem, 96; auth, Bringing Forth Fruit: Luther on Social Welfare, in Rosin, ed, A Cup of Cold Water: A Look at Biblical Charity, Concordia Sem, 97; auth, Reformers, The Preacher, and Skepticism: Luther, Brenz, Melanchthon, and Ecclesiastes, Verlag Philipp von Zabern, 97. **CONTACT ADDRESS** Concordia Sem, 801 DeMun Ave, Saint Louis, MO 63105. **EMAIL** rosinr@csl.edu

ROSKILL, MARK
PERSONAL Born London, England, m, 3 children **DISCIPLINE** ART HISTORY **EDUCATION** Trinity Col, BA, 56, MA, 61; Harvard Univ, MA, 57; Princeton Univ, PhD, 61. **CAREER** Princeton, 59-61; Harvard, 61-68; assoc prof, 68-73, prof, 73-99, Univ Mass Amherst. **RESEARCH** English painting; Victorian studies; European art of 19th and 20th centuries; history of photography; theory of modern art; contemporary art; criticism of modern art. **SELECTED PUBLICATIONS** Co-auth, Truth and Falsehood in Visual Images, 83; auth, What is Art History?, 89; The Interpretation of Cubism, 85; The Interpretation of Pictures, 89; Klee, Kandinsky and the Thought of their Time: A Critical Perspective, 92; The Languages of Landscape, 97. **CONTACT ADDRESS** Art History Dept, Univ of Massachusetts, Amherst, 325 Bartlett Hall, Amherst, MA 01003. **EMAIL** mroskill@arthist.umass.edu

ROSNER, DAVID
DISCIPLINE UNITED STATES HISTORY **EDUCATION** Univ Mass, MS; Harvard Univ, PhD. **CAREER** Prof. **SELECTED PUBLICATIONS** Auth, Children, Race, and Power: Kenneth and Mamie Clark's Northside Center,Univ Va, 96; co-auth, Deadly Dust: Silicosis and the Politics of Occupational Disease in Twentieth Century America, Princeton Univ, 94; co-ed, Hives of Sickness, Rutgers, 95; Health Care in America: Essays in Social History: Dying for Work, Ind Univ, 87; Slaves of the Depression, Cornell Univ, 87. **CONTACT ADDRESS** Dept of History, Columbia Col, New York, 2960 Broadway, New York, NY 10027-6902.

ROSS, DOROTHY RABIN
PERSONAL Born 08/13/1936, Milwaukee, WI, m, 1958, 2 children **DISCIPLINE** AMERICAN HISTORY **EDUCATION** Smith Col, AB; Columbia Univ, MA, 59, PhD, 65. **CAREER** Lectr hist, George Washington Univ, 71; special asst on women, AHA, 71-72; asst prof, Princeton Univ, 72-76; spec asst to secy, HEW, 77; from assoc prof to prof hist, Univ Va, Charlottesville, 78-90; Arthur O Lovejoy Prof Hist, Johns Hopkins Univ, 90-; bd ed, J Hist Ideas, 92; chemn, dept hist, Johns Hopkins Univ, 93-96. **HONORS AND AWARDS** Res fel psychiat & hist psychiat, Payne Whitney Clinic, Med Col, Cornell Univ, 65-67; res fel hist psychol, George Washington Univ, 67-68; Natl Sci Found res fel, 80-81; fel Ctr for Advanced Stud in Behavioral Sci, Stanford, 92-93; Elect, Soc of Am Hist, 93; fel Woodrow Wilson Intl Ctr for scholar, DC, 96-97; Spencer Found Mentor Awd, 97-99; fel, Rockefeller Study and Conference Center, Bellagio, 99. **MEMBERSHIPS** AHA; Orgn Am Historians; Int Soc Hist Behav & Soc Sci; Hist Sci Soc; Am Studies Assn. **RESEARCH** American intellectual, social and behavioral sciences history. **SELECTED PUBLICATIONS** Auth, G. Stanley Hall: The Psychologist as Prophet, Univ Chicago Pr, 72; auth, Historical Consciousness in 19th Century America, AHR 89, 84; auth, The Origins of American Social Science, Cambridge Univ Press, 91; ed, Modernist Impulses in the Human Sciences, 1870-1930, Johns Hopkins Univ Press, 94; auth, Grand Narrative in American Historical Writing, AHR 100, 95. **CONTACT ADDRESS** 2914 33rd Pl NW, Washington, DC 20008. **EMAIL** doross1@ibm.net

ROSS, ELLEN
PERSONAL Born 06/06/1942, Detroit, MI, m, 1991, 2 children **DISCIPLINE** HISTORY **EDUCATION** Univ Chicago, BA, 64; Columbia Univ, MA, 65; Univ Chicago, PhD, 75. **CAREER** Asst prof, Conn Col, 71-76; asst prof, Ramapo Co., 76-82; assoc prof, 82-91; prof, 92- . **HONORS AND AWARDS** Phi Beta Kappa, 64; Woodrow Wilson Fel, 64-65; NEH fel, 90-

91. **MEMBERSHIPS** Am Hist Asoc; Berkshire Conf of Women Hist. **RESEARCH** Britain, 1870-1940; social history. **SELECTED PUBLICATIONS** Co-auth with Rayna Rapp, Sex and Society: Notes from the Intersection of Anthropology and Social History, Comparative Studies in Soc and Hist, 81; auth, Love and Toil: Motherhood in Outcast London 1870-1918, 93; auth, Human Commnion or a Free Lunch: School Dinners in Victorian and Edwardian London, Giving: Western Ideas of Philanthropy, 96; auth, Lady Explorers In Darkest London, 98; auth, Ladies Write the London Slums, The Historical Archeology of Urban Slums, 99. **CONTACT ADDRESS** School of Social Sciences, Ramapo Col of New Jersey, Mahwah, NJ 07430. **EMAIL** eross@ramapo.edu

ROSS, RONALD JOHN
PERSONAL Born 09/24/1935, St. Paul, MN, m, 1971 **DISCIPLINE** MODERN EUROPEAN HISTORY **EDUCATION** Univ MN, Minneapolis, AB, 61, MA, 63; Univ CA, Berkeley, PhD(hist), 71. **CAREER** From instr to asst prof, 68-74, chm dept hist, 76-78, assoc prof, 74-95, prof hist, Univ WI-Milwaukee, 96-. **MEMBERSHIPS** AHA;German Studies Asn. **RESEARCH** Modern German history; political and social history of modern Europe. **SELECTED PUBLICATIONS** Auth, Heinrich Ritter von Srbik and Gesamtdeutsch History, Rev Politics, 1/69; Beleaguered Tower: The Dilemma of Political Catholicism in Wilhelmine Germany, Univ Notre Dame, 76; Critic of the Bismarckian Constitution: Ludwig Windthorst and the Relationship Between Church and State in Imperial Germany, J Church & State, 3/79; Enforcing the Kulturkampf: The Bismarckian State and the Limits of Coercion in Imperial Germany, J Modern Hist, 3/84; Catholic Plight in the Kaiserreich: A Reappraisal, in Another Germany: A Reconsideration of the Imperial Era, Westview, 88; The Kulturkampf and the Limitations of Power in Bismarck's Germany, J Ecclesiastical Hist, 4/95; The Kulturkampf: Restrictions and Controls on the Practice of Religion in Bismarck's Germany, in Freedom and Religion in the Nineteenth Century, Stanford, 97; The Failure of Bismarck's Kulturkampf: Catholicism and the State Power in Imperial Germany, 1871-1887, Catholic Univ Am Press, 98. **CONTACT ADDRESS** Dept Hist, Univ of Wisconsin, Milwaukee, PO Box 413, Milwaukee, WI 53201-0413. **EMAIL** rjross@csd.uwm.edu

ROSS, STEPHANIE A.
DISCIPLINE AESTHETICS, FEMINISM **EDUCATION** Smith Col, BA, 71; Harvard Univ, MA, 74, PhD, 77. **CAREER** Assoc prof, Univ Mo, St Louis. **HONORS AND AWARDS** UMSL summer res fel, 78; NEH summer sem, 80; Weldon Spg grant, Univ Mo, St Louis, 81; UMSL summer res fel, 84; trustee, Am Soc for Aesthet, 86-89; Huntington Libr NEH fel, 89; fel, Yale Ctr for Brit Art, 90; Univ Mo Res Bd grant, 94; NEH summer inst, 95. **MEMBERSHIPS** Am Philos Asn; Am Soc for Aesthet; Soc for Women in Philos. **RESEARCH** Misguided marriage. **SELECTED PUBLICATIONS** Auth, Conducting and Musical Interpretation, Brit J of Aesthet, Vol 36, No 1, 96. **CONTACT ADDRESS** Univ of Missouri, St. Louis, Saint Louis, MO 63121.

ROSS, STEVEN
PERSONAL Born 05/08/1949, New York, NY, m, 1984, 2 children **DISCIPLINE** HISTORY **EDUCATION** Columbia Univ, BA, 71; Oxford Univ, BPhil, 73; Princeton Univ, MA, 75; PhD, 80. **CAREER** Asst Prof to Prof, Univ S Calif, 75-. **HONORS AND AWARDS** Theater Library Asn Book Awd, 99; LA Times Best Non-fiction Book of 98; Phi Kappa Phi Book Awd, 99, 87; Reubenheimer Awd, 98; Hewlett Foundation, 98; covert Awd, 92; USC Asn Awd, 92; Graves Fel, 91; Haynes Fel, 86; Burlington Northern Awd, 87; Fletcher Green Prize, 80. **MEMBERSHIPS** AHA, OAH, ASA. **RESEARCH** American South History; Working Class History; Popular Culture; Film History. **SELECTED PUBLICATIONS** Auth, Working-class Hollywood: Silent film and the Shaping of Class in America, Princeton Univ Press, 98; auth, Workers on the Edge: Work, Leisure, and Politics in Industrializing Cincinnati, 1788-1890, Columbia Univ Press, 85; auth, "Silent Film and the Shaping of American Political Culture," in Before Television: Mass Media and Political Cultures in Western Europe and the United States, 1900-1950, Cambridge, forthcoming; auth, "How Hollywood Became Hollywood: Money, Politics, and Movies," in Metropolis in the Making: Los Angeles in the 1920s, Univ Calif Press, forthcoming; auth, "A Journey of Discovery: Researching and Writing Working Class Hollywood," Stanford Humanities Review, (990: 50-71; auth, "The Revolt of the Audiences: Reconsidering Audiences and Reception During the Silent Era," in American Movie Audiences: From the Turn of the Century to the Sound Era, British Film Inst, (99): 88-107; auth, "Get Me Rewrite: Class Warfare on Titanic," Los Angeles Times, (98); 3; auth, "Beyond the Screen: History, Class, and the Movies," in The Hidden Foundation: Cinema and the Question of Class, 96; auth, "America's Labor Day: The Dilemma of a Workers' Celebration," Journal of American History, (92): 1294-1323; auth, "Struggles for the Screen: Workers, Radicals, and the Political Uses of Silent film," American Historical Review, (91): 333-367. **CONTACT ADDRESS** Dept Hist, Univ of So California, 3502 Tousdale Pkwy, Los Angeles, CA 90089-0034. **EMAIL** sjross@usc.edu

ROSSI, JOHN P.
PERSONAL Born 04/07/1936, Philadelphia, PA, m, 1966, 1 child **DISCIPLINE** MODERN BRITISH HISTORY **EDUCATION** LaSalle Col, BA, 58; Univ Notre Dame, MA, 60; Univ Pa, PhD(19th century Brit hist), 65. **CAREER** Asst instr hist, Univ Pa, 60-62; from instr to assoc prof, 62-75,prof hist, La Salle Col, 75-, chmn dept, 74-81. **MEMBERSHIPS** AHA; Conf Brit Studies; Am Coun Irish Studies; Soc of Am Baseball Research (SABR). **RESEARCH** Internal history of the British Liberal party in 1870's; career of the 1st Marquis of Ripon; British reaction to McCarthyism; career of George Orwell; History of Baseball. **SELECTED PUBLICATIONS** Auth, Orwell's Reception in America, Four Quarters, winter 73; Liberal Leadership and the Second Afghan War, Can J Hist, 9/73; Home Rule and the Liverpool by Election of 1880, Irish Hist Studies, 9/74; Selection of Lord Hartington as Liberal leader, Proc Am Philos Soc, 8/75; Orwell and Catholicism, Commonweal, 6/76; Transformation of the Liberal Party 1873-1880, Transaction Am Philos Soc, 7/78; America's view of George Orwell, Rev Polit, 10/81; Catholic Opinion of the Eastern Question, 1876-1878, Church Hist, 3/82; Farewell to Fellow-Traveling: The Waldorf Conference of March 1949, Continuity, Nu 10, spring 85; Churchill's Iron Curtain Speech: the American Reception, Modern Age, XXX, Nu 2, spring 86; The British Reaction to McCarthyism, LXX, nu i, Mid-America, Jan 88; Orwell and Chesterton, LXIII, nu 251, Thought, Dec 88; A Glorified Form of Rounders: Baseball in Britain February 1914, in Alvin Hall, ed, Cooperstown: Symposium on Baseball and American Culture, 1990, Meckler Press, 91; The Iron Curtain: A Premature Anti-Communist Film, Film and History, XXIV, No 3-4, 101-112, 94; A Baseball Myth Exploded: Bill Veeck and the 1943 Sale of the Phillies, co-authored with David Jordan and Larry Gerlach; The National Pastime: A Review of Baseball History #18, 98; auth, A Whole New Game: off the Field Changes in Baseball, 1946-1960, McFarland, 99; auth, The National Game: Baseball and American Culture, Ivan R. Dee publishers, Chicago, 00. **CONTACT ADDRESS** Dept of Hist, La Salle Univ, 1900 W Olney Ave, Philadelphia, PA 19141-1199. **EMAIL** Rossi@lasalle.edu

ROSSI, MONICA
PERSONAL Born 12/18/1962, Ravenna, Italy, m, 1997 **DISCIPLINE** ITALIAN STUDIES **EDUCATION** Universite Degli Studi di Bologna, 89; Univ Wash, MA, 89; NY Univ, PhD, 00. **CAREER** Asst Prof, Univ Wash, 87-89; Grad Instr, NYork Univ, 89-91; Vis Lect, Vassar Col, 93-00. **HONORS AND AWARDS** Dean's Travel Fund Awd, NY Univ, 90-91, 95; Vassar Col Res Grant, 96-97. **MEMBERSHIPS** PMLA, MLA, AAIS, AATI. **RESEARCH** Feminist criticism, 20th-century Italian literature, post-colonial Italophone literature, Italian cinema. **SELECTED PUBLICATIONS** Auth, "Ma io dissento: intervista con Noam Chomsky," Panorama (90); auth, "Apologia della differenza: uno sguardo dall'esterno alla condizione degli immigrati africani in Italia in 'Pummaro' de Michele Placido e 'L'articolo 2' di Maurizio Zaccaro," Canadian J of Ital Studies, 20th Anniversary Vol 1977-1997 and spec issue: Ital Cinema, vol 20, no 54 (97); auth, "Re-Thinking History: Women's Transgression," in La Briganta, Gendering Italian Fiction, Feminist Revisions of Italian History, (WI: Farleigh Dickinson Univ Pr, 99). **CONTACT ADDRESS** Dept Lang, Vassar Col, 124 Raymond Ave, PO Box 196, Poughkeepsie, NY 12604. **EMAIL** morossi@vassar.edu

ROSSITER, MARGARET W.
PERSONAL Born 07/08/1944, Malden, MA, s **DISCIPLINE** HISTORY OF SCIENCE & MEDICINE **EDUCATION** Radcliffe Col, Harvard Univ, AB, 66; Univ Wis, MS, 67; Yale Univ, MPhil, 69, PhD, 71; Regis Col, ScD, 97. **CAREER** Actg Asst Prof & Lectr, 73-74, 75-76, Res Assoc, Univ Calif - Berkeley, 76-82; Res Assoc, Am Acad Arts & Sci, 77-86; Dir, Hist & Philos Sci Prog, Nat Sci Found, 82-83; Vis Lectr & Vis Schol, Harvard Univ, 83-86; NSF Vis Prof, 86-88, Prof, 88-93, The Marie Underhill Noll Prof Hist & Sci, Cornell Univ, 93-; Ed, Osiris, 93-01; Ed, Isis, 94-. **HONORS AND AWARDS** Silver Medal, Justus-Liebig Univ, 79; Berkshire Prize, 83; Wilbur Cross Medal, Yale Univ Grad Sch, 84; Hoopes Teaching Awd, Harvard Univ, 84; Res Prize, Justus-Liebig Univ, 85; Kreeger-Wolf Distinguished Vis Prof, Northwestern Univ, 85; Regents Lectr, Univ Calif - Riverside, 86; Sarton Lectr, Am Asn Advancement Sci, 90; Arthur Holly Compton Distinguished Lectr, Wash Univ, 97; Hist of Women in Sci Prize, Hist Sci Soc, 97; Pfizer Prize, Hist Sci Soc, 97; recipient of numerous grants and fellowships, inc Guggenheim, Rockefeller, and MacArthur Prize Fels. **MEMBERSHIPS** Hist Sci Soc; Int Comn Hist Women Sci, Technol, & Med; Phi Bet Kappa; Am Asn Advancement Sci. **RESEARCH** History of women in science; American science; history of agriculture. **SELECTED PUBLICATIONS** Auth, The Emergence of Agricultural Science -- Justus Liebig and the Americans, 1840-1880, Yale Univ Press, 75; Women Scientists in America, Struggles and Strategies to 1940, Johns Hopkins Univ Press, 82; co-ed, Historical Writing on American Science, Johns Hopkins Univ Press, 86; Science at Harvard, 1636-1945, Lehigh Univ Press, 92; auth, Women Scientists in America: Before Affirmative Action, 1940-1972, Johns Hopkins Univ Press, 95; ed, Catching Up with the Vision, Essays on the Occasion of the 75th Anniversary of the Founding of the History of Science Society, 99; author of numerous articles and other publications. **CONTACT ADDRESS** Cornell Univ, 726 University Ave., #201, Ithaca, NY 14850. **EMAIL** mw4@cornell.edu

ROSZAK, THEODORE
PERSONAL Born 11/15/1933, Chicago, IL, m, 1 child **DISCIPLINE** HISTORY **EDUCATION** UCLA, BA, 55; Princeton Univ, PhD, 58. **CAREER** Stanford Univ, 59-62; Calif State Univ, Hayward, 62-. **HONORS AND AWARDS** Guggenheim Fel, 71-72. **SELECTED PUBLICATIONS** Auth, Flicker, 90, The Memoirs of Elizabeth Frankenstein, 95; The Voice of the Earth, 92; America the Wise, 98. **CONTACT ADDRESS** History Dept, California State Univ, Hayward, Hayward, CA 94542.

ROTH, JONATHAN
PERSONAL Born 12/06/1955, Redwood City, CA, m, 1993 **DISCIPLINE** ANCIENT HISTORY **EDUCATION** Columbia Univ, PhD, 91. **CAREER** Vis asst prof, Tulane Univ, 90-91; tchg fel, New York Univ, 91-94; from asst prof to assoc prof, San Jose State Univ, 94-. **HONORS AND AWARDS** Fulbright-Hayes scholar, 79-80; Dorot fel, 91-94. **MEMBERSHIPS** APA; Soc of Ancient Mil Hist. **RESEARCH** Roman military history. **SELECTED PUBLICATIONS** Coauth, Nine Unpublished Inscriptions in the Collection of Columbia University, Zeitschrift fur Papyrologie und Epigraphik, 88; coauth, Greek Ostraka from Mons Porphyrites, Bull of the Am Soc of Papyrologists, 92; auth, The Size and Organization of the Imperial Roman Legion, Historia, 94; auth, The Length of the Siege of Masada, Scripta Classica Israelica, 95; auth, P.Col.263-264, Sales of Donkeys, in Bagnall, ed, Columbia Papyri X, Columbia Univ, 97; auth, Early Kingdoms of Western Asia and Northern Africa, and Greece, in Stearns, ed, Langer Encyclopedia of World History, Houghton Mifflin, forthcoming; auth, George Willis Botsford, in Kornegay, ed, American National Biography, Oxford Univ, 1998; auth, The Logistics of the Roman Army at War, (264 BC-AD 235), EJ Brill, 1999. **CONTACT ADDRESS** History Dept, San Jose State Univ, 1 Washington Sq, San Jose, CA 95192-0117. **EMAIL** jroth@email.sjsu.edu

ROTH, MITCHEL
DISCIPLINE HISTORY **EDUCATION** Univ Md, BA, 75; Univ Calif, Santa Barbara, MA, 87; PhD, 93. **CAREER** Graduate Teachng Asst, Univ of Calif, 90-92; Lecturer, Sam Houston State Univ, 93-94; Vis Asst Prof, Sam Houston State Univ, 94-95; Asst prof, 95-00; Assoc prof, 00-, Sam Houston State Univ. **RESEARCH** American western history; history of crime and policing; organized crime; comparative criminal justice. **SELECTED PUBLICATIONS** Auth, Courtesy, Service and Protection: A History of the Texas Department of Public Safety, Taylor Publishing Co. (Dallas), 95; auth, Historical Dictionary of War Journalism, Greenwood Press (Westport), 97; auth, Fulfilling a Mandate: A History of the Sam Houston State University Criminal Justice Center, Sam Houston Univ Press, 97; auth, "From Matron to Cop: A Historical Comparison of Perceptions of Female Police Officers in the 1920s and 1980s," in To Research, To Read, To Reason, To Write, To Report, ed. By Diane Dowdey (New York, Simon and Schuster Custom Publishing, 98); auth, Reading the American West: Primary Source Readings in American History, Addison Wesley Longman (New York), 98; auth, "Organized Crime in the Balkans," Crime and Justice International (00); auth, "Mounted Police," Crime and Justice International (00); auth, "The Emerging Yardie Problem," Crime and Justice International (00); auth, Historical Dictionary of Law Enforcement, Greenwood Press (Westport), 00; auth, "Drugs in the Classroom: A Historical Approach to Drug Education," Journal of Criminal Justice Education (01). **CONTACT ADDRESS** Col of Criminal Justice, Sam Houston State Univ, Huntsville, TX 77341.

ROTH, MOIRA
PERSONAL Born 07/24/1933, London, England, d **DISCIPLINE** ART HISTORY **EDUCATION** New York Univ, BA, 59; Univ Calif, Berkeley, MA, 66, PhD, 74. **CAREER** Asst/assoc prof, Univ Calif, San Diego, 74-85; Prof, Art Hist, Mills Coll, 85-. **HONORS AND AWARDS** Frank Jewlett Mather Awd for lifetime achievement in art criticism. **MEMBERSHIPS** Coll Art Asn **RESEARCH** Contemporary American Art; Feminism; Multiculturalism. **SELECTED PUBLICATIONS** edr/contrib, Connecting Conversations: Interviews with 28 Bay area woemn Artists, Eucalyptus Press, 88; edr, We Flew Over the Bridge; the Memoirs of Faith Ringgold, LittleBrown, 95; edr, Rachel Rosenthal, John Hopkins Univ Press, 97. **CONTACT ADDRESS** Art Dept, Mills Col, 5000 MacArthur Blvd, Oakland, CA 94613.

ROTH, RANDOLPH A.
PERSONAL Born San Francisco, CA, m, 1977, 1 child **DISCIPLINE** HISTORY **EDUCATION** Stanford, Univ, BA, 73; Yale Univ, PhD, 81. **CAREER** Instr, hist Grinnell; asst prof Hist, Grinnell Col, 78-85. **MEMBERSHIPS** Am Antiquarian Soc. **RESEARCH** Social hist, relig, crime. **SELECTED PUBLICATIONS** Auth, "The First Radical Abolitionists: The Reverend James Milligan and the Reformed Presbyterians of Vermont," New Eng Quart 55, 82; auth, The Democratic Dilemma: Religion, Reform, and the Social Order in Vermont, 1791-1850, 87; auth, "Is History a Process? Revitalization Theory, Nonlinearity, and the Central Metaphor of Social Science History,"

Soc Sci Hist 16, Summer 92; auth, "The Other Masonic Outrage: The Death and Transfiguration of Joseph Burnham," Jour of the Early Rep 14, Spring 94; auth, "The Generation Conflict Reconsidered," in American Vistas, Oxford Univ Press, 95; auth, "Blood Calls for Vengeance!: The History of Capital Punishment in Vermont," Vermont Hist 65, 97; auth, "Child Murder in New England," Social Sci Hist, 25, 01; auth, "Spousal Murder in Northern New England, 1775-1865," in Christine Daniels, ed., Over the Threshold: Intimate Violence in Early American, (99). **CONTACT ADDRESS** Dept of Hist, Ohio State Univ, Columbus, Columbus, OH 43210. **EMAIL** roth.5@osu.edu

ROTHBLATT, SHELDON

PERSONAL Born 12/14/1934, Los Angeles, CA, m, 1956, 3 children **DISCIPLINE** MODERN ENGLAND, GEORGIAN AND VICTORIAN CULTURAL HISTORY, HISTORY OF UNIVERSITIES **EDUCATION** Univ Calif, Berkeley, BA, 56; MA, 59; King's Col, Cambridge Univ, 61-63; PhD(Hist), 65. **CAREER** From instr to assoc prof, 63-74, assoc dir, Ctr Study Higher Educ, 77-82, prof Hist, Univ Calif, Berkeley, 74-, dean Fresh & Soph Studies, Lett & Sci, 82-; Dept of Hist at UC Berkeley, 83-87; stint prof Hist, Royal Instit Tech, Stockholm, Sweden, 97-99; visitor, Nuffield Col, Oxford Univ, 77; scholar in residence, Rockefeller Ctr, Bellagio, 79; **HONORS AND AWARDS** Soc Sci Res Coun fac res fel, 66-67; Davis fel, Princeton Univ, 69-70; Guggenheim fel, 72-73; Am Coun Learned Soc fel, 81-83; Fel at the Swedish Collegium for Advanced Studies in the Social Sciences, 88; Berkeley Citation, 86; Hon Doctorate, Gothenburg Univ (Sweden), 99; Nat Academy of Educ, 96; Fel Royal Hist Soc of Britain. **MEMBERSHIPS** AHA, Conf Brit Studies (pres, Pac Coast Br, 78-80), Hist Educ Soc. **RESEARCH** University history, elites, professional groups; cultural and intellectual history. **SELECTED PUBLICATIONS** Auth, The Revolution of the Dons: Cambridge and Society in Victorian England, Faber & Faber, London & Basic Bks, 68 & Cambridge Univ Press, 81; coauth, Tradition and Change in English Liberal Education, Faber & Faber, 76; Nineteenth-Century London, In: People and Communities in the Western World, Dorsey Press, 79; G M Young: England's Historian of Culture, Victorian Studies, Summer 79; co-ed, The European and American University Since 1800, Cambridge University Press, 93; The Modern University and Its Discontents, Cambridge University Press, 97. **CONTACT ADDRESS** Dept of History, Univ of California, Berkeley, 3229 Dwinelle Hall, Berkeley, CA 94720-2551. **EMAIL** srotnbla@uclink4.berkeley.edu

ROTHENBERG, GUNTHER ERIC

PERSONAL Born 07/11/1923, Berlin, Germany, m, 1995 **DISCIPLINE** CENTRAL & EAST EUROPEAN HISTORY; MILITARY HISTORY **EDUCATION** Univ Ill, BA, 54, PhD, 58; Univ Chicago, MA, 56. **CAREER** Instr hist, Ill State Normal Univ, 58; asst prof, Southern Ill Univ, 58-62; from assoc prof to prof, Univ NMex, 63-73; Prof Mil Hist, Purdue Univ, 73-, Am Philos Soc grants, 61, 65, 67, 70 & 75; Am Coun Learned Soc & Soc Sci Res Coun grants, 62, 68, 73 & 77; Guggenheim fel, 62-63; mem, Hist Evaluation & Res Orgn, 63-68; fel, Interuniv Sem Armed Forces & Soc, 72-; prof emer, Purdue, 98; professional fel, Australian Defence Force Acedemy, 00-. **MEMBERSHIPS** AHA; Renaissance Soc Am; Am Asn Advan Slavic Studies; Conf Group Cent Europ Hist; Co Mil Hist. **RESEARCH** Habsburg military history; military history; national security affairs. **SELECTED PUBLICATIONS** Auth, The Austrian Military Border in Croatia, Univ Ill, 60; The Military Border in Croatia, 1740-1881, Univ Chicago, 66; The nationality problem in the Habsburg army, Austrian Hist Yearbk, 67; The Austrian army in the age of Metternich, J Mod Hist, 6/68; The Army of Francis Joseph, Purdue Univ, 76; The Art of Warfare in the Age of Napoleon, Batsford, 77 & Ind Univ, 78; The Anatomy of the Israeli Army, Batsford, 79 & Hippocrene, 79; Napoleon's Great Adversaries: The Archduke Charles and the Austrian Army, 1792-1814, Batsford, 82 & Ind Univ, 82; auth, The Austro-Hungarian Campaign afianst Serbia in 1914, The J of Milit Hist 53, 89; auth, Soldiers and the Revolution: The French Army, Society, and the State, 1788-1789, Hist J 32, 89; auth, The Austrian Military Response to the French Revolution and Napoleon, Essays in European Hist, 89; auth, Military Intelligence Gathering in the Second Half of the Eighteenth Century, Go Spy the Land: Military Intelligence and History, Praeger, 92; auth, Armies and Warfare during the Last Century of the Ancien Regime, Readings in Military Art and Science, Colo Springs, 92; auth, The Age of Napoleon, The Laws of War, Constraints on Wardare in the Western Wold, Yale Univ, 95; auth, The Napoleonic Wars, London: Cassel, 99. **CONTACT ADDRESS** Dept of Hist, Australian Defence Academy, Campbell, Australia ACT 2600. **EMAIL** gunther.rothenberg@arts.monash.edu.au

ROTHENBERG, MARC

PERSONAL Born 10/13/1949, Philadelphia, PA, m, 1985, 2 children **DISCIPLINE** HISTORY OF SCIENCE, HISTORY AND ASTRONOMY **EDUCATION** Villanova Univ, BA, 70; Bryn Mawr Col, PhD, 74. **CAREER** Res assoc, pub mus, Acad of Natural Sci of Philadelphia, 74-75; asst ed, Joseph Henry Papers, 75-83; assoc ed, Joseph Henry Papers, 83-85; ed, Joseph Henry Papers, Smithsonian Inst, 85-. **MEMBERSHIPS** Hist of Sci Soc; Soc for Hist in the Fed Govt; Soc for the Hist of Tech; Orgn of Amer Hist. **RESEARCH** History of American science; History of astronomy; Documentary Ed. **SELECTED PUBLICATIONS** Coed, The Papers of Joseph Henry Vol 3: 1836-1837: The Princeton Years, Smithsonian Inst Press, 79; co-ed, A Scientist in American Life: Essays and Lectures of Joseph Henry, Smithsonian Inst Press, 80; asst ed, The Papers of Joseph Henry. Vol 4: 1838-1840: The Princeton Years, Smithsonian Inst Press, 81; auth, The History of Science and Technology in the United States: A Critical and Selective Bibliography, Garland Publ, 82; assoc ed, The Papers of Joseph Henry. Vol 5: 1841-1843: The Princeton Years, Smithsonian Inst Press, 85; co-ed, Scientific Colonialism: A Cross Cultural Comparison, Smithsonian Inst Press, 87; ed, The Papers of Joseph Henry. Vol 6: 1844-1846: The Princeton Years, Smithsonian Inst Press, 92; auth, The History of Science and Technology in the United States: A Critical and Selective Bibliography, vol 2, Garland Publ, 93; Ed, The Papers of Joseph Henry, Volume 7: 1847-1849: The Smithsonian Years, Smithsonian Inst Press, 96; ed, The Papers of Joseph Henry, Vol 8:1850-1853:The Smithsonian Years, Smithsonian Inst Press, 98. **CONTACT ADDRESS** Arts and Industries 2188, Smithsonian Inst, Joseph Henry Papers, Washington, DC 20560-0429. **EMAIL** rothenbergm@osia.si.edu

ROTHFELD, ANNE

PERSONAL Born 01/12/1967, MD, s, 1 child **DISCIPLINE** ARCHIVES HISTORY **EDUCATION** Catholic Univ Am, MSLS, 98. **CAREER** Archives Techn, US Holocaust Memorial Museum, 93-98; Infor spec, Univ Md, 98-99; Archivist/Historians, 99-. **MEMBERSHIPS** Am History Asn; Orgn of Am History; Am Libr Asn; Special Libr Asn; Am Asn State and Local Hist; Society Hist Progressive and Gilded Age. **RESEARCH** Local and public history; late 19th/early 20th century American and German history; archives and special collections. **SELECTED PUBLICATIONS** Auth, rev, Economics of Digital Information: Collection, Storage, and Delivery, 99; auth, rev, Louis Shores: Defining Educational Librarianship, 99; auth, rev, More Than the Facts: The Research Division of the National Education Association, 1922-1997; auth, "A Source of Holocaust Research: The United Restitution Organization," Perspectives, 00; auth, "Electronic Reference Desk," The History Highway 2000: A guide to internet resources, 00. **CONTACT ADDRESS** 3806 Stepping Stone Ln, Burtonsville, MD 20866. **EMAIL** arothfeld@usmint.treas.gov

ROTHMAN, DAVID

DISCIPLINE UNITED STATES HISTORY **EDUCATION** Columbia Univ, MA, 58; Harvard Univ, PhD, 64. **CAREER** Prof. **SELECTED PUBLICATIONS** Auth, The Discovery of the Asylum: Social Order and Disorder in the New Republic, 71; Conscience and Convenience: The Asylum and Its Alternatives in Progressive America, 80; The Willowbrook Wars, 84; Strangers at the Bedside: A History of How Law and Bioethics Transformed Medical Decision-making, 91; Beginnings Count: The Technological Imperative in American Health Care, 97. **CONTACT ADDRESS** Dept of History, Columbia Col, New York, 2960 Broadway, New York, NY 10027-6902.

ROTHMAN, HAL K.

DISCIPLINE HISTORY **EDUCATION** Univ Tex Austin, PhD, 85. **CAREER** Prof, Univ Nev Las Vegas. **RESEARCH** Environmental history; public history. **SELECTED PUBLICATIONS** Auth, Devil's Bargains: Tourism in the Twentieth Century American West, 98; The Greening of Nation? Environmentalism in the U.S. Since 1945, 97; I'll Never Fight Fire With My Bare Hands Again, 94; On Rims and Ridges: The Los Alamos Area Since 1880, 92; Preserving Different Pasts The American National Monuments, 89; ed, Reopening the American West, 98; co-ed, Out of the Woods: Essays in Environmental History, 97. **CONTACT ADDRESS** History Dept, Univ of Nevada, Las Vegas, 4505 Md Pky, Las Vegas, NV 89154.

ROTHMAN, ROGER

PERSONAL Born 06/23/1967, New York, NY, m, 1996, 1 child **DISCIPLINE** ART **EDUCATION** Princeton Univ, BA, 89; Hunter Col, MFA, 92; Columbia Univ, MA, 95; PhD, 00. **CAREER** Pub lectr adj prof, Parsons Sch of Design, 95-97; adj prof, Sarah Lawrence Col, 96; instr, Columbia Univ, 97; adj prof, Sch of Visual Arts, 98; instr, Barnard Col, 96-99; asst prof, Agnes Scott Col, 00-. **HONORS AND AWARDS** Whiting Found Fel, 99-00; Dissertation Fel, Columbia Univ, 98-99; Matisse Fel for Dissertation, Columbia Univ, 97-98; Fel, Columbia Univ, 93-96; Harriet Eagleson Fel, Hunter Col, 89; Seitz Prize, Princeton Univ, 89. **MEMBERSHIPS** Col Art Asn. **RESEARCH** European modernism 1900-1940. **CONTACT ADDRESS** Dept Art, Agnes Scott Col, 141 E College Ave, Atlanta, GA 30030. **EMAIL** rrothman@agnesscott.edu

ROTHNEY, GORDON O.

PERSONAL Born 03/15/1912, Richmond, PQ, Canada **DISCIPLINE** HISTORY **EDUCATION** Univ Bishop's Col, BA, 32; Univ London, MA, 34, PhD, 39. **CAREER** Bishop's Col Sch, Lennoxvile, Que, 39-41; soc sci fac, 41-52, prof hist, Sir George Williams Col, 41-52; prof & head hist, Memorial Univ Nfld, 52-63; dean arts, Lakehead Univ, 63-68; vis prof hist, Univ Western Ont, 69-70; prof hist, Univ Man, 70-79 (Retired). **HONORS AND AWARDS** Que gov post-grad scholar, 32-34; Can Coun sr res fel, 59-60, 68-69; Centennial Medal, 67; fel, Royal Hist Soc, London, 69; LLD(hon), Memorial Univ Nfld, 87. **MEMBERSHIPS** Institut d'histoire de l'Amerique francaise; Can Hist Asn; Hum Res Coun. **SELECTED PUBLICATIONS** Auth, Newfoundland: A History; auth, Canada In One World. **CONTACT ADDRESS** 333 Vaughan St, Ste 904, Winnipeg, MB, Canada R3B 3J9.

ROTHNEY, JOHN ALEXANDER

PERSONAL Born 09/27/1935, Boston, MA **DISCIPLINE** MODERN FRENCH HISTORY, WORLD HISTORY **EDUCATION** Johns Hopkins Univ, AB, 57; Harvard Univ, AM, 58, PhD(hist), 64. **CAREER** Teaching fel hist, Harvard Univ, 61-64, instr, 64-66; from asst prof to assoc prof, Univ MO, Columbia, 66-70; assoc prof, 70-74, PROF HIST, OH STATE UNIV, 74-; Sr resident fel, Humanities Res Inst, Reed Col, 68; Am Coun Learned Socs fel, 71-72; ed, Fr Hist Studies, 76-85. **HONORS AND AWARDS** Co-Pres, Soc for French Hist Studies, 90-91. **MEMBERSHIPS** AHA; Soc Fr Hist Studies; Soc Hist Mod, France. **RESEARCH** Right-wing movements in modern France; the Second Empire in France; modernization and political change; 20th-century world history. **SELECTED PUBLICATIONS** Auth, Bonapartism after Sedan, Cornell Univ, 69; ed, The Brittany Affair and the Crisis of the Ancien Regime, Oxford Univ, 69; auth, (with Carter V. Findley) 20th-Century World, Houghton Mifflin, 86, 4th ed, 98. **CONTACT ADDRESS** Dept of Hist, Ohio State Univ, Columbus, 230 W 17th Ave, Columbus, OH 43210-1361. **EMAIL** rothney.1@osu.edu

ROUSE, JACQUELINE ANNE

PERSONAL Born 02/01/1950, Roseland, VA, s **DISCIPLINE** HISTORY **EDUCATION** Howard University, Washington, DC,, 1968-72; Atlanta University, Atlanta, GA, MA, 1972-73; Emory University, Atlanta, GA, PhD, 1983. **CAREER** Pal, Beach Jr College, Lake Worth, Florida, senior instructor, 73-80; Georgia Institute of Teachers, Atlanta, GA, guest lecturer, 83; Morehouse College, Atlanta, GA, associate professor, 83-; American University/Smithsonian Institute, Landmarks professor of history, 89; Georgia State Univ, prof of history, currently. **HONORS AND AWARDS** FIPSE, Curriculum on Black Women's History, Spellman College, 1983-84; NEH Summer Grant for College Teachers, 1984; UNCF Strengthening the Humanities Grant, 1985. **MEMBERSHIPS** Assistant editor, Journal of Negro History, 1983-89; advisor/reference, Harriet Tubman Historial & Cultural Museum, Macon, GA, 1985; panelist, American Association University of Women, 1985-; principal scholar/member, Steering Committee, National Conference of Women in Civil Rights Movement, 1988; panelist, Jacob Javits Fellowship, Department of Education, 1989; national vice director, Assistant of Black Women Historians, 1989-; first vice president, Association of Social & Behavorial Scientists, 1989-; consultant/advisor, Atlanta Historical Society, 1989; historian consultant, Apex Collection of Life & Heritage, 1989. **CONTACT ADDRESS** Dept. of History, Georgia State Univ, Atlanta, GA 30303.

ROUTLEDGE, MARIE I.

PERSONAL Born 08/23/1951, Toronto, ON, Canada **DISCIPLINE** ART HISTORY **EDUCATION** Univ Toronto, BA, 75. **CAREER** Res & cur, 75-79, res & doc coordr, Inuit art sect, Indian & Northern Affairs Can, 81-84; mgr, Theo Waddington Gallery, NY, 79-81; asst cur, 85-93, Assoc Curator Inuit Art, Nat Gallery of Canada, 93-. **MEMBERSHIPS** Native Art Stud Asn Can; Ottawa Native Art Stud Gp. **RESEARCH** Inuit art. **SELECTED PUBLICATIONS** Auth, Inuit Art in the 1970's, 79; auth, Pudlo: Thirty Years of Drawing, 90; ed, Inuit Arts Crafts mag, 81-84. **CONTACT ADDRESS** National Gallery of Canada, PO Box 427, Stn A, Ottawa, ON, Canada K1N 9N4.

ROWAN, STEVEN

PERSONAL Born 04/04/1943, Bremerton, WA, m, 1966, 2 children **DISCIPLINE** HISTORY **EDUCATION** Univ Wash, BA, 65; Harvard Univ, AM, 66, PhD, 70. **CAREER** Prof, Univ Mo, St. Louis, 70-; temp lectr, Kings Col, London, 75-76. **HONORS AND AWARDS** Phi Beta Kappa, 64; Humboldt Fel, 79-80; Inst. for Adv Studies, Princeton, 88-89. **MEMBERSHIPS** Am Hist Asn; Medieval Acad Am. **RESEARCH** Late-medieval Germany; Roman law; Germans in America. **SELECTED PUBLICATIONS** Auth, Germans for a Free Missouri: Translations from the St. Louis Radical Press, 1856-1862, 83; auth, Ulrich Zasius: A Jurist in the German Renaissance, 1561-1535, 87; auth, Memoirs of a Nobody: The Missouri Years of an Austrian Radical, 98. **CONTACT ADDRESS** Dept of History, Univ of Missouri, St. Louis, 8001 Natural Bridge Rd, Saint Louis, MO 63121. **EMAIL** srowan@umsl.edu

ROWE, D. L.

PERSONAL Born 05/05/1947, Syracuse, NY **DISCIPLINE** HISTORY **EDUCATION** Ithaca College, BA, 69; Univ Virginia, MA, 72, PhD, 72. **CAREER** Hist Prof, 81, Middle Tenn State Univ; exec Dir, 77-81, Landmarks Assoc NY; res writer, 74-77, County Hist Planner NY. **HONORS AND AWARDS** Outstanding Honors Fac Mem, 97,95,92; Cannonsburgh Awd for Res. **RESEARCH** Amer Religious History; Primitive Baptists; Millenarianism. **SELECTED PUBLICATIONS** Auth, Tending the Garden: The Stewardship Commission and the

Southern Baptist Convention, 1961-1997, 98; auth, Thunder and Trumpets: The Millerite Movement and Apocalyptic Thought in Upstate NY, 1800-1850, Chico CA, Scholars Press, 85; auth, The Millerites: A Shadow Portrait, in: The Disappointed: Millerism and Millenarianism in the Nineteenth Century, ed by Ron Numbers, Jonathan M Butler, Knoxville, Univ of Tenn, 93. **CONTACT ADDRESS** 800 E Burton, Murfreesboro, TN 37130. **EMAIL** drowe@acad1.mtsu.edu

ROWE, GAIL STUART
PERSONAL Born 12/02/1936, Los Angeles, CA, m, 1957, 2 children **DISCIPLINE** AMERICAN HISTORY **EDUCATION** Fresno State Col, AB, 59; Stanford Univ, MA, 60, PhD(hist), 69. **CAREER** From asst prof to assoc prof, 69-77, prof hist, Univ Northern CO, 77-. **MEMBERSHIPS** Inst Early Am Hist & Cult; Orgn Am Historians; Soc Historians Early Am Repub. **RESEARCH** Early Am legal hist; Am colonial hist, soc & polit; Am Revolution. **SELECTED PUBLICATIONS** Auth, A Valuable Acquisition in Congress: Thomas McKean, Delegate from Delaware to the Continental Congress, 1774-1783, PA Hist, 7/71; Thomas McKean and the Coming of the Revolution, PA Mag Hist & Biog, 1/72; The Travail of John McKinley, First President of Delaware, Del Hist, spring-summer 76; Outlawry in Pennsylvania, 1782-88, and the Achievement of an Independent Judiciary, Am J Legal Hist, 7/76; Rev V John Clowes, Jr, and the Shape of Politics in Pre-Revolutionary Sussex, Del Hist, fall-winter, 77; Thomas McKean: The Shaping of an American Republican, CO Assoc Univ, 78; Alexander Addison: The Disillusionment of a Republican Schoolmaster, W Pa Hist Mag, 7/79; Power, Justice, and Foreign Relations in the Confederation Period: The Marbois-Longchamps Affair, 1784-1786, PA Mag Hist & Biog, 7/80; Infanticide, Its Judicial Resolution, and Criminal Code Revision in Early Pennsylvania, Proceedings of the Am Philos Soc, 135, 91; Judicial Tyrant and Vox Populi: Pennsylvanians View Their State Supreme Court, 1777-1799, PA Mag of Hist and Biog, 118, Jan/Apr 94; Embattled Bench: The Pennsylvania Supreme Court and the Forging of a Democratic Society, 1684-1809, DE Univ Press, 94. **CONTACT ADDRESS** Dept Hist, Univ of No Colorado, 501 20th St, Greeley, CO 80639-0001. **EMAIL** growe@bentley.univnorthco.edu

ROYSTER, CHARLES WILLIAM
PERSONAL Born 11/27/1944, Nashville, TN **DISCIPLINE** HISTORY **EDUCATION** Univ Calif, Berkeley, AB, 66; MA, 67; PhD, 77. **CAREER** Asst prof hist, Col William & Mary, 77-79; asst prof hist, Univ Tex, Arlington, 79-81; assoc prof hist, La State Univ, 81-83; prof hist, 84-85; T. Harry Williams Prof Am Hist, 85-92; Boyd Prof Hist, 92-. **HONORS AND AWARDS** Francis Parkman Prize, 80; Book Prize, Nat Hist Soc, 81; Bancroft Prize, 92; Lincoln Prize, 92; Charles S. Sydnor Awd, 92; fel hist, Inst Early Am Hist & Cult, 77-79; John Simon Guggenheim Fellow, 82-83; National Humanities Center Fellow, 84-85; vis fel, Henry E. Huntington Library, 89, 96, 98. **MEMBERSHIPS** AHA **RESEARCH** United States Civil War; American Revolution; war and society. **SELECTED PUBLICATIONS** Auth, The Nature of Treason: Revolutionary Virtue and Americans' Reactions to Benedict Arnold, William & Mary Quart, 4/79; A Revolutionary People at War: The Continental Army and American Character, 1775-1783, Univ NC, Chapel Hill, Press, 79; Light-Horse Harry Lee and the Legacy of the American Revolution, Alfred A Knopf, 81; The Destructive War: William Tecumseh Sherman, Stonewall Jackson, and the Americans, Alfred A. Knopf, 91. **CONTACT ADDRESS** Dept of Hist, Louisiana State Univ and A&M Col, Baton Rouge, LA 70803-0001.

ROYSTER, PHILIP M.
PERSONAL m **DISCIPLINE** AFRICAN-AMERICAN STUDIES **EDUCATION** University of Illinois, 1960-62; DePaul University, BA, 1965, MA, 1967; Roosevelt University, Black Cultures Seminar, 1969; Loyola University, PhD, American and British Literature, 1974. **CAREER** Dept of African/Afro-Amer Studies, SUNY Albany, asst prof, 75-78; English Dept, Fisk Univ, asst prof, 74-75, instructor, 70-74; Syracuse University, Department of Afro-American Studies, associate professor, 78-1981; Kansas State University, Department of English, associate professor, 81-85, professor, 85-88, American Ethnic Studies Program, coordinator, 84-88; Bowling Green State University, Department of Ethnic Studies, professor, 87-92, assistant chair, 90-91; University of Illinois at Chicago, Department of English, professor, 91-, Department of African-American Studies, professor, 91-, African-American Cultural Center, director, 91-. **HONORS AND AWARDS** Bowling Green State University, Faculty Research Committee Basic Grant Awd, 1988, Black Student Union and Board of Black Cultural Activities, Certificate of Appreciation, 1988; the Seaton Third Poetry Awd, 1983; Kansas State University, Faculty Research Grant, 1981, 1982; Mellon Foundation, Mellon Project, 1980; Syracuse University, Senate Research Committee Grant, 1979; Fisk University, Study Grant, 1971, 1974; Loyola University, Assistantship, 1967-68, Fellowship, 1968-69; DePaul University, Arthur J Schmitt Scholarship, 1967. **MEMBERSHIPS** Society for New Music, board member, 1979-81; The African-American Drum Ensemble, 1987-; Honor Society of Phi Kappa Phi, 1992-; Illinois Committee of Black Concerns in Higher Education, 1992-; University of Illinois at Chicago Black Alumni Association, 1992-; Association of Black Cultural Centers, 1991-, National Steering Committee, 1991-, Constitution Bylaws Subcommittee, 1991-; Popular Culture Association, 1976-; Modern Language Association; College Language Association; National Council of Black Studies; National Association of the Church of God Summit Meeting Task Force; Emerald Avenue Church of God, Historical Committee, chairperson. **SELECTED PUBLICATIONS** Author, "The Rapper as Shaman for a Band of Dancers of the Spirit: U Can't Touch This," The Emergency of Black and the Emergence of Rap Special Issue of Black Sacred Music: A Journal of Theomusicology, pages 60-67, 1991, "The Sky is Gray: An Analysis of the Story," American Short Stories on Film: A Series of Casebooks, Langenscheidt-Longman, "The Curse of Capitalism in the Caribbean: Purpose and Theme in Lindsay Barrett's Song for Mumu," Perspectives in Black Popular Culture, The Popular Press, pages 22-35, 1990; Literary & Cultural Criticism: "In Search of Our Fathers' Arms: Alice Walker's Persona of the Alienated Darling," Black American Literature Forum, 20.4, 347-70, 1986; "The Spirit Will Not Descend Without Song: Cultural Values of Afro-American Gospel Tradition," Folk Roots: An Exploration of the Folk Arts & Cultural Traqditions of Kansas, Ed Jennie A Chinn, Manhattan: Univ for Man, 19-24, 1982; "Contemporary Oral Folk Expression," Black Books Bulletin, 6.3, 24-30, 1979; "A Priest and a Witch Against the Spiders and the Snakes: Scapegoating in Toni Morrison's Sula," Umoja 2.2, 149-68, 1979; "The Bluest Eye: The Novels of Toni Morrision," First World, 1.4, 34-44, 1977; Suggestions for Instructors to Accompany Clayers' and Spencer's Context for Composition, Co-authored with Stanley A Clayes, New York: Appleton-Century-Crofts, 1969; Books of Poetry: Songs and Dances, Detroit, Lotus Press, 1981; The Back Door, Chicago, Third World Press, 1971; Photography: A Milestone Sampler: Fifteenth Ann Anthology, Detroit, Lotus Press, "Samuel Allen," 10, "Jill Witherspoon Boyer," 22, "Beverley Rose Enright," 40, "Naomi F Faust," 44, "Ray Fleming," 50, "Agnes Nasmith Johnston," 56, "Delores Kendrick," 68, "Pinkie Gordon Lane," 74, "Naomi Long Madgett," 80, "Haki R Madhubuti," 86, "Herbert Woodward Martin," 92, "May Miller," 104, "Mwatabu Okantah," 110, "Paulette Childress White," 122, 1988; Master Drummer & Percussionist: "Earth Blossom," The John Betsch Society, Strata-East Recording Co, #SES-19748, 1975; Received a four and a half star review in Downbeat, 24-26, May 1975; "A White Sport Coat and a Pink Crustacean," Jimmy Buffet, Dunhill ABC, DSX 50150, 1973; "Hanging Around the Observatory," John Hiatt, Epic KE 32688, 1973; "We Make Spirit (Dancing in the Moonlight)," John Hiatt, Epic, 5-10990, ZSS 157218, 1973; "Backwoods Woman," Dianne Davidson, Janus, JLS 3043, 1972; "The Knack," The Interpreters, Cadet LP 762, 1965. **CONTACT ADDRESS** African-American Cultural Center, Univ of Illinois, Chicago, Rm 208 Addams Hall, 830 S Halsted Street, Chicago, IL 60607-7030.

ROZBICKI, MICHAL J.
PERSONAL Born 06/24/1946, Gdynia, m, 1991, 1 child **DISCIPLINE** ENGLISH LITERATURE, HISTORY **EDUCATION** Warsaw Univ, Poland, MA, 70, PhD, 84; Maria Curie-Sklodowska Univ, Poland, 75. **CAREER** Asst prof to assoc prof, 76-92, Warsaw Univ; asst prof to assoc prof, 92-, St Louis Univ. **HONORS AND AWARDS** Free Univ Berlin Fel, 82, 89; Oxford Univ Fel, 84; Rockefeller Found Fel, 90; John Carter Brown Libr Fel, 86; Huntington Libr Fel, 91; Amer Coun of Learned Soc Fel, 79-80. **MEMBERSHIPS** AAUP; Org Amer Hist. **RESEARCH** Cultural hist of colonial British Amer **SELECTED PUBLICATIONS** Auth, Transformation of English Cultural Ethos in Colonial America: Maryland 1634-1720, Univ Press Amer, 88; auth, The Birth of a Nation: History of the United States of American to 1860, Interim Publ House, Warsaw, 91; art, Between East-Central Europe and Britain: Reformation, Science, and the Emergence of Intellectual Networks in Mid-Seventeenth Century, E Europe Quart, 96; art, The Curse of Provincialism: Negative Perceptions of Colonial American Plantation Gentry, J S Hist, 97; auth, A Bridge to a Barrier to American Identity? The Uses of European Taste among Eighteenth Century Plantation Gentry in British American, Amerikastudien, Heidelberg, 98; auth, The Complete Colonial Gentleman: Cultural Legitimacy in Plantation America, Univ Press Va, 98. **CONTACT ADDRESS** Dept of History, Saint Louis Univ, 3800 Lindell Blvd, PO Box 56907, Saint Louis, MO 63156-0907. **EMAIL** rozbicmj@slu.edu

RUBERT, STEVEN
PERSONAL Born 11/12/1947, Houston, TX, m, 1996, 2 children **DISCIPLINE** HISTORY **EDUCATION** Calif State Univ, BA, 72; Calif State Univ at Northridge, BA, 73; Univ Calif at Santa Barbara, MA, 77; Univ Calif at Los Angeles, PhD, 90. **CAREER** Res assoc, Univ Zimbabwe, 84-85; book rev ed, Ufahamu, 86-90; teaching assoc, Univ Calif at Los Angeles, 86-88; vis lectr, Rutgers Univ, 89; vis asst prof, Pacific Lutheran Univ, 90; vis prof, Wash Community Col System, 90-91; from asst prof to assoc prof, Ore State Univ, 91-. **HONORS AND AWARDS** Outstanding Academic Book, Choice, 99. **MEMBERSHIPS** African Studies Asn, Hist Asn of Zimbabwe, Asn of Concerned Africa Scholars. **RESEARCH** Public Health in Zimbabwe, Colonial Disease. **SELECTED PUBLICATIONS** Coauth, Historical Dictionary of Zimbabwe, Scarecrow Press, 79, 90 & forthcoming; auth, "Tobacco Farmers and Wage Laborers in Colonial Zimbabwe," in White Farms, Black Labor: Agrarian Transition in Southern Africa 1910-1950, eds. Jonathan Crush and Alan Jeeves (James Currey Publ, 97); auth, A Most Promising Weed: A History of Tobacco Farming and Labor in Colonial Zimbabwe, 1890-1945, Ohio Univ Ctr for Int Studies (Athens, OH), 98. **CONTACT ADDRESS** Dept Hist, Oregon State Univ, 306 Milam Hall, Corvallis, OR 97331-8558. **EMAIL** srubert@orst.edu

RUBIN, JAMES HENRY
PERSONAL Born 05/04/1944, Cambridge, MA **DISCIPLINE** HISTORY OF ART **EDUCATION** Yale Univ, BA, 65; Univ Paris, Institute d'art, license-es-lettres, 67; Harvard, PhD, 72. **CAREER** Asst Prof, Boston Univ, 72-73; Asst Prof, Princeton Univ, 73-79; Assoc Prof, Stony Brook, The State Univ of NY, 79-87; Prof, Stony Brook, State Univ of NY, 87-; Dir of Graduate Studies, 89-89; Department Chair, 89-; Adjunct Prof, The Cooper Union, 79-. **HONORS AND AWARDS** Ford Found Fel, 67-72; Wrightsman Fel, 69; Travel Grant, Am Coun of Learned Societies, 89. **MEMBERSHIPS** CAA; AHNCA. **RESEARCH** 19th century art. **SELECTED PUBLICATIONS** Auth, Eighteenth-Century French Life Drawing, Princeton, 77; auth, Realism and Social Vision in Courbet and Proudhon, Princeton, 81; auth, Eugene Delacroix, Die Dantebarke, Frankfurt, 87; Manet's Silence and the Poetics of Bouquets, Essays in Art and Culture, Harvard Univ Press, 94; Courbet, Art and Ideas, London Phaidon Press, 97; Impressionism, Art and Ideas, London Phaidon Press, 99. **CONTACT ADDRESS** Dept Art, SUNY, Stony Brook, 2221 Staller Center for the Arts, Stony Brook, NY 11794-5400. **EMAIL** jrubin@ms.cc.sunysb.edu

RUBINCAM, CATHERINE I.
PERSONAL Born 08/23/1943, Belfast, Northern Ireland, m, 1974, 4 children **DISCIPLINE** GREEK HISTORY **EDUCATION** Univ Toronto, BA, 64; Oxford Univ, BA, 66; Harvard Univ, PhD, 69. **CAREER** Asst prof then assoc prof, classics, Erindale Col, Univ Toronto, 69- . **MEMBERSHIPS** Am Philol Asn. **RESEARCH** Graeco-Roman History and Historiography; Classical Tradition; History of Women in the Professoriate. **SELECTED PUBLICATIONS** Auth, "Qualification of Numerals in Thucydides," AJAH , (79): 77-95; auth, "The Organization and Composition of Diodoros' Bibliotheke," EMC/CV, no. 6, (87): 313-328; auth, "Cross-references in the Bibliotheke of Diodoros,' Phoenix 43, (89): 39-61; auth, "Casualty Figures in Thucydides Descriptions of Battle," TAPA 121, (91): 181-198; auth, "The Nomenclature of Julius Caesar and the Later Augustus in the Triumviral Period," Historia 41, (92): 88-103; auth, Mary White and Women Professors of Classics in Canadian Universities, Class World, 96-97; auth, The Organization of Material in Graeco-Roman World Histories, in, Pre-Modern Encyclopedic Texts: Proceedings of the Second COMERS Congress, 97; auth, Did Diodorus Siculus Take Over Cross-References from His Sources? Am J of Philol, 98; auth, How Many Books Did Diodorus Siculus Originally Intend to Write? Class Q, 98. **CONTACT ADDRESS** Dept of Classics, Univ of Toronto, Mississauga, ON, Canada L5L 1C6. **EMAIL** rubincam@chass.utoronto.ca

RUCKER, BRIAN
PERSONAL Born 05/22/1961, Pensacola, FL, d, 1 child **DISCIPLINE** HISTORY **EDUCATION** Pensacola Jr Col, AA, 81; Univ W Fla, BA, 83; MA, 85; Fla State Univ, PhD, 90. **CAREER** Teaching asst, Fla State Univ, 86-90; adj prof, Univ W Fla, 93-96; adj prof, 90-96, assoc prof hist, 96- , Pensacola Jr. Col. **HONORS AND AWARDS** Acad Teaching Exc, 00. **MEMBERSHIPS** Fla Hist Soc; Gulf S Hist Asn; Pensacola Hist Soc; Soc Com Archaeol. **RESEARCH** Gulf South history, Florida history, Antebellum/frontier. **SELECTED PUBLICATIONS** Ed, From Pensacola to Belize: An American Odyssey Through Mexico in 1903, Patagonia Press, 97; auth, "It Can't Happen Here(?): A History of Earthquakes in West Florida, Pensacola Hist Illus 5 (97): 14-27; auth, Encyclopedia of Education in Antebellum Pensacola, Patagonia Press, 99; auth, "Nixon's Raid and Other Precursors to Jackson's 1814 Invasion of Spanish West Florida, Gulf S Hist Rev 14 (99): 33-50. **CONTACT ADDRESS** Dept Lib Arts, Pensacola Junior Col, 5555 W Highway 98, Pensacola, FL 32507-1015.

RUDDY, T. MICHAEL
PERSONAL Born 07/17/1946, Kansas City, KS, m, 1970, 3 children **DISCIPLINE** TWENTIETH CENTURY UNITED STATES & DIPLOMATIC HISTORY **EDUCATION** Rockhurst Col, AB, 68; Creighton Univ, MA, 70; Kent State Univ, PhD(hist), 73. **CAREER** Asst prof, Kent State Univ, Tuscarawas Campus, 73-77; assoc prof to prof hist, St Louis Univ, 77-. **HONORS AND AWARDS** Fulbright Lectureship, Joensuu Finland, 83-84. **MEMBERSHIPS** Soc Historians Am Foreign Rels; Orgn Am Historians. **RESEARCH** US relations with Europe's neutrals, especially Finland and Sweden; NATO; European integration. **SELECTED PUBLICATIONS** The Cautious Diplomat: Charles E Bohlen and the Soviet Union, 1929-1969, Kent State Univ Press; Damning the Dam: The St Louis District Corps of Engineers and the Controversy over the Meramec Basin Project from Its Inception to Its Deauthorization (GPO); ed, Charting an Independent Course: Finland's Place in the Cold War and in US Foreign Policy; articles on US foreign policy in the Cold War. **CONTACT ADDRESS** Hist Dept, Saint Louis Univ, 3800 Lindell Blvd, PO Box 56907, Saint Louis, MO 63156-0907. **EMAIL** ruddytm@slu.edu

RUDIN, RONALD
DISCIPLINE HISTORY **EDUCATION** Univ Pittsburgh, BA; Univ York, MA, PhD. **CAREER** Prof. **SELECTED PUBLICATIONS** Auth, four books and numerous articles dealing with the economic and social history of Quebec in the nineteenth and twentieth centuries; Making History in Twentieth-Century Quebec. **CONTACT ADDRESS** Dept of Hist, Concordia Univ, Montreal, 1455 de Maisonneuve W, Montreal, QC, Canada H3G 1M8. **EMAIL** rudin@vax2.concordia.ca

RUDNICK, LOIS P.
PERSONAL Born 06/18/1944, Boston, MA, m, 1965, 1 child **DISCIPLINE** AMERICAN STUDIES **EDUCATION** Tufts Univ, BA, 66; MA, 68; Brown Univ, PhD, 77. **CAREER** Asst to Assoc to Prof English & Am Stud, Univ Mass, 77-; Dir, Am Stud Prog, Univ Mass, 83-. **HONORS AND AWARDS** Phi Beta Kappa; Mary C Turpie Awd, Am Stud Assoc, 97. **MEMBERSHIPS** Am Stud Asn; MELUS. **RESEARCH** Modern American culture; Southwest literature & culture. **SELECTED PUBLICATIONS** Auth, Mabel Dodge Luhan: New Woman, New Worlds, Univ NMex Press, 84; co-ed, 1915, The Cultural Moment: The New Politics, The New Woman, The New Psychology, The New Art, and The New Theatre in America, Rutgers Univ Press, 91; auth, Utopian Vistas: The Mabel Dodge Luhan House and the American Counterculture, Univ NMex Press, 96; ed, Intimate Memories: The Autobiography of Mabel Dodge Luhan, Univ of NMex Press, 99. **CONTACT ADDRESS** 220 Wolomolopoag St, Sharon, MA 02067. **EMAIL** Lois.Rudnick@umb.edu

RUDOLPH, CONRAD
PERSONAL Born 01/26/1951, Rock Island, IL, m, 1980, 2 children **DISCIPLINE** HISTORY OF ART **EDUCATION** Univ Calif, Los Angeles, BA, 77; MA, 81, PhD, 85. **CAREER** Visting asst prof, Gustavus Adolphus Col, 85-86; asst prof, Univ Notre Dame, 88-91; assoc prof, 91-97, Prof, Univ Calif, Riverside, 97-. **HONORS AND AWARDS** Andrew W. Mellon Postdoctoral Reasearch fel,86-87; J. Paul Getty Postdoctoral fel, 87-88; John Simon Guggenheim fel, 94-95; Mellon fel, Univ Pittsburgh, 86-87; Getty fel Getty Ctr The Getty Research Inst, 87- 88. **MEMBERSHIPS** College Art Assoc; International Center of Medieval Art; Medieval Academy of America. **RESEARCH** The medieval attitude toward art, the ideological use of art, monasticism and art. **SELECTED PUBLICATIONS** Auth, " Heterodoxy and the Twelve Great Feasts of the Eastern Church," Comitatus 12, (81), 13-30; auth, " The 'Principal Founders' and the Early Artistic Legislation of C teaux," Studies in Cistercian Art and Architecture 3, Cistercian Studies Series 89, Kalamazoo, (81), 1-45; auth, " The Scholarship on Bernard of Clairvaux's Apologia," Citeaux: Commentarii Cistercienses 40, (89), 69-111; auth, " Bernard of Clairvaux's Apologia as a Description of Cluny and the Controversy Over Monastic Art," Gesta 27 (88), 125-132; auth, Artistic Change at St-Denis: Abbot Suger's Program and the Early Twelfth-Century Controversy over Art, Princeton Univ Press, Princeton, 90; auth, The " Things of Greater Importance": Bernamd of Clairvoux's Apologia and the Medieval Attitude Toward Art, Univ Pennsylvania Press, Philadelphia, 90; auth, Violence and Daily Life: Reading, Art, and Polemics in the Citeaux Moralia in Job, Princeton Univ Press, Princeton, 97; auth, " Building-Miracles as Artistic Justification in the Early and Mid-twelfth Century," Radical Art History: Internationale Athologie, Subject: O K Werckmeister, Zip Verlag, Zurich, (97), 398-410; auth, : In the Beginning: Theories and Images of Creation in Northern Europe in the Twelfth Century," Art History 22 (99), 3-55; auth, " La Resistenza su l' arte nel Occidentale, " Arti e storia nel Medioevo, Turin, 00. **CONTACT ADDRESS** Dept Hist Art, Univ of California, Riverside, Riverside, CA 92521-0319. **EMAIL** conrad.rudolph@ucr.edu

RUDOLPH, FREDERICK
PERSONAL Born 06/19/1920, Baltimore, MD, m, 1949, 2 children **DISCIPLINE** HISTORY **EDUCATION** Williams Col, BA, 42; Yale Univ, MA, 49, PhD(hist), 53. **CAREER** Instr, 46-47, 51-53, from asst prof to assoc prof, 53-61, prof hist 61-82, Prof Emer, 82- , Williams Col. vis lectr hist & educ, Harvard Univ, 60-61; vis prof Univ Calif, Berkeley, 83; exec ed, Change, 80-84 . **HONORS AND AWARDS** Guggenheim fel, 58-59, 68-69; Frederick W Ness Awd, Asn Am Col, 78; LittD, Williams Col, 85; LHD, Univ Rochester, 94; LHD, Wilkes Univ, 98. **MEMBERSHIPS** Nat Acad Ed, AHA; Org Am Historians; Am Studies Asn. **RESEARCH** American intellectual history; higher education in the United States; American national character. **SELECTED PUBLICATIONS** Auth, Mark Hopkins and the Log, Yale Univ, 56; American College and University: A History, Knopf, 62; ed, Essays on Education in the Early Republic, Harvard Univ, 65; auth, Neglect of Students as a Historical Tradition, Col & Students, 66; Curriculum: A History of the American Undergraduate Course of Study Since 1636, Jossey-Bass, 77; Heritage and Tradition in Carnegie Foundation for the Advancement of Teaching, In: Common Learning: A Carnegie Colloquium on General Education, 81; ed, Perspectives: A Williams Anthology, 83. **CONTACT ADDRESS** PO Box 515, Williamstown, MA 01267.

RUDY, WILLIS
PERSONAL Born 01/25/1920, New York, NY, m, 1948, 3 children **DISCIPLINE** HISTORY **EDUCATION** City Col New York, BSS, 39; Columbia Univ, MA, 40, PhD, 48. **CAREER** Instr hist, City Col New York, 39-49; instr hist educ, Harvard Univ, 49-52; prof hist, Mass State Col, Worcester, 52-63; prof hist, 63-, prof emeritus, Fairleigh Dickinson Univ; res historian, Qm Corps, US Dept Army, 52; res consult, Nat Citizens Comn Pub Schs, 52-53; vis prof, NY Univ, 53; consult, Educ Policies Comn, Nat Educ Asn, 55; vis lectr, Harvard Univ, 53, 57-58. **HONORS AND AWARDS** Cromwell Medal. **MEMBERSHIPS** AHA; Orgn Am Historians. **RESEARCH** History of higher education in America; social and intellectual history of the United States; history of learning. **SELECTED PUBLICATIONS** Auth, The Universities of Europe 1100-1914, Fairleigh Dickinson, 84; auth, Total War and Twentieth Century Higher Learning, Fairleigh Dickinson, 91; coauth, Higher Education in Transition: A History of American Higher Education, 1636-1976, Transaction, 96; auth, The Campus and a Nation in Crisis, Fairleigh Dickinson, 96; auth, The College of the City of New York, A History, Harper, 49,77, Harper, 55, 68, 76. **CONTACT ADDRESS** 161 W Clinton Ave, Tenafly, NJ 07670.

RUEBEL, JAMES
PERSONAL Born 08/18/1945, Cincinnati, OH, m, 1966, 2 children **DISCIPLINE** ANCIENT ROMAN HISTORY, CLASSICAL LANGUAGES **EDUCATION** Yale Univ, BA, 67; Univ Cincinnati, MA, 70, PhD, 72. **CAREER** Instr Greek & Latin, Classics Dept, Univ Cincinnati, 72-73; asst prof, Classics Dept, Univ MN, 73-78; asst prof, 78-81, Assoc Prof, 81-93, Prof Classics, for Lang & Lit, IA State Univ, 93-00; dean, honors dol, Ball State Univ, 00-. **MEMBERSHIPS** Am Philol Asn; Asn Ancient Historians; Class Asn Midwest & South; Am Class League; Archaeol Inst Am. **RESEARCH** Roman republican history; Roman culture from Hannibal to Horace. **CONTACT ADDRESS** Honors College, Ball State Univ, 104 Carmichael, Muncie, IN 47306. **EMAIL** jruebel@bsu.edu

RUEDY, JOHN D.
PERSONAL Born 04/28/1927, Alameda, CA, m, 1953, 3 children **DISCIPLINE** MIDDLE EAST HISTORY **EDUCATION** Univ Calif, Berkeley, AB, 48; San Diego State Col, MA, 61; Univ Calif, Los Angeles, PhD(hist), 65. **CAREER** Asst English, Lycee Henri IV, Paris, France, 48-49; asst prof, 65-68, assoc prof, 68-92, Prof Hist, Georgetown Univ, 92- , Chmn Arab Studies Prog, 75-88, Lectr, Johns Hopkins Univ Sch Advan Int Studies, 70-75; Fulbright scholar, Tunisia, 72-73. **MEMBERSHIPS** Mid E Inst; Mid E Studies Asn of N Am; AHA. **RESEARCH** Colonial North Africa; 20th century Syria and Palestine. **SELECTED PUBLICATIONS** Auth, Land Policy in Colonial Algeria, Univ Calif, 67; contrib, Palestine: A Search for Truth, Pub Affairs, 70; The Transformation of Palestine, Northwestern Univ, 71; auth, Modern Algeria: The Origins and Development of a Nation, Indiana; ed & contribr, Islamism & Secularism in North Africa, St Martins, 94. **CONTACT ADDRESS** Dept of History, Georgetown Univ, Washington, DC 20007.

RUESTOW, EDWARD G.
PERSONAL Born 09/30/1937, Honolulu, HI, m **DISCIPLINE** HISTORY **EDUCATION** Univ Pa, BA, 59; MFA, 60; George Wash Univ, MA, 65; Univ Ind Bloomington, PhD, 70. **CAREER** Prof. **RESEARCH** History of science in the early modern period. **SELECTED PUBLICATIONS** Auth, The Microscope in the Dutch Republic: The Shaping of Discovery, Cambridge, 96; auth, Physics at 17th and 18th-Century Leiden: Philosophy and the New Science in the University, Martinus Nijhoff, 73. **CONTACT ADDRESS** History Dept, Univ of Colorado, Boulder, Campus Box 234, Boulder, CO 80309.

RUFF, JULIUS R.
PERSONAL Born 08/28/1946, Staten Island, NY, m, 1972, 2 children **DISCIPLINE** HISTORY **EDUCATION** Guilford Col, AB 68; Lehigh Univ, MA, 70; Univ NC, PhD, 93. **CAREER** Istructor, Less-McRae Col, 76-77; instr to asst prof, Averett Col, 77-80; asst to assoc prof, Marquette Univ, 80-. **HONORS AND AWARDS** Georges Lurcy Fel, NC, 75; Nat Endowment for the Humanities, 87; Awd for Teaching Excellence, Marquette Univ, 93. **MEMBERSHIPS** Am Hist Asn, Am Soc for Legal Hist, Coun for European Studies, Intl Asn for the Hist of Crime and Criminal Justice, Soc for French Hist Studies, Soc for the Study fo French Hist, Western Soc for French Hist. **RESEARCH** Seventeenth and eighteenth-century French social and legal history. **SELECTED PUBLICATIONS** Auth, Crime, Justice and Public Order in Old regime France: The Senechaussees of Libourne and Bazas, 1696-1789, Croom Helm: London, 84; auth, Discovering the Western Past, 2 vols, Houghton Mifflin: Boston, 00. **CONTACT ADDRESS** Dept History, Marquette Univ, PO Box 1881, Milwaukee, WI 53201-1881. **EMAIL** julius.ruff@marquette.edu

RUGGIERO, GUIDO
PERSONAL Born 05/24/1944, Danbury, CT **DISCIPLINE** HISTORY **EDUCATION** Univ Co, BA, 66, Univ Calif Los Angeles, MA, 67, PhD, 72. **CAREER** Vis prof to assoc prof, Univ Cincinnati, 71-87; assoc prof to prof, Univ Ct, 87-94; prof, Univ Miami, 94-97; Josephine Berry Weiss Chair, prof, Pa St Univ, 97- . **HONORS AND AWARDS** Inst Adv Study, Princeton, 81-82, 91; Ateneo Veneto, Socio Straniero; Harvard Villa I Tatti Fel, 90-91; NEH Fel, 81-82,90-91; John Simon Guggenheim Mem Found Fel, 91. **MEMBERSHIPS** Amer Hist Assoc, Renaissance Soc of Amer; Sixteenth Century Stud Assoc. **RESEARCH** Renaissance & early modern Italy history & lit; premodern sex & gender; culture & early sci. **SELECTED PUBLICATIONS** Auth, The Boundaries of Eros: Sex Crime and Sexuality in Renaissance Venice, Oxford Univ Press, 85; auth, Binding Passions: Tales of Magic, Marriage, and Power at the End of the Renaissance, Oxford Univ Press, 93; Deconstructing the Body, constructing the Body Politic: Ritual Execution in the Renaissance, in Riti e rituali nelle societa medievali, Centro Italiano di Studi sull'Alto Medioevo, 94; Sexuality, & The Italian Renaissance, entries in The Encyclopedia of Social History, Garland Press, 94; coauth, Introduction: The Crime of History, & Afterword: Crime and the Writing of History, in History from Crime, Selections from Quaderni Storici, Johns Hopkins Univ Press, 94; auth, Politica e giustizia, in Storia di Venezia dalle origini alla caduta della Serenissima, Istituto della Encilopedia Italiana fondata da Giovanni Trecanni, 97; ed, Studies in the History of Sexuality, Oxford Series. **CONTACT ADDRESS** Dept of History, Pennsylvania State Univ, Univ Park, University Park, PA 16802-5500. **EMAIL** gxr12@psu.edu

RUGGLES, STEVEN
DISCIPLINE HISTORY **EDUCATION** Univ Pa, PhD, 84. **CAREER** Prof **HONORS AND AWARDS** Sharlin Prize, 88; William J. Goode Awd, 89. **RESEARCH** Historical demography. **SELECTED PUBLICATIONS** Auth, Prolonged Connections: The Rise of the Extended Family in Nineteenth Century England and America, Univ Wis, 87; pubs on fertility, living arrangements of the elderly, race and ethnicity, family reconstitution, life-course analysis, and demographic methods. **CONTACT ADDRESS** History Dept, Univ of Minnesota, Twin Cities, 614 Social Sciences Tower, 267 19th Ave S, Minneapolis, MN 55455. **EMAIL** ruggles@atlas.socsci.umn.edu

RUGOFF, MILTON
PERSONAL Born 03/06/1913, New York, NY, m, 1937, 1 child **DISCIPLINE** HISTORY, ENGLISH **EDUCATION** Columbia Col, BA, 33; Columbia Univ, MA, 34, PhD, 40. **CAREER** Ed, Alfred E Knopf, Inc, 42-47; assoc ed, 47-48, Mag of the Year; ed, 53, Readers Subscription Bk Club; ed, vice pres, 48-93, Chanticleer Press, Inc, NY. **HONORS AND AWARDS** Literary Lion medal, NY Pub Lib, 90; Ohioana Bk Awd, 82. **MEMBERSHIPS** Soc Amer Hist; Authors' Guild. **RESEARCH** American Biography; Elizabethan literature; history of traveland exploration. **SELECTED PUBLICATIONS** Auth, The Penguin Book of World Folk Tales, Viking, 49; ed & intro, The Great Travelers, S and S, 61; auth, Donne's Imagery: A Study in Creative Sources, Atheneum, 62; auth, Marco Polo's Adventures in China, Caravel Bks, 64; auth, Prudery and Passion: Sexuality in Victorian America, Putnam, 71; ed, Britannica Encycl of American Art, Simon, 73; auth, The Beechers: An American Family in the Nineteenth Century, Harper & Row, 81; auth, America's Gilded Age: Intimate Portraits from an Era of Extravagance and Change, Holt & Co, 89. **CONTACT ADDRESS** 18 Ox Ridge Rd, Elmsford, NY 10523.

RUIZ, TEOFILO FABIAN
PERSONAL Born 01/02/1943, Habana, Cuba, m, 1998, 2 children **DISCIPLINE** HISTORY **EDUCATION** City Col NYork, BA, 69; NYork Univ, MA, 70; Princeton Univ, PhD, 74. **CAREER** Instr hist, 73-74, asst prof, 74-80, assoc prof hist, 81-85, prof hist, 85-98, Dir Ford Colloquium, 92-95, Brooklyn Col; 80-, Mellon fel humanities, Aspen Inst Humanistic Studies, 75-76; Res Found City Univ NYork fac res award, 75-76 & 76-77; Danforth assoc, 78-84; Am Coun Learned Soc fel, 79-80; prof Span Medieval lit, 88-98, prof hist 95-98, CUNY; vis prof distinguished tchg, Princeton Univ, 97-98; prof hist UCLA, 98-. **HONORS AND AWARDS** Dir Studies, Ecole des Hautes Etudes en Science Sociales, (Paris), 93; Outstanding Master's Univ & Col Prof of Year, Carnegie Found for Advan Teaching, 94-95; Premio del Rey, Am Hist Asn Biennial Awd for Best Bk Span Hist, 95; PSC-CUNY Res Awd, 96-97; Wolfe Inst Fel, 96-97. **MEMBERSHIPS** Soc Span Port Hist Studies; Acad Res Historians Medieval Spain; Medieval Acad. **RESEARCH** Castilian history late medieval (social and economic). **SELECTED PUBLICATIONS** Representacion de uno mismo, representacion de otros y por otros: Castilla, Los castellanos y el Nuevo Mundo a finales de la edad media, Temas Medievales, 93; Goodby Columbus and All That: History and Textual Criticism, New W Indian Guide, 93; Jew, Conversos, and the Inquisition, 1391-1492: The Ambiguities of History, in Jewish-Christian Encounters Over the Centuries: Symbiosis, Prejudice, Holocaust, Dialogue, ed M Perry & F M Schweitzer, NY, Peter Lang Inc, 94; Elite and Popular Culture in Late Fifteenth-Century Castilian Festivals: The Case of Jaen, In City and Spectacle in Medieval Europe, ed B A Hanawalt & K L Reyerson (Minn: Univ Mn, 94; Judios y cristianos en el ambito urbano bajomedieval: Avila Y Burgos, 1200-1350 Xudeos e conversos na historia, Actas do Congreso Internacional de Judios Y Conversos en la Historia, 2 vols Santiago de Compostela: Deputacion de Orense, 94; Crisis and Continuity: Land and Town in Late Medieval Castile, Univ Pa: Phil, 94; La fromazione della monarchia non consacrata: simboli e realta di potere nella Castiglia

mediovale, in Federico II e il mondo mediterraneo, a cura di Pierre Toubert e Agostino Paravicino Bagliani, 3 vols, Palermo: Sellerio editore, 95; Representacion: Castilla, los castellanos y el Nuevo Mundo a finales de la edad media y principios de la moderna, in Historia a debate, Medieval, Santiago de Compostela, 95; Violence in Late Medieval Castile: The Case of the Rioja, Revista de Historia, 95; Teaching as Subversion: in Inspiring Teaching: Carnegie Professors of the Year Speak, ed John K Roth, Jaffrey, NH: Anker, 96; Propietat i llengua: Canvis d valors a la Castella medieval, L'Avenc, 97;Women, Work and Daily Life in Late Medieval Castile, in Women at Work in Spain: From the Middle Ages to Early Modern Times, ed M Stone & C Benito-Vessels, NY, 98; The Peasantries of Iberia, 1400-1800, in The Peasantries of Europe, From the Fourteenth to the Eighteenth Centuries, ed Tom Scott, (Longman: London) 98; auth, Spanish Society, 1400-1600, Longman, 01. **CONTACT ADDRESS** 1557 S. Beverly Glen Blvd. Apt 304, Los Angeles, CA 90024. **EMAIL** tfruiz@history.ucla.edu

RUMMEL, ERIKA
DISCIPLINE SOCIAL; INTELLECTUAL HISTORY OF EARLY MODERN EUROPE **EDUCATION** Univ Toronto, PhD. **CAREER** Prof **SELECTED PUBLICATIONS** Auth, Erasmus and His Catholic Critics, De Graaf, 89; Erasmus on Women, U of Toronto P, 96; The Humanist-Scholastic Debate in the Renaissance and Reformation, Harvard UP, 95; Erasmus, 96; The Importance of Being Doctor: The Quarrel over Competency between Humanists and Theologians, 96. **CONTACT ADDRESS** Dept of History, Wilfrid Laurier Univ, 75 University Ave W, Waterloo, ON, Canada N2L 3C5. **EMAIL** erummel@mach1.wlu.ca

RUNYAN, TIMOTHY J.
PERSONAL Born 08/09/1941, Gary, IN, m, 1964, 2 children **DISCIPLINE** HISTORY **EDUCATION** Capital Univ, BS, 63; Univ Md, MA, 65; PhD, 71; Univ London Inst Hist Res, 67-69. **CAREER** Instr to prof, Cleveland State Univ., 69-97; instr, Univ of Md, 69; asst dean, Col of arts and sci, Cleveland State Univ, 76-79; dir of classical and medieval studies prof, Cleveland State Univ., 78-86; acting chemn of dept of art, Cleveland State Univ, 81-82; acting chemn of dept of modern lang, Cleveland State Univ, 82-86; vis prof, Oberlin Col, 89; vis prof & dir prog in maritime studies, E Carolina Univ, 94-96; prof & dir prog of maritime studies, E Carolina univ, 97-. **HONORS AND AWARDS** Fel, Maryland Univ, 67-69; Penrose Fund Awd, Am Philos Soc, 73 & 76; John Lyman Book Awd, N Am Soc for Oceanic Hist, 88; First Place, Museum Category of Northern Ohio Live Mag, 91; listed in Who's Who in the Midwest, Who's Who in America, and Who's Who in the World. **MEMBERSHIPS** Nat Maritime Alliance, N Am Soc for Oceanic Hist, Int Comn for Maritime Hist, Great Lakes Hist Soc, Asn for Great Lakes maritime Hist, Soc for Hist Archaeol, Royal Hist Soc, Midwest Medieval Hist Confr, Medieval Acad of Am, Ohio Acad of Hist. **RESEARCH** Maritime History and Archaeology, Medieval Europe. **SELECTED PUBLICATIONS** Auth, "The constabulary of Bordeaux: The Accounts of John Ludham (1372-73) and Robert de Wykford (1373-75)," Medieval Studies XXXVI (74): 215-258, XXXVII (75): 42-84; auth, "The Laws of Oleron and the Admiralty Court in Fourteenth Century England," Am J of Legal Hist XIX (75):95-111; auth, "Ships and Mariners in Later Medieval England," J of British Studies XVI (77): 1-17; auth, "Shipwreck Legislation and the Preservation of Submerged Artifacts," J of Int Law 22 (90): 31-45; auth, "The Relationship of Northern and Southern Seafaring Traditions in Late Medieval Europe," in Medieval Ships and the Birth of Technological Societies, eds. C. Villain-Gandossi, S. Busuttil, P. Adam (Malta: European Center for Documentation in the Soc Sci, 91), 197-209; auth, "Naval Logistics in the Hundred Years War," in Feeding Mars: Essays on Logistics and Resource Mobilization in Western Warfare from the Middle Ages to the Present, ed. John Lynn (CO: Westview Press, 93); auth, "Wine and War: The Anglo-Gascon Wine Trade in the Later Middle Ages," in Maritime Food Transport, ed. Klaus Friedland (Koln: Bohlau Verlag, 94), 245-255; auth, "The Cog as a Warship," in Cogs, Caravels and Galleons: The Sailing Ship 1000-1630, ed. R. W. Unger (London: Conway Maritime Press, 94), 47-58; co-ed, To Die Gallantly: The Battle of the Atlantic, Westview Press (Boulder, CO), 94. **CONTACT ADDRESS** Maritime Studies Prog, East Carolina Univ, Admiral Eller House, Greenville, NC 27858-4353.

RUNYON, RANDOLPH PAUL
PERSONAL Born 02/13/1947, Maysville, KY, m, 1983, 2 children **DISCIPLINE** FRENCH LITERATURE, AMERICAN STUDIES **EDUCATION** Johns Hopkins Univ, PhD(French), 73. **CAREER** Asst prof, Case Western Reserve Univ, 74-76; asst prof to assoc prof, 77-84, Prof French, Miami Univ, 84-. **MEMBERSHIPS** MLA; Soc des Amis de Montaigne; Am Studies Asn; SAtlantic Mod Lang Asn; Robert Penn Warren Circle. **RESEARCH** Sixteenth century French literature; 20th century French literature; literary criticism; 20th century American literature. **SELECTED PUBLICATIONS** Auth, Fowles, Irving, Barthes: Canonical Variations on an Apocryphal Theme, Ohio State Univ Press, 81; The Braided Dream: Robert Penn Warren's Late Poetry, Univ Press of Ky, 90; The Taciturn Text: The Fiction of Robert Penn Warren, Ohio State Univ Press, 90; Reading Raymond Carver, Syracuse Univ Press, 92; Delia Webster and the Underground Railroad, Univ Press of Ky, 96; auth, In La Fontaine's Labyrinth: A Thread through the Fables, Charlottesville, Va, Rookwood Press, 00. **CONTACT ADDRESS** Dept of French & Ital, Miami Univ, Oxford, OH 45056-1602. **EMAIL** runyonr@muohio.edu

RUPP, LEILA J.
PERSONAL Born 02/13/1950, Plainfield, NJ **DISCIPLINE** HISTORY, WOMEN'S STUDIES **EDUCATION** Bryn Mawr Col, AB, 72, PhD(hist), 76. **CAREER** Vis lectr hist, Univ Pa, 76-77; asst prof, 77-82, assoc prof, 82-87, prof, Ohio State Univ, 87-. **HONORS AND AWARDS** Ohio Acad of Hist Outstand Tchg Awd **MEMBERSHIPS** Berkshire Conf Women Historians; AHA; OHA **RESEARCH** Women's history; hist of sexuality. **SELECTED PUBLICATIONS** Auth, Mobilizing Women for War: German and American Propaganda, 1939-1945, Princeton Univ, 78; co-ed, Nazi Ideology Before 1933: A Documentation, Univ Tex, 78; coauth, Survival in the Doldrums: The American Women's Rights Movement, 1945 to the 1960s, Oxford Univ, 87; auth Wolrds of Women: The Making of an International Women's Movement, Princeton Univ, 97; auth, A Desired Past: A Short Hist of Same-Sex Love in Am, Chicago Univ, 99. **CONTACT ADDRESS** 230 W 17th Ave, Columbus, OH 43210-1361. **EMAIL** rupp.1@osu.edu

RUPP, TERESA
PERSONAL Born 10/15/1958, New York, NY, m, 1976, 2 children **DISCIPLINE** HISTORY, MEDIEVAL HISTORY **EDUCATION** Santa Clara Univ, BA, 80; Cornell Univ, MA, 83; PhD, 88. **CAREER** Assoc prof, Mount St. Mary's Col, 88-. **HONORS AND AWARDS** BA, summa cum laude, 80; Phi Beta Kappa, 80. **MEMBERSHIPS** Am Hist Asn, Medieval Acad Am. **RESEARCH** Medieval political thought, medieval Italy. **SELECTED PUBLICATIONS** Auth, "Common'='Of the Commune': Private Property and Individualism in Remigio dei Girolami's De bono pacis," Hist of Political Thought 14, 41-56 (93); auth, "Damnation, the Individual, and the Community in Remigio dei Girolami's De bono communi," Hist of Political Thought (forthcoming). **CONTACT ADDRESS** Dept Hist, Mount Saint Mary's Col and Sem, 16300 Old Emmitsburgh Rd, Emmitsburg, MD 21727-7700. **EMAIL** rupp@msmary.edu

RUSCH, SCOTT M.
PERSONAL Born 11/28/1956, Ft. Rucker, AL **DISCIPLINE** ANCIENT HISTORY, GREECE, ROME **EDUCATION** State Univ New York, Albany, BA, 78; Univ PA, MA, 89, PhD, 97. **CAREER** Three semesters as teaching asst at Univ PA, 79-81. **HONORS AND AWARDS** New York State Regents Scholarship, 74; Univ Fel from Univ PA, 81. **MEMBERSHIPS** Am Philol Asn; Classical Asn of the Atlantic States; Am Hist Asn; Asn of Ancient Hist; Friends of Ancient Hist; Soc of Ancient Military Hist. **RESEARCH** Ancient warfare; Thucydides; the history of the Peloponnesian War. **SELECTED PUBLICATIONS** Auth, Poliorcetic Assault in the Peloponnesian War, Univ PA, dissertation, 97. **CONTACT ADDRESS** 4224 Osage Ave, Apt 43, Philadelphia, PA 19104. **EMAIL** rusch@ccat.sas.upenn.edu

RUSSELL, EDMUND PAUL, III
DISCIPLINE HISTORY OF SCIENCE, ENVIRONMENTAL HISTORY **EDUCATION** Stanford Univ, BA, 80; Univ Mich, Ann Arbor, PhD, 93. **CAREER** Writer, ed, and appropriate technology project leader with Volunteers in Asia, Int Inst of Rural Reconstruction, Silang, Cavite, Philippines, 80-82; teacher, Duchesne Academy, Omaha, Nebraska, 82-83; Lou Henry Hoover House Manager, Stanford Univ, 84-86; prof lectr, American Univ, 94; asst prof, Univ of Va, Charlottesville, 94-. **HONORS AND AWARDS** Arthur W. Bocock Scholar, 75; Nat Merit Scholar, 75; Fulbright Fel to the Philippines (declined), 90; Am Asn for the Advancement of Science-Environmental Protection Agency Science and Engineering Fel, 93; Distinguished Dissertation Awd, Univ Mich, 94; Nat Sci Found CAREER Awd, 95-99; Alumni Bd of Trustees Teaching Awd, Univ Va, 98; State Coun on Higher Ed in Va Outstanding Fac Awd, 99. **MEMBERSHIPS** Am Soc for Engineering Educ, Am Soc for Environmental Hist, Org of Am Hists, Soc for the Hist of Technol. **SELECTED PUBLICATIONS** Auth, "Science and the Environment," in Topical Essays for Teachers, ed. Henry Steffens (WA: Hist of Sci Soc, 95), 111-134; auth, " 'Speaking of Annihilation': Mobilizing for War against Human and Insect Enemies, 1914-1945," J of Am Hist, 82 (March 96): 1505-1529; auth, " 'Lost Among Parts Per Billion': Ecological Protection at the United States Environmental Protection Agency, 1970-1993," Environmental Hist 2 (Jan 97): 29-51; auth, "L. O. Howard Promoted War Metaphors as a Rallying Cry for Economic Entomology," Am Entomologist, 45 (summer 99): 74-78; auth, "The Strange Career of DDT: Experts, Federal Capacity, and 'Environmentalism' in World War II," Technol and Culture (99): 770-796; auth, "Peaceful Warfare: Fighting Humans and Insects with Chemicals from World War I to Silent Spring, NY: Cambridge Univ Press (forthcoming spring 2001); rev of Jessica Wang, American Science in an Age of Anxiety: Scientists, Anticommunism, and the Cold War, Technology and Culture (forthcoming). **CONTACT ADDRESS** Div of Technol, Culture, and Commun, Univ of Virginia, 351 McCormick Rd, PO Box 400744, Charlottesville, VA 22904-4744. **EMAIL** epr5d@virginia.edu

RUSSELL, FREDERICK
PERSONAL Born 11/01/1940, Syracuse, NY, m, 1968 **DISCIPLINE** HISTORY **EDUCATION** Swarthmore Col, BA, 62; Johns Hopkins Univ MA, 64; PhD, 69; Univ Chicago, MA, 75. **CAREER** Instr through Assoc Prof, Rutgers Univ, 69-. **HONORS AND AWARDS** Adams prize, Am Hist Asn, 76. **MEMBERSHIPS** Phi Beta Kappa, Am Hist Asn, am Soc for Legal Hist, Medieval Acad, N Am patristics soc, Del Valley Medieval Asn. **RESEARCH** Augustine, especially his political thought, Canon law, Crusades and warfare. **SELECTED PUBLICATIONS** Auth, The Just War in the Middle Ages, Cambridge Univ Press, 75; auth, "Only Something Good Can Be Evil: the Genesis of Augustine's Secular Ambivalence," Theological Studies, (90): 698-716; auth, "The Bifurcation of Creation: Augustine's Attitudes Toward Nature," Sewanee Mediaeval Studies, (95): 83-96; auth, "Augustine: Conversion by the Book," in Varieties of Religious Conversion in the Middle Ages, 97; auth, "Persuading the Donatists: Augustine's Coercion by Words," in the Limits of Ancient Christianity. Essays on Late Antique Thought and Culture in Honor of R.A. Markus, Univ Mich Press, 99. **CONTACT ADDRESS** Dept Hist, Rutgers, The State Univ of New Jersey, Newark, 175 Univ Ave, Newark, NJ 07102-1803. **EMAIL** frussell@andromeda.rutgers.edu

RUSSELL, HILARY A.
PERSONAL Born 10/24/1947, Kingston, Jamaica **DISCIPLINE** HISTORY **EDUCATION** Carleton Univ, BA, 69. **CAREER** Staff Historian, Nat Hist Sites Directorate, 70-; co-dir conf, Bethune: His Times and His Legacy/son epoque et son message, McGill Univ, 79; proj hist, Elgin and Winter Garden Theatres, 85-89. **HONORS AND AWARDS** City Toronto Bk Awd, 90. **SELECTED PUBLICATIONS** Auth, All That Glitters: A Memorial to Ottawa's Capitol Theatre and its Predecessors, 75; auth, Double Take: The Story of the Elgin and Winter Garden Theatres, 89; contribur, American National Biography; contribur, The Canadian Encyclopedia; contribur, The Dictionary of Canadian Biography; contribur, The Oxford Companion to Theatre History. **CONTACT ADDRESS** 25 Eddy St, F5, Hull, QC, Canada K1A 0M5.

RUSSELL, JAMES M.
PERSONAL Born 12/27/1944, Atlanta, GA, m, 1968, 2 children **DISCIPLINE** HISTORY **EDUCATION** Wesleyan Univ, BA, 66; Princeton Univ, MA, 68, PhD, 72. **CAREER** Prof. **HONORS AND AWARDS** Phi Beta Kappa, 65; Fulbright Senior Lectureship, Genova Italy, 88. **MEMBERSHIPS** Southern Hist Asn; Organization of Am Hist; Urban Hist Asn. **RESEARCH** Urban History; Southern Homicide. **SELECTED PUBLICATIONS** Auth, Atlanta, 1847-1890: City Building in the Old South and the New, Baton Rouge and London, 88; auth, International Cotton Exposition of 1881, Greenwood, 90; The Phoenix City and the Civil War: Atlanta's Economic Miracle, J Ga and S, 90; Using the Computer to Teach Undergraduates Quantitative Methodologies in Historical Research, Int J Soc Edu, 90; Regional and National Perspectives on American Urban History, Can Rev Am Studies, 90; Depicting the Battle of Chancellorsville on a Macintosh Computer, Hist Microcomputer Rev, 94; Economic Factors as Causes of the Civil War, Westport, 96. **CONTACT ADDRESS** Dept of History, Univ of Tennessee, Chatanooga, 615 McCallie, Chattanooga, TN 37403. **EMAIL** univrel@cecasun.utc.edu

RUSSELL, PAUL A.
PERSONAL Born 04/25/1949, Ogdensburg, NY, s **DISCIPLINE** HISTORY **EDUCATION** State Univ NY, BA, 71; Boston Col, MA, 72; PhD, 78. **CAREER** Asst prof, Am Univ in Cairo, 79-84; asst prof to prof, Anna Maria Col, 86-. **HONORS AND AWARDS** Town-Gown Awd, Paxton, 90. **MEMBERSHIPS** Am Hist Asn, Am Soc for Church Hist, Renaissance Soc of Am. **RESEARCH** Renaissance Medicine, 19th Century European-American persons **SELECTED PUBLICATIONS** Ed, Paxton, Massachusetts: History & Vital Statistice, 1748-1850, Heritage Books, 96; auth, Lay Theology in the Reformation: Popular Pamphleteers in Southwest Germany, 1521-1525, Cambridge Univ Press, 86; trans, Abu Mina: A Guide to the Ancient Pilrimage Center, Cairo, 86; auth, "Ficino's Consiglio Contro La Pestilentia in the European Tradition: in Verbum Analecta Neolatina, Vol 1, (99): 85-96; auth, "Andreas von Stuttgart." in Die Deutsche Literatur, (Bern, 94): 482-483. **CONTACT ADDRESS** Dept History, Anna Maria Col, 50 Sunset Lane, Paxton, MA 01612-1106. **EMAIL** prussell@annamaria.edu

RUSSELL-WOOD, A. J. R.
PERSONAL Born 10/11/1939, Corbridge-on-Tyne, United Kingdom, m, 1972, 2 children **DISCIPLINE** HISTORY **EDUCATION** Oxford Univ, BA, 63; MA, 67; DPhil, 67. **CAREER** From Assoc Prof to Prof, Johns Hopkins Univ, 72-. **HONORS AND AWARDS** Herbert E Bolton Prize, 69; Arthur P Whitaker Prize, 83; Dom Joao de Castro Int Prize, 92. **MEMBERSHIPS** RGS, EAAS, RHS, Inst Hist e Geog Brasileiro. **RESEARCH** Colonial Latin America, Portuguese Empire 1415-1825, comparative colonialism. **SELECTED PUBLICATIONS** Auth, Society and Government in Colonial Brazil 1500-1822, 92; auth, A World on the Move. The Portuguese in Africa, Asia and America 1415-1808, 92; auth, "Portugal and the Sea: A World

Embraced" (97); co-ed, "The Portuguese Empire 1415-1808" (98); auth, "Local Government in European Overseas Empires 1450-1800," 2 vols (99); co-ed, "Government and Governance of European Empires 1415-1800," 2 vols (00); auth, "Robert Chester Smith: Research Scholar and Historian," in Robert C Smith: A investigacao na historia da arte (Lisbon: Gulbenkian Found Pr, 00); auth, "Acts of Grace: Portuguese Monarchs and Their Subjects of African Descent in Eighteenth-Century Brazil," J of Latin Am Studies, vol 32.1 (00). **CONTACT ADDRESS** Dept Hist, Johns Hopkins Univ, Baltimore, 3400 N Charles St, Baltimore, MD 21218-2608. **EMAIL** russwood@jhuvms.hcf.jhu.edu

RUSSO, DAVID J.
DISCIPLINE HISTORY **EDUCATION** Univ Mass, BA; Yale Univ, MA, PhD. **RESEARCH** United States hist **SELECTED PUBLICATIONS** Auth, Families and Communities: A New View of American History, 74; auth, Keeper's of our Past: Local Historical Writing in the United States, 1820's-1930's, 88; auth, Clio Confused, 95. **CONTACT ADDRESS** History Dept, McMaster Univ, 1280 Main St W, Hamilton, ON, Canada L8S 4L9. **EMAIL** russod@mcmaster.ca

RUST, ERIC C.
PERSONAL Born 12/24/1950, Lubeck, Germany, m, 1978, 2 children **DISCIPLINE** HISTORY **EDUCATION** Wilfrid Laurier Univ, BA, 74; Lamar Univ, MA, 78; Univ Tex at Austin, PhD, 87. **CAREER** From lectr to assoc prof, Baylor Univ, 84-. **MEMBERSHIPS** AHA, S Hist Asn, SW Hist Asn, Soc for Mil Hist. **RESEARCH** German naval history, early modern Europe. **SELECTED PUBLICATIONS** Auth, Naval Officers Under Hitler: The Story of Crew 34, Praeger (New York), 91; trans and ed, Erich Topp, The Odyssey of a U-Boat Commander: Recollections of Erich Topp, Praeger (New York), 92. **CONTACT ADDRESS** Dept Hist, Baylor Univ, Waco, PO Box 97306, Waco, TX 76798-7306. **EMAIL** Eric_Rust@Baylor.edu

RUTHERFORD, DONALD P.
DISCIPLINE HISTORY OF MODERN PHILOSOPHY **EDUCATION** Univ CA, PhD, 88. **CAREER** Philos, Emory Univ. **SELECTED PUBLICATIONS** Auth, Leibniz and the Rational Order of Nature. **CONTACT ADDRESS** Dept of Hist, Emory Univ, Atlanta, GA 30322-1950. **EMAIL** phildr@emory.edu

RUTHERFORD, PAUL F. W.
PERSONAL Born 02/22/1944, Middlesex, England **DISCIPLINE** HISTORY, MEDIA STUDIES **EDUCATION** Carleton Univ, BA, 65; Univ Toronto, MA, 66, PhD, 73. **CAREER** Lectr, 69-73, asst prof, 73-75, assoc prof, 75-82, chmn, 82-87, Prof History, Univ Toronto, 82-. **HONORS AND AWARDS** SSHRC res grant, 90-91; SSHRC res grant, 93-96; SSHRC res grant, 99-02. **RESEARCH** Cultural history, canadian history, and the study of twentieth century popular culture. **SELECTED PUBLICATIONS** Auth, The Making of the Canadian Media, 78; auth, A Victorian Authority: The Daily Press in Late Nineteenth Century Canada, 82; auth, When Television Was Young: Primetime Canada 1952-1967, 90; auth, The New Icons? The Art of Television Advertising, 94; ed, Saving the Canadian City: The First Phase 1880-1920, 74. **CONTACT ADDRESS** Dept of History, Univ of Toronto, Toronto, ON, Canada M5S 1A1. **EMAIL** prutherf@chass.utoronto.ca

RUTKOFF, PETER
DISCIPLINE HISTORY **EDUCATION** St Lawrence Univ, AB, 64; Univ Pa, MA 65; PhD, 71. **CAREER** Prof hist, NEH Distinguished Tchg Prof Hist, 97-00; prof, 85-; assoc prof, 78-85; asst prof, 71-77, Kenyon Coll; visiting instr, Union Col, 70-71; visiting assoc prof, Grad Fac New School for Social Research, 79-82; prof and dir of Am Studies, 00-. **HONORS AND AWARDS** Dir, NEH Summer Sem, 97; prof yr, Carnegie Found and Coun Advancement and Support Educ, 93; dir, NEH Summer Sem Sec Tchg(s), 93; Outstanding Fac Award: Black Student Union, 90, 98; Martin Luther King, Jr. Award, , 90; Publication Award, New York Modern, Best Book, 00; Ohio Academy of Hist; fel, smithsonian, 87-88, 92-93; grant, neh, 93; proj grant, nah, 87-89; mellon grant coord, 87-88. **RESEARCH** Modern Am, Am studies, Western cultural hist. **SELECTED PUBLICATIONS** Auth, Revanche and Revision: The Origins of the Radical Right in France 1880-1900, Ohio Univ Press, 81; auth, New School: A History of the New School for Social Research, 1886; New York Baseball, The City Speaks, Prospects, 96; contrib, New York Encyclopedia, Yale Univ Press, 95; Golemby's Running, Crab Orchard Rev, 97;coauth, Appalachian Spring: An Artistic Collaboration, Prospects, 96; The Origins of Bebop, Kenyon Rev, 96; auth, New York Modern: The Arts and the City, 99; auth, "Down By the Riverside," Story Quarterly, 00; auth, Shadow Ball: A Novel of Baseball and Chicago, 01. **CONTACT ADDRESS** Dept of Hist, Kenyon Col, Gambier, OH 43022. **EMAIL** rutkoff@kenyon.edu

RUTLAND, ROBERT ALLEN
PERSONAL Born 10/01/1922, Okmulgee, OK, m, 1947, 2 children **DISCIPLINE** HISTORY **EDUCATION** Univ Okla, BA, 47; Cornell Univ, AM, 50; Vanderbilt Univ, PhD, 53. **CAREER** Res assoc hist, State Hist Soc Iowa, 52-54; from instr to prof jour, Univ Calif, Los Angeles, 54-69; bicentennial coordr, Libr Congr, 69-71; ed-in-Chief, Papers James Madison, 71-87, prof hist, 77-87; Univ Va; prof hist, Univ Tulsa, 87-98; Fulbright prof, Univ Innsbruck, Austria, 60-61; vis prof, Univ E Anglia, 80. **MEMBERSHIPS** Orgn Am Historians; Am Antiq Soc. **RESEARCH** History of Constitution and Bill of Rights. **SELECTED PUBLICATIONS** Auth, James Madison and the Search for Nationhood, Libr Cong, 81; ed, Papers of James Madison, Vols 8-14, Univ Chicago & Univ Va, 73-86; auth, James Madison, The Founding Father, Macmillan, 87; auth, The Presidency of James Madison, Kansas, 90; auth, Boyhood in the Dust Bowl, Colorado, 95; auth, The Republicans, Missouri, 96. **CONTACT ADDRESS** History Dept, Univ of Tulsa, Tulsa, OK 74104. **EMAIL** robert-rutland@utulsa.edu

RWIZA, KATETEGEILWE MOSESKATETEGEILWE MOSESKATETEGEILWE MOSES
PERSONAL Born 12/15/1957, Bukoba, Tanzania, m, 1995, 3 children **DISCIPLINE** GEOGRAPHY **EDUCATION** Leningrad Mining Inst, MSc, 87; ITC Enschede, Netherlands, MSc, 92. **CAREER** Asst lect, Univ Col Lands and Arch Studies, 87; lect, 92; vis schl, Univ ID, 98-99. **HONORS AND AWARDS** Fulbright, 98-99. **RESEARCH** Environmental planning and management. **SELECTED PUBLICATIONS** Auth, "Geoinformatics the Future for Land Surveyors," J Survey World (London, 99); auth, "Energy for Sustainable Development In Tanzania," J Energy and Devel (CO, 99): vol 24, no 1. **CONTACT ADDRESS** Dept Geography, Univ of Idaho, 375 s Lane St, Moscow, ID 83844-0001. **EMAIL** rwiz2091@uidaho.edu

RYAN, HERBERT JOSEPH
PERSONAL Born 02/19/1931, Scarsdale, NY **DISCIPLINE** THEOLOGY, HISTORY **EDUCATION** Loyola Univ, Ill, AB, 54, MA, 60, PhL, 56; Woodstock Col, Md, STL, 63; Gregorian Univ, STD, 67. **CAREER** From asst prof to assoc prof hist theol, Woodstock Col, Md, 67- 74; assoc prof relig studies, 74-79, Prof Theol, Loyola Marymount Univ, 79-, Off Roman Cath observer, Lambeth Conf, 68; mem joint comn Anglican-Roman Cath relat, Roman Cath Bishops Comn Ecumenical, Affairs, 68-; convenor joint comn ministry & off observer Roman Cath Church, Gen Conv Episcopal Church, 69, 71 & 73; secretariat for promoting Christian unity, Anglican-Roman Cath Int Comn, 69-; vis lectr hist theol, Union Theol Sem, NY, 71-74; vis prof ecumenical & ascetical theol, Gen Theol Sem, 73-74. **HONORS AND AWARDS** Int Christian Unity Awd, Graymoor Ecumenical Inst, 74; Medal Order St Augustine, Archbishop Canterbury, London, 81; std, gen theol sem, 73. **MEMBERSHIPS** Am Acad Relig; Cath Hist Soc; Cath Theol Soc Am; Church Hist Soc; N Am Acad Ecumenists; Mediaeval Acad Am. **RESEARCH** Anglican theological tradition; influence of St Augustine on Christian theology; methodology of ecumenical theology. **SELECTED PUBLICATIONS** Auth, Wolsey - Church, State And Art - Gunn,Sj, Lindley,Pg, Editors/, Theol Studies, Vol 0053, 1992; The Synods For The Carolingian Empire From Ad721 To Ad090 Held In France And In Italy - Ger - Hartmann,W/, Speculum-A J Of Medieval Studies, Vol 0067, 1992; The Renewal Of Anglicanism - Mcgrath,Ae/, Theol Studies, Vol 0055, 1994. **CONTACT ADDRESS** Dept of Theological Studies, Loyola Marymount Univ, 7900 Loyola Blvd, Los Angeles, CA 90045.

RYAN, JAMES D.
PERSONAL Born 11/29/1938, Buffalo, NY, m, 1963, 3 children **DISCIPLINE** HISTORY **EDUCATION** NYork Univ, PhD, 72. **CAREER** From Instr to prof, Bronx Commun Col, CUNY, 79- ; Chm Dept Hist, 91- . **HONORS AND AWARDS** NEH fel, 81; ACLS grant, 90; PCS/CUNY res awards, 91, 92, 96, 97, 98; BCC found res grant, 93; AAC/NEA award, 96. **MEMBERSHIPS** Medieval Acad of Am; Medieval Club of NY; Am Hist Asn; Am Catholic Hist Asn; World Hist Asn; Am Acad of Polit and Soc Sci; ECCSSA. **RESEARCH** History of Crusades and Mission; Church history; medieval travel; cross cultural contacts. **SELECTED PUBLICATIONS** Auth, Nicholas IV and the Evoloution of the Eastern Missionary Effort, in Archivum Pontificiae Historiae, 81; auth For Christ of Christendom: Contrasting Western Missionary Goals in the Morea and Asian Mission Lands in the Late Thirteenth and Early Fourteenth Centuries, in Transactions of the 17th Internatl Congress of Hist Sci, 92; auth, Missionary Objectives in China and India in the Fourteenth Century, in Proceedings of the Am Hist Asn, 92; auth, European Travelers before Columbus: The Fourteenth Century's Discovery of India, in Cath Hist Rev, 93; auth, Conversion vs. Baptism? European Missionaries in Asia in the Thirteenth and Fourteenth Centuries, in Varieties of Religious Conversion in the Middle Ages, Univ Pr Florida, 97; auth, Christian Wives of Mongol Khans: Tartar Queens and Missionary Expectations in Asia, in J of Royal Asiatic Soc, 98; auth, Preaching Christianity along the Silk Route: Missionary Outposts in the Tartar Middle Kingdom, in J of Early Mod Hist, 98. **CONTACT ADDRESS** Dept of History, Bronx Comm Col, CUNY, University Ave & West 181st St, Bronx, NY 10453. **EMAIL** jdrbx@cunyvm.cuny.edu

RYAN, JAMES G.
PERSONAL Born 01/31/1947, Wilmington, DE, d **DISCIPLINE** AMERICAN POLITICAL HISTORY **EDUCATION** Univ Del, BA, 70; MA, 73; Univ Notre Dame, MA, 75; PhD, 81. **CAREER** Adj exploit, 76-87; vis asst prof, Drexel Univ, 85; vis asst prof, Muhlenburg Col, 87-90; asst prof, Texas AM Univ, 90-96; ten assoc prof, 96-. **HONORS AND AWARDS** Fac Res Gnts, Muhlenburg Coll, Texas AM Univ; Intl Res, Texas AM Univ. **MEMBERSHIPS** AHA; OAH; HS; HAC; SHGAPE; TFA. **RESEARCH** Twentieth century political history; nineteenth century political history; radicalism and radical movements. **SELECTED PUBLICATIONS** Auth, "American Communism and Anticommunism: Availability of New Documents and the Beginnings of an Academic Reassessment," Historian 60 (98): 366-71; auth, Earl Browder: The Failure of American Communism (Tuscaloosa: Univ AL Press, 97); auth, "Earl Browder and American Communism," in American Reform and Reformers, eds. Randall M Miller, Paul A Cimbala (Westport: Greenwood Press, 96). **CONTACT ADDRESS** Dept General Academics, Texas A&M Univ, Galveston, PO Box 1675, Galveston, TX 77553-1675. **EMAIL** ryanj@tamug.tamu.edu

RYAN, THOMAS JOSEPH
PERSONAL Born 05/28/1942, Brooklyn, NY **DISCIPLINE** LATIN AMERICAN & UNITED STATES HISTORY **EDUCATION** Fla Southern Col, BS, 63; Univ Ala, MA, 66; NOVA Southeastern Univ, EdD, 87. **CAREER** Teacher & coach hist, Charlotte Sr High, 64-65; prof hist, Broward Community Col, 66-; Dir Camp BCC, 79-94; lectr Latin Am, World Campus Afloat, 75; tour guide, Broward Community Col 74-98. **HONORS AND AWARDS** Salvation Army Family Awd, 85; USMC Semper Fi Awd, 89 & 91; J.C. Penny Volunteer of the Year, 90; South Fla Manufacturer's Exemplary Practice, 91; Buick Volunteer Spirit, 94; SPD History Grant, 94 & 95; Teach Learn CTN, 95 & 96; BCC Boyr Awd, 97; Intercollegiate Hall of Fame, 97; Prof of the Year, 98. **MEMBERSHIPS** South Eastern Conf Latin Am; Nat Asn Student Personel Admin; Am Camp Asn; Fla State Elks Assoc. **RESEARCH** Latin American travel study programs; Mayan experience; Caribbean pirates, Fidel Castro. **CONTACT ADDRESS** Broward Comm Col, 3501 Davie Rd, Fort Lauderdale, FL 33314-1604.

RYANG, KEY S.
PERSONAL Born 12/19/1930, Korea, m, 1962, 2 children **DISCIPLINE** AMERICAN STUDIES **EDUCATION** Trinity Univ, BA, 56; Columbia Univ, MA, 60; PhD, 72. **CAREER** Instr, US State Dept, For Ser Inst, 68; asst prof, assoc prof, prof, Mary Washington Col, 73-. **HONORS AND AWARDS** Ed, J Mod Kor Stud. **MEMBERSHIPS** AAS; TSS; AHA. **RESEARCH** Modern Korean intellectual history; China's Tiang history; law. **SELECTED PUBLICATIONS** Auth, "Sin Ch'ae-ho ui Kundae Sakwanui Kunjae wa Paijon: The Qrigin and Development of Sin Ch'ae-ho's Modern Historiography," Tanjae Sin Ch'ae-ho Yun'gu Ronjip, Chunqpuk Univ Press, 95; auth, "Koun Ch'oe Ch'i-won Yun'gu: A Study of Koun Ch'oe Ch'i-won," Korean-French Culture Press (Seoul), 95; rev, "Silla Sasan P'imyony," by Ch'oe Ch'i-won, J Modern Korean Studies 6 (96); rev, "Koryo Taechangkyongpan pochon-ul uihan kich'o haksul yon'yu: Studies of the Conservation for Koryo Tripitaka Printing Blocks in the Hasein Monastery," J Mod Kor Stud 6 (96); auth, "Ch'oe Ch'i-won's T'ang Poetry and Its Modern Interpretation," J Modern Korean Studies 7 (00). **CONTACT ADDRESS** Dept History, Mary Washington Col, 1301 College Ave, Fredricksburg, VA 22401-5300. **EMAIL** kryang@mwc.edu

RYBCZYNSKI, WITOLD
PERSONAL Born 03/01/1943, Edinburgh, United Kingdom, m, 1974 **DISCIPLINE** ARCHITECTURE **EDUCATION** Loyloa Col High Sch, 60; McGill Univ, B Arch, 66, M Arch, 72. **CAREER** Asst prof, McGill Univ, 75-80, assoc prof, 80-86, prof, 86-93; Meyerson Prof of Urbanism, Univ of Pa, 94-. **HONORS AND AWARDS** Qspell Literary Prize, 88, 89; P/A Awd, 91; Alfred Jurzykowski Found Awd, 93; Hon Fel, AIA, 93; Philadelphia Athoneaum Prize, 97; Christopher Awd, 2000; 2000 Notable Book Awd, ALA. **RESEARCH** Architecture, urbanism, technology and culture. **SELECTED PUBLICATIONS** Auth, Paper Heroes: A Review of Appropriate Technology (80); auth, Taming the Tiger: The Struggle to Control Technology (83); auth, Home: A Short History of an Idea (86); auth, The Most Beautiful House in the World (89); auth, Waiting for the Weekend (91); auth, Looking Around: A Journey Through Architecture (92); auth, A Place for Art (93); auth, City Life: Urban Expectations in a New World (95); auth, A Clearing in the Distance: Frederick Law Olmsted and America in the Nineteenth Century (99); auth, One Good Turn: A Natural History of the Screwdriver and the Screw (2000). **CONTACT ADDRESS** Dept Architecture-Meyerson, Univ of Pennsylvania, 210 S 34th St, Philadelphia, PA 19104-3804. **EMAIL** rybczyns@pobox.upenn.edu

RYDELL, ROBERT WILLIAM
PERSONAL Born 05/23/1952, Evanston, IL, m, 1982, 2 children **DISCIPLINE** AMERICAN HISTORY & STUDIES **EDUCATION** Univ Calif, Berkeley, AB, 74, Los Angeles, MA, 75, CPhil, 77, PhD(hist), 80. **CAREER** Asst Prof Hist, Mont State Univ, 80-84, Vis asst prof, Univ Calif, Los Angeles, summer, 81; Assoc Prof Hist, 84-89; Prof Hist, 89-. **HONORS AND AWARDS** Phi Beta Kappa, 74; Allan Nevins Prize, 81;

Fel Smithsonian Inst, 82-83; fel Netherlands Inst for Advanced Study, 91-92; John Adams, Univ of Amsterdam, 85-86. **MEMBERSHIPS** AHA, ASA. **RESEARCH** United States intellectual history; United States cultural history; history of technology. **SELECTED PUBLICATIONS** Auth, All the World's a Fair, 84; auth, World of Fairs, 93; ed, Cultural Transmissions and Receptions, 93; auth, Natures Metropolis - Chicago And The Great-W - Cronon,W/, Southwestern Hist Quart, Vol 0097, 1993; Capitalism On The Frontier - Billings And The Yellowstone-Valley In The 19th-Century - Vanwest,C/, Montana-The Mag Of Western Hist, Vol 0044, 1994; The Birth Of The Museum - History, Theory, Politics - Bennett,T/, Cult Studies, Vol 0011, 1997; Wild W Shows And The Images Of Am-Indians, 1883-1933 - Moses,Lg/, Pac Hist Rev, Vol 0066, 1997; ed, The Reason why the Colored American is Not in the Columbian Exposition, 99; coauth, Fair America, 00. **CONTACT ADDRESS** Dept of Hist & Philos, Montana State Univ, Bozeman, Bozeman, MT 59717-0001. **EMAIL** rwrydell@montana.edu

RYNDER, CONSTANCE
DISCIPLINE AMERICAN SOCIAL HISTORY AND BRITISH HISTORY **EDUCATION** Univ Toledo, BA, 67; Univ NE, MA,70, PhD, 73. **CAREER** Prof; past pres, AAUP, Fla Conf. **HONORS AND AWARDS** Louise Loy Hunter Awd, 92. **RESEARCH** Women in hist; Native Am; western civilization, US hist since 1877; ancient hist and Irish hist. **SELECTED PUBLICATIONS** Auth, The education of a Progressive Reformer: William and Amy Maher, NW Ohio Quart, 91. **CONTACT ADDRESS** Dept of Hist, Univ of Tampa, 401 W. Kennedy Blvd, Tampa, FL 33606-1490. **EMAIL** crynder@alpha.utampa.edu

RYON, RODERICK NAYLOR
PERSONAL Born 07/11/1938, Washington, DC **DISCIPLINE** AMERICAN HISTORY **EDUCATION** Western Md Col, AB, 60; Pa State Univ, AM, 63, PhD(hist), 66. **CAREER** From asst prof to assoc prof, 65-73, Prof Hist, Towson Col, 73- **RESEARCH** Society and politics of the Jacksonian era; labor and reform movements. **SELECTED PUBLICATIONS** Auth, Public sponsorship of special education in Pennsylvania from 1818 to 1834, Pa Hist, 7/67; Moral reform and Democratic politics: The dilemma of Robert Vaux, Quaker Hist, spring 70. **CONTACT ADDRESS** Dept of Hist, Towson State Univ, Baltimore, MD 21204.

RYZL, MILAN
PERSONAL Born 05/22/1928, Prague, Czechoslovakia, m, 1951, 3 children **DISCIPLINE** PHYSICS, CHEMISTRY **EDUCATION** Charles' Univ Prague, Czech Republic, RNDr, equiv to PhD, 92. **CAREER** Instr Biol, Czechoslovak Acad Sci, 67; Corr Res Assoc Parapsychology Lab, Duke Univ Durham NC; Tchg Psotions: San Diego State Univ, San Jose State Univ, Univ of California, Santa Barbara, CA, J F Kennedy Univ Orinda, CA, retired. **HONORS AND AWARDS** Wm McDougall Awd, parasychological Res, 92. **MEMBERSHIPS** Parapsychol Assoc. **RESEARCH** Extra-sensory perception, its develo in hypnosis and its soc significance. **SELECTED PUBLICATIONS** Over 100 res papers; Parapsychologh; A scientific Approach, Hawthorn, NY 70; Das grosse Handbuch der Parapsychologie, Ariston Verlag, Munchen Germany, 97; as of Agust 98: total of 15 books(including 3 text books) on experimental parapsycholog and its relation to religion; published in 15 languages. **CONTACT ADDRESS** Westgate Station, PO Box 9459, San Jose, CA 95157.

S

SAAB, E. ANN POTTINGER
PERSONAL Born 12/18/1934, Boston, MA, d, 2 children **DISCIPLINE** MODERN EUROPEAN & MIDDLE EASTERN HISTORY **EDUCATION** Wellesley Col, BA, 55; Radcliffe Col, MA, 57, PhD(hist), 62. **CAREER** Instr hist, Middlebury Col, 62-64; lectr, 65-66, from asst prof to assoc prof, 66-75, Prof Hist, Univ NC, Greensboro, 75-, Head Dept, 78-84, assoc Dean Grad School, 90-98; Soc Sci Res Coun fel, Turkey, 64-65. **MEMBERSHIPS** Mid E Studies Asn NAm; AHA. **RESEARCH** French policy towards the German states in the 1860's; origins of the Crimean War with relation to Ottoman politics; British attitudes toward the ottoman Empire. **SELECTED PUBLICATIONS** Auth, Napoleon III and the German Crisis, 1865-66, Harvard Univ, 66; The Origins of the Crimean Alliance, Univ VA, 77; transl, Winifred Baumgart, The Peace of Paris, 1856, ABC-Clio, 81; Reluctant Icon: Gladstone, Bulgaria, and the Working Classes, 1856-1878, Harvard Univ, 91. **CONTACT ADDRESS** Dept of Hist, Univ of No Carolina, Greensboro, Greensboro, NC 27412. **EMAIL** annsaab@earthlink.net

SACHAR, HOWARD M.
PERSONAL Born 02/10/1928, St Louis, MO, m, 1964, 3 children **DISCIPLINE** HISTORY **EDUCATION** Swarthmore Col, BA, 47; Harvard Univ, MA, 50; PhD, 53. **CAREER** George Washington Univ, 65-. **HONORS AND AWARDS** Dr of Humanee Letters, Honoris Causa, Hebrew Union Col, 96. **RESEARCH** Modern European History, Modern Jewish History. **SELECTED PUBLICATIONS** Auth, Farewell Espana, 96; auth, Europe and Israel, 99. **CONTACT ADDRESS** Dept Hist, The George Washington Univ, 2035 H St NW, Washington, DC 20052-0001. **EMAIL** sachar@gwu.edu

SACHS, WILLIAM L.
PERSONAL Born 08/23/1947, Richmond, VA, m, 1986, 1 child **DISCIPLINE** HISTORY OF CHRISTIANITY **EDUCATION** Baylor, BA, 69; Vanderbilt Univ, MDiv, 72; Yale Univ, STM, 73; Univ Chicago, PhD, 81. **CAREER** Dir of Res, Episcopal Church Found; vis fel, Yale Univ. **RESEARCH** English and American evangelicism; religious leadership; Anglican communion. **SELECTED PUBLICATIONS** Auth, The Transformation of Anglicanism, Cambridge; auth, Of One Body, John Knox. **CONTACT ADDRESS** Episcopal Church Foundation, 815 Second Ave, New York, NY 10017. **EMAIL** bsachs@episcopalfoundation.org

SACK, JAMES J.
PERSONAL Born 12/04/1944, Monroe, MI **DISCIPLINE** HISTORY **EDUCATION** Univ Notre Dame, BA, 67; Univ Mich, PhD, 73. **CAREER** Prof Hist, Univ Ill, Chicago. **MEMBERSHIPS** AHA; N Am Conf on British Stud; Midwest Victorian Stud Asn. **RESEARCH** Eighteenth and nineteenth century British politics. **SELECTED PUBLICATIONS** Auth, The Grenvillites: Party Politics and Factionalism in the Age of Pitt and Liverpool, Illinois, 79; auth, From Jacobite to Conservative: Reaction and Orthodoxy in Britain, 1760-1832, Cambridge, 93. **CONTACT ADDRESS** History Dept, Univ of Illinois, Chicago, 601 S Morgan St, Chicago, IL 60607. **EMAIL** JSack@uic.edu

SACK, RONALD H.
PERSONAL Born 11/23/1943, Chicago, IL, s **DISCIPLINE** HISTORY **EDUCATION** Univ Wis, BA, 65; Univ Minn, MA, 67; PhD, 70. **CAREER** From asst prof to prof, NC State Univ, 71-. **HONORS AND AWARDS** Deutscher Akademischer Austauschdienst Fel, 69-90. **MEMBERSHIPS** Am Oriental Soc. **RESEARCH** Chaldean Mesopotamia, Ancient Near East, Historiography. **SELECTED PUBLICATIONS** Auth, Images of Nebuchadnezzar--The Emergence of a Legend, 91; auth, Neriglissan--King of Babylon, 94; auth, Cuneiform Documents from The Chaldean and Persian periods, 94. **CONTACT ADDRESS** Dept Hist, No Carolina State Univ, PO Box 8108, Raleigh, NC 27695-0001. **EMAIL** ronald_sack@ncsu.edu

SACKS, DAVID HARRIS
PERSONAL Born 12/14/1942, Brooklyn, NY, m, 1971 **DISCIPLINE** HISTORY **EDUCATION** Brooklyn Col, BA, 63; Harvard Univ, AM, 65; PhD, 77. **CAREER** From Asst Prof to Prof, Reed Col, 89-. **HONORS AND AWARDS** Burlington-Northern Found Fac Achievement Awd, Reed Col, 91; Woodrow Wilson Fel, 92-93; Guggenheim Fel, 92-93; John Ben Snow Found Prize, 92; Fel, Australian Nat Univ, 93; Fel, Royal Hist Soc, 96; Vollum Fac Awd, Reed Col, 97. **MEMBERSHIPS** AHA, ASLH, EHS, NACBS, PPS, RSA, RHS, SSA, SCSA. **RESEARCH** Early modern British and European history, history of the Atlantic world, history of political and ethical discourse, cultural history, urban history. **SELECTED PUBLICATIONS** Auth, Trade, Society and Politics in Bristol 1500-1640, Garland Publ (New York), 85; auth, The Widening Gate: Bristol and the Atlantic Economy 1450-1700, Univ Calif Pr (Berkeley, CA), 91; auth, "The Countervailing of Benefits: Monopoly, Liberty and Benevolence in Elizabethan England," in Tudor Polit Cult (Cambridge: Cambridge UP, 95), 272-291;auth, "Political Culture,' in A Companion to Shakespeare (Oxford: Blackwell, 99), 117-136; co-ed, The Historical Imagination in Early Modern Britain: History, Rhetoric and Fiction 1500-1800, Cambridge UP (Cambridge), 97; **CONTACT ADDRESS** Dept Hist, Reed Col, 3203 SE Woodstock Blvd, Portland, OR 97202 8199.

SADLIER, ROSEMARY
PERSONAL Born Toronto, ON, Canada **DISCIPLINE** HISTORY **EDUCATION** York Univ, BA; Univ Toronto, MSW, BEd. **CAREER** Pres, Bd Dirs, Ontario Black History Society. **HONORS AND AWARDS** Cert Recognition, Women PACE-Project Advan Childhood Educ, 96; Volunteer Awd 10 Years Serv, Min Citizenship, 94; Volunteer Awd, Ont Black Hist Soc. **MEMBERSHIPS** Writers' Union Can; CAN:BAIA. **SELECTED PUBLICATIONS** Auth, Leading the Way: Black Women in Canada, 95; auth, Mary Ann Shadd: Publisher, Editor, Teacher, Lawyer, Suffragette, 95; auth, Harriet Tubman and the Underground Railroad, Her Life in Canada and the United States, 96. **CONTACT ADDRESS** Ontario Black Hist Society, 10 Adelaide St E, Toronto, ON, Canada M5C 1J3.

SAEGER, JAMES SCHOFIELD
PERSONAL Born 08/19/1938, Columbus, OH, d, 1964, 2 children **DISCIPLINE** HISTORY **EDUCATION** Ohio State Univ, BA, 60; MA, 63; PhD, 65. **CAREER** Instr hist, Ohio State Univ, 65-67; instr to prof hist, Lehigh Univ, 67- . **HONORS AND AWARDS** Fulbright; NEH; res grant Orgn Am States. **MEMBERSHIPS** AHA; CLAH; MACLAS; RMCLAS. **RESEARCH** Ethnohistory, Paraguay, Argentina. **SELECTED PUBLICATIONS** Auth, "Survival and Abolition: The Eighteenth entury Paraguayan Encomienda," The Americas, 38, p59-85, (81); auth, "Another View of the Mission as a Frontier Institution: The Guaycuruan Missions of Santa Fe, 1743-1810," Hispanic Am Hist Rev, 65, no 3, p 493-517, (85); auth, "Eighteenth-Century Guaycuruan Missions in Paraguay," Indian-Relig Relations in Colonial Span Am, p 55-86, Syracuse NY (89); auth, "The Mission and Historical Missions: Film and the Writing of History, " The Americas: A Quarterly Rev of Inter-American Cultural History, 51, p 393-415, (95); auth, "Warfare, Reorganization, and Readaption at the Margins of Spanish Rule-The Chaco and Paraguay (1573-1882), Cambridge History of Native Peoples of the Americas, Cambridge and NY, (99); auth, The Chaco Mission Frontier: The Guaycuruan Experience, (Tuscon AZ), (00). **CONTACT ADDRESS** Dept Hist, Lehigh Univ, Maginnes #9, Bethelem, PA 19015. **EMAIL** JSS@LEHIGH.EDU

SAFFORD, FRANK ROBINSON
PERSONAL Born 06/04/1935, El Paso, TX, m, 1959, 2 children **DISCIPLINE** LATIN AMERICAN HISTORY **EDUCATION** Harvard Univ, AB, 57; Columbia Univ, MA, 59, PhD(Latin Am hist), 65. **CAREER** From instr to asst prof Latin Am & US hist, Dartmouth Col, 62-66; from asst prof to assoc prof, 66-77, Prof Latin Am Hist, Northwestern Univ, Evanston, 77-, Vis assoc prof hist, Univ Tex, Austin, 72-73; assoc ed, Hisp Am Hist Rev, 72-73. **MEMBERSHIPS** Conf Latin Am Hist; Latin Am Studies Asn. **RESEARCH** Nineteenth-century Latin America; social and economic history of Latin America; Colombian history. **SELECTED PUBLICATIONS** Auth, Foreign and national enterprise in nineteenth-century Colombia, Bus Hist Rev, winter 65; Significacion de los antioquenos en el desarrollo economico colombiano, Anuario Colombiano Hist y Cult, 67; Latin America, Allyn & Bacon, 70; Social aspects of politics in nineteenth-century Spanish America: New Granada, 1825-1850, J Social Hist, 3/72; contribr, New Approaches to Latin American History, 74 & auth, The Ideal of the Practical: Colombia's Struggle to Form a Technical Elite, 76, Univ Tex; Aspectos del siglo XIX en Colombia, Ediciones Hombre Nuevo, 77. **CONTACT ADDRESS** Dept of Hist, Northwestern Univ, Evanston, IL 60201.

SAFFORD, JEFFREY JAEGER
PERSONAL Born 05/14/1934, Greenwich Village, NY, m, 1957, 4 children **DISCIPLINE** UNITED STATES HISTORY **EDUCATION** Wagner Col, AB, 56, MSEduc, 59; Rutgers Univ, PhD(hist), 68. **CAREER** Instr phys educ, Wagner Col, 56-57; US Army, 57-59; instr lang arts social studies, Plainfield Pub Schs, NJ, 59-61; instr English & jour & asst dir pub rels, Susquehanna Univ, 61-62; dir pub rels, Wagner Col, 62-65; from asst prof to assoc prof, 68-77, Prof Hist, Mont State Univ, 77-, Vis lectr hist, Munson Inst Maritime Hist, 70-73, 92-99. **HONORS AND AWARDS** Wylie Meritorious Res Awd, Montana State Univ, 80; John Lyman Book Awd; N. Atlantic Soc for Oceanic Hist, 99 as co-author of American and The Sea. **MEMBERSHIPS** NAtlantic Soc Oceanic Historians; Soc Historians Am Foreign Rels; Orgn Am Historians. **RESEARCH** United States foreign affairs; United States maritime history; Western Mining History 19th c. **SELECTED PUBLICATIONS** Auth, Wilsonian Maritime Diplomacy, 1913-1921, Rutgers Univ, 78; auth, World War I Maritime Policy and National Security, in: America's Maritime Legacy, Westview, 79; auth, Anglo-American Maritime Relations during the two World Wars, Am Neptune, 81; auth, The Decline of the American Merchant Marine, 1850-1914: An Historiograhaphical Appraisal, in: Change and Adaptation in Maritime History, Memorial Univ, 84; auth, The United States Merchant Marine in Foreign Trade, 1800-1939, in: Business History of Shipping, Univ of Tokyo, 85; auth, United States Maritime Policy and Diplomacy During the Phony War, 1939-1940, Internat'l Journal of Maritime History, 89; co-auth, In The People's Interest: A Centennial History of Montana State Univ, 1893-1993, MSU, 93; auth, The United States Merchant Marine During World War II, in: Oxford Companion to the Second World War, 95; auth, Connecticut Capital at Work in the Gold Fields of Montana, 1865-68, Montana: The Magazine of Western History, 97; coauth, America and the Sea, Mystic Seaport Foundation, 98. **CONTACT ADDRESS** Dept of Hist, Montana State Univ, Bozeman, Bozeman, MT 59717-2320. **EMAIL** js50bach@aol.com

SAGE, MICHAEL
PERSONAL Born 12/04/1944, New York, NY, m, 2 children **DISCIPLINE** ROMAN HISTORY & CLASSICS **EDUCATION** Univ Mich, BA, MA (hist); Univ Toronto, MA (classics), PhD. **CAREER** Univ Waterloo, asst prof (hist), 74-75; Univ Cincinnati, asst prof (classics), 75-81, assoc prof, 81-90, prof, 90-. **HONORS AND AWARDS** Canada Coun, Province of Ontario, Semple Fel. **MEMBERSHIPS** Am Philological Asn; Soc Promotion Roman Studies. **RESEARCH** Late Roman hist; Christianity; ancient mil hist. **SELECTED PUBLICATIONS** Ancient Greek Warfare, London, 96. **CONTACT ADDRESS** Univ of Cincinnati, 407 Blegen Libr, Cincinnati, OH 45221. **EMAIL** Michael.Sage@uc.edu

SAGINI, MESHACK
PERSONAL Born 11/30/1944, Kisii, Kenya, m, 1973, 4 children **DISCIPLINE** EDUCATION ADMINISTRATION, HISTORY **EDUCATION** West Indies, BEd, 79; Andrews, MA, 82; MSU, PhD, 87. **CAREER** Elementary school teacher, 67; high school deputy principal, 71-75; Col lecturer, 89-97; asst prof to res prof, Langston Univ, 98-. **HONORS AND AWARDS** Excellence in Teaching, Am Pol Sci Asn, 97; Excellence in Res and teaching, Langston Univ, 97. **MEMBERSHIPS** OK Pol Sci Asn, am Pol Sci Asn, MAAAS, Ok League of Pol Sci, African Professionals Asn. **RESEARCH** Organizational behavior, Public policy, Africans in higher education. **SELECTED PUBLICATIONS** Auth, The African and the African-American University: a Historical and Sociological Analysis, Univ Press of America, 96. **CONTACT ADDRESS** Dept Soc Sci & Humanities, Langston Univ, PO Box 157, Langston, OK 73050-0728. **EMAIL** mmsagini@lunet.edu

SAILLANT, JOHN D.
PERSONAL Born 07/25/1957, Providence, RI, m, 3 children **DISCIPLINE** EARLY AMERICAN LITERATURE; HISTORY **EDUCATION** Brown Univ, BA, 79; MA, 81; DPhil, 89. **CAREER** Assoc prof, English, W Mich Univ. **HONORS AND AWARDS** NEHGrant, 97; Ames Fel, Univ Mass, 97; Am Acad Relig Grant, 96; The Huntington & British Acad Grant; RI Comt Hum Grant, 96; Va Hist Soc Mellon Res Grant, 94, 96; Am Counc Learned Socs Fel, 92-93; **MEMBERSHIPS** Am Acad Relig; Am Hist Asn; Am Soc Eighteenth-Century Studies; Am Studies Asn; Forum Eu Expansion & Global Interaction; Great Lakes Am Studies Asn; New England Hist Asn; Soc of Early Amists; Soc Historians Early Republic. **SELECTED PUBLICATIONS** Auth, The Black Body Erotic and the Republican Body Politic, 1790-1820, Jour Hist Sexuality, 95; Slavery and Divine Providence in New England Calvinism: The New Divinity and a Black Protest, New England Quart, 95; Explaining Syncretism in African American Views of Death: An Eighteenth-Century Example, Cult & Tradition, 95; Hymnody in Sierra Leone and the Persistence of an African American Faith, The Hymn, 97; The American Enlightenment in Africa: Jefferson's Colonizationism and Black Virginians' Migration to Liberia, 1776-1840, Eighteenth-Century Studies, 98. **CONTACT ADDRESS** Dept of Engl, Western Michigan Univ, Sprau Tower, Kalamazoo, MI 49008-5092. **EMAIL** john.saillant@wmich.edu

SAINSBURY, JOHN
DISCIPLINE EARLY MODERN BRITISH HISTORY **EDUCATION** Cambridge Univ, BA, MA; McGill Univ, PhD. **CAREER** Assoc prof; ch. **RESEARCH** John Wilkes. **SELECTED PUBLICATIONS** Auth, Disaffected Patriots: London Supporters of Revolutionary America, McGill-Queen's UP. **CONTACT ADDRESS** Dept of Hist, Brock Univ, 500 Glenridge Ave, Saint Catharines, ON, Canada L2S 3A1. **EMAIL** jsainsbu@spartan.ac.BrockU.CA

SAKIHARA, MICHAEL MITSUGU
PERSONAL Born 02/26/1928, Okinawa, Japan, m, 1962, 1 child **DISCIPLINE** HISTORY **EDUCATION** Univ Oregon, BA, 55, BA, 60; Univ Hawaii, PhD, 71. **CAREER** Assoc prof, Univ Hawaii, 74-95; Pres, Hawaii Int Col, 95-. **HONORS AND AWARDS** Fulbright Res Scholarship, 87-88. **MEMBERSHIPS** Hosei Univ Fel, Okinawa Int Univ Fel. **RESEARCH** Dictionary of the Okinawan language and culture, Chinese investiture mission to Ryukyu in 1800. **SELECTED PUBLICATIONS** Auth, A Brief History of Early Okinawa (87). **CONTACT ADDRESS** Hawaii Pacific Univ, 2322 Fern St #204, Honolulu, HI 96826. **EMAIL** KHIC@aol.com

SAKMYSTER, THOMAS LAWRENCE
PERSONAL Born 10/06/1943, Perth Amboy, NJ, m, 1967, 2 children **DISCIPLINE** MODERN & DIPLOMATIC HISTORY **EDUCATION** Dartmouth Col, BA, 65; Ind Univ Bloomington, MA, 67, PhD, 71. **CAREER** From asst prof to prof hist, 71-97, Walter Langsam Prof Mod Europ Hist, Univ Cincinnati, 97-. **HONORS AND AWARDS** Article Prize, Am Asn Study Hungarian Hist, 76; Book Prize, Am Asn Study Hungarian Hist, 85. **MEMBERSHIPS** AHA; Am Asn Advan Slavic Studies; Am Asn Study Hungarian Hist (secy, 73-75, pres, 79-80). **RESEARCH** Modern Hungary; East European diplomatic history; European military elites; film and history. **SELECTED PUBLICATIONS** Auth, Hungary, the Great Powers, and the Danubian Crisis, 1936-1939, Univ Ga Press, 80; Hungary's Admiral on Horseback: Miklos Horthy, 1918-1944, Columbia Univ Press, 94. **CONTACT ADDRESS** Dept of Hist, Univ of Cincinnati, PO Box 210373, Cincinnati, OH 45221-0373. **EMAIL** tom.sakmyster@uc.edu

SAKU, JAMES C.
PERSONAL Born Ghana, West Africa, m, 1988, 3 children **DISCIPLINE** GEOGRAPHY **EDUCATION** Univ Cape Coast, Ghana, BA; Wilfred Laurier Univ, MA, 90; Univ Saskatchewan, PhD, 95. **CAREER** Adjunct fac, Trent Univ, 95-96; asst prof, Frostburg State Univ, 96-. **MEMBERSHIPS** Asn of Am Geog, Can Asn of Geog. **RESEARCH** Native Canadians, Third and Fourth World Development. **SELECTED PUBLICATIONS** Coauth with R. M. Bone and T. Johnson, "Economic Growth, Community Development and Income Distribution: Northwest Territories, Canada," Ontario Geog, 38 (92): 1-11; auth, "Map Use Teaching and Experience," Cartographica, 29 (92): 3 & 4, 38-45; coauth wirh R. M. Bone,"Transportation Bibliography for the Mackenzie Basin," Dept of Geog, Univ Saskatchewan, Saskatoon (94); coauth with R. M. Bone and P. D. McPherson,"Settlement Study," in Mackenzie Basin Impact Study (MBIS) Interim Report #2, Cohen Stewart, ed, Atmospheric Environ Service, Environ Can, Downsview, Ont (94); coauth with R. M. Bone and S. Long, "Non-Renewable Resource Study: Final Report," Mackenzie Basin Impact Study, Saskatoon: Signe Res Assocs, Ltd (95); coauth with R. M. Bone and S. Long, "Settlement Study: Final Report," Mackenzie Basin Impact Study, Saskatoon: Signe Res Assocs, Ltd (95); coauth with A. Akkerman and R. M. Bone, "Qualitative Indicators of Multi-regional Demographic Change: Potential for Developing Countries," in Demographic Transition: The Third World Scenario, A. Ahmad, D. Noin, and H. N. Sharma, eds, New Delhi: Rawat Pubs (97); coauth with R. M. Bone and G. Duhaime, "Towards an Institutional Understanding of Comprehensive Land Claim Agreements in Canada," Inuit/Etudes/Studies, 22 (98): 109-121; auth, "Aboriginal Census Data: An Appraisal," The Can J of Native Studies, 20 (2000): 1; auth, "Looking for Solutions in the Canadian North: Modern Treaties as a New Strategy," The Can Geog, 44 (2000): 1. **CONTACT ADDRESS** Dept Geography, Frostburg State Univ, 101 Braddock Rd, Frostburg, MD 21532. **EMAIL** Jsaku@frostburg.edu

SALEM, JAMES M.
PERSONAL Born 11/15/1937, Portage, WI, m, 1958, 4 children **DISCIPLINE** AMERICAN STUDIES **EDUCATION** Univ Wis, BS, 61; La State Univ, PhD, 65. **CAREER** Asst Prof, Kent State Univ, 65-67; From Asst Prof to Prof, Univ Ala, 67-. **HONORS AND AWARDS** Outstanding Ref Work Awd, 70; Outstanding Educr of Am Awd, 72; Cert of Excellence for Distinguished Achievement in Commun Arts, 77; Outstanding Commitment to Teaching Awd, Univ Ala, 98. **MEMBERSHIPS** Am Cult Asn, ASA Int Asn for the Study of Popular Music, SAM, Southeastern Am Studies Asn. **RESEARCH** The 1950's, American youth culture, African-American culture, American drama. **SELECTED PUBLICATIONS** Auth, A Guide to Critical Reviews: Part I: American Drama 1909-1982, 3rd Ed, The Scarecrow Pr, 84; auth, Drury's Guide to Best Plays, 4th Ed, The Scarecrow Pr, 87; auth, A Guide to Critical Reviews: Part II: The Musical 1909-1982, 3rd Ed, The Scarecrow Pr, 91; auth, "Johnny Ace: A Case Study in the Diffusion and Transformation of Minority Culture," Propects: An Annual of Am Cult Studies, 17 (92): 211-241; auth, "Death and the Rhythm-and-Bluesman: The Life and Recordings of Johnny Ace," Am Music (93): 316-367; auth, The Late Great Johnny Ace and the Transition from R&B to Rock 'N' Roll, Univ Ill Pr, 99. **CONTACT ADDRESS** Dept Am Studies, Univ of Alabama, Tuscaloosa, Box 870214, Tuscaloosa, AL 35487-0214. **EMAIL** jsalem@tenhoor.as.ua.edu

SALIH, HALIL IBRAHIM
PERSONAL Born 02/26/1939, Kyrenia, Cyprus, m, 1989, 4 children **DISCIPLINE** POLITICAL SCIENCE, GOVERNMENT, AREA STUDIES, MIDDLE EAST AREA STUDIES, INTERNATIONAL STUDIES, INTERNATIONAL ORGANIZATIONS AND LAW **EDUCATION** Univ of Pacific, BA, 63; Am Univ, MA, 65, PhD, 67. **CAREER** Asst prof, 68-71, assoc prof, 71-81, Chr Polit Sci Dept, 73-95, Chr Soc Sci Dept, 95, prof of Political Science, 81-, Texas Wesleyan Col, 68-; Hall of Nations Scholar, 65-66; Pi Sigma Alpha, 67; Danfort Assoc, 79; Malone fel, 95. **HONORS AND AWARDS** Outstanding Educ Am, 72; Texas Wesleyan Fac Recog Award, 81 & 94; Mortar Board, 96. **MEMBERSHIPS** Mid East Inst; Am Asn Univ Prof; W Soc Sci Asn; SW Sco Sci Asn; Int Studies Asn. **RESEARCH** International law and organizations; Middle East; Greco-Turkish crisis; Cyprus. **SELECTED PUBLICATIONS** Auth Cyprus: An Analysis of Cypriot Political Discord, 68; Cyprus: The Impact of Diverse Nationalism on a State, 78. **CONTACT ADDRESS** Dept of Social Science, Texas Wesleyan Univ, 1201 Wesleyan St, Fort Worth, TX 76105. **EMAIL** salihi@txwes.edu

SALISBURY, JOYCE E.
PERSONAL Born 12/10/1944, Tucson, AZ, d, 2 children **DISCIPLINE** HISTORY **EDUCATION** Rutgers Univ, BA, 73; MA, 75; PhD, 81. **CAREER** Prof, Univ of Wis Green Bay, 81-. **HONORS AND AWARDS** Frankenthal chair of History; CASE Teacher of the Year, WI, 91. **RESEARCH** Early medieval and late antique history of religion and sexuality. **SELECTED PUBLICATIONS** Auth, Church Fathers, Independent Virgins, Verso Pr, (London), 91; ed, Sex in the Middle Ages, Garland (NY), 91; ed, Medieval World of Nature, Garland (NY), 93; auth, The Beast Within: Animals in the Middle Ages, Routledge, Chapman and Hall (NY), 94; auth, Perpetua's Passion: Death and Memory of a Young Roman Woman, Routledge, Chapman and Hall, 97; auth, The West in the World: A Mid-Length History, McGraw Hill, (NY), 00; auth, An Encyclopedia of Women in the Ancient World, (forthcoming). **CONTACT ADDRESS** Dept Hist, Univ of Wisconsin, Green Bay, 2420 Nicolet Dr, Green Bay, WI 54311-7003. **EMAIL** salisbuj@uwgb.edu

SALISBURY, NEAL
PERSONAL Born 05/07/1940, Los Angeles, CA, m, 1970, 1 child **DISCIPLINE** HISTORY **EDUCATION** Univ Of Calif at LA, BA, 63, MA, 66, PhD, 72. **CAREER** PROF, HIST, SMITH COLL **HONORS AND AWARDS** Fel, Smithsonian Institution, 72-73; fel, Center for the Hist of the Am Indian, Newberry Libr, 77-78; fel, Nat Endowment for the Humanities, 84-85; fel, Charles Warren Center for Studies in Am Hist, Harvard Univ, 89; fel, Nat Humanities Center, 91-92; fel, Am Antiquarian Soc, 95-96; fel, Am Coun of Learned Societies, 00-01. **MEMBERSHIPS** Am Antiquarian Soc; Am Historical Asn; Am Soc for Ethnohistory; Associates of the Omohundro Inst of Early Am Hist and Culture; Orgn of Am Historians; Soc of Early Americanists. **RESEARCH** Native peoples of North Am; Colonial North Am. **SELECTED PUBLICATIONS** Auth, Manitou and Providence: Indians, Europeans, and the Making of New England, 1500-1643, Oxford Univ Press, 82; auth, "The Indians' Old World: Native Americans and the Coming of Europeans," Wm & Mary Quart 53, 96; ed with introd, The Sovereignty and Goodness of God, Bedford Books, 97; coauth, Enduring Vision: A Hist of the Am People, Houghton Mifflin, 00. **CONTACT ADDRESS** Dept of Hist, Smith Col, Northampton, MA 01063. **EMAIL** nsalisbu@smith.edu

SALISBURY, RICHARD VANALSTYNE
PERSONAL Born 10/12/1940, Oswego, NY, m, 1966, 3 children **DISCIPLINE** LATIN AMERICAN HISTORY **EDUCATION** Hamilton Col, AB, 62; Univ Wis, MA, 63; Univ KS, PhD, 69. **CAREER** Asst prof hist, State Univ NY Col Geneseo, 69-76; assoc prof, 76-80; prof hist, Western KY Univ, 80, Vis asst prof hist, AZ State Univ, 73-74. **HONORS AND AWARDS** Distinguished Univ Prof. **MEMBERSHIPS** Latin Am Studies Asn; Conf Latin Am Hist; Soc Historians Am For Rels. **RESEARCH** Central Am international rel, espec in the 20th century; for influence in Central Am. **SELECTED PUBLICATIONS** Auth, The Anti-Imperialist Career of Alejandro Alvarado Quiros, Hisp Am Hist Rev, 11/77; Costa Rica and the 1924 Honduran Crisis, Revista de Historia, 1/78; Jorge Volio and Isthmian Revolutionary Politics, Red River Valley Hist J World Hist, summer, 80; Good Neighbors? The United States and Latin America in the Twentieth Century, In: American Foreign Relations, A Historiographical Review, Greenwood Press, 81; The Middle American Exile of Victor Raul Maya de La Torre, The Americas, 7/83; Mexico, The United States, and the 1926-1927 Nicaraguan Crisis, Hisp Am Hist Rev, 5/86; Revolution and Recognition: A British Perspective on Isthmian Affairs During the 1920's, The Americas, 1/92; Great Britain, The United States, and the 1909-1910 Nicaraguan Crisis, The Americas, 1/97; Costa Rica y el Istmo, 1900-1934, Editorial de Costa Rica, 84; Anti-Imperialism and International Competition in Central America, 1920-1929, Sch Resources, 89. **CONTACT ADDRESS** Dept of Hist, Western Kentucky Univ, 1 Big Red Way St, Bowling Green, KY 42101-3576. **EMAIL** richard.salisbury@wku.edu

SALLER, RICHARD
PERSONAL Born 10/18/1952, NC, m, 1974, 2 children **DISCIPLINE** CLASSICAL HISTORY **EDUCATION** Univ Ill, BA, 74; Cambridge Univ, PhD, 78. **CAREER** Asst prof, Swarthmore Col, 79-84; assoc to full prof, Univ Chicago, 84-, DEAN, SOC SCI DIV, UNIV CHICAGO, 94-. **MEMBERSHIPS** Am Philol Asn, Am Hist Asn **RESEARCH** Roman soc and econ hist. **SELECTED PUBLICATIONS** Auth, Patriarchy, Property, and Death in the Roman Family, 94, Cambridge Press; co-ed, The Family in Italy from Antiquity to the Present, 91, Yale Univ Press; auth, "The Social Dynamics of Consent to Marriage and Sexual Relations: The Evidence of Roman Comedy," in Consent and Coercion to Sex and Marriage in Ancient and Medieval Societies, 93; coauth, "Foucault on Sexuality in Greco-Roman Antiquity," in Foucault and the Writing of History," 94; auth, "The Hierarchical Household in Roman Society: A Study of Domestic Slavery," in Serfdom and Slavery, 96; auth, "Roman Kinship: Structure and Sentiment," in The Roman Family in Italy: Status, Sentiment, Space, 97. **CONTACT ADDRESS** Dept of Classics, Univ of Chicago, 1126 E 59th St, Chicago, IL 60637. **EMAIL** sall@midway.uchicago.edu

SALLIS, CHARLES
DISCIPLINE SOUTHERN HISTORY AND ETHNIC AND CULTURAL DIVERSITY **EDUCATION** Univ Ky, PhD. **CAREER** Prof & past dept ch and past dir, Heritage Prog; fac, Millsaps Col, 68-; past tutor, Brit Stud Prog, Oxford Univ, 5 summers sessions. **HONORS AND AWARDS** Millsaps Distinquished prof, 73; 2 Nat Endowment for the Humanities fel(s); Southern Reg Council's Lillian Smith awd, 75. **SELECTED PUBLICATIONS** Coauth, Mississippi: Conflict and Change. **CONTACT ADDRESS** Dept of History, Millsaps Col, 1701 N State St, Jackson, MS 39210. **EMAIL** salliwc@okra.millsaps.edu

SALMON, JOHN HEARSEY MCMILLAN
PERSONAL Born 12/02/1925, Thames, New Zealand **DISCIPLINE** EARLY MODERN HISTORY, FRENCH LITERATURE **EDUCATION** Victoria Univ Wellington, BA, 50, MA, 52, LittD(hist), 70; MLitt, Cambridge Univ, 57. **CAREER** Approved lectr hist, Cambridge Univ, 55-57; lectr, Victoria Univ

Wellington, 57-60; prof, Univ NSW, 60-65 & Univ Waikato, NZ, 65-69; prof, 69-71, Marjorie Walter Goodhart Prof Hist, Bryn Mawr Col, 71-, Ed bds, Fr Hist Studies, Sixteenth Century J & J Mod Hist. **MEMBERSHIPS** AHA; fel Royal Hist Soc; Soc Fr Hist Studies. **RESEARCH** Early modern French history; French literature in the early modern period; French political theory. **SELECTED PUBLICATIONS** Auth, The French Religious Wars in English Political Thought, Clarendon, 59 & Greenwood Press, 81; A History of Goldmining in New Zealand, NZ Govt Printer, 63; ed, The French Wars of Religion: How Important Were Religious Factors, Heath, 67; auth, Cardinal de Retz, Weidenfeld & Nicholson, 69; co-ed, Francogallia by Francois Hotman, Cambridge Univ, 72; Society in Crisis: France in the Sixteenth Century, St Martin's, 75 & Methuen, 2nd ed, 79; French satire in the late sixteenth century, Sixteenth Century J, 75; Cicero and Tacitus in sixteenth-century France, Am Hist Res, 80. **CONTACT ADDRESS** Dept of Hist, Bryn Mawr Col, Bryn Mawr, PA 19010.

SALOMON, RICHARD
PERSONAL Born 08/12/1948, New York, NY, m, 1970, 1 child **DISCIPLINE** SANSKRIT **EDUCATION** Univ Pa, PhD, 75. **CAREER** From Asst Prof to Prof, Univ Wash, 81-. **HONORS AND AWARDS** Guggenheim Feel; Saionji For Area Studies Feel; 3 NEH Fels. **MEMBERSHIPS** Am Orient Soc, Int Assoc. of Buddhist Studies, Am Acad of Relig, Royal Asiatic Soc. **RESEARCH** Sanskrit language and literature, Indian epigraphy, Gandharon studies. **SELECTED PUBLICATIONS** Auth, "Five Kharosthi Inscriptions," Bull of the Asia Inst 10 (96): 233-246; auth, "South Asia Writing Systems: Introduction," in The World's Writing Systems (NY: Oxford Univ Pr, 96), 371-372; auth, "An Inscribed Silver Buddhist Reliquary of the Time of King Kharaosta and Prince Indravarman," J of the Am Orient Soc 116 (96): 418-452; auth, "A Preliminary Survey of Some Early Buddhist Manuscripts Recently Acquired by the British Library," J of the Am Orient Soc 117 (97): 353-358; auth, Indian Epigraphy: A Guide to the Study of Inscriptions in the Indo-Aryan Languages, Oxford Univ Pr (New York, NY), 98; auth, Ancient Buddhist Scrolls from Gandhara: The British Library Kharosthi Fragments, Univ Wash Pr/British Libr (Seattle, WA/London, UK), 99. **CONTACT ADDRESS** Dept Lang, Univ of Washington, PO Box 353521, Seattle, WA 98195. **EMAIL** rsalomon@u.washington.edu

SALVAGGIO, RUTH
PERSONAL Born 04/25/1951, New Orelans, LA **DISCIPLINE** AMERICAN STUDIES **EDUCATION** Rice Univ, PhD, 79. **CAREER** Prof, Univ NMex Albuquerque, 90-. **MEMBERSHIPS** MLA, Am Studies Asn. **SELECTED PUBLICATIONS** Auth, "Druden's Dualities," Englidh Lit Studies Ser, Univ of Victoria, 83; auth, Enlightened Absence: Neoclassical Configurations of the Feminine, Univ of Ill Press (Urbana), 88; co-ed, Women Critics, 1660-1820, Ind Univ Press (Bloomington), 95. **CONTACT ADDRESS** Dept Am Studies, Univ of New Mexico, Albuquerque, 1 Univ Campus, Albuquerque, NM 87131-0001. **EMAIL** salvagio@unm.edu

SALVATORE, NICHOLAS ANTHONY
PERSONAL Born 11/14/1943, Brooklyn, NY, m, 1974, 2 children **DISCIPLINE** HISTORY **EDUCATION** Hunter Col, BA, 68; Univ Calif, Berkeley, MA, 69, PhD, 77. **CAREER** Instr, Col Holy Cross, 76-77, asst prof hist, 77-81; from Asst Prof to Assoc Prof Hist, 81-92, Prof Hist, NY State Sch Indust & Labor Res, Cornell Univ, 93-, Prof Am Studies, Cornell Univ, 95-. **HONORS AND AWARDS** Batchelor fel hist, Col Holy Cross, 78; NEH fel, 79-80; Bancroft Prize in American History, 83; Outstanding Academic Book, Choice Magazine, 83; John H. Dunning Prize, 84; NEH fel, 88-89; New England Hist Asn Outstanding Book Awd, 96; Senior Fel, Inst for Adv Study of Rel, Yale Univ, 99-00. **MEMBERSHIPS** AHA; Orgn Am Historians; Soc Am Hist. **RESEARCH** American labor history; American socialism; Afro-American history. **SELECTED PUBLICATIONS** Auth, Eugene V Debs: Citizen and Socialist, Univ Ill Press, 82; ed, Seventy Years of Life and Labor, ILR Press, 84; auth, We All Got History: The Memory Books of Amos Webber, Times Books/Random House, 96. **CONTACT ADDRESS** American Studies and ILR, Cornell Univ, 290 Ives Hall, Ithaca, NY 14853-0001. **EMAIL** nas4@cornell.edu

SALVUCCI, LINDA KERRIGAN
PERSONAL Born 05/28/1951, Pittston, PA, m, 1973, 2 children **DISCIPLINE** HISTORY **EDUCATION** Villanova Univ, BA, 73; Princeton Univ, MA, 79, PhD, 85. **CAREER** Asst prof, 85-91, assoc prof, hist, 91- , Trinity Univ. **HONORS AND AWARDS** Hubert Herring Awd, Pacific Coast Coun on Latin Am Stud, 85; NEH fel, 88-89; vis scholar, center for Latin Am Stud, Univ Calif, Berkeley, 88-89; Lydia Cabrera Awd for Cuban Hist Stud, Conf on Latin Am Hist, 95; Am Philos Soc grant, 97. **MEMBERSHIPS** Am Hist Asn; Nat Counc on Hist Educ; Conf on Latin Am Hist; Omohundro Inst of Early Am Hist and Culture. **RESEARCH** Early America; Atlantic empires; colonial Cuba; U.S. history textbooks. **SELECTED PUBLICATIONS** Coauth, The Politics of Protection: Interpreting Commercial Policy in Late Bourbon and Early National Mexico, in Andrien, ed, The Political Economy of Spanish America in the Age of Revolution, 1750-1850, New Mexico, 94; auth, Did NAFTA Rewrite History? Recent Mexican Views of the United States Past, J of Am Hist, 95; coauth, Call to Freedom: Beginnings to 1914, Holt, Rinehart & Winston, 98; coauth, "Cuba and the Latin American Terms of Trade: Old Theories, New Evidence," Journal of Interdisciplinary History, XXXI: 2, Autumn, 00, 197-222, coathored with Richard Salvucci. **CONTACT ADDRESS** Dept of History, Trinity Univ, 715 Stadium Dr, San Antonio, TX 78212-7200. **EMAIL** lsalvucc@trinity.edu

SALYER, LUCY
DISCIPLINE HISTORY HISTORY **EDUCATION** Univ Calif, Berkeley, PhD. **CAREER** Assoc prof, Univ NH, 89-. **HONORS AND AWARDS** NEH fel; Am Coun for Learned Soc fel; Louis Pelzer Mem Awd, J of Am Hist; Theodore Saloutos Mem Awd, Immigration Hist Soc, 96. **RESEARCH** Social and legal history of American citizenship. **SELECTED PUBLICATIONS** Auth, "Captives of Law: Judicial Enforcement of the Chinese Exclusion Laws," J of Am Hist 76 (89); auth, Laws Harsh as Tigers: Chinese Immigrants and the Shaping of Modern Immigration Law, 95; contribur, Entry Denied: Exclusion and the Chinese Community in America, 1882-1943, 91. **CONTACT ADDRESS** Univ of New Hampshire, Durham, Durham, NH 03824. **EMAIL** les@christa.unh.edu

SALZMAN, MICHELE
PERSONAL Born 08/02/1952, Brooklyn, NY, m, 1985, 2 children **DISCIPLINE** HISTORY **EDUCATION** CUNY, Brooklyn, BA, 73; Bryn Mawr Col, MA, 75; PhD, 81. **CAREER** Lectr, Swarthmore Col, 80; asst prof, Columbia Univ, 80-82; asst to assoc prof, Boston Univ, 82-95; assoc prof, Univ of Calif, 95-; chair, 99-. **HONORS AND AWARDS** Phi Beta Kappa; Massenzia Fel, Rome, 77-78; Whiting Fel, 78-79; Res Grants, Columbia Univ, 81, 82; Res Grant, Boston Univ, 83; Res Fel, ACLS, 83; Mellon Fel, 86-87; Richard Krautheimer Fel, 87; ACLS Grant, 90. **MEMBERSHIPS** Am Philog Assoc; Assoc of Ancient Hist; N Am Patristic Soc. **RESEARCH** Late Antiquity, Roman Religion, The History of Greece and Rome, Women in the Ancient World **SELECTED PUBLICATIONS** Auth, On Roman Time: The Codex-Calendar of 354 and the Rhythms of Urban Life in Late Antiquity, Univ of Calif Pr, 90; auth, The Making of a Christian Aristocracy: Religious and Social Change in the Later Roman Empire, Harvard Univ Pr, (forthcoming); auth, The Select Letters of Symmachus: Text and Translation, Univ of Liverpool Pr, (forthcoming). **CONTACT ADDRESS** Dept Hist, Univ of California, Riverside, 900 University Ave, Riverside, CA 92521-0001. **EMAIL** michele.salzman@ucr.edu

SALZMAN, NEIL
PERSONAL Born 10/25/1940, Brooklyn, NY, m, 1986, 3 children **DISCIPLINE** HISTORY **EDUCATION** City Col NYork, BA, 62, MA, 65; Grad Ctr CUNY, MA, 77; NYork Univ, PhD, 73. **CAREER** Instr of Hist, 70-75, Asst prof Polit Sci, 75-80, Assoc prof Polit Sci, 80-91, Prof Polit Sci & Hist, Fairleigh Dickinson Univ, 91- . **HONORS AND AWARDS** NY State Regents Scholar, 58-62; NY State Scholar Incentive Awd, 65-69; Grad Fel, CUNY, 68; Univ Res Grant-in-Aid, 88-89; Tchg Released Time for Res, 88, 89, 93, 96, 97; Univ Res Grant-in-Aid, 93-94; Tchr of the Year, 94-95. **RESEARCH** Am Polit Sci Asn; Am Hist Asn; Am Asn Univ Prof; Orgn Am Hist. **SELECTED PUBLICATIONS** Rev, Alternative Paths: Soviets and Americans, 1917-1920, 'Festschrift for N V Riasanovsky, Russian Hist, 93; rev, War Revolution and Peace in Russia: The Passages of Frank Golder, 1914-1917, "Festschrift for N V Riasanovsky, Russian Hist, 93; auth, Reform and Revolution: The Life and Times of Raymond Robins, Kent State Univ Press, 94; The Jewish Currents Reader: 1986-1996, Asn Promotion Jewish Secularism, 98; Russia in War and Revolution: General William V. Judson's Accounts from Petrograd, 1917-1918, Kent State Univ Press, 98. **CONTACT ADDRESS** 147 Old Camby Road, Verbank, NY 12585-5215. **EMAIL** grnsalzman@worldnet.att.net

SAMAHA, JOEL
DISCIPLINE HISTORY **EDUCATION** Northwestern Univ, JD; PhD. **CAREER** Prof **RESEARCH** Criminal justice history. **SELECTED PUBLICATIONS** Auth, Law and Order in Historical Perspective, 74; Sedition in Elizabethan Essex, 79; A Case of Murder: The Rule of Law in Minnesota, 1860, 76; Hanging for Felony: The Rule of Law in Elizabethan Colchester, 79; The Recognizance in tudor Law Enforcement, 80; Descretion and the Anglo-Saxon Books of Penitentials, 83; John Winthrop and the Criminal Law, 89; Criminal Law, 90; Criminal Justice, 89; Criminal Procedure, 90. **CONTACT ADDRESS** History Dept, Univ of Minnesota, Twin Cities, 614 Social Sciences Tower, 267 19th Ave S, Minneapolis, MN 55455. **EMAIL** jsamaha@tc.umn.edu

SAMATAR, ABDI I.
DISCIPLINE GEOGRAPHY **EDUCATION** Univ Calif at Berkeley, PhD, 85. **CAREER** Assoc Prof, Univ of Minn, 93-; Chief Res Assoc, Human Sci Res Coun, Pretoria Safrica, 97-. **HONORS AND AWARDS** Sr Fulbright Fel; MacArthur Found Res Grant; Excellence in Teaching Awd. **RESEARCH** Development, Public Institutions, Ethnicity, Africa. **SELECTED PUBLICATIONS** Auth, The State and Rural Transformation, UW Press (Madison), 89; auth, "Leadership and Ethnicity in the Making of African State Models: Botswana Versus Somalia," Third World Quart 18-4 (97): 687-707; auth, "Development Geography and the Third World State," Progress in Human Geog 21-2 (97); auth, "Industrial Strategy and the African State: The Botswana Experience," Can J of African Studies 31-2 (97): 268-299; auth, An African Miracle: Botswana, Heineman (Portsmouth), 99. **CONTACT ADDRESS** Geog, Univ of Minnesota, Twin Cities, 267 19th Ave S, 414 Soc Sci Bldg, Minneapolis, MN 55455. **EMAIL** samat001@maroon.tc.umn.edu

SAMUDIO, JEFFREY
PERSONAL Born 10/03/1966, San Gabriel, CA, s **DISCIPLINE** ARCHITECTURE **EDUCATION** Univ of Southern Calif, Bachelor of Archit; Archit Licensing, 98; Nat Trust for Historic Preservation Leadership Training, 93. **CAREER** Student asst slide libr curator, Archit & Fine Arts Image Center, 84-87, Freeman House Fel, School of Archit Frank Lloyd Wright Historic Site, 92-93, guest lectr, School of Archit, 92-95, assoc dir &co-founder, Prog in Historic Preservation, 93-96, instr, School of Archit & School of Urban Planning and Development, USC; instr, Los Angeles Trad-Tech Col and Rio Hondo Col, 89-97; VP of Acquistions and Project Development, Northeast Design and Development Group, Inc, 89-90; INSTR, 95, ADVISORY BOARD MEMBER, 97-, CAL POLY POMONA SCHOOL OF ENVIRONMENTAL DESIGN, 97-; ASSOC PROF, 97-, ENVIROMENTAL DESIGN DEPT, AM INTERCONTINENTAL UNIV; DIR & FOUNDER, CENTER FOR PRESERVATION ED AND PLANNING, 94-; PARTNER, DESIGN AID, ARCHIT PLANNING PRESERVATION, 87-. **HONORS AND AWARDS** Awd of Honor, Am Inst of Archits; 1995 Hist Preservation Awd, Los Angeles Conservancy, 95; Certificate of Appreciation, City of Los Angeles, 84 & 89; Outstanding Service to the Profession Awd, AIA, 91; Phi Kappa Phi Res Mentorship Awd, USC Grad School, 91; Freeman House Res Grant, Graham Found, 91; Grants for Diversity, Nat Trust for Hist Preservation & Getty Found, 92 & 96; Nat Trust for Hist Preservation Grant, 93; Getty Grant, USC Prog in Hist Preservation, 93; Nat Trust for Hist Preservation Grant, 93; Nat Park Service, USC Prog in Hist Preservation-Training Center, 95-96; Loyola Found of Washington-Marist Convent Fiji, 97; World Monuments Fund-Preservation Management, 97; Co-Sponsor for Confr on His Roads in Am, Nat Park Service, 98. **MEMBERSHIPS** Am Inst of Archits; Am Planning Asn; Soc of Archit Historians/SCC; Los Angeles City Hist Soc; Int Commt on Monuments and Sites; Nat Main St Roundtable; Nat Preservation Forum of the Nat Trust for Hist Preservation; Los Angeles Conservancy Asn for Preservation Tech APT. **RESEARCH** Historic preservation. **SELECTED PUBLICATIONS** Auth, Why the Heritage of the South Pacific is Important in a Eurocentric World, Soc of Archit Historians Rev, 97; auth, Preservation in Culturally Diverse Communities, Diversity and Architects, 95. **CONTACT ADDRESS** Design Aid Architects, 1722 N Whitley Ave, Hollywood, CA 90028. **EMAIL** daid@pacbell.net

SANABRIA, SERGIO LUIS
PERSONAL Born 10/14/1944, Havana, Cuba, m **DISCIPLINE** ARCHITECTURAL HISTORY **EDUCATION** Princeton Univ, PhD, 84. **CAREER** Assoc prof, Miami Univ, 80- . **HONORS AND AWARDS** Samuel Kress Publication Awd, Archit Hist Found; Miami Univ fac res grants. **MEMBERSHIPS** SAH, SHOT, CAA. **RESEARCH** Gothic and Renaissance architecture in France and Spain. **SELECTED PUBLICATIONS** Auth, From Gothic to Renaissance Sterotomy: Design Methods of Philibert de l'Orme and Alonso de Vandelvira, Technol and Cult, 89; auth, A Late Gothic Drawing of San Juan de los Reyes in Toledo at the Prado Museum in Madrid, Jour of the Soc of Archit Historians, 92; auth, La Lave de la Catedral Neuva de Salamanca, El Siglo de Oro en Salamanca, 95; auth with Kristina Luce, The Rayonnant Gothic Buttresses at Metz Cathedral, The Cathedral, the Mill, and the Mine: Essays on Medieval Technology, 97; Rodrigo Gil and the Classical Transformation of Gothic Architecture in the Spanish Golden Age, 99. **CONTACT ADDRESS** Dept of Archit, Miami Univ, Oxford, OH 45056. **EMAIL** sanabrsl@muohio.edu

SANCHEZ, GEORGE J.
DISCIPLINE HISTORY **EDUCATION** Harvard Col, BA, 81; Stanford Univ, MA, 84, PhD, 89. **CAREER** Dir, Chicano/Latino Stud Prog; assoc prof, Univ Southern Calif, 97-; assoc prof, Univ Mich, 93-97; asst prof, UCLA, 88-93; Andrew Norman Lect, Colo Col, 96; William Andrews Clark Mem Libr prof, UCLA, 93-94; Ford Found post-doc fel, 90-91; dir, Prog in Amer Cult, Univ Mich, 94-97. **HONORS AND AWARDS** Local History awd, Southern Calif Hist Soc, 97; Theodore Saloutus Mem Bk awd, Immigration Hist Soc, 94; Bk awd, Pac Coast Branch, Amer Hist Asn, 94; Robert Athearn Bk prize, Western Hist Asn, 94; J.S. Holliday awd, Calif Hist Soc, 94; New Scholar awd, Amer Educ Res Asn, 95. **MEMBERSHIPS** Amer Stud Asn, 97-; Latino Adv Comt, National Mus of Amer Hist, Smithsonian Inst, 95-; Comt on Int Migration, Soc Sci Res Coun, 94-. **SELECTED PUBLICATIONS** Auth, Becoming Mexican American: Ethnicity, Culture and Identity in Chicano Los Angeles, 1900-1945, NY: Oxford UP, 93; Face the Nation: Race, Immigration, and the Rise of Nativism in Late Twentieth Century America, Int Migration Rev 31:4, 97; Ethnicity, in A

Companion to American Thought, Blackwell, 97; Reading Reginald Denny: The Politics of Whiteness in Late Twentieth Century America, in Amer Quart 47:3, 95; The 'New Nationalism,' Mexican Style: Race and Progressivism in Chicano Political Development during the 1920s, in Calif Progressivism Revisited, Berkeley: Univ Calif Press, 94; Assessing Relations Between Mexican Americans and the Japanese, in Relations Between American Ethnic Groups and Japan, Tokyo: NIRA, 94; coauth, Contemporary Peoples/Contested Places, in The Oxford Hist of the Amer West, NY: Oxford UP, 94; ser co-ed, American Crossroads: New Works in Ethnic Studies, Univ Calif Press. With Earl Lewis, Univ Mich, George Lipsitz, UC, San Diego, Peggy Pascoe, Univ Oregon, and Dana Takagi, UC, Santa Cruz, 94-: Pages from History: Documentary Series for Secondary Schools, Oxford UP, With Sarah Deutsch, Clark Univ, Emily Honig, UC, Santa Cruz, Carol Karlsen, Univ Mich, and Robert Moeller, UC, Irvine. 94-. **CONTACT ADDRESS** Dept of History, Univ of So California, University Park Campus, Los Angeles, CA 90089. **EMAIL** georges@rcf.usc.edu

SANCHEZ, JOSE MARIANO
PERSONAL Born 11/01/1932, Santa Fe, NM, m, 1956, 5 children **DISCIPLINE** 20TH CENTURY EUROPEAN HISTORY **EDUCATION** St Louis Univ, BS, 54, AM, 57; Univ NMex, PhD, 61. **CAREER** From instr to assoc prof, 60-69, chmn dept, 71-74, prof hist, St. Lous Univ, 69-. **MEMBERSHIPS** AHA; Am Cath Hist Assn; Soc Span & Port Hist Studies. **RESEARCH** Modern Spanish history; 20th century Europe. **SELECTED PUBLICATIONS** Auth, Reform and Reaction: The Politico-Religious Background of the Spanish Civil War, Univ NC, 64;auth, Anticlericalism: A Brief History, Univ Notre Dame, 72; coauth & contribr, Great Events From History: Modern Europe, Salem, 73; auth, The Spanish Civil War As A Religious Tragedy, University of Notre Dame Press, 87. **CONTACT ADDRESS** Dept of History, Saint Louis Univ, 221 N Grand Blvd, Saint Louis, MO 63103-2097. **EMAIL** sanchejm@slu.edu.

SANDAGE, SCOTT A.
DISCIPLINE HISTORY **EDUCATION** Univ Iowa, BA, 85; Rutgers Univ, MA, 92, PhD, 95. **CAREER** ASST PROF, HIST, CARNEGIE MELLON UNIV **HONORS AND AWARDS** NE Assn of Grad Schools Prize, 95-96. **MEMBERSHIPS** Am Antiquarian Soc **SELECTED PUBLICATIONS** Auth, "A Marble House Divided: The Lincoln Memorial, the Civil Rights Movement, and the Politics of Memory, 1939-1963," Jour of Am Hist 80, 93, repr in Race and the Invention of Modern Nationalism, Garland Press; auth, Defeats and Dreams: A Cultural History of Failure in Nineteenth-Century America, Harvard Univ Press; auth, "The Gaze of Success: Failed Men and the Sentimental Marketplace, 1873-1893," in Sentimental Men: Sentimentality and Masculinity in American Fiction and Culture. **CONTACT ADDRESS** Dept of Hist, Carnegie Mellon Univ, BH240, Pittsburgh, PA 15213-2878. **EMAIL** sandage@andrew.cmu.edu

SANDERS, LIONEL
PERSONAL Born 05/21/1942, Hitchin, United Kingdom, d, 1 child **DISCIPLINE** HISTORY; CLASSICS **EDUCATION** McMaster, PHD **CAREER** Lect, 70-71, Univ Kingston, Ont; Asst Prof, 72-74, Loyola Col, Montreal; Assoc Prof, 76-96, Concordia Univ, Montreal; Full Prof, 96-pres, Concordia Univ **MEMBERSHIPS** Hellenic Soc; Canadian Class Assoc; Am Philol Assoc **RESEARCH** History and Historiography of Greek Sicily **SELECTED PUBLICATIONS** Auth, "Plato's First Visit to Sicily," Kokalos, 79, 207-19; auth, "Dionysius I of Syracuse and the Validity of the Hostile Tradition," SCI, 79, 64-84; auth, "Diodorus Siculus and Dionysius I of Syracuse," Historia, 81, 394-411. **CONTACT ADDRESS** Dept. Of Classics Modern Langs, Concordia Univ, Montreal, 1435 De Maisonneuve Blvd W, Montreal, QC, Canada H3G 1M8. **EMAIL** sanders@alcor.concordia.ca

SANDFORD, GEORGE W.
PERSONAL Born 07/31/1947, Elizabeth, NJ, m, 1974, 2 children **DISCIPLINE** HISTORY **EDUCATION** Denison Univ, BA, 70; Univ Wis Madison, MA, 75; PhD, 79. **CAREER** For Serv Officer, US State Dept For Serv, 80-98; Asst Prof, Principia Col, 98-. **MEMBERSHIPS** Am Coun on Ger, Am For Serv Asn. **RESEARCH** German Democratic Republic (Former East Germany). **SELECTED PUBLICATIONS** Auth, From Hitler to Ulbricht: The Communist Reconstruction of East Germany, 1945-46, Princeton, 83; coauth, Grenada: The Untold Story, Madison Books, 84. **CONTACT ADDRESS** Dept of Hist, Principia Col, Elsah, IL 62028. **EMAIL** gws@prin.edu

SANDLER, LUCY FREEMAN
PERSONAL Born 06/07/1930, New York, NY, m, 1958, 1 child **DISCIPLINE** ART HISTORY **EDUCATION** Queens Col, BA, 51; Columbia Univ, MA, 57; NYork Univ, PhD, 64. **CAREER** Asst ed, Art Bull, 63-67; from asst prof to prof, hist of art, Washington Sq Col, NY Univ, 64-; ed, Col Art Asn Am Monogr Ser, 70-75, 86-89; chemn, dept Fine Arts, NYork Univ, 75-88. **HONORS AND AWARDS** Nat Endowment for Humanities fel for independent study & res, 67-68,77; Nat Found Arts & Humanities grant, 67-68; Guggenheim fel, 88-89; Fel of the Soc of Antiquaries of London, 91-; fel, Medieval Acad of Am, 97-. **MEMBERSHIPS** Col Art Asn Am (secy, 78-80, vpres, 80-81, pres, 81-); Int Ctr Medieval Art; AAUP; Medieval Academy of Am. **RESEARCH** Medieval art; illuminated manuscripts. **SELECTED PUBLICATIONS** Auth, The Peterborough Psalter in Brussels and Other Fenland Manuscripts, London and NYork, 74; auth, The Psalter of Robert de Lisle in the British Libr, London and NYork, 83; auth, Gothic Manuscripts, 1285-1385 (A Survey of Manuscripts Illuminated in the British Isles, Vol V), London and NYork, 86; auth, The Age of Chivalry, English Art 1200-1400, Royal Academy (London), 87); auth, Omne bonum: A Fourteenth Century Encyclopedia of Universal Knowledge, London, 96; auth, The Ramsey Psalter, Graz, 97; auth, The Ramsey Psalter, Graz, 99; auth, The Psalter of Robert de Lisle in the British Libr, London, revised ed, 99; auth, "Psalter," in Enciclopedia dell'arte medievale (Rome), in press. **CONTACT ADDRESS** Dept of Fine Arts, New York Univ, 100 Washington Sq E, New York, NY 10003-6688. **EMAIL** ls5@is2.nyu.edu

SANDOR, MONICA A.
PERSONAL Born 12/06/1960, Montreal, QC, Canada **DISCIPLINE** HISTORY **EDUCATION** Queen's Univ, BA, 83; Univ Toronto, MA, 84; PhD, 91. **CAREER** Manuscript ed, Univ Toronto Pr, 86-91; asst prof, Queen's Univ, 91-. **HONORS AND AWARDS** Mellon Fel, 83-86; Ont Grad Scholar, 86-87. **MEMBERSHIPS** Medieval Acad; CSM; SSCS; EHS. **RESEARCH** Medieval spirituality; popular piety; monastic history; female spirituality; church history. **CONTACT ADDRESS** Hist Dept, Queen's Univ at Kingston, Kingston, ON, Canada K7L 3N6. **EMAIL** sandorm@qsilver.queensu.ca

SANDOS, JAMES A.
DISCIPLINE HISTORY **EDUCATION** Univ Calif Berkeley, PhD, 78. **CAREER** Prof, Univ Redlands. **RESEARCH** Latin America history; California Indian history; Vietnam and Guerrilla warfare in the 20th century. **SELECTED PUBLICATIONS** Auth, From 'Boltonlands' to 'Weberlands' The Borderlands Enter American History, Am Quarterly, 94; Rebellion in the Borderlands: Anarchism and the Plan of San Diego, 1904-1923, Univ Okla, 92; Christianization Among the Chumash: An Ethnohistoric Perspective, Am Indian Quarterly, 91. **CONTACT ADDRESS** History Dept, Univ of Redlands, 1200 E Colton Ave, Box 3090, Redlands, CA 92373-0999. **EMAIL** sandos@uor.edu

SANDWEISS, MARTHA
PERSONAL Born St. Louis, Missouri, m, 2 children **DISCIPLINE** AMERICAN HISTORY **EDUCATION** Yale Univ, doctorate. **CAREER** Cur, Amon Carter Mus, Ft Worth, 79-89; prof, Amherst Col, 89-; dir, Mead Art Mus, Amherst Col, 89-97. **RESEARCH** The cult hist of photography in the Am West during the 19th-century. **SELECTED PUBLICATIONS** Auth, Laura Gilpin: An Enduring Grace, 86; coauth, Eyewitness to War: Prints and Daguerreotypes of the Mexican War,1846-1848, 89; ed, Photography in Nineteenth-Century America, 91; coed, Oxford History of the American West, 94. **CONTACT ADDRESS** Amherst Col, Amherst, MA 01002-5000.

SANDY, KITY
PERSONAL Born 03/17/1950, Chicago, IL, s **DISCIPLINE** HISTORY OF ART **EDUCATION** Northwestern Univ, BA, 71; Univ Chicago, MA, 74, PhD, 81. **CAREER** Univ Md, Col Pk, 96-. **HONORS AND AWARDS** Curated, A Hidden Treasure: Japanese Woodblock Prints from the James Austin Collection, travelling exhibition, Carnegie Mus Art, Det Inst Art, Mus Middlebury Coll, opened Sep 97. **SELECTED PUBLICATIONS** Auth, A Hidden Treasure: Japanese Prints in the James Austin Collection, Carnegie Inst, 95; auth, The Last Tosa: Iwasa Katsumochi Matabei, Bridge to Ukiyo-e, Univ Hawaii Press, 99; auth, Kaikoku michi no ki, a 17th cen travelogue by Iwasa Matabei, Monumenta Serica XLV, 97; auth, A Court Painting of a Fast Bull in the Cleveland Museum of Art, Orientations, Sept 91; entries on Hiroshige and Munakata Shiko in the Handbook of the Carnegie Museum of Art, Carnegie Museum of Art, 95; review of Ukiyo-e Paintings in the British Museum by Timothy Clark, J Asian Stud, 94; The Bulls of Chomyo-Ji A joint work by Sotatsu and Mitsuhiro, Monumenta Nipponica vol 47, no 7, Winter, 1992; The Elvehjem Museum Yanone Goro: A late Example of the Torii tradition Oriental Art XXXIV; No. 2 (Summer 1988). **CONTACT ADDRESS** 2601 Park Ctr Dr, Alexandria, VA 22302. **EMAIL** sk150@umail.umd.edu

SANFORD, DANIEL
DISCIPLINE INTERNATIONAL STUDIES **EDUCATION** Univ Denver, PhD. **CAREER** Dir, Grad Sch Intl Mg, Whitworth col; prof-. **HONORS AND AWARDS** Fulbright scholar, Univ Kiemyung, Daegu, Korea; res fel, Univ Calif, Berkeley.; former pres, world trade coun; northwest intl edu assn. **MEMBERSHIPS** Mem, Spokane Mayor's Comm Intl Devel; Spokane Chamber of Com Intl Steering Comm. **RESEARCH** International political economy with focus on trade politics in Northeast Asia. **SELECTED PUBLICATIONS** Auth, South Korea and the Socialist Countries; The Politics of Trade. **CONTACT ADDRESS** Dept of Hist, Whitworth Col, 300 West Hawthorne Rd, Spokane, WA 99251. **EMAIL** dsanford@whitworth.edu

SANNEH, LAMIN
DISCIPLINE HISTORY **EDUCATION** Union Col, AB, 67; Univ Birmingham, England, MA, 68; Univ London, PhD, 74. **CAREER** Prof, Harvard Univ, 81-88; prof, Yale Univ, 89-. **HONORS AND AWARDS** Commandeur de l'Ordre National du Lion, Senegal; Who's Who in Am; Honorary Res Prof, Sch of Oriental and African Studies; Life Mem, Clare Hall, Cambridge Univ, England. **MEMBERSHIPS** Bd of the Inst for Advanced Christin Studies. **RESEARCH** History of religion; history of Islam; history of Christianity; African-American religious history. **SELECTED PUBLICATIONS** Auth, The Crown and the Turban: Muslims and West African Pluralism, Denver: Westview Press (96); auth, Religion and the Variety of Culture: A Study in Origin and Practice, Valley Forge, Pa: Trinity Press Int (96); auth, Piety and Power: Muslims and Christians in West Africa, Orbis Books (96); auth, Het Evangelie is Niet Los Verkrijgbaar, Uitgeverij Kok--Kampen, Netherland (96); coauth, Faith and Power: Christianity and Islam in "Secular" Britain, London: SPCK (98). **CONTACT ADDRESS** Dept Hist, Yale Univ, PO Box 208324, New Haven, CT 06520-8324. **EMAIL** lamin.sanneh@yale.edu

SANSON, JERRY P.
PERSONAL Born 03/13/1952, Alexandria, LA, m, 1991, 1 child **DISCIPLINE** HISTORY, POLITICAL SCIENCE **EDUCATION** La Col, BA, 74; La State Univ, MA, 75; PhD, 84. **CAREER** Instr to prof, La State Univ, 86-. **HONORS AND AWARDS** Huie-Dellmon Trust Prof, La State Univ, 98-00. **MEMBERSHIPS** La Hist Assoc; N La Hist Assoc; La Polit Sci Assoc; La Acad of Sci; Gulf S Hist Assoc. **RESEARCH** New Deal - World War II Era. **SELECTED PUBLICATIONS** Auth, Louisiana State and Local Government, Prentice-Hall, (Englewood Cliffs, NJ), 92; auth, Louisiana During World War II, La State Univ Pr, (Baton Rouge), 99. **CONTACT ADDRESS** Dept Lib Arts, Louisiana State Univ, Alexandria, 8100 Hwy 71 S, Alexandria, LA 71302-9119. **EMAIL** jsanson@pobox.lsua.edu

SANTIAGO, MYRNA
PERSONAL Born 02/26/1960, Chula Vista, CA, m, 1998, 1 child **DISCIPLINE** HISTORY **EDUCATION** Princeton Univ, BA, 78; Univ of Calif at Berkeley, MA, 93, PhD, 97. **CAREER** Lectr, Mills Col, 98; lectr, Univ of Calif at Berkeley, 98; Asst Prof, St. Mary's Col. **HONORS AND AWARDS** Ford Found fel; fulbright scholar. **MEMBERSHIPS** LASA; AHA; ASEH. **RESEARCH** Latin American history; Environment; labor. **CONTACT ADDRESS** Hist Dept, Saint Mary's Col, California, Moraga, CA 94574. **EMAIL** msantiag@stmarys-ca.edu

SAPERSTEIN, MARC E.
PERSONAL Born 05/09/1944, Brooklyn, NY, m, 1970, 2 children **DISCIPLINE** HISTORY **EDUCATION** Harvard Univ, BA, 66; Hebrew Univ, MA, 72; Harvard Univ, PhD, 77. **CAREER** Lectr, Harvard Univ, 77-79; assoc prof, Harvard Div Sch, 79-86; prof, Wash Univ, 86-97; Charles E Smith Prof, George Washington Univ, 97-. **HONORS AND AWARDS** Phi Beta Kappa; Herzog Fel; Kent Fel; ACLS Fel; Penn Cen Judaic Fel; Nat Jewish Bk Awd; AAJR. **MEMBERSHIPS** AHA. **RESEARCH** History of Jewish preaching; medieval and early modern Jewish cultural history; Christian-Jewish relations. **SELECTED PUBLICATIONS** Auth, Decoding the Rabbis: A Thirteenth-Century Commentary on the Aggadah, Harvard Univ Press (Cambridge), 80; auth, Jewish Preaching 1200-1800, Yale Univ Press (New Haven), 80; auth, Moments of Crisis in Jewish-Christian Relations, SCM -Trinity Press Intl (London and Philadelphia), 89; auth, Essential Papers on Messianic Movements and Personalities in Jewish History, NYU Press (NY), 96. **CONTACT ADDRESS** Dept History, The George Washington Univ, 2142 G Street NW, Washington, DC 20052. **EMAIL** msaper@gwu.edu

SAPPER, NEIL GARY
PERSONAL Born 02/15/1941, Denver, CO, m, 1965, 2 children **DISCIPLINE** HISTORY **EDUCATION** Univ Denver, BA, 63; Eastern NMex Univ, MA, 65; Tex Tech Univ, PhD(hist), 72. **CAREER** Instr hist, Black Hawk Col, 65-67; asst prof, 72-76, assoc prof, 76-79, prof Soc Sci, Amarillo Col, 79-; co-ed, H-Survey, 95-; co-ed, H-Texas, 97-. **HONORS AND AWARDS** Grant recipient, Pub Policy & Inter-scholastic Athletics in Tex, Tex Comt Humanities & Pub Policy, 76. **MEMBERSHIPS** Orgn Am Historians; Tex State Hist Asn. **RESEARCH** United States social history; African-American people in Texas. **SELECTED PUBLICATIONS** Auth, Aboard the Wrong Ship in the Right Books: Doris Miller and Historical Accuracy, E Tex Hist Rev XVIII, Winter 80; Black Culture in Texas: A Lone Star Renaissance, Red River Valley Hist Rev, Spring 81; For a Graybeard, Things Change, Community and Jr Col J LIII, 10/82; The Fall of the NAACP in Texas, The Houston Rev VII, Winter 85; coauth, Amarillo's Centenial Plaza: Public/Private Funding, Tex Recreation and Park Soc J, 10-12/87; auth, Telecourses Serve the Gifted and the Talented in Two Small Texas High Schools, The Agenda VII, Fall 92; Antonio Maceo Smith, Doris Miller, and Lonnie E. Smith, In: The New Handbook of Texas, Austin: Tex State Hist Asn, 95. **CONTACT ADDRESS** Dept of Social Sci, Amarillo Col, PO Box 447, Amarillo, TX 79178-0001. **EMAIL** sapper-ng@actx.edu

SAPPOL, MICHAEL
PERSONAL Born 04/18/1953, New York, NY, d, 2 children **DISCIPLINE** HISTORY **EDUCATION** City Col NYork, BA, 78; Columbia Univ, PhD, 97. **CAREER** Curator-historian, Natl Library of Medicine. **MEMBERSHIPS** AHA; OAH; AAHM. **SELECTED PUBLICATIONS** Auth, "Sammy Tubbs and Dr. Hubbs: Anatomical Dissection, Minstrelsy and the Technology of Self-Making in Postbellum America," Configurations 4 (96); auth, A Traffic of Dead Bodies; Princeton Univ Press. GEN **CONTACT ADDRESS** National Libr of Med, 8600 Rockville Pike, Bldg 38, Rm 1E-21, Bethesda, MD 20894. **EMAIL** michael_sappol@nlm.nih.gov

SARANTAKES, NICK
PERSONAL Born 07/16/1966, St Helena, CA, s **DISCIPLINE** HISTORY **EDUCATION** Univ Tex, BA, 89; Univ Kentucky, MA, 91; Univ Southern Calif, PhD, 97. **CAREER** Asst prof, Texas A & M Univ, 97- . **HONORS AND AWARDS** Libr Congress Jr Fel; Marine Corps Diss fel, 95-96; W Point Mil Hist Sum fel, 99; H. Bailey Carroll Awd SW Hist Quart, 00. **MEMBERSHIPS** Am Hist Asn; Soc Hist Am For Relations. **RESEARCH** US-Japanese diplomatic relations, British participation in the invasion of Japan, Richard Nixon and his interest and political use of sports. **SELECTED PUBLICATIONS** Auth, "Continuity through Change: The Return of Okinawa and Iwo Jima, 1967-1972, " J Am E-Asian Rel vol 3, no 1, pp34-53, (94); auth, "Richard Nixon, Sportswriter: The President, His Historical All-Star Baseball Team, and the Election of 1972," J Sport Hist, vol 27, no 1, pp 192-202, (97); auth, "The Politics and Poetry of Advice and Consent: Congress Confronts the Roosevelt Administration during the State Department Confirmation Incident of 1944," Pres Stud Quart, vol 28, no 2, pp 153-168, (98); auth, "Political Football: Nixon Meets the Longhorns," Texas Alcalde, pp 95-96, (98); auth, " Interservice Relations: The Army and the Marines at the Battle of Okinawa, April-June, 1945," Infantry, pp 12-15, (99); auth, "In the Service of the Pharaoh? The US and the Deployment of Korean Troops in Vietnam, 1965-1968," Pac Hist Rev, vol 68, no 3, pp 425-449, (99); auth, "Lyndon Johnson, Foreign Policy, and the Election of 1960," SW Hist Quart, (99); auth, Keystone: The American Occupation of Okinawa and US-Japanese Relations, 1945-1972, Texas A & M Univ Press, (00). **CONTACT ADDRESS** Dept Hist, Texas A&M Univ, Commerce, PO Box 3011, Commerce, TX 75429-3011. **EMAIL** Nick_Sarantakes@tamu-commerce.edu

SARASON, RICHARD SAMUEL
PERSONAL Born 02/12/1948, Detroit, MI **DISCIPLINE** RELIGIOUS STUDIES, HISTORY OF RELIGIONS **EDUCATION** Brandeis Univ, AB, 69; Hebrew Union Col, MAHL, 74; Brown Univ, PhD(relig studies), 77. **CAREER** Instr relig studies, Brown Univ, 76-77, asst prof, 77-79; asst prof, 79-81, Assoc Prof Rabbinic Lit & Thought, Hebrew Union Col, 81- **MEMBERSHIPS** Am Acad Relig; Soc Bibl Lit; Asn Jewish Studies; Am Sch Orient Res; Soc Values Higher Educ. **RESEARCH** Judaism in late antiquity; early rabbinic Judaism, Mishnah-Tosefta, rabbinic midrash and liturgy. **SELECTED PUBLICATIONS** Transl, Joseph Heinemann's Prayer in the Talmud, Walter de Gruyter & Co, 77; auth, A History of the Mishnaic Law of Agriculture: Demai, E J Brill, 78; contribr, Approaches to Ancient Judaism, Scholars, 78 & 80; Joseph Heinemann Memorial Volume, Magnes, 81; ed, The Tosefta: An English Translation, I The Order of Seeds, Ktav, 83. **CONTACT ADDRESS** Hebrew Union Col-Jewish Inst of Religion, Ohio, 3101 Clifton Ave, Cincinnati, OH 45220.

SARDESAI, D. R. (DAMODAR RAMAJI)
PERSONAL Born 01/05/1931, Goa, India, m, 1960, 2 children **DISCIPLINE** SOUTH AND SOUTHEAST ASIAN HISTORY **EDUCATION** Univ Bombay, BA, 52, MA, 65, Univ Calif at Los Angeles, PhD, 65. **CAREER** Vice Chair of Dept of Hist, Univ of Calif at Los Angeles, 82-84; Chair of Dept of Hist, Univ of Calif at Los Angeles, 84-85; Chair of S & Southeast Asian Studies and prof, Univ of Calif at Los Angeles, 86-93; dir, Univ of Calif Educ Abroad Prog, 93-95; Emeritus Prof of Hist and Navin Pratima Doshi Chair in Indian Hist, Univ of Calif at Los Angeles, 98-. **HONORS AND AWARDS** Sir William Wedderburn Prize, Univ of Bombay, 65. **MEMBERSHIPS** Soc Sci Res Coun, Royal Hist Soc, Father Heras Soc, Asiatic Soc of Bombay. **RESEARCH** South and Southeast Asia. **SELECTED PUBLICATIONS** Coauth, India Through the Ages (sixth edition), Allied Pub (New Delhi, India), 80; co-ed, Patterns of Development and Defense in Asia, Praeger (New York, NY), 80 & Allied Pub (New Delhi, India), 81; auth, Vietnam. Trials and Tribulations of a Nation, Promilla Pub (New Delhi, India) & Long Beach Pub, 89; co-ed, The Legacy of Nehru: A Centennial Assessment, Promilla Pub (New Delhi, India), & Nataraj Pub (Washington, DC), 92; auth, Vietnam. The Struggle for a National Identity, Westview Press (Boulder, CO), 92; co-ed, Environmental Challenges, Wiley Eastern (New Delhi, India), 93; auth, Vietnam: Past and Present (third edition), Westview Press (Boulder, CO), 98. **CONTACT ADDRESS** Dept Hist, Univ of California, Los Angeles, PO Box 951473, Los Angeles, CA 90095-1473. **EMAIL** sardesai@ucla.edu

SARETZKY, GARY D.
PERSONAL Born 06/26/1946, Newton, MA, m, 1980, 3 children **DISCIPLINE** HISTORY **EDUCATION** Thomas Edison Col, BA, 86; Univ Wis, MA, 69; BA, 68. **CAREER** Archivist, Educational Testing Service, 69-93; Archivist, Menmouten County, 94-; Coordinator Public Hist Internship Prog, Rutgers Univ, 94-; Instr to Assoc Prof, Mercer County Community Col, 77-. **HONORS AND AWARDS** Recognition Awd, NJ Hist commission, 99. **MEMBERSHIPS** SAA, MARAC, AIG, DVAG **RESEARCH** History of photography. **SELECTED PUBLICATIONS** Auth, Index to ETS Research Report Series and Related Publications, 1948-1992, Princeton, 93; auth, A Guide to the Ben D. Wood Paper, Princeton, 92; auth, "Margaret Bourke-White: Eyes on Russia," The Photo Review, (99): 3-4; auth, "Carl Campbell Brigham," American national Biography, 98; auth, "Elias Goldenshky: Wizard of Photography," Pennsylvania History, (97): 206-272; auth, "North American Business Archives: A Developmental Perspective," Business History Bulletin, (91): 6-8; auth, "Photographic conservation," conservation Administration news, (88): 4-5; auth, "Recent Photographic conservation and Preservation Literature," Picturescope, (87): 117-132; auth, "The Effects of electrostatic copying on Modern Photographs," Picturescope, (86): 64-65; auth, "Oral History in American Business Archives," American Archivist, (81): 353-355; auth, "North American Business Archives: Results of a Survey," American Archivist, (77): 413-419. **CONTACT ADDRESS** Dept Hist, Rutgers, The State Univ of New Jersey, New Brunswick, PO Box 5059, New Brunswick, NJ 08903-5059.

SARFOH, KWABWO A.
PERSONAL Born 11/17/1936, Ghana, m, 1971, 4 children **DISCIPLINE** AFRICAN STUDIES **EDUCATION** Unjiv Ghana, BA, 62, MA, 65; Univ Cincinnati, PhD, 76. **CAREER** Lectr, Univ Sci & Technol, Kumass, Ghana, 65-72; vis asst prof, Tenn Technol Univ, Cookville, 76-77; asst prof, SUNY, Albany, 80-91, assoc prof, 91-. **MEMBERSHIPS** African Studies Asn, Asn of African Studies Progs, Nat Coun of Black Studies. **SELECTED PUBLICATIONS** Auth, Hydropower Development in West Africa, Peter Lang (90); auth, Energy Development in West Africa, Greenwood Press (92). **CONTACT ADDRESS** Dept Africana Studies, SUNY Albany, 1400 Washington Ave, Albany, NY 12222-0100. **EMAIL** js829@cas.albany.edu

SARGENT, JAMES E.
PERSONAL Born 03/17/1941, Flint, MI, m, 1986, 2 children **DISCIPLINE** US HISTORY **EDUCATION** Flint Junior Col, AA, 60; E Mich Univ, BS, 64; Mich State Univ, MA, 68; PhD, 72. **CAREER** Prof, Clemson Univ, 70-75; Ball State Univ, 75-77; Va W Community Col, 77-; chair, Va W Community Col, 94-. **HONORS AND AWARDS** NDEA Fel, Mich State Univ, 67-70; Phi Kappa Phi, 69. **MEMBERSHIPS** Org of Am Hist; Soc for Am Baseball Res; Pro Football Res Assoc. **RESEARCH** 20th Century U.S. History as well as baseball, football, basketball and hockey since the 1930's. **SELECTED PUBLICATIONS** Auth, Roosevelt and the Hundred Days of 1933: Struggle for the Early New Deal, Garland, 81. **CONTACT ADDRESS** Dept Soc Sci, Virginia Western Comm Col, PO Box 14007, Roanoke, VA 24038-4007. **EMAIL** jsargent@vw.cc.va.us

SARLOS, ROBERT KAROLY
PERSONAL Born 06/06/1931, Budapest, Hungary, m, 1962, 2 children **DISCIPLINE** THEATRE HISTORY **EDUCATION** Occidental Col, BA, 59; Yale Univ, PhD(hist of theatre), 65. **CAREER** Instr English, Mitchell Col, 62-63; from lectr to acting asst prof, 63-65, asst prof, 66-70, assoc prof, 70-79, Prof Dramatic Art, Univ Calif, Davis, 79-, Vpres, Woodland Opera House Inc, 80- **MEMBERSHIPS** Int Fed Theatre Res; Am Soc Theatre Res. **RESEARCH** Elizabethan, Baroque and American theatre. **SELECTED PUBLICATIONS** Auth, Development and operation of the first Blackfriars theatre, In: Studies in the Elizabethan Theatre, 61; Two outdoor productions of Giuseppe Galli Bibiena, Theatre Surv, 5/64; coauth, The Woodland Opera House: The end of an era in California theatre, Calif Hist Soc Quart, 12/69; auth, Jig Cook and the Provincetown Players: Theatre in Ferment, Univ Mass Press, 82. **CONTACT ADDRESS** Dept of Dramatic Art, Univ of California, Davis, Davis, CA 95616.

SARNA, JONATHAN D.
PERSONAL Born 01/10/1955, Philadelphia, PA, m, 1986, 2 children **DISCIPLINE** AMERICAN JEWISH HISTORY **EDUCATION** Brandeis Univ, BA, 75, MA, 75; Yale Univ, MA, 76, MPhil, 78, PhD, 79. **CAREER** Joseph H. & Belle R. Braun Prof Amer Jewish Hist, 90- , Dept ch, 92-95, 98, Brandeis Univ; Prof Amer Jewish Hist, 88-90, assoc prof, 84-88, asst prof, 80-84, vis lectr, 79-80, Hebrew Union Col-Jewish Inst Rel; Ch of the Board, Judaica On-Line Network (H-Judaic), 96- ; Ch, Acad Coun, Amer Jewish Hist Soc, 92-95; Dir Boston Jewish Hist Proj, 92-95; Dir, Ctr Stud The Amer Jewish Experience, 86-90, Acad dir, 84-86, acad adv, 81-84; vis assoc prof, Hebrew Univ, 86-87; vis asst prof Judaic Stud, Univ Cincinnati, 83-84; asst Amer Hist, Yale Univ, 78; Dir, Am Jewish Experience Curriculum Proj, 82-90; assoc ed, Amer Natl Biog, ed J. Garraty; Consultant, Amram Nowak Assoc, Amer Jewish Hist Film Proj, 94- ; Consulting ed, Am: The Jewish Experience, by Sondra Leiman, UAHC Press, 92-94; Publ Committee, Jewish Publ Soc, 85-90; Ed Board, Univ Press New England, 92- ; ed, North Amer Judaism sec, Rel Stud Rev, 84-94; ed comm, Queen City Heritage, 85- ; ed board, Am Jewish Hist, 88- ;ed board, Rel and Amer Cult, 89-96; ed board, Contemporary Jewry, 92- ; ed board, Patterns of Prejudice, 94- ; ed committee, Jewish Soc Stud, 93- ; acad comm, Touro Natl Heritage Trust, 93- ; adv comm, Ctr for Amer Jewish Hist, Temple Univ, 91; adv comm, Ctr Stud N Amer Jewry, Ben-Gurion Univ, Israel, 91- ; Wexner Found Grad Fel Comm, 89-92; Adv board, Maurice Amado Found, 90-95. **HONORS AND AWARDS** NEH Sr fel, 96; Lilly Endow grants, 84-93; Pew Endow grant, 91-94; Lady Davis Endow 86-87; Amer Coun Learned Soc, 82; Mem Found Jewish Cult, 82-83; Bernard and Audre Rapoport Fel in Amer Jewish Hist, Amer Jewish Archives, 79-80; Mem Found Jewish Cult, 77-79; Natl Found Jewish Cult, 77-79; Loewenstein-Wiener Fel, Amer Jewish Archives, 77; Howard F. Brinton Fel, Yale Univ, 77-78; Seltzer-Brodsky Prize Essay, YIVO Inst, 77; Charles Andrews Fel, Yale Univ, 76-77; Hebrew Free Loan Assn Fel, Amer Jewish Hist Soc, 74-75. **MEMBERSHIPS** Amer Acad Rel; Amer Hist Assn; Amer Jewish Hist Soc; Assn Jewish Stud; Can Jewish Hist Soc; Cincinnati Hist Soc; Immigration Hist Soc; Org Amer Hist; Phi Beta Kappa; Soc Hist Early Am Rep. **RESEARCH** Judaism. **SELECTED PUBLICATIONS** Ed, Jews in New Haven, Jewish Hist Soc New Haven, 78; Mordecai Manuel Noah: Jacksonian Politician and American Jewish Communal Leader-A Biographical Study, PhD Theis, Yale Univ, 79; Jacksonian Jew: The Two Worlds of Mordecai Noah, Holmes & Meier, 81; People Walk on Their Heads: Moses Weinberger's Jews and Judaism in New York, Holmes & Meier, 82; co-ed, Jews and the Founding of the Republic, Markus Wiener, 85; The American Jewish Experience: A Reader, Holmes and Meier, 86, 2nd ed, 97; American Synagogue History: A Bibliography and State-of-the-Field Survey, with Alexandria S. Korros, Markus Wiener, 88; Yahadut Amerika: American Jewry: An Annotated Bibliography of Publications in Hebrew, with Janet Ljss, Hebrew Univ, 91; JPS: The Americaniztion of Jewish Culture (A history of the Jewish publication Soc, 1888-1988), JPS, 89; The Jews of Cincinnati, with Nancy H. Klein, Ctr for the Stud Am Jewish Experience, 89; A Double Bond: The Constitutional Documents of American Jewry, ed with Daniel J. Elazar and Rela Geffen Monson, Univ Press of Am, 92; Ethnic Diversity and Civic Identity: Patterns of Conflict and Cohesion in Cincinnati Since 1820, ed with Henry D. Shapiro, U of Illinois P, 92; Yehude Artsot Ha-Berit, ed with Lloyd Gartner, Merkaz Shazar, 92; Observing America's Jews by Marshall Sklare, ed, with forword and head-notes, UP of New England, 93; The Jews of Boston, with Ellen Smith, Combined Jewish Philanthropies/Northeastern Univ Press, 95; The Evolution of the American Synagogue, in The Americanization of the Jews, ed Robert M. Seltzer & Norman J. Cohen, New York, NYU Press, 95, 215-229; When Jews Were Bible Experts, Moments, Oct 95, 4, 55.80; Perched Between Continuity and Discontinuity: American Judaism at a Crossroads, Proceedings of the Rabbinical Assembly, 56, 95, 74-79; Current Trends and Issues in American Jewish Religious Life, Gesher, 42, 132, 95, 111-117, in Hebrew; contribution to Rebuilding Jewish Peoplehood: Where Do We Go From Here? A Symposium in the Wake of the Rabin Assassination, Amer Jewish Comm, 96, 86-87; The American Jewish Community's Crisis of Confidence, Pamphlet, World Jewish Congress, 96; From Antoinette Brown Blackwell to Sally Priesand: An Historical Perspective on the Emergence of Women in the American Rabbinate, Women Rabbis: Exploration and Celebration, ed Gary P. Zola, Cincinnati, American Jewish Archives, 96, 43-53; A Projection of America as it Ought to Be: Zion in the Mind's Eye of American Jews, in Allon Gal, ed, Envisioning Israel: The changing Ideals and Images of North American Jews, Jerusalem & Detroit, Magnes Press & Wayne State Univ Press, 96, 41-59; If You Lend Money to My People, Learning Torah With. .3:18, Feb 8, 97, 1-4; Minority Faiths and the American Protestant Mainstream, ed. U of Illinois P, 97; Abba Hillel Silver and American Zionism, co-ed with Mark A. Raider and Ronald W. Zwelg, Frank Cass, 97; Religion and State in the American Jewish Experience, with David G. Dalin, U of Notre Dame P, 97; Masterworks of Modern Jewish Writing, gen ed, 11 vol, Markus Wiener Publ; Amer Jewish Life, co-ed, 8 vol, Wayne State Univ Press; Brandeis Series in American Jewish History, Cult and Life, gen ed, 10 vol, Brandeis Univ Press/UP of New England; Contribution to One Year Later: The Rabin Symposium, Am Jewish Comm, 97; Two Traditions of Seminary Scholarship, in Jack Werheimer, ed, Tradition Renewed: A History of the Jewish Theological Seminary, Jewish Theol Sem, 97, 54-80; Structural Challenges to Jewish Continuity, American Jewry: Portrait and Prognosis, ed David M. Gordis and Dorit P. Gray, Wilstein Inst Behrman House, 97, 404-408; Back to the Center: The Plain Meaning of A Statement on Jewish Continuity, Am Jewish Comm, 97; Jacob Rader Marcus, Am Jewish Year Bk, 97, 97, 633-640; Martha Wolfenstein, in Paula Hyman and Deborah D. Moore, eds, Jewish Women in Am, Routledge, 97, 1486-1487; Foreword to Gerry Cristol, A Light in the Prairie: Temple Emanu-El of Dallas, 1872-1997, TCU Press, 98; Committed Today, Divorced Tomorrow, JTS Mag, 7, Winter 98, 12, 23; Ten Ways That Israel Liberated American Jewry, Hadassah Mag, 79, June 98, 14-15; American Jewish Education in Historical Perspective, Jour Jewish Ed, 64, Fall 98, 8-21; **CONTACT ADDRESS** Dept of Near East and Judaic Studies, Brandeis

Univ, MS 054, Waltham, MA 02454. **EMAIL** sarna@brandeis.edu

SARTI, ROLAND
DISCIPLINE HISTORY **EDUCATION** Rutgers Univ, PhD, 67. **CAREER** Prof, Univ MA Amherst . **HONORS AND AWARDS** Howard Marraro Prize, 86. **MEMBERSHIPS** New England Hist Asn, Soc Italian Hist Studies. **RESEARCH** Italian and Europ soc hist. **SELECTED PUBLICATIONS** Auth, Fascism and the Industrial Leadership in Italy 1919-1940, 71; HisLong Live the Strong: A History of Rural Society in The Appenine Mountains, 85; Giuseppe Mazzini entitled Mazzini: A Life for the Religion of Politics, 97; ed, The Ax Within: Italian Fascism in Action, 74. **CONTACT ADDRESS** Dept of Hist, Univ of Massachusetts, Amherst, Mass Ave, Amherst, MA 01003.

SASSON, JACK MURAD
PERSONAL Born 10/01/1941, Aleppo, Syria **DISCIPLINE** ASSYRIOLOGY, HEBREW SCRIPTURE **EDUCATION** Brooklyn Col, BA, 62; Brandeis Univ, MA, 63, PhD, 66. **CAREER** From asst prof to assoc prof, 66-77, Prof Relig, Univ NC, Chapel Hill, 77-91; assoc ed, J Am Orient Soc, 77; Mary Jane Werthan prof of Judaic and Bibl Studies, Divinity School, Vanderbilt Univ. **HONORS AND AWARDS** Soc Relig Higher Educ fel, 69-70. **MEMBERSHIPS** Soc Bibl Lit; Am Orient Soc; Israel Explor Soc; Dutch Orient Soc. **RESEARCH** Ancient Near Eastern societies. **SELECTED PUBLICATIONS** Auth, Circumcision in the ancient Near East, J Bibl Lit, 66; The Military Establishments at Mari, 69 & contribr, Hebrew-Ugaritic Studies, 71, Pontif Bibl Inst; Archive keeping at Mari, Iraq, 72; Literary motif in . . . Gilgamesh epic, Studies Philol, 72; Commentary to Ruth, Johns Hopkins Univ, 78; ed, Civilizations of the Ancient Near East, 95. **CONTACT ADDRESS** Divinity School, Vanderbilt Univ, Nashville, TN 37240. **EMAIL** jack.m.sasson@vanderbilt.edu

SASSON, SARAH DIANE HYDE
PERSONAL Born 08/27/1946, Asheville, NC, m, 1969, 3 children **DISCIPLINE** AMERICAN LITERATURE & HISTORY **EDUCATION** Univ NC, BA, 68, PhD(Eng), 80; Univ IL, Urbana, MA, 71. **CAREER** Instr Eng, 80-81, lectr Am studies, 81-82, Dir, Master of Arts in Lib Studies Prog, Duke Univ, 87-; Dir, Univ MAT Prog, Duke Univ, 91-95; Assoc of Graduate Lib Studies, Pres, 94-96. **HONORS AND AWARDS** Am Coun Learned Soc Fel. **MEMBERSHIPS** Am Folklore Soc; Am Studies Asn; MLA. **RESEARCH** Shaker lit; Am autobiography; Am relig lit. **SELECTED PUBLICATIONS** Auth, The Shaker Personal Narrative, Univ TN Press (in prep). **CONTACT ADDRESS** Duke Univ, Box 90095, Durham, NC 27708.

SATO, ELIZABETH SELANDERS
PERSONAL Born 03/17/1942, Philadelphia, PA, m, 1966, 2 children **DISCIPLINE** HISTORY **EDUCATION** Muskingun Col, BA, 65; Univ Mich, MA, 67, PhD(hist), 76. **CAREER** Fulbright res fel, Historiographical Inst, Tokyo Univ, 70-71; teaching fel, East Asia, Univ Mich, 71-72; vis asst prof, Univ Cincinnati, 72-73, asst prof hist, 73-80. **MEMBERSHIPS** Asn Asian Studies; AAUP. **RESEARCH** Social and economic history of medieval Japan; Japanese cultural history; women in Japan. **SELECTED PUBLICATIONS** Auth, Hired Swords - The Rise Of Private Warrior Power In Early Japan - Friday,Kf/, Am Hist Rev, Vol 0098, 1993. **CONTACT ADDRESS** Dept of Hist, Univ of Cincinnati, Cincinnati, OH 45221.

SATRE, LOWELL JOSEPH
PERSONAL Born 11/15/1942, Veblen, SD, m, 1965, 4 children **DISCIPLINE** MODERN ENGLISH HISTORY **EDUCATION** Augustana Col, SDak, BA, 64; Univ SC, MA, 67, PhD(hist), 68. **CAREER** Asst prof, 68-75, assoc prof hist, Youngstown State Univ, 75-82, prof hist 82-. **MEMBERSHIPS** AHA; Conf Brit Studies; World Hist Asn; Midwest Victorian Studies Asn. **RESEARCH** British empire history; English social history. **SELECTED PUBLICATIONS** Auth, St John Brodrick and Army reform 1901-1903, J Brit Studies, spring 76; Mafeking relieved, Brit Hist Illus, 10/75; After the Match Girls' Strike: Bryant and May in 1890's, in Victorian Studies, pp.7-31, autumn 82; Biographical entry of Thomas Burt, Vol II of Biographical Dictionary of Modern British Radicals, ed by Joseph Baylen and Norbert Gossman, pp. 111-115, 84; Thomas Burt and the Crisis of Late-Victorian Liberalism in the North-East, in Northern History, pp. 174-193, Univ of Leeds, England, 87; Education and Religion in the Shaping of Thomas Burt, Miner's Leader, Bulletin of the North East History Labour Society, Bulletin No 26, pp. 87-104, 92; Diamond Jubilee (Queen Victoria's) entry in England in the 1890's: An Encyclopedia of British Literature, Art, and Culture, Garland Press, 93; Biography/biographical entry on Lord Castlereagh in Statesmen Who Changed the World, pp 73-84, Greenwood Press, 93; Great Depression entry in Events That Changed the World, pp 67-80, Greenwood Press, 95; A Note on the Northumberland Miners' Association Annual Picnic, North East History, 97. **CONTACT ADDRESS** Dept of Hist, Youngstown State Univ, One University Plz, Youngstown, OH 44555-3452. **EMAIL** lesatre@ix.netcom.com

SATYA, LAXMAN D.
PERSONAL Born Hyderabad, India, s **DISCIPLINE** HISTORY **EDUCATION** Osmania Univ, Hyderabad, India, BA, 75, MA, 77; Univ Ill, Chicago, MA, 86; Tufts Univ, PhD, 94. **CAREER** Teaching asst, Tufts Univ, 90-91; vis asst prof, Ball State Univ, 92-93; asst prof, Brookdale Community Col, 93-94; asst prof, Lock Haven Univ, Pa, 94-97, assoc prof, 98-. **HONORS AND AWARDS** Bell Fel, Forest Hist Soc, Durham, NC, 91; Pre-Doctoral Fel, Smithsonian Inst, Washington, DC, 90-91; NEH grants, 95, 98; Prof Fac Develop Coun grant, 97; Southeast Asia Workshop, Slippery Rock Univ, Pa, 98; vis guest fel, Centre for Modern Oriental Studies, Berlin, Germany, 98; participant, Annual Conf of the Foreign Policy Res Inst, Philadelphia, Pa, 99; vis guest scholar, Osaka City Univ, Japan, 99; vis fel, Inst of Oriental Culture, Univ of Tokyo, Japan, 99/ **MEMBERSHIPS** Agricultural Hist Soc, Am Hist Asn, Asn of Asian Studies, Mid-Atlantic Regional Asn of Asian Studies, Mid-Atlantic World Hist Asn, Pa Asn of Scholars and Teachers, War and Soc in South Asia Group, World Hist Asn. **SELECTED PUBLICATIONS** Auth, Cotton and Famine in Berar (Central India): 1850-1900, Manohar Pubs, New Delhi (97); auth, "Colonial Sedenterisation and Subjugation: The Case of the Banjaras of Berar: 1850-1900," J of Peasant Studies, vol 24, no 4 (July 97): 314-336; auth, "Colonial Encroachment and Popular Resistance: Land Survey and Settlement Operations in Berar: 1860-1877," Agricultural Hist, vol 72, no 1 (winter 98): 55-76; auth, "Commercialization, Environment, and Ecological Change in the Purna River Valley in Behrar in Central Deccan: 1850-1900," South Asia: Institutions, Changes and Networks, Quart J of the Univ of Tokyo, vol 2, no 1 (Sept 22, 99): 102-112; auth, Debunking the Myth: An Essay Review of Frances Wood's book 'Did Marco Polo Go To China'," Educ About ASIA, vol 4, no 3 (winter 99): 48-51; auth, Historical Geography, Agrarian Ecology, and the Forest Dwellers of the Purna River Valley: Central India in the Nineteenth Century (forthcoming); auth, A Social History of Colonial Berar: A Nineteenth Century Profile (forthcoming); auth, "Colonial Modernization and Popular Resistance in Central India: A Nineteenth Century Story," Scholars (forthcoming); rev, "Paul Erik Baak. Plantation Production and Political Power: Plantation Development in Southwest India in a Long Term Historical Perspective, 1743-1963," J of Asian Studies (forthcoming); rev, "Kate Brittlebank. Tipu Sultan's Search for Legitimacy: Islam and Kingship in a Hindu Domain," J of Am Oriental Sociol (forthcoming); rev, "Chetan Singh. Natural Premises: Ecology and Peasant Life in Western Himalayas: 1800-1950," Environmental Hist (forthcoming). **CONTACT ADDRESS** Dept Hist, Pol Sci & Econ, Lock Haven Univ of Pennsylvania, 401 N Fairview St, Lock Haven, PA 17745-2342. **EMAIL** Isatya@eagle.Ihup.edu

SAUDER, ROBERT A.
PERSONAL Born 10/11/1943, Santa Maria, CA, m, 1975 **DISCIPLINE** GEOGRAPHY **EDUCATION** Calif State Univ, BA; Univ Ore, MA, 69; PhD, 73. **CAREER** Instructor to Prof, Univ New Orleans, 70-. **HONORS AND AWARDS** Excellence in Teaching Awd, Univ New Orleans, 88; Outstanding Teacher-Scholar in Geog, Asn of Am Geog, 94. **MEMBERSHIPS** Asn of Am Geog; Asn of Pacific Coast Geog. **RESEARCH** Historical geography of the American West; Historical geography of western cities; Goeography of New Orleans. **SELECTED PUBLICATIONS** Co-ed, A Field Guidebook for Louisiana, Asn of Am Geog, 78; auth, The Lost Frontier--Water Diversion in the Growth and Destruction of Owens Valley Agriculture, Univ AZ Press, 94; auth, "Mountains and Lowlands: Human Adaptation in the Owens Valley, California," in The Mountainous West: Explorations in Historical Geography, (Lincoln, 95), 305-330; auth, "New Orleans' Ethnic Landscapes," in Ethnic Persistence and Change in Europe and America: Traces in Landscape and Society, (Innsbruck, 96), 7-27; co-auth, "Introduction," in Ethnic Persistence and Change in Europe and America: Traces in Landscape and Society, (Innsbruck, 96), 1-4; co-ed, Ethnic Persistence and Change in Europe and America: Traces in Landscape and Society, Innsbruck, 96; auth, "State v. Society: Public Land Law and Mormon Settlement in the Sevier Valley, Utah," Agricultural History, (96): 57-89. **CONTACT ADDRESS** Dept Geog, Univ of New Orleans, 2000 Lakeshore Dr, New Orleans, LA 70148-0001. **EMAIL** rsauder@uno.edu

SAUER, ANGELIKA
PERSONAL Born Erlanger, Germany **DISCIPLINE** GERMAN-CANADIAN STUDIES **EDUCATION** Univ Augsburg, MA, 86; Carleton Univ, MA, 88; Univ Waterloo, PhD, 94. **CAREER** Ch, German Can Studs, Univ Winnipeg, 94-. **HONORS AND AWARDS** Beaverbrook Prize, Carleton Univ, 87; Awd Foreign Nats, Gov Can, 88-92. **MEMBERSHIPS** Can Inst Int Affairs; Comt Hist Second World War; Org Stud Nat Hist Can. **RESEARCH** Canadian-German Relations in the 1940s and 1950s; Immigration and Multiculturalism Policies in Canada and Australisa since World War II; The Involvment of the Private Sector and Social Groups in Immigrant Recruitment and Adaptation. **SELECTED PUBLICATIONS** Auth, "A Matter of Domestic Policy? Canadian Immigration Policy and the Admission of Germans, 1945-50," in Can Hist Rev 74 2, 93; auth, "Christian Charity, Government Policy and German Immigration to Canada and Australia, 1947 to 1952," in Immigration and Ethnicity in Canada, 96; auth, "Hopes of Lasting Peace: Canada and Post-Hostilities Germany, 1945," in 1945 in Canada and Germany: The Past Viewed Through the Present, 96; auth, "Goodwill and Profit: Mackenzie King and Canadian Appeasement," A Country of Limitations: Canada and the World in 1939, Ottawa, 96; auth, "So Untimely a Retreat: The Decision to Withdraw the Canadian Force of Occupation from Germany," Uncertain Horizons: Canadians and their World in 1945, Ottawa, 97; auth, "Being Germaan in Western Canada," Journal of the West, 98. **CONTACT ADDRESS** Dept of German-Canadian Studies, Univ of Winnipeg, Winnipeg, MB, Canada R3B 2E9. **EMAIL** angelika.sauer@uwinnipeg.ca

SAUL, NORMAN E.
PERSONAL Born 11/26/1932, La Fontaine, IN, m, 1959, 3 children **DISCIPLINE** HISTORY, INTERNATIONAL RELATIONS **EDUCATION** Ind Univ, BA, 54; Columbia Univ, MA, 57; PhD, 65. **CAREER** Instr, Purdue Univ, 62-65; asst prof, Brown Univ, 65-68; Univ Kans, 70-. **HONORS AND AWARDS** Higuchi Res Awd, 97; Kans Humanities Coun Public Service Awd, 97; Inst for Advanced Study member, 00; IREX and Kennan Awds. **MEMBERSHIPS** Am Hist Asn, Am Asn for Advancement of Slavic Studies, Kans State Hist Soc. **RESEARCH** Russian-American Relations, Immigration of Germans from Russia, Russian Revolution. **SELECTED PUBLICATIONS** Auth, Russia and the Mediterranean 1797-1807, 70; auth, Sailors in Revolt in 1917, 78; auth, Distant Friends: The US and Russia 1763-1867; auth, Concord and Conflict: The US and Russia 1867-1914, 96. **CONTACT ADDRESS** Dept Hist, Univ of Kansas, Lawrence, Lawrence, KS 66045-0001. **EMAIL** normsaul@falcon.cc.ukans.edu

SAUNDERS, ELMO STEWART
PERSONAL Born 04/03/1936, Bradenton, FL, m, 1969, 2 children **DISCIPLINE** EARLY MODERN EUROPEAN HISTORY **EDUCATION** DePauw Univ, BA, 59; Ball State Univ, MA, 62; Ind Univ, MA, 64; Ohio State Univ, PhD(hist), 80. **CAREER** Instr bibliog, Ohio State Univ Libr, 65-77; Asst Prof Hist Res Methods, Purdue Univ Libr, 78-, Chercheur en Mission, Inst Nat de Recherche en Sci Humaines, Niger, 72-73. **MEMBERSHIPS** Soc French Hist Studies; Asn Col Res Libr. **RESEARCH** Science, technology and bureaucracy in 17th century France; bibliography of 17th century science and technology; cultural policies of early modern France. **SELECTED PUBLICATIONS** Auth, Library Circulation Of Univ Press Publ/, J Of Scholarly Publ, Vol 0027, 1996. **CONTACT ADDRESS** General Libr, Purdue Univ, West Lafayette, West Lafayette, IN 47907. **EMAIL** ssaunder@purdue.edu

SAUNT, CLAUDIO
PERSONAL Born 10/18/1967, San Francisco, CA **DISCIPLINE** HISTORY **EDUCATION** Columbia Univ, BA, 89; Duke Univ, MA, 91; PhD, 96. **CAREER** Lectr, Columbia Univ, 96-98; asst prof, Univ of Ga, 98-. **HONORS AND AWARDS** NEH Fel, 95; Mellon Fel, 96-98; Bolton-Komand Prize, 98. **MEMBERSHIPS** AHA; Am Soc for Ethnohistory; S Hist Assoc; Omohundro Inst of Early Am Hist and Cult. **RESEARCH** Southeastern Indians, the Early South. **SELECTED PUBLICATIONS** Auth, "Domestick.. Quiet being broke: Gender Conflict among Creek Indians in the Eighteenth Century", Contact Points: North American Frontiers from the Mohawk Valley to the Mississippi, 1750-1830, eds Fredrick J. Teute and Andrew R.L. Cayton, Univ of NC, 98; auth, "The English has now a Mind to make Slaves of them all: Creeks, Seminoles, and the Problem of Slavery", Am Indian Quarterly 22 (98): 157-181; auth, A New Order of Things: Property, Power, and the Transformation of the Creek Indians, 1733-1816, Cambridge Univ Pr (NY), 99; auth, "Taking Account of Property: Social Stratification among the Creek Indians in the Early Nineteenth Century", William and Mary Quarterly, (forthcoming). **CONTACT ADDRESS** Dept Hist, Univ of Georgia, Athens, GA 30602-0002. **EMAIL** csaunt@arches.uga.edu

SAVAGE, DAVID WILLIAM
PERSONAL Born 01/01/1937, Cincinnati, OH, m, 1959, 3 children **DISCIPLINE** MODERN BRITISH HISTORY **EDUCATION** Denison Univ, BA, 59; Princeton Univ, MA, 61, PhD, 63. **CAREER** Instr hist, 62-63, Princeton Univ & Stanford Univ, 63-65, asst prof, 65-67; asst prof, 67-73, dir spec progs, 72-73, Clark Univ; assoc dean fac, , 73- Lewis & Clark Col; assoc prof, 81-; Dean of Arts of Humanities, 95-98. **HONORS AND AWARDS** PBK. **MEMBERSHIPS** AHA; Conf Brit Studies. **RESEARCH** 19th & 20th century Britain; British colonialism; India. **SELECTED PUBLICATIONS** Auth, The Attempted Home Rule Settlement of 1916, Eire-Ireland, 67; ed, The Imprint of Roman Institutions, Holt, 70; auth, The Parnell of Wales has Become the Chamberlain of England: auth, Lloyd George and the Irish Question, J Brit Studies, 72; auth, Evangelical Education Policy in Britain and India, 1857-60; Journal of Imperial and Commonwealth Hist, 94; auth, Missionaries of the Development of the Colonial Ideology of Female Education in India, Gender and Hist, 97. **CONTACT ADDRESS** Lewis and Clark Col, 0615 SW Palatine Hill Rd, Portland, OR 97219-7879. **EMAIL** savage@lclark.edu

SAVAGE, MELISSA
PERSONAL Born 04/27/1945, CT, 2 children **DISCIPLINE** GEOGRAPHY **EDUCATION** Russell Sage Col, BA, 66; Univ

Pa, MA, 68; Univ Colo, PhD, 89. **CAREER** Vis sci, Nat Center for Atmospheric Res, 89-90; asst prof to assoc prof emerita, UCLA, 90-98. **MEMBERSHIPS** Asn of Am Geogr. **RESEARCH** Biogeography; Conservation; Dendroecology; Resource conservation. **SELECTED PUBLICATIONS** Co-auth, "Early and persistent decline in fire frequency in a pine forest of the American Southwest," Ecology, (90): 2374-2378; auth, "Structural dynamics of a southwestern pine forest under chronic human disturbance," Annals of the Asn of Am Geogr, (91): 271-289; co-auth, "Diversity and disturbance in a Colorado subalpine forest," Physical Geog, (92): 240-249; auth, "Ecological disturbance and nature tourism," Geog Rev, (93): 231-232; auth, "Structural dynamics of a montane pine forest: effects of land use change in northern Thailand," Mountain Res and Develop, (94): 245-250; auth, "Anthropogenic and natural disturbance and patterns of mortality in a mixed conifer forest in California," Can J of Forest Res, (94): 1149-1159; co-auth, "The role of climate in a pine forest regeneration pulse in the Southwestern United States," Ecoscience, (96): 310-318; auth, "The role of anthropogenic disturbance in a mixed conifer morality episode," J of Vegetation Sci, (97): 95-104; co-auth, "Community dynamics: What happens when we rerun the tape?," J of Theoretical Biol, (00): 515-526; co-auth, "Ecological Restoration of Southwestern Ponderosa Pine Forests: Ecosystems: A Broad Framework," Ecological Restoration, 00. **CONTACT ADDRESS** Dept of Geog, Univ of California, Los Angeles, 1255 Bunche, Box 951524, Los Angeles, CA 90095-1524. **EMAIL** forests@ucla.edu

SAVAGE, WILLIAM W., JR.
PERSONAL Born 10/13/1943, Richmond, VA, m, 1 child **DISCIPLINE** HISTORY **EDUCATION** Univ of SC, BA, 64, MA, 66; Univ of Okla, PhD, 72. **CAREER** From asst prof to prof, Univ of Okla, 73-. **MEMBERSHIPS** Western Hist Asn; Okla Hist Soc; Southern Historical Assn. **RESEARCH** Am Frontier; Popular Culture. **SELECTED PUBLICATIONS** Auth, The Cherokee Strip Live Stock Association, 73; The Cowboy Hero, 79; Singing Cowboys And All That Jazz, 83; Comic Books And America, 1945-1954, 90; ed, Cowboy Life, 75; Indian Life, 77. **CONTACT ADDRESS** Dept of History, Univ of Oklahoma, 455 W. Lindsey, Rm. 406, Norman, OK 73019.

SAWATSKY, RODNEY JAMES
PERSONAL Born 12/05/1943, Altona, MB, Canada, m, 1965, 3 children **DISCIPLINE** RELIGION, HISTORY **EDUCATION** Can Mennonite Bible Col, Winnipeg, B Christian Ed, 64; Bethel Col, Kans, BA, 65; Univ Minn, MA, 72; Princeton Univ, MA, 73 & Phd(relig), 77. **CAREER** Instr hist, Can Mennonite Bible Col, Winnipeg, 67-70; asst prof relig, 74-80, Dir Acad Affairs, Conrad Grabel Col, Univ Waterloo, 74-89, assoc prof Relig, Univ of Waterloo, 81-94; pres, Conrad Grebel Col, 89-94; pres, Messiah Col, 94-. **MEMBERSHIPS** Am Soc Church Hist; Am Acad Relig; Can Soc Study Relig; Can Protection Relig Freedom (pres, 78-). **RESEARCH** Mennonite history; evangelical and new religions; Canadian religious history. **SELECTED PUBLICATIONS** Coauth, Evangelical-Unification Dialogue, Rose of Sharon Pr (New York, NY), 79; co-ed, The Limits of Perfection, Inst of Anabaptist-Mennonite Studies (Waterloo, ON), 93. **CONTACT ADDRESS** President's Office, Messiah Col, One Col Ave, Grantham, PA, Canada 17027. **EMAIL** sawatsky@messiah.edu

SAWKINS, ANNEMARIE
PERSONAL Born 06/15/1965, Durham, England, m, 1996 **DISCIPLINE** ART HISTORY **EDUCATION** McGill Univ, MA 93; PhD 98; Colgate Univ, BA 88. **CAREER** Assoc Curator, Haggerty Museum of Art, 99-; Univ Wis Mil, lect, adj prof, 95-98; McGill Univ, instr 94. **HONORS AND AWARDS** Villard de Honnecourt Res Prize; 2 Max Binz Fel; Women's Cent McGill Fel; Max Stern Major Fel. **MEMBERSHIPS** CAA; AVISTA; ICMA; SAH; 16th Century Studies; MAM; AFM. **RESEARCH** Late gothic; medieval; renaissance. **SELECTED PUBLICATIONS** Auth, A Renaissance Treasury: The Flagg Collection of European Decorative Arts and Sculpture, entries Hudson Hills Press, 98; auth, Royal and Imperial Emblematics in the Architecture of Francois I, Architecture and the Emblem, ed, Peter M Daly, 98; Byzantine Influence at Saint-Front at Perigueux, The Avista Forum Jour, 98; auth, Giovanni Battista Piranesi, in: From Durer to Daumier: European Prints from the Collection of McGill Univ, ed Carol Solomon-Kiefer, Montreal, McGill Univ Press, 93. **CONTACT ADDRESS** Haggerty Museum of Art, Marquette Univ, P O Box 1881, Milwaukee, WI 53202. **EMAIL** a.sawkins@marquette.edu

SAWYER, DANA
PERSONAL Born 07/04/1951, Jonesport, ME, d, 2 children **DISCIPLINE** ART **EDUCATION** West Conn State Univ, BA, 73; Univ Hawaii, MA, 78; Univ Iowa, MA, 88. **MEMBERSHIPS** American Academy of Religion. **RESEARCH** North Indian Hindu ascetics. **SELECTED PUBLICATIONS** Auth, Monastic Structure of Banarsi Dandi Sadhus, in Hertel and Humes (eds); auth, Living Banaras, (Buffalo: SUNY Press, 1993); Transl, Yabshas: Essays in the Water Cosmology, by A.K. Coomaraswamy; ed, Paul Schroeden, Oxford University Press, 94. **CONTACT ADDRESS** Dept Liberal Arts, Maine Col of Art, 97 Spring St, Portland, ME 04101-3933. **EMAIL** dsawyer@meca.edu

SAWYER, JEFFREY K.
DISCIPLINE HISTORY **EDUCATION** San Francisco Art Inst, BFA, 72; Univ Calif Berkley, AB, 75, MA, 78, PhD, History, 82. **CAREER** Part-time Fac, Univ Calif, 78-83; Asst prof, Univ Richmond, 83-86; Assoc prof, Univ Balt, Dir, Jurisprudence Prog, 96-; Div Chair, 95-; Dir, Master Arts Legal & Ethical Studies, 91-95; Assoc prof, 92. **RESEARCH** Chair, Board of Trustees, Harford Comm College, member; Selden Society, Phi Beta Kappa. **SELECTED PUBLICATIONS** Maryland Legal History, Auth, Judicial Corruption and Legal Reform in Early Seventeenth-Century France, Law & Hist Rev, 88; auth, 'Benefit of Clergy' in Maryland and Virginia, Am Jour Legal Hist, 90; auth, Printed Poison: Pamphlets, Faction Politics, and the Public Sphere in Early Seventeenth-Century France, Univ Calif Press, 90; auth, Distrust of the Legal Establishment in Perspective: Maryland During the Early National Years, GA Jour S Legal Hist, 93; auth, "Women, Law, and the Pursuit of Happiness in Early Harford County" Harford Historical Bulletin 81 (1999): 3-41. **CONTACT ADDRESS** College of Liberal Arts, Univ of Baltimore, 1420 N. Charles Street, Baltimore, MD 21201. **EMAIL** jsawyer@ubmail.ubalt.edu

SAX, BENJAMIN
PERSONAL Born 01/07/1950, Boston, MA, s **DISCIPLINE** HISTORY **EDUCATION** Univ Chicago, BA, 73; MA 73; PhD, 78. **CAREER** From asst prof to assoc prof, Univ of Kans, 79-. **HONORS AND AWARDS** Vis Fel, Inst for Advanced Study, Princeton. **MEMBERSHIPS** Int Soc for Study in Europ Ideas, Int Asn for Philos & Lit. **RESEARCH** Intellectual & cultural history of Europe, philosophy of history. **SELECTED PUBLICATIONS** Auth, Images of Identity; auth, Cultural Visions. **CONTACT ADDRESS** Dept Hist, Univ of Kansas, Lawrence, Lawrence, KS 66045-0001. **EMAIL** bensax@falcon.cc.ukans.edu

SAXON, ARTHUR HARTLEY
PERSONAL Born 03/24/1935, Pittsburgh, Pa, m, 1957, 2 children **DISCIPLINE** HISTORY OF THE THEATRE **EDUCATION** Univ Pittsburgh, BA, 56; Columbia Univ, MA, 61; Yale Univ, PhD(hist of theatre), 66. **CAREER** Asst prof speech, theatre & English, Univ Pittsburgh, 66-69; assoc prof theatre, Univ Conn, 69-7; City Col New York & Grad Sch, City Univ New York, 71-76; Temple Univ, 78-81; gen ed, Archon Bks on Popular Entertainments, Shoe String Press, Inc, 77-80, Auth, Ed & Lectr, 76-, Am ed, Theatre Res/Rech Theatrales, 70-73; Guggenheim fel, 71-72, 82-83; Am Coun Learned Socs fel, 77-78; vis prof Am studies, Yale Univ, 81; mem bd Barnum Mus, 80- **HONORS AND AWARDS** Medal Barnum Festival Soc, 80; Membre d'Honneur, Club du Cirque, 80; "Key to the City" of Bridgeport, CT, 83; Barnard Hewitt Awd for "P.T. Barnum: The Legend and the Man," 90. **MEMBERSHIPS** Club du Crique. **RESEARCH** History of the circus and popular entertainments. **SELECTED PUBLICATIONS** Auth, A brief history of the Claque, Theatre Surv, 64; Enter Foot and Horse: A History of Hippodrama in England and France, Yale Univ, 68; contribr, Le Grand Livre du Cirque, Edito-Serv, 78; auth, The Life and Art of Andrew Ducrow & The Romantic Age of the English Circus, 78 & ed, The Autobiography of Mrs Tom Thumb, 79, Archon; Selected Letters of P. T. Barnum, Columbia Univ, 83; trans, As Barnum par Lui-Meme, Editions de la Gardine, 86; auth, P.T. Barnum: The Legend and the Man, Columbia Univ, 89; auth, Letters I Wish P.T. Barnum Had Written, Jumbo's Press, 94; auth, Barnumiana: A Select, Annotated Bibliog of Works By or Relating to P.T. Barnum, Jumbo's Press, 95; auth, Circus Language: A Glossary of Circus Terms, Jumbo's Press, 00. **CONTACT ADDRESS** 166 Orchard Hill Dr., Fairfield, CT 06430.

SAYWELL, JOHN T.
PERSONAL Born 04/03/1929, Weyburn, SK, Canada **DISCIPLINE** HISTORY, ENVIRONMENTAL STUDIES **EDUCATION** Victoria Col Univ BC, BA, MA; Harvard Univ, PhD. **CAREER** Lectr, Univ Toronto, 54; asst prof, 57, assoc prof, 62, Prof History & Environmental Stud, Dean, York Univ, 63-73. **MEMBERSHIPS** Mem, Can Hist Asn; mem, Can Pol Sci Asn. **SELECTED PUBLICATIONS** Auth, Canada: Pathways to the Present, Toronto: Stoddart, 99; auth, "The Illusory Concensus," in National History; auth, "Mitch Hepburn and Willie King's War," in N. Hillmer et al ed., A Country of Limitations: Cnadda and the World in 1939, (Canadian Committee for the History of the Second World War, 96): 120-137. **CONTACT ADDRESS** 158 Fulton Ave, Toronto, ON, Canada M4K 1Y3. **EMAIL** jsaaywell@yorku.ca

SBACCHI, ALBERTO
PERSONAL Born Palermo, Italy, m, 1963, 2 children **DISCIPLINE** AFRICAN AND MODERN EUROPEAN HISTORY **EDUCATION** Columbia Union Col, BA, 62; Pac Union Col, MA, 63; Univ Ill, Chicago Circle, PhD, 75. **CAREER** Head social sci dept hist, Ethiopian Adventist Col, 63-68; res asst hist, Univ Ill, Chicago Circle, 68-74; Prof Hist, Atlantic Union Col, 74-, Fel hist, Univ Ill, Chicago Circle, 70-71; res grant, Amitaly Soc, 70-71, Ital Ministry Foreign Affairs, Rome, 70-72, Am Coun Learned Soc, 76-77 & Atlantic Union Col Fac Res Grant, 78-79; Sec Brd of Dirs, Weidner Found, 94-; VP Brd of Dirs, Thayer Conservatory Orchestra, 85-87; Brd of Contributing eds, Morn of Africa Journal, 99-. **HONORS AND AWARDS** Knight of the Order of the Merit of the Italian Republic; Outstand Svc and Ded as Fac Adv, Phi Alpha Theta; Recognition for Acad Ach, Atlantic Union Col; Student Asn Awd for Teach Excel, Atlantic Union Col; Fulbright-Mays grant, 81-82; Fulbright Travel grant, 88; American Phils Soc grant, 91; Brooklyn Col Found grant, 98; John H. Weidner Found grant, 00. **MEMBERSHIPS** AHA; African Studies Asn; Soc Ital Hist Studies; Asn Seventh Day Adventist Historians (exec secy, & pres, 75-77); Afro-Ital Inst; Clinton Hist Soc; Phi Alpha Theta; Inst Storicc della resistenza e dell'Eta Moderna' Asn des Amis des Archives Diplomatiques. **RESEARCH** Italian colonialism in Ethiopia; European expansion; imperialism; diplomatic history. **SELECTED PUBLICATIONS** Auth, Legacy of bitterness: Poison gas and atrocities in the Italo-Ethiopian War 1935-1936, Geneva-Africa, 2/74; Secret talks for the submission of Haile Selassie and Asfaw Wassen, 1936-1939, Int J African Hist Studies, 4/74; Italian mandate or protectorate over Ethiopia, 1935-1936, Rivista di Studi Politici Internazionali, 4/75; The Italians and the Italo-Ethiopian War, 1935-1936, TransAfrican J Hist, 2/76; Italy and the treatment of the Ethiopian aristocracy, 1936-1939, Int J African Hist Studies, 2/77; Italian plans and projects for the colonization of Ethiopia, 1936-1940, Africa, 4/77; Governor John Clarkson's diary and the origin of Sierra Leone, J African Studies, 1/78; Il Colonialismo Italiano in Ethiopia, 1936-1940, Milan: Mursia, 80; auth, Legacy of Bitterness: Ethiopia and Fascist Italy, 1935-1941, Red Sea Press, 97; auth, Ethiopia Under Mussolini, Zed Books, 85, 2nd ed 89;auth, marcus Gravey and Ethiopia 1920-1940, Proced of the IX Int Conf of Ethiopian Stu, USSR Acad of Sci and African Inst, 86; auth, The Consolata Mission Archives and Italian Colonialism, Atti del Cenvegno Internazionale, Fonti e Problemi della Politica Coloniale Italiana, Messina-Taermina, 89; auth, Ital-Ethiopian Relations 1935-1941; Le Guerre Coloniali del Fascismo, Laterza Rowe, 91; auth, The Late R.L. Hess and the Memoirs of Giacomoe Maretti at the Court of Yohannes IV of Ethiopia, Proceedof the XII Int Conf of Ethiopian Stu, Mich St Univ, 95; auth, The Recognition of the Italian Empire 1936-1938, Proceed of the XIII Int Conf of Ethiopian Stu, Univ of Kyoto, 97. **CONTACT ADDRESS** Atlantic Union Col, PO Box 1000, South Lancaster, MA 01561-9999.

SCAGLIA, GUSTINA
PERSONAL Born Glastonbury, CT **DISCIPLINE** HISTORY, ART **EDUCATION** NYork Univ, Inst of Fine Art, MA, 52, PhD, 60. **CAREER** Asst prof, 62, prof, 70-90, Queens Col, CUNY. **HONORS AND AWARDS** Amer Asn of Univ Women Fulbright Grand to Rome. **RESEARCH** Drawings of machines; arch drawings of antiquities by XV-XVI century artists. **SELECTED PUBLICATIONS** Auth, Il Vitruvio Magliabechiano di Francesco di Giorgio, Documenti inediti di cultura Toscana, Vol VI, 85; auth, Francesco di Giorgio, Checklist and History of Manuscripts and Drawings in Autographs and Copies. Lehigh Univ Press, 92, Architectural Drawings of Antonio Da Sangallo - the Younger, 94. **CONTACT ADDRESS** 400 Central Park West, 5A, New York, NY 10025.

SCALISE, CHARLES J.
PERSONAL Born 07/25/1950, Baltimore, MD, m, 1980, 2 children **DISCIPLINE** CHURCH HISTORY, CHRISTIAN THEOLOGY **EDUCATION** Princeton Univ, AB, summa cum laude, 72; Yale Div Sch, MDiv, magna cum laude, 75; S Baptist Theol Sem, PhD, 87; Univ Oxford, postgrad, 90-91. **CAREER** Baptist Chaplain, Yale, 75-82; lectr, Pastoral Theol, Yale Div Sch, 76-80; dir, dept Christian higher educ, Baptist Conven New Eng, 82-84; asst prof, S Baptist Theol Sem, 87-94; assoc and mang ed, Rev and expositor, 91-94; assoc prof, Fuller Theol Sem, 94- . **HONORS AND AWARDS** Sloan Scholar, 68-72; Ger bk prize, 71; Albert G. Milband mem scholar prize, 71; Phi Beta Kappa, 72; Tew prize, 73; Oliver Ellsworth Daggett prize, 74; Julia A. Archibald high scholar prize, 75; Outstanding young men Am, 75; Who's Who S and SW, 93-94. **RESEARCH** Theological hermeneutics; History of exegesis; History of doctrine; pastoral Theology. **SELECTED PUBLICATIONS** Auth, Allegorical Flights of Fancy: The Problem of Origen's Exegesis, The Greek Orthodox Theol Rev, 32, 87, 69-88; Origen and the Sensus Literalis, in Origen of Alexandria, Notre Dame, 88, 117-129; Developing a Theological Rationale for Ministry: Some Reflections on the Process of Teaching Pastoral Theology to MDiv Students, Jour Pastoral Theol, 1, 91, 53-68; Hermeneutics as Theological Prolegomena: A Canonical Approach, Mercer UP, 94; Canonical Hermeneutics: Childs and Barth, Scotish Jour Theol, 47, 94, 61-88; Teresa of Avila: Teacher of Evangelical Women? Cross Currents: The Jour of the Asn for Rel and Intel Life, 46, 96, 244-249; From Scripture to Theology: A Canonical Journey into Hermeneutics, InterVarsity Press, 96; Agreeing on where We Disagree: Lindbeck's Postliberalism and Pastoral Theology, Jour Pastoral Theol, 8, 98, 43-51. **CONTACT ADDRESS** Fuller Theol Sem, 101 Nickerson St, Ste 330, Seattle, WA 98109-1621. **EMAIL** cscalise@fuller.edu

SCALLEN, CATHERINE B.
DISCIPLINE NORTHERN BAROQUE ART **EDUCATION** Wellesley Col, BA; Williams Col, MA, Princeton Univ PhD, 90. **CAREER** Vis prof, CWRU, 91-92; Fairfield uviv, Conn, 92-95; assist prof, CWRU, 95-. **HONORS AND AWARDS** Co-cur, Cubism and American Photography, 1910-1930. **SE-**

LECTED PUBLICATIONS Auth, Catalog ed, exhib catalog Passion and Patience: The Joys of Collecting; Old Masters from the Arnold;Seena Davis Collection. **CONTACT ADDRESS** Case Western Reserve Univ, 10900 Euclid Ave, Cleveland, OH 44106. **EMAIL** cbs2@po.cwru.edu

SCAMEHORN, HOWARD LEE
PERSONAL Born 02/27/1926, Kalamazoo, MI **DISCIPLINE** UNITED STATES ECONOMIC HISTORY **EDUCATION** Western Mich Univ, AB, 49; Univ Ill, MA, 52, PhD(hist), 56. **CAREER** Prof Hist, Univ Colo, 56-, Dir, Western Bus Hist Res Ctr, Denver, 67- **MEMBERSHIPS** Orgn Am Historians; Western Hist Asn. **RESEARCH** Business, industry, mining in the American west; mining; transportation. **SELECTED PUBLICATIONS** Auth, Thomas Scott Baldwin, Ill State Hist Soc J, 56; Balloons to Jets, Regnery, 57; American air transport and air power doctrine, Air Power Historian, 61; The Buckeye Rovers, Ohio Univ, 65; John C Osgood and the Western steel industry, Ariz & West, 73; Pioneer Steelmaker in the West: CF&L, Pruett, 76; coauth, University of Colorado, 1876-1976, Jovanovich, 76. **CONTACT ADDRESS** Dept of Hist, Univ of Colorado, Boulder, Boulder, CO 80309.

SCANLAN, J. T.
DISCIPLINE EIGHTEENTH-CENTURY ENGLISH LITERATURE, LEGAL HISTORY **EDUCATION** Rutgers Col, A.B.; Univ Mich, A.M.; PhD. **CAREER** Vis asst prof, Vassar Col; assoc prof Eng, Providence Col. **RESEARCH** Eighteenth-century writing; legal history, contemporary non-fiction. **SELECTED PUBLICATIONS** Writes on eighteenth-century English literature, legal history, and contemporary non-fiction. **CONTACT ADDRESS** Dept of Eng, Providence Col, Providence, RI 02918-0001. **EMAIL** hambone@providence.edu

SCANLON, JAMES EDWARD
PERSONAL Born 05/20/1940, Steubenville, OH **DISCIPLINE** HISTORY **EDUCATION** Georgetown Univ, AB, 62; Univ Wis, MA, 65; Univ Va, PhD(hist), 69. **CAREER** Prof Hist, Randolph-Macon Col, 79-, Chmn Dept, 81-, Consult, Choice Mag, 69- **MEMBERSHIPS** Orgn Am Historians; AAUP. **RESEARCH** Colonial history, New York and West Indies. **SELECTED PUBLICATIONS** Auth, A sudden conceit, La Hist, 68; British politics and appointment of Robert Hunter, NY Hist Soc Quart, 73; History of Randolph-Macon College, Univ Press Va (in prep). **CONTACT ADDRESS** Dept of Hist, Randolph-Macon Col, 200 Henry St, Ashland, VA 23005-1697.

SCARBOROUGH, WILLIAM
PERSONAL Born 01/17/1933, Baltimore, MD, m, 1954, 2 children **DISCIPLINE** HISTORY **EDUCATION** Univ NC at Chapel Hill, AB, 54; PhD, 62; Cornell Univ, MA, 57. **CAREER** Asst prof, Millsaps Col, 61-63; asst prof, Univ La at Monroe, 63-64; from assoc prof to Charles W. Moorman Distinguished Alumni Prof in the Humanities, Univ Southern Miss, 64-; dept of hist chemn, Univ Southern Miss, 80-90. **HONORS AND AWARDS** Excellence in Teaching Awd, Univ Southern Miss, 81 & 84; Fac Res Awd, Univ Southern Miss, 89; Jules & Frances Landry Awd, LSU Press, 89. **MEMBERSHIPS** Southern Hist Asn, Agr Hist Soc, Miss Hist Soc, SC Hist Soc, St George Tucker Soc, The Hist Soc. **RESEARCH** Antebellum South (Plantation System, Slavery, Agriculture), The Civil War. **SELECTED PUBLICATIONS** Auth, The Overseer: Plantation Management in the Old South, 66 & 84; ed, The Diary of Edmund Ruffin (3 vols), 72-89; auth, "Heartland of the Cotton Kingdom," in A History of Mississippi, ed. R. A. McLemore, 73; auth, "Science on the Plantation," in Science and Medicine in the Old South, eds. Ronald L. Numbers & Todd L. Savitt, 89. **CONTACT ADDRESS** Dept Hist, Univ of So Mississippi, 2805 Hardy St, Hattiesburg, MS 39406-0001.

SCARDAVILLE, MICHAEL CHARLES
PERSONAL Born 02/05/1948, Newark, NJ, m, 1970, 2 children **DISCIPLINE** APPLIED & LATIN AMERICAN HISTORY **EDUCATION** Rutgers Univ, BA, 70; Univ Fla, MA, 72, PhD(hist), 77. **CAREER** Oral historian, Nat Geographic, 74; historian, Hist St Augustine Preservation Bd, 77-81; Assoc Prof & Dir Appl Hist Prog, Univ SC, 81-, Consult, Fla Endowment for the Humanities, 79-80, Pub Broadcasting Syst, 79, Riverside-Avondale Preservation, 80-81, City of Palatka, 80-82 & City of Arcadia, 82. **MEMBERSHIPS** Nat Coun Pub Hist; Nat Trust for Hist Preservation; Am Asn for State & Local Hist; Conf of Latin Am Historians; Southeast Borderlands Asn. **RESEARCH** Historic preservation; the effect of urban development on the built environment; urban development of southeastern and circum-Caribbean coastal communities. **SELECTED PUBLICATIONS** Auth, Economic growth and the urban poor: Mexico City in the late colonial period, Latinamericanist, 77; coauth, Florida in the late first Spanish period: The 1756 Grinan report, El Escribano, 79; auth, Alcohol abuse and tavern reform in late colonial Mexico City, Hisp Am Hist Rev, 80; coauth, Historic Sites and Buildings Survey of St Augustine, Florida, 80 & Cultural Resource Survey of Palatka, Florida, 81, Fla Div of Archives and Hist; auth, Approaches to the study of the southeastern borderlands, In: Alabama and the Borderlands, Univ Ala Press (in prep). **CONTACT ADDRESS** Dept of Hist, Univ of So Carolina, Columbia, Columbia, SC 29208.

SCHAAR, STUART H.
PERSONAL Born 09/26/1937, New York, NY **DISCIPLINE** COMPARATIVE HISTORY **EDUCATION** City Col NYork, BA, 58; Princeton Univ, PhD, 66. **CAREER** Asst prof hist, Univ WI, Madison, 64-69; Fac assoc, Am Univs Field Staff, 67-69; assoc prof hist, Brooklyn Col, 69-97, Prof, 96. **HONORS AND AWARDS** John D and Catherine T MacArthur, $23,600 Grant (June 95) to organize a conference at the Center of International Studies, Princeton Univ on the present Algerian crisis; John D and Catherine T MacArthur $22,500. Grant (June 95) to produce a film on the Algerian crisis with the Algerian film director Merzac Allouache, receipient of the 1994 International Film Critics Awd at Cannes, Paris, Shown in Aug 97; Swiss Foundation for Peace and Development Grants-tot, $45,000, Jan 95, two conferences, one with 18 North African Women re violence against North African Women and the second, co-sponsored by the Institute for the Transregional study of the Contemporary Middle East, North Africa and Central Asia, Princeton Univ; John D and Catherina T MacArthur Foundation $43,000, Dec 97, international conference on the present Algerian crisis, London, Feb 98; John D and Catherine T MacArthur Foundation $25,000 Grant, projects aimed at fortifying civil society in North Africa, Apr 98. **MEMBERSHIPS** Fel Mid E Studies Asn NAm; AHA; World Hist Assoc. **RESEARCH** Comp Islamic hist. **SELECTED PUBLICATIONS** Auth, Rebellion, revolution and religious intermediaries in some nineteenth century Islamic states; Co-ed, The Shaping of the Modern World from the Enlightenment to the Present, 3d ed, Minn St Paul, West Publishing Co, 95; In: Churches and States: The Religious Institution and Modernization, Am Univs Field Staff, 67; The Barbary Coast (c 500 BC-AD 639), In: The Horizon History of Africa, Am Heritage, 71; King Hassan's alternatives, In: Man, State and Society in the Contemporary Maghreb, Praeger, 73; Le jeu des forces politiques en Tunisie, Maghreb-Machrek, 10-12/77; coauth, M'hamed Ali and the Tunisian labour movement, Race & Class, winter 78. **CONTACT ADDRESS** Dept Hist, Brooklyn Col, CUNY, 2901 Bedford Ave, Brooklyn, NY 11210-2813. **EMAIL** sschaar@brooklyn.cuny.edu

SCHACHT, JOHN N.
PERSONAL Born 02/24/1943, Chicago, IL, m, 1972, 2 children **DISCIPLINE** HISTORY **EDUCATION** Wesleyan Univ, BA, 1964; MA, 1966, PhD, 1977, Univ Iowa; Univ Illinois, MS, 1977. **CAREER** Researcher, Communication Workers of America-Univ Iowa Oral History Project, 68-72; Libr, Univ Iowa, 77-. **HONORS AND AWARDS** Herbert Hoover Library Assoc Scholar, 89-90. **MEMBERSHIPS** ALA; Assoc for Bibliography of History **RESEARCH** U.S. labor history; Iowa history; World War II; bibliography of history. **SELECTED PUBLICATIONS** Auth, The Making of Telephone Unionism 1920-1947, New Brunswick, NJ: Rutgers Univ Press, 85; auth, Labor History in the Academy: A Layman's Guide to a Century of Scholarship, Labor's Heritage, 94. **CONTACT ADDRESS** Reference Dept, Library, Univ of Iowa, Iowa City, IA 52242. **EMAIL** john_schacht@uiowa.edu

SCHADE, ROSEMARIE
DISCIPLINE HISTORY **EDUCATION** York Univ, BA, MA; Univ York, PhD. **CAREER** Assoc prof. **RESEARCH** German bourgeois feminist movement. **SELECTED PUBLICATIONS** Auth, co-ed, eight volume bibliography, Gender Balancing History: Towards an Inclusive Curriculum; Ein weibliches Utopia: Organisationen und Ideologien der Madchen und Frauen in der burgerlichen Jugendbewegung, 1905-1933. **CONTACT ADDRESS** Dept of Hist, Concordia Univ, Montreal, 1455 de Maisonneuve W, Montreal, QC, Canada H3G 1M8. **EMAIL** rschade@vax2.concordia.ca

SCHAEFER, JEAN OWENS
DISCIPLINE ART HISTORY **EDUCATION** Stanford Univ, BA, 68; Univ CA-Berkeley, MA, 71, PhD, 77. **CAREER** Prof, adj prof, Women's Stud, Univ of WI, Parkside. **SELECTED PUBLICATIONS** Auth, Kaethe Kollwitz in America: Tides in the Reception of the Work, Women's Art J, vol 15, 94; Gossaert's Vienna St. Luke Portraying the Virgin: An Early Response to Iconoclasm, Source: Notes in the Hist of Art, XII, 92; Restructuring for Innovative Undergraduate Education, J Prof Stud, 90. **CONTACT ADDRESS** Dept of Art, Univ of Wyoming, PO Box 3964, Laramie, WY 82071-3964. **EMAIL** Jeans@uwyo.edu

SCHAFER, ELIZABETH D.
PERSONAL Born 09/26/1965, Opelika, AL **DISCIPLINE** HISTORY **EDUCATION** Auburn Univ, BA, 86, MA, 88, PhD, 93. **CAREER** Independent Scholar, 93-. **HONORS AND AWARDS** Shirley Henn Memorial Awd for Critical Scholar, 98, Hollins Univ; Four Honorable Mentions in Writer's Digest writing competition for poetry, fiction and non-fiction, 94, 97, 98. **MEMBERSHIPS** Am Hist Asn; Org Am Hist; Southern Hist Asn; Soc Hist Technol; Hist Science Soc; Childrens Lit Asn. **RESEARCH** History of science and technology; history of women; history of African Americans. **SELECTED PUBLICATIONS** Coauth, Women Who Made a Difference in Alabama, Tuscaloosa AL: Alabama League of Women Voters, 95; auth, entry, Biographical Encyclopedia of Mathematicians, 98; Biographical Encyclopedia of Scientists, 98; auth, entry, Science Supplement: Spring 1998, 98; auth, Beacham's Sourcebook for Exploring Young Adult Fiction: Harry Potter, Beacham Publishing, Washington D.C., 00. **CONTACT ADDRESS** PO Box 57, Loachapoka, AL 36865. **EMAIL** edschafer@reporters.net

SCHAFER, JUDITH
PERSONAL Born 12/12/1942, New Orleans, LA, m, 1963, 2 children **DISCIPLINE** HISTORY **EDUCATION** Newcomb Col, BA, 63; Tulane Univ, MA, 78; PhD, 85. **CAREER** Vis assoc prof to assoc prof, Tulane Univ, 90-. **HONORS AND AWARDS** Peter T. Cominos Prize, 82; John T. Monroe Fel, 83-84; William r. Hogun Awd, 83; Col of Arts and Sci Exemplary Serv Awd, 91; Newcomb Mortar Board Fac Teaching Awd, 92, 95; Fel, St. George Tucker Soc, 92; Francis Butler Simkins Prize, 93-94; General L. Kemper Williams Prize, 95; Barbara Greenbaum Newcomb Fel Res Stipend, 95; paul Tulane Col Student Senate Awd, 95; Fel, Grady McWhinney Found, 98. **MEMBERSHIPS** Org of Am Hist; S Hist Assoc; Am Soc for Legal Hist; Soc for Hist of the Early Am Republic; La Hist Assoc; Supreme Court of La Hist Soc; Caribbean Studies Assoc. **RESEARCH** U.S. Legal History, Southern History, Louisiana. **SELECTED PUBLICATIONS** Auth, "The Immediate Impact of Nat Turner's Insurrection on New Orleans", La Hist 21, (80): 361-376; auth, "New Orleans Slavery as Seen in Advertisements", J of Southern Hist 47, (Feb 81): 35-56; auth, "The Long Arm of the Law: Slave Criminals and the Supreme Court in Antebellum Louisiana", Tulane Law Rev 60, (June 86): 1247-68; auth, "Open and Notorious Concubinage", The Emancipation of Slave Mistresses by Will and the Supreme Court in Antebellum Louisiana", La Hist 28, (Spring 87): 165-82; auth, Slavery, the Civil Law, and the Supreme Court of Louisiana, La State Univ Pr, 94; auth, "Forever Free from the Bonds of Slavery: Emancipation and Voluntary Enslavement in New Orleans, 1846-1862, (forthcoming); auth, "Slaves and Crime in New Orleans, 1846-1862", Race, Crime and the Law, eds Donald Nieman and Christopher Waldrep, Univ of Ga Pr, (forthcoming); coauth, Louisiana Lives: People Who shaped the Destiny of the Pelican State, (forthcoming); auth, "The Murder of a Lewd and Abandoned Woman: State v Abraham Parker", Am J of Legal Hist (forthcoming). **CONTACT ADDRESS** Dept Hist, Tulane Univ, 6823 St Charles Ave, New Orleans, LA 70118-5665. **EMAIL** jschafer@mailhost.tcs.tulane.edu

SCHAFFER, RONALD
PERSONAL Born 04/22/1932, New York, NY, m, 1957, 2 children **DISCIPLINE** MILITARY & AMERICAN HISTORY **EDUCATION** Columbia Col, BA, 53; Princeton Univ, AM, 55, PhD, 59. **CAREER** Instr hist, Columbia Col, 58-60; from instr to asst prof, Ind Univ, 60-65; from asst prof to assoc prof, 65-75, prof hist, CA State Univ, Northridge, 75-, Grants, Am Philos Soc, 60 & 78; res grants, CA State Univ, Northridge, 68, 78 & 81; Nat Endowment Hum fel, 82. **MEMBERSHIPS** Orgn Am Historians; Soc Military Hist **RESEARCH** Recent US hist, espec mil hist. **SELECTED PUBLICATIONS** Auth, The Montana Woman Suffrage Campaign, 1911-1914, Pac NW Quart, 1/64; The War Department's Defense of ROTC, 1920-1940, Wis Mag Hist, winter 69-70; The 1940 Small Wars Manual and the Lessons of History, 4/72 & General Stanley D Embick: Military Dissenter, 10/73, Mil Affairs; The Problem of Consciousness in the Woman Suffrage Movement: A California Perspective, Pac Hist Rev, 11/76; auth, The United States in World War I: A Selected Bibliography, Clio Press, 78; American Military Ethics in World War II: The Bombing of German Civilians, J Am Hist, 9/80; Wings of Judgment: American Bombing in World War II, Oxford Univ Press, 85; America in the Great World War: The Rise of the War Welfare State, Oxford Univ Press, 91. **CONTACT ADDRESS** Dept of Hist, California State Univ, Northridge, 18111 Nordhoff St, Northridge, CA 91330-8250. **EMAIL** ronald.schaffer@csun.edu

SCHALLER, MICHAEL
PERSONAL Born 06/02/1947, New York, NY, 3 children **DISCIPLINE** HISTORY OF UNITED STATES FOREIGN RELATIONS **EDUCATION** State Univ NYork, Binghamton, BA, 68 Univ Mich, MA, 69, PhD(hist), 74. **CAREER** Asst prof, 74-79, assoc prof hist, Univ Az, 79-84, prof hist 84-, Nat Endowment for Humanities fel, 80-81; Guggenheim Mem fel, 81-82; Fulbright Fellowship, 83-84. **HONORS AND AWARDS** Bernath Book Prize, Soc Historians Am Foreign Rel, 80. **MEMBERSHIPS** Orgn Am Historians; Soc Hist Am Foreign Rel. **RESEARCH** United States-China relation, World War II period; post World War II United States-East Asian policies; United States-Japan relations. **SELECTED PUBLICATIONS** Auth, The United States Crusade in China, 1938-1945, Columbia Univ, 79; The United States and China in the 20th Century, Oxford Univ, 79; The American Occupation of Japan, Oxford Univ Press, 85; Douglas MacArthur--The Far Eastern General, Oxford Univ Press, 89; Reckoning with Reagan, Oxford Univ Press, 92; Altered States--The U.S. and Japan Since the Occupation, Oxford Univ Press, 97. **CONTACT ADDRESS** Dept of Hist, Univ of Arizona, Tucson, AZ 85721-0001. **EMAIL** schaller@u.arizona.edu

SCHAMA, SIMON
DISCIPLINE HISTORY OF ART **EDUCATION** Cambrdge Univ, PhD, 69. **CAREER** Prof. **HONORS AND AWARDS**

Art critic, New Yorker. **RESEARCH** Biography of Rembrandt. **SELECTED PUBLICATIONS** Auth, Patriots and Liberators: Revolution in the Netherlands, 1780-1813, 77; Two Rothschilds and the Land of Israel, 78; The Embarrassment of Riches: an Interpretation of Dutch Culture in the Golden Age, 87; Citizens: a Chronicle of the French Revolution, 89; Dead Certainties: Unwarranted Speculations, 91; Landscape and Memory, 95. **CONTACT ADDRESS** Dept of Hist, Columbia Col, New York, 2960 Broadway, New York, NY 10027-6902.

SCHANTZ, MARK S.
DISCIPLINE HISTORY **EDUCATION** Geo Wash Univ, BA, 77; Yale Div Sch, MDiv, 81; Emory, PhD, 91. **CAREER** ASSOC PROF, HIST, HENDRIX COLL **MEMBERSHIPS** Am Antiquarian Soc **SELECTED PUBLICATIONS** Auth, "Religious Tracts, Evangelical Reform, and the Market Revolution in Antebellum America," Jour of the Early Rep, 97; auth, Piety in Providence: The Class Dimensions of Religious Experience in Providence, Rhode Island, 1790-1860, Cornell Univ Press, 00. **CONTACT ADDRESS** Dept of Hist, Hendrix Col, Conway, AR 72031. **EMAIL** schantzms@hendrix.edu

SCHAPSMEIER, EDWARD LEWIS
PERSONAL Born 02/08/1927, Council Bluffs, IA **DISCIPLINE** RECENT AMERICAN & DIPLOMATIC HISTORY **EDUCATION** Concordia Teacher's Col, Nebr, BA, 49; Univ Nebr, Omaha, MA, 52; Univ Southern Calif, PhD(hist), 65. **CAREER** Lectr hist, Univ Southern Calif, 64-65; instr, Ohio State Univ, 65-66; assoc prof, 66-67, prof to dist prof emer, Ill State Univ, 67-, Vis prof hist, Ill Wesleyan Univ, 68-69; regional ed, J West, 70-78. **MEMBERSHIPS** AHA; Orgn Am Historians; Oral Hist Asn; Am Studies Asn; Agr Hist Soc. **RESEARCH** Recent American history; diplomatic and agricultural history. **SELECTED PUBLICATIONS** Coauth, Henry A Wallace of Iowa, The Agrarian Years, 1910-40, 68 & Prophet in Politics: Henry A Wallace and the War Years, 1940-65, 69, Iowa State Univ; Walter Lippmann: Philosopher-journalist, Pub Affairs, 69; Abundant Harvests: Story of American Agriculture, Forum, 73; Encyclopedia of American Agricultural History, Greenwood, 76; Ezra Taft Benson and the Politics of Agriculture, Interstate, 76; Dictionary of Political Parties, Greenwood, 81; co-ed, Senator Everett M Dirksen of Illinois: The Politics of Minority Leadership, Univ Ill Press, 82. **CONTACT ADDRESS** Dept of Hist, Illinois State Univ, Normal, IL 61790. **EMAIL** eschap@ilstu.edu

SCHARF, PETER M.
PERSONAL Born 06/14/1958, New Haven, CT, s **DISCIPLINE** SANSKRIT LANGUAGE & LITERATURE, INDIAN PHILOSOPHY, LINGUISTICS **EDUCATION** Weslyan Univ, BA, 81; Brown Univ, 82-83; Univ Penn, PhD, 90. **CAREER** Comp prog, Microtex,81; comp prog, Real Dec Corp, 81-82; comp prog, Lang Sys, 82-83; teach asst, Univ Pa, 85-86; vis lectr, Univ Vir, 92; vis lectr, 92-94; SAF comm, 92-; chair, 95-96; FAC comp, 94-97; lectr, 94-, Brown Univ. **HONORS AND AWARDS** Outstand HS Sr Sems Schl; Foreign Lang Area Stud Fel; AIIS, Res Fel; Mellon Grad Fel; UP Dean Fel; NEH Fel; Post Doc Fel; APS Gnt. **MEMBERSHIPS** BORI; AOS; AAS; APA; BLS; Dharam Hinduja Indic Res Cen. **RESEARCH** Indian philosophy of language and linguistics; Indian philosophy; concepts of the self; Vedic interpretation in Indian literature; text encoding and computational analysis of Sanskrit. **SELECTED PUBLICATIONS** Auth, The Denotation of Generic Terms in Ancient Indian Philosophy: Grammar, Nyaya, and Mimamsa, Trans Am Philo Soc 86 APS (Philadelphia), 96; auth, "Pan mi, vivaksa, and karaka-rule-ordering," in Madhav Deshpande, ed. George Cardona, in press; auth "The term 'akrti' and the Concept of a Class Property in the Mahabhasya," Wiener Zeitschrijtfur die Kunde Sudasiens 36 (92): 31-48; auth, "Assessing Sabara's Arguments for the Conclusion that a Generic Term Denotes Just a Class Property, " J Indian Philo 21 (93): 1-10; auth, "Does Panini prohibit prohibitive compounds? An analysis of negation in the term anupasarge," Wiener Zeitschrififtir die Kunde Sudasiens 39 (95): 15-24; auth, "Early Indian Grammarians on a speaker's intention," J Am Oriental Soc 115 (95): 66-76; auth, "Clause-initial dvayam: One less case of an extra posed adverb," Indo-Iranian J 40 (97): 327-338; rev of, "Panini Re-Interpreted," by Charu Deva Shastri, Hist Ling 18 (91): 399-402; rev of, "Sanskrit Syntax: A Volume in Honor of the Centennial of Speijer's Sanskrit Syntax," ed, Hans Henrich Hock, J Am Oriental Soc 114 (94): 485-487; rev of, "Ideology and Status of Sanskrit: Contributions to the History of Sanskrit Language," ed. Jan E M Houben, Anthro Ling 40 (98): 167-174. **CONTACT ADDRESS** Dept Classics, Brown Univ, 1 Prospect St, Providence, RI 02912-9100. **EMAIL** Peter_Scharf@Brown.edu

SCHARNAU, RALPH WILLIAM
PERSONAL Born 10/22/1935, Woodstock, IL, m, 1960, 3 children **DISCIPLINE** UNITED STATES HISTORY **EDUCATION** Beloit Col, BA, 57; Univ Ill, MA, 59; Northern Ill Univ, PhD, 70. **CAREER** Instr hist, Northern Ill Univ, 63-64; asst prof, McKendree Col, 65-69, assoc prof, 69-70; assoc prof, 70-75, prof hist, 75- , Univ Dubuque; prof hist, Univ Dubuque, 75-99; hist lectr, Univ of Wis-Platteville, 99-00; part-time inst, NE IA Com Col, Peosta, 00-. **HONORS AND AWARDS** Participant, Wye Fac Sem, 87; NEH summer inst for col and univ faculty, 94; Throne-Aldrich Awd, 94; mem, scholar and grant comt, Hoover Presidential Library Asn, 99. **MEMBERSHIPS** AHA; Orgn Am Historians. **RESEARCH** American social and cultural history; American labor history; American environmental history. **SELECTED PUBLICATIONS** Auth, Thomas J Morgan and the United Labor Party of Chicago, J Ill State Hist Soc, spring 73; Elizabeth Morgan, crusader for labor reform, Labor Hist, summer 73; auth, Workers and Politics: The Knights of Labor in Dubuque, Iowa, 1885-1890, Annals of IA, 87; auth, The Knights of Labor in Iowa, Annals of IA, 91; auth, Workers, Unions, and Workplaces in Dubuque, 1830-1990, annals of IA, 93; auth, Street Car Strike 1903: Dubuque Walks, Labor's Heritage, 95; auth, The Labor Movement in Iowa, 1900-1910, J of the West, 96. **CONTACT ADDRESS** Dept of History, Northeast Iowa Comm Col, Peosta, 10250 Sundown Rd, Peosta, IA 52068. **EMAIL** rrscharnau@aol.com

SCHAUB, MARILYN MCNAMARA
PERSONAL Born 03/24/1928, Chicago, IL, m, 1969, 1 child **DISCIPLINE** RELIGIOUS STUDIES, CLASSICAL LANGUAGES **EDUCATION** Rosary Col, BA, 53; Univ Fribourg, PhD(class philos), 57. **CAREER** Asst prof class lang, 57-62, assoc prof relig studies & class lang, 62-69, Rosary Col; assoc prof, 73-77, prof theol, 77-80, Duquesne Univ; hon assoc, Am Schs Orient Res, Jerusalem, 66-67; admin dir, expedition to the southeast end of the Dead Sea, Jordan, 77, 79, 81, 89-90. **HONORS AND AWARDS** Pres Awd for Faculty Excellence in Teaching, Duquesne Univ, 90. **MEMBERSHIPS** Soc Bibl Lit; Cath Bibl Asn; Am Acad Relig; Archaeol Inst Am. **RESEARCH** Old Testament; New Testament; early Bronze Age settlements at the southeast end of the Dead Sea, Jordan. **SELECTED PUBLICATIONS** Co-translr, Agape in the New Testament, Herder, 63-67; auth, Friends and Friendship in St Augustine, Alba, 65; contribr, Encyclopedic Dictionary of Religion, Corpus, 78; contrib, Harper Collins Bible Dictionary, 96; contrib, Collegeville Pastoral Dictionary of Biblical Theology, 96. **CONTACT ADDRESS** Theol Dept, Duquesne Univ, Pittsburgh, PA 15282. **EMAIL** schaub@duq3.cc.duq.edu

SCHAUS, GERALD
DISCIPLINE GREEK ARCHAEOLOGY **EDUCATION** Alberta, PhD. **CAREER** Prof; Dept Ch. **MEMBERSHIPS** Greek Symposia Assn Waterloo. **RESEARCH** Greek Archaeol with a special interest in Archaic Greek pottery; Greek hist; Greek colonization. **SELECTED PUBLICATIONS** Coauth, "Notes on the Topography of Eresos," Am Journal of Archaeol 98, (94): 411-430; coauth, Corpus Vaasorum antiquorum, The Univ Museum, Philadelphia, 95; auth, "An Archaeologcal Field Survey at Eresos, Lesbos," Echoes du Monde Classique/Classical Views 15, (96): 27-74. **CONTACT ADDRESS** Dept of Classics, Wilfrid Laurier Univ, 75 University Ave W, Waterloo, ON, Canada N2L 3C5. **EMAIL** gschaus@mach1.wlu.ca

SCHEIBER, HARRY N.
PERSONAL Born New York, NY, m, 1958, 2 children **DISCIPLINE** UNITED STATES HISTORY **EDUCATION** Columbia Univ, AB, 55; Cornell Univ, MA, 57, PhD, 62. **CAREER** From instr to prof hist, Dartmouth Col, 60-71; prof hist, Univ Calif, San Diego, 71-80; Stefan A Riesenfeld prof of law & hist, Univ Calif, Berkeley, 80-. **HONORS AND AWARDS** Moses Coit Tyler Prize, 59 & Messenger Prize, 60, Cornell Univ; Ohio Univ Press Awd, 70; MA (Hon) Dartmouth, 65; JD (Hon), Uppsala Univ, Sweden, 98; Hon Fel Am Soc for Legal Hist, 99; Am Coun Learned Socs fel studies law, 66-67; fel, Ctr Advan Studies Behav Sci, 66-67, vis scholar, 70-71; pres, NH Civil Liberties Union, 69-70; mem, Beveridge-Dunning Prize Comn, AHA, 70-73, chmn, 73; mem comt US hist, Col Entrance Exam Bd, 70-80; pres, Coun Res Econ Hist, 72-75; Guggenheim fel, 70-71; dir, Nat Endowment for Humanities Sem, 78, 79 & 81; Rockefeller fel, 80; Project 87 fel, 80. **MEMBERSHIPS** Agr Hist Soc; Am Soc Legal Hist; Law & Soc Asn; Econ Hist Asn; AHA; Ocean Governance Study Group; Calif Supreme Ct Hist Soc. **RESEARCH** Am legal hist; 19th & 20th Century US hist; Am econ hist; ocean law and marine resources. **SELECTED PUBLICATIONS** Auth, Wilson Administration and Civil Liberties 1917-21, Cornell Univ Pr, 60; auth, The Condition of American Federalism, US Congress print, 65; auth, Ohio Canal Era: A Case Study of Government and the Economy 1820-61, Ohio Univ Pr, 70, 2nd ed, 87; auth, American Economic History, Harper & Row, 76; auth, American Law and the Constitutional Order, Harvard Univ Pr, 2nd ed, 87; auth, Legal Culture and the Legal Profession, Westview, 97; auth, The State and Freedom of Contract, Stanford Univ Pr, 99; auth, Inter-Allied Conflict and Ocean Law: The Occupation Command's Revival of Japanese Fisheries and Whaling, Acad Sinica Pr, 01; ed & contrib, Law of the Sea, The Common Heritage & Emerging Challenges, Kluwer Law Intl, 01; **CONTACT ADDRESS** Sch of Law, Univ of California, Berkeley, Boalt Hall, Berkeley, CA 94720-2150. **EMAIL** scheiber@uclink.berkeley.edu; scheiber@law.berkeley.edu

SCHEIDE, FRANK MILO
PERSONAL Born 04/01/1949, Redwing, MN, m, 1993 **DISCIPLINE** FILM HISTORY AND MASS MEDIA CRITICISM **EDUCATION** Univ Wisc, BS, 71, MA, 72, PhD, 90. **CAREER** Lect, Univ Wisc, 73; Tchg asst, Univ Wisc, 73-75; Instr, Univ Wisc, 75-76; Asst prof, Ball State Univ, 76-77; Instr, Univ Ark, 77-83; 84-91; Asst prof, Univ Ark, 91-. **RESEARCH** Silent Film, Cherokee History and Culture. **SELECTED PUBLICATIONS** Auth, Introductory Film Criticism: A Historical Perspective, Kendall/Hunt Publ Co, 94; **CONTACT ADDRESS** KH 417 Dept Comm, Univ of Arkansas, Fayetteville, Fayetteville, AR 72701. **EMAIL** fscheide@comp.uark.edu

SCHEIFELE, ELEANOR L.
DISCIPLINE MEDIEVAL ART **EDUCATION** Univ Wash, PhD. **CAREER** Vis asst prof. **RESEARCH** Sculpture at Moissac; Cluniac Patronage; Visigothic and Mozarabic Spain; images of beasts and demons; medieval iconography; medieval court art. **SELECTED PUBLICATIONS** Auth, pubs on French Romanesque sculpture and patronage of Richard II, Oxford. **CONTACT ADDRESS** Grand Rapids Comm Col, 143 Bostwick Ave, NE, Grand Rapids, MI 49503. **EMAIL** escheife@grcc.cc.mi.us

SCHEINBERG, STEPHEN
DISCIPLINE 20TH CENTURY U.S. HISTORY **EDUCATION** Chicago Univ, BS; Univ Wis, MA, PhD. **CAREER** Vis prof, San Diego State Univ; Northeastern Ill Univ; prof; ch, dept of Hist, Concordia Univ. **RESEARCH** 20th Century U.S. hist, right wing extremism, and anti-semitism in North Am. **SELECTED PUBLICATIONS** Auth, Right Wing Extremism: Threats to International Peace and Security, 97. **CONTACT ADDRESS** Dept of Hist, Concordia Univ, Montreal, 1455 de Maisonneuve W, Montreal, QC, Canada H3G 1M8. **EMAIL** drsteve@alcor.concordia.ca

SCHEINER, IRWIN
PERSONAL Born 05/22/1932, New York, NY, m, 1965, 2 children **DISCIPLINE** MODERN JAPANESE HISTORY **EDUCATION** Queens Col, NYork, BA, 53; Univ Mich, Ann Arbor, MA, 58, PhD(Hist), 66. **CAREER** Actg instr, 63-65, lectr, 65-66, from asst prof to assoc prof, 66-73, prof Japanese Hist, Univ Calif, Berkeley, 73-, Soc Sci res fel, 68 & 69; Fulbright res fel, Japan, 68-69; Soc Sci Res Coun travel grant, 73-74; Univ Humanities res prof grant, Univ Calif, Berkeley, 74; Nat Humanities Inst fel, Univ Chicago, 77-78; Japan Found Fel, 81-82; 87-88. **MEMBERSHIPS** Assn Asian Studies. **RESEARCH** Japanese social-intellectual history of Tokugwa and Meiji Periods; comparative social and intellectual history. **SELECTED PUBLICATIONS** Auth, Christian Samurai and Samurai values, In: Modern Japanese Leadership, Univ Ariz, 66; Christian Converts and Social Protest in Meiji Japan, Univ Calif, 70; The mindful peasant: A sketch for the study of peasant rebellion, J Asian Studies, 8/73; ed, Modern Japan: An Interpretive Anthology, Macmillan, 74; auth, Benevolent lords and honorable peasants, In: Japanese Thought in the Tokugawa Period, Univ Chicago, 78; The Japanese Village: Imagined, Real, contested, Mirror of Modernity, Stephan Vlastos, ed, University of California Press, 98; auth, "Socialism, Liberalism, & Martisor," in Modern Japanese Thought, ed. Bob T. Wakabayashi, Cambridge Univ Press, 98. **CONTACT ADDRESS** Dept of History, Univ of California, Berkeley, 3229 Dwinelle Hall, Berkeley, CA 94720-2551.

SCHELBERT, LEO
PERSONAL Born 03/16/1929, Kaltbrunn, Switzerland, m, 1965, 4 children **DISCIPLINE** AMERICAN IMMIGRATION HISTORY **EDUCATION** Fordham Univ, MA, 61; Columbia Univ, PhD(Am hist), 66. **CAREER** Asst instr western civilization, Rutgers Univ, 63-64, from instr to asst prof hist, 64-69; Swiss Nat Found scholar res fel, 69-70; lectr Swiss emigration, Univ Zurich, 70-71; asst prof, 71-73, chmn dept, 77-79, assoc prof Am immigration hist, 73-79, actg chmn dept, 81-82, Prof Am Immigration Hist, Univ Ill, at Chicago, 79-, Guest prof, Univ Dusseldorf, 76, emer 99. **MEMBERSHIPS** Orgn Am Historians; Swiss Am Hist Soc (secy, 68-69, pres, 75-80). **RESEARCH** American immigration; European emigration. **SELECTED PUBLICATIONS** Ed, New Glarus 1845-1970: The Making of a Swiss American Town, Tschudi, Glarus, Switz, 70; Einfuhrung in die schweig Auswanderungsgeschichte der Neuzeit, Leemann, Zurich, 76; Alles ist ganz anders hier: Auswandererschicksale in Briefen, Walter, Olten, Switz, 77; auth, America Experienced Eighteenth and Nineteenth Century Accounts of Swiss Immigrants, Camden, ME, 96; auth, Switzerland Under Siege 1939-1945, auth, A Neutral Nation's Stuggle for Survival, Rockport, ME, 00. **CONTACT ADDRESS** Dept of Hist, Univ of Illinois, Chicago, Chicago, IL 60680. **EMAIL** lschelbe@uic.edu

SCHENCK, MARY JANE
DISCIPLINE FRENCH, ENGLISH, MEDIEVAL STUDIES **EDUCATION** Eckerd Col, BA, 66; Univ NC Chapel Hill, MA, 68; Pa State Univ, PhD, 73. **CAREER** Prof, St. Andrews Col, 72-74; prof, Univ Tampa, 76-. **HONORS AND AWARDS** Fel, School of Criticism and Theory, 79; Fulbright Lectr Togo, 89-90; S Africa, 97; McArthur Distinguished Alumni Awd, Eckerd Col, 89; David Delo Res Grant, Univ Tampa, 99. **MEMBERSHIPS** MLA; CCCC; WPA; Societe Reneesvals; Int Courtly Lit Soc. **RESEARCH** Literature and the law - medieval, short narrative - medieval. **SELECTED PUBLICATIONS** Auth, The Fabliaux: Tales of Wit and Deception, Purdue Univ Monographs, Benjamins, 87; auth, Read Write Revise: An ESL Writing Text, St Martin's Pr, 88; auth, Echoes of the Epic: Essays

in Honor of F.J. Brault, Summa, 98. **CONTACT ADDRESS** Dept English, The Univ of Tampa, 410 W Kennedy Blvd, Tampa, FL 33606-1450. **EMAIL** mschenck@alpha.utampa.edu

SCHERER, IMGARD S.
PERSONAL Born 01/14/1937, Berlin, Germany, m, 1958, 4 children **DISCIPLINE** HISTORY OF PHILOSOPHY **EDUCATION** Amer Univ, PhD, 91. **CAREER** Asst Prof, 92-, Loyola Coll, MD; Vis Prof, 92, Amer Univ; Vis Prof, 88-91, George Mason Univ. **HONORS AND AWARDS** Amer Philos Assoc; North Amer Kent Soc. **MEMBERSHIPS** ASA, Phi Sigma Tan, IHSP. **RESEARCH** Science of Aesthetics, Theory of Judgement applied to Science, Morality and Art. **SELECTED PUBLICATIONS** Auth, The Crisis of Judgement in Kant's Three Critiques, In Search of a Science of Aesthetics, NY, Peter Lang Pub Co, 95; The Problem of the A Priori in Sensibility, Revisiting Kant's and Hegel's Theories of the Senses, forthcoming, The Review of Metaphysics; co-auth, Kant's Critique of Judgement and the Scientific Investigation of Matter, Universitat Karlsruhe, Germany, Inst Of Philos, Vol 3, 97; Kant's Eschatology in Zum ewigen Frieden: The Concept of Purposiveness to Guarantee Perpetual Peace, Proceedings of the 8th International Kant Congress, Memphis, 95. **CONTACT ADDRESS** Dept of Philosophy, Loyola Col, 4501 N Charles St, Baltimore, MD 21210-2699. **EMAIL** ischerer@loyola.edu

SCHERER, PAUL HENRY
PERSONAL Born 10/12/1933, Sedalia, MO, m, 1959, 2 children **DISCIPLINE** MODERN EUROPEAN DIPLOMATIC HISTORY **EDUCATION** Midland Lutheran Col, AB, 55; Univ Wis, MS, 56, PhD(hist), 64. **CAREER** From instr to asst prof, Colo State Univ, 61-64; from asst prof to assoc prof, 64-77, asst chmn dept, 66-68, chmn, 70-73, Prof Hist, Ind Univ, South Bend, 77-97, Colo State Univ fac res grants, 62-63; Ind Univ Found res grant, 66-67, 71-73; Am Philos Found grant, 68. **MEMBERSHIPS** AHA **RESEARCH** Lord John Russell; 19th century Anglo-French diplomacy; 20th century European diplomacy. **SELECTED PUBLICATIONS** auth, The Orsini Affair and the Decay of the Anglo-French Allimo, Rocky Mountain Social Science Journal, March 1965; Auth, Influence of the American Revolution on European History, Indiana Social Studies Quarterly Winter 74-75; Auth, Collision Of Empires - Britain In 3 World-Wars, 1793-1945 - Harvey,Ad/, Albion, Vol 0025, 1993; Palmerstons Foreign-Policy - 1848 - Billy,Gj/, Historian, Vol 0057, 1994; Defense And Diplomacy - Britain And The Great-Powers, 1815-1914 - Bartlett,Cj/, Albion, Vol 0026, 1994; auth, Lord John Russell, 99 Susquehanna U. Press I European Diplomacy 1900 to the Present, 66, Review Publications; auth, Partner or Puppet? Lord John Russell at the Foreign Office, 1859-1862, Albion, vol. 19, no. 3; auth, Ingmar Bergman's The Touch, Scandinavian Studies. **CONTACT ADDRESS** Dept of Hist, Indiana Univ, South Bend, South Bend, IN 46615.

SCHERR, ALBERT E.
PERSONAL Born 01/05/1963, Florence, Italy, s **DISCIPLINE** US HISTORY **EDUCATION** NYork Univ, PhD, 98. **CAREER** Asst prof, hist dept, CUNY-BCC, 98-. **HONORS AND AWARDS** Mazzini Soc fel; Smith Col Amer Studies, Diploma fel; NY Univ Hist teaching award; NY Univ dean's dissertation award. **MEMBERSHIPS** OAH; AHA. **RESEARCH** U.S. twentieth century cultural history; Popular culture; Film studies; New Deal. **SELECTED PUBLICATIONS** Auth, Did Private Nolan Get His Glory? Movies Press and Audiences during the Spanish American War, Columbia Jour of Amer Studies, 98; auth, In the Land of Milk and Honey: European Anti-Fascist Exiles in Hollywood, Hist Jour of Film, Radio and Television, 98; co-auth, Ambiguous Sovereignties: Notes on the Suburbs in Italian Cinema, Suburban Discipline, Princeton Archit Press, 97; auth, Shoot the Right Thing: African American Filmmakers and the Contemporary American Public Discourse, Toward a New American nation?, Keele Univ Press, 95; auth, Fritz Lang, I Moguls e altri recent citizens, Lo straniero interno, Ponte all Grazie, 94; auth, Facsimili storici, Corsari del tempo, Ponte alle Grazie, 94. **CONTACT ADDRESS** Dept Hist, Franklin Pierce Law Ctr, 2 White St, Concord, NH 03301-4197. **EMAIL** sqg0700@isz.nyu.edu

SCHICK, JAMES BALDWIN MCDONALD
PERSONAL Born 10/03/1940, Lafayette, IN, m, 1963, 1 child **DISCIPLINE** HISTORY **EDUCATION** Univ Wis-Madison, BS, 62, MS, 63; Ind Univ, Bloomington, PhD(hist), 71. **CAREER** Asst prof, 67-71, assoc prof, 71-77, Prof Hist, Pittsburg State Univ, 77-, Ed, Practice of Hist J, 77-78; ed, Midwest Quart, 81-; ed, Hist Comput Rev, 85-. **MEMBERSHIPS** Orgn Am Historians; Southern Hist Soc; Inst Early Am Hist & Cult. **RESEARCH** Antifederalism and the Constitution; North Carolina in the revolution. **SELECTED PUBLICATIONS** Coauth, The future as history: An experimental approach to introductory history for the general student, Hist Teacher, 74; auth, Microfilmed newspapers in the classroom, Masthead, 77; Vehicular religion and the gasoline service station, Midwest Quart, 77; Using the microfilmed Virginia Gazette in class, History Teacher, 80; coauth, The Early American Republic revisited: Textbook perceptions of American history, 1789-1848, J Early Repub, 81; auth, E Pluribus Unum (software); auth, Teaching History with a Computer, Lyceum Books, 90. **CONTACT ADDRESS** Dept of History, Pittsburg State Univ, 1701 S Broadway St, Pittsburg, KS 66762-7500. **EMAIL** jschick@pittstate.edu

SCHIEFEN, RICHARD JOHN
PERSONAL Born 05/09/1932, Rochester, NY **DISCIPLINE** MODERN CHURCH HISTORY, HISTORY OF RELIGION **EDUCATION** Univ Toronto, BA, 56, MA, 62; Univ St Michael's Col, STB, 61; Univ Rochester, MEd, 58; Univ London, PhD, 70. **CAREER** From asst prof to assoc prof hist, Univ St Thomas, Tex, 65-72, chmn dept, 70-72; assoc prof church hist, St Michael's Col, Univ Toronto, 72-81; Dean Sch Theol, Univ St Thomas, 81- **MEMBERSHIPS** AHA; Am Cath Hist Asn; Can Cath Hist Asn; Ecclesiastical Hist Soc. **RESEARCH** Victorian religion; 19th century Roman Catholicism. **SELECTED PUBLICATIONS** Auth, A Hist Commentary On The Major Catholic Works Of Newman,Cardinal - Griffin,Jr/, Cath Hist Rev, Vol 0080, 1994; Trial Of Strength, Furtwangler,Wilhelm In The Third-Reich - Prieberg,Fk/, Biog-An Interdisciplinary Quart, Vol 0018, 1995; Cath Devotion In Victorian Eng - Heimann,M/, Cath Hist Rev, Vol 0083, 1997. **CONTACT ADDRESS** Sch of Theol, Univ of St. Thomas, Texas, Houston, TX 77024. **EMAIL** schiefen@stthom.edu

SCHIERLE, GOTTHILF GOETZ
PERSONAL Born 04/10/1934, m, 1971, 1 child **DISCIPLINE** ARCHITECTURAL DESIGN, STRUCTURAL DESIGN BUILDING SCIENCE **EDUCATION** Dipl-Ing, Stuttgart, Ger, 59; Univ CA, Berkeley, MA, 75, PhD, 75. **CAREER** Prof, 92-, assoc prof, 78-92, vis assoc prof, 76-78, Univ Southern CA; found dir, 85-95, Grad Building Sci Prog; lectr & ch Struct Sequence, Univ CA, Berkeley, 66-78; vis prof, UCLA, 96-97; lectr, Stanford Univ, 68. **HONORS AND AWARDS** Fel, Am Inst Arch, 94; Bund Deutscher Baumeister, Ger; ACSA Creative Acheivements Awd, 98; FEAMA Grant, 99-01; NSF Grants, 90, 91, 92; found dir, master bldg sci prog, 85-96. **MEMBERSHIPS** Col fellows, Am Inst Arch; Am Inst Arch; Bund Deutscher Baumeister, Ger; ed bd, J for Arch Educ, 95-98 & Fabrics & Arch, 95-; sci comt, Int Symp, 96; mem, NSF workshop, seismic res policy plan, DC, 93; chr, CA State Comn, Arch License Exams for Gen & Long-Span Struct, 86-89. **RESEARCH** Consortium seismic. **SELECTED PUBLICATIONS** Auth, Membranes under Prestress, Fabrics in Architecture, 96; Quality Control in Seismic Design and Construction, J Performance Constructed Fac, 96; Span/Depth Tables for Structure Systems and Elements, Guidelines for the Design of Double-Layer Grids, 96; Quality Control for Seismic Safety, ATC US-Japan Workshop, 94; Quality Control for Seismic Safety, LA Architect, 94; Computer Aided Seismic Design, J Arch and Plan Res, 94; Computer Aided Design for Wind and Seismic Forces, Comput Supported Design in Arch, ACADIA, 92; Dynamic Editing Computer Aided Design, Symp Proc Baden-Baden, 91; Computer Aided Seismic Design, Developments in Structural Engg, 90; coauth, Computer-Aided Design of Membrane Structures, Proc Int Symp Conceptual Design of Structures, Stuttgart, Ger, 96; Vernacular Forms: Wind Tunnel Tests and Computer Simulation, Proc Int Conf on Wind Engg, New Delhi, 95. **CONTACT ADDRESS** School of Archit, Univ of So California, University Park Campus, Los Angeles, CA 90089. **EMAIL** schierle@usc.edu

SCHIFERL, ELLEN
DISCIPLINE ART **EDUCATION** Grinnell Col, BA; Univ Minn, MA, PhD. **CAREER** Assoc prof. **RESEARCH** Interactive multimedia educational software; visual environment and visualization; visual representation of space and time. **SELECTED PUBLICATIONS** Auth, pubs on medieval and renaissance art history, computer based instruction and art criticism. **CONTACT ADDRESS** Dept of Art, 37 Col Ave, Gorham, MA 04038-1083.

SCHIFFHORST, GERALD JOSEPH
PERSONAL Born 10/13/1940, St. Louis, MO, m, 1987 **DISCIPLINE** ENGLISH, ART HISTORY **EDUCATION** St Louis Univ, BS, 62, MA, 63; Wash Univ, PhD(English), 73. **CAREER** Instr English, Univ Mo-St Louis, 66-67; asst prof to prof English, Univ Cent Fla, 70-, Nat Endowment for Humanities fel art hist, Southeastern Inst Medieval & Renaissance Studies, Duke Univ, 74; . **MEMBERSHIPS** MLA; Shakespeare Asn Am; Milton Soc Am; SAtlantic Mod Lang Asn. **RESEARCH** Milton; Renaissance iconography of patience; teaching English composition. **SELECTED PUBLICATIONS** Ed & coauth, The Triumph of Patience: Medieval and Renaissance Studies, Fla Univ, 78; coauth, Short English Handbook, Scott, 79, 2nd ed, 82, 3rd ed, 86; auth, Patience & the Humbly Exalted Heroism of Milton's Messiah (art), Milton Studies, XVI, 82; auth, John Milton, 90; Short Handbook for Writers, McGraw Hill, 91, 97; co-ed, The Witness of Times, Duquesne Univ Press, 93; assoc ed, Seventeenth-Century News, 96-99. **CONTACT ADDRESS** Dept of English, Univ of Central Florida, PO Box 161346, Orlando, FL 32816-1346. **EMAIL** schiffhg@mail.ucf.edu

SCHIFFMAN, JOSEPH
PERSONAL Born 06/13/1914, New York, NY, m, 1942, 2 children **DISCIPLINE** ENGLISH, AMERICAN STUDIES **EDUCATION** LI Univ, BA, 37; Columbia Univ, MA, 47; NYork Univ, PhD, 51. **CAREER** From instr to assoc prof English, LI Univ, 45-58, coordr grad prog Am studies, 56-58; chmn dept English, 59-68, prof English, 58-68, James Hope Caldwell prof Am studies, 68-79, EMER PROF ENGLISH & PROF CONTINUING EDUC, DICKINSON COL, 79-86, 90-96; Acting ed, Am Quart, 60; head Am lit, Int Bibliog Comt, 61-64; founding dir, Am Studies Res Ctr, India, 64; vis Fulbright prof, Univ Bordeaux, France, 65-66; vis prof, Univ South Fla, 81; Fulbright-Hays vis prof, Univ of Indonesia, 81-82. **HONORS AND AWARDS** Lindback Found Distinguished Teaching Awd, 62. **MEMBERSHIPS** MLA; Am Studies Asn. **RESEARCH** American literature and civilization. **SELECTED PUBLICATIONS** Auth, Introduction to Lindsay Swift's Brook Farm, Corinth, 61; ed, Three Shorter Novels of Herman Melville, Harper, 62; Edward Bellamy's Duke of Stockbridge, Harvard Univ, 62; coauth, A critical history of American literature: from its beginning to the present, In: Cassell's Encyclopedia of World Literature, 73. **CONTACT ADDRESS** Dickinson Col, Carlisle, PA 17013.

SCHILCHER, LINDA
DISCIPLINE HISTORY **EDUCATION** Oxford Univ, DPhil. **CAREER** Assoc prof. **RESEARCH** Islamic history; modern Middle East history. **SELECTED PUBLICATIONS** Auth, Der Nahe Osten in the Zwischenkriegszeit 1919-1939, Steiner Verlag, 89; co-auth, Families in Politics, Steiner Verlag, 85. **CONTACT ADDRESS** Dept of History, Univ of California, Center for Near East Studies, CA 90025. **EMAIL** schilcherl@mciworld.com

SCHILLING, DONALD
PERSONAL Born 01/04/1942, Stevens Point, WI, m, 2 children **DISCIPLINE** HISTORY **EDUCATION** DePauw Univ, BA, 64; Univ Wis-Madison, MA, 96, PhD, 72. **CAREER** Denison Univ, asst prof, 72-78, assoc prof, 79-87, prof, 88-, dean, first-year students, 97-. **HONORS AND AWARDS** Fel, Summer Inst on the Holocaust and Jewish Civilization, Northwestern Univ, June, 96; Inst of Europ Stud Fel, Berlin, June, 93; Holocaust Educ Found: course develop grant, 92; Fulbright-Hays sem abroad: Soc and Econ Change in S Africa, 91; Denison Univ res found grant 94, 87, 84, 72; Dension Univ fac develop grant, 91, 81, 79, 77, 74, 73; NEH, summer sem fel, 76. **MEMBERSHIPS** Am Hist Asn; German Studies Asn; Ohio Acad of Hist. **RESEARCH** Mod German hist; Holocaust; historiography; pedagogy; educ policy in Africa. **SELECTED PUBLICATIONS** The Dynamics of Educational Policy Formation in Kenya, 1928-1934, Hist of Ed Quart, 80, 51-76; Local Native Councils and the Politics of African Education in Kenya, 1924-1939, Int Jour African Hist Stud, IX, 2, 76, 218-247; How Much War Should Be Included in a Course on World War II?, Teaching Hist: A Jour of Methods, 18:1, 93, 14-21; Modernization and the Origins of National Socialism: the Case of Middle Franconia, in Proceedings of the Citadel Symposium on Hitler and National Socialism, Charleston: Citadel Univ Press, 81, 60-70; The Politics of Education in Colonial Algeria and Kenya, Athens: Ohio Univ Press, 83; Politics in a New Key: the Transformation of Politics in Northern Bavaria, 1890-1914, Ger Stud Rev, XVII:1, 94, 33-57; The Dead End of Demonizing: Dealing with the Perpetrators in Teaching the Holocaust, in Perspectives on the Holocaust: A Guide for Teachers and Scholars, NY Univ Press, 96; Histories of the War in Europe and the Pacific," in World War II in Europe, Africa, and the Americas, with General Sources: A Handbook of Literature and Research, Greenwood Press, 97, 3-21; Ed, Lessons and Legacies II: Teaching the Holocaust in a Changing World, Evanston: Northwestern Univ Press, 98. **CONTACT ADDRESS** Denison Univ, Granville, OH 43023. **EMAIL** schilling@denison.edu

SCHLAFLY, DANIEL L.
PERSONAL Born 09/24/1940, St Louis, MO, m, 1966, 2 children **DISCIPLINE** HISTORY **EDUCATION** Geotwn Univ, AB, 61; Colum Univ, MA, 65; PhD, 72; St Lou Univ, MBA, 98. **CAREER** Instr, 64-66, 69-72; St Louis Univ; asst prof, 72-78; assoc prof, 78-98; prof, 98-. **HONORS AND AWARDS** Adenauer Schlp. **MEMBERSHIPS** AHA; AAASS; ACHA. **RESEARCH** 18th Century Russia; Roman Catholic Church in Russia. **SELECTED PUBLICATIONS** Auth, "Iezuity V Rossii V tsarstvovanie Ekateriny II, Pavla I I Aleksandra I (Jesuits in Russia during the Reigns of Catherine II, Paul I, and Alexander I)," Rodina 5 (93): 16-19; ed, transl of, The Rule of Catherine the Great, 1768-1770: Turkey and Poland, in History of Russia (Gulf Breeze, FL: Acad Intl Press, 94); auth, "Filippo Balatri in Peter the Great's Russia," J fur Gesch Osteuropas 45 (97): 181-98; auth, "Fr. Demetrius Gallitzin: Son of the Russian Enlightenment," Cath Hist Rev 83 (97): 716-725; auth, "The First Russian Diplomat in America: Andrei Dashkov on the New Republic," Hist 60 (97): 39-57; auth, "Roman Catholicism in Today's Russia: The Troubled Heritage," J Church and State 39 (97): 681-96; auth, "'True to the Ratio Studiorum?' Jesuit Colleges in St. Petersburg," Hist Edu Quart 37 (97): 421-34; auth, "A Muscovite Boiarynia Faces Peter the Great's Reforms: Dar'ia Golitsyna between Two Worlds," Can-Am Slavic Stud 39 (97): 249-68; ed, transl of, Catherine the Great in Power: Domestic and Foreign Affairs, 1763-1764, in History of Russia (Gulf Breeze, FL: Acad Intl Press, 94); auth, :The Ratio Studiorum on Alien Shores: Jesuit Colleges in St Petersburg and Georgetown," Rev Port de Filos 55 (99): 253-274. **CONTACT ADDRESS** Dept History, Saint Louis Univ, 221 North Grand Blvd, Saint Louis, MO 63103-2006. **EMAIL** daniel@slu.edu

SCHLATTER, FREDRIC WILLIAM
PERSONAL Born 06/16/1926, Tacoma, WA **DISCIPLINE** CLASSICAL LANGUAGES, HISTORY **EDUCATION** Gonzaga Univ, AB, 49, MA, 50; Alma Col, Calif, STL, 57; Princeton Univ, PhD(classics), 60. **CAREER** Instr classics, Gonzaga Prep, 50-52; instr, St Francis Xavier Div, 52-53, from asst prof to assoc prof, 61-74, dean, 62-65, Prof Classics, Gonzaga Univ, 74-, Chmn Dept Class Lang, 68-, Prof Hist, 76- **HONORS AND AWARDS** Prof Emeritus, 98; Festschrift: Nova Doctrina Veturque, 99. **MEMBERSHIPS** Am Philol Asn; Archaeol Inst Am; Asn Ancient Historians. **RESEARCH** Justin's Epitome of Pompeius Trogus. **SELECTED PUBLICATIONS** Auth, A Mosaic Interpretation Of Jerome, 'In Hiezechielem'/, Vigiliae Christianae, Vol 0049, 95; The 2 Women In The Mosaic Of Santa-Pudenziana, J Of Early Christian Studies, Vol 0003, 95; The Clash Of Gods - A Reinterpretation Of Early-Christian Art - Mathews,Tf/, Heythrop J-A Quart Rev Of Philos And Theol, Vol 0037, 96; auth, G.M. Hopkins: The Dublin Notes of Homer; The Hopkins Quart, Vol 0024, 97. **CONTACT ADDRESS** Dept of Class Lang, Gonzaga Univ, 502 E Boone Ave, Spokane, WA 99258-0001.

SCHLAUCH, WOLFGANG T.
PERSONAL Born 07/05/1935, Plochingen, Germany, m, 1964, 2 children **DISCIPLINE** MODERN EUROPEAN HISTORY **EDUCATION** Univ Freiburg, Staatsexamen, 62, PhD, 65. **CAREER** Teacher Ger, 62-65; asst prof hist, Converse Col, 65-67; assoc prof, Univ Miss, 67-69; assoc prof, 69-73, prof hist, Eastern Ill Univ, 73-98, prof emer, 7/98-; vis prof, Univ Southern Queensland, spring 96; adjunct prof, New Mexico State Univ, 99. **HONORS AND AWARDS** Oustanding Fac Awd, Eastern Ill Univ, 85. **MEMBERSHIPS** Ger Studies Asn; Conf Group Ger Politics. **RESEARCH** Twentieth century Europe; modern Germany; diplomatic history. **SELECTED PUBLICATIONS** Co-auth, The United States and the Federal Republic of Germany, Contacts and Relations in Historical and Cultural Perspective, Am Asc of Teachers, 77; Dissent in Eastern Europe:Rudolfo Bahro's Criticism of Eastern European Communism, Nationalities Papers, 81; West Germany: Reliable Part ner? Perspectives on Recent American-German Relations, Ger Studies Rev, 85; Ruestungshilfe der USA 1939-1945, 2nd ed, Bernard & Graefe, 86; The Atlantic Alliance at the Crossroads: A Changing Relationship, in War and Peace, Perspective in the Nuclear Age, Tex Tech Univ Press, 88; Defense and Security: The SPD and East-West Relations and Society in Germany, Austria and Switzerland, 90; The German Social Democrats and the Greens: A Challenge to the Western Alliance, Peace and Change, 90; Foreign Minister Genscher's Foreign Policy: Continuity or Ambiguity, European Studies J, 94. **CONTACT ADDRESS** 821 Raleigh Rd, Las Cruces, NM 88005. **EMAIL** wolfgang@zianet.com

SCHLEIFER, JAMES THOMAS
PERSONAL Born 11/15/1942, Rochester, NY, m, 1964, 2 children **DISCIPLINE** AMERICAN HISTORY **EDUCATION** Hamilton Col, BA, 64; Yale Univ, MA, 66; MPhil, 68, PhD(hist), 72. **CAREER** From instr to assoc prof, 69-83, Prof Am Hist, Col New Rochelle, 83-; Dean Gill Library Col New Rochelle, 87-; vis prof, Univ Paris, 86; vis lect, Yale Univ, 83, 84, 95; Am Coun Learned Soc fel, 74-75 & 81-82; vis fel, Hist Dept, Yale Univ, 81-82; res grant, Am Philos Soc, 79, 85; Nat Endowment for Humanities res grant, 82-83. **HONORS AND AWARDS** George Washington Egleston Prize, Yale Univ, 72; Gilbert Chinard Incentive Award, Soc Fr Hist Studies, 74; Merle Curti Award, Orgn Am Hist, 81. **MEMBERSHIPS** French Nat Comm for Publication of Complete Works of Tocqueville, 86-; Am Hist Asn; Orgn Am Historians; Tocqueville Soc. **RESEARCH** Alexis de Tocqueville; European-American intellectual and cultural relations; American intellectual history; hist Am Higher Educ. **SELECTED PUBLICATIONS** Contribr, Writing History, Appleton, 2nd ed, 67; auth, Alexis de Tocqueville describes the American character: two previously unpublished portraits, S Atlantic Quart, spring 75; Images of America after the Revolution: Tocqueville and Beaumont visit the early Republic, 1/77 & How democracy influences preaching: a previously unpublished chapter from Tocqueville's Democracy in America, 10/77 & Tocqueville and American literature: A newly acquired letter, 1/80, & Tocqueville and Centrailization, 10/83, Yale Univ Libr Gazette; The Making of Tocqueville's Democracy: How Alexis de Tocqueville's Famous Work on America Developed, Univ NC, 80; Spanish translation, Fondo de Cultura Economica, 85 and rev ed, Liberty Fund, 00; contribr, Dictionary of French History, Greenwood, 86; auth, Tocqueville, Bouquin ed, Laffont, 86; auth, Reconsidering Tocqueville's Democracy in America, Rutgers, 88; auth, A Passion for Liberty: Tocqueville in Democracy and Revolution, Library of Congress, 89; Liberty of Expression in America and in France, Wilson Center, 88; auth, Interpreting Tocqueville's Democracy in America, Univ Press of Am, 91; auth, Liberty/Liberte: The American and French Experiences, Johns Hopkins, 92; Liberty, Equality, Democracy, NY Univ Press, 92; co-ed, De la Democratie en Amerique, Pleiade Edition, Gallimard, 92; auth, The College of New Rochelle: An Extraordinary Story, Donning, 94. **CONTACT ADDRESS** Gill Library, Col of New Rochelle, New Rochelle, NY 10805. **EMAIL** jschleifer@cnr.edu

SCHLERETH, THOMAS J.
PERSONAL Born 03/23/1941, Pittsburgh, PA, m, 1973, 1 child **DISCIPLINE** AMERICAN HISTORY & STUDIES **EDUCATION** Univ Notre Dame, BA, 63; Univ Wisc, MA, 65; Univ Iowa, PhD, 69. **CAREER** Newberry Libr jr fel hist, 67-69; asst prof, hist & amer studies, Grinnell Col, 69-72; asst prof, 72-77, assoc prof, amer studies & chairman dept, 77-78, Univ Notre Dame; vis prof, faculty of design, Univ of Calgary, 85-86; contri ed., The Journal of Am Hist, 87-98; gen ed., Midwest Hist and Cult Publication Series, Indiana Univ Press, 84-; Nat fac fel, Nat Fac Found, 94-. **HONORS AND AWARDS** Fac fel, The Reilly Ctr for Sci, Tech and Values, Univ Notre Dame; Newberry Libr fac fel hist, 70-71; Nat Endowment for Humanities fel archit hist, 77-78; assoc, Danforth Found, 77-83; Newberry Libr fel hist, 78; Henry Francis DuPont Winterthur Mus scholar, 77, 83; The Public Historian, 86; Best Scholarly Article, 85-86; Presidential award, Univ Notre Dame, 86; Nat Endow for the Humanities Res fel, 77, 87; Rodger D. Branigin Scholar award, Franklin Col, 87; sr res fel, Smithsonian Inst, 88; Elsie Crews Parson prize, Ctr for Amer Cult Studies, 90; Henry H. Douglas Distinguished Scholar award, 94. **MEMBERSHIPS** Amer Studies Asn; Soc Archit Hist; Orgn Amer Hist; Amer Studies Asn Advan Humanities. **RESEARCH** American cultural history; Material culture studies; Urban architectural history; Landscape history. **SELECTED PUBLICATIONS** Auth, Victorian America: Transformations in Everyday Life, 1876-1915, Harper & Row, 91; auth, Cultural History and Material Culture, UMI Res Press, 90; University of Virginia Press, 92; auth, Reading the Road, Univ Tenn Press, 97; auth, A Dome of Learning: The University of Notre Dame's Main Building, Univ Notre Dame Alumni Asn, 91; co-ed, American Home Life, 1890-1930: A Social History of Spaces and Services, Univ Tenn Press, 92, 94; co-auth, Sense of Place: American Regional Cultures, Univ Press of Ky, 90, 94; auth, The Industrial Belt, Garland Publ, 87; auth, U.S. 40: A Roadscape of the American Experience, Ind Univ Press, 84; auth, Material Culture Studies in America, Amer Asn for State and Local Hist, 82; auth, Artifacts and The American Past, Amer Asn for State and Local Hist, 82; auth, The Cosmopolitan Ideal in Enlightenment Thought, Univ Notre Dame Press, The University of Notre Dame, A Portrait of Its History and Campus, Univ Notre Dame Press, 76, 79, 92. **CONTACT ADDRESS** Dept. of American Studies, Univ of Notre Dame, 303 O'Shaughnessy Hall, Notre Dame, IN 46556. **EMAIL** schlereth.2@nd.edu

SCHLESINGER, ROGER
PERSONAL Born 12/23/1943, London, England, m, 1998 **DISCIPLINE** HISTORY **EDUCATION** Univ Ill, PhD, 69. **CAREER** Prof & dept chair, Hist Dept, Washington State Univ, 68-. **MEMBERSHIPS** Am Hist Asn; Soc Hist Discoveries. **RESEARCH** Renaissance exploration; European-American Indian contact. **SELECTED PUBLICATIONS** Coauth, Andre Thevet's North America: A Sixteenth Century View, McGill-Queens, 86; auth, Portraits from the Age of Exploration, Univ Ill Press, 93; auth, In the Wake of Columbus, Harlan-Davidson, 96. **CONTACT ADDRESS** Dept Hist, Washington State Univ, Pullman, WA 99164-4030. **EMAIL** schlesin@wsu.edu

SCHLEUNES, KARL ALBERT
PERSONAL Born 04/21/1937, Kiel, WI, m, 1964 **DISCIPLINE** MODERN GERMAN HISTORY **EDUCATION** Lakeland Col, BA, 59; Univ Minn, MA, 61, PhD(Ger hist), 66. **CAREER** Asst prof mod Europ hist, Univ Ill, Chicago, 65-71, res fel, 67; Assoc Prof Mod Europ Hist, Univ NC, Greensboro, 71-, Soc Sci Res Coun grant, 71-72; Nat Endowment for Humanities res grant, 73. **MEMBERSHIPS** AHA; Hist Kommission der Deutschen Ges fur Erziehungswissenschaft. **RESEARCH** Nineteenth- and 20th-century Germany; Holocaust. **SELECTED PUBLICATIONS** Auth, the Twisted Road to Auschwitz, 70; auth, Schooling and Society: the Politics of Education in Prussia and Bavaria, 89. **CONTACT ADDRESS** Dept of History, Univ of No Carolina, Greensboro, 1000 Spring Garden, Greensboro, NC 27402-6170. **EMAIL** kaschleu@uncg.edu

SCHLOTTERBECK, JOHN THOMAS
PERSONAL Born 02/29/1948, Lynn, MA, m, 1973, 1 child **DISCIPLINE** AMERICAN HISTORY **EDUCATION** Johns Hopkins Univ, BA, 70, MA, 74, PhD(Am hist), 80; Univ Mich, MA, 72. **CAREER** Instr Am hist, Western Md Col, 74-75, asst prof, 76; instr, Oberlin Col, 77-78; instr, 78-80, Asst Prof Am Hist, Depauw Univ, 80- **MEMBERSHIPS** Orgn Am Historians; Southern Hist Asn; Inst Early Am Hist & Cult. **RESEARCH** Nineteenth century Southern society; rural and agricultural history; American slavery. **SELECTED PUBLICATIONS** Contribr, The social economy of an upper South community: Orange and Greene Counties, Virginia, 1815 to 1860, In: Class, Conflict and Consensus: Antebellum Southern Community Studies, Greenwood Press, 82. **CONTACT ADDRESS** Dept of Hist, DePauw Univ, 313 S Locust St, Greencastle, IN 46135-1736.

SCHLUNZ, THOMAS PAUL
PERSONAL Born 08/15/1941, Clinton, IA **DISCIPLINE** MEDIEVAL EUROPEAN HISTORY **EDUCATION** Belmont Abbey Col, AB, 65; Univ Ill, Urbana, AM, 67, PhD(hist), 73. **CAREER** Instr hist, Ohio Univ, Portsmouth, 67-69; instr, 73-74, asst prof, 74-84, Univ New Orleans, assoc prof, 84-. **MEMBERSHIPS** Haskins Soc. **RESEARCH** Anglo-Norman ecclesiastical history. **SELECTED PUBLICATIONS** Auth, Church and state in Normandy at the time of the Becket controversy, McNeese Rev, Vol XXIV, 58 & 75-75. **CONTACT ADDRESS** Dept of History, Univ of New Orleans, 2000 Lakeshore Dr, New Orleans, LA 70148-0001. **EMAIL** tschlunz@uno.edu

SCHMANDT, RAYMOND HENRY
PERSONAL Born 09/20/1925, Indianapolis, IN, m, 1949, 2 children **DISCIPLINE** EUROPEAN HISTORY **EDUCATION** St Louis Univ, AB, 47, AM, 49; Univ Mich, AM & PhD(hist), 52. **CAREER** Instr Ger, St Louis Univ, 46-50; from instr to asst prof hist, DePaul Univ, 52-58; from asst prof to assoc prof, Loyola Univ, Ill, 58-66; chmn dept, 73-76, Prof Hist, St Joseph's Col, PA, 66-, Ed, Records Am Cath Hist Soc Phila, 68-73. **MEMBERSHIPS** AHA; Am Cath Hist Asn; Mediaeval Acad Am; Am Soc Reformation Res; Am Soc Church Hist. **RESEARCH** Medieval German and ecclesiastical history. **SELECTED PUBLICATIONS** Coauth, History of the Catholic Church, Bruce, 57; Leo XIII and the Modern World, Sheed, 61; ed, Popes Through History (3 vols), Newman, 61-69; The Election and Assassination of Albert of Louvain, Bishop of Liege, 1191-92, Speculum, SLII: 639-660; Public Opinion, the Schism and the Fourth Crusade, Diakonia, 3: 284-299; auth, The fourth crusade and the just-war theory, Cath Hist Rev, 75; The Gotland Campaign of the Teutonic Knights, J Baltic Studies, 75; coauth, History of the Archdiocese of Philadelphia, Archdiocese, 76. **CONTACT ADDRESS** Dept of Hist, Saint Joseph's Univ, Philadelphia, PA 19131.

SCHMAUS, WARREN STANLEY
PERSONAL Born 04/02/1952, Staten Island, NY, m, 1979, 2 children **DISCIPLINE** PHILOSOPHY & HISTORY OF SCIENCE **EDUCATION** Princeton Univ, AB, 74; Univ Pittsburgh, MA, 75, PhD(Hist & Philos of Sci), 80. **CAREER** Asst prof Philos, Ill Inst Technol, 80-, res assoc, Study Ethics in Professions, Ill Inst Technol, 80-; asst prof Phil, Ill Inst Technol, 80-85; from assoc prof to prof, 85-95; prof, 95-. **HONORS AND AWARDS** Vis fel, Center for Philosophy of Science, Univ of Pittsburgh, 96-97; vis scholar, Univ Chicago, 87-88. **MEMBERSHIPS** Am Philos Asn; Philos Sci Asn; Hist Sci Soc; Cheiron; Soc Social Studies Sci; HOPOS, Hist of the Philos of Science Working Group. **RESEARCH** Hist and philos of the social sciences. **SELECTED PUBLICATIONS** Auth, Durkheim's Philosophy of Science and the Sociology of Knowledge, Univ of Chicago Press, 94; auth, "Functionalism and the Meaning of Social Facts," Philosophy of Science 66, (99): 314-323; co-ed, Emile Durkheim: Critical Assessments, London, Routledge, 01; some 50 articles and reviews. **CONTACT ADDRESS** Dept of Humanities, Illinois Inst of Tech, 3301 S Dearborn, Chicago, IL 60616-3793. **EMAIL** schmaus@iit.edu

SCHMELLER, HELMUT JOHN
PERSONAL Born 09/02/1932, Baernau, m, 1963, 2 children **DISCIPLINE** EUROPEAN HISTORY **EDUCATION** Univ Erlangen, AB, 58; Ft Hays State Univ, MA, 68; Kans State Univ, PhD(hist), 75. **CAREER** Prof Hist, Ft Hays State Univ, 66- **MEMBERSHIPS** Western Asn Ger Studies; Soc Ger Am Studies (first vpres, 81-83). **RESEARCH** National socialism; anti-Semitism; German-American studies. **SELECTED PUBLICATIONS** Auth, Hitler and Keitel, Ft Hays State Univ, 70; coauth & ed, Early Pioneer Families in Decatur County, 79 & auth, The Germans from Russia, 81, Ethnic Heritage Studies. **CONTACT ADDRESS** Dept of Hist, Fort Hays State Univ, Hays, KS 67601.

SCHMIDT, GREG
DISCIPLINE AMERICAN HISTORY **EDUCATION** Univ Ill, BA, MA, PhD. **CAREER** Prof; **MEMBERSHIPS** NCTE, MLA, TESOL, Dep Comp Comt. **RESEARCH** American social, intellectual and Constitutional history. **SELECTED PUBLICATIONS** Rev, Colonial Life, Am Studies, 79; Book Culture in Post-Revolutionary Virginia, Jour Early Republic, 86. **CONTACT ADDRESS** Winona State Univ, PO Box 5838, Winona, MN 55987-5838.

SCHMIDT, HANNS-PETER
PERSONAL Born 07/30/1930, Berlin, Germany **DISCIPLINE** INDO-IRANIAN STUDIES **EDUCATION** Univ Hamburg, PhD(Indo-Iranian studies), 57. **CAREER** Asst prof Indo-Iranian studies, Univ Saugar, 59-61; asst Indology, Univ Tubingen, 61-64, dozent, 65-67; from asst prof to assoc prof, 67-70, Prof Indo-Iranian Studies, Univ Calif, Los Angeles, 70-, Res fel, Deccan Col Post-Grad & Res Inst, Poona, India, 57-59 & Ger Res Asn, 61; prof Sanskrit, Rijksuniversiteit te Leiden, Netherlands, 74-76. **MEMBERSHIPS** Am Orient Soc; Ger Orient Soc. **RESEARCH** Sanskrit; Avesta; Middle Persian. **SELECTED PUBLICATIONS** Auth, Vedischvrata Undawestisch Urvata, 58; auth, Brhaspati und Indra, 68; auth, Form and Meaning of Yasna 33, 85; auth, Some Women's Rites and Rights in the Veda, 87. **CONTACT ADDRESS** Dept of Near Eastern Lang & Cult, Univ of California, Los Angeles, Los Angeles, CA 90024. **EMAIL** hschmidt@ucla.edu

SCHMIDT, HENRY CONRAD
PERSONAL Born 05/07/1937, Southampton, NY, m, 1966 **DISCIPLINE** LATIN AMERICAN HISTORY **EDUCATION** Univ Tex, Austin, BA, 60, MA, 69, PhD(Latin Am hist), 72. **CAREER** Asst prof, 72-78, Assoc Prof Hist, Tex A&M Univ, 78- **MEMBERSHIPS** Latin Am Studies Asn. **RESEARCH** Latin American culture and thought. **SELECTED PUBLICATIONS** Auth, Toward The Innerscape Of Mexican Historiology - Liberalism And The History Of Ideas/, Mexican Studies-Estudios Mexicanos, Vol 0008, 1992; Heretic Texts - Spa - Krauze,E/, Historia Mexicana, Vol 0043, 1993; South Of The Border - Mexico In The Am Imagination, 1914-1947 - Oles,J/, Southwestern Hist Quart, Vol 0098, 1994; The Latin-Americans - Spirit And Ethos - Dealy,Gc/, Hisp Am Hist Rev, Vol 0074, 1994. **CONTACT ADDRESS** Dept of Hist, Texas A&M Univ, Col Station, 1 Texas A and M Univ, College Station, TX 77843. **EMAIL** hcschmidt@tamu.edu

SCHMIDT, MARTIN EDWARD
PERSONAL Born 04/24/1935, Hartford, CT, 2 children **DISCIPLINE** HISTORY **EDUCATION** Kent State Univ, BS, 59, MA, 60; Univ PA, PhD(Hist), 66. **CAREER** Asst prof hist, Univ WI-Oshkosh, 66-69; asst chemn grad affairs, 76-78, asst prof hist, 70-74, assoc prof to assoc prof emer hist, Univ Wis-Milwaukee, 74-, asst chemn undergrad affairs, 81-. **HONORS AND AWARDS** Am Philos Soc res fel, 70 & 74. **MEMBERSHIPS** Western Soc Fr Hist. **RESEARCH** Modern France; European diplomatic. **SELECTED PUBLICATIONS** Auth, Prelude to intervention: Madagascar and the failure of Anglo-French diplomacy, 1890-95, Hist J, 4/72; Le Parlement and the definition of the liberal Third Republic, 1879-1883, Can J Hist, 2/74; Alexandre Ribot: Odyssey of a Liberal in the Third Republic, Martinus Nijhoff, 74. **CONTACT ADDRESS** 2214 W Daphne Rd, Glendale, WI 53209. **EMAIL** schmdt@uwm.edu

SCHMIDT, WILLIAM JOHN
PERSONAL Born 05/22/1926, Green Bay, WI, m, 1949 **DISCIPLINE** CHURCH HISTORY **EDUCATION** N Cent Col, BA, 51; Evangel Theol Sem, BD, 54; Columbia Univ, PhD (church hist), 66. **CAREER** Pastor, Wis Conf Evangel United Brethren Church, 52-62; tutor, Union Theol Sem, 62-65; from asst prof to assoc prof church hist, NY Theol Sem, 67-70; adj assoc prof church hist, 67-70, assoc prof, 70-78, Prof Theol, St Peter's Col, NJ, 78-, Res writer with Samuel McCrea Cavert on The American Churches in the Ecumenical Movement, 00-1968, 65-67; mem Gen Prog Coun, Reformed Church Am, 70-76. **MEMBERSHIPS** Am Soc Church Hist; N Am Acad Ecumenists (secy-treas, 68-72). **RESEARCH** American church history; history of the ecumenical movement; religous syncretism. **SELECTED PUBLICATIONS** Auth, COCU in the crucible, Cath World, 8/68; The morphology of ecumenism, Foundations, 7-9/69; Samuel McCrea Cavert: American bridge to the German church 1945-46, J Presby Hist, spring 73; The sheep market, New Pulpit Digest, 7-8/77; Evolution of an American mind, J Ecumenical Studies, spring 77; The Conciliar Renaissance, Mid-Stream, 4/78; Interpreters of the faith: Samuel McCrea Cavert, A D Mag, 5/78; Architect of Unity: A Biography of Samuel McCrea Cavert, Friendship, 78. **CONTACT ADDRESS** Dept of Theol, Saint Peter's Col, Kennedy Blvd, Jersey City, NJ 07306.

SCHMITT, HANS ADOLF
PERSONAL Born 06/06/1921, Frankfurt am Main, Germany, m, 1944, 3 children **DISCIPLINE** HISTORY **EDUCATION** Washington & Lee Univ, AB, 40; Univ Chicago, MA, 43, PhD(hist), 53. **CAREER** Asst prof hist, Ala State Teachers Col, Florence, 48-50; from asst prof to assoc prof, Univ Okla, 53-59; from assoc prof to prof, Tulane Univ, 59-67; prof, NY Univ, 67-71; mem, Ctr Advan Studies, 71-73, Prof Hist, Univ VA, 71-91; Prof Emeritus, Univ VA, 91-; Fulbright Scholar, Belgium & Luxembourg, 56-57; Tulane Univ Fac Res Coun fel, 63 & 65-66; Sesqui-centennial assoc, Ctr Advan Studies, Univ Va, 77. **HONORS AND AWARDS** Louis G Beer Prize, AHA, 63. **MEMBERSHIPS** AHA; Southern Hist Asn (exec coun, 74-77); Soc Fr Hist Studies (pres, 66-67); Conf Group Cent Europ Hist. **RESEARCH** French intellectual history; problems of political integration on the national and international level; German constitutional history. **SELECTED PUBLICATIONS** Auth, "The Path to European Union," LSU Press, 62; auth, "Charles Peguy, the Decline of an Intellectual," Ibid., 67; auth, "European Union from Hitler to DeGaulle, Van Nostrand, 69; ed., "Historians of Modern Europe, LSU Press, 71; coauth & ed, with John L. Snell, "The Democratic Movement in Germany 1789-1914," Unsarolina Press, 76; ed. & intr., U.S. Occupation in Europe after World War II," Kansas 78; ed & contr., "Neutral Europe between War and Revolution 1917-23," Univ Press of VA, 88; auth, "Lucky Victim," LSU Press, 89; auth, "Quakers and Nazis," U. of Missouri, 97. **CONTACT ADDRESS** Dept of Hist, Univ of Virginia, 1711 Old Forge Rd., Charlottesville, VA 22901-2111.

SCHMITTER, AMY
DISCIPLINE HISTORY OF EARLY MODERN PHILOSOPHY, HISTORY OF METAPHYSICS, PHILOSOPHY OF A **EDUCATION** Bryn Mawr Col, AB, 84; grad work, Univ Bonn, 88-89; Univ Pittsburgh, PhD, 93. **CAREER** Asst prof, Univ NMex. **SELECTED PUBLICATIONS** Auth, Representation, Self-Representation, and the Passions in Descartes, Rev of Metaphysics, Vol XVII, No 2, Dec 94; Formal Causation and the Explanation of Intentionality in Descartes, The Monist, Jl 96. **CONTACT ADDRESS** Univ of New Mexico, Albuquerque, Albuquerque, NM 87131. **EMAIL** amys@unm.edu

SCHNEIDER, JEFFREY A.
PERSONAL Born 07/07/1963, Erie, PA **DISCIPLINE** GERMAN STUDIES **EDUCATION** Bates Col, BA, 85; Cornell Univ, MA, 92; PhD, 97. **CAREER** Asst prof, Vassar Col, 97-. **HONORS AND AWARDS** DAAD Fel, 92-94. **MEMBERSHIPS** MLA, GSA, WiG, AHA. **RESEARCH** German militarism, gender, sexuality, popular culture, foreign language pedagogy, media studies. **CONTACT ADDRESS** Vassar Col, 124 Raymond Ave, PO Box 501, Poughkeepsie, NY 12604. **EMAIL** jeschneider@vassar.edu

SCHNEIDER, JOANNE
PERSONAL Born Fargo, ND, m, 1980 **DISCIPLINE** GERMAN HISTORY, MODERN EUROPEAN HISTORY, WOMEN'S HISTORY **EDUCATION** St Olaf Col, BA; Brown Univ, MA, PhD. **CAREER** Prof, RI Col. **MEMBERSHIPS** AHA, NEHA, CCWH. **RESEARCH** 18th and 19th century Ger soc, intellectual, cult hist. **SELECTED PUBLICATIONS** Co-comp, Women in Western European History. **CONTACT ADDRESS** Rhode Island Col, Providence, RI 02908. **EMAIL** joanne.schneider@hotmail.com

SCHNEIDER, LAURENCE
DISCIPLINE CHINA **EDUCATION** Wash Univ, AB, 58, Univ Calif, MA, 60, PhD, 68. **CAREER** Asst prof to prof, State Univ NY, Buffalo, 66-91; Assoc dean, soc sci, 87-91; Prof, Wash Univ, 91- ; Dir, Int Studies fice, 91-93; Chair, Hist Grad Comt, 94. **HONORS AND AWARDS** Nat Endowment Hum fel, 69-70; Soc Sci Res Coun grants, 73-74, 81-82; Nat Sci Found grant, 78-79; NY Coun Hum grant, 85. **SELECTED PUBLICATIONS** Auth, The Rockefeller Foundation, the China Foundation, and the Development Modern Science in China, Soc Sci & Med, 82; Ed, Lysenkoism In China: Profoceedings The 1956 Qingdao Genetics Symposium, Sharpe, 86; Genetics in Republican China, 1920-1949; Science And Medicine In Twentieth Century China: Research And Education, Univ Mich Ctr Chinese Studies, 88; Learning from Russia: Lysenkoism and the Fate Genetics in China, 1950-1986, Sci & Technol In Post-Mao China, Harvard Univ Profess,89. **CONTACT ADDRESS** Washington Univ, 1 Brookings Dr, Saint Louis, MO 63130.

SCHNEIDER, ROBERT A.
PERSONAL Born 03/12/1949, Manchester, NH, m, 1990, 2 children **DISCIPLINE** HISTORY **EDUCATION** Yale, BA, 71; Wesleyan Univ, MA, 74; Univ Mich, PhD, 82. **CAREER** Prof, Catholic Univ, 96; Assoc Prof, 90-96; Asst Prof, Brandeis Univ, 81-89. **HONORS AND AWARDS** NEH Fellowship; All Souls College; Oxford Visiting; Guggenheim Fellowship. **MEMBERSHIPS** AHA; Society for the Study of French History. **RESEARCH** Early Modern France Europe **SELECTED PUBLICATIONS** Auth, "The Ceremonial City," Princeton UP 95; Paperback, 97; auth, " Public Life in Toulouse 1463-1789," Cornell UP 89. **CONTACT ADDRESS** Dept History, Catholic Univ of America, 620 Michigan Ave Northeast, Washington, DC 20064-0001. **EMAIL** schneidr@cua.edu

SCHNEIDER, ROBERT W.
PERSONAL Born 05/28/1933, Londonville, OH, m, 1955, 3 children **DISCIPLINE** INTELLECTUAL HISTORY **EDUCATION** Col Wooster, BA, 55; Western Reserve Univ, MA, 56; Univ Minn, PhD, 59. **CAREER** Asst hist, 56-58, instr, Univ Minn, 58-59; instr, Col Wooster, 59-61; from asst prof to assoc prof, 61-73, Prof Hist, Northern Ill Univ, 73-98; Freelance writer & res, 98; Am Philos Soc res grant, 62, 64; Fulbright teaching fel, Regensburg Univ, Ger, 93-94. **MEMBERSHIPS** AHA; Am Studies Asn; Orgn Am Historians. **RESEARCH** Am concepts of man; Am Thought and Culture since WWII. **SELECTED PUBLICATIONS** Auth, Stephen Crane and the drama of transition: A study in historical continuity, J Cent Miss Valley Am Studies Asn, 61; Frank Norris: The naturalist as Victorian, Midcontinent Am Studies J, 62; The American Winston Churchill, Midwestern Quart, 62; Five Novelists of the Progressive Era, Columbia Univ, 65; Novelist to a Generation: The Life & thought of Winston Churchill, Popular Press, 76. **CONTACT ADDRESS** Dept of Hist, No Illinois Univ, 801 Woodlawn Dr, De Kalb, IL 60115. **EMAIL** td0rws1@corn.cso.niu.edu

SCHNEIDER, TAMMI J.
PERSONAL Born 12/28/1962, Detroit, MI, m, 1998 **DISCIPLINE** ANCIENT HISTORY **EDUCATION** Univ PA, PhD (Ancient Hist), 91. **CAREER** From asst prof relig to assoc prof, Claremont Graduate Univ, 93-. **MEMBERSHIPS** ASOR; SBL **RESEARCH** Ancient history; bible; archaeology; Assyriology. **SELECTED PUBLICATIONS** Auth, New Dissertations: A New Look at the Campaign Annals of Shalmaneser III, Mar Shipri: News letter of the Comm on Mesopotamian Civilization, 94; Did King Jehu Kill His Own Family?, Biblical Archaeology Rev, 95; Rethinking Jehu, Biblica, 96; New Project: Tel Safi, Israel, 97; Review of Mesopotamian Civilizations: The Material Foundations, by D. T. Potts, Cornell Univ Press, 97, RSR 23/4, 97; Statistical Consulting in Archaeology: Digging for Real Data, with Jim Bentley and Donald Bentley, Proceedings of the Fifth International Conference on Teaching of Statistics, vol 1, ed, Lionel Pereira-Mendoza, Int Asn for Statistical Ed, Singapore: JCS Office Supplies & Services Pte Ltd, 98; Field Report for Area G, Part !, with William Krieger, The Eighth Season of Excavation at Tel Harassim (Nahal Barkai) 1997, ed Edith Shmuel Givon, preliminary report 8, Tel-Aviv: Bar-Ilan Univ, 98; Assyria, Assurbanipal, Assurnasirpal, and Sargon II, in Eerdmans Dictionary of the Bible, Wm B. Eerdmans Pub Co, forthcoming; Judges, The Everlasting Covenant: Studies in Hebrew Narrative and Poetry, Liturgical Press, 00. **CONTACT ADDRESS** Inst Antiquity & Christianity, Claremont Graduate Sch, 831 N. Dartmouth Ave., Claremont, CA 91711. **EMAIL** Tammi.Schneider@cgu.edu

SCHNELL, GEORGE ADAM
PERSONAL Born 07/13/1931, Philadelphia, PA, m, 1958, 3 children **DISCIPLINE** GEOGRAPHY **EDUCATION** Pa State Col, Soc Sci, BS, 58; Pa State Univ, MS, Geog, 60; Pa State Univ, PhD, 65. **CAREER** Lectr, Pa State Univ, 62; asst prof, SUNY-New Paltz, 62-65; assoc prof, SUNY-New Paltz, 65-68; vis assoc prof, Univ Hawaii, 66; prof, SUNY-New Paltz, 68; chm, Dept Geog, SUNY-New Paltz, 69-94; adj prof, Empire State Coll, 74-81; PROF, GEOG, SUNY-NEW PALTZ. **MEMBERSHIPS** Asn Am Geog; Pa Acad Sci; Pa Geog Soc; Nat Coun Geog Educ **RESEARCH** Population growth; Migration & mortality of the aging **SELECTED PUBLICATIONS** "Pennsylvania's Aged Population: Problems and Prospects," Proceedings of the Annual Mtg of the Pa Geog Soc, 97; "Physiography and Cultural Landscape, A Study of Carbon County, Pa," Jour Pa Acad Sci, 97; contribur, "Protecting Freshwater Wetlands in New York: State Mapping and Local Response," Ecology of Wetlands and Associated Systems, Pa Acad Sci, 98. **CONTACT ADDRESS** Geography Dept., SUNY, New Paltz, 75 S Manheim Blvd, New Paltz, NY 12561-2499. **EMAIL** georgeschnell@msn.com

SCHNIEDEWIND, WILLIAM M.
PERSONAL Born 09/05/1962, New York, NY, m, 1990, 2 children **DISCIPLINE** NEAR EASTERN STUDIES **EDUCATION** Brandeis Univ, PhD 92. **CAREER** UCLA, assoc prof, 94-; Chair, Dept of Near Eastern Languages and Cultures. **MEMBERSHIPS** ASOR; SBL. **RESEARCH** Social History of Israel; Early Biblical Interpretation. **SELECTED PUBLICATIONS** Auth, Society and the Promise to David: The Reception History of the 2 Samuel 7:1-17, Oxford Univ Press; A Social History of the Hebrew Language: From Its Origins to the Rabbinic Period, in progress; auth, The Word of God in Transition: From Prophet to Exegete in the Second Temple Period, Jour Stud Old Testament, Sheffield, JSOT Press, 95; auth, Qumran Hebrew as an Antilanguage, Jour of Biblical stud; The Davidic Dynasty and Biblical Interpretation in the Qumran Community, proceedings of Intl Congress on Dead Sea Scrolls, Jerusalem, Israel; Manasseh King, in: Encycl of the Dead Sea Scrolls, Oxford Univ Press; auth, The Dialect of the Elisha-Elijah Narratives: A Case Study in Northern Hebrew, coauth, Jewish Quart Rev, 97; The Problem With Kings: Recent Study of the Deuteronomistic History, Rel Stud Rev, 96; auth, Are We His People?, Biblical Interpretation During Crisis, Biblica, 95; auth, History and Interpretation: The Religion of Ahab and Manasseh in the Book of Kings, Cath Biblical Quart, 93. **CONTACT ADDRESS** Univ of California, Los Angeles, 405 Hilgard, Los Angeles, CA 90095-1511. **EMAIL** williams@ucla.edu

SCHNUCKER, ROBERT VICTOR
PERSONAL Born 09/30/1932, Waterloo, IA, m, 1955, 3 children **DISCIPLINE** EARLY MODERN EUROPEAN HISTORY **EDUCATION** Northeast Mo State Univ, AB, 53; Univ Bubuque, BD, 56; Univ Iowa, MA, 60, PhD, 69. **CAREER** Pastor, First Presby Church, Springville, Iowa & United Presby Church, US, 56-63; from asst prof to assoc prof soc sci, 63-70, admin intern, 70-71, prof hist & religion, Northeast Mo State Univ 70-, Chmn Dept Philos & Relig, 71-86; Europ hist consult, Educ Media Inc, 71-76; managing ed & bk rev ed, Sixteenth Century J, 72-97; ed, Network News Exchange, Soc Hist Educ, 76-86; ed, Historians of Early Mod Europe, 76-97; vpres, Learning-Instr Facilitators, 76-86; UNI, 98-; Board of Humanities Iowa, 99-; Pastor, Bethany Presbyterian Church Grundy Center, 00. **HONORS AND AWARDS** Recipient of numerous grants from Mo Comt for the Humanities, NEH, J. Paul Getty Trust, Huguenot Soc Am, and Diefale Gout; Certificate of Appreciation from the Serials Industry Systems Comt, 87; Fel, Soc Sci Study of Relig, 90; Sixteenth Century Studies Conf Medal, 97. **MEMBERSHIPS** Fel Soc Values in Higher Educ; Sixteenth Century Studies Conf (secy, 70-72, pres, 72-73, exec secy, 75-97); AHA; Am Soc Church Hist; Soc Reformation Res; Am Acad Relig; Mo Hist Conf; Am Asn Univ Prof (organized local chapter); numerous other organizations. **RESEARCH** Social history of Puritan England to 1645; Reformation history; theory of learning. **SELECTED PUBLICATIONS** Auth, Child Raising Principles Among the Puritans, in Mothers in Pre-Industrial England, Routledge, 90; Using the Internet in Journal Publishing, Schol Publ, 90; ed, Early Osteopathy in the Words of A.T. Still, TJUP, 92; auth, Welcome to the Electronic World, SEMS, 95; author of numer-

ous other journal articles and book chapters. **CONTACT ADDRESS** 23582 Railroad St, Parkersburg, IA 50665. **EMAIL** rvs@cedarnet.org

SCHOENAUER, NORBERT
PERSONAL Born 01/02/1923, Reghin, Romania **DISCIPLINE** ARCHITECTURE, HISTORY **EDUCATION** Royal Hungarian Tech Univ, Budapest; Royal Acad Fine Arts, Copenhagen; McGill Univ, MArch, 59. **CAREER** Dir, Sch Arch, 72-75, Macdonald Emer Prof Architecture, Mcgill Univ; Can Del UN Econ Comn Europe, Budapest, 76, Ottawa, 77. **HONORS AND AWARDS** La Medaille du Merite, 95. **MEMBERSHIPS** Fel, Royal Arch Inst Can; Royal Acad Arts; Order Archs Que. **SELECTED PUBLICATIONS** Auth, Introduction to Contemporary Housing, 73; auth, 6000 Years of Housing Vols 1-3, 81; auth, History of Housing, 92; auth, Cities, Suburbs, Dwellings, 94; auth, Arts & Crafts and Art Nouveau Dwellings, 96; coauth, The Court-Garden House, 62; coauth, Grassroots Greystones & Glass Towers, 89; ed, John Bland at Eighty: A Tribute, 91. **CONTACT ADDRESS** 815 Sherbrooke St, W, Rm 201, Montreal, QC, Canada H3A 2K6. **EMAIL** nschoe@po-box.mcgill.ca

SCHOENBRUN, D. L.
PERSONAL Born 10/25/1958, Boston, MA, m, 1989 **DISCIPLINE** HISTORY **EDUCATION** UCLA, MA 83, PhD 90; Lewis & Clark Col, BA 80. **CAREER** Univ Georgia, asst prof 90-95, assoc prof 95-98. **HONORS AND AWARDS** Fulbright-Hays Fel; Soc Sci Res Coun Fel; Amer Coun of LS Gnt. **MEMBERSHIPS** ASA; BIEA **RESEARCH** Precolonial African History. **SELECTED PUBLICATIONS** Auth, A Green Place, A Good Place: Agrarian Change, Gender, and Social Identity in the Great Lakes Region to the 15th Century, Social Hist of Africa, eds, A. Issacmanand J. Allman, Portsmouth, NH, Heinman and James Curry, 98; The Historical Reconstruction of Great Lakes Bantu Cultural Vocabulary: Etymologies and Distributions, Rudiger Koppe Verlag, Koln, 97; Special Issue of the African Archaeological Rev: Papers in Honor of Merrick Posnansky, co-ed, 93; The (IN)Visible Roots of Bunyoro-Kitara and Buganda in the Lakes Region: 800-1300, in: Susan K. McIntosh, Pathways To Complexity: Intermediate Societies in Africa, Cambridge, Cam UP,99; Some Thoughts on Ancient Historical Dimensions of Current Conflicts in the Greater Kivu Region, Uganda Jour, 96; An Intellectual History of Power: Usable Pasts From the Great Lakes Region, eds Gilbert Pwiti, Robert Soper, Aspects of African Archaeology, Harare Zim, U of Zimbabwe Press, 96; Gendered Histories Between the Great Lakes: Varieties and Limits, Intl Jour of African Hist Stud, 96. **CONTACT ADDRESS** Dept of History, Univ of Georgia, Athens, GA 30602-1602. **EMAIL** dschoenb@arches.uga.edu

SCHOENL, WILLIAM J.
PERSONAL Born 02/15/1941, Buffalo, NY, m, 1966, 3 children **DISCIPLINE** HISTORY **EDUCATION** Canisias Col, BS, 63; Columbia Univ, MA, 64; PhD, 68. **CAREER** Asst Prof, Michigan State Univ, 68-; Assoc Prof, 72; Prof, 78. **HONORS AND AWARDS** Global Competence Grant, Michigan State University; Kiwanis Club of Okemos Foundation Grant; National Endowment for the Humanities Grant; American Philosophical Society Grant; New York State Regents Teaching Fellowships for Graduate Study. **MEMBERSHIPS** Michigan State Univ Peace & Justice Initiative; Michigan State Univ Center for Advanced Study of International Development; Center for Jung Studies of Detroit. **RESEARCH** New Internationa perspectives on the Vietnam War; Life and Work of C.G. Jung. **SELECTED PUBLICATIONS** Auth, "C.G. Jung: His Friendships with Mary Mellon and J.B. Priestley, 98; auth, "Major issues in The Life and Work of C.G. Jung, 96; auth, "The Intellectual Crisis in English Catholicism," 82. **CONTACT ADDRESS** Dept History, Michigan State Univ, 301 Morrill Hall, East Lansing, MI 48824-1036. **EMAIL** schoenl@pilot.msu.edu

SCHOFIELD, H.
PERSONAL Born 07/09/1931, Minneapolis, MN, d, 2 children **DISCIPLINE** EUROPEAN HISTORY **EDUCATION** Univ Minn, BA, 53, PhD, 60; Univ Conn, MA, 56. **CAREER** Asst to assoc prof, Univ Wisc-Eau Claire, 60-66; assoc to full prof, Col Wom Col, 66-81; vis prof, Mentrop State Col, 91- . **HONORS AND AWARDS** Univ Minn fel, 58; Tozer fel, 59. **RESEARCH** Modern French history. **SELECTED PUBLICATIONS** Auth, Red Light Red Light, Tor Books, (88); auth, A Private Kind of War, Tor Books, (90). **CONTACT ADDRESS** Dept Hist, Metropolitan State Col of Denver, PO Box 173362, Denver, CO 80217-3362.

SCHOFIELD, KENT
PERSONAL Born 03/12/1938, San Bernardino, CA, m, 1960, 2 children **DISCIPLINE** MODERN AMERICAN HISTORY **EDUCATION** Univ Calif, Riverside, BA, 61, PhD(hist), 66; Claremont Grad Sch, MA, 62. **CAREER** Asst prof hist, Harvey Mudd Col, 65-66; from asst prof to assoc prof, 66-74, assoc dean acad planning, 72-76, Prof Hist, Calif State Col, San Bernardino, 74-, Chmn Dept, 77- **MEMBERSHIPS** AHA; Orgn Am Historians; Am Studies Asn. **RESEARCH** Modern American history. **SELECTED PUBLICATIONS** Auth, The public image of Herbert Hoover in the 1928 campaign, Mid Am, 10/69. **CONTACT ADDRESS** Dept of Hist, California State Univ, San Bernardino, 5500 University Pky, San Bernardino, CA 92407-7500.

SCHOFIELD, ROBERT EDWIN
PERSONAL Born 06/01/1923, Milford, NE **DISCIPLINE** HISTORY OF SCIENCE **EDUCATION** Princeton Univ, BA, 44; Univ Minn, MS, 48; Harvard Univ, PhD, 55. **CAREER** Res asst physics, Knolls Atomic Power Lab, Gen Elec Co, 48-50; teaching fel gen ed, Nat Sci, Harvard Univ, 50-53, 54-55; from asst prof to assoc prof hist & hist sci, Univ Kans, 55-59; from assoc prof to prof, 60-72, Lynn Thorndike prof, 72-79; Prof to prof emer Hist Tech & Sci, Iowa State Univ, 79-. **HONORS AND AWARDS** Pfizer Prize, Hist Sci Soc, 64; Guggenheim fels, 59-60 & 67-68; mem sch hist studies, Inst Advan Studies, 67-68 & 74-75; assoc, Ctr d'Hist des idees dans LeMonde Angle-Am, Univ Paris-Sorbonne, 77-. **MEMBERSHIPS** Am Phys Soc; Hist Sci Soc; Soc Hist Technol; Am Soc 18th Century Studies; fel Royal Soc Arts. **RESEARCH** History of 18th century English science and technology; life and work of Joseph Priestly; scientific societies. **SELECTED PUBLICATIONS** Auth, Roller,Duane,Henry,Dubose, 14 March 1920 22 August 1994/, Isis, 1995. **CONTACT ADDRESS** Dept of Hist, Iowa State Univ of Science and Tech, Ames, IA 50011.

SCHOLNICK, ROBERT JAMES
PERSONAL Born 06/22/1941, Boston, MA, m, 1964, 1 child **DISCIPLINE** AMERICAN LITERATURE & STUDIES **EDUCATION** Univ Pa, AB, 62; Brandeis Univ, MA, 64, PhD(English & Am lit), 69. **CAREER** Asst prof, 67-72, assoc prof, 73-80, PROF ENGLISH, COL WILLIAM & MARY, 80- **MEMBERSHIPS** MLA **RESEARCH** American literature; American poetry; Walt Whitman. **SELECTED PUBLICATIONS** Auth, The Original Eye, Whitman, Schelling And The Return To Origins/, Walt Whitman Quart Rev, Vol 0011, 1994; Cult Or Democracy - Whitman, Benson,Eugene, And The Galaxy/, Walt Whitman Quart Rev, Vol 0013, 1996. **CONTACT ADDRESS** Dept of English, Col of William and Mary, Williamsburg, VA 23185.

SCHOONOVER, THOMAS DAVID
PERSONAL Born 05/27/1936, Winona, MN, m, 1966, 1 child **DISCIPLINE** AMERICAN HISTORY **EDUCATION** Univ Minn, BA, 59, PhD(hist), 70 La State Univ, MA, 61. **CAREER** Instr hist, Univ Wis-La Crosse, 62-63; lectr, Europ Div, Univ Md, 63-67; from instr to asst prof, 69-75, Assoc Prof Am Hist, Univ Southwestern LA, 75-, Nat Endowment for Humanities younger humanist fel, 72-73; area ed, The Americas: A Quart Rev of Inter-Am Hist, 73-; Deutscher Akademischer Austauschdiens grant 75; Am Philos Soc grants, 79 & 80; Southern Regional Educ Bd grant, 80; Nat Endowment for Humanities, summer sem, 80; Fulbright sr lectr, Univ of Bielefeld, 81-82; Fritz Thyssen Stiftung grant, 82. **MEMBERSHIPS** AHA; Orgn Am Hist; Soc Historians Am Foreign Rel; Soc Sci Hist Asn. **RESEARCH** United States relations with Latin America; 19th century United States; United States foreign relations. **SELECTED PUBLICATIONS** Auth, Dollars over Dominion: The Triumph of Liberalism in Mexican-United States Relations, 1861-1867. Baton Rouge: Louisiana State Univ Press, 78; auth, The Mexican Lobby: Matoutias Romero in Washington, 1861-1867, Lexington: Univ of Kentucky Press, 86; auth, A Mexican View of American in the 1860s: A Foreign Diplomat Describes the Civil War and Reconstruction, Rutherford, NJ: Fairleigh Dickinson Univ Press, 91; auth, The United States in Central America, 1860-1911: Episodes in Social Imperialism and Imperial Rivalry in the World System, Durham, NC: Duke Univ Press, 91; auth, The Banana Men: American Mercenaries and Entrepreneurs in Central America, 1880-1930, Durham, NC: Duke Univ Press, 91; auth, Germany in Central Ameica, 1821-1929: Competive Imperialism, Univ, AL: Univ of Alabama Press, 98; auth, France in Central America, 1821-1929: Culture and Commerce, Willmington, DE: Scholarly Resources, 00. **CONTACT ADDRESS** Dept of Hist, Univ of Southwestern Louisiana, 200 Hebrard Blvd, Lafayette, LA 70504-8401. **EMAIL** tds@louisiana.edu

SCHOPPA, ROBERT KEITH
PERSONAL Born 11/20/1943, Vernon, TX, m, 1968, 2 children **DISCIPLINE** MODERN CHINESE HISTORY **EDUCATION** Valparaiso Univ, BA, 66; Univ Hawaii, MA, 68; Univ Mich, PhD(mod Chinese hist), 75. **CAREER** Instr, 68-71 & 74-75, asst prof, 75-80, Assoc Prof Hist, Valparaiso Univ, 75-, Chmn, 80-, Assoc ctr, Ctr Far Eastern Studies, Univ Chicago, 76-; res prof, Valparaiso Univ, 77-79. **MEMBERSHIPS** Asn Asian Studies; Soc Ch'ing Studies; AHA; Social Sci Hist Asn. **RESEARCH** Twentieth century Chinese social and political elites and institutions; Chinese social and political development from 1850-1949. **SELECTED PUBLICATIONS** Auth, The composition and functions of the local elite in Szechwan, 1851-1874, Ch'ing-Shih Wen-t'i, 11/73; Local self-government in Zhekiang, 1909-1927, Mod China, 10/76; province and nation: The Chekiang provincial autonomy movement, 1917-1927, J Asian Studies, 8/77; Chinese Elites and Political Change: Zhejiang Province in the Early Twentieth Century, Harvard Univ Press, 82. **CONTACT ADDRESS** Dept of Hist, Valparaiso Univ, 651 College Ave, Valparaiso, IN 46383-6493.

SCHORSCH, ISMAR
PERSONAL Born 11/03/1935, Hanover, Germany, m, 1960, 3 children **DISCIPLINE** JEWISH HISTORY **EDUCATION** Ursinus Col, BA, 57; Columbia Univ, MA, 61, PhD(hist), 69; Jewish Theol Sem, MHL, 62. **CAREER** Instr Jewish hist, Jewish Theol Sem Am, 67-68; instr, Columbia Univ, 68, asst prof, 68-70; assoc prof, 70-76, prof, 76-80, Rabbi Herman Abramovitz Prof Jewish Hist, Jewish Theol Sem Am, 80-, Dean, Grad Sch, 75-; Mem Found Jewish Cult grant, 73-76. **HONORS AND AWARDS** Ansley Awd, Columbia Univ Press, 69; Litt D (hon), Wittenberg Univ, 89, Ursinus Col, 90, Gratz Col, 95, Russian State Univ, 96. **MEMBERSHIPS** Leo Baeck Inst (pres); fel Am Acad Jewish Res. **RESEARCH** Modern German Jewish history; Jewish historiography; modern Jewish history. **SELECTED PUBLICATIONS** Auth, The philosophy of history of Nachman Krochmal, Judaism, 61; Moritz Gudemann: Rabbi, historian and apologist, Leo Baeck Inst Yearbk, 66; Jewish Reactions to German Anti-Semitism, 1870-1914, Columbia Univ, 72; German antisemitism in the light of post-war historiography, Leo Baeck Inst Yearbk, Vol XIX, 74; translator & ed, Heinrich Graetz's, The Structure of Jewish History and Other Essays, Jewish Theol Sem Am, 75; auth, From Wolfenbuttel to Wissenschaft: The divergent careers of Isaac M Jost and Leopold Zunz, Leo Baeck Inst Yearbk, Vol XXI, 76; Historical reflections on the Holocaust, Conservative Judaism, fall-winter 76-77; auth, From Text to Context: The Turn to History in Modern Judaism, 94. **CONTACT ADDRESS** Dept of Hist, Jewish Theol Sem of America, 3080 Broadway, New York, NY 10027-4650. **EMAIL** isschorsch@jtsa.edu

SCHOTT, LINDA
PERSONAL Born 06/07/1957, Hondo, TX, d, 2 children **DISCIPLINE** HISTORY **EDUCATION** Baylor Univ, BA, 79; Stanford Univ, MA, 82, PhD, 86. **CAREER** Instr, Stanford Univ, 84-85; asst prof, Southwest Tex State Univ, 85-86; asst prof, Tex Lutheran Col, 86-89; asst prof to assoc prof, Univ of Tex San Antonio, 89-. **HONORS AND AWARDS** Phi Beta Kappa; David M. Potter Prize, Stanford Univ, 83; James Birdsall Weter Fel, Stanford Univ, 83-84; School of Lib Arts Nominee, Presidential Awd for Excellence in Teaching, Southwest Tex State Univ, 86; First Runner-Up Berkshire Sum Fel, Radcliffe, Col, 86; Fac Res Awd, Univ of Tex, San Antonio, 91; Who's Who of Am Women, 97-98; Headliner Awd, Women In Commun Inc. 98. **RESEARCH** Women's history in the U.S. since 1860, intellectual history. **SELECTED PUBLICATIONS** Auth, "The Woman's Peace Party and The Moral Basis for Women's Pacifism", Frontiers VIII.2 (Spring 85): 19-24; auth, "Engendered Philosophical Perspectives: Jane Addams and William James on Alternatives to War", J of the Hist of Ideas, (Apr 93): 241-254; auth, "Middle-of-the-Road Pacifists: Carrie Chapman Catt and the National Committee on the Cause and Cure of War", Peace and Change (Jan 96): 1-21; coauth, "My Mother Was a Mover: African-American Seminole Women in Brackettville, Texas 1914-1964", Writing the Range: Race, Class, and Culture in the Women's West, eds Sue Armitage and Elizabeth Jameson, Univ of Okla Pr, 97; auth, Reconstructing Women's Thoughts: The Women's International League for Peace and Freedom before World War II, Stanford Univ Pr, 97. **CONTACT ADDRESS** Dept Behav Sci, Univ of Texas, San Antonio, 6900 N Loop 1604 W, San Antonio, TX 78249-1130. **EMAIL** lschott@utsa.edu

SCHRADER, WILLIAM C.
PERSONAL Born 08/06/1940, Louisville, KY, d, 3 children **DISCIPLINE** HISTORY **EDUCATION** Bellarmine Col, AB, 62; Cath Univ Am, MA, 66; PhD, 72. **CAREER** Asst prof to prof, Tex Tech Univ, 66-. **HONORS AND AWARDS** Fulbright Awd, 62-63; Woodrow Wilson Awd, 63-64; NEH Fel, 78-79; Outstanding Fac Awd, 70-71; 92-93. **MEMBERSHIPS** AHA; ACHA; SEASECS; ASECS; AAUP. **RESEARCH** Early Modern Germany. **SELECTED PUBLICATIONS** Auth, "Families and Factions in the Cathedral Chapter of Munster", Tenn Tech J XVII (82): 33-40; auth, "Careers in the Church and the Extinction of Noble Families in Westphalia, 1648-1806", Cath Hist Rev LXXIII.3 (87): 424-29; auth, "The Cathedral Chapter at Minden and Its Members, 1650-1803", Westfalische Zeitschrift 139, (89): 83-122; auth, "The Catholic Revival in the Cathedral Chapters of Osnarbruck and Minden, 1591-1651", Cath Hist Rev LXXVIII.1 (92): 35-50; auth, "The Creation of the Kingdom of Sicily", Chronology of European History, Salem Pr, (97); auth, "Der sieg des Reform-Katholizismus in Osnarbrucker Domkapitel, 1585-1623", Osnabrucker Mitteilunge, 102, (97); 65-76; auth, "Adrian IV, 1154-1159", "Investiture Controversy", Encycl of the Vatican and Papacy, ed Frank J Coppa, Greenwood Pr, (Westport, CT), 99. **CONTACT ADDRESS** Dept Hist, Tennessee Tech Univ, 900 N Dixie Ave, Cookeville, TN 38505-0001. **EMAIL** wcschrader@tntech.edu

SCHRECKER, ELLEN
PERSONAL Born 08/04/1938, Philadelphia, PA, m, 1981, 2 children **DISCIPLINE** HISTORY **EDUCATION** Radcliffe Col, BA, 60; Harvard, PhD, 74. **CAREER** Preceptor, Expository Writing, Harvard Univ, 75-81; Adj Asst Prof, NYork Univ, 83-85; Prog Officer, NYork Coun for Humanities, 84-85; Lectr, Princeton Univ, 85-87; Adj Prof, Columbia Univ, 96; The Union Inst, 91-95; Asst to Full Prof, Yeshiva Univ, 87-; Ed, Academe, 98-. **HONORS AND AWARDS** Bunting Inst Fel, 77-

78; Res Fel, Harry S. Truman Libr, 87; Outstanding Book Awd, Hist of Educ Soc, 87; Fel Nat Humanities Center, 94-95; Outstanding Acad Book "Choice", 98. **MEMBERSHIPS** OAH, AHA, PEN, SHAFR. **RESEARCH** US since 1945. **SELECTED PUBLICATIONS** Auth, Mrs. Chiang's Szechwan Cookbook, Harper and Row (NY), 76, 87; auth, The Hired Money: The French Debt to the United States, 1917-1929, Arno Press (NY), 79; auth, co-ed, Regulating the Intellectuals: Perspectives on Academic Freedom in the 1980s, Praeger (NY), 83; auth, No Ivory Tower: McCarthyism and the Universities, Oxford Univ Press (NY), 86; auth, The Age of McCarthyism: A Brief History with Documents, Bedford Books (Boston), 94; auth, Many Are the Crimes: McCarthyism in America, Little, Brown (NY), 98, Princeton Univ Press, 99; auth, "The Spies Who Loved Us," The Nation (May 24, 99); auth, "Left, Right, and Labor," Working USA (Jan-Feb 00); auth, "McCarthyism and Democracy," in War and Democracy: The Peloponnesian War and the Korean War, ed. David McCann and Barry Strauss (M.E. Sharpe, forthcoming); auth, "McCarthyism: The Myth and the Reality," in McCarthyism in America, ed. Douglas Brinkley and Sam Tanenhaus (Yale Univ Press, forthcoming). **CONTACT ADDRESS** Dept Hist, Stern Col for Women, 245 Lexington Ave, New York, NY 10016-4605. **EMAIL** schrecker@ymail.yu.edu

SCHREIBER, ROY
PERSONAL Born 03/13/1941, Newark, NJ **DISCIPLINE** HISTORY **EDUCATION** Univ Calif at LA, BA, 64, MA, 65; Univ London, PhD, 67. **CAREER** Asst prof, hist, Upsala Col, 67-68; asst to assoc to Prof, Hist, Indiana Univ S Bend, 68-. **HONORS AND AWARDS** Fel, Inst Hist Res, London, 66-67; co-ed, conf British Stud Bio Series, 77; fel, Royal Hist Soc, 81; Authors' Guild, 89; Indiana Univ, S Bend Teaching Award, 89; All Univ Fac Coloquim Exc in Teaching, 90; Dramatists Guild, 93. **MEMBERSHIPS** Am Hist Asn; N Am Conf British Stud **RESEARCH** 17th & 18th cent Great Britain, 18th cent Pacific exploration; Australia, 1789-1810. **SELECTED PUBLICATIONS** Auth, The Fortunate Adversities of William Bligh, 91; "Triumphant Reason," Authors, 94-95; "Indiana University History Departments Talk About Teaching," Perspectives, 36, 98; auth, Some Food for Thought in History, Teching History, forthcoming; auth, James Hay, Earl of Carlisle, New Dictionary of National Biogrpahy, Oxford Univ Press, forthcoming; Wayward Souls, Raconteur, 1:9, Apr 94; Triumphant Reason, Authors, July 94-Feb 95. **CONTACT ADDRESS** Dept of History, Indiana Univ, South Bend, South Bend, IN 46634.

SCHRIER, ARNOLD
PERSONAL Born 05/30/1925, Bronx, NY, m, 1949, 4 children **DISCIPLINE** HISTORY **EDUCATION** Northwestern Univ, PhD 56. **CAREER** Univ Cincinnati, asst prof. assoc prof, prof, dir of grad studies, 56-78, Walter C Langsam Prof 72-95, Walter C Langsam Prof Emeritus 95-. **HONORS AND AWARDS** SSRC Fell 56 and 63; Vis Assoc Prof IN Univ; Vis Lect Duke Univ; Dist Vis Prof US Airforce Acad; Dist Ser Awd. **MEMBERSHIPS** AHA; WHA; AAASS; OAH; IHRA; NCSS. **RESEARCH** Russian Hist; World Hist; Immigration Hist **SELECTED PUBLICATIONS** Auth, Ireland and the American Emigration, 1850-1900, Univ Minnesota, 58, re-issued, Russell and Russell 70, pbk, Dufour 97; Living World History, coauth, Pub Scott, Foresman, 64, rev 93; History and Life: The World and Its People, Pub Scott, Foresman, 77, rev 93; a Russian Looks At America, Chicago, 79. **CONTACT ADDRESS** Dept of History, Univ of Cincinnati, 10 Diplomat Dr, Cincinnati, OH 45215. **EMAIL** hope.earls@uc.edu

SCHROEDER, JOHN H.
PERSONAL Born 09/13/1943, Twin Falls, ID, m, 1965, 2 children **DISCIPLINE** HISTORY **EDUCATION** Lewis and Clark Col, BA, 65; Univ Va, MA, 67; PhD, 71. **CAREER** From Asst Prof to Prof, Univ Wis, 71-. **HONORS AND AWARDS** Uhrig Awd for Distinguished Teaching, Univ Wis, 74; AMOCO Awd for Distinguished Teaching, Univ Wis, 75; ACE Fel, Am Coun of Educ, 82-83. **MEMBERSHIPS** OAH, SHER, SHAFR, SHSW. **RESEARCH** 19th Century United States, naval, maritime and diplomatic history. **SELECTED PUBLICATIONS** Auth, Mr. Polk's War: American Opposition and Dissent 1846-1848, Univ Wis Pr, 73; auth, Shaping the American Empire: The Commercial and Diplomatic Role of the American Navy 1829-1861, Greenwood Pr, 85; auth, Commodore Matthew C Perry 1794-1858: A Biography, U S Naval Inst Pr, forthcoming. **CONTACT ADDRESS** Dept Hist, Univ of Wisconsin, Milwaukee, PO Box 413, Milwaukee, WI 53201-1413. **EMAIL** jhs@uwm.edu

SCHROEDER, PAUL W.
DISCIPLINE HISTORY **EDUCATION** Tex Christian Univ, MA, 56; Univ Tex Austin, PhD, 58. **CAREER** Prof, Univ Ill Urbana Champaign, 64-; assoc prof, 63-64. **HONORS AND AWARDS** Fulbright Scholar, 56-57; Fel, NEH, 73; Fel, Am Council of Learned Societies, 76-77; Fel, Woodrow Wilson International Center for Scholars, 83-84; Honorary Doctor of Letters, Valparaiso Univ, 93. **RESEARCH** Late sixteenth to twentieth century European international politics; theory of history. **SELECTED PUBLICATIONS** Auth, Austria, Great Britian, and the Crimean War: The Destruction of the European Concert, Ithaca, NY: Cornell Univ Press, 72; auth, "Did the Vienna Settlement Rest on Balance of Power?", Am Hist Rev, 97, 2, (92): 683-706, 733-5; auth, "The Transformation of Political Thinking, 1787-1848," in Coping with Complexity in the International System, eds. Jack Snyder and Robert Jervis, (Boulder, CO: Westview Press, 93): 47-70; auth, "System and Systemic Thinking in International History," Journal of International Hist Rev, 1, (93): 116-34; auth, "Economic Intergration and the European International System in the Era of World War I," Am Hist Rev 94, 4, (93): 1130-37; auth, "Historical Reality vs Neo-Realist Theory," International Security 19, 2, (94): 108-48; auth, The Transformation of European Politics, 1763-1848, Oxford Clarendon, 94. **CONTACT ADDRESS** History Dept, Univ of Illinois, Urbana-Champaign, 52 E Gregory Dr, Champaign, IL 61820. **EMAIL** pschroed@uiuc.edu

SCHROEDER, SUSAN P.
DISCIPLINE HISTORY **EDUCATION** UCLA, PhD. **CAREER** Hist, Loyola Univ. **RESEARCH** Latin American history; Mexico Cuba. **SELECTED PUBLICATIONS** Auth, Society and Politics in Mexico Tenochtitlan, Tlatelolco, Texcoco, Culhuacan, and Other Nahua Altepetl in Central Mexico, Codex Chimalpahin, 97; Indian Women in early Mexico, Univ Okla Press, 97; Encyclopedia of Mexico. Three items, biographies: Chimalpahin and Juan de Tovar, S J; essay: Indian Women, Chicago and London: Fitzroy Dearborn Pub, 97; The Pax Colonial and Native Resistance in New Spain, Univ Nebr Press, 98; Chimalpahin y los reinos de Chalco, Colegio Mexiquense, 94; Looking Back at the Conquest: Nahua Perceptions of Early Encounters from the Anns of Chimalpahin, in Chipping Away on Earth: Stud in Prehispanic and Colonial Mexico in Honor of Arthur J.O. and Charles E. Dibble, Labryinthos Press, 94; Father Jose Maria Luis Mora, Libism, and the British and Foreign Bible Society in Nineteenth-Century Mexico, The Americas, 94. **CONTACT ADDRESS** Fine Arts Dept, Loyola Univ, Chicago, 6525 N. Sheridan Rd., Chicago, IL 60626. **EMAIL** sschroe@wpo.it.luc.edu

SCHROEDER-LEIN, GLENNA R.
PERSONAL Born 09/23/1951, Pasadena, CA, m, 1990 **DISCIPLINE** HISTORY **EDUCATION** Univ GA, PhD 91; Univ AZ, MLS 81; Cal State Univ, Fullerton, MA 78, BA 75. **CAREER** Univ TN, 90-00, asst ed, pprs of Andrew Johnson, 93-, adj lectr hist; Washington Coll, 90, vis asst prof; World Vision, CA, 82-84, phto lib; South W Museum, CA, 77-81, archivist. **HONORS AND AWARDS** McClung Awd, best journal art. **MEMBERSHIPS** SHA; Conf on Faith Hist; OAH. **RESEARCH** Antebellum, civil war, reconst US. **SELECTED PUBLICATIONS** Confederate Hospitals on the Move: Samuel H Stout & The Army of Tennessee, 94; The Papers of Andrew Johnson, asst ed, 92-00; various artl and bk revs. **CONTACT ADDRESS** Univ of Tennessee, Knoxville, Knoxville, TN 37996-4000.

SCHROTH, SARAH W.
DISCIPLINE ART HISTORY **EDUCATION** NYork Univ, PhD. **CAREER** Adj asst prof, Univ NC, Chapel Hill; assoc cur and prof, Duke Univ Museum of Art. **RESEARCH** Span baroque painting. **SELECTED PUBLICATIONS** Auth, 36 Women Artists: Dissolving the Separation Between Art and Life, Atlanta Women's Art Collective, 78; Burial of the Court of Orgaz, Stud in the Hist of Art, Vol II, 82; Early Collectors of Still-Life Painting in Castile, Spanish Still Life in the Golden Age, 85; David Roberts in Context, Duke UP, 96. **CONTACT ADDRESS** Museum of Art, Duke Univ, Room 121, Box 90732, Durham, NC 27708. **EMAIL** fiii@acpub.duke.edu

SCHUFREIDER, GREGORY
DISCIPLINE HISTORY OF PHILOSOPHY, RECENT CONTINENTAL PHILOSOPHY, THE PHILOSOPHY OF ART **EDUCATION** Northwestern Univ, BA, 69; Univ Calif, Santa Barbara, MA, PhD, 75. **CAREER** Prof, La State Univ. **RESEARCH** Heidegger. **SELECTED PUBLICATIONS** Auth, An Introduction to Anselm's Argument, Temple UP, 78; The Metaphysician as Poet-Magician, in Metaphilosophy, 79; Art and the Problem of Truth, Man and World, 81; Heidegger on Community, Man and World, 81; The Logic of the Absurd, in Philos and Phenomenol Res, 83; Overpowering the Center: Three Compositions by Modrian, in JAAC, 85; Heidegger Contribution to a Phenomenology of Culture, 86; Confessions of a Rational Mystic: Anselm's Early Writings, Purdue Univ ser, in the Hist of Philos, 94. **CONTACT ADDRESS** Dept of Philos and Relig Stud, Louisiana State Univ and A&M Col, 106 Coates Hall, Baton Rouge, LA 70803.

SCHUKER, STEPHEN A.
PERSONAL Born 02/16/1939, New York, NY, m, 1998, 2 children **DISCIPLINE** HISTORY **EDUCATION** Cornell Univ, AB, 59; Harvard Univ, AM, 62; Harvard Univ, PhD, 69. **CAREER** From Instr to Asst Prof, Harvard Univ, 68-75; Adj Prof, Johns Hopkins Univ, 78-83; From Assoc Prof to Prof, Brandeis Univ, 77-91; Prof, Univ Va, 91-. **HONORS AND AWARDS** Who's Who in Am; Who's Who in the E; Who's Who in the Southeast; Who's Who in Am Educ; John D and Catherine T MacArthur Found Fel, 87-88; Secy of the Navy Sen Res Fel, Naval War Col, 92-93; Stipendiat, Hist Kolleg, 96-97; Res Fel, Ger Marshall Fund of the U S, 98-99. **RESEARCH** 20th-Century diplomatic, economic and political history of Europe and the United States. **SELECTED PUBLICATIONS** Auth, The End of French Predominance in Europe: The Financial Crisis of 1924 and the Adoption of the Dawes Plan, Univ NC Pr (Chapel Hill, NC), 76; auth, "Bayern und der rheinische Separatismus 1923-1924," in Jahrbuch des Historischen Kollegs, No 3 (Munich, 98), 75-111; auth, "Dwight Whitney Morrow," in Am Nat Biog 15 (New York: Oxford UP, 99), 926-928; auth, "The Gold-Exchange Standard: A Reinterpretation," in The Int Financial Syst: Past and Present (New York: Cambridge UP, forthcoming); auth, "The European Union: From Jean Monnet to the Euro: A Historical Overview," in The European Union: From Jean Monnet to the Euro (Athens, OH: Ohio UP, forthcoming). **CONTACT ADDRESS** Dept Hist, Univ of Virginia, 216 Randall Hall, Charlottesville, VA 22903-3244. **EMAIL** sas4u@virginia.edu

SCHULMAN, BRUCE J.
PERSONAL Born 12/16/1959, New York, NY, m, 1989, 2 children **DISCIPLINE** HISTORY **EDUCATION** Yale Univ, BA, 81; Stanford Univ, MA, 82; PhD, 87. **CAREER** Asst Prof to Assoc Prof, Univ Calif, 87-93; Assoc Prof and Dir, Boston Univ, 94-. **HONORS AND AWARDS** Grad Fel, Stanford Univ, 81-85; Giles Whiting Fel, 85; Mabelle McLeod Lewis Mem Fel, 86; Fac Development Grant, UCLA, 89; NEH Fel, 92; Outstanding Teaching, UCLA Mortar Board, 90, 92; Eby Awd, 93; Harriet and Charles Luckman distinguished Teaching Awd, 93; Fel, Charles Warren Ctr, 96; Fulbright Sen Prof, 99. **SELECTED PUBLICATIONS** Auth, From Cotton Belt to Sunbelt; Federal Policy, Economic Development, and the Transformation of the South, 1938-1980, Oxford Univ Press, 91; auth, Lyndon B. Johnson and American Liberalism, Bedford Books, 94; auth, "Forget the Framers: Lower Bar on Impeachment," Los Angeles Times, Jan 99; auth, "As American As Hating Intellectuals," Los Angeles Time, Feb 99; auth, "Out of the Streets and Into the Classroom?: The New Left and the Counterculture in U.S. History Textbooks," Journal of American History, 99; auth, "Some Recent Peaks in Crisis Management," Bostonia, (99): 70-73; auth, "Hate Crimes Amid the Prosperity," Los Angeles Times, Apr 99; auth, "The Historic Power of Special Interests," Los Angeles Times, Jun 99; auth, "In Praise of Parities," Los Angeles Times, Oct 99; auth, This Ain't No Party: The 1970s and the Making of Modern America, 1969-1984, Free Press, forthcoming. **CONTACT ADDRESS** Dept Hist, Boston Univ, 226 Bay State Rd, Boston, MA 02215-1403. **EMAIL** bjschulm@bu.edu

SCHULTE, JOSEPHINE HELEN
PERSONAL Born 05/09/1929, Foley, AL **DISCIPLINE** COLONIAL & MODERN LATIN AMERICAN HISTORY **EDUCATION** Spring Hill Col, BS, 57; Univ Southern Miss, MA, 61; Loyola Univ Chicago, PhD(hist), 69; Trinity Univ, MA, 76. **CAREER** Transl, Gulf Steamship Agency, Ala, 49-58; res asst Mobile metrop area audit, Southern Inst Mgt, 59-60; spec lectr hist, Spring Hill Col, 60-62; asst prof, Univ of the Americas, 67-70; assoc prof, 70-79, Prof Hist, St Mary's Univ, Tex, 79-, Grad Adv Hist, 73-, Dir Latin Am Studies Prog, 74-, Teacher Ger info & educ, Brookley Field AFB, Ala, 51-62; teacher English & Span, Prichard Jr High Sch, Ala, 62; mem bd dirs, Southwestern Conf Latin Am Studies, 77-82; Orgn Am States grant, Mexico, 66-67; Orgn Am States & Spanish government res fel, Spain, 81-82. **MEMBERSHIPS** Latin Am Studies Asn; Cath Hist Asn. **RESEARCH** Mexico in the 19th century; Spanish borderlands in North America; Colonial Latin America. **SELECTED PUBLICATIONS** Auth, Mission And Might - The Political Religious Clash Between The Dominican Order In Peru And The Viceroy Francisco De Toledo 1561-1581 - Ger - Hehrlein,Y/, Cath Hist Rev, Vol 0079, 1993; Ger-Bohemians - The Quiet Immigrants - Rippley,Lj, Paulson,Rj/, Cath Hist Rev, Vol 0082, 1996; Manuscript Sources For The Hist Of Iberian Am - A Guide To Research Tools - Spa - Hilton,Sl, Gonzalescasasnovas,I/, Hisp Ame Hist Rev, Vol 0076, 1996; Origins Of The Cath-Church In The Caribbean-Islands - The Hist Of The Dioceses Of Santo-Domingo, Concepcion-De-La-Vega, San-Juan-De-Puerto-Rico And Santiago-De-Cuba From Their Establishments Up To The Mid-17th-Century - Ger, Cath Hist Rev. **CONTACT ADDRESS** 6623 Callaghan Rd Apt 1703, San Antonio, TX 78229.

SCHULTENOVER, DAVID, SJ
PERSONAL Born 08/19/1938, Sauk Rapids, MN, s **DISCIPLINE** HISTORICAL THEOLOGY **EDUCATION** Spring Hill Col, BS, 63; Loyola Univ, MS, 66; St. Louis Univ, PhD, 75 **CAREER** Prof, 94-pres, Assoc Prof, 85-94, Adj Asst Prof, 78-83, Creighton Univ; Asst Prof, 75-78, Marquette Univ; Book review editor for Theological Studies, 00. **HONORS AND AWARDS** Nat Endowm for the Humanities Fel; Alpha Sigma Nu Ntl Bk Awd; Deutscher Akademischer Austauschdienst Fel; Alpha Sigma Nu **MEMBERSHIPS** Am Acad of Relig; Am Soc Church History; Cath Theolog Soc of Am **RESEARCH** Christology; Roman Catholic Modernism; Models and Images of the Church **SELECTED PUBLICATIONS** Auth, George Tyrrell: In Search of Catholicism, Patmos Press, 81; Auth, A View from Rome: The Eve of the Modernist Crisis, Fordham University Press, 93. **CONTACT ADDRESS** Jesuit Community, Creighton Univ, 2500 California Plaza, #Jesuit, Omaha, NE 68178-0001. **EMAIL** dnover@creighton.edu

SCHULTHEISS, K.
PERSONAL Born 02/19/1962, New Haven, CT, m, 1992, 3 children **DISCIPLINE** Yale Univ, BA, 84; Harvard Univ, MA, 90; PhD, 94. **CAREER** Vis lectr, Lake Forest Col, 93-94; vis lectr, Northwestern Univ, 95-96; vis asst prof, Univ Ill, 96-98; asst prof, 98-. **HONORS AND AWARDS** Fulbright Res Grant; Phi Beta Kappa. **MEMBERSHIPS** AHA; SFHS. **RESEARCH** History of women; history of France; European Social and Cultural history; history of medicine. **SELECTED PUBLICATIONS** Auth, "Bodies and Souls: Politics and the Professionalization of Nursing in France," Harvard UP, forthcoming. **CONTACT ADDRESS** Dept History, Univ of Illinois, Chicago, 851 S Morgan St, Chicago, IL 60607-7042. **EMAIL** kschulth@uic.edu

SCHULTZ, MARVIN
PERSONAL Born 10/08/1949, Albuquerque, NM **DISCIPLINE** HISTORY **EDUCATION** Ang State Univ, BA, 71; SW Tex State Univ, MA, 84; Tex Christ Univ, PhD, 94. **CAREER** Instr, Oua Tech Col, 94-; dir, 98-. **HONORS AND AWARDS** McWhinney Res Found, Found Fel; Who's Who Am Teach. **MEMBERSHIPS** Hist Soc; SHA; SSSA; AHA. **RESEARCH** Southern culture; local history. **SELECTED PUBLICATIONS** Ed, United States History Documents to Accompany Liberty, Equality, and Power: A History of the American People, Harcourt Brace (Ft Worth, TX) 96, 2 vol; coauth, Instructor's Resource Manual with Video Guide to Accompany A People and A Nation, Houghton Mifflin (Boston), 93, 4th ed; auth, "Running the Risks of Experiments: The Politics of Penal Reform in Tennessee, 1807-1829," Tenn Hist Quart (93). **CONTACT ADDRESS** Dept General Education, Ouachita Technical Col, PO Box 816, Malvern, AZ 72104-0816. **EMAIL** mschultz@otcweb.org

SCHULTZ, ROBERT
PERSONAL Born 04/04/1955, Los Angeles, CA, m, 1985, 1 child **DISCIPLINE** HISTORY **EDUCATION** Calif State Univ, BA, 84; Univ Minn, MA, 87; PhD, 91. **HONORS AND AWARDS** Kaiser Family Found Grant, 89; NEH, Germany, 95. **MEMBERSHIPS** Orgn of Am Hist. **RESEARCH** Social, cultural and intellectual history of the United States. **SELECTED PUBLICATIONS** Auth, "No Longer an Island: Exploring the Significance of Atlantic Trade to the Industrial Revolution", The Industrial Revolution in comparative Perspective, eds Christine Roder and Michael Thompson, Krueger, (99): 63-83; auth, Conflict and Change: Minneapolis Truck Drivers Make a Dent in the New Deal, Waveland Pr, (Prospect Heights, IL), 00. **CONTACT ADDRESS** Dept Hist, Illinois Wesleyan Univ, PO Box 2900, Bloomington, IL 61702-2900. **EMAIL** rschultz@titan.iwu.edu

SCHULTZ, STANLEY KENTON
PERSONAL Born 07/12/1938, Los Angeles, CA, m, 1991, 3 children **DISCIPLINE** AMERICAN HISTORY, URBAN STUDIES **EDUCATION** Occidental Col, AB, 60; Univ Kans, MA, 63, Univ Chicago, PhD(Am hist), 70. **CAREER** From instr to assoc prof Am hist, 67-76, assoc prof, 76-80, Prof Hist, Univ Wis-Madison, 80-, Chmn Am Inst Prog, 69-79, Lib Arts fel, Harvard Law Sch, 71-72; Res Training fel, Soc Sci Res Coun, 71-72; Rockefeller Found Hum Fel, 81-82. **HONORS AND AWARDS** Pelzer Prize, Orgn Am Historians, 65; Abel Wolman Awd, 90. **MEMBERSHIPS** Am Studies Asn; Orgn Am Historians. **RESEARCH** Interdisciplinary urban studies; American social history; history of American education. **SELECTED PUBLICATIONS** Auth, The Old West, Digital Book Series in History and Society, 00. **CONTACT ADDRESS** Dept of Hist, Univ of Wisconsin, Madison, 455 North Park St, Madison, WI 53706-1483. **EMAIL** skschult@facstaff.wisc.edu

SCHULZ, ANNE MARKHAM
PERSONAL Born 03/03/1938, New York, NY, 1 child **DISCIPLINE** HISTORY OF ART **EDUCATION** Radcliffe Col, BA, 59; NYork Univ, MA, 62, PhD, 68. **CAREER** Instr, 63-65, Smith Col; asst prof, 67-68, Univ Ill, Chicago Circle; lectr, 68-70 & 75, vis asst prof, 77-79, res assoc, 81-83, vis prof, 92-93, Brown Univ; vis prof, 87, Universita degli Studi, Naples Italy; asst cur, Mus Art, RI Sch Design, 68-69; Am Coun of Learned Socs & Am Philos Soc grants-in-aid, 74-75; Howard Found fel, 72-73; Kress Found fel, 74-75; Am Coun Learned Socs travel grant, 75; Delmas Found fel, 78; NEH fel, 82-83, res grant, 82-. **HONORS AND AWARDS** Assoc, Villa Itatti, Florence, 83-84; Am Coun Learned Soc Sr frl, 87-88; IREX Travel grants, 92, 96; Fulbright Sr Res Fel, 97-97; Pro Helvetia grant, 97; NEH Sr Indep Stud Grant, 98. **MEMBERSHIPS** Col Art Assn; Renaissance Soc Am; Soc of Archit Hist; Istituto di Storia dell'ante Lombarda. **RESEARCH** Italian painting and sculpture of the early Renaissance; Renaissance painting in Northern Europe. **SELECTED PUBLICATIONS** Auth, Giambatista and Larenzo Bregno: Venetian Sculpture in the High Renaissance, Cambridge Univ Press, 91; auth, Nanni di Bartolo e il portale della Bisilica di San Nicola a Tolentino, Centro Di Florence, 97; auth, Giammario Mosca called Padovano: A Renaissance Sculptor in Italy and Poland, Penn St Press, 98. **CONTACT ADDRESS** Dept of Art, Brown Univ, Providence, RI 02912.

SCHULZ, JUERGEN
PERSONAL Born 08/18/1927, Kiel, Germany, m, 1968, 3 children **DISCIPLINE** HISTORY OF ART **EDUCATION** Univ Calif, Berkeley, BA, 50; Univ London, PhD, 58. **CAREER** From instr to assoc prof hist of art, Univ Calif, Berkeley, 58-68; Prof hist art, 68-90, Andrea V. Rosenthal prof hist of art & archit, 90-94, Brown Univ, Providence; Guggenheim fel, 66-67; Inst Advan Study, 72-73; NEH fel 72-73 & 78-79, Fulbricht res scholar (Comm Educ & Cult Exch between Italy & US, 82-83; Samuel H. Kress Prof, 00-01, Nat Gallery of Art. **HONORS AND AWARDS** Grande Ufficiale, Stella della Solidarieta dell Repubblica Italiana, 69. **MEMBERSHIPS** Col Art Asn; Renaissance Soc Am; Kunsthist Inst Florenz; Soc Archit Historians; Centro Internaz Studi Architettura, Vicenza, membro Cons. Sci, 84- ; Ateneo Veneto, Venice, socio 89- . **RESEARCH** History of Italian, late Medieval and Renaissance art and architecture. **SELECTED PUBLICATIONS** Auth, Vasari at Venice, Burlington Mag, 61; Pinturicchio and the revival of antiquity, J Warburg & Courtauld Insts, 62; Pordenone's cupolas, Study Renaissance & Baroque Art Presented to Anthony Blunt, 67; Venetian Painted Ceilings of the Renaissance, Univ Calif, 68; Printed plans .., of Venice, 1486-1797, Saggi e Memorie di Storia dell' Arte VII, 70; Jacopo de Barbaris view of Venice, Art Bull, 78; auth, La cartografia tra scienza e arte, Modena (Panini) 1990 Piazz medievale di San Marco, Annali Architettura, 92/93, Early Plans of the Fondaco dei Turchi, Memoirs Am Academy in Rome, 97. **CONTACT ADDRESS** Dept of History of Art and Architecture, Brown Univ, Box 1855, Providence, RI 02912.

SCHULZE, FRANZ
PERSONAL Born 01/30/1927, Uniontown, PA, d **DISCIPLINE** ART; ARCHITECTURE **EDUCATION** Univ Chicago, PhB 45; Sch Art Inst Chicago, MFA 50. **CAREER** Lake Forest College, Hollender Prof, 52-91. **HONORS AND AWARDS** Graham Foun Fel; NEH; Ford Foun Fel; Skidmore Owings & Merrill Foun Fel; Alice Hitchcock Davis Awd; Hon Mention biography of Mies Van der Rohe 1586. **MEMBERSHIPS** SAH **RESEARCH** Architectural history and biography. **SELECTED PUBLICATIONS** Auth, Mies Van der Rohe: A Critical Biography, 86; Mies Van der Rohe: Critical essays, ed, 89; Mies Van der Rohe Archive, Museum of Mod Art, ed, 93; Philip Johnson: Life and Work, 94. **CONTACT ADDRESS** Lake Forest Col, Lake Forest, IL 60045. **EMAIL** schulze@lfc.edu

SCHULZINGER, ROBERT D.
DISCIPLINE HISTORY **EDUCATION** Columbia Univ, BA, 67; Yale Univ, MPhil, 69; PhD, 71. **CAREER** Prof. **SELECTED PUBLICATIONS** Auth, A Time for War: The United States and Vietnam, 1945-1975, Oxford, 97; American Diplomacy in the Twentieth Century, Oxford, 94; co-auth, Present Tense: The United States since 1945, Houghton-Mifflin, 92. **CONTACT ADDRESS** History Dept, Univ of Colorado, Boulder, Boulder, CO 80309. **EMAIL** schulzin@spot.colorado.edu

SCHUNK, THOM
DISCIPLINE MODERN BRITAIN AND IRELAND, ANCIENT AND MEDIEVAL, U.S. HISTORY **EDUCATION** Univ Wis-Oshkosh, BA, 72; Univ Wis-Whitewater, MA, 75; Marquette Univ, PhD, 86. **CAREER** Dept Hist, Univ of WI **HONORS AND AWARDS** Smith Family Res fel, 84-85 & 85-86 ;Ocean County Col Res Grant, 93-94. **RESEARCH** Anglo-Irish hist; Northern Ireland 1945-present. **SELECTED PUBLICATIONS** Auth, Irish-Americans, Pasadena, 92. **CONTACT ADDRESS** Dept of Hist, Univ of Wisconsin, Parkside, 900 Wood Rd, PO Box 2000, Kenosha, WI 53141-2000.

SCHUSTER, LESLIE
DISCIPLINE EUROPEAN SOCIAL AND LABOR HISTORY, COMPARATIVE HISTORY **EDUCATION** Roosevelt Univ, BA; Northern IL Univ, MA, PhD. **CAREER** Instr, RI Col. **RESEARCH** French labor and soc hist. **SELECTED PUBLICATIONS** Auth, Workers and Community: The Case of the Peat-Cutters and the Shipbuilding Industry in Saint-Nazaire, J of Soc Hist. **CONTACT ADDRESS** Rhode Island Col, Providence, RI 02908.

SCHUTTE, ANNE JACOBSON
PERSONAL Born 04/24/1940, Palo Alto, CA, d **DISCIPLINE** HISTORY **EDUCATION** Pembroke Col, BA, 62; Stanford Univ, AM, 63; PhD. 69. **CAREER** Instr to prof, Lawrence Univ, 66-91; prof, Univ of Va, 92-. **HONORS AND AWARDS** Fulbright Travel Grant, 65-66; Pro Helvetia Found Grant, 66; Am Philos Soc Grant, 71; Newberry Libr Fel, 78; NEH Fel, 79-80; 88-89, 95; Gladys Krieble Delmas Found Fel, 85, 96; Sesquicentennial Grant, Univ of Va, 99-00. **MEMBERSHIPS** AHA; Am Soc of Church Hist; Renaissance Soc of Am; Sixteenth Century Studies Conf; Soc for Confraternity Studies; Soc for Ital Hist Studies; Soc for Reformation Res. **SELECTED PUBLICATIONS** Auth, Pier Paolo Vergerio: The Making of an Italian Reformer, Droz (Geneva), 77; auth, Printed Italian Vernacular Religious Books, 1465-1550: A Finding List, Droz, (Geneva), 83; auth, "Vergerio, Pier Paolo", Encycl of the Reformation, ed Hans Hillerbrand, Oxford Univ Pr, (96): 228-29; auth, "Prefazione", L'Inquisizione nel patriarcato e diocesi di Aquileia, 1557-1559, Centro Studi Storicic Menocchio, (98); auth, "Palazzo del Sant'Uffizio: The Opening of the Roman Inquisition's Central Archive", Perspectives 37.5 (99): 25-28; auth, "Gregorio Barbarigo e le donne. Buone cristiane e false sante", Gregorio Barbarigo, ed Liliana Billanovich and Pierantonio Gios, Inst per la Storia Ecclesiastica Padovana, (Padua), (99): 845-66; auth, "Little Women, Great Heroines: Simulated and Genuine Female Holiness in Early Modern Italy", Women and Faith: Catholic Religious Life in Italy from Late Antiquity to the Present, eds Lucetta Scaraffia and Gabriella Zarri, Harvard Univ Pr, (99): 144-58; auth, Aspiring Saints: Pretense of Holiness, Inquisition, and Gender in the Venetian Republic, 1618-1750, Johns Hopkins Univ Pr, (forthcoming); auth, "Saints and Witches in Early Modern Italy: Stepsisters or Strangers?", Space, Time, and Women's Lives in Early Modern Europe, ed Anne Jacobson Schutte, thomas Kuehn, and Silvana Seidel Menchi, Truman State Univ Pr, (forthcoming). **CONTACT ADDRESS** Dept Hist, Univ of Virginia, Charlottesville, VA 22903-3244. **EMAIL** ajs5w@virginia.edu

SCHUYLER, DAVID
PERSONAL Born 04/09/1950, Albany, NY, m, 1985, 1 child **DISCIPLINE** AMERICAN HISTORY **EDUCATION** Am Univ, BA, 71; Univ NC, MA, 76; Univ DE, MA, 76; Columbia Univ, PhD(hist), 79. **CAREER** Asst prof to PROF AM STUDIES, FRANKLIN & MARSHALL COL, 79-92; editorial bd, 92-. **HONORS AND AWARDS** Richard B Morris Prize, Columbia Univ, 81; Christian F. and Mary R. Lindback Found Awd for Distinguished Teaching, Franklin & Marshall Col, 94. **MEMBERSHIPS** Orgn Am Historians; Am Studies Asn; Soc Archit Historians; Urban Hist Asn; PA Hist Asn (coun); Soc Am City and Regional Planning Hist (pres). **RESEARCH** Urban history; American cultural history. **SELECTED PUBLICATIONS** Auth,The New Urban Landscape: The Redefinition of City Form in Nineteenth-Century America, Johns hopkins, 86; Apostle of Taste: Andrew Jackson Downing, 1815-1852, Johns Hopkins Univ Press, 96; co-ed, The Papers of Frederick Law Olmsted, vol II: Slavery and the South, 1852-1857, 81, vol III: Creating Central Park, 1857-1861, 83, vol IV: The Years of Olmsted, Vaux & Company 1865-1874, 92; auth, A City Transformed: Race, Renewal and Suburbanization in Lancaster, Pennsylvania, 1940-1980, Penn State Univ Press, 01. **CONTACT ADDRESS** Am Studies Prog, Franklin and Marshall Col, PO Box 3003, Lancaster, PA 17604-3003. **EMAIL** D_Schuyler@fandm.edu

SCHUYLER, MICHAEL WAYNE
PERSONAL Born 09/05/1941, Winfield, KS, m, 1969, 2 children **DISCIPLINE** AMERICAN HISTORY **EDUCATION** Southwestern Col, Kans, BA, 63; Univ Kans, MA, 65, PhD(Am hist), 69. **CAREER** From asst prof to assoc prof, 69-78, prof hist, Kearney State Col, 78-, chm dept, 82-, Humanist Am Agr, Buffalo County Hist Soc, 78-; vis prof, Southwest Tex State Univ, 80-81. **MEMBERSHIPS** Orgn Am Historians; Nat Educ Asn; Am Hist Asn; Buffalo County Hist Soc; Ctr for the Study of the Presidency; Nebr State Council for the Social Studies; Nebr State Educ Asn; Nebr State Hist Soc; Popular Cult Asn. **RESEARCH** The 1920's and 1930's; Great Plains agriculture 1920 to 1930; the Kennedy assassination. **SELECTED PUBLICATIONS** Auth, Watergate in Historical Perspective: Conservative Achievement or Liberal Failure, Platte Valley Rev, spring 74; Drought and Politics 1936: Kansas as a Test Case, Great Plains J, fall 75; The Hair-Splitters: Reno and Wallace, 1932-1933, Ann Iowa, fall 76; Drought Relief in Kansas, 1934, Kans Hist Quart, winter 76; auth & contribr, Great Plains Agriculture in the 1930's, in: The Great Plains Experience, Univ Mid-Am, 78; The Assassination of John F Kennedy: The Search for Conspiracies, Platte Valley Rev, 79; auth, The Politics of Change: The Battle for the Agricultural Adjustment Act of 1938, Prologue: A Jour of the Nat Arch, Fall 83; The Ku Klux Klan in Nebraska -- 1920-1930, Nebr Hist: A Quart Magazine, Fall 85; The Bitter Harvest: Lyndon B. Johnson and the Assassination of John F. Kennedy, J Am Cult, Fall 85; Ghosts in the White House: LBJ, RFK, and the assassination of JFK, Presidential Studies Quart, Summer 87; The Dread of Plenty: Agricultural Relief Activities of the Federal Government in the Middle West, 1933-1939, Sunflower Univ Press, 89; New Deal Farm Policy in the Middle West: A Retrospective View, J of the West, October 94. **CONTACT ADDRESS** Dept of Hist, Univ of Nebraska, Kearney, 905 W 25th St, Kearney, NE 68849-4238.

SCHWALLER, JOHN
PERSONAL Born 07/02/1948, Aays, KS, m, 1970, 2 children **DISCIPLINE** COLONIAL LATIN AMERICAN HISTORY AND LITERATURE **EDUCATION** Grinnell Col, BA, 69; Univ Kans, MA, 71; Ind Univ, PhD, 78. **CAREER** Assoc instr, Univ of Kans, 69-71; teaching asst, Ind Univ, 73-74; instr, Ind Univ, 74 & 77; asst prof, Hays State Univ, 78-79; asst prof to assoc prof, Fla Atlantic Univ, 79-86; coord of Curriculum in Latin Am Studies, Fla Atlantic Univ, 79-93; acting chemn dept of hist, Fla Atlantic Univ, 84 & 88; vis prof, Inst Nac de Antropologia e Hist, 85-86; prof, Fla Atlantic Univ, 86-93; asst dean of col of humanities, Fla Atlantic Univ, 89-90; assoc dean of The Schmidt Col of Arts and Humanities, Fla Atlantic Univ, 90-93; acting chemn dept of lang and ling, Fla Atlantic Univ, 90, 92, & 93; adj prof, Regional Sem of St Vincent de Paul, 90-93; vis scholar, Franciscan Sch of Theol, 93-95; dir of Acad of

Am Franciscan Hist, Franciscan Sch of Theol, 93-; assoc provost and assoc vpres for Academic Affairs, Univ of Mont, 95-; prof of hist, Univ of Montana, 95-. **HONORS AND AWARDS** Benito Juarez-Abraham Lincoln Fel, Mexican Secretaria de Relaciones Exteriores, 75-76; res fel, Org of Am States, 76-77; James A. Woodburn Fel, Ind Univ, 77; Am Philos Soc Res Grant, 82; Newberry Libr Associates' Fel, 82; Fla Atlantic Univ Seed Grant, 80-81 & 82; NEH summer sem, 80 & 84; Fac Equipment Grant, Fla Atlantic Univ, 83; Andrew W. Mellon Fel, Tulane Univ Libr, 83; Fulbright-Hays Fel, U.S. Dept of Educ, 82-83; Libr Development Awd for Res, Univ of Fla, 84; Distinguished Teacher of the Year, Fla Atlantic Univ, 83-84; Tinker Postdoctoral Fel, Tinker Found, 84-86; res grants, NEH, 89-90 & 93-95; listed in Who's Who in the South and Southwest; listed in Who's Who in the West; distinguished adminr, Univ of Mont, 99-00. **MEMBERSHIPS** AHA, CLAH, RMCLAS, ACHA. **RESEARCH** 16th Century Latin America. **SELECTED PUBLICATIONS** Auth, Partidos y parrocos bajo la real corona en la Nueva Espana siglo XVI, Inst Nac de Antropologia e Hist (Mexico), 81; auth, Origins of Church Wealth in Mexico: Ecclesiastical Finances and Church Revenues 1523-1600, Univ of NMex Press (Albuquerque, NM) 85; auth, The Church and Clergy in Sixteenth-Century Mexico, Univ of NMex Press (Albuquerque, NM), 87; co-ed, A Guide to Confession Large and Small in the Mexican Language (1634), Univ of Okla Press, 99; auth, "Encoded Behaviors: Society, the Church, and Cultural History in Early Colonial Latin America," Latin Am Res Rev (99): 246-270; auth, The Church in Colonial Hispanic America: A Reader, forthcoming; auth, "Don Luis de Velasco," Guide to Documentary Sources for Andean Art and Archeology, Nat Gallery of Art (Washington, DC), forthcoming; auth, "Don Luis de Velasco" and "Archives and Libraries," Oxford Encycl of Mesoamerican Cultures, Oxford Univ Press (New York), forthcoming; auth, "Juan de Zumarraga" and "Inquisition: New World," Encycl of the Renaissance, Charles Scribner's Sons (New York), forthcoming. **CONTACT ADDRESS** Office of the Provost, Univ of Montana, Missoula, MT 59812. **EMAIL** schwallr@selway.umt.edu

SCHWALM, LESLIE A.

PERSONAL Born 02/18/1956, Washington, DC **DISCIPLINE** HISTORY **EDUCATION** Univ Mass, BA, 79; Univ Wis, PhD, 91. **CAREER** Fel, NHPRC, Univ Maryland, 87-88; assoc prof, Univ Iowa, 91-. **HONORS AND AWARDS** Willie Lee Rose Bk Awd; Letitia Woods Brown Pub Prize; Fac Schl Awd, UI; NEH Fel; May Brodbeck Hum Fel; Res Enhan Awd, UICIF; Dev Lv, UI; NEH, Stp; AAUW, Diss Found; Woodrow Wilson Nat Fel. **MEMBERSHIPS** AHA; OAH; SHA; SAWH. **RESEARCH** 19th century US social history; US women's history; slavery; Civil War; emancipation. **SELECTED PUBLICATIONS** Auth, A Hard Fight For We: WomenÛs Transition from Slavery to Freedom in Lowcountry South Carolina, Univ Ill Press (97); auth, "Sweet Dreams of Freedom: Freedwomen's Reconstruction of Life and Labor in Lowcountry South Carolina," J Wom Hist 9 (97): 9-38; rev of, "More Than Chattel: Black Women and Slavery in the Americas," eds. David Barry Gaspar, Darlene Clark Hine, J Soc Hist (97); rev of "Civil War Disobedience," in Yankee Women: Gender Battles in the Civil War, by Elizabeth D Leonard, Wom Rev Books 3 (94): 29-30; rev of, A Confederate Lady Comes of Age: The Journal of Pauhne Decaradeuc Heyward, 1863-1888, ed. Mary D Robertson (Columbia: University of South Carolina Press, 92); rev of "Rebel Belle," in The Civil War Diaries of Sarah Morgan, ed. Charles East (Univ Georgia Press, 91). **CONTACT ADDRESS** Dept History, Univ Iowa, Iowa City, IA 52242. **EMAIL** leslie-schwalm@uiowa.edu

SCHWARTZ, GERALD

DISCIPLINE MODERN AMERICAN HISTORY **EDUCATION** WA State Univ, PhD. **CAREER** Hist Dept, Western Carolina Univ **SELECTED PUBLICATIONS** Auth, A Woman Doctor's Civil War: Esther Hill Hawks' Diary, 89. **CONTACT ADDRESS** Western Carolina Univ, Cullowhee, NC 28723.

SCHWARTZ, JOEL

PERSONAL Born 09/12/1942, New York, NY, m, 1969, 2 children **DISCIPLINE** URBAN & SOCIAL HISTORY **EDUCATION** Univ Chicago, BA, 62, MA, 65, PhD, 72. **CAREER** Asst prof, 69-77, assoc prof, 77-86; prof hist, Montclair State Univ, 86-, adj prof, Columbia Univ; Assoc, Columbia Univ Sem in the City, 73. **MEMBERSHIPS** Orgn Am Historians. **RESEARCH** Nineteenth century urban neighborhoods and families; suburbanization; progressivism. **SELECTED PUBLICATIONS** Auth, Evolution of suburbs In: Suburbia: The American Dream and Dilemma, Doubleday, 76; ed, Cities of the Garden State, Kendall/Hunt, 77; The New York Approach, OH State Univ Pres, 93. **CONTACT ADDRESS** Dept of Hist, Montclair State Univ, 1 Normal Ave, Montclair, NJ 07043-1699. **EMAIL** schwartzj@mail.montclair.edu

SCHWARTZ, PETER

PERSONAL Born 03/14/1948, Washington, DC, m, 1972, 3 children **DISCIPLINE** MEDIEVAL HISTORY **EDUCATION** Mt. St. Mary's Col, BA, 70; Wash State Univ, MA, 72; Bowling Green State. Univ, PhD, 78. **CAREER** Assoc prof, Elmira Col, 76-. **HONORS AND AWARDS** Josef Stein; Teaching Scholarship, McGraw-Rock. **MEMBERSHIPS** NCTE; NYSTE. **RESEARCH** Arthurian Legend (Malory). **SELECTED PUBLICATIONS** Auth, "The Mansion of Many Rooms: Spatial Imagery in Keats' Hyperion: A Fragment", CCFL Jour 8, 88; auth, "Thirteen Ways of Looking at the Destruction of the Round Table", CCFL 13, 91; auth, "Malory's Tristram: Courtly Love Exposed", CCFL, 14, 92; auth, Malory's Errant Knights", Malory Newsletter (forthcoming). **CONTACT ADDRESS** Dept Humanities, Elmira Col, 1 Park Pl, Elmira, NY 14901-2085. **EMAIL** pswtz@aol.com

SCHWARTZ, SHULY RUBIN

PERSONAL Born 03/26/1953, Brooklyn, NY, m, 1973, 4 children **DISCIPLINE** JEWISH HISTORY **EDUCATION** Barnard Col, BA; Jewish Theol Sem Am, MA, PhD. **CAREER** Rabbi Irving Lehrman Res Asst Prof Am Jewish Hist; dean, Albert A. List Col Jewish Studies. **HONORS AND AWARDS** Doctoral Dissertation Scholarship, 85-86; Doctoral Scholarship, 85-86, 82-83; Honorable Mention Awd, 99; Rabbi Levi A. Oln Memorial Fel, 99-00; Josoeph H. Fichter Res Awd, 99-00. **MEMBERSHIPS** Am Hist Asn; Am Jewish Hist Soc; Asn for Jewish Studies; Asn for the Sociology of Relig. **RESEARCH** Image and role of the Rebbetzin, (rabbi's wife), in American Jewish life, American Jewish Religious Movements; Jewish women. **SELECTED PUBLICATIONS** Auth, The Emergence of Jewish Scholarship in America: The Publication of the Jewish Encyclopedia, Hebrew Union Col Press, 91; Camp Ramah: The Early Years, 1947-1952, Conser Judaism, 87; Ramah Philosophy and the Newman Revolution, Studies in Jewish Education and Judaica in Honor of Louis Newman. **CONTACT ADDRESS** Jewish Theol Sem of America, 3080 Broadway, New York, NY 10027. **EMAIL** shschwartz@jtsa.edu

SCHWARTZ, STUART

PERSONAL Born 09/04/1940, Springfield, MA **DISCIPLINE** COLONIAL LATIN AMERICA **EDUCATION** Middlebury Col, AB, 62; Columbia Univ, MA, 63, PhD(hist), 68. **CAREER** From instr to assoc prof Latin Am hist, 67-73, chmn dept, 76-79, Prof Hist, Univ Minn, 73-, Vis asst prof Latin Am hist, Univ Calif, Berkeley, 69-70; adv, Conf Latin Am Soc Sci, Mex, 72-; vis prof, Fed Univ Bahia, Brazil, 74; Am Coun Learned Soc fel, 74-75; Guggenheim fel, 78-79. **MEMBERSHIPS** AHA; Conf Latin Am Hist; Latin Am Studies Asn. **RESEARCH** Colonial Latin America; Brazil; social history. **SELECTED PUBLICATIONS** Auth, Africa And The Africans In The Making Of The Atlantic World, 1400-1680 - Thornton,J/, Hisp Am Hist Rev, Vol 0073, 1993; Family, Inheritance And Power In Sao-Paulo - 1765-1855 - Port - Bacellar,Cda/, J Of Interdisciplinary Hist, Vol 0024, 1994. **CONTACT ADDRESS** Dept of Hist, Yale Univ, PO Box 208324, New Haven, CT 06520-8324.

SCHWARZ, MARC LEWIS

PERSONAL Born 02/19/1938, Cambridge, MA, m, 1963 **DISCIPLINE** ENGLISH HISTORY **EDUCATION** Bates Col, AB, 59; Harvard Univ, MAT, 60; Univ Calif, Los Angeles, PhD(hist), 65. **CAREER** Asst prof hist, Univ Mass, Amherst, 65-67; asst prof, 67-72, assoc prof, hist, Univ NH, 72-. **HONORS AND AWARDS** Nat Endowment for the Humanities, 96. **MEMBERSHIPS** Conf Brit Studies. **RESEARCH** Private research libraries in Renaissance England; Joan Bocher and the treatment of heresy under Edward VI. **SELECTED PUBLICATIONS** Contrib ed, Private Libraries in Renaissance England, Vol 2. **CONTACT ADDRESS** Dept of Hist, Univ of New Hampshire, Durham, 125 Technology Dr, Durham, NH 03824-4724. **EMAIL** mschwarz@hopper.unh.edu

SCHWARZ, PHILIP JAMES

PERSONAL Born 11/12/1940, New York, NY, m, 1970, 2 children **DISCIPLINE** AMERICAN HISTORY **EDUCATION** Brown Univ, AB, 62; Univ Conn, MA, 65; Rutgers Univ, MLS, 65; Cornell Univ, PhD, 73. **CAREER** From Asst Prof to Assoc Prof, 72-90, prof Am hist, Va Commonwealth Univ, 90-. **HONORS AND AWARDS** Fel, Va Ctr for the Humanities, Spring 93. **MEMBERSHIPS** Am Soc Legal Hist; Southern Hist Asn; Am Hist Asn; Henrico County Hist Soc; Nat Coun Hist Educ; Org Am Hist; Phi Kappa Phi, VCU Chapter; Soc Hist Early Repub; Va Coun Hist Educ; Va Hist Soc. **RESEARCH** Colonial America; slavery; constitutional history. **SELECTED PUBLICATIONS** Auth, The Jarring Interests: New York's Boundary Makers, 1664-1776, State Univ NY Press, 79; Twice Condemned: Slaves and the Criminal Laws of Virginia, LSU Press, 88; Slave Laws in Virginia, Univ Ga Press, 96. **CONTACT ADDRESS** Dept of Hist, Virginia Commonwealth Univ, Box 842001, Richmond, VA 23284-2001. **EMAIL** pschwarz@saturn.vcu.edu

SCHWARZBACH, FREDRIC S.

PERSONAL Born New York, NY **DISCIPLINE** ENGLISH LITERATURE, URBAN STUDIES **EDUCATION** Columbia Univ, AB, 71, MA, 72; London Univ, PhD(English), 76. **CAREER** Res asst English, Univ Col London, 74-77; ASST PROF ENGLISH, WASH UNIV, ST LOUIS, 77-, Am Coun Learned Soc fel, 80. **MEMBERSHIPS** MLA **RESEARCH** Nineteenth century literature; social context of literature; literature and the city. **SELECTED PUBLICATIONS** Auth, Dickens And The 1830s - Chittick,K/, Victorian Studies, Vol 0036, 1992. **CONTACT ADDRESS** Dept of English, Washington Univ, Saint Louis, MO 63130. **EMAIL** fschwarz@kent.edu

SCHWEIKART, LARRY EARL

PERSONAL Born 04/21/1951, Mesa, AZ, m, 1987, 1 child **DISCIPLINE** HISTORY **EDUCATION** Ariz State Univ, BA, 72, MA, 80; Univ Calif-Santa Barbara, PhD, 84. **CAREER** Asst prof to prof, Univ Dayton, 85-. **RESEARCH** US economic, business, military & industrial relations. **SELECTED PUBLICATIONS** Ed, Encyclopedia of American Business History, "Banking and Finance to 1913," Calif Bankers, Simon & Schuster, 94; "Abraham Lincoln and Growth of Government in the Civil War Era," Continuity 21, 97; coauth, "Banking in the Golden State from the Gold Rush to the 1990's," Calif Hist, 97; "Banking and Finance in North America, 1607-1997," Banking, Trade & Industry, Cambridge Univ Press, 97; auth, "The Entrepreneurial Adventure: A History of Business in the United States," Harcourt, 00. **CONTACT ADDRESS** Dept Hist, Univ of Dayton, Dayton, OH 45469. **EMAIL** schweika@checkov.hm.udayton.edu

SCHWENINGER, LOREN LANCE

PERSONAL Born 01/07/1941, Culver City, CA, m, 1965, 4 children **DISCIPLINE** AFRICAN AMERICAN HISTORY **EDUCATION** Univ of Colo, BA, 62, MA, 66; Univ of Chicago, PhD, 72. **CAREER** Instr, 71-73, asst prof, 73-78, assoc prof, 78-85, prof, 85-, Univ NC, Greensboro. **HONORS AND AWARDS** Fulbright Senior lectr, Univ of Geneva, Italy, 91; NEH Res Grant, 95-97, 97-99; NHPRC Res Grant, 91-99; Charles Stewart Mott Found Res Grant, 97-99. **MEMBERSHIPS** OAH; AHA; SHA; ASALH. **RESEARCH** Slavery. **SELECTED PUBLICATIONS** Auth, Black Property Owners in the South, Ill Press, 91, Ill Paperback, 97. **CONTACT ADDRESS** 807 Rankin Pl., Greensboro, NC 37412.

SCHWIEDER, DOROTHY ANN

PERSONAL Born 11/28/1933, Presho, SD, m, 1955, 2 children **DISCIPLINE** IOWA & WOMAN'S HISTORY **EDUCATION** Dakota Wesleyan Univ, BA, 55; Iowa State Univ, MA, 68; Univ Iowa, PhD, 81. **CAREER** Instr Am govt, Dakota Wesleyan Univ, 60-62; instr, 69-81, Asst Prof Am Hist, Iowa State Univ, 81- **MEMBERSHIPS** Orgn Am Hist; AAUP; Am Asn Univ Women. **RESEARCH** Communitarian studies; woman's economic history and ethnic history. **SELECTED PUBLICATIONS** Coauth, A paradox of change in the life style of Iowa's old order Amish, Int Rev Mod Sociol, spring 76; contribr, Reader's Encycl of the American West, Thomas Crowell, 77; Labor roles of Iowa farm women, Proceedings Nat Archives Conf, 4/77; coauth, The Granger Homestead project, Palimpsest, 9-10/77; The Beachy Amish in Iowa: A case study, Mennonite Quart Rev, winter 77; Frontier brethern, Mont Mag Western Hist, winter 78; Italian-Americans in Iowa's coal camps, Annals of Iowa, spring, 82; Early exploration and settlement, In: Iowa's Natural Heritage, 82. **CONTACT ADDRESS** Dept of Hist, Iowa State Univ of Science and Tech, Ames, IA 50010.

SCHWOERER, LOIS GREEN

PERSONAL Born 06/04/1927, Roanoke, VA, w, 1 child **DISCIPLINE** EUROPE; ENGLISH HISTORY; RENAISSANCE **EDUCATION** Smith Col, BA, 49; Bryn Mawr Col, MA, 52, PhD(hist), 56. **CAREER** Teacher, Shipley Sch, Pa, 49-51; instr hist, Bryn Mawr Col, 54-55; lectr, Univ Pittsburgh, 61-63; from lectr to assoc prof, 64-76, dept chmn, 79-81, Prof Hist, George Washington Univ, 76-92, Am Philos Soc Grant, 71-72; Nat Endowment Humanities sr fel, 75, 88-91; sr fel, Folger Shakespeare Libr, 78; fel, Royal Hist Soc, 80-; Elmer Louis Kayser, prof, 92-96; now emer. **HONORS AND AWARDS** Best Bk Awd, Berkshire Conf Women Historians, 75; Honorable mention, John Ben Snow prize, 83; Love prize, 85. **MEMBERSHIPS** AHA; Conf Brit Studies; Int Comn Hist Rep & Parliamentary Insts. **RESEARCH** English political and intellectual history, 17th and 18th centuries; the Revolution of 1688-89; 17th & 18th century English women, especially Lady Rachel Russell, print culture English background to Second Amendment to U.S. Bill of Rights. **SELECTED PUBLICATIONS** Auth, No Standing Armies! The Antiarmy Ideology in Seventh Century England, Baltimore and London, The Johns Hopkins Univ Press, 74; auth, "A Jornall of the Convention at Westminster begun the 22 of January 1688/9," Bulletin of the Institute of Historical Research 49 (76): 242-63; auth, The Declaration of Rights, 1689, Baltimore and London, The Johns Hopkins Univ Press, 81; auth, "The Transformation of the Convention into a Parliament, February 1689," Parliamentary Hist 3 (fall 84): 57-76; auth, Lady Rachel Russell 1637-1723: One of the Best of Women, Baltimore and London, The Johns Hopkins Univ Press, 88; auth, "Images of Queen Mary II, 1688-95," Renaissance Quarterly 42 (89): 717-748; auth, "Locke, Lockean Ideas and the Glorious Revolution," Journal of the History of Ideas 51 (Oct-Dec. 90): 31-48; auth, The Revolution of 1688-89: Changing Perspectives, ed. Lois G. Schwoerer, Cambridge Univ Press, 92; auth, "The Attempted Impeachment of Sir William Scroggs, Lord Chief Justice of the Court of King's Bench, November 1680-March 1681, The Historical Journal 38.4, (Dec. 95): 843-874; auth, "British Lineages, American Choices," in Bill of Rights Government Proscribed, ed by Ronald Hoffman and Peter J. Albert, (Charlottesville, Va., Univ Press of Virginia, 97); auth, Women's Public Political Voice in England: 1640-1700," in Women, Intellect and Politics, Their Intersection in Early-Modern Britain, ed. Hilda Smith, (Cambridge Univ Press, 98); auth, "To Hold and Bear Arms: The English Perspective," Chicago-Kent Law Review, Illinois Institute of Technology, vol. 76, no. 1, (00); auth, The Ingenious Mr. Henry Care, A Restoration Publicist, Baltimore and London, The Johns Hopkins Univ Press, 01. **CONTACT ADDRESS** Dept of Hist, The George Washington Univ, Washington, DC 20052. **EMAIL** lgsch101@msn.com

SCIONTI, JOSEPH NATALE
PERSONAL Born 09/25/1931, Boston, MA, m, 1955, 2 children **DISCIPLINE** EARLY MODERN EUROPEAN HISTORY **EDUCATION** Suffolk Univ, BA, 60; Tufts Univ, MA, 61; Brown Univ, PhD(reformation) 67. **CAREER** Prof Hist, Univ Mass Dartmouth, 65-; Mem, Community Leaders Am, 72-; prog dir, New Eng Renaissance Conf, 73. **MEMBERSHIPS** AHA; Renaissance Soc Am **RESEARCH** Reformation in Germany, especially Luther's opponents; Renaissance in Italy, especially Florentine humanism; 19th century Italy, especially Risorgimento. **SELECTED PUBLICATIONS** Contribr, Historical Abstracts, Am Bibliog Ctr-Clio, 71-; Encyclopedia World Biography, McGraw, 73; Giuseppe Mazzini, Giuseppe Garibaldi, Huldreich Zwingli, In: Research Guide to European Historical Biography. **CONTACT ADDRESS** Dept of Hist, Univ of Massachusetts, Dartmouth, 285 Old Westport Rd, North Dartmouth, MA 02747-2300.

SCOBIE, INGRID WINTHER
PERSONAL Born 01/02/1943, Bloomington, IN, 4 children **DISCIPLINE** AMERICAN & WOMEN'S HISTORY **EDUCATION** Brown Univ, BA, 64; Univ Rochester, MA, 65; Univ Wis, PhD(Am hist), 70. **CAREER** Vis lectr hist, Princeton Univ, 75; sr Fulbright Hays prof, Univ El Salvador & Nat Inst Teacher Training, Buenos Aires, 76; lectr US hist & res assoc, Univ Calif, San Diego, 77-79 & 81-82; Asst Prof US Hist, Tex Woman's Univ, 82-, Ed & interviewer, Regional Oral Hist Off, Bancroft Libr, Univ Calif, Berkeley, 77-81; panelist & reviewer, Nat Endowment for Humanities, 79-, res grant, 81-84; Eleanor Roosevelt Inst grant, 80. Am Philos Soc grant, 80. **MEMBERSHIPS** AHA; Orgn Am Historians; Oral Hist Asn; Nat Coun Pub Hist. **RESEARCH** California; legislative activity; 20th century social and political history, especially women in politics. **SELECTED PUBLICATIONS** Auth, Las distintas interpretaciones del progresivismo norteamericano como resultado de la vision historica de sus autores, In: Actas de las Terceras Jornadas de Investigacion de la Historia y Literatura Rioplatense y de los Estados Unidos, Mendoza, Argentina, 70; Jack B Tenney and the parasitic menace: Anti-communist legislation in California, 1940-49, Pac Hist Rev, 5/74; Helen Gahagan Douglas and her 1950 senate race with Richard M Nixon, Southern Calif Hist Quart, spring 76; Ella Reeve Bloor, In: Dict of American Biography, suppl 5, 77; Family and community history through oral history, Pub Historian, summer 79. **CONTACT ADDRESS** Dept of Hist & Govt, Texas Woman's Univ, P O Box 425889, Denton, TX 76204-5889.

SCORGIE, GLEN G.
PERSONAL Born 03/29/1952, Vancouver, BC, Canada, m, 1978, 3 children **DISCIPLINE** HISTORICAL THEOLOGY **EDUCATION** Univ of St Andrews, Scotland, PhD, 86. **CAREER** Data-processing marketing asst, 74-76; IBM Canada, Toronto; adjunct prof of theology, 84-91, Canadian Theological Seminary; dir of admissions, 76-79, asst prof, 84-88, acting dean of faculty, Jan-May 89, assoc prof 88-91, Canadian Bible Col; academic dean and vice-pres, 91-96, prof 95-96, North Amer Baptist Col; prof, Bethel Theological Seminary, 96-. **HONORS AND AWARDS** Who's Who in America; British Government Overseas Research Student Scholarship; Regent College Church History Prize; Delta Epsilon Chi Honor Society. **MEMBERSHIPS** American Academy of Religion; Canadian Evangelical Theological Assn; Conference on Faith and History; Evangelical Theological Society. **RESEARCH** Key Determinants of Spirtual Resilience: An Interdisciplinary Perspective; Movie Theology: Thinking Christianly about Contemporary Film and Cinema; Asian theology and spirituality, Christology and pluralism. **SELECTED PUBLICATIONS** Auth, A Call for Continuity: The Theological Contribution of James Orr, 88; Directionary of Twentieth Century Christian Biography, 95; auth, A.B. Simpson, Holiness and Modernity, in Studies in Canadian Evangelical Renewal, Faith Today, 96; coauth, Human Life is Not Sheep: An Ethical Perspective on cloning, Journal of the Evangelical Theological Society, Dec 97; auth, Yearning for God: The Potential and Poverty of the Catholic Spirituality of Francis de Sales, Journal of the Evangelical Theological Society, Sept 98. **CONTACT ADDRESS** 6116 Arosa St, San Diego, CA 92115-3902. **EMAIL** gscourgie@bethel.edu

SCOTT, ALISON M.
PERSONAL Born 02/01/1956, Dugway, UT **DISCIPLINE** AMERICAN STUDIES **EDUCATION** Whitman Coll, BA, 78; Univ Chicago, Grad Library Sch, AM, 82, Divinity Sch, AM, 82; Boston Univ, PhD, 95. **CAREER** Ref libn, Columbia Univ, Rare Book & Manuscript Library, 83-85; asst curator, rare books, Smith Coll, 85-90; head libn, Popular Culture Library, 93-00, asst prof, 95-98, assoc prof, Dept Popular Culture, Bowling Green State Univ, 98-00; Charles Warren Bibliographer for American Hist, Harvard Coll Library, Harvard Univ, 00-. **HONORS AND AWARDS** Livrarian of The Year, Romance writers of America, 99. **MEMBERSHIPS** Amer Lib Assn; Soc History Authorship, Reading, and Publishing; Soc Historians Early Amer Republic; Popular Culture Assn. **RESEARCH** History of the book in the early American republic; popular literature. **SELECTED PUBLICATIONS** Referred jour articles: "Why Aren't You Here? Postcards in the Popular Culture Library," Popular Culture in Libraries, vol 3, no 2, 95, simultaneous pub in Postcards in the Library: Invaluable Visual Resources, 95; "They Came from the Newsstand: Pulp Magazines and Vintage Paperbacks in the Popular Culture Library," Primary Sources & Their Original Works, vol 4, 96, simultaneous publication in Pioneers, Passionate Ladies, and Private Eyes: Dime Novels, Series Books, and paperbacks, 96; auth, "Vincent Starrett (26 October 1886-4 January 1974," American Book Collectors and Bibliographers, vol, 187, Dictionary of Literary Biography, 97; editor, The Writing on the Cloud: American Culture Confronts the Atomic Bomb, 97; auth, "The Paper They're Printed On," in Pulp Art: Original Cover Paintings for the Great American Pulp Magazines, 97. **CONTACT ADDRESS** Widener Library, Harvard Univ, Cambridge, MA 02138. **EMAIL** alisonms@yahoo.com

SCOTT, CLIFFORD H.
PERSONAL Born 07/21/1937, Independence, IA, m, 1960, 2 children **DISCIPLINE** AMERICAN HISTORY **EDUCATION** Univ Northern Iowa, BA, 59; Univ Iowa, MA, 60, PhD, 68. **CAREER** Instr hist, Webster City Iowa Jr Col, 60-62; asst prof, Southeast Mo State Col, 65-68; asst prof hist, 68-75, assoc prof am hist, 75-, In Univ-Purdue Univ; proj dir, Nat Sci Found fel, 74; proj dir, Ind Comt Humanities, 77. **MEMBERSHIPS** AHA; Orgn Am Historians; AAUP. **RESEARCH** American intellectual history; gilded age America; American ethnic history. **SELECTED PUBLICATIONS** Auth, A Naturalistic Rationale For Women's Reform, Historian, winter 70; art, Images of Blackest Africa in American fiction, NDak Quart, fall 72; auth, Lester Frank Ward, Twayne, 76; auth, Fort Wayne German-Americans in WWI, Old Fort News, 77; art, Hoosier Kulturkampf, J Ger-Am Studies, 79; art, Assimilation in a German-American community, Northwest Ohio Quart, 80; art, Mission to Africa: Changing Ideas On Race And Culture, Proc Ind Acad Soc Sci, 80; art, The Amana colony: Communal Escape To The Middle Border, Proc Univ Wyo, 82. **CONTACT ADDRESS** Dept of History, Indiana Univ-Purdue Univ, Fort Wayne, 2101 Coliseum Blvd E, Fort Wayne, IN 46805-1445. **EMAIL** scottc@ipfw.edu

SCOTT, DARYL
DISCIPLINE UNITED STATES HISTORY **EDUCATION** Marquette Univ, BA, 84; Stanford Univ, PhD, 94. **CAREER** Assoc prof. **SELECTED PUBLICATIONS** Auth, Contempt and Pity: Social Policy and the Image of the Damaged Black Psyche 1880-1996, 97. **CONTACT ADDRESS** Dept of History, Columbia Col, New York, 2960 Broadway, New York, NY 10027-6902.

SCOTT, DONALD M.
DISCIPLINE HISTORY **EDUCATION** Harvard Univ, BA, 62; Univ Wis, MS, 64, PhD, 68. **CAREER** Assoc prof, hist, NC State Univ; PROF, HIST & DEAN FAC, DIV SOC SCI, QUEENS COLL, CUNY. **MEMBERSHIPS** Am Antiquarian Soc **SELECTED PUBLICATIONS** Auth, From Office to Profession: New England Ministry, 1750-1850, 78; auth, "The Popular Lecture and the Creation of a Public in Mid-Nineteenth Century America," Jour of Am Hist 66, 80; auth, America's Families: A Documentary History, 82; auth, "Print and the Public Lecture System, 1840-1860," in Printing and Society in Early America, AAS 83; auth, "Itinerant Lectures and Lecturing in New England, 1800-1850," in Hierarchy in New England and New York, 86; auth, "Knowledge and the Marketplace," in The Mythmaking Frame of Mind: Social Imagination and American Culture, 93. **CONTACT ADDRESS** Dean of the Social Sciences, Queens Col, CUNY, 6530 Kissena Blvd, Flushing, NY 11367-1597. **EMAIL** Donald_Scott@QC.edu

SCOTT, REBECCA JARVIS
PERSONAL Born 07/18/1950, Athens, GA, m, 1978, 2 children **DISCIPLINE** LATIN AMERICAN HISTORY **EDUCATION** Harvard Univ, BA, 71; London Sch Econ, MPhil, 73; Princeton Univ, PhD(hist), 82. **CAREER** Prof Hist, Univ of Mich, 80- . **MEMBERSHIPS** AHA; Latin Am Studies Asn. **RESEARCH** Slave emancipation and transition to free labor in Cuba, 1868-1895; comparative study of emancipations and postemancipation societies, Cuba, Brazil, Louisiana; race and citizenship in comparative perspective. **SELECTED PUBLICATIONS** Auth, Defining The Boundaries Of Freedom In The World Of Cane - Cuba, Brazil, And Louisiana After Emancipation, Am Hist Rev, Vol 0099, 1994; coauth, Beyond Slavery: Explorations of Race, Labor and Citizenship in Postemancipation Societies, Univ of NC Press (Chapel Hill), 00. **CONTACT ADDRESS** Dept Hist, Univ of Michigan, Ann Arbor, 555 S State St, 1029 Tisch Hall, Ann Arbor, MI 48109-1003. **EMAIL** rjscott@umich.edu

SCOTT, ROY V.
PERSONAL Born 12/26/1927, Wrights, IL, m, 1959, 3 children **DISCIPLINE** AMERICAN HISTORY **EDUCATION** Iowa State Univ, BS, 52; Univ Ill, MA, 53, PhD, 57. **CAREER** Asst prof hist, Univ Southwestern La, 57-58; res assoc, Bus Hist Found 58-59; asst prof hist, Univ Mo, 59-60; from asst prof to assoc prof, 60-64, prof hist, Miss State Univ, 64-98, assoc, Bus Hist Found, 63-64; William L Giles distinguished prof of hist, 74-98; prof emer, 98-. **HONORS AND AWARDS** Cert Commendation, Am Asn State & Local Hist, 77; fel, Agricultural His Soc, 99. **MEMBERSHIPS** AHA; Orgn Am Historians; Agr Hist Soc (vpres, 77-78, pres, 78-79); Econ Hist Asn; Miss Hist Soc, pres, 89-90. **RESEARCH** Farm life in the Middle West. **SELECTED PUBLICATIONS** Auth, Agrarian Movement in Illinois, 1880-1896, Univ Ill, 62; American railroads and agricultural extension, 1900-1914, Bus Hist Rev, spring 65; The Reluctant Farmer: The Rise of Agricultural Extension to 1914, Univ Ill, 71; coauth, The Public Career of Cully A Cobb: A Study in Agricultural Leadership, Univ Miss, 73; co-ed, Southern agriculture since the Civil War, Agr Hist Soc, 79; auth, Railroad development Programs in the Twentieth Century, Iowa State Univ Press, 85; Eugene Beverly Ferris and Agricultural Science in the Lower South, Center for the Study of Southern Culture, 91; coauth, The Great Northern Railway: A History, Harvard Business School Press, 88; Wal-Mart: A History of Sam Walton's Retail Phenomenon, Twayne, 94; Old Main: Images of a Legend, Miss State Univ Alumni Asn, 95. **CONTACT ADDRESS** Dept of History, Mississippi State Univ, PO Box H, Mississippi State, MS 39762-5508.

SCOTT, SAMUEL FRANCIS
PERSONAL Born 01/10/1938, Quincy, MA, m, 1961, 2 children **DISCIPLINE** MODERN EUROPEAN & FRENCH HISTORY **EDUCATION** Boston Col AB, 59; Univ Wis-Madison, MA, 62, PhD(hist), 68. **CAREER** From instr to asst prof, 67-76, assoc prof, 76-81, Prof Hist, Wayne State Univ, 81-, Wayne State Univ fac res award, 70 & 76; Soc Sci Res Coun fac res grant, 71; Nat Endowment for Humanities res grant, 76. **MEMBERSHIPS** AAUP; Soc Etudes Robespierristes; Soc Fr Hist Studies; fel Inter-Univ Sem Armed Forces & Soc; Am Soc 18th Century Studies. **RESEARCH** French Revolution; social history; military history. **SELECTED PUBLICATIONS** Auth, Regeneration of line army during the French Revolution, J Mod Hist, 70; The French Revolution and the professionalization of the Officer Corps, In: On Military Ideology, 71; Soldats de L'armee de Ligne en 1793, Ann Hist Revolution Francaise, 72; Problems of law and order during 1790, Am Hist Rev, 75; French Aid to the American Revolution, Willaim L Clements Libr, 76; Response of Royal Army to French Revolution, Clarendon, Oxford, 78; Soldiers of Rochambeau's Expeditionary Corps, In: La Revolution Americaine Et L'Europe, CNRS, Paris, 79; Gentlemen Soldiers at Time of French Revolution, Military Affairs, 81. **CONTACT ADDRESS** Dept of Hist, Wayne State Univ, 838 Mackenzie, Detroit, MI 48202-3919.

SCOTT, SUSAN C.
PERSONAL Born 07/13/1942, Drexel Hill, PA, s **DISCIPLINE** ART HISTORY; ARCHITECTURAL HISTORY **EDUCATION** Penn St Univ, BS, 64; Penn St Univ, MA, 78; Penn St Univ, PhD, 95 **CAREER** Teacher public schools, Pa & Delaware, 64-70; instr, Penn St Univ, 85-94; asst prof, Penn St Univ, 95 **HONORS AND AWARDS** Founding Member, Intl Soc Study of Chinese Archit Hist; Penn St Univ Panhellenic Soc Awd for outstanding teaching; Louise Purcell/Knight Ridder Travel Grant; **MEMBERSHIPS** College Art Assoc; Amer Soc for 18th Cent Studies; British Soc for Eighteenth Cent Stud; Soc of Architectural Historians; American Fulbright Soc; Int Soc for Chinese Architectural Studies **RESEARCH** Asian Art and Architecture; Baroque Architecture in Italy; Renaissance Architecture in Italy **SELECTED PUBLICATIONS** Co-ed, Rembrandt, Rubens, and the Art of their Time: Recent Perspectives, Pa State Univ, 97 (and 9 earlier vols); review of Elisabeth Blair MacDougall, "Fountains, Statues, and Flowers: Studies in Italian Gardens of the Sixteenth and Seventeenth Centuries," Jrnl Soc Archit Historians, 97; co-ed, The Art of Interpreting, Pa State Univ, 96; The Triumph of the Baroque: Architecture in Europe 1600-1750, catalogue of the exhibition, ed by Henry A. Millon, Turin, 99, eleven entries in the English and Italian eds, six entries in the French ed. **CONTACT ADDRESS** Dept Art Hist, Pennsylvania State Univ, Univ Park, 229 Arts Building, University Park, PA 16802. **EMAIL** ssm117@psu.edu

SCOTT, WILLIAM BUTLER
PERSONAL Born 02/27/1945, Charleston, SC, m, 1966 **DISCIPLINE** HISTORY **EDUCATION** Presby Col, BA, 67; Wake Forest Univ, MA, 68; Univ Wis, Madison, PhD(hist), 73. **CAREER** Asst prof, 73-80, Assoc Prof Hist, Kenyon Col, 80- **MEMBERSHIPS** AHA; Orgn Am Historians; Southern Hist Asn; Inst Early Am Hist & Cult. **RESEARCH** American intellectual and legal history. **SELECTED PUBLICATIONS** Auth, In Pursuit of Happiness: American Conceptions of Property, Ind Univ, 77; J Waters Waring: The advocate of Another South, South Atlantic Quart, 78. **CONTACT ADDRESS** Kenyon Col, Seitz House, Gambier, OH 43022-9623.

SCOTT, WILLIAM R.
DISCIPLINE AFRICAN-AMERICAN HISTORY **EDUCATION** PhD, Princeton Univ. **CAREER** Prof, Lehigh Univ; Dir of the African-American Studies Prog. **MEMBERSHIPS** Inst Int Educ S African Educ Prog; dir, United Negro Col Fund/ Mellon Minorities Fels Prog. **RESEARCH** Black American thought; African-U.S. interaction. **SELECTED PUBLICATIONS** Auth, Sons of Sheba's Race: African-Americans and the Italo-Ethiopian War; co-ed, Americans from Africa. **CONTACT ADDRESS** African American Studies Prog, Lehigh Univ, Bethlehem, PA 18015. **EMAIL** wrs4@lehigh.edu

SCRANTON, PHILIP
PERSONAL Born 09/11/1946, New Brighton, PA, m, 1983, 1 child **DISCIPLINE** AMERICAN HISTORY, HISTORY OF TECHNOLOGY **EDUCATION** Univ Penn, BA, 68, MA, 71, PhD, 75. **CAREER** Instr to assoc prof, Phil Col of Textiles and Science, 74-84; assoc prof to prof, 84-97, Univ Bd of Gov prof, 99-, Rutgers Univ, Camden; Kranzberg Prof, Georgia Inst Tech, 97-99 ; dir, Ctr Hist Bus, Hagley Mus and Lib, 92- ; ed, Stud in Industry and Soc, Rutgers Univ Pr, 94- . **HONORS AND AWARDS** President's Awd for Tchg Excellence, PCT&S; Soc for the Hist of the Early Republic book awd; Taft Prize in labor hist book awd; Newcomen prize in bus hist, article awd; NEH fel; Mellon res fel. **MEMBERSHIPS** Am Hist Asn; Org of Am Hist; Soc for the Hist of Tech; Bus Hist Conf; So Hist Asn. **RESEARCH** American industrialization, 1860-1980. **SELECTED PUBLICATIONS** Auth, Proprietary Capitalism: the Textile Manufacture at Philadelphia, 1800-1885, Cambridge Univ Pr, 83; coauth, Work Sights: Industrial Philadelphia, 1890-1950, Temple Univ Pr, 86; auth, Figured Tapestry: Markets, Production, and Power in Philadelphia Textiles, 1885-1941, Cambridge Univ Pr, 89; auth, Diversity in Diversity: Flexible Production and American Industrialization; 1870-1930, in Bus Hist Rev, 91; auth, Large Firms and Industrial Restructuring: the Philadelphia Region, 1900-1980, in Pa Mag of Hist and Bio, 92; auth, Manufacturing Diversity: Production Systems, Markets, and American Consumer Society, Tech and Culture, 94; auth, Determinism and Indeterminacy in the History of Technology, in Machines and History, MIT, 94; auth, Have a Heart for the Manufacturers, in Flexibility and Mass Production in Western Industrialization, Cambridge, 97; auth, Endless Novelty: Specialty Production and American Industrialization, 1865-1925, Princeton, 97. **CONTACT ADDRESS** Dept of Hist, Rutgers, The State Univ of New Jersey, Camden, 311 N Fifth St, Armitage Hall, Camden, NJ 08102. **EMAIL** scranton@cam.rutgers.edu

SCULLY, PAMELA F.
PERSONAL m, 1987, 2 children **DISCIPLINE** HISTORY **EDUCATION** Univ Cape Town, BA, 85; MA, 87; Univ Mich, PhD, 93. **CAREER** Vis instr, 92-93, Kenyon Col; vis scholar, Stanford Univ, 94-95; asst prof, 93- Kenyon Coll; asst prof, Denison Univ, 99-. **HONORS AND AWARDS** Fac Devel Grant, Kenyon Col, 94; NEH Fel, 95-96; Fac Devel Grant, 96-97. **MEMBERSHIPS** African Studies Asn; Am Hist Asn. **RESEARCH** South African History; Sub-Saharan African History; Race, Sexuality and Empire; Comparative Slavery and Emancipation in the Atlantic World. **SELECTED PUBLICATIONS** Auth, Narratives of Infanticide in the Aftermath of Slave Emancipation in the Rural Western Cape, South Africa, 1838-1848, Can Jour of African Studies, 96; Rape, Race, and Colonial Culture: The Sexual Politics of Identity in the Nineteenth Century Cape Colony, South Africa, Am Hist Rev, 95; Liquor and Labor in the Western Cape, Liquor and labor in Southern Africa, Ohio Univ Press, 92; rev, Elizabeth Schmidt, Peasants, Traders, and Wives, Soc Hist 21, 96; P.J. van der Merwe, The Migrant Farmer in the History of the Cape Colony, 1657-1842, Soc Hist 20, 95; Les Switzer, Power and Resistance in an African Society, Intl Jour of African Hist Studies 28, 95; Elizabeth Eldredge and Fred Morton, Slavery in South Africa, IJAHS 30, 96; Robert C-H Shell, Children of Bondage, Am Hist Rev 101, 96; auth, Liberating the Family? Gender and British Slave Emancipation in the Rural Western Cape, South Africa, 1823-1853, Heinmann (Portsmouth), 97. **CONTACT ADDRESS** Dept of Hist, Denison Univ, Granville, OH 43023. **EMAIL** scully@DENISON.EDU

SEADLE, MICHAEL S.
DISCIPLINE HISTORY; LIBRARY SCIENCE **EDUCATION** Earlham Col, BA, 72; Univ Mich, MS, 97; Univ Chicago, MA, 73, PhD, 77. **CAREER** Asst dir, Acad Computing Svcs, E Mich Univ, 87-89; online oper mgr, asst dir, Libr Tech Dept, Cornell Univ, 89-92; pres, Seadle Consult, 92-96; digital info assoc, Univ Mich, 96-97; DIGITAL SVCS LIBRN, MICH STATE UNIV, 98-. **SELECTED PUBLICATIONS** Ed, Library Hi Tech, 97-. **CONTACT ADDRESS** Michigan State Univ, 100 Library, East Lansing, MI 48224-1048. **EMAIL** seadle@mail.lib.msu.edu

SEAGER, SHARON HANNUM
PERSONAL Born 10/24/1938, Amarillo, TX **DISCIPLINE** HISTORY **EDUCATION** Trinity Univ, BA, 60; Rice Univ, PhD(hist), 65. **CAREER** Asst prof hist, Southeast Mo State Col, 64-66; assoc prof, 66-80, Prof Hist, Ball State Univ, 80; actg dir, women and gender studies prog, Ball State Univ, 91-92. **MEMBERSHIPS** Orgn Am Historians; Southern Hist Asn; Southern Asn for Women Hist. **RESEARCH** Ideology of the Southern Confederacy; history of the South; women in American history. **SELECTED PUBLICATIONS** Auth, Thomas Chilton--lawyer, politician, preacher, Filson Club Hist Quart, 64; contribr, History from a feminist perspective, In: Conspectus of History, Cambridge Univ, 78. **CONTACT ADDRESS** Dept of History, Ball State Univ, Muncie, IN 47306-0002. **EMAIL** sseager@gw.bsu.edu

SEALE, WILLIAM
PERSONAL Born 08/07/1939, Beaumont, TX, m, 1966, 2 children **DISCIPLINE** AMERICAN HISTORY **EDUCATION** Southwestern Univ, BA, 61; Duke Univ, MA, 64, PhD, 65. **CAREER** Lectr US hist, 64-65, Univ Houston; lectr, Univ SC, 69-71; asst prof hist, 65-69, Lamar State Univ; adj prof archit, 79-, Columbia Univ; curator, 74-75, Smithsonian Institution; free-lance writer & consult on hist restor & proj in Am hist, 77-. **MEMBERSHIPS** AHA; Soc Archit Historians; Assn Preservation Technol. **RESEARCH** American cultural history, particularly as it relates to architecture and customs of living. **SELECTED PUBLICATIONS** Auth, The President's House: A History, White House Hist Assn, 87; auth, Of Houses and Time, Harry Abrams, 91; auth, The White House; History of an American Idea, Am Inst of Archit Press, 92; auth, The White House Garden, White House Hist Assn, 95. **CONTACT ADDRESS** 805 Prince St, Alexandria, VA 22314. **EMAIL** oeconomy@aol.com

SEALEY, RAPHAEL
PERSONAL Born 08/14/1927, Middlesbrough, United Kingdom, d, 1 child **DISCIPLINE** HISTORY **EDUCATION** Univ Oxford, BA, 47; MA, 51. **CAREER** Prof, Univ Calif at Berkeley, 67-. **MEMBERSHIPS** Am Philol Asn, Asn of Ancient Historians. **RESEARCH** Greek History, Comparative Law. **SELECTED PUBLICATIONS** Auth, Demosthenes and his Time, Oxford Univ Press, 93; auth, The Justice of the Greeks, Univ of Mich Press, 94. **CONTACT ADDRESS** Dept Hist, Univ of California, Berkeley, 3229 Dwinelle Hall, Berkeley, CA 94720-2550. **EMAIL** squiley@socrates.berkeley.edu

SEARS, ELIZABETH ANN
PERSONAL Born 06/06/1949, m, 1981 **DISCIPLINE** AMERICAN MUSIC HISTORY, AFRICAN-AMERICAN MUSIC, AMERICAN MUSICAL THEATER, PIANO PERFORMANCE **EDUCATION** New Eng Conserv Mus, BM; Ariz State Univ, MM; Cath Univ Am, PhD. **CAREER** Music, Wheaton, Col. **RESEARCH** European and American art song, piano performance; American music; opera and art song; piano literature and piano performance. **SELECTED PUBLICATIONS** Ed, bk of essays on Amer pop song; co-writer, textbook on Amer musical theater; articles on piano music and sing by block composers; articles on musical theater, esp. Rodgers and Hammerstein; impact discs of art song and spiritual arrangements by block composers. **CONTACT ADDRESS** Dept of Mus, Wheaton Col, Massachusetts, 26 East Main St, Norton, MA 02766. **EMAIL** asears@wheatonma.edu

SEATON, DOUGLASS
PERSONAL Born 06/08/1950, Baltimore, MD, m, 1972 **DISCIPLINE** HISTORICAL MUSICOLOGY **EDUCATION** Columbia Univ, PhD, 77. **CAREER** Fla State Univ, 78- . **MEMBERSHIPS** Am Musicol Soc; The Col Mus Soc; 19th Cent Stud Asn; Lyrica Soc Word-Music Rel. **RESEARCH** Felix Mendelssohn Bartholdy, song, criticism. **SELECTED PUBLICATIONS** The Art Song: A Research and Information Guide, 87; Ideas and Styles in the Western Musical Tradition, 91. **CONTACT ADDRESS** School of Music, Florida State Univ, Tallahassee, FL 32306-1180. **EMAIL** seaton_d@cmr.fsu.edu

SEAVER, PAUL SIDDALL
PERSONAL Born 03/19/1932, Philadelphia, PA, m, 1956, 2 children **DISCIPLINE** ENGLISH HISTORY **EDUCATION** Haverford Col, BA, 55; Harvard Univ, MA, 56, PhD(hist), 65. **CAREER** Instr hist, Reed Col. 62-64; asst prof, 64-70, Assoc Prof Hist, Stanford Univ, 70-, John Simon Guggenheim Mem Found fel, 70-71; prof, 82-. **HONORS AND AWARDS** British Council Prize in the Humanities, 86. **MEMBERSHIPS** AHA; Hist Asn, Eng; Am Soc Church Hist; Royal Hist Soc. **RESEARCH** 16th and 17th century London **SELECTED PUBLICATIONS** Auth, "The English Reformation," Reformation Europe: A Guide to Research, St Louis, (82): 271-296; auth, Wallingtons World: A Puritan Artisan in Seventeenth Century London, Stanford, 85; auth" A Geographic Perspective in History in Microcosm: An Artisanal Case Study," Geographic Perspectives in History, Basil Blackwell, 89; auth, " A Social Contract? Master Against Servant in the Court of Requests," History Today, 39,(89), 50-56; Declining Status in an Aspiring Age: The Problem of the Gentle Apprentice in Seventeenth-Century London" Court, Country, and Culture: Essays on Early Modern British History In Honor of Perez Zagorin, Boydel and Brewer, (92), 129-147; auth, '"Thomas Dekker's Shoemaker's Holiday and the world of London artisans and apprentices," David L Smith , Richard Strier and David Bevington, ,The Theatrical City: London Culture, Theatre and Literature, 1576-1649 (Cambridge U P,95): 87-100; auth, " Work Discipline and the Apprentice in Early Modern London," Penelope Gouk, Wellsprings of Achievement, (Aldershot: Variorum,95)m159-179; auth, "Laud and the Livery Companies," Charles Carlton, State, Sovereigns and Society: Essays in Early Modern English History in Honor of A J Slavin, (Sutton, 97): 219-234; " Recent Studies of the English Reformation," Religious Studies Review, 24/1 (98): 31-36; " Symposium: Controlling (Mis) Behavior: Introduction," Journal of British Studies, 37 (98): 231-245. **CONTACT ADDRESS** Dept of Hist, Stanford Univ, Stanford, CA 94305-1926. **EMAIL** seaver@leland.standford.edu

SEBESTA, JUDITH LYNN
PERSONAL Born Chicago, IL **DISCIPLINE** CLASSICAL LANGUAGES AND LITERATURE, ANCIENT HISTORY, WOMEN IN ANTIQUITY **EDUCATION** Univ Chicago, AB, 68; Stanford Univ, PhD, 72. **CAREER** From instr to asst prof, 72-77, Assoc Prof Classics, Univ S Dak, 77-, Dir, Integrated Humanities Prof, Univ SDak, 81, Dir Classics, 81, Chair, Dept Hist, 97-. **HONORS AND AWARDS** Phi Beta Kappa, 67; Harrington Lectr, Col Arts & Sci, 94. **MEMBERSHIPS** Am Philol Asn; Class Asn Midwest & South; Am Classical League. **RESEARCH** The Roman army; provinces of the Roman empire; classical philology. **SELECTED PUBLICATIONS** Auth, Carl Orff Carmina Burana, Bolchazy-Carducci Publ, 84, 96; Mantles of the Gods and Catullus 64, Syllectu Classica 5, 93; coauth, The World of Roman Costume, Univ Wis Press, 94; auth, Women's Costume and Feminine Civic Morality in Augustan Rome, Gender & Hist 9, 97; Aliquid Sem per Novi: New Challenges & New Approaches, in Latin for the 21st Century, Addison-Wesley, 97. **CONTACT ADDRESS** Dept of Hist, Univ of So Dakota, Vermillion, 414 E Clark St, Vermillion, SD 57069-2390. **EMAIL** jsebesta@sunbird.usd.edu

SECKINGER, DONALD SHERMAN
PERSONAL Born 02/01/1933, New York, NY, m, 1955, 3 children **DISCIPLINE** PHILOSOPHY & HISTORY OF EDUCATION **EDUCATION** Univ Calif, Los Angeles, AB, 54, MA, 56, EdD, 65. **CAREER** From asst prof to assoc prof educ, Calif State Univ, Los Angeles, 64-70; assoc prof educ found, 70-77, Prof Educ Found, Univ Wyo, 77-, Vis lectr educ, Univ Calif, Los Angeles, 68-69. **MEMBERSHIPS** Fel Philos Educ Soc; Am Educ Studies Asn; fel Far Western Philos Educ Soc(-secy-treas, 74-77, vpres, 77 & pres, 78-). **RESEARCH** Philosophical anthropology; existential philosophy. **SELECTED PUBLICATIONS** Auth, Tombaugh,Clyde - Discoverer Of The Planet Pluto - Levy,D/, J Of The W, Vol 0032, 1993. **CONTACT ADDRESS** Dept of Educ Founds, Univ of Wyoming, Laramie, WY 82070.

SEDGWICK, ALEXANDER
PERSONAL Born 06/08/1930, Boston, MA, m, 1961, 2 children **DISCIPLINE** EARLY MODERN AND MODERN EUROPEAN HISTORY **EDUCATION** Harvard Univ, AB, 52, PhD(hist), 63. **CAREER** Instr hist, Dartmouth Col, 62-63; from asst prof to assoc prof, 63-74, Prof hist, Univ VA, 74-95, Univ prof 95-97, Dept ChPerson, 79-85, Dean Col A&S, 85-90; Dean GSAS 90-95; Emer prof, 97-. **HONORS AND AWARDS** Am Coun Learned Soc grant-in-aid, 67-68, Am Phil Soc grant-in-aid, 71. **MEMBERSHIPS** AHA; Soc Fr Hist Studies (execsecy, 79-84, pres 84); AAUP (nat coun 76-79). **RESEARCH** Early and mod French hist. **SELECTED PUBLICATIONS** Auth, The Ralliement in French Politics, 1890-98, Harvard Univ, 65; The Third French Republic, 1870-1914, Crowell, 68; Jansenism in 17th Century France: Voices from the Wilderness, Univ VA, 77; Seventeenth-Century French Jansenism and the Enlightenment, Fr Relig & Soc, 82; Voltaire: I'd Rather Be in Philadelphia, 85; The Nuns of Port-Royal, A Study in Female Spirituality, 90; The Gentle Strength, 90; Prophets Without Honor, 90; La revolutionn francaise et le caractere de la Democratie francaise, 90; La famille Arnauld a travers le Port-Royal de Saaainte-Beuve, Chroniques de Port Royal, 95; Travails of Conscience, Harvard Univ, 98; auth, The Travails of Conscience: The Arnauld Family and the Ancien Regime, Harvard, 98. **CONTACT ADDRESS** Dept of History, Univ of Virginia, Randall Hall, Charlottesville, VA 22903. **EMAIL** as6d@virginia.edu

SEDLAR, JEAN WHITENACK
PERSONAL Born 02/02/1935, South Milwaukee, WI, d, 2 children **DISCIPLINE** EUROPEAN & WORLD HISTORY **EDUCATION** Univ Chicago, MA, 56, PhD(hist), 70. **CAREER** Lectr hist, Ill Inst Technol, 71-72; asst prof to prof hist, Univ Pittsburgh, Johnstown, 72-. **HONORS AND AWARDS** NEH Inst 87, 89; summer Fulbright to Germany, 92. **MEMBERSHIPS** Am Asn Advan Slavic Studies; Midwest Slavic Asn. **RESEARCH** East-central Europe; history from medieval period to present; cross cultural influences in history; East-Central Europe: World War II. **SELECTED PUBLICATIONS** Co-ed, The Origins of Civilization, Vol I, The Ancient Near East, Vol II, The Classical Mediterranean World, Vol III, Classical India, Vol IV, Classical China, Vol V & India, China and Japan: The Middle Period, Vol VII, In: Readings in World History, Oxford Univ Press, 69-71; auth, India and the Greek World: A Study in the Transmission of Culture, Rowman & Littlefield, 80; India in the Mind of Germany: Schelling, Schopenhauer and Their Times, Univ Press Am, 82; auth, East Central Europe in the Middle Ages, 1000-1500, In: Vol III of History of East Central Europe, Univ Wash Press, 94. **CONTACT ADDRESS** Dept of Hist, Univ of Pittsburgh, 450 Schoolhouse Rd, Johnstown, PA 15904-2912. **EMAIL** sedlar@pitt.edu

SEE, SCOTT W.
PERSONAL Born 10/12/1950, Washington, DC, m, 1978, 2 children **DISCIPLINE** HISTORY **EDUCATION** Muskingum Col, BA, 72; Univ Maine, MA, 80; PhD, 84. **CAREER** Instr, Canterbury Sch, 83-85; asst prof, Univ Vermont, 85-91; act dir, 92-93; assoc prof, 91-97; prof, 97; assoc prof, Univ Maine, 97-00; prof, 00-. **HONORS AND AWARDS** Kroepsch-Maurice Awd; Fulbright Res Fel; Fel, Cen Res, Ver; Phi Alpha Theta Nat Hon Soc; Sir John A Macdonald Prize. **MEMBERSHIPS** CHA; AHA; ACSUS; AAH; MANECCS; FA. **RESEARCH** History of Canadian collective violence and nineteenth-century immigration patterns. **SELECTED PUBLICATIONS** Auth, Riots in New Brunswick: Orange Nativism and Social Violence in the 1840s, Univ Tor Press (Toronto), 93, 2nd printing 99; auth, "Nineteenth-Century Collective Violence: Toward a North American Context," Labour/Le Travail 39 (97): 1-26; auth, "The Orange Order and Social Violence in Mid-Nineteenth Century Saint John," in Readings in Canadian History: Pre-Confederation, eds. R Douglas Francis, Donald B Smith (Harcourt Brace: 98); auth, "The Orange Order and Social Violence in Mid-Nineteenth-Century Saint John," A Nation of Immigrants: Women, Workers, and Communities in Canadian History, 1840s-1960s, eds. Franca Iacovetta, Paula Draper, Robert Ventresca (Univ Tor Press, 98); auth, "'Mickies and Demons' vs. 'Bigots and Boobies': The Woodstock Riot of 1847," Acad 21 (91): 110-131; auth, "Polling Crowds and Social Violence: New Brunswick's 'Fighting Elections' of 1842-43," Can Hist Rev 72 (91): 127-156. **CONTACT ADDRESS** Dept History, Univ of Maine, 200A Stevens Hall, Orono, ME 04469. **EMAIL** scottsee@maine.maine.edu

SEED, PATRICIA
PERSONAL Born 09/20/1949, Baltimore, MD, m, 1984, 2 children **DISCIPLINE** LATIN AMERICAN HISTORY **EDUCATION** Fordham Univ, BA, 71; Univ Tex, Austin, MA, 75; Univ Wis-Madison, PhD(Latin Am hist), 80. **CAREER** Anthropology and History (INAH), 76-78; Vis Investigator, Urban Hist Sem, Nat Inst of Anthrop and Hist (INAH), 76-78; Consult, dir, Nat Archives of Mex, 78; Vis Lectr, Ohio Univ, 79; Asst prof, Col of Charleston, 80-82; Adj Assoc Prof, Med Univ of South Carolina, 90-94; Asst prof, Rice Univ, 82-87, Assoc prof, 87-94, Prof, 94-; Vis Scholar, Dept of Hist and Ctr for Gender Studies, Universidade de Campinas, Campinas, Brazil, 93. **HONORS AND AWARDS** Fulbright-Hays Dissertation Fel, 76-77; Soc Sci Res Coun Int Doctoral Dissertation Fel, 76-78; Nat Endowment for the Humanities, Summer Res Stipend for res in Spain on church/state relations, 81; Tinker Found Fel for mathematical physics at Inst for Mathematical Physics, Univ of Maryland, 84; Nat Endowment for the Humanities Fel, Newberry Libr, 86; Bryce Wood Bk Awd, Honorable Mention, 89; Herbert Eugene Bolton Prize, 89; Conference on Latin Am Hist Prize, Honorable Mention, 92; Nominated for Berkshire Prize, 94; Vasco Da Gama Lectureship (from Portuguese government, Commiso para a Histria dos Decobrimentos), 95. **MEMBERSHIPS** AHA, 72-; Latin Am Studies Asn, 73-; Conf on Latin Am Hist, 73; World Hist Asn, 92-; Associates of the Omohundro Inst for Early Am Hist and Cult, 94-; Forum on European and Global Interaction, 95-; Soc for Judeo-Greek Studies, 96-; Latin Am Subaltern Studies (Founding Mem). **RESEARCH** History of European colonialism in the New World. **SELECTED PUBLICATIONS** Auth, To Love Honor and Obey in Colonial Mexico: Conflicts over Marriage Choice, 1574-1821, Stanford Univ Press, 88; auth, Amar, honrar, y obedecer en el Mxico colonial [Spanish translation of To Love, Honor and Obey] Mexico: Editorial Patria, 91 serialized in Suplemento Dominical (Sunday Cultural Supplement) La Jornada (Mexico City) Nov. 96-June 97; auth, Ceremonies of Possession In Europe's Conquest Of The New World, 1492-1640, Cambridge Univ Press, 95; auth, "The Conquest of the Americas, 1500-1650," chapter 9 Cambridge Illustrated History of Warfare, ed. By Geoffrey Parker, (95); auth, "Afterword: Further Perspectives on Culture, Limits, and Borders," in Border, Theory, Limits eds. Scott Michaelsen and David Johnson (Minneapolis: University of Minnesota, 97); auth, "The Key to the House" in Home, Exile, Homeland: Film, Media, and the Politics of Place ed. Hamid Naficy (London: Routledge Press, 98); auth, "The Church and the Patriarchal Family: Marriage Conflicts in Sixteenth-and Seventeenth-Century Mexico," in Mara Beatriz Nizza da Silva, ed. Families in the Expansion of Europe, 1500-1800 (Brookfield, Vt: Ashgate, 98); auth, "Charles V, Gold, and Chocolate," (Re)Legitimating the Past (Brussels, 99); auth, American Pentimento: The Invention of Indians and the Pursuit of Riches, 1492-1640, Univ of Minnesota Press, 00; auth, "Caliban and Native Title: This Island's Mine," in Peter Hulme and William Sherman, eds. The Tempest and its Travels (London, 00). **CONTACT ADDRESS** Dept of Hist MS-42, Rice Univ, PO Box 1892, Houston, TX 77251-1892. **EMAIL** Seed@rice.edu

SEEDORF, MARTIN F.
PERSONAL Born 03/09/1943, Spokane, WA, m, 1966, 2 children **DISCIPLINE** HISTORY **EDUCATION** Eastern Wash Univ, BA, 64; BAE, 65; Univ Wash, MA, 68; PhD, 74. **CAREER** Instr, Big Bend Community Col, 72-87; vis prof, Wash State Univ, 87-89; prof, Eastern Wash Univ, 89-. **HONORS AND AWARDS** Outstanding Instr Awd, 75-76; NEH Summer Inst, 82. **MEMBERSHIPS** N Am Conf on British Studies; Am Conf on Irish Studies; British Polit Group. **RESEARCH** Modern British History, British-Irish Relations. **SELECTED PUBLICATIONS** Auth, "The Lloyd George Government and the Strickland Report on the Burning of Cork, 1920, Albion, (Summer 72); auth, "The Lloyd George Government and the Anglo-Irish War 1919-1921", Proc of the AHA 1978, (79); coauth, "Army Air Bases: The Effects of World War II on Grant County, Washington", Proc of a Conf on Military Influences on Washington History, (Mar 84); coauth, "Era of Drought and Depression: The Columbia Basin in the 1920's", Pacific Northwest Forum (Fall 89); coauth, "James O'Sullivan, the Pumpers' and the Fight for Grand Coulee Dam, 1918-1933", Pacific Northwest Forum, (Spring 90); auth, "Defending Reprisals: Sir Hamar Greenwood and the Troubles, 1920-1921", Eire-Ireland XXV.4 (Winter 91); auth, "Education Reform in England and Wales, 1988-1993", British Politics Group Newsletter (Spring 94); coauth, "Runways and Reclamation", Wash State Hist Soc, (June 94); auth, "James O'Sullivan", American National Biography, ACLS/Oxford Univ Pr, 99; auth, "Greenwood, Hamar, 1st Viscount (1870-1948)", New Dictionary of National Biography, Oxford Univ Pr, (forthcoming). **CONTACT ADDRESS** Dept Hist, Eastern Washington Univ, M/S 27, Cheney, WA 99004. **EMAIL** mseedorf@mail.ewu.edu

SEELY, BRUCE E.
PERSONAL Born 01/10/1953, Chicago, IL, m, 1985, 2 children **DISCIPLINE** HISTORY **EDUCATION** St. Lawrence Univ, BA, 75; Univ Delaware, MA, 77; PhD, 82. **CAREER** US Dept of the Interior, NPS, historian, 76-78; Texas A&M Univ, asst prof, 81-86; Mich Tech Univ, asst prof, assoc prof, prof, 86-, Pres Univ Senate, 97-; prog dir, Sci and Technology Studies, Nat Sci Found, 00. **HONORS AND AWARDS** Soc Indust Archeo, Norton Prize, 84; Rail & Loco Hist Soc, Rail Hist Awd, 85-86; Soc Hist of Tech, Abbott Payson Usher Awd, 87; PWHS & APWA, Abel Wolman Awd, 88; MTU, Omicron Delta Kappa, Copper Scroll Awd, 90; MIT, Dibner Inst, Fellow, 96; Wickenden Awd, Am Soc for Engineering Educ, 00. **MEMBERSHIPS** SHT, SIA, OAH, PWHS, BHC. **RESEARCH** Hist of tech and eng; eng edu; rail and hwy transport; iron and steel indust. **SELECTED PUBLICATIONS** Auth, Building the American Highway System: Engineers as Policy Makers, Temp Univ Press, 87; auth, The Diffusion of Science into Engineering: Highway Research at the Bureau of Public Roads, in: The Transfer and Transformation of Ideas and Material Culture, Tex A and M Univ Press 88; ed and contribur, Encyclopedia of American Business History and Biography: The Iron and Steel Industry in the Twentieth Century, Bruccoli Clark Layman Inc, 94; auth, "Teaching the History of Technology," in Studies in History of Sciences, The Asiatic Society, 97; auth, "Visions of Am Highways, 1900-1980," in Geschicte des Zukunft des Verkehors, Campus Verlog, 97. **CONTACT ADDRESS** Dept of Social Sciences, Michigan Tech Univ, 1400 Townsend Dr, Houghton, MI 49931-1295. **EMAIL** bseely@mtu.edu

SEELY, GORDON M.
PERSONAL Born 04/14/1930, San Mateo, CA, m, 1958, 2 children **DISCIPLINE** HISTORY OF EDUCATION **EDUCATION** Stanford Univ, AB, 51, MA, 54 & 58, PhD, 63. **CAREER** Teacher, High Schs & Jr Col, Calif, 54-55, 56-57, 59-60; from asst prof to assoc prof, 60-69, prof History, San Francisco State Univ, 69-. **RESEARCH** American social and intellectual history, especially education; California history. **SELECTED PUBLICATIONS** Ed, Education and Opportunity, Prentice-Hall, 1st ed, 71, 2nd ed, 75. **CONTACT ADDRESS** Dept Hist, San Francisco State Univ, 1600 Holloway Ave, San Francisco, CA 94132-1740. **EMAIL** evgor@worldnet.att.net

SEELYE, JOHN D.
DISCIPLINE HISTORY **CAREER** GRAD RES PROF, UNIV FLA **MEMBERSHIPS** Am Antiquarian Soc **SELECTED PUBLICATIONS** Auth, Melville: The Ironic Diagram, 70; auth, Prophetic Waters: The River in Early American Life and Literature, 77; auth, "Rational Exultation: The Erie Canal Celebration of 1825," Procs of the AAS 84, 84; auth, Monumental Trivia: The Rhetorical History of Plymouth Rock," paper, SE AM Stud Asn, 87; auth, Beautiful Machine: Rivers and the Republican Plan, 1755-1828, Oxford Univ Press, 91. **CONTACT ADDRESS** PO Box 2199, Hawthorne, FL 32640.

SEEMAN, ERIK R.
DISCIPLINE HISTORY **EDUCATION** Harvard Univ, AB, 89, Univ MIch, PhD. **CAREER** Asst Prof, Hist, State Univ NY Buffalo **MEMBERSHIPS** Am Antiquarian Soc **SELECTED PUBLICATIONS** Auth, "She Died Like Good Old Jacob, Deathbed Scenes and Inversions of Power in New England, 1675-1775," Procs of the AAS 104; auth, The Spiritual Labour of John Barnard: An Eighteenth-Century Artisan Constructs His Piety, Rel & Am Cult: A Jour of Interp 5, Summer 95; auth, "Sarah Prentice and the Immortalists: Sexuality, Piety, and the Body in Eighteenth-Century New England," Sex and Sexuality in Early America, New York University Press, 98; auth, "Lay Conversion Narratives: Investigating Ministerial Intervention," New England Quarterly, 98; auth, "Justise Must Take Plase: Three African Americans Speak of Religion in Eighteenth-Century New England," William and Mary Quarterly, 99; auth, "It Is Better To Marry Than To Burn: Anglo-American Attitudes Toward Celibacy, 1600-1800," Journal of Family History, 99; auth, "Pious Persuasions: Laity and Clergy in Eighteenth Century New England," Johns Hopkins University Press, 99; auth, "To Die a Triumphant Death: Deathbed Scenes as Cultural Scripts in Colonial New England," St. Martin's Press, 01; auth, "Reading Indians' Deathbed Scenes: Ethnohistorical and Representational Approaches," Journal of American History, 01; **CONTACT ADDRESS** Dept of History, SUNY, Buffalo, Park Hall, Buffalo, NY 14260. **EMAIL** seeman@buffalo.edu

SEFTON, JAMES EDWARD
PERSONAL Born 07/29/1939, San Francisco, CA **DISCIPLINE** UNITED STATES HISTORY **EDUCATION** Univ Calif, Los Angeles, AB, 61, PhD, 65. **CAREER** From instr to assoc prof, 65-73, Prof Hist, Calif State Univ, Northridge, 73-, Nat Col Athletics Asn, Fac Athletics Rep, 81-90; Am Philos Soc Penrose Fund grant, 68-69. **HONORS AND AWARDS** Distinguished Teaching Awd, Calif State Univ, Northridge, 70. **MEMBERSHIPS** AHA; Southern Hist Asn; Orgn Am Historians; US Naval Inst. **RESEARCH** Military and naval history; Civil War and Reconstruction; United States constitutional history; Fine arts and historical photography. **SELECTED PUBLICATIONS** Auth, The United States Army and Reconstruction, 1865-77, La State Univ, 67; The impeachment of President Johnson: A century of historical writing, 6/68 & Aristotle in blue and braid: General John M Schofield's essays on Reconstruction, 3/71, Civil War Hist; Black slaves, red masters, white middlemen: A congressional debate of 1852, Fla Hist Quart, 10/72; Tribute pennies and tribute clauses: Religion in the first constitutions of Trans-Mississippi States, 1812-1912, in The American West and the Religious Experience, 74; auth, Andrew Johnson and the Uses of Constitutional Power, Little, 80; Admiral Royal Eason Ingersoll, in Dictionary of American Military Biography, Greenwood Press, 84; Ulysses S Grant, in Encyclopedia of the American Presidency, Simon & Schuster, 94; Reconstruction, Photography and War, and Naval Operations in the Pacific in World War II, in: Oxford Companion to American Military History, 98; exhib, " My L A/My Berlin," Berlin Academy of Fine Arts, 99; exhib, " California 166," Allan Hancock College, Santa Maria, CA and California State Univ, Bakersfield, 99-00; exhib, " Textures of the Night," Cal State univ, Northridge, 00. **CONTACT ADDRESS** Dept of Hist, California State Univ, Northridge, 18111 Nordhoff St, Northridge, CA 91330-8250.

SEGAL, ALAN FRANKLIN
PERSONAL Born 08/02/1945, Worcester, MA, m, 1970, 2 children **DISCIPLINE** JUDAICA, HISTORY OF RELIGION **EDUCATION** Amherst Col, BA, 67; Brandeis Univ, MA, 69; Hebrew Union Col, BHL, 70; Yale Univ, MPhil, 72, PhD(Judaica), 75. **CAREER** Asst prof Judaica, Princeton Univ, 74-78; assoc prof, Univ Toronto, 78-81; Assoc Prof Judaica, Barnard Col & Grad Fac, Columbia Univ, 81-, Woodrow Wilson fel, 67-68; Jewish Mem Found fel, 73 & 78; Guggenheim fel, 78; chairperson Judaica Sect IAHR, Winnipeg, 80; Mellon fel, Aspen Inst, 81; chmn relig dept, Barnard Col, 81; Ingeborg Rennert Prof of Judaic Studies. **HONORS AND AWARDS** Woodrow Wilson Fel; Guggenheim Fel; NEH Fel; NEH Grant; Jerome Malino Awd; Mellon Fel; Annenberg Fel. **MEMBERSHIPS** Soc Bibl Lit; SNTS, Asn Jewish Studies; Asn Sci Study Relig; Am Acad of Relig; CSBS; ATS. **RESEARCH** Judaica; early Christianity. **SELECTED PUBLICATIONS** Auth, Two Powers in Heaven: Rabbinic Polemics Against Christianity and Gnosticism, Brill, 77; coauth, Philo and the Rabbis on the name of God, J Study Judaism, 79; Heavenly ascent in Hellenistic Judaism, early Christianity and their environments, 23: 2 & Rabbinc Polemic and the radicalization of Gnosticism, 23:2, ANRW; Ruler of this world: Attitudes towards mediator figures and the problem of a sociology of Gnosticism, In: Jewish and Christian Self-Definition II, Fortress, 81; Hellenistic magic: Some questions of definition, In: Studies in Gnosticism Presented to Gilles Quispel on the Occasion of his 65th Birthday, Brill, Leiden, 81; auth, Rebecca's Children, Harvard, 86; auth, Paul the Convert, Yale, 90. **CONTACT ADDRESS** Dept of Relig, Barnard Col, New York, NY 10027. **EMAIL** asegal@barnard.columbia.edu

SEGEL, EDWARD BARTON
PERSONAL Born 12/25/1938, Boston, MA **DISCIPLINE** HISTORY **EDUCATION** Harvard Univ, AB, 60; Univ Calif, Berkeley, MA, 62, PhD(hist), 69. **CAREER** Actg asst prof hist, Univ Calif, Berkeley, 65-67, from lectr to asst prof, 67-73, humanities res fel, 70-71; asst prof hist, Reed Col, 73-76, prof hist & humanities, Reed Col, 76-. **HONORS AND AWARDS** Teaching Awd, Univ Calif, Berkeley, 67. **MEMBERSHIPS** AHA; SHAFR **RESEARCH** European diplomatic history, 19th and 20th centuries; British foreign policy, 1919-1939; Cold War. **SELECTED PUBLICATIONS** Auth, A J P Taylor and history, Rev Politics, 10/64 & In: The Origins of the Second World War: A J P Taylor and His Critics, Wiley, 72; Paul Tillich and the unbelievers, Humanity, 12/65. **CONTACT ADDRESS** Dept of History, Reed Col, 3203 SE Woodstock Blvd, Portland, OR 97202-8199. **EMAIL** Edward.Segel@reed.edu

SEGGER, MARTIN
PERSONAL Born 11/22/1946, United Kingdom, m, 1970, 3 children **DISCIPLINE** ART HISTORY **EDUCATION** Univ Victoria Canada, BA, 69, DspEd, 70; London Univ, UK, M.

Phil, 73. **CAREER** Royal British Columbia Museum, 74-77; adj prof, dir, 77-, Maltwood Art Museum & Gallery, Univ of Victoria. **HONORS AND AWARDS** Harvey J McKee/Apr; Natl Comm Awd 7 Lieut Gov's Awd, Heritage Canada Found; AASLH Awd of Merit; elected a fel of the Royal Soc of Arts, 82. **MEMBERSHIPS** ICOM/ICTOP; Soc for Stud of Arch in Canada; Asn for Preservation Tech; ICOMOS-Canada; Can Museum Dir Org. **RESEARCH** Architectural history 19th century, European & Amer, Europe dec arts, cult resource management. **SELECTED PUBLICATIONS** Auth, Victoria, An Architectural History, 79; ed, The British Columbia Parliament Buildings, 79; auth, This Old House, 82; auth, This Old Town, 84; auth, The Bulidings of Samuel Maclure: In Search of Appropriate Form, 86; auth, Exploring Victoria's Architecture 1842-1997, 97. **CONTACT ADDRESS** Hartwood Gallery, Univ of Victoria, PO Box 3025, Victoria, BC, Canada V8W 3P2. **EMAIL** msegger@uvic.ca

SEGRE, CLAUDIO GIUSEPPE
PERSONAL Born 03/02/1937, Palermo, Italy, m, 1967, 2 children **DISCIPLINE** MODERN HISTORY **EDUCATION** Reed Col, BA, 57; Stanford Univ, MA, 61; Univ Calif, Berkeley, MA, 64, PhD(hist), 70. **CAREER** Instr hist, Stanford Univ, 67-70 asst prof, 70-77, Assoc Prof Hist, Univ Tex, Austin, 77-, Nat Endowment for Humanities fel, 73-74; Air Force Hist Found grant, 76. **HONORS AND AWARDS** Marraro Prize, Soc Ital Hist Studies, 75. **MEMBERSHIPS** Soc Ital Hist Studies. **RESEARCH** Modern Italy; fascism; imperialism. **SELECTED PUBLICATIONS** Auth, Italo Balbo and the coolonization of Libya, J Contemp Hist, 72; Fourth Shore: La Parola del Popolo, 7/76. **CONTACT ADDRESS** Dept of Hist, Univ of Texas, Austin, Austin, TX 78712.

SEHLINGER, PETER J.
PERSONAL Born 08/18/1940, Louisville, KY, m, 1977 **DISCIPLINE** HISTORY **EDUCATION** Univ of South, BA, 62; Tulane Univ, MA, 64; Univ Ky, PhD(hist), 69. **CAREER** Assoc dean overseas study, Ind Univ, Bloomington, 76-79; assoc prof hist, 69-79, prof hist, Ind Univ, Indianapolis, 79-; prof hist, 79-99; prof emeritus, Ind Univ Indianapolis, 99-. **MEMBERSHIPS** Andean Sect, Coun Latin Am Hist; Latin Am Studies Asn; AHA; Midwest Asn Latin Am Studies; Soc Iberian & Latin Am Thought; Ind Asn of Historians. **RESEARCH** Chilean intellectual history; international investment and the War of the Pacific; US Diplomatic History. **SELECTED PUBLICATIONS** Auth, A Select Guide to Chilean Libraries and Archives, Ind Univ Latin Am Studies Series, 79; auth, Oral Hist Projects in Argentina, Chile, Peru, and Bolivia, Intl Jour of Oral Hist, 84; auth, Ricardo Donoso, Revista Chilena de Historia y Geografia, 85; auth, At the Moment of Victory . . . The Battle of Shiloh, Filson Club Hist Quarterly, 97; auth, Gen Wm Preston, Register of the Ky Hist Soc, 95; auth, National Archive of Chile, Inter-Am Rev of Bibliography, 98; coauth, Magazine of Hist, 87; Holman Hamilton, Spokesman for Democracy: Claude G Bowers, Ind Hist Soc, 00; coed, ky Profiles, Ky Hist Soc, 82. **CONTACT ADDRESS** 2129-A Rome Dr, Indianapolis, IN 46228. **EMAIL** psehling@iupui.edu

SEIBERLING, GRACE
DISCIPLINE ART HISTORY, VISUAL AND CULTURAL STUDIES **EDUCATION** Yale Univ, PhD, 76. **CAREER** Assoc prof, Univ of Rochester. **RESEARCH** 19th century painting and photography, espec Impressionism; early Brit photography; mus(s). **SELECTED PUBLICATIONS** Auth, Monet in London, Atlanta: High Mus, 88; Amateurs, Photography, and the Mid-Victorian Imagination, Chicago, Univ Chicago Press, 86 & Naturaleza y tecnica en las series de Monet, In Claude Monet, Madrid, Museo Espanol de Arte Comtemporaneo, 86; coauth, A Vision Exchanged: Amateurs and Photography in Mid- Victorian England, London Victoria and Albert Mus, 85. **CONTACT ADDRESS** Dept of Art and Art Hist, Univ of Rochester, 601 Elmwood Ave, Ste. 656, 422 Morey , Rochester, NY 14642. **EMAIL** seib@troi.cc.rochester.edu

SEIDEL, ROBERT H.
PERSONAL Born 09/06/1945, Kansas City, KS, m, 1993, 1 child **DISCIPLINE** HISTORY OF SCIENCE **EDUCATION** Westmar Col, BA, 67; Univ Calif, MA, 68; PhD, 78. **CAREER** Museum dir, Bradbury, 85-90; proj leader, Los Alamos Nat Lab, 90-92; sr analyst, 92-94; prof, Univ Minn, 94-. **HONORS AND AWARDS** Woodrow Wilson Fel; NSTA First Prize Essay; Dibner Inst Sr Fel. **MEMBERSHIPS** HSS; SHT; AAUP. **RESEARCH** Modern Physical Sciences and their Technical Applications. **SELECTED PUBLICATIONS** Auth, Lawrence and His Laboratory: vol 1 of A History of the Lawrence Berkeley Laboratory, 89; auth, Los Alamos and the Making of the Atomic Bomb, 94. **CONTACT ADDRESS** Dept Physics, Univ of Minnesota, Twin Cities, 150 Amundson Hall, Minneapolis, MN 55455-0149. **EMAIL** rws@umn.edu

SEIDEL, ROBERT NEAL
PERSONAL Born 10/10/1936, New York, NY, m, 1957, 3 children **DISCIPLINE** HISTORY **EDUCATION** State Univ NYork, Cortland, BA, 68; Cornell Univ, MA, 71, PhD, 73. **CAREER** Lectr hist, Cornell Univ, 72-73; from asst prof to prof, 74-90, Distinguished Teaching Prof Hist, Empire State Col, Rochester, 90-, actg assoc dean, 81-82, interim dean, 90-91; res assoc policy studies, Prog Policies Sci & Technol in Develop Nations, Cornell Univ, 73-74. **HONORS AND AWARDS** Earhard Found, Ann Arbor, Mich fel res grant, 78. **MEMBERSHIPS** AHA; OAH; APSA. **RESEARCH** History of American foreign relations; United States-Latin American relations; 20th century United States history. **SELECTED PUBLICATIONS** Auth, American reformers abroad: The Kemmerer Missions in South America, in J Econ Hist, 6/72; Progressive Pan Americanism: Development and United States Policy Toward South America, 1906-1931, 73 & Toward an Andean Common Market for Science and Technology, 74, Cornell Univ; Latin America: The Burden of Derivative Modernization, in Third World Rev, fall 76; coauth, Learning Contracts as Aids to Independent Study in History, in Teaching Hist: J Methods, spring 77; Neighborly Affection and the Common Good, Saratoga Springs, 90. **CONTACT ADDRESS** SUNY, Empire State Col, 1475 Winton Rd N, Rochester, NY 14609-5803. **EMAIL** rseidel@sescva.esc.edu

SEIDMAN, MICHAEL
PERSONAL Born Philadelphia, PA **DISCIPLINE** HISTORY **EDUCATION** Swarthmore Col, BA, 72; Univ Calif Berkeley, MA, 77; Univ Amsterdam, PhD, 82. **CAREER** Asst prof, Rutgers Univ, 83-90; asst prof to prof, Univ NC Wilmington, 90-. **SELECTED PUBLICATIONS** Auth, Workers against Work: Labor in Paris and Barcelona during the Popular Fronts, 1936-38, Univ of Calif Pr, (Berkeley), 91; auth, "Women's Subversive Individualism in Barcelona during the 1930s", Int Rev of Soc Hist, XXXVII, (92): 161-176; auth, "Workers in a repressive Society of Seduction: Parisian Metallurgists in May-June 1968", Fr Hist Studies, (93): 255-278; auth, "The Artist as Populist: Hemingway and the Spanish Civil War", Mediterranean Studies, Thomas Jefferson Univ Pr, (94); 157-164; auth, "Individualisms In Madrid during the Spanish Civil War", J of Mod Hist, (96): 63-82; auth, "Revolutionary Collectivism: Parisian Post Art in 1968", Contemp Fr Civilization, (96): 145-167; auth, "Quiet Fronts in the Spanish Civil War", Historian 61.4, (99): 821-841; auth, "Agrarian Collectives during the Spanish Revolution and Civil War", Europ Hist Quarterly, 30.2, 209-235; auth, "The Libertarian Pre-Revolution of 1968", China Scholar 1.2 (forthcoming). **CONTACT ADDRESS** Dept Hist, Univ of No Carolina, Wilmington, 601 S College Rd, Wilmington, NC 28403-3201. **EMAIL** seidmanm@uncwil.edu

SEIGLE, CECELIA
PERSONAL Born 12/13/1931, Japan, m, 1963 **DISCIPLINE** ASIAN STUDIES **EDUCATION** Miami Univ, AB, 57; Bryn Mawr Col, MA, 59; Univ Penn, PhD, 71. **CAREER** Lectr, 85, sr lectr, assoc prof, 95, prof emer, 99-, Univ Pa. **HONORS AND AWARDS** Provost Awd, Dist Teach. **MEMBERSHIPS** MAR; AAS. **RESEARCH** Japanese literature and cultural history. **SELECTED PUBLICATIONS** Transl, Yoshiwara - The Glittering World of the Japanese Courtesan (Univ Hawaii Press, 93); co-transl, The Temple of Dawn, by Yukio Mishima (Alfred Knopf, 73; London: Secker & Warbury, 74); transl, Darkness in Summer by Takeshi Kaiko (Alfred Knopf, 73; London: Peter Owen, 88; Tokyo: Charles E. Tuttle Co); transl, Into a Black Sun, by Takeshi Kaiko (Kodansha International, 80; Charles E Tuttle, 85); transl, Five Thousand Runaways, by Takeshi Kaiko (Dodd Mead, 87; London: Peter Owen, 90; Charles E. Tuttle Co); rev, Women of the Pleasure Quarter, ed. Elizabeth de Sabato Swinton (Worcester: Worcester Art Museum, and New York: Hudson Hill Press, 95; J Japanese Studies, 98); auth, Shogun's Ladies in Edo Castle, forthcoming; auth, Aru kojo to sono kazoku no shazo: Shinanomiva Chikako to shuhen no hitobito Iwanami (Shoten, forthcoming). **CONTACT ADDRESS** Dept Asian Studies, Univ of Pennsylvania, Williams Hall 847, Philadelphia, PA 19104-6305. **EMAIL** cseigle@sas.upenn.edu

SEIP, TERRY
PERSONAL Born 10/26/1944, Pawnee City, NE, m, 1966, 3 children **DISCIPLINE** HISTORY **EDUCATION** Kans State Univ, BA, 67; La State Univ, MA, 70; PhD, 74. **CAREER** From asst prof to assoc prof, Univ S Calif, 74-. **HONORS AND AWARDS** Warrick Memorial Fund Dissertation Fel, 73; La State Univ Dissertation Year Fel, 73-74; USC Dept of Hist Travel and Res Funds, 75, 77, 81, 83, 84, 88, 89; Haynes Found Summer Fel for Fac, 77; Award for Distinguished Teaching, USC, 81; Am Philos Soc Grant-in-Aid for Basic Res, 83; USC Phi Kappa Phi Fac Recognition Bk Award, 85; USC President's Circle Award, 85; USC President's Circle Fac Award for Teaching, Res, and Service, 85-86; USC Associates Award for Excellence in Teaching, 90; USC Skull and Dagger Initiate, 94; Am Hist Asn Nancy Lyman Roelker Mentorship Award for Undergraduate Teaching, 97; USC Latter-Day Saint Student Asn, Teacher of the Year, 98-99; USC Gamma Sigma Alpha, Prof of the Year, 98-99; USC Col Fac Res Account, 98, 99; USC Ctr for Excellence in Teaching, Fac Fel, CET Professorship, 97-99. **MEMBERSHIPS** Am Hist Asn, Orgn of Am Historians, Southern Hist Asn, Soc for Hist Educ. **RESEARCH** American Civil War and Reconstruction, American South, Teaching. **SELECTED PUBLICATIONS** Auth, The South Returns to Congress, 83; auth, Men, Economic Measures, and Intersectional Relationships, 1868-1879, 83; auth, "We Shall Gladly Teach": Preparing History Graduate Students for the Classroom, 99. **CONTACT ADDRESS** Dept Hist, Univ of So California, 3502 Trousdale Pkwy, Los Angeles, CA 90089-0034. **EMAIL** tseip@usc.edu

SEIPP, DAVID J.
PERSONAL Born 10/19/1955, Dubuque, IA, m, 1994 **DISCIPLINE** LEGAL HISTORY **EDUCATION** Harvard Col, AB, 77; Merton Col Oxford, BA, 79; St. Johns' Col Cambridge, LLB, 80; Harvard Law Sch, JD, 82. **CAREER** Law clerk, U.S. Court of Appeals, 82-83; assoc, Foley, Hoag, and Eliot, 83-86; assoc prof, Boston Univ Sch Law, 86-92; prof, 92- . **MEMBERSHIPS** Selden Soc; Am Soc for Legal Hist; Am Law Inst. **RESEARCH** Legal history. **SELECTED PUBLICATIONS** Auth, The Concept of Property in the Early Common Law, Law and Hist Rev, 94; auth, Crime in the Year Books, Law Reporting in Britain: Proceedings of the Eleventh British Legal History Conference, 95; auth, The Distinction Between Crime and Tort in Early Common Law, Boston Univ Law Rev, 96; auth, Holmes's Path, Boston Univ Law Rev, 97; auth, The Mirror of Justices, Learning the Law: Proceedings of the Thirteenth British Legal History Conference, 99. **CONTACT ADDRESS** School of Law, Boston Univ, 765 Commonwealth Ave, Rm 934B, Boston, MA 02215. **EMAIL** dseipp@bu.edu

SELBY, JOHN EDWARD
PERSONAL Born 01/01/1929, Boston, MA, m, 1954, 4 children **DISCIPLINE** EARLY AMERICAN HISTORY **EDUCATION** Harvard Univ, AB, 50; Brown Univ, MA, 51, PhD(hist), 55. **CAREER** From instr to asst prof hist, Univ Ore, 55-61; asst dir res, Colonial Williamsburg, 61-65; assoc prof, 65-70, actg dean grad studies, 68-70, grad dean arts & sci, 71-81, Prof Hist, Col William & Mary, 70-, Book rev ed, William & Mary Quart, 65-70, 71-99, actg ed, 70-71; Prof Emeritus, 99-. **MEMBERSHIPS** AHA **RESEARCH** The American Revolution; 18th century Virginia. **SELECTED PUBLICATIONS** Auth, The Revolution in Virginia, 1775-1783, 88; coauth, Colonial Virginia: A History, 86. **CONTACT ADDRESS** Dept of Hist, Col of William and Mary, Williamsburg, VA 23185. **EMAIL** jeselb@wm.edu

SELBY, JOHN G.
PERSONAL Born 12/06/1955, Detroit, MI, m, 1990, 1 child **DISCIPLINE** HISTORY **EDUCATION** Univ Ariz, BA, 80; Duke Univ, MA, 81; PhD, 84. **CAREER** Visiting Asst Prof, Guilford Col, 84-85; Visiting Asst Prof, Duke Univ, 85-86; Visiting Prof to Prof, Roanoke Col, 86-. **HONORS AND AWARDS** Albert J Beveridge Grant, AHA, 83-84; NATO Discussion Series Travel Grant, 89; Roanoke Col Fac Scholar, 97-. **MEMBERSHIPS** OAH, SHA, VHS. **RESEARCH** Civil War; 19th Century South; Social History. **CONTACT ADDRESS** Dept Hist, Roanoke Col, 221 Col Lane, Salem, VA 24153-3747. **EMAIL** selby@roanoke.edu

SELINGER, SUZANNE
PERSONAL Born 01/31/1940, New York, NY **DISCIPLINE** HISTORY **EDUCATION** Vassar Col, BA, 60; Yale Univ, MA, 61, PhD, 65; Columbia Univ, MSLS, 74. **CAREER** Asst prof, hist, Douglass Col, 66-70; ref librn, Yale Univ Libr, 74-81; asst ed, Frederick Douglass Papers, Yale Univ, 83-84; theol librn, assoc prof, hist theol, Drew Univ, 87- . **MEMBERSHIPS** AHA; Karl Barth Soc of N Am; Am Theological Library Asn. **RESEARCH** Twentieth-century theology; twentieth-century intellectual and cultural hist; feminist theory. **SELECTED PUBLICATIONS** Auth, Calvin Against Himself: An Inquiry in Intellectual History, Archon, 84; asst ed, The Frederick Douglass Papers, Series One: Speeches, Debates, and Interviews, v.4, 1864-80, Yale, 91; auth, Charlotte von Kirschbaum and Karl Barth: A Study in Biography and the History of Theology, Penn State, 98. **CONTACT ADDRESS** University Library, Drew Univ, Madison, NJ 07940. **EMAIL** sselinge@drew.edu

SELLER, MAXINE SCHWARTZ
PERSONAL Born 05/23/1935, Wilmington, NC, m, 1956, 3 children **DISCIPLINE** AMERICAN HISTORY **EDUCATION** Bryn Mawr Col, BA, 56; Univ Pa, MA, 57, PhD(hist), 65. **CAREER** From instr to asst prof hist, Temple Univ, 64-66; from assoc prof to prof, Bucks County Community Col, 66-74; asst prof, 74-77, assoc prof, 77-82, Prof Social Educ, State Univ NY, Buffalo, 82-, Mem teaching div, Am Hist Asn, 74-77; secy, Hist Educ Div, Am Educ Res Asn, 78-79. **MEMBERSHIPS** Am Hist Asn; Am Educ Res Asn; Immigration Hist Soc; Orgn Am Historians; Am Jewish Hist Soc. **RESEARCH** History of ethnic groups in United States; history of women in United States; history of education of women and minorities in United States. **SELECTED PUBLICATIONS** Auth, Isaac Leeser's views on the restoration of a Jewish Palestine, Am Jewish Hist Quart, 9/68; Beyond the stereotype: A new look at the immigrant women 1880-1924, J Ethnic Studies, spring 75; The education of Polish, Italian and Jewish immigrant children in Buffalo, NY, 1890-1916, NY Hist, 4/76; To Seek America: A History of Ethnic Life in the United States, Jerome Ozer, 77; The education of the immigrant woman, 1890-1930, J Urban Hist, 5/78; ed, Immigrant Women, Temple Univ Press, 81; Ethnic Theatre in the United States, Greenwood Press, 82; auth, G Stanley Hall and Edward Thorndike on the education of women: Theory and policy in the Progressive Era, Educ Studies, winter 81. **CONTACT ADDRESS** Dept Social Found, SUNY, Buffalo, PO Box 601000, Buffalo, NY 14260-1000.

SELYA, ROGER M.
PERSONAL Born 06/21/1942, Newton, MA, m, 1970, 3 children **DISCIPLINE** GEOGRAPHY **EDUCATION** Boston Univ, AB, 64; Harvard Univ, AM, 66; Univ Min, PhD, 71. **CAREER** Vis Schl, Inst Econ, Taipei, 91; assoc prof, Univ Cinci, 81-92; vis schl, Harvard Univ, 99-00; prof, Univ Cinci, 92-. **HONORS AND AWARDS** Excel Univ Teach Awd. **MEMBERSHIPS** AAG; AAS; AAAG. **RESEARCH** Economic development of East Asia and its consequences. **SELECTED PUBLICATIONS** Auth, "Where Do We Go Now? Issues in Establishing a New Jewish "Center" in Cincinnati, Ohio," in Land and Community, Geography in Jewish Studies, ed. Harold Brodsky (College Park: Univ Maryland Press, 97); auth, "Economic Restructuring and Spatial Changes in Manufacturing in Taiwan, 1971-1986," Geoforum 24 (93): 115-26; auth, "Abnormally Elevated Sex Ratios in Taiwan: An Exploratory Review," Am Asian Rev 12 (94): 201-22; auth, "Taiwan as a Service Economy," Geoforum 25 (94): 305-22, reprinted in: Econ Geog Reader: Producing and Consuming Global Capitalism, eds. J Bryson, N Henry, D Keeble, R Martin (Chichester: John Wiley and Sons Ltd, 99). **CONTACT ADDRESS** Dept Geography, Univ of Cincinnati, PO Box 210131, Cincinnati, OH 45221-0131. **EMAIL** selyarm@uc.edu

SEMONCHE, JOHN ERWIN
PERSONAL Born 02/09/1933, Alpha, NJ, m, 1962, 1 child **DISCIPLINE** AMERICAN HISTORY **EDUCATION** Brown Univ, AB, 54; Northwestern Univ, MA, 55, PhD, 62; Duke Univ, LLB, 67. **CAREER** Instr hist, Univ Conn, 60-61; from instr to asst prof hist & mod civilization, 61-68, assoc prof, 68-73, Prof Hist, Univ NC Chapel Hill, 73-, Lectr sch law, Univ NC, Chapel Hill, 67-78; attorney, 67- **HONORS AND AWARDS** Phi Beta Kappa, Order of the Coif, 1988 EDUCOM/NCRIPTAL Awd for Distinguished Software. **RESEARCH** American legal and constitutional history; jurisprudence. **SELECTED PUBLICATIONS** Auth, Keeping the Faith: A Cultural History of the U.S. Supreme Court, 98; auth, Religion and Constitutional Government in the United States, 85; auth, Charting the Future: The Supreme Court Respondes to a Changing Society, 1890-1920, 78; auth, Ray Stannard Baker: A Quest for Democracy in Modern America, 1870-1918, 69. **CONTACT ADDRESS** Dept of Hist, Univ of No Carolina, Chapel Hill, Chapel Hill, NC 27599-3195. **EMAIL** semche@email.unc.edu

SENGUPTA, GUNJA
PERSONAL Born Calcutta, India, s **DISCIPLINE** HISTORY **EDUCATION** Univ Bombay, BA, 85; Tulane Univ, PhD, 91. **CAREER** Assoc prof, Tex A & M Univ, 96-98; asst prof, Brooklyn Col CUNY, 98-. **HONORS AND AWARDS** Paul Barrus Distinguished Fac Awd for Teaching, Tex A & M Univ, 98. **MEMBERSHIPS** AHA, Orgn of Am Historians. **RESEARCH** US Civil War, African American social history. **SELECTED PUBLICATIONS** Auth, Evangelicals & Entrepreneurs, Masters & Slaves in Territorial Kansas, Univ of Georgia Pr, 96. **CONTACT ADDRESS** Dept Hist, Brooklyn Col, CUNY, 2901 Bedford Ave, Brooklyn, NY 11210-2813. **EMAIL** sengupta@brooklyn.cuny.edu

SENIE, HARRIET F.
PERSONAL Born 09/23/1943, New York, NY, d, 1 child **DISCIPLINE** ART HISTORY, CONTEMPORARY ART **EDUCATION** Brandeis Univ, BA, 64; Hunter Col, MA, 71; Inst of Fine Arts, PhD, 81. **CAREER** Gallery dir, asst prof of art hist, SUNY at Old Westbury, 79-82; assoc dir, The Art Museum, Princeton Univ, 82-85; Visting Prof, 94-97; Prof, Cuny Grad Center, 97-; Dir, Museum Studies Prog, Prof of Art Hist, City Col, NY, 86-. **HONORS AND AWARDS** PSC CUNY Res Grant, 88, 91, 94, & 96; Rifkind Scholars Awd, City Col, 93; Eisner Scholars Awd, 89; NEA Museum Studies Grant, 87; Pres Grant for Innovative Teaching, 86; Princeton Univ Spears Fund Res Grant, 83; Kress Found Res Grant, 78-79; Inst of Fine Arts, 74 78; NY Univ, 73 74. **MEMBERSHIPS** Col Art Asn; Am Studies Asn; Am Asn of Museums; Art Table; Coun of SUNY Gallery and Exhibition Dirs. **SELECTED PUBLICATIONS** coed & contrib, Public Art and the Legal System, Public Art Rev, 94; auth, Eden Revisited: The Contemporary Garden as Public Art, Urban Paradise, Public Art Issues, 94; contribur, Encycl of New York City, Yale Univ Press, 95; contrib, Dictionary of Women Artists, Fitzroy Dearborn Pub, 97; Public Art in Brazil, Sculpture, 98; Smithsonian 98; auth, "In Pursuit of Memory: Berlin, Bamberg, & the Specter of History," Sculpture Apr 99; auth, "Disturbances in the Fields of Marmon: Towards a History of Artists' Billboards," in Laura Heon, ed., Billboard: Art on the Road, Met Press, 99; auth, "Mourning in Protest Spontaneous Memorials and the Sacralization of Public Space," Harvard Design Magazine, Octoer 99; auth, "Perpetual Tension: Considering Richard Serras Jewish Identity," in Matthew Bargeel & Melly Heyd, eds., Complex: Jewish Consciousness & Modern Art, Rutgers, 00. **CONTACT ADDRESS** 215 Sackett St., Brooklyn, NY 11231-3604. **EMAIL** hfsenie@interport.net

SENN, ALFRED ERICH
PERSONAL Born 04/12/1932, Madison, WI, m, 1957, 3 children **DISCIPLINE** MODERN EUROPEAN HISTORY **EDUCATION** Univ Pa, BA, 53; Columbia Univ, cert & MA, 55, PhD(mod Europ hist), 58. **CAREER** Lectr hist, Hunger Col, 58; from instr to asst prof, Newark Col Arts & Sci, Rutgers Univ, 58-61; from asst prof to assoc prof, 61-67, chmn Russ area studies prog, 66-69, Prof Hist, Univ Wis-Madison, 67-, Vis lectr, Princeton Univ, 60; adj asst prof, Fordham Univ, 61; Fulbright res fel, Ger, 63-64; Guggenheim Found fel, 69-70. **MEMBERSHIPS** Am Asn Advan Slavic Studies. **RESEARCH** Twentieth century Eastern Europe. **SELECTED PUBLICATIONS** Auth, Emergence of Modern Lithuania, Columbai Univ, 59; The Great Powers, Lithuania and the Vilna question, E J Brill, Leiden 66; The Russian Revolution in Switzerland, 1914-1917, Univ Wis, 71; Diplomacy and Revolution, Notre Dame Univ, 74. **CONTACT ADDRESS** Dept of Hist, Univ of Wisconsin, Madison, 455 North Park St, Madison, WI 53706-1483.

SENTILLES, RENEE M.
DISCIPLINE HISTORY **EDUCATION** Mt. Holyoke Col, BA, 88; Utah State Univ, MA, 91; Wm & Mary Col, PhD, 97. **CAREER** VIS ASST PROF, HIST, FRANKLIN & MARSHALL COLL **MEMBERSHIPS** Am Antiquarian Soc **RESEARCH** Adah Isaacs Menken **CONTACT ADDRESS** Hist & Am Stud, Franklin and Marshall Col, PO Box 3003, Lancaster, PA 17604-3003.

SERAILE, WILLIAM
PERSONAL Born 03/12/1941, New Orleans, LA, m, 1970, 2 children **DISCIPLINE** AFRICAN-AMERICAN & AMERICAN HISTORY **EDUCATION** Cent Wash State Univ, BA, 63; Columbia Univ, MA, 67; City Univ New York, PhD(Am hist), 77. **CAREER** Assoc ed, Silver Burdette Company, Morristown, 70-71; from lectr to prof African-Am hist, Herbert H Lehman Col, 71-; contrib ed, Afro-Am NY Life & Hist, 82-. **MEMBERSHIPS** Asn Study Afro-Am Life & Hist. **RESEARCH** African-American politics. **SELECTED PUBLICATIONS** Auth, The Voice of Dissent: Theophilus Gould Steward and Black Am, Carlson Publ (Brooklyn, NYork), 91; rev, Bright Radical Star - Black-Freedom And White Supremacy On The Hawkeye Frontier - Dykstra,Rr/, Montana-The Mag Of Western Hist, Vol 0045, 1995; auth, Fire in His Heart: Bishop Benjamin Tucker Tanner and the Am Church, Univ Tenn Pr (Knoxville), 98. **CONTACT ADDRESS** Dept Black Studies, Lehman Col, CUNY, 250 Bedford Park W, Bronx, NY 10468-1527.

SEREBRENNIKOV, NINA EUGENIA
DISCIPLINE ART HISTORY **EDUCATION** George Washington Univ, BA; Univ NC Chapel Hill, MSLS, MA, PhD. **CAREER** Assoc prof, Davidson Col. **RESEARCH** Medieval, Renaissance, and Baroque art; issues of gender. **SELECTED PUBLICATIONS** Auth, publ(s) about 16th-century Flemish painting, espec the work of Peter Bruegel the Elder. **CONTACT ADDRESS** Davidson Col, 102 N Main St, PO Box 1719, Davidson, NC 28036. **EMAIL** niserebrennikov@davidson.edu

SERELS, M. MITCHELL
PERSONAL Born 01/12/1948, New York, NY, m, 1979, 4 children **DISCIPLINE** PSYCHOLOGY; HISTORY **EDUCATION** Yeshiva Univ, BA, 67, MS, 70; Hunter Col, MA, 71; NYork Univ, PhD, 90. **CAREER** Assoc Dir, Jacob E Safea Inst of Sephardic Stud, Yeshiva Univ, 73-; Univ Dir of Foreign Stud Svcs, Yeshiva Univ, 92-99; Chair, Dept of History, Berkely College. **HONORS AND AWARDS** Knighted, Caballero de order de Merito Civil, by King Juan Carlos I of Spain. **MEMBERSHIPS** Am Soc of Sephardic Stud; Nat Asn of Foreign Stud Advisors. **RESEARCH** Jews of Spanish origin; Morocco; W Africa. **SELECTED PUBLICATIONS** Auth, Sephardim and the Holocaust, NY, 94; auth, Historia de los Judios de Tanger, Caracos, 96; auth, Jews of Cape Verde: A Brief History, NY, 97; auth, Studies on the History of Portuguese Jews. **CONTACT ADDRESS** Berkeley Col, White Plains, 40 Red Oak Lane, White Plains, NY 10604. **EMAIL** mitchser@aol.com

SERVLNIKOV, SERGIO
PERSONAL Born 05/09/1961, Argentina **DISCIPLINE** HISTORY **EDUCATION** Universidad de Buenos Aires, Licencido, 98; New York State Univ, PhD, 98 **CAREER** Asst prof, Univ Ky **HONORS AND AWARDS** James D. Robertson Memorial Prize; Conference of Latin Am Hist **MEMBERSHIPS** Am Hist Asn **RESEARCH** Latin Am Hist **SELECTED PUBLICATIONS** Auth, art, When Looting Became a Right. Food Riots and Urvan Poverty in Argentina, 94; Auth, art, Disputed Images of Colonialism. Spanish Rule in Indian Subversion in Northern Potosi, 1777-1780, 96; auth, art, Su verdad y su justicia. Tomas Katari y la in **CONTACT ADDRESS** Dept of History, Univ of Kentucky, Lexington, KY 40506-0027. **EMAIL** sseruln@pop.uky.edu

SESSIONS, KYLE CUTLER
PERSONAL Born 07/06/1934, Malad, ID, m, 1959, 3 children **DISCIPLINE** REFORMATION & RENAISSANCE HISTORY **EDUCATION** Ohio State Univ, BA, 56, MA, 59, PhD(Reformation hist), 63. **CAREER** Lectr hist, Huron Col, Ont, 63-64, asst prof, 64-67; dir honors, 73-78, assoc prof 67-88; prof hist, Ill State Univ, 88-99, ret. 99. **MEMBERSHIPS** Conf on Faith & Hist; Am Soc Reformation Res; 16th Century Studies Conf (pres, 69-71); Western Assoc for Ger Studies. **RESEARCH** Lutheran Reformation; music of the Reformation; Peasants' revolt; music, printing of the Reformation. **SELECTED PUBLICATIONS** Ed., Reformation and Authority: The Meaning of the Peasants' Revolt, 68; auth, Faces in the Peasants' Revolt, 76; coed, Pietas et Societas: New Trends in Reformation Social History, 88; auth, The Ger Peasants War And Anabaptist Community Of Goods - Stayer,Jm/, Am Hist Rev, Vol 0097, 1992; Germania-Illustrata - Essays On Early-Modern Germany Presented To Strauss,Gerald - Fix,Ac, Karant-nunn,Sc/, Cath Hist Rev, Vol 0080, 1994; auth, Looking Back: A 75th Anniversary History of Phi Eta Sigma National Honor Society, 98. **CONTACT ADDRESS** Dept of Hist, Illinois State Univ, Normal, IL 61790-4420.

SEWELL, RICHARD HERBERT
PERSONAL Born 04/11/1931, Ann Arbor, MI, m, 1971, 1 child **DISCIPLINE** AMERICAN HISTORY **EDUCATION** Univ Mich, AB, 53; Harvard Univ, MA, 54, PhD(hist), 62. **CAREER** Asst prof hist, Northern Ill Univ, 62-64; vis lectr, Univ Mich, 64-65; from asst prof to assoc prof, 65-74, Prof Hist, Univ Wis-Madison, 74-95; Prof Emer, 95-. **HONORS AND AWARDS** PBK **MEMBERSHIPS** Southern Hist Asn; Soc of Civil War Historians; State Hist Soc of Wis. **RESEARCH** United States political and social history, 1815-1877. **SELECTED PUBLICATIONS** Auth, A House Divided: Sectionalism and Civil War, 1848-1865, Johns Hopkins Univ, 88; auth, Sherman - Merchant Of Terror, Advocate Of Peace - Vetter,Ce/, J Of Southern H, Vol 0059, 1993; When The Yankees Came - Conflict And Chaos In The Occupied South, 1861-1865 - Ash,Sv/, Revs In Am Hist, Vol 0024, 1996; The Hard Hand Of War - Union Policy Toward Southern Civilians, 1861-1865 - Grimsley,M/, Revs In Am Hist, Vol 0024, 1996. **CONTACT ADDRESS** Dept of Hist, Univ of Wisconsin, Madison, Madison, WI 53706. **EMAIL** rhsewell@facstaff.wisc.edu

SEXTON, DONAL J.
PERSONAL Born 07/13/1939, Buffalo, NY, m, 1962, 2 children **DISCIPLINE** HISTORY **EDUCATION** Univ of Tenn, PhD, 75; Mich State Univ, MA, 65, BA, 63 **CAREER** Teaching asst, Univ Tenn, 72-73; Asst Prof to Full Prof, Tusculum Col, 65-. **HONORS AND AWARDS** Nat Alumni Facul Awd, 98; Moncado Prize awd, 94; Tenured, 70 **MEMBERSHIPS** WW2 Studs Asn; SHAFR. **RESEARCH** Intelligence, especially signals on communications intelligence, and covert and deception operations. **SELECTED PUBLICATIONS** Coauth, Glimpses of Tusculum Col, 94; auth, Signals Intelligence in World War II, 96. **CONTACT ADDRESS** Tusculum Col, Greenville, TN 37743-6126. **EMAIL** dsexton@tusculum.edu

SEYMOUR, JACK L.
PERSONAL Born 10/27/1948, Kokomo, IN, m, 1997, 2 children **DISCIPLINE** HISTORY AND PHILOSOPHY OF EDUCATION **EDUCATION** Ball State Univ, BS; Vanderbilt Divinity School, DMin & MDiv; George Peabody Col of Vanderbilt, PhD. **CAREER** Asst prof Church & Ministry, Vanderbilt Univ 74-78; Dir Field Educ, Chicago Theol Sem, 78-82; prof Christian Educ, assoc prof, asst prof, Scarritt Grad School, 82-88; prof Relig Educ, 88-, acad dean, 96-, Garrett-Evangelical Theol Sem, 88-. **RESEARCH** Theology of people of God; Ethnographic Research in education; Theological education. **SELECTED PUBLICATIONS** Coauth Educating Christians: The Intersection of Meaning, Learning, and Vocation, Abdington Press, 93; For the Life of a Child: The 'Religious' in the Education of the Public, Relig Educ, 94; Contemporary Approaches to Christian Education, Theological Perspectives on Christian Formation, W B Eerdmans, 96; The Ethnographer as Minister: Ethnographic Research in the Context of Ministry Vocations, Relig Educ, 96; Temples of Meaning: Theology and the People of God, Lib Relig Educ, 96; rev Essays on Religion and Education: An Issue in Honor of William Bean Kennedy, Relig Educ, 96; The Cry for Theology: Laity Speak about the Church, and The Cry for Theology: Laity Speak about Theology, PACE: Professional Approaches for Christian Education, 96; auth Mapping Christian Education: Approaches to Congregational Learning, Abingdon Press, 97; Thrashing in the Night: Laity Speak about Religious Knowing, Relig Educ, 97. **CONTACT ADDRESS** Garrett-Evangelical Theol Sem, 2121 Sheridan Rd, Evanston, IL 60201. **EMAIL** Jack-Seymour@garrett.edu

SHABAZZ, AMILEAR
PERSONAL Born 02/11/1960, TX, m, 2 children **DISCIPLINE** HISTORY **EDUCATION** Univ Tex, BA, 82; Lamar Univ, MA, 90; Univ Houston, PhD, 96. **CAREER** Lecturer, Lamar Univ, 89-91; Adj Instructor, Lee Col, 92; Instructor, Houston Cmty Col, 92; Instructor, Prairie View A & M Univ, 93-94; Res Assoc to Lecturer and Instructor, Univ Houston, 92-97; Asst Prof, Univ Ala, 97-. **HONORS AND AWARDS** NEH Summer Fel, Univ Calif; Mellon Fel, Univ Tex. **MEMBERSHIPS** Org of Am Hist, Nat Coun on Black Studies, Am Studies Asn, S Conf on African Am Studies. **SELECTED PUBLICATIONS** Co-ed, The Forty Acres documents: What Did the United States Really Promise the People Freed from Slavery?, Songhay, 94; auth, The Desegregation of Higher Education in Texas: A Statistical Summary and Research Report,

Univ Houston press, 92; rev, of "A Walk to Freedom: The Reverend Fred Shuttlesworth and the Alabama Christian Movement for Human Rights, 1956-1964," by Marjorie White, The Alabama Review, forthcoming; rev, of "From Selma to Sorrow: The Life and Death of Viola Liuzzo," by Mary Stanton, The Journal of Mississippi History, forthcoming; auth, "What is the Value and Meaning of Black History Month?," Mobile Register, 99; auth, "One for the Crows, One for the Crackers: The Strange Career of Public Higher Education in Houston, Texas," The Houston Review, (98): 124-143; auth, "The African American Educational Legacy in Beaumont, Texas: A Preliminary Analysis," Texas Gulf Historical and Biographical Record, (91): 56-76. **CONTACT ADDRESS** Dept Am Studies, Univ of Alabama, Tuscaloosa, PO Box 870214, Tuscaloosa, AL 35487-0154. **EMAIL** amil@bama.ua.edu

SHADBOLT, DOUGLAS
PERSONAL Born 04/18/1925, Victoria, BC, Canada **DISCIPLINE** ARCHITECTURE, HISTORY **EDUCATION** Univ BC; McGill Univ; Univ Ore, BArch, 57. **CAREER** Asst to assoc prof, McGill Univ, 58-61; prof & founding dir, sch archit, NS Tech Col, 61-68; prof & founding dir, sch archit, Carleton Univ, 68-79; dir, sch archit, 79-90, Prof Emer Architecture, Univ BC, 90-. **HONORS AND AWARDS** DEng(hon), NS Tech Col, 69; DEng(hon), Carleton Univ, 82; ACSA Distinguished Prof, 87. **SELECTED PUBLICATIONS** Auth, Ron Thom, The Shaping of an Architect, 95. **CONTACT ADDRESS** 4525 Gothard St, Vancouver, BC, Canada V5K 3K8.

SHADE, WILLIAM G.
PERSONAL Born 04/05/1939, Detroit, MI, m, 1962, 2 children **DISCIPLINE** AMERICAN HISTORY **EDUCATION** Brown Univ, AB, 61, MAT, 62; Wayne State Univ, PhD, 66. **CAREER** Instr hist, Temple Univ, 66-67; from instr to assoc prof, 67-76, prof hist Lehigh Univ, 76-, ed, Pa Hist, 68-72; mem adv bd nat parks, monuments & hist sites, Secy Interior, 71-77; vis assoc prof, Univ Va, 72-73. **HONORS AND AWARDS** Avery O Craven Awd, Org of Am Hist, 97; Eleanor and Joseph F Libsch Res Awd, Lehigh Univ, 97. **MEMBERSHIPS** AHA; Orgn Am Historians; Survey Studies Habits & Attitudes. **RESEARCH** Civil War and Reconstruction; American political development; 19th century social history. **CONTACT ADDRESS** Dept of History, Lehigh Univ, 9 W Packer Ave, Bethlehem, PA 18015-3081.

SHAFFER, ARTHUR
PERSONAL Born 03/18/1936 **DISCIPLINE** HISTORY **EDUCATION** Univ Calif Los Angeles, BA, 59; MA, 62; PhD, 66. **CAREER** From asst prof to assoc prof, 66-76, Prpf Hist, Univ MO, St. Louis, 76-, Nat Endowment for Humanities fel, 72-73. **HONORS AND AWARDS** SC Hist Soc Awd, 91. **SELECTED PUBLICATIONS** Auth, The Politics of History: Writing the History of the American Revolution, 1783-1815, 75; To Be An American: David Ramsay and the Making of an American National Consciousness, 91; Edmund Randolph's History of Virginia, Univ Va, 70; co-ed, Politics and Patronage in the Gilded Age: The Garfield-Henry Correspondence, Univ Wis Madison, 70. **CONTACT ADDRESS** History Dept, Univ of Missouri, St. Louis, 484 Lucas Hall, Saint Louis, MO 63121. **EMAIL** Shaffer@umslvma.umsl.edu

SHAFFER, NANCY E.
PERSONAL Born Los Angeles, CA **DISCIPLINE** THE HISTORY AND PHILOSOPHY OF SCIENCE **EDUCATION** Graceland Col, BS, 85; Rice Univ, MA, 87; Ariz State Univ, MA, 91; Univ Calif, Davis, PhD, 96. **CAREER** Instr, Concordia Univ, Montreal, Quebec; asst prof, Univ Nebr, Omaha. **MEMBERSHIPS** Philos of Sci Asn; Am Asn of Philos Tchr. **RESEARCH** Biased reasoning and error, Contextualism and Naturalism, Philosophy of the cognitive and social sciences. **SELECTED PUBLICATIONS** Auth, Bias in Scientific Practice, Philos of Sci; auth, "What is Bias," (forthcoming); auth, "Teaching Critical Thinking skills via the Internet," (forthcoming). **CONTACT ADDRESS** Dept of Philos and Relig, Univ of Nebraska, Omaha, Omaha, NE 68182-0265. **EMAIL** nshaffer@unomaha.edu

SHAFFER, THOMAS LINDSAY
PERSONAL Born 04/04/1934, Billings, MT, m, 1954, 8 children **DISCIPLINE** HISTORY **EDUCATION** Univ Albuquerque, BA, 58; Univ Notre Dame, JD, 61; St. Mary's Univ, Tex, LLD (honorary), 84. **CAREER** Univ Notre Dame, asst prof of law, 63-66, prof of law, 66-80, assoc dean, 69-71, dean, 71-75, Robert and Marion Short prof of law, 88-97, Robert and Marion Short prof of law emer, 97-, supv atty, Notre Dame Legal Aid Clinic, 91-; Univ Calif Los Angeles, visiting prof of law, 70-71; Univ Va, visiting prof of law, 75-76; Washington and Lee Univ, Frances Lewis scholar, fall 79, prof of law, 80-87, Robert E. R. Huntley prof of law, 87-88, dir, Frances Lewis Law Ctr, 83-85; Univ Maine, visiting prof of law, summer 82 & 86, fall 98; Boston Col, Richard Huber Distinguished Visiting Prof of Law, fall, 92; **HONORS AND AWARDS** Phi Beta Kappa; Order of the Coif; Emil Brown Prize in preventive law, 66; pres citation, Univ Notre Dame, 75; Gallagher lectr, Soc for Adolescent Med, 76; Or Emet lectr, York Univ, 79; Rightor Lectr, Loyola Univ, 79; Seegers lectr, Valparaiso Univ, 81; Sullivan lectr, Capital Univ, 82; Cunningham lectr, Queen's Univ, 84; Burch lectr, Vanderbilt Univ, 84; Blankenbaker lectr, Univ Mont, 85; Law Forum lectr, Oh State Univ, 88; Currie lectr, Univ Miss, 89; Vasey Sumposium lectr, Univ Dayton, 89; Lichtenstein lectr, Hofstra Univ, 89; Tabor lectr, Valparaiso Univ, 97; Law and Soc lectr, William Mitchell Col of Law, 91; St. Thomas More award and honorary doctorate, St. Mary's Univ of Tex, 83; Law medal, Gonzaga Univ, 91; Reinhold Niebuhr award, Univ Notre Dame, 91; Teacher of the year, Notre Dame Law Sch, 91; Jour of Law and Relig award, 93; Hon Order of Ky Colonels; Admiral of the Tex Navy; Honorary Oakie From Muskogee. **MEMBERSHIPS** Nat Lawyers Asn; Amer Law Inst; Amer Col of Probate Coun; Amer Bar Asn; Asn of Amer Law Sch; Univ of Miami Sch of Law; Practicing Law Inst; Bar Asn of the Seventh Fed Circuit; Soc for Values in Higher Educ; Christ Legal Soc; Ind State Bar Asn; Cath Comn on Intellectual and Cultural Affairs; St. Joseph County Bar Asn; Soc of Christ Ethics; Jewish Law Asn. **RESEARCH** Property, ethics, law and poverty. **SELECTED PUBLICATIONS** Auth, Sermon, Red Mass for the judges and lawyers of the Twin Cities, St. Paul, 28 sep, 97; auth, The Christian Jurisprudence of Robert E. Rodes, Jr.; auth, Professor Frank Booker: A Colleague's Reflection, Notre Dame Lawyer, 12, spring, 97; auth, On Living One Way in Town and Another Way at Home, Inaugural Glenn Tabor Lecture in Legal Ethics, Valparaiso Univ, 31 feb, 97; auth, The Ethical Preparation of Lawyers, Seventh Circuit Judicial Conf, 13 oct, 96; auth, Morality in the Practice of Law, Faith and Ethics Series, First Presbyterian Church, Bethlehem, Penn, 29 sep, 96; auth, Stories of Legal Order in American Business, Univ Notre Dame, 30 sep-1 oct, 96; auth, H. Jefferson Powell on The American Constitutional Tradition: A Conversation, 72, Notre Dame Law Rev, 11, 96; rev, Greenawalt, Private Consciences and Public Reasons, 38, Jour of Church and State, 413, 96; auth, Surprised by Joy on Howard Street, CSC, Labors from the Heart: Mission and Ministry in a Catholic Univ, 96; auth, On Teaching Legal Ethics in the Law Office, 71, Notre Dame Law Rev, 605, 96; co-auth, Is This Appropriate?, 46, Duke Law Jour, 781, 97; co-auth, A Reply to Professor Sammons: Lawyers As Strangers and friends, 18, Univ Ark Little Rock Law Rev, 69, 95; auth, Maybe a Lawyer Can Be a Servant; If Not.., 27, Tex Tech Law Rev, 1345, 96; auth, On Lying for Clients, Conference on Legal Ethics, Hofstra Univ, mar, 96; rev, Kellerman, A Keeper of the Word, Christ Legal Soc Quart, summer, 95; rev, Kronman, The Lost Lawyer: Failing Ideals of the Legal Profession, 41, Loyola Univ Law Rev, 387, 95. **CONTACT ADDRESS** Law School, Univ of Notre Dame, Notre Dame, IN 46556.

SHAHID, IRFAN ARIF
PERSONAL Born 01/15/1926, Nazareth, Palestine, m, 1976 **DISCIPLINE** HISTORY, LITERATURE **EDUCATION** Oxford Univ, BA, 51; Princeton Univ, PhD, 54. **CAREER** Jr fel Arab-Byzantine rel, Ctr Byzantine Studies, 59-60; assoc prof, Ind Univ, Bloomington, 60-62; assoc prof, 62-66, prof Arabic, Georgetown Univ, 66-, Fulbright-Hays fel Arabic-Am lit, US Off Educ, 68-69; vis fel, Inst Advan Studies, Princeton, 76; Sultanate of Oman prof Arabic & Islamic lit, Georgetow Univ, 81- **HONORS AND AWARDS** Andrew W Mellon Fund Distinguished Lectureship in Lang & Ling, Sch Lang & Ling, Georgetown Univ, 77-79. **MEMBERSHIPS** Am Orient Soc; Mediaeval Acad Am; Mid East Studies Asn NAm; Mid East Inst; Am Asn Tchr(s) Arabic; Life mem, Clare Hall, Cambridge Univ, Engl, 89. **RESEARCH** Arab hist; Arab-Byzantine rel; Arabic lit. **SELECTED PUBLICATIONS** Auth, The martyrs of Najran: new documents, In: Subsidia Hagiographica, 71; Epistula de re publica genereda, In: Themistii Orationes, Vol III, Teubner Class Ser, 74; Rome and the Arabs, 84, Byzantium and the Arabs in the Fourth Century, 84, Byzantium and the Arabs in the Fifth Century, 89, Byzantium and the Arabs in the Sixth Century, 95, Dumbarton Oaks. **CONTACT ADDRESS** Dept of Arab Lang, Lit & Ling, Georgetown Univ, Washington, DC 20057-1046. **EMAIL** shahidi@gunet.georgetown.edu

SHALHOPE, ROBERT E.
PERSONAL Born 02/24/1941, Kansas City, MO, m, 1963, 2 children **DISCIPLINE** HISTORY **EDUCATION** DePauw Univ, BA, 63; Univ MO, MA, 64, PhD, 67. **CAREER** Univ OK, 67-, George Lynn Cross prof of History, 91-. **HONORS AND AWARDS** Fel, Charles Warren Center for Studies in American History, Harvard Univ; NEH fel; Am Antiquarian Soc; NEH summer fel. **MEMBERSHIPS** Org of Am Hist; Omohunduo Inst of Am Hist and Culture; Am Antiquarian Soc. **RESEARCH** American political culture throughout the period 1760-1876. **SELECTED PUBLICATIONS** Auth, The Roots of Democracy: American Culture and Thought, 1760-1800, Twayne, 90; Bennington and the Green Mountain Boys: The Emergence of Liberal Democracy in Vermont, 1760-1850, Johns Hopkins Univ Press, 96. **CONTACT ADDRESS** Dept of History, Univ of Oklahoma, W Lindsey, Rm. 403A, Norman, OK 73019. **EMAIL** robert-shalhope@ou.edu

SHANAFELT, GARY
PERSONAL Born 08/03/1947, Orange, CA, m, 1983, 1 child **DISCIPLINE** HISTORY **EDUCATION** Univ Calif at Irvine, BA, 69; Univ Calif at Berkeley, MA, 70; PhD, 77. **CAREER** Vis asst prof, Univ of Wyo, 79-80; vis asst prof, Wash Univ in St Louis, 80-81; vis asst prof to prof, McMurry Univ, 81-. **HONORS AND AWARDS** Ford Career Fel, 69-74; Fulbright Fel, 75-76. **MEMBERSHIPS** Am Hist Asn, Ger Studies Asn. **RESEARCH** Austria-Hungary, World War I. **SELECTED PUBLICATIONS** Auth, The Secret Enemy: Austria-Hungary and the German Alliance 1914-1918, E Europ Monographs/ Columbia Univ Press, 85. **CONTACT ADDRESS** Dept Hist, McMurry Univ, PO Box 638, Abilene, TX 79697-0001. **EMAIL** gshan@mcmurry.mcm.edu

SHANK, WESLEY I.
PERSONAL Born 03/01/1927, San Francisco, CA, m, 1949, 3 children **DISCIPLINE** ARCHITECTURE **EDUCATION** Univ Calif - Berkeley, BA, 51; McGill Univ, MArch, 65. **CAREER** Draftsman, architect, architectural specifications writer in San Francisco Bay area, 51-63; Prof, 64-92, Prof Archit Emeritus, Iowa State Univ, 92-; architect and architectural historian, Nat Park Service, Historic Am Buildings Survey field offices across the U.S., 67-82. **MEMBERSHIPS** Soc Archit Hist; Am Inst Archit. **RESEARCH** Historic American architecture and architects. **SELECTED PUBLICATIONS** Auth, Hugh Garden in Iowa, Prairie Sch Rev 5, 68; The Residence in Des Moines, J Soc Archit Hist 29, 70; Eighteenth-Century Architecture of the Upper Delaware River Valley of New Jersey and Pennsylvania, J Soc Archit Hist 31, 72; compiler, The Iowa Catalog: Historic American Buildings Survey, Univ Iowa Press, 79; Cochrane & Piquenard, Edmond Jacques Eckel, Edward Townsend Mix, and John Francis Rague, entries in: Macmillan Encyclopedia of Architects, The Free Press, 82; The Demise of the County Courthouse Tower in Iowa: A Study in Early Twentieth Century Cultural and Architectural Change, The Annals of Iowa, Spring 92; Eckel & Mann, In: Dictionary of Art, Grove, 96; Iowa's Historic Architects: A Biographical Dictionary, Univ Iowa Press, 99; Edward Townsend Mix, In: American National Biography, Oxford Univ Press (forthcoming 99). **CONTACT ADDRESS** 1904 Northcrest Cir, Ames, IA 50010-5113. **EMAIL** wshank@iastate.edu

SHANNON, CATHERINE BARBARA
PERSONAL Born Hingham, MA **DISCIPLINE** HISTORY **EDUCATION** Univ Toronto, BA, 60; Nat Univ Ireland, Dublin, MA, 63; Univ Mass, 63, PhD(hist), 75. **CAREER** Teacher hist, Holbrook High Sch, 64-67; Prof, Brit & Irish Hist, Westfield State Col, 67- . **HONORS AND AWARDS** Westfield State Col fac res grant, 74; Solas Awd from Irish Immigration Center, 94; Irish American Partnership Heritage Cup Awd, 98; "Dreamer of Dreams Awd", 99; Westfeld St College Foundation Research Awd, 00. **MEMBERSHIPS** AHA; Irish Hist Soc; Am Comt Irish Studies; New England Conference for Irish Studies. **RESEARCH** Political and social history of modern Ireland; Northern Ireland 1820-1922; British Unionist party politics, 1820-1922-. **SELECTED PUBLICATIONS** Auth, Ulster Liberal Unionists and Local Government Reform, 1885-1898, Irish Hist Studies, 3/73; auth, Arthur J. Balfour and Ireland, 1874-1922, Catholic Univ of Am Press, 88. **CONTACT ADDRESS** 577 Western Ave, Westfield, MA 01085-2501. **EMAIL** cbs38@aol.com

SHANNON, SYLVIA C.
DISCIPLINE HISTORY **EDUCATION** Georgetown Univ, AB, 74; Boston Univ, PhD, 88. **CAREER** Asst prof to assoc prof, St Anselm Col, 91-. **RESEARCH** Early mod Europ hist, espec Renaissance and Reformation hist; confessional struggle between Calvinists and Cath(s) in France on the colonial efforts made by the French Crown in Brazil. **SELECTED PUBLICATIONS** Auth, Military Outpost or Religious Refuge?: the Expedition of Villegagnon to Rio de Janeiro in 1555, Proceedings Fr Colonial Hist Soc, 96; auth, "Villegagnon, Polyphemus and Cain of America: Religion and Polemics in the French New World," in Changing Identities in Early Modern France, ed. Michael Wolfe (Duke Univ Press, 96); auth, "Military Outpost of Protestant Refuge: the Expedition of Villegagnon to Brazil in 1555," in Essays in French Colonial History, ed. J. Johnston (Mich State Press, 97). **CONTACT ADDRESS** Dept of Hist, Saint Anselm Col, 100 Saint Anselm Dr, Manchester, NH 03102-1310. **EMAIL** sshannon@anselm.edu

SHANNON, TIMOTHY J.
PERSONAL Born 07/31/1964, Morristown, NJ, m, 1989, 2 children **DISCIPLINE** AMERICAN HISTORY **EDUCATION** Northwestern Univ PhD, 93. **CAREER** Asst Prof hist, Gettysburg College. **HONORS AND AWARDS** Recipient of Dixon Ryan Fox Prize, New York State Historical Assoc; 98. **MEMBERSHIPS** OAH **RESEARCH** Native American History; American Colonial History. **SELECTED PUBLICATIONS** Auth, The Crossroads of Empire: Indians Colonists and the Albany Congress of 1754, Cornell Univ Press, forthcoming; auth, Dressing for Success on the Mohawk Frontier: Hendrick William Johnson and the Indian Fashion, William and Mary Qtly, 96; This Unpleasant Business: The Transformation of Land Speculation in the Ohio Country, in: The Pursuit of Public Power: The Origins of Politics in Ohio, eds, Jeffrey P Brown, Andrew R L Clayton, Kent State Univ Press, 94; auth, The Ohio Company and the Meaning of Opportunity in the American West, New Eng Qtly, 91; auth, Change, forthcoming, 00. **CONTACT ADDRESS** History Dept, Gettysburg Col, Gettysburg, PA 17325. **EMAIL** tshannon@gettysburg.edu

SHANTZ, DOUGLAS H.
PERSONAL Born 01/11/1952, Kitchener, ON, Canada, m, 1974, 4 children **DISCIPLINE** HISTORY **EDUCATION**

Wheaton Col, BA, 73; Westminster Theological Sem, MA; Univ of Waterloo, MA, 80, PhD, 87. **CAREER** Asst Prof of Theol, 83-86, NW Baptist Theol; Assoc Prof of Relig Studies, 86-98, Trinity West Univ; assoc prof, Univ of Calgary, Endowed Chair of Christian Thought, 99-. **HONORS AND AWARDS** SSHRC Small Grant; **MEMBERSHIPS** AAR; Soc for Reformation Res; Am Soc of Church Hist **RESEARCH** Radical Reform; German Pietism and Millenialism **SELECTED PUBLICATIONS** Auth, "Crautwald, Valentin," Oxford Encyclopedia of the Reformation, Oxford Univ Press, 96; Auth, "The Crautwald-Bucer Correspondence 1528 A Family Feud Within the Zwingli Circle," Mennonite Quarterly Review, 94, 79-94 **CONTACT ADDRESS** Trinity Western Univ, 7600 Glove, Langley, BC, Canada V2Y 1Y1. **EMAIL** shantz@twu.ca

SHAPERE, DUDLEY
PERSONAL Born 05/17/1928, Harlingen, TX, m, 4 children **DISCIPLINE** PHILOSOPHY, HISTORY **EDUCATION** Harvard Univ, BA, 49; Ma, 54; PhD, 57. **CAREER** Instr, Ohio St Univ, 57-60; Asst Prof to Prof, Univ Chicago, 60-72; Prof, Univ Ill, 72-75; Prof, Univ Md, 75-84; Prof, Wake Forest Univ, 84-. **HONORS AND AWARDS** Fel, Am Asn for the Advan of Sci, 70; Nat Sci Found Grants, 70-72, 73, 74-75, 76-78, 85-86; Res Fel, Universidad Autonoma de Mexico, 81, 86; Otto G Neugebauer Fel, Inst for Advan Study, forthcoming. **MEMBERSHIPS** APA, PSA, Hist of Sci Soc, APA, Am Asn for the Advan of Sci. **CONTACT ADDRESS** Dept Philos & Hist, Wake Forest Univ, Drawer 7229, Reynolds Station, Winston-Salem, NC 27109. **EMAIL** shapere@wfu.edu

SHAPIRO, BARBARA JUNE
PERSONAL Born 08/07/1934, Chicago, IL, m, 1955, 1 child **DISCIPLINE** ENGLISH HISTORY **EDUCATION** Univ Calif, Los Angeles, BA, 56; Radcliffe Col, MA, 58; Harvard Univ, PhD(Hist), 66. **CAREER** Asst prof Hist, Occidental Col, 65-66; from asst prof to assoc prof, Pitzer Col, 66-70; lectr, Univ Calif, Berkeley, 70-71; prof & dean fac, Wheaton Col, 71-73; assoc prof, Univ Calif, San Diego, 73-76; prof Rhectoric, Univ Calif, Berkeley, 77-94, vis assoc Hist, Wellesley Col, 69-70; Prof, Grad School, Univ of Cal, Berkeley, 94-. **MEMBERSHIPS** Conf Brit Studies; Am Soc Legal Hist. **RESEARCH** English intellectual history 1500-1700; European intellectual history 1400-1700. **SELECTED PUBLICATIONS** Auth, Latitudinarianism and science in 17th century England, Past & Present, 68; John Wilkins: An Intellectual Biography, Univ Calif Press, 69; Law and science in 17th century England, Stanford Law Rev, 69; Law reform in 17th century England, 78 & Bacon & law reform, 81, Am J Legal Hist; History and Natural History in 17th Century England, Univ Calif Press, 81; Probability and Certainty in 17th century England: The Relationships between Science, Religion, History, Law and Literature, Princeton Univ Press, 83; Beyond Reasonable Doubt and Probable Cause Studies in the Anglo-American Law of Culture, Univ of California Press, 91; The Culture of Fact in Early Modern England (in progress). **CONTACT ADDRESS** Dept of Rhetoric, Univ of California, Berkeley, 2125 Dwinelle Hall, Berkeley, CA 94720-2671. **EMAIL** bshapiro@socrates.berkeley.edu

SHAPIRO, EDWARD S.
PERSONAL Born 01/14/1938, Washington, DC, m, 1965, 4 children **DISCIPLINE** HISTORY **EDUCATION** Georgetown Univ,BA 59; Univ NC; Harvard Univ PhD 68. **CAREER** St John's Univ, instr asst prof 65-69. **HONORS AND AWARDS** Oxford Cen Fell; Ecumenical Res Fell. **MEMBERSHIPS** AHA; AMJHS; OAH. **RESEARCH** Am Jewish hist, 20th century Am hist, Am ethnic hist. **SELECTED PUBLICATIONS** The Letters of Sydney Hook: Democracy, Communism and the Cold War; A Time for Healing: American Jewry Since World War II. **CONTACT ADDRESS** 4 Forest Dr, West Orange, NJ 07052. **EMAIL** shapired@lanmailshu.edu

SHAPIRO, H. ALAN
PERSONAL Born 08/03/1949, New York, NY, s **DISCIPLINE** CLASSICAL ARCHAEOLOGY **EDUCATION** Princeton Univ, PhD, 77. **CAREER** Asst Prof, Columbia Univ, 77-78; Mellon Fel & Asst Prof, Tulane Univ, 78-81; Asst Prof to Assoc Prof, Stevens Inst Technol, 81-92; Prof, Univ Canterbury, 94-96; Prof, Johns Hopkins Univ, 97-. **HONORS AND AWARDS** Phi Beta Kappa; NEH grant, 89; Parker Vis Scholar, Brown Univ, 90; Vis Scholar, Deutsches Archaologisches Institut, 92; Guggenheim Fel, 92-93. **MEMBERSHIPS** Archaeol Inst Am; Am Philol Asn. **RESEARCH** Greek art and archaeology; mythology. **SELECTED PUBLICATIONS** Auth, Myth into Art. Poet and Painter in Classical Greece, Routledge, 94; coauth, Women in the Classical World, Oxford, 94; co-ed, The Archaeology of Athens and Attica under the Democracy, Oxbow Bks, 94; Mother City and Colony. Classical Athenian and South Italian Vases in New Zealand and Australia, Exhibition Catalogue, Robert MacDougall Art Gallery, Christchurch, 95; Greek Vases in the San Antonio Museum of Art, 96; series ed, Cambridge Studies in Classical Art and Iconography, 92-; transl, The Mask of Socrates, Univ Calif, 95; auth, Art and Cult under the Tyrants in athens, von Zabern 1989, supplement, 95. **CONTACT ADDRESS** Classics Dept, Johns Hopkins Univ, Baltimore, 3400 N Charles St, Baltimore, MD 21218-2690. **EMAIL** ashapiro@jhu.edu

SHAPIRO, HENRY D.
PERSONAL Born 05/07/1937, New York, NY, m, 1963, 3 children **DISCIPLINE** AMERICAN INTELLECTUAL HISTORY **EDUCATION** Columbia Col, AB, 58; Cornell Univ, MA, 60; Rutgers Univ, PhD(hist), 66. **CAREER** Teaching asst hist, Cornell Univ, 58-60; asst instr, Rutgers Univ, 60-62; instr, Ohio State Univ, 63-66; asst prof, 66-71, assoc prof, 71-80, Prof Hist, Univ Cincinnati, 80-, Co-Dir, Ctr Neighborhood & Community Studies, 81-, Charles Warren fel, Harvard Univ, 71-72; Fulbright sr lectr Am hist, John F Kennedy Inst Am Studies, Free Univ Berlin, 77-78. **HONORS AND AWARDS** Moses Coit Tyler Prize, Cornell Univ, 61; W D Weatherford Prize, Berea Col, 79. **MEMBERSHIPS** Am Studies Asn. **RESEARCH** American intellectual history; history of American culture; American science in the 19th century. **SELECTED PUBLICATIONS CONTACT ADDRESS** Dept of Hist, Univ of Cincinnati, Cincinnati, OH 45221.

SHAPIRO, HENRY L.
PERSONAL Born New York, NY **DISCIPLINE** ANCIENT PHILOSOPHY, AESTHETICS **EDUCATION** Univ Toronto, BA, 60; Columbia Univ, PhD, 69. **CAREER** Preceptor philos, Columbia Univ, 64-66; actg asst prof, Univ Calif, Riverside, 66-68; chmn dept, 70-73, Asst Prof Philos Univ Mo-St Louis, 68-. **RESEARCH** Greek philosophy; 19th century continental philosophy; philosophy of literature. **SELECTED PUBLICATIONS CONTACT ADDRESS** Dept of Philos, Univ of Missouri, St. Louis, 8001 Natural Bridge, Saint Louis, MO 63121-4499.

SHAPIRO, HERBERT
PERSONAL Born 06/14/1929, Jamaica, NY, m, 1957, 2 children **DISCIPLINE** AMERICAN HISTORY **EDUCATION** Queens Col, BA, 52; Columbia Univ, MA, 58; Univ Rochester, PhD(hist), 64. **CAREER** Asst prof hist, Morehouse Col, 62-66; from Asst Prof to Assoc Prof, 66-88, Prof Hist, Univ Cincinnati, 88-. **MEMBERSHIPS** AHA; Orgn Am Historians; Southern Hist Asn. **RESEARCH** The populist-progressive period; African-American history. **SELECTED PUBLICATIONS** Coauth, The World of Lincoln Steffens, Hill & Wang, 62; auth, The Ku Klux Klan during Reconstruction--South Carolina episode, J Negro Hist, 1/64; The Muckrakers in American Society, Heath, 68; The Populists and the Negro: A reconsideration, In: The Making of Black America, Atheneum, 68; Steffens, Lippmann and Reed: The muckraker and his proteges, Pac Northwest Quart, 10/71; Muckracking in America, Forum, 76; Lincoln Steffens and the McNamara Case, Am J Econ & Sociol, 10/80; Eugene Genovese, Marxism and the Study of Slavery, J Ethnic Studies, Vol 9, No 4; White Violence and Black Response: From Reconstruction to Montgomery, 88; co-ed, American Communism and Black Americans, 1930-1934, 91; I Belong to the Working Class: The Unfinished Autobiography of Rose Pastor Stokes, 92; Northern Labor and Antislavery: A Documentary History, 94; ed, African American History and Radical Historiography: Essays in Honor of Herbert Aptheker, 98. **CONTACT ADDRESS** Dept of Hist, Univ of Cincinnati, PO Box 210373, Cincinnati, OH 45221-0373. **EMAIL** shapirh@ucbeh.san.uc.edu

SHAPIRO, STANLEY
PERSONAL Born 10/16/1936, New York, NY, m, 1964 **DISCIPLINE** RECENT AMERICAN HISTORY **EDUCATION** Brooklyn Col, AB, 58; Univ CA, Berkeley, AM, 59, PhD, 67. **CAREER** Instr, 65-67, Asst prof hist, Wayne State Univ, 68-, dir, honors prog, Wayne State Univ, 94. **MEMBERSHIPS** AHA; Orgn Am Historians; Labor Historians, 70. **RESEARCH** Polit, soc, and intellectual hist of the First World War period. **SELECTED PUBLICATIONS** Auth, The great war and reform: Liberals and labor, 1917-1919, Labor Hist, 71; The twilight of reform: Advanced liberals after the armistice, Historian, 71; The passage of power: Labor and the new social order, Proc Am Philos Soc, 12/76; auth, "Hand and Brain: The Farmer Labor Party of 1920," in Labor History, 26, Summer, 85. **CONTACT ADDRESS** Dept of Hist, Wayne State Univ, 3139 FAB, Detroit, MI 48202-3919. **EMAIL** aa1357@wayne.edu

SHARFMAN, GLENN
PERSONAL Born 09/06/1961, Chicago, IL, m, 1985, 3 children **DISCIPLINE** HISTORY **EDUCATION** Univ Miami, BA, 83; Univ NC, MA, 85, PhD, 89. **CAREER** Assoc Prof History, Hiram Col, 90-. **HONORS AND AWARDS** Michael Starr Awd; Paul Martin Awd. **MEMBERSHIPS** AHA; Leo Baeck Inst; Ohio Acad Hist. **RESEARCH** Modern Jewish; modern German; Holocaust. **SELECTED PUBLICATIONS** The Dilemma of Jewish Youths in Nazi Germany, Shafer, 92; Various Solutions to the Juderfrage: A Look back at 19th century antisemitism, Festschift for Richard Rubenstein; "Integration or Exclusion?: Bavarian Jews in the 19th Century," Jour Relig Hist, 95; Jewish Emancipation in 1848, Revolutions of 1848, 96; auth, "The Quest for Justice: The Reaction of The Ukranian-American Community to The John Demjanjuk Trials," J of Genocide Res 2 (00): 65-87; auth, "The Reaction of the Jewish Community to the Trial of John Demjanjuk," The Historian (fall, 00). **CONTACT ADDRESS** Dept. Of History, Hiram Col, Pendleton House, Hiram, OH 44234. **EMAIL** sharfmangr@hiram.edu

SHARMA, JAGDISH P.
PERSONAL Born 01/04/1934, m, 1962, 2 children **DISCIPLINE** ANCIENT HISTORY & RELIGION **EDUCATION** Agra Univ, BA, 55; Univ London, BA(hons), 59, PhD(ancient hist), 62. **CAREER** Vis asst prof Indian hist, Univ Va, 63-64; vis asst prof sch int serv, Am Univ, 64; asst prof, 64-68, assoc prof, 68-76, prof Indian hist, Univ Hawaii, Manoa, 76-; dir undergrad majors in Asian studies, Univ Hawaii, 69-71, chm hist forum, Hist Fac Res Sem, 69-75, 97-; adv, Jainas Am. **MEMBERSHIPS** Asn Asian Studies; life fel Royal Asiatic Soc; Am Orient Soc; AAUP. **RESEARCH** Ancient republics; ancient politics and democracy in the ancient world; Jainism; comparative religions. **SELECTED PUBLICATIONS** Auth, Republics in Ancient India, c 1500 BC-500 BC, E J Brill, Leiden, 68; coauth, Hinduism, Sarvodaya and Social Change, In: Religion and Political Modernization, Yale Univ, 74; auth, Jaina and Buddhist Traditions Regarding the Origins of Ajatasattu's War within Vajjians: A New Interpretation, Shramana, Vol 25, No 9 & 10; Hemacandra: The Life and Scholarship of a Jaina Monk, Asian Profile, Vol 3, No 2; Jainas as a Minority in Indian Society and History, Jain J, Vol 10, No 4; coauth, Dream-Symbolism in the Sramanic Tradition, Firma KLM-Calcutta, 80; ed & contribr, Individuals and Ideas in Modern India; auth, Nine Interpretative Studies, Firma KLM-Calcutta, 82; Time Perspective in the Study of Culture, J Soc Res, 3/79; Life-Pattern of the Jinas in Bibliography: East & West, ed by Carol Ramalb, Hon, 89; Jawaharlal Nehru--A Biographical Sketch, in Foreign Visitors to Congress: Speeches and History for US Capitol Society, Wash, DC, Millwood, NY, Karaus Int Pubs, 2 vols, 89; August 15 (1947)-India in Book of Days-1987: An Encyclopedia, Ann Arbor: The Reirian Press, 88; Japan as Seen From America and India: My First Impressions in Japanese with Eng Summary in Japan in the World Vol XIII Takushoku Univ, Tokyo, 94; Indian Thinking and Thinkers in Perspectives on History & Culture (in honor of Prof D P Singhal), ed by Arvind Sharma, Indian Books Centre, Delhi, 92; Individuals and Ideas in Traditional India, ed with contribution, MRML, New Delhi (in press); Jaina Yakshas, Kusumanjali, Meerut, India, 89, 93; The Jinasattvas: Class and Gender in the Social Origins of Jaina Heroes, ed by N. K. Wagle, Univ Toronto Press, (99): 72-85; Political History in the Historiography of Ancient India: New Trends and Prospects in Political History in a Changing World, ed by G C Pande, et al Kusumanjali, Jodhpur, 92; Ambapali's Vesali about 500 B C in City in Pre-Modern Asia, ed by Leslie Gunawardana (forthcoming). **CONTACT ADDRESS** Dept Hist, Univ of Hawaii, Manoa, 2530 Dole St, Honolulu, HI 96822-2383. **EMAIL** jpsharma@hawaii.edu

SHARMA, R. N.
PERSONAL Born 10/22/1944, Punjab, India, m, 1972, 2 children **DISCIPLINE** LIBRARY AND INFORMATION SCIENCE; HIGHER EDUCATION; HISTORY **EDUCATION** Univ Delhi, BA, 63, MA, 66; N TX State Univ, MLS, 70; SUNY, Buffalo, PhD, 82. **CAREER** Asst librn, Col Ozarks, 70-71; ref librn, Colgate Univ, 71-81; head librn, Penn State Univ, Beaver Campus, 81-85; asst dir, Univ WI, 85-89; dir, Univ Evansville, 89-95; dir, WV State Col, 96-. **HONORS AND AWARDS** Who's Who Among Asian Am, 92-94; advisory bd, 94-98, Asian Lit; Humprhy/OCLC/Forest Press Awd, 97, ALA; chair, Am Librns Delegation to Palestine, 97; Am Librns Delegation to Northern Ireland, 97; Benjamin Franklin Awd, 98, Publishers Marketing Asn; Editor-in-Chief, Library Times International 84; President, Asian/American Libraries Association, 93-94. **MEMBERSHIPS** Am Libr Asn; Asn Col Res Libr; Int Relations Round Table; Indian Libr Asn; Asian/Pacific Am Librn Asn. **RESEARCH** International librarianship; history of libraries; library administration; reference services. **SELECTED PUBLICATIONS** Auth, "Indian Librarianship: Perspectives and Prospects," Kalayni 81; auth, Indian Academic Libraries and Dr. S. R. Ranganathan: A Critical Study, Sterling, 86; Ranganathan and the West, Sterling, 92; Research and Academic Librarians: A Global View, Resources in Education, 92; Changing Dimensions: Managing Library and Information Services for the 1990's: A Global Perspective, Ed Resources Infor Center, 94; Linking Asian/Pacific Collections to America, Educational Resources Infor Center, 95; auth, "Libraries and Education in Palestine, Near East and South Asia," Subcommittee/International Relations/ALA, 99. **CONTACT ADDRESS** Drain-Jordan Library, West Virginia State Col, PO Box 1002, Institute, WV 25112-1002. **EMAIL** sharmarn@mail.wvsc.edu

SHARONI, SIMONA
DISCIPLINE MIDDLE EASTERN STUDIES **EDUCATION** George Mason Univ, PhD. **CAREER** Prof, Am Univ. **RESEARCH** Conflict resolution, gender; Israeli-Palestinian conflict. **SELECTED PUBLICATIONS** Auth, Gender and the Israeli-Palestinian Conflict: The Politics of Women's Resistance, Syracuse Univ Press, 95. **CONTACT ADDRESS** American Univ, 4400 Massachusetts Ave, Washington, DC 20016.

SHARP, BUCHANAN
PERSONAL Born 09/25/1942, Dumbarton, Scotland, m, 1964, 2 children **DISCIPLINE** BRITISH & DUTCH HISTORY **EDUCATION** Univ Calif, Berkeley, AB, 64, PhD(hist), 71; Univ Ill, Urbana-Champaign, MA, 65. **CAREER** Asst prof, 70-77, Assoc Prof Hist, Univ Calif Santa Cruz, 77- **MEMBERSHIPS** Econ Hist Soc; Past & Present Soc, Eng; Scottish Hist Soc;

AHA. **RESEARCH** Economic and social history of Tudor-Stuart England; economic and social history of the Dutch Republic in the 16th and 17th centuries. **SELECTED PUBLICATIONS** Auth, In Contempt of All Authority: Rural Artisans and Riot in the West of England, 1586-1660, Univ Calif Press, 80. **CONTACT ADDRESS** Dept of Hist, Univ of California, Santa Cruz, 1156 High St, Santa Cruz, CA 95064-0001.

SHARP, JAMES ROGER
PERSONAL Born 08/08/1936, Troy, KS, m, 1957, 2 children **DISCIPLINE** AMERICAN HISTORY **EDUCATION** Univ Mo, BA, 58, MA, 60; Univ Calif, Berkeley, PhD(hist), 66. **CAREER** Asst prof, 66-70, assoc prof, 70-81, Prof Hist, Syracuse Univ, 79-, Chairperson Dept, 76-, Soc Sci Res Coun res grant, 69; Nat Endowment for Humanities fel, 70-71; consult, Nat Endowment for Humanities Panel for Younger Humanist Fels, 71 & 72; Am Coun Learned Soc fel, 79-80. **MEMBERSHIPS** AHA; Orgn Am Historians; Southern Hist Asn. **RESEARCH** Early national and middle periods of United States history. **SELECTED PUBLICATIONS** Auth, The Jacksmians Versus the Banks, Columbia U Press, 70; auth, American Politics in the Early Republic, Yale Univ Press, 93,95; auth, The Origins Of Jeffersonian Commercial-Policy And Diplomacy - Benatar,Ds/, J Of Southern Hist, Vol 0060, 1994; Original Intentions - On The Making And Ratification Of The United-States Constitution - Bradford,Me/, J Of Interdisciplinary Hist, Vol 0026, 1995; Clinton,George - Yeoman Politician Of The New Republic - Kaminski,Jp/, Am Hist Rev, Vol 0100, 1995; The Papers Of Jackson, Andrew, Vol 4, 1816-1820 - Moser,Hd, Hoth,Dr, Hoeman,Gh, Eds/, Penn Mag Of Hist And Biog, Vol 0119, 1995; The Presidency Of Jackson,Andrew - Cole,Db/, Penn Mag Of Hist And Biog, Vol 0119, 1995; Devising Liberty - Preserving And Creating Freedom In The New Am Republic - Konig,Dt/, William And Mary Quart, Vol 0053, 1996; Jefferson And Madison - 3 Conversations From The Founding - Banning,L/, J Of Am Hist, Vol 0082, 1996; The Jacksonian Promise - Am 1815-1840 - Feller,D/, Am Hist Rev, Vol 0102, 1997; The Papers Of Madison, James, Secretary-Of-State Series, Volume 3 - March 1, 1802 October 6, 1802 - Mattern, Db, Stagg, Jca, Cross, Jk, Perdue,Sh/, Penn Mag Of Hist And Biog, Vol 0121, 1997. **CONTACT ADDRESS** Dept of Hist, Syracuse Univ, Syracuse, NY 13210. **EMAIL** jrsharp@maxwell.syr.edu

SHARRER, GEORGE TERRY
PERSONAL Born 12/30/1944, Baltimore, MD, m, 1982, 2 children **DISCIPLINE** UNITED STATES AND MEDICAL HISTORY **EDUCATION** Univ Md, College Park, BA, 66, MA, 68, PhD(hist), 75. **CAREER** Technician agr, 69-72, specialist mfg, 72-75, Smithsonian Inst, 75-, ed, Living Historical Farm Bull, 76-85; cur, health sciences, Smithsonian Inst, 93-. **MEMBERSHIPS** Nat Found for Cancer Res, Carilion Biomedical Inst Fund for Inherited Diseases Res. **RESEARCH** History of Medicine. **SELECTED PUBLICATIONS** Auth, Marylanders United States Patents, 1790-1830, spring 76 & Flour milling and the growth of Baltimore, 1750-1830, fall 76, Md Hist Mag; Commerce and industry, In: Alexandria: A Town in Transition, 1800-1900, Alexandria Hist Soc, 77; The search for naval policy, 1783-1812, In: In War and Peace, Greenwood, 78; Agricultural museums in developing countries, In: 1977 Annual, Living Hist Farms & Agr Mus, 78; 1001 References for the History of American Ford Technology, Agr Hist Ctr, Davis, Calif, 78; Hitching history to the plow, Historic Preservation, 11-12/80; Naval stores, In: Material Culture of the Woods Agriculture, Hollow Press, 81; auth, The Kind of Fate, Ames, IA, 00. **CONTACT ADDRESS** Mus of Am Hist, Smithsonian Inst, Rm 5031, Washington, DC 20650. **EMAIL** sharrert@nmah.si.edu

SHARY, TIMOTHY
PERSONAL Born 08/17/1967, Cheverly, MD, s **DISCIPLINE** FILM HISTORY **EDUCATION** Hampshire Col, BA, 91; Ohio Univ, MA, 93; Univ of Mass, PhD, 98. **CAREER** Lectr, Univ Mass Amherst; Vis Lectr, Clark Univ, 97-. **HONORS AND AWARDS** Phi Kappa Phi. **MEMBERSHIPS** Soc for Cinema Studies; Univ Film & Video Asn. **RESEARCH** Contemporary American cinema and media; East European cinema; the phenomenology of film and video; new media technology; Films of Alfred Hitchcok, Ingmar Bergman, and Atom Egoyan. **SELECTED PUBLICATIONS** Auth, Reification and Loss in Postmodern Puberty: The Cultural Logic of Fredric Jameson and Young Adult Movies, Postmodernism in the Cinema, Berghahn Books, 98; The Teen Film and its Methods of Study, J of Popular Film and Television, 97; The Only Place To Go Is Inside: Confusions of Sexuality and Class in Clueless and Kids, Pictures of a Generation on Hold: Youth in Film and Television of the 90s, Media Studies Working Group, 96; Exotica: Atom Egoyan's Neurotic Thriller, Point of View, 95; Video as Accessible Artifact and Artificial Access: The Early Films of Atom Egoyan, Film Criticism, 95; Viewing Experience: Structures of Subjectivity in East and West European Films, Echoes and Mirrors, 94; Present Personal Truths: The Alternative Phenomenology of Video in I've Heard the Mermaids Singing, Wide Angle, 93. **CONTACT ADDRESS** Dept of Visual & Performing Arts, Clark Univ, 950 Main St., Worcester, MA 01610. **EMAIL** tshary@clarku.edu

SHASHKO, PHILIP
PERSONAL Born 03/27/1936, m, 1971, 2 children **DISCIPLINE** RUSSIAN & BALKAN HISTORY **EDUCATION** Mich State Univ, BA, 60; Univ Calif, Berkeley, MA, 61; Univ Mich, Ann Arbor, cert Russ studies, 63, PhD(hist), 69. **CAREER** Asst prof, 68-74, assoc prof, 74-82, Prof Hist, Univ Wis-Milwaukee, 82-, Int Res & Exchanges Bd fel, Bulgaria, 69-70; Univ Wis Grad Sch res grant, 69-70; Am Coun Leraned Socs travel grant, Warsaw, 73; Nat Endowment for Humanities grant, 78. **HONORS AND AWARDS** Standard Oil Teaching Excellence Awd, Univ Student Govt, 73. **MEMBERSHIPS** Am Asn Advan Slavic Studies; AHA; Am Asn Southeast Europ Studies; Bulgarian Studies Asn (vpres, 75-78). **RESEARCH** Russian intelligentsia; modern Balkans; Russian-Balkan relations. **SELECTED PUBLICATIONS** Auth, Voices from the mountain: The image of the Ottoman-Turk in Bulgarian literature, Balkanistika, 75; General Ivan Kishelsky's program for the liberation of Bulgaria, In: Bulgaria Past and Present, 76; Subitiiata v Bulgariia ot 1923 g prez pogleda na Amerikanskia pechat, In: Akademik Christo Christov: Izsledvaniia po sluchai 60 godini ot rozhdenieto mu, Sofia, 76; ed, The Bulgarian Uprising of April, 1876 and the Eastern Question, Tempe, 77; auth, From Mt Athos to the Shipka Pass: Slavic consciousness among the Bulgarian Renaissance intelligentsia, Les Cultures Slaves et les Balkans, Vol II, Sofia, 78; Vestnik New York Times za Ruskoturskata voina i osvobozhdenieto na Bulgariia, Istoricheski pregled, 78; ed, The Russo-Turkish War of 1877-1878 and the Liberation of Bulgaria, Tempe, 79; auth, Studies in Ethnicity: The East European Experience in America, 80. **CONTACT ADDRESS** Dept of Hist, Univ of Wisconsin, Milwaukee, Po Box 413, Milwaukee, WI 53201-0413.

SHAW, BARTON CARR
PERSONAL Born 06/06/1947, Annapolis, MD, m, 1982, 1 child **DISCIPLINE** AMERICAN HISTORY **EDUCATION** Elon Col, AB, 69; Univ Wis-Milwaukee, MA, 72; Emory Univ, PhD, 79. **CAREER** Asst prof hist, Ga Inst Technol, 79-80; from Asst Prof to Prof Hist, Cedar Crest Col, 80-; Fulbright Sr Lectr, Univ Sheffield (UK), 87. **HONORS AND AWARDS** Ford Found Fel, 72-76; Frederick Jackson Turner Awd, Org Am Hist, 85; Cedar Crest Col Alumnae Awd for Excellence in Tchg, 89; NEH Summer Inst on the Southern Civil Rights movement, Harvard Univ, 97. **MEMBERSHIPS** Orgn Am Historians; Southern Hist Asn. **RESEARCH** Hist of the Am South; hist of Am populism. **SELECTED PUBLICATIONS** Auth, The Hobson Craze, US Naval Inst Proc, 2/76; From the user's perspective: Research in Georgia archives, Ga Archive, spring 80; The wool-hat boys: A history of the populist party in Georgia, 1892 to 1910, Proc Ninty-Fifth Annual Meeting Am Hist Asn, 80; The Wool-Hat Boys: Georgia's Populist Party, LSU Press, 84. **CONTACT ADDRESS** Dept of Hist, Cedar Crest Col, 100 College Dr, Allentown, PA 18104-6196. **EMAIL** bcshaw@cedarcrest.edu

SHAW, DANIEL
PERSONAL Born 10/28/1951, Aurora, IL, m, 1992, 2 children **DISCIPLINE** AESTHETICS, 19TH AND 20TH CENTURY CONTINENTAL PHILOSOPHY **EDUCATION** Northern Ill Univ, BA, 72, MA, 75; Ohio State Univ, PhD, 81. **CAREER** Lectr, Ohio State Univ, 79-81; asst prof, Gettysburg Col, 81-86; assoc prof, 86-, Perf Arts comt, 88-90, treas, 92-94, Prof Develop Comt, 88-91, 92-94, fac adv, WLHU Radio Station, Philos Club, ch, APSCUF Presidential Eval Comt, 89, ch, APSCUF Honors Comt, 89-90, 90-91, APSCUF Gender Issues Comt, ch, APSCUF Comt to Revise the Prom Doc, Lock Haven Univ, 95. **HONORS AND AWARDS** NEH, summer sem, Univ Calif, Riverside, 85; Deut Academisches Austauschdienst (DAAD) scholar prog, 86; NEH summer sem, Yale Univ, 94. **SELECTED PUBLICATIONS** Auth, The Survival of Tragedy: Dostoevsky's The Idiot, Dialogue: J of the Nat Honor Soc for Philos, Oct, 75; Absurdity and Suicide: A Reexamination, Philos Res Arch, Mar, 86; A Kuhnian Metatheory for Aesthetics, J of Aesthet and Art Criticism, Fall, 86; Nietzsche as Sophist: A Polemic, Int Philos Quart, Dec, 86; Rorty and Nietzsche: Some Elective Affinities, Int Stud in Philos, Nov, 89; The American Democratic Ideology, The Lock Haven Int Rev, Fall, 90; Thelma and Louise: Liberating or Regressive? in Film, Individualism and Community, Ronald Dotterer, ed, Susquehanna UP, 94; Lang Contra Vengeance: The Big Heat, J of Value Inquiry, Dec 95; auth, "Existential Implications of 'Dead Ringers'," Film and Philos 3 (97); auth, "Nietzche's Sophistic Aesthetics," Jrnl of Nietzsche Stud, Special Nietzsche and Post-Analytic Philos Conf Ed (forthcoming); auth, book note on John Gedo's "The Artist and the Emotional Life," in Jrnl of Aesthetics and Art Crit (forthcoming). **CONTACT ADDRESS** Lock Haven Univ of Pennsylvania, R.D. 2, 190A, Mill Hall, PA 17751. **EMAIL** dshaw@eagle.1hup.edu

SHAW, DONALD LEWIS
PERSONAL Born 10/27/1936, Raleigh, NC, m, 1960, 4 children **DISCIPLINE** MASS COMMUNICATIONS HISTORY **EDUCATION** Univ NC, Chapel Hill, AB, 59, MA, 60; Univ Wis, PhD(mass commun), 66. **CAREER** From asst prof to assoc prof, 66-76, prof jour, 76- , Kenan Prof, 92- , Univ NC, Chapel Hill. **MEMBERSHIPS** Asn Educ in Jour; AJHA; AAPOR; WAPOR. **RESEARCH** Relationship among technology, mass communication and culture. **SELECTED PUBLICATIONS** Coauth, The Agenda-Selling Function of Mass Media, Publ Opinion Quart, summer 72; coauth (with McCombs), The Emergence of American Political Issues: The Agenda-Setting Function of the Press, West Pub Co, 77; coauth, Communication and Democracy. **CONTACT ADDRESS** Sch of Journalism, Univ of No Carolina, Chapel Hill, Chapel Hill, NC 27514.

SHAW, JOSEPH WINTERBOTHAM
PERSONAL Born 07/06/1935, Chicago, IL, m, 1965, 2 children **DISCIPLINE** BRONZE AGE AEGEAN & CLASSICAL GREEK ARCHEOLOGY **EDUCATION** Brown Univ, BA, 57; Wesleyan Univ, MAT, 59; Univ Pa, PhD(classical archaeol), 70. **CAREER** Excavation architect Greek architecture, Kenchreai Excavations, Univ Chicago, 63-70 & Kato Zakros Excavations, Greek Archaeol Serv, 64-70; from asst prof to assoc prof, 70-77, assoc chmn dept, 77-79, prof Fine Art, Univ Toronto, 77-, Adj prof underwater archaeol, Am Inst Nautical Archaeol, 72-; adv ed, Am J Field Archaeol, 73-; dir Aegean archaeol, Kommos Excavations, ROM & Univ Toronto, 75-; numerous res grants and fels in Can & Am. **HONORS AND AWARDS** Fel, Soc of Antiquaries of London, 80; Honorary degree Doctor of Humane Letters, Brown Univ, 87; Fel, Royal Soc of Canada, 93. **MEMBERSHIPS** Archaeol Inst Am; Can Mediter Inst. **RESEARCH** Minoan archaeology; Aegean architecture and archaeology; investigation of prehistoric and historic harbors and harbor works in the Aegean and Eastern Mediterranean. **SELECTED PUBLICATIONS** Auth, Excavations At Kommos Crete During 1986-1992/, Hesperia, Vol 0062, 1993; Excavations In The Southern Area At Kommos, Crete, 1993/, Am J Of Archaeol, Vol 0098, 1994; 2 3-Holed Stone Anchors From Kommos, Crete - Their Context, Type And Origin/, Int J Of Nautical Archaeol, Vol 0024, 1995; ed, An ecavation on the South Coast of Crete: The Kommos Region, Ecology, and Minoan Industries, Princeton Univ Press, 95, 96. **CONTACT ADDRESS** Dept of Fine Art, Univ of Toronto, 100 St. George St, Sidney Smith Hall , Rm 6036, Toronto, ON, Canada M5S 1A1. **EMAIL** jwshaw@scar.utoronto.ca

SHAY, ROBERT
DISCIPLINE MUSIC HISTORY, CHORAL MUSIC **EDUCATION** Wheaton Col, BMus; NEngl Conserv Mus, MMus; Univ NC, Chapel Hill, MA, PhD. **CAREER** Assoc prof, Lyon Col. **SELECTED PUBLICATIONS** Auth, Henry Purcell: The Early Manuscript Sources, Cambridge UP. **CONTACT ADDRESS** Dept of Music, Lyon Col, 300 Highland Rd, PO Box 2317, Batesville, AR 72503. **EMAIL** shay@lyon.edu

SHEA, EMMETT A.
PERSONAL Born 10/24/1931, Worchester, MA, m, 1961, 1 child **DISCIPLINE** POLITICAL SCIENCE, GOVERNMENT, HISTORY **EDUCATION** Boston Univ, BS, 55, Ed M, 56, AM, 61; Boston Col, AM, 71; Boston Col/Int Inst for Advanced Studies, PhD, 82. **CAREER** Prof, Worchester State Col, 62-, chair, Dept of Hist & Political Sci, 70-79, coordr, grad prog, 70-; lectr, Wellesley Col, 57-62; vis prof, Regis Col, 65-70; vis prof, Col of the Holy Cross, 63-73. **HONORS AND AWARDS** Pi Gamma Mu (Nat Soc Sci Honor Soc); Phi Alpha Theta (Nat Hist Honor Soc); Certificate of Meritorious Service, Commonwealth of Mass. **MEMBERSHIPS** Am Hist Asn, New England Hist Asn, Asn for the Advancement of Slavic Studies, N E Slavic Asn, Am Asn for Asian Studies. **RESEARCH** 19th and 20th century Russia, Soviet Union, Russian Federation, American-Russian/Soviet relations, U.S.-East Asia relations. **CONTACT ADDRESS** Dept Hist & Govt, Worcester State Col, 486 Chandler Sr, Worcester, MA 01602-2832.

SHEA, WILLIAM LEE
PERSONAL Born 08/22/1948, Breaux Bridge, LA, m, 1971, 1 child **DISCIPLINE** AMERICAN HISTORY **EDUCATION** La State Univ, Baton Rouge, BA, 70; Rice Univ, PhD(hist), 75. **CAREER** Assoc Prof Hist, Univ Ark, Monticello, 74- **HONORS AND AWARDS** Moncado Prize, Am Military Inst, 78. **MEMBERSHIPS** AHA; Southern Hist Asn; Am Military Inst; Civil War Round Table Assoc. **RESEARCH** Early American history; military history; American Civil War. **SELECTED PUBLICATIONS** Auth, Virginia at war, 1644-1646, Military Affairs, 77; coauth, The Afrika Korps in Arkansas, 1942-1946, 78 & auth, Battle at Ditch Bayou, 80, Ark Hist Quart; auth, The first American militia, Military Affairs, 82; The Virginia Militia in the 17th Century, La State Univ Press, 83. **CONTACT ADDRESS** Social Sci Dept, Univ of Arkansas, Monticello, Monticello, AR 71655.

SHEDD, D.
PERSONAL Born 08/04/1922, New Have, CT, m, 1946, 4 children **DISCIPLINE** HISTORY OF MEDICINE **EDUCATION** Yale Univ, BS, 44; Yale Univ Sch Med, MD, 46 **CAREER** Inst, asst prof, assoc prof, dept surgery, Yale Univ Sch Med, 53-67; chief, dept head, neck surgery, Roswell Pk Cancer Inst, 67-96; res prof, dept surgery, 67-97, emer, State Univ NY, Buffalo, 97-. **HONORS AND AWARDS** Markle Scholar Med, 53-58; Alpha Omega Alpha Hon Med Soc,; Sigma Xi hon sci soc. **MEMBERSHIPS** Soc Univ Surgeons; New England Surgical Soc; Soc Head, Neck Surgeons; Am Col Surgeons; Soc Surgical Oncology; Am Asn Hist Med; Am Head, Neck Soc. **RESEARCH** Hist of Medicine. **SELECTED PUBLICATIONS** Coauth, Nicholas Senn: Outrider of Modern Head and

Neck Oncology, Bull Am Col Surgeons, 81:20-24, 96; auth, The Work of Henry T. Butlin, an Early Head and Neck Surgeon, Am J Surgery, 173: (97): 234-236; coauth, The Work of George Washington Crile in Head and Neck Surgery, Bull Am Col Surgeons, 81:27; coauth, Contributions of Grant E. Ward to Head and Neck Oncology, Bull Am Col Surgeons, 82:18, 97. **CONTACT ADDRESS** Roswell Park Mem Inst, Elm & Carlton Sts, Buffalo, NY 14263. **EMAIL** donshedd@prodigy.net

SHEDEL, JAMES P.
PERSONAL Born 04/10/1947, Oakland, CA, m, 1983, 1 child **DISCIPLINE** HISTORY, ART & SOCIETY **EDUCATION** Univ of Calif at Santa Cruz, BA, 69; Univ of Rochester, MA, 70, PhD, 78. **CAREER** Lectr, Univ of Rochester, 75; tchg/res fel, Stanford Univ, 76-77; vis asst prof, Northwestern Univ, 78-79; Asst Prof to Assoc Prof, Georgetown Univ, 79-. **HONORS AND AWARDS** Fulbright fel, 73-74. **MEMBERSHIPS** Am Hist Asn; Am Catholic Hist Asn; German Studies Asn; Soc of Architectural Historians. **RESEARCH** Austria (18th-20th centuries); Germany; art and society. **SELECTED PUBLICATIONS** Auth, Art and Society, the New Art Movement in Vienna: 1897-1914, The Soc for the Promotion of Sci and Scholar, 81; Austria and Its Polish Subjects, 1866-1914: A Relationship of Interests, Austrian Hist Yearbook, 89; A Question of Identity: Kokoschka, Austria, and the Meaning of the AnschluB, 1938: Undertanding the Past, Overcoming the Past, Ariadne Press, 91; Art and Idnetity: The Wiener Secession 1897-1938, Sucession: Permanence of an Idea, Verlag Gerd Hatje, 97. **CONTACT ADDRESS** Dept of Hist, Georgetown Univ, Washington, DC 20057. **EMAIL** shedelj@georgetown.edu

SHEEHAN, BERNARD W.
PERSONAL Born 02/24/1934, New York, NY, m, 1957, 3 children **DISCIPLINE** HISTORY **EDUCATION** Fordham Univ, BS, 57; Univ Mich, MA, 58; Univ Va, PhD, 65. **CAREER** Instr hist, Regis Col, 58-62; asst prof, Univ Ala, 65-66; asst prof, Col William & Mary, 66-69, fel, Inst Early Am Hist & Cult, 66-69; assoc prof, 69-80, prof hist, IN Univ, Bloomington, 80, Assoc ed, J Am Hist, 69-73, actg ed, 73-74; Henry E Huntington Libr fel, 75-76; adj scholar, Heritage Found; ed, Ind Mag Hist, 96-. **HONORS AND AWARDS** Earhart Found fels, 77, 78, 81 & 82; dir, Nat Endowment Hum Summer Sem, 80. **RESEARCH** The Indian in early Am hist; Am intellectual hist. **SELECTED PUBLICATIONS** Auth, Indian-White Relations in Early America: A Review Essay, 4/69 & Paradise and the Noble Savage in Jeffersonian Thought, 7/69, William & Mary Quart; Seeds of Extinction: Jeffersonian Philanthropy and the American Indian, Chapel Hill, 73; Savagism and Civility: Indians and Englishmen in Colonial Virginia, Cambridge, 80; The Problem of moral Judgements in History, SAtlantic Quart 84, 85; The Indian Problem in the Northwest: From Conquest to Philanthropy, In: Launching the Extended Republic: The Federalist Era, 96. **CONTACT ADDRESS** Dept. of History, Indiana Univ, Bloomington, Ballantine 822, Bloomington, IN 47405.

SHEEHAN, JAMES JOHN
PERSONAL Born 05/31/1937, San Francisco, CA, m, 1989, 1 child **DISCIPLINE** MODERN EUROPEAN HISTORY **EDUCATION** Stanford Univ, AB, 58; Univ Calif, Berkeley, MA, 59, PhD(hist), 64. **CAREER** Instr hist, Stanford Univ, 62-64; from asst prof to assoc prof, Northwestern Univ, Evanston, 64-72, prof, 72-79; Prof Hist, Stanford Univ, 79-, Vis fel, Inst Advan Studies, 73-74 & Wolfson Col, Oxford, 81; fels, Nat Endowment for Humanities, summer, 72 & Am Coun Learned Soc, 81-82. **MEMBERSHIPS** AHA **RESEARCH** German social and political history. **SELECTED PUBLICATIONS** Auth, The destruction of German democracy, In: Major Crises in Western Civilization, Harcourt, 64; Political leadership in the German Reichstag, Am Hist Rev, 68; Liberalism and the city in the 19th century Germany, Past & Present, 71; Liberalism and society in Germany, 1815-1848, J Mod Hist, 73; ed, Industrialization and Industrialization and Industrial Labor in 19th Century Europe, Wiley, 74; Imperial Germany, Watts, 76; auth, German Liberalism in the Nineteenth Century, Univ Chicago, 78; What is German History?, J Mod Hist, 81; auth, German History, 1770-1866, 89; auth, Museums in the German, Artworld, 00. **CONTACT ADDRESS** Dept of Hist, Stanford Univ, Stanford, CA 94305-1926. **EMAIL** sheehan@stanford.edu

SHEIDLEY, HARLOW W.
PERSONAL Born 12/18/1941, San Francisco, CA, m, 1962, 2 children **DISCIPLINE** HISTORY **EDUCATION** Stanford Univ, AB, 63; Univ Conn, MA, 78, PhD, 90. **CAREER** ASST PROF, HIST, UNIV COLO, COLO SPRINGS, 92-99, Asso prof, hist, Univ Colo, Colo Springs, 99-. **HONORS AND AWARDS** Phi Beta Kappa, Woodrow Wilson Found Charlotte W. Newcombe Fel, Am Antiquariam Soc Frances Hieatt Fel. **MEMBERSHIPS** Soc for Historians of the Early Am Republic; Am Historical Assoc; Organization of Am Historians; Omohundro Inst of Early Am History and Cult. **RESEARCH** Nineteenth-century New England; Boston elite men; Boston elite women. **SELECTED PUBLICATIONS** Auth, Dialogues of a New Republic: An Exhibition of Selected Items from the Pierce Welch Gaines Collection of Americana, 80; auth, "Preserving the Old Fabrick: The Massachusetts Conservative Elite and the Constitutional Convention of 1820-1821," Procs of the Mass Hist Soc 103, 91; auth, "The Webster-Hayne Debate: Recasting New England's Sectionalism," New Eng Quart 67, 94; auth, Sectional Nationalism: Massachusetts Conservative Leaders and America, 1815-1836, Northeastern Univ Press, 98. **CONTACT ADDRESS** Dept of Hist, Univ of Colorado, Colorado Springs, 1420 Austin Bluffs Pkwy., Colorado Springs, CO 80933-7150. **EMAIL** hsheidley@gateway.net

SHELDON, MARIANNE BUROFF
PERSONAL Born 07/16/1946, Brooklyn, NY, 1 child **DISCIPLINE** AMERICAN HISTORY **EDUCATION** Rutgers Univ, BA, 68; Univ Mich, MA, 70, PhD, 75. **CAREER** Instr Hist, Univ Mich, 75; asst prof, 75-81, from assoc prof to prof Hist, Mills Col, 81-88. **MEMBERSHIPS** AHA; Southern Hist Asn; Orgn Am Historians. **RESEARCH** American history ot 1820; Antebellum South; American urban history. **SELECTED PUBLICATIONS** Auth, Black-White relations in Richmond, Virginia, 1782-1820, J Southern Hist, XLV: 27-44; Social stratification in Richmond, Virginia, 1788-1817, SAtlantic Urban Studies, IV: 177-197; Women in the Labor Force, with Nancy Thornborrow in Women: A Feminist Perspective, ed, Jo Freeman, 5th edition, 95. **CONTACT ADDRESS** Mills Col, 5000 MacArthur Blvd, Oakland, CA 94613-1000. **EMAIL** mshel@mills.edu

SHELDON, ROSE MARY
DISCIPLINE ANCIENT HISTORY **EDUCATION** Col NJ, BA; Hunter Col, MA; Univ Mich, PhD. **CAREER** Prof, VMI; ed bd, Int J Intel and Counterintel. **HONORS AND AWARDS** Nat Intel Bk Awd, 87; Rome Prize, 80. **SELECTED PUBLICATIONS** Contribu, Stud in Intel, Intel and Nat Security, Amer Intel J, Intel Quart, Foreign Intel Lit Scene, Small Wars and Insurgenies, J Mil Hist, The Washington Post. **CONTACT ADDRESS** Dept of History, Virginia Military Inst, Lexington, VA 24450. **EMAIL** rms@umi.edu

SHELLEY, BRUCE
DISCIPLINE HISTORICAL THEOLOGY **EDUCATION** Columbia Bible, BA; Fuller Sem, M.Div; Iowa Univ, Ph.D. **CAREER** Sr prof, Denver Sem. **HONORS AND AWARDS** Ed adv bd, Christian Hist; consult ed, InterVarsity's popular Dictionary of Christianity in Am. **SELECTED PUBLICATIONS** Auth, Church History in Plain Language; All the Saints Adore Thee; The Gospel; and the American Dream and The Consumer Church; corresponding ed, Christianity Today; pub(s), articles in Encycl Am; Evangel Dictionary of Theol; New Intl Dictionary of the Christian Church. **CONTACT ADDRESS** Denver Conservative Baptist Sem, PO Box 10000, Denver, CO 80250. **EMAIL** bruces@densem.edu

SHELMERDINE, CYNTHIA WRIGHT
PERSONAL Born 01/07/1949, Boston, MA **DISCIPLINE** CLASSICS; CLASSICAL ARCHAEOLOGY **EDUCATION** Bryn Mawr Col, AB, 70; Cambridge Univ, BA, 72, MA, 80; Harvard Univ, AM, 76, PhD, 77. **CAREER** Asst prof Classics, Univ Tex, Austin, 77-84; assoc prof, 84-97; prof, 97-; chair, 98-. **HONORS AND AWARDS** Marshall scholar, 70-72; Ctr. for Hellenic Studies, jr fel, 81-82; Pres assocs tchg award, Univ of Texas, 88. **MEMBERSHIPS** Archaeol Inst Am; Am Philol Asn; Am Sch Class Studies Athens Alumni Asn; Class Asn Middle West & South. **RESEARCH** Mycenaean Greek; Bronze Age Archaeology. **SELECTED PUBLICATIONS** Auth, The Pylos Ma tables reconsidered, Am Jour Archaeol, 73; contribur, Excavations at Nichoria (vol II), Univ Minn, (in press); Nichoria in context, Am Jour Archeol, 81; coauth, The Pylos Regional Archaeological Project. Part1: Overview and the Archaeological Survey, Hesperia 66, 97; auth, Review of Aegean Prehistory VI: The Palatial Bronze Age of the Central and Southern Greek Mainland, Am Jour of Archeol 101, 97; contribur, Sandy Pylos. From Nestor to Navarino, Univ Texas, 98. **CONTACT ADDRESS** Dept of Classics, Univ of Texas, Austin, Austin, TX 78712-1181. **EMAIL** cwshelm@mail.utexas.edu

SHELTON, JO-ANN
DISCIPLINE ROMAN AND GREEK HISTORY **EDUCATION** Univ Calif, Berkeley, PhD, 74. **CAREER** Prof, Univ Calif, Santa Barbara. **RESEARCH** Roman and Greek tragedy; Roman social hist; Roman epistol. **SELECTED PUBLICATIONS** Auth, Seneca's Hercules Furens: Theme, Structure, and Style, Gottingen, 78; As the Romans Did, Oxford, 88; The Madness of Hercules, Lawrence, 91. **CONTACT ADDRESS** Dept of Classics, Univ of California, Santa Barbara, Santa Barbara, CA 93106-7150. **EMAIL** jshelton@humanitas.ucsb.edu

SHEN, QING
PERSONAL Born 04/05/1962, China, m, 1989, 1 child **DISCIPLINE** URBAN PLANNING **EDUCATION** Zhejiang Univ, BS, 82; Univ British Columbia, MA, 86; Univ Cal Berkeley, PhD, 93. **CAREER** Asst prof, MIT, 93-99; assoc prof, 99-. **HONORS AND AWARDS** Emerge Schl Paper Awd; AAG, MMQM Spec Grp; Horwood Crit Prize; Min Edu China Grad Stud Fel. **MEMBERSHIPS** ACSP; AAG; URISA; TRB. **RESEARCH** Urban planning; spatial modeling and analysis; GIS. **SELECTED PUBLICATIONS** Auth, "An Application of GIS to the Measurement of Spatial Autocorrelation," Computers, Enviro Urban Sys 18 (94): 167-191; auth, "Spatial Impacts of Locally Enacted Growth Controls: The San Francisco Bay Region in the 1980s," Enviro Planning B: Plan and Design 23 (96): 61-91; auth, "Urban Transportation Problems in Shanghai, China: Problems and Planning Implications," Intl J Urban and Region Res 21 (97): 589-606; coauth, "Job Accessibility in the San Juan Metropolitan Region -Implications for Rail Transit Benefit Analysis," Trans Res Rec 1618 (98): 22-31; auth, "Location Characteristics of Inner-City Neighborhoods and Employment Accessibility of Low-Wage Workers," Enviro and Planning B: Plan and Design 25 (98): 345-365; auth, "Spatial Technologies, Accessibility, and the Social Construction of Urban Space," Computers, Enviro and Urban Sys 22 (98): 447-464; auth, "Transportation, Telecommunications, and the changing Geography of Opportunity," Urban Geog 20 (99): 334-355; coauth, "Strategies to Improve Job Accessibility - A Case Study of Tren Urbano in the San Juan Metropolitan Region," Trans Res Rec 1669 (99): 53-60; auth, "Spatial and Social Dimensions of Commuting," J Am Plan Asn 66 (00): 68-82; auth, "New Telecommunications and Residential Location Flexibility," Environ and Plan Asn (forthcoming); auth, "A Spatial Analysis of Job Openings and Access in a U.S. Metropolitan Area," J Am Plan Asn (forthcoming). **CONTACT ADDRESS** Dept Urban Planning, Massachusetts Inst of Tech, 77 Massachusetts Ave, Room 9-526, Cambridge, MA 02139. **EMAIL** qshen@mit.edu

SHEN, XIAOPING
DISCIPLINE GEOGRAPHY **EDUCATION** Univ Ottawa, Phd, 95; Beijing Normal Univ, MSC, 86; Beijing Normal Univ, BSC, 83. **CAREER** Lecturer, Beijing Normal Univ, 86-89; Cantographer, Univ of Ottawa, 93-95; Asst Prof, Central Connecticut State Univ, 95-. **MEMBERSHIPS** Assoc of Amer Geographers, Chmese Prof GIS. **RESEARCH** Economic geography GIS; China and East Asia; Cartography. **SELECTED PUBLICATIONS** Auth, "The Distribution of the Aluminium Industry of the Loess Plateau," Proceedings, International Symposium on Environmental Control and Resources Development in China's Loess Plateau Region, Ed. Commission for Integrated Survey of Natural Resources, Beijing: the Chinese Academy of Science; auth, "Chinese Student Encyclopedia," Beijing: Guangming Publishing House, 91; auth, "Manufacturing Key Sectors," in National Atlas of Canada, Fifth Edition, Ottawa: Energy Mines and Resources Canada, Fifth Edition, Ottawa; Energy Mines and Resources Canada, 93; auth, "Manufacturing Productivity," in National Atlas of Canada, Fifth Edition, Ottawa: Energy Mines and Resources Canada; auth, "Geomorphology Research of Professor Shen Yuchang, Beijing: Environmental Sciences Press; auth, "Spatial Inequality of Rural Industrial Development in China, 89-94, Journal of Rural Studies, 15, 2: 179-199; auth, "Transistion in Regional Geographic Education in the United States: Case Study of Asian Geography, In: Geographic Research at the Turn of the Century, Taiwan: Taiwan Normal University; auth, "In: Facts about China, Ji, Xiao-bin," Ed. New York: H.W. Wilson, 00. **CONTACT ADDRESS** Dept Geography, Central Connecticut State Univ, 1615 Stanley St, New Britain, CT 06053. **EMAIL** shenx@ccsu.edu

SHENTON, JAMES
DISCIPLINE UNITED STATES HISTORY **EDUCATION** Columbia Univ, BA, 49; PhD, 55. **CAREER** Prof. **RESEARCH** Immigration and ethnic history. **SELECTED PUBLICATIONS** Auth, Robert John Walker: A Politician from Jackson to Lincoln, 61; The Reconstruction: A Documentary History of the South after the Civil War, 63; The Historian's History of the United States, 66; Free Enterprise Forever!, 77; Ethnic Groups in American Life, 78. **CONTACT ADDRESS** Dept of History, Columbia Col, New York, 2960 Broadway, New York, NY 10027-6902.

SHEON, AARON
PERSONAL Born 10/07/1937, Toledo, OH, d, 1963, 2 children **DISCIPLINE** HISTORY OF ART **EDUCATION** Univ Mich, AB, 59, MA, 60; Princeton Univ, MFA, 62, PhD(hist of art), 66. **CAREER** Staff officer, UNESCO, Paris, 63-66; asst prof, 66-68, assoc prof, 69-78, prof Hist of Art & Actg chmn dept, Univ Pittsburg, 79-, vis exhib cur, Mus Art, Carnegie Inst, Pittsburgh, 77-81; prog consult, Nat Endowment for Arts & Humanities, 78-; vis prof, Carnegie-Mellon Univ, 81; consult, Pa Arts Coun, 81-; Nat Endowment Humanities grant, 79. **HONORS AND AWARDS** Chancellor Bowman Awd, 76. **MEMBERSHIPS** Col Art Asn Am; Soc Hist Fr Art. **RESEARCH** Nineteenth century French art; art and scientific thought. **SELECTED PUBLICATIONS** Auth, The Gosman Collection, Univ Pittsburgh, 69; Monticelli, His Contemporaries, His Influence, Mus Art, Pittsburgh, 78; Organic Vision, the Architecture of Peter Berndtson, Horizon Press, 80; Octave Tassaert's Le Suicide: Early realism and the plight of women, Arts, 5/81; Monticelli Centennial, Marseille Museum, 86; Van Gogh's Understanding of Theories of Neurosis and Degeneration, 96. **CONTACT ADDRESS** Dept of Fine Arts, Univ of Pittsburgh, 104 Frick Fine Arts, Pittsburgh, PA 15260-7601. **EMAIL** ash2+@pitt.edu

SHEPARDSON, DONALD E.
PERSONAL Born 05/14/1936, Port Huron, MI, s **DISCIPLINE** HISTORY **EDUCATION** Eastern Ill Univ, BS, 61; Univ Ill, MA, 64; PhD, 99. **CAREER** Instr, Bowling Green

State Univ, 66-69; Instr, Va Polytech Inst, 69; From Asst Prof to Prof, Univ N Iowa, 69-. **HONORS AND AWARDS** Distinguished Teaching Awd, Col of Soc and Behav Sci, 95; Awds for Fac Excellence, Iowa Board of Regents, 99. **MEMBERSHIPS** Soc for Military Hist. **RESEARCH** Modern diplomatic and military history. **SELECTED PUBLICATIONS** Auth, Rosa Luxemburg and the Noble Dream, Peter Lang Publ, 96; auth, "The Fall of Berlin and the Rise of a Myth," J of Military Hist, vol 62 (98): 135-153; auth, Conflict and Diplomacy from the Great War to the Cold War, Peter Lang Publ, 99. **CONTACT ADDRESS** Dept Hist, Univ of No Iowa, Cedar Falls, IA 50614-0027. **EMAIL** donald.shepardson@uni.edu

SHEPHERD, JOHN
DISCIPLINE HISTORY OF POPULAR MUSIC **EDUCATION** Carleton Univ, BA, BM; Royal Col of Mus, ARCM; Univ York, UK, DPhil. **CAREER** Prof; ch of Editorial Bd and managing ed, the Encyclopedia of Popular Music of the World, Cassell. **HONORS AND AWARDS** Davidson Dunton res lectrship, 92; adj res prof, grad prog in musicology, york univ; dept of mus, univ ottawa. **RESEARCH** Sociology and aesthetics of music, popular music stud, theory and method in musicology, cultural stud, and the sociology of music education. **SELECTED PUBLICATIONS** Auth, Music as Social Text, Polity Press, 91; co-auth, Rock and Popular Music: Politics, Policies, Institutions, Routledge, 93; Music and Cultural Theory, Polity Press of Cambridge, 97; Popular Music Studies: A Select International Bibliography, 97; co-ed, Relocating Cultural Studies: Developments in Theory and Research, Routledge, 93. **CONTACT ADDRESS** Carleton Univ, 1125 Colonel By Dr, Ottawa, ON, Canada K1S 5B6.

SHEPPARD, THOMAS FREDERICK
PERSONAL Born 06/05/1935, Indianapolis, IN **DISCIPLINE** HISTORY, MODERN EUROPE **EDUCATION** Vanderbilt Univ, AB, 57; Univ Nebr, MA, 62; Johns Hopkins Univ, PhD(hist), 69. **CAREER** Instr hist, Western Ky Univ, 62-65; from asst prof to assoc prof, 69-77, chmn dept, 75-81, Prpf Hist, Col William & Mary, 77-, Nat Endowment for Humanities younger humanists fel, France, 72-73; mem coun, Inst Early Am Hist & Cult, 78-81. **MEMBERSHIPS** AHA; Soc Fr Hist Studies. **RESEARCH** French Social and economic history, local history. **SELECTED PUBLICATIONS** Auth, Justice In The Sarladais 1770-1790 - Reinhardt,Sg/, Am Hist Rev, Vol 0098, 1993. **CONTACT ADDRESS** Dept of Hist, Col of William and Mary, Williamsburg, VA 23185.

SHERIFF, CAROL
DISCIPLINE HISTORY **EDUCATION** Wesleyan, BA, 85; Yale Univ, MA, 88, PhD, 93. **CAREER** Assoc prof, hist, Coll Wm & Mary. **HONORS AND AWARDS** NY State Hist Asn Prize, 96; Awd For Excellence in Res using holdings of the NY State Arch, 96. **MEMBERSHIPS** OAH, AHA, SHEAR. **SELECTED PUBLICATIONS** Auth, The Artificial River: The Erie Canal and the Paradox of Progress, 1817-1862, Hill & Wang, 96. **CONTACT ADDRESS** Hist Dept, Col of William and Mary, Box 8795, Williamsburg, VA 23187-8795. **EMAIL** cxsher@wm.edu

SHERIFF, MARY D.
DISCIPLINE ART HISTORY **EDUCATION** Univ DE, PhD. **CAREER** Prof, Univ NC, Chapel Hill. **RESEARCH** 18th and 19th century art; critical theory. **SELECTED PUBLICATIONS** Auth, J.-H. Fragonard: Art and Eroticism, Univ Chicago Press, 90; coed, Eighteenth-Century Studies (1993-1998) The Exceptional Woman: Elisabeth Vigee-Lebrun and the Cultural Politics of Art, Univ Chicago Press, 96. **CONTACT ADDRESS** Univ of No Carolina, Chapel Hill, Chapel Hill, NC 27599. **EMAIL** msheriff@email.unc.edu

SHERMAN, RICHARD B.
PERSONAL Born 11/16/1929, Somerville, MA, m, 1952, 2 children **DISCIPLINE** AMERICAN HISTORY **EDUCATION** Harvard Univ, AB, 51, PhD, 59; Univ PA, MA, 52. **CAREER** Instr hist, PA State Univ, 57-60; from asst prof to assoc prof, 60-70, prof Hist, 70-87, Chancellor Prof Hist, 87-92, :Pullen Prof Hist, 92-94, PROF EMERITUS, COL WILLIAM & MARY, 94-; Fulbright prof hist, Univ Stockholm, 66-67. **HONORS AND AWARDS** PBK **MEMBERSHIPS** AAUP. **RESEARCH** Recent American history. **SELECTED PUBLICATIONS** Ed, The Negro and the City, Prentice-Hall, 70; auth, The Republican Party and Black America, from McKinley to Hoover, 1896-1933, Univ VA, 73; The Case of Odell Wallen and Virginia Justice, 1940-1942, Univ TN, 92; co-auth, The College of William and Mary: A History, King and Queen Press, 93; articles in New England Quart, Mid-America, Polit Sci Quart, PA Hist, J Negro Hist, Historian, Proloque, J Southern Hist, VA Mag Hist and Biography. **CONTACT ADDRESS** Dept of Hist, Col of William and Mary, Williamsburg, VA 23187. **EMAIL** rbsher@wm.edu

SHERMAN, WILLIAM LEWIS
PERSONAL Born 04/09/1927, Pasadena, CA, m, 1960, 3 children **DISCIPLINE** COLONIAL LATIN AMERICAN HISTORY **EDUCATION** Univ of the Americas, MA, 58; Univ NMex, PhD(hist), 67. **CAREER** Foreign serv, US Dept State, 51-53; instr & asst to pres, Mex City Col, 59-60; coord Latin Am area studies, Peace Corps, Univ NMex, 63-65; asst prof hist, Calif Western Univ, 65-66 & Colo State Univ, 66-68; from asst prof to assoc prof, 68-76, Prof Hist, Univ Nebr-Lincoln, 76-, Fac Improv Comt res grant, Spain, 67; Woods res grant, Cent Am, 70; Nebr Found res grant, Cent Am, 72; Del Amo grant, Spain, 64-65; Univ Nebr grant, Spain, 80. **MEMBERSHIPS** Int Cong Americanists; Int Congr Americanists; corresp mem Geog & Hist Soc Guatemala. **RESEARCH** Central America and Mexico in the 16th century. **SELECTED PUBLICATIONS** Auth, Tlaxcalans in post-conquest Guatemala, Tlalocan, summer 68; Abusos contra los indios de Guatemala: Relaciones del obispo, 1602-1605, Caravelle, 12/68; Indian slavery and the Cerrato reforms, Hisp Am Hist Rev, 2/71; coauth, The Course of Mexican History, Oxford Univ, 78; Forced Native Labor in Sixteenth Century Central America, Univ Nebr Press, 79. **CONTACT ADDRESS** Dept of Hist, Univ of Nebraska, Lincoln, Lincoln, NE 68508.

SHERRICK, REBECCA LOUISE
PERSONAL Born 05/28/1953, Carthage, IL **DISCIPLINE** AMERICAN HISTORY, WOMEN'S STUDIES **EDUCATION** IL Wesleyan Univ, BA, 75; Northwestern Univ, PhD(hist), 80. **CAREER** Asst prof hist to provost, Carroll Col, 80-. **MEMBERSHIPS** AHA; Orgn Am Historians. **RESEARCH** Father-daughter relationship as a factor in identity formation; female friendships among late-Victorian women; autobiography and womens identity. **SELECTED PUBLICATIONS** Auth, Toward Universal Sisterhood, Women's Studies Int Forum, 9/82. **CONTACT ADDRESS** Dept Hist, Carroll Col, Wisconsin, 100 N East Ave, Waukesha, WI 53186-5593.

SHERRY, MICHAEL STEPHEN
PERSONAL Born 01/08/1945, Indianapolis, IN, 2 children **DISCIPLINE** AMERICAN HISTORY **EDUCATION** Washington Univ, BA, 67; Yale Univ, MA, 69, PhD(hist), 75. **CAREER** Teacher hist, Hamden Hall Country Day Sch, Conn, 69-71 & Yale Psychiat Inst, Yale Univ, 74-76; assoc visit prof, Am hist, Northwestern Univ, 76-79; Nat Endowment for Humanities res fel, 79-80; Asst Prof Am Hist, 80-82, Assoc Prof, Hist, 82-87, prof, history, 87-, asst dean for freshman, College for Arts and Sciences, 94-97, assoc dean, Weinberg College of Arts and Sciences, Northwestern Univ, 98-01; Lectr Am hist, Yale Univ, 75-76. **HONORS AND AWARDS** Richard W. Leopold Prof of History, Northwestern Univ, 01-; Humanities Research Awd, Northwestern Univ, 89-90; Bancroft Prize for Distinguished Books in American History and Diplomacy, for The Rise of American Air Power, 88; Rockefeller Foundation Humanities Fellowship, 83-84; NEH Fellowship, 79-80. **MEMBERSHIPS** Orgn Am Historians; Am Hist Assn. **RESEARCH** Modern U.S. History. **SELECTED PUBLICATIONS** Auth, The Rise of American Air Power: The Creation of Armageddon, Yale Univ Pr, 87; The Origins Of Sdi, 1944-1983 - Baucom,Dr/, Diplomatic Hist, Vol 0018, 1994; Cardinal Choices - Presidential Sci Advising From The Atomic-Bomb To Sdi - Herken,G/, Diplomatic Hist, Vol 0018, 1994; The Devil We Knew - Americans And The Cold-War - Brands,Hw/, J Of Am Hist, Vol 0081, 1994; We Value Teaching Despite - And Because Of - Its Low Status/, J Of American Hist, Vol 0081, 1994; Projections Of War - Hollywood, Am Cult, And World-War-Ii - Doherty,T/, Diplomatic Hist, Vol 0019, 1995; auth, In the Shadow of War: The United States Since the 1930s, Yale Univ Pr, 95; Untitled/, J Of Am Hist, Vol 0083, 1996; The New Winter Soldiers - Gi And Veteran Dissent During The Vietnam Era - Moser,R/, Revs In Am Hist, Vol 0025, 1997; Masters Of War - Military Dissent And Politics In The Vietnam Era - Buzzanco,R/, Revs In Am Hist, Vol 0025, 1997. **CONTACT ADDRESS** Dept of Hist, Northwestern Univ, Evanston, IL 60208-2220. **EMAIL** m-sherry@northwestern.edu

SHERWIN, MARTIN J.
PERSONAL Born 07/02/1937, Brooklyn, NY, m, 1963, 2 children **DISCIPLINE** HISTORY **EDUCATION** Dartmouth Col, BA, 59; UCLA, PhD, 71. **CAREER** Walter S. Dickson prof of Hist, Tufts Univ. **HONORS AND AWARDS** Bernath Bk Prize; Am Hist Bk Prize; Guggenheim Fel; NEH Fel; Rockefeller Found Fel; MacArthur Found Peace Fel; Soc Am Hist; Arms Control Fel; UNESCO Distinguished Fel; Prof of the Year, 85, 86; Silver Medal, Coun for the Advancement and Support of Education. **MEMBERSHIPS** AHA; OAH; ASA; SHAFR; CPRH. **RESEARCH** Cold War. **SELECTED PUBLICATIONS** A World Destroyed: Hiroshima and the Origins of the Arms Race. **CONTACT ADDRESS** Tufts Univ, Medford, Medford, MA 02155. **EMAIL** martin.sherwin@tufts.edu

SHESGREEN, SEAN NICHOLAS
PERSONAL Born 12/05/1939, Derry City, Ireland, d, 2 children **DISCIPLINE** ENGLISH LITERATURE, ART HISTORY **EDUCATION** Loyola Univ Chicago, BA, 62, MA, 66; Northwestern Univ, PhD(English), 70. **CAREER** Teaching asst English, Northwestern Univ, 68-69; asst prof, 69-74, assoc prof, 74-82, Prof English, Northern IL Univ, 82-, Presidential Res Prof, 90-95; Vis fac mem, Univ CA, Riverside, 74-75; Am Philos Soc grant-in-aid, 76; exchange prof English, Xian Foreign Lang Inst, People's Repub China, 81-82. **HONORS AND AWARDS** Huntington Library Summer fel, 98; Yale Univ Center for Art fel, 90; Ball Brothers Found fel, Lilly Library, IN Univ, Bloomington; NEH Newberry Library Sr fel, 98-99; Houghton Lib Fel, 95. **MEMBERSHIPS** MLA; Am Soc 18th Century Studies. **RESEARCH** Eighteenth century novel with emphasis on Henry Fielding; 18th century graphic art with emphasis on William Hogarth; cries of London. **SELECTED PUBLICATIONS** Auth, Literary Portraits in the Novels of Henry Fielding, Northern Ill Univ, 72; ed, Engravings by Hogarth, Dover, 73; auth, A Harlot's Progress and the Question of Hogarth's Didacticisms, 18th Century Life, 75; Hogarth's Industry and Idleness, 18th Century Studies, 76; Hogarth and the Times-of-the-Day Tradition, Cornell Univ Press, 82; Marcellus Laroon's Cryer of the City of London, Studies Bibliog, 82; The Crier and Hawkers of London, Stanford Univ Press, 90. **CONTACT ADDRESS** No Illinois Univ, 1425 W Lincoln Hwy, De Kalb, IL 60115-2825. **EMAIL** shesgreen@niu.edu

SHEWMAKER, KENNETH EARL
PERSONAL Born 06/26/1936, Los Angeles, CA, m, 1960, 2 children **DISCIPLINE** AMERICAN DIPLOMATIC HISTORY **EDUCATION** Concordia Teachers Col, BS, 60; Univ Calif, Berkeley, MA, 61; Northwestern Univ, PhD(US-Chinese rels), 66. **CAREER** Instr hist, Northwestern Univ, 65-66; asst prof, Col William & Mary, 66-67; from asst prof to assoc prof, 67-78, prof hist, Dartmouth Col, 78-, Soc Sci Res Coun/Am Coun Learned Soc Joint Comt Contemp China res grant, 67-68; Nat Hist Publ Comn res grant, 72-73; Dartmouth Col sr fac grant, 82. **HONORS AND AWARDS** Stuart L Bernath Prize, Soc Hist Am Foreign Rels, 72; Distinguished Teaching Awd, Dartmouth Col, 86 & 96; Honorary membership in Phi Beta Kappa, 99. **MEMBERSHIPS** New Hampshire Hist Soc; Orgn Am Historians; Soc Hist Am Foreign Rels. **RESEARCH** American diplomatic history; United States-China relations; Daniel Webster and American foreign policy. **SELECTED PUBLICATIONS** Auth, Americans and Chinese Communists, 1927-1945: A Persuading Encounter, Cornell Univ Press, 71; auth, Daniel Webster and the Politics of Foreign Policy, Journal of American History, September 76; auth, The war of words: The Cass-Webster Debate of 1842-43, Diplomatic Hist, spring 81; auth, Daniel Webster and the Oregon Question, Pacific Historical Review, May 82; ed, The Papers of Daniel Webster, Diplomatic Paper, 2 vols, Univ Press of New England, 83-87; auth, Daniel Webster and American Conservatism, in Traditions and Values, ed. Norman A. Graebner, Univ Press of America, 85; auth, Congress only can declare war and the President is Commander in Chief: Daniel Webster and the War Power, Diplomatic History, Fall 88; Daniel Webster, Angler, The American Fly Fisher, Fall 92; Forgeing the Great Chain: Daniel Webster and the Origins of American Foreign policy Toward East Asia and the Pacific 1841-1852, Proceedings of the Am Philos Soc, 85; Hook and line, and bob and sinder: Daniel Webster and the Fisheries Dispute of 1852, Diplomatic History, Spring 85; contribur, Encyclopedia of US Foreign Relations, Oxford Univ Press, 97; Commercial Expansionism in China, Hawaii, and Japan, Major Problems in American Foreign Relations Vol 1: To 1920, 00; ed, Daniel Webster: The Completest Man, Univ Press New England, 90; auth, Untaught Diplomacy: Daniel Webster and the Lobos Islands Controversy, Diplomatic History, Fall 97; auth, Missiia Neila Brauna v Rossii 1850-1852, Americana, 98; auth, This Unblessed War: Daniel Webster's Opposition to the War of 1812, Historical New Hampshire, Spring/Summer 98. **CONTACT ADDRESS** Dept of History, Dartmouth Col, 6107 Reed Hall, Hanover, NH 03755-3506. **EMAIL** shewmaker@dartmouth.edu

SHI, MINGZHENG
PERSONAL Born 11/03/1963, Beijing, China, m, 1994, 1 child **DISCIPLINE** HISTORY **EDUCATION** Peking Univ, BA, 86; Univ of Conn, MA, 88; Columbia Univ, PhD, 93. **CAREER** Asst prof, Univ of Houston, 92-97; asst prof, Univ of Haw, 97-. **HONORS AND AWARDS** ACLS, 90-91; NEH, 95-96. **MEMBERSHIPS** Asia Soc, Houston Center, 92-95, Urban Hist Asn, 00-02. **RESEARCH** Chinese social and cultural history, history of cities. **SELECTED PUBLICATIONS** Auth, Remaking Beijing, Peking Univ Press, 95; auth, "America as an Idea: a Historical Inquiry of the Chinese Perceptions of the United States," The Jour of Am Studies 28 (96); auth, "Rebuilding the Chinese Captial: Beijing in the Early Twentieth Century," Urban Hist 25 (98); auth, "From Imperial Gardens to Public Parks: The Transformation of Space in Early Twentieth Century Beijing," Modern China 24 (98); auth, "Must the Walls Be Torn Down? The Cultural Dimension of Urban Planning in Twentieth Century China," Planning Hist 22 (00). **CONTACT ADDRESS** Dept Hist, Univ of Hawaii, Manoa, 2530 Dole St, Honolulu, HI 96822-2303. **EMAIL** mingzhen@hawaii.edu

SHIELDS, JOHANNA NICOL
PERSONAL Born 07/12/1942, Mobile, AL, m, 1968, 2 children **DISCIPLINE** AMERICAN HISTORY **EDUCATION** Univ Ala, BA, 64; MA, 65; PhD, 72. **CAREER** Instr, Univ Ala, Huntsville, 67-69, 70-72; from asst prof to prof emer, Univ Ala, Huntsville, 72-; chair, Dept Hist, Univ Ala, Huntsville, 91-95; dir, Humanities Center, Univ Ala, Huntsville, 92-93, 98-. **HONORS AND AWARDS** Res Fel, AAUW, 69-70; Gabriel Awd, Am Studies Asn, 82. **MEMBERSHIPS** Orgn Am Historians; Southern Hist Asn; The Hist Soc; Soc Historians Early Am Repub. **RESEARCH** Antebellum United States history; 19th century Southern history. **SELECTED PUBLICATIONS** Auth, The Line of Duty: Maverick Congressmen and the Devel-

opment of American Political Culture, 1836-1860, Greenwood Press, 85; auth, "Whigs Reform the 'Bear Garden': Representation and The Apportionment Act of 1842," J of the Early Repub (10/85): 335-382; auth, "A Social History of Antebellum Alabama Writers," Ala Rev (7/89): 163-191; auth, "A Sadder Simon Suggs: Freedom and Slavery in the Humor of Johnson Hooper," J of Southern Hist (11/90): 641-664; auth, "White Honor, Black Humor, and the Making of a Southern Style," Southern Cult (Summer, 95): 420-430. **CONTACT ADDRESS** Humanities Center, Univ of Alabama, Huntsville, Rm 322 Roberts Hall, Huntsville, AL 35899. **EMAIL** shieldsj@email.uah.edu

SHIELS, RICHARD DOUGLAS
PERSONAL Born 04/05/1947, Detroit, MI, m, 1972 **DISCIPLINE** AMERICAN AND RELIGIOUS HISTORY **EDUCATION** Hope Col, BA, 68; Yale Univ, MAR, 71; Boston Univ, PhD, 76. **CAREER** Asst prof, Boston Univ, 75-76; asst prof, 76-82, assoc orof hist, Ohio St Univ, Newark, 82-. **MEMBERSHIPS** Orgn Am Historians; AHA. **RESEARCH** American intellectual and social history. **SELECTED PUBLICATIONS** Auth, "Second Great Awakening in Connecticut," Church History, Vol 49, 80; Feminization of American congregationalists, 1730-1835, Am Quart, Vol 33, 81. **CONTACT ADDRESS** History Dept, Ohio State Univ, Newark, 1179 University Dr, Newark, OH 43055-1797. **EMAIL** shiels.1@osu.edu

SHIFF, RICHARD
DISCIPLINE ART AND ART HISTORY **EDUCATION** Yale Univ, PhD. **CAREER** Prof; Effie Marie Cain Regents Chr in Art & dir, Ctr Study Modernism. **RESEARCH** Mod art from the early 19th century to the present, with emphasis on French painting and post-war Am art. **SELECTED PUBLICATIONS** Auth, Cezanne and the End of Impressionism & stud of critical and methodological issues; publ on, artists Edouard Manet, Willem de Kooning, Richard Serra, Vija Celmins, Jasper Johns, Roger Fry's social theories, and on Walter Benjamin's theory of aura. **CONTACT ADDRESS** Dept of Art and Art Hist, Univ of Texas, Austin, 2613 Wichita St, FAB 2.106, Austin, TX 78705.

SHINER, LARRY
PERSONAL Born 05/06/1934, Oklahoma City, OK, m, 1980, 2 children **DISCIPLINE** PHILOSOPHY, HISTORY **EDUCATION** Northwestern Univ, BA, 56; Universite de Strasbourg, Doctorate, 61. **CAREER** Asst prof, Univ of Tampa, 61; assoc prof, Cornell Col, 62-71; prof, Univ of IL Springfield, 71-. **HONORS AND AWARDS** William S. Pilling Fel, 59; Danforth Cross-Disciplinary Fel, 67. **MEMBERSHIPS** Am Soc for Aesthetics. **RESEARCH** Philosophy of Art, 18th Century Studies. **SELECTED PUBLICATIONS** Auth, The Secularization of History, Abingdon Pr, 68; auth, The Secret Mirror: Literary Form and History in Tocqueville; Cornell Univ, 98. **CONTACT ADDRESS** Dept Hist, Univ of Illinois, Springfield, PO Box 19243, Springfield, IL 62794-9243. **EMAIL** shiner.larry@uis.edu

SHINGLETON, ROYCE GORDON
PERSONAL Born 10/25/1935, Stantonsburg, NC, m, 1962, 2 children **DISCIPLINE** HISTORY **EDUCATION** East Carolina Univ, BS, 58; Appalachian St Univ, MA, 64; Fla State Univ, PhD, 71. **CAREER** Ga State Univ, 68-74; Oglethorpe Univ, 74-77; Darton Col, 77-. **HONORS AND AWARDS** Darton Col Found Commun Service Awd, 79; SE Writers' Asn award for best non-fiction manuscript, 81; Atlanta Foundation Grant, 85; Atlanta Hist Soc Franklin Garrett Awd, 85; Darton Col Foundation Advising Awd, 93; Nat Inst for Staff and Org Dev Awd for Excellence in Tchng, 94; recipient of the Clarendon Awd, 95. **MEMBERSHIPS** US Civil War Ctr; Ga Asn of Hist; Univ System of Ga Advisory Comt on Hist; Thronateeska Heritage Ctr of Albany. **RESEARCH** Civil War and Reconstruction; 19th century US; Southern hist; US Survey. **SELECTED PUBLICATIONS** Auth, John Taylor Wood, Sea Ghost of the Confederacy, Univ GA Press, 79, 81; auth, Richard Peters: Champion of the New South, Mercer Univ Press, 85; High Seas Confederate, The Life and Times of John Newland Maffitt, Univ SC Press, 94, 95; auth, co-auth, The Confederate States Navy: The Ships, Men and Organization, 1861-65, Naval Inst Press & Conway Maritime Press, 97; and numerous articles and book reviews. **CONTACT ADDRESS** Soc Sci Div, Darton Col, Albany, GA 31707. **EMAIL** rshingle@mail.dartnet.peachnet.edu

SHIPLEY, NEAL ROBERT
PERSONAL Born Pittsburgh, PA **DISCIPLINE** HISTORY **EDUCATION** Grove City Col, AB, 59; Harvard Univ, AM, 60, PhD(hist), 67. **CAREER** Asst prof hist, Univ Tenn, Knoxville, 67-78; assoc prof, 68-85, Prof Hist, Univ Mass, Amherst, 85-, assoc dean, humanities & fine arts, 85-92; dir, UMass Amherst-Trinity Col, Oxford, Oxford Summer Seminar Brit Studies, 87-92. **RESEARCH** Tudor-Stuart history; Victorian studies **SELECTED PUBLICATIONS** Auth, Full hand and worthy purposes: The foundation of Charter House, 1606-1616, Guildhall Studies, 4/75; History of a manor: Castle Campes, 1580-1629, Bull Inst Hist Res, 11/75; Thomas Sutton: Tudor-Stuart moneylender, Bus Hist Rev, winter 76; London's City Lands Committee, 1592-1644, Guildhall Studies, spring 77. **CONTACT ADDRESS** Dept of Hist, Univ of Massachusetts, Amherst, Amherst, MA 01003-0002. **EMAIL** nrs@oitunix.oit.umass.edu

SHIRAZI, FAEGHEH S.
PERSONAL Born 01/02/1952, Abadan, Iran, d, 2 children **DISCIPLINE** MIDDLE EAST STUDIES **EDUCATION** Univ Houston, BA, 75; Kans State Univ, MS, 76; Ohio State Univ, PhD, 86. **CAREER** Instructor, Collin County Col, 88-90; Res Assoc to Asst Prof, Univ Tex, 90-. **HONORS AND AWARDS** Univ Fac Summer Res Grant, Univ Houston, 98; Dean's Fel, Univ Tex, 01. **RESEARCH** Women's studies; Middle Eastern cultures/Muslim cultures. Interested in the material cultures especially textiles and clothing as it effects gender relationship and social/cultural lives of people in the Muslim and/or Middle Eastern societies. **SELECTED PUBLICATIONS** Auth, The Veil Unveiled: Visual, Political and Literary Dynamics of the Veil, Univ Press of Fla, in press; auth, "Tools of Persuasion: Images of Iranian Women," Studies in Contemporary Islam, in press; auth, "Visions of Paradise; Persian and Anatolian Textiles in the Collection of the Harry Ransom Center," The Library Chronicle of the Univ of Tex at Austin, 97; auth, "Hijab (Veiling), from a Dramaturgical perspective in Post Revolutionary Iran," Journal of the Critical Studies in the Middle East, (95): 54-63; auth, "The Politics of Clothing in the Middle East; The Case of Hijab in Post-Revolution Iran," Journal of the Critical Studies in the Middle East, 93. **CONTACT ADDRESS** Dept Middle East Studies, Univ of Texas, Austin, Austin, TX 78712-1013. **EMAIL** fshirazi@uts.cc.utexas.edu

SHLAPENTOKH, DMITRY V.
PERSONAL Born 05/31/1950, Kiev, Russia, m, 1994, 2 children **DISCIPLINE** HISTORY **EDUCATION** Univ Moscow, BA; Mich St Univ, MA; Univ Chicago, PhD, 88. **CAREER** Vis Asst Prof, St Univ NY (SUNY), 88; Assoc Prof, Ind Univ, 91-. **HONORS AND AWARDS** Fel, Int Napoleanic Soc; Who's Who in the World; Lady Davis Fel, Hebrew Univ; Hoover Fel, 92; Mellon Grant-in-Aid for Res, Ind Univ, 95; Travel Grant, ACLS, 95; NEH Fel, Columbia Univ, 97. **MEMBERSHIPS** INS, ACLS. **RESEARCH** Russia: past and present, European history, comparative history. **SELECTED PUBLICATIONS** Auth, The French Revolution in Russian Intellectual Life (1865-1905), Praeger (Westport, CT), 96; auth, The French Revolution and the Anti-Democratic Tradition in Russia, Rutgers UP, 97; auth, The Counterrevolution in Revolution, Macmillan (UK), 99; auth, "The Post-Soviet History and NATO Expansion," Humboldt J of Soc Rel, vol 25 (99); auth, "The Illusions and Realities of Russian Nationalism," Wash Quart, vol 23 (00); auth, "The Problem with Russian Democracy: Can Russia Rise Again?" in Democracy (Cambridge UP, 00); auth, "Soviet Movie Industry," in The Int Movie Indust (SIU Pr, forthcoming). **CONTACT ADDRESS** Dept Hist, Indiana Univ, South Bend, PO Box 7111, South Bend, IN 46634-7111.

SHLOSSER, FRANZISKA E.
DISCIPLINE MEDIEVAL HISTORY **EDUCATION** McGill Univ, MA, PhD. **CAREER** Assoc prof. **RESEARCH** History of costume and interiors. **SELECTED PUBLICATIONS** Pub(s), ancient Greek Numismatics, Late Antiquity and Byzantine History; auth, The Reign of the Emperor Maurikios (582-602): A Reassessment, Hist Monogr 14, Athens: Hist Publ St D Basilopoulos, 94. **CONTACT ADDRESS** Dept of Hist, Concordia Univ, Montreal, 1455 de Maisonneuve W, Montreal, QC, Canada H3G 1M8. **EMAIL** shlosse@vax2.concordia.ca

SHNEIDMAN, J. LEE
PERSONAL Born 06/20/1929, New York, NY, m, 1961, 2 children **DISCIPLINE** MEDIEVAL HISTORY **EDUCATION** NYork Univ, BA, 51, MA, 52; Univ Wis, PhD, 57. **CAREER** Vis instr hist, 56-57, CUNY; lectr hist & govt, 57-58, Univ Md Overseas Prog; from instr to asst prof hist, 57, 58-62, Fairleigh Dickinson Univ; asst prof, 62-63, Brooklyn Col, 62-63; from asst prof to assoc prof, 63-71, prof hist, 71-, Adelphi Univ; mem ed bd, Indice Historico Espanol. **MEMBERSHIPS** AHA; Mediaeval Acad Am; Group for Use of Psychol in Hist; chmn, Columbia Univ Seminar; Hist of Legal and Polit Thought and Institutions. **RESEARCH** Political thought and nationalism in the Middle Ages; psychohistory; psychobiography of Aaron Burr. **SELECTED PUBLICATIONS** Auth, Rise of the Anagonese-Cafalan Empire, 1200-1350, New York Univ Press, 70; coauth, Kennedy, Twayne, 73; auth, "Spain and France, 1940-1950," Facts on File, 75; Auth, Eastern Europe and the Soviet Union, Spain in the Twentieth Century World, Greenwood, 80; coauth, The Burr-Hamilton Duel: Suicide or Murder?, J Psychohist, vol 8, 80. **CONTACT ADDRESS** 161 W 86th St, New York, NY 10024.

SHOCKEY, GARY C.
PERSONAL Born 11/07/1959, New London, CT **DISCIPLINE** MEDIEVAL STUDIES **EDUCATION** Hartwick Col, BA, 81; Middlebury Col, MA, 82; Univ Calif, PhD, 98. **CAREER** Vis asst prof, John Carroll Univ, 97-. **MEMBERSHIPS** MLA; ALSC; AATG; MAP. **RESEARCH** Post-classical courtly romances of the 13th century; medieval law political discourse; status of peasantry in medieval courtly romance; Minnesang. **CONTACT ADDRESS** John Carroll Univ, 20700 N Park Blvd, OC 142, University Heights, OH 44118. **EMAIL** gshockey@jcu.edu

SHOEMAKER, RAYMOND LEROY
PERSONAL Born 02/11/1942, Lawton, Okla, m, 1981, 4 children **DISCIPLINE** HISTORY **EDUCATION** US Mil Acad, BS, 64; Ind Univ, MA, 71, PhD(hist), 76. **CAREER** Admin Dir, 94-; Asst Exec Secy, Ind Hist Soc, 76-94, Bus Mgr, 79-. **MEMBERSHIPS** Orgn Am Historians; Ind Hist Soc. **RESEARCH** Diplomatic history; Indiana history; naval history. **SELECTED PUBLICATIONS** Auth, Lew Wallace and the Mexican connection, the United States and the French intervention in Mexico, 1861-1867, Ind Mil Hist J, 1/78; Diplomacy from the Quarterdeck: The Navy in the Caribbean, 1815-1830, In: Changing Interpretations and New Sources on Naval History, Garland Press, 79; Henry Lane Wilson and Republican Policy toward Mexico, 1913-1920, Ind Mag Hist, 6/80; co-producer, Indiana Ragtime: A Documentary Album, Ind Hist Soc, 81; co-prod, The Classic Hoagy Carmichael, 10/88; contrib, Biographical Directory of the Union, 6/96; co-prod, You're the Top: Cole Porter in the 1930's, 4/92; co-prod, You're Sensational: Cole Porter in the '20s, '30s, and '40s. **CONTACT ADDRESS** Indiana Historical Society, 450 W Ohio St, Indianapolis, IN 46202. **EMAIL** rshoemaker@indianahistory.org

SHOEMAKER, REBECCA SHEPHERD
PERSONAL Born 05/10/1947, Franklin, NC, m, 1981, 1 child **DISCIPLINE** US HISTORY **EDUCATION** Berea Col, BA, 69; Ind Univ, MA, 70; PhD, 76. **CAREER** Instr, Univ NC at Wilmington, 73-74; asst prof, Ill State Univ, 74-77; asst prof, Ind State Univ, 79-82; assoc prof, 82-92; prof, 92-. **HONORS AND AWARDS** HIS CLIO Grant; IHC Res Fel. **MEMBERSHIPS** OAH; IAH; HIS. **RESEARCH** 20th Century US Constitutional History; Civil Liberties History in 20th Century US. **SELECTED PUBLICATIONS** Co-ed, A Biographical Directory of the Indiana General Assembly, vol 1, 1816-1899 (Indianapolis), 80; auth, "Indiana Civil Liberties Union," in An Encyclopedia of Indianapolis, eds. David Bodenhamer, Robert G Barrows (Bloomington, IN, 94); auth, "Justice Willis VanDevanter," in A Biographical Directory of US Supreme Court Justices, ed. Melvin I Urofsky (NY, 94); auth, "James D Williams," Traces of Ind and Midwestern Hist 5 (96); auth, "James Britt Donovan," (6: 735-736) and "Edith Spurlock Sampson," (19: 231-232) in American National Biography, eds. John A Garraty, Mark C Carnes (NY: Oxford UP, 99). **CONTACT ADDRESS** Dept History, Indiana State Univ, 210 North 7th St, Terre Haute, IN 47809-0001. **EMAIL** hishoema@ruby.indstate.edu

SHORROCK, WILLIAM IRWIN
PERSONAL Born 06/16/1941, Milwaukee, WI, m, 1964, 2 children **DISCIPLINE** MODERN EUROPEAN & EUROPEAN DIPLOMATIC HISTORY **EDUCATION** Denison Univ, BA, 63; Univ Wis, MA, 65, PhD, 68. **CAREER** From instr to asst prof Europ hist, Univ Wis, Marathon County Campus, 67-69; assoc prof, 69-82, prof hist, Cleveland State Univ, 82- **HONORS AND AWARDS** Fulbright Scholar, 83. **MEMBERSHIPS** AHA; Fr Colonial Hist Soc. **RESEARCH** Nineteenth and twentieth century French diplomatic history; Third Republic French political history. **SELECTED PUBLICATIONS** Auth, The French presence in Syria and Lebanon before the First World War, 1900-1914, in Historian, 2/72; Anticlericalism and French policy in the Ottoman Empire, in Europ Studies Rev, 1/74; France and the rise of facism in Italy, 1919-1923, in J Contemp Hist, 10/75; French Imperialism in the Middle East: The Failure of Policy in Syria and Lebanon, 1900-1914, Univ Wis, 76; French suspicion of British policy in Syria, 1900-1914, in J Europ Studies, 76; La France, l'Italie fasciste et la question de l'Adriatique, 1922-1924, in Rev d'hist diplomatique, 80; Prelude to empire: French Balkan policy, 1878-1881, in East Europ Quart, 81; The Jouvenel mission to Rome and the origins of the Laval-Mussolini accords, 1933-1935, in Historian, 82; From Ally to Enemy: The Enigma of Fascist Italy in French Diplomacy, 1920-1940, Kent State Univ Press, 88. **CONTACT ADDRESS** Office Acad Affairs, Cleveland State Univ, 1983 E 24th St, Cleveland, OH 44115-2440. **EMAIL** w.shorrock@csuohio.edu

SHORTRIDGE, JAMES R.
PERSONAL Born 03/14/1944, Kansas City, MO, m, 1967, 2 children **DISCIPLINE** GEOGRAPHY **EDUCATION** Dartmouth Col, AB 66; Univ Kansas, MA 68, PhD 72. **CAREER** Univ Kansas, asst prof 72-77, assoc prof 77-84, prof 84-. **HONORS AND AWARDS** OBK 66; Guggenheim fel 79-80. **MEMBERSHIPS** AAG; Kansas State Hist Soc. **RESEARCH** Historical and cultural geography of US. **SELECTED PUBLICATIONS** Raw Valley Landscapes, Univ Pr Kansas, 88; The Middle West, Univ Kansas Press, 89; Peopling the Plains, Univ Press Kansas, 96; The Taste of American Place, with Barbara G Shortridge and James R Shortridge, Rowman Littlefield, 98; Our Town on the Plains, Univ Pr Kansas, 00. **CONTACT ADDRESS** Dept Geography, Univ of Kansas, Lawrence, Lawrence, KS 66045. **EMAIL** shortrid@ukans.edu

SHOWALTER, DENNIS
PERSONAL Born 02/12/1942, Delano, MN **DISCIPLINE** HISTORY **EDUCATION** St John's Univ, BA, 63; Univ of Minn, MA, 65; PhD, 69. **CAREER** From asst prof to prof, The Colo Col, 69-; distinguished vis prof, USAFA, 91-93; distinguished vis prof, USMA, 92-98. **HONORS AND AWARDS**

Paul Birdsall Prize, Am Hist Asn, 92. **MEMBERSHIPS** Soc for Military Hist, Ger Studies Asn. **RESEARCH** Military history, modern Germany. **SELECTED PUBLICATIONS** Auth, "The Political Soldiers of Imperial Germany: Myths and Realities," Ger Studies Rev XVI (94): 59-77; auth, "Hubertusberg to Auerstaedt: The Prussian Army in Decline?" Ger Hist XII (94): 308-333; auth, The Wars of Frederick the Great, Longmans (London, Eng), 96; auth, "Past and Future: The Military Crisis of the Weimar Republic," War and Soc XIV (96): 49-72; auth, "German Military Elites in the Twentieth Century," Military Elites in War and Peace, Praeger, 96; auth, "Dien Bien Phu in Three Cultures," War and Soc XVI (98); auth, "Deterrent to Doomsday Machine: The Imperial German Army, 1890-1914," The J of Military Hist LXVI (00). **CONTACT ADDRESS** Dept Hist, Colo Col, 14 E Cache La Poudre St, Colorado Springs, CO 80903-3243. **EMAIL** dshowalter@coloradocollege.edu

SHRADER, CHARLES R.
PERSONAL Born 07/03/1943, Nashville, TN, m, 1963, 2 children **DISCIPLINE** HISTORY **EDUCATION** Vanderbilt Univ, BA, 64; Columbia Univ, MA, 70, MPhil, 74, PhD, 76; US Army Command and Gen Staff Col, 78; US Army War Col, 82; NATO Defense Col, 84. **CAREER** Comn Off, US Army 64-87; asst prof, US Mil Acad; fac, US Army Command and Gen Staff Col, 77-80; act dir/dep dir, Combat Stud Inst, 78-80; chief, Oral Hist Br/asst dir, US Army Mil Hist Inst, 80-84; Fac, US Army War Col, 80-84; Fac, NATO Defense Col, 84-85; chief, Hist Svcs Div, US Army Ctr Mil Hist, 85-87; adj fac, Univ Md, 74-76; adj fac, Elizabethtown Col, 88-89; adj fac, Pa State Univ, Harrisburg, 88-90; Independent Scholar, 87-; Exec Dir, Soc Mil Hist, 92-00. **HONORS AND AWARDS** Army War Col Fac Writing Prize, 82; Harold L. Peterson Awd hon men, 93; Marshall Chair of Mil Stud, US Army War Col, 83-84. **MEMBERSHIPS** AHA; Phi Beta Kappa; Medieval Acad Am; US Comn Mil Hist; Soc Historians For Rel; Nat Coalition Independent Scholars. **RESEARCH** Am mil biography; ins and intellectual his of US Army; hist mil logistics; medieval ms stud; ecclesiastical, intellectual, mil hist Middle Ages. **SELECTED PUBLICATIONS** Gen ed, Reference Guide to United States Military History, Facts on File, 91-94; auth, U.S. Military Logistics, 1607-1990: A Research Guide, Greenwood Press, 92; auth, Friendly Fire: The Inevitable Price, Parameters: US Army War Col Q, XXII:3, Autumn 92; auth, Communist Logistics in the Korean War, Greenwood Press, 95; auth, From Vietnam to the Gulf and After: Logistics and US Army Strategic Planning Since 1945, in Serving Vital Interests: Australia's Strategic Planning in Peace and War, DARA, 96; auth, United States Army Logistics, 1775-1992: An Anthology, US Army Ctr of Mil Hist, 97; auth, The First Helicopter War: Logistics and Mobility in Algeria, 1954-1962, Praeger, 00; auth, The Withered Vine: Logistics and the Communist Insurgency in Greece, 1945- 1949, Praeger, 99. **CONTACT ADDRESS** 910 Forbes Rd, Carlisle, PA 17013. **EMAIL** Heriger@aol.com

SHRESTHA, MOHAN N.
PERSONAL Born 03/22/1939, Kathmandu, Nepal, m, 1959, 2 children **DISCIPLINE** GEOGRAPHY **EDUCATION** Patna Univ, BA, 57; Tribhuuan Univ, B ED, 61; MA, 63; Univ Iowa, PhD, 69. **CAREER** Lectr, Tribhuvan Univ, 69-71; asst prof to prof, Bowling Green State Univ, 71-. **HONORS AND AWARDS** Chancellor's Gold Medal, Tribhuvan Univ, 63; Mahendra Vidaya Bhusan, 63, 70; Ford-Rockefeller Found Grant, 79-81. **MEMBERSHIPS** Assoc of Am Geog; Nepal Studies Assoc; Am Sociol Assoc. **RESEARCH** Environment, population migration and public policy. **SELECTED PUBLICATIONS** Auth, "Human Resources" in Nepal: Development and Change in a Landlocked Himalayan Kingdom, Inst for the Study of Lang and Cultures of Asia and Africa, Tokyo Univ of Foreign Studies, 94; auth, "Nepalese in America: A Historical Perspective" in Nepalese American Perspectives: The First National Convention of Nepalese and Friends of Nepal in N Am, 95; ed, Nepalese American Perspectives: Proceedings of the First Nat Convention of Nepalese and Friends of Nepal in N Am, ANMA (Cincinnati), 95; auth, "Population Growth and Urbanization" in Nepal: Himalayan Kingdom in Transition, United Nations Univ Press, 96. **CONTACT ADDRESS** Dept Geog, Bowling Green State Univ, 1001 E Wooster St, Bowling Green, OH 43403-0001. **EMAIL** mshrest@bgnet.bgsu.edu

SHRIMPTON, G. S.
DISCIPLINE GREEK HISTORY **EDUCATION** Univ Brit Col, BA, 63, MA, 65; Stanford Univ, PhD, 70. **CAREER** Prof, 67-. **HONORS AND AWARDS** Pres, Fac Assn, 82-83, 83-84; CUFA/BC, 83-84, 92-93; Victoria Choral Soc, 86-87; Class Assn of Pacific Northwest, 88-89; act ch, Hisp and Ital dept, 84-85. **RESEARCH** History and historians of fifth and fourth-century Greece. **SELECTED PUBLICATIONS** Ed, Classical Contributions: Essays in Honour of M.F. McGregor, Toronto, 81; auth, Theopompus the Historian, Montreal, 91. **CONTACT ADDRESS** Dept of Greek and Roman Studies, Univ of Victoria, PO Box 1700 STN CSC, Victoria, BC, Canada V8W 2Y2. **EMAIL** gshrimpt@uvic.ca

SHRIVER, GEORGE HITE
PERSONAL Born 10/26/1931, Jacksonville, FL, m, 1986, 4 children **DISCIPLINE** WESTERN RELIGIOUS HISTORY **EDUCATION** Stetson Univ, AB, 53; Southeastern Baptist Theol Sem, NC, BD, 56; Duke Univ, PhD(hist & church hist), 61. **CAREER** Instr relig, Duke Univ, 58-59; assoc prof church hist, Southeastern Baptist Theol Sem, NC, 59-68, prof hist, 68-73; assoc prof, 73-76, Prof Hist, GA Southern Col, 76-99, Emer, 99; Am Asn Theol Schs fel & Swiss-Am exchange scholar, 65-66; consult, Choice, 70- **HONORS AND AWARDS** Prof of the Yr, GSU, 75; Ruffin Cup Awd, GSU, 98. **MEMBERSHIPS** Am Soc Church Historians; AHA; Am Acad Relig; AAUP. **RESEARCH** Philip Schaff and Mercersburg theology; American religious dissent; the ecumenical movement. **SELECTED PUBLICATIONS** Auth, The changed concept of religious liberty in Roman Catholics, Outlook, 8/66; Renewal and the dynamic of the provisional, Christian Century, 12/67; The Teilhardian tradition and the theological quest, Relig in Life, autumn 68; American Religious Heretics, 66, transl, From Science to Religion, 68 & The Humanness of John Calvin, 91, Abindon; contrib ed, Contemporary Reflections on the Medieval Christian Tradition, Duke Univ, 73; auth, Philip Schaff: Christian Schader and Ecumenical Prophet, Mercer Press, 87; auth, Dictionary of Henry Trials in American Christianity, Greenwood Press, 98; auth, Encyclopedia of Religious Controversier in the U.S., Greenwood Press, 98; auth, Pilgrims Through the Years, Providence House, 99. **CONTACT ADDRESS** 106 Benson Dr, Statesboro, GA 30458. **EMAIL** cshriver@frontiernet.net

SHUBERT, HOWARD
PERSONAL Born 11/15/1954, Montreal, Canada, m, 1986, 2 children **DISCIPLINE** HISTORY OF ARCHITECTURE **EDUCATION** McGill Univ, BComm, 77, BA, 79; Univ Toronto, MA, 80, MPhil, 83. **CAREER** Assoc cur, Can Ctr for Archit, 85- . **MEMBERSHIPS** Soc of Archit Hist; Soc for the Stud of Archit in Can. **RESEARCH** Sports architecture. **SELECTED PUBLICATIONS** Auth, Toys and the Modernist Tradition, Canadian Centre for Architecture, 93; auth, Richard Henriquez: Memory Theatre, Canadian Centre for Architecture, 93; auth, Frank Lloyd Wright and Quebec, ARQ, 96; auth, making History Become Memory: The Architecture of Richard Henriquez, Soc for the Stud of Archit in Can, Bull, 96; auth, Introducing Other Soundings, Archit and Urbanism, 97; auth, The Architects and Designers of Lincoln Center, New York, Casabella, 98; auth, Sports Facilities in Canada, in, 1999 Canadian Encyclopedia World Edition, CD-ROM, McClelland & Stewart, 98. **CONTACT ADDRESS** 1920 Baile St, Montreal, QC, Canada H3H 2S6. **EMAIL** howards@cca.qc.ca

SHUMSKY, NEIL LARRY
PERSONAL Born 05/28/1944, Dayton, OH, m, 1966, 2 children **DISCIPLINE** AMERICAN URBAN & SOCIAL HISTORY **EDUCATION** Univ Calif, Los Angeles, AB, 66; Univ Calif, Berkeley, PhD(hist), 72. **CAREER** Instr hist, San Francisco State Col, 68-72; asst prof, 72-78, Assoc Prof Hist, VA Polytech Inst & State Univ, 78-. **HONORS AND AWARDS** Fulbright Fellow, Austria, 70-71. **MEMBERSHIPS** AHA; Am Studies Asn; Orgn Am Historians. **RESEARCH** American urban and social history; American ethnic relations. **SELECTED PUBLICATIONS** Auth, The Market Revolution - Jacksonian Am, 1815-1846 - Sellers,C/, J Of Interdisciplinary Hist, Vol 0024, 1993; The Metropolitan Frontier - Cities In The Modern Am-W - Abbott,C/, Pac Histl Rev, Vol 0064, 1995. **CONTACT ADDRESS** Dept of Hist, Virginia Polytech Inst and State Univ, Blacksburg, VA 24061. **EMAIL** yksmvhs@rt.edu

SIBALIS, MICHAEL
DISCIPLINE CULTURE; HISTORY OF MODERN FRANCE **EDUCATION** McGill, BA; Sir George Williams, MA; Concordia, PhD. **CAREER** Prof. **RESEARCH** Parisian labour movement from 1789 to 1834, the political police under Napoleon I, and the hist of sexuality in Modern France. **SELECTED PUBLICATIONS** Auth, "Andre Troncin, ouvrier (1802-1846): Une victime de la prison politique," 1848: Bulletin de la Societe d'histoire de la Revoution de 1848 et des Revolutions du XIXe siecle, 8, (91): 83-91; auth, "Prisoners by Mesure de haute police under Napoleon I: Reviving the Lettres de cachet," Proceedings of the Western Soc for French History 18, (91): 83-91; auth, "Un aspect de la legende noire de Napoleon Ier: Le mythe de l'enfemement d'opposants politiques comme fous," 'Revue de l'Institut Napoleon 156, (91): 8-24; auth, "La Cote-d'or, terre d'exil: Les residents sous surveillance pendant le Consulat et l'Empire," Annales de Bourgogne 64, (92): 39-51; auth, "Internal Exile in Napoleonic France, 1789-1815," Proceedings of the Western society for French Hist 20, (93): 189-98; auth, "Jan Czynski: Jalons pour la biographie d'un fourieriste de la Grande emigration polonaise," Cahiers Charles Fourier 6, (95): 58-85; auth, "The Regulation of Male Homosexuality in Revolutionary and Napoleonic France," in Homosexuality in Modern France, ed. Jeffrey Merrick and Bryant T. Ragan, (Oxford Univ Press: New York, 96): 80-81; auth, "Paris-Babylone/Paris-Sodome: Images of Homosexuality in the Nineteenth Century City," in Images of the City in Nineteenth-Century France, ed. John West-Sooby, (Boombana Publications: Mount Nebo, Queensland, Australia, 98): 13-22; auth, "The Parisian Tailors in 1848: The Association fraternelle des ouvriers tailleurs (The Atelier de Clichy)," in The Sphinx in the Tuileries and Other Essays in Modern French History: Papers Presented at the Eleventh George Rude Seminar, ed., Robert Aldrich and Martyn Lyons, (Univ of Sydney: Sydney, Australia, 99): 154-68; auth, "Paris," in Queer Sites: Gay Urban Histories since 1600, ed. David Higgs, (Routledge: London, 99): 10-37. **CONTACT ADDRESS** Dept of History, Wilfrid Laurier Univ, 75 University Ave W, Waterloo, ON, Canada N2L 3C5. **EMAIL** msibalis@mach1.wlu.ca

SICHER, ERWIN
PERSONAL Born 12/05/1935, Kuhnsdorf, Austria, m, 1959, 3 children **DISCIPLINE** HISTORY **EDUCATION** Collonges-Sous-Saleve, THB, 57; Pacific Union Col, MA, 59; Univ South Calif, PhD, 70; Texas Women Univ, PhD, 91. **CAREER** From assoc prof to prof to chem, 70-, Andrews Univ. **HONORS AND AWARDS** Tchr Year, SWAU, 81; Presidential citation for service to SWAU, 82; Zapara Awd for excellence in tchg, 88; pres, asn sda historians; secy, keene independent sch district; chemn, odyssey harbor. **MEMBERSHIPS** Am Hist Asn **RESEARCH** Twentieth Century Europe, Third Reich. **SELECTED PUBLICATIONS** Auth, art, Adult Education in the Third Reich, 95. **CONTACT ADDRESS** Southwestern Adventist Univ, Keene, TX 76059. **EMAIL** sichere@swau.edu

SICIUS, FRANCIS
DISCIPLINE WESTERN CIVILIZATION **EDUCATION** State Univ, BA, MA, Loyola Univ Chicago PhD, 89. **CAREER** History, St. Thomas Univ. **SELECTED PUBLICATIONS** Area: Cath soc. **CONTACT ADDRESS** St. Thomas Univ, 16400 N.W. 32nd Ave, Miami, FL 33054-9913. **EMAIL** fsicius@stu.edu

SIDBURY, JAMES
PERSONAL Born 05/26/1958, Baltimore, MD, s **DISCIPLINE** HISTORY **EDUCATION** Johns Hopkins Univ, BA, 80; MA, 87; PhD, 91. **CAREER** Asst prof to assoc prof, Univ Tex, 91-. **HONORS AND AWARDS** Rockefeller Found Fel, 93. **MEMBERSHIPS** Am Hist Asn; Org of Am Hist; S Hist Asn; Omohundro Inst for Early Am Hist and Culture. **RESEARCH** Early American Race and Slavery **SELECTED PUBLICATIONS** Auth, "Slave Artisans in Richmond, Virginia, 1780-1810," in American Artisans: Crafting Social Identity, 1750-1850, Baltimore, 95; auth, Ploughshares into Swords: Race, Rebellion, and Identity in Gabriel's Virginia, 1730-1810, Cambridge, 97; auth, "Saint Domingue in Virginia: Ideology, Local Meanings, and Resistance to Slavery, 1790-1800," J of Southern Hist, 97; auth, "Reading, Revelation, and Rebellion: The Textual Communities of Gabriel, Denmark Vesey and Nat Turner," in Judgment Day: Nat Turner, Oxford Univ Press, 01; auth, "E Pluribus Unum: Race Formation in the Era of the American Revolution," in Empire and Nation: Essays in Honor of Jack P. Greene, Baltimore, (forthcoming). **CONTACT ADDRESS** Dept Hist, Univ of Texas, Austin, Campus MC B7000, Austin, TX 78712. **EMAIL** sidbury@mail.utexas.edu

SIDEBOTHAM, STEVEN EDWARD
PERSONAL Born 03/23/1951, Berlin, Germany, d, 1981 **DISCIPLINE** ANCIENT HISTORY, CLASSICAL ARCHEOLOGY **EDUCATION** Univ Pa, BA, 74; Univ Mich, MA(class archeol) & MA(hist), 77, PhD(hist), 81. **CAREER** From Asst Prof to Prof, Hist, Univ Del, 81- **MEMBERSHIPS** Archaeol Inst Am; Soc for the Promotion Hellenic Studies; Soc for the Promotion Roman Studies; Assoc of Ancient Historians; Explorers Club. **RESEARCH** Roman economic and trade policy in the Red Sea, Persian Gulf and Indian Ocean; Roman numismatics; Roman lamps and terra sigillata stamps. **SELECTED PUBLICATIONS** Auth, Berenike 1994, 1995, 1996, 1997, 1998 Reports; auth, Abu Sha'ar reports in JARCE 1989, 1994 and Dumbarton Oaks 1994; auth, Abu Sha'ar Nile Road survey in AJA 1991; Via Hadriana Survey in BIFAO 1997, 1998, JARCE 2000; auth, Quseir-Nile road survey in JEA 1989. **CONTACT ADDRESS** Dept of Hist, Univ of Delaware, Newark, DE 19716. **EMAIL** ses@udel.edu

SIDRAN, BEN H.
PERSONAL Born 08/14/1943, Chicago, IL, m, 1969, 1 child **DISCIPLINE** AMERICAN STUDIES **EDUCATION** Univ Wis, BA, 65; Univ Sussex, MA philos, 67, PhD, 70. **CAREER** Author **HONORS AND AWARDS** Fel, Wisc Acad Arts Sci Winner, ACE Awd. **MEMBERSHIPS** ASCAP; NARAS; AFTRA; AF of M. **SELECTED PUBLICATIONS** Talking Jazz, Da Capo Press; Black Talk, Da Capo Press. **CONTACT ADDRESS** Box 763, Madison, WI 53701. **EMAIL** bensidran@aol.com

SIEBER, GEORGE WESLEY
PERSONAL Born 11/16/1930, Evansville, IN, m, 1961, 2 children **DISCIPLINE** HISTORY **EDUCATION** Carroll Col (Wis), BA, 52; Univ Wis, MS, 53; Univ Iowa, PhD, 60. **CAREER** Asst prof hist, Lakeland Col, 59-62; from asst prof to assoc prof, 62-66, Prof Hist, Univ Wis-Oshkosh, 66-, Chmn Dept, 74-. **MEMBERSHIPS** Econ Hist Asn; Nat Asn Interdisciplinary Ethnic Studies; Forest Hist Soc. **RESEARCH** Sawmilling in the Mississippi Valley; Indians of Wisconsin. **SELECTED PUBLICATIONS** Auth, Sawlogs for a Clinton sawmill, summer 64 & The relationship between an Iowa sawmill firm and the Chicago and Northwestern Railway, summer 67, Ann Iowa; Wisconsin pine land and logging management, Trans Wis Acad Sci, Arts & Lett, summer 68; Lumbermen at Clinton: 19th century sawmill center, Ann Iowa, fall 71. **CONTACT ADDRESS** Dept of History, Univ of Wisconsin, Oshkosh, Oshkosh, WI 54901.

SIEBER, ROY
DISCIPLINE AFRICAN AND OCEANIC ART **EDUCATION** Univ Iowa, PhD. **CAREER** Prof emer. **RESEARCH** Northern Nigeria and western Ghana; exhibiting African art; the roles of conoisseurship. **SELECTED PUBLICATIONS** Auth, African Textiles and Decorative Arts; African Furniture and Household Objects and African Art in the Cycle of Life. **CONTACT ADDRESS** Hist of Art Dept, Indiana Univ, Bloomington, 1201 E 7th St, Fine Arts 132, Bloomington, IN 47405. **EMAIL** sieber@indiana.edu

SIEGEL, ADRIENNE
PERSONAL Born 06/10/1936, New York, NY, m, 1972 **DISCIPLINE** AMERICAN HISTORY, POPULAR LITERATURE **EDUCATION** Univ Pa, BS, 57; Columbia Univ, MA, 59; New York Univ, PhD(hist), 73. **CAREER** Teacher, James Madison High Sch, 62-82; asst prof hist, Long Island Univ, 77-93: Fel, New York Univ, 71-72; assoc, Danforth Found, 72-82; Fulbright fel India, 78; fel, Inst Res in Hist, 81-82; Asst Prof, City Univ NY, Col Staten Island, 93-. **HONORS AND AWARDS** Phi Delta Kappa Scholarship, 90; Phi Delta Kappa Chapter Editor & Fdn Rep, 88-93; Phi Delta Kappa Cert Rec, 89; NY Univ Alumnae Awd, 74; Bronx Educ Endowment Fund Board 84-93. **MEMBERSHIPS** Orgn Am Historians; Popular Cult Asn. **RESEARCH** History of the American city. **SELECTED PUBLICATIONS** Auth, When Cities Were Fun, J Popular Cult and in Twentieth Cent Lit Crit, 75; Philadelphia: A Chronological and Documentary History, Oceana, 75; Brothels, Bets and Bars, NDak Quart, 76; The Image of the American City in Popular Literature, Kennikat, 81; auth, The Marshall Court, Associated Faculty Press, 87; auth, Visions for the Reconstruction of the NYC School System, in Urban Education, Jan 86; auth, Incubator of Dreams: Directing College Guidance at America's Most Elite Minority High School, Education, Winter 89; auth, A Case for Colaboratives: Turning Around Bronx Public Schools, Urban Review, 88; auth, Mission Possible: The Rescue of Bronx Public Schools, Phi Delta Kappa Fastback, 88; auth, Don't Wait, Communicate: Helping Teachers to Talk Shop, The Effective School Report, 87; auth, Collective Dreams or Urban Realities: Psychohistory, Persons & Communities, 83; auth, The Myth of Mobility in the Media of Another Century, in The Many Faces of Psychohistory, Intl. Psychohistorical Assn, 84. **CONTACT ADDRESS** 330 W Jersey St, Elizabeth, NJ 07202. **EMAIL** siegel@postbox.csi.cuny.edu

SIEGEL, JERROLD
PERSONAL Born 06/09/1936, St Louis, MO, m, 1966, 2 children **DISCIPLINE** HISTORY **EDUCATION** Harvard Univ, AB, 58; Princeton Univ, MA, 60; PhD, 64. **CAREER** Instr to prof, Princeton Univ, 62-88; prof, NYork Univ, 88-; William J. Kenan Prof, 94-. **HONORS AND AWARDS** Phi Beta Kappa, 58; Fulbright Fel, Italy, 61-62; Old Dominion Fel, 66-67; MEH Fel 79-80, 87-88; Selma V. Forkosch Prize, 87; Resident, Am Acad, Rome, 00. **SELECTED PUBLICATIONS** Auth, Rhetoric and Philosophy in Renaissance Humanism, Princeton Univ Pr, 68; coed, Action and Conviction in Early Modern Europe, Princeton Univ Pr, 69; auth, Marx's Fate: The Shape of a Life, Princeton Univ Pr, 78; auth, Bohemian Paris. Culture, Politics and the Boundaries of Bourgeois Life, 1830-1930, Elisabeth Sifton Books, (NY), 86; ed, Figures on the Horizon, Univ of Rochester Pr, 93; auth, The Private Worlds of Marcel Duchamp: Desire, Liberation and the Self in Modern Culture, Univ of Calif Pr, 95; auth, "Boundaries", Salmagundi 111 (96); auth, "Introduction" to Marcel Gauchet and Gladys Swain, Madness and Democracy (Princeton), 99; auth, "Problematizing the Self", Beyond the Cultural Turn, eds Lynn Hunt and Victoria Bonnell, (Berkeley and Los Angeles), 99. **CONTACT ADDRESS** Dept Hist, New York Univ, 19 University Pl, New York, NY 10003-4556.

SIEKHAUS, ELISABETH
DISCIPLINE GERMAN STUDIES **EDUCATION** Univ Calif, Berkeley, BA, 65, MA, 67, PhD, 72. **CAREER** Prof; Mills Col, 77. **RESEARCH** German culture and literature; German poetry and music; Age of Goethe and the 19th century; interdisciplinary studies. **SELECTED PUBLICATIONS** Auth, Die lyrischen Sonette der Catharina Regina von Greiffenberg, Berner Beitraege zur Barockgermanistik: Peter Lang, Bern/ Frankfurt, 82; Europaeische Hochschulschriften: Peter Lang, Bern/ Frankfurt, 82 double-publ; Six Hundred Years of German Women's Poetry; introduced and ed, articles by Mills Col Ger majors, 92-94, 95; Strategies to Enhance the Foreign Language Learning Experience of Adult Beginners, In: The Canberra Linguist, Vol XVIII, 89. **CONTACT ADDRESS** Dept of German Studies, Mills Col, 5000 MacArthur Blvd, Oakland, CA 94613-1301. **EMAIL** siekhaus@mills.edu

SIERRA-MALDONADO, RODRIGO
PERSONAL Born 08/04/1954, Guayaquil, Ecuador, m, 1989, 2 children **DISCIPLINE** GEOGRAPHY **EDUCATION** Catholic Univ Ecuador, 86; Ohio State Univ, MS, 89; MA, 91; PhD, 94. **CAREER** Asst Prof to Assoc Prof, Catholic Univ of Ecuador, 86-87; Asst Prof, Ariz State Univ, 95-. **HONORS AND AWARDS** Tessie Smith Noyes Fel, 87-89. **MEMBERSHIPS** AAG. **RESEARCH** Land cover change, Tropical Andean region, Biodensity conservation. **SELECTED PUBLICATIONS** Auth, "Dynamics and Patterns of Deforestation in the Western amazon: The Napo Deforestation Front, 1986-1996," Applied Geography, (00): 1-16; auth, "Traditional resource use systems and tropical deforestation in a multi-ethnic region in Northwest Ecuador," Environmental Conservation, (99): 136-145; auth, "Forest Resource Use Change During Early market Integration: Hypothesis and empirical analysis of the Huaorani in Upper amazonia," Ecological Economics, (99): 107-119; auth, Areas Prioritarias para la Conservacion de la Biodiversidad en el Ecuador continental. Un Estudio Basado en la Biodiversidad de Ecosistemas y su Ornitofauna, Wildlife Conservation Soc, 99; ed, Propuesta Preliminar de un sistema de clasificacion de Vegetacion para el Ecuador continental, Quite, Ecuador, 99; auth, "The dynamics and human organization of tropical deforestation in Northwest Ecuador, 1983-1995," Human Ecology, (98): 135-161; auth, LaDeforestacion en el Noroccidente del Ecuador, 1983-1993, EcoCiencia, 96; auth, "Urban System Development, Ecuador's Amazon region and Generalization," in Frontiers in Regional Development, Rowman & Littlefield pub, 96; auth, "Urban System Evolution in Frontier Settings: General Frameworks and the Ecuadorian Amazon," Geographical Review, (94): 251-265. **CONTACT ADDRESS** Dept Geog, Arizona State Univ, PO Box 870104, Tempe, AZ 85287.

SIES, MARY CORBIN
DISCIPLINE AMERICAN CULTURE, HISTORY **EDUCATION** MI State Univ, BA, 74; Univ MI, MA, 77, PhD, 87. **CAREER** Dir, grad stud; assoc prof; affil fac mem, women's stud dept; mem, Hist Preservation fac. **RESEARCH** Material culture studies, planning history, architectural history, urban history, and cultural and social history of the U.S. in the 19th and 20th centuries. **SELECTED PUBLICATIONS** Auth, God's Very Kingdom on the Earth: The Design Program for the American Suburban Home, 1877-1917, Mod Arch in Am: Visions and Revisions, Iowa State UP, 91; Toward a Performance Theory of the Suburban Ideal, 1877- 1917, Perspectives in Vernacular Architecture IV, Univ Mo Press, 91; Planning the American City Since 1900, (Johns Hopkins UP, 96; George W. Maher's Planning and Architecture, An Inquiry Into the Ideology of Arts & Crafts Design, The Substance of Style: New Perspectives on the Amer Arts and Crafts Movement, Winterthur Mus, 96; Paradise Retained: An Analysis of Persistence in Planned, Exclusive Suburbs, 1880-1980, Planning Perspectives 12, 97. **CONTACT ADDRESS** Am Stud Dept, Univ of Maryland, Col Park, Taliaferro Hall, Rm 2117, College Park, MD 20742-8821. **EMAIL** ms128@umail.umd.edu

SIEVENS, MARY BETH
DISCIPLINE HISTORY **EDUCATION** Mt Holyoke, BA, 86; Boston, MA, 92, PhD, 97. **CAREER** Instr, Champlain Col; asst prof, Fredonia Univ. **MEMBERSHIPS** Am Antiquarian Soc **RESEARCH** Gener relations and marriage in the early republic. **SELECTED PUBLICATIONS** Co-ed, Yankee Correspondence: Civil War Letters between New England Soldiers and the Home Front, 96. **CONTACT ADDRESS** Dept of Hist, Fredonia Univ, E332 Thompson Hall, Fredonia, NY 14063. **EMAIL** marybeth.sievens@fredonia.edu

SIL, NARASINGHA P.
PERSONAL Born 12/11/1937, Calcutta, India, m, 1965, 1 child **DISCIPLINE** HISTORY **EDUCATION** Univ of Calcutta, MA, 61; Univ of Ore, MA, 73; MEd, 74; PhD, 78. **CAREER** Lectr, Vidyasagar, 62-63; lectr, Chandernagore, Col, 63-64; teaching fel, Univ of Ore, 71-74, 77-78; asst prof, Univ of Benin, Nigeria, 80-86; prof, Western Ore Univ, 87-. **HONORS AND AWARDS** Faculty Honors Awd, Western Ore Univ, 92. **MEMBERSHIPS** AHA; Phi Kappa Phi; N Am Conf on British Studies; Am Acad of Relig; Inst of Hist Studies; Renaissance Soc of America. **RESEARCH** History of Tudor England, History of Religious Movements in Nineteenth Century Bengal, History of Modern Africa, History of Modern Europe. **SELECTED PUBLICATIONS** Auth, "Bengal", "Ganesha", "Jallianwala Bagh Incident", "Karma", "Nirvana", "Reformist Hindu Sects", "Vedanta Movement", Asian-American Encyclopedia (Marshall Cavendish, (NY), 95; auth, Swami Vivekananda: A Reassessment, Susquehanna Univ Pr, 97; auth, "Asceticism and Misogyny: Vivekananda's concept of Women", Asian Culture quarterly, XXV.2 (97): auth, "Mahendranath Gupta (1854-1932)" and "Sarada Devi (1853-1920)", Encyclopedia of Hinduism and Indic Religions, Univ of SC, (Columbia), 98; auth, "Saradamani's Holy Motherhood: A Reappraisal", Asian J of Women's Studies, IV.1 (98): auth, "Tagore's Broken Next vs. Ray's Charulata: A Critique", Asian Cinema X.2 (99); auth, Tudor Placemen and Statesmen: Select Case History (forthcoming). **CONTACT ADDRESS** Dept Soc Sci, Western Ore Univ, 345 Monmouth Ave N, Monmouth, OR 97361-1314. **EMAIL** siln@wou.edu

SILBER, NINA
PERSONAL Born 06/12/1959, New York, NY, m, 1989, 2 children **DISCIPLINE** U.S. HISTORY **EDUCATION** Univ of CA, Berkeley, PhD, 89. **CAREER** Vis asst prof, Univ of Delaware, 89-90; from asst prof to assoc prof, Boston Univ, 90-; dir of Women's Stud at BU, 94-96, 98-99. **HONORS AND AWARDS** Smithsonian fel, 87-89; Charles Warren fel, Harvard Univ, 96-97; Sr Fulbright Scholar, Czech Republic, 99-00. **MEMBERSHIPS** Org of Am Hists; Southern Hist Asn. **RESEARCH** Civil War; Women. **SELECTED PUBLICATIONS** Auth, The Romance of Reunion: Northerners and the South, 1865-1900, 93; Yankee Correspondence: Civil War Letters between New England Soldiers and the Homefront, 96; introd to new ed of M. Livermore, My Story of the War, 95; The Northern Myth of the Rebel Girl, Women of the American South: A Multicultural Reader, Christie Anne Farnham; coed, Divided Houses: Gender and the Civil War, 92. **CONTACT ADDRESS** Dept of History, Boston Univ, 226 Bay State Rd., Boston, MA 02215. **EMAIL** nsilber@bu.edu

SILBEY, JOEL H.
PERSONAL Born 08/16/1933, Brooklyn, NY, m, 1959, 2 children **DISCIPLINE** AMERICAN HISTORY **EDUCATION** Brooklyn Col, BA, 55; Univ Iowa, MA, 56, PhD, 63. **CAREER** Asst prof hist, San Francisco State Col, 60-64; vis asst prof, Univ Pittsburgh, 64-65; asst prof, Univ Md, 65-66; from asst prof to assoc prof, 66-68, prof Am History, 68-86, Pres White Prof History, 86- , Cornell Univ, 68-, Soc Sci Res Coun & Am Philos Soc fel, 69-70; NSF fel, 70-74; Nat Endowment for Humanities sr fel, 80-81; vis fel Ctr Advan Study in Behav Sci, 85-86; vis scholas Russell Sage Found, 88-89; John Simon Guggenheim Mem fel, 89-90. **MEMBERSHIPS** AHA; Orgn Am Historians; Southern Hist Asn. **RESEARCH** Political history; slavery controversy; Civil War and reconstruction. **SELECTED PUBLICATIONS** Auth, The Civil War synthesis in American political history, Civil War Hist, 6/64; The Shrine of Party: Congressional Voting Behavior, 1841-1852, Univ Pittsburgh, 67 & Greenwood, 81; The Transformation of American Politics, 1840-1860, Prentice Hall, 67; co-ed, Voters, Parties and Elections, Xerox, 72; Clio and computers: moving into Phase II, 1970-1972, Comput & Humanities, 11/72; Political Ideology and Voting Behavior in the Age of Jackson, Prentice-Hall, 73; A Respectable Minority: The Democratic Party in the Civil War Era, Norton, 77; co-ed, A History of American Electoral Behavior, Princeton Univ, 78; The Partisan Imperative: The Dynamics of American Politics Before the Civil War, Oxford, 85; The American Political Nation, 1838-1893, Stanford, 91; ed Encycl of Am Legis System, Scribners, 93; auth, "The State and Practice of American Political History at the Millennium," Journal of Policy History (99). **CONTACT ADDRESS** Dept of Hist, Cornell Univ, McGraw Hall, Ithaca, NY 14853-0001.

SILCOX, DAVID P.
PERSONAL Born 01/28/1937, Moose Jaw, SK, Canada **DISCIPLINE** ART HISTORY **EDUCATION** Univ Toronto, BA, 59, MA, 66; Courtauld Inst, Univ London, 62-63. **CAREER** Arts off, Can Coun, 65-70; asst to assoc dean fine arts, 70-73, assoc prof, York Univ, 70-77; dir cultur affairs, Municipality Metro Toronto, 74-83; asst to deputy min, Dept Communications, Ottawa, 83-91; Sr Resident and Assoc Fellow, Massey Col, Univ Toronto, 91-98; dir, Univ of Toronto Art Centre, 98-. **HONORS AND AWARDS** Sir Frederick Banting Awd, 62; Can Coun arts bursary, 62, res grant, 73, res fel, 74-75; McLean Found res grant, 70; York Univ res grant, 72. **SELECTED PUBLICATIONS** Auth, Christopher Pratt, 82, 95; auth, Painting Place: The Life and Work of David B. Milne, 96; coauth, Tom Thomson: The Silence and the Storm, 77; contribur, Jack Bush, 84; guest ed, Canadian Art, 62; int ed bd, Studio Int, 68-75. **CONTACT ADDRESS** Univ Col, Univ of Toronto, 15 King's College Circle, Toronto, ON, Canada M5S 3H7.

SILK, GERALD
PERSONAL Born 12/29/1947, Fall River, MA, m, 1983, 1 child **DISCIPLINE** ART HISTORY **CAREER** Asst prof, Columbia Univ, 76-83; asst prof, Univ Pennsylvania, 83-87; assoc prof, Tyler Sch of Art, Temple Univ, 98-. **HONORS AND AWARDS** Amer Acad in Rome Prize, 81-82; Ailsa Mellon Bruce Senior Fel CASUA, Natl Gallery of Art, 87-88; NEH Summer Stipend 91. **MEMBERSHIPS** Coll Art Assn; Soc of Fel the Amer Acad in Rome; Amer Culture/Popular Culture Assn. **RESEARCH** Modern and contemporary art. **SELECTED PUBLICATIONS** Auth, Museums discovered: The Wadsworth Atheneum, 82; Automobile and Culture, 84; Refrains and Reframes: Artists Rethink Art History, Art Journal, Fall 95; Fascist Modernism and the Photo-Collages of Bruno Munari, in Studies: Cultural and Artistic Upheavals in Modern Europe, 1848-1945, 96; Censorship and Controversy in the Career of Edward Kienholz, in Suspended License: Essays in the History of Censorship and the Visual Arts, 97; All by Myself: Piero Manzoni's Autobiographical Use of his Body, its Parts, and its Products, in True Relations: Essays on Autobiography and the Postmodern, 98 **CONTACT ADDRESS** Dept of Art Hist, Temple Univ, Philadelphia, PA 19122. **EMAIL** gsilk@nimbus.ocis.temple.edu

SILLIMAN, ROBERT HORACE
PERSONAL Born 01/26/1935, Waterbury, CT, m, 1956 **DISCIPLINE** HISTORY OF SCIENCE **EDUCATION** Cornell Univ, BA, 56, MA, 59; Princeton Univ, MA, 64, PhD(hist), 68. **CAREER** From instr to asst prof hist, 64-71, Assoc Prof Hist, Emory Univ, 71- **MEMBERSHIPS** Hist Sci Soc. **RESEARCH** European intellectual history; history of optics; early 19th century physics. **SELECTED PUBLICATIONS** Auth, William Thomson: Smoke rings and 19th century atomism, Isis, 12/63; Fresnel, In: Dictionary of Scientific Biography, Scribner, 72. **CONTACT ADDRESS** Dept of History, Emory Univ, 1364 Clifton Rd N E, Atlanta, GA 30322-0001.

SILVER, MARK H.
PERSONAL Born 12/27/1964, Tokyo, Japan **DISCIPLINE** ASIAN STUDIES **EDUCATION** Haverford Col, BA, 87; Yale Univ, MA, 93; M Philos, 95; PhD, 99. **CAREER** From Instr to Asst Prof, Colgate Univ, 97-. **MEMBERSHIPS** Asn for Asian Studies. **RESEARCH** Japanese Popular Lit 1868-1941. **SELECTED PUBLICATIONS** Auth, "Matsumoto Seicho" and coauth, "Japan, Crime and Mystery Writing in," in The Oxford Companion to Crime and Mystery writing, ed. Rosemary Herbert (99). **CONTACT ADDRESS** Dept Asian Lang and Lit, Colgate Univ, 13 Oak Dr, Hamilton, NY 13346-1338.

SILVERA, ALAIN
PERSONAL Born 09/19/1930, Alexandria, Egypt, m, 1955, 1 child **DISCIPLINE** MODERN HISTORY **EDUCATION** Cornell Univ, AB, 52; Ecole Normale Superieure, Paris, 55; Harvard Univ, AM, 53, PhD, 63. **CAREER** Lectr govt, Univ Md, Paris, France, 56-57; tutor hist & lit, Harvard Univ, 58-59; lectr, 61-63, from asst prof to assoc prof, 63-74, Prof Hist, Chr Hist, 93-, Bryn Mawr COL, 74-, Am Asn Mid East Studies traveling fel, Cairo, 63; Fulbright vis prof, Univ Lille, 66-67, 68-69; vis prof, Bryn Mawr Inst Avignon, 67, 69 & 71; fels, Am Philos Soc, 71 & Am Coun Learned Socs, 74-75; vis prof, Temple Univ, 74-75; sr fel, Am Res Ctr Egypt, Cairo, 77-78, sr Fulbright, Egypt, 82-83. **MEMBERSHIPS** AHA; Fr Soc Mod Hist; MidE Studies Asn NAm. **RESEARCH** Modern Near East; 19th and 20th century France. **SELECTED PUBLICATIONS** Auth, Daniel Halevy and His Times, Cornell Univ, 66; Jomard and Egyptian reforms in 1839, Mid Eastern Studies, 71; The French Revolution of May 1968, Va Quart Rev, 71; ed, The End of the Notables, Wesleyan Univ, 74; auth, The origins of the French Expedition to Egypt, Islamic Quart, 74; The first Egyptian student mission to France under Muhammad Ali, Mod Egypt, Frank Cass, London, 80; Kemalism and the origins of Egyptian Nationalism, Atatnrk, Istanbul, 81; Egypt and the French Revolution, Revue Francaise d'histoire d'outre-Mer, 82; Colonizing Egypt, Victorian Studies, 89; The Guide to the Labyrinth, Times Lit Suppl, 96; Of Caliphs and Sultans, The New Criterion, 96; North African Jewry, The Jewish Jour Sociol, 96; ed The Encyclopedia of Revolution and Revolutionaries: from Anarchism to Zhou en Lai, Facts on File, 96; The Jews of Egypt, Mid E Stud, 99; Elie Kedourie, politique et moraliste, Frank Cass, 97; Moshe Sharett, Mid E Stud, 98; auth, "The Eastern Question," Mid E Stud (00). **CONTACT ADDRESS** Dept of Hist, Bryn Mawr Col, 101 N Merion Ave, Bryn Mawr, PA 19010-2899. **EMAIL** alainasilvera@aol.com

SILVERMAN, DEBORAH
PERSONAL Born 05/04/1954, Tacoma, WA, m, 1983, 1 child **DISCIPLINE** HISTORY **EDUCATION** Princeton Univ, BA, 75; PhD, 83. **CAREER** Asst prof to prof, UCLA, 81-. **HONORS AND AWARDS** Guggenheim Fel; NEH Fel; Phi Beta Kappa; Getty Res Inst Scholar. **RESEARCH** Modernism in comparative fin-de-siecles; Early abstraction in painting; Van Gogh and Gauguin; Art Nouveau; Brussels 1900. **SELECTED PUBLICATIONS** Auth, "Vincent Von Gogh Portrait of the Artist as a Young Man," Barbican Gallery London, 92; auth, Van Gogh and Gauguin: The Search for Sacred Art, Farrar Straus and Giroux Pub, 00. **CONTACT ADDRESS** Dept Hist, Univ of California, Los Angeles, 6265 Bunche, PO Box 951473, Los Angeles, CA 90095-1473. **EMAIL** silverma@history.ucla.edu

SILVERMAN, JASON H.
PERSONAL Born 05/26/1952, Brooklyn, NY, m, 1986, 1 child **DISCIPLINE** HISTORY **EDUCATION** Univ Va, BA, 74; Colo state Univ, MA, 76; Univ Ky PhD, 81. **CAREER** Lecturer to Acting Asst Prof, Yale Univ, 80-84; Asst Prof to Prof, Winthrop Univ, 84-. **HONORS AND AWARDS** Student Govt Asn Outstanding Prof Awd, 94; Panhellenic Outstanding Fac Awd, 94, 93; Winthrop Col Distinguished Prof Awd, 91; Governor's Prof of the Year Awd, 90; Presidential Distinguished service Awd, 90; Phi Kappa Phi Excellence in Teaching Awd, 90, 88, 86; Winthrop Col Outstanding Jun Prof Awd, 85; Res Fel, Inst for southern Studies, 85. **MEMBERSHIPS** Southern Hist Soc, Soc of Civil War Hist, St. George Tucker Soc. **RESEARCH** American Civil War, Old South, Civil War Society. **SELECTED PUBLICATIONS** Co-auth, Shanks: the Life and Letters of General Nathan George Evans, CSA, Savas Pub Co., forthcoming; co-auth, A rising star of Promise: The civil War Odyssey of David Jackson Logan, 17th South Carolina Infantry, 1861-1864, Savas Pub Co, 98; co-auth, Relief and Recovery in Post civil War south Carolina: a Death by Inches, Mellen Press, 97; auth,, "The Peopling of America: A synoptic History," in Americans All: A National Education Program, Beltsville, MD, 94; auth, America Before 1877: a Synoptic History, McGraw-Hill Book co, 89; auth, Unwelcome Guests: Canada West's Response to American Fugitive Slaves, 1800-1865, Assoc Fac Press, 85; co-ed The Frederick Douglass Papers. Series One: Speeches, Debates, and Interviews. Vol III: 1855-1863, Yale Univ Press, 85; co-ed, The Frederick Douglass papers. Series One: Speeches, Debates, and Interviews. Vol II: 1847-1854, Yale Univ Press, 82. **CONTACT ADDRESS** Dept Hist, Winthrop Univ, 701 W Oakland Ave, Rock Hill, SC 29733-0001. **EMAIL** silvermanj@winthrop.edu

SILVERMAN, KENNETH EUGENE
PERSONAL Born 02/05/1936, New York, NY, 2 children **DISCIPLINE** ENGLISH, AMERICAN STUDIES **EDUCATION** Columbia Univ, BA, 56, MA, 58, PhD(English), 64. **CAREER** Instr English, Univ WY, 58-59; preceptor, Columbia Col, 62-64; PROF ENGLISH, NY UNIV, 64-, Danforth assoc, 68-71; Nat Endowment for Humanities Bicentennial grant, 72-74; Am Coun Learned Soc grant-in-aid, 86; Am Philos Soc grant, 86. **HONORS AND AWARDS** Ambassador of Honor Book Awd, 84; Bancroft Prize in Am Hist, 85; Pulitzer Prize for Biography, 85; John Simon Guggenheim Memorial Found fel, 89-90; Edgar Awd, The Mystery Writers of America, 92; Christopher Literary Awd, Soc of Am Magicians, 97. **MEMBERSHIPS** Fel, Am Antiqn Soc; The Authors' Guild; fel, Soc Am Hist; The Century Asn; Soc Am Magicians. **RESEARCH** American culture. **SELECTED PUBLICATIONS** Ed, Colonial American Poetry, Hafner, 68; auth, Timothy Dwight, Twayne, 69; ed, Literature in America I: The Founding of a Nation, Free Press, 71; Selected Letters of Cotton Mather, La State Univ, 71; auth, A Cultural History of the American Revolution, Crowell, 76; A Cultural History of the American Revolution, Thomas Y. Crowell, 76; co-ed, Adventures in American Literature, Harcourt Brace Jovanovich, 80, rev eds, 85, 89; auth, The Life and Times of Cotton Mather, Harper & Row, 84; Edgar A. Poe. Mournful and Never-ending Remembrance, HarperCollins, 91; ed, New Essays on Poe's Major Tales, Cambridge Univ Press,93, with intro; HOUDINI!!! The Career of Ehrich Weiss, HarperCollins, 96. **CONTACT ADDRESS** Dept of English, New York Univ, 19 University Pl, New York, NY 10003-4556. **EMAIL** ks2@is2.nyu.edu

SILVERMAN, SHERMAN E.
PERSONAL Born 12/07/1937, Baltimore, MD, m, 1966, 3 children **DISCIPLINE** GEOGRAPHY **EDUCATION** Towson State Teachers Col, BS, 63; Cath Univ Am, MA, 66; Univ Md Col Park, ABD, 76. **CAREER** prof, Prince George's Cmty Col, 68-. **HONORS AND AWARDS** Distinguished Teaching Achievement Awd, Nat coun for Geog Educ, 93; Distinguished teacher-scholar, Asn of Am Geogr. **MEMBERSHIPS** nat coun for Geog Educ, Asn of am Geogr, Penn Geogr soc, E Cmty Col Soc Sci Asn. **RESEARCH** The evolution of cultural landscapes in N Am (Historical geography). **SELECTED PUBLICATIONS** Auth, "Settling the Prairie Frontier," ECCSSA Journal, (86): 25-44; auth, "An Ecological Study of the Northwest Branch within the Chesapeake Bay Watershed," in An Interdisciplinary Approach to the Chesapeake Bay Watershed, Largo, (93): 45-82; auth, "Cultural Geography in a Lionel Layout," O-Gauge Railroading, (91): 43-45; auth, "Early Jewish Neighborhoods in Washington, DC: Insights from the 1900 Manuscript Census," in Land and Community, Bethesda, (97): 245-255; auth, Physical Geography as a Synthesis, Ann Arbor, MI, 97; auth, Physical Geography as a Synthesis, 2nd Ed, Ann Arbor, MI, 98; auth, Introduction to Geography as a Social Science, Ann Arbor, MI, 99; auth, "The Independent Jewish High School Fraternity: The Example of Sigma alpha Rho," ECCSSA Journal, (99): 27-45; auth, "The Persistence of Mount Savage, Maryland: An Historical Geography," in Pittsburgh and the Alleghenies, Washington, 00; auth, "Brownsville, PA and Brockport, NY: A Contrast in Town Development as Influenced by Transportation," The Pennsylvania Geographer, 00. **CONTACT ADDRESS** Dept Hist & Govt, Prince George's Comm Col, 301 Largo Rd, Upper Marlboro, MD 20774-24109. **EMAIL** silverse@pg.cc.md.us

SILVERMAN, VICTOR
PERSONAL Born New York, NY **DISCIPLINE** HISTORY **EDUCATION** Univ CA, Berkeley, BA, 84, MA, 86, PhD, 90. **CAREER** Lectr, St. Mary's Col of CA, 92; vis prof, SAIS-Nanjing Univ, China, 92-93; Asst Prof, Pomona Col, 93-98; assoc prof, Pomona Col, 99-. **HONORS AND AWARDS** Fulbright fel; Excellence in European Studies fel; Kaiser Found Awd; Horizon's Found Grant; Calif Coun for Humanities Grant. **MEMBERSHIPS** OAH; AHA; Soc for Historians of Am Foreign Relations; Southwest Labor Studies Asn; Social Sci Hist Asn. **RESEARCH** US labor; diplomacy; sexuality; CA/San Francisco; film. **SELECTED PUBLICATIONS** Auth, Popular Bases of the International Labor Movement in the United States and Britain, 1939-1949, Int Rev of Social Hist 38, 93; Is National History a Thing of the Past?: On the Growing Reality of World History in the 20th Century, European Legacy 1:2, summer 96; Imagining Internationalism in America and British Labor, 1939-1949, Univ IL Press, forthcoming 99; Insider-Outsider-No-Sider: Life and Death of Rose Cohen, The Stanger/Lo Straniero, forthcoming, 99; reviews and opinion pieces in a variety of academic and popular publications, film and creative work; auth, "The Failures of Jewish Americanization," in Jewish Locations, Bat Ami Bar On and Lisa Tessman, eds., Rowman & Littlefield, 01; auth, "Looking for Compton's: The Lost History of Transsexuals in San Franciso's Tenderloin," documentary film in production, 01. **CONTACT ADDRESS** Dept of Hist, Pomona Col, 551 N. College Ave., Claremont, CA 91711. **EMAIL** vsilverman@pomona.edu

SILVERS, ANITA
PERSONAL Born 11/01/1940, New York, NY **DISCIPLINE** PHILOSOPHY, AESTHETICS **EDUCATION** Sarah Lawrence Col, BA, 62; Johns Hopkins Univ, PhD(philos), 67. **CAREER** Prof Philos, San Francisco State Univ, 67-, Vis lectr philos, Sussex Univ, 72-73; assoc ed, J Aesthetics & Art Criticism, 79-; mem, Nat Coun Humanities, 80-; Exec Secy, Coun Philos Studies, 79-82. **MEMBERSHIPS** Am Philos Asn; Am Soc Aesthetics; Asn Advan Humanities. **RESEARCH** Philosophy of the arts; ethics; journalism ethics. **SELECTED PUBLICATIONS** Auth, Vincent Story, The Importance Of Centextualism For Art Educ/, J Of Aesthetic Educ, Vol 0028, 1994. **CONTACT ADDRESS** 15 Otsego Ave, San Francisco, CA 94112.

SIMMONS, JEROLD LEE
PERSONAL Born 08/30/1941, Lexington, NE, m, 1967 **DISCIPLINE** AMERICAN HISTORY **EDUCATION** Kearney State Col, BA, 63; Univ Nebr, Omaha, MA, 67; Univ Minn, PhD(hist), 71. **CAREER** Instr US hist, Ill Col, 71-72; lectr, Univ Ill, 72-73; asst prof, Bellevue Col, 73-79, chair, Div Soc & Behav Sci, 74-79; prof US hist, Univ Nebr, Omaha, 79-. **RESEARCH** History of American civil liberties; local history; film history. **SELECTED PUBLICATIONS** Ed, La Belle Vue: Studies in the History of Bellevue, Nebraska, Walsworth, 76; auth, Operation Abolition: The Campaign to Abolish the House Un-American Activities Committee, 1938-1965, Garland, 86; auth, The Dame in the Kimono: Hollywood, Censorship and the Production Code from the 1920s to the 1960s, Weidenfeld, 90, Expanded edition, Kentucky, 01. **CONTACT ADDRESS** Dept of Hist, Univ of Nebraska, Omaha, 6001 Dodge St, Omaha, NE 68182-0002.

SIMMONS, MICHAEL
PERSONAL Born 06/15/1952, Raleigh, NC, m, 1973, 2 children **DISCIPLINE** ANCIENT HISTORY **EDUCATION** Univ S AL, BA, 76; Duke, MDiv, 80; Yale, STM, 82; New Col Univ of Edinburgh, PhD, 85 **CAREER** Asst Prof, Auburn Univ **HONORS AND AWARDS** Res Grant Oxford Univ, 95; Res Grant Oxford Univ, 99 **MEMBERSHIPS** Assoc Internationale des Etudes Patristiques; Am Philo Assoc; Am Hist Assoc; N Am Patristics Assoc **SELECTED PUBLICATIONS** Auth, Arnobius of Sicca, in Religious Conflict & Competition in the Age of Diocletian, Oxford, 95 **CONTACT ADDRESS** History Dept, Auburn Univ, Montgomery, PO Box 244023, Montgomery, AL 36124-4023. **EMAIL** mbsimmons@1-a-net.net

SIMON, JANICE
DISCIPLINE ART HISTORY **EDUCATION** SUNY, Buffalo, BA, 78; Univ Mich, MA, 81, PhD, 90. **CAREER** Asst prof to ASSOC PROF, ART, UNIV GEORGIA **MEMBERSHIPS** Am Antiquarian Soc **SELECTED PUBLICATIONS** Auth, "Imaging a New Heaven on a New Earth: The Crayon and Nineteenth-Century America Periodical Covers," Am Per 1, 91; "Seeking to Keep that Earlier, Wilder Image Bright," Winterthur Portfolio 27, 92; auth, Sanford R Gifford's Kaaterskill Falls: A Place of Intimate Immensity," Bull Det Inst of Arts 67, Spring 93; auth, "Glimpses of Eternity: The Mythic Late Paintings of Charles Burchfield," Extending the Golden Year: The Charles Burchfield Centenary, Hamilton College, 93; co-ed, "Introduction, The Promise of 1893;" Crosscurrents in American Art at the Turn of the Century, Georgia Mus Art, 94; cont, essays Am Paintings in the Det Inst of Arts v 2, Fall, 97; auth, "Nature's Forest Volume: The Aldine, The Adirondacks, and the Sylvan Landscape" in The Call of the Wild: Printmakers in the Adirondacks, Syracuse Univ Press, 98; auth, essays on The Aldine and The Crayon for Am & Intl Art Per, Greenwood Press, 98; "Naked wastes..glorious woods: The Forest View of the White Mountains," in Images of the Hills: The Visual Arts and the White Mountains, New Hampshire Hist Soc and N.E. Press, 98. **CONTACT ADDRESS** School of Art, Univ of Georgia, Visual Arts Bldg., Athens, GA 30602. **EMAIL** jsimon@uga.cc.uga.edu

SIMON, JOHN Y.
PERSONAL Born 06/25/1933, Highland Park, IL, m, 1956, 2 children **DISCIPLINE** AMERICAN HISTORY **EDUCATION** Swarthmore Col, BA, 55; Harvard Univ, MA, 56, PhD, 61. **CAREER** Instr hist, OH State Univ, 60-64; assoc prof, 64-71, Prof Hist, S IL Univ, Carbondale, 71-, Exec Dir Ulysses S Grant Asn, 62. **MEMBERSHIPS** AHA; Orgn Am Historians. **RESEARCH** Am Civil War. **SELECTED PUBLICATIONS** Auth, Ulysses S Grant Chronology, Ohio Hist Soc, 63; ed, General Grant by Matthew Arnold with a rejoinder by Mark Twain, 66 & The Papers of Ulysses S Grant, vol 1-24, Southern Ill Press, 67-00; The Personal Memoirs of Julia Dent Grant, Putnam, 75. **CONTACT ADDRESS** Ulysses S Grant Asn Morris Libr, So Illinois Univ, Carbondale, Carbondale, IL 62901-6632. **EMAIL** jsimon@lib.siu.edu

SIMON, PAUL L.
PERSONAL Born 07/05/1936, Cincinnati, OH, m, 1965, 3 children **DISCIPLINE** MODERN UNITED STATES HISTORY **EDUCATION** Villa Madonna Col, BA, 58; Xavier Univ, OH, MA, 59; Univ Notre Dame, PhD, 65. **CAREER** From instr to assoc prof, 63-73, Prof Hist, Xavier Univ, OH, 73-, Chmn Dept, 65. **MEMBERSHIPS** MALAS **RESEARCH** Mexico, Central Am, Caribbean. **SELECTED PUBLICATIONS** Auth, The appointing powers of the President, Cithara, 63; Frank Walker, New Dealer, 1933-1935, Univ Microfilms, 65; Cincinnati's unique immigrant experience, Ill Quart, sprig 72; Source Book: Cincinnati's Ethnic Heritage, Xavier Univ, Ohio, 78. **CONTACT ADDRESS** Dept of Hist, Xavier Univ, Ohio, 3800 Victory Pky, Cincinnati, OH 45207-1092. **EMAIL** simon@admin.xu.edu

SIMON, ROGER DAVID
PERSONAL Born 07/05/1943, Indianapolis, IN, m, 2 children **DISCIPLINE** AMERICAN HISTORY **EDUCATION** Rutgers Univ, New Brunswick, AB, 65; Univ Wis-Madison, MA, 66, PhD, 71. **CAREER** From instr to prof, 70-86, Prof hist, Lehigh Univ, 86. **MEMBERSHIPS** AHA; Orgn Am Historians; Soc Hist Technol; Urban Hist Asn. **RESEARCH** Urban hist; soc hist. **SELECTED PUBLICATIONS** Auth, Housing and services in an immigrant neighborhood, J Urban Hist, 76; The City-Building Process, Am Philos Soc, 78, rev ed 96; coauth, Migration, Kinship, and Urban Adjustment: Blacks and Poles in Pittsburgh, 1900-1930, J Am Hist, 79; Lives of Their Own, Univ IL Press, 82. **CONTACT ADDRESS** Dept of Hist, Lehigh Univ, 9 W Packer Av, Bethlehem, PA 18015-3081. **EMAIL** rds2@lehigh.edu

SIMON, ROLAND HENRI
PERSONAL Born 10/07/1940, Haiphong, North Vietnam **DISCIPLINE** LITERARY SEMIOTICS, FRENCH CIVILIZATION **EDUCATION** Univ Wis, MA, 67 Stanford Univ, PhD(French & humanities), 76. **CAREER** Instr French, Middlebury Col, 72-75, dean French sch, 73-76, asst prof, 75-76; Asst Prof French, Univ VA, 76-. **MEMBERSHIPS** MLA; Am Asn Teachers French; NEastern Mod Lang Asn; SAtlantic Mod Lang Asn. **RESEARCH** Theory of literature; autobiography; French civilization. **SELECTED PUBLICATIONS** Auth, Le role de l'ecriture dans La Chute de Camus et Quelqu'un de Pinget, 74 & Les Prologues du Quart Livre de Rabelais, 74, French Rev; Langage et authenticate dans Biffures de Michel Leiris, Stanford French Rev, 78; Pour une nouvelle pedagogie du theatre classique, Australian J French Studies, 78. **CONTACT ADDRESS** Dept of French & Gen Ling, Univ of Virginia, 1 Cabell Hall, Charlottesville, VA 22903-3125.

SIMON, STEPHEN JOSEPH
PERSONAL Born 07/02/1939, Clay Center, OH, m, 1970, 2 children **DISCIPLINE** ANCIENT HISTORY **EDUCATION** Xavier Univ (Ohio), BA,61; Loyola Univ of Chicago, PhD(hist), 73. **CAREER** Instr hist, St Procopius Col, 67-69 & Loyola Univ, Italy, 69-70; asst prof, 70-77, dir foreign studies, 72-73, Prof Hist, Appalachian State Univ, 77-. **MEMBERSHIPS** AHA; Class Asn Atlantic States; Am Philol Asn. **RESEARCH** Roman religion; the Roman Empire; Etruscan art. **SELECTED PUBLICATIONS** Auth, Euripides defense of women & Domitianpatron of letters, 11/73, Class Bull; The Boeotian concept of democracy, Tertesius, spring 74. **CONTACT ADDRESS** Dept of History, Appalachian State Univ, 1 Appalachian State, Boone, NC 28608-0001.

SIMPSON, CHRIS
DISCIPLINE EARLY ROMAN IMPERIAL HISTORY **EDUCATION** Alberta, PhD. **CAREER** Assoc prof. **RESEARCH** Archaeol of Roman Italy and the monuments, lit, and hist of early imperial Rome. **SELECTED PUBLICATIONS** Auth, The Excavations of San Giovanni di Ruoti, 77; Caligula's cult: immolation, immortality, intent, 96; The Original Site of the Fasti Capitolini, 93s; auth, Caesar Divi Filius, Athenaeum 86, (98): 419-37; auth, The Curia Iulia and the Ara Victoriae in August 29 B.C., in C. Deroux, ed., Studies in Latin Literature and Roman History 9, Latomus 244, (Brussels, 98): 225-30. **CONTACT ADDRESS** Dept of Classics, Wilfrid Laurier Univ, 75 University Ave W, Waterloo, ON, Canada N2L 3C5. **EMAIL** csimpson@wlu.ca

SIMS, AMY R.
PERSONAL Born New York, NY, m, 1972, 2 children **DISCIPLINE** MODERN EUROPEAN HISTORY, EUROPEAN INTELLECTUAL HISTORY, POLITICAL THEORY **EDUCATION** Queens Col, BA, Magna Cum Laude; Cornell Univ, MA, PhD. **CAREER** Instr, asst to dir of Overseas Stud, Stanford Univ; instr, Boston Col; asst prof Hist, Golden Gate Univ; tchg fel, Harvard Univ, Cornell Univ. **MEMBERSHIPS** Am Hist Asn; German Stud Assoc; Phi Beta Kappa. **SELECTED PUBLICATIONS** Auth of article on historians in Nazi Germany. **CONTACT ADDRESS** Golden Gate Univ, 536 Mission St., San Francisco, CA 94105-2968. **EMAIL** asims@ggu.edu

SIMS, HAROLD DANA
PERSONAL Born 10/19/1935, Fort Myers, FL, m, 1965, 2 children **DISCIPLINE** LATIN AMERICAN HISTORY **EDUCATION** Stetson Univ, BA, 62; Univ Fla, MA, 63, PhD, 68. **CAREER** From instr to asst prof, 66-72, assoc prof, 72-82, prof hist, Univ of Pittsburgh; Whitaker Prize for best book, MACLAS, 91. **RESEARCH** Nineteenth century Mexican social history; Japanese immigration to Latin America; Napoleonic Latin American policy. **SELECTED PUBLICATIONS** Auth, A House Divided: Ideological Divisions in Cuban Labor and the U.S. Role, 1944-1949, Cuban Studies 21, 91; The Expulsion of Mexico's Spaniards, 1821-1836, Pittsburgh, 91; Cuba, in Latin America Between the Second World War and the Cold War, Cambridge Univ Press, 93; coauth, Las minas de plata en el distrito minero de Guanajuato, Guanajuato, 93; co-ed, MACLAS Latin American Essays Vols 8-12, 95-99; author of numerous other articles and chapters. **CONTACT ADDRESS** Dept of Hist, Univ of Pittsburgh, 3K38 Forbes Quad, Pittsburgh, PA 15260-0001. **EMAIL** dana1@pitt.edu

SIMS, LOWERY STOKES
PERSONAL Born 02/13/1949, Washington, DC, s **DISCIPLINE** ART HISTORY **EDUCATION** Queens Coll, BA 1970; Johns Hopkins Univ, MA 1972; CUNY, New York, NYork, MA, philosophy, 1990, PhD, 1995. **CAREER** Metro Museum of Art, asst museum educ 1972-75; Queens Coll Dept Art, adjunct instructor 1973-76; Sch Visual Arts, instructor 1975-76, 81-86; Metro Museum of Art, assoc curator beginning 1979-, Curator, currently. **HONORS AND AWARDS** Fellowship for Black Dr Students, Ford Found, 1970-72; Employee Travel Grant, Metro Museum Art, 1973; numerous publications; Amer Artists & Exhibition Catalogs; Hon Doctor of Humane Letters, Maryland Inst Coll of Art, 1988; Frank Jewett Mather Awd, College Art Association, 1991; One of Crain's Magazine Top 100 Minortiy Executives, 1998; Lifetime Achievement in the Arts, Queens Museum of Art, 1998. **MEMBERSHIPS** Mem grants comm, Metro Museum Art, 1975-77; museum aid panel, NY State Council on Arts, 1977-79; mem, Art Table, College Art Assn 1983-, Assn of Art Critics, Amer Sect Intl Art Critics Assn 1980-, Natl Conf of Artists; visual arts panel, New York State Council on Arts 1984-86; council mem, New York State Council on Arts, 1987-92; bd, College Art Association, 1994-97; bd, Tiffany Foundation, 1995-97; advisory bd, Center for Curational Studies, 1995-; chair, Forum of Curators and Conservator, Metro Museum of AA, 1996-97. **CONTACT ADDRESS** Dept of 20th Century Art, The Studio Museum, 144 W 125th St, New York, NY 10027.

SIMS, ROBERT CARL
PERSONAL Born 12/26/1936, Ft Gibson, OK, m, 1963, 3 children **DISCIPLINE** UNITED STATES HISTORY **EDUCATION** Northeastern Okla State Col, BA, 63; Univ Okla, MA, 65; Univ Colo, PhD(hist), 70. **CAREER** Assoc prof, 70-80, Prof Hist, Boise State Univ, 80-, Nat Endowment for Humanities fel race & ethnicity, Columbia Univ, 77-78, Dean, College of Social Sciences and Public Affairs, 85-95. **MEMBERSHIPS** AHA; Orgn Am Historians. **RESEARCH** Japanese-Americans; Idaho and Pacific Northwest history; United States economic history. **SELECTED PUBLICATIONS** Auth, Idaho's Governors, 91; " Historians and Minorities," Interpreting Local History and Culture, 91. **CONTACT ADDRESS** Dept of Hist, Boise State Univ, 1910 University Dr, Boise, ID 83725-0399. **EMAIL** rsims@boisestate.edu

SINCLAIR, LAWRENCE A.
PERSONAL Born 09/19/1930, Chicago, IL, w, 1955, 3 children **DISCIPLINE** ARCHAEOLOGY **EDUCATION** Carroll Col, Waukesha Wis, BA, 52; McCormick Theol Sem, Chicago Ill, BD, 55; Johns Hopkins Univ, Baltimore Md, 58. **CAREER** Asst Field Supvr, Drew-McCormick Excavation of Shechem, Jordan, 57; From Asst Prof to Prof, Carroll Col, 58-96; Consultant, Am Libr Asn, 60-; Vis Lectr, Univ of Wis Madison, 62; Vis Lectr, Univ of Wis Milwaukee, 67-68; Chair of Dept Relig Studies, Carroll Col, 67-96; Vis Lectr, Marquette Univ, 91-96. **HONORS AND AWARDS** N.F. McCormick Grad Fel, 55-58; The Johns Hopkins Univ Scholar, 55-58; The Presbyterian Grad Fel, 58; Uhrig Found Excellent Teacher Awd, 66; Fel to the Inst for Ecumenical and Cult Res, St. Johns Univ, 70; Vis Prof Res Grant, Marquette Univ, 77; Carroll Col Res Grant, 87; MacAllister Travel grant to the Middle E, 96. **MEMBERSHIPS** Am Sch of Orient Res, The Cath Bibl Soc, The Chicago Soc of Bibl Res, Milwaukee Are Bibl Archaeol Soc, The Soc of Bibl Lit. **RESEARCH** Old Testament History, Literature and Archaeology, The Prophets of the Old Testament, Dead Sea Scrolls, Climate and History of the ancient Near East. **SELECTED PUBLICATIONS** Auth, "David," "Diaspora," in Theologische Realenzyklopadie Vol 8: 378-388, 709-712; auth, "A Qumran Biblical Fragment: Hosea 4Q XIId (Hosea 1:7-2:5)," Bul of Am Sch of Orient Res 239 (80): 61-65; auth, "Hebrew Text of the Qumran Micah Pesher and the Textual Traditions of the Minor Prophets," Reveu de Qumran 42-11 (83): 253-263; auth, "A Qumran Biblical Fragment: 4QEzeka (Ezek. 10:17-11:11)," Reveu de Qumran 53-14 (89): 99-106; co-ed, The Psalms and Other Studies of the Old Testament, Nashotah House, 90; auth, "11QPsa: A Psalm Scroll from Qumran: Text and Canon," The Psalms and other Studies of the Old Testament: 109-115; auth, "Preliminary Results of Joint Historical and Climatological High Resolution Modeling Study of E. Mediterranean Area: Egypt, Mesopotamia and Palestine," forthcoming; 12 articles in Eerdmans Dictionary of the Bible, forthcoming. **CONTACT ADDRESS** Dept Rel Studies, Carroll Col, Wisconsin, 100 N E Ave, Waukesha, WI 53186-3103. **EMAIL** sinclair@execpc.com

SINCLAIR, MICHAEL LOY
PERSONAL Born 08/13/1939, Hendersonville, NC, m, 1961, 1 child **DISCIPLINE** MODERN CHINA, CHINA AND THE WEST **EDUCATION** Wake Forest Univ, BA, 63; Stanford Univ, AM, 65, PhD, 73. **CAREER** Instr, 68-73, asst prof, 73-76, assoc prof, 76-84, prof horf hist, Wake Forest Univ, 84-; Woodrow Wilson Fel, 63, Ford Found East Asian Studies Fel, 66-68. **MEMBERSHIPS** Asn Asian Studies. **RESEARCH** China and the West; the French settlement of Shanghai; Sino-French War 1883-85; computers in historical research. **SELECTED PUBLICATIONS** Auth, Through the Bamboo Curtain: Changing European conceptions of China from Marco Polo to the present, In: Asian Studies III, 78; How China Sees the World, In: China: The Challenge of the '80s, Charlotte, NC, 80. **CONTACT ADDRESS** Dept of Hist, Wake Forest Univ, Box 7806, Winston-Salem, NC 27109-7806. **EMAIL** sinclair@wfu.edu

SINGAL, DANIEL JOSEPH
PERSONAL Born 11/17/1944, Boston, MA, m, 1969, 2 children **DISCIPLINE** AMERICAN INTELLECTUAL HISTORY **EDUCATION** Harvard Col, BA, 66; Columbia Univ, MA, 67, PhD(hist), 76. **CAREER** Mellon fel hist, Tulane Univ, 77-79, asst prof, 79-80; Asst Prof Hist, Hobart & William Smith Col, 80-83; assoc prof history, 83-89; prof hist, 89; NIMH fel social hist, Columbia Univ, 66-70. **HONORS AND AWARDS** Charles W Ramsdell Awd, 81; Ralph Waldo Emerson award, 83; Francis B. Simkins Prize, 83; Fred W. Morrison award in Southern Studies, 83; John Simon Guggenheim Found Fellow, 84-85; George A. and Eliza Gardner Howard Found Fellow, 99-00. **MEMBERSHIPS** Orgn Am Historians; Am Hist Asn. **RESEARCH** Intellectual and cultural history of the U.S.; American historiography; Modernist culture. **SELECTED PUBLICATIONS** Auth, Ulrich B Phillips: The Old South as the New, J Am Hist, 3/77; Broadus Mitchell and the Persistence of New South Thought, J Southern Hist, 8/79; The War Within: From Victorian to Modernist Thought in the South, Univ NC Press, 82; ed, Beyond Consensus: Richard Hofstadter and American Histriography, American Historical Review, 84; ed, Towards a Definition of American Mosernism, American Quarterly, 87; ed, Modernist Culture in America, Wadsworth, 89; ed, Let Them Eat Images, Reviews in America History, 95; William Faulkner: The Making of a Modernist, Univ NC Press, 10/97. **CONTACT ADDRESS** Dept of History, Hobart & William Smith Cols, 300 Pulteney St, Geneva, NY 14456-3382. **EMAIL** singal@hws.edu

SINGER, DAVID G.
PERSONAL Born 04/23/1932, Cleveland, OH, m, 1975, 2 children **DISCIPLINE** UNITED STATES HISTORY **EDUCATION** Loyola Univ of Chicago, PhD, 73. **CAREER** Instr, hist, Spertus Inst of Judaica, De Vry Tech Inst; instr, ESL, CRT Tech Inst, De Vry Tech Inst. **HONORS AND AWARDS** Teaching fel, Loyola Univ of Chicago. **MEMBERSHIPS** Midwest Jewish Stud Asn; National and Illinois Teachers of Eng as a Second Lang. **RESEARCH** Judaism, Amer Jewish Hist. **SELECTED PUBLICATIONS** Auth, From St. Paul's Abrogation of the Old Covenant to Hitler's War Against the Jews, Anti-Semitism in American History, Urbana, 87; auth, The Christian Search for a New Zion: Christian Love and Hate of the Jews and Judaism from the Time of St. Paul to the Present, Huntington (WV), 99. **CONTACT ADDRESS** 6749 Drake, Lincolnwood, IL 60712. **EMAIL** glenngo@aol.com

SINGER, MARTIN
DISCIPLINE HISTORY OF EAST ASIA **EDUCATION** Hunter Col, BA; Univ Mich, MA, PhD. **CAREER** Assoc prof; dept ch, 94-97; dean, Fac Arts and Sci, Concordia Univ, 97-. **HONORS AND AWARDS** Ass provost, 77-80; provost, 80-85; founding dir, Concordia Univ Coun Intl Coop, 86-89. **RESEARCH** China and Japan. **SELECTED PUBLICATIONS** Auth, Educated Youth and the Cultural Revolution in China, 71; The Revolutionization of Youth in The People's Republic of China, 77; Canadian Academic Relations with the People's Republic of China Since 1970, 2 vol(s), 86; China's Academic Relations With Canada: Past, Present and Future, 92; Academic Relations Between Canada and China, 1970-1995, 96. **CONTACT ADDRESS** Dept of Hist, Concordia Univ, Montreal, 1455 de Maisonneuve W, Montreal, QC, Canada H3G 1M8. **EMAIL** msinger@vax2.concordia.ca

SINGER, WENDY F.
DISCIPLINE SOUTH ASIAN HISTORY **EDUCATION** Univ Va, BA, 82; MA,84; PhD, 91. **CAREER** Assoc prof, Kenyon Coll; dir of International Studies. **HONORS AND AWARDS** Fel, A. N. Sinha Institute, India, 86; NEH travel grant, 93; Fulbright Fac Res Abroad, 95-96; Visiting Res, Moscow, 94; PEW Grant, 94. **RESEARCH** British imperialism, oral history methodology. **SELECTED PUBLICATIONS** Auth, Creating History: Oral Narrative and Political Resistance, Oxford Univ Press, 97; Indian Peasants and the Communist International International Communism and the Communist International, Manchester Univ Press, 97; In Pursuit of Dignity, Jour of Women's Hist, 96; rev, Eldrid Mageli, Organizing Women's Protest; A Study of Political Styles in Two South Indian Activist Groups, Curzon Press, 97. **CONTACT ADDRESS** Dept of Hist, Kenyon Col, Gambier, OH 43022. **EMAIL** singerw@kenyon.edu

SINGLETON, GREGORY HOLMES
PERSONAL Born 10/04/1940, Florence, AL, m, 1995 **DISCIPLINE** AMERICAN HISTORY **EDUCATION** San Fernando Valley State Col, BA, 67; Univ CA, Los Angeles, PhD, 76. **CAREER** Instr hist, Northwestern Univ, 70-72; from Asst Prof to Assoc Prof, 72-83, prof hist, Northeastern IL Univ, 83. **HONORS AND AWARDS** Fel, Univ Chicago, 77; sr res fel, Inst for Advan Study Relig, Divinity Sch, Univ Chicago, 81-82. **MEMBERSHIPS** AHA; Orgn Am Historians; Am Studies Asn; Am Soc Church Hist. **RESEARCH** Am cult hist Am soc hist; hist of Christianity. **SELECTED PUBLICATIONS** Auth, Mere middle-class institutions: Urban protestantism in nineteenth

century America, J Social Hist, summer 73; The genesis of suburbia: A complex of historical trends, In; The Urbanization of the Suburbs, Sage, 73; Fundamentalism and urbanization; a quantitative critique of impressionist interpretation, In; The New Urban History, Princeton, 75; Protestant voluntary associations and the shaping of Victorian America, Am Quart, winter 76; Popular culture or the culture of the populace?, J Popular Cult, summer 77; Religion in the City of Angels: American Protestant Culture and Urbanization, Los Angeles 1850-1930, UMI, Studies in Am Hist and Culture 2, 79; Ecumenism Revisited: Eulogy for the '60s, Ekklesia, Spring 97. **CONTACT ADDRESS** Dept of Hist, Northeastern Illinois Univ, 5500 N St Louis Ave, Chicago, IL 60625-4625. **EMAIL** g-singleton@neiu.edu

SIPORIN, STEVE
DISCIPLINE ENGLISH; HISTORY **EDUCATION** Stanford Univ, BA, 69; Univ Ore, MA, 74; Ind Univ, PhD, 82. **CAREER** Lectr, Ind Univ, 76; folklore consult to Iowa Arts Coun, 77-78; folk arts coordr, Ore Arts Comn, 80-81; folk arts coordr, Idaho Comn on the Arts, 82-86; from asst prof to assoc prof, Utah State Univ, 90-. **HONORS AND AWARDS** Conference Fel, Institute of the Am West, 83; Res Fel, Memorial Found for the Jewish Culture, 84-85; Res Fel, Hebrew Univ of Jerusalem, 85; Travel Fel, 85; Fac Res Fel, Utah State Univ, 88-89; Fund for the Translation of Jewish Lit Grant, 88; Fulbright Lectureship, 92-93; Honorable Mention, Giuseppe Pitre International Folklore Prize, 93; Humanist of the Year, Utah State Univ, 94; Res Fel, Memorial Found for the Jewish Culture, 99-00. **MEMBERSHIPS** Int Soc for Folk Narrative Res; Am Folklore Soc; Folklore Soc Utah; Int Conf Group on Portugal. **SELECTED PUBLICATIONS** Public Folklore: A Bibliographic Introduction, Public Folklore, Wash., D.C.: Smithsonian Inst. Press, 92; Folklife and Survival: The Italian- Americans of Carbon County, Utah, Old Ties, New Attachments: Italian-American Folklife in the West, Wash., D.C.: Libr. Of Congress, 92; American Folk Masters: The National Heritage Fellows, 92; The Sephardim: Field Report From Portugal, Jewish Folklore and Ethnology Review 15, 93; Memories of Jewish Life, New Horizons in Sephardic Studies, Albany: State Univ of NY Press, 93; From Kashrut to Cucina Ebraica: The Recasting of Italian Jewish Foodways, Jour of Am Folklore 107, 94; Halloween Pranks: Just a Little Inconvenience, Halloween and Other Festivals of Death and Life, Knoxville: Univ of Tenn. Press, 94; National Heritage Fellows, Am Folklore: An Encyclopedia, New York: Garland, 96; auth, " County Football Scholarships," Foaftale News: Newsletter of The International Society for Contemporary Legend Research 45 (99): 2-4; auth, "On Scapegoating Public Folklore," Journal of American Folklore, 00; auth, "Tall Tales and Sales," in Worldview and the American West: The Life of the Place Itself, (Utah State Univ Press, 00); auth, Introduction to Worldview and American West: The Life of Place Itself, Utah State Univ Pr, 00. **CONTACT ADDRESS** Dept of English, Utah State Univ, Logan, UT 84322-3200. **EMAIL** siporin@cc.usu.edu

SIPRESS, JOEL M.
PERSONAL Born 06/13/1964, Summit, NJ **DISCIPLINE** HISTORY **EDUCATION** Princeton Univ, AB, 86; Univ NC, MA, 89; PhD, 93. **CAREER** Instr, Univ of NC, 93-94; asst to assoc Prof, Univ Wis, 94-. **HONORS AND AWARDS** Teaching Performance Awd, Univ of Wis, 97; Wis Teaching Fel, Univ of Wis, 00. **MEMBERSHIPS** Am Hist Asn, Orgn of Am Historians, Soc for Hist Ed, Southern Hist Assoc. **RESEARCH** History of the Amercan South, Race and Ethnicity. **SELECTED PUBLICATIONS** Auth, "From the Barrel of a Gun: The Politics of Murder in Grant Parish, Louisiana", Louisiana History (forthcoming); auth, "Relearning Race & Teaching Race as a Cultural Construction," The History Teacher, (97). **CONTACT ADDRESS** Dept Hist & Soc Sci, Univ of Wisconsin, Superior, PO Box 2000, Superior, WI 54880.

SIRHANDI, MARCELLA
DISCIPLINE CONTEMPORARY AND 20TH CENTURY SOUTH ASIAN ART **EDUCATION** Ohio State Univ, PhD, 95. **CAREER** Assoc prof, Okla State Univ, 95-. **SELECTED PUBLICATIONS** Auth, Contemporary Painting in Pakistan, 92. **CONTACT ADDRESS** Dept of Art, Oklahoma State Univ, Stillwater, 108 Bartlett Center for Studio Arts, Stillwater, OK 74078-4085. **EMAIL** marcela@okstate.edu

SISHAGNE, SHUMET
PERSONAL Born 01/20/1950, Ethiopia, m, 1980, 1 child **DISCIPLINE** HISTORY **EDUCATION** Haile Selassie Univ, BA, 73; Addis Ababa Univ, MA, 84; Univ Ill, Urbana-Champaign, PhD, 92. **CAREER** Lect, Addio Ababa Univ, Ethiopia, 84-86; asst prof, Christopher Newport Univ, 91-98, assoc prof, 98-. **HONORS AND AWARDS** Swedish Agency for Res Cooperation with the Develoing Countries, SAREC Awd, 83; Istito Italo-Africano Fel, Rome, 90; Arms Control, Disarmament and Int Security, MacArthur Fel, 90. **MEMBERSHIPS** Third World Studies. **RESEARCH** Ethiopia, Eritrea. **SELECTED PUBLICATIONS** Auth, "Ethiopian Irredentism in Eteben," Dialogue: The J of Ethiopian University Teachers Association (Aug 92); auth, "The Genius of Adwa: Menelik II, Consensus Builder and Master Mobilizer," Proceedings of the Adwa Century Conference, Mich State Univ (96). **CONTACT ADDRESS** Dept Hist, Christopher Newport Univ, 1 Univ Pl, Newport News, Va 23606-2949.

SITKOFF, HARVARD
DISCIPLINE HISTORY **EDUCATION** Columbia Univ, PhD. **CAREER** Prof, Univ NH, 76. **HONORS AND AWARDS** Charles Warren Ctr fel, Harvard Univ; Mary Ball Washinton Prof Am Hist in Ireland; NEH fel; Allen Nevins Awd, Columbia Univ; John Adams Prof Am Civilization in the Neth; Nat Fac of Hum, Arts and Sci; Rutgers Ctr for Hist Anal Scholar-in-Residence; Fletcher M Green Awd, Southern Hist Asn; Robert Starobin Mem fel. **RESEARCH** Race riots of the 1960s. **SELECTED PUBLICATIONS** Auth, A New Deal for Blacks, 78; The Struggle for Black Equality, 81, 93; Fifty Years later: The New Deal Evaluated, 85; coauth, The Enduring Vision: A History of the American People, 90, 92, 96; ed, A History of Our Time, 82, 87, 91,95. **CONTACT ADDRESS** Univ of New Hampshire, Durham, Durham, NH 03824. **EMAIL** his@christa.unh.edu

SIVIN, NATHAN
PERSONAL Born 05/11/1931, Clarksburg, WV, m, 1962 **DISCIPLINE** HISTORY OF SCIENCE **EDUCATION** Mass Inst Technol, BS, 58; Harvard Univ, AM, 60, PhD(hist of sci), 66. **CAREER** Vis lectr, Univ Singapore, 62-63; instr humanities, Mass Inst Technol, 64-65, from asst prof to assoc prof hist sci, 66-73, prof hist of sci & Chinese cult, 73-77; prof, Chinese Cult & Hist of Sci, Univ Pa, 77-; res assoc, Res Inst Humanistic Studies, Kyoto Univ, 67-68 & 71-72, vis prof, 74 & 79-80; ed & publ, Chinese Sci, 75; gen ed, Science, Medicine & Technology in East Asia, monogr series, Univ Mich, 80. **HONORS AND AWARDS** Nat Sci Found res grant, 67-70 & 79-81; Guggenheim Found fel, 71-72; Hon prof, Chinese Academy of Sciences; res grant, Nat Libr of Medicine, 74-76; Nat Program for Advanced Study and Res in China, 86-87; sr scholar res grant, Chiang Ching-kuo Found for Int Scholarly Exchange, 98-99; ma, univ pa, 78. **MEMBERSHIPS** Fel Am Acad Arts & Sci; Hist Sci Soc; Am Soc Study Relig; full mem Int Acad Hist Sci. **RESEARCH** Traditional Chinese science & medicine; comparative hist of science. **SELECTED PUBLICATIONS** Auth, Science and Medicine in Twentieth-Century China: Res and Educ, Ctr for Chinese Studies, Univ Mich (Ann Arbor), 89; auth, Science in Ancient China, Researches and Reflections, Variorum Collected Studies Series, Aldershot, Hants: Variorum, 95; auth, Medicine, Philos and Religion in Ancient China, Researches and Reflections, Variorum Collected Studies Series, 95; auth, Science and Civilisation in China, Vol 6, pt 6, Medicine, Cambridge Univ Pr, 00. **CONTACT ADDRESS** Dept of Hist and Sociology of Science, Univ of Pennsylvania, Philadelphia, PA 19104-6304. **EMAIL** msiviu@sas.upeuu.edu

SKAGGS, DAVID CURTIS
PERSONAL Born 03/23/1937, Topeka, KS, m, 1961, 2 children **DISCIPLINE** HISTORY **EDUCATION** Univ Kans, MS, 59; MA, 60; Georgetown Univ, PhD, 66. **CAREER** Instructor to Prof, Bowling Green State Univ, 65-98; Visiting Prof, Air War Col, 90-91, 95-96. **HONORS AND AWARDS** John Lyman Book Awd, 97; Edwin B. Hooper Res Grant, 99; John Nicholas Brown Fel, Brown Univ, 98. **MEMBERSHIPS** Org of Am Hist; Soc for Military Hist; Soc of Hist of the Early Am Rep; Omohundro Inst of Early Am Hist & Culture. **RESEARCH** Colonial. **SELECTED PUBLICATIONS** Auth, Roots of Maryland Democracy, 1754-1776, Greenwood Press, 73; ed, Poetic Writing of Thomas Craddock, Univ Delaware Press, 83; co-ed, Johann Ewald, Treatise on Partisan Warfare, Greenwood, 91; co-auth, A Signal Victory: the Lake Erie Campaign, 1812-1813, Naval Inst Press, 97. **CONTACT ADDRESS** Dept Hist, Bowling Green State Univ, Bowling Green, OH 43403-0220. **EMAIL** dskaggs@bgnet.bgsu.edu

SKAGGS, JIMMY M.
PERSONAL Born 06/13/1940, Gorman, TX, 3 children **DISCIPLINE** AMERICAN STUDIES, ECONOMICS **EDUCATION** Sul Ross State Col, Tex, BS, 62; Tex Tech Univ, MA, 65, PhD(hist), 70. **CAREER** From asst prof to assoc prof econ, 70-77, assoc prof Am studies, 75-77, Chmn Dept Am Studies, Wichita State Univ, 75-, Prof Am Studies & Econ, 77-. **MEMBERSHIPS** Southwestern Soc Sci Asn; Mid-Continent Am Studies Asn. **SELECTED PUBLICATIONS** Auth, Chisholm,Jesse - Ambassador Of The Plains - Hoig,S/, J Of The W, Vol 0032, 1993; The Frontier World Of Fort-Griffin - The Life And Death Of A Western Town - Robinson,C/, Pac Hist Rev, Vol 0062, 1993; Tex Crossings - The Lone Star State And The Am Far W, 1836-1986 - Lamar,Hr/, Pac Hist Rev, Vol 0062, 1993; Imagining Development - Economic Ideas In Peru Fictitious Prosperity Of Guano, 1840-1880 - Gootenberg,P/, Agricultural Hist, Vol 0069, 1995. **CONTACT ADDRESS** Dept of Am Studies, Wichita State Univ, Wichita, KS 67208.

SKALITZKY, RACHEL IRENE
PERSONAL Born 02/07/1937, Waterloo, WI **DISCIPLINE** COMPARATIVE LITERATURE, MEDIEVAL STUDIES **EDUCATION** Mt Mary Col, BA, 62; Fordham Univ, MA, 66, PhD(class lang & lit), 68. **CAREER** Teacher 6th grade, St Boniface Sch, Milwaukee, 58-62; teacher Latin & music, St Anthony High Sch, Detroit, 62-63; instr classics, Mt Mary Col, 68-69, asst prof & chmn, 69-72; lectr classics, 72-73, asst prof, 73-76, Assoc Prof Comp Lit, Univ WI-Milwaukee, 76-, Coordr Women's Studies, 75-82. **MEMBERSHIPS** Am Comp Lit Asn; Am Philol Asn; Nat Women's Studies Asn; MLA; Am Asn Univ Women. **RESEARCH** Classical philology; literary criticism; patristic lit. **SELECTED PUBLICATIONS** Auth, Good wine in a new vase, Horace, Epistles 1.2, Trans & Proc Am Philol Asn, 68; Annianus of Celeda: His Text of Chrysostom's Homilies on Matthew, Aevum, 71; Horace on travel, Epistles 1.11, Class J, 73; Plotinian Echoes in Peri Hypsous 7.2 and 9.7-10, Class Bull, 2/77. **CONTACT ADDRESS** Dept of Comp Lit, Univ of Wisconsin, Milwaukee, Po Box 413, Milwaukee, WI 53201-0413. **EMAIL** rachelsk@uwm.edu

SKEEN, C. EDWARD
PERSONAL Born 07/28/1937, Williams Mountain, WV, m, 1961, 2 children **DISCIPLINE** HISTORY **EDUCATION** Ohio Univ, BS, 59; Ohio State Univ, MA, 60; PhD, 66. **CAREER** Asst prof, Ohio State Univ, 66-67; asst prof to prof, Univ Memphis, 68- . **HONORS AND AWARDS** Fel Advan Ed-Nat his Publ Comn, 67-68; Distinguished Tchg Serv Awd, 83-84; Distinguished Book Awd Army Hist Found, 98. **MEMBERSHIPS** Soc Hist of Early Repub. **RESEARCH** Early Republic (US). **SELECTED PUBLICATIONS** Auth, John Armstrong, Jr.: A Biography, Syracuse, (80); auth, Citizen Soldiers in the War of 1812, Lexington, (98). **CONTACT ADDRESS** Dept Hist, Univ of Memphis, Campus Box 526120, Memphis, TN 38152-6120. **EMAIL** ceskeen@memphis.edu

SKELTON, WILLIAM B.
PERSONAL Born 05/14/1939, Syracuse, NY, m, 1968, 1 child **DISCIPLINE** MODERN HISTORY **EDUCATION** Bowdoin Col, BA, 61; Northwestern Univ, MA, 63, PhD, 68. **CAREER** Instr hist, Ohio State Univ, 65-69; assoc prof, 69-80, prof Us hist, Univ Wis-Stevens Point, 80-. **HONORS AND AWARDS** Soc Mil 1st Distinguished Book Awd, 94. **MEMBERSHIPS** Orgn Am Historians; AHA. **RESEARCH** US hist, 19th century; soc hist US Army, 19th century. **SELECTED PUBLICATIONS** Auth, The commanding general and the problem of command in the US Army, 1821-1841, Mil Affairs, 12/70; Professionalization in the US Army Officer Corps during the Age of Jackson, Armed Forces & Soc, summer 75; Army officers' attitudes toward Indians, 1830-1860, Pacific Northwest Quart, 7/76; An American Profession of Arms: The Army Officer Corps, 1783-1861, 92; The Confederation's Regulars: A Social Profile of Enlisted Service in America's First Standing Army, William and Mary Quart, 89; High Army Leadership in the Era of the War of 1812: The Making and Reamking of the Officer Corps, William & Mary Quart, 94; Samuel P. Huntington and the Roots of the American Military Tradition, Jour Mil Hist, 96. **CONTACT ADDRESS** Dept of History, Univ of Wisconsin, Stevens Point, 2100 Main St, Stevens Point, WI 54481-3897. **EMAIL** wskelton@uwsp.edu

SKEMP, SHEILA LYNN
PERSONAL Born 08/21/1945, Melrose Park, IL, m, 1999 **DISCIPLINE** AMERICAN HISTORY **EDUCATION** Univ MT, BA, 67; Univ IA, MA, 70, PhD, 74. **CAREER** Asst prof hist, Ripon Col, 75-76; asst prof, Western CT State Col, 77-79; asst prof, Univ IA, 79-80; asst prof hist, Univ MS, 80-88, assoc prof, Univ MS, 88-97, prof hist, Univ MS, 97-, Consult, Univ Mid-Am, 77. **HONORS AND AWARDS** Outstanding Tchr in Lib Art, Univ MS, 93; Mortar Board Outstanding Faculty Women, Univ MS, 97. **MEMBERSHIPS** Am Studies Asn; Southern Asn Women Historians. **RESEARCH** Am colonial puritanism; Am revolution-RI; 18th century Am; Am Women's/Gender Hist to 1877. **SELECTED PUBLICATIONS** Auth, George Berkeley's Newport experience, RI Hist, 5/78; coed, Foundations of Am Nationalism, Univ Mid-Am Press, 78; Co-ed, Sex, Race, & the Role of Women in the South, Univ Press MS, 83; Co-ed, Race & Family in the South, Univ Press MS, 99; Auth, William Franklin: Son of a Patriot, Servant of a King, Oxford, 90; Auth, Benjamin & William Franklin: Patriot & Loyalist, Father & Son, Bedford Press, 94; Auth, Judith Sargent Murray: A Brief Biography with Documents, Bedford Press, 98. **CONTACT ADDRESS** Hist Dept, Univ of Mississippi, General Delivery, University, MS 38677-9999. **EMAIL** sskemp@olemiss.edu

SKLAR, KATHRYN KISH
PERSONAL Born 12/16/1939, Columbus, OH, m, 2 children **DISCIPLINE** HISTORY **EDUCATION** Radcliffe Col, BA, 65; Univ Mich, PhD, 69. **CAREER** Asst prof, Univ Mich, 69-74; assoc prof, Univ Calif, Los Angeles, 74-81; prof hist, Univ Calif, LA, 81-88; DIST PROF HISTORY, SUNY, BINGHAMTON, 88-. **HONORS AND AWARDS** Berkshire Conf Book Prize, 74, 95; Asn Res on Nonprofit Orgs and Vol Action, Outstanding Contr award. **MEMBERSHIPS** Berkshire Conf Women Historians; Org Am Historians; AHA. **RESEARCH** Hist Am women and social movements. **SELECTED PUBLICATIONS** Co-ed, Social Justice Feminists in the United States and Germany: A Dialogue in Documents, 1885-1933, Cornell Univ Press, 98; auth, Florence Kelley and the Nation's Work: the Rise of Women's Political Culture, 1830-1900, Vol I, Yale Univ Press, 95; co-ed U.S. History as Women's History: New Feminist Essays, Univ NC Press, 95; auth, The Consumers' White Label of the National Consumers' League, 1898-1918, in Getting and Spending: American and European Consumption in the Twentieth Century, Cambridge Univ Press, 98; auth, Hull House Maps and Papers: Social Science as Women's Work in the 1890's, in The Social Survey Movement in Historical Per-

spective, Cambridge Univ Press, 92, reprint in Gender and American Social Science: The Formative Years, Princeton Univ Press, 98; auth, Women Who Speak for an Entire Nation: American and British Women Compared at the World Anti- Slavery Convention, London, 1840, in The Abolitionist Sisterhood: Women's Political Culture in Antebellum America, Cornell Univ Press, 94. **CONTACT ADDRESS** Dept of History, SUNY, Binghamton, Binghamton, NY 13902. **EMAIL** kksklar@binghamton.edu

SKLAR, ROBERT ANTHONY
PERSONAL Born 12/03/1936, New Brunswick, NJ, m, 1958, 2 children **DISCIPLINE** CINEMA STUDIES, CULTURAL HISTORY **EDUCATION** Princeton Univ, AB, 58; Harvard Univ, PhD, 65. **CAREER** From asst prof to prof hist, Univ Mich, Ann Arbor, 65-76; PROF CINEMA STUDIES & CHMN DEPT, NY UNIV, 77-, Rackham fel, 67; Fulbright lectr, USEC, Japan, 71; distinguished vis prof, Bard Col, 75-76; Rockefeller Found humanities fel, 76-77; contribr ed, Am Film Mag, 77- **HONORS AND AWARDS** Theatre Libr Asn Awd, 75. **MEMBERSHIPS** Am Studies Asn (vpres, 71); Soc Cinema Studies; Nat Film Preserv Bd; New York Film Fest Selec Cmt; Mich Am Stu Asn; ed bd, Am Qrt. **RESEARCH** American movies and television; twentieth century American culture and society. **SELECTED PUBLICATIONS** Auth, F Scott Fitzgerald, Oxford Univ, 67; ed, The Plastic Age: 1917-1930, Braziller, 70; auth, Movie-Made America: A Cultural History of American Movies, Random House, 75; auth, Prime Time America: Life On and Behind the Television Screen, Random House, 82; co-ed, Resisting Images: Essays on Cinema and History, Temple Univ, 90; auth, City Boys: Cagney, Bogart, Garfield, Princeton Univ, 92; auth, Film: An International History of the Medium, Prentice Hall, 93; auth, Movie-Made AmericaL A Cultural History of American Movies, Vintage Bks, 94; co-ed, Frank Capra: Authorship and the Studio System, Temple Univ, 98. **CONTACT ADDRESS** Dept of Cinema Studies, New York Univ, 721 Broadway, Rm 600, New York, NY 10003-6807. **EMAIL** rs9@is2.nyu.edu

SLANE, ANDREA
DISCIPLINE FILM HISTORY **EDUCATION** Rutgers Univ, BA; Univ Calif, PhD. **CAREER** Engl, Old Dominion Univ. **RESEARCH** Video and Multimedia. **SELECTED PUBLICATIONS** Area: Kinks in the System: Six Shorts About People Left to their own Devices; Six short videos on the human processing of information received by machines; Irresistible Impulse (feature length video); Research on images of fascism. **CONTACT ADDRESS** Old Dominion Univ, 4100 Powhatan Ave, Norfolk, VA 23058. **EMAIL** ASlane@odu.edu

SLATER, PETER GREGG
PERSONAL Born 06/03/1940, New York, NY, m, 1963, 1 child **DISCIPLINE** AMERICAN SOCIAL & INTELLECTUAL HISTORY **EDUCATION** Cornell Univ, BA, 62; Brown Univ, MA, 65; Univ Calif, Berkeley, PhD(hist), 70. **CAREER** Actg instr hist, Univ Calif, Berkeley, 66-67; from instr to asst prof, Dartmouth Col, 68-77; assoc prof, 77-81, prof Hist, Mercy Col, NY, 81-, Chmn Dept, 77-89, Special Asst to Provost, 93-94, Dean, White Plains Campus, 94-; assoc provost, 98-. **HONORS AND AWARDS** Phi Beta Kapp, 62; Sears-Roebuck Fnd Teaching Excellence, 90; M Pedis Mercy Col, 98. **MEMBERSHIPS** Am Studies Asn; Council Col Arts Scis White Plains Bus Dev Corp. **RESEARCH** Family history; cultural modernism. **SELECTED PUBLICATIONS** Auth, Ben Lindsey and the Denver Juvenile Court: A Progressive look at human nature, Am Quart, summer 68; Ethnicity in the Great Gatsby, Twentieth Century Lit, 1/73; Children in the New England Mind: In Death and in Life, Archon Bks, 77; From the cradle to the coffin: Patental bereavement and the shadow of infant damnation in Puritan society, Psychohistory Rev, Fall-winter 77-78; The negative secularism of the modern temper: Joseph Wood Krutch, Am Quart, summer 81; auth, The Egg, Modernsense, Spring-Summer, 84; auth, Joseph Wood Krutch, A Companion to American Thought, 95; High Wire column, White Plains Watch, 97-. **CONTACT ADDRESS** Mercy Col, 277 Martine Ave, White Plains, NY 10601. **EMAIL** pslater@mercynet.edu

SLATERY, WILLIAM PATRICK
PERSONAL Born 01/10/1943, Watts Bar Dam, TN, m, 1969, 2 children **DISCIPLINE** ART **EDUCATION** Univ Chattanooga, AB, 65; E Tenn St Univ, MA, 67 **CAREER** SR instr, art, 68-, Palm Beach Comm Col; adj art instr, 67-68, Univ Tenn, Chattanooga; profes News Photographer, 78-, Chattanooga Free Press; chmn, 78-, Town Council, Cloud Lake, FL. **RESEARCH** Computer graphics & Univ studio applications **CONTACT ADDRESS** PO Box 42, Lake Worth, FL 33460. **EMAIL** slateryp@pbcc.cc.fl.us

SLATTA, RICHARD W.
PERSONAL Born 10/22/1947, Powers Lake, ND, m, 1982, 1 child **DISCIPLINE** HISTORY **EDUCATION** Pacific Lutheran Univ, BA, 69; Portland State Univ, MA, 74; Univ Tex at Austin, PhD, 80. **CAREER** Vis res, Inst Torcuato di Tella, 77-78; lectr, Concordia Lutheran Col, 78-80; vis instr, Univ Colo, 79-80; from asst prof to prof, NC State Univ, 80-; grad adminr of Hist Dept, NC State Univ, 90-93. **HONORS AND AWARDS** Fel, Fulbright-Hays Doctoral Dissertation Prog, 77-78; Fel, Res Inst Torcuato di Tella, 77-78; Int Doctoral Res Fel, Soc Sci Res Coun, 77-78; Fac Res Grant, NC State Univ, 81-82; Postdoctoral Fel, Tinker Found, 84-85; Hubert Herring Book Prize, Pacific Coast Coun on Latin Am Studies, 84; Grand Prize Winner, Computer Learning Month Higher Educ Fac Papers, 88; Western Heritage Awd, Nat Cowboy Hall of Fame, 91; Best Ref Source Awd, Libr J, 94; Outstanding Ref Awd, Am Libr Asn, 95. **MEMBERSHIPS** Am Hist Asn, Western Writers of Am, Confr on Latin Am Hist, Western Hist Asn, Sigma Delta Pi, South Eastern Confr on Latin Am Hist, Sigma Iota Rho. **RESEARCH** Comparative Frontiers, Nineteenth-Century Argentina, Cowboys of the Americas, Educational Computing. **SELECTED PUBLICATIONS** Auth, Gouchos and the Vanishing Frontier, Univ Nebr Press, 83 & 92; ed & contribur, Bandidos: The Varieties of Latin American Banditry, Greenwood Press (Westport, CT), 87; auth, Cowboys of the Americas, Yale Univ Press, 90 & 94; auth, The Cowboy Encyclopedia, ABC-CLIO 94 & W. W. Norton, 96; auth, Comparing Cowboys and Frontiers, Univ Okla Press (Norman, OK), 97. **CONTACT ADDRESS** Dept Hist, No Carolina State Univ, PO Box 8108, Raleigh, NC 27695-0001. **EMAIL** slatta@ncsu.edu

SLATTERY, M. C.
PERSONAL Born 11/05/1964, Cape Town, South Africa, m, 1988 **DISCIPLINE** GEOGRAPHY, GEOLOGY **EDUCATION** Univ Witwatersrand, BA, 88, BA (Hons), 89; Univ Toronto, MSc, 90; Univ Oxford, DPhil, 94. **CAREER** Asst prof, 94-97, Dir Grad Studies, East Carolina Univ, 97; asst and assoc prof, Tex Christian Univ, 98-. **HONORS AND AWARDS** Awarded $250,000 USDA Res Grant; Awded Arts and Sciences Col Res Awd, East Carolina Univ; Awded the Stanley Jackson Gold Medal, Univ Witwatersrand. **MEMBERSHIPS** Asn Am Geog, British Geomorphological Res Group. **RESEARCH** Drainage basin hydrology, soil erosion and conservation, fluvial sediments. **SELECTED PUBLICATIONS** Coauth with T. P. Burt, "On the complexity of sediment delivery in fluvial systems," in M. G. Anderson and S. Brooks, eds, Advances in Hillscope Processes, John Wiley & Sons, Chichester (96); coauth with T. P. Burt, "Particle size characteristics of suspended sediment in hillslope runoff and stream flow," Earth Surface Processes and Landforms, 2, 705-719 (97); coauth with T. P. Burt and P, A. Gares, "Dramatic erosion of a tobacco field at Vanceboro, North Carolina, USA," Southeastern Geog, 37, 85-90 (97); coauth with J. Walden and T. P. Burt, "Use of mineral magnetic measurements to fingerprint suspended sediment sources: approaches and techniques for data analysis," J of Hydrology, 202, 353-372 (97); coauth with P. A. Gares and J. D. Phillips, "Quantifying soil erosion and sediment delivery on North Carolina Coastal Plain croplands," Conservation Voices, 1(2), 20-25 (98); coauth with J. D.119-140 (99); coauth with J. D. Phillips and P. A. Gares, "Agricultural soil redistribution and landscape complexity," Landscape Ecology, 14, 197-211 (99); coauth with K. Cappiella, "Spatial and temporal patterns of sediment and nutrient flux in a coastal plain agricultural basin, North Carolina," NC Geog, 7, 39-46 (99); coauth with P. Gares and J. D. Phillips, "Multiple Modes of storm runoff generation in a North Carolina coastal plain watershed," Water Resources Res (under rev); coauth with J. Walden and T. P. Burt,"Fingerprinting suspended sediment sources using mineral magnetic measurements: a qualitative approach," in I. Foster, ed, Tracers in Geomorphology, John Wiley & Sons, Chichester (in press). **CONTACT ADDRESS** Dept Geol, Texas Christian Univ, PO Box 298830, Fort Worth, TX 76129-0001. **EMAIL** m.slattery@tcu.edu

SLAUGHTER, THOMAS PAUL
DISCIPLINE EARLY AMERICAN HISTORY **EDUCATION** Univ Md, BA, 76, MA, 78; Princeton Univ, MA, 80, PhD(hist), 82. **CAREER** Asst Prof Hist, Rutgers Univ, 82-, Fel, Am Bar Found, 82- **MEMBERSHIPS** Orgn Am Historians; Soc for Historians Early Am Repub. **RESEARCH** Whiskey rebellion; social banditry in the era of the American Revolution; the case of Aaron Burr. **SELECTED PUBLICATIONS CONTACT ADDRESS** Hist Dept, Rutgers, The State Univ of New Jersey, New Brunswick, P O Box 5059, New Brunswick, NJ 08903-5059.

SLAVIN, ARTHUR J.
PERSONAL Born 02/15/1933, Brooklyn, NY, m, 1968, 5 children **DISCIPLINE** ENGLISH LITERATURE, HISTORY **EDUCATION** La State Univ, BA, 58; Univ NC, PhD, 61. **CAREER** Asst prof hist, Bucknell Univ, 61-65; from asst prof to prof, Univ Calif, Los Angeles, 65-73; prof & chmn dept, Univ Calif, Irvine, 73-74; dean col arts & sci, Univ Louisville, 74-77, Justus Bier Distinguished Prof Humanities & prof hist, Univ Louisville, 77-98, Emeritus, 98-; mem, Bd Consults, Nat Endowment Humanities, 76-; Clark lectr, William A Clark Libr, 77-78; distinguished lectr hist, Brigham Young Univ, 80; distinguished lectr, NC Asn Col Universities, 82. **HONORS AND AWARDS** Guggenheim fel, 67-68; fel, Royal Hist Soc of Great Britain, 69; sr res fel, Fogler Libr, 70-71; Henry Huntington Libr res fel, 75; Nat Endowment for Humanities fel, 80-81. **MEMBERSHIPS** AHA; Conf Brit Studies; Medieval Acad Am; Am Soc Reformation Res; Renaissance Soc Am. **RESEARCH** Tudor England; The Holocaust and imaginative literature; literature, politics and modern culture. **SELECTED PUBLICATIONS** Auth, Politics and Profit, Cambridge Univ Pr, 66; auth, Henry VII and the English Reformation, 68; auth, Thomas Cromwell on Reform and Reformation, 69; auth, Tudor Men and Institutions, 72; auth, The Precarious Balance, 73; auth, The Ways fo the West, 3 vols, 73-75; auth, The Tudor Age and Beyond, 86; auth, Politics and Ideology in the Sixteenth Century, 94; auth, State Sovereigns and Society, 98. **CONTACT ADDRESS** 502 Club Lane, Louisville, KY 40207. **EMAIL** ajslav01@athena-louisville.edu

SLAWEK, STEPHEN
PERSONAL Born 05/01/1949, W. Chester, PA, m, 2 children **DISCIPLINE** MUSIC AND ASIAN STUDIES **EDUCATION** Univ IL at Urbana-Champaign, PhD. **CAREER** Prof; Univ TX at Austin, 83-. **RESEARCH** Musical traditions of South Asia. **SELECTED PUBLICATIONS** Auth, Sitar Technique in Nibaddh Forms, Delhi, Motilal Banarsidass, 87; coauth, Musical Instruments of North India: Eighteenth century Portraits by Baltazard Solvyns, Delhi, Manohar Publ, 97. **CONTACT ADDRESS** School of Music, Univ of Texas, Austin, 2613 Wichita St, Austin, TX 78705. **EMAIL** slawek@mail.utexuas.edu

SLIND, MARVIN G.
DISCIPLINE MODERN EUROPEAN, SCANDINAVIAN AND WORLD HISTORY **EDUCATION** Wash State Univ, PhD, 78. **CAREER** Asst prof, Luther Col, Decorah, IA. **HONORS AND AWARDS** Fulbright Scholarship, 75-76; Fac of the Year Awd, Washington State Univ, 91. **MEMBERSHIPS** Norwegian-Am Hist Asn; Soc for the Advancement of Scandinavian Study; soc of Hist of Scandinavia; Fulbright Asn. **SELECTED PUBLICATIONS** Coauth, Norse to the Palouse: Sagas of the Selbu Norwegians; co-ed, NAFSA's Guide to Education Abroad for Advisers and Administrators. **CONTACT ADDRESS** Dept of History, Luther Col, 700 Col Dr, Decorah, IA 52101. **EMAIL** slindmar@luther.edu

SLOAN, DAVID
DISCIPLINE HISTORY **EDUCATION** Univ Calif Santa Barbara, PhD. **CAREER** Assoc prof. **RESEARCH** Colonial America; early national period. **SELECTED PUBLICATIONS** Auth, The Expedition of Hernando de Soto: A Post-Mortem Report, Part I, Ark Hist Quarterly, 92; The Expedition of Hernando de Soto: A Post-Mortem Report, Part II, Ark Hist Quaterly, 92. **CONTACT ADDRESS** History Dept, Univ of Arkansas, Fayetteville, 408 Old Main, Fayetteville, AR 72701. **EMAIL** dsloan@comp.uark.edu

SLOAN, EDWARD WILLIAM
PERSONAL Born 10/19/1931, Cleveland, OH, m, 5 children **DISCIPLINE** HISTORY **EDUCATION** Yale Univ, BA 53, MA 54; Harvard Univ, MA 60, PhD 63. **CAREER** Trinity College, inst to Charles P. Northam Prof of Hist, 63 to present. **HONORS AND AWARDS** Phi Beta Kappa. **MEMBERSHIPS** AHA; OAH; ASA; US Naval Inst; IMEHA; BHC; NASOH. **RESEARCH** Maritime and Naval Hist; Business and Entrepreneuria Hist; Hist of Technology. **SELECTED PUBLICATIONS** Auth, America and the Sea, coauth, Mystic CT, Mystic Seaport Press, 98; Glasgow's Response to New Yorks Challenge: The Cunard Steamship Persia Confronts America's Collins line in the Race for Transatlantic Supremacy, paper pres at Bus Hist Conf Glasgow, Scotland, 97; Diving in to History: Unraveling the Mystery of a Lost Transatlantic Liner, Conn Acad of Arts and Sciences, Hartford CT, 95; The Wreck of the Collins Liner Pacific: A Challenge for Maritime Historians and Nautical Archaeologists, Bermuda Jour of Archae and Maritime Hist, 93; The Nightingale and the Steamship: Jenny Lind and the Collins Liner Atlantic, The Amer Neptune, 91. **CONTACT ADDRESS** Dept of History, Trinity Col, Connecticut, 300 Summit ST, Hartford, CT 06106. **EMAIL** edward.sloan@mail.trincoll.edu

SLOAN, HERBERT
DISCIPLINE UNITED STATES HISTORY **EDUCATION** Stanford Univ, BA, 69; Columbia Univ, PhD, 88. **CAREER** Assoc prof. **SELECTED PUBLICATIONS** Auth, Principle and Interest: Thomas Jefferson and the Problem of Debt, 95; The Earth Belongs to the Living, 93. **CONTACT ADDRESS** Dept of History, Columbia Col, New York, 2960 Broadway, New York, NY 10027-6902.

SLOAN, PHILLIP R.
DISCIPLINE HISTORY **EDUCATION** Univ Utah, BS, 60; Scripps Inst of Ocean, MS, 64; Univ Calif San Diego, MA, 67, PhD, 70. **CAREER** Prof, 74-. **RESEARCH** History of biology; Buffon studies; history of natural history; evolution; recent human genetics. **SELECTED PUBLICATIONS** Auth, The Gaze of Natural History, 95; Lamarck from an English-Language Perspective, 97; Lamarck in Britain: Trans-forming Lamarck's Transformism, 97; ed, Richard Owen's Hunterian Lectures at the Royal College of Surgeons, 92. **CONTACT ADDRESS** History and Philosophy of Science Dept, Univ of Notre Dame, Notre Dame, IN 46556. **EMAIL** Phillip.R.Sloan.1@nd.edu

SLOAN, THOMAS
DISCIPLINE ART HISTORY **EDUCATION** Univ NE, BFA, 60; Northwestern Univ, MA, 62, PhD, 72. **CAREER** Instr, Princeton Univ; Northwestern Univ; Univ VA; Northeastern IL, Univ; ch, assoc prof, 86-. **HONORS AND AWARDS** Fel grant, Northwestern Univ; travel grant, Fulbright-Hays. **SELECTED PUBLICATIONS** Pub(s), Arts mag; Scandinavian Rev; Psychoanalytic Perspectives On Art. **CONTACT ADDRESS** Dept of Art Hist, Sch of the Art Inst of Chicago, 37 S Wabash Ave, Chicago, IL 60603.

SLOTKIN, RICHARD S.
PERSONAL Born 11/08/1942, Brooklyn, NY, m, 1963, 1 child **DISCIPLINE** AMERICAN STUDIES **EDUCATION** Brooklyn Col, BA, 63; Brown Univ, PhD, 67. **CAREER** Teaching assoc , Brown Univ, 65-66; instr, Peace Corps Trainee Prog, Brown Univ, 65; asst prof, Wesleyan Univ, 66-73, assoc prof, 73-76, prof, 76-82, Olin Prof, 82-; vis assoc prof, Yale Univ, 74. **HONORS AND AWARDS** NEH Younger Humanist Fel, 73-74; Albert J. Beveridge Awd, AHA, 73; Nat Book Awd finalist, 73; Honorary degree, MA, ad eundum gradum, Wesleyan Univ, 76; Rockefeller Found Fel, 77-78; Guggenheim Fel, 77-78 (declined); NEH Summer Stipend, 81; Don D. Walker Prize, Western Am Lit, 82; Little Big Horn Assocs Literary Awd, 85; Nat Book Awd Finalist, 93; Mary C. Turpie Prize, Am Studies Asn, 95; Regents' Lectr, Univ Calif, Davis, May 96; Excellence in Teaching, Wesleyan Univ, 97. **MEMBERSHIPS** ASA, AHA, OAH, AAUP, Soc of Am Hists. **RESEARCH** American cultural history, literature, film, violence. **SELECTED PUBLICATIONS** Auth, Regeneration Through Violence: The Mythology of the American Frontier, 1600-1860, Middletown: Wesleyan Univ Press (73); coauth, So Dreadfull a Judgement: Puritan Responses to King Philip's War, 11675-1677, Middletown: Wesleyan Univ Press (78, 88); auth, The Crater, NY: Atheneum (80, 81); auth, The Fatal Environment: The Myth of the Frontier in the Age of Industrialization, 1800-1890, NY: Atheneum Pubs (85); auth, The Return of Henry Starr, NY: Atheneum (88); auth, Gunfighter Nation: The Myth of the Frontier in Twentieth Century America, NY: Atheneum Pubs (92); auth, "The Movie Western," in Updating the Literary West, eds. Thomas Lyon, Christine Bold, et al (TX: TCU Press, 97), 873-83; auth, Abe: A Novel of the Young Lincoln. A John Macrae Book, NY: Henry Holt and Co, Inc (2000); auth, "Visual Narrative and American Myth, from Thomas Cole to John Ford," in The American Victorians and Virgin Nature, eds. T. J. J. Lears, Boston: Elizabeth Stewart Gardner Mus (2000). **CONTACT ADDRESS** Center for the Americas, Wesleyan Univ, 255 High St, Middletown, CT 06459. **EMAIL** rslotkin@wesleyan.edu

SLOUFFMAN, JAMES W.
PERSONAL Born 04/01/1950, Dayton, OH, m, 1981 **DISCIPLINE** FINE ARTS **EDUCATION** Wright State Univ, BFA, 72; Univ Cincinnati, MFA, 76. **CAREER** Dir, dept chemn, 79-; Antonelli Col. **HONORS AND AWARDS** Catholic Kolping Society Service Awd; 1996 tchr year award; 22 years tenure **MEMBERSHIPS** IGIA; Alpha Beta Kappa Nat Honor Society. **RESEARCH** The operas of Richard Wagner. **CONTACT ADDRESS** 124 E 7th St, Cincinnati, OH 45202. **EMAIL** jims@antonellic.com

SMAIL, DANIEL LORD
PERSONAL Born 10/05/1961, Ithaca, NY, m, 1985, 3 children **DISCIPLINE** HISTORY **EDUCATION** Univ Wis, BA, 84; Univ Mich, PhD, 94. **CAREER** Asst prof of History, Fordham Univ, 95-. **HONORS AND AWARDS** Phi Beta Kappa; fels from NEH and ACLS; William Koren Awd, Soc for French Hist Studies; President's Book Awd, Soc Sci Hist Asn. **MEMBERSHIPS** Am Hist Asn, Medieval Acad of Am, Soc for French Hist Studies, Western Soc for French Hist, Soc Sci Hist Asn. **RESEARCH** History and anthropology of law and justice, 1200-1600; urban history and demography, southern France, Italy, Mediterranean; ways of knowing, forms of documentation, and memory in medieval Europe. **SELECTED PUBLICATIONS** Auth, "Notaries, Courts, and the Legal Culture of Late Medieval Marseille," in Urban and Rural Communities in Medieval France: Provence and Languedoc, 1000-1500, ed, Kathryn L. Reyerson and John Drendel, Leiden: E. J. Brill (98): 23-50; auth, "The General Taille of Marseille, 1360-1361: A Social and Demographic Study," Provence historique, 49 (99): 473-85; auth, Imaginary Cartographies: Possession and Identity in Late Medieval Marseille, Ithca, NY: Cornell Univ Press (99); auth, "Geographies of Power in Angevin Marseille," The Medieval Practices of Space, ed Barbara Hanawalt and Michal Kobialka, Minneapolis: Univ of Minn Press (2000); auth, "Making the Law in Mediterranean Europe," (in progress); auth, "La topography socioprofessionelle de Marseille au quatorzieme siecle," Actes du colloque de Marseille (forthcoming 2000); co-ed with Susanne Pohl, "Vengeance, Peacemaking, and the Law in Medieval Europe: A Source Book" (in progress). **CONTACT ADDRESS** Dept Hist, Fordham Univ, Bronx, NY 10458. **EMAIL** smail@fordham.edu

SMALL, JOCELYN PENNY
DISCIPLINE GREEK, ETRUSCAN AND ROMAN ART **EDUCATION** Princeton Univ, PhD. **CAREER** Prof, Rutgers, The State Univ NJ, New Brunswick. **HONORS AND AWARDS** Guggenheim Fel, 00 **RESEARCH** Etruscan and Roman art, mythology and iconography; cognitive studies. **SELECTED PUBLICATIONS** Auth, SIBYL: The US Database of Classical Iconography: Issues of Simplicity and Complexity of Design, in Rev Informatique et Statistique dans les Sci humaines 29, 93; The Etruscan View of Greek Art, in Boreas 14/15, 94; Scholars, Etruscans, and Attic Painted Vases, J of Roman Archaeol 7, 94; Wax Tablets of the Mind: Cognitive Studies of Literacy and Memory in Classical Antiquity, Routledge, 97; coed, Murlo and Etruscan Studies. Essays in Memory of Kyle Meredith Phillips, Jr, Univ of Wis Press, 94; auth, "Time in Space: Narrative in Classical Art," Art Bulletin 81, (99): 562-575. **CONTACT ADDRESS** Dept of Art Hist, Rutgers, The State Univ of New Jersey, New Brunswick, 71 Hamilton St, Brunswick Voorhees Hall, New Brunswick, NJ 08901-1248. **EMAIL** jpsmall@rci.rutgers.edu

SMALL, LAWRENCE FARNSWORTH
PERSONAL Born 12/30/1925, Bangor, ME, m, 1947, 4 children **DISCIPLINE** HISTORY, POLITICAL SCIENCE **EDUCATION** Univ Maine, BA, 48, MA, 51; Bangor Theol Sem, BD, 48; Harvard Univ, PhD, 55. **CAREER** Asst minister, All Souls Church, Lowell, Mass, 50-52 & First Congregational Church, Winchester, Mass, 52-55; minister, Paramus Congregational Church, NJ, 55-59; assoc prof hist & polit sci, 59-61, dean & registr, 61-65, actg pres, 65-66, Prof Hist, Rocky Mountain Col, 61-, Pres, 66-75, retired, 90. **HONORS AND AWARDS** D.H.L. hon. Rocky Mountain Col. **MEMBERSHIPS** AHA; Am Polit Sci Asn. **RESEARCH** American intellectual and religious history, especially Unitarianism and Fundamentalism. **SELECTED PUBLICATIONS** Ed & contribr, History of Religion in Montana, 2 vols; Trails Revisited, The Story of the Montana/Northern Wyoming Conference, U.C.C.; A Century of Politics on the Yellowstone, Journey With the Law, the Life of Judge William J. Jameson; Montana Passage, A Homesteader's Heritage; Courageous Journey, the Road to Rocky Mountain College. **CONTACT ADDRESS** 7320 Sumatra Pla, Billings, MT 59102.

SMALL, MELVIN
PERSONAL Born 03/14/1939, New York City, NY, m, 1958, 2 children **DISCIPLINE** HISTORY **EDUCATION** Dartmouth, BA, 60; Univ of Michigan, MA, 61; PhD, 65. **CAREER** Asst Prof, Wayne State Univ, 65; Assoc 69; Prof 76; Chair 79-86; Visiting Prof U, 72-74, 83. **HONORS AND AWARDS** ACLS Study Fellowship, 69; Enrichment Grant; Canadian Govt, 87; Kuchl Prize, SHAFR, 89; NATO Fellowship, 96; Fellow Center for Behavioral. **MEMBERSHIPS** AHA; OAH; SHAFR; Peace History; Society. **RESEARCH** Amer Foreign Relations; Peace History; Vietnam War. **SELECTED PUBLICATIONS** Auth, "The Presidency of Richard Nixon," 99; auth, "Democracy and Diplomacy, 96; auth, "Covering Dissent, 94; auth, "Johnson, Nixon & The Doves, 88. **CONTACT ADDRESS** Dept History, Wayne State Univ, 3119 Fab, Detroit, MI 48202. **EMAIL** m.small@wayne.edu

SMALLS, JAMES
DISCIPLINE MODERN ART, AFRICAN-AMERICAN ART **EDUCATION** UCLA, PhD. **CAREER** Asst prof, Rutgers, The State Univ NJ, Univ Col-Camden. **RESEARCH** Nineteenth-century French art with special interest in the representation of blacks, women, colonized peoples; nineteenth and twentieth-century African-American art and culture. **SELECTED PUBLICATIONS** Auth, Public face, Private Thoughts: Fetish, Interracialism, and the Homoerotic in Some Photographs by Carl Van Vechten, in Sex Positives?: The Cultural Politics of Dissident Sexualities, Yale UP, 91; Food for Thought: African-American Visual Narration, in Dream Singers, Story Tellers: An African-American Presence, exh cat, Fukui Fine Art Mus, Japan, and NJ State Mus, 92; America the Beautiful, America the Ugly, Benny Andrews, The Am Ser, exh cat, NJ State Mus, 93; A Ghost of a Chance: Invisibility and Eli sion in African-American Art Historical Practice, in Art and Doc 13, 94; Separating the Men from the Men: (Re)defining Masculinity in and out of the Artist's Studio, in Semiotics, 94; Making Trouble for Art History: The Queer Case of Girodet, in Art J 55, no 4, 96. **CONTACT ADDRESS** Dept of Art Hist, Rutgers, The State Univ of New Jersey, New Brunswick, Voorhees Hall, 71 Hamilton St, New Brunswick, NJ 08903.

SMALLWOOD, ANDREW
PERSONAL Born New York, NY, s **DISCIPLINE** BLACK STUDIES **EDUCATION** Pa State Univ, BS, 88; ME, 92; Northern IL Univ, DEd, 98. **CAREER** Instr, Northern IL Univ, 94-96; instr to asst prof, Univ of Nebr, 96-. **HONORS AND AWARDS** Charter G Woodson Scholar, 92-94; Excellence in Teaching, Univ of Nebr, 98. **MEMBERSHIPS** Nat Coun for Black Studies. **RESEARCH** African American: History, Psychology and Policy Studies. **SELECTED PUBLICATIONS** Rev, of "Making Malcolm: The Myth and Meaning of Malcolm X", by Michael E Dyson, Western J of Black Studies 20.4 (96); auth, "Malcolm X: An Intellectual Aesthetic to Black Adult Education", Black Lives: Essays in African American Biography, ed James L Conyers, M.E. Sharpe Pub, (Armonk, NY), 98; auth, "Culture, Leadership and Intellectual Thought: A Critical Examination of Selected Historical Adult Education Ideologies by African American Educators", African American Sociology: A Social Study of the Pan African Diaspora, eds, James L. Conyers, Jr and Alva P Barnett, Nelson-Hall Pub, (Chicago), 98; auth, "Leadership under Fire: A Critical Examination of Chairs in Black Studies Departments and Programs", Black Intellectualism and Culture, ed James L Conyers Jr, JAI Pr, (Greenwich, CT), 99; auth, "Black Nationalism and the Call for Black Power", African Am Res Perspectives 5.1, Univ of Mich, 99; auth, "Leadership, Adult Education and Malcolm X: An Afrocentric Analysis", Thresholds in Education, Northern IL Univ, (forthcoming). **CONTACT ADDRESS** Dept Black Studies, Univ of Nebraska, Omaha, 6001 Dodge St, Omaha, NE 68182-0001. **EMAIL** andrew_smallwood@unomaha.edu

SMALLWOOD, ARWIN
PERSONAL Born 07/19/1965, Windsor, NC, m, 1993, 2 children **DISCIPLINE** HISTORY **EDUCATION** NC Central Univ, BA, 88; MA, 90; Ohio State Univ, PhD, 97. **CAREER** Vis instr, NC A & T State Univ, 93-94; asst prof, Bradley Univ, 95-; dir, African-American Studies Prog, Bradley Univ, 95-. **HONORS AND AWARDS** Outstanding Service Awd, Foreign Service Inst, U.S. Dept of State; Fac Res Mentor, Bradley Univ, 96-97 & 97-98; First Year Fac Teaching Awd, Bradley Univ, 95-96; Archie K. Davis Fel, Bradley Univ, 00-01. **MEMBERSHIPS** AHA, OAH, SHA: ASALH, OIEAHC. **RESEARCH** Southern history, African-American history, Native American history, Colonial American history, black indians in Colonial North Carolina. **SELECTED PUBLICATIONS** Auth, The Bart F. Smallwood Papers, Univ NC Chapel Hill; auth, The Atlas of African-American History and Politics: From the Slave Trade to Modern Times, McGraw-Hill (Boston, MA), 97. **CONTACT ADDRESS** Dept Hist, Bradley Univ, 1501 W Bradley Ave, Peoria, IL 61625-0001. **EMAIL** arwin@bradley.edu

SMALLWOOD, JAMES MILTON
PERSONAL Born 07/10/1944, Terrell, TX, m, 2 children **DISCIPLINE** HISTORY, POLITICAL SCIENCE **EDUCATION** ETex State Univ, BS, 67, MA, 69; Tex Tech Univ, PhD(hist, polit sci), 74. **CAREER** Instr hist, ETex State Univ, 67-69, Southeastern Okla State Univ, 69-70 & Tex Tech Univ, 70-74; dir Will Rogers Res Proj, 76-81, Prof Hist, Okla State Univ, 75-, Consult, Okla Humanities Coun & Okla Heritage Asn, 77-**MEMBERSHIPS** AHA; Orgn Am Historians; Southern Hist Asn; Western Hist Asn. **RESEARCH** Recent United States history; Southern United States history; Civil War, Reconstruction. **SELECTED PUBLICATIONS** Auth, And Gladly Teach, Univ Okla, 76; Blacks in Reconstruction Texas, ETex Hist J, 76; Disaffection in Confederate Texas, Civil War Hist, 76; Urban Builder: The Life and Times of Stanley Draper, Univ Okla, 77; Black self-help and education in Reconstruction Texas, Bull Negro Hist, 78; Banquo's ghost and the Paris Peace Conference, East Europ Quart, 78; Will Rogers's Daily Telegrams (4 vols), Okla State Univ, 78; Time of Hope, Time of Despair: Black Texans During Reconstruction, Kennikat Press, 81. **CONTACT ADDRESS** Dept of Hist, Oklahoma State Univ, Stillwater, Stillwater, OK 74074.

SMARR, JANET L.
PERSONAL Born 05/20/1949, Chicago, IL, m, 1973, 2 children **DISCIPLINE** DRAMA, LITERATURE, ITALIAN STUDIES **EDUCATION** Brown Univ, BA, 70; Princeton Univ, PhD, 75. **CAREER** Instr, Princeton Univ, 75-76; instr, Univ of Mass, 76-77; asst prof, Yale Univ, 79-80; asst prof to prof, Univ of Ill, 80-00; prof, Univ of CA San Diego, 00- **HONORS AND AWARDS** AAUW Fel, 74-75; SE Inst of Medieval and Renaissance Studies, 76; Mellon Fel, 77-78, Fel, Univ of Ill, 86, 99; Awd, Am Asn of Ital Studies, 84; ALTHE Awd, 96. **MEMBERSHIPS** MLA, Renaissance Soc of Am, Am Assoc of Ital Studies, Am Soc for Theatre Res, Am Boccaccio Assoc. **RESEARCH** Renaissance, Italian and Comparative Literature, Renaissance Women writers. **SELECTED PUBLICATIONS** Auth, "Petrarch: A Vergil Without a Rome," Rome in the Renaissance, the City and the Myth, (82); ed and transl, Italian Renaissance Tales, Solaris Pr, 83; auth, Boccaccio and Fiammetta: the Narrator as Lover, Univ of Ill Pr, 86; transl, Boccaccio's Eclogues, Garland Publ, 87; auth, "Poets of Love and Exile," Dante and Ovid: Essays in Intertextuality, (91); auth, "Boccaccio and Renaissance Women Writers," Studi sul Boccaccio, (91-92); ed, Historical Criticism and the Challenge of Theory, Univ of Ill Pr, 93; auth, "A dialogue of dialogues: Tullia d-Aragona and sperone Speroni," MLN, (98); auth, Other Races, Other Spaces: Boccaccio's Representation of non-Christian People and Places in the Decameron, Studi sul Boccaccio, 99; auth, Substituting for Laura: Objects of Desire for Renaissance Women Poets, Comp Lit Studies, 00. **CONTACT ADDRESS** Dept Theatre and Dance, Univ of California, San Diego, La Jolla, CA 92093-0344. **EMAIL** jsmarr@ucsd.edu

SMART, NINIAN
PERSONAL Born 05/06/1927, Cambridge, United Kingdom, m, 1954, 4 children **DISCIPLINE** HISTORY, PHILOSOPHY **EDUCATION** Oxford Univ, BA, 51, B Phil, 54. **CAREER** Univ of Wales, 52-55; Univ of London, 56-61; Chair, Univ of Birmingham, 61-67; Lancaster Univ, 67-89; Univ of Calif Santa Barbara, 77-99. **HONORS AND AWARDS** Honorary Doctorates from Chicago Loyola Univ, Glasgow Univ, Sterling Univ, Kelamya Univ, Lancaster Univ. **MEMBERSHIPS** AAR; ASSR; BSRS; Aristotelian Soc. **RESEARCH** Philosophy of

Religion, Comparative Study of Religion, Indian Religions, Chinese Religions, Religion and Politics. **SELECTED PUBLICATIONS** Auth, Religions and Faith, 58, 00; auth, The World's Religions, 88, 97; auth, Dimensions of Religions, 97; auth, World Philosophies, 99. **CONTACT ADDRESS** Dept Relig Studies, Univ of California, Santa Barbara, 552 University Rd, Santa Barbara, CA 93106-0002.

SMEINS, LINDA
DISCIPLINE ART HISTORY **EDUCATION** Univ Denver, BFA; Calif State, MA; Univ Brit Columbia, PhD. **CAREER** Dept Art, Western Wash Univ **MEMBERSHIPS** Mem, Col Art Assn; Soc Arch Hist(s). **SELECTED PUBLICATIONS** Auth, Stopovers in the Flight of Time, Jet Dreams Art of the Fifties in the Northwest Seattle/London: Univ Washn Press, Tacoma Art Museum, 95; National Rhetoric, Public Discourse, and Spatialization: Middle Class America and the Pattern Book House, Nineteenth-Century Contexts, 92. **CONTACT ADDRESS** Dept of Art, Western Washington Univ, 516 High St, Bellingham, WA 98225. **EMAIL** lsmeins@cc.wwu.edu

SMETHURST, RICHARD JACOB
PERSONAL Born 10/05/1933, Carlisle, PA, m, 1956 **DISCIPLINE** JAPANESE HISTORY **EDUCATION** Dickinson Col, AB, 55; Univ Mich, Ann Arbor, MA, 61, PhD, 68. **CAREER** From Asst Prof to Assoc Prof, 67-85, prof hist, Univ Pittsburgh, 85-, Dept Chair, Univ Ctr for Int Studies Res Prof, 88-. **MEMBERSHIPS** Asn Asian Studies; Columbia Univ Mod Japan Seminar. **RESEARCH** Japanese social and economic history; Japanese rural history; comparative military history. **SELECTED PUBLICATIONS** Auth, The Military Reserve Association and the Minobe Crisis of 1935, in Crisis Politics in Prewar Japan, Sophia Univ, 70; The Creation of the Military Reserve Association in Japan, J Asian Studies, 8/71; A Social Basis for Prewar Japanese Militarism: The Army and the Rural Community, Univ Calif, 74; Agricultural Development and Tenancy Disputes in Japan, 1870-1940, Princeton, 87; Japan's First Experiment with Democracy, 1870-1940, in The Social Meaning of Democracy, NYU, 95; The Self-Taught Bureaucrat: Takahashi Korekiyo and Economic Policy during the Great Depression, in Learning in Likely Places: Varieties of Apprenticeship in Japan, Cambridge, 98. **CONTACT ADDRESS** Dept History, Univ of Pittsburgh, 3P01 Forbes Quad, Pittsburgh, PA 15260-0001. **EMAIL** rsmet@pitt.edu

SMILEY, DAVID LESLIE
PERSONAL Born 03/17/1921, MS, m, 1945, 1 child **DISCIPLINE** HISTORY **EDUCATION** Baylor Univ, AB, 47, MA, 48; Univ Wis, PhD, 53. **CAREER** Asst prof, 50-56, assoc prof, 57-63, Prof Hist, 63-91, prof emer, Wake Forest Univ, 91- .Fulbright lectr, Univ Strasbourg, 68-69. **RESEARCH** United States history, especially the national period; the South in American history; the southern antislavery movement. **SELECTED PUBLICATIONS** Coauth, The South in American History, Prentice-Hall, 2nd ed, 60; auth, Lion of White Hall: Life of C M Clay, Univ Wis, 62; coauth, Southern politics, In: Le Sud au Temps de Scarlett, Hachette, Paris, 66. **CONTACT ADDRESS** 1060 Polo Rd NW, Winston-Salem, NC 27106.

SMILEY, RALPH
PERSONAL Born 03/24/1927, New York, NY, m, 1964, 4 children **DISCIPLINE** EUROPEAN HISTORY, THE MIDDLE EAST **EDUCATION** Brooklyn Col, BA, 51; Rutgers Univ, MA, 63, PhD(mod Europe), 71. **CAREER** Asst hist, Rutgers Univ, 63-65, teaching asst, Douglass Col, 65-66; assoc prof, Indiana Univ of Pa, 66-69; assoc prof, 69-80, Prof Hist, Bloomsburg State Col, 80-, Adj Prof Mass Commun, 77-, Instr film, Pa State Univ, 76-77. **MEMBERSHIPS** Am Film Inst; AHA; Conf Group Cent Europ Hist; Am Asn Advan Slavic Studies; MidE Inst. **RESEARCH** Twentieth century European inter-war period, 1919-1939; European imperialism; film semiotics. **SELECTED PUBLICATIONS** Producer, dir & ed, The Monkey's Paw (film), 77. **CONTACT ADDRESS** Dept of Hist, Bloomsburg Univ of Pennsylvania, Bloomsburg, PA 17815.

SMIT, J. W.
DISCIPLINE EARLY MODERN EUROPEAN HISTORY **EDUCATION** Univ Utrecht, MA, 53, PhD, 58. **CAREER** Queen Wilhelmina prof. **RESEARCH** Social and economic history of the 16th and 17th-centuries. **SELECTED PUBLICATIONS** Fruin en de Partijen Tijdens de Republiek, 58; History of Art, Art in History, History in Art, Stud in 17th Century Dutch Cult, 91. **CONTACT ADDRESS** Dept of Hist, Columbia Col, New York, 2960 Broadway, New York, NY 10027-6902.

SMITH, BILLY G.
DISCIPLINE HISTORY **EDUCATION** UCLA, BA, 71, MA, 73, PhD, 81. **CAREER** PROF, HIST, MONTANA STATE UNIV **MEMBERSHIPS** AM Antiquarian Soc **SELECTED PUBLICATIONS** Auth, "The Vicissitudes of Fortune: The Careers of Laboring Men in Philadelphia, 1750-1800," Univ NC Press, 88; auth, The Lower Sort: Philadelphia's Laboring People, 1750-1800, Cornell Univ Press, 1990; coauth, Blacks Who Stole Themselves: Advertisements for Runaways in the Pennsylvania Gazette, 1728-90, Univ Penn, 89; auth, coauth, The Unfortunate: The Voyage and Adventures of William Moraley, an Indentured Servant, Penn State Press, 91; auth, Life in Early Philadelphia: Documents from the Revolutionary and Early National Periods, Penn State Univ Press, 95; coauth, "A Melancholy Scene of Devastation": The Public Response to the 1793 Philadelphia Yellow Fever Epidemic, 97; auth, "Runaway Slaves in the Mid-Atlantic Region during the Revolutionary Era," in The Transforming Hand of Revolution: Reconsidering the American Revolution as a Social Movement, Univ Press Va. **CONTACT ADDRESS** Hist & Phil, Montana State Univ, Bozeman, Bozeman, MT 59717. **EMAIL** uhibs@msu.oscs.montana.edu

SMITH, C. SHAW, JR.
DISCIPLINE ART HISTORY **EDUCATION** Univ NC Chapel Hill, AB, MA, PhD. **CAREER** Assoc prof and dept chr, Davidson Col. **RESEARCH** 18th and 19th-century painting; mod and contemp art; art and theory; French art hist. **SELECTED PUBLICATIONS** Auth, publ(s) in Eugene Delacroix and French Romanticism, Southern cult, art criticism. **CONTACT ADDRESS** Davidson Col, 102 N Main St, PO Box 1719, Davidson, NC 28036. **EMAIL** shsmith@davidson.edu

SMITH, CARL
PERSONAL 2 children **DISCIPLINE** AMERICAN STUDIES **EDUCATION** Yale Univ, PhD. **CAREER** Cur, Chicago Historical Society exhibitions; The Great Chicago Fire & Web of Memory; Prof, Franklyn Bliss Snyder; The Dramas of Haymarket. **HONORS AND AWARDS** CAS outstanding tchg awd; McCormick tchg professorship; awd(s), Best Book in North Am Urban History; Soc of Midland Authors' first prize for non-fiction, 94. **SELECTED PUBLICATIONS** Auth,Chicago and the American Literary Imagination, 1880-1920 ,84; Urban Disorder and the Shape of Belief: The Great Chicago Fire, the Haymarket Bomb, and the Model Town of Pullman, 94. **CONTACT ADDRESS** Dept of English, Northwestern Univ, 1897 Sheridan, 215 Univ Hall, Evanston, IL 60208. **EMAIL** cjsmith@northwestern.edu

SMITH, CHARLES
PERSONAL Born 04/14/1936, Fall River, MA, m, 1981, 1 child **DISCIPLINE** HISTORY **EDUCATION** Williams Col, BA, 58; Harvard Univ, MA, 60; Univ Mich, PhD, 68. **CAREER** Asst prof, San Diego Univ, 67-71; assoc prof, 72-76; prof, 77-92; prof, dept hd, Wayne State Univ, 92-94; prof, dept hd, Univ Ariz, 94-. **HONORS AND AWARDS** Fulbright Grant; SSRC/ACLS Diss Grant; ARC Egypt Res Grants; APS Res Grants; IAS Fel, Hebrew Univ; Fel, Vir Cen Human; Udall Cen Fel; Pres, Am Res Cen, Egypt, 96-99. **MEMBERSHIPS** AHA; MEI; MESA; ARCE; ISA. **RESEARCH** World War I and the Middle East; Palestine and Arab-Israeli conflict; Nationalism; modern Egypt. **SELECTED PUBLICATIONS** Auth, Islam and the Search for Social Order in Modern Egypt, 83; auth, Palestine and the Arab-Israeli Conflict, 88, 4th ed 00; auth, "The Arab-Israeli Conflict," The Encyclopedia of the Palestines (00); auth, "Secularism and Islam," Oxford Encyclopedia of the Modern Islamic World, (95); auth, "Imagined Identities, Imagined Nationalisms: Print Culture and Egyptian Nationalism in Light of Recent Scholarship," Intl J Middle Eastern Studies (97); auth, "The Intellectual and Modernization, Definitions and Reconsiderations: the Egyptian Experience," Comparative Studies In Soc and Hist (80); auth, "The Crisis of Orientation: The Shift of Egyptian Intellectuals to Islamic Subjects in the 1930s," Intl J Islamic Studies (73). **CONTACT ADDRESS** Dept Near Eastern Studies, Univ of Arizona, PO Box 210080, Tucson, AZ 85721-0080. **EMAIL** cdsmith@u.arizona.edu

SMITH, CHARLIE CALVIN
PERSONAL Born 06/12/1943, Brickeys, AR, m **DISCIPLINE** HISTORY **EDUCATION** AM & N Coll Pine Bluff AR, BA, 66; AR State Univ Jonesboro, MSE, 71; Univ of AR Fayetteville, PhD, 78. **CAREER** AR State Univ, asst prof of History 1978-; AR State Univ, instructor in History 1970-78; Lee Co Public School Marianna AR, Social Studies teacher, asst football coach 1966-70; Arkansas State Univ, assoc prof of History, 82-86, asst dean 1986-. **HONORS AND AWARDS** Endowment for the Humanities 1980; Presidential Fel, ASU, 1982, Outstanding Black Fac Mem/Teacher, Black Student Body, 1984-86, 88. **MEMBERSHIPS** Southern Conf Afro-Am Studies. **RESEARCH** 20th century US history; African American history. **SELECTED PUBLICATIONS** Auth, The Oppressed Oppressors Negro Slavery among the choctaws of OK Red River Valley History Review vol 2, 75; The Civil War Letters of John G Marsh, Upper OH Valley History Review, 79; The Diluting of an Inst the Social Impact of WWII on the AR family" AR history quarter (spring) 80; biographical sketches of AR Governors J Marion Futrell & Homer M Adkins; War and Wartime Changes: The Transformation of Arkansas, 1940-45, U of A Press, 1986; auth, African Americans: Their History, Heritage, 97. **CONTACT ADDRESS** Prof of Hist, Arkansas State Univ, PO Box 1030, State University, AR 72467. **EMAIL** csmith@toltec.astate.edu

SMITH, DALE CARY
PERSONAL Born 07/02/1951, Orlando, FL, m, 1973, 1 child **DISCIPLINE** HISTORY OF MEDICINE **EDUCATION** Duke Univ, BA, 73; Univ Minn, PhD, 79. **CAREER** Instr & res fel hist med, Univ Minn, 79-81, Asst Prof, 81-82; from Asst Prof to Assoc Prof, 82-97, Prof and Chair Med Hist, Uniformed Serv Univ of the Health Sci, 97-; Book rev ed, J Hist Med & Allied Sci, 79-82, Assoc ed, 83-87; Ed, Am Asn Hist Med Newsletter, 97-. **HONORS AND AWARDS** Laurance D. Redway, MD, Awd for Excellence in Medical Writings of the Med Soc of the State of NY, 87; named Outstanding Teacher by 1st year med students: 96, 97, 98. **MEMBERSHIPS** Am Asn Hist Med; AHA; Orgn Am Historians; AAAS; Soc Mil Hist; U.S. Naval Inst. **RESEARCH** Changing concepts of disease; development of clinical medicine and surgery; history of military medicine. **SELECTED PUBLICATIONS** Auth, Quinine and fever: The development of the effective dosage, J Hist Med, 76; The rise and decline of typhomalarial fever, J Hist Med, 82; ed, On the Causes of Fever by William Budd, Johns Hopkins Univ Press, 84; auth, An Historical Overview of the Recognition of Appendicitis, NY State J Med, 86; Military Medicine, in Encyclopedia of the American Military, Charles Scribners Sons, 94; Appendicitis Appendectomy and the Surgeon, Bull Hist Med, 96; The American Gastroenterological Association: A Centennial History, Am Gastroenterological Asn. 99. **CONTACT ADDRESS** Dept of Med Hist, Uniformed Services Univ of the Health Sciences, 4301 Jones Bridge Rd, Bethesda, MD 20814-4799. **EMAIL** dcsmith@usuhs.mil

SMITH, DANIEL B.
PERSONAL Born 08/12/1950, Kansas City, MO, s, 1 child **DISCIPLINE** HISTORY **EDUCATION** Okla State Univ, BA, 72; Univ Va, PhD, 78. **CAREER** Prof, Univ Ky, 78-. **HONORS AND AWARDS** NEH Screenwriting Fel, 85, 90, 95; Emmy, Alamance, 96. **RESEARCH** Early America; history of the family; film and history. **SELECTED PUBLICATIONS** Auth, Inside the Great House: Planter Family Life in Eighteenth-Century Chesapeake Society, 80; auth, art, Cotton Mather and Children in the Puritan Heart, 95; auth, art, This Heaven in Idea: Image and Reality on the Kentucky Frontier, 98. **CONTACT ADDRESS** Dept of History, Univ of Kentucky, Lexington, KY 40506. **EMAIL** dbsmit0l@pop.uky.edu

SMITH, DANIEL SCOTT
PERSONAL Born 09/24/1942, Galesburg, IL, d, 2 children **DISCIPLINE** AMERICAN & DEMOGRAPHIC HISTORY **EDUCATION** Univ Fla, BA, 63; Univ Calif, Berkeley, MA, 65, PhD(hist), 73; Princeton Univ, cert demog, 74. **CAREER** From instr to asst prof hist, Univ Conn, 71-74; asst prof, 74-77, Assoc Prof Hist, Univ Ill, Chicago, 77-, Instr, Newberry Libr Inst Quant Hist, 72-; Pop Coun fel, Off Pop Res, Princeton, 73-74; assoc dir, Family & Community Hist Ctr, Newberry Libr, 74-; Am Coun Learned Socs fel, 77-78; Ed, Historical Methods, 80- **MEMBERSHIPS** Pop Asn Am; AHA; Econ Hist Asn; Orgn Am Historians. **RESEARCH** American historical demography. **SELECTED PUBLICATIONS** Auth, Life Course, Norms, and the Family System of Older Americans in 1900, J of Family Hist, Vol 4, 1979; Historical Change in the Household Structure of the Elderly in Economically Developed Societies, in Robert W. Fogel, et al., eds., Aging:Stability and Change in the Family, 1981; Differential Mortality in the United States before 1900, J of Interdisciplinary Hist, Vol 13, 1983; All in Some Degree Related to Each Other: A Demographic and Comparative Resolution of the Anomaly of New England Kinship, Amer Hist Rev, Vol 94, 1989; The Meanings of Family and Household: Change and Continuity in the Mirror of the American Census, Population and Development Rev, Vol 18, 1992; American Family and Demographic Patterns and the Northwest European Model, Continuity and Change, Vol 8, 1993; Continuity and Discontinuity in Puritan Naming: Massachusetts, 1771, William and Mary Quart, Vol 51, 1994; Cultural Demography: New England Deaths And The Puritan Perception Of Risk, J Of Interdisciplinary Hist, Vol 26, 1996; The Number And Quality Of Children: Education and Marital Fertility in Early 20th-Century Iowa, J Of Soc Hist, Vol 30, 1996; Population and Political Ethics: Thomas Jefferson's Demography of a Generation, William and Mary Quart, Vol 56, 1999. **CONTACT ADDRESS** Dept of Hist, Univ of Illinois, Chicago, 601 S. Morgan St., 921 University Hall, Chicago, IL 60607-7109. **EMAIL** dan.smith@uic.edu

SMITH, DAVID CLAYTON
PERSONAL Born 11/14/1929, Lewiston, ME, m, 1953, 2 children **DISCIPLINE** MODERN & AGRICULTURAL HISTORY **EDUCATION** Farmington State Col, BS, 55; Univ ME, M Ed, 56, MA, 58; Cornell Univ, PhD(hist), 65. **CAREER** Instr hist, Hobart & William Smith Col, 60-63, instr hist & econ, 63-65; from asst prof to assoc prof, 65-75, prof hist, Univ ME, Orono, 75-, chemn dept, 80-, Mem & chemn, Maine Hist Preserv Comn, 70-75; pres, Penobscot Heritage Mus Living Hist, 72-76; coop prof, Inst Quaternary Studies, 78-. **HONORS AND AWARDS** James Madison Prize, 94. **MEMBERSHIPS** AHA; Orgn Am Historians; Forest Hist Soc; Agr Hist Soc; Asn Can Studies US. **RESEARCH** Forest hist; agr hist; climate hist; H.G. Wells; World War II. **SELECTED PUBLICATIONS** Auth, Lumbering and the Maine Woods: A Bibliography, Maine Hist Soc, 70; History of United States Papermaking 1690-1970, Lockwood, 71; History of Maine Lumbering 1869-

1960, 72, A History of the Univ ME, 78, History of the Maine Agricultural Experiment Station, 80 & Long Time Series Temperature and Precipitation Maine 1808-1980, 81, Univ ME; auth, Desperately Mortal: A Life of H.G. Wells, 86; coauth, Miss You, 90; coauth, Since You Went Away, 92; coauth, We're In This War, Too, 93; ed, Collected Correspondence of H.G. Wells, 98. **CONTACT ADDRESS** Dept of History, Univ of Maine, Orono, ME 06973. **EMAIL** dcsmith@maine.maine.edu

SMITH, DAVID FREDRICK
PERSONAL Born 06/11/1941, Liverpool, England, m, 1998, 1 child **DISCIPLINE** MODERN BRITISH HISTORY **EDUCATION** Bristol Univ, BA, 63; Wash Univ, AM, 65; Univ Toronto, PhD, 72. **CAREER** Lectr hist, Webster Col, 65-67; lectr, Univ Toronto, 71-72; asst prof, 72-80, from assoc prof history to prof, Univ Puget Sound, 80-. **MEMBERSHIPS** Conf Brit Studies. **RESEARCH** British policy in Germany 1945-1951. **CONTACT ADDRESS** Dept Hist, Univ of Puget Sound, 1500 N Warner St, Tacoma, WA 98416-0005. **EMAIL** DFSMITH@ups.edu

SMITH, DENNIS P.
PERSONAL Born 02/09/1949, Kittery, ME, m, 1982, 4 children **DISCIPLINE** HISTORY **EDUCATION** Northeastern St Univ, BA, 85, MS, 87. **CAREER** Asst prof, Ok St Univ **HONORS AND AWARDS** Regents Distinguished Teaching Awd, 97; estab ok film repository, usao, 90; actively worked with st teacher training in the arts; campus co-ord for cooperative agreements with st vocational tech inst. **MEMBERSHIPS** Comm Col Humanities Assoc; Nat Assoc for Humanities Educ. **RESEARCH** Biblical hist; oral hist; visual arts. **CONTACT ADDRESS** Dept Humanities, Oklahoma State Univ, Oklahoma City, 900 N Portland, Oklahoma City, OK 73107-6195. **EMAIL** smithdp@okway.okstate.edu

SMITH, DUANE ALLAN
PERSONAL Born 04/20/1937, San Diego, CA, m, 1960, 1 child **DISCIPLINE** UNITED STATES HISTORY **EDUCATION** Univ Colo, BA, 59, MA, 61, PhD(Hist), 64. **CAREER** From asst prof to assoc prof, 64-72, prof Hist, Ft Lewis Col, 72-, Am Asn State & Local Hist grant-in-aid, 67; Huntington Libr res grant, 68, 73 & 78. **HONORS AND AWARDS** Colorado Prof of Year, 90. **MEMBERSHIPS** Mining Hist Assoc; Western Hist Asn. **RESEARCH** Western mining camps; mining history; Colorado history. **SELECTED PUBLICATIONS** Auth, Rocky Mountain Mining Camps: The Urban Frontier, Ind Univ 67; coauth, A Colorado History, Pruett, 72, 76, 88, 95; auth, Horace Tabor, His Life and the Legend, Colo Assoc Press, 73; Silver Saga, Pruett, 74; Colorado Mining, Univ NMex, 77; Rocky Mountain Boom Town, Univ NMex, 80; Secure the Shadow, Colo Sch Mines, 80; coauth, A Land Alone, Pruett, 81; Mining America Univ Press Kansas, A Tale of Two Towns, Univ Press Colo, 97; auth, The Legendary Line: Durango to Silverton, Western Reflections, 99. **CONTACT ADDRESS** Southwest Center, Fort Lewis Col, 1000 Rim Dr, Durango, CO 81301-3999. **EMAIL** smith_d@fortlewis.edu

SMITH, DWIGHT L.
DISCIPLINE HISTORY **EDUCATION** Indiana Central Univ, AB, 40; Indiana, AM, 41, PhD, 49; Indianapolis, LittD, 87. **CAREER** Prof to Prof Emer, Hist, Miami University Ohio **MEMBERSHIPS** Am Antiquarian Soc **RESEARCH** War of 1812 **SELECTED PUBLICATIONS** Auth, Indians of the United States and Canada: A Bibliography, vol 1, 74, vol 2, 83; auth, The War of 1812: An Annotated Bibliography, Garland, 85; The History of Canada: An Annotated Bibliography, 83; coauth, The Colorado River Survey: Robert B. Stanton and the Denver, Colorado Canyon & Pacific Railroad, 87; auth, Survival on a Westward Trek, 1858-1859: The John Jones Overlanders, Ohio Univ Press, 89; coauth, A Journey through the West: Thomas Rodney's 1803 Journey from Delaware to the Mississippi Territory, Ohio Univ Press, 97. **CONTACT ADDRESS** 6195 Fairfield Rd., No. 12, Oxford, OH 45056.

SMITH, ELIZABETH BRADFORD
DISCIPLINE WESTERN MEDIEVAL ART AND ARCHITECTURE **EDUCATION** Inst Fine Arts, NYork, MA, PhD; lisc, Univ Strasborg, France. **CAREER** Assoc prof, Pa State Univ, 82-. **RESEARCH** Structure of French Romanesque and Italian Gothic architecture. **SELECTED PUBLICATIONS** Auth, Medieval Art in America; patterns of Collecting, Palmer Museum, 1800-1940; arts, Romanesque sculpture in France, England and the Low Countries. **CONTACT ADDRESS** Pennsylvania State Univ, Univ Park, 201 Shields Bldg, University Park, PA 16802. **EMAIL** exs11@psu.edu

SMITH, F. TODD
PERSONAL Born 11/21/1957, New Orleans, LA, m, 1996 **DISCIPLINE** HISTORY **EDUCATION** Univ Mo, BA, 79; Univ SD, MA, 83; Tulane Univ, PhD, 89. **CAREER** Asst prof, Xavier Univ La, 91-96; asst prof, Univ W Fl, 96-97; asst prof, Univ of N Tx, 97-. **HONORS AND AWARDS** Ray A. Billington Awd, Western His Assoc, 92; Ottis Lock Awd, East Tx Hist Assoc, 96. **MEMBERSHIPS** Amer Hist Assoc **RESEARCH** Southern plains native amer; colonial Tx & La. **SELECTED PUBLICATIONS** Auth, The Kadohadacho Indians and the Louisiana-Texas Frontier, 1803-1815, Southwestern Hist Quart, 91; The Red River Caddos: A Historical Overview to 1835, Bull of the Tx Archeol Soc, 94; A Native Response to the Transfer of Louisiana: The Red River Caddos and Spain, 1762-1803, La Hist, 96; The Caddo Indians: Tribes at the Convergence of Empires, 1542-1854, Tx A & M Univ Press, 95; The Caddos, the Wichitas, and the United States, 1846-1901, Tx A& M Univ Press, 96; The Wichita Indians: Southern Plains Farmers, Hunters, and Traders, 1541-1845, forthcoming. **CONTACT ADDRESS** History Dept, Univ of No Texas, Denton, TX 76203. **EMAIL** ftsmith@unt.edu

SMITH, GENE A.
PERSONAL Born 09/07/1963, Fort Payne, AL, m, 1998 **DISCIPLINE** HISTORY **EDUCATION** Auburn Univ, BA, 87; MA, 87; PhD, 91. **CAREER** Adj instr, Central Ala Community Col, 87-88; adj instr, Southern Union State Jr Col, 88-91; TA, Auburn Univ, 85-91; asst prof, Mont State Univ Billings, 91-94; asst prof to assoc prof, Tex Christian Univ, 94-. **HONORS AND AWARDS** NEH Grant, 92; Eastern Mont Col Fac Merit Awd, 93; Vice Admiral Edwin B. Hooper Res Grant, 93-94; USMA-ROTC Mil Hist Fel, 94; General Jay A. Matthews, Jr. Prize, 94; Va Hist Soc Mellon Res Fel, 93, 97; C. Allan and Majorie Braun Fel, 97-98; Presenter, Ford Chair Lectures, Southeastern La Univ, 00. **MEMBERSHIPS** Soc for Hist of the Early Am Repub; Soc for Mil Hist; S Hist Assoc; Va Hist Soc; Gulf S Hist Assoc; N Am Soc for Oceanic Hist; SW Soc Sci Assoc. **RESEARCH** American history 1789-1820, Naval and Maritime History. **SELECTED PUBLICATIONS** Auth, For the Purposes of Defense: The Politics of the Jeffersonian Gunboat Program, Univ of Dela Pr, (Newark), 95; auth, "To Effect a Peace through the Medium of War: Jefferson and the Circumstances of Force in the Mediterranean", Consortium on Revolutionary Europe, 1750-1850: Selected Papers 1996 (96): 155-160; auth, Iron and Heavy Guns: Duel Between the Monitor and Merrimac, McWhieney Found Pr, (Abilene, TX), 97; auth, "Griffin Dobson: Virginia Slave, California Freeman", Va Cavalcade 46, (Autumn 97): 278-287; coauth, Filibusters and Expansionists: Jeffersonian Manifest Destiny, 1800-1821, Univ of Ala Pr, (Tuscaloosa), 97; auth, "A Little Sharp Looking Frenchman and his Battle of New Orleans", Hist New Orleans Collection Quarterly 16, (Winter 98): 2-6; auth, "Experimenting with Reform: Thomas ap Catesby Jones and the First Ordnance Survey, 1833-1834", New Interpretations in Naval History: Selected Papers from the 13th Naval History Symposium, eds William M. McBride and Eric P. Reed, Naval Inst Pr, (Annapolis, MD, 98): 81-92; auth, "Our Flag was display'd within their Works: The Treaty of Ghent and the Conquest of Mobile", Ala Rev 52 (Jan 99): 3-21; ed, Historical Memoir of the War in West Florida and Louisiana in 1814-15: With an Atlas, by Arsene Lacarriere Latour (1816), Univ Pr of Fla, 99; auth, Thomas ap Catesby Jones: Commodore of Manifest Destiny, Naval Inst Pr, (Annapolis, MD), 00. **CONTACT ADDRESS** Dept Hist, Texas Christian Univ, Fort Worth, TX 76129. **EMAIL** gsmith@tcu.edu

SMITH, HAROLD L.
PERSONAL Born 11/25/1942, Ottumwa, IA **DISCIPLINE** MODERN BRITISH HISTORY **EDUCATION** Univ Northern Iowa, BS, 65; Univ Iowa, MA, 67, PhD, 71. **CAREER** Asst prof hist, Univ Mo-Kansas City, 71, Univ Mont, 72-73, Univ Iowa, 75-76; from Asst Prof to Assoc Prof, 76-84, Prof Hist, Univ Houston-Victoria, 85-, asst to chancellor acad affairs, 81-82. **HONORS AND AWARDS** Nat Endowment for Humanities fel, 77, 93; Am Philos Soc grant, 79, 85, 94; NEH Grant, 90; Vis Fel, Univ Oxford, 94; Elected Fel of the Royal Hist Soc of Great Britain, 00. **MEMBERSHIPS** AHA; Western Conf Brit Studies (pres 87-88). **RESEARCH** British women's history; 20th century Britain. **SELECTED PUBLICATIONS** Ed, War and Social Change: British Society in the Second World War, Manchester Univ Press, 86; British Feminism in the Twentieth Century, Univ Mass Press, 90; auth, Britain in the Second World War: A Social History, Manchester Univ Press, 96; The British Women's Suffrage Campaign, 1866-1928, Longman, 98; author of several journal articles. **CONTACT ADDRESS** Dept of Hist, Univ of Houston, Victoria, 2506 E Red River, Victoria, TX 77901-4450. **EMAIL** smithh@cobalt.vic.uh.edu

SMITH, HELMUT
PERSONAL Born 12/10/1962, Freiburg, Germany, m, 1998 **DISCIPLINE** HISTORY **EDUCATION** Cornell Univ, BA, 84; Yale Univ, PhD, 91. **CAREER** Vanderbilt Univ, 91- . **HONORS AND AWARDS** DAAD fel; NEH fel; Volkswagen Found fel; Nordhaus Awd Tchg. **MEMBERSHIPS** Am Hist Asn. **RESEARCH** Modern German history. **SELECTED PUBLICATIONS** Auth, German Nationalism and Religious Conflict, 1870-1914, Princeton Univ Press, 95. **CONTACT ADDRESS** Dept History, Vanderbilt Univ, 2201 W End Ave, Nashville, TN 37235-0001. **EMAIL** Helmut.W.Smith@Vanderbilt.edu

SMITH, HENRY
DISCIPLINE JAPANESE HISTORY AND ART **EDUCATION** Yale Univ, BA, 62; Harvard Univ, PhD, 70. **CAREER** Prof. **SELECTED PUBLICATIONS** Ed, Learning from Shogun: Japanese History and Western Fantasy, 80. **CONTACT ADDRESS** Dept of Hist, Columbia Col, New York, 2960 Broadway, New York, NY 10027-6902.

SMITH, JAMES DAVID
PERSONAL Born 06/23/1930, Monroe, LA, m **DISCIPLINE** ART **EDUCATION** So U, BA 1952; Univ CA, 1954-55; Univ So CA, MFA 1956; Chouinard Art Inst, 1962; CO Coll, 1963; Univ OR, PhD 1969. **CAREER** Santa Barbara County Schools, consultant, 70, 74, 75; Univ of CA, Dept of Studio Art, prof, 69-, Dept of Black Studies, chmn, 69-73; Univ OR, vis asst prof 1967-69; Santa Barbara HS, instr 1966-67; So Univ, asst prof 1958-66; Prairie View Coll, instr 1956-58; So Univ, vis prof 1954-55. **HONORS AND AWARDS** Selected John Hay Whitney Fellow in the Humanities 1963; exhibited in Dallas Mus of Art; Santa Barbara Mus of Art 1973; Awd of Merit, CA Art Educ, 1983; Eugene J Grisby Jr Art Awd, Natl Art Educ Assn, 1981; CA Art Educ of the Year, Natl Art Educ Assn, 1986; numerous shows in galleries throughout US; University Distinguished Professor in the Arts & Humanities, 1992-93. **MEMBERSHIPS** Nat Art Educ Assn 1963-; past pres CA Art Educ Assn 1977-79; mem Kappa Alpha Psi; Phi Delta Kappa; NAACP; bd dir Self Care Found of Santa Barbara 1974-; bd dir Children's Creative Proj Santa Barbara 1975-84; pres CA Art Educ Assn 1975-77; co-orgnr Spl Art Exhibition for Hon Edmond Brown Jr, Governor of the State of California, 1975. **CONTACT ADDRESS** Dept of Studio Art, Univ of California, Santa Barbara, Santa Barbara, CA 93106.

SMITH, JAMES HOWELL
PERSONAL Born 07/17/1936, Farmersville, TX, m, 1958, 2 children **DISCIPLINE** AMERICAN HISTORY **EDUCATION** Baylor Univ, BA, 58; Tulane Univ, MA, 61; Univ Wis, PhD, 68. **CAREER** Faculty, WAKE FOREST UNIV, 65-, ch dept hist, 87-95; So Fel Fund Col Tchg Fel, 58-61; Duke Univ Lilly Found Schol 77-78; Tx Christian Univ Res Leave Adjunct Fac, 97-98; **HONORS AND AWARDS** NEH Summer Fel, Howard Univ, 69; ODK Award Contrib Stud Life, 89; Schoonmaker Fac Prize Contrib Comm Serv, 97; Leadership Winston-Salem, 98-99. **MEMBERSHIPS** AHA; Orgn Am Historians. **RESEARCH** Afro- Am hist; hist of Am philanthropy; 20th century Am hist; Presidential Disability and the 25th Amendment. **SELECTED PUBLICATIONS** Auth, Mrs Ben Hooper: Peace worker and politician, Wis Mag Hist, winter 62-63; Texas, 1893, Southwestern Hist Quart, 10/66; Industry and Commerce 1896-1975: Winston-Salem in History, Vol VIII, 77; coed Disability in US Presidents: Report, Recommendations and Commentaries by the Working Group, Bowman Gray Sci Press, 97. **CONTACT ADDRESS** PO Box 7806, Winston-Salem, NC 27109-7806. **EMAIL** smithhow@wfu.edu

SMITH, JAMES MORTON
PERSONAL Born 05/28/1919, Bernie, MO, m, 1945, 2 children **DISCIPLINE** HISTORY **EDUCATION** Univ Southern Ill, BEd, 41; Univ Okla, MA, 46; Cornell Univ, PhD(hist), 51. **CAREER** Instr hist, Butler Univ, 46-48; res assoc int indust & labor rels, Cornell Univ, 51-52; instr hist, Ohio State Univ, 52-55, Howard fac fel, 54-55; lectr hist & ed pub, Inst Early Am Hist & Cult, Col William & Mary, 55-66; prof AM hist, Cornell Univ, 66-70; prof, Univ Wis-Madison, 70-76; Prof Am Hist, Univ Del, 76-; Dir, Winterthur Mus, 76-, Grants-in-aid, Inst Early Am Hist & Cult, 52, Soc Sci Res Coun, 53, Am Philos Soc, 54, Fund for Republic, 55, Thomas Jefferson Mem Found, 59 & Am Coun Learned Soc, 60; consult, Conf Nature & Writing of Hist, Kans, 55; Guggenheim fel, 60-61; vis prof Am hist, Duke Univ, 62-63 & Univ Wis, 64-65; chmn, Coun Inst Early Am Hist & Cult, 70-76; dir, State Hist Soc Wis, 70-76; prin investr proj, Nat Endowment for Humanities, 72-73; mem admin bd, Papers John Marshall, 72-74; bd mem, Papers of James Madison & Black Abolitionist Ed Proj; gen ed, Bicentennial State Hist. **MEMBERSHIPS** Orgn Am Historians; Southern Hist Asn; Am Asn Mus; Asn Art Mus Dirs; Am Asn State & Local Hist. **RESEARCH** Early American constitutional development and civil liberties. **SELECTED PUBLICATIONS** Auth, Freedom's Fetters: The Alien and Sedition Laws and American Civil Liberties, Cornell Univ, 56; coauth, Liberty and Justice: A Historical Record of American Constitutional Development, Knopf, 58; ed, Seventeenth Century America: Essays in Colonial History, Univ NC, 59; auth, George Washington: A Profile, Hill & Wang, 69; ed, The Constitution, Harper, 71; Politics and Society in American History (2 vols), Prentice-Hall, 73. **CONTACT ADDRESS** Winterthur Mus, Winterthur, DE 19735.

SMITH, JEFFREY A.
PERSONAL Born 01/25/1958, Valparaiso, IN **DISCIPLINE** ENGLISH, AMERICAN STUDIES **EDUCATION** Valparaiso Univ, BA, English/Humanities, 80; Univ Chicago, MA, English, 81; Univ Calif, Los Angeles, MFA, film/theater/television, 93. **CAREER** Lectr, English, Univ Illinois-Chicago, 81-82; instructor, Dept of Popular Culture, Bowling Green State Univ, 86-87; lecturer, writing programs, Univ Calif-Los Angeles, 87-99; lectr, Marshall School of Business, Univ Southern Calif, 99-. **HONORS AND AWARDS** Fulbright Fellowship to Great Britain, 84-86; honorable mention, Danforth Graduate Fellowship, 80. **MEMBERSHIPS** Natl Coun of Teachers of English, Conf on Coll Composition and Commun; Modern Lan-

guage Assn. **RESEARCH** Writing; commun and pedagogy; Amer culture; politics; popular arts and media. **SELECTED PUBLICATIONS** Auth, "Students' Goals, Gatekeeping, and Some Questions of Ethics," College English, Mar 97; "The L.A. Riots: A Case Study of Debate Across the Political Spectrum," in Writing and Reading Across the Curriculum, 97; "Why College," College English, Mar 96; "Against 'Illegeracy': Toward a New Pedagogy of Civic Understanding," College Composition and Commun, May 94; coauth, "In Search of Lost Pedagogical Synthesis," College English, Nov 93. **CONTACT ADDRESS** 8533 Cashio St., 5, Los Angeles, CA 90035-3650. **EMAIL** smith@humnet.ucla.edu

SMITH, JEFFREY CHIPPS
PERSONAL Born 04/21/1951, Plainfield, NJ, m, 1973, 3 children **DISCIPLINE** ART OF NORTHERN EUROPE FROM 1400 UNTIL 1700 **EDUCATION** Columbia Univ, MA, MPhil, PhD. **CAREER** Prof; Univ TX at Austin, 79-; fel 3 occasions, Zentralinstitut f r Kunstgeschichte in Munich; Kay Fortson Chair in European Art, 00-. **HONORS AND AWARDS** Alexander von Humboldt-Stiftung of Bonn, Ger, 24 month fel; ACLS, NEH, & Getty grant Prog; Guggenheim, 98-99. **MEMBERSHIPS** Bd dir, Historians Netherlandish Art, 89-94 & bd of dir, Cole Art Asn, 96-2000. **RESEARCH** Jesuit contrib to Ger art and on Ger sculpt from 1400until 1648. **SELECTED PUBLICATIONS** Auth, Nuremberg, A Renaissance City, 1500-1618, Austin, 83 & German Sculpture of the Later Renaissance, c. 1520-1580: Art in an Age of Uncertainty, Princeton, 94, ed, New Perspectives on the Art of Renaissance Nuremberg: Five Essays, Austin, 85. **CONTACT ADDRESS** Dept of Art and Art Hist, Univ of Texas, Austin, Austin, TX 78712. **EMAIL** chipps@mail.utexas.edu

SMITH, JOANNA S.
PERSONAL Born 07/17/1965, Brooklyn, NY **DISCIPLINE** ARCHAEOLOGY **EDUCATION** Princeton Univ, BA, 87; Bryn Mawr Col, MA, 89, PhD, 94. **CAREER** Inst, Brookline Adult Ed, 95; res fel, lectr, dept archaeol, Boston Univ, 95; Archaeol res, Leventis Found, Cyprus, 96-98; res fel, archaeol, Boston Univ, 98; vis asst prof, archaeol, Bryn Mawr Col, 99-00; asst prof, Columbia Univ, 00-. **HONORS AND AWARDS** Summa Cum Laude, 87; Seeger grant, Am School of Class Stud, Athens, 87; Fulbright grant, 91-92; Jacob K Javits fel, 88-91, 92-93; Whiting fel, 93-94; NEH fel, 96; Kress fel, 97. **MEMBERSHIPS** Am Philol Asn; Am Sch of Class Stud, Athens; Am Sch of Oriental Res; Archaeol Inst Am; Cyprus Am Archaeol Res Inst. **RESEARCH** The Eastern Mediterranean in the Bronze and Iron Ages; Cyprus; socio- economic and administrative structures; cult and ritual; cylinder and stamp seals; linear scripts (Cypro-Minoan, Linear B, Cypriot Syllabic); metal, textile, and ceramic technology; spatial, contextual, and functional analysis; co-auth, "The Cypro-Minoan Corpus Project Takes An Archaeological Approach," Arti-facts in Near Eastern Archaeology 61 (99): 129-130; co-auth, "The Cypro-Minoan Corpus Project wins Best of Show Award for the Poster Display at the 1998 Annual Meeting of the Archaeological Institute of America," CAARI News 18 (99): 5. **SELECTED PUBLICATIONS** Auth, The Cylinder Seal and the Inscribed Sherd, in Todd, ed, Excavations at Sanida, Report of the Dept of Antiquities, Cyprus, 92; auth, From Writing to Weaving, CAARI News, 93; auth, The Pylos Jn Series, Minos, 92/93; auth, Preliminary Comments on a Rural Cypro-Archaic Sanctuary in Polis-Peristeries, Bull of the Am Sch of Oriental Res, 97; auth, Cylinder Seal, in South, ed, Vasilikos Valley Project 4: Kalavasos- Ayios Dhimitrios III: Tombs 8, 9, 11-20, Stud in Mediterranean Archaeol, 98. **CONTACT ADDRESS** Dept of Art Hist & Archaeology, Columbia Univ, 826 Schermerhorn Hall, Mail Code 5517, New York, NY 10027. **EMAIL** JoSamSmith@aol.com

SMITH, JOHN DAVID
PERSONAL Born 10/14/1949, Brooklyn, NY, m, 1989, 3 children **DISCIPLINE** HISTORY **EDUCATION** Baldwin-Wallace Col, AB, 71; Univ Ky, AM, 73; PhD, 77. **CAREER** Grad Teaching asst, Univ Ky, 71-74; curator, Louis A. Warren Lincoln Libr & Museum, 77-79; assoc fac, Ind University-Purdue Univ, 78-79; dir, Historic Columbia Found, 79-80; lectr, Univ SC, 79-80; instr, Southeast Mo State Univ, 80-81; vis asst prof, Univ Ky, 81; asst prof, Southeast Mo State Univ, 81-82; from vis asst prof to Graduate Alumni Distinguished Prof, NC State Univ, 86-; Fulbright Prof of Am Studies, Ludwig-Maximilians-Universitat, 98-99. **HONORS AND AWARDS** Fel, ACLS, 81-82; James Still Fel, Andrew W. Mellon Found, 82; Fel, Project 87 Sem, Stanford Univ, 83; Albert J. Beveridge Travel Grant, Am Hist Asn, 83; Outstanding Academic Book, Am Libr Asn, 83; Travel to Collections Grant, NEH, 86; Albert J. Beveridge Travel Grant, Am Hist Asn, 87; Richard H. Collins Prize, Ky Hist Soc, 89; Outstanding Reference Book, Am Libr Asn, 89; Outstanding Academic Book, Choice, 89; Best Reference Book, Libr J, 89; Hilbert T. Ficken Memorial Awd, Baldwin-Wallace Col, 94; Distinguished Am Speaker, United States Info Services, 94; Myers Ctr Awd for the Stud of Human Rights in N Am, Myers Ctr for the Study of Intolerance in the United States at the Univ Ark, 96. **MEMBERSHIPS** Am Hist Asn, Orgn of Am Historians, Southern Hist Asn, Hist Soc of NC, Soc of Am Archivists, Soc of NC Archivists. **RESEARCH** Southern History, Slavery and Emancipation, Civil War. **SELECTED PUBLICATIONS** Auth, Anti-Black Thought 1863-1925: "The Negro Problem" An Eleven-Volume Anthology of Racist Writings, Garland Pub, Inc. (New York), 93; auth, Black Voices from Reconstruction 1865-1877, Millbrook Press (Brookfield, CT), 96 & Univ Press of Fla, (Gainesville, FL), 97; coauth, A Mythic Land Apart: Reassessing Southerners and Their History, Greenwood Press, 97; coauth, This Wilderness of War: The Civil War Letters of George W. Squire, Hoosier Volunteer," Univ Tenn Press (Knoxville, TN), 98; auth, Slavery, Race, and American History: Historical Conflict, Trends, and Method, 1866-1953, M. E. Sharpe (Armonk, NY), 99; auth, Black Judas: William Hannibal Thomas and "The American Negro," Univ Ga Press (Athens, GA), 00; coauth, A Union Woman in Civil War Kentucky: The Diary of Frances Peter, Univ Ky (Lexington, KY), 00. **CONTACT ADDRESS** Dept Hist, No Carolina State Univ, PO Box 8108, Raleigh, NC 27695-0001. **EMAIL** smith_jd@unity.ncsu.edu

SMITH, JOHN K., JR.
DISCIPLINE HISTORY OF TECHNOLOGY AND BUSINESS HISTORY **EDUCATION** PhD,Univ Del. **CAREER** Asso prof, Lehigh Univ. **RESEARCH** History of industrial research and development and the chemical industry. **SELECTED PUBLICATIONS** Co-auth, Science and Corporate Strategy: DuPont R&D,1902-1980. **CONTACT ADDRESS** Lehigh Univ, Bethlehem, PA 18015.

SMITH, JONATHAN ZITTELL
PERSONAL Born 11/21/1938, New York, NY, m, 1964, 2 children **DISCIPLINE** HISTORY OF RELIGION, HELLENISTIC RELIGIONS **EDUCATION** Haverford Col, BA, 60; Yale Univ, PhD(hist relig), 69. **CAREER** Instr relig, Dartmouth Col, 65-66; actg asst prof, Univ Calif, Santa Barbara, 66-68; asst prof, 68-73, William Benton prof relig & human sci, 74-82, dean col, 77-82, Robert O Anderson Distinguished Serv Prof Humanities, Univ Chicago, 82-, Co-ed, Hist Relig, 68-81. **HONORS AND AWARDS** McGill Univ, DD, (honoris causa), 96; Fellow, Am Acad of Arts & Sciences, 00; Pres, North Am Assoc for the Study of Religion, (1996-2002). **MEMBERSHIPS** Soc Bibl Lit; Am Acad Relig; Am Soc Study Relig; North Am Assoc for the Study of Religion. **RESEARCH** Hellenistic religions; anthropology of religion; method and theory of religion. **SELECTED PUBLICATIONS** Auth, Map is not Territory: Studies in the History of Religions, E J Brill, 78; Imagining Religion: From Babylon to Jonestown, Univ Chicago, 82; auth, To Take Place: Toward Theory in Ritual Univ Chicago, 87; auth, Drudgery Divine: On the Comparison of Early Christianities and the Religions of Late Antiquity, Univ Chicago, 90; gen.ed., The Harper Collins Dictionary of Religion, Harper Collins, 95. **CONTACT ADDRESS** Univ of Chicago, 1116 E 59th St, Chicago, IL 60637.

SMITH, JUDITH
PERSONAL Born 06/03/1948, Kansas City, MO, m, 1975, 3 children **DISCIPLINE** AMERICAN STUDIES **EDUCATION** Radcliffe Col, BA, 70; Brown Univ, MA, 74; PhD, 80. **CAREER** Vis Instr, Univ RI, 76; vis asst prof, Univ RI, 78 & 79; from asst prof to assoc prof, Boston Col, 81-93; dir of Am Studies, Boston Col, 86-87 & 91-93; assoc prof & dir of Grad Prog in Am Studies, Univ Mass at Boston, 93-. **HONORS AND AWARDS** Award for Excellence in Grad Teaching, Northeastern Asn of Grad Schs Awd, 98. **MEMBERSHIPS** Am Studies Asn, Orgn of Am Historians, Am Historical Asn, Soc for Cinema Studies. **RESEARCH** Twentieth-Century US Social and Cultural History, Contested Representations of Race and Ethnicity in Postwar Popular Culture. **SELECTED PUBLICATIONS** Coauth, Nothing Left to Lose: Case Studies of Street People, Beacon Press (Boston, MA), 72; auth, Family Connections: A History of Italian and Jewish Immigrant Lives in Providence, Rhode Island, 1900-1940, State Univ NY Press (Albany, NY), 85; coauth, The Evolution of American Urban Society 3rd, 4th, & 5th revised editions, Prentice Hall (Englewood Cliffs, NJ), 87, 93, & 99; auth, "The Transformation of Family and Community Culture in Immigrant Neighborhoods, 1900-1940," in The New Labor History and the New England Working Class, eds. Herbert Gutman and Donald Bell (IL: Univ Ill Press, 87), 159-183; auth, "The Marrying Kind: Working Class Courtship and Marriage in 1950s Hollywood," in Multiple Voices in Feminist Film Criticism, eds. Diane Carsen, Linda Dittmar, and Janice Welsch (MN: Univ Minn Press, 94), 226-242. **CONTACT ADDRESS** Dept Am Studies, Univ of Massachusetts, Boston, 100 Morrissey Blvd, Boston, MA 02125. **EMAIL** judith.smith@umb.edu

SMITH, LACEY BALDWIN
PERSONAL Born 10/03/1922, Princeton, NJ **DISCIPLINE** HISTORY **EDUCATION** Bowdoin Col, BS, 46; Princeton Univ, MA, 49, PhD(hist), 51. **CAREER** Instr hist, Princeton Univ, 51-53; asst prof, Mass Inst Technol, 53-55; assoc prof, 55-62, chmn dept, 71-72, 74-77, Prpf Hist, Northwestern Univ, Evanston, 62-, Sr Fulbright scholar & Guggenheim fel, 63-64; Nat Endowment for Humanities sr fel, 73-74 & 82-83; chmn grad rec exam comt, Educ Testing Serv, 73-75; chmn, Ill Humanities coun, 82. **HONORS AND AWARDS** Lit Awd, Chicago Found, 76; littd, bowdoin col, 77. **MEMBERSHIPS** Midwestern Conf Brit Studies (pres, 70-72); Conf Brit Studies (pres, 77-79); fel Royal Hist Soc; fel Royal Soc Lit UK; AHA. **RESEARCH** English history, especially 16th century. **SELECTED PUBLICATIONS** Auth, English treason trials and confessions in the 16th century, J Hist Ideas, 10/54; A Tudor Tragedy, the Life and Times of Catherine Howard, Jonathan Cape, London, 61; The Elizabethan Epic, Jonathan Cape, London, 66; This Realm of England, 1399-1689, Heath, 66, 4th ed, 83; Henry VIII, the Mask of Royalty, Houghton, 71; Elizabeth Tudor, Portrait of a Queen, Little Brown, 75; Elizabeth I: Problems in Civilization, Forum Press, 80; The Past Speaks, Sources and Problems in English History to 1688, Heath, 81. **CONTACT ADDRESS** 225 Laurel Ave, Wilmette, IL 60091.

SMITH, LAURENCE D.
PERSONAL Born 10/28/1950, Iowa City, IA, m, 1981 **DISCIPLINE** HISTORY OF PSYCHOLOGY **EDUCATION** Univ New Hampshire, PhD 83. **CAREER** Univ Maine, asst prof, assoc prof, 83 to 98-. **MEMBERSHIPS** HSS; CS; APA; APS **RESEARCH** History of psychology; philosophy of science; graphical data displays. **SELECTED PUBLICATIONS** Auth, Behaviorism and logical positivism: A reassessment of the alliance, Stanford, CA: Stanford Univ Press, 86; auth, On prediction and control: B.F. Skinner and the technological ideal of science, Am Psychologist, 47, (92): 216-223; co-ed with W. R. Woodward, B. F. Skinner and Behaviorism in American Culture, Beth PA, Lehigh Univ Press, 96; The role of data and theory in co-variation assessment: Implications for the theory-ladenness of observation, Coauth, Jour of Mind and Behav, 96; Behaviorism, in: R. Fox and J. Kloppenberg, eds, A companion to American thought, Cambridge MA, Blackwell, 95; coauth, Psychology without p values: Data analysis at the turn of the 19th century, Am Psychologist, 55, (00): 260-263; coauth, Scientific graphs and the hierarchy of the sciences: A Latourian survey of inscription practices, Social Studies of Science, 30, (00): 73-94. **CONTACT ADDRESS** Dept of Psychology, Univ of Maine, Orono, ME 04469. **EMAIL** ldsmith@maine.maine.edu

SMITH, MARK
DISCIPLINE PRE-MODERN EUROPEAN HISTORY **EDUCATION** Westmont Col, BA, summa cum laude; Denver Sem, MDiv; Univ Calif, Santa Barbara, MA, PhD. **CAREER** Instr, Albertson Col, 89-; bd supvr, Bethsaida Excavations, Israel. **SELECTED PUBLICATIONS** Auth, A Hidden Use of Porphyry's History ofPhilosophy in Eusebius' Praeparatio Evangelica, J of Theol Stud, 88; In Search of Santa, Timeline, 91; Ancient Bisexuality and the Interpretation of Romans 1:26-27, J of Am Acad of Relig, 96; Eusebius and the Religion of Constantius I, Studia Patristica, 97; A Tale of Two Julias: Julia, Julias and Josephus, in Bethsaida Excavations Rpt, Vol 2; Paul and Ancient Bisexuality, J of Am Acad of Relig, 97. **CONTACT ADDRESS** Dept of History, Albertson Col of Idaho, 2112 Cleveland Blvd., Caldwell, ID 83605-4432. **EMAIL** msmith@albertson.edu

SMITH, MERRITT ROE
PERSONAL Born 11/14/1940, Waverly, NY **DISCIPLINE** HISTORY OF TECHNOLOGY **EDUCATION** Georgetown Univ, AB, 63; Pa State Univ, MA, 65, PhD, 71. **CAREER** Asst prof, Ohio State Univ, 70-75, assoc prof hist, 75-78; Prof hist technol , Prof Science Tech & Soc, MIT, 78-, Adv ed, Technol & Cult, 72-; Am Philos Soc res grant, 74; Harvard-Newcomen fel, Grad Scb Bus Admin, Harvard Univ, 74-75; fel, Regimal Econ Hist Res Ctr, Eleutherian Mills Libr, 78-79. **HONORS AND AWARDS** F J Turner Awd, Orgn Am Historians, 77; Pfizer Awd, Hist Sci Soc, 78; Hon Mention, Thomas Newcomen Awd in Bus Hist, Newcomen Soc North Am & Bus Hist Rev, 80; Guggenheim Fel, 83; NSF Scholar, NSF, 84; Regents Fel, Smithsonian Inst, 84-85; Leonardo da Vinci Medal, Soc Hist Technol, 94; Hon Dr Humane Lett, Rensselaer Polytechnic Inst, 97. **MEMBERSHIPS** Soc Hist Technol; Orgn Am Historians; Soc Indust Archaeol; Hist Sci Soc; Am Hist Asm; Am Antiq Soc; Ma Hist Soc. **RESEARCH** Nineteenth century metalworking technologies; transfer of technology; comparative study of early industrial communities; role of the military in technological and industrial development. **SELECTED PUBLICATIONS** Auth, George Washington and the establishment of the Harpers Ferry Armory, Va Mag Hist & Biog, 10/73; From craftsman to mechanic, Technological Innovation and the Decorative Arts, Univ Va, 73; The American Precision Museum, Technol & Cult, 74; Harpers Ferry Armory and the New Technology, Cornell Univ, 77; contribr, Military arsenals and industry before World War I, War Business and American Society, Kennikat, 77; Eli Whitney and the American system, Technology in America, VOA Forum Ser, 78; Does Technology Drive History, MIT Press, 94; Major Problems in the History of American Technology, Houghton Mifflin, 98. **CONTACT ADDRESS** Dept Hist, Massachusetts Inst of Tech, 77 Massachusetts Ave, Cambridge, MA 02139-4307. **EMAIL** Roesmith@MIT.edu

SMITH, MICHAEL MYRLE
PERSONAL Born 11/02/1940, Springfield, IL, m, 1982, 3 children **DISCIPLINE** HISTORY **EDUCATION** Southern Ill Univ, BA, 63, MA, 67; Tex Christian Univ, PhD(hist), 71. **CAREER** Asst prof, 70-76, Assoc Prof Hist, Okla State Univ, 76-93, Actg Chmn Dept, 78-79; Prof, 93- **RESEARCH** Mexico; Mexican-American. **SELECTED PUBLICATIONS** Auth, The real expedicion maritima de la Vacuna in New Spain and

Guatemala, Am Philos Soc, 74; auth, The Mexicans in Oklahoma, Univ of Oklahoma, 80; Carrancista Propaganda And The Print Media In The United-States--An Overview Of Institutions, Americas, Vol 52, 95. **CONTACT ADDRESS** Dept of Hist Life Sci West, Oklahoma State Univ, Stillwater, Stillwater, OK 74074. **EMAIL** mms7334@okway.okstate.edu

SMITH, NEIL
PERSONAL Born 07/18/1954, Leith, Scotland, m, 1996 **DISCIPLINE** GEOGRAPHY **EDUCATION** St Andrews Univ, BSc, 77; Johns Hopkins Univ, PhD, 82. **CAREER** Asst prof to prof, Rutgers Univ, 86-99; Distinguished Prof, CUNY Grad Center, 00-. **HONORS AND AWARDS** Asn of Am Geogr; John Simon Guggenheim Fel, 95, Honors for Distinguished Scholar, 00. **MEMBERSHIPS** Am Anthrop Assoc; Assoc of Am Geogr. **RESEARCH** Social Theory, Geography, Native and Culture, Urban Space and Culture. **SELECTED PUBLICATIONS** Auth, New Urban Frontier, Routledge, (London), 96. **CONTACT ADDRESS** Graduate Sch and Univ Ctr, CUNY, 365 Fifth Ave, New York, NY 10016-4309.

SMITH, PAMELA H.
PERSONAL Born 11/30/1957, CA, m **DISCIPLINE** HISTORY, HISTORY OF SCIENCE **EDUCATION** Univ of Wollongong, New Wales, Australia, BA, 79; The Johns Hopkins Univ, PhD, 91. **CAREER** Asst prof, Pomona Col, 90-97, assoc prof, 97-; Dir, European Studies, Claremont Grad Univ, 96-. **HONORS AND AWARDS** German Academic Exchange Service (DAAD) Grad Res Fel, 86-88; Long & Widmont Memorial Found Awd, 89; Pew Liberal Arts Enrichment Prog, 92; Pfizer Prize for The Business of Alchemy, Hist of Sci Soc, 95; NEH Res Assistance Grants, 92, 96, 97, 99; Sidney NM. Edelstein Int Fel, 97-98; NEH Res Fel, 997-98; John S. Guggenheim Fel, 97-98; Getty Res Inst Fel, 2000-2001. **MEMBERSHIPS** Am Hist Asn, Hist of Sci Soc, West Coast Hist of Sci Soc, British Asn for the Hist of Sci, Am Asn for Netherlandic Studies, Hists of Netherlandish Art. **SELECTED PUBLICATIONS** Auth, The Business of Alchemy: Science and Culture in the Holy Roman Empire, Princeton: Princeton Univ Press (94); auth, "Science and Taste: Pining, the Passions, and the New Philosophy in Seventeenth-century Leiden," Isis, 90 (99): 420-461; auth, "Artists as Scientists: Nature and Realism in Early Modern Europe," Endeavour, 24 (2000): 13-21; auth, "Vital Spirits: Alchemy, Redemption, and Artisanship in Early Modern Europe," in Rethinking the Scientific Revolution," ed by Margaret J. Osler, Cambridge Univ Press (2000); co-ed, Commerce and the Representation of Nature in Early Modern Europe, Routledge (forthcoming); auth, "Giving Voice to the Hands: The Articulation of Material Literacy in the Sixteenth Century," Popular Literacy: Caught Between Art and Crime, ed by John Trimbur, Univ Pittsburgh Press (forthcoming); auth, "Laboratories," The Cambridge Hist of Sci, Vol 3: Early Modern Europe, ed Lorraine Daston and Katharine Park, Cambridge Univ Press (forthcoming); auth, Scholars, Scientists, Merchants, and Kings: Kunstkammern in the Making of Social Status in Early Modern Europe," Looking Through the Hapsburg Glasses: America's Presence in Seventeenth-Century Art and Science, ed Ineke Phaf-Rheinberger (under review). **CONTACT ADDRESS** Dept Hist, Pomona Col, 333 N Col Way, Claremont, CA 91711-4429. **EMAIL** pamela_smith@pomona.edu

SMITH, PATRICK
DISCIPLINE MODERN AND CONTEMPORARY ART **EDUCATION** Notre Dame Univ, BA; Univ NC, MA; Northwestern Univ, PhD. **CAREER** Assoc prof **RESEARCH** American modern and post-modern art. **SELECTED PUBLICATIONS** Publ, Andy Warhol's Art and Films; Warhol: Conversations about the Artist. **CONTACT ADDRESS** Dept of art., Wichita State Univ, 1845 Fairmont, Wichita, KS 67260-0062.

SMITH, PAUL
DISCIPLINE VISUAL ARTS **EDUCATION** Kent Univ, PhD. **CAREER** Assoc prof. **RESEARCH** Cultural theory and criticism; film and visual studies; gender studies; Marxism. **SELECTED PUBLICATIONS** Auth, Clint Eastwood: A Cultural Production, 93; Madonnarama: On Sex and Popular Culture, 93; Discerning the Subject, 88. **CONTACT ADDRESS** Dept of Film and Media Studies, George Mason Univ, Fairfax, 4400 University Dr, Fairfax, VA 22030.

SMITH, PAUL HUBERT
PERSONAL Born 06/21/1931, East Sparta, OH, m, 1954, 2 children **DISCIPLINE** AMERICAN HISTORY **EDUCATION** Bowling Green State Univ, BA, 54, MA, 55; Univ Mich, PhD, 62. **CAREER** Asst prof hist, Memphis State Univ, 60-62; from asst prof to assoc prof, Univ Nev, 62-66, chmn dept, 65-66; assoc prof, Univ Fla, 66-69; ed, Letters Of Delegates To Cong, 1774-89, Libr Cong, 69-96. **HONORS AND AWARDS** Butterfield Awd, Assn for Doc Ed, 88; Jefferson Prize, Soc for Hist Fedl Govt, 98. **MEMBERSHIPS** AHA; Orgn Am Historians; Am Studies Asn; Inst Early Am Hist & Cult; Asn for Doc Ed. **RESEARCH** American colonial and revolutionary history; 18th century British history. **SELECTED PUBLICATIONS** Auth, Loyalists and Redcoats, Univ NC, 64; Sir Guy Carleton, George Washington's Opponents, Morrow, 68; ed, English Defenders of American Freedoms, Libr Congr, 72; ed, Manuscript Sources..on the American Revolution, Libr Congr, 75; ed, Letters of Delegates to Congress, 26 v., US Govt Printing Off, 76-99. **CONTACT ADDRESS** 15320 Pine Orchard Dr, Silver Spring, MD 20906.

SMITH, PHILIP CHADWICK FOSTER
PERSONAL Born 02/17/1939, Salem, MA, 2 children **DISCIPLINE** MARITIME HISTORY **EDUCATION** Harvard Col, BA, 61. **CAREER** Asst cur, 63-66, cur maritime hist, Peabody Mus, Salem, 66-78; managing ed, Am Neptune, 69-79; ed mus publ, 78-79; CUR, PHILADELPHIA MARITIME MUS, 79-, Curator Maritime hist, Bostonian Soc, 67-78; mem bd ed, Hist Collections, Essex Inst, Salem, 75-; consult, Seafarers ser, Time-Life Bks Inc, 77-; assoc ed, Colonial Soc Mass, 78-; pres & chmn, Corinthian Historical Found, 81; ed, Am Neptune, 80-; vis lectr, Univ Pa, 81- **MEMBERSHIPS** US Comn Maritime Hist; Coun N Am Soc Oceanic Hist; Coun Am Maritime Mus; Soc Nautical Res; Int Cong Maritime Mus. **RESEARCH** Maritime history. **SELECTED PUBLICATIONS** Ed, The Journals of Ashley Bowen (1728-1813) of Marblehead (2 vols), Colonial Soc Mass & Peabody Mus Salem, 73; auth, The Frigate Essex Papers: Building the Salem Frigate, 1798-1799, Peabody Mus Salem, 74; Captain Samuel Tucker (1747-1833), Continental Navy, Essex Inst, 76; Fired by Manley Zeal: A Naval Fiasco of the American Revolution, 77, The Artful Roux, Marine Painters of Marseille, 78 &; More Marine Paintings and Drawings in the Peabody Museum, Peabody Mus Salem, 79; ed, Seafaring in Colonial Massachusetts, 80; Sibley's Heir: A Volume in Memory of Clifford Kenyon Shipton, Colonial Soc Mass, 82. **CONTACT ADDRESS** Philadelphia Maritime Mus, 321 Chestnut St, Philadelphia, PA 19106.

SMITH, REUBEN W.
DISCIPLINE HISTORY **EDUCATION** Univ CA, BA, 51; MA, 52; Harvard Univ,PhD, 63. **CAREER** Prof emer, Univ Pacific. **RESEARCH** Islamic civilization; Near and Middle East. **SELECTED PUBLICATIONS** Auth, publ(s) on Islam. **CONTACT ADDRESS** Hist Dept, Univ of the Pacific, Stockton, Pacific Ave, PO Box 3601, Stockton, CA 95211.

SMITH, RICHARD CANDIDA
PERSONAL Born 09/27/1946, San Francisco, CA, m, 2 children **DISCIPLINE** HISTORY **EDUCATION** Univ Calif, BA, 69; MA, 90, PhD, 92. **CAREER** Assoc dir/ed, Univ of Calif, 84-93; asst prof to assoc prof, Univ of Mich, 93-. **HONORS AND AWARDS** James V Mink Awd, 93; Dean's Awd for Excellence in Res, 98; Janet and William Cassebaum Fac Awd, 98; Ecole des Hautes Etudes en Les Sciences Sociales Fel, 99; CIC Acad Leadership Fel, 99-00. **MEMBERSHIPS** Org of Am Hist; AHA; Oral Hist Assoc; Am Studies Assoc; Soc for Fr Hist Studies. **RESEARCH** Nineteenth and twentieth century US and European intellectual history, aesthetic theory, memory, personal narrative, and representations of identity, oral history theory. **SELECTED PUBLICATIONS** Auth, "Exquisite Corpse: The Sense of the Past in Oral History Interviews with California Artists", Oral Hist Rev 17, (89); auth, "Imitation and Invention: Tradition and the Advant-Garde in the Work of Two Jewish Émigr¤ American Artists", Int J of Oral Hist 10, (89); auth, "Frank Lloyd Wright as Educator: The Taliesin Fellowship Program 1932-1959", Architecture and the Sites of History, ed David Dunster and Iain Borden, Butterworths, (London, 95); auth, Utopia and Dissent: Art, Poetry, and Politics in California, Univ of Calif Pr, 95; auth, "The Elusive Quest of the Moderns", On the Edge of America: Modernist Art in California, ed Paul J. Karlstrom, Univ of Calif Pr, 96; auth, "Junk into Art: Noah Purifoy's Assemblage of Experience", Noah Purifoy: Outside and In the Open, ed Lizzetta Le-Falle-Collins, Calif African Am Museum, (Los Angeles, 97); auth, Mallarme's Children: Symbolism and the Renewal of Experience, Univ of Calif Pr, 99; auth, "Analytic Strategies for Oral History Interviews", Handbook of Interviewing, ed Jaber F Gubrium and James A Holstein, Sage, (Beverly Hills), (forthcoming). **CONTACT ADDRESS** Dept Hist, Univ of Michigan, Ann Arbor, 435 S State St, Ann Arbor, MI 48109-1003. **EMAIL** candidas@umich.edu

SMITH, RICHARD J.
PERSONAL 1 child **DISCIPLINE** HISTORY, CHINESE CULTURE **EDUCATION** Univ CA, Davis, PhD, 72. **CAREER** Master, Hanszen Col, 82-87; adj prof, Ctr for Asian Studies, Univ TX, Austin; prof, 73-, dir, Asian Stud and Asian Outreach, Rice Univ; George and Nancy Rupp Prof of Humanities; prof hist. **HONORS AND AWARDS** Phi Beta Kappa Teaching Awd, 78; George R. Brown Superior Teaching Awd, 80, 82, 83, 90; George R. Brown Awd for Excellence in Teaching, 85, 90; George R. Brown Certificate of Highest Merit, 92; Minnie Stevens Piper Prof Awd, 87; Rice Univ Student Assoc Mentor Awd, 87; Allison Sarofim Distinguished Teaching Prof, 94-96; Nicholas Salgo Distinguished Teaching Prize, 96; Carnegie Found for the Advancement of teaching "Texas Teacher of the Year," 98. **MEMBERSHIPS** Advirosry Board of Chinese Historians in the United States; Nat Advisory Comt of the Asia Society's Asian Educational Resource Ctr, NYork; Nat Comt on the U.S.-China Relations; Nat Commission on Asia in the Schools. **RESEARCH** Contemp Chinese cult. **SELECTED PUBLICATIONS** Auth, China's Cultural Heritage: The Qing Dynasty, 1644-1912, 83; Fortune-tellers and Philosophers: Divination in Traditional Chinese Society, 91; Chinese Almanacs, 92; Chinese Maps: Images of All Under Heaven, 96; coauth, Robert Hart and China's Early Modernization, 91; H.B. Morse, Customs Commissioner and Historian of China, 95; coed, Cosmology, Ontology, and Human Efficacy: Essays in Chinese Thought, 93. **CONTACT ADDRESS** Dept Hist, Rice Univ, MS-42, PO Box 1892, Houston, TX 77005. **EMAIL** smithrj@rice.edu

SMITH, ROBERT FREEMAN
PERSONAL Born 05/13/1930, Little Rock, AR, m, 1951, 2 children **DISCIPLINE** UNITED STATES HISTORY **EDUCATION** Univ Ark, BA, 52, MA, 53; Univ Wis, PhD(Hist), 58. **CAREER** Instr Hist, Univ Ark, 53; assoc prof, Tex Lutheran Col, 58-62; from asst prof to assoc prof, Univ RI, 62-66; vis assoc prof, Univ Wis, 66-67; assoc prof, Univ Conn, 67-69; prof Hist, Univ Toledo, 69-; disting univ prof, 86; Tom L Evans res award, Harry S Truman Libr Inst, 76-77. **HONORS AND AWARDS** Tex Writer's Roundup Awd, 61; Bk Awd, Ohio Acad Hist, 73. **MEMBERSHIPS** Orgn Am Historians; Soc Historians Am Foreign Rels; Am Mil Inst; US Naval Inst; Southern Hist Asn. **RESEARCH** United States diplomatic history; history of inter-American relations; American military history. **SELECTED PUBLICATIONS** Auth, United States and Cuba: Business and Diplomacy, 1917-1960, 60 & What Happened in Cuba?, 63, Twayne; Background to Revolution: The Development of Modern Cuba, Knopf, 66; The United States and Revolutionary Nationalism in Mexico, 1916-1932, Univ Chicago, 72; Republican policy and the Pax Americana, 1921-1933, In: From Colony to Empire: Essays in the History of American Foreign Relations, Wiley, 72; The good neigbor policy: The liberal paradox in United States relations with Latin America, In: Watershed of Empire: Essays on New Deal Foreign Policy, Inst Humane Studies, 76; Reciprocity, In: Dictionary of the History of American Foreign Policy, Scribner, 78; auth, Era of Caribbean Intervention, Vol I, In: The United States and the Latin American Sphere of Influence, Kreiger Publ Co, 81; The Caribbean World and the United States: Mixing Rum and Coca Cola, Twayne Publ, 94; Estados Unidos y la Revolucion Mexicana, 1921-1959, in: Mitos en las Relaciones Mexico-Estados Unidos, Secretaria de Relaciones Exteriores de Mexico, 95. **CONTACT ADDRESS** Dept of History, Univ of Toledo, 2801 W Bancroft St, Toledo, OH 43606-3390.

SMITH, ROBERT J.
DISCIPLINE HISTORY **EDUCATION** Yale Univ, BA, 57; Univ Pa, MA, 61, PhD, 67. **CAREER** Prof. **RESEARCH** Capitalism; education in Europe. **SELECTED PUBLICATIONS** Auth, The Ecole Normale Superieure and the Third Republic, SUNY, 82; The Making of the Modern World, St Martin's; Patron, Famille, et Entreprise: Bouchayer et Viallet De Grenoble, 96. **CONTACT ADDRESS** Dept of History, SUNY, Col at Brockport, Brockport, NY 14420. **EMAIL** rjsmith@acspr1.acs.brockport.edu

SMITH, ROBERT W.
PERSONAL Born 04/17/1960, Cincinnati, OH, m, 1986, 4 children **DISCIPLINE** HISTORY **EDUCATION** Cincinnati Bible Col, BA, 82; Cincinnati Christian Sem, MA, 87; M DIV, 88, Miami Univ, MA, 88, PhD, 94. **CAREER** Instr, Miami Univ, 90-94; assoc prof, Fla Christian Col, 94-. **HONORS AND AWARDS** Endowment for Bibl Res Travel Grant, 92; Diss Fel, Miami Univ, 94. **MEMBERSHIPS** Am Schools of Oriental Res; Inst for Bibl Res; Near East Archaeol Soc. **RESEARCH** Ancient History of the Levent, Archaeology of Jordon. **SELECTED PUBLICATIONS** Auth, "New Evidence Regarding Early Christian Chronology: A Reconsideration", Chronos, Kairos, Christos II, Mercer Univ Pr, 98. **CONTACT ADDRESS** Dept Gen Ed, Florida Christian Col, 1011 Bill Beck Blvd, Kissimmee, FL 34744-4402. **EMAIL** bob.smith@fcc.edu

SMITH, SHERRY L.
PERSONAL Born 03/19/1951, Hammond, IN, m, 1986 **DISCIPLINE** HISTORY **EDUCATION** Purdue Univ, BA, 72, MA, 74; Univ of Washington, PhD, 84. **CAREER** Asst prof to assoc prof, Univ Texas, 85- . **HONORS AND AWARDS** NEH fel for Col Tchrs, 96-97; NEH Summer Stipend, 94; Fulbright Found Sr lecturship, NZ, 93. **MEMBERSHIPS** AHA; Western Hist Asn; Am Soc for Ethnohistory. **RESEARCH** American Indians; American West. **SELECTED PUBLICATIONS** Auth, Sagebrush Soldier: William Earl Smith's View of the Sioux War of 1876, Univ Oklahoma Pr, 89; auth, The View from Officers' Row: Army Perceptions of Indians, Univ Arizona Pr, 91; auth, A Woman's Life in the Teton Country: Geraldine A. Lucas, in Montanam, the Mag of West Hist, 94; auth, Reimagining the Indian: Charles Erskine Scott Wood and Frank Linderman, in Pacific Northwest Q, 96; auth, Frontier Army: Military Life on the Frontier, Women and the Frontier Army, and, George Crook, in Encyclopedia of the American West, Macmillan, 96; auth, Lost Soldiers: Re-Searching the Military in the West, in Western Hist Q, 98; auth, Introduction, Covered Wagon Women, Univ Nebraska, forthcoming. **CONTACT ADDRESS** Dept of History, So Methodist Univ, Dallas, TX 75205. **EMAIL** sherrys@mail.smu.edu

SMITH, STEVEN G.
PERSONAL Born 07/28/1953 **DISCIPLINE** PHILOSOPHY OF RELIGION; PHILOSOPHY OF HUMAN NATURE; GENDER; HISTORY OF PHILOSOPHY AND RELIGIOUS THOUGHT **EDUCATION** Fla State Univ, BA, 73; Vanderbilt Univ, MA, 78; Duke Univ, PhD, 80. **CAREER** Dept Philos, Millsaps Col **RESEARCH** Ethics, aesthetics, metaphysics. **SELECTED PUBLICATIONS** Auth, The Argument to the Other: Reason Beyond Thought in Karl Barth and Emmanuel Levinas, 83; The Concept of the Spiritual: An Essay in First Philosophy, 88 & Gender Thinking, 92; auth, "Sympathy, Scruple, and Piety: The Moral and Religious Valuation of Nonhumans," Journal of Religious Ethics, 21, (93): 319-342; auth, "Bowl Climbing: The Logic of Religious Question Rivalry," International Journal for Philosophy of Relig, 36, (94): 27-43; auth, "Greatness in Theism and Atheism: The Anselm-Feuerbach Conversation," Modern Theology, 12, (96): 385-403; auth, "Abraham's Family in Children of Gebelawi," Literature and Theology, 11, (97): 168-184; auth, "Can I Know Your IQ," Public Affairs Quarterly, 11, (97): 365-382; auth, "Kinds of Best World," International Journal for Philosophy of Religion, 44, (98): 145-162; auth, "Three Religious Attitudes," Philosophy and Theology, 11, (98): 3-24. **CONTACT ADDRESS** Dept of Philosophy, Millsaps Col, 1701 N State St, Jackson, MS 39210. **EMAIL** smithsg@millsaps.edu

SMITH, THOMAS G.
PERSONAL Born 11/10/1945, Binghampton, NY, m, 1968, 4 children **DISCIPLINE** HISTORY **EDUCATION** SUNY, Cortland, BA, 67; Univ Connecticut, MA, 69, PhD, 77. **CAREER** Nichols Col, asst prof, 75-81, assoc prof, 82-86, prof, 87-. **HONORS AND AWARDS** Nichols Col ser awd for contrib to the college, 86. **MEMBERSHIPS** Org Am Historians; Environmental Hist Asn. **RESEARCH** US Foreign Policy; Environ Hist. **SELECTED PUBLICATIONS** Robert Frost, Stuart Udall, and the Last Go-Down, New Eng Quart, 97; John Kennedy, Stuart Udall, New Frontier Conservation, Pacific Hist Rev, 95; Negotiating With Castro: The Bay of Pigs Prisoners and a Lost Opportunity, Diplomatic Hist, 95; The Canyon Lands National Park Controversy, 1961-1964, Utah Hist Quart, 91; Independent: A Biography of Lewis W Douglas, with Robert Browder, NY, Knopf, 86; auth, "Voice for Wild and Scenic Rivers: John P. Saylor of Pennsylvania," Pa Hist, 99. **CONTACT ADDRESS** Dept History, Nichols Col, Dudley, MA 01570. **EMAIL** smithtg@nichols.edu

SMITH, TOM W.
PERSONAL Born, PA, m, 1969, 3 children **DISCIPLINE** AMERICAN HISTORY **EDUCATION** Univ Chicago, PhD, 79. **CAREER** Dir of General Social Survey, Nat Opinion Res Center, Univ Chicago, 80-; Secretary General, Int Social Survey Prog, 97-. **HONORS AND AWARDS** Worcestor Prize, 94; AAPOR Innovators Awd, 00. **MEMBERSHIPS** Am Asn for Public Opinion Res; A, Soc Asn; Mid-West Asn for Public Opinion Res. **RESEARCH** Social change; survey methods. **SELECTED PUBLICATIONS** Auth, Holocaust Denial: What the Survey Data Reveal, Working Papers in Contemporary Anti-Semitism, Am Jewish Committee, 95; A Political Profile of Italian Americans: 1972-1994, Nat Italian Am Found, 96; Annotated Bibliography of Papers Using the General Social Survey, 11th ed, with James A Davis, NORC, 96; General Social Surveys, 1972-1996: Cumulative Codebook, with James A Davis, NORC, 96; Marriage and Divorce, American Demographics, 19, Oct 97; Tall Oaks from Little Acorns Grow: The General Social Surveys, 1971-1997, The Public Perspective, 8, Feb/March 97; Why Our Neck of the Woods is Better Than the Forest, The Public Perspective, 9, June/July 98; The 1997-1998 National Gun Policy Survey of the National Opinion Research Center: Research Findings, NORC Report, March 98; Standard Definitions: Final Disposition of Cases Codes and Outcome Rates for RDD Telephone Surveys and In-Person Household Surveys, AAPOR, 98; National Pride: A Cross-National Analysis, GSS Cross-National Report no 19, with Lars Jarkko, NORC, 98; numerous other publications. **CONTACT ADDRESS** Nat Opinion Research Center, Univ of Chicago, 1155 E 60th St, Chicago, IL 60637. **EMAIL** smitht@norcmail.uchicago.edu

SMITH, W. WAYNE
PERSONAL Born 11/30/1936, Laurel, DE, m, 1960, 2 children **DISCIPLINE** AMERICAN HISTORY **EDUCATION** Md State Teachers Col, Salisbury, BS, 58; Univ Md, MA, 61, PhD(hist), 67. **CAREER** Instr hist, Frostburg State Col, 61-63; asst prof, Southern Conn State Col, 66-68; assoc prof, 68-71, PROF HIST, IND UNIV PA, 71-, Nat Endowment for Humanities fel, 76; Newberry fel, 77. **MEMBERSHIPS** AHA; Orgn Am Historians; Southern Hist Asn. **RESEARCH** Jacksonian America; Civil War. **SELECTED PUBLICATIONS CONTACT ADDRESS** Dept Hist, Indiana Univ of Pennsylvania, Indiana, PA 15701.

SMITH, WALLACE CALVIN
PERSONAL Born 05/12/1941, Pembroke, GA, m, 1964, 2 children **DISCIPLINE** AMERICAN HISTORY **EDUCATION** Emory Univ, AB, 63; Univ NC, Chapel Hill, MA, 65, PhD, 71. **CAREER** Asst prof hist, LaGrange Col, 65-67; teaching assoc, Univ NC, 67-71; asst prof, Jacksonville Univ, 71-72; asst prof, 72-75, assoc prof, 75-83, , Prof Hist Univ SC Aiken, 83-, Chmn Social & Behav Sci Div, 81-85. **HONORS AND AWARDS** Phi Beta Kappa, Pi Gamma Mu, Phi Alpha Theta, Who's Who Among American Teachers. **MEMBERSHIPS** Southern Hist Asn; Soc Hist Early Am Repub; GA Hist Soc; SC Hist Asn. **RESEARCH** Colonial American history; revolution and early national era; Antebellum Southern Unitarians, William Gregg. **SELECTED PUBLICATIONS** Auth, Utopia's last chance? The Georgia silk boomlet of 1751, GA Hist Quart, spring 75; Habersham Family, In: Encycl of Southern History, 79; James Habersham et al, articles, in Dictionary of Georgia Biography, 83; The Habershams in Forty Years of Diversity, UGA Press, 84; David Wallace & Graniteville Centennial, proceedings of SCHA, 97; co-auth, African-Americans and the Palmetto State, 94. **CONTACT ADDRESS** Dept of Hist and Political Science, Univ of So Carolina, Aiken, 471 University Pky, Aiken, SC 29801. **EMAIL** Calvins@aiken.sc.edu

SMITH, WILSON
PERSONAL Born 01/23/1922, Malden, MA, m, 1949, 2 children **DISCIPLINE** HISTORY **EDUCATION** Amherst Col, AB 47; Univ Cal Berk, MA 48; Columbia Univ, PhD 55. **CAREER** Princeton Univ, inst 53-58; John Hopkins Univ, asst prof, assoc prof, 58-64; Univ Cal Davis, prof, 64-90; Univ Cal Acad Sen, vice ch, ch, Ac Rep to Regents, 83-85; Phillip D. Reed Found, member, 90-96. **HONORS AND AWARDS** Beveridge Awd; SSRC res awards; Henry Huntington Libr Grant. **MEMBERSHIPS** AHA; OAH; HES; AAUP **RESEARCH** US intellectual history; history of Amer higher EDU. **SELECTED PUBLICATIONS** Auth, Professors and Public Ethics, Cornell Univ Pr, 55; ed, Am Higher Educ, 61; auth, Essays in American Intellectual History, Dryden 75; Theories of Education in Early America, Bobbs, 73; articles, book revs, encyc essays and contributions to American National Biography. **CONTACT ADDRESS** 1215 West 8th St, Davis, CA 95616.

SMITH, WOODRUFF DONALD
PERSONAL Born 03/22/1946, Missoula, MT, m, 1967, 2 children **DISCIPLINE** MODERN EUROPEAN & AFRICAN HISTORY **EDUCATION** Harvard Univ, AB, 67; Univ Chicago, AM, 68, PhD(hist), 72. **CAREER** Asst prof hist, Roosevelt Univ, 68-69; sr analyst, Sparcom, Inc, Va, 72-73; asst prof, 73-77, assoc prof, 77-81, PROF HIST, UNIV TEX, SAN ANTONIO, 81-, Am Philos Soc grant, 76-77; Ger Acad Exchange Serv grant, 78; Fulbright fel, Netherlands, 80; Nat Endowment for Humanities grant, 81. **MEMBERSHIPS** AHA **RESEARCH** Modern German history; history of imperialism; African history. **SELECTED PUBLICATIONS** Coauth, The social and political origins of German diffusionist ethnology, J Hist Behav Sci, 78; The German Colonial Empire, Univ NC, 78; The emergence of German urban sociology, 1900-1910, J Hist Soc, 80; European Imperialism in the 19th and 20th Centuries, Nelson-Hall, 82; The German Experience Of Professionalization--Modern Learned Professions And Their Organizations From The Early 19th-Century To The Hitler Era, J Of Interdisciplinary Hist, Vol 23, 93; Nicolai,Helmut And Nazi Ideology, Am Hist Rev, Vol 98, 93 **CONTACT ADDRESS** Dept Hist, Univ of Massachusetts, Boston, 100 Morrissey Blvd, Boston, MA 02125-3300.

SMITH-ROSENBERG, CARROLL
DISCIPLINE HISTORY & PSYCHIATRY **EDUCATION** Conn Col for Women, BA, 75; Columbia Univ, MA, 58; PhD, 68. **CAREER** Assoc prof, hist & psych, Univ Penn; PROF, HIST & WOMEN'S STUD, GRAD CH, AM CULT PROG, UNIV MICH. **MEMBERSHIPS** Am Antiquarian Soc **RESEARCH** Gender & class in 19th cent Am; Am identity & the US Constitution. **SELECTED PUBLICATIONS** Auth, "Sex as Symbol in Jacksonian America," Am Jour of Soc 84, 78; auth, "Davy Crockett as Trickster: Pornography, Liminality and Perversion in Victorian America," Jour of Contemp Hist 17, 82; auth, Disorderly Conduct; Visions of Gender in Victorian America, Alfred A. Knopf, 85; auth, "Domesticating Virtue: Coquettes and Rebels in Young America," in Literature and the Body, Johns Hopkins Univ Press, 88; auth, "Dis-covering the Subject of the Great Constitutional Discussion 1786-1789," Jour of Am Hist 79, 91; auth, "Subject Female: Engendering American Identity," Am Lit Hist, 93. **CONTACT ADDRESS** Prog in Am Culture, Univ of Michigan, Ann Arbor, 2402 Mason Hall, Ann Arbor, MI 48109-1027. **EMAIL** csmithro@umich.edu

SMITHER, HOWARD ELBERT
PERSONAL Born 11/15/1925, Pittsburg, KS, m, 1946, 2 children **DISCIPLINE** HISTORICAL MUSICOLOGY **EDUCATION** Hamline Univ, AB, 50; Cornell Univ, MA, 52, PhD(musicol), 60. **CAREER** From instr to asst prof music, Oberlin Col, 55-60; asst prof, Univ Kans, 60-63; assoc prof, Tulane Univ, 63-68; assoc prof, 68-71, prof music, 71-79, dir grad studies music, 77-79, HANES PROF OF HUMANITIES IN MUSIC, UNIV NC, CHAPEL HILL, 79-, Fulbright res grant, Italy, 65-66; Nat Endowment for Humanities sr res fel, Italy, 72-73 & England, 79-80, Prof Emeritus, 91. **HONORS AND AWARDS** Deems Taylor Awd, Am Soc Composers, Authors & Publ, 78. **MEMBERSHIPS** Am Musicol Soc (pres, 80-82); Libr Asn; Int Musicol Soc. **RESEARCH** History of the oratorio; music in the Italian baroque; rhythmic techniques in 20th century music.; jazz history and performance. **SELECTED PUBLICATIONS** Auth, The rhythmic analysis of twentieth century music, J Music Theory, 64; The Latin dramatic dialogue, J Am Musicol Soc, 67; Narrative and dramatic elements in the Laude Filippine, 1563-1600, Acta Musicologica, 69; Domenico Alaleona's Studi su la storia dell'oratorio, Notes, 75; Carissimi's Latin oratorios, Analecta Musicologica, 76; The baroque oratorio: A report on research, Acta Musicologica, 76; A History of the Oratorio (vols 1 & 2), Univ NC, 77, vol 3, 87, vol 4, 00; Oratorio and sacred opera, 1700-1825, Proc Royal Musicol Asn, 79-80; Il-Tempio-Armonico--Music From The Oratorio-Dei-Filippini Of Rome: 1575-1705, Music & Letters, Vol 74, 93. **CONTACT ADDRESS** Dept of Music, Univ of No Carolina, Chapel Hill, Chapel Hill, NC 27514. **EMAIL** hes@email.unc.edu

SMOCOVITIS, VASSILIKI B.
PERSONAL Born 11/15/1955, El Mansura, Egypt, s **DISCIPLINE** HISTORY OF SCIENCE **EDUCATION** Univ Western Ont, BS, 79; Cornell Univ, PhD, 88. **CAREER** Vis asst prof to assoc prof, Univ of Fla, 88-. **HONORS AND AWARDS** Mellon Fel, 90-92; Choice Outstanding Acad Book Awd, 97. **MEMBERSHIPS** Hist of Sci Soc; Soc for the Study of Evolution; Botanical Soc of Am; AAAS. **RESEARCH** History of Evolutionary Biology, History of Botany. **SELECTED PUBLICATIONS** Auth, Unifying Biology: The Evolutionary Synthesis and Evolutionary Biology, Princeton Univ Pr, 96. **CONTACT ADDRESS** Dept Hist, Univ of Florida, PO Box 117320, Gainesville, FL 32611-7320. **EMAIL** bsmocovi@history.ufl.edu

SMOOT, RICK
PERSONAL Born 07/14/1956, Ashland, KY, s **DISCIPLINE** HISTORY **EDUCATION** Marshall Univ, BA, 78; MA, 81; Univ Ky, PhD, 88. **CAREER** Asst to the dir, Oral Hist of Appalachia Prog, Marshall Univ, 80-81; microcomputer coord, First Am Bank, 82-83; project interviewer, Univ of Ky, 83-85; teaching asst, Univ of Ky, 83-85; historian, Univ of Ky, 85-88; asst prof McNeese State Univ, 88-89; adj fac, Marshall Univ, 89-93; res ed, Marshall Univ, 89; dir, Economic Development Admin Technical Assistance Prog, Marshall Univ, 89-90; dir, Inst for Int Trade Development, Marshall Univ, 90-93; freelance writer, ed, consult, 93-; from adj fac to asst prof, Ky Lexington Community Col, 95-. **HONORS AND AWARDS** Sigma Tau Delta, Marshall Univ, 78; listed in Who's Who Among Students in Am Universities and Colleges, 79 & 81; Colonial Dames Awd, Marshall univ, 81; Gamma Beta Phi Soc, Marshall Univ, 82; Alpha Tau Omega Found Resident Schol, Univ of Ky, 83-85; Outstanding Young Men of Am, 81 & 85; Omicron Delta Kappa, Univ of Ky, 85; grant, Ky Oral Hist Comn, 87; A.D. Kirwin Fel Awd, Univ of Ky, 88; listed in Who's Who in Am Educ, 94. **MEMBERSHIPS** Southern Historical Asn, Oral Hist Asn, Appalachian Studies Asn, Ky Asn of Teachers of Hist. **RESEARCH** Social and Political History of the United States, Southern History, History of Appalachia, Institutional History, Kentucky History. **SELECTED PUBLICATIONS** Auth, "John Sherman Cooper: The Early Years, 1901-1927," The Register of the Ky Historical Soc 93 (95: 133-158; auth, "Medical History Notes from Appalachia," Appalachian Heritage 23 (95): 21-28; auth, "Head for the hills," Compendium, the Magazine of Appalachian Regional Healthcare, Inc., (96): 11-12, 20; auth, "Parting the Waters," Compendium, the Magazine of Appalachian Regional Healthcare, Inc., (97): 10-11; auth, "The Gavel and the Sword: Experiences Shaping the Life of John Sherman Cooper," A Mythic Land Apart: Reassessing Southerners and Their History, Greenwood Press (Westport, CT), 97; auth, "Dreams, Brick, and Mortar: John Sharpe Chambers and the Origins of the University of Kentucky Medical Center," Fislon Club Hist Quart 72 (98): 42-75. **CONTACT ADDRESS** Dept Soc Sci, Lexington Community Col, Oswald Bldg, Lexington, KY 40506-0001. **EMAIL** smoot@pop.uky.edu

SMUTS, MALCOLM R.
PERSONAL Born 02/15/1949, New York, NY, m, 1972, 2 children **DISCIPLINE** HISTORY **EDUCATION** Yale Univ, BA, 71; Princeton Univ, PhD, 76. **CAREER** Asst Prof to Prof, Univ Mass, 76-. **MEMBERSHIPS** N Am Soc for Court Stud; Nat Conf of British Studies. **RESEARCH** Culture and Politics in Britain, ca. 1585-1640; International courts. **CONTACT ADDRESS** Dept Hist, Univ of Massachusetts, Boston, 100 Morrissey Blvd, Dorchester, MA 02125-3300. **EMAIL** malcolmsmuts@umb.edu

SMYLIE, JAMES HUTCHINSON
PERSONAL Born 10/20/1925, Huntington, WV, m, 1952, 3 children **DISCIPLINE** AMERICAN CHURCH HISTORY **EDUCATION** Washington Univ, BA, 46; Princeton Theol Sem, BD, 49, ThM, 50, PhD(church hist), 58. **CAREER** Asst minister, First Presby Church, St Louis, 50-52; instr church hist, Princeton Theol Sem, 56-59, asst prof, 59-62, dir studies, 60-62; alumni vis prof church hist, 62-64, assoc prof, 64-67, PROF AM CHURCH HIST, UNION THEOL SEM, VA, 67-95, Advan Relig Studies Found grant, 67; ed, J Presby Hist, 68-95. **MEMBERSHIPS** AHA; Am Cath Hist Asn; Am Studies Asn; Am Soc Church Historians (secy, 63-). **RESEARCH** Religion and politics; religion and culture. **SELECTED PUBLICATIONS** Auth, Into All the World, 65; auth, A Cloud of Witnesses, John Knox, 65; ed, Presbyterians and the American Revolu-

tion: A documentary account, 74; Presbyterians and the American Revolution: An interpretive account, J Presby Hist, 76; auth, A Brief History of Presbyterians, Geneva Press, 96. **CONTACT ADDRESS** 3211 Noble, Richmond, VA 23222.

SMYTHE, KATHLEEN
DISCIPLINE HISTORY, AFRICAN **EDUCATION** Wooster Col, BA, 88; Univ Wis, MA, 91; PhD, 97. **CAREER** Asst prof , Xavier Univ, 97-. **HONORS AND AWARDS** Fulbright Doct Diss Fel, 95-96; Wenner-Gren Anthropol Foundation grant, 94-95. **MEMBERSHIPS** African Studies asn, Am Hist Asn. **RESEARCH** Colonial African history, Christianity in Africa, East African history, Social history. **SELECTED PUBLICATIONS** Auth, "Church and State in Nkansi, 1880-1980," Tanzania Zamani, (forthcoming); auth, "Where one slept mattered: Fipa socialization and cultural markers of growth in Nkansi, Ufipa," in Rethinking Age in Africa: Colonial and Post-Colonial Interpretations of Cultural Processes, (forthcoming); auth, "Child of the Clan or Child of the Priests: Life Stories of Two fipa Nuns," Journal of Religious History; auth, The Creation of a Catholic fipa Society: conversion in Nkansi District, Ufipa," East African Expressions of Christianity, (99): 129-149. **CONTACT ADDRESS** Dept Hist, Xavier Univ, Ohio, 3800 Victory Pkwy, Cincinnati, OH 45207-1035. **EMAIL** smythe@xu.edu

SNADEN, JAMES N.
PERSONAL Born 12/19/1937, Ann Arbor, MI, m, 1959, 2 children **DISCIPLINE** GEOGRAPHY **EDUCATION** Eastern Mich Univ, BS, 59; Univ Mich, MA, 64; PhD, 74. **CAREER** Prof, Central Conn State Univ, 66-. **HONORS AND AWARDS** Gamma Theta Upsilon; Res Fel, Org of Am States. **MEMBERSHIPS** Assoc of Am Geog; Nat Coun for Geog Educ. **RESEARCH** Geography of Latin America. **SELECTED PUBLICATIONS** Auth, "Puerto Rico", Latino Encyclopedia, 96; auth, "Colombia", "Panama", "Nicaragua", and "El Salvador", Lands and Peoples, Grolier's, 97; auth, "South American", "Brazil", and "Mexico", Grolier Multi-Media Encyclopedia. **CONTACT ADDRESS** Dept Geog, Central Connecticut State Univ, 1615 Stanley St, New Britain, CT 06053. **EMAIL** snaden@ccsu.edu

SNEAD, DAVID L.
PERSONAL Born 02/21/1969, Charleston, SC, m, 1991, 2 children **DISCIPLINE** HISTORY **EDUCATION** Virginia Tech, BA, 90; MA, 91; Univ Virginia, PhD, 97. **CAREER** Vis Asst Prof, Randolph-Macon Col, 94-99; Vis Asst Prof; 96-99, Univ of Richmond; Asst prof,Tex Tech Univ, 99-. **HONORS AND AWARDS** J. Ambler Johnston Awd for Top Graduating Undergraduate Hist Major at Virginia Tech, 90; Graduate Assistantship Funding at Virginia Tech, 90-91; Eisenhower World Affairs Inst Travel Grant, 95; Delta Gamma Sorority Certificate of Recognition, Outstanding Prof at the Univ of Richmond, 98; Phi Beta Kappa. **MEMBERSHIPS** Soc of Historians of Am Foreign Relations; Am Hist Asn; Soc for Military Hist; Coun for Social Studies Educ. **RESEARCH** Diplomatic and military history **SELECTED PUBLICATIONS** Auth, The Gaither Committee, Eisenhower, and the Cold War, Ohio State Univ Pr (Columbus, OH), 99; auth, Commentary on Kenneth A. Osgood, "Form before Substance: Eisenhower's Commitment to Psychological Warfare and Negotiations with the Enemy," Diplomatic History, 00; auth, "Russell Island" in World War II in the Pacific: An Encyclopedia, ed. Stanley Sandler (Florence, KY, Garland Publishing, 00). **CONTACT ADDRESS** Dept of Hist, Texas Tech Univ, Box 41013, Lubbock, TX 79409-1013. **EMAIL** david.snead@ttu.edu

SNEDEGAR, KEITH
DISCIPLINE MEDIEVAL HISTORY, HISTORY OF SCIENCE **EDUCATION** Univ Mich, AB, 83; Univ Edin, MSc, 84; Oxford Univ, D Phil. **CAREER** Adj asst prof, Grand Valley State Univ, 89-93; asst prof, Ut Valley State Col, 94-00; assoc prof, 00-. **HONORS AND AWARDS** Postdoc Res Fel, Univ CapeTwn, 94-95. **MEMBERSHIPS** ASA; AHA; HSS; MAA. **RESEARCH** History of astronomy. **SELECTED PUBLICATIONS** Auth, "The Works and Days of Simon Bredon, a fourteenth-century astronomer and physician," in Between Demonstration and Imagination, eds. Lodi Naufa, Arjo Vanderjagt (99). **CONTACT ADDRESS** Dept History, Political Science, Utah Valley State Col, 800 Univ Mall, Orem, UT 84097-8295. **EMAIL** snedegke@uvsc.edu

SNETSINGER, JOHN
PERSONAL Born 05/12/1941, Santa Barbara, CA **DISCIPLINE** AMERICAN HISTORY **EDUCATION** Univ Calif, Los Angeles, AB, 63; Univ Calif, Berkeley, MA, 66; Stanford Univ, PhD(hist), 69. **CAREER** Instr hist, San Jose State Univ, 67-70; PROF HIST, CALIF POLYTECH STATE UNIV, SAN LUIS OBISPO, 70-, Researcher, Harry S Truman Inst Nat & Int Affairs, 68 & 73. **RESEARCH** Recent American foreign policy; ethnic history. **SELECTED PUBLICATIONS** Auth, Truman, the Jewish Vote and the Creation of Israel, Hoover Inst, Stanford Univ, 74. **CONTACT ADDRESS** Dept of Hist, California Polytech State Univ, San Luis Obispo, San Luis Obispo, CA 93407.

SNOW, GEORGE EDWARD
PERSONAL Born 01/13/1939, Miami, FL, m, 1958, 4 children **DISCIPLINE** MODERN EUROPEAN HISTORY **EDUCATION** Ohio State Univ, BA, 62, MA, 64; Ind Univ, PhD(hist), 70. **CAREER** From asst prof to assoc prof, 67-73, PROF HIST, SHIPPENSBURG STATE COL, 73-, CHMN DEPTS HIST & PHILOS, 80-, Am Philos Soc res grant, 73; co-holder Nat Endowment for Humanities prog develop grant, 76-77. **MEMBERSHIPS** Soc Sci-Hist Asn; AHA; Am Asn Advan Slavic Studies; Can Asn Slavists. **RESEARCH** Imperial Russian bureaucracy under Nicholas II; imperial Russian labor policy in the 19th and 20th centuries. **SELECTED PUBLICATIONS** Auth, The Kokovtsov Commission: An abortive attempt at labor reform in Russia in 1905, Slavic Rev, 12/72; The Peterhof Conference and the Bulygin Duma, Russ Hist/Hist Russe, 75. **CONTACT ADDRESS** Dept of Hist, Shippensburg Univ of Pennsylvania, 1871 Old Main Dr, Shippensburg, PA 17257-2299.

SNOW, VERNON F.
PERSONAL Born 11/25/1924, Milwaukee, WI, m, 1949 **DISCIPLINE** ENGLISH HISTORY **EDUCATION** Wheaton Col, BA, 48; Univ Chicago, MA, 49; Univ Wis, PhD, 53. **CAREER** Instr western civilization, Univ Ore, 53-56; vis lectr English hist, Univ Wis, 56-57; asst prof western civilization, Univ Ore, 57-60; from asst prof to assoc prof English hist, Mont State Univ, 60-66; prof hist, Univ Nebr, Lincoln, 66-74, chmn dept, 70-71; prof hist, Syracuse Univ, 74-. **HONORS AND AWARDS** Am Philos Soc grant, 58; vpres, Snow Found, 69-74, pres, 74-. **MEMBERSHIPS** AHA; Conf Brit Studies; Int Comn Hist Rep & Parliamentary Insts; Midwest Conf Brit Studies; fel Royal Hist Soc. **RESEARCH** English constitutional history, Stuart period; English legal history. **SELECTED PUBLICATIONS** Auth, The Grand Tour diary of Robert C Johnson, Proc Am Philos Soc, 58; Parliamentary Reapportionment Proposals in the Puritan Revolution, English Hist Rev, 60; The Concept of Revolution in Seventeenth Century England, Hist J, 62; Essex the Rebel, Univ Nebr, 70; J B S: The Biography of John Ben Snow, NY Univ, 74; ed, Holinshead's Chronicles, AMS Press, 76; auth, Parliament in Elizabethan England, Yale Univ, 77; Private Member Journals of the Long Parliament, Yale, 82; The Teenage Diary Of Snow, Charles 1850, Ny Hist, Vol 74, 93. **CONTACT ADDRESS** 6216 Royal Birkdale, Jamesville, NY 13078.

SNYDER, ARNOLD C.
DISCIPLINE HISTORY **EDUCATION** Univ Waterloo, BA, 74; McMaster Univ, MA, 75; PhD, 81. **CAREER** Prof of Hist, Conrad Grebel Col. **HONORS AND AWARDS** Ed, Conrad Grebel Rev. **RESEARCH** Anabaptist history and thought, spirituality and peace, and themes related to church history. **CONTACT ADDRESS** Dept of History, Univ of Waterloo, Conrad Grebel Col, 200 Westmount Rd, Waterloo, ON, Canada N2L 3G6. **EMAIL** casnyder@uwaterloo.ca

SNYDER, LEE DANIEL
PERSONAL Born 06/04/1933, Waterbury, CT, m, 1961, 2 children **DISCIPLINE** MEDIEVAL-RENAISSANCE STUDIES **EDUCATION** Williams Col, AB, 55; Harvard Univ, AM, 56, PhD(Europ hist), 66; Union Theol Sem, MDiv, 61. **CAREER** Asst prof hist, Ithaca Col, 63-64 & Ohio Wesleyan Univ, 64-69; assoc prof hist, 69-80, Prof History,NEW COL, UNIV S FLA, 80-, DIR MEDIEVAL-RENAISSANCE STUDIES, 77-, Vis prof, Methodist Theol Sch Ohio, 68. **HONORS AND AWARDS** Phi Beta Kappa , 54; Danforth Grad Fel, 55-63; Fulbright, Germany, 56-57; Florida Teaching Awd, 94, **MEMBERSHIPS** Mediaeval Acad Am; Am Soc Church Hist; Soc Values Higher Educ; Am Soc Reformation Res; International Society fo Comparative Study of Civilizaition; 16th Century St Soc. **RESEARCH** Renaissance and Reformation church history; Christian devotion in 14th- centuries; Historical Theory. **SELECTED PUBLICATIONS** Auth, Seeking insight on insight, Soundings, 74; Some thoughts on a theology of resurrection, Encounter, 75; Erasmus on prayer, Renaissance & Reformation, 76; auth, " Gerson's Veonacular Advice on Prayer," 15th C Studies, vol X, 84; auth, " Ancient History Expanded, 1200 BCE to 600 CE," World History, Markus Weiner, 85; auth, The Social Dimension Of Piety--Associative Life And Devotional Change In The Penitent Confraternities Of Marseilles: 1499-1792, Church Hist, Vol 65, 96; Patronage In Renaissance Italy From 1400 To The Early 16th-Century, Church Hist, Vol 66, 1997; Religion, Political-Culture And The Emergence Of Early-Modern Society --Essays In German And Dutch History, Church Hist, Vol 64, 95; translator, Macrobius,Ambrosius,Aurelius,Theodosius--Commentary On The Dream Of Scipio, Church Hist, Vol 61, 92; auth, " Non-Processional Procession in DonQuixote," Indiana Journel of Hispanic Literatures, 94; auth, Macro-History , A Theoretical Approach to Comparative World History, Edwin Mellon Press, 99. **CONTACT ADDRESS** Div of Soc Sci, New Col of the Univ of So Florida, 5700 N Tamiami Trail, Sarasota, FL 34243. **EMAIL** lsnycer@sar.usf.edu

SNYDER, ROBERT EDWARD
PERSONAL Born 03/27/1943, Amsterdam, NY, m, 1961, 2 children **DISCIPLINE** AMERICAN HISTORY **EDUCATION** Union Col, BA, 67, MA, 71; Syracuse Univ, PhD(Am Studies), 80. **CAREER** ASST PROF AM STUDIES, UNIV SOUTH FLA, 80- **HONORS AND AWARDS** General L. Kemper Williams Prize, 74; Robert L. Brown Awd, 75; Charlton W. Tebeau Awd, 93; D.B. McKay Awd, 93; Certificate of Commendtion AASLH, 93. **MEMBERSHIPS** AHA; OAH; SHA; ASA; FHS. **RESEARCH** Modern America; American South; Popular culture; Photography. **SELECTED PUBLICATIONS** Auth, Huey Long and the presidential election of 1936, La Hist, spring 75; The concept of demagoguery: Huey P Long and his literary critics, La Studies, spring 76; Huey Long and the Cotton Holiday Plan of 1931, La Hist, spring 77; The Cotton Holiday Movement in Mississippi, J Miss Hist, 2/78; Women, Wobblies, and workers' rights: The 1912 textile strike in Little Falls, New York, NY Hist, 1/79; contribr, At the Point of Production, Greenwood Press, 81; auth, Cotton Crisis, Univ of N.C. Press, 84; auth, History of Women, Meckler Corp, 90; auth, Pioneer Commercial Photography, Univ Press of Florida, 92; auth, Developing Dixie, Greenwood Press, 98; auth, Companion to Southern Literature, LSW, 01. **CONTACT ADDRESS** Dept of Am Studies, Univ of So Florida, Tampa, FL 33620.

SOCHEN, JUNE
PERSONAL Born 11/26/1937, Chicago, IL **DISCIPLINE** HISTORY **EDUCATION** Univ Chicago, AB, 58; Northwestern Univ, AM, 60, PhD(hist), 67. **CAREER** Ed, Carnegie Corp Proj on Guide & Motivation Super Studies, 60-61; teacher English & hist, NShore Country Day Sch, Ill, 61-64; PROF HIST, NORTHEASTERN ILL UNIV, 64-, Nat Endowment for Humanities younger humanist grant, 71-72. **MEMBERSHIPS** AHA; Am Studies Asn. **RESEARCH** Women's history; 20th century United States intellectual history; popular culture. **SELECTED PUBLICATIONS** Ed, The New Feminism in Twentieth Century America, Heath, 71; The Black Man and the American Dream, 1900-1930, 71 & auth, The New Woman: Feminism in Greenwich Village, 1910-1920, 72, Quadrangle; co-ed, Destroy to Create: Readings on the American Environment, Dryden, 72; auth, The Unbridgeable Gap: Blacks and Their Quest for the American Dream, 1900-1930, Rand McNally, 72; Movers and Shakers: American Women Thinkers and Activists, 1900-1970, Quadrangle, 73; Her story: A Woman's View of American History, Alfred, 74, 2nd ed, 81; Consecrate Every Day: The Public Lives of Jewish American Women, 1880-1980, State Univ NY, 81; Enduring Values: Women in Popular Culture, Praeger Publ, 87; Cafeteria America: New Identities in Contemporary Life, Iowa State Univ Press, 88; ed, Women's Comic Visions, Wayne State Univ Press, 91; auth, She Who Laughs Lasts: The Life and Times of Mae West, Harlan Davidson, Inc, 92; auth, From Mae to Madonna: Women Entertainers in 20th c America, Univ Press of Kent, 99. **CONTACT ADDRESS** Dept of History, Northeastern Illinois Univ, 5500 N St Louis Ave, Chicago, IL 60625-4625. **EMAIL** jsochen@neiu.edu

SOCOLOFSKY, HOMER EDWARD
PERSONAL Born 05/20/1922, Tampa, KS, m, 6 children **DISCIPLINE** HISTORY **EDUCATION** Kans State Univ, BS, 44, MS, 47; Univ Mo, PhD, 54. **CAREER** Asst, 46, from instr to assoc prof, 47-63, Prof Hist, KS State Univ, 63-92, emeritus prof, 92-, Vis asst prof, Yale Univ, 54-55; Woods fel, Nebr Hist Soc, 61-; actg chmn dept, Kans State Univ, 64-65 & 69-70; comnr, Kans Am Revolution Bicentennial Comn, 75-76; sr context consult, Univ Mid-Am, 75; Fulbright lectr, India, 81-82. **MEMBERSHIPS** Orgn Am Historians; Agr Hist Soc (vpres, 67-68, pres, 68-69); Western Hist Asn; Great Plains Hist Asn. **RESEARCH** Agricultural history; public land disposal and land policy; history of the Great Plains. **SELECTED PUBLICATIONS** co-auth, The presidency of Benjamin Harrison, 87; auth, Kansas Governor, 90; co-comp, Kansas History: An Annotated Bibliography, 92; auth, Biography of the Honorable Richard Dean Rogers, Senior United States District Judge, 95. **CONTACT ADDRESS** Dept of Hist, Kansas State Univ, Manhattan, KS 66506. **EMAIL** hesocol@ksu.edu

SOCOLOW, SUSAN M.
PERSONAL Born New York, NY, m, 1965, 2 children **DISCIPLINE** HISTORY **EDUCATION** Barnard Col, BA, 62; Columbia Univ, MA, 64, PhD, 73. **CAREER** Samuel Candler Dobbs Prof Lat Am Hist. **MEMBERSHIPS** Am Hist Assoc, Conf on Latin Am Hist, Assoc of Caribbean Historians, Soc for Spanish and Portuguese Historical Studies. **RESEARCH** Latin American social history. **SELECTED PUBLICATIONS** Auth, The Merchants of Viceregal Buenos Aires: Family and Commerce; The Bureaucrats of Buenos Aires, 1769-1810: Amor Al Real Servicio; Women in Colonial Latin America; ed, The Atlantic Staple Trade; co-ed, Cities and Society in Colonial Latin America; The Countryside in Colonial Latin America. **CONTACT ADDRESS** Dept History, Emory Univ, 221 Bowden Hall, 561 Kilgo Cir, Atlanta, GA 30322. **EMAIL** socolow@emory.edu

SODEN, DALE
PERSONAL Born 05/04/1951, Spokane, WA, m, 1974, 2 children **DISCIPLINE** HISTORICAL, POLITICAL, AND INTERNATIONAL STUDIES **EDUCATION** Univ Wash, MA, 76; PhD, 80. **CAREER** Asso dean acad aff; assoc prof, 85-; Prof of Hist, Whitworth Col. **HONORS AND AWARDS** Corp

bd, YMCA; bd of trustees, Pacific Lutheran theol sem, Berkeley. **MEMBERSHIPS** St Mark's Lutheran Church. **RESEARCH** Relationship between religion and public policy in the history of the Pacific Northwest. **SELECTED PUBLICATIONS** Auth, history of Whitworth College; articles for scholarly jour(s) on topics in American religious history; The Reverend Mark Matthews: Activist in the Progressive Era. **CONTACT ADDRESS** Dept of Hist, Whitworth Col, 300 West Hawthorne Rd, Spokane, WA 99251. **EMAIL** dsoden@whitworth.edu

SODERLUND, JEAN
PERSONAL Born 01/17/1947, Philadelphia, PA, m, 1967 **DISCIPLINE** HISTORY **EDUCATION** Douglass Col, AB, 68; Rowan Col of NJers, MA, 71; Temple Univ, PhD, 82. **CAREER** Teacher, Deptford Township High School, 68-72; Instr, Camden County Col, 72-75; Graduate Asst, Temple Univ, 76-77; Papers of William Penn, Historical Society of PA, 80-83; Swarthmore Col Peace, Curator, 83-88; Asst Prof, 88-90, Univ of Maryland; Asst Prof, Univ of Maryland, 90-94; Prof of History, Lehigh Univ, 94-; Co-directory, Lawrence Henry Gipson Institute for Eighteenth-Century Studies, 96-; Chair, History Dept, Lehigh Univ, 98-. **HONORS AND AWARDS** Summer Fellowships, Temple Univ, 77, 79, Fellowship, Temple Univ, 75-78, Andrew W. Mellon Dissertation Fellowship, PCEAS, Univ of PA, 79-80, Kramer Awd in American History, Temple Univ, 80, Bernard C. Watson Dissertation Awd, Temple Univ, 82, Alfred E. Driscoll Publication Prize, New Jersry Commission, 83, Postdoctoral Fellowship, Philadelphia Ctr for Early American Studies, Univ of PA, 88, Summer Faculty Fellowship, Graduate School, UMBC, 89, Research Grant, New Jersey Historical Commission, 90-91, Research Grants, Gipson Institute, 97, 98, Research Grant, New Jersey Historical Commission, 98. **SELECTED PUBLICATIONS** Auth, The Papers of William Penn, Univ of PA Press, 81; 82; auth, William Penn and the Founding of PA, 1680-1684: A Documentary History, Univ of PA Press, 93; auth, Quakers and Slavery: A Divided Spirit, Princeton Univ Press (Princeton, NJ), 85; coauth, with Gary B. Nash, Freedom by Degrees: Emancipation in Pennsylvania and Its Aftermath, Oxford Univ Press (New York), 91; coauth, with Lewis Gould, David Oshinsky, and Edward Ayers, American Passages: A History of the United States, Harcourt College Publishers, 99. **CONTACT ADDRESS** Dept History, Lehigh Univ, 9 W Packer Ave, Unit 1, Bethlehem, PA 18015-3082. **EMAIL** jrsa@lehigh.edu

SOFFER, REBA NUSBAUM
PERSONAL Born 12/22/1934, Nashville, TN, m, 1956, 1 child **DISCIPLINE** MODERN EUROPEAN HISTORY **EDUCATION** Brooklyn Col, BA, 55; Wellesley Col, MA, 57; Radcliffe Col, PhD, 62. **CAREER** From instr to assoc prof, 61-71, PROF HIST, CALIF STATE UNIV, NORTHRIDGE, 71-, Vis lectr, Univ Calif Los Angeles, 67-68, vis prof, 80; fel, Nat Endowment Humanities, 71 & 81-82, Am Counc Learned Soc, 72, Am Philos Soc, 74; Munro Humanities lectr, Calif Inst Technol, 77; vis fel, Mansfield Col, Oxford & vis prof, Selwyn Col, Cambridge, 81; lectr, Northern Ariz Univ, 80, Inst Educ, Univ Calif, Berkeley, 82. **HONORS AND AWARDS** Pac Coast Br Awd, AHA, 78. **MEMBERSHIPS** AHA; Conf Brit Studies (assoc exec secy, 78-83); Pac Coast Conf Brit Studies (pres, 76-78); Inst Hist Res; Soc Hist Soc Sci. **RESEARCH** British history of the 19th and 20th centuries: intellectual, social and institutional. **SELECTED PUBLICATIONS** Auth, Attitudes and allegiances in the Unskilled North, 1830-1850, Int Rev Soc Hist, Vol X, 65; New Elitism: Social Psychology in Prewar England, J Brit Studies, 5/69; The revolution in English social thought, 1880-1914, Am Hist Rev, 12/70; various biographical essays, In: The Encycl of World Biography, 73; Ethics and Society in England: The Revolution in the Social Sciences, 1870-1914, Univ Calif, 78. **CONTACT ADDRESS** Dept of Hist, California State Univ, Northridge, Northridge, CA 91324.

SOKAL, MICHAEL MARK
PERSONAL Born 10/06/1945, Brooklyn, NY, m, 1968, 2 children **DISCIPLINE** HISTORY OF SCIENCE & TECHNOLOGY **EDUCATION** Cooper Union, BE, 66; Case Western Reserve Univ, MA, 68, PhD, 72. **CAREER** Res asst Hist of Sci, Ctr Hist Physics, Am Inst Physics, New York, 66; asst prof, 70-75, assoc prof, 75-81, prof Hist, Worchester Polytech Inst, 81-, vis res fel, Div Med Sci, Nat Mus Hist & Technol, Smithsonian Inst, 73-74; affil assoc prof Hist of Sci & Technol, Clark Univ, 75-80; nat lectr, Sigma Xi, 79-81; vis scholar Hist of Sci, Harvard Univ, 81-82; Program Officer, National Endowment for the Humanitties, 95; Program Officer, National Science Foundation, 98-00. **HONORS AND AWARDS** WPI Paris Fletcher Disting Prof in Humanities, 93-95; chmn elect, chmn & Immediate Chmn Section on Hist and Philo of Science, Am Assn for the Advan of Science, 97-99. **MEMBERSHIPS** Hist Sci Soc; Soc for Hist of Tech; Cheiron; Am Asn Advan Sci. **RESEARCH** History of psychology; history of American science and technology. **SELECTED PUBLICATIONS** Auth, Science and James McKeen Cattell, 1894 to 1945, Science, 80; ed, An education in psychology: James McKeen Cattell's journal and letters from Germany and England, 1880-1888, Mass Inst Tech Press, 81; auth, ed, Psychological Testing and Am Soc, 1890-1930, Rutgers Univ Press, 87; coauth, The Establishment of Science in America: 150 Years of the American Association for the Advancement of Science, Rutgers Univ Press, 99. **CONTACT ADDRESS** Dept of Humanities and Arts, Worcester Polytech Inst, 100 Institute Rd, Worcester, MA 01609-2247. **EMAIL** msokal@wpi.edu

SOKOL, DAVID M.
PERSONAL Born 11/03/1942, New York, NY, m, 1963, 2 children **DISCIPLINE** ART HISTORY **EDUCATION** NYork Univ, PhD. **CAREER** Prof, Univ IL at Chicago. **RESEARCH** Am art; mod art; museology. **SELECTED PUBLICATIONS** Auth, American Vision: Paintings from a Century of Collecting; Life in 19th Century America; co-auth, American Art: Painting-Sculpture-Architecture-Decorative Arts-Photography. **CONTACT ADDRESS** Art Hist Dept, Univ of Illinois, Chicago, 935 W. Harrison, Chicago, IL 60607-7039. **EMAIL** dmsokol@uic.edu

SOLBERG, WINTON UDELL
PERSONAL Born 01/11/1922, Aberdeen, SD, m, 1952, 3 children **DISCIPLINE** AMERICAN HISTORY **EDUCATION** Univ SDak, AB, 43; Harvard Univ, MA, 47, PhD, 54. **CAREER** From instr to asst prof soc sci, US Mil Acad, 51-54; from instr to asst prof hist, Yale Univ, 54-58; James Wallace prof Am hist, Macalester Col, 58-62; vis prof, 61-62, assoc prof, 62-67, chmn dept hist, 70-72, Prof Am Hist, Univ Ill, Urbana, 67-, Morse fel, Yale Univ, 57-58; consult & lectr, US Army War Col, Carlisle Barracks, 59, 60 & 62; res fel, Ctr Study Hist of Liberty in Am, Harvard Univ, 62-63; Fulbright-Hays lectr, Johns Hopkins Sch Adv Int Studies, Bologna, 67-68; mem, Ill Coun Humanities, 73-75; Nat Endowment Humanities sr fel, 74-75; dir, Nat Endowment Humanities Residential Sem, 76-77; vis prof, Konan Univ, Kobe, Japan, 81; vis lectr, Korea and Malaysia, 85, Korea, 92; vis prof, Univ Calcutta, India, 93. **HONORS AND AWARDS** Fulbright-Hays lectr, Moscow Univ, USSR, 78. **MEMBERSHIPS** Orgn Am Hist; Am Studies Asn; Southern Hist Asn; AHA; AAUP (first vpres, 74-76). **RESEARCH** American intellectual history; American religious and scientific thought; political and constitutional thought. **SELECTED PUBLICATIONS** Auth, A History of American Thought and Culture, Kinseido, 83; auth, "Cotton Mather, The Christian Philosopher, and the Classics," Proceedings of the Am Antiq Soc 96 (86): 323-366; auth, "Science and Religion in Early America: Cotton Mather's Christian Philosopher," Church Hist 56 (87): 73-92; auth, "Primitivism and the American Enlightenment," in The American Quest for the Primitive Church, ed. Richard Hughes (Urbana: Univ Ill Press, 88), 50-68; auth, The Constitutional Convention and the Formation of the Union, Univ Ill Press (Urbana, IL), 90; auth, "The Sabbath on the Overland Trail to California," Church Hist 59 (90): 340-355; auth, "The Catholic Presence at the University of Illinois," Cath Hist Rev 76 (90): 765-812; auth, "The Early Years of the Jewish Presence at the University of Illinois," Relig and Am Cult 2 (92): 215-245; auth, Cotton Mather, The Christian Philosopher, Univ Ill Press (Urbana, IL), 94; auth, The University of Illinois, 1894-1904: The Shaping of the University, Univ Ill Press (Urbana, IL), 00. **CONTACT ADDRESS** Dept of Hist, Univ of Illinois, Urbana-Champaign, Urbana, IL 61801. **EMAIL** wsolberg@uiuc.edu

SOLDON, NORBERT C.
PERSONAL Born 08/04/1932, Nanticoke, PA, m, 1959, 3 children **DISCIPLINE** MODERN EUROPEAN HISTORY **EDUCATION** Pa State Univ, BA, 54, MA, 59; Univ Del, PhD(hist), 69. **CAREER** Teacher soc sci, High Sch, Del, 59-63; from asst prof to assoc prof, 63-69, PROF EMER EUROP HIST, WEST CHESTER UNIV, 69-99. **HONORS AND AWARDS** Distinguished Fac Awd, 80. **MEMBERSHIPS** AHA; Conf Brit Studies; Res Soc Victorian Periodicals; Soc Study Labour Hist; Study Group Int Labor & Working Class Hist. **RESEARCH** British history, 1815 to the present; European economic history; European intellectual history; comparative women's trade union history. **SELECTED PUBLICATIONS** Auth, Victorian periodicals: The crisis of late Victorian liberalism, Victorian Periodical News, 12/73; Laissez-faire as dogma: The story of the liberty and property defence league, In: Essays in Anti-Labour History, Macmillan, 74; Women in British Trade Unions, 1874-1976, Gill & Macmillan, 78; On Her Their Lives Depend--Munitions Workers In The Great-War, Am Hist Rev, Vol 100, 95; ed, The World of Women's Trade Unions, Greenwood Press, 85; ed, John wilkinson 1728 - 1868 English Ironmaster and Inventor, Melleh Press, 98; ed, " Emma Patterson, Lord Wemyss," Dictionary of National Biography, 01. **CONTACT ADDRESS** 957 Cloud Lane, West Chester, PA 19380.

SOLHEIM, BRUCE
PERSONAL Born 09/03/1958, Seattle, WA, m, 1996, 4 children **DISCIPLINE** HISTORY **EDUCATION** Bowling Green State Univ, PhD; Pacific Lutheran Univ, MA; Campbell Univ, BS. **CAREER** Prof of History, Citrus Col, 98-; Adjunct instr, Green River Community Col, 93-98; vis Asst Prof, Pacific Lutheran Univ, 94-95. **HONORS AND AWARDS** Eisenhower Institute Grant; Norwegian Ministry Foreign Affairs Grant. **MEMBERSHIPS** Society for Historians of Amer Foreign Relations; Amer Historical Assoc. **RESEARCH** Vietnam War; Scandanavian-US relations. **SELECTED PUBLICATIONS** Auth, "On Top of the World," Greenwood, 00; auth, "Nordic Nexus," Praeger, 94. **CONTACT ADDRESS** Dept Social Science, Citrus Col, 1000 W Foothill Blvd, Glendora, CA 91741-1885. **EMAIL** brucesolheim@yahoo.com; bsolheim@citrus.cc.ca.us

SOLIDAY, GERALD
PERSONAL Born 11/25/1939, OH, d, 2 children **DISCIPLINE** HISTORY **EDUCATION** Harvard Univ, PhD, 69. **CAREER** Assoc prof; assoc prof, Univ Texas-Dallas. **RESEARCH** European social and cultural history; social history of literature; historiography. **SELECTED PUBLICATIONS** Auth, A Community in Conflict: Frankfurt Society in the Seventeenth and Early Eighteenth Centuries, Brandeis Univ, 74; Principal Editor and one contribution, The History of Kinship and the Family: A Select International bibliography, Kraus Int, 80; Stadtische Fuhrungsschichten in Marburg 1560-1800, Marburg, 80; Aus schlechten Christen werden gemeiniglich auch schlechte Unterthanen: Die Schulbildung der Marburger Handwerker in der fruhen Neuzeit, Hessisches Jahrbuch fur Landesgeschichte, 93. **CONTACT ADDRESS** Historical Studies, Univ of Texas, Dallas, P O Box 830688, Richardson, TX 75083-0688. **EMAIL** soliday@utdallas.edu

SOLLORS, WERNER
PERSONAL m, 2 children **DISCIPLINE** ENGLISH; AMERICAN STUDIES **EDUCATION** Freie Universitaet Berlin, Germany, PhD, 75. **CAREER** Asst prof, Berlin, 75-78; Columbia Univ, 78-82; assoc prof, Columbia Univ, 82-83; prof, Harvard Univ, 83- . **HONORS AND AWARDS** Guggenheim fel; Andrew W. Mellon fel; Constance Rouske Prize. **MEMBERSHIPS** MLA; ASA; OAH; ACLA. **RESEARCH** Am Studies; Comp Lit. **SELECTED PUBLICATIONS** Auth, Beyond Ethnicity: Consent and Descent in American Culture, 86; The Return of Thematic Criticism, 93; Theories of Ethnicity: A Classical Reader, 96; Neither Black Nor White Yet Both: Thematic Explorations of Interracial Literature, 97; Multilingual America: Transnationalism, Ethnicity, and the Languages of American Literature, 98; The Multilingual Anthology of American Literature: A Reader of Original Texts with English Translations, 00; Interracialism: Black-White Inter marriage il American History, Literature, and Law, 00. **CONTACT ADDRESS** Barker Center, Harvard Univ, 12 Quincy Ave, Cambridge, MA 02138. **EMAIL** amciv@fas.harvard.edu

SOLOMON, HOWARD MITCHELL
PERSONAL Born 06/27/1942, New Castle, PA **DISCIPLINE** HISTORY OF STEREOTYPING, LESBIAN AND GAY HISTORY, EARLY MODERN EUROPE **EDUCATION** Univ Pittsburgh, AB, 64; Northwestern Univ, Evanston, MA, 67, PhD, 69. **CAREER** Teaching asst hist, Northwestern Univ, 65-67; from instr to asst prof, NY Univ, 68-71; asst prof, 71-74, assoc prof, 74-92, dean undergrad studies & acad affairs, 78-82, academic dean, Center for European Studies (Talloires, France), 92; dir, writing across the cirriculum, 92-94; Prof Hist, Tufts Univ, 92-. **HONORS AND AWARDS** Lesbian/Gay Campus Service Awd, 92. **MEMBERSHIPS** AHA; Soc Fr Hist Studies; Nat Coalition Bldg Inst; Center for Millennial Studies. **RESEARCH** History of stereotyping; lesbian/gay history; health and medicine; early modern France. **SELECTED PUBLICATIONS** Auth, Public Welfare, Science and Propaganda in 17th Century France, Princeton Univ, 72; The Gazette and Anti-statist Propaganda: the Medium of Print in the First Half of the 17th century, CAN J Hist, 74; Teaching about Health in Preindustrial Europe, Radical Teacher, 81; What a Shame You Don't Publish: Crossing the Boundaries as a Public Intellectual Activist, Dangerous Territories: Struggles for Difference and Equality in Education, Routledge, 97; Nebuchadnezzar, the Cripple, and Ground Hog Day: a Mediation on Tu B'Shvat, Tu B'Shvat Anthology, Jewish Pub Soc, 98. **CONTACT ADDRESS** Dept of Hist, Tufts Univ, Medford, Medford, MA 02155. **EMAIL** hsolom01@emerald.tufts.edu

SOLOWAY, RICHARD ALLEN
PERSONAL Born 03/04/1934, Boston, MA, m, 1957 **DISCIPLINE** HISTORY **EDUCATION** Univ Iowa, BA, 55; Univ Wis, MA, 56, PhD(hist), 60. **CAREER** Asst prof hist, Univ Mich, 62-68; assoc prof, 68-71, Prof Hist, Univ NC, Chapel Hill, 71-; Eugen Merzbacher Distinguished Prof, 94-. **HONORS AND AWARDS** John Bell Snow Prize, 83 for outstanding book in the socl sci (Birth Control and the Population Question in England, 1877-1930. Univ of N Carolina Press, 82. **MEMBERSHIPS** AHA; Conf British Studies; Royal Historical Society. **RESEARCH** Modern English history; European social and intellectual history. **SELECTED PUBLICATIONS** Auth, Prelates and People: Ecclesiastical Social Thought in England, 1783-1852, London, 69; auth, Birth Control and the Population Question in England, 1877-1930, Univerisity of North Carolina Press, 82; auth, Demography and Degeneration: Eugenics and the Declining Birth Rate in Twentieth Century England, Chapel Hill, 92, new ed. 95; auth, Darwinism, War And History--The Debate Over The Biology Of War From The Origin Of Species To The First-World-War, Histoire Sociale-Social Hist, Vol 29, 96; The Perfect Contraceptive, Eugenics And Birth-Control Research In Britain And Am In The Interwar Years, J Of Contemporary Hist, Vol 30, 95; Measuring The Mind--Education And Psychology In England, C.1860-C.1990, Amn Hist Rev, Vol 101, 96; Fertility, Class And Gender In Britain, 1860-1940, Albion, Vol 29, 97; Contraception And Abortion From The Ancient-World To The Renaissance, J Of Interdisciplinary Hist, Vol 24, 94; The Facts Of Life, The Creation Of Sexual Knowledge In Britain, 1650-1950, Albion, Vol 28, 96. **CONTACT ADDRESS** Dept of Hist, Univ of No Carolina, Chapel Hill, Chapel Hill, NC 27599-3195. **EMAIL** soloway@email.unc.edu

SOLTOW, JAMES HAROLD
PERSONAL Born 07/01/1924, Chicago, IL, m, 1946 **DISCIPLINE** HISTORY **EDUCATION** Dickinson Col, AB, 48; Univ Pa, AM, 49, PhD(hist), 54. **CAREER** Asst hist, Univ Pa, 50-52; lectr, Hunter Col, 52-55; res assoc, Colonial Williamsburg, Inc, 55-56; instr hist & sociol, Russell Sage Col, 56-58; fel bus hist, Grad Sch Bus Admin, Harvard Univ, 58-59; from asst prof to assoc prof, 59-68, chmn dept, 70-75, PROF HIST, MICH STATE UNIV, 68-, Nat Rec Mgt Coun res fel, 54; Found Econ Educ fel, 60; Fulbright res fel, Univ Louvain, 65-66. **MEMBERSHIPS** AHA; Econ Hist Asn; Orgn Am Historians; Econ & Bus Hist Soc; Bus Hist Conf. **RESEARCH** American economic and social history. **SELECTED PUBLICATIONS** Auth, Foundations of Regional Industrialization, In: Regional Economic History: The Mid-Atlantic Area Since 1700, Hagley Found, 76; coauth, The Evolution of the American Economy: Growth, Welfare, and Decision Making, Basic Books, 79; Origins of Small Business and the Relationships Between Large and Small Firms, In: Small Business in American Life, Columbia Univ Press, 80; Cotton As Religion, Politics, Law, Economics And Art, Agricultural Hist, Vol 68, 94; A Hist Of Small Business In Am, J Of Am Hist, Vol 80, 93; Cotton As Religion, Politics, Law, Economics And Art, Agricultural Hist, Vol 68, 94. **CONTACT ADDRESS** Dept of Hist, Michigan State Univ, East Lansing, MI 48823.

SOMERVILLE, JAMES KARL
PERSONAL Born 05/02/1935, Racine, WI, m, 1960 **DISCIPLINE** AMERICAN HISTORY **EDUCATION** Univ Wis, Milwaukee, BS, 57; Univ Wis, Madison, MS, 59; Western Reserve Univ, PhD, 65. **CAREER** Teacher, high sch, Ill, 59-61; instr hist, Ohio State Univ, 65-67; asst prof, 67-90, Assoc Prof Hist, State Univ NY Col Geneseo, 90-97, Prof Emer, 97-. **MEMBERSHIPS** Inst Early Am Hist & Cult; AHA; Orgn Am Historians. **RESEARCH** The colonial family; Women in colonial America; Childhood and adolescence in American history; The Vietnam War. **SELECTED PUBLICATIONS** Auth, Family demography and the published record: An analysis of the vital statistics of Salem, Massachusetts, Essex Inst Hist Collections, 10/70; The Salem (Massachusetts) woman in the home, 1660-1770, Eighteenth Century Life, 9/74; Homesick in upstate New York: The sala of Sidney Roby, 1843-1847, NY Hist, 4/91. **CONTACT ADDRESS** Dept of Hist, SUNY, Col at Geneseo, 1 College Cir, Geneseo, NY 14454-1401. **EMAIL** somerville@uno.cc.geneseo.edu

SOMKIN, FRED
PERSONAL Born 05/12/1924, Detroit, MI, m, 1959 **DISCIPLINE** AMERICAN HISTORY **EDUCATION** Wayne Univ, BA, 46; Columbus Law Sch, LLB, 52; Am Univ, MA, 62; Cornell Univ, PhD, 67. **CAREER** Lawyer, Washington, DC, 52-59; lectr hist, Queen's Univ, Ont, 62-65, from asst prof to assoc prof, 65-68; assoc prof history, 68-91, prof, 92-94, PROF EMER, 94- , CORNELL UNIV, 68-, Res fel, Charles Warren Ctr Study Am Hist, Harvard Univ, 67-68; pub mem, Prof Standards Rev Comt, NY State Psychol Asn, 77-79. **MEMBERSHIPS** Am Soc Legal Hist; Am Cult Asn; Jean Bodin Soc; Asn Jewish Stud. **RESEARCH** American intellectual history; Jewish immigrant culture; American legal history. **SELECTED PUBLICATIONS** Auth, The contributions of Sir John Lubbock, FRS, to the origin of species, Royal Soc London Notes & Rec, 12/62; Unquiet Eagle: Memory and Desire in the Idea of American Freedom, 1815-60, Cornell Univ, 67; Sir John Lubbock (Lord Avebury), In: Dictionary of Scientific Biography, (16 vols), Scribners, 70-78; Love's body, USA, Rev Am Hist, 12/79; Scripture notes to Lincoln's second inaugural, Civil War Hist, 6/81; How Vanzetti said goodbye, J Am Hist, 9/81; The Strange Careet of Fugitivity in the History of Interstate Extradition, Utah Law Rev, 84; Zions Harp by the East River: Jewish-American Popular Songs in Columbus's Golden Land, 1890-1914, Perspectives in Am Hist, 85; Where have all the Chazonim gone?, Kolenu, 86; HO-WA-HO-SA-WA-KA: Chief Wolf Paw on the Airwaves, A Memoir and Meditation, Consumable Goods: Papers fron the NE Pop Cult Asn Mtg, 86; A Constitutional Parable, The Cresset, 88; A Note on the Wit of the Hermit of Prague, Notes and Queries, 94; Joseph Campbells Old Woman and Ben Sirahs Wisdom, ANQ, 98; auth, Was Capt. Gueeg good for the Jews?, Midstream, 99. **CONTACT ADDRESS** Dept of Hist, Cornell Univ, McGraw Hall, Ithaca, NY 14853-4601.

SOMMERFELDT, JOHN R.
PERSONAL Born 02/04/1933, Detroit, MI, m, 1956, 4 children **DISCIPLINE** HISTORY **EDUCATION** Univ Mich, AB, MA, PhD. **CAREER** Prof, Dallas Univ. **HONORS AND AWARDS** Phi Eta Sigma; Phi Beta Kappa; Phi Alpha Theta; Kappa Delta Pi; Who's Who in America, 75. **MEMBERSHIPS** Medieval Academy of America; American Catholic Historical Association; American Society of Church History; American Historical Assoc. **RESEARCH** Medieval intellectual history; medieval spirituality and ecclesiastical history. **SELECTED PUBLICATIONS** Ed., "Studies in Medieval Culture, I-XII 69-78; ed., "Studies in Medieval Cistercian History," 77; ed., "Cistercian Ideals and Reality," 78; ed., "The Chimaera of His Age," 80; ed., "Abba," 81; ed., "Erudition at God's Service," 87; auth, The Spiritual Teachings of Bernard of Clairvaux, 91;ed., "Bernardus Magister," 92; auth, "Studiosorum Speculum," 92; ed., "Studies in the Theology of St. Thomas Aquinas, 95. **CONTACT ADDRESS** Dept of History, Univ of Dallas, 1845 E Northgate Dr, Braniff 236, Irving, TX 75062. **EMAIL** jrsommer@acad.udalbs.edu

SOMMERVILLE, CHARLES JOHN
PERSONAL Born 08/15/1938, Lawrence, KS, m, 1964, 2 children **DISCIPLINE** ENGLISH CULTURAL HISTORY **EDUCATION** Univ Kansas, BA, 60, MA, 63; Univ Iowa, PhD, 70; Univ Reading, ND UK. **CAREER** Prof, 71- Univ FA; Instr, 68-70, Stanford Univ. **HONORS AND AWARDS** Ids Mem; SWR Sr Fel. **RESEARCH** Secularization; Popular Religion. **SELECTED PUBLICATIONS** Auth, The News Revolution in England: Cultural Dynamics of Daily Information, 96; The Secularization of Early Modern England: From Religious Culture to Religious Faith, 92; The Discovery of Childhood in Puritan England, 92; The Rise and Fall of Childhood, 90; Popular Religion in Restoration England, 77. **CONTACT ADDRESS** History Dept, Univ of Florida, Box 117320, Gainesville, FL 32611. **EMAIL** jsommerv@history.ufl.edu

SOMMERVILLE, JOHANN
PERSONAL Born 12/18/1953, Carshalton, Surrey, England, m, 1977 **DISCIPLINE** HISTORY **EDUCATION** Cambridge Univ, BA, 76; MA, 80; PhD, 81. **CAREER** Fel, St John's Col Cambridge, 80-84; Asst Prof to Prof, Univ Wisc, 88-. **HONORS AND AWARDS** Joseph Hodges Choate Memorial Fel, Harvard Univ, 76-77; R. Stanton Avery Distinguished Fel, Huntington Library, 98-99. **MEMBERSHIPS** Royal Hist Soc, N Am Conf of British Studies. **RESEARCH** Early modern Britain and Europe; History of political thought. **SELECTED PUBLICATIONS** auth, royalists and Patriots: Politics and Ideology in England, 1603-1640, 2nd ed, 99; auth, Thomas Hobbes: Political Ideas in Historical Context, 92. **CONTACT ADDRESS** Dept Hist, Univ of Wisconsin, Madison, 455 N Park St, Madison, WI 53706-1405.

SONN, RICHARD D.
DISCIPLINE HISTORY **EDUCATION** Univ Calif Berkeley, PhD. **CAREER** Assoc prof. **RESEARCH** France history; modern European history. **SELECTED PUBLICATIONS** Auth, Culture and Anarchy, Drunken Boat, 94; Anarchism, Twayne, 92; Anarchists, Artists and Aesthetes (rev), Nineteenth C Contexts, 91; The Early Political Career of Maurice Barres: Anarchist, Socialist, or Protofascist?, Clio, 91; British Anarchism, Garland, 93. **CONTACT ADDRESS** History Dept, Univ of Arkansas, Fayetteville, 416 Old Main, Fayetteville, AR 72701. **EMAIL** rsonn@comp.uark.edu

SORELLE, JAMES MARTIN
PERSONAL Born 02/01/1950, Waco, TX, m, 1973 **DISCIPLINE** AMERICAN HISTORY **EDUCATION** Univ Houston, BA, 72, MA, 74; Kent State Univ, PhD(hist), 80. **CAREER** Asst prof Afro-Am hist, Ball State Univ, 79-80; LECTR AM HIST, BAYLOR UNIV, 80- **MEMBERSHIPS** Orgn Am Historians; Southern Hist Asn. **RESEARCH** Afro-American history; urban history; 20th century United States. **SELECTED PUBLICATIONS** Auth, An de po cullud man is in de wuss fix uv awl: Black occupational status in Houston, Texas, 1920-1940, Houston Rev, spring 79; The Waco horror: The lynching of Jesse Washington, Southwestern Hist Quart (in prep). **CONTACT ADDRESS** Dept of Hist, Baylor Univ, Waco, Waco, TX 76798.

SORIA, REGINA
PERSONAL Born 05/17/1911, Rome, Italy, m, 1936 **DISCIPLINE** ITALIAN, ART **EDUCATION** Univ Rome, LittD, 33. **CAREER** From instr to assoc prof foreign lang, 42-61, prof Ital, 61-76, Emer Prof Mod Lang, Col Notre Dame, MD, 76. Instr Span, McCoy Col, 50-52; field researcher, Arch Am Art, 60-63, archivist, Rome Off, 63-64. **MEMBERSHIPS** MLA; Am Studies Asn; Am Asn Teachers Ital; AAUP. **RESEARCH** Biography and catalogue of the works of Elihu Vedder-American painter; American artists in Italy, 1760-1914; Italian participation in the visual arts of 18th and 19th century America. **SELECTED PUBLICATIONS** Auth, Washington Allston's lectures on art, the first American art treatise, J Aesthet & Art Criticism, 3/60; Some background for Elihu Vedder's Cumean Sibyl and Young Marysays, spring 60 & Elihu Vedder's mythical creatures, summer 63; Art Quart; Mark Twain and Vedder's Medusa, Am Quart, winter 64; Life of Elihu Vedder & spring, 76; Elihu Vedder, American Old Master, Ga Mus Art Bull, spring 76; Hendrik Andersen: American Sculptor, Ny Rev Of Books, Vol 40, 93. **CONTACT ADDRESS** 1609 Ramblewood Rd, Baltimore, MD 21239.

SORIN, GERALD
PERSONAL Born 10/23/1940, Brooklyn, NY, m, 1962, 1 child **DISCIPLINE** AMERICAN HISTORY **EDUCATION** Columbia Univ, BA, 62, PhD(Am hist), 69; Wayne State Univ, MA, 64. **CAREER** From asst prof to assoc prof, 65-77, prof hist, State Univ NY Col New Paltz, 77-, Danforth assoc, 70-; John Adams Distinguished Chair in American History (Fulbright, Netherlands), 98; Distinguished Teaching Prof, 94-. **MEMBERSHIPS** Orgn Am Historians; Am Jewish Hist Soc. **RESEARCH** Abolitionism; 19th century radicalism; Civil War; American Jewish experience. **SELECTED PUBLICATIONS** Auth, New York Abolitionists, Greenwood, 71; Abolitionism: A New Perspective, Praeger, 72; The Prophetic Minority, Indiana, 85; The Nurturing Neighborhood, New York Univ, 90; A Time for Building, John Hopkins, 92; Tradition Transformed, John Hopkins, 97. **CONTACT ADDRESS** Dept of Hist, SUNY, New Paltz, 75 S Manheim Blvd, New Paltz, NY 12561-2400. **EMAIL** soring@matrix.newpaltz.edu

SORKIN, DAVID
PERSONAL Born 09/22/1953, Chicago, IL, m, 1976, 4 children **DISCIPLINE** HISTORY **EDUCATION** Univ Wis Madison, BA, 75; Univ Cal Berkeley, MA, 77; PhD, 83. **CAREER** Asst Prof of Judaic Studies; Brown Univ, 83-86; Junior Research Fellow to Lecturer and Fellow, St. Anthony's College & Centre for Hebrew for Hebrew & Jewish Studies, Oxford Univ, 86-92; Frances & Laurence Weinstein Prof of Jewish Studies, Univ of Wisconsin-Madison, 92. **HONORS AND AWARDS** Tense/Joel H. Cavior Awd for the Best Book in History, 88; British Academy Grant, 91; National Endowment for the Humanities 94-5. **MEMBERSHIPS** Amer Historical Assoc; Assoc for Jewish Studies. **RESEARCH** Modern Jewish History; European Cultural and Religious History. **SELECTED PUBLICATIONS** Auth, "The Transformation of German Jewry, 1780-1840," 87; auth, "Moses Mendelssohn and the Religious Enlightenment," 96; auth, "The Berlin Haskalah and German Religious Though," 00. **CONTACT ADDRESS** Dept History, Univ of Wisconsin, Madison, 3211 Humanities; 455 N. Park St., Madison, WI 53706. **EMAIL** djsorkin@facstaff.wisc.edu

SORRENSON, RICHARD J.
DISCIPLINE HISTORY OF PHILOSOPHY **EDUCATION** Auckland Univ, MS, 84; Princeton Univ, PhD, 93. **CAREER** Asst prof, Ind Univ. **HONORS AND AWARDS** Res fel, Nat Sci Found; res fel, Ind Univ; res fel, Am Philos Soc. **MEMBERSHIPS** Am Philos Soc. **RESEARCH** Voyages of scientific discovery, history of technology, science and gender, the chemical revolution, science and enlightenment. **SELECTED PUBLICATIONS** Auth, The ship as a scientific instrument in the eighteenth century, Osiris. 96; Towards a history of the Royal Society of London in the 18th century, 96. **CONTACT ADDRESS** Dept of Hist and Philos of Sci, Indiana Univ, Bloomington, Goodbody 130, Bloomington, IN 47405. **EMAIL** rjs@indiana.edu

SORTOR, M.
PERSONAL Born 07/25/1957, New York, NY, m, 1981 **DISCIPLINE** HISTORY **EDUCATION** Univ CAL SD, PhD, 89. **CAREER** Assoc Prof, Asst Prof, teach/res, 89 to 95-, Grinnell College; Fel, 87-89, Stanford. **HONORS AND AWARDS** NEH Fel; Best Article in Urban Hist; Harris Fel. **MEMBERSHIPS** AHA; MA; RSA; SCS; SLCS; UHA. **RESEARCH** France and Flanders, 1250-1550; Urban History; Economic History. **SELECTED PUBLICATIONS** Coed, The Other side of Western Civilization, 92, 5th ed, 99; auth, The Ieperleet Affair: The Struggle for Market Position in Late Medieval Flanders, Speculum, 98; auth, Saint-Omer and Its Textile Trades in the Late Middle Ages: A Contribution to the Proto-Industrialization Debate, Amer Hist Rev, 98. **CONTACT ADDRESS** Dept of History, Grinnell Col, Grinnell, IL 50112. **EMAIL** sortor@grinnell.edu

SOSIN, JACK MARVIN
PERSONAL Born 04/17/1928, Hartford, CT, m, 1965, 1 child **DISCIPLINE** AMERICAN COLONIAL HISTORY **EDUCATION** Univ Conn, BA, 50, MA, 51; Ind Univ, PhD, 58. **CAREER** Lectr hist, Ind Univ, 57-58; from instr to assoc prof, 58-65, prof hist, Univ Nebr, Lincoln, 65-. **MEMBERSHIPS** AHA; Orgn Am Historians; Conf Brit Studies; fel Royal Hist Soc. **RESEARCH** British imperial history and administration. **SELECTED PUBLICATIONS** Auth, Whitehall and the Wilderness, Univ Nebr, 61; The proposal in the pre-Revolutionary decade for establishing bishops in the colonies, J Ecclesiastical Hist, 4/62; The Massachusetts Acts of 1774, Huntington Libr Quart, 5/63; Imperial regulation of colonial paper money, Penn Mag Hist, 4/64; Agents and Merchants, Univ Nebr, 65; The Revolutionary Frontier, Holt, 67. **CONTACT ADDRESS** Dept Hist, Univ of Nebraska, Lincoln, Lincoln, NE 68508.

SOSNOWSKI, THOMAS C.
PERSONAL Born 09/28/1945, MI, m, 1980, 2 children **DISCIPLINE** HISTORY **EDUCATION** Univ Detroit, BA, 67; Kent State Univ, MA, 70, PhD, 75; Laval Univ Quebec, 70. **CAREER** ASSOC PROF HIST, KENT STATE UNIV, STARK CAMPUS, 76-. **HONORS AND AWARDS** Dist Teaching Awd, Kent State Univ, 78, 85. **MEMBERSHIPS** Soc Fr Hist Stud; Western Soc Fr Hist; Ohio Acad Hist; Ohio Hist Soc; Stark County Hist Soc. **RESEARCH** Fr revolution; emigres; Ohio hist. **SELECTED PUBLICATIONS** various **CONTACT ADDRESS** 6000 Frank Ave NW, Canton, OH 44720. **EMAIL** tososnowski@stark.kent.edu

SOTO, SHIRLENE
PERSONAL Born San Luis Obispo, CA, m **DISCIPLINE** HISTORY **EDUCATION** San Francisco State Univ, BA, 69; Univ N Mex, MA, 71; PhD, 77. **CAREER** Instructor, Univ N

Mex, 76-77; Asst Prof, Calif Polytech State Univ, 77-80; Admin Fel to Prof and Asst Vice Pres, Calif State Univ, 80-. **HONORS AND AWARDS** Fel, Calif state Univ, 80-86; Fel, UCLA, 85-86; Deans Res Fund, 87-88; Grant, 91-96. **MEMBERSHIPS** Latin Am Studies Asn, Pacific Coast Coun on Latin Am Studies, Nat Asn for Chicana and Chicano Studies, W Asn of Women Hist, Mijeres Activas en Letras y Cambio Social. **RESEARCH** Mexico; Women in Mexico 20th Century; The Chicana; Women in Latin Am. **SELECTED PUBLICATIONS** Auth, Emergence of the Modern Mexican Woman: Her Participation in Revolution and Struggle for Equality 1910-1940, 90; contrib, "Latinas in the United States," in World History, 97; auth, Notable Hispanic American Women, 93. **CONTACT ADDRESS** Dept Chicano Studies, California State Univ, Northridge, 18111 Nordhoff St, Northridge, CA 91330-0001.

SOUCY, ROBERT J.
PERSONAL Born 06/25/1933, Topeka, KS, m, 1957, 2 children **DISCIPLINE** MODERN EUROPEAN HISTORY **EDUCATION** Washburn Univ, AB, 55; Univ Kans, MA, 57; Univ Wis, PhD(hist), 63. **CAREER** Instr hist, Harvard Univ, 63-64; asst prof, Kent State Univ, 64-66; asst prof, 66-76, assoc prof, 76-79, PROF HIST, OBERLIN COL, 79- **MEMBERSHIPS** AHA; Soc Fr Hist Studies. **RESEARCH** French fascism; late 19th and early 20th century French intellectual history. **SELECTED PUBLICATIONS CONTACT ADDRESS** Dept of Hist, Oberlin Col, Oberlin, OH 44070.

SOUTHARD, EDNA CARTER
PERSONAL Born 02/09/1945, Cairo, Egypt, m, 1969, 2 children **DISCIPLINE** RENAISSANCE ART HISTORY **EDUCATION** Barnard Col, BA, 66; Univ Chicago, MA, 73; Ind Univ, PhD(art hist-Renaissance), 78. **CAREER** Asst & researcher, New York Times, Brussels Bur, 67-69; asst manuscript ed, Univ Chicaago Press, 70-71; adj instr jour & art hist, Earlham Col, 74-76; adj assoc prof, Wright State Univ, 79-80; educ & prog coordr, 80-82; assoc curator, 82-86; ASST PROF ART HIST, curator of collections and exhibition, and MIAMI UNIV, 82-, Proj dir, Democracy in Peace & War: Great Books in Political Values, 78-79; adj asst prof, Ind Univ, 80-81 & Miami Univ, 81; US rep, Conf Int Negociants Oeuvres Art Competition, 79 & 80. **HONORS AND AWARDS** US rep, Conf Int Negociants Oeuvres Art Competition, 79 & 80; John Anson Kittredge Education Fundgrant, 95; Miami Univ Faculty Development grant, 95 and 83; Am Philosophical Society grant, 80; Am Council of Learned Soceities, grant-in-aid, 79. **MEMBERSHIPS** Col Art Asn; Am Asn Mus; Renaissance Soc Am; International Council of Museums. **RESEARCH** Italian Renaissance painting; 19th and 20th century European art; Sienese art and the Palazzo Pubblico; Jewish act. **SELECTED PUBLICATIONS** Auth, The earliest known decorations for the Palazzo Pubblico, Siena, Burlington Mag, 8, 79; The Frescoes in Siena's Palazzo Pubblico, 1289-1539, Garland, 79; Simone Martini's lost Marcus Regulus: Document rediscovered and a subject clarified, Zeitschrift f?r Kunstgeschichte, XLII, No 2-3, 79; Ambrogio Lorenzetti's Frescoes in the Sala della Pace: a change of names, Mitteilungen des Kunsthistorischen Institutes in Florenz, No 3, 80; auth, Reflections on the Documented Works by Simone Martini in the Palazzo Pubblico, Siena, in Simone Martinii Atti del Convegno, ed. Luciano Bellosi, Centro Di, 88; Kings And Connoisseurs--Collecting Art In 17th-Century Europe, Sixteenth Century J, Vol 27, 96; The Sienese Trecento Painter Bartolo-Di-Fredi, Sixteenth Century J, Vol 26, 95; auth, George Bottin: Painter of Montmartre, Miami Univ 84; auth, George Bottini in The Dictionary of Art, Macmillan, 95. **CONTACT ADDRESS** Art Mus, Miami Univ, 801 Patterson Ave, Oxford, OH 45056. **EMAIL** southael@muohio.edu

SOUTHARD, ROBERT FAIRBAIRN
PERSONAL Born 07/27/1945, Baltimore, MD, m, 1969, 2 children **DISCIPLINE** MODERN EUROPEAN HISTORY **EDUCATION** Columbia Univ, BA, 66; Univ Chicago, PhD, 74. **CAREER** Asst prof, 71-77, assoc prof, 77-81, prof hist, Earlham Col, 81- **MEMBERSHIPS** AAUP; AIS; MWJSA. **RESEARCH** History; European historiography; modern Jewish history. **SELECTED PUBLICATIONS** Auth, Marxist Rhetoric, Fascist Behavior, Alternative, 6-7/76; Theology in Droysen's early political historiography: Free will, necessity, and the historian, Hist & Theory, Vol XVIII, No 3; Droysen and the Prussian School of History, Lexington, 94. **CONTACT ADDRESS** Dept of Hist, Earlham Col, 801 National Rd W, Richmond, IN 47374-4095. **EMAIL** bobs@earlham.edu

SOUTHERLAND, JAMES EDWARD
PERSONAL Born 06/14/1942, Houston County, AL, m, 1964, 2 children **DISCIPLINE** LATIN AMERICAN HISTORY **EDUCATION** Univ Ga, AB, 65, MA, 67, PhD(Hist), 70. **CAREER** Asst prof, 69, assoc prof Hist, Brenau Univ, 82-, chmn, Humanities, 99-, 71-89; Nat Endowment for Humanities grants, 73-74. **HONORS AND AWARDS** BFA Outstanding faculty, 83; Outstanding faculty, 84; Panhellemc faculty Member of the year, 91; grant to participate in Freeman Found ASIANetwork Summer Inst in Asia Prog, 99. **MEMBERSHIPS** Southern Hist Asn; Southeast Council Latin Am Studies; AHA; ODK, 93. **RESEARCH** Mexican-United States relations. **SELECTED PUBLICATIONS** Auth, John Forsyth and the frustrated 1857 loan and land grab, WGa Col Studies in Soc Sci, 6/72; Samuel Adams in American Portraits, Vol I to 1877, Kendall/Hunt Publishing Co, 93; Biographical sketches of Eugene McCarthy, Joseph and Daniel Berrigan in The Vietnam War: An Encyclopedia, Garland Press, 96. **CONTACT ADDRESS** Dept of Humanities, Brenau Univ, One Centennial Circle, Gainesville, GA 30501-3697. **EMAIL** jsoutherland@lib.brenau.edu

SOUTHERN, DAVID WHEATON
PERSONAL Born 02/19/1938, Great Bend, KS, m, 1961, 1 child **DISCIPLINE** AMERICAN HISTORY **EDUCATION** Alderson-Broaddus Col, BA, 64; Wake Forest Univ, MA, 65; Emory Univ, PhD, 71. **CAREER** Instr hist, NC Wesleyan Col, 65-67; from asst prof to assoc prof, 70-86, prof hist, Westminster Col, Mo, 86-. **HONORS AND AWARDS** NEH fel, 82-83; res grant, Am Coun Learned Soc, 85, Am Philos Soc, 88; Cushwa Grant, Univ Notre Dame, 87; Gustavus Myers Awd - an outstanding book on intolerance, 87 & 96. **MEMBERSHIPS** Orgn Am Historians; AHA; Southern Hist Asn; Asn for Study of Negro Life and Hist. **RESEARCH** Black-white relations in America since the Civil War; American politics and reform, 1890 to 2000. **SELECTED PUBLICATIONS** Auth, An American Dilemma: Gunnar Myrdal and the civil rights cases of 1944-1954, J Hist Soc, spring 81; Beyond Jim Crow liberalism: Judge Waring and the fight against segregation in South Carolina, 1942-1952, J Negro Hist, fall 81; Gunnar Myrdal and Black-White Relations: The Use and Abuse of An American Dilemma, 1944-1969, Baton Rouge, 87; An American Dilemma after Fifty Years: Putting the Myrdal Study and Black-White Relations in Perspective, Hist Teacher, 2/95; John LaFarge and the Limits of Catholic Interracialism, 1911-1963, Baton Rouge, 96; But Think of the Kids: Catholic Interracialists and the Great American Taboo of Race Mixing, U.S. Cath Hist (forthcoming Fall 98); author of a number of book chapters and reviews. **CONTACT ADDRESS** Dept of Hist, Westminster Col, Missouri, 501 Westminster Ave, Fulton, MO 65251-1299. **EMAIL** southed@jaynet.wcmo.edu

SOWARDS, JESSE KELLEY
PERSONAL Born 05/12/1924, Clintwood, VA, m, 1946, 2 children **DISCIPLINE** EARLY MODERN EUROPEAN HISTORY **EDUCATION** Univ Wichita, AB, 47; Univ Mich, MA, 48, PhD(hist), 52. **CAREER** Instr hist, William Woods Col, 50-51; assoc prof hist & humanities, Northwest Mo State Col, 51-56; from asst prof to prof, 56-73, DISTINGUISHED PROF HIST, WICHITA STATE UNIV, 73-, DEAN LIB ARTS & SCI, 65-, Ford Found fac res grant, 53-54. **MEMBERSHIPS** AHA; Renaissance Soc Am; Mediaeval Acad Am; Cent Renaissance Conf (pres, 72). **RESEARCH** Renaissance and Reformation, especially intellectual history; Erasmus studies. **SELECTED PUBLICATIONS** Auth, Interpretations Of Erasmus C. 1750-1920--Man On His Own, Renaissance Quarterly, Vol 47, 94; Annotated Catalog Of Early Editions Of Erasmus At The Center-For-Reformation-And-Renaissance-Studies, Toronto, Sixteenth Century J, Vol 27, 96; Erasmus Annotations On The New-Testament, Galatians To The Apocalypse, Sixteenth Century J, Vol 25, 94; Historia And Fabula--Myths And Legends In Hist Thought From Antiquity To The Modern-Age, Sixteenth Century J, Vol 27, 96; Bibliotheca-Erasmiana-Bruxellensis--Catalog Of Erasmus Works Published In The 16th-Century Belonging To The Bibliotheque-Royale-Albert-1er, Sixteenth Century J, Vol 24, 93. **CONTACT ADDRESS** Dept of Hist, Wichita State Univ, Wichita, KS 67208.

SOWARDS, STEVEN W.
DISCIPLINE HISTORY, LIBRARY SCIENCE **EDUCATION** Stanford Univ, BA, 73; Ind Univ, MA, 76, PhD, 81, MLS, 86. **CAREER** Ref librn, Hanover Col, 86-88; hum librn, Swarthmore Col, 88-96; soc scis & hum ref, 96-98, head, main libr ref, Mich State Univ librs, 98-. **HONORS AND AWARDS** Fulbright res fel, Vienna, 77-78 **MEMBERSHIPS** ALA, Libr Hist Round Table, MLA. **RESEARCH** Mod Balkan hist; hist librs; web-based ref tools. **SELECTED PUBLICATIONS** Auth, Austria's Policy of Macedonian Reform, East European Monographs, 89; auth, Historical Fabrications in Library Collections, Collection Management 10/3- 4, 88; auth, Save the Time of the Surfer: Evaluating Web Sites for Users, Library Hi Tech 15/3-4, 97; auth, A Typology for Ready Reference Web Sites in Libraries, First Monday: Peer-Reviewed J on the Internet 3/5. May 98; auth, "Novas, Niches and Icebergs: Practical Lessons for Small-Scale Web Publishers," in JEP: The J of Electronic Publishing, vol 5, 99. **CONTACT ADDRESS** Libraries, Michigan State Univ, 100 Library, East Lansing, MI 48224. **EMAIL** sowards@msu.edu

SOYER, DANIEL
DISCIPLINE AMERICAN IMMIGRATION AND ETHNICITY **EDUCATION** NYork Univ, PhD. **CAREER** Asst prof, 97, Fordham Univ. **HONORS AND AWARDS** Thomas J Wilson prize, Harvard UP, 97, Co-winner, Viener Prize. **MEMBERSHIPS** Am Jeweish Historical Soc, Academic Council, Am Jewish Historical Soc. **RESEARCH** Documentation of immigrant lives through autobiography. **SELECTED PUBLICATIONS** Auth, Jewish Immigrant Associations and American Identity in New York, 1880-1939, Harvard UP, 97 **CONTACT ADDRESS** Dept of Hist, Fordham Univ, Rose Hill Campus, Bronx, NY 10458.

SPALL, RICHARD
PERSONAL Born 12/01/1952, Logansport, IN, m, 1972, 2 children **DISCIPLINE** HISTORY OF BRITAIN **EDUCATION** Wittenberg Univ, BA, 77; Univ Ill, AM, 79; Univ Ill, PhD, 85. **CAREER** Grad teaching asst, Univ Ill, 78-82; Babcock res fel, Univ Ill, 82-83; grad col fel/Von Mises Fel, 83; vis lectr, Univ Ill, 83-84; vis instr, OWU, 84-85; vis asst prof, OWU, 85-86; asst prof, OWU, 85-89; assoc prof, OWU, 89-96; book review ed, The Historian, 93-; Cornelia Coles Fairbanks prof of hist, 96-. **HONORS AND AWARDS** Cornelia Coles Fairbanks Endowed Professorship, Ohio Wesleyan Univ; Sherwood Dodge Shanklin Teaching Award, Ohio Wesleyan Univ; All-Campus Award for Excellence in Teaching, Univ Ill; Col of Humanities Outstanding Teaching Award, Univ Ill; Phi Kappa Phi Academic Honor Soc; Laurence Marcellus Larson Prize, Univ Ill; Joseph Ward Swain Prize, Univ Ill; Margaret S. Ermarth Award, Wittenberg Univ; Paul F. Bloomhardt Award, Wittenberg Univ; Phi Alpha Theta. **MEMBERSHIPS** Anglo Am Conference of Historians; British History Asn; Conference of Historical Journals; Healey Institute; Historical Asn; Inst of Historical Res; Midwest Conference on British Studies; Ohio Academy of History; Phi Alpha Theta. **RESEARCH** Free trade radicalism; Victorianism; 19th-Century British political and social reform. **SELECTED PUBLICATIONS** Auth, "John Bright", in Research Guide to European Historical Biography 1450 to the Present, Beacham, 93; auth, "Anthony Ashley Cooper, 7th earl of Shaftsbury", "Henry John Temple, 3rd Viscount Palmerston", "Sir Robert Peel", in Historical Leaders of the World, Gale Research, 94; auth, "Review of the 'Victorian World Picture'", in Albion 30, Rutgers Univ Press, 97. **CONTACT ADDRESS** Ohio Wesleyan Univ, 400 Elliott Hall, Delaware, OH 43015. **EMAIL** rfspall@cc.owu.edu

SPANGLER, MAY
PERSONAL Born 04/24/1956, Boulogne Billahcourt, France, m, 1980, 3 children **DISCIPLINE** FRENCH LITERATURE, ARCHITECTURE, ART **EDUCATION** Ecole des Beaux-Arts, MA, 82; Emory Univ, MA, 92; PhD, 96. **CAREER** Intern architect, Ateliers Remondet and Taieb, 79; intern architect, Helfrich and Briles Architects, 80-83; intern architect, Rabun and Hatch Architects, Inc., 85-89; free-lance architect, 85-89; instr, Agnes Scott Col; instr, Emory Univ. **HONORS AND AWARDS** Scholar, Ga Inst of Technol Col of Archit, 78; Traveling Scholar, Ga Inst of Technol Col of Archit, 78; Traveling Grant, Ecole des Beaux-Arts, 79; Grad Sch Fel, Emory Univ, 91-96; Anne Amari Perry Awd, 95. **MEMBERSHIPS** MLA. **RESEARCH** Cultural Studies: Literature, Architecture and Art (with an emphasis on Paris), Eighteenth-Century French Literature and History of Ideas (with an emphasis on Diderot and Natural Science). **SELECTED PUBLICATIONS** Auth, "Science, philosophie et litterature: le polype de Diderot," Recherches sur Diderot et sur l'Encyclopedie 23 (97); auth, "L'accident du moderne dans l'ubanisme parisien," Orage 11 (97); rev, of "Denis Diderot: Extravagance et genialite," by Marie-Helene Chabut, Symposium (forthcoming). **CONTACT ADDRESS** Dept Fr & Ital, Emory Univ, 1364 Clifton Rd NE, Atlanta, GA 30322-1061. **EMAIL** mspangl@emory.edu

SPANN, EDWARD K.
PERSONAL Born 04/12/1931, Fairlawn, NJ, m, 1961, 4 children **DISCIPLINE** HISTORY **EDUCATION** Iona Col, BA, 52; NYork Univ, MA, 53; PhD, 57. **CAREER** Researcher, Sleepy Hollow Restorations, 58; lectr, Hunter Col, 58-60; instr, NYork Univ, 60; asst ed, Albert Lallatin Papers, 61; from asst prof to prof, Ind State Univ, 61-. **HONORS AND AWARDS** Dixon Ryan Fox Manuscript Awd, 77; Research/Creativity Awd, Ind State Univ, 83; Distinguished Alumni Awd, Iowa Col, 83; Distinguished Prof, Ind State Univ Col of Arts and Sci, 98. **MEMBERSHIPS** Urban Hist Asn, Ind Hist Soc. **RESEARCH** History, Nineteenth-century U. S., Urban Utopianism. **SELECTED PUBLICATIONS** Auth, Ideals of Politics, 72; auth, The New Metropolis, 81 & 83; auth, Brotherly Tomorrows, 89; auth, Hopedale, 92; auth, Designing Modern America, 96. **CONTACT ADDRESS** Dept Hist, Indiana State Univ, 210 N 7th St, Stalker Hall, Terre Haute, IN 47809-0001. **EMAIL** spann@indynet.com

SPARKS, ESTHER
DISCIPLINE AMERICAN WORKS ON PAPER, FOLK ART OF THE AMERICAS **EDUCATION** Univ Chicago, BA; Northwestern Univ, MA, PhD. **CAREER** Dir, W Graham Arader III Gallery, Chicago; cur, Northwestern Univ; cur, Art Inst of Chicago; Vis Prof, Univ Miss. **SELECTED PUBLICATIONS** Auth, Universal Limited Art Editions: A History of the First 25 Years, Harry N Abrams, 89. **CONTACT ADDRESS** Art Dept, Univ of Mississippi, 205 Bryant Hall, University, MS 38677. **EMAIL** esparks@olemiss.edu

SPATZ, NANCY
PERSONAL Born 03/05/1961, Chicago, IL **DISCIPLINE** MEDIEVAL STUDIES **EDUCATION** Northwestern Univ, BA, 83; Cornell Univ, MA, 86, PhD, 92 **CAREER** Lect, 90-91, Alfred Univ; Asst Prof, 91-96, Univ of N Colo; Visit Asst Prof, 94-95, Colo Col; Assoc Prof, Univ of N Colo, 96-99; lectr, Santa Clara Univ, 99- . **HONORS AND AWARDS** NEH Summer Seminar in Rome **MEMBERSHIPS** Medieval Acad of Am **RESEARCH** Medieval Hist **SELECTED PUBLICA-**

TIONS Auth, "Evidence of Inception Ceremonids in the Twelfth-Century schools of Paris," Hist of Univ 13 (94): 3-19; auth, "Church Porches and the Liturgy and Twelfth-Century Rome," in the Medieval Liturgy: A Volume for Teaching, eds Thomas Heffernan & E. Ann Matter (Kalamazoo, MI, 01). **CONTACT ADDRESS** Hist Dept, Santa Clara Univ, 500 El Camino Real, Santa Clara, CA 95053. **EMAIL** nancyspatz@aol.com

SPEAR, ALLAN H.
DISCIPLINE HISTORY **EDUCATION** Yale Univ, MA, PhD. **CAREER** Assoc prof **RESEARCH** Recent American history; Afro-American history; Minnesota history. **SELECTED PUBLICATIONS** Auth, Black Chicago: The Making of a Negro Ghetto, 1890-1920, 67. **CONTACT ADDRESS** History Dept, Univ of Minnesota, Twin Cities, 614 Social Sciences Tower, 267 19th Ave S, Minneapolis, MN 55455. **EMAIL** spear001@tc.umn.edu

SPECHT, NEVA JEAN
PERSONAL Born 01/31/1967, Marshalltown, IA **DISCIPLINE** HISTORY **EDUCATION** Grinnell Col, BA, 89; Univ Del, MA, 91; PhD, 97. **CAREER** Instr, Univ of Del, 95-96; lectr to asst prof, Appalachian State Univ, 96-. **MEMBERSHIPS** AHA; OAH; AAM; SHEAR. **RESEARCH** Early American social and cultural history, religion, migration and Society of Friends. **CONTACT ADDRESS** Dept Hist, Appalachian State Univ, PO Box 32072, Boone, NC 28607. **EMAIL** spechtnj@appstate.edu

SPECTOR, DANIEL E.
PERSONAL Born 12/19/1942, Pensacola, FL, m, 1964, 2 children **DISCIPLINE** HISTORY **EDUCATION** George Washington Univ, BA, 63; Univ Tex, MA, 72; PhD, 75. **CAREER** Chemical Corps Historian, 88-94; Adj Prof, Univ Ala, 88-. **HONORS AND AWARDS** Fel, Univ FL; Fel, Univ TX. **MEMBERSHIPS** Am Hist Asn; MESA; MEI; Soc for Military Hist. **RESEARCH** Middle East; Military history. **CONTACT ADDRESS** Dept Hist, Univ of Alabama, Birmingham, 1530 3rd Ave S, Birmingham, AL 35294-0001. **EMAIL** spectord@aol.com

SPECTOR, JACK
DISCIPLINE MODERN ART **EDUCATION** Columbia Univ, PhD. **CAREER** Prof II, Rutgers, The State Univ NJ, Univ Col-Camden. **SELECTED PUBLICATIONS** Auth, Surrealist Art and writing, 1919 to 1939, The Gold of Tome, Cambridge UP, 96; Medusa on the Barricades, in Am Image, Vol 53, no 1, 96; Delacroix's Liberty on the Barricades in 1815 and 1830, in Source, Notes on the Hist of Art, vol xv no 3, 96; ed, American Image, Vol 53, nos 1 and 2, 96. **CONTACT ADDRESS** Dept of Art Hist, Rutgers, The State Univ of New Jersey, New Brunswick, Voorhees Hall, 71 Hamilton St, New Brunswick, NJ 08903.

SPECTOR, RONALD H.
PERSONAL Born 01/17/1943, Pittsburgh, PA, m, 1970, 2 children **DISCIPLINE** HISTORY **EDUCATION** Johns Hopkins Univ, AB, 64; Yale Univ, MA, 66; PhD, 67. **CAREER** Instr, Yale Univ, 66-67; Asst Prof, La St Univ, 69-71; Assoc Prof, Univ Ala, 86-90; Prof, George Wash Univ, 90-. **HONORS AND AWARDS** Fulbright Hays Lectr, New Delhi, India, 77-78; USIA Vis Lectr, Philippines, Thailand, 77; AHA Rep, U S St Dept, 89-91; Guest Scholar, Woodrow Wilson Int Ctr, 90; Sr Fel, Rutgers Univ, 94. **MEMBERSHIPS** SMH, Ctr for Strategic and Int Studies. **RESEARCH** Researching Viet Nam experience, George Dewey, American military history. **SELECTED PUBLICATIONS** Auth, Advice and Support: The Early Years 1941-1960 (The U S Army in Vietnam), paperback ed, MacMillan/Free Pr, 83; auth, Eagle Against the Sun: The American War with Japan, Free Pr/MacMillan (New York), 84; auth, "How Do You Know if You're Winning? Perception and Reality in America's Military Performances in Vietnam," in The Vietnam War (London: Macmillan Pr, 93); auth, "Seizing Japan's Strategic Points," in From Pearl Harbor to Hiroshima (London: MacMillan Pr, 94); auth, After Tet: The Bloodiest Year in Vietnam, Free Pr (New York), 92. **CONTACT ADDRESS** Dept Hist, The George Washington Univ, 2035 H St NW, Washington, DC 20052-0001. **EMAIL** spector@gwu.edu

SPECTOR, SCOTT
DISCIPLINE HISTORY **EDUCATION** John Hopkins Univ, PhD, 93 **CAREER** Asst Prof, Univ MI, 00-. **SELECTED PUBLICATIONS** Auth, Prague Territories: National Conflict and Cultural Innovation in Kafka's Fin de Siecle, Berkeley and Los Angeles: Univ Cal Press, 00. **CONTACT ADDRESS** Dept of History, Univ of Michigan, Ann Arbor, Ann Arbor, MI 48109-1003. **EMAIL** spec@umich.edu

SPECTOR, SHERMAN DAVID
PERSONAL Born 05/07/1927, Andover, MA, m, 1955, 3 children **DISCIPLINE** HISTORY OF RUSSIA & EAST CENTRAL EUROPE **EDUCATION** Bowdoin Col, AB, 49; Columbia Univ, AM, 51, PhD, 60. **CAREER** Lectr polit sci, George Washington Univ, 53-55; lectr hist, Pace Col, 56-57; asst prof, State Univ NY, Albany, 57-60; asst prof, 60-68, coordr spec events, 77-82, PROF HIST, RUSSELL SAGE COL, 68-, State Univ NY Res Found grant-in-aid, 57; consult foreign area studies, NY State Educ Dept, 63-70; Fulbright-Hays prof hist, Univ Bucharest, 70; dir, Sage Soviet Summer Sem, E Europe, 71 & 72. **MEMBERSHIPS** AHA **RESEARCH** History of modern Rumania; 20th century Russia. **SELECTED PUBLICATIONS** Auth, Rumania at the Paris Peace Conference, Twayne, 62; Rumania, Encycl American, 64-76; ed, A History of the Balkan Peoples, Twayne, 72; auth, Rumania & Bulgaria at (the) Paris Peace Conference, In: A History of First World War, Purnell, London, 72; ed, A History of the Romanian Peoples, GK Hall, 74; auth, Soviet Moldavia, In: Nationalism in the USSR, Univ Detroit, 77. **CONTACT ADDRESS** Dept of Hist, Russell Sage Col, Troy, NY 12180.

SPEIDEL, MICHAEL PAUL
PERSONAL Born 05/25/1937, Pforzheim, Germany, m, 1966, 2 children **DISCIPLINE** ROMAN HISTORY **EDUCATION** Univ Freiburg, PhD, 62. **CAREER** Lectr hist & Ger, Chulalongkorn Univ, Bangkok, 62-64; dir studies, Ger lang, Goethe House, Montreal, 65-68; assoc prof, 68-73, prof ancient hist, Univ Hawaii, Manoa, 73-, Chmn, Dept of History, Univ of Hawaii; lectr Ger, McGill Univ, 66-68; Am Coun Learned Soc grant-in-aid, 73-74; vis prof Roman Hist, Univ S Africa, 75; Nat Endowment for Humanities res tool grant, 76; vis prof Univ Wien/Austria. **MEMBERSHIPS** Ger Archaeol Inst. **RESEARCH** Greek and Roman epigraphy and papyrology; history of the Roman Empire; history of the Roman Army. **SELECTED PUBLICATIONS** Auth, Equites Singulares Augusti, Bonn, 65; auth, Guards of the Roman Armies, Bonn, 78; auth, Mithras-Orion, Leiden, 80; auth, Iuppiter Dolichenus, Aalen, 80; auth, Roman Army Studies I and II, Amsterdam and Stuttgart, 84 & 92; auth, Die Denkmaler der Kaiserreiter, Cologne, 94; auth, Riding for Caesar: The Roman Emperors' Horse Guard, Harvard Univ Press, 94; auth, Wolf Warriors (forthcoming). **CONTACT ADDRESS** Dept of Hist, Univ of Hawaii, Manoa, 2530 Dole St, Honolulu, HI 96822-2303. **EMAIL** Speidel@hawaii.edu

SPELLMAN, PAUL
PERSONAL Born 12/08/1948, Corpus Christi, TX, m, 1972, 2 children **DISCIPLINE** HISTORY **EDUCATION** SW Univ, BA, 71; Univ Tex-Austin, MA, 87; Univ Houston, PhD, 97. **CAREER** Instr, hist, Texas A & I Univ, 91-94, Houston Commun Col, 94-98, Wharton Jr Col, 98- . **MEMBERSHIPS** Texas State Hist Asn; Texas Storytellers Asn. **RESEARCH** Texas history, Southwest. **SELECTED PUBLICATIONS** Auth, Race tp Velasio, Hendrick-Long, (95); auth, Forgotten Texas Leader, Texas A & M Press, (99); auth, Spindletop Boom Daysm Texas A & M Press, (00). **CONTACT ADDRESS** Dept Soc Sci, Wharton County Junior Col, 911 E Boling Highway, Wharton, TX 77488-3252. **EMAIL** Drpaulspellman@hotmail.com

SPENCE, CLARK CHRISTIAN
PERSONAL Born 05/25/1923, Great Falls, MT, m, 1953, 2 children **DISCIPLINE** AMERICAN HISTORY **EDUCATION** Univ Colo, BA, 48, MA, 51; Univ Minn, PhD(hist), 55. **CAREER** Instr hist, Carleton Col, 54-55; from instr to assoc prof, Pa State Univ, 55-60; vis lectr, Univ Calif, Berkeley, 60-61; assoc prof, 61-64, chmn dept, 67-70,prof hist, Univ IL, Urbana, 64-90, emeritus, 90-, Ford Found fac fel, soc sci res on bus, 63-64; Guggenheim fel, 70-71. **HONORS AND AWARDS** Beveridge Awd, AHA, 56; Bk Awd, Agr Hist Soc, 59. **MEMBERSHIPS** AHA; Orgn Am Historians; Agr Hist Soc; Western Hist Asn(Pres, 69-70). **RESEARCH** Western American; agricultural and mineral history. **SELECTED PUBLICATIONS** Auth, God Speed the Plow: The Coming of Steam Cultivation to Great Britain, Univ IL, 60; auth, The Sinews of American Capitalism, Hill & Wang, 64; auth, Mining Engineers and the American West: The Lace-Boot Brigade, 1849-1933, Yale Univ, 70; auth, Territorial Politics and Government in Montana, 1864-1889, Univ IL, 75; auth, Montana: A Bicentennial History, Norton, 78; auth, The Rainmakers: American 'Pluviculture' to World War II, Univ NE, 80; auth, The Salvation Army Farm Colonies, Univ AZ, 85; auth, The Conrey Placer Mining Company: A Pioneer Gold Dredging Enterprise in Montana, 1897-1922, Mont Hist Soc, 89; auth, The Northern Gold Fleet: Twentieth-Century Gold Dredging in Alaska, Univ IL, 96; auth, For Wood River or Bust: Idaho's Silver Boom of the 1880s, Moscow & Boise, Univ ID, 99. **CONTACT ADDRESS** Dept of HIst, Univ of Illinois, Urbana-Champaign, Urbana, IL 61801. **EMAIL** c-spence@wuc.edu

SPENCE, JONATHAN DERMOT
PERSONAL Born 08/11/1936, Surrey, England, m, 1993, 2 children **DISCIPLINE** HISTORY OF CHINA **EDUCATION** Cambridge Univ, BA, 59; Yale Univ, PhD, 65. **CAREER** Mem fac, 56-71, prof hist, Yale Univ, 71-, chmn, coun E Asian studies, 77-, Ed, Ch'ing-shih wen-t'i, 66-73; rev ed, J Asian Studies, 73-75; dir, Nat Endowment for Humanities Sem, 77. **HONORS AND AWARDS** Guggenheim fel; McArthur fel; Am Philos Soc; Am Acad of Arts and Sciences; fel of the British Acad. **MEMBERSHIPS** Asn Asian Studies; AHA. **RESEARCH** History of China since 1600. **SELECTED PUBLICATIONS** Auth, The Death of Woman Wang, Viking, 78; auth, The Gate of Heavenly Peace, Viking, 80; auth, The Memory Palace of Matteo Ricci, Viking, 84; auth, The Question of Hu, Knopf, 87; auth, The Search for Modern China, Norton, 90; auth, Cinese Roundabout, Norton, 92; auth, God's Chinese Son, Norton, 97; auth, The Chan's Great Continent, Norton, 99; auth, Mao Zedong, Penguin-Lipper, 00; auth, Treason by the Book, Viking-Penguin, 01. **CONTACT ADDRESS** Dept of Hist, Yale Univ, P O Box 208324, New Haven, CT 06520-8324. **EMAIL** jonathan.spence@yale.edu

SPENCE, MARY LEE
PERSONAL Born 09/04/1927, Kyle, TX, m, 1953, 2 children **DISCIPLINE** AMERICAN HISTORY **EDUCATION** Univ Tex, BA, 47; MA, 48; Univ Minn, PhD, 57. **CAREER** From instr to asst prof soc sci, Southwest Tex State Univ, 48-53; lectr, Pa State Univ, 55-58; from asst prof to prof emer, Univ Ill, Urbana-Champaign, 73-. **HONORS AND AWARDS** Nat Hist Pub & Rec Com grants, 77-78, 87-90; Huntington Libr fel, 92. **MEMBERSHIPS** Orgn Am Historians; Asn Doc Edit; Western Hist Asn (pres, 81-82). **RESEARCH** Western America, women's history. **SELECTED PUBLICATIONS** Coed, The Expeditions of John Charles Fremont, 5 vols, Univ of Ill Press, 70-84; coauth, Fanny Kelly's Narrative of her Captivity Among the Sioux Indians, Donnelly, 90; coauth, The Letters of Jessie Benton Fremont, Univ of Ill Press, 93; auth, The Arizona Diary of Lily Fremont, 1878-1881, Univ of Ariz Press, 97. **CONTACT ADDRESS** Dept of Hist, Univ of Illinois, Urbana-Champaign, Urbana, IL 61801. **EMAIL** c-spence@uiuc.edu

SPENCER, ELAINE GLOVKA
PERSONAL Born 09/17/1939, Rice Lake, WI, m, 1966, 1 child **DISCIPLINE** HISTORY **EDUCATION** Lewis & Clark Col, BA, 61; Univ Calif, Berkeley, MA, 62, PhD(hist), 69. **CAREER** Asst prof 69-81, assoc prof, 81-91, prof, Northern Ill Univ, 92-, dept chmn, 95-99. **HONORS AND AWARDS** Newcomen Special Award, Bus Hist, 79; Hermann E Krooss Prize, Bus Hist Conf, 81. **MEMBERSHIPS** AHA **RESEARCH** Modern German social history. **SELECTED PUBLICATIONS** Auth, Managers and Labor in Impaerial Germany: Rughr Industrialists as Employers 1896-1914, Rutgers Univ Press, 84; auth, State Power and Local Interests in Prussian Cities: Police in the Dusseldorf district 1848-1914," Central European Hist 19, (86), 293-313; auth, Prussia's Rhine Province 1815-1914," Journal of Urvan Hist 16, (90), 366-385; Workers Culture In Imperial Germany--Leisure And Recreation In Rhineland And Westphalia, Histoire Sociale-Social Hist, Vol 26, 93; Regimenting Revelry--Rhenish Carnival In The Early-19th-Century, Central European Hist, Vol 28, 95; auth, "Custom, Commerce, and Contention: Rhenish Carnival Celabratiuons 1890-1914," German Studies Review 20, (97), 323-2341. **CONTACT ADDRESS** Dept of Hist, No Illinois Univ, 1425 W Lincoln Hwy, De Kalb, IL 60115-2825. **EMAIL** espencer@niu.edu

SPENCER, GEORGE W.
PERSONAL Born 08/30/1939, Wooster, OH, m, 1966, 1 child **DISCIPLINE** SOUTH ASIAN HISTORY **EDUCATION** Univ Md, BA, 61; Univ Calif, Berkeley, MA, 63, PhD, 67. **CAREER** Asst Prof, 67-73, Assoc Prof, 73-84, Prof Hist, Northern Ill Univ, 84-, asst chair, dir grad stud, 85-90, Dept Chair, 90-95, 99-. **MEMBERSHIPS** Asn Asian Studies; AHA. **RESEARCH** Political, social and economic implications of religious movements and institutions in early South India. **SELECTED PUBLICATIONS** Auth, The Politics of Expansion: The Chola Conquest of Sri Lanka and Sri Vijaya, Madras: New Era Publications, 83; ed, Temples, Kings and Peasants: Perceptions of South India's Past, Madras: New Era Publications, 87; auth, "Trade, Prestige and the State in Medieval South India: Some Characteristics," in Proceedings of the Thirteenth International Symposium on Asian Studies, 1991 (Hong Kong: Asian Research Service, 92), 447-57; auth, "Snapshots of South Indian Studies in the United States," IATR Newsletter, International Association of Tamil Research (97): 4-8; auth, "In Search of Change: Reflections on the Scholarship of Noboru Karashima," in Kenneth R. Hall ed., Structure and Change in Early South India: Essays in Honor of Professor Noboru Karashima, (Delhi: Oxford Univ Press, 99), 28-43. **CONTACT ADDRESS** Dept of History, No Illinois Univ, De Kalb, IL 60115-2893. **EMAIL** gspencer@niu.edu

SPENCER, HEATH A.
PERSONAL Born 09/26/1966, Seattle, WA, m, 1988, 3 children **DISCIPLINE** HISTORY **EDUCATION** Univ Ky, BA, 88, MA, 92, PhD, 97 **CAREER** Asst prof, Ks Wesleyan Univ, 95- **MEMBERSHIPS** German Stud Assoc; Conf Group on Cent Eur Hist; Phi Alpha Theta. **RESEARCH** German social & religious hist in the nineteenth & twentieth cent **CONTACT ADDRESS** Dept of History, Kansas Wesleyan Univ, Salina, KS 67401. **EMAIL** spencerh@kwu.edu

SPERBER, JONATHON
PERSONAL Born 12/26/1952, New York, NY, m, 1990, 1 child **DISCIPLINE** HISTORY **EDUCATION** Cornell Univ, AB, 73; Univ Chicago, MA, 74, PhD, 80. **CAREER** Archivist, Leo Baeck Inst, New York, 79-82; vis asst prof, Northwestern Univ, 82-84; Asst prof to assoc prof to prof, Univ Mo Columbia, 84- . **HONORS AND AWARDS** Fel, Alexander von Hum-

boldt-Stiftung, 87-88; Fel, John Simon Guggenheim Memorial Found, 88-89; Herbert Baxter Adams Prize, Amer Hist Assoc, 85; German Stud Assoc/German Acad Exchange Svc book prize, 93; Allan Sharlin Memorial Awd, Soc Sci Hist Assoc, 98; NEH Fel, 01-02; phi beta kappa, 73; grad student fel of the german acad exchange svc, 76-78. **MEMBERSHIPS** Amer Hist Assoc; German Stud Assoc. **RESEARCH** Soc, polit & relig hist of nineteenth century Germany & modern Europe. **SELECTED PUBLICATIONS** Auth, Popular Catholicism in Nineteenth Century German, Princeton Univ Press, 84; Rhineland Radicals: The Democratic Movement and the Revolution of 1848-1849, Princeton Univ Press, 91; The European Revolutions, 1848-1851, Cambridge Univ Press, 94; The Kaiser's Voters: Electors and Elections in Imperial Germany, Cambridge Univ Press, 97; auth, Revolutionayr Europe 1780-1850, Longman, 00. **CONTACT ADDRESS** Dept of History, Univ of Missouri, Columbia, Read Hall, Columbia, MO 65211. **EMAIL** sperberj@missouri.edu

SPERRY, KIP
PERSONAL Born 05/24/1940, Chardon, OH, m, 1973, 1 child **DISCIPLINE** HISTORY **EDUCATION** Brigham Young Univ, AS, 70; BS, 71; MLS, 74. **CAREER** Asst/Assoc Prof, Brigham Young Univ, 91-. **HONORS AND AWARDS** Fel, Am Soc of Genealogist; Fel, Nat Geneal Soc; Fel, Ut Geneal Asn. **MEMBERSHIPS** Am Soc of Genealogist, Nat Geneal Soc, New England Hist Geneal Soc. **RESEARCH** Teaching American genealogy and family history, Research in United States, Canada, England, Scotland, and Isle of Man, Writing and editing, Paleography. **SELECTED PUBLICATIONS** Auth, New England Genealogical Research: A Guide to Sources, (Bowie, Md), 88; auth, Genealogical Research in Ohio, (Baltimore, Md), 97; auth, Reading Early American Handwriting, (Baltimore, Md), 98; auth, Abbreviations & Acronyms: A Guide for Family Historians, (Orem, Ut), 00. **CONTACT ADDRESS** Brigham Young Univ, 210E JSB, Provo, UT 84602-5644. **EMAIL** Kip_Sperry@byu.edu

SPETTER, ALLAN BURTON
PERSONAL Born 12/24/1939, Brooklyn, NY, m, 1966 **DISCIPLINE** AMERICAN DIPLOMATIC HISTORY **EDUCATION** Rutgers Univ, BA, 60, MA, 61 PhD(hist), 67. **CAREER** Asst prof hist, 67-71, asst dean, Col Lib Arts, 71-74, ASSOC PROF HIST, WRIGHT STATE UNIV, 71- **MEMBERSHIPS** AHA; Orgn Am Historians; Soc Hist Am Foreign Rels. **RESEARCH** American diplomacy, 1865-1900. **SELECTED PUBLICATIONS** Auth, The Presidency of Benjamin Harrison, Univ Press of Kansas, 87. **CONTACT ADDRESS** 731 Torrington Pl, 466 Millett Hall, Dayton, OH 45406. **EMAIL** allan.spetter@wright.edu

SPIEGEL, GABRIELLE MICHELE
PERSONAL Born 01/20/1943, New York, NY, m, 1965, 2 children **DISCIPLINE** MEDIEVAL HISTORY, HISTORIOGRAPHY **EDUCATION** Bryn Mawr Col, BA, 64; Harvard Univ, MAT, 65; John Hopkins Univ, MA, 70; PhD(hist), 74. **CAREER** Lectr hist, Bryn Mawr Col, 72-73; asst prof, 74-79, assoc prof hist, 79-92, prof, 92-93, Univ MD; prof, 93-, Johns Hopkins Univ. **HONORS AND AWARDS** Elected fel of the Medieval Acad, 96; Nat Endowment for the Humanities Travel to Collections grant, 91; Center for Advanced Study in the Behavioral Sciences, Stanford Univ, fel (NEH and Mellon), 89-90; William Koren Jr. Prize, 88; John Simor Guggenheim found, fel, 88; Hon Rockefeller Residency fel, 87-88; Nat Endowment for the Humanities Summer Stipend, 79, summer res grant, 76. **MEMBERSHIPS** Medieval Acad Am; Southeastern Medieval Asn; AHA; Berkshire Conf Women Historians (pres, 81-83). **RESEARCH** Capetian history; historiography; French historiography. **SELECTED PUBLICATIONS** auth, Romancing rhe Past: The Rise of Vernacular Prose Historiography in Thirteenth-Century France, Univ of Calif Press (Berkeley), 95; auth, The Past as Text: The Theory and Prcatice of Medieval Historiography, Johns Hopkins Univ Press (Baltimore), 97, auth, Il Passato come Testo. Teoria e pratica della storiografia medievale, Picola biblioteca di storia, Instituti Editoriali e Poligrafici Internaziionali (Pisa-Roma), 98; auth, "In the Mirror's Eye: The Writing of Medieval History in North America," in Imagined Histories: The State of Historical Wiritng in North America, ed. Anthony Molho and Gordon S. Wood (Princeton Univ Press, 98), 238-262; auth, "Theory into Practice: Reading Medieval Chronicles," The Medieval Chronicle Proceedings of the First Int Conference on the Medieval Chronicle (Amsterdam, Atlanta, 99): 1-12; cotrans, Stories of a Historian: Kantorowicz by Alain Boureau, Johns Hopkins Univ Press, forthcoming. **CONTACT ADDRESS** Dept of Hist, Johns Hopkins Univ, Baltimore, 3400 N. Charles St., Baltimore, MD 21218. **EMAIL** spiegel@jhunix.hcf.jhu.edu

SPILLER, ROGER JOSEPH
PERSONAL Born 10/19/1944, Bonham, TX, m, 1971 **DISCIPLINE** AMERICAN MILITARY HISTORY **EDUCATION** Southwest Tex State Univ, BA, 69, MA, 71; La State Univ, PhD(Am hist), 77. **CAREER** Instr US hist, Southwest Tex State Univ, 74-78; vis assoc prof, 78-80, ASSOC PROF MIL HIST, US ARMY COMMAND & GEN STAFF COL, 80-, Command historian, US Army Combined Arms Ctr & Ft Leavenworth, 80- **MEMBERSHIPS** Orgn Am Historians; Am Mil Inst; Southern Hist Asn. **SELECTED PUBLICATIONS** Auth, Some implications of Ultra, Mil Affairs, 4/76; Assessing Ultra, Mil Rev, 8/79; Calhoun's expansible army; The history of a military idea, SAtlantic Quart, winter 80; ed, S L A Marshall at Leavenworth: Five lectures presented at the US Army Command and General Staff College, 80, ed & contribr, A Brief History of the US Army Command and General Staff College, 81 & auth, Not war but like war: The American intervention in Lebanon, 1958, In: Leavenworth Paper No 3, 81, US Army Command & Gen Staff Col; ed, Dict of American Military Biography, Greenwood Press; auth, Soldiers Of The Sun, The Rise And Fall Of The Imperial Japanese Army, J Of Military Hist, Vol 57, 93; Crossing The Deadly Ground--United-States-Army Tactics, 1865-1899, J Of Southern Hist, Vol 62, 96. **CONTACT ADDRESS** PO Box 3173, Fort Leavenworth, KS 66027.

SPINDEL, DONNA JANE
PERSONAL Born 07/13/1949 **DISCIPLINE** EARLY AMERICAN HISTORY **EDUCATION** Mount Holyoke Col, AB, 71; Duke Univ, PhD(hist), 75. **CAREER** Ed asst, NC State Arch, 74, admin asst to dir, 75-76; ASST PROF HIST, MARSHALL UNIV, 76-, Res grants, Am Philos Soc & Marshall Univ, 78. **MEMBERSHIPS** Orgn Am Historians; Am Soc Legal Hist. **RESEARCH** Early American legal history; colonial American history. **SELECTED PUBLICATIONS** Auth, Anchors of empire: Savannah, Halifax and the Atlantic frontier, Am Rev Can Studies, autumn 76; ed, North Carolina Indian Records, NC Div Arch & Hist, 77; auth, The Stamp Act crisis in the British West Indies, J Am Studies, 8/77; Law and disorder: The North Carolina Stamp Act crisis, NC Hist Rev, (in press). **CONTACT ADDRESS** Dept of Hist, Marshall Univ, Huntington, WV 25701.

SPINK, WALTER M.
PERSONAL Born 02/16/1928, Worcester, MA, m, 1952, 3 children **DISCIPLINE** HISTORY OF ART **EDUCATION** Amherst Col, BA, 49; Harvard Univ, MA, 50, PhD, 54. **CAREER** U.S. Army Medical Corps, 54-56; vis lectr, Univ of Chicago, 72; vis lectr, Brown Univ, 60; Instr, Brandeis Univ, 56-58; asst prof, Brandeis Univ, 58-61; assoc prof, Univ of Mich, 61-70; prof, Univ of Mich, 70-. **HONORS AND AWARDS** Fulbright Grantee, Dept of Anthrop, 52-53; Master of Ceremonies, Dayton Art Museum, 90; Fac Recognition Grant for NEH Fel, 90; Fac Recognition grant for Guggenheim Fel, 91; Invited to speak on my theories by Indira Gandhi National Center for the Arts, New Delhi, 92; Hooker Distinguished Vis Prof, McMaster Univ, 93; Various notices and/or articles of work in Indian Express, Lokmat Times, and other papers in India, 92-93; Delgate to International Conference: "The Future of Asia's Past," Thailand, 95. **MEMBERSHIPS** Asn for Asian Studies; Col Art Asn; Bharat Itihasa Samshodhaka Mandala, Poona; Bhandarkar Oriental Res Institute, Poona; Am Comt for South Asian Art; Indian Asn of Art Hist; Soc for South Indian Studies; Indian Archaeol Soc. **RESEARCH** Indian sculpture and archit of early Buddhist, Gupta, and early medival periods; the God Krishna; art and worship. **SELECTED PUBLICATIONS** Auth, Ajanta to Ellora, Univ of Mich, 67; auth, The Quest for Krishna, Ann Arbor, 72; auth, Krishnamandala, Univ of Mich, 71; auth, The Axis of Eros, New York: Schocken Books, 73; auth, A Scholar's Guide to the Ajanta Caves, U of Mi, 92; auth, Ajanta, A Brief History and Guide, Lavanya Publishers, 93; auth, "The Ecology of Art," (forthcoming, 94); auth, "The Caves at Ellora," enciclopedia Italiana, 94; auth, "A New Vakataka Chronology, Ajanta, (forthcoming, 94); auth, "The Vakataka Caves at Ajanta and Their Successors," in Art of the Gupta-Vakataka Age, by S.R. Goyal, New Delhi, 94. **CONTACT ADDRESS** Dept of Hist of Art, Univ of Michigan, Ann Arbor, 2 Geddes Heights, Ann Arbor, MI 48104. **EMAIL** wspink@umich.edu

SPITZ, LEWIS W.
PERSONAL Born 12/14/1922, Bertrand, NE, m, 1948, 2 children **DISCIPLINE** HISTORY **EDUCATION** Concordia Col, AB, 44; Concordia Sem, BD, 47; Univ Mo, AM, 48; Harvard Univ, PhD, 54. **CAREER** Asst prof hist, Univ Mo, 53-60; assoc prof, 60-65, PROF HIST, STANFORD UNIV, 65-, WILLIAM R KENAN, JR CHAIR HIST, 74-, Soc Relig Higher Educ Kent fel; Guggenheim fel, 56; Huntington Libr fel, 59; Am Coun Learned Soc fel & Fulbright prof, Univ Mainz, 60-61; Am ed, Arch Reformation Hist, 67-; Nat Endowment for Humanities sr fel, 68-69; pres, Friends of Reformation Res, 76-; sr fel, Inst Advan Study, Princeton, 79-80; vis prof, Columbia Univ, 80-81. **HONORS AND AWARDS** Trenholme Award, 48; dd, concordia theol sem, 77; lld, valparaiso univ, 78. **MEMBERSHIPS** AHA; Am Soc Church Hist (pres, 76-); Am Soc Reformation Res (pres, 63-64); Renaissance Soc Am; Cent Renaissance Conf (pres, 56-57). **RESEARCH** Renaissance and Reformation. **SELECTED PUBLICATIONS** Auth, Conrad Celtis: The German Arch-Humanist, 57; auth, The Religious Renaissance of the German Humanists, 63; auth, Life in Two Worlds: A Biography of William Sinler, 68; auth, The Renaissance and Reformation Movements, 2 vols, 87; auth, Humanismus und Reformationin der Deutschen Geschichte, 80; auth, The Protestant Reformation, 1517-1559, 85; contribr, The Harvest of Humanism in Central Europe: Essays in Honor of Lewis W. Spits, 92; coauth, Johann Sturm on Education, 95; auth, Luther and German Humanism, 96; auth, The Reformation: Education and History, 97; ed, The Protestant Reformation: Major Documents, 97. **CONTACT ADDRESS** Dept of Hist, Stanford Univ, Stanford, CA 94305.

SPITZER, ALAN B.
PERSONAL Born 03/27/1925, Philadelphia, PA, m, 1950, 2 children **DISCIPLINE** MODERN EUROPEAN & FRENCH HISTORY **EDUCATION** Swarthmore Col, BA, 48; Columbia Univ, MA, 49, PhD(hist), 55. **CAREER** Instr gen educ, Boston Univ, 53-54, asst prof, 55-57; from asst prof to assoc prof, 57-63, PROF HIST, UNIV IOWA, 63- **MEMBERSHIPS** AHA; Conf Fr Studies; AAUP. **RESEARCH** The social history of 19th century France; the politics of the French Restoration. **SELECTED PUBLICATIONS** Auth, The Revolutionary Theories of La Blanqui, Columbia Univ, 57; The good Napoleon III, Fr Hist Studies, 62; Anarchy and culture: Fernand Pelloutier and the dilemma of revolutionary syndicalism, Int Rev Social Hist, 63; The bureaucrat as proconsul: The restoration prefect and the police generale, Comp Studies Soc & Hist, 65; Old Hatreds and Young Hopes: The French Carbonari Against the Bourbon Restoration, Harvard Univ, 71; The historical problem of generations, Am Hist Rev, 73; Victer Cousin and the French generation of 1820, In: Essays in Honor of Jacques Barzun, Harper & Row, 76. **CONTACT ADDRESS** Dept of Hist, Univ of Iowa, Iowa City, IA 52240.

SPITZER, LEO
PERSONAL Born 09/11/1939, La Paz, Bolivia, 1 child **DISCIPLINE** AFRICAN HISTORY, COMPARATIVE WORLD HISTORY **EDUCATION** Brandeis Univ, BA, 61; Univ Wis, Madison, MA, 63, PhD(African hist), 69. **CAREER** From instr to asst prof, 67-75, assoc prof, 75-81, PROF HIST, DARTMOUTH COL, 81-, Mem, Nat Humanities Fac, 70-74; Dartmouth fac fel, 71 & 78; Soc Sci Res Coun fel, Brazil, 72; consult, Inst Contemp Curric Develop, 73-; Comp World Hist Prog fel, Univ Wis, 74-75; Am Coun Learned Soc grant, 78; Nat Endowment Humanities fel, 81. **MEMBERSHIPS** African Studies Asn; AHA. **RESEARCH** African and Afro-Brazilian reactions to Western culture; assimilation and identity--a comparative historical inquiry; Sierra Leone, Brazil; Austria. **SELECTED PUBLICATIONS** Contribr, Africa and the West, Univ Wis, 72; auth, Interpreting African intellectual history: A critical review of the past decade, African Studies Rev, 72; coauth, ITA Wallace-Johnson and the West African Youth League (2 parts), Int J African Hist Studies, 73; auth, The Sierra Leone Creoles, Univ Wis, 74; Assimilation and identity in comparative perspective, Biography, 80; Os Dois Mundos de Andre Rebongas, Cornelius May, e Stefan Zweig, Estudos Afro-Asiatices, 80; Into the bourgeoisie: A study of Stefan Zweig and Jewish social mobility, 1750-1880, In: Stefan Zweig's Time, Life and Work, State Univ NY Press, 82. **CONTACT ADDRESS** Dept of Hist, Dartmouth Col, 6107 Reed Hall, Hanover, NH 03755-3506.

SPRAGUE, PAUL EDWARD
PERSONAL Born 02/28/1933, Cumberland, MD, m, 1956, 2 children **DISCIPLINE** ARCHITECTURAL & ART HISTORY **EDUCATION** Rutgers Univ, BA, 54; Princeton Univ, MFA, 62; PhD, 69. **CAREER** Asst prof art hist, Lake Forest Univ, 63-64; asst prof archit hist, Univ Notre Dame, 64-68; asst prof art & archit hist, Univ Chicago, 68-74; adj asst prof archit hist, Univ Ill, Chicago, 74-77; Assoc Prof, 77-84; Prof Archit Hist, 84-97, Prof Emer, 97- , Univ Wis, Milwaukee; vis prof, Univ Cincinnati, 80; vis prof, Seijo Univ, Tokyo, 90. **MEMBERSHIPS** Soc Archit Historians; Victorian Soc in Am; Midwest Art Hist Soc; Soc for Industrial Archaeol; Frank Lloyd Wright Conservancy; Southeast Chapter Soc of Archit Hist. **RESEARCH** Early modern architecture in the Midwest; Sullivan-Wright, their students and colleagues; conservation of historic architecture (historic preservation). **SELECTED PUBLICATIONS** Auth, Adler & Sullivan's Schiller Building, 65; auth, The National Farmer's Bank, Prarie Sch Rev, 67; auth, Griffin Rediscovered in Beverly, Prarie Sch Rev, 73; auth, Frank Lloyd Wright and Prarie School Architecture in Oak Park, Oak Park Landmarks Comn, 76; auth, The Drawings of Louis Sullivan, Princeton, 79; auth, The Origin of Baloon Framing, J Soc Archit Historians, 81; auth, Chicago Baloon Frame, The Technology of Historic American Buildings, 84; auth, Louis Sullivan and Adler & Sullivan, in Macmillan Encyclopedia of Architecture, 82; ed, contribur, Frank Lloyd Wright in Madison, Elvehjem Museum, 90; auth, Frank Lloyd Wright, in The Dictionary of Art, Macmillan, 96; coauth, Two American Architects in India: Walter B. Griffin and Marion M. Griffin, 1935-1937, Univ Ill, 97; auth, Marion Mahony as Originator of Griffin's Mature Style: Fact or Myth? in Beyond Architecture: Marion Mahony and Walter Griffin, Powerhouse Museum, Sydney, 98. **CONTACT ADDRESS** 624 Bertram Dr, Rockledge, FL 32955. **EMAIL** spraquep@earthlink.net

SPRAGUE, STUART SEELY
PERSONAL Born 06/24/1937, Norwalk, CT, m, 1966, 4 children **DISCIPLINE** AMERICAN URBAN HISTORY **EDUCATION** Yale Univ, BA, 60, MAT, 62; NYork Univ, PhD(hist), 72. **CAREER** Master hist, Hatch Sch, Newport, RI, 60-61; teacher, Jurupa Jr High Sch, Riverside, Calif, 62-63; from asst prof to assoc prof, 68-75, PROF HIST, MOREHEAD STATE UNIV, 75- **MEMBERSHIPS** Spelean Hist Asn. **RESEARCH** Early national period; Appalachian history; Kentucky history.

SELECTED PUBLICATIONS Auth, The names the thing: Ohio town promotion in the Era of Good Feelings, Names, 77; The great Appalachian iron and coal town boom, 1889-1893, Appalachian J, 77; contribr, The lure of the city: New York's great hotels in the Golden Age, 1873-1907, Conspectus of Hist, Cities in Hist, 78; auth, Postcard Ancestors, Family Heritage, 79; Kentucky politics and the heritage of the American Revolution: The early years, 1783-1788, Regist Ky Hist Soc, 80; Yale of yore: Learning by osmosis, a hidden curriculu, Yale Alumni Mag, 80; coauth (with E Perkins), Frankfort: A Pictorial History, 80; auth, Eastern Kentucky: A Pictorial History, spring 82. **CONTACT ADDRESS** Dept of Hist, Morehead State Univ, UPO 846, Morehead, KY 40351.

SPRENG, RONALD
PERSONAL Born 06/16/1948, Denison, IA, m, 1976 **DISCIPLINE** HISTORY **EDUCATION** S Dak State Univ, BS, 72; Oak Hills Christian Col, 87; Bemidji State Univ, MSEd, 91; Univ, N Dak, DA, 94. **CAREER** Faculty, Fridley High School, 72-80; Administrator, Heartland Christian Acad, 80-85; Pastor, Northern Bible Church, 83-86; Faculty, Oak Hills Christian Col, 86-. **HONORS AND AWARDS** UND Doct Res Fel. **MEMBERSHIPS** MN Hist Soc, Phi Alpha Theta, AHA. **RESEARCH** US Social/Environmental History. **CONTACT ADDRESS** Dept Hist & Env Studies, Oak Hills Bible Col, 1600 Oak Hills Rd SW, Bemidji, MN 56601-8826. **EMAIL** rspreng@hotmail.com

SPRING, DAVID
PERSONAL Born 04/29/1918, Toronto, ON, Canada **DISCIPLINE** HISTORY **EDUCATION** Univ Toronto, BA, 39; Harvard Univ, AM, 40, PhD, 48. **CAREER** Lectr hist, Univ Toronto, 46-48; from asst prof to assoc prof, 49-62, PROF HIST, JOHNS HOPKINS UNIV, 62-, Vis prof Victorian studies, Univ Leicester, 68-69; Nat Endowment for Humanities sr fel, 76-77. **HONORS AND AWARDS** Guggenheim fel, 57-58; Tawney Mem lectr, Brit Econ Hist Soc, 81. **MEMBERSHIPS** AHA; Conf Brit Studies; fel Royal Hist Soc. **RESEARCH** Modern English history; English landed classes in the 19th century; English social and political thought of 19th and 20th centuries. **SELECTED PUBLICATIONS** Auth, English Landed Estate in the 19th Century: Its Administration, Johns Hopkins Univ, 63; contrib, Land and Industry: The Landed Estate and the Industrial Revolution, David & Charles, 71; Great Landowners of Great Britain and Ireland, Univ Leicester, 71; co-ed, Ecology and Religion in History, Harper & Row, 74; coauth, The First Industrial Society, Macmillan, 75; ed & contrib, European Landed Elites in 19th Century, Johns Hopkins Univ, 77; contribur, Jane Austen: New Perspectives, Holmes & Meier, 83; contrib, Land and Society in Britain, 1700-1914, Manchester, 96. **CONTACT ADDRESS** Dept of History, Johns Hopkins Univ, Baltimore, 3400 N Charles St, Baltimore, MD 21218.

SPRINGER, HASKELL SAUL
PERSONAL Born 11/18/1939, New York, NY, m, 1993, 2 children **DISCIPLINE** AMERICAN LITERATURE & STUDIES **EDUCATION** Queens Col, NYork, BA, 61; Ind Univ, MA, 65, PhD, 68. **CAREER** Instr, Univ Va, 66-68; from asst prof to assoc prof, 68-78, prof Eng, 78-, Univ Kans; Fulbright prof Am lit, Universidade Catolica & Universidade Fed, Rio de Janeiro, Brazil, 75-76; vis prof, amer lit, Sorbonne, Paris, 85-86. **MEMBERSHIPS** MLA; AAUP; Melville Soc; Amer Cult Assn. **RESEARCH** Classic American literature; hypertext literature; textual scholarship. **SELECTED PUBLICATIONS** Ed, America and the Sea: A Literary History, University of Georgia, 95; auth, The Captain's Wife at Sea, Iron Men, Wooden Women: Gender and Seafaring in the Atlantic World, 1700-1920, Johns Hopkins, 96. **CONTACT ADDRESS** Dept of English, Univ of Kansas, Lawrence, Lawrence, KS 66045-0001. **EMAIL** springer@ukans.edu

SPRUNGER, KEITH L.
PERSONAL Born Berne, IN, m, 1959, 3 children **DISCIPLINE** HISTORY **EDUCATION** Wheaton Col, BA, 57; Univ Ill, MA, 57; PhD, 63. **CAREER** Asst to prof of history, Bethel Col, North Newton, Kans, 63-, Oswald H. Wedel Prof of Hist. **HONORS AND AWARDS** Soc Sci Res Coun Fel, Sabbatical 69-70; Am Philos Soc Fel, Sabbatical 69-70, 83-84; Am Coun of Learned Soc Fel, Sabbatical, 76-77; E. Harris Harbinson Awd for Gifted Teaching, Danforth Found, 72; Fel, Z.W.O. (Netherlands Org for the Advancement of Pure Res), Univ Leiden, 83; AAHE: "50 Fac Leader," Change, July/Aug 86. **MEMBERSHIPS** Am Hist Asn, Am Soc of Church Hist, Conf on Faith and Hist, Oral Hist Asn, Doopsgezinde Hist Kring (Netherlands), AAUP. **SELECTED PUBLICATIONS** Auth, The Learned Doctor William Ames (72); auth, Voices Against War (73); auth, Dutch Puritanism: A History of English and Scottish Churches of the Netherlands in the 16th and 17th Centuries (82); auth, The Auction Catalogue of the Library of William Ames (88); auth, Trumpets from the Tower: English Puritan Printing in the Netherlands 1600-1640 (94); auth, Campus, Congregation, and Community: The Bethel College Mennonite Church 1897-1997 (97). **CONTACT ADDRESS** Dept Hist, Bethel Col, Kansas, 300 E 27th St, North Newton, KS 67117-8061. **EMAIL** sprunger@bethelks.edu

SPRY, IRENE
PERSONAL Born Transvaal, South Africa **DISCIPLINE** ECONOMIC HISTORY **EDUCATION** London Sch Econ, 24-25; Girton Col, Cambridge, BA, 28; Bryn Mawr Col, MA, 29. **CAREER** Lectr, asst prof, Univ Toronto, 29-38; lectr, writer & reviewer, 45-67; assoc prof/prof, 68-73, Prof Emer, Univ Ottawa, 74-. **HONORS AND AWARDS** Res Fel, Can Plains Res Ctr; Can Coun Res Awd, 65; Distinguished Can Citizen Awd, Univ Regina, 87; Off, Order Can, 93; LLD Univ Toronto, 71; DU Univ Ottawa, 85. **SELECTED PUBLICATIONS** Auth, The Palliser Expedition, 64; auth, The Papers of the Palliser Expedition, 1857-1860, 68; auth, The Transition from a Nomadic to a Settled Society in Western Canada, 1856-1896, in Trans Royal Soc Can, 68. **CONTACT ADDRESS** Univ of Ottawa, Ottawa, ON, Canada K1N 6NS.

SPURLOCK, JOHN C.
PERSONAL Born 05/20/1954, Riverside, CA, m, 1979, 2 children **DISCIPLINE** AMERICAN HISTORY **EDUCATION** Univ Calif-Riverside, BA, 76; MA, 77; Rutgers Univ, PhD, 87. **CAREER** Asst Prof, Bloomsburg Univ, 87-89; Asst Ed, Papers of Albert Gallatin, Baruch Col, CUNY, 89-90; Asst Prof to Assoc Prof, Seton Hill Col, 90-. **MEMBERSHIPS** Am Hist Asn; Org Am Hist. **RESEARCH** Social and cultural history. **SELECTED PUBLICATIONS** Auth, Free Love: Marriage and Middle-Class Radicalism in America, 1825-1860, NY Univ, 88; coauth, New and Improved: The Transformation of American Women's Emotional Culture, NY Univ, 98. **CONTACT ADDRESS** Hist Dept, Seton Hill Col, Greensburg, PA 15601. **EMAIL** jspurloc@setonhill.edu

SPYRIDAKIS, STYLIANOS V.
PERSONAL Born 01/27/1937, Crete, Greece, 2 children **DISCIPLINE** ANCIENT HISTORY **EDUCATION** Univ Calif, Los Angeles, BA, 60, PhD(ancient hist), 66. **CAREER** Instr ancient hist, Univ Calif, Santa Barbara, 64-65; asst prof, Calif State Univ, Los Angeles, 65-66; asst prof, Univ Nebr, Lincoln, 66-67; asst prof to prof Ancient History, Univ Calif, Davis, 67-, vis prof, Univ Crete, Greece, 79-80. **HONORS AND AWARDS** Walter Lowey Fel, Heidelberg, 63-64; elector, Univ of Crete, 80-; Distinguished Teaching Awd, Univ Calif, Davis, 70; Honorary Member, Cretan Hist and Archaeol Soc; Board of Dir, S. B. Vryonis Center for the Study of Hellenism, Sacto, Calif, 89-. **MEMBERSHIPS** Cretan Hist & Archaeol Soc; Asn Ancient Hist. **RESEARCH** Hellenistic history; Crete and the Aegean. **SELECTED PUBLICATIONS** Auth, Ptolemaic Itanos and Hellenistic Crete, Univ Calif, 70; Cretica: Studies on Ancient Crete, New Rochelle, 92; Mantinades: Selected Love Distichsof Crete, New Rochelle, 97; coauth and translator, Ancient Greece: Documentary Perspectives, Kendall-Hunt, 85; Ancient Rome: Documentary Perspectives, Kendall-Hunt, 90; numerous journal articles and monographs. **CONTACT ADDRESS** Dept of Hist, Univ of California, Davis, Davis, CA 95616-5200. **EMAIL** svspyridakis@ucdavis.edu

ST CLAIR HARVEY, ARCHER
DISCIPLINE ART HISTORY **EDUCATION** Princeton Univ, PhD. **CAREER** Assoc prof, Rutgers Univ. **HONORS AND AWARDS** Assoc dir, Am Acad Rome/Soprintendenza Archeologica di Roma Palatine East Excavation. **RESEARCH** Early Christian and Byzantine art; late antique art; Byzantine influence on Western art; liturgical and topographical influence on Early Christian and Medieval art. **SELECTED PUBLICATIONS** Auth, A Byzantine Source for the San Paolo Bible, Festschrift Kurt Weitzmann, Princeton, 95; coauth, A Late Roman Domus with Apsidal Hall on the Northeast Slope of the Palatine, Rome Papers (Jour Roman Archaeol), 94; Scavi di un complesso tardo romano sul versante nord ovest dei Palatino, Bolletino di archeologia, 91. **CONTACT ADDRESS** Dept of Art Hist, Rutgers, The State Univ of New Jersey, Rutgers Col, Voorhees Hall, 71 Hamilton St, New Brunswick, NJ 08903. **EMAIL** astch@rci.rutgers.edu

ST. GEORGE, ROBERT B.
DISCIPLINE AMERICAN HISTORY **EDUCATION** Hamilton, AB, 76; Delaware, MA, 78; Univ of Penn, MA, 80, PhD, 82. **CAREER** Assoc prof, Univ Penn. **HONORS AND AWARDS** Fred Kniffer Prize, 88; George Wittenborn Awd of the Art Libraries of North America, 88; Charles F. Montgomery Prize, 88. **MEMBERSHIPS** Am Antiquarian Soc. **RESEARCH** Lit and reading in Mass, 1640-1720. **SELECTED PUBLICATIONS** Auth, "From Nature to Culture," Portfolio: The Mag of the Fine Arts 4, 82; auth, "Set Thine House in Order: The Domestication of the Yeomanry in Seventeenth-Century New England," in New England Begins: The Seventeenth Century, Museum of Fine Arts, 82; auth, "Heated Speech and Literacy in Seventeenth-Century New England," in 17th-Century New Eng, 84; auth, Material Life in America, 1600-1860, Northeastern Univ Press, 88; ed, American Seating Furniture, 1630-1730: An Interpretive Catalogue of the Winterthur Collection, W W Norton, 88; auth, "Bawns and Beliefs: Architecture, Commerce, and Conversion in Early New England," Winterthur Portfolio, Winter 90; Conversing by Signs: Place and Performance in Early New England Culture, 95. **CONTACT ADDRESS** Dept of Hist, Univ of Pennsylvania, 3401 Walnut St, Ste 352B, Philadelphia, PA 19104-6228. **EMAIL** stgeorge@sas.upenn.edu

STABILE, DONALD ROBERT
PERSONAL Born 03/07/1944, New York, NY **DISCIPLINE** ECONOMIC HISTORY AND HISTORY OF ECONOMIC THOUGHT **EDUCATION** Univ of MA, Amherst MA, 72; PhD, 79. **CAREER** Prof of Econ, St. Mary's College of MD, 89-; Chair Dept of Econ , St. Mary's Coll of MD, 98-; Assoc Provst for Academic Services, St. Mary's Coll of MD, 96-98; Assoc Prof of Econ, St Mary's Coll of MD, 85-89; Asst Prof of Econ, St. Mary's Coll of MD, 80-85; Asst Prof of Econ, Drury Coll, 78-80. **HONORS AND AWARDS** G. Thomas and Martha Myers Yeager Endowed Chair in Liberal Arts, St. Mary's College of Md. **MEMBERSHIPS** Econ and Bus Hist Soc; Assoc for Evolutionary Econ; Assoc for Soc Econ. **RESEARCH** Hist of Econ Thought; Political Economy; Hist of Federal Fin; Interdisciplinary Soc Sci **SELECTED PUBLICATIONS** The Origins of American Public Finance: The Debates Over Money, Debts and Taxes in the Costitutional Era,1776-1836, Greenwood Press, 98; Work and Welfare: The Social Costs of Labor in the History of Economic Thought, Greenwood Press 96; Activist Unionism: The Institutional Econimics of Solomon Barkin, M.E.Sharpe, Inc 93; Adam Smith and the Natural Wage: Sympathy,Subsistence and Social Distance, Review of Social Economy, 97; Thorstein Veblen's Intellectual Antecedents: A Case for John Bates Clark, Journal of Economic Issues, 97; Therories of Consumption and Waste: Institutional Foreshadowings in Classical Writings, Journal of Economic Issues, 96; Pigou, Clark and Modern Economics, Cambridge Journal of Economic Issues, 96; Pigou's Influence on Clark: Work and Welfare, Journal of Economic Issues, 95; Henry George's Influence on John Bates Clark, American Journal of Economics and Sociology, 95; auth, Community Associations: The Emergence and Acceptance of a Quiet Innovation in Housing, Greenwood Press, 00. **CONTACT ADDRESS** St. Mary's Col of Maryland, Saint Mary's City, MD 20686. **EMAIL** drstabile@osprey.smcm.edu

STACKHOUSE, JOHN G., JR.
DISCIPLINE THEOLOGY; PHILOSOPHY OF RELIGION; CHURCH HISTORY **EDUCATION** Queen's Univ Kingston, BA, 80; Wheaton Col Grad Sch, 82; Univ Chicago, PhD, 87. **CAREER** Instr, Wheaton Col Grad Sch, 84-86; Asst Prof, NWestern Col, Iowa, 87-90; from Asst Prof to Prof Religion, Univ Manitoba, 90-98; Sangwoo Youtong Chee Prof Theology, Regent Col, Vancouver, 98-. **HONORS AND AWARDS** Prof of the Year (Awd for Teaching Excellence), NWestern Col, 89; Rh Found Awd for Outstanding Contributions to Schol and Res in the Humanities, Univ Manitoba, 93; Outreach Awd for Community Service, Univ Manitoba, 97; First Place for Editorial Writing, Canadian Church Press, 98. **MEMBERSHIPS** Am Acad Relig; Am Soc Church Hist; Canadian Soc Church History; Canadian Evangelical Theol Asn. **RESEARCH** Epistemology; philosophy of religion; religion in North America. **SELECTED PUBLICATIONS** Auth, Canadian Evangelicalism in the Twentieth Century: An Introduction to Its Character, Univ Toronto Press, 93; Can God Be Trusted? Faith and the Challenge of Evil, Oxford Univ Press, 98; author of over 200 journal articles and reviews. **CONTACT ADDRESS** Regent Col, 5800 University Blvd., Vancouver, BC, Canada V6T 2E4. **EMAIL** jgs@regent-college.edu

STACKLEBERG, J. RODERICK
PERSONAL Born 05/08/1935, Munich, Germany, m, 1991, 3 children **DISCIPLINE** HISTORY **EDUCATION** Harv Univ, AB, 56; Univ Ver, MA, 72; Univ Mass, PhD, 74. **CAREER** Lectr, San Diego State Univ, 74-76; vis asst prof, Univ Ore, 76-77; asst prof, Univ Dak, 77-78; asst prof, 78-81; assoc prof, 81-89; prof, 89-, Gonzaga Univ. **HONORS AND AWARDS** Fulbright Awd, 82; Burlington N Schl, 90. **MEMBERSHIPS** AHA; Phi Alpha Theta; GSA; NANS. **RESEARCH** National socialism; Volkisch ideology; Nietzschean thought; modern Germany. **SELECTED PUBLICATIONS** Auth, "Teaching Mann's Short Fiction: A Historian's Perspective," in Approaches to Teaching Thomas Mann's "Death in Venice" and Other Short Fiction, ed. Jeffrey B Berlin (NY: MLA, 92), 29-38; auth, "The Philosopher of Fascism? Nietzsche Through the Eyes of Ernst Nolte," Platte Valley Rev 22 (94): 38-47; auth, "Revision and Revival of the Past: The 'New Conservatism' of Ernst Nolte," Alphabet City (95): 64-67; auth, "Ernst Haeckel," "Hans F K Gunther," "Social Darwinism," "Racism, 1870-1990," and "Volkisch Ideology" in Modern Germany: An Encyclopedia of History, People, and Culture, 1871-1990, 2 vol, ed. Dieter K Buse, Juergen C Doerr (NY: Garland, 98): 423, 427-8, 812-13, 920-1, 1036-8; auth, "The Federal Republic of Germany," "The Frankfurt School," "Historikerstreit," "The Spiegel Affair," "Bitburg," "Walter Ulbricht," and "Franz Josef Strauss" in Europe Since 1945: An Encyclopedia, ed. Bernard Cook (Garland, forthcoming). **CONTACT ADDRESS** Dept History, Gonzaga Univ, 502 East Boone Ave, Spokane, WA 99258-1774.

STADTWALD, KURT
PERSONAL Born 12/03/1957, Omaha, NE, m, 1990, 2 children **DISCIPLINE** HISTORY **EDUCATION** William Jewell Col, BA, 80; Univ Nebr, MA, 82; Univ Minn, PhD, 91. **CAREER** Vis Prof, Denison Univ, 90-91; assoc prof, 91-, chemn, 96-, Concordia Univ. **HONORS AND AWARDS** Who's Who in Am Cols and Univs, 80; grad fel, ctr austrian stud, 85-86; fulbright fel, austria, 87-88; disseration fel, univ minn, 89-90. **MEMBERSHIPS** Sixteenth Century Society; Friends of the

Society of Reformation Res. **RESEARCH** German Humanism; the Holy Roman Empire; sixteenth century political opinions. **SELECTED PUBLICATIONS** Auth, article, Pope Alexander III's Humiliation of Emperor Frederick Barbarossa as an Episode in Sixteenth-Century German History, 93; auth, article, Patriotism and Antipapalism in the Politics of Conrad Celtis's Vienna Circle, 93; auth, book Roman Popes and German Patriots, 96. **CONTACT ADDRESS** Dept of History, Concordia Univ, Illinois, 7400 Augusta St, River Forest, IL 60305. **EMAIL** crfstadtwkw@curf.edu

STAFFORD, BARBARA MARIA
PERSONAL Born 09/16/1941, Vienna, Austria, m **DISCIPLINE** ART HISTORY **EDUCATION** Northwestern Univ, BA, 64, MA, 66; Sorbonne, 61-62; Univ Chicago, PhD, 72. **CAREER** Instr, Nat Coll of Educ, 69-70, 71-72; asst prof, Loyola Univ, 72-73; from asst to assoc prof, Univ Del, 73-81; Prof, Univ Chicago, 81-. **HONORS AND AWARDS** Univ Del Excellence-in-Teaching Awd, 76; ACLS Summer Grant, 76; Univ Del Summer Grants, 74, 78; NEH Fel, 79-80; Am Soc for 18th Century Studies Clifford Prize, 79; Ctr for Adv Stud in the Visual Arts Fel, 79-80; Millard Meiss Publ Awd, CAA, 83; Smithsonian Inst Fel, 84-85; Joh Simon Guggenheim Fel, 89-90; Alexander von Humboldt Sr Fel, 89-91; Univ Cal Humanities Res Inst Fel, 91; Co-recip Gottschalk Prize for best book on an 18th century topic, 92; Univ Mich Fel, 93; Getty Ctr Schol, 95-96; Honorary Doctorate, Maryland Inst, 96. **MEMBERSHIPS** Amer Soc for 18th-Century Studies; Brit Assn for 18th-Century Studies; Coll Art Assn; Hist of Sci Soc; Int Soc for 18th Century Studies; Soc francaise de l'histoire de la dermatologie; Soc de l'hsitoire d'art francais; Soc of Archit Hist; Society for Sci, Lit & Soc. **SELECTED PUBLICATIONS** Auth, Symbol and Myth: Humber de Superville's Essay on Absolute Signs in Art, Associated Univ Presses, 79; Voyage into Substance: Art Science, Nature and the Illustrated Travel Account, 1760-1840, MIT, 84; Body Criticism: Imaging the Unseen in Enlightenment Art and Medicine, MIT, 91; Artful Science, Enlightenment Entertainment and the Eclipse of Visual Education, MIT, 91; Good Looking: Essays on the Virtue of Images, MIT, 96; catalogues: Imaging the Body: From Fragment to Total Display, Art Inst of Chicago, 92; Metaphors of Biological Structure/Architecture Construction, Art Inst of Chicago, 92; Depth Studies: Illustrated Anatomies from Vesalius to Vicqd'Azyr, Univ Chicago, 92; coed: The Blackwell Companion to the Enlightenment, Blackwell, 91; European Cultures, Studies in Literature and the Arts, DeGruyter, 93-; consulting ed: Advances in Visual Semiotics, Univ Ind, 95; coed, Reflecting Senses, Perception and Appearance in Literature, Culture and the Arts, DeGruyter, 95; articles: Art of Conjuring, or How the Romantic Virtuoso Learned from the Enlightened Charlatan, Art J, summer 92; Present Image, Past Text, Post Body: Educating the Late Modern Citizen, Semiotica, 92; Presuming Images and Consuming Words: The Visualization of Knowledge from the Enlightenment to Postmodernism, Consumption and the World of Goods, Routledge, 93; Images of Ambiguity: Eighteenth-Century Microscopy and the Neither/Nor, Visions of Empire, Cambridge Univ, 93; Instructive Games: Apparatus and the Experimental Aesthetics of Imposture, Reflecting Senses, Perception and Appearance inLiterature, Culture and the Arts; Critic's Voice, Sculpture Mag, 95; Medical Ethics as Postmodern Aesthetics: Reflections on Biotehnological Utopia, Utopian Visions, Univ Mich, 95; Eighteenth-Century at the End of Modernity: Towards the Re-Enlightenment, Past Prologue, AMS Press, 94; Making Images Real: Toward a Pragmatic Aesthetics and an Applied Interdisciplinarity, J. Pual Getty Trust Newsletter, spring 94; Interview, Sculpture Mag, May 94; Pain under Pane, Beyond Ars Medica, Thread Waxing Space, 95-96; Cross-Cortical Romance: Analogy, Art, and Consciousness, Art Issues, Mar/Apr 96; Display and the Rhetoric of Contamination, Visualization in the Sciences, Princeton Univ, 96; Digital Imagery and the Practices of Art History, Art Bulletin, 97. **CONTACT ADDRESS** Dept of Art, Univ of Chicago, Cochrane-Woods Art Ctr, Chicago, IL 60637. **EMAIL** bms6@midway.uchicago.edu

STAFFORD, WILLIAM SUTHERLAND
PERSONAL Born 11/09/1947, San Franciso, CA, m, 1969, 4 children **DISCIPLINE** CHURCH HISTORY **EDUCATION** Stanford Univ, BA, 65-69; Yale Univ, MA, Mphil, 69-74, PhD, 75; Univ de Strasbourg: Fac de theol protestante, 73-74. **CAREER** Tchg fel, Yale Col, 71-73; vis asst prof, Brown Univ, 74-76; asst prof, 76-82; assoc prof, Va Theol Sem, 82-90; David J. Ely prof, 90-; associate dean for Acad Aff, VP. **MEMBERSHIPS** ASCH, ACHA **RESEARCH** Late Medieval-Reformation Church History. **SELECTED PUBLICATIONS** Auth, Disordered Loves: Healing the Seven Deadly Sins, Cowley Publ, 94; Sexual Norms in the Medieval Church, A Wholesome Example: Sexual Morality in the Episcopal Church, 91; The Eve of the Reformation: Bishop John Fisher, 1509, Hist Mag Protestant Episcopal Church, 85. **CONTACT ADDRESS** Virginia Theol Sem, 3737 Seminary Rd, Alexandria, VA 22304. **EMAIL** wstafford@vts.edu

STAGER, LAWRENCE E.
PERSONAL Born 01/05/1943, Kenton, OH, m, 1970, 1 child **DISCIPLINE** NEAR EASTERN ARCHEOLOGY & HISTORY **EDUCATION** Harvard Univ, BA, 65, MA, 72, PhD(Syro-Palestinian archaeol & hist), 75. **CAREER** Instr, 73-74, asst prof, 74-75, ASSOC PROF SYRO-PALESTINIAN ARCHAEOL, ORIENT INST, UNIV CHICAGO, 76-, Co-dir, Am Exped Idalion, Cypress, 72-74; ed, Am Schs Orient Res Newslett, 75-76; dir, UNESCO Save Carthage Proj, Am Pumic Archaeol Exped, 75-80; assoc trustee, Am Schs Orient Res, 77-80; assoc ed, Bull Am Schs Orient Res, 78- **MEMBERSHIPS** Am Schs Orient Res; Archaeol Inst Am; Am Orient Soc; Soc Bibl Lit. **RESEARCH** Phoenician colonization; agriculture in the Bronze and Iron Age Levant; Bronze Age urbanization in the eastern Mediterranean. **SELECTED PUBLICATIONS** Auth, Farming in the Judean Desert during the Iron Age, Bull Am Schs Orient Res, 76; coauth, A metropolitan landscape: The late Punic port of Carthage, World Archaeol, 77; auth, The rite of child sacrifice at Carthage, In: New Light on Ancient Carthage, Univ Mich Press, 80; Highland village life in Palestine some three thousand years ago, Orient Inst News & Notes, 81; The archaeology of the east slope of Jerusalem and the terraces of the Kidron, J Near Eastern Studies, 82; The first fruits of civilization, In: Olga Tufnell Festschrift, Inst Archeol Occasional Papers, 82; The Dating Of Ancient Water-Wells By Archaeological And 14c Methods--Comparative-Study Of Ceramics And Wood, Israel Exploration J, Vol 44, 94; coauth, Production and commerce in temple courtyards, Bull Am Schs Orient Res, 82. **CONTACT ADDRESS** Dept of Near Eastern Lang & Civilizations, Harvard Univ, 6 Divinity Ave, Cambridge, MA 02138. **EMAIL** stager@fas.harvard.edu

STAHL, ALAN MICHAEL
PERSONAL Born 08/07/1947, Providence, RI **DISCIPLINE** MEDIEVAL HISTORY, NUMISMATICS **EDUCATION** Univ Calif, Berkeley, BA, 68; Univ Pa, MA, 73; PhD(hist), 77. **CAREER** Asst cur, 80-82, ASSOC CUR MEDIEVAL COINS, AM NUMISMATIC SOC, 82-86. **HONORS AND AWARDS** Gladys K. Delmas Foundation, Grant for Research, 81, 83, 85; Robinson-Kraay Fel, Oxford Univ, 94. **MEMBERSHIPS** Am Academy of Res Historians of Medieval and Renaissance Spain; Am Historical Asn; Am Medallic Sculpture Asn; Am Numismatic Asn; Am Numismatic Soc; Charles Homer Haskins Soc; Columbia Univ Medieval Studies Seminar; Federation Internationale de la Medaille; International Cneter of Medieval Art; Italian Art Soc; Medieval Academy of Am; National Sculpture Soc; New York Numismatic Club; Soc for the Study of the Crusades and the Latin East. **RESEARCH** Medieval numismatics; European economic history. **SELECTED PUBLICATIONS** Auth, The Merovingian Coinage of the Region of Metz, 82; auth, The Venetian Tornesello: A Medieval Colonial Coinage, Am Numismatic Soc, Numismatic Notes and Monographs 163, New York, 85; ed, The Medal in America, Coinage of the Americas Conference, New York, 88; auth, Merovingiens et royaumes barbares, Fonds Bourgey, Paris: Errance, 94; ed, The Medal in America, Vol 2, Coinage of the Americas Conference, New York, 99; ed, The Documents of Angelo de Cartura and Donato Fontanella: Venetian Notaries in Fourteenth-Century Crete, Dumbarton Oaks Res Library and Collection, Washington DC, 00; auth, Zecca; The Mint of Venice in the Middle Ages, Baltimore: Johns Hopkins Univ Press, 00; auth, "The Circulation of Medieval Venetian Coinages," in Lucia Travaini, ed. Moneta locale, moneta straniera: Italia ed Europa XI-XV secolo, Societa Numismatica Italiana, Collana di Numismatica e Scienze Affini 2, Milan, (99): 87-111; auth, "The Grosso of Enrico Dandolo," in Melanges Tony Hackens, Revue Belge de Numismatique, 145, (99): 261-68; ed, "Mint and Medal in the Renaissance," in Perspectives on the Renaissance Medal, Stephen K. Scher, ed., Garland Studies in the Renaissance, New York: Garland, (00): 137-47. **CONTACT ADDRESS** Am Numismatic Soc, Broadway & 155th St, New York, NY 10032. **EMAIL** mistrasparta@atsearthlink.net

STALEY, ALLEN
PERSONAL Born 06/04/1935, Mexico, MO, m, 1968, 2 children **DISCIPLINE** HISTORY OF ART **EDUCATION** Princeton Univ, BA, 57; Yale Univ, MA, 60, PhD(Art Hist), 65. **CAREER** Lectr, The Frick Collection, 62-65; asst cur Paintings, Phila Mus Art, 65-68; from asst prof to assoc prof Art Hist, 69-76, prof Art Hist & Archaeol, Columbia Univ, 76-. **RESEARCH** English painting. **SELECTED PUBLICATIONS** Coauth, Romantic Art in Britain: 1760-1860, Phila Mus Art, 68; ed, From Realism to Symbolism: Whistler & Hist World, Columbia Univ, 71; auth, The Pre-Raphaelite Landscape, Oxford Univ, 73; The Post-Pre-Raphaelite Print: Etching, Illustration, Reproductive Engraving, and Photography in England in and around the 1860's, Wallach Art Gallery, Columbia University, 95. **CONTACT ADDRESS** Dept of Art History, Columbia Univ, 2960 Broadway, New York, NY 10027-6900.

STALLS, M.
PERSONAL Born 10/22/1947, Metropolis, IL **DISCIPLINE** AFRICAN-AMERICAN STUDIES; FOUNDATION OF EDUCATION **EDUCATION** Southern IL Univ, BA 1970, MS 1976, PhD 1991. **CAREER** IL Dept of Children & Family Svcs, child welfare worker 1970-75; IL Farmers Union, manpower coordinator 1976-78; SIU-C School of Tech Careers, researcher/service coord 1978-80; SIU-C Ctr for Basic Skills, coord of supple inst, developmental skills specialist/instructor, visiting assistant professor, Black American studies, developmental skills training specialist, currently. **HONORS AND AWARDS** Serv Awd Eurma C Hayes Comp Child Care Services/PAC 1977; Fel IL Comm on Black Concerns in Higher Educ 1984; Cert of Appreciation SIU-C HEADSTART Carbondale, IL 1986; Iota Phi Theta Quintessence Awd 1984; SIU-C-BAC Acad Excellence Awd 1987, Paul Robeson Awd; Fac Staff Awd 1988; 5 Poems published in Literati 1989; coord Southern Region ICBCHE Regional Fall Sem 1988; George S. Counts Doctoral Awd 1990; ICBCHE, Dedicated Serv Awd, 1990; Alton Metropolitan Human Development Recognition Awd, 1991; Humanitarian Awd, SIUC Black Affairs Coun, 1996; Southern Illinois Univ at Carbondale, Acad Excellence Awd, Black Affairs Coun, 1991; nominee, Outstanding Prof, Grad & Prof Educ, 1994, Univ Woman of Distinction Awd, Univ Administrative/Prof, 1998. **MEMBERSHIPS** Founder/coord Black Women's Coalition 1983; mentor SIU-C Proj Magic 1984-; consultant Jack Co Public Housing Initiatives Training Prog 1985; IL Comt on Black Concerns in Higher Educ steering comt mem, 1985-, vice chair, Southern Region, 1997, 1998; consultant SIU-C Women's Studies Film Proj 1986-; Am Asn of Counseling and Devel; Nat Coun of Black Studies; exe dir Star Human Serv Devel Corp Inc, 1987-; Founder/convener Assembly of African, African-Am Women, 1989, Kappa Delta Pi, 1987; Am Asn of Univ Women; Asn of Black Women in Higher Educ ABWHE. **RESEARCH** Ethnic history, education; Black Women's Issues; Human welfare. **CONTACT ADDRESS** Center for Basic Skills, So Illinois Univ, Carbondale, Woody Hall, C-7, Carbondale, IL 62901. **EMAIL** mstalls@notes.siu.edu

STAMBROOK, FRED
PERSONAL Born 11/16/1929, Vienna, Austria **DISCIPLINE** HISTORY **EDUCATION** Oxford Univ, BA, 50; Univ London, BS, 51, PhD, 60. **CAREER** Educ Off, RAF, 50-52; mem, Ger War Doc Proj, 54-59; lectr hist, Univ Sydney, 60-68; Prof History, Univ Manitoba, 68-, assoc dean, arts, 75-77, dean 77-82, vice pres acad, 82-91; vis prof, Univ Ky, 67. **HONORS AND AWARDS** Queen's Silver Jubilee Medal, 77; Canada 125 Medal, 92. **SELECTED PUBLICATIONS** Auth, European Nationalism in the Nineteenth Century, 69; co-ed, Documents on German Foreign Policy 1918-1945, Ser C & D, 56-66; co-ed, A Modern History Sourcebook, 66. **CONTACT ADDRESS** Dept History, Univ of Manitoba, Winnipeg, MB, Canada R3T 2M8.

STAMP, ROBERT M.
PERSONAL Born 02/11/1937, Toronto, ON, Canada **DISCIPLINE** HISTORY **EDUCATION** Univ Western Ont, BA, 59, PhD, 70; Univ Toronto, MA, 62. **CAREER** Tchr, London Sec Sch, 60-65; asst prof, Univ Western Ont, 65-69; assoc prof 69-73, prof 73-83, dir Can stud 80-83, prof, Univ Calgary, 95. **RESEARCH** Alberta and Canadian educational history; alternatives in education; teacher education; modernist studies; post-1945 Calgary. **SELECTED PUBLICATIONS** Auth, School Days: A Century of Memories, 75; auth, The Schools of Ontario 1876-1976, 82; auth, The World of Tomorrow, 85; auth, QEW: Canada's First Superhighway, 87; auth, Kings, Queens and Canadians, 87; auth, Royal Rebels, 88; auth, Riding the Radials, 89; auth, Early Days in Richmond Hill, 91; auth, Bridging the Border, 92; auth, Turning 100 Together, 94. **CONTACT ADDRESS** Dean's Office: Education, 123 - 34A St NW, Calgary, AB, Canada T2N 2Y4. **EMAIL** stamp@ucalgary.ca

STANDRING, TIMOTY
DISCIPLINE ITALIAN RENAISSANCE AND BAROQUE **EDUCATION** Univ Chicago, PhD, 82. **CAREER** Assoc prof-. **RESEARCH** Pousiin, Castiglione, Cassiano dal Pozzo, British landscape painting. **SELECTED PUBLICATIONS** Pub(s), Burlington Mag, Print Quart, Art Jour, Sixteenth Century Stud, Renaissance Quart. **CONTACT ADDRESS** Dept of Art Hist, Univ of Denver, 2199 S Univ Blvd, Denver, CO 80208.

STANISLAWSKI, MICHAEL
DISCIPLINE JEWISH, RUSSIAN, AND EUROPEAN INTELLECTUAL HISTORY **EDUCATION** Harvard Univ, 73, PhD, 79. **CAREER** Nathan J Miller prof. **SELECTED PUBLICATIONS** Auth, Tsar Nicholas I and the Jews, 83; For Whom Do I Toil?, 88; Psalms for the Tsar, 88; co-auth, Heritage: Civilization and the Jews: Study Guide, 84; ed, Heritage: Civilization and the Jews: Source Reader, 84. **CONTACT ADDRESS** Dept of Hist, Columbia Col, New York, 2960 Broadway, New York, NY 10027-6902.

STANLEY, DELLA M. M.
PERSONAL Born 08/21/1950, Kingston, ON, Canada **DISCIPLINE** CANADIAN STUDIES **EDUCATION** Mt Allison Univ, BA, 73; Univ NB, MA, 74, PhD, 80. **CAREER** Asst prof, Queen's Univ, 78-81; Asst prof, Saint Mary's Univ, 84-90; asst prof, 82-92, Coordr, Canadian Studies Programme, 88-, Assoc Prof, 92-, Chair, Political & Canadian Studies, Mt St Vincent Univ, 97-. **MEMBERSHIPS** Asn Can Stud; Can Hist Asn; Adminrs Can Stud Progs; Osgoode Soc; Heritage Can. **SELECTED PUBLICATIONS** Auth, Au Service de deux peuples: Pierre Landry, 76; auth, Louis Robichaud: A Decade of Power, 84; auth, A Man for Two Peoples: Judge Pierre Landry, 88; auth, A Victorian Lady's Album: Kate Shannon's Halifax and Boston Diary of 1892, 94. **CONTACT ADDRESS** Can Stud Prog, Mount Saint Vincent Univ, 106 Shore Dr, Bedford, NS, Canada B4A 2E1. **EMAIL** dellaStanley@msvu.ca

STANLEY-BLACKWELL, LAURIE
PERSONAL Born Kingston, ON, Canada **DISCIPLINE** HISTORY **EDUCATION** Mt Allison Univ, BA, 77; Dalhousie Univ, MA, 80; Queen's Univ, PhD, 89. **CAREER** Instr, Queen's Univ, 86-88; Asst Prof, 89-94, Assoc Prof Hist, St Francis Xavier Univ, 94-. **HONORS AND AWARDS** Federated Alumni Life Mem Prize, 77; Tweedle Memorial Gold Medal, 77; Groiler Award Hist, 78, Outstanding Tchr Award, Fac Arts, Mt Allison Univ, 95,; Killam Memorial Scholar, Dalhousie Univ, 78-79. **MEMBERSHIPS** Can Hist Asn; Asn Can Studs; Atlantic Asn Hist. **RESEARCH** History of Maritime Canada, as well as Canadian culture and religious history. **SELECTED PUBLICATIONS** Auth, Unclean! Unclean! Leprosy in New Brunswick 1844-1880, 82; auth, The Well-Watered Garden: The Presbyterian Church in Cape Breton 1798-1860, 83; contribur, Dictionary of Canadian Biography, coauth, Canadian Studies: a guide to the Sources; coauth, Changing roles of women within the Christian Church in Canada; coauth, the Contrubution of Presbyterianism to the Maritime Provinces of Canada; coauth, St George's Cathedral: Two Hundred Years of Community; coauth, Les abeilles pillotent. **CONTACT ADDRESS** Dept of History, St. Francis Xavier Univ, Antigonish, NS, Canada B2G 2W5. **EMAIL** lstanley@juliet.stfx.ca

STANSIFER, CHARLES LEE
PERSONAL Born 12/13/1930, Garden City, KS, m, 1954, 4 children **DISCIPLINE** LATIN AMERICAN HISTORY **EDUCATION** Wichita State Univ, BA, 53, MA, 54; Tulane Univ, PhD, 59. **CAREER** Ed asst, Miss Valley Hist Rev, 55-58; asst prof hist, Univ Southwestern La, 58-63; asst prof, 63-65, dir jr year prog, Costa Rica, 66 & 74, assoc prof, 65-79, prof hist, Univ KS, 79-, Dir, Ctr Latin Am Studies, 75-89, Doherty Found fel, 62-63; dir, Tri-Univ Ctr Latin Am Studies, KS, 76-82. **MEMBERSHIPS** Conf Latin Am Hist; Lat Am Studies Asn. **RESEARCH** Central Am and Mex hist; US-Latin Am diplomatic rel(s). **SELECTED PUBLICATIONS** Auth, E George Squier and the Honduras Interoceanic Railroad Project, Hisp Am Hist Rev, 2/66; Application of the Tobar Doctrine to Central America, The Americas, 1/67; E George Squier: Varios aspectos de su carrera in Centro America, Rev Pensamiento Centroam, 68; National Latin America: A topical approach, Univ Kans, 74; Jose Santos Zelaya: A new look at Nicaragua's liberal dictator, Rev Interam, fall 77; Ruben Dario and his relationship to the Dictator Zelaya, Ann, Southeastern Asn Latin Am Studies, 3/79; The Nicaraguan national literacy crusade, No 6, 81 & Cultural Policy in the old and the new Nicaragua, No 41, 81, Am Univs Field Staff Reports; Costa Rica, Clio Press, 91; Nicaragua's prolonged contra war, In: Prolonged war: a post-nuclear challenge, Air Univ Press, 94; Elections and democracy in Central America: the cases of Costa Rica and Nicaragua, In: Assessing democracy in Latin America, Westview Press, 98; coauth, La Universidad de Costa Rica of Universidad de Kansas: Origenes de sus relaciones academicas Nvestra Tierra Editorial (San Jose, Costa Rica) (00), 115 . **CONTACT ADDRESS** Dept of Hist, Univ of Kansas, Lawrence, Lawrence, KS 66045-0001. **EMAIL** cstan@ukans.edu

STANSKY, PETER D. L.
PERSONAL Born 01/18/1932, New York, NY, s **DISCIPLINE** HISTORY **EDUCATION** Yale Univ, BA, 53; Kings Col, BA, 55; MA, 59; Harvard Univ, PhD. **CAREER** Asst prof, Harvard Univ, 61-68; assoc prof, to prof, Stanford, 68-. **HONORS AND AWARDS** NEH, 83, 98; Guggenheim, 66, 73; ACLS, 78. **MEMBERSHIPS** AHA; NACBS; PCCBS; RSVP; William Morris Soc. **SELECTED PUBLICATIONS** Ed, Left and War: The British Labour Party and the First World War (69); ed, John Morley: Nineteenth Century Essays (70); ed, On Churchill: A Profile (73); ed, Victorian Revolution: Government and Society in Victoria's Britain (73); ed, Nineteen Eighty-Four (83); co-ed, The Aesthetic Movement and the Arts and Crafts Movement (76, 79); On or About December 1910: Early Bloomsbury and its Intimate World (96); auth, The Book that Never Was: William Morris, Charles Gere and the Mouse of the Wolfings (98); coauth, Journey to the Frontier: Julian Bell and John Cornford, Their Lives and the 1930's (66); coauth, The Unknown Orwell (72); coauth, The Transformation (79). William Abraham's) London's Burning (1994) **CONTACT ADDRESS** Dept History, Stanford Univ, Bldg 200, Stanford, CA 94305. **EMAIL** stansky@stanford.edu

STANTON, EDWARD F.
PERSONAL Born 10/29/1942, Colorado Springs, CO, m, 1996, 2 children **DISCIPLINE** HISPANIC STUDIES **EDUCATION** UCLA, BA, 64; MA, 69; PhD, 72. **CAREER** Asst prof, 72-78; assoc prof, 79-89; prof, 89-; Bingham prof, 98-; Univ Ken; vis prof, Univ Comp, Spn, 96; vis prof, Univ, Intl Mend, Spain, 99. **HONORS AND AWARDS** Sr Fulbright Lectr; SMC Res Gnt; Phi Eta Sigma; Phi Beta Kappa; NEH Gnt; Innov Teach Awd; Nat Def Res Fel; Del Amo Found Res Fel; Dict Am Schl, Contemp Auth, Intl Biog. **MEMBERSHIPS** Hemingway Soc; FGL. **RESEARCH** Modern Spanish literature film and culture; comparative literature. **SELECTED PUBLICATIONS** Auth, The Tragic Myth: Lorca and Cante Jondo, Univ Press Kentucky (Lexington, KY), 78; auth, Hemingway and Spain: A Pursuit, Univ Wash Press, 89; auth, Road of Stars to Santiago, Univ Press Kentucky (Lexington, KY), 94; auth, Hemingway y el Pais Vasco, Centro Vasco de las Artes y las Letras (Bilbao, Spain), 97; auth, Handbook of Popular Spanish Culture, Greenwood Press (Westport, CT), 99; auth, Culture and Customs of Spain, Greenwood Press (Westport, CT), forthcoming; auth, Notable Hispanic Quotations, Greenwood Press (Westport, CT), forthcoming. **CONTACT ADDRESS** Dept Spanish, Italian, Univ of Kentucky, 500 S Limestone St, Lexington, KY 40506-0001. **EMAIL** stanton@pop.uky.edu

STANTON, PHOEBE BAROODY
PERSONAL Born 12/05/1914, Freeport, IL, w, 1948, 1 child **DISCIPLINE** HISTORY, ART HISTORY **EDUCATION** Mt Holyoke Col, BA, 37; Radcliffe Col, MA, 38; Univ London, PhD, 50. **CAREER** Instr humanities, Reed Col, 45-46; cult affairs asst, US Embassy, London, 50-51, cult affairs off, 51-53; lectr hist of art, Bryn Mawr Col, 53-54; educator, Walters Gallery, Baltimore, Md, 54-55; lectr, Goucher Col, Towson, Md, 55-56; lectr hist of art, eve col, 55-80, from asst prof to prof, 62-71, William R Kenan, Jr prof hist of art, Johns Hopkins Univ, 71-80; consult urban design, Dept Housing & Community Develop & Charles Ctr-Inner Harbor Mgt Admin, City of Baltimore, 70-. **HONORS AND AWARDS** Calvert Prize for Historic Preservation, 76; Emmarv Awd, critical writing, 76; Col Art Assoc Distinguished teaching award, 80; Am Council of Learned Societies Grant, 46-49; Nat Endow for the Humanities, 67-68, 72-72; Chapel Brook Found Grant, 67-68; Phi Beta Kappa, Mt. Holyoke Col, 37; Honorary Doctorates, Mt. Holyoke Col, 71, Towson State Univ, 80. **MEMBERSHIPS** Col Art Asn Am; Victorian Soc; Soc Archit Hist, Gt Brit; Soc Archit Historians. **RESEARCH** History of architecture in Great Britain and the United States; history of urban design. **SELECTED PUBLICATIONS** Auth, The Gothic Revival and American Church Architecture: An Episode in Taste 1840-1856, Johns Hopkins Univ, 68; auth, Pugin, Thames & Hudson, 71; auth, 50 various articles on architecture and urban design for the Baltimore Sun, 71-80; auth, The George Peabody Library, in Cast Iron in Baltimore, ed J. Dilts; contrib, The Houses of Parliament, Yale, 76; auth, approx 20 articles in various peer reviewed publications. **CONTACT ADDRESS** 100 W University Pkwy, Baltimore, MD 21210. **EMAIL** pabstanton@aol.com

STAPLES, A.
PERSONAL Born 01/02/1969, Buffalo, NY, m, 1992 **DISCIPLINE** HISTORY **EDUCATION** St. Bona Venture Univ, BA, 91; Ohio State Univ, MA & PhD, 93, 98. **CAREER** Asst, Prof of History, Middle Tenn State Univ, 98-; Asst Ed, Diplomatic History, 93-95. **HONORS AND AWARDS** Stuart L. Bernath Dissertation Grant of the Society for Historians of Am Foreign Relations, 96; CLIO Awd for Distinguished Teaching of the Zeta Chapter of Phi Alpha Theta, 94. **MEMBERSHIPS** AHA; OAH; SHAFR; Phi Alpha; Theta. **RESEARCH** UN Specialized Agencies; Economic Development; International Identity. **SELECTED PUBLICATIONS** Auth, "Norris E Dodd and the Connections Between Domestic and International and International Agricultural Policy," Agricultural History, 74 (Spring, 00). **CONTACT ADDRESS** Dept History, Middle Tennessee State Univ, PO Box 23, Murfreesboro, TN 37132-0001. **EMAIL** astaples@mtsu.edu

STARK, GARY DUANE
PERSONAL Born 06/27/1948, St. Paul, MN **DISCIPLINE** MODERN GERMAN HISTORY **EDUCATION** Hamline Univ, BA, 70; Johns Hopkins Univ, MA, 72, PhD(hist), 74. **CAREER** Vis asst prof hist, Dalhousie Univ, 74-75; asst prof, 75-81, ASSOC PROF HIST, UNIV TEX, ARLINGTON, 81- **MEMBERSHIPS** AHA; Southern Hist Asn; Conf Group Cent Europ Hist; Western Asn Ger Studies. **RESEARCH** German cultural history; German social and political history; sociology of knowledge. **SELECTED PUBLICATIONS** Auth, Der Verleger als Kulturunternehmer, Archiv fur Geschichte des Buchwesens, 76; Publishers and cultural patronage in Germany, 1890-1933, Ger Studies Rev, 78; The ideology of the German Burschenschaft generation, Europ Studies Rev, 78; Entrepreneurs of Ideology: Neoconservative Publishers in Germany 1890-1933, Univ NC, 81; ed, Essays in Culture and Society in Modern Germany, Tex A&M Univ, 82. **CONTACT ADDRESS** Dept of Hist, Univ of Texas, Arlington, Arlington, TX 76019.

STARKEY, ARMSTRONG
PERSONAL m, 1962, 1 child **DISCIPLINE** HISTORY **EDUCATION** Hiram Col, BA, 60; Univ Ill, MA, 62; PhD, 68. **CAREER** Adelphi Univ, 68-. **MEMBERSHIPS** Soc of Military Hist. **RESEARCH** 18th Century Military and Cultural History. **SELECTED PUBLICATIONS** Auth, "War and Culture, A Case Study: The English and the Conduct of the British Army in America, 1755-1781," War and Society, (90), auth, "Paol: to Stony Poiul: An essay on military ethics and weaponry during the American Revolution," Jour of Military Hist, (94); auth, "European and Native American Warfare, 1675-1815," Oklahoma, (98). **CONTACT ADDRESS** Dept Hist, Adelphi Univ, Garden City, NY 11530. **EMAIL** starkey@adelphi.edu

STARN, RANDOLPH
PERSONAL Born 04/03/1939, Modesto, CA, m, 1960, 2 children **DISCIPLINE** EARLY MODERN EUROPEAN HISTORY **EDUCATION** Stanford Univ, BA, 60; Univ Calif, Berkeley, MA, 61; Harvard Univ, PhD(Hist), 67. **CAREER** Asst prof, 66-71, assoc prof, 71-78, prof Hist, Univ Calif, Berkeley, 78-; Marian E Koshland Disting prof and dir Townsend Cen for Humanities, 96; prof Italian Studies; Fulbright lectr, Univ Perugia, 73-74; vis mem, Inst Advan Study, Princeton Univ, 79-80; Guggenheim Fel, 84; dir Ecole des Hautes Etudes, Paris, 86. **MEMBERSHIPS** AHA; Renaissance Soc Am. **RESEARCH** Renaissance Italy; historiography; history. **SELECTED PUBLICATIONS** Auth, Donato Giannotti and His Epistolae, Droz, Geneva, 68; A Renaissance Likeness: Art and Culture in Raphael's Julius II, 80 & Contrary Commonwealth: The Theme of Exile in Medieval and Renaissance Italy, 82, Univ Calif; Arts of Power 92, Univ Calif, Ambrogio Lorenzetti Soc, 94. **CONTACT ADDRESS** Dept of History, Univ of California, Berkeley, 3229 Dwinelle Hall, Berkeley, CA 94720-2551.

STARR, CHESTER G.
PERSONAL Born 10/05/1914, Centralia, MO, m, 1940, 4 children **DISCIPLINE** ANCIENT HISTORY **EDUCATION** Univ Mo, AB, 34, AM, 35; Cornell Univ, PhD, 38. **CAREER** Am Acad Rome fel, 38-40; from instr to prof hist, Univ Ill, Urbana-Champaign, 40-70; PROF HIST, UNIV MICH, ANN ARBOR, 70-, BENTLEY PROF, 73-, Guggenheim fel, 50-51, 58-59. **HONORS AND AWARDS** Citation of Merit, Univ Mo, 63; lld, univ mo, 81. **MEMBERSHIPS** AHA; Soc Promotion Roman Studies; Asn Ancient historians (pres, 74-78); fel, Am Acad Arts & Sci. **RESEARCH** Roman Empire; ancient civilization; early Greece. **SELECTED PUBLICATIONS** Auth, Civilization and the Caesars, Cornell Univ, 54; Origins of Greek Civilization, Knopf, 61; Roman Imperial Navy, Heffer, Cambridge, 2nd ed, 61; History of the Ancient World, Oxford Univ, 65, 3rd ed, 82; Awakening of the Greek Historical Spirit, Knopf, 68; Athenian Coinage, 480-449 BC, Clarendon, 70; Political Intelligence in Classical Greece, Brill, 74; Economic and Social Growth in Early Greece, Oxford Univ, 77; Beginnings of Imperial Rome, Univ Mich, 80; Essays on Ancient History, Brill, 79; The Roman Empire: A Study in Survival, Oxford Univ, 82; Ships And Sea-Power Before The Great-Persian-War--The Ancestry Of The Ancient Trireme, Am Hist Rev, Vol 99, 94. **CONTACT ADDRESS** Dept of Hist, Univ of Michigan, Ann Arbor, 555 S State St, 1029 Tisch Hall, Ann Arbor, MI 48109-1003.

STARR, KEVIN
DISCIPLINE HISTORY **EDUCATION** PhD. **CAREER** Prof, Sch Urban and Regional Plan, Univ Southern Calif. **RESEARCH** History of California & the West. **SELECTED PUBLICATIONS** Auth, Americans & the California Dream, 1850-1915, Oxford, 73; Inventing the Dream: California Through the Progressive Era, Oxford, 85; Material Dreams: Southern California Through the 1920s, Oxford, 90; The Dream Endures: California Through the Great Depression, Oxford, 96. **CONTACT ADDRESS** Dept of History, Univ of So California, University Park Campus, Los Angeles, CA 90089. **EMAIL** kstarr@library.ca.gov

STARR-LEBEAU, GRETCHEN D.
DISCIPLINE HISTORY **EDUCATION** Univ Va, BA, 90; Univ Mich, MA, 92; PhD, 96. **CAREER** Asst prof, Univ Ky, 97-. **MEMBERSHIPS** Am Hist Asn, Soc for Span & Port Hist Studies, Sixteenth-century Studies, Am Acad of Res Historians of Medieval Spain. **RESEARCH** Fifteenth- through Seventeenth-century Spanish History, Religious and Cultural History. **SELECTED PUBLICATIONS** Ed, American Eras: Early American Civilizations and Exploration to 1600, Gale Pr, 97; auth, "Mari Sanchez and Irez Gonzalez: Conflict and Cooperation Among New Christians," in Women in the Inquisition, ed. Mary Giles (Johns Hopkins Univ Pr, 98). **CONTACT ADDRESS** Dept Hist, Univ of Kentucky, 500 S Limestone St, Lexington, KY 40506-0001. **EMAIL** starrle@pop.uky.edu

STARTT, JAMES DILL
PERSONAL Born 07/26/1932, Baltimore, MD, m, 1960, 2 children **DISCIPLINE** BRITISH COMMONWEALTH & BRITISH HISTORY **EDUCATION** Univ Md, BA, 57, MA, 61, PhD(hist), 65. **CAREER** Asst prof hist, Murray State Univ, 64-66; assoc prof, 66-71, PROF HIST, VALPARAISO UNIV, 71- **MEMBERSHIPS** AHA; MidWest Conf Brit Studies; Am Comt Irish Studies. **RESEARCH** History of Journalism; British history. **SELECTED PUBLICATIONS** Auth, Early press reaction to Wilson's league proposal, Jour Quart, summer 62; Wilson's mission to Paris: The making of a decision, Historian, summer 68; Wilson's trip to Paris: Profile of press response, Jour Quart, winter 69; The uneasy partnership: Wilson and the press at Paris, Mid-Am, 1/70; A perspective on historians in twentieth century America, Cresset, 9/75; Into the Thirties with J L Garvin: Private thoughts of a great publicist, Libr Chronicle, 78; Journalism's Unofficial Ambassador: A Biography of Edward Price Bell, 1869-1943, Ohio Univ Press, 79. **CONTACT ADDRESS** 822 Brosn St, Valparaiso, IN 46383.

STAUDENMAIER, JOHN M.
DISCIPLINE HISTORY OF AMERICA **EDUCATION** St Louis Univ, BA, MA; Univ Pa, PhD. **CAREER** Prof, 81. **HONORS AND AWARDS** Bannon scholar, Santa Clara Univ; Dibner fel, MIT; Gasson Prof, Boston College. **MEMBERSHIPS** Soc History of Technology, Am Historians, Amnesty Int. **RESEARCH** Historiography of Technology, Technologi-

cal Ethics. **SELECTED PUBLICATIONS** Auth, Technology's Storytellers: Reweaving the Human Fabric; ed, Technology and Culture. **CONTACT ADDRESS** Dept of Hist, Univ of Detroit Mercy, 4001 W McNichols Rd, PO BOX 19900, Detroit, MI 48219-0900.

STAUFFER, GEORGE B.
PERSONAL Born 02/18/1947, Hershey, PA, m, 1986, 1 child **DISCIPLINE** MUSIC HISTORY, LITERATURE, PERFORMANCE **EDUCATION** Columbia Univ, PhD. **CAREER** Prof & dean ch; gen ed, Monuments Western Mus ser at Macmillan. **HONORS AND AWARDS** Guggenheim, Fulbright, ACLS, and IREX fellowships. **MEMBERSHIPS** Pres, Amer Bach Soc. **RESEARCH** Baroque music; works and life of J.S. Bach in particular. **SELECTED PUBLICATIONS** Auth, J.S. Bach as Organist; Bach Perspectives 2 & Bach: The Mass in B Minor; articles in, Early Mus, Mus Quart, J Musicol, Bach-Jahrbuch. **CONTACT ADDRESS** Rutgers, The State Univ of New Jersey, New Brunswick, Mason Gross School of the Arts, 33 Livingston Ave, New Brunswick, NJ 08901-1959. **EMAIL** stauffer@rci.rutgers.edu

STAVE, BRUCE M.
PERSONAL Born 05/17/1937, New York, NY, m, 1961, 1 child **DISCIPLINE** AMERICAN HISTORY **EDUCATION** Columbia Univ, AB, 59, MA, 61; Univ Pittsburgh, PhD(hist), 66. **CAREER** From instr to asst prof hist, Univ Bridgeport, 65-70; from asst prof to assoc prof, 70-75, res found grants, 70-, dir, oral hist proj, 79-81, prof hist, 75- , chemn, 85-94, Univ CT, dir, Ctr Oral Hist, 81-, Fulbright lectr, India, 68-69; Nat Endowment Hum fel, 74; dir, Peoples CT Oral Hist Proj, 74-76; guest fel & vis lectr, Yale Col, 76; ed, Oral Hist Rev, 96-99, assoc ed, J Urban Hist, 76-; Fulbright prof, New Zealand, Australia & Philippines, 77, Fulbright prof, Peoples Rep of China, 84-85; Board of Trustees Distinguished Prof, 00-. **HONORS AND AWARDS** Harvey Kantor Mem Awd for Significant Work in Oral Hist, New Eng Asn Oral Hist, 77; Homer Babbidge Jr Awd for best bk, Asn for Study of CT Hist, 95. **MEMBERSHIPS** AHA; Orgn Am Historians; Oral Hist Asn; Soc Sci Hist Asn; Immigrant Hist Soc; New Eng Hist Asn; CT Acad of Arts & Sci; New Eng Asn of Oral Hist; CT Coord Comt for the Promotion of Hist. **RESEARCH** Am urban hist; recent Am hist; oral hist. **SELECTED PUBLICATIONS** Auth, The New Deal and the Last Hurrah, Univ Pittsburgh, 70; ed, Urban Bosses, Machines and Progressive Reformers, Heath, 72; co-ed, The Discontented Society, Rand McNally, 72; auth, Urban bosses and reform, In: The Urban Experience, Wadworth, 73; Series of oral history conversations on urban history, J Urban Hist, 74-; ed & contribr, Socialism & the Cities, Kennikat, 75, 77; auth, The Making of Urban History, 77 & ed, Modern Industrial Cities: History, Policy & Survival, 81, Sage; co-ed, Talking about Connecticut: Oral History in the Nutmeg State, Conn Humanities Council, 85, rev, 90; coauth, Mills and Meadows: A Pictorial History of Northeastern Connecticut, Donning Co, 91; coauth, From the Old Country: An Oral History of European Migration to America, Twayne, 94; coauth, Witnesses to Nuremberg: An Oral History of American Participants at the War Crimes Trials, Twayne, 98. **CONTACT ADDRESS** Dept of History, Univ of Connecticut, Storrs, Storrs, CT 06269-2103. **EMAIL** stave@uconnvm.uconn.edu

STAVIG, WARD
PERSONAL Born 11/30/1948, Ukiah, CA, m, 1986, 2 children **DISCIPLINE** HISTORY **EDUCATION** Univ Calif Davis, PhD, 91 **CAREER** Instr, Sacramento City Col, 75-78; lectr, Calif St Univ Hayword, 89; vis lectr, Univ Calif Santa Cruz, 91; lectr, Univ Calif Davis, 90, 92; vis prof, Universidad Catolica Boliviana, 93; asst prof to assoc prof, Univ S Fl, 93- . **HONORS AND AWARDS** Fulbright Fel, 83-84, 92-93. **MEMBERSHIPS** AHA; CLAH. **RESEARCH** Colonial Andes; indigenous society. **SELECTED PUBLICATIONS** Auth, " Ladrones, Cuatreros Y Salteadores: Indios Criminales en el Cuzco Rural a fines de la Colonia," Bandoleros, Abiigeos Y Montoneros, Criminalidad y Vilolencia en el Peru, Siglos XVII-XX, Lima, 90; auth, " The Past Weighs on the Minds of the Living: Culture Ethnicity, and the Rural Lower Class," Latin American Speech Review, Vol XXVI, no 2, 91; auth," Living in Offense of Our Lord" : Indigenous Sexual Values and Marital Life in the Colonial Crucible," Hispanic American Historical Review, Vol 75, no, 4, 95; auth, Conflict, Violence, And Resistance, in The Countryside in Colonial Latin America, Univ NM Press, 96; America and the People Truly Without History, review essay, Colonial Latin American, 97; Culture, Technology and Social Change: Selected Proceedings of the Third Biennial conf, Univ S Fl, 96; Amor y Violencia Sexual, Valores indigenas en la sociedad colonial, Instituto de Estudios Peruanos, 96; The World of Tupac Amaru: Cultural Identity, community and Conflict in Colonial Peru, Univ Nb Press, 99; auth, " Ambiguous Visions: Nature, Law, and Culture in Indigenouys-Spanish Land Relations in Colonial Peru," HAHR 80:1, 00; auth, " Continuing The Bleeding of These Pueblos Will Shortly Make Them Cadavers: The Potosi Mita, Cultural Identity, and Communal Survival in Colonial Peru," The Americas Vol 56:4, 00. **CONTACT ADDRESS** Dept of History, Univ of So Florida, 4202 E Fowler Ave, Tampa, FL 33620-8100. **EMAIL** stavig@lluna.cas.usf.edu

STAVRIANOS, LEFTEN STAVROS
PERSONAL Born 02/05/1913, Vancouver, BC, Canada **DISCIPLINE** HISTORY **EDUCATION** Univ BC, AB, 33; Clark Univ, AM, 34, PhD, 37. **CAREER** Lectr, Queen's Univ, Can, 37-38, instr, Smith Col, 39-43, asst prof, 43-44, 45-46; from assoc prof to prof, 46-73, EMER PROF HIST, NORTHWESTERN UNIV, 73-; ADJ PROF, UNIV CALIF, SAN DIEGO, 76-, Royal Soc Can fel, Europe, 38-39; Guggenheim fel, 51-52; fel, Ctr Advan Study Behav Sci, 72-73. **MEMBERSHIPS** AHA; Nat Educ Asn. **RESEARCH** World history; modern Balkan history. **SELECTED PUBLICATIONS** Auth, Balkan Federation; The Balkans Since 1453; World Since 1500, 66, World to 1500, 70 & Man's Past and Present, 70, Prentice-Hall; The Promise of the Coming Dark Age, W H Freeman, 76; Global Rift: The Third World Comes of Age, William Morrow, 81. **CONTACT ADDRESS** Dept Hist, Univ of California, San Diego, La Jolla, CA 92093.

STAVROS, STEVE
DISCIPLINE HISTORY **EDUCATION** Cal Poly Pomona, BA, 90; Claremont Grad School, MA, 92. **CAREER** Adj instr, Chaffey Col, 94-. **HONORS AND AWARDS** Teacher of Distinction, Riverside Community Col. **MEMBERSHIPS** Calif Part Time Fac Asn. **RESEARCH** Anti-bellum US history. **SELECTED PUBLICATIONS** Auth, "F.B. Warder: Letters to Home from the USS Seawolf", Submarine Rev, Oct (99). **CONTACT ADDRESS** Sch Soc & Behav Sci, Chaffey Col, 5885 Haven Ave, Alta Loma, CA 91737-3002. **EMAIL** sjstav@aol.om

STAYER, JAMES MENTZER
PERSONAL Born 03/15/1935, Lancaster, PA, m, 1958, 3 children **DISCIPLINE** HISTORY **EDUCATION** Juaniata Col, AB, 57; Univ Va, AM, 58; Cornell Univ, PhD(hist), 64. **CAREER** Instr hist, Ithaca Col, 59-61; asst prof, Bridgewater Col, 62-65; asst prof early mod Europ hist, Bucknell Univ, 65-68; asst prof Renaissance & Reformation hist, 68-72, assoc prof, 72-78, PROF HIST, QUEEN'S UNIV, ONT, 78-, Am Philos Soc grant-in-aid, 67-68; Alexander von Humboldt Found res grant, Ger, 67-67 & 79-80; publ subvention, Humanities Res Coun Can, 72; Can Coun leave fel, 74-75; Soc Sci Humanities Res Coun Can, 82-83. **MEMBERSHIPS** Sixteenth Century Studies Conf; Am Soc Reformation Res. **RESEARCH** Ulrich Zwingli; Renaissance and Reformation history; radical reformation. **SELECTED PUBLICATIONS** Auth, The German Peasants' War and Antibaptist Community of Goods, 94; auth, Martin Luther: German Saviour, German Evangelical Theological Factions and Interpretation of Luther, 1917-1933, McGill-Queen's Press, 00. **CONTACT ADDRESS** Dept of Hist, Queen's Univ at Kingston, Kingston, ON, Canada K7L 3N6. **EMAIL** jms2@post.queensu.ca

STEADY, FILOMINA
DISCIPLINE AFRICAN AMERICAN STUDIES **EDUCATION** Smith Col, BA, 65; Boston Univ, MA, 66; Oxford Univ, BLiH, 68; PhD, 74. **HONORS AND AWARDS** Otelia Cromwell Distinguished Alumni Awd, Smith Col, 82. **MEMBERSHIPS** African Studies Asn; Asn of Black Women Hist. **RESEARCH** Africana Studies (Gender Studies); Gender and Development; African diaspora, theory and methodology. **SELECTED PUBLICATIONS** Ed, Activities of the United Nations System on Women in Environment and Development, UNCED Res Paper, 92; ed, National Reports: Selected Case Studies on the Role of Women in Sustainable Development, UNCED Res Paper, 92; ed, Women and Children First: Environment, Poverty and Sustainable Development, Schenkman Books, 93; co-ed, Women and the United Nations: Reflections and New Horizons, Schenkman Books, 95; auth, Women and the Amistad Connection: Sierra Leone Krio Society, Schenkman Books, 00; auth, "African Feminism," Encyclopaedia of Feminism, Routledge, 00; auth, "Women in Africa and in the Diaspora: Linkages and Influences," in Global Dimensions of the African Diaspora, Howard Univ Press, forthcoming; auth, "The Gender Factor in the African Social Situation," The African Social Situation, forthcoming; auth, "Unity and Disunity: The Challenge of Ethnicity to Africa's Development," in Ethnicity, Citizenship, Stability and Socioeconomic Development in Africa, forthcoming; auth, "Gender, Democratic Culture and Practice in Africa," AAWORD, forthcoming. **CONTACT ADDRESS** African Am Studies, Wellesley Col, 106 Central St, Wellesley, MA 02481.

STEALEY, JOHN E.
PERSONAL Born 10/28/1941, Clarksburg, WV, m, 1963 **DISCIPLINE** HISTORY **EDUCATION** WVa Univ, AB, 63; WVa Univ, MA, 65; WVa Univ, PhD, 70. **CAREER** Asst Prof, Glenville State Col, 67-69; Asst Prof, Shepherd Col, 69-71; Prof, Shepherd Col, 74-. **HONORS AND AWARDS** Nat Defense Grad Fel, 63-66, Ford Found Travel-Study Grant, 73; Fel, WVa Humanities Coun, 96. **MEMBERSHIPS** SHA, Orgn of Am Historians, Agr Hist Soc. **RESEARCH** American economic history, American legal history, Southern Appalachia, reconstruction in border states. **SELECTED PUBLICATIONS** Auth, The Antebellum Kanawha Salt Business and Western Markets, UP Ky (Lexington, KY), 93; auth, Kanawhan Prelude to Nineteenth-Century Monopoly in the United States, Hist Soc (Richmond, VA), 00. **CONTACT ADDRESS** Dept Hist, Shepherd Col, PO Box 3210, Shepherdstown, WV 25443. **EMAIL** jstealey@shepherd.edu

STEARNS, PETER N.
PERSONAL Born 03/03/1936, London, England, m, 1998, 4 children **DISCIPLINE** MODERN HISTORY **EDUCATION** Harvard Univ, AB, 57, AM, 59; PhD, 63. **CAREER** From instr to assoc prof hist, Univ Chicago, 62-68; prof, Rutgers Univ, New Brunswick, 68-73, chmn dept, 69-73; HENIZ PROF, CARNEGIE-MELLON UNIV, 73-, DEAN, COL OF HUMANITIES AND SOCIAL SCIENCES, 91-; Vis asst prof, Northwestern Univ, 65; managing ed, J Social Hist, 67-; Am Philos Soc & Soc Sci Res Coun grants, 67-68; vis prof, Sir George William Univ, 70; Guggenheim fel, 73-74; vis prof polit sci, Univ Houston, 78. **HONORS AND AWARDS** Koren Prize, Soc Fr Hist Studies, 66; Newcomen Spec Awd Bus Hist, Newcomen Soc, 67; Guggenheim fellowship, 72-74 **MEMBERSHIPS** AHA, vice-pres, 95-98; Soc Fr Hist Studies; Soc Sci Hist Asn. **RESEARCH** Modern social history; comparative European history; applied history; world history. **SELECTED PUBLICATIONS** Auth, European Society in Upheaval, Macmillan, 67, rev ed, 75; 1848: The Tide of Revolution in Europe, Norton, 74; Lives of Labor: Works in Maturing Industial Society, 75 & Old Age in European Society, 77, Holmes & Meier; Paths to Authority, Middle Class Consciousness, Univ IL, 78; Be a Man! Males in Society, 80 & Old Age in Preindustrial Society, 82, Holmes & Meier; Anger: the Struggle for Emotional Control in America's History, Chicago, 86; World History: Patterns of Change and Continuity, Harper & Row, 87; Jealousy: The Evolution of an Emotion in American History, NYU, 89; Meaning Over Memory: Recasting the Teaching of Culture and History, NC, 93; The Industrial Revolution in World History, Westview, 93; American Cool: Developing the Twentieth-Century Emotional Style, NYU, 94; Millenium III, Century XXI: A Retrospective on the Future, Westview, 96; Fat History: Bodies and Beauty in Western Society, NYU, 97. **CONTACT ADDRESS** Dept of Hist, George Mason Univ, Fairfax, 4400 University Dr., Fairfax, VA 22030. **EMAIL** pstearns@gmu.edu

STEARNS, STEPHEN
PERSONAL Born 12/24/1935, Boston, MA, w, 4 children **DISCIPLINE** HISTORY **EDUCATION** Harvard Univ, BA, 57; Columbia Univ, MA, 59; Univ Calif, Berkeley, PhD, 67. **CAREER** Instr, Vassar Col, 65-67; asst prof, CUNY, Richmond Col, 67-74; assoc prof, CUNY, Col of Staten Island, 74-. **HONORS AND AWARDS** Fulbright Grant, UK, 62063; Renewal Awd, 63-64; Moncado Prize, Am Military Inst. **MEMBERSHIPS** AHA; Conf on British Studies. **RESEARCH** Early modern Britain; Military History. **SELECTED PUBLICATIONS** Auth, "Conscription and English Society in the 1620's", Jour of British Studies, 72; auth, "Leonard Woolf and the Long Journey for Peace", Peace and Change, 74; auth, "a Problem of Logistics in the Early 17th Century: the Siege of Re", Military Affairs, 78. **CONTACT ADDRESS** Dept History, Col of Staten Island, CUNY, 2800 Victory Blvd, Staten Island, NY 10314-6609.

STEBBINS, ROBERT E.
PERSONAL Born 07/28/1931, Lima, OH, m, 1954, 3 children **DISCIPLINE** MODERN EUROPEAN HISTORY **EDUCATION** Bowling Green State Univ, BA, 53; Yale Univ, BD, 56; Univ Minn, MA, 60, PhD(hist), 65. **CAREER** Assoc prof, 63-71, prof Hist, Eastern KY Univ, 71-. **MEMBERSHIPS** AHA **RESEARCH** Nineteenth century France; European intellectual history. **CONTACT ADDRESS** Dept of Hist, Eastern Kentucky Univ, 521 Lancaster Ave, Richmond, KY 40475-3102. **EMAIL** Hisstebb@acs.eku.edu

STEBENNE, DAVID
PERSONAL Born 07/04/1960, Providence, RI, s **DISCIPLINE** HISTORY, LAW **EDUCATION** Yale Univ, BA, 82; Columbia Univ, JD, MA, 86, PhD, 91. **CAREER** Lectr, Hist, Yale Univ, 91-93; asst prof, Hist, Ohio State Univ, 93-97; Assoc Prof, Hist, Ohio State Univ, 97-. **MEMBERSHIPS** Am Hist Asn; Org Am Hist; Bus Hist Conf; Md Bar **RESEARCH** Modern US history; politics, economics, labor & legal history **SELECTED PUBLICATIONS** Arthur J. Goldberg: New Deal Liberal, Oxford Univ Press, 96. **CONTACT ADDRESS** Hist Dept, Ohio State Univ, Columbus, 106 Dulles Hall, 230 w 17th, Columbus, OH 43210-1367. **EMAIL** stebenne.1@osu.edu

STEEGER, WILLIAM P.
PERSONAL Born 05/26/1945, Brooklyn, NY, m, 1968, 4 children **DISCIPLINE** OLD TESTAMENT ARCHEOLOGY **EDUCATION** Univ Florida, BA, 67; Southern Baptist Theol Sem, Louisville, Mdiv 70, PhD, 83; Univ of Louisville, KY, MA, 72. **CAREER** Instr, 69-73, Univ of Louisville; Prof, 76-86, Baptist Theol of Southern Africa, Johannesburg, S Africa; Prof, 78-86, Die Theol Sem van die Baptist; Prof, 83-84, Oakland City Coll; Prof, 86, Ouachita Baptist Univ, Arkadelphia, AR, Chr Div of Rel and Philos, prof to retire prof, So Baptist Theol Sem. **HONORS AND AWARDS** Phi Kappa Phi; Phi Alpha Theta; Amer Ed, KY, South; Biblical Stud and Archaeol; Man of Achievement; Vis Prof of OT-Southern Baptist Theol Sem, KY. **MEMBERSHIPS** Soc of Biblical Lit; Evangelical Theol Soc; Inst of Biblical Res; Natl Assoc of Baptist Prof of Rel. **RESEARCH** Old Testament; Biblical Archaeology. **SELECTED PUBLICATIONS** Contrib auth, Anchor Bible Dictionary, Doubleday & Co; Contrib auth, Mercer Commentary of the Bible, Mercer

Univ Press; auth, Joshua: An Exposition, Baptist Theological College of Southern Africa, Johannesburg, South Africa; Psalms: An Exposition, Old Testament Theology, Old Testament Introduction, Baptist Theo College of S Africa, Johannesburg, S Africa. **CONTACT ADDRESS** Dept Old Testament, So Baptist Theol Sem, 2825 Lexington Rd., Louisville, KY 40280. **EMAIL** steeger@alpha.edu

STEELE, JANE
PERSONAL Born 04/27/1955, Salisbury, NC, s **DISCIPLINE** US HISTORY **EDUCATION** Livingstone Col, BA, 77; NC Central Univ, MLS, 80; MA, 86. **CAREER** Govt Documents Libr, Forsyth County Pub Libr, 83-84; Ref Libr, Barber-Scotia Col, 80; Historian, Old Salem, Inc, 86-. **HONORS AND AWARDS** NCCU SLS/IS fel, 78-79; MESCA Scholar, 90. **MEMBERSHIPS** Early Music Am; Special Libr Assoc; Phi Gamma Mu; Phi Alpha Theta. **RESEARCH** Multiculturalism in the 18th Century, the Relationship between Native American and African Communites on the Atlantic Coast of North America, The Black Middle Class, Ancient Egypt (18th Dynasty), African and Native American Military History and Hawaiian History. **CONTACT ADDRESS** 1565 US Hwy 601 S, Mocksville, NC 27028. **EMAIL** jat50@hotmail.com

STEELE, RICHARD WILLIAM
PERSONAL Born 01/28/1934, New York, NY, m, 1957, 2 children **DISCIPLINE** AMERICAN HISTORY **EDUCATION** Queens Col, NYork, AB, 56; Univ Wis, MA, 59; Johns Hopkins Univ, MA, 66, PhD(Am hist), 69. **CAREER** Archivist, Nat Arch, 60-61; historian, Off Joint Chiefs Staff, 62-63; from asst prof to assoc prof hist, 67-75, PROF HIST, SAN DIEGO STATE UNIV, 75- **MEMBERSHIPS** AHA; Orgn Am Historians. **RESEARCH** World War II American home front; Franklin D Roosevelt and public opinion; Roosevelt subversion and dissent. **SELECTED PUBLICATIONS** Auth, "The War on Intolerance, The Reformation of American Nationalism, 1939-1941," J of Am Ethnic Hist 9 (89); auth, "Arming Military-Justice--The Origins Of The United-States-Court-Of-Military-Appeals, 1775-1950," Historian 56 (93); auth, "The Propaganda Warriors--American Crusade Against Nazi Germany," Int Hist Rev 19 (97); auth, "America Unbound, World-War-2 And The Making Of A Superpower," Pacific Hist Rev 63 (94); auth, "Fear Of The Mob And Faith In Government In Free Speech Discourse, 1919-1941," Am J of Legal Hist 38 (94); auth, Free Speech in the Good War, St Martin's Press, 99. **CONTACT ADDRESS** Dept of Hist, San Diego State Univ, San Diego, CA 92182.

STEELMAN, JOSEPH F.
PERSONAL Born 12/22/1922, Wilkesboro, NC, m, 1947, 2 children **DISCIPLINE** AMERICAN HISTORY **EDUCATION** Univ NC, AB, 43, MA, 47, PhD, 55. **CAREER** Instr hist, Univ NC, 47-52; instr hist & govt, Tex A&M Univ, 52-53; asst prof hist, State Univ NY Cortland, 53-54; from asst prof to assoc prof, 55-63, Southern fel, 58, PROF HIST, E CAROLINA UNIV, 63-, Pres, NC Lit & Hist Asn, 70- & Hist Soc NC, 76- **HONORS AND AWARDS** R D W Connor Award, 66, 67, 70; Christopher Crittenden Award, 96. **MEMBERSHIPS** AHA; Orgn Am Historians; Southern Hist Asn; North Carolina Literary and Historical Asn; The Historical Soc of North Carolina. **RESEARCH** North Carolina in the Progressive Era, 1884-1917; Republican Party politics in North Carolina, 1884-1917; Joseph Hyde Pratt and North Carolina Conservation Movements, 1884-1917. **SELECTED PUBLICATIONS** Auth, Republicanism in North Carolina: John Motley Morehead's Campaign to Revive a Moribund Party, 1908-1910, Vol XLII: 153-168; The Trials of a Republican State Chairman: John Motley Morehead and North Carolina Politics, 1910-1912, Vol XLIII: 31-42; Richmond Pearson, Roosevelt Republicans, and the Campaign of 1912 in North Carolina, Vol XLIII: 122-139; The Progressive Democratic Convention of 1914 in North Carolina, Vol XLVI: 83-104; Republican Party Strategists and the Issue of Fusion with Populists in North Carolina, 1893-1894, Vol XLVII: 244-269; Edward J Justice: Profile of a Progressive Legislator, 1899-1913, Vol XLVIII: 147-160 &; Origins of the Campaign for Constitutional Reform in North Carolina, 1912-1913, Vol LVI: 396-418, NC Historical Rev; auth, Essays in American History, 64; auth, Essays in Southern Biography, 65; auth, Studies in the History of the South 1875-1922, 66; ed, Of Tar Heel Towns, Shipbuilders, Reconstructionists, and Alliancemen: Papers in NC Hist, 81; The Papers Of William,Alexander Graham, Vol 8, 1869-1875, J Of Southern Hist, Vol 60, 94; **CONTACT ADDRESS** Dept of Hist, East Carolina Univ, Greenville, NC 27834.

STEELY, MELVIN T.
PERSONAL Born 05/09/1939, Atlanta, GA, 3, 2 children **DISCIPLINE** HISTORY **EDUCATION** Vanderbilt Univ, PhD, 71. **CAREER** Prof. **RESEARCH** Modern German history; Cold War; 20th century Europe; oral history. **SELECTED PUBLICATIONS** Auth, pubs on East Germany; Versailles Treaty, and the Nazis in the Spanish Civil War; auth, The Gentleman from Georgia: A Biography of Newt Gingrich, Mercer Univ Pr (Macon, Ga), 00. **CONTACT ADDRESS** History Dept, State Univ of West Georgia, Carrollton, GA 30118. **EMAIL** msteely@westga.edu

STEEN, IVAN DAVID
PERSONAL Born 09/06/1936, New York, NY, m, 1958, 2 children **DISCIPLINE** AMERICAN HISTORY **EDUCATION** NYork Univ, BA, 57, MA, 59, PhD(hist), 62. **CAREER** Instr hist, Hunter Col, 62-65; ASST PROF HIST, STATE UNIV NY ALBANY, 65-, Consult historian, Historic Rome Develop Proj, NY, 66-67; Dir, Oral History Program, State Univ NY Albany, 82-; Dir, Graduate Program in Public History, State Univ NY Albany, 83-; Assoc Prof, Hist, State Univ NY Albany, 85-. **MEMBERSHIPS** Orgn Am Historians; Nat Coun on Public Hist; Oral Hist Assoc. **RESEARCH** American social history; history of the American city. **SELECTED PUBLICATIONS** Auth, America's first World's Fair, NY Hist Soc Quart, 7/63; Philadelphia in the 1850's: As described by British travelers, Pa Hist, 1/66; Palaces for travelers: New York City's hotels in the 1850's as viewed by British visitors, NY Hist, 4/70; Cleansing the Puritan city: The Reverend Henry Morgan's anti-vice crusade in Boston, New Eng Quart, 9/81; Before The Mayor Was Mayor--The Education And Early Career Of Erastus Corning, Ny Hist, Vol 073, 92. **CONTACT ADDRESS** Dept of History, SUNY, Albany, RD 1 Box 196G, Albany, NY 12222. **EMAIL** oralhis@csc.albany.edu

STEETS, CHERYL
PERSONAL Born 10/02/1954, Warwick, RI, m, 1992 **DISCIPLINE** INDO-IRANIAN STUDIES **EDUCATION** Univ RI, BA, 77; UCLA, PhD, 93. **CAREER** Tchg asst, tchg fel, UCLA, 84-91. **HONORS AND AWARDS** Univ Calif Fel, 89; Mabel Wilson Richards Found Scholar, 91. **MEMBERSHIPS** Am Oriental Soc, APA. **RESEARCH** Comparative mythology and Indo-European literature; Indo-Iranian studies; Indo-Iranian linguistics. **SELECTED PUBLICATIONS** Auth, "Sun Maiden's Wedding," UMI, 93 (diss); "Ajahad u dva mithuna," Studies in Honor of Jean Puhvel, pt 1, Ancient Languages; Institute for the Study of Man, 97. **CONTACT ADDRESS** 6755 Mira Mesa Blvd, #123-168, San Diego, CA 92121. **EMAIL** nad@earthlink.net

STEEVES, PAUL DAVID
PERSONAL Born 06/20/1941, Attleboro, MA, m, 1962, 2 children **DISCIPLINE** RUSSIAN MODERN & ECCLESIASTICAL HISTORY **EDUCATION** Washington Univ, AB, 62; Univ Kans, MA, 72, PhD(Russ hist), 76. **CAREER** Asst instr Western civilization, Univ Kans, 66-68; vis lectr hist, Kans State Teachers Col, 71-72; asst prof, 72-78, PROF HIST, STETSON UNIV, 78-, DIR RUSS STUDIES, 76-, DIR HONORS PROG, 78-, Ed, Newsletter, Conf Faith & Hist, 79. **HONORS AND AWARDS** O P Backus Awd, Univ Kans, 76; W H McInery Awd, Stetson Univ, 79. **MEMBERSHIPS** AHA; Conf Faith & Hist; Am Asn Advan Slavic Studies; Soc Study Relig Under Communism; Southern Conf Slavic Studies. **RESEARCH** Evangelical Baptist movement in Russia. **SELECTED PUBLICATIONS** Auth, Baptists as subversives in the contemporary Soviet Union, In: God and Caesar, Conf Faith & Hist, 71; ed, Church and State in USSR, A sourcebook, Stetson Univ, 73; auth, Alexander Karev, evangelical in a Communist land, Fides et Historia, 76; Amendment of Soviet law concerning religious association, J Church & State, 77. **CONTACT ADDRESS** Dept of Hist, Stetson Univ, De Land, 421 N Woodland Blvd, Deland, FL 32720-3761.

STEFFEL, R. VLADIMIR
PERSONAL Born 10/10/1937, New York, NY, m **DISCIPLINE** HISTORY **EDUCATION** Case West Res, AB, 57; Ohio State, MA, 59; BS, 61; PhD, 69. **CAREER** Teach, Strang HS, 61-62; asst prof, Dalh Univ, 66-67; instr, 68-70; asst prof, 70-74; assoc prof, 74-; Oh State Univ. **HONORS AND AWARDS** NEH Fel; Dist Ser Awd; Alum Dist Teach Awd. **MEMBERSHIPS** AHA; APSA; AAASS; CBS; SHS; OAH; NCSS; CHC; ACM; NCHE. **RESEARCH** Modern British history; social and economies. **SELECTED PUBLICATIONS** Auth, "The Growth of Slum Control in the East End (of London), 1889-1907," East Lon Papers (70): 25-35; auth, "The Slum Question: The London County Council and Decent Dwellings for the Working Classes, 1880-1914," Albion 5 (73): 314-25; auth, "The Boundary Street Estate, An Example of Urban Redevelopment By the London County Council, 1880-1914," Town Plan Rev (76): 161-173; auth, "The Housing Question and Urban History: Britain, 1740-1918," J Urb Hist 6 (79): 112-118; auth, "Colonial and Indian Exhibition, 1886," in Historical Dictionary of World's Fairs and Expositions, ed. John E Finding, Kimberly D Pelle (Westport, CT: Greenwood Press, 90); auth, "The Housing Question in the East End of London Revisited, 1840-1919," Ohio Acad Hist NL (98): 1-6. **CONTACT ADDRESS** Dept History, Ohio State Univ, Marion, 1465 Mount Vernon Ave, Marion, OH 43302-5628. **EMAIL** steffel.1@osu.edu

STEFFEN, JEROME ORVILLE
PERSONAL Born 02/26/1942, WI, m, 1966, 2 children **DISCIPLINE** AMERICAN HISTORY **EDUCATION** Univ Wis, BS, 66; Eastern Michigan Univ, MA, 68; Univ Mo-Columbia, PhD(hist), 71. **CAREER** Assoc prof, Univ Okla, 74-99; prof & ch, Dept of Hist, Ga Southern Univ, 99- . **MEMBERSHIPS** Org Am Historians; Western Historical Asn. **RESEARCH** American frontier; comparative frontiers. **SELECTED PUBLICATIONS** Ed, Mid-American Frontiers Ser, 47 vols, Arno Press, 75; auth, William Clark Jeffersonian Man on the Frontier, 77, co-ed, Frontiers: A Comparative Approach, 77, auth, Comparative Frontiers: A Proposal for Studying the American West, 80, ed, American West: New Perspectives New Dimensions, 81 & auth, Stages of development in Oklahoma history, In: Oklahoma: New Viewpoints, 82, Univ Okla Press; Gold Seeking--Victoria And California In The 1850s, Pacific Hist Rev, Vol 65, 96; Were In The Money--Depression Am And Its Films, J Of The West, Vol 34, 95; Cycles Of Myth Restoration--One Approach To Understanding Amn Culture, J Of Am Culture, Vol 16, 93. **CONTACT ADDRESS** Dept of Hist, Georgia So Univ, PO Box 8054, Statesboro, GA 30460-8054. **EMAIL** jsteffen@gasou.edu

STEFFEN, KONRAD
PERSONAL Born 01/02/1952, Zurich, Switzerland, m, 1983, 2 children **DISCIPLINE** GEOGRAPHY **CAREER** Assoc Prof to Prof and Assoc Dir, Univ Colo, 91-. **MEMBERSHIPS** Deutsche Gesellschaft fur Polarforschung; Schweizerische Geog Gesellschaft; Asn Am Geog; Intl Glacial Soc; Am Geophysical Union; Am Meteorol Soc. **SELECTED PUBLICATIONS** Co-auth, "AVHRR surface temperature and narrow-band albedo comparison with ground measurements for the Greenland ice sheet," Annals of Glaciology, (93): 49-54; auth, "Surface energy exchange during the onset of melt at the equilibrium line altitude of the Greenland ice sheet," Annals of Glaciology, (95): 13-18; co-auth, "Snow melt on the Greenland ice sheet as derived from passive microwave satellite data," Journal Climate, (97): 1795-1797; co-auth, "A new monthly climatology of global radiation for the Arctic and comparison with NCEP-NCAR reanalysis and ISCCP-C2 fields," Journal Climate, (98): 11, 121-136. **CONTACT ADDRESS** Dept Geog, Univ of Colorado, Boulder, Box 260, Boulder, CO 80309-0260.

STEFFENSEN-BRUCE, INGRID A.
PERSONAL Born 05/12/1967, Lewisburg, PA, m, 1992, 1 child **DISCIPLINE** HISTORY OF ART AND ARCHITECTURE **EDUCATION** Univ VA, BA, 88; Yale Univ, MA, 89; Univ DE, PhD, 94. **CAREER** Instr (Tenure Track), Brookdale Col, 96-. **HONORS AND AWARDS** Wilbur Owen Sypherd Awd for Outstanding Dissertation in the Humanities, Univ DE, 95; Phi Beta Kappa, Univ VA, 95. **MEMBERSHIPS** Col Art Asn; Soc of Architectural Hist; Am Culture Asn. **RESEARCH** 19th century Am art and architecture. **SELECTED PUBLICATIONS** Auth, The World's Columbian Exposition and Its Influence on the Milwaukee Public Library and Museum Competition, 1893, Nineteenth Century, spring 97; Portrait of the PhD as a Young Woman, in On the Market: Surviving the Academic Job Search, eds Christina Boufis and Victoria Olsen, Riverhead Books, 97; Nineteenth-Century Women as Architects: the Ladder Question, Nineteenth Century, spring 98; Marble Palaces, Temples of Art: Art Museums, Architecture, and American Culture, 1890-1930, Bucknell Univ Press, 98; auth, "Classic Serenity or Oriental Splendor: Cass Gilbert's Designs for the Louisiana Purchase Expositions, 1904," Nineteenth Century Fall 99; "Cass Gilbert's St. Louis: Public Architecture, Civic Ideals," in Cass Gilbert, Life and Work, Architect of the Public Domain eds, Barbara Christen and Steven Aardens, W.W. Norton, 00. **CONTACT ADDRESS** 64 Whitney Rd, Short Hills, NJ 07078. **EMAIL** isteffensen@home.com

STEGGLES, MARY ANN
DISCIPLINE ART **EDUCATION** Univ Manitoba, BA, 87, MA, 90; Univ Leicester, PhD. **CAREER** Asst prof, Acadia Univ. **RESEARCH** Art and politics nineteenth century art public monuments; patronage indian art and architecture. **SELECTED PUBLICATIONS** Auth, The Myth of the Monuments, 94; Bombay: A City of Imperial Statues, 96. **CONTACT ADDRESS** Dept of Art, Acadia Univ, Wolfville, NS, Canada B0P 1XO. **EMAIL** mary.steggles@acadiau.ca

STEGMAIER, MARK JOSEPH
PERSONAL Born 08/27/1945, Cumberland, MD, m, 1971, 2 children **DISCIPLINE** AMERICAN HISTORY **EDUCATION** Univ Santa Clara, BA, 67; Univ Calif, Santa Barbara, MA, 70, PhD(hist), 75. **CAREER** Asst prof, 75-82, assoc prof am hist, Cameron Univ, 82-. **MEMBERSHIPS** AHA; Orgn Am Historians. **RESEARCH** United States History, 1840-1860. **SELECTED PUBLICATIONS** Auth, "Maryland's Fear of Insurrection at the Time of Braddock's Defeat," Maryland Historical Magazine 71, (76): 467-486; auth, "Intensifying the Sectional Conflict: William Seward vs James Hammond in the Lecompton Debate of 1858." Civil War History 31, (85): 197-221; auth, " The Case of the Coachman's Family: An Incident of President Filmore's Administration,"Civil War History 32, (86): 318-324; auth, " Zachary Taylor Versus the South," Civil War History 33, (87): 219-241; auth, "Treachery or Hoax? The Rumored Southern Conspiracy to Confederate with Mexico," Civil War History 35, (89): 28-38; coauth, James F Milligan: His Journal of Fremont's Fifth Expedition, 1853-1854; His Adventurous Life on Land and Sea, Glendale, Arthur H Clark Co., 88: 300; auth, Texas, New Mexico, and the Compromise of 1850: Boundary Dispute and Sectional Crisis Kent: Kent State Univ Press, 96; auth, ' Window on Washington in 1850: Tracking Newspaper Letter-Writers," American Journalism 15, (98): 69-82; auth, "The Guadeloupe Hidalgo Treaty as a Factor in the New Mexico-Texas Boundary Dispute," The Treaty of Guade-

loupe Hidalgo, 1848: Papers of the Sesquicentennial Symposium, 1848-1998, Las Cruces: Dona Ana County Historical Society and Yucca Tree Press, 99. **CONTACT ADDRESS** Dept of Soc Sci, Cameron Univ, 2800 Gore Blvd, Lawton, OK 73505-6377. **EMAIL** markst@cameron.edu

STEIMAN, LIONEL BRADLEY
PERSONAL Born 07/12/1941, Winnipeg, MB, Canada, m, 1967, 1 child **DISCIPLINE** EUROPEAN HISTORY **EDUCATION** Univ Man, BA, 64; Univ Pa, MA, 65, PhD(hist), 70. **CAREER** Lectr, 70-72, asst prof, 72-78, ASSOC PROF HIST, UNIV MAN, 78- **MEMBERSHIPS** Western Asn Ger Studies. **RESEARCH** German exile studies. **SELECTED PUBLICATIONS** Auth, Franz Werfel: The Faith of an Exile: From Prague to Beverly Hills; auth, Paths to Genocide: Antisemitism in Western History. **CONTACT ADDRESS** Dept of Hist, Univ of Manitoba, 403 Fletcher Argue Bldg, Winnipeg, MB, Canada R3T 5V5. **EMAIL** lsteimn@cc.umanitoba.ca

STEIN, KENNETH W.
PERSONAL Born 07/15/1946, New York, NY, s, 3 children **DISCIPLINE** HISTORY **EDUCATION** Franklin Marshall Col, BA, 68; Univ Mich, MA, 69/71, PhD 76. **CAREER** Prof/ Dir Mid East Res Prog. **HONORS AND AWARDS** Carter Ctr Mid East Fellow. **RESEARCH** Modern Near-Eastern history; social and economic history of Palestine in the twentieth century; inter-Arab political history; the Arab-Israeli peace process and the Mediterranean littoral states of the Near East. **SELECTED PUBLICATIONS** Auth, The Intifadah and the 1936-39 Uprising: A Comparison; The Study of Middle Eastern History in the United States; auth, The Land Question in Palestine 1917-1939: The Blood of Abraham; Making Peace Between Arabs and Israelis: Lessons from Fifty Years of Negotiating Experience; coauth, Heroic Diplomacy: Sadat, Kissinger, Curtel, Begin The Quest for Arab-Israeli Peace, 99. **CONTACT ADDRESS** Dept History, Emory Univ, 121 Bowden Hall, 561 Kilgo Cir, Atlanta, GA 30322-1950. **EMAIL** kstein@emory.edu

STEIN, LEON
PERSONAL Born 03/28/1941, New York, NY, m, 1965, 1 child **DISCIPLINE** EUROPEAN INTELLECTUAL HISTORY **EDUCATION** NYork Univ, BA, 62, MA, 64, PhD(hist), 66. **CAREER** Instr hist, NY Univ, 65-66; asst prof, 66-70, assoc prof, 70-80, PROF HIST, ROOSEVELT UNIV, 80- **MEMBERSHIPS** AHA; Conf Group Cent Europ Historians. **RESEARCH** Modern European intellectual history; Germany 1500-1815. **SELECTED PUBLICATIONS** Auth, Patriotism and religion in the Thirty Years' War, Cent Europ Hist, 72; A Desperate Embrace-The Holocaust And The Ideas Of Existentialism, Proteus, Vol 12, 95. **CONTACT ADDRESS** Dept of Hist, Roosevelt Univ, 430 S Michigan, Chicago, IL 60605.

STEINBERG, LEO
PERSONAL Born 07/09/1920, Moscow, USSR **DISCIPLINE** HISTORY OF ART **EDUCATION** NYork Univ, PhD(art), 60. **CAREER** Prof art hist, Hunter Col, 61-75; BENJAMIN FRANKLIN PROF HIST OF ART & UNIV PROF, UNIV PA, 75-, Soc Fels, Am Acad in Rome. **HONORS AND AWARDS** DFA, Philadelphia Col Art, 81. **MEMBERSHIPS** Col Art Asn Am. **RESEARCH** Renaissance, baroque and contemporary art. **SELECTED PUBLICATIONS** Auth, The Philosophical Brothel (Picasso's Demoiselles d' Avignon), Art News, 9-10/72; Other Criteria, Confrontations with Twentieth-Century Art, Oxford Univ, 72; Leonardo's Last Supper, Art Quart, 73; Michelangelo's Last Judgment as Merciful Heresy, Art in Am, 11-12/75; Michelangelo's Last Paintings, Phaidon & Oxford Univ, 75; Borromini's San Carlo alle quattro Fontane, Garland, 77; A corner of the Last Judgment, Daedalus, spring 80; The Line of Fate in Michelangelo's painting, Critical Inquiry, spring 80. **CONTACT ADDRESS** Univ of Pennsylvania, Philadelphia, PA 19104.

STEINBERG, MARK D.
DISCIPLINE HISTORY **EDUCATION** Univ Cal Santa Cruz, BA, 78, Univ Calif Berkeley, PhD; MA, 87. **CAREER** Asst Prof, Assoc Prof, Yale Unvi, 89-94, 94-96, Asst Prof, Harvard Univ, 87-89, Vist Instr, Univ Ore, 87, Assoc prof, Univ Ill Urbana Champaign, 96-. **HONORS AND AWARDS** Dir, Russian E Europ Center. **RESEARCH** Cultural and social history of the nineteenth and twentieth centuries. **SELECTED PUBLICATIONS** Auth, Moral Communities: The Culture of Class Relations in the Russian Printing Industry 1867-1907, Univ Calif, 92; co-ed, Cultures in Flux: Lower Class Values, Practices and Resistance in Late Imperial Russia, Princeton, 94; auth, the Fall of the Romanovs: Political Dreams and Personal Struggles in a Time of Revolution, with Vladimir Khrustalev, Yale Univ Press, 95; coauth, Biographical dictionary of European Labor Leaders, Greenwood Press, 95; coauth, International Labor and Working-Class History Journal, 96; coauth, "Stories and Voices: History and Theory," Russian Rev, (96); auth, "The Urban Landscape in Workers' Imagination," Labor, Thought and Society in Russia in the late 19th and Early 20th Centuries, (96), ed, "Predstavlenie o lichnosti v srede rabochikh intelligentov," Rabochi I intelligentsia rossii v epokhu reform I revoliutsii, (97), 96-113; ed, "The Injured and Insurgent Self: The Moral Imagination of Russia's Lower Class Writers," Workers and Intelligentsia in Late Imperial Russia, (99); auth, "Reforming the Area Studies curriculum," Newsnet: Newsletter of the AAASS, (99). **CONTACT ADDRESS** History Dept, Univ of Illinois, Urbana-Champaign, 810 S. Wright St, 309 Gregory Hall, Champaign, IL 61820. **EMAIL** steinb@uiuc.edu

STEINBERG, MICHAEL P.
DISCIPLINE HISTORY **EDUCATION** Princeton Univ, AB, 78; Univ Chicago, MA, 81; PhD, 85. **CAREER** Vis Asst prof, Cornell Univ, 88; Vis Prof, Nat Tsinghua Univ, 94; Asst Prof, Colgate Univ, 86-89; Asst Prof to Assoc Prof, Cornell Univ, 89-99; Vis Assoc Prof, Univ Chicago, 95. **SELECTED PUBLICATIONS** Auth, Listening to Reason: Music and Subjectivity in the Long Nineteenth Century, forthcoming; auth, "Mendelssohn's Music and German-Jewish Culture," The Musical Quarterly, 99; auth, "The Materiality of the Baroque," in Intellectual Tradition in Movement, ASCA Yearbook, Amsterdam, 98; auth, "1921: Walter Benjamin and Gershom Scholem," in Yale Handbook of 'German-Jewish Writing', Yale Univ Press, 97; auth, "Das Mendelssohn-Bach Verhaltnis als asthetischer Diskurs der Moderne," in Felix Mendelssohn-Mitwelt und Nachwelt, , Leipzig, 96; auth, "Felix Mendelssohn-Bartholdy: Musik, Geschichte, Allegorie," in Das aufgesprengte Kontinuum: Ober die Geschichtsfahigkeit der Musik, Graz, 96; ed, "Walter Benjamin and the Demands of History," Cornell Univ Press, 96; ed, Aby Warburg, Images from the Region of the Pueblo Indians of North America, Cornell Univ Press, 95; ed, "History and Theory Beiheft: The Presence of the Historian: Essays in memory of Arnaldo Momigliano, 91; auth, The Meaning of the Salzburg Festival: Austria as Theater and Ideology, 1890-1938, Cornell Univ Press, 90. **CONTACT ADDRESS** Dept Hist, Cornell Univ, McGraw Hall, Ithaca, NY 14853.

STEINBERG, SALME HARJU
PERSONAL Born 02/21/1940, New York, NY, m, 1963, 2 children **DISCIPLINE** AMERICAN HISTORY **EDUCATION** Hunter Col, City Univ New York, BA, 60, MA, 62; Johns Hopkins Univ, PhD(hist), 71. **CAREER** Instr hist, Towson State Col, 64-66; lectr, Goucher Col, 71-72; asst prof, Northwestern Univ, 72-75; asst prof, 75-78, ASSOC PROF HIST, NORTHEASTERN ILL UNIV, 78- **MEMBERSHIPS** Orgn Am Historians; Bus Hist Conf; Econ Hist Asn. **RESEARCH** United States economic and social history; United States business history; non-profit institutions. **SELECTED PUBLICATIONS** Auth, Reformer in the Marketplace: Edward W Bok and the Ladies Home Journal, La State Univ Press, 79. **CONTACT ADDRESS** 2708 Harrison St, Evanston, IL 60201.

STEINER, BRUCE E.
DISCIPLINE HISTORY **EDUCATION** St Thomas, AB, 56; Univ Virg, MA, 59, PhD, 62. **CAREER** PROF, HIST, OHIO UNIV **MEMBERSHIPS** Am Antiquarian Soc **SELECTED PUBLICATIONS** Auth, "Anglican Office-Holding in Pre-Revolutionary Connecticut: The Parameters of New England Community," Wm & Mary Quart 31, 74; auth, Connecticut Anglicans in the Revolutionary Era: A Study in Communal Tensions, 79. **CONTACT ADDRESS** Dept of Hist, Ohio Univ, Athens, OH 45701.

STEINHARDT, NANCY SHATZMAN
PERSONAL Born 07/14/1954, St. Louis, MO, m, 1979, 4 children **DISCIPLINE** EAST ASIAN ART; ARCHAEOLOGY **EDUCATION** Wash Univ, AB, 74; Harvard Univ, AM, 75, PhD, 81. **CAREER** Lectr, Bryn Mawr Col, 81-83; lectr, Univ Pa, 82-86; asst prof, 86-91, assoc prof, 91-98, prof, 98-, Univ Pa. **HONORS AND AWARDS** Am Phlos Soc grant, 99; Soc Sci Res Found fel, 97; Nat Endow for the Humanities fel, 94; Asian Cultural Coun grant, 93; Amer Philos Soc grant, 92; Getty Grant Prog Sr fel, 90; Amer Coun of Learned Soc fel, 89; Graham Found for Adv Studies in the Fine Arts, grant, 89. **MEMBERSHIPS** Col Art Asn; Asn of Asian Studies; Soc of Archit Hist; Hist of Islamic Art; Soc of East Asian Archaeol; Northeast China Studies Asn. **RESEARCH** Chinese art and architecture from Han through Yuan; Central Asian art & archaeology; Northeast Asian art & architecture. **SELECTED PUBLICATIONS** Article, The Temple to the Northern Peak in Quyang, Artibus Asiae, 58, 1/2, 69-90, 98; auth, Liao Architecture, Univ Hawaii Press, 97; article, Chinese Cartography and Chinese Calligraphy, Oriental Art, 43, 1, 10-20, 97; article, Chinese Architecture, Chinese City Planning, Dict of Art, vol 6, 646-666, 96; article, Chinese Architecture, 963-966, Orientations, 26, 2, 46-52, 95; article, Liao: An Architectural Tradition in the Making, Artibus Asiae, 54, 1/2, 5-39, 94; article, The Tangut Royal Tombs near Yinchuan, Essays in Honor of Oleg Grabar, Muqarnas, 10, 369-381, 93; auth, Chinese Imperial City Planning, Univ Hawaii Press, 90; auth, Chinese Traditional Architecture, China Inst, 84. **CONTACT ADDRESS** Dept. of Asian & Middle Eastern Studies, Univ of Pennsylvania, 847 Williams Hall, Philadelphia, PA 19104-6305. **EMAIL** nssteinh@sas.upenn.edu

STEINMETZ, DAVID CURTIS
PERSONAL Born 06/12/1936, Columbus, OH, m, 1959, 2 children **DISCIPLINE** CHURCH HISTORY **EDUCATION** Wheaton Col, Ill, AB, 58; Drew Univ, BD, 61; Harvard Univ, ThD(church hist), 67. **CAREER** From asst prof to assoc prof church hist, Lancaster Theol Sem, 66-71; assoc prof, 71-79, Prof Church Hist & Doctrine, Divinity Sch, Duke Univ, 79-, Am Asn Theol Schs fac fel, Oxford Univ, 70-71; vis prof church hist, Harvard Univ, 77; Guggenheim fel, Cambridge Univ, 77-78. **MEMBERSHIPS** Am Soc Church Hist; Am Soc Reformation Res; Mediaeval Acad Am; Renaissance Soc Am; Soc Bibl Lit. **RESEARCH** History of Christian thought in the late Middle Ages and Reformation. **SELECTED PUBLICATIONS** Auth, Misericordia Dei, The Theology of Johannes von Staupitz in Its late Medieval Setting, Brill, Leiden, 68; Reformers in the Wings, Fortress, 71 & Baker, 81; Libertas Christiana: Studies in the Theology of John Pupper of Goch (1475), Harvard Theol Rev, 72; Late Medieval Nominalism and the Clerk's Tale, Chaucer Rev, 77; The Baptism of John and the Baptim of Jesus in Huldrych Zwingli, Balthasar Hubmaier and Late Medieval Theology, In: Continuity and Discontinuity in Church History, Brill, Leiden, 79; The Superiority of Pre-Critical Exegesis, Theol Today, 80; Luther and Staupitz: An Essay in the Intellectual Origins of the Protestant Reformation, Duke, 80; Calvin on Isaiah 6: A Problem in the History of Exegeis, Interpretation, 82. **CONTACT ADDRESS** Divinity Sch, Duke Univ, Durham, NC 27706.

STEINWEIS, ALAN
DISCIPLINE EUROPEAN, JEWISH HISTORY **EDUCATION** Univ NC, Chapel Hill, PhD, 88. **CAREER** Hyman Rosenberg Assoc Prof Hist, dir, Judaic Stud, Univ Nebr, Lincoln. **HONORS AND AWARDS** Fulbright award, 96. **SELECTED PUBLICATIONS** Art, Ideology, and Economics in Nazi Germany, Univ NC Press, 93. **CONTACT ADDRESS** Univ of Nebraska, Lincoln, 637 Oldfat, Lincoln, NE 68588-0417. **EMAIL** aes@unlserve.unl.edu

STENECK, NICHOLAS H.
PERSONAL Born 05/08/1940, Jersey City, NJ, m, 1963, 2 children **DISCIPLINE** HISTORY OF SCIENCE, SCIENCE POLICY **EDUCATION** Rutgers Univ, BS, 62; Univ Wis-Madison, MA, 69, PhD(hist, hist sci), 70. **CAREER** Asst prof, 70-76, ASSOC PROF HIST, UNIV MICH, ANN ARBOR, 76-, Am Coun Learned Soc study fel, 72-73. **MEMBERSHIPS** Hist Sci Soc. **RESEARCH** Scientific revolution, 17th century England; contemporary science-values disputes. **SELECTED PUBLICATIONS** **CONTACT ADDRESS** Dept of Hist, Univ of Michigan, Ann Arbor, Ann Arbor, MI 48104.

STEPENOFF, BONITA M.
DISCIPLINE HISTORY **EDUCATION** Ohio State Univ at Columbus, BA, 71; Univ Mo at Columbia, MA, 78; MLS, 81; PhD, 92. **CAREER** Acquisitions specialist, State Hist Soc of Mo, 78-84; cultural resource preservationist, Mo Dept of Natural Resources, 84-92; from asst prof to assoc prof, Southeast Mo State Univ, 93-. **HONORS AND AWARDS** Bryant Spann Mem Prize, Eugene V. Debs Found; Sullivan Fel, Museum of Am Textile Hist. **MEMBERSHIPS** Sigma Pi Kappa, Nat Coun for Preservation Educ, Labor and Working Class Hist Asn, Nat Coun on Public Hist. **RESEARCH** Labor History, Historic Preservation, Missouri History. **SELECTED PUBLICATIONS** Auth, Their Fathers' Daughters: Silk Mill Workers in Northeastern Pennsylvania, 1880-1960, Susquehanna Univ Press, 99. **CONTACT ADDRESS** Dept Hist, Southeast Missouri State Univ, 1 University Plaza, Cape Girardeau, MO 63701-4710. **EMAIL** bstepenoff@semovm.semo.edu

STEPHAN, JOHN JASON
PERSONAL Born 03/08/1941, Chicago, IL, m, 1963 **DISCIPLINE** RUSSIAN & EAST ASIAN HISTORY **EDUCATION** Harvard Univ, AB, 63, MA, 64; Univ London, PhD(hist), 69. **CAREER** Res assoc int rel, Soc Sci Res Ctr, Waseda Univ, Japan, 69-70; from asst prof to assoc prof; 70-77, chmn EAsian studies comt, Asian Studies Prog, 73-74, PROF HIST, UNIV HAWAII, MANOA, 77-; Trustee, Libr Int Rels, Chicago, 75-; Japan Found prof fel, 77; sr assoc mem, St Antony's Col, Oxford Univ, 77; vis prof, Inst Far E, Moscow, 82; Sanwa Distinguished Scholar in Residence, Fletcher School of Law and Diplomacy, Tufts Univ, 89. **HONORS AND AWARDS** Kenneth W. Baldridge Prize, Hawaii Chapter, Phi Alpha Theta, 96. **MEMBERSHIPS** Asn Asian Studies; Am Asn Advan Slavic Studies; AHA; Canadian Hist Asn. **RESEARCH** Modern Japanese foreign relations, especially Soviet-Japanese relations; history of Soviet Far East and northern Japan; Japanese-Americans in East Asia. **SELECTED PUBLICATIONS** Auth, Sakhalin: A History, Oxford, 71; Korean Minority in the Soviet Union, Mizan, 12/71; Japanese Studies in the Soviet Union, Asian Studies Prof Rev, spring 73; The Kuril Islands: Russo-Japanese Frontier in the Pacific, Oxford, 74; Japan and the Soviet Union: The Distant Neighbours, Asian Affairs, 10/77; The Russian Fascists, Harper & Row, 78; Asia in the Soviet Conception, In: Soviet Policy in Asia, Yale, 82; Hawaii Under the Rising Sun, Univ HI Press, 84; Soviet-American Horizons on the Pacific, with V. P. Chichkanov, Univ HI Press, 86; The Russian Far East: A History, Stanford Univ Press, 94; Highjacked in Utopia: American Nikkei in Manchuria, Amerasia J, vol 23, no 3, winter 97-98. **CONTACT ADDRESS** Dept of Hist, Univ of Hawaii, Manoa, 2530 Dole St, Honolulu, HI 96822-2303. **EMAIL** stephan@hawaii.edu

STEPHANSON, ANDERS
DISCIPLINE UNITED STATES HISTORY **EDUCATION** Gothenburg Univ, BA, 75; Columbia Univ, PhD, 86. **CAREER** Assoc prof. **SELECTED PUBLICATIONS** Auth, Kennan and the Art of Foreign Policy, 89; Manifest Destiny, 95. **CONTACT ADDRESS** Dept of History, Columbia Col, New York, 2960 Broadway, New York, NY 10027-6902.

STEPHEN, ELIZABETH H.
DISCIPLINE DEMOGRAPHY **EDUCATION** Colo Women's Col, BA, 75; Georgetown Univ, MA, 82; Univ Tex Austin. PhD, 85. **CAREER** Assoc Prof to Asst Prof, Georgetown Univ, 87-. **MEMBERSHIPS** Pop Asn of Am, Am Sociol Asn **RESEARCH** Infertility and reproductive health. **SELECTED PUBLICATIONS** Coauth, "Patterns of Intermarriage of Guestworker Populations in the Federal Republic of Germany: 1960-1985," Zeitschrift fur Bevolkengswissenschaft 14-2 (88): 187-204; auth, At the Crossroads: Fertility of Mexican American Women, Garland Press (NY), 89; coauth, "Marital Non-Cohabitation: Separation does not Make the Heart Grow Fonder," J of Marriage and the Family 52 (Feb 90): 259-270; coauth, "Intergenerational Transfers: A Question of Perspective," The Gerontologist 31-5 (91): 640-647; coauth, "Assimilation, Disruption and the Fertility of Mexican-Origin Women in the Unites States," Int Migration Rev 26 (Spring 92): 67-88; coauth, "Near and Far: Contact on Nom-residential Fathers with their Children," J of Divorce and Remarriage 20-3/4 (93): 171-191; coauth, "Order Amidst Disorder: Marital Transitions of Young Adults," J of Divorce and Remarriage 20-3/4 (95): 1-21; auth, "Projections of Impaired Fecundity among Women in the United States: 19950-2020," Fertility and Sterility 66-2 (96): 205-209; coauth, "Impaired Fecundity in the United States: 1982-1995," Family Planing Perspectives 30-1 (98): 34-42; coauth, "Updated Projections of Infertility in the United States: 1995-2020," Fertility and Sterility 70-1 (98): 30-34. **CONTACT ADDRESS** Dept Demog, Georgetown Univ, PO Box 571214, Washington, DC 200557-1214.

STEPHENS, LESTER DOW
PERSONAL Born 02/18/1933, Gatesville, TX, m, 2 children **DISCIPLINE** HISTORY **EDUCATION** Univ Corpus Christi, BS, 54; Univ Tex, MEd, 59; Univ Miami, PhD, 64. **CAREER** Teacher pub schs, Tex, 54-57; asst prof hist, Univ Corpus Christi, 57-61; social studies ed, 63-66, assoc prof, 66-67, assoc prof social studies, educ & hist, 67-69, assoc prof hist, 69-78, prof, 78-98, dept hd, 81-91, emeritus prof, Univ Ga, 98-. **HONORS AND AWARDS** Eight awards for distinguished teaching, Univ Ga. **MEMBERSHIPS** AHA; Orgn Am Hist; Hist of Sci Soc; Soc Stu of Natural Hist; Southern Hist Asn. **RESEARCH** History of science, historiography **SELECTED PUBLICATIONS** Auth, Probing the Past: A Guide to the Study and Teaching of History, Allyn & Bacon, 74; Historiography: A Bibliography, Scarecrow, 75; Evolution and woman's rights in the 1890's, Historian, 76; Joseph LeConte on evolution, education and the structure of knowledge, J Hist Behav Sci, 76; Farish Furman's formula: Scientific farming and the new South, Agr Hist, 76; Joseph LeConte's evolutional idealism, J Hist Ideas, 78; Joseph LeConte and the development of the physiology and psychology of vision in the United States, Anals of Sci, 80; Joseph LeConte: Gentle prophet of evolution, La State Univ Press, 82; The Evolution Controversy In America, J Of Southern Hist, Vol 62, 96; Ancient Animals and other Wondrous Things, Charleston Museum, 88; Scientific Societies in the Old South, Sci and Med in the Old South, La State Univ, 89; John Edwards Holbrook and Lewis R. Gibbes, Col Bldg in Ichthyology and Heptetology, Am Soc of Ichthyologists and Herpetologists, 97. **CONTACT ADDRESS** Dept of Hist, Univ of Georgia, Georgia University, Athens, GA 30602-0001. **EMAIL** lsteohen@arches.ugov.edu

STEPHENS, THOMAS M.
PERSONAL Born 11/15/1951, Spartanburg, SC **DISCIPLINE** LATIN AMERICAN STUDIES **EDUCATION** Univ SC, BA, 74; MA, 76; Univ Mich, PhD, 84. **CAREER** Asst Prof, Rutgers Univ, 81-90; Assoc Prof, Rutgers Univ, 90-. **MEMBERSHIPS** MLA, AATSP. **RESEARCH** Race, language, ethnicity in Latin America. **SELECTED PUBLICATIONS** Auth, "Renegotiating Ethnonymy: Constructs for 'mulatto' in Iberian America," Critica Hispanica 22 (00); auth, "Anglicisms in Spanish American Ethnonymy: Identity and Lexical Renegotiation," La Coroniza 26.1 (97): 165-177; auth, "Complexities of Ethnic and Racial Terminology in Latin America and the Caribbean," in Africana: The Encycl of the African and African-American Experience, (NY: Basic Civitas Books, 99), 499-501; auth, Dictionary of Latin American Racial and Ethnic Terminology, 2nd ed, Univ Pr Fla (Gainesville, FL), 99. **CONTACT ADDRESS** Dept Lang, Rutgers, The State Univ of New Jersey, New Brunswick, 105 George St, New Brunswick, NJ 08901-1414. **EMAIL** tstephns@rci.rutgers.edu

STEPHENS, WILLIAM RICHARD
PERSONAL Born 01/02/1932, Ashburn, MO, m, 1952, 3 children **DISCIPLINE** AMERICAN SOCIAL & EDUCATIONAL HISTORY **EDUCATION** Greenville Col, BS, 53; Univ Mo, Columbia, MEd, 57; Wash Univ, EdD, 64. **CAREER** Assoc prof, Greenville col, 57-61; assoc prof, Ind State Univ, 64-70; prof, Ind Univ, Bloomington, 70-71; vpres & dean fac, 71-77, pres, 77-93, Greenville Col; retired as Pres Emeritus, 93; dir of Pres Fel Inst, 95-; senior advisor, Council for Christian Colleges and Univ. **HONORS AND AWARDS** Awd of Merit, Nat Voc Guid Assn, 73; Distinguished Alumnus Awd, Greenville Col, 81. **MEMBERSHIPS** Hist Educ Soc; Philos Educ Soc. **RESEARCH** Social and intellectual sources of American educational theory and systems, 1885-1920; progressive and reform values in American public education, 1890-1920. **SELECTED PUBLICATIONS** Coauth, Jesse Hewlon, Educ Forum, 11/67; Schools and wars, Teachers Col J, 5/67; The junior high school, a product of reform values, 1890-1920, 11/67, Teachers Col J; Social Reform and the Origins of Vocational Guidance, 1890-1925, Nat Voc Guid Assn, 70; coauth, Education in American Life, Houghton, 71; auth, Careers in Criminal Justice, 99. **CONTACT ADDRESS** Greenville Col, 321 8th St NE, Washington, DC 20002. **EMAIL** wstephen@greenville.edu

STERCKX, ROEL
PERSONAL Born 05/13/1969, Turnhout, Belgium, s **DISCIPLINE** CHINESE PHILOSOPHY, HISTORY **EDUCATION** Katholieke Univ Leuven, Lic Sinology, 91; Cambridge Univ, MPhil, 93; PhD, 97. **CAREER** Asst prof, Univ of Ariz, 01-. **HONORS AND AWARDS** Allen and Amy Mary Preston Read Scholar, Cambridge Univ, 93; Spalding Scholar, 95; Fel, Wolfson Col, Univ of Oxford, 97. **MEMBERSHIPS** Assoc for Asian Studies. **RESEARCH** Thought, religion and cultural history of China during the Warring States and early imperial periods. **SELECTED PUBLICATIONS** Auth, "An Ancient Chinese Horse Ritual," Early China 21 (96): 47-79; auth, "Transcending Habitats: Authority, Territory, and the Animal Realm in Warring States and Early Imperial China," Bull of the Brit Assc for Chinese Studies, (96): 9-19; auth, "Transforming the Beasts. Animals and Music in Early China," Toung Pao 86, 1-3, (00): 1-46; auth, The Animal and the Daemon in Early China, SUNY Pr, (Albany) in press. **CONTACT ADDRESS** Dept of E Asian Studies, Univ of Arizona, Franklin Bldg 404, Tucson, AZ 85721. **EMAIL** sterckx@email.arizona.edu

STERLING, DAVID L.
PERSONAL Born 07/04/1929, Brooklyn, NY, m, 1963 **DISCIPLINE** AMERICAN HISTORY **EDUCATION** NYork Univ, BA, 51, MA, 52, PhD, 58; Ohio State Univ, JD, 67. **CAREER** Asst prof Am hist, Albany State Teachers Col, 57-59; instr, Ohio State Univ, 59-64; asst prof, 64-69, ASSOC PROF AM HIST, UNIV CINCINNATI, 69- **MEMBERSHIPS** AAUP **RESEARCH** Life of John Pintard, 1759-1844. **SELECTED PUBLICATIONS CONTACT ADDRESS** Dept of Hist, Univ of Cincinnati, Cincinnati, OH 45221.

STERN, FRITZ
PERSONAL Born 02/02/1926, Breslau, Germany, m, 1996, 2 children **DISCIPLINE** MODERN EUROPEAN AND GERMAN HISTORY **EDUCATION** Columbia Univ, BA, 46; Columbia Univ, Phd, 53. **CAREER** Univ Prof, Emeritus. **HONORS AND AWARDS** Hon Degrees: Oxford, New School for Social Research; Columbia Univ Peace Prize, German Book Trade, 99. **MEMBERSHIPS** Poure le merite, Am Philosophical Society, American Acad of Arts and Sciences. **RESEARCH** European History (modern). **SELECTED PUBLICATIONS** Ed, The Varieties of History, 56; The Politics of Cultural Despair, 61; The Failure of Illiberalism: Essays on the Political Culture of Modern Germany, 72; Gold and Iron: Bismarck, Bleichroder and the Building of the German Empire, 77; Dreams and Delusions: the Drama of German History, 87; auth, Einstein's German World, 99. **CONTACT ADDRESS** Dept of Hist, Columbia Col, New York, 15 Claremont Ave, New York, NY 10027.

STERN, MARVIN
DISCIPLINE HISTORY **EDUCATION** Brandeis Univ, AB; AM; PhD; Harvard Univ, AM; Yale Univ, AM. **CAREER** Assoc prof, Lawrence Tech Univ, 94-. **HONORS AND AWARDS** Vis fel, Cambridge Univ, England, 01-02. **MEMBERSHIPS** MHS; Am Soc 18th Century Studies; The Authors Guild. **RESEARCH** 18th Century England; Edward Gibbon; Clinton; Lord Sheffield; Catherine Maria Fanshawe; Military History. **SELECTED PUBLICATIONS** Auth, Death, Grief, and Friendship in the Eighteenth Century: Edward Gibbon and Lord Sheffield, 84; auth, Thorns and Briars: Bonding, Love, and Death, 1764-1870, 91; auth, "The Colonel's Curse," BBC Hist Magazine, 01; auth, "From America to the Crimea: Three Generations of British Officers," Contemporary Rev (forthcoming); auth, "Lady Maria Josepha Stanley," in New Dictionary of National Biography (forthcoming); auth, "Loyalty Knows No Shame," Ideas, Aesthetics, Inquiries, in the Early Modern Era (forthcoming). **CONTACT ADDRESS** Dept Humanities, Lawrence Tech Univ, 21000 W 10 Mile Rd, Southfield, MI 48075-1051. **EMAIL** mn@post.harvard.edu

STERN, NANCY B.
PERSONAL Born 07/15/1944, NY, m, 1964, 2 children **DISCIPLINE** HISTORY OF SCIENCE, COMPUTER INFO SYS **EDUCATION** SUNY, Stony Brook, PhD, 77. **CAREER** Brodlieb Distinguished Prof Business, Hofstra Univ, 77-. **HONORS AND AWARDS** Beta Gamma Sigma; Citibank, Hist Comp; IFIP Pioneer Day. **MEMBERSHIPS** ACM; ISIS. **RESEARCH** Multimedia, hist of computing. **SELECTED PUBLICATIONS** Computers and Information Processing, Cobol Programming, 8th ed, John Wiley and Sons, Inc. **CONTACT ADDRESS** BCIS Dept, Hofstra Univ, Hempstead, NY 11550. **EMAIL** nancy.stern@hofstra.edu

STERN, ROBIN
DISCIPLINE ART HISTORY **EDUCATION** State Univ NYork, AB, 74; Univ Chicago, AM, 77, PhD, 84. **CAREER** Instr, DePaul Univ; Univ Chicago; Northwestern Univ; vis asst prof, 84-. **HONORS AND AWARDS** Wrtg fel, Univ Chicago; res grant, Metropolitan Ctr Far E Art Stud. **SELECTED PUBLICATIONS** Auth, Emaki; Masterworks in Wood: China and Japan by Donald Jenkins. **CONTACT ADDRESS** Dept of Art Hist, Sch of the Art Inst of Chicago, 37 S Wabash Ave, Chicago, IL 60603.

STERN, STEVE JEFFEREY
PERSONAL Born 12/28/1951, Brooklyn, NY **DISCIPLINE** LATIN AMERICAN HISTORY **EDUCATION** Cornell Univ, BA, 73; Yale Univ, MPhil, 76, PhD, 79. **CAREER** Asst prof hist, Univ Wis-Madison, 79-, Vis asst prof hist, Yale Univ, 82. **MEMBERSHIPS** Latin Am Studies Asn; Conf Latin Am Hist. **RESEARCH** History of indigenous peoples--Andean South America; colonial Latin American history. **SELECTED PUBLICATIONS** Auth, The rise and fall of Indian-White alliances: A regional view of conquest history, Hisp Am Hist Rev, 81; contribur, chap, In: The Inca and Aztec States, 1400-1800, Acad Press, 82; auth, Peru's Indian Peoples and the Challenge of Spanish Conquest: Huamanga to 1640, Univ Wis, 82. **CONTACT ADDRESS** Dept of History, Univ of Wisconsin, Madison, 455 North Park St, Madison, WI 53706-1483.

STEVENS, DONALD G.
PERSONAL Born 02/14/1939, Boston, MA, m, 1964, 2 children **DISCIPLINE** MODERN EUROPEAN HISTORY **EDUCATION** St Anselm's Col, BA, 60; Niagara Univ, MA, 62; St Johns Univ, NYork, PhD, 67. **CAREER** Asst, Niagara Univ, 61; Asst Prof to Prof Hist, 64-90, John Whitman Distinguished Service Prof, King's Col, Pa, 90-. **MEMBERSHIPS** AHA; SHAFR; WWII Studies Asn. **RESEARCH** American relations with the League of Nations; Anglo-American relations WWII; economic warfare. **CONTACT ADDRESS** Dept of Hist, King's Col, 133 N River St, Wilkes-Barre, PA 18711-0801. **EMAIL** dgsteven@rs01.kings.edu

STEVENS, KEVIN M.
DISCIPLINE HISTORY **EDUCATION** Univ Wis - Madison, PhD, 92. **CAREER** Asst Prof Hist, Univ Nev, 90-. **MEMBERSHIPS** Soc Ital Hist Studies. **RESEARCH** Printing/publishing - 16th century Italy. **SELECTED PUBLICATIONS** Auth, Printing and Politics: Carlo Borromeo and the Seminary Press of Milan, Stampa, libri e letture a Milan nell'eta di Carlo Borromeo, Vita e Pensiero, 92; coauth, Giovanni Battista Bosso and the Paper Trade in late Sixteenth-Century Milan, La Bibliofilia, XCVI, 94; auth, Printing and Patronage in Sixteenth-Century Milan: The Career of Francesco Moscheni (1547-66), Gutenberg-Jahrbuch, 95; Vinceno Girardone and the Popular Press in Counter-Reformation Milan: A Case Study (1570), 16th Century J 3, 95; A Bookbinder in Early Seventeenth-Century Milan. The Shop of Pietro Martire Locarno, The Library, Univ Oxford Press, 96; Liturgical Publishing in mid-Sixteenth-Century Milan: The Contracts for the Breviarium Humiliatorum (1548) and the Breviarium Ambrosianum (1556), La Bibliofilia 2, 97. **CONTACT ADDRESS** History Dept, Univ of Nevada, Reno, Reno, NV 89557-0037. **EMAIL** kstevens@scs.unr.edu

STEVENS, M.
PERSONAL Born San Francisco, CA, m, 1979 **DISCIPLINE** HISTORY **EDUCATION** Univ San Francisco, BA, 76; Univ Calif Berkeley, MA, 80; PhD, 97. **CAREER** Lectr, Calif State Univ, 97-99; Lectr, San Francisco State Univ, 99-. **HONORS AND AWARDS** Mellow Fel; Distinguished Teaching Asst; Marion Brown Mem Scholar; Eugene Irving McCormac Grad Scholar; Archbishop Riordan Scholar. **MEMBERSHIPS** AHA. **RESEARCH** Bioethics, Post World War II Society and Culture. **SELECTED PUBLICATIONS** Auth, Bioethics in America: Origins and Cultural Politics, 00. **CONTACT ADDRESS** Dept of Hist, San Francisco State Univ, 1600 Holloway, San Francisco, CA 94132. **EMAIL** mltstevens@aol.com

STEVENSON, JOHN A.
PERSONAL Born 11/06/1952, Clinton, SC, m **DISCIPLINE** ENGLISH AND HISTORY **EDUCATION** Duke Univ, BA, 75; Univ Va, PhD, 83. **CAREER** Asst prof, 82-90, assoc prof, 90-, chair, 96-, Eng, Univ Colo. **HONORS AND AWARDS** Nat Merit Scholar; AB Duke Scholar; Phi Beta Kappa; Boulder Facul Teaching Awd, 90. **MEMBERSHIPS** MLA. **RESEARCH** 18th century British literature. **SELECTED PUBLICATIONS** Auth, Tom Jones and the Stuarts, ELH, 94; auth, The British Novel, Defoe to Austen, 90; auth, A Vampire in the Mirror, PMLA, 88; auth, Clarissa and the Harlowes Once More, ELH, 81. **CONTACT ADDRESS** Dept. of English, Univ of Colorado, Boulder, Box 226, Boulder, CO 80309. **EMAIL** john.stevenson@colorado.edu

STEVENSON, LOUISE L.
PERSONAL Born 06/11/1948, NY, m, 2 children **DISCIPLINE** AMERICAN STUDIES **EDUCATION** Columbia Univ, BA, 70; New York Univ, MA, 73; Boston Univ, PhD, 81. **CAREER** Assoc teacher Am studies, Mass Bay Communities Col, 75; lectr Am hist & studies, Univ NH, 76; admin dir, Am & New England Studies Prog, Boston Univ, 77-79; vis lectr hist, Univ NH, Durham, 79-82; PROF HIST & AM STUDIES DEPT, FRANKLIN & MARSHALL COL, 82-, chair, dept of hist, 91-94, chair, women's stud, 94-00. **HONORS AND AWARDS** Morgan Fel, Library Co of Philadelphia, 00; Stephen Botein Fel, 00; Winterthur Fel, 00; Andrew W. Mellon Fel, 94; Spencer Fnd Grant, 94, 89; Bradley R. Dewey Awd for Scholarship and Teaching, Franklin and Marshall Col, 92; H.F. DuPont Scholar, 88. **MEMBERSHIPS** AHA, ASA, OAH, SHARP. **RESEARCH** Intellectual history, women's history. **SELECTED PUBLICATIONS** Auth, "Women antisuffragists in the 1915 Massachusetts campaign," New England Quart 52, (79): 80-93; auth, "Sarah Porter Educates Useful Ladies, 1847-1900," Winterthur Portfolio 18, no. 1 (83): 39-59; auth, Scholarly Means to Evangelical Ends: The New Haven Scholars and the Transformation of Higher Learning in America, 1830-1890, Baltimore, 86; auth, Miss Porter's School: A History in Documents, 2 vols, New York," 87; auth, "It's Come to America: The History of the Book," Reviews in Am Hist 18 (90): 337-42; auth, "Prescription and Reality: Reading Advisers and Reading Practice, 1860-1880," Book Research Quart (Winter 90-91): 43-61; auth, The Victorian Homefront: American Thought and Culture, 1860-1880, New York, 91; auth, "Women's Intellectual History: A New Direction," Newsletter of the Intellectual History Group 15 (93): 32-8; "Reading Circles," Oxford Companion to Women's Writing in the U.S. (95): 746-49; ed, Women's History: Selected Reading Lists and Course Outlines from American Colleges and Universities, 4th ed, New York, 98. **CONTACT ADDRESS** Hist & Am Studies Dept, Franklin and Marshall Col, PO Box 3003, Lancaster, PA 17604-3003. **EMAIL** l_stevenson@fandm.edu

STEVER, SARAH S.
DISCIPLINE ANCIENT, MEDIEVAL, RENAISSANCE HISTORY **EDUCATION** Sarah Lawrence Col, AB; Univ Mich, PhD. **CAREER** Ch; assoc prof, Hist, Univ Detroit Mercy, 81. **HONORS AND AWARDS** Fel(s), Danforth Found; Renaissance Soc Am; dir, lib arts summer stud, volterra, italy. **RESEARCH** History of Italy in the Renaissance and early modern France. **SELECTED PUBLICATIONS** Auth, articles on Renaissance humanism and philology. **CONTACT ADDRESS** Dept of Hist, Univ of Detroit Mercy, 4001 W McNichols Rd, PO BOX 19900, Detroit, MI 48219-0900. **EMAIL** steversn@audmercy.edu

STEWARD, DICK HOUSTON
PERSONAL Born 12/11/1942, Jefferson City, MO, m, 1969, 2 children **DISCIPLINE** AMERICAN DIPLOMATIC HISTORY **EDUCATION** Southeast Mo State Col, BS, 64; Univ Mo-Columbia, MA, 65, PhD(Hist), 69. **CAREER** Instr Hist, Univ Mo-Columbia, 68-69; asst prof, 71-75, assoc prof Hist, Lincoln Univ, 75-. **RESEARCH** Recent United States history; Latin American history; United States economic diplomacy; Western and Southern hist. **SELECTED PUBLICATIONS** Contribr, It Actually Costs Us Nothing: US-Colombian Economic Policy, Houghton, 73; auth, Trade a Hemisphere: The Good Neighbor Policy & Reciprocal Trade, Univ Mo, 75; Money, Marines, and Mission: Recent US-Latin American Policy, Univ Press Am, 80; auth, Frontier Swashbuckler: The Life and Legend of John Smith T, Univ Missouri Pr, 00; auth, Duels and the Roots of Violence in Missouri, Univ Missouri Pr, 00. **CONTACT ADDRESS** Dept of Soc Sci, Lincoln Univ, Missouri, 820 Chestnut St, Jefferson City, MO 65101-3500.

STEWART, CHARLES CAMERON
PERSONAL Born 12/19/1941, Evanston, IL, 3 children **DISCIPLINE** AFRICAN HISTORY, ISLAMIC HISTORY **EDUCATION** Hanover Col, BA, 63; Univ Ghana, MA, 65; Oxford Univ, DPhil(Orient Studies), 70. **CAREER** Asst prof, 71-74, actg dir African Studies Prog, 77-78 & 80-81, assoc prof Hist, Univ Ill, Urbana-Champaign, 74- & dir African Studies Prog, 81-84, from lectr to sr lectr Hist, Ahmadu Bello Univ, Nigeria, 73-76; chmn Dept Hist, Univ Ill, Urbana-Champaign 92-97; exec assoc dean, Coll Lib Arts, 97-. **MEMBERSHIPS** African Studies Asn. **RESEARCH** Recent Mauritanian history; history of Islamic Africa; historiography of Northern Nigeria. **SELECTED PUBLICATIONS** Auth, Notes on North and West African manuscript material, Res Bull Ctr Arabic Doc, 68; New source on the book market in Morocco in 1830, Hesperis-Tamuda, 70; co-ed, Julien, History of North Africa, Routledge/Praeger, 70; auth, Political authority and social stratification in Mauritania, In: Arabs and Berbers, Heath, 72; coauth, Islam and Social Order in Mauritania, Clarendon, 73; auth, Southern Saharan scholarship and the bilad al-sudan & Frontier disputes and problems of legitimation, J African Hist, 76; co-ed, Modes of Production in Africa, Sage, 81; co-ed Imagining the Twentieth Century, U Ill Press, 97. **CONTACT ADDRESS** Dept of History, Univ of Illinois, Urbana-Champaign, 810 S Wright St, Urbana, IL 61801-3611. **EMAIL** cc@uiuc.edu

STEWART, GORDON THOMAS
PERSONAL Born 07/06/1945, Newport-on-Tay, Scotland, m, 1967, 2 children **DISCIPLINE** MODERN HISTORY **EDUCATION** Univ St Andrews, MA, 67; Queen's Univ, Ont, PhD(mod hist), 70. **CAREER** Asst prof, 70-73, ASSOC PROF HIST, MICH STATE UNIV, 73- **RESEARCH** British Empire since the 18th century; Canadian-American studies; American colonial history. **SELECTED PUBLICATIONS** Coauth, A People Highly Favoured of God, the Nova Scotia Yankees and the American Revolution, Archon Bks, 72; Documents Relating to the Great Awakening in Nova Scotia 1760-1791, The Champlain Soc (Toronto), 82; The Origins of Canadian Politics: A Comparative Approach, Univ of Brit Columbia Press, 86; The American Response to Canada since 1776, MSU Press, 92; Jute and Empire: The Calcutta Jute Wallahs and the Landscapes of Empire, Manhattan Univ Press, 98; The Contribution Of Methodism To Atlantic Canada, Canadian Hist Rev, Vol 74, 93; The Siege Of Fort Cumberland, 1776--An Episode In The American-Revolution William And Mary Quart, Vol 54, 97; Canada And The United-States--Ambivalent Allies, Am Hist Rev, Vol 101, 96; Revolution Downeast--The War For Amn Independence In Maine, Am Hist Rev, Vol 100, 95; After The Rebellion--The Later Years Of William Lyon Mackenzie , NY Hist, Vol 73, 92. **CONTACT ADDRESS** Dept of Hist, Michigan State Univ, 301 Morrill Hall, East Lansing, MI 48824-1036.

STEWART, JAMES BREWER
PERSONAL Born 08/08/1940, Cleveland, OH, m, 1965, 2 children **DISCIPLINE** AMERICAN HISTORY **EDUCATION** Dartmouth Col, BA, 62; Case Western Reserve Univ, MA, 66, PhD(hist), 68. **CAREER** Asst prof, Carroll Col, Wis, 68-69; from asst prof to James Wallace Prof Hist, Macalester Col, 69-; vis dist prof hist, Univ S Carolina, 78-79; provost, Macalester Col, 87-90. **HONORS AND AWARDS** Res & teaching fel, Newberry Libr, 72-73; Fel, Am Coun of Learned Soc, 80; Soc of Midland Authors Best Biography Awd, 86; fel Am Coun Learned Socs. **MEMBERSHIPS** Orgn Am Historians; Southern Hist Asn; Soc Hist of Early Am Republic. **RESEARCH** Pre-civil War U.S. political and social history; antislavery and African American history; comparative slavery and emancipation. **SELECTED PUBLICATIONS** Auth, Joshua R. Giddings and the Tactics of Radical Politics, Case Western Reserve Univ, 70; Holy Warriors: The Abolitionists and American Slavery, Hill & Wang, 76, rev ed, 97, Japanese transl, 94; Wendell Phillips: Liberty's Hero, La State Univ, 86; ed, The Constitution and the Problem of Freedom of Expression, Southern Ill Univ, 86; William Lloyd Garrison and the Challenge of Emancipation, Harlan Davidson, 92; coauth, To Heal the Scourge of Prejudice: The Life and Writings of Hosea Easton, Univ Mass, 99; ed & contribur, Race and the Making of the Republican Nation, Madison House, 00. **CONTACT ADDRESS** Dept of History, Macalester Col, 1600 Grand Ave, Saint Paul, MN 55105-1899. **EMAIL** stewart@macalester.edu

STIEBING, WILLIAM H., JR
PERSONAL Born 12/21/1940, New Orleans, LA, m, 1965, 1 child **DISCIPLINE** ANCIENT HISTORY, ARCHAEOLOGY **EDUCATION** Univ New Orleans (formerly La State Univ), BA, 62; Univ Pa, PhD, 70. **CAREER** Instr, Univ New Orleans, 67-70; asst prof, 70-73; assoc prof, 73-85; prof, 85-. **HONORS AND AWARDS** Nat Def Edu Act Fel; Dist Fac Awd. **MEMBERSHIPS** AHA; AIA; SBL. **RESEARCH** Late Bronze Age in the Eastern Mediterranean; Ancient Israelite Religion; history of archaeology; pseudoscientific or 'cult' archaeology and its proponents. **SELECTED PUBLICATIONS** Auth, Ancient Astronauts, Cosmic Collisions, and Other Popular Theories About Man's Past, Prometheus Books (Buffalo, NY), 84; auth, Out of the Desert: Archaeology and the Exodus/Conquest Narratives, Prometheus Books (Buffalo, NY), 89; auth, Uncovering the Past: A History of Archaeology, Prometheus Books (Buffalo, NY), 93, ppbk Oxford UP, 94. **CONTACT ADDRESS** Dept History, Univ of New Orleans, 2000 Lakeshore Dr, New Orleans, LA 70148-2550. **EMAIL** wstiebing@msn.com

STIEGLITZ, ROBERT R.
PERSONAL Born 04/14/1943, Bershad, Ukraine, m, 1975, 2 children **DISCIPLINE** ANTHROPOLOGY, ARCHAEOLOGY **EDUCATION** City Col of NYork, BA, 67; Brandeis Univ, MA, 69; PhD, 71. **CAREER** Chemn, Hebraic Studies Dept, Rutgers Univ, Newark, NJ, 81-84; Vis Prof, Jewish Theol Sem of NY, 95-98; Assoc Prof, Rutgers Univ, Newark, NJ, 83-. **HONORS AND AWARDS** Archaeol Inst of Am Fel. **MEMBERSHIPS** Am Sch of Orient Res, Archaeol Inst of Am, Israel Explor Soc, Hellenic Inst of Marine Archaeol. **RESEARCH** Biblical Archaeology, Ancient Seafaring, West-Semitic Epigraphy. **SELECTED PUBLICATIONS** Coauth, Phoenicians on the Northern Coast of Israel, Haifa: Necht Museum, Univ of Haifa, 93; auth, "The Minoan Origin of Tyrian Purple," Bibl Archaeologist 57 (94): 46-54; auth, "Stratonos Pyrgos - Migdal Sar - Sebastos: History and Archaeology," in Caesarea Maritima: A Retrospective after Two Millennia, ed. A. Raban and K. G. Holum (Leiden: Brill, 96), 593-608; auth, "Ptolemy IX Soter II Lathyrus on Cyprus and the Coast of the Levant," in Res Maritima: Cyprus and the Eastern Mediterranean from Prehistory to Late Antiquity, CAARI Monograph Ser Vol I, ed. S Swiny et al (Atlanta: Scholar's Press, 97), 301-306; coauth, Illustrated Dictionary of Bible Life and Times, Reader's Digest (NY), 97; auth, "The Phoenician-Punic Menology," in Boundaries of the Ancient Near Eastern World: A Tribute to Cyrus H. Gordon, ed. M. Lubetski et al (Sheffield: Sheffield Acad Press, 98), 211-221; auth, "A Late Byzantine Reservoir and 'Piscina' at Tel Tanninim, " Israel Explor J 48 (98): 54-65; auth, "Phoenician Ship Equipment and Fittings," in Tropis V: International Symposium on Ship Construcion in Antiquity, ed. H. Tzalas (Anthens: Hellenic Inst for the Preserv of Nautical Tradition, 99), 409-420; auth, "Straton's Tower and Demetrias again: one town or two?," in Caesare Papers 2, ed. K. G. Holum et al (Portsmouth, RI: JRA, 99), 359-360. **CONTACT ADDRESS** Classical and Modern Languages and Literatures Dept, Rutgers, The State Univ of New Jersey, Newark, 175 Univ Ave., Newark, NJ 07102-1814. **EMAIL** stieglit@andromeda.rutgers.edu

STILES, KRISTINE
DISCIPLINE ART HISTORY **EDUCATION** Univ CA Berkeley, PhD. **CAREER** Assoc prof, Duke Univ. **RESEARCH** Contemp art. **SELECTED PUBLICATIONS** Auth, Theories and Documents of Contemporary Art, 96. **CONTACT ADDRESS** Dept of Art and Art Hist, Duke Univ, East Duke Building, Durham, NC 27706.

STILLMAN, DAMIE
PERSONAL Born 07/27/1933, Dallas, TX, m, 1960, 2 children **DISCIPLINE** ART HISTORY **EDUCATION** Northwestern Univ, BS, 54; Univ Del, MA, 56; Columbia Univ, PhD(art hist), 61. **CAREER** Asst librn, W P Beklnap, Jr, Res Libr Am Painting, H F duPont Winterthur Mus, 57-59; asst prof art hist, Oakland Univ, 61-65; assoc prof, 65-68, prof art hist, Univ Wis-Milwaukee, 68-77, chm dept, 75-77; PROF ART HIST, 77-89, JOHN W SHIRLEY PROF ART HIST, UNIV DEL, 89-00 & CHM DEPT, 81-86, 93-98; John W. Shirley Prof of Art History, emeritus, 00- ed-in-chief, Buildings of the United States, 96- . **HONORS AND AWARDS** Am Coun Learned Soc grant-in-aid, 68; Nat Endowment for Humanities younger humanist fel, 70-71; Am Philos Soc res grant, 73; Soc Archit Historians Founders Awd, 75; NEH fel, 86-87; Univ Del Ctr for Advanc Stud fel, 88-89; Gottschalk Prize, Am Soc Eighteenth Century Stud, 88. **MEMBERSHIPS** Col Art Asn Am; Soc Archit Historians (pres, 82-84); Soc Archit Hist, Gt Brit; Am Soc Eighteenth Century Studies; Northeast Am Soc for Eighteenth Century Stud, (pres 95-96); Victorian Soc in Am. **RESEARCH** Eighteenth century English and American architecture; American and English art; neo-classical architecture and decoration. **SELECTED PUBLICATIONS** Auth, New York City Hall: Competition and Execution, J Soc Archit Hist, 11/64; The Decorative Work of Robert Adam, Tiranti, London, 66; English Painting: The Great Masters, 1730-1860, McGraw, 66; The Gallery at Lansdowne House: International Architecture and Decoration in Microcosm, Art Bull, 3/70; British Architects and Italian Architectural Competitions, 1758-1780, J Soc Archit Hist, 3/73; The Pantheon Redecorated, VIA III, 77; Death Defied and Honor Upheld: the Mausoleum in Neo-Classical England, Art Quart, 78; Church Architecture in Neo-Classical England, J Soc Archit Hist, 5/79; auth, English Neo-Classical Architecture, Zwemmer, 88; auth, The Neo-Classical Transformation of the English Country House, in Stud in the Hist of Art, 89; auth, City Living Federal Style, in Everyday Life in the Early Republic, Winterthur, 94; auth, British Architectural Books in the Eighteenth Century, Avery's Choice, 97; auth, From the Ancient Roman Republic to the American New One, A Republic for the Ages, 99; auth, Architectural Books in New York: From Lacomb to Lafever, Architects and Their Books in Early America, 2000. **CONTACT ADDRESS** Dept of Art Hist, Univ of Delaware, Newark, DE 19716.

STILLMAN, NORMAN (NOAM) ARTHUR
PERSONAL Born 07/06/1945, New York, NY, w, 2 children **DISCIPLINE** ORIENTAL STUDIES, MIDDLE EASTERN HISTORY **EDUCATION** Univ Pa, BA, 67, PhD(Orient studies), 70. **CAREER** Asst prof Near Eastern lang & lit, NY Univ, 70-73; From Assoc prof to Prof Hist & Arabic, State Univ NY Binghamton ON, 73-95, Jewish Theol Sem fel, 70-71; consult, Soc Sci Res Coun, 72-77 & Nat Geog Soc, 79-80; vis assoc prof Mid Eastern & Jewish hist, Haifa Univ, 79-80; Schusterman/Josey Prof of Judaic Hist, Univ of Okla, 95-. **HONORS AND AWARDS** Distinguished Humanist, Ohio State Univ, 00. **MEMBERSHIPS** Am Orient Soc; Mid East Studies Asn NAm; Asn Jewish Studies; Conf Jewish Social Studies; Societe de l'histoire du Maroc. **RESEARCH** History of the Jews under Islam; North African history; semitic languages and literatures. **SELECTED PUBLICATIONS** Auth, The Jews of Arab Lands, Jewish Publ Soc Am, 79; co-ed, Studies in Judaism and Islam, 81 & asst ed, Studies in Geniza and Sepharad: Heritage, 81, Magnes Press; auth, Jews of Sefrou, Univ of Manchester Press, 88; co-trans, Travail in an Arab Land, Univ of Alabama Press, 89; auth, The Jews of Arab Lands in Modern Times, JPS, 91; auth, Sephardi Religious Responses to Modernity, Harwood Acad Press, U.K., 95; co-ed, From Iberia to Diaspora, Brill, 99. **CONTACT ADDRESS** Dept of Hist, Univ of Oklahoma, Norman, OK 73019. **EMAIL** nstillman@ou.edu

STINGER, CHARLES LEWIS
PERSONAL Born 03/19/1944, Waverly, NY, m, 1968, 2 children **DISCIPLINE** ITALIAN RENAISSANCE HISTORY **EDUCATION** Hobart Col, BA, 66; Stanford Univ, MA, 67, PhD(hist), 71. **CAREER** Instr Europ social & cult prog, Stan-

ford Univ, 70-72; Harvard Ctr Renaissance Study fel, Villa I Tatti, Florence, Italy, 72-73; asst prof, 73-77, ASSOC PROF HIST, STATE UNIV NY BUFFALO, 77-, Am Coun Learned Socs grant-in-aid, 77. **MEMBERSHIPS** Renaissance Soc Am; Am Soc Reformation Res; AHA. **RESEARCH** The Renaissance in Rome; religious thought in Italian Renaissance humanism. **SELECTED PUBLICATIONS** Auth, Humanism and the Church Fathers: Ambrogio Traversari (1386-1439) and Christian Antiquity in the Italian Renaissance, State Univ NY, 77; Roma Triumphans: Triumphs in the thought and ceremonies of Renaissance Rome, Medievalia et Humanistica, 81. **CONTACT ADDRESS** Dept of Hist, SUNY, Buffalo, Buffalo, NY 14261.

STINSON, ROBERT WILLIAM

PERSONAL Born 09/12/1941, Elmhurst, IL, m, 1966, 2 children **DISCIPLINE** AMERICAN HISTORY, HISTORIOGRAPHY, FILM HISTORY, MUSICOLOGY **EDUCATION** Allegheny Col, BA, 64; Ind Univ, MA, 66, PhD(hist), 71. **CAREER** From Asst Prof to Assoc Prof, 70-88, PROF HIST, MORAVIAN COL, 88-. **HONORS AND AWARDS** Lindback Awd for Distinguished Teaching, Christian and Mary Lindback Found, 72. **RESEARCH** United States, 1865 to the present; history of journalism; history of film; historiography. **SELECTED PUBLICATIONS** Auth, S S McClure's My autobiography: The progressive as self-made man, Am Quart, summer 70; McClure's road to McClure's: How revolutionary were the 1890's magazines?, Jour Quart, summer 70; Ida Tarbell and the ambiguities of feminism, Pa Mag Hist & Biog, 4/77; Lincoln Steffens' Shame of the Cities reconsidered, New Republic, 7/77; How they kept the trust: Ida Tarbell's John D Rockefeller, Nation, 11/77; On the death of a baby, Atlantic Monthly, 7/79; Lincoln Steffens, Ungar, 79; The Long Dying of Baby Andrew, Little, Brown, 83; The Faces of Clio, Nelson-Hall, 87. **CONTACT ADDRESS** Dept of History, Moravian Col, 1200 Main St, Bethlehem, PA 18018-6650. **EMAIL** merws01@moravian.edu

STITES, FRANCIS NOEL

PERSONAL Born 12/25/1938, Indianapolis, IN, m, 1966, 2 children **DISCIPLINE** AMERICAN CONSTITUTIONAL HISTORY **EDUCATION** Marian Col, Ind, BA, 60; Ind Univ, MA, 65, PhD(hist), 68. **CAREER** Instr hist, Eastern Ind Ctr, Earlham Col, 66-67; from asst prof to assoc prof, 68-77, PROF HIST, SAN DIEGO STATE UNIV, 77- **MEMBERSHIPS** Orgn Am Historians; AHA; Am Soc Legal Hist. **RESEARCH** Early American legal and social history. **SELECTED PUBLICATIONS** Auth, Private Interest and Public Gain, the Dartmouth College Case, 1819, Univ Mass, 72; John Marshall: Defender of the Constitution, Little, Brown & Co, 81. **CONTACT ADDRESS** Dept of Hist, San Diego State Univ, 5500 Campanile Dr, San Diego, CA 92182-8147. **EMAIL** fstites@mail.sdsu.edu

STOCKMAN, ROBERT H.

PERSONAL Born 10/06/1953, Meriden, CT, m, 1992, 1 child **DISCIPLINE** HISTORY OF RELIGION **EDUCATION** Wesleyan Univ, BA, 75; Brown Univ, MSc, 77; Harvard Divinity School, MTS, 82, ThD, 90. **CAREER** Grad res asst, Brown Univ, 75-77; instr, Geology and Oceanography, Comm Col of RI, 77-80; instr, Geology, Boston State Col, 80-82; instr, Geology, Univ Lowell, 83-84; instr, Geology and Astronomy, Bentley Col, 83-90; teaching asst, Harvard Univ, 86-89; asst prof relig, DePaul Univ, 95-96; Instr Relig, DePaul Univ, 90-95, 96-98. **MEMBERSHIPS** Amer Academy Relig; Middle East Studies Assoc; Soc Iranian Studies; Assoc Baha i Studies, member, ex comm, 90-98, member and chair, Study of Religions Section, 89-. **RESEARCH** Amer Bahai hist; Amer relig hist. **SELECTED PUBLICATIONS** Auth, The Bahai Faith in America, vol 1, Origins, 1892-1900, Baha'i Pub Trust, 85, vol 2, Early Expansion, 1900-1912, George Ronald, 95; The Baha'i Faith in America: One Hundred Years, in World Order, vol 25, no 3, spring 94; Paul Johnson's Theosophical Influence in Baha'i History: Some Comments, in Theosophical Hist, vol 5, no 4, Oct 94; The Baha'i Faith: A Portrait, in Joel Beversluis, ed, A Sourcebook for the Earth's Community of Religions, 2nd ed, CoNexus Press, 95; The Baha i Faith in the 1990's, article in Dr Timothy Miller, ed, America's Alternative Religions, SUNY Press, 95; The Vision of the Baha' i Faith, in Martin Forward, Ultimate Visions: Reflections on the Religions We Choose, One World, 95; The Baha'i Faith in England and Germany, 1900-1913, in World Order, vol 27, no 3, spring 96; The Baha'i Faith section of the Pluralism Project, CD Rom, Columbia Univ Press, 97; many other articles, several forthcoming publications. **CONTACT ADDRESS** Institute for Baha'i Studies, 224 Swanson Cir, South Bend, IN 46615. **EMAIL** rstockman@usbnc.org

STODDARD, ROBERT

PERSONAL Born 08/29/1928, Auburn, NE, m, 1955, 3 children **DISCIPLINE** GEOGRAPHY **EDUCATION** NE Wesleyan Univ, BA, 50; Univ NE, MA, 60; Univ IA, PhD, 66. **CAREER** Asst prof, NE Wesleyan Univ, 61-63; vis prof, Tribhuvan Univ Kathmandu, 75-76; asst to full prof, Univ of NE, 67-. **HONORS AND AWARDS** Distinguished Teaching Achievement Awd. **MEMBERSHIPS** Asn of Am Geog. **RESEARCH** Geography of religion. **SELECTED PUBLICATIONS** Ed, Sacred Places, Sacred Spaces: The Geography of Pilgrimages, LA State Univ Press, 97; auth, "Major Pilgrimage Places in the World,", in Pilgrimage in the Old and New World (Berlin: Dietrich Reimer Verlag, 94), 17-36; auth, "Trends in Published Research in India," in The Roots of Indian Geography: Search and Research; Homage to S. P. Chatterjee(Banaras Hindu Univ, 92), 159-166; auth, The Disaster of Deforestation in the Brazilian Rainforest,," in Natural and Technological Disasters: Causes, Effects and Preventative Measures, (Penn Acad of Sci, 92), 527-535; auth, Field Techniques and Research Methods in Geography, 92 Auth, Human Geography: People, Places, and Cultures, 2nd ed, Prentice-Hall, Inc, 89. **CONTACT ADDRESS** Dept Geography, Univ of Nebraska-Lincoln, PO Box 880135, Lincoln, NE 68588.

STODDARD, WHITNEY S.

PERSONAL Born 03/25/1913, Greenfield, MA, m, 3 children **DISCIPLINE** ART HISTORY **EDUCATION** Williams, BA, 35; Harvard Univ, MA, 36; PhD, 41. **CAREER** Instr, Williams Col, 38; asst prof, 43; assoc prof, 49; prof, 55. **HONORS AND AWARDS** Col Art Asoc, Outstanding Teacher Awd, 89. **MEMBERSHIPS** Col Art Asoc; Soc of Archit Hist **RESEARCH** Middle Ages--France **SELECTED PUBLICATIONS** The West Portals of Saint-Denis and Chartres, 52; Adventure in Architecture, 58; Monastery and Cathedral in France, 66; The Facade of Saint-Gilles du-Gard, 73; The Sculptors of the West Portals of Chartres, 87. **CONTACT ADDRESS** 1611 Cold Spring Rd., Apt. 227, Williamstown, MA 01267-2777.

STODDARD-HAYES, MARLANA

PERSONAL Born 11/05/1957, IA, m, 1993 **DISCIPLINE** PAINTING, DRAWING **EDUCATION** Colo State Univ, BA, 80; Wichita State Univ, MA, 83; MAIS Candidate, Marylhurst Univ, Ore, 97-. **CAREER** Artist-In-Residence, USD #395, Rush Co, Kans, 83-86; Artist-In-Residence, Dodge City Community Col, 86-95; Prof, Dodge City Community Col, 96-00. **HONORS AND AWARDS** Artist in Residence Grant, Kans Arts Commission, 83-89; Nat Endowment for The Arts, Underserved Communities; Weskowin Corst Found Fel, 90; Who's Who Am Teachers, 00. **MEMBERSHIPS** Col Art Asn, Kans Watercolor Soc. **RESEARCH** Painting, Interdisciplinary studies, Mixed media approaches. **SELECTED PUBLICATIONS** Auth, "Artist's Communities," in Alliance of Artist's Communities (Stanley Kunitz, 96), 135. **CONTACT ADDRESS** Dept Humanities and Soc Sci, Dodge City Comm Col, 2501 N 14th Ave, Dodge City, KS 67801-2316. **EMAIL** marlana@dccc.dodge-city.ks.us

STOEFFLER, FRED ERNEST

PERSONAL Born 09/27/1911, Happenbach, West Germany, m, 1941, 2 children **DISCIPLINE** RELIGION, HISTORY OF CHRISTIANITY **EDUCATION** Temple Univ, BS, 38, STM, 45, STD, 48; Yale Univ, BD, 41. **CAREER** Pastor, Methodist Church, 39-51; from asst prof to prof hist Christianity, 51-62, Prof Relig, Temple Univ, 62-, Mem coun, Am Soc Church Hist, 77-79. **MEMBERSHIPS** Am Soc Church Hist; Am Soc Reformation Res; AHA; Acad Polit Sci; Am Acad Relig. **RESEARCH** Reformation; mysticism; pietism. **SELECTED PUBLICATIONS** Auth, Mysticism in the Devotional Literature of Colonial Pennsylvania, Pa Ger Folklore Soc, 49; The Rise of Evangelical Pietism, Brill, Leiden, 65; transl, B Lohse, History of Doctrine, Fortress, 66; auth, German Pietism During the 18th Century, Brill, Leiden, 73; ed & contribr, Continental Pietism and Early American Christianity, Wm B Eerdmans, 76; Anton Wilhelm Bohme: Studies On The Ecumenical Thought And Dealings Of A Pietist From Halle, Church Hist, Vol 61, 92. **CONTACT ADDRESS** Dept of Relig, Temple Univ, Philadelphia, PA 19122.

STOETZER, O. CARLOS

PERSONAL Born 06/28/1921, Buenos Aires, Argentina, d, 1955, 2 children **DISCIPLINE** HISTORY OF LATIN AMERICA & AFRICA **EDUCATION** Univ Perugia, cert Ital civ, 42; Debrecen Univ, cert Hungarian civ, 43; Freiburg Univ, Dr iur(law), 45; Georgetown Univ, PhD(int rels), 61. **CAREER** Asst cult dept, Pan Am Union, Orgn Am States, DC, 50-51, philatelic div, 51-53, travel div, 53-56, coun, 56-61; actg secy, Inter-Am Inst Agr Sci, 58-61; assoc prof polit sci, Manhattanville Col, 61-63, 64-66; chief div law & hist, Inst Latin Am Studies, Hamburg, Ger, 63-64; assoc prof, 66-79, Prof Hist, Fordham Univ, 79-91, RETIRED PROF EMERITUS. **HONORS AND AWARDS** Knight Comdr Order Isabella the Catholic, Span Govt, 59; prof honorario Universidad del Salvador, Buenos Aires, Argentina, 82. **MEMBERSHIPS** Soc for Iberian & Latin Am Thought (pres, 77-79); Latin Am Studies Asn; Caribbean Studies Asn; Conf Latin Am Hist; Argentine Asn Am Studies. **RESEARCH** Hispanic world, especially intellectual history and international relations. **SELECTED PUBLICATIONS** Auth, The Organization of American States, an Introduction, Praeger, 65, 93; El Pensamiento Politico en la America Espanola Durante el Periodo de la Emancipacion, 1789-1825 (2 vols), Inst Estud Polit, Madrid, 66; Die geistigen Grundlagen der spanischamerikanischen Unabhangigkeit, In: Idee und Wirklichkeit in Iberoamerika, Beitrage zur Politik und Geistesgeschichte, Hoffman & Campe, Hamburg, 69; Grundlagen des spanischamerikauischen Verfassungsdenkens, Verfassung und Recht in Ubersee, 69; Nineteenth-century traditionalism in Spanish America, Int Philos Quart, 78; Benjamin Constant and the Doctrinaire Liberal Influence in Hispanic America, Verfassung und Recht in Ubersee, 78; The Scholastic Roots of the Spanish-American Revolution, Fordham Univ, 79; Positivism and Idealism in the Hispanic World: The Positivist Case of Brazil and the Krausean Influence in Spanish America, Rev Interam, summer 79; numerous entries, Historical Dictionary of the Spanish Empire, 1402-1975, Westport, CT: Greenwood Press, 92; Complejidades regionales en la formacion de las naciones de la America Central y del Caribe, South Eastern Latin Americanist, XXXVII, 4, spring 94; The HispanicTradition, Latin American Revolutions, 1808-1826, Old and New World Origins, ed and with an intro by John Lynch, Univ OK Press, 94; Der mittelamerianische Indigo und Echo in Europa in der Fruhen Neuzeit, Jahrbuch fur Geschichte von Staat, Wirtschaft und Geschichte Lateinamerikas, Cologne, GER, vol 32, 95; Krausean Philosophy as a Major Political and Social Force in Modern Argentina and Guatemala, Bridging the Atlantic. Toward a Reassessment of Iberian and Latin American Cultural Ties, ed and with intro by Marina Perez de Mendiola, Albany, State Univ NY Press, 96; Iberoamerica. Historia politica y cultural, vol I: Los Gobiernos Peninsulares (1492/1500-1808), vol II: Periodo de la Independencia (1808-1826), vol III: Organizacion y constitucion de las naciones iberoamericanas (1826-1880), Buenos Aires: Fundacion Universidad a Distancia Hernandarias, Editorial Docencia, 96; vol IV: Marco politico de Iberoamerica en el siglo XX (1880-1945), vol V: De la posguerra a fines del milenio, Buenos Aires: Fundacion Universidad a Distancia Hernandarisa, Editorial Docenica, 20; numerous other articles including a collection of seventeen Haitian presidential biographies that appeared in Haiti Philately, Port Townsend, WA, from June 95 through Sept. 99; Karl Christian Friedrich Krause and his Influence in the Hispanic World, Cologne: Bohlau Verlag, 98. **CONTACT ADDRESS** PO Box 7484, Wilton, CT 06897.

STOEVER, WILLIAM K. B.

PERSONAL Born 06/20/1941, Riverside, CA, m, 1971 **DISCIPLINE** HISTORY OF RELIGION **EDUCATION** Pomona Col, BA, 63; Yale Univ, MDiv, 66, MPhil, 69, PhD(relig studies), 70. **CAREER** Asst prof, 70-75, assoc prof, 76-80, prof humanities, Western Wash Univ, 80-, Chemn, Dept Lib Studies 78-, Nat Endowment for Humanities res fel, 74-75. **MEMBERSHIPS** AHA; Am Soc Church Hist; Am Acad Relig; Am Studies Asn. **RESEARCH** History and historiography of religion in Amica; 17th century Puritanism; Jonathan Edwards; religion and cultural change. **SELECTED PUBLICATIONS** Auth, Henry Boynton Smith and the German theology of history, Union Sem Quart Rev, fall 69; Nature, grace, and John Cotton: The theological dimension in the New England antinomian controversy, Church Hist, 3/75; A Faire and Easie Way to Heaven: Covenant Theology and Antinomianism in Early Massachusetts, Wesleyan Univ Press, 78; The Godly Will's Discerning: Shepard, Edwards, and the Identification of True Godliness, Jonathan Edwards's Writings: Text, Context, Interpretation, Ind Univ Press, 97. **CONTACT ADDRESS** Dept of Lib Studies, Western Washington Univ, M/S 9084, Bellingham, WA 98225-5996. **EMAIL** bristow@wwu.edu

STOFF, MICHAEL B.

PERSONAL Born 05/12/1947, New York, NY, 2 children **DISCIPLINE** HISTORY **EDUCATION** Rutgers College, BA, 69; Yale Univ, MPhil, 72, PhD, 77. **CAREER** Act instr, 74-75, lectr, 76-79, Yale Univ; asst prof, 79-86, ASSOC PROF HIST, UNIV TEX, AUSTIN, 86-; dir of graduate studies in history, 98-. **HONORS AND AWARDS** Lane Cooper Scholar, Rutgers, 67-69; Univ fel, Yale Univ, 69-74; res grant, Concilium Int, Area Stud, Yale Univ, 73-74; summer res award, Univ Res Inst, Univ Tex, Austin, 80-81; acad dev grant, Univ Tex, Austin, 80-81; Summer Inst Grant, NEH, Bard Col, Vassar Col, Franklin D Roosevelt Libr, 86, 88, 90, 92; Walter Prescott Webb fel, Univ Tex, Austin, 89; Friars' Centennial Teaching Excellence Awd, 96; Dean's fel, Col Lib Arts, Univ Tex, Austin, 97. **SELECTED PUBLICATIONS** auth, Oil, War, and American Security, Yale Press, 80; coed, The Manhattan Project: A Documentary Introduction to the Atomic Age, Mcgraw Hill, 90; Co-auth, Nation of Nations: A Narrative History of the American Republic, McGraw Hill, 98-, 99; co-auth, American Journey: The Quest for Liberty, Prentice Hall, 94; co-auth, The American Nation, Prentice Hall, 96; auth, 1945: auth, Herbert Hoover, in The Reader's Companion to the American Presidency, Houghton Mifflin & Co, 00. **CONTACT ADDRESS** History Dept, Univ of Texas, Austin, Campus Mail Code B7000, Austin, TX 78712. **EMAIL** mbstoff@mail.utexas.edu

STOIANOVICH, TRAIAN

PERSONAL Born 07/23/1921, Yugoslavia, m, 1945, 2 children **DISCIPLINE** HISTORY **EDUCATION** Univ Rochester, BA, 42; NYork Univ, MA, 49. **CAREER** Instr hist, NY Univ, 52-55; from instr to assoc prof, 55-67, fel, 65-66, prof I, 67-75, PROF II HIST, RUTGERS UNIV, 75-, Am Philos Soc res fel, Paris & Belgrade, 58; Fulbright res fel, Salonika, Greece, 58-59; vis asst prof, Univ Calif, Berkeley, 60 & Stanford Univ, 60-61; vis assoc prof, NY Univ, 63 & 66-67; Am rep, Comn Econ & Social Hist, Int Asn SE Europe Studies, 66-71; Fulbright res fel, Paris, 77. **MEMBERSHIPS** AHA; Econ Hist Asn; Am Asn Advan Slavic Studies; AAUP. **RESEARCH** Modern European history; economic history; social history. **SELECTED PUBLI-**

CATIONS Auth, An Economic And Social-Hist of The Ottoman-Empire, 1300-1914, Historian, Vol 59, 96; The Uskoks of Senj--Piracy, Banditry, And Holy-War In The 16th-Century Adriatic, Am Hist Rev, Vol 98, 93; Social-History of Siberia 1815-1941--Sustainable Progress During Industrialization, Am Hist Rev, Vol 101, 96; Elementary-Education In Yugoslavia: 1918-1941--Social Modernization, Am Hist Rev, Vol 102, 97. **CONTACT ADDRESS** Dept of Hist, Rutgers, The State Univ of New Jersey, New Brunswick, New Brunswick, NJ 08903.

STOKES, GALE
PERSONAL Born 09/05/1933, Orange, NJ, m, 1958, 2 children **DISCIPLINE** HISTORY **EDUCATION** Colgate Univ, BA, 54; IN Univ, MA, 65, PhD, 70. **CAREER** To Mary Gibbs Jones prof of History, Rice Univ, 68-; Intrim Dean of Humanities, 00-01. **HONORS AND AWARDS** Wayne S Vucinich Prize, AAASS, 94; Russ E Europe Inst, IN Univ, Distinguished Alumnus, 95. **MEMBERSHIPS** Am Hist Asn (member, res coun, 98-); Am Asn for Advancement of Slavic Studies (bd, 97-98). **RESEARCH** 19th and 20th century Eastern Europe; Balkans; Natsanacism; world hist. **SELECTED PUBLICATIONS** Auth, The Politics of Development: the Emergence of Political Parties in Nineteenth Century Serbia, Duke Univ Press, 90; The Walls Came Tumbling Down: The Collapse of Communism in Eastern Europe, Oxford Univ Press, 93; From Stalinism to Pluralism, 2nd ed, Oxford Univ Press, 95; Three Eras of Political Change in Eastern Europe, Oxford Univ Press, 97; The West Transformed, with Warren Hollister and Sears McGee, Harcourt Brace, 99. **CONTACT ADDRESS** History Dept MS-33, Rice Univ, 6100 S Main St, Houston, TX 77005-1892. **EMAIL** gstokes@rice.edu

STOKES, LAWRENCE DUNCAN
PERSONAL Born 01/10/1940, Toronto, ON, Canada, m, 1964, 2 children **DISCIPLINE** MODERN EUROPEAN & GERMAN HISTORY **EDUCATION** Univ Toronto, BA, 62; Johns Hopkins Univ, MA, 64, PhD(hist), 72. **CAREER** Asst prof, 67-73, ASSOC PROF HIST, DALHOUSIE UNIV, 73-, Can Coun res grant, 73, 76, fel, 74-75; Humboldt fel, 79-80. **MEMBERSHIPS** Can Hist Asn; Conf Group Cent Europe Hist; Hist Asn, England; Can Comt Hist 2nd World War; Interuniv Ctr Europ Studies. **RESEARCH** Twentieth century German history; history of European fascist movements. **SELECTED PUBLICATIONS** Auth, "The German People and the Destruction of the European Jews," Central European Hist 6, (73), 167-91; auth, Medieval and Reformation Germany (to 1648): a select biography; co-ed, The Silence of the Sea, 92. **CONTACT ADDRESS** Dept of Hist, Dalhousie Univ, 1411 Seymour St, Halifax, NS, Canada B3H 3J5.

STOKSTAD, MARILYN JANE
PERSONAL Born 02/16/1929, Lansing, MI **DISCIPLINE** ART HISTORY **EDUCATION** Carleton Col, BA, 50; Mich St Univ, MA, 53, PhD, 57; Oslo Univ, post grad, 51-52. **CAREER** Instr, 56-58, Univ Mich; fac mem, 58-, assoc prof, 61-66, dir, mus art, 61-67, prof, 66-80, res assoc, sum, 65-66, 67, 71, 72, assoc dean, Col Liberal Arts & Sci, 72-76, Univ Kans; res cur, 69-80, bd dir, 72-75, 81-84, 88-96, dist prof, art, 80-94, Nelson-Atkins Mus Art; consult curator, medieval art, 80, vice pres, 90-93, pres, 93-96, Judith Harris Murphy dist prof, 94-, sr adv, 96-97, Intl Ctr Medieval Art. **HONORS AND AWARDS** Fulbright Fel, 51-52; NEH grantee, 67-68; Dist Svc Awd, Alumni Assn Carleton Col, 83; Fel AAUW; Kans Gov's Arts Awd, 97; James D Burke Prize in Fine Arts, St. Louis Museum of Art, 99; Balfour Jeffery Awd for Res in Humanities and Soc Sci; Univ of Kansas Rex Achievement Awd, 00. **MEMBERSHIPS** AAUW; Midwest Col Art Conf; Col Art Assn; Soc Archit Hist; Int Center of Medieval Art; Medieval Acad of Am, Mediterranen Studies Assoc, Am Soc for Hispanic Art Hist Studies; Historians of British Art; Italian art Soc. **RESEARCH** Medieval art. **SELECTED PUBLICATIONS** Auth, Santiago de Compostela, 78; auth, The Scottish World, 81; coauth, Gardens of the Middle Ages, 83; auth, Medieval Art, 86; auth, Art History, 95; auth, Art History, revised ed, 99; auth, Art, A Brief History, 00; auth, Art History, 2nd ed, 01. **CONTACT ADDRESS** Dept of Art History, Univ of Kansas, Lawrence, Lawrence, KS 66045. **EMAIL** stokstad@eagle.cc.ukans.edu

STOLER, MARK A.
PERSONAL Born 03/02/1945, New York, NY, m, 1991, 1 child **DISCIPLINE** HISTORY **EDUCATION** City Col of New York, BA, 66; Univ Wis, Madison, MA, 67, PhD, 71. **CAREER** Lect, Univ WI, Milwaukee, 68-69; Prof Hist, Univ VT, 70-; vis prof, Strategy Dept, US Naval War Col, 81-82; vis prof Hist, Univ Haita, Israel, 84-85; vis prof Hist, US Military Academy, 94-95. **HONORS AND AWARDS** Phi Alpha Theta; Army Civilian Service Awd and Commander's Awd for Public Service, 81, 95; Kidder Outstanding Faculty Awd, Univ VT, 84; Dean's Lecture Awd, Univ VT, 92; Univ Scholar Awd, Univ VT, 93; Phi Beta Kappa. **MEMBERSHIPS** Soc for Historians of Am Foreign Relations; Am Hist Asn; Org of Am Historians; Soc for Military Hist; World War II Studies Asn; Vermont Historical Soc; Committee on Peace Res in History; Center for Res on VT. **RESEARCH** US diplomatic and military history. **SELECTED PUBLICATIONS** Auth, The Politics of the Second Front: American Military Planning and Diplomacy in Coalition Warfare, 1941-1943, Greenwood Press, 77; The Origins of the Cold War (ed Microfiche collection), Scholarly Resources, 82; Explorations in American History: A Skills Approach, 2 vols, with Marshall True, IDC Pubs, 80, 2nd ed, Alfred A. Knopf, 86; George C. Marshall: Soldier-Statesman of the American Century, Twayne Pubs, 89; George C. Marshall, Robert Murphy, Edmund Muskie, and Lend-Lease, in Encyclopedia of US Foreign Relations, ed Bruce W. Jentleson and Thomas G. Paterson, Council of Foreign Relations, Oxford Univ Press, 97; Why George C.Marshall: A Biographical Assessment, in The Marshall Mission to China, ed Larry I. Bland, George C. Marshall Found, 98; Allied Summit Diplomacy, in World War II in Asia and the Pacific and the War's Aftermath, with General Themes: A Handbook of Literature and Research, ed Lloyd Lee. Greenwood Press, 98; George Marshall and Henry Stimson, in Oxford Companion to United States History, Oxford Univ Press, 98; George C. Marshall, Joint Chiefs of Staff and Diplomatic and Military Course of World War II, in The Oxford Companion to American Military History, ed John Whiteclay Chambers II, Oxford Univ Press, 98; The Joint Chiefs of Staff Assessment of Soviet-American Relations in the Spring of 1945, in Victory in Europe, 1945: the Allied Triumph over Germany and the Opening of the Cold War, ed Arnold A. Offner and Theodore A. Wilson, Univ Press KS, forthcoming 00; auth, "Allies and Advensarces! the Joint chiefs of Staff, the Grand Alliance, and U.S. Strategy in World War II," Univ of North Carolina Press, (forthcoming), 00. **CONTACT ADDRESS** Dept of Hist, Univ of Vermont, Wheeler House- 442 Main St., Burlington, VT 05405. **EMAIL** mstoler@zoo.uvm.edu

STOLL, STEVEN
DISCIPLINE HISTORY **EDUCATION** Univ Calif, Berkeley, BA, 88; Yale Univ, MA, 90, MPhil, 92, PhD, 94. **CAREER** ASST PROF, HIST, YALE UNIV **MEMBERSHIPS** Am Antiquarian Soc **CONTACT ADDRESS** Hist Dept, Yale Univ, PO Box 208234, New Haven, CT 06520-8324.

STOLTZFUS, NATHAN
DISCIPLINE MODERN EUROPE **EDUCATION** Harvard, MDiv, 84; PhD, 93. **CAREER** Assoc prof, Fla State Univ. **HONORS AND AWARDS** H. F. Guggenheim Fel; Fulbright; IREY; Friedrick Ebert Stiftung Fraenkel Prize in Contemp Hist; listed in Who's Who in the World. **RESEARCH** Twentieth-Century Europe. **SELECTED PUBLICATIONS** Auth, Resistance of the Hearth, W. W. Norton, 96; co-ed, Social Outsiders in Nazi Germany, Princeton Univ Press, 01. **CONTACT ADDRESS** Dept Hist, Florida State Univ, PO Box 3062200, Tallahassee, FL 32306-2200. **EMAIL** nstoltzfus@worldnet.att.net

STONE, ANDREA JOYCE
DISCIPLINE ART HISTORY **EDUCATION** Univ Fla, BA, 74; Univ Tex, MA, 77, PhD, 83. **CAREER** Asst prof, 84-91; assoc prof, 91-. **SELECTED PUBLICATIONS** Auth, Images from the Underworld: Naj Tunich and the Tradition of Maya Cave Painting, Univ Tex, 95; The Petroglyphs in the Guianas and Adjacent Areas of Brazil and Venezuela (rev), 89; A Dream of Maya (rev), Univ NMex, 89; The Mesoamerican Ballgame (rev), Univ NMex, 89; Arte rupestre colonial y republicano de Bolivia y paises vecinos, Latin Am Indian Lit, 89. **CONTACT ADDRESS** Dept of Art History, Univ of Wisconsin, Milwaukee, PO Box 413, Milwaukee, WI 53201. **EMAIL** stone@csd.uwm.edu

STONE, BAILEY S.
PERSONAL Born 06/08/1946, Schenectady, NY, s **DISCIPLINE** HISTORY **EDUCATION** Bowdoin Col, BA, 68; Princeton Univ, PhD, 73. **CAREER** From asst prof to prof, Univ Houston, 75- . **MEMBERSHIPS** AHA; Soc for French Hist Stud; Phi Alpha Theta. **RESEARCH** Eighteenth-century and Revolutionary Europe; modern revolutions. **SELECTED PUBLICATIONS** Auth, The Parliament of Paris, 1774-1789, Univ N Carolina, 81; auth, The French Parliaments and the Crisis of the Old Regime, U N Carolina, 86; auth, The Genesis of the French Revolution: A Global-Historical Interpretation, Cambridge, 94. **CONTACT ADDRESS** Dept of History, Univ of Houston, Houston, TX 77204-3785. **EMAIL** BSStone@jetson.uh.edu

STONE, DAVID M.
DISCIPLINE SOUTHERN BAROQUE ART **EDUCATION** Harvard Univ, PhD. **CAREER** Assoc prof. **SELECTED PUBLICATIONS** Auth, Guercino, Master Draftsman: Works from North American Collections, Harvard, 91; Guercino: Catalogo completo dei dipinto, Cantini, 91. **CONTACT ADDRESS** Dept of Art Hist, Univ of Delaware, 318 Old College, Newark, DE 19716. **EMAIL** dmstone@udel.edu

STONE, KAREN
PERSONAL Born 05/03/1957, Langdale, AL, m, 1976 **DISCIPLINE** HISTORY **EDUCATION** Auburn Univ, BA, 75; MA, 84; PhD, 98. **CAREER** Instr hist, S Union State Commun Col, 84- . **HONORS AND AWARDS** Who's Who Among America's Teachers, 95, 96, 98, 00; Phi Theta Kappa. **MEMBERSHIPS** Ala Asn Hist; Ala Baptist Hist Soc; Delta Kappa Gamma; Orgn Am Hist; Phi Alpha Theta; S Baptist Hist Asn; S Hist Asn. **RESEARCH** Southern history, Religious history, Modern US. **SELECTED PUBLICATIONS** Auth, A History of the First Baptist Church of Prattville, Alabama: 1839-1989, (90); auth, A History of the First Baptist Church of Wetumpka, (95). **CONTACT ADDRESS** Dept Sco Sci & Math, So Union State Comm Col, 1226 63 Ave SW, Lanett, AL 36863. **EMAIL** kstone@suscc.cc.al.us

STONE-MILLER, REBECCA
PERSONAL Born 07/17/1958, Manchester, NH, m, 1989, 2 children **DISCIPLINE** ART HISTORY **EDUCATION** Yale Univ, PhD, 87. **CAREER** Asst Prof, 90-96, Assoc Prof, Emory Univ, 96-. **HONORS AND AWARDS** Getty Grant for Catalogue Preparation, 98-99. **MEMBERSHIPS** Inst Andean Studies; Phi Beta Kappa; Col Art Asn. **RESEARCH** Andean art; textiles; Central American art; shamanism. **SELECTED PUBLICATIONS** Auth, To Weave for the Sun: Ancient Andean Textiles, Thames & Hudson, 94; Art of the Andes, Thames & Hudson (World of Art Series), 96. **CONTACT ADDRESS** Art Hist Dept, Emory Univ, Carlos Hall, Atlanta, GA 30322. **EMAIL** rstonem@emory.edu

STONE-RICHARDS, MICHAEL
DISCIPLINE 20TH CENTURY EUROPEAN ART **EDUCATION** Courtauld Inst Art, PhD. **CAREER** Prof, Northwestern Univ. **RESEARCH** 20th-century European art from symbolism to Viennese Actionism; Situationist International with special emphasis on surrealism in its international dimension, art and phenomenology in post-World War II Europe. **SELECTED PUBLICATIONS** Auth, essays in Ger & Engl on, Picasso; Breton; Reverdy. **CONTACT ADDRESS** Dept of Art History, Northwestern Univ, 1801 Hinman, Evanston, IL 60208.

STORCH, NEIL T.
PERSONAL Born 05/15/1940, New York, NY **DISCIPLINE** HISTORY **EDUCATION** Seton Hall Univ, AB, 63; Univ Wis-Madison, MA, 64, PhD(hist), 69. **CAREER** Asst prof, 69-75; from assoc prof hist to prof, Univ Minn, Duluth, 75-. **MEMBERSHIPS** Orgn Am Historians; Am Cath Hist Asn; Am Cath Hist Soc, Amer Cath Hist; Amer Academy of Rel; College Theol Soc. **RESEARCH** Diplomatic history; American Catholic history. **SELECTED PUBLICATIONS** Auth, "John Ireland and the Modernist Controversy," Church Hist (85); auth, "Catholic Universities are Facing an Academic Feedom Dilemma," Chronicle of Higher Educ (87); coauth, A Hist of Duluth Diocese, 89; coauth, UMD Comes of Age: The Firs One Hundred Years, 96. **CONTACT ADDRESS** Dept of History, Univ of Minnesota, Duluth, 10 University Dr, Duluth, MN 55812-2496. **EMAIL** mstorch@d.umn.edu

STORRS, LANDON R. Y.
PERSONAL Born 05/29/1962 **DISCIPLINE** HISTORY **EDUCATION** Yale Univ, BA, 83; Univ Wisc, Madison, MA, 89, PhD, 94. **CAREER** Tchg asst, Univ Wisc, Madison, 90-93; vis asst prof, Middlebury Col, 94-95; asst prof, hist, Univ Houston, 95- . **HONORS AND AWARDS** Magna cum laude, 83; Univ Wisc Grad Sch fel, 89-90; Mellon fel, 87-88, 88-89, 92; Univ Houston Res Initiation grant, 96; finalist, Lerner-Scott Prize, Orgn of Am Hist, 96; limited grant-in-aid, Univ Houston, 98. **MEMBERSHIPS** Orgn of Am Hist; AHA; Coord Coun for Women in Hist; Social Sci Hist Asn; S Hist Asn; S Asn for Women Hist; AAUP. **SELECTED PUBLICATIONS** Auth, An Independent Voice for Unorganized Workers: The Consumers' League Speaks to the Blue Eagle, Labor's Heritage, 95; auth, Gender and the Development of the Regulatory State: The Controversy over Restricting Women's Night Work in the Depression-Era South, J of Policy Hist, 98; auth, Civilizing Capitalism: The National Consumers' Leagues Women's Activism, and Labor Standards in the New Deal Era, Univ N Carolina, 00. **CONTACT ADDRESS** Dept of History, Univ of Houston, Houston, TX 77204-3785.

STORTZ, GERRY
DISCIPLINE HISTORY **EDUCATION** Univ Waterloo, BA, 73; MA, 76; Univ Guelph, PhD, 80. **CAREER** Assoc prof; chair hist dept; St Jerome's Univ; Asst Prof, Univ Western Ontario; Assoc Prof, York Univ; Asst Prof, Wilfrid Laurier Univ; asst Prof, St Jerome's Univ; Assoc Prof, St Jerome's. **MEMBERSHIPS** Canadian Catholic Hit Assoc, Canadian Histo Assoc, Soc for Canada's Nat Hist, Waterloo Heritage Found. **RESEARCH** Canadian religious history; Canadian labour history; immigration history. **SELECTED PUBLICATIONS** Auth, A Canadian Veterinarian Overseas in the First World War; Archbishop Lynch and New Ireland: An Unfulfilled Dream for Canada's Northwest; Archbishop Lynch and the Knights of Labor; Archbishop Lynch and Toronto's Anglicans; Arthur Palmer: Founder and First Rector of St. George's Anglican Church, Guelph; auth, Creed and Culture: The Place of English Speaking Catholics in Canadian Society. **CONTACT ADDRESS** Dept of History, St. Jerome's Univ, Waterloo, ON, Canada N2L 3G3. **EMAIL** gjtortz@watarts.uwaterloo.ca

STORTZ, MARTHA ELLEN
DISCIPLINE HISTORICAL THEOLOGY; ETHICS **EDUCATION** Carleton Col, BA; Univ Chicago, MA, PhD. **CAREER** Prof **HONORS AND AWARDS** Mem, convener, GTU Core Dr fac; adv comm, LCA Study on Issues Concerning Homosexuality, 86; bd mem,, Ctr for Women and Rel, GTU;

ELCA rep, Intl Consult of Lutheran Women Theologians, Helsinki, 91. **MEMBERSHIPS** Mem, Ctr for Global Edu, Augsburg Col; ELCA Task Force on Theol Edu; ELCA Commn for Church in Soc Bd. **SELECTED PUBLICATIONS** Auth, PastorPower, Abingdon Press, 93. **CONTACT ADDRESS** Dept of Historical Theology and Ethics, Pacific Lutheran Theol Sem, 2770 Marin Ave, Berkeley, CA 94708-1597. **EMAIL** mstortz@autobahn.org

STORY, RONALD
DISCIPLINE HISTORY **EDUCATION** NYork State Univ, PhD, 72. **CAREER** Prof, Univ MA Amherst. **SELECTED PUBLICATIONS** Auth, Forging of an Aristocracy: Harvard and the Boston Upper Class 1800-1870, 80; co-auth, Generations of Americans: A History of the United States, 76; co-ed, A More Perfect Union: Documents in American History, 84; Sports in Massachusetts: Historical Essays, 91; Five Colleges: Five Histories, 93. **CONTACT ADDRESS** Dept of Hist, Univ of Massachusetts, Amherst, Mass Ave, Amherst, MA 01003.

STOTT, ANNETTE
DISCIPLINE ART **EDUCATION** Boston Univ, PhD, 86; Univ of Wis-Madison, MA, 80; Concordia Col, BA, 77 **CAREER** Assoc prof, 94-, Asst Prof, 91-94, Univ of Denver; Asst Prof, 87-91, Winthrop Univ; Asst Prof, 86-87 Univ of Maine-Orono; dir, Shool of Art and Art Hist, 99-. **HONORS AND AWARDS** NEH Fel, 97-98; Fulbright Fel, Netherlands, 83-84; summa cum laude; boston univ fel **MEMBERSHIPS** Col Art Asn; Am Culture Assoc; Am Studies Asn **RESEARCH** Am Art and Architecture; Women's Studies **SELECTED PUBLICATIONS** Auth, Holland Mania: The Unknown Dutch Period in American Art and Culture, New York: Overlook Press, 98; Transformative Triptychs in Multicultural America, The Art Journal, 98 **CONTACT ADDRESS** Sch of Art, Univ of Denver, 2121 E Asbury Ave, Denver, CO 80208. **EMAIL** astott@du.edu

STOTT, WILLIAM MERRELL
PERSONAL Born 06/02/1940, New York, NY, d, 2 children **DISCIPLINE** AMERICAN STUDIES, ENGLISH **EDUCATION** Yale Univ, AB, 62; MPh, 70; PhD, 72. **CAREER** Foreign serv officer, US Info Agency, 64-68; asst prof, 71-74; assoc dean, Div Gen & Comp Studies, 75-77; assoc prof, 74-80; prof, Univ Tex, Austin, 80-01; dir, Am Studies Prog, 81-84; Guggenheim Mem Found Fel, 78; Fulbright lectr, Polytechnic of Cent London, 80-81; Univ of Leiden, 86-87. **MEMBERSHIPS** Am Studies Asn. **RESEARCH** Journalism; mass culture; autobiography. **SELECTED PUBLICATIONS** Auth, Documentary Expression and Thirties America, Oxford Univ, 73, Chicago UP, 86; coauth, On Broadway, Univ Tex, 78; auth, Write to the Point, Columbia UP, 90; auth, Facing the Fire: Experiencing and Expressing Anger Appropriately, Doubleday, 93. **CONTACT ADDRESS** Dept of Am Studies, Univ of Texas, Austin, GAR 303, B7100, Austin, TX 78712-1026. **EMAIL** wstott@mail.utexas.edu

STOUT, HARRY S.
DISCIPLINE HISTORY **EDUCATION** Calvin Coll, BA, 69; Kent State Univ, MA, 72, PhD, 74. **CAREER** Assoc prof, hist, Univ Conn; MASTER, BERKELEY COLL & JONATHAN EDWARDS PROF, AM CHRISTIANITY, YALE UNIV **MEMBERSHIPS** Am Antiquarian Soc **SELECTED PUBLICATIONS** Auth, The New England Soul: Preaching and Religious Culture in Colonial New England, Oxford, 86; co-ed, Jonathan Edwards and the American Experience, Oxford, 88; auth, The Divine Dramatist: George Whitefield and the Rise of Modern Evangelicalism, Eardmans Press, 91. **CONTACT ADDRESS** Berkeley Col, Yale Univ, 403 Yale Station, New Haven, CT 06520.

STOUT, JOSEPH A.
PERSONAL Born 05/27/1939, Sioux City, IA, m, 1975, 2 children **DISCIPLINE** HISTORY **EDUCATION** Angelo State Univ, BA, 67; Tex A&M Univ, MA, 89; Okla State Univ, PhD, 71. **CAREER** Asst prof, Mo Southern State Col, 71-72; asst prof, to prof, Ok State Univ, 72-. **HONORS AND AWARDS** NDEATitle V Fel, Tex A&M Univ, 78. **MEMBERSHIPS** SW Coun on Latin Am Studies, Tex State Hist Asn, W Hist Asn. **RESEARCH** Mexico-U.S. frontiers, Mexican history, U.S. military history. **SELECTED PUBLICATIONS** Auth, Border Conflict: Villistas, Carrancistas, and the Punitive Expedition, 1915-1920, Tex Christian Univ, Press, 99; auth, "The United States Army and the Native Americans," The American Military Tradition: From Colonial Times to the Present, Scholarly Resources, 93; auth, "Apache Menace on the Frontier, 1876-1886," La Ciudad y el Camp en la historia de Mexico, San Diego, 92; auth, "Historiography and Sources in Mexico for Frontier History,"Cinco Siglos in la historia de Mexico, 92; auth, Frontier Adventurers: American Exploration in Oklahoma, Oklahoma Historical Soc, 76; auth, Apache Lightning: The Last Great Battle of the Ojo Calientes, New York, 74; auth, A Short History of the American West, New York, 74; auth, The Liberators: The filibustering Expeditions into Mexico, 1848 and the Last Thrust of Manifest Destiny, Los Angeles, 73; ed, The Mexican War: Changing Interpretations, Chicago, 73. **CONTACT ADDRESS** Dept Hist, Oklahoma State Univ, Stillwater, Stillwater, OK 74078. **EMAIL** jas1624@okstate.edu

STOUT, NEIL R.
PERSONAL Born 08/12/1932, Marietta, OH, m, 1956, 2 children **DISCIPLINE** AMERICAN HISTORY **EDUCATION** Harvard Univ, AB, 54; Univ Wis, MS, 58, PhD, 62. **CAREER** From instr to asst prof hist, Agr & Mech Col Tex, 61-64; from asst prof to assoc prof, 64-72, prof hist, Univ Vermont, 72-00; prof emer, 00- . **MEMBERSHIPS** New Eng Hist Asn (vpres, 78-79, pres, 79-80); Orgn Am Historians; VT Hist Soc, AHA. **RESEARCH** Am Revolution; biography; Sir John Temple, 1731-98. **SELECTED PUBLICATIONS** Auth, Spies who went out in the cold, Am Heritage, 2/72; Royal Navy in America, 1760-1775, US Naval Inst, 73; The Perfect Crisis, NY Univ, 76; auth, History Student's Vade Mecum, 90, 93, 94, 96. **CONTACT ADDRESS** 129 Robinson Pkwy, Burlington, VT 05401. **EMAIL** nstout@zoo.uvm.edu

STOVER, JOHN FORD
PERSONAL Born 05/16/1912, Manhattan, KS, m, 1937, 3 children **DISCIPLINE** HISTORY **EDUCATION** Univ Nebr, AB, 34, MA, 37; Univ Wis, PhD(Am hist), 51. **CAREER** From instr to assoc prof, 47-59, prof, 59-78, prof emer, Purdue Univ, 78-, Mem, Ind Sesquicentennial Comn Exec Comt & chmn, Educ Comt, 62; consult, Midwest Prog Airborn TV Instr, 63-64; consult & contribr suppl, Dictionary Am Biog, 66-67. **MEMBERSHIPS** AHA; Orgn Am Historians; Southern Hist Asn; Soc Am Hist; Western Hist Asn. **RESEARCH** American transportation history; American social history; Civil War and Reconstruction. **SELECTED PUBLICATIONS** Auth, Railroads of the South, 1865-1900, Univ NC, Chapel Hill, 55; American Railroads, Univ Chicago, 61; A History of American Railroads, 67 & Turnpikes, Canals, and Steamboats, 69, Rand McNally; The Life and Decline of the American Railroad, Oxford Univ, 70; Transportation in American History, Am Hist Asn, 70; History of the Illinois Central Railroad, Macmillan, 75; Iron Road to the West, Columbia Univ, 78; Politics And Industrialization--Early Railroads In The United-States And Prussia, J Of Am Hist, Vol 82, 95. **CONTACT ADDRESS** Dept Hist, Purdue Univ, West Lafayette, Lafayette, IN 47907.

STOW, GEORGE BUCKLEY
PERSONAL Born 03/17/1940, Camden, NJ, m, 1974, 2 children **DISCIPLINE** MEDIEVAL ENGLISH HISTORY **EDUCATION** Lehigh Univ, BA, 67; Univ Southern Calif, MA, 68; Univ Ill, Urbana, PhD(hist), 72. **CAREER** From instr to assoc prof, 72-83, Prof Hist, La Salle Univ, 83- **HONORS AND AWARDS** Phi Beta Kappa, Phi Kappa Phi; Phi Alpha Theta; Eta Sigma Phi; Joseph Ward Swain Prize, 70; Lawrence M Larsen Awd, 70; NDEA Fel 68; Woodward Wilson Dissertation Fel, 70; La Salle Univ Summer Res Grant, 75, 85 & 88; La Salle Univ Res Leave Sabbatical 88; Amer Philos Soc Res Grant, 88 & 89. **MEMBERSHIPS** Fel Royal Hist Soc. **RESEARCH** Medieval Europe; Ancient Rome; England to 1688. **SELECTED PUBLICATIONS** Auth, The Vita Ricardi Secundi as a Source for the Reign of Richard II, Vale Evesham Hist Soc Res Papers, 73; Some New Manuscripts of the Vita Ricardi Secundi, 1377-1402, Manuscripta, 75; Thomas Walsingham, John Malvern and the Vita Ricardi Secundi, 1377-1381, Mediaeval Studies, 77; auth, Historia Vitae et Regni Ricardi Secundi, Univ Pa, 77; auth, Bodleian Library Ms Bodley 316 and the Dating of Thomas Walsingham's Literary Career, Manuscripta, 81; Richard II in Thomas Walsingham's Chronicles, Speculum, 84; Richard II in Jean Foissart's Chroniques, J of Medieval Hist, 85; Chronicles versus Record Sources: The Character of Richard II, Documenting the Past, 89; Richard II in John Gower's Confessio Amantis: Some Historical Perspectives, Mediaevalia, 93; Richard II Leader and Tyrant, Great Leaders, Great Tyrants, Greenwood, 1995; Richard II and the Invention of the Pocket Handkerchief, Albion, 95; Stubbs, Steel, and Richard II as Insane: The Origin and Evolution an English Historiographical Myth, Proceedings of the Amer Philos Soc, 99. **CONTACT ADDRESS** Dept of History, La Salle Univ, 1900 W Olney Ave, Philadelphia, PA 19141-1199. **EMAIL** stow@lasalle.edu

STOWERS, STANLEY KENT
PERSONAL Born 02/24/1948, Munice, IN, m, 1968, 2 children **DISCIPLINE** HISTORY OF EARLY CHRISTIANITY **EDUCATION** Abilene Christian Univ, AB, 70; Princeton Theol Sem, MA, 74; Yale Univ, PhD(relig studies), 79. **CAREER** Asst prof relig studies, Phillips Univ, 79-80; Asst Prof Relig Studies, 81-91, PROF REL STUDIES, BROWN UNIV, 91-. **HONORS AND AWARDS** Sheridan Teaching Awd, 97; Woodrow Wilson fel, 92; NEH fel, 91; FIAT fel, 90. **MEMBERSHIPS** Am Acad Relig; Soc Bibl Lit. **RESEARCH** Early Christianity; Hellenistic philosophy; early Christian literature; Greek Religion. **SELECTED PUBLICATIONS** Auth, The Diatribe and Paul's Letter to the Romans, Scholars Press, 81; auth, A Rereading of Romans, Yal Univ Press, 94; auth, Letter Writing in Greco-Roman Anqiquity, Westminster Press, 86. **CONTACT ADDRESS** Dept of Relig Studies, Brown Univ, Box 1927, Providence, RI 02912-9127. **EMAIL** Stanley_Stowers@brown.edu

STRAIT, JOHN B.
PERSONAL Born 03/22/1968, Gellipalis, OH, s **DISCIPLINE** GEOGRAPHY **EDUCATION** Wittenberg Univ, BA, 91; GA State Univ, MA, 93; Univ GA, PhD, 99. **CAREER** Instr, Kinnesaw State Univ96-98; instr, Univ GA, 97-99; instr, Emmanuel Col, 99; asst prof, Longwood Col, 99-2000. **HONORS AND AWARDS** Graduation with Honors, Wittenberg Univ, 81; Outstanding Teaching Awd, Dept Geography, Univ GA, 98. **MEMBERSHIPS** Asn Am Geographies; Southeast Division of Asn Am Geographers; Nat Coun for Geographic Ed; Urban Affairs Asn. **RESEARCH** Urban poetry, geography of race and ethnicity, residential segregation, Latin America and the Caribbean, geographical history of music and sport, urban-economic change. **SELECTED PUBLICATIONS** Coauth with Thomas Mulleady, "Environmental Impact of and Economic Potential for Hillside Agriculture: The Yallahs River Watershed," Inter-American Institute for Cooperation on Agriculture (97); auth, "An Examination of Extreme Urban Poverty: The Impact of Metropolitan Employment and Demographic Dynamics, 1970-1990," Urban Geography (forthcoming). **CONTACT ADDRESS** Dept Natural Science, Longwood Col, 201 High St, Farmville, VA 23909-1801.

STRANAHAN, PATRICIA
PERSONAL Born 10/07/1949, New Castle, PA **DISCIPLINE** MODERN CHINESE & JAPANESE HISTORY **EDUCATION** Westminster Col, BA, 71; Univ Pa, MA, 74, PhD(Orient studies), 79. **CAREER** Asst prof Hist, Tex A&M Univ, 80-86; assoc prof, Tex A&M Univ, 86-97; prof, Dept of Hist, Univ of Pittsburgh, 97-; dir, of the Asian Stud Program, 97-. **MEMBERSHIPS** Asn Asian Stud. **RESEARCH** Hist of Chinese Communist Party; dev of policy for women in Yanan (1937-1947). **SELECTED PUBLICATIONS** Auth, Molding the Medium: the Chinese Communist Party and the Liberation Daily, Armonk, NY: M.E. Sharpe, 90; auth, The Last Battle: Mao and the Internationalists Fight for the Liberation Daily," China Quarterly, 123, 90; auth, "Strange Bedfellows: The Communist Party and Shanghai's Elite in the National Salvation Movement," China Quarterly, 129, 92; auth, "The Politics of Persuasion: Communist Rhetoric and the Revolution," Indiana East Asian Working Paper Series 4, 94; ed and transl, "The Communist Party in Shanghai," Chinese Studies in History, Vol. 28, No. 2, 94; auth, Underground: the Shanghai Communist Party and the Politics of Survival, 1927-1937, Boulder, CO: Rowman & Littlefield, 98. **CONTACT ADDRESS** Dept of Asian Stud, Univ of Pittsburgh, 4E95 Forbes Quadrangle, Pittsburgh, PA 15260. **EMAIL** stranahan@ucis.pitt.edu

STRANGE, JAMES F.
PERSONAL Born 02/02/1938, Pampa, TX, m, 1960, 4 children **DISCIPLINE** BIBLICAL STUDIES, ARCHEOLOGY **EDUCATION** Rice Univ, BA, 59; Yale Univ, MDiv, 64; Drew Univ, PhD, 70. **CAREER** Asst prof, 72-75, assoc prof, 75-80, prof relig studies, Univ S Fla, Tampa, 80-, dean col arts & lett, 81-89, Montgomery fel, William F Albright Inst Archaeol Res, Jerusalem, 70-71; fel Off Judeo-Christian Studies, Duke Univ, 71-72; asoc dir, Joint Exped to Khirbet Shema', Israel, 71-73; assoc dir, Meiron Excavation Proj, Israel, 73-78; vis lectr, Univ of the Orange Free State, Repub S Africa, 79; Nat Endowment for Humanities fel, Jerusalem, 80; dir, Survey in Galilee, 82; dir USF Excavations at Sepphoris, Israel, 83; dir, Excavations Qumran, 96; Benjamin Meaker vis prof Inst Advan Stud, Univ Bristol, 97. **HONORS AND AWARDS** Samuel Robinson Lect, Wake Forest Univ, 81; ; Herbert G. May Memorial Lecture, Oberlin Col, 88; The Parkhurst Lectures, Southwestern Col, 91; McMannis Lect, Wheaton Col, 96. **MEMBERSHIPS** Soc Bibl Lit; Israel Explor Soc; Am Schs Orient Res; NY Acad Sci; Soc Sci Explor. **RESEARCH** Archaeology of Israel in Roman to Arab times; Roman and Byzantine ceramics in the Eastern Mediterranean; computer models for Roman-Byzantine archaeology and historical geography. **SELECTED PUBLICATIONS** Coauth, Archaeology and rabbinic tradition at Khirbet Shema, the 1970 and 1971 campaigns, Bibl Archaeologist, 72; Excavations at Meiron in Upper Galilee--1971, 1972, 74 & auth, Late Hellenistic and Herodian ossuary tombs at French Hill, Jerusalem, 75, Bull of Am Schs of Orient Res; coauth, Ancient Synagogue Excavations at Khirbet Shema, Upper Galilee, Israel 1970-1972, Duke Univ, 76; auth, Capernaum, Crucifixion, Methods of, & Magdala, Interpreter's Dictionary of Bible, suppl vol, 76; Excavations at Meiron, in Upper Galilee--1974, 1975: A second preliminary report, 78 & coauth, Excavations at Meiron, 81, Am Schs of Orient Res; Archaeology and the religion of Judaism, Aufstieg und Niedergang der Roemischen Welt, 81; coauth, The Excavations at the Ancient Synagogue of Gush Halav, Israel, 90; co-ed, "Ancient Texts, Archaeology as Text, and the Problem of the First Century Synagogue," The Evolution of the Synagogue, Valley Forge: Trinity Press International, 00. **CONTACT ADDRESS** Dept Relig Studies, Univ of So Florida, 4202 Fowler Ave, CPR 107, Tampa, FL 33620-9951. **EMAIL** strange@chuma1.cas.usf.edu

STRANGES, ANTHONY N.
PERSONAL Born 09/28/1936, Niagara Falls, NY, m, 1963, 2 children **DISCIPLINE** HISTORY OF SCIENCE **EDUCATION** Niagara Univ, BS, 58; MS, 64; Univ Wis, PhD, 77. **CAREER** Instr, Notre Dame High School, 59-63; instr, Lewiston Porter High School, 63-69; archivist, Univ of Wis Madison, 74-77; prof, Tex A&M Univ, 77-. **HONORS AND AWARDS** Nat Sci Found Fel; Tex A&M Univ Teaching Awd. **MEMBERSHIPS** Hist of Sci Soc; Soc for the Hist of Tech; Hist of Chemistry. **RESEARCH** History of chemistry, History of energy - alternative energy, synthetic fuels. **SELECTED PUBLICATIONS** Auth, Electrons and Valance: Development of the The-

ory, 1900-1925, 82. **CONTACT ADDRESS** Dept Hist, Texas A&M Univ, Col Station, College Station, TX 77843-4236. **EMAIL** astranges@tamu.edu

STRATER, HENRY A.
PERSONAL Born 10/28/1934, Cleveland, OH, m, 3 children **DISCIPLINE** ENGLISH, CLASSICAL LANGUAGES **EDUCATION** John Carroll Univ, AB, 56, MA; Case Western Univ, MA, 59; Ohio State Univ, PhD, 71. **CAREER** Tchr, Shaker Heights Sch, Ohio, 56-84; holder of Waldron ch in Classics, Univ Sch, 84- . **HONORS AND AWARDS** Good tchr awd, Class Asn Mid W and S; Seelbach awd for excel in tchg. **MEMBERSHIPS** Amer Class League; Ohio Class Conf; Amer Philol Asn; Class Asn Mid W and S. **RESEARCH** Vergil; Methods of teaching Classical Languages. **SELECTED PUBLICATIONS** Auth, Greek to Me: An Introduction to Classical Greek. **CONTACT ADDRESS** Univ Sch, 1131 Blanchester Rd, Lyndhurst, OH 44124. **EMAIL** hastrater@aol.com

STRAUSBERG, STEPHEN FREDERICK
PERSONAL Born 09/03/1943, Brooklyn, NY **DISCIPLINE** ECONOMIC HISTORY **EDUCATION** Brooklyn Col, BA, 64; Cornell Univ, PhD(hist), 70. **CAREER** Res historian, US Pub Land Law Rev Comn, 66-67; asst prof, 68-82, ASSOC PROF HIST, UNIV ARK, FAYETTEVILLE, 82-, Proj planner, Ark Humanities Prog, 76-78. **HONORS AND AWARDS** Outstanding Humanist, Ark Humanities Prog, 76. **MEMBERSHIPS** AHA; Orgn Am Historians. **RESEARCH** Southern economic history; history of public lands; Arkansas history. **SELECTED PUBLICATIONS** Contribr, History of the Public Domain, US Govt Printing Off, 69; Historical Abstracts, 72-76 & America, 73-76, ABC-Clio; auth, Federal Stewardship on the Frontier, Arno, 78; Swamplands in Indiana, Ind J Hist, 78; The New Deal in Arkansas, The Depression in the Southwest, Kennikat Press, 80. **CONTACT ADDRESS** Dept of Hist, Univ of Arkansas, Fayetteville, Fayetteville, AR 72701-1202.

STRAUSS, DAVID
PERSONAL Born 07/19/1937, St. Louis, MO, m, 1994, 3 children **DISCIPLINE** HISTORY **EDUCATION** Amherst Col, BA, 59; Columbia Univ, MA, 63, PhD, 68. **CAREER** Vis prof, Univ Lyon, France, 70-71; Instr, 67-68, asst prof, 68-74, Colgate Univ; vis prof, 83-84, vis scholar, 88, Waseda Univ, Tokyo; assoc prof, 74-80, Prof Hist, 80-, Kalamazoo Col. **MEMBERSHIPS** Am Studies Assoc; History of Science Society. **RESEARCH** US Cultural and Intellectual History; Victorian America. **SELECTED PUBLICATIONS** Auth, "Menace in the West: The Rise of French Anti-Americanism in Modern Times," Westport, CT: Greenwood Press, 78; auth, "Percivel Lowell: The Culture and Science of a Gorton," Cambridge, MA. Harvard University Press, 00. **CONTACT ADDRESS** Dept of History, Kalamazoo Col, 1200 Academy St, Kalamazoo, MI 49006. **EMAIL** strauss@kzoo.edu

STRAUSS, GERALD
PERSONAL Born 05/03/1922, Frankfurt am Main, Germany **DISCIPLINE** HISTORY **EDUCATION** Boston Univ, AB, 49; Columbia Univ, AM, 50, PhD, 57. **CAREER** Instr hist, Phillips Exeter Acad, 51-57; asst prof, Univ Ala, 57-59; from asst prof to assoc prof, 59-71, prof hist, Ind Univ, Bloomington, 71-. **HONORS AND AWARDS** Am Coun Learned Soc grants-in-aid, 60, 62; Fulbright exchange prof, Trinity Col, Univ Dublin, 61-62; Guggenheim fel, 65-66, 72-73; mem, Inst Advan Study, Princeton Univ, 75-76. **RESEARCH** Early modern European history; German humanism. **SELECTED PUBLICATIONS** Auth, Martin Bucer--Reforming Church And Community, Central European Hist, Vol 28, 95; Religion, Political-Culture And The Emergence Of Early-Modern Society--Essays In German And Dutch Hist, J Of Modern Hist, Vol 66, 94; Wondrous In His Saints--Counterreformation Propaganda In Bavaria, J Of Modern Hist, Vol 67, 95; The Harvest Of Humanism In Central-Europe--Essays In Honor of Lewis W. Sptitz, Catholic Hist Rev, Vol 79, 93. **CONTACT ADDRESS** Dept of Hist, Indiana Univ, Bloomington, Bloomington, IN 47405.

STRAUSS, WALLACE PATRICK
PERSONAL Born 03/17/1923, St. Louis, MO, m, 1951, 1 child **DISCIPLINE** AMERICAN HISTORY **EDUCATION** Occidental Col, AB, 48; Stanford Univ, MA, 49; Columbia Univ, PhD, 58. **CAREER** Historian, Peabody Mus Exped, Polynesia, 51; lectr Am hist, Columbia Univ, 58; instr soc sci, San Francisco State Col, 58-60; asst prof hist, Dakota State Col, 60-61; asst prof Am thought & lang, Mich State Univ, 61-66; assoc prof, 66-70, Prof Am Hist, Oakland Univ, 70-, Fulbright lectr, Univ Hong Kong, 64-65, sr Fulbright lectr Am hist, 70-71. **MEMBERSHIPS** Am Studies Asn; AHA; Soc Historians Am Foreign Rels. **RESEARCH** Nineteenth century American diplomatic history; American naval history; international rivalries in the Pacific in the 19th century. **SELECTED PUBLICATIONS** Auth, Preparing the Wilkes Expedition: A study in disorganization, Pac Hist Rev, 8/59; Americans in Polynesia, 1783-1842, Mich State Univ, 63; Paradoxical cooperation: Sir Joseph Banks and the London Missionary Society, Hist Studies Australia & NZ, 4/64; ed, Stars and Spars: The American Navy in the Age of Sail, Blaisdell, 68; auth, Isolation and Involvement: An Interpretive History of American Diplomacy, Xerox, 72; coauth, Lands below the Horn, In: America Spreads Her Sails, Naval Inst, 73; The Voyage Of The Peacock--A Journal By Benajah Ticknor Naval Surgeon, Pacific Hist Rev, Vol 61, 92. **CONTACT ADDRESS** Dept of Hist, Oakland Univ, Rochester, MI 48063.

STRAYER, ROBERT WILLIAM
PERSONAL Born 10/22/1942, Pittsburgh, PA **DISCIPLINE** SOVIET, WORLD, & AFRICAN HISTORY **EDUCATION** Wheaton Col, Ill, BA, 64; Univ Wis-Madison, MA, 66, PhD(hist), 71. **CAREER** Prof Hist, State Univ NY Col Brockport, 70-. **HONORS AND AWARDS** Chancellor's Awd for Excellence in Teaching. **MEMBERSHIPS** African Studies Asn. **RESEARCH** Modern imperialism in Africa; missionary history in Africa; the recruitment of chiefs in colonial Kenya. **SELECTED PUBLICATIONS** Auth, The dynamics of mission expansion, Int J African Hist Studies, 73; The making of mission schools in Kenya, Comp Educ Rev, 73; Mission history in Africa, African Studies Rev, 76; The Making of Mission Communities in East Africa, State Univ NY, 78; Kenya: Focus on Nationalism, Prentice-Hall, 75; The Making of the Modern World, St. Martin's Press, 95; Why Did the Soviet Union Collapse, M.E. Sharpe, 98. **CONTACT ADDRESS** Dept of Hist, SUNY, Col at Brockport, 350 New Campus Dr., Brockport, NY 14420-2914. **EMAIL** rstrayer@po.brockport.edu

STREETS, HEATHER
PERSONAL Born 09/27/1968, Bogota, Colombia, m, 1986, 2 children **DISCIPLINE** MODERN BRITISH HISTORY **EDUCATION** Duke Univ, PhD, 98. **CAREER** Asst prof, Washington State Univ. **MEMBERSHIPS** AHA, NACBS. **RESEARCH** Britain, British Empire, India, Gender. **SELECTED PUBLICATIONS** Auth, Side By Side in Generous Rivalry: Highlanders, Sikhs, and the Making of Modern Martial Race Ideology in the 1857 Indian Uprising, J Brit Stud; auth, "A Century After the Union: Scottis Identity in the Highland Regiments in the Late Eighteenth and Nineteenth Centuries," in Steve Murdoch and Andrew Mackillop, eds The Scottish Military Experience, c. 1600-c. 1800, Brill Press; rev, "Military Spin Doctors in Late Victarian Society? The Case of Frederick Roberts," Journal of Victorian Culture. **CONTACT ADDRESS** Dept of History, Washington State Univ, 301 Wilson Hall, PO Box 644030, Pullman, WA 99164-4030. **EMAIL** streetsh@wsu.edu

STRICKER, FRANK A.
PERSONAL Born 05/10/1943, Evanston, IL, m, 1984, 2 children **DISCIPLINE** HISTORY, LABOR STUDIES **EDUCATION** Loyola Univ, BA; Princeton Univ, MA; PhD. **CAREER** Chemn Hist Dept, Calif State Univ Dominguez Hills, 82-84 & 92-93; coord Labor Studies Prog, Calif State Univ Dominguez Hills, 86-; co-chemn Hist Dept, Calif State Univ Dominguez Hills, 96-99; Advising Center Advisor and Mentor, Calif State Univ Dominguez Hills, 97-. **MEMBERSHIPS** Calif Fac Asn, Interdisciplinary Studies/PACE, Soc Sci Hist Asn, Southwest Labor Studies Asn , Los Angeles Soc Hist Res Sem, Asn for the Study of Netherlandish Art. **RESEARCH** U.S. labor, poverty, film history. **SELECTED PUBLICATIONS** Auth, "Cookbooks and Law Books: The Hidden History of Career Women in Twentieth-Century America," J of Soc Hist 10 (76): 1-19; auth, "The Wages of Inflations: Workers" Earnings in the World War One Era," Mid-America 63 (81): 93-105; auth, "Jobs and Power," WAMH Newsletter (83): 18-19; auth, "Causes of the Great Depression," Econ Forum 14 (winter 83-84): 41-58; auth, "Affluence for Whom: Another Look at Prosperity and the Working Classes in the 1920s," Labor Hist 24 (83) 5-23; auth, "Economic Success and Academic Professionalization: Questions from Two Decades of U.S. History (1908-1929)," Soc Sci Hist 12 (88): 143-170; auth, "American Professors in the Progressive Era: Incomes, Aspirations, and Professionalism," J of Interdisciplinary Hist 19 (88): 231-257; auth, "Repressing the Working Class: Individualism and the Masses in Frank Capra's Films," Labor Hist 31 (90): 454-467; auth, "An American Middle Class Meets the Consumer Age: Pelxotto's Rational Professor in the 1920s," Amerikastudien/American Studies 34 (90): 311-331; auth, "Why History? Thinking about the Uses of the Past," The Hist Teacher 25 (92): 293-312. **CONTACT ADDRESS** Dept Hist, California State Univ, Dominguez Hills, 1000 E Victoria St, Carson, CA 90747-0001.

STRICKLAND, ARVARH E.
PERSONAL Born 07/06/1930, Hattiesburg, MS, m, 1951, 2 children **DISCIPLINE** HISTORY **EDUCATION** Tougaloo Coll, Tougaloo, MS, BA, history, English, 1951; Univ of Illinois, Urbana, IL, MA, education, 1953, PhD, history 1962. **CAREER** Chicago State Coll, asst prof, 62-65, assoc prof, 65-68, prof, 68-69; Univ of Missouri at Columbia, prof, 69-95, prof emeritus, 95-, chmn dept of history, 80-83, interim dir black studies program, 86, 94-95, Office of the Vice President for Academic Affairs, sr faculty assoc, 87-88; interim assoc vice pres for academic affairs, 89, assoc vice pres for academic affairs, 89-91. **HONORS AND AWARDS** Kappa Delta Pi (education), 1953; Phi Alpha Theta (history), 1960; Kendric C Babcock Fellow in History, Univ of Illinois, 1961-62; Distinguished Serv Awd, Illinois Historical Soc, 1967 Honor Soc of Phi Kappa Phi, Univ of Missouri, 1973; Assoc of the Danforth Found, 1973; Omicron Delta Kappa Natl Leadership Honor Soc, 1978; Martin Luther King Memorial Comm Awd for Outstanding Community Serv, 1982; Faculty-Alumni Awd, Alumni Assn of the Univ of Missouri, 1983; Serv Appreciation Awd, Missouri Comm for the Humanities, 1984; Thomas Jefferson Awd, Univ of Missouri, 1985; Office of Equal Opportunity Awd for Exemplary Serv in Enhancing the Status of Minorities, Univ of Missouri, 1985; Distinguished Alumni Awd (Tougaloo Coll), Natl Assn for Equal Opportunity in Higher Educ, 1986; N Endowment for the Humanities, Travel to Collections Grant, 1986; Byler Distinguished Professor Awd, Univ of Missouri, Columbia, 1994; St Louis American's Educator of the Year Awd, 1994. **MEMBERSHIPS** Amer Assn of Univ Prof; Missouri Advisory Commn on Historic Preservation, 1976-80; Gen Bd of Higher Educ and Ministry, The United Methodist Church, 1976-80, mem exec comm; commr, Columbia Planning and Zoning Comm, 1977-80; Assn for the Study of Afro-Amer Life and History; Southern Historical Assn; bd of trustees, State Historical Soc of Missouri; co-chmn, Mayor's Steering Comm for Commemorating the Contribution of Black Columbians, Columbia, MO, 1980; mem, Fed Judicial Merit Selection Comm for the Western Dist of Missouri, 1982; Kiwanis Club of Columbia; Missouri Historical Records Advisory Bd; commr, Peace Officers Standards and Training Commn, 1988-89. **SELECTED PUBLICATIONS** History of the Chicago Urban League, Univ of Illinois Press, 1966; Building the United States, author with Jerome Reich and Edward Biller, Harcourt, Brace Jovanovich Inc, 1971; The Black American Experience, co-author with Jerome Reich, Harcourt, Brace Jovanovich Inc, 1974; Vol I, From Slavery through Reconstruction to 1877; Vol 11, From Reconstruction to the Present Since 1877; Edited with an Introduction, Lorenzo J Greene, Working With Carter G Woodson, The Father of Black History: A Diary, 1928-30, Louisiana State Univ Press, 1989; Edited with an introduction, Lorenzo J Greene, Selling Black History for Carter G Woodson: A Diary, 1930-33, Univ of Missouri Press, 1996. **CONTACT ADDRESS** Department of History, Univ of Missouri, Columbia, 101 Read Hall, Columbia, MO 65211.

STRICKLIN, DAVID
PERSONAL 2 children **DISCIPLINE** HISTORY **EDUCATION** Baylor Univ, BA, MA; Tulane Univ, PhD. **CAREER** Asst prof, Lyon Col. **HONORS AND AWARDS** CASE/Carnegie Arkansas Prof of the Yr, 99. **MEMBERSHIPS** OAH, OHA, Southern Hist Soc, Ark Hist Assoc. **RESEARCH** Southern cult; Am relig; vernacular music. **SELECTED PUBLICATIONS** Auth, A Genealogy of Dissent: The Culture of Southern Baptist Protest in the Twentieth Century, UP KY. **CONTACT ADDRESS** Division of Humanities, Lyon Col, 300 Highland Rd, PO Box 2317, Batesville, AR 72503. **EMAIL** dstricklin@lyon.edu

STRIKER, CECIL LEOPOLD
PERSONAL Born 07/15/1932, Cincinnati, OH, m, 1968 **DISCIPLINE** HISTORY OF ART, ARCHAEOLOGY **EDUCATION** Oberlin Col, BA, 56; NYork Univ, MA, 60, PhD, 68. **CAREER** From instr to asst prof hist of art, Vassar Col, 62-68; assoc prof, 68-78, prof hist of art, Univ Penn, 78-; field rep, Dumbarton Oaks Ctr Byzantine Studies, 66-85, vis fel, 70-71; co-dir, Kalenderhane Archaeol Proj, Turkey, 66-; art historian in residence, Am Acad Rome, 70-71; co-investr, Greek Medieval Dendrochronological Proj, 76-88; pres, Am Res Inst Turkey, 77-84. **HONORS AND AWARDS** Am Acad Rome, Art Historian in Residence; Koldewey Gesellschaft, 80; German Archaeol Inst, corresp mem, 85. **MEMBERSHIPS** Col Art Asn Am; Archaeol Inst Am; Koldewey Gesellschaft. **RESEARCH** Early Christian, Byzantine and early medieval art, architecture and archaeology. **SELECTED PUBLICATIONS** Auth, Applied Proportions in Later Byzantine Architecture, Studien zur Byzantinischen Kunstgeschichte, Amsterdam, 95; ed, Architectural Studies in Memory of Richard Krautheimer, Mainz, 96; auth, Richard Krautheimer and the Study of Early Christian and Byzantine Architecture, In Memoriam Richard Krautheimer: Relazioni della Giornata di Studi, Roma, Palazzo dei Conservatori, 97; auth and co-ed, Kalenderhane in Istanbul: The Buildings, Their history, Architecture and Decoration, Mainz, 97. **CONTACT ADDRESS** Dept of Hist of Art, Univ of Pennsylvania, 3405 Woodland Walk, Philadelphia, PA 19104-6208. **EMAIL** cstriker@sas.upenn.edu

STROCCHIA, SHARON T.
DISCIPLINE HISTORY **EDUCATION** Stanford Univ, BA, 72; Univ Calif Berkeley, MA, 73, PhD, 81. **CAREER** Assoc prof **HONORS AND AWARDS** Nat Humanities Ctr, Fel; Am Philosophical Soc Res Grant, 87; Harvard Univ Ctr for Italian Renaissance Studies, 84-85, Folger Library Fel; Newberry Library, Fel. **RESEARCH** Social and cultural history of Renaissance Italy; women, gender, and family in 15th-century Florence; the use of feminist theory for Renaissance studies; social history of nuns and nunneries in Renaissance Florence. **SELECTED PUBLICATIONS** Auth, Death and Ritual in Renaissance Florence. **CONTACT ADDRESS** Dept History, Emory Univ, 221 Bowden Hall, 561 Kilgo Cir, Atlanta, GA 30322-1950. **EMAIL** sstrocc@emory.edu

STROKANOV, ALEXANDRE
PERSONAL Born 04/26/1957, m **DISCIPLINE** HISTORY **EDUCATION** Penn State Univ, Diploma with Excellence, 79; PhD, 87. **CAREER** Asst Prof, Perm State Univ, 79-84; Lectur-

er, Central Committee of the All-Union Komsomol Organization, 84-90; Vis Lecturer, Inst of Youth Moscow, 85-93; Vis Lecturer, Acad of Soc Sci, Moscow, 87-93; Vice-chairman, Intl Federation of Children Organization, Moscow, 90-93; Vis Prof to Prof, Gardner-Webb Univ, 93-. **RESEARCH** Russian political life; The development of the multiparty system, participation of the major political parties and movements in elections; Reasons for the failure of President Yeltsin's political and economic reform; Commonwealth of Independent states primarily concentrating on their contemporary political and cultural history. **SELECTED PUBLICATIONS** Auth, "The Collapse of the Soviet Union and the Human Rights Issue," 1999 Southeastern World Affairs Inst, 99; auth, "The conflict in Kosovo and its Impact on the World Politics," Gardner-Webb Univ Press, 99; auth, "Cultural Diversity in the Marketplace," Inst of Management Accountants, 98; auth, "The current Russian Crisis: Reasons and the Ways of future Development," Gardner-Webb Univ, 98; auth, "The Present and future of Russia," Univ SC, 98; auth, "What led Russia into this Crisis?," The Charlotte Observer, (98): 15A; auth, "The Chechen War and the future of Caucasus, unpublished; auth, "Yeltsin's move a step away from democratic order," Shelby Star, 93; auth, "Zvat kogo-to na barrikady ne nashe tsel," Uchitel'skaya Gazeta, 91. **CONTACT ADDRESS** Dept Soc Sci, Gardner-Webb Univ, Boiling Springs, NC 28017.

STROM, SHARON HARTMAN
PERSONAL Born 12/24/1941, Oakland, CA, 4 children **DISCIPLINE** AMERICAN SOCIAL HISTORY **EDUCATION** Whittier Col, BA, 63; Cornell Univ, MA, 69, PhD(hist), 70. **CAREER** Lectr hist, State Univ NY Stony Brook, 69-70; asst prof, 70-75, assoc prof hist, Univ RI, 75-80, full prof, 80-, dept chair. **MEMBERSHIPS** Orgn Am Historians. **RESEARCH** Labor history; history of women. **SELECTED PUBLICATIONS** Auth, Leadership and Tactics in the American Woman Suffrage Movement, J Am Hist, 9/75; coauth, Moving the Mountain: Women Working for Social Change, Feminist Press, 80; Beyond the Typewriter: Gender, Class, and Office Work, Univ of Ill, 92. **CONTACT ADDRESS** Dept of Hist, Univ of Rhode Island, 80 Upper Col Rd, Ste 3, Washburn Hall Room 113, Kingston, RI 02881. **EMAIL** shstrom@uri.edu

STRONG, DOUGLAS HILLMAN
PERSONAL Born 10/07/1935, San Francisco, CA, m, 3 children **DISCIPLINE** AMERICAN & ENVIRONMENTAL HISTORY **EDUCATION** Univ Calif, Berkeley, BA, 58, MA, 59; Syracuse Univ, PhD(soc sci), 64. **CAREER** From asst prof to assoc prof, 64-68, Prof Hist, San Diego State Univ, 71- **RESEARCH** California environmental history; national park history. **SELECTED PUBLICATIONS** Auth, The Sierra Forest Reserve: The movement to preserve the San Joaquin Valley watershed, Calif Hist Soc Quart, 3/67; Trees--or Timber? The Story of Sequoia and Kings Canyon National Parks, Sequoia Natural Hist Asn, 68; The Conservationists, Addison-Wesley, 71; These Happy Grounds: A History of the Lassen Region, Loomis Mus, 73; Teaching American environmental history, Social Studies, 10/74; Ethics or expediency: An environmental question, Environ Affairs, spring 76; Ralph H Cameron and the Grand Canyon, Arizona & the West, spring/summer 78; Preservation efforts at Lake Tahoe, Forest Hist, 4/81. **CONTACT ADDRESS** Dept of Hist, San Diego State Univ, San Diego, CA 92182.

STRONG, DOUGLAS M.
PERSONAL Born 09/27/1956, Buffalo, NY, m, 1986, 2 children **DISCIPLINE** HISTORY OF CHRISTIANITY **EDUCATION** Houghton Col, BA, 78; Princeton Theological Seminary, Mdiv, 81, PhD, 90. **CAREER** PROF OF HIST OF CHRISTIANITY, WESLEY THEOLOGICAL SEMINARY, 89-. **HONORS AND AWARDS** President, Wesleyan Theological Society, 97-99. **MEMBERSHIPS** Am Acad of Religion; Am Soc of Church Hist; Am Hist Asn; Wesleyan Theological Soc. **RESEARCH** 19th Century American religious history. **SELECTED PUBLICATIONS** Auth, Reading Christian Ethics: A Historical Sourcebook, Westminster John Knox, 96; auth, They Walked in the spirit: Personal Faith and Social Action in America, Westminster John Knox, 97; auth, Perfectionist Politics: Abolitionism and the Religious Tensions of American Democracy. **CONTACT ADDRESS** Wesley Theol Sem, 4500 Massachusetts Ave NW, Washington, DC 20016. **EMAIL** gnorts@erols.com

STRONG, JOHN A.
PERSONAL Born 10/03/1935, Cooperstown, NY, m, 1961, 2 children **DISCIPLINE** HISTORY **EDUCATION** Syracuse Univ, MA, 59, PhD(hist), 68. **CAREER** Assoc prof, 65-80, Prof Hist & Am Studies, Southampton Col, Long Island Univ, 80- **MEMBERSHIPS** AHA; African Studies Asn. **RESEARCH** African history; American social and cultural history. **SELECTED PUBLICATIONS** Auth, Indian-White relations in seventeenth century Virginia, Maxwell Rev, 12/64; Emerging ideological patterns among Southern African refugees, Africa Today, summer 67; The Imposition Of Colonial Jurisdiction Over The Montauk Indians Of Long-Island, Ethnohist, Vol 41, 94. **CONTACT ADDRESS** Dept of Soc Sci, Long Island Univ, Southampton Col, 239 Montauk Hwy, Southampton, NY 11968-4198.

STRONG-BOAG, VERONICA
PERSONAL Born 07/05/1947, Scotland **DISCIPLINE** HISTORY, WOMEN'S STUDIES **EDUCATION** Univ Toronto, BA, 70; Carleton Univ, MA, 71; Univ Toronto, PhD, 75. **CAREER** Hist/Women's Stud School, dept hist, Trent Univ, 74-76; Concordia Univ, 76-80; dept hist & women's stud prog, Simon Fraser Univ, 80-91; dir, Ctr Res Women's Stud & Gender Rel, 91-97, Prof Educational Studies, Univ BC, 91-. **HONORS AND AWARDS** John A. Macdonald Prize, Can Hist Asn **MEMBERSHIPS** Can Hist Asn (pres, 93-93) **RESEARCH** Women's History Family and Education Canadian History Gender. **SELECTED PUBLICATIONS** Co-ed, Rethinking Canada, (Toronto: Copp clark, Pitman, 91), 455; co-ed, british colubmia reconsidered: Essays on Women in B.C., (Vancouver Press Gang), 92; auth, "A History of the Canadian Peoples: 1867 to the Present," vol 2, (Tornonto: Copp Clark Pitman, 93), 2 chap; auth, "Janey Canuck: Women in Canada Between Two World Wars, 1919-1939," CHA Hist Booklet, 94; auth, Their Side of the Story: Women'sw Vioces from Ontario Suburbs, 1945-1960, (Toronto: Univ of Toronto Press, 95); auth, "Too Much and Not Enough-- The Pradox of Power for Feminnist Adaemics Working with Community Feminist on Issues Related to Violence," Violence: A Collectgive Responsibility, (Ottawa: Soc Sci Fed of Can, 95); auth, "Chapter 11 B.C. Society in th 20th Century," the Pacific Provice, (Vancover: Douglas & McIntyre, 96); co-auth, "Constructing Canada: An Intoduction," in Painting the Maple: Essays on Race, Gender and the Construction of Canada, (Vancouver: UBC Press, 98); auth, "A Red Girl's Reasoning: E. Pauline Johnson constructs the New Nation," in Painting the Maple, (Vancover: UBC Press, 98); auth, "What Women's Space?: Changing Suburbs: Foundation, Form and Function, (London: E & FNSPON, 99). **CONTACT ADDRESS** Dept Educ Stud, Univ of British Columbia, 2125 Main Mall, Vancouver, BC, Canada V6T 1Z4. **EMAIL** veronica.strong-boag@ubc.ca

STROUP, RODGER EMERSON
PERSONAL Born 10/04/1946, St. Louis, MO, m, 1968, 1 child **DISCIPLINE** AMERICAN HISTORY **EDUCATION** Wofford Col, BA, 68; Univ SC, MA, 72, PhD(hist), 80. **CAREER** Grad asst Am hist, Univ SC, 70-72, teaching asst world & US hist, 72-74; dir & cur, Hist Columbia Found, 74-79; Cur Hist, SC State Mus, 79-, Consult, Am Asn State & Local Hist, 79- **RESEARCH** South Carolina material culture studies. **SELECTED PUBLICATIONS** Auth, Before and after: Three letters from E B Heyward, SC Hist Mag, 4/73; The naval policy of England's liberal government 1906, 73 & John L McLaurin: Independent Tillmanite, 75, Proc SC Hist Asn; Upcountry patron: Wade Hampton II, In: Artist in the Lives of South Carolina, Carolina Art Asn, 78; Columbia And Richland County--A South-Carolina Community, 1740-1990, J Of Am Hist, Vol 81, 94. **CONTACT ADDRESS** So Carolina Dept of Archives and History, 8301 Parklane Rd., Columbia, SC 29223-4905. **EMAIL** stroup@scdah.state.sc.us

STROZIER, CHARLES B.
PERSONAL Born 02/16/1944, Athens, GA, m, 1985, 4 children **DISCIPLINE** HISTORY **EDUCATION** Harvard Univ, BA, 66; Univ Chicago, MA, 67; Univ Chicago, PhD, 71; Chicago Inst Psychoanalysis, 72-81. **CAREER** Co-Dir, Center on Violence and Human Survival, John Jay Col of Criminal Justice, 86-; Prof, John Jay Col of Criminal Justice, 86; Fac Mem, New York Inst for Psychoanalytic Self Psychol, 95-; Supv Psychoanalyst, Training and Res Inst in Self Psychol, 97-. **HONORS AND AWARDS** Writer of the Year Awd, Lincoln Libr, 82; Distinguished Merit Awd, Ill State Hist Asn, 87; Awd of Achievement, Abraham Lincoln Asn, 91; Cert of Hon, Int Psychohistorical Asn, 96; Vision Awd, Nat Asn for the Advan of Psychoanalysis, 97; Diplomate, Am Psychotherapy Asn, 99. **RESEARCH** Psychohistory. **SELECTED PUBLICATIONS** Coed, The Public and Private Lincoln: Contemporary Perspectives, Southern Ill Univ Pr (Carbondale, IL), 79: auth, Lincoln's Quest for Union: Public and Private Meanings, Basic Books (New York, NY), 82; coauth, The Leader: Psychohistorical Studies, Plenum Pr (New York, NY), 84; ed, Heinz Kohut, Self Psychology and the Humanities: Reflections on a New Psychoanalytic Approach, Norton Publ Co (New York, NY), 85; auth, Apocalypse: On The Psychology of Fundamentalism in America, Beacon Pr, 94; ed, Genocide, War and Human Survival and Trauma and Self, Roman and Littlefield, 96; ed, The Year 2,000: Essays on the End, New York Univ Pr (New York, NY), 97; auth, "Death and Self," Progress in Self Psychology 15 (99): 321-342; auth, "Heinz Kohut and 'The Two Analyses of Mr. Z': The Use (and Abuse?) of Case Material in Psychoanalysis," The Psychoanalytic Rev 86 (99): 569-586; auth, Heinz Kohut: His Life and Work, Farrar, Straus & Giroux (forthcoming) **CONTACT ADDRESS** Dept Hist, John Jay Col of Criminal Justice, CUNY, 445 W 59th St, New York, NY 10019. **EMAIL** chuckstrozier@juno.com

STRUEVER, NANCY SCHERMERHORN
PERSONAL Born La Salle, IL **DISCIPLINE** RENAISSANCE INTELLECTUAL HISTORY **EDUCATION** Univ Rochester, BA, 54, MA, 57, PhD(hist), 66. **CAREER** Inst hist, Rochester Inst Technol, 62-63; from instr to assoc prof, Hobart & William Smith Cols, 64-73; assoc prof, 73-78, Prof Hist, Johns Hopkins Univ, 78-, Am Coun Learned Soc fel, 72-73; fel, Ctr Humanities, Wesleyan Univ, 73. **MEMBERSHIPS** AHA **RESEARCH** Linguistics and history. **SELECTED PUBLICATIONS CONTACT ADDRESS** Dept of Hist, Johns Hopkins Univ, Baltimore, 3400 N Charles St, Baltimore, MD 21218.

STRUVE, WALTER
PERSONAL Born 05/06/1935, Somers Point, NJ, m, 1959 **DISCIPLINE** HISTORY **EDUCATION** Yale, PhD, 63; MA, 57; Lafayette College, AB, 55. **CAREER** Instr hist, Princeton Univ, 61-64; from instr to assoc prof, 64-82, prof hist, City College NY, 82-. **HONORS AND AWARDS** German Fulbright Fellow, Kiel Univ, 55-56; German Academic Exchange Service (DAAD) Fellow, Free Univ of Berlin, 60-61; Research Fulbrights, 90, 78-79; Fritz Thyssen Foundation Research Grant, 79-80; German Academic Exchange Servicce (DAAD) Research Grant, 78; American Philosophical Society Research Grant, 68-69; City University and City College of New York Research Grants and Fellowships, 98 (Rifkind), 92; 83-84; 81-82; 74-76; 73; 71; 67. **MEMBERSHIPS** Amer Historical Assoc; German Studies Assoc; Immigration and Ethnic History Society; Society for German Amer Studies. **RESEARCH** Germany since 1815; German emigration since 1815. **SELECTED PUBLICATIONS** Auth, Elites against Democracy, Leadership Ideals in Bourgeois Political Thought in Germany, 1890-1933, Princeton Univ, 73; auth, "Die Republik Texas, Bremen und das Hildesheimische, Ein Beitraq zur Geschichte von Auswanderung, Handel und gesellschaftlichem Wandel im 19 Jahrhundert, Quellen und Darstellungen zur Geschichte Niedersachsens 96, Hildesheim: Verlag August Lax, 83; auth, "Aufsteg und Herrschaft des Nationalsozialismus in einer industriellen Kleinstadt, Osterode am Harz 1918-1945," The Rise and Rule of Nazism in a Small Industrial Town, Osterode am Harz, 1918-1945, Essen: Klartext Verlag, 92; auth, Germans and Texands, Commerce, Migration, and Culture in the Days of the Lone-Star Republic, University of Texas Press, 96. **CONTACT ADDRESS** Dept of German, City Col, CUNY, Convent Ave. at 138th St., New York, NY 10031.

STUARD, SUSAN M.
PERSONAL Born 04/15/1935, Rochester, NY, m, 1957, 3 children **DISCIPLINE** HISTORY **EDUCATION** Smith Col, BA, 57; Univ Rochester, MA, 61; SUNY Geneseo, MS, 61; Yale Univ, PhD, 70. **CAREER** Assoc Prof, SUNY Brockport, 70-85; Vis Assoc Prof, Haverford Col, 83-88; Prof, Haverford Col, 88-. **HONORS AND AWARDS** SUNY Found Awd, Delmans Found Grant, Berkshire Prize for Best Article, 95. **MEMBERSHIPS** AHA, Med Acad of Am, Econ Hist Asn, Soc for Ital Hist Studies, Berkshire Conf. **RESEARCH** Medieval history, women, social and economic history. **SELECTED PUBLICATIONS** Auth, Women in Medieval Society (Philadelphia, PA), 92; ed, Becoming Visible, 2nd & 3rd ed (Boston, MA), 87, 98; auth, Women in Medieval History and Historiography (Philadelphia, PA), 87; auth, A State of Deference (Philadelphia, PA), 92; auth, "Ancillary Evidence on the Decline of Medieval Slavery," Past and Present 149 (95): 3-32; auth, Gilding the Market in Fourteenth-Century Italy, (forthcoming). **CONTACT ADDRESS** Dept Hist, Haverford Col, 370 Lancaster Ave, Haverford, PA 19041-1336. **EMAIL** sstuard@haverford.edu

STUEWER, ROGER H.
PERSONAL Born 09/12/1934, Shawano, WI, m, 1960, 2 children **DISCIPLINE** HISTORY OF PHYSICS **EDUCATION** Univ Wis, PhD(hist sci & physics), 68. **CAREER** Instr physics, Heidelberg Col, 60-62; from asst prof to assoc prof hist physics & physics, Univ Minn, Minneapolis, 67-71; assoc prof hist sci, Boston Univ, 71-72; assoc prof hist physics & physics, 72-74, prof hist sci, Univ Minn, Minneapolis, 74-00, prof emer,00-, Am Coun Learned Soc fel, 74-75, 83-84; hon res assoc, Harvard Univ, 74-75; ed, Physics in Perspective, Am J Phyics Resource Letters. **HONORS AND AWARDS** AAAS fel, 83; Am Phts Soc fel, 91; George Taylor Distinguised Service Awd, Univ Minnesota, 90; Am Assn Phy Teachers Distinguished Service Citation, 90; Sigma Xi Distinguished Lecturer, 97-99; Am Phys soc Centennial Lecturer, 98-99. **MEMBERSHIPS** Hist Sci Soc (secy, 72-77); Am Physics Soc; Am Assn Phys Teachers; Brit Soc Hist Sci; AAAS. **RESEARCH** History of 19th and 20th century physics; history of quantum theory; optics; nuclear physics. **CONTACT ADDRESS** Sch of Physics and Astron, Univ of Minnesota, Twin Cities, 116 Church St SE, Minneapolis, MN 55455-0149. **EMAIL** rstuewer@physics.spa.umn.edu

STUNKEL, KENNETH REAGAN
PERSONAL Born 09/08/1931, Ft Worth, TX, m, 1971, 3 children **DISCIPLINE** ASIAN & EUROPEAN INTELLECTUAL HISTORY **EDUCATION** Univ Md, BA, 54, MA, 59, PhD, 66. **CAREER** Assoc prof, 65-75, Prof Hist, Monmouth Col NJ, 75-, Dean, Sch Humanities & Soc Sci, 81-86, 93-; Lectr hist & philos, Univ Col, Far E Div & Univ Md, 73-74. **MEMBERSHIPS** Asn Asian Studies; AHA; Int Studies Asn. **RESEARCH** Impact of Sanskrit scholarship on European culture, 1785-1840; comparative Chinese and European intellectual history, especially with respect to science; Japanese environmental problems; Skepticism in early Modern Europe; The Thought of Lewis Mumford; Coherence in the humanities. **SELECTED PUBLICATIONS** Auth, Economic Super Powers and the Environment, 76; auth, Indian, Greek, and Christian Thought in

Antiquity, 79; authored and co-author of five books and some 25 articles. **CONTACT ADDRESS** Dept of Hist, Monmouth Univ, 400 Cedar Ave, West Long Branch, NJ 07764-1898. **EMAIL** kstunkel@mondec.monmouth.edu

STURGEON, MARY C.

PERSONAL Born 12/06/1943, Los Angeles, CA, s s **DISCIPLINE** ART HISTORY **EDUCATION** Bryn Mawr Col, PhD. **CAREER** Prof, ch, dept Art, Univ NC, Chapel Hill; visting prof, Elizabeth A Whitehead, 98-99. **HONORS AND AWARDS** Woodrow Wilson Fel; Fulbright Fel, Greece, 98-99. **MEMBERSHIPS** Am Sch of Classical Studies; Managing Committee; Archaeological Institute of Am; Col Art Assoc; Inter Assoc of Classical Archaeology; ASMOSIA; SECAC **RESEARCH** Archaic, class and hellenistic sculpture; Greek painting. **SELECTED PUBLICATIONS** Auth, The Reliefs from the Theater in Ancient Corinth, Princeton Univ, 77; Sculptures from the Sanctuary of Poseidon at Isthmia, Princeton Univ, 87; coed, Stephanos: Studies in Honor of Bunilde S. Ridgway, K Hartswick, 98; auth, "A Peloponnesian Aphrodite: The corinth Theater type," stephonos, 223-233; auth, "Hellenistic Sculpture at Corinth: The State of the Question," Regional Schools on Hellenistic Sculpture, O Palagia and WDE Coulson, Oxford, (98), 1-13; The Corinth Amazon: Formation of a Roman Classical Sculpture, Am J of Archaeol 99, 95; auth, Scuopture of the Classical Style at Corinth 1896-1996, Forthcoming; auth, Sixth-century Athens and the Cyclades, Forthcoming. **CONTACT ADDRESS** Univ of No Carolina, Chapel Hill, Chapel Hill, NC 27599. **EMAIL** sturgeon@email.unc.edu

STURGILL, CLAUDE C.

PERSONAL Born 12/09/1933, Glo, KY **DISCIPLINE** EARLY MODERN EUROPE **EDUCATION** Univ Ky, AB, 56, MA, 59, PhD, 63. **CAREER** Instr, Univ Ky, 61; asst prof Europ hist, Western Ky State Col, 62-64; asst prof early mod Europe, Wis State Univ, Oshkosh, 64-66; assoc prof French hist, E Carolina Univ, 66-69; assoc prof, 69-77, Prof 18th Century Europ Hist, Univ, Fla, 77-, Wis State Univ Regents' grant, 64-65; Nat Endowment for Humanities fel, 68; councilor, Int Comn Mil Hist, 71-; secygen, US Comn Mil Hist, 73-79; Fulbright prof, France 80; prof Centre de Recherches sur la Civilisation de l'Europe Moderne, Univ de Paris IV (Sorbonne), 80. **HONORS AND AWARDS** Int Comn Mil Hist medal for fostering int cooperation, 76. **MEMBERSHIPS** AHA; Soc Hist France; US Comn Mil Hist. **RESEARCH** Administrative history of the French army, 1700-1730. **SELECTED PUBLICATIONS** Auth, Marshal Villars in the War of the Spanish Succession, Univ Ky, 65; coauth, A Guidebook to the History of the Western World, Heath, 67, 69 & 76; ed-in-chief, Proceedings on the Interuniversity Consortium on Revolutionary Europe, 1750-1850, 73, 74, 75 & auth, Claude Le Blanc: Civil Servant of the King, 76, Univ Fla; La Formation de la Milice Permanente en France, 1726-1730, Ser Hist de l'Armee, Paris, 77; ed, Rolle's Petition, Univ Fla, 78; L'Organisation et l'Administration de la Marechaussee et de la Justice Prevotale, 1720-1730, Ser Hist de l'Armee, Paris, 80; Soldiers--Disciplinary Laboratory--The Army Of Piedmont In The 18th-Century, Am Hist Rev, Vol 98, 93; The War Of The Austrian Succession, Am Hist Rev, Vol 100, 95. **CONTACT ADDRESS** Div of Humanities Dept of Hist, Univ of Florida, 4131 GPA, Gainesville, FL 32611.

STURSBERG, PETER

PERSONAL Born 08/31/1913, Chefoo, China **DISCIPLINE** CANADIAN STUDIES **EDUCATION** McGill Univ **CAREER** Journalist, 34-40; ed & war correspondent, CBC, 41-45; foreign correspondent, var publs, 45-57, 73-80; commentator, CTV, 60-73; instr, Can stud, 80-88, adj prof, Simon Fraser Univ, 82-88 (Retired). **HONORS AND AWARDS** Can Radio Awd, 50; mem, Order Can, 96. **RESEARCH** Canadian studies; communications; political history. **SELECTED PUBLICATIONS** Auth, Journey Into Victory, 1944; auth, Agreement in Principle, 61; auth, Those Were The Days, 69; auth, Mister Broadcasting, 71; auth, Diefenbaker Leadership Gained 1956-62, 75; auth, Diefenbaker Leadership Lost 1962-67, 76; auth, Lester Pearson and the American Dilemma, 80; auth, EXTRA! When the Papers Had the Only News, 82; auth, Gordon Shrum, 86; auth, The Golden Hope, 87; auth, Roland Michener: The Last Viceroy, 89; auth, The Sound of War, 93. **CONTACT ADDRESS** 5132 Alderfield Pl, West Vancouver, BC, Canada V7W 2W7.

STURTEVANT, DAVID REEVES

PERSONAL Born 09/20/1926, Zanesville, OH, m, 1947, 3 children **DISCIPLINE** HISTORY **EDUCATION** Muskingum Col, BA, 50; Stanford Univ, MA, 51, PhD, 58. **CAREER** From Asst Prof to Prof, 55-94, Prof Emeritus Hist, Muskingum Col, 94-; conducted grad seminars, Ataneo de Manila Univ & Univ Philippines; vis prof Philippine hist, Univ Hawaii, 76-77. **HONORS AND AWARDS** Fulbright res grant, Philippines, 65-66; Am Coun Learned Soc-Soc Sci Res Coun res grant, Asia, 70. **MEMBERSHIPS** Asn Asian Studies. **RESEARCH** East Asian history, especially southeast Asia, particularly the Philippine Islands. **SELECTED PUBLICATIONS** Auth, Sakdalism and Philippine radicalism, J Asian Studies, 2/62; Guardia de Honor: Revitalization within the revolution, Asian Studies, 8/66; No uprising fails, Solidarity, 10/66; Epilog for an old Colorum, Solidarity, 8/68; Agrarian Unrest in the Philippines, Ctr Int Studies, Ohio Univ, 69; Popular Uprisings in the Philippines, 1840-1940, Cornell Univ, 76. **CONTACT ADDRESS** Dept of Hist, Muskingum Col, 153 Stormont St, New Concord, OH 43762-1199.

SUAREZ-VILLA, LUIS

PERSONAL m **DISCIPLINE** URBAN PLANNING **EDUCATION** Univ Florida, BA, 69; MA, 72; Cornell Univ, MRP; 75; PhD, 81. **CAREER** Prof, Univ California Irv, 82-. **HONORS AND AWARDS** Fulbright Fel; Robert Donaldson Memor Prize. **MEMBERSHIPS** RSA; ASA; AEA; AAS; AAG. **RESEARCH** Regional economic development; technology. **SELECTED PUBLICATIONS** Coauth, "The Development of Sweden's R&D-intensive Electronics Industries: Exports, Outsourcing and Territorial Distribution," Envir Plan 28 (96):783-818; coauth, "Outsourcing, R&D and the Pattern of Intrametropolitan Location: The Electronics Industries of Madrid," Urb Stud (96); coauth, "Globalizacion y Localizacion: Las Estrategias Cooperativas y Ia Competitividad de Ia Empresa" in Tendencias Actuales de Ia Economia V de las Orcianizaclones, ed. Consejo General de Colegios de Economistas de Espana (Las Palmas, Spain, 96); coauth, "Operational Strategy, R&D, and Intrametropolitan Clustering in a Polycentric Structure: The Advanced Electronics Industries of the Los Angeles Basin." Urban Studies 34 (97):1343-1380; auth, "California's Recovery and the Restructuring of the Defense Industries," in Regional Resilience and Defense Conversion in the United States, ed. RD Norton (Greenwich, CT: JAI Press, 97); auth, "The Structures of Cooperation: Downscaling, Outsourcing and the Networked " Alliance, Small Bus Econ 10 (98):5-16; coauth, "Losses from the Northridge Earthquake: Disruptions to High Technology Industries in the Los Angeles Basin," J Disaster Stud 23 (98):19-44. **CONTACT ADDRESS** School of Social Ecology, Univ of California, Irvine, Irvine, CA 92697-7075. **EMAIL** lsuarez@uci.edu

SUCHLICKI, JAIME

PERSONAL Born 12/08/1939, Cuba, 3 children **DISCIPLINE** MODERN HISTORY, INTERAMERICAN STUDIES **EDUCATION** Univ Miami, BA, 64; MA, 65; Tex Christian Univ, 68. **CAREER** Res asst, Ctr Advan Int Studies, 64-65, asst prof Hist & res assoc, 67-70, lectr; assoc prof & assoc dir, Inst Inter Am Studies, 70-76, prof Hist & dir Latin Am Studies, Univ Miami, 76-; Dir, Inst for Cuban and Cuban-Am Studies, 99-. **HONORS AND AWARDS** Selected as one of "Outstanding Acad Books of 1971", Am Libr Assoc; Emilio Bacardi Moreau Prof of Hist, Univ of Miami. **MEMBERSHIPS** Advisory Board on Bilingual Educ; Univ Lectureship Comm; Cuban Studies Assoc. **RESEARCH** Interamerican studies, Caribbean, Central America, especially Cuba. **SELECTED PUBLICATIONS** Auth, Mexico: From Mentezuma to NAFTA; auth, Cuba: From Columbus to Castro; auth, Cuban Communism; auth, The Cuban Economy; auth, The cuban Military: Status and Outlooks; auth, "Cuba Beyond Castro", Transaction Pub; auth, "Castro's Uneven Trading Field", J of Comm. **CONTACT ADDRESS** Dept Hist, Univ of Miami, PO Box 248107, Miami, FL 33124-8107. **EMAIL** jsuchlicki@sis.miami.edu

SUELLEN, HOY

PERSONAL Born 08/14/1942, Chicago, IL, m, 1986 **DISCIPLINE** AMERICAN HISTORY **EDUCATION** St. Mary's Col, Notre Dame, IN, BA, 65; Indiana Univ, Bloomington, MA, 71; Indiana Univ, Bloomington, PhD, 75. **CAREER** Guest Prof, Dept of History, Univ of Notre Dame, 99-; vis Assoc Prof, History, Notre Dame, 87-98; Asst Dir, North Carolina Division of Archives and History, Raleigh, 81-87; Dir, Public Works Historical Society, 75-81; Asst Prof, History, State Univ of New York at Plattsburgh, 75-81. **HONORS AND AWARDS** Louisville Institute Research Grant, 99-00; Spencer Foundation Research Grant, 96-97; Abigail Quigley McCarthy Ctr for Women's Research Fel, 95-96; National Endowment for the Humanities Senior Research Fel, 92-93; Hibernian Awd, Cushwa Ctr for the Study of Am Catholicism, Univ of Nortre Dame, 92; Irish Am Cultural Institute Fel, 91-92; Newberry Library Summer Fel, Aug. 89; British Academy (London) and Henry E. Huntington Library Exchange Fellow, May-June 89; National Endowmentt for the Humanities and Henry E. Huntington Library Senior Research Fel, 86-87; Am Hisotorical Association, Albert Beveridge Grant for Research in Am History, 84; Am Philosophical Society Research Grant, 77. **MEMBERSHIPS** Amer Catholic Historical Assoc; Amer Historical Ass; Amer Society of Church History; and Organization of Amer Historians. **RESEARCH** Amer Women; Religion; and Race. **SELECTED PUBLICATIONS** Auth, "History of Public Works History in the US, 76; coauth, "Public Works History in the United States: A Guide to the Literature, 82; auth, "The Garbage Disposer, the Public Health, and the Good Life," Technology and Culture, 26, Oct. 85. auth, "Bullettin of the History of Medicine," 63, summer 89; auth,"From Dublin to New Orleans: The Journey of Nora and Alice, 94; auth, "Chasing Dirt: The American Pursuit of Cleanliness, 95; auth, "The Journey Out: The recruitment and Emigration of Iris Religious Women to the United states, 1812-1914," Journal of Women's History, 6/7, Winter/Sring 95; auth, "Caring for Chicago's Women and Girls: The Sister of the Good Shepherd, 1859-1911, Journal of Urban History, 23, Mar 97; auth, "Walking Nuns: Chicago's Irish Sisters of Mercy," in Ellen Skerrett, ed., At the Crossroads: Old St. Patrick's and the Chicago Irish, 97; **CONTACT ADDRESS** Dept History, Univ of Notre Dame, 347 Mission Hills, Chesterton, IN 46304.

SUGRUE, THOMAS J.

PERSONAL Born 07/24/1962, Detroit, MI, m, 1993, 1 child **DISCIPLINE** HISTORY **EDUCATION** Columbia Univ, BA, 84; Cambridge Univ, BA, 86; MA, 89; Harvard Univ, MA, 87; PhD, 92. **CAREER** Asst prof, 92-97; assoc prof, 97-99; prof, 00-, Univ Pa. **HONORS AND AWARDS** Bancroft Prize; Philip Taft Prize; Pres Bk Awd; Urban Hist Asn Prize; Choice Outs Acad Bk. **MEMBERSHIPS** OAH; AHA; ASA; SSHA; Phi Beta Kappa. **RESEARCH** 20th C US; urban; political; race relations. **SELECTED PUBLICATIONS** Auth, The Origins of the Urban Crisis: Race and Inequality in Postwar Detroit, Princeton Univ Press, 94; coed, W.E.B. DuBois, Race, and the City: The Philadelphia Negro and Its Legacy (Univ of Pennsylvania Press, 98); auth, "Carter's Urban Policy Crisis," in The Carter Presidency: Policy Choices in the Post New Era, ed. Gary Fink, Hugh Davis Graham (Lawrence: Univ Press of Kansas, 98), 137-57; auth, "Poor Families in the Era of Urban Transformation: The 'Underclass' in Myth and Reality," in Families: A Multicultural Reader, ed. Stephanie Coontz (New York and London: Routledge, 99), 243-57; auth, "Segmented Work, Race-Conscious Workers: Structure, Agency, and Division in the CIO Era," Intl Rev of Social Hist (96), 389-406; auth, "Reassessing the History of Postwar America," Prospects: An Annual of American Culture Studies (95), 493-509; auth, "'Forget about Your Inalienable Right to Work': Deindustrialization and Its Discontents at Ford, 1950-1953," Intl Labor and Working-class Hist 48 (95), 112-30. **CONTACT ADDRESS** Dept History, Univ of Pennsylvania, 3401 Walnut St, Philadelphia, PA 19104-6228. **EMAIL** tsugrue@sas.upenn.edu

SULLIVAN, CHARLES R.

PERSONAL Born Washington D.C., m, 2 children **DISCIPLINE** HISTORY **EDUCATION** George Mason Univ, BA; Columbia Univ, MA; MPil; PhD. **CAREER** Assoc prof, Dallas Univ. **RESEARCH** Modern European intellectual history; history of political economy and classical Liberalism. **SELECTED PUBLICATIONS** Auth, The First Chair of Political Economy in France: Alexandre Vandermonde and the Principles of Sir James Steuart at the Ecole Normale of the Year III, Fr Hist Stud, 97; auth, Western Histories in Invitation to the Classics, Baker, 98. **CONTACT ADDRESS** Dept of History, Univ of Dallas, 1845 E Northgate Dr, Irving, TX 75062. **EMAIL** sullivcr@acad.udallas.edu

SULLIVAN, DENIS

DISCIPLINE GREEK, LATIN, CLASSICAL PHILOLOGY AND ANCIENT HISTORY **EDUCATION** Tufts Univ, AB, 66; Univ NC Chapel Hill, PhD, 72; Cath Univ, MS, 75. **CAREER** Libr staff, Univ Md, 75-78; asst dean, Univ Md, Univ Col, 78-82; asst prof, Univ Md Col Pk, 82-88; assoc prof, Univ Md Col Pk, 88-. **HONORS AND AWARDS** Phi Beta Kappa; NDEA Title IV Fel; Woodrow Wilson Dissertation Fel; Dumbarton Oaks Byzantine Fel, 91-92 and 98-99. **MEMBERSHIPS** Amer Philol Asn; US Nat Comt on Byzantine Studies. **RESEARCH** Byzantine studies; Textual criticism. **SELECTED PUBLICATIONS** Auth, The Life of St. Ioannikios in Byzantine Defenders of Images, ed A. M. Talbot, Dumbarton Oaks, Wash, DC, 243-351, 98; Tenth Century Byzantine Offensive Siege Warfare: Instructional Prescriptions and Historical Practice, Byzantium at War, Athens, Nat Hellenic Res Foun, 179-200, 97; Was Constantine VI Lassoed at Markellai?, Greek, Roman and Byzantine Studies, 35, 3, 287-291, 94; Legal Opinion of Eustathios (Romaios) the Magistros, A. Laiou, Consent and Coercion to Sex and Marriage in Ancient and Medieval Societies, Wash, 175-175, 93; The Life of Saint Nikon: Text, Translation and Commentary, Brookline, Ma, Hellenic Col Press, 87; The Versions of the Vita Niconis, Dumbarton Oaks Papers, 32, 157-173, 78; auth, Siegecraft: Two Tenth-Century Instructional Manuals by "Heron of Byzantium," Dumbarton Oaks (Wash, DC), 00. **CONTACT ADDRESS** EDCI, Univ of Maryland, Col Park, Benjamin Bldg, College Park, MD 20742. **EMAIL** ds77@umail.umd.edu

SULLIVAN, DONALD DAVID

PERSONAL Born 05/11/1930, Denver, CO, m, 1964, 3 children **DISCIPLINE** MEDIEVAL & RENAISSANCE HISTORY **EDUCATION** Univ Chicago, BA, 56, MA, 57; Univ Colo, PhD(hist), 67. **CAREER** Asst prof hist, San Diego State Col, 65-67; Asst Prof Hist, Univ Nmex, 67- **MEMBERSHIPS** AHA; Renaissance Soc Am; Mediaeval Acad Am; Am Soc Church Hist. **RESEARCH** German religious and ecclesiastical history of the 15th century; early humanism in Northern Europe, especially Nicholas of Cusa; periodization. **SELECTED PUBLICATIONS** Auth, Nicholas of Cusa as Reformer, Mediaeval Studies, 74; Innuendo & the Weighted Alternative in Tacitus, Class J, 76; The end of the Middle Ages, Hist Teacher, 81. **CONTACT ADDRESS** Dept Hist, Univ of New Mexico, Albuquerque, Albuquerque, NM 87110.

SULLIVAN, MICHAEL J.

PERSONAL Born 06/12/1941, Newport, RI, m, 1969, 2 children **DISCIPLINE** HISTORY **EDUCATION** Holy Cross, BA, 62; Univ Virginia, PhD, 69. **CAREER** Asst prof, assoc prof, prof, Drexel Univ, 70-. **HONORS AND AWARDS** NATO Fel; Excell Teach, Linback Awd. **MEMBERSHIPS** ISA. **RESEARCH** US Foreign policy; comparative government. **SELECTED PUBLICATIONS** Auth, Measuring Global Values: The Ranking of 162 Countries, Greenwood Press (Westport, CT), 91; auth, Comparing State Policies: A Framework for Analyzing 100 Governments, Greenwood Press (Westport, CT), 96, 2nd printing 99. **CONTACT ADDRESS** Dept History, Politics, Drexel Univ, 3141 Chestnut St, Philadelphia, PA 19104-2816.

SUMIDA, JON T.
PERSONAL Born 07/07/1949, Washington, DC, m, 1975, 2 children **DISCIPLINE** HISTORY **EDUCATION** Univ of Calif, Santa Cruz, BA, 71; Univ of Chicago, MA, 74; PhD, 82. **CAREER** From Asst Lectr to Assoc Prof, Univ of Md, Col Park, 80-. **HONORS AND AWARDS** Fel, Wilson Center Wash DC, 86, 95-96; Guggenheim Fel, 90-91; Naval Hist Author of the Year, US Naval Inst, 96; Moncado Prize, Soc of Mil Hist, 93, 95. **MEMBERSHIPS** AHA, Int Naval Res Orgn, Int Trumpet Guide. **RESEARCH** Naval History, Strategic Theory. **SELECTED PUBLICATIONS** Auth, The Pollen Papers, George Allen & Unwin, 84; auth, In Defense of Naval Supremacy: Finance, Technology and British Naval Policy, 1889-1914, Unwin Hyman/Routledge, 89/93; auth, Inventing Grand Strategy and Teaching Command: The Classic Works of Alfred Thayer Mahan Reconsidered, Johns Hopkins, 97/99. **CONTACT ADDRESS** Dept Hist, Univ of Maryland, Col Park, 2115 F S Key Hall, College Park, MD 20742-0001. **EMAIL** js130@umd.edu

SUMNER, GREGORY D.
DISCIPLINE AMERICAN HISTORY & CULTURE **EDUCATION** Ind Univ, BA, MA, PhD; University Mich Law Sch, JD. **CAREER** Assoc prof, 93. **HONORS AND AWARDS** Fel(s), Andrew Mellon Found; John D and Catherine T MacArthur Found; NEH. **SELECTED PUBLICATIONS** Auth, Dwight Macdonald and the Politics Circle: The Challenge of Cosmopolitan Democracy, Cornell Univ Press, 96. **CONTACT ADDRESS** Dept of Hist, Univ of Detroit Mercy, 4001 W McNichols Rd, PO BOX 19900, Detroit, MI 48219-0900. **EMAIL** SUMNERGR@udmercy.edu

SUN, RAYMOND
DISCIPLINE EUROPEAN HISTORY **EDUCATION** Johns Hopkins Univ, PhD, 91. **CAREER** Asst prof, Washington State Univ. **SELECTED PUBLICATIONS** Auth, Catholic-Marxist Competition in the Working-Class Parishes of Cologne during the Weimar Republic, in Cath Hist Rev 83, 97 & Arbeiter Priester und die 'Roten': Kulturelle Hegemonie im Katholischen Milieu, 1885-1933, Workers, Priests and 'Reds': Cultural Hegemony in the Catholic Milieu, 1885-1933, in Geschichte zwischen Kultur und Gesellshaft: Beitrage zur Theoriedebatte, History Between Culture and Society: Contributions to the Debate Over Theory, Munich: Beck Verlag, 97. **CONTACT ADDRESS** Dept of History, Washington State Univ, 301 Wilson Hall, PO Box 644030, Pullman, WA 99164-4030. **EMAIL** sunray@wsu.edu

SUNDBERG, WALTER
DISCIPLINE CHURCH HISTORY **EDUCATION** S.t Olaf Col, BA, 69; Princeton Theol Sem, MDiv, 73, PhD, 81; Univ Tubingen, Ger, 71-72. **CAREER** Vis instr, Augsburg Col, 80; instr, Augsburg Col, 81-84; US Army Chaplains prog, 77; Lutheran Theol Sem, Philadelphia, 76; vis prof, Col St. Catherine, 85-86; asst prof, 84; assoc prof, 86; prof, 94-; act ch, hist dept, 87-88. **HONORS AND AWARDS** Rockefeller Theol fel; grad fel; Amer Lutheran Church; asst minister, como park lutheran church; ed bd(s), lutheran quart; lutheran commentator; bd mem, great commn network; lutheran bible ministries; lutheran bible inst; alc inter-church relations comm. **MEMBERSHIPS** Mem adv coun, Interpretation. **SELECTED PUBLICATIONS** Contrib, Ministry in 19th Century European Lutheranism, Called and Ordained: Lutheran Perspectives on the Office of Ministry, 90; pub(s), articles in First Things, Lutheran Quart, Lutheran Forum; coauth, The Bible in Modern Culture: Theology and Historical Critical Method from Spinoza to Kasemann, 95. **CONTACT ADDRESS** Dept of Church History, Luther Sem, 2481 Como Ave, Saint Paul, MN 55108. **EMAIL** wsundber@luthersem.edu

SUNDSTROM, ROY ALFRED
PERSONAL Born 02/24/1934, Mineola, NY, m, 1963, 2 children **DISCIPLINE** ENGLISH & EARLY MODERN EUROPEAN HISTORY **EDUCATION** Univ Mass, Amherst, AB, 56; Western Mich Univ, MA, 66; Kent State Univ, PhD(Hist), 72. **CAREER** Asst prof, 69-73, assoc prof, 73-79, prof Hist, Humboldt State Univ, 79-, Am Philos Soc res grant, 74 & 75. **MEMBERSHIPS** AHA; Conf Brit Historians; Huguenot Soc London. **RESEARCH** Late Stuart England; biography of Sidney Godolphin, 1645-1712. **SELECTED PUBLICATIONS** Auth, Some original sources relating to Huguenot refugees in England, 1680-1727, Brit Studies Monitor, Summer 76; The French Huguenots and the Civil List, 1696-1727: A study of alien assimilation in England, Albion, Fall 76; Sidney Godolphin: Servant of the State, Univ of Delaware, Press, 92. **CONTACT ADDRESS** Dept of History, Humboldt State Univ, 1 Harps St, Arcata, CA 95521-8299.

SUNSERI, ALVIN RAYMOND
PERSONAL Born 02/11/1925, New Orleans, LA, m, 1952, 6 children **DISCIPLINE** HISTORY OF WARS & REVOLUTIONS **EDUCATION** Southeast La Univ, BA, 53; La State Univ, MA, 55, PhD(hist), 73. **CAREER** Instr hist, St Paul's Col, 54-56 & NMex Mil Inst, 56-59; asst prof, Col Santa Fe, 59-61 & NMex Highlands Univ, 61-63; teaching asst, La State Univ, 63-65; asst prof, Western State Col Colo, 65-67; from asst prof to assoc prof, 67-75, Prof Hist, Univ Northern Iowa, 75-. **MEMBERSHIPS** AHA; Orgn Am Historians; Southern Hist Asn; Hist Asn England. **RESEARCH** Military-industrial complex; Civil War & reconstruction. **SELECTED PUBLICATIONS** Auth, Baron von Steuben and the reeducation of the American Army, Armor, 65; The Ludlow Massacre, American Chronicle, 1/72; Anglo-American attitudes toward the Hispanos, 1946-1961, J Mex-Am Hist, 12/73; The army and the economy: Iowa as a case study, In: The United States Army in Peacetime: Essays in Honor of the Bicentennial 1775-1975, 75; The Chicano studies program in Northern New Mexico: Broken promises and future prospects, In: Identitiy and Awareness in the Minority Experience, La Crosse, 75; The migrant workers of Iowa, In: Essays on Minority Cultures, Univ Wis-La Crosse, 76; The Military-Industrial Complex in Iowa, In: War, Business and American Society, Kennikat, 77; Seeds of Discord: New Mexico Following the Anglo-American Conquest, 1846-1861, Nelson-Hall, 78. **CONTACT ADDRESS** Dept of Hist, Univ of No Iowa, Cedar Falls, IA 50613.

SUNY, RONALD GRIGOR
PERSONAL Born 09/25/1940, Philadelphia, PA, m, 1971, 2 children **DISCIPLINE** RUSSIAN & ARMENIAN HISTORY **EDUCATION** Swarthmore Col, BA, 62; Columbia Univ, MA & Russ Inst Cert, 65, PhD(hist), 68. **CAREER** Spec lectr hist, Columbia Univ, 67-68; asst prof, Oberlin Col, 68-72, assoc prof, 72-81; Alex Manogian Prof Mod Armenian Hist, Univ Mich, Ann Arbor, 81-, Int Res & Exchanges Bd grant, USSR, 71-72; prof mod Armenian hist, Univ Mich, Ann Arbor, 77-78. **MEMBERSHIPS** Am Asn Advan Slavic Studies; Study Group Hist Europ Labor & Working Class Hist; Soc Armenian Studies. **RESEARCH** Russian social history; labor movement and social democracy in Transcaucasia; nationality problems in the USSR. **SELECTED PUBLICATIONS** Auth, Journeyman for the revolution: Stalin and the labour movement in Baku, Soviet Studies, 1/72; The Baku Commune, 1917-1918: Class and Nationality in the Russian Revolution, Princeton Univ, 72; Armenia in the Twentieth Century, Columbia Armenian Studies. **CONTACT ADDRESS** 1723 Wells, Ann Arbor, MI 48104.

SURRENCY, ERWIN C.
PERSONAL Born 05/11/1924, Jesup, GA, m, 1945, 2 children **DISCIPLINE** LEGAL HISTORY **EDUCATION** Univ Ga, AB, 47, AM, 48, LLB, 49; George Peabody Col, MALS, 50. **CAREER** Librn, Charles Klein Law Libr, Temple Univ, 50-78, from asst prof to assoc prof law, 54-60, prof, 60-78; Prof Law & Dir Law Libr, Univ Ga, 79-, Ed, Am J Legal Hist, 57-; lectr, Queen's Univ, Belfast, 63-64; mem, Asn Am Law Schs; consult, Nigerian Govt on Law Libr, 75-76. **MEMBERSHIPS** Am Soc Legal Hist (pres, 57-59); Am Hist Asn; Stair Soc; Selden Soc; Am Asn Law Libr (pres, 73-74). **RESEARCH** History of the legal profession in America; history of the federal courts; legal history of Georgia. **SELECTED PUBLICATIONS** Auth, Marshall Reader, 55; How The United-States Perfects An International Agreement, Law Libr J, Vol 85, 93; coauth, Research in Pennsylvania Law, 55; Guide to Legal Research, 59, Oceana. **CONTACT ADDRESS** Dept of Law, Univ of Georgia, Athens, GA 30601.

SURRIDGE, MARIE
PERSONAL Born London, England **DISCIPLINE** FRENCH STUDIES **EDUCATION** Oxford Univ, BA, 53, MA, 57, PhD, 62. **CAREER** Tchr, part-time, Oxford Univ, 55-67; asst prof, 70-77, assoc prof, 77-87, head Fr dept, 83-93, Prof, Queen's Univ, 87-. **SELECTED PUBLICATIONS** Auth, Le ou la? The Gender of French Nouns, 95. **CONTACT ADDRESS** Dept of French Studies, Queen's Univ at Kingston, Kingston, ON, Canada K7L 3N6.

SUTHERLAND, DANIEL E.
PERSONAL Born 03/05/1946, Detroit, MI, m, 1993, 3 children **DISCIPLINE** HISTORY **EDUCATION** Wayne St Univ, BS, 68, MA, 73, PhD, 76. **CAREER** Vis asst prof, 76, Univ Alabama; adj asst prof, 76-77, Wayne St Univ; asst prof, 77-83, assoc prof, 83-86, prof, 88-89, dept head, 83-89, McNeese St Univ; assoc prof, 89-91, prof, 91-, dept chmn, 92-98, Univ Arkansas; **HONORS AND AWARDS** NEH Stipends (1978, 1988, 2000); USMA Fellow (1983), AASLH Grant (1984), Jefferson Davis Medal (1990), Mellon Fellow (1995), Laney Prize (1996), Freeman Prize (1996), AASLH Certificate of Merit (1996). **MEMBERSHIPS** Southern Historical Assoc., Society of Civil War Historians, Society for Military History, The Historical Society, St. George Tucker Society, Assoc. for Preservation of Civil War Sites. **RESEARCH** 19th century US hist **SELECTED PUBLICATIONS** Forty articles and book chapters; twelve books, including Americans and Their Servants (1981), The Confederate Carpetbaggers (1988), Expansion of Everday Life (1989), Seasons of War (1996), Fredericksburg and Chancellorsville (1998), Guerrillas, Unionists, and Violence on the Confederate Home Front, editor (1999). **CONTACT ADDRESS** Dept of History, Univ of Arkansas, Fayetteville, Old Main 416, Fayetteville, AR 72701. **EMAIL** dsutherl@comp.uark.edu

SUTTON, DONALD SINCLAIR
PERSONAL Born 11/08/1938, London, England, m, 1987, 2 children **DISCIPLINE** HISTORY **EDUCATION** Cambridge Univ, BA, 62, PhD(Orient studies), 71; Columbia Univ, MA, 64. **CAREER** Instr, 69-71, asst prof, 71-77, Assoc Prof Hist, Carnegie-Mellon Univ, 77-. **HONORS AND AWARDS** SSRC/ACLS Joint Comm on Contemporary China res grant, 71-72; ACLS Comm on Chinese Civilization, 80-81, res grant; Inter-Univ Prog, Taipei, retraining grant, 86-87; Chiang Ching-kuo Found res grant, 91-92; St. Johns Col Cambridge, res grant, 00; Fulbright res grant, 01. **MEMBERSHIPS** Asn Asian Studies. **RESEARCH** Ritual religion in Chinese history; ethnicity and China's southwestern frontier. **SELECTED PUBLICATIONS** Auth, The Ma Yuan Cult, in Chinese Literature: Essays, Articles, Reviews, 89; auth, Festival Troupe of Taiwan, Jour of Asian Studies, 90; auth, Ritual and Culture of Cannibalism, Comparative Studies in Society and History, 95; auth, Confucians Confront Spiritual Mediums, Late Imperial China, 00; auth, Myth Making on an Ethnic Frontier, Modern China, 00; auth, Chinese Folk Religion in Motion: A Taiwan Performance Troupe in the Twentieth-century, Harvard Univ Asia Center (forthcoming); coed, Empire at the Margins: Culture, Ethnicity, and Frontier in Early Modern China, Univ Calif (forthcoming). **CONTACT ADDRESS** Dept of Hist, Carnegie Mellon Univ, 5000 Forbes Ave, Pittsburgh, PA 15213-3890. **EMAIL** ds27@andrew.cmu.edu

SUTTON, PAUL
PERSONAL Born 12/10/1961, CA, m, 1985, 1 child **DISCIPLINE** GEOGRAPHY **EDUCATION** Union Col, BS, 83; Univ Calif Santa Barbara, MA, 95; MA, 97; PhD, 99. **CAREER** Teacher, Anacap High School, 83-93; Lecturer and Teaching Asst, Univ Calif Santa Barbara, 92-98; Asst Prof, Univ Denver, 98-. **HONORS AND AWARDS** Honorable Mention, Excellence in Teaching Awd, Univ CA, 96; Fel, SUCSB; Fel, NASA; Excellence in Res Awd, UCSB. **RESEARCH** Quantitative urban geography; Techniques and methods of remote sensing and digital image processing; Spatial analysis and applied statistics; Geographic information science; Research methods in human geography. **SELECTED PUBLICATIONS** Co-auth, "Multimedia Guided Writing Modules for Introductory Human Geography," Journal of Geography, (95): 571-577; co-auth, "Color Your World: An Introduction to ArcView education Modules," NCGIA, 95; co-auth, "A comparison of Nighttime Satellite Imagery and Population Density for the continental United States," Photogrammetric Engineering and Remote Sensing, (97): 1303-1313; co-auth, "Lab Manual for Geog 176-B: Introduction the technical issues of GIS using Arc/INFO," NCGIA, 97; co-auth, "The Value of the World's Ecosystem Services and Natural Capital," Nature, 97; auth, "Modeling Population Density using Nighttime Satellite Imagery and GIS," computers, Environment and Urban Systems, (97): 227-244; auth, Unit #11 Registration and conflation of the NCGIA's Core Curriculum Technical Program, 98; co-auth, "Radiance calibration of DMSP-OLS low-light imaging data of human settlements, 98. **CONTACT ADDRESS** Dept Geog & Geol, Univ of Denver, 2199 S University, Denver, CO 80210. **EMAIL** psutton@du.edu

SUTTON, ROBERT F.
PERSONAL Born 04/06/1947, Philadelphia, PA, m, 1969, 1 child **DISCIPLINE** CLASSICAL ARCHAEOLOGY **EDUCATION** Haverford Col, AB, 69; Univ NC Chapel Hill, PhD, 81. **CAREER** TA, Univ of NC Chapel Hill, 72-74, 76-77, vis asst prof, Univ of Fla, 77-78; asst prof, Loyola Univ, 81-89; instr Aegean Inst, Greece, 80, 93, prof, Ind Univ, 89-. **HONORS AND AWARDS** Woodrow Wilson Fel, 69; Fac Serv Awd, IUPUI, 98. **MEMBERSHIPS** Archaeol Inst of Am; Am Philog Assoc; Classic Assoc of Middle W and S; Ind Classical Conf; Ind Foreign Lang Teachers Assoc. **RESEARCH** Art and archaeology of ancient Greece and Rome, Social History, Gender and Sexuality, Iconography. **SELECTED PUBLICATIONS** Auth, "The Populonia Coinage and the Second Punic War", Studi introduttivi alla monetazione etrusca, Supplemento Annalle 22, (75): 199-211; ed, Daidalikon: Studies in Memory of Raymond V. Scholder, S.J., Bolchazy-Carducci, (Wauconda, IL), 89; auth, "Ceramics of the Historic Period", in The Nemea Valley Archaeological Project 1984-1987: An Interim Report, eds J. Wright, J. Cherry, J. Davis, E. Mantzourani, S. Sutton, R. Sutton, Hesperia 59 (90): 579-659; auth, "Ceramic evidence for Settlement and Land Use in the Geometric to Hellenistic Periods", in Landscape Archaeology as Long-term History; Northern Keos in the Cycladic Islands, ed J.F. Cherry, J.L. Davis and E.M. Mantzourani, Inst of Archaol, UCLA, (91): 245-263; auth, "Pornography and Persuasion on Attic Pottery", in Pornography and Representation in Greece and Rome, ed Amy Richlin, Oxford Univ Pr, (NY, 92): 3-35; auth "Making the Scruffy Sherds Speak: Intensive Surface Survey in Greece", Ind Archaeol 1 (97): 144-59; auth, "Nuptial Eros. The Visual Discourse of the Wedding in Classical Athens", J of the Walters Art Gallery 55.56 (97/98): 27-48; auth, "The Good, the Base, and the Ugly: the Drunken Orgy in Attic Vase Painting and the Athenian Self", in Not the Classical Ideal: Athens and the Construction

of the Other in Greek Art, ed Beth Cohen, Brill (Leiden), 00. **CONTACT ADDRESS** Dept Foreign Lang and Cult, Indiana Univ-Purdue Univ, Indianapolis, 425 University Blvd, Indianapolis, IN 46202-5208. **EMAIL** rfsutton@iupui.edu

SUTTON, ROBERT PAUL
PERSONAL Born 09/21/1940, Altoona, PA, m, 1963, 3 children **DISCIPLINE** UNITED STATES HISTORY **EDUCATION** Juniata Col, BA, 62; Col William & Mary, MA, 64; Univ Va, PhD(hist), 67. **CAREER** Lectr hist, Christopher Newport Col, 62-64; instr, Univ Va, 64-67; assoc prof, Mansfield State Col, 67-70, chmn dept, 68-70; dir local & regional arch/collections, 76-79, from assoc prof to prof hist, Western Ill Univ, 70-82; dir Ctr Icarian Studies, 79-; Bd Dir communcal Studies Assoc, 93-; Nat Endowment for Humanities fel, 70. **HONORS AND AWARDS** Western Ill Univ Faculty Excellence Awds 76-77, 86-95; Western Ill Univ Outstanding Research Awd, College of Arts & Sciences, 94; Communal Studies Assoc Distinguished Service Awd, 98. **MEMBERSHIPS** AHA; Southern Hist Asn; Am Soc Legal Hist; Soc Am Archivists. **RESEARCH** Intellectual and social history of early national era, History of American Law, Communcal Societies. **SELECTED PUBLICATIONS** Auth, Nostalgia, pessimism, and malaise: the doomed aristocrat in late-Jeffersonian Virginia, 1/68 & Sectionalism and social structure: a case study of Jeffersonian democracy, 1/72, Va Mag Hist & Biog; ed, The Prairie State: A Documentary History of Illinois (2 vols), Eerdmans, 76; co-ed, Mon Cher, Emile: The Cabet Baxter Letters, 1854-55, Western Ill Regional Studies, spring 79; Voyage in Icaria: A message to the world, In: Humanistic Values of the Icarian movement, Ill Humanities Coun, 81; Morris Birkbak and Prairre Albion: A Critical Bibliography, Midwest Bibliography, Univ Iowa Press, 81; Les Icariens: The Utopian Dream in Europe and America, 94; **CONTACT ADDRESS** Dept of History, Western Illinois Univ, 1 University Cir, Macomb, IL 61455-1390. **EMAIL** Robert_Sutton@ccmail.wiu.edu

SUTTON, SHARON EGRETTA
PERSONAL Born 02/18/1941, Cincinnati, OH **DISCIPLINE** ARCHITECTURE **EDUCATION** Univ of Hartford, B Mus 1963; Columbia Univ, March 1973; City Univ of NYork, M Phil 1981, MA Psychology 1982, PhD Psychology 1982. **CAREER** Musician, orchestras of "Fiddler on the Roof," "Man of La Mancha," the Bolshoi, Moiseiyev and Leningrad Ballet Companies 1963-68; architect, Pratt Institute, visiting asst prof 1975-81; Columbia Univ, adj asst prof 1981-82; Univ of Cincinnati, asst prof 1982-84; SE Sutton Architect, private practice 1976-; Univ of MI, assoc prof, 84-94, prof of architecture and urban planning, 94-97; founder/director, The Urban Network; Univ of Washington, prof of architecture, dir CEEDS; fine artist, Exhibitions, The Evans-Tibbs Collection in Washington, DC, 85; Your Heritage House in Detroit, MI 1986, June Kelly Gallery in NYC 1987, Univ of MI Musuem of Art 1988; Art included in collections of, The Mint Museum, The Baltimore Museum of Art, Baltimore, MD, The Wadsworth Atheneum, Hartford, CT. **HONORS AND AWARDS** Danforth Foundation, Post baccalaureat Awd 1979-81; Design Rsch Recognition Awd Natl Endowment for the Arts 1983; group VII Natl Fellowship, WK Kellogg Foundation, 1986-1989; project director Natl Endowment for the Arts, "Design of Cities" Grant; American Planning Assn Education Awd, 1991; University of Michigan Regent's Awd for Distinguished Public Service; first African-American woman to be named a full professor of architecture in the US, 94; Second African-American Woman to be advanced to fellowship in the Amer Inst of Architects, 95; Distinguished Professor, Association of Collegiate Schools of Architecture; Life Achievement Awd, Michigan Women's Hall of Fame, 1997. **MEMBERSHIPS** Amer Institute of Architects; Amer Psychological Assn; American Educational Research Association; National Architectural Accrediting Board; Assoc of Collegiate Schools of Architecture. **RESEARCH** Youth, culture, environment. **SELECTED PUBLICATIONS** Auth, Learning through the Built Environment: An Ecological Approach to Child Development, Irvington Publishers, NYork, 85; auth, "Weaving a Tapestry of Resistance: The Places, Power and Poetry of a Sustainable Society," in Critical Studies in Educ and Culture Series, ed. Giroux and Freire (Westport: Bergin and Garvey Publishers, 96). **CONTACT ADDRESS** Prof of Architecture, Univ of Washington, 208 T Gould Hall, PO Box 355720, Seattle, WA 98195-5720. **EMAIL** sesut@u.washington.edu

SVEJDA, GEORGE J.
PERSONAL Born 03/12/1927, Horni Vilimec, Czechoslovakia, m, 1967, 4 children **DISCIPLINE** MODERN MEDIEVAL, DIPLOMATIC & IMMIGRATION HISTORY **EDUCATION** St Procopius Col, BA, 52; Georgetown Univ, PhD, 59; postdoc study, Univ Penn, 61-63. **CAREER** Res assoc polit sci, Columbia Univ, 58-59; European exchange specialist, Libr Cong, 59-61; tech writer sci, Franklin Inst, Pa, 62; historian, US Dept Interior, 62-80; res analyst, Dept of Justice, Dept of Navy. **HONORS AND AWARDS** Phi Alpha Theta; Dict of Int Biog, 72; Who's Who Among Authors and Journalists, 74. **MEMBERSHIPS** Orgn Am Historians; Am Acad Polit & Soc Sci. **RESEARCH** Modern, medieval and United States diplomatic and immigration history. **SELECTED PUBLICATIONS** Auth, Carl Sandburg: Literary Liberty Bell, Nat Park Serv, 71; auth, Furnishing Study for the Castle Clinton Officer's Quarters, 72, Nat Park Serv; art, The Czech Catholic immigration to the United States of America, Czech Catholics at the 41st International Eucharistic Congress Philadelphia, 76; art, George Washington, Encycl Southern History, La State Univ, 79. **CONTACT ADDRESS** 1007 Cliftonbrook Lane, Silver Spring, MD 20905. **EMAIL** Svejda@erols.com

SVINGEN, ORLAN J.
PERSONAL Born 07/21/1947, Glendive, MT, m, 1970, 3 children **DISCIPLINE** UNITED STATES HISTORY **EDUCATION** Univ Toledo, PhD,82. **CAREER** Assoc prof, Washington State Univ. **HONORS AND AWARDS** Ceremonial Blanket and Certificate of Awd, Pawnee Tribe of Oklahoma, 89; William F. Mullen Awd for Excellence in Teaching, 99. **RESEARCH** American Indian history, Public history. **SELECTED PUBLICATIONS** Auth, The Northern Cheyenne Indian Reservation 1877-1900, UP Colo, 94; ed, The History of the Idaho National Guard, ID Mil dept, 95 articles in Western Historical Quarterly, American Indian Quarterly, American Indian Culture and Research Journal, Montana: The Magazine of Western History. **CONTACT ADDRESS** Dept of History, Washington State Univ, 301 Wilson Hall, PO Box 644030, Pullman, WA 99164-4030. **EMAIL** svingen@wsu.edu

SWAIN, CHARLES W.
PERSONAL Born 07/30/1937, Des Moines, IA, m, 1958, 2 children **DISCIPLINE** HISTORY OF RELIGION **EDUCATION** State Univ Iowa, AB, 59; Brown Univ, PhD(relig), 65. **CAREER** Instr relig, Oberlin Col, 63-65; from asst prof to assoc prof, 65-77, Prof Relig, Fla State Univ, 77-, Soc Relig Higher Educ Asian relig fel, 67-68; vis lectr, Ctr Study World Relig, Harvard Univ, 67-68; Helmsley lectr, Brandeis Univ, 68. **MEMBERSHIPS** Am Acad Relig; AAUP; Soc Values Higher Educ. **RESEARCH** History of western religious thought; history of western philosophy; phenomenology of religion. **SELECTED PUBLICATIONS CONTACT ADDRESS** Dept of Relig, Florida State Univ, 600 W College Ave, Tallahassee, FL 32306-1096.

SWAIN, MARTHA HELEN
PERSONAL Born 06/21/1929, Cape Girardeau, MO, s **DISCIPLINE** HISTORY **EDUCATION** Miss State Univ, BS, 50; Vanderbilt Univ, MA, 54, PhD(hist), 75. **CAREER** Teacher social studies, pub schs, Miss & Fla, 50-69; from instr to asst prof hist, 74-78, chmn dept, 78-81, Assoc Prof, Tex Woman's Univ, 78-, Asst prof social studies, Fla State Univ, 63-64; Cornaro Prof Emerita, 95-; Prof, Mississippi St Univ, 95-98. **MEMBERSHIPS** AHA; Orgn Am Historians; Southern Hist Asn; Southern Asn Women Historians. **RESEARCH** New Deal; social welfare history; 20th century Mississippi. **SELECTED PUBLICATIONS** Auth, The lion and the fox: Franklin D Roosevelt and Senator Pat Harrison, J Miss Hist, 76; Pat Harrison and the Social Security Act, Southern Quart, 77; Joseph H Short, In: Dictionary of American Biography, Suppl V, Scribners, 77; The Harrison Education Bills, 1935-1941, Miss Quart, 78; Pat Harrison: The New Deal Years, Univ Press Miss, 78; Ellen Woodward, In: Notable American Women, Harvard Univ, 80; auth, Ellen S. Woodward: New Deal Advocate for Women, Univ Press MS, 95. "New Deal in Libraries." in Libraries and Culture, 30; "Dialogue on Southern Women's History" Journal of Women's History, 8. **CONTACT ADDRESS** Dept History-Cms 9707, Mississippi State Univ, PO Box 6130, Mississippi State, MS 39762. **EMAIL** mswain@ra.msstate.edu

SWANSON, MAYNARD WILLIAM
PERSONAL Born 09/04/1929, Worcester, MA, m, 1958, 3 children **DISCIPLINE** MODERN HISTORY, AFRICAN HISTORY **EDUCATION** Amherst Col, BA, 52; Harvard Univ, MA, 57, PhD(hist), 65. **CAREER** Lectr hist, Univ Natal, 62; instr, Yale Univ, 63-65, asst prof, 65-70; Assoc Prof Hist, Miami Univ, 70-, Morse fel, Yale Concilium Int Studies, 67-68, travel & res grants, 69; Am Philos Soc travel & res grant, 69; Soc Sci Res Coun & Am Coun Learned Soc res grant, SAfrica, 74; vis lectr, Univ Natal, 82. **MEMBERSHIPS** AHA; African Studies Asn. **RESEARCH** South Africa, history of native policy; race relations; urban history. **SELECTED PUBLICATIONS** Auth, South West Africa, in trust, 1915-1939, In: Britain and Germany in Africa: Imperial Rivalry and Colonial Rule, Yale Univ, 67; Urban origins of separate development, Race, 68; Reflections on urban history in South Africa, In: Focus on Cities, Inst Social Res, Univ Natal, 70; The Durban System: Roots of urban apartheid in colonial Natal, African Studies, 12/76; The sanitation syndrome: Bubonic Plaque and urban native policy in the Cape Colony, 1900-1909, J African Hist, 77; The Views of Mahlathi: Writings of a Black South African, Natal Univ Press, 82; The Making Of Modern South-Africa--Conquest, Segregation And Apartheid, J Of African Hist, Vol 36, 95. **CONTACT ADDRESS** Dept of Hist, Miami Univ, Oxford, OH 45056.

SWANSON, RANDY
PERSONAL Born 03/13/1953, Chicago, IL, m, 1974, 2 children **DISCIPLINE** ARCHITECTURE **EDUCATION** Univ Ill-Urbana-Champaign, BS, 76, MA, 81; Univ Penn, MS, 87, PhD, 93. **CAREER** Archit, Sole Proprietor; assoc Prof Archit, UNC-Charlotte. **MEMBERSHIPS** HCARB; SHOT; SBSE; SAH **RESEARCH** Hist and theory technology and design; scientific facilities. **SELECTED PUBLICATIONS** Auth, Two Directions of Technical Innovation in Late 19th Century Laboratory Design, Architecture: Design Implementation, ACSA Press, 93; Changing Concepts of Early Twentieth-Century Laboratory Design: Technological Risk and Innovation at New Haven, Ct and Blackley, England, Int Conf London, 96; l'Observatoire de Paris, (1667-1672) by Claude Perrault: A Preliminary Report of an Architectural Examination, Nat Conf Baltimore, 98; coauth, "Educational Research in the 3rd Year Design Curriculum: Visualizing the Design Sciene Process with Information Technology," for International ACSA/ARCC Science and Technology Conference, Universite de Montreal, 99; coauth, Undergraduate Research Training in Design: Using Issue Dualities and Concept Modeling, for Research by Design, Internationall Conference EAAE/AEEA and Delft Univ of Technology, 00; coauth, Developing A Process-Oriented Assessment System for Architectural Design Studio Courses, Seattle, 01. **CONTACT ADDRESS** College of Architecture, Univ of No Carolina, Charlotte, Charlotte, NC 28223. **EMAIL** RSWANSON@EMAIL.UNCC.EDU

SWART, PAULA
PERSONAL Born The Hague, Netherlands **DISCIPLINE** ASIAN STUDIES **EDUCATION** Lang Inst, Beijing, Chinese Lang, 78; Univ Leiden, BA, 79; Univ Nanjing, China, 79; Univ Amsterdam, MA, 82. **CAREER** Participant, res proj Witte Leeuw, 79-81; res asst, Montreal Mus Fine Arts, 83-89; Curator, Asian Studies, Vancouver Museum, 89-. **HONORS AND AWARDS** Undergrad Scholar, 74-77; Holland China Exchange Scholar, 77-78; Grad Scholar, 79-81, Dutch Gov. **MEMBERSHIPS** Japan Sword Appreciation Soc; Can Soc Asian Art; Am Museum Asn. **SELECTED PUBLICATIONS** Auth, Bronze Carriages from the Tomb of China's First Emperor, in Archaeol, Vol 37, 84; auth, Art from the Roof of the World: Tibet, 89; coauth, In Search of Old Nanking, 82; coauth, Chinese Jade Stone for the Emperors, 86. **CONTACT ADDRESS** Curator Asian Studies, Vancouver Mus, 1100 Chestnut St, Vancouver, BC, Canada V6J 3J9.

SWARTZ, MARVIN
PERSONAL Born 07/28/1941, Boston, MA, m, 1984, 2 children **DISCIPLINE** HISTORY MODERN EUROPE **EDUCATION** AB, Princeton Uni, 63; MA, PhD, Yale Univ, 64, 69. **CAREER** Inst Hist, Univ Mass, Boston, 67-68; Asst Prof, Assoc Prof, Prof Hist, Univ Mass, Amherst, 70-. **HONORS AND AWARDS** Danforth Fel; Woodrow Wilson Fel; Univ Mass for Res and Tchg. **RESEARCH** Europe, 1870-1945; British Poli and Foreign Policy; the Holocaust. **SELECTED PUBLICATIONS** The Union of Democratic Control in British Politics during the First Workd War, Oxford: Clarendon Press, 71; Disraeli's Reminiscences, London: Hamish Hamilton, 75; NY: Stein & Day, co-ed, 76; The Politics of British Foreign Policy in the Era of Disraeli and Gladstone, London: Macmillan; NY: St Martin's Press, 85. **CONTACT ADDRESS** Dept Hist, Univ of Massachusetts, Amherst, Herter Hall, Amherst, MA 01003. **EMAIL** mswartz@history.umass.edu

SWEARER, DONALD K.
PERSONAL Born 08/02/1934, Wichita, KS, m, 1964, 2 children **DISCIPLINE** HISTORY OF RELIGION **EDUCATION** Princeton Univ, BA, cum laude 56, MA, 65, PhD, 67; Yale Univ, BD, 62, STM, 63. **CAREER** Assoc Prof 70-75, Prof 75-, Eugene M Lang Res Prof 87-92, Charles and Harriet Cox McDowell Prof of Religion 92-, Swarthmore College; Instr, Asst Prof 65-70, Oberlin College. **HONORS AND AWARDS** Phi Beta Kappa; Lent Fel; 3 NEH Fels; Fulbright Fel; Guggenheim Fel; 2 Fulbright Fels. **MEMBERSHIPS** AAAS; AAR; ASSR; SBCS; AAUP. **RESEARCH** Buddhism; Comparative Religious Ethics. **SELECTED PUBLICATIONS** Auth, Holism and the Fate of the Earth, Rel and Ecology: Forging an Ethic Across Traditions, forthcoming; Center and Periphery: Buddhism and Politics in Modern Thailand, Buddhism and Politics in Modern Asia, ed, Ian Harris, Cassell's 98; Buddhist Virtue Voluntary Poverty and Extensive Benevolence, J of Rel Ethics, 98; The Worldliness of Buddhism, Wilson Qtly, 97; Bhikkhu Buddhadasa's Interpretation of the Buddha, J of the American Acad of Religion, 96; Hypostasizing the Buddha: Buddha: Image Consecration in Northern Thailand, Hist of Religions, 95; coauth, The Legend of Queen Cama, Camadevivamsa, Albany NY, SUNY Press, 98; auth, The Buddhist World of Southeast Asia, Albany, SUNY Press, 95; Ethics Wealth and Salvation, A Study in Buddhist Social Ethics, coed, Columbia, Univ S Carolina Press, pbk ed, 92. **CONTACT ADDRESS** Dept of Religion, Swarthmore Col, Swarthmore, PA 19081. **EMAIL** dsweare1@swarthmore.edu

SWEENEY, JERRY K.
PERSONAL Born 07/13/1941, Pratt, KS, w, 3 children **DISCIPLINE** HISTORY **EDUCATION** Ft. Hays Kansas State Col, BA, 62; Kansas State Univ, MA, 67; Kent State Univ, Phd, 70. **CAREER** Prof and Head, Dept of History, South Dakota State Univ, 70-. **HONORS AND AWARDS** Teacher of the Year, College of Arts and Science, 76, 98, 00; Danforth Assoc, 77-85, ROTC Workshop in the Military Art, 81; Teacher of the Year, College of Arts & Science, 76; Danforth Assoc, 77-85; Senior Sabbatical, 78, 87 & 94; ROTC Workshop in the Military Art, 81; Scholar-Diplomat Seminar, US Dept of State, 82;

Administrative Assoc, College of Home Economics, SDSU, 87; Teacher of the Year, Arts & Science, 98. **MEMBERSHIPS** Society of Historians for American Foreign Relations; Conference Group on Modern Portugal and Society of Military History. **RESEARCH** Portuguese-American Diplomatic Relations, Hugh James Campbell; Eleanor roosevelt Institute, 75; Amer Council of Learned Societies, 76 & 78; Harry S Truman Foundation, 78; S.D.S.U. Research Fund, 78, 80 & 90; Danforth Foundation, 80; S.D. Committee on the Humanities, 83, 85, 86, 87 & 91. **SELECTED PUBLICATIONS** Auth, "Flint's Island," Masterplots II: Juvenile and Young Adult Fiction," Salem Press, 91; auth, "Gary's Player," The Twentieth Century: Great Athletes," Salem Press, 92; auth, "Bjorn Borg," The Twentieth Century: Great Athletes, Salem Press, 92; auth, "Casey Tibbs," the Twentieth Century: Great Athletes, Salem Press, 92; auth, "Corporatism comes to Paraguay and the Americas," Great Events from History II: Human Rights, Vol. 1, Salem Press, 92; auth, "East Timor Declares Independence, But Is Annexed by Indonesia," Great Events from History II: History Rights, Vol. II, Salem Press, 92; auth, "Rita Mae Brown," Identities and Issues in Literature," Salem Press, 97; auth, "Southern Discomfort," Identities and Issues in Literature," Salem Press, 97; auth, "Rubyfruit Jungle," Identities and Issues in Literature," Salem Press, 97; auth, Unwanted Alliance: Portugal and the US," The Romance of History: Essays in Honor of Lawrence S. Kaplan, Kent State Univ Press, 97. **CONTACT ADDRESS** Dept History, So Dakota State Univ, PO Box 504, Brookings, SD 57007-0001. **EMAIL** sweeney_57006@yahoo.com

SWEENEY, KEVIN
DISCIPLINE COLONIAL AMERICAN HISTORY **EDUCATION** Yale Univ, PhD, 86. **CAREER** Instr, Amherst Col, 89. **RESEARCH** The hist and material cult of 17th and 18th-century New Engl. **SELECTED PUBLICATIONS** His writing has focused on the hist and material cult of seventeenth and eighteenth-century New Engl. **CONTACT ADDRESS** Amherst Col, Amherst, MA 01002-5000.

SWEET, PAUL ROBINSON
PERSONAL Born 03/14/1907, Willow Grove, PA, m, 1937, 2 children **DISCIPLINE** HISTORY **EDUCATION** DePauw Univ, AB, 29; Univ Wis, PhD, 34. **CAREER** Mem fac, Birmingham-Southern Col, 34-36, Bates Col, 36-46, Univ Chicago, 46-47 & Colby Col, 47-48; US ed-in-chief, Documents Ger Foreign Policy, 18-1945, US Dept State, 48-59, first secy polit affairs, Am Embassy, Bonn, 59-63, consul gen, US Consulate Gen, Stuttgart, 63-67; prof hist, 68-76, Emer Prof Hist, Mich State Univ, 76-, Chmn Atlantic affairs sem, Foreign Serv Inst, US Dept State, 67-68. **MEMBERSHIPS** AHA **RESEARCH** Modern German and Austrian history; European diplomatic history. **SELECTED PUBLICATIONS** Coauth, The Tragedy of Austria, Gollancz, London, 48; Festschrift fur Heinrich Benedikt, Vienna, 57; auth, Friedrich von Gentz: Defender of the Old Order, Greenwood, 70; The historical writing of Heinrich von Srbik, Hist & Theory, 70; Wilhelm von Humboldt (1767-1835): His legacy to the historian, Centennial Rev, 71; Young Wilhelm von Humboldt's writings reconsidered, J Hist Ideas, 73; Wilhelm von Humboldt: A Biography 1767-1808, Ohio State Univ, Vol I, 78; The Windsor File + British Government Efforts To Suppress Publication Of Documents From The German-Foreign-Ministry-Archives, Historian, Vol 59, 97; Fichte And The Jews--A Case Of Tension Between Civil-Rights And Human-Rights, German Studies Rev, Vol 16, 93. **CONTACT ADDRESS** Dept of Hist, Michigan State Univ, East Lansing, MI 48824.

SWEETS, JOHN FRANK
PERSONAL Born 07/18/1945, Knoxville, TN, m, 1992, 1 child **DISCIPLINE** MODERN EUROPEAN HISTORY **EDUCATION** Fla State Univ, BA, 67; Duke Univ, MA, 69, PhD, 72. **CAREER** Asst prof, 72-77, assoc prof, 77-84, Prof Hist, Univ Kans, 85-; Ed, Proc Western Soc Fr Hist, 81-; NEH fel, 78-79 & 87-88 **MEMBERSHIPS** AHA; Soc Fr Hist Studies; Western Soc Fr Hist. **RESEARCH** Social and political history of 20th century France; lacemakers of LePuy in 19th Century; resistance and occupation in France 1940-1944; Vichy France. **SELECTED PUBLICATIONS** Auth, The Politics of Resistance in France, Northern Ill Univ Press, 76; Choices in Vichy France, Oxford Univ Press, 86 & 94; Clermont-Ferrand a l'heure allemande, Plon, 96 **CONTACT ADDRESS** Dept of Hist, Univ of Kansas, Lawrence, Lawrence, KS 66045-0001. **EMAIL** jfsweets@falcon.cc.ukans.edu

SWERDLOW, AMY
PERSONAL Born New York, NY, 4 children **DISCIPLINE** AMERICAN HISTORY **EDUCATION** New York Univ, BA, 63; Sarah Lawrence Col, MA, 73. **CAREER** Assoc dir, 73-76, Prof Women's Hist, Sarah Lawrence Col, 81-, Fel, Rutgers Univ & Woodrow Wilson Found, 80. **MEMBERSHIPS** AHA; Orgn Am Historians. **RESEARCH** Women's history; peace movements. **SELECTED PUBLICATIONS** Coauth, Household & Kin: Families in Flux, Feminist Press, McGraw Hill, 81; co-ed, Class, Race & Sex: The Dynamics of Control, G K Hall, 83; Ladies Day at the Capitol, Women Strike for Peace, Feminist Studies, fall 82; Polite Protesters--The Amn Peace Movement Of The 1980s, J Of Am Hist, Vol 81, 95; The Women And The Warriors--The US Section Of The Womens-International-League-For-Peace-And-Freedom, 1911-1946, J Of Am Hist, Vol 83, 96. **CONTACT ADDRESS** Dept Women's Hist, Sarah Lawrence Col, 80 CPW, New York, NY 10023.

SWETNAM, SUSAN
PERSONAL Born 06/15/1950, Abingdon, PA, m, 1985 **DISCIPLINE** ENGLISH LITERATURE, AMERICAN LITERATURE, AMERICAN STUDIES **EDUCATION** Univ Mich, PhD, 79. **CAREER** Prof of Eng, Idaho State Univ. **HONORS AND AWARDS** Rackham Scholar, Univ of Mich; Phi Beta Kappa; Phi Kappa Phi; Distinguished Teacher, Idaho State Univ; Distinguished Public Servant, Idaho State Univ; Outstanding Res, Idaho State Univ. **RESEARCH** Fiction and Nonfiction narrative; personal essay; Intermountain West stud. **SELECTED PUBLICATIONS** Auth, Lives of the Saints in Southeast Idaho: An Introduction to Mormon Pioneer Life Story Writing; pubs in Tough Paradise, Idaho and the American West, Journal of the West, Frontiers: A Journal of Women Studies, and Northwest Folklore; auth, Home Muontains: Reflections from a Western Middle Age, Washington State Univ Press, 00; auth, Ring of Fire: Writers of the Greater Yellowstone Region, Rendezvous, many popular national and regional magazines. **CONTACT ADDRESS** Dept of English and Philosophy, Idaho State Univ, Pocatello, ID 83209. **EMAIL** swetsusa@isu.edu

SWIDLER, LEONARD
PERSONAL Born 01/06/1929, Sioux City, IA, m, 1957, 2 children **DISCIPLINE** RELIGION; HISTORY **EDUCATION** St Norbert Col, BA, 50; Marquette Univ, MA, 55; Univ Tubingen, STL, 59; Univ Wis, PhD(hist), 61. **CAREER** From asst prof to assoc prof hist, Duquesne Univ, 60-66; Prof Relig, Temple Univ, 66-, Founder & co-ed, J Ecumenical Studies, 64-; mem, Comt Educ for Ecumenism & Presby/ Reformed and Roman Cath Consultation, 65-; fel, Inst Ecumenical & Cult Res, 68-69; Fulbright res grant, Ger, 72-73; guest prof Cath & Protestant theol, Univ Tubingen, 72-73; guest prof Philos, Nankai, Tianjin, 87; Co-Founder/Dir, Global Dialogue Institute, 95-. **HONORS AND AWARDS** LLD, La Salle Col, 77. **MEMBERSHIPS** Am Soc Church Hist; Am Acad Relig; Cath Theol Soc, Am; Church Hist Soc. **RESEARCH** Inter-religious dialogue; modern church history; women in religion and society; global ethics. **SELECTED PUBLICATIONS** Ed, Ecumenism, the Spirit and Worship, 66; auth, The Ecumenical Vanguard, 66; Freedom in the Church, 69; coauth, Bishops and People, 71; Isj en Isjah, 73; auth, Women in Judaism, 76; Blood Witness for Peace and Unity, 77; coauth, Women Priests, 77; Yeshua: A Model for Moderns, 87; After the Absolute, 90; Toward a Catholic Constitution, 96; THEORIA-PRAXIS, 98; auth, The Study of Religion in the Age of Dialogue, 00. **CONTACT ADDRESS** Dept of Religion, Temple Univ, 1114 W Berks St, Philadelphia, PA 19122-6090. **EMAIL** dialogue@vm.temple.edu

SWIERENGA, ROBERT PETER
PERSONAL Born 06/10/1935, Chicago, IL, m, 1956, 5 children **DISCIPLINE** AMERICAN HISTORY **EDUCATION** Calvin Col, AB, 57; Northwestern Univ, MA, 58; State Univ Iowa, PhD(hist), 65. **CAREER** Instr high sch, Iowa, 58-61; instr hist, Calvin Col, 61-62, asst prof, 65-68; assoc prof, 68-72, Prof Hist, Kent State Univ, 72-, Am Coun Learned Soc grant-in-aid, 67-68; managing ed, Soc Sci Hist, 76; Fulbright-Hays Silver Opportunity res scholar, Netherlands, 76; Am Coun Learned Soc fel, 81. **MEMBERSHIPS** Orgn Am Historians; Econ Hist Asn; Agr Hist Soc; Soc Sci Hist Asn; Immigration Hist Soc. **RESEARCH** American land, immigrant, and quantitative history. **SELECTED PUBLICATIONS** Auth, Bright Radical Star--Black-Freedom and White Supremacy on the Hawkeye Frontier, Agricultural Hist, Vol 68, 94; Evangelicals and Politics in Antebellum America, Civil War Hist, Vol 40, 94; Untitled, J Am Hist, Vol 83, 96; Odyssey-Of-Woe--The Journey of the Immigrant Ship April from Amsterdam to New-Castle, 1817-1818, Penn Magazine Hist Biography, Vol 0118, 94; Out on the Wind--Poles and Danes in Lincoln County, Minnesota, 1880-1905, Historian, Vol 55, 93; Born in the Country--A History Of Rural America, J Am Hist, Vol 83, 96; Strategic Factors in 19th-Century American Economic-History--A Volume to Honor Robert Fogel, J Interdisciplinary Hist, Vol 24, 94. **CONTACT ADDRESS** Dept of Hist, Kent State Univ, Kent, OH 44242.

SWIETEK, FRANCIS ROY
PERSONAL Born 04/17/1946, La Salle, IL, s **DISCIPLINE** MEDIEVAL HISTORY, LATIN **EDUCATION** St John's Univ, Minn, BA, 68; Univ Ill, Urbana-Champaign, MA, 71, PhD(hist), 78. **CAREER** Libr manuscript cataloguer & asst to dir 8 St John's Univ, Minn, 71-74; Asst Prof Hist, Univ Dallas, 78-. **MEMBERSHIPS** Medieval Acad Am; AHA; AAUP. **RESEARCH** Medieval intellectual and ecclesiastical history; Medieval Latin literature; Latin paleography. **SELECTED PUBLICATIONS** Auth, Ab Antiquo Alterius Ordinis Fuerit: Alexander III on the Reception of Savigny into the Cistercian Order, Rev Hist, Vol 89; Trans, Bernard of Clairvaux, The Sentences, Cist Faths Series 55, Kalamazoo, 00. **CONTACT ADDRESS** Dept of Hist, Univ of Dallas, Irving, TX 75061. **EMAIL** swietek@acad.udallas.edu

SWIFT, MARY GRACE
PERSONAL Born 08/03/1927, Bartlesville, OK **DISCIPLINE** RUSSIAN HISTORY & GOVERNMENT **EDUCATION** Creighton Univ, BS, 56, MA, 60; Notre Dame Univ, PhD(Soviet area studies), 67. **CAREER** Assoc Prof Hist, Loyola Univ, LA, 66- **HONORS AND AWARDS** De la Torre Bueno Prize, 73. **MEMBERSHIPS** Am Asn Advan Slavic Studies. **RESEARCH** Dance history, especially Russian ballet. **SELECTED PUBLICATIONS** Auth, Sisters in Arms--Catholic Nuns Through 2 Millennia, New Orleans Rev, Vol 23, 97. **CONTACT ADDRESS** Dept of Hist, Loyola Univ, New Orleans, New Orleans, LA 70118.

SWINNEY, EVERETTE
PERSONAL Born 09/09/1933, Lima, OH, m, 1953, 4 children **DISCIPLINE** AMERICAN HISTORY **EDUCATION** OH Northern Univ, BA, 55; PA State Univ, MA, 57; Univ TX, PhD, 66. **CAREER** Grad asst, PA State Univ, 55-57; from instr to assoc prof, 57-67, prof hist, Southwest TX State Univ, 67-96, prof emeritus, 96-, chmn dept, 67-80. **MEMBERSHIPS** Orgn Am Historians; Southern Hist Asn. **RESEARCH** Civil War and reconstruction; computers and hist; historiography. **SELECTED PUBLICATIONS** Auth, Enforcing the Fifteenth Amendment, 1870-1877, J Southern Hist, 5/62; United States v Powell Clayton, Ark Hist Quart, summer 67, Suppressing the Klu Klux Klan: Re Enforcement of the Reconstruction Amendments 1870-1877, garland pub, 87. **CONTACT ADDRESS** Dept of Hist, Southwest Texas State Univ, 601 University Dr, San Marcos, TX 78666-4685. **EMAIL** es08@swt.edu

SWINTH, KIRSTEN
PERSONAL Born 06/09/1964, Pittsburgh, PA, m, 1994, 1 child **DISCIPLINE** HISTORY **EDUCATION** Stanford Univ, BA, 86; Yale Univ, PhD, 95. **CAREER** Teaching Fel to Instructor, Yale Univ, 89-91; Adj Prof, Univ Md, 92; Visiting Asst Prof, George Washington Univ, 95-97; Asst Prof, Fordham Univ, 97-. **HONORS AND AWARDS** Ames Fund Grant, 98-00; John Paul Getty Fel, 97-98; Spec Dissertation Fel, Yale Univ, 92-93; John F. Enders Res Grant, 92; Harry S. Truman Scholarship, 89-90; Fel, Yale Univ, 88-91; Phi Beta Kappa, 85. **SELECTED PUBLICATIONS** Auth, "Metropolitan Lives: The Ashcan Artists and their New York," The Public Historian, (96): 132-134; auth, "Florence Levy," in Jewish Women in America, Carlson Pub, 97; auth, "Cultural Leadership in America: Art Matronage and Patronage," American Studies Intl, 99; auth, "Emily Sartain and Harriet Judd Sartain: Female Influence and A Community of Women Professionals," in The Sartain Family and Philadelphia's Cultural Landscape, Temple Univ Press, 00; auth, "The American Century at the Whitney Museum of American Art," American Quarterly, 00; auth, Painting Professionals: Women Artists and the Development of American Art, 1870-1920, Univ NC Press, 00. **CONTACT ADDRESS** Dept Hist, Fordham Univ, 441 E Fordham Rd, Bronx, NY 10458-5149. **EMAIL** Swinth@fordham.edu

SWINTON, GEORGE
PERSONAL Born 04/17/1917, Vienna, Austria **DISCIPLINE** HISTORY OF ART **EDUCATION** McGill Univ, BA, 46; Montreal Sch Art Design, 46-47; Art Students' League, 49-50. **CAREER** Cur, Saskatoon Art Ctr, 47-49; instr, Smith Col, 50-53; artist-in-res, Queen's Univ, 53-54; prof art, Univ Man, 54-74; prof, 73-81, adj prof, 81-85, PROF EMER ART HISTORY, CARLETON UNIV, 86-; vis prof, Simon Fraser Univ, 72; vis prof, Univ Wisconsin, 74; vis prof, Univ Leningrad, 81. **HONORS AND AWARDS** Centennial Medal, 67; mem, Order of Can, 79; Canada 125 Medal; LLD(hon), Univ Man, 87. **SELECTED PUBLICATIONS** Auth, Eskimo/Sculpture/Esquimaude, 65; auth, Sculpture of the Eskimo, 72, 2nd ed 75, 3rd ed 82; auth, Sculpture Esquimaude, 76; auth, Sculpture of the Inuit, 92; coauth, What is Good Design?, 54; illusr/des, Red River of the North, 69. **CONTACT ADDRESS** School for Studies in Art & Culture, Carleton Univ, 1125 Colonel By Drive, Ottawa, ON, Canada K1S 5B6.

SWINTON, KATHERINE E.
PERSONAL Born 08/14/1950, East York, ON, Canada **DISCIPLINE** LAW, HISTORY **EDUCATION** Univ Alta, BA, 71; Osgoode Hall Law Sch, York Univ, LLB, 75; Yale Univ, LLM, 77. **CAREER** Parliamentary intern, House of Commons, 71-72; law clerk, Supreme Court Can, 75-76; asst prof, Osgoode Hall Law Sch, 77-79; asst prof, 79-82, assoc prof, 82-87, prof fac law, Univ Toronto, 88-97; JUSTICE, ONTARIO COURT (GENERAL DIVISION), 97-. **SELECTED PUBLICATIONS** Auth, The Supreme Court and Canadian Federalism: The Laskin-Dickson Years, 90; co-ed, Studies in Labour Law, 83; co-ed, Competing Constitutional Visions: The Meech Lake Accord, 88; co-ed, Rethinking Federalism, 95. **CONTACT ADDRESS** Ontario Court, 361 University Ave, Toronto, ON, Canada M5G 1T3.

SYLIOWICZ, JOSEPH S.
PERSONAL Born 12/07/1931, Belgium, m, 1960, 2 children **DISCIPLINE** INTERNATIONAL STUDIES **EDUCATION** BA Univ of Denver, 53; MA School of Adv Intl Studies, John Hopkins Univ, 55; PhD Columbia Univ, 61. **CAREER** Univ MD, Extension Div, 60; Hunter Col, 61-62; Brooklyn Col, 61-64; Long Island Univ, 66; Univ Mich 80; Univ Utah, 80; Oxford

Univ, Michaelmas Term, 84; founder, Intermodal Trans Inst and Prof, Graduate School of Intl Studies, Univ Denver, present. **HONORS AND AWARDS** Outstanding Educator of the Year, Colo Transportation Comm, 99; Intl Awd for Dci and Ethics in Trans Res, Alliance for Trans Res, 97; Outstanding Scholar, Burlington Northern Found Awd, 86; Sr Assoc St Anthony's Col and Fel Dept of External Studies, Oxford Univ, 84-85; Fulbright Sr Res Fellowship, 83; Soc Sci Res Council, 68-69. **MEMBERSHIPS** Phi Beta Kappa; Pi Gamma Mu; Tau Kappa Alpha; Phi Delta Rho; Am Men of Sci; Who's Who in the West; Dictionary of Intl Bio; Intl Scholars Dir; Intl Auth; Writer Who's Who. **RESEARCH** Transportation and sustainable development; Middle East education. **SELECTED PUBLICATIONS** Denver International Airport: Lessons Learned, McGraw Hill,96, Co-auth; Politics, Technology and Development: Decision Making in the Turkish Iron and Steel Industry, NY: St Martins Press and London: The Manmillan Press Ltd/St Antony's College Series, 91; Education in L C Brown, ed, The Imperial Legacy: The Ottoman Imprint on the Balkans and the Middle East, NY, Coumbia Univ Press, 95; Education and Political Development in M Heper ed, Politics in the 3rd Turkish Republic, Westview, 93; Revisiting Transportation Planning and Decision Making Theory, co-auth, 74. **CONTACT ADDRESS** Graduate School of Intl Studies, Univ of Denver, Denver, CO 80210. **EMAIL** JSZYLIOW@DU.EDU

SYLLA, EDITH DUDLEY
PERSONAL Born 08/15/1941, Cleveland, OH, m, 1963, 2 children **DISCIPLINE** HISTORY OF SCIENCE, MEDIEVAL PHILOSOPHY **EDUCATION** Radcliffe Col, AB, 63; Harvard Univ, AM, 64, PhD(hist of sci), 71. **CAREER** Instr social studies, 68-70, asst prof hist, 70-75, assoc prof, 75-81, Prof Hist, NCar State Univ, 81-; Reviewer, Zentralblatt fur Math, 73. **HONORS AND AWARDS** NSF res grant, Oxford, Eng, 75-76; fel, Andrew D White Ctr for Humanities, Cornell Univ, 78-79, Inst Advan Studies, Princeton, 82-83. **MEMBERSHIPS** Hist Sci Soc; Mediaeval Acad Am; AAAS; AHA; Int Soc Study Mediaeval Philos. **RESEARCH** History of 14th century philosophy; medieval logic, mathematics and science. **SELECTED PUBLICATIONS** Auth, Medieval quantifications of qualities: The Merton School, Arch Hist Exact Sci, 71; Medieval concepts of the latitude of forms: The Oxford calculators, Arch Hist Doctrinale et Litteraire Moyen Age, 74; co-ed, The Cultural Context of Medieval Learning, Reidel, 75; auth, Autonomous and handmaiden science: St Thomas Aquinas and William of Ockham on the physics of the eucharist, In: The Cultural Context of Medieval Learning, Reidel, 75; coauth, Richard Swineshead, In: Dict of Scientific Biography (vol 13), Scribner's, 75; The science of motion, In: Science in the Middle Ages, Univ Chicago. **CONTACT ADDRESS** Dept of Hist, No Carolina State Univ, Box 8108, Raleigh, NC 27695. **EMAIL** edith_sylla@ncsu.edu

SYLVESTER, JOHN ANDREW
PERSONAL Born 12/20/1935, Springfield, MA **DISCIPLINE** UNITED STATES HISTORY & DIPLOMACY **EDUCATION** Harvard Univ, AB, 57; Univ Wis, MA, 59; PhD(hist), 67. **CAREER** U.S. Army, 58-62; asst prof, 66-70, assoc prof Hist, Okla State Univ, 70-95, retired. **HONORS AND AWARDS** Three awards for teaching from student groups. **MEMBERSHIPS** Orgn Am Historians; Soc Historians Am Foreign Rel. **RESEARCH** United States History; United States Foreign Relations; World War II. **SELECTED PUBLICATIONS** Auth, "Who is Still Wearing the Emperor's Clothes?: The Unwitting Radical as a Marxist-Leninist," Coninuity: A Journal of History 17 (93); auth, "Taft, Dulles and Ike--New Faces For 1952," Mid-Am Hist Rev 76 (94); auth, "On the Teaching of America Diplomatic History: A Consideration of Values in American Foreign Relations," Free Inquiry in Creative Sociology 23 (95) **CONTACT ADDRESS** 4 Belden Court, Agawam, MA 01001.

SYLWESTER, HAROLD JAMES
PERSONAL Born 09/23/1934, Roseburg, OR, m, 1965, 2 children **DISCIPLINE** AMERICAN DIPLOMATIC HISTORY **EDUCATION** Concordia Teachers Col, BS, 56: Univ Ore, MEd, 60; Univ Kans, MA, 64, PhD(Am hist), 70. **CAREER** Instr Am hist, Concordia Teachers Col, 64-65; asst prof, 69-75, Assoc Prof Hist, Cent MO State Univ, 75-; Prof of Hist, 84-99. **HONORS AND AWARDS** Res grant, Harry S Truman Inst, 70, Kansas City Regional Coun Higher Educ, 70 & Am Philos Soc, 71; US Dept Educ grant, 81-82; NEH fel, 79, 88; Constitution - Bicentennial Commission, 89; Fel, Mid-America Japan in the school, U.S.-Japan Found, Univ Kans, 92; Fulbright-Hayes, Russia and the Baltic States, 94. **MEMBERSHIPS** Orgn Am Historians; Soc for Hist of Am For Policy; Nat Coun for the Soc Studies; Concordia Hist Inst; Nat Coun of Geog Educ. **RESEARCH** Focus on the Truman administration; public opinion and American foreign policy; relationship between domestic developments and foreign affairs. **SELECTED PUBLICATIONS** Auth, The Swedish Lutherans on the Delaware and their interest in schools, Concordia Hist Quart, 7/67; The Kansas press and the coming of the Spanish-American War, Historian, 2/69. **CONTACT ADDRESS** Dept of History, Central Missouri State Univ, 4509 Range Ct, Lawrence, KS 66049. **EMAIL** jksyl@sunflower.com

SYMCOX, GEOFFREY
PERSONAL Born 11/08/1938, Swindon, England, m, 1971, 2 children **DISCIPLINE** HISTORY **EDUCATION** Oxford Univ, BA, 60; Univ Stockholm, MA, 62; UCLA, PhD, 67. **CAREER** Asst prof to prof, UCLA, 69-. **HONORS AND AWARDS** Guggenheim Fel, 77-78; Res fel, Am Philos Soc; Fel, Max Planck Inst. **MEMBERSHIPS** Am Hist Asn; Urban Hist Asn; World Hist Asn; Soc for Court Studies; Deputazione Subalpina di Storia Patria; Soc for Italian Hist; Soc di Studi Valdesi. **RESEARCH** French and Italian History 1550-1800, especially Piedmont; History of architecture and urban planning; State institutions and Armed forces. **SELECTED PUBLICATIONS** Auth, Victor Amadeus II. Absolutism in the Savoyard State 1675-1730, London, 83. **CONTACT ADDRESS** Dept Hist, Univ of California, Los Angeles, 6265 Bunche, PO Box 951473, Los Angeles, CA 90095-1473. **EMAIL** symcox@history.ucla.edu

SYMEONOGLOU, SARANTIS
PERSONAL Born 02/14/1937, Athens, Greece, m, 1965, 2 children **DISCIPLINE** CLASSICAL ARCHEOLOGY **EDUCATION** Univ Athens, Greece, BA, 61; Columbia Univ, PhD(archaeol), 71. **CAREER** Asst cur archaeol, Greek Archaeol Serv, 63-66; asst prof, 69-76, Assoc Prof Archaeol, WA Univ, 77-, Field dir excavation, Columbia Univ Archaeol Exped, 70-74; WA Univ res fel archaeol, 73-74; Am Philos Soc fel archaeol, 76; Founder and Dir, Odyssey Project, 84-; Prof, 85-. **HONORS AND AWARDS** Nat Geographic Grants, excav Ithaka, 84-85; Packard Humanities inst, excav Ithaka, 98. **MEMBERSHIPS** Archaeol Inst Am; Asn Field Archaeol; Am Schs Oriental Res; Am Oriental Soc. **RESEARCH** Arch Soc Athens **SELECTED PUBLICATIONS** Auth, Excavations in Boeotia, 1965, 66; coauth, Antiquities and monuments of Boeotia, 67, Archaeologikon Deltion; auth, A chart of Minoan and Mycenaean pottery, Am J Archaeol, 70; Archaeological survey in the area of Phlamoudhi Cyprus, Report Dept Antiq Cyprus, 72; Thebes, Greece: an archaeological and sociological problem, Architectura, 72; coauth, Ancient Collections in WA Univ, WA Univ, 73; auth, Kadmeia I; Mycenaean Finds from Thebes, Greece, Studies Mediterranean Archaeol, 73; contribr, Excavations at Phlamoudhi & the form of the Sanctuary in Bronze Age Cyprus, Archaeol Cyprus, Recent Develop, 75; The Topography of Thebes, Princeton Univ Press, 85; The Island of Odysseus, in The Sciences, Nov-Dec, 88. **CONTACT ADDRESS** Dept of Art & Archaeol, Washington Univ, 1 Brookings Dr, Box 1189, Saint Louis, MO 63130-4899. **EMAIL** ssymeono@artsci.wustl.edu

SYMONDS, CRAIG LEE
PERSONAL Born 12/31/1946, Long Beach, CA, m, 1969, 1 child **DISCIPLINE** AMERICAN HISTORY **EDUCATION** Univ Calif, Los Angeles, BA, 67; Univ Fla, MA, 69, PhD, 76. **CAREER** Asst prof strategy, US Naval War Col, 74-75; from Asst Prof to Assoc Prof, 76-86, prof hist, US Naval Acad, 86-, Chair, Dept Hist, 88-92. **HONORS AND AWARDS** Teaching Excellence Awd, USNA, 88; John Lyman Book Awd, NASOH, 95 and 97; S.A. Cunningham Awd for Literary Achievement, 97; Research Excellence Awd, USNA, 98; Superior Civilian Service Awd (2 awards); Civilian Meritorious Service Awd. **MEMBERSHIPS** Am Mil Inst; US Naval Inst; North Am Soc Oceanic Hist; Soc Historians Early Am Repub. **RESEARCH** 19th century American Naval Policy; United States Civil War. **SELECTED PUBLICATIONS** Ed, Charleston Blockade, NNC Press, 76; auth, Navalists and Antinavalists, Univ Del Press, 80; ed, A Year on a Monitor, USC Press, 88; Civil War Reminiscences of William H. Parker, Naval Inst Press, 90; auth, Joseph E. Johnston: A Civil War Biography, W.W. Norton, 92; U.S. Naval Institute's Historical Atlas of the U.S. Navy, 95; Stonewall of the West: Patrick Cleburne and the Civil War, Univ Press Kans, 97; Confederate Admiral:The Life and Wars of Franklin Buchanan, Naval Institute Press, 99. **CONTACT ADDRESS** Dept of Hist, United States Naval Acad, Annapolis, MD 21402. **EMAIL** symonds@nadn.navy.mil

SYMONS, T. H. B.
PERSONAL Born 05/30/1929, Toronto, ON, Canada, m, 1963, 3 children **DISCIPLINE** MODERN HISTORY **EDUCATION** Univ Toronto, BA, 51; Oxford Univ, MA, 53. **CAREER** Instr mod hist & dean men, Trinity Col, Univ Toronto, 54-56, instr & dean, Devonshire House, 56-63; asst prof, 63-66, founding pres & vchancellor, 61-72, Assoc Prof to Vanier Prof Emer, Trent Univ, 66-, Charter mem, World Univ Serv Can; mem, Adv Comt Confederation to Prime Minister Ont, 65-72; chmn, Ministerial Comn Fr Lang Educ Ont, 71-72; chmn, Asn Commonwealth Univs, 71-72; chmn, Nat Comn Can Studies, 72-; mem, Ont Arts Coun, 74-76; chmn, Ont Human Rights Comn, 75-78; spec adv higher educ to Govt of Can, 76; mem, Can Coun, 76- **HONORS AND AWARDS** Officer of Order of Can, 76; lld, waterloo lutheran univ, 71, univ nb, 72, york univ, 73, trent univ, 75 & lawrentian univ, 77; du, univ ottawa, 74. **MEMBERSHIPS** Fel Royal Soc Arts; Can Hist Asn; Champlain Soc; Asn Can Studies US; fel Royal Soc Can. **RESEARCH** Canadian history and contemporary Canadian studies; local history; Canadian-American relations. **CONTACT ADDRESS** Symons Campus, Trent Univ, 1600 West Bank Dr, Peterborough, ON, Canada K9J 7B8.

SYMONS, VAN J.
PERSONAL Born 06/05/1945, Logan, UT, m, 1971, 5 children **DISCIPLINE** HISTORY **EDUCATION** Brigham Young Univ, AB, 70; Brown Univ, PhD, 75. **CAREER** Asst prof, Whittier Col, 74-78; vis Mansfield Prof, The Maureen and Mike Mansfield Center, Univ of Mont, 90-91; Asst to Full Prof of Hist, 78-, Dir of Asian Studies Prog, 78-90, Chemn of Hist Dept, Augustana Col, 83-86 & 92-95. **HONORS AND AWARDS** Board Chair, ASIANetwork, 97-98; Executive Dir, ASIANetwork 99-present; NEH summer inst, Univ of Mich, 94, Univ of Mont, 95. **MEMBERSHIPS** Asn for Asian Studies; ASIANetwork. **RESEARCH** Late Ming-Early Qing Chinese dynastic history. **SELECTED PUBLICATIONS** Co-ed, Asia in the undergraduate curriculum, M.E. Sharpa Inc., 00; Auth, Moral Judgment in War and Crimes Against Humanity, America's Wars in Asia: A Cultural Approach to Hist and Memory, M.E. Sharpe Inc., 98; Near the Vortex of the Storm: Ming Chinese Frontier Politics and the 1627 Manchu Invasion of Korea, Ch'ing-chu Cha-ch'I Ssu-ch'in chiao-shou pa-shih shou-ch'en hsueh-shu lun-wen chi, 95; Peace, War, and Trade Along the Great Wall: Nomadic-Chinese Interaction Through Two Millennia, Ind Univ Press, 89; Ch'ing Ginseng Management: Ch'ing Monopolies in Microcosm, Az State Univ, Center for Asian Studies, 81. **CONTACT ADDRESS** Dept of Hist, Augustana Col, Illinois, Rock Island, IL 61201. **EMAIL** ASAINetwork@Augustana.edu

SYNAN, VINSON
PERSONAL Born 12/01/1934, Hopewell, VA, m, 1960, 4 children **DISCIPLINE** CHURCH HISTORY **EDUCATION** Univ Richmond, BA; Univ Ga, MA, PhD. **CAREER** Dean; prof, 94. **MEMBERSHIPS** Soc for Pentecostal Studies, Founder. **RESEARCH** Pentecostal/charismatic movements. **SELECTED PUBLICATIONS** Auth, Emmanuel Col:The First Fifty Years, MA thesis, N Wash Press, 68; The Holiness-Pentecostal Movement in the U.S., PhD dissertation, Eerdmans, 71; The Old-Time Power: History of the Pentecostal Holiness Church, Advocate Press, 73; Charismatic Bridges, Word of Life, 74; Aspects of Pencostal/Charismatic Origins, Logos, 75; Azusa Street, Bridge Publ, 80; In the Latter Days, Servant, 85; The Twentieth-Century Pentecostal Explosion, Creation House, 87; Launching the Decade of Evangelization, N Amer Renewal Srv Comm, 90; Under His Banner: A History of the FGBMFI, Gift Publ, 92; The Spirit Said Grow, MARC, World Vision, 92; auth, The Century of the Holy Spirit, Thomas Nelson, 01. **CONTACT ADDRESS** Sch of Divinity, Regent Univ, 1000 Regent Univ Dr, Virginia Beach, VA 23464-9831. **EMAIL** vinssyn@regent.edu

SYNNOTT, MARCIA G.
PERSONAL Born 07/04/1939, Camden, NJ, m, 1979, 2 children **DISCIPLINE** HISTORY **EDUCATION** Radcliffe Col, AB, 61; Amherst, AM, 64; Univ of Mass, PhD, 74. **CAREER** Asst prof to prof, Univ of SC, 74-. **HONORS AND AWARDS** Fulbright Awd, Univ of Oslo, 88. **MEMBERSHIPS** AHA; OAH; S Hist Assoc; NCPH; Hist of Educ Soc. **RESEARCH** Higher education, anti-Semitism, desegregation, Southern women's history, historic site interpretation. **SELECTED PUBLICATIONS** Auth, The Half-Opened Door: Discrimination and Admissions at Harvard, Yale and Princeton 1970-1970 (74); auth, "Alice Spearman Wright: Curl Rights Apostle to South Carolinians", in Beyond Image and Convention, ed Janet Conjell et al (98)> **CONTACT ADDRESS** Dept Hist, Univ of So Carolina, Columbia, Columbia, SC 29225. **EMAIL** synnott@gwm.sc.edu

SYRETT, DAVID
PERSONAL Born 01/08/1939, White Plains, NY, m, 1962, 3 children **DISCIPLINE** BRITISH EIGHTEENTH CENTURY NAVAL HISTORY **EDUCATION** Columbia Univ, BA, 61, MA, 64; Univ London, PhD(hist), 66. **CAREER** Asst prof, 66-71, assoc prof, 71-80, Prof Hist, Queens Col, NY, 80- **MEMBERSHIPS** Navy Rec Soc, Eng; Royal Hist Soc; Soc Nautical Res; AHA. **RESEARCH** British naval history in the 18th century. **SELECTED PUBLICATIONS** Auth, Shipping and the American War, Univ London, 70; Siege and Capture of Havana, Navy Rec Soc, 70. **CONTACT ADDRESS** Dept of Hist, Queens Col, CUNY, 6530 Kissena Blvd, Flushing, NY 11367-1597.

SZABO, FRANZ A. J.
DISCIPLINE HISTORY **EDUCATION** Univ Montreal, BA; Univ Alberta, MA, 70; PhD, 76. **CAREER** Prof, Carleton Univ. **HONORS AND AWARDS** Barbara Jelavich prize, AAASS. **RESEARCH** Enlightened Absolutism in the Habsburg Monarchy. **SELECTED PUBLICATIONS** Auth, Kaunitz an dEnlightened Absolutism, 1753-1780, Cambridge Univ Press, 94; ed, Staaskanzler Wenzel Anton von Kaunitz-Rietberg, 1711-1794: Neue Perspektiven und Kuitur der europaischen Aufklarung, with Grete Klingenstein, Graz: Schnider Verlag, 96; ed, A History of the Austiran Migration to Canada, with Frederick C. Engelmann and Manfred Prokop, Ottawa: Carleton Univ Press, 96; ed, Austrian Immigration to Canada: Selected Essays, Ottawa: Carleton Univ Press, 96; ed, "Wenzel Anton Kaunitz-Rietberg und Seine Zeit: Bemerkungen zum 200, Todestag des Staatskanzlers," in Grete Klingenstein and Franz A.J. Szabo, eds., (Graz: Schnider Verlag 96): 6-28; ed,

"Reflections on the Austrian identity in the Old World and the New," in Frederick C. Englemann, Manfred Prokop and Franz A.J. Szabo, eds., A History of the Austrain migration to Cnaada, (Ottawa: Carleton Univ Press, 96): 7-23; auth, "Innere Staatsbildung und soziale Modernisierung: Uberschreiten von Grenzen?" Das Achzente Jahhundert und Osterreich, vol. XIII, (99): 31-48. **CONTACT ADDRESS** Dept of Hist, Carleton Univ, 1125 Colonel By Dr, Ottawa, ON, Canada K1S 5B6. **EMAIL** fszabo@ccs.carleton.ca

SZABO, JOYCE
DISCIPLINE ART **EDUCATION** Wittenberg Univ, BA, 73; Vanderbilt Univ, MA, 78; Univ NMex, PhD, 83. **CAREER** Assoc prof, Univ N Mex. **SELECTED PUBLICATIONS** Co-ed, "New Places and New Spaces: Nineteenth-Century Plains Art in Florida," New Mexico Archaeological Society Papers in Honor of J.J. Brody, Archaeological Society of New Mexico, 18, (92): 193-201; auth, "Howling Wolf: An Autobiography of a Plains Warrior-Artist," Allen Memorial Art Museum Bulletin 46:1, 92; auth, "Howling Wolf: An Autobiography of a Plains Warrior-Artist," Univ Art Museum, Gallery Guide, Univ of New Mexico, Albuquerque, 94; auth, "Chief Killer and a New Reality: Narration and Description in Fort Marion Art," American Indian Art Magazine 19:2, (9): 50-57; auth, "Sheilds and Lodges, Warriors and Chiefs: Kiowa Drawings as Historic Records," Ethnohistory 41:1, (94): 1-24; auth, "People of the Mimbres--Exhibition Review," Museum Anthropology, 18:3, (94): 61-64; auth, Howling Wold and the Hisotyr of Ledger Art, Univ of New Mexico Press, 94; ed, Plains Indian Drawings 1865-1935: Pages from a Visul History, New York: Harry N. Abrams, Inc., 96; auth, "Mapped Battles and Visual Narratives: The Arrest and Killing of Sitting Bull," American Indian Art Magazine 21:4, (96): 64-75. **CONTACT ADDRESS** Art Dept, Univ of New Mexico, Albuquerque, 1805 Roma NE, Albuquerque, NM 87131. **EMAIL** szabo@unm.edu

SZARMACH, PAUL E.
DISCIPLINE ENGLISH & MEDIEVAL STUDIES **EDUCATION** Canisius Col, AB, 63; Harvard Univ, AM 64; PhD, 68. **CAREER** Tchg fel, Harvard Univ, 66;Instr, US Military Acad, 68-70; Asst prof, 70-75, assoc prof, 75-83; dir, Center for Medieval and Early Renaissance Studies, SUNY, 75-86, 88-92; prof, SUNY, 83-94; acting Vice-Povost, Graduate Studies and Res, SUNY, 86-87; Prof, Western Mich Univ, 94-. **MEMBERSHIPS** Member, Executive committee of Centers and Regional Asn (sub-committee of the Mediaeval Acadamy), 80-83; member, SUNY Res Foundation Board of Directors. **RESEARCH** Old English literature with special reference to Old English porse and its Latin backgrounds. **SELECTED PUBLICATIONS** Co-ed, ACTA 4: The Fourteenth Century, CEMERS, 77; ed, Aspects of Jewish Culture in the Middle Ages, SUNY Press, 78; The Old English Homily and Its Backgrounds, SUNY Press, 78; Vercelli Homilies IX-XXIII, Toronto Univ Press, 81; The Alliterative Tradition in the Fourteenth Century, Kent State Univ Press, 81; co-ed, Mediaevalia 6, Festschrift for Bernard F. Hupp, 80; An Introduction to the Mediaeval Mystics of Europe; SUNY Press, 84; Studies in Earlier Old English Prose, SUNY Press, 86; Sources of Anglo-Saxon Culture, Studies in Medieval Culture, 20, The Medieval Inst, 86; Sources of Anglo-Saxon Literary Culture: A Trial Version, Medieval and Renaissance Texts and Studies 74; Suffolk: Boydell and Brewer; 94; Holy Men and Holy Women: Old English Prose Saints' Lives and Their Contexts, SUNY Press, 96; gen ed, Medieval England: An Encyclopedia, Garland Publ, 98. **CONTACT ADDRESS** Dept Medieval Institute, Western Michigan Univ, 1903 W Michigan Ave, Kalamazoo, MI 49008. **EMAIL** paul.szarmach@wmich.edu

SZASZ, FERENC
PERSONAL Born 02/14/1940, Davenport, IA, m, 1969, 3 children **DISCIPLINE** HISTORY **EDUCATION** Ohio Wesleyan Univ, BA, 62; Univ of Rochester, PhD, 69. **CAREER** Vis instr to prof, Univ of N Mex. **HONORS AND AWARDS** Fulbright Scholar, England, 84-85. **MEMBERSHIPS** OAH; WHA; NMHS; ASCH. **RESEARCH** Early history of the Atomic Age, Religion in America, Scots in America. **SELECTED PUBLICATIONS** Auth, The Divided Mind of Protestant America, 1880-1930, 82; ed, Religion in the West, 84; auth, The Day the Sun Rose Twice: The Story of the Trinity Site Nuclear Explosion, July 16, 1945, 84; auth, The Protestant Clergy in the Great Plains and Mountain West, 1865-1915, 88; auth, The Brit Scientists and the Manhattan Project: the Los Alamos Years, 92; coed, Religion in Modern New Mexico, 97; ed, Great Mysteries of the West, 93; auth, Scots and the North American West, 00; Religion in the Modern American West, 00. **CONTACT ADDRESS** Dept History, Univ of New Mexico, Albuquerque, 1 University Campus, Albuquerque, NM 87131-0001.

SZASZ, MARGARET CONNELL
PERSONAL Born Pasco, WA, 3 children **DISCIPLINE** UNITED STATES HISTORY **EDUCATION** Univ Wash, BA, 57, MA, 68; Univ N Mex, PhD(hist), 72. **CAREER** Prof, Univ of New Mexico, 87-. **MEMBERSHIPS** Western Hist Asn; Orgn Am Historians. **RESEARCH** History of American Indian education; American Indian ethnohistory; scottish history. **SELECTED PUBLICATIONS** Auth, Education and the American Indian, 74, 77, 99; auth, Indian Education In the American Colonies; auth, Between Indian & White Worlds: The Cultural Broker. **CONTACT ADDRESS** Hist Dept, Univ of New Mexico, Albuquerque, 1312 Lafayette Dr NE, Albuquerque, NM 87131-1181.

SZUCHMAN, MARK DAVID
PERSONAL Born 06/21/1948, Havana, Cuba, m, 1969, 2 children **DISCIPLINE** LATIN AMERICAN HISTORY **EDUCATION** Brandeis Univ, BA, 69; Univ Tex, Austin, MA, 71, PhD(hist), 76. **CAREER** Asst prof, 76-81, Assoc Prof Hist, Fla Int Univ, 81-, Soc Sci Res Coun res grant family hist, 78-79. **MEMBERSHIPS** Conf Latin Am Hist; Latin Am Studies Asn; Soc Sci Hist Asn; Chile-Rio Plata Studies Comt. **RESEARCH** Latin American urban history; 19th century Argentina; the family. **SELECTED PUBLICATIONS** Coauth, Educating Immigrants: Voluntary Associations in the Acculturation Process, In: Educational Alternatives in Latin America: Social Change and Social Stratification, Univ Calif, Los Angeles, 75; Occupational Stratification Studies In Argentina: A Classificatory Scheme, Latin Am Res Rev, spring 76; auth, The Limits of the Melting Pot in Urban Argentina: Marriage and Integration in Cordoba, 1869-1909, Hisp Am Hist Rev, 2/77; Aliens in Latin America: Functions, Cycles and Reactions, In: European Exiles and Latin America: A Comparative View (in press); coauth, City and Society: Their Connection in Latin American Historical Research, Latin Am Res Rev, 79; auth, Visions of the Melting Pot in the American City: European and Native Expectations in the United States and Argentina in the Period of Mass Immigration, In: Ethnicity in a Changing World (in prep); Mobility and Integration in Urban Argentina: Cordoba in the Liberal Era, Univ Tex Press, 80. **CONTACT ADDRESS** Dept of Hist, Florida Intl Univ, 1 F I U South Campus, Miami, FL 33199-0001.

T

TABBERNEE, WILLIAM
PERSONAL Born 04/21/1944, Rotterdam, Netherlands, m, 3 children **DISCIPLINE** EARLY CHURCH HISTORY **EDUCATION** Coburg Tchrs Col, TPTC, 65; Melbourne Col of Divinity, DipRE, 68, LTh, 68; Univ Melbourne, BA, 72, PhD, 79; Yale Divinity Sch, STM, 73. **CAREER** Lectr, Church history and systematic theol, 73-76, chemn Dept of Christian Thought and Hist, 77-80, Col of the Bible, Melbourne, Australia; dean, Evangelical Theol Asn, Melbourne, Australia, 79-80; prin, Col of the Bible of Churches of Christ in Australia, 81-91; pres, prof of Christian Thought and Hist, 91-94, Stephen J. England prof of Christian Thought and History, 95-, Phillips Theol Sem. **HONORS AND AWARDS** DDiv, Phillips Univ, 93. **MEMBERSHIPS** AAR; NAPS; Australian and New Zealand Soc for Theol Stud. **RESEARCH** Early Christianity; Montanism. **SELECTED PUBLICATIONS** Auth, Montanist Regional Bishops: New Evidence from Ancient Inscriptions, Jour of Early Christian Stud, 93; auth, Evangelism Beyond the Walls, Impact, 95; auth, Lamp-bearing Virgins: An Unusual Episode in the History of Early Christian Worship based on Mt25:1-13, Europ Evangel Soc, 95; auth, Paul of Tarsus: Church Planter Par Excellence, Australian Christian, 96; auth, 25 December, Christmas? Australian Christian, 96; auth, Unfencing the Table: Creeds, Councils, Communion and the Campbells, Mid-Stream, 96; auth, Augustine: Doctor of Love, Australian Christian, 97; auth, Archaeology; Revelation Revelations, Australian Christian, 97; auth, Athanasius: Champion of Orthodoxy, Australian Christian, 97; auth, Eusebius' Theology of Persecution: As Seen in the Various Editions of His Church History, Jour of Early Christian Stud, 97; auth, Ignatius, the Letter- Writing Martyr, Australian Christian, 97; auth, Learning to Handle the Gospel and the Fire Simultaneously: Ministerial Education for the Twenty-First Century, in Exploring Our Destiny, World Convention of Churches of Christ, 97; auth, Montanist Inscriptions and Testimonia: Epigraphic Sources Illustrating the History of Montanism, Patristic Monograph Ser, Mercer Univ, 97; auth, Our Trophies Are Better Than Your Trophies: The Appeal to Tombs and Reliquaries in Montanist- Orthodox Relations, Studia Patristica, 97; auth, Perpetua; The First Woman Journalist, Australian Christian, 97; auth, Eusebius: Chronicler of a Golden Age, Australian Christian, 98; auth, Francis of Assisi: Preacher to the Birds, Australian Christian, 98; auth, Mary Magdalene: A Saint with an Undeserved Reputation, Australian Christian, 98; auth, Restoring Normative Christianity: Episkope and the Christian Church, Mid-Stream, 98. **CONTACT ADDRESS** Phillips Theol Sem, 4242 S Sheridan Rd, Tulsa, OK 74145. **EMAIL** ptspres@fullnet.net

TABILI, LAURA
PERSONAL Born, WI **DISCIPLINE** HISTORY **EDUCATION** Univ Wisconsin, Milwaukee, BS, 78, MA, 82; Rutgers Univ, PhD, 88. **CAREER** Asst prof, 88-94, assoc prof, 94- , Univ Arizona. **HONORS AND AWARDS** Am Philos Soc res grant, 97; German Marshall Found res grant, 98. **MEMBERSHIPS** Am Hist Asn; N Am Conf on British Stud; Coun for European Stud. **RESEARCH** Migration; British and European history; women's hist; race; hist explanations for racial confilct in British and European societies. **SELECTED PUBLICATIONS** Auth, "Keeping the Natives Under Control" Race Segration and the Domestic Dimensions of Empire, 1920-1939," International Labor and Working Class History 44, (93): 141-177; auth, "Social Networks and Orgainization Building in Britain's Interwar Black Communities," in Gabriela Hauch, ed., Geschlecht-Klasse-Ethnizitt: 28er Tagung der Historikerinnen und Historiker der Arbeiterinnen-und Arbeiterbewegung, (Wien: Europaverlag, 93): 171-188; auth, "We Ask for British Justice,": Workers and Racial Difference in Lte Imperial Britain, Ithaca, New York: Cornell Univ Press, 94; auth, "The Construction of Racial Difference in Twentieth Cnetury Britain: The Speical Restirction (Coloured Alen Seamen) Order, 1925," Journal of British Studies 33, 1, 94; auth, "Labour Migration, Racial Formation, and Class Identity: Some Reflections on the British Case," North West Laabour Hist, 95; auth, A Maritime Race: Masculinity and the Racial Division of Labor in British Merchant Ships, 1900-1939," in Margaret S. Creighton and Lisa Norling, eds., Baltimore, Maryland: The Johns Hopkins Univ Press, 96): 169-188; auth, "Women of a Very Low Type: Crossing Racial Boundaries in Late Imperial Britain," in Laura Frader and Sonya Rose, eds., Ithaca, New Yorrk: Cornell Univ Press, 96): 165-190. **CONTACT ADDRESS** History Dept, Univ of Arizona, Tucson, AZ 85721. **EMAIL** tabili@u.arizona.edu

TACKETT, TIMOTHY
PERSONAL Born 08/30/1945, Santa Monica, CA, m, 1998 **DISCIPLINE** HISTORY **EDUCATION** Pomona Col, BA, 67; Stanford Univ, MA, 69; PhD, 73. **CAREER** Asst Prof, Marquette Univ, 74-79; Prof, Catholic Univ, 79-88; Prof, Univ Calif, 88-. **HONORS AND AWARDS** Nat Humanities Ctr Fel, 00; Leo Gershoy Prize, 98; Pres Fel, Univ Calif, 96-97; NEH Fel, 90-91; Woodrow Wilson Intl Ctr Guest Scholar, 88; Camargo Foundation Fel, 87; Guggenheim Foundation Fel, 86-87; Chester Higby Prize, 84; Koren Prize, 83; Fulbright Fel, 82-83; Am Philos Soc Res Grant, 75, 81; Phi Alpha Theta Awd, 78; Shea Prize, 78; ACLS Fel, 77-78; SSRC Fel, 70-73; NDEA Fel, 69-70; Ford Foundation Fel, 67-68; Fulbright Fel, 67-68; Phi Beta Kappa, 67. **MEMBERSHIPS** Soc fro French Hist studies, French Hist Soc, Societe des etudes robespierristes. **RESEARCH** French Revolution; French religious culture (18th Century). **SELECTED PUBLICATIONS** Auth, Becoming a Revolutionary: The Deputies of the French National Assembly and the Emergence of a Revolutionary Culture (1789-1790), Princeton Univ Press, 96; auth, Atlas de la Revolution francaise, Vol. 9 Religion, Editions de l'EHESS, 96; auth, The French Revolution Research Collection, Religion, Pergamon Press, 90; auth, Religion, Revolution, and regional Culture in eighteenth Century France, Princeton Univ Press, 86; auth, Priest and Parish in Eighteenth Century France: A social and Political Study of the Cures in a diocese of Dauphine, Princeton Univ Press, 77. **CONTACT ADDRESS** Dept Hist, Univ of California, Irvine, Irvine, CA 92697. **EMAIL** ttackett@uci.edu

TAGER, JACK
PERSONAL Born 10/18/1936, Brooklyn, NY, m, 1969, 2 children **DISCIPLINE** MODERN UNITED STATES & URBAN HISTORY **EDUCATION** Brooklyn Col, BA, 58; Univ CA, Berkeley, MA, 59; Univ Rochester, PhD(hist), 65. **CAREER** Asst prof hist, OH State Univ, 64-67; asst prof, 67-70, assoc prof, 70-77, Prof hist, Univ MA, Amherst, 77-, Dir honors, Univ MA, Amherst, 78-82. **MEMBERSHIPS** Orgn Am Historians. **SELECTED PUBLICATIONS** Auth, The Intellectual as Urban Reformer: Brand Whitlock and the Progressive Movement, Case Western Reserve Univ, 68; co-ed, The Urban Vision: Selected Interpretations of the Modern American City, Dorsey, 70; Massachusetts and the Gilded Age, Umass Press, 85; co-ed, Historical Atlas of Massachusetts, Umass Press 1991; coed, Massachusetts Politics, Inst for Mass Studies, 98; coauth, Massachusetts: A Concise History, Umass Press, 00; auth, Boston Riots, New York Univ Press, 00. **CONTACT ADDRESS** Dept of Hist, Univ of Massachusetts, Amherst, Amherst, MA 01002. **EMAIL** patjack@history.edu.umass

TAGG, JAMES
DISCIPLINE HISTORY **EDUCATION** Western Mich Univ, BA, 64; Wayne State Univ, MA, 68; PhD, 73. **CAREER** Prof, Univ of Lethbridge. **RESEARCH** Early American Republic; the American response to the French Revolution. **SELECTED PUBLICATIONS** Auth, Benjamin Franklin Bache and the Philadelphia Aurora, Univ Pa, 91. **CONTACT ADDRESS** Dept of History, Univ of Lethbridge, 4401 University Dr W, Lethbridge, AB, Canada T1K 3M4. **EMAIL** tagg@hg.uleth.ca

TAGG, JOHN
DISCIPLINE ART HISTORY **EDUCATION** Royal Col Art London. **CAREER** Art Dept, SUNY, Bingham **RESEARCH** Hist and theory of photography; mod Europ and Am cult hist; contemp critical theory (Marxism, semiotics, poststructuralism); curatorial practice. **SELECTED PUBLICATIONS** Auth, The Discontinuous City: Picturing and the Discursive Field in Visual Culture: Images and Interpretations, 94; The Pencil of History in Fugitive Images: From Photography to Video, 95; A Discourse (With Shape of Reason Missing) in Vision and Textuality, 95; The Currency of the Photograph in Representation and Photography: The Screen Education Reader, vol II; A Change of Skin in (Un)Fixing Representation; The World of Photography or Photography of the World? in Camerawork: A Reader. **CONTACT ADDRESS** Dept. of Art History, SUNY, Binghamton, PO Box 6000, Binghamton, NY 13902-6000. **EMAIL** jtagg@binghamton.edu

TAKAKI, RONALD TOSHIYUKI
PERSONAL Born 04/12/1939, Honolulu, HI, m, 1961, 3 children **DISCIPLINE** UNITED STATES HISTORY, MULTICULTURALISM **EDUCATION** Col Wooster, BA, 61; Univ Calif, Berkeley, MA, 62; PhD(hist), 67. **CAREER** Instr Am hist, Col San Mateo, 65-67; asst prof hist, Univ Calif, Los Angeles, 67-72; prof ethnic studies, Univ Calif, Berkeley, 72-; Nat Humanities Found fel, 70-71; Rockefeller Found fel, 81-82. **HONORS AND AWARDS** Distinguished Teaching Awd, Berkeley, 81; Messenger Lecturer, Cornell Univ, 93; fel, Soc Am Hist, 95; honorary doctorates from Wheelock Col, The Col of Wooster, Macalester Col, and Northeaster Univ. **RESEARCH** Ethnic studies; race relations; American social and intellectual history. **SELECTED PUBLICATIONS** Auth, A Pro-Slavery Crusade: The Agitation to Reopen the African Slave Trade, Free, 71; auth, Violence in the Black Imagination, Putnam, 72; auth, Iron Cages: Race and Culture in 19th Century America, Knopf, 79; auth, Strangers from a Different Shore: A History of Asian Americans, Little, Brown, 95; auth, A Different Mirror: A History of Asian Americans, Little, Brown, 93; auth, Hiroshima: Why America Dropped the Atomic Bomb, Little, Brown, 95; auth, A Larger Memory: A History of Our Diversity, with Voices, Little, Brown, 98; auth, Double Victory: A Multicultural History of America in World War II, Little, Brown, 00. **CONTACT ADDRESS** Dept Ethnic Studies, Univ of California, Berkeley, 506 Barrows Hall, Berkeley, CA 94720-2571. **EMAIL** rtakaki@uclink4.berkeley.edu

TALBOT, ALICE MARY
PERSONAL Born 05/16/1939, Washington, DC, m, 1964, 2 children **DISCIPLINE** BYZANTINE STUDIES **EDUCATION** Radcliffe Col, AB, 60; Columbia Univ, MA, 65; PhD, 70. **CAREER** Exec ed, Oxford Dict of Byzantium, 84-91; vis sr res assoc, Dumbarton Oaks, 91-92; adv, 92-97; dir, 97-. **HONORS AND AWARDS** R.L. Hawkins Awd, 91; CNRS Fel, 93. **MEMBERSHIPS** Byzantine Studies Conf; Medieval Acad of Am; US Nat Comm for Byzantine Studies. **RESEARCH** Monashcism, Hagiography, Women's Studies. **SELECTED PUBLICATIONS** Auth, The Correspondence of Athanasius I, Patriarch of Constantinople: Letters to the Emperor Andronicus II, Members of the Imperial Family and Officials, An Edition, Translation and Commentary, (Washington, DC), 75; auth, Faith Healing in Late Byzantium: The Posthumous Miracles of the Patriarch Athanasios I of Constantinople by Theoktistos the Stoudite, (Brookline, MA), 83; auth, "Old Age in Byzantium", Byzantinische Zeitschrift 77 (84): 37-48; auth "A Comparison of the Monastic Experience of Byzantine Men and Women", Greek Orthodox Theol Rev 30, (85): 1-20; auth, "Old Wine in New Bottles: The Rewriting of Saint's Lives in the Palaiologan Period", The Twilight of Byzantium, ed S. Curcic and D. Mouriki, (Princeton, NJ, 91): 15-26; coed, Oxford Dictionary of Byzantium, (NY), 91; auth, "La donna", L'Umo bizantino, ed G. Cavallo (Rome-bari, 92): 165-207; ed, Holy Women of Byzantium: Ten Saints' Lives in English Translation, (Wash, DC), 96; auth, "Women's Space in Byzantine Monasteries", DOP 52, (98): 113-127; ed, Byzantine Defenders of Images. Eight Saint's Lives in English Translation, (Wash, DC), 98. **CONTACT ADDRESS** Dumbarton Oaks, 1703 32 St NW, Washington, DC 20007.

TALBOT, CHARLES
DISCIPLINE NORTHERN EUROPEAN ART OF THE GOTHIC, RENAISSANCE, AND BAROQUE **EDUCATION** Yale Univ, PhD. **CAREER** Alice Pratt Brown distinguished prof. **SELECTED PUBLICATIONS** Pub(s), area of Ger art; Span Colonial Art and Arch in Mex and Latin Am. **CONTACT ADDRESS** Dept of Art Hist, Trinity Univ, 715 Stadium Dr, San Antonio, TX 78212.

TALBOTT, JOHN EDWIN
PERSONAL Born 09/25/1940, Grinnell, IA, 4 children **DISCIPLINE** MODERN EUROPEAN HISTORY **EDUCATION** Univ Mo, BA, 62; Stanford Univ, MA, 63, PhD(hist), 66. **CAREER** From instr to asst prof hist, Princeton Univ, 66-71; assoc prof, 71-79, Prof Mod Europ Hist, Univ Calif, Santa Barbara, 79-, Class of 1931 bicentennial preceptor, Princeton Univ, 69-71; mem bd human resources, Nat Acad Sci, 71-74; mem, Inst Advan Study, 75-76; vis prof hist, Stanford Univ, 80-81; vis prof strategy, Naval War Col, 81-82. **HONORS AND AWARDS** Best Book Awd, Pac Coast Branch AHA, 81, Best Article Awd, U.S. Navy, 85. **MEMBERSHIPS** AHA; Soc Fr Hist Studies; Univ of CA President's Fellowship in the Humanities, 93-94; ACLS Fellowship, 93-94; Andrew Mellon Award, Huntingtn Library, 94; MacArthur Foundation Research Grant, 94-95; Rockefeller Foundation Fellowship, 96-97. **RESEARCH** Modern France; history of education; European social history; War and Society. **SELECTED PUBLICATIONS** Auth, Soldiers, Psychiatrists, and Combat Trauma, J Interdisciplinary Hist, Vol 27, 97; auth, The Pens and Ink Sailor, Charles Middleton and the King's Navy, 1778-1813, London, 98. **CONTACT ADDRESS** Dept of Hist, Univ of California, Santa Barbara, 552 University Rd, Santa Barbara, CA 93106-0001. **EMAIL** talbott@humanitas.ucsb.edu

TALBOTT, ROBERT DEAN
PERSONAL Born 02/18/1928, Centralia, IL, m, 1957, 1 child **DISCIPLINE** LATIN AMERICAN HISTORY **EDUCATION** Univ Ill, BA, 50; MA, 55; PhD, 59. **CAREER** Teaching asst, Univ Ill, 55-58; instr hist, Kans State Teachers Col, Emporia, 58-59; assoc prof soc sci, NDak State Teachers Col, Valley City, 59-62; assoc prof hist, Kearney State Col, 62-67; from asst prof to assoc prof, Univ of Northern Iowa, 67-74; Prof, Latin Am Hist, Univ Northern Iowa, 74-00; Prof Emer, Univ Norther Iowa, 00-. **MEMBERSHIPS** Conf Latin Am Hist; AHA; Latin Am Studies Asn; Midwest Asn Lat Am Studies (pres, 81-82). **RESEARCH** Chilean boundaries and associated political problems. **SELECTED PUBLICATIONS** Auth, A History of the Chilean Boundaries, Iowa State Univ Press. **CONTACT ADDRESS** Dept of Hist, Univ of No Iowa, Cedar Falls, IA 50613. **EMAIL** robert.talbott@uni.edu

TAMBS, LEWIS
PERSONAL Born 07/07/1927, San Diego, CA, d, 7 children **DISCIPLINE** LATIN AMERICAN & IBERIAN HISTORY **EDUCATION** Univ Calif, Berkeley, BS, 53, Santa Barbara, MA, 62, PhD, 67. **CAREER** Asst plant engr, Standard Brands, Calif, 53-54; pipeline engr, Creole Petroleum Corp, Caracas, Venezuela, 54-57; gen mgr, CACYP, Instalaciones Petroleras, Maracaibo, 57-59; from instr to asst prof hist, Creighton Univ, 65-69; assoc prof, 69-75, dir, Ctr Latin Am Studies, 72-75, prof hist, Ariz State Univ, 75-80 & 87-; vis prof mod Brazil, Am Grad Sch Int Mgt, 72-79; consult NSC, 82-83; US Ambassador Colombia, 83-85; US Ambassador Costa Rica, 85-87. **HONORS AND AWARDS** Fac res grant, Amazon, 70 & Washington, DC & Madrid, 71; Outstanding Honor Awd of the Drug Enforcement Administration, 85; America's Best Friends of the Americas, 85; Outstanding Alumnus, Univ of Californis, Santa Barbara, 86. **MEMBERSHIPS** Coun Foreign Rels; Pac Coast Coun Latin Am Studies. **RESEARCH** Amazon rubber boom, 1890-1912; geopolitics of the Pacific basin; conflict in the southern cone of South America. **SELECTED PUBLICATIONS** Auth, "Latin American: Geopolitics and the New World Order," Global Affairs, VII (92): 59-73; auth, "The Expulsion of the Jews From Spain, 1492," in 1492 (NY: Weathersfield Institute, 93), 38-58; co-auth, Santa Fe III: Making Demography Work in the Americas, Washington, D.C.: New World Institute, 94; auth, "Expulsion of the Jewish Community from the Spains, 1492," in Religion in the Age of Exploration: The Case of Spain and New Spain (Creighton Univ Press, 96), 1-23; auth, "Demography, Geopolitics and the Decline of the West," in Humanism and the Good Life: Proceedings of the Fifteenth Congress of the World Federation of Humanists, 1994, Peter Horwath, Editor (NY: Peter Lang, 98), 57-64. **CONTACT ADDRESS** Dept Hist, Arizona State Univ, PO Box 872501, Tempe, AZ 85287-2501. **EMAIL** lewis.tambs@asu.edu

TAMINIAUX, PIERRE S.
PERSONAL Born 03/19/1958, Brussels, Belgium, m, 1999 **DISCIPLINE** FRENCH STUDIES **EDUCATION** Univ Libre Bruxelles, BA, 81; Univ Calif Santa Barb, MA, 86; Univ Calif Berkeley, PhD, 90. **CAREER** Asst prof, Miami Univ, 90-91; asst to assoc prof, Georgetown Univ, 91-. **HONORS AND AWARDS** FLL Res Grant, 95, 99; Belgian Am Educ Found. **MEMBERSHIPS** MLA; SCS. **RESEARCH** 20th century French literature and culture; literature and the visual arts; cultural and national identities film. **SELECTED PUBLICATIONS** Auth, Robert Pinget, Le Seuil, 94; auth, Spectres de Nations, 96; auth, Sacred Text/Scared Nation, Camden House, 96; auth, The Show Must Not Go On, Lignes, 97; auth, "Nation et Insurrection," Les Temps Mod (97; auth, Poetique de la Negation, L'Harmattan, 98; auth, Faire Ou Ne Pas Faire: Telle N'est Pas la Question, Jean-Michel Place, 00; auth, Pour une Poetique Cinematographique de la Lecture, L'Harmattan, 01. **CONTACT ADDRESS** Fr Dept, Georgetown Univ, Washington, DC 20057. **EMAIL** taminiap@gunet.georgetown.edu

TANENBAUM, JAN KARL
PERSONAL Born 12/21/1936, Chicago, IL, m, 1958, 3 children **DISCIPLINE** MODERN EUROPEAN HISTORY **EDUCATION** Univ Mich, BA, 58; Univ Calif, Berkeley, MA, 60, PhD, 69. **CAREER** From instr to asst prof, 66-74, assoc prof, 74-79, prof history, Fla State Univ, 79-. **MEMBERSHIPS** AHA; Soc Fr Hist Studies; Soc Histoire Moderne; Fr Colonial Hist Soc. **RESEARCH** Modern French history. **SELECTED PUBLICATIONS** Auth, General Maurice Sarrail 1856-1929, The French Army and Left-Wing Politics, Univ NC, 74; France and the Arab Middle East, 1914-1920, Am Philos Soc, 78; The French army and the Third Republic, In: Trends in History, winter 81; French Estimates of Germany's Operational War Plans in Knowing One's Enemies, Princeton Univ Press, 84. **CONTACT ADDRESS** Dept of History, Florida State Univ, 600 W College Ave, Tallahassee, FL 32306-1096.

TANKARD, JUDITH B.
PERSONAL Born 02/18/1942, New York, NY, m, 1969 **DISCIPLINE** ART HISTORY **EDUCATION** Univ NC, BA, 63; NYork Univ, MA, 67. **CAREER** Instr Landscape Hist, Radcliffe Seminars, 87-; independent scholar, writer, lecturer, editor, and consultant on historic gardens. **HONORS AND AWARDS** Am Horticultural Soc Bk Awd, 98. **MEMBERSHIPS** Soc Archit Hist; Garden Writers Asn Am; New England Garden Hist Soc; The Garden Hist Soc; The Southern Garden Hist Soc; SPNEA. **RESEARCH** Anglo-American historic gardens and garden makers. **SELECTED PUBLICATIONS** Coauth, Gertrude Jekyll: A Vision of Garden and Wood, Sagapress-Abrams, 89; Gertrude Jekyll at Munstead Wood, Sutton-Sagapress, 96; auth, The Gardens of Ellen Biddle Shipman, Sagapress-Abrams, 97; author of numerous articles; coauth, A Place of Beauty: Artists and Gardens of The Cornish Colony, Tenspeed Press, 00. **CONTACT ADDRESS** 1452 Beacon St., Newton, MA 02468. **EMAIL** judith@tankard.net

TANNENBAUM, REBECCA J.
DISCIPLINE HISTORY **EDUCATION** Wesleyan, BA, 84; Yale Univ, MA, 93, PhD, 96. **CAREER** Asst prof History, Univ Ill, Chicago. **RESEARCH** Practice of medicine in American history. **SELECTED PUBLICATIONS** Fel Publ, A Woman's Calling: Women Medical Practitioner in New England, 1650-1750, Yale, 96; auth, Earnestness, Temperance, Industry: The Definitions and Uses of Professional Character Among Nineteenth Century American Physicians, Jour of the Hist of Med and Life Sci 49, 94; What is Best to be Done for these Fevers: Elizabeth Davenport's Medical Practice in New Haven Colony, The New Eng. Quart, 97. **CONTACT ADDRESS** Dept of History, M/L 198, Univ of Illinois, Chicago, 913 University Hall, 601 S Morg, Chicago, IL 60607-7109. **EMAIL** rtannen@uic.edu

TANNER, HELEN HORNBECK
PERSONAL Born 07/05/1916, Northfield, MN, w, 1940, 3 children **DISCIPLINE** ETHNOHISTORY **EDUCATION** Swarthmore Col, AB, 37; Univ Fla, MA, 49; Univ Mich, PhD, 61. **CAREER** Vis lectr, Univ of Mich, 65; lectr, Univ of Mich Extensin Service, 74; acting dir, D'Arcy McNickle Ctr for Am Indian Hist, 84-85; res assoc, 81-95; sr res fel, 95-. **HONORS AND AWARDS** Am Asn of Univ Women, Nat Fel, 58-59; Grant form NEH for, Atlas of Great lakes Indian History,", 76; Recipient, Illinois Hist Soc Book Award, 87; Recipient, Erminie Wheeler-Voegelin Award from the Am Soc of Ethnohistory for best book in the filed published previous year, 88; Independent Scholar Fel from the Nat Endowment for the Humanities, 89; Travel Grant, Am Ocun for Learned Societies, 90. **MEMBERSHIPS** Can Cartographic Asn; Conf Latin Am Historians; Am Soc Ethnohist; Soc Hist Discoveries; Am Soc Ethnohist (pres, 82-). **RESEARCH** Indian history of Great Lakes; Spanish borderlands; historical cartography. **SELECTED PUBLICATIONS** Auth, Zespedes in East Florida, 1784-1790, (Coral Gables: Univ of Miami Press, 63; auth, The Ojibwas: A Critical Bibliography, Bloomington & London, Indiana Univ Press, 76; auth, "The Glaize in 1792, a Composite Community," in American Encounters, ed. James Merrell and Peter Mancall, (New York and London: Routledge Press, 00); reprint from Ethnohistory, vol. 25, no. 1, (78): 15-38; ed, Atlas of Great Lakes Indian History, Norman: Univ of Oklahoma Press, 87; auth, The Ojibwas, New York: Chelsea House Publishing Co., 92; coauth, "The Ojibwa-Jesuit Debate at Walpole Island, 1844," Ethnohistory, vol. 41, no. 2, 94; co-ed, "The Career of Joseph La Frane Coureur de Bois in the Upper Lakes," The Fur Trade Revisited: Selected Papers of the Sixth Fur Trade Conference in Mackinc Island 1991, (East Lansing, and Mackinac Island: Michigan State Univ and Mackinac Island Commission, (94): 171-188; ed, The Settling of North America, New York: Macmillan Books, 95; auth, "History vs. The Law: Proccessing Indians in the American Legal System," Univ of Detroit Mercy Law Review, Vol. 76, No. 3, 99; auth, "The Mille Lacs Band and the Treaty of 1855," in Fish in the Lakes, Wild Rice, and Gme in Abundance, (East Lansing, Mich State Univ Press, 00). **CONTACT ADDRESS** Newberry Library, 5178 Crystal Dr, Beulah, MI 49617.

TAO, TIEN-YI
PERSONAL Born 01/24/1919, China **DISCIPLINE** CHINESE HISTORY **EDUCATION** Nat Taiwan Univ, BA, 52, MA, 56; Univ Chicago, PhD(Chinese hist), 73. **CAREER** Res assoc Chinese hist, Inst Hist & Philol, Academia Sinica, 57-60; Asst Prof Hist, Hist Dept, Univ Hawaii, 68- **MEMBERSHIPS** Asn Asian Studies. **RESEARCH** China government and China bureaucracy. **SELECTED PUBLICATIONS** Auth, 'Yen Tieh Lun' Discourses on Salt and Iron--As a Historical Source, Bul Inst Hist Philol Acad Sinica, Vol 67, 96. **CONTACT ADDRESS** Dept of Hist, Univ of Hawaii, Manoa, 2530 Dole St, Honolulu, HI 96822-2303.

TAPPY, RON E.
DISCIPLINE NEAR EASTERN LANGUAGES AND CIVILIZATIONS **EDUCATION** Harvard Univ, PhD, 90. **CAREER** Res assoc, Harvard Univ, 90-91; vis asst prof, Univ Mich, 90-92; assoc prof, Westmont Col, 92-. **RESEARCH** Archaeology of Ancient Syria-Palestine; Biblical Archaeology **SELECTED PUBLICATIONS** Auth, Samaria, Encycl Near Eastern Archaeol, Oxford UP, 96; Review of Ancient Jerusalem Revealed, Jour of Near Eastern Stud, 96; Did the Dead Ever Die in Biblical Judah, Bulletin of the Amer Sch of Oriental Res, 95; Psalm 23: Symbolism and Structure, The Cath Bibl Quart, 95; Ahab, Hazor, Megiddo, The Oxford Companion to the Bible, Oxford UP, 93. **CONTACT ADDRESS** Dept of Rel, Westmont Col, 955 La Paz Rd, Santa Barbara, CA 93108-1099. **EMAIL** tappy@westmont.edu

TARANOW, GERDA
PERSONAL Born New York, NY, s **DISCIPLINE** THEATRE HISTORY & ENGLISH **EDUCATION** NYork Univ, BA, 52; MA, 55; Yale Univ, PhD, 61. **CAREER** From instr to asst prof, Univ KY, 63-66; asst prof, Syracuse Univ, 66-67; from asst prof to assoc prof, 67-76, prof English, Conn Col, 76-; fel, Yale Univ, 62-63; NEH fel, 80-81, referee, 72-. **HONORS AND AWARDS** Delta Phi Alpha. **MEMBERSHIPS** MLA; Am Soc Theatre Res; Int Fed Theatre Res; Asn Recorded Sound Collections; Societe d'histoire du Theatre (France); Soc for Theatre Res (England). **RESEARCH** Shakespeare; drama; performance. **SELECTED PUBLICATIONS** Auth, Sarah Bernhardt: The Art Within the Legend, Princeton Univ, 72; The Bernhardt Hamlet: Culture and Context, Peter Lang, 97. **CONTACT ADDRESS** 292 Pequot Ave, Apt 2L, New London, CT 06320. **EMAIL** gtar@conncoll.edu

TARBELL, ROBERTA K.
PERSONAL Born 01/06/1944, d, 3 children **DISCIPLINE** RENAISSANCE, BAROQUE, 19TH AND 20TH CENTURY ART AND ARCHITECTURE **EDUCATION** Cornell Univ, BS, 65; Univ Del, MA, 68; PhD, 76 **CAREER** Asst cur, Del Art Mus, 67-69; guest dir, Whitney Mus of Am Art, Nat Mus of Am Art, Rutgers Univ Art Gallery, Jewish Mus, 74-85; asst prof Art Hist, 84-90, actg chp 90-92, 96; assoc prof, Rutgers, State Univ NJ, Camden Col of Arts and Sci, 90-; adj asso prof Art Hist, Winterthur Mus/Univ Del, 86-. **HONORS AND AWARDS** Grad fel, Univ Del, 69-72; Smithsonian Inst predoctoral fel, 72-74; NEH res summer stipend 82-84; John Sloan Mem Found res grant, 85; Rutgers Univ res coun grant, 85-92; fac acad stud prog, Rutgers Univ, 88, 89, 93, 97; Smithsonian Inst sr postdoctoral fel, Hirshhorn Mus and Sculpture Garden, Wash, DC, 89; John Sloan Mem Found res grant, 89-90; Spec Award, Bd of Gov, Rutgers Univ, 90. **MEMBERSHIPS** Bd mem, Walt Whitman Asn, 89-; bd mem, Ctr of the Creative Arts, Yakys, Del, 95-; Col Art Asn; Catalogue RaisonnQ Scholars' Asn; Asn of Hist of Am Art; Soc of Archit Hist; Women's Caucus for Art. **RESEARCH** Twentieth-century sculpture. **SELECTED PUBLICATIONS** Auth, Marguerite Zorach, Smithsonian Inst, 73; auth, Peggy Bacon, Smithsonian Inst, 75; auth, Hugo Robus, Smithsonian Inst, 80; coauth, Vanguard American Sculpture, Rutgers Univ, 80; auth and co-ed, Walt Whitman and the Visul Arts, Rutgers Univ, 92; auth, Robert Laurent and American Figurative Sculpture, Univ Chicago, 94; auth, "Primitivism" in The Human figure in American Sculpture, (Univ Wash Press and the Los Angeles County Mus of Art, 95); auth, "Walt Whitman and the Visual Arts," in a Historical Guide to Walt Whitman, (Oxford Univ, 00); auth, Scupture in Ency of American Studies, 01. **CONTACT ADDRESS** Dept of Fine Arts, Rutgers, The State Univ of New Jersey, New Brunswick, Camden Col of Arts and Sci, 250 Fine Arts Bldg, New Brunswick, NJ 08903-2101. **EMAIL** tarbell@camden.rutgers.edu

TARR, JOEL A.
PERSONAL Born 05/08/1934, Jersey City, NJ, m, 4 children **DISCIPLINE** AMERICAN HISTORY **EDUCATION** Rutgers Univ, BS, 56, MA, 57; Northwestern Univ, PhD(hist), 63. **CAREER** Teaching asst, Northwestern Univ, 57-59; lectr hist, Chicago campus, 59-61; from instr to asst prof, Calif State Col Long Beach, 61-66; vis prof Am hist, Univ Calif, Santa Barbara, 66-67; from asst prof to prof hist & urban affairs, 67-76, prof hist, technol & urban affairs, 76-79, Prof Hist & Pub Policy, 79-90, Richard S. Caliguiri Prof Hist & Policy, Carnegie-Mellon Univ, 90-, dir, Prog Technol & Humanities, 75-, co-dir, Prog Applied Hist & Soc Sci, 77-. **HONORS AND AWARDS** Am Philos Soc grant, 64-65; Scaife fel, Carnegie-Mellon Univ, 67-69; Nat Endowment for Humanities jr fel, 69-70; Gen Elec Found grant, 72-73; NSF grant, 75 & 78; Exxon Found, 81-82; Andrew W Mellon Found grant, 75-80 & 80-85; NSF grants, 85, 95; Abel Wolman Prize of the Public Works Hist Soc for the Best Book Published in Public Works Hist, 88; Carnegie-Mellon Univ Robert Doherty Prize for "Substantial and Sustained Contributions to Excellence in Education", 92; Choice Distinguished Academic Book Awd, 97. **MEMBERSHIPS** Org Am Hist; Am Soc Environmental Hist; Soc Hist Tech; Urban Hist Asn (pres-elect, 97). **RESEARCH** Technology and the city; urban environmental history. **SELECTED PUBLICATIONS** Auth, A Study in Boss Politics: William Lorimer of Chicago, Univ Ill, 71; coauth, Technology and the Rise of the Networked City in Europe and America, Temple Univ Press, 88; auth, The Search for the Ultimate Sink: Urban Pollution in Historical Perspective, Series in Technology and the Environment, Univ Akron Press, 96; Searching for a Sink for an Industrial Waste, In: Out of the Woods: Essays in Environmental History, Univ Pittsburgh Press, 97; coauth, "The Centrality of the Horse to the Nineteenth-Century American City," The Making of Urban American, (NY: SR Publ, 97), 105-130; coauth, "Women as Home Safety Managers: the Changing Perception of the Home as a Place of Hazard and Risk 1870-1940," The Wellcome Institute Series in the Hist of Med, (Amsterdam: Rodopi, 97), 196-233; coauth, "The Struggle for Smoke Control in St Louis: Achievement and Emulation," Andrew Hurley, (St Louis: Missouri Historical Society, 97), 199-220; coauth, "At the Intersection of Histories: Technology and the Environment," Tech and Culture, (98), 601-640; auth, "Transforming An Energy System: The Evolution of the Manufactured Gas Industry and the Transition to Natural Gas in the United States 1807-1954, " Olivier Coutard, (London: Routledge, 99), 19-37; coauth, "Environmental Activism Locomotive Smoke, and the Corporate Response: the Case of the Pennsylvania Railroad and Chicago Smoke Control," 73 Business History Review, (99), 677-704. **CONTACT ADDRESS** Prog in Technol & Soc, Carnegie Mellon Univ, 5000 Forbes Ave, Pittsburgh, PA 15213-3890. **EMAIL** jt03@andrew.cmu.edu

TARR, ZOLTAN
PERSONAL Born, Hungary **DISCIPLINE** SOCIOLOGY, HISTORY **EDUCATION** Univ Ill, PhD, 74. **CAREER** CUNY; New School; Rutgers Univ. **HONORS AND AWARDS** Two Fullbright fel; two NEH fel. **MEMBERSHIPS** ASA; APSA; AHA. **RESEARCH** Intellectual history; history of European Jewry. **SELECTED PUBLICATIONS** Auth and coeditor, ten books, fifty articles. **CONTACT ADDRESS** 134 West 93rd St., #5-B, New York, NY 10025.

TARTER, BRENT
PERSONAL Born 10/06/1948, Austin, TX **DISCIPLINE** HISTORY OF VIRGINIA, AMERICAN REVOLUTION **EDUCATION** Angelo State Col, San Angelo, BA, 70; Univ Va, MA, 72. **CAREER** Hist ed, Va Independence Bicentennial Comn, 74-82. **MEMBERSHIPS** Southern Hist Asn. **RESEARCH** History of Virginia; history of the United States, 1900-1945; American revolution. **SELECTED PUBLICATIONS** Auth, David Humphrey Life of General Washington, with Washington,George Remarks, J Southern Hist, Vol 59, 93. **CONTACT ADDRESS** Va State Libr, Richmond, VA 23219.

TARVER, H. MICHAEL
PERSONAL Born Baton Rouge, LA, s **DISCIPLINE** HISTORY **EDUCATION** Univ Southwest La, BA; MA; Bowling Green State Univ, PhD. **CAREER** Doctoral teaching fel, Bowling Green State Univ, 90-94; instr Hist, Greenville Technol Col, SC, 94-95; asst prof, McNeese State Univ, 95-. **HONORS AND AWARDS** Phi Alpha Theta, Phi Beta Delta, Pi Gamma Mu; Amos E. Simpson Awd, Univ SW La, 89; Joe Gray Taylor Fac Res Awd, McNeese State Univ, 96-97; Shearman Res Initiative Fel, McNeese State Univ, 97-98; J. William Fulbright Sr Scholar, Univ de Los Andes, 99; La Endowment for the Humanities Grants, 97. 98, 99, 2000. **MEMBERSHIPS** Conf on Latin Am Hist, Southeast World Hist Asn, La Hist Asn. **SELECTED PUBLICATIONS** Assoc ed, The Cambridge World History of Human Disease, NY: Cambridge Univ Press (93), Kenneth F. Kiple, ed; auth of four entries in The Historical Encyclopedia of World Slavery, 2 vols, ed by Junius P. Rodriguez, Santa Barbara, Ca: ABC-CLIO Press (97); auth, "A Historical Perspective of Massage," Ch 1 of Massage Principles and Practices, Susan Salvo, ed, Philadelphia: W. B. Saunders (98); auth, "Garcilasco de la Vega," and "Louis A. Perez, Jr," in Encyclopedia of Historians and Historical Writing, ed by Kelly Boyd, London: Fitzroy Dearborn (99); auth, "Latin and South America," History Highway 2000: A Guide to Internet Resources, Dennis Trinkle and Scott Meriman, eds, NY: M. E. Sharpe (2000); auth, The Rise and Fall of Carlos Andres Perez: A Brief History, Lewiston, NY: Edwin Mellon Press (2000); assoc ed, Cambridge Encyclopedia of Food and Nutrition, Kenneth F. Kiple, Cambridge Univ Press (2000); coauth with Alan Austin, "The History of Sago," in Cambridge Encyclopedia of Food and Nutrition, ed by Kenneth F. Kiple, Cambridge Univ Press (2000). **CONTACT ADDRESS** Dept Hist, McNeese State Univ, PO Box 92860, Lake Charles, LA 70609.

TATA, ROBERT J.
PERSONAL Born 03/03/1935, New Britain, CT, m, 1958, 3 children **DISCIPLINE** GEOGRAPHY **EDUCATION** Syracuse Univ, AB, 57; MA Geog, 61; PhD, 68; Fla Atlantic Univ, MA Economics, 79. **CAREER** Grad Teaching Asst, Syracuse Univ, 57-58; Res Asst, Syracuse Univ, 61-64; Chemn of Geog Dept, Fla Atlantic Univ, 70-76; From Asst Prof to Prof Emeritus, Fla Atlantic Univ, 64-. **MEMBERSHIPS** Asn of Am Geogr. **SELECTED PUBLICATIONS** Coauth, "The MID(S): Are We Destroying an Irreplaceable Asset?," Mil Intel 11-2 (Apr/June 85): 13-16; auth, "Course Outline for Regional Studies," in Internationalizing the Undergraduate Curriculum, Spec Publ of Asn of Am Geogr (Washington, DC, 85); coauth, "Racial Separation Versus Social Cohesion: The Case of Trinidad-Tobago," Revista Geografica 104 (Julio-Decembre 86): 23-31; coauth, "World Variations in Human Welfare: A New Index of Development Status," Ann of the AAG 78-4 (Dec 88): 580-593; auth, "Puerto Rico," in West Indies Section, Encyclopedia Britannica Vol 39 Macropaedia 15th Ed (89): 755-758; coauth, "World Variation in Human Welfare: A New Index of Development Status: A Reply," Ann of the AAG 79-4 (89): 614-615; coauth, "The Urban Areas of Haiti," in Handbook of Latin American Urbanization: Historical Profiles of Major Cities, ed. Gerald M. Greenfield (Westport, CT: Greenwood Press, 90); auth, World Geography: Student Notebook/Guide, Privately Publ, 92; auth, "Haiti," in Microsoft Encarta, Microsoft Corp, 95; auth, World Geography: Student Notebook/Guide Second Ed, Privately Publ, 96. **CONTACT ADDRESS** Dept Geog and Geol, Florida Atlantic Univ, PO Box 3091, Boca Raton, FL 33431. **EMAIL** b33bacchus@earthlink.net

TATAREWICZ, JOSEPH N.
DISCIPLINE HISTORY **EDUCATION** IN Univ, PhD. **CAREER** Asst prof, Univ MD Baltimore County. **RESEARCH** Hist of sci; sci policy; public hist. **SELECTED PUBLICATIONS** Auth, Space Technology and Planetary Astronomy. **CONTACT ADDRESS** Dept of Hist, Univ of Maryland, Baltimore, Hilltop Circle, PO Box 1000, Baltimore, MD 21250. **EMAIL** tatarewicz@.umbc.edu

TATE, MICHAEL LYNN
PERSONAL Born 01/24/1947, Big Spring, TX, m, 1972, 2 children **DISCIPLINE** AMERICAN HISTORY **EDUCATION** Austin Col, BA, 69; Univ Toledo, MA, 70, PhD(Am hist), 74. **CAREER** Asst prof Am hist, Concordia Col, MN, 73-74 & Austin Col, summer, 74; from asst prof to prof, Univ NE, Omaha, 74-; Contrib ed, Am Indian Quart, 76-; exec ed hist, Govt Publ Rev, 81-. **HONORS AND AWARDS** Muriel H. Wright Awd from OK Hist Soc; Diamond Professorship, Univ NE at Omaha; Burlington Northern Faculty Achievement Awd; Univ NE Great Teacher Awd. **MEMBERSHIPS** Orgn Am Historians; Western Hist Asn; Soc Am Indian Studies & Res; Center for Great Plains Study. **RESEARCH** American Indian history and legal questions; Am frontier. **SELECTED PUBLICATIONS** Auth, The Indians of Texas, Scarecrow Press, 86; auth, The Upstream People: An Annotated Research Bibliography of the Omaha Tribe, Scarecrow Press, 91; auth, Nebraska History: An Annotated Bibliography, Greenwood Press, 95; auth, The Frontier Army in the Settlement of the West, Univ OK Press, 99. **CONTACT ADDRESS** Dept of Hist, Univ of Nebraska, Omaha, 6001 Dodge St, Omaha, NE 68182-0002.

TATE, THAD W.
PERSONAL Born 05/27/1924, s **DISCIPLINE** EARLY AMERICAN HISTORY **EDUCATION** Univ NC, AB, 47, MA, 48; Brown Univ, PhD, 60. **CAREER** Retired. **MEMBERSHIPS** AHA, OAH, SHA, Mass Hist Soc, Am Antiq Soc, VA Hist Soc, Am Soc Environmental History, Hist Soc, Epis Church, **RESEARCH** Colonial Virginia, Am Revolution, Environmental History. **SELECTED PUBLICATIONS** Fel Publ, The Discovery and Development of the Southern Colonial Landscape, Procs of the AAS 92, 83; auth, The Negro in Eighteenth-Century Williamsburg, Univ Va, 66, repr 85; co-ed and contrib, The Chesapeake in the Seventeenth Century, Univ NC Press, 79; coauth, Colonial Virginia: A History, KTO Press, 86; auth, Transformation of the Land in Colonial America, In: Our American Land: 1987 Yearbook of Agriculture, US Govt Printing Off, 87; coauth and ed, The College of William and Mary: A History, King and Queen Press, 93. **CONTACT ADDRESS** 313 1/2 Burns Lane, Williamsburg, VA 23185-3908.

TATHAM, DAVID FREDERIC
PERSONAL Born 11/29/1932, Wellesley, MA, m, 1979 **DISCIPLINE** ART HISTORY **EDUCATION** Univ Mass, AB, 54; Syracuse Univ, MA, 60, PhD(humanities), 70. **CAREER** Lectr fine arts, 62-71, dean students, 66-71, assoc prof, 72-78, Prof Art Hist, Syracuse Univ, 78-, Chmn, 73-77, 80-86. **HONORS AND AWARDS** Henry A Moe Prize, 91; John Ben Snow Awd, 96; Am Philos Soc fel; NEH fel; life fel, Atheneum of Philadelphia. **MEMBERSHIPS** Col Art Asn Am; Am Antiqn Soc. **RESEARCH** American painting and graphic arts of 19th and 20th centuries. **SELECTED PUBLICATIONS** Auth, Lure of the Striped Pig: The Illustration of Popular Music in America 1820-1870, Imprint Soc, 73; Winslow Homer's Library, 5/77, Am Art J; Winslow Homer and the New England Poets, Proceedings of the Am Antiquarian Soc, 10/79; Samuel F B Morse's Gallery of the Louvre, Am Art J, fall 81; auth, Prints and Printmakers of New York State, Syracuse, 86; auth, Winslow Homer and the Illustrated Book, Syracuse, 92; auth, Winslow Homer in the Adirondacks, Syracuse, 96; auth, Winslow Homer and this Pictoral Press," 01. **CONTACT ADDRESS** Dept of Fine Arts, Syracuse Univ, Syracuse, NY 13244. **EMAIL** dftatham@syr.edu

TATUM, GEORGE B.
PERSONAL Born 08/01/1917, Cleveland, OH, m, 1942, 3 children **DISCIPLINE** ART AND ARCHAEOLOGY **EDUCATION** Princeton Univ, AB, 40; MFA, 47; PhD, 50. **CAREER** Prof, Univ Pa, 48-68; prof, Univ Del, 68-78; visiting prof, Williams Col, 81; adj prof, Columbia Univ, 79-82. **HONORS AND AWARDS** Phi Beta Kappa; Sr Fel in Landscape Archit, Dumbarton Oaks (Harvard Univ), 67-68. **MEMBERSHIPS** Am Inst of Archit (Hon.); Athenaeum of Philadelphia; Soc of Archit Historians. **RESEARCH** American architecture (eighteenth and nineteenth centuries); history of garden design (American and English). **SELECTED PUBLICATIONS** Auth, Penn's Great Town; Two Hundred Fifty Years of Philadelphia Architecture in Prnts and Drawings, 61; auth, Architecture, The Arts in America: The Colonial Period, 66; auth, Philadelphia Georgian: The City House of Samuel Powel and Some of its Eighteenth-Century Neighbors, 76; ed with E.B. MacDougall, Prophet with Honor: The Career of Andrew Jackson Downing, 1815-1852, 89; auth with William Alex, Calvert Vaux: Architect and Planner, 94. **CONTACT ADDRESS** 9102 Chester Village West, Chester, CT 06412-1047. **EMAIL** george@cshore.com

TATUM, NANCY R.
PERSONAL Born 08/14/1930, Pittsburg, KS **DISCIPLINE** ENGLISH LITERATURE & HISTORY **EDUCATION** Univ Ark, BA, 52; Bryn Mawr Col, MA, 54, PhD, 60. **CAREER**

Instr English & asst to dean, Lake Erie Col, 58-59; from instr to assoc prof, 60-69, Prof English, Washingotn Col, 69-, Ernest A Howard Prof, 79-99; Ernest A Howard, Prof Emerita, 99. **MEMBERSHIPS** MLA; Shakespeare Asn Am. **RESEARCH** Restoration drama; Shakespearean stage technique; seventeenth century English social and economic history. **CONTACT ADDRESS** Dept of English, Washington Col, 300 Washington Ave, Chestertown, MD 21620-1197.

TAUBER, ALFRED I.
PERSONAL Born 06/24/1947, Washington, DC, m, 2000, 4 children **DISCIPLINE** PHILOSOPHY; HISTORY OF SCIENCE **EDUCATION** BS, 69, Tufts Univ; MD, 73, Tufts Univ School of Medicine **CAREER** Instr, 78-80, Asst Prof, 80-82, Harvard Medical School; Assoc Prof Medicine, 82-86, Assoc Prof Biochemistry, 82-86; Assoc Prof Pathology, 84-87, Prof of Medicine, 86-, Prof of Pathology, 87-, Boston Univ School of Medicine; Prof Philosophy, 93-, College of Arts and Sciences, Boston Univ. **RESEARCH** Philosophy and the history of science **SELECTED PUBLICATIONS** Coauth, Metchnikoff and the Origins of Immunology: From Metaphor to Theory, 91; Auth, The Immune Self: Theory or Metaphor, 94; Coauth, The Generation of Diversity: Clonal Selection Theory and the Rise of Molecular Immunology, 97; Auth, Confessions of A Medicine Man: An Essay in Popular Philosophy, 99. **CONTACT ADDRESS** Center for Philosophy and History of Science, Boston Univ, Boston, MA 02115. **EMAIL** ait@bu.edu

TAURA, GRACIELLA CRUZ
DISCIPLINE HISTORY **EDUCATION** Univ Miami, PhD. **CAREER** Assoc prof. **MEMBERSHIPS** Am Hist Asn; Cuban Studies Asn; Latin Am Studies Asn. **RESEARCH** Latin American intellectual history; Cuban and Cuban American Studies; women's history. **SELECTED PUBLICATIONS** Auth, Annexation and National Identity: The Issues of Cuba's Mid-Nineteenth Century Debate, 97; Women's Rights and the Cuban Constitution of 1940, 94; co-ed, Outside Cuba/Fuera de Cuba: Contemporary Cuban Visual Artists, 89. **CONTACT ADDRESS** History Dept, Florida Atlantic Univ, 777 Glades Rd, Boca Raton, FL 33431.

TAYLOR, ALAN S.
DISCIPLINE HISTORY **EDUCATION** Colby, BA, 77; Brandeis, PhD, 86. **CAREER** Prof History, Univ Calif, Davis. **HONORS AND AWARDS** Winner Bancroft, Beveridge, and Pulitzer Prizes for 'William Cooper's Town,' 96. **RESEARCH** Canada and the United States; American Frontier and West **SELECTED PUBLICATIONS** Fel publ, From Fathers to Friends of the People, Jour of the Early Repub 11, 91; auth, Liberty Men and Great Proprietors: The Revolutionary Settlement on the Maine Frontier, Univ NC, 90; Who Murdered Judge William Cooper? NY Hist, 91; William Cooper's Town: Power and Persuasion on the Frontier of the Early Republic, Knopf, 95. **CONTACT ADDRESS** Dept of History, Univ of California, Davis, Davis, CA 95616. **EMAIL** astaylor@ucdavis.edu

TAYLOR, ARNOLD H.
PERSONAL Born 11/29/1929, Regina, VA **DISCIPLINE** HISTORY **EDUCATION** VA Union U, BA cum laude 1951; Howard U, MA 1952; The Cath Univ of Am, PhD 1963. **CAREER** Howard Univ, prof History 1972-; Univ of CT at Sterrs, prof history 1970-72; NC Central Univ, prof History 1965-70; So Univ in New Orleans, prof history chmn div of soc sci 1964-65; Benedict Coll, instr to prof of history 1955-64. **HONORS AND AWARDS** Recip post doc res grants Nat Endowment on the Humanities 1968, Am Council of Learned Societies 1969, Ford Found 1969-70, Univ of CT res found 1971-72. **MEMBERSHIPS** Mem assn for the study of Afro Am Life & History; So Historical Assn; Am Historical Assn; Orgn of Am Historians; author Am Diplomacy & the Narcotics Traffic 1900-39, A Study in InternatlHumanitarian Reform Duke Univ Press 1969, "Travail & Triumph Black Life & Culture in the South Since the Civil War" Greenwood Press 1976; author several articles in scholarly journals Fulbright Hays Sr Lectr, Am Hist at Jadavpur Univ Calcutta India 1967-68. **CONTACT ADDRESS** Prof of History & Dept Chrmn, Howard Univ, Washington, VT 20059.

TAYLOR, CLEDIE COLLINS
PERSONAL Born 03/08/1926, Bolivar, AR **DISCIPLINE** ART HISTORY **EDUCATION** Wayne State U, BS 1948, MA 1957; L'Universita Per Stranieri, Cert etruscology 1968; Wayne State U, SP cert humanities/art/hist 1970; Union Grad Sch, PhD art hist 1978. **CAREER** Detroit Pub Sch, art tchr 1979, Supr of Art 1980-; Metal Processes WSU, instructor fashion design 1981; Arts Extended Gallery Inc, dir, currently; Pri Jewelry Design, practicing metal craftsperson; Children's Museum, asst dir, 87-91. **HONORS AND AWARDS** Contribution to Black Artist Nat Conf of Artist 1984, 1994; Spirit of Detroit Awd City of Detroit 1983; curator "African Tales in Words And Wood" 1984; curator "Tribute to Ernest Hardman" Exhibit Scarab Club 1985; award, Spirit of Detroit, City of Detroit for Small Business 1988; One Hundred Black Women for Art and Literature 1989; Governor's Awd for Contribution to Art Education, 1989. **MEMBERSHIPS** 1st chmn Detroit Cncl of the Arts 1977-81; 1st chmn Minority Arts Advisory Panel MI Cncl for the Arts 1982-; mem bd of trustees Haystack Mountain Sch of Crafts 1982-; mem Detroit Scarab Club 1983-; DPS advisor/liason Detroit Art Tchrs Assn 1983-; mem/art advisor Nat Assn of the African Diaspora 1980-; dir Art Symposium Surinam NAAD Conf 1982; mem Berea Lutheran Ch; mem Alpha Kappa Alpha Sor; dir Art Symposium Barbados; appointed Michigan Council for the Arts 1987-; Board of Michigan Arts Foundation, 1988-. **SELECTED PUBLICATIONS** Publ "Journey to Odiamola" 1978; "Words in a SketchBook" 1985; **CONTACT ADDRESS** Arts Extended Gallery, 1553 Woodward, Ste 212, Detroit, MI 48226.

TAYLOR, DAVID VASSAR
PERSONAL Born 07/13/1945, St Paul, MN, m, 1976, 2 children **DISCIPLINE** HISTORY **EDUCATION** Univ of Minnesota, BA 1967; Univ of Nebraska, MA 1971, PhD 1977; Harvard Univ, IEM Program 1985. **CAREER** St Olaf Coll, Northfield MN, dir Amer minority studies program 1974-76; State Univ of New York New Paltz Campus, chairperson black studies dept 1977-78; Hubert Humphrey Collection Minnesota Historical Soc, curator 1978-79; Macalester Coll, dir minority/special serv program 1979-83; The Coll of Charleston, dean of undergraduate studies 1983-86; Minnesota State Univ System Office, assoc vice chancellor for academic affairs 1986-89; Univ of Minnesota Gen Coll, Minneapolis MN, dean 1989-. **HONORS AND AWARDS** Research Fellow-Dissertation Fellowship Fund for Black Americans 1975-77; consultant historian "Blacks in Minnesota" film for Gen Mills 1980. **MEMBERSHIPS** Bd of dirs Hallie Q Brown Comm Center St Paul 1978-79; bd of advisors Perrie Jones Library Fund St Paul 1979-80, Minnesota Quality of Life Study 1979-80; vestry St Phillip's Episcopal Church 1978-81; bd of trustees Seabury Western Theological Seminary 1985-90; chairman, board of directors, Penumbra Theatre Co; board, Friends of the Saint Paul Public Libraries; treasurer, Jean Covington Foundation; brd mem Hope Community; brd mem, Healtheast. **SELECTED PUBLICATIONS** Author bibliography/14 articles/chapter in book. **CONTACT ADDRESS** Dean, General College, Univ of Minnesota, Twin Cities, 128 Pleasant St, SE, Minneapolis, MN 55455. **EMAIL** taylor@mailbox.mail.umn.edu

TAYLOR, DORCETA E.
DISCIPLINE ENVIRONMENTAL HISTORY **EDUCATION** Yale Univ, MFS, 85; MA, M Phil, 88; PhD, 91. **CAREER** Asst prof, Wash State Univ, 95-98; Asst prof, Univ of Mich, 92-95, 98-. **HONORS AND AWARDS** Distinguished Serv to the Univ and Higher Ed, NE IL Univ, 93; Outstanding Environ Achievement, NE IL Univ, 93; Leadership Awd, Forest Congress Board, 96. **MEMBERSHIPS** Am Sociol Assoc. **RESEARCH** Environmental history and ideology, Environmental inequality, social movements, gender, poverty, Environmental activism in the U.S., Britain and Canada. **SELECTED PUBLICATIONS** Rev, of "Environmental Sociology: A Social Constructionist Perspective", by John Hannigan, Contemporary Sociol 26, (Nov 97):733-734; auth, "The Urban Environment: The Intersection of White Middle Class and White Working Class Environmentalism (1928-1920s), Advances in Human Ecology, Vol 7, (98):207-292; auth, "Mobilizing for Environmental Justice in Communities of Color: An Emerging Profile of People of Color Environmental Groups" in Ecosystem Management: Adaptive Strategies for Natural Resource Orgns in the 21st Century, ed J. Aley, W. Burch, B. Canover and D. Field (Wash, DC: Taylor & Francis, 99), 33-67; auth, "Central Park as a Model for Social Control: Urban Parks, Social Class and Leisure Behavior in Nineteenth-Century America", Jour of Leisure Res 31 (99):420-477; auth, "The Rise of the Environmental Justice Paradigm: Injustice Framing and the Social Construction of Environmental Discourses, Am Behav Scientist 43, (00):408-580; ed, "Advances in Environmental Justice: Research, theory and Methodology", Am Behav Scientist 43 (Jan 00); auth, "Meeting the Challenge of Wild Land Recreation Management: Demographic Shifts and Social Inequality", Jour of Leisure Res 32 (00); coed, Environmental Justice (New Orleans: S Univ of New Orleans Pr, 00; auth, ed, "Race, Class Gender and the American Environment: 1820-1995" in Environ Justice, ed R. Bullard, D. Taylor, G. Johnson (New Orleans: S Univ of New Orleans Pr) (forthcoming). **CONTACT ADDRESS** Sch Natural Res, Univ of Michigan, Ann Arbor, 430 E Univ Ave, Ann Arbor, MI 48109-1115. **EMAIL** dorceta@umich.edu

TAYLOR, IRA DONATHAN
PERSONAL Born 08/12/1962, Hot Springs, AR, m, 1986, 3 children **DISCIPLINE** HISTORY **EDUCATION** Hardin-Simmons Univ, BFA, 85, MA, 89; Univ Ark, Fayetteville, PhD, 97. **CAREER** Asst prof, Hardin-Simmons Univ, 95-; Chmn, Dept of Hist. **HONORS AND AWARDS** Phi Kappa Phi, Alpha Chi, Nat Scholar Soc. **MEMBERSHIPS** Asn Ancient Hist; W Tex Hist Asn; Taylor County Hist Commission; Tex Medieval Asn; World Hist Asn; Hist Soc. **RESEARCH** Ancient, medieval and military history. **SELECTED PUBLICATIONS** Auth, A Comparitive Study of the Post-Alexandrian Macedonian Phalanx and the Roman Manipular Legend to the Battle of Pydna, 93; coauth, Along the Texas Forts Trail, 97; auth, Some Living Conditions at Forts in the American Southwest, 98; auth, "Battle of Carrhae", "Battle of Cynoscephalae", "Battle of Pharsalus", " Battle of Thapsus", "Battle of Magnesia," in The Encyclopedia of The Ancient World. **CONTACT ADDRESS** Hardin-Simmons Univ, Box 16125, Abilene, TX 79698. **EMAIL** dtaylor@hsutx.edu

TAYLOR, JAMES S.
DISCIPLINE HISTORY **EDUCATION** Stanford Univ, PhD, 66. **CAREER** Prof. **RESEARCH** Britain history; modern Europe; world history. **SELECTED PUBLICATIONS** Auth, pubs on English philanthropy and the Poor Law system. **CONTACT ADDRESS** History Dept, State Univ of West Georgia, Carrollton, GA 30118. **EMAIL** jtaylor@westga.edu

TAYLOR, JEROME
PERSONAL Born 01/26/1940, Waukegan, IL, m **DISCIPLINE** AFRICAN-AMERICAN STUDIES **EDUCATION** Univ of Denver, BA 1961; IN Univ, PhD 1965. **CAREER** Mental Health Unit Topeka, dir 1968-69; Univ of Pittsburgh Clinical Psych Ctr, dir 1969-71; Univ of Pittsburgh, assoc prof of black studies and education, dir, Inst for the Black Family, currently. **HONORS AND AWARDS** Postdoctoral fellow, Menninger Found, 1965-67. **MEMBERSHIPS** Mem Amer Psychol Society, Assoc of Black Psych, Omicron Delta Kappa, Sigma Xi, Psi Chi; member, National Black Child Development Institute; member, National Council on Family Relations. **CONTACT ADDRESS** Dir, Inst for the Black Family, Univ of Pittsburgh, Pittsburgh, PA 15260.

TAYLOR, KAREN
DISCIPLINE HISTORY **EDUCATION** Univ Utah, BA, 80; Clark, MA, 82; Duke Univ, PhD, 88. **CAREER** Assoc prof. **SELECTED PUBLICATIONS** Auth, Moral Motherhood and the Suppression of Corporal Punishment, Jour Psychohistory, 87; The Cult of True Motherhood and the Expansion of the Domestic Sphere, The Study of Women: History, Religion, Literature and the Arts, Greenwood Press, 89. **CONTACT ADDRESS** Dept of Hist, The Col of Wooster, Wooster, OH 44691.

TAYLOR, KENNETH LAPHAM
PERSONAL Born 05/16/1941, Los Angeles, CA, m, 1969, 3 children **DISCIPLINE** HISTORY OF SCIENCE **EDUCATION** Harvard Col, AB, 62; Harvard Univ, AM, 65, PhD(hist of sci), 68. **CAREER** Asst prof, 67-72, assoc prof hist of sci, Univ Okla, 72-, dept chemn, 79-92, 99, Nat Ctr Sci Res fel, 73-74. **HONORS AND AWARDS** S T Friedman Medal, Geol Soc London, 98; pres, Hist of Earth Sci Soc, 97-98; chair, Geol Soc of Am, Hist of Geol Div, 99. **MEMBERSHIPS** Brit Soc Hist Sci; Hist Sci Soc; Soc Hist Technol; Hist of Earth Sci Soc; Geol Soc Am; Soc Hist Nat Hist. **RESEARCH** History of geology; science in the 18th century. **CONTACT ADDRESS** Dept of Hist of Sci, Univ of Oklahoma, 601 Elm Ave, Norman, OK 73019-3106. **EMAIL** ktaylor@ou.edu

TAYLOR, LARISSA JULIET
PERSONAL Born Philadelphia, PA **DISCIPLINE** HISTORY **EDUCATION** Harvard Univ, ALB, 81; Brown Univ, MA, 82; PhD, 90. **CAREER** Instructor, MIT, 87; Lecturer, Harvard Univ, 91-92; Asst Prof, Wellesley Col, 88-93; Asst Prof, Assumption Col, 93-94; Assoc Prof, Colby Col, 94-. **HONORS AND AWARDS** John Nicholas Brown Prize, Medieval Acad of Am, 96; NEH Grant; Herzog August Bibliothek Grant. **MEMBERSHIPS** AHA; Renaissance Soc; French Hist Soc; Soc for Reformation Research; Am Catholic Hist Asn. **RESEARCH** Medieval/Reformation preaching; Religion; Mary Magdalene. **SELECTED PUBLICATIONS** Auth, Soldiers of Christ: Preaching in Late Medieval and Reformation France, Oxford Univ press, 92; auth, "Images of Women in the Sermons of Guillaume Pepin," Journal of the Canadian Hist Asn, (94): 265-276; auth, "Comme un chien mort: Preaching About Kingship in France, 1460-1572," Proceedings of the Western Soc for French History, (95): 157-170; co-auth, "He Could have mad Marvels in this Language: A Nahuatl Sermon by Father Juan de Tovar, S.J.," Estudios de cultura Nahuatl, (96): 212-244; auth, "The Influence of Humanism on Post-Reformation Catholic Preachers in France," Renaissance Quarterly, (97): 115-130; auth, "The Good Shepherd: Francois LePicart (1504-1556), sixteenth Century Journal, (97): 793-810; auth, Heresy and Orthodoxy in Sixteenth-Century Paris: Francois Le Picart and the beginnings of the Catholic reformation, 99; ed, Preacher and Audience: Sermons in the Reformation and Early Modern Period, Brill Pub, 01. **CONTACT ADDRESS** Dept Hist, Colby Col, 150 Mayflower Hill Dr, Waterville, ME 04901-4799. **EMAIL** ljtaylor@colby.edu

TAYLOR, QUINTARD, JR.
PERSONAL Born 12/11/1948, Brownsville, TN **DISCIPLINE** HISTORY **EDUCATION** St Augustine's Coll, BA 1969; Univ of MN, MA 1971, PhD 1977. **CAREER** Univ of MN, instructor 1969-71; Gustavus Adolphus Coll, instructor 1971; WA State U, asst prof 1971-75; CA Polytechnic State U, prof of history; Univ of Lagos, Akoka Nigeria, visiting Fulbright prof 1987-88; Univ of OR, prof, 90-96, dept head, 97-. **HONORS AND AWARDS** Carter G Woodson Awd ASALH 1980; Kent Fellowship The Danforth Found 1974-77; Bush Fellowship Univ of MN 1971-77; NEH Travel & Collections Grant, National Endowment for the Humanities 1988; The Emergence of Afro-American Communities in the Pacific Northwest 1865-1910; Carter G Woodson Awd for best article published in the Journal of Negro History 1978-79. **MEMBERSHIPS** Consult Great Plains Black Museum 1980-85; consult Afro-Am Cultural Arts Ctr 1977-78; reviewer Nat Endowment for the Humanities 1979-83; pres Martin Luther Fund 1983-85,

mem 1979-; mem Endowment Comm "Journal of Negro History" 1983-; mem, California Black Faculty Staff Assn 1985-, Golden Key Natl Honor Society 1987-, Phi Beta Delta Society for International Scholars 1989-; bd of governors, Martin Luther King Vocational-Technical Coll, Owerri Nigeria 1989-, African-American Vocational Institute, Aba Nigeria 1989-. **SELECTED PUBLICATIONS** Written: In Search of the Racial Frontier: African Americans in the American West, 1528-1990; The Forgiving of A Black Community Seattles, Central District from 1870 Through the Civil Rights Era; auth, Seeking El Dorado: African Americans in California. **CONTACT ADDRESS** Dept of History, Univ of Washington, Seattle, WA 98195-0001. **EMAIL** qtaylor@u.washington.edu

TAYLOR, RICHARD STUART
PERSONAL Born 06/24/1942, Chicago, IL **DISCIPLINE** AMERICAN HISTORY, HISTORY OF RELIGION **EDUCATION** Wheaton Col, Ill, BA, 64; Northern Ill Univ, MA, 70, PhD(hist), 77. **CAREER** Publ ed, 78-80, Dir Off Res & Publ, Hist Sites Div, Ill Dept Conserv, 80- **MEMBERSHIPS** AHA; Am Soc Church Hist; Orgn Am Historians; Soc Historians Early Am Repub. **RESEARCH** Evangelicalism in 19th century America; antebellum reform; new thought in the 1920s. **SELECTED PUBLICATIONS** Auth, Preachers--Billy Sunday, and Big-Time American Evangelism, J Am Hist, Vol 80, 93; Between Memory and Reality--Family and Community in Rural Wisconsin, 1870-1970, J Interdisciplinary Hist, Vol 26, 95. **CONTACT ADDRESS** Illinois Historical Preservation Agency, 523 W Monroe Apt 1, Springfield, IL 62704.

TAYLOR, ROBERT
PERSONAL Born 05/02/1958, Pittsburgh, PA, m, 2000 **DISCIPLINE** HISTORY **EDUCATION** Univ S Fla, BA, 83; MA, 85; Fla State Univ, PhD, 91. **CAREER** Instr, Univ of S Ala, 90-91; instr, Fla Atlantic Univ, 92-96; instr, Univ of St Francis, 92-98; instr Indian River Community Col, 92-99. **HONORS AND AWARDS** Diss Fel, Fla State Univ, 87-90. **MEMBERSHIPS** OAH; SHA; Fla Hist Soc. **RESEARCH** 19th Century U.S., the American Civil War, the South, Florida history, U.S. military history, 20th Century Europe, political science. **SELECTED PUBLICATIONS** Auth, This War So Horrible: The Civil War Diary of Hiram Smith Williams, Univ of Ala Pr, 93; auth, Rebel Storehouse: Florida in the Confederate Economy, Univ of Ala Pr, 95; auth, A Pennsylvanian in Blue: The Civil War Diary of Thomas Beck Walton, White Mane Pub, 95; auth, World War II in Fort Pierce, Arcadia Pr, 99; coauth, This Cruel War: The Civil War Letters of Grant and Malinda Taylor, Mercer Univ Pr, 00. **CONTACT ADDRESS** Dept Humanities, Florida Inst of Tech, 150 W University Blvd, Melbourne, FL 32901-6982. **EMAIL** rotaylor@fit.edu

TAYLOR, ROBERT R.
DISCIPLINE TWENTIETH-CENTURY EUROPE HISTORY **EDUCATION** Brit Columbia Univ, BA, MA; Stanford Univ, PhD. **CAREER** Prof. **RESEARCH** History of the Welland Canals. **SELECTED PUBLICATIONS** Auth, The Word in Stone: The Role of Architecture in the National Socialist Ideology, Univ Calif Press; Hohenzollern Berlin: Construction and Reconstruction, Meany. **CONTACT ADDRESS** Dept of Hist, Brock Univ, 500 Glenridge Ave, Saint Catharines, ON, Canada L2S 3A1. **EMAIL** rtaylor@spartan.ac.BrockU.CA

TAYLOR, SANDRA C.
PERSONAL Born Sacramento, CA, m **DISCIPLINE** AMERICAN FOREIGN RELATIONS **EDUCATION** Stanford Univ, AB, 58; Univ Colo, MA, 63, PhD(hist), 66. **CAREER** Teacher social studies, Denver Pub Schs, 59-62; instr hist, Univ Colo, Denver Ctr, 63; instr, Colorado Springs Ctr, 66; asst prof, 66-72, asst dean lib educ, 76-78, assoc dean lib educ, 78-81, Assoc Prof Hist, Univ Utah, 73-, Vis asst prof hist & Asian studies, Univ Hawaii, Hilo Col, 72-73. **MEMBERSHIPS** Orgn Am Historians; Soc Historians of Am Foreign Rels; Asn for Asian Studies. **RESEARCH** American relations with Meiji Japan; biography of Sidney L Gulick; relocation of Japanese Americans. **SELECTED PUBLICATIONS CONTACT ADDRESS** Dept of Hist, Univ of Utah, 217 Carlson Hall, Salt Lake City, UT 84112-3124.

TAYLOR, SARAH E.
PERSONAL Born 09/00/1974, Mobile, AL, s **DISCIPLINE** HISTORY **EDUCATION** Univ W Ala, BS, 95; MAT, 96. **CAREER** Instr, Bishop State Community Col; campus life coordr & adj instr, Meridian Community Col; staff, Univ W Ala Student Development Ctr. **MEMBERSHIPS** Am Hist Asn, Southern Hist Asn, Ala Hist Asn. **RESEARCH** Social History, Women's History. **CONTACT ADDRESS** Dept Soc Sci, Bishop State Comm Col, 351 N Broad St, Mobile, AL 36603-5833.

TAYLOR, SUE
DISCIPLINE ART HISTORY **EDUCATION** Roosevelt Univ, BA; Univ Chicago, MA, PhD. **HONORS AND AWARDS** Am Asn of Univ Women; Am Fel, 94. **SELECTED PUBLICATIONS** Auth, Lessons in Hysteria: Louise Bourgeois in the Nineties, New Art Examiner, 97; auth, Hans Bellmer: The Anatomy of Anxiety, MIT Press, 00. **CONTACT ADDRESS** Portland State Univ, PO Box 751, Portland, OR 97207-0751. **EMAIL** taylorsc@pdx.edu

TAYLOR, THOMAS TEMPLETON
PERSONAL Born 01/08/1955, Columbia, SC, m, 1975, 3 children **DISCIPLINE** HISTORY **EDUCATION** UnivNC-Greensboro, BA, 76, MA, 78; Univ Ill at Urbana-Champaign, PhD, 88. **CAREER** Lect, Residential Col, Univ NC-Greensboro, 84-88; asst prof, 88-93, assoc prof, 93- ,Wittenberg Univ. **HONORS AND AWARDS** Phi Alpha Theta, 75; Univ Diss Fellow, Univ Ill, 82-83; ODK Disting Tchg Awd Wittenberg, 91. **MEMBERSHIPS** Am Soc Legal Hist; Soc Cinema Stud; Am Soc Church Hist; Assoc Inst for Early Am Hist and Culture; Conf Faith and Hist. **RESEARCH** Legal, film, religious, early American history. **SELECTED PUBLICATIONS** Law and Justice, in Jessica Kross, ed., American Eras, 1600-1754, Gale Res, 98. **CONTACT ADDRESS** Dept of History, Wittenberg Univ, PO Box 720, Springfield, OH 45501. **EMAIL** ttaylor@wittenberg.edu

TAYLOR, TOM
DISCIPLINE HISTORY **EDUCATION** St John's Univ, BA, 78; Univ MN, MA, 83, PhD, 88. **CAREER** Hist, Seattle Univ. **MEMBERSHIPS** AHA; Ger Stud Asn; Soc Sci Hist Asn. **SELECTED PUBLICATIONS** Auth, Children in Mod German History, Children in Historical and Comparative Perspective; Images of Youth and the Family in Wilhelmne Germany: Toward a Reconsideration of the German Sondring, Ger Stud Rev, 92. **CONTACT ADDRESS** Dept of Hist, Seattle Univ, 900 Broadway, Seattle, WA 98122-4460. **EMAIL** twtaylor@seattleu.edu

TAYLOR-MITCHELL, LAURIE
PERSONAL Born 06/01/1956, Houston, TX, m, 1990, 1 child **DISCIPLINE** HISTORY OF ART **EDUCATION** Univ MI, PhD, 88 **CAREER** Asst prof, 91-96, Univ of Incarnate Word, San Antonio, TX; independent scholar, 96-. **HONORS AND AWARDS** Phi Beta Kappa **MEMBERSHIPS** Coll Art Assn; Italian Art Soc; Midwest Art Hist Soc; ICMA; South Central Renaissance Conf **RESEARCH** Painting and sculpture, 14th and 15th century, Florence and Tuscany **SELECTED PUBLICATIONS** Auth, Images of St. Màtthew Commissioned by the Arte del Cambio for Orsanmichele in Florence: Some Observations on Conservatism in Form and Patronage, Gesta, 92; Guild Commissions at Orsanmichele: Some Relationships Between Interior and Exterior Imagery in the Trecento and Quattrocento, Explorations in Renaissance Culture, 94; A Florentine Source for Verrocchio's Figure of St. Thomas at Orsanmichele, Zeitschrift fur Kunstgeschichte, 94; Botticelli's San Barnaba Altarpiece: Guild Patronage in a Florentne Context, The Search for a Patron in the Middle Ages and the Renaissance, 96. **CONTACT ADDRESS** 110 Sunnycrest Dr, San Antonio, TX 78228-2913.

TEAFORD, JON C.
PERSONAL Born Columbus, OH **DISCIPLINE** HISTORY **EDUCATION** Oberlin Col, BA, 69; Univ of Wis, MA, 70, PhD, 73. **CAREER** Vis asst prof of Hist, Iowa State Univ, 73-75; asst prof, 75-79, assoc prof, 79-84, prof, Purdue Univ, 84-. **MEMBERSHIPS** Urban Hist Asn; Soc of Am City & Regional Planning Hist. **SELECTED PUBLICATIONS** Auth, The Municipal Revolution in America, 75; City and Suburb: The Political Fragmentation of Metropolitan America, 79; The Unheralded Triumph: American Urban Government 1870-1900, 84; The Twentieth-Century American City, 86; The Rough Road to Renaissance: Urban Revitalization in America 1940-1985, 90; Cities of the Heartland: The Rise and Fall of the Industrial Midwest, 93; Post-Suburbia: The Politics and Government of Edge Cities, 97. **CONTACT ADDRESS** History Dept, Purdue Univ, West Lafayette, West Lafayette, IN 47907.

TEBBENHOFF, EDWARD H.
PERSONAL Born 04/14/1949, Suffren, NY, m, 1980, 1 child **DISCIPLINE** HISTORY **EDUCATION** Univ Minn, PhD, 92 **CAREER** Assoc prof, Luther Col. **RESEARCH** Early Amer, hist methods **CONTACT ADDRESS** History Dept, Luther Col, 700 College Dr, Decorah, IA 52101.

TEGEDER, VINCENT GEORGE
PERSONAL Born 10/01/1910, La Crosse, WI **DISCIPLINE** HISTORY POLITICAL SCIENCE **EDUCATION** St John's Univ, Minn, BA, 33; Univ Wis, MA, 42, PhD, 49. **CAREER** Prof hist, 46-79, Emer Prof Hist, St John's Univ, Minn, 79-, Archivist, 75-96, Vis prof hist, Sacramento State Col, 65-66 & 67 & Int Div, Sophia Univ, Tokyo, 73-74. **HONORS AND AWARDS** NCAIS, India, 70. **MEMBERSHIPS** Am Cath Hist Asn. **RESEARCH** American West during the Civil War; culture on the frontier; colonization. **SELECTED PUBLICATIONS** Auth, "Lincoln," MVHR, Vol 35, 77; auth, Obituary (rev), Cath Hist Rev, Vol 80, 94. **CONTACT ADDRESS** St. John's Univ, Archives Collegeville, MN 56321. **EMAIL** vtegeder@csbsju.edu

TEICH, ALBERT HARRIS
PERSONAL Born 12/17/1942, Chicago, IL, m, 1989, 3 children **DISCIPLINE** SCIENCE AND TECHNOLOGY POLICY **EDUCATION** PhD, MIT, 69; BS, MIT 64. **CAREER** Dir Directorate for Sci and Policy Programs, Amer Asso for the Advancement of Sci, 90-; Head Office of Public Sector ProgramS, Amer Assoc for the Advancement of Sci, 84-89; Manager Sci Policy Studies Amer Assoc for the Advancement of Sci, 80-84; Deputy Dir, Graduate Program in Sci Tech and Public Policy, Assoc Prof, Public Affairs George Washington Univ, 76-80; Vis Res Prof, Graduate School of Publc Affairs, State Univ NY, Albany, 75-76; Dir of Res Inst for Public Policy Alternatives, State Univ NY, 74-75. **MEMBERSHIPS** Amer Assoc for the Advancement of Sci Elected Fellow, 86; Elected Chm Section X, 88-89; Tech Transfer Soc Elected VP, 86-91; Elected Member Board of Dir, 91-95; Assoc for Public Policy, Analysis and Mgt Elected Member, Policy Board, 96-99; Amer Soc for Public Admin Member, Ed Board Pub, Admin Rev, 83-86; Sigma Xi. **RESEARCH** US and Intl Sci and Tech policy; budgeting and priority setting; Sci Tech and Soc; mutual impacts of Tech and Soc; Soc and ethical aspects of Info Tech and computer networking. **SELECTED PUBLICATIONS** Albert H.Teich, Science and Society in The World Book Science Year 00, Chicago World Book Publishng Co, 99; Albert H. Teich, The Political Context of Science Priority Setting, in the United States, chapter 1, in Mark S.Frankel and Jane Cave eds; Evaluating Science and Scientists, Budapest, Central Euro Univ Press, 97; Albert H.Teich ed, Conpetitiveness in Academic Research, AAAS, 97 ; Albert H.Teich, Cost, Funding and Budget Issues in Mega-science Projects; The Case of the United States Chapter 5 in Organization for Economic Cooperation and Development Mega-science Policy Issues, OECD, 95; Albert H.Teich, ed, Technology and the Future, St.Martin's Press, first published, 72, 8th ed, 99; Albert H.Teich, US Science Policy in the 1990s: New Institutional Arrangements, Procedures and Legitmations, in Susan E.Cozzens et al, The Research System in Transition, Kluwer Academic Publ 90. **CONTACT ADDRESS** Am Asn for the Advancement of Sci, 1200 New York Ave NW, Washington, DC 20005. **EMAIL** ateich@aaas.org

TELESCA, WILLIAM JOHN
PERSONAL Born 08/01/1931, Port Chester, NY, m, 1958, 4 children **DISCIPLINE** MEDIEVAL HISTORY, CLASSICAL CIVILIZATION **EDUCATION** Fordham Univ, BA, 58, MS, 61, PhD(medieval hist), 68. **CAREER** Teacher soc studies, Port Chester High Sch, NY, 58-67; asst prof medieval hist, 67-80, prof hist, Le Moyne Col, NY, 80-00; Prof Emer, 00-. **HONORS AND AWARDS** Regents War Service Scholar, 58-61; Fulbright Scholar in Rome, 66-67. **MEMBERSHIPS** Mediaeval Acad Am; Asn Cistercian Studies; AAUP. **RESEARCH** Western monasticism; 15th century French monarchy and the papacy. **SELECTED PUBLICATIONS** Auth, The Problem of the Commendatory Monasteries and the Order of Citeaux, Citeaux, 71; The Cistercian Dilemma at the Close of the Middle Ages: Gallicanism or Rome, In: Studies in Medieval Cistercian History, 71 & Jean de Cirey, an Abbot General of the Fifteenth Century, In: Studies in Medieval Cistercian History, Vol II, 73, Cistercian Publ; Papal Reservations and Provisions of Cistercian Abbeys, Citeaux, 75; The Cistercian Abbey in Fifteenth Century France: A Victim of Competing Jurisdictions of Sovereignty, Suzerainty, and Primacy in Cistercians in the Late Middle Ages, Cistercian Publ, 81; The Order of Citeaux during the Council of Basel, 1431-1449, In: Citeaux Com Cist, Vol II, 17-36; Cistercian 'Transfers' and Papal Provisions in the Fifteenth Century, Citeaux, pp279-293, 90; Tasse pagate dagli ordini religiosi alla Santa Sede nel medioevo, in Dizionario degli istituti di perfezione, pp 27-39, 94. **CONTACT ADDRESS** Dept of Hist, Le Moyne Col, 1419 Salt Springs Rd, Syracuse, NY 13214-1300.

TEN GROTENHUIS, ELIZABETH
PERSONAL Born 10/01/1948, Manila, Philippines, m, 1977, 2 children **DISCIPLINE** ART HISTORY **EDUCATION** Harvard Univ, AB, 70; AM, 72; PhD, 80. **CAREER** Assoc Prof, Boston Univ. **HONORS AND AWARDS** Japan Found Fel, 78; Res Grant, Metro Ctr for Far E Art Studies, 93, 98; Sen Vis Fel, Nat Univ of Singapore, 00; Intl Who's Who of Prof and Bus Women. **MEMBERSHIPS** Cambridge Buddhist Asn; Col Art Asn; Asn for Asian Studies; Japan Art Hist Asn. **RESEARCH** History of Japanese Art, especially religious painting; Pan-Asian Buddhist tradition; Silk Road Studies; East Asian Garden Design. **SELECTED PUBLICATIONS** Auth, "Visions of a Transcendent Realm: Pure Land Images in the Cleveland Museum of Art," The Bulletin of the Cleveland Museum of Art Vol 78, (91): 274-300; auth, "Chujohime: The Weaving of Her Legend," in Flowing Traces: Buddhism in the Literary and Visual Arts of Japan, (Princeton Univ Press, 92), 180-200; auth, "The White Path Crossing Two Rivers: A Contemporary Japanese Garden Represents the Past," J of Garden History, (95): 1-18; auth, Japanese Mandalas: Representations of Sacred Geography, Univ Haw, 99; ed, The Silk Road, Univ Wash Press, in press. **CONTACT ADDRESS** Dept Art Hist, Boston Univ, 725 Commonwealth Ave, Boston, MA 02215. **EMAIL** eteng@bu.edu

TENENBAUM, SERGIO
DISCIPLINE ETHICS, HISTORY OF MODERN PHILOSOPHY, PRACTICAL REASON **EDUCATION** Hebrew Univ Jerusalem, BA, 88; Univ Pittsburgh, MA, 93, PhD, 96. **CAREER** Asst prof, Univ NMex. **SELECTED PUBLICATIONS** Auth, Hegel's Critique of Kant in the Philosophy of Right, in Kant Studien; Realists without a Cause: Deflationary Theories of Truth and Ethical Realism, Can J of Philos. **CONTACT ADDRESS** Univ of New Mexico, Albuquerque, Albuquerque, NM 87131. **EMAIL** sergio@unm.edu

TENG, TONY
PERSONAL m, 1 child **DISCIPLINE** EAST ASIAN HISTORY, MODERN CHINA AND JAPAN **EDUCATION** Tunghai Univ, Taiwan, BA; Occidental Col, MA; Univ Wis, Madison, PhD. **CAREER** Prof, RI Col. **RESEARCH** Mod Chinese diplomatic hist. **SELECTED PUBLICATIONS** Publ entries in National Dictionary of Revolutionary China, 1838-1926 and Nationalism in East Asia, an Encyclopdia Study. **CONTACT ADDRESS** Rhode Island Col, Providence, RI 02908. **EMAIL** tteng1@juno.com

TENKOTTE, PAUL A.
PERSONAL Born 06/30/1960, Covington, KY **DISCIPLINE** HISTORY **EDUCATION** Thomas More Col, BA, 82; Univ Cincinnati, MA, 83; PhD, 89. **CAREER** Asst prof to Prof and director of Intl Studies, Thomas More Col, 87-. **HONORS AND AWARDS** Cultural Exchange Grant, 91; Charles P Taft Fel, Cincinnati, 82, 84, 85; Lenore McGrane Fel, Univ Cincinnati, 86-87; Dr. John Pine Nat Scholarship, 85; Excellence in Teaching Awd, Cincinnati, 90. **MEMBERSHIPS** Phi alpha Theta Intl Honor Soc, Am Hist Asn, Wilson Center Assoc. **RESEARCH** Urban History (American); History of American Architecture; History of the Catholic Church in the US; World History. **SELECTED PUBLICATIONS** Auth, A Heritage of Art and Faith; Downtown Covington Churches, 86. **CONTACT ADDRESS** Dept Hist & Govt, Thomas More Col, 333 Thomas More Pkwy, Crestview Hills, KY 41017-3428. **EMAIL** paul.tenkotte@thomasmore.edu

TEORIO-TRILLO, MAURICIO
PERSONAL Born 10/18/1962, Mexico City, Mexico, m, 1995, 1 child **DISCIPLINE** HISTORY **EDUCATION** Univ At Metropolitana, Licenciatura, 85; Stanford Univ, MA, 87; PhD, 92. **CAREER** Prof, Centro de Investigacion y Docencia Econ Mexico, 94-; Assoc Prof, Univ Tex, 95-; Fel, Wissenschaftskolleg zu Berlin, 00-01. **MEMBERSHIPS** Am Hist Soc **SELECTED PUBLICATIONS** Auth, Mexico at the World's fairs: Crafting a Modern Nation, Univ Calif Press, 96; auth, Artilugio de la Nacion Moderna, El Fondo de Cultura Economica, Mexico, 98; auth, Argucias de la Historia, Editorial Paidos, Mexico City, 99; auth, De Como Ignorar, Ed Fondo de Cultura Economica, Mexico, 00. **CONTACT ADDRESS** Dept Hist, Univ of Texas, Austin, 5414 Av H, Austin, TX 78751. **EMAIL** metnorio@mail.utexas.edu

TEPASKE, JOHN J.
PERSONAL Born 12/08/1929, Grand Rapids, MI, m, 1951, 2 children **DISCIPLINE** LATIN AMERICAN HISTORY **EDUCATION** Mich State Univ, BA, 51; Duke Univ, MA, 53, PhD, 59. **CAREER** Asst prof hist, Memphis State Univ, 58-59; from instr to assoc prof, Ohio State Univ, 59-67; assoc prof, 67-69, prof hist, Duke Univ, 69-; Foreign area training fel & res fel, Univ Calif, Berkeley, 62-63; Tinker Found fel, 75-77; Nat Endowment for Humanities fel, 77; Am Philos Soc fel, 81; chmn, Conf Latin Am Hist, 81; Soc Sci Res Coun Fel, 85-86; Bank Spain Fel, 86-87; Nat Hum Ctr Fel, 89-90; Guggenheim Fel, 95-96; Distinguished Serv Award, Conf Latin Am Hist, 96. **MEMBERSHIPS** AHA; Conf Latin Am Hist; Latin Am Studies Asn; Soc Span & Port Studies. **RESEARCH** Quantitative history; vice-royalty of Peru; comparative colonial history. **SELECTED PUBLICATIONS** Auth, The Governorship of Spanish Florida, 1700-1763, Duke Univ, 63; Three American Empires, Harper, 67; auth, La Real Hacienda de Nueva Expana: La Real Caja de Mexico, 1576-1816, Inst Nacional de Antropologia e Historia, 76; ed, Discourse and Political Reflections on the Kingdoms of Peru, Univ Okla Press, 78; Research Guide to Andean History: Bolivia, Chile, Ecuador and Peru, Duke Univ Press; coauth, The Royal Treasuries of the Spanish Empire in America, Peru 1; Upper Peru 2; Chile and the Rio de la Plata, Duke Univ Press, 82; coauth, The Royal Protomedicato: The Regulation of the Medical Professions in the Spanish Empire, Duke Univ Press, 95; coauth, Ingresos y egresos de la Real Hacienda de Nueva Espana, Instituto Nacional de Antropologia e Historia, 86 & 88; coauth The Royal Treasuries of the Spanish Empire in America, Eighteenth-Century Ecuado, Duke Univ Press, 90. **CONTACT ADDRESS** Dept of History, Duke Univ, PO Box 90719, Durham, NC 27708-0719. **EMAIL** jjay@acpub.duke.edu

TERAOKA, ARLENE
DISCIPLINE GERMAN STUDIES **EDUCATION** Yale Univ, BA, 76; Stanford, MA, 77; PhD, 83. **CAREER** Asst Prof, Univ of Wash, 83-85; Asst Prof, Princeton Univ, 85-89; Assoc Prof/Prof, Univ of Minn, 89-. **HONORS AND AWARDS** ACLS/SSRC E Europ Studies, 86-87; DDAD Prize for Distinguished Scholar in Ger Studies, 99. **MEMBERSHIPS** MLA, GSA, AATG, Int Brecht Soc, Women in Ger. **RESEARCH** 20th-century German Literature, culture, politics. **SELECTED PUBLICATIONS** Auth, The Silence of Entropy or Universal Discourse: The Postmodernist Poetics of Heiner Mueller, 85; auth, East, West, and Others: The Third World in Postwar German Literature, 96. **CONTACT ADDRESS** Dept German, Univ of Minnesota, Twin Cities, 9 Pleasant St SE, 205 Folwell Hall, Minneapolis, MN 55455-0194. **EMAIL** terao001@tc.umn.edu

TERBORG-PENN, ROSALYN M.
PERSONAL Born 10/22/1941, Brooklyn, NY, d, 1 child **DISCIPLINE** HISTORY **EDUCATION** Queens Coll CUNY, BA 1963; George Washington U, MA 1967; Howard U, PhD 1977. **CAREER** Morgan State U, prof of history, coordinator of graduate programs in history, 86-. **HONORS AND AWARDS** Grad History Essay Awd Rayford Logan, Howard Univ 1973; Grad Fellowship in History Howard Univ 1973-74; Post Doct Fellowship for Minorities Ford Found 1980-81; Visiting Scholar Grant Smithsonian Inst 1982, 1994; Travel to Collections Grant Nat Endowment for the Humanities 1984; Association of Black Women Historians, Letitia Woods Brown Awd for Best Article Published on Black Women, 1987-88, for Best Anthology, 1995, for Best Book, 1998; Lorraine A Williams Leadership Awd, 1998; The Sage Womens Educational Press, Anna Julia Cooper Awd for Distinguished Scholarship, 1995. **MEMBERSHIPS** History editor Feminist Studies, 1984-89; commr Howard Cty MD Commn for Women 1980-82; chair, American Historical Association Comm on Women Historians, 1991-93; Research & Publications Comm, Maryland Historical Soc, 1989-96; Alpha Kappa Alpha Sorority, Inc; Association of Black Women Historians, founder, 1978. **SELECTED PUBLICATIONS** Author: Afro-American Woman-Struggles and Images, 1978, 1981, 1997; Women in Africa and the African Dispora, 1987, 1996; African-American Women in the Struggle for the Vote, 1998. **CONTACT ADDRESS** Professor of History, Morgan State Univ, Baltimore, MD 21251. **EMAIL** rmterborg@aol.com

TERRILL, ROSS
PERSONAL Born Melbourne, Australia **DISCIPLINE** ASIAN STUDIES **EDUCATION** Weley Col Melbourne, 56; BA, First Class Hon, Univ of Melbourne, 62; PhD, Polit Sci, Harvard Univ, 70; Welsey Col, Asia Soc, 96-00. **CAREER** Austalian Army, 57-58; Tutor in Polit Sci, Univ of Melbourne, 62-63; Staff Sec Australian Student Christian Movement, 62, 64-65; Res Fel Asia Sic, 68-70, Lectr on Govt, 70-74, Dir Student Prog in Intl Affairs, 74-77, Assoc Prof Govt, Harvard Univ, 74-78; Vis Prof, Monash Univ, 96-98; Res Assoc, Fairbank Center for East Asian Res, Harvard Univ 70-; vis prof, Univ of Tex, 67-01. **HONORS AND AWARDS** Natl Mag Awd for Reporting Excellence, 72; George Polk Memoria Awd for Outstanding Mag Reporting, 72; Summer Prize for PhD Thesis, Harvard Univ, 70; Exhibition in Polit Sci, Univ of Melbourne, 57; Frank Knox Memorial Fellowship, Harvard Univ, 65-66. **MEMBERSHIPS** Author's League; PEN Am Ctr; Asn of Asian Studies. **SELECTED PUBLICATIONS** China in Our Time, Simon & Schuster, 92; The Australians, Simon & Schuster, 87; The White-Boned Demon: A Biography of Madame Mao Zedong, William Morrow, 84; Mao in History, The Natl Interest, 98; China Under Deng, Foreign Affairs, Vol 73 No 5, 94; China Quarterly, No 139, 94; Journal of Asian Studies, Vol 48, No 4, 89; Bulletin of Australian Political Studies Associations, Vol 8 No 2, Political Sci Quarterly, No 40, 69; Mao: A Biography, Stanford, 00; The Australians: The Way We Live Now, Doubleday, 00. **CONTACT ADDRESS** Fairbank Ctr for East Asian Res, Harvard Univ, Cambridge, MA 02138. **EMAIL** terr@compuserve.com

TERRILL, TOM E.
PERSONAL Born 09/15/1935, Oklahoma City, OK, m, 1961, 2 children **DISCIPLINE** AMERICAN HISTORY **EDUCATION** Westminster Col, Mo, BA, 57; Princeton Theol Sem, BD, 61; Univ Wis-Madison, MA, 63, PhD(Am hist), 66. **CAREER** Vis asst prof Am & African hist, Hiram Col, 65-66; asst prof Am hist, 66-70, assoc prof, 70-80, Prof Hist, Univ SC, 80-, Vis lectr, Allen Univ, 67 & 70; vis prof church hist, Lutheran Southern Theol Sem, 72; Nat Endowment for Humanities younger humanist fel, 73-74; grant, SC Comt for Humanities, 73, 76 & 78-; Rockefeller Found Humanities fel, 79-80. **MEMBERSHIPS** AHA; Econ Hist Asn; Southern Hist Asn; Orgn Am Historians. **RESEARCH** Late 19th century United States; Southern textile workers; Southern economic and labor history. **SELECTED PUBLICATIONS** Auth, The South--A Bibliographical Essay, Am Studies Int, Vol 31, 93. **CONTACT ADDRESS** Dept of Hist, Univ of So Carolina, Columbia, Columbia, SC 29208.

TERRY, ANN R.
DISCIPLINE ART HISTORY **EDUCATION** Eastern Mich Univ, BFA, 71; Univ Ill, MA, PhD. **CAREER** Independent scholar **HONORS AND AWARDS** Fel(s): Int Res & Exchanges Bd; The Kress Found; Am Philos Soc; Dumbarton Oaks Fel; Omicron Delta Kappa Awd. **RESEARCH** Archaeology,art and architecture of early Christian period. **CONTACT ADDRESS** 5 Riding Club Rd, Danvers, MA 01923. **EMAIL** terreich@massmed.org

TERRY, JANICE J.
PERSONAL Born 03/29/1942, Cleveland, OH, m **DISCIPLINE** MODERN MIDDLE EAST HISTORY **EDUCATION** Col Wooster, BA, 64; Am Univ Beirut, MA, 66; Univ London, PhD, 68. **CAREER** Assoc prof hist, 68-76, assoc prof hist & philos, 76-80, prof hist, Eastern Mich Univ, 80-, US Dept Health, Educ & Welfare res grant, Egypt, 73. **MEMBERSHIPS** Mid East Studies Asn N Am; Brismes AAUG. **RESEARCH** Modern Egypt. **SELECTED PUBLICATIONS** Auth, Official British reaction to Egyptian nationalism, al-Abhath, 68; Israel's policy toward the Arab states, in The Transformation of Palestine, Northwestern Univ, 71; co-ed, The Arab World From Nationalism to Revolution, Medina Univ, 71; auth, Struggle for independence in Aden, MidE Forum, winter & summer 73; The consequences of economic abstention: The Aswan Dam, in Intervention or Abstention, Univ Press Ky, 75; Zionist Attitudes Toward Arabs: Palestine Studies, 76; The Wafd 1919-1952: Cornerstone of Egyptian Political Power, Third World Ctr, 82; coauth (with professors Goff, Moss & Upshur), The World in the 20th Century, McGraw Hill, 5th ed; coauth, World History, West, 3rd ed. **CONTACT ADDRESS** Dept of Hist, Eastern Michigan Univ, 701 Pray Harrold, Ypsilanti, MI 48197-2201.

TERRY, SEAN
PERSONAL Born 03/04/1965, San Diego, CA, m, 1993, 1 child **DISCIPLINE** GEOGRAPHY **EDUCATION** Southwest Miss State Univ, BS, 88; MS, 91; Univ Okla, PhD, 95. **CAREER** Adj prof, Rose State Col, 95-98; instr, Univ of Okla, 94-98; vis asst prof, Drury Univ, 98-. **HONORS AND AWARDS** Olson Awd, Univ of Okla, 93; 1st place Nat Student Paper Competition, CA AAG, 94; Grant, Univ of Okla, 95; Excellence in Teaching Awd, Rose State Col, 97-98. **MEMBERSHIPS** Assoc of Am Geogr; Nat Coun for Geog Educ; Nat Assoc of Environ Prof. **RESEARCH** Water quality, geography of food, environmental conservation, geographic education. **SELECTED PUBLICATIONS** Coauth, Geography 1003: Introduction to the Geosciences, Middlesex Res Corp, 95; auth, Geography 2603, World Regional Geography, Univ of Okla, (Norman), 96; auth, Geography 4913, Regional Geography of the United States and Canada, Univ of Okla, (Norman), 96; auth, Laboratory Manual for Physical Geography 1114, King Pub, (Norman, OK), 96; rev, of "River of Promise, River of Peril" by John Thorson, Soc Sci Quarterly (96): auth, "Historical Impacts and Recovery in the Healdton Oil Field, Oklahoma", Proceedings of the Nat Assoc of Environ Prof, 96: auth, "Effects of Wastewater Disposal on an Oil Field Landscape", Environ Geosciences, 3.3 (96): auth, Physical Geography, Navy Pace Prog, (Baltimore, Md): 97; auth, Environmental Conservation, Univ of Okla Ind Studies Dept, (Norman), 98; auth, "Production History of the Healdton Field, Oklahoma", Okla Geology Notes 56.5, (99). **CONTACT ADDRESS** Dept Hist and Govt, Drury Col, 900 N Benton Ave, Springfield, MO 65802. **EMAIL** sterry@drury.edu

TEUTE, FREDRIKA J.
PERSONAL Born 10/16/1947, Rochester, NY, m, 1985 **DISCIPLINE** AMERICAN HISTORY **EDUCATION** Radcliffe Col, BA, 69; Col of William & Mary, MA, 76; Johns Hopkins Univ, PhD, 88. **CAREER** Assoc ed, Papers of James Madison, 71-76; Ed of Publ, Virginia Hist Soc, 81-84; assoc ed, Papers of John Marshall, 84-89; Ed of Publ, Omohundro Inst of Early Am Hist and Cult, 89- . **HONORS AND AWARDS** Butler Prize, Johns Hopkins Univ; Bunting Inst Fel; Mellon fel; NEH-Am Antiq Soc Fel. **MEMBERSHIPS** Am Antiq Soc; AHA; OAH; ASECS; SHA; ASA; ADE; SEA. **RESEARCH** Early American frontiers; early Kentucky; early national political culture. **CONTACT ADDRESS** Omohundro Inst of Early American History and Culture, PO Box 8781, Williamsburg, VA 23187-8781. **EMAIL** fjteut@wm.edu

TEVIOTDALE, ELIZABETH C.
PERSONAL Born 11/15/1955, New York, NY, s **DISCIPLINE** ART HISTORY **EDUCATION** BA, State Univ of NYork at Buffalo, 79; MA, Univ of NC, 81; MA, Tulane Univ, 85; PhD, Univ of NC, 91. **CAREER** 97-, Assoc Curator of Manuscripts, The J. Paul Getty Mus 92-97, Asst Curator of Manuscripts, The J. Paul Getty Mus 91-92, vis asst prof, Davidson Col Spring 91, vis instru, Univ of IA. **HONORS AND AWARDS** Samuel H. Kress Found Predoctoral Fel Summer 88-90; Swedish Institute Guest Scholarship 89; Fulbright Travel Grant 83-84; For Exchange Fel, Freie Universitat Berlin, 83-84; DAAD Res Grant, 99. **MEMBERSHIPS** UCLA Center of Medieval and Renaissance Studies Am Musicological Soc Col Art Assoc International Center of Medieval At Medieval Acad of Am. **RESEARCH** Western medieval liturgical manuscripts and their illumination. **SELECTED PUBLICATIONS** A Pair of Franco-Flemish Cistercian Antiphonals of the 13th Century and Their Programs of Illumination in Interpreting and Collecting Fragments of Medieval Books, Anderson-Lovelace, (00): 231-258; An Episode in the Medieval Afterlife of the Caligula Troper, in Anglo-Saxon Manuscripts and Their Heritage, ed Phillip Pulsiano and Elaine Treharne, Ashgate, 98, pp 219-226; Latin Verse Inscriptions in Anglo-Saxon Art, Gesta 35, 96, 99-110; 750 Years in the Life of a Pair of Cistercian Antiphonals Pastoral Music 20/2, 96, 38-40; The Invitation to the Puy d'Evreux, Current Musicology 52, 93, 7-26; Some Classified Catalogues of the Cottonian Library, The British Library Jour 18, 92, 74-87; Music and Pictures in the Middle Ages, in Companion to Medieval and Renaissance Music, ed Tess Knighton and David Fallows, JM Dent, 92, pp 179-188; The Filiation of the Music Illustrations in a Boethius in Milan and in the Piacenza Codice magno, Imago Musicae 5, 88, 7-22; A Speculation on an Affinity between Ruskin's Seven Lamps of Architecture and Monet's Cathedrals, The Rutgers Art Review 4, 83, 68-77. **CONTACT ADDRESS** J. Paul Getty Mus, 1200 Getty Center Drive, Ste. 1000, Los Angeles, CA 90049-1687. **EMAIL** eteviotdale@getty.edu

THACKER, JACK W.
PERSONAL Born 09/10/1940, Atlanta, GA, m, 1978 **DISCIPLINE** HISTORY **EDUCATION** Ga State Univ, BA, 61; Univ SCar, MA, 63; PhD, 66. **CAREER** Instructor, Univ SCar, 64; Asst Prof to Prof, W Ky Univ, 64-; Visiting Prof, US Military Acad, 82. **HONORS AND AWARDS** NDEA Fel, 61-64; Teaching Awd, W KY Univ, 71; Library Awd, W KY Univ, 91; Commanders Awd for Public Service, US Army, 96; Outstanding Educator in Am, 71-74. **MEMBERSHIPS** Soc of Military Hist; Am Hist Asn. **RESEARCH** 20th Century Military History **CONTACT ADDRESS** Dept Hist, Western Kentucky Univ, 1 Big Red Way St, Bowling Green, KY 42101-5730. **EMAIL** jack.thacker@wku.edu

THACKERAY, FRANK W.
PERSONAL Born 03/16/1943, Pittsburgh, PA, m, 1971, 2 children **DISCIPLINE** RUSSIAN & EASTERN EUROPEAN HISTORY **EDUCATION** Dickinson Col, BA, 65; Temple Univ, MA, 71; PhD, 77. **CAREER** Asst Prof to Prof, Ind Univ SE, 77-. **HONORS AND AWARDS** Fulbright Hayes Fel; Distinguished Res and Creativity Awd, IN Univ SE. **MEMBERSHIPS** Am Hist Asn; Am Asn for the Adv of Slavic Studies; Polish Inst of Arts and Sci in Am; Fulbright Alumni Asn. **RESEARCH** Ninteenth Century Russia; Nineteenth Century Poland. **SELECTED PUBLICATIONS** Ed, The Greenwood Histories of Modern Nations, Greenwood Pub Group; co-ed, Events That Changed the World, Greenwood Pub Group; co-ed, Events That Changed America, Greenwood Pub Group; auth, Antcedents of Revolution: Alexander I and the Polish Congress Kingdom, East European Monographs. **CONTACT ADDRESS** Div Soc Sci, Indiana Univ, Southeast, 4201 Grant Line Rd, New Albany, IN 47150-2158. **EMAIL** fthacker@ius.edu

THADEN, EDWARD C.
PERSONAL Born 04/24/1922, Seattle, WA, m, 1950 **DISCIPLINE** HISTORY **EDUCATION** Univ Wash, BA, 44; Univ Zurich, Cert, 48; Univ Paris, PhD, 50. **CAREER** Instr to prof, Pa State Univ, 52-68; vis prof, Univ Marburg, 65; from prof to prof emeritus, Univ Ill, 68-; vis prof, Martin Luther Univ, 88; vis res prof, Moscow, 88, 90. **HONORS AND AWARDS** Fulbright Fel, Finland, 57-58, Germany, 65, Poland/Finland, 68; Carnegie Grant; ACLS Res Awds, 63, 75; IREX/USSR Acad Awds, 75, 88, 90; Woodrow Wilson Int Ctr Scholar, 80; pres, comm internationale des etudies historques slaves, 95-00. **MEMBERSHIPS** Am Hist Asn; Asn Adv Baltic Stud; Am Asn Adv of Slavic Studies; Com Int des Etudes Historique Slaves. **RESEARCH** Russian; Balkan; Baltic and Scandinav history. **SELECTED PUBLICATIONS** Auth, The Western Borderland of Russia, 1710-1870, 84; auth, Interpretting History: collected Essays on the Relations of Russia with Europe, 90; auth, Essays in Russian and East European History: Festschrift in Honor of Edward C. Thaden, 95; auth, art, Der Sowjetische Historismus und Ostmitteleuropa Nach 1939, 95; auth, The Rise of Historicism in Russia, 99. **CONTACT ADDRESS** PO Box 31786, Seattle, WA 98103-1786. **EMAIL** engvik@worldnet.att.net

THAL, SARAH
PERSONAL Born 07/06/1966, Toledo, OH, s **DISCIPLINE** HISTORY **EDUCATION** Georgetown Univ BSc, 88; SOAS Univ London, BA, 90; Columbia Univ, MA, 91; MPhil, 93; PhD, 99. **CAREER** Asst prof, Rice Univ, 99-. **HONORS AND AWARDS** Marshall Scholar, 88; Mellon Fel in the Humanities, 88. **MEMBERSHIPS** Am Hist Asn, Asn for Asian Studies, Soc for the Study of Japanese Relig. **RESEARCH** Modern Japan, Religion and Society. **SELECTED PUBLICATIONS** Auth, Rearranging the Landscape of the Gods: A History of Kompira Pligrimage in the Meiys Period, Columbia Univ, 99. **CONTACT ADDRESS** Dept Hist, Rice Univ, 6100 Main St, Houston, TX 77005-1827. **EMAIL** thal@rice.edu

THAYER, JOHN A.
DISCIPLINE HISTORY **EDUCATION** Univ Wis, PhD, 60. **CAREER** Prof **RESEARCH** Nineteenth and twentieth century Italian and European cultural-political history. **SELECTED PUBLICATIONS** Auth, Italy and the "Great War": Politics and Culture, 1870-1915, 73; History As Logic and As Explanation, Studies Modern Italian Hist, 86. **CONTACT ADDRESS** History Dept, Univ of Minnesota, Twin Cities, 614 Social Sciences Tower, 267 19th Ave S, Minneapolis, MN 55455. **EMAIL** thaye001@tc.umn.edu

THEILE, KARL H.
PERSONAL Born St. Louis, MO **DISCIPLINE** HISTORY; INTERNATIONAL RELATIONS **EDUCATION** Univ Rochester, BS, 61; Calif State Univ, LA, MA, 63; Univ Southern Calif, PhD, 81. **CAREER** Prof, dept chemn, LA T-TCC, 70-. **MEMBERSHIPS** Hum Asn Calif **RESEARCH** World War II **SELECTED PUBLICATIONS** Auth, Beyond Monsters and Clowns, 96. **CONTACT ADDRESS** 3940 Fairway Ave, Studio City, CA 91604.

THEODORE, CHARMANT
PERSONAL Born 11/03/1953, Haiti, m, 1978, 3 children **DISCIPLINE** ART, SCIENCES **EDUCATION** Univ South Florida, BA, 88; Univ South Florida, MA, 91. **CAREER** Lecturer, Center for Latin American Studies; Univ of Florida, 89-93; Lecturer, African & Asian Languages & Literatures, Univ of Florida, 93-96; Lecturer, Romance Languages and Literatures, Univ of Florida, 96-00. **RESEARCH** Translation; Courtroom Interpretation; Haitian Creole Grammar; Literary Criticism. **SELECTED PUBLICATIONS** Auth, "Haitian Creole, English/English-Haitian Creole Dictionary; auth, "Edition Critique De La Famille Des Pitite-Caille (MA Thesis) (Critical Edition of La Famille Des Pitite-Caille). **CONTACT ADDRESS** 4301 Ashby Ln, Tampa, FL 33624. **EMAIL** theodore@typhoon.coedu.usf.edu

THEOHARIS, ATHAN
PERSONAL Born 08/03/1936, Milwaukee, WI, m, 1966, 2 children **DISCIPLINE** RECENT UNITED STATES HISTORY **EDUCATION** Univ Chicago, AB, 56, AB, 57, AM, 59, PhD, 65. **CAREER** Instr hist, Tex A&M Univ, 62-64; asst prof, Wayne State Univ, 64-68; assoc prof, Staten Island Community Col, 68-69; from assoc prof to prof hist, Marquette Univ, 69-; Thomas P Lockwood prof Am hist, State Univ NY, Buffalo, 82-83. **HONORS AND AWARDS** Fac res fel, Wayne State Univ, 67; Certificate of Merit, Am Bar Asn, 72; grant, Johnson Found, 77; grant, Nat Endowment for Humanities, 76; Binkley-Stephenson Awd, 79; grant, Warsh-Mott Fund, 80; grant, Field Found, 80; res grant, Albert Beyeridge, 80; fel, Investigative journalism, 80. **MEMBERSHIPS** AHA; Orgn Am Historians; Acad Polit Sci. **RESEARCH** Truman administration; the cold war; civil liberties in the years and after and federal surveillance policy. **SELECTED PUBLICATIONS** Auth, The Yalto Myths, 70; auth, Seeds of Repression, 70; coed, The Specter, 74; auth, Spying on Americans, 78; ed, Beyond the Hiss Case, 82; coauth, The Boss, 88; ed, From the Secret Files of J. Edgar Hoover, 91; ed, The FBI: An Annotated Bibliography and Res Guide, 94; auth, J. Edgar Hoover, Sex and Crime, 95; ed, A Culture of Secrecy, 98; ed, The FBI: A Comprehensive Reference Guide, 99. **CONTACT ADDRESS** Dept of Hist, Marquette Univ, Milwaukee, WI 53201.

THERIAULT, MICHEL
PERSONAL Born 12/02/1942, Toronto, ON, Canada **DISCIPLINE** CANON LAW, HISTORY **EDUCATION** Univ Montreal, Bphil, 62; McGill Univ, MLS, 76; Pontif Univ St Thomas (Rome), JCD, 71. **CAREER** Head acquisitions dept, Univ Montreal Libr, 69-75; chief, Retrospective Nat Biblio Div, Nat Libr Can, 75-85; asst prof, 85-92, Assoc Prof Canon Law, St Paul Univ, 92-. **MEMBERSHIPS** Can Canon Law Soc (secy-treas, 88-90, vice-pres, 95-97); Soc Law Eastern Churches (deleg Can, 87-97); Bibliog Soc Can (assoc secy, 81-86). **SELECTED PUBLICATIONS** Auth, Neo-vagin et impuissance, 71; auth, Le livre religieux au Quebec depuis les debuts de l'imprimerie jusqu'a la Confederation 1764-1867, 77; auth, The Institutions of Consecrated Life in Canada from the Beginning of New France up to the Present, 80; ed, Choix et acquisition des documents au Quebec, vol 1, 77; co-ed, Proceedings of the 5th International Congress of Canon Law, 86; co-ed, Code de droit canonique, 90; co-ed, Canonical Studies Presented to Germain Lesage, 91; co-ed, Studia Canonica, Index 1-25 1967-1991, 92; co-ed, Code of Canon Law Annotated, 93; transl, A Manual for Bishops, 94. **CONTACT ADDRESS** Faculty of Canon Law, Saint Paul Univ, 223 Main St, Ottawa, ON, Canada K1S 1C4. **EMAIL** theriaul@fox.nstn.ca

THERNSTROM, STEPHAN ALBERT
PERSONAL Born 11/05/1934, Port Huron, MI, m, 1959, 2 children **DISCIPLINE** AMERICAN HISTORY **EDUCATION** Northwestern Univ, BS, 56; Harvard Univ, AM, 58, PhD, 62. **CAREER** Instr hist & lit, Harvard Univ, 62-66, asst prof hist, 66-67; assoc prof, Brandeis Univ, 67-69; prof, Univ Calif, Los Angeles, 69-73; prof, 73-81, Winthrop Prof Hist, Harvard Univ, 81-, Res mem, Mass Inst Technol-Harvard Univ Joint Ctr Urban Studies, 62-69; Am Coun Learned Soc fel, 65-66; Guggenheim Found fel, 69-70; mem hist adv comt, Math Soc Sci Bd, 72-; bd dirs, Soc Sci Res Coun, 77-80; Pitt prof Am hist, Cambridge Univ, 78-79; dir, Charles Warren Ctr for Study Am Hist, 80-83. **HONORS AND AWARDS** Bancroft Prize Am Hist, 74; Harvard Univ Press Faculty Prize, 74; Leland Prize, Am Hist Asn, 81. **MEMBERSHIPS** Soc Am Historians. **RESEARCH** American social, urban and ethnic history. **SELECTED PUBLICATIONS** Auth, Poverty and Progress, Harvard Univ, 64; Poverty, Planning and Politics in the New Boston, Basic Bks, 68; co-ed, Nineteenth Century Cities: Essays in the New Urban History, Yale Univ, 69; auth, Reflections on the new urban history, Daedalus, 9/71; coauth, Men in motion: Urban population mobility in 19th century America, J Interdisciplinary Hist, fall 71; ed, The Harvard Studies in Urban History, 71, auth, The Other Bostonians: Poverty and Progress in the American Metropolis, 1880-1970, 73 & ed, The Harvard Encyclopedia of American Ethnic Groups, Harvard Univ, 79; coauth, America in Black and White: One Nation, Indivisible, 97; coauth, "Reflections on the Shape of the River," UCLA Rev, 99. **CONTACT ADDRESS** 1445 Massachusetts Ave, Lexington, MA 02420. **EMAIL** thernstr@fas.harvard.edu

THOLFSEN, TRYGVE RAINONE
PERSONAL Born 04/05/1924, Philadelphia, PA, m, 1947, 3 children **DISCIPLINE** MODERN EUROPEAN & ENGLISH HISTORY **EDUCATION** Yale Univ, BA, 48, MA, 49, PhD(hist), 52. **CAREER** From instr to asst prof hist, Univ Calif, Los Angeles, 52-59; assoc prof & chmn dept, La State Univ, 59-62; assoc prof, 62-67, Prof Hist, Teachers Col, Columbia Univ, 67-, Guggenheim fel, 68-69. **MEMBERSHIPS** AHA; Conf Brit Studies. **RESEARCH** Victorian England; history and philosophy of history. **SELECTED PUBLICATIONS** Auth, Origins of the Birmingham Caucus, Hist J, 59; Transition to democracy in Victorian England, Int Rev Soc Hist, 61; Historical Thinking, Harper, 67; The intellectual origins of Mid-Victorian stability, Polit Sci Quart, 71; ed, Sir James Kay-Shuttleworth on Popular Education in England, Teachers Col, 73 & auth, Working Class Radicalism in Mid-Victorian England, 77, Columbia Univ; The ambiguous virtues of the study of history, Teachers Col Rec, 77; Moral education in the Victorian sunday school, Hist Educ Quart, 80. **CONTACT ADDRESS** Teachers Col, Columbia Univ, Box 217, New York, NY 10027.

THOMAIDIS, SPERO T.
PERSONAL Born 12/14/1928, Highland Falls, NY **DISCIPLINE** MODERN EUROPEAN HISTORY **EDUCATION** City Col NYork, BA, 47; Columbia Univ, MA, 48, PhD(Hist), 65. **CAREER** Assoc prof Hist, Bemidji State Univ, 65-. **MEMBERSHIPS** AHA. **RESEARCH** German Reformation; modern European intellectual history. **CONTACT ADDRESS** Dept of History, Bemidji State Univ, 1500 Birchmont Dr NE, Bemidji, MN 56601-2699.

THOMAS, CARL ERIC
PERSONAL Born 10/16/1955, Jacksonville, FL, m, 2 children **DISCIPLINE** HISTORY **EDUCATION** Jacksonville Univ, BA, 76; Univ Fla, MA, 78. **CAREER** Asst Prof to Prof and Div Chair, Jacksonville Univ, 87-. **MEMBERSHIPS** AHA; OAH; AAUP; S Hist Asn; FL Hist Soc; Nat Coun for Soc Studies. **CONTACT ADDRESS** Div of Soc Sci, Jacksonville Univ, 2800 Univ Blvd N, Jacksonville, FL 32211. **EMAIL** ethomas@cju.edu

THOMAS, CAROL G.
PERSONAL Born 08/11/1938, Oak Park, IL, m, 1960 **DISCIPLINE** ANCIENT HISTORY **EDUCATION** Northwestern Univ, AM, 61, PhD(hist), 65. **CAREER** Instr hist, 64-65, acting asst prof, 65-67, asst prof, 67-71, assoc prof, 71-81, Prof Ancient Hist, Univ Wash, 81-, Am Coun Learned Soc study fel, 75. **MEMBERSHIPS** Soc Prom Hellenic Studies; Am Philol Asn. **RESEARCH** Greek political institutions, especially Homeric period; continuity between Mycenaean Age and classical Greek history; the Greek polis. **SELECTED PUBLICATIONS** **CONTACT ADDRESS** Dept of Hist, Univ of Washington, Seattle, WA 98195.

THOMAS, DIANA
PERSONAL Born Phoenix, AZ **DISCIPLINE** ARCHITECTURAL HISTORIAN **EDUCATION** York Univ, BA(Art Hist), 79; Ariz State Univ, MA (Archit Hist), 83. **CAREER** Consultant & Archit Hist, 83-85; archit hist, Alta Community Dev, 85-92; archit hist, Preservation Office, State of Ariz, 92-94; Preservation Planner, City Phoenix, 94-. **MEMBERSHIPS** Soc Stud Archit Can; Am Soc Archit Hist; Edmonton Soc Urban & Archit Studs. **SELECTED PUBLICATIONS** Auth, Traditions in a New World: Ukrainian-Canadian Churches in Alberta, in Soc Stud Archit Can Bull, 88; auth, Ukrainian Churches in Alberta: A Look at Tradition in Transition, in Proc Ukrainian Festival, 88; auth, The Alberta Inventory of Historic Sites: Recording Ukrainian Church Architecture, in Pamiatky Ukrainy, 92. **CONTACT ADDRESS** Soc Study Architecture Canada, PO Box 2302, Stn. D, Ottawa, ON, Canada K1P 5W5.

THOMAS, DONALD E.
DISCIPLINE HISTORY **EDUCATION** Univ Mich, BA; Univ Chicago, MA, PhD. **SELECTED PUBLICATIONS** Auth, Diesel: Technology and Society in Industrial Germany, Univ Ala Press, 87; articles on, 19th and 20th century Ger technologival history. **CONTACT ADDRESS** Dept of History, Virginia Military Inst, Lexington, VA 24450.

THOMAS, EMORY M.
PERSONAL Born 11/03/1939, Richmond, VA, m, 1962, 2 children **DISCIPLINE** AMERICAN HISTORY **EDUCATION** Univ Va, BA, 62; Rice Univ, PhD, 66. **CAREER** From asst prof to assoc prof, 67-77, Prof Hist, Univ GA, 77-87, Regents Prof Hist, Univ Ga, 87-; Douglas Southall Freeman Prof Hist, Univ Richmond; Lamar lectr, Wesleyan Col, 72. **HONORS AND AWARDS** John S Longscope Prize, Rice Univ, 66; Fulbright sr lectr, Univ Genoa, 74; Albert Christ-Janer Awd, Creativity Res, Univ GA, 80; Univ GA Alumni Soc, Fac Serv Awd, 82; Sea Grant, Oral hist Georgia coast, 82-84; Joseph H Parks-Alf A Heggoy Awd, Excellence Teaching, 88; Mellon res fel, VA Hist Soc, 89. **MEMBERSHIPS** Southern Hist Asn; Orgn Am Historians; Ctr Study Southern Cult. **RESEARCH** Southern history; Confederacy; Maritime history. **SELECTED PUBLICATIONS** Auth, "Marse Robert at Midlife," in The Confederate High Command & Related Topics (White Mane Press, 90); auth, "The Confederacy as a Revolutionary Experience," in Major Problems in the Civil War and Reconstruction (D C Heath, 90); Everyone's War, in Touched By Fire, vol 2, Little Brown, 90; God and General Lee, Anglican and Episco-

pal Hist, 3/91; ed bd, Encyclopedia of the Confederacy, 4 vol, Simon & Schuster, 93; Secession, Succession, and Sumter: the Crisis of 1860-61, in The Davis A Sayre History Symposium: Collected Essays, 1985-89, Sayre School, 93; Rethinking Robert E Lee, Douglas Southall Freeman Hist Rev, Univ Richmond, spring 94; Introduction, Georgia Hist Quart, special ed, spring 95; Robert E Lee: A Biography, W W Norton, 95; Eggs, Aldie, Shepherdstown and J E B Stuart, in the Gettysburg Nobody Knows, Oxford Univ Press, 97; Killing Yankees: Confederate Strategy and Military Policy, in Writing the Civil War: The Quest to Understand, Univ SC Press, 10/98; The Lees, in Intimate Strategies: Military Marriages of the Civil War, Oxford Univ Press, in press; Ambivalent Visions of Victory: Jefferson Davis, Robert E Lee, and Confederate Grand Strategy, in Jefferson Davis and His Generals, Oxford Univ Press, in press. **CONTACT ADDRESS** Dept of Hist, Univ of Georgia, 202 LeConte Hall, Athens, GA 30602-1602. **EMAIL** et68@webtv.net

THOMAS, GERALD EUSTIS
PERSONAL Born 06/23/1929, Natick, MA, m, 1954, 3 children **DISCIPLINE** HISTORY **EDUCATION** Harvard Univ, BA 1951; George Washington Univ, MS 1966; Yale Univ, PhD 1973. **CAREER** US Navy, commanding officer USS Impervious, 62-63; College Training Programs Bureau of Naval Personnel, head, 63-65; US Navy, commanding officer USS Bausell, 66-68; Prairie View A&M Coll Naval ROTC Unit, prof of naval science & commanding officer, 68-70; US Navy, commander Destroyer Squadron Five, 73-75, rear admiral, 74-81; US Dept of Defense, acting deputy asst sec of defense for intl security affairs & dir of Near East, South Asia, & Africa Region, 76-78, Comtrapac, US Pacific Fleet, 78-81, retired, 81; State Dept, US ambassador to Guyana 81-83, US ambassador to Kenya 83-86; Yale Univ, Lecturer, Davenport College, Master, currently. **MEMBERSHIPS** Overseer, Bd of Overseers, Harvard Univ, 1981-88; bd of trustees, Univ of San Diego, 1981-86; life mem, Org of Amer Historians. **CONTACT ADDRESS** Master of Davenport Col, Yale Univ, 271 Park St, New Haven, CT 06511-4751.

THOMAS, JACK RAY
PERSONAL Born 12/23/1931, Youngstown, OH, m, 1957 **DISCIPLINE** LATIN AMERICAN HISTORY **EDUCATION** Youngstown Univ, BA, 54; Kent State Univ, MA, 60; Ohio State Univ, PhD(hist), 62. **CAREER** Asst prof Latin Am hist, Univ Wis-Eau Claire, 62-65; asst prof, 65-69, assoc prof, 69-79, Prpf Latin Am Hist, Bowling Green State Univ, 79-, Nat Found Arts & Humanities res fel, 68. **MEMBERSHIPS** AHA; Midwest Coun Latin Am Studies; Conf Latin Am Hist; Latin Am Studies Asn; Soc Hist Am Foreign Rel. **RESEARCH** Nineteenth century Latin American historiography; Latin American accounts of travels in the United States in the 19th century; United States-Chilean relations, 1891-1945. **SELECTED PUBLICATIONS** Auth, The role of private libraries and public archives in 19th century Spanish American historiography, J Libr Hist, 10/74; Generation of '42, Americas, 5/75; The Chilean gerneration of 1842 and the concept of Latin American union, Revista/Rev Interamericana, summer 76; The role of the press in the Chilean Rebellion of 1851, Americas: Quart Rev Inter-Am Cult Hist, 7/79; The impact of the generation of 1842 on Chilean historiography, The Historian, 8/79; coauth (with Louis Patsouras), Varieties and Problems of Twentieth Century Socialism, Nelson Hall, 81; Biographical Dictionary of Latin American History: Historians and Historiography from the Colonial Period to 1920, Greenwood Press, 82. **CONTACT ADDRESS** Dept of Hist, Bowling Green State Univ, Bowling Green, OH 43402.

THOMAS, JEAN D'AMATO
PERSONAL Born 07/20/1945, Boston, MA, m, 1989, 3 children **DISCIPLINE** CLASSICAL TRADITION **EDUCATION** Tufts Univ, BA, 67; Middlebury Col, MA, 69; Johns Hopkins Univ, PhD, 76. **CAREER** Vis lectr, Univ Pittsburgh, 74-75; vis lectr Williams Col, 75-76; dir, Vergillian Soc of Am summer sessions, Rome, 78; asst prof, Univ So Calif, 76-81; dir, prof-in-charge, Intercollegiate Ctr for Class Stud, Rome, 82-83; adj asst prof, Brandeis Univ, 83; lectr, NEH funding, Summer Inst for High Sch Tchrs, 83, 84; adj instr, Univ Md, 87; humanist adm, NEH, 84-87; dir, lib arts progs for adults, Tufts Univ, 87-88; columnist, Natchitoches Times, 96- ; assoc prof, prof, Louisiana Scholars Col, Northwestern State Univ, 88-; co-dir, Athens in the Fifth Century, 92; co-dir Art and Science, 94; co-dir Companie Felix: Nature, Art and the Works of Men, 00. **HONORS AND AWARDS** Diss fel, AAU, 72; Am Council of Learned Soc fel, 77; NEH travel grant, 89; APA res grant, 91 Louisiana Endow Hum grant, 92; Il Premio Giornalistico Theodor Mommsen, 93; Athens in the Fifth Century, LEH funding, Summer Inst for High Sch Teachers, 92; Co-Dir, Art and Science LEH funding, 94; Co-Dir, Felix Nature, Art, and the Works of Men, NEH funding, 00. **MEMBERSHIPS** Am Philol Asn; Int Inst for Class Tradition; Louisiana Class Asn; Vergillian Soc Am. **RESEARCH** Classical tradition, both in literature and art and archaeology, as it applies to the Phlegraean Fields near Naples; the classical tradition in the United States. **SELECTED PUBLICATIONS** Auth, Cicero's Property in the Phlegraean Fields and Antiquarian Investigation in the Naples Area, VIATOR, 93; auth, The Apocryphal Lighthouse at Capo Miseno: A Creation of Medieval Scholarship, VIATOR, 96. **CONTACT ADDRESS** 332 Henry Ave, Natchitoches, LA 71457. **EMAIL** damato@alpha.nsula.edu

THOMAS, JOHN LOVELL
PERSONAL Born 10/28/1926, Portland, ME, m, 1951, 2 children **DISCIPLINE** AMERICAN HISTORY **EDUCATION** Bowdoin Col, BA, 47; Columbia Univ, MA, 50; Brown Univ, PhD(Am civilization), 60. **CAREER** Lectr English, Barnard Col, Columbia Univ, 50-52; instr Am civilization, Brown Univ, 54-56, asst prof hist, 61-62; asst prof, Harvard Univ, 62-64; assoc prof, 64-72, Prof Hist, Brown Univ, 72- **RESEARCH** American intellectual history. **SELECTED PUBLICATIONS** Auth, Alternative America, 83; auth, All Over the Map--Rethinking American Regions, J Am Hist, Vol 83, 96; Positivist Republic--Auguste Comte and the Reconstruction of American Liberalism, 1865-1920, Am Hist Rev, Vol 0101, 96; Through the Avenue of Art (rev), William Mary Quart, Vol 53, 96; auth, A Country in the Mind: Bernard DeVoto, Wallace Stegner, History and the American Land, 00. **CONTACT ADDRESS** Dept of Hist, Brown Univ, 1 Prospect St, Providence, RI 02912-9127.

THOMAS, MARK
PERSONAL Born 11/17/1954, Hampton Court, England, m, 1985, 2 children **DISCIPLINE** HISTORY **EDUCATION** Oxford, BA, 76; MA, 80; DPhil, 84; Cornell, MA, 79. **CAREER** Asst/Assoc, Prof of History, Univ of Virginia, 92. **HONORS AND AWARDS** T.S. Ashton Prize, Economic Histroy Society, 84; Alexander Gerschenkron Prize, Economic History Assoc, 85; Visiting Fellow, Institute for Advanced Studies, Australian National Univ, 84,93,95. **MEMBERSHIPS** Vis Fellow, All Souls College, 97; Economic Visitor Society, Economic History Assoc, Cliometric Society. **RESEARCH** Economic History (UK, US, Australia. **SELECTED PUBLICATIONS** Auth, Income Distribution in Historical Perspective, ed. With Y.S. Brenner and H. Kaelble, (Cambridge: Cambridge Univ Press and Paris: Maison des Sciences de l'Homme), 91; auth, Capitalism in Context: Essays in economic development and cultural change in honor of R. M. Hartwell, ed. With J.A. James (Chicago: Univ of Chicago Press), 94; auth, The Disintegration of the World Economy between the Wars, ed. Cheltenham: Edward Elgar, 96; auth, Economic Challenges of the 21st Century in Historical Perspective, ed. With Paul A. David and Peter Solar (London: British Academy), forthcoming; auth, "The Trade Deficit in Historical Perspective," in Second Thoughts: The Uses of American Economic History, ed, D. McCloskey (New York: Oxford Univ Press, 93), 88-95, auth, "Wages in Interwar Britain: a skeptical inquiry," in Labour Market Evolution, ed. G. Grantham and M.E. McKinnon (London: Routledge, 94), 245-69; auth, "A substantial Australian superiority?" Anglo-Australian comparisons of consumption and income in the comparisons of consumption and income in the late nineteenth century," Australian Economic History Review 35 (95): 10-38, "Laboring hoarding, skills and productivity during depressions: microeconomic evidence from the United States in the 1890's , with John A. James), in C.E. Nunez, Microeconomic analysis of the household and the labor market, 1880-1939 (Seville, Spain: International Economic History Assoc), 98; auth, "Retirement saving before Social Security, " with John A. James and Michael Palumbo, National Tax Journal 91 (99): 361-370; auth, "Paying for Old Age: past, present, future," with Paul Johnson, in P. Solar and M. Thomas ed., Economic Challenges of the 21st Century in Historical Perspective (London: British Academy, 00). **CONTACT ADDRESS** Dept History, Univ of Virginia, Randall Hall, Charlottesville, VA 22903-3244. **EMAIL** mark.thomas@virginia.edu

THOMAS, NIGEL J. T.
PERSONAL Born 02/07/1952, Rochester, United Kingdom, m, 1992, 2 children **DISCIPLINE** HISTORY AND PHILOSOPHY OF SCIENCE **EDUCATION** Leeds Univ, PhD, 87. **CAREER** Instr, Calif Inst Techol, 90-92; instr, Rio Hondo Coll, 96-97; adj asst prof Calif State Univ, 95-. **MEMBERSHIPS** Am Philos Asn; Soc for Philos and Psychol; Cognitive Sci Soc; Hist of Sci Soc; Soc for Machines and Mentality; Cheiron; Am Psychol Asn; Asn for the Scientific Study of Consciousness, Soc for the Multidisciplinary Study of Consciousness. **RESEARCH** Philosophy of Mind; Imagination; Cognitive Science; History of Psychology. **SELECTED PUBLICATIONS** Rev, The Imagery Debate, 94; auth, Imagery and the coherence of Imagination: a Critique of White, J of Philos Res, 97; A Stimulus to the Imagination, Psyche, 97; Mental Imagery, the Stanford Encycl of Philos, 97; entries on Sir Frederick Gowland Hopkins and Marshall W Nirenberg, The Biographical Encycl of Sci, 98; auth, "Experience and Theory as Determinants of Attitudes Towards Mental Representation," American J of Psychology, 102, (89), 395-412; auth, Imagery and the Coherence of Imagination: a Critique of White, J of Philosophical Res, 22, (97), 95-127; auth, A Stimulus to the Imagination, Psyche 3, 97; auth, Enries on Sir Frederick Gowland Hopkins, and Marshall W. Nirenberg-in Richard Olson & Roger Smith, eds. The Biographical Encyclopedia of Scientists, New York: Marshall Cavendish Corp., 98; auth, Zombie Killer--in S.R. Hameroff, A.W. Kaszniak, & A.C. Scott eds., Toward a Science of Consciousness II, Cambridge, MA: MIT Press, 98; auth, Zombie Killer--in S.R. Hameroff, A.W. Kaszniak, & A.C. Scott, eds., Toward a Science of Consciousness II, Cambridge, MA: MIT Press, 98; auth, Mental Imagery in E. Zalta, ed. The Stanford Encyclopedia of Philosophy, 99; auth, Imagination in C. Eliasmith, ed. Dictionary of Philosophy of Mind, 99; auth, Are Theories of Imagery Theories of Imagination? An Active Perception Approach to Conscious Mental Content,--Cognitive Science, 23, (99), 207-245; auth, Mental Imagery, Philosophical Issues About, forthcoming in Encyclopedia of Cognitive Science, Macmillan: London; Auth, Are Theories of Imagery Theories of Imagination? An Active perception Approach to Conscious Mental Content, Cognitive Sci, forthcoming. **CONTACT ADDRESS** 86 South Sierra Madre Blvd #5, Pasadena, CA 91107. **EMAIL** n.j.thomas70@members.leeds.ac.uk

THOMAS, ORLAN E.
DISCIPLINE MUSIC HISTORY AND LITERATURE, MUSIC THEORY **EDUCATION** Univ NE, BME, MM; Eastman Sch Mus, DMA. **CAREER** Assoc prof Mus, TX Tech Univ. **SELECTED PUBLICATIONS** Auth, So You Want to Write a Song? Fundamentals of Songwriting. **CONTACT ADDRESS** Dept of Music, Texas Tech Univ, MS 2033, Lubbock, TX 79409. **EMAIL** othomas@ttacs.ttu.edu

THOMAS, SAMUEL JOSEPH
PERSONAL Born 09/06/1941, Cleveland, OH, m, 1965, 3 children **DISCIPLINE** AMERICAN & MODERN EUROPEAN HISTORY **EDUCATION** Kent State Univ, BA, 64; MI State Univ, MA, 66, PhD, 71. **CAREER** Asst instr, 66-69, instr, 70-71, asst prof, 71-77, assoc prof, 77-, prof Am hisy, MI State Univ, 77. **HONORS AND AWARDS** Cushwa res travel grants; M Thomas Inge Awd for Comic Arts Scholarship, 97. **MEMBERSHIPS** Am Cath Hist Asn; Orgn Am Historians; Am Soc Church Hist; Am Immig Soc; Soc for Hist Ed. **RESEARCH** Nineteenth and 20th century Am relig hist; role of the press in Am relig hist; Am Cath hist.; Political cartoons of the Gilded Age. **SELECTED PUBLICATIONS** Auth, The American Press and the Church-State Pronouncements of Pope Leo XIII, U S Cath Hist, 80; The American Press and the Encyclical Longinqua Oceani, Jour Church State, 80; Catholic Journalists and the Ideal Woman in Late Victorian American, Int Jour Women's Studies, 1, 81; Nostrum Advertising and the Image of Woman as Invalid in Late Victorian America, Jour Am Culture, 82; Portraits of a Rebel Priest: Edward McGlynn in Caricature, 1886-1893, Jour Am Culture, 84; The Tattooed Man Caricatures and the Presidential Campaign of 1884, Jour Am Culture, 87; After Vatican II: The American Catholic Bishops and the Syllabus from Rome, 1966-1968, Cath Hist Rev, 4, 97; auth, Maligning Poverty's Prophet: Puck, Henry George and the Mayoral Campaign of 1886, Jour Am Culture, 98; auth, Dissent and Due Process After Vatican II: An Early Case Study in American Catholic Leadership, U.S. Catholic Historian, 99; auth, Not an Inquisition: Alexander Zaleski and the Bishops Committee on Doctrine, 1966-1970, Polish American Studies, 00. **CONTACT ADDRESS** Dept of Hist, Michigan State Univ, 301 Morrill Hall, East Lansing, MI 48824-1036. **EMAIL** thomass1@pilot.msu.edu

THOMASSON, GORDON C.
PERSONAL Born 12/28/1942, Santa Monica, CA, m, 1975, 4 children **DISCIPLINE** HISTORY, RELIGION **EDUCATION** UCLA, AB, 66; UCSB, AM, 72; Cornell Univ, PhD, 87. **CAREER** Asst prof, 80-82, Cuttington Univ; world stud fac, 88-93, Marlboro Col & Schl for Intl Training; asst prof, 93-, Broome Com Col (SUNY); intl stud adj, 96-98, CCNY **RESEARCH** Globval hist, world relig, anthropology of development, Liberia, Southeast Asia, Mormonism. **CONTACT ADDRESS** 280 Academy Dr., Vestal, NY 13850. **EMAIL** thomasson_g@mail.sunybroome.edu

THOMPSON, ALAN SMITH
PERSONAL Born 01/13/1939, Mobile, AL, m, 1966, 2 children **DISCIPLINE** AMERICAN HISTORY **EDUCATION** Auburn Univ, BA, 61; Univ AL, MA, 63, PhD, 79. **CAREER** Tchr Am hist, Vigor High Sch, 63-64; tchg asst, Univ AL, 65-66, 67-68 & instr, 66-67; instr, 68-70, asst prof, 70-80, assoc prof, 80-86, prof Am hist, La State Univ, Shreveport, 86-, dir, LSUS Oral Hist Prog, 85-90, 93-97, ed, North LA Hist Asn Jour, 90. **HONORS AND AWARDS** NEH Summer Inst Grants, 77 & 87; LSUS Res Grant, 82; LSUS Am Studies Grant, 85, 87 - 88; Community Found Shreveport-Bossier Grants, 85-88, 90-92 & 95; Cath Diocese of Alexandria-Shreveport Grant, 83-84; LA Div of Arts Grant, 94. **MEMBERSHIPS** Southern Hist Asn; LA Hist Asn; North LA Hist Asn; Nat Trust Hist Preserv; Ala Hist Asn; Nat Coun on Pub Hist; LA Pres Alliance. **RESEARCH** Antebellum south; Antebellum Ala; Shreveport; Antebellum Mobile; Am archit hist; Caddo Indians. **SELECTED PUBLICATIONS** Auth, The Caspiana Big House: Its history and restoration, NLa Hist Asn J, summer 78; Historic and cultural resources of Coushatta, Louisiana, Red River Bridge and Approaches, Coushatta, La, Report 2, 2/79; Physical impacts: Historic background of Coushatta, environmental assessment for Red River Bridge and Approaches, Coushatta, La, 3/81, La Dept Transp; Southern rights and nativism as issues in Mobile politics, 1850-1861, Ala Rev, Ala Hist Asn, 4/82; Shreveport 1878-1900, Shreveport Jour, 9/85; Shreveport Transportation: Riverboats & Railroads, Glimpses of Shreveport, 85; thomas Jefferson-President, The Rating Game in American Politics, 86; Populism in Shreveport, North La Hist Asn Jour, winter 86; The Shreveport Rate Case, Grassroots Constitutionalism, 88; History of Community Foundation of Shreveport-Bossier, 96. **CONTACT ADDRESS** Dept Hist & Social Sci, Louisiana State Univ and A&M Col, 1 University Pl, Shreveport, LA 71115-2301. **EMAIL** athompso@pilot.lsus.edu

THOMPSON, BRUCE
PERSONAL Born 09/24/1955, New York, NY, s **DISCIPLINE** HISTORY **EDUCATION** Princeton Univ, BA, 77; Stanford Univ, MA, 81; Stanford Univ, PhD, 87. **CAREER** Lect, Stanford Univ, 87-91; Lect, Univ Calif, 91-00. **HONORS AND AWARDS** Excellence in Teaching Awd, Univ Calif, 77; Georges Lorce Fel, 82-83; Alumni Asn Favorite Prof Awd, Univ Calif, 91, 93;. **MEMBERSHIPS** Am Hist Assoc. **RESEARCH** Modern European intellectual history. **SELECTED PUBLICATIONS** Ed, "Critical History: The Career of Ian Watt, Stanford Humanities Rev, 8.1(00). **CONTACT ADDRESS** Dept Hist, Univ of California, Santa Cruz, 1156 High St, Santa Cruz, CA 95064-1077. **EMAIL** brucet@cats.ucsc.edu

THOMPSON, DOROTHY GILLIAN
PERSONAL Born 02/25/1943, Duncan, BC, Canada **DISCIPLINE** MODERN FRENCH HISTORY **EDUCATION** Univ BC, BA, 64, PhD(Fr hist), 72; Stanford Univ, MA, 65. **CAREER** Instr Europ Hist, Purdue Univ, 68-70; lectr, Univ Windsor, 71-72; asst prof, 72-77, Assoc Prof Europ Hist, Univ NB, Fredericton, 77- **MEMBERSHIPS** AHA; Soc Fr Hist Studies. **RESEARCH** Confiscation of ecclesiastical property in 18th century France; 18th century French Jesuits. **SELECTED PUBLICATIONS** Coauth, "France Oveseas," in New Oxford History of France Vol IX, 1660-1788; ed, William Doyle, Oxford: Oxford Univ Press, 01. **CONTACT ADDRESS** Dept of Hist, Univ of New Brunswick, Fredericton, PO Box 4400, Fredericton, NB, Canada E3B 5A3.

THOMPSON, G. RAY
PERSONAL Born 12/21/1943, Almena, KS, m, 1969, 2 children **DISCIPLINE** HISTORY **EDUCATION** Fort Hays State Univ, AB, 65; MA, 67; PhD, 72, Univ Kansas; graduate certs from Am Acad of Classical Studies in Rome, 69, and Am School of Classical Studies in Athens, 70. **CAREER** Asst/Assoc/Full Prof, 72-, Salisbury State Univ. **HONORS AND AWARDS** Outstanding Fac Awd, 88; assoc chair of hist dept, 76-89; chair, 89-; Fall Opening Convocation speaker, 91, SSE; cofounder, Res Center for Delmarva Hist and Culture, Salisbury State Univ; pres of local chapter of Phi Kappa Phi, 75-77, 83-87, 90-98. **MEMBERSHIPS** Exec boards of Wicomico Hist Soc; Pemberton Hall Found; Nabb Res Center for Delmarva Hist and Cult; Delmarva Adv Coun; Pres of Preservation Trust of Icomico, Inc.; Salisbury Hist Dist Comn; Lower Eastern Shore Hertiage Comt; Wimcomico Heritage Comt; Lower Shore Delmarva Genealogical Soc; Wimcomico County Free Libr, City Hall Mus; Md Hist Trust Award, 94; Am Hist Asn; Archaeological Inst of Am. **RESEARCH** Colonial Chesapeake history; Ancient Greece and Rome; Numismatics; Propography. **SELECTED PUBLICATIONS** Auth, "The Coinage of the Emperor Elagabalus," Journal of the Society for Ancient Numismatics (75); auth, "The Rule of Gordian III (235-244 AD): Numismatic and Epigraphical Evidence," Journal of the Society for Ancient Numismatics (76); auth, Minturno: Study of a Maritime Colony of Rome from the Third Century BC; auth, "Religious Revolution in the Early Third Century AD Roman World," The Ancient World: Journal of Graeco-Roman Antiquities; auth, "A Study in Imperial Marriage: Humismatic and Epigraphic Evidence of the Wives of Elagabalus (218-222 AD)," Journal of the Society for Ancient Numismatics (81); auth, Mapping Delmarva's Past, 90; auth, Historic Salisbury, 91; auth, "Mosaic of Education," Academically Speaking (91); auth, Inventories of Women of old Somerset on Maryland's Eastern Shore, 1677-1726, 95; auth, Assorted Wills and Deeds of Gift of the Lower Eastern Shore of Maryland and Virginia 1648-1845, 97. **CONTACT ADDRESS** Salisbury State Univ, Salisbury, MD 21801. **EMAIL** grthompson@ssu.edu

THOMPSON, GLEN L.
PERSONAL Born 04/14/1950, LaCrosse, WI, m, 1977, 2 children **DISCIPLINE** ANCIENT HISTORY **EDUCATION** Northwestern Col, BA, 72; Wisconsin Lutheran Sem, MDiv, 77; Columbia Univ, MA, 84, PhD, 90. **CAREER** Prof, Michigan Lutheran Sem, 92-96; prof, Martin Luther Col, 97- . **MEMBERSHIPS** Soc Bibl Lit; Am Philol Asn; N Am Patristics Soc; Asn Ancient Historians; Inst for Bibl Res; Evangel Theol Soc. **RESEARCH** Roman social history; early Christian Church; Greek and Latin manuscripts. **SELECTED PUBLICATIONS** Auth, A Dike Certificate from Tebtunis, Bul of Am Soc of Papyrologists, 91; auth, Jesus and the Historical Jesus, Wisc Lutheran Q, 95; auth, Teaching the Teachers: Pastoral Training in the Early Church, Wisc Lutheran Q, 97. **CONTACT ADDRESS** Martin Luther Col, 1995 Luther Ct, New Ulm, MN 56073. **EMAIL** thompsgl@mlc-wels.edu

THOMPSON, JANET ANN
PERSONAL Born 08/01/1944, Balboa, Panama Canal Zone **DISCIPLINE** HISTORY **EDUCATION** Univ Cincinnati, BA, 74, MA, 76, PhD, 87; Case Western Reserve Univ, MSLS, 84. **CAREER** Asst prof librarianship, Univ New Mexico, 86-88; asst prof hist, Southwest Texas State Univ, 88-90; hist fac, Tallahassee Commun Col, 90- . **RESEARCH** Women; witchcraft; English West country. **SELECTED PUBLICATIONS** Auth, Wives, Widows, Witches and Bitches: Women in 17th Century Devon, Peter Lang, 93. **CONTACT ADDRESS** Div of History and Social Sciences, Tallahassee Comm Col, Tallahassee, FL 32304. **EMAIL** thompsja@mail.tallahassee.cc.fl.us

THOMPSON, JOHN H.
PERSONAL Born 09/18/1946, Winnipeg, MB, Canada **DISCIPLINE** HISTORY **EDUCATION** Univ Winnipeg, BA, 68; Univ Man, MA, 69; Queen's Univ, PhD, 75. **CAREER** Prof hist, McGill Univ, 71-90; exch prof, Simon Fraser Univ, 82-83; exch prof, 87-88, Prof History, Duke Univ, 90-; Distinguished Vis Prof, Univ Alta, 97-. **HONORS AND AWARDS** Margaret McWilliams Medal, Man Hist Soc, 68; W L Morton Gold Medal, Univ Man, 69; Can Hist Asn Reg Hist Prize, 81. **MEMBERSHIPS** Can Hist Asn **SELECTED PUBLICATIONS** Auth, Ethnic Minorities During Two World Wars, 91; auth, The Harvests of War: the Prairie West, 1914-1918, 78; sr auth, Canada 1922-39: Decades of Discord, 85; auth, Forging the Prairie West, 98; co-ed, Loyalties in Conflict: Ukrainians in Canada During the Great War, 83. **CONTACT ADDRESS** 6420 Ada Blvd, Edmonton, AB, Canada T5W 4P2. **EMAIL** jhtl@gpu.srv.ualberta.ca

THOMPSON, LARRY
PERSONAL Born 02/09/1967, El Paso, TX, m, 1996 **DISCIPLINE** ART **EDUCATION** Univ Tx San Antonio, BFA, 93; Univ N Tx, MFA, 95. **CAREER** Teaching Fel, Univ N Tx, 93-95; Art Teacher, Irving Independent Sch Distr, Irving, Tx, 96-98; Asst prof, La Col, 98-. **HONORS AND AWARDS** Best of Show, 94; Juror's Awd, 93, 95, 96; univ tx san antonio dean's list 90-93. **MEMBERSHIPS** Col Art Assoc. **RESEARCH** Painting **CONTACT ADDRESS** 4 Lark Pl, Apt. 2, Arkadelphia, AR 71923-2943. **EMAIL** thompson@lacollege.edu

THOMPSON, LAURENCE G.
PERSONAL Born 07/09/1920, Ichowfu, China, m, 1943, 5 children **DISCIPLINE** ASIAN STUDIES, SINOLOGY **EDUCATION** Univ Calif, Los Angeles, BA, 42; US Navy Japanese Lang Sch, dipl, 43; Claremont Grad Sch, MA, 47, PhD(Orient studies), 54. **CAREER** Teacher pub & pvt schs, Calif & Colo, 46-51; cult attache, Am Embassy, Taipei, 51-53; staff off, US Foreign Serv Tokyo, Singapore, Manila & Hong Kong, 54-56; rep Asian Found, Korea, 56-58 & Taiwan, 58-59; prof music, Taiwan Norm Univ, 59-62; asst prof Chinese lang & lit, Pomona Col, 62-65; from asst prof to assoc prof, 65-70, dir East Asian Studies Ctr, 72-74, chmn dept East Asian lang & cult, 68-70 & 72-76, PROF EAST ASIAN LANG & CULT, UNIV SOUTHERN CALIF, 70- **MEMBERSHIPS** Am Orient Soc; Royal Asiatic Soc; Asn Asian Studies; Am Acad Relig; Soc Study Chinese Relig. **RESEARCH** Chinese thought and religion; history of Taiwan. **SELECTED PUBLICATIONS** **CONTACT ADDRESS** Dept of E Asian Lang & Cult, Univ of So California, Los Angeles, CA 90007.

THOMPSON, MARGARET SUSAN
PERSONAL Born 01/25/1949, Brooklyn, NY **DISCIPLINE** HISTORY, POLITICAL SCIENCE **EDUCATION** Smith Col, AB, 70; Univ Wis-Madison, MA, 72, PhD(hist), 79. **CAREER** Instr, Knox Col, 77-78, asst prof, 79-81; Asst Prof Hist, Syracuse Univ, 81-, Nat Endowment for Humanities res grant, summer, 80; J Franklin Jameson fel, AHA, 80-81. **HONORS AND AWARDS** Ford Foundation Graduate Fel, 72-74; Newberry Library (Chicago) Res Fel, 75; Alice Smith Fel, Wisconsin State Historical Soc, 75-76; Russell Sage Foundation Postdoctoral Fel in the Social Sciences, 83-84; Cushwa Center for Study of American Catholicism, Univ of Notre Dame, Res Grant, 84; Rockefeller Foundation Humanities Fel, 85-86. **MEMBERSHIPS** Orgn Am Historians; Am Polit Sci Asn; Soc Sci Hist Asn; AHA. **RESEARCH** American political history; Civil War and Reconstruction; 20th century politics. **SELECTED PUBLICATIONS** Auth, Cultural Conundrum--Sisters, Ethnicity, and the Adaptation of American-Catholicism, Mid Am Hist Rev, Vol 74, 92; Rose Hawthorne Lathrop--Selected-Writings, Cath Hist Rev, Vol 81, 95; auth, "The Ministry of Women and the Transformation of Catholicism in the 19th-Century America," History of European Ideas, 95; auth, Concentric Circles of Sisterhood," Claiming Our Roots: Sesquecentennial History of the IHM Sisters, 95. **CONTACT ADDRESS** Syracuse Univ, 145 Eggers Hall, Syracuse, NY 13244-1090. **EMAIL** msthomps@syr.edu

THOMPSON, ROBERT FARRIS
PERSONAL Born 12/30/1932, El Paso, TX, m **DISCIPLINE** AFRICAN-AMERICAN HISTORY **EDUCATION** Yale U, BA 1955, MA 1961, PhD 1965. **CAREER** African & Afro-Amer Art History Yale Univ, prof 1964-. **SELECTED PUBLICATIONS** Authored "African Influence on the Art of the United States" 1969; "Black Gods & Kings" 1971; "African Art in Motion" 1974; "Four Moments of the Sun" 1981; "Flash of the Spirit" 1983. **CONTACT ADDRESS** Professor History of Art, Yale Univ, 63 Wall St, New Haven, CT 06510.

THOMPSON, STEPHEN A.
PERSONAL Born, OK, m, 1 child **DISCIPLINE** GEOGRAPHY **EDUCATION** Univ Calif, Los Angeles, BA, 74; Univ Colo Boulder, MA, 80; PhD, 83. **CAREER** Univ of NMex, 84-91; Millersville Univ of Pa, 91- **MEMBERSHIPS** Am Water Resources Asn, Am Geophysical Union. **RESEARCH** Water resources. **SELECTED PUBLICATIONS** Auth, Hydrology for water management, A.A. Balkema Publ (Rotterdam), 99; auth, Water use, Management and Planning in the United States, Acad Press (San Diego), 99. **CONTACT ADDRESS** Dept Geog, Millersville Univ of Pennsylvania, PO Box 1002, Millersville, PA 17551. **EMAIL** Stephen.Thompson@millersville.edu

THOMPSON, VICTORIA E.
PERSONAL Born 06/03/1964, Brooklyn, NY **DISCIPLINE** HISTORY **EDUCATION** Univ Calif Berkeley, BA, 87; Univ Pa, PhD, 93. **CAREER** Asst prof, Xavier Univ, 93-99; asst prof, Ariz State Univ, 99-. **HONORS AND AWARDS** Mellon Found Fel, 92-93; Chateaubriand Fel, 91-92; Am Philos Soc Res Grant, 97. **MEMBERSHIPS** Am Hist Asn; French Hist Studies; W Soc for French Hist. **RESEARCH** Nineteenth-Century France: culture, urban, travel, gender and sexuality. **SELECTED PUBLICATIONS** Auth, "Creating Boundaries: Homosexuality and the Changing Social Order in France, 1830-1870," in Homosexuality in Modern France, (Oxford Univ Press, 96), 102-127; auth, The Virtuous Marketplace: Women and Men, Money and Politics in Paris, 1830-1870, Johns Hopkins Univ Press, 00. **CONTACT ADDRESS** Dept Hist, Arizona State Univ, PO Box 872501, Tempe, AZ 85287. **EMAIL** victoria.thompson@asu.edu

THORMANN, GERARD CHARLES
PERSONAL Born 09/30/1922, Frankfurt, Germany, m, 1953, 4 children **DISCIPLINE** HISTORY **EDUCATION** Univ Aix-Marseille, BesL, 41; Columbia Col, BA, 46; Columbia Univ, MA, 47, PhD(hist), 51. **CAREER** From instr to assoc prof hist, Notre Dame Col Staten Island, 48-59; assoc prof, 59-68, Prof Hist, Manhattanville Col, 68- **MEMBERSHIPS** AHA; Am Cath Hist Asn; Soc Fr Hist Studies. **RESEARCH** Modern European history; Christian democratic parties; Christian trade unionism. **SELECTED PUBLICATIONS** Auth, History of French Christian trade unionism, 1887-1951; History of the Belgian-Christian Workers Movement, Cath Hist Rev, Vol 0082, 96; The Thought of Pottier, Antoine 1849-1923 in Contribution to the History of Christian Democracy in Belgium, Cath Hist Rev, Vol 0080, 94. **CONTACT ADDRESS** Dept of Hist, Manhattanville Col, Purchase, NY 10577.

THORNTON, ARCHIBALD PATON
PERSONAL Born 10/21/1921, Glasgow, Scotland, m, 1948, 2 children **DISCIPLINE** HISTORY **EDUCATION** Glasgow Univ, MA, 47; Oxford Univ, DPhil(hist), 52. **CAREER** Lectr hist, Oxford Univ, 48-50; lectr, Aberdeen Univ, 50-57; prof and chmn, Univ W Indies, 57-60, dean fac arts, 59-60; chmn dept, 67-72, Prof Hist, Univ Toronto, 60-, Her Majesty's Colonial Serv App Bd, 52-57; Smuts fel, Cambridge Univ and Commonwealth fel, St John's Col, 65-66 and 70. **MEMBERSHIPS** AHA; Can Hist Asn; fel Royal Hist Soc; fel Royal Soc Can. **RESEARCH** British history; commonwealth history; imperial history. **SELECTED PUBLICATIONS** Auth, In the City of the Heart--Reflections on Jerusalem, A Unique Imperial City Beyond Europe, Queens Quart, Vol 0103, 96; A Summer Crossing--The Landing-Craft Tank which Crossed the English-Channel on Sunday June 4, 1944 to Invade and Liberate Hitler-Occupied Europe, Queens Quart, Vol 0101, 94; The Travelers Tale, Queens Quart, Vol 0101, 94; Rights As A European Export, Queens Quart, Vol 0102, 95. **CONTACT ADDRESS** Dept of Hist, Univ of Toronto, Toronto, ON, Canada M5S 1Aa.

THORNTON, JOHN K.
PERSONAL Born Fort Monroe, VA, m, 1981, 2 children **DISCIPLINE** AFRICA AND WORLD HISTORY **EDUCATION** Univ Mich, BA, 71; UCLA, MA, PhD. **CAREER** Prof; taught at,Univ Zambia in Lusaka, 80-81; part time, Allegheny Col, 81-84 & Univ Va, 84-86; Millersville Univ, 86-. **RESEARCH** Central Africa particularly on the Kingdom of Kongo, northern Angola during the period 1500-1800. **SELECTED PUBLICATIONS** Auth, The Kingdom of Kongo: Civil War and Transition, 1641-1718, Univ Wis Press, 83; Africa and Africans in the Making of the Atlantic World, 1400-1680, Cambridge UP, 92, 2nd ed, 98; auth, Kongolese Saint Anthony Comb, UP, 98; auth, Warfare in Atlantic Africa, USU of London P, 99. **CONTACT ADDRESS** Dept of History, Millersville Univ of Pennsylvania, PO Box 1002, Millersville, PA 17551-0302. **EMAIL** lin@cldc.howard.edu

THORNTON, RICHARD C.
PERSONAL Born 03/22/1936, Camden, NJ, m, 1981, 2 children **DISCIPLINE** HISTORY, INTERNATIONAL AFFAIRS **EDUCATION** Colgate Univ, BA, 61; Univ WA, PhD, 66. **CAREER** Res assoc hist, Univ WA, 66-67; prof hist & int affairs, George Washington Univ, 67. **RESEARCH** US foreign policy; Sino-Soviet relations. **SELECTED PUBLICATIONS** Auth, The Comintern and Li Li-san Line in 1930, The China Quart, 64; Soviet Histoirans and China's Past, Problems of Communism, 68; The Comintern and the Chinese Communists: 1928-1931, Univ of Wash Press, 69; China and the Communist World, In: Communist China, 1949-1968: A Twenty Year Assessment (Frank Trager and William Henderson, ed), NY Univ Press, 70; Bear and Dragon: Sino-Soviet Relations, 1949-1971, Am-Asian Educ Exchange Monogr Series, 71; The Structure of Communist Politics, World Politics, 7/72; The Soviet Policy Toward China, In: Soviets in Asia (Norton L Dodge, ed), Washington, DC, 72; China, the Struggle for Power, 1917-1972, Ind Univ Press, 73; Problems and Prospects for Research on China, Int Studies Newsletter, Univ Pittsburgh, winter 73; Soviet Strat-

egy in the Vietnam War, Asian Affairs, 74; South Asia: Imbalance on the Subcontinent, Orbis, fall 75; Teng Hsiao-ping and Peking's Current Political Crisis: A Structural Interpretation, Issues and Studies, 7/76; Toward a New Equilibrium? Tripolar Politics, 1964-1976, Naval War Col Rev, winter 77; Soviet Strategy in Asia since World War II, In: The USSR/US Defense: A Critical Comparison, Am Inst of Aeronautics and Astronautics, 77; The Political Succession to Mao Tse-tung, Issues and Studies, 6/78; The Chinese Revolution in Global Perspectives, In: China, A Balance Sheet (Jurgen Domes, ed), Univ Saarbrucken, 79; Sino-Soviet Rivalry in Southeast Asia, Issues and Studies, 10/80; US-Soviet Strategic Balance in the Middle East, 1977-1981, Korea and World Affairs, winter 81; China: A Political History, 1917-1980, Westview Press, 82; Arms Control and Heavy Missiles, The Naval War Col Rev, 84; Distant Connections: US-Soviet Rivalry in the Middle East and Southeast Asia, Asian Affairs, fall 84; Is Detente Inevitable?, Wash Inst for Values in Public Policy, 85; Soviet Asian Strategy in the Brezhnev Era and Beyond, Wash Inst for Values in Public Policy, 85; Strategic Change and American Foreign Policy: Perceptions of the Sino-Soviet conflict, Jour of Northeast Asian Studies, spring 86; The Grand Strategy Behind Renewed Sino-Soviet Ties, The World and I, 12/86; Nuclear Superiority, Geopolitics and State Terrorism, Global Affairs, fall 86; Detente II-SALT III, American Dream or Nightmare? The World and I, 1/87; The Nixon-Kissinger Years, The Reshaping of American Foreign Policy, Paragon House, 11/89; Defense/Aerospace: The United States in an Emerging New World, The Wash Res Group, 7/90; Deng's Middle Kingdom Strategy, In: The Broken Mirror: China after Tiananmen (George Hicks, ed), Longman Group UK Ltd, 90; Middle East Oil: Dividing the Spoils, Defense and Diplomacy, 90; The Carter Years: Toward a New Global Order, Paragon House, 91; Co-auth (with Alan Capps), New Light on the Iran Hostage Rescue Mission, Marine Corps Gazette, 12/91; Co-auth (with John Newman), A Comparative Plitical-Economic History of the Peoples Republic of China: A Short Course, In Depth, 12/92; John King Fairbank: An Assessment, The World and I, 6/92; Co-auth (with Bruce A Babcock), Japan's Response to Crisis: Not with a Bang but with a Buck, Global Affairs, winter 93; Mikhail Gorbachev: A Preliminary Strategic Assessment, The World and I, 1/93; Co-auth (with Alan Capps), Somalia's Iranian Connection, Washington Commentary, 10/8/93; Nixon's Foreign Policy was Undercut by Kissinger, The Wash Times, 5/3/94; The Sino-Russian Struggle for Hegemony in Northeast Asia, Problems of Post-Communism, 95; China at the Crossroads, The World and I, 4/96; Russo-Chinese Detente and the Emerging New World Order, In: The Roles of the United States, Russia and China in the New World Order (Hafeez Malik, ed), St Martin's Press, 97; The Secretary's History Lesson, The Wash Post, 6/29/97; Reagan Versus Volcker: Economic Policy Conflict in the First Year, In: Kurt London Occasional Papers, Inst for European, Russian and Eurasian Studies, George Wash Univ, 98; The Falklands Sting: Reagan, Thatcher and the Argentine Bomb, Brassey's, 98; Odd Man Out: Truman, Stalin, Mao and the Origin of the Korean War, Brassey's, 00. **CONTACT ADDRESS** Inst for Europ, Russ & Eurasian Studies, The George Washington Univ, 2013 G St N W, Ste. 401, Washington, DC 20052-0001.

THORNTON, S. A.
PERSONAL Born 12/18/1950, Munich, Germany **DISCIPLINE** HISTORY **EDUCATION** Univ Calif Berkeley, BA, 72; San Francisco State Univ, MA, 78; Univ Cambridge, MA, 83; PhD, 88. **CAREER** Asst Prof, St Lawrence Univ, 91-94; Asst Prof to Assoc Prof, Ariz State Univ, 94-. **RESEARCH** Jishu; Japanese epic; Japanese cinema. **SELECTED PUBLICATIONS** Auth, "Charisma and Community Formation in Medieval Japan: The Case of the Yugyo-ha (1300-1700)," Cornell E Asia Prog, 99. **CONTACT ADDRESS** Dept Hist, Arizona State Univ, 1636 S River Dr, Tempe, AZ 85281. **EMAIL** sybil.thornton@asu.edu

THORPE, WAYNE L.
DISCIPLINE HISTORY **EDUCATION** Univ Wash, BA; Portland State Univ, BA; Univ Colo, MA; Univ British Columbia, PhD. **HONORS AND AWARDS** Vis res fel, Intl Inst Soc Hist, Amsterdam. **RESEARCH** European hist. **SELECTED PUBLICATIONS** Auth, The Workers Themselves: Revolutionary Syndicalism and International Labour 1919-1923; co-ed, Revolutionary Syndicalism: An International Perspective. **CONTACT ADDRESS** History Dept, McMaster Univ, 1280 Main St W, Hamilton, ON, Canada L8S 4L9. **EMAIL** thorpew@mcmaster.ca

THRASHER, WILLIAM
PERSONAL Born 06/08/1934, Foreman, AR, s **DISCIPLINE** ART **EDUCATION** Boston Univ, MFA, 61; Henderson St niv, BA, 56 **CAREER** Independent cur. **HONORS AND AWARDS** John E Thayer Awd, 97; Fulbright Fel, 91; Japan Found Fel, 97. **RESEARCH** Contemporary Japanese craftmanship **SELECTED PUBLICATIONS** Auth, The Way of Tea: American Art for the Japanese Tea Ceremony, 85; auth, Tribute to Kojiro Tomita: Asian Art from the Permanent Collection, 90; auth, Kindred Spirits: The Eloquence of Function in American Shaker and Japanese arts of Daily Life, 95; contrib, Shaped with a passion: The Carl W. Weyerhaeuser Collection of Japanese Ceremics, 98. **CONTACT ADDRESS** Wellesley, MA 02481. **EMAIL** wmthras@aol.com

THURBER, TIM
PERSONAL Born 08/28/1967, Kenosha, WI, m, 1997 **DISCIPLINE** HISTORY **EDUCATION** Gustavus Adolphus Col, BA, 89; Univ NC, Chapel Hill, MA, 91, PhD, 96. **CAREER** Asst prof History, SUNY Oswego. **HONORS AND AWARDS** Phi Beta Kappa. **MEMBERSHIPS** Org of Am Hist, Am Hist Asn. **RESEARCH** Race, politics, liberalism, conservatism, post 1945 U.S. history. **SELECTED PUBLICATIONS** Auth, The Politics of Equality: Hubert H. Humphrey and the African American Freedom Struggle, Columbia Univ Press (98). **CONTACT ADDRESS** Dept Hist, SUNY, Oswego, 7060 State Route 104, Oswego, NY 13126-3560. **EMAIL** Thurber@oswego.edu

THURSBY, GENE ROBERT
PERSONAL Born 05/08/1939, Akron, OH, m, 1963 **DISCIPLINE** INDIC RELIGION, HISTORY OF RELIGIONS **EDUCATION** Oberlin Col, BA, 61, BDiv, 64; Duke Univ, PhD(-relig), 72. **CAREER** Asst prof, 70-76, ASSOC PROF RELIG, UNIV FLA, 76-, CONSULT, CHOICE: J ASN COL AND RES LIBR, 70-; scholar-diplomat, US Dept State Sem SAsia, 72 and Sem Pop Matters, 73. **MEMBERSHIPS** Am Acad Relig; Am Orient Soc; Royal Asiatic Soc Gt Brit and Ireland; Asn Asian Studies; Soc Asian and Comp Philos. **RESEARCH** Interreligious relations in South Asia; history of Hindu religious and social movements in the 20th century; philosophical analysis for religious uses of language. **SELECTED PUBLICATIONS** Auth, Some Resources for History of Religions, Bull Am Acad Relig, 67; coauth, South Asian Proscribed Publications, 1907-1947, Indian Arch, 69; Hindu-Muslim Relations in British India, Brill, 75; Religious Nationalism in Hindus And Muslims In India, J Asian Hist, Vol 0030, 96. **CONTACT ADDRESS** Dept of Relig, Univ of Florida, P O Box 117410, Gainesville, FL 32611-7410.

THURSTON, GARY J.
PERSONAL Born 03/05/1941, Spencer, IO, s **DISCIPLINE** HISTORY OF MODERN EUROPE AND OF RUSSIA **EDUCATION** Columbia Univ, PhD, 73. **CAREER** Dept Hist, Univ of RI **RESEARCH** Juxtaposition of public and private space in Russian theater in the half-century before the revolution of 1917. **SELECTED PUBLICATIONS** Auth, bk on the hist of Russ popular theater. **CONTACT ADDRESS** Dept of Hist, Univ of Rhode Island, 8 Ranger Rd, Ste. 1, Kingston, RI 02881-0807. **EMAIL** thurston@uri.edu

THURSTON, ROBERT
DISCIPLINE MODERN RUSSIAN HISTORY **EDUCATION** Univ Mich, PhD, 80. **CAREER** Miami Univ, prof hist, 96-. **RESEARCH** Mod Russian hist; Europ witch hunts; Am lynching. **SELECTED PUBLICATIONS** Liberal City, Conservative State: Moscow and Russia's Urban Crisis, 1906-1914, Oxford Univ Press, 87; Life and Terror in Stalin's Russia, 1934-1941, Yale Univ Press, 96; ed & contrib, The People's War: Popular Response to World War II in the Soviet Union, forthcoming, Univ Ill Press, 00; auth, The Witch Hunts in Europe and North America, 1400-1700, Longman Press, (forthcoming). **CONTACT ADDRESS** Miami Univ, Oxford, OH 45056. **EMAIL** thurstrw@muohio.edu

THYRET, ISOLDE
PERSONAL Born 02/11/1955, Stuttgart, Germany **DISCIPLINE** HISTORY **EDUCATION** Univ of WA, PhD, 92, MA, 86, BA, 85, BA, 81 **CAREER** Asst Prof, 94-, Kent St Univ; Visit Prof, 93-94, CO Col **HONORS AND AWARDS** Lib and media Svcs Res Collection Awd, 98 **MEMBERSHIPS** Am Hist Asn; Assn for Women in Slavic Studies; Hagiography Soc **RESEARCH** Women and Relig in medieval Russia **SELECTED PUBLICATIONS** Auth, Muscovite Miracle Stories as Sources for Gender-specific Religious Experience, DeKalb: N IL Press, 97; Blessed is the Tsarisa's Womb: The Myth of Miraculous Birth and Royal Motherhood in Muscovite Rusia, Russian Review, 94 **CONTACT ADDRESS** Dept of History, Kent State Univ, Kent, OH 44242. **EMAIL** ithyret@kent.edu

TICHENOR, IRENE
PERSONAL Born 12/21/1942, Marshall, MO, m, 1971, 2 children **DISCIPLINE** HISTORY **EDUCATION** Univ Mo, MS, 63; Columbia Univ, MLS, 73; PhD, 83. **CAREER** Asst Ref Librn, Union Theol Sem, 72-73; Tech Servs Librn, Brooklyn Col, 73-76; Head Librn, Brooklyn Hist Soc, 88-96; Dir, Brooklyn Hist Soc, 96-97; Prof, State Univ NYork (SUNY), 97-. **MEMBERSHIPS** Am Printing Hist Assoc, METRO Libr Consortium, Am Libr Assoc, Bibliog Soc of Am, Soc for the Hist of Authorship, Reading and Publ, Organization of Am Historians. **RESEARCH** History of printing and allied arts, Nineteenth-Century America. **SELECTED PUBLICATIONS** Auth, Introduction to Reprint of Theodore Low De Vinne's 1871 "Printers' Price List", Garland Publ Co (New York, NY), 80; auth, "Master Printers Organize: The Typothetae of the City of New York, 1865-1906," in Small Bus in Am Life (NY: Columbia Univ Pr, 80); auth, "The Life of the Printer in 19th-Century New York," in Billheads & Broadsides: Job Printing in the 19th-Century Seaport (NY: South St Seaport Museum, 85). **CONTACT ADDRESS** Dept Hist, SUNY, 794 Carroll St, Brooklyn, NY 11215. **EMAIL** itichenor@earthlink.net

TIERNEY, BRIAN
PERSONAL Born 05/07/1922, Scunthorpe, England, m, 1949, 4 children **DISCIPLINE** HISTORY **EDUCATION** Cambridge Univ, BA, 48, PhD(hist), 51. **CAREER** From instr to assoc prof hist, Cath Univ Am, 51-59; prof, 59-67, Goldwin Smith prof medieval hist, 67-77, Bryce & Edith M Bowmar Prof Humanistics Studies, Cornell Univ, 77-92, Guggenheim fel, 55-57; vis lectr, Univ Calif, Los Angeles, 56; mem Inst Advan Study, Princeton, 61-62; Am Coun Learned Soc fels, 61-62 & 66-67; Soc Relig Higher Educ fel, 66-67; Nat Endowment for Humanities fel, 77-78 & 85-86. **HONORS AND AWARDS** DTh, Uppsala Univ, 64; DHL, Cath Univ Am, 81. **MEMBERSHIPS** AHA; Am Cath Hist Asn (pres, 64); fel Mediaeval Acad Am; fel Am Acad Arts & Sci; fel Am Philos Soc; Corresponding fel British Academy. **RESEARCH** Mediaeval representative government; mediaeval law; mediaeval church history. **SELECTED PUBLICATIONS** Auth, Foundations of the Conciliar Theory, Cambridge Univ, 55; Crisis of Church and State 1050-1300, Prentice-Hall, 64; Origins of Papal Infallibility, E J Brill, 72; Religion, Law, and the Growth of Constitutional Thought, 1150-1650, Cambridge Univ, 82; The Idea of Natural Rights, Scholars Press, 97. **CONTACT ADDRESS** Dept of History, Cornell Univ, Ithaca, NY 14853. **EMAIL** bt20@cornell.edu

TIERSTEN, LISA
DISCIPLINE MODERN EUROPEAN CULTURAL HISTORY **EDUCATION** Univ Mass, BA; Yale Univ, PhD, 91. **CAREER** Asst prof, Bernard Col. **SELECTED PUBLICATIONS** Auth, Consumer Culture and the European Bourgeoisie, Il Bollettino del diciannovesimo secolo, 97. **CONTACT ADDRESS** Dept of Hist, Columbia Col, New York, 2960 Broadway, New York, NY 10027-6902.

TIGNOR, ROBERT L.
PERSONAL Born 11/20/1933, Philadelphia, PA, m, 1956, 1 child **DISCIPLINE** MIDDLE EASTERN HISTORY **EDUCATION** Col Wooster, BA, 55; Yale Univ, MA, 56, PhD, 60. **CAREER** From instr to assoc prof, 60-76, Prof Hist, Princeton Univ, 76-, Chmn Dept, 77- **MEMBERSHIPS** Mid E Studies Asn. **RESEARCH** Modern African and Middle Eastern history. **SELECTED PUBLICATIONS CONTACT ADDRESS** Dept of Hist, Princeton Univ, Princeton, NJ 08540.

TIJERINA, ANDRES
PERSONAL Born, TX **DISCIPLINE** HISTORY **EDUCATION** Tex A & M Univ, BA, 67; Tex Tech Univ, MA, 73; Univ Tex at Austin, PhD, 77. **CAREER** Assoc prof, Tex A & M Univ, 90-95; assoc prof, Incarnate Word Col, 95-96; assoc prof, UTSA, 96-97; assoc prof, Austin Community Col, 97-98. **HONORS AND AWARDS** Kate Brookes Bates Awd, TSHA; Presidio La Bahia Prize, Sons of the Republic of Tex; T.R. Fehrenbach Awd, Tex Hist Comn; Grad Fel, Univ of Tex, 76-77; Choice Book Awd, MLA, 95; Excellence in Teaching Awd, Phi Theta Kappa Honor Soc, 99. **MEMBERSHIPS** Tex State Hist Asn, Am Hist Asn, Phi Alpha Theta Hist Honor Soc. **RESEARCH** Nineteenth-Century Texas history. **SELECTED PUBLICATIONS** Auth, History of Mexican Americans in Lubbock, Tex Tech Univ Press, 78; auth, Tejanos and Texas Under the Mexican Flag 1821-1836, Tex A & M Univ Press, 94; auth, Tejano Empire: Life on the South Texas Ranchos, Tex A & M Univ Press, 98. **CONTACT ADDRESS** Dept Soc & Behav Sci, Austin Comm Col, 1555 Cypress Creek Rd, Cedar Park, TX 78613-3607. **EMAIL** andrest@austin.cc.tx.us

TILLMAN, HOYT CLEVELAND
PERSONAL Born 07/08/1944, Crestview, FL, m, 1970, 2 children **DISCIPLINE** HISTORY, CHINESE THOUGHT **EDUCATION** Belhaven Col, BA, 66; Univ Va, MA, 68; Harvard Univ, PhD(hist and East Asian lang), 76. **CAREER** From sophomore tutor to head tutor East Asian studies, Harvard Univ, 74-76; asst prof, 76-81, assoc prof, 81-88, prof, 88-, hist, Ariz State Univ; vis prof, Peking Univ, 82-84; Princeton Univ, 90; Univ Hawaii, 94; Academia Sincia, 93, 94, 96, 00; Univ Washinton, 96. **HONORS AND AWARDS** Fulbright-Hays Fac Res Abroad Prog, 82-83; Nat Acad of Science, Comm for Scholarly Communications with China, 82-84; Nat Endowment for the Humanities, 88-89; Am Council of Learned Societies, 89-90; Humboldt Res Award, 00-01. **MEMBERSHIPS** AHA; Asn Asian Studies; Soc Asian and Comp Philos. **RESEARCH** History of Chinese Thought, Culture, and Medicine. **SELECTED PUBLICATIONS** Auth, "Proto-nationalism in 12th Century China? The Case of Ch'en Liang," Harvard Jour Asiatic Studies (79); auth, Utilitarian Confucianism: Ch'en Liang's Challenge to Chu Hsi, Harvard, 82; auth, Confucian Discourse and Chu Hsi's Ascendancy, Hawaii, 92; auth, "A New Direction in Confucian Scholarship: Approaches to Examining the Differences Between Neo-Confucianism and Tao-hsueh," Philos E and W (92); auth, Ch'en Liang on Public Interest and the Law, Hawaii, 94; auth, "The Uses of Neo-Confucianism Revisited," Philos E and W (94); coed, China Under Jurchen Rule: Essays on Chin Intellectual and Cultural History, State Univ of NYork, 95; auth, "One Significant Rise in Chu-ko Liang's Popularity: The Impact of the Jurchen Invasion," Hanxue yanjiu (Chinese Studies) (96); auth, Zhu Xi de siwei shijie (Chu Hsi's World of Thought), Taipei, 96; trans, Business as a Vocation: The Autobiography of Mr Wu Ho-su, Harvard, 00. **CONTACT ADDRESS** Dept of Hist, Arizona State Univ, Tempe, AZ 85287-2501. **EMAIL** HTillman@asu.edu

TILLSON, ALBERT H., JR.
PERSONAL Born 11/12/1948, Arlington, VA, m, 1988 **DISCIPLINE** HISTORY **EDUCATION** George Mason Univ, BA, 71; John Hopkins Univ, MA, 74; Univ Texas, PhD, 86. **CAREER** Lecturer, Northern Virginia Community Col, 75-76, 85; Teaching Asst, Asst Instr, Univ of Tex, 77-79, 81-83; Asst Prof, 86-92, Assoc Prof, 92-, Univ Tampa; Instr, 86, Pan Amer Univ; Instr, 84-85, St Norbert College. **HONORS AND AWARDS** Waltr Prescott Webb Fel, Univ of Tex, 77; Hist Scholarship, Colonial Dames of Am, 78, 79; Univ Fel, Univ of Tex, 80-81; Fac Development Grants, Univ of Tampa, 87-94, 97-00; Andrew Mellon Res Fel, Virginia Histol Soc, 91, 92, 95; Travel to Collections Grant, Nat Endowment for the Humanities, 91; David Delo Res Professorship, Univ of Tampa, 99-00; Travel grant for CIEEa conference on Cuba at the Millenium, Havana from Col of Business, Univ of Tampa, 00. **MEMBERSHIPS** Am Histol Asn, Inst of Early Am Hist and Culture, Southern Histol Asn, Virginia Histol Soc, Southeastern Am Soc for Eighteenth Century Studies. **RESEARCH** Colonial and revolutionary US history, esp the 18th century Chesapeake slavery in the early British and Spanish America. **SELECTED PUBLICATIONS** Auth, "The Militia and Popular Political Culture in the Upper Valley of Virginia, 1740-1775," Virginia Magazine of Hist and Biography, 86; auth, "The Localist Roots of Backcountry Loyalism: An Examination of Popular Political Culture in Virginia's New River Valley, Journal of Southern Hist, 88; auth, "The Southern Backcountry: A Survey of Current Research," Virginia Magazine of History and Biography, 90; auth, Gentry and Common Folk: Political Culture on a Virginia Frontier, 1740-1789, Univ Pr of Ky, 91; auth, The American Revolution, 1775-1783: An Encyclopedia, edited by Richard L. Blanco and Paul J. Sanborn, Garland Publishing, Inc., 93; auth, "The Maintence of Revoluntionary Consensus: Treatment of Tories in Southwestern Virginia, 1775-1790." in the Loyalists and Community in North America, edited by Timothy M. Barnes, Robert M. Calhoon, and Geoge A. Rawlyk, Greenwood Pr, 94; auth, American National Biography, edited by John A. Garraty and Mark C. Carnes, Oxford Univ Pr, 99; auth, The New Dictionary of National Biography, forthcoming on Oxford Univ Pr. **CONTACT ADDRESS** Dept of History, Univ of Tampa, Box 2F, Tampa, FL 33606-1490. **EMAIL** atillson@alpha.utampa.edu

TILLY, LOUISE A.
DISCIPLINE HISTORY **EDUCATION** Univ Toronto, PhD, 55. **CAREER** Michael E Gellert Prof Hist and Sociol and chr Comm on Hist Studies. **RESEARCH** Global perspectives on industrialization and gender inequality. **SELECTED PUBLICATIONS** Auth, The European Experience of Declining Fertility, 92; Politics and Class in Milan, 1881-1901, 92; coauth, Women, Work, and Family, 78; The Rebellious Century, 75; co-ed, Women, Politics, and Change, 90; co-ed and co-trans, Meme Santerre, A French Woman of the People, 85. **CONTACT ADDRESS** Eugene Lang Col, New Sch for Social Research, 66 West 12th St, New York, NY 10011.

TIMBERLAKE, CHARLES E.
PERSONAL Born 09/09/1935, Greenup County, KY, m, 1958, 3 children **DISCIPLINE** HISTORY **EDUCATION** Berea Col, BA, 57; Claremont Grad Sch, MA, 62; Univ Wash, PhD, 68. **CAREER** Teach asst, Univ Wash, 61-64; asst, assoc, prof, dist prof, chair, Univ Missouri, 67-; vis prof, Univ Manchester, 87-88; asst dir, Honors Col, 88-90; edu dir, San Francisco, 91-; consult, St Petersburg, 92-95; vis prof, Joensu Univ, 96, 98, 00. **HONORS AND AWARDS** Dist Fac Awd; Byler Dist Prof Awd; Fulbright-Hays Fac Res Awd; IREB Awds; NSF Awd; Who's Who in Am, Midwest; Hon Prof, Lanzhou Univ, China; Hon Prof in Lanzhou, China Univ, 91; Dis Prof Awd, MU Alumni Assoc, 00. **MEMBERSHIPS** IAI; AAU; AAASS; AHA; CSC; MCH; SHSM; MO Fulbright Asn. **RESEARCH** Modern Russian history; socio-economic and religious history of rural Russia 1861 to present. **SELECTED PUBLICATIONS** Auth, "The Tsarist Government's Preoccupation with 'The Liberal Party' in Tver Province, 1890-1905," in The Emergence of Democracy in Late Imperial Russia, ed. Mary Schaeffer Conroy (Niwot, Co: UP Colo, 98): 30-59; coauth, Services and Quality of life in Rural Villages in the Former Soviet Union: Data from 1991 and 1993 Surveys, UP of Am (Lanham, Md, NY, Oxford, UK), 98; auth, The Fate of Russian Orthodox Monasteries and Convents Since 1917. The Donald W. Treadgold Papers in Russian, East European, and Central Asian Studies, #3. Jackson School of International Studies, Univ of Washington, 95; auth, "N. A. Korf (1834-83): Designer of the Russian Elementary School Classroom," in School and Society in Tsarist and Soviet Russia, ed. Ben Eklof (London & NY: Macmillan Pub, 93): 12-35; auth, "The Middle Classes in Late Tsarist Russia," in Social Orders and Social Classes in Europe since 1500: Studies in social stratification, ed. Michael Bush (London & NY: Longman Pub, 92): 86-113; auth, "The Zemstvo and the Development of a Russian Middle Class," in Between Tsar and People: Educated Society and the Quest for Public Identity in Late Imperial Russia, eds. Edith Clowes et al (Princeton: Princeton UP, 91): 164-179; auth, "Higher Learning, the State, and the Professions in Russia," in The Transformation of Higher Learning, 1860-1930, ed. Konrad Jarausch, vol 13 in the series: Historisch Sozialwissenschaftliche Forschungen (Klett Cotta Verlag: Stuttgart, Federal Republic of Germany, 82): 321-345, and by Univ of Chicago Press, 83, Konrad Jarausch, ed. **CONTACT ADDRESS** Dept Hist, Univ of Missouri, Columbia, 101 Read Hall, Columbia, MO 65211-7500. **EMAIL** timberlakec@missouri.edu

TIMBIE, JANET ANN
PERSONAL Born 10/17/1948, San Francisco, CA, m, 1969, 2 children **DISCIPLINE** HISTORY OF CHRISTIANITY, COPTIC LANGUAGE **EDUCATION** Stanford Univ, AB, 70; Univ Pa, PhD(relig studies), 79. **CAREER** Reader hist and relig, Am Univ, 71-72 and prof lectr relig, 80-81; Dumbarton Oaks Ctr for Byzantine Studies fel, 78-79; Mellon fel, Cath Univ, 79-80; Catholic Univ 93-; RES AND WRITING, 82-, Ed and transl, US Cath Conf Bishops, 79-82. **MEMBERSHIPS** Cath Bibl Asn; Soc Bibl Lit; Am Acad Relig; Int Asn Coptic Studies; N Amer Patristic Soc. **RESEARCH** Christianity in Egypt through 5th century; development of early Christian monasticism; Coptic language and literature. **SELECTED PUBLICATIONS** Auth, The dating of a Coptic-Sahidic Psalter codex from the University Museum in Philadephia, Le Museon, 75; Dualism and the Concept of Orthodoxy in the Thought of the Monks of Upper Egypt, Edwin Mellen P; The Status of Women and Gnosticism in Irenaeus and Tertullian, Cath Biblical Quart, Vol 0058, 96; coauth, The Nag Hammadi library in English, Religious Studies Rev, 82; co-ed, The Testament of Job, Scholars Press, 75. **CONTACT ADDRESS** 4608 Merivale Rd, Chevy Chase, MD 20815. **EMAIL** jtimbie@worldnet.att.net

TINDALL, GEORGE BROWN
PERSONAL Born 02/26/1921, Greenville, SC, m, 1946, 2 children **DISCIPLINE** AMERICAN HISTORY **EDUCATION** Furman Univ, AB, 42; Univ NC, MA, 48, PhD(hist), 51. **CAREER** Asst prof hist, Eastern Kent State Col, 50-51, Univ Miss, 51-52, Woman's Col Univ NC, 52-53 and La State Univ, 53-58; assoc prof, 58-64, prof hist, 64-69, Kenan Prof, Univ NC, Chapel Hill, 69-, Guggenheim fel, 57-58; Soc Sci Res Coun fac res grant, 59-60; mem, Inst Advan Study, Princeton, 63-64; Fulbright Gast prof, Interpreters Inst, Univ Vienna, 67-68; vis prof, Kyoto Am Studies summer sem, 77; Nat Endowment for Humanities and Ctr Adv Study Behav Sci fels, 79-80. **HONORS AND AWARDS** LittD, Furman Univ, 72. **MEMBERSHIPS** AHA; Orgn Am Historians; Southern Hist Asn (vpres, 72, pres, 73); Soc Am Historians. **RESEARCH** United States history; history of the South. **SELECTED PUBLICATIONS** Auth, South Carolina Negroes, 1877-1900, Univ SC, 52; ed, The Pursuit of Southern History, La State Univ, 64; auth, Mythology: A New Frontier in Southern History, In: The Idea of the South, Univ Chicago, 64; ed, A Populist Reader, Harper Torchbks, 66; auth, The Emergence of the New South, 1913-1945, La State Univ, 67; The Disruption of the Solid South, Univ Ga, 72 & Norton, 72; The Persistent Tradition in New South Politics, 75 & The Ethnic Southerners, 76, La State Univ. **CONTACT ADDRESS** Dept Hist, Univ of No Carolina, Chapel Hill, Chapel Hill, NC 27514.

TINGLEY, DONALD FRED
PERSONAL Born 03/13/1922, Marshall, IL, m, 1944, 1 child **DISCIPLINE** HISTORY **EDUCATION** Eastern Ill State Col, BS, 47; Univ Ill, MA, 48, PhD(hist), 52. **CAREER** Hist res ed, Ill State Hist Soc, 52-53; asst prof soc sci, 53-56, assoc prof, 56-62, Prof Hist, Eastern Ill Univ, 62- **MEMBERSHIPS** Orgn Am Historians. **RESEARCH** Intellectual, religious and social history of the United States; Illinois history. **SELECTED PUBLICATIONS** Auth, Flower, Eliza Julia--Letters Of An English Gentlewoman in Life on the Illinois-Indiana Frontier, 1817-1861, J Am Hist, Vol 0079, 93; coauth and ed, Essays in Illinois History, Southern Ill Univ, 68; The Emerging University, Eastern Ill Univ, 74; Social History of the United States, Gale Res, 79; The Structuring of a State: The History of illinois, 1899-1928, Univ Ill, 80; Women and Feminism in American History, Gale Res, 81. **CONTACT ADDRESS** 401 Burwash Dr., Apt. 146, Savoy, IL 61874-9574.

TINSLEY, JAMES AUBREY
PERSONAL Born 01/02/1924, Haynesville, LA, m, 1948, 3 children **DISCIPLINE** AMERICAN HISTORY **EDUCATION** Baylor Univ, BA, 47; Univ NC, MA, 48; Univ Wis, PhD, 54. **CAREER** Instr Am hist, Agr and Mech Col Tex, 48-49; instr, NTex State Col, 49-50, asst prof, 51-52; from asst prof to assoc prof, 53-61, chmn dept hist, 67-69, Prof Am Hist, Univ Houston, 61-, Assoc Dean Col Arts and Sci, 69-, Ed, Publisher Tex Gulf Coast Hist Asn, 56-; vis prof, Vanderbilt Univ, 63-64. **MEMBERSHIPS** Orgn Am Historians; Southern Hist Asn; Am Studies Asn; Am Asn State and Local Hist. **RESEARCH** Progressive movement in Texas; United States business and economic history. **SELECTED PUBLICATIONS** Auth, Historical organizations as aids to history, In: In Support of Clio, State Hist Soc Wis, 58; Texas Society of Certified Public Accountants: A History, Tex Soc Cert Pub Acct, 62. **CONTACT ADDRESS** Dept of Hist, Univ of Houston, Houston, TX 77004.

TINSLEY, JAMES R.
PERSONAL Born 02/15/1944, Shreveport, LA, w, 1944 **DISCIPLINE** HISTORY; FRENCH **EDUCATION** Centenary Col, BA, 66; E Tex State Univ, MA, 67; Univ Ala, MLS, 75; Univ St Anne, Dipl Fr. **CAREER** Instr, Wm Carey Col, 67; asst prof, Morehead State Univ, 68-74; arch, St Mary Parish, 76-79; Acad Sacred Heart, 80-81; prefect, Trinity Heights Acad, 82-86; asst headmaster, Grawood School, 88-90; teacher, Glenbrook School, 90-94; Caddo Parish School, 94- . **HONORS AND AWARDS** Gorgas Fel, Univ Ala; Conofil Fel, Univ Ste Anne. **MEMBERSHIPS** S Hist. **RESEARCH** Edward Irving, Catholic Apostolic Church, GOA. **SELECTED PUBLICATIONS** Auth, The Church in the War-A History of St. Marks Cathedral in WW II. **CONTACT ADDRESS** Dept Behav Sci, Bossier Parish Comm Col, 2719 Airline Dr, Bossier City, LA 71111-5801.

TIRADO, ISABEL A.
DISCIPLINE HISTORY **EDUCATION** Hunter Col, CUNY, BA, 69; MA, 73; Univ Calif-Berkeley, PhD, 85. **CAREER** Assoc prof & ch, Hist Dept, William Paterson Col, 85-; ch, Hist dept, 93-96; mem, Provost Search Comt, 95; mem, Comprehensive Anal Ranking Comt, 94-95; Hist Dept Exec Coun, 90-91 & 92-93; Freshman Sem instr, 92-93; Search Comt, Distinguished Vis Hisp Scholar, 93; Search Comt, Acad Coordr, Off of Minority Educ, 93; Campus-wide Sabbatical Comt, 92; Local Arrangements Comt, AHA, 90; ch, Curric Comt, 89-91; Search Comt for Assoc VP, WPC, 87; ch, Western Civilization Comt, 87-89; fac adv, Stud Advisement Ctr, WPC, 87; NJ Humanities Grant, 86-87; Writing Across Curric prog, 86-87; fac mentor to minority stud, 86-87; NJ Endowment for the Humanities, 86; Curric & Activ Comt, 85-86; act instr, Univ Calif-Berkeley, 85; grad instr, Univ Calif-Berkeley, 82-84; lectr, Lehman Col, CUNY, 71-72; coordr, Women's and Minorities' Proj, Grad Assembly, Univ Calif-Berkeley, 82-83; res asst, Univ Ccalif-Berkeley, 77-78. **HONORS AND AWARDS** NEH, Columbia Univ, 96; IREX Individual Advan Res Opportunities in Eurasia grant, 96-97; Amer Philos Soc travel grant, 95; IREX Short Term Travel Grants, 93, 94 & 95; IREX Collab Grant, 92; NEH, Stanford Univ 92; Nat Coun for Soviet and E Europ Res fel, 91-92; sr fel, Harriman Inst, Columbia Univ, 91-92; Fulbright-Hays fel, 90; IREX sr scholar exchange, Soviet Acad Sci, Inst Hist, 90; Ford Found Postdr fel, 88-89; vis sch, Harriman Inst, Columbia Univ, 85-86 & 88-89; NEH, Fordham Univ, 86; Mellon Found Dissertation fel, 84-85; Dean's fel, Univ Calif-Berkeley, 83-84; IREX-Leningrad State Univ Exchange, 82; IREX Dissertation Grant, 80-81; Ford Found Doctoral fel, 77-79; Michael Gurevich Awd, 75; Dean's List, Hunter Col, 67-69. **MEMBERSHIPS** Amer Asn for the Advan of Slavic Stud; AHA; Asn of Women in Slavic Stud; Peasant Consortium; Lat Amer Network of Col Empls. **SELECTED PUBLICATIONS** Auth, Books Young Guard: The Petrograd Komsomol Organizations 1917-1920, Greenwood Press, 88; The Komsomol and Young Peasant Women: The Polit Mobilization of Young Women in the Russian Village, 1921-1927, Russ Hist, 23, 96; Nietzschean Images in the Komsomol's Vanguardism, in Nietzsche and Soviet Culture: Ally and Adversary, Cambridge Univ Press, 94; The Village Voice: Women's Views of Themselves and Their World in Russian Chastushki of the 1920s, The Carl Beck Papers, 93; The Komsomol and Young Peasants: the Dilemma of Rural Expansion, 1921-1925, Slavic Rev, 93; The Revolution, Young Peasants, and the Komsomol's Anti-Religious Campaigns 1920-1928, Can-Amer Slavic Stud, 92; rev, Peasant Icons: Representations of Rural People in Late 19th Century Russia, Slavic Rev, 94; New Directions in Soviet History, Cambridge Univ Press, 94; Russia's Women: Accommodation, Resistance, Transformation, Amer Hist Rev, 93; Peasant Russia, Civil War: The Volga Countryside in Revolution, 1917-1921, The Historian, 90. **CONTACT ADDRESS** Dept of History, William Paterson Col of New Jersey, 300 Pompton Rd., Wayne, NJ 07470. **EMAIL** tirado@frontier.wilpaterson.edu

TIRADO, THOMAS C.
DISCIPLINE LATIN AMERICAN HISTORY, COLUMBUS AND THE AGE OF DISCOVERY **EDUCATION** Univ Ill, BA, 61; Georgetown Univ, MA, 66; Temple Univ, PhD, 77. **CAREER** Prof; Millersville Univ, 65-; rural commun develop, Peace Corps, 62-63, Proj Colombia; tchg asst, Univ Ill; dir, Comput Information Retrieval Syst on Columbus & the Age of Discovery. **SELECTED PUBLICATIONS** Auth, Publication of Celsa's World: Conversations with a Mexican Peasant Woman, Ctr for Latin Amer Stud, Ariz State UP, 91; Celsa's World: Conversations with a Mexican Peasant Woman, Ariz State Univ, 95; rev, Cristoforo Colombus: God's Navigator, Hisp Amer Hist Rev, 95; Portugal and Columbus--Old Drives in New Discoveries, Mediter Stud, 93; Not 'Just Another Reader,' rev Marvin Lunenfeld's 1492: Discovery, Invasion, Encounter: Sources and Interpretations, in the Int Columbian Quincentenary Alliance Newsl, 91; Discovery Five Hundred, Newsle Int Columbian Quincentenary Alliance, Inc, rev Marvin Lunenfeld's 1492: Discovery, Invasion, Encounter: Sources and Interpretations, 91; Bul, Soc for Span and Portuguese Hist Stud, Not 'Just Another Reader,' rev Marvin Lunenfeld's 1492: Discovery, Invasion, Encounter: Sources and Interp(s), 91; auth, Alfonso Lopez Pumarejo: Concialdor, Planeta Press (Bogota, Colombia), 86. **CONTACT ADDRESS** Dept of History, Millersville Univ of Pennsylvania, PO Box 1002, Millersville, PA 17551-0302. **EMAIL** tct225@yahoo.com

TITLEY, E. BRIAN
PERSONAL Born 01/08/1945, Cork, Ireland **DISCIPLINE** HISTORY **EDUCATION** Nat Univ Ireland, BA, 66; Univ Man, BEd, 70, MEd, 75; Univ Alta, PhD, 80. **CAREER** Sec

sch tchr, Man, 67-70; elem sch prin, Dept Indian Affairs, 71-74; lectr, 80-86, asst prof, 86-89, assoc prof, Univ Alta, 89-90; assoc prof, 91-93, Prof Education, Univ Lethbridge, 93-. **MEMBERSHIPS** Can Hist Asn; Can Hist Educ Asn (pres, 90-92); Can Soc Study Educ; Writers Guild Alta. **SELECTED PUBLICATIONS** Auth, Church, State and the Control of Schooling in Ireland, 1900-1944, 83; auth, A Narrow Vision: Duncan Campbell Scott and the Administration of Indian Affairs in Canada, 86; auth, Dark Age: The Political Odyssey of Emperor Bokassa, 97; ed, Canadian Education: Historical Themes and Contemporary Issues, 90; co-ed, Education in Canada: An Interpretation, 82. **CONTACT ADDRESS** Dept of Educ, Univ of Lethbridge, 4401 University Dr, Lethbridge, AB, Canada T1K 3M4. **EMAIL** brian.titley@uleth.ca

TITON, JEFF TODD
PERSONAL Born 12/08/1943, Jersey City, NJ, 1 child **DISCIPLINE** AMERICAN STUDIES **EDUCATION** Amherst College, BA, 65; Univ Minn, MA, 70, PhD, 71. **CAREER** Prof music, 86-, Brown Univ; vis Prof at: 85, Carleton College, 90, Berea College, 93, Amherst College; Asst Prof, Assoc Prof, 71-86, Tufts Univ. **HONORS AND AWARDS** NEH Fels; ASCAP Deems Taylor Awd. **MEMBERSHIPS** Soc for Ethnomusicology; AFS; ASA. **RESEARCH** American Music, old time fiddle and string band music, blues; Lined-out hymnody of Old Regular Baptists; Black Preaching. **SELECTED PUBLICATIONS** Auth, Knowing Fieldwork, Shadows in the Field, ed, Gregory Barz, Timothy Cooley, NY, Oxford Univ Press, 96; ed, Worlds of Music: An Introduction to Music of the World's Peoples, NY Schirmer Books, 84, rev 2nd edition, 92, 3rd ed, 96; Text, J Amer Folklore, 95; Bi-musicality as Metaphor, J Amer Folklore, 95; Blues and Franklin Rev CL, Encyc of African-American Culture and History, ed, Jack Saltzman, David L Smith, Cornel West, NY, MacMillan, 95; Early Downhome Blues: A Musical and Cultural Analysis, Urbana IL, Univ IL Press, 77, pbk, Illini Books 79, Winner ASCAP Deems Taylor Award, rev 2nd ed, Univ N C Press, 95; auth, Powerhouse for God, Univ Texas Press, 88. **CONTACT ADDRESS** Dept of Music, Brown Univ, Box 1924, Providence, RI 02912. **EMAIL** Jeff_Titon@brown.edu

TITTLER, ROBERT
PERSONAL Born 12/07/1942, New York, NY **DISCIPLINE** HISTORY **EDUCATION** Oberlin Col, BA, 64; New York Univ, MA, 65; PhD, 71. **CAREER** Asst prof, 69-74, assoc prof, Loyola Col, 74-75; assoc prof, 75-81, chmn hist, Loyola campus, 76-77, co-chmn, united dept, 77-78, Prof History, Concordia Univ, 81-, dir, hist grad prog, 86-89; Andrew H. Mellon lectr, Princeton, 87; vis prof, Yale Univ, 98. **HONORS AND AWARDS** Haskell fel & Penfield fel, England, 68-69; Can Coun leave fel, 74-75; SSHRC res grants 82-83, 87-89, 91-94, 97-99; NEH fel, 91. **MEMBERSHIPS** Ctr Renaissance Reformation Stud; Inst Hist Res; N Am Conf Brit Stud; Econ Hist Soc; Soc 16th Century Stud; Rec Early Eng Drama; Past Present Soc. **RESEARCH** Politics and political culture of Tudor and Stuart England; English towns and cities; the interplay between at (especially architectue and portraiture), politics and society; and the implications of the English Refomation. **SELECTED PUBLICATIONS** Auth, Nicholas Bacon, The Making of a Tudor Statesman, 76; auth, The Reign of Mary I, 83, 2nd ed, 91; auth, Architecture and Power, the Town Hall and the English Urban Community 1500-1640, 91; auth, The Reformation and the Towns, 98; Acad ed-in-chief, History of Urban Society in Europe, 5 vol ser; auth, "Townspeople and Nationa, Biogaphical Essays in the English Urban Expeience, 1500, 1650," (Standford U.P., 2000). **CONTACT ADDRESS** Dept of History, Concordia Univ, Montreal, 7141 Sherbrooke St W, Montreal, QC, Canada H4B 1R6. **EMAIL** tittler@vax2.concordia.ca

TIYAMBE ZELEZA, PAUL
PERSONAL Born 05/25/1955, Zimbabwe **DISCIPLINE** HISTORY **EDUCATION** Univ of Malawi, BA, 72-76; Univ of London, MA, 77-78; Dalhousie Univ, PhD, 78-82. **CAREER** Lectr, Kenyatta Univ, 84-87; visiting prof, Dalhousie Univ, 90; assoc prof, Trent Univ, 90-95; prof, Trent Univ, 95; acting dir, Trent Univ, 94-95. **HONORS AND AWARDS** Social Science and Humanities Res Council, 94-97; UIUC Col of Liberal Arts and Sciences, 95-00; Univ of Ill Res Board, 96; Univ of Ill Res Board, 96-97; Center's NRC programs and FLAS fellowships for, 97-00; dir, center african studies. **MEMBERSHIPS** Founder member of the Malawian Writers' Series Editorial Board, 74; Asn of Caribbean Historians, 83-84; Canadian Asn of African Studies, 81-84, 90-; The Writers' Union of Canada, 92-; The Canadian Center for International Pen, 92-; Canadian Asn of African Studies Executive, 91-95; Canadian Asn for the Study of International Dev, 91-4. **RESEARCH** Kenyan and African economic and labor hist, imperialism an dcolonialism, Kenyan and African economic, labor, environmental, and gender hist African studies and lit. **SELECTED PUBLICATIONS** Auth, Night of darkness and Other Stories, Limbe: Montfort Press, (76): 217; auth, Labour, Unionization and Women's Participation in Kenya: 1963-1987; Nairobi: Friedrich Ebert Foundation, (88): 207; auth, Smouldering Charcoal, Oxford: Heinemann International, (92): 183; auth, A Modern Economic History of Africa, Vol 1: The Nineteenth Century, Dakar: Codesria, (93): 501; auth, The Joys of Exile: Stories, Toronto: House of Anansi Press, (94): 194; auth, Manufacturing African Studies and Crises, Dakar Book Series, (97): 650; ed, The Creation and Consumption of Leisure in Urban Africa, with Dan Williams, (forthcoming); ed, Space, Society, and Culture in Africa, with Ezekiel Kalipeni, Univ of Ill Press, (forthcoming); ed, Beyond Cirsis in Africa: Sturggles and Transformations, with M.C. Diop, Dakar: Codesria Book Series, (forthcoming); auth, A Modern Economic History of Africa, Vol 2: The Twentieth Century, Dakar: Codesria Book Series and other publishers, (forthcoming); **CONTACT ADDRESS** History Dept, Univ of Illinois, Urbana-Champaign, isb, mc 485, 910 s fifth, Champaign, IL 61820. **EMAIL** zeleza@staff.uiuc.edu

TOBEY, RONALD CHARLES
PERSONAL Born 10/25/1942, Plymouth, NH, 2 children **DISCIPLINE** HISTORY OF SCIENCE AND TECHNOLOGY **EDUCATION** Univ NH, BA, 64; Cornell Univ, MA, 66, PhD, 69. **CAREER** Vis asst prof Am hist, Univ Pittsburgh, 69-70; asst prof, 70-75; assoc prof, 75-81, prof hist of sci, Univ CA, Riverside, 81, dir prog hist resources mgt, 72, Nat Endowment for Hum fel, 75; mem adv coun, Nat Arch Region 9, 76-77; mem bd trustees, Riverside Munic Mus, 77-83; Pres, Board of Dir, Mission Inn Found, 85-93. **MEMBERSHIPS** AHA; Orgn Am Historians; Hist Sci Soc; Soc Hist Tech. **RESEARCH** Hist of Am sci; Am soc hist; Hist Am Sci & Tech. **SELECTED PUBLICATIONS** Auth, American Ideology of National Science, 1919-1930, Univ Pittsburgh, 71; How Urbane is the Urbanite? An Historical Model of the Urban Hierarchy and The Social Motivation of Service Classes, Hist Methods Newslett, 9/74; Theoretical Science and Technology in American Ecology, Technol & Cult, 10/76; American Grassland Ecology, 1895-1955: The Life Cycle of a Professional Research Community, In: History of American Ecology, Arno, 77; Technology and culture, Vol 17, 76; Saving the Prairies, In: The Life Cycle of the Founding of American Plant Ecology, 1895-1955, Univ Calif, 81; The Citrus Industry and the Revolution of Corporate Capitalism in Southern California, 1887-1944, California History p6-21, 95; Moving Out and Settling In: Residential Mobility, Home Owning and The Public Enframing of Citizenship, 1921-1950, American Historical Review p13595-1422, 90; Technology as Freedom: The New Deal and the Electrical Modernization of the American Home, Univ CA, 96. **CONTACT ADDRESS** Dept Hist, Univ of California, Riverside, 900 University Ave, Riverside, CA 92521-0204. **EMAIL** rtobey@lucknow.com

TOBIN, EUGENE MARC
PERSONAL Born 03/23/1947, Newark, NJ, m, 1979, 2 children **DISCIPLINE** AMERICAN HISTORY **EDUCATION** Rutgers Univ, BA, 68; Brandeis Univ, MA, 70, PhD(Am hist), 72. **CAREER** Instr hist, Jersey City State Col, 72-75; asst prof, Kutztown State Col, 75-76; vis asst prof, Miami Univ, 77-79 & Ind Univ, Bloomington, 79-80; asst prof hist, Hamilton Col, 80-, Nat Endowment for Humanities fel hist, Vanderbilt Univ, 76-77; Am Philos Soc res grant, 78 & 82; Miami Univ Fac res appointment, 78; dir, Am Studies, Hamilton Col, 83-88; asst prof, 80-83; assoc prof, 83-88; prof hist, 88-; publius virgilius Rogers prof Am hist, 88-90. **HONORS AND AWARDS** William Adee Whitehead Awd, NJ Hist Soc, 76. **MEMBERSHIPS** AHA; Orgn Am Historians; Natl Assoc Independent Colleges & Univ; Commission of Independent Coll and Univ, New York. **RESEARCH** Recent American political history. **SELECTED PUBLICATIONS** Auth, The progressive as politician: Jersey City 1896-1907, NJ Hist, spring 73; Mark Fagan, the progressive as single taxer, 7/74 & In pursuit of equal taxation: Jersey City's struggle against corporate arrogance, 4/75, Am J Econ & Sociol; The progressive as humanitarian: The search for social justice in Jersey City 1890-1917, NJ Hist, fall-winter, 75; The political economy of George L Record: A progressive alternative to socialism, Historian, 8/77; co-ed, The Age of Urban Reform: New Perspectives on the Progressive Era, Kennikat, 77; Direct action and conscience: The 1913 Paterson strike as example of the relationship between labor radicals and liberals, Labor Hist, winter 79; George L Record and the progressive spirit, NJ Hist Comn; America's Independent Progressives, 1913 1933, Greenwood Press, 1986; co-editor, The National Lawyers Guild: From Roosevelt through Reagan, Temple University Press, 88. **CONTACT ADDRESS** President's Office, Hamilton Col, New York, 198 College Hill Rd, Clinton, NY 13323-1292. **EMAIL** etobin@hamilton.edu

TOBY, RONALD P.
PERSONAL Born 12/06/1942, White Plains, NY, m, 1987 **DISCIPLINE** HISTORY, ANTHROPOLOGY **EDUCATION** Columbia Univ, BA, 65, MA, 74, PhD, 77. **CAREER** Preceptor, 72-73, Columbia Univ; lectr, 77-78, Univ Calif Berkeley; asst prof to prof, dept head, 78-, Univ Il Urbana-Champaign; vis prof, 84-85, Keio Univ; vis prof, 95-96, Kyoto Univ; prof, Tokyo Univ, 00-. **HONORS AND AWARDS** Fulbright-Hays Fel, 74-76, 84-85; Univ Scholar Univ Il, 86-89; LAS Faculty Fel, 87-88; Nat Endow for the Human Sr Fel, 88-89; Japan Found Prof Fel, 89-90; Toyota Found Res Grant, 89-91; JSPS Sr Res Fel, 93; Nat Endow for the Humanities Summer Res Fel, 94. **MEMBERSHIPS** Amer Hist Asn; Asn for Asian Stud; Early Modern Japan Group; Chosen Gakkai(Korean Stud Asn); Int Soc for Ryukyuan Stud. **RESEARCH** Ethinicity & identity, cultural hist & international relations. **SELECTED PUBLICATIONS** Auth, State and Diplomacy in Early Modern Japan: Asia in the Development of the Tokugawa Bakufu, Stanford, 91; co-auth, Gyoretsu to misemono (Parades & Entertainments), Asahi Shinbunsha, 94; auth, " On the appearance of the " Hairy barbarian": ideas of Other and imagination of the foreign in early-modern Japan," A history of Japan at the boundary, Yamakawa shuppan, 97; auth, Imagining and Imaging 'Anthropos' in Early-modern Japan, Visual Anthrop Rev, 98; auth, Gazing at 'Man': the Early-Modern Japanese Imaginary and the Birth of a Visual Anthropology, Wanami world history, Iwanami Shoten, 99; auth, From 'sangoku' to 'bankoku': The Iberian Irruption and Japanese cosmology, Mare Liberum, forthcoming. **CONTACT ADDRESS** Dept of History, Univ of Illinois, Urbana-Champaign, 309 Gregory Hall, 810 S Wright St, Urbana, IL 61801. **EMAIL** rptoby@uiuc.edu

TODD, IAN ALEXANDER
PERSONAL Born 09/24/1941, West Kirby, England, m, 1981 **DISCIPLINE** ARCHAEOLOGY **EDUCATION** Univ Birmingham, BA, 63, PhD(archaeol), 67. **CAREER** Asst prof, 69-77, Assoc Prof Archaeol, Brandeis Univ, 77-, Dir archeol excavation at Neolithic Cypriote site, Kalavasos-Tenta, 76-; comt mem and chmn, Cyprus Archaeol Res Inst sect, Am Schs Orient Res, 78; dir, Cyprus Am Archaeol Res Inst, 79-80. **MEMBERSHIPS** Brit Inst Archaeol Ankara; Brit Inst Persian Studies; Int Inst Conserv Hist and Artistic Works; Prehist Soc; Israel Explor Soc. **RESEARCH** Early prehistory of Near and Middle East and archaeology of areas of the Aegean, Near and Middle East; archaeology of Anatolia; archaeology of Cyprus. **SELECTED PUBLICATIONS** Auth, Asikli Huyuk: A Protoneolithic Site in Central Anatolia, Anatolian Studies, 66; Preliminary Report on a Survey of Neolithic Sites in Central Anatolia, Turk Arkeoloji Dergisi, 66; Anatolia and the Khirbet Kerak Problem, Alter Orient Altes Testament, 73; Catal Huyuk in Perspective, Cummings, 76; Vasilikos Valley Project: First Preliminary Report, 1976, Report Dept Antiq Cyprus, 77; Vasilikos Valley Project: Second Preliminary Report, 1977, 79 and Vasilikos Valley Project: Third preliminary report, 1978, 79, J Field Archaeol; The Neolithic Period in Central Anatolia, 80; Neutron-Activation Analysis of Obsidian from Kalavasos-Tenta, J Field Archaeol, Vol 0022, 95. **CONTACT ADDRESS** Dept of Class and Orient Studies, Brandeis Univ, Waltham, MA 02254.

TODD, MARGO
PERSONAL Born 07/24/1950, Peoria, IL, m, 1970, 3 children **DISCIPLINE** HISTORY **EDUCATION** Tufts, BA, 72; Washington Univ, MA, 77, PhD, 81. **CAREER** Vanderbilt Univ, asst prof, 81-87, assoc prof, 87-. **HONORS AND AWARDS** Royal Hist Soc, Fel; Univ of Edinburg, St. Andrews Univ, NEH & ACLS Fel. **MEMBERSHIPS** NACBS, 16th Century Studies Soc. **RESEARCH** Hist early modern England and Scotland; Reformation and culture of protestantism. **SELECTED PUBLICATIONS** Auth, Christian Humanism and the Puritan Social Order, Cambridge Press, 87; auth, "Profane Pastimes and the Reformed Community: The Persistence of Popular Festivities," in Early Modern Scotland Journal of British Studies, vol 39, (00), "The English Reformation After 1558," in the Reformation World, ed, A. Pettegree (London, 00); A Captive's Story: Puritans, Pirates, and the Drama of Reconciliation, The Seventeenth Century, 97; All One With Tom Thumb: Arminianism, Popery and the Story of the Reformation in Early Stuart Cambridge, Church Hist, 95; Puritan Self-fashioning: The Diary of Samuel Ward, Jour of Brit Stud, 92; Providence, Chance and the New Science in Early Stuart Cambridge, The Hist J, 86. **CONTACT ADDRESS** Dept of History, Vanderbilt Univ, PO Box 1802, Sta B, Nashville, TN 37235. **EMAIL** margo.todd@vanderbilt.edu

TODD, MARY
PERSONAL Born 11/18/1947, Berwyn, IL, m, 1999, 4 children **DISCIPLINE** HISTORY **EDUCATION** Valparaiso Univ, BA, 69; Roosevelt, Univ, MGS, 90/ Univ IL Chicago, PhD, 96. **CAREER** Lectr, Roosevelt Univ, 89-97; vis asst prof, Univ of Il Chicago, 96-97; assoc prof, Concordia Univ, 97-. **HONORS AND AWARDS** Tue Schelbert Awd, 93-96; Who's Who Among America's Teachers, 96, 98. **MEMBERSHIPS** AHA; Orgn of Am Hist; Nat Col Honors Coun; Coordinating Coun for Women in Hist. **RESEARCH** Religion and Gender, Fundamentalism and Feminism. **SELECTED PUBLICATIONS** Auth, Authority Vested: A Story of Identity and Change in the Lutheran Church - Missouri Synod, Eerdman, 00. **CONTACT ADDRESS** Dept Hist, Concordia Univ, Illinois, 7400 Augusta St, River Forest, IL 60305-1499. **EMAIL** crftoddml@curf.edu

TODOROVA, M.
PERSONAL Born 01/05/1949, Sofia, Bulgaria, m, 1976, 2 children **DISCIPLINE** HISTORY **EDUCATION** Sofia Univ Bulgaria, PhD 77. **CAREER** Univ Sofia, asst prof, assoc prof, 73-92; Univ Florida, asst, assoc, full prof, 92 to 96-. **HONORS AND AWARDS** Wilson Cen Sch fel, 88&94; Mellon Dist Prof; Fulbright Prof, 88-89; Nat Humanities Center, 00-01; Guggenheim Awd, 00-01. **MEMBERSHIPS** AHA; AAASS **RESEARCH** Balkan; East European Hist; Anthropology. **SELECTED PUBLICATIONS** Auth, Imagining the Balkans, Oxford Univ Press, 97; Balkan Family Structure and the European Pattern, Amer Univ Press, 93; English Travelers' Accounts on the Balkans, Sofia, 87. **CONTACT ADDRESS** Dept of History, Univ of Florida, Gainesville, FL 32611. **EMAIL** mtodorv@history.ufl.edu

TOKER, FRANKLIN K.
PERSONAL Born 04/29/1944, Montreal, PQ, Canada, m, 1972, 3 children **DISCIPLINE** ARCHITECTURAL HISTORY, MEDIEVAL ARCHEOLOGY **EDUCATION** McGill Univ, BA, 64; Oberlin Col, AM, 66; Harvard Univ, PhD(fine arts), 72. **CAREER** Dir archaeol excavation, Cathedral of Florence, 69-74; vis Mellon prof archit, Carnegie-Mellon Univ, 74-76, assoc prof hist of archit, 76-80; prof Hist Of Art, Univ Pittsburgh, 80-, Harvard Univ Ctr Ital Renaissance Studies fel, 72-74; vis prof, Univ Florence, 88-89, Univ Rome, 91-, Univ Reggio Calabria, 96; mem, Inst for Advanced Study, Princeton, NJ, 85. **HONORS AND AWARDS** Kress Fel, 65; Can Coun Fel, 66; Fel Comt to Rescue Italian Art, Florence, 69; Alice Davis Hitchcock Bk Awd, Soc Archit Historians, 70; fel I Tatti-Harvard Univ Ctr for Italian Renaissance Studies, Florence, 72; Guggenheim fel, 79; NEH grants, 79, 92; Arthur Kingsley Porter Prize, Col Art Asn, 80; NEH sr fel, 85; Pittsburgh Hist and Landmarks Found award for Pittsburgh: An Urban Portrait, 87; fel Bellagio Study and Conf Ctr, Rockefeller Found, 94; life mem Col Art Asn, Arthur Kingsley Porter prize, 80; life mem, Medieval Acad; life mem Soc Archit Hist (pres 93-94, board dir 85-88). **MEMBERSHIPS** Col Art Asn; Nat Trust Hist Preserv; Soc Archit Historians; Int Ctr Medieval Art. **RESEARCH** Medieval architecture in Italy; architecture of the nineteenth century; history of the architectural profession. **SELECTED PUBLICATIONS** Auth, The Church of Notre-Dame in Montreal, McGill-Queen's Univ, 70, Fr ed, 81, rev ed, 91; James O'Donnell: An Irish Georgian in America, J Soc Archit Historians, 70; coauth, An Umbrian Abbey: San Paolo di Valdiponte, Papers Brit Sch Rome, 73; S Reparata: L'Antica Cattedrale Fiorentina, Bonechi, Florence, 74; auth, Excavations below the Cathedral of Florence, Gesta, 75; A baptistery below the Baptistery of Florence, Art Bull, 76; Richardson en concours: The Pittsburgh courthouse, Carnegie Mag, 77; Florence Cathedral: The design stage, Art Bull, 78; Pittsburgh: An Urban Portrait, 86, 2nd ed, 95. **CONTACT ADDRESS** Dept of History and Art, Univ of Pittsburgh, 104 Frick Fine Arts, Pittsburgh, PA 15260-7601. **EMAIL** ftoker@pitt.edu

TOKUNAGA, EMIKO
PERSONAL Born 09/28/1939, San Francisco, CA, s **DISCIPLINE** HISTORY OF DANCE **EDUCATION** Harvard, Admin Fel, 95-96; NYork Univ, MA, 66; Univ UT, BFA, 61. **CAREER** Coord, 94-98, Harvard-Radcliffe; art dir, Summer Dance98-, Boston Conserv; adj assoc prof, Hofstra Univ, 93-94. **HONORS AND AWARDS** 2,000 Performances with Tokunaga Dance. **RESEARCH** Dance dialogues. **CONTACT ADDRESS** PO Box 1008 Astor Sta, Boston, MA 02123.

TOLLES, BRYANT F.
PERSONAL Born 03/14/1939, Hartford, CT, m, 1962, 2 children **DISCIPLINE** MUSEUM STUDIES **EDUCATION** Yale Univ, BA, 91; MAT, 62; Boston Univ, PhD, 70. **CAREER** Asst Dean, Instructor in History, Tufts Univ, 65-71; Asst Dir and Librarian, New Hampshire Historical Society, 72-74; Exec Dir, Essex Institute, 74-84; Associate Prof of History and Art History; Dir, Museum Studies Program, Univ of Delaware, 84. **MEMBERSHIPS** Organization of American Historians; Society of Architectural Historians; American Assoc for State and Local History; National Council on Public History. **RESEARCH** 19th-century New England architectural, social, cultural and economic history; history of tourism. **SELECTED PUBLICATIONS** Auth, New Hampshire Architecture: An Illustrated Guide, Univ Press of New England (Hanover, NH), 79; auth, Architecture in Salem: An Illustrated Guide, Essex Institute (Salem, MA), 83; auth, Leadership for the Future: Changing Directorial Roles in American History Museums and Historical Societies, American Association for State and Local History (Nashville, TN), 91; auth, The Grand Resort Hotels of the White Mountains: A Vanishing Architectural Legacy, David R. Godine, Publisher, Inc. (Boston), 98; auth, Summer Cottages in the White Mountains: The Architecture of Leisure and Recreation, Univ Press of New England (Hanover, NH), 00. **CONTACT ADDRESS** Museum Studies Program, Univ of Delaware, 301 Old College, Newark, DE 19716. **EMAIL** bftolles@udel.edu

TOLMACHEVA, MARINA
PERSONAL 1 child **DISCIPLINE** ISLAMIC CIVILIZATION AND MIDDLE EAST HISTORY **EDUCATION** Inst Ethnog, Acad Sci USSR, Leningrad, PhD, 70. **CAREER** Prof & dir Asia Prog, Washington State Univ. **SELECTED PUBLICATIONS** Auth, The Pate Chronicle, Mich State UP, 93; The Muslim Women in Soviet Central Asia, Central Asian Survey, 93 & Ibn Battuta on Women's Travel in the Dar al-Islam, Women and the Journey, Wash State UP, 93. **CONTACT ADDRESS** Dept of History, Washington State Univ, 301 Wilson Hall, PO Box 644030, Pullman, WA 99164-4030. **EMAIL** tolmache@wsu.edu

TOLSON, ARTHUR
PERSONAL Born 10/15/1924, Sweet Springs, MO, d, 1 child **DISCIPLINE** HISTORY **EDUCATION** Wiley Col, AB, 46; Okla State Univ, MA, 52; Univ of Okla, PhD, 66. **CAREER** Prof, Harvis Col, 62-67; prof, Southern Univ, 67-. **MEMBERSHIPS** Southern Conf on African Am Hist; Assoc for the Study of Afro-Am Life and Hist. **RESEARCH** African American History. **SELECTED PUBLICATIONS** Auth, "Booker T. Washington's Philosophy and Oklahoma's African American Towns", Booker T. Washington - Interpretive Essays, ed Tundle Adeleke, 98. **CONTACT ADDRESS** Dept Hist, So Univ and A&M Col, 500 Jesse Stone, Baton Rouge, LA 70813-5000.

TOLZMANN, DON HEINRICH
PERSONAL Born 08/12/1945, Granite Falls, MN, m, 1971, 3 children **DISCIPLINE** HISTORY; GERMAN-AMERICAN STUDIES **EDUCATION** Univ Minnesota, BA; United Theologisic Seminary; Univ Kentucky, MA; Univ Cincinnati, PhD. **CAREER** Curator, German Am Collection and Director German Am Studies Prog, Univ Cincinnati, 74-. **HONORS AND AWARDS** Fed Ser Cross, (FRG); German Am Tricent Medal; German Am of the year award. **MEMBERSHIPS** Soc for Ger Am Studies **SELECTED PUBLICATIONS** German-Americans and the World Wars, Muenchen, K G Saur, 95; In der Neuen Welt, Deutsche-Amerikanische Festschrift fuer die 500-Jahrfeier der Entdeckung von Amerika, NY, Peter Lang, 92; Cincinnati's German Heritage, Bowie, MD, Heritage Books Inc, 94; The First Germans in America, with NY Germans, Bowie, MD, Heritage Books, 92; The Cincinnati Germans after the Great War, NY, Peter Lang, 87; German American Literature, Metuchen, NJ, Scarecrow Pr, 77; German-Americana, Metuchen, NJ, Scarecrow Pr, 75; auth, The German-American Experience, Amherst, NY, Humanity Books, 01. **CONTACT ADDRESS** Univ of Cincinnati, PO Box 210113, Cincinnati, OH 45221. **EMAIL** Don.Tolzmann@uc.edu

TOMASEK, KATHRYN
DISCIPLINE U.S. HISTORY **EDUCATION** Rice Univ, BA; Univ Wisconsin-Madison, MA, PhD,95. **CAREER** Ch. **RESEARCH** US women's history, 19th-century US, African-American history. **SELECTED PUBLICATIONS** Publ, on women and utopia, Alcott's March family trilogy; Children and family, Fourierist communities. **CONTACT ADDRESS** Dept of Hist, Wheaton Col, Massachusetts, 26 East Main St, Norton, MA 02766. **EMAIL** ktomasek@wheatonma.edu

TOMASINI, WALLACE JOHN
PERSONAL Born 10/19/1927, Brooklyn, NY, m, 1953, 2 children **DISCIPLINE** ART HISTORY **EDUCATION** Univ Mich, BA, 49, MA, 50, PhD(hist), 53; Post Doctorate, NYU Inst of Fine Arts, 53-57; Univ of Florence, Italy, 50-52. **CAREER** Finch Col, 54-57; from asst prof to assoc prof, 57-64, prof Art Hist, 64- , dir Sch Art & Art Hist, 72-94, Univ Iowa; Belg-Am Found fel, 53; Am Philos Soc grant, 57-58; Univ Iowa fac res grants, 59-60 & 66-68; Ford FU Grant, 74-77. **MEMBERSHIPS** Am Numis Soc; AHA; Col Art Asn Am; Midwest Art Hist Soc; Renaissance Soc Am; HCIF/HCREF. **RESEARCH** Visigothic numismatics; social and economic status of Renaissance artists; Giotto studies; Lirages Porcelain. **SELECTED PUBLICATIONS** Auth, The Barbaric Tremissis in Spain and Southern France; Anastasivs to Leoviglild, Am Numis Soc, 64; Drawing and the Human Figure, 1400-1964, Univ Iowa, 64; coauth, Paintings From Midwestern University Collections, Comt Instnt Coop, 73; E. Dreweloue Ptgs, 89; Haviland China, 92. **CONTACT ADDRESS** Sch of Art & Art Hist, Univ of Iowa, 100 Art Building, Iowa City, IA 52242-1706. **EMAIL** wallace.tomasini@uiowa.edu

TOMAYKO, JAMES EDWARD
PERSONAL Born 07/08/1949, Charleroi, PA, m, 1972 **DISCIPLINE** CHINESE LANGUAGE, HISTORY OF TECHNOLOGY **EDUCATION** Carnegie-Mellon Univ, BA, 71, DA, 80; Univ Pittsburgh, MA, 72. **CAREER** Headmaster, Self-Directed Learning Ctr, 75-80; instr hist, Garden City Community Col, 80-81; tech pub specialist, NCR Corp, 81; ASST PROF COMP SCI, HIST AND CHINESE, WICHITA STATE UNIV, 82- **MEMBERSHIPS** Soc for the Hist of Technol; Asn Comput Mach; Chinese Lang Teachers Asn; Am Asn Artificial Intelligence; Asn Comput Ling. **RESEARCH** History of computing; Chinese natural language processing. **SELECTED PUBLICATIONS** Auth, The Ditch Irrigation Boom in Southwest Kansas, J West, fall 82; A Simple, Comprehensive Input/Output System for Chinese Natural Language Processing, Comp Sci Dept, Wichita State Univ, 5/82; The Relationship Between the N-BU-N and V-BU-V Constructions in Chinese, Proc of the Mid-Am Ling Conf, 82; Memories of Turing, Alan in Annals of the History of Computing, Vol 0015, 93. **CONTACT ADDRESS** 828 S Holyoke, Wichita, KS 67218. **EMAIL** jet=@ux6.sp.cs.cmu.edu

TOMES, NANCY JANE
PERSONAL Born 10/25/1952, Louisville, KY, m, 1979 **DISCIPLINE** AMERICAN HISTORY **EDUCATION** Univ Ky, BA, 74; Univ Pa, PhD(hist), 78. **CAREER** Asst Prof Am Hist, Hist Dept, State Univ NY Stony Brook, 78-, NIMH trainee, Rutgers and Princeton Prog Ment Health Res, 81- **MEMBERSHIPS** AHA; Orgn Am Historians; Social Sci Hist Asn. **RESEARCH** Medical history; history of women in the professions. **SELECTED PUBLICATIONS** Auth, A Torrent of Abuse, J Social Hist, Spring 78; Little World of Our Own, J Hist Med and Allied Sci, 10/78; A Generous Confidence in Madhouses, Mad Doctors and Madmen, Univ Pa P, 81; The Quaker Connection in Friends and Neighbors, Temple Univ P, 82; Am Attitudes toward the Germ theory of Disease, J Hist Med Allied Sci, Vol 52, 97; Introduction to Special Issue on Rethinking the Reception of the Germ Theory of Disease--Comparative Perspectives, J Hist Med Allied Sci, Vol 52, 97. **CONTACT ADDRESS** Dept of Hist, SUNY, Stony Brook, 100 Nicolls Rd, Stony Brook, NY 11794-0002.

TOMLINS, CHRISTOPHER L.
PERSONAL Born 04/02/1951, Beaconsfield, England, m, 1980, 2 children **DISCIPLINE** HISTORY; LEGAL STUDIES **EDUCATION** Oxford Univ, BA, 73; Sussex Univ, MA, 74; Oxford Univ, MA, 77; Jonhs Hopkins Univ, MA, 77; PhD, 81. **CAREER** La Trobe Univ, lectr, 80-85; sr lectr, 86-88; reader, 89-94; res fel, Am Bar Found, 92-96; sr res fel, 96- . **HONORS AND AWARDS** Fulbrigh Fel, 75; Am Bar Found Legal Hist Fel, 84; Am Hist Asoc Littleton-Griswold Fund Fel, 88; Erwin W. Surrency Prize, Am Soc for Legal Hist, 89; James willard Hurst Pirze of the Law and Soc Asoc, 94; Littleton-Griswold Prize of the Am Hist Asoc and the Am Soc for Legal Hist, 94. **MEMBERSHIPS** Am Hist Asoc; Orgn of Am Hist; Econ Hist Asoc; Am Soc for Legal Hist. **RESEARCH** American legal history and the history of legal culture, 16th-20th centuries; history of work and labor. **SELECTED PUBLICATIONS** Auth, Law, Labor, and Ideology in the Early American Republic, 93; auth, How Who Rides Whom: Recent 'New' Histories of American Labor Law and What They May Signify, Social Hist, 95; auth, Subordination, Authority, Law: Subjects in Labor History, Int Labor and Working Class Hist, 95; auth, Why Wait for Industrialism? An Historiographical Argument, Labor Hist, 99; co-ed with Bruce H. Mann, The Many Legalities of Early American, forthcoming. **CONTACT ADDRESS** American Bar Foundation, 750 N Lake Shore Dr, Chicago, IL 60611. **EMAIL** clt@abfn.org

TOMLINSON, ROBERT
PERSONAL Born 06/26/1938, Brooklyn, NY **DISCIPLINE** ART **EDUCATION** Pratt Inst, Brooklyn, BFA 1961; Columbia Univ Teachers Coll NYork, 1963; CUNY Graduate Center NYork, PhD 1977. **CAREER** Emory Univ Atlanta, asst prof 1978-84, assoc prof, 84-93, prof, 94-; Hunter Coll NY, adj asst prof 1972-78; HS of Art & Design NY, French instr 1968-72; Ministere de l'Education Nationale Paris, Eng instr 1963-68; This Week Mag, asst art dir 1961-63. **HONORS AND AWARDS** Number 1 man exhibit of Painting Paris, London, NY, Washington 1968, 1971, 1979, 1984; rep in private coll; Advanced Study Fellow Ford Found, 1972-76; fellow, CUNY 1975-77; Amer Council of Learned Societies Grant 1979. **MEMBERSHIPS** Mem Am Soc for Eighteenth Cent Stud mem Mod Lang Assoc; chmn Emory Univ Commn on the Status of Minorities 1980-81, 1984-85. **CONTACT ADDRESS** Emory Univ, Atlanta, GA 30322.

TOMPSON, RICHARD STEVENS
PERSONAL Born 01/21/1935, Glen Ridge, NJ, m, 1960, 3 children **DISCIPLINE** BRITISH & IRISH HISTORY **EDUCATION** Yale Univ, BA, 57; Villanova Univ, MA, 62; Univ Mich, PhD(hist), 67. **CAREER** Lectr Hist, Univ Mich, 66-67; chmn dept, 75-80; prof Hist, Univ Utah, 76-00. **MEMBERSHIPS** Conf Brit Studies. **RESEARCH** British legal hist. **SELECTED PUBLICATIONS** Auth, The Leeds grammar school case, J Educ Admin & Hist, 70; Classics or Charity? The Dilemma of the 18th Century Grammar School, Manchester Univ, 71; The Charity Commission and the Age of Reform, Routledge, 79; auth, Justices of the Peace and the United Kingdom in the Age of Reform, J Legal Hist, 86; auth, The Atlantic Archipelago: A Political History of the British Isles, Mellen, 86; Scottish Judges and the Birth of British Copyright, Juridical Review, 92; auth, Islands of Law: A Legal History of the British Isles, Peter Lang, 00. **CONTACT ADDRESS** Dept of History, Univ of Utah, 1560 Indian Hills Dr, Salt Lake City, UT 84108. **EMAIL** richard.tompson@m.cc.utah.edu

TOOLEY, T. HUNT
PERSONAL Born 02/19/1955, Vernon, TX, m, 1977, 3 children **DISCIPLINE** HISTORY **EDUCATION** Tex A&M Univ, BA, 77; MA, 78; Univ of Va, PhD, 86. **CAREER** Instr, Univ Va, 85-86; vis asst prof, Univ of NC, 86-87; asst prof, Erskine Col, 87-91; asst prof to assoc prof, Austin Col, 91-. **HONORS AND AWARDS** Pres Scholar, Tex A&M, 73-77; DuPont Fel, Univ Va; DAAD Grant, 82-83; Excellence in Teaching Awd, Erskine Col, 88. **MEMBERSHIPS** Hist Soc; Ger Studies Assoc; Southern Hist Assoc; Assoc Int d'histoire contemporaine de l'Europe. **RESEARCH** Modern Europe, Twentieth Century Germany, War and Peacemaking in the Modern World. **SELECTED PUBLICATIONS** Auth, "Nazi Technocracy and Coerced Labor: A Case Study of the Synthetic Fuel Industry", Red River Valley Hist J of World Hist 3 (78): 161-172; auth, "German Political Violence and the Border Plebiscite in Upper Silesia, 1919-1921", Central Europ Hist 21, (88): 56-98; auth, "The Internal Dynamics of Changing Frontiers: The Plebiscites on Germany's Borders, 1919-1921", The Establishment of European Frontiers After the Two World Wars, eds Carole Fink and Peter Baechler, Peter Lang, (96): 149-165; auth, "The Polish-German Ethnic Dispute in the 1921 Upper Silesian Plebiscite", Can Rev of Studies in Nationalism 24 (97): 13-20; auth, National Identity and Weimar Germany: Upper Silesia and The Eastern Border, 1918-1922, Univ of Nebr Pr, 97; auth, "The

Hindenburg Program of 1916: A Central Experiment in Wartime Planning", Quarterly J of Austrian Econ 2 (99): 51-62. **CONTACT ADDRESS** Dept Hist, Austin Col, 900 N Grand Ave, Sherman, TX 75090-4440. **EMAIL** htooley@austinc.edu

TOPLIN, ROBERT B.
PERSONAL Born 09/26/1940, Philadelphia, PA, m, 1962, 2 children **DISCIPLINE** UNITED STATES AND LATIN AMERICAN HISTORY **EDUCATION** Pa State Univ, BA, 62; Rutgers Univ, MA, 65, PhD, 68. **CAREER** Teaching asst hist, Rutgers Univ, 64-67; from asst prof to assoc prof hist, Denison Univ, 68-78; assoc prof, 78-79, Prof Hist, Univ NCar, Wilmington, 80-; ed, Film Reviews, J of Am Hist, 87-; proj dir, PBS Television ser Slavery in America. **HONORS AND AWARDS** Nat Endowment for Humanities younger humanist fel, 70-71, sr fel, 77, media grant, 78, production grant, 80 and script grant, 82; Fel, Va Ctr Hum, 94; fel, ACLS, 91; UNC-W summer res initiative, 96; NEH summer inst, Brazil, 92; NEH prod grant, 91. **MEMBERSHIPS** Orgn Am Historians; AHA; Southern Hist Asn, Lat Am Stud Asn; IAMHIST. **RESEARCH** Film and history **SELECTED PUBLICATIONS** Auth, Upheaval, Violence, and the Abolition of Slavery in Brazil: The Case of Sao Paulo, Hisp Am Hist Rev, 11/69; Reinterpreting Comparative Race Relations: the United States and Brazil, J Black Studies, 12/71; The Abolition of Slavery in Brazil, Atheneum, 72; The Specter of Crisis: Slaveholder Reactions to Abolitionism in the United States and Brazil, Civil War Hist, 6/72; ed, Slavery and Race Relations in Latin America, 74 and auth, Unchallenged Violence: An American Ordeal, 75, Greenwood; Between Black and White: Attitudes Toward Southern Mulattoes, 1830-1861, J Southern Hist, 79; Freedom and Prejudice: The Legacy of Slavery in the United States and Brazil, Greenwood, 81; auth, Hollywood as Mirror; Changing Views of Outsiders and Enemies in American Movies, Greenwood Press, 82; ed, Ken Burns' The Civil War, Oxford Univ Press, 96; auth, History by Hollywood: The Use and Abuse of the American past, Univ Ill Press, 96; ed, Oliver Stone's USA: Film, Hist, and Controversey, 00. **CONTACT ADDRESS** Dept of Hist, Univ of No Carolina, Wilmington, Wilmington, NC 28403. **EMAIL** toplinrb@uncwil.edu

TOPPIN, EDGAR ALLAN
PERSONAL Born 01/22/1928, New York, NY, m **DISCIPLINE** AFRICAN AMERICAN STUDIES **EDUCATION** Howard Univ, AB cum laude 1949, MA 1950; Northwestern Univ, PhD 1955. **CAREER** AL State Coll, instr 1954-55; Fayetteville State Coll, chmn Soc Sci Div 1955-59; Univ Akron, asst assc prof 1959-64; VA State Coll, full prof 1964-; NC Coll, vis prof 1959, 63; Western Res Univ, 62; Univ Cincinnati, 64; San Francisco State Coll, 69; IN Univ, 71. **HONORS AND AWARDS** Grad flwshps from Howard Univ 1949-50; Hearts Fnd 1950-51, 1952-53; John Hay Whitney Fnd opport Flwship History 1964; research grants from Amer Assn State Local History 1964; Old Dominion Fnd 1968; Ford Fnd 1970; Comtemporary Authors. **MEMBERSHIPS** Natl Pres Assc study Afro-Amer life & history 1973-76; editorial bd Journal Negro History 1962-67; exec bd Orgn Amer Historians 1971-74; mem Natl Hist Pub Commn 1972- 1st black mem; adv bd Natl Parks Historic Sites Bldgs & Monuments 1st black mem; bd dir So Flwshps Fund 1966-; World Book Encyclopedia Socl Sci Adv Com 1968-; vice pres bd Akron Urban League 1961-64; bd dir Fayetteville United Fund 1957-59. **SELECTED PUBLICATIONS** Author books, Pioneer Patriots 1954; Mark Well Made 1967; Unfinished March 1967; Blacks in Amer 1969; Biog History of Black in Amer 1971; Black Amer in US 1973; 30 lesson educ TV Course Amer from Africa. **CONTACT ADDRESS** Virginia State Univ, Petersburg, VA 23803.

TORBENSON, CRAIG L.
DISCIPLINE HISTORICAL-CULTURAL GEOGRAPHY, HISTORIC PRESERVATION **EDUCATION** Brigham Young Univ, BS, 82; MS, 85; Univ Okla, PhD, 92. **CAREER** Dept Hist, Wichita State Univ **RESEARCH** Norwegian-American nigration and settlement; historical and cultural geography. **SELECTED PUBLICATIONS** Auth, A Geography of Social Fraternities and Sororities, Nat Soc Sci Jour, 97; Themes in Geography: An Interactive Study Guide, Kendall/Hunt, 94; World Regional Geography; An Atlas Study Guide, Kendall/Hunt. **CONTACT ADDRESS** Dept of Hist, Wichita State Univ, 1845 Fairmont, Wichita, KS 67260-0062.

TORODASH, MARTIN
PERSONAL Born 03/13/1928, Brooklyn, NY, m, 1967 **DISCIPLINE** AMERICAN AND LATIN AMERICAN HISTORY **EDUCATION** Univ Pa, AB, 50; NYork Univ, MA, 55, PhD(hist), 66. **CAREER** From asst prof to assoc prof, 61-73, Prof Hist, Fairleigh Dickinson Univ, 73-, Assoc, Columbia Univ sem Early Am hist and cult, 67- **MEMBERSHIPS** AHA; Orgn Am Historians; Hakluyt Soc; Soc Hist Discoveries. **RESEARCH** Woodrow Wilson's Administration; Discovery and Exploration: Samoa. **SELECTED PUBLICATIONS** Auth, The American Presidency since 1789, Wheeler's Rev, fall 60; Columbus historiography since 1939, 11/66 & Magellan historiography, 5/71, Hisp Am Hist Rev. **CONTACT ADDRESS** Dept of Hist and Polit Sci, Fairleigh Dickinson Univ, Teaneck-Hackensack, Teaneck, NJ 07666.

TORREY, GLENN E.
PERSONAL Born 12/04/1930, Yuba City, CA, m, 1959, 3 children **DISCIPLINE** MODERN EUROPEAN HISTORY **EDUCATION** Univ Ore, BS, 53, MA, 57, PhD, 60. **CAREER** From asst prof to assoc prof, 59-65, Prof Hist, Emporia State Univ, 65-; assoc ed, Yearbk Romanian Studies, 68-; Int Res and Exchanges Bd res prof, Romania, 72 and 76. **HONORS AND AWARDS** US Dept State exchange scholar, Romania, 61-62, sr res award, 66-67; Am Coun Learned Soc Slavic and EEurop grant, 61-62; Am Philos Soc grant-in-aid, 62, grant, 76; Am Coun Learned Soc-Soc Sci Res Coun Slavic and EEurop grant, 66-67. **MEMBERSHIPS** AHA; Am Asn Advan Slavic Studies. **RESEARCH** German-Romanian relations, 1914-1918, Romania during the First World War, Central and Eastern European history. **SELECTED PUBLICATIONS** Auth, Romania and the Belligerents, 1914-1916, J Contemp Hist, 6/66; The Central Powers and Romania, August-November 1914, Suedost-Forsch, 66; Romania's Decision to Intervene: 1916 in Yearbook of Romanian Studies, Vol II, 72; Romania and the Allied Offensive at Salonika, August 1916, Rev Roumaine d'Hist, 75; The Entente and the Romanian campaign of 1916 in Romanian Studies, Vol IV, 77; The Romanian Campaign of 1916: Its Impact on the Belligerents, Slavic Rev, Vol 39, 80; auth, General Henri Berthelot and Romania 1916-1919, Columbia Univ Press, 87; auth, When Treason was a Crime: The Case of Colonel Alexander Sturdza of Romania, Emporia State Studies, 92; auth, The Revolutionary Russian Army and Romania 1917, Univ of Pittsburg Press, 95. **CONTACT ADDRESS** 1301 100th Ave NE, Bellevue, WA 98004. **EMAIL** torreygl@juno.com

TOTTEN, GEORGE OAKLEY, III
PERSONAL Born 07/21/1922, Washington, DC, m, 1976, 2 children **DISCIPLINE** POLITICAL SCIENCE; ASIAN COMPARATIVE GOVERNMENT; ASIAN POLITICAL THOUGHT. **EDUCATION** Univ Mich, U.S. Military Intelligence Japanese Lang School, Certificate, 43; Columbia, AB, 46, AM, 49; Yale Univ, MA, 50, PhD, 54; Univ Stockholm, Docentur-i-Japanologi, 77. **CAREER** Lect in Govt, Columbia Univ, E Asian Inst, 54-55; res assoc E Asian Affairs, Fletcher School Law & Dipl, 55-58; asst prof Political Science, MIT, 58-59; asst prof Political Science & History, Boston Univ, 59-61; assoc prof Political Science, Univ Rhode Island, 61-64; assoc to full prof Political Science, 65-92, Distinguished Prof Emer, 95-, USC, 65-; vis prof, Univ Stockholm, 77-79 & 85-88, Waseda Univ, 70-73, Univ Hawaii, 92. **HONORS AND AWARDS** Plaque for promoting Korean studies at USC, Consul General of Korea, 75; Plaque for Leadership, Service, and Contributions, USC Department of Political Science, 92; Distinguished Professor Emeritus, President of USC, 96; Plaque for the Promotion of Korean Studies, Asn for Korean Studies in North Am, 98; Honorary Pres, Huaxiu Private School, Anyang City, Henan Province, China, 99-. **MEMBERSHIPS** Am Polit Sci Asn; Int Polit Sci Asn; Asn for Asian Studies; Asn Korean Polit Sci NA; Los Angeles-Guangzhan Sister City Asn; Japan Soc S Calif; US-China Peoples Friendship Asn; Comt US-China Rel. **RESEARCH** Peaceful reunification of North and South Korea and Taiwan and Mainland China; Creating a stable peace in Northeast Asia among China, Japan, Korea, Russia, and the U.S.; Romanization in Chinese, Japanese, and Korean. **SELECTED PUBLICATIONS** Auth, The Social Democratic Movement in Prewar Japan, 66, Chinese edition, 87, Korean edition, 97; coauth, Socialist Parties in Postwar Japan, 66; co-ed and coauth, Developing Nations; Quest for a Model, 70, Japanese edition, 1975; ed, Helen Foster Snow's Song of Ariran, 73, Korean edition, 91; co-ed and co-transl, Ch'ien Mu's Traditional Government in Imperial China, 82, paperback 00; coauth, Japan and the New Ocean Regime, 84; co-ed, China's Economic Reform: Administering the Introduction of the Market Mechanism, 92; co-ed, Community in Crisis: The Korean American Community After the Los Angeles Civil Unrestl, 92, 94; ed, Kim Dae-jung's A New Beginning, 96; ed, Lee Hee-ho's, Praying for Tomorrow, 00. **CONTACT ADDRESS** Dept of Political Science, Univ of So California, VKC 327, Los Angeles, CA 90089-0044. **EMAIL** totten@usc.edu

TOULOUSE, MARK G.
PERSONAL Born 02/01/1952, Des Moines, IA, m, 1976, 3 children **DISCIPLINE** AMERICAN RELIGIOUS HISTORY **EDUCATION** Howard Payne Univ, BA, 74; Southwestern Baptist Theol Sem, MDiv, 77; Univ Chicago, PhD, 84. **CAREER** Instr, relig stud, Ill Benedictine Col, 80-82, asst prof, 82-84; asst prof of hist, Phillips Univ Grad Sem, 84-86; asst prof, Brite Divinity Sch, Texas Chr Univ,86-89, assoc prof, 89-91, assoc dean, 91-94, prof, 94- 99; Prof and Dean, 99-. **HONORS AND AWARDS** Henry Luce III Fel, 97-98; Who's Who in Relig, 89-90, 92-93; Men of Achievement, 93; Who's Who in Am Educ, 96-97. **MEMBERSHIPS** Am Acad Relig; Am Soc of Church Hist; Disciples of Christ Hist Soc. **RESEARCH** American theology; American religion and culture; history of Christian Church (Disciples of Christ). **SELECTED PUBLICATIONS** Auth, The Christian Century and American Public Life: The Crucial Years,1956-1968, in New Dimensions in Modern American Religious History, 93; auth, A Case Study: Christianity Today and American Public Life, in J of Church and State, 93; auth, W.A. Criswell, in Dictionary of Baptists in America, 94; auth, The Braunschweiger-Bibfeldts: the Metaphysical Incarnation of Wo/Man, in The Unrelieved Paradox, 94; auth, The Christian Church (Disciples of Christ), in Encyclopedia Americana, 94; auth, What is the Role of a Denomination in a Post-Denominational Age, in Lexington Theol Q, 94; auth, Sojourners, in Popular Religious Magazines of the United States, 95; auth, several entries in Encylopedia of Religious Controversies in the United States, 97; auth, The Problem and Promise of Denominational History, in Discipliana, 97; auth, Joined in Discipleship: The Shaping of Contemporary Disciples Identity, Chalice, rev ed, 97; coed, Makers of Christian Theology in America, Abingdon, 97; auth, "The Transformation of John Foster Dulles," Mercer University Press, 85; coed, "Sources of Christian Theology in America," Abingdon, 99; ed, "Walter Scott: A Nineteenh-Century Evangelical, Chalice," 99. **CONTACT ADDRESS** Brite Divinity School, Texas Christian Univ, TCU Box 298130, Fort Worth, TX 76129. **EMAIL** m.toulouse@tcu.edu

TOUPIN, ROBERT
PERSONAL Born 02/05/1924, Montreal, PQ, Canada **DISCIPLINE** MODERN HISTORY **EDUCATION** Univ Montreal, BA, 52; Immaculate-Conception Col, Montreal, LPh, 53, LTh, 60; Univ Toronto, MA, 56; Sorbonne, DUniv(hist), 65. **CAREER** From lectr to asst prof, 61-69; Assoc Prof Hist, Laurentian Univ, 69-; Dir and ed-in-chief, Laurentian Univ Rev, 73-77 and 79-. **MEMBERSHIPS** Asn Int des Docteurs de l'Univ Paris; Renaissance Soc Am; Soc d'etudes de la Renaissance. **RESEARCH** Relations between church and state in France in late 16th century; documents relating to the Jesuits in New France in the 18th century; French society and intellectual life. **SELECTED PUBLICATIONS** Ed, Correspondance du nonce en France G B Castelli, 1581-1583, Pontif Gregorian Univ and DeBoccard, Paris, 67; co-ed, Correspondance du nonce en France A M Salviati, t II 1574-1578, Pontif Gregorian Univ, Rome, 75. **CONTACT ADDRESS** Dept of Hist, Archives de la compagnie de Jesus, CP 130, Saint-Jerome, QC, Canada J7Z 5T8.

TOURE, DIALA
PERSONAL Born 07/17/1965, Paris, France, m, 1996 **DISCIPLINE** ART HISTORY **EDUCATION** Univ Saint-Denis, Paris, BA, 90; Univ La Sorbonne, MA, 92; PhD, 98. **CAREER** Res Asst, Nat Museum of African and Oceanic Arts, Paris, France, 93-94; Asst Prof, Europ Inst of Arts and Design, Paris, France, 95-97; Teach Assoc, Northwestern Col, Saint-Paul, Minn, 98-99; Lectr, Univ of Minn Minneapolis, 98-99. **HONORS AND AWARDS** Ctr of Studies and Res on Contemp Art Awd, 92; Fidelca Predoctoral Fel, 94-95; Agence de Cooperation Culturelle et Technique Publ Grant, 96. **MEMBERSHIPS** Soc of Archit Historians, African Studies Asn, The Arts Coun on the African Studies Asn, Asn for Art Hist, Col Art Asn. **RESEARCH** Post-colonial architecture in West Africa, Islamic architecture in Africa, African visual arts, history and cultures. **SELECTED PUBLICATIONS** Auth, "Modern Architecture in West Africa," in Napoli Europea Africa (Napoli, 93); auth, Contemporary issues in West African Architecture, ACCT (Paris), 94; auth, "Vallees du Niger," in exhibit catalog Reunion des Musees Nationaux (Paris), 93; auth, "Henri Chomette," in Dictionnare de l'Architecture du Xxe siecle (Paris: Hazan, 96), 194; auth, "Modern architectures in West Africa from the 1950s to 1990s," La Revue Noire (Dec 98); auth, "Emergence of the Sudanese Style in French colonies of West Africa 1920-1940," Rutgers Art Rev 19 (June 99); auth, "Architecture in West African countries," Am Visions (Apr/May 99). **CONTACT ADDRESS** 320 7th St SE Apt 215, Minneapolis, MN 55414.

TOVELL, ROSEMARIE
PERSONAL Born Lima, Peru **DISCIPLINE** ART HISTORY **EDUCATION** Queen's Univ, BA, 68; Univ Toronto, MA, 72. **CAREER** Cur asst, 72-73, asst cur, 73-82, Curator, Prints Drawings, Nat Gallert Can, 82-. **MEMBERSHIPS** Print Coun Am; Can Eskimo Arts Coun. **SELECTED PUBLICATIONS** Auth, Reflections in a Quiet Pool: The Prints of David Milne, 80; auth, Berczy, 91; auth, A New Class of Art: the Artist's Print in Canadian Art, 1877-1920, 96; coauth, An Engraver's Pilgrimage: James Smillie Jr. in Quebec 1821-1830, 89. **CONTACT ADDRESS** National Gallery of Canada, 380 Sussex Dr, Ottawa, ON, Canada K1N 9N4.

TOWNSEND, GAVIN
PERSONAL Born 06/16/1956, Santa Monica, CA, m, 1981, 1 child **DISCIPLINE** ART HISTORY **EDUCATION** Hamilton Col, Clinton, NYork, BA, 78; Univ CA, Santa Barbara, MA, 81, PhD, 86. **CAREER** Asst prof, 86-92, assoc prof of Art, UTC, 92-; dir, Univ Honors Prog, Univ TN at Chattanooga, 97-. **HONORS AND AWARDS** Outstanding Prof Awd, Student Govt Asn, UTC; Samuel Kress Found Fel. **MEMBERSHIPS** Soc of Am Architectural Historians. **RESEARCH** Architectural hist. **SELECTED PUBLICATIONS** Auth, The Tudor Houses of the Prairie School, Arris, 3, 92; Helmut Jahn, for the 20th Century Supplement to the Encyclopedia of World Biography, Jack Heraty & Assoc, 94; Frank Forster and the French Provincial Revival in America, Arris, 6, 95; Max von Pettenkofer, The Macmillan Dictionary of Art, Macmillan, 96; Lamb and Rich, and Kirby, Petit and Green, in Robert MacKay, ed, Long Island Country Estates and Their Architects, 1860-1940, Norton, 97; several other publications. **CONTACT ADDRESS** Dept of Art, Univ of Tennessee, Chattanooga, Chattanooga, TN 37403. **EMAIL** Gavin-Townsend@utc.edu

TOWNSEND, RICHARD
DISCIPLINE HISTORY OF ART **EDUCATION** Univ New Mex, BA, 64; Univ of the Amer, Mex City, MA, 66; Harvard Univ, PhD, 75. **CAREER** Instr, art hist, Univ Neb, 67-69; asst prof, art hist, Univ Tex Austin, 74-79; cur, dept of African and Amerindian Arts, Art Inst of Chicago, 82-. **HONORS AND AWARDS** Fulbright, 64-65; Grand Prize Fel, Harvard, 67-75. **MEMBERSHIPS** CAA, NMAI, SAA. **RESEARCH** Pre-Columbian fields, especially the Aztecs; West Mexico; The United States southwestern peoples; Ancient North American Woodlands. **SELECTED PUBLICATIONS** Ed, The Ancient Americas: Art from Sacred Landscapes, Landscape and Symbol, The Renewal of Nature at the Temple of Tlaloc, Art Inst of Chicago, 92; auth, The Aztecs, Thames and Hudson, 91; auth, Sacred Geography, Sacred Lakes, Encycl of World Relig, MacMilland and Co, 86; auth, Coronation at Tenochtitlan, The Aztec Templo Mayor, Dumbarton Oaks Ctr for Pre-Columbian Studies, 86; auth, Deciphering the Nazca World: Ceramics Images from Ancient Peru, Mus Studies, Art Inst and the Univ of Chicago Press, 85; auth, The Art of Tribes and Early Kingdoms: Selections from Chicago Collections, Art Inst of Chicago, 84; auth, Pyramid and Sacred Mountain, Ethnoastronomy and Archaeoastronomy in the American Tropics, NY Acad of Sic, v 385, 82; auth, Malinalco and the Lords of Tenochtitlan, The Art and Iconography of Late Post-Classic Central Mexico, Dumbarton Oaks Ctr for Pre-Columbian Studies, 82; auth, State and Cosmos in the Art of Tenochtitlan, Dumbarton Oaks Ctr for Pre-Columbian Studies, 79; ed, Ancient West Mex: Art and Archaeology of the Unknown Past, Thames and Hudson, 98. **CONTACT ADDRESS** Dept of African and Amerindian Arts, Art Inst of Chicago, 111 S. Michigan Av., Chicago, IL 60603. **EMAIL** rtownsend@artic.edu

TRACEY, DONALD RICHARD
PERSONAL Born 01/24/1932, Baltimore, MD, m, 1962, 2 children **DISCIPLINE** MODERN EUROPEAN HISTORY **EDUCATION** Univ Md, BA, 54, MA, 62, PhD(hist), 67. **CAREER** From instr to asst prof hist, Temple Univ, 65-72; assoc prof and chmn dept hist and polit sci, 72-77, Prof Hist, Ill Col, 77- **MEMBERSHIPS** Conf Group Cent Europ Hist. **RESEARCH** Modern European history; German history. **SELECTED PUBLICATIONS** Auth, Reform in the early Weimar Republic: The Thuringian example, J Mod Hist, 6/72; Development of national socialist party in Thuringia, Cent Europ Hist, 3/75. **CONTACT ADDRESS** Dept of Hist and Polit Sci, Illinois Col, Jacksonville, IL 62650.

TRACHTENBERG, ALAN
PERSONAL Born 03/22/1932, Philadelphia, PA, m, 1952, 3 children **DISCIPLINE** ENGLISH, AMERICAN STUDIES **EDUCATION** Temple Univ, AB, 54; Univ Minn, PhD(Am studies), 62. **CAREER** Instr English, Gen Col, Univ Minn, Minneapolis, 56-61; from instr to assoc prof, Pa State Univ, University Park, 61-69; assoc prof, 69-71, PROF AM STUDIES and ENGLISH, YALE UNIV, 72-, CHMN DEPT AM STUDIES, 80-, Am Coun Learned Soc grant-in-aid, 64-65, study fel, 68-69; fel, Ctr Adv Studies Behav Sci, 68-69. **MEMBERSHIPS** MLA; Am Studies Asn. **RESEARCH** American literature; American cultural history. **SELECTED PUBLICATIONS** Auth, Brooklyn Bridge: Fact and Symbol, Oxford, 65; The American scene: Versions of the city, Mass Rev, spring 67; The journey back: Myth and history in Tender is the Night, English Inst Essays, 68; ed, Democratic Vistas, 1860-1880, Braziller, 70; auth, The form of freedom in Huck Finn, Southern Rev, 71; ed, Memoirs of Waldo Frank, Univ Mass, 73. **CONTACT ADDRESS** Am Studies Prog, Yale Univ, P O Box 208302, New Haven, CT 06520-8302.

TRACHTENBERG, MARC
PERSONAL Born 02/09/1946, New York, NY, m, 1973, 1 child **DISCIPLINE** HISTORY **EDUCATION** Univ Calif, Berkeley, AB, 66, MA, 67, PhD(hist), 74. **CAREER** Asst prof, 74-80, Assoc Prof Hist, Univ Pa, 80-. **HONORS AND AWARDS** Social Sci Res Coun res training fel econ, 77-78. **MEMBERSHIPS** AHA; Societe d'Histoire Moderne. **RESEARCH** International politics 1914 to present. **SELECTED PUBLICATIONS** Auth, Etienne Clementel and French economic diplomacy during the First World War, French Hist Studies, 77. **CONTACT ADDRESS** Dept of Hist, Univ of Pennsylvania, Philadelphia, PA 19174. **EMAIL** cram@sas.upenn.edu

TRACY, JAMES
PERSONAL Born 02/14/1938, St. Louis, MO, m, 1997, 3 children **DISCIPLINE** HISTORY **EDUCATION** St. Louis Univ, BA, 59; Johns Hopkins Univ, MA, 60; Notre Dame, MA, 61; Princeton Univ, PhD, 67. **CAREER** From instr to prof, Univ Minn, 66- . **HONORS AND AWARDS** Fel, Netherlands Inst for Advanc Stud, 93-94. **MEMBERSHIPS** Am Hist Asn; Am Cath Hist Asn; Soc for Reformation Res; Sixteenth Century Stud Conf. **RESEARCH** Sixteenth century Europe; Low Countries; Europeans overseas. **SELECTED PUBLICATIONS** Co-ed, Handbook of European History in the Late Middle Ages, Renaissance and Reformation, 2 v, Brill, 93-94; auth, Studies in Eighteenth Century Mughal and Ottoman Trade, J of the Econ and Soc Hist of the Orient, 94; auth, Lords, Peasants, and The Beginnings of Calvanist Preaching in Holland's Noorderkwartier, in Thorpe, ed, Politics, Religion and Diplomacy in Early Modern Europe: Essays in Honor of De La Mar Jensen, St Louis, 94; auth, Erasmus among the Post-Modernists: Dissimulatio, Bonae Literae, and Docta Pietas Revisited, in Pagel, ed, Erasmus' Vision of the Church, St. Louis, 95; auth, Liberation through the Philosophia Christi: Erasmus as a Reformer of Doctrine, Luther Jahrbuch, 95; auth, Erasmus of the Low Countries, California, 96; auth, Die Civitates in der Christlicher Rechtsordnung bei Erasmus von Rotterdam, in Blickle, ed, Theorien Kommunaler Ordnung, Munich, 96; auth, Erasmus, Coornhert, and the Acceptance of Religious Disunity in the Body Politic: A Low Countries Tradition? in Berkvens-Stevelink, ed, The Emergence of Tolerance in the Dutch Republic, Leiden, 97; auth, Europe's Reformations, 1450-1650, 99; ed, City Walls: The Urban Enceinic in Global Perspective, 00. **CONTACT ADDRESS** History Dept, Univ of Minnesota, Twin Cities, 614 Social Sciences, Minneapolis, MN 55455. **EMAIL** tracy001@tc.umn.edu

TRACY, PATRICIA JUNEAU
PERSONAL Born 03/09/1947, Hartford, CT, m, 1969 **DISCIPLINE** AMERICAN HISTORY **EDUCATION** Smith Col, BA, 69; Univ Mass, Amherst, PhD, 77. **CAREER** Asst Prof to Prof Am Hist, Williams Col, 78-. **RESEARCH** Social hist of colonial New England; cross cultural family hist; gender. **SELECTED PUBLICATIONS** Auth, Jonathan Edwards, Pastor: Religion and Society in 18th Century Northampton, Hill & Wang, 80. **CONTACT ADDRESS** Dept of Hist, Williams Col, Stetson Hall, Williamstown, MA 01267-2600. **EMAIL** patricia.j.tracy@williams.edu

TRAFZER, CLIFFORD EARL
PERSONAL Born 03/01/1949, Mansfield, OH **DISCIPLINE** AMERICAN INDIAN AND AMERICAN HISTORY **EDUCATION** Northern Ariz Univ, BA, 70, MA, 71; Okla State Univ, PhD(hist), 73. **CAREER** Archivist, Northern Ariz Univ Libr, 70-71; mus cur, Ariz Hist Soc, 73-76; instr Am Indian hist, Navajo Community Col, 76-77; asst prof Am Indian hist, 77-82, Assoc Prof Am Hist, Wash State Univ, 82- **MEMBERSHIPS** Western Hist Asn; Am Indian Hist Soc; Orgn Am Historians. **RESEARCH** American Indian history; the Southwest and the Columbia Plateau. **SELECTED PUBLICATIONS** Auth, Garces, Anza, and the Yuma Frontier, Yuma County Hist Soc, 75; The Judge: The Life of Robert A Hefner, Okla Univ, 75; Dine and Bilagaana, 78, Navajos and Spaniards, 78 & Navajo Raiders and Anglo Expanisionist, 78, Navajo Community Col; The Volga Germans: Pioneers of the NW, Univ Press Idaho, 81; Yuma: Frontier Crossing of the Far SW, Western Heritage Press, 81; The Kit Carson Campaign: The Last Great Navajo War, Okla Univ, 81. **CONTACT ADDRESS** Native Am Prog Dept of Hist, Washington State Univ, Pullman, WA 99163.

TRANI, EUGENE PAUL
PERSONAL Born 11/02/1939, Brooklyn, NY, m, 1962, 2 children **DISCIPLINE** AMERICAN HISTORY **EDUCATION** Univ Notre Dame, BA, 61; Ind Univ, MA, 63, PhD(hist), 66. **CAREER** Instr hist, Ohio State Univ, 65-67; from asst prof to prof hist, Southern Ill Univ, Carbondale, 67-76; prof and vpres acad affairs, Univ Nebr-Lincoln, 76-80; Prof Hist and Vchancellor Acad Affairs, Univ MO-Kansas City, 80-, Southern Ill Univ Off Res and Proj grant, 67-69 and 70-72; vis res assoc, Papers of Woodrow Wilson, Princeton Univ, 69-70; Nat Endowment for Humanities younger humanist award, 72-73; Woodrow Wilson Int Ctr Scholars fel, 72-73; Lilly Endowment fel, 75-76. **HONORS AND AWARDS** Sr Fulbright lectr, Moscow State Univ, USSR, 81. **MEMBERSHIPS** AHA; Orgn Am Historians; Am Asn Advan Slavic Studies; Soc Historians Am Foreign Rels; Coun Foreign Rels. **RESEARCH** American diplomatic history; recent American history. **SELECTED PUBLICATIONS** Auth, Notes for Charles Sawyer's Concerns of a Conservative Democrat, Southern Ill Univ, 68; Russia in 1905: The view from the American Embassy, Rev Politics, 69; The Treaty of Portsmouth: An Adventure in American Diplomacy, Univ Ky, 69; Woodrow Wilson, China, and the missionaries, 1913-1921, J Presby Hist, 71; coauth, The American YMCA and the Russian Revolution, Slavic Rev, 74; auth, The Secretaries of the Department of the Interior, 1849-1969, Smithsonian Inst, 75; Woodrow Wilson and the decision to intervene in Russia: A reconsideration, J Mod Hist, 76; coauth, The Presidency of Warren G Harding, Regents Press Kans & Lawrence, 77; The foreign policy of Nebraska, Washington Quart, summer 80. **CONTACT ADDRESS** Office of VChancellor, Univ of Missouri, Kansas City, Kansas City, MO 64110.

TRASK, DAVID F.
PERSONAL Born 05/15/1929, Erie, PA, m, 1965 **DISCIPLINE** AMERICAN HISTORY **EDUCATION** Wesleyan Univ, BA, 51; Harvard Univ, AM, 52, PhD, 58. **CAREER** Instr polit econ, Boston Univ, 56-58; from instr to assoc prof hist, Wesleyan Univ, 58-62; from asst prof to assoc prof, Univ Nebr, Lincoln, 62-66; from assoc prof to prof hist, State Univ NY Stony Brook, 66-76, chmn dept, 69-74; dir, Off Historian, Dept State, Washington, DC, 76-81; Chief Historian, US Army Ctr Mil Hist, Washington, DC, 81-, Dir, NDEA Inst, 65; mem, Nat Hist Publ and Rec Comn, 76-81 and Senate Hist Off Adv Comt, 77-78. **MEMBERSHIPS** AHA; Orgn Am Historians; Soc Historians of Am Foreign Rel; Soc Hist Fed Govt; Nat Coun Pub Hist. **RESEARCH** Recent American history; American diplomatic history; American military history. **SELECTED PUBLICATIONS** Auth, General Tasker Howard Bliss and the Sessions of the World, 1919, Am Philos Soc, 66; Victory Without Peace: American Foreign Relations in the Twentieth Century--World War I at Home: Readings on American Life 1914-1920, 70, Wiley; Captains and Cabinets: Anglo-American Naval Relations 1917-1918, Univ Mo, 72; The War with Spain in 1898, Macmillan, 81; The Spanish-American War--Conflict in the Caribbean and the Pacific, 1895-1902,, Int Hist Rev, Vol 17, 95; Trial By Friendship--Anglo-American Relations, 1917-1918, J Mil Hist, Vol 57, 93; coauth, A Bibliography for the Study of United States-Latin American Relations Since 1810, Univ Nebr, 68; The Unfinished Century: America Since 1900, 73 and The Ordeal of World Power: American Diplomacy Since 1900, 75, Little, Brown. **CONTACT ADDRESS** 3223B Sutton Pl NW, Washington, DC 20016.

TRASK, KERRY A.
PERSONAL Born 10/17/1941, Orillia, ON, Canada, d, 2 children **DISCIPLINE** HISTORY **EDUCATION** Hamline Univ, St. Paul, MN, BA (Hist, cum laude), 65; Univ MN, MA (Hist), 68, PhD (Hist), 71. **CAREER** Asst, Assoc, Prof, Univ WI Colleges, Stationed at Univ WI, Manitowoc, 72-. **HONORS AND AWARDS** Teacher of the Year, Univ WI, Manitowoc, 76; Coun for WI Writers, Leslie Cross Book-Length Nonfiction Awd, 96; State Hist Soc of WI Distinguished Service to History Book Awd of Merit; WI Library Asn Literary Awd of Outstanding Achievement by a WI Author, 96. **MEMBERSHIPS** Am Soc Ethnohistory; Inst of Early Am Hist and Culture; State Hist Soc of WI. **RESEARCH** Ethnohistory of the early Great Lakes region; Colonial Am; early WI and the Am Civil War. **SELECTED PUBLICATIONS** Auth, In the Pursuit of Shadows: Massachusetts, Millelialism, and the Seven Years War, Garland Pub, Inc, 89; Fire Within: A Civil War Narrative From Wisconsin, Kent State Univ Press, 95; I Have Been Brave But Wicked-Pray For Me, Voyageur, spring/summer, 98; numerous articles published before 90, and many book reviews for MI Hist Rev, Ethnohistory, William and Mary Quart, Voyageur, and The Old Northwest. **CONTACT ADDRESS** Univ of Wisconsin Ctr, Manitowoc County, 705 Viebauh St., Manitowoc, WI 54220. **EMAIL** ktrask@uwc.edu

TRASK, ROGER R.
PERSONAL Born 09/14/1930, Erie, PA, m, 1956, 3 children **DISCIPLINE** AMERICAN HISTORY **EDUCATION** Thiel Col, BA, 52; Pa State Univ, MA, 54, PhD(hist), 59. **CAREER** From instr to asst prof hist, Upsala Col, 59-62; asst prof, Thiel Col, 62-64; from asst prof to prof US hist, Macalester Col, 64-74; Prof US Hist, Univ S Fla, 74-, Vis lectr US diplomatic hist, Univ Ill, Champaign, 67-68; chief historian, US Nuclear Regulatory Comn, 77-78. **MEMBERSHIPS** AHA; Orgn Am Historians; Soc Historians Am Foreign Rels. **RESEARCH** United States diplomatic history, 20th century; Turkish-American relations; United States-Latin American relations. **SELECTED PUBLICATIONS CONTACT ADDRESS** Dept of Hist, Univ of So Florida, Tampa, FL 33620.

TRATTNER, WALTER IRWIN
PERSONAL Born 07/26/1936, New York, NY, m, 1958, 3 children **DISCIPLINE** AMERICAN HISTORY **EDUCATION** Williams Col, AB, 58; Harvard Univ, AMT, 59; Univ Wis, MS, 61, PhD, 64. **CAREER** Teaching asst, Univ Wis, 60-62, res asst, 62-63; asst prof hist, Northern Ill Univ, 63-65; asst prof hist, 65-67, assoc prof hist and social welfare, 67-71, prof to prof emer Hist, Univ Wis Milwaukee, 71-, Dept Health, Educ and Welfare grant, 68-69. **HONORS AND AWARDS** Outstanding Educator of Am, Outstanding Educr Am, 71 and 75. **MEMBERSHIPS** Nat Conf Social Welfare; AHA; Orgn Am Historians; Social Welfare Hist Group. **RESEARCH** American social history; history of social welfare in America; recent American history. **SELECTED PUBLICATIONS** Auth, Homer Folks: Pioneer in Social Welfare, Columbia Univ, 68; Crusade for the Children: A History of the National Child Labor Committee and Child Labor Reform in America, Quadrangle, 70; The fight against child labor, Welfare Rev, 9-10/70; Homer Folks's The care of destitute, neglected and delinquent children, Child Welfare, 6/72; Social work and economic dependence, 1872-1972, In: A Century of Concern, 1873-1973, Nat Conf Social Welfare, 73; From Poor Law to Welfare State: A History of Social Welfare in America, Free Press, 74, rev ed, 79; The Federal Government and social welfare in early nineteenth century America, Social Serv Rev, 6/76; ed, Social welfare or social control: Some historical reflections on regulating the poor, Univ Tenn Press, 82. **CONTACT ADDRESS** 10639 N Magnolia Dr, Mequon, WI 53092. **EMAIL** wit@uwm.edu

TRAUTMANN, THOMAS ROGER
PERSONAL Born 05/27/1940, Madison, WI, m, 1962, 2 children **DISCIPLINE** HISTORY OF ANCIENT INDIA **EDUCATION** Beloit Col, BA, 62; Univ London, PhD(hist), 68. **CAREER** Lectr early hist S Asia, Sch Orient & African Studies, Univ London, 65-68; from asst prof to assoc prof, 68-77, prof hist, Univ Mich, Ann Arbor, 77-; prof anthro 84-; chair, dept hist, 87-90; dir, Institute for the Humanities, 97-, ed, Comparative in Society and History, 97-. **HONORS AND AWARDS** Marshall D. Sahlins Colligiate Prof of History and

Anthropology 97-; Mary Fair Croushore Prof of Humanities, 97-. **MEMBERSHIPS** Asn Asian Studies. **RESEARCH** India, Kinship and marriage; statecraft. **SELECTED PUBLICATIONS** auth, Dravidain Kinship, Cambridge, 81; auth, Lewis Henry Morgan and the Invention of Kinship, California, 87; auth, Aryans and British India, California, 97; Hullabaloo about Telugu, South Asia Research, 99. **CONTACT ADDRESS** Dept Hist, Univ of Michigan, Ann Arbor, 435 S State St, Ann Arbor, MI 48109-1003. **EMAIL** ttraut@umich.edu

TREADGOLD, WARREN
PERSONAL Born 04/30/1949, Oxford, United Kingdom, m, 1982 **DISCIPLINE** HISTORY, CLASSICS **EDUCATION** Harvard Univ, AB, 70; PhD, 77. **CAREER** Lectr, UCLA, 77-78; Univ Munich, Free Univ Berlin, 78-80; 82-83; Lectr, Standford Univ, 80-82; asst prof, Hillsdale Col, 83-88; vis prof, Univ Calif at Berkeley, 86; asst prof, Fla Int Univ, 88-97; prof, St Louis Univ, 97- **HONORS AND AWARDS** Woodrow Wilson Int Center for Scholars Fel; NEH Fel (2); Visiting Fel, All Souls Col, Oxford; Alexander von Humboldt Fel; Outstanding Achievements and Performance awards, Fla Int Univ. **MEMBERSHIPS** AHA; Am Philos Assoc; Medieval Acad of Am; AAUP. **RESEARCH** Byzantine history and literature. **SELECTED PUBLICATIONS** Auth, The Nature of the Bibliotheas of Photrus, 80; auth, The Byzantine State Finances in the Eighth and Ninth Centures, 82; ed, Renaissances Before the Renaissance, 84; auth, The Byzantine Revivial, 88; auth, Byzantium and It's Army, 95; auth, A History of the Byzantine State and Society, 97; auth, A Concise History of Byzantium, 00. **CONTACT ADDRESS** Dept Hist, St. Louis Univ, 221 N Grand Boulevard, Saint Louis, MO 63103-2006. **EMAIL** treadgw@slu.edu

TRECKEL, PAULA ANN
PERSONAL Born 03/15/1953, Youngstown, OH, m, 1980 **DISCIPLINE** COLONIAL AMERICAN HISTORY **EDUCATION** Kent State Univ, BA, 73; Syracuse Univ, MA, 76, PhD(Am studies), 78. **CAREER** Asst prof hist, Col St Benedict, 78-81; Asst Prof Hist, Allegheny Col, 81-, Consult, American Women Writers Prog, Ungar Publ Co, Inc, 79-81. **MEMBERSHIPS** Orgn Am Historians. **RESEARCH** Women and families on the colonial American frontier; women and medicine in Early America; Ida Tarbell and the age of reform. **SELECTED PUBLICATIONS** Auth, An historiographical essay: Women on the American frontier, The Old Northwest, 12/75; Critique of James Axtell's The White Indians of Colonial America, William & Mary Quart, 1/76; contribr, Narcissa Whitman, Ann Eliza Webb, Eliza Roxey Snow, Fanny Stenhouse, Alice Earle, Emily Putnam & Lucy Salmon, American Women Writers, Vols 1-4, Ungar Publ Co, 79-81; auth, Jane Grey Swisshelm and feminism in Minnesota territory, Midwest Rev, spring 80. **CONTACT ADDRESS** Dept of Hist, Allegheny Col, Box 131, Meadville, PA 16355.

TREDWAY, JOHN THOMAS
PERSONAL Born 09/04/1935, North Tonawanda, NY, m, 1950, 2 children **DISCIPLINE** CHURCH & INTELLECTUAL HISTORY **EDUCATION** Augustana Col, BA, 57; Univ Ill, MA, 58; Garrett Theol Sem, BD, 61; Northwestern Univ, PhD, 64. **CAREER** From asst prof to prof hist, 64-75, dean col, 70-75, pres, 75-, Augustana Col, Ill; vis prof, Waterloo Luther-an Sem, 67-68; chmn, Nat Lutheran-Methodist Theol Dialogs, 77-. **MEMBERSHIPS** Am Soc Church Historians; AHA. **RESEARCH** Nineteenth century American and British church history; modern European intellectual history. **SELECTED PUBLICATIONS** Auth, Newman: Patristics, ecumenics and liberalism, Christian Century, 65; co-ed, The Immigration of Ideas, Augustana Hist Soc, 68. **CONTACT ADDRESS** Augustana Col, Illinois, Rock Island, IL 61201.

TREFOUSSE, HANS L.
PERSONAL Born 12/18/1921, Frankfurt, Germany, w, 1947, 1 child **DISCIPLINE** HISTORY **EDUCATION** City Col NYork, BA, 42; Columbia Univ, MA, 47, PhD(hist), 50. **CAREER** Instr hist, Hunter Col, 47-48; instr, Adelphi Col, 49-50; from instr to assoc prof, 50-65, Prof Hist, Broolyn Col, 66-, Mem grants-in-aid selection comt, Am Coun Learned Soc, 62-64; Prof Hist, Grad Ctr, City Univ NY, 64-; Assoc, Sem Am Civilization, Columbia Univ, 68-; Guggenheim fel, 77-78. **HONORS AND AWARDS** Dintinguished Prof. 86-; Emeritus, 98-. **MEMBERSHIPS** AHA; Orgn Am Historians; Southern Hist Asn. **RESEARCH** American history; Civil War and Reconstruction; international relations. **SELECTED PUBLICATIONS** Auth, The Spirit of 1848--German Immigrants, Labor Conflict, and the Coming of the Civil-War, Revs Am Hist, Vol 21, 93; Let Us Have Peace--Grant, Ulysses S. and the Politics of War and Reconstruction, 1861-1868, J Southern Hist, Vol 59, 93; The Culture of Sentiment--Race, Gender, and Sentimentality in 19th-Century America, Historian, Vol 56, 94; The Papers of Johnson, Andrew, Vol 10--February-July 1866, Civil War Hist, Vol 40, 94; The Jewel of Liberty--Lincoln,Abraham Re-Election and the End of Slavery, J Southern Hist, Vol 62, 96; The Capture of New Orleans, 1862, Civil War Hist, Vol 42, 96; The Papers of Johnson,andrew, Vol 11, August 1866 January 1867, Civil War Hist, Vol 42, 96; The Federal Impeachment Process--A Constitutional and Historical-Analysis, Am Hist Rev, Vol 102, 97; State of Rebellion--Reconstruction in South-Carolina, J Am Hist, Vol 84, 97; Lincoln,Abraham--From Skeptic to Prophet, Civil War Hist, Vol 43, 97. **CONTACT ADDRESS** Dept of Hist, Brooklyn Col, CUNY, 2901 Bedford Ave, Brooklyn, NY 11210-2813.

TREGOUET, ANNIE D.
DISCIPLINE FRENCH STUDIES **EDUCATION** Univ Montpellier, BA, 86; MA, 87; Univ Colo Boulder, PhD, 00. **CAREER** Vis asst prof, Case Western Reserve Univ, 00-01; vis asst prof, Oberlin Col, 01-. **MEMBERSHIPS** MLA; LFA. **RESEARCH** Film and literary theory; modern and contemporary French and Francophone literature; French and Francophone cinema; European cinema. **SELECTED PUBLICATIONS** Auth, "Une Adaptation d'Auteur: Les Miserables de Claude Lelouch," Etudes Romances (98); auth, "The Male Gaze Subverted: Germaine Dulac's Le Belle Dame sans Merci," WVa Univ Philol (01). **CONTACT ADDRESS** Dept Romance Lang, Oberlin Col, 173 West Lorain St, Oberlin, OH 44074. **EMAIL** adrmtregouet@yahoo.com

TRELEASE, ALLEN WILLIAM
PERSONAL Born 01/31/1928, Boulder, CO, 2 children **DISCIPLINE** HISTORY **EDUCATION** Univ IL, AB, 50, MA, 51; Harvard Univ, PhD(hist), 55. **CAREER** Teaching fel, Harvard Univ, 53-55; from instr to prof hist, Wells Col, 55-67, acting dean fac, 62-63, dept head, 63-67; prof hist, Univ NC, Greensboro, 67-94, head dept, 84-92, , Retired 94. **HONORS AND AWARDS** Charles S Sydnor Awd, Southern Hist Asn, 72. **MEMBERSHIPS** AHA; Orgn Am Historians; Southern Hist Asn. **RESEARCH** American history; Southern history; Civil War and Reconstruction periods. **SELECTED PUBLICATIONS** Auth, Indian Affairs in Colonial New York: The 17th Century, Cornell Univ, 60; The Iroquois and the Western fur trade, Miss Valley Hist Rev, 6/62; Who were the scalawags?, J Southern Hist, 11/63; contribr, Attitudes of Colonial Powers Toward the American Indian, Univ Utah, 69; auth, White Terror: The Ku Klux Klan Conspiracy and Southern Reconstruction, 71 & Reconstruction: The Great Experiment, 71, Harper & Row; Republican Reconstruction in North Carolina, J Southern Hist, 8/76; The Fusion Legislatures of 1895 and 1897: A roll-call analysis of the North Carolina House of Representatives, NC Hist Rev, 7/80; The North Carolina Railroad, 1849-1871, and the Modernization of North Carolina, Univ NC Press, 91; Changing Assignments: A Pictorial History of the University of North Carolina, Univ NC G, 91. **CONTACT ADDRESS** 307 Kirk Rd, Greensboro, NC 27455. **EMAIL** treleasea@worldnet.att.net

TRENNERT, ROBERT ANTHONY
PERSONAL Born 12/15/1937, South Gate, CA, m, 1965, 2 children **DISCIPLINE** AMERICAN HISTORY **EDUCATION** Occidental Col, BA, 61; Los Angeles State Col, MA, 63; Univ Calif, Santa Barbara, PhD(hist), 69. **CAREER** From instr to asst prof hist, Temple Univ, 67-74; asst prof, 74-76, assoc prof, 76-81, Prof Hist, Ariz State Univ, 81-. **MEMBERSHIPS** Western Hist Asn; Minine History Assoc; Westerners Int. **RESEARCH** American Indian policy; American Indian education; popular images of the American Indian. **SELECTED PUBLICATIONS** Auth, The Federal-Government and Indian Health in the Southwest--Tuberculosis and the Phoenix-East-Farm-Sanatorium, 1909-1955, Pacific Hist Rev, Vol 0065, 96; auth, White Man's Medicine: Government Doctors and the Navajo, 1863-1955, Univ of New Mexico Press, 98; auth, "Superwomen in Indian Country: U.S.I.S. Field Nurses in Arizona and New Mexico, 1928-1940," Journal of AZ History, vol 41, 31-56. **CONTACT ADDRESS** Dept of Hist, Arizona State Univ, Tempe, AZ 85287-2501. **EMAIL** robert.trennert@asu.edu

TRENTMANN, FRANK
DISCIPLINE HISTORY **EDUCATION** London Sch for Economics and Political Sci, Univ London, BA, 88; Harvard Univ, MA, 91; PhD, 99. **CAREER** Instr, Princeton Univ, 97, asst prof, 99-. **HONORS AND AWARDS** Leverhulme Trust Fel, UK; Scouloudi Fel, Inst of Hist Res, London, UK; Krupp Found Fel, USA; Hans-und-Gretchen Tietje Stiftung, Hamburg (Germany); Friedrich-Ebert-Stiftung, Fel (Germany). **SELECTED PUBLICATIONS** Auth, "The Strange Death of Free Trade: the Erosion of 'Liberal Concensus' in Great Britain, c. 1903-32" in Citizenship and community: Liberals, radicals and collective identities int the British Isles, 1865-1931, ed E. Briagini, Cambridge Univ Press (96); auth, "The Transformation of Fiscal Reform: Reciprocity, Modernization, and the Fiscal Debate within the Business Community in Early Twentieth-Century Britain," Hist HJ, XXXIX, 4 (96): 1005-48; auth, "Wealth versus Welfare: the British Left between Free Trade and National Political Economy before the First World War," Hist Res, LXX (97): 70-98; auth, "Civil Society, Commerce, and the 'Citizen-Consumer': Popular Meanings of Free Trade in late nineteenth- and early twentieth-century Britain," Center for European Studies, Harvard Univ, Working Paper Series, No 66 (summer 97); auth, "Political Culture and Political Economy," Rev of Int Political Economy (RIPE), 5:2 (98): 217-251; auth, "Fiscal Politics in Modern Britain," in Reader in British History (forthcoming); auth, "Leisure in Modern Britain," historiographical survey for Reader in British History, gen ed, Prof D. M. Loades, 2 vols, Fitzroy Dearborn Pub, London (forthcoming); auth, "Bread, Milk, and Democracy in Modern Britain," in The Politics of Consumption, eds, Martin Daunton and Matthew Hilton, Oxford and New York: Berg Pubs (forthcoming); co-ed with Mark Bevir, Beyond Markets: Non-Marxist and Post-Marxist Critiques of the Market--Historical and Theoretical Perspectives (forthcoming); ed and auth of "Paradoxes of Civil Society," and "Civil Society, Commerce, and Consumption," in Paradoxes of Civil Society: New Perspectives on the Evolution of Civil Society in Modern Britain and Germany, Oxford and New York: Berghahn Books (2000): 3-46, 306-31. **CONTACT ADDRESS** Dept Hist, Princeton Univ, 130 Dickinson Hall, Princeton, NJ 08544-0001.

TREVELYAN, AMELIA M.
PERSONAL Born 02/21/1946, Marshall, MI, d, 2 children **DISCIPLINE** VISUAL ARTS **EDUCATION** Univ Mich, BA; MA; Univ Calif, PhD, 87. **CAREER** Instructor, Rhode Island Col, 70-73; Asst Prof, Center for the Creative Studies Col of Art and Design, 81-83; Assoc Prof, Gettysburg Col, 86-. **HONORS AND AWARDS** NEA Heritage and Preservation Grant, 00; Richard Florsheim Art Fund Grant, 99; Central PA Consortium Grant, 99; ELCA Grant, 98; NEH Summer Inst, 97; PEW Trust Grants, 93-96; PA Coun for Humanities Grant, 93; Can Embassy Prog Grants, 90, 91. **MEMBERSHIPS** Col Art Asn, Native Am Studies Asn, Can Native Art Studies Asn. **RESEARCH** Art of the First Nations; Early metallurgy; Tribal arts; Feminist art. **SELECTED PUBLICATIONS** Auth, "Jaune Quick-to-See Smith," in Contemporary Masters: the Eiteljorg Fellowship for Native American Fine Art, Vol I, 99; auth, "Jaune Quick-to-See smith," Native Peoples, 99; auth, "Copper and the Bi-lobed Arrow at Etowah," in Iconography of the Southeastern Ceremonial Complex, Univ Tex Press, 99; co-auth, St. James Guide to Native North American Artists, St. James Press, 98; auth, "American Indian Metalwork: Woodlands," in The Dictionary of Art, Macmillan Pub, 96; auth, "The Pawnee and the Southern Cult: A comparison of Ritual Traditions in the Southeast and on the Plains," in Celebration of Indigenous Thought and Expression, Lake Superior State Univ Press, 96; auth, Seeing a New World: the Art of Carl Beam and Frederic Remington, Cumberland press, 93; auth, The Columbus Boat, Corpus Christi State Univ Press, 92; auth, Robert Houle: Lost Tribes, Hood College Press, 91; auth, "Continuity of form and function in the Art of the Eastern Woodlands," Canadian Journal of Native American Studies, 90. **CONTACT ADDRESS** Dept Visual Arts, Gettysburg Col, 300 N Washington St, Gettysburg, PA 17325. **EMAIL** atrevely@gettysburg.edu

TREXLER, RICHARD C.
PERSONAL Born 03/27/1932, Philadelphia, PA, 2 children **DISCIPLINE** HISTORY **EDUCATION** Baylor Univ, AB; Johan Goethe Univ, Frankfurt, PhD, 64. **CAREER** Asst prof, UTEP, 64-6; asst prof, Occidental Col, 66-68; assoc prof, Univ Ill, Champaign-Urbana, 70-78; PROF, 78-, DISTING PROF, 95-, SUNY, BINGHAMTON. **HONORS AND AWARDS** Harvard Univ., Villa I Tatti (1968-70); Institute for Advanced Study (73-74); Ecole des Hautes Etudes, (1980, 1984); CASVA (84-85); J. Simon Guggenheim (1985-86); Art Council Chair, UCLA (1987); Wissenschaftskolleg zu Berlin (93-94); J. Paul Getty Senior Research Grant in the History of Art (96-97); National Humanities Center (97-98). **MEMBERSHIPS** Medieval Acad of Am. **RESEARCH** Italian History; Behavioral History; Native Am History; Gender History. **SELECTED PUBLICATIONS** Auth, Synodal Law in Florence and Fiesole, 1306-1518; auth, The Spiritual Power: Republican Florence under Interdict, 74; auth, Public Life in Renaissance Florence (80, 91); auth, Church and Community: Studies in the History of Florence and New Spain, 87; auth, The Christian at Prayer: an Illustrated Prayer Manual of Peter the Chanter, 87; auth, Naked Before the Father: the Renunciation of Francis of Assisi, 89; auth, Sex and Conquest: Gendered Conquest, Political Order, and the European Conquest of the Americas, 95; auth, The Journey of the Magi: Meanings in History of a Christian Story, 97. **CONTACT ADDRESS** Dept of History, SUNY, Binghamton, Binghamton, NY 13902-6000. **EMAIL** trexler@binghamton.edu

TRIBE, IVAN MATHEWS
PERSONAL Born 05/01/1940, Albany, OH, m, 1966 **DISCIPLINE** AMERICAN HISTORY **EDUCATION** Ohio Univ, BSEd, 62, MA, 66; Univ Toledo, PhD(hist), 76. **CAREER** Lectr, 76-77, asst prof history, Rio Grande Col, 77-84, assoc prof, 84-90, prof, 90-, Fel, Berea Col Appalachian Studies, 80. **MEMBERSHIPS** Appalachian Studies Assn; Orgn Am Historians. **RESEARCH** Appalachian culture; industrial communities; Ohio and Midwest. **SELECTED PUBLICATIONS** Auth, Rise and Decline of Private Academies in Albany, Ohio, Ohio Hist, 69; coauth, Molly O'Day and the Cumberland Mountain Folks, John Edwards Memorial Found, Univ Calif, Los Angeles, 75; auth, West Virginia Country Music During the Golden Age of Radio, Goldenseal, 77; Dream and Reality in Southern Ohio: The Development of the Columbus and Hocking Railroad, The Old Northwest, 78; Songs of the Silver Bridge, Goldenseal, 79; co-ed, An Encyclopedia of East Tennessee, Children's Mus Oak Ridge, 81; Mountaineer Jamboree: Country Music in West Virginia, Lexington: Univ Press of Kentucky, 84; The Stonemans: An Appalachian Family and the Music That Shared Their Lives, Univ of Illinois Press, 93; co-auth, Definitive Country: The Ultimate Encyclopediaof Country Music and Its Performers, Perigee Books, 95. **CONTACT ADDRESS**

Dept of Hist, Univ of Rio Grande, Rio Grande, OH 45674-9999. **EMAIL** itribe@urgrgcc.edu

TRICKEL, JOHN
PERSONAL Born 08/25/1942, Tulsa, OK, m, 2000, 2 children **DISCIPLINE** US HISTORY **EDUCATION** Univ Tulsa, BA, 64; MA, 66; Univ North Tex, Ed D, 80. **CAREER** Instr, Westark Comm Col, 67-69; prof, Richland Col, 73-. **HONORS AND AWARDS** NOEA Title IV Scholar; Hist Series Awd. **MEMBERSHIPS** TCCTA; DCCCFA. **RESEARCH** Teaching American History. **SELECTED PUBLICATIONS** Auth, Telecourse Guide for the American Adventure, 86, 91, 95, 98; auth, Adventures in America, 89, 90, 95; auth, Perspectives on America, in Readings in US History, 97. **CONTACT ADDRESS** Dept Humanities, Richland Col, 12800 Abrams Rd, Dallas, TX 75243-2173. **EMAIL** jat8470@dcccd.edu

TRIMBLE, RICHARD M.
PERSONAL Born 03/05/1949, PA, m, 1971, 3 children **DISCIPLINE** HISTORY **EDUCATION** Univ Bridgeport, BS; Seton Hall Univ, MA; Brookdale Community Col, AS; Rutgers Univ, EdS. **CAREER** adj prof, Brookdale Cmty Col. **HONORS AND AWARDS** Teacher of the Year, Manasquan District, 83; Governors Teacher Recognition Prog, 86; Outstanding Sec Sch Teacher Awd, Princeton, 84; NJ State Teacher of the Year in Am Hist, 95. **SELECTED PUBLICATIONS** Auth, In the Classroom: Suggestions & Ideas for the Beginning Teacher, Univ Press, 90; auth, Brothers 'Til Death: The Civil War Letters of Thomas, William & Maggie Jones, West Farms, NJ 1861-86, 98; auth, The Ultimate Hockey Drill Book, 97. **CONTACT ADDRESS** Dept History & Govt, Brookdale Comm Col, 765 Newman Springs Rd, Lincroft, NJ 07738-1543.

TRIMBLE, STANLEY W.
PERSONAL Born 12/08/1940, Columbia, TN, m, 1964, 2 children **DISCIPLINE** GEOGRAPHY **EDUCATION** Univ N Ala, BS, 63; Univ Ga, MA, 69; PhD, 73. **CAREER** Asst Prof, Univ Wis, 72-75; Asst Prof to Prof, UCLA, 75-; Res Hydrologist, USGS, 73-84; Vis Prof, Univ Chicago, 78, 81, 90; Vis Prof, Univ Col London, 85; Guest Prof, Univ Vienna, 94, 99; Vis Prof, Univ Durham, 98. **HONORS AND AWARDS** Fel, NSF, 67-71; Fel, Univ Calif Regents, 76; Fulbright Fel, 95; Sigma Xi; Frost Lectureship; Who's Who. **MEMBERSHIPS** Asn Am Geog; Am Geophys Union; Nat Asn Scholars. **RESEARCH** Historical Geography; Human-induced changes of hydrology and geomorphology. **SELECTED PUBLICATIONS** Auth, "Stream Channel Erosion," Science, 97; auth, "Decr. Sed Storage Rates," Science, 99; co-auth, "U.S. Soil Erosion Rates," Science, 00. **CONTACT ADDRESS** Dept Geog, Univ of California, Los Angeles, 295 Edmundson Rd, Prospect, TN 38477. **EMAIL** trimble@geog.ucla.edu

TRIMMER, JOSEPH FRANCIS
PERSONAL Born 08/04/1941, Cortland, NY, m, 1966, 1 child **DISCIPLINE** AMERICAN LITERATURE & STUDIES **EDUCATION** Colgate Univ, BA, 63; Purdue Univ, MA, 66, PhD, 68. **CAREER** Tchg asst Eng, Purdue Univ, 65-68; asst prof, 68-72, assoc prof, 72-80, prof eng, Ball State Univ, 80, coordr gen educ eng,, 72, Adv ed, Alfred Publ Co, 78. **MEMBERSHIPS** MLA Conf Col Comp & Commun; Am Studies Asn. **RESEARCH** Am lit; Am studies; writing. **SELECTED PUBLICATIONS** Auth, Black American Notes on the Problem of Definition, Ball State Univ Monogr, 71; ed, A Casebook on Ralph Ellison's Invisible Man, Crowell, 72; auth, Ralph Ellison's Flying Home, Studies Short Fiction, spring 72; The Virginian: Novel and films, Ill Quart, 12/72; V K Ratliff: A portrait of the artist in motion, Mod Fiction Studies, winter 74; coauth, American Oblique: Writing About the American Experience, Houghton, 76; auth, Memoryscape: Jean Sheperd's midwest, Old Northwest, 12/76; ed, The National Book Award for Fiction: An Index to the First Twenty-Five Years, G K Hall, 78; Narration as Knowledge, Heinemann, 98; Fictions, Harcourt Brace, 98; Writing With a Purpose, Houghton Mifflin, 98. **CONTACT ADDRESS** Dept of Eng, Ball State Univ, 2000 W University, Muncie, IN 47306-0002. **EMAIL** jtrimmer@bsu.edu

TRIPP, LUKE S.
PERSONAL Born 02/06/1941, Atoka, TN, m, 1989, 3 children **DISCIPLINE** COMMUNITY STUDIES **EDUCATION** Wayne State Univ, BS, 66; Univ Mich, MA, 74; PhD, 80. **CAREER** Sem leader, Wayne State Univ, 68; teacher, Santa Maria Educ Center, 69-70; Instr, Wayne County Col, 71-72; Dir, Univ of Mich, 77-80; vis asst prof, Univ of IL, 81-82; asst prof, Southern Il Univ, 82-89; prof, St. Cloud State Univ, 89-. **HONORS AND AWARDS** Who's Who Among Black Americans, 87; Int. Dir of Distinguished Leadership, 88; Marcus Garvey Peace and Liberation Awd, 88; Mary B. Craik Awd for Equality and Justice Awd, 90; Distinguished Teacher Awd, St. Cloud State Univ, 90; Outstanding Fac Awd, St Cloud State Univ, 91; Outstanding Work as Human Rights Activist Awd, St. Cloud State Univ, 92; Awd for Outstanding Work in Human Rights, 93; Professor of the Year, St Cloud State Univ, 93; 96; Awd, Student Coalition Against Racism, 93; Awd for Contributions and Service to the Students of Color and Department of Minority Student Prog, St Cloud Statre Univ, 95. **MEMBERSHIPS** Am Assoc of Behav and Soc Sci; IL Counc for Black Studies; Nat Counc for Black Studies; Soc of Ethnic and special Studies. **RESEARCH** Black radicalism and student activism, and the various influences of Afro-American culture on American culture. **SELECTED PUBLICATIONS** Auth, "Black Students, Ideology, and Class", Afro-Scholar Working Paper Series 9 , Univ of IL, (83): 1-55; auth, "Community Leadership and Black Former Student Activists of the 1960s", Western J of Black Studies 10.2 (86): 86-89; auth, Black Student Activists: Transition to Middle Class Professionals, Univ Pr of Am, (Lanham, MD), 87; auth, "Race Consciousness Among African-American Students, 1980s", Western J of Black Studies 15.3 (91): 159-168; auth, "The Political Views of Black Students During the Reagan Era", Black Scholar 22.3 (92): 45-52; auth, "The Intellectual Roots of the Controversy around Cultural Diversity and Political Correctness", Western J of Black Studies 18.4 (94): 227-230; auth, "Blacks in America: American Mythology and Miseducation", Oppression and Social Justice: Critical Frameworks, ed J. Andrezjewski, Simon & Schulster, (Needham Heights, MA, 96): 316-321; auth, "Celebrating Diversity Through Community Events, Minnesota Cities 82.11, (Nov 97): auth, "Emphasizing Critical thinking In Studying Race, Class, And Gender", Excellence in Teaching, St Cloud State Univ, Vol 4, (Sept 98). **CONTACT ADDRESS** Dept Community Studies, St. Cloud State Univ, 720 4th Ave S, Saint Cloud, MN 56301-4442. **EMAIL** ltripp@stcloudstate.edu

TRISCO, ROBERT FREDERICK
PERSONAL Born 11/11/1929, Chicago, IL, s **DISCIPLINE** HISTORY & RELIGION **EDUCATION** St. Mary of the Lake Seminary, BA, 51; Pontifical Gregorian Univ, STL, 55, Hist. Eccl.D, 62. **CAREER** Inst, 59-63, Asst Prof, 63-65, Assoc Prof, 65-75, Prof, 75-96, Vice-Rector for Academic Affairs, 66-68, Chemn, Dept of Church Hist, 75-78, Prof, Dept of Church Hist, Kelly-Quinn Distinguished Professor of Church Hist, 99-; The Catholic Univ of Am, 76-. **HONORS AND AWARDS** Honorary degree, Doctor of Humane Letters, Belmont Abbey Col, 92; Honorary Prelate of His Holiness (Monsignor), 92. **MEMBERSHIPS** Am Catholic Hist Asn, Sec 1961-, Sec and Treas 1983-; Am Soc of Church Hist; Pontifical Commt for Hist Sci. **RESEARCH** History of the Catholic Church in the United States and in the British Isles; history of the modern Papacy. **SELECTED PUBLICATIONS** Ed, The Catholic Hist Rev, 63-. **CONTACT ADDRESS** Catholic Univ of America, Curley Hall, Washington, DC 20064. **EMAIL** TRISCO@cua.edu

TRITLE, LAWRENCE
PERSONAL Born 10/13/1946, Glendale, CA, m, 1970 **DISCIPLINE** HISTORY **EDUCATION** Univ Calif at Los Angeles, AB, 68; Univ S Fla, AM, 72; Univ Chicago, PhD, 78. **CAREER** Asst prof to prof, Loyola Marymount Univ, 78-; vis prof, Univ Calif, Los Angeles, 92. **HONORS AND AWARDS** NEH Fel, 79; Marie Chilton Chair of Humanities, Loyola Univ, 87. **MEMBERSHIPS** Am Hist Asn, Am Philol Asn, Asn of Ancient Hist, Friends of Ancient Hist. **RESEARCH** Ancient History (Greece and Rome), Comparative history, Vietnam. **SELECTED PUBLICATIONS** Auth, From Melos to My Lai War and Survival, 00; auth, Text and Tradition: Studies in Greek History and Historiography in Honor of Mortimer Chambers, 99; auth, Balkan Currents. Studies in the History, Culture and Society of a Divided Land, 98; auth, The Greek World in the Fourth Century BC, 97; auth, Phocion the Good, 88. **CONTACT ADDRESS** Dept Hist, Loyola Marymount Univ, 7900 Loyola Blvd, Los Angeles, CA 90045-2659. **EMAIL** ltritle@lmumail.lmu.edu

TROLANDER, JUDITH ANN
PERSONAL Born 05/31/1942, Minneapolis, MN **DISCIPLINE** AMERICAN HISTORY **EDUCATION** Univ Minn, BA, 64; Case Western Reserve Univ, MSLS, 66, MA, 69, PhD(hist), 72. **CAREER** Lectr US hist, Cleveland State Univ, spring, 71; instr, Univ Akron, summer, 71; asst prof, Western Ill Univ, 71-75; from assoc prof to prof US Hist, Univ Minn, Duluth, 75-, Dir, Northeast Minn Hist Ctr, 76-87. **MEMBERSHIPS** Orgn Am Historians; Social Welfare Hist Group. **RESEARCH** Social history in the United States. **SELECTED PUBLICATIONS** Auth, Twenty years at Hiram House, Ohio Hist, winter 69; The response of settlements to the Great Depression, Social Work, 9/73; Settlement Houses and the Great Depression, Wayne State Univ Press, 75; Anna Lane Lingelbach, 77, Lavinia Lloyd Dock, 80, Lillie Peck, 80 & Emily Greene Balch, 81, In: Dict of American Biography; Social action: Settlement houses and Saul Alinsky, 1939-65, Social Serv Rev, 9/82; auth, Professionalism and Social Change: From the Settlement House Movement to Neighborhood Centers, 1886 to the Present, Columbia Univ Press, 87; Fighting Racism and Sexism: The Council on Social Work Education, Social Service Review, March, 97. **CONTACT ADDRESS** Dept of History, Univ of Minnesota, Duluth, 10 University Dr, Duluth, MN 55812-2496. **EMAIL** jtroland@d.umn.edu

TRONZO, WILLIAM
PERSONAL Born 03/06/1957, Detroit, MI, m, 1985, 1 child **DISCIPLINE** MEDIEVAL ART, EARLY CHRISTIAN AND BYZANTINE ART **EDUCATION** Haverford Col, BA, 73; Harvard Univ, PhD, 82. **CAREER** Instr, Dumbarton Oaks and Am Univ, 82-84; Johns Hopkins, 84-90; Duke Univ, 92-96; Williams Col, 96-97; Tulane Univ, 97-. **HONORS AND AWARDS** Robert Woods Bliss fel, Dumbarton Oaks, 75-76; Arthur Lehman fel, Harvard, 76-77; Rome prize fel, 76-77; 1977-79; Inst for Adv Study Princeton, 90-91; CASVA, NGA, 91-92. **MEMBERSHIPS** CAA; SAH; Associazione Italiana Degli Storici Dell'Arte Medioevale; ICMA; US Nat Comm for Byzantine Studies. **SELECTED PUBLICATIONS** Auth, The Prestige of St. Peters. Observations on the Function of Monumental Narrative Cycles in Italy, Stud Hist of Art of the Nat Gallery of Art, 16, 85; The Medieval Object-Enigma, and the Problem of the Cappella Palatina in Palermo, Word & Image, 9, 93; Mimesis in Byzantium: Notes Towards a History of the Function of the Image, RES: Jour Anthrop and Aesthet, 25, 94; I grandi cicli pittorici romani e la loro influenza, La Pittura in Italia: L'Altomedioevo, Milan, 94; auth, The Cultures of His Kingdom. Roger II and the Cappella Palatina in Palermo, Princeton, 97. **CONTACT ADDRESS** Dept of Art, Tulane Univ, 6823 St Charles Ave, New Orleans, LA 70118. **EMAIL** wtronzo@mailhost.tcs.tulane.edu

TROXLER, CAROLE WATTERSON
PERSONAL Born 02/22/1943, LaGrange, GA, m, 1967, 2 children **DISCIPLINE** HISTORY **EDUCATION** Univ Ga, AB, 64; Univ NC at Chapel Hill, MA, 66; PhD, 74. **CAREER** Instr, Davidson County Community Col, 66-68; from asst prof to prof, Elon Col, 70-. **HONORS AND AWARDS** Woodrow Wilson Fel; Career Teaching Fel; Gertrude Carraway Awd, Hist Preservation Soc of NC; Herbert Clarence Bradshaw Awd, Sons of the Am Revolution; Donald Hoffman Fac Advisor Awd, Phi Alpha Theta Int; Excellence in Teaching Awd, United Church of Christ Board for Homeland Ministries; Phil Beta Kappa; Phi Kappa Phi; Phi Alpha Theta. **MEMBERSHIPS** Am Hist Asn, Isle of Man Natural Hist and Antiquarian Soc, Am Soc for Eighteenth Century Studies, S E Council for Canadian Studies, Asn for Canadian Studies in the United States, Southern Confr on British Studies, N Am Confr on British Studies, Southern Hist Asn, Hist Soc of NC, NC Lit and Hist Asn. **RESEARCH** Eighteenth-century Southern Backcountry, Loyalist Settlements in Greater Nova Scotia, Loyalists and Loyalist Migration from Southern States, David Fanning, Sallie Stockard, Alamance County, North Carolina. **SELECTED PUBLICATIONS** Auth, "A Loyalist Life: John Bond of South Carolina and Nova Scotia," Acadiensis: J of the Hist of the Atlantic Region (90): 72-91; auth, "'The Great Man of the Settlement:' North Carolina's John Legett at Country Harbour, Nova Scotia, 1784-1812," NC Hist Rev (90); auth, "Community and Cohesion in the Rawdon Loyalist Settlement," Nova Scotia Hist Rev (92): 41-66; auth, "Hidden from History: Black Loyalists at Country Harbour, Nova Scotia," in Moving On: Black Loyalists in the Afro-Atlantic World, ed. John Pulis (99); auth, Shuttle & Plow: A History of Alamance County, North Carolina (99). **CONTACT ADDRESS** Dept Hist, Elon Col, Campus Box 2145, Elon College, NC 27244-2020. **EMAIL** carole.troxler@elon.edu

TROY, NANCY J.
DISCIPLINE MODERN ART **EDUCATION** Yale Univ, PhD. **CAREER** Prof, Univ Southern Calif; past ed-in-ch and bd mem, Art Bull; organizes, Getty Res Institute's Work in Progress lect ser. **RESEARCH** Relationship between art, theater & haute couture fashion in early 20th-century France & America. **SELECTED PUBLICATIONS** Co-ed, Architecture and Cubism, MIT Press, 97. **CONTACT ADDRESS** Col Letters, Arts & Sciences, Univ of So California, University Park Campus, Los Angeles, CA 90089.

TROY, VIRGINA GARDNER
PERSONAL Born Albuquerque, NM, m, 1990, 1 child **DISCIPLINE** ART HISTORY **EDUCATION** W Wa Univ, BA, 79; Univ Wa Seattle, MA, 86; Emory Univ, PhD, 97. **CAREER** Instr, 80-83, Bellevue Art Museum Sch; teaching asst, 84-86, Univ Wa; instr, 89-91, Brenau Univ; instr, 89-93, Art Inst Atlanta; instr, 89-93, Amer Col Applied Art; teaching asst to teaching assoc, 92-96, Emory Univ; adj faculty, 95-97, Atlanta Col Art; adj faculty, 97-98, N Ga Col & St Univ, Dahlonega; adj faculty, 89-98, Kennesaw St Univ Ga; asst prof, 98-, Berry Col. **HONORS AND AWARDS** Betty Park Awd, 96,98; Berry Col Overseas Summer Res Grant, 99. **MEMBERSHIPS** Col Art Assoc; SE Col Art Assoc; Hist Central & E Europ Art. **RESEARCH** Bauhaus; Anni Albers; Mary Hambidge. **SELECTED PUBLICATIONS** Auth, Anni Albers at Black Mountain College, Mid-Atlantic Col Art Conf, 98; art, Anni Albers and the Andean Textile Paradigm, Josef and Anni Albers: Europa und Amerika, Kunstmuseum Bern, 98; art, The Great Weaver of Eternity: Dynamic Symmetry and Utopian Ideology in the Art and Writing of Mary Hambidge, Surface Design J, 99. **CONTACT ADDRESS** PO Box 6083, Rome, GA 30162. **EMAIL** vtroy@berry.edu

TRUDEL, MARCEL
PERSONAL Born 05/29/1917, St-Narcisse de Champlain, Canada, m, 1970, 3 children **DISCIPLINE** HISTORY OF CANADA **EDUCATION** Seminaire des Trois-Rivieres, AB, 38; Laval Univ, BA, 38; Lic es Lettres, 41; Dr es Lettres, 45. **CAREER** Prof, Bourget Col, 41-45; postdoc res fel, Harvard Univ, 45-47; prof, Laval Univ, 47-65; dir, Inst of Hist and Geog, 54-55; dir, Inst of Hist, 55-64; prof, Carleton univ, 65-66; dir, Inst of Can Studs, 65-66; res prof, Univ of Ottawa, 66-82; dir, Hist Dept, Univ of Ottawa, 66-68. **HONORS AND AWARDS**

Fel, Royal Society of Can; Prix David, Govt of QC, 45, 51; Leo-Pariseau Medal, Asn Canadienne-Francaise pour l'Avancement des Scis, 60; Prix Casgrain, Laval Univ, 61; Prix Concours Litteraire du Quebec, Govt of QC, 63, 66; Tyrrell Medal, Can Hist Asn, 64; Prix Duvernay, Societe Saint-Jean-Baptiste, 66; Gov-Gen of Can Priz, 67; mem, Order of Can, 71; Molson Awd, Molson Co, 80. **MEMBERSHIPS** Inst Fr-Am Hist; Can Hist Asn (pres); Fr-Can Acad. **SELECTED PUBLICATIONS** Auth, Vezine, 46, 62; auth, L'Influence de Voltaire au Canada, 45; auth, Louis xvi, le Congres americain et le Canada (1774-1789), 76; auth Histoire de la Nouvelle-France, Fides, Vol I, 63, Vol II, 66, Vol III part 1, 80, Vol III part 2, 82, Vol IV, 97. **CONTACT ADDRESS** 5 Dollard, Aylmer, QC, Canada J9H 1G1.

TRUMBACH, RANDOLPH
PERSONAL Born 12/06/1944, Belize City, Belize **DISCIPLINE** ENGLISH & EUROPEAN HISTORY **EDUCATION** Univ New Orleans, BA, 64; Johns Hopkins Univ, MA, 66, Ph-D(hist), 72. **CAREER** Intern hist, Univ Chicago, 69-71; asst prof, 73-78, assoc prof hist, 78-84, prof, 85-, Baruch Col & CUNY Grad School, CUNY res awards, 73-74, 77-80, & 85-86; Nat Endowment Humanities fel, 79. **HONORS AND AWARDS** Baruch Col Distinguished Schol Awd, 79, 99. **MEMBERSHIPS** AHA; Am Soc 18th Century Studies; Soc Sci Hist Asn; Conf Brit Studies. **RESEARCH** 18th century English social history; the family, sex, religion. **SELECTED PUBLICATIONS** Auth, London's sodomites, J Social Hist, 9/77; The Rise of the Egalitarian Family, Acad Press, 78; Sex and the Gender Revolution Vol 1, Univ Chicago Press, 98. **CONTACT ADDRESS** Dept of History, Baruch Col, CUNY, 17 Lexington Ave, New York, NY 10010-5518. **EMAIL** randolph_trumbach@baruch.cuny.edu

TRUMPENER, ULRICH
PERSONAL Born 03/24/1930, Berlin, Germany, m, 1954, 3 children **DISCIPLINE** MODERN EUROPEAN HISTORY **EDUCATION** Univ Ore, BA, 54; Univ Calif, Berkeley, MA, 57, PhD(hist), 60. **CAREER** Instr hist, Stanford Univ, 60-61; asst prof, Univ Iowa, 61-66; from asst prof to assoc prof, 66-71, Prof Hist, Univ Alta, 71-, Can Coun fel, 70-71, res grant, 74. **MEMBERSHIPS** AHA; Conf Group Cent Europ Hist; Can Hist Asn. **RESEARCH** Modern German history; military history; international relations. **SELECTED PUBLICATIONS** Auth, Germany and the Ottoman Empire 1914-1918, Princeton Univ Pr, Princeton, NJ, 68; auth, "Junkers and Others: The Rise of Commoners in the Prussian Army, 1871-1914, Canadian J of Hist, 14, (79): 29-47. **CONTACT ADDRESS** Dept of Hist & Classics, Univ of Alberta, 2-28 Henry Marshall Tory Bldg, Edmonton, AB, Canada T6G 2H4.

TRUSS, RUTH SMITH
PERSONAL Born 04/21/1960, m, 1982, 1 child **DISCIPLINE** HISTORY **EDUCATION** Univ Ala, PhD, 92. **CAREER** ASST PROF HIST, UNIV MONTEVALLO, 98-. **MEMBERSHIPS** OAH: SHA, Ala Hist Asn; Ala Asn of Hist. **SELECTED PUBLICATIONS** Auth, "The Alabama Nationall Guard and the Protection of Prisoners," in The Alabama Review, 96; auth, "Progress Toward Professionalism: The Alabama National Guard on the Mexican Border, 1916-1917," in Millitary History of the West, (00). **CONTACT ADDRESS** Univ of Montevallo, Station 6180, Montevallo, AL 35115. **EMAIL** trussr@um.montevallo.edu

TRUSTY, NORMAN LANCE
PERSONAL Born 09/26/1933, Ancon, m, 1956, 2 children **DISCIPLINE** AMERICAN HISTORY **EDUCATION** Col William & Mary, AB, 56; Boston Univ, AM, 57, PhD, 64. **CAREER** Instr Hist, Ohio State Univ, 60-64; from asst prof to assoc prof, 64-77, chmn Dept Hist & Polit Sci, 67-74, prof Hist, Purdue Univ, Calumet Campus, 77-, dir, Regional Studies Inst, Purdue Univ, Calumet Campus. **HONORS AND AWARDS** Distinguished Teacher Ancon, Canal Zone; Alumni Teacher Awd, Panama. **MEMBERSHIPS** Orgn Am Historians. **RESEARCH** Antislavery: Revolutionary War; Northwest Indiana. **SELECTED PUBLICATIONS** Ed, Black America: A Bibliography, Purdue Univ, 76; auth, War by the book: the defense of Yorktown, IASS Proc, 77; contribr, Calumet region since 1930, In: The Calumet Region, Ind Hist Bur, 77. **CONTACT ADDRESS** Dept of History, Purdue Univ, Calumet, 2233 171st St, Hammond, IN 46323-2094. **EMAIL** trustyl@aol.com

TRUTTY-COOHILL, PATRICIA
PERSONAL Born 04/20/1940, Uniontown, PA, m, 1962, 3 children **DISCIPLINE** ART **EDUCATION** Univ Toronto, BA, 62; Penn State Univ, MA, 66; PhD, 82. **CAREER** Lecturer to Prof, West Ky Univ, 80-. **MEMBERSHIPS** Col Art Assoc, World Phenomenology Inst, Sixteenth Century Studies. **RESEARCH** Leonardo da Vinci. **SELECTED PUBLICATIONS** Auth, The Drawings of Leonardo da Vinci and His School in America, Florence, 93; auth, "Visualizing Tymieniecka's", Poetica Nova, 303-315. **CONTACT ADDRESS** Dept Art, Western Kentucky Univ, 1 Big Red Way St, Bowling Green, KY 42101-5730. **EMAIL** trutty@coohill.com

TSAI, SHIH-SHAN HENRY
PERSONAL Born 02/01/1940, Chia-yi, Taiwan, m, 2 children **DISCIPLINE** ASIAN STUDIES **EDUCATION** Nat Taiwan Normal Univ, BA, 62; Univ Ore, MA, 67, PhD, 70. **CAREER** Vis assoc prof, Nat Taiwan Univ, 70-71; vis assoc prof, Univ Calif, Los Angeles, 79; vis assoc prof, Univ Calif, Berkely, 81; PROF, DIR ASIAN STUDIES, UNIV ARK, 83-. **HONORS AND AWARDS** Ark Alumni Asn, Disinguished Achievement for Res and Teaching, Grant from Walton Family Charitable Foundation. **RESEARCH** Chinese Emigration, Ming Dynasty, Eunch Power in Imperial China. **SELECTED PUBLICATIONS** Auth, China and the Overseas Chinese in the United States, Univ of Arkansas Press, 83; auth, The Chinese Experience in America, Indiana Univ Press, 86; auth, The Eunuchs in the Ming Dynasty, SUNY, 96; auth, The Ming Emperor Yongle (1360-1424): A Biography, Univ of Washington Press, 00; auth, The Story of the Ming Eunuch Admiral Zheng He, Yaun-Liou Publishing, 01. **CONTACT ADDRESS** History Dept, Univ of Arkansas, Fayetteville, 505 Old Main, Fayetteville, AR 72703. **EMAIL** HTSAI@comp.uark.edu

TSEO, GEORGE
PERSONAL Born 09/28/1958, Utica, NY, m, 1992, 1 child **DISCIPLINE** GEOGRAPHY **EDUCATION** Penn State Univ, Bs, 80; Univ Adelaide, PhD, 87. **CAREER** Postdoc fel, Lan Inst, 88-89; prof, Pa State Univ, 89-. **RESEARCH** Enterprise privatization through employee ownership. **SELECTED PUBLICATIONS** Auth, The China Trade Manual Thompson Pub Gp (NY), 95; auth, "Employee empowerment: Solution to a burgeoning crisis?" Challenge Mag (95): 25-31; auth, "Jiang strengthens his political position, but threats still lurk," China Trade Bul 11 (95): 3-7; auth, "English-language directory of Chinese businesses now available," China Trade Bul 10 (95): 6-8; auth, "Reforming China's township and village enterprises: A feasibility study on the applicability of the Mondragon cooperative model," J Rur Coop, Israel 23(95): 31-65; auth, "Destabilization of the Chinese countryside and rural industrial development" J Contemp Asia 25 (95): 492-523; auth, "Chinese economic reform and employee ownership," J Emp Own Law Fin 7 (95): 159-191; auth, "Joy Luck: The perils of transcultural 'translation'," Film/Lit Quart 5 (96): 338-343; auth, "Employee ownership in Chinese rural industry and lessons from comparison to the Russian Case," J Rur Coop 26 (98): 97-118. **CONTACT ADDRESS** Dept Science, Pennsylvania State Univ, Hazleton, Hazleton, PA 18201. **EMAIL** gkt1@psu.edu

TSIN, MICHAEL
DISCIPLINE CHINESE HISTORY **EDUCATION** Univf Essex, BA, 82; Princeton Univ, PhD, 91. **CAREER** Asst prof. **RESEARCH** Cultural history of revolution in twentieth-century China. **SELECTED PUBLICATIONS** Auth, Imagining Society' in Early Twentieth-Century China, The Idea of the Citizen, 97; Nation, Governance and Modernity in Early Twentieth-Century China. **CONTACT ADDRESS** Dept of Hist, Columbia Col, New York, 2960 Broadway, New York, NY 10027-6902.

TSIRPANLIS, CONSTANTINE NICHOLAS
PERSONAL Born 03/18/1935, Cos, Greece **DISCIPLINE** HISTORY, PHILOSOPHY **EDUCATION** Greek Theol Sch Halki, Istanbul, Lic theol, 57; Harvard Univ, STM, 62; Columbia Univ, AM, 66; Fordham Univ, PhD(hist), 73. **CAREER** Instr mod Greek, NY Univ, 64-70; teacher classics and chmn dept, Collegiate Sch, NY, 67-69; instr mod Greek, New Sch Social Res, 68-70; res and writing, 70-72; adj prof world hist, NY Inst Technol, 72-75; Assoc Prof Church Hist and Greek Studies, Unification Theol Sem, 76-, Lectr class philol, Hunter Col, 66-67; lectr medieval and ancient hist, Mercy Col, 72; adj prof Western civilization, Delaware County Community Col, 75, Dutchess County Community Col, 76. **HONORS AND AWARDS** Nat Medal Greek Rebirth, Greek Govt, 72. **MEMBERSHIPS** NAm Acad Ecumenists; Am Soc Neo-Hellenic Studies (exec vpres, 67-69), Am Philol Asn, Medieval Acad Am; NAm Patristic Soc. **RESEARCH** Late Byzantine intellectual history and theology; early Byzantine theology and philosophy; Greek patristics. **SELECTED PUBLICATIONS** Auth, The Incarnation in St Athanasius' Thought, 63 & The Theology of History in Clement of Alexandria, 64, Athens; The imperial administration in John Lydus, Byzantinische Zeitschrift, Ger, 73; Mark Eugenicus and the Council of Florence, Salonica, 74; The Liturgical and Mystical Theology of N Cabasilas, Athens, 76; A Modern Greek Idiom and Phrase Book, Barrons, 78; Greek Patristic Theology, 79; Studies in Byzantine History, 80. **CONTACT ADDRESS** Unification Theol Sem, 10 Dock Rd, Barrytown, NY 12507.

TSUNODA, ELIZABETH
DISCIPLINE MODERN JAPAN **EDUCATION** Univ Ill, BA, 62, Columbia Univ, MA, 84, MPhil, 86; PhD, 93. **CAREER** Vis adj prof, NY Univ, 85-87; Vis adj prof, Smith Col, 87; Proeceptor, Columbia Univ, 91; Asst prof, Washington Univ, 93 **SELECTED PUBLICATIONS** Coed & contribr, Contemporary Japan: Teaching Workbook, Columbia Univ, 88; auth, Rationalizing Japan's Political Economy: The Business Community's Initiative, 1920-1945, (forthcoming). **CONTACT ADDRESS** Washington Univ, 1 Brookings Dr, Saint Louis, MO 63130. **EMAIL** etsunoda@artsci.wustl.edu

TSURUMI, E. PATRICIA
PERSONAL Born 02/19/1938, North Vancouver, BC, Canada **DISCIPLINE** JAPANESE HISTORY **EDUCATION** Univ BC, BA, 59; Tenri Univ, Nara Japan, cert Japanese lang, 61; Harvard Univ, AM, 66, PhD(hist and E Asian lang), 71. **CAREER** Asst prof hist, Univ Western Ont, 71-72; asst prof, 72-77, Assoc Prof Hist, Univ Victoria, 77-, Res assoc Japanese hist, EAsian Res Ctr, Harvard Univ, 74-75; Can Coun leave fel, 74-75; Japan Soc Prom Sci fel, 79; Soc Sci and Humanities Res Coun Can leave fel, 79-80. **HONORS AND AWARDS** Kyoto Nat Essay Prize foreign scholars, Int Cult Asn, Japan, 79. **MEMBERSHIPS** Can Soc Asian Studies; Comp and Int Educ Soc Can; Asn Asian Studies; BC Women's Studies Asn; Anarcho Inst. **RESEARCH** Japanese colonialism; Japanese education; history of Japanese women in a comparative focus. **SELECTED PUBLICATIONS** Ed, The Other Japan: Postwar Realities, M.E. Sharpe, Armonk, NY, 88; auth, Factory Girls: Women in The Thread Mills of Meiji Japan, Princeton Univ Pr, Princeton, NJ, 92. **CONTACT ADDRESS** Dept of Women's Stud, Univ of Victoria, PO Box 3045, Stn CSC, Victoria, BC, Canada V8W 3P4.

TU, CHING-I
PERSONAL Born 05/13/1935, Nanking, China, m, 1970, 2 children **DISCIPLINE** CHINESE LITERATURE, CHINESE HISTORY **EDUCATION** Nat Taiwan Univ, BA, 58; Univ Wash, PhD, 67. **CAREER** Asst prof to assoc prof to prof to chemn, 66-, Rutgers Univ; vis assoc prof, Univ Hawaii, 71-72; vis prof, Nat Taiwan Univ, 74-75. **HONORS AND AWARDS** Res grant, US Dept Educ; res grant, Chiang Ching-Kuo Found; grants, Korean Found; found dir, chinese prog, found chair, dept e asian lang and cultures, rutgers univ. **MEMBERSHIPS** Asn Asian Stud; Am Asn Chinese Stud; MLA. **RESEARCH** Chinese literary criticism; Chinese intellectual history; cultural changes in Asia. **SELECTED PUBLICATIONS** Auth, Anthology of Chinese Literature, 72-; auth, Readings in Classical Chinese Literature, 81; auth, Tradition and Creativity: Essays on East Asian Civilization, 88; auth, Essays on East Asian Humanities; 91; auth, Classics and Interpretations: The Hermeneutic Traditions in Chinese Culture, 00. **CONTACT ADDRESS** Dept of Asian Lang and Cultures, Rutgers, The State Univ of New Jersey, New Brunswick, New Brunswick, NJ 08903. **EMAIL** citu@rci.rutgers.edu

TU, WEI-MING
PERSONAL Born 02/26/1940, Kunming, China, m, 1963, 1 child **DISCIPLINE** HISTORY, RELIGIOUS PHILOSOPHY **EDUCATION** Tunghai Univ, Taiwan, BA, 61; Harvard Univ, MA, 63, PhD(hist), 68. **CAREER** Vis lectr humanities, Tunghai Univ, Taiwan, 66-67; lectr EAsian studies, Princeton Univ, 67-68, asst prof, 68-71; from asst prof to assoc prof hist, Univ Calif, Berkeley, 71-77, prof, 77-81; Prof Chinese Hist and Philos, Harvard Univ, 81-, Consult-panelist, Nat Endowment for Humanities, 75; Am Coun Learned Soc fel, 77; mem bd dirs, Chinese Cult Found San Francisco, 79- **MEMBERSHIPS** Asn Asian Studies; Soc Asian and Comp Philos; Am Acad Polit Sci. **RESEARCH** Chinese intellectual history; Confucianism in East Asia; religious philosophy. **SELECTED PUBLICATIONS** Auth, Introduction--Cultural Perspectives, Daedalus, Vol 0122, 93; Destructive Will and Ideological Holocaust--Maoism as a Source of Social Suffering in China, Daedalus, Vol 0125, 96. **CONTACT ADDRESS** Dept of EAsian Lang and Civilizations, Harvard Univ, Cambridge, MA 02138.

TUCK, DONALD RICHARD
PERSONAL Born 04/24/1935, Albany, NY, m, 1957, 2 children **DISCIPLINE** HISTORY OF RELIGIONS, ASIAN STUDIES **EDUCATION** Nyack Col, BS, 57; Wheaton Col, MA, 65; Univ Iowa, PhD(relig and cult), 70. **CAREER** Minister of youth, Presby Church, Ill, 63-65; interim minister, Methodist Church, Fed Church and United Church of Christ, Iowa, 65-69; teaching and res asst, Sch Relig, Univ Iowa, 67-68; from instr to assoc prof relig, 69-78, PROF RELIG, WESTERN KY UNIV, 78-, Fac res grant, Radhakrishnan and Tagore, 70; fac res grant, Tagore, 72; consult, Choice, 76-, Nat Endowment Humanities, 77- and South Asia in Rev, 78-; fac res grant, Santal Relig, 76 and soc aspects, Bhagavata, Purana, 78. **MEMBERSHIPS** Am Acad Relig; Asn Asian Studies. **RESEARCH** Religion and culture of Modern India; Sarvepalli Radhakrishnan and Rabindranath Tagore; Bengal Vaisnavism-Caitanya. **SELECTED PUBLICATIONS** Auth, Lacuna in Sankara Studies--A Thousand Teachings Upadesasahasri, Asian Philos, Vol 0006, 96. **CONTACT ADDRESS** Dept of Relig and Philos, Western Kentucky Univ, 1 Big Red Way St, Bowling Green, KY 42101-3576.

TUCKER, BRUCE
DISCIPLINE HISTORY **EDUCATION** Univ Toronto, BA, 70, MA, 72; Brown Univ, PhD, 79. **CAREER** Assoc prof and dept ch; taught at, Dalhousie Univ; Univ Cincinnati and Univ Windsor; assoc ed, Can Rev of Amer Stud. **MEMBERSHIPS** Pres, Can Assn for Amer Stud. **RESEARCH** American cultural and intellectual history; urban history and historiography. **SELECTED PUBLICATIONS** Auth, Beyond Synthesis: The Problem of Coherence in American History, Can Rev Amer Stud 26, 96; The New American Intellectual History: A Review Essay, Can Rev Amer Stud, vol 22, 91; Oral History: An Inter-

view with Virginia Rock, Can Rev Amer Hist 27, 97; The Politics of Culture in Provincial New England, Reviews in Amer Hist 25, 97;Oral History: An Interview with Robert Martin, Can Rev Amer Stud 26, 96; Oral History: An Interview with Bruce Daniels, Can Rev Amer Stud 25, 95 & Assessing the Field: An Oral History Interview, Can Rev Amer Stud 23, 92; coauth, Changing Plans for America's Inner Cities: Cincinnati's Over-the-Rhine and Twentieth-Century Urbanism, Ohio UP, 98; contrib, Roscoe Giffin and the First Cincinnati Workshop on Urban Appalachians, in Phillip Obermiller, Down Home, Downtown: Urban Appalachians Today, Dubuque, Iowa: Kendall/Hunt, 96; Michael T. Maloney, rep in Interviewing Appalachia, Knoxville: U of Tennessee P, 94 & Towards a New Ethnicity: Urban Appalachian Ethnic Consciousness in Cincinnati, 1950-1987, Ethnic Diversity and Civic Identity: Patterns of Conflict and Cohesion in Cincinnati Since the Nineteenth Century, Chicago and Urbana: U of Illinois P, 92. **CONTACT ADDRESS** Hist Dept, Univ of Windsor, 401 Sunset Ave, Windsor, ON, Canada N9B 3P4. **EMAIL** TUCKER1@uwindsor.ca

TUCKER, DAVID MILTON

PERSONAL Born 11/28/1937, Pottsville, AR, m, 1966, 2 children **DISCIPLINE** AMERICAN HISTORY **EDUCATION** Col Ozarks, BA, 59; OK State Univ, MA, 61; Univ IA, PhD(hist), 65. **CAREER** PROF HIST, MEMPHIS STATE UNIV, 65-. **MEMBERSHIPS** Orgn Am Historians; Am Hist Asn. **RESEARCH** Recent American history; African American history. **SELECTED PUBLICATIONS** Auth, Justice Horace Harmon Lurton: the Shaping of a National Progressive, Am J Legal Hist, 7/69; Black pride and Negro business in the 1920's, Bus Hist Rev, winter 69; Lieutenant Lee of Beale Street, Vanderbilt Univ, 71; Black Pastors and Leaders, Memphis State Univ, 75; Memphis Since Crump: Bossism, Blacks and Civic Reformers, Univ TN, 81; Arkansas: A People, Memphis State, 85; Decline of Thrift in America, Praeger, 90; Kitchen Gardening in America, IA State, 93; Mugwumps: Public Moralists of the Gilded Age, MO, 98. **CONTACT ADDRESS** Dept of Hist, Univ of Memphis, Memphis, TN 38152-6120. **EMAIL** dtucker@cc.memphis.edu

TUCKER, LOUIS LEONARD

PERSONAL Born 12/06/1927, Rockville, CT, m, 1953, 2 children **DISCIPLINE** EARLY AMERICAN HISTORY **EDUCATION** Univ Wash, BA, 52, MA, 55, PhD, 57. **CAREER** Instr hist, Univ Calif, Davis, 57-58; instr, Col William and Mary, 58-60; dir, Cincinnati Hist Soc, 60-66; asst comnr state hist and state historian, State Educ Dept NY, 66-76; Dir, Mass Hist Soc, Boston, 77-, Fel hist, Inst Early Am Hist and Cult, Williamsburg, Va, 58-60; lectr, Univ Cincinnati, 60-65; Churchill fel, English Speaking Union, 69; adj prof, Boston Univ, 77-; Nat Archiv Adv Coun, 77-; Emeritus Dir, MA History Society, 98. **MEMBERSHIPS** Am Asn State and Local Hist (pres, 72-74). **RESEARCH** Colonial American and New York State history. **SELECTED PUBLICATIONS** Auth, The New-York-Historical-Society--Lessons from One Nonprofits Long Struggle for Survival, NY Hist, Vol 0077, 96. **CONTACT ADDRESS** 328 Harvard St, No 2, Cambridge, MA 02139.

TUCKER, MARK

PERSONAL Born 10/25/1945, Natchez, MS, m, 1968 **DISCIPLINE** LIBRARY AND INFORMATION SCIENCE, HISTORY **EDUCATION** Lipscomb Univ, BA, 67; George Peabody Col Teach, Vanderbilt Univ, MLS, 68, EdS, 72; Univ Ill, Urbana-Champaign, PhD, 83. **CAREER** Head Librarian, Fred-Hardeman Univ, 68-71; ref librn, Wabash Col, 73-79; ref librn, Purdue Univ, 79-82; asst prof, libr sci, Purdue Univ, 79-85; sen ref librn, Purdue Univ, 82-90; assoc prof, libr sci, Purdue Univ, 85-89; PROF, LIBR SCI, 89-, HUM, SOC SCI, EDUC LIBRN, 90-, PURDUE UNIV. **HONORS AND AWARDS** Council on Library Resources Research Fellow, 90; Frederick B. Artz Research Grantee, Oberlin College Archives, 91; Grantee Committee on Institutional Cooperation, NEH, 91-94. **MEMBERSHIPS** American Library Asn; Sons of Confederate Veterans; Asn for the Bibliography of History; Asn of College and Research libraries; Disciples of Christ Historical Society; Society for Historians of the Guilded Age and Progressive Era; Southern Historical Asn; Friends of the Univ of Illinois Library; Phi Kappa Phi, Beta Phi Mu. **RESEARCH** Hist, biog, related to librarianship and higher educ. **SELECTED PUBLICATIONS** Auth, Sabin, Joseph (6 Dec 1821-5 June 1991), Am Nat Biography, 18: 168-69, Oxford Univ Press, 99; auth, Work, Monroe Nathan (1866-1945), in Notable Black American Men, 1262-66, Gale Research, 98; auth, Editor Untold Stories: Civil Rights, Libraries, and Black Librarianship, 98; auth, Wide Awakening: Political and Theological Impulses for Reading and Libraries at Oberlin College, 1883-1908, Univ Ill Occasional Papers, 207, 97; co-auth, Change and Tradition in Land Grant University Libraries, in For the Good of the Order: Essays Written in Honor of Edward G. Holley, JAI Press, 94; auth, American Library History: A Comprehensive Guide to the Literature, 89; auth, User Instruction in Academic Libraries: A Century of Selected Readings, 86; auth, co-ed, Reference Services and Library Education: Essays in Honor of Frances Neel Cheney, 83. **CONTACT ADDRESS** Hum, Soc Sci & Educ Libr, Purdue Univ, West Lafayette, Stewart Ctr, West Lafayette, IN 47907. **EMAIL** jmark@purdue.edu

TUCKER, MARY EVELYN

PERSONAL Born 06/24/1949, New York, NY, m, 1978 **DISCIPLINE** RELIGION, HISTORY **EDUCATION** Trinity Col, BA, 71; SUNY, Fredonia, MA, 72; Fordham Univ, MA, 77; Columbia Univ, PhD, 85. **CAREER** Lectr, Eng, Erie Commun Col, 72; lectr Eng, Notre Dame Seishin Univ, Japan, 73-75; lectr relig, Elizabeth Seton Col, 76-78; preceptor, Columbia Univ, 79-80, 83; asst prof hist, Iona Col, 84-89; assoc prof relig, Bucknell Univ, 89-98; prof religion, Bucknell Univ, 99- . **HONORS AND AWARDS** Phi Beta Kappa; HEW fel, 71-72; NEH fel, 77; Columbia Pres fel, 80-81, 81-82; Japan Found fel, 83-84; Mellon fel, 85-86; Columbia Univ postdoctoral res fel, 87-88; Person of the Year Awd, Bucknellian, 92; NEH Chair in the Hum, 93-96; sr fel, Center for the Study of World Relig, Harvard Univ, 95-96; Trinity Col Centennial Alumnae Awd for Academic Excellence, 97; assoc in res, Reischaur Inst of Japanese Stud, Harvard Univ, 95-00. **MEMBERSHIPS** Neo-Confucian Stud, Columbia Univ. Regional Sem on Japan, Columbia Univ; Am Teilhard Asn; Environ Sabbath, UN Environ Prog; AAR; Asn Asian Stud; Soc for Values in Higher Educ; Asn for Relig and Intellectual Life. **SELECTED PUBLICATIONS** Auth, Moral and Spiritual Cultivation in Japanese Neo-Confucianism: The Life and Thought of Kaibara Ekken (1630-1714), SUNY, 89; co-ed, Worldviews and Ecology, Bucknell Univ, 93; co-ed, Buddhism and Ecology: The Interaction of Dharma and Deeds, Harvard Univ, 97; co-ed, Confucianism and Ecology: The Interrelation of Heaven, Earth, and Humans, Harvard Univ, 98; Hinduism and Ecology:The Intersection of Earth, Sky, and Water, Harvard Univ, 99. **CONTACT ADDRESS** Dept of Religion, Bucknell Univ, Lewisburg, PA 17837. **EMAIL** mtucker@bucknell.edu

TUCKER, MELVIN JAY

PERSONAL Born 03/03/1931, Easthampton, MA, m, 1953, 3 children **DISCIPLINE** HISTORY **EDUCATION** Univ Mass, BA, 53, MA, 54; Northwestern Univ, PhD, 62. **CAREER** Instr, Colby Col, 59-60; instr, MIT, 60-63; dir of grad studies, SUNY at Buffalo, 79-85; from asst to assoc prof, SUNY at Buffalo, 63- . **HONORS AND AWARDS** Certificate of Merit, Buffalo and Erie Co Hist Soc, 74. **MEMBERSHIPS** ABH; AHA: Alpha Phi Theta; Conf of Brit Studies. **RESEARCH** Meditation; prayer in late medieval, early modern hist; John Skelton. **SELECTED PUBLICATIONS** Auth, The Life of Thomas Howard, Earl of Surrey and Second Duke of Norfolk, 1433-1524, Moulton & Co (The Hague), 64; auth, "The Child as Beginning and End: 15th and 16the Centruy English Childhood, in The History of Childhood, NY, ed Lloyd de Mause, PschoHistory Pr, 74; coauth, Centering: Your Guide to Inner Growth, Warner Destiny (NY), 78; coauth, "Historians and Using Tomorrow's Research Libraries: Research Teaching and Training," History Teacher 17 (May 84): 385-444; auth, "Joel Hurstfield: Historian for All Seasons," in Recent Historians of Great Britain: Essays on the Post 1945 Generation, ed Walter Arnstein (Ames, IA: Iowa State Univ Pr, 90), 37-56. **CONTACT ADDRESS** 107 Willow Green Dr, Tonawanda, NY 14228. **EMAIL** mjtucker@acsu.buffalo.edu

TUCKER, NANCY BERNKOPF

PERSONAL Born New York, NY, m **DISCIPLINE** HISTORY **EDUCATION** Hobart & William Smith Col, BA, 70; Columbia Univ, MA, 73, MAPhil, 76, PhD, 80. **CAREER** Asst Prof, 80-86, assoc prof, 86-87, Colgate Univ; assoc prof, 87-94, prof, 94-, Georgetown Univ. **RESEARCH** Amer foreign rel; Amer East Asian rel, esp rels with China, Taiwan, Hong Kong & Korea. **CONTACT ADDRESS** Dept of History, Georgetown Univ, Washington, DC 20057-1058. **EMAIL** tuckern@gerogetown.edu

TUCKER, RICHARD PHILIP

PERSONAL Born 09/17/1938, Morristown, NJ **DISCIPLINE** MODERN ASIAN HISTORY **EDUCATION** Oberlin Col, AB, 60; Harvard Univ, MA, 61, PhD(hist), 66. **CAREER** Asst prof, 66-72, assoc prof, 72-82, Prof Hist, Oakland Univ, 82-, Mem bd trustees, Am Inst Indian Studies, 68-71 and 76-83, fac fel, 69-70 and 80-82; Am Coun Learned Soc res grant, 69-70; mem, Nat Humanities Fac, 71-74, chmn, Maharashtra Study Group, 71-73. **MEMBERSHIPS** Asn Asian Studies; Soc Relig Higher Educ; Am Asn Advan Sci; Am Soc Environmental Hist; Forest Hist Soc. **RESEARCH** South Asian and comparative environmental history. **SELECTED PUBLICATIONS** Auth, The proper limits of agitation: The crisis of 1879-80 in Bombay presidency, J Asian Studies, 2/69; The redefinition of orthodoxy in Maharashtra, 1830-57, Maratha Hist Sem Papers, 70; From Dharmashastra to politics, Indian Econ & Social Hist Rev, 9/70; Ranadc and thc Roots of Indian Nationalism, Univ Chicago, 72; Hindu traditionalism and nationalist ideologies in nineteenth-century Maharashtra, Mod Asian Studies, 76; ed, International Economy and Forest Use in Nineteenth Century, Duke Univ Press, 82. **CONTACT ADDRESS** Dept of Hist, Oakland Univ, Rochester, MI 48063.

TUCKER, SPENCER C.

DISCIPLINE HISTORY **EDUCATION** Va Mil Inst, BA, 59; Univ NC, hapel Hill, MA, 62; PhD, 66. **CAREER** John Biggs ch Mil Hist, Va Mil Inst, 97-; Fulbright fel, Univ Bordeaux, 59-60; capt, Army Intel, 65-67; prof, Tex Christian Univ, 67-97, ch hist dept, 92-97; vis res assoc, Smithsonian Inst, 69-70. **SELECTED PUBLICATIONS** Auth, Arming the Fleet: US Naval Ordnance in the Muzzle-Loading Era, Naval Inst Press, 89; The Jeffersonian Gunboat Navy, Univ SC Press, 93; Raphael Semmes and the Alabama, Ryan Place, 96; coauth, Injured Honor: The Chesapeake-Leopard Affair of June 22, 1807, Naval Inst Press, 96; The Great War, 1914-18, Univ Col London Press, 98; The Big Guns, Civil War Siege, Seacoast and Naval Cannon, Mus Restoration Serv, 98; ed, The European Powers in the First World War, An Encycl, Garland, 96; ed, Encyclopedia of the Vietnam War, 3 vols, ABC-CLIO, 98; auth, Vietnam, Univ Pr of Kentucky, 99; ed, Encyclopedia of the Vietnam War, Oxford Univ Pr, 00; auth, Andrew H. Foore, Civil War Admiral on Western Waters, Naval Institute Pr, 00; ed, Encyclopedia of the Korean War, 3 vol, ABC-CLIO, 00; auth, Handbook of Nineteenth-Century Naval Warfare, Naval Institute Pr, 00. **CONTACT ADDRESS** Dept of History, Virginia Military Inst, Lexington, VA 24450. **EMAIL** tuchersc@vmi.edu

TUCKER, WILLIAM E.

PERSONAL Born 06/22/1932, Charlotte, NC, m, 1955, 3 children **DISCIPLINE** AMERICAN RELIGIOUS & CHURCH HISTORY **EDUCATION** Atlantic Christian Col, BA, 53, LLD, 78; Tex Christian Univ, BD, 56; Yale Univ, MA, 58, PhD(relig), 60. **CAREER** From assoc prof to prof relig & philos, Atlantic Christian Col, 59-66, chmn dept, 62-66; assoc prof church hist & asst dean, Brite Divinity Sch, Tex Christian Univ, 66-69, prof church hist, 69-76, assoc dean, 69-71, dean, 71-76; pres, Bethany Col, 76-79; chancellor, Tex Christian Univ, 79-98, trustee, Disciples of Christ Hist Soc, 69-; mem bd, Christian Church (Disciples of Christ), 71-, dir bd higher educ, 73-, chmn bd, 75-77; pres, Coun Southwestern Theol Schs, 75-76; vpres, WVa Found Independent Cols, 77-. **HONORS AND AWARDS** LLD, Atlantic Christian Col, 78; DHL, Chapman Col, 81; DHu, Bethany Col, 82. **RESEARCH** American church history since 1865; history and thought of the Christian Church (Disciples of Christ) and related religious groups; Fundamentalism and the Church in America. **SELECTED PUBLICATIONS** Auth, J H Garrison and Disciples of Christ, Bethany, 64; contribr, The Word We Preach, Tex Christian Univ, 70; Westminster Dictionary of Church History, Westminster, 71; Dictionary of American Biography, suppl 3, Scribner's, 73; coauth, Journey in Faith: A History of the Christian Church (Disciples of Christ), Bethany, 75; contribr, Encycl of Southern History, La State Univ Press, 79. **CONTACT ADDRESS** Chancellor Emeritus, 100 Throckmorton St, Ste 416, Fort Worth, TX 76102-2870. **EMAIL** w.tucker@tcu.edu

TUCKER, WILLIAM F.

PERSONAL Born 04/27/1941, Whiteville, NC, m, 1967, 1 child **DISCIPLINE** HISTORY **EDUCATION** Univ NC Chapel Hill, AB, 64; Ind Univ, MA, 66, PhD, 71. **CAREER** Asst prof to assoc prof, 71-99, Univ Ark; assoc prof, 00-. **HONORS AND AWARDS** Fulbright-Hayes Faculty Res Abroad, 74-75; dean's list. **MEMBERSHIPS** Middle East Stud Asn; Middle East Medievalists. **RESEARCH** Shiite Islam; ecological & soc hist; pre-modern Islamic world. **SELECTED PUBLICATIONS** Auth, Ibn Battuta, Abu Abd Allah Muhammad (1304-1377), Arab Traveler, The Discoverers: an Encyclopedia of Explorers and Exploration, McGraw Hill Co, 80; art, Abd Allah ibn Mauwiya and the Janahiyya: Rebels and Ideologues of the Late Umayyad Period, Studia Islamica, 80; contr, Charismatic Leadership and Shiite Sectarianism, Middle East and Islamic societies, Amana Books, 87; contr, The Emergence of Kurdish Nationalism and the Sheikh Said Rebellion, 1880-1925, Univ Tx Press, 89; art, Environmental Hazards, Natural Disasters, Economic Loss and Mortality in Mamiuk Syria, Mamluk Stud Rev, 99. **CONTACT ADDRESS** 108 Hartman Ave, Fayetteville, AR 72701. **EMAIL** wtucker@comp.uark.edu

TULCHINSKY, GERALD J. J.

PERSONAL Born 09/09/1933, Brantford, ON, Canada **DISCIPLINE** HISTORY **EDUCATION** Univ Toronto, BA, 57; McGill Univ, MA, 60; Univ Toronto, PhD, 71. **CAREER** Lectr, Loyola Col (Montreal), 60-62; asst prof, Univ Sask, 65-66; asst prof, 66-73, assoc prof, 73-83, Prof History, Queen's Univ, 83-. **SELECTED PUBLICATIONS** Auth, River Barons: Montreal Business Men and Development of Industry and Transportation 1837-1953, 77; auth, Taking Root: The Origins of the Canadian Jewish Community, 92; ed, Immigration in Canada; To Preserve and Defend; contribur, Dictionary of Canadian Biography; contribur, Canadian Encyclopedia; auth, Branching Out: the Transformation of the Canadian Jewish Community was published by Stoddart in November, 98. **CONTACT ADDRESS** Dept of History, Queen's Univ at Kingston, Kingston, ON, Canada K7L 3N6. **EMAIL** tulchins@post.queensu.ca

TULL, CHARLES JOSEPH

PERSONAL Born 08/28/1931, Runnemede, NJ, m, 1953, 6 children **DISCIPLINE** UNITED STATES HISTORY **EDUCATION** Creighton Univ, BS, 55; Univ Notre Dame, MA, 57, PhD(hist), 62. **CAREER** Instr hist, St Vincent Col, 59-61; asst prof, DePaul Univ, 61-65; assoc prof US hist, 66-71, chmn dept hist, 68-70, Prof Hist, Ind Univ, South Bend, 71-, Vis assoc prof, Univ Notre Dame, 65-66, 67-68. **MEMBERSHIPS** Oral Hist Asn; AHA; Am Cath Hist Asn; Orgn Am Historians;

Southern Hist Asn. **RESEARCH** Recent United States political and diplomatic history, Vietnam War **SELECTED PUBLICATIONS** Auth, The Coughlin-Fahey Connection--Coughlin, Charles,E., Fahey,Denis, Cssp, and Religious Anti-Semitism in the United-States, 1938-1954, Cath Hist Rev, Vol 0079, 93. **CONTACT ADDRESS** 118 Wakewa Ave, South Bend, IN 46617.

TULL, HERMAN
PERSONAL Born 10/27/1955, Philadelphia, PA, m, 1978, 2 children **DISCIPLINE** HISTORY AND LITERATURE OF RELIGIONS **EDUCATION** Hobart Col, BA, 78; Northwestern Univ, PhD, 85. **CAREER** Asst prof, Rutgers Univ; lectr, Princeton Univ. **HONORS AND AWARDS** Univ fel, Northwestern Univ; Getty Postdoctoral fel. **RESEARCH** Vedic ritual; Gnomic literature in Sanskrit. **SELECTED PUBLICATIONS** Auth, Hinduism, Harper's Dictionary of Religious Education, 90; auth, F. Max Muller and A.B. Keith: 'Twaddle,' the 'Stupid' Myth, and the Disease of Indology, NUMEN, 91; auth, The Tale of 'The Bride and the Monkey': Female Insatiability, Male Impotence, and Simian Virility in Indian Literature, J Hist of Sexuality, 93; auth, The Killing That Is Not Killing: Men, Cattle, and the Origins of Non-Violence (ahimsa) in the Vedic Sacrifice, Indo-Iranian J, 96; auth, The Veduic Origins of Karma: Cosmos as Man in Ancient Indian Myth and Ritual. **CONTACT ADDRESS** 228 Terhune Rd., Princeton, NJ 08540. **EMAIL** hwtull@msn.com

TULLOS, ALLEN E.
DISCIPLINE HISTORY **EDUCATION** Univ Ala, BA, 72; Univ NC, MA, 76; Yale Univ, MA, 79, PhD, 85. **CAREER** Affl prof dept hist/Grad Inst Lib Arts. **HONORS AND AWARDS** Charles S. Syndor Prize, So Hist Assn; coprod, A Singing Stream: Chronicle of a Black Family; Best Indep Prod, Corp Pub Broadcasting. **RESEARCH** US popular culture; American regional cultures; 19th- and 20th-century Southern studies, history and film; geography and justice in the Black Belt region of the American South since the civil rights movement. **SELECTED PUBLICATIONS** Auth, Habits of Industry: White Culture and the Transformation of the Carolina Piedmont; **CONTACT ADDRESS** Dept History, Emory Univ, 221 Bowden Hall, 561 Kilgo Cir, Atlanta, GA 30322-1950. **EMAIL** ilaat@emory.edu

TUMASONIS, ELIZABETH
PERSONAL Born Charleston, WV **DISCIPLINE** ART HISTORY **EDUCATION** Col William & Mary, BA, 63; New York Univ, MA, 67; Univ Calif Berkley, PhD, 79. **CAREER** Instr, Univ Missouri, 66-67; instr, DePauw Univ, 67-69; tchg assoc, Univ Calif Berkeley, 69-72; instr, Univ S Calif, 73-75; prof, Calif State Univ, 78-81; asst prof, 81-91, ch, 91-94, Adjunct Prof, Hist Art, Univ Victoria, 91-. **HONORS AND AWARDS** Awd Excellence Tchg, Univ Victoria Alumni, 89; Tchg Fel, 3M, 92. **MEMBERSHIPS** Univ Art Asn Can; German Studs Asn; Victoria Horticultural Soc. **SELECTED PUBLICATIONS** Auth, The Image of the Centaur in the Painting of Arnold Bocklin, in New Mexico Studs Fine Arts, 78; auth, The Piper Among the Ruins: The Image of the God Pan in the Painting of Arnold Bocklin, in RACAR: The Can Art Rev, 91; auth, Max Klinger's Christ on Olympus: The Confrontation between Christianity and Paganism, in RACAR: The Can Art Rev, 95. **CONTACT ADDRESS** Dept of History in Art, Univ of Victoria, PO Box 1700 STN CSC, Victoria, BC, Canada V8W 2Y2. **EMAIL** dpouliot@finearts.uvic.ca

TURK, ELEANOR L.
PERSONAL Born 09/09/1935, Charlottesville, VA, d, 1958, 1 child **DISCIPLINE** HISTORY **EDUCATION** Oh Wesleyan Col, BA, 57; Univ Ill, Urbana, MA, 70; Univ Wis, Madison, PhD, 75. **CAREER** Asst Dean, Col of Liberal Arts and Scis, Univ Kans, 77-78; Asst Dean, Sch of Humanities and Scis, Ithaca Col, 78-83; assoc prof, Indiana Univ East, Richmond, 83-90, prof, 90-. **HONORS AND AWARDS** Phi Beta Kappa; Phi Alpha Theta; Pi Sigma Alpha; Alpha Sigma Lambda; Who's Who in Educ; Res Travel Fel, Germany, 73; Indiana Univ East Fac Prof Develop Fund Grant, 84; NEH Travel Grant, 85; Indiana Univ East Chancellor's "Gold Star" Awd for Excellence, for North Central Self-Study Report, May 92; Participant: Fulbright Sommer Sem: Deutsche Landeskunde, 92; Indiana Univ East Teaching Excellence Recognition Awd, 99; Indiana Univ East Certificate of Recognition, Martin Luther King Multicultural and Diversity Awd, 2000; Indiana Univ East Summer Fac fel, 2000. **MEMBERSHIPS** Am Asn of Univ Profs; Central European Caucus, Am Hist Soc; Asn for German Studies; Soc for German-Am Studies; World Hist. **SELECTED PUBLICATIONS** Auth, "Charles V (1500-1558)," in Frank W. Thackeray and John E. Findling, eds, Statesmen Who Have Changed the World: A Bio-Bibliographical Dictionary of Diplomacy, Greenwood Press (93): 120-128; auth, "Charles V" and "Wilhelm II," in Arnold Blumberg, ed Great Leaders, Great Tyrants: Contemporary Views of World Rulers Who Have Made History, Greenwood Press (95): 45-51, 327-333; auth, "The United States, Germany, and the Future of Europe: Designing Overseas Study for Commuter Students," Proceedings: 13th International Conference of the International Coun for Innovation in Higher Education--Global Inter-Networking and Higher Education (Oct 95); auth, "The Unification of Germany, 1871," in Frank W. Thackeray and John E. Findling, eds, Events That Changed the World in the Nineteenth Century, Greenwood Press (96): 139-150; auth, "The United States, Germany, and the Future of Europe: Designing Overseas Study for Commuter Students," Int J of Innovative Higher Educ, Vol 12 (96): 119-28; auth, "Prince Henry's Royal Welcome: German-American Response to the Visit of the Kaiser's Brother, 1902," Yearbook of German-American Studies, Vol 34 (99); auth, The History of Modern Germany, Westport, Ct: Greenwood Pub Co (99). **CONTACT ADDRESS** Dept Humanities and Fine Arts, Indiana Univ, East, Richmond, IN 47374. **EMAIL** eturk@indiana.edu

TURK, RICHARD WELLINGTON
PERSONAL Born 02/10/1938, Ann Arbor, MI, m, 1963, 2 children **DISCIPLINE** AMERICAN NAVAL AND DIPLOMATIC HISTORY **EDUCATION** Albion Col, BA, 60; Fletcher Sch Law, MA, 61, MALD, 62, PhD(int affairs), 68. **CAREER** Asst prof, 68-76, assoc prof, 76-80, Prof Hist, Allegheny Col, 80-. **MEMBERSHIPS** AHA; Soc Historians Am Foreign Rels. **RESEARCH** American Naval Nistory, 1865-1914. **SELECTED PUBLICATIONS** Auth, The Ambiguous Relationship, Greenwood, 1987. **CONTACT ADDRESS** Dept of Hist, Allegheny Col, 520 N Main St, Meadville, PA 16335-3902. **EMAIL** rturk@alleg.edu

TURNER, B. L., II
PERSONAL Born 12/22/1945, Texas City, TX, m, 1968, 2 children **DISCIPLINE** GEOGRAPHY **EDUCATION** Univ Tex, Austin, BA, 68, MA, 69; Univ Wisc, Madison, PhD, 74. **CAREER** Asst prof, Univ Md, Baltimore, 74-76; res assoc, Univ Okla, 75-76, asst prof, 76-79; asst prof, Clark Univ, 80-81, assoc prof, 81-85, prof, 85-, Dir, Grad Sch of Geog, 83-88 & 97-98, Milton P. and Alice C. Higgins Prof of Environment and Soc, 96-. **HONORS AND AWARDS** John Simon Guggenheim Mem Fel, 81-82; Carl O. Sauer Distinguished Scholar Awd, Conference of Latin Am Geogrs, 87; Fel, Ctr for Advanced Study in the Behav Scis, Stanford, Calif, 94-95; Distinguished Res Honors, Asn of Am Geogrs, 95; Nat Acad of Scis, 95-; Centenary Medal, Royal Scottish Geog Soc, 96; Am Acad of Arts and Scis, 98-. **MEMBERSHIPS** Asn of Am Geogrs, Soc for Am Archaeol, Am Asn for the Advan of Sci, Conference of Latin Am Geogrs. **RESEARCH** Nature-society relationships, land-use change. **SELECTED PUBLICATIONS** Co-ed with P. D. Harrison, Pre-Hispanic Maya Agriculture, Albuquerque: Univ New Mex Press (78); co-ed with W. C. Clark, R. W. Kates, J.F. Richards, J. T. Matthews, and W. B. Meyer, The Earth as Transformed by Human Action: Global and Regional Changes in the Biosphere over the Past 300 Years, Cambridge: Cambridge Univ Press (90); co-ed with W. B. Meyer, Changes in Land Use and Land Cover: A Global Perspective, Cambridge: Cambridge Univ Press (94); co-ed with J. X. Kasperson and R. E. Kasperson, Regions at Risk: Comparisons of Threatened Environments, Tokyo: United Nations Univ (95); coauth with T. M. Whitmore, On the Eve of Conquest: Cultivation and Cultivated Landscapes in Fifteenth Century Middle America, Oxford Geog Series, Oxford: Oxford Univ Press (in press). **CONTACT ADDRESS** Grad Sch of Geography, Clark Univ, 950 Main St, Worcester, MA 01610. **EMAIL** bturner@black.clarku.edu

TURNER, DORIS J.
PERSONAL Born St Louis, MO **DISCIPLINE** LATIN AMERICAN STUDIES **EDUCATION** Stowe Coll St Louis, BA 1953; Universidade da Bahia Salvador Bahia Brazil, 1963; St Louis U, PhD 1967. **CAREER** Kent State Univ, asso prof & coordinator, Latin American Studies, currently. **HONORS AND AWARDS** Fulbright Fellowship Brazil 1962-64; Research Grant to Brazil, Kent State Univ 1976; Danforth Assn 1976; NEH Summer Fellwshp Brown Univ 1979; Postdoctoral Fellowship, Ford Foundation, 1987-88; Outstanding Teaching Awd, College of Arts & Sciences, Kent State Univ, 1986. **MEMBERSHIPS** Field reader US Ofc of Educ (HEW) 1976-77, 79; elected mem & past chmn Nat Ofc Steering & Com of Consortium of Latin Am Studies Prog 1973-76. **CONTACT ADDRESS** Romance Languages & Literatures, Kent State Univ, 101 Satterfield Hall, Kent, OH 44242.

TURNER, ELDON R.
DISCIPLINE HISTORY **EDUCATION** Washburn, BA, 63; Univ Kans, MA, 67, PhD, 73. **CAREER** Asst prof History, Univ Fla. **RESEARCH** Early New England. **SELECTED PUBLICATIONS** Auth, Gender, Abortion, and Testimony: A Textual Look at the Martin Cases, Middlesex County, Massachusetts, 1681-83, Procs of Mass Hist Soc, 87; Statute for the Times: Two Hundred Years of Virginia's Statute for Religious Liberty, Amer Hist Today, 87. **CONTACT ADDRESS** Dept of History, Univ of Florida, 4131 Turlington Hall, Gainesville, FL 32611.

TURNER, FRANK MILLER
PERSONAL Born 10/31/1944, Springfield, OH **DISCIPLINE** BRITISH & MODERN INTELLECTUAL HISTORY **EDUCATION** Col William & Mary, AB, 66; Yale Univ, PhM, 70, PhD, 71. **CAREER** Instr to asst prof, 71-77, dir undergrad studies, 75-78, assoc prof, 77-82, prof hist, Yale Univ, 82-; dir, spec humanities prog, 80-. **HONORS AND AWARDS** Nat Endowment for Humanities fel younger humanist, 74-75, fel independent study, 78-79; Mellon fel, Aspen Inst, 75. **MEMBERSHIPS** AHA; Conf Brit Studies, Royal Hist Soc. **RESEARCH** Victorian intellectual history; science and religion; influence of classical thought; The Oxford Monument. **SELECTED PUBLICATIONS** Auth, Lucretius among the Victorians, Victorian Studies, 73; auth, Between Science and Religion: The Reaction to Scientific Naturalism in Late Victorian England, Yale Univ, 74; art, Rainfall, plagues and the Prince of Wales: A chapter in the conflict of science and religion, J Brit Studies, 74; art, Victorian scientific naturalism and Thomas Carlyle, Victorian Studies, 75; art, The Victorian conflict between science and religion in professional dimension, Isis, 78; coauth, The Western Heritage, Macmillan, 79; art, Public Science in Britain, 1880-1919, Isis, 80; auth, The Greek Heritage in Victorian Britain, Yale Press, 81; auth, Contesting Cultural Authority: Essays in Victorian Intellectual Life, Cambridge Univ Press, 93; coauth, The Western Heritage, 5th ed, Prentiss Hall, 95; auth, The Idea of a University, John Henry Newman (Rethinking the Western Tradition), Yale Univ Press, 96. **CONTACT ADDRESS** Dept of Hist of Med and Sci, Yale Univ, 333 Cedar St, New Haven, CT 06510. **EMAIL** frank.turner@yale.edu

TURNER, HENRY ASHBY, JR.
PERSONAL Born 04/04/1932, Atlanta, GA, m, 1958, 3 children **DISCIPLINE** HISTORY **EDUCATION** Washington and Lee Univ, BA, 54; Princeton Univ, MA, 57; PhD, 60. **CAREER** Instructor to Prof, Yale Univ, 58-. **HONORS AND AWARDS** Phi Beta Kappa; Commander's Cross of Order of Merit, Fed Rep of Germany; Honorary LLD, Washington and Lee Univ. **RESEARCH** Modern European History. **SELECTED PUBLICATIONS** Auth, Stresemann and the Politics of the Weimar Republic, Princeton Univ Press, 63; auth, German Big Business and the Rise of Hitler, New York, 85; auth, Faschismus und Kapitalismus in Deutschland, Gottingen, 72; auth, Germany from Partition to Reunification, New Have, 92; auth, Hitler's Thirty Days to Power: January 1933, Reading MA, 96. **CONTACT ADDRESS** Dept Hist, Yale Univ, PO Box 208324, New Haven, CT 06520-8324. **EMAIL** henry.turner@yale.edu

TURNER, JAMES
PERSONAL Born 06/25/1946, Knoxville, TN **DISCIPLINE** HISTORY **EDUCATION** Harvard Univ, BA, 68, AM, 71, PhD, 75. **CAREER** Prof. **RESEARCH** British and American intellectual history; history of academic knowledge. **SELECTED PUBLICATIONS** Auth, Reckoning with the Beast: Animals, Pain, and Humanity in the Victorian Mind, 80; Without God, Without Creed: The Origins of Unbelief in America, 85; auth, The Liberal Education of Charles Eliot Norton, Johns Hopkins Univ Press, 99; coauth, The Sacred and the Secular Univ, with Jon H. Roberts, Princeton Univ Press, 00. **CONTACT ADDRESS** History Dept, Univ of Notre Dame, Notre Dame, IN 46556.

TURNER, JOHN D.
PERSONAL Born 07/15/1938, Glen Ridge, NJ, m, 1992, 2 children **DISCIPLINE** HISTORY OF RELIGION **EDUCATION** Dartmouth Col, AB, 60; Union Theol Sem, BD, 65, ThM, 66; Duke Univ, PhD, 70. **CAREER** Asst prof, Univ Montana, 71-75; Cotner Col Prof Relig, 76- , Assoc prof History, 76-83, Chr, Prog Relig Stud, 78- , Prof Classics & History, 84- , Univ Nebraska-Lincoln. **HONORS AND AWARDS** Rockefeller Doctoral fel, 68, Phi Beta Kappa, 69, Duke Univ; Am Soc Learned Soc fel, 76. **MEMBERSHIPS** Soc Bibl Lit; Studiorum Novi Testamenti Soc; Int Soc Neoplatonic Stud; Int Asn Coptic Stud; Corresp Inst Antiq & Christianity. **RESEARCH** Biblical studies; History of Hellenistic/Graeco-Roman Religion and Philosophy; Gnosticism; History of Later Greek Philosophy; Codicology and Papyrology; Greek, Coptic, Egyptian and Hebrew language and literature. **SELECTED PUBLICATIONS** Auth, Typologies of the Sethian Gnostic Treatises from Nag Hammadi, Les textes de Nag Hammadi et le probleme de leur classification: Actes du colloque tenu a Quebec du 15 au 22 Septembre, 1993, Peeters and Univ Laval, 95; ed, The Nag Hammadi Library After Fifty Years: Proceedings of the 1995 Society of Biblical Literature Commemoration, E.J. Brill, 97; auth, To See The Light: A Gnostic Appropriation of Jewish Priestly Practice and Sapiential and Apocalyptic Visionary Lore, Mediators of the Divine: Horizons of Prophecy and Divination on Mediterranean Antiquity, Scholars Press, 98; The Gnostic Seth, Biblical Figures Outside the Bible, Trinity Int Press, 98; Introduction & Commentaire, Zostrien, Presses de l'Universite Laval/Editions Peeters, 99; ed, Gnosticism and Later Platonism: Themes, Figures, Texts, Society of Biblical Literature, 00; auth, Marsanes (NHX,1), Presses de l'Universite Laval, edition peeters, 00; auth, Gnosticism and the Platonic Tradition, Presses de l'Universite Laval, editions peeters, 00. **CONTACT ADDRESS** Dept of Classics, Univ of Nebraska, Lincoln, 238 Andrews Hall, Lincoln, NE 68588-0337. **EMAIL** jturner2@unl.edu

TURNER, RALPH V.
PERSONAL Born 08/27/1935, Forrest City, AR **DISCIPLINE** MEDIEVAL HISTORY **EDUCATION** Univ Ark, BA, 57, MA, 58; Johns Hopkins Univ, PhD, 62. **CAREER** Jr instr hist, Johns Hopkins Univ, 60-62; from instr to asst prof, Fla State Univ, 62-66; from asst prof to assoc prof, Ohio Univ,

66-70; assoc prof, 70-73, Prof Hist, Fla State Univ, 73-, Am Bar Found legal hist fel, 80-81; vis fel, St Edmund's House, Cambridge Univ, 80-81. **MEMBERSHIPS** AHA; Conf Brit Studies; Am Soc Legal Hist; Selden Soc; Pipe Roll Soc. **RESEARCH** Medieval English constitutional and legal history; the judiciary in late 12th and early 13th century England. **SELECTED PUBLICATIONS** Auth, The English Judiciary in the Age of Glanvill and Bracton (Cambridge Univ Pr, 1985); auth, Man Raised from the Dust (Univ of Pennsylvania Press, 88); auth, John-Lackland 1199-1216--Military Reputation Reconsidered-, Jour Medieval Hist, Vol 0019, 93; auth, King John (Longman U.K., 94); auth, The Problem of Survival for the Angevin Empire--Henry-II and His Sons Vision Versus Late 12th-Century Realities, Amer Hist Rev, Vol 0100, 95; John, King Concept of Royal Authority, History of Political Thought, Vol 0017, 96; Richard-Lionheart and English Episcopal Election, Albion, Vol 0029, 97. **CONTACT ADDRESS** Dept of Hist, Florida State Univ, Tallahassee, FL 32306. **EMAIL** rvtu1066@aol.com

TURNER, THOMAS REED
PERSONAL Born 08/19/1941, Cambridge, MA, m, 1969, 2 children **DISCIPLINE** CIVIL WAR HISTORY **EDUCATION** Boston Univ, BA, 63, MA, 64, PhD(hist), 71. **CAREER** Assoc prof, 71-80, Prof Hist, Bridgewater State Col, 81-. **MEMBERSHIPS** AHA; Orgn Am Historians. **RESEARCH** Lincoln and Civil War; American assassinations; American foreign relations. **SELECTED PUBLICATIONS** Auth, Public opinion and the assassination of Abraham Lincoln, Part 1, spring 76 & 78 & Part 2, summer 76 & 78, Lincoln Herald; Did Weichmann turn state's evidence to save himself?: A critique of a true history of the assassination of Abraham Lincoln, Lincoln Herald, winter 79; Beware the People Weeping: Public Opinion and the Assassination of Abraham Lincoln (in press). **CONTACT ADDRESS** Dept of Hist, Bridgewater State Col, Bridgewater, MA 02324.

TURNER, WES
DISCIPLINE EARLY CANADA AND THE NINETEENTH-CENTURY BRITISH EMPIRE HISTORY **EDUCATION** Univ Toronto, BA, MA; Duke Univ, PhD. **CAREER** Assoc prof. **RESEARCH** Canadian immigration history. **SELECTED PUBLICATIONS** Auth, The War of 1812: the War that Both Sides Won, Dundurn, 90; The Early Settlement of Niagara, Niagara's Changing Landscape, Carleton UP, 94. **CONTACT ADDRESS** Dept of Hist, Brock Univ, 500 Glenridge Ave, Saint Catharines, ON, Canada L2S 3A1. **EMAIL** wturner@spartan.ac.BrockU.CA

TURSHEN, MEREDETH
DISCIPLINE URBAN STUDIES **EDUCATION** Sussex Univ, UK, PhD, 75. **CAREER** Assoc prof, Rutgers Univ. **HONORS AND AWARDS** Fel, The Population Coun, 72-73; Fel, Inst for Policy Studies, Washington, DC, 76-77; Residency, Nat Sci Found, 77-78; NJIT Alumni Asn Authors Citation for The Political Ecology of Disease in Tanzania, Awded at 18th Annual NJ Writers Conf, March 23, 1985; residency, Va Ctr for the Creative Arts, Jan 87; Rutgers Univ Fac Academic Study Prog Awd, fall 85, fall 89, spring 94, fall 97; Institut Nat de la Sante et de la Res Medicale (INSERM), Paris, Fel, 89-90; Rutgers Univ Fac Merit Awd, 84, 85, 86, 87, 90, 91, 93, 95, 98, 99; residency, Hirsch Farm Project, Hillsboro, Wisc, July 92; Fulbright-Hays Seminars Abroad: Continuity and Change in Morocco and Tunisia, June-July 93; Ctr for the Critical Analysis of Contemporary Culture Fac Fel, 95-96. **RESEARCH** Third World social policy, African health policy. **SELECTED PUBLICATIONS** Auth, Political Ecology of Disease in Tanzania, New Brunswick: Rutgers Univ Press (84), Ch 1 reprinted in P. J. Brown, ed, Understanding and Applying Medical Anthropology, Mayfield Pub Co (99); auth, Thr Politics of Public Health, New Brunswick: Rutgers Univ Press (89), UK ed, Zed Books, London (89); ed, Women and Health in Africa, Trenton, NJ: Africa World Press (91); ed with B. Holcomb, Women's Lives and Public Policy: The International Experience, Westport, CT: Greenwood Press (93); auth, "US Aid to AIDS in Africa," in AIDS in Africa and the Caribbean, ed by G. C. Bond, J. Kreniske, I. S. Susser, and J. Vincent, Boulder, CO: Westview Press (97): 181-188; auth, "The Political Ecology of AIDS in Africa," in The Political Economy of AIDS, ed by M. Singer, Amityville, NY: Baywood (97); auth, "Rationalizing Health Care Provision in Zimbabwe: The Role of the Public Sector in Treating the Malaise of Inefficiency," in Development at a Crossroads: Uncertain Paths to Sustainability after the Neo-Liberal Revolution, ed by M. R. Carter, J. Carson, and F. Zimmerman, Madison: Univ Wisc Global Studies Prof (98); ed with C. Twagiramariya, What Women Do in Wartime: Gender and Conflict in Africa, London: Zed Books (98); auth, "The Ecological Crisis inTanzania," in Dangerous Intersections: Feminist Perspectives on Population, Environment, and Development, ed by Jael Silliman and Ynestra King, Boston: South End Press/London: Zed Books (99); auth, Privatizing Health Services in Africa, New Brunswick: Rutgers Univ Press (99). **CONTACT ADDRESS** Dept Urban Studies, Rutgers, The State Univ of New Jersey, New Brunswick, PO Box 1958, New Brunswick, NJ 08903.

TUSA, MICHAEL
DISCIPLINE 19TH CENTURY MUSIC **EDUCATION** Princeton Univ, PhD. **CAREER** Assoc prof; Univ TX at Austin, 81-; served as, bk review ed, Beethoven Forum & J Am Musicol Soc. **RESEARCH** 19th-century opera; the study of the compos process; the hist of piano music. **SELECTED PUBLICATIONS** Auth, Euryanthe' and Carl Maria von Weber's Dramaturgy of German Opera Oxford, Clarendon Press, 91; publ on Weber, Wagner, Schubert & Beethoven in 19th-century Music, J Amer Musicol Soc, Archiv Fuer Musikwissenschaft, Music Rev, Beethoven Forum & New Grove. **CONTACT ADDRESS** School of Music, Univ of Texas, Austin, 2613 Wichita St, Austin, TX 78705.

TUSHINGHAM, ARLOTTE DOUGLAS
PERSONAL Born 01/19/1914, Toronto, ON, Canada, m, 1948, 2 children **DISCIPLINE** ARCHAEOLOGY **EDUCATION** Univ Toronto, BA, 36; Univ Chicago, BD, 41, PhD(Near East studies), 48. **CAREER** Instr Old Testament, Pine Hill Divinity Hall, NS, 41-42, 46; instr, Univ Chicago, 48-50; ann prof, Am Sch Orient Res, Jerusalem, 51-52, dir, 52-53; assoc prof, Queen's Univ, Ont, 53-55; assoc prof, 55-64, prof Near Eastern studies, Univ Toronto, 64-79; chief archaeologist, 64-79, Consult, Royal Ont Mus, 79-, Head art and archaeol div, Royal Ont Mus, 55-64. **HONORS AND AWARDS** Gold Medal, Iran, 66. **MEMBERSHIPS** Can Mus Asn (pres, 63-65); fel Royal Soc Can; fel Soc Antiq London. **RESEARCH** Near Eastern archaeology, particularly Palestine. **SELECTED PUBLICATIONS** Auth, The Walls of Jerusalem--From the Canaanites to the Mamlukes, Jour Amer Oriental Soc, Vol 0116, 96. **CONTACT ADDRESS** Royal Ontario Mus, 100 Queen's Park, Toronto, ON, Canada M5S 2C6.

TUSHNET, MARK VICTOR
PERSONAL Born 11/18/1945, Newark, NJ, m, 1969, 2 children **DISCIPLINE** LAW, AMERICAN LEGAL HISTORY **EDUCATION** Harvard Col, BA, 67; Yale Univ JD & MA, 71. **CAREER** Asst prof, 73-76, assoc prof, 76-79, prof law, Univ Wis, 79-; prof law, Georgetown Univ Law Ctr, 81-. **MEMBERSHIPS** Orgn Am Historians; Am Soc Legal Hist; Am Hist Assn; Conf Critical Legal Studies. **RESEARCH** Constitutional law; federal jurisdiction; American legal history. **SELECTED PUBLICATIONS** Auth, The Warren Court in Historical Perspective, ec, University of Press of Virginia, 93; auth, Making Civil Rights Law: Thurgood Marshall and the Supreme Court, 1936-1961, Oxford University Press, 94; auth, Brown v Board of Education, Franklin Watts, 95; coauth, Remnants of Belief: Contemporary Constitutional Issues, Oxford University Press, 96; auth, Making Constitutional Law: Thurgood Marshall and the Supreme Court, 1961-1991, Oxford University Press, 97; auth, Taking the Constitution Away from the Courts, Princeton Univ Press, 99. **CONTACT ADDRESS** Law Ctr, Georgetown Univ, 600 New Jersey NW, Washington, DC 20001-2022. **EMAIL** tushnet@law.georgetown.edu

TUTTLE, RICHARD J.
PERSONAL Born 06/22/1941, Oakland, CA, d, 1 child **DISCIPLINE** HISTORY OF ART **EDUCATION** Stanford Univ, PhD, 76. **CAREER** Asst Prof, Assoc Prof, 77 to 83-, Tulane Univ; res Asst, 72-76, Bibliothela Hertziana, Rome. **HONORS AND AWARDS** SAH Founders Awd; Rome Prize Fel. **MEMBERSHIPS** SAH **RESEARCH** Italian Renaissance Architecture and Urbanism. **SELECTED PUBLICATIONS** Auth, Piazza Design Strategies in Renaissance Bologna: Piazza Maggiore, Annali di Archi, 94; The Basilica of S Petronio in Bologna, in: The Renaissance from Brunelleschi to Michelangelo: The Representation of Architecture, ed, H A Millon, V Magnago Lampugnani, Milan, Bompiani, 94; Jacopo Vignola, in: The Dictionary of Art, London and NY, MacMillan, 96; Vignola and Villa Giulia: the White drawing, Casabella, 97; auth, On Vignola's Rule of the Five Orders, in:" Paper Palaces: The Rise of the Renaissance Architectural Treatise, ed, Vaughn Hart, Peter Hicks, London, Yale, 98; Bologna in: Storia dell'architettura italiana: il Quattrocento, ed, Paolo Fiore, Milan, Electa, 98. **CONTACT ADDRESS** Newcomb Art Dept, Tulane Univ, New Orleans, LA 70118-5698. **EMAIL** rjtuttle@mailhost.tcs.tulane.edu

TUTTLE, WILLIAM M.
PERSONAL Born 10/07/1937, Detroit, MI, m, 1995, 4 children **DISCIPLINE** HISTORY **EDUCATION** Denison Univ, BA, 59; Univ Wis, MA, 64; PhD, 67. **CAREER** From asst prof to prof, Univ of Kans, 67-; vis prof, Univ of SC, 80; intra-university prof, Univ of Kans, 82-83; res assoc, Inst of Human Development, Univ of Calif at Berkeley, 86-88. **HONORS AND AWARDS** Sr Fel in Southern and Negro Hist, Inst of Southern Hist, Johns Hopkins Univ, 69-70; Awd of Merit for State Hist, Ill State Hist Soc, 71; Awd of Merit, Am Asn for State and Local Hist, 72; Fel, Charles Warren Ctr for Studies in Am Hist, Harvard Univ, 72-73; Younger Humanist Fel, NEH, 72-73; John Simon Guggenheim Memorial Fel, 75-76; Tom L. Evans grant, Truman Libr Inst, 75-76; Albert J. Beveridge Grant, Am Hist Asn, 82; NEH Fel, 83-84; Stanford Humanities Ctr Fel, Stanford Univ, 83-84; Projects Res Grant, NEH, 86-89; Fel, Hall Ctr for the Humanities, 90; Grant, John F. Kennedy Libr Found, 92; Denison Univ Alumni Citations, 95; W.T. Kemper Fel for Teaching Excellence, 98. **MEMBERSHIPS** Soc of Am Historians, Am Hist Asn, Orgn of Am Historians, Asn for the Study of African Am Life and Hist, Am Studies Asn. **RESEARCH** Recent American History, African American History, American Social History. **SELECTED PUBLICATIONS** Auth, W.E.B. Du Bois, Prentice-Hall, 73; coauth, Plain Folk: The Life Stories of Undistinguished Americans, Univ of Ill Press, 82; auth, "Daddy's Gone to War": The Second World War in the Lives of America's Children, Oxford Univ Press, 93; auth, Race Riot: Chicago in the Red Summer of 1919 2nd ed, Univ of Ill Press, 96; coauth, A People and a Nation: A History of the United States 6th ed, 00. **CONTACT ADDRESS** Dept Hist, Univ of Kansas, Lawrence, Lawrence, KS 66045-0001. **EMAIL** tuttle@falcon.cc.ukans.edu

TWETON, D. JERONE
PERSONAL Born 05/08/1933, Grand Forks, ND, m, 1957, 3 children **DISCIPLINE** AMERICAN HISTORY **EDUCATION** Gustavus Adolphus Col, BA, 55; Univ NDak, MA, 56; Univ Okla, PhD(hist), 64. **CAREER** From asst prof to prof hist, Dana Col, 59-65; from asst prof to assoc prof, 65-71, Prof Hist, Univ N Dak, 71-, Chmn Dept, 65-, Vis scholar, Gen Beadle State Col, 67. **MEMBERSHIPS** AHA; Orgn Am Historians; Econ Hist Asn; Western Hist Asn; Agr Hist Soc. **RESEARCH** The American West; the Populist era. **SELECTED PUBLICATIONS** **CONTACT ADDRESS** Dept of Hist, Univ of No Dakota, Grand Forks, ND 58202.

TWINAM, ANN
PERSONAL Born 04/23/1946, Cairo, IL, m, 1973 **DISCIPLINE** LATIN AMERICAN HISTORY **EDUCATION** Northern Ill Univ, BA, 68; Yale Univ, MPhil, 71, PhD(hist), 76. **CAREER** Teaching asst, Yale Univ, 71-72; from asst prof to prof, Univ Cincinnati, 74-. **HONORS AND AWARDS** Thomas F. McGann Prize; Rocky Mountain Coun Latinamericanists for Public Lives, Private Secrets. **MEMBERSHIPS** Latin Am Studies Asn; Conf Latin Am Hist; Midwest Asn Latin Americanists; AAUP; Rocky Mountain Coun Latin Americanists; Am Hist Asn **RESEARCH** Colonial Latin America, Gender, Family, Social hist; sixteenth to eighteenth century Spain, gender, social history. **SELECTED PUBLICATIONS** Auth, Miners, Merchants, and Farmers in Colonial Columbia, Univ Tex Press (Austin, Tex), 82; transl, Mineros, Comerciantes y Labradores: Las Raices del Espiritu Empresarial en Antioquia: 1763-1810, (Colombia: Fundacion Antioquena para los Estudios Sociales, 85); auth, "Honor, Sexuality and Illegitimacy in Colonial Spanish Am," in Sexuality and Marriage in Colonial Latin Am (Univ Nebr Pr, 89); auth, "The Negotiation of Honor: elites, Sexuality, and Illegitimacy in Eighteenth-Century Spanish Am," in the Faces of Honor: Sex, Shame and Violence in Colonial Latin Am, eds. Sonya Lipsett-Rivera and Lyman Johnson (Albuquerque: Univ of New Mexico Pr, 98); auth, Public Lives, Private Secrets: Gender, Honor, Sexuality and Illegitimacy in Colonial Spanish Am, Stanford Univ Pr, 99; auth, "Death on an Eighteenth-Century Ecuadorian Hacienda. Was Don Joseph de Grivjalva y Recalde, Guilty or Not Guilty?" Colonial Lives: Documents on Latin Am Hist, 1550-1850, eds., Richard Boyer and Geoff Spurling, Oxford Univ Pr, 99. **CONTACT ADDRESS** Dept Hist, Univ of Cincinnati, ML 373, Cincinnati, OH 45221. **EMAIL** Ann.Twinam@uc.edu

TWOHIG, DOROTHY ANN
PERSONAL Born 05/10/1927, Charleston, WV **DISCIPLINE** AMERICAN AND ECONOMIC HISTORY **EDUCATION** Morris Harvey Col, BA, 52; Columbia Univ, MA, 54. **CAREER** Ed staff, Dict American Biography, Columbia Univ, 57-59, asst ed, Papers of Alexander Hamilton, 59-69; Assoc Prof, Univ VA, 80-, Assoc Ed, Papers of George Washington, 69-, Lectr, Dept Hist, Univ Va, 78-; co-ed, The Diaries of George Washington, 6 vols, Univ Press Va, 76-79. **HONORS AND AWARDS** Philip M Hamer Awd, Soc Am Archivists, 77. **MEMBERSHIPS** AHA; Soc Historians Early Am Repub. **RESEARCH** George Washington; history of early American public finance; Colonial economic history. **SELECTED PUBLICATIONS** contribr, Dict American History, Scribner's, 78; ed, J Proc of the President, Univ Press Va, 81. **CONTACT ADDRESS** Papers of George Washington, Univ of Virginia, 1 Randall Hall, Charlottesville, VA 22903-3244.

TWOMBLY, ROBERT C.
PERSONAL Born 11/16/1940, Boston, MA, m, 1988, 2 children **DISCIPLINE** HISTORY **EDUCATION** Harvard Univ, BA, 62; Univ Wis, MA, 64; PhD, 68. **CAREER** Prof, City Col of NY. **RESEARCH** US and European Architecture: 19th and 20th Centuries. **SELECTED PUBLICATIONS** Ed, Blacks in White America Since 1865: Issues and Interpretations, David McKay, 71; auth, Frank Lloyd Wright: An Interpretive Biography, Harper & Row, 73, 74; Frank Lloyd Wright: His Life and His Architecture, Wiley, 79, 80; ed, Louis Sullivan: The Public Papers, Univ of Chicago Press, 88; auth, Power & Style: A Critique of Twentieth-Century Architecture in the United States, Hill & Wang, 95, 97; coauth, Louis Sullivan: The Poetry of Architecture, in press. **CONTACT ADDRESS** Dept Hist, City Col, CUNY, 160 Convent Ave, New York, NY 10031-9101.

TYLER, DANIEL
PERSONAL Born 08/09/1933, Abington, PA, m, 1955, 3 children **DISCIPLINE** HISTORY **EDUCATION** Harvard Univ,

AB, 55; Colo State Univ, MA, 67; Univ NMex, PhD(hist), 70. **CAREER** Prof Hist, Colo State Univ, 70-, Fulbright lectr, Univ Autonoma de Mexico, 74-76, Univ de Cuyo, Argentina, 79. **MEMBERSHIPS** Western Hist Asn. **RESEARCH** Mexico period of the American Southwest, 1821-1848; Colorado since 1932. **SELECTED PUBLICATIONS** Contribr, The Mexican War: Changing Interpretations, Swallow, 73; ed, Western American History in the Seventies, Robinson, Ft Collins, 73; Red Men and Hat Wearers, Pruett, 77; Destino Manifiesto, Univ Ibero-Am, Mexico, 77; Uso y Abuso de Poder, UIA and El Caballito, Mexico, 82. **CONTACT ADDRESS** Dept of Hist, Colorado State Univ, Fort Collins, CO 80523-0001.

TYLER, JOHN W.
PERSONAL Born 05/21/1951, Wilmington, DE **DISCIPLINE** EARLY AMERICAN HISTORY **EDUCATION** Trinity Col, BA, 73; Princeton Univ, MA, 75, PhD(hist), 80. **CAREER** Chmn Hist Dept, Groton Sch, 78-. **MEMBERSHIPS** AHA; Orgn Am Historians; Inst Study Early Am Hist and Culture. **RESEARCH** 18th century mercantile history; causation of the American revolution; 18th century social history and material culture. **SELECTED PUBLICATIONS** Auth, The Secret-6--The True Tale of the Men Who Conspired with Brown, John, New Eng Quart-Hist Rev of New Eng Life and Letters, Vol 0068, 95; In Public Houses, Drink and the Revolution of Authority in Colonial Massachusetts, , New Eng Quart-Hist Rev of New Eng Life and Letters, Vol 0069, 96. **CONTACT ADDRESS** Groton Sch, Farmers Row, Groton, MA 01450. **EMAIL** jtyler@groton.org

TYLER, PAMELA
DISCIPLINE HISTORY **EDUCATION** Tulane Univ, PhD, 89 **CAREER** Asst prof, 90-96, Assoc Prof, 96-, NC State Univ. **HONORS AND AWARDS** Gen L Kemper Williams Prize in La Hist, 96 **MEMBERSHIPS** Southern Asn Women Historians; Southern Hist Asn. **RESEARCH** Women in 20th cent Am South **SELECTED PUBLICATIONS** Auth, Silk Stockings and Ballot Boxes: New Orleans Women and Politics, 1920-1963, Univ Ga Press, 96. **CONTACT ADDRESS** No Carolina State Univ, Box 8108, Raleigh, NC 27695-8108.

TYLER MAY, ELAINE
DISCIPLINE HISTORY **EDUCATION** Univ Calif Los Angeles, PhD. **CAREER** Prof. **HONORS AND AWARDS** Pres, Am Studies Asn. **RESEARCH** Family history; gender issues; 20th century Am political culture; Cold War era. **SELECTED PUBLICATIONS** Auth, Great Expectations: Marriage and Divorce in Post-Victorian America, Univ Chicago, 80; Homeward Bound: American Families in the Cold War Era, Basic Bk, 88; Pushing the Limits: American Women, 1940-1961, Oxford, 94; Barren in the Promised Land: Childless Americans and the Pursuit of Happiness, Harvard Univ Press, 97; auth, Homeward Bound, 99; co-ed, Here, There, and Everywhere: The Foreign Politics of American Popular Culture. **CONTACT ADDRESS** History Dept, Univ of Minnesota, Twin Cities, 104 Scott Hall, 72 Plesant St, Minneapolis, MN 55455. **EMAIL** mayxx002@tc.umn.edu

U

UBBELOHDE, CARL
PERSONAL Born 11/04/1924, Waldo, WI, d, 4 children **DISCIPLINE** HISTORY **EDUCATION** Wis State Col, Oshkosh, BS, 48; Univ Wis, MS, 50, PhD, 54. **CAREER** From instr to assoc prof hist, Univ Colo, 54-65; from assoc prof to prof, 65-75, actg chmn dept, 67-68, chmn dept, 73-76, Henry Eldridge Bourne Prof Hist, Case Western Reserve Univ, 75-, Chmn Dept, 80-93. **HONORS AND AWARDS** Harfurth Awd, Univ Wis, 55; Carl Frederick Wittke Distinguished Teacher, Case Western Reserve Univ, 67-69 and 73. **MEMBERSHIPS** Orgn Am Historians; AHA; Asn Can Studies in US. **RESEARCH** American Colonial and Revolutionary history. **CONTACT ADDRESS** Dept of Hist, Case Western Reserve Univ, 2300 Overlook Rd., No. 819, Cleveland, OH 44106. **EMAIL** carlubbelohde@compuserve.com

UDOVITCH, ABRAHAM L.
PERSONAL Born 05/31/1933, Winnipeg, MB, Canada, m, 1956, 2 children **DISCIPLINE** ISLAMIC HISTORY **EDUCATION** Columbia Univ, BS, 58, MA, 59; Jewish Theol Sem, BHL, 59; Yale Univ, PhD, 65. **CAREER** Asst prof Islamic studies, Brandeis Univ, 64-65 and Cornell Univ, 65-67; chmn dept, Near Eastern Studies, 73-76, assoc prof, 67-71, Prof Islamic Hist, Princeton Univ, 71-, Soc Sci Res Coun res grant, 67-68; Guggenheim fel, 70-71; Fulbright-Hays grant, 71-72. **MEMBERSHIPS** Am Orient Soc; Mid E Studies Asn; Am Res Inst Turkey. **RESEARCH** Economic and social history of the medieval Islamic world. **SELECTED PUBLICATIONS** Auth, Credit as investment in medieval Islamic trade, J Am Orient Soc, 67; Partnership and Profit in Medieval Islam, Princeton Univ, 70; Theory and practice of Islamic law: Some evidence from the Geniza, Studies Islamica, 71; ed, The Middle East: Oil, Conflict and Hope, D C Heath, 76; The Islamic Middle East 700-1900, Darwin Press, 80. **CONTACT ADDRESS** Dept of Near Eastern Studies, Princeton Univ, 110 Jones Hall, Princeton, NJ 08540.

UEDA, REED T.
PERSONAL Born 09/14/1949, Honolulu, HI, m, 1970, 2 children **DISCIPLINE** AMERICAN HISTORY **EDUCATION** Univ Calif, Los Angeles, BA, 70; Univ Chicago, MA, 73; Harvard Univ, MA, 76, PhD, 81. **CAREER** Res ed, Harvard Encycl Am Ethnic Groups, Harvard Univ, 77-79; instr hist, 80-81; vis prof, Brandeis Univ, 85; vis prof, Harvard Univ, 87-89, 96; asst prof, 81-88, Assoc prof hist, Tufts Univ, 88-98; Issue ed, Harvard Educ Rev, fall, 77; co-ed, J Interdisciplinary Hist; assoc, Charles Warren Ctr Studies in Am Hist, 98; prof of hist, Tufts Univ, 98-; Migration Comt, MIT, 96- **HONORS AND AWARDS** Woodrow Wilson Intl Ctr fel; NEH fel; Am Counc Learned Soc fel; Resident Mem, Mass Hist Soc, 99; Fel, Charley Warren Ctr Studies in Am Hist, 99. **MEMBERSHIPS** AHA; Orgn Am Hist. **RESEARCH** History of immigration; history of urbanization; history of ethnic groups. **SELECTED PUBLICATIONS** Auth, West Indians & naturalization and citizenship & coauth, Central and South Americans & policies against prejudice and discrimination, Harvard Encycl American Ethnic Groups, Harvard Univ Press, 80; West End House 1906-1981, West End House, 81; Avenues to Adulthood, 87; Postwar Immigrant American, 94; auth, "The Progressive State and Immigrant Identities," in Progressive Era Policies (99). **CONTACT ADDRESS** Dept of Hist, Tufts Univ, Medford, 520 Boston Ave, Medford, MA 02155-5555. **EMAIL** rueda@emerald.tufts.edu

UFFORD, LETTIA W.
PERSONAL Born 07/30/1936, Durham, NC, m, 1961, 3 children **DISCIPLINE** HISTORY **EDUCATION** Radcliffe Col, AB, 58; Columbia Univ, MA, 62, PhD, 77. **CAREER** Independent **HONORS AND AWARDS** NDEA Title IV fel, 59-61 **MEMBERSHIPS** Middle East Stud Asn; Am Hist Asn; Princeton Res Forum. **RESEARCH** 19th cent Middle East **SELECTED PUBLICATIONS** Auth, Imperialists at Work and Play: The Papers of General Sir John and Lady Maxwell, Princeton Univ Library Chronicle, No LI:2; Winter 90. **CONTACT ADDRESS** 150 Mercer St., Princeton, NJ 08540. **EMAIL** cufford@aol.com

UHR, HORST
PERSONAL Born 01/03/1934, Wiesbaden, Germany **DISCIPLINE** HISTORY OF ART **EDUCATION** Wayne State Univ, BA, 69; Columbia Univ, MA, 70, PhD(art hist), 75. **CAREER** Asst prof, 75-80, assoc prof, 81-87, Prof Renaissance Art & Archit, Wayne State Univ, 87-. **MEMBERSHIPS** Col Art Asn Am **RESEARCH** Northern painting 15th and 16th centuries; 19th century German painting **SELECTED PUBLICATIONS** Auth, The Late Drawings of Lovis Corinth: The Genesis of his Expressionism, Arts Mag, 11/76; Pink Clouds Walchensee: The apotheosis of a mountain landscape, Bull Detroit Inst Arts, 12/77; Lovis Corinth's Formation in the Academic Tradition: The evidence of the Kiel sketchbook and other related student drawings, Arts Mag, spring 78; coauth, Aureola and Fructus: Distinctions of beatitude in scholastic thought and the meaning of some crowns in early Flemish painting, Art Bull, 6/78; auth, Masterpieces of German Expressionism in the Detroit Institute of Arts, Hudson Hill Press, 82; auth, Lovis Corinth, Univ Calif Press, Berkeley-London, 90; auth, "Patrons and Painters in Quest of an Iconographic Program: The Case of the Signorelli Frescoes in Orvieto," Zeitschrift fur Kunstgeschichte 61/2, 92; auth, "Das Kronenmotiv bei Maria und anderen Heiligen in der Altkolner Malerei, Wallraf-Richartz-Jahrbuch LVI, 95. **CONTACT ADDRESS** Dept of Art & Art Hist, Wayne State Univ, 150 Art, Detroit, MI 48202-3103. **EMAIL** aa5202@wayne.edu

ULBRICH, DAVID J.
PERSONAL Born 03/02/1971, Dayton, OH, s **DISCIPLINE** HISTORY **EDUCATION** Univ Dayton, BA, 93; Ball State Univ, MA, 96; Kan State Univ, PhD, in progress. **CAREER** Vis instr, Univ Dayton, 95, 96, 97; res, NASA, 97; instr, gta, Kans State Univ, 97-00. **HONORS AND AWARDS** US Mar Corp Fel; Recog Teach Cert; Logis Edu Found Schlp. **MEMBERSHIPS** Hist Soc; SMH; AMSA. **RESEARCH** American history; Military history, esp strategy, logistics and policy; gender studies. **SELECTED PUBLICATIONS** Auth, "A Male-Conscious Critique of All Quiet On the Western Front," J Mens Stud 3 (95): 229-40; auth, "A Kantian Critique of Machiavelli's 'Ethic of Power,'" in Philosophical Perspectives on Power and Domination: Theories and Practices, eds. Laura Duhan Kaplan, Laurence F Bove (Amsterdam, Holland, Atlanta GA: Rodopi Press, 97); auth, "Clarifying the Origins and Strategic Mission of the US Marine Corps Defense Battalion, 1898-1941," War and Soc 17 (99): 81-109. **CONTACT ADDRESS** Dept History, Kansas State Univ, 206 Eisenhower Hall, Manhattan, KS 66506-1000. **EMAIL** ulbrich@ksu.edu

ULLMAN, JOAN CONNELLY
PERSONAL Born 07/08/1929, New York, NY, m, 1982, 0 child **DISCIPLINE** MODERN SPANISH HISTORY **EDUCATION** Univ Calif, Berkeley, AB, 51; Bryn Mawr Col, MA, 53, PhD(hist and mod Spanish lit), 63. **CAREER** Polit asst foreign serv, US Dept State, 53-57; dir, Int Inst for Girls, Spain, 58-61 and 78-79; dean students and asst prof hist, Elbert Covell Col, Univ of the Pac, 63-66; from asst prof to assoc prof, 66-74, Prof Hist, Univ Wash, 74-95; ed, Soc Spanish and Poruguese Hist Studies Bull, 73-77. **HONORS AND AWARDS** Guggenheim Found fel, 72-73; Real Academia de la Historia: Madrid. Corresponding Mem: Election on Merit, 80. **MEMBERSHIPS** AHA; SSPHS; AARHMS; ASHAHS. **RESEARCH** Spanish history, especially restoration, 1875-1923; labor history, both socialism, anarcho-syndicalism, 19th and 20th century, and anticlericalism; socialism; Jews in Spanish history; 19th and 20th century historiography. **SELECTED PUBLICATIONS** Aut, "The Warp and Woof of Spanish Parlimentary Politics, 1808-1939. Anticlericalism versus neo-Catholicism," European Studies Review 13 (83): 145-176; auth, "Complex History, Rich Legacy," in Scenes of a Sephardic Life (Seattle, Washinton State Jewish Historical Society, 92); auth, "A Social-History of Modern Spain," Hist Soc-Soc Hist (93); "The Jews in the History of Spain, Antiquity to the Present," in Sephardic Studies in the University, ed. Jane Gerber (NYork, 95), 125-140. **CONTACT ADDRESS** Dept of Hist, Univ of Washington, Box 353560, Seattle, WA 08195-353560.

ULRICH, HOMER
PERSONAL Born 03/27/1906, Chicago, IL, m, 1934, 3 children **DISCIPLINE** HISTORY OF MUSIC, MUSICOLOGY **EDUCATION** Univ Chicago, MA, 39. **CAREER** Cellist and bassoonist, Chicago Symphony Orchestra, 29-35; head music dept, Monticello Col, 35-38; from assoc prof to prof music lit, Univ Tex, 39-53; prof and head dept music, 53-72, Emer Prof Music Lit and Music, Univ MD, College Park, 72-, Ed, Am Music Teacher, 72- **MEMBERSHIPS** Music Teachers Nat Asn; Am Musicol Soc. **RESEARCH** Music history, chamber music; symphonic music. **SELECTED PUBLICATIONS** Auth, Chamber Music, Columbia Univ, 48 & 66; The Education of a Concert-Goer, Dodd, 49; Symphonic Music, Columbia Univ, 52; Famous Women Singers, Dodd, 53; Music: A Design for Listening, 57, 62 & 70 & A History of Music and Musical Style, 63, Harcourt; A Centennial History of the Music Teachers National Association, Music Teachers Nat Asn, 76. **CONTACT ADDRESS** 3587 S Leisure World Blvd, Silver Spring, MD 20906.

ULRICH, LAUREL THATCHER
PERSONAL Born 07/11/1938, Sugar City, ID, m, 1958, 5 children **DISCIPLINE** AMERICAN HISTORY **EDUCATION** Univ Utah, BA, 60; Simmons Col, MA, 71; Univ New NH, PhD(hist), 80. **CAREER** Instr English, 72-73, instr hist, 76-80, Asst Prof Hist, Humanities Prog, Univ NH, 80-. **MEMBERSHIPS** Orgn Am Historians; Mormon Hist Asn; Nat Women Studies Asn. **RESEARCH** Women and family in America; early American cultural history; women and religion. **SELECTED PUBLICATIONS** Auth, Cole, Robert World--Agriculture and Society in Early Maryland, Jour Interdisciplinary Hist, Vol 0023, 93. **CONTACT ADDRESS** Humanities Prog, Univ of New Hampshire, Durham, 125 Technology Dr, Durham, NH 03824-4724. **EMAIL** ulrich@fas.harvard.edu

ULTEE, MAARTEN
PERSONAL Born 01/13/1949, Utrecht, Netherlands, M, 1994, 1 child **DISCIPLINE** EUROPEAN HISTORY **EDUCATION** Reed Col, BA, 69; Johns Hopkins Univ, MA, 72; PhD, 75. **CAREER** Lectr, Stanford Univ, 74-75; asst prof, Hobart and Wm Smith Col, 75-78; vis asst prof, Davidson Col, 79-80; asst prof to prof, Univ Ala, 80-. **HONORS AND AWARDS** Woodrow Wilson Fel; NEH Fel, 78-79; DAAD, 84; Bankhead fund, 84, 98, 00; Col of Physicians of Philadelphia fel, 96; Huntington Libr, 01-02. **MEMBERSHIPS** Am Asn for the Hist of Med, Am Cath Hist Asn, Southern Asn for the Hist of Med and Sci, Western Soc for Fr Hist. **RESEARCH** History of surgery, France and the Nethlands, 1500-1800. **SELECTED PUBLICATIONS** Auth, The Abbey of St Germain des Pres in the Seventeenth Century, Yale Univ Pr, 81; auth, Adapting to Conditions: War and Society in the Eighteenth Century, Univ Ala Pr, 86; auth, The Course of French History, Franklin Watts, 88; auth, "The Politics of Professorial Appointment at Leiden," Hist of Univ 9, (90); auth, Plain Lives in a Wolters Kluwer, 95; auth, Worldwide Banking, ABN-AMRO Bank, 99. **CONTACT ADDRESS** Dept Hist, Univ of Alabama, Tuscaloosa, PO Box 870212, Tuscaloosa, AL 35487-0212. **EMAIL** multee@bama.ua.edu

UMEMOTO, KAREN
PERSONAL Born Los Angeles, CA **DISCIPLINE** URBAN STUDIES **EDUCATION** San Francisco State Univ, BS, 83; Univ Calif, MA, 89; Mass Inst Technol, PhD, 98. **CAREER** Instr, Univ Calif, Los Angeles, 95; Acting Asst Prof, Univ Haw, 96-98; Vis School, Univ Calif, 99; Asst Prof, Univ Hawaii, 98-. **HONORS AND AWARDS** Grant, Univ Res Coun, 98-99; Grad Fel, Mass Inst of Technol, 91-93; Res Grant, Inst of Am Cultures, 84-85. **MEMBERSHIPS** Urban Scholars Group, Nat Inst Against Hate Crimes, Papakolea Community Asn, Malama Nanakuli Ahupua'a, Asn of Col Schools of Planning, Nat Asn of Asian Am Studies, Nat Women's Studies Asn. **SELECTED PUBLICATIONS** Auth, "From Vincent Chin to Joseph Ileto: Asian Pacific Americans and Hate Crime Policy, "in The State of Asian Pacific America: Transforming Race Relation, UCLA, 00; co-auth, "A Profile of Race-bias Hate Crimes in Los Angeles County," Western Criminology Review, (99): 2; co-auth, "LA Story: Partnering Psychology and Law Enforcement Responding to Hate Crimes," The California Psychologist, 99; co-auth, "Moving Forward to Care for Hawaii: Holomua I Malama

Hawaii," Service Learning Handbook, Campus Compact National Center for Community Colleges, 99; auth, "Blacks and Koreans in Los Angeles: The Case of LaTasha Harlins and Soon Ja Du," in Blacks, Latinos, and Asians in Urban America: Status and Prospects for Politics and Activism, Praeger Pub, 94; co-auth, "Life and Work in the Inner City" and "Diversity Within a Common Agenda," in The State of Asian Pacific America: Economic Diversity, Issues & Policies, UCLA, 94. **CONTACT ADDRESS** Dept Urban Studies & Planning, Univ of Hawaii, Honolulu Comm Col, 2424 Maile Way, Honolulu, HI 96822. **EMAIL** kumemoto@hawaii.edu

UNDERWOOD, TED LEROY
PERSONAL Born 07/22/1935, Agra, KS, m, 1958, 2 children **DISCIPLINE** EARLY MODERN EUROPEAN HISTORY **EDUCATION** Univ Calif, Berkeley, BA, 59; Berkeley Baptist Divinity Sch, BD, 62; Univ London, PhD, 65. **CAREER** Asst prof ecclesiastical hist, Bishop Col, 65-67; from asst prof to assoc prof, 67-73, Prof Hist, Univ Minn, Morris, 73-00, Chmn Soc sci Div, 78-87; Asst Academic Dean, 98-99. **HONORS AND AWARDS** H.T. Morse Distinguished Teaching Professorship, 74. **MEMBERSHIPS** Am Soc Church Hist; Friends Hist Soc; Conf British Studies. **RESEARCH** Seventeenth century English Puritanism. **SELECTED PUBLICATIONS** Auth, Miscellaneous Works of John Bunyan, vol 1, 80, vol 4, 89; auth, Bunyan in Our Time, Church Hist, Vol 0063, 94; 1st Among Friends--Fox, George and the Creation of Quakerism, Cath Hist Rev, Vol 0081, 95; auth, Primitivism, Radicalism, and the Lamb's War, 97; auth, The Acts of the Witnesses, 99. **CONTACT ADDRESS** Dept of Hist Soc Sci Div, Univ of Minnesota, Morris, 600 E 4th St, Morris, MN 56267-2134. **EMAIL** underwtl@mrs.umn.edu

UNGER, IRWIN
PERSONAL Born 05/02/1927, Brooklyn, NY, m, 1970, 3 children **DISCIPLINE** HISTORY **EDUCATION** City Col New York, BSS, 48, Columbia Univ, MA, 49, PhD, 58. **CAREER** Instr hist, Columbia Col, 56-58; spec lectr, Univ PR, 58-59; asst prof, Long Beach State Col, 59-62; asst prof, assoc prof, Univ Calif, Davis, 62-66; Prof Hist, Wash Sq Col, NY Univ, 66-, Grants-in-aid, Soc Sci Res Coun, 59. **HONORS AND AWARDS** Pulitzer Prize Hist, 65; Am Philos Soc, 60, 62; Am Coun Learned Soc fel, 65-66; Guggenheim fel, 72-73; Rockefeller Humanities Found fel, 80-81; Harry Frank Guggenheim fel, 86-87. **MEMBERSHIPS** AHA; Orgn Am Historians; Econ Hist Asn. **RESEARCH** Civil War and Reconstruction; United States economic history; U.S. in the 1960s. **SELECTED PUBLICATIONS** Auth, The business community and the origins of the 1875 Résumption Act, Bus Hist Rev, 61; The Greenback Era: A Social and Political History of American Finance, 1865-1879, Princeton Univ, 64; The New Left and American history, Am Hist Rev, 7/67; A History of the New Left, Dodd, 74; coauth, The Vulnerable Years: The United States, 1896-1917, Holt, 77; with Debi Unger, Turning Point, 68, Scribners, 88, Best of Intentions, Doubleday, 97; LBJ: A Life, Wiley, 99. **CONTACT ADDRESS** Dept of Hist, New York Univ, 19 University Pl, New York, NY 10003-4556. **EMAIL** ungerclio@aol.com

UNGER, NANCY
PERSONAL Born 07/22/1956, Seattle, WA, m, 1983, 2 children **DISCIPLINE** HISTORY **EDUCATION** Gonzaga Univ, BA, 78; Univ S Calif, MA, 81; PhD, 85. **CAREER** Lectr, San Francisco State Univ, 86-94; adj to asst prof, Santa Clara Univ, 94-. **HONORS AND AWARDS** John Randolph Haynes Fel, Univ of S Calif, 78-79; Student Recognition of Excellent Teaching, San Francisco State Univ, 92. **MEMBERSHIPS** Org Am Historians, Soc for Hist of the Gilded Age and Progressivisim, Am His Asn, Am Soc for Environmental Hist. **RESEARCH** Progressive era, U.S. environmental history, U.S. women and gender. **SELECTED PUBLICATIONS** Auth, Fighting Bob La Follette: The Righteous Reformer, Univ of NC Press (Chapel Hill, NC), 00. **CONTACT ADDRESS** Dept Hist, Santa Clara Univ, 500 El Camino Real, O'Connor Hall 16, Santa Clara, CA 95053-0001. **EMAIL** nunger@scu.edu

UNRAU, WILLIAM ERROL
PERSONAL Born 08/19/1929, Goessel, KS, m, 1952, 2 children **DISCIPLINE** AMERICAN HISTORY **EDUCATION** Bethany Col, Kans, BA, 51; Univ Wyo, MA, 56; Univ Colo, PhD, 63. **CAREER** Assoc prof hist and chmn dept, Bethany Col, Kans, 57-64; assoc prof, 65-68, Prof Hist, Wichita State Univ, 68-. **MEMBERSHIPS** AHA; Orgn Am Historians; Western Hist Asn. **RESEARCH** American Indian and federal Indian policy; settlement and economic development of the Great Plains and American west. **SELECTED PUBLICATIONS** Auth, Indian Law Race Law--A 500-Year History, Historian, Vol 0055, 93; Tribal Wars of the Southern Plains, West Hist Quart, Vol 0024, 93; Bloody Dawn--The Story of the Lawrence Massacre, Jour So Hist, Vol 0059, 93; State and Reservation--New Perspectives on Federal Indian Policy, Pacific Hist Rev, Vol 0063, 94; Between Indian and White Worlds--The Cultural Broker, Montana-Mag West Hist, Vol 0045, 95; The White Earth Tragedy--Ethnicity and Dispossession at a Minnesota-Anishinaabe-Reservation, 1889-1920, Amer Hist Rev, Vol 0100, 95; The Northern Cheyenne Indian Reservation, 1877-1900, Amer Hist Rev, Vol 0100, 95; Our Hearts Fell to the Ground--Plains Indian Views of How the West Was Lost, Jour Early Rep, Vol 0017, 97. **CONTACT ADDRESS** Dept of Hist, Wichita State Univ, Wichita, KS 67208.

UNTERBERGER, BETTY MILLER
PERSONAL Born 12/27/1923, Scotland, m, 1944, 3 children **DISCIPLINE** HISTORY **EDUCATION** Syracuse Univ, AB, 43; Radcliffe Col, MA, 46; Duke Univ, PhD(Hist), 50. **CAREER** Asst prof Hist, ECarolina Col, 48-50; dir Lib Arts Ctr Adults, Whittier Col, 54-57, assoc prof Hist, 57-61; from assoc prof to prof, Calif State Col, Fullerton, 61-68, grad coordr, 66-68; prof Hist, Tex A&M Univ, 68-, Ford Found res grant, 59; Am Philos Soc res grants, 60-61; nat examr, Advan Placement Am Hist; Tex A&M Univ Orgn Res Fund grant, 69-70; partic, Nat Security Forum, US Air Force, 73; mem Adv Comt on Foreign Rels of US, State Dept, 78-81, chmn, 81; comnr, Nat Hist Publ & Records Comn, 81-83. **HONORS AND AWARDS** Asn of Former Students Distinguished Achievement Awd for Teaching, 75. **MEMBERSHIPS** AHA; Rocky Mountain Asn Slavic Studies (vpres, 72-); Soc Historians Am Foreign Rels; Orgn Am Historians; Conf Peace Res Hist. **RESEARCH** American diplomatic history; Soviet American relations; American Far Eastern relations. **SELECTED PUBLICATIONS** Auth, Woodrow Wilson and the decision to send American troops to Siberia, Pac Hist Rev, 55; America's Siberian Expedition, 1918-1920: A Study of National Policy, Duke Univ, 56, Greenwood, 69; Russian revolution and Wilson's Far Eastern policy, Russ Rev, 57; American Intervention in the Russian Civil War, Heath, 68; The arrest of Alice Masaryk, Slavic Rev, 74; The American image of Mohamed Ali Jinnah, Pakistan Affairs, 12/76; National self-determination, In: Dictionary of the History of American Foreign Policy, Scribner's, 78; American Image of Mohammed Ali Jinnah another Pakistan Liberation Movement, Diplomatic Hist, 81; The United States and National Self Determination, Presidential Studies Quarterly, Fall, 96; Woodrow Wilson and the Cold War, in the Liberal Persuasion: Arthur Schlesinger, Jr and the Challenge of the American Past, ed, John Patrick Digging, Princeton University Press, 97. **CONTACT ADDRESS** Dept of History, Texas A&M Univ, Col Station, College Station, TX 77843. **EMAIL** bettymu@tamu.edu

UPSHUR, JIU-HWA LO
DISCIPLINE HISTORY **EDUCATION** Univ Mich, PhD. **CAREER** Prof, Eastern Michigan Univ. **RESEARCH** Modern China. **SELECTED PUBLICATIONS** Coauth, The Twentieth Century: A Brief Global history; World History; co-ed, Lives and Times: A World History Reader. **CONTACT ADDRESS** Dept of History and Philosophy, Eastern Michigan Univ, 701 Pray-Harrold, Ypsilanti, MI 48197.

UPTON, DELL
PERSONAL Born 06/24/1949, Ft. Monmouth, NJ, d **DISCIPLINE** HISTORY, ENGLISH, AMERICAN CIVILIZATION **EDUCATION** Colgate Univ, BA, 70; Brown Univ, MA, 75; PhD, 80. **CAREER** Archit Hist, Va Hist Landmarks Commission, 74-79; Museum and Hist Preservation Consultant, 79-82; asst prof, Case Western Reserve Univ, 82-83; asst, full, prof Univ Calif Berkeley, 83-. **HONORS AND AWARDS** Summer Res Fel, 87; Alice Davis Hitchock, Soc of Archit Hist, 87; John Hope Franklin Awd, Am Studies Asn, 87; Abbott Lowell Cummings Awd, 87, 99; Rachal Awd Va Hist Soc, 88; Vis Sr Fel, Nat Gallery of Art, 88; Guggenheim Fel, 90-91; Getty Sr Res Grant in Art Hist, 90-91; Louisiana Lit award, 96. **MEMBERSHIPS** Soc of Archit Hist; Vernacular Archit Forum; Orgn of Am Hist; Am Hist Asn; Am Studies Asn; Urban Hist Asn. **RESEARCH** Vernacular architecture; Cultural landscapes; Material culture; Urban cultural landscapes of the early republic; Black main streets in the early 20th-century South. **SELECTED PUBLICATIONS** Auth, Madaline: Love and Survival in Antebellum New Orleans, 96; Architecture in the United States, 98. **CONTACT ADDRESS** Dept of Architecture, Univ of California, Berkeley, Berkeley, CA 94720-1800. **EMAIL** Upton@socrates.berkeley.edu

URBAN, MICHAEL A.
PERSONAL Born Chicago, IL **DISCIPLINE** GEOGRAPHY **EDUCATION** Elmhurts Col, BS, 91; Univ Okla, MA, 94; Univ Ill, 00. **CAREER** Asst Prof, Univ of Mo, 98-. **MEMBERSHIPS** Asn of Am Geogr, Am Geophysical Union, Geological Soc of Am. **RESEARCH** Fluvial geomorphology, environmental ethics, environmental history, environmental management. **SELECTED PUBLICATIONS** Coauth, "Interaction between scientists and nonscientists in community-based watershed management: Emergence of the concept of stream naturalization," Environ Management 24-3 (99): 297-308. **CONTACT ADDRESS** Dept Geog, Univ of Missouri, Columbia, 3 Stewart Hall, Columbia, MO 65211-6170. **EMAIL** urbanm@missouri.edu

URBAN, WILLIAM LAWRENCE
PERSONAL m, 1965, 3 children **DISCIPLINE** MEDIEVAL HISTORY **EDUCATION** Univ Tex, BA, 61, MA, 63, PhD(hist), 67 **CAREER** Asst prof hist, Univ Kans, 65-66; asst prof, 66-71, chmn dept, 70-74, assoc prof, 71-78, Prof Hist, Monmouth Col, IlL, 78-, Chmn Dept, 81-, Lee L Morgan Prof Hist; Vis prof, Knox Col, 71 & 73; dir Florence prog, Assoc Cols Midwest, 74-75; dir Zagreb prog, ACM, 86; dir, Olomouc prog, ACM, 91; Fulbright res fel, Ger, 75-76; fac fel, Univ Chicago, 76-77; Nat Endowment for Humanities grants, 77, 78-79 & 81. **MEMBERSHIPS** AHA; Mediaeval Acad Am; AAUP **RESEARCH** Crusades; medieval Baltic. **SELECTED PUBLICATIONS** Co-auth, A History of Monmouth College, 79; The Samogitian Crusade, 89; Dithmarschen, A Medieval Peasant Republic, Mellen, 91; The Baltic Crusade, 2nd ed, 94; auth, Tannenberg and After, 99; auth, The Prussian Crusade, 2nd ed, 00. **CONTACT ADDRESS** Dept of Hist, Monmouth Col, 700 E Broadway, Monmouth, IL 61462-1963. **EMAIL** urban@monm.edu

URNESS, CAROL
PERSONAL Born 04/08/1936, Wilmington, CA **DISCIPLINE** HISTORY **EDUCATION** Univ Minn, Minneapolis, BA, 57, MA, 60. **CAREER** From jr librn to sr librn, Univ Libr, 59-64, Asst Cur Rare Bks, James Ford Bell Libr, Univ Minn, Minneapolis, 64-. **MEMBERSHIPS** Soc Hist Discoveries; Hakluyt Soc; Soc Bibliog Natural Hist; Asn Bibliog Hist. **RESEARCH** Geographical exploration to 1800; history of science. **SELECTED PUBLICATIONS** Auth, A Naturalist in Russia: Letters of Peter Simon Pallas to Thomas Pennant, Univ Minn, 67; co-ed (with John Parker), The American Revolution: A Heritage of Change, 75; compiler (with John Parker), The James Ford Bell Library: An annotated catalog, 81. **CONTACT ADDRESS** 1026 23rd Ave NE, Minneapolis, MN 55418.

UROFSKY, MELVIN IRVING
PERSONAL Born 02/07/1939, New York, NY, m, 1961, 2 children **DISCIPLINE** AMERICAN HISTORY **EDUCATION** Columbia Univ, AB, 61, MA, 62, PhD(hist), 68. **CAREER** Instr hist, Ohio State Univ, 64-67; asst prof, State Univ NY, Albany, 67-70, dean innovative educ, 70-72, asst prof hist, Allen Ctr, 72-74; chmn dept, 74-81, Prof Hist, VA Commonwealth Univ, 74-, Nat Endowment for Humanities grant, 67-74, sr fel, 76; consult, Inst Advan Urban Educ, 71-72; co-chmn, Am Zionist Fedn Ideological Comt, 76-78; chmn, Zionist Acad Coun, 77-79; chmn, Acad Coun Am Jewish Historical Soc, 79. **HONORS AND AWARDS** Kaplan Awd, Jewish Bk Coun, 76. **MEMBERSHIPS** Orgn Am Historians; AHA; Am Jewish Hist Soc. **RESEARCH** American history; history of American Jewry. **CONTACT ADDRESS** 1500 Careybrook Dr, Richmond, VA 23233. **EMAIL** murofsky@saturn.vcu.edu

URY, M. WILLIAM
PERSONAL Born 04/05/1956, Cleveland, OH, m, 1984, 4 children **DISCIPLINE** SYSTEMIC & HISTORICAL THEOLOGY **EDUCATION** Asbury Col, BA, 78; Asbury/Theolog Seminary, M.Div, 83; Drew Univ, PhD, 91. **CAREER** Prof, Wesley Theolog Seminary, 89-00, **HONORS AND AWARDS** Tchr of the Year, 94-95; Who's Who in Amer Univ & Col; Phi Alpha Theta; Theta Phi. **MEMBERSHIPS** Amer Acad Relig; Evangel Theolog Seminary; Wesley Theolog Soc. **RESEARCH** Theology; Historical Theology; Philosophy; Languages. **SELECTED PUBLICATIONS** Coauth, Loving Jesus: A Guidebook for Mature Discipleship, Discipleship Manual Vol III, 98; coauth, Following: A Guidebook for Mature Discipleship Vol II, Discipleship Manual, 97; The World is Still Our Parish, Good News Mag, 96. **CONTACT ADDRESS** Wesley Biblical Sem, Box 9928, Jackson, MS 39286. **EMAIL** bury@wbs.edu

USILTON, LARRY
PERSONAL Born 11/11/1946, Lake Wales, FL, m, 1966, 3 children **DISCIPLINE** MEDIEVAL ENGLAND, MEDIEVAL EUROPE, ANCIENT GREECE AND ROME **EDUCATION** Miss State Univ, BA, MA, PhD. **CAREER** Instr, Univ NC, Wilmington. **MEMBERSHIPS** Medieval Acad Am; Royal Hist Soc London. **RESEARCH** English monasticism. **SELECTED PUBLICATIONS** Auth, The Worlds of Medieval Women, Creativity, Influence, and Imagination, WVa Univ Press, 85; The Kings of Medieval England, C.560-1485: A Survey and Research Guide, Scarecrow Press, 96; articles on corrodies in The American Benedictine Rev, June, 80. **CONTACT ADDRESS** Univ of No Carolina, Wilmington, 234 Morton Hall, Wilmington, NC 28403-3297. **EMAIL** usiltonl@uncwil.edu

UTLEY, ROBERT MARSHALL
PERSONAL Born 10/31/1929, Bauxite, AR, m, 1956, 2 children **DISCIPLINE** MODERN HISTORY **EDUCATION** Purdue Univ, BS, 51; Ind Univ, MA, 52. **CAREER** Historian, Joint Chiefs Staff, US Dept Defense, 54-57; historian, Nat Surv Hist Sites and Bldgs, Southwest Region, Nat Park Serv, 57-62, regional historian, 62-64, chief historian, 64-72, dir off archeol and hist preserv, 72-73, asst dir park hist preserv, 73-76; dep exec dir, Adv Coun Hist Preserv, 77-80; Writing and Consult, 80- **HONORS AND AWARDS** Distinguished Serv Awd, Dept Interior, 71; littd, purdue univ, 74, univ nmex, 76. **MEMBERSHIPS** Orgn Am Historians; Western Hist Asn(vpres, 66-67, pres, 67-68). **RESEARCH** American frontier; American Indian; historic preservation. **SELECTED PUBLICATIONS** Auth, Maclean and Custer, Montana-Mag West Hist, Vol 0043, 93; Desert Lawmen--The High Sheriffs of New-Mexico and Arizona, 1846-1912, NMex Hist Rev, Vol 0069, 94; Untitled, Montana-Mag West Hist, Vol 0045, 95. **CONTACT ADDRESS** 5 Vista Grande Ct Eldorado, Santa Fe, NM 87501.

V

VADNEY, THOMAS EUGENE
PERSONAL Born 07/01/1939, Lowville, NY **DISCIPLINE** RECENT AMERICAN AND WORLD HISTORY **EDUCATION** Univ Toronto, BA, 63; Univ Wis, MA, 65, PhD(Am hist), 68. **CAREER** Vis asst prof Am hist, Univ Minn, Minneapolis, 68-70; asst prof, 70-72, Assoc Prof Am Hist, Univ Man, 72-, Can Coun res grants, 71-72, 74 and leave fel, 76-77; Univ Man Res Bd res grants, 72-74; co-ed, Can Rev Am Studies, 77-78. **MEMBERSHIPS** Orgn Am Historians; AHA; Can Hist Asn; Can Asn Univ Teachers. **RESEARCH** Recent American history; post-1945 world history; Canadian-American urban history. **SELECTED PUBLICATIONS** Auth, The World Since 1945, Thomas E. Vadney, Paperback, 99; auth, The wayward liberal; a political biography of Donald Richberq, Thomas E. Vadney. **CONTACT ADDRESS** Dept of Hist, Univ of Manitoba, 403 Fletcher Argue Bldg, Winnipeg, MB, Canada R3T 5V5. **EMAIL** vadney@cc.umanitoba.ca

VALAIK, J. DAVID
PERSONAL Born 06/09/1935, Hazleton, PA, m, 1960, 3 children **DISCIPLINE** AMERICAN HISTORY **EDUCATION** Univ Notre Dame, BA, 57; Univ Rochester, PhD, 64. **CAREER** From asst prof to assoc prof, 60-71, dean continuing studies, 70-80, prof hist, Canisius Col, 71-. **MEMBERSHIPS** AHA; Am Cath Hist Asn; Orgn Am Historians. **RESEARCH** Twentieth century and United States diplomatic history; Latin American relations. **SELECTED PUBLICATIONS** Auth, Catholics, Neutrality and the Spanish Embargo, 1937-39, in J Am Hist, 6/67; American Catholic Dissenters and the Spanish Civil War, in Cath Hist Rev, 1/68; American Catholics and the Spanish Republic 1931-1936, in J Church & State, winter 68; Col Paul D Bunker, Assembly, US Military Acad, 12/80; Theodore Roosevelt: An American Hero in Caricature, Western NY Inst Press, 93; A History of the Diocese of Buffalo, Western NY Heritage Press, 97. **CONTACT ADDRESS** Dept of Hist, Canisius Col, 2001 Main St, Buffalo, NY 14208-1098. **EMAIL** valaik@canisius.edu

VALDES, DENNIS N.
PERSONAL Born 08/30/1946, Detroit, MI, s **DISCIPLINE** HISTORY, CHICANO STUDIES **EDUCATION** Univ Mich, PhD, 78. **CAREER** Asst prof, Wayne St Univ, 78-80; assoc prof, Univ of Wis-Madison, 90-91; asst, assoc prof, prof, Univ Minn, 80-. **HONORS AND AWARDS** Rockefeller Minority Postdoctoral Fel, UCLA, 83-84; Rockefeller Residency in the Humanities, Walter Reuther Libr of Labor and Urban Affairs, 87-88. **MEMBERSHIPS** Labor and Working Class History Asn; Nat Asn for Chicana and Chicano Studies. **RESEARCH** Chicano/Mexican labor & social hist. **SELECTED PUBLICATIONS** Auth, Al Norte: Agricultural Workers in the Great Lakes Regions, Univ Tex, 91; auth, Barrios Nortenos: St. Paul and Midwestern Mexican Communities in the Twentieth Century, Univ Tex, 00; coed, Voices of a New Chicana/o History, Mich State Univ Press, 00. **CONTACT ADDRESS** Dept of Chicano History, Univ of Minnesota, Twin Cities, 2 Scott Hall, Minneapolis, MN 55455. **EMAIL** valde001@tc.umn.edu

VALENZE, DEBORAH
DISCIPLINE 18TH AND 19TH-CENTURY BRITISH HISTORY **EDUCATION** Brandeis Univ, PhD, 82. **CAREER** Assoc prof, Bernard Col. **RESEARCH** Commoditization of culture in eighteenth-century Britain. **SELECTED PUBLICATIONS** Auth, Prophetic Sons and Daughters: Female Preaching and Popular Religion in Industrial England, Princeton, 85; The First Industrial Woman, Oxford, 95. **CONTACT ADDRESS** Dept of Hist, Columbia Col, New York, 2960 Broadway, New York, NY 10027-6902.

VALKENIER, ELIZABETH KRIDL
PERSONAL Born 11/13/1926, Warsaw, Poland, m, 1951, 1 child **DISCIPLINE** RUSSIAN HISTORY **EDUCATION** Smith Col, BA, 48; Yale Univ, MA, 49; Columbia Univ, PhD, 73. **CAREER** Ref Asst & Res Assoc, Couns on Foreign Rel, 53-62; European Inst Res Asst to P.E. Mosely, Dir, 62-72; Asst Curator, Bakhmeteff Archive, 75-78; Res Scholar, Harriman Inst, 81-; Adj Prof, Political Science, 82-, Columbia Univ. **HONORS AND AWARDS** Phi Beta Kappa; BA Cum Laude; PhD with dist, MacArthur Fdn, Fac Res Prog, 85-86; Natl Coun for Soviet & Europe Res, 79-81, 89-90; IREX Sr Scholar Res & Trvl Grants, 74-98; Pew Fdn, 91, Kennan Inst , 91. **MEMBERSHIPS** AAASS; Pol Inst of Arts and Sci; Mid Atl Slavic Stud Assn; SHERA. **RESEARCH** Russian Central Asian Relations, Biography, Valentin Serov (1865-1911), Russian Painter **SELECTED PUBLICATIONS** Auth,The Soviet Union and the Third World: An Economic Bind, Praeger, 83&85; Auth, The Wanderers, Master of the 19th Century Russian Painting, Univ of Tx Press, 91; Auth, Art and Culture in Nineteenth Century Russia, Ind Univ Press, 83; Auth, East-West Tensions in the Third World, W.W. Norton, 86; Auth, Russian Realist Art, the State of Society, The Peredvizhniki and Their Tradition, Columbia Univ Press, 89; Auth, Ilya Repin and the World of Russian Art, Columbia Univ press , 90; Stalinizing Polish History: What Soviet Archives Disclose, E Europ Pol and Soc, V 7, No 1, 93; The Writer an Artist's Model: Repin's Portrait of Garshin, Metro Mus of Art J, V28, 93; Contr, Russian Art and Architecture, Acad Amer Encl, 93; Contr, The Birth of Realism, The Move Toward Decorativism, Cambridge Ency of Russia and Soviet Union, 93; The Changing Face of Oriental Studies in Russia, Central Asia Monitor, 4/94; The Birth of National Style, The Russian Stravinsky (Brklyn Acad Music, 94); Repin Tetrospective, Tretiakov Gallery, Slavic Rev, V54 No1, 94; Repin za rubezhom , Nashe Nasledi/Moscow/ No31, 94; Repin in Emigration, Har Inst Rev, V8 No4, 95; Contrib, Russian 19th Century Painters, Dict of Art, 95; Contrib, Russian Art and Architecture, Collier Ency, 95. **CONTACT ADDRESS** Columbia Univ, Harriman Inst, 420 West 1, New York, NY 10027.

VALLETTA, CLEMENT LAWRENCE
PERSONAL Born 07/31/1938, Easton, PA **DISCIPLINE** AMERICAN CIVILIZATION, ENGLISH **EDUCATION** Univ Scranton, BA, 61; Univ Pa, MA, 62, PhD(Am Civilization), 68. **CAREER** From instr to assoc prof, 64-77, chmn dept, 71-80, prof English, King's Col, PA, 77-. **MEMBERSHIPS** MLA; Am Studies Asn; Am Folklore Soc; Christianity and Literature. **RESEARCH** Americanization of ethnic groups; influence of relativity physics in non-scientific aspects; American civilization, folk, rhetorical, literary aspects. **SELECTED PUBLICATIONS** Auth, Friendship and games in Italian American life, Keystone Folklore Quart, 70; Einstein, Edison and the conquest of irony, Cithara, 72; contrib, The ethnic experience in Pennsylvania, Bucknell Univ, 73; Studies in Italian American social history, Rowman & Littlefield, 75; auth, A study of Americanization in Carneta, Arno, 75; ed, Ethnic Drama: Video-Text and Study Guide, ERIC, 81; Pennsylavania History, 92; with Robert Paoletti In-Determindcy in Science and Discourse, Technical Writing and Communication, 95; Caring and Christian Irony in Ann Tyler's Novels, Repis Collage Proceedings, 96; A Christian Dispersion in Don DeLillo's The Names, Christianity and Literature, 98. **CONTACT ADDRESS** Dept of English, King's Col, 133 N River St, Wilkes-Barre, PA 18711-0801. **EMAIL** clvallet@kings.edu

VALOIS, RAYNALD
PERSONAL Born 05/19/1935, Sorel, PQ, Canada, m, 1970, 1 child **DISCIPLINE** AESTHETICS, LOGIC **EDUCATION** Col de St Hyacinthe, Que, BA, 55; Univ du Latran, Rome, BTh, 64; Laval Univ, PhD(philos), 73. **CAREER** Prof philos, Laval Univ, 68-76; secretaire particulier, Ministre Des Richesses Naturelles, Govt Que, 76-78; PROF PHILOS, LAVAL UNIV, 78-. **RESEARCH** Aesthetics of plastic arts. **SELECTED PUBLICATIONS** Auth, Definition and Demonstration in the Logic of Aristotle, Laval Theol et Philos, Vol 0050, 94. **CONTACT ADDRESS** Dept of Philos, Univ of Laval, Quebec, QC, Canada G1K 7P4. **EMAIL** raynald.valois@fp.ulaval.ca

VALONE, CAROLYN
DISCIPLINE ITALIAN RENAISSANCE ART **EDUCATION** Northwestern Univ, PhD. **CAREER** Prof, Trinity Univ. **SELECTED PUBLICATIONS** Pub(s), area of Roman and Venetian art and patronage of the sixteenth and seventeenth centuries. **CONTACT ADDRESS** Dept of Art Hist, Trinity Univ, 715 Stadium Dr, San Antonio, TX 78212.

VALONE, JAMES S.
PERSONAL Born 12/29/1934, Warren, PA, m, 1959, 4 children **DISCIPLINE** EARLY MODERN EUROPEAN HISTORY **EDUCATION** Pa State Univ, AB, 56, MA, 58; Univ Mich, PhD, 65. **CAREER** From instr to asst prof, 61-68, assoc prof hist, Canisius Col, 68-, assoc dean, sch bus, 80-. **MEMBERSHIPS** AHA; Soc Fr Hist Studies; Am Cath Hist Soc. **RESEARCH** The political affairs of the Huguenots from 1598-1629. **SELECTED PUBLICATIONS** Auth, The Huguenots and the War of the Spanish Marriages: 1615-1616, Univ Microfilms, 66; Huguenot Politics, 1601-1622, The Edwin Mullen Press, 94. **CONTACT ADDRESS** Dept of Hist, Canisius Col, 2001 Main St, Buffalo, NY 14208-1098. **EMAIL** valone@canisius.edu

VAN BROEKHOVEN, DEBORAH
PERSONAL Born 02/15/1950, Toccoa, GA, m, 1978 **DISCIPLINE** AMERICAN STUDIES; HISTORY **EDUCATION** Barrington Col, BA, 72 Bowling Green State Univ, MA, 73, PhD, 77. **CAREER** Grand Rapids Baptist Col, asst prof of hist, 76-78; Barrington Col, asst prof, 78-85; Pembroke Center, Brown Univ, vis assoc prof, 85-87; OH Wesleyan Univ, assoc prof, 87-98; Am Baptist Hist Soc, exec dir, 98-. **HONORS AND AWARDS** NEH Fel, 86-87, Am Antiquarian Soc. **MEMBERSHIPS** Soc for Historians of the Early Am Republic, Friends Hist Assoc, OH Acad of Hist, Southern Hist Assoc, Organization of Am Historians, Am Hist Assoc. **RESEARCH** Relig, Soc and Cult Hist. **SELECTED PUBLICATIONS** Articles: Better than a Clay Club; The Organization of Women's Anti-Slavery Fairs, 1835-60, Slavery & Abolition 19, 98; 24-45; Needles, Pens and Petitions: Reading Women into Antislavery History, in The Meaning of Slavery in the North, Garland, 98, 125-155; Suffering with Slaveholders: Francis Wayland and the Politics of Baptist Antislavery Positions, Religion and the Antebellum Debate Over Slavery, Univ of GA Press, 98; Abolitionists Were Female: Rhode Island Women and the Antislavery Network, 1830-1860, Urbana and Chicago: Univ of IL Press, 99. **CONTACT ADDRESS** American Baptist Hist Soc, Valley Forge, PA 19482-0851. **EMAIL** dbvanbro@abc-usa.org

VAN DE MIEROOP, MARC
DISCIPLINE ANCIENT NEAR EASTERN HISTORY **EDUCATION** Katholieke Universiteit, BA, 78; Yale, PhD, 83. **CAREER** Hist, Columbia Univ **SELECTED PUBLICATIONS** Auth, Society and Enterprise in Old Babylonian Ur, 92. **CONTACT ADDRESS** Columbia Univ, 2960 Broadway, New York, NY 10027-6902.

VAN DEBURG, WILLIAM L.
PERSONAL Born 05/08/1948, Kalamazoo, MI, m, 1967, 2 children **DISCIPLINE** AFRO-AMERICAN HISTORY **EDUCATION** Western Mich Univ, BA, 70; Mich State Univ, MA, 71, PhD, 73. **CAREER** Asst prof, 73-79, assoc prof Afro-Amer studies, 79-85, dept chmn, 81-84, prof 85-, Univ Wis-Madison; Danforth assoc, Danforth Found, 75-81. **HONORS AND AWARDS** Gustavus Myers Center, Outstanding Book Awd, 93. **MEMBERSHIPS** Southern Hist Assn. **RESEARCH** Black Popular cultural studies, Black Nationalism; Slavery and plantation studies. **SELECTED PUBLICATIONS** Auth, Slavery and Race in American Popular Culture, Univ Wis Press, 84; auth, The Slave Drivers: Black Agricultural Labor Supervisors in the Antebellum South, Oxford Univ Press, 88; ; auth, New Day in Babylon: The Black Power Movement and American Culture, 1965-1975, Univ Chicago Press, 92; auth, Modern Black Nationalism: From Marcus Garvey to Louis Farrakhan, New York, University Press, 97; auth, Black Camelot: African-American Culture Heroes in Their Times, 1960-1980, University of Chicago Press, 97. **CONTACT ADDRESS** Afro-Am Studies Dept, Univ of Wisconsin, Madison, 600 N Park St, Madison, WI 53706-1403. **EMAIL** wlvandeb@facstaff.wisc.edu

VAN DER MERWE, NIKOLAAS JOHANNES
PERSONAL Born 08/11/1940, Cape Province, South Africa, m, 1973, 2 children **DISCIPLINE** ARCHAEOLOGY **EDUCATION** BA, 62, MA, 65, PhD, 66, Yale. **CAREER** Curatorial and Lab Asst, Yale Uni, 62-66; Asst Prof Anthro, 66-69, Assoc Prof Anthro, 69-74, State Univ NY, Binghamton; Prof Archeol, 74-, Dir African Studies, 76-78, Dir Archeometry Res Unit, Found for Res Devel, 93-98, Univ Cape Town; Clay Orof of Sci Archaeol, Dept Anthro, 88-, Prof, Dept Earth and Planetary Sci, Harvard Univ. **HONORS AND AWARDS** Telemecanique Conservation Award, 91; John F. W. Herschel Medal for achievement in science, Royal Society of South Africa, 94; Pomerance Medal for scientific contributions to archaeology, Archaeological Institute of America, 98. **MEMBERSHIPS** Fel, Am anthrop Asn; Am Asn for the Advan of Science; Explorers Club; Royal Soc of South Africa; Soc of Antiquaries; Univ of Cpe Town; British Institute in Eastern Africa; Pan African Asn of Prehistory and Quaternary Studies; Sigma Xi; Soc for Am Archaeology; Soc for Archaeol Science; South African Archaeol Soc; South African Soc for Quaternary Res; Southern African Asn of Archaeologists; West African Archaeol Asn. **RESEARCH** Isotopic dietary chemistry, Metallurgical hist; African Iron Age. **SELECTED PUBLICATIONS** A L Cohen, J E Parkington, G B Brundit & N J van der Merwe, 92, A Holocene marine climate record in mollusc shells from the southwest African coast, Quanternary Research 38, 379-385; N J van der Merwe, J A Lee-Thorp & J S Raymond, 93, Light stable isotopes and the subsistence base of Formative cultures at Valdivia, Ecuador in J B Lambert and G Grupe eds, Prehistoric Human Bone-Archaeology at the Molecular Level, pp 63-98, Berlin: Springer-Verlag; Lee-Thorp, N J van der Merwe, & C K Brain, 94, Diet of Australopithecus robustus at J A Swartkrans from stable carbon siotope analysis, J Human Evolution 27, 361-372. **CONTACT ADDRESS** Peabody Museum, Harvard Univ, Cambridge, MA 02138. **EMAIL** vanderme@fas.harvard.edu

VAN DER MIEROOP, MARC
DISCIPLINE ANCIENT NEAR EASTERN HISTORY **EDUCATION** Katholieke Univ, Leuven, BA, 78; Yale Univ, PhD, 83. **CAREER** Prof. **RESEARCH** Imperialism in the ancient Near East. **SELECTED PUBLICATIONS** Auth, Society and Enterprise in Old Babylonian Ur, 92. **CONTACT ADDRESS** Dept of Hist, Columbia Col, New York, 2960 Broadway, New York, NY 10027-6902.

VAN HARTESVELDT, FRED R.
PERSONAL Born 03/29/1945, Centralia, IL, m, 1968, 1 child **DISCIPLINE** HISTORY **EDUCATION** Mryvil Col, BA, 67; Auburn Univ, MA, 69; PhD, 75. **CAREER** Vis asst prof, Coker Col, 75-76; assoc prof, Val City Col, 76-80; prof, Ft Val State Univ, 80-. **HONORS AND AWARDS** Auburn Univ Fel, 67, 70; Nat Teach Fel, 75; NEH Gnt, 79, 87; GA Gov Teach Fel, 99-00. **MEMBERSHIPS** SCBS; GAH; NACBS; SHA. **RESEARCH** Modern British history; Military history, esp World War I and the Boer War; medical history, esp the influenza pandemic of 1918-1919. **SELECTED PUBLICATIONS** Auth, The Battles of the Somme, 1916: Historiography and Annotated Bibliography, Greenwood Press (Westport, CT), 96; auth, The Dardanelles Campaign, 1915: Historiography and Annotated Bibliography Greenwood Press (Westport, CT), 97; auth, The Boer War, in Sutton Pocket Histories, ed. Asa Briggs (Thrupp Stroud, Gloucestershire: Alan Sutton Pub, 00); auth, The Boer War: Historiography and Annotated Bibliography, Greenwood Press (Westport, CT), 00; ed, The 1918-1919 Pandemic of In-

fluenza: The Urban Impact in the Western World The Edwin Mellen Press (Lewiston, NY), 92; auth, "The Personal Factor in the Negotiation of the Clayton-Bulwer Treaty," Georgia Asn Hist (93): 158-68; auth, "The Undergraduate Research Paper and Electronic Sources: A Cautionary Tale," Teach Hist 23 (98): 51-59; auth, "Caring for Workers; The Health and Welfare Programs of the British Ministry of Munitions, 1916-1918," Maryland Hist (forthcoming), auth, "Burke's Political Philosophy," in Survey of Social Science: Government and Politics Series, ed. Frank N Magill (Salem Press, 95); auth, "King George's War," in Great Events From History: North American Series, rev ed (Salem Press, 97). **CONTACT ADDRESS** Dept History, Political Science, Fort Valley State Univ, 1005 State Univ Dr, Fort Valley, GA 31030-4313. **EMAIL** vanhart@mto.infi.net

VAN HELDEN, ALBERT
PERSONAL Born 03/07/1940, The Hague, Netherlands **DISCIPLINE** HISTORY OF SCIENCE **EDUCATION** Univ London Imp College, PhD, 70. **CAREER** Prof, Institute for the History and Philosophy of Science, Univ of Utrecht, 70-. **MEMBERSHIPS** AAAS; HSS. **RESEARCH** History of Astronomy **SELECTED PUBLICATIONS** Auth, A Catalog of Early Telescopes, Isituto e Museo di Storia della Scienza, Florence, 98; coauth, The History of Science in the Netherlands, Leiden, Brill, 98; The Galileo Project, http://www.rice.edu/Galileo, 95, hypertext resource on the life and work of Galileo Galilei 1564-1642; coed, Scientific Instruments, Osiris, 94; coed, Julian Huxley 1887-1975: Biologist and Statesman of Science, RUP 93. **CONTACT ADDRESS** Dept of History, Rice Univ, Box 1892, Houston, TX 77251-1892. **EMAIL** helden@rice.edu

VAN LIERE, FRANS
PERSONAL Born 01/27/1964, Zierikzee, Netherlands, m, 1994, 2 children **DISCIPLINE** MEDIEVAL STUDIES **EDUCATION** Univ Groningen, M.Div, 88; MA, 89; PhD, 96. **CAREER** Asst prof, Col of Charleston, 95-98; asst prof, Calvin Col, 98-. **MEMBERSHIPS** AHA, SEMA, SSBMA. **RESEARCH** Medieval Biblical Exegesis, Church History. **SELECTED PUBLICATIONS** Auth, "Was the Medieval Church Corrupt?," Misconceptions about the Middle Ages, online, 99; auth, "The School of St. Victor in Perspective," Medieval Perspectives 11 (96): 209-222; auth, Andreae de Sancto Victore opera, vol.2, Expositio hystorica in librum Regum, Brepols, 96; auth, Andrew of St Victor and the Gloss on Samuel and Kings," Instrumenta Patristica 28 (95): 249-253. **CONTACT ADDRESS** Dept History, Calvin Col, 3201 Burton St SE, Grand Rapids, MI 49546-4301. **EMAIL** fvliere@calvin.edu

VAN MIEGROET, HANS J.
DISCIPLINE ART HISTORY **EDUCATION** Univ CA, PhD. **CAREER** Assoc prof, Duke Univ. **RESEARCH** Economic, soc and polit hist of early mod Europ art with emphasis on Burgundy, France, the Netherlands and Germany. **SELECTED PUBLICATIONS** Auth, on Konrad Witz and Gerard David; co-auth, studies on econ arts, 96; Markets and Novelty, 98. **CONTACT ADDRESS** Dept of Art and Art Hist, Duke Univ, East Duke Building, Durham, NC 27706. **EMAIL** hvm@acpub.duke.edu

VAN NUS, WALTER
DISCIPLINE HISTORY **EDUCATION** Univ Toronto, BA, MA, PhD. **CAREER** Assoc prof; acting assoc dean, Concordia. **HONORS AND AWARDS** Dir, undergrad hist prog(s); act assoc dean. **RESEARCH** Canadian urban development and urban architecture. **SELECTED PUBLICATIONS** Pub(s), series of papers on urban aesthetics, the history of urban planning thought in Can, urban development in Montreal; auth, Intellectual underpinnings of architectural modernism in Canada. **CONTACT ADDRESS** Dept of Hist, Concordia Univ, Montreal, 1455 de Maisonneuve W, Montreal, QC, Canada H3G 1M8. **EMAIL** vannus@vax2.concordia.ca

VAN PATTEN, JAMES J.
PERSONAL Born 09/09/1925, North Rose, NY, m, 1961 **DISCIPLINE** HISTORY, PHILOSOPHY **CAREER** Asst, assoc prof, 62-69, Cent Mo St Univ; assoc, Soc for Hist/Philos of Educ; prof, 69-71, Univ Okla; assoc, prof, 71-99, Univ Ark; Adj Prof, Fla Atlantic Univ, 00; Emer Prof, Univ of Arkansas, 00-. **MEMBERSHIPS** APA, Amer Ed Res Assn, Ed Law Assn, Phil of Ed Soc, Amer Ed Stud Assn, Am Philos Soc, World Future Soc. **RESEARCH** Futurism, history of Amer educ, global educ, phil/history. **SELECTED PUBLICATIONS** Auth, What's Really Happening in Education, Univ Press Amer, 97; auth, The Culture of Higher Education, Univ Press Amer, 96; auth, Watersheds in Higher Education, Mellon Press NY, 97; coauth, History of Education in America, Prentice Hall/Merrill, 99; auth, A New Century in Retrospect and Prospect, Univ Pr of Am, 00; auth, Higher Education Culture, Case Studies and a New Century, Univ Pr of Am, 00. **CONTACT ADDRESS** Education Leadership, Univ of Arkansas, Fayetteville, GE 303 Education, Fayetteville, AR 72701. **EMAIL** jvanpatt@aol.com

VAN TINE, WARREN R.
PERSONAL Born 08/28/1942, Philadelphia, PA, m, 1983, 1 child **DISCIPLINE** HISTORY **EDUCATION** Baldwin-Wallace Col, BA, 65; Northern Ill Univ, MA, 67; Univ Mass, PhD,72. **CAREER** From asst prof to assoc prof to prof, 70-, Ohio State Univ. **HONORS AND AWARDS** Fulbright Sen Lectr, 78; Ctr Labor Res Grant, 90-91; Univ Distinguished Affirmation Action Awd, 93; Outstanding Tchg Awd, Sigma Chi Fraternity, 94-95; Ctr Labor Res Grant, 96-97. **MEMBERSHIPS** Ohio Acad Hist; Labor and Working Class Hist Asn. **RESEARCH** US labor, African American, Ohio. **SELECTED PUBLICATIONS** Auth, The Making of the Labor Bureaucrat: Union Leadership in the United States, 1870-1920, 73; coauth, John L. Lewis: A Bibliography, 77; coauth, In the Workers' Interests: A History of the Ohio AFL-CIO, 1958-1998, 98. **CONTACT ADDRESS** 230 W 17th Ave, Columbus, OH 43202. **EMAIL** vantine.1@osu.edu

VAN ZANTEN, DAVID
DISCIPLINE HISTORY **EDUCATION** Vis student Courtauld Inst of Art, London, 63-64; Princeton Univ, BA, 65; Harvard Univ, MA, 66, PhD, 70. **CAREER** Vis Prof, 76, Cornell Univ; Vis Prof, 79, Univ of California/Berkley; Vis Prof, 80, Columbia Univ; Asst Prof, 70-71, McGill Univ; Asst Prof/Assoc Prof, 71-79, University of Pennsylvania; Assoc Prof/Prof, 79-, Northwestern Univ. **HONORS AND AWARDS** NEH Sr Fel, 97-98/89-90; Chevalier of the Ordre des Arts et des Lettres, France, 95; Alice Davis Hitchcock Awd, 88; Prix Bernier Academie des Beaux-Arts, Paris; Fulbright Fel, Paris, 68-69. **SELECTED PUBLICATIONS** Auth, Walter Burley Griffin Selected Designs, 70; auth, The Architectural Polychromy of the 1830s, Garland, 77; auth, The Beaux-Arts tradition in French Architecture, Princeton, 82; auth, Designing Paris The Architecture of Duban Labrouste Vaudoyer and Duc, MIT Press, 87; auth, Building Paris Architectural Institutions and the Transformation of the French Capital 1830-1870, Cambridge, 95. **CONTACT ADDRESS** Dept of Art History, Northwestern Univ, Evanston, IL 60208. **EMAIL** d-van@nwu.edu

VANAUKEN, SHELDON
DISCIPLINE HISTORY, ENGLISH **EDUCATION** Oxford Univ, BLitt, 57. **CAREER** From asst prof to assoc prof, 48-73, Prof Hist and English, Lynchburg Col, 73- **RESEARCH** Nineteenth century England. **SELECTED PUBLICATIONS** Auth, Employment Law Survey, Denver Univ Law Rev, Vol 0072, 95. **CONTACT ADDRESS** 100 Breckenbridge, Lynchburg, VA 24501.

VANDERMEER, PHILIP
PERSONAL Born 04/10/1947, Grand Rapids, MI, m, 1969, 2 children **DISCIPLINE** HISTORY **EDUCATION** Calvin Col, BA, 69; Univ Ill, MA, 71; PhD, 76. **CAREER** Prof, Purdue Univ, 76-83; prof, Univ Tex, 83-85; prof, Ariz State Univ, 85-. **MEMBERSHIPS** Org of Am Hist; Soc Sci Hist Asn; Soc of Hist of the Gilded Age and Progressive Era. **RESEARCH** The Rise of Phoenix since 1940; The Legal Profession in the Midwest, 1830-1930. **SELECTED PUBLICATIONS** Co-ed, Belief and Behavior: Essays in the New Religious History, Rutgers Univ Press, 91; auth, "Congress and Other Legislatures," in Encyclopedia of the American Legislative System, (Charles Scribners, 94), 1546-1567; auth, "Hiram Johnson and the Dilemmas of California Progressivism," in The Human Tradition in the Gilded Age and Progressive Era, (Scholarly Resources, 00), 169-186. **CONTACT ADDRESS** Dept Hist, Arizona State Univ, MC 2501, Tempe, AZ 85287. **EMAIL** p.vander.meer@asu.edu

VANDERPOOL, HAROLD YOUNG
PERSONAL Born 06/28/1936, Port Arthur, TX, m, 1960, 3 children **DISCIPLINE** AMERICAN HISTORY, ETHICS **EDUCATION** Harding Col, BA, 58; Abilene Christian Univ, MA, 60; Harvard Univ, BD, 63, PhD(relig & hist), 71, ThM, 76. **CAREER** From instr to asst prof relig & Am studies, Wellesey Col, 66-75; Harvard Univ Interfac Prof Med Ethics fel, 75-76; Assoc Prof Hist Med & Med Ethics, Univ Tex Med BR, Galveston, 76- **HONORS AND AWARDS** Kennedy Fnd Fel; Outstand Acad Bk, Assn of Col and Res Lib; Special Govt Emp for the NIH and US FDA **MEMBERSHIPS** Am Asn for Hist Med; AHA; Am Soc Church Hist; Soc Health & Human Values; Am Studies Asn. **RESEARCH** Ethics of reseach with Human Subjects; medical ethics; hisoty of medicine in American society; religion and society. **SELECTED PUBLICATIONS** Auth, The ethics of terminal care, JAMA, 78; auth, Responsibility of Physicians Toward Dying Patients, Medical Complications in Cancer Patients, Raven, 81; auth, Medicine and Religion: How Are They Related? J Relig & Health, 90; auth, Death and Dying: Euthanasia and Sustaining Life: Historical Perspective, Ency of Bioethics, Simon & Schuster MacMillan, 95; coauth, The Ethics of Research Involving Human Subjects, U Pub Group, 96; auth, Doctors and the Dying of Patients in American History, Physician Assisted Suicide, Indiana Univ, 97; auth, Critical Ethical Issues in Clinical Trials with Xenotransplants, The Lancet, 98. **CONTACT ADDRESS** Inst of Med Humanities, Univ of Texas, Med Branch at Galveston, 301 University Blvd, Galveston, TX 77555-1311. **EMAIL** hvanderp@utmb.edu

VANDERVORT, BRUCE
PERSONAL Born 04/28/1940, Sparta, WI, m, 1985, 4 children **DISCIPLINE** HISTORY **EDUCATION** Univ Va, PhD, 89. **CAREER** Prof, Va Mil Inst. **HONORS AND AWARDS** Editor, J Mill Hist; asst ed, j mil hist. **MEMBERSHIPS** Am Historical Assoc.; French Colonial Historical Society; Society for Military Bestory. **RESEARCH** Modern French history after1789; the history of European imperialism. **SELECTED PUBLICATIONS** Auth, Victor Griffuelhes and French Syndicalism, 1895-1922, La State Univ Press, 96; Wars of Imperial Conquest in Africa, 1830-1914, Univ Col London Press, 98. **CONTACT ADDRESS** Dept of History, Virginia Military Inst, Lexington, VA 24450. **EMAIL** vandervortb@vmi.edu

VANDERWOOD, PAUL JOSEPH
PERSONAL Born 06/03/1929, Brooklyn, NY **DISCIPLINE** LATIN AMERICAN HISTORY **EDUCATION** Bethany Col, BA, 50; Memphis State Univ, MA, 57; Univ Tex, Austin, PhD(hist), 70. **CAREER** Journalist, Memphis Press Scimitar, 54-63; evaluator, US Peace Corps, 63-64; Prof Hist, San Diego State Univ, 69-95. **HONORS AND AWARDS** Nat Asn State and Local Hist Awd, 71; Hubert B Herring Awd, Pac Coast Coun Latin Am Studies, 76 and 81; Thomas F. McGann Memorial Awd, 98. **MEMBERSHIPS** AHA; Conf Latin Am Hist; Am Film Inst; Pac Coast Coun Latin Am Studies; AHA. **RESEARCH** Popular Catholicism; tourism. **SELECTED PUBLICATIONS** Auth, War Scare on the Lower Rio Grande: Robert Runyon's Plutos of Border Conflict, 1913-1916, Austin: Texas Historical Assn, 91; auth, Disorder and Progress: Bandits, Police, and Mexican Development, Wilmington: Scholarly Resources, 92; auth, Los rostros de la batalla: Furia en la Prantera Mexico-Estados Unidos, 1910-1917, Mexico: Grijalbo, 93; auth, The Power of God Against the Guns of Government, Stanford: Stanford Univ Press, 98. **CONTACT ADDRESS** Dept of Hist, San Diego State Univ, 8705 Jefferson, LaMesa, CA 91941. **EMAIL** vanderwo@mail.sdsu.edu

VANDIVER, FRANK EVERSON
PERSONAL Born 12/09/1925, Austin, TX, m, 1955 **DISCIPLINE** HISTORY **EDUCATION** Univ Tex, MA, 49; Tulane Univ, PhD(hist), 51. **CAREER** Historian, US Civil Serv, Tex, 44-45; Air Force historian, Ala, 51-52; instr hist, exten, Univ Ala, 52; from instr to asst prof, Wash Univ, 52-55; from asst prof to prof, 55-65, chmn dept hist, 62 and 68-69, acting pres, 69-70, Harris Masterson, Jr prof hist, Rice Univ, 65-79, provost, 70-79, vpres, 75-79; pres, North Tex State Univ, 79-81; PRES, TEX AandM UNIV, 81-, Am Philos Soc res grants, 54, 55 and 60; Guggenheim fel, 55-56; lectr, Va Civil War Centennial Comn, Richmond, 62; Harmon Mem lectr, US Air Force Acad, 63, mem, Harmon Mem Lect Serv Selection Comt, 71-; Harmsworth prof, Oxford Univ, 63-64; pres, Jefferson Davis Asn, 63-, chief adv ed, Papers of Jefferson Davis; master, Margarett Root Brown Col, 64-66; mem adv coun, Off Chief Mil Hist, Dept Army, 69-74, selection comt, Ft Leavenworth Hall of Fame Asn of US Army, 71-80; chmn, US Army Mil Hist Res Collection Adv Comt, 72-; mem, Nat Coun on Humanities, 72-78, chmn educ subcomt, 73-76, chmn planning and analysis subcomt, 76-78, vchmn, 76-78; vis prof mil hist, US Mil Acad, 73-74; bd dirs, Inst Civil War Studies, 75-; Fulbright-Hays fel, 76; hon chmn, Pershing Mem Mus, 77- **HONORS AND AWARDS** Carr P Collins Prize, Tex Inst Lett, 58; Harry S Truman Awd, 66; Jefferson Davis Awd, Confederate Mem Lit Soc, 71; Fletcher Pratt Awd, NY Civil War Round Table, 71; Best Bk Awd for Non-fiction, Tex Bks Rev, 77; ma, oxford univ, 63. **MEMBERSHIPS** Orgn Am Historians; AHA (vpres, 74-75, pres, 75-76); Southern Hist Asn; Fel Soc Am Historians; Am Comt Hist 2nd World War. **RESEARCH** American history; military history; Civil War history. **SELECTED PUBLICATIONS** Auth, Lee and Jackson--Confederate Chieftains, Jour Amer Hist, Vol 0080, 93; Lee Considered--Lee,Robert,E. and Civil-War History, Jour So Hist, Vol 0059, 93; Uncertain Warriors--Johnson,Lyndon and His Vietnam Advisers, Jour So Hist, Vol 0061, 95; Pay Any Price--Johnson,Lyndon and the Wars for Vietnam, Jour So Hist, Vol 0063, 97; Burns,Ken the Civil War--Historians Respond, Jour So Hist, Vol 0063, 97; Fulbright--A Biography, Jour So Hist, Vol 0063, 97. **CONTACT ADDRESS** Texas A&M Univ, Col Station, College Station, TX 77843-3400. **EMAIL** f-vandiver@tamu.edu

VANN, RICHARD T.
PERSONAL Born 06/25/1931, Belton, TX, m, 1954, 1 child **DISCIPLINE** SOCIAL AND INTELLECTUAL HISTORY **EDUCATION** Southern Methodist Univ, BA, 52; Oxford Univ, BA, 54, MA, 58; Harvard Univ, MA, 57, PhD(hist), 59. **CAREER** Instr hist, Harvard Univ, 59-61; asst prof, Carleton Col, 61-64; assoc prof, 64-69, Prof Hist and Lett, Wesleyan Univ, 69-, **HONORS AND AWARDS** Exec ed, Hist and Theory, 65-; Soc Relig Higher Educ cross-disciplinary fel, 66-67; Soc Sci Res Coun grant, 66-67 and fel, 70-71; Am Coun Learned Socs grant, 66-68; prin investr, Nat Endowment for Humanities grant, 74-77; Guggenheim fel, 76-77; Vpres, Am Hist Asn, 87-89. **MEMBERSHIPS** Fel Royal Hist Soc. **RESEARCH** Historical demography; theory of history; history of the family. **SELECTED PUBLICATIONS CONTACT ADDRESS** Dept of Hist, Wesleyan Univ, Middletown, CT 06457. **EMAIL** rvann@wesleyan.edu

VANN, ROBERT LINDLEY
PERSONAL Born 08/08/1945, Greenville, TX **DISCIPLINE** ARCHITECTURE **EDUCATION** Univ Tex, Austin, BS, 67; Am School of Classical Studies, 72; Cornell Univ, PhD, 76. **CAREER** Lectr, 74-75, asst prof archit, Univ Md, College Park, 75-, vis mem archit, Cornell Summer Prog in Rome, 79-80. **MEMBERSHIPS** Soc Archit Historians; Archaeol Inst Am; Soc Hist Archaeol; Asn Field Archaeol. **RESEARCH** Aspects of construction in Roman archaeology; underwater archaeology; architecture of the Roman provinces. **SELECTED PUBLICATIONS** Auth, A discussion of the cisterns, Excavations at Carthage, Vol III, 77; auth, A note on the building mortars at Carthage, Excavations at Carthage, 1976,Vol IV, 78; auth, Problems and procedures in architectural recording at Carthage, Roman cisterns in the Michigan field, Univ Mich, 77; auth, Byzantine street construction in the southwest quarter, Caesarea Studies, 82. **CONTACT ADDRESS** Sch of Architecture, Univ of Maryland, Col Park, Architecture Bldg, Rm 1208, College Park, MD 20742-1411. **EMAIL** rv6@umail.umd.edu

VANSINA, JAN
PERSONAL Born 09/14/1929, Antwerp, Belgium, m, 1954, 1 child **DISCIPLINE** AFRICAN HISTORY & ANTHROPOLOGY **EDUCATION** Univ Leuven, PhD(mod hist), 57. **CAREER** Resrchr, Inst Cent African Res, Belgium, 52-60, dir ctr, 57-60; vis lectr, Univ Lovanium, Leopoldville, 57-59; vis lectr, Northwestern Univ, 62-63; vis prof, Univ Lovanium Kinshasha, 66-67, prof, 71; vis prof, Univ Pa, 82; vis prof, Paris Sorbonne, 84-85; assoc prof, 60-64, prof, 64-73, 75-77, Vilas Res and JD MacArthur Prof, Univ Wis-Madison, 77- . **HONORS AND AWARDS** Quinquennial Prize, 67; Herskovits Prize, African Studies Asn, 67 . **MEMBERSHIPS** Fel African Studies Asn; Royal Acad Overseas Sci, Belgium; AHA; Int African Inst; Int Soc Folk Narrative Res. **RESEARCH** General social anthropology; African history; techniques and methods in culture history. **SELECTED PUBLICATIONS** Auth, Catastrophe and Creation--The Transformation of an African Culture, Jour African Hist, Vol 0034, 93; Ethnography and the Hist Imagination, Intl Jour African Hist Stud, Vol 0026, 93; Bantu Roots--French and English, Intl Jour African Hist Stud, Vol 0026, 93; History Making in Africa, Intl Jour African Hist Stud, Vol 0027, 94; Africa and the Disciplines--The Contribution of Research in Africa to the Social-Sciences and the Humanities, Intl Jour African Hist Stud, Vol 0027, 94; History in Popular Songs and Dances--The Bemba Cultural Zone of Upper Shaba Zaire--French, Jour African Hist, Vol 0035, 94; Valleys of the Niger--French, Jour African Hist, Vol 0036, 95; New Linguistic Evidence and the Bantu Expansion, Jour African Hist, Vol 0036, 95; Iron, Gender, and Power--Rituals, of Transformation in African Societies, Amer Hist Rev, Vol 0100, 95; African Masterworks in the Detroit-Institute-of-Arts, Jour African Hist, Vol 0038, 97; South-Pacific Oral Traditions, Jour Interdisciplinary Hist, Vol 0027, 97. **CONTACT ADDRESS** 2810 Ridge Rd, Madison, WI 53705.

VANTINE, WARREN
PERSONAL Born 08/28/1942, Philadelphia, PA, m, 1942, 1 child **DISCIPLINE** US HISTORY **EDUCATION** Baldwin-Wallace Col, BA, 65; Northern Ill Univ, MA, 67; Univ Mass, PhD, 72. **CAREER** Asst to prof, Ohio State Univ, 70- . **HONORS AND AWARDS** Fulbright Sr lectr, 78; Distinguished Affirmative Action Awd, 73; Outstanding Teacher Awd, 95. **RESEARCH** US since 1875, American labor, African-American. **SELECTED PUBLICATIONS** Auth, Making of the Labor Bureaucrat, 73; co-auth, John L. Lewis, 77; auth, In the Workers' Interest, 98. **CONTACT ADDRESS** Dept Hist, Ohio State Univ, Columbus, 230 W 17 Ave, Columbus, OH 43210-1361. **EMAIL** Vantine.1@osu.edu

VAPORIS, CONSTANTINE N.
DISCIPLINE HISTORY **EDUCATION** Princeton Univ, PhD. **CAREER** Assoc prof, Univ MD Baltimore County. **HONORS AND AWARDS** Fulbright Sch Awd. **RESEARCH** Japanese and East Asian hist. **SELECTED PUBLICATIONS** Auth, Breaking Barriers: Travel and the State in Early Modern Japan. **CONTACT ADDRESS** Dept of Hist, Univ of Maryland, Baltimore, Hilltop Circle, PO Box 1000, Baltimore, MD 21250. **EMAIL** vaporis@research.umbc.edu

VARDAMAN, JAMES WELCH
PERSONAL Born 11/26/1928, Dallas, TX, m, 1955, 3 children **DISCIPLINE** MODERN EUROPEAN HISTORY **EDUCATION** Baylor Univ, BA, 51; Univ Minn, MA, 52; Vanderbilt Univ, PhD, 57. **CAREER** Instr Hist, La Col, 54-56; asst prof, Howard Payne Col, 56-58 & Tex Christian Univ, 58-62; assoc prof, Va Mil Inst, 62-66; prof Hist, Baylor Univ 66-; Jo Murphy chairholder, Int Ed; dir Cen Int Affairs. **MEMBERSHIPS** AHA; Southern Hist Asn; Nat Assn for Foreighn Student Affairs; Assn of Int Ed Admin. **RESEARCH** English history; 20th century European history; 17th century Europe. **CONTACT ADDRESS** Dept of History, Baylor Univ, Waco, PO Box 97306, Waco, TX 76706-7306. **EMAIL** James_Vardaman@baylor.edu

VARDY, STEVEN BELA
PERSONAL Born 07/03/1936, Hungary, m, 1962, 3 children **DISCIPLINE** HISTORY, EAST EUROPEAN STUDIES **EDUCATION** John Carroll Univ, BS, 59; Indiana Univ, MA, 61, PhD, 67. **CAREER** Instr, Washburn Univ, 63-64; from asst prof to distinguished prof, Duquesne Univ, 64-; IREX vis scholar, Hung Acad of Scis & Univ of Budapest, 69-70, 75-76; adj prof, Univ of Pittsburgh, 78-96; chemn, Dept of Hist, Duquesne Univ, 83-86. **HONORS AND AWARDS** Res Grants from IREX, NEH, Ford Found, Hunkele Found, Noble J. Dick Found, W. Penn Asn, German Am Nat Cong; Hillman Found, 63-97; Presidential Awd for Excellence in Scholar, Duquesne Univ, 84; Hungary's Berzsenyi Prize, 92; Elected Mem of the Hungarian Writers' Found, 97; Gold Medal for Hist Scholar, Arpad Acad of Arts and Scis, 97; McAnulty Distinguished Prof of Hist, Duquesne Univ, 98. **MEMBERSHIPS** Am Asn for the Advan of Slavic Studies; Am Asn for the Study of Hungarian Hist; AHA; Am Hungarian Educators' Asn; Arpad Acad of Arts and Scis; Hungarian Writers' Fedn; Int Asn of Hungarian Hists; Int Asn of Hungarian Lang and Cult; Int PEN. **RESEARCH** Central European/Hungarian historiography; modern central European/Habsburg/Hungarian history; immigration history with emphasis on Hungarian immigration. **SELECTED PUBLICATIONS** Auth, Hungarian Historiography and the "Geistesgeschichte" School, 74; auth, Society in Change: Studies, 83; auth, Modern Hungarian Historiography, 76; Clio's Art in Hungary and in Hungarian-America, 85; The Hungarian-Americans, 85; auth, Louis The Great: King of Hungary and Poland, 86; Baron Joseph Eoetvoes: A Literary Biography, 87; auth, Triumph in Adversity: Studies in Hungarian Civilization, 88; auth, Hungarian Americans: The Hungarian Experience in North America, 89; The Austro-Hungarian Mind: At Home and Abroad, 89; Attila the Hun, 90; Historical Dictionary of Hungary, 97; Hungarians in the New World, 00. **CONTACT ADDRESS** Dept of History, Duquesne Univ, Pittsburgh, PA 15282. **EMAIL** Svardy@aol.com

VARG, PAUL ALBERT
PERSONAL Born 03/20/1912, Worcester, MA, m, 1936, 1 child **DISCIPLINE** HISTORY **EDUCATION** Clark Univ, BA, 35, MA, 37; Univ Chicago, PhD, 47. **CAREER** Teacher, Publ Schs, Iowa, 36-37; critic teacher hist, Nebr State Teachers Col, Kearney, 37-38; instr, NPark Col, 39-43; assoc prof, Ohio State Univ, 46-58; prof, 58-62, Dean, Col Arts and Lett, 62-69, Prof Hist, Mich State Univ, 69-, Fulbright lectr, Univ Stockholm, 55-56; vis prof, Univ Ore, 57-58. **MEMBERSHIPS** AHA; Orgn Am Historians. **RESEARCH** American diplomatic history. **SELECTED PUBLICATIONS** Auth, Encountering the Dominant Player--United-States Extended Deterrence Strategy in the Asia-Pacific, Intl Hist Rev, Vol 0014, 92; United-States Attitudes and Policies Toward China--The Impact of American Missionaries, Cath Hist Rev, Vol 0079, 93. **CONTACT ADDRESS** Dept of Hist, Michigan State Univ, East Lansing, MI 48824.

VARGA, NICHOLAS
PERSONAL Born 09/13/1925, Elizabeth, NJ, m, 1951, 3 children **DISCIPLINE** AMERICAN HISTORY **EDUCATION** Boston Col, BS, 51, MA, 52; Fordham Univ, PhD, 60. **CAREER** From instr to prof, 55-92, chmn dept, 62-67, prof emer hist, Loyola Col, Md, 92-, archivist, 77-. **MEMBERSHIPS** AHA; NY State Hist Asn. **RESEARCH** New York colonial history; 19th and 20th century Baltimore. **SELECTED PUBLICATIONS** Auth, The New York Restraining Act .., in NY Hist, 7/56; Robert Charles, New York agent, 1748-1770, in William & Mary Quart, 4/61; The Reverend Michael Houdin (1706-1776) .., in Hist Mag Protestant Episcopal Church, 12/64; Crisis in the Great Republic, Fordham Univ, 69; Town and County, Weslyan Univ, 78; Baltimore's Loyola, Loyola's Baltimore, Md Hist Soc, 90. **CONTACT ADDRESS** Dept of Hist, Loyola Col, 4501 N Charles St, Baltimore, MD 21210-2694.

VARNELIS, KAZYS
PERSONAL Born 09/20/1967, Chicago, IL, m, 1995 **DISCIPLINE** HISTORY OF ARCHITECTURE AND URBANISM **EDUCATION** Simon's Rock Col, AA; Cornell Univ, BS, MA, PhD. **CAREER** Fac Coordinator, Hist/Theory, Southern Calif Inst of Archit, 99-. **HONORS AND AWARDS** JAE/ACSA Article of the year, 98. **MEMBERSHIPS** Soc of Architectural Historians. **RESEARCH** Modern architecture. **SELECTED PUBLICATIONS** Auth, The Education of the Innocent Eye, Jour of Archit Educ, 98; auth, You Cannot Not Know History: Philip Johnson's Politics and Cynical Survival, Jour of Archit Educ, 95. **CONTACT ADDRESS** So California Inst of Architecture, 350 Merrick St, Los Angeles, CA 90013. **EMAIL** kazys@sciarc.edu

VARNER, ERIC R.
DISCIPLINE ANDEAN ART AND ARCHITECTURE **EDUCATION** Yale Univ, PhD, 93. **CAREER** Art, Emory Univ. **SELECTED PUBLICATIONS** Auth, Damnatio Memoriae and Roman Imperial Portraiture. **CONTACT ADDRESS** Emory Univ, Atlanta, GA 30322-1950. **EMAIL** evarner@emory.edu

VASSBERG, DAVID ERLAND
PERSONAL Born 03/13/1936, Harlingen, TX, m, 1962, 2 children **DISCIPLINE** SPANISH & LATIN AMERICAN HISTORY **EDUCATION** Univ Tex, Austin, BA, 58, MA, 66, PhD(Hist), 71. **CAREER** Asst prof, 71-77, assoc prof Hist, 77-83, Univ Tex-Pan Am, 83-98; vis scholar Univ Texas, Austin, 86, 94-96; vis research prof, Univ of Valladolid, Spain, 91; Nat Endowment for Humanities fel, 74-75; Joint Hispano-American Council fel, 78-79; Nat Institutes for Health fel, 95-96; Span Ministry of Foreign Affairs fel, 95. **HONORS AND AWARDS** Europ Hist Prize, Southwestern Social Science Assn, 77; Pan American Distinguished Faculty Awds, 83, 85. **MEMBERSHIPS** Soc Span & Port Hist Studies; American Hist Assn; Soc Science Hist Assn; Asociacion de Demografia Historica, Spanish. **RESEARCH** Early modern Spanish history; rural history; family history. **SELECTED PUBLICATIONS** Auth, The Tierras Baldias: community property and public lands in 16th century Castile, Agr Hist, 7/74; Villa-Lobos as pedagogue: music in the service of the state, J Res Music Educ, Fall 75; The sale of Tierras Baldias in 16th century Castile, J Mod Hist, 12/75; African influences on the music of Brazil, Luso-Brazilian Rev, Summer 76; coauth, Regionalism and the musical heritage of Latin America, Inst Latin Am Studies, Univ Tex Austin, 80; El campesino castellano frente al sistema comunitaro: Usurpaciones de tierras concejiles y baldias durante el siglo XVI, Boletin de la Real Academia de la Historia, Spring 78; auth, Concerning Pigs, the Pizzaros, and the agro-pastoral background of the conquerors of Peru, Latin Am Res Rev, Fall 78; The Village and the Outside World in Golden Age Castile: Mobility and Migration in Everyday Rural Life, Cambridge Univ Press, 96. **CONTACT ADDRESS** Dept of History, Univ of Texas, Pan American, 1201 W University Dr, Edinburg, TX 78539-2999. **EMAIL** vassberg@prc.utexas.edu

VAUGHAN, ALDEN T.
PERSONAL Born 01/23/1927, Providence, RI, m, 1983, 2 children **DISCIPLINE** HISTORY **EDUCATION** Amherst Col, BA, 50; Columbia Univ, MEd, 56; MA, 58; PhD, 64. **CAREER** Teacher, Hackley School, NY, 50-51; ABDavis High School, NY, 56-60; instructor, 61-64, asst prof, 64-67, assoc prof, 67-69, prof, 69-94, prof emeritus, Columbia Univ, 94-. **HONORS AND AWARDS** Grants from Am Coun Learned Socs, Huntington Library, & Folger Shakespeare Library; fellowships from Guggenheim Found, 73-74, Charles Warren Center of Harvard Univ, 74, Folger Sh. Library 77, 89, Am Antiquarian Soc, 83; teaching awards from Columbia Univ, 81, 94. **MEMBERSHIPS** Org Am Hist, Am Soc for Ethnohistory, Shakespeare Asn of Am, Soc Am Historians. **RESEARCH** Col. North America, American Race Rel., Shakespeare's "The Tempest." **SELECTED PUBLICATIONS** Auth, New England Frontier (Little, Brown, 65; 3rd ed, Univ Okla, 95); auth, American Genesis: Captain John Smith and the Founding of Virginia (Little, Brown, 75); co-ed, Puritans Among the Indians (Harvard Univ, 81); coauth, Shakespeare's Caliban (Cambridge Univ, 91); auth, Roots of American Racism (Oxford Univ, 95); co-ed, The Tempest (Arden Shakespeare, 99); ed, New England Encounters (Northeastern Univ, 99). **CONTACT ADDRESS** Columbia Univ, New York, NY 10027-6900. **EMAIL** aldenvaughan@aol.com

VAUGHN, BARRY
PERSONAL Born 10/29/1955, Mobile, AL, s **DISCIPLINE** CHURCH HISTORY **EDUCATION** Harvard Univ, BA, 78; Yale Univ, MDiv, 82; Univ of St Andrews, UK, PhD, 90. **CAREER** Asst prof, Samford Univ, 88-90; asst prof, 90-91, adj prof, 93-98, Univ Alabama. **HONORS AND AWARDS** Day fel, 82; Rotary Grad Fel, 84-85. **MEMBERSHIPS** AAR; AHA. **SELECTED PUBLICATIONS** Auth, Benjamin Keach's The Gospel Minister's Maintenance Vindicated and the Status of Ministers among Late Seventeenth Century Baptists, Baptist Rev of Theol, 93; auth, Reluctant Revivalist: Isaac Watts and the Evangelical Revival, Southeastern Comn on the Study of Relig, 93; auth, Resurrection and Grace: The Sermons of Austin Farrer, Preaching, 94; auth, Sermon, Sacrament, and Symbol in the Theology of Karl Rahner, Paradigms, 95; auth, The Glory of a True Church: Benjamin Keach and Church Order among Late Seventeenth Century Particular Baptists, Baptist Hist and Heritage, 95; auth, The Pilgrim Way: A Short History of the Episcopal Church in Alabama, in, Our Church: The Diocese of Alabama in history and Photographs, 96; auth, Gospel Songs and Evangelical Hymnody: Evaluation and Reconsideration, Am Organist, 96; auth, When Men Were Numbered, Anglican Dig, 97; auth, Sermons for Advent and Christmas, Clergy J, forthcoming. **CONTACT ADDRESS** 4041 Ridge Ave, #4-303, Philadelphia, PA 19129-1550. **EMAIL** anglcan@aol.com

VAUGHN, STEPHEN LEE
PERSONAL Born 01/03/1947, Poplar Bluff, MO, m, 1974, 1 child **DISCIPLINE** AMERICAN HISTORY **EDUCATION** Southeast Mo State Univ, BA, 68; Ind Univ, MA, 69; Ind Univ, PhD, 77. **CAREER** Lectr Am hist, Ind Univ, 77-78, asst prof, 78-79; assoc ed, J Am Hist, 79-80; asst prof diplomatic hist, Univ Ore, Eugene, 80-81; asst prof hist jour & mass commun, Univ of Wis-Madison, 81-, Hist asst to exec secy, Orgn Am Historians, 77-80, actg exec secy, 82-; asst prof, Ind Univ, 81. **MEMBERSHIPS** Orgn Am Historians; AHA; Asn Educ Jour. **RESEARCH** Late 19th and 20th century America, social, intellectual, diplomatic history; nationalism; history of mass communications. **SELECTED PUBLICATIONS** Auth, Holding Fast the Inner Lines: Democracy, Nationalism and the Committee on Public Information, Univ NC Press, 80; ed, The Vital Past: Writings on the Uses of History, Univ Ga Press, 85; auth, Morality and Entertainment, J Am Hist, 6/90; Ronald Reagan

in Hollywood: Movies and Politics, Cambridge Univ Press, 94; assoc ed, Dictionary of American History, Scribner's, 96. **CONTACT ADDRESS** Univ of Wisconsin, Madison, 821 University Ave, Madison, WI 53706-1497. **EMAIL** slvaughn@facstaff.wisc.edu

VAZQUEZ, OSCAR E.
DISCIPLINE ART HISTORY **EDUCATION** Univ CA Santa Barbara, PhD, 89. **CAREER** Assoc prof/dir undergrad studies, SUNY Binghamton. **RESEARCH** Mod Europ art, collections, patronage and art market systems; 18th and 19th century art criticism and theory; Span art and cult hist; Latin Am 19th and 20th century art. **SELECTED PUBLICATIONS** Auth, Beauty Buried in its own Cemetery: Santiago Rusinol's 'Jardins d'Espanya'" as Reliquaries of Aristocratic History, Word & Image, 95; Defining Hispanidid: Allegories, Genealogies and Cultural Politics in the Madrid Academy Competitions of 1893, Art Hist, 97. **CONTACT ADDRESS** SUNY, Binghamton, PO Box 6000, Binghamton, NY 13902-6000. **EMAIL** frances@binghamton.edu

VECOLI, RUDOLPH JOHN
PERSONAL Born 03/02/1927, Wallingford, CT, m, 1959, 3 children **DISCIPLINE** AMERICAN SOCIAL HISTORY **EDUCATION** Univ Conn, BA, 50; Univ Pa, MA, 51; Univ Wis, PhD, 63. **CAREER** For affairs officer, US Info Agency, US Dept State, 51-54; instr hist, Ohio State Univ, 57-59 and Pa State Univ, 60-61; lectr Am civilization, Rutgers Univ, 61-63, asst prof hist, 63-65; assoc prof Am hist, Univ Ill, Urbana, 65-67; Prof Am Hist and Dir, Immigration Hist Res Ctr, Univ Minn, Minneapolis, 67-, Mem bd dirs, Am Immigration and Citizenship Conf, 69-; Am Coun Nationalities Serv; vis prof Am hist, Univ Uppsala, 70; Am-Scand Found fel, 70; sr res scholar, Fulbright-Hays Prog, Italy, 73-74. **HONORS AND AWARDS** Gold Medal, Lucchesi che hanno onorato l'Italia nel mondo, 71; Medallion from City Coun Ljubljana, 81; Cavaliere Ufficiale nell'Ordine al Merito della Repubblica Italiana, Pres Ital repub, 82. **MEMBERSHIPS** AHA; Orgn Am Historians; Am Ital Hist Asn (pres, 66-70); Immigration Hist Soc (pres, 82-). **RESEARCH** History of American immigration and ethnic groups; Italian American history; history of the American labor movement. **SELECTED PUBLICATIONS** Auth, "The Invention of Ethnicity: A Perspective from the USA," Altreitalie (Turin), 90; auth, "Italian Immigrants and Working Class Movements in the United States: A Personal Reflection on Class Ethnicity," Journal of the Canadian Historical Association (93): 293-305; auth, "Etnia, internazionalism e protezionismo operaio: gli immigrati italiani e I movimento operai negli USA, 1880-1950," in La Riscoperta delle Americhe Lavoratori e Sindacato nell'emigrazione in America Latina, 1870-1970, Vanni Belengino, Emilio Franzina, Adolfo Pepe, eds. Milan (94): 507-525; auth, "The Lady and the Huddle Masses: The Statue of Liberty as a Symbol of Immigration," in The Statue of Liberty Revisited, Wilton S. Dillon and Neil G. Kotler, eds. (Washington: Smithsonian Institution Press, 94), 39-69; auth, "The Italian diaspora, 1876-1976," Cambridge Survey of World Migration, Robin Cohen, ed. (Cambridge, 95), 114-22; auth, "The Significance of Immigration in the Formation of an American Identity," The History Teacher, 30 (96): 9-27; auth, "Primo Maggio: May Day Observances among Italian Immigrant Workers, 1890-1920," Labor's Heritage 7 (96): 28-41; auth, "Are Italian Americans Just White Folks?," Italian Americana, XIII (95): 149-61; auth, "The Italian Immigrant Press and the Construction of Social Reality, 1850-1920," in Print Culture in a Diverse America, eds. James P. Danky and Wayne A. Wiegand, Urbana and Chicago: University of Illinois Press, 1998, 17-33; auth, "Immigrants in the Twin Cities: Melting Pot or Mosaic?" in Swedes in the Twin Cities, ed. Philip J. Anderson (St. Paul: Minnesota, Historical Society), 00. **CONTACT ADDRESS** Immigration Hist Res Ctr, Univ of Minnesota, Twin Cities, 311 Elmer L. Andersen Library, 222-21st Ave S, Minneapolis, MN 55455. **EMAIL** vecol001@tc.umn.edu

VECSEY, CHRISTOPHER
PERSONAL Born 12/07/1948, New York City, NY, m, 1980, 1 child **DISCIPLINE** RELIGION, NATVE AMERICAN STUDIES **EDUCATION** PhD, 77, Northwestern Univ. **CAREER** Prof, Colgate Univ. **RESEARCH** American Indian Religions. **SELECTED PUBLICATIONS** Auth, American Indian Environments, Syracuse Univ, 80, auth, Traditional Ojibwa Religion and Its Historical Changes, American Philosophical Society, 83; auth, Imagine Ourselves Richly, Corssroad/Continuum, 88; auth, Where the Two Roads Meet, The paths of Kateri's Kin, Iroquois Land Claims, Syracuse Univ, 88; auth, auth, American Indian Catholics, Padres' Trail, Univ Notre Dame Press, 96, 97, 99; ed, Religion in Native North America, Idaho Press, 90; Handbook of American Indian Religious Freedom, Crossroad/Continuum, 91. **CONTACT ADDRESS** Dept of Philos and Relig, Colgate Univ, 13 Oak Drive, Hamilton, NY 13346. **EMAIL** wkelly@mail.colgate.edu

VEENKER, RONALD ALLEN
PERSONAL Born 05/13/1937, Huntington Park, CA, m, 1960, 1 child **DISCIPLINE** OLD TESTAMENT; ANCIENT NEAR-EASTERN STUDIES **EDUCATION** Bethel Col, Minn, BA, 59; Bethel Theol Sem, BDiv, 63; Hebrew Union Col, PhD(Ancient NE), 68. **CAREER** Asst prof, Univ Miami, 67-68; assoc prof, 68-76, Prof Bibl Studies, Western KY Univ, 76-, Fel, Hebrew Union Col, Jewish Inst Relig, 77-78. **MEMBERSHIPS** Am Orient Soc; Soc Bibl Lit. **RESEARCH** Old Babylonian economic and legal texts; computer assisted analysis of Old Babylonian economic texts. **SELECTED PUBLICATIONS** Auth, Stages in the Old Babylonical legal process, Hebrew Union Col Annual, 76; contribr, Interpreter's Dictionary of the Bible: Supplement, Abingdon, 76; auth, Gilgamesh and the Magic Plant, Bibl Archaeol, Fall 81; A Response to W.G. Lambert, Bibl Archaeol, Spring 82; Noah, Herald of Righteousness, Proceedings of the Eastern Great Lakes and Midwest Bibl Soc, vol VI, 86; coauth, Me m, the First Ur III Ensi of Ebla, In: Ebla 1975-1985: Dieci anni di studi linguistici e fililogici, Atti del Convegno Internazionale, Napoli, 10/85; auth, Texts and Fragments: The Johnstone Collection, J of Cuneiform Studies, vol 40, no 1, 88; A critical review of Karl van Lerberghe, Old Babylonian Legal and Administrative Texts from Philadelphia, Orientalia Lovaniensia Analecta 21, Uitgeverij Peeters, 86, for the J of the Am Orient Soc, 92; Texts and Fragments: Collection of the Erie Historical Museum, J of Cuneiform Studies, vol 43, no 1, 93. **CONTACT ADDRESS** Dept of Philos & Relig, Western Kentucky Univ, 1 Big Red Way St, Bowling Green, KY 42101-3576. **EMAIL** ronald.veenker@wku.edu

VEHSE, CHARLES T.
PERSONAL Born 03/07/1961, Huntington, WV, m, 1984, 1 child **DISCIPLINE** HISTORY OF RELIGIONS **EDUCATION** Univ of Chicago, PhD, 98, MA, 85; Brown Univ, AB, 83. **CAREER** Vis Asst Prof, 96-, West VA Univ; lectr, 88-91, Dept of Theo, Loyola Univ Chicago; Tutor for German Lang, 82-83, Brown Univ. **HONORS AND AWARDS** Dean's Prof Travel Grant; Solomon Goldman Lecture; Vis Res Fellow; Fellow, Interuniversity Prog for Jewish Stud; Arie and Ida Crown Mem Res Grant; Lucius N. Littauer Found Res Grant; Bernard H. and Blanche E. Jacobson Found Res Grant; Stipendium des Landes Baden-Wurtemberg. **RESEARCH** Religious and Judaic Studies, German Judaism of the modern era, History and Methods in the History of Religion, Ritual Studies and Comp Liturgy, History and Interpretaion of the Hebrew Bible; Humanities and Social Sciences, German Language and Literature. **SELECTED PUBLICATIONS** Auth, Religious Practice and Consciousness, A Case Study of Time from the 19th century, Consciousness Research Abstracts, Thorverton, UK, J of Consci Stud, 98; Were the Jews of Modern Germany as Emancipated and Assimilated as We Think?, The Solomon Goldman Lectures, 96-97, Spertus Institute of Jewish Studies; Long Live the King, Historical Fact and Narrative Fiction in 1 Samuel 9-10, The Pitcher Is Broken, Memorial Essays for Gosta WW. Ahlstrom, Sheffield Academic Press, 95. **CONTACT ADDRESS** 252 Stansbury, PO Box 6312, Morgantown, WV 26506. **EMAIL** cvehse@wvu.edu

VENARDE, BRUCE L.
PERSONAL Born 09/14/1962, Philadelphia, PA **DISCIPLINE** HISTORY, LITERATURE **EDUCATION** Swartmore Col, BA, 84; Harvard Univ, AM, 85, PhD, 92. **CAREER** Lectr, Harvard Univ, 92-95; vis asst prof, Tufts Univ, 94-96; asst prof, Univ Pittsburgh, 96-99, assoc prof, 99-. **MEMBERSHIPS** Medieval Acad of Am, Am Hist Asn. **RESEARCH** Medieval European history and culture, France, Christianity, Latin literature, gender and sexuality. **SELECTED PUBLICATIONS** Auth, " La reforme a Apt (X-XII siecles): Patrimoine, patronage et famille," Provence historique 38 (98): 131-147; auth, "Praesidentes Negotiis: Abbesses as Managers in Twelfth-Century France," in Samuel K. Cohn Jr. and Steven A. Epstein, eds, Portraits of Medieval and Renaissance Living: Essays in Memory of David Herlihy, Univ Mich Press (96); auth, Women's Monasticism and Medieval Society: Nunneries in France and England, 890-1215, Cornell Univ Press (97, paperback, 99); auth, "Drogo of Sint-Winoksbergen, Life of Godelieve, in Thomas F. Head, ed, Medieval Hagiography: An Anthology, Garland Pub (2000); auth, Robert of Arbrissel: A Reader, Cath Univ Press Am (forthcoming). **CONTACT ADDRESS** Dept Hist, Univ of Pittsburgh, WPHH 3M26, Pittsburgh, PA 15260. **EMAIL** bvenarde@pitt.edu

VERBA, ERICKA K.
DISCIPLINE LATIN AMERICAN HISTORY **EDUCATION** Brown Univ, BA, 82; Univ Calif at Los Angeles, MA, 89; PhD, 99. **CAREER** Pres performer, Sabia Inc, 76-89; dir perf, Desborde, 89-99; res asst, CA, 90; teach asst, Univ Calif, Los Angeles, 90-91; instr, Univ de Santiago, Chile, 92; teach fel, Univ Calif, Los Angeles, 94-95; teach asst, Univ Calif, Los Angeles, 95; res asst, Univ Calif, Los Angeles, 96; tutor, Univ Calif, Los Angeles, 96-97; dir perf, concert, 96; pt fac, Santa Monica Col, 97-; pt fac, Chicano Stud Dept, Univ Calif, Los Angeles, 98-; lectr, Univ Calif, Los Angeles, 99-00. **HONORS AND AWARDS** William Leopold Fichter Prem; Arnold Bennett Prize; Univ Calif, Los Angeles, Teach Fel; Fulbright Gnt; SSRC Diss Fel; Mellon Fel; LAC Res Gnt; Mabel Wilson Richards Schl; Univ Calif, Los Angeles, Trav Gnt. **MEMBERSHIPS** LASA; AHA; CCWHP. **RESEARCH** Women in Latin America; Latin America popular culture; Latin American Feminism. **SELECTED PUBLICATIONS** Auth, "The Circulo de Lectura de Senoras and the Club de Senoras of Santiago, Chile: Middle- and Upper-class Feminist Conversations 1915-1920," J Woman's Hist 7 (95); ; auth, :Las Hojas Suelts: Nineteenth-Century Chilean Popular Poetry as a Source for the Historian," Stud Latin Am Pop Cult 11 (93). **CONTACT ADDRESS** Dept Social Studies, Santa Monica Col, 1900 Pico Blvd, Santa Monica, CA 90405-1628. **EMAIL** everba@ucla.edu

VERBRUGGE, MARTHA HELEN
PERSONAL Born 07/19/1949, Northfield, MN **DISCIPLINE** MEDICAL AND AMERICAN SOCIAL HISTORY **EDUCATION** Carleton Col, BA, 71; Harvard Univ, PhD(sci hist), 78. **CAREER** Asst Prof Med and Sci Hist, Bucknell Univ, 78-, Nat Endowment for Humanities grant, summer, 79; Am Coun Learned Soc grant, 80; res fel, Charles Warren Ctr Studies for Am Hist, Harvard Univ, 81-82; prof, med and sci hist, Bucknell, 78-. **HONORS AND AWARDS** NEH Fel, 91-92; Spencer Found Grant, 95-96; ACOG Res Fel, 98; His of Women in Sci Prize, 91; Teaching Awd: Class of 1956 Lectureship, Bucknell Univ. **MEMBERSHIPS** AHA; Am Asn Hist Med; Hist Sci Soc; Orgn Am Historians. **RESEARCH** History of women's health and exercise in America; history of popular health and hygienic habits; history of non-orthodox systems of medicine and personal health. **SELECTED PUBLICATIONS** Auth, Recreating the Body--Womens Physical-Education and the Science of Sex-Differences in America, 1900-1940, Bulletin Hist Med, Vol 0071, 97; "Gym Periods and Monthly Periods: Concepts of Menstruation in American Physical Education 1900-1940," in Body Talk, Univ of Wisc Press, 00; auth, Able-Bodied Womanhood, Oxford Univ Press, 88. **CONTACT ADDRESS** Dept of Hist, Bucknell Univ, Lewisburg, PA 17837-2029. **EMAIL** verbrgge@bucknell.edu

VERGE, ARTHUR C.
PERSONAL Born 03/14/1956, Santa Monica, CA, s **DISCIPLINE** HISTORY **EDUCATION** Univ Calif, Santa Barbara, BA, 78; Univ Southern Calif, MA, MPA, 84, PhD, 88. **CAREER** Prof, El Camino, 89-. **HONORS AND AWARDS** Presidential Leadership Awd, 95, Doane Col. **MEMBERSHIPS** Am Hist Asn; Calif Hist Soc; Southern Calif Hist Soc. **RESEARCH** California history; second world war; beach and surf culture. **SELECTED PUBLICATIONS** Auth, art, The Scandinavian-Americans, 90; auth, Paradise Transformed: Los Angeles During the Second World War, 93; auth, art, The Impact of the Second World War on Los Angeles, 94; auth, art, Daily Life in Wartime California, 99. **CONTACT ADDRESS** Dept of History, El Camino Col, 16007 Crenshaw Blvd, Torrance, CA 90506.

VERKERK, DOROTHY HOOGLAND
DISCIPLINE ART HISTORY **EDUCATION** Rutgers Univ, PhD. **CAREER** Asst prof, Univ NC, Chapel Hill. **RESEARCH** Late antique, Celtic, early medieval art and cult. **SELECTED PUBLICATIONS** Auth, Exodus and Easter Vigil in the Ashburnham Pentateuch, Art Bull 77, 95. **CONTACT ADDRESS** Univ of No Carolina, Chapel Hill, Chapel Hill, NC 27599. **EMAIL** dverkerk@email.unc.edu

VERNON, JAMES
PERSONAL Born 03/02/1965, Melton, United Kingdom, m, 1991, 2 children **DISCIPLINE** HISTORY **EDUCATION** Manchester Univ, BA, 87; PhD, 91. **CAREER** Postdoc fel to sen lectr, Manchester Univ, 91-00; asst prof to assoc prof, Univ Calif Berkeley, 00-. **HONORS AND AWARDS** Brit Acad Postdoc Fel, 91-94; Brit Acad Personal Res Grant, 93-94; Enterprise in Higher Educ Grant, 95-96; Econ and Soc Res Coun Res Fel, 99-01. **MEMBERSHIPS** Royal Hist Soc; N Am Conf on Brit Studies. **RESEARCH** Modern British social, cultural and political history; Hunger and citizenship in the first half of the twentieth century. **SELECTED PUBLICATIONS** Auth, Politics and the people: a study in English political culture, c. 1815-1867, Cambridge Univ Press, 93; auth, "Who's afraid of the 'linguistic turn'? The politics of social history and its discontents," Soc Hist, (94): 81-97; ed, Re-reading the constitution: new narratives in the political history of England's long nineteenth century, Cambridge Univ Press, 96; auth, "Border Crossings: Cornwall and the English (Imagi)Nation," in Imagining Nations, (Manchester, 98), 153-172; auth, "For some queer reason. The trials and tribulations of Colonel Barker's masquerade in interwar Britain," Signs, (00): 37-62. **CONTACT ADDRESS** Dept Hist, Univ of California, Berkeley, 3229 Dwinelle Hall, Berkeley, CA 94720. **EMAIL** jvernon@socrates.berkeley.edu

VERRETT, JOYCE M.
PERSONAL Born 05/26/1932, New Orleans, LA, m **DISCIPLINE** HISTORY **EDUCATION** Dillard U, BA 1957; NYork Univ, MS 1963; Tulane U, PhD 1971. **CAREER** Orleans Parsih LA, hs teacher 1958-63; Dillard Univ Div of Ntrl Sci, instr prof chmn. **HONORS AND AWARDS** HS Vldctn 1948; Alpha Kappa Mu Nat Hon Soc 1956; Beta Kappa Chi Nat Sci Hon Soc 1956; Grad Summa Cum Laude Dillard Univ 1957; NSF Fllwshp for Adv Study 1960-62; 1st blk wmn to recv PhD in Bio from Tulane Univ 1971; Otstndng Educ of Am 1972. **MEMBERSHIPS** Ent Soc Am; Nat Inst Sci; Beta Beta Beta Bial & Hon Soc; Beta Kappa Chi Sci Hon Soc Cncr Assn Grtr ND 1974; LA Hrt Assn 1973-; NAACP 1960-; Reg 9 Sci Fair 1958-. **CONTACT ADDRESS** Dillard Univ, 2601 Gentilly Blvd, New Orleans, LA 70122.

VERVOORT, PATRICIA
PERSONAL Born Boston, MA **DISCIPLINE** ART HISTORY **EDUCATION** St. Mary's Univ, BA, 63; Univ Iowa, MA, 70. **CAREER** Lectr, art hist, 75-89, asst prof, 89-92, ch, dept visual arts, 90-95, Assoc Prof, Art History, Lakehead Univ, 92-. **MEMBERSHIPS** Univ Art Asn Can; Soc Stud Archit Can. **SELECTED PUBLICATIONS** Auth, Meaning in Old Buildings, in Thunder Bay Hist Mus Soc Papers and Records V, 77; auth, Sunrise on the Saguenay: Popular Literature and the Sublime, in Mosaic: J Interdisciplinary Stud Lit, 88; auth, Lakehead Terminal Elevators: Aspects of Their Engineering History, in Can J Civil Engg, 90; auth, Re-Constructing van Gogh: Paintings as Sculptures in Low Countries and Beyond, 93. **CONTACT ADDRESS** Dept of Visual Arts, Lakehead Univ, Thunder Bay, ON, Canada P7B SE1. **EMAIL** pat.vervoort@lakeheadu.ca

VETROCQ, MARCIA E.
DISCIPLINE ART HISTORY **EDUCATION** Princeton Univ, BA; Stanford Univ, MA, PhD; Columbia Univ, postdoctoral work. **CAREER** Prof, Univ New Orleans; corresp ed, Art in Am. **HONORS AND AWARDS** Wolfsonian Found sr fel, Am Acad, Rome, 96. **MEMBERSHIPS** Int Asn of Art Critics. **SELECTED PUBLICATIONS** Articles on art history and contemporary criticism in Europe and the United States in Art in America; catalogue essay for the Guggenheim Museum's exhibition The Italian Metamorphosis, 1943-1968, NY, 94; a major article on contemporary American art for the Encyclopedia Italiana, Rome, 96. **CONTACT ADDRESS** Univ of New Orleans, New Orleans, LA 70148. **EMAIL** clrfa@uno.edu

VIAULT, BIRDSALL SCRYMSER
PERSONAL Born 09/20/1932, Mineola, NY, m, 1970 **DISCIPLINE** NINETEENTH & TWENTIETH CENTURY EUROPEAN HISTORY **EDUCATION** Adelphi Univ, BS, 55, MA 56; Univ Tubingen, dipl, 54; Duke Univ, MA, 57, PhD, 63. **CAREER** From instr to asst prof hist, Adelphi Univ, 59-68; assoc prof, 68-72, Prof Hist, Winthrop Col, 72-97, Prof Emer, 98-, Chmn, 79-89; vis assoc prof, Duke Univ, 70. **HONORS AND AWARDS** Ford Found coop prog Humanities postdoctoral fel, Univ NC, Duke Univ, 69-70. **MEMBERSHIPS** Am Cath Hist Asn; Southern Hist Asn; SC Hist Asn; Phi Kappa Phi, Phi Alpha Theta, Zeta Beta Tau. **RESEARCH** German history, 1919-1945; European diplomatic history, 1919-1940; the Cold War. **SELECTED PUBLICATIONS** Auth, Les demarches pour le retablissemennt de la paix (Septembre 1939-Aout 1940), 7/67 & Mussolini et la Recherche d'une Paix Negociee (1939-1940), 7/77, Rev d'Hist de la Deuxieme Guerre Mondiale; World History in the 20th Century, 69; American History since 1865, 89, rev ed, 93; Western Civilization since 1600, 90; Modern European History, 90; English History, 92. **CONTACT ADDRESS** Dept of Hist, Winthrop Univ, 701 W Oakland Ave, Rock Hill, SC 29733-0001. **EMAIL** viaultb@charlotte.infi.net

VIERECK, PETER
PERSONAL Born 08/05/1916, New York, NY, m, 1972, 2 children **DISCIPLINE** POETRY, HISTORY **EDUCATION** Harvard Univ, BS, 37, AM, 39, PhD, 42. **CAREER** Instr hist and lit, Harvard Univ, 46-47; asst prof hist, Smith Col, 47-48; assoc prof, 48-49, assoc prof Europ and Russ hist, 49-55, alumni found prof Europ and Russ hist, 55-80, William R Kenan Jr Prof Hist, Mt Holyoke Col, 80-; Vis lectr, Smith Col, 48-49; Guggenheim fels, 49 and 55; vis lectr, Poet's Conf, Harvard Univ, 53 and Univ Calif, Berkeley, 57 and 64; Whittal lectr poetry, Libr Cong, 54 and 63; Fulbright prof Am poetry, Univ Florence, 55; Elliston poetry lectr, Univ Cincinnati, 56; US Dept State cult exchange poet, USSR, 61; Twentieth Century Fund travel and poetry res grant, Russia, 62; lectr poetry, City Col New York and New Sch Social Res, 64; dir poetry workshop, NY Writer's Conf, 65-67. **HONORS AND AWARDS** Garrison Prize for Poetry, Phi Beta Kappa, 36; Harvard Bowdoin Medal for Prose, 39; Tietjens Prize for Poetry, 48; Pulitzer Prize for Poetry, 49; dhl, olivet col, 59. **MEMBERSHIPS** AHA **RESEARCH** Modern European and Russian history; Anglo-American poetry; modern Russian culture. **SELECTED PUBLICATIONS** Metrics, Not Hour Hand, Parnassus Poetry In Rev, Vol 18, 93; My Seventy-Seventh Birthday, Parnassus Poetry Rev, Vol 18, 93; Slack A While, Parnassus Poetry Rev, Vol 18, 93; .. and Sometimes Not, Parnassus Poetry Rev, Vol 18, 93; Invocation, Parnassus Poetry Rev, Vol 18, 93; Threnody Reversals, Parnassus Poetry Rev, Vol 18, 93; Moon Ode, Parnassus Poetry Rev, Vol 18, 93; Second Moon Ode, Parnassus Poetry Rev, Vol 18, 93; Topsy Turvy, Parnassus Poetry Rev, Vol 18, 93; Why I Sometimes Believe in God, Parnassus Poetry Rev, Vol 18, 93; auth, Tide and Continuities, Poems New & Old, Univ of Ark, 95. **CONTACT ADDRESS** 12 Silver St., South Hadley, MA 01075.

VIETOR, RICHARD HENRY KINGSBURY
PERSONAL Born 04/22/1945, Minneapolis, MN, m, 1968, 3 children **DISCIPLINE** HISTORY **EDUCATION** Union Col, NYork, BA, 67; Hofstra Univ, MA, 71; Univ Pittsburgh, PhD (hist), 75. **CAREER** Vis asst Am hist, Va Polytechnic Inst and State Univ, 75; asst prof recent US hist, Univ Mo-Columbia, 75-78; Assoc Prof Bus Admin, Harvard Bus Sch, 78-; Consult energy policy, Hudson Inst, 75-77; prof, 84; Senior Assoc Dean, 00. **HONORS AND AWARDS** Newcomen Award, 81. **MEMBERSHIPS** Orgn Am Historians. **RESEARCH** Twentieth century American energy policy and environmental policy. **SELECTED PUBLICATIONS** Auth, Energy policy in America, Cambridge Univ Press, 84; auth, Strategic Manage hunt in the Regulated Environment, 88; auth, Contrived Competition: Regulation and Deregulation in America, Harvard Univ Press, 94; auth, Containing the Atom in Nuclear Regulation in a Changing Environment, 63-71, Am Hist Rev, Vol 99, 94; coauth, Business Management and the Natural Environment, Southwestern Publishing, 96; coauth, Globalization and Growth, Harcourt, 01. **CONTACT ADDRESS** Business Sch, Harvard Univ, 232 Baker, Boston, MA 02163. **EMAIL** rvietor@hbs.edu

VIGIL, RALPH HAROLD
PERSONAL Born 09/06/1932, Vigil, CO, m, 1969, 2 children **DISCIPLINE** COLONIAL LATIN AMERICAN HISTORY, SOUTHWESTERN HISTORY **EDUCATION** Pac Lutheran Univ, BA, 58; Univ NMex, MA, 65, PhD (hist), 69. **CAREER** Instr hist, Washburn Univ, 65-69; asst prof, Fresno State Col, 69-71; assoc prof, Univ Tex, El Paso, 71-72; Assoc Prof Hist, Univ Nebr, Lincoln, 73-87; prof, 87-97; prof emeritus, 97-. **HONORS AND AWARDS** John Hay Whitney Found Opportunity fel, 59-60; Dept of State grant for the study of Latin Am lit in Mexico, 62-63; Washburn Univ Res grant, 68-69; Washburn Univ Libr honors lecturer, 68; Phi Alpha Theta (hon); Fulbright Commision fel, Spain, 67-68; biographical sketch in Reading Excersises on Mexican Americans, 77; Certificate of Merit from the G.I. Forum of Bebraska for contributions, leadership, and service to the Hispanic Community, 79; Manuscript, "Bartolome de Las Casas, Judge Alonso de Zorita, and the Franciscans: A Collaborative Effort for the Spiritual Conquest of the Borderlands," judged the best presented in Latin Am His, 79; Certificate of Appreciation in recognition of service to learning disabled students at Univ of Nebraska, Lincoln, 87; Prize Spain and America in the Quincentennial of the Discover for manuscript, "Alonso de Zorita, Royal Judge and Christian Humanist, 1512-1585," 87. **MEMBERSHIPS** AHA; Asn Borderlands Scholars; Conf Latin am Hist. **RESEARCH** Sixteenth century Spanish New World Society; Spanish borderlands. **SELECTED PUBLICATIONS** Auth, "Negro Slaves and Rebels in the Spanish Posessions," Historian (71); auth, "The New Borderlands History: A Critique," NMex Hist Rev (73); auth, "The Hispanic Heritage and the Borderlands," J San Diego Hist (73); auth, "A Reappraisal of the Expedition of Panfilo de Narvaez to Mexico in 1520," Rev Hist Am (74); auth, "Willa Cather and Historical Reality," NMex Hist Rev (75); auth, Alonso de Zorita, Early and Last Years, The Americans, 76; auth, "The Way West: John Nichols and Historical Reality," Journal of the West (85); auth, "Alonso de Zorita and the Indians of the Golden and Iron Ages," Proceedings, Rocky Mountain Council on Latin American Studies (87); auth, "Spanish Exploration and the Great Plains in the Age of Discovery," Great Plains Quarterly (90); auth, "Oidores Letnados and the Idea of Justice, 1480-1570," The Americas, 90. **CONTACT ADDRESS** Dept of Hist, Univ of Nebraska, Lincoln, 637 Oldfather Hall, Lincoln, NE 68588-0327. **EMAIL** RalphHVigil@aol.com

VILES, PERRY
PERSONAL Born 10/19/1932, Boston, MA, m, 1959, 5 children **DISCIPLINE** EARLY MODERN EUROPEAN HISTORY **EDUCATION** Harvard Univ, AB, 54, MA, 57, PhD(hist), 65. **CAREER** From instr to asst prof hist, Univ Pa, 63-71; asst prof, 71-74, chmn dept, 73-74, asst to pres develop, 74-78, asst dean, Lyndon State Col, 78-, Am Antiq Soc vis fel, 72; Gov's Comn Admin Justice, State Vt, 74-77. **RESEARCH** European and American social history, 1700-1850; family and adolescent in Western society. **SELECTED PUBLICATIONS** Auth, The slaving interest in the Atlantic ports, 1763-1792, Fr Hist Studies, fall 72. **CONTACT ADDRESS** Off of the Dean, Vail Ctr, Lyndon State Col, Lyndonville, VT 05851.

VINCENT, CHARLES
PERSONAL Born 10/19/1945, Hazlehurst, MS, m, 1971, 3 children **DISCIPLINE** MODERN HISTORY **EDUCATION** Jackson State Univ, BA, 66; La State Univ, Baton Rouge, MA, 68, PhD, 73. **CAREER** Instr soc sci, TJ Harris Jr Col, 67-68; instr, 68-69, asst prof, 69-70, 73-75, assoc prof, 75-78, Prof History, Southern Univ, Baton Rouge, 78-, Moton Ctr Independent Studies fel, 78-. **HONORS AND AWARDS** Eminent Scholar, Va State Univ, 90-91; Pres Fac Excellence Awd, 94; Found Hist La Preserv Awd, 96. **MEMBERSHIPS** Asn Study Afro-Am Life & Hist; Southern Hist Asn; Orgn Am Historians. **RESEARCH** Reconstruction history; Southern history; Afro-American history. **SELECTED PUBLICATIONS** Auth, Two Articles, Dictionary of Negro Biography, Crowell, 75; Laying the cornerstone at Southern University, La Hist, summer 76; Louisana's Black Legislators and Their Efforts to Pass a Blue Law during Reconstruction, J Black Studies, 9/76; Black Legislators in Louisana during Reconstruction, La State Univ, 76; Southern University and World War I: Aspects of the University and its Leadership, J Soc & Behav Scientists, 79; Antoine Dubuclet: Louisana's Black State Treasure, 1868-1978, J Negro Hist, spring 81; Booker T Washington's tour of Louisiana, April 1915, La Hist, spring 81; A Centennial History of Southern University & A&M College, 1880-1980, Moran Industs, 81; Black Constitution Makers: In Search of Fundamental Law, Lafayette), 93; Blacks in Louisiana, in Vol 3, Encyclo of African-American Culture & History, (NY) 96; auth, "Anlebettum N.O. Black Busines" and P.B.S. Pinchback," in Encyclopedia of African American Business History ed Juliet E.K. Walker, 99; auth, The African American Experience in Louisiana: Part A from Africa to the Civil War, Lafayette, 99; auth, "Civil Rights in LA," in Waldo Martin & Patricia Sullivan, ed Civil Rights in the U.S., NY 00; auth, "Hiram Revels"; auth, "T. Thomas Fortune". **CONTACT ADDRESS** Dept Hist, So Univ and A&M Col, PO Box 9491, Baton Rouge, LA 70813.

VINCENT, K. STEVEN
PERSONAL Born 11/13/1947, Hot Springs, AR, m, 1 child **DISCIPLINE** HISTORY **EDUCATION** Univ Calif at Berkeley, BA, 70; MA, 72; PhD, 81. **CAREER** From asst prof to prof, NC State Univ, 81-. **HONORS AND AWARDS** Nat Humanities Ctr Fel, 86-87. **MEMBERSHIPS** French Historical Studies, Western Soc for French Hist, Confr for the Study of Polit Thought, Asn des Amis de Benoit Malon. **RESEARCH** Modern European Intellectual History, Modern French History. **SELECTED PUBLICATIONS** Auth, Between Marxism and Anarchism: Benoit Malon and French Reformist Socialism, 92; auth, Pierre-Joseph Proudion and the Rise of French Republican Socialism, 84; ed, The Human Tradition in Modern France, 00. **CONTACT ADDRESS** Dept Hist, No Carolina State Univ, PO Box 8108, Raleigh, NC 27695-0001.

VINIKAS, VINCENT
PERSONAL Born 03/29/1951, PA **DISCIPLINE** HISTORY **EDUCATION** Pa State Univ, BA, 72; Columbia Univ, MA, 74; MPhil, 76; PhD 83. **CAREER** Prof, Univ Ark at Little Rock. **HONORS AND AWARDS** Phi Beta Kappa; Phi Alpha Theta; Phi Kappa Phi; NEH Inst Fel, 84, 93, & 98. **RESEARCH** Modern American culture. **SELECTED PUBLICATIONS** Auth, Soft Soap, Hard Sell: American Hygiene in an Age of Advertisement, 92; auth, "Specters in the Past: The Saint Charles, Arkansas, Lynching of 1904 and the Limits of Historical Inquiry," J of S Hist (99). **CONTACT ADDRESS** Dept Hist, Univ of Arkansas, Little Rock, 2801 S Univ Ave, Little Rock, AR 72204-1000. **EMAIL** vxvinikas@ualr.edu

VINOVSKIS, MARIS A.
PERSONAL Born 01/01/1943, Riga, Latvia, m, 1966, 1 child **DISCIPLINE** AMERICAN HISTORY **EDUCATION** Wesleyan Col, BA, 65; Harvard Univ, AM, 66, PhD, 75. **CAREER** Asst prof hist, Univ Wis, 72-74; asst prof, 74-77, assoc prof, 77-80, prof hist, 80-, A.M & H.P. Bentley Prof of Hist, 97-, fac mem, School of Public Policy, 98-, Univ Mich; mem demog, Ctr Demog & Ecol, Univ Wis, 72-74; Clark Univ & Am Antiqn Soc fel family hist, 73-74; Harvard Ctr Population Studies res fel, 73-75; fac assoc polit sci, Inst Social Res, Univ Mich, 74-81; asst staff dir pop, US House Select Comt on Pop, 77-78; res scientist, Inst Soc Res, Univ Mich, 81-; Guggenheim fel, 81; res advisor to OERI, US Dept of Educ, 92-93. **HONORS AND AWARDS** Elected mem Nat Acad of Educ, 96; elected pres Hist of Educ Soc, 94-95. **MEMBERSHIPS** AHA; Social Sci Hist Asn; Econ Hist Asn; Orgn Am Historians; Pop Asn Am. **RESEARCH** Demographic history; family history; educational history. **SELECTED PUBLICATIONS** Coauth, Religion, Family, and the Life Course: Explorations in the Social History of Early America, Michigan, 92; co-ed, Learning from the Past: What History Teaches Us About School Reform, Johns Hopkins, 95; auth, Education, Society, and Economic Opportunity: A Historical Perspective on Persistent Problems, Yale, 95; auth, History and Educational Policymaking, Yale, 99. **CONTACT ADDRESS** Dept of History, Univ of Michigan, Ann Arbor, 1029 Tisch Hall, Ann Arbor, MI 48109-1003. **EMAIL** vinovski@umich.edu

VINYARD, JOELLEN
PERSONAL Born Ottawa, KS, m, 2 children **DISCIPLINE** HISTORY **EDUCATION** Univ Mich, PhD. **CAREER** Prof, coop and internship adv Graduate Program Coordinator, Eastern Michigan Univ. **HONORS AND AWARDS** Outstanding Faculty Teaching Awd, 98; Faculty Scholarship Awd, 99; Outstanding Scholar. **RESEARCH** US Michigan,US, Urban. **SELECTED PUBLICATIONS** Auth, The Irish on the Urban Frontier: Nineteenth-Century Detroit; Michigan: The World Around Us; auth, "For Faith and Fortune: Education of Immigrants in Detroit," Univ of Illinois Press, 99. **CONTACT ADDRESS** Dept of History and Philosophy, Eastern Michigan Univ, 701 Pray-Harrold, Ypsilanti, MI 48197. **EMAIL** his_vinyard@online.emich.edu

VIOLA, HERMAN JOSEPH
PERSONAL Born 02/24/1938, Chicago, IL, m, 1964, 3 children **DISCIPLINE** AMERICAN HISTORY **EDUCATION** Marquette Univ, BA, 60, MA, 64; Ind Univ, Bloomington, PhD (hist), 70. **CAREER** Archivist, Nat Arch, 67-72; Nat Hist Publ Comn, 68; ed, Prologue, J Nat Arch, 68-72; Dir Nat Anthrop Arch, Smithsonian Inst, 72-87; Dir, Human Studies Film Arch, Smithsonian Inst, 82-; curator emer, Natl Mus of Nat Hist. **HONORS AND AWARDS** Marquette Univ, 84; Merit Awd for distinguished professional achievement; One of three finalists for the position of Archivist of the United States, 87; hon doctor of letters degree, Wittenberg Univ, 88. **MEMBERSHIPS** Soc Am Archivists; Orgn Am Historians; Western Hist Asn. **RESEARCH** The Civil War; the American West; and the

American Indian. **SELECTED PUBLICATIONS** Auth, Magnificent Voyagers: The U.S. Exploring Expedition of 1838-1841, Smithsonian Institution Press, 86; auth, Exploring the West, Smithsonian Exposition Books, 87; auth, After Columbus: The Chronicle of America's Indian Peoples Since 1492, Smithsonian Institution Press, 90; ed, Seeds of Change, Smithsonian Institution, 91; auth, Ben Nighthorse Campbell: An American Warrior, Random House, 93; auth, The Memoirs of Charles Henry Veil, Random House, 93; auth, The North American Indians, Crown Books, 96; auth, Warrior Artists, The National Geographic Soc, 98; auth, It is a Good Day to Die, Crown Books, 98; auth, Little Bighorn Remembered: The Untold Indian Story of Custer's Last Stand, Random House, 99. **CONTACT ADDRESS** National Museum of Nat Hist, Smithsonian Inst, Washington, DC 20560.

VIOLAS, PAUL CONSTANTINE
PERSONAL Born 05/04/1937, Rochester, NY, m, 1957, 4 children **DISCIPLINE** HISTORY OF EDUCATION **EDUCATION** Univ Rochester, BA, 59, MA, 66, EdD 69. **CAREER** Teacher US hist, Canandaigua Acad, 59-66; Prof Hist of Educ, Univ Ill, 68-; Assoc Dean, 82-; Assoc ed, Educ Theory, 70-. **MEMBERSHIPS** Hist Educ Soc. **RESEARCH** History of urban education United States; history of working class; class consciousness. **SELECTED PUBLICATIONS** Auth, Fear and freedom, Educ Theory, winter 70; The indoctrination debate & the Great Depression, Hist Teacher, 5/71; coauth, Roots of Crisis, Rand McNally, 73; auth, The Training of the Urban Working Class, Rand McNally, 78; Reflections on theories of human capital, skills, training and vocational education, Educ Theory, spring 82; co-ed, Readings in American Public Schooling, Ginn, 82. **CONTACT ADDRESS** Univ of Illinois, Urbana-Champaign, 375 Educ Bldg, Urbana, IL 61801.

VIOLETTE, AURELE J.
PERSONAL Born 07/11/1941, ME, m, 1967, 2 children **DISCIPLINE** HISTORY **EDUCATION** Ohio State Univ, PhD, 71. **CAREER** Prof. **RESEARCH** Russian history. **SELECTED PUBLICATIONS** Auth, French in Peopling Indiana: the Ethnic Experience, 96; pubs in Slavonic and East European Review, European Studies Review, Indiana Magazine of History; auth, Fort Wayne, 99. **CONTACT ADDRESS** Dept of History, Indiana Univ-Purdue Univ, Fort Wayne, E 2101 Coliseum Blvd, Fort Wayne, IN 46805. **EMAIL** violetta@ipfw.edu

VIPOND, MARY
DISCIPLINE HISTORY **EDUCATION** Queen's Univ, BA; Univ Toronto, MA, PhD. **CAREER** Prof. **MEMBERSHIPS** Mem, Concordia's Ctr for Broadcasting Stud. **RESEARCH** Twentieth century English Canadian intellectual, cultural and media history. **SELECTED PUBLICATIONS** Auth, The Mass Media in Canada, 89; 2nd ed, 92; Listening In: The First Decade of Canadian Broadcasting, 1922-1932. **CONTACT ADDRESS** Dept of Hist, Concordia Univ, Montreal, 1455 de Maisonneuve W, Montreal, QC, Canada H3G 1M8. **EMAIL** vipond@vax2.concordia.ca

VIPPERMAN, CARL
PERSONAL Born 03/27/1928, Sophia, WV, m, 1957, 1 child **DISCIPLINE** AMERICAN HISTORY **EDUCATION** Univ NC, Chapel Hill, AB, 55; Univ Ga, MA, 61; Univ Va, PhD (hist), 66. **CAREER** From asst prof to assoc prof Am hist, Col Charleston, 64-67; asst prof, 67-79, Assoc Prof Am Hist, Univ GA, 79-. **MEMBERSHIPS** Southern Hist Asn. **RESEARCH** Middle period of American history; Lowndes family in colonial and antebellum South Carolina politics; Georgia politics and Indian removal. **CONTACT ADDRESS** Dept of Hist, Univ of Georgia, 202 LeConte Hall, Athens, GA 30602-1602.

VISSER, DERK
DISCIPLINE HISTORY **EDUCATION** Bryn Mawr Col, PhD. **CAREER** Prof, Ursinus Col. **HONORS AND AWARDS** Lindback Awd for Excellence in Tchg; Laughlin Prof Achievement Awd. **RESEARCH** Medieval European history; the history of the Renaissance and Reformation. **SELECTED PUBLICATIONS** Published widely on the Reformation in Germany and the Netherlands, including the standard biography of Zacharius Ursinus as well as several books and numerous articles on medieval church history. **CONTACT ADDRESS** Ursinus Col, Collegeville, PA 19426-1000.

VITA, STEVEN
PERSONAL Born 07/16/1960, Chicago, IL, s **DISCIPLINE** ART **EDUCATION** Univ of Chicago Lab Sch, 74-76; Latin Sch of Chicago, 76-78; Denison Univ, BA, 78-82 **CAREER** Ed and Founder, 91-pres, Veery Journ **MEMBERSHIPS** Am Philos Assoc **CONTACT ADDRESS** Veery, Suite 2044, Chicago, IL 60602.

VITZ, ROBERT C.
PERSONAL Born 12/26/1938, Minneapolis, MN, m, 1964, 3 children **DISCIPLINE** HISTORY **EDUCATION** Depauw Univ, BA, 60; Miami Univ, MA, 67; Univ NC at Chapel Hill, PhD, 71. **CAREER** Vis asst prof, Purdue Univ, 71-72; from asst prof to prof & chemn, Northern Ky Univ, 72-. **HONORS AND AWARDS** NEH Summer Fel, 77. **MEMBERSHIPS** Cincinnati Museum Ctr, Ky Asn of Teachers of Hist, Inst for Studies in Am Music. **RESEARCH** American Cultural History, Urban History, Cincinnati. **SELECTED PUBLICATIONS** Auth, "Painters of Reform: Robert Henri, John Sloan, and The New York Realists," in Reform and Reformers in The Progressive Era, 82; auth, The Queen and the Arts: Cultural Life in Nineteenth-Century Cincinnati, 89; auth, "The Troubled Life of James Handasyd Perkins," Queen City Heritage 53 (93); auth, "Introduction," in Cincinnati Symphony Orchestra: Centennial Portraits, 94. **CONTACT ADDRESS** Dept Hist & Geog, No Kentucky Univ, Newport, KY 41099-0001. **EMAIL** ritz@nku.edu

VIVIAN, JAMES FLOYD
PERSONAL Born 08/25/1934, Phoenix, AZ, m, 1964, 2 children **DISCIPLINE** US HISTORY, LATIN AMERICAN & UNITED STATES DIPLOMATIC HISTORY **EDUCATION** Coe Col, BA, 60; Univ Nebr-Lincoln, MA, 64; Am Univ, PhD(US Diplomacy), 71. **CAREER** Archivist, Nat Arch, Washington, DC, 69-70; asst prof US & Latin Am Hist, Univ Wis-Platteville, 70-73; assoc prof Hist, 73-80, prof Hist, Univ NDak, 80-. **MEMBERSHIPS** AHA; Orgn Am Historians; Soc Historians Am Foreign Rels: AAUP; Conf Latin Am Hist. **RESEARCH** US political, Inter-American affairs; United States-Latin American relations. **SELECTED PUBLICATIONS** Auth, The Taking of Panama Canal Zone: Myth and reality, Diplomatic Hist, Winter 80; US Policy during Brazilian Naval Revolt, 1893-94: Case for American neutrality, Am Neptune, 10/81; ed, William Howard Taft: Collected Editorials, 1917-1921, NY: Praeger Publishers, 90; The President's Salary: A Study in constitutional Declension, 1789-1990, NY: Garland Press, 93. **CONTACT ADDRESS** Dept of History, Univ of No Dakota, Box 8096, Grand Forks, ND 58202-8096.

VLAM, GRACE A. H.
PERSONAL Born 12/17/1930, Netherlands, s **DISCIPLINE** ART HISTORY **EDUCATION** Univ Utah, MA, 60; Univ Mich, Ann Arbor, PhD, 76. **CAREER** Cur and Actg Dir, Salt Lake Art Ctr, 66-68; instr, Univ Utah, 69-70; tchg fel, Univ Mich, 71-73; vis asst prof, SUNY Buffalo, 76-77; indep res, Yale Univ, 77-78; vis asst prof, Weber State Col, 81-82; adj instr, 82-88, assoc instr, 89- , Univ Utah; Assoc Prof Art Hist and Hum, Salt Lake Commun Col. **HONORS AND AWARDS** Plantin-Moretus Mus Res Grant, Antwerp, Belgium, 72; Samuel B. Kress grant, 73-74; Horace Rackham res grant, 74-75; A. and S. Krissoff Res Grant, 74-75; NEH summer stipend, 77, 83. **MEMBERSHIPS** Col Art Asn of Am. **RESEARCH** Archaeo-Art history. **SELECTED PUBLICATIONS** Coauth, The Poet-Painters: Buson and His Followers, Univ Michigan, 74; coauth, Namban Byobu (Namban Screens), Kodansha, 79; contribur, Muller, ed, Encyclopedia of Dutch Art, 97; numerous articles in The Aet Bulletin, Aetibus Asiae, Kokka, Zeitschrift fuer Kunstgeschiekte. **CONTACT ADDRESS** Humanities Dept, Salt Lake Comm Col, 4600 S Redwood Rd, PO Box 30808, Salt Lake City, UT 84130-0808.

VLASICH, JAMES ANTHONY
PERSONAL Born 04/19/1944, Hillsboro, IL, 2 children **DISCIPLINE** AMERICAN INDIAN HISTORY, AMERICAN WEST, SPORTS HISTORY. **EDUCATION** Southern Ill Univ, BA, 67; Ft Lewis Col, BA, 75; Univ Utah, MA, 77, PhD, 80. **CAREER** Assoc engr & comput programmer, McDonnel Douglas Corp, 67-68; United States Army, 68-69; Comput Programmer, State of Colo, 70-73; asst US hist, Univ Utah, 75-77, res asst Am Indians, Am West Ctr, 78-79; instr US hist, Westminster Col, 79; historian Western hist, Archaeol Ctr, Univ Utah, 80-81; asst prof Indians, Southern Utah Univ, Lake City, Utah, 74-77. **HONORS AND AWARDS** Teacher of the Year, Southern Utah Univ, 86; Southern Utah Univ Awd for best published article of the year (Alexander Cleland and the Origin..), 92; Distinguished Educator, Southern Utah Univ, 98. **MEMBERSHIPS** Orgn Am Historians; Western Hist Asn; Soc Am Baseball Res. **RESEARCH** Southwest Indians; New Mexico history. **SELECTED PUBLICATIONS** Auth, Transitions in pueblo agriculture, 1938-1948, NMex Hist Rev, 1/80; The history of the Bayhorse mining district, 9/80, History of the Elko and Ely districts, 4/81 & History of the Escalante Desert, 8/81, Univ Utah Archaeol Ctr; Assimilation or extermination: A cooperative study of Indians of the US in 19th century and Brazilian Indians in the 20th century, Occas Papers, No 19, Am West Ctr, Univ Utah, 81; A Legend for the Legendary: The Origin of the Baseball Hall of Fame, Bowling Green Univ Press, 90; Alexander Cleland and the Origin of the Baseball Hall of Fame, in Cooperstown Symposium on Baseball and American Culture, Meckler Publ, 89; Bob Broeg, in The Dictionary of Literary Biography: Twentieth Century Sportswriters, Gale Res, 96. **CONTACT ADDRESS** So Utah Univ, 225 Centrum, Cedar City, UT 84720-2470. **EMAIL** vlasich@suu.edu

VOEGELI, VICTOR JACQUE
PERSONAL Born 12/21/1934, Jackson, TN, m, 1956, 2 children **DISCIPLINE** UNITED STATES HISTORY **EDUCATION** Murray State Col, BS, 56; Tulance Univ, MA, 61, PhD(hist), 65. **CAREER** Instr US Hist, Tulane Univ, 63-65, asst prof, 65-67; from asst prof to assoc prof, 67-73, chmn dept, 73-75, prof Hist, Vanderbilt Univ, 73-, dean, Col Arts & Sci, 76-92; acting dean, Col Arts & Sciences, 96-97; Nat Endowment for Humanities res grant, 69-70 & 72; prof-dean, emer, 98. **MEMBERSHIPS** Southern Hist Asn Orgn Am Historians. **RESEARCH** Southern Hist; Civil War and reconstruction; 19th century United States. **SELECTED PUBLICATIONS** Auth, The Northwest and the race issue, 1861-1862, Miss Valley Hist Rev, 9/63; Free But Not Equal: The Midwest and the Negro During the Civil War, Univ Chicago, 67. **CONTACT ADDRESS** Vanderbilt Univ, Box 1863, Nashville, TN 37240-0001. **EMAIL** jacque.voegeli@vanderbilt.edu

VOELTZ, RICHARD ANDREW
PERSONAL Born 12/04/1948, Chicago, IL **DISCIPLINE** MODERN EUROPEAN HISTORY **EDUCATION** Univ Calif, Santa Cruz, BA, 71; Univ Ore, MA, 74; Univ Calif, Los Angeles, PhD (hist), 80. **CAREER** Teaching asst western civilization, Univ Calif, Los Angeles, 79-80; Lectr Hist, Calif State Univ, Fullerton, 80-. **MEMBERSHIPS** AHA; NAm Soc Sport Hist. **RESEARCH** British and German colonial companies; South Africa; comparative social history. **SELECTED PUBLICATIONS** Auth, Sport, culture and society in late Imperial and Weimar Germany: Some suggestions for future research, J Sport Hist, fall 77; The question of British participation in the Bagdad railway and imperial reaction in the Persian Gulf, 1899-1906, J Hist Studies, Am Univ, fall 81. **CONTACT ADDRESS** 11005 Sardis Ave, Los Angeles, CA 90064.

VOGEL, ROBERT
PERSONAL Born 11/04/1929, Vienna, Austria, 1 child **DISCIPLINE** MODERN HISTORY **EDUCATION** Sir George Williams Univ, BA, 52; McGill Univ, MA, 54, PhD (hist), 59. **CAREER** Lectr, 58-61, from asst prof to assoc prof, 61-69, chmn dept, 66-71, Prof Hist, McGill Univ, 69-; Dean Fac Arts, 71-. **MEMBERSHIPS** AHA; Orgn Hist Asn. **RESEARCH** British foreign policy in the nineteenth and twentieth centuries; war and society in modern Europe. **SELECTED PUBLICATIONS** Auth, Earthworms, Smithsonian, Vol 24, 93; From Consecutio Temporum to Aktionsart, Lingua E Stile, Vol 31, 96; Alienation in Studies on the Early Works of Boll, Etudes Germaniques, Vol 52, 97. **CONTACT ADDRESS** Fac of Arts, McGill Univ, 853 Sherbrooke St, Montreal, QC, Canada H3A 2T6.

VOGELER, MARTHA SALMON
PERSONAL Born New York, NY, m, 1962 **DISCIPLINE** ENGLISH LITERATURE, INTELLECTUAL HISTORY **EDUCATION** Jersey City State Col, BA, 46; Columbia Univ, MA, 52, PhD (English), 59. **CAREER** Lectr French Columbia Univ, 55-60; lectr, NY Univ, 56-59; instr, Vassar Col, 59-62; asst prof, Long Island Univ, 62-66; assoc prof, 69-73, Prof English, Calif State Univ, Fullerton, 73-; Am Coun Learned Soc grant, 67; Am Philos Soc grants, 67 and 70. **MEMBERSHIPS** MLA; AAUP; Tennyson Soc; Res Soc Victorian Periodicals; Pac Coast Conf British Studies. **RESEARCH** Victorian biography, aesthetics and religious thought. **SELECTED PUBLICATIONS** **CONTACT ADDRESS** Dept of English, California State Univ, Fullerton, Fullerton, CA 92831.

VOGT, DANIEL
PERSONAL Born 08/08/1943, Haledon, NJ, s **DISCIPLINE** HISTORY **EDUCATION** Bob Jones Univ, BA, 65; Univ NY Binghampton, MA, 67; Univ Southern Miss, PhD, 80. **HONORS AND AWARDS** Willie D. Halzell Prize, Miss Hist Soc, 87. **MEMBERSHIPS** OAH; SHA; Miss Hist Soc. **RESEARCH** Mississipi History. **SELECTED PUBLICATIONS** Auth, "Poor Relief in Frontier Mississippi, 1798-1832", J of Miss Hist 49, (89): 181-199; coauth, Mississippi: A Portrait of an American State, Clairmont Pr, 99. **CONTACT ADDRESS** Dept Hist, Jackson State Univ, 1400 Lynch St, Jackson, MS 39217-0002. **EMAIL** dcvogt@ccaix.jsums.edu

VOGT, GEORGE LEONARD
PERSONAL Born Belleville, IL **DISCIPLINE** AMERICAN HISTORY **EDUCATION** Yale Univ, AB, 66; Univ Va, MA, 70 PhD (hist), 78. **CAREER** From asst to exec dir, 74-78, Asst Dir Publ, Nat Hist Publ and Rec Comn, 78-. **MEMBERSHIPS** Asn State and Local Hist; Southern Hist Asn; Manuscript Soc (vpres, 81-); Nat Micrographics Asn. **RESEARCH** Twentieth century southern politics; historical editing; American cultural history. **SELECTED PUBLICATIONS** **CONTACT ADDRESS** Nat Hist Publ and Rec Comn, National Archives, Washington, DC 20408.

VOIGT, DAVID QUENTIN
PERSONAL Born 08/09/1926, Reading, PA, m, 1951, 2 children **DISCIPLINE** HISTORY, SOCIOLOGY, ANTHROPOLOGY **EDUCATION** Albright Col, BS (history), 48; Columbia Univ, MA (Am hist), 49; Syracuse Univ, PhD (Hist, Socl Sci), 62. **CAREER** Teacher, state of NY, social studies, 50-56; assoc prof hist and social science, Millerville State Univ, PA, 56-63; assoc prof, sociology & anthroplogy, Muskingum Col, New Concord, OH, 63-64; prof of sociology & anthropology at Albright Col, Reading, PA, 64-95, prof Emeritus, 96-. **HONORS AND AWARDS** Winner of Lindback Distinguished Teaching Awd; Alumnus of the Year, Milton Hershey School, PA, 93. **MEMBERSHIPS** PA Sociol Soc (past pres); Am An-

thropol Asn; Am Sociol Asn; Soc for Am Baseball Res (past pres); North Am Soc for Sports Hist. **RESEARCH** Am baseball studies--author of seven books on Am major league baseball; leisure in AM; Civil War hist. **SELECTED PUBLICATIONS** Auth, Thenk God for Nuts, in The Perfect Game, Marl Alvarez, ed, Dallas, TX, 93; The History of Major League Baseball, in 3rd ed of Total Baseball, 93; The League That Failed, Scarecrow Press of MD, 98. **CONTACT ADDRESS** Dept of Sociol, Albright Col, Reading, PA 19603.

VOIGTS, LINDA EHRSAM
PERSONAL Born 05/09/1942, Abilene, KS, m, 1963, 1 child **DISCIPLINE** OLD AND MIDDLE ENGLISH, HISTORY OF MEDICINE **EDUCATION** William Jewell Col, BA, 63; Univ Mo-Kansas City, MA, 66; Univ Mo-Columbia, PhD (English), 73. **CAREER** Teacher Ger and English, North Kansas City High Sch, 63-65; instr English, William Jewell Col, 65-69; instr compos, Univ Mo-Columbia, 72; vis asst prof English, William Jewell Col, 73-74 and Univ Mo-Columbia, 74-75; asst prof, 75-79, Assoc Prof English, Univ MO-Kansas City, 79-; Am Coun Learned Soc grant-in-aid, 75; Andrew W Mellon fac fel humanities, Harvard Univ, 78-79; vis instr, Harvard Univ, summer, 80. **HONORS AND AWARDS** Zeitlin-VerBrugge Prize, Hist of Sci Soc, 81. **MEMBERSHIPS** Mediaeval Acad Am; MLA; Hist of Sci Soc; Am Asn Hist Med; New Chaucer Soc. **RESEARCH** Old English; Middle English. **SELECTED PUBLICATIONS** Auth, A new look at a manuscript containing the Old English translation of the Herbarium Apulei, Manuscripta, 76; One Anglo-Saxon view of the classical Gods, Studies in Iconography, 78; The significance of the name Apuleius to the Herbarium Apulei, Bull Hist of Med, 78; Anglo-Saxon Plant Remedies and the Anglo-Saxons, Isis, 79; A Boece fragment, Studies in the Age of Chancer, 79; coauth, A missing leaf from Douce 250, Bodleian Libr Record, 81; A Letter from a Middle English Dictaminal Formulary in Harvard Law Library MS.43, Speculum, 81; Editing Middle English medical texts, In: Editing Texts in the History of Science and Medicine, Garland, 82. **CONTACT ADDRESS** Dept of English, Univ of Missouri, Kansas City, 5100 Rockhill Rd, Kansas City, MO 64110-2499.

VOLL, JOHN OBERT
PERSONAL Born 04/20/1936, Hudson, WI, m, 1965, 2 children **DISCIPLINE** MIDDLE EASTERN HISTORY **EDUCATION** Darmouth Col, AB, 58; Harvard Univ, AM, 60, PhD (hist and Mid E studies), 69. **CAREER** From instr to asst prof, 65-73, Assoc Prof Hist, Univ NH, 73-; Nat Endowment for Humanities younger humanist fel, 71-72. **MEMBERSHIPS** Mid E Studies Asn NAm; Am Orient Soc; Mid E Inst; African Studies Asn; New Eng Hist Asn (secy 75-78). **RESEARCH** Modern Islamic history; Sudanese history; methodology of world history. **SELECTED PUBLICATIONS** Auth, Historical Discord in the Nile Valley, Int J African Hist Stud, Vol 27, 94; Islam as a Special World System, J World Hist, Vol 5, 94; The Sufi Brotherhoods in the Sudan, Int J African Hist Stud, Vol 29, 96; Civil War in the Sudan, Int J African Hist Stud, Vol 29, 96; Islam in the View from the Edge, Int Hist Rev, Vol 18, 96; Merchants and Faith in Muslim Commerce and Culture in the Indian Ocean, J World Hist, Vol 8, 97. **CONTACT ADDRESS** Dept of Hist, Georgetown Univ, PO Box 571035, Washington, DC 20057-1035.

VOLPE, VERNON L.
PERSONAL Born 03/24/1955, New Orleans, LA, m, 1982, 2 children **DISCIPLINE** HISTORY **EDUCATION** Youngstown State Univ, BA, 77; MA, 79; Univ Neb, PhD, 84. **CAREER** Vis prof, Tex AM Univ, 86-87; prof, Univ Neb, 87-00; ch, 93-96, 99-00. **HONORS AND AWARDS** Pratt-Hines Found Fac Awd; UNK Teach Awd. **MEMBERSHIPS** OAH; SHA; SHEAR. **RESEARCH** Nineteenth century politics; Civil War and reconstruction; antislavery movement; western exploration and expansion. **SELECTED PUBLICATIONS** Auth, Forlorn Hope of Freedom: The Liberty Party in the Old Northwest, Kent St Univ (Kent, OH), 90; auth, "The Anti-Abolitionist Campaign of 1840," Civ War Hist 56 (86): 325-339; auth, "The Fremonts and Emancipation in Missouri," Hist 56 (94): 339-354; auth, "The Liberty Party and Polk's Election, 1844" Hist 53 (91): 691-710; auth, "The Origins of the Fremont Expeditions," Hist 62 (00): 245-263. **CONTACT ADDRESS** Dept History, Univ of Nebraska, Kearney, 905 W 25th St, Kearney, NE 68849-1285. **EMAIL** volpev@unk.edu

VON ARX, JEFFERY P.
PERSONAL Born 05/12/1947, Bellefonte, PA, s **DISCIPLINE** HISTORY **EDUCATION** Princeton Univ, AB, 69; Yale Univ, MA, 73, Mphil, 74, PhD, 80; Weston Sch of Theol, Mdiv, 81. **CAREER** Asst Prof History, Assoc Prof, Dept Chair, Georgetown Univ, 82-98; Dean, Fordham Coll, 98-. **HONORS AND AWARDS** Visiting Fel, Research Sch of the Social Sci, Australian Natl Univ, 90; Georgetown Univ Summer Academic Grant, 86; Grant-in-Aid, Concilium on Area and Internatl Studies, Yale Univ, 75; Phi Beta Kappa, Princeton Univ, 69; Natl Merit Scholar, Princeton Univ, 65-69. **MEMBERSHIPS** Amer Hist Assoc; Amer Catholic Hist Assoc; member, Joint Commission of Bishops and Scholars; North Amer Conf on British Studies; Amer Conf for Irish Studies; Australian Studies Assoc of North Amer. **RESEARCH** British and Irish 19th century hist; church hist, Australian hist. **SELECTED PUBLICATIONS** auth, Victorian Faith in Crisis, The Victorian Crisis of Faith as Crisis of Vocation, Macmillan, London, 90; Recusant Studies, Archbishop Manning and the Kulturkampf, Oct 92; ed, Varieties of Ultramontanism, Catholic Univ Press, Washington D.C., 97; auth, Progress and Pessimism, Havard UP, 85; auth, "Catholics and Politics," in From Without the Flaminian Gate, Darnton, Longman and Todd (London), 99. **CONTACT ADDRESS** Dean's Office, Fordham Univ, Bronx, NY 10458. **EMAIL** jvonarx@fordham.edu

VON BAEYER, EDWINNA L.
PERSONAL Born 08/22/1946, Detroit, MI **DISCIPLINE** HISTORY **EDUCATION** Univ Mich, BA, 68; Univ Pa, MA, 70. **CAREER** Independent writer, researcher & editor, Canada, 78- . **HONORS AND AWARDS** Can Coun Explor grant, 81; SSHRCC grant, 83. **MEMBERSHIPS** Bd dir, Ottawa Independent Writers Asn, 89-94; Friends of Cent Exp Farm, 96-. **RESEARCH** Canadian landscape history. **SELECTED PUBLICATIONS** Auth, Rhetoric and Roses: A History of Canadian Gardening, 1900-1930, Fitzhenry & Whiteside (Markham, ON), 84; auth, Garden of Dreams: Kingsmere and Mackenzie King, Dundurn Pr (Toronto, ON), 90; co-auth, The Reluctant Gardener: A Beginners Guide, Random House, 92; co-auth, The No-Garden Gardener: Gardening on Balconies, Decks, Patios and Porches, Random House, 93; co-auth, Garden Voices: Two Centuries of Canadian Garden Writing, Random House, 95; auth, 100 Years of Community Service: History of the May Court Club, May Court Club, 99. **CONTACT ADDRESS** 131 Sunnyside Ave, Ottawa, ON, Canada K1S 0R2.

VON HAGEN, MARK L.
DISCIPLINE HISTORY **EDUCATION** Georgetown Univ, BSFS, 76; Indiana Univ, MA, Slavic Lang aand Lit, 78; Stanford Univ, MA, Hist, 80, PhD, 85. **CAREER** Instr, Assoc Dir, Indiana Univ, 81-82; Visiting Prof, Yale Univ, Jan 88-May 88; Asst Prof, Columbia Univ, Jan 85- June 89; Visiting Prof, Osteuropa-Inst, Sept 91-Dec 91; Assoc Dir, Columbia Univ, W. Averell Harriman Inst for the Advanced Study of the Soviet Union, July 89-June 92; Visiting Assoc Prof, Stanford Univ, Jan 95-June 95; Dir, The Harriman Inst, Columbia Univ, July 95-present; Prof, Columbia Univ, July 89-present. **SELECTED PUBLICATIONS** Auth, Post-Soviet Political Order: Conflict and State Building, The Great War and the Mobilization of Ethnicity in the Russian Empire, 98; ConAuth, Forging the Sword: Selecting, Educating and Training Cadets and Junior Officers in the Modern World, Confronting Backwardness: Dilemmas of Soviet Officer Education in the Interwar Years, 1918-1941, forthcoming 1998; Peoples, Nations, Identies: The Russian-Ukrainian Encounter, Introduction and States, Nations and Identities: The Russian-Ukrainian Encounter in the First Half of the 20th Century, forthcoming 1998; Kazan, Moscow, St. Petersburg: Multiple Faces of the Russian Empire, Writing the History of Russia as Empire, 97. **CONTACT ADDRESS** The Harriman Institute, Columbia Univ, 420 W. 118, New York, NY 10027. **EMAIL** mlv2@columbia.edu

VONFALKENHAUSEN, L.
DISCIPLINE ART HISTORY **EDUCATION** Harvard Univ, PhD 88. **CAREER** Stanford Univ vis prof; Univ Cal Riverside, asst prof, assoc prof; U of Calif LA, prof. **HONORS AND AWARDS** Andrew W Miller Postdoc Fel; Getty Rex Fel. **MEMBERSHIPS** AAA; AAS; CAA. **RESEARCH** Chinese Bronze Age Archaeology. **SELECTED PUBLICATIONS** Auth, Suspended Music: Chime-Bells in the Culture of Bronze Age China, Berk and LA, U of Calif Press, 93; auth, The Waning of the Bronze Age: Material Culture and Social Developments, 770-481 bc, The Cambridge History og Bronze Age China, Edward L Shaughnessy, Michael Loewe, eds, Cambridge, Cambridge U Press, forthcoming; auth, Reflections on the Political Role of Spirit Mediums in Early China: The wu Officials in the Zhou li, Early China, 95; auth, The Moutuo Bronzes: New Perspectives on the Late Bronze Age in Sichuan, Arts Asiatiques, 96, auth, The Concept of wen in the Ancient Chinese Ancestral Cult, Chin Lit: Essays Article and Rev, 96; auth, Inscribed and Decorated Objects, coauth, in: Down by the Station: The Los Angeles Chinatown 1850-1933, by Roberta S Greenwood, LA, UCLA Inst of Archaeol, 96; rev, Monumentally in Early Chinese Art and Architecture, by Wu Hung, Early China, 96; auth, Early Chinese Texts: A Bibliographic Guide, ed, Michael J. Loewe, China Rev Intl, 96; auth, Art and Political Expression in Early China, by Martin Powers, Harvard Jour of Asiatic Stud, 95; translations from Chinese, Teng Shu-p'ing, The Original Significance of bi Disks: Insights Based on Liangzhu Jade bi with Incised Symbolic Motifs, co-ed, Jour of East Asian Archaeol, forthcoming. **CONTACT ADDRESS** Dept of Art History, Univ of California, Los Angeles, Los Angeles, CA 90095-1417. **EMAIL** lothar@humnet.ucla

VOSPER, JIM M.
PERSONAL Born 03/29/1947, Centralia, WA, s **DISCIPLINE** HISTORY, EDUCATION, PHILOSOPHY **EDUCATION** Saint Martin's Col, BA, 68; Univ Nebr, Lincoln, MA, 73, PhD, 76. **CAREER** Part-time instr, Centralia Col, 77-; part-time instr, South Puget Sound Community Col, 84-. **HONORS AND AWARDS** McNair Scholar Mentor, 96. **MEMBERSHIPS** Am Fedn of Teachers, Nat Educ Asn. **RESEARCH** Pacific Northwest history, educational history, religion in history. **SELECTED PUBLICATIONS** 19 biographical sketches for the three volume Biographical Dictionary of American Educators, 78. **CONTACT ADDRESS** Dept Humanities & Soc Sci, Centralia Col, 600 W Locust St, Centralia, WA 98531-4035. **EMAIL** jvosper@centralia.ctc.edu

VRYONIS, SPEROS, JR.
PERSONAL Born 07/18/1928, Memphis, TN, m, 3 children **DISCIPLINE** HISTORY (ANCIENT, BYZANTINE, BALKAN, ISLAMIC, TURKISH) **EDUCATION** Southwestern Col (now Rhodes Col), BA, 50; Harvard, MA, 52, PhD, 56. **CAREER** Jr Fulbright fel, Am, School of Classical Studies Athens, 50-51; jr fel, Dumbarton Oaks, Washington, DC, 54-56; instr, Harvard Univ, 56-60; prof, UCLA, 60-88; prof, Univ Athens, 76-83; Alexander S Onassis Prof of Hellinic Civilization & Culture, New York Univ; dir, G E von Grunebaum Center of Near Eastern Studies UCLA, dir, Onassis Center for Hellenic Studies, NYU, dir, Vryonis Center, Sacramento, 96-. **HONORS AND AWARDS** Fel, Medieval Academy of Am; fel, Am Philos Soc; fel, Am Academy of Arts and Scirnces; Haskins Medal, Am Med Academy; Kokkinos Awd, Academy of Athens. **RESEARCH** Classical antiquity; Byzantium; Ottoman-Turkish hist; Islamic hist; hist of Balkans; immigration hist. **SELECTED PUBLICATIONS** Auth, Byzantium and Europe, London, 70; The Decline of Medieval Hellenism in Asia Minor and the Process of Islamization from the Eleventh through the Fifteenth Century, Berkeley, 71; Byzantium: Its Internal History and Relations with the Muslim World, London, 71; ed, The Past in Medieval and Modern Greek Culture, Malibu, 78; auth, Studies on Byzantium, Seljuks and Ottomans, Malibu, 81; St. George Greek Community of Memphis, Malibu, 82; The Turkish State and History. Cleo Meets the Grey Wolf, Thessalonika, 91; ed, Greece on the Road to Democracy: From the Junta to PASOK 1974-1986; ed, The Greeks and the Sea, New Rochelle, 93; auth, Byzantine Institutions, Society and Culture, vol I, The Imperial Institution and Society, New Rochelle, 97. **CONTACT ADDRESS** 3140 Gold Camp Dr, Ste 50, Rancho Cordova, CA 95670-6023.

VUCINICH, WAYNE S.
PERSONAL Born 06/23/1913, Butte, MT **DISCIPLINE** HISTORY **EDUCATION** Univ Calif, AB, 36, AM, 37, PhD, 41. **CAREER** Res analyst, Off Strategic Serv, 41-45 and US Dept State, 45-46; From instr to prof hist, 46-77, cur and dir Russ and East Europe studies, Hoover Inst, 74-77, Robert and Florence McDonnell Prof Eastern Europ Studies, Stanford Univ, 77-; Dir Ctr Russ and Eastern Europ Studies, 72-. **HONORS AND AWARDS** Festschrift in my honor, entitled Nation and Ideology; George Louis Beer Prize, 55; Dean's Awd for Distinguished Teaching, 77; The Vucinich Prize, AAASS, 82; Presented an engraved plaque by the Stanford Alumni and the Univ for 42 years of service as a teacher and scholar, 88; Commendation by Donald Kennedy, Pres of Stanford Univ for dedication and contribution to Stanford Univ and Stanford Alumni Asn, 88; AAASS Awd for Distinguished Contributions to Slavic Studies, 89; **MEMBERSHIPS** AHA; Am Asn Adv Slavic Studies (pres). **RESEARCH** East Europe and Near East history. **SELECTED PUBLICATIONS** Auth, Serbia Between East and West: The Events of 1903-1908, Stanford, 54; auth, The Ottoman Empire: Its Record and Legacy, Van Nostrand, 65; auth, "Ausgleich and Vojvodina," in Der Osterreichisch-Ungarische Ausgleich, Slovensska Akademia ved Historicky ustav, Bratislava, (71): 831-859; auth, A Study in Social Survival: Katun in Bileca Rudine, Univ of Denver, Graduate School in Social Studies, 75; auth, "Croatian Illyrism: Its Background and Genesis," in Stanley B. Winters and Joseph Held eds, Intellectual and Social Development in the Habsburg Empire, (New York: Columbia Univ, 75); auth, "A Zadruga in Bileca Rudine," in Robert F. Byrnes ed, Communal Families in the Balkans: The Zadruga, Univ of Notre Dame Press, (76): 162-186; auth, "Mlada Bosna and the First World War," in Robert A. Kann, et al. Eds, The Habsburg Empire in World War I, Columbia Univ, (77): 45-70; ed and contrib, "The First Serbian Uprising," in series War and Society in East Central Europe, (Columbia Univ Press, 82); ed and contrib, "The Tito-Stalin Split: At the Brink of War and Peace," in series War and Society in East Central Europe, (Columbia Univ Press, 82); ed, Ivo Andric Revisited: The Bridge Still Stands ed, Univ of California, (Berkeley), 95. **CONTACT ADDRESS** Dept of Hist, Stanford Univ, Stanford, CA 94305.

W

WABUDA, SUSAN
PERSONAL Born 01/22/1957, Derby, CT **DISCIPLINE** HISTORY **EDUCATION** Southern Conn State Univ, BA, 79; Wesleyan Univ, MA, 80; Cambridge Univ, PhD, 92. **CAREER** Asst Prof, Fordham Univ, 93-. **HONORS AND AWARDS** Fel, Royal Hist Soc, 99. **MEMBERSHIPS** Ecclesiastical Hist Soc, Am Hist Asn. **RESEARCH** The history of the English Reformation. **SELECTED PUBLICATIONS** Co-ed, Belief and Practice in Reformation England: A Tribute to Patrick Collinson from His Students, Aldershot and Brookfield, 98; auth, "Fruitful Preaching in the Diocese of Worcester: Bishop Hugh Latimer and His Influence, 1535-1539," in Religion and the En-

glish People 1500-1640: New Voices, New Perspectives, 98; auth, "Revising the Reformation," Journal of British Studies, (96): 257-262; auth, "Bibliography of the Published Writings of Patrick Collinson, 1957-1992,: in Religion, Culture, and Society in Early Modern Britain: Essays in Honour of Collinson, Cambridge Univ Press, 94; auth, "Bishops and the Provision of Homilies, 1520 to 1547," The Sixteenth Century Journal, (94): 551-566; auth, Preaching During the English Reformation, Cambridge Univ Press, forthcoming. **CONTACT ADDRESS** Dept Hist, Fordham Univ, 441 E Fordham Rd, Bronx, NY 10458-5159. **EMAIL** wabuda@fordham.edu

WACHOLDER, BEN ZION
PERSONAL Born 09/21/1924, Dzarow, Poland, m, 1993, 4 children **DISCIPLINE** ENGLISH LITERATURE; CLASSICS; HISTORY **EDUCATION** Yeshiva Univ, BA, 51; UCLA, PhD, 60. **CAREER** Prof, Hebrew Union Col, 56-98. **HONORS AND AWARDS** Pursuing the Text: Studies in Honor of Ben Zion Wacholder on the Occasion of his Seventieth Birthday **MEMBERSHIPS** Soc of Bibl Lit; Asoc of Jewish Studies **RESEARCH** Judaism during the second temple period; Hellenistic Judaism; Dead Sea Scrolls; Talmudic Studies; ancient historiography, ancient calendars **SELECTED PUBLICATIONS** auth, Nicolaus of Damascus, 62; auth, Eupolemus, 74; Essays in Jewish Chronology and Chronography, 84; The Dawn of Qumran, 84; A Preliminary Edition of the Unpublished Dead Sea Scrolls, 96. **CONTACT ADDRESS** 7648 Greenland Pl., Cincinnati, OH 45237. **EMAIL** ben648@aol.com

WACK, JOHN THEODORE
PERSONAL Born 12/18/1934, South Bend, IN **DISCIPLINE** AMERICAN HISTORY **EDUCATION** Univ Notre Dame, AB, 55, MA, 57, PhD, 67. **CAREER** From instr to assoc prof, 61-79, prof hist, Wheeling Col, 79- chmn dept, 75-; prof emer, 00. **MEMBERSHIPS** AHA; Orgn Am Historians. **RESEARCH** Am social hist; native Am hist; hist of Appalachia. **CONTACT ADDRESS** Dept of Hist, Wheeling Jesuit Col, 316 Washington Ave, Wheeling, WV 26003-6243. **EMAIL** jtwack@wju.edu

WADDAMS, STEPHEN M.
PERSONAL Born 09/30/1942, England **DISCIPLINE** HISTORY **EDUCATION** Trinity Col, BA, 63; King's Col, Cambridge, MA, 69, PhD, 94; Univ Toronto, LLB, 67; Univ Michigan, LLM, 68, SJD, 72. **CAREER** Asst prof, Univ Toronto, 68; assoc prof, 71; prof law, Univ Toronto, 76-. **HONORS AND AWARDS** Hurst Prize in Law, 65; Angus MacMurchy Gold Medal, 67; Law Reform Comn Can Awd, 89; David W Mundell Medal, 96; Visiting Sr Res Fel; Jesus Col, Oxford; Visiting Sr Lectr, Univ of Otago, Dunedin, New Zealand; Visiting Fel, All Souls Col, Oxford; Fel of Trinity Col, Univ of Toronto; Fel of the Royal Soc of Canada, 88, 89; Canadian Asn of Law Teachers/Law Reform Commmission of Canada Awd for Outstanding Contribution to Legal Research and Law Reform. **MEMBERSHIPS** Mem, Law Soc Upper Can; Can Bar Asn: Can Asn Law Tchrs; fel, Royal Soc Can, 88. **SELECTED PUBLICATIONS** Auth, Products Liability; auth, The Law of Contarcts; auth, The Law of Damages; auth, Introduction to the Study of Law; auth, Law, Politcs and the Church of England; auth, Sexual Slander in Nineteenth-Century England; auth, "New Directions in Products Liability," in Torts tomorrow: a tribute to John Fleming (ed Allen Linden and Nicholas Mullany, Law Book Company) (98): 119; auth, "Damages: Assessment of Uncertainties," 13 Journal of Contract Law 55, 98; auth, "Crossing Conceptual Boundaries: Liability for Product Defects," 14 Journal of Contract Law 28, 99; auth, "Causation, physicians, and disclosure of risks," 7 Tort Law Review 5, 99. **CONTACT ADDRESS** Fac of Law, Univ of Toronto, 78 Queen's Park, Toronto, ON, Canada M5S 2C5. **EMAIL** s.waddams@utoronto.ca

WADDELL, JAMES
PERSONAL Born, WV, m **DISCIPLINE** HISTORY, PHILOSOPHY **EDUCATION** Duke Univ, AB, 60; BD, 63; Oxford Univ, PhD, 65. **CAREER** Instructor, Princeton Univ, 65-68; Prof and Assoc Dean, Stephens Col, 72-79; Prof, Dean and Vice Pres, Col of Santa Fe, 79-82; Prof and Dean, Western N Mex Univ, 82-85; Prof, Dean and Assoc Vice Pres, Univ Redlands, 85-93; Academic Dean to President, Menlo Col, 94-. **HONORS AND AWARDS** NEH Grant, 84; Roswell Messing Fel, Oxford Univ, 74; Woodrow Wilson Fac Fel, Princeton Univ, 66068; Scholarship, Duke Univ, 56-60. **MEMBERSHIPS** Am Asn of Higher Educ, Am Asn of Univ Prof, Am Philos Soc, Am Acad of Relig, N Mex Coun of Art Educ, Inst for Adv Philos Res, Royal Inst of Philos. **RESEARCH** Philosophy and sexuality; History and philosophy of education, Relation of philosophy, religion and literature. **SELECTED PUBLICATIONS** Auth, "Philosophies Make Philosophers," Falling in Love with Wisdom: American Philosophers Talk About their calling, Oxford Univ Press, 93; auth, "Serious Educators and Self-directed Adults: an alliance for Success," Journal of Self-directed Education, (88): 7-10; auth, "Keble and the Reader's Imagination," Christianity and Literature, (85): 39-56; auth, "The Abandonment of Authority," Research Bulletin, (83): 2-3; co-ed, Art and Religion as Communication, John Knox Press, 74; auth, **CONTACT ADDRESS** President, Menlo Col, 1000 El Camino Real, Atherton, CA 94027-4300. **EMAIL** jwaddell@menlo.edu

WADDELL, LOUIS MORTON
PERSONAL Born 03/19/1931, Bronxville, NY, m, 1958, 2 children **DISCIPLINE** HISTORY **EDUCATION** Princeton Univ, AB, 53; NYork Univ, MA, 61; Univ NC, Chapel Hill, PhD, 71. **CAREER** Instr hist and polit sci, Davis and Elkins Col, 61-63; assoc prof social sci, La Polytech Inst, 66-68; asst prof, Paul D Camp Community Col, 72-73; assoc historian, PA Hist and Mus Comn, 73-, assoc ed, PA Heritage, 92-. **MEMBERSHIPS** PA Hist Soc; Hist Soc of PA; NACBS. **RESEARCH** Pennsylvania history; lmilitary history; political history. **SELECTED PUBLICATIONS** Ed, Papers of Henry Bouquet, Vol 306, PA Hist Mus Comn, 76-94; auth, Comp and Ed Unity from Diveristy: Extracts from Selected PA Colonial Documents, PA Hist Mus Comn, 80; auth, To Secure the Blessings of Liberty: PA and the Changing US Constitution, PA Hist Mus Comn, 86; auth, "Defending the Long Perimeter: Forts on the PA, MD, and VA Frontier, 1755-1765," Pennsylvania History (95); coauth, French and Indian War in PA, 1753-1763, PA Hist Mus Comn, 96. **CONTACT ADDRESS** Div of Archives and Manuscripts, Pennsylvania Historical and Mus Commission, PO Box 1026, Harrisburg, PA 17108-1026. **EMAIL** Lwaddell@phmc.state.pa.us

WADE, JACQUELINE E.
PERSONAL Born 09/07/1940, Murfreesboro, TN **DISCIPLINE** AFRICAN-AMERICAN STUDIES **EDUCATION** Fisk Univ, BA 1962; Univ of PA, MSW 1972, PhD 1983. **CAREER** Univ of PA, dir Penn Children's Ctr 1973-80, assoc dir of student life 1980-84, faculty school of social work 1973-88, dir Afro Amer studies prog 1984-88; Bennett College, Women's Research Training and Development, director, 88-90; Ohio State University, National Council for Black Studies, exec dir, 90-. **HONORS AND AWARDS** Challenge Grant, St Peter's Coll Urban Educ, 1988-. **MEMBERSHIPS** Consultant Trenton State Coll AFAMS Dept 1984-, Philadelphia Sch Dist Desegregation Office 1985-, Benj Bannekar Honors Coll Prairie View A&M 1985-, Conrad Hilton Foundation 1985-88. **CONTACT ADDRESS** Executive Director, Natl Council for Black Studies, Ohio State Univ, Columbus, 208 Mount Hall, 1050 Carmack Rd, Columbus, OH 43210.

WADE, LOUISE CARROLL
PERSONAL Born 02/22/1928, Toledo, OH **DISCIPLINE** AMERICAN SOCIAL & URBAN HISTORY **EDUCATION** Wellesley Col BA, 48; Univ Rochester, PhD(hist), 54. **CAREER** Lectr hist, Univ Rochester, 55-60 & Univ Chicago, 63-67; assoc prof hist,75-80, prof hist, 80-93, prof emer, Univ Ore, 93-, adv counc, Ill Bicentennial Publ, 74-75, mem Social Welfare Hist Group (secy-treas, 62-66); AHA; Orgn Am Historians; Fulbright Award, Australia, 80. **HONORS AND AWARDS** Newberry Lib Fel, 89-90. **MEMBERSHIPS** AHA; Orgn Am Historians; Western Asn Women Historians. **RESEARCH** American Urban social and labor history. **SELECTED PUBLICATIONS** Auth, Graham Taylor: Pioneer for Social Justice, 1851-1938, Univ Chicago, 64; The social gospel impulse and Chicago settlement-house founders, Chicago Theol Sem Regist, 4/65; coauth, A History of the United States, Houghton Mifflin, 66; auth, The heritage of Chicago's early settlement houses, J Ill State Hist Soc, winter 67; Julia Lathrop, Florence Kelley, Mary McDowell & Margaret Haley, In: Notable American Women: A Biographical Dict, Harvard Univ, 71; We are something more than packers, Chicago Hist, fall-winter 73; Graham Taylor, Mary McDowell & Mary Church Terrell, In: Dict of American Biography, Scribner, 74; Burnham & root's stockyards connection, Chicago Hist, fall 75; Chicago's Pride: The Stockyards, Packing Town, and Environs in the Nineteenth Century, Univ of Ill Press, 87; The Problem with Classroom use of Upton Sinclair's The Jungle, Am Studies, 91. **CONTACT ADDRESS** Dept of History, Univ of Oregon, Eugene, OR 97403-1288. **EMAIL** lwade@darkwing.uoregon.edu

WADE, MICHAEL G.
PERSONAL Born 10/01/1946, Oakland, CA, m, 1970, 3 children **DISCIPLINE** HISTORY **EDUCATION** Maryland, BA, 68; SW LA, MA, 71, PhD, 78 **CAREER** Inst, 78-83, MS Co Cmnty Col; Asst Prof, 83-87, Assoc Prof, 87-92, Prof, 92-95, Chair, 95-, Appalachain St Univ; **HONORS AND AWARDS** Beveridge Res Grant, 84; phi alpha theta; phi kappa phi; pi gamma mu; sigma tau delia **MEMBERSHIPS** LA Hist Asn; Southern Hist Asn **RESEARCH** College desegregation; New Deal **SELECTED PUBLICATIONS** Ed, Education in Louisiana through the Integration Era, CLS, 99; Auth, Sugar Dynasty: M.A. Patout and Son, ltd., 1791-1993, CLS, 95 **CONTACT ADDRESS** Dept of History, Appalachian State Univ, Boone, NC 28608. **EMAIL** wademg@appstate.edu

WADE, REX ARVIN
PERSONAL Born 10/09/1936, Piedmont, KS, m, 1957, 3 children **DISCIPLINE** RUSSIAN HISTORY **EDUCATION** Southwestern Col, BA, 58; Univ Nebr, MA, 60, PhD, 63. **CAREER** From asst prof to prof hist, Wis State Col, La Crosse, 63-68; chmn dept, 77-80; Prof Hist, Univ Hawaii, 68-; Dean Fac Arts and Humanities, 80-; Nat Defense Foreign Lang fel, 61; vis prof, Univ NC, 71, Nat Endowment for Humanities sr fel, 72, Univ Nebr, 73 and Portland State Univ, 76; Fulbright-Hays fel, Findland, 72; Am Coun Learned Soc Sr fel, 74-75; Int Res and Exchanges Bd, 75 and 82. **MEMBERSHIPS** AHA; Am Asn Advan Slavic Studies; AAUP. **RESEARCH** Russian Revolution. **SELECTED PUBLICATIONS** Auth, Argonauts of peace, Slavic Rev, 9/67; Irakli Tsereteli and Siberian Zimmerwaldism, J Mod Hist, 12/67; The triumph of Siberian Zimmerwaldism, Can Slavic Studies, 67; Why October?, Soviet Studies, 68; The Russian search for Peace, 1917, Stanford Univ, 69; The Rajonnye Sovety of Petrograd: The role of the political bodies in the Russian Revolution, Jahrbucher fur Geschichte Osteuropas, 6/72; Red Guards and Militiamen: Spontaneity and Leadership in the Russian Revolution, Stanford Univ Press, 82. **CONTACT ADDRESS** Fac Arts and Humanities, Univ of Hawaii, Manoa, Honolulu, HI 96822.

WADE, WILLIAM JUNIUS
PERSONAL Born 10/12/1927, Little Rock, AR, m, 1953, 3 children **DISCIPLINE** AMERICAN HISTORY **EDUCATION** Southwestern at Memphis, BA, 49; Univ NC, MA, 50, PhD, 59. **CAREER** Asst prof, 52-53, dean fac, 62-77, prof hist, King Col, 53-; assoc ed, Journal Presby Hist, 69-77. **MEMBERSHIPS** AHA; Orgn Am Historians; Southern Hist Assn; Am Soc Church Hist. **RESEARCH** History of the Presbyterian Church in the United States; religion in American culture. **CONTACT ADDRESS** Dept of History, King Col, 1350 King College Rd, Bristol, TN 37620-2635.

WAGAR, W. WARREN
PERSONAL Born 06/05/1932, Baltimore, MD, m, 1953, 4 children **DISCIPLINE** HISTORY **EDUCATION** Franklin & Marshall Col, AB (magna cum laude), 53; Ind Univ, MA, 54; Yale Univ, PhD, 59. **CAREER** Inst to assoc prof of hist, Wellesley Col, 58-66; assoc prof to prof of hist, Univ of NMex, 66-71; Prof of Hist, 71-86, Distinguished Tchg Prof of Hist, SUNY-Binghamton, 86-. **HONORS AND AWARDS** Fulbright Scholar, 57-58; ACLS Fel, 63-64; NEH Sr Fel, 74-75; Univ and Chancellor's Awds for Excellence in Tchg, SUNY, 85; honorary Doctor of Humane Letters, Univ of Maine, 96. **MEMBERSHIPS** Am Hist Asn; Soc for Utopian Studies; Sci-Fiction Res Asn; H.G. Wells Soc. **RESEARCH** European intellectual history; futures studies; world history. **SELECTED PUBLICATIONS** Auth, World Views: A Study in Comparative History, Dryden Press & Holt Rinehart, 77; Terminal Visions: The Lit of Last Things, Ind Univ Press, 82; The Next Three Futures: Paradigms of Things to Come, Praeger, 91, Adamantine Press, 92, Greenwood Press, 91; ed, The Secular Mind: Transformations of Faith in Modern Europe, Holmes & Meier, 82; auth, "A Short History of the Future," Univ of Chicago Press, 89, 2nd ed., 92, 3rd ed., 99. **CONTACT ADDRESS** Dept of Hist, SUNY, Binghamton, PO Box 6000, Binghamton, NY 13902. **EMAIL** wwagar@binghamton.edu

WAGENAAR, LARRY
PERSONAL Born 06/11/1962, Grand Rapids, MI, d, 2 children **DISCIPLINE** HISTORY **EDUCATION** Hope Col, BA, 87; Kent State Univ, MA, 92. **CAREER** Asst Prof to Assoc Prof and Dir of the Joint Archives of Holland, Hope Col, 94-. **MEMBERSHIPS** Soc of Am Archivists, Org of Am Hist, Midwest Archives Conf. **RESEARCH** Dutch American immigration; Archival science **SELECTED PUBLICATIONS** Co-ed, The Dutch American Experience, forthcoming; ed, Dutch Enterprise: Alive and Well in North America, Hope Col Press, 99; co-auth, Campus alive: A Walking Tour of Hope College, Hope Col Press, 99; co-ed, The sesquicentennial of Dutch Immigration: 150 Years of Ethnic Heritage, Hope Col Press, 98; asst ed, In Christ's Service: The Classis of Holland, Michigan and Its congregations 1847-1997, Holland, 97; co-auth, Albertus C. Van Raalte: Dutch leader and American Patriot, Hope Col Press, 96. **CONTACT ADDRESS** The Joint Archives of Holland, Hope Col, PO Box 9000, Holland, MI 49422-9000. **EMAIL** wagenaar@hope.edu

WAGENHEIM, OLGA
PERSONAL Born 09/24/1941, Camuy, PR, m, 1961, 2 children **DISCIPLINE** HISTORY **EDUCATION** Inter Am Univ, San Juan, PR, BA, 70; State Univ NY Buffalo, MA, 71; Rutgers Univ Brunswick NJ, PhD, 81. **CAREER** Instr, Puerto Rican Studies Prog, 77-81; from Asst Prof to Assoc Prof, Rutgers Univ Newark Campus, 81-; Dir, Puerto Rican Studies Prog, 81-. **HONORS AND AWARDS** Ford Found Fel, 73-76; Fulbright Lectr, Arg, 91; Outstanding Teacher of the Year, Newark Col of Arts and Sci, Rutgers Univ, 91. **MEMBERSHIPS** Oral Hist Asn, Latin Am Studies Asn. **RESEARCH** Puerto Rico, Puerto Ricans in the US, Caribbean Migration to the US. **SELECTED PUBLICATIONS** Auth, El Grito de Lares: Sus Causas y Sus Hombres, Ediciones Huracan (Rio Peidras, PR), 84; auth, Puerto Rico's Revolt for Independence: El Grito de Lares, Westview Press (Boulder, CO), 85 and Markus Wiener Publ (Princeton), 93; co-ed, The Puerto Ricans: A Documentary History, Praeger Publ (NY), 73, Doubleday Anchor (NY), 75, and Markus Wiener Publ (Princeton), 94; auth, Puerto Rico: An Interpretive History: From Pre-Columbian Times to 1990, Markus Wiener Publ (Princeton), 98. **CONTACT ADDRESS** Dept Hist, Rutgers, The State Univ of New Jersey, Newark, 180 Univ Ave, Newark, NJ 07102-1803. **EMAIL** OJWagenheim@cs.com

WAGNER, ROY
PERSONAL Born 10/02/1938, Cleveland, OH, d, 2 children **DISCIPLINE** MEDIEVAL HISTORY, CULTURAL AN-

THROPOLGY **EDUCATION** Harvard Col, AB, 61; Univ Chicago, AM, 62, PhD, 66. **CAREER** Asst prof, South Ill Univ, 66-68; assoc prof, Northwest Univ, 68-74; Prof, Univ VA, 74-. **MEMBERSHIPS** Am Anthrop Asn **RESEARCH** Myth, cultural & religious conceptualization; Holographic world perspectives in Melanesia. **SELECTED PUBLICATIONS** The Curse of Souw, Chicago Press, 67; Habu, Chicago, 72; Lethal Speech, Cornell, 78; The Invention of Culture, Chicago Press, 81; Asiwinarong, Princeton, 86. **CONTACT ADDRESS** Dept Anthrop, Univ of Virginia, Brooks Hall, Charlottesville, VA 22903.

WAGNER, WILLIAM GILSON
PERSONAL Born 05/28/1950, Erie, PA, m, 1972, 1 child **DISCIPLINE** RUSSIAN AND EUROPEAN HISTORY **EDUCATION** Haverford Col, BA, 72; Oxford Univ, BPhil, 74, DPhil-(mod hist), 81. **CAREER** Res lectr, Christ Church, Oxford Univ, 78-80; Asst Prof Hist, Williams Col, 81-87; Exam hist, Oxford and Cambridge Sch Exam Bd, 75-80; grad adv, Inter-Fac Liason Comt Russ and East Europ Studies, Oxford Univ, 78-80, tutor hist, Balliol Col, 78-80; assoc prof, 87-94; prof, 94-. **MEMBERSHIPS** AHA; Am Asn Advan Slavic Studies. **RESEARCH** Russian socio-legal and religious history; general socio-legal history, particularly in property, inheritance, and family law; women's and family history; women and religion. **SELECTED PUBLICATIONS** Auth, "Tsarist Legal Policies at the End of the Nineteenth Century: A Study in Inconsistencies," Slavonic and East European Review, LIV:3 (76): 371-94; auth, "Legislative Reform of Inheritance in Russia, 1861-1914," in W.E. Butler, ed., Russian Law: Historical and Political Perspective, A.w. Sijthoff, Leyden, (77): 143-78; auth, "The Civil Cassation Department of the Senate as an Instrument of Progressive Reform in Post Emancipation Russian," Slavic Review, XLII:1 (83): 36-59; Annotated, Nikolai Chernyshevsky, What is to Be Done?, Cornell Press, Ithaca, 89; auth, "Chernyshevsky, What is to Be Done? and the Russian Intelligentsia" with M. Katz, Cornell Univ Press, Ithaca, (89): 1-36; auth, "The Trojan Mare: Women's Rights and Civil Rights in Prerevolutionary Russia," in O. Crisp and L. Edmondson, eds., Civil Rights in Prerevolutionary Russia, Oxford Univ Press, Oxford (89): 65-84; auth, "Ideology, Identity, and the Emergence of a Middle Class," in E.W. Clowes, J.L. West, and S.D. Kassow, eds., The Search for Civil Consciousness in Late Imperial Russia, Princeton Univ Press, Princeton, (91): 149-63; auth, Marriage, Property, and Law in Late Imperial Russia, Oxford Historical Monographs, Clarendon Press, Oxford, 94; auth, "Family Law, the Rule of Law, and Liberalism in Late Imperial Russia," Juhrbucher fur Geschichte Osteuropas, XLIII 4 (95): 519-35; auth, "Civil Law, Individual Rights, and Judicial Activism in Late Imperial Russia," in P.H. Solomon, Jr., ed. Reforming Justice in Russia, 1864-1994: Power, Culture, and the Limits of Legal Order, M.E. Sharpe, Armonk, NY (97): 21-44; **CONTACT ADDRESS** Hist Dept, Williams Col, 880 Main St, Williamstown, MA 01267-2600. **EMAIL** williamg.wagner@williams.edu

WAHL, JIM
DISCIPLINE HISTORY **EDUCATION** Univ Western Ontario, BA, 62; Louis Univ, MA, 64; PhD, 68. **CAREER** Assoc prof, St. Jerome's Univ; asst dean, St. Jerome's Univ; academic dean, St. Jerome's Univ; ch, dept of Hist, St. Jerome's Univ; lectr, St. Jerome's Univ. **RESEARCH** Legal history; nineteenth century religious history. **SELECTED PUBLICATIONS** Auth, Baldus de Ubaldis and the Foundations of the Nation-State; Baldus de Ubaldis: A Study in Reluctant Conciliarism; Father Louis Funcken's Contribution to German Catholicism: in Waterloo County, Ontario; Looking Back: The Early Days, Louis Funcken and St. Jerome's College; auth, Dictionary of American Resurrectionists: 1865-1990; auth, Outline of Medieval History; auth, "Reflections on the History of the Congregation of the Resurrection,". **CONTACT ADDRESS** Dept of History, St. Jerome's Univ, Waterloo, ON, Canada N2L 3G3.

WAIBEL, PAUL R.
PERSONAL Born 12/15/1944, Bay City, MI, m, 1980, 2 children **DISCIPLINE** HISTORY **EDUCATION** Lynchburg Col, BA, 68; Va Polytechnic Inst, MA, 72; W Va Univ, PhD, 77. **CAREER** Asst prof, Union Univ, 78-83; asst prof, Trinity Col, 84-88; assoc prof, Liberty Col, 89-93; prof, Belhaven Col, 89-. **HONORS AND AWARDS** Fulbright-hayes Scholar, Ger, 71-72; NEH Fel, 80. **MEMBERSHIPS** Conf on Faith and Hist; Europ Sec, S Hist Assoc; Int Dietrich Bonhoeffer Soc; Hist Soc. **SELECTED PUBLICATIONS** Auth, Politics of Accommodation, 83; auth, Twentieth-Century Europe: A Brief History, 99; auth, Quiknotes: Church History, 00. **CONTACT ADDRESS** Dept Hist and Govt, Belhaven Col, 1500 Peachtree St, Jackson, MS 39202-1754. **EMAIL** pwaibel@mail.belhaven.edu

WAITE, ROBERT GEORGE LEESON
PERSONAL Born Cartwright, MB, Canada, m, 1943, 2 children **DISCIPLINE** MODERN HISTORY **EDUCATION** Macalester Col, BA, 41; Univ Minn, MA, 46; Harvard Univ, PhD (hist), 49. **CAREER** From asst prof to prof, 49-60, chmn dept, 68-73, Brown Prof Hist, Williams Col, 60-; Fulbright and Guggenheim scholars, 53-54; Am Coun Learned Soc and Soc Sci Res Coun grants, 66-67, 68 and 82; Mem Col Entrance Bd, Bd Exam for Advan Placement in Europ Hist, 67-; sr mem hist, St Antony's Col, Oxford Univ, 78 and 82. **MEMBERSHIPS** AHA **RESEARCH** Modern German history; psychoanalysis and history--the case of Kaiser William II. **SELECTED PUBLICATIONS CONTACT ADDRESS** 1659 Main St., Glastonbury, CT 06033-2961.

WAJDA, SHIRLEY
PERSONAL Born 05/28/1958, Warren, OH **DISCIPLINE** HISTORY **EDUCATION** Boston Univ, BA, 84; Univ Pa, AM, 89; PhD, 92. **CAREER** Instr, Clarion Univ Pa, 89-91; Asst Prof, Boston Univ, 91-94; Vis Asst Prof, Univ Iowa, 95; Asst Prof, Kent State Univ, 96-. **HONORS AND AWARDS** Smithsonian Inst Grad Student Fel, Nat Mus of Am Hist, 88; Andrew Mellon Found Res Fel, Mass Hist Soc, 91; Jr Fac Fel, Boston Univ, 93-94; Nat Endowment for the Humanities Fel, 93-94; Richard F. Morgan Res Fel, Western Reserve Hist Soc, 96; Hagley-Winterthur Arts and Industs Res Fel, 97; Andrew Mellon Found Res Fel, Libr Co of Philadelphia, 97. **MEMBERSHIPS** ASA, Organization of Am Historians, Soc for the Hist of Authorship Reading and Publ, Soc for Historians of the Early Am Republic, Vernacular Archit Forum, Nineteenth-Century Studies Asn, Am Asn of Mus, Asn of Historians of Am art. **RESEARCH** Nineteenth-Century American social, cultural and intellectual history, American art and material culture studies, history of consumption and consumerism, photography. **SELECTED PUBLICATIONS** Auth, "A Room with a Viewer: The Parlor Stereoscope, Comic Sterographs and the Psychic Role of Play in Late Victorian America," in Hard at Play: Leisure in America, 1840-1940 (Amherst: Univ Mass Pr, 92), 112-138; auth, "The Artistic Portrait Photograph," in The arts and the American Home. 1890-1930 (Knoxville: Univ Tenn Pr, 94), 165-182; auth, "The Commercial Photographic Parlor, 1839-1889," Shaping Communities: Perspectives in Vernacular Achit, VI, Univ Tenn Pr (97): 216-230; auth, "'And a Little Child Will Lead Them': Children's Cabinets of Curiosities, 1790-1860," Reader: Essays in Reader-Oriented Theory, Criticism and Pedagogy, 38-39 (97-98): 5-9. **CONTACT ADDRESS** Dept Hist, Kent State Univ, PO Box 5190, Kent, OH 44242-0001. **EMAIL** swajda@kent.edu

WAKELYN, JON L.
PERSONAL Born 08/19/1938, Tampa, FL, m, 1990, 2 children **DISCIPLINE** HISTORY **EDUCATION** Long Island Univ, BA, 62; Rice Univ, PhD, 66. **CAREER** Asst to assoc prof, Washington Col, 66-70; asst to prof, Cath Univ Am, 70-96; vis prof, Univ Md, 74-75; vis prof, Maynoth Col, Ireland, 92, 94; PROF, KENT STATE UNIV, 96-. **HONORS AND AWARDS** NDEA fel; NEH fel, 68; ALA outstanding ref work, 78; outstanding teach, Cath Uni, 83. **MEMBERSHIPS** Org Am Historians; So Hist Asn. **RESEARCH** 19th cent U.S.; Old South. **SELECTED PUBLICATIONS** Auth, Politics of A Literary Man, 73; Biographical Dictionary of the Confederacy, 78; auth, Catholics in the Old South, 83, 99; auth, Web of Southern Social Relations, 85, 87; auth, Biographical Dictionary of State Leaders, 89; auth, Southern Pamphlets on Secession, 96; auth, Leaders of the American Civil War, 98; auth, Southern Unionist Pamphlets in Civil War, 00 **CONTACT ADDRESS** 126 E Stretsboro St, Hudson, OH 44236. **EMAIL** jwakelyn@kent.edu

WAKEMAN, FREDERIC EVANS, JR.
PERSONAL Born 12/12/1937, Kansas City, KS, 3 children **DISCIPLINE** CHINESE HISTORY **EDUCATION** Harvard Col, BA, 59; Univ Calif, Berkeley, MA, 62, PhD, 65. **CAREER** Asst prof, 65-67, assoc prof, 69-71, prof, hist, 71- , Univ Calif, Berkeley; dir, Inter-Univ Prog for Chinese Lang Stud, Taipei, 67-68; pres, Social Sci Res Coun, 86-89; Walter and Elise Haas Prof Asian Stud, Univ Calif, Berkeley, 89- ; dir, Inst of East Asian Stud, 90- . **HONORS AND AWARDS** Phi Beta Kappa; Levenson Prize, Berkeley Prize, 87; pres, Am Hist Asn, 92; Phi Beta Kappa Vis Scholar, 94-95. **MEMBERSHIPS** Am Hist Asn; Asn of Asian Stud; Am Acad of Arts and Sci; APA. **RESEARCH** History of early Republican China; Shanghai history. **SELECTED PUBLICATIONS** Auth, Strangers at the Gate: Social Disorder in South China, 1839-1861, Univ Calif, 66; auth, Nothing Concealed: Essays in Honor of Liu Yu-yun, Taipei: CMRASC, 70; auth, History and Will: Philosophical Perspectives of the Thought of Mao Tse-tung, Univ Calif, 73; coauth, Conflict and Control in Late Imperial China, Univ Calif, 75; auth, The Fall of Imperial China, Free Press, 75; auth, The Great Enterprise: The Manchu Reconstruction of Imperial Order in Seventeenth-Century China, Univ Calif, 85; co-ed, Perspectives on Modern China: Four Anniversaries, M.E. Sharpe, 91; co-ed, Shanghai Sojourners, Institute of East Asian Studies, 92; auth, Policing Shanghai, 1927-1937, Univ Calif, 95; auth, The Shanghai Badlands: Wartime Terrorism and Urban Crime, 1937-1941, Cambridge, 96; co-ed, China's Quest for Modernization, Institute of East Asian Studies, 97. **CONTACT ADDRESS** Institute of East Asian Studies, Univ of California, Berkeley, 2223 Fulton St, No 2318, Berkeley, CA 94720-2318. **EMAIL** jingcha@socrates.berkeley.edu

WALBANK, MICHAEL BURKE
PERSONAL Born 04/14/1933, Bristol, England, m, 1978 **DISCIPLINE** CLASSICS, ARCHEOLOGY **EDUCATION** Univ Bristol, BA, 54; Univ BC, MA, 65, PhD (classics), 70. **CAREER** Asst prof, 70-76, Assoc Prof Classics, Univ Calgary, 76-; Can Coun fels, 71-72 and 76-77; consult, BBCOpen Univ Prod, 78. **MEMBERSHIPS** Am Sch Class Studies Athens; Class Asn of Can; Archaeol Inst of Am; Soc Prom Hellenic Studies; Soc Prom of Roman Studies. **RESEARCH** Greek epigraphy; Greek archaeology; ancient science and technology. **SELECTED PUBLICATIONS** Auth, A Lex Sacra of the State and of the Deme of Kollytos, Hesperia, Vol 63, 94; Greek Inscriptions from the Athenian Agora in Lists of Names, Hesperia, Vol 63, 94; Greek Inscriptions from The Athenian-Agora in Building Records, Hesperia, Vol 64, 95; An Inscription from the Athenian Agora in Thasian Exiles at Athens, Hesperia, Vol 64, 95; Greek Inscriptions from the Athenian Agora Financial Documents, Hesperia, Vol 65, 96; Greek Inscriptions from the Athenian Agora, Hesperia, Vol 66, 97. **CONTACT ADDRESS** 14 Harcourt Rd SW, Calgary, AB, Canada T2V 5J1.

WALBERG, GISELA
DISCIPLINE ANCIENT HISTORY **EDUCATION** Univ Stockholm, Fil Kand, 66; Univ Uppsala, PhD, 76. **CAREER** Asst, Medelhavsmuseet, 64-67, 69-70; asst, Swedish Inst, Athens, 67-69; asst prof, Uppsala Univ, 76-78; asst prof, Univ Cincinnati, 79-82; assoc prof, Univ Cincinnati, 82-84; prof, Univ Cincinnati, 84-; Marion Rawson prof of Prehistory, 93-. **HONORS AND AWARDS** Alexander von Humboldt-Stiftung Grant; Alexander-von-Humboldt-Stiftung Fel; Swedish Nat Endowment Hum; Lerici-Found. **SELECTED PUBLICATIONS** Auth, Kamares, A Study of the Character of Palatial Middle Minoan Pottery, Almkvist & Wiksell, Uppsala, 76; auth, Kamares Style, The Overall Effects of Palatial Middle Minoan Pottery, Almkvist & Wiksell, Uppsala, 78; auth, Provincial Middle Minoan Pottery, von Zabern, Mainz, 83; auth, Tradition and Innovation, Essays in Minoan Art, von Zabern, Mainz, 86; auth, Middle Minoan III, A Time of Transition, (SIMA XCVII) Gothenburg, 92; auth, The Nelson and Helen Glueck Collection of Cypriot Pottery with a Biography of Nelson Glueck by R. G. Bullard (SIMA Pocketbook 111), Gothenburg, 92; auth, Illustration Volume to Furumark, The Mycenaen Pottery, Mycenaean Pottery III, Stockholm, 92; auth, Excavations on the Acropolis of Midea I. Results of the Greek-Swedish Excavations, Vol I: 1-2, The Excavations on the Lower Terraces 1985-1991, Stockholm, 98; auth, "The Excavations of the Midea Megaron," BICS 42, 98; auth, "The Date and Origin of the Kamares Cup form Tell el Dab'a," Agypten und Levante VIII, 98. **CONTACT ADDRESS** Dept of Classics, Univ of Cincinnati, PO Box 210226, Cincinnati, OH 45210-0226. **EMAIL** Giswalberg@aol.com

WALCH, TIMOTHY G.
PERSONAL Born 12/06/1947, Detroit, MI, m, 1978, 2 children **DISCIPLINE** US HISTORY **EDUCATION** Univ Notre dame, BA 70; Northwester Univ, PhD 75. **CAREER** Assoc dir, Soc Amer Archivists, 75-79; prog analy, Nat Archive Records Admin, 79-83; Ed Br Chief, Nat Archive Rec Admin, 83-88; Asst dir Herbert Hover Pres Lib, 88-93; and Director, 93. **MEMBERSHIPS** OAH; US Cath Hist Soc. **RESEARCH** Hist of the US Presidency, Hist of Amer Catholicism. **SELECTED PUBLICATIONS** Herbert Hoover and Franklin D Roosevelt: A Documentary History, 98; At the President's Side: The Vice Presidency in the Twentieth Century, 97; Parish School: American Catholic Parochial Education from Colonial times to the Present, 96. **CONTACT ADDRESS** Herbert Hoover Library, PO BOX 488, West Branch, IA 52358. **EMAIL** timothy.walch@hoover.nara.gov

WALCOTT, ROBERT
PERSONAL Born 01/24/1910, Boston, MA **DISCIPLINE** HISTORY **EDUCATION** Harvard Univ, AB, 31, AM, 32, PhD, 38. **CAREER** Asst hist, Harvard Univ, 36-38, instr and tutor, 38-41; instr, Westminster Col, Pa, 41-42 and Black Mountain Col, 45-46; From asst prof to prof, 46-75, Emer Prof Hist, Col Wooster, 75-; Fulbright award, UK, 53-54; Soc Sci Res Coun fel, 55-56. **MEMBERSHIPS** Fel Royal Hist Soc. **RESEARCH** English history; European history, especially 17th and 18th centuries; economic history. **SELECTED PUBLICATIONS** Auth, Out of The Kumbla in Morrison, Toni Jazz and Pedagogical Answerability, Cult Studies, Vol 9, 95. **CONTACT ADDRESS** 14 Whig Rd, Dennis, MA 02638.

WALD, ALAN MAYNARD
PERSONAL Born 06/01/1946, Washington, DC, w, 1975, 2 children **DISCIPLINE** AMERICAN STUDIES, ENGLISH LITERATURE **EDUCATION** Antioch Col, BA, 69; Univ Calif, Berkeley, MA, 71, PhD(English), 74. **CAREER** Lectr English, San Jose State Univ, 74; teaching assoc, Univ Calif, Berkeley, 75; asst prof English Lit & Am Cult, Univ Mich, Ann Arbor, 75-, from assoc prof to prof, 81-86; Full Prof of English, 87-; Dir, Program in Am Culture, 00. **HONORS AND AWARDS** ACLS Natl Fel, 83-84; Beinecke llow, Yale, 89; Michigan Humanities fell, 85; Excellence in Research Awd from UM, 96; A Bartlett Giamatti Faculty fel at UM Instit for Humanities, 97-98; Guggenheim Fel, 99-00. **MEMBERSHIPS** MLA, ASA. **RESEARCH** American literary radicalism; Marxist aesthetics; the New York intellectuals. **SELECTED PUBLICATIONS** Auth, James T. Farrell: The Revolutionary Socialist Years, 78; auth, The Revolutionary Imagination, 83; auth, The New York Intellectuals, 87; The Responsibility of In-

tellectuals, 92; Writing From the Left, 94. **CONTACT ADDRESS** Dept of English, Univ of Michigan, Ann Arbor, 3187 Angell Hall, Ann Arbor, MI 48109-10003. **EMAIL** awald@umich.edu

WALDBAUM, JANE C.
PERSONAL Born 01/28/1940, New York, NY, m, 1995 **DISCIPLINE** CLASSICAL ARCHEOLOGY, ANCIENT ART **EDUCATION** Brandeis Univ, AB, 62; Harvard Univ, AM, 64, PhD, 68. **CAREER** From asst prof to prof art hist, Univ Wis-Milwaukee, 73-; vis assoc prof art hist, IN Univ, Bloomington, 78-79; Chemn dept, Univ Wis-Milwaukee, 82-85, 86-89, 91-92; exec comt, Archaeol Inst Am, 74-77; chemn, comt on mem prog, 77-81; nominating comt, 84; chemn, comt on lecture prog, 85-87; academic trustee, 93-98; comt prof responsibilities, 93-; fellowship comt, 93-98; gold metal comt, 93-, chair, 96-97; ancient near east comt, 93, first vice-president 99-; chair, annual meeting comt, 99-; **HONORS AND AWARDS** Res fel class art & archaeol, Harvard Univ, 68-70 & 72-73; Am Philos Soc grant, 72; Nat Endowment for Hum fel, summer, 75; vis schol, Univ Penn, 85-86; vis schol, Inst of Archaeol, Hebrew Univ of Jerusalem, Israel, 89-90 and 90-91; Am Sch(s) of Oriental Research-NEH Post Doct Research Fel, 89-90; Dorcot Research Prof, W F Albright Inst of Archaeol Research, 90-91; **MEMBERSHIPS** Archaeol Inst Am, National, Boston Society, Pres, Milwaukee Soc, 83-85, 91-95, 97-99; Am Schs Orient Res; Soc for Archaeol Sci; Asn for Field Archaeol; Soc for Archaeol Sciences; Israel Exploration Soc; Milwaukee Area Biblical Archaeol Soc, Bd of Dir, 87-; WI Soc for Jewish Learning, Bd member, 93-99. **RESEARCH** Early Iron Age in the Eastern Mediterranean; ancient metalwork and metallurgy; archaeol of Sardis. **SELECTED PUBLICATIONS** Auth, Philistine tombs from Tell Fara and their Aegean prototypes, Am J Archaeol 70 (66): 331-340; coauth, New excavations at Sardis and some problems in Western Anatolian archaeology, In: Near Eastern Archaeology in the Twentieth Century, Studies in Honor of Nelson Glueck, Doubleday, 70; auth, A bronze and iron Iranian axe in the Fogg Art Museum, In: Studies Presented to George M A Hanfmann, Philipp von Zabern, 71; The Luristan bronzes, Princeton Mus Rec, 73; coauth, A survey of Sardis and major monuments outside the city walls, Sardis Report 1, Harvard Univ, 75; auth, From bronze to iron: The Transition from the Bronze Age to the Iron Age in the Eastern Mediterranean, Paul Astroms Forlag, Studies in Mediter Archaeol, 78; The first archaeological appearance of iron and the transition to the Iron Age, In: The Coming of the Age of Iron, A Festschrift for Cyril Stanley Smith, 80; Sardis Monograph 8, Metalwork from Sardis, the finds through 1974, Harvard Univ Press, 83; Bimetallic objects fron the eastern Mediterranean and the question of the dissemination of iron, In: Proc the Archaeol Symposium, Early Metallurgy on Cyprus, Larnaca, 82; Metalwork and Metalworking at Sardis, in Sardis Twenty-Seven Years of Discovery, 87; The Coming of Iron, Wisconsin Academy Rev 33 (87); Metalwork from Idalion, 1971-1980, in Am Expedition to Idalian, Cyprus, 1973-1980, ed. L E Stager and A M Walker, 89, 328-355; Copper, Iron, Tin, Wood: The Start of the Iron Age in the Eastern Mediterranean, Archeomaterials 3 (89): 111-122; Early Greek Contacts with the Southern Levant, c 1000-600BC: The Eastern Perspective, Bulletin of the Am Schs of Oriental Research 293 (94): 53-67; The Chronology of Early Greek Pottery: New Evidence from Seventh Century BC Destruction Levels in Israel, with Jodi Magness, Am J Archaeol 101, pp 23-40, 97; "Greeks in the East or Greeks and the East? A Study in the Definition and Recognition of Presence," Bulletin of the Am Schools of Oriental Res 305 (97): 1-17. **CONTACT ADDRESS** Dept Art Hist, Univ of Wisconsin, Milwaukee, PO Box 413, Milwaukee, WI 53201-0413. **EMAIL** jcw@uwm.edu

WALDMAN, MARTIN
PERSONAL Born 03/10/1940, Brooklyn, NY, m, 1962 **DISCIPLINE** HISTORY OF MODERN FRANCE **EDUCATION** Brandeis Univ, BA, 60; Syracuse Univ, PhD (hist), 68. **CAREER** Asst Europ hist, Syracuse Univ, 62-64; lectr, 66-68, asst prof, 68-80, Assoc Prof Europ Hist, City Col New York, 80-; City Univ Res Found fel, 74-75. **MEMBERSHIPS** AHA; Soc Fr Hist Studies; Soc Mod Hist, France. **RESEARCH** French social history; the Paris Commune of 1871. **SELECTED PUBLICATIONS** Auth, Eliminating the Market for Secondhand Goods in an Alternative Explanation for Leasing, J Law Econ, Vol 40, 97. **CONTACT ADDRESS** Dept of Hist, City Col, CUNY, 138th St and Convent Ave, New York, NY 10031.

WALDREP, CHRISTOPHER
PERSONAL Born 11/19/1951, Oak Ridge, TN, m, 1976, 2 children **DISCIPLINE** HISTORY **EDUCATION** Eastern Ill Univ, BS, 73; Purdue Univ, MA, 74; Ohio State Univ, PhD, 90. **CAREER** Teacher, Washington Ohio City Schools, 74-90; Asst Prof to Prof, Eastern Ill Univ, 90-. **HONORS AND AWARDS** Ruth Higgins Awd, Ohio State Univ Dept, 88-89; Rest Grant, Eastern Ill Univ Coun, 90-91, 91-92; Grant, commission on the Bicentennial of the US Constitution, 91; Grant, Ill Humanities Coun, 91; NEH Summer Seminar, 91; Littleton-Griswold Grant, Am Hist Asn, 91-92. **MEMBERSHIPS** Am Hist Asn, Org of Am Hist, Southern Hist Asn, am Soc for Legal Hist, Ky Hist Soc, Soc of Hist of the Early Am Republic, Miss Hist Soc, Ill State Hist soc. **RESEARCH** Racial violence; US South; Law and constitution, Civil war/Reconstruction. **SELECTED PUBLICATIONS** Auth, Night riders: Defending community in the black Patch: 1890-1915, Duke Univ Press, 93; auth, roots of disorder: Race and Criminal Justice in the American south, 1817-1880, Univ Ill Press, 98; auth, "Creating a Metaphor for the Past: Uniting History and computing in the classroom" Perspectives, (95): 13-15; auth, "Substituting Law for the Lash: emancipation and Legal formalism in a Mississippi county Court," Journal of American History, (96): 1425-1451; auth, "Opportunity on the frontier south of the Green," in The Buzzel About Kentucky: Settling the Promised Land, Univ Press of Ky, 98; auth, "Word and deed: The Language of Lynching, 1820-1953," in Lethal Imagination: violence and Brutality in American History, NY Univ Press, 99; auth, "Review Essay: For Cause and comrades: Why Men fought in the civil War," Journal of the Abraham Lincoln Association, (99): 85-97; auth, "Women, the Civil War, and Legal Culture in Vicksburg, Mississippi," Journal of Mississippi History, (99): 137-148; auth, "War of Words: The controversy over the Definition of Lynching, 1899-1940," Journal of southern History, (00): 75-100. **CONTACT ADDRESS** Dept Hist, Eastern Illinois Univ, 600 Lincoln Ave, Charleston, IL 61920-3011. **EMAIL** cfcrw@eiu.edu

WALDSTREICHER, DAVID L.
DISCIPLINE HISTORY **EDUCATION** Yale Univ, PhD, 94. **CAREER** Asst prof American Studies, Yale Univ. **SELECTED PUBLICATIONS** Fel Publ, In the Midst of Perpetual Fetes: The Making of American Nationalism, 1776-1820, IEAHAC & UNC Press, pending; auth, 'Fallen under My Observation: Vision and Virtue in The Coquette, Early Amer Lit 27, 92; Federalism and the Politics of Style, In: Federalism Revisited, pending. **CONTACT ADDRESS** Dept of American Studies, Yale Univ, PO Box 208236, New Haven, CT 06520-8236. **EMAIL** david.waldstreicher@yale.edu

WALKEN, CHRISOPHER
DISCIPLINE HISTORY OF AFRICAN-AMERICAN MUSIC **EDUCATION** Hamilton Col, BA; Rutgers Univ, MA, PhD. **CAREER** Assoc prof. **HONORS AND AWARDS** Summer stipend and a travel-to-collections grant, NEH; fel, media grants, W Va Hum Coun; res grants, W Va Univ fac senate. **RESEARCH** Jazz; Multicultural study of the history of art music. **SELECTED PUBLICATIONS** Publ, articles in Black Mus Res Jour, Col Mus Symposium, Contrib to Mus Edu, Mus and Letters, The New Grove Dictionary of Mus and Musicians; George Crumb: Profile of a Composer; and Oratorios of the Italian Baroque. **CONTACT ADDRESS** Dept of Mus, West Virginia Univ, Morgantown, PO Box 6009, Morgantown, WV 26506-6009. **EMAIL** cwilkin2@wvu.edu

WALKER, DAVID ALLAN
PERSONAL Born 04/14/1941, Alexandria, VA, m, 1967, 2 children **DISCIPLINE** AMERICAN HISTORY **EDUCATION** Missouri Valley Col, BA, 63; La State Univ, MA, 65; Univ Wis-Madison, PhD (hist), 73. **CAREER** Instr hist, Lakeland Col, 66-68; asst prof hist, Mankato State Univ, 71-75; asst prof, 75-78, Assoc Prof Hist, Univ Northern Iowa, 78-; Minn Hist Soc res fel hist, 73-74; vis prof Univ Wyoming, 81-82. **HONORS AND AWARDS** Charles J Kennedy Awd, Econ and Bus Hist Soc, 477. **MEMBERSHIPS** Western Hist Asn; Orgn Am Historians; Econ and Bus Hist Soc; Social Sci Hist Asn. **RESEARCH** American West: mining, conservation, territorial. **SELECTED PUBLICATIONS** Auth, Lake Vermilion gold rush, Minn Hist, summer 74; coauth, Duluth-Superior Harbor Cultural Resources Study, Corps Engr Report, 76; auth, Entrepreneurial conflict on an iron range frontier, Essays in Econ & Bus Hist 81; Iron Range Frontier, Minn Hist Soc, 79; coauth, Biographical Directory of the Territorial Governors, Meckler (in prep). **CONTACT ADDRESS** Dept of Hist, Univ of No Iowa, Cedar Falls, IA 50613.

WALKER, ERNESTEIN
PERSONAL Born 05/26/1926, McDonough, GA, m **DISCIPLINE** HISTORY **EDUCATION** Spelman Coll, AB 1949; Atlanta U, MA 1953; Univ Edinburgh, 1958; Western Res U, PhD 1964. **CAREER** Morgan State U, prof hist 1965-; SC State Coll, instr prof 1956-65; Fort Valley State Coll, instr 1955-56; KY State U, 54-55. **MEMBERSHIPS** Mem Am Hist Assn; Assn Study Afro Life & Hist; So Hist Assn; medieval acad pres Baltimore Chap Nat Alumnae Assn, Spelman Coll Publ, "Disestablishment of the Ch of Ireland", Jour Social Sci 1960; "Age of Metternick a study in nonmenclature" exploration educ 1962; "the influence of Lord Liverpool 1815-1827" Jour Higher Educ 1967; "The Struggle for Parliamentary Reform" 1977; "The Black Woman" The Black Am Ref Book 1976. **CONTACT ADDRESS** Morgan State Univ, Baltimore, MD 21239.

WALKER, FORREST A.
PERSONAL Born 10/08/1929, Pittsburg, KS, m, 1956, 2 children **DISCIPLINE** AMERICAN HISTORY **EDUCATION** Tex Col Arts and Indust, BA, 51, MA, 52; Univ Okla, PhD (hist), 62. **CAREER** Asst prof hist, Florence State Col, 61-63; assoc prof, 63-70, chmn dept, 70-76, Prof Hist, Eastern NMex Univ, 70-; Chmn Dept Hist, 80-. **MEMBERSHIPS** Orgn Am Historians. **RESEARCH** Twentieth century American history. **CONTACT ADDRESS** Dept of Hist, Eastern New Mexico Univ, Portales, Portales, NM 88130. **EMAIL** forrest.walker@enmu.edu

WALKER, GEORGE KONTZ
PERSONAL Born 07/08/1938, Tuscaloosa, AL, m, 1966, 2 children **DISCIPLINE** LAW, HISTORY **EDUCATION** Univ AL, BA, 59; Vanderbilt Univ, LLB, 66; Duke Univ, MA, 68; Univ VA, LLM, 72. **CAREER** From asst prof to assoc prof, 72-76, Prof Law, Wake Forest Univ, 77-, Woodrow Wilson fel, Duke Univ, 62-63; Sterling fel, Yale Law Sch, 75-76; vis prof law, Marshall-Wythe Sch Law, Col William & Mary, 79-80; vis prof Law, Univ Ala Sch Law, 85; Charles H Stockton Prof Intl Law, Naval War Col, 92-93. **HONORS AND AWARDS** Phi Beta kappa, Order of Barristers (hon), Order of the Coif (hon), Am Law Inst. **MEMBERSHIPS** Virginia, North Carolina Bars; Am Soc Int law; Int law Asn, Am Bar Asn; Maritime Law assoc, VA, NC Bar Asns; admitted to practice in federal courts. **RESEARCH** International law; federal jurisdiction; admiralty; conflict of laws; civil procedure; alternative dispute resolution. **SELECTED PUBLICATIONS** Ed, of 10 bks, over 40 bk chpts, articles. **CONTACT ADDRESS** Sch of Law, Wake Forest Univ, PO Box 7206, Winston-Salem, NC 27109-7206.

WALKER, HUGH D.
PERSONAL Born 02/21/1934, Plymouth, NH, m, 1957, 5 children **DISCIPLINE** KOREAN HISTORY **EDUCATION** Univ NH, BA, 56; Univ Calif, Los Angeles, MA, 60, PhD, 71. **CAREER** Lectr hist & Chinese, Far East Div, Univ Md, 62-65; from asst prof to assoc prof hist & Chinese, 65-76, Prof Hist, Univ Wis Stevens Point, 76-, Mem, Korean Res Ctr, Seoul, 62-. **MEMBERSHIPS** Asn Asian Studies; Korean Hist Asn. **RESEARCH** Korean history; Sino-Korean diplomatic relations; East Asian history. **SELECTED PUBLICATIONS** Auth, Korea and the Chinese imperium, Orient-West, 3-4/64; Traditional Sino-Korean diplomatic relations, Monumenta Serica, 65; The weight of tradition, in Korea's Response to the West, Korean Res Publ, 68. **CONTACT ADDRESS** Dept of Hist, Univ of Wisconsin, Stevens Point, 2100 Main St, Stevens Point, WI 54481-3897.

WALKER, JULIET ELISE KIRKPATRICK
PERSONAL Born 07/18/1940, Chicago, IL, d, 2 children **DISCIPLINE** AFRO-AMERICAN HISTORY **EDUCATION** Roosevelt Univ, BA, 63; Univ Chicago, AM, 70, PhD(US hist), 76. **CAREER** Teacher hist & curric writer, Chicago Bd Educ, 63-69; lectr, dept of hist, Roosevelt Univ, 72-73; instr Black Studies, Univ Wis-Milwaukee, 73-76; asst prof Am Hist, Univ Ill, Urbana, 76-82, assoc prof, 82-90, prof, 90-; vis prof, Univ Tx Austin, spring 79; consult, Nat Endowment for Humanites, 76-78 & People's Heritage, Milwaukee, 77-78; Newberry Libr Chicago fel, 77; Harvard Univ, W. E. B. DuBois Institute, research assoc, 86-87; Princeton Univ, Shelby Cullom Davis Center for Hist Studies, fel, fall 94; Univ Witwatersrand, Johannesburg, South Africa, vis senior Fulbright prof, dept of hist, 95. **HONORS AND AWARDS** Newberry Lib Fellowship for the Study of State and Local Hist, summer 77; Karl E Mundt educational and Historical Found Prize, 78; Univ Illinois Undergraduate Instructional Awd, 81; Nat Endowment for the Humanities (NEH) Fellowship for Independent Study and Research, 82-83; Am Hist Asn, Albert J. Beveridge Grant for Research in Am Hist, April, 84; Honorable Mention, Otto A. Rothert Awd for best article published in each vol of The Filson Club History Quart, Jan 84; Asn of Black Women Historians Brown Publication Prize, Special Citation for Free Frank, Oct 85; Berkshire Fellowship in Hist, Radcliffe Col Mary Ingraham Bunting Institute, summer 85; Newcomen Prize for the best article "Racism, Slavery, and Free Enterprise: Black Entrepreneurshipo in the United States before the Civil War," to be published in the Harvard Business History Review for 1986; Asn of Black Women Historians, Brown Publication Prize for the best article "Racism, Slavery, and Free Enterprise," published by or on Black Women in 1986; Rockefeller Found Fellowship, 86-87; E. Franklin Frazier Vis Scholar for 88-89 at Clark Univ, Worchester, Ma, declined; Ralph Metcalfe Prof, Oct 3-6, 89, Marquette Univ, Milwaukee, WI; Ga Interdepartmental Univ Hist Program Vis Distinguished Scholar, 90; George Rogers Clark Awd, Sept 90; Key to the City of Barry, Ill, Oct 90; Carter G. Woodson Awd forbest article punblished 1983-1985, Journal of Negro Hist, Oct 91; Incomplete List of Faculty Rated as Excellent, 91; Finalist, Oakley-Kunde Awd for Excellence to Undergraduate Education, 93; Princeton Univ, Shelby Cullom Davis Center for Hist Studies, Fellowship, fall semester, 94; Fulbright Fellowship for Teaching and Research, South Africa, 95; United States Information Agency Fulbright Certificate of award, 96; and numerous grants from the Univ of Ill at Urbana from 85-94. **MEMBERSHIPS** Asn for Study Afro-Am Life & Hist; AHA; Southern Hist Asn; Orgn Am Historians. **RESEARCH** African American business history, Black Intellectual History, Black Women and Peace Activism. **SELECTED PUBLICATIONS** Auth, Occupational Distribution of Frontier Towns in Pike County: An 1850 Census Survey, Western Ill Regional Studies 5, 2: 146-171, fall 82; Black Entrepreneurship: An Historical Inquiry, Essays in Economic and Business Hist, 1: 37-55, 83; Pioneer Slave Entrepreneurship on the Kentucky Pennyroyal Frontier, Journal of Negro Hist 68, 2: 289-308, summer 83; Entrepreneurial Ventures in the Origin of Agricultural Towns in Nineteenth Century Illinois, Ill Hist Journal 78, 1: 289-303, spring 83; Legal Processes and Judicial Challenges: Black Land Ownership on the Western Illinois Frontier, Western Ill Reg Studies 6, 2: 22-38, fall 83, reprinted, ed Paul Finkelman, Race and Law Before Emancipation, Hamden, Ct: Gar-

land Pubs, 91;The Legal Status of Free Blacks in Early Kentucky, 1792-1825, the Filson Club Hist Quart 57: 383-395, Oct 83, reprinted, ed Paul Finkelman,. Race and Law Before Emancipation, Hamden, Ct: Garland Pubs, 91; Racism, Slavery, and Free Enterprise: Black Entrepreneurship in the United States before the Civil War, Harvard Business Hist Rev 60, 3: 343-382, autumn 86; Whither Liberty, Legality, or Equality: Slavery, Race, Property and the 1787 American Constitution, New York Law School Journal of Human Rights 6, 2: 299-352, spring 89; Prologue to Capitalism: Free Enterprise and Black Entrepreneurship. A Comparative History of Black Business in the United States and South Africa, Johannesburg, South Africa: Univ of the Witwatersrand, Institute for Advances Social Research, 95; Entrepreneurs, Jack Salzman, David Lionel Smith and Cornel West, eds, Encyclopedia of African-American Culture and History, vol 2, New York: Simon & Schuster Macmillan, 96; Banking, Jack Salzman, David Lionel Smith and Cornel West, eds, Encyclopedia of African-American Culture and History, vol 1, New York: Simon & Schuster Macmillan, 96; The Promised Land: The Chicago Defender and the Black Press in Illinois, 1862-1970, in H. Lewis Suggs, ed, The Black Press in the Midwest, Westport Ct: Greenwood Press Pubs Group, 96; Promoting Black Entrepreneurship and Business Enterprise in Antebellum America: The National Negro Convention, 1830-1855, in Thomas D. Boston, ed, A Different Vision: Race and Public Policy: 2 vols, London: Routledge Press, 97; Trade and Markets in Precolonial West and West Central Africa: The Cultural Foundation of the African American Business Tradition, in Thomas D. Boston, ed, A Different Vision: Race and Public Policy, 2 vol, London: Routledge Press, 97; African Americans, in Elliot Barkan, ed, A Nation of Peoples: A Sourcebook on America's Multicultural Heritage, Westport, Cn: Greenwood Pub, 98; ed, African Americans in Business: The Path Towards Empowerment, Washington, D. C.:The Assoc Pubs, Inc, 98;ed, Encyclopedia of African American Business History, Westport, Cn: Greenwood Pub Group, forthcoming 98; auth, The History of Black Business in America: Capitalism, Race, Entrepreneurship, New York: Macmillan/Twayne. 98; Free Frank: A Black Pioneer on the Antebellum Frontier, Lexington: The Univ Press of Ky, 83, 85, paper, 95; War, Peace, and Structural Violence: Peace Activism and the African American Experience, Bloomington: Indiana Univ , Center on Global Change and World Peace, 92; African-American Business and Entrepreneurship: Critical Historiographical Assessments in the Economic and Cultural Life of Blacks and Capitalism, contract, Westport, Ct: Greenwood, forthcoming 99. **CONTACT ADDRESS** Dept of Hist, Univ of Illinois, Urbana-Champaign, 810 S Wright St, Urbana, IL 61801-3611. **EMAIL** jewalker@uiuc.edu

WALKER, LAWRENCE DAVID
PERSONAL Born 10/04/1931, Las Animas, CO, m, 1954, 2 children **DISCIPLINE** EUROPEAN HISTORY **EDUCATION** Stanford Univ, AB, 53, MA, 57; Univ Calif, Berkeley, PhD, 65. **CAREER** Instr hist Western civilization, Stanford Univ, 61-63; asst prof mod Europ hist, Univ Southern Calif, 64-69; assoc prof, 69-81, prof to prof emer Hist, Ill State Univ, 81-. **HONORS AND AWARDS** Nat Endowment for Humanities younger humanist fel, 71-72; Nat Endowment for Humanities residential fel, Northwestern Univ, 81-82. **MEMBERSHIPS** AHA; Group Use Psychol Hist; Cath Hist Asn. **RESEARCH** Historiography; quantitative history. **SELECTED PUBLICATIONS** Auth, Marc Bloch's Feudal Society, Hist & Theory, 63; Hitler youth and Catholic youth, 1933-1936: A study in totalitarian conquest, Cath Univ Am, 71; Le concordat avec le Reich et les organisations de jeunesse, La revue d'histoire de la deuxieme guerre mondiale, 1/74; Psychological dimensions of historiography, Psychohist Rev, summer 78; Young priests as opponents: Factors associated with clerical opposition to the Nazis, Bavaria, 1933, Cath Hist Rev, 79; Schematismen as sources in the study of German social history, Hist Methods, 79; Historical linguistics and the comparative method of Marc Bloch, Hist & Theory, 80; The Nazi youth cohort, the missing variable, Psychohist Rev, fall 80. **CONTACT ADDRESS** Dept of Hist, Illinois State Univ, Campus Box 4420, Normal, IL 61761. **EMAIL** lwalke@ilstu.edu

WALKER, MACK
PERSONAL Born 06/06/1929, Springfield, MA, m, 1954, 3 children **DISCIPLINE** MODERN EUROPEAN HISTORY **EDUCATION** Bowdoin Col, AB, 50; Harvard Univ, PhD, 59. **CAREER** Instr hist, RI Sch Design, 57-59; from instr to asst prof, Harvard Univ, 59-66; from assoc prof to prof, Cornell Univ, 66-74; prof of hist, Johns Hopkins Univ, 74-99, dept chm, 79-82; Emer, 89-. **HONORS AND AWARDS** Fel, Inst Advan Study, 77. **MEMBERSHIPS** Am Acad Arts & Sci. **RESEARCH** German social and political history. **SELECTED PUBLICATIONS** Auth, Germany and the emigration, 1816-1885, Harvard Univ, 64; ed, Metternich's Europe, Harper, 68; Plombieres, Oxford Univ, 68; auth, German Home Towns, Cornell Univ, 71, 98; auth, Johann Jakob Moser and the Holy Roman Empire of the German Nation, NC Univ, 81; auth, The Salzburg Transaction, NC Univ, 92; auth, Der Salzburger Handel Vandenhoeck and Rupprecht, 97. **CONTACT ADDRESS** 2212 W Rogers Ave, Baltimore, MD 21209. **EMAIL** reklaw_m@email.msn.com

WALKER, MELISSA
PERSONAL Born 09/13/1962, Blount, CO, m, 1999 **DISCIPLINE** HISTORY **EDUCATION** Maryville Col, BA, 85; Providence Col, MA, 93; Clark Univ, PhD, 96. **CAREER** Office Manager, Maryville Col, 85-86; dir, 86-87; assoc dir to asst dir, Bryant Col, 87-96; asst prof, Converse Col, 96-. **HONORS AND AWARDS** Malone Fel, Nat Coun on US, 98; Outstanding Student Org, Converse Col, 00; Fel, Baylor Univ, 00. **MEMBERSHIPS** S Hist Assoc; S Assoc of Women Hist; Rural Women's Studies Assoc; Tenn Hist Soc; SC Hist Assoc; Appalachian Studies Assoc. **RESEARCH** Rural Women's Hist; S Hist. **SELECTED PUBLICATIONS** Auth, "Lillian Smith", in Feminist Writers, ed P. Kester-Shelton, St. James Pr, 96; auth, "Home Extension Work Among African Americans in East Tennessee, 1920-1939", Agr Hist, Summer 96; auth, "Making Do and Doing Without: East Tennessee Farm Women Cope with Economic Crisis: 1920-1941", Jof E Tenn Hist, Spring 97; auth, "Home Extension Work" and "Home Economics", in Hist Dict of Women's Educ, ed Linda Eisenmann, Greenwood Pr, 98; auth, "African Americans and TVA Reservoir Property Removal: Race in a New Deal Program", Agr Hist, Spring 98; auth, "Farm Wives and Commercial Farming: The Case of Loudon County, Tennessee", Tenn Hist Quart, Summer 98; auth, "Narrative Themes in the Oral Histories of Farming Folk", Agr Hist, Spring 00; auth, "Culling Out the Men From the Boys: Concepts of Success in the Recollections of a Southern Farmer", Oral Hist Rev; Winter/Spring 00; auth, "All We Knew Was to Farm: 'Farm Women and Change in the Upcountry South, 1919-1941", Johns Hopkins Univ Pr, May, 00; auth, "Lucy Mercer Rutherfurd" and "American Student Union", in the Eleanor Roosevelt Encycl, ed Maurine H. Beasley, Greenwood Pr (forthcoming). **CONTACT ADDRESS** Dept Hist and Govt, Converse Col, 580 E Main St, Spartanburg, SC 29302-1931. **EMAIL** melissa.walker@converse.edu

WALKER, PAMELA J.
DISCIPLINE NINETEENTH-CENTURY BRITISH HISTORY **EDUCATION** Concordia Univ, BA, 82; York Univ, MA, 84; Rutgers Univ, PhD, 91. **CAREER** Assoc prof, Carleton Univ. **RESEARCH** Trans-Atlantic religious and cultural movements; Nineteenth-century British hist, women's hist. **SELECTED PUBLICATIONS** Ed, "I Live But Yet Not I For Christ Liveth in Me: Men and Masculinity in the Salvation Army, 1865-1890," in Asserting Manliness, John Tosh and Michael Roper, eds., London: Routledge, (91): 92-112; auth, "Proclaiming Women's Right to Preach," Harvard Divinity Bulletin, vol xxii, (94): 20-23, 35; co-ed, Voices of the Spirit: Womens Preachers and Prophets through Two Milennia of Christianity, with Beverly Mayne Kienzel, The Univ of Calif Press, (forthcoming 98); auth, "A Carnival of Equality: The Salvation Army and the Politics of Religion in Working-Class Communities," Journal of Victorian Culture, 5, 00. **CONTACT ADDRESS** Dept of Hist, Carleton Univ, 1125 Colonel By Dr, Ottawa, ON, Canada K1S 5B6. **EMAIL** pjwalker@ccs.carleton.ca

WALKER, PHILIP ALFRED
PERSONAL Born 11/16/1919, Winston-Salem, NC, m, 1957, 4 children **DISCIPLINE** MODERN EUROPEAN HISTORY **EDUCATION** Univ NC, AB, 40, PhD (recent Europe), 55; Emory Univ, MA, 42. **CAREER** Instr hist, Emory Univ, 47-48; From asst prof to assoc prof, Univ Southern Miss, 51-58; assoc prof, La Polytech Inst, 58-63; chmn div humanities, 66-71, Prof Hist and Head Dept, Univ NC, Asheville, 63-80; Fel, Inst Asian Studies, Duke Univ, 67; prof emer, 90. **HONORS AND AWARDS** OBK; Fulbright Scholar to France, 49-50. **MEMBERSHIPS** AHA; Southern Hist Asn. **RESEARCH** Paris peace conference of ; general intellectual history. **CONTACT ADDRESS** 5 Northwood Rd., Asheville, NC 28804. **EMAIL** gwalk1227@aol.com

WALKER, RENEE B.
PERSONAL Born 04/30/1968, Allentown, PA, m, 1994, 1 child **DISCIPLINE** ARCHAEOLOGY **EDUCATION** Ind Univ Pa, BA, 90; Univ Tenn, MA, 93; PhD, 98. **CAREER** Vis Asst Prof, Skidmore Col, 98-. **HONORS AND AWARDS** Grad Student Teaching Awd, 96. **MEMBERSHIPS** Soc for Am Anthrop, Southeast Archaeol Conf. **RESEARCH** Archaeology of eastern North America. **SELECTED PUBLICATIONS** Coauth, "Regress What on What?: Paleodemographic Age Estimation as a Calibration Problem," in Integrating Archaeological Demography: Multidisciplinary Approaches to Prehistoric Population, ed. R.R. Paine (Carbondale, IL: Center for Archaeol Investigations, Occasional Paper 24, 97); coauth, "A Preliminary Report on the Archaeology of a Mississippian Cave Art Site from East Tennessee," Southeastern Archaeol 16-1 (97): 51-73; auth, "Book note on 'Dogan Point: A Shell Matrix Site in the Lower Hudson Valley' ed. Cheryl Claassen," Southeastern Archaeol 16-1 (97): 95; auth, "Late-Paleo-Indian Faunal Remains from Dust Cave, Alabama," Current Res in the Pleistocene 14 (97): 85-87; auth, "Early Holocene Ecological Adaptations at Dust Cave, Alabama," in Sustaining Appalachia's Environment: The Human Dimension, ed. Benita Howell (Springfield: Univ of Ill Press, 00). **CONTACT ADDRESS** Dept Anthrop and Sociol, Skidmore Col, 815 N Broadway, Saratoga Springs, NY 12866.

WALKER, ROBERT HARRIS
PERSONAL Born 03/15/1924, Cincinnati, OH, m, 1953, 3 children **DISCIPLINE** AMERICAN CIVILIZATION **EDUCATION** Northwestern Univ, BS, 45; Columbia Univ, MA, 50; Univ Pa, PhD (Am civilization), 55. **CAREER** Educ spec, US War Dept, Shizuoka, Japan, 46-47; instr English, Carnegie Inst Technol, 50-51; instr Am civilization and ed, Am Quart, Univ Pa, 53-54; asst prof, Univ Wyo, 55-59, actg dir Am studies, 56-59; assoc prof Am lit, 59-63, dir Am Studies Prog, 59-65 and 68-70, Prof Am Civilization, George Washington Univ, 63-; Ed, Am Quart, 53-54, Am Studies Int, 70-81 and Contrib in Am Studies Ser, 70-; consult, US Info Agency and US Foreign Serv Inst, 59-66 and Peace Corps, 61-62; dir, Div Educ and Pub Prog, Nat Endowment for Humanities, 66-68; fels, Woodrow Wilson Int Ctr, 72-73, Rockefeller Ctr, Bellagio, 79, Huntington Libr, 80 and Hoover Inst, 80; comnr, Japan-US Friendship Comn, 77-81; Am Coun Learned Soc Deleg to Unesco, 78-; Am specialist grants, Thailand, Greece and Iran, 79, Israel, 80 and Brazil, 81. **MEMBERSHIPS** Am Studies Asn (pres, 70-71); Orgn Am Historians; Cosmos Club. **RESEARCH** Reform; literature and society. **SELECTED PUBLICATIONS** Auth, Crossings in the Great Transatlantic Migrations, 1870-1914, Am Studies Int, Vol 31, 93; Cincinnati, Queen City of the West, 1819-1838, Am Studies Int, Vol 31, 93; Bode, Carl in In Memoriam, Am Quart, Vol 45, 93; Sporting with the Gods in The Rhetoric of Play and Game in american Culture in Oriard, M, Am Studies Int, Vol 31, 93; Small Craft Advisory, Am Studies Int, Vol 31, 93; The American Pacific in from the Old China Trade to the Present, Am Studies Int, Vol 31, 93; Remembering Bode, Carl, 1911-1993, Am Studies Int, Vol 31, 93; Too Marvelous For Words in The Life and Genius of Tatum, Am Studies Int, Vol 32, 94; Beyond the Rising Sun in Nationalism in Contemporary Japan, Am Studies Int, Vol 33, 95. **CONTACT ADDRESS** 3915 Huntington St NW, Washington, DC 20015.

WALKER, ROBERT MILLER
PERSONAL Born 12/10/1908, Flushing, NY **DISCIPLINE** ART HISTORY **EDUCATION** Princeton Univ, AB, 32, MFA, 36; Harvard Univ, PhD, 41. **CAREER** Instr fine arts, Williams Col, 35-38; asst, Harvard Univ, 39-40; From asst prof to prof, 41-74, chmn dept, 41-71, Emer Prof Art Hist, Swarthmore Col, 74-; Lectr, Pa Acad Fine Arts, 46 and 47 and Johns Hopkins Univ, 49. **MEMBERSHIPS** Col Art Asn Am; Soc Archit Hist (treas, 55-63); Archaeol Inst Am; Print Coun Am. **RESEARCH** Art history; architecture; prints and drawings. **SELECTED PUBLICATIONS** Auth, 2 Unpublished Portuguese Sonnets on the Battle of Ameixial and June 8 1663, Port Studies, Vol 9, 93; Fanshawe,Richard Lusiad and Fariaesousa, Manuel, De Lusiadas Comentadas and The Probable Source in Castilian Prose of the 1st English Translation of Camoes Os Lusiadas in New Documentary Evidence, Port Studies, Vol 10, 94. **CONTACT ADDRESS** Six Fox Hollow, Wayland, MA 01778.

WALKER, SUE SHERIDAN
PERSONAL Born 08/11/1935, Chicago, IL, m, 1959, 1 child **DISCIPLINE** MEDIEVAL HISTORY **EDUCATION** Loyola Univ, BA, 58, MA, 61; Univ Chicago, PhD(hist), 66. **CAREER** Asst prof hist, Univ Windsor, 66-68; asst prof, 68-71, assoc prof, 71-79, prof hist, Northeastern Ill Univ, 79-, Am Asn Univ Women fel, 65-66; chmn, Northeastern Ill Univ & Am Soc Legal Hist Conf on English Plea Rolls, 73, 86; bk rev ed, Am J Legal Hist, 77-82; Nat Endowment for Humanities fel, 82-83. **HONORS AND AWARDS** Elected a Fellow of the Royal Historical Society, 86; named to the Council of the Pipe Roll Society, 96; Newberry Library/National Endowment for the Humanities Fellowship, 90-91. **MEMBERSHIPS** Am Soc for Legal Hist; AHA; Medieval Acad Am; Selden Soc. **RESEARCH** Medieval English Family Law and Society: Inheritance, dower and wardship; rights of women and legal process in the royal courts esp concerning widows as litigants in dower pleas and the impact of an increasingly professional royal court. **SELECTED PUBLICATIONS** Auth, "Violence and the exercise of Feudal guardianship: The action of ejectio custodia," Am J Legal Hist 16 (72); Proof of age of Feudal heirs in Medieval England, Mediaeval Studies, Vol XXXV, 73; Widow and ward: The Feudal Law of child custody in Medieval England, Feminist Studies No 3, 34/76; ed, Checklist of Research in British Legal Manuscripts, Vol I & II, Northeastern Ill Univ; The Action of Waste in the Early Common Law, Legal Records and the Historian, Royal Hist Soc, 78; Feudal Constraint and Free Consent in the Making of Marriages in Medieval England: Widows in the King's Gift, Can Hist Soc, 79; ed & transl, Court Rolls of the Manor of Wakefield, Oct 1331 to Sept 1333, W.C. R.S., YAS, Leeds, 83; Wife and Widow in Medieval England, Univ Mich Press, 93; a series of articles on Wardship, Marriage and Legal Remedies including Free Consent and Marriage of feudal wards in medieval England, J of Medieval Hist 8, pp 123-134, 92; Punishing convicted ravishers: statutory strictures and actual practice.., J of Medieval Hist 13, pp 237-250, 87; guest ed and contrib to an issue of family law (papers from one session of the 1986 Conference on British Legal Manuscripts), J of Medieval Hist 14, no 1, 88; Common Law Juries and Feudal Marriage Customs.., Univ of Ill Law Review 1984, no 3, pp705-718; Wrongdoing and Compensation: The Pleas of Wardship.., The J of Legal Hist 9, 88; Wager of Law and Judgment by Default in Pleas of Dower in the Royal Courts of Late Thirteenth-and Fourteenth Century England, The Life of the Law, ed Peter Birks, London, 93. **CONTACT ADDRESS** Dept of Hist, Northeastern Illinois Univ, 5500 N St Louis Ave, Chicago, IL 60625-4625. **EMAIL** SS-Walker@neiu.edu

WALKOWITZ, DANIEL JAY
PERSONAL Born 11/25/1942, Paterson, NJ, m, 1965, 1 child **DISCIPLINE** HISTORY **EDUCATION** Univ Rochester, BA, 64; PhD, 72. **CAREER** Instr hist, Rensselaer Polytech Inst, 69-71; lectr univ col, Rutgers Univ, New Brunswick, 71-72, asst prof, Rutgers Univ, 72-78; asst prof, 78-80, assoc prof, NYork Univ, 80-88; codir grad prog pub hist, 81-88; prof hist, NY Univ, 88-; dir, Metropolitan studies, 89-; proj dir, Nat Endowment for Humanities Media Grant, 76-78 and 80; consult, Cabin Creek Films, 78-81, the Wobblies, 79, Saratoga Co Hist Mus, 79, Red Hill Films, 80, Am Film inst, 80-81, Chinatown Hist Proj, 81-82. **HONORS AND AWARDS** Fel, Rutgers Univ Res Council, 73; Rutgers Univ Res Council grants, 71, 72, 73, 74; Nat Endowment for the Humanities, Media Development Grant, 76-77; Nat Endowment for the Humanities, Media Production Grant, 77-78; Mellon Fel, Univ of Pennsylvania, 78-79; Nat Endowment for the Humanities, Media Development Grant, 80; NYork Council for the Humanities, Chairman's grant, 82; NYork Council for the Humanities, Chairman's grant, 85-86; NYork Univ Res Challenge Fund Grant, 86-87; IREX, res travel grant for Donetsk Video proj, 89; Nat Council for Soviet and East European Res, 89; Nat Council for Soviet and East European Res, 90; Channel 4 (Britain) production grant, 89-90; NYork Council for the Humanities, Chairman's grant, "State and Representation: Representations of the State Conference; Nat Council for Soviet and East European Res, 92-93; NYork Council for the Humanities, Chairman's grant, 94; NYork Council for the Humanities, Chairman's grant, 96; T. Backer Fund, 99; Gadd/Merril Fund, 99. **MEMBERSHIPS** Orgn Am Historians; Soc Sci Hist Asn; AHA; Nat Council on Pub Hist; Oral Hsitory Asn. **RESEARCH** Working-class history; comparative urban and social history. **SELECTED PUBLICATIONS** Proj dir, "The Molders of Troy," 80; auth, "The Historian as Filmmaker: A Manifesto," Historical Jour of Film, Radio, and Television (84); auth, "Visual History: The Craft of the Historian-Filmamker," The Public Historian (84-85); auth, "Corporate History, or Giving History the Business," in Presenting the Past, ed. S. Benson, et al. (Philadelphia, Temple Univ Press, 86), 223-236, 393-395; auth, "New York: A Tale of Two Cities," in Snowbelt Cities, ed. Richard M. Bernhard (Indiana Univ Press, 89), 189-208; cowriter, dir, producer, "Perestroika From Below," Channel 4, England, 90; cowriter, producer, "Public History Today," Nat Council for Public History, 90; coauth, "Sub/versions of History: A Meditation on Film and Historical Narrative," History Workshop Jour 38 (94): 203-214; coauth, Workers of the Donbass Speak: Survival and Identity in the New Ukraine, SUNY Albany press, 95; auth, Working with Classs: Social Workers and the Politics of Middle-Class Identity, Univ of NC Press, 99; **CONTACT ADDRESS** Public History Program, New York Univ, 285 Mercer St., New York, NY 10003-6607. **EMAIL** daniel.walkowitz@nyu.edu

WALL, BENNETT HARRISON
PERSONAL Born 12/07/1914, Raleigh, NC, m, 3 children **DISCIPLINE** HISTORY **EDUCATION** Wake Forest Col, AB, 33; Univ NC, AM, 41, PhD, 46. **CAREER** From instr to assoc prof hist, Univ Ky, 44-65; assoc prof, 65-69, head dept, 68-73, prof hist, Tulane Univ, 69-80; Lectr Hist, Univ GA, 81-. **MEMBERSHIPS** Econ Hist Asn; Agr Hist Soc; Orgn Am Historians; Southern Hist Asn (secy-treas, 52-); Newcomen Soc. **RESEARCH** Southern history; United States business and economic history, 00-72; United States local and regional politics, 1865-20. **SELECTED PUBLICATIONS** Auth, Kentucky and the Bourbons in The Story of Allen Dale Farm, J Southern Hist, Vol 59, 93; The History of Belle Meade in Mansion, Plantation, and Stud, J Southern Hist, Vol 59, 93. **CONTACT ADDRESS** Dept of Hist, Univ of Georgia, Athens, GA 30602.

WALL, HELENA M.
PERSONAL Born 11/22/1955, New York, NY **DISCIPLINE** HISTORY **EDUCATION** Brandeis Univ, BA (Hist), 77; Harvard Univ, MA (Hist), 78, PhD (Hist), 83. **CAREER** Lect in Hist and Hist and Lit, Harvard Univ, 83-84; asst prof Hist, 84-90, assoc prof Hist, 90-98, Prof of Hist, Pomona Coll, 98-. **HONORS AND AWARDS** NEH fel for Coll Teachers; NEH Summer fel; fel, Charles Warren Center, Harvard Univ; Phi Beta Kappa. **MEMBERSHIPS** AHA; OAH. **RESEARCH** Colonial Am; Am social hist; early modern hist. **SELECTED PUBLICATIONS** Auth, Fierce Communion: Family and Community in Early America, Harvard Univ Press, 90. **CONTACT ADDRESS** Dept of Hist, Pomona Col, Claremont, CA 91711. **EMAIL** hwall@pomona.edu

WALL, IRWIN M.
PERSONAL Born 04/21/1940, New York, NY, m, 1961, 1 child **DISCIPLINE** FRENCH, EUROPEAN, AND INTERNATIONAL HISTORY **EDUCATION** Columbia Univ, BA, 61, MA, 62, PhD, 68. **CAREER** PROF HIST, Univ of Calif, Riverside, 70-. **MEMBERSHIPS** Western Soc Fr Hist (pres, 94-95) **RESEARCH** French Left; French-American relations. **SELECTED PUBLICATIONS** Auth, French Communism in the Era of Stalin, 83; L'Influence Americaine sur la politique francaise, Paris, 89; The United States and the Making of Postwar France, 91; France, the United States, and the Algerian War, 1954-1962, 00; numerous book chapters and articles on French history and politics. **CONTACT ADDRESS** Dept of Hist, Univ of California, Riverside, 900 University Ave, Riverside, CA 92521-0001. **EMAIL** irwin.wall@ucr.edu

WALLACE, ANDREW
PERSONAL Born 11/18/1930, Springfield, IL, m, 1958, 2 children **DISCIPLINE** AMERICAN HISTORY **EDUCATION** Univ Ariz, BA, 53, PhD (hist), 68. **CAREER** Ed, J Ariz Hist, Ariz Pioneers Hist Soc, 64-68; asst prof, 68-80, Asspc Prof Hist, Northern Ariz Univ, 80-. **MEMBERSHIPS** AHA; Orgn Am Historians; Western Hist Asn. **RESEARCH** Nineteenth century United States history; history of the American West; American military history. **SELECTED PUBLICATIONS** Auth, Dedication to Will Croft Barnes, Ariz & the West, autumn 60; Pumpelly's Arizona, Palo Verde, 65; The Image of Arizona, Univ NMex, 71. **CONTACT ADDRESS** Dept of Hist, No Arizona Univ, Flagstaff, AZ 86001.

WALLACE, CARL M.
DISCIPLINE HISTORY **EDUCATION** Univ New Brunswick, MA; Univ Alberta, PhD. **CAREER** Prof. **RESEARCH** Communities in Northern Ontario: An Hist Comparative Study. **SELECTED PUBLICATIONS** Auth, Communities in the Northern Ontario Frontier, Dundern, 92; co-ed, Reappraisals in Canadian History: Pre-Confederation, Scarborough, 92; co-ed, Reappraisals in Canadian History: Post-Confederation, Scarborough, 92; co-ed, Sudbury: Railtown to Regional Capital, Dundurn, 93. **CONTACT ADDRESS** Dept of History, Laurentian Univ, 935 Ramsey Lake Rd, Sudbury, ON, Canada P3E 2C6. **EMAIL** wallace@nickel.laurentian.ca

WALLACE, PATRICIA D.
PERSONAL Born 04/14/1938, Streetman, TX, d, 1 child **DISCIPLINE** HISTORY **EDUCATION** Southern Methodist Univ, BA, 60; Univ Tex, MA, 62; PhD, 75. **CAREER** Prof, Baylor Univ, 73-. **HONORS AND AWARDS** Phi Beta Kappa; Woodrow Wilson Fel. **MEMBERSHIPS** Am Hist Asn, Southern Women Historians. **RESEARCH** Cold War, U.S. Foreign Relations, History of the American Woman. **SELECTED PUBLICATIONS** Auth, Politics of Conscience: A Biography of Margaret Chase Smith; auth, Threat of Peace: James F Byrnes and the Council of Foreign Ministers; auth, Waco: Texas Crossroads; auth, A Spirit So Rare: A History of the Women of Waco; auth, Our Land, Our Lives: A Pictorial History of McLennon County: auth, Centennial: An Illustrated History of the Methodist Home. **CONTACT ADDRESS** Dept Hist, Baylor Univ, Waco, PO Box 97306, Waco, TX 76798-7306.

WALLACE, WILLIAM E.
PERSONAL Born 07/30/1952, Oakland, CA, m, 1976, 2 children **DISCIPLINE** PAINTING, SCULPTURE, AND ARCHITECTURE ITALY FROM 1300 TO 1700 **EDUCATION** Columbia Univ, PhD, 83. **CAREER** Art Historian Washington Univ. **HONORS AND AWARDS** Robert Sterling Clark Distinguished Prof, 99; Am Academy in Rome, 96-97; Villa I Tatti, Florence, 90-91. **SELECTED PUBLICATIONS** Auth, ; Michelangelo at San Lorenzo: The Genius as Entreprepreneur, Cambridge Univ Press, 94; Michelangelo: Selected Scholarship in English, 5 volumes, Garland Press, 95; auth, Michalangelo: A Complete Sculpture Painting, Architecture, Levin, 98; auth, Michaelangelo: Selected Readings, Garland, 99. **CONTACT ADDRESS** Dept of Art History and Archaeology, Washington Univ, 1 Brookings Dr, P O Box 1589, Saint Louis, MO 63130-4899. **EMAIL** wwallace@artsci.wrstl.edu

WALLACH, ALAN
PERSONAL Born 06/08/1942, Brooklyn, NY, m, 1988 **DISCIPLINE** ART HISTORY **EDUCATION** Columbia Univ, PhD, 73. **CAREER** Asst to Assoc Prof, Kean Col, 74-88; Ralph H Wark Prof of Art & Art Hist, Prof Am Stud, Col of William & Mary. **HONORS AND AWARDS** Smithsonian Inst Sr Postdoctoral Fellow, 85-86. **MEMBERSHIPS** Col Art Asn; Am Stud Asn; Board of Dir, College Art Assoc, 96-00. **RESEARCH** 9th century American art; museums & art institutions. **SELECTED PUBLICATIONS** Auth, Making a Picture of the View from Mt Holyoke, American Iconology: New Approaches to Nineteenth Century Art and Literature, Yale Univ Press, 80-91, 310-312, 93; co-ed, auth, Thomas Cole: Landscape into History, Yale Univ Press, 94; auth, Wadsworth's Tower: An Episode in the History of American Landscape Vision, Am Art, 10:3, 8-27, 96; auth, Long-term Visions, Short-term Failures: Art Institutions in the United States, 1800-1860, Art in Bourgeois Society, 1790-1850, Cambridge Univ Press, 303-319, 98; Exhibiting Contradiction: Essays on the Art Museum in the United States, Univ Mass Press, 98. **CONTACT ADDRESS** Dept of Art/Art Hist, Col of William and Mary, PO Box 8795, Williamsburg, VA 23187. **EMAIL** axwall@wm.edu

WALLENSTEIN, PETER
PERSONAL Born 05/22/1944, East Orange, NJ, m, 1986 **DISCIPLINE** U.S. HISTORY **EDUCATION** Columbia Univ, BA, 66; Johns Hopkins Univ, PhD, 73. **CAREER** Instr and asst prof, Sarah Lawrence Col, 70-75; vis asst prof, Univ Toronto, 75-77; asst prof, Univ Maryland in East Asia, 79-82; asst prof and assoc prof, Va Polytechnic Inst and State Univ, 83-. **HONORS AND AWARDS** E Merton Coulter Awd, George Historical Socity, 86; McClung Awd, East TN Historical Society, 92; Mario D Zamora Distinguished Service Awd, VA School Science Asn, 96. **MEMBERSHIPS** Southern Hist Asn; Orgn Amer Hist. **RESEARCH** Southern History; Virginia; Race and Policy: Higher Education. **SELECTED PUBLICATIONS** Auth, Virginia Tech, Land-Grant University, 1872-1997: History of a School, a State, a Nation, Blacksburg, Va, Pocahontas Press, 97; From Slave South to New South: Public Policy in Nineteenth-Century Georgia, Chapel Hill, Univ NC Press, 87; essays, Laissez Faire and the Lunatic Asylum: State Welfare Institutions in Georgia-The First Half Century, 1830s-1880s, ed Elna C. Green, Before the New Deal: Essays in Southern Social Welfare History, 1830-1930, Athens, Univ Ga Press, 98; Indian Foremothers: Race, Sex, Slavery, and Freedom in Early Virginia, eds Catherine Clinton and Michele Gillespie, The Devil's Lane: Sex and Race in the Early South, New York, Oxford Univ Press, 57-73, 97; Helping to Save the Union: The Social Origins, Wartime Experience, and Military Impact of White Union Soldiers from East Tennessee, eds Kenneth W. Noe and Shannon H. Wilson, Appalachia in the Civil War, Knoxville, Univ of Tenn Press, 1-29, 97; Incendiaries All: Southern Politics and the Harpers Ferry Raid, ed Paul Finkelman, His Soul Goes Marching On: Responses to John Brown and the Harpers Ferry Raid, Charlottesville, Univ Press of Va, 149-73, 95; Race, Marriage, and the Law of Freedom: Alabama and Virginia, 1860s-1960s, Chicago-Kent Law Rev, 70, no 2, special issue The Law of Freedom, 371-437, 94; Flawed Keepers of the Flame: The Interpreters of George Mason, Va Mag of Hist and Bio, 102, April, 229-60, 94; These New and Strange Beings: Women in the Legal Profession in Virginia, 1890-1990, Va Mag of Hist and Bio, 101, April, 193-226, 93; Cartograms and the Mapping of Virginia History, 1790-1990, Va Soc Sci Jour, 28, 90-110, 93. **CONTACT ADDRESS** History Dept., Virginia Polytech Inst and State Univ, Blacksburg, VA 24061. **EMAIL** pwallens@vt.edu

WALLOT, JEAN-PIERRE
PERSONAL Born 05/22/1935, Valleyfield, PQ, Canada **DISCIPLINE** HISTORY **EDUCATION** Univ Montreal, BA, 54, LL, 57, MA, 57, PhD, 65. **CAREER** Lectr & asst prof, Univ Montreal, 61-66; hist, Mus Man, 66-69; assoc prof, Univ Toronto, 69-71; prof, Concordia Univ, 71-73; chmn, 73-75, vice dean arts & sci, 75-82, vice pres, 82-85, Univ Montreal; guest lectr, Univ Sherbrooke, 67, 68; guest lectr, Univ Que Montreal, 72; guest lectr, Univ BC, 72; guest lectr, Laval Univ, 73, 77; guest lectr, Univ Ottawa, 86-98; ; Nat Archivist, 85-97; mem, secy, Acad I, Royal Soc Can (sect pres, 85-87, pres-elect, 96-97, pres, 97-99). **HONORS AND AWARDS** Fel, Royal Soc Can, 78; Tyrrell Medal Royal Soc, 82; Acad des lettres du Quebec, 83; Doctorate hon) & Univ Medal, Univ Rennes (France), 87; Off, Ordre des Arts et Lettres de la Republique francaise, 87; Am Antiquarian Soc, 87; Off, Order Can, 91; Centenary Medal, Royal Soc, 94; Doctorate (hon), Univ Ottawa, 96; Jacques-Ducharme Prize, Asn Archivistes Que, 97. **MEMBERSHIPS** Can Hist Asn; Inst d'histoire de l'amerique francaise; Chevaliers de colomb. **RESEARCH** Economic and social history of Quebec **SELECTED PUBLICATIONS** Auth, Intrigues francaises et americaines au Canada 1800-1802, 65; auth, Un Quebec qui bougeait 1801-1810, 73; coauth, Les Imprimes dans le Bas-Canada 1794-1812, 73; ed, Memoires d'un Bourgeois de Montreal, 80; ed, France de l'Ouest et Quebec, 82; ed, Evolution et eclatement du monde rural, 86. **CONTACT ADDRESS** Inst of Canadian Stud, Univ of Ottawa, 52 Univ Private, Rm 103, Ottawa, ON, Canada K1A 0N3. **EMAIL** jpwallot@uottawa.ca

WALSH, DAVID A.
DISCIPLINE ART AND ART HISTORY **EDUCATION** Univ MN, PhD, 74. **CAREER** Assoc prof, Univ of Rochester. **HONORS AND AWARDS** NEH res grant, 89-91. **RESEARCH** Medieval art; archaeology; hist; art hist. **SELECTED PUBLICATIONS** auth, "Bordesley Abbey: A Guide to the Church," (84); The Excavations of Cluny III by K.J. Conant, Le gouvernement d'Hugues de Semur Cluny, Actes du Colloque scientifique int, Cluny, 88; The Iconography of the Bronze Doors of Barisanus of Trani, Gesta, XXI/2; Regionalism and Localism in Early Cistercian Architecture in England, Arte Medievale, II, vol 2; coauth, Architecture of Cowdery's Down: a Reconsideration, Archaeol J, 150, 93; auth, Reconstructions of the Mill Buildings, In A Medieval Industrial Complex and its Landscape: The Metalworking, Watermills, and Workshops of Bordesley Abbey, York: Counc for Brit Archaeol Res Report, 93; **CONTACT ADDRESS** Dept of Art and Art Hist, Univ of Rochester, 414 Morey Hall, Rochester, NY 14642. **EMAIL** dwls@db1.cc.rochester.edu

WALT, JOSEPH W.
PERSONAL Born 04/21/1924, Los Angeles, CA **DISCIPLINE** MODERN EUROPEAN HISTORY **EDUCATION** Univ Tenn, AB, 47, AM, 51; Northwestern Univ, PhD, 60. **CAREER** Teacher, High Sch, Tenn, 50-52; instr Europ hist, Univ Tenn, 52-63; teaching asst, Northwestern Univ, 53-55; from asst prof to assoc prof, 55-64, prof hist, 64-94, emer, Simpson Col, 94-. **MEMBERSHIPS** AHA; Mid E Inst; Hist Asn Liechtenstein. **RESEARCH** Modern Middle East; Swiss-Liechtenstein. **SELECTED PUBLICATIONS** Auth, Don Berry, Iowan, Herzberg, 74; Era of Levere, Banta, 75; ed, The Phoenix, Benson, 76; Beneath the Whispering Maples: The History of Simpson College, Simpson Col Press, 95. **CONTACT ADDRESS** Dept of History, Simpson Col, Iowa, 701 N C St, Indianola, IA 50125-1297.

WALTER, HARTMUT S.
PERSONAL Born 07/13/1940, Stettin, Germany, m, 1969, 2 children **DISCIPLINE** GEOGRAPHY **EDUCATION** Univ Bonn, PhD, 67. **CAREER** Prof, UCLA, 72-. **HONORS AND AWARDS** Harkness Fel, UCLA, 67-69; Fel, Am Ornithologists Union, 87. **MEMBERSHIPS** Am Asn for the Adv of Sci. **RESEARCH** Conservation of Nature; Biogeography; Ornithology. **SELECTED PUBLICATIONS** Co-ed, Environmental hazards and bioresource management in the United States-Mexico borderlands, UCLA, 90; auth, "Driving forces of island biodiversity: An appraisal of two theories," Physical Geog, (98): 351-377; auth, "Land use conflicts in California," in Landscape Degradation in Mediterranean-type Ecosystems, (Berlin, 98), 107-126. **CONTACT ADDRESS** Dept Geog, Univ of California, Los Angeles, 1255 Bunche Hall, 405 Hilgard St, Los Angeles, CA 90095-1524. **EMAIL** walter@geog.ucla.edu

WALTER, JOHN CHRISTOPHER
PERSONAL Born 05/05/1933, Oracabessa, Jamaica **DISCIPLINE** HISTORY **EDUCATION** Ark AM&N Coll, BS; Univ of Bridgeport, MA; Univ of Maine at Orono, PhD. **CAREER** From instr to asst prof hist, Purdue Univ, 70-73; chmn dept Black studies, John Jay Col Criminal Justice, 73-76; asst prof hist, 76-80, Assoc Prof Afro-Am Studies, 80-; Chmn, Ind Higher Educ Comt Afro-Am Studies, Ind State Dept Educ, 73. **MEMBERSHIPS** Asn Studies Afro-Am Life and Hist; Southern Hist Asn; AHA; Orgn Am Historians; Caribbean Hist Asn. **RESEARCH** Role of West Indians in american Black Leadership, 1900-2970; blacks and technology, 00-60; race and American foreign relations in the 20th century. **SELECTED PUBLICATIONS** Auth, A Passion for Equality, 77, Politics & Africanity in West Indian Soc Brown Univ, 83, The Black Immigrant & PoliticalRadicalism in the Harlem Renaissance 61st Annual Conf of the Assoc for the Study of Afro-Amer Life & History, 76, Franklin D. Roosevelt & the Arms Limitation 1932-41 Hofstra Univ Conf, 82, Politics & Africanity in West Indian Soc Brown Univ, 83, The Transformation of Afro-Amer Politics, The Contribs of the West Indian Immigrant Colby Coll, 83, Women & Identity in the Caribbean Smith Coll Women's Studies Cluster Comm Sem 83, Enterprise Zones, Conservative Ideology or Free-Floating Political Fantasy? Simon's Rock of Bard Coll Bulletin, 84. **CONTACT ADDRESS** Afro-Am Ctr, Bowdoin Col, Brunswick, ME 04011.

WALTER, RICHARD JOHN
PERSONAL Born 05/03/1939, Champaign, IL, m, 1969, 1 child **DISCIPLINE** HISTORY **EDUCATION** Duke Univ, BA, 61; Stanford Univ, PhD(hist), 66. **CAREER** From asst prof to assoc prof, 68-77, prof hist, Wash Univ, 77-, consult Latin Am hist, Fulbright-Hays Prog, 72-76. **MEMBERSHIPS** Latin Am Studies Asn; Conf Latin Am Hist. **RESEARCH** Latin American political history, with special concentration on Argentina. **SELECTED PUBLICATIONS** Auth, Student Politics in Argentina, Basic Bks, 68; The intellectual background of the 1918 University Reform in Argentina, Hisp Am Hist Rev, 5/69; Municipal politics and government in Buenos Aires: 1918-1930, J InterAmerican Studies & World Affairs, 5/74; The Socialist Party of Argentina, 1890-1930, Univ Tex, 77; Elections in the city of Buenos Aires during the first Yrigoyen Administration, Hisp Am Hist Rev, 78; Politics and Urban Growth in Buenos Aires, 1910-1942, Cambridge, 93; The Province of Buenos Aires and Argentine Politics, 1912-1943, Cambridge, 85. **CONTACT ADDRESS** Dept of History, Washington Univ, 1 Brookings Dr, Saint Louis, MO 63130-4899. **EMAIL** rjwalter@artsci.wustl.edu

WALTERS, E. GARRISON
PERSONAL Born 02/07/1944, Atlantic City, NJ, m, 1976 **DISCIPLINE** HISTORY **EDUCATION** Boston Univ, BA, 67, MA, 68; Ohio State Univ, PhD (hist), 72. **CAREER** Spec asst Provost admin, 72-74, Asst Dean Humanities, 74- and Lectr Int Studies, Ohio State Univ, 75-; Asst dir, Ctr Slavic and East European Studies, Ohio State Univ, 77-78; Adj Asst Prof, Slavic and East Europ Lang and Lit, Ohio State Univ, 78-; Ed, Balkanistica, 80-. **RESEARCH** Contemporary Eastern Europe; the history of Southeastern Europe; Romanian history. **SELECTED PUBLICATIONS CONTACT ADDRESS** Col of Humanities, Ohio State Univ, Columbus, Columbus, OH 43210.

WALTERS, ELIZABETH J.
DISCIPLINE ANCIENT EGYPTIAN, GREEK AND ROMAN ART AND ARCHITECTURE **EDUCATION** Vasaar Col, BA; Inst Fine Arts, NYork, MA, PhD. **CAREER** Assoc prof, Pa State Univ, 82-. **HONORS AND AWARDS** Norbert Schimmel fel, Metropolitan Museum Art; dir, Temple-Town Hierakonpolis Proj, Egypt. **MEMBERSHIPS** Assoc mem, Am Scho Class Stud, Athens. **RESEARCH** Greek sculpture for the Agora excavations. **SELECTED PUBLICATIONS** Auth, Attic Grave Reliefs that Represent Women in the Dress of Isis; Hesperia Supp XXII, Princeton. **CONTACT ADDRESS** Pennsylvania State Univ, Univ Park, 201 Shields Bldg, University Park, PA 16802. **EMAIL** DrWalters@aol.com

WALTERS, GWENFAIR
DISCIPLINE CHURCH HISTORY **EDUCATION** Wellesley Col, BA; Gordon-Conwell Theol Sem, MDiv; Cambridge Univ, PhD. **CAREER** Consult, hist archv proj, Cambridge Univ; asst prof, 93-; adv to Women; dir, Edu Tech Develop, Gordon-Conwell Theol Sem, 93-. **RESEARCH** History of worship, spirituality, media, technology, and the arts in the Church. **SELECTED PUBLICATIONS** Ed, Towards Healthy Preaching. **CONTACT ADDRESS** Gordon-Conwell Theol Sem, 130 Essex St, South Hamilton, MA 01982.

WALTERS, RONALD
PERSONAL Born 07/20/1938, Wichita, KS, m **DISCIPLINE** AFRICAN-AMERICAN STUDIES **EDUCATION** Fisk Univ, BA History 1963; Amer Univ, MA 1966, PhD 1971. **CAREER** Georgetown & Syracuse Univ, instr; Brandeis Univ African & Afro-Amer Studies, chmn 1969-71; Howard Univ, chmn pol sci 1971-74, prof of pol sci; Univ of Maryland, prof and sr fellow, currently. **HONORS AND AWARDS** The Ida B Wells Barnett Awd Natl Alliance of Black School Educators 1985; Rockefeller Foundation Rsch Grant 1985; The Congressional Black Associates Awd 1986. **MEMBERSHIPS** Past pres African Heritage Studies Assoc; mem bd Natl Black Election Study, Inst of Social Rsch, Univ of MI; mem adv bd Southern Christian Leadership Conf; founder Natl Black Independent Political Party; secty/founding mem Natl Black Leadership Roundtable; founder/past mem Bd of TransAfrica; consultant United Nations Special Comm Against Apartheid of the Security Cncl. **SELECTED PUBLICATIONS** Speaks & writes on US Foreign Policies toward Africa & Black Amer Politics; over 70 articles in several scholarly jrnls; three books in press; Disting CommServ Awd Howard Univ 1982; Disting Scholar/Activists Awd The Black Scholar Magazine 1984. **CONTACT ADDRESS** Afro-American Studies Program, Univ of Maryland, Col Park, Lefrak Hall, Ste 2169, College Park, MD 20742. **EMAIL** rwalters@bss2.umd.edu

WALTERS, RONALD GORDON
PERSONAL Born 04/23/1942, Sacramento, CA, m, 1965, 1 child **DISCIPLINE** AMERICAN SOCIAL & CULTURAL HISTORY **EDUCATION** Stanford Univ, AB, 63; Univ CA, Berkeley, MA, 65, PhD, 71. **CAREER** Actg instr hist, Univ CA, Berkeley, 67-68; from instr to asst prof, 70-75, assoc prof, 75-81, prof hist, Johns Hopkins Univ, 81-, Nat Endowment for Humanities younger humanist fel, 74-75; Rockefeller Found hum fel, 77-78. **MEMBERSHIPS** Southern Hist Asn; AHA; Orgn Am Historians. **RESEARCH** Am reform movements; sexual attitudes and behavior; popular entertainment. **SELECTED PUBLICATIONS** Ed, Primers for Prudery: Sexual Advice to Victorian America, Prentice-Hall, 73; The Antislavery Appeal: American Abolitionism After 1830, Johns Hopkins Univ, 76; American Reformers: 1815-1860, Hill & Wang, 78, rev ed, 97; Signs of the times: Clifford Geertz and historians, Social Res, autumn 80; Popular Culture, In: Encyclopedia of the United States in the Twentieth Century (Kutler, ed), Scribner's, 96; ed, Scientific Authority in Twentieth-Century America, Johns Hopkins Univ, 97. **CONTACT ADDRESS** Dept Hist, Johns Hopkins Univ, Baltimore, 3400 N Charles St, Baltimore, MD 21218-2680. **EMAIL** rgw1@jhu.edu

WALTHER, THOMAS ROBERT
PERSONAL Born 02/26/1938, Placedo, TX, m, 1963, 3 children **DISCIPLINE** HISTORY **EDUCATION** Tex A&I Univ, BA, 59, MA, 64; Univ Okla, PhD(hist), 71. **CAREER** Field worker, State Dept Pub Welfare, Tex, 61-62; investr, US Civil Serv Comn, Tex, 62-64; from asst prof to assoc prof, 68-79, Prof Hist and Dept Chmn, Pittsburg State Univ, 79-. **MEMBERSHIPS** Orgn Am Historians; Western Hist Asn; Southern Hist Asn; Kans State Hist Soc. **RESEARCH** The American West; American economic history; 19th century United States history. **SELECTED PUBLICATIONS** Auth, Some aspects of economic mobility in Barrett Township of Thomas County, 1885-1905, Kans Hist Quart, autumn 71; Native white American emigrants to Kansas, Bull Kans State Col Pittsburg, 12/75; coauth, Crawford County: From coal to soybeans, 1900-1941, Heritage of Kans, spring 78; Industrialization in southeastern Kansas, 1870-1915, Heritage Great Plains, spring 81; Industrialization on the Frontier: A Case Study, Crawford County, Kansas, 1870-1915, Red River Hist Rev, Fall 81; Two Architects of Industrialization in Southeast Kansas: Morris Cliggitt and George Nicholson, The Little Balkans Rev, Winter 82-83; 100 Years of Excellence, A History of the Pittsburg & Midway Coal Company, 1885-1985, P&M Coal Company, 85; auth, The Governors and Lieutenent Governors from Southeast Kansas, The Little Balkans Rev, Winter 88-89. **CONTACT ADDRESS** Dept of History, Pittsburg State Univ, 1701 S Broadway St, Pittsburg, KS 66762-7500. **EMAIL** twalther@pittstate.edu

WALTNER, ANN
DISCIPLINE HISTORY **EDUCATION** Univ Calif Berkeley, PhD. **CAREER** Assoc prof **RESEARCH** Chinese fiction. **SELECTED PUBLICATIONS** Auth, The Grand Secretary's Family: Three Generations of Women in the Family of Wang Hsi-Chueh, 92; Learning from a Woman: Ming Literati Responses to Tanyangzi, Int J Am Oriental Hist, 90; On Not Becoming a Heroine: Lin Dai-Yu and Cui Ying-ying, Signs, 89; The Moral Status of the Child in Late Imperial China: Childhood in Ritual and Law, Social Res, 86. **CONTACT ADDRESS** History Dept, Univ of Minnesota, Twin Cities, 614 Social Sciences Tower, 267 19th Ave S, Minneapolis, MN 55455. **EMAIL** waltn001@tc.umn.edu

WALTON, BRIAN G.
DISCIPLINE JACKSONIAN PERIOD **EDUCATION** Vanderbilt Univ, PhD. **CAREER** Hist Dept, Western Carolina Univ **HONORS AND AWARDS** Coordr, Hist Day. **SELECTED PUBLICATIONS** Auth, The Greek and Roman Worlds, 80. **CONTACT ADDRESS** Western Carolina Univ, Cullowhee, NC 28723.

WALTON, GUY E.
PERSONAL Born 10/18/1935, New York, NY, m, 1970, 1 child **DISCIPLINE** ART HISTORY **EDUCATION** Wesleyan Univ, BA, 57; NYork Univ, MA, 62, PhD(art hist), 67. **CAREER** Prof, fine arts, Col of Arts and Sci, NY Univ. **HONORS AND AWARDS** Knight, 1st class, Royal Order of the Polar Star, Sweden. **MEMBERSHIPS** Col Art Asn; Soc of Archit Hist; Soc de l'histoire de l'art francais. **RESEARCH** 17th century France, Italy, Sweden and Russia. **SELECTED PUBLICATIONS** Auth, Versailles, the view from Sweden, NY, 88; Louis XIV's Versailles, Chicago, 86. **CONTACT ADDRESS** 100 Bleecker St., Apt 23A, New York, NY 10012. **EMAIL** gw1@is3.nyu.edu

WANDYCZ, PIOTR STEFAN
PERSONAL Born Krakow, Poland **DISCIPLINE** MODERN EUROPEAN HISTORY **EDUCATION** Univ Grenoble, cert, 42; Cambridge Univ, BA, 48, MA, 52; Col of Europe, cert and London Sch Econ, PhD, 51. **CAREER** Res assoc, Mid-Europ Studies Ctr, 52-54; From instr to assoc prof hist, Ind Univ, 54-66; assoc prof, 66-68, Prof Hist, Yale Univ, 68-; Soc Sci Res Coun grant, 58; Am Philos Soc grants, 60, 64 and 81; Ford Int Prog grant, 63; res fel, Russ Ctr, Harvard Univ, 63-65; Rockefeller Found grant, 63; vis prof, Columbia Univ, 67, 69 and 75; partic acad exchange with Poland and Czech, Int Res and Exchange Bd, 72-73; Guggenheim Mem Found fel, 77-78. **HONORS AND AWARDS** George L Beer Prize, AHA, 62; Alfred Jutzykowski Found Prize, 76; ma, yale univ, 68. **MEMBERSHIPS** AHA; Polish Hist Asn Gt Brit; Int Free Acad Sci and Lett, Paris; Polish Inst Arts and Sci in am; Czech Soc Arts and Sci in am. **RESEARCH** Twentieth century East European diplomatic history. **SELECTED PUBLICATIONS** Auth, the Popular Front and Central Europe in the Dilemmas of French Impotence, 1918-1940, Am Hist Rev, Vol 98, 93; Untitled, Am Hist Rev, Vol 99, 94; Untitled, Am Hist Rev, Vol 102, 97. **CONTACT ADDRESS** Dept of Hist, Yale Univ, New Haven, CT 06520. **EMAIL** pswand@pantheon.yale.edu

WANG, AIHE
DISCIPLINE HISTORY; LANGUAGE **EDUCATION** Higher Education Examination Committee, P.R.C., BA, 83; Chinese Acad of Social Sciences, MA, 86; MA, 90, PhD, Harvard Univ **CAREER** Asst prof, Purdue Univ, 95-. **CONTACT ADDRESS** Dept of Hist, Purdue Univ, West Lafayette, 1 Purdue Univ, West Lafayette, IN 47907-1968. **EMAIL** aihewang@purdue.edu

WANG, DI
DISCIPLINE HISTORY, MODERN CHINA **EDUCATION** Sichuan Univ, China, BA, 82, MA, 85; Johns Hopkins Univ, MA, 97, PhD, 98. **CAREER** Lectr, Sichuan Univ, China, 85-87, assoc prof, 87-92; res fel, Center for Chinese Studies, Univ Mich, 91-92; asst prof, Tex A & M Univ, 98-. **HONORS AND AWARDS** The Young Chinese Scholar Fel, Am Coun of Learned Socs, 91-92; Sun Yat-sem Culture and Ed Found, Taiwan, 98; Dean's Teaching Fel, Johns Hopkins Univ, 98; over a dozen fellowships and Awds. **MEMBERSHIPS** Am Hist Asn, Asn for Asian Studies. **RESEARCH** Chinese popular culture, urban history, social history, and public life in the 19th and 20th-century China. **SELECTED PUBLICATIONS** Auth, "Jinnian Meiguo guanyu jindai Zhongguo chengshi de yanjui," [Chinese urban history: A review article on recent studies in America], Lishi yanjui, No 1 (96): 171-186; auth, "Wanqing Changjiang shangyou diqu gonggong lingyu de fazhan," [A study on public sphere in the upper Yanzi region in the late Qing], Lishi yanjui, No 1 (96): 5-16; auth, "Jinnian Meiguo guanyu jindai Zhong-Mei guanxi de yanjui," [Modern Sino-American relations: A review article on recent studies in America], Lishi yanjui (Hist res, Beijing), No 2 (97): 170-183; auth, "Developments in the Public Sphere Along the Upper Reaches of the Yangtze River During the Late Qing Period," Soc Scis in China XVIII, No 2 (97): 125-130; auth, "Street Culture: Public Space and Urban Commoners in Late-Qing Chendu," Modern China 24.1 (Jan 98): 34-72; auth, "Dazhong wenhua yanjui yu jindai Zhongguo shehui: dui jinnian Meiguo youguan yanjiu de shuping," [Popular culture and modern Chinese society: A review article on recent studies in the US], Lishi yanjui (Hist Res), No 5 (99): 174-186; auth, "The Idle and the Busy: Teahouses and Public Life in Early Twentieth-Century Chengdu," J of Urban Hist 26.4 (May 2000): 411-437. **CONTACT ADDRESS** Dept Hist, Texas A&M Univ, Col Station, 1 Tex A & M Univ, College Station, TX 77843-0001. **EMAIL** di-wang@tamu.edu

WANG, K. W.
PERSONAL Born 11/22/1954, Taipei, Taiwan **DISCIPLINE** HISTORY **EDUCATION** Stanford Univ, PhD, 85. **CAREER** Vis Assoc Prof, 96-97, Ntl Chengchi Univ Taiwan; vis Lectr, 93, Hong Kong Univ. **MEMBERSHIPS** AAS; Soc Stud 20th

Century China in NA; AACS. **RESEARCH** Nationalist Party; Wartime China, 1937-1945. **SELECTED PUBLICATIONS** Auth, Modern China: An Encyclopedia of History Culture and Nationalism, NY, Garland Pub, 98. **CONTACT ADDRESS** History Dept, Saint Michael's Col, Colchester, VT 05439. **EMAIL** kwang@smcvt.edu

WANG, LIPING
DISCIPLINE HISTORY **EDUCATION** Univ Calif San Diego, PhD, 97. **CAREER** Asst prof **RESEARCH** Social and cultural history of the Late Imperial China and the Republican China (1911-1949). **SELECTED PUBLICATIONS** Auth, Tradition as a Modern Invention: Tourism and Spatial Changes in Hangzhou: 1900-1927, Univ Hawaii. **CONTACT ADDRESS** History Dept, Univ of Minnesota, Twin Cities, 614 Social Sciences Tower, 267 19th Ave S, Minneapolis, MN 55455. **EMAIL** lipin003@tc.umn.edu

WANG, Q. EDWARD
PERSONAL Born 06/25/1958, Shanghai, China, m, 1987 **DISCIPLINE** MODERN CHINESE AND JAPANESE HISTORY, CHINESE CULTURAL HISTORY **EDUCATION** East China Normal Univ, Shanghai, BA, MA; Syracuse Univ, PhD, 92. **CAREER** Instr, chp, dept Hist, coordr, Asian/Asian Am Stud prog, Rowan Univ. **RESEARCH** Chinese cultural and intellectual history; comparative historiography. **SELECTED PUBLICATIONS** Boks and articles on Chinese cultural and intellectual history and comparative historiography in both Chinese and English. **CONTACT ADDRESS** Rowan Univ, Glassboro, NJ 08028-1701. **EMAIL** wangq@rowan.edu

WANK, SOLOMON
PERSONAL Born 03/16/1930, Brooklyn, NY, m, 1955, 2 children **DISCIPLINE** MODERN EUROPEAN HISTORY **EDUCATION** NYork Univ, BA, 51; Columbia Univ, MA, 52, PhD (hist), 61. **CAREER** Lectr hist, Brooklyn Col, 57-58, 59-60; lectr, City Col New York, 60-61; From asst prof to assoc prof hist, 61-73, chmn dept, 65-71, Prof Hist, Franklin and Marshall Col, 73-91; Leww Audenreid prof of hist, 86-91, emeritus, 91-; Lectr, Pace Col, 57-58, 59; Franklin and Marshall Col fac res grant, 64, 73-75 and 76-78; Am Philos Soc res grants, 65, 78; Fulbright fel, Vienna, 58-59, 64-65; Am Coun Learned Soc fel, 67-68; mem Mid Atlantic Regional Evaluating Comt for younger scholar fels and summer stipends, Nat Found for Humanities, 67-71; vis scholar, Inst ECent Europe, Columbia Univ, 79-80; distinguished vis prof liberal arts, Concordia Univ, 81-82; Austrian History yearbook ed, 89-96; fel, Japan center for Area Studies, Osaka Univ, 99. **HONORS AND AWARDS** Lindback Awd for Distinguished Teaching, Franklin and Marshall Col, 85. **MEMBERSHIPS** AHA; Conf Group Cent Europ Hist; Peace Hist Soc; AAUP; Conf Group for Study Nationalism; Czechoslovakia Hist Conference; Soc for Austrian and Habsburg Hist. **RESEARCH** Europe in the th and 20th centuries; diplomatic history of Europe, 1871-14; Habsburg monarchy, 1867-18. **SELECTED PUBLICATIONS** Auth, the Habsburg Monarchy Among the Great Powers, Ctrl European Hist, Vol 26, 93; auth, The Decline and Fall of the Habsburg Empire 1815-, Ctrl European Hist, Vol 26, 93; auth, Desperate Counsel in Vienna in July 14 And Full-Text of Promemoria with Translation ApPENded - Molden,Berthold Unpublished Memorandum, Ctrl European Hist, Vol 26, 93; The Protocols of the Ministerial Council of the Austro Hungarian Monarchy 1896-1907, J Modern Hist, Vol 66, 94; auth, Vienna Washington in a J of Diplomatic Relations, 1838-1917, Ctrl European Hist, Vol 27, 94; auth, Between Berlin and St Petersburg in Foreign Policy of the Austro Hungarian Empire Under Kalnoky, Gustave, 1881-1895, Ctrl European Hist, Vol 28, 95; auth, "The Disintegration of the Habsburg and Ottoman Empires," in The End of Empire? The Transformation of the USSR in Comparative Perspective (M.E. Sharpe, 97). **CONTACT ADDRESS** Dept of Hist, Franklin and Marshall Col, Lancaster, PA 17604. **EMAIL** s_wank@acad.fandm.edu

WARD, ALLEN M.
PERSONAL Born 04/18/1942, Lawrence, MA **DISCIPLINE** HISTORY **EDUCATION** Brown Univ, AB, 64; Princeton Univ, AM, 66; PhD, 68. **CAREER** Asst Prof, Columbia Univ, 67-69; Asst Prof to Prof Emeritus, Univ Conn, 69-. **HONORS AND AWARDS** NEH Summer Stipend, 73; Grant, Am Coun of Learned Soc, 77; Visiting Res Fel, Univ New Eng Australia, 84; Distinguished Service Awd, Classical Asn of CT, 94; Distinguished Service Awd, Classical Asn of New Eng, 97; Phi Beta Kappa, 63; Woodrow Wilson Fel, 64-65; Woodrow Wilson Dissertation Fel, 66-67. **MEMBERSHIPS** Classical Asn of CT; Classical Asn of New Eng; Am Classical League; Friends of Ancient Hist; Am Philol Asn; Asn of Ancient Hist. **RESEARCH** Hellenistic Greece; Republican Rome. **SELECTED PUBLICATIONS** Co-auth, A History of the Roman People, Prentice Hall, 99; co-auth, Ancient History: Recent Trends and New Directions, Regina Books, 97; auth, A Brief History of Rome's Multicultural Civilization, Amherst, 96; auth, "The Catilinarian Orations in Their Context: Politics and Values," New England Classical Newsletter and Journal, (92): 1-5; co-auth, A History of the Roman People, 2nd ed, Prentice-Hall, 84. **CONTACT ADDRESS** Dept Hist, Univ of Connecticut, Storrs, 241 Glenbrook Rd, Storrs, CT 06269-9005. **EMAIL** ward@uconnvm.uconn.edu

WARD, DAVID
PERSONAL Born 07/08/1938, Manchester, United Kingdom, m, 1964, 2 children **DISCIPLINE** GEOGRAPHY **EDUCATION** Univ Leeds, UK, BA, MA; Univ Wisconsin Madison, MSc, PhD. **CAREER** Univ Wis Mad, Andrew H Clark Prof, geog, 69-, Chanc, 93-. **HONORS AND AWARDS** Guggenheim fel, ACL fel, Fulbright fel. **MEMBERSHIPS** Asn Am Geog. **RESEARCH** Hist geog, urban geog. **SELECTED PUBLICATIONS** Cities and Immigrants: A Geography of change in Nineteenth Century America, NY, Oxford Univ Press, 71; Poverty, Ethnicity and the American City, Changing Conceptions of the Slum and the Ghetto, 1840-1920, NY, Cambridge Univ Press, 89; numerous articles and dissertations. **CONTACT ADDRESS** WISCAPE, 1000 Bascom Mall, 409 Education Bldg., Madison, WI 53706. **EMAIL** ward@mail.bascom.wisc.edu

WARD, HARRY M.
PERSONAL Born 07/30/1929, Lafayette, IN **DISCIPLINE** AMERICAN HISTORY **EDUCATION** William Jewell Col, BA, 51; Columbia Univ, MA, 54, PhD, 60. **CAREER** Asst prof hist, Georgetown Col, 59-61; from asst prof to assoc prof, Morehead State Univ, 61-65; assoc prof hist, 65-78, chmn dept, Univ Col, 70-74, Prof Am Hist, Univ Richmond, 78-, Wm Binford Vest prof his, 93-99, emer, 99, Vis assoc prof, Southern Ill Univ, 67-68; res grants, Plimoth Plantation, 68-69, Va Soc Cincinnati, 70, 73 & City of Richmond, 73; mem comt Am hist, col level exams, Educ Testing Serv, Princeton, NJ, 69; mem Richmond Bicentennial Comn, 72-80; consult, US Bicentennial Media Corp, 74-76. **HONORS AND AWARDS** Fraunces Tavern Museum Book Awd, 90; Va Soc Sci Asn Scholar Awd, 92. **MEMBERSHIPS** AHA; Southern Hist Asn; Orgn Am Historians; Va Hist Soc; fel Pilgrim Soc. **RESEARCH** American colonial and Revolutionary history; American frontier; early Virginia history. **SELECTED PUBLICATIONS** Auth, The United Colonies of New England, 1643-90, Vantage, 61; Department of War, 1781-1795, Univ Pittsburgh, 62; Dominion interlude, In: The Colonial Experience, Houghton, 66; Unite or Die: Intercolony Relations, 1690-1763, 71 & Statism in Plymouth Colony, 73, Kennikat; Search for American identity: Early historians of New England, In: Perspectives On Early American History, Harper, 73; coauth, Richmond During the Revolution, 1775-1783, Univ Va, 77; Auth, Duty, Honor or Country: General George Weedon and the American Revolution, Am Philos Soc, 79; auth, Richmond: An Illustrated History, Windsor, 85; auth, Charles Scott and the Spirit of 76, University of Virginia, 88; auth, Major General Adam Stephen and the Cause of America Liberty, Univ Va, 89; auth, Colonial America, 1607-1763, Prentice Hall, 91; auth, The American Revolution: Nationhood Achieved, 1763-1788, St. Martin's, 95; auth, General William Maxwell and the New Jersey Continentals, Greenwood Press, 97; auth, The War for Independence and The Transformation of American Society, Univ Col of London, 99. **CONTACT ADDRESS** Dept of Hist, Univ of Richmond, 28 Westhampton Way, Richmond, VA 23173-0002.

WARD, JAMES A.
PERSONAL Born 06/09/1941, Buffalo, NY, w, 1965, 1 child **DISCIPLINE** HISTORY **EDUCATION** Purdue Univ, BA, 64, MA, 65; La State Univ, PhD, 69. **CAREER** Prof. **SELECTED PUBLICATIONS** Auth, That Man Haupt: A Biography of Herman Haupt Baton, La State Univ, 73; Edgar Thomson: Master of the Pennsylvania, Greenwood, 80; Railroads and the Character of America, Univ Tennessee, 86; coauth, American History: A Brief View, Brown, 78; ed, Southern Railroadman: Conductor Nimrod I. Bell's Memoirs, Northern Ill Univ, 93; The Fall of the Packard Motor Car Company, Stanford, 95; co-ed, Railroads in America, Northern Ill Univ. **CONTACT ADDRESS** Dept of History, Univ of Tennessee, Chatanooga, 615 McCallie, Chattanooga, TN 37403. **EMAIL** James-ward@utc.edu

WARD, JAMES R.
PERSONAL Born 10/14/1939, Jacksonville, TX, d, 2 children **DISCIPLINE** AMERICAN HISTORY **EDUCATION** Tex Christian Univ, BA, 61; MA, 63; PhD, 72. **CAREER** Instr hist, Navarro Jr Col, 63-67; asst to prof, Angelo State Univ, 70- . **HONORS AND AWARDS** Univ Teacher Yr Awd, 83, 84, 88. **MEMBERSHIPS** Orgn Am Hist; Texas State His Asn; Phi Alpha Theta. **RESEARCH** American frontier history, American diplomatic history, Texas history. **SELECTED PUBLICATIONS** Co-auth, Ten Texans in Gray, Hill Col Press, (68); auth, "Establishing Law and Order in the Oil Fields: The 1924 Ranger Raids in Navarro County, Texas," Texana, (70); auth, "Richard William Dowling," New Handbook of Texas, Texas State Hist Asn, (96). **CONTACT ADDRESS** Dept Hist, Angelo State Univ, San Angelo, TX 76909-0001. **EMAIL** James.Ward@angelo.edu

WARD, JOHN WILLIAM
PERSONAL Born 12/21/1922, Boston, MA, m, 1949, 3 children **DISCIPLINE** AMERICAN CIVILIZATION **EDUCATION** Harvard Col, AB, 45; Univ Minn, MA, 50, PhD (Am civilization), 53. **CAREER** From instr to assoc prof English and Am civilization, Princeton Univ, 52-57, assoc prof hist, 58-64, chmn Am civilization prog, 61-64; prof hist, Amherst Col, 64-79, pres, 71-79; Pres, Am Coun Learned Soc, 82-; Coun Humanities fel, Princeton Univ, 54-55; Guggenheim fels, 58 and 68; fel, Inst Advan Studies Behav Sci, 63-64; Fulbright lectr Am hist, Univ Reading, 67-68; Phi Betta Kappa distinguished lectr, 70-71. **HONORS AND AWARDS** LLD, Amherst Col, 79. **MEMBERSHIPS** Am Studies Asn; AHA: Soc Am Historians. **RESEARCH** Relation of ideas and expressive forms to social forces in america. **SELECTED PUBLICATIONS** Auth, Down Deep in Dixie in Black South Fiction in the Privileged Place of Story, African Am Rev, Vol 27, 93; Black South Literature in Before Day Annotations for Jackson, Blyden, African Am Rev, Vol 27, 93; Southern Visions in What We Seen, What We Foresee in from the Lions View, African Am Rev, Vol 27, 93; Black Southern Culture in 1st Words, African Am Rev, Vol 27, 93; Afterword and Black Southern Culture and the Reason Its Music Was Not Examined in This Issue in Why No Music, African Am Rev, Vol 27, 93; Introduction and the Culture of the Black South in Seeing Instead of Just Looking, African Am Rev, Vol 27, 93; Sayings, Sermons, Tall Tales and Lies in Contemporary Black Poetry, African Am Rev, Vol 27, 93; Reading South in Poets Mean and Poems Signify, A Note on Origins, African Am Rev, Vol 27, 93; We Aint Playing and the Concept of a Black Theater of the South, African Am Rev, Vol 27, 93; Serious, Georgia Rev, Vol 48, 94; Denizens Vieux Carre, Mississippi Quart, Vol 48, 95; Triangulation, Lit Med, Vol 15, 96; The Norton Anthology of African American Literature, Am Book Rev, Vol 18, 97. **CONTACT ADDRESS** Am Coun Learned Soc, 800 Third Ave, New York, NY 10022.

WARF, BARNEY
PERSONAL Born 12/28/1956, Los Angeles, CA, s, 1 child **DISCIPLINE** GEOGRAPHY **EDUCATION** Univ WA, PhD, 85. **CAREER** Economic Analyst, New York, 86-89; Asst Prof, Kent State Univ, 89-94; Prof and Chair, Fla State Univ, 94-. **HONORS AND AWARDS** SEDAAG Res Honors; FSU Teaching Improvement Awd. **MEMBERSHIPS** Asn Am Geog. **RESEARCH** Telecommunications; Services; Political economy. **CONTACT ADDRESS** Dept Geog, Florida State Univ, PO Box 3062190, Tallahassee, FL 32306. **EMAIL** bwarf@coss.fsu.edu

WARGA, RICHARD G., JR.
DISCIPLINE GREEK, LATIN, MYTHOLOGY, SCIENTIFIC TERMINOLOGY **EDUCATION** Univ Ill, Urbana-Champaign, PhD, 88. **CAREER** Instr Classics, coordr, elem Lat crse, La State Univ. **RESEARCH** Epigraphy; papyrology; Coptic studies. **SELECTED PUBLICATIONS** Auth, A Coptic-Greek Stele from Memphis, Tennessee, in Chronique d'Egypte LXVI, 91; A Repayment of a Loan, in Zeitschrift f(r Papyrologie und Epigraphik 100, 94. **CONTACT ADDRESS** Dept of For Lang and Lit, Louisiana State Univ, 122 A Prescott Hall, Baton Rouge, LA 70803. **EMAIL** warga@lsu.edu

WARING, STEPHEN P.
PERSONAL Born 10/04/1958, NE, m, 1999 **DISCIPLINE** HISTORY **EDUCATION** Doane Col, BA, 80; Univ Iowa, MA, 82, PhD, 88. **CAREER** Asst prof, 88-94, ASSOC PROF HIST, 94-, UNIV ALA, HUNTSVILLE **HONORS AND AWARDS** SIRS Intellectual Freedom Awd, 93; Fel Aerospace hist, Outstanding , UAH Alumni Fdn, 97-98; Research Awd, UAH Alumni Fnd, 99-00; AIAA Manuscript Awd in Aerospace History, 01 **RESEARCH** Hist tech; labor hist; intellectual hist; policy hist; technological history. **SELECTED PUBLICATIONS** Auth, Taylorism Transformed: Scientific Management Theory Since 1945, Univ NC Press, 91; auth, The Challenger Investigations: Engineering Knowledge, and Politics, 1971-1988, forthcoming; Peter Drucker, MBO, and the Corporatist Critique of Scientific Management in A Mental Revolution: The Scientific Management Movement After Taylor, Ohio State Univ Press, 92; Cold Calculus: The Impact of the Cold War on Operations Research, in Radical History Review 63, 95; auth, At the Center: The History of NASA's Marshall Space Flight Center, 1960-1990, under rev by NASA-MSFC CHAND TO Power to Explore: The History of NASA's Marshall Space Fight Center, 1960-1990, US GPO, 99. **CONTACT ADDRESS** History Dept, Univ of Alabama, Huntsville, Huntsville, AL 35899. **EMAIL** warings@email.uah.edu

WARK, ROBERT RODGER
PERSONAL Born 10/07/1924, Edmonton, AB, Canada **DISCIPLINE** HISTORY OF ART **EDUCATION** Univ Alta, BA, 44, MA, 46; Harvard Univ, MA, 49, PhD (fine arts), 52. **CAREER** Scssional instr English, Univ Alta, 46-48; teaching fel fine arts, Harvard Univ, 50-51, instr, 52-54; instr hist art, Yale Univ, 54-56; Cur, Art Collections, Huntington Libr and Art Gallery, 56-; Lectr art, Calif Inst Technol, 60 and Univ Calif, Los Angeles, 67-81. **MEMBERSHIPS** Col Art Asn Am; Asn Art Mus Dir. **RESEARCH** British art of the Georgian period. **SELECTED PUBLICATIONS** Auth, the Gentle Pastime of Extra Illustrating Books and Relationships Between Visual and Verbal Communication and the Increase of Book Illumination in Mid 18th Century, Huntington Libr Quart, Vol 56, 93; Thackeray Drawings for Cornhill To Cairo in the Huntington Library, Huntington Libr Quart, Vol 57, 94. **CONTACT ADDRESS** Huntington Libr and Art Gallery, San Marino, CA 91108.

WARLICK, M. E.
DISCIPLINE 18TH THROUGH 20TH CENTURY EUROPEAN ART, CONTEMPORARY ART **EDUCATION** Univ Md, PhD, 84. **CAREER** Assoc prof-. **RESEARCH** Max Ernst, Gustav Klimt, alchemy, surrealism, contemporary women artists. **SELECTED PUBLICATIONS** Publ, Art Jour, Leonardo, Art Bulletin, The Philosopher's Stones. **CONTACT ADDRESS** Dept of Art Hist, Univ of Denver, 2199 S Univ Blvd, Denver, CO 80208.

WARMBRUNN, WERNER
PERSONAL Born 07/03/1920, Frankfurt, Germany, m, 1984, 2 children **DISCIPLINE** HISTORY **EDUCATION** Cornell Univ, BA; Stanford Univ, MA, PhD. **CAREER** Prof emer; dir, Pitzer Hist and Archiv Proj. **RESEARCH** German History, History of the Second World War. **SELECTED PUBLICATIONS** Auth, The Dutch under German Occupation 1940-1945, Stanford Univ Press, 63; auth, The German Occupation of Belgium 1940 - 1944, Peter Lang, 93. **CONTACT ADDRESS** Dept of Hist, Pitzer Col, 1050 N. Mills Ave., Claremont, CA 91711-6101.

WARNER, ROBERT MARK
PERSONAL Born 06/28/1927, Montrose, CO, m, 1954, 2 children **DISCIPLINE** AMERICAN HISTORY **EDUCATION** Muskingum Col, BA, 49; Univ Mich, MA, 53, PhD, 58. **CAREER** Teacher high sch, Colo, 49-50; asst cur, 57-61, asst dir, 61-66, dir, Mich Hist collections, Univ Mich, Ann Arbor, 66-71, from lectr to prof hist, 71-96, prof libr sci, 74-96; Archivist of US, 80-85, Mem, Int Coun Arch, 76-; bd dirs, Woodrow Wilson Int Ctr Scholars; LHD DePaul Univ, 83; Exec Comt 84-88. **HONORS AND AWARDS** HHD, Westminster Col, 81; LLD, Muskingum, 81; LHD, DePaul, 83; Dean, Univ of Mich, Sch of Infor, 85-92; Univ Hist, 95-; Dean Emeritus, 96-; Prof Emeritus of Infor, 96-; Prof Emeritus of Hist, 96-. **MEMBERSHIPS** AHA; Orgn Am Historians; fel Soc Am Archivists (vpres, 75-76, pres, 76-77). **RESEARCH** Progressive movement; Michigan history; archival management. **SELECTED PUBLICATIONS** Auth, Profile of a Profession: A History of the Michigan State Dental Association, Wayne State Univ, 63; coauth, The Modern Manuscript Library, Scarecrow, 66; co-ed, A Michigan Reader: 1865 to the Present, Eerdmans, 74; auth, Diary of a Dream, A History of the National Archives Independence Movement, 1980-85, Scarecrow, 95. **CONTACT ADDRESS** School of Information, Univ of Michigan, Ann Arbor, 550 E University Ave, Ann Arbor, MI 48109-1092. **EMAIL** archlib@umich.edu

WARNER, TED J.
PERSONAL Born 03/02/1929, Ogden, UT, m, 1953, 3 children **DISCIPLINE** WESTERN AMERICAN HISTORY **EDUCATION** Brigham Young Univ, BS, 55, MS, 58; Univ NMex, PhD (hist), 64. **CAREER** Instr hist, Col Eastern Utah, 56-58; spec col librn, Univ NMex, 60-62; assoc prof, 62-72, Prof to Prof Emer Hist and Chmn Dept, Brigham Young Univ, 72-; Mem, Colonial NMex Hist Found and Mem, Bd Utah State Hist, 77-. **MEMBERSHIPS** Western Hist Asn; AHA; Orgn Am Historians; Mormon Hist Asn. **RESEARCH** Spanish borderlands; Indian in american history. **SELECTED PUBLICATIONS** Auth, Spanish emigration records in the Archive General de Indias, Seville, Spain, Utah Geneal Soc, 69; Don Felix Martinez and the Santa Fe Presidio, 1693-1730, NMex Hist Rev, 70; coauth, The Goshute Indians in pioneer Utah, Utah Hist Quart, 71; auth, The significance of the Dominguez-Velez de Escalante Expedition, Charles Redd Monographs, No 5, 75; ed, The Dominguez Escalante Journal: Their Expedition Through Colorado, Utah, Arizona and New Mexico, in 1776, Brigham Young Univ, 76. **CONTACT ADDRESS** Dept of Hist, Brigham Young Univ, Provo, UT 84602. **EMAIL** tjw4@email.byu.edu

WARNICKE, RETHA MARVINE
PERSONAL Born 10/05/1939, McLean Co, KY, m, 1961, 2 children **DISCIPLINE** TUDOR-STUART HISTORY **EDUCATION** Ind Univ, Bloomington, BA, 61; Harvard Univ, MA, 63, PhD (hist), 69. **CAREER** From lectr to full prof, Ariz State Univ, 69-. **MEMBERSHIPS** AHA; Royal Hist Soc. **RESEARCH** Constitutional history; women's history; funeral sermons. **SELECTED PUBLICATIONS** Auth, William Lambare: Elizabethan Antiquay, Phillimore Press, 73; auth, Women of The English Renaissance and Reformation, Greenwood Press (Westport, CT), 83; auth, The Rise and Fall of Ann Boleyn: Family Politics of the Court of Henry VIII, Cambridge Univ Press, 89; auth, "The Fall of Boleyn, Anne Revisited," Eng Hist Rev 108 (93); auth, "Henry VIII Greeting of Anne of Cleves and Early Modern Court Protocol," Albion 28 (96); auth, The Marrying of Anne of Cleves: Royal Protocol in Tudor England, Cambridge Univ Press, 00. **CONTACT ADDRESS** Dept of Hist, Arizona State Univ, Tempe, AZ 85281. **EMAIL** rwarnicke@asu.edu

WARREN, ANN KOSSER
PERSONAL Born 04/13/1928, Jersey City, NJ, m, 1949, 5 children **DISCIPLINE** MEDIEVAL AND RELIGIOUS HISTORY **EDUCATION** City Univ New York, BA, 49; Case Western Reserve Univ, MA, 76, PhD (hist), 80. **CAREER** Lectr Hist, Case Western Reserve Unvi, 80-; Vis asst prof, Hiram Col, fall, 80. **MEMBERSHIPS** Mediaeval Acad Am; AHA; Soc Church Hist; Midwest Medieval Asn. **RESEARCH** Medieval English recluses: anchorites and hermits; medieval spirituality: pilgrimage phenomena; medieval social history: will studies and family history. **SELECTED PUBLICATIONS** Auth, the Black Death and Pastoral Leadership in the Diocese of Hereford in the 14th Century, Church Hist, Vol 65, 96; A History of Canterbury Cathedral, Albion, Vol 28, 96; Contemplation and Action in the Other Monasticism, Cath Hist Rev, Vol 83, 97. **CONTACT ADDRESS** Dept of Hist, Case Western Reserve Univ, Cleveland, OH 44106.

WARREN, DONALD R.
PERSONAL Born 09/27/1933, Waco, TX, m, 1957, 3 children **DISCIPLINE** HISTORY OF EDUCATION **EDUCATION** Univ Tex, BA, 56; Harvard Univ, ThM, 60; Univ Chicago, PhD (hist educ), 68. **CAREER** Prog dir social serv, Cambridge Neighborhood House, 56-60; dean students tutorials and social issues, College House, 60-62; dir studies adult educ, Ecumenical Inst, 62-64; asst prof hist and philos educ, Chicago State Univ, 65-69; assoc prof, Univ Ill, Chicago, 69, head dept policy studies, 70-79; Prof and Chmn Dept Educ Policy, Planning and Admin, Univ MD, College Park, 79-; Consult educ res, US Office Educ, 71-73; consult educ policy and hist educ, Holt, Rinehart, and Winston Inc, 72-79; chmn, Task Force Acad Stand, Am Educ Studies Asn, 76-78; Assoc ed, Educ Theory, 76-69; bd scholars, Potomac Educ Resources, 80-. **MEMBERSHIPS** Am Educ Studies Asn (pres, 75-76); Am Educ Res Asn (secy, 74-76); Ctr Study Democratic Inst; AHA; Hist Educ Soc. **RESEARCH** History of American education; history of federal education policy; education policy. **SELECTED PUBLICATIONS** Auth, Run for Office, Trial, Vol 29, 93. **CONTACT ADDRESS** Dept of Educ Policy Planning and Admin, Univ of Maryland, Col Park, College Park, MD 20742.

WARREN, J. BENEDICT
PERSONAL Born 06/30/1930, Waterflow, NM, m, 1968 **DISCIPLINE** COLONIAL MEXICAN AND LATIN AMERICAN HISTORY **EDUCATION** Duns Scotus Col, BA, 53; Univ NMex, MA, 60, PhD (hist), 63. **CAREER** Ed, Americas, Acad Am Franciscan Hist, Washington, DC, 63-66; From asst prof to assoc prof, 68-77, Prof Hist, Univ MD, College Park, 77-93; Fel, John Carter Brown Libr, Brown Univ, 65; consult, Hisp Found, Libr Cong, 67-72; Fulbright res award, Mexico, 81-82; prof emer, Univ Md-College Park; prof-investigador, Colegio de Michoacan, Mexico. **HONORS AND AWARDS** Acad Mexicana de la Historia, 96; Presea Vasco de Quiroga, City of Patzcuaro, Michoacan, Mexico, 00; decoration of the Mexican Order of the Aguila Azteca, Govt of Mexico, 01. **MEMBERSHIPS** Conf Latin am Hist; Latin am Studies Asn. **RESEARCH** Sixteenth century Michoacan; Bishop Vasco de Quiroga; intellectual history of 16th century Mexico. **SELECTED PUBLICATIONS** Auth, Chimalpahin and the Kingdoms of Chalco, Am, Vol 49, 93; The Encomenderos of New Spain, 1521-1555, Am, Vol 50, 93; Mexico and the Spanish Conquest, Hist, Vol 57, 95; Lascasas in Mexico in Unknown History and Work, Cath Hist Rev, Vol 81, 95. **CONTACT ADDRESS** Dept of Hist, Univ of Maryland, Col Park, College Park, MD 20742. **EMAIL** bpwarren@prodigy.net.mx

WARREN-FINDLEY, JANELLE
PERSONAL Born 03/15/1945, Tucson, AZ, m, 1973, 1 child **DISCIPLINE** HISTORY **EDUCATION** Tex Woman's Univ, BA, 68; George Wash Univ, MPhil, 72; PhD, 73. **CAREER** Fulbright Am Lectr, Univ Goteborg, Swed, 73-76; Lectr, Univ Md, London, 76-78; Asst Lectr, George Wash Univ, 78-80; Res Consult, Wash DC, 80-89; Adj Assoc Res Prof, George Wash Univ, 89-91; Sen Hist, CEHP, 91-94; Assoc Prof and Co-Dir of Grad Prog, Ariz State Univ, 93-. **HONORS AND AWARDS** James Madison Prize of the Soc for Hist in the Fed Govt, 87; Michael Robinson Prize for Hist Anal, Nat Coun on Pub Hist, 91; Sen Fulbright Fel, New Zealand, 97; Ian Axford Fel in Pub Policy, New Zealand, 00. **MEMBERSHIPS** Org of Am Hist; Nat Coun on Pub Hist. **RESEARCH** Public cultural policy; The cultural meanings of tangible and intangible culture in the U.S.; Twentieth century American cultural history; Human heritage management worldwide. **SELECTED PUBLICATIONS** Co-auth, Technologies for Prehistoric and Historic Preservation, Krieger Publishing Co, 86, reprint ed, Krieger Pub Col, 88; co-auth, "Technology and Historic Preservation: the Cultural Context," Public Historian, 91; co-ed, Exploring the Unknown: Selected Comments in the History of the U.S. Civil Space Program, Vol I, Govt Printing Off, 95; co-auth, Training Cold Warriors: An Historical Perspective and Consideration of the Build Environment at Luke AFB and the Gila Bend AFAF, 1946-1989, Dames and Moore, Inc, 96; auth, "Public History in the United States: An Overview Report from the Field," Public History Rev, 98; auth, "International Public History: A Report from the Field," Public Historian, 98; auth, "The Collier as Commemoration: The Project Mercury Astronauts and the Collier Trophy, 1962," in From Engineering Science to Big Science, Govt Printing Office, 98; auth, "Historical Consulting," in Public History: Essays from the Field, Krieger Press, 99; auth, Human Heritage Management in New Zealand in the Year 2000 and Beyond, Ian Axford New Zealand Fel in Public Policy, 01. **CONTACT ADDRESS** Dept Hist, Arizona State Univ, 1515 E Bell de Mar Dr, Tempe, AZ 85283. **EMAIL** janelle.warren-findley@asu.edu

WARTH, ROBERT DOUGLAS
PERSONAL Born 12/16/1921, Houston, TX **DISCIPLINE** HISTORY **EDUCATION** Univ Ky, BS, 43; Univ Chicago, AM, 45, PhD, 49. **CAREER** Instr hist, Univ Tenn, 50-51; instr, Rutgers Univ, 51-54, asst prof, 54-58; vis prof, Paine Col, 60; assoc ed, Grolier Soc, 60-62 and 63-64; lectr hist, Hunter Col, 62-63; assoc prof, Staten Island Community Col, 64-68; Prof Hist, Univ KY, 68-. **MEMBERSHIPS** AHA; Am Asn Advan Slavic Studies; Southern Conf Slavic Studies (pres, 82-83). **RESEARCH** Modern Russian history; Soviet foreign relations; international communism. **SELECTED PUBLICATIONS** Auth, Leon Trotsky, writer and historian, J Mod Hist, 3/48; The Allies and the Russian Revolution, Duke Univ, 54; Soviet Russia in World Politics, Twayne, 63; On the historiography of the Russian Revolution, Slavic Rev, 6/67; Joseph Stalin, Twayne, 69; Diplomacy from the inside: Russia in the Civil War of 1918-1920, In: Civil Wars in the Twentieth Century, Univ Ky, 72; Lenin, 73 & Leon Trotsky, 77, Twayne. **CONTACT ADDRESS** Dept of Hist, Univ of Kentucky, Lexington, KY 40506.

WARTLUFT, DAVID J.
PERSONAL Born 09/22/1938, Stouchsbung, PA, d, 4 children **DISCIPLINE** AMERICAN LUTHERAN HISTORY **EDUCATION** BA, Muhlenberg Col, 1960; MDiv, LTSP, 1964; MA, Univ Pa, 1964; MS in Library Science, Drexel Univ, 1968; Pastorate in Pa, 1964-65. **CAREER** Dir of the Library; cord, Formation Group prog. **HONORS AND AWARDS** Bd of dir(s), treasurer, Lutheran Hist Conf; exec sec, Amer Theol Library Assn. **RESEARCH** Exploring the Lutheran heritage. **SELECTED PUBLICATIONS** Pub(s), on American Lutheranism. **CONTACT ADDRESS** Dept of Practical Theology, Lutheran Theol Sem at Philadelphia, 7301 Germantown Ave, Philadelphia, PA 19119-1794. **EMAIL** Dwartluft@ltsp.edu

WASERMAN, MANFRED
PERSONAL Born 03/21/1933, Free City of Danzig, Poland, 1 child **DISCIPLINE** AMERICAN HISTORY, LIBRARY SCIENCE **EDUCATION** Univ Md, BA, 59, MA, 61; Cath Univ Am, MS, 63, PhD (hist), 82. **CAREER** Teacher hist, Prince Geofe's County, Md, Pub Sch, 60-62; librn, Library, Yale Univ, 63-65; Curator, Mod Manuscripts, Nat Libr Med, 65-. **MEMBERSHIPS** Am Asn Hist Med; AHA; Am Libr Asn; Oral Hist Asn. **RESEARCH** History of medicine and public health; history of child health care; primitive medicine and ethnology. **SELECTED PUBLICATIONS** Auth, Montefiore, Moses, A Hebrew Prayer Book, and Medicine in the Holy Land, Judaism, Vol 45, 96. **CONTACT ADDRESS** Hist Med Div, National Libr of Med, Bethesda, MD 20209.

WASSERMAN, MARK
PERSONAL Born 01/29/1946, Boston, MA, m, 1968, 2 children **DISCIPLINE** HISTORY **EDUCATION** Univ of Chicago, PhD **CAREER** Asst prof, Northern Ill Univ, 76-77; from asst prof to prof, Rutgers Univ, 78-. **HONORS AND AWARDS** Arthur P. Whitaker Awd, 84, 87. **MEMBERSHIPS** AHA; LASA; MACLAS; PCCLAS; RMCLAS. **RESEARCH** Mexico **SELECTED PUBLICATIONS** Auth, Persistent Oligarchs: Elites and Politics in Chihuahua, Mexico, 1910-1949, 93; auth, Everyday Life and Politics in Nineteenth Century Mexico: Men, Women and War, 00. **CONTACT ADDRESS** Dept of History, Rutgers, The State Univ of New Jersey, New Brunswick, 16 Seminary Place, New Brunswick, NJ 08901. **EMAIL** wasserm@rci.rutgers.edu

WASSON, ELLIS ARCHER
PERSONAL Born 12/31/1947, Rye, NY **DISCIPLINE** HISTORY **EDUCATION** Johns Hopkins Univ, BA, 72, MA, 72; Univ Cambridge, PhD (hist), 75. **CAREER** Chmn dept hist, 77-78, Hist Master, Rivers Sch, Mass, 76-; Dean Fac, 78-. **MEMBERSHIPS** AHA; Eng Hist Asn; New Eng Hist Teachers (secy-treas, 78). **RESEARCH** Nineteenth century English history. **SELECTED PUBLICATIONS** Auth, The Coalitions of 1827 and the Crisis of Whig Leadership, Hist J, fall 77; The Kendall Whaling Museum, New England Social Studies Bull, 70; The Third Earl Spencer and agriculture, 1818-1845, Agr Hist Rev, summer 78; The Spirit of Reform, 1832-1867, Albion, 80. **CONTACT ADDRESS** Rivers Sch, 333 Winter St, Weston, MA 023.

WASWO, ANN
PERSONAL Born 05/17/1940, Los Angeles, CA, m, 1964 **DISCIPLINE** JAPANESE HISTORY **EDUCATION** Stanford Univ, BA, 61, MA, 64, PhD (hist), 69. **CAREER** Lectr East Asian civilization, Stanford Univ, 68-69, actg asst prof hist, 69-70; asst prof, Univ Va, 71-76; Asst Prof, Princeton Univ, 79-. **MEMBERSHIPS** Asn Asian Studies. **RESEARCH** Social history of modern Japan. **SELECTED PUBLICATIONS** Contribr, Japan in Crisis, Princeton Univ, 74; auth, Japanese Landlords: The Decline of a Rural Elite, Univ Calif, 77. **CONTACT ADDRESS** East Asian Studies, Princeton Univ, Princeton, NJ 08540.

WATANABE, MORIMICHI
PERSONAL Born 08/08/1926, Yamagata, Japan, m, 1954, 1 child **DISCIPLINE** LATE MEDIEVAL HISTORY, POLITICAL SCIENCE **EDUCATION** Univ Tokyo, LLB, 48; Colum-

bia Univ, MA, 56, PhD (polit theory), 61. **CAREER** Lectr polit sci, Meiji Gakuin Jr Col, Tokyo, 48-50, prof, 50; instr, Meiji Gakuin Col, 49-51, lectr, 51-54; vis asst prof, Kans State Col Pittsburg, 60-61; instr, Queens Col, NY, 61-63; From asst prof to assoc prof, 63-71, Prof Hist and Polit Sci, C W Post Ctr, Long Island Univ, 71-; Am Philos Soc res grants, 64, 70 and 77; Am Coun Learned Soc res grant, 66; Found Reformation Res grant-in-aid, 70; vis prof, Fac Law, Univ Tokyo, 76 and Fac Law, Keio Univ, 76. **MEMBERSHIPS** AHA; Mediaeval Acad Am; Renaissance Soc Am; Am Cath Hist Asn; Am Soc Church Hist. **RESEARCH** History of legal and political thought; Conciliar Movement; Nicholas of Cusa. **SELECTED PUBLICATIONS** Auth, The Political Ideas of Nicholas of Cusa, with Special Reference to his De Concordantia Catholica, Libr Droz, Geneva, Switz, 63; The Episcopal election of 1430 in Trier and Nicholas of Cusa, Church Hist, 39: 229-316; Nicholas of Cusa and the idea of tolerance, In: Nicolo' Cusano agli inizi del Mondo Moderno, Sansoni Ed, Florence, 70; Authority and consent in church government: Panormitanus, Aeneas Sylvius, Cusanus, J Hist Ideas, 33: 217-236; Humanism in the Tyrol: Aeneas Sylvius, Duke Sigmund and Gregor Heimburg, J Medieval & Renaissance Studies, 4: 177-202; Gregor Heimburg and early humanism in Germany, In: Philosophy & Humanism: Renaissance Essays in Honor of Paul O Kristeller, Brill, Leiden, 76; translr (into Japanese), Paul O Kristeller, Renaissance Thought, Univ Tokyo, 77; auth, Imperial reform in the mid-fifteenth century: Gregor Heimburg and Martin Mair, J Medieval & Renaissance Studies, 9: 209-235. **CONTACT ADDRESS** C W Post Ctr, Long Island Univ, C.W. Post, 720 Northern Blvd, Greenvale, NY 11548-1300.

WATELET, HUBERT

PERSONAL Born 09/14/1932, La Louviere, Belgium, m, 1958, 5 children **DISCIPLINE** MODERN EUROPEAN HISTORY **EDUCATION** Univ Louvain, MA, 57, PhD (mod hist), 69. **CAREER** Librn, Univ Lovanium, Kinshasa, 58-61; archivist, State Archiv, Belg, 62-64; lectr Europ hist, 64-67, asst prof, 67-71, Assoc Prof Hist, Univ Ottawa, 71-. **MEMBERSHIPS** Can Hist Asn; Soc for Fr Hist Studies. **RESEARCH** Industrial revolution; 20th century French historiography. **SELECTED PUBLICATIONS** Auth, Une industrialisation sans developpement, 80; coed, La philosophie de l'historire et la pratique historienne d'aujourd'hui, 82; auth, Le Grand-Hornu, joyau de la revolution industrielle et du Boinagge, 89, 93; auth, L'entreprise privee en periode de crise economique, 97. **CONTACT ADDRESS** Dept of Hist, Univ of Ottawa, 147 Seraphin-Marion, Ottawa, ON, Canada K1N 6N5. **EMAIL** hwatelet@uottawa.ca

WATERS, JOHN J.

PERSONAL Born 04/22/1937, New York, NY, m, 2 children **DISCIPLINE** AMERICAN COLONIAL HISTORY **EDUCATION** Manhattan Col, AB, 57; Columbia Univ, PhD (hist), 65. **CAREER** Res asst John Jay papers, Columbia Univ, 61-65; asst prof, 65-69, assoc prof, 69-77, Prof Hist, Univ Rochester, River Campus, 78-; Mem, Inst Early Am Hist and Cult, Williamsburg, Va and Jamestown Prize, 68; John Carter Brown res fel, Brown Univ, 68; Charles Warren fel, Harvard Univ, 70-71. **MEMBERSHIPS** AHA; Orgn Am Historians; Soc Sci Hist Asn. **RESEARCH** Social history of pre-industrial America; historical and quantitative methodology. **SELECTED PUBLICATIONS CONTACT ADDRESS** Dept of Hist, Univ of Rochester, 500 Joseph C Wilson, Rochester, NY 14627-9000.

WATERS, NEIL L.

PERSONAL Born 03/08/1945, Portland, OR, m, 1968 **DISCIPLINE** JAPANESE HISTORY, US-JAPAN RELATIONS, EAST ASIAN CIVILIZATION **EDUCATION** Pac Lutheran Univ, BA; Wash State Univ, MA; Univ Hawaii, PhD. **CAREER** Prof, 90-; Kawashima prof Japanese Stud, 90; dept ch; Dir of International Studies, 98-00. **MEMBERSHIPS** Research Fellow, Reischaner Institute, Harvard Univ; Assoc for Asian Studies; Am Assoc of Univ Professors; Am Historical Assoc. **RESEARCH** Japanese social, intellectual and regional history in the Meiji and Taisho eras. **SELECTED PUBLICATIONS** Auth, Japan's Local Pragmatists Council on East Asian Studies, Harvard UP, 83; The Second Transition: Early to Mid-Meiji in Kanagawa Prefecture, J Asian Stud, 49 2, 90 & The Village Consolidation of 1889: theInstitutionalization of Contradiction, Asian Cult Stud 18, 92; ed, Beyond the Area Studies Wars: Toward a New International Studies Univ Press of New England, 01. **CONTACT ADDRESS** Dept of History, Middlebury Col, Middlebury, VT 05753. **EMAIL** neil.waters@middlebury.edu

WATKINS, THOMAS H.

PERSONAL Born 03/02/1943, Ithaca, NY, m, 1969, 1 child **DISCIPLINE** ANCIENT HISTORY **EDUCATION** Cornell Univ, BA, 65; Univ NC, MA, 67; PhD, 72. **CAREER** Instr to prof, Western Ill Univ, 70-. **HONORS AND AWARDS** Phi Kappa Phi; Visiting Scholar, Rome,97. **MEMBERSHIPS** Soc Promotion Roman Studies, Asn of Ancient Historians, Classical Asn Middle West & South, Ill Class Conf. **RESEARCH** Roman History **SELECTED PUBLICATIONS** Auth, L. Munatius Plancus: Serving and surviving in the roman Revolution, Scholars Press: Atlanta, 97. **CONTACT ADDRESS** Dept Hist, Western Illinois Univ, 1 University Circle, Macomb, IL 61455-1367. **EMAIL** tom_watkins@ccmail.wiu.edu

WATKINS-OWENS, IRMA

PERSONAL Born Jackson, MS, m, 1975, 2 children **DISCIPLINE** AFRICAN-AMERICAN HISTORY **EDUCATION** Univ MI, PhD. **CAREER** Assoc prof, Fordham Univ. **HONORS AND AWARDS** Ford Found Fel; NEH Fel; SUNY Fac Summer Fel, Fordham Fac Fel. **MEMBERSHIPS** OAH; Black Women Historians; ASALH. **RESEARCH** Study of African American women; Dispora Studies. **SELECTED PUBLICATIONS** Auth, Blood Relations: Caribbean Immigrants and the Harlem Community, 1900-1930, Ind UP, 96. **CONTACT ADDRESS** Dept of Hist, Fordham Univ, 113 W 60th St, New York, NY 10023. **EMAIL** watkinsowens@forham.edu

WATROUS, LIVINGSTON V.

DISCIPLINE ART HISTORY **EDUCATION** Univ PA, PhD. **CAREER** Fac, SUNY Buffalo; to chr art hist dept and dir grad studies; Whitehead Prof, Am Schl Class Studies Athens, 93-94; prof, present, SUNY Buffalo. **HONORS AND AWARDS** Grants, Archaeol Inst Am, NEH, Nat Geog Soc, Fulbright comm, and Inst Aegean Studies; dir, gournia survey project; elizabeth a. whitehead prof, am schl classical studies athens, 93-94. **RESEARCH** Greek art and archaeol; Bronze Age Aegean art; archaeol. **SELECTED PUBLICATIONS** Auth, The Sanctuary of Zeus at Psychro, 96; The Plain of Phaistos; Kommos III: The Late Bronze Age Pottery, Princeton UP, 92. **CONTACT ADDRESS** Dept Art, SUNY, Buffalo, 202 Center for the Arts, Buffalo, NY 14260-6010.

WATROUS, MARY A.

DISCIPLINE LATIN AMERICA AND WORLD HISTORY **EDUCATION** Wash State Univ, PhD, 91. **CAREER** Asst prof, Washington State Univ. **RESEARCH** Food and cuisines in world history. **SELECTED PUBLICATIONS** Auth, Mexican Banking and Finance, 1940-96 & Short Term Miracles: Long Term Paradox, in The Encyclopedia of Mexico: History, Society, and Culture, Fitzroy Dearborn Publ, 98. **CONTACT ADDRESS** Dept of History, Washington State Univ, 301 Wilson Hall, PO Box 644030, Pullman, WA 99164-4030. **EMAIL** watrous@wsu.edu

WATSON, ALAN DOUGLAS

PERSONAL Born 05/03/1942, Rocky Mount, NC, m, 1964, 3 children **DISCIPLINE** COLONIAL AMERICAN HISTORY **EDUCATION** Duke Univ, AB, 64; E Carolina Univ, MA, 66; Univ SC, PhD(hist), 71. **CAREER** Instr hist, Danville Div, Va Polytech Inst, 66-68; asst prof, 71-74, assoc prof, 74-79, Prof Hist, Univ NC, Wil ington, 79-. **MEMBERSHIPS** NC Hist Asn; Southern Hist Asn. **RESEARCH** Colonial American society and economy; United States economic history. **SELECTED PUBLICATIONS** Auth, Society and economy in colonial Edgecombe County, NC Hist Rev, summer 73; Orphanage in Colonial North Carolina: Edgecombe County as a case study, NC Hist Rev, 4/75; Society in Colonial North Carolina, NC Archives, 75; ed, A letter from Charles Williamos to Lord Dartmouth, July 1766, SC Hist Mag, 1/76; auth, The Quitrent System in Royal South Carolina, William & Mary Quart, 4/76; auth, A History of New Bern and Craven County NC, Tryon Palace Commission, 87; auth, Wilmington: Port of North Carolina, Univ SC Press, 92; auth, A Brief History of Onslow County (NC), NC Arch, 95. **CONTACT ADDRESS** Dept of Hist, Univ of No Carolina, Wilmington, 601 S College Rd, Wilmington, NC 28403-3201. **EMAIL** watsona@uncwil.edu

WATSON, HARRY L.

PERSONAL Born 07/10/1949, Greensboro, NC, m, 1977, 2 children **DISCIPLINE** HISTORY **EDUCATION** Brown Univ, AB, 71; Northwestern Univ, PhD, 76. **CAREER** Asst prof to prof, Univ of NC, 76-; Dir, Center for the Study of the Am South, 99-. **HONORS AND AWARDS** Woodrow Wilson Int Center Fel, 84-85; James Harvey Robinson Prize, AHA, 84; Grant, Inst for Res in Soc Sci, UNC-CH; Brinkley-Stephenson Awd, Orgn of Am Hist, 98. **MEMBERSHIPS** AHA; Orgn of Am Hist; S. Hist Assoc; Soc for Hist of the Early Am Republic; St. George Tucker Soc. **RESEARCH** Antebellum South, Jacksonian America. **SELECTED PUBLICATIONS** Auth, Jacksonian Politics and Community Conflict: The Emergence of the Second American Party System in Cumberland County, North Carolina, La State Univ Pr (Baton Rouge), 81; auth, An Independent People: The Way We Lived in North Carolina, 1770-1820, Univ of NC Pr, (Chapel Hill), 83; auth, "Old Hickory's Democracy", Wilson Quart 9, (85): 101-133; auth, "Conflict and Collaboration: Yeomen, Slaveholders, and Politics in the Antebellum South", Social Hist 10.3 (85): 273-298; auth, Liberty and Power: the Politics of Jacksonian America, Hill & Want (NY), 90; auth, "The Ambiguous Legacy of Jacksonian Democracy" in Democrats and the America Idea: A Bicentennial Appraisal, ed Peter B. Kovler, Center for Nat Policy Pr, (Washington, 92), 53-75; auth, "Slavery and Development in a Dual Economy: The South and the Market Revolution" in The Market Revolution in America, ed Melvyn Stokes, Univ Pr of Va, (Charlottesville, 96), 43-73; auth, "The Common Rights of Mankind: Subsistence, Shad, and Commerce in the Early Republican South", Jof Am Hist, 83.1 (June 96): 13-43; auth, "Humbug? Bah! Altschuler and Blumin and the Riddle of the Antebellum Electorate", Jof Am Hist 84 (Dec 97): 886-893; ed, Andrew Jackson vs Henry Clay: Democracy and Development in Antebellum America, Bedford/St. Martins, (Boston), 98. **CONTACT ADDRESS** Dept Hist, Univ of No Carolina, Chapel Hill, 440 W Franklin St, CB #3195, Hamilton Hall, Chapel Hill, NC 27599-2319. **EMAIL** hwatson@email.unc.edu

WATSON, JUDGE

PERSONAL Born 06/12/1926, Carver, KY, m, 1952, 3 children **DISCIPLINE** AMERICAN SOUTH, MEDIEVAL EUROPEAN HISTORY **EDUCATION** Asbury Col, BA, 52; Ind Univ, Bloomington, MA, 57, PhD (hist), 63. **CAREER** Asst prof hist, Glenville State Col, 58-64; assoc prof, Asbury Col, 64-67; lectr, Ariz State Univ, 67-68; assoc prof, ETex State Univ, 68-69; mem fac hist, Fla Southern Col, 71-78. **MEMBERSHIPS** Orgn Am Historians; AHA; Southern Hist Soc; AHA; Southern Hist Soc. **RESEARCH** Broad form mineral deed: its impact on the coal fields of Eastern North America; Eastern Kentucky: a subregion of Appalachia in the 20th century. **SELECTED PUBLICATIONS** Coauth, Centennial history: First United Methodist Church Cooper, Texas, First United Methodist Church, Tex, 70; auth, Josiah Stoddard Johnston, John Young Brown & Black Patch War, In: Dictionary of Southern History, 77. **CONTACT ADDRESS** 5604 Scott Lake Rd, Lakeland, FL 33803.

WATSON, PATTY JO

PERSONAL Born 04/26/1932, Superior, NE, m, 1955, 1 child **DISCIPLINE** ARCHAEOLOGY **EDUCATION** Univ Chicago, MA, 56, PhD (anthrop), 59. **CAREER** Archeol field asst, Iraq-Jarmo Proj, Orient Inst, Univ Chicago, 54-55, archeologist and ethnographer, Iranian Prehist Proj, 59-60; res assoc, Orient Inst, Univ Chicago, 64 and 67; From asst prof to assoc prof, 69-73, actg chmn dept anthrop, 71-72, Edward Mallinckrodt Distinguished, Prof Anthrop, Washington Univ, 73-; NSF grant, Univ ChicagoOrient Inst Exped, Iran, 59-60; Ill State Mus Soc grant, Ky, 63; proj assoc and unit dir, Anthrop Curric Study Proj, Am Anthrop Asn, 65-67; NSF res grants, Univ ChicagoOrient Inst-Istanbul Univ, Turkey, 68 and 70; NSF sr res grant and NSFUndergrad Res Partic Proj grant, Ky and NMex, 69-72; fel, Cave Res Found; ed, Am Anthropologist, 73-77; mem adv panel, NSF, 74-76; Nat Endowment for Humanities res grant, 77; Ctr Advan Study in Behav Sci fel, 81-82, 91-92. **HONORS AND AWARDS** Honorary Life Mem Nat Speleological Soc; Fryxell Medal, Soc for Am Arch, 90; Distinguished Serv Award Am Anth Assoc, 96; Gold Medal Archaeological Inst of Am, 99. **MEMBERSHIPS** Fel Am Anthrop Asn; Soc Am Archaeol; Archaeol Inst Am; Am Schs Orient Res; Mid East Studies Asn; Am Acad Arts & Sciences; Am Philosophical Soc. **RESEARCH** Ethnoarcheology; archeological theory and method; beginnings of food production in the Old World and in the Eastern United States. **SELECTED PUBLICATIONS** Coauth, Man and Nature, Harcourt, 69; Systematic, intensive surface collection, Am Antiquity, 70; Explanation in Archaeology, Columbia Univ, 71; A comparative statistical analysis of painted pottery from seven Halafian sites, Paleorient, 73; auth, The future of archaeology in anthropology: culture history and social science, In: Research and Theory in Current Archaeology, Wileym 73; ed & contribr, Archaeology of the Mammoth Cave Area, Academic, 74; auth, Archaeological Ethnography in Western Iran, Univ Ariz, 79; Method and Theory in Shipwreck Archaeology, In: Shipwrecks as Anthropology, Univ Nmex, 83; "Archaeological Interpretation: 1985," In: American Archaeology, Past & Future, (SI Press, 96); auth, "Explaining the Transition to Agriculture," In: Last Hunters, First Farmers, (SAR, 95); auth, "From the Hilly Flanks of the Fertile Crescent to the Eastern Woodlands of North America," In: Grit Tempered: Early Women Archaeologists in the Southeastern United States, (Univ Florida, 99). **CONTACT ADDRESS** Dept of Anthrop, Washington Univ, 1 Brookings Dr, Saint Louis, MO 63130-4899. **EMAIL** pjwatson@artsci.wustl.edu

WATSON, RICHARD L.

PERSONAL Born 06/27/1945, Washington, DC, m, 1983, 2 children **DISCIPLINE** AFRICAN HISTORY **EDUCATION** Duke Univ, BA, 67; Boston Univ, MA, 69; PhD, 74. **CAREER** Prof, NC Wesleyan Col, 72-. **HONORS AND AWARDS** Lilly Found Scholarship, 76; Am Philos Soc Res Grant, 84; Jefferson Pilot Prof, 86; Alumni distinguished Prof, 91; Am Philos Soc Res Grant, 98; United Methodist Awd for Exemplary Teaching 92. **MEMBERSHIPS** SE Reg Sem in African Studies. **RESEARCH** 19th Century South Africa, Slavery. **SELECTED PUBLICATIONS** Auth, "Missionary Influence at Thaba Nchu: A Reassessment", Int Jof African Hist Studies 10, (77): 394-407; auth, "Review Essay: American Scholars and the Continuity of African Culture in the United States", Jof Negro Hist, LXII (78): 375-386; auth, "The Subjection of a South African State", Jof African Hist 21, (80): 357-373; auth, "Slavery and Ideology: The South African Case", Int Jof African Hist Studies 20, (87): 27-43; auth, South Africa in Pictures, Lerner Pub (Minneapolis), 88; auth, The Slave Question: Liberty and Property in South Africa, Univ Pr of New England, 90. **CONTACT ADDRESS** Dept Soc Sci, No Carolina Wesleyan Col, 3400 N Wesleyan Blvd, Rocky Mount, NC 27804-8699. **EMAIL** rwatson@ncwc.edu

WATSON, THOMAS DAVIS

PERSONAL Born 10/29/1929, Lake Charles, LA, m, 1953, 2 children **DISCIPLINE** LATIN AMERICAN & UNITED STATES HISTORY **EDUCATION** N Mex State Univ, BA,

51; Univ Southwestern La, MA, 69; Tex Tech Univ, PhD(hist), 72. **CAREER** Asst prof, 72-76, assoc prof, 76-80, Prof Hist, Mcneese State Univ, 80-, Mem, La Bicentennial Comn, 73-77. **MEMBERSHIPS** Western Hist Asn; Southern Hist Asn; Conf Latin Am Hist. **RESEARCH** Spanish Colonial Louisiana and Florida; United States diplomacy. **SELECTED PUBLICATIONS** Auth, The PWA comes to the Red River Valley, Red River Valley Hist Rev, summer 74; A scheme gone awry: Bernardo do Galvez, Gilberto Antonio de Maxent and the Southern Indian trade, La Hist, winter 76; Continuity in commerce: Development of the Panton, Leslie and Company trade monopoly in West Florida, Fla Hist Quart, 4/76; The troubled advance of Panton, Leslie and Company into Spanish West Florida, In: Eighteenth Century Florida and the Revolutionary South, Univ Press Fla, 78; Strivings for sovereignty: Alexander McGillivary, creek warfare and diplomacy, 1783-1790, Fla Hist Quart, 4/80; coauth (with Samuel Wilson Jr), A lost landmark revisited: The William Panton House of Pensacola, Fla Hist Quart, 7/81. **CONTACT ADDRESS** Dept of Hist, McNeese State Univ, Lake Charles, LA 70609.

WATT, JEFFREY R.

PERSONAL Born 04/25/1958, Connellsville, PA, m, 1987, 2 children **DISCIPLINE** EUROPEAN HISTORY **EDUCATION** Grove City Col, BA, 80; Ohio Univ, MA, 82; Univ Wisc, Madison, PhD, 87. **CAREER** Lectr, hist, Univ Wisc, Madison, 87-88; asst prof, 88-94, assoc prof, 94- , hist, Univ Miss. **HONORS AND AWARDS** Cora Lee Graham Awd for Outstanding Teacher of Freshmen, 91; NEH summer stipend, 92. **MEMBERSHIPS** Am Hist Asn; Calvin Stud Soc; Renaissance Soc of Am; Soc for Reformation Res. **RESEARCH** Early modern Europe; social history. **SELECTED PUBLICATIONS** Auth, The Making of Modern Marriage: Matrimonial Control and the Rise of Sentiment in Neuchatel, 1550-1800, Cornell Univ, 92; auth, Women and the Consistory in Calvin's Geneva, Sixteenth Century J, 93; auth, The Control of Marriage in Reformed Switzerland, 1600-1800, in Graham, ed, Later Calvinism: International Perspectives, Sixteenth Century Journal Publ, 94; auth, The Marriage Laws Calvin Drafted for Geneva, in Neuser, ed, Calvinus Sacrae Scripturae Professor, Eerdman's, 94; auth, The Family, Love, and Suicide in Early Modern Geneva, J of Family Hist, 96; auth, Calvin on Suicide, Church Hist, 97; auth, Reformed Piety and Suicide in Geneva, 1550-1800, in Roney, ed, The Identity of Geneva: The Christian Commonwealth, 1564-1864, Greenwood, 98; auth, Suicide in Reformation Geneva, Archive for Reformation Hist, 98; auth, The Impact of the Reformation and the Counter-Reformation, in Barbagli, ed, The History of the European Family, v.1: Family Life in Early Modern Times, Yale Univ, forthcoming; auth, Choosing Death: Suicide and Calinism in Early Modrn Geneva, Kirksville, MO, Truman State Univ Press, 01 forthcoming. **CONTACT ADDRESS** Dept of History, Univ of Mississippi, University, MS 38677. **EMAIL** hswatt@olemiss.edu

WATTS, JILL

PERSONAL Born Pomona, CA **DISCIPLINE** HISTORY **EDUCATION** Univ Calif, BA, 81; MA, 83; PhD, 89. **CAREER** Asst Prof, Weber State Univ, 89-91; Assoc Prof to Dept Director, Calif State Univ, 92-. **HONORS AND AWARDS** Fel, Soc for the Humanities, Cornell Univ, 94-95. **MEMBERSHIPS** Am Hist Asn, Org of am Hist, Am Studies Asn. **RESEARCH** US Cultural History; African-American History; Film. **SELECTED PUBLICATIONS** Auth, Go; Harlem USA: The Father Divine Story, Univ Calif Press, 92; auth, Mae West: an Iron in Black and White, Oxford Univ Press, forthcoming. **CONTACT ADDRESS** Dept Hist, California State Univ, San Marcos, 333 S Twin Oaks Vlly, San Marcos, CA 92096-0001.

WATTS, SYDNEY

PERSONAL Born 12/03/1965, Brussels, Belgium, m, 2000 **DISCIPLINE** HISTORY **EDUCATION** Sarah Lawrence Col, BA, 87; Cornell Univ, MA, 94; PhD, 99. **CAREER** Asst Prof, Univ Richmond, 99-. **MEMBERSHIPS** AHA; FHS; WSFH. **RESEARCH** History of 18th Century France; Food History; Social and Cultural History. **CONTACT ADDRESS** Dept Hist, Univ of Richmond, 28 Westhampton Way, Richmond, VA 23221. **EMAIL** swatts@richmond.edu

WAUGH, DANIEL CLARKE

PERSONAL Born 12/12/1941, Philadelphia, PA **DISCIPLINE** MEDIEVAL & EARLY MODERN RUSSIAN HISTORY **EDUCATION** Yale Univ, BA, 63; Harvard Univ, AM, 65, PhD(hist), 72. **CAREER** Asst prof, 72-80, Assoc Prof Hist & Russ & East Europ Studies, Univ Wash, 80-. **MEMBERSHIPS** Am Asn Advan Slavic Studies; Int Asn Paper Historians. **RESEARCH** Cultural history of Muscovite Russia; Russian diplomatics; paleography and codicology; filigranology. **SELECTED PUBLICATIONS** Contribr, Appendix I, In: The Kurbskii-Groznyi Apocrypha, Harvard Univ, 71; auth, Neizvestnyi pamiatnik drevnerusskoi literatury, Arkheograficheskii ezhegodnik za 1971 god, 72; K izucheniiu istorii rukopisnogo sobraniia P M Stroeva, Trudy Otdela drevnerusskoi literatury, 76 & 77; Slavianskie rukopisi Sobraniia Grafa F A Tolstogo, Inter Doc Co, 77; The lessons of the Kurbskii Controversy regarding the study and dating of old Russian manuscripts, In: Russian and Slavic History, 77 & The Great Turkes Defiance: On the History of the Apocryphal Correspondence of the Ottoman Sultan in Its Muscovite and Russian Variants, 78, Slavica; Two Unpublished Muscovite Chronicles, Oxford Slavonic Papers, 79; News of the False Messiah: Reports on Shabbetai Zevi in Ukraine and Muscovy, Jewish Social Studies, 79. **CONTACT ADDRESS** Dept of Hist, Univ of Washington, Seattle, WA 98195.

WAUGH, EARLE HOWARD

PERSONAL Born 11/06/1936, Regina, SK, Canada, m, 1970, 3 children **DISCIPLINE** HISTORY OF RELIGION **EDUCATION** McMaster Univ, BA, 59, MA, 65; Univ Chicago, MA, 68, PhD(hist relig), 72. **CAREER** Lectr, Indiana Univ, 70-71; Asst Prof, Univ of Alberta, 74-76; Assoc Prof, Univ of Alberta, 76-85; Prof, Univ of Alberta, 86-; Guest Prof, St. Thomas Univ, 92-93; Acting Chair, Univ of Alberta, 97-98. **HONORS AND AWARDS** Alberta Film Awd, 78; Gold Medal, Houston International Film Festival, 79; Silver Medal, Educational Houston International Film Festival, 79. **MEMBERSHIPS** Am Acad of Relig; Mid East Studies Asn; Can Soc Study Relig; Boreal Circle Soc; Am Res Center in Egypt; Soc for Medieval Studies; International Soc for the Study of Non-Traditional Medicine; Asn for Canadian Studies; Canadian Mediterranean Institute. **RESEARCH** Islam in North Am; Middle Eastern Sufism, Alberta Cree Traditions, Religious Interaction in Alberta. **SELECTED PUBLICATIONS** Auth, The Munshidin of Egypt, Their World and Their Song, Univ of South Carolina Press, Columbia, South Carolina, 89; auth, Dissonant Worlds: Rogier Vandersteene; auth, Among the Cree Wilfrid Laurier Univ Press, Waterloo, 96; coed, The Muslim Family in North America, Univ of Alberta Press, Edmonton, 91; coed, The Shaping of an American Islamic Discourse: A Memorial to Fazlur Rahman, Scholar's Press, Istanbul, (94): 129-143; auth, "Alexander in Islam: the Sacred Persona in Muslim Rulership adab," in Subject and Ruler: The Cult of the Ruler in Classical Antiquity, Alastair Small, ed, Journal of Roman Archeology, Supplementary Series 17, (96): 237-253; auth, "Wach and the Double Truth," in Teaching Theology and Religion, Vol 1, (97): 20-25; transl, "In Praise of the Prophet, Muhammad," Trans. & comm in Windows on the House of Islam, Univ of California Press, Berkeley, CA, (98): 120-123; auth, "Introduction," and "Beyond Scylla and Kharybdis: The Discourses of Isalmic Idenity in Fazlur Rahman," in The Shaping of an American Islamic Discourse: A Memorial to Fazlur Rahman, Earle H. Waugh and Frederic M Den, ed, Scholar's Press, Atlanta, Gerogia, (99): 1-; auth, "Dead Men in sultry Darkness': Western Theory the Problematic of a Baseline Cultural Motif in Islamic Ascetic Tradition," in Journal of Asian and African Studies, Vol 34, 1, (99): 1-20. **CONTACT ADDRESS** Dept of Comp Lit, Relig, & Film/Media Stud, Univ of Alberta, 347 Arts, Edmonton, AB, Canada T6G 2E6. **EMAIL** earle.waugh@ualberta.ca

WEAKLAND, JOHN EDGAR

PERSONAL Born 05/11/1932, Mansfield, OH, m, 1960, 3 children **DISCIPLINE** MEDIEVAL & RENAISSANCE HISTORY **EDUCATION** John Carroll Univ, BSS, 54; Kent State Univ, MA, 60; Western Reserve Univ, PhD, 66. **CAREER** Instr hist, Kent State Univ, 60-66; from asst prof to assoc prof, 66-73, prof hist, Ball State Univ, 73; vis scholar, St Edmund's House, Cambridge, 73, 83; dir, London Ctr, Ball State Univ, 74-75; ed, Int J Soc Educ, 84-98. **HONORS AND AWARDS** Am Philos Soc res grant, 68-69 & 71-72; Andrew W Mellon fel, 82; Outstanding Fac Serv Awd, Ball State Univ, 96. **MEMBERSHIPS** AHA; Am Cath Hist Asn; Mediaeval Acad Am; Renaissance Soc Am; Am Soc Church Hist. **RESEARCH** Early Renaissance church; Avignon Papacy; medieval witchcraft. **SELECTED PUBLICATIONS** Auth, John XXII before his pontificate, 1244-1316: Jacques Duese and his family, Archivum Hist Pontificiae, 72; ed & contribr, Society in ferment: medieval and modern, 72 & Focus on religion, 72, Ind Soc Studies Quart; auth, Renaissance Paideia: some ideals in Italian humanism and their relevance today, Social Studies, 4/73; ed & contribr, Myths-past and present, Indians Social Studies Quart, 75; auth, Pastorelli, Pope and persecution, Jewish Social Studies, 76; coauth, Wing Chun: Sil Lim Tao, Crompton, London, 76; coauth, Wing Chun: Chum Kil, Crompton, London, 81; Wang Chun: Bil Jee, Crompton, 83. **CONTACT ADDRESS** Dept of Hist, Ball State Univ, 2000 W University, Muncie, IN 47306-0480. **EMAIL** 00jeweakland@bsu.edu

WEARE, WALTER BURDETTE

PERSONAL Born 12/26/1938, Denver, CO, m, 1955, 2 children **DISCIPLINE** UNITED STATES HISTORY **EDUCATION** Univ Colo, BA, 63, MA, 64; Univ NC, PhD(hist), 70. **CAREER** From instr to asst prof, 68-74, assoc prof hist, Univ Wis-Milwaukee, 74-, Nat Endowment for Humanities fel Afro-Am hist & cult, Stanford Univ, 70-71; Am Coun Learned Soc fel, 76-77. **MEMBERSHIPS** Southern Hist Asn; Asn Study Afro-Am Life & Hist; Orgn Am Historians. **RESEARCH** History of the South; Afro-American history; United States social and intellectual history since 1865. **SELECTED PUBLICATIONS** Auth, Black Business in the New South: A Social History of the North Carolina Mutual Life Insurance Company, Univ Ill, 73. **CONTACT ADDRESS** Dept of History, Univ of Wisconsin, Milwaukee, PO Box 413, Milwaukee, WI 53201-0413. **EMAIL** BWeare@csd.uwm.edu

WEARING, J. P.

PERSONAL Born Birmingham, England **DISCIPLINE** ENGLISH LITERATURE, THEATRE HISTORY **EDUCATION** Univ Wales, Swansea, BA, 67, PhD(English), 71; Univ Sask, MA, 68. **CAREER** Lectr English, Univ Alta, 71-74; asst prof, 74-77, assoc prof English, Univ Ariz, 77-84, Killam fel English, Univ Alta, 71-73; ed, Nineteenth Century Theatre Res, 72-; Guggenheim fel Theatre Hist, 78-79; prof English, Univ Ariz, 84-. **HONORS AND AWARDS** NEH Research Grant 87-91. **MEMBERSHIPS** Nineteenth Century Theatre Res; English Lit Transition. **RESEARCH** English theatre history; 19th and 20th century English drama; Shakespeare. **SELECTED PUBLICATIONS** Auth, Two early absurd plays in England, Mod Drama, 73; ed, The Collected Letters of Sir Arthur Pinero, Univ Minn, 74; auth, The London Stage 1890-1899: A Calendar of Plays and Players, Scarecrow, 76; The West End London Stage in the 1890's, Educ Theatre J, 77; coauth, English Drama and Theatre, 1800-1900, Gale Res, 78; auth, American and British Theatrical Biography: A Directory, Scarecrow, 78; Henry Arthur Jones: An Annotated Bibliography of Writings about Him, English Lit in Transition, 79; The London Stage 1900-1909: A Calendar of Plays and Players, Scarecrow, 81; The London Stage 1950-1959: A Calendar of Plays and Players, 2 vols, Metuchen, NJ & London: the Scarecrow Press, 93. **CONTACT ADDRESS** Dept of English, Univ of Arizona, 472 Modern Lang Bldg, PO Box 210067, Tucson, AZ 85721. **EMAIL** jpwearing@aol.com

WEART, SPENCER R.

PERSONAL Born 03/08/1942, Detroit, MI, m, 1971, 2 children **DISCIPLINE** HISTORY OF SCIENCE **EDUCATION** Cornell Univ, BA, 63, Univ Colo, PhD, 68. **CAREER** Fel solar physics, Calif Inst Technol, 68-71; res specialist hist, Univ Calif, Berkeley, 71-74; Dir, Ctr Hist Physics, Am Inst Physics, 74-. **MEMBERSHIPS** Am Astron Soc; Hist Sci Soc; Soc Social Studies Sci. **RESEARCH** History of nuclear physics, astronomy and French science. **SELECTED PUBLICATIONS** Co-ed, Leo Szilard: His Version of the Facts, MIT Press, 78; Scientists in Power, Harvard Univ Press, 79; Global Warming, Cold-War, And The Evolution Of Research Plans/, Historical Studies In The Physical And Biological Sciences, Vol 0027, 1997; Global Warming, Cold-War, And The Evolution Of Research Plans/, Historical Studies In The Physical And Biological Sciences, Vol 0027, 1997. **CONTACT ADDRESS** Am Inst of Physics, Center for History of Physics, One Physics Ellipse, College Park, MD 20740-3843. **EMAIL** sweart@aip.org

WEAVER, DOUG

PERSONAL Born 04/22/1956, Fredericksburg, VA, m, 1979, 2 children **DISCIPLINE** CHURCH HISTORY **EDUCATION** Miss Col, BA, 78; Southern Baptist Theol Sem, M Div, 81; PhD, 85. **CAREER** Asst prof, Bluefield Col, 86-88; prof, Chair, Brewton-Parker Col, 89-. **HONORS AND AWARDS** Jordan Teacher Excellence Awd, Brewton Parker Col **MEMBERSHIPS** AAR; ASCH; NABPR. **RESEARCH** American Religion: Pentecostalism, Baptist History. **SELECTED PUBLICATIONS** Auth, The Healer Prophet: William Marrion Branham, Mercer Univ Pr, 87; auth, A Cloud of Witnesses, Smyth & Helwyn Publ, 93; auth, From Our Christian Heritage, Smyth & Helwys Publ, 98; ed, The Whitsitt Journal; auth, Every Town Needs a Downtown Church: A Hist of FBC Gainesville, Fl, Southern Baptist Hist Soc, 00. **CONTACT ADDRESS** Dept Relig and Philos, Brewton-Parker Col, PO Box 2120, Mount Vernon, GA 30445-0197. **EMAIL** dweaver@cybersouth.com

WEAVER, GARRETT F.

PERSONAL Born 06/17/1948, Durham, NC, s **DISCIPLINE** HISTORY **EDUCATION** NC Cntrl, Attend; Univ of NC, PhD 1987. **CAREER** Univ of NC, lectr Afro-Amer studies 1985; Univ of WI, 73-74; St Augustine Coll, 72-73; NC St Univ, 72-73; Rio Grande Coll; Marshall Univ; WV Univ, 68-72; Afro-Amer & African Studies, 85; Jackson State Univ, asst prof of history 1975-88. **MEMBERSHIPS** Mem Am Historical Assn; Assn for Study of Afro-Am & Life & History; Nat Geo Soc; pres NAACP Charleston; mem Kanawha Co Div Comm Wlfr Bd; NASALH Biecennial Com; Phi Beta Sigma Frat; Afro-Am Studies Cons; Black Geneological Rsrchr; dir Public & Applied History Prop; dir of history English Link Proj Jackson State Univ. **CONTACT ADDRESS** Univ of No Carolina, Chapel Hill, 301 Peabody, Chapel Hill, NC 27514.

WEAVER, JOHN C.

PERSONAL Born 05/11/1946, Stratford, ON, Canada, m, 1971, 1 child **DISCIPLINE** URBAN & CANADIAN HISTORY **EDUCATION** Queens Univ, BA Hons, 69; Duke Univ, MA, 70, PhD(hist), 73. **CAREER** Lectr hist, Queens Univ, 72-74; asst, 74-77, Assoc Hist, Mcmaster Univ, 78-, Res assoc urban studies, Inst Local Gov, Queens Univ, 73-74. **MEMBERSHIPS** Can Hist Asn. **RESEARCH** Urban land use; urban social. **SELECTED PUBLICATIONS** Auth, The reconstruction of the Richmond District: An episode in Canadian planning and public housing, Plan Can, 75; Tomorrow's metropolis revisited: A critical assessment of Canadian urban reform, Can City, 77; Shaping the Canadian City, 1890-1920, Inst Pub Affairs, Can, 77; Policing Morals, The Metropolitan Police And The Home-Office - Petrow,S, Urban History Review-Revue D

Histoire Urbaine, Vol 0023, 1995; Beyond The Fatal Shore - Pastoral Squatting And The Occupation Of Australia, 1826 To 1852, American Historical Review, Vol 0101, 1996. **CONTACT ADDRESS** Dept Hist, McMaster Univ, Hamilton, ON, Canada L8S 4L8.

WEBB, GEORGE ERNEST
PERSONAL Born 06/17/1952 **DISCIPLINE** AMERICAN HISTORY, HISTORY OF SCIENCE **EDUCATION** Univ AZ, BA, 73, MA, 74, PhD, 78. **CAREER** Asst Prof Hist, TN Technol Univ, 78-83; Assoc Prof Hist, TN Technol Univ, 83-88; Prof Hist, TN Technol Univ, 88-. **HONORS AND AWARDS** Phi Beta Kappa, Phi Kappa Phi, Outstanding Fac Awd in Tchg, TN Technol Univ, 90; Caplenor Faculty Research Awd, TN Technol Univ, 93. **MEMBERSHIPS** AHA; Hist Sci Soc; West Hist Assoc; AAAS. **RESEARCH** Hist of Am science. **SELECTED PUBLICATIONS** Auth, Tree Rings and Telescopes: The Scientific Career of A.E. Douglass, Univ AZ, 83; The Evolution Controversy in America, KY Univ, 94; various articles in scholarly journals and encyclopedias. **CONTACT ADDRESS** Dept of History, Tennessee Tech Univ, Cookeville, TN 38505. **EMAIL** gwebb@tntech.edu

WEBB, LYNNE M.
PERSONAL Born 03/20/1951, Shamokin, PA, m, 1984, 3 children **DISCIPLINE** COMMUNICATION AND COMMUNITY DEVELOPMENT **EDUCATION** Pa State Univ, BS, 72; Univ Ore, MS, 75, PhD, 80. **CAREER** Instr, Berea Col, 78-80; vis assoc prof, Univ Hawaii, 90; assoc prof, Univ Fla, 80-91; assoc prof, Univ Memphis, 91-99; Prof., Univ Arkansas, 99-**HONORS AND AWARDS** Who's Who in America; Who's Who of Amer Women; Who's Who in the South and Southwest; Who's Who in the Media and Commun; Who's Who in Amer Educ; Outreach award, Southern States Commun Asn, 97; top res paper award, 98, 90, 86; teaching award, Col of Liberal Arts & Sci, 89-90, 85-86, 83-84; teaching award, Alpha Lambda Delta, 86-87; American Communication Asn, 99-00. **MEMBERSHIPS** Intl Commun Asn; Nat Commun Asn; Southern States Commun Asn; Tenn Commun Asn. **RESEARCH** Commun theory; Interpersonal commun; Family commun; Commun and aging. **SELECTED PUBLICATIONS** Co-auth, Applied family commun res: Casting light upon the demon, Jour of Applied Commun Res, 95; co-auth, Maintaining effective interaction skills, Communication in Later Life, Butterworth-Heinemann, 95; co-auth, Socially constructing the aging experience: A review essay on the Handbook of Communication and Aging Research, Health Comm, 96; auth, Proactive collegiality: Stalking the demon where he lives, Spectra, 96; auth, A proactive stance, Connections, 95; Auth, Convention financing: Theft or misunderstanding, Connections, 97. **CONTACT ADDRESS** 417 Kimpel Hall, Fayetteville, AR 72701. **EMAIL** lynnewebb320@cs.com

WEBB, ROBERT KIEFER
PERSONAL Born 11/23/1922, Toledo, OH, m, 1957, 2 children **DISCIPLINE** HISTORY **EDUCATION** Oberlin Col, AB, 47; Columbia Univ, AM, 48, PhD, 51. **CAREER** Instr hist, Wesleyan Univ, 51-53; from asst prof to prof, Columbia Univ, 53-70; ed, Am Hist Rev, 68-75; Prof hist, Univ MD, Baltimore County 75-93, Guggenheim fel, 59-60, 73-74; Am Coun Learned Soc fel, 66-67; ed, AAUP Bull, 75-81; Nat Endowment for Humanities res grant, 78-80; Mem, Instit for Ad Stud, 82-83; Vis fel, Australian Natl Univ, 86; Christensen Res Fel, St. Catherine's Coll, Oxford, 92; Emer Prof, 93-. **HONORS AND AWARDS** Hon fel, Australian Acad of the Hum; Hon fel, Harris Manchester Col, Oxford. **MEMBERSHIPS** Fel Royal Hist Soc. **RESEARCH** Nineteenth century Brit soc hist. **SELECTED PUBLICATIONS** Auth, The British Working Class Reader, 1790-1848, 55 & Harriet Martineau, A Radical Victorian, 60, Columbia Univ; Modern England, 68, 2nd ed, 80 & coauth, Modern Europe, 73, Harper. **CONTACT ADDRESS** Dept of History, Univ of Maryland, Baltimore, 1000 Hilltop Cir, Baltimore, MD 21250.

WEBB, ROSS ALLAN
PERSONAL Born 07/22/1923, Westchester, NS, Canada, m, 1954, 2 children **DISCIPLINE** AMERICAN DIPLOMATIC RECONSTRUCTION & BRITISH HISTORY **EDUCATION** Acadia Univ, BA, 49; Univ Pittsburgh, MA, 51, PhD, 56. **CAREER** Lectr hist, Univ Pittsburgh, 50-56; from asst prof to assoc prof, Univ Ky, 56-57; dean fac, 68-75, vpres acad affairs, 71-75, chmn dept hist, 67-68; Prof Emeritus and Univ Historian, Winthrop Univ. **HONORS AND AWARDS** Distinguished Prof Awd, Winthrop Univ, 77; Algernon Sydney Sullivan Awd, 81. **MEMBERSHIPS** AHA; Southern Hist Asn; Kentucky Historical Society. **RESEARCH** The British provincial press and the coming of the American Revolution. **SELECTED PUBLICATIONS** Auth, The Alaskan Boundary Dispute, 1779-1903, US Dept State, 51; coauth, A Book of Remembrance, Univ Pittsburgh, 56; auth, A Yankee from Dixie: Benjamin Helm Bristow, 3/64 & Benjamin H Bristow, civil rights champion, 1866-1872, Civil War Hist, 69; Benjamin Helm Bristow, Border State Politician, Univ Ky, 69; contribr, Radicalism, Racism and Party Realignment: The Border States During Reconstruction, Johns Hopkins Univ, 69; auth, Kentucky in the Reconstruction Era, Univ Press Ky, 79. **CONTACT ADDRESS** Dept of History, Winthrop Univ, 701 W Oakland Ave, Rock Hill, SC 29733-0001. **EMAIL** webbr@winthrop.edu

WEBB, STEPHEN SAUNDERS
PERSONAL Born 05/25/1937, Syracuse, NY, m, 1985, 5 children **DISCIPLINE** HISTORY **EDUCATION** Williams Col, BA, 59; Univ Wisc, MS, 61; PhD, 64. **CAREER** Asst Prof, St Lawrence Univ, 64-65; Asst Prof, Col of William & Mary, 65-68; Asst Prof to Prof, Syracuse Univ, 68-. **HONORS AND AWARDS** Fel, Inst if Early Am History & Culture; Fel, NEH. **MEMBERSHIPS** Royal Hist Soc. **RESEARCH** Imperial Adminstrators; Ward Society; The History of the Hodenosaunee. **SELECTED PUBLICATIONS** Auth, The Governors-General the English Army and the Definition of the Empire, 1569-1681, Univ NC Press, 87; auth, Lord Churchill's Coup The Anglo-Armeican Empire and the Glorious Revoltuion Reconsidered, Syracuse, 98. **CONTACT ADDRESS** Dept Hist, Syracuse Univ, 145 Eggers, Syracuse, NY 13244-1020. **EMAIL** sswebb@maxwell.syr.edu

WEBBER, RANDALL C.
PERSONAL Born 11/28/1961, Oak Ridge, TN, s **DISCIPLINE** HISTORY; RELIGIOUS STUDIES, SOCIOLOGY **EDUCATION** Furman Univ, BA, 82; Southern Baptist Theological Seminary, MDiv, 85, PhD, 89. **CAREER** Manuscript editor, 87-89, Paradigms; asst ed, 89-92, Univ MI; dir, emergency housing, Salvation Army, 92- ; proprietor, Webber Church Consulting, 97- . **HONORS AND AWARDS** Who's Who in Bibl Studies and Archaeol, 93. **MEMBERSHIPS** Soc of Bibl Lit; Am Acad of Bereavement; Nat Bd of Cognitive Behavioral Therapists. **RESEARCH** Early Christianity; Grief; Politics. **SELECTED PUBLICATIONS** Auth, Successful Grief and Chronic Homelessness: Is There a Relationship? Grief Work, 95; auth, Kentucky Reader Proposes Ethics Code for Churches, Baptist Today, 95; auth, Reader-Response Analysis of the Epistle of James, 96; auth, An Idealistic Reading of the Apocalypse, 99. **CONTACT ADDRESS** 325 E Kentucky St, Louisville, KY 40203-2709. **EMAIL** rcwbbb@juno.com

WEBER, DAVID J.
PERSONAL Born 12/20/1940, Buffalo, NY, m, 1962, 2 children **DISCIPLINE** LATIN AMERICAN & AMERICAN SOUTHWEST HISTORY **EDUCATION** State Univ NYork Col, Fredonia, BS, 62; Univ NM, MA, 64, PhD, 67. **CAREER** From asst prof to prof hist, San Diego State Univ, 67-76; Prof Hist, Southern Methodist Univ, 76-, Dept Chmn, 79-86, Robert and Nancy Dedman Prof Hist, 86-, Dir, William P. Clements Center for Southwest Studies, 95-; Fulbright-Hays lectr, Univ Costa Rica, 70; Danforth Assoc, 73; NEH Younger Humanist fel hist, 74-75; Am Coun Learned Soc fel, 80; Fellow, Center for Advanced Study in the Behavioral Sciences, Stanford Univ, 86-87, NEH Fellowship, 90-91. **HONORS AND AWARDS** Herbert E Bolton Awd, Western Hist Asn, 81; Ray Allen Billington Awd from the Org of Am Hist for the best book to appear on the American frontier in the previous two years, 83; elected to membership in the Academia Mexicana de la Historia, 83; Outstanding Art Book Awd from the Nat Cowboy Hall of Fame and Western Heritage Center, 85; elected a Fellow of the Soc of Am Hist, 86; Honorary President, 8th Conference of Mexican and North American Historians, San Diego, Oct 90; Caughey Western History Asn Prize, for the outstanding book on the American West in 92; Premio Espana y America, from the Spanish Ministry of Culture, 92. **MEMBERSHIPS** Orgn Am Historians; Conf Latin Am Hist; Western Hist Asn, pres 90-91; AHA. **RESEARCH** Spanish-Mexican borderlands; Chicano history; fur trade. **SELECTED PUBLICATIONS** Ed, The Extranjeros: Selected Documents from the Mexican Side of the Trail, 1825-1828, Stagecoach Press, 67; The Lost Trappers, Univ NM, 70; auth, The Taos Trappers: The Fur Trade in the Far Southwest, 1540-1846, Univ OK, 71; Foreigners in Their Native Land: Historical Roots of the Mexican Americans, Univ NM, 73; ed, Northern Mexico on the Eve of the United States Invasion: Rare Imprints Concerning California, Arizona, New Mexico and Texas, 1821-1846, Arno, 76; co-ed, Fortunes are for the Few: Letters of a Forty-Niner by Charles William Churchill, San Diego Hist Soc, 77; ed, New Spain's Far Northern Frontier: Essays on Spain in the American West, 1540-1821, 79 & auth, The Mexican Frontier, 1821-1846: The American Southwest Under Mexico, 82, Univ NM; Richard H. Kern: Expeditionary Artist in the Far Southwest, 1848-1853, Univ of NM Press, 85; Myth and the History of the Hispanic Southwest: Essays by David J. Weber, Univ of NM Press, 88, paperback reprint 90; The Californios vs. Jedediah Smith: A New Cache of Documents, Arthur H. Clark Co, 90; The Spanish Frontier in North America, Yale Univ Press, 92; co-ed, Trading in Santa Fe: John Kingsbury's Correspondence with James Josiah Webb, 1853-1861, SMU Press for the DeGolyer Lib, 96; On the Edge of Empire: The Taos Hacienda of Los Martinez, Museum of NM Press, 96. **CONTACT ADDRESS** Hist Dept, So Methodist Univ, Dallas, TX 75275-0176. **EMAIL** dweber@mail.smu.edu

WEBER, RALPH E.
PERSONAL Born 04/19/1926, St Cloud, MN, m, 1952, 9 children **DISCIPLINE** HISTORY **EDUCATION** St John's Univ, AB, 48; Univ Notre Dame, MSEd, 50; PhD, 56. **CAREER** U.S. Navy, 44-46; instr, Univ of Notre Dame, 53-54; asst dean, Marquette Univ, 54-57; registrar & dir of admissions, Marquette Univ, 57-61; from asst prof to prof, Marquette Univ, 69-. **HONORS AND AWARDS** Fac Awd for Teaching Excellence, Marquette Univ, 69; Scholar in Residence, Central Intelligence Agency, 87-88; Scholar in Residence, Nat Security Agency, 91-92. **MEMBERSHIPS** Soc for Historians of Am For Relations, Asn of Former Intelligence Officers. **RESEARCH** American Foreign Intelligence, American Code and Ciphers. **SELECTED PUBLICATIONS** Auch, United states Diplomatic Codes and Ciphers, 79; ed, From the Foreign Press (2 vols), 80; ed, The Final Memorandum, 88; auth, Masked Dispatches, 93; ed, Spymaters: Ten CIA Officers in Their Own Words, 99. **CONTACT ADDRESS** Dept Hist, Marquette Univ, PO Box 1881, Milwaukee, WI 53201-1881.

WEBER, RONALD
PERSONAL Born 09/21/1934, Mason City, IA, m, 3 children **DISCIPLINE** AMERICAN STUDIES **EDUCATION** Univ Notre Dame, BA, 57; Univ Iowa, MFA, 60; Univ Minn, PhD, 67. **CAREER** Instr, Loras Col, 60-62; asst prof, 63-66, assoc prof, 67-76, prof, Am Stud, 76- , chemn, 70-77, Univ Notre Dame. **HONORS AND AWARDS** Fulbright lectr, Univ Coimbra, Portugal, 68-69, 82, Univ Lisbon, 82; res fel, NEH, 72-73; Faculty Awd, 76; CHOICE Outstanding Academic Book of 81-82; res award, Univ Notre Dame 83, 88; res fel, Freedom Forum Center for Media Stud, Columbia Univ, 85-86; Bronze Medal, Council for Advancement and Support of Ed, 88; exec committee, Catholic Comn on Intellectual and Cult Affairs, 93-96; Kaueb Teaching Awd, 99. **RESEARCH** American Lit. **SELECTED PUBLICATIONS** Auth, O Romance Americano, Libraria Almedina, 69; ed and contribur, America in Change: Reflections on the 60s and 70s, Univ Notre Dame, 72; ed and contribur, The Reporter as Artist: A Look at The New Journalism Controversy, Hastings, 74; co-ed and contribur, An Almost Chosen People: The Moral Aspirations of Americans, Univ Notre Dame, 76; auth, The Literature of Fact: Literary Nonfiction in American Writing, Ohio Univ, 80; auth, Seeing Earth: Space Exploration in American Writing, Ohio Univ Pr, 84; auth, Company Spook, St Martins, 86; auth, Troubleshooter, St Martins, 88; auth, Hemingway's Art of Nonfiction, St Martins, 90; auth, The Midwestern Ascendancy in American Writing, Indiana Univ, 92; auth, Hired Pens: Professional Writers in America's Golden Age of Print, Ohio Univ, 97; auth, The Aluminum Hatch, Write Way, 98; Auth, Catch and Keep, Write Way, 2000. **CONTACT ADDRESS** Dept of American Studies, Univ of Notre Dame, Notre Dame, IN 46556. **EMAIL** h.r.weber.z@nd.edu

WEBER, SHIRLEY NASH
PERSONAL Born 09/20/1948, Hope, AR, m **DISCIPLINE** AFRICAN-AMERICAN STUDIES **EDUCATION** Univ of CA LA, BA 1966-70, MA 1970-71, PhD 1971-75. **CAREER** Episcopal City Mission Soc LA, caseworker 69-72; CA State Coll LA, instructor 72; San Diego State Univ, Prof 72-; San Diego City Schools, San Diego, CA, president, board of education, 90-91. **HONORS AND AWARDS** Fellow Woodrow Wilson Fellowship 1970; Black Achievement Action Enterprise Develop 1981; Women of Distinction Women Inc 1984; Natl Citation Awd, Natl Sorority of Phi Delta Kappa, Inc. July 1989; Citizen of the Year, Omega Psi Phi Fraternity, 1989; Carter G Woodson Education Awd, NAACP, San Diego, 1989. **MEMBERSHIPS** Bd mem CA Black Faculty & Staff 1976-80; pres Black Caucus Speech Comm Assoc 1980-82; pres Natl Comm Assn 1983-85; regional editor Western Journal of Speech 1979-; adv bd Battered Women's Serv YWCA 1981-; Council of 21 Southwestern Christian Coll 1983-; 1st vice pres Natl Sor of Phi Delta Kappa Delta Upsilon Chapt; trustee Bd of Educ San Diego Unified School District 1988-96. **CONTACT ADDRESS** Afro-American Studies, San Diego State Univ, San Diego, CA 92182.

WEBER, TIMOTHY P.
PERSONAL Born 05/25/1947, Los Angeles, LA, m, 1968, 2 children **DISCIPLINE** CHURCH HISTORY **EDUCATION** UCLA, BA, 69; Fuller Theol Sem, M Div, 72; Univ Chicago, MA, 74, PhD, 76. **CAREER** Asst, assoc, prof, 76-92, Denver Sem; David T Porter Prof, Church hist, 92-96, S Baptist Theol Sem; vice pres, acad affairs, dean of sem, prof, 97-, N Baptist Theol Sem. **RESEARCH** General hist of Christianity; Amer relig hist, evangelicalism, fundamentalism, millennial movements. **SELECTED PUBLICATIONS** Auth, "Living in the Shadow of the Second Coming," U of Chicago Press, 87. **CONTACT ADDRESS** No Baptist Theol Sem, 660 # Butterfield Rd, Lombard, IL 60148. **EMAIL** tpweber@seminary.edu

WEBRE, STEPHEN
PERSONAL Born 10/13/1946, Baton Rouge, LA, m **DISCIPLINE** HISTORY **EDUCATION** Univ Southwestern La, BA, 68; Tulane Univ, MA, 75, PhD, 80. **CAREER** Cur Manuscript, La State Mus, 80-82; asst prof hist, 82-85, assoc prof hist, 85-90, prof hist, La Tech Univ, 90-. **MEMBERSHIPS** Am Hist Asn; Latin Am Studies Asn; La Hist Asn; N La Hist Asn; SW Hist Asn; Southwestern Soc Sci Asn. **RESEARCH** Soc and polit hist of Colonial Latin Am; emphasis on Central Am; 20th-century polit movements in Mod Latin Am. **SELECTED PUBLICATIONS** Auth, Jose Napoleon Duarte and the Christian Democratic Party in Salvadoran Politics, 1960-1977, 79; auth, La sociedad colonial en Guatemala: Estudios locales y regionales, 89. **CONTACT ADDRESS** Dept of Hist, Louisiana Tech Univ, PO Box 8548, Ruston, LA 71272. **EMAIL** swebre@gans.latech.edu

WEBSTER, DONALD B.
PERSONAL Born 10/14/1933, Rochester, NY **DISCIPLINE** HISTORY, ART **EDUCATION** Univ Maine, BA, 59; Univ RI, MA, 61. **CAREER** NY State Hist Asn, 61-63; Robertson Mus Arts & Sci, 63-66; PROF, UNIV TORONTO, 66-; CURATOR EMER, CANADIANA DEPT, ROYAL ONT MUS; ch, Nat Portrait Gallery. **HONORS AND AWARDS** Fel, Royal Soc Arts **MEMBERSHIPS** Co Mil Hist; Am Ceramic Cir; Soc Hist Archaeol; Soc Post-Medieval Archaeol. **SELECTED PUBLICATIONS** Auth, Georgian Canada, Conflict & Culture, 84; auth, Military Bolt Action Rifles 1841-1918, 93; auth, Canfake, 97; ed, Book of Canadian Antiques, 74. **CONTACT ADDRESS** Canadiana Dept, Royal Ontario Mus, 100 Queen's Park, Toronto, ON, Canada M5S 2C6.

WEBSTER, GERALD R.
PERSONAL Born 06/02/1953, Bremerton, WA, m, 1982, 1 child **DISCIPLINE** GEOGRAPHY **EDUCATION** Univ Colo Denver, BA, 76; W Wash Univ, MS, 80; Univ Ky, PhD, 84. **CAREER** Vis asst prof, Univ Miami, 84-85; asst prof, Univ Wyo, 85-89; prof and dept chair, Univ Ala, 89-. **HONORS AND AWARDS** Res Honors Award, Asn Am Geogr, 00. **MEMBERSHIPS** Asn of Am Geogr; Am Geog Soc; Nat Coun for Geog Educ. **RESEARCH** Political geography; Electoral geography; Districting. **SELECTED PUBLICATIONS** Auth, "Cuba: Moving Back to the Future with Tourism," J Geog, (92): 226-233; co-auth, "The Power of an Icon," Geog Rev, (94): 131-143; auth, "Partisan Shifts in Presidential and Gubernatorial Elections in Alabama, 1932-1994," Prof Geogr, (96): 379-391; co-auth, "On Enlarging the U.S House of Representatives," Polit Geog, (98): 319-329; co-auth, "The Electoral Geography of Anti-Gay Rights Referenda in Oregon," Prof Geogr, (98): 498-515; auth, "Playing a Game with Changing Rules: Geography, Politics and Redistricting in the 1990s," Polit Geog, (00): 141-161; auth, "Women, Politics, Elections and Citizenship," J Geog, (000: 1-10; co-auth, "Place and Region in American Legal Culture," Hist Geog, (00): 127-148; auth, "Changing Geographical Patterns of Religious Denomination Affiliation in Georgia, 1970-1990," SE Geogr, (00): 25-51; co-auth, "Whose South is it Anyway?: Debating the Confederate Battle Flag in South Carolina," Polit Geog, (01): 271-299. **CONTACT ADDRESS** Dept Geog, Univ of Alabama, Tuscaloosa, PO Box 870322, Tuscaloosa, AL 35487-0322. **EMAIL** gwebster@bama.ua.edu

WEBSTER, JILL
PERSONAL Born 09/29/1931, London, England **DISCIPLINE** HISTORY **EDUCATION** Univ Liverpool, BA, 78, post-grad cert educ, 65; Univ Nottingham, MA, 64; Univ Toronto, PhD, 69. **CAREER** Prof, 68-95, assoc dean arts & sci, 78-81, dir ctr medieval stud, 89-94, ch grad dept Span & Port, 93-94, Prof Emer, Univ Toronto, 95-. **HONORS AND AWARDS** Fel, Royal Soc Can, 91. **MEMBERSHIPS** Pres, Am Acad Res Hist Medieval Spain, 90-95; Corres mem, Seccio Historica-Arqueologica, Inst d'Estudis Catalans, Barcelona, 96-. **SELECTED PUBLICATIONS** Auth, Els Menorets: The Franciscans in the Realms of Aragon from St. Francis to the Black Death(1348), 93. **CONTACT ADDRESS** Dept of Span and Port, Univ of Toronto, 91 Charles St West, Toronto, ON, Canada M5S 1K7. **EMAIL** jwebster@epas.uoftoronto.ca

WEBSTER, NIAMBI DYANNE
DISCIPLINE HISTORY **EDUCATION** Drake Univ, BA, English/drama, 1973; Mankato State Coll, MS, curriculum & instruction, 1975; University of Iowa, PhD, curriculum & instruction, 1991. **CAREER** Des Moines Public Schools, instructor 75-78; Iowa Bystander, freelance writer, associate editor, 76-80; Univ of IA, coord minority progs 78-83, grad asst instructor 80-83; IA Arts Council, touring music/theatre folk artist 78-; Coe Coll, instr dir special servs; dir, multicultural & international student affairs, Skidmore College, 89-91; Sonoma State University, Asst Prof, American Multucultural Studies Dept, currently. **HONORS AND AWARDS** Comm Service in the Fine Arts NAACP Presidential 1978; Black Leadership Awd Univ of IA 1979; Social Action Awd Phi Beta Sigma Frat 1980; Outstanding Young Woman in the Arts NAACP Natl Women Cong 1981; Women Equality & Dedication Comm on the Status of Women 1981; Trio Achievers Awd Natl Cncl of Educ Oppor Assoc 1985; Outstanding Woman of the Year Awd Linn Co Comm 1986. **MEMBERSHIPS** Outreach counselor YMCA Des Moines 1974-78; instr Gateway Oppor Pageant 1975-78; press & publicity chair NAACP Des Moines Chap 1976-78; founder/dir Langston Hughes Co of Players 1976-82; co-chair Polk Co Rape/Sexual Assault Bd 1977-80; artist-in-the schools IA Arts Council 1978-; 6th Judicial Dist Correctional Serv CSP & News Editor Volunteer 1984-; chairperson Mid-Amer Assoc of Ed Oppty Prog Personnel Cultural Enrichment Comm 1984-; mem Delta Sigma Theta Sor, Berkeley Alumnae; Iowa City Comm Schools Equity Comm mem 1985-87. **CONTACT ADDRESS** American Multicultural Studies Department, Sonoma State Univ, 1801 E Cotati Ave, Rohnert Park, CA 94928-3613.

WEBSTER, RICHARD J.
PERSONAL Born 04/28/1939, Towanda, PA, m, 1966, 1 child **DISCIPLINE** AMERICAN CIVILIZATION **EDUCATION** Lafayette Col, AB, 61; Univ of Delaware, MA, 63; Univ of Pennsylvania, MA, 65, PhD, 77. **CAREER** Inst, 63-67, Temple Univ; Asst Prof, 67-69, Assoc Prof, 69-78, Prof, 78-, West Chester Univ. **HONORS AND AWARDS** Pi Delta Epsilon (Journalism) Awd, Lafayette Col; Winterthur Fel, Univ of Del. **MEMBERSHIPS** Soc of Architectual Historians, Vernacular Architecture Forum, Penn Hist Assoc **RESEARCH** American architecture and material culture, Pennsylvania in particular. **SELECTED PUBLICATIONS** Auth, Philadelphia Preserved Catalog of the Historic American Buildings Survey, Temple Univ Press, 76 rev ed 81; CoAuth Philadelphia Three Centuries of American Art, Phil Musuem of Art, 76; Introduction Philadelphia A Guide to the Nations Birthplace, Univ of Penn Press, 88; Cultural Stability on a Moving Frontier Germanic Domestic Architecture from Eighteenth Century Pennsylvania to Nineteenth Century Missouri, Proc of Soc for the Interdisciplinary Stud of Soc Imagery, Univ of South Colorado, 97; Coauth, Pennsylvania Catalog Historic American Buildings Survey, Penn Hist and Museum Com, 99; auth, Pennsylvania Architecture: The Historic American Buildings Survey, 1990-1993, 00. **CONTACT ADDRESS** 1249 Surrey Rd, West Chester, PA 19382. **EMAIL** rwebster@wcupa.edu

WECKMAN, GEORGE
PERSONAL Born 03/20/1939, Philadelphia, PA **DISCIPLINE** HISTORY OF RELIGION **EDUCATION** Philadelphia Lutheran Sem, BD, 63; Univ Chicago, PhD, 69. **CAREER** Asst prof Philos, 68-72, assoc prof, 72- , Ohio Univ. **MEMBERSHIPS** AAR. **RESEARCH** Monasticism. **SELECTED PUBLICATIONS** Auth, My Brothers' Place: An American Lutheran Monastery, Lawrenceville, VA, Brunswick Publ Corp, 92; Reduction in the Classroom, in Religion and Reductionism: essays on Eliade, Segal, and the Challenge of the Social Sciences for the Study of Religion, ed, Thomas A. Idinopulos and Edward Yonan, Leiden, E.J. Brill, 94, 211-219; Respect of Others' Sacreds, in The Sacred and its Scholars, ed Thomas A. Idinopulos and Edward Yonan, Leiden, E.J. Brill, 96. **CONTACT ADDRESS** Dept of Philosophy, Ohio Univ, 19 Park Pl, Athens, OH 45701. **EMAIL** weckman@ohio.edu

WEEKS, THEODORE R.
PERSONAL Born 09/05/1959, Okinawa, Japan, s **DISCIPLINE** HISTORY **EDUCATION** Univ Colo, BA, 80; MA, 84; Univ Calif Berkeley, PhD, 92. **CAREER** Asst prof to assoc prof, S Ill Univ Carbondale, 93-. **HONORS AND AWARDS** Golda Meir Fel, 92-93; Fel, Woodrow Wilson Ctr, 93; SSRC Fel, 94-96; IREX Grant, 95, 96-97, 98; Fel, Hoover Inst, 97; Grant, Mem Found for Jewish Cult, 98-99; George S and Gladys W Queen Awd for Excellence in Teaching, SIUC, 00; Fulbright Grant, 00-01. **MEMBERSHIPS** AHA, Am Assoc for the Advan of Slavic Studies, Assoc for the Study of Nationality. **RESEARCH** Nationalism, Minority Nationalities in East-Central Europe, the Russian Empire and the USSR, National Movements in East Central Europe and Russia, Ethnic Relations and Assimilations. **SELECTED PUBLICATIONS** Auth, "The End of the Uniate Church in Russia: The Vozoedinenie of 1875," Jahbucher fur Geschichte Osteuropas XLIV, (95): 1-13; auth, "Polish Progressive Anti-Semitism, 1905-1914," E Europ Jewish Affairs XXV.2 (95): 49-68; auth, "Defending Our Own: Government and the Russian Minority in the Kingdom of Poland, 1905-1914," Russ Rev LIV.4, (95): 539-551; auth, Nation and State in Late Imperial Russia: Nationalism and Russification on Russia's Western Frontier 1863-1914, N Ill Univ Pr, (DeKalb), 96; auth, "Our Muslims' - The Lithuanian Tatars and the Russian Imperial Government," Jour of Baltic Studies 30.1, (99): 5-17; auth, "Poles, News, and Russians, 1863-1914: The Death of the Ideal of Assimilation in the Kingdom of Poland," Polin: A Jour of Polish-Jewish Studies, 12, (99): 242-256; Faith, "Monuments and Memory: Immortalizing Count MN Muraviev in Vilna, 1898," Nationalities Papers 27.4, (99): 551-564; auth, "Russification and the Lithuanians, 1863-1905," Slavic Rev 60.1, (01): 96-114; auth, "Between Rome and Tsargrad: The Uniate Church in Imperial Russia," in Of Religion and Empire: Missions, Conversion, and Tolerance in Tsarist Russian, eds Robert B. Geraci and Michael Khodarkovsky, Cornell UP, (Ithaca, 01): 70-91. **CONTACT ADDRESS** Dept Hist, So Illinois Univ, Carbondale, MC4519, Carbondale, IL 62901. **EMAIL** tadeusz@siu.edu

WEGS, JAMES ROBERT
PERSONAL Born 04/23/1937, Quincy, IL, m, 1964, 1 child **DISCIPLINE** MODERN EUROPEAN SOCIAL HISTORY **EDUCATION** Western Ill Univ, BA, 64; Northern Ill Univ, MA, 66; Univ Ill, PhD, 70. **CAREER** Asst prof Europ hist, New York Univ, 69-76; asst prof, Vanderbilt Univ, 76-77; Assoc Prof Europ Hist, Univ Notre Dame, 77-. **MEMBERSHIPS** AHA **RESEARCH** Modern European social history; working class history. **SELECTED PUBLICATIONS** Auth, Europe Since 1945, St Martin's Press, 77; Die sterreichische Kriegswirtschaft, 1914-1918, Verlag A Schendl, 79; Working class respectability: The Viennese experience, J Social Hist, summer 82; auth, Growing Up Working Class: Viennese Working Class Youth, 1890-1940, Penn State, 89; Images Of Youth - Age, Class, And The Male Youth Problem 1880-1920 - Hendrick,H, Journal Of Social History, Vol 0027, 1993; Fascism And The Working-Class In Austria, 1918-1934 - The Failure Of Labor In The 1st Republic - Lewis,J, Journal Of Modern History, Vol 0066, 1994; auth, Europe Since 1945, St Martins, 96. **CONTACT ADDRESS** Dept of History, Univ of Notre Dame, 219 O'Shaughnessy Hall, South Bend, IN 46617. **EMAIL** james.r.wegs.1@nd.edu

WEHTJE, MYRON FLOYD
PERSONAL Born 10/21/1938, Longview, WA, m, 1962, 3 children **DISCIPLINE** EARLY AMERICAN HISTORY **EDUCATION** Andrews Univ, BA, 62, MA, 63; Univ Va, PhD, 78. **CAREER** Instr hist, Plainview Acad, SDak, 63-64 & Can Union Col, 64-67; from instr to asst prof, 68-71, assoc prof, 71-79, prof hist, Atlantic Union Col, 79-. **HONORS AND AWARDS** Thomas Jefferson Found Fel, 68-69; ZAPARA Excellence in Teaching Awd, 88. **MEMBERSHIPS** The Soc for Hist of the Early Am Repub. **RESEARCH** Boston in the Revolutionary and early national periods; the age of Jefferson; American church history. **SELECTED PUBLICATIONS** Auth, The Congressional Elections of 1799 in Virginia, WVa Hist, 7/68; Charles Willson Peale and his Temple, Pa Hist, 4/69; Opposition in Virginia to the War of 1812, Va Mag Hist & Biog, 1/70; approx 20 articles for Hist J of Mass, including: Boston's Response to Disorder in the Commonwealth, 1/84; Boston and the Calling of the Federal Convention of 1787, 6/87; The Ideal of Virtue in Post-Revolutionary Boston, winter/89; Controversy over the Legal Profession in Post-Revolutionary Boston, summer/92; Factionalism in Post-Revolutionary Boston, summer/95. **CONTACT ADDRESS** Dept of Hist, Atlantic Union Col, Box 1000, South Lancaster, MA 01561-9999.

WEI, C. X. GEORGE
PERSONAL Born Shanghai, China, d, 1 child **DISCIPLINE** HISTORY **EDUCATION** Henan Univ China, MA; Wash Univ, MA; PhD, 96. **CAREER** Asst prof, Shanghai Acad Soc Sci, 83-88; Instr, Wash Univ, 93-94; Vis Asst prof, Univ Toledo, 94-96; Vis Asst prof, Whitman Col, 96-97; Asst Prof, Susquehanna Univ, 97-. **HONORS AND AWARDS** Specially Invited Prof, Inst Hist Res, China, 99; Res Grant, Taiwan, 98-99; Fac Res Grant, Susquehanna Univ, 98-99; Pub Grant, Pac Cultural Foundation, Taiwan, 97-98; Res Grant, Pac Cultural Foundation, Taiwan, 94-95; Teaching and Res Fel, Wash Univ, 88-93. **RESEARCH** Modern Chinese history, Traditional Chinese history, China's foreign relations, US foreign policy since 1900, US-Asia relations, Sino-American Economic relations, Traditional East Asian history, Modern East Asian history, Japanese history, Women history of East Asia, Modern World history. **SELECTED PUBLICATIONS** Auth, "The Cold War and Taiwan's Reconstruction: The Changing Economic Policy of the Economic Cooperation administration of the US toward the Nationalist Government," (in Chinese) in The Theses on Taiwan by Chinese Historians in the United States, Hong Kong press, forthcoming; auth, "An Economic chance to be Lost: The Conflicting Approaches of the ECA and the State Department toward China in 1948-1949," Pacific Historical Review, forthcoming; auth, "The Nationalistic Root and Nature of the Nationalist Reconstruction Policy," in An Examination of Chinese Nationalism from the Past to the Present, Greenwood Pub, forthcoming; auth, "Chinese Nationalism in the Age of Globalization," in Collaboration and Confrontation: Chinese Society and Nationalism, Greenwood Publishing, forthcoming; rev, of "America's Wars in Asia: A Cultural Approach to History and Memory," by Philip West, Education About Asia, forthcoming; auth, "Cold War attitudes poison US foreign relations," Daily Local News, Dec 98; auth, "Cold War over, mentality remains," Joplin Globe, Dec 98; auth, "Cold War Mentality," Daily Messenger, New York, Dec 98; rev, of "Heterodox Thoughts during the Cultural Revolution," by Song, Yongyi, Chinese Culture, 98. **CONTACT ADDRESS** Dept Hist, Susquehanna Univ, Selinsgrove, PA 17870-1002. **EMAIL** wei@roo.susqu.edu

WEI, WILLIAM
PERSONAL Born 01/18/1948, Dinghai, China, m, 1 child **DISCIPLINE** HISTORY **EDUCATION** Marquette Univ, BA, 69; Univ Mich, MA, 71; PhD, 78. **CAREER** Prof and director of the Sewall Acad Prog. **HONORS AND AWARDS** Boulder Fac Assembly Awd for Excellence in Service, 98. **RESEARCH** Modern Chinese history and Asian American history. **SELECTED PUBLICATIONS** Auth, Counterrevolution in China: The Nationalists in Jiangxi During the Soviet Period, Mich Studies on China Series, Univ Mich, 85; auth, The Asian American Movement, Asian American History and Culture Series, Temple Univ, 93; auth, "1990's China: The Winds of Change," in The People of Russia and China: Facing the Dawn of a New Century, ed. Max J. Okenfuss and Ann Blaisdell Rothery (St. Louis, Oasis Institute, 99); auth, "The Politicization and Nationalization of Hong Kong During the Asian Financial Crisis," International Journal 55(1) (99-00): 45-56. **CONTACT ADDRESS** Hist Dept, Univ of Colorado, Boulder, Boulder, CO 80309. **EMAIL** william.wei@colorado.edu

WEIGEL, RICHARD DAVID
PERSONAL Born 02/01/1945, Teaneck, NJ, m, 1968, 1 child **DISCIPLINE** HISTORY, CLASSICS **EDUCATION** Dickinson Col, BA, 66; Univ Del, MA, 68, PhD, 73. **CAREER** From instr to asst prof hist, Univ Del, 72-76; asst prof, Univ RI, 75; from Asst Prof to Assoc Prof, 76-84, Prof Hist, Western Ky Univ, 84-, Dept Head Hist, 98-. **HONORS AND AWARDS** Nat Endowment for Humanities summer sem grants, 77 & 80; Vis Schol, Wolfson Col, Oxford Univ, 93-; Am Acad in rome Advisory Coun, 94-. **MEMBERSHIPS** Am Philol Asn; Am

Numismatic Soc; Assn Ancient Historians; Soc Prom Roman Studies; Royal Numismatic Soc. **RESEARCH** Roman Republic; ancient numismatics; Roman religion. **SELECTED PUBLICATIONS** Coauth, Peace in the Ancient World, McFarland, 81; auth, Lepidus: The Tarnished Triumvir, Routledge, 92; Roman History in the Age of Enlightenment: The Dassier Medals, Revue Numismatique 36, 95; Roman Coins: An Iconographical Approach, Annali dell Istituto di Numismatica 42, 95; auth, "Roman Republican Generals and the Vowing of Temples," Classica et Medievalia 49 (98); auth, "The Anonymous Quadrantes Reconsidered," Annotazioni Numismatich Suppl 11 (98); author of numerous other articles. **CONTACT ADDRESS** Dept of Hist, Western Kentucky Univ, 1 Big Red Way, Bowling Green, KY 42101-3576. **EMAIL** Richard.Weigel@wku.edu

WEIGLEY, RUSSELL F.

PERSONAL Born 07/02/1930, Reading, PA, m, 1963, 2 children **DISCIPLINE** HISTORY **EDUCATION** Albright Col, BA, 52; Univ of Pa, MA, 53; PhD, 56. **CAREER** Inst, Univ of Pa, 56-58; asst prof to assoc prof, Drexel Inst of Tech, 58-62; assoc prof to dist prof emer, Temple Univ, 62- ; vis prof, Dartmouth Col, 67-68; vis prof of Mil Hist, U S Army War Col, 73-74. **HONORS AND AWARDS** John Simon Guggenheim Mem Found Fell, 68-69; Pres, AMI, 75-78; Pres Penn AHA, 76-77; Awd Dist Wk, Non-fict Phil Author, 83; Samuel Elliot Morison Awd, AMI, 89; Dist Bk Awd, Non-Am Mil Hist, SMH, 92; George C Marshall Memor Found Lectr, SMH, 95. **MEMBERSHIPS** APS, SAH, AHA, OAH, SHA, SMH, PHA, HSPACW. **RESEARCH** US and European military history, World War II military history. **SELECTED PUBLICATIONS** Auth, Quartermaster General of the Union Army: A Biography of M C Meigs, 59; auth, Towards an American Army: Military Thought from Washington to Marshall, 62; auth, History of the United States Army, 67; auth, The Partisan War: The South Carolina Campaign of 1780-1782, 70; auth, The American Way of War: A History of United States Military Strategy and Policy, 73; auth, Eisenhower's Lieutenants: The Campaign of France and Germany, 1944-1945, 81; ed, Philadelphia: A 300 Year History, 82; auth, The Age of Battles: The Quest for Decisive Warfare from Breitenfeld to Waterloo, 91; auth, A Great Civil War: A Military and Political History, 1861-1865, 00. **CONTACT ADDRESS** Dept of Hist, Temple Univ, 1115 West Berks St, Gladfelter Rm 913, Philadelphia, PA 19122-6006.

WEIKART, RICHARD

PERSONAL Born 07/21/1958, MA, m, 1983, 5 children **DISCIPLINE** HISTORY **EDUCATION** Tex Christian Univ, BA, 80; MA, 89; Univ Iowa, PhD, 94. **CAREER** From asst prof to assoc prof, Calif State Univ at Stanislaus, 94-. **HONORS AND AWARDS** Fel, Univ of Iowa, 89-92; Fulbright Fel, 92-93; Forkosch Prize for best article, 93; Forum for Hist of Human Sci Dissertation Prize, 96. **MEMBERSHIPS** Am Hist Asn, Ger Studies Asn, Hist of Sci Soc. **RESEARCH** Social Darwinism (especially in Germany), Eugenics, Biomedical Ethics. **SELECTED PUBLICATIONS** Auth, "The Origins of Social Darwinism in Germany," J of the Hist of Ideas 54 (93): 469-488; auth, The Myth of Dietrich Bonhoeffer, 97; auth, Socialist Darwinism: Evolution in German Socialist Thought from Marx to Bernstein, 99. **CONTACT ADDRESS** Dept Hist, California State Univ, Stanislaus, 801 W Monte Vista Ave, Turlock, CA 95382-0256.

WEIKEL, ANN

PERSONAL Born 12/26/1935, New York, NY **DISCIPLINE** ENGLISH & MEDIEVAL HISTORY **EDUCATION** Mt Holyoke Col, AB, 57; Yale Univ, MA, 59, PhD(hist), 66. **CAREER** Instr hist, Mt Holyoke Col, 63-64; from instr to asst prof, Knox Col, 64-67; asst prof, 67-70, assoc prof, 70-79, Prof Hist, Portland State Univ, 80-. **MEMBERSHIPS** Mediaeval Acad Am; Conf Brit Studies. **RESEARCH** Tudor England; Med-Tudor government and society. **SELECTED PUBLICATIONS** Auth, The Mariau Council Revisited, The Med-Tudor Politie 1540-1560, Macmillan, 80. **CONTACT ADDRESS** Dept of Hist, Portland State Univ, PO Box 751, Portland, OR 97207-0751.

WEIL, MARK S.

PERSONAL Born 05/26/1939, St. Louis, MO, m, 2 children **DISCIPLINE** NORTHERN RENAISSANCE ART, RENAISSANCE ARCHITECTURE **EDUCATION** Colgate Univ, AB, Washington Univ, MA; Ph D, Columbia Univ. **CAREER** Asst Prof, Univ of Missouri, 68, Asst Prof, Washington Univ St Louis, 68-74, Assoc Prof, Washington Univ St Louis, 74, Dept Chm, Washington Univ St Louis, 82-88, Prof, Washington Univ St Louis, 85, Dept Chm, Washington Univ, 95-99, Prof Collab Arts, Washington Univ St Louis, 98, Dir, Washington Univ Gallery of art, 98-, Dir, Washington Univ Visual Arts and Design Center, 99. **HONORS AND AWARDS** Fellow, Nat Endowment for the Humanities, 72; Research Fellow, American Academy in Rome, 85. **MEMBERSHIPS** CAA, SAH. **RESEARCH** Italian Baroque Sculpture, Renaissance Prints. **SELECTED PUBLICATIONS** Auth, "The Devotion of the Forty Hours and Roman Baroque Illusions," Journal of the Warburg and Courtald Institutes, 37 (74), 218-48; co-auth, "The Pamphili Chapel in Sant 'Agostino," Roemisches Jahrbuch fuer Kunstgeschichte 15, (74), 183-98; auth, "IL Sacro Bosco di Bomarzo: A Literary and Antiquarian Interpretation," Journal of Garden Hist 4, (84) 1-94; auth, "Un fauno molestato da cupidi: forma e significato," Gian Lorenzo Bernini e le arti visive, (Rome , 87), 73-84; auth, "A Bronzetto of Scipione Borghese by Bernini," Source, Notes in the Hist of Art 8-9, (89), 34-39; auth, "The Relationship of the Cornaro Chapel to Mystery Plays and Italian Court Theatre," Art and Pagentry in the Renaissance and Barogue, (Penn State Univ, Vol 6, 90), 159-178; auth, "Art and Pageantry in the Renaissance and Baroque," Papers in Art Hist from the Pennsylvania State Univ, vol 6, (90), 458-486; auth, "Love, Monsters, Movement and Machines: The Marvelous," (91), 159-78; auth, "Love , Monsters, Movement and Machines: The Marvelous in Theaters, Festivals and Gardens," Hood Museum of Art, Dartmouth Col, (91), 159-178; auth, "L'orazione delle Quarant' Ore come guida allo sviluppo del linguaggio barocco," Centri e periferie del barocco, (Rome, 92), 675-694; auth, " Men, Women , and God: German Renaissance Prints," St Louis exhibition catalog, (St Louis Art Museum, 97), ed, "Conversation Pieces," Intro to a Catalog of recent work by Michael Eastman, 97; auth, "Bozzetti for the Ponte Sant Angelo: a New Look," Bulletin of the Harvard Univ art Museums, 99. **CONTACT ADDRESS** Gallery of Art, Washington Univ, 1 Brookings Dr., PO Box 1189, Saint Louis, MO 63130. **EMAIL** mark_weil@aismail.wustl.edu

WEINBERG, GERHARD LUDWIG

PERSONAL Born 01/01/1928, Hanover, Germany, 1 child **DISCIPLINE** HISTORY **EDUCATION** State Univ NYork Albany, BA, 48; Univ Chicago, MA, 49, PhD, 51. **CAREER** Res asst hist, Univ Chicago, 51; res analyst, Columbia Univ, 51-54; lectr mod hist, Univ Chicago, 54-55; vis lectr hist, Univ Ky, 55-56, asst prof, 57-59; dir, Am Hist Asn Microfilm Proj, Alexandria, Va, 56-57; from assoc prof to prof hist, Univ Mich, Ann Arbor, 59-74; Kenan Prof Hist, Univ NC, 74-99, Consult war doc, AHA, 57-60; Rockefeller Found Int Rel Prog & Soc Sci Res Coun fel, 62-63; Am Coun Learned Soc fel, 65-66; Guggenheim fel, 71-72; Nat Endowment for Humanities fel, 78-79; vpres res, AHA, 82-84. **HONORS AND AWARDS** George Louis Beer Prize, AHA, 71 & 94; Halverson Prize, Western Asn Ger Studies, 81; Dr Hum Letters, Univ Albany, 89; **MEMBERSHIPS** AHA; Conf Group Cent Europ Hist; Am Comt Hist of Second World War; Coord Comt Women Hist Profession; Am Acad Arts & Sci; German Stud Asn. **RESEARCH** Modern German history; modern diplomatic history; World Wars I and II. **SELECTED PUBLICATIONS** Auth, Guide to Captured German Documents, Maxwell AFB, 52; Germany and the Soviet Union, Brill, 54; ed, Hitlers Zweites Buch, Deut Verlags-Anstalt, 61; coauth, Soviet Partisans in World War II, Univ Wis, 64; auth, The Foreign Policy of Hitler's Germany, 1933-36, Univ Chicago, 70; The Foreign Policy of Hitler's Germany, 1937-39, Univ Chicago, 80; World in the Balance: Behind the Scenes of World War II, New England Univ Press, 81; A World at Arms: A Global History of World War II, Cambridge Univ Press, 94; Germany Hitler, and World War II, Cambridge Univ Press, 95. **CONTACT ADDRESS** 1416 Mt. Willing Rd., Efland, NC 27243. **EMAIL** gweinbe@email.unc.edu

WEINBERGER, STEPHEN

PERSONAL Born 09/03/1942, Boston, MA, m, 1966, 2 children **DISCIPLINE** MEDIEVAL HISTORY **EDUCATION** Northeastern Univ, BA, 65; Univ Wis-Madison, MA 66, PhD, 69. **CAREER** Asst prof, 69-73, assoc prof hist, Dickinson Col, 73-83, prof hist, 83, dir, Ctr int Studies, Bologna, Italy, 73-75. **MEMBERSHIPS** Mediaeval Acad Am; AHA. **RESEARCH** Medieval soc and economic hist; medieval demography. **SELECTED PUBLICATIONS** Auth, Peasant households in Provence, ca 800-1100, Speculum; Les conflicts entre clercs et laics dans la Provence du XIe siecle, Annales du Midi, 92:269-279; Nobles et noblesse dans la Provence medievale (ca 850-1100), Annales: econ, soc, civilisations, 81; Aristocratic families and social stability in eleventh century Provence, J Medieval Hist; Law courts, justice, and social responsibility in Medieval Provence, Revue Hist. **CONTACT ADDRESS** Dept of Hist, Dickinson Col, 1 Dickinson Col, Carlisle, PA 17013-2897.

WEINER, LYNN

PERSONAL Born 02/08/1951, Detroit, MI, m, 1974, 2 children **DISCIPLINE** HISTORY; AMERICAN STUDIES **EDUCATION** Univ Mich, AB, 72; Boston Univ, MA, 75, PhD, 81. **CAREER** Vis Prof, Northwestern Univ, 90-91; Prof Hist, Roosevelt Univ, 91-, Assoc Dean, Col Arts & Sci, 93-. **HONORS AND AWARDS** NEH Fel, 89; Binkley-Stephansen Awd, Org Am Hist, 95. **MEMBERSHIPS** Am Hist Asn; Org Am Hist; Am Studies Asn; Coord Comt Women Hist. **RESEARCH** U.S. social history; women's history; history of the family. **SELECTED PUBLICATIONS** Auth, Our Sister's Keepers': The Minneapolis Woman's Christian Association & Housing for Working Women, Minn Hist, Spring 79; Sisters of the Road: Women Transients & Tramps, Walking to Work: Tramps in America, 1790-1935, Nebraska, 84; From Working Girl to Working Mother: The Female Labor Force in the United States, 1920-1980, NC, 85; Women and Work, Reclaiming Our Past: Landmarks of Women's History, Ind, 92; Reconstructing Motherhood: The La Leche League in Postwar America, J Am Hist, 3/94; There's a Great Big Beautiful Tommorrow: Historic Memory and Gender in Walt Disney's Carousel of Progress, J Am Cult, Spring 97; Domestic Constraints, Voices of Women's Historians, Ind (99); author of numerous encyclopedia entries, book reviews, and other publications. **CONTACT ADDRESS** History Dept, Roosevelt Univ, 430 S. Michigan Ave., Chicago, IL 60605. **EMAIL** lweiner@roosevelt.edu

WEINGARTNER, JAMES JOSEPH

PERSONAL Born 08/21/1940, Bethlehem, Pa, m, 1966, 2 children **DISCIPLINE** HISTORY **EDUCATION** Muhlenberg Col, AB, 62; Univ Wis, MS, 63, PhD(hist), 67. **CAREER** Proj asst, Univ Wis, 64-65, teaching asst, 65-67; asst prof hist, Univ NH, 67-69; from asst prof to assoc prof, 69-77, Prof Hist, Southern Ill Univ, Edwardsville, 77- **HONORS AND AWARDS** Air Force Hist Res Agen Res Assoc **MEMBERSHIPS** AHA; Conf Group Cent Europ Hist; Am Comt Hist 2nd World War. **RESEARCH** Twentieth century Germany; recent military history. **SELECTED PUBLICATIONS** Auth, "War Against Subhumans," Historian, (58); auth, "Unconventional Allies: Willis Everett and Joachim Peiper," Historian, (62); auth, Sepp Dietrich, Heinrich Himmler, and the Leibstandarte SS Adolf Hitler, Cent Europ Hist, 9/68; Hitler's Guard: The Story of the Leibstandarte SS Adolf Hitler, 1933-1945, Southern Ill Univ, 74; Crossroads of Death: The Story of the Malmedy Massacre and Trial, Univ Calif, 78; auth, Law and Justics in the Nazi SS: The Case of Konrad Morgen, Cent Europ Hist, 83; auth, Massacre at Biscari: Patton and an American War Crime, Historian, 89; auth, Otto Skorzeny and the Laws of War, Jou of Milit Hist, 91; auth, Trophies of War: US Troops and the Mutiliation of Japanese War Dead, Pacific Hist Rev, 92; auth, Crusade: Willis M. Everett and the Malmedy Massacre, New York Univ Press, 00. **CONTACT ADDRESS** Dept of Hist, So Illinois Univ, Edwardsville, 6 Hairpin Dr, Edwardsville, IL 62026-0001. **EMAIL** jweinga@siue.edu

WEINRIB, ERNEST JOSEPH

PERSONAL Born 04/08/1943, Toronto, ON, Canada, m, 1970 **DISCIPLINE** LAW, ANCIENT HISTORY **EDUCATION** Univ Toronto, BA, 65, LLB, 72; Harvard Univ, PhD(classics), 68. **CAREER** Asst prof classics, 68-70, asst prof law, 72-75, assoc prof, 75-81, Prof Law, Fac Law, Univ Toronto, 81-. **HONORS AND AWARDS** Killam Res Fel, 86-88; Connaught Sr Fel, 90-91; Fel of the Royal Soc of Canada. **MEMBERSHIPS** Class Can Asn; Asn Can Law Teachers. **RESEARCH** Tort law; Roman law; jurisprudence; legal theory. **SELECTED PUBLICATIONS** Auth, Judiciary law of M Livius Drusus, Historia, 70; Obnuntiatio: two problems, Z Savigny-Stuftung, 70; A step forward in factual causation, Mod Law Rev, 75; The fiduciary obligation, 75 & Illegality as a tort defense, 76, Univ Toronto; Contribution in a contractual setting, Can Bar Rev, 76; Utilitarianism, Economics, and Legal Theory, Univ Toronto Law J, 80; The Case for a Duty to Rescue, Yale Law J, 80; Obedience to the Law in Plato's Crito, Am J Jurisprudence, 82; The Jurisprudence Of Legal Formalism, Harvard Journal Of Law And Public Policy, Vol 0016, 1993; auth, The Idea of Private Law, Harvard Univ Press, 95. **CONTACT ADDRESS** Fac of Law, Univ of Toronto, Toronto, ON, Canada M5S 1A1. **EMAIL** e.weinrib@utoronto.ca

WEINSTEIN, FRED

PERSONAL Born 10/19/1931, Brooklyn, NY, m, 1962, 5 children **DISCIPLINE** MODERN HISTORY **EDUCATION** Brooklyn Col, BA, 54, MA, 57; Univ Calif, Berkeley, PhD, 62. **CAREER** Instr hist, Univ Calif, Berkeley, 63-65; asst prof Russ hist, Univ Ore, 65-66; asst prof humanities & Russ hist, San Jose State Col, 66-69; assoc prof, State Univ of New York, 69-73, Prof Hist, State Univ Ny Stony Brook, 73-, Fel, Inst Advan Study, 70-71; Bd of Advisors Psy Review, 74-00; Prof Emer, Suny Stony Brook, 00-. **MEMBERSHIPS** AHA; Group for Uses of Psychol in Hist. **SELECTED PUBLICATIONS** Coauth, The Wish to be Free, Univ Calif, Berkeley, 69; Psychoanalytic Sociology, Johns Hopkins Univ, 73; auth, The Dynamics of Nazism, Acad Press, 80; auth, History and Theory After the Fall, Univ of Chicago, 90; The Powers Of The Past - Reflections On The Crisis And The Promise Of History - Kaye,Hj, American Historical Review, Vol 0098, 1993; Mythical Past, Elusive Future - History And Society In An Anxious Age - Furedi,F, American Historical Review, Vol 0099, 1994; The Fin-De-Siecle Culture Of Adolescence - Neubauer,J, Journal Of Interdisciplinary History, Vol 0024, 1994; Freud Russia - National Identity In The Evolution Of Psychoanalysis - Rice,Jl, Russian Review, Vol 0053, 1994; Psychohistory And The Crisis Of The Social-Sciences, History And Theory, Vol 0034, 1995; Fantasy And Reality In History - Loewenberg,P, American Historical Review, Vol 0102, 1997; Freud Pscychoanalysis, Social Theory, SUNY Press, 01. **CONTACT ADDRESS** Dept of Hist, SUNY, Stony Brook, Stony Brook, NY 11790. **EMAIL** fweinstein@ms.cc.sunysb.edu

WEINSTEIN, STANLEY

PERSONAL Born 11/13/1929, Brooklyn, NY, m, 1952, 1 child **DISCIPLINE** BUDDHIST & EAST ASIAN STUDIES **EDUCATION** Komazawa Univ, Japan, BA, 58; Univ Tokyo, MA, 60; Harvard Univ, PhD(Far Eastern lang), 66. **CAREER** Lectr Far Eastern Buddhism, Univ London, 62-68; assoc prof Buddhist studies, 68-74, Prof Buddhist Studies, Yale Univ, 74-; NEH sr fel, 74-75. **MEMBERSHIPS** Am Orient Soc; Asn Asian Studies **RESEARCH** Buddhist studies; East Asian languages and history. **SELECTED PUBLICATIONS** Auth, The Kanjin kakumusho: A Compendium of the Teachings of the

Hosso Sect, Komazawa Daigaku Kenkyu Kiyo, 60; contr ed, Japanese-English Buddhist Dictionary, Tokyo, 65; Buddhism, In: The Cambridge Encyclopedia of China, Cambridge Univ Press, 82; 38 medium length and 82 short articles In: The Encylcopedia of Japan, Kodansha, Tokyo, 82; Alayavijnana and Buddhism, Schools of: Chinese Buddhism, In: The Encyclopedia of Religion, Macmillang Publ Co, 87; Buddhism Under the T'ang, Cambridge Univ Press, 87; Nihon Bukkyo to ichi Amerikajin Bukkyo kenkyuka no setten: Todai no Bukkyo no hakkan ni chinande, Komazawa Daigaku Bukkyo gakubu ronshu, 88; tangdae Pulgyo chongp'a hyongsong e issoso hwangsil ui huwon (in Korean)(Imperial Patronage in the Formation of the Tang Buddhist Schools), Chonggyo wa munhwa (Relgion and Culture), 12/95; Rennyo shiso ni okeru renzokusei to henka (Continuity and Change the Thought of Rennyo Shonin [1415-1499], In: rennyo no sekai (The World of Rennyo), Bun'eido, Kyoto, Japan, 98; auth, "Aristocratic Buddhism," in The Cambridge History of Japan, vol. 2, ed. Donald H. Shively and William H. McCollough (Cambridge Univ Press, 99); transl, Tangdai fojiao, Foguang Wenhua Shiye (Taipei, Japan), 99. **CONTACT ADDRESS** Dept of Relig Studies, Yale Univ, PO Box 208287, New Haven, CT 06520-8287. **EMAIL** stanley.weinstein@yale.edu

WEIR, DAVID A.
PERSONAL Born 07/24/1958, Bronxville, NY, m, 1989, 3 children **DISCIPLINE** HISTORY **EDUCATION** Haverford, BA, 80; Princeton, MA, 83, PhD, 92; St. Andrews, PhD, 84. **CAREER** Asst prof of History, 87-94; assoc prof of history, Centenary Col, 94-00; elected chair, Dept of Soc and Behav Scis, 94-95. **HONORS AND AWARDS** Bronxville Public Schs Parent-Teacher Asn, Freshman Year Scholar, 76-77, St. Andrew's Soc of the State of Nyork, Grad Fel for study in Scotland, 80-81; Princeton Univ, Univ Fel, 81-85; Am Soc of Church Hist, Frank S. and Elizabeth D. Brewer Prize, 83; Univ of St Andrews, Samuel Rutherford Distinguished Thesis Award, 84; Am Antiquarian Soc, Frances Hiatt Fel, 84; Woodrow Wilson Nat Fel Found, Charlotte W. Newcombe Doctoral Dissertation Fel, 84-85; Ctr of Theol Inquiry, Post-Doctoral Fel, 85-87; Fac Grant for developing skills in comput work using the Res Libraries Infor Network, Centenary Col Alumni Asn; Fac grants, Centenary Col Fac Res and Dev Fund. **MEMBERSHIPS** Am Acad of Relig; Am Hist Asn; Am Soc of Church Hist; Am Studies Asn; Calvin Studies Soc; Columbia Univ Sem on Early Am Hist and Cult; Conf on Faith and Hist; Inst of Early Am Hist and Cult; Organization of Am Hist; Presbyterian Hist Soc; Sixteenth Century Studies Soc; Soc for Values in Higher Educ. **SELECTED PUBLICATIONS** Auth, "The Relevance of the Reformation for Reformed Presbyterians Today," Covenanter Witness, 102, (86): 4-6; auth, "A Puritan Christmas," Eternity Magazine, 37, (86): 20-1; auth, The Origins of the Federal Theology in Sixteenth-Century Reformation Thought, Oxford: The Clarendon Press of the Oxford Univ Press, 90; auth, "Dictionary of Christianity in America, Downers Grove, Ill: InterVarsity Press, 90; auth, "Here Lies History Revealed,' Hackettstown, New Jersey, (93): 4; **CONTACT ADDRESS** Dept of Hist and Political Science, Nyack Col, 1 S Blvd, Nyack, NY 10960. **EMAIL** weir@nyack.edu

WEIR, ROBERT MCCOLLOCH
PERSONAL Born 08/26/1933, Philadelphia, PA, m, 1955, 2 children **DISCIPLINE** MODERN HISTORY **EDUCATION** Pa State Univ, BA, 58; Western Reserve Univ, MA, 61, PhD(hist), 66. **CAREER** From instr to asst prof hist, Univ Houston, 65-67; from asst prof to assoc prof, 67-78, Prof Hist, Univ, SC, 78-, Nat Endowment for Humanities fel, 67-68. **HONORS AND AWARDS** Annual Essay Awds, William & Mary Quart, 69 & Southeastern Am Soc Eighteenth Century Studies, 80. **MEMBERSHIPS** Am Antiquarian Soc; AHA; Orgn Am Historians; Southern Hist Asn. **RESEARCH** American colonial and revolutionary history. **SELECTED PUBLICATIONS** Auth, An interpretation of pre-revolutionary South Carolina politics, 69; auth, William & Mary Quart, The South Carolinian as extremist, S Atlantic Quart, winter 75; ed, The Letters of Freeman, Etc., by William Henry Drayton & others, Univ SC Press, 77; auth, Portrait of a hero, Am Heritage, 76; auth, The role of the newspaper press in the southern colonies on the eve of the revolution: An interpretation, In: The Press and the American Revolution, Am Antiquarian Soc, 80; auth, Colonial South Carolina: A History, KTO, Ltd., 83, Univ SC Press, 97; auth, The Last of American Freemen, Studies in the Political Culture of the Colonial and Revolutionary South, Mercer Univ Press, 86; auth, South Carolina: Slavery and the structure of the union, In: Ratifying the Constitution, Univ Press Kansas, 89; auth, Shaftesbury's Darling: The Carolinas in the seventeenth century, In: Oxford History of the British Empire, Oxford Univ Press, 98. **CONTACT ADDRESS** Dept of Hist, Univ of So Carolina, Columbia, Columbia, SC 29208. **EMAIL** weir@gwm.sc.edu

WEISBERG, DAVID B.
PERSONAL Born 11/15/1938, New York, NY, M, 1958, 3 children **DISCIPLINE** ASSYRIOLOGY **EDUCATION** Columbia Col, AB, 60; Jewish Theol Sem Am, BHL, 60; Yale Univ, PhD, 65. **CAREER** Res Assoc Assyriol, Orient Inst, Univ Chicago, 65-67; from asst prof to assoc prof, 67-71, Prof Bible & Semitic Lang, Hebrew Union Col, Ohio, 71- **HONORS AND AWARDS** Guggenheim Fel, 98-99; Rockerfeller/Bellagio, Fel, 96. **MEMBERSHIPS** Am Orient Soc; Soc Bibl Lit, MLA, AALS, Law & Humanities Institute. **RESEARCH** Bible; Assyriology. **SELECTED PUBLICATIONS** Auth, Guild Structure and Political Allegiance in Early Achaemenid Mesopotamia, Near Eastern Res, No. 1, Yale Univ, 67; A neo-Babylonian temple report, J Am Orient Soc, 67; Rare accents of the 21 books, Jewish Quart Rev, 67; Texts from the Time of Nebuchadnezzar, Yale, Vol 17, 80; auth, When Lawyers Write, Little Brown, 87; auth, The Failure of the Word, Yale U Press, 84; auth, Poethics, Columbia U Press, 92; Uruk - Late Babylonian Economic Texts From The Eanna Archive, Pt 1, Texts Of Varied Contents - German And Akkadian - Gehlken,E, Journal Of Near Eastern Studies, Vol 0055, 96; auth, Vichy Law and the Holocaust in france, NYU Press, 96. **CONTACT ADDRESS** Dept of Bible & Semitic Lang, Hebrew Union Col-Jewish Inst of Religion, Ohio, Cincinnati, OH 45220.

WEISBERGER, BERNARD A.
PERSONAL Born 08/15/1922, Hudson, NY, 3 children **DISCIPLINE** UNITED STATES HISTORY **EDUCATION** Columbia Univ, AB, 43; Univ Chicago, MA, 47, PhD(US hist), 50. **CAREER** Asst prof hist, Antioch Col, 52-54 & Wayne State Univ, 54-59; assoc prof, Univ Chicago, 59-63; prof, Univ Rochester, 63-68; assoc ed, 70-72, Contrib Ed, Am Heritage Co, New York, 72-; Res & Writing, 79-, Am Coun Learned Soc fel, 59-60; vis prof hist, Vassar Col, 72-79. **HONORS AND AWARDS** Ramsdell Prize, Southern Hist Asn, 62. **RESEARCH** American journalism; United States, 1877-1917. **SELECTED PUBLICATIONS** Auth, The American heritage history of the American people, Am Heritage, 71; Pathways to the Present, Harper, 76; The Dream-Maker: William C Durant, Founder of General Motors, Little, Brown, 79; Speaking Of Speakers + Some Former Great Speakers-Of-The-House, American Heritage, Vol 0046, 1995; The Fbi Unbound - How The Bureau Got Those Restrictions That So Many People Today Want To See Abolished, American Heritage, Vol 0046, 1995; Genes, Brains, And Bunk + The Dillingham-Commission Report Findings Of 1910, American Heritage, Vol 0046, 1995; What Makes A Marriage + The Courts Are Taking Up The Question Of What Can And Cannot Constitute Legal Wedlock, American Heritage, Vol 0047, 1996; Election In Silver And Gold + The Bryan,William,Jennings Mckinley,William Electoral Contest Of 1896, American Heritage, Vol 0047, 1996; The Frozen Republic - How The Constitution Is Paralyzing Democracy - Lazare,D, American Heritage, Vol 0047, 1996; Big-Bang At Bikini + Worries Surrounded These Early Atomic-Bomb Tests, American Heritage, Vol 0047, 1996; The Mckinley Era Mega-Merger - Our Century Ends As It Began, With Corporations Rushing Into Wedlock, American Heritage, Vol 0047, 1996; Old Years New Years + History Of Some New Years Traditions In The United-States, American Heritage, Vol 0047, 1996; The Amateur Diplomats + Morrow,Dwight, Daniels,Josephus, And Us-Mexican Relations, 1927-1941, American Heritage, Vol 0048, 1997; Righteous Fists + The Boxer Rebellion And The Light It Casts On America Long, Complex Relationship With China, American Heritage, Vol 0048, 1997; The Kids Judge + Juvenile-Delinquency Corrections History, American Heritage, Vol 0048, 1997; What Made The Government Grow + Some Interesting Facts Concerning American History, American Heritage, Vol 0048, 1997; Terms Of No Endearment + The Usually Difficult 2nd Terms Of 2-Term American Presidents, American Heritage, Vol 0048, 1997; The Bank War + Jackson,Andrew And The 2nd-Bank-Of-The-United-States, American Heritage, Vol 0048, 1997. **CONTACT ADDRESS** 55 W 55th St, New York, NY 10019.

WEISBERGER, WILLIAM
PERSONAL Born 06/25/1942, Steubenville, OH, m, 1968, 1 child **DISCIPLINE** EUROPEAN INTELLECTUAL HISTORY **EDUCATION** Georgetown Univ, BSFS, 64; Duquesne Univ, Masters, 67; Univ Pittsburgh, PhD(Europ cult hist), 80. **CAREER** Assoc Prof Europ Hist & Sociol, Butler Community Col, 69-. **MEMBERSHIPS** Am Hist Asn. **RESEARCH** The Enlightenment and Freemasonry in London, Paris, Prague and Vienna. **SELECTED PUBLICATIONS** Auth, Enlightened Men, Standard Press, 67; Studies in Central European Freemasonry, Iowa Res Lodge, 73; The World of John T Desaguliers, Pfeifer Press, 80. **CONTACT ADDRESS** 107 Crosslands Rd, Butler, PA 16001.

WEISBORD, ROBERT G.
DISCIPLINE AFRICAN-AMERICAN HISTORY AND THE HISTORY OF THE EUROPEAN HOLOCAUST **EDUCATION** NYork Univ, PhD, 66. **CAREER** Dept Hist, Univ of RI **HONORS AND AWARDS** URI Tchg & Res Excellence awd(s). **SELECTED PUBLICATIONS** Publ on, Jewish-Black relations; Pan-Africanism & the Papacy's polit position during WWII. **CONTACT ADDRESS** Dept of Hist, Univ of Rhode Island, 8 Ranger Rd, Ste. 1, Kingston, RI 02881-0807.

WEISBROT, ROBERT S.
PERSONAL Born New York, NY, m, 1995 **DISCIPLINE** HISTORY **EDUCATION** Harvard Univ, PhD 80, MA 75; Princeton Univ grad fell 73-74; BrandeisUniv BA 73. **CAREER** Colby Col, prof 80-, Christian A Johnson Dist Prof, 93. **RESEARCH** Civil rights, for policy, Am polit reform. **SELECTED PUBLICATIONS** Freedom Bound: A History of America's Civil Rights Movement, W W Norton, 90, reprint, Penguin, 91; Father Divine and the Struggle for Racial Equality, Univ IL Press, 83, reprint Beacon Press, 84; The Jews of Argentina: From the Inquisition to Peron, Jewish Pub Soc, 79; Hercules: The Legendary Journeys: The Official Companion, NY, Doubleday, 98; Xena: Warrior Princess: The Official Guide to the Xenaverse, NY, Doubleday, 98; Cry for Them: The Roots of Argentie Anti-Semitism, The New Repub, 94. **CONTACT ADDRESS** Dept of Hist, Colby Col, Waterville, ME 04901. **EMAIL** rsweisbr@colby.edu

WEISS, ELLEN B.
DISCIPLINE HISTORY OF ARCHITECTURE **EDUCATION** Univ Ill, PhD, 84. **CAREER** Prof, Tulane Univ, 87- . **MEMBERSHIPS** Soc of Archit Hist; Vernacular Archit Forum. **RESEARCH** American architecture and urbanism; camp meetings; African-American architects. **SELECTED PUBLICATIONS** Auth, North Kingstown, R I , 79; auth, An Annotated Bibliography on African American Architects and Builders, 93; auth, City in the Woods: The Life and Design of an American Camp Meeting, 98. **CONTACT ADDRESS** School of Architecture, Tulane Univ, New Orleans, LA 70118. **EMAIL** eweiss@mailhost.tcs.tulane.edu

WEISS, JAMES MICHAEL
PERSONAL Born 12/02/1946, Chicago, IL **DISCIPLINE** HISTORICAL & CONTEMPORARY SPIRITUALITY; RENAISSANCE & REFORMATION HISTORY **EDUCATION** Loyola Univ, Chicago, BA, 67; Univ Chicago, MA, 70, PhD(hist), 79. **CAREER** Instr, Ludwig- Maximilians Univ, Munich, 75-76; vis instr humanities, Univ Notre Dame, 78-79; assoc Prof Church Hist, Boston Col, 79-, Res fel, Inst Europ Geschichte, Mainz, WGer, 74-78. **HONORS AND AWARDS** Mellon Fel, Harvard Univ, 83-84; Fel, Nat Human Ctr, NCarolina, 86-87. **MEMBERSHIPS** Am Soc Church Hist; Am Soc Reformation Res; Cath Hist Soc; Renaissance Soc Am; 16th Century Conf; Episocal Soc for Ministry in Higher Educ. **RESEARCH** Hist of sprituality; hist of biographical writing. **SELECTED PUBLICATIONS** Auth, Ecclesiastes and Erasmus, Arch Reformationsgeshichte, 74; auth, The Six Lives of Rudolph Agricola: Forms & Functions of Humanis Biography, Humanistica Lovaniensia, 81; auth, Technique of Faint Praise: Johann Sturm's Life of Beatus Rhenanus, Biblioteque d'Humanisme et Renaissance, 81; auth, Erasmus at Luther's Funeral: Melanchthon's Eulogy of Luther, Sixteenth Century Studies, 85; auth, German Humanist Lives of the Saints, J of Med & Renaissance Studies, 85; auth, Luther & His Colleagues on the Lives of the Saints, Harvard Lib Bull, 85/86; auth, Melanchthon's Life of Erasmus, Acta Conventus Neo Latini, 90; auth, Varieties of Biography in the Italian Renaissance, in Cultural Visions, ed Benjamin Sax (Amsterdam, 00); auth, "Humanism," in Oxford Encycl of the Reformation, 96; auth, "Renaissance," in Oxford Encycl of the Reformation, 96. **CONTACT ADDRESS** Dept of Theol, Boston Col, Chestnut Hill, 140 Commonwealth Ave, Chestnut Hill, MA 02467. **EMAIL** james.weiss@bc.edu

WEISS, JOHN
PERSONAL Born 03/31/1927, Dearborn, MI, m, 1952, 2 children **DISCIPLINE** HISTORY **EDUCATION** Wayne State Univ, BA, 50; Columbia Univ, MA, 53, PhD, 58. **CAREER** Asst prof Europ hist, Wayne State Univ, 56-68; Prof Mod Europ Hist, Lehman Col, 69-. **RESEARCH** Modern European intellectual, political and social history; history of ideas and ideologies. **SELECTED PUBLICATIONS** Auth, Moses Hess: Utopian Socialist, Wayne State Univ, 60; The university as corporation, New Univ Thought, 9-10/62; Lorenz Von Stein and dialectical idealism, Int Rev Social Hist, 63; ed, The Origins of Modern Consciousness, Wayne State Univ, 65; auth, The Fascist Tradition, Radical Right Wing Extremism in Modern Europe, Harper, 67; Adam Smith and the philosophy of antihistory, In: The Uses of History, 68; ed, Nazis and Fascists in Europe, Quadrangle, 70; auth, Conservatism in Europe: Traditionalsim, Reaction and Counter-Revolution, Harcourt, Brace & Jovanovich, 77; The Readers Repentance - Women Preachers, Women-Writers, And 18th-Century Social Discourse - Krueger,Cl, Journal Of American History, Vol 0081, 1995. **CONTACT ADDRESS** Dept of Hist, Lehman Col, CUNY, Bronx, NY 10468.

WEISSBACH, LEE SHAI
PERSONAL Born 05/14/1947, Haifa, Israel, m, 1968, 2 children **DISCIPLINE** HISTORY **EDUCATION** Univ Cincinnati, BA, 69; Harvard Univ, AM, 70; PhD, 75. **CAREER** Lecturer, Boston Col, 75-76; res assoc, Harvard Univ, 76-78; lecturer, Regis Col, 77-78; asst prof, Univ Louisville, 78-84; vis scholar, Harvard Univ, 85-86; assoc prof to prof, Univ Louisville, 90-. **HONORS AND AWARDS** Dist Career of Service Awd, Louisville, 99; Sen Scholar Fel, 95-96; Rapoport Fel, 90-91. **MEMBERSHIPS** Am Jewish Hist Soc, Soc for Fr Hist Studies, Southern Jewish Hist Soc, Asn for Jewish Studies, Filson Club Hist Soc. **RESEARCH** Modern Jewish Hist, Modern French Hist. **SELECTED PUBLICATIONS** Auth, The Synagogues of Kentucky: Architecture and History, Univ Press: Lexington, 95; auth, Child Labor Reform in Nineteenth-Century France: Assuring the Future Harvest, LA State Univ Press: Baton Rouge, 89; auth, "Decline in an Age of Expansion: Disappearing Jewish Communities in the Era of Mass Migra-

tion: in American Jewish Archives 49, 99; auth, "Unexplored Terrain: The History of Small Jewish Communitis in Western Society: in Shofar 17, 98. **CONTACT ADDRESS** Dept History, Univ of Louisville, 2301 South 3rd St, Louisville, KY 40292-0001. **EMAIL** weissbach@louisville.edu

WEISSER, HENRY G.
PERSONAL Born 05/21/1935, New York, NY, d, 4 children **DISCIPLINE** BRITISH & IRISH HISTORY **EDUCATION** Hartwick Col, BA, 57; Columbia Univ, MA, 58, PhD, 65. **CAREER** Teacher, Clymer Cent Sch, 57, Robert Louis Stevenson Sch, 60-61 & East Brunswick High Sch, 61-62; instr hist, Luther Col, Iowa, 62-64; from asst prof to assoc prof, 65-74, prof hist,, Colo State Univ 74-, Fac Improve Comt grants, Colo State Univ, 67-68, 68-69 & 72; res assoc, Grad Sch Int Studies, Soc Sci Found, Univ Denver, 68-69; Am Philos Soc res grant, 72; vis fel, Univ Warwick, 80-81; Nat Endowment for Humanities fel, 80-81. **MEMBERSHIPS** AHA; Rocky Mountain Conf Brit Studies (pres, 79-80); Am Conf Irish Studies. **RESEARCH** British working class history, especially Chartism; Victorian social history. **SELECTED PUBLICATIONS** Auth, British Working Class Movements and Europe, 1815-1848, Manchester Univ, 75; auth, April 10: Cahllenge and Respone in England in 1848, Univ Pr of Am, 83; auth, Understadnign the U.K.: A Guide to British Culture, Politics, Geography, Economics and Hist, Hippocrene Books (New York), 87; auth, Hippocrene Companion Guide to Ireland: Travel, Culture, Society, Politics and History, Hippocrene Books (New York), 90, 2nd ed, 94; auth, Hippocrene USA Guide to Rocky Mountain States, Hippocrene Books (New York), 92; auth, Hippocrene Companion Guide to Britain: England, Scotland, Wales, Hippocrene Books (New York), 93; auth, Ireland: And Illustrated Hist, Hippocrene Books (New York), 99. **CONTACT ADDRESS** Dept of Hist, Colorado State Univ, Fort Collins, CO 80523-0001. **EMAIL** hweisser@vines.colostate.edu

WEISSMAN, NEIL BRUCE
PERSONAL Born 12/10/1948, Rome, NY, m, 1970, 1 child **DISCIPLINE** RUSSIAN & COMPARATIVE HISTORY **EDUCATION** Colgate Univ, BA, 70; Princeton Univ, MA, 72, PhD(hist), 76. **CAREER** Asst prof, 75-82, Assoc Prof Hist & Comp Civilizations, Dickinson Col, 82-. **MEMBERSHIPS** Am Asn Advan Slavic Studies; Int Soc Comp Study Civilizations. **RESEARCH** Russian history and government; comparative bureaucracy. **SELECTED PUBLICATIONS** Auth, Rural crime in Tsarist Russia: The question of hooliganism, Slavic Rev, 6/78; Reform in Tsarist Russia, Rutgers Univ Press, 81. **CONTACT ADDRESS** Dept of Hist, Dickinson Col, 1 Dickinson College, Carlisle, PA 17013-2897.

WELCH, ASHTON WESLEY
PERSONAL Born 06/17/1947, m, 1976 **DISCIPLINE** AFRICAN-AMERICAN STUDIES **EDUCATION** Univ of Hull, UK, 1966-67; Wilberforce Univ, BA, 1968; Univ of Wisconsin, Madison, certificate, 1971, MA, 1971; Univ of Birmingham, UK, PhD, 1979. **CAREER** Richmond College, UK, 87-88; Creighton Univ, coordinator of black studies, 75-, history chairman, 86-93, assoc prof, 75-. **HONORS AND AWARDS** Creighton Univ, Robert F Kennedy Awd, 1992; Creighton Univ, College of Arts and Sciences, Dean's Awd, 1993; AK-SAR-BEN, Nebraska Educator Awd, 1992. **MEMBERSHIPS** African Studies Assn, 1971-; Assn for the Study of Afro-Amer Life & Culture, 1973-; Natl Council on Black Studies, Committee on Ethics, 1976-; Natl Assn of Ethnic Studies, bd of dirs 1977-; Great Plains Black Museum, bd of dirs, 1975-88; Creighton Federal Credit Union, bd of dirs, 1986-. **SELECTED PUBLICATIONS** "The National Archives of the Ivory Coast," 1982; "Omaha: Positve Planning for Peaceful Integration," 1980; "The Making of an African-American Population: Omaha," 1993; "Emancipation in the United States," 1993; "Jihad," Just War: Three Views, 1991; "The Civil Rights Act of 1968," 1992; "Ethnic Definitions as Reflections of Public Policy," 1983. **CONTACT ADDRESS** Dept of Hist, Creighton Univ, 2500 California Plaza, 341 Administration, Omaha, NE 68178.

WELCH, JUNE R.
DISCIPLINE HISTORY **EDUCATION** Tex Christian Univ, BA; Univ Tex Arlington, BA; Tex Technol Col, MA; George Washington Univ, JD. **CAREER** Assoc prof, Dallas Univ. **RESEARCH** Texas and Southwest, American Indian, 19th-century America. **SELECTED PUBLICATIONS** Auth, O Ye Legendary Texas Horned Frog, 93; A Family History, 66; The Texas Courthouse, 71; Texas: New Perspectives, 71; Historic Sites Of Texas, 72; Dave's Tune, 73; People And Places In The Texas Past, 74; And Here's To Charley Boyd, 75; The Glory That Was Texas, 75; Going Great In The Lone Star State, 76; The Texas Governor, 77; The Texas Senator, 78; All Hail The Mighty State, 79; The Colleges Of Texas, 81; Riding Fence, 83; The Texas Courthouse Revisited, 84; A Texan's Garden Of Trivia, 85; Tell Me a Texas Story, 91. **CONTACT ADDRESS** Dept of History, Univ of Dallas, 1845 E Northgate Dr, Braniff 204, Irving, TX 75062. **EMAIL** jwelch@acad.udallas.edu

WELKE, BARBARA Y.
DISCIPLINE HISTORY **EDUCATION** Univ Chicago, PhD, 95. **CAREER** Asst prof **HONORS AND AWARDS** Erwin C. Surrency Prize, 97; Lerner-Scott Prize, 96. **RESEARCH** Twentieth-century U.S. history; U.S. legal and constitutional history. **SELECTED PUBLICATIONS** Auth, When All the Women Were White, and All the Blacks Were Men: Gender, Class, Race, and the Road to Plessy, 1855-1914, Law Hist Rev, 95; Unreasonable Women: Gender and the Law of Accidental Injury, 1870-1920, Law Social Inquiry, 94. **CONTACT ADDRESS** History Dept, Univ of Minnesota, Twin Cities, 614 Social Sciences Tower, 267 19th Ave S, Minneapolis, MN 55455. **EMAIL** welke004@tc.umn.edu

WELLER, CECIL
PERSONAL Born 03/03/1961, Tuscaloosa, AL, m, 1986, 1 child **DISCIPLINE** HISTORY **EDUCATION** Tex Christian Univ, BA, 83; MA, 86; PhD, 93. **CAREER** Teaching asst, Tex Christian Univ, 86-89; adj, univ of Tex at Dallas, 89; instr to prof, San Jacinto Col S, 89-. **HONORS AND AWARDS** Ottis Locke Teaching Awd, E Tex Hist Asn, 94; NISOD Excellence in Educ Awd, Univ of Tex, 95. **MEMBERSHIPS** Am Hist Asn, Southern Hist Asn, Southwestern Soc Sci Asn, E Tex Hist Asn, Tex State Hist Asn. **RESEARCH** Politicl history, 1890-1940, Southern history, the Civil War. **SELECTED PUBLICATIONS** Auth, Always a Loyal Democrat: The Life of Joe T. Robinson, Univ of Ark Press (Fayetteville, AR), 98; co-ed, Our Legacy: Articles and Documents in American History (2 vols), AHCP (New York, NY). **CONTACT ADDRESS** Dept Soc & Behavioral Sci, San Jacinto Col, South, 13735 Beamer Rd, Houston, TX 77089-6099. **EMAIL** ewelle@south.sjcd.cc.tx.us

WELLMAN, JUDITH
DISCIPLINE HISTORY **EDUCATION** Univ VA, PhD. **CAREER** Prof, SUNY Oswego. **RESEARCH** Local and soc hist; Women's hist, 19th century US. **SELECTED PUBLICATIONS** Auth, Landmarks Of Oswego County, Syracuse UP, 88; many articles on women's history. **CONTACT ADDRESS** Dept Hist, SUNY, Oswego, 109 Mahar Hall, Oswego, NY 13126.

WELLS, CAMILLE
DISCIPLINE ARCHITECTURAL HISTORY **EDUCATION** Wake Forest Univ, BA, 74; Univ Va, MA, 76; William and Mary Col, PhD, 94. **CAREER** Asst prof. **RESEARCH** Architecture and historic landscapes of early America. **SELECTED PUBLICATIONS** Auth, pubs on emphasizes Virginia from early settlement to the Civil War. **CONTACT ADDRESS** Dept of Architectural History., Univ of Virginia, Charlottesville, VA 22903. **EMAIL** cwells@virginia.edu

WELLS, DAVID FALCONER
PERSONAL Born 05/11/1939, Bulawayo, Zimbabwe, m, 1965, 2 children **DISCIPLINE** SYSTEMATIC THEOLOGY, CHURCH HISTORY **EDUCATION** Univ London, EngL, BD, 66; Trinity Evangel Divinity Sch, ThM, 67; Univ Manchester, PhD, 69. **CAREER** From asst prof to prof church hist, Trinity Evangel Divinity Sch, 69-77, prof syst theol, 78-79; Prof Syst Theol, Gordon-Conwell Theol Sem, 79-, Acad dean, Gordon-Conwell Theol Sem, Charlotte, 98-; Res fel, Divinity Sch, Yale Univ, 73-74; mem, Int Evangel Roman Cath Dialog Missions, 81-; chmn, Task Force Roman Cath, World Evangel Fel Theol Comn, 81-84. **HONORS AND AWARDS** Distinguished lectr, London Inst for Contemp Christianity, London, 85. **RESEARCH** Contextualization; Christology; Roman Cath modernism. **SELECTED PUBLICATIONS** Ed, Toward a Theology for the Future, Creation House, 71; auth, Revolution in Rome, Inter-Varsity Press, 73; ed, The Evangelicals, Abingdon Press, 75; auth, Search for Salvation, Inter-Varsity Press, 78; The Prophetic Theology of George Tywell, Scholars Press, 81; ed, The Eerdmans Handbook of American Christianity, Eerdmans, 83; auth, The Person of Christ: A Biblical and Historical Analysis of the Incarnation, Crossway, 84; ed, Reformed Theology in America: A History of Its Modern Development, Eerdmans, 85; ed, God the Evangelist: How the Holy Spirit Words to Bring Men and Women to Faith, Eerdmans, 87; ed, Christian Faith and Practice in the Modern World: Theology from an Evangelical Point of View, Eerdmans, 88; ed, Turning to God: Biblical Conversion in the Modern World, Baker, 89; ed, The Gospel in the Modern World: A Tribute to John Stott, InterVarsity, 91; auth, No Place for Truth, Or, Whatever Happened to Evangelical Theology, Eerdmans, 93; auth, God in the Wasteland: The Reality of Truth in a World of Fading Dreams, Eerdmans, 94; auth, Losing Our Virtue: Why the Church Must Recover Its Moral Vision, Eerdmans, 98. **CONTACT ADDRESS** Gordon-Conwell Theol Sem, 130 Essex St, South Hamilton, MA 01982-2395.

WELLS, ROBERT VALE
PERSONAL Born 07/14/1943, Bridgeport, CT, m, 1964, 2 children **DISCIPLINE** AMERICAN COLONIAL HISTORY **EDUCATION** Denison Univ, BA, 65; Princeton Univ, PhD(hist), 69. **CAREER** From instr to assoc prof, 69-80, Prof Hist, Union Col, NY, 80-, US Dept Health, Educ & Welfare grant, 72-73; fel, Charles Warren Ctr for Studies Am Hist, Harvard Univ, 74-75; John Simon Guggenheim Found fel, 77-78. **MEMBERSHIPS** AHA; Orgn Am Historians. **RESEARCH** Demographic history; American demographic history. **SELECTED PUBLICATIONS** Auth, Family size and fertility control in eighteenth century America, Pop Studies, 71; auth, "Demographic change and the life cycle of American families," J Interdisciplinary Hist, 71; auth, "Quaker marriage patterns in a colonial perspective," William & Mary Quart, 72; auth, The Population of the British Colonies in America Before 1776, Princeton Univ, 75; auth, "Family history and demographic transition," J Social Hist, 75; auth, "On the dangers of constructing artificial cohorts in times of rapid social change," J Interdisciplinary Hist, 78; auth, "Population dynamics in the eighteenth-century Mississippi River Valley," J Soc Hist, 78; Revolutions in Americans' Lives, Greenwood, 82; auth, "The Mortality Transition In Schenectady, New-York, 1880-1930," in Social Science History, Vol 0019, 1995; auth, Facing the 'King of Terrors,' Cambridge Univ, 00. **CONTACT ADDRESS** Dept of Hist, Union Col, New York, 807 Union St, Schenectady, NY 12308-3107. **EMAIL** wellsr@union.edu

WELLS, WALTER
PERSONAL Born 12/13/1937, New York, NY, m, 1961, 3 children **DISCIPLINE** ENGLISH, AMERICAN STUDIES **EDUCATION** NYork Univ, BS, 60, MA, 63; Univ Sussex, DPhil, 71. **CAREER** Instr lang arts, CA State Polytech Col, 63-66; from asst prof to assoc prof, 67-77, prof English & Am Studies, 77-98, chmn Am Studies, 71-85, Prof Emeritus, CA State Univ, Dominguez Hills, 98-; gen consult ed in humanities, Educulture, Inc, 77-80. **RESEARCH** Twentieth century Am; narrative nonfiction; stylistics. **SELECTED PUBLICATIONS** Auth, Communications in Business, Wadsworth, 68, 2nd ed, 77; Tycoons and Locusts: A Regional Look at Hollywood Fiction of the 1930's, Southern IL Univ, 73; Mark Twain's Sure-Fire Programmed Guide to Backgrounds in American Literature, Educulture, 77-80. **CONTACT ADDRESS** Dept of English, California State Univ, Dominguez Hills, 1000 E Victoria, Carson, CA 90747-0005. **EMAIL** wwells@dhvx20.csudh.edu

WELSH-OVCHAROV, BOGOMILA M.
PERSONAL Born Sofia, Bulgaria **DISCIPLINE** FINE ART **EDUCATION** Univ Toronto, BA, 64, MPhil, 71; Univ Utrecht, PhD, 76. **CAREER** Prof Fine Arts Univ Toronto. **HONORS AND AWARDS** Chevalier, L'Ordre Palmes Acad, 94. **RESEARCH** Vincent Van Gogh. **SELECTED PUBLICATIONS** Auth, The Early Work of Charles Amgrand and his Contact with Van Gogh, 71; auth, Van Gogh in Perspective, 73; auth, Van Gogh: His Paris Period: 1886-88, 76; auth, Vincent Van Gogh and the Birth of Cloisonism, 81; auth, Emile Bernard: Bordellos and Prostitutes in Turn-of-the-Century French Art, 88; auth, Charles Pachter, 92. **CONTACT ADDRESS** Dept of Fine Art, Univ of Toronto, 100 St George St, 6036 Sidney Smith Hall, Toronto, ON, Canada M5S 3G3. **EMAIL** bogomila.welsh@utoronto.ca

WEMPLE, SUZANNE FONAY
PERSONAL Born 00/00/1927, Veszprem, Hungary, m, 1957, 3 children **DISCIPLINE** MEDIEVAL HISTORY **EDUCATION** Univ Calif, Berkeley, BA, 53; Columbia Univ, MLS, 55, PhD(medieval hist), 67. **CAREER** Instr hist, Stern Col Women, 62-64; lectr soc sci, Teachers Col, Columbia Univ, 64-68; instr hist, 66-67, asst prof, 68-72, assoc prof, 72-80, chair women's studies, 78-80, actg chair dept, 81, Prof Hist, Barnard Col, 80-, Dir, Nat Endowment for Humanities grants medieval & renaissance studies, 77-78 & 78-81; actg chair medieval & renaissance studies, Barnard Col, 78-79; Fulbright travel grant, Italy, spring, 82; Spivack grant, Barnard Col, 81. **HONORS AND AWARDS** Best Bk Prize, Berkshire Conf Women Historians, 82. **MEMBERSHIPS** Mediaeval Acad Am; AHA; AAUP; Inst Res Hist. **RESEARCH** Middle Ages; medieval women; law. **SELECTED PUBLICATIONS** Coauth (with JoAnn McNamara), The power of women through the family, Feminist Studies, I: 726-741; auth, Metaphor or the Carolingian doctrine of corporations, Speculum, 49: 222-237; coauth (with JoAnn McNamara), Sanctity and power: The pursuit of medieval women, In: Becoming Visible: History of European Women, Houghton & Mifflin, 76; auth, Claudius of Turin's Organic, Edizioni di Storia e Letteratura, Rome, 79; Women in Frankish Society: Marriage and the Cloister, 500-900, Univ Pa Press, 81. **CONTACT ADDRESS** Dept of Hist, Barnard Col, New York, NY 10027.

WENDELKEN, CHERIE
DISCIPLINE ARCHITECTURAL HISTORY OF JAPAN, ART HISTORY OF JAPAN **EDUCATION** BA, 77; MArch, 80; PhD, 94. **CAREER** Asst prof, Harvard Univ. **MEMBERSHIPS** CAA; SAH. **RESEARCH** Japanese architecture and art, 1868 to present. **CONTACT ADDRESS** Dept of History of Art and Architecture, Harvard Univ, 480 Broadway, Cambridge, MA 02138. **EMAIL** wendelk@fas.harvard.edu

WENDORFF, LAURA C.
PERSONAL 1 child **DISCIPLINE** AMERICAN CULTURE **EDUCATION** Univ Wis, BA, 81; Univ Mich, MA, 84, PhD, 92. **CAREER** Tchg asst, Univ Mich, 83-84; asst prof, Univ Wis, 94-00; to assoc prof, 00-. **SELECTED PUBLICATIONS** Auth, Demonic Males: Apes and the Origins of Human Violence (rev), 98; Eric Heiden, Pierian, 88. **CONTACT ADDRESS** Dept of Humanities, Univ of Wisconsin, Platteville, 1 University Plaza, Platteville, WI 53818-3099. **EMAIL** wendorff@uwplatt.edu

WENGERT, TIMOTHY J.
DISCIPLINE REFORMATION HISTORY **EDUCATION** Univ Mich, BA, 72, MA, 73; Luther Sem, MDiv, 77; Duke Univ, PhD, 84. **CAREER** Prof **HONORS AND AWARDS** Melanchthon Prize, City of Bretten, 00. **SELECTED PUBLICATIONS** Auth, Philip Melanchthon's interpretation of John's Gospel; ed, Telling the Churches' Stories, Eerdmans; co-ed, The Book of Concord, Augsburg Fortress Publ; transl, Luther's Small Catechism; auth, Human Freedom, Christian Righteousness, Oxford UP; Law and Gospel, Baker Bk(s). **CONTACT ADDRESS** Dept of Hisory and Systematic Theology, Lutheran Theol Sem at Gettysburg, 7301 Germantown Ave, Philadelphia, PA 19119-1794. **EMAIL** Twengert@ltsp.edu

WENTE, EDWARD FRANK
PERSONAL Born 10/07/1930, New York, NY, m, 1970 **DISCIPLINE** EGYPTOLOGY **EDUCATION** Univ Chicago, AB, 51, PhD(Egyptol), 59. **CAREER** Dir Egyptol, Am Res Ctr Egypt, 57-58; res assoc, 59-63, from asst prof to assoc prof, 63-70, chmn, Dept Near Eastern Lang & Civilization, 75-79, Prof Egyptol; Orient Inst, Univ Chicago, 70-95; prof emeritus, Univ Chicago, 96-; mem, Am Res Ctr Egypt, 57-; field dir epigraphic surv, Orient Inst, Luxor, Egypt, 72-73; mem archeol adv coun, Smithsonian Inst, 79-82. **RESEARCH** Epigraphy; Egyptian philology; history of the Egyptian New Kingdom. **SELECTED PUBLICATIONS** Coauth, Medinet Habu, Vol VI, 63, Vol VII, 64; auth, Late Ramesside Letters, 67 & coauth, The Beit el-Wali Temple of Ramesses II 67, Univ Chicago; The Literature of Ancient Egypt, Yale Univ, 72; A chronology of the New Kingdom, In: Studies in Honor of George R Hughes, Univ Chicago, 76; The Temple of Khonsu, Vol I, 79, Vol II 81; The Tomb of Kheruef, 80; co-ed, An X-Ray Atlas of the Royal Mummies, Univ Chicago, 80; Letters from Ancient Egypt, Soc Biblical Lit, 90. **CONTACT ADDRESS** Orient Inst, Univ of Chicago, 1155 E 58th St, Chicago, IL 60637. **EMAIL** e-went@uchicago.edu

WERCKMEISTER, O. K.
DISCIPLINE ART HISTORY **EDUCATION** Freie Universitat Berlin, PhD. **CAREER** Mary Jane Crowe distinguished prof, Northwestern Univ. **RESEARCH** Political history of art in the middle ages and during the decade of the Great Depression, especially the art of totalitarian regimes in the Soviet Union, Germany, and Italy. **SELECTED PUBLICATIONS** Auth, The Making of Paul Klee's Career, 1914-1920; Citadel Culture. **CONTACT ADDRESS** Dept of Art History, Northwestern Univ, 1801 Hinman, Evanston, IL 60208.

WERLICH, DAVID P.
PERSONAL Born 11/02/1941, Minneapolis, MN, m, 1960, 3 children **DISCIPLINE** LATIN AMERICAN HISTORY **EDUCATION** Univ Minn, BA, 63, MA, 67, PhD(hist), 68. **CAREER** Asst prof, 68-78, Assoc Prof 78-84; Hist, 78-; Prof, 84-; Chair, 88-00, Southern Ill Univ, Carbondale. **HONORS AND AWARDS** Delta Awd, 91; OAS fellow, 82. **MEMBERSHIPS** Conf Latin Am Hist; Midwestern Asn Latin Am Studies. **RESEARCH** Peruvian history; Amazonian history, U.S. Naval history, Latin American History. **SELECTED PUBLICATIONS** Auth, Peru: A Short History, Southern Ill Univ, 78; Research Tools for Latin American Historians: A Select, Annotated Bibliography, Garland, 80; rev, Peru, auth, Admiral of the Amazon: John Randolph Tusker, His Confederate Colleagues and Peru, Univ Press of Virginia, 90; rev, The Evolution Of A Crisis - Rudolph,Jd, Hispanic American Historical Review, Vol 0073, 1993; rev, Militarism And Politics In Latin-America - Peru From Sanchezcerro To Sendero-Luminoso - Masterson,Dm, Hispanic American Historical Review, Vol 0075, rev, 1995; Mirages Of Transition - The Peruvian Altiplano, 1780-1930 - Jacobsen,N, Historian, Vol 0057, 1995; rev, Amazonian Indians From Prehistory To The Present - Anthropological Perspectives - Roosevelt,A, Historian, Vol 0058, 1996. **CONTACT ADDRESS** Dept of Hist, So Illinois Univ, Carbondale, Mailcode 4519, Carbondale, IL 62901-4519. **EMAIL** elmaximo@siu.edu

WERLY, JOHN MCINTYRE
PERSONAL Born 11/06/1939, Rochester, NY, m, 1961, 3 children **DISCIPLINE** UNITED STATES HISTORY **EDUCATION** Trinity Col, CT, BA, 61, MA, 66; Syracuse Univ, PhD(hist), 72. **CAREER** Teacher hist, Robinson Sch, West Hartford, Conn, 63-68; teaching asst, Syracuse Univ, 69-70; instr, State Univ NY Cortland, 70-72; asst prof, 72-78, assoc prof Hist, Southeastern MA Univ, 78-84; full prof hist, Univ MA Dartmouth, 84-. **HONORS AND AWARDS** Leo Sullivan Teacher of Yr Awd, Southeastern MA Univ Fac Fedn, 77; Who's Who in the East; Commonwealth Citation for Outstanding Performance, 87; Col of Arts and Sciences Distinguished Teaching Awd, 92; Who's Who in America. **MEMBERSHIPS** Orgn Am Historians. **RESEARCH** American nativist movements; American millenarian movements. **SELECTED PUBLICATIONS** Auth, The Millenarian Right, SAtlantic Quart, 72; The Irish of Manchester, 1832-49, Irish Hist Studies, 73; Premillennialism and the Paranoid Style, Am Studies, 77; The Reform and Radical Millenial Alternatives in Colonial New England, Amerika Studien/Am Studies , 84. **CONTACT ADDRESS** Dept Hist, Univ of Massachusetts, Dartmouth, 285 Old Westport Rd, North Dartmouth, MA 02747-2300. **EMAIL** jwerly@umassd.edu

WERNER, JOHN M.
DISCIPLINE HISTORY **EDUCATION** Evansville Col, BA, 64; Ind Univ, AM, 67; Ind Univ, PhD, 73. **CAREER** From Asst Prof to Prof, Western Ill Univ, 69-. **HONORS AND AWARDS** Distinguished Teaching Awd, 80. **RESEARCH** The dissolution of religious institutions in the British Isles. **SELECTED PUBLICATIONS** Auth, "David Hume in America," J of the Hist of Ideas (72); auth, 'Reaping the Bloody Harvest": Race Riots in the United States During the Age of Jackson 1824-1849, Garland Pr, 86. **CONTACT ADDRESS** Dept Hist, Western Illinois Univ, 1 University Circle, Macomb, IL 61455-1367.

WERT, HAL E.
PERSONAL Born 04/17/1940, Detroit, MI, d, 3 children **DISCIPLINE** HISTORY **EDUCATION** Univ Iowa, BA, 66; Univ Kan, MA, 74; Mph, 75; PhD, 91. **CAREER** From Instr to Prof, Kan City Art Inst, 71-. **HONORS AND AWARDS** Phi Alpha Theta; Herbert Hoover Presidential Libr Travel Awd, 94-95; IREX Short-Term Travel Grant, 95; Travel Grant, Novosibirsk, Russ, 95; Outstanding Proj Grant, Kan City Art Inst, 95; Fulbright-Hays Group Proj Awd, 96; Who's Who Among Am Teachers, 98; Pilot Proj Awd, Kan City Art Inst, 98; Excellence in Teaching Awd, Kan City Art Inst, 99; Herbert Hoover Presidential Libr Travel Awd, 99; Who's Who Among Am Teachers, 00. **MEMBERSHIPS** AABS, OAH, RMASS, SHAFR, SMH, World War II Studies Asn. **RESEARCH** World War I, World War II, The Presidencies of Roosevelt, Hoover, and Truman, emphasis on foreign policy. **SELECTED PUBLICATIONS** Auth, "Flight and Survival: American and British Aid to Polish Refugees in the Fall of 1939," Polish Rev, vol XXXIV, no 3 (89): 227-248; auth, "Hoover, Roosevelt and the Politics of Aid to Finland 1939-1940," in World War II: A Fifty year Perspective on 1939 (Albany, NY: Sienna Col Pr, 92), 89-112; auth, "U S Aid to Poles Under Nazi Domination 1939-1941," The Historian, vol 51, no 3 (95): 511-524; auth, "The Dissolution of Yugoslavia: A Balkan Tragedy," Southeast European Monitor, vol III, no 4 (96): 3-25; auth, "Freedom From Want: The Dutch Hunger Winter 1944-1945," in Victory in Europe 1945: From World War II to the Cold War (Lawrence, KS: Univ Iowa Pr, 00); auth, "Years of Frustration: Herbert Hoover and World War II," in Uncommon Americans: The Lives and Legacies of Herbet and Lou Henry Hoover (Univ Iowa Pr, forthcoming). **CONTACT ADDRESS** Dept Hist, Kansas City Art Inst, 4415 Warwick Blvd, Kansas City, MO 64111-1820. **EMAIL** hwert@aol.com

WERTHEIMER, JACK
DISCIPLINE JEWISH HISTORY **EDUCATION** Queens Col CUNY, BA, MA; Columbia Univ, MPhil; PhD, 78. **CAREER** Adj lectr, City Col and Queens Col CUNY; vis asst prof, Vassar College; adj assoc prof, US Mil Acad West Point; dir, Joseph and Miriam Ratner Ctr Study Conser Judaism; provost/chief acad off, Jewish Theol Sem Am; Joseph and Martha Mendelson Prof Am Jewish Hist. **HONORS AND AWARDS** Grant, Pew Charitable Trusts; Nat Jewish Bk Awd, 93-94. **RESEARCH** History and the contemporary state of Conservative Judaism. **SELECTED PUBLICATIONS** Auth, Unwelcome Strangers East European Jews in Imperial Germany, Oxford Univ Press, 87; A People Divided: Judaism in Contemporary America, Basic Bks and Univ Press New England, 97; ed, The American Synagogue--A Sanctuary Transformed, Cambridge Univ Press, 87; The Uses of Tradition: Jewish Continuity in the Modern Era, JTS/Harvard,93; The Modern Jewish Experience--A Reader's Guide, NYU Press, 93. **CONTACT ADDRESS** Jewish Theol Sem of America, 3080 Broadway, New York, NY 10027. **EMAIL** jawertheimer@jtsa.edu

WERTHEIMER, JOHN
PERSONAL Born 06/14/1963, Washington, DC, m, 1994, 2 children **DISCIPLINE** HISTORY **EDUCATION** Oberlin Col, BA, 85; Princeton Univ, MA, 94; Princeton Univ, PhD, 92. **CAREER** Assoc Prof of History, Davidson Col, 99-; Asst Prof of History, Davidson Col, 93-99; Lecturer, Princeton Univ, 91-93. **HONORS AND AWARDS** George Abernathy Research Fel, 99; Friends of the Princeton Univ Library Visiting Fel, 97; Mrs. Giles Whiting Foundation Honorific Fellowship in the Humanities, 90--91; John O'Cannon Awd, 90; Golieb Fellowship in Legal History, NYU Law School, 89-90. **MEMBERSHIPS** Am. Society for Legal History; Organization of Amer Historian. **RESEARCH** Amer Legal History. **SELECTED PUBLICATIONS** Auth, "The Antisatellite Negotiations," in Albert Carnesale and Richard N. Haass, eds., Superpower Arms Control: Setting the Record Straight, Cambridge, MA: Balinger, 87: 139-64; auth, "The Green and the Black: Irish Nationalism and the Dilemma of Abolitionist," New York Irish History, vol. 5, 90-91: 5-15; auth, "Mutual Film Reviewed: The Movies, Censorship, and Free Speech in Progressive America," The American Journal of Legal History, 37:2, April 93: 158-89; auth, "Freedom of Speech: Zechariah Chafee and Free-Speech History," Reviews in American History, vol. 22, no. 2, June 94: 365-77; auth, "Escape of the Match-Strikers': Disorderly North Carolina Women, the Legal System, and the Samarcand Arson Case of 1937," North Carolina Historical Review, 75: 4, October 98: 435-60. **CONTACT ADDRESS** Dept History, Davidson Col, PO Box 1719, Davidson, NC 28036-1719. **EMAIL** jowertheimer@davidson.edu

WESSEL, THOMAS ROGER
PERSONAL Born 09/28/1937, Belmond, IA, m, 1964, 1 child **DISCIPLINE** AMERICAN HISTORY, ANTHROPOLOGY **EDUCATION** Iowa State Univ, BS, 63; Univ Md, MA, 68, PhD(hist), 72. **CAREER** Res asst hist, Smithsonian Inst, 65-68; asst prof, 72-75, head dept hist & philos, 79, Assoc Prof Hist, Mont State Univ, 75-79, Prof, Nat Endowment for Humanities fel anthrop, 73-74; Nat Prof, 80. **HONORS AND AWARDS** Res Achievement, Smithsonian Inst, 74. **MEMBERSHIPS** Agr Hist Soc; Orgn Am Historians; Western Hist Asn. **RESEARCH** American agricultural history; American Indian history. **SELECTED PUBLICATIONS** Auth, Prologue to the Shelterbelt, 1870-1934, J West, 68; Roosevelt and the Great Plains Shelterbelt, Great Plains J, 69; Agriculture and Iroquois hegemony in New York, 1604-1779, Md Historian, 70; A History of the Rocky Boy's Reservation, Bur Indian Affaris, 74; Agriculture, Indians and American history, Agr Hist, 76; Agriculture in the Great Plains, 1876-1930, Agr Hist Soc, 77; 4-H, An American Idea, 1900-1980, Nat 4-H Counc, 82; Centennial West - Essays On The Northern Tier States - Lang,Wl, Montana-The Magazine Of Western History, Vol 0043, 1993; The Northern-Cheyenne Indian Reservation, 1877-1900 - Svingen,Oj, Western Historical Quarterly, Vol 0025, 1994; Rooted In Dust - Surviving Drought And Depression In Southwestern Kansas - Rineykehrberg,P, Great Plains Quarterly, Vol 0016, 1996. **CONTACT ADDRESS** Dept of Hist, Montana State Univ, Bozeman, Bozeman, MT 59715.

WESSER, ROBERT F.
PERSONAL Born 02/18/1933, Buffalo, NY, m, 2 children **DISCIPLINE** UNITED STATES HISTORY **EDUCATION** Univ Buffalo, BA, 54, MA, 56; Univ Rochester, PhD(hist), 61. **CAREER** From instr to asst prof Am studies, State Univ NY Buffalo, 59-66, dir Am studies prog, 63-66, asst dean, Col Arts, & Sci, 65-66; assoc prof, 66-72, dir grad studies hist, 75-77 & 79-80, prof hist, 72-95, chmn dept, 80-83, 87-90, prof emeritus, 95- , SUNY Albany; Am Asn State & Local Hist grant-in-aid, 64; consult, Albany Inst Hist & Art & NY State Senate, 77-78. **HONORS AND AWARDS** Chancellor's Awd for Excellence in Teaching, State Univ NY, 74. **MEMBERSHIPS** AHA; Orgn Am Historians. **RESEARCH** Twentieth century United States history; latter 19th century United States history; New York State history. **SELECTED PUBLICATIONS** Auth, Charles Evans Hughes and the urban sources of political progressivism, NY Hist Soc Quart, 10/66; Charles Evans Hughes: Politics and Reform in New York, 1905-1910, Cornell Univ, 67; Conflict and compromise: The workmen's compensation movement in New York, 1890 s-1913, Labor Hist, summer 71; Election of 1888, In: History of American Presidential Elections, 1789-1968 (4 vols), Chelsea House & McGraw, 71; contribr ed (with David M Ellis), Two Hundred Years of the New York state legislature, Albany Inst of Hist and Art, 78; auth, The impeachment of a governor: William Sulzer and the politics of excess, NY Hist, 10/79; Woman suffrage, prohibition, and the New York experience in the progressive era, In: An American Historian: Essays to Honor Selig Alder, State Univ NY, Buffalo, 80; New York state and regulation of the insurance industry, In: American Industrialization, Economic Expansion, and the Law: 1870-1914, Sleepy Hollow Press, 81; auth, A Response to Progressivism: The Democratic Party in New York Politics, 1902-1918, NY Univ, 86. **CONTACT ADDRESS** 235 Lenox Ave, Albany, NY 12208.

WESSLEY, STEPHEN EUGENE
PERSONAL Born 10/29/1944, Mahopac, NY, m, 1966, 2 children **DISCIPLINE** MEDIEVAL HISTORY **EDUCATION** St John's Univ, BA, 66; Columbia Univ, MA, 67, PhD(medieval hist), 76. **CAREER** Instr hist, State Univ NY, New Paltz, 70-73; asst prof, 73-80, assoc prof, Hist, York Col Pa, 80- **HONORS AND AWARDS** Lehman Fel; Fulbright Res Fel; Gladys Krieble Delmas Fdn Fel; Am Coun of Learned Soc Grant-in-Aid; Am Phil Soc Grant; Prog for Cultural Cooperation Bet Spain's Min of Culture and Educ and U.S. Univ Grant. **MEMBERSHIPS** Medieval Acad Am; AHA; Ecclesiastical Hist Soc; Soc Ital Hist Studies. **RESEARCH** Medieval heresy; history of women. **SELECTED PUBLICATIONS** Auth, The thirteenth-century Guglielmites: Salvation through women, In: Medieval Women, Oxford, 78; The composition of Georgius' Disputatio inter Catholicum et parterinum hereticum, Archivum Fratrum Praedicatorum, 78; Bonum est Benedicto mutare locum: The role of the life of Saint Benedict in Joachim of Fiore's monastic reform, Rev Benedictine, 80; auth, Joachim of Fiore and Monastic Reform, New York, 90; auth, Study Guide, 2 Vols, 98; Western Civilizations, Norton Study Guide. **CONTACT ADDRESS** Dept of History, York Col, Pennsylvania, PO Box 15199, York, PA 17405-7199. **EMAIL** swessley@ycp.edu

WEST, C. S'THEMBILE
PERSONAL Born 05/21/1949, Harlem, NY **DISCIPLINE** AFRICAN AMERICAN STUDIES **EDUCATION** City College, CUNY, BS, 71; Columbia Univ Teachers Col, MA, 74; Temple Univ, PhD, 94. **CAREER** Guest prof, Bryn Mawr, 92, 94, 97; adj prof, instr, Temple Univ, 97-99; adjunct prof, asst prof, Theatre, LeHigh Univ, 98-99; Asst Prof, Visiting Prof, FL International Univ, 00. **HONORS AND AWARDS** Fulbright-Hays Awd, 91; Faculty Recognition Awd, CUNY, 91; St. Louis Public Schools, Role Model Experiences Awd, 93; Pan-African Stud Educ Prog, Temple Univ, Appreciation Awd, 97. **MEM-**

BERSHIPS Am Acad Relig; Women in Relig and Soc Group; Natl Assn of Black Journalists. **RESEARCH** African American women; social protest movements; womanism; women and religion; African American religious expression; performance and prayer. **SELECTED PUBLICATIONS** Auth, Dianne McIntyre: Twentieth Century African American Griot, in African Dance: A Historical and Philosophical Inquiry, African World Press, 96; auth, **CONTACT ADDRESS** 1030 Derry Ln, Apt 27, Macomb, IL 61455. **EMAIL** thama2u@aol.com

WEST, CARROLL V.
PERSONAL Born 01/29/1955, Murfreesboro, TN, m, 1980, 2 children **DISCIPLINE** HISTORY **EDUCATION** Middle Tenn State Univ, BA; Univ Tenn, MA; Col William Mary, PhD. **CAREER** Hist consult, MHS, 83-85; hist consult, WHC, 82-83, 89-00; MTSU Cen Hist Prev, 85-00; sr ed, Tenn Hist Quart, 93-00. **HONORS AND AWARDS** Hilton Smith Fel, 77-78; AASLH Cert Commend, 96; AASLH Merit Awd, 99; Tenn Hist Bk Awd, 99. **MEMBERSHIPS** OAH; AASLH; SHA; WHA; Tenn Hist Soc; NTHP; VAF; SESAH; SHEAR. **RESEARCH** American South; American West; Historic Preservation. **SELECTED PUBLICATIONS** Auth, Capitalism on the Frontier (univ NE Press, 93); auth, Tennessee's Historical Landscapes (Univ Tenn Press, 95); ed, Tennessee History: The Land, the People, the Culture (univ Tenn Press, 98); ed, Tennessee Encyclopedia of History and Culture (Tenn Hist Soc, 98); auth, New Deal Landscape of Tennessee (Univ Tenn Press, 00). **CONTACT ADDRESS** Middle Tennessee State Univ, PO Box 80, Murfreesboro, TN 37132-001. **EMAIL** cwest@mtsu.edu

WEST, ELLIOTT
PERSONAL Born 04/19/1945, Dallas, TX, m, 1983, 5 children **DISCIPLINE** UNITED STATES HISTORY **EDUCATION** Univ Texas, Austin, BA, 67; Univ Colorado, MA, 69, PhD, 71. **CAREER** Asst prof, 71-75, assoc prof, 75-79, Univ Tex, Arlington; assof prof, 79-81, prof, 81-00, dist prof, Univ Ar, 00-. **HONORS AND AWARDS** Western Heritage Awd, best nonfiction book, 90, 96; Arkansas Prof of the Year, Carnegie Found for Advancement of Tchg, 95; George Perkins Marsh Prize, 97; Francis Parkman Pr, 99; Ray Allen Billington Awd, 99; PEN Center West Awd, 99; Caughey Western History Assoc Pr, 99. **MEMBERSHIPS** Western Hist Asn; Am Soc of Environ Hist. **RESEARCH** American West and Frontier; Environmental History; Native American History; History of the Family. **SELECTED PUBLICATIONS** Auth, Growing Up With the Country, 89; auth, The Way West: Essays on the Central Plains, New Mexico, 95; auth, Growing Up in Twentieth Century America: A History and Resource Guide, Greenwood, 96; auth, The Contested Plains: Indians, Goldseekers and the Rush to Colorado, Kansas, 98. **CONTACT ADDRESS** Dept of History, Univ of Arkansas, Fayetteville, Fayetteville, AR 72701. **EMAIL** ewest@comp.uark.edu

WEST, FRANKLIN CARL
PERSONAL Born 08/17/1934, Portland, OR, m, 1963, 1 child **DISCIPLINE** MODERN GERMAN HISTORY **EDUCATION** Reed Col, BA, 56; Univ Ore, MA, 58; Univ Calif, Berkeley, PhD(hist), 70. **CAREER** Instr hist, Northwestern Univ, 63-64; instr & asst prof humanities, Reed Col, 64-66; from instr to asst prof, 66-75, assoc prof, 75-80, Prof Hist, Portland State Univ, 81-96, emeritus, 96-. **RESEARCH** Political and cultural history of the Weimar Republic. **SELECTED PUBLICATIONS** Auth, A Crisis of the Weimar Republic: A Study of the German Referendum of 20 June 1926, American Philosophical Soc, Philadelphia, 85; auth, "Success Without Influence. Emil Ludwig During the Weimar Years," Leo Baeck Year Book XXX (85): 169-189; auth, "On the Significance of a Once Fashionable Trend: 'Modern' Biography," Monatshefte 79.2 (87): 199-209; ed and compiler, Emil Ludwig, Fur die Weimarer Republik un Europa: Ausgewahlte Zeitungs- und Zeitschriftenartikel 1919-1932, Peter Lang (Frankfurt am Main), 91; auth, "'World Historical Chatter' Leo Lowenthal's Critique of German Popular Biography," Zeitschrift fur Literaturwissenschaft und Linguistik 105 (97): 159-168. **CONTACT ADDRESS** Dept of Hist, Portland State Univ, Portland, OR 97207.

WEST, HUGH A.
PERSONAL Born 08/16/1946, Broken Arrow, OK, m, 1971, 2 children **DISCIPLINE** HISTORY **EDUCATION** Stanford Univ, BA, 68; MA, 71; PhD, 80. **CAREER** Teach res fel, Stanford Univ, 75-77; instr, 78-80, asst prof, 80-87, assoc prof, 87-, assoc dean, dir, 87-93, chair, 98-, Univ Richmond. **HONORS AND AWARDS** Maxwell Prize, 88; Alfred P Sloan, Schl; Phi Beta Kappa; Kent Fel, 72-75; DAAD Fel, 74-75. **MEMBERSHIPS** AHA; ASECS; GSA. **RESEARCH** German enlightenment; Georg Forster. **SELECTED PUBLICATIONS** Transl, The Historical Essays of Otto Hintze, ed. Felix Gilbert (Oxford, 75); auth, "Gottinger and Weimar: The Organization of Knowledge and Social Theory in Eighteenth-Century Germany," Cen Euro Hist 11 (78): 150-161; auth, "Georg Forster and the Meaning of the French Revolution," Pro Thirteenth Consort Revolut Euro (83): 288-305; auth, "The Limits of Enlightenment Anthropology: Georg Forster and the Tahitians," Hist Euro Ideas 10 (89): 147-160; auth, "The Political Ambiguity of Brotherhood: Georg Forster and the Rosicrucians," Pro Twenty-First Consort on Revol Euro (91): 67-74. **CONTACT ADDRESS** Dept History, Univ of Richmond, 28 Westhampton Way, Richmond, VA 23173-0001. **EMAIL** hwest@richmond.edu

WEST, JAMES L.
PERSONAL Born 01/20/1944, Vallejo, CA, d, 2 children **DISCIPLINE** HISTORY **EDUCATION** Princeton Univ, AB, MA, PhD. **CAREER** Vis prof, 95-; prof, Trinity Waterford 71-95; Middebury 95-; prof of Humanities, 99-. **RESEARCH** Peasant cultures; European and Russian cultural history; Historiography, Philosophy of History. **SELECTED PUBLICATIONS** Ed, Between Tsar and People: Educated Society and the Quest for Public Identity in Late Imperial Russia; ed, Merchant Moscow: Visions of Russia's Vanished Bourgeoisie. **CONTACT ADDRESS** Dept of History, Middlebury Col, Middlebury, VT 05753. **EMAIL** west@middlebury.edu

WEST, MARTHA S.
PERSONAL Born 02/05/1946, Pomona, CA, 3 children **DISCIPLINE** HISTORY; LAW **EDUCATION** Brandeis Univ, BA, 67; Indiana Univ, JD, 74. **CAREER** Atty, 74-82; asst prof, Univ Calif Davis Law Sch, 82-88; prof and assoc dean, 88-92; prof, 92- . **HONORS AND AWARDS** The 1981 Redding Scholar, Indianapolis Chamber of Com, Lacy Exec Leadership Series, 81-82; The Ruth E. Anderson Awd from Women's Res and Resources Ctr and Women's Studies Prog, UC Davis, for outstanding service on behalf of campus women, 90; Sacramento YWCA Outstanding Woman of the Year in Educ, 91; The Deanna Falge Awd for diversity and affirmative action, UC Davis, 96; The William & Sally Rutte Distinguished Teaching Awd, UCD Law Sch, 97. **MEMBERSHIPS** AAUP; NLG; ABA. **RESEARCH** Women's legal rights; sex discrimination in higher education. **SELECTED PUBLICATIONS** Auth, Gender Bias in Academic Robes: The Law's Failure to Protect Women Faculty, Temple Law Rev, 94; auth, Women Faculty: Frozen in Time, Academe, 95; auth, History Lessons: Affirmative Action, The Women's Rev of Books, 96; auth, The Historical Roots of Affirmative Action, La Raza Law J, 96; co-auth with H.H. Kay, Sex-Based Discrimination: Text, Cases, and Materials, 96; auth, Equitable Funding of Public Schools under State Constitutional Law, J Gender, Race, and Justice, 98. **CONTACT ADDRESS** School of Law, Univ of California, Davis, Davis, CA 95616. **EMAIL** mswest@ucdavis.edu

WESTERKAMP, MARILYN J.
PERSONAL Born Cincinnati, OH, 2 children **DISCIPLINE** HISTORY **EDUCATION** Brandeis Univ, BA, 76; Univ Pa, MA, 78; PhD, 84. **CAREER** Vis asst prof, Univ of Wyo, 84-85; asst prof, Clarion Univ of Pa, 85-89; asst prof to prof, Univ of Calif at Santa Cruz, 89-. **HONORS AND AWARDS** Phila Ctr for Early Am Studies, 80-81; Penfield Overseas Res Fel, 81-82; ACLS Fel, 93-94. **MEMBERSHIPS** Am His Asn, Am Soc of Church Historians, Org Am Hist, Omohundro Inst of Early Am Soc and Culture. **RESEARCH** Colonial America, American religion and culture, early modern gender and culture. **SELECTED PUBLICATIONS** Auth, Triumph of the Laity: Scots Irish Piety and the Great Awakening, Oxford Univ Press, 88; auth, Women and Religion in Early America 1600-1850, Routledge, 99. **CONTACT ADDRESS** Dept Hist, Univ of California, Santa Cruz, Merrill Col, Santa Cruz, CA 95064. **EMAIL** mjw@cats.ucsc.edu

WESTERLUND, JOHN S.
PERSONAL Born 07/26/1945, Ontario, CA, m, 1980, 2 children **DISCIPLINE** HISTORY **EDUCATION** US Military Acad, BS, 68; Ut State Univ, MA, 77; US Army For Area Officer's Course, 84; N Ariz Univ, PhD, 01. **CAREER** Instructor, US Army West Point, 79; Asst Prof, Ut State Univ, 77-80; Prof, French Army War Col Paris, 87-90; Chair and Adj Fac to Teaching Asst, N Ariz Univ, 90-. **HONORS AND AWARDS** Intl Fel, Paris, 85-86; Grand Canyon Pioneers Soc Scholarship Awd, 99; Phi Alpha Theta SW Reg Conf, 98; G.M. Farley Scholarship, N AZ Univ, 98; Francis McAllister Fel, 98. **MEMBERSHIPS** Soc of Military Hist; W Hist Asn; AZ Hist Soc. **RESEARCH** American West; Military; Women in America; Recent Europe. **SELECTED PUBLICATIONS** Auth, "The French Army of the 1990s," Military Review, 90; auth, "The Gulf War: The Military Engagement," in The New World Order: Rethinking America's Global Role, (AZ Honors Acad Press, 92); auth, "Rommel's Afrika Korps in Northern Arizona: Austrian Prisoners of War at Navajo Ordinance Depot," Journal of Arizona History, 98. **CONTACT ADDRESS** Dept Hist, No Arizona Univ, PO Box Nau, Flagstaff, AZ 86011-0001. **EMAIL** john.westerlund@nau.edu

WESTERMANN, MARIET
DISCIPLINE ART HISTORY **EDUCATION** Williams Col, BA, 84; NYork Univ, Inst Fine Arts, MA, 89, PhD, 97. **CAREER** Res asst, Metrop Mus Art, 89; adj lectr, NY Univ, 89; adj lectr, Goldsmiths' Col, Univ London, 93; ASST PROF ART HIST, RUTGERS UNIV, 95-. **CONTACT ADDRESS** Dept of Art History, Rutgers, The State Univ of New Jersey, New Brunswick, Voorhees Hall, New Brunswick, NJ 08901. **EMAIL** mwestermann@home.com

WESTFALL, CARROLL W.
PERSONAL Born 12/23/1937, Fresno, CA, m, 1982, 2 children **DISCIPLINE** ART HISTORY **EDUCATION** Univ Calif, BA, 61; Univ Manchester, MA, 63; Columbia Univ, PhD, 67. **CAREER** Amherst Col, 66-72; Univ Ill Chicago, 72-82; Univ Va, 82-98; Frank Montana prof and chair, Sch of Archit, Univ Notre Dame, 98-. **MEMBERSHIPS** Col Art Asn; Soc of Archit Hist; Congress for New Urbanism. **RESEARCH** History of urbanism; Theory of classical and traditional architecture; History of the classical tradition. **SELECTED PUBLICATIONS** Auth, Renewing the American City, Urban Renaissance, Intl Conf on Innovative Urban and Archit Policies: A Vision of Europe, Univ Bologna, Italy, 52-69, 96; auth, The Classical American City in Image and in Chicago, Modulus 23: The Archit Rev at the Univ of Va, 52-71, 95; auth, Allan Greenberg and the Difficult Whole of Architecture, Allan Greenberg: Selected Works, Archit Monogr, no 39, London, Acad Editions, 6-10, 95; auth, Thinking about Modernism and Classicism, The Classicist, I, 6-10, 94-95; auth, The True American City, The New City: The American City, Univ Miami Sch of Archit, II, 8-25, 93-94; "Architecture and Democracy, Democracy and Architecture," Democracy and the Arts, ed A. Melzed, J. Weinberger, M. Zinman, Symposium on Science, Reason, and Modern Democracy, Michigan State Univ, 94-95, Ithaca and London (Cornell Univ Press, 99) 73-91. **CONTACT ADDRESS** Univ of Notre Dame, 110 Bond Hall, Notre Dame, IN 46617. **EMAIL** westfall.z@nd.edu

WESTHAUSER, KARL E.
DISCIPLINE HISTORY **EDUCATION** Cornell Univ, BA, 83; Brown Univ, AM, 85, PhD, 94. **CAREER** Assoc Prof Hist, ALA STATE UNIV, 93. **CONTACT ADDRESS** Alabama State Univ, Campus Box 25, Montgomery, AL 36101. **EMAIL** kwesthauser@alasu.asunet.edu

WESTON, CORINNE COMSTOCK
PERSONAL Born 12/08/1919, Castle Hill, ME, m, 1947 **DISCIPLINE** HISTORY **EDUCATION** Univ Maine, BA, 41; Columbia Univ, MA, 44, PhD, 51. **CAREER** Instr hist, Univ Maine, 46-47; instr, Columbia Univ, 47-48; instr, Univ Maine, 48-49; lectr, Columbia Univ, 49-51; instr, Brooklyn Col, 51-52; prof, Univ Houston, 52-63; from vis assoc prof to assoc prof, Hunter Col, 64-68, assoc prof, Lehman Col, 68-69, Prof Hist, Lehman Col, 69-, Am Coun Learned Soc grant, 62; grants in United Kingdom, 74, 75, 78; mem, Inst Hist Res, Univ London. **HONORS AND AWARDS** Fac Res Awd, City Univ New York, 70-72, 76-77, 79-80. **MEMBERSHIPS** AHA; Conf Brit Studies; Am fel Royal Hist Soc. **RESEARCH** British constitutional theory and history; Stuart and Victorian England. **SELECTED PUBLICATIONS** Auth, Beginnings of the classical theory of the English constitution, Proc Am Philos Soc, 4/56; The Royal mediation in 1884, English Hist Rev, 4/67; Liberal leadership and the Lords' veto, Hist J, 68; Concepts of estates in Stuart political thought, In: Representative Institutions in Theory and Practice, Vol XXXIX, Studies Presented to the International Commission for History of Representative and Parliamentary Institutions, Libr Encycl, Brussels, 70; Legal sovereignty in the Brady Controversy, Hist J, 72; coauth, Subjects and sovereigns: The grand controversy over legal sovereignty in Stuart England, Cambridge Univ Press, 81; auth, The authorship of the Freeholders Grand Inquest, English Hist Rev, 1/80; Sir Robert Holbourne, Henry Powle & Thomas Hunt, In: Biographical Dict of British Radicals in the Seventeenth Century, Vol 1, Harvester Press, 82; auth, The House of Lords and Ideological Politics: Lord Salisbury's Referendal Theory and the Conservative Party, 1846-1922, Am Phil Soc, 95; auth, Lord Selborne, Bonar Law, and the Tory Revolt, in Lords of Parliament: Studies, 1714-1914, Stanford Univ Press. **CONTACT ADDRESS** 200 Central Park S, New York, NY 10019.

WESTON, TIMOTHY B.
DISCIPLINE HISTORY **EDUCATION** Univ Wis Madison, BA, 86; Univ Calif Berkeley, MA, 89; PhD, 95. **CAREER** Prof. **SELECTED PUBLICATIONS** Auth, Corrupt Capital, Reformed Academy: Beijing and the Identity of Beijing University, 1898-1919, Kluwer, 98; America must face true cost of China Policy, 97; New Beijing Municipal Archives Building Welcomes Researchers, Chinese Urban Hist News, 96; Anarchism and Chinese Political Culture (rev), 94; co-auth, U.S., China Face Future In Which Fates Intertwine, Rocky Mountain News, 97. **CONTACT ADDRESS** History Dept, Univ of Colorado, Boulder, Boulder, CO 80309. **EMAIL** weston@stripe.colorado.edu

WETHERELL, CHARLES W.
DISCIPLINE HISTORY **EDUCATION** St Lawrence, BA, 69; Univ NH, PhD, 80. **CAREER** Dir, Lab for Hist Res, Univ Calif, Riverside. **SELECTED PUBLICATIONS** Fel Publ, 'For These and Such Like Reasons': John Holt's Attack on Benjamin Franklin, Procs of the AAS 88, 78; coauth, The New Hampshire Committees of Safety and Revolutionary Republicanism, 1775-1784, Hist of NH 35, 80; coauth, Wealth and Renting in Pre-Revolutionary Philadelphia, Jour of Amer Hist 71, 85; coauth, The Kinship Domain in an Eastern European Peasant Community: Pinkenhof, 1833-50, Amer Hist Rev 93, 88; coauth, The Measure of Maturity: The Pennsylvania Gazette, 1728-65, William and Mary Quart, 89. **CONTACT ADDRESS** Dept of History, Lab for Hist Res, Univ of California, Riverside, Riverside, CA 92121.

WETZELL, RICHARD
PERSONAL Born 08/05/1961, Hannover, Germany, s **DISCIPLINE** GERMAN STUDIES **EDUCATION** Swarthmore Col,

BA, 84; Columbia Univ, MA, 85; Fordham Univ, PhD, 91. **CAREER** Asst prof, Univ Maryland, 91-93; postdoc fel, Harvard Univ, 93-95; asst prof, Univ Maryland, 95-00; res fel, Ger Hist Inst, 00-. **HONORS AND AWARDS** James Bryant Conant Postdoc Fel; Guggenheim Res Gnt. **MEMBERSHIPS** AHA; GSA; HSS. **RESEARCH** Modern German, intellectual, political; legal history; history of science. **SELECTED PUBLICATIONS** Auth, Inventing the Criminal: A History of German Criminology, 1880-1945, Univ NC Press (Chapel Hill), 00; auth, "The Medicalization of Criminal Law Reform in Imperial Germany," in Institutions of Confinement: Hospitals, Asylums and Prisons in Western Europe and North America, 1500-1950, ed. Norbert Finzsch, Robert Jutte (Cambridge Univ Press, 96). **CONTACT ADDRESS** Dept Research, German Historical Institute, 1607 New Hampshire Ave, Washington, DC 20009.

WEXLER, ALICE RUTH
PERSONAL Born 05/31/1942, New York, NY **DISCIPLINE** AMERICAN HISTORY **EDUCATION** Stanford Univ, BA, 64; Georgetown Univ, MA, 66; Ind Univ, PhD(hist), 72. **CAREER** Asst to assoc prof, hist, Sonoma State Univ, 72-82; vis scholar, Univ Calif, Riverside, 82-85, 87; lectr Univ Calif, Riverside, 85-86; vis lectr, Calif Inst Technol, 93; adj lectr, hist, Claremont Grad Sch, 94; adj lectr, hist, Occidental Col, 94-95; lectr, UCLA, 94, 96, 97; res scholar, Ctr for the Study of Women, UCLA, 94- . **HONORS AND AWARDS** Fulbright fel, 64-65; NEH summer stipends, 79, 86; NEH fel, 87; fel, ACLS, 97-98; John Simon Guggenheim Memorial Fel, 99-00; Guggenheim Fel. **MEMBERSHIPS** AHA; West Coast Asn of Women Historians; PEN; Am Stud Asn. **RESEARCH** Medical History; History of Huntington's Disease; Gender; Science; and Medicine. **SELECTED PUBLICATIONS** Auth, Pain and prejudice in the Santiago campaign of 1898, J Inter-Am Studies & World Affairs, 2/76; The early life of Emma Goldman, Psychohist Rev, spring 80; Emma Goldman on Mary Wollstonecraft, Feminist Studies, spring 81; Emma Goldman: A Radical in America, Pantheon, 89; auth, Emma Goldman in Exile, Beacon, 89; auth, Mapping Fate: A Memoir of Family, Risk, and Genetic Research, Times, 95; auth, Mapping Fate, Time Books/Univ of Calif Press, 95. **CONTACT ADDRESS** 1930 Ocean Ave, No. 315, Santa Monica, CA 90405. **EMAIL** arwexler@ucla.edu

WEXLER, VICTOR G.
PERSONAL Born 11/26/1941, New York, NY **DISCIPLINE** EUROPEAN INTELLECTUAL HISTORY **EDUCATION** Univ Mich, UA, 63; Columbia Univ, MA, 65, PhD(hist), 71. **CAREER** Instr humanities, Stevens Inst Technol, 69-71; asst prof, 72-77, Assoc Prof Hist, Univ Md, Baltimore County, 77-, Nat Endowment Humanities fel, 78-79, 82; assoc dean, Col of Arts and Sci, 94-. **MEMBERSHIPS** AHA; Am Soc 18th Century Studies; East Cent Soc (pres). **RESEARCH** Eighteenth-century France and Britain. **SELECTED PUBLICATIONS** Auth, David Hune and the History of England, 79. **CONTACT ADDRESS** Dept of Hist, Univ of Maryland, Baltimore, 1000 Hilltop Circle, Baltimore, MD 21250. **EMAIL** wexler@umbc.edu

WHARTON, ANNABEL JANE
DISCIPLINE ART HISTORY **EDUCATION** London Univ, PhD. **CAREER** Prof, Duke Univ. **HONORS AND AWARDS** Fel from the ACLS, Nat Humanities Center and CASVA; Grants from the NEH and Graham Found. **RESEARCH** Early Christian and Byzantine art and architecture; modern architecture. **SELECTED PUBLICATIONS** Auth, Art of Empire, Penn State Press, 88; auth, Refiguring the Post Classical City: Dura, Jerash, Jerusalem and Ravenna, Cambridge, 95; Art of Empire treat Early Christian and Byzantine painting and architecture as an expression of the social and cultural assumptions of their audiences; auth, Building the Cold War: Hilton International Hotels and Modern Architecture, Univ of Chicago Press, 01. **CONTACT ADDRESS** Dept of Art and Art Hist, Duke Univ, East Duke Building, Durham, NC 27706. **EMAIL** wharton@acpub.duke.edu

WHAYNE, JEANNIE
PERSONAL Born 05/23/1948, Memphis, TN, m, 1989 **DISCIPLINE** HISTORY **EDUCATION** Univ Calif San Diego, BA, 79, MA, 81, PhD, 89. **CAREER** Asst prof, 90-96, assoc prof, Univ Ark, 96-. **SELECTED PUBLICATIONS** Auth, A New Plantation South: Land, Labor, and Federal Favor in Twentieth Century Arkansas, Univ Va, 96; The Significance of Race, Class, and Family in the Battle for Prohibition in Small Town Arkansas, Locus, 95; ed, Cultural Encounters in the Early South: Indians and Europeans in Arkansas, Univ Ark, 95; co-ed, The Governors of Arkansas, Univ Ark, 95; auth, The Arkansas Delta: Land of Paradox, Fayetteville, Univ of Arkansas Press, 93; auth, Shadows Over Sunnyside: Evolution of a Plantation in Arkansas, 1830-1945, Fayetteville, Univ of Arkansas Press, 93; co-ed, The Governors of Arkansas, Fayetteville, Univ of Arkansas Press, 95; auth, Arkansas Biography: A Collection of Notable Lives, Fayetteville: Univ of Arkansas Press, 00. **CONTACT ADDRESS** History Dept, Univ of Arkansas, Fayetteville, 411A Old Main, Fayetteville, AR 72701. **EMAIL** jwhayne@comp.uark.edu

WHEALEY, ROBERT H.
PERSONAL Born 05/16/1930, Freeport, NY, m, 1954, 3 children **DISCIPLINE** HISTORY **EDUCATION** Univ Del, BA, 52; Univ Mich, MA, 54; PhD, 63. **CAREER** Teaching Fel, Univ Mich, 58-59; Instr, Univ Maine, 61-64; Assoc Prof, Ohio Univ, 64-. **HONORS AND AWARDS** Phi Kappa Phi, 52; Fulbright Fel, Spain, 66; Fel Madrid, 77-78; Travel grant, Joint US-Spanish committee of Educational and Cultural affairs, 80. **MEMBERSHIPS** AHA, German Studies Asn, Soc Spanish Portuguese Studies. **RESEARCH** Diplomacy and international relations, 1914 to present. **SELECTED PUBLICATIONS** auth, "Hitler and the Spanish Civil War: a Shifting balance of Power," in The Lion and the Eagle, Berghan Books, 00; auth, "Nazi Propagandist Joseph Goebbels and the Spanish Civil War," The Historian, (99): 341-360; auth, "Francisco Franco y Bahamonde, 1892-1975," in Great Leaders, Great tyrants?, Greenwood Press, 95; auth, "War and Peace" in ready Reference: Ethics vol III, Salem Press, 94; auth, "Selected biographies and Interpretations of Hitler," in Holocaust Literature: A Handbook of critical, Historical and Literary Writings, Greenwood Press, 93; auth, "Wilhelm Canaris 1887-1945," in Research Guide to European Historical biography 1450-Present, Beacham Pub, 92; auth, auth, "communist Party in Spain, partido comunista espanol," in Historical Dictionary of Modern Spain, Greenwood Press, 90; auth, Hitler and Spain: the nazi Role in the Spanish civil War 1936-1939, Univ Press of Kentucky, 89; auth, "Anglo-American Oil confronts Spanish Nationalism, 1927-1931: A Study of Economic Imperialism," Diplomatic History, (88): 11-126; auth, "G.D.G. Cole," in biographical Dictionary of Modern peace Leaders, Greenwood Press, 85. **CONTACT ADDRESS** Dept Hist, Ohio Univ, 1 Ohio Univ, Athens, OH 45701-2942. **EMAIL** whealey@ouvaxa.cats.ohiou.edu

WHEATON, BRUCE R.
DISCIPLINE HISTORY OF SCIENCE **EDUCATION** Stanford Univ, BS; Univ Cal-Berkeley, MA; Princeton Univ, MA & PhD. **CAREER** Tchr Science & Tech, Univ Cal-Berkeley; Prin, Technol & Phys Sci Hist Assoc; George Mayr Educ Found Schol. **MEMBERSHIPS** US Hist Sci Soc **RESEARCH** Cultural history of science and technology **SELECTED PUBLICATIONS** auth The Tiger and the Shark: Empiricial roots of wave-particle dualism, Cambridge, 91; Inventory of Sources for History of Twentieth-Century Physics: Report and Microfiche Index to 700,000 Letters. **CONTACT ADDRESS** Technol & Phys Sci Hist Assn, 1136 Portland Ave, Albany, CA 94706. **EMAIL** wheaton@tapsha.edu

WHEELER, DOUGLAS L.
PERSONAL Born 07/19/1937, St Louis, MO, m, 1964, 2 children **DISCIPLINE** HISTORY **EDUCATION** Dartmouth Col, AB, 59; Boston Univ, MA, 60; PhD, 63. **CAREER** Part-time instr: Morgan State Col, Boston Univ, Univ Col of Rhodesia, 67; res assoc, Harvard Univ, 84-86, Center for Int Affairs; asst prof, Univ of New Hampshire, 65-69, assoc prof, 69-75, full prof, 75-. **HONORS AND AWARDS** High Distinction in Major Awd, Dartmouth Col, 59; Awded NDEA Fel, African Hist, 59-61; Boston Univ, 62-63; Fulbright Student grantee, Univ of Lisbon, 61-62; Fulbright-Hays Grantee, 69-70; res grants from Univ of NH, various foundations in Lisbon (including FLAD, Gulbenkian, Orient, Cameos Inst) and USA (Tinker Found), for Portuguese studies work; Awded Portuguese Hist Prof (Chair), Univ of NH; Medal/decoration from government of Portugal, Grand Officer, Order of Prince Henry, 93. **MEMBERSHIPS** Am Hist Asn, ICG on Portugal, SSPHS. **RESEARCH** History of Portugal and the Portuguese Empire since 1415; history of contemporary espionage. **SELECTED PUBLICATIONS** Auth, Republican Portugal, 78; auth, Angola, 81; auth, A Diadura Militar, 88; auth, Historical Dictionary of Portugal, 1st ed, Scarecrow Press (93), 2nd ed (forthcoming 200-2001); coed, In Search of Modern Portugal. **CONTACT ADDRESS** Dept Hist-Horton Soc Sci, Univ of New Hampshire, Durham, 125 Technology Dr, Durham, NH 03824-3586. **EMAIL** dwheeler@christa.unh.edu

WHEELER, GERALD EVERETT
PERSONAL Born 08/16/1924, Everett, WA, m, 1948, 1 child **DISCIPLINE** AMERICAN HISTORY **EDUCATION** Univ Calif, Berkeley, AB, 48, MA, 49, PhD(Am & Far Eastern hist), 54. **CAREER** Instr hist, Col Holy Names, 50; teaching asst, Univ Calif, Berkeley, 50-52; asst prof, US Naval Acad, 52-57; assoc, 57-80, Prof Hist, San Jose State Univ, 80-, Dean Soc Sci, 76-, Ed jour, Am Aviation Hist Soc, 59-60; Fulbright-Hays teaching grant, Philippines, 63-64; prof hist, Univ Calif, Berkeley, 64-65; E J King prof maritime hist, US Naval War Col, 68-69; ed, Newslett, Soc Hist Am Foreign Rels, 69-72. **MEMBERSHIPS** AHA; Orgn Am Historians; Am Aviation Hist Soc (pres, 66-67); Soc Hist Am Foreign Rels; Am Mil Inst. **RESEARCH** American diplomatic history, 1920-1970; American naval history, 1900-1970; Philippine history, 1900-1946. **SELECTED PUBLICATIONS** Coauth, Outline of world naval history, Acad Press, 56; auth, Prelude to Pearl Harbor: US Navy and the Far East, 1921-1931, Univ Mo, 63; National policy planning between the World Wars, Naval War Col Rev, 69; Admiral William Veazie Pratt, US Govt Printing Off, 74; The Road to War: The United States and Japan, 1931-1941, Forum Press, 77; Edwin Denby, 1921-1924 and Charles Francis Adams III, 1929-1933, In: The American Secretaries of the Navy (2 vols), US Naval Inst, 80. **CONTACT ADDRESS** Dept of Hist, San Jose State Univ, San Jose, CA 95192.

WHEELER, RACHEL
PERSONAL Born 09/11/1969, Fondulac, WI, s **DISCIPLINE** HISTORY **EDUCATION** Yale Univ, PHD, 98 **CAREER** Asst Prof, 98-pres **MEMBERSHIPS** AAR; AHA **RESEARCH** Religious Hist; Missions; Colonial America; Native American History **CONTACT ADDRESS** Dept of Relig Studies, Lewis and Clark Col, 0615 SW Palatine Hill Rd, Portland, OR 97219. **EMAIL** rwheeler@lclark.edu

WHEELER, WILLIAM BRUCE
DISCIPLINE HISTORY **EDUCATION** Univ Va, PhD, 67. **CAREER** Prof, Hist, Univ Tenn. **RESEARCH** Early national period; American urban history. **SELECTED PUBLICATIONS** Co-auth, Knoxville, Tennessee: Continuity and Change in an Appalachian City, Univ Tenn Pr (Knoxville), 82; co-auth, TVA and the Tellico Dam: A Bureaucratic Crisis in Post-Industrial America, Univ Tenn Pr (Knoxville), 86; co-auth, Discovering the American Past, 2 vols., 5th ed, Houghton Mifflin (Boston), forthcoming 01; co-auth, Discovering the Global Past, 2 vols., 2d ed, Houghton Mifflin (Boston), forthcoming 01. **CONTACT ADDRESS** Dept of History, Univ of Tennessee, Knoxville, 915 Volunteer Blvd, 6th Fl, Dunford Hall, Knoxville, TN 37996-4065. **EMAIL** wwheele1@utk.edu

WHEELOCK, ARTHUR K., JR.
PERSONAL Born 05/13/1943 **DISCIPLINE** ART HISTORY **EDUCATION** Williams Col, BA, 65; Harvard Univ, PhD, 73. **CAREER** Harvard Univ, 68-69, 70-71; Lectr, Univ of Maryland, 74, asst prof, 74-84; assoc prof, 84-88; prof of art hist, 88-; Res Cur, Nat Gallery of Art, 74-75; Cur of Dutch and Fleming painting, 76-84; Cur of Northern Baroque Painting, 84-. **HONORS AND AWARDS** Harvard Fellowships, 67-68, 69-71; Nat Defense Title IV Fel, 69-70; Nat Gallery of Art: David E. Finley Fel, 71-74; Nat Endowment for the Arts, 79-80; Nat Gallery of Art Ailsa Mellon Bruce Curatorial Fel from the Ctr for Advanced Study in the Visual Arts, 83, 87; Robert H. Smith Curatorial Res Leave Fel, 90; Col Art Asn/Nat Inst for Conservation Awd for Distinction in Scholarship and Conservation, 93; Robert H. Smith Curatorial Res Leave Fel, 93; Minda de Gunzburg Prize for the best exhibition catalogue of 95; Johannes Vermeer Prize for outstanding achievement in Dutch art, 96; Bicentennial Medal, Williams Col, 96; Am Achievement Awd, 96. **SELECTED PUBLICATIONS** Auth, Perspective, Optics and Delft Artists around 1650, Garland Press, 77; auth, Jan Vermeer, Harry N. Abrams, Inc., 81; co-ed, Van Dyck 350, National Gallery of Art, 94; auth, Dutch Paintings of the 17th Century, National Gallery of Art and Oxford Univ Press, 95; auth, Vermeer and the Art of Painting, Yale Univ Press, 95; auth, Johannes Vermeer: The Complete Works, Harry N. Abrams, Inc., 97; auth, Vermeer's The Art of Painting, National Gallery of Art, Washington, D.C., 99; co-ed, The Public and Private in Dutch Culture of the Golden Age, 00; co-auth, Gerrit Dou (1613-1675): Master Painter in the Age of Rembrandt, National Gallery of Art, 00; co-auth, Small Northern European Portraits from the Walters Art Gallery, Baltimore, National Gallery of Art, 00. **CONTACT ADDRESS** Dept Northern Baroque Painting, National Gallery of Art, Washington, DC 20565. **EMAIL** a-wheelock@nga.gov

WHELAN, STEPHEN T.
PERSONAL Born 07/28/1947, Philadelphia, PA, m, 1971, 1 child **DISCIPLINE** LAW, HISTORY **EDUCATION** Princeton Univ, BA, 68; Harvard Univ, JD, 71. **CAREER** Atty, 75-, partner, 78, Thacher Proffitt & Wood, Mudge Rose Guthrie & Alexander. **HONORS AND AWARDS** Magna cum laude, Princeton Univ; Outstanding Sr, student pol org, Princeton Univ. **MEMBERSHIPS** Amer Bar Asn; Fel, Amer Col of Investment Counsel; The Economic Club, NY. **RESEARCH** Financial law, econ history **SELECTED PUBLICATIONS** Auth, New York's Uniform Commercial Code New Article 2A, Matthew Bender & Co., 94; art, American Bar Association Annual Survey: Leases, Bus Lawyer, Vol 49, 94 & Vol 50, 95 & Vol 51, 96 & Vol 52, 97; art, Securitization of Medical Equipment Finance Contracts, Med Finance & Tech Yearbook, Euromoney Pub, 95; art, Securitization of Medical Equipment Finance Contracts, World Leasing Yearbook, Euromoney Pub, 96; coauth, The ABC's of the UCC: Article 2A (Leases), Amer Bar Asn, 97; art, Asset Securitization, Comm Finance Guide, Matthew Bender, 98. **CONTACT ADDRESS** Thacher Proffitt & Wood, 2 World Trade Ctr, New York, NY 10048. **EMAIL** swhelan@thacherproffitt.com

WHELCHEL, MARIANNE
DISCIPLINE AMERICAN LITERATURE AND WOMEN'S STUDIES **EDUCATION** LaGrange Col, BA; Purdue Univ, MA; Univ CT, PhD. **CAREER** Prof, Antioch Col. **HONORS AND AWARDS** NEH grant, 82-83. **RESEARCH** Alice Carr. **SELECTED PUBLICATIONS** Wrote on letters, jour(s), and oral testimony; publ on Adrienne Rich, and Alice Carr, a 1904 Antioch graduate who nursed in World War I and became internationally known for public health work in Greece during the 1920s. and 1930s. **CONTACT ADDRESS** Antioch Col, Yellow Springs, OH 45387.

WHISENHUNT, DONALD W.
PERSONAL Born 05/16/1938, Meadow, TX, m, 1960, 2 children **DISCIPLINE** HISTORY **EDUCATION** McMurray Col, BA, 60; Tex Tech Univ, PhD, 62. **CAREER** Asst to assoc prof, Murray State Univ, 66-69; assoc prof, Thiel Col, 69-73; prof, Eastern NMex Univ, 73-77; prof, Tex Eastern Univ, 77-83; prof, Wayne State Col, 83-91; prof, Western Wash Univ, 91-. **HONORS AND AWARDS** Fulbright, China, 95, Korea, 99. **MEMBERSHIPS** Org of Am Hist. **RESEARCH** 20th Century US history - especially 1930s. **SELECTED PUBLICATIONS** Auth, Poetry of the People: Poems to the President, 1929-1945, Bowling Green State Univ Popular Pr, 96; ed, American Portraits: History through Biography, Kendall/Hunt Pub, (Dubuque, IA), 93; coed, Selected Letters of Eleanor Roosevelt, 1912-1962, Univ Pr of Ky, (forthcoming). **CONTACT ADDRESS** Dept Hist, Western Washington Univ, M/S 9056, Bellingham, WA 98225.

WHITE, BARBARA EHRLICH
PERSONAL Born New York, NY, m, 1961, 2 children **DISCIPLINE** ART HISTORY **EDUCATION** Smith, BA, 58; Columbia, MA, 60, PhD, 65. **CAREER** Adj prof, 65-, Tufts Univ. **HONORS AND AWARDS** NEH; Kress. **MEMBERSHIPS** Col Art Asn. **RESEARCH** Impressionism; P.A. Renoir. **SELECTED PUBLICATIONS** Ed, Impressionism in Perspective, Prentice-Hall, 78; auth, Renoir: His Life, Art, and Letters, Abrams, 85; auth, Impressionists Side by Side: Their Friendships, Rivalries, and Artistic Exchanges, Knopf, 96 **CONTACT ADDRESS** Dept of Art History, Tufts Univ, Medford, Medford, MA 02155. **EMAIL** artbew@rcn.com

WHITE, CHARLES SIDNEY JOHN
PERSONAL Born 09/25/1929, New Richmond, WI **DISCIPLINE** HIST OF RELIGIONS, HINDUISM & MEDIEVAL & MODERN HINDI POETRY **EDUCATION** Univ Wis, BA, 51; Univ of the Am, MA, 57; Univ Chicago, MA, 62, PhD, 64. **CAREER** Asst prof Indian studies, Univ WI, 65-66; asst prof, relig thought & S Asian studies, Univ PA, 66-71; coordr, ctr Asian Studies, 73-76, assoc prof, Am Univ, 71-78, Dir Ctr Asian Studies, 76-78, Prof Philos & Relig, Am Univ 78-94, Prof Emer Philos & Relig, 95-, chmn dept philos & relig, 84-87 & 88-94, Dir Inst Vaishnava Studies, 71-; Vis lectr Hist Relig, Princeton Univ, 68; Vis prof world relig, Lakehead Univ, Thunder Bay, Ontario, 74, 77, 80, 82, 84 & 88 (summers); Vis prof, Wesley Sem, Fall 85; Jr fel, Am Inst Indian Studies, Poona, India, 64-65 & res fel, Agra, 68-69, trustee, 73-; Kern Found Fel, 72. **HONORS AND AWARDS** Inst Int Educ graduate award, Span lang and lit, Universidad nacional de Mexico; Rockefeller Doctoral fel, relig, hon, Univ Chicago, 61; NDEA fel, Hindu-Urdu, Univ Chicago 61-64; Am Philos Soc fel, 66-67; Summer res grant, Univ PA, India, 70; Col Arts & Sci travel res grant, summer 74; Am Univ travel grant, India, summer 76; Center for Asian Studies, Am Univ, summer grant, 78; Smithsonian Grant, prin investigator, India, 82-83; Am Univ Col Arts & Sci Awd fro Outstanding Scholar, 84; Am Univ Senate Comt Res, India, summer 87; CAS Mellon Awd; Am Inst Indian Studies fac res fel, India, 95, spring 97. **MEMBERSHIPS** Am Asn Asian Studies; Am Acad Relig; Am Orient Soc; Soc Sci Study Relig. **RESEARCH** Hist of relig methodology; Hindu lit; Islam. **SELECTED PUBLICATIONS** Auth, Sufism in Hindi literature, 64 & Krishna as divine child, 70, Hist Relig; Heaven, In: The Encyclopedia Britannica, 65; Resources for the study of Medieval Hindu devotional religion,, Am Philos Soc Yearbk 67; A Note Toward Understanding in Field Method, In: Understanding in History of Relition, Univ Chicago Press, 67; Bhakti, In: The Encyclopedia Britannica, 68; Devi, Dharma, Dayanand Saraswati, Durga, Diwali, The Encyclopedia Americana, 68; Krsna as divine child, Hist Relig, 70; The Sai Baba movement, J Asian Studies, 72; Henry S Olcott: A Buddhist apostle, Theosophist, 4/73; co-auth, Responses to Jay J Bim on Bernard Meland, Jour Relig, 4/73; Swami Muktananda, Hist Relig, 74; Caurasi Pad of Sri Hit Harivams (transl), Univ Hawaii, 77; Structure in history of religions, Hist Relig, 78; Ramayana, Ramanuja, Ram Mohan Roy, Ramakrishna, Encyclopedia Americana, 79; Ramakrishna's Americans, Yugantar Prakashan, 79; Madhva, Mahavira, Mantra, Mandala, Manu, Encyclopedia Americana, 79; Mother Guru: Jnanananda of Madras, India, In: Unspoken Worlds: Women's Religious Lives, Harper and Row, 80, 2nd ed, Wadsworth, 88; The Hindu Holy Person, Ramakrishna, Satya Sai Baba, J Krishnamurti, Ramana Maharshi, Sadhu, Guru, Rsi, Acarya, Meher Baba, In: Abingdon Dictionary of Living Religions, 81, Perennial Dictionary of World Religions, Harper and Row, 89; Untouchables, Parsis, Encyclopedia Americana, 81; Kuan Yin, Juggernaut, Kali, Kama Sutra, Karma, Kautilya, Krishna, Jiddu Krishnamurti, Kshatriya, Kumbha Mela, Lakshmi, In: Encyclopedia Americana, 82; co-auth, The Religious Quest, Univ Md. 83, 2nd ed, 85; Religion in Asia, In: Funk and Wagnall's Yearbook, 85-93, and Collier's International Yearbook; Almsgiving, Gift Giving, Jiddu Krishnamurti: A Biograhy, In: Encyclopedia of Religion, Macmillan Co, 86; Inwardness and privacy: Last bastions of religious life, Theosophis, 86 & Holistic Human Concern for World Welfare, 87; Indian developments: Sainthood in Hinduism, In: Sainthood: Its Manifestations in World Religions, Univ Calif Press, 88, paperbk, 8/90; co-auth, Joseph Campbell: Transformations of Myth Through Time, and An Anthology of Readings, Harcourt Brace Jovanovich, 89; co-ath (with David Haberman), rev, Sonic Theology: Hinduism and Sacred Sound by Guy L Beck, Jour Vaisnava Studies, spring 94; Nimbarka Sampradaya, Anandamayi Ma, Ramana Marsi, Sadhu, Swami, svamin, In: HarperCollins Dictionary of Religion, 95; The remaining Hindi works of Sri Hit Harivams, Jour Vaisnava Studies, fall 96; Mircea Eliade, Bengal Nights .. Maitreyi Devi, It Does Not Die, rev, Love and Politics for Eliade, Annals of Scholarship, summer 97; Muhammad as Spiritual Master, In: The Quest, 8/98. **CONTACT ADDRESS** Dept of Philos & Relig, American Univ, 4400 Massachusetts Ave NW, 123 McCabe Hall, Washington, DC 20016-8056.

WHITE, DAN SELIGSBERGER
PERSONAL Born 05/30/1939, Oakland, CA, m, 1963, 2 children **DISCIPLINE** MODERN EUROPEAN HISTORY **EDUCATION** Stanford Univ, BA, 61; Harvard Univ, MA, 63, Ph-D(hist), 67. **CAREER** Instr hist, Harvard Univ, 66-69; from asst prof to assoc prof, Mass Inst Technol, 69-76; lectr hist, Univ Mass, Boston, 76-77; assoc prof, 77-93, chrm dept, 94- , Prof Hist, Univ at Albany, 93- . **MEMBERSHIPS** AHA **RESEARCH** Modern German history; modern European history; state and society since1750. **SELECTED PUBLICATIONS** Co-ed, The Thirteenth of May: The Advent of de Gaulle's Republic, Oxford Univ, 68; auth, The Splintered Party: National Liberalism in Hessen and the Reich 1867-1918, Harvard Univ, 76; auth, Lost Comrades: Socialists of The Front Generation 1918-1945, Harvard, 92. **CONTACT ADDRESS** Dept of History, SUNY, Albany, Ten Broeck 105, Albany, NY 12222. **EMAIL** dwhite@cas.albany.edu

WHITE, DAVID ANTHONY
PERSONAL Born 02/17/1937, Boston, MA, m, 1985, 2 children **DISCIPLINE** LATIN AMERICAN & MODERN SPANISH HISTORY **EDUCATION** Stanford Univ, BA, 58; Univ Calif, Berkeley, MBA, 61; Univ Calif, Los Angeles, PhD, 68. **CAREER** PROF HIST, SONOMA STATE UNIV, 68-, Danforth Found assoc, 69-; Fel Col Teachers, Nat Endowment for Humanities, 81. **MEMBERSHIPS** AHA; Conf Latin Am Hist; Pac Coast Coun Latin Am Studies. **RESEARCH** Mexico in the 20th Century; Modern Mexican Art, American Ex-patriots in Mexico, 1920s-1930s; United States-Latin American relations. **SELECTED PUBLICATIONS** Creative history: Writing historical fiction, Proc Pac Coast Coun Latin Am Studies, Vol VII, 80-81; Siqueiros: A Biography, Floricanto Press, 94. **CONTACT ADDRESS** Dept Hist, Sonoma State Univ, 1801 E Cotati Ave, Rohnert Park, CA 94928-3609. **EMAIL** tony.white@sonoma.edu

WHITE, DONALD
PERSONAL Born 04/02/1935, Boston, MA, m, 1968, 3 children **DISCIPLINE** CLASSICAL ARCHAEOLOGY **EDUCATION** Harvard Univ, AB, 57; Princeton Univ, MA, 61, PhD(-class archaeol), 64. **CAREER** From instr to assoc prof class archaeol, Univ Mich, 63-73; assoc prof class archaeol & assoc curator, Univ Museum, Univ Pa, 73-87; prof class archaeol and curator, Univ Mus, Univ Pa, 88-, Dir, Excavations, Apollonia and Cyrene, eastern Libya, Marsa Matruh, NW Egypt. **HONORS AND AWARDS** Honorary fellow, Wolfson Col, Oxford. **MEMBERSHIPS** Life member, Archaeol Inst Am; Associazione Internazione di Archeologia Classica, Philadelphia; numismatic and Antiquarian Soc. **RESEARCH** Excavation and publication of 3 N African sites, ancient architecture, curating greek and Roman collections. **SELECTED PUBLICATIONS** Coauth, Apollonia, the Port of Cyrene, 77; The Extramural Sanctuary of Demeter and Persephone at Cyrene I 1984 and V 1993; 70 articles and reviews. **CONTACT ADDRESS** Mus of Archaeol and Anthropol, Univ of Pennsylvania, 33 and Spruce Sts, Philadelphia, PA 19104. **EMAIL** donwhite@sas.upenn.edu

WHITE, DONALD WALLACE
PERSONAL Born Summit, NJ **DISCIPLINE** AMERICAN HISTORY, INTERNATIONAL RELATIONS **EDUCATION** Hartwick Col, BA, 69; City Col, City Univ New York, MS, 72; NYork Univ, MA, 72, PhD(hist), 79. **CAREER** Asst res scientist, 76-80, Assoc Res Scientist, NY Univ, 80-87, Instr NY Univ, 72-73 & 79, asst ed, Papers William Livingston, 76-79, assoc ed, 79-80, asst to McGeorge Bundy, nuclear weapons hist, 79-87, adj asst prof and instructor, 82-. **HONORS AND AWARDS** Outstanding Teaching Awd, New York Univ, Postdoctoral res grants from the Dept of Hist; NEH; Res Grant from the New Jersey Historical Commission; Service Awd of the Morris County Historical Soc. **MEMBERSHIPS** Am Historical Asn. **RESEARCH** Culture and ideas of post-World War II United State foreign affairs; global history patterns of the rise and decline of civilizations; local history. **SELECTED PUBLICATIONS** Auth, "A Local History Approach to the American Revolution: Chatham, New Jersey," New Jersey History 96 Spring-Summer (78): 49-64; assoc ed, The Paper of William Livingston, Trenton, NJ: Rutgers University Press and the New Jersey Historical Commission, vol 1, 79, vol 2, 80; auth, "A Local History Approach to the American Revolution: Chatham, New Jersey, New Jersey History 96 (78): 49-64; auth, A Village at War: Chatham, New Jersey, and the American Revolution, Fairleigh Dickinson Univ Press (Rutherford, NJ), 79; auth, "Census-Making and Local History: In Quest of the People of a Revolutionary Village," Prologue: Journal of the National Archives 14 (82): 157-68; auth, "Census-Making and Local History: In Quest of the People of a Revolutionary Village," Prologue: Journal of the National Archives 14 (82): 157-68; auth, "It's a Big Country: Writers on Internarionalism and the American Landscape after World War II," Journal of the West 26 (87): 80-86; auth, "The Nature of World Power in American History: An Evaluation at the End of World War, Diplomatic History 11 (87): 181-202; auth, "History and American Internationalism: The Formulation from the Past after World War II," Pacific Historical Review 58 (89): 145-72; auth, "The American Century in World History," Journal of World History 3 (92): 105-27; auth, The American Century: The Rise and Decline of the United States As a World Power Yale Univ Press (New Haven and London), paperback ed, 99, Chinese language edition, forthcoming; auth, "Mutuable Destiny: The End of the American Century?" Harvard International Review 20 (97/98): 42-47; **CONTACT ADDRESS** Gallatin School, New York Univ, 715 Broadway, New York, NY 10003.

WHITE, ELIZABETH
PERSONAL Born 07/22/1964, Boston, m, 1994, 2 children **DISCIPLINE** HISTORY **EDUCATION** Yale Univ, PhD, 95. **CAREER** Asst prof, Univ Nev Las Vegas. **MEMBERSHIPS** OAH; ASA. **RESEARCH** 19th Century Market Culture; Sentmentalism. **SELECTED PUBLICATIONS** Auth, "American culture." **CONTACT ADDRESS** History Dept, Univ of Nevada, Las Vegas, 4505 Md Pky, Las Vegas, NV 89154. **EMAIL** eaw@nevada.edu

WHITE, G. EDWARD
PERSONAL Born 03/19/1941, Northampton, MA, m, 1966, 2 children **DISCIPLINE** LAW, HISTORY **EDUCATION** Amherst Coll, BA, 63; Yale Univ, MA, 64; PhD, 67; Harvard Univ, JD, 70. **CAREER** Prof, Univ Virginia, 72-. **HONORS AND AWARDS** AAAS Fel; Tri Coif Awd, Dist Schl; SAH Fel. **MEMBERSHIPS** ALI; ASLH. **RESEARCH** Constitutional history; legal history; constitutional law. **SELECTED PUBLICATIONS** Auth, Earl Warren: A Public Life, Oxford, 82; auth, The Marshall Court and Cultural Change, Oxford, 91; auth, Justice Oliver Wendell Holmes: Law and the Inner Self, Oxford, 93; auth, Creating the National Pastime: Baseball Transforms Itself, Princeton, 96; auth, Intervention and Detachment: Essays on Legal History and Jurisprudence, Oxford, 94; auth, The Constitution and the New Deal, Harvard, 00. **CONTACT ADDRESS** School of Law, Univ of Virginia, 580 Massie Rd, Charlottesville, VA 22903-3244. **EMAIL** gewhite@law5.law.virginia.edu

WHITE, JOHN CHARLES
PERSONAL Born 04/14/1939, Washington, DC, m, 1963 **DISCIPLINE** MODERN HISTORY **EDUCATION** Washington & Lee Univ, BA, 60; Duke Univ, MA, 62, PhD(hist), 64. **CAREER** From asst prof to assoc prof, 67-76, Prof Hist, Univ Ala, Huntsville, 76-, Chmn Dept, 70-, Duke Univ res grant, 64; mem bd dirs, Consortium Revolutionary Europe, 73. **MEMBERSHIPS** Am Soc 18th Century Studies; AHA. **RESEARCH** French colonial policy in 18th century; careers of P V Malouet and Marechal de Castries; Fifth French Republic. **SELECTED PUBLICATIONS** Auth, L'Hopital Maritime de Toulon, Annales du Midi, 12/71; Aspects of reform of the French Navy under Castries: A case for humanity and justice, Univ GA, 75; ed, Proceedings Consortium on Revolutionary Europe, Univ GA, 77. **CONTACT ADDRESS** Dept of Hist, Univ of Alabama, Huntsville, Huntsville, AL 35807.

WHITE, JOHN HOXLAND
PERSONAL Born 11/10/1933, Cincinnati, OH **DISCIPLINE** AMERICAN RAILROAD HISTORY **EDUCATION** Miami Univ, BA, 58. **CAREER** Curator Transp, Smithsonian Inst, 58-, Lectr, Univ Pa, 66, Univ Calif, 70 & Univ Moscow, 73; consult, Calif State RR Mus, 70- & Pa State RR Mus, 68-; ed, RR Hist, 70-79. **HONORS AND AWARDS** Doctor of Letters Miami Univ, 96; DEXTER PRIZE, 94; Book award by SOC. HIST. OF TECH; RR Hist Awd, RR & Locomative Hist Soc, 82; Dexter Prize, 94; Doctor of Letters Miami Univ, 96; Book award by Soc Hist of Tech. **MEMBERSHIPS** Soc Hist Technol; RR & Locomotive Hist Soc. **RESEARCH** Railroad technology, particulary 19th century. **SELECTED PUBLICATIONS** Auth, Cincinnati Locomotive Builders, Smithsonian Inst Pres, 65; American Locomotives, 1830-1880, Johns Hopkins Univ Press, 68; ed, Development of the Locomotive Engine, Mass Inst Technol Press, 70; auth, Early American Locomotives, 72 & Horse Cars, Cable Cars and Omnibuses, 74, Dover Publ; American Railroad Passenger Car, Johns Hopkins Press, 78; John Bull: 150 Years a Locomotives, Smithsonian Inst Press, 81; auth, A Short History of American Locomotive Builders, Boss Books, 82; auth, The American Railroad Freight Car, Johns Hopkins Press, 93. **CONTACT ADDRESS** History Dept, Miami Univ, Oxford, OH 45056.

WHITE, KEVIN
DISCIPLINE AQUINAS, MEDIEVAL PHILOSOPHY **EDUCATION** Univ Ottawa, PhD. **CAREER** Philos, Catholic Univ Am. **RESEARCH** Thomistic psychology; Aquinas; Augustine. **SELECTED PUBLICATIONS** Auth, The Meaning of Phantasia in Aristotle's De anima, III, 3-8, Dialogue 24, 85; St Thomas Aquinas and the Prologue to Peter of Auvergne's Quaestiones super De sensu et sensato, Documenti e studi sulla

tradizione filosofica medievale 1, 90; three previously unpublished chapters from St Thomas Aquinas's Commentary on Aristotle's Meteora: Sentencia super Meteora 2;13-15, Mediaeval Studies 54 , 92; The Virtues of Man the Animal sociale: Affabilitas and Veritas in Aquinas, The Thomist 57, 93; Individuation in Aquinas's Super Boetium De Trinitate, Q;4, American Catholic Philosophical Quarterly 69, 95; Aquinas on the Immediacy of the Union of Soul and Body, in Paul Lockey, ed;, Studies in Thomistic Theology, Houston: Center for Thomistic Studies, 96; Ed, Hispanic Philosophy in the Age of Discovery, Catholic Univ Am Press, 97; Coed, Jean Capreolus et son temps, Cerf, 97. **CONTACT ADDRESS** Catholic Univ of America, 620 Michigan Ave Northeast, Washington, DC 20064. **EMAIL** whitek@cua.edu

WHITE, LONNIE JOE

PERSONAL Born 02/12/1931, Knox City, TX, m, 1951, 2 children **DISCIPLINE** AMERICAN HISTORY **EDUCATION** WTex State Col, BA, 50; Tex Tech Col, MA, 55; Univ Tex, PhD(Am hist), 61. **CAREER** Teaching asst hist, Univ Tex, 57-61; from asst prof to assoc prof, 61-67, Prof Am Hist, Memphis State Univ, 67- **MEMBERSHIPS** AHA; Western Hist Asn; Southern Hist Asn. **RESEARCH** American frontier; military history of the Southwest. **SELECTED PUBLICATIONS** Auth, Politics on the southwestern frontier: Arkansas territory, 1819-1936, Memphis State Univ, 64; White women captives of Southern Plains Indians 1866-1875, J of West, 7/69; Indian raids the Kansas frontier, 1869, Kans Hist Quart, winter 71; coauth, Hostiles and horse Soldiers: Indian Battles and Campaigns in the West, Pruett, 72; co-ed, By Sea to San Francisco, 1849-50: The Journal of Dr James Morison, Memphis State Univ, 77; auth, Indian soldiers of the 36th division, Mil Hist of Tex & Southwest, 79; From Desert To Bayou - The Civil-War Journal And Sketches Of Merrick,Morgan,Wolfe - Thompson,Jd, Journal Of The West, Vol 0032, 1993. **CONTACT ADDRESS** Dept of Hist, Univ of Memphis, Memphis, TN 38152.

WHITE, PHILIP LLOYD

PERSONAL Born 07/31/1923, Akron, OH, m, 1958, 5 children **DISCIPLINE** AMERICAN HISTORY **EDUCATION** Baldwin-Wallace Col, AB, 47; Columbia Univ, MA, 49, PhD(Am Hist & Govt), 54. **CAREER** Lectr World Hist, City Col New York, 54-55; asst prof Am Hist, Univ Tex, 55-58; Fulbright lectr, Univ Nottingham, Eng, 58-59; asst prof, Univ Chicago, 59-62; assoc prof, 62-75, prof Hist, Univ Texas, Austin, 75-, Mem, inst Early Am Hist & Cult, Williamsburg, Va; fel, Charles Warren Ctr, Harvard Univ, 64-65. **MEMBERSHIPS** Orgn Am Historians; Soc Historians Early Am Repub. **RESEARCH** Commerce of pre-revolutionary New York; origins of American nationality; frontier community development in New York and Pennsylvania. **SELECTED PUBLICATIONS** Auth, Beekmans of New York in Politics and Commerce & ed, Beekman Mercantiel Papers (3 vols) NY Hist Soc, 56; coauth, A History of the American People, McGraw, 70; contribr, Perspectives on Early American History, Harper, 73; auth, Beekmantown, New York, Univ Tex, 79. **CONTACT ADDRESS** Dept of History, Univ of Texas, Austin, Austin, TX 78712-1026. **EMAIL** philwhite@mail.utexas.edu

WHITE, RONALD C.

PERSONAL Born 05/22/1939, Minneapolis, MN, m, 1991, 2 children **DISCIPLINE** HISTORY, RELIGIOUS STUDIES **EDUCATION** Univ Calif at Los Angeles, BA, 61; Princeton Theol Sem, M Div, 64; Princeton Univ, MA, 70; PhD, 72. **CAREER** Lectr, Colo Col, 65-66; Instr, Princeton Univ, 70-71; Asst Prof, Rider Col, 72-74; Asst/Assoc Prof, Whitworth Col, 74-81; Vis Prof, San Francisco Theol Sem, Grad Theol Union, 79; Vis Lectr/Lectr, Princeton Theol Sem, 81-88; Ed, Princeton Sem Bul, 83-88; Reader, Huntington Libr, 88-; Prof, Fuller Theol Sem, 89-93; Vis Prof, The Sch of Theol at Claremont, 90-91; Vis Prof, Occidental Col, 91-92; Lectr, Univ Calif, Los Angeles, 91-95; Vice-Pres for Acad Affairs, Dean, Prof, San Francisco Theol Sem, 96-. **HONORS AND AWARDS** World Coun of Churches Scholar, Lincoln, Eng, 66-67; Princeton Univ Fel, 68-70; Ford Found Fel in Ethnic Studies, 70-72; Rider Col Fac Fel, 73; Princeton Univ Vis Fel, 86; Haynes Fel, Huntington Libr, 89; Louisville Inst Fel, 92-94; Lilly Endowment Fel, 94-95. **MEMBERSHIPS** Am Acad of Rel, AHA, Am Soc of Church Hist, Asn of Case Teaching. **RESEARCH** African-American Religious History, Abraham Lincoln, The Social Gospel, Youth Ministry. **SELECTED PUBLICATIONS** Coauth, The Social Gospel: Religion and Reform in Changing America, Temple Univ Press (Philadelphia), 76; coauth, American Christianity: A Case Approach, Eerdmans (Grand Rapids), 86; co-ed, Partners in Peace and Education, (Grand Rapids), 88; co-ed, An Unsettled Arena: Religion and the Bill of Rights, Eerdmans (Grand Rapids), 90; auth, Liberty and Justice for All: Racial Reform and the Social Gospel, Harper and Row (San Francisco), 90; auth, "Youth Ministry at the Center: A Case Study of Young Life," in Reforming the Center: American Protestantism, 1900 to the Present (Grand Rapids: Eerdmans, 98); auth, "Lincoln's Sermon on the Mount: The Second Inaugural," in Religion and the American Civil War, ed. Randall M. Miller, Harry S. Stout, and Charles Reagan Wilson (NY: Oxford Univ Press, 98). **CONTACT ADDRESS** Vice-Pres Acad Affairs, Dean Church Hist, San Francisco Theol Sem, 2 Kensington Rd, San Anselmo, CA 94960-2905.

WHITE, STEVEN D.

DISCIPLINE HISTORY **EDUCATION** Harvard Col, AB, 65; PhD, 72. **CAREER** Asa G. Candler Prof Medieval Hist. **RESEARCH** Medieval French and English history; pre-modern European legal history. **SELECTED PUBLICATIONS** Auth, Custom, Kinship, and Gifts to Saints: the Laudatio Parentum in Western France, 1050-1150; Sir Edward Coke and the Grievances of the Commonwealth, 1621-1628. **CONTACT ADDRESS** Dept History, Emory Univ, 221 Bowden Hall, 561 Kilgo Cir, Atlanta, GA 30322-1950. **EMAIL** histsdw@emory.edu

WHITEHEAD, JOHN S.

DISCIPLINE WESTWARD MOVEMENT **EDUCATION** Yale Univ, PhD, 71. **CAREER** Univ Alaska **SELECTED PUBLICATIONS** Auth, The Separation of College and State: Columbia, Dartmouth, Harvard, and Yale, 1776-1876, 73; Alaska Statehood: The Memory of the Battle, 93. **CONTACT ADDRESS** Univ of Alaska, Fairbanks, PO Box 757480, Fairbanks, AK 99775-7480. **EMAIL** ffjsw@aurora.alaska.edu

WHITEHEAD, RUTH

PERSONAL Born Charleston, SC **DISCIPLINE** ART HISTORY **EDUCATION** Apprentice, The Charleston Museum, 61-65; registr, 70-71, cur asst, hist, staff ethnologist, 72-86, Asst Cur, History, & Staff Ethnologist, Nova Scotia Museum, 87-. **HONORS AND AWARDS** Awd Merit, Am Asn State Local Hist, 81; Reg'l Hist Cert Merit, Can Hist Soc, 82; Awd Merit, Can Museums Asn, 82, 89. **MEMBERSHIPS** Bata Shoe Museum Found. **SELECTED PUBLICATIONS** Auth, Leonard Paul: Portrait of a People/Traditional Micmac Crafts, 78; auth, International Inventory of Micmac, Maliseet and Beothuk Material Culture, 5 vols, 88; auth, The Old Man Told Us: Excerpts from Micmac History, 1500-1950, 91. **CONTACT ADDRESS** Dept of History & Staff Ethnologist, Nova Scotia Mus, Halifax, NS, Canada.

WHITEHOUSE, DAVID BRYN

PERSONAL Born 10/15/1941, Worksop, England **DISCIPLINE** ARCHAEOLOGY **EDUCATION** Cambridge Univ, Eng, BA, 63; MA, 65, PhD, 67. **CAREER** Wainwright Fel, Oxford Univ, 66-73; dir, Brit Inst Afghan Stud, 73-74; dir, Brit Sch at Rome, 74-84; chief cur, Corning Museum Glass, 84-87; dep dir, Corning Museum Glass, 87-92; DIR, CORNING MUSEUM GLASS, 92-. **MEMBERSHIPS** Int Asn Hist Glass; Soc Antiq London; Am Asn Museums **RESEARCH** Early glass & glassmaking; Late antiquity; Islamic art & archaeology **SELECTED PUBLICATIONS** "Byzantine Gilded Glass," Gilded and Enamelled Glass from the Middle East, Brit Mus Press, 98; Excavations at d-Dur (Umm al-Qaiwain, United Arab Emirates), The Glass Vessels, Peeters, 98; rev, "The Islamic Baths of Palestine," Bibliotheca Orientalis, 98; rev, "The Von Post Collection of Cypriote Late Byzantine Glazed Pottery," Bibliotheca Orientalis, 98. **CONTACT ADDRESS** Corning Mus of Glass, One Museum Way, Corning, NY 14830-2253. **EMAIL** director@cmog.org

WHITEHOUSE, EUGENE ALAN

PERSONAL Born 07/15/1931, Augusta, ME, m, 1955, 1 child **DISCIPLINE** MODERN EUROPEAN HISTORY **EDUCATION** Pa State Univ, BA, 53; Univ Mich, MA, 56, PhD, 62. **CAREER** Prof Europ Hist, Nothern Mich Univ, 59-, assoc dean sch Arts & Sci, 67-74. **MEMBERSHIPS** AHA **RESEARCH** Germany in the 1860's. **CONTACT ADDRESS** Sch Arts & Sci, No Michigan Univ, 1401 Presque Isle Ave, Marquette, MI 49855-5301. **EMAIL** ewhiteho@nmu.edu

WHITESIDE, JAMES B.

DISCIPLINE HISTORY **EDUCATION** Colo State Univ, BA, 72; Colo State Univ, MA, 80; Univ Colo at Boulder, PhD, 86. **CAREER** Instr to assoc prof, Univ of Colo at Denver, 90-. **HONORS AND AWARDS** Leroy Hofen Awd, Colo Hist Soc, 85; Teaching Excellence Awd, Univ of Colo at Denver Col of Liberal Arst & Sci, 96; Pub Prize, Colo Endowment for the Humanities, 99. **MEMBERSHIPS** Org of Am Historians, Western Hist Asn, N Am Soc for Sprots Hist. **RESEARCH** United States, labor, diplomacy, sports. **SELECTED PUBLICATIONS** Auth, Regulating Danger: The Struggle for Mine Safety in the Rocky Mountain Coal Industry, 99; auth, Colorado: A Sports History, 99. **CONTACT ADDRESS** Dept History, Univ of Colorado, Denver, PO Box 173364, Denver, CO 80217-3364.

WHITFIELD, STEPHEN JACK

PERSONAL Born 12/03/1942, Houston, TX, m, 1984 **DISCIPLINE** AMERICAN STUDIES **EDUCATION** Tulane Univ, BA, 64; Yale Univ, MA, 66; Brandeis Univ, PhD, 72. **CAREER** Instr hist, 66-68, Southern Univ New Orleans; asst prof, 72-79, assoc prof, 79-85, prof, 85-, am studies, Brandeis Univ **HONORS AND AWARDS** Kayden Prize in the Humanities, 81. **MEMBERSHIPS** Am Studies Assn; Orgn Am Historians; Am Jewish Hist Soc. **RESEARCH** American political and intellectual history in 20th century; post-WW II US hist, Amer Jewish Hist. **SELECTED PUBLICATIONS** Auth, Voices of Jacob, Hands of Esau, Archon, 84; auth, A Critical American: The Politics of Dwight Macdonald, Archon, 84; auth, A Death in the Delta: The Story of Emmett Till, Free Press, 88; auth, American Space, Jewish Time, Archon, 88; auth, The Culture of the Cold War, John Hopkins Univ, 91. **CONTACT ADDRESS** Dept of Am Studies, Brandeis Univ, Waltham, MA 02454-9110. **EMAIL** switfield@brandeis.edu

WHITING, CECILE

PERSONAL Born 04/02/1958, Providence, RI, m, 1983, 2 children **DISCIPLINE** ART HISTORY **EDUCATION** Swarthmore Col, BA, 80; Stanford Univ, MA, 83; PhD, 86. **CAREER** Asst prof to prof, UCLA, 88-; vis asst prof, Duke Univ, 87-88 **HONORS AND AWARDS** Grant, UCLA Center for the Study of Women, 92-93, 96-97; Fel, UCLA, 94-95; Merrillyn Pace Award, UCLA 93; Career Develop Award, UCLA, 90. **MEMBERSHIPS** Col Art Asn; Am Studies Asn. **RESEARCH** Art and politics in the 1930s; Pop art; High art and popular culture; Gender theory. **SELECTED PUBLICATIONS** Auth, "Figuring Marisol's Femininities," RACAR, (91): 73-90; AUTH, "Regenerate Art: The Reception of German Expressionism in the United States, 1900-1945," Art Criticism, (93): 72-92; auth, "Pop At Home," in Domesticity and Modernism, (London, 96), 81-94; auth, "Trompe L'il and the Counterfeit Civil War," The Art Bulletin, (97): 251-168; auth, A Taste for Pop: Pop Art, Gender, and Consumer Culture, Cambridge Univ Press, 97; auth, "Decorating with Stettheimer and the Boys," Am Art, (00): 25-49; auth, "More than Meets the Eye: Archibald Motley and Debates on Race in Art," in Prospects: An Annual of American Cultural Studies, (forthcoming). **CONTACT ADDRESS** Dept Art Hist, Univ of California, Los Angeles, 100 Dodd Hall, Los Angeles, CA 90095-1417. **EMAIL** Whiting@humnet.ucla.edu

WHITING, PETER

PERSONAL Born 09/16/1960, Washington, DC, m, 1990, 2 children **DISCIPLINE** GEOLOGY **EDUCATION** Carleton Col, BA, 82; Univ Calif, PhD, 90. **CAREER** Fac Res Assoc, Univ Md, 82-83; Res Asst, Univ Calif, 84-90; Visiting Fac Researchers, Univ Genoa, 90; Geomorphologist, EA Engineering, 90-91; Visiting Scientist, Univ WA, 90-91; Visiting Asst Prof to Assoc Prof, Case Western Reserve Univ, 91-. **HONORS AND AWARDS** Aldo Leopold Leadership Fel, 00; George Mayer Chair, 95-98; Lilly Foundation Teaching Fel, 93-94; Sigmi Xi. **MEMBERSHIPS** Am Geophysical Union; Am Geomorphological Field Group; Geol Soc of Am; Great Lakes Aquatic Ecosystem Research Consortium. **RESEARCH** Rivers; Streams; Sediment; Water rights. **SELECTED PUBLICATIONS** Co-auth, "A Numerical Study of Bank Storage and its Contribution to Streamflow," Journal of Hydrology, v202 (97): 121-136; auth, "Floodplain maintenance flows," Rivers 6 (98): 160-170; co-auth, "Annual hysteresis in bedload rating curves," Water Resources Research 34 (98): 2393-2399; co-auth, "Equations and transformations for extension of streamflow records," Water Resources Research 35 (99): 243-254; co-auth, "Fine sediment residence times in rivers determined using fallout radionuclides (Bc, Cs, Pb)," Geomorphology 27 (99): 75-92; co-auth, "Sediment transporting flows in headwater streams," Bull Geol Soc America 111 (99): 450-466; co-auth, "Computing effective discharge with S-Plus," Computers and Geosciences 25 (99): 559-565; co-auth, "Alluvial architecture in headwater streams with special emphasis on step-pool topography," Earth Surface Processes and Landforms, in press; co-auth, "Flow measurement and characterization," in Tools in Fluvial Geomorphology, in press; co-auth, "The geometric, sedimentologic and hydrologic attributes of spring-dominated streams," Geomorphology, forthcoming. **CONTACT ADDRESS** Dept Geol, Case Western Reserve Univ, 10900 Euclid Ave, Cleveland, OH 44106. **EMAIL** pjw5@po.cwru.edu

WHITLEY, DAVID S.

PERSONAL Born 03/05/1953, Williams AFB, AZ, m, 1987, 1 child **DISCIPLINE** ANTHROPOLOGY, ARCHAEOLOGY **EDUCATION** UCLA, PhD, 82. **CAREER** Chiel Archaeologist, Inst of Archaeology, UCLA, 83-87; post-doc res fel, Archaeology dept, Univ of the Witwatersrand, 87-89; principle, WIS Consultants, 89-. **HONORS AND AWARDS** Special appreciation awards: CA Indian Found, 93; Simi Valley Hist Soc, 91; Canadian Tribal Coun, 89. **MEMBERSHIPS** Fel, Am Antropological Asn; Soc for Am Archaeology; Soc of Prof Archaeologists; Int Coun of Monuments and Sites. **RESEARCH** Western, northern Am archaeology; prehistoric religion; rock art; neuropsychology. **SELECTED PUBLICATIONS** Auth, New Light in Old Art: Recent Advances in Hunter-Gatherer Rock Art Research, co-ed with L L Loendorf, UCLA Inst of Archaeology, Monograph 36, 94; Guide to Rock Art Sites: Southern California and Southern Nevada, Mountain Press Pub Co, 96; Following the Shaman's Path, Maturango Museum, 98; Reader in Gender Archaeology, co-ed with K Hayes-Gilpen, Routledge, 98; ed, Reader in Archaeological Theory: Post-processual and Cognitive Approaches, Routledge, 98; Les Chamanes de Californie: Art Rupestre Amerindien de Californie, Editions du Seuil, in press; numerous other scholarly articles, book reviews, and other publications. **CONTACT ADDRESS** 447 Third St, Fillmore, CA 93015. **EMAIL** huitli@impulse.net

WHITMAN, T. STEPHEN

PERSONAL Born 02/08/1950, Rexmont, PA, m, 1997 **DISCIPLINE** HISTORY **EDUCATION** Mich State Univ, BA, 71;

Drexel Univ, MS, 73; Johns Hopkins Univ, MA, 90, PhD, 93. **CAREER** Adj Prof, Univ Houston, 83; Human Resources Mgr, US Dept State, 75-90; Mem, Comn US State Dept Personnel Mgt, 92-93; Asst Prof Hist, St. Mary's Col, 94-; Consult, US State Dept, 97. **HONORS AND AWARDS** Superior Honor Awd, US Dept State, 90; Md Hist Soc Bk Awd, 97. **SELECTED PUBLICATIONS** Auth, Industrial Slavery at the Margin: The Maryland Chemical Works, J Southern Hist, 93; Diverse Good Causes: Manumission and the Transformation of Urban Slavery, Soc Sci Hist, 95; The Price of Freedom: Slavery and Manumission in Baltimore and Early National Maryland, Univ Press Ky, 97. **CONTACT ADDRESS** History Dept, Mount Saint Mary's Col and Sem, Emmitsburg, MD 21727. **EMAIL** whitman@msmary.edu

WHITNEY, ELSPETH
DISCIPLINE HISTORY **EDUCATION** City Univ NYork, PhD, 85. **CAREER** Assoc prof, Univ Nev Las Vegas; 90-; chair History dept, 95-98. **RESEARCH** Medieval Europe history; science and technology history; European women history; environment history. **SELECTED PUBLICATIONS** Auth, Paradise Restored: The Mechanical Arts from Antiquity Through the Thirteenth Century, 90; auth, articles in Environmental Ethics and Journal of Women's History. **CONTACT ADDRESS** History Dept, Univ of Nevada, Las Vegas, 4505 Md Pky, Las Vegas, NV 89154.

WHITTAKER, CYNTHIA HYLA
PERSONAL Born 05/15/1941, Niagara Falls, NY, m, 2 children **DISCIPLINE** RUSSIAN HISTORY **EDUCATION** Marymount Col, NYork, BA, 62; Ind Univ, Bloomington, MA, 64, PhD(Russ hist), 72. **CAREER** Asst Prof Russ Hist, Baruch Col, 73-, Res grant & partic, Young Fac Exchange Prog with Soviet Union, 73; City Univ New York fac res award, 74-75; ed, Slavic & Europ Educ Rev, 76-. **MEMBERSHIPS** AHA; Am Asn Advan Slavic Studies. **RESEARCH** Conservatism and education in Imperial Russia. **SELECTED PUBLICATIONS** Auth, The white Negro: Russian and American abolition, NDak Quart, 65; co-ed, The American bibliography of Russian and East European studies for 1963, 66 & The American bibliography of Russian and East European studies for 1964, 66, Ind Univ; auth, The women's movement during the reign of Alexander II: A case study in Russian liberalism, J Mod Hist, 76; The ideology of Sergei Uvarov: An interpretive essay, Russ Rev, 78; The impact of the Oriental Renaissance in Russia, Jahrbuecher fuer Geschichte Osteuropas, 78; One use of history in education: A translation and analysis of Uvarov's speech of 1818, Slavic & Europ Educ Rev, 78; From promise to purge: The first years of St Petersburg University, Paedagogica Historica, 79; To The Editor + Cracraft,James Review Of Alexander,John Biography Of Catherine-The-Great, Slavic Review, Vol 0053, 1994; Political-Ideas And Institutions In Imperial Russia - Raeff,M, Slavic Review, Vol 0054, 1995; Scenarios Of Power - Myth And Ceremony In Russian Monarchy, Vol 1, From Peter-The-Great To The Death Of Nicholas-I - Wortman,Rs, American Historical Review, Vol 0101, 1996. **CONTACT ADDRESS** Dept of Hist, Baruch Col, CUNY, 531 Main St, New York, NY 10044. **EMAIL** cynthia_whittaker@baruch.cuny.edu

WHITTENBURG, CAROLYN
PERSONAL Born 10/03/1946, Danville, VA, m, 1970, 2 children **DISCIPLINE** HISTORY **EDUCATION** Averett Jr Col, AA, 67; Meredith Col, BA, 69; Wake Forest Univ, MA, 71; William & Mary Col, EdN, 97. **CAREER** From Instr to Asst Prof, Hampton Univ, 86-. **HONORS AND AWARDS** Distinguished Teaching Awd, 91; Fel, Wake Forest Univ; Kappa Delta Pi; Who's Who in the S, 99; Who's Who in Am, 00. **MEMBERSHIPS** AHA, SHA, WHA. **RESEARCH** Virginia history, history of women in higher education. **SELECTED PUBLICATIONS** Rev, James Madison and the American Nation 1751-1836: An Encyclopedia, 94; auth, "Abner Anderson," Dict of Va Biog, Va St Libr Publ (98): 123; auth, "Dr Thomas Pleasants Atkinson," Dict of Va Biog, Va St Libr Publ (98): 243-244; auth, "Bishop James Madison," Am Nat Biog, Oxford UP (99):; auth, "The Huguenots in North Carolina," The Encycl of NC Hist, Univ NC Pr (forthcoming); auth, "North Carolina in the Continental Congress," The Encycl of NC Hist, Univ NC Pr (forthcoming). **CONTACT ADDRESS** Dept Hist, Hampton Univ, Hampton, VA 23668. **EMAIL** cswhit@mail.wm.edu

WHITTENBURG, JAMES PENN
PERSONAL Born 10/26/1946, Rome, GA, m, 1970, 1 child **DISCIPLINE** AMERICAN HISTORY **EDUCATION** Univ Chattanooga, AB, 69; Wake Forest Univ, MA, 71; Univ Ga, PhD(hist), 74. **CAREER** Asst prof hist, Univ Mo-Columbia, 74-77; asst prof, 77-80, Assoc Prof Hist, Col William & Mary, 80-. **MEMBERSHIPS** Southern Hist Asn; Orgn Am Historians. **RESEARCH** Colonial America; Southern history; quantification. **SELECTED PUBLICATIONS** Auth, The computer as a teaching aid: a report on two class projects, Hist Teacher, 5/76; coauth, Measuring inequality: a FORTRAN Program for the Gini Index, Schutz Coefficient, and Lorenz Curve, Hist Methods Newsletter, spring 77; auth, Planters, lawyers, and merchants: social change and the origins of the North Carolina Regulation, 4/77 & The common farmer: Herman Husband's plan for peace between the United States and the Indians, 1792, 10/77, William & Mary Quart; Primal Forces, 3 Interlocking Themes In The Recent Literature On 18th-Century Virginia, Virginia Magazine Of History And Biography, Vol 0104, 1996. **CONTACT ADDRESS** Dept of Hist, Col of William and Mary, Williamsburg, VA 23185. **EMAIL** jpwhitt@wm.edu

WICKBERG, DANIEL
PERSONAL Born 04/11/1960, Oakland, CA **DISCIPLINE** HISTORY **EDUCATION** Yale Univ, PhD, 93. **CAREER** Asst prof. **RESEARCH** Modern American cultural and intellectual history; American studies; history of social thought; historiography **SELECTED PUBLICATIONS** Auth, The Senses of Humor: Self, Laughter and Bourgeois Consciousness in Modern America, Cornell, 97; auth, "Homophobia: On the Cultural History of an Idea," Critical Inquiry 27, (00): 42-57; auth, "Sambo and the Sympathetic Imagination: racial Characterology and the Meaning of Laughter in Nineteenth-Century America," Intellectual History Newsletter 23, 01; auth, "Intellectual History vs. the Social History of Intellectuals," Rethinking History 5, 01. **CONTACT ADDRESS** Dept of Arts and Humanities, Univ of Texas, Dallas, Richardson, TX 75083-0688. **EMAIL** wickberg@utdallas.edu

WICKER, NANCY L.
PERSONAL Born, IN, m, 1991 **DISCIPLINE** ARCHAEOLOGY **EDUCATION** Eastern IL Univ, BA, 75; Univ Minn, MA, 79; PhD, 90. **CAREER** Asst prof, Mankato State Univ, 90-95; assoc prof to prof, Minn State Univ, Mankato, 95-. **HONORS AND AWARDS** Kress Art Hist Fel, 77-78; Minneapolis Found Fel, 82; Am Scandinavian Found Thord-Gray Fel, 82; Sigma Xi Res Grant, 86; Aurora Borealis Prize, 88; Birka Int Scholar, 92; NEH, 95, 00; Berit Wallenberg Found Grant 97; IREX Grant, 97. **MEMBERSHIPS** Am Anthrop Assoc; Am Assoc of Univ Women; Am Scandinavian Found; Archaeol Inst of Am; Europ Assoc of Archaeol; Medieval Acad of Am; Soc for Am Archaeol; Soc for Medieval Archaeol. **RESEARCH** Early Medieval art and archaeology in northern Europe, especially Scandinavia. **SELECTED PUBLICATIONS** Auth, "Swedish-Anglian Contacts Antedating Sutton Hoo: The Testimony of the Scandinavian Gold Bracteates", Sutton Hoo: 50 Years After, ed Robert Farrell and Carol Neuman de Vegvar, Miami Univ, (Oxford, OH, 92): 149-171; auth, "The Organization of Crafts Production and the Social Status of the Migration Period Goldsmith", The Archaeol of Gundme and Lundeborg, ed Poul-Otto Nielsen, Klavs Randsborg and Henrik Thrane, Univ I Kobenhavn, (94): 145-150; auth, "Bracteate Workshops and Runic Literacy: Testimony from the Distribution of Inscriptions", Proceedings of the Third Int Symposium on Runes and Runic Inscriptions, ed James K. Knirk, Institutionen for nordiska sprak, Upsalla Universitet, (94): 59-81; auth, "On the Trail of the Elusive Goldsmith: Tracing Individual Style and Workshop Characteristics in Migration Period Metalwork", Gesta, (94): 65-70; auth, "Selective Female Infanticide as Partial Explanation for the Dearth of Women in Viking Period Scandinavia", Violence and Society in Early Medieval Western Europe: Private, Public and Ritual, ed Guy Halsall, Boydell Pr, (Woodbridge, Suffolk, 98): 205-221; auth, "Production Areas and Workshops for the Manufacture of Bracteates", Runeninschriften als Quellen interdisziplinarer Forschung. Ed Klaus Kuwel, de Gruyter, (Berlin/NY, 98): 254-267; auth, "Infanticide in Late-Iron-Age Scandinavia", The Loved Body's Corruption: Archaeological Contributions to the Study of Human Morality, ed Jane Downes and Tony Pollard, Cruithen Pr, (Glasgow, 99): 106-119; coed, From the Ground Up: Beyond Gender Theory in Archaeology, Proceedings of the Fifth Gender and Archaeology Conference in 1998, Archaeopress (Oxford), 99; auth, "Archaeology and Art History: A Search for Common Ground", Medieval Archaeol 43, (00): 161-171. **CONTACT ADDRESS** Dept Art, Minnesota State Univ, Mankato, Nelson 136, Mankato, MN 56001. **EMAIL** nancy.wicker@mankato.msus.edu

WICKSTROM, JOHN B.
PERSONAL Born 07/23/1941, Lansing, MI, m, 1996 **DISCIPLINE** HISTORY **EDUCATION** Mich St Univ, BA, 59; Yale Univ, MA, 64, PhD, 69. **CAREER** Asst prof to assoc prof to prof, 68-, Kalamazoo Col. **HONORS AND AWARDS** Lucasse Lectorship Awd, 82. **MEMBERSHIPS** Medieval Acad; Medieval Acad of Midwest. **RESEARCH** Medieval church hist; monastic hist. **SELECTED PUBLICATIONS** Auth, ICS MS 34: A 15th Cent Cistercian Breviary, Manuscripta, 84; auth, The Antiphons ad psalmos of Carthusian Lauds, Analecta Cartusiana, 88; auth, The Humiliati: Liturgy and Identity, Archivum Fratres Praedicatorum, 92; auth, St. Maurus of Glanfueil: Text and Image in the Making of a Holy Man, Stud in Iconography, 94; auth, Pope Gregory's Life of Benedict and the Illustrations of Abbot Desiderius of Monte Cassino, Stud in Iconography, 98. **CONTACT ADDRESS** Dept of History, Kalamazoo Col, 1200 Academy St, Kalamazoo, MI 49006. **EMAIL** wickstro@kzoo.edu

WICKWIRE, MARY BOTTS
PERSONAL Born 02/13/1935, Carthage, MO, m, 1957, 2 children **DISCIPLINE** MODERN HISTORY **EDUCATION** Wellesley Col, BA, 56; Yale Univ, MA, 57, PhD(hist), 63. **CAREER** Am Philos Soc res grant, 65-66; asst prof, 72-73, assoc prof, 73-81, prof, Univ Mass, Amherst, 81-. **MEMBERSHIPS** Conf Brit Studies; Soc Am Historians; List & Index Soc. **RESEARCH** Eighteenth century British history; British imperial history; Canadian history. **SELECTED PUBLICATIONS** Coauth, Cornwallis: The American Adventure, Houghton, 70; Cornwallis and the War of Independence, Faber & Faber, 71; Cornwallis: The Imperial Years, 80. **CONTACT ADDRESS** Dept of Hist, Univ of Massachusetts, Amherst, Amherst, MA 01003-0002. **EMAIL** wickwire@history.umass.edu

WIDENOR, WILLIAM C.
DISCIPLINE HISTORY **EDUCATION** Univ Calif Berkeley, PhD, 75. **CAREER** Prof, Univ Ill Urbana Champaign. **RESEARCH** History of the foreign relations of the United States. **SELECTED PUBLICATIONS** Auth, American Planning for the United Nations: Have We Been Asking the Right Questions?, Dipl Hist, 82; Henry Cabot Lodge and the Search for an American Foreign Policy, Univ Calif, 83; The Role of Electoral Politics in American Foreign Policy Formulation: Are Historians Meeting the Conceptual Challenge?, Soc Hist Am For Rel Newsletter, 85. **CONTACT ADDRESS** History Dept, Univ of Illinois, Urbana-Champaign, 52 E Gregory Dr, Champaign, IL 61820. **EMAIL** wwidenor@staff.uiuc.edu

WIDER, SARAH ANN
PERSONAL Born 06/07/1959, Albuquerque, NM **DISCIPLINE** AMERICAN RENAISSANCE, MUSIC AND LITERATURE **EDUCATION** Univ NM, BA, 81; Cornell Univ, MA, PhD, 84, 86. **CAREER** Assoc prof, Colgate Univ, 86. **MEMBERSHIPS** Phi Beta Kappa; Phi Kappa Phi; The Emerson Society. **RESEARCH** Emerson, congregation response to early 19th century Am sermons. **SELECTED PUBLICATIONS** Auth, Anna Tilden, Unitarian Culture and the Problem of Self-Representation, Georgia, 97; auth, The Critical Reception of Emerson: Unsettling All Things, Camden House, 00. **CONTACT ADDRESS** Dept of Eng, Colgate Univ, 13 Oak Drive, Hamilton, NY 13346. **EMAIL** swider@mail.colgate.edu

WIECEK, WILLIAM MICHAEL
PERSONAL Born 01/31/1938, Cleveland, OH, m, 2000, 3 children **DISCIPLINE** UNITED STATES LEGAL & CONSTITUTIONAL HISTORY **EDUCATION** Cath Univ Am, BA, 59; Harvard Univ, LLB, 62; Univ Wis-Madison, PhD(hist), 68. **CAREER** From asst prof to assoc prof, 68-77, Prof Hist, Univ MO-Columbia, 77-85; Congdon Prof of Publoc Law & Prof of Hist, Syracuse Univ Col of Law, 85-. **HONORS AND AWARDS** Phi Beta Kappa **MEMBERSHIPS** Orgn Am Historians; Am Law Inst; Am Historical Asn. **RESEARCH** American legal and constitutional development; slavery; U.S. Supreme Court. **SELECTED PUBLICATIONS** Auth, The reconstruction of federal judicial power, 1863-1875, Am J Legal Hist, 69; The great writ and reconstruction: The Habeas Corpus Act of 1867, J Southern Hist, 70; The Guarantee Clause of the US Constitution, Cornell Univ, 72; Somerset: Lord Mansfield and the legitimacy of slavery in the Anglo-American World, Univ Chicago Law Rev, 74; The law of slavery and race in the thirteen mainland colonies of British America, William & Mary Quart, 77; The Sources of Antislavery Constitutionalism in America, 1760-1848, Cornell Univ Press; Equal Justice Under Law: Constitutional Development, 1835-1875, Harper & Row; auth, Lost World of Classical Legal Thought, Oxford Univ Press, 98. **CONTACT ADDRESS** Col of Law, Syracuse Univ, Syracuse, NY 13244. **EMAIL** wmwiecek@law.syr.edu

WIECZYNSKI, JOSEPH LEON
PERSONAL Born 04/13/1934, Baltimore, MD, m, 1962, 4 children **DISCIPLINE** HISTORY OF RUSSIA **EDUCATION** St Mary's Sem & Univ, BA, 56; Georgetown Univ, PhD, 66. **CAREER** Analyst Soviet studies, 64-66, US Libr Cong; asst prof hist, 66-68, Edgewood Col; from asst prof to assoc prof, 68-74, prof hist, 74-, Va Polytech Inst & State Univ; Am Philos Soc res grants, 69-70, 71 & 73; res grants, Va Polytech Inst & State Univ, 71-72 & 74-75; vis prof, 76-77, Oxford Univ; vis prof, 89, Univ London; pres, Southern Conf on Slavic Stud, 89; vice pres, 89-92, Amer Catholic Hist Assn; ed, 90-95, J Soviet and Post Soviet Review, retired 99. **MEMBERSHIPS** AHA; Am Asn Advan Slavic Studies; Am Cath Hist Asn; Southern Slavic Conf; Am Renaissance Soc. **RESEARCH** Russian intellectual history; early Russian history. **SELECTED PUBLICATIONS** Auth, Economic Consequences of Disarmament: The Soviet View, Russ Rev, 68; auth, Donation of Constantine in Medieval Russia, Cath Hist Rev, 69; auth, Archbishop Gennadius and the West, Can-Am Slavic Studies, 72; ed, Moscow and the West, 72 & Ivan the Terrible, 74, Acad Int; auth, Hermetism and Cabalism in The Heresy of the Judaizers, Renaissance Quart, 75; auth, The Russian Frontier, Univ Va, 76; ed, The Modern Encyclopedia of Russian and Soviet History, Acad Int, 76-90; ed, 54 vols, The Gorbachev Encyclopedia, Ross, 93; ed, The Gorbachev Reader, Ross, 93; ed, The Gorbachev Bibliography, Ross, 96. **CONTACT ADDRESS** 3398 W. Chelmsford Ct, Sarasota, FL 34235-0947. **EMAIL** j.wieczynski@home.com

WIENER, JOEL H.
PERSONAL Born 08/23/1937, New York, NY, m, 1961, 3 children **DISCIPLINE** BRITISH HISTORY **EDUCATION** NYork Univ, BA, 59; Cornell Univ, PhD, 65. **CAREER** From instr to asst prof hist, Skidmore Col, 64-67; asst prof, 67-72,

from asst prof hist to assoc prof, 72-78, prof hist, 78-, chemn dept, 81-85, City Col NY; vis lectr hist, Univ York, Eng, 71-73; Prof Emeritus History, 00-. **MEMBERSHIPS** AHA; Conf Brit Studies; fel Royal Hist Soc; Res Soc Victorian Periodicals (pres 83-85)-, Am Journalism Historians Asn. **RESEARCH** Modern British history; history of journalism. **SELECTED PUBLICATIONS** Auth, Radicalism and Freethought in Nineteenth-Century England: The Life of Richard Carlile, Greenwood, 82; ed, Innovators and Preachers: The Role of the Editor in Victorian England, Greenwood, 85; ed, Papers for the Millions; The New Journalism in Britain, 1850s to 1914, Greenwood, 88; auth, William Lovett. **CONTACT ADDRESS** 267 Glen Ct, Teaneck, NJ 07666. **EMAIL** jwiener@idt.net

WIENER, JONATHAN M.
PERSONAL Born 05/16/1944, St. Paul, MN **DISCIPLINE** SOCIAL HISTORY **EDUCATION** Princeton Univ, BA, 66; Harvard Univ, PhD(govt), 72. **CAREER** Actg asst prof polit, Univ Calif, Santa Cruz, 72; lectr sociol & polit sci, Univ Calif, Los Angeles, 72-73; asst prof, 73-77, prof hist, Univ Calif, Irvine, 84- ; Am Coun Learned Socs fel, 78; Rockefeller Found humanities fel, 78. **RESEARCH** Social history of American South; history and social theory; recent United States history. **SELECTED PUBLICATIONS** Auth, Planter-merchant conflict in reconstruction Alabama, Past & Present, 75; Social origins dictatorship and democracy, Hist & Theory, 76; Social Origins of the New South, La State Univ, 78; Class Structure and Economic Development in the American South, Am Hist Rev, 79; auth, Come Together: John Lennon in His Time, Random, 84; auth, Professors, Politics & Pop, Verso, 94; auth, Gimme Some Truth: The John Lennon FBI Files, Univ Calif, 99. **CONTACT ADDRESS** Dept of History, Univ of California, Irvine, Irvine, CA 92697. **EMAIL** jmwiener@uci.edu

WIENER, MARTIN J.
PERSONAL Born 06/01/1941, Brooklyn, NY, 2 children **DISCIPLINE** MODERN BRITISH HISTORY **EDUCATION** Brandeis Univ, BA, 62; Harvard Univ, MA, 63, PhD(hist), 67. **CAREER** Asst prof, 67-72, assoc prof, 72-80, Prof Hist, Rice Univ, 80-, Nat Endowment for Humanities younger humanist fel, 73-74; Am Coun Learned Soc fel, 82; Nat Endowment for Humanities Senior Fel, 86-87; Woodrow Wilson Intl Ctr Fel, 92-98. **HONORS AND AWARDS** Schuyler Prize, Am Hist Asn, 81; Honorable Mention, Snow Prize, NACBS, 91. **MEMBERSHIPS** AHA; Conf Brit Studies; Am Soc for Legal Hist; Soc Hist Soc; Int Assoc for Hist of Times & Criminal Justice. **RESEARCH** Nineteenth and 20th century British social and intellectual history; criminal justice history. **SELECTED PUBLICATIONS** Auth, Between Two Worlds: The Political Thought of Graham Wallas, Clarendon, Oxford, 71; English Culture and the Decline of the Industrial Spirit 1850-1980, Cambridge, 81; Reconstructing the Criminal: Culture, Law, and Policy in Enlgand, 1830-1914, Cambridge, 90; Gentlemen Capitalists, The Social And Political World Of The Victorian Businessman - Malchow,Hl, Victorian Studies, 93; Crime In 19th-Century Wales - Jones,Djv, Victorian Studies, 93; Women, Crime And Custody In Victorian England - Zedner,L, Victorian Studies, 93; The Unloved State - 20th-Century Politics In The Writing Of 19th-Century History, Journal Of British Studies, 94. **CONTACT ADDRESS** Dept of Hist, Rice Univ, Houston, TX 77251. **EMAIL** wiener@rice.edu

WIGEN, KAREN
DISCIPLINE HISTORY **EDUCATION** Univ MI Ann Arbor, BA, 80; Univ CA Berkeley, PhD, 90. **CAREER** Assoc prof, Duke Univ. **HONORS AND AWARDS** Ford Foundation grant, 97; John K. Fairbank book prize, 95; fellowships, from the Japan Foundation, NEH, Fulbright-Hays, and FLAS **RESEARCH** Processes and patterns of Japan's modernization; regional identities in East Asia during the nineteenth and twentieth centuries, temporal and spatial frameworks used by Japanese historians **SELECTED PUBLICATIONS** Auth, The Making of a Japanese Periphery 1750-1920, Univ Ca, 95; Politics and piety in Japanese native-place studies: The rhetoric of solidarity in Shinano, 96; co-auth, The Myth of Continents: A Critique of Meta-Geography, Univ Ca, 97; ed, Mirror of Modernity: Japan's Invented Traditions, Univ Ca, 98; auth, "Culture, Power, and Place: The New Landscapes of Regionalism in East Asia," American Historical Review, (fall 99); auth, "Teaching About Home: Geography At Work in the Prewar Negano Classroom," Journal of Asian Studis, (August 00) **CONTACT ADDRESS** Dept of Hist, Duke Univ, 1440 Franklin Center, Box 90405, Durham, NC 27708. **EMAIL** kwigen@acpub.duke.edu

WIGGINS, JAMES BRYAN
PERSONAL Born 08/24/1935, Mexia, TX, m, 1956, 2 children **DISCIPLINE** RELIGION; HISTORY **EDUCATION** Tex Wesleyan Col, BA, 57; Southern Methodist Univ, BD, 59; Drew Univ, PhD(hist theol), 63. **CAREER** Instr English, Union Jr Col, 60-63; from asst prof to assoc prof relig, 63-75, Prof Relig, Syracuse Univ, 75-, Eliaphalet Remington Prof of Rel, 98, Chmn, 81-, Soc Relig Higher Educ fel; Found Arts, Relig & Cult fel; AAUP. **MEMBERSHIPS** Am Acad Relig; Am Soc Church Hist. **RESEARCH** Interaction of theology with other strands of intellectual history, particularly since Reformation; Narrative language in religious discourse; religion and Culture studies. **SELECTED PUBLICATIONS** Auth, The Methodist episcopacy: 1784-1900, Drew Gateway, 63; John Fletcher: The embattled saint, Wesleyan Col, 65; coauth, The foundations of Christianity, Ronald, 69; auth, Theological reflections on reflecting on the future, Crosscurrents, winter 71; Story, In: Echoes of the Wordless Word, Am Acad Relig, fall 73; ed, Religion as Story, Harper & Row, 75; auth, Re-visioning psycho-history, Theology Today, 76; contribr, Death and Eschatology, In: Introduction to Study of Religion, Harper & Row, 78; Christianity: A Cultural Perspective, Prentice Hall, 84; In Praise of Religion Diversity, Routledge, 96. **CONTACT ADDRESS** Dept of Religion, Syracuse Univ, 501 HL, Syracuse, NY 13244. **EMAIL** jbwiggru@syr.edu

WIGGINS, SARAH W.
PERSONAL Born 06/29/1934, Montgomery, AL, w, 1967, 1 child **DISCIPLINE** HISTORY **EDUCATION** Huntingdon Col, BA, 56; La State Univ, MA, 58; PhD, 65. **CAREER** Instr, S Sem Jr Col, 59-61; from instr to prof, Univ of Ala, 61-95; retired 95. **HONORS AND AWARDS** UDC Mrs Simon Baruch Awd, 74; Ramsey Awd for Teaching, Ala Asn of Historians, 95; ODK Serv Awd, 95. **MEMBERSHIPS** Ala Hist Asn, S Hist Asn, Asn for Documentary Editing, Orgn of Am Historians, La Hist Asn. **RESEARCH** Southern and Alabama history. **SELECTED PUBLICATIONS** Auth, The Scalawag in Alabama Politics, 1865-1881, Univ of Ala Press, 77; compiler, From Civil War to Civil Rights, 1860-1960, Univ of Ala Press, 87; ed, The Journals of Josiah Gorgas, 1857-1878, Univ of Ala Press, 95. **CONTACT ADDRESS** Dept Hist, Univ of Alabama, Tuscaloosa, PO Box 870212, Tuscaloosa, AL 35487-0154. **EMAIL** swiggins@bama.ua.edu

WIKLE, THOMAS A.
PERSONAL Born 01/26/1962, Pasadena, CA, m, 1989, 2 children **DISCIPLINE** GEOGRAPHY **EDUCATION** Univ Cal, Santa Barb, BA, 83; Cal State Univ, MA, 85; S Ill Univ, PhD, 89. **CAREER** Asst prof, Okla State Univ, 89-93; assoc prof, 93-98; dept hd, 94-00; prof, 98-. **HONORS AND AWARDS** Doct Fel, S Ill Univ; Phi Beta Kappa; Regents Dist Teach Awd; NCGE Dist Teach Awd. **MEMBERSHIPS** AAG. **RESEARCH** Natural resources management; dialect geography. **SELECTED PUBLICATIONS** Coauth, "The Focus of Linguistic Innovation In Texas," English Worldwide 12 (91): 195-214; coauth, "The Apparent Time Construct," Lang Variation and Change 3 (91): 241-64; coauth, "Methodology of a Survey of Oklahoma Dialects," SECOL Rev 21 (97): 1-29; coauth, "The Effects of Methods on Results In Dialectology," Eng Worldwide 18 (97): 35-63; coauth, "Using Apparent Time Data to Chart Linguistic Diffusion," Lang Variation and Change 5 (93): 359-90; auth, "Evaluating the Acceptability of Recreation Rationing Policies Used on Rivers," Environ Manage 15 (91): 389-94; auth, "Comparing Rationing Policies Used on Rivers," J Park Rec Admin 9 (91): 73-80; auth, "Quantitative Mapping Techniques for Displaying Language Variation and Change," in Language Variety In the South Revisited, eds. Cynthia Berstein, Thomas Nunnally, Robin Sabino (Tuscaloosa, AL: Univ Alabama Press, 97); auth, "Those Benevolent Boosters: Spatial Patterns of Kiwanis Membership in the U.S," J Cultural Geog 17 (97): 1-19; auth, "Continuing Education and Competency Programs in GIS," Intl J Geog Info Sci 12 (98): 491-507; auth, "International Expansion of the American-Style Service Club," J Am Culture 22 (99): 51-58. **CONTACT ADDRESS** Dept Geography, Oklahoma State Univ, Stillwater, Stillwater, OK 74078-0001.

WILCOX, DEAN
PERSONAL Born 04/20/1964, Mt. Kisco, NY, m, 1987, 1 child **DISCIPLINE** THEATRE HISTORY, THEORY, AND CRITICISM **EDUCATION** Glasboro State College (now Rowan Univ), NJ, BA (Theatre Arts), 86; Univ SC, MFA (Lighting Design), 89; Univ WA School of Drama, Seattle, PhD (Theatre Hist, Theory, and Criticism), 94. **CAREER** Teaching asst, Dept of Drama, Univ WA, 91-94; lect, Theatre Hist, Univ CA, San Diego, spring 95; vis asst prof, Dartmouth Col, June-Aug 98; Asst Prof, Theatre Histroy, Theory, and Criticism, TX Tech Univ, 96-. **HONORS AND AWARDS** Univ WA Fowler Graduate travel grant, 93; Univ WA Grad School Dissertation Fel, 93; Mellon Postdoctoral Fel at Cornell Univ, 95-96; accepted to Teaching Academy at TX Tech Univ, April 98. **MEMBERSHIPS** Asn of Theatre in Higher Ed; Int Federation for Theatre Res; Am Soc for Theatre Res; Am Soc for Aesthetics. **RESEARCH** Performance studies; postmodernism; semiotics; deconstruction; design hist and theory; chaos theory; performance art. **SELECTED PUBLICATIONS** Auth, book review of Phillip B. Zarilli's Acting (Re)Considered and Mariellen R. Sanford's Happenings and Other Acts, Theatre Survey, Vol 37, no 2, Nov 96; Political Allegory or Multimedia Extravaganza? A Historical Reconstruction of the Opera Company of Boston's Intolleranza, Theatre Survey, Vol 37, no 2, Nov 96; What Does Chaos Theory Have to Do with Art?, Modern Drama, Vol XXXIX, no 4, winter 96; book review of Alma Law and Mel Gordon's Meyerhold, Eisenstein and Biomechanics, Theatre Res Int, Vol 22, no 2, Autumn 97; book review of Marvin Carlson's Performance: A Critical Introduction and Richard Schechner's The Future of Ritual, Theatre Survey, Vol 38, no 2, Nov 97; Karen Finley's Hymen, Theatre Res Int, Vol 22, no 1, spring 97; A Complex Tapestry of Text and Imagery: Karen Finley, The American Chestnut, Cornell University, May 10, 1996, The Jour of Dramatic Theory and Criticism, Vol XII, no 1, fall 97; book review of Colin Counsell's Signs of Performance and Walter Gropius' The Theatre of the Bauhaus, Theatre Jour, Vol 50, no 3, Oct 98; book review of William Demastes' Theatre of Chaos: Beyond Absurdism, Into Orderly Disorder, Theatre Survey, Vol 39, no 2, Nov 98; book review of Arthur Holmberg's The Theatre of Robert Wilson, Theatre Res Int, Vol 23, no 3, Autumn 98; book review of Jonathan Kalb's The Theatre of Heiner Muller, Theatre Res Int, forthcoming; The Historical Nature of Time: Dramatic Criticism and New Historicism, Theatre Insight, forthcoming. **CONTACT ADDRESS** Dept of Theatre and Dance, Texas Tech Univ, Box 42061, Lubbock, TX 79409-2061. **EMAIL** thdea@ttu.edu

WILCOX, LARRY DEAN
PERSONAL Born 09/03/1942, West Lafayette, OH, m, 1960, 2 children **DISCIPLINE** MODERN GERMAN HISTORY, WW II, & HOLOCAUST **EDUCATION** Ohio Univ, AB, 64; Univ Va, MA 66, PhD(hist), 70. **CAREER** From instr to asst prof, 68-75, assoc prof hist, Univ Toledo, 75-, prof, 85-; ch, Univ of Toledo Fac Senate, 91-92. **HONORS AND AWARDS** Phi Beta Kappa, 63; NDEA, 64-7; DAAD Study Awards, 76, 83, 94; Outstanding Teacher Award, 85; Fel, Institute on the Holocaust and Jewish Civilization, Northwestern Univ, 96; Holocaust Educational Found East European Travel Seminar, 97; Univ of Toledo Ctr for Teaching Excellence Fel Award, 99. **MEMBERSHIPS** AHA; Conf Group Cent Europ Hist; Ger Studies Asn; Ohio Acad of Hist. **RESEARCH** Twentieth century Germany; press and propaganda in the rise of National Socialism; visual representations of WW II & the Holocaust. **SELECTED PUBLICATIONS** Auth, Hitler and the Nazi Concept of the Press, J of Newspaper and Periodical History, Winter 85; coed, Germany and Europe in the Era of Two World Wars, Univ Press of Virginia, 86; The Nazi Press Before the Third Reich, in Germany & Europe; auth, "Oron J. Hale, 1902-1991, Central European History, II-4, (90); auth, "Did the 'Real War' Get Into the Pictures: An Analysis of WW II Documentary Films, " in Thomas O. Kelly, ed., World War II: Variants and Visions, (Siena Col, 99); auth, "Shadows of a Distant Nightmare: Visualizing the Unimaginable Holocaust in Early Documentary Films,' in Remembering for the Future: The Holocaust in the Age of Genocide, 01. **CONTACT ADDRESS** Dept of History, Univ of Toledo, 2801 W Bancroft St, Toledo, OH 43606-3390. **EMAIL** lwilcox@uoft02.utoledo.edu

WILHELMSEN, ALEXANDRA
DISCIPLINE HISTORY **EDUCATION** Univ Dallas, BA, 67; Rice Univ, MA, 69; Univ Navarra, PhD, 71. **CAREER** Adj prof, Dallas Univ, 71-. **HONORS AND AWARDS** Luis Hernando de Larramendi awd in Spain, 95. **RESEARCH** Spanish history, Spain's Camino de Santiago, Catholic Church, monarchy, and romanesque art. **SELECTED PUBLICATIONS** Auth, La formacion del pensamiento politico del Carlismo 1810-1875, Madrid, Editorial Actas. **CONTACT ADDRESS** Dept of History, Univ of Dallas, 1845 E Northgate Dr, 206 Carpenter Hall, Irving, TX 75062. **EMAIL** awilhel@acad.udallas.edu

WILKIE, JACQUELINE S.
PERSONAL Born 11/28/1956, Albany, NY, s, 1 child **DISCIPLINE** HISTORY **EDUCATION** Col of St Rose, BA, 78; Northeastern Univ, MA, 79; Carnegie-Mellon Univ, PhD, 82. **CAREER** Tchng, res asst, Northeastern Univ, 78-79; curr designer, 79-81, exec asst, Dept of History, Northeastern Univ, 81-82; 81-82, proj soc hist, Exec Asst., Carnegie-Mellon Univ; 81, adj asst prof, 82-83, Carnegie-Mellon Univ; asst prof, hist, 83-87-91; Central Mich Univ; women's stud coord, 92-97; Prof, Hist, 92-00; asst prof, hist, 87-91, Luther Coll.; Full Prof, 00-; Assoc Prof of History, 92-00; History Dept Head, 98-; Women Studies Coor, 92-97. **HONORS AND AWARDS** Mortar Board Commendation for contributions to academic excellence, Central MI Univ, 85; Women's History Research Grant Recipient, Minnesota Historical Society, 91; Joyce Foundation Scholar-in-Residence, Luther College, 91. **MEMBERSHIPS** Organization of Am Historians, National Women's Studies Assn, Am Society for the History of Medicine. **RESEARCH** US popular medicine & nursing, oral hist. **SELECTED PUBLICATIONS** Auth, Submerged Sensuality: Technology and Perceptions of Bathing, Journal of Social History, 86; auth, Hygiene in the Oxford Companion on the Body, Forthcoming; Cleanliness in Encyclopedia of Social History, 93; auth, The Staying Power of a Little Known Novella: Ann Petry's 'In Darkness and Confusin," with David Faldet in Tradition and Innovation, edited by Scott Lee and Allen Speight, Univ Press of Am, 99. **CONTACT ADDRESS** History Dept, Luther Col, Decorah, IA 52101-1045. **EMAIL** wilkieja@luther.edu

WILKIE, JAMES WALLACE
PERSONAL Born 03/10/1936, Idaho Falls, ID, m, 1963, 2 children **DISCIPLINE** LATIN AMERICAN HISTORY **EDUCATION** Mex City Col, BA, 58; Univ Calif, Berkeley, MA, 59, PhD(hist), 65. **CAREER** Teacher, High Sch, Calif, 59-60; instr hist, Mex City Col, 60; from asst prof to assoc prof, Ohio State Univ, 65-68; assoc prof, 68-71, assoc dir Latin Am Ctr, 70-76, Prof Hist, Univ Calif, Los Angeles, 71-, Dir, Latin Am Oral Hist Res Proj, 63-; Ohio State Univ fac res grant, 66-67; pres, Hist Res Found, 68-; mem, Robertson Prize Comt, Conf Latin Am Hist, 68, comt on activities & proj, 68-; Ford Found

grant, 68-69; mem orgn & prog comt, Third Int Cong Mex Hist, 69, distinguished serv award comt, 70; fel, Latin Am Ctr, Univ Calif, Los Angeles, 70, 72 & 73; Soc Sci Res Coun-Am Coun Learned Soc grant, 71; chmn comt Mex studies & cochmn, Fourth Int Cong Mex Hist, 73; chmn, Conf Latin Am Studies Asn, 76; Univ wide coordr, Consortium Mex & US, Univ Calif, 81-83; ed, Statistical Abstract of Latin America, 77-; pres and founder, PROFMEX, 82-. **HONORS AND AWARDS** Ohio Acad Hist Bk Awd, 67; Bolton Prize, 68. **MEMBERSHIPS** Latin Am Studies Asn; Conf Latin Am Hist Asn. **RESEARCH** Mexico, Bolivia, Costa Rica, and Venezuela; comparative Latin American historical statistics; oral history of twentieth-century Latin America. **SELECTED PUBLICATIONS** Auth, The Mexican Revolution: Federal Expenditure and Social Change Since 1910, Univ Calif, 67, rev ed, 70; coauth, Mexico en el Siglo XX: Entrevistas de Historia Oral, Instituto Mex Investigationes Econ, 69; auth, Elitelore, 73, Measuring Land Reform 74 & Statistics and State Policy in Latin America, 74, UCLA Latin Am Ctr; coed, Contemporary Mexico, Univ Calif, 75; ed, Money and Politics in Latin America, UCLA Latin Am Ctr, 77; auth, Intelectuales: Luis Chavez Orozco, Daniel Cosio Villegas, Jose Munoz Cota, Jesus Silva Herzog, 95. **CONTACT ADDRESS** Prog on Mexico, Univ of California, Los Angeles, 11361 Bunche Hall, Los Angeles, CA 90095. **EMAIL** wilkie@ucla.edu

WILKIE, NANCY C.
PERSONAL Born 12/27/1942, Milwaukee, WI, m **DISCIPLINE** GREEK ARCHEOLOGY, CLASSICS **EDUCATION** Stanford Univ, AB, 64; Univ Minn, MA, 67, PhD(Greek), 75. **CAREER** Instr classics, Macalester Col, 72-75; adj instr, 74-75, adj asst prof classics, 75-79, Prof Classics & Socioanthrop, Carleton Col, 79-, Field dir, Phocis-Doris Exped, Loyola Univ, Chicago, 77-80; Dir, Grevena Project, 88-. **MEMBERSHIPS** Archaeol Inst Am, Pres, 98-; Am Philol Asn; Soc Prof Archaeologists; Soc Am Archaeol; Register of Professional Archaeologists. **RESEARCH** Prehistoric Greek archaeology; archeological sampling. **SELECTED PUBLICATIONS** Auth, The Nichoria Tholos & Area-IV-6, Hesperia, 75; Area I, Evacuations at Nichoria in Southwest Greece, Vol I, Minn, 78; Early Helladic Pottery from Phokis and Doris, Teiresias, 79; Shaft Graves at Nichoria, Temple Univ Aegean Symp, 81; ed. With W.D.E. Coulson Contributions to Aegean Archaeology, CAS, U of MN, 85; auth, Excavations at N. Choria. Vol 2 (U of MN Press) editor with W.A. McDonald, 92; The Earliest Farmers In Macedonia, Antiquity, Vol 0071, 1997; **CONTACT ADDRESS** Carleton Col, 1 N College St, Northfield, MN 55057-4044. **EMAIL** nwilkie@carleton.edu

WILKIE, WILLIAM E.
PERSONAL Born 01/19/1936, Marshalltown, IA **DISCIPLINE** HISTORY **EDUCATION** Cath Univ Am, MA, 57; Univ Fribourg, PhD, 66; Cambridge Univ, MA, 72. **CAREER** From Instr to Assoc Prof, 57-80, Prof Hist, Loras Col, 80-; Vis fel, Cambridge Univ, 72-73, 81. **HONORS AND AWARDS** NEH jr res fel, Italy, 72-73; Mellon Fel Humanities, Kans Univ, 82; Fulbright Fel Ger, 84, 89; Cert Comm, Am Asn State & Local Hist Soc. **MEMBERSHIPS** Fel Royal Hist Soc. **RESEARCH** History of Mississippi valley 1500-. **SELECTED PUBLICATIONS** Auth, Rome and the Tudors Before the Reformation, Cambridge Univ, 74 ; Dubuque on the Mississippi 1788-1988. **CONTACT ADDRESS** Dept Hist, Loras Col, PO Box 178, Dubuque, IA 52004-0178.

WILKINS, MIRA
PERSONAL Born 06/01/1931, New York, NY **DISCIPLINE** BUSINESS HISTORY **EDUCATION** Radcliffe Col/Harvard Univ, AB, 53; Cambridge Univ England, PhD, 57. **CAREER** Res assoc, Weyerhaeuser Enterprises Hist, Columbia Univ, 57-58, res assoc, Ford Motor Co Hist, 58-60, co-dir, Ford Overseas Hist Proj, 60-62, proj dir Hist Am Bus Abroad, Grad Sch Bus, 62-66, adj asst prof, 64-66; assoc prof Hist & Indust Admin, Union Col, 66-68; vis lectr Hist, Smith Col, 68-70; prof Econ, Fla Int Univ, 74-, supvr, Corpus Christi Col, Cambridge Univ, 56-57; instr, Wayne State Univ, 58-59; lectr Econ Hist, Univ Mass, Amherst, 72; dir, Foreign Investment Fla Proj, 75-80; Guggenheim fel, 81-82. **HONORS AND AWARDS** Fla Int Univ Prof Exc Awd, 94; 93 Cass Prize for best article in Business History, 92. **MEMBERSHIPS** Am Econ Asn; AHA; Acad Int Bus; Bus Hist Conf; Econ Hist Assn. **RESEARCH** International business history; economic history; history of foreign investment in the United States. **SELECTED PUBLICATIONS** Auth, American Business Abroad: Ford on Six Continents, Wayne State Univ, 64; The Emergence of Multinational Enterprise: American Business Abroad from the Colonial Era to 1914, Harvard Univ, 70; The role of private business in the international diffusion of technology, J Econ Hist, 3/74; Multinational oil companies in South America in the 1920s: In Argentina, Bolivia, Brazil, Chile, Colombia, Ecuador, Peru, Bus Hist Rev, Fall 74; The Maturing of Multinational Enterprise: American Business Abroad from 1914 to 1970, Harvard Univ, 74; The oil companies in perspective, In: Daedalus, Fall 75; Modern European economic history and the multinationals, J Europ Econ Hist, Winter 77; Multinational automobile enterprises and regulation: An historical overview, In: Government, Technology, and the Future of the Automobile, McGraw-Hill, 80; The History of Foreign Investment in the United States to 1914, Cambridge, Mass: Harvard Univ Press, 1989. **CONTACT ADDRESS** Dept of Economics, Florida Intl Univ, Miami, FL 33199-0001. **EMAIL** Wilkinsm@fiu.edu

WILLEN, DIANE
PERSONAL Born 05/19/1943, Hartford, CT, 1 child **DISCIPLINE** ENGLISH HISTORY **EDUCATION** Conn Col, BA, 65; Harvard Univ, MA, 66; Tufts Univ, PhD(hist), 72. **CAREER** Asst prof hist, Kalamazoo Col, 72; from asst prof to assoc prof, 72-91, Prof Hist, GA State Univ, 91-, Chair, Hist Dept, 98-; vis prof, Oxford Univ, Summer 91. **HONORS AND AWARDS** Phi Beta Kappa, 64; Winthrop Schol, 64; Conn Col Hist Prize and Honors in Hist, 65; Rosemary Park Fel, 65; Omicron Delta Kappa, 75; Dale Somers Memorial Awd, 82, 89; Ga State Univ Res Grants, 84, 89, 95; Am Hist Asn, Bernadotte E. Scmitt Grant for Res, 88; Am Philos Soc Res Grant, 89. **MEMBERSHIPS** AHA; Conf Brit Studies; Southern Asn Women Historians. **RESEARCH** Tudor-Stuart England, especially political, social and religious history; women's history, especially the pre-industrial period. **SELECTED PUBLICATIONS** Auth, Lord Russell and the Western Countries, J Brit Studies, autumn 75; Robert Browne and the Dilemma of Religious Dissent, J United Reformed Church Hist Soc, 10/80; John Russell, First Earl of Bedford. One of the King's Men, Royal Hist Soc, 81; Godly Women in Early Modern England: Puritanism and Gender, J of Ecclesiastical Hist, 10/92; Communion of the Saints: Spritual Reciprocity and the Godly Comunity in Early Modern England, Albion, Spring 95; author of numerous other journal articles and book reviews. **CONTACT ADDRESS** Dept Hist, Georgia State Univ, 33 Gilmer St SE, Atlanta, GA 30303-3080. **EMAIL** hisddw@panther.gsu.edu

WILLETT, DONALD E.
DISCIPLINE HISTORY **EDUCATION** St. Edwards Univ, BA, 72; Stephen F. Austin State Univ, MA, 76; Tex A & M Univ, PhD, 85. **CAREER** Instr, Blinn Col, 82-85; asst prof to assoc prof, Tex A & M Galveston, 85-. **HONORS AND AWARDS** Teaching Excellence Awd Awd, Tex A & M Univ, 86; Ottus Lock Teaching Excellence, E Tex Hist Assoc, 92; C.K. Chamberlain Awd, 94, Edmond Eikel Outstanding Fac Awd, 96. **MEMBERSHIPS** E Tex Hist Assoc; Gulf S Hist Assoc; Tex State Hist Assoc. **RESEARCH** United States Maritime Labor, Texas Maritime History. **SELECTED PUBLICATIONS** Auth, "The Galveston Dock Wars, 1936-1937", E Tex Hist Assoc J; auth, "The 1939 Tanker Strike", Int J of Maritime Hist. **CONTACT ADDRESS** Dept Gen Educ, Texas A&M Univ, Galveston, PO Box 1675, Galveston, TX 77553-1675.

WILLEY, GORDON R.
PERSONAL Born 03/07/1913, Chariton, IA, m, 1938, 2 children **DISCIPLINE** ANTHROPOLOGY, ARCHAEOLOGY **EDUCATION** Univ AZ, AB, 35, AM, 36; Columbia Univ, PhD, 42. **CAREER** Sr anthropologist, Smithsonian Inst, 43-50; Bowdirch Prof of Archaeology, 50-87, prof Emeritus, Harvard Univ, 87-. **HONORS AND AWARDS** Litt D (honorary), Cambridge Univ, 77, Univ AZ, 81, Univ NM, 84; Gold Medal, Archaeol Inst of Am, 71; Huxley Medal, Royal Anthropol Inst, 84; Gold Medal, Society of Fantiquaries, London. **MEMBERSHIPS** Am Anthropol Asn; Soc for Am Archaeology; National Academy of Science; American Philosophical Soc. **RESEARCH** Mexican and Central American archaeology. **SELECTED PUBLICATIONS** Auth, Archaeology of the Florida Gulf Coast, Smithsonian Misc Colls, vol 113, Smithsonian Inst, 49; Prehistoric Settlement Patterns in the Viru Valley, Peru, Bul 155, Bureau of Am Ethnology, Smithsonian Inst, 53; Method and Theory in American Archaeology, with Phillip Phillips, Univ Chicago Press, 58; Prehistoric Maya Settlements in the Belize Valley, with W R Bullard, J B Glass, and J C Gifford, Peabody Museum Papers, Harvard Univ, 65; An Introduction to American Archaeology: Vol I North and Middle America, 66, Vol II, South America, 71, Prentice-Hall; The Altar de Sacrificios Excavations: General Summary and Conclusions, Peabody Museum Papers, vol 64, no 3, Harvard Univ, 73; A History of American Archaeology, with J A Sabloff, Thames and Hudson, Ltd, and W H Freeman and Co, 74, 80, 93; New World Archaeology and Culture History: Collected Essays and Articles, republished with intro comments and annotations, Univ NM Press, 90; Excavations at Seibal, Department of Peten, Guatemala: General Summary and Conclusions, Memoirs, vol 17, no 4, Peabody Museum, Harvard Univ, 90; The Copan Residential Zone: Ceramics and Artifacts, with R M Leventhal, A A Demarest, and W L Fash, Jr, Papers Peabody Museum, vol 80, Harvard Univ, 94. **CONTACT ADDRESS** Peabody Museum, Harvard Univ, Cambridge, MA 02138.

WILLIAMS, ALAN JOHN
PERSONAL Born 01/16/1944, Ossining, NY **DISCIPLINE** FRENCH HISTORY **EDUCATION** Stanford Univ, BA, 66; Yale Univ, PhD(hist), 74. **CAREER** Asst Prof French Hist, Wake Forest Univ, 74-. **HONORS AND AWARDS** Excellence in Teaching Awd, Wake Forest Univ, 78. **MEMBERSHIPS** Soc French Hist Studies. **RESEARCH** Parisian police; 18th century charlatans; the relationship between political structures and systems of patronage or protection in 18th century France. **SELECTED PUBLICATIONS** Auth, The police and public health in eighteenth century Paris, Soc Sci Quart, 75; The police and the poor of Paris, In: Transactions of the Fourth International Congress on the Enlightenment, Voltaire Found, Oxford, 76; The police and the administration of eighteenth century Paris, J Urban Hist, 78; The Police of Paris, 1718-1789, La State Univ, spring 79. **CONTACT ADDRESS** 95 Beechwood Dr, Lewisville, NC 27023.

WILLIAMS, BERNARD D.
PERSONAL Born 07/16/1930, Philadelphia, PA **DISCIPLINE** MODERN EUROPEAN HISTORY **EDUCATION** LaSalle Col, BA, 54; Niagara Univ, MA, 55. **CAREER** Niagara Univ, 56-60, instr hist, 56-61, asst prof and acting chair dept mil sci, 60-61, Univ of Scranton, asst prof, 62-68, dir adv stud adv stud off, 66-68, assoc prof, 68-76, prof hist, 76-97, prof emeritus, 97-, vis prof Univ Ottawa, 62. **MEMBERSHIPS** AHA; Acad Polit Sci; Am Mil Inst; US Naval Inst; Soc Historians of Am Foreign Rels. **RESEARCH** Diplomatic and military history of World War I and World War II; diplomatic history of the 19th century; the drought in West Africa, 1968-1975. **SELECTED PUBLICATIONS** Auth, BS degree in military science, Army, 12/67. **CONTACT ADDRESS** Dept of Hist, Univ of Scranton, Scranton, PA 18510.

WILLIAMS, BRUCE
DISCIPLINE FILM THEORY, HISTORY, HISPANIC LANGUAGES & LITERATURES **EDUCATION** Univ Calif-Los Angeles, PhD, 86. **CAREER** Assoc prof. **RESEARCH** Film theory and cinema history and aesthetics. **SELECTED PUBLICATIONS** Publ on res interest. **CONTACT ADDRESS** Dept of Language and Cultures, William Paterson Col of New Jersey, 300 Pompton Rd., Wayne, NJ 07470. **EMAIL** williamsb@wpunj.edu

WILLIAMS, C. FRED
PERSONAL Born 12/24/1943, Allen, OK, m, 1971, 3 children **DISCIPLINE** AMERICAN WEST **EDUCATION** E Cent State Col, BAE, 65; Wichita State Univ, MA, 66; Univ OK, PhD, 70. **CAREER** From asst prof to assoc prof, 69-78, head dept, 73-80, prof hist, Univ AR, Little Rock, 78, assoc dean, Col Lib Arts, 80-83; Assoc vice chancellor for edu prog, 83-88. **HONORS AND AWARDS** Exec secretary-treasurer, Agricultural Hist Soc, 00-. **MEMBERSHIPS** Orgn Am Historians; Western Hist Asn; Agr Hist Soc. **RESEARCH** Agricult; AR state hist; historical novels. **SELECTED PUBLICATIONS** Auth, William M Jardine: Secretary of Agriculture for the business side of farming, Wichita State Studies, 70; The bear state image: Arkansas in the nineteenth century, Ark Hist Quart, 80; ed, A Documentary History of Arkansas, 84; Arkansas: An Illustrated History of the Land of Opportunity, 86. **CONTACT ADDRESS** Dept of Hist, Univ of Arkansas, Little Rock, 2801 S University Av, Little Rock, AR 72204-1099. **EMAIL** cfwilliams@ualr.edu

WILLIAMS, DANIEL
PERSONAL Born 05/11/1955, St Louis, MO, m **DISCIPLINE** THEOLOGY, HISTORICAL THEOLOGY, PATRISTICS **EDUCATION** Northeastern Col, BA, 78; Trinity Evangelical Divinity Sch, MDiv, 81; Princeton Theol Sem, ThM, 85; Univ Toronto, MA, 86. **CAREER** Asst prof, Loyola Univ, Chicago, 94-2000, assoc prof, 2000-. **HONORS AND AWARDS** NEH Fel for Univ Teachers, 200-01. **MEMBERSHIPS** Am Soc of Church Hist, Ecclesiastical Hist Soc, Groupe Suisse d'Etudes Partristiques, Int Asn for Patristic Studies, Midwest Patristics Sem, North Am Patristic Soc. **RESEARCH** Latin early fathers; orthodoxy and heresy; doctrinal development of Trinity. **SELECTED PUBLICATIONS** Co-ed and contribur, Arianism After Arius: Essays on the Development of the Fourth Century Trinitarian Conflicts, Edinburgh: T & T Clark (93); auth, Ambrose of Milan and the End of the Nicene-Arian Conflicts, Oxford Univ Press (95); auth, "Another Exception to Later Fourth Century 'Arian' Typologies: The Case of Germinius of Sirmium," The J of Early Christian Studies, 4 (96): 335-357; auth, "Historical Portrait or Polemical Portrayal?: The Alignment between Pagans and Arians in the Later Fourth Century," Studia Patristica XXIX (97): 178-194; auth, "Politically Correct in Milan: A Response to P. Kaufman's 'Diehard Homoians and the Election of Ambrose'," J of Early Christian Studies, 5 (97): 441-46; auth, "Constantine, Nicaea and the 'Fall' of the Church," in Christian Origins: Theology, Rhetoric and Community, eds, L. Ayres and G. Jones, London: Routledge Press (98): 117-136; auth, "The Search for Sola Scriptura in the Early Church," Interpretation, 52 (98): 338-350. **CONTACT ADDRESS** Dept Theol, Loyola Univ, Chicago, 6525 N Sheridan Rd, Chicago, IL 60626-5344. **EMAIL** dwilli1@orion.it.luc.edu

WILLIAMS, DAVID R.
PERSONAL Born 02/28/1923, Kamloops, BC, Canada **DISCIPLINE** HISTORY **EDUCATION** Univ BC, BA, 48, LLB, 49. **CAREER** Adj Prof/Writer-in-Residence, Fac Law, Univ Victoria 80-. **HONORS AND AWARDS** Univ BC Medal Can Bibliog, 78; Crime Writers Can Awd, 93. **MEMBERSHIPS** Law Soc BC; Writers Union Can. **SELECTED PUBLICATIONS** Auth, 100 Years at St Peter's Quamichan, 77; auth, The Man for a New Country: Sir Matthew Baillie Begbie, 77; auth, Duff: A Life in the Law, 84; auth, Pioneer Parish: The Story of St Peter's Quamichan, 91; auth, With Malice Aforethought: Six Spectacular Canadian Trials, 93. **CONTACT ADDRESS** Faculty of Law, Univ of Victoria, 3355 Gibbins Rd, Duncan, BC, Canada V9L 1N9.

WILLIAMS, GERHILD SCHOLZ
PERSONAL Born 09/18/1942, Perleberg, Germany, d **DISCIPLINE** EARLY MODERN STUDIES **EDUCATION** Univ Wash, BA, 69, MA, 71, PhD(comp lit), 74. **CAREER** Asst prof, 75-81, Assoc Prof Ger, Wash Univ 81-86, prof, 86-. **HONORS AND AWARDS** Barbara Schaps Thomas and David M. Thomas, prof in the Humanities. **MEMBERSHIPS** Medieval Acad Am; MLA, Am Asn Teachers Ger; Midwestern Mod Lang Asn; 16th c. Studies Asn; Renaissance Soc of Am. **RESEARCH** French, German, literature of the early modern period. **SELECTED PUBLICATIONS** Auth, The vision of death, A study of the memento mori expressions in some Latin, German and French Didactic texts of the 11th and 12th centuries, Kummerle Goppingen W Ger, 10/76; auth, Das Weiterleben des Mittelalters in der deutschen Literatur, Konigstein: Athenaum, 83; auth, Literatur und Kosmos: Innen-und Aussenwelten in der deutschen Literatur des 15. Bis 17. Jahrhunderts, Amsterdam: Rodopi, 86; auth, Alte Texte lesen: Textlinguistische Zugange zur alteren deutsche Literatur, Bern/Stuttgart: Paul Haupt, 88; auth, Defining Dominion: The Discourses of Magic and Witchcraft in Early Modern France and Germany, Ann Arbor: Michigan UP, 95, Paperback edition 99; auth, Knowledge, Science, and Literature in Early Modern Germany, Chapel Hill: North Carolina UP, 96; trans, "Hexen und Herrschaft: Die Diskurse der Magie und Hexerei" im fruhneuzeitlichen Frankreich und Deutschland, (Munchen: Fink, 98) **CONTACT ADDRESS** Dept of Ger, Washington Univ, One Brookings Dr, Campus Box 1104, Saint Louis, MO 63130-4899. **EMAIL** gerhild_williams@aismail.wustl.edu

WILLIAMS, HARRY M.
DISCIPLINE HISTORY **EDUCATION** Lincoln, BA, 71; Univ Mo, MA, 82; Brown, MA, 84, PhD, 88. **CAREER** Assoc prof History, Carleton Col. **RESEARCH** Charles Lenox Remond, female abolitionists. **SELECTED PUBLICATIONS** Diss, When Black Is Right: The Life and Writings of George S. Schuyler, Brown, 88. **CONTACT ADDRESS** Dept of History, Carleton Col, Northfield, MN 55057.

WILLIAMS, JAMES CALHOUN
PERSONAL Born 09/24/1942, San Francisco, CA, s, 1 child **DISCIPLINE** HISTORY OF AMERICAN TECHNOLOGY **EDUCATION** Univ Ore, BA, 64; San Jose State Univ, MA, 71; Univ Calif at Santa Barbara, PhD, 84. **CAREER** Prof, Gavilan Col, 71-85; expert witness and historical consultant, 78-; exec dir, Calif Hist Ctr Foundation, 85-93; prof, De Anza Col, 93-. **HONORS AND AWARDS** Certificate of Commendation for the book Energy and the Making of Modern California, Am Asn for State and Local Hist; Distinguished Service Awd, Calif Council for the Promotion of Hist; Awd of Distinction, Calif Council for the Promotion of Hist; Sourisseau Academy Local History Awd; Rockefeller Fel, Univ Calif at Santa Barbara; Summer Studies Fel, Nat Endowment for the Humanities, Univ of Calif at Los Angeles. **MEMBERSHIPS** AHA; Am Soc for Environmental Hist; Calf Council for the Promotion of Hist; Calif Historical Soc; Int Committee for the Hist of Technology; Nat Council on Public Hist; Org of Am Historians; Soc for the Hist of Technology. **RESEARCH** Technology and the environment; earthquake engineering; energy systems; technology and gender. **SELECTED PUBLICATIONS** Auth, "The Trolley: Technology and Values in Retrospect", in San Jose Studies, 3, 77; auth, "Cultural Conflict: The Origins of American Santa Barbara", in The Southern Calif Quart, 60, 78; auth, "Television--Reflection of American Society", in The Evolution of Mass Culture in America, 1877 to Present, Forum Press, 82; auth, "Otherwise a Mere Clod: California Rural Electrification", in IEEE Technology and Society Mag, 7, 88; auth, "Standards of Professional Conduct in California", in Ethics and Public History: An Anthology, in Robert E. Krieger Publ Co., 90; auth, "Engineering California Cities", in Science-Technology Relationships/Relations Science-Technique, San Francisco Press, 93; auth, "Earthquake Engineering: Designing Unseen Technology against Invisible Forces", in ICON: Journal of the Int Committee for the Hist of Technology, 1, 95; auth, "Fuel at Last: Oil and Gas for California, 1860s-1940s" in Calif Hist 75, 96; auth, "California's First High-Head Turbine Installation", in IA: The Journal of the Soc for Industrial Archeology, 22:1, 96; auth, Energy and the Making of Modern California, University of Akron Press, 97; auth, "Energy, conservation, and Modernity: The Failure to Electrify Railroads in the American West", in Technology and Western Landscapes, Halcyon Imprint, 98; auth, "Frederick E. Terman and the Rise of Silicon Valley", in Int Journal of Technology Management, 16:8. 98; auth, "Getting Housewives the Electric Message: Gender and Energy Marketing in the Early Twentieth Century", in His & Hers: Gender, Consumption, and Technology, Univ of Va Press, 98. **CONTACT ADDRESS** De Anza Col, 21250 Stevens Creek Blvd., Cupertino, CA 95014. **EMAIL** JCW1@netcom.com

WILLIAMS, JOAN C.
DISCIPLINE HISTORY **EDUCATION** Yale Univ, BA, 74; Harvard Law Sch/Mass Inst Technol, JD/MS, 80. **CAREER** Asst Planner, SOM Environmental Study Group, 74-75; Project Hist, Nat Park Service, Hist Am Engineering Record, Puerto Rico, 76; Law Clerk, Legal Action Ctr, 77; Law Clerk to Lawyer, Lane & Edson, P.C., 79-82; Prof Law, Am Univ, 82-; Vis Prof, Univ Va Law Sch, 92; Vis Prof, Harvard Law Sch, 93-94; dir, Gender, Work & Family Project at American Univ Washington Col of Law, 98-. **HONORS AND AWARDS** Deconstructing Gender cited as one of the most cited law review articles ever written, The Most-Cited Law Review Articles Revisited, Chicago-Kent Law Rev 751, 96; cited as one of the most prolific law professors in the country, The Most Prolific Law Professors and Faculties, Chicago-Kent Law Rev 751, 96; Am Univ Annual Oustanding Scholarship Contributions of the Year Awd, 99-00. **MEMBERSHIPS** DC Bar, 80. **SELECTED PUBLICATIONS** Auth, Unbending Gender: Why Family and Work Conflict and What to Do About It, Oxford Univ Press, 00; auth, " Derechos iguales a la propiedad: si mujeres no fueran pobres," ILANUD, 99; auth, " Igualdad sin discriminacion," Genero y derecho, 99; auth, Trabajo familiar y en el mercado de trabajo," IV Curso: Mujer y Derechos Humanos, 99; auth, " Deconstructing Gender," 87 Michigan Law Review 797, 89; coauth, Land Ownership and Use 4th ed, Aspen Law & Business, 97; auth," Is Coverture Dead? Beyond a New Theory of Alimony," 82 Georgetown Law Review 2227, 94. **CONTACT ADDRESS** Washington Col Law, American Univ, 4801 Massachusetts Ave. NW, Washington, DC 20016-8181. **EMAIL** swolfe@wcl.american.edu

WILLIAMS, JOANNA
PERSONAL Born Bloomington, IN, d, 1 child **DISCIPLINE** ART HISTORY **EDUCATION** Swarthmore Col, BA, 60; Radcliffe Col, MA, 61; Harvard Univ, PhD, 69. **CAREER** Lectr to prof, Univ Calif Berkeley, 67-. **HONORS AND AWARDS** Guggenheim Fel, 79. **MEMBERSHIPS** Col Art Asn; Asn of Asian Studies; Am Committee for S Asian Art. **RESEARCH** Indian sculpture, painting; Southeast Asian Arts. **SELECTED PUBLICATIONS** Co-auth, Palm-leaf Miniatures: The Art of Raghunath Prusti of Orissa, Univ Calif Press, 96; auth, "Construction of Gender in the Paintings and Graffiti of Sigiriya," in Representing the Body: Gender issues in Indian art, (New Delhi, 97), 56-67. **CONTACT ADDRESS** Dept Hist of Art, Univ of California, Berkeley, 416 Doe Library, Berkeley, CA 94720-6020. **EMAIL** ptusty@socrates.berkeley.edu

WILLIAMS, JOHN ALEXANDER
PERSONAL Born 04/12/1938, Galveston, TX, d, 3 children **DISCIPLINE** HISTORY **EDUCATION** Tulane Univ, BA, 61; Yale Univ, MA, 62; PhD, 66. **CAREER** Asst prof, Univ of Notre Dame, 66-71; asst prof, Univ of IL Chicago, 71-72; assoc prof to prof, WV Univ, 72-79; asst dir, NEH, 79-86; dir, Christopher Columbus Quincentenary Jubilee Comm, 86-88; prof, Appalachian State Univ, 89-. **HONORS AND AWARDS** Woodrow Wilson Fel, 61-62, 63-65; Literary Merit Awd, WV Libr Assoc; 76; Rockefeller Archives Ctr Grant, 77; NEH Res Awd, 78; Am Asn for State and Local Hist Grants, 68, 76; Awd of Merit, 96. **RESEARCH** American regionalism and regional history, Appalachian history, history of mining, historiography. **SELECTED PUBLICATIONS** Auth, West Virginia and the Captains of Industry, WV Univ Pr, (Morgantown), 76; auth, West Virginia: A History, WW Norton, (NY), 76; coed, Old Ties and New Attachments: Italian-American Folklife in the West, Libr of Congress Am Folklife Center, (Washington), 92; auth, West Virginia: A History for Beginners, Appalachian Editions, (Charleston), 93; coauth, Sinking Columbus: Contested History, Cultural Politics and Mythmaking in the 1992 Quincentenary, Univ Pr of Fla, (forthcoming). **CONTACT ADDRESS** Dept Hist, Appalachian State Univ, Boone, NC 28608-0001.

WILLIAMS, JOHN W.
PERSONAL Born 02/25/1928, Memphis, TN, m, 1955, 6 children **DISCIPLINE** ART HISTORY **EDUCATION** Yale Univ, BA, 52; Univ MI, MA, 53, PhD, 62. **CAREER** From instr to assoc prof art hist, Swarthmore Col, 60-72; Prof Art Hist, Univ Pittsburgh, 72-, Fulbright res grants, Spain, 63-64, 68-69; proj grant, Nat Endowment for Hum, 71-73. **HONORS AND AWARDS** Distinguished Service Prof, 94. **MEMBERSHIPS** Col Art Asn Am; Int Ctr Medieval Art. **RESEARCH** Span medieval art. **SELECTED PUBLICATIONS** Auth, A Spanish tradition of Bible illustration, J Warburg & Courtald Insts, 65; The Monastery of Valeranica, Madrider Mitteilungn, 70; San Isidoro de Leon, Art Bull, 73; Marcialis Pincerna, In: Hortus Imaginum, Univ KS, 74; Generationes Abrahae: Reconquest iconography in Leon, Gesta, 77; Early Spanish Manuscript Illumination, Braziller, 77; A Spanish Apocalypse, Braziller, 91; The Illustrated Beatus, 5 vols, Harvey Miller, 94; ed, Imaging the Early Medieval Bible, Penn St, 99. **CONTACT ADDRESS** Dept of Hist of Art & Archit, Univ of Pittsburgh, 104 Frick Fine Arts, Pittsburgh, PA 15260-7601. **EMAIL** jww23@pitt.edu

WILLIAMS, L. PEARCE
PERSONAL Born 09/08/1927, Marmon, NY, m, 1949, 4 children **DISCIPLINE** HISTORY OF SCIENCE **EDUCATION** Cornell Univ, BA, 49, PhD, 52. **CAREER** Instr hist, Yale Univ, 52-56; asst prof, Univ Del, 56-59; from asst prof to prof, 60-71, chmn dept, 69-74, John Stambaugh Prof Hist, Cornell Univ, 71-, Assoc historian, Nat Found Infantile Paralysis, 56-57; Nat Sci Found fel, 59-60; pres comn teaching, Int Union Hist & Philos Sci, 64-80. **HONORS AND AWARDS** Pfizer Awd, Hist Sci Soc, 66. **MEMBERSHIPS** AHA; Hist Sci Soc; Royal Inst Gr Brit; Acad Int Hist Sci. **RESEARCH** Science during the French Revolution and First Empire; physical sciences in the 19th century. **SELECTED PUBLICATIONS** Auth, Michael Faraday, A Biography, Chapman & Hall, London & Basic Bk, 65; The Origins of Field Theory, 66 & coauth, Great Issues in Western Civilization, 67, Random; ed, Selected Correspondence of Michael Faraday (2 vols), Cambridge Univ, 72; coauth, A History of Science in Western Civilization (3 vols), Univ Press Am, 77-78; auth, Album of Science: The Nineteenth Century, Scribner, 78; Faraday,Michael - Sandemanian And Scientist - A Study Of Science And Religion In The 19th-Century - Cantor,G, Isis, Vol 0085, 1994; Faraday,Michael And The Royal-Institution - The Genius Of Man And Place - Thomas,Jm, Isis, Vol 0085, 1994; The Biographical Dictionary Of Scientists - Porter,R, Isis, Vol 0086, 1995. **CONTACT ADDRESS** Dept of STS, Cornell Univ, Ithaca, NY 14853. **EMAIL** lpw3@cornell.edu

WILLIAMS, LAWRENCE H.
PERSONAL Born 09/14/1943, Louisville, KY, m, 1965, 3 children **DISCIPLINE** HISTORY **EDUCATION** Univ Iowa, PhD, 85. **CAREER** Prof, 85-99, Africana stud & hist, Luther Col. **RESEARCH** African Amer hist from slavery to contemporary. **SELECTED PUBLICATIONS** Auth, Black Higher Feb. in Kentucky, 1879-1930. **CONTACT ADDRESS** Luther Col, 700 College Dr, Decorah, IA 52101. **EMAIL** williala@martin.luther.edu

WILLIAMS, LEE ERSKINE, II
PERSONAL Born 04/02/1946, Jackson, MS, m, 1973, 1 child **DISCIPLINE** HISTORY **EDUCATION** Knoxville Col, TN, BA, 68; East TN State Univ, MA, 70; MS State Univ, PhD, 75. **CAREER** Instr, Middle TN State Univ, 69-72; prof, History, UAH, 74-, dir, Multicultural Affairs, 91-. **MEMBERSHIPS** AL Hist Asn; AL Asn of Historians; Southern History Asn. **RESEARCH** African-Am hist; AL hist; Southern hist. **SELECTED PUBLICATIONS** Auth, Anatomy of Four Race Riots, 73; Post-War Riots in America, 91. **CONTACT ADDRESS** History Dept, Univ of Alabama, Huntsville, Huntsville, AL 35807. **EMAIL** Willial@email.UAH.edu

WILLIAMS, LEROY THOMAS
PERSONAL Born 10/20/1944, Camden, AR, m, 1969, 1 child **DISCIPLINE** AMERICAN HISTORY, AFRO-AMERICAN STUDIES **EDUCATION** Ark AM&N Col, BS, 70; Univ Toledo, MA, 71, PhD(Am hist), 77. **CAREER** Asst prof hist, Cleveland State Univ, 76-77; asst prof, 77-81, assoc prof hist, Univ Ark, Little Rock, 81-. **MEMBERSHIPS** Asn Study Afr-Am Life & Hist; Nat Asn Black Prof. **RESEARCH** American social history; Afro-American urban history; Afro-American social history. **SELECTED PUBLICATIONS** Auth, Newcomers to the city, Ohio Hist, 81; ed, A Documentary History of Arkansas, 82. **CONTACT ADDRESS** Dept Hist, Univ of Arkansas, Little Rock, 2801 S University Ave., Little Rock, AR 72204-1000.

WILLIAMS, LYNN BARSTIS
PERSONAL Born 07/10/1946, Detroit, MI, United States, D **DISCIPLINE** COMPARATIVE LITERATURE, ART HISTORY **EDUCATION** Univ of IL, PhD, 74; SUNY-Albany, MLS, 76 **CAREER** Librn III, 89-, Auburn Univ; Assoc Prof, 76-89, Volun St Comnty col **HONORS AND AWARDS** AL Libr Asn Col and Univ Div awd for outstand contrib to prof lit **MEMBERSHIPS** Am Libr Asn; AL Hist Asn; AL Libr Asn **RESEARCH** AL art colonies, Southern Prints. **SELECTED PUBLICATIONS** Auth, Printmaking as a Bozart of the South, 1914-1947, Southern Quarterly, 98; American Printmakers, 1880-1945: An Index to Reproductions and Biocritical Information, Scarecrow, 93; Images of Scottsboro Souther Cultures 6:1 (Spring 00), 50-65 Another Provincetown? Alabama's Gulf Coast Art Colonies at Bayou La Batre and Coden Gulf South Historical Review 15:2 (00) 41-58. **CONTACT ADDRESS** Reference Dept, Auburn Univ, Auburn, AL 36849-5606. **EMAIL** willily@auburn.edu

WILLIAMS, MICHAEL
PERSONAL Born 07/30/1960, Mobile, AL, m, 1987, 3 children **DISCIPLINE** HISTORY **EDUCATION** Troy State Univ, BS, 82; Auburn Univ, MACt, 84; Southwestern Baptist Theol Sem, MDiv, 87; PhD, 93. **CAREER** From asst prof to assoc prof, Dallas Baptist Univ, 95-; dean of humanities and soc sci, Dallas Baptist Univ, 96-. **HONORS AND AWARDS** Prof of the Year, Dallas Baptist Univ, 95-96; Church Hist Awd, TBHS, 97; Church Hist Awd, Tex Baptist Hist Soc, 99; Piper Outstanding Prof Awd, Dallas Baptist Univ, 99-00; **MEMBERSHIPS** Southern Hist Asn, Am Soc of Church Hist, Southern Baptist Hist Soc, Tex Baptist Hist Soc, Confr on Faith and Hist. **RESEARCH** Nineteenth-Century American South, American Christianity, Baptist History. **SELECTED PUBLICATIONS** Auth, Victory Through Faith: A History of the Rosen Heights Baptist Church 1906-1996, Rosan Heights Baptist Church (Fort Worth, TX), 96; auth, To God Be the Glory: The Centennial History of Dallas Baptist Univ 1898-1998, Legacy Books (Arlington, TX), 98. **CONTACT ADDRESS** Dept Humanities & Soc Sci, Dallas Baptist Univ, 3000 Mountain Creek Pkwy, Dallas, TX 75211-9209. **EMAIL** mikew@dbu.edu

WILLIAMS, NUDIE EUGENE
PERSONAL Born 10/16/1936, Fairfield, AL, 1 child **DISCIPLINE** MINORITY AND AFRICAN HISTORY **EDUCATION** Clark Col, BS, 59; Okla State Univ, MA, 73, PhD(hist), 77. **CAREER** Instr, 76-77, Asst Prof Hist, Univ Ark, 77-, Coord Black studies, Univ Ark. **MEMBERSHIPS** Western Hist Soc; Southern Hist Asn; Orgn Am Historians; Asn Study Negro Life & Hist; Assoc Soc & Behav Sci. **RESEARCH** American minorities in the Southwest (Black lawmen); Black Western newspapers; West African comparative history. **SELECTED PUBLICATIONS** Auth, Cassius McDonald Barnes, governor of Oklahoma Territory, 1897-1901, Chronicles Okla, spring 75 & chap IV, In: Territorial Governors of Oklahoma, Okla Hist Soc, 75; A summary: Black newspapers in Oklahoma, 1889 to 1929, Okla Publ, 3/78; Black men who wore the star, The Chronicles of Oklahoma, Vol LIX, No 1; Black men who wore white hats: Grant Johnson, United States Deputy Marshall, Red River Valley Historical Rev, Vol V, No 3; Bass Reeves: Lawman in the Western Ozarks, Negro Hist Bull, Vol 42, No 2; A summary: Black newspapers in Oklahoma, 1889-1929, The Okla Publ, 678; Cassius McDonald Barnes, 1897-1901, Chronicles of Okla, Vol LII, No 1. **CONTACT ADDRESS** Main Campus, Univ of Arkansas, Fayetteville, Fayetteville, AR 72701-1202.

WILLIAMS, ORA
PERSONAL Born 02/18/1926, Lakewood, NJ, s **DISCIPLINE** AFRICAN-AMERICAN STUDIES **EDUCATION** Virginia Union University, Richmond, VA, AB, 1950; Howard University, Washington, DC, MA, 1953; University of California, Irvine, CA, PhD, 1974. **CAREER** Southern University, Baton Rouge, LA, instructor, 53-55; Tuskegee Institute, Tuskegee, AL, instructor, 55-57; Morgan State University, Baltimore, MD, instructor, 57-65; Camp Fire Girls, Inc, New York, NY, program advisor, 65-68; California State Univ, Long Beach, CA, prof, 68-88, Prof Emerita, 88-; Virginia Union University, visiting professor, 90-91. **HONORS AND AWARDS** Second Annual Achievement Awd in Humanities and Performing Arts Research, Virginia Union University Alumni Association of Southern California, 1983; Pillar of the Community Awd, Long Beach Community Improvement League, 1988; Outstanding Service Awd, Mayor of Long Beach, 1988; Consortium of Doctors, Savannah, GA, 1993. **MEMBERSHIPS** College Language Association; BEEM-Black Experience as Expressed in Music, board of directors, 1982; NAACP; Afro-American Youth Association, 1984; Delta Sigma Theta Sorority: **SELECTED PUBLICATIONS** Co-author of article "Johnny Doesn't/Didn't Hear," Journal of Negro History, spring, 1964; author, American Black Women in the Arts and Social Sciences: A Bibliographical Survey, Scarecrow Press, 1973, 1978, 1994; Author: Just Like Meteor: A Bio-Bibliography of the Life and Works of Charles William Williams. **CONTACT ADDRESS** English Dept, California State Univ, Long Beach, 1250 Bellflower Blvd, Humanities Office Bldg, Long Beach, CA 90840.

WILLIAMS, PATRICK RYAN
PERSONAL Born 12/08/1970, Rutland, VT, m, 1993, 3 children **DISCIPLINE** ARCHAEOLOGY **EDUCATION** Northwestern Univ, BA, 93; Univ Fla, MA, 95, PhD, 97. **CAREER** Vis asst prof, Univ Fla, 98-2000; asst prof, Boston Univ, 2000-. **HONORS AND AWARDS** Phi Beta Kappa, 91; Nat Science Found Fel, 93; Fulbright Fel, 95; GA Bruno grant, 97; Heinz Family grant, 98. **MEMBERSHIPS** Soc for Am Archaeol, Register of Prof Archaeol, Registro Nacional de Archaeologos del Peru. **RESEARCH** GIS and remote sensing in archaeology, archaeology of empires, agriculture, Andean South America. **SELECTED PUBLICATIONS** Coauth with M. Mo, "Empires of the Andes..," Discovering Archaeology (March/April 2000); auth, "Construction, chronology, and reorganization at the Wari Administrative Center of Cerro Baul," Latin American Antiquity, 11, 3, (in press); auth, "Excavations Aquologica en al Centre Administrative Wari de Carro Baul," Gaceta Aquologica Andina Set (in Press). **CONTACT ADDRESS** Dept Archaeol, Boston Univ, 675 Commonwealth Ave, Boston, MA 02215.

WILLIAMS, QUEEN J.
PERSONAL Born 12/16/1946, Pembroke, KY, m, 1965, 3 children **DISCIPLINE** AFRICAN HISTORY **EDUCATION** Univ Louisville, BA, 69; Murray St Univ, MA, 78. **CAREER** Lang specialist, 69-71, Louisville Bd of Ed; ABE instr, 80-82, Kirkwood Col; paideia instr, 88-, Luther Col. **RESEARCH** African-Amer women's hist. **CONTACT ADDRESS** 601 West Water St, Decorah, IA 52101. **EMAIL** williaqu@luther.edu

WILLIAMS, RICHARD HAL
PERSONAL Born 10/07/1941, Beeville, TX, m, 1963, 2 children **DISCIPLINE** HISTORY **EDUCATION** Princeton Univ, AB, 63; Yale Univ, MA, 64, PhD, 68. **CAREER** From asst prof to assoc prof hist, Yale Univ, 68-75; prof & chmn dept hist, 75-79, dean, Dedman Col, Southern Methodist Univ, 80, Morse fel, Yale Univ, 71-72; res grant, Southern Methodist Univ, 77, 79-80; evaluator/prin investr, Nat Endowment Hum, 76-78; Am Philos Soc grant, 79-80; fel, Univ Col, Oxford, 80. **HONORS AND AWARDS** Everett Eugene Edwards Awd, Agr Hist Soc, 67; Outstanding Prof, Southern Methodist Univ, 77, 79, 94. **MEMBERSHIPS** AHA; Orgn Am Historians; Western Hist Asn; Southwestern Soc Sci Asn. **RESEARCH** Gilded Age; Progressive Era. **SELECTED PUBLICATIONS** Auth, George W Julian and land reform in New Mexico, 1885-1889, Agr Hist, 1/67; Dry bones and dead language: The Democratic Party, In: The Gilded Age, Syracuse Univ, 70; The Democratic Party and California Politics, 1880-1896, Stanford Univ, 73; Years of Decision: American Politics in the 1890s, John Wiley & Sons, 78; co auth, The Manhattan Project, Temply, 91; auth, Dear Tom, Dear Theodore: The Letters of Theodore Roosevelt and Thomas B. Reed, Theodore Roosevelt Association Journal, 95; auth, The Politics of the Gilded Age, Essays in Honor of Vincent P. DeSantis, Univ Notre Dame, 97; co auth, America: Past and Present, Addison Wesley, 5th ed, 98. **CONTACT ADDRESS** Dept of Hist, So Methodist Univ, PO Box 750001, Dallas, TX 75275-0001. **EMAIL** hwilliam@mail.smu.edu

WILLIAMS, RICHARD S.
DISCIPLINE HISTORY OF ANCIENT GREECE, ROME AND MEDIEVAL EUROPE **EDUCATION** Mich State Univ, BA, 66, MA, 69, PhD, 73. **CAREER** Vis asst prof, Univ of Kentucky, 73-74; asst to assoc prof, Wash State Univ, 74-. **HONORS AND AWARDS** President's Fac Excellence Awd for Instruction, 92; 2 NEH Summer Inste awards. **RESEARCH** Roman Republican Politics, Roman Mathematics. **SELECTED PUBLICATIONS** Auth, "The Role of Amicitia in the Career of A. Gabinius (Cos. 58)," Phoenix: The J of the Class Assoc of Can 32 (78): 195-210; auth, "The Appointment of Glabrio (Cos. 67) to the Eastern Command," Phoenix: The J of the Class Assoc of Can, 38 (84): 221-234; auth, "Rei Publicae Causa: Gabinius' Defense of His Restoration of Ptolemy Auletes," The Class J, 81 (85): 25-38; auth, "Good King Priam," Liverpool Class Monthly 11.10 (86): 162; auth, "God Bless Ye Archaeologists," Liverpool Class Monthly 12 (87): 127; coauth, "Cn. Pompeius Magnus and L. Afranius: Failure to Secure the Eastern Settlement," Class J 83 (88): 198-206; auth, "Caesar BG 1.1.1 Once Again," Liverpool Class Monthly 14 (89): 156; auth, "The Red and the Black Figure," Liverpool Class Monthly 16 (91): 145; coauth, "Finger Numbers in the Greco-Roman World and the Early Middle Ages," Isis 86 (95): 587-608. **CONTACT ADDRESS** Dept of History, Washington State Univ, 301 Wilson Hall, PO Box 644030, Pullman, WA 99164-4030. **EMAIL** sarek@wsu.edu

WILLIAMS, ROBERT CHADWELL
PERSONAL Born 10/14/1938, Boston, MA, m, 1960, 2 children **DISCIPLINE** MODERN HISTORY **EDUCATION** Wesleyan Univ, BA, 60; Harvard Univ, AM, 62, PhD(hist), 66. **CAREER** From lectr to asst prof hist, Williams Col, 65-70; assoc prof, 70-77, Prof Hist, Washington Univ, 77-, Dean, Univ College, 81-, Kennan Inst Advan Russ Studies sr fel, 76-77. **MEMBERSHIPS** Am Asn Advan Slavic Studies. **RESEARCH** Russian-German relations; origins of Bolshevism; nuclear energy history. **SELECTED PUBLICATIONS** Auth, Russians in Germany: 1900-1914, J Contemp Hist, 10/66; Russian wars prisoners and Soviet-German relations 1918-1921, Can Slavic Papers, 10/67; Changing landmarks in Russian Berlin: 1922-1924, Slavic Rev, 69; Culture in Exile: Russian Emigres in Germany, 1881-1941, Cornell Univ, 72; Artists in Revolution: Portraits of the Russian Avante-Garde, 1905-1925, Ind Univ, 77; Russian Art and American Money: 1900-1940, Harvard Univ, 80. **CONTACT ADDRESS** Dept of Hist, Washington Univ, Saint Louis, MO 63130.

WILLIAMS, ROBIN B.
DISCIPLINE ARCHITECTURAL HISTORY; MODERN **EDUCATION** Univ Penn, PhD 93, MA 90; Univ Toronto, BA 87. **CAREER** Savannah Col Art & Design, dir, VHS project 97-, Ch dept arch hist, 96-, prof, dept art/hist, 93-96; Univ Penn, tchg asst, 87-90. **HONORS AND AWARDS** GA Humanities Coun Gnt; Who's Who Amer Tchrs; Sch Arts Sci Diss Fel; Mellon Fel; Soc Sci Hum Res Coun Canada Doctoral Fel; Isaac Perry essay Prize; Thom Ustick Walter Essay Prize. **MEMBERSHIPS** SAH; SCSAH; CAA; IAS; GHS. **RESEARCH** 19TH CENTURY ARCH AND URBANISM IN Italy, US and Canada; Savannah arch and urbanism; City sqs; computer tecno for stud of archi and urbanism. **SELECTED PUBLICATIONS** Auth, The Image of Secular Power: The romanita of Italian State Architecture under the Sinistra, 1876-1890, in: Guglielmo Calderini: La costruzione di un architettura nel progetto di una Capitale, ed Giorgio Muratore, Perugia, 96; Creating the National Capital: the Urban Works of the Royla Italian Government, Can Med Inst Bull, 92. **CONTACT ADDRESS** Dept of Architectural History, Savannah Col of Art and Design, PO Box 3146, Savannah, GA 31402-3146. **EMAIL** rwilliam@scad.edu

WILLIAMS, VERNON J., JR.
PERSONAL Born 04/25/1948, Marshall, TX, d, 2 children **DISCIPLINE** HISTORY **EDUCATION** Univ Tex at Austin, BA, 69; Brown Univ, AM, 73; PhD, 77. **CAREER** Asst prof, Rhode Island Col, 85-90; lectr, Afro-American Studies Prog, 89-90; res assoc, Afro-Am Studies Ctr at Boston Univ, 89-90; from assoc prof to prof, Purdue Univ, 90-. **HONORS AND AWARDS** NEH Summer Sem, Yale Univ, 89; ACLS Grant in Aid, 90-91; Clio Grant, Ind Hist Soc, 94-95. **MEMBERSHIPS** Afro-American Hist Asn of the Niagara Frontier, Inc., Orgn of Am Historians, Immigrant and Ethnic Hist Soc, Southern Hist Asn, Asn of Black Sociologists, Asn of Soc and Behav Sci. **RESEARCH** History of the American Social Sciences, African American History, American Studies. **SELECTED PUBLICATIONS** Auth, "Franz Boas and the African American Intelligentsia," The Western J of Black Studies 19 (95): 81-89; auth, "W.E.B. DuBois and E. Franklin Frazier: Exposing the Pitfalls of Prejudiced Social Science," The Riot: The J of Black Heritage 15 (96): 14-21; auth, Rethinking Race: Franz Boas and His Contemporaries, Univ Press of Ky (Lexington, KY), 96; auth, "Monroe N. Work's Contribution to Booker T. Washington's Nationalist Legacy," The Western J of Black Studies 21 (97): 85-91; auth, "Booker T. Washington--Myth Maker," in A Different Vision: African American Economic Thought (2 vols), ed. Thomas D. Boston (London: Routledge, 97), 194-212; auth, "Franz Boas's Paradox and the African American Intelligentsia," in African Americans and Jews in the Twentieth Century: Studies in Convergence and Conflict, ed.s V. P. Franklin, Nancy Grant, Harold M. Kletnick, and Genna R. McNeil (MO: Univ Mo Press, 98), 54-86. **CONTACT ADDRESS** Dept Hist, Purdue Univ, West Lafayette, West Lafayette, IN 47907. **EMAIL** vjwmsjr@purdue.edu

WILLIAMS, WILLIAM HENRY
PERSONAL Born 06/09/1936, Port Jervis, NY, m, 1959, 2 children **DISCIPLINE** EARLY AMERICAN HISTORY **EDUCATION** Drew Univ, AB, 58; Yeshiva Univ, MA, 59; Univ Del, PhD(hist), 71. **CAREER** Instr, 67-71, asst prof, 71-77, assoc prof hist, 77-85, Prof Hist, 85- , Paralell Prog, Univ Del; southern coord, Master of Arts in Liberal Stud, Univ Del, 88- . **HONORS AND AWARDS** Consult, Pa Hosp, 75-76; chmn, Del Humanities Forum, 76-77, consult, 77-81; proposal reviewer, Nat Endowment Humanities, 79- . **MEMBERSHIPS** Orgn Am Historians. **RESEARCH** Early American social history. **SELECTED PUBLICATIONS** Auth, Early Days of the Anglo-Americans First Hospital, J Am Med Asn, 3/65; The Industrious Poor and the Founding of the Pennsylvania Hospital, Pa Mag Hist & Biog, 10/73; ed, Sixteen Miles from Anywhere: A History of Georgetown, Delaware, Countian Press, 76; auth, Independence and Early American Hospitals, Bicentenary Issue, J Am Med Asn, 5/7/76; Anglo-Americas First Hospital: The Pennsylvania Hospital, 1751-1841, Haverford House, 76; A Means to an End: Oregon's Protestant Missionaries View the Indian, Pac Historian, Summer 76; ed, Oral History Project: Education in Sussex County, Delaware, Sussex County Bicentennial Comt, 78; contrib, Dict American Medical Biography & Dict of American Biography; auth, The Garden of American Methodism: The Delmarva Peninunsula, 1769-1820, Scholarly Resources, 84; auth, The First State: An Illustrated History of Delaware, Windsor, 85; auth, Slavery and Freedom in Delaware, 1639-1865, Scholarly Resources, 96; auth, The Delmarva Chicken Industry: 75 Years of Progress, Delmarva Poultry Industry, 98. **CONTACT ADDRESS** 238 W Pine, Georgetown, DE 19947.

WILLIAMS-MYERS, ALBERT J.
PERSONAL Born 03/10/1939, Edison, GA, m, 1962 **DISCIPLINE** AFRICAN-AMERICAN STUDIES **EDUCATION** Wagner College, BA, 1962; UCLA, life-time teaching certificate, 1969, MA, 1971, PhD, 1978. **CAREER** Mobilization for Youth, work group leader, 62-63; All Saints Parish School, teacher, 8th thru 11th grade, 63-64; College of the Virgin Islands, head resident, director of activities, 64-65; New York City Youth Board, street club worker, 65-66; US Peace Corps, Malawi, Africa, volunteer, 66-68; Carleton College, prof, 76-79; SUNY Albany African-American Institute, exec dir, 90-91; SUNY Coll at New Paltz, Prof, currently. **HONORS AND AWARDS** Ford Foundation, Research in Africa & the Middle East Graduate Fellowship, 1973-74; Historic Hudson Valley, Distinguished African-American Researcher Awd, 1992. **MEMBERSHIPS** African Studies Association, 1971-80; New York African Studies Association, president, 1985-88; NAACP, Ellenville, Chapter, 1985-. **SELECTED PUBLICATIONS** Writer, "Slavery, Rebellion and Revolution in The Americas: A Historiographical Scenario on the Theses of Genovese and Others," Journal of Black Studies 26, 4 March 1996; Making The Invisible Visible: African-Americans in New York History, 1994; "A Portrait of Eve: History of Black Women in Hudson Valley," 1987; NY City, African Americans and Selected Memory: An Historiographical Assessment of a Black Presence Before 1877; Journal of Afro-Americans in New York Life and History, July 1997; Books Published: "Long Hammering: Essays on the forging of an African American Presence in the Hudson River Valley to the Early Twentieth Century," Africa World Press, 1994; "Destructive Impulses: An Examination of An American Secret in Race Relations: White Violence," University Press of America, 1995. **CONTACT ADDRESS** SUNY, New Paltz, College Hall F-106, New Paltz, NY 12561.

WILLIAMSON, ARTHUR H.
PERSONAL Born 12/14/1943, Cleveland, OH, m, 1970, 1 child **DISCIPLINE** HISTORY **EDUCATION** Carleton Col, BA, 65; Wash Univ, St Louis, MA, 68, PhD, 74. **CAREER** Vis asst prof of Hist, Wash Univ-St Louis, 74-75; Asst prof of Hist, Univ Chicago, 75-78; Asst Dean Grad School Arts & Sci, NY Univ, 78-88; Dean Grad Stud, 88-91, Prof Hist, 88- , Calif State Univ-Sacramento. **HONORS AND AWARDS** Fulbright Sr Schol, 93-94; Hon prof Hist, Dept Hist, Univ Aberdeen (UK); Brit Acad Travel grant, 98; Sr fel, Inst Advan Stud, Univ Edin-

burgh, 93-94; Danforth Tchg fel, 65-68; Woodrow Wilson Diss fel, 68-69; Univ (Ford) grant, 69-70. **MEMBERSHIPS** Am Hist Asn; 16th Century Conf; Pac Coast Conf Brit Stud. **RESEARCH** Early modern Britain; History of political thought; Reformation. **SELECTED PUBLICATIONS** Auth, Scottish National Consciousness in the Age of James VI, Humanites, 79; coed, The Expulsion of the Jews: 1492 and After, Garland Press, 94; auth, "Union with England Traditional, Union with England Radical: Sir James Hope and the Mid 17th-Century British State," Engl Hist Rev (95); auth, "Images of Blood: Ethnic Identity and the Destruction of the Left in Europe and America, 1972-1992," CSUS (95); auth, "Scots, Indians, and Empire: The Scottish Politics of Civilization, 1519-1609," in Past and Present (96); auth, "Patterns of British Identity: 'Britain' and its Rivals in the 16th and 17th Centuries," in The New British History: The Founding of a Modern State, 1603-1715 (I.B. Tauris, 99); coed, George Buchanan the Political Poetry, Scottish Hist Soc, 00; coed, The British Union: David Hume of Godscroft's De unione insulae Britannicae, Ashgate, 01; auth, "Britain, Race, and the Iberian World Empire," in The Stuart Kingdoms in the 17th Century (01); auth, "Britain and the Beast: The Apocalypse and the 17th-Century Debate about the Creation of British State," in The Millenarian Turn (Kluwer, 01); **CONTACT ADDRESS** Dept of Hist, California State Univ, Sacramento, Sacramento, CA 95819-6059. **EMAIL** williamsonah@csus.edu

WILLIAMSON, CHRIS
PERSONAL Born 08/06/1956, PA **DISCIPLINE** GEOGRAPHY **EDUCATION** Pa State Univ, BS, 77; Univ Va, MS, 81; Univ S Calif, PhD, 86. **CAREER** Census Bureau, 79-88; Planning Consultant, 89-92; City Planner, 92-95; Assoc Prof,Univ of Southern Calif, 95-. **HONORS AND AWARDS** Res Fel, Am Inst of Certified Planers. **MEMBERSHIPS** Am Planning Asn. **RESEARCH** Census 2000, Redistricting, Urban Planning. **SELECTED PUBLICATIONS** Auth, Making Sense of Census 2000, forthcoming. **CONTACT ADDRESS** Dept Geog, Univ of So California, 3620 S Vermont Ave, Los Angeles, CA 90089-0255. **EMAIL** cbwillia@usc.edu

WILLIAMSON, JOEL R.
PERSONAL Born 10/27/1929, Anderson Cty, SC, m, 1986, 3 children **DISCIPLINE** HISTORY **EDUCATION** Univ SC, AB, 49; MA, 51; Univ Calif, PhD, 64. **CAREER** Instr to Prof, Univ NC, 60-. **HONORS AND AWARDS** The Mayflower Cup, 94; Nominated for the Pulitzer Prize in Hist, 94, 85; Res Fel, Rockefeller Ctr, Italy, 88; NEH Fel, 87-88; Francis Parkman Prize, soc of Am Hist, 85; Frank L and Harriet C Owsley Awd, 85; Ralph Waldo Emerson Awd, Phi Beta Kappa, 85; Guggenheim Fel, 70-71. **MEMBERSHIPS** Soc of am Hist, Southern Hist Asn, Am Hist Asn, Org of Am Hist. **RESEARCH** Black-White Relations; Southern Culture; William Faulkner, Margaret Mitchell; Elvis Presley; Tennessee Williams. **SELECTED PUBLICATIONS** Auth, William Faulkner and Southern History, Oxford Univ Press, 93; auth, a Rage for Order, Oxford Univ Press, 86; auth, The Crucible of race: black-White relations in the American South since emancipation, Oxford Univ Press, 84; auth, New People: Miscegenation and Mulattoes in the United States, The Free Press, 80; auth, The Origins of Segregation, D.C. Heath, 68; auth, After slavery: The Negro in south Carolina during reconstruction, 1861-1877, Univ NC Press, 65; auth, The Feminine Elvis, forthcoming; auth, Elvis Presley: The Cultural Roots, forthcoming; auth, The Souls of White folk: The Evolution of southern White culture in the Twentieth Century, forthcoming. **CONTACT ADDRESS** Dept Hist, Univ of No Carolina, Chapel Hill, 440 W Franklin St, Chapel Hill, NC 27599-2319.

WILLIS, ALFRED
PERSONAL Born 06/07/1955, Atlanta, GA, s **DISCIPLINE** ART HISTORY AND ARCHAEOLOGY **EDUCATION** Clemson Univ, BA, 76; Columbia Univ, PhD, 84; Univ Chicago, MA, 86. **CAREER** Asst prof, Syracuse Univ, 84-85; adj instr, Univ Ill at Chicago, 85-86; res, Canadian Ctr fro Archit, 86-87; actg dir, Resource Ctr, Univ Ill at Chicago, 87-88; librn, Found for Doc of Archit, Nat Gallery of Art, 88-89; cataloger, 89-90; archit librn, Kent State Univ, 90-93; head, Art Libr, Univ Cal Los Angeles, 93- . **HONORS AND AWARDS** Columbia Univ Pres Fel, 79-81; Belgian-American Educ Found Fel, 81-82; Belgian Minsitry for Netherlandish Cult Fel, 83-84. **MEMBERSHIPS** Art Libr Soc of North Am; Asoc of Archit Librns; ALA; Col Art Asoc; Sco of Archit Hist. **RESEARCH** Belgian architecture and decorative arts; theosophical architecture; Los Angeles architecture; architectural drawings; aesthetics of architecture; library science. **SELECTED PUBLICATIONS** Auth, The Exoteric and Esoteric Functions of Le Corbsier's Mundanem (1929), Modulus, 81; auth, The Gates in the Brialmont Fortifications of Antwerp as Architectural Monuments, Revue belge d'histoire militaire, 83; auth, Mannerism, Nature, and Abstraction in the Early Architectural Designs of Victor Horta, Horta: Art Nouveau to Modernism, 96; auth, The Place of Archives in the Universe of Architectural Documentation, Am Archivist, 96; auth, L'Ommegang de Bruxelles en 1930: Le contexte historique d'un cortege historique, Pleins feux sur l'Ommegang, 97. **CONTACT ADDRESS** Univ of California, Los Angeles, 2250 Dickson Art Center, 405 Hilgard Ave, Los Angeles, CA 90024-1392. **EMAIL** awillis@library.ucla.edu

WILLIS, FRANK ROY
PERSONAL Born 07/25/1930, Prescot, England, m, 1959, 3 children **DISCIPLINE** MODERN HISTORY **EDUCATION** Cambridge Univ, BA, 52; Stanford Univ, PhD, 59. **CAREER** Instr hist civilization, Stanford Univ, 59-60; from instr to assoc prof hist, Univ Wash, 60-64; assoc prof, 64-67, Prof Hist, Univ Calif, Davis, 67-, Am Coun Learned Soc grant-in-aid, 61; Rockefeller Found res grant int rels, 62-63; Guggenheim Found fel, 66-67; vis prof int rels, Stanford Univ, 71-72; Soc Sci Res Coun res training fel, 73-74. **MEMBERSHIPS** AHA **RESEARCH** France since 1750; Germany and Italy since 1945; European integration. **SELECTED PUBLICATIONS** Auth, The French in Germany, 1945-1949, 62 & France, Germany and the New Europe, 1945-1963, 65, rev ed, 68, Stanford Univ; Europe in the Global Age: 1939 to the Present, Dodd, 68; Italy Chooses Europe, Oxford Univ, 71; Western Civilization: An Urban Perspective, Heath, 73; ed, European Integration, Watts, 75; World Civilizations, Heath, 82; The French Paradox, Hoover, 82. **CONTACT ADDRESS** Dept of Hist, Univ of California, Davis, Davis, CA 95616.

WILLIS, JAMES F.
PERSONAL m, 1 child **DISCIPLINE** HISTORY **EDUCATION** Southern State Col Magnolia, BA, 67; Duke Univ, MA, 68, PhD, 76. **CAREER** Instr, Little Rock Univ, 68-69; instr, 69-71; asst prof, Southern State Col, 73-74; asst prof, 74-93; prof polit sci, Southern AR Univ, 93-. **HONORS AND AWARDS** Best Paper Prize, 94. **MEMBERSHIPS** Ark Hist Asn; Ark Polit Sci Asn; Ark Asn Col Hist Tchr; Soc Hist Am For Rel; Int Studies Asn; Southern Polit Sci Asn; SW Soc Sci Asn; Am Hist Asn; Am Polit Sci Asn; Orgn Am Hist; Am Asn Univ Prof. **RESEARCH** Am for rel(s); international Law; Latin Am hist; East Asia hist. **SELECTED PUBLICATIONS** Auth, Breckinridge Clifton Rodes, Oxford, Univ, 95; The SAU Poll, Southern AR Univ; The SAU Poll # 2, Southern AR Univ. **CONTACT ADDRESS** Hist Dept, So Arkansas Univ, Magnolia, East University, PO Box 100, Magnolia, AR 71753-5000. **EMAIL** jfwillis@saumag.edu

WILLS, GREGORY A.
PERSONAL 3 children **DISCIPLINE** CHURCH HISTORY **EDUCATION** Duke Univ, BS; Gordon-Conwell Theol Sem, MDiv; Duke Univ, ThM; Emory Univ, PhD. **CAREER** Archives and spec coll(s) libn, Boyce Centennial Lib, Assoc Prof, S Baptist Theol Sem. **SELECTED PUBLICATIONS** Auth, dissertation, Democratic Religion: Freedom, Authority, and Church Discipline in the Baptist South, 1785-1900, Oxford UP; entries on Basil Manly, Jr. and Jesse Mercer, Amer Nat Biography. **CONTACT ADDRESS** Dept of Church History, So Baptist Theol Sem, 2825 Lexington Rd, Louisville, KY 40280. **EMAIL** gwills@sbts.edu

WILLS, JOHN E., JR.
PERSONAL Born 08/08/1936, Urbana, IL, m, 1958, 5 children **DISCIPLINE** HISTORY **EDUCATION** Univ Ill, AB, 56; Harvard Univ, MA, 58; PhD, 67. **CAREER** Instr, Stanford Univ, 64-65; instr, Univ Southern Calif, 65-67; asst prof, 67-72; assoc prof, 72-84; prof, 84- . **MEMBERSHIPS** Asoc for Asian Studies; Am Hist Asoc. **RESEARCH** The Ming-Qing transition in 17th-century China; pre-modern Chinese foreign relations; China's coastal regions and their overseas connections; the maritime interconnections of Europeans and Asians in early modern times; comparative history; philosophy of history. **SELECTED PUBLICATIONS** Auth, Pepper, Guns, and Parleys: The Dutch East India Company and China, 1662-1681, 74; co-ed with Jonathan D. Spence, From Ming to Ch'ing: Conquest, Region, and Continuity in Seventeenth-Century China, 79; Embassies and Illusions: Dutch and Portuguese Envoys to K'ang-his, 1666-1687, 84; auth, Mountain of Fame: Portraits in Chinese History, 94. **CONTACT ADDRESS** History Dept, Univ of So California, Los Angeles, CA 90089-0034. **EMAIL** jwills@usc.edu

WILLUMSON, GLENN GARDNER
PERSONAL Born 06/22/1949, Glendale, CA, m, 1970, 2 children **DISCIPLINE** ART HISTORY; ENGLISH **EDUCATION** St. Mary's Col, BA, 71; Univ Calif Davis, MA, 84; Univ Calif Santa Barbara, PhD, 88. **CAREER** Teacher, Calif Secondary Sch, 71-81; cur, Amer Art and Photog, Getty Res Inst, 88-92; affil prof, Dept of Art Hist, Pa State, 93-; Senior Cur, Palmer Mus of Art, Pa State, 92-. **HONORS AND AWARDS** Nat Endow for the Humanities fel, 97-98; Haynes fel, Huntington Libr, fac res grant, 94; J. Paul Getty Publ grant, 91; Annette Baxter prize, Amer studies, 87; Kress found fel, 87; Nat Writing Proj fel, 87; teaching resources grant, 84. **MEMBERSHIPS** Col Art Asn; Amer Studies Asn; Asn of Hist of Amer Art; Asn of Univ Mus and Galleries. **RESEARCH** History of photography; American art. **SELECTED PUBLICATIONS** Auth, "The Shifting Audience of the University Museum," Museum International; auth, The Getty Research Institute: Materials for a New Photo-History, Hist of Photog, XXII, 1, 31-39, Spring, 98; auth, Clement Greenberg, Encycl of World Bio, Jan, 95; auth, A Family Album: Portraits by John Sloan, Amer Art Rev, 116-117, June-July, 94; auth, Collecting with a Passion: Selections from the Pincus Collection of Contemporary Art, Univ Pk, Palmer Mus of Art, 93; auth, Silver Salts and Blueprints, London Times Lit Suppl, 19 Mar, 93; auth, W. Eugene Smith and the Photographic Essay, NY, Cambridge Univ Press, 92; essays, Van Dyck's Iconographie, Mus Plantin-Moretus, Stedelijk Prenteenkabinet, 376-387, 91; auth, Alfred Hart: Photographer of the Transcontinental Railroad, Hist of Photog, XII, 1, 61-75, Jan-Mar, 88. **CONTACT ADDRESS** Palmer Museum of Art, Pennsylvania State Univ, Univ Park, University Park, PA 16802-2507. **EMAIL** ggw2@psu.edu

WILMARTH, ARTHUR E.
PERSONAL Born 02/16/1951, Olean, NY, m, 1983, 2 children **DISCIPLINE** HISTORY **EDUCATION** Yale Univ, BA, 72; Harvard Univ, JD, 75 **CAREER** Assoc, Arent, Fox, Kinter, Plotkin & Kahn, 75-79; assoc, Jones, Day, Reavis & Pogue, 79-85; partner, Jones, Day, Reavis & Pogue, 79-85; assoc prof law, George Washington Univ, 86-; partner, Barley, Snyder, Senft & Cohen, 92-94. **HONORS AND AWARDS** Phi Beta Kappa, Yale Univ; Who's Who in American Law; Who's who in the East; rated "av" by Martindale-Hubbell. **MEMBERSHIPS** ABA; District of Columbia Bar. **RESEARCH** Banking law; corporate law; Am legal hist. **SELECTED PUBLICATIONS** Auth, "The Case for the Validity of State Regional Banking Laws", in 18 Loyola of Los Angeles Law Review, 85; auth, "The Original Purpose of the Bill of Rights: James Madison and the Founders' Search for a Workable Balance between Federal and State Power", in 26 Am Criminal Law Review, 89; auth, "The Expansion of State Bank Powers, the Federal Response and the Case for Preserving the Dual Banking System", in 58 Fordham Law Review, 90; auth "The Potential Risks of Nationwide Consolidation in the Banking Industry: A Reply to Professor Miller", in 77 Iowa Law Review, 92; auth "Too Big to Fail, Too Few to Serve? The Potential Risks of Nationwide Banks", in 77 Iowa Law Review, 92; auth, "Too Good to be True? The Unfulfilled Promises Behind Big Bank Mergers", in 2 Stanford Journal of Law, Business & Finance, 95; coauth, Corporations and Alternative Business Vehicles, 4th ed, 97. **CONTACT ADDRESS** Law School, The George Washington Univ, 720 20th St, NW, Washington, DC 20052. **EMAIL** awilmarth@main.nlc.gwu.edu

WILMETH, DON B.
PERSONAL Born 12/15/1939, Houston, TX, m, 1963, 1 child **DISCIPLINE** THEATRE HISTORY, POPULAR CULTURE **EDUCATION** Abilene Christian Col, BA, 61; Univ AR, MA, 62; Univ IL, PhD, 64. **CAREER** Asst prof theatre, Eastern NM Univ, 64-65, head dept drama, 65-67; from asst prof to The Asa Messer Prof, theatre & English, Brown Univ, 67-, actg chmn theatre arts prog, 72-73, exec officer, Theatre Arts Dept, 73-, Chmn Dept, 79-87, 98-01; honorary curator, H. Adrian Smith Collection of Conjuring Books & Magiciana (In Brown Special Collections); consult, Asn Col & Res Libr, 70-; theatre ed, Intellect Mag, 74-; bk rev ed, The Theatre J, 78-80; assoc ed, Mod Lang Studies, 80; coordr, Grad Prog in Theatre Studies, 87-95; consult, Libr Congress Am theatre project, 92-94; Vis Schol, Osaka Univ and Japan Found, Summer 93; Selection Comt, Robert Lewis Medal for Lifetime Achievement in Theater Res, 94-99; O.R. and Eva Mitchell Distinguished Vis Prof, Trinity Univ, 95; Dean, Col Fels Am Theatre, 96-98; Corresponding Schol, Shaw Festival, Ontario, 98. **HONORS AND AWARDS** Eastern NM Univ res grants, 66-68; George Freedley Theatre Bk Awd, Theatre Libr Asn, 71-72; Bernard Hewitt Awd, 81, 99; Guggenheim fel, 82; Outstanding Theatre Alum, Univ Arkansas, 98; Special Awd, New England Theatre Conference, 98; Betty Jean Jones Awd, 99; Special Jury Awd, Theatre Libr Asn, 99; ma, brown univ, 70. **MEMBERSHIPS** Theatre Libr Asn (vpres, 81); Am Theatre Asn; Am Soc Theatre Res (pres 91-94, secy 95-01); Int Fedn Theatre Res (exec comt 94-97); New Engl Theatre Conf; Am Theatre & Drama Soc (exec bd 95-99). **RESEARCH** Popular entertainment; life and art of the 19th century actor, G F Cooke; Am theatre of the 19th century. **SELECTED PUBLICATIONS** Contribr, Drama/theatre, In: Books for College Libraries, 2nd ed, Am Libr Asn, 74; auth, The American Stage to World War I, 78 & American and English Popular Entertainment, 80, Gale Res Co; The Language of American Popular Entertainment, 81 & Variety Entertainment and Outdoor Amusements, 82, Greenwood Press; co-ed, Plays by William Hooker Gillette, Cambridge Univ Press, 83; auth, Mud Show: American Tent Circus Life, Univ NMex Press, 88; co-ed and contribr, Cambridge Guide to World Theatre, Cambridge Univ Press, 88; contribr, Theatre in the Colonies and United States, 1750-1915: A Documentary History, Cambridge Univ Press, 96; co-ed, The Cambridge Guide to the American Theatre, Cambridge Univ Press, 93; auth, Staging the Nation: Plays from the American Theatre, 1787-1909, Bedford Bks, 98; co-ed, The Cambridge History of American Theatre, Beginnings to 1870, Cambridge Univ Press, 98, vol 2, 99, vol 3, 00. . **CONTACT ADDRESS** Dept of Theatre Arts, Brown Univ, 1 Prospect St, Providence, RI 02912-9127. **EMAIL** donwilmeth@brown.edu

WILSON, B.
PERSONAL Born 03/30/1947, Tampa, FL, d, 3 children **DISCIPLINE** HISTORY **EDUCATION** Benedictine Col, BA 69; MSU, MA 72, PhD. **CAREER** General Motors Inst, assoc prof, 75; Western Mich Univ, prof, 90. **HONORS AND AWARDS** Who's Who in: The Midwest, Amer, The World. **MEMBERSHIPS** Assoc for the Study of African Amer Life and History. **RESEARCH** The Afri/Amer Experience; topics in Pan African **SELECTED PUBLICATIONS** Auth, Some Thoughts on the

Black Roots of American Pop Culture, in: Amer Pop Cult at Home and Abroad, 96; African Americans in Michigan, in: Ethnic Mich, 96. **CONTACT ADDRESS** Dept of Black Americana Studies, Western Michigan Univ, 331 Moore Hall, Kalamazoo, MI 49008-5093. **EMAIL** benjamin.wilson@wmich.edu

WILSON, CARTER
PERSONAL Born 12/27/1941, Washington, DC, s **DISCIPLINE** COMMUNITY STUDIES **EDUCATION** Harvard Univ, BA, 63; Syracuse Univ, MA, 66. **CAREER** Lectr, Harvard Univ, 66-69; Lectr, Tufts Univ, 69-72; From Asst Prof to Prof, Univ Calif, 72-. **HONORS AND AWARDS** Soc Sci Res Coun Awd, 94; Ruth Benedict Prize, SOGLA, 96. **RESEARCH** Maya people, Mexico, gay movements, family dynamics. **SELECTED PUBLICATIONS** Auth, Crazy February, 66; auth, On Firm Ice, 68; auth, I Have Fought the Good Fight, 69; auth, A Green Tree and a Dry Tree, 72; auth, Treasures on Earth, 81; auth, Hidden in the Blood, 95. **CONTACT ADDRESS** Dept Community Studies, Univ of California, Santa Cruz, 1156 High St, Santa Cruz, CA 95064-1077. **EMAIL** georgec@cats.ucsc.edu

WILSON, CHARLES REAGAN
PERSONAL Born 02/02/1948, Nashville, TN **DISCIPLINE** AMERICAN HISTORY, RELIGION **EDUCATION** Univ Tex, El Paso, BA, 70, MA, 72; Univ Tex, Austin, PhD(hist), 77. **CAREER** Vis prof Am studies, Univ Wuerzburg, West Ger, 77-78; lectr, Univ Tex, El Paso, 78-80; vis prof, Tex Tech Univ, 80-81; Asst Prof Am Hist, Univ Miss, 81-, Co-ed, Encycl Southern Cult, 81- **RESEARCH** Southern culture; American religion; popular culture. **SELECTED PUBLICATIONS** Auth, Bishop Thomas Frank Gailor: Celebrant of Southern tradition, Tenn Hist Quart, fall 79; The religion of the lost cause: Southern civil religion, J Southern Hist, 5/80; Baptized in Blood: The Religion of the Lost Cause, 1865-1920, Univ Ga Press, 80; Robert Lewis Dabney: Religion and the Southern holocaust, Va Mag Hist & Biog, 1/81; Southern funerals, cemeteries, the lost cause, Thomas Frank Gailor and Charles Todd Quintard, Encycl Southern Relig (in prep). **CONTACT ADDRESS** Univ of Mississippi, Box 6640, University, MS 38655.

WILSON, CHRISTOPHER M.
PERSONAL Born 12/23/1951, Iowa City, IA **DISCIPLINE** ARCHITECTURAL HISTORY **EDUCATION** Univ New Mex, MA, 81. **CAREER** J.B. Jackson, prof of cultural landscape studies, 99- ; Adj Assoc Prof, 87-99, Univ NM, Sch Archit Plan; Consulting Archit Historian, 83-. **HONORS AND AWARDS** Cummings and Villagra Awds for Best Book, Myth of Santa Fe. **MEMBERSHIPS** VAF; SAH; ASA; WHA; NTHP. **RESEARCH** Historic and contemporary architecture and cultural landscapes of the US-Mexico borderlands; the history and politics of cultural tourism and historic preservation. **SELECTED PUBLICATIONS** Auth, The Myth of Santa Fe: Creating a Modern Regional Tradition, Albuquerque, Univ New Mexico Press, 97; Tierra Amarilla: Its History, Architecture and Cultural Landscape, Museum of New Mexico Press, 91; Spatial Mestizaje on the Pueblo-Mexicano-Anglo Frontier, J Sch of Archit and Plan, 94; When a Room is the Hall, MASS 84, reprinted in: Images of an American Land: Vernacular Architecture in the Western US, ed, Thomas Carter, Albuquerque, U of NM Press 97. **CONTACT ADDRESS** School of Architecture and Planning, Univ of New Mexico, Albuquerque, Albuquerque, NM 87131. **EMAIL** chwilson@unm.edu

WILSON, CONSTANCE MARALYN
PERSONAL Born 10/07/1937, Woonsocket, RI **DISCIPLINE** SOUTHEAST ASIAN AND ASIAN HISTORY **EDUCATION** Swarthmore Col, BA, 59; Cornell Univ, PhD(hist), 70. **CAREER** Instr Asian hist, San Francisco State Col, 66-67; instr, 67-68, asst prof, 68-79, Assoc Prof Southeast Asian Hist, Northern Ill Univ, 79-, Ford Found Southeast Asia fel, 71-72; Nat Endowment for Humanities younger humanist fel, 73- ; assoc prof 79-88; full prof, Southeast Asian Hist, Northern Ill Univ, 88- . **MEMBERSHIPS** Asn Asian Studies (vchairperson prog comt, 80-81, chairperson, 81-82); ed, Cormosea Bulletin 82-91; Siam Soc; Burma Res Soc; AHA. **RESEARCH** Economic and social history of Thailand. **SELECTED PUBLICATIONS** Auth, Toward a Bibliography of the Life and Times of Mongkut, King of Thailand, 1851-1868, In: Southeast Asian History and Historiography: Essays Presented to DGE Hall, Ithaca and London, Cornell Univ, 76; coed (with C S Smith & G V Smith), Royalty and Commoners: Essays in Thai Administrative, Economic and Social History, In: Contributions to Asian Studies, Vol 15, 80; Thailand: A Handbook of Historical Statistics, Boston: G.K. Hall & Co., 83; co-ed (with Lucien M. Hanks); The Burma-Thailand Frontier over Sixteen Decades: Three descriptive documents, Athens, OH: OH Univ, Southeast Asia Series, no 70, 85; "Revenue Farming, Economic Development, and Government Policy in the Early Bangkok Period, 1830-1892"; In the Rise and Fall of Revenue Farming, St. Martins, 93. **CONTACT ADDRESS** Dept of Hist, No Illinois Univ, 1425 W Lincoln Hwy, De Kalb, IL 60115-2825.

WILSON, DANIEL JOSEPH
PERSONAL Born 12/19/1949, Wausau, WI **DISCIPLINE** AMERICAN INTELLECTUAL HISTORY **EDUCATION** Univ Wis, Whitewater, BA, 72; Johns Hopkins Univ, MA, 74, PhD(Hist), 76. **CAREER** Instr, Univ Md, Baltimore County, 76-77, Johns Hopkins Univ, 77-78; asst prof US Hist, Muhlenberg Col, 78-, from assoc prof to prof, 85-94; res asst, Papers of Benjamin Henry Latrobe, 78; fel, Am Coun Learned Soc, 81-82. **HONORS AND AWARDS** Class of 1932 Res Prof, 86-87; Phi Beta Kappa, 77. **MEMBERSHIPS** AHA; Orgn Am Historians; Am Studies Asn; Am Philos Asn; Am Assoc for the His of Medicine. **RESEARCH** The impact of science and professionalization of American philosophy; history of American philosophy; a cultural hist of the polio epidemics in Am; hist of disability. **SELECTED PUBLICATIONS** Auth, Nature in Western popular literature from the dime novel to Zane Grey, NDak Quart, 76; Professionalization and organized discussion in the APA, 1900-1922, J Hist Philos, 79; Arthur O Lovejoy and the moral of The Great Chain of Being, J Hist Ideas, 80; Arthur O Lovejoy and the Quest for Intelligibility, Univ NC Press, 80; co-ed, The Cause of the South: Selections from De Bow's Review, La State Univ Press, 82; auth, Arthur O Lovejoy: An Annotated Bibliography, Garland Publ, 82; Covenants of Work and Grace; Themes of Recovery and Redemption in Polio Narratives, Literature and Medicine, 94; A Crippling Fear: Experiencing Polio in the Era of FDR, Bulletin of the History of Medicine, 98. **CONTACT ADDRESS** Dept of History, Muhlenberg Col, 2400 W Chew St, Allentown, PA 18104-5586. **EMAIL** dwilson@muhlenberg.edu

WILSON, DAVID B.
PERSONAL Born 02/12/1941, Louisville, KY, m, 1964, 1 child **DISCIPLINE** HISTORY OF SCIENCE **EDUCATION** Wabash Col, AB, 63; Johns Hopkins Univ, PhD(hist sci), 68. **CAREER** Asst prof hist sci, Univ Okla, 67-71; archivist, Libr, Cambridge Univ, 71-75; Asdoc Prof Hist & Mech Eng, Iowa State Univ, 75-87; prof, 87-. **MEMBERSHIPS** Hist Sci Soc; British Soc for the Hist of Sci. **RESEARCH** Nineteenth century British science; Scottish Englightenment. **CONTACT ADDRESS** Dept of Hist, Iowa State Univ of Science and Tech, Ames, IA 50011-0002.

WILSON, DAVID L.
PERSONAL Born 06/04/1943, Fort Wayne, IN, 2 children **DISCIPLINE** AMERICAN HISTORY **EDUCATION** Univ Kans, BA, 65, MA, 67; Univ Tenn, PhD(hist), 74. **CAREER** Res, Ulysses S Grant Asn, 73-74; vis asst prof hist, Southern Ill Univ, Carbondale, 76-78; asst ed, 78-81, Assoc Ed, Ulysses S Grant Asn, 82-, Instr Am hist, John A Logan Col, 73-80; adj asst prof hist, Southern Ill Univ, Carbondale, 74-76 & 78-; Nat Hist Publ & Records Comt fel, 75-76; consult, US Dept State Hist Off, 79. **MEMBERSHIPS** Asn Doc Ed; Soc Historians Am For Rel; Orgn Am Historians. **RESEARCH** American Civil War era; Sino-American relations. **SELECTED PUBLICATIONS** Auth, The Lloyd Lewis-Bruce Catton research notes, Ulysses S Grant Asn, 73; coauth, The Presidency of Warren G Harding, Regents Press of Kans, 77; asst-ed, The Papers of Ulysses S Grant, Vol 8, April 1-July 6, 1863, 74, Vol 9, July 7-Dec 31, 1863, 82 & Vol 10, Jan 1-May 31, 1864, 82, Southern Ill Univ Press, 79; contribr, Encycl of Southern History, La State Univ Press, 79; coauth, Samuel H Beckwith: Grant's Shadow, Ulysses S Grant: Essays & Doc, 81; co-ed, Ulysses S Grant: Essays & Documents, Southern Ill Univ Press, 81. **CONTACT ADDRESS** Ulysses S Grant Asn, So Illinois Univ, Carbondale, Carbondale, IL 62901.

WILSON, DONALD E.
PERSONAL Born 01/04/1931, Corbin, KY, m, 1953, 3 children **DISCIPLINE** HISTORY, POLITICAL SCIENCE **EDUCATION** Univ Louisville, BA, 53; WVa Univ, MA, 61; Univ Denver, PhD, 79. **CAREER** Off, US Air Force, 53-79; From Fac to Prof, Samford Univ, 79-. **HONORS AND AWARDS** Phi Kappa Phi; Phi Alpha Theta; Pi Gamma Mu. **MEMBERSHIPS** SHA, Ala Asn Historians, NAS. **RESEARCH** Military history, World War II, the air war, Vietnam. **SELECTED PUBLICATIONS** Auth, In Search of Patriots in World War II Britain, Samford UP, 98. **CONTACT ADDRESS** Dept Hist & Polit Sci, Samford Univ, 800 Lakeshore Dr, Birmingham, AL 35229-0001. **EMAIL** dewilson@samford.edu

WILSON, GEORGE M.
PERSONAL Born 04/27/1937, Columbus, OH, m, 1960, 2 children **DISCIPLINE** HISTORY **EDUCATION** Princeton Univ, AB, 58; Harvard Univ, MA, 60; PhD, 65. **CAREER** Asst Prof of History, Univ of Illinois at Urbana-Champaign, 64-67; Assoc Prof of History, Indiana Univ, Bloomington, 67-76; Prof of History, Indiana Univ, Bloomington, 76-; Dean for International Programs, Indiana Univ, 75-78; Dir, East Asian Studies Center, Indian Univ, 87-. **HONORS AND AWARDS** Fulbright-Hayes Sr Fel; Japan Found Professional Fel. **MEMBERSHIPS** Am Historical Asn; Asn for Asian Studies; Indiana Asn of Historians. **RESEARCH** Nationalism in Japan; the Meiji Restoration; Japanese intellectual history; modern East history; Meiji Restoration. **SELECTED PUBLICATIONS** Auth, "Patriots and Redeemers in Japan: Motives in the Meiji Restoration," Univ of Chicago Press, 92; auth, "Radical Nationalist in Japan: Kita Ikki, 1883-1937," Harvard Univ press, 69; auth, "Crisis Politics in Prewar Japan, Monumenta Nipponica Monograph Series," Sophia Univ Press, 70. **CONTACT ADDRESS** Dept History, Indiana Univ, Bloomington, 1020 East Kirkwood Ave., Bloomington, IN 47405-7103. **EMAIL** gmw@indiana.edu

WILSON, GLEE EVERITT
PERSONAL Born 11/25/1935, Webb City, MO, m, 1959 **DISCIPLINE** ANCIENT HISTORY, ROMANIAN CIVILIZATION **EDUCATION** Univ Kans, BA, 59, MA, 63; Univ Washington, PhD(hist), 71. **CAREER** Asst prof hist, Okla State Univ, 66-69; asst prof, 69-79, Assoc Prof Hist, Kent State Univ, 79-, Coordr, Romanian Studies Prog, Kent State Univ. **MEMBERSHIPS** Archaeol Inst Am; Soc Romanian Studies; Am Asn Southeast Europ Studies. **RESEARCH** Athenian topography and monuments; Greek cities and shores of the Black Sea; Graeco-Roman world in the third century AD. **CONTACT ADDRESS** Dept of Hist, Kent State Univ, PO Box 5190, Kent, OH 44242-0001.

WILSON, HAROLD STACY
PERSONAL Born 06/22/1935, Neva, TN, m, 2 children **DISCIPLINE** AMERICAN HISTORY **EDUCATION** King Col, BA, 57; John Hopkins Univ, MA, 59; Emory Univ, PhD, 66. **CAREER** Asst prof hist, Wesleyan Col, Ga, 63-66; asst prof, 66-68, Col Found grant, 67-68, Assoc Prof hist, Old Dominion Univ, 68-, Assoc ed, Textile Hist Rev, 62-64, ed, 64-66; assoc ed, Wesleyan Quart Rev, 64-67; Fulbright sr lectr, Comt Int Exchange of Persons, Taiwan, 71-72, Singapore, 78-80; coordr, First Ann Urban S Conf, 74-75, chair, local arrange, committ, SHA, 88; chair, hist dept, 91-98. **HONORS AND AWARDS** Sigma Delta Chi book award, 70. **MEMBERSHIPS** AHA; Southern Hist Asn; Civil War Hist Asn. **RESEARCH** Civil War and Reconstruction; American South; progressive era; Res proj, A Very Peculiar Institution: Cotton Manufacturing in the Slave States during the Era of the Civil War. **SELECTED PUBLICATIONS** Auth, Basil Manly: Apologist for slavocracy, Ala Rev, 1/62; The role of Carter Glass in the disfranchisement of the Virginia Negro, Historian, 1/69; McClure's Magazine and the Muckrakers, Princeton Univ, 70; President Jimmy Carter and a philosophy of the sea-- Mahonist Doctrines in a modern setting, Commentary, 12/78; The chastening of the imperial president, J Hist Soc, 6/79; Mary White Ovington, First Person Singular, Whiston, 80; Circulation and Survival: McClure's Magazine and the Strange Death of Muckraking Journalism, W IL Reg Stud, 88; contrib, The Historical Dictionary of the Progressive Era,1890-1920, Greenwood,88; Matthew Fontaine Maury, The Encyclopedia of Southern Culture, UNC Press, 89; The Cruise of the C.S.S. Alabama in Southeast Asian Waters, The Journ of Confed Hist, 90. **CONTACT ADDRESS** Dept of History, Old Dominion Univ, Norfolk, VA 23529-0091. **EMAIL** hwilson@odu.edu

WILSON, IAN E.
PERSONAL Born 04/02/1943, Montreal, PQ, Canada **DISCIPLINE** HISTORY, ARCHIVAL STUDIES **EDUCATION** Queen's Univ, BA, 67, MA, 74. **CAREER** Univ archv, Queen's Univ, 70-76; archv, City Kingston, 72-76; prov archv, Sask Arch Bd, 76-86; chmn, Sask Heritage Adv Bd, 78-83; Archivist of Ont, 86-; dir gen, Info Rsrc Mgt Div, Ont Ministry Cult Commun, 90-93; Adj Prof, Info Stud, Univ Toronto, 93-. **HONORS AND AWARDS** Woodrow Wilson fel(hon), 67; W. Kaye Lamb Prize, 83. **MEMBERSHIPS** Secy & vice pres, Kingston Hist Soc, 67-76; pres, Ont Hist Soc, 75-76; Ont dir, Forum Young Can, 95-; pres, Champlain Soc, 95-. **SELECTED PUBLICATIONS** Coauth, Heritage Kingston, 73; coauth, Canadian Archives, 80; ed, Kingston City Hall, 75; ed, Regina Before Yesterday, 78. **CONTACT ADDRESS** Ontario Archives, 77 Grenville St, Unit 300, Toronto, ON, Canada M5S 1B3.

WILSON, JAMES HUGH
PERSONAL Born 04/17/1934, Charleston, MO, m, 1958, 2 children **DISCIPLINE** MODERN EUROPEAN HISTORY **EDUCATION** Southeast Mo State Col, BSEd, 59; Univ Mo, MA, 60, PhD(hist), 66. **CAREER** Asst prof hist, Bemidji State Col, 66-68; Assoc Prof Hist, Newberry Col, 68-, Chmn, Dept Hist, 72-, Chmn, Dept Educ, 81-. **MEMBERSHIPS** Soc French Hist Studies; AHA. **RESEARCH** Modern France; French revolutionary tribunal. **CONTACT ADDRESS** Dept of Hist, Newberry Col, Newberry, SC 29108.

WILSON, JEAN C.
DISCIPLINE ART HISTORY **EDUCATION** The Johns Hopkins Univ, PhD, 84. **CAREER** Assoc prof/dir grad studies, SUNY Binghamton. **RESEARCH** Renaissance and early mod visual cult in Italy and Northern Europe (1300-1700); art markets and socio-economic circumstances of production. **SELECTED PUBLICATIONS** Auth, Painting in Bruges at the Close of the Middle Ages in Studies in Society and Visual Culture, The Pennsylvania State P; Adriaen Isenbrant and the Problem of his Oeuvre: Thoughts on Authorship, Style, and the Methodology of Connoisseurship, Oud Holland, 95; Enframing Aspirations: Albrecht Durer's Self-Portrait of 1493 in the Musee du Louvre, Gazette des Beaux-Arts, 95; Reflections on St Luke's Hand: Icons and the Nature of Aura in the Burgundian Low Countries during the Fifteenth Century in The Sacred Image, East and West, Univ IL P, 95. **CONTACT ADDRESS** SUNY, Binghamton, PO Box 6000, Binghamton, NY 13902-6000. **EMAIL** jcwilson@binghamton.edu

WILSON, JOHN
PERSONAL Born 02/16/1944, Vancouver, BC, CANADA, m, 1967, 2 children **DISCIPLINE** HISTORY **EDUCATION** UC Santa Barbara, BA, 64; Northwestern Univ, PhD, 71. **CAREER** Minot State College, 66-74; Federal Aviation Admin, 74-76; MidAmerica Nazarene College, 76-89; Prof, Southern CA Col, 89-99; renamed Vanguard Univ, 99-. **HONORS AND AWARDS** Hearst Fellow, Northwestern, 64-65; Danforth Fellow, 80-86; Teacher of the Year, MANC, 84; SCC, 95; Phi Alpha Theta, Phi Delta Lambda. **MEMBERSHIPS** Org of Am Hist, Am Hist Asn, The Hist Society, Society of Hist of Am Foreign Relations, Conference on Faith and History. **RESEARCH** Aviation hist; mil hist hist of Am for policy; 20th Century US especially baseball. **SELECTED PUBLICATIONS** Auth, Research Guide in History, 74; auth, Turbulence Aloft: The Civil Aeronautics Administrations Amid Wars and Rumors of War, 1938-1953, 79; auth, A New Research Guide in History, 86; auth, Herbert Hoover and the Armed Forces, 93; auth,c Forging the American Character: Readings in United States History, 91, 97, 00; auth, A New Research Guide in History, Turbulence Aloft: The Civil Aeronautics Administration Amid Wars and Rumors of Wars, 1938-1953; Herbert Hoover and the Armed Forces; Forging the American Character: Readings in United States History. **CONTACT ADDRESS** Dept of Hist and Polit Sci, So California Col, Vanguard Univ, 55 Fair Dr, Costa Mesa, CA 92626. **EMAIL** jwilson@vanguard.edu

WILSON, JOHN BARNEY
PERSONAL Born 03/12/1930, Gainesville, FL, m, 1952, 2 children **DISCIPLINE** RUSSIAN AND EUROPEAN HISTORY **EDUCATION** Univ Fla, BA, 53; Boston Univ, AM, 54, PhD(hist), 66. **CAREER** From instr to assoc prof, 57-73, Prof Hist, DePauw Univ, 73-, Great Lakes Col Asn res grant, USSR, 65; vis prof, Ill State Univ, summer, 68, Univ RI, summer, 72 & Butler Univ, summer 79. **MEMBERSHIPS** AHA; Am Asn Advan Slavic Studies; Midwest Asn Latin Am Studies. **RESEARCH** Soviet and 19th century Russian history; Central Asia; eastern Europe. **CONTACT ADDRESS** Dept of Hist, DePauw Univ, Greencastle, IN 46135.

WILSON, JOHN ELBERT
PERSONAL m, 3 children **DISCIPLINE** CHURCH HISTORY **EDUCATION** Emory Univ, BA, 64; Drew Univ, MDiv, 67; Claremont Grad Univ, PhD, 75. **CAREER** PD, church hist, Univ of Basel, Switzerland, 83-84; PROF OF CHURCH HIST, PITTSBURGH THEOLOGICAL SEMINARY, 84-. **MEMBERSHIPS** Am Acad of Relig; Am Soc of Church Hist; Int Schelling Soc. **SELECTED PUBLICATIONS** Auth, Schellings Mythologie. Zur Auslegung der Philosophie der Mythologie und der Offenbarung, Frommann-Holzboog, 93; auth, Schelling und Nietzsche. Zur Auslegung der freuhen Werke Friedrich Nietzsches, W. de Gruyter, 96. **CONTACT ADDRESS** Pittsburgh Theol Sem, 616 N Highland Ave, Pittsburgh, PA 15206-2596. **EMAIL** jwilson@pts.edu

WILSON, JOHN FREDERICK
PERSONAL Born 04/01/1933, Ipswich, MA, m, 1954, 4 children **DISCIPLINE** AMERICAN RELIGIOUS HISTORY **EDUCATION** Harvard Col, AB, 54; Union Theol Sem, NYork, MDiv, 57, PhD, 62. **CAREER** Lectr relig, Barnard Col, 57-58; from instrto prof, 60-77,asst dean, 65-72, chmn dept, 74-81, COLLORD PROF RELIG, PRINCETON UNIV, 77-, dean of graduate school, 94-; Mem bd dirs, Union Theol Sem, NY, 77-. **HONORS AND AWARDS** Guggenheim Fellowship, 99. **MEMBERSHIPS** AHA; Am Soc Church Hist (pres, 76); Soc Values Higher Educ; Asn Document Editing; Am Studies Asn. **RESEARCH** Puritan studies; religion in American history; Jonathan Edwards. **SELECTED PUBLICATIONS** Auth, Pulpit in Parliament, 69; auth, Public Religion in American Culture, 79; ed, Jonathan Edwards: A History of the Work of Redemption, 89; auth, The Churching of America, 1776-1990, J Church and State, Vol 0035, 93; When Time Shall be no More, J Interdisciplinary Hist, Vol 0024, 94; A New Denominational Historiography + The Importance of Continuing Study of Denominations for American Religious History, Relig and Amer Culture J of Int, Vol 0005, 95; Cosmos in the Chaos, Theol Today, Vol 0053, 96; Religious Melancholy and Protestant Experience in America, J Interdisciplinary Hist, Vol 0026, 96; The Politics of Revelation and Reason, J Interdisciplinary Hist, Vol 0028, 97. **CONTACT ADDRESS** Dept of Relig, Princeton Univ, 13 1879 Hall, Princeton, NJ 08544. **EMAIL** jfwilson@princeton.edu

WILSON, LEONARD GILCHRIST
PERSONAL Born 06/11/1928, Orillia, ON, Canada, m, 1969, 1 child **DISCIPLINE** HISTORY OF MEDICINE **EDUCATION** Univ Toronto, BA, 49; Univ London, MSc, 55; Univ Wis, PhD(hist of sci), 58. **CAREER** Vis instr, Univ Calif, Berkeley, 58-59; asst prof, Cornell Univ, 59-60; from asst prof to assoc prof hist of sci & med, Yale Univ, 60-67; prof hist of med & head dept, 67-98, prof emer hist of med, Univ Minn, Minneapolis, 98-; ed, J Hist Med & Allied Sci, 73-82. **MEMBERSHIPS** AAAS; Am Asn Hist Med; Int Acad Hist Sci; Geol Soc Am; Brit Soc Hist Sci. **RESEARCH** Charles Lyell, hist of concepts of fever; hist of physiology. **SELECTED PUBLICATIONS** Coauth, Selected Readings in the History of Physiology, C C Thomas, 66; auth, Sir Charles Lyell's Scientific Journals on the Species Question, 70 & Charles Lyell, the Years to 1841: The Revolution in Geology, 72, Yale Univ Press; ed, Benjamin Silliman and His Circle, Sci Hist Publ, 79; auth, Medical Revolution in Minnesota, St. Paul Midewiwin Press, 89; Lyell in America: Transatlantic Geology, 1841-1853, Johns Hopkins Univ Press, 98. **CONTACT ADDRESS** Dept of Hist of Med, 797 Goodrich Ave, Saint Paul, MN 55105-3344. **EMAIL** wilso004@maroon.tc.umn.edu

WILSON, LEWIS
DISCIPLINE HISTORY **EDUCATION** Univ CA at Berkeley, PhD. **CAREER** Prof, Southern CA Col. **SELECTED PUBLICATIONS** Auth, A History of the Western World, Revive Us Again; contrib(s) to, Dictionary of the Pentecostal & Charismatic Movement. **CONTACT ADDRESS** Dept of Hist and Polit Sci, So California Col, 55 Fair Dr., Costa Mesa, CA 92626.

WILSON, LISA H.
DISCIPLINE HISTORY **EDUCATION** Franklin and Marshall Col, BA; Temple Univ, MA, PhD. **CAREER** Assoc prof; Conn Col, 87-; past actg dir, Gender and Women's Stud Prog, Conn Col. **HONORS AND AWARDS** Richard L. Morton awd; Andrew W. Mellon Fac fel Hum, Harvard Univ & Charles Warren Ctr fel, Harvard Univ;Homer D babbidge, Jr, Book Awd, 99; Phi Alpha theta Book Awd, 00. **RESEARCH** Early Amer hist; Gender studies. **SELECTED PUBLICATIONS** A 'Man of Business': The Widow of Means in Southeastern Pennsylvania, 1750-1850, William and Mary Quart, 87; Auth, Life After Death: Widows in Pennsylvania, 1750-1850, 91; auth, Ye Heart of a Man: The Dometid Life of Men in Colocnial New England, New Haven: yale Unvi Press, 99; auth, Ye heart of a Father: Male Parenting in Colonial New England," J of family Hist, (99), 255-274; auth, A Marriage Well-Orderd: Love, Power, and Partnership in Colonial New England, A Shared Experience: Men, Women, and the History of Gender. **CONTACT ADDRESS** Dept of History, Connecticut Col, 270 Mohegan Ave, Box 5526, New London, CT 06320. **EMAIL** lhwil@conncoll.edu

WILSON, MAJOR L.
PERSONAL Born 08/26/1926, Vilonia, AR, m, 1956, 2 children **DISCIPLINE** UNITED STATES SOCIAL AND INTELLECTUAL HISTORY **EDUCATION** Vanderbilt Univ, BA, 50; Univ Ark, MA, 53; Univ Kans, PhD(hist), 64. **CAREER** Assoc prof, 64-67, assoc prof, 67-70, Prof Hist, Memphis State Univ, 70-. **MEMBERSHIPS** Southern Hist Asn; Orgn Am Historians; Soc Historians Early Am Repub. **RESEARCH** United States intellectual history, 1800-1865; Jacksonian period. **SELECTED PUBLICATIONS** Auth, The concept of time and the political dialogue in the United States, 1828-1848, winter 67 & The free soil concept of progress and the irrepressible conflict, winter 70, Am Quart; The repressible conflict: Seward's concept of progress and the free-soil movement, J Southern Hist, 11/71; Space, Time and Freedom: The Quest for Nationality and the Irrepressible Conflict, Greenwood, 74; Paradox lost: order and progress in evangelical thought, Church Hist, 75; The Presidency of Martin Van Buren, Kansas, 82. **CONTACT ADDRESS** Dept of Hist, Univ of Memphis, Memphis, TN 38152.

WILSON, MARY
PERSONAL Born 08/18/1953, Eastman, GA, m, 1986 **DISCIPLINE** HISTORY **EDUCATION** Middle Ga Col, AS, 72; Mercer Univ, BA, 74; Fla State Univ, MA, 75; PhD, 83. **CAREER** Asst prof, Tift Col, 80-81; prof, Middle Ga Col, 83-. **HONORS AND AWARDS** Teacher of the Year, Gamma Beta Phi, 87; Alumni Asn Awd, Ga Col, 95; Governor's Teaching Fel, Ga, 99-00. **MEMBERSHIPS** Am Soc for Environmental Hist, Am Asn of Univ Professors, Delta Kappa Gamma, Ga Asn of Historians, Ga Historical Soc, Southern Hist Asn. **RESEARCH** Southern History, Environmental History, CD-ROM Technology. **SELECTED PUBLICATIONS** Auth, "The Heyday of Georgia's Longleaf Pine Lumber Industry," Ga Hist Quart (95); auth, "Using CD-ROM Technology to Teach the Process of History," Syllabus (99). **CONTACT ADDRESS** Dept Soc Sci, Middle Georgia Col, 1100 2nd St SE, Cochran, GA 31014-1564. **EMAIL** mwilson@warrior.mgc.peachnet.edu

WILSON, MARY C.
DISCIPLINE HISTORY **EDUCATION** Oxford Univ, PhD, 84. **CAREER** Prof, Univ MA Amherst . **SELECTED PUBLICATIONS** Auth, King Abdullah Britain and the Making of Jordan, 87; The Modern Middle East: A Reader, 94. **CONTACT ADDRESS** Dept of Hist, Univ of Massachusetts, Amherst, Mass Ave, Amherst, MA 01003.

WILSON, MICHAEL
DISCIPLINE HISTORY **EDUCATION** Cornell Univ, PhD, 93. **CAREER** Asst prof. **RESEARCH** Modern European cultural; intellectual and social history; history of gender and sexuality; historiography. **SELECTED PUBLICATIONS** Auth, Consuming History: The Nation, the Past and the Commodity of L'Exposition Universelle de 1900, Am Jour Semiotics, 91; Gender and Transgression in Bohemian Montmartre, Routlege, 91; Lessons of the Master: The Artist and Sexual Identity in Henry James, Henry James Rev, 93. **CONTACT ADDRESS** Dept of History, Univ of Texas, Dallas, Richardson, TX 75083-0688. **EMAIL** mwilson@utdallas.edu

WILSON, NORMAN J.
PERSONAL Born 07/31/1958, Racine, WI, m, 1986, 3 children **DISCIPLINE** HISTORY **EDUCATION** Univ Wis, BA, 81; Univ Calif, Los Angeles, MA, 87; PhD 94. **CAREER** Asst prof of hist, Xavier (Ohio), 92-98; coord of international studies, Methodist Col, 98-. **HONORS AND AWARDS** Ger Acad Exchange Service Fel; Theodore Saloutos Awd. **MEMBERSHIPS** Am Hist Asn, Sixteenth Century Studies, Phi Alpha Theta Hist Honor Soc. **RESEARCH** Reformation Europe and Historiography. **SELECTED PUBLICATIONS** Auth, History in Crisis? Recent Directions in Historiography, Prentice Hall (Upper Saddle River, NJ), 99; auth, The European Renaissance and Reformation (1350-1600), The Gale Group (Farmington Hills, MI), forthcoming. **CONTACT ADDRESS** Dept Hist and Govt, Methodist Col, 5400 Ramsey St, Fayetteville, NC 28311-1420. **EMAIL** nwilson@methodist.edu

WILSON, PHILIP
PERSONAL Born 07/13/1961, Wichita, KS, m, 1989, 2 children **DISCIPLINE** HISTORY OF SCIENCE **EDUCATION** Univ Kans, BGS, 83; Johns Hopkins Univ, MA, 88; Univ London, PhD, 92. **CAREER** Historian, Univ Haw, 92-93; Res Aff, Yale Univ, 93-94; Historian , Truman State Univ, 94-99; Faculty, Shimen Col, 99-00; Historian, Penn State, 00-. **HONORS AND AWARDS** Zakon Hist of Medicine Essay Awd; Fel, Wellcome History of Medicine, 84-92; Fel, Temkin History of Medicine, 85-87; Fel, Clemdenning History of Medicine, 84; Fel, Folger Library, 84. **MEMBERSHIPS** Am Asn History of Medicine; Hist of Sci Soc; Arthur Conan Doyle Soc; Am Soc 18th Century Studies. **RESEARCH** 18th Century British Medicine and Surgery; 19th Century Swiss-American Geology and Geography; 20th Century American Eugenics. **SELECTED PUBLICATIONS** Auth, Surgery, Skin and Syphilis: Daniel Turner's London (1667-1741), 99; auth, Childbirth: Changing Ideas and Practices in Britain and America 1600 to the present, 96. **CONTACT ADDRESS** Dept Humanities, Penn State Col of Medicine, 500 Univ Dr, Hershey, PA 17033-2390.

WILSON, RAYMOND
PERSONAL Born 04/11/1945, New Kensington, PA, m, 1970, 1 child **DISCIPLINE** HISTORY **EDUCATION** Ft Lewis Col, BA, 67; Univ Nebr, MA, 72; Univ NMex, PhD, 77. **CAREER** Grad Asst, Univ Nebr, 67-68, 71-72; Grad Asst, Univ NMex, 74-77; From Asst Prof to Prof, Ft Hays State Univ, 79-. **HONORS AND AWARDS** Excellence in Teaching Awd, Kans Coun for the Soc Studies; Governor's Medal of Merit, 86; President's Distinguished Scholar, Ft Hays State Univ, 92. **MEMBERSHIPS** Western Hist Asn, Kans Coun for the Soc Studies. **RESEARCH** American West, American Indian, Kansas history. **SELECTED PUBLICATIONS** Auth, Ohiyesa: Charles A Eastman: Santee Sioux, Univ Ill Pr (Urbana, IL), 83, 99; auth, Indian Lives: Essays on Nineteenth and Twentieth-Century Native American Leaders, Univ NMex Pr (Albuquerque, NM), 85, 93; auth, Native Americans in the Twentieth-Century, Univ Ill Pr (Urbana, IL), 86; auth, Kansas Land, Gibbs Smith Publ (Layton, UT), 88; **CONTACT ADDRESS** Dept Hist, Fort Hays State Univ, 600 Park St, Hays, KS 67601-4009. **EMAIL** rwilson@fhsu.edu

WILSON, RICHARD GUY
PERSONAL Born 05/16/1940, m, 2 children **DISCIPLINE** HISTORY OF ARCHITECTURE; ART HISTORY **EDUCATION** Univ Co, BA, 63; Univ Mi, MA, 68, PhD, 72. **CAREER** Teaching asst hist of art, Univ Mich, 69 & 70; from asst prof to assoc prof archit, Ia State Univ, 72-76; Assoc Prof Commonwealth Prof Archit Hist, Univ Va, 76 & Chemn Archit Hist, 79-, NSF res grant, 74; Iowa State Design Ctr grant, 73-74 & 75; Iowa Arts Coun, Nat Endowment Arts grant, 75-76; asst ed newslett, Soc Archit Historians, 75-78; guest cur, Brooklyn Mus, 77-80; Univ Va res grant, 78; Am Philos Soc res grant, 81; vis lectr, Polytechnic South Bank, London, 81. **HONORS AND AWARDS** Phi Beta Phi, 70, Hon mem AIA, 86; Am Hist Asn, Pac Coast Br, Best Article, 86; W Hist Asn, Best Article, 86; Charles Montgomery Prize, Most Distinguished Contrib Decorative Arts Soc, 87; Best Book of Year, Am Libr Asn, 87; Soc of Archit Hist Catalogue Awd, 93; Awd Excellence, 93; Best Essay of Year, S Libr Asn, 93. **MEMBERSHIPS** Soc Archit Historians; Nat Trust Hist Preserv; Col Art Asn. **RESEARCH** The architecture of McKim, Mead and White; the American Renaissance; design in the 1920s and 1930s; Rustic design in the Am wilderness, and the Colonial Revival in Am. **SELECTED PUBLICATIONS** The Making of Virginia Architecture, Univ Va, 92; Thomas Jefferson's Academical Village: The Making of an Architectural Masterpiece, Univ Va, 93; auth, "Richmond's Monument Avenue," Univ of NC Press, 01; auth, "Buildings of the United States: Eastern Virginia," Oxford Univ Press, 01. **CONTACT ADDRESS** Dept Archit Hist, Univ of Virginia, Campbell Hall, Charlottesville, VA 22903. **EMAIL** rgw4h@virginia.edu

WILSON, ROBERT ARDEN
PERSONAL Born 07/17/1910, Des Moines, IA, m, 1940, 3 children **DISCIPLINE** HISTORY **EDUCATION** Willamette Univ, BA, 39; Univ Wash, MA, 42, PhD, 49. **CAREER** Instr US & Far Eastern hist, Willamette Univ, 39-41; from instr to assoc prof, 49-72, prof far eastern hist, 72-80, Emer Prof Hist, Univ Calif, Los Angeles, 80-, Fulbright res scholar, Japan, 52-

53. **MEMBERSHIPS** Asn Asian Studies; AHA. **RESEARCH** Japanese political history, especially late Tokugawa and early Meiji periods. **SELECTED PUBLICATIONS** Auth, Genesis of the Meiji Government, Univ Calif; J of Henry Heusken, Rutgers, 63. **CONTACT ADDRESS** Dept of Hist, Univ of California, Los Angeles, Los Angeles, CA 90024.

WILSON, ROBERT SYDNEY
PERSONAL Born 07/23/1943, Moncton, NB, Canada, m, 1965, 2 children **DISCIPLINE** HISTORY **EDUCATION** Gordon Col, BA, 64; Univ Guelph, MA, 67, PhD(Brit hist), 73. **CAREER** Lectr Brit hist, Univ Guelph, 70-71; Lectr Hist & Dean Arts, Atlantic Baptist Col, 71-. **MEMBERSHIPS** Am Soc Church Hist; Can Soc Church Hist; Conf Faith & Hist. **RESEARCH** Nineteenth century British history; nineteenth and twentieth century Atlantic Baptist history. **SELECTED PUBLICATIONS** Contribr, Thirty-six articles, In: New International Dictionary of the Christian Church, Zondervan, 74; auth, The decline of preaching, Atlantic Baptist, 74; Alexander Crawford, In: Scottish Tradition, Univ Guelph, Ont, 82. **CONTACT ADDRESS** Atlantic Baptist Col, Salisbury Rd, Box 1004, Moncton, NB, Canada E1C 8P4.

WILSON, THEODORE A.
PERSONAL Born 09/27/1940, Evansville, IN, m, 1962, 2 children **DISCIPLINE** UNITED STATES DIPLOMATIC, MILITARY HISTORY **EDUCATION** Ind Univ, AB, 62, MA, 63, PhD(hist), 66. **CAREER** Actg asst prof, 65-66, from asst prof to assoc prof, 66-73, chmn dept, 79-81, Prof Hist, Univ Kans, 73-, Assoc Dean, Col Lib Arts & Sci, 76-79, Sr res assoc, Harry S Truman Libr Inst Nat & Int Affairs, 69-72; Nat Endowment for Humanities Younger fel, 71-72; Guggenheim fel, 72-73; vis prof Am hist, Univ Col, Dublin, 75-76; pres, Past & Present Inc, 79-88; Chair, Dept of History, 79-81; Dir, Hall Ctr for Humanities, 83-89; John Morrison Prof, CGSC, 83-84; General Ed, Modern War Studies, Univ Press Of Kansas, 86-. **HONORS AND AWARDS** Francis Parkman Prize, Soc Am Historians, 69; Ctr for Military History Sr Res Fel, 89-91. **MEMBERSHIPS** Orgn Am Historians; AHA; Soc Historians Am Foreign Rels; Soc Am Historians. **RESEARCH** United States diplomacy, 1933-1953; history of the Second World War, Society of Military Historians. **SELECTED PUBLICATIONS** Ed, WWZ: Critical Issue, 74; auth, Makers of America Diplomacy, 75; auth, The Marshall Plan, 1947-1951, 78; coauth, Three Generations in 20th Century America, 76, rev-ed, 81; auth, The First Summit, 69, rev ed, 91; auth, D-Day, 94; auth, Victory in Europe 1945, 00. **CONTACT ADDRESS** Dept of Hist, Univ of Kansas, Lawrence, Lawrence, KS 66045. **EMAIL** tawilson@flacon.cc.ukans.edu

WILSON, WILLIAM HENRY
PERSONAL Born 11/03/1935, St. Joseph, MO, m, 1960, 2 children **DISCIPLINE** UNITED STATES HISTORY **EDUCATION** Univ Mo, BJ, 57, MA, 58, PhD, 62. **CAREER** Instr, Univ Mo, 58-60; res assoc, Hist Kansas City Res Proj, 60-62; asst prof hist, Univ SDak, 62-63; from asst prof to assoc prof, Univ Alaska, 63-67; from assoc prof to Regents prof hist, North Tex State Univ, 68-. **HONORS AND AWARDS** Turman Libr Inst grant, 64; Am Philos Soc grant, 66, 75; Am Asn State & Local Hist grant, 66; NEH Younger Scholars fel, 68; Lewis Mumford Prize, 89. **MEMBERSHIPS** Orgn Am Historians; Southern Hist Asn; Soc Am City & Regional Planning; Tex State Hist Asn; Wash State Hist Asn. **RESEARCH** U S Urban history. **SELECTED PUBLICATIONS** Auth, The City Beautiful Movement in Kansas City, Univ Mo, 64; Coming of Age: Urban America, 1915-1945, Wiley, 74; Railroad in the Clouds: The Alaska Railroad in the Age of Steam, 1914-1945, Pruett, 77; The City Beautiful Movement, Johns Hopkins, 89; co-auth, Carl F Gould: A Life in Architecture in the Arts, Washington, 95; Hamilton Park: A Planned Black Community in Dallas, Johns Hopkins, 98. **CONTACT ADDRESS** Dept of Hist, Univ of No Texas, P O Box 310650, Denton, TX 76203-0650. **EMAIL** bwilson@unt.edu

WILSON, WILLIAM JERRAM
PERSONAL Born 06/04/1928, Salt Lake City, UT, m, 1959, 2 children **DISCIPLINE** ARABIC, MIDDLE EAST HISTORY **EDUCATION** Univ UT, BA, 46, MA, 59, PhD, 65. **CAREER** Asst prof, 65-70, actg head dept, 76-77, 88-89, Assoc Prof Near Eastern Studies, Univ AZ, 70-; Univ Az subsistence & travel res grant, 66, res grant, 68; vis asst prof Arabic, Univ UT, 67. **MEMBERSHIPS** Mid E Studies Asn; Am Asn Teachers Arabic; Royal Asiatic Soc. **RESEARCH** Arabic contribution to the life sciences. **CONTACT ADDRESS** Dept of Near Eastern Studies, Univ of Arizona, Franklin 509, Tucson, AZ 85721-0001. **EMAIL** wjw@u.arizona.edu

WILT, ALAN FREESE
PERSONAL Born 05/14/1937, Nappanee, IN, m, 1963, 2 children **DISCIPLINE** MODERN EUROPEAN HISTORY **EDUCATION** DePauw Univ, BA, 59; Univ Mich, MA, 60, PhD(hist), 69. **CAREER** Instr hist, Midwestern Univ, 61-62; from instr to asst prof, 67-76, assoc prof, 76-81, Prof Hist, Iowa State Univ, 81-, Vis prof, Air War Col, 82-83. **MEMBERSHIPS** AHA; Conf Group Cent Europ Hist; Am Comt Hist 2nd World War; Western Asn Ger Studies. **RESEARCH** Twentieth century Europe; military history; German history. **SELECTED PUBLICATIONS** Auth, Hitler Panzers East, Amer Hist Rev, Vol 0098, 93; Riviera to the Rhine, J Mil Hist, Vol 0057, 93; Churchill, J Mod Hist, Vol 0066, 94; D-Day June 6, 1944, Amer Hist Rev, Vol 0100, 95; Why the Allies Won, J Mil Hist, Vol 0060, 96; Frontsoldaten, Amer Hist Rev, Vol 0102, 97. **CONTACT ADDRESS** Dept of Hist, Iowa State Univ of Science and Tech, Ames, IA 50011-0002.

WILTENBURG, JOY
DISCIPLINE EARLY MODERN EUROPE AND WOMEN'S HISTORY **EDUCATION** Univ Rochester, BA; Univ Va, PhD, 84. **CAREER** Instr, Rowan Col of NJ. **RESEARCH** Social history, especially in early modern Germany and England. **SELECTED PUBLICATIONS** Published a book and several articles on social history in early modern Germany and England. **CONTACT ADDRESS** Rowan Univ, Glassboro, NJ 08028-1701.

WIMBERLY, DAN
PERSONAL Born 01/06/1948, Shreveport, LA, m, 1987 **DISCIPLINE** HISTORY **EDUCATION** La Col, BA, 69; Baptist Misionary Asn Theol Sem, MDiv, 72; Univ Tex at Tyler, MA, 89; Tex Tech Univ, PhD, 95. **CAREER** Teacher, Chapel Hill High Sch, 81-82; teacher, Canton High Sch, 83-89; teacher, Lindale High Sch, 89-90; instr, Bartlesville Wesleyan Col, 96-00. **MEMBERSHIPS** Okla Hist Soc, Nat Coun for the Soc Studies, Phi Alpha Theta. **RESEARCH** American frontier religion. **SELECTED PUBLICATIONS** Auth, Biography of Elder Daniel Parker. **CONTACT ADDRESS** Dept Soc and Behavioral Sci, Bartlesville Wesleyan Col, 2201 Silver Lake Rd, Bartlesville, OK 74006-6233. **EMAIL** dwimberly@bwc.edu

WINCH, JULIE P.
DISCIPLINE HISTORY **EDUCATION** Cambridge, BA, 75; London, MA, 76; Bryn Mawr, MA, 79, PhD, 82. **CAREER** Assoc prof History and Black Studies, Univ Mass, Boston. **RESEARCH** Black studies, American free blacks, emigration to Haiti. **SELECTED PUBLICATIONS** Fel Publ, Philadelphia's Black Elite: Activism, Accommodation, and the Struggle for Autonomy, 88; auth, Philadelphia and the Other Underground Railroad, Penn Mag of Hist and Biog 3, 87; Virginia Pindell Trotter, Trotter Inst Rev 2,88; auth, paper, American Free Blacks and Emigration to Haiti, Eleventh Carib Cong, Carib Inst and Stud Ctr for Latin Amer, 88; You Have Talents - Only Cultivate Them: Philadelphia's Black Female Literary Societies and the Abolitionist Crusade, In: The Abolitionist Sisterhood: Women's Political Culture in Antebellum America, Cornell Univ, 94. **CONTACT ADDRESS** Dept of History, Univ of Massachusetts, Boston, 100 Morrissey Blvd., Boston, MA 02125. **EMAIL** winch@umbsky.cc.umb.edu.

WIND, BARRY
DISCIPLINE ART HISTORY **EDUCATION** City Col NYork, BA, 62; Univ NYork, MA, 64, PhD, 72. **CAREER** Asst instr, Rutgers, 65-66; asst prof, Univ Ga, 67-71; asst prof, 71-77; assoc prof, Univ Wis, 77-87; vis assoc prof, Newberry Libr, 85; prof, 87-. **HONORS AND AWARDS** Distinguished Schr Awd. **SELECTED PUBLICATIONS** Auth, Genre in the Age of the Baroque, Garland, 91; Piccolo Ridicolo: A Little Bit on Bocchi, 94; A Quaker in Jan Steen, 95; auth, "Velazuez's Bodegones: A Studyin 17th Century Spanish Genre Painting," Fairfat, 6; auth, "A Foul and Congregation: Images of Freaks in Baroque AA," London 98. **CONTACT ADDRESS** Dept of Art History, Univ of Wisconsin, Milwaukee, PO Box 413, Milwaukee, WI 53201. **EMAIL** bwind@uum.edu

WINDSOR-LISCOMBE, RHODRI
PERSONAL Born 02/05/1946, Rhiwbina, Wales, m, 1990, 2 children **DISCIPLINE** ART HISTORY **EDUCATION** Clifton Col, Univ of London, BA, PhD, 72. **CAREER** Lectr, Univ London, extra-mural stud, 68-74; asst prof, McGill Univ, 74-76; asst, assoc, prof, Univ British Columbia, 76- . **HONORS AND AWARDS** Campden Charities Scholar, 68-72; fel, Soc of Antiquaries; sr fel, Green Col, Univ British Columbia; Vancouver Book Awd, Int Writers Festival, 98. **MEMBERSHIPS** Soc for Stud of Archit in Canada; Soc of Archit Hist; Walpole Soc. **RESEARCH** Introduction to art and design history and theory 18th-19th Century Art; Architecture and Engineering and 19th-20th Century Art, Architecture and engineering and 19th-20th Century North American Architecture and Engineering. The creative processes of architects, technical arsthetics, concepts and practices in Applied Scintific Design. **SELECTED PUBLICATIONS** Auth, William Wilkins, Cambridge, 80; coauth, Francis Rattenbourg and British Columbia, British Columbia, 83; auth, The Church Architecture of Robert Mills, Southern Historical, 85; auth, Nationalism or Cultural Imperialism: The Chateau Style in Canada, Archit Hist, 93; auth, Altogether American: Robert Mills Architect and Engineer, Oxford, 94; auth, The New Spirit Modern Architecture in Vancouver, 1938-1965, Canadian Center for Architecture, MIT, 97; auth, Practicing Interdisciplinary, Univ of Toronto Press, 98; auth, A Cultural Archaeology of the Greek Revival, Choice, 99. **CONTACT ADDRESS** Dept of Fine Arts, Univ of British Columbia, 6333 Memorial Rd, Vancouver, BC, Canada V6T 1W5. **EMAIL** rhodri@mercury.ubc.ca

WINELAND, JOHN D.
PERSONAL Born 11/09/1958, Gary, IN, m, 1993, 1 child **DISCIPLINE** ANCIENT HISTORY, ARCHAEOLOGY **EDUCATION** Valparaiso Univ, BS, 80; Cincinnati Christian Sem, MA, 87, MDiv, 88; Miami Univ, MA, 88, PhD, 96. **CAREER** Assoc prof, Bibl Stud and Archaeol, Roanoke Bible Col, 95-98; assoc prof Hist, Ky Christian Col, 98- ; adj instr, Cincinnati Bible Col, 91, 94; adj instr, N Ky Univ, 93-94; adj instr, Miami Univ, Middletown Campus, 91-94, Hamilton Campus, 91-94. **HONORS AND AWARDS** Who's who of Bibl Stud and Archael, 1993; Grad Acievement Awd, Miami Univ, 89-90; Endow BiblRes Travel Grant, 88, 90; Editor, Near East Archaeol Soc Bulletin, 96- ; Trustee, near East Archaeol Soc, 92- . **MEMBERSHIPS** AHA; ASOR; NEAS; CFH; AAH; SBL; IBR. **RESEARCH** Near Eastern History and Archaeology. **SELECTED PUBLICATIONS** Auth, Area A, Tell Abil: Preliminary Report of the 1988 Excavation Season, Near East Archaeological Soc Bull, 32-33, Winter 89; The 1990 Excavation Season Area A Tell Abil: Preliminary Report, Near East Archaeol Soc Bull, 35-36, winter 90; The Sixthe Season of Excavation, Area A, Tell Abila: Area Supervisor Preliminary Report, Near East Archaeol Soc Bull, 38, 93, 2-10; Tiberius, in Historic World Leaders, vol 3, 1250-1253, Detroit, Gale, 94; Anchor Bible Dictionary, 18 minor entries, including: Adramyttium, Amphipolis; Attalia; Beroea; Cauda; Cimmerians; Derbe; Fair Havens; Forum of Appius; Lasea; Mitylene; Patara; Phaselius; Thegium; Salome; Samos; Sepharad; Three Taverns, New York, Doubleday, 92; Archaeological and Numismatic Evidence of Greco-Roman Religions of the Decapolis, with Particular Emphasis on Gerasa and Abila, ARAM, 4, 92, 329-342, proceedings frfrom the Third Intl Conf of ARAM Soc for Syro-Mesopotamian Stud, The Oriental Inst, Univ Oxford, Eng; Oxford Encyclopedia of Near Eastern Archaeology, two biographical entries, K. A.C. Creswell, George Adam Smith, New York, Oxford Univ Press, 97. **CONTACT ADDRESS** Dept of History, Kentucky Christian Col, 100 Academic Pkwy, Grayson, KY 41143-2205. **EMAIL** wineland@email.kcc.edu

WINES, ROGER
DISCIPLINE HISTORY **EDUCATION** Columbia Univ, PhD **CAREER** Prof, Fordham Univ. **MEMBERSHIPS** New York Historical Soc; Bronz County Historical Soc. **SELECTED PUBLICATIONS** Auth, Enlightened Despotism: Reform or Reaction?, Heath, 67; ed, Leopold von Ranke's The Secret of World History: Selected Writings on the Art and Science of History Fordham UP, 81; publ, articles on the hist of the Bronx; auth, articles on Long Island, Bronx history and on history archaeology. **CONTACT ADDRESS** Hist Dept, Fordham Univ, Bronx, NY 10458.

WINK, ANDRE
PERSONAL Born 09/18/1953, Hollandia, Netherlands, s **DISCIPLINE** HISTORY **EDUCATION** PhD, Univ Leiden, Netherlands, 94. **CAREER** Prof, hist, Univ Wisc Madison, 89-. **HONORS AND AWARDS** CSC Huygens award, Netherlands. **RESEARCH** South and southeast Asia. **SELECTED PUBLICATIONS** Auth, Al-Hind: The making of the Indo-Islamic world, vol 1-2, 90-97. **CONTACT ADDRESS** Dept. of History, Univ of Wisconsin, Madison, 3211 Humanities Bldg., 455 North , Madison, WI 53706. **EMAIL** awink@facstaff.wisc.edu

WINKLE, KENNETH
DISCIPLINE U. S. 19TH CENTURY HISTORY **EDUCATION** Univ Wis, Madison, PhD, 84. **CAREER** Assoc prof, Univ Nebr, Lincoln. **HONORS AND AWARDS** Cora Friedline fac summer fel, 91; NEH summer stipend, 92. **RESEARCH** Social history of Abraham Lincoln and his Illinois roots. **SELECTED PUBLICATIONS** Auth, The Politics of Community: Migration and Politics in Antebellum Ohio, Cambridge UP, 88. **CONTACT ADDRESS** Univ of Nebraska, Lincoln, 617 Oldfat, Lincoln, NE 68588-0417. **EMAIL** kwinkle@unlinfo.unl.edu

WINKLER, ALLAN M.
PERSONAL Born 01/07/1945, Cincinnati, OH, m, 1992, 2 children **DISCIPLINE** AMERICAN HISTORY **EDUCATION** Harvard Univ, BA, 66; Columbia Univ, MA, 67; Yale Univ, MPhil, 72; PhD, 74. **CAREER** Instr to asst prof, Yale Univ, 73-78; asst prof to assoc prof, Univ of Ore, 79-86; prof, Miami Univ, 86-. **HONORS AND AWARDS** Mellon Fel, 78; Fulbright Grant, 78-79, 95-96; NEH Fel, 81-82; Bicentennial Chair, Finland, 78-79; John Adams Chair, The Netherlands, 84-85; Am Coun on Educ Fel, 91-92; Distinguished Educ Awd, Miami Univ, 98. **MEMBERSHIPS** AHA; Org of Am Hist; Am Studies Assoc. **RESEARCH** American Social and Political History, 20th Century America, World War II, The Nuclear Age. **SELECTED PUBLICATIONS** Auth, The Politics of Propaganda: The Office of War Information, 1942-1945, Yale Univ Pr, 78; auth, Modern America: The United Stated from World War II to the Present, Harper and Row, 85; auth, "Home Front, USA: America during World War II, Harlan Davidson, 86; ed, The Recent Past: Readings on America Since World War II, Harper and Row, 89; coauth, The American People: Creating a Nation and a Society, Harper & Row, 86; auth, Cassie's War, Royal Fireworks Pr, 94; coauth, America: Pathways to the Present, Prentice Hall, 94; auth, Life Under a Cloud:

American Anxiety about the Atom, Oxford Univ Pr, 93; auth, The Cold War, Oxford Univ Pr, (forthcoming). **CONTACT ADDRESS** Dept Hist, Miami Univ, Upham Hall 254, Oxford, OH 45056-1879. **EMAIL** winkleam@muohio.edu

WINKLER, HENRY RALPH
PERSONAL Born 10/27/1916, Waterbury, CT, m, 1940, 3 children **DISCIPLINE** HISTORY **EDUCATION** Univ Cincinnati, AB, 38, AM, 40; Univ Chicago, PhD, 47. **CAREER** From asst prof to assoc prof, Rutgers Univ, 47-58, chmn dept hist, 60-64, dean fac lib arts, 67-71, vprovost, 68, vpres acad affairs, 71-72, sr vpres acad affairs, 73-76, prof hist, 58-77, exec vpres, 76-77; exec vpres, 77, Univ Prof Hist & Pres, Univ Cincinnati, 77-, Info analyst, Off War Info, 42-43; Fulbright vis prof, London Sch Econ, 53-54; vis prof, Bryn Mawr Col, 59-60; chmn Europ hist, Nat Col Entrance Exam, 60-64; fac mem, Hays Fels Summer Inst Humanities, Williams Col, 60, 62 & Colo Col, 61; managing ed, Am Hist Rev, 64-68; mem, Joint Comt Bibliog Aids to Hist, 66-; mem Comn Humanities in Schs, 67-; adv comt foreign copying, Libr Cong, 67-; mem bd trustees, Nat Humanities Fac, 69-, pres, 71-; mem exec comt, Nat Asn State Univ & Lang-Grant Col, 78-81; bd dirs, Am Coun Educ, 79-81; prof emer. **HONORS AND AWARDS** Lindbach Awd Distinguished Teaching, Rutgers Univ, 63; littd, lehigh univ, rutgers univ & st thomas inst; lhd, nky univ, hebrew union col & city univ manila; lld, xavier univ. **MEMBERSHIPS** AHA; Orgn Am Historians; Conf Brit Studies. **RESEARCH** British diplomacy and foreign relations; British history in the nineteenth and twentieth centuries. **SELECTED PUBLICATIONS** Auth, National Crisis and National Government--British Politics, the Economy, and Empire, 1926-1932, Amer Hist Rev, Vol 0098, 93; auth, The League of Nations Movement in Great Britian, 1914-49, 1952 Great Britain in the Twentieth Century, 1960, 2nd ed, 66; coed, Great Problems in European Civilization, 1954, 2nd ed, 66, Twentieth Century Britain, 77; auth, Paths Not Taken: British Labous and International Policy in the Nineteen Twenties, 94. **CONTACT ADDRESS** Off of the Pres Emer, Univ of Cincinnati, 571 Langsam Library, Cincinnati, OH 45221.

WINKS, ROBIN WILLIAM EVERT
PERSONAL Born 12/05/1930, West Lafayette, IN, m, 1952, 2 children **DISCIPLINE** COMPARATIVE IMPERIAL & DIPLOMATIC HISTORY **EDUCATION** Univ Colo, BA, 52; MA, 53; Johns Hopkins Univ, PhD, 57. **CAREER** Instr, Univ of Colo, 53; instr hist, Conn Col Women, 56-57; Smith-Mundt prof, Univ Malaya, 62; instr, Commonwealth Studies, Univ London, 66-67; master, Berkeley Coll, Yale Univ, 77-90; dir, off of spec proj & founds, Yale Univ, 74-76; from instr to Randolph W. Townsend prof hist, Yale Univ, 57- ; ch, hjist dept, Yale Univ, 87-90; Eastman prof, Oxford Univ, 92-93; ch, studies in environ, 93-96; Harmsworth prof, Oxford Univ, 99-00. **HONORS AND AWARDS** Morse Fel, 59-60; Soc Sci Res Coun Awd, 59-60; Smith-Mundt Fel, 62-63; sr fac fel, Yal Univ, 65-66; Hon MA, Yale Univ, 67; DLitt, Univ Neb, 76, Univ Colo, 87, Westminster Coll, 89; Fel, Royal Hist Soc; Fel, Explorer's Club; Guggenheim fel, 76-77; mem, Nat Park Serv adv bd, 80- , chmn, 81- ; ma, yale univ, 67; dlitt, univ nebr, 76. **MEMBERSHIPS** AHA; Org of Am Historians; Canadian Hist Asn; Asia Soc; Athenaeum Ref Club; Royal Commonwealth Soc; Yale Club. **RESEARCH** Canadian-American diplomatic and cultural relations; Australia, New Zealand Britain in the Pacific; comparative history race relations. **SELECTED PUBLICATIONS** Auth, The Blacks in Canada, Yale Univ, 71; ed, Slavery: A Comparative Perspective, NY Univ, 72; auth, An American's Guide to Britain, Scribner's, 77; Other Voices, Other Views, Greenwood, 78; Western Civilization, 79 & Detective Fiction, 80, Prentice-Hall; The Relevance of Canadian History, Macmillan, 79; Modus Operandi, Godine, 82; auth, Cloak and Gown: Scholars in the Secret War, Morrow, 87; auth, Asia in Western Language Fiction, Manchester, 90; auth, Frederick Billings, Oxford, 91; auth, Laurance S. Rockefells, Island, 97. **CONTACT ADDRESS** Dept of Hist, Yale Univ, P O Box 208324, New Haven, CT 06520-8324. **EMAIL** robin.winks@yale.edu

WINNIK, HERBERT CHARLES
PERSONAL Born 08/19/1938, Hartford, CT, m, 1994, 2 children **DISCIPLINE** HISTORY OF AMERICAN SCIENCE & THOUGHT **EDUCATION** Purdue Univ, BS, 60; Yale Univ, MA, 61; Univ Wis, Madison, PhD(Am hist), 68. **CAREER** Asst prof hist, Va Polytech Inst, 65-69; assoc prof hist, St Mary's Col, MD, 69-; consult to dean of arts & sci, Slippery Rock State Col, 68-. **MEMBERSHIPS** Orgn Am Historians; AHA; Soc Hist Sci; AAUP. **RESEARCH** American intellectual history; history of science and of American science. **SELECTED PUBLICATIONS** Auth, Summary View of AFOSR Solid State Science Program, Air Force Off Sci Res, 61; Science and Morality in TC Chamberlin, J Hist Ideas, 7-9/70; A Reconsideration of Henry A Rowland: The Man, Ann Sci, 6/72. **CONTACT ADDRESS** Dept Hist, St. Mary's Col of Maryland, Box 384, Leonardtown, MD 20650. **EMAIL** hcwinnik@osprey.smcm.edu

WINPENNY, THOMAS R.
PERSONAL Born 07/23/1941, Philadelphia, PA, m, 1967, 2 children **DISCIPLINE** HISTORY **EDUCATION** Pa State Univ, BA, 64; MA, 65; Univ Del, PhD, 72. **CAREER** Adj Prof, Franklin and Marshall Col, 78; Instr to Prof, Elizabethtown Col, 68-. **HONORS AND AWARDS** NDEA, Princeton Univ, 66; Hagley Fel, 70-72; NEH Fel, Princeton, 81; NEH Fel, Ind Univ, 84; NEH Fel, Iowa State Univ, 90; Res Grant, Eleutherian Mills Hist Library, 77, Exceptional Book Awd, Gordon and Breach Pub, 98, John F. Steinman Foundation Awd, Elizabethtown Col, 84. **SELECTED PUBLICATIONS** Auth, "Hard Drinking, Murder, and Violence along French Creek: worker's Celebrations as chronicled in The Phoenix Works diary," Pennsylvania History, 98; auth, "The Subtle Demise of Industry in a Quiet City: the Deindustrialization of Philadelphia, 1965-1995," Essays in Economic and Business History, 98; auth, "Milton S. Hershey Ventures into Cuban Sugar," Pennsylvania History, 95; auth, "The Lancaster Artisan As Businessman: The View from R.G. Dun and Company," Journal of the Lancaster County Historical Society, 94; auth, "Who Needs Engineers to Improve an Urban Water System? Lancaster's Bursting reservoir Provided Plenty of Water," Journal of the Lancaster County Historical Society, 92; auth, "Antebellum Communities Coveting a National Foundry: A Self-Serving Non-Answer to An Ongoing Problem," Essays in Economic and Business History, 92; auth, "Competing in the Medical Marketplace in Jacksonian America: The Creative Strategy of Dr. George Barrett Kerfoot," Pennsylvania Magazine of History and biography, 92; auth, Without Fitting, Filing, or chipping: a History of the Phoenix Bridge company, 96; auth, Bending is not Breaking: Adaptation and Persistence Among 19th Century Lancaster Artisans, 90; auth, Industrial Progress and Human Welfare: The Rise of the Factory System in 19th Century Lancaster, 82. **CONTACT ADDRESS** Dept History, Elizabethtown Col, 1 Alpha Dr, Elizabethtown, PA 17022-2298. **EMAIL** winpentr@acad.etown.edu

WINQUIST, ALAN
PERSONAL Born 06/07/1942, Astoria, NY **DISCIPLINE** HISTORY **EDUCATION** Wheaton Col, BA, 64; Northwestern Univ, MAT, 65; NYork Univ, PhD, 76. **CAREER** Instr, Nassau Community Col, 70-73; Prof, Taylor Univ, 73-. **HONORS AND AWARDS** The Sears-Roebuck Found Teaching Excellence and Campus Leadership Awd, 91; Fund for Fac Scholar, Taylor Univ, 3 times. **MEMBERSHIPS** AHA, Conf on Faith and Hist, Ind Hist Soc, Ind Asn of Historians. **RESEARCH** Scandinavian immigration history, Modern South Africa. **SELECTED PUBLICATIONS** Auth, Scandinavians and South Africa, A.A. Balkema (Cape Town), 78; auth, Swedish American Landmarks, Where to go and what to see, Swedish Coun of Am (Minneapolis), 95; coauth, God's Ordinary People: No Ordinary Heritage, Taylor Univ Press (Upland, IN), 96. **CONTACT ADDRESS** Dept Hist, Taylor Univ, Upland, 236 W Reade Ave, Upland, IN 46989-1001. **EMAIL** alwinquis@tayloru.edu

WINROTH, ANDERS
PERSONAL Born 08/17/1965, Ludvika, Sweden, m **DISCIPLINE** HISTORY **EDUCATION** Stockholm Univ, BA, 90; Columbia Univ, PhD, 96. **CAREER** Sir James Knott Fellow, Univ of Newcastle, 96-98; Asst Prof, Yale Univ, 98-. **RESEARCH** Medieval cultural, Intellectual and legal history, Scandinavian history. **SELECTED PUBLICATIONS** Auth, The Making of Gratian's Decretum, Cambridge UP, 00. **CONTACT ADDRESS** Dept History, Yale Univ, PO Box 208324, New Haven, CT 06520-8324. **EMAIL** anders.winroth@yale.edu

WINSHIP, PETER
PERSONAL Born Pensacola, FL, m, 1966, 2 children **DISCIPLINE** HISTORY; LITERATURE (18TH -20TH CENTURIES-EUROPE) **EDUCATION** Harvard, AB, 64, LLB, 68; London Univ, London Sch of Economics and political sci, LLM, 73. **CAREER** Lectr, 70-72, Addis Ababa Univ; 74-present, Southern Methodist Univ **MEMBERSHIPS** American Law Inst. **RESEARCH** Legal history; Comparative law; International law **SELECTED PUBLICATIONS** Auth, The U.N. Sales Convention and the Emerging Caselaw, in EMPTIO-VENDITIO INTER NATIONES: IN ANERKENNUNG FUR LEHRTATIGKEIT KARL HEINZ NEUMAYER, 97; auth, Selected Security Interests in the United States, Emerging Financial Markets and Secured Transactions, Kluwer, 98; auth, Karl Llewellyn in Rome, 98. **CONTACT ADDRESS** Dallas, TX 75275-0116. **EMAIL** pwinship@mail.smu.edu

WINSLOW, RICHARD E., III
PERSONAL Born 12/21/1934, Boston, MA, s **DISCIPLINE** AMERICAN HISTORY **EDUCATION** Union Col, BS, 57; Univ NH, MA, 65; Pa State Univ, PhD, 70. **CAREER** Asst Prof, Pa State Univ, 70-71, Behrend Col, 71-77; Adjunct Assoc Prof, Univ Md, 78-79; Assoc Ed, Univ Ky, 79-81; Lib, Rochester Pub Lib, 81-83; Lib, Portsmouth Pub Lib, 83-. **HONORS AND AWARDS** Fellow, Civil War Rnd Table, 70. **MEMBERSHIPS** Portsmouth Marine Soc; Thoreau Soc; Melville Soc; Naval Hist Fnd. **RESEARCH** Marine/maritime/naval history; Henry David Thoreau; Herman Melville. **SELECTED PUBLICATIONS** Auth, Constructing Munitions of War: The Portsmouth Navy Yard Confronts the Confederacy, 1861-1865, Portsmouth Marine Soc, 95; auth, "Do Your Job!": An Illustrated Bicentennial History of the Portsmouth Naval Shipyard, 1800-2000, 00; contrib, various periodicals, including Portsmouth Herald, Historical New Hampshire. **CONTACT ADDRESS** 1 Harborview Dr, Rye, NH 03870.

WINSOR, MARY PICKARD
PERSONAL Born 08/25/1943, New York, NY, m, 1975 **DISCIPLINE** HISTORY OF SCIENCE **EDUCATION** Radcliffe Col, AB, 65; Yale Univ, PhD(hist sci), 71. **CAREER** Lectr, 69-70, asst prof, 70-74, Assoc Prof Hist Biol, Inst Hist & Philos Sci & Technol, Univ Toronto, 74-. **MEMBERSHIPS** Hist Sci Soc; Can Soc Hist & Philos Sci. **RESEARCH** History of taxonomy; history of the Museum of Comparative Zoology at Harvard Univ; history of invertebrate zoology. **SELECTED PUBLICATIONS** Auth, Starfish, Jellyfish and the Order of Life, 76; auth, Reading the Shape of Nature: Comparative Zoology at the Agassiz Museum, 91. **CONTACT ADDRESS** Inst Hist and Philosophy Sci and Tech, Univ of Toronto, 91 Charles St W, Rm 316, Toronto, ON, Canada M5S 1K7. **EMAIL** mwinsor@chass.utoronto.ca

WINSTON, MICHAEL R.
PERSONAL Born 05/26/1941, New York, NY, m, 1963, 2 children **DISCIPLINE** HISTORY **EDUCATION** Howard Univ, BA 1962; Univ CA, MA 1964, PhD 1974. **CAREER** Howard Univ, instr 64-66; Inst Serv Edn, exec asst & assoc dir 65-66; Educ Asso Inc, educ consult 66-68; Langston Univ, devel consult 66-68; Howard Univ, asst dean liberal arts 68-69, dir res hist dept 72-73; Moorland-Spingarn Res Ctr, dir 73-83; Howard Univ, vice pres academic affairs 83-90, Alfred Harcourt Foundation, vice president, 92-93, president, 93-. **HONORS AND AWARDS** Moten fel, Univ Edinburgh; Wilson Fel, Univ of Calif, 62; Ford fel, 69-70; Woodrow Wilson Internat, Ctr Scholars fel, 79-80. **MEMBERSHIPS** Exec bd Nat Capital Area coun Boy Scouts Am, 88-90; Nat Coun for Hist Standards; bd overseers com to visit dept hist, Harvard Univ, 96-; Commn on Col and Univ Nonfrofl Studies, ABA; Nat Ctr for Hist in the Schools, UCLA/NEH; Nat adv comm and coun of scholars Libr of Congress; nat adv bd Protect Historic Am; An Hist Asn; Orgn An Hist; Am Antiquarian Soc; Hist Soc Washington; Atlantic Counc of U.S.; Coun on Fgn Rels; Nat Coun for Hist Standards; Epsilon Boule; Sigma Pi Phi; Phi Beta Kappa. **SELECTED PUBLICATIONS** Coauth, The Negro in the United States, 70; auth, The Howard University Department of History, 1913-73, 73; co-ed, Dictionary of American Negro Biography, 82; coauth, Historical Judgements Reconsidered, 88. **CONTACT ADDRESS** President, 8401 Colesville Rd, Silver Spring, MD 20910-3312. **EMAIL** mwinston@erols.com

WINTER, ROBERT W.
PERSONAL Born 07/17/1924, Indianapolis, IN, s **DISCIPLINE** HISTORY **EDUCATION** Dartmouth, AB, 47; Johns Hopkins, PhD, 57. **CAREER** Inst, 51-53, Bowdoin Col; inst, 54-56, Dartmouth; asst prof, 56-63, UCLA; prof, 63-94, Occidental Col. **HONORS AND AWARDS** Pres Awd, CA Preserv Found. 96; Pflueger Awd, local history, Historical Soc of S CA; Pres Awd, Amer Inst of Architects, LA, 79. **MEMBERSHIPS** Soc of Architect Hist; Natl Trust for Historic Preserv; Victorian Soc; Hist Soc of S CA; CA Hist Soc, Pasadena Hist Musuem. **RESEARCH** Architectural history; arts & crafts movement. **SELECTED PUBLICATIONS** Auth, American Bungalow Style, 96; ed, Toward a Simpler Way of Life, 97; auth, Hidden LA, 98. **CONTACT ADDRESS** 626 South Arroyo Blvd., Pasadena, CA 91105.

WINTERS, DONALD
PERSONAL Born 04/15/1945, Albany, NY, m, 1969, 1 child **DISCIPLINE** AMERICAN CULTURE, POETRY **EDUCATION** Long Beach State Univ, BA, 68; Univ Mich, MA, 70; Univ Minn, PhD, 81. **CAREER** Instr, Col of St Francis, 89, 91; Instr, Minn Community and Tech Col. **HONORS AND AWARDS** Diss Fel, 80-81; Ralph Gabriel Diss Awd, 82; NEH Summer Sem, Yale Univ, 86. **MEMBERSHIPS** Am Studies Assoc; Minn Educ Assoc; Community Col Humanities Assoc. **RESEARCH** I.W.W. and radical labor history, popular culture, rock music, music and poetry of Bob Dylan. **SELECTED PUBLICATIONS** Auth, Soul of the Wobblies, greenwood Pr, 85; auth, "Covington Hall: The Utopian Vision of a Wobbly Poet", Labor's Heritage 4.2, 92. **CONTACT ADDRESS** Dept Humanities, Minneapolis Comm and Tech Col, 1501 Hennepin Ave, Minneapolis, MN 55403-1710.

WINTERS, DONALD LEE
PERSONAL Born 08/11/1935, Ft Dodge, IA, m, 1960, 2 children **DISCIPLINE** UNITED STATES ECONOMIC HISTORY **EDUCATION** Univ Northern Iowa, BA, 57, MA, 63; Univ Wis, Madison, PhD(hist), 66. **CAREER** From asst prof to assoc prof hist, Univ Northern Iowa, 66-70; assoc prof, 70-79, Prof Hist, Vanderbilt Univ, 79-. **HONORS AND AWARDS** Agr Hist Soc Bk Awd, 69. **MEMBERSHIPS** Orgn Am Historians; Southern Hist Asn; Agr Hist Soc; Econ Hist Asn; Soc Sci Hist Asn. **RESEARCH** United States economic and agricultural history. **SELECTED PUBLICATIONS** Auth, The persistence of progressivism: Henry Cantwell Wallace and the movement for agricultural economics, Agr Hist, 4/67; Henry Cantwell Wallace as Secretary of Agriculture, 1921-1924, Univ Ill, 70; Tenant farming in Iowa, 1860-1900: An analysis of farm leases, Agr Hist, 1/74; Tenancy as an economic institution: The growth and distribution of agricultural tenancy in Iowa, 1850-1900, J Econ Hist, 6/77; Farmers Without Farms: Agricultural Tenancy in Nineteenth Century Iowa, Greenwood, 78; Agricultural tenancy in the nineteenth century Middle West: The historiographical debate, Ind Mag hist, 6/82. **CONTACT ADDRESS** Dept of Hist, Vanderbilt Univ, Nashville, TN 37240.

WINTERS, STANLEY B.
PERSONAL Born 06/05/1924, New York, NY, m, 1970, 2 children **DISCIPLINE** MODERN HISTORY **EDUCATION** NYork Univ, AB, 48; Columbia Univ, AM, 50; Rutgers Univ, PhD(hist), 66. **CAREER** Instr hist, NY Univ, 49-50; from instr to assoc prof, 57-68, assoc chmn dept humanities, 65-72, Prof Hist, NJ Inst Technol, 68-, Res assoc, Rutgers Univ Urban Studies Ctr, 61-62; NSF Workshop Environ & Technol fel, 69; assoc ed, Studies E Europ Soc Hist, 71-81; consult, Newark Off Pub Info, 72-80; managing ed, E Cent Europe, 75-; NJ Comt for Humanities grant, 76; S & H Found grant, 77; Co-Adj Prof Hist, Grad Fac, Rutgers Univ, 80-. **HONORS AND AWARDS** Overseers Pub Serv Awd, NJ Inst Technol Found, 82. **MEMBERSHIPS** AHA; Am Asn Advan Slavic Studies; Czech Soc Arts & Sci; Soc Hist of Technol; OAH; UHA. **RESEARCH** Habsburg monarchy and modern Czechoslavakia; Euro-American urban history. **SELECTED PUBLICATIONS** Co-auth, co-ed, Intellectual and Social Developments in the Habsburg Empire from Maria Theresa to World War I, Columbia Univ, 75; comp, co-auth, ed, From Riot to Receovery: Newark after Ten Years, Univ Press of Am, 79; auth, Jan Otto, T.G. Masaryk, and the Czech National Encyclopedia, Jahrbucher fur Geschichte Osteuropas, vol. 31, 83; auth, The Forging of a Historian. Robert A Kann in American, 1939-1976, Austrian History Yearbook, vol. 17-18, 84; comp, ed, Dynasty, Politics and Culture. Selected Essays by Robert A. Kann, Social Science Monographs, 91; auth, Josef Hlavka, Zdenek Nejedly, and the Czech Academy of Sciences and Arts, 1891-1952, Minerva, vol. 32, 94; auth, Science and Politics: The Rise and Fall of the Czechoslovak Academy of Sciences, Bohemia, col. 35, 94; auth, The Beginnings of American Scholarship on Czech and Slovak History, in Czech and Slovak History: An American Bibliography, comp, George J. Kovtun, Library of Congress, 96. **CONTACT ADDRESS** 22365 Queens Ave, Port Charlotte, FL 33952-8433.

WINTLE, THOMAS
DISCIPLINE CHURCH HISTORY **EDUCATION** Chicago Theol Sem, DMN, 75 **CAREER** Par Minist, 75-95, Par Minist, 95-pres **MEMBERSHIPS** AAR; ASCH **RESEARCH** New England Church Hist **SELECTED PUBLICATIONS** Auth, A New England Village Church, 85 **CONTACT ADDRESS** 3 Conant Rd, Weston, MA 02193-1625.

WINTZ, CARY DECORDOVA
PERSONAL Born 02/12/1943, Houston, TX, m, 1974, 1 child **DISCIPLINE** HISTORY **EDUCATION** Rice Univ, BA, 65; Kansas St Univ, MA, 68, PhD, 74. **CAREER** Instr, 71-74, asst prof, 74-77, assoc prof, 77-82, prof, 82-, chmn, dept hist, geography & econ, 95, dir, acad comput, 88-94, Texas So Univ; asst dir, fac instruct & support, Frederick Douglass Inst, 87-88; staff, Southwestern Social Sci Asn. **HONORS AND AWARDS** Phi Alpha Theta, Hist Hon Soc; Who's Who in S & SW, 89, 91, 94; Who's Who in the W, 90; Dist Svc Awd, 88, Res Scholar of Year, 96, Texas Southern Univ; Mobil Fac Fel, Intl Fac Develop Sem, Ghana, 98. **MEMBERSHIPS** AHA; Org of Amer Hist; So Hist Assn. **RESEARCH** African-Amer hist; Texas hist; late 19th & early 20th century US. **SELECTED PUBLICATIONS** Auth, The Politics and Poetry of Claude McKay, Claude McKay: Centennial Stud, Sterling Pub, 92; co-ed, Black Dixie: Essays on Afro-Texan History and Culture in Houston, Texas A&M Univ Press, 92; coauth, The Economic Impact of Residential Desegregation on Historically Black Neighborhoods in Houston, Texas 1950-1990, J of Econ & Bus Hist Soc 13, 95; ed, The Harlem Renaissance 1920-1940: Interpretation of an African American Literary Movement, Garland Pub, 96; ed, African American Political Thought, 1890-1930: Washington, DuBois, Garvey, and Randolph, Sharpe, 96; auth, W.E.B. DuBois, The NAACP, and the Struggle for Racial Equality, Amer Reform & Reformers, Greenwood Pub, 96; auth, Women in Texas, Texas Heritage, 97. **CONTACT ADDRESS** Exhibits and Publisher Relations, Southwestern Social Science Asn, 2001 Holcomb #602, Houston, TX 77030. **EMAIL** aashcdwintz@tsu.edu

WIRTH, JOHN DAVIS
PERSONAL Born 06/17/1936, Dawson, NM, m, 1960, 3 children **DISCIPLINE** MODERN LATIN AMERICAN HISTORY **EDUCATION** Harvard Univ, BA, 58; Stanford Univ, PhD(Latin Am hist), 66. **CAREER** Teacher hist, Putney Sch, Vt, 59-61; asst prof, 65-71, vchmn dept, 72-74, assoc prof, 71-77, Prof Hist, Stanford Univ, 77-, Gildred prof of Latin American Studies, 91-, Dir, Ctr Latin Am Studies, 75-83, Soc Sci Res Coun res fels, 69-70 & 72; Fulbright res grant, 80; chair, Spanish & Portuguese Dept, 86-88; vice provost, 88-91; Wildred prof of Latin Am Studies, 91-. **HONORS AND AWARDS** Bolton Prize, Conf Latin Am Hist, 71; Bolton Prize honorable mention, 78. **MEMBERSHIPS** AHA; Conf Latin Am Hist; Latin Am Studies Asn; Am Asn for Environmental Hist. **RESEARCH** Brazilian regionalism in the Old Republic; transfrontier migration in modern Latin America; comparative history of Latin America; North American integration; environmental history of the Americas. **SELECTED PUBLICATIONS** Auth, The Politics of Brazilian Development, 1930-1954, Stanford Univ, 70; A politica do Desenvolvimento na era de Vargas, Fundacao Getulio Vargas, 72; Minas Gerrais in the Brazilian Federation, 1889-1937, 77 & co-ed, Manchester and Sao Paulo: Problems of Rapid Urban Growth, 78, Stanford Univ; O Fiel da balanca: Minas Gerais na Federacao brasileira, 1889-1937, Paz e Terra, 80; auth, Smoke in North America, Kansas Press, 00. **CONTACT ADDRESS** Dept of Hist, Stanford Univ, Stanford, CA 94305-1926. **EMAIL** jdwirth@stanford.edu

WISE, EDWARD MARTIN
PERSONAL Born 08/08/1938, New York, NY, 2 children **DISCIPLINE** LAW, LEGAL HISTORY **EDUCATION** Univ Chicago, BA, 56; Cornell Univ, LLB, 59; NYork Univ, LLM, 60. **CAREER** Res assoc, Comparative Criminal Law Proj, 63-64; res fel, Inst Judicial Admin, 64-65; assoc prof, 65-68, prof Law, Wayne State Univ, 68-; assoc dean 86-92; Vis prof, NY Univ Sch Law, 68; gen coun, Am Civil Liberties Union Mich, 77-86; vis prof, Univ Utrecht, 79-98. **MEMBERSHIPS** Am Soc Legal Hist; Am Soc Int Asn Penal Law (pres, 89-); Am Soc Int Law; Selden Soc; Am Law Inst; Int Acad of Comparative Law; Int Law Assoc. **RESEARCH** International and comparative criminal law; legal history. **SELECTED PUBLICATIONS** Auth, International Criminal Law, 65; auth, Anglo-American Criminal Justice, 67; Studies in Comprative Criminal Law, 75; auth, The Italian Penal Code, 78; auth, Criminal Science in a Global Society, 94; auth, Art Dedere Art Judicare, 95; Comparative Law-Cases-Text-Materials, 98. **CONTACT ADDRESS** Law Sch, Wayne State Univ, 468 Ferry Mall, Detroit, MI 48202-3698. **EMAIL** E.M.Wise@Wayne.edu

WISE, STEVE
PERSONAL Born 01/30/1952, Toledo, OH, m, 1997 **DISCIPLINE** HISTORY **EDUCATION** Wittenberg Univ, BA, 74; Bowling State Univ, MA, 77; Univ SC, PhD, 83. **CAREER** Dir, Parris Island Mus, 83-; Adj Prof, Univ of SC at Beaufort, 84-. **HONORS AND AWARDS** "Gate of Hell" Best book Awd for SC Hist, SC Hist Soc, 95; Daughters of the Am Revolution Hist Medal for Serv in Promoting Am Hist, 96. **MEMBERSHIPS** Beaufort Hist Soc, Charleston Preservation Soc, Coun on Am Mil Past, Hist Beaufort Found, SC Battleground Trust, SC Soc, SC Hist Soc, Mil Order of the Loyal Legion of US. **RESEARCH** American Civil War, United States Navy, United States Fortifications, Reconstructions, Beaufort, SC. **SELECTED PUBLICATIONS** Auth, Lifeline of the Confederacy: Blockade Running During the Civil War, Univ of SC Press (Columbia), 88; auth, Gate of Hell: Campaign or Chaleston Harbor, 1863, Univ of SC Press (Columbia), 94. **CONTACT ADDRESS** Dept Hist and Govt, Univ of So Carolina, Beaufort, 801 Carteret St, Beaufort, SC 29902-4601. **EMAIL** wsiesr@mcrdpi.usme.mil

WISE, SYDNEY F.
PERSONAL Born Toronto, ON, Canada **DISCIPLINE** HISTORY **EDUCATION** Univ Toronto, BA, 49, BLS, 50; Queen's Univ, MA, 53; Univ Guelph, LLD, 87. **CAREER** Lectr, Royal Mil Col, 50-55; lectr to prof hist, 55-66, Queen's Univ, R. Samuel McLaughlin res prof, 64-65; dir hist, Dept Nat Defence, 66-73; prof to prof emer, 73-, dir, Inst Can Stud, Carleton Univ, 78-81, dean grad stud & res, Carleton Univ, 81-90, dir, univ press, 83-90, gov, 80-83. **HONORS AND AWARDS** Cruickshank Gold Medal, Ont Hist Soc; fel, Royal Soc Can; mem, Order Can. **MEMBERSHIPS** Can Hist Asn; UN Asn Can; Ont Hist Soc. **RESEARCH** War & military history. **SELECTED PUBLICATIONS** Coauth, Men in Arms: a history of the inter-relationships of warfare and western society, 56, 2nd ed 62, 3rd ed 70, 4th ed 79, 5th ed 91; coauth, Task Force Report to Federal Cabinet on Sport for Canadians, 69; coauth, Canada's Sporting Heroes: Their Lives & Times, 74; coauth, Canadian Airmen in the First World War, vol 1 80; coauth, God's Peculiar Peoples, Essays in the Political Culture of 19th Century Canada, 93; coauth, The Valour and the Horror Revisited, 94; coauth, East to Adventure: The Flight of Wild Oats 1933, 97. **CONTACT ADDRESS** Dept of Hist, Carleton Univ, 1125 Colonel By Dr, 400 Paterson Hall, Ottawa, ON, Canada K1S 5B6.

WISEMAN, JOHN BAILES
PERSONAL Born 02/10/1938, Alliance, NE, m, 1964, 2 children **DISCIPLINE** AMERICAN HISTORY **EDUCATION** Linfield Col, BA, 60; Univ Md, MA, 62, PhD(Am hist), 67. **CAREER** Asst prof Am hist, Keene State Col, 66-69 & Morgan State Col, 69-71; assoc prof, 71-77, Prof Am Hist, Frostburg State Col, 77-, Danforth Found fel Black studies, 70-71. **MEMBERSHIPS** Orgn Am Historians; AHA; Asn Studies Afro-Am Life & Hist. **RESEARCH** Twentieth-century American history; Afro-American history. **SELECTED PUBLICATIONS** Auth, Racism in Democratic Party Politics, 1904-1912, Mid-America, 1/69; collabr, Allegany County, Maryland: A History, McClain, 76; auth, Dilemmas of a Party Out of Power: the Democracy, 1904-1912, Garland, 88; coauth, Maryland: Unity in Diversity, 90. **CONTACT ADDRESS** Dept of History, Frostburg State Univ, Frostburg, MD 21532-1715. **EMAIL** jwiseman1@mindspring.com

WISEMAN, MARY BITTNER
PERSONAL Born 08/21/1936, Philadelphia, PA, m, 1989, 1 child **DISCIPLINE** AESTHETICS; FEMINISM **EDUCATION** St John's Col, Md, AB, 59; Harvard Univ, AM, 63; Columbia Univ, PhD, 74. **CAREER** From Instr to Prof Philos, Brooklyn Col of the City University of New York, 72-98, Prof of Philos and Comparative Lit, Grad Sch of the City Univ of New York; Prof Emerita, 98-; Dep exec officer, Humanities Inst, Brooklyn Col, 81-83. **HONORS AND AWARDS** CUNY Research Grants; NEH Summer Stipend. **MEMBERSHIPS** Am Philos Asn; Am Soc Aesthet; Soc Women Philos; Col Art Asn. **RESEARCH** Philosophy of art; interpretation; theory of criticism. **SELECTED PUBLICATIONS** Auth, The Ecstasies of Roland Bartles, Routledge, 89; numerous articles in Am Philos Quart, Brit J of Aesthetics, J Aesthetics & Art Criticism, and others. **CONTACT ADDRESS** Dept of Philos, Brooklyn Col, CUNY, 4936 Curley Hill Rd., Doylestown, PA 18901. **EMAIL** hagold@aol.com

WISER, VIVIAN
PERSONAL Born 06/17/1915, Lyndonville, NY **DISCIPLINE** AMERICAN HISTORY **EDUCATION** Univ Md, BA, 38, MA, 39, PhD, 63. **CAREER** Archivist, Nat Arch, 43-46, 48-56; Historian, USDA, 56-. **MEMBERSHIPS** Soc Am Archivists; AHA; Agr Hist Soc; Orgn Am Historians; Soc Personnel Admin. **RESEARCH** History of the United States Department of Agriculture; agricultural changes in antebellum Maryland; history of agricultural marketing. **SELECTED PUBLICATIONS** Auth, History of the Flower Bulb Industry in Washington State, Agr Hist, Vol 0068, 94. **CONTACT ADDRESS** Agr Hist, Group ES CS USDA, Washington, DC 20250.

WISHNE, BRIAN
PERSONAL Born 01/06/1950, Chicago, IL, m, 1995, 1 child **DISCIPLINE** ARCHITECTURE **EDUCATION** Knox Col, BA, 71; Princeton Univ, 80. **CAREER** Tchg asst, Princeton Univ, 79-80; vis prof, Univ Miami, 85; asst prof, Univ Cinn, 81-86; assoc prof, Univ of Wis, 88-. **HONORS AND AWARDS** Architecture Destin Awds. **MEMBERSHIPS** ACSA; Soc Archit Hist, AIA. **RESEARCH** Architectural Design, Landscape Architecture, Historic Preservation. **SELECTED PUBLICATIONS** Auth, The Architecture of Herbert W. Tullgren 1889-1944: Modern Apartments in Depression-Era Milwaukee, 93; Magazine, 1993; The Architecture of Connection: Spatial Formation in the Public Architecture of Louis I. Kahn, 92; International Paradox: An Examination of the Boundary Between Architecture and Sculpture, 92. **CONTACT ADDRESS** Sch of Architecture and Urban Planning, Univ of Wisconsin, Milwaukee, PO Box 413, Milwaukee, WI 53201. **EMAIL** bwishne@uwm.edu

WITCOMBE, CHRISTOPHER L. C. E.
DISCIPLINE ART HISTORY **EDUCATION** Univ MA, BA; MA; Bryn Mawr Col, PhD. **CAREER** Fac, 83-; Chr and prof art hist, Sweet Briar Col. **RESEARCH** Ancient Greek and Roman art; Renaissance and Baroque art; 16th century Italian art. **SELECTED PUBLICATIONS** Auth, publ(s) about painting, archit and prints of 16th century Italian art in Journal of the Society of Architectural Historians, The Burlington Magazine, and Gazette des Beaux-Arts. **CONTACT ADDRESS** Sweet Briar Col, Sweet Briar, VA 24595. **EMAIL** witcombe@sbc.edu

WITEK, JOHN W.
PERSONAL Born 09/13/1933, Chicago, IL **DISCIPLINE** EAST ASIAN HISTORY **EDUCATION** Loyola Univ, IL, AB, 57, PhL, 59, MA, 64, STL, 66; Georgetown Univ, PhD, 73. **CAREER** Asst prof hist, Xavier Univ, 73-75; asst prof, 75-81, Asoc prof History, Georgetown Univ, 81-. **HONORS AND AWARDS** Phi Beta Kappa; Eugene Asher Distinguished Teaching Awd (Hon Mention), AHA, 91. **MEMBERSHIPS** AHA; Am Oriental Soc; Asia Soc; Asn Asian Studies; Soc Ch'ing Studies; Pres, Mid-Atlantic Reg/Asn Asian Studies, 89-90. **RESEARCH** China and Japan, 16th to 18th centuries; Christian missions in China and Japan; Chinese intellectual history, 16th century to the present. **SELECTED PUBLICATIONS** Auth, Manchu Christians at the Court of Peking in the Early Eighteenth Century, ed, E Malatesta & Y Raguin, Succes et echecs de la rencontre Chine et Occident du XVIe au XXe siecle Varietes sinologiques, Nouvelle, serie, col 74 (Taipei & Paris) 93; Eliminating Misunderstandings: Antoine de Beauvollier (1657-1708) and his Eclaircissements sur les controverses de la Chine D E Mungello, ed, The Chinese Rites Controversy: Its History and Meaaning, Monumenta Serica Monograph Series (Nettetal) 94; J Witek, ed, Ferdinand Verbiest (1623-1688), Jesuit Missionary, Scientist, Engineer and Diplomat, Monumenta Serica Monograph Series XXX (Nettetal) 94; The Seventeenth-Century Advance into Asia: A Review Article, Journal of Asian Studies, 94; Claude Visdelou and the Chinese Paradox, Images de la Chine: Le Contexte occidental de la sinologie naissante, Varietes sinologiques, Nouvelle serie, vol 78 (Taipei & Paris: Institut Ricci) 95; Reporting to Rome: Some Major Events in the Christian Community in Peking, 1686-1687, Echanges culturels et religieux entre la Chine et l'Occident, Varietes sinologiques, Nouvelle serie, vol 83 (San Francisco, Taipei & Paris, Institut Ricci) 95; A Dialogue on Astronomical Phenomena and Natural Theology in Early Eighteenth-Century China, F Masini ed, Western Humanistic Culture Presented to China by Jesuit Missionaries (XVII-XVIII) Centuries (Rome) 96; The Jesuits in China During the Seventeenth and Eighteenth Centuries, Archivum Historicum Societatis Jesu, 96; Principles of Scholasticism in China: A Comparison of Giulio Aleni's Wanwu zhenyuan with Matteo Ricci's Tianzhu shiyi, Tiziana

Lippiello & R Malek, ed, Scholar from the East, Giulio Aleni SJ (1582-1649) and the Dialogue between Christianity and China (Nettetal) 97. **CONTACT ADDRESS** Dept Hist, Georgetown Univ, PO Box 571035, Washington, DC 20057-1035.

WITHINGTON, ANN F.
PERSONAL Born Boston, MA, s **DISCIPLINE** HISTORY **EDUCATION** Harvard, BA, 66; Univ Calif, MA, 72; Yale Univ, PhD, 83. **CAREER** Assoc prof History, SUNY, Albany. **RESEARCH** American political history. **SELECTED PUBLICATIONS** Auth, The Trial of Anne Hutchinson: A Political Trial, New Eng Quart, 78; Republican Bees: The Political Economy of the Beehive in Eighteenth Century America, Studies in Eighteenth-Century Culture 18, 88; Consumption and Republican Ideology in the Early Republic, In: Everyday Life in the Early Republic, Norton, 94; auth, Toward a More Perfect Union: Virtue and the Formation of American Republics, Oxford Univ Press, 91. **CONTACT ADDRESS** Dept of History, SUNY, Albany, Albany, NY 12222. **EMAIL** withingtona@hotmail.com

WITHINGTON, WILLIAM ADRIANCE
PERSONAL Born 02/17/1924, Honolulu, HI, m, 1955, 2 children **DISCIPLINE** GEOGRAPHY **EDUCATION** Harvard Univ, BA 46; Northwestern Univ, MA 48, PhD 55. **CAREER** Geo Washington Univ, inst, asst prof, 48-53; Univ Kentucky, inst, asst prof, assoc prof, 55-89; Nommenson Univ North Sumatra Indonesia, vis Ford Foun prof, 57-59. **HONORS AND AWARDS** Ford Foun Fel. **MEMBERSHIPS** AAS; AAG; AGS; NCGE; SF Div; SE Div AAG; Sigma Xi. **RESEARCH** Sumatra Indonesia; Southeast Asia; Human cultural geog; urban geog. **SELECTED PUBLICATIONS** Auth, Editor for Indonesia entries for Gazetteer, Columbia Univ Press, 98; Kentucky Encycl, contributor, Lexington KY, Univ Press KY, 92; Southeast Asia, Grand Rapids MI, Fideler, editor from 61-80's. **CONTACT ADDRESS** 113 Johnston Blvd, Lexington, KY 40503-2028.

WITHROW, WILLIAM
PERSONAL Born 09/30/1926, Toronto, ON, Canada **DISCIPLINE** ART HISTORY **EDUCATION** Univ Toronto, BA, 50, Art Spec, OCE, 51, BEd, 55, MEd, 58, MA, 61. **CAREER** Art dept head, Earl Haig Col, 51-59; prin & res dir, Ont Dept Educ, 57-59; dir, 61-91, Dir Emer, Art Gallery Ontario. **HONORS AND AWARDS** Mem, Order Can, 80. **MEMBERSHIPS** Fel, Can Mus Asn; fel, Ont Col Art; life mem, Asn Art Mus Dirs; past pres, Can Art Mus Dir Orgn. **SELECTED PUBLICATIONS** Auth, Sorel Etrog/Sculpture, 67; auth, Contemporary Canadian Painting, 72. **CONTACT ADDRESS** 7 Malabar Pl, Don Mills, ON, Canada M3B 1A4.

WITT, RONALD GENE
PERSONAL Born 12/23/1932, Wayne, MI, m, 1965, 3 children **DISCIPLINE** RENAISSANCE AND REFORMATION HISTORY **EDUCATION** Univ Mich, BA, 54; Harvard Univ, PhD(hist), 65. **CAREER** Fulbright lectr Am civilization, Univ Strasbourg, 55-56; from instr to asst prof hist, Harvard Univ, 65-71; assoc prof, 71-80, Prof Hist, Duke Univ, 80-, Old Dom Fund fel, 68-69; mem univ sem Renaissance, Columbia Univ, 72-; Nat Endowment for Humanities grant, 74; Guggenheim Found fel, 77; Coun Learned Soc grant, 79. **HONORS AND AWARDS** "Coun of Learned Soc grant, 79", read N.E.H. 83-84; Fulbright Research Fellowship, 85-86; N.E.H., 90-91; Rome Prize, 96-97. **MEMBERSHIPS** Mediaeval Acad Am; Renaissance Soc Am; AHA; Soc Ital Hist Studies. **RESEARCH** Italian humanism. **SELECTED PUBLICATIONS** Auth, Coluccio Szalutati and His Public Letters (Geneva: Droz, 76); auth, The Earthly Republic of the Italian Humanitis, ed B. Kohl and Ronald Witt (Philadelphia: Univ of PA, 78); auth, Hercules at the Crossroads, The Life, Works and Thought of Coluccio Salutati, 1331-1406, Durham, Duke Press, 83; auth, Cultural Roots and Continuities, 4th ed, with M. Witt, F. Tirro, A Dunbar and C. Brown, 6th ed, Boston, Houghton-Mifflin, 00; auth, "In the Footsteps of the Ancient." Origins of Italian Humanism form Lovato to Bruni, 1250-1420, Leiden: Brill. 00. **CONTACT ADDRESS** Dept of Hist, Duke Univ, Durham, NC 27706. **EMAIL** rwitt@duke.edu

WITTIG, JOSEPH SYLVESTER
PERSONAL Born 08/18/1939, Pittsburgh, PA, m, 1969 **DISCIPLINE** ENGLISH, MEDIEVAL STUDIES **EDUCATION** Wheeling Col, BA, 63; Univ Scranton, MA, 65; Cornell Univ, PhD(English, medieval studies), 69. **CAREER** Asst prof, 69-76, assoc prof, 76-88, prof, English, Univ NCar-Chapel Hill, 88- . **MEMBERSHIPS** MLA; Mediaeval Acad Am; New Chaucer Soc; AAUP; Southern Atlantic Mod Lang Asn. **RESEARCH** Middle English literature; Old English literature; medieval studies. **SELECTED PUBLICATIONS** Auth, Homiletic fragment II and the Epistle to the Ephesians, Traditio, 69; auth, The Aeneas-Dido allusion in Chretien's Erec et Enide, Comp Lit, 70; Piers Plowman B, Passus IX-XII: Elements in the design of the inward journey, Traditio, 72; The dramatic and rhetorical development of Long Will's Pilgrimage, Neuphilologische Mitteilungen, 76; auth, Figural Narrative in Cynewulf's Juliana, Anglo-Saxon England, No 4; auth, William Langland Revisted, NY, 97. **CONTACT ADDRESS** Dept of English, Univ of No Carolina, Chapel Hill, Chapel Hill, NC 27514. **EMAIL** jwittog@unc.edu

WITTNER, LAWRENCE STEPHEN
PERSONAL Born 05/05/1941, Brooklyn, NY, m, 1999, 1 child **DISCIPLINE** AMERICAN FOREIGN POLICY, MODERN AMERICAN HISTORY **EDUCATION** Columbia Col, AB, 62; Univ Wis, MA, 63; Columbia Univ, PhD, 67. **CAREER** Asst prof hist, Hampton Inst, 67-68 & Vassar Col, 68-73; Fulbright sr lectr, Japan, 73-74; lectr, 74-76, from asst to assoc prof, hist, 76-83, prof Hist, 83-, SUNY Albany; vis assoc prof, Columbia Univ, 76; res grants, Harry Truman Libr, 75 & Eleanor Roosevelt Inst, 77; fel & grant, Res Found, State Univ NY, 77-78 & 80-81; Nat Endowment for Humanities fel, 80-81; co-exec ed, Peace and Change: A Journal of Peace Res, 84-87. **HONORS AND AWARDS** Univ Awd for Excellence in Research, SUNY Albany, 85; SUNY Albany Fac Res Awds Program grant, 86-87; ACLS/Ford fel, 87-88; NEH grant, 88; Council on peace Res in Hist, Charles DeBenedetti prize, 89; NY State/United Univ Professions Excellence Awd, 90; US Int of Peace res grant, 90-92; Am Philos Soc res grant, 92; Soc for Hist of Am For Rel, Warren F. Kuehl prize, 95; NEH stipend 98; SUNY Albany Fac Res Awds, 98-99; Nonprofit Sector Research Fund, Aspen Institute, grant, 98-99. **MEMBERSHIPS** Conf Peace Res in Hist (pres, 77-79); Soc Historians Am Foreign Rels; Orgn Am Historians. **RESEARCH** History of American foreign policy; international history. **SELECTED PUBLICATIONS** Auth, Blacklisting Schweitzer, Bull of the Atomic Scientists, 95; auth, The Menace of the Maidens, Fellowship, 95; auth, Resisting the Bomb: A History of the World Nuclear Disarmament Movement, 1954-1970, Stanford, 97; auth, Merle Curti and the Development of Peace History, Peace and Change, 98; auth, The Nuclear Threat Ignored: How and Why the Campaign Against the Bomb Disintegrated in the Late 1960s, 1968: The World Transformed, Cambridge, 98; coauth, "Lifting the Iron Curtain: The Peace March to Moscow of 1960-61," Int Hist Rev, 99; auth, "Gender Roles and Nuclear Disarmament Activism, 1954-1965," Gender & History, 00; auth, "Reagan and Nuclear Disarmament," Boston Review, 00. **CONTACT ADDRESS** Dept of History, SUNY, Albany, 1400 Washington Ave, Albany, NY 12222. **EMAIL** wittner@csc.albany.edu

WOBST, H. MARTIN
PERSONAL Born 12/12/1943, Eickelborn, Germany, m, 1981, 2 children **DISCIPLINE** EUROPEAN PRE-HISTORY **EDUCATION** Univ Mich, Ann Arbor, BA, 66, MA, 68, PhD(anthrop), 71. **CAREER** Asst, prof, 71-77, assoc prof, 77-84, prof 84-, chrmn dept anthrop, Univ Mass, Amherst, 74-80, ed, Memoirs, Soc Am Archaeol, 71-75. **MEMBERSHIPS** Fel Am Anthrop Asn; Soc Am Archaeol; fel Royal Anthrop Inst; member, Am Anthrop Asn, 90-92; Pres, Northeastern Anthrop Asn, 90-92; member, Exec Comt, 92-01. **RESEARCH** Pre-history of Eastern Europe and the Union of Soviet Socialist Republics; computer simulations of Paleolithic societies; archaeological theory and cultural ecology; the social articulations of material culture, indigenous archaeologies. **SELECTED PUBLICATIONS** Auth, The Butterfield Site, Mich Anthrop Papers, 68; Boundary Conditions for Paleolithic Cultural Systems, Am Antiq, 74; The Demography of Finite Populations and the Origins of the Incest Taboo, Am Antiq, 75; Locational Relationships in Paleolithic Society, J Human Evolution, 76; Stylistic Behavior and Information Exchange, Mich Anthrop Papers, 77; ed, Research Reports, Dept of Anthrop, Univ of Mass, 78-84; co-ed, Agency in (spite of) material culture, In Agency in archaeology, (Routledge: London, 99): 40-50; ed, Style in archaeology, or archaeologists in style, In Material meanings: Critical approaches to the interpretation of material culture, (Univ of Utah Press: Salt Lake City, 99): 118-132; auth, Regions and Late Pleistocene Hunter-Gatherers, IN Regional Approaches to Adaptation in Late Pleistocene Western Europe, Oxford, (00): 221-229. **CONTACT ADDRESS** Dept of Anthrop, Univ of Massachusetts, Amherst, Machmer, Amherst, MA 01003-4805. **EMAIL** wobst@anthro.umass.edu

WOEHRMANN, PAUL JOHN
PERSONAL Born 04/01/1939, Lakewood, OH, m, 1965, 1 child **DISCIPLINE** AMERICAN HISTORY **EDUCATION** Ohio State Univ, BA, 61, MA, 62; Kent State Univ, PhD, 67. **CAREER** Asst, Kent State Univ, 62-66; asst prof hist, WVa Wesleyan Col, 66-68 & Univ Tenn, Nashville, 68-70; res fel, Papers of Henry Clay, Univ Ky, Nat Hist Publ Comn, 70-71; Librn Hist & Marine Collection, Milwaukee Pub Libr, 72-, Milwaukee Area Tech Col, 89-; WVa Wesleyan Col res grant, 68; proj dir, Nat Endowment for Humanities, The Papers of Carl & Frank Ziedlen, 81-. **MEMBERSHIPS** Orgn Am Historians; Soc Historians Early Am Repub. **RESEARCH** Early national period, United States history; military history. **SELECTED PUBLICATIONS** Auth, At the Headwaters of the Maumee, a History of the Forts of Fort Wayne, Ind Hist Soc, 71; National Response to the Sack of Washington, Md Hist Mag, 71; ed, A Guide to the Socialist Party-Social Democratic Federation Collection of the Milwaukee Public Library, Milwaukee Pub Libr, 76; ed, The autobiography of Abraham Snethen, frontier preacher, Filson Club Hist Quart, 10/77. **CONTACT ADDRESS** Milwaukee Pub Libr, 814 W Wisconsin Ave, Milwaukee, WI 53233-1443. **EMAIL** p.woehr@mpl.org

WOHL, ANTHONY STEPHEN
PERSONAL Born 03/28/1937, London, England, m, 1964, 2 children **DISCIPLINE** HISTORY **EDUCATION** Cambridge Univ, BA, 58; Brown Univ, PhD(hist), 66. **CAREER** Teaching asst hist, Brown Univ, 59-62; from instr to assoc prof, 63-77, Prof Hist, Vassar Col, 77-, Vis lectr hist, Leicester Univ, Eng, 68-69; chmn nat prog, Conf Brit Studies, 77-. **MEMBERSHIPS** Conf Brit Studies; NE Victorian Studies Asn. **RESEARCH** Social history, Victorian England; housing reform and policy; public health. **SELECTED PUBLICATIONS** Auth, The bitter cry of outcast London, Int Rev Soc Hist, 69; ed, The Bitter Cry of Outcast London, Leicester Univ, 70; auth, Octavia Hill and the homes of the London poor, J Brit Studies, 71; The housing of the working classes in London, 1815-1914, In: The History of Working Class Housing, David & Charles, 71; Unfit for human habitation, In: The Victorian City, Routledge Kegan, Paul, 73; The Eternal Slum, Edward Arnold, 77; ed, The Victorian Family, Croom Helm, 77. **CONTACT ADDRESS** Dept of Hist, Vassar Col, Poughkeepsie, NY 12601.

WOHL, ROBERT
PERSONAL Born 02/13/1936, Butte, MT, m, 1966, 1 child **DISCIPLINE** MODERN HISTORY **EDUCATION** Univ Calif, Los Angeles, AB, 57; Princeton Univ, AM, 59, PhD(hist), 63. **CAREER** From instr to asst prof hist, Univ Southern Calif, 61-64; from asst prof to assoc prof, 64-69, chmn dept, 70-73, Prof Hist, Univ Calif, Los Angeles, 69-, Soc Sci Res Coun grant, 68-69; Nat Endowment for Humanities fel, 78-. **HONORS AND AWARDS** George Louis Beer Prize, 67. **MEMBERSHIPS** AHA; Soc Ital Hist Studies. **RESEARCH** International communism; modern Italy; comparative European intellectual and social history 1870 to the present. **SELECTED PUBLICATIONS** Auth, French communism in the making, 1914-1924, Stanford Univ, 66; The Generation of 1914, Harvard Univ, 78. **CONTACT ADDRESS** Dept of Hist, Univ of California, Los Angeles, Los Angeles, CA 90024.

WOLF, GEORGE D.
PERSONAL Born 06/04/1923, Corry, PA, m, 1948, 3 children **DISCIPLINE** AMERICAN CIVILIZATION **EDUCATION** Muskingum Col, BA, 47; Bucknell Univ, MA, 53; Univ Pa, PhD(Am civilization), 64. **CAREER** High sch teacher, Pa, 48-56; Lycoming Col, 54-56; assoc prof Am hist, Lock Haven State Col, 57-64, Danford Assoc, 60-72; prof hist, 64-66; fac fel, Nat Ctr Educ Polit, 65-66; spec asst to Gov Pa, 65-66; assoc prof, 66-69; historian, Pa Const Conv, 67-68; Prof, 69-83; Instr; consult to Lt Gov Pa, 67-70; mem, Bd State Col & Univ Dir, 70-71; head div humanities, soc sci & educ, 71-73; dean fac, 73-78; Emeritus Prof, Penn State Harrisburg, 83-. **MEMBERSHIPS** Orgn Am Historians; AAUP; Am Studies Asn. **RESEARCH** Pennsylvania history and politics: the Scranton administration, 1963-1967; Pennsylvania constitutional convention, 1967-1968; politics in America. **SELECTED PUBLICATIONS** Auth, The Politics of Fair Play, Pa Hist, 1/65; The Scranton Papers, Western Pa Hist Mag, 10/68; State Constitutional Revision, Dept Pub Instr, 68; The Fair Play Settlers of the West Branch Valley, 1769-1784, Pa Hist & Mus Comn, 69; Constitutional Revision in Pennsylvania, Nat Munic League, 69; Introd & Index for Debates of the Pennsylvania Constitutional Convention, Publ Bur, 69; The fair play settlers of the West Branch Valley, In: Pennsylvania 1776, 75 & William Scranton Pennsylvania Statesman, 81, Pa State Univ Press. **CONTACT ADDRESS** 304 Deerfield Rd, Camp Hill, PA 17011. **EMAIL** gwolf@paonline.com

WOLF, KENNETH BAXTER
PERSONAL Born 06/01/1957, Santa Barbara, CA, 2 children **DISCIPLINE** HISTORY, RELIGIOUS STUDIES **EDUCATION** Stanford, BA (Religious Studies), 79, PhD (History), 85. **CAREER** Asst prof, 85-92, Assoc Prof, Pomona Col, 92-, chair, Hist Dept, 95-98. **HONORS AND AWARDS** Phi Beta Kappa; Inst for Advanced Study, member 89-91; Wig Distinguished Prof, Pomona Col, 88, 93, 98. **MEMBERSHIPS** Medieval Academy; Medieval Asn of the Pacific; Assoc Members of the Inst for Advanced Study. **RESEARCH** Medieval Mediterranean hist; late antique/medieval Christianity; saints. **SELECTED PUBLICATIONS** Auth, The Earliest Spanish Christian Views of Islam, Church Hist 55, 86; Conquerors and Chroniclers of Early Medieval Spain, Liverpool Univ Press, 90, revised ed, forthcoming; The Earliest Latin Lives of Muhammad, in Michael Gervers and Ramzi Jibran Bikhazi, eds, Conversion and Continuity: Indigenous Christian Communities in Islamic Lands, Eighth to Eighteenth Centuries, Pontifical Inst of Mediaeval Studies, 90; Crusade and Narrative: Bohemond and the Gesta Francorum, J of Medieval Hist, 17, 91; The 'Moors' of West Africa and the Beginnings of the Portuguese Slave Trade, J of Medieval and Renaissance Studies 24, 94; Making History: The Normans and Their Historians in Eleventh-century Italy, Univ PA Press, 95; Christian Views of Islam in Early Medieval Spain, in John Tolan, ed, Medieval Christian Perspectives of Islam: A Collection of Essays, Garland, 96; Christian Martyrs in Muslim Spain, Cambridge Univ Press, 88, Japanese ed, K. Hayashi, trans, Tosui Shobou Press, 98; Muhammad as Antichrist in Ninth-century Cordoba, in Mark Meyerson, ed, Christians, Muslims and Jews in Medieval and Early Modern Spain: Interaction and Cultural Change, Univ Notre Dame Press, forthcoming. **CONTACT ADDRESS** 551 N. College Ave., Claremont, CA 91711. **EMAIL** kwolf@pomona.edu

WOLF, REVA J.
PERSONAL Born 06/17/1956, Denver, CO **DISCIPLINE** ART HISTORY **EDUCATION** Brandeis Univ, BA, 78; NY Univ, MA, 81; PhD, 87. **CAREER** Asst prof, Boston Col, 88-95; asst to assoc prof, SUNY New Paltz, 96-. **HONORS AND AWARDS** J Clawson Mills Fel, 85-86; Yale Center for Brit Art Fel, 89; Mellon Fel, 90-91; NEA Grant, 91; Inst for Advan Study Fel, 95-96; Citation, Reader's Catalogue, 97. **MEMBERSHIPS** MLA, Col Art Asn. **RESEARCH** The history of the interview with the artist, interpretation and contradiction, word-image relationships, social history of art. **SELECTED PUBLICATIONS** Auth, "Onlooker, Witness, and Judge in Goya's Disasters of War," Callot, Goya, and the Horrors of War, Hood Museum, (90); auth, Goya and the Satirical Print in England and on the Continent, 1730 to 1850, David R Godine, 91; auth, "Collaboration and Social Exchange: Screen Tests/A Diary by Gerard Malanga and Andy Warhol," Art Journal, (93); auth, "Writing New Histories in the Interview," New Histories, (Inst of Contemp Art, 96); auth, "The Word Transfigured as Image: Andy Warhol's Responses to Art Criticism," Smart Museum Bull of Art, (97); auth, Andy Warhol, Poetry, and Gossip in the 1960s, Univ of Chicago Pr, 97; auth, "The Uses of Foucault's History of Sexuality in the Visual Arts," Philos Today, (98); auth, "Thinking You Know," Poetics Jour, (98); auth, "Progress is very important in everything except food," Andy Warhol Photography, (Hamburger Kunsthalle, Andy Warhol Museum, 99); auth, "Goya: Image, Reality, and History," Goya's Realism, (Statens Museum, 00). **CONTACT ADDRESS** Dept Art Hist, SUNY, New Paltz, 75 S Manheim Blvd, New Paltz, NY 12561. **EMAIL** wolfr@matrix.newpaltz.edu

WOLFE, MICHAEL
PERSONAL Born 09/30/1956, Sarasota, FL, m, 1980, 2 children **DISCIPLINE** HISTORY **EDUCATION** Boston Univ, BA, 79; MA, 80; Johns Hopkins Univ, MA, 82; PhD, 86. **CAREER** Instr, Univ of Md, 85-86; instr, Univ of Dallas, 86-88; instr, Univ of Southern Calif, 88-89; asst prof to prof, Pa State Altoona Col, 89-. **MEMBERSHIPS** Soc Fr Hist Studies; Western Soc Fr Hist. **RESEARCH** French history, religious history, urban history. **SELECTED PUBLICATIONS** Auth, The Conversion of Henry IV: Politics, Power, and Religious Belief in Early Modern France, Harvard Univ Press, 93; coed, The Medieval City Under Siege, Boydell and Brewer, 95; ed, Changing Identities in Early Modern France, Duke Univ Press, 97; coed, Technology and Resource Use in Medieval Europe: Cathedrals, Mills, and Mines, Aldershot, 97; coed, The Medieval City Under Siege, Boydell and Brewer, 99; coed, Senses of Place: Inventing Landscape in Medieval Western Europe, Univ Press of Fla, 01. **CONTACT ADDRESS** History Dept, Pennsylvania State Univ, Altoona, 3000 Ivyside Park, Altoona, PA 16601-3760. **EMAIL** mww4@psu.edu

WOLFF, GERALD W.
PERSONAL Born 05/16/1939, Cleveland, OH, m, 1989, 6 children **DISCIPLINE** HISTORY **EDUCATION** Bowling Green State Univ, BS, 61; MA, 62; Univ Iowa, PhD, 69. **CAREER** Asst Prof, Calif State Univ Long Beach, 66-69; From Asst to Full Prof, Univ of SDak, 69-95; Adj Prof, SDak Sch of Mines and Technology, 95-98; Adj Prof, Western Iowa Tech Community Col, 98-00. **HONORS AND AWARDS** Edward Eugene Edwards Awd, Agr Hist; Robinson Awd SDak Hist; Outstanding Teacher Awd, Univ of SDak. **MEMBERSHIPS** Orgn of Am Hist, Southern Hist Asn, Soc for Historians of the Early Am Repub. **RESEARCH** 19th Century Political History, South Dakota History, Oral History. **SELECTED PUBLICATIONS** Auth, "The Slavocracy and the Homestead Problem of 1854," Agr Hist 40 (Apr 66): 101-111; auth, The Ottawa People, Phoenix: Indian Tribal Series, 76; auth, The Kansas-Nebraska Bill: Party, Section, and the Coming of the Civil War, Revisionist Press (NY), 77; auth, "Father Sylvester Eiserman and Marty Mission," SDak Hist 5 (Fall 79): 360-389; auth, "Mark Hanna's Goal: American Harmony," Ohio Hist 79 (Summer/Autumn 70): 138-151; auth, "First Protestant Epsicopal Bishop of Dakota: William Hobart Hare," in South Dakota Leaders: From Pierre Chariteau, Jr. to Oscar Howe, ed. Herbert T. Hoover (Vermillion, SD: Univ of SDak Press, 89), 81-105. **CONTACT ADDRESS** Univ of So Dakota, Vermillion, Vermillion, SD 57069.

WOLFF, JANET
DISCIPLINE ART HISTORY, VISUAL AND CULTURAL STUDIES **EDUCATION** Univ Birmingham, UK, PhD. **CAREER** Dir, grad prog in Visual and Cult Stud & prof. **HONORS AND AWARDS** Guggenheim fel, 93-94. **RESEARCH** Sociology of art and cult; gender and cult; memoir, soc hist, and cult theory; modernism and modernity. **SELECTED PUBLICATIONS** Auth, Resident Alien: Feminist Cultural Criticism, New Haven: Yale UP, 95; Feminine Sentences: Essays on Women and Culture, Berkeley: Univ Calif Press, 90; Aesthetics and the Sociology of Art, London and Boston: Allen & Unwin, 83, 2nd ed, Ann Arbor: Univ Mich Press, 93; The Social Production of Art, NY UP, 81, 2nd ed, 93 & Hermeneutic Philosophy and the Sociology of Art, London and Boston: Routledge & Kegan Paul, 75. **CONTACT ADDRESS** Dept of Art and Art Hist, Univ of Rochester, 601 Elmwood Ave, Ste. 656, 423A Morey, Rochester, NY 14642. **EMAIL** jwlf@nail.rochester.edu

WOLLMAN, DAVID HARRIS
PERSONAL Born 06/20/1936, Boston, MA, m, 1967, 2 children **DISCIPLINE** BRITISH & EARLY MODERN EUROPEAN HISTORY **EDUCATION** Northeastern Univ, AB, 58; Univ Wis-Madison, MA, 61, PhD, 70. **CAREER** Instr Europ hist, Univ Md, Europ Div, 64; instr to asst prof hist, Knox Col, Ill, 67-71; asst prof to assoc prof, 71-78, coordr humanities courses, 73-76, prof hist, Geneva Col, 78-, Chmn Dept, 74-. **HONORS AND AWARDS** Nat Endowment for Humanities grant, summer 80 **MEMBERSHIPS** Conf Faith & Hist; Conf Brit Studies; Exec Dir, Beaver Co Ind Museum **RESEARCH** Stuart England, especially parliament and foreign policy; Amer Indus Hist **SELECTED PUBLICATIONS** Auth, Portraits in Steel: An Illustrated History of Jones and Lenghlin Steel Corporation, Kent State Univ Press (Kent, OH), 99. **CONTACT ADDRESS** Dept of History, Geneva Col, 3200 College Ave, Beaver Falls, PA 15010-3599. **EMAIL** dwollman@geneva.edu

WOLOCH, ISSER
PERSONAL Born 10/16/1937, New York, NY, m, 1962, 2 children **DISCIPLINE** MODERN EUROPEAN HISTORY **EDUCATION** Columbia Col, AB, 59; Princeton Univ, MA, 61, PhD, 65. **CAREER** Lectr hist, IN Univ, 63-64, asst prof, 65-66; asst prof, Univ CA, Los Angeles, 66-69; assoc prof, 69-75, Prof Hist, Columbia Univ, 75-98, Moore Collegiate Prof of Hist, 98-; Fel comt int & comp studies, Univ CA, Los Angeles, 68; Am Coun Learned Soc fel, 73-74; mem, Inst Advan Studies, 73-74, 88; NEH fel, 80-81; Guggenheim fel, 81-82; Ecole des Hautes Etudes Fellow, 86; Fellow, Center for the History of Freedom, 94. **HONORS AND AWARDS** Leo Gershoy Awd (Am Hist Asn), 95; Leo Gershoy award, AHA, 95. **MEMBERSHIPS** AHA; Soc Fr Hist Studies. **RESEARCH** Eighteenth and nineteenth centuries; French Revolution; French social history. **SELECTED PUBLICATIONS** Auth, Jacobin Legacy: The Democratic Movement Under the Directory, Princeton Univ, 70; ed, The Peasantry in the Old Regime: Conditions and Protests, Holt, 70; auth, French economic and social history, J Interdisciplinary Hist, 74; coauth, The Western Experience, Knopf, 74, 7th ed, 99; auth, The French Veteran, from the Revolution to the Restoration, Univ NC, 79; Eighteenth-Century Europe: Tradition and Progress, 1715-1789, W W Norton, 82; The New Regime: Transformations of the French Civic Order, 1789-1820's, W. W. Norton, 94; ed, Revolution and the Meanings of Freedom in the Nineteenth Century, Stanford Univ Press, 96; auth, Napoleon and his Collaorators: The Making of a Dictatorship, W W Norton, 00. **CONTACT ADDRESS** Dept of Hist, Columbia Univ, New York, NY 10027-6900. **EMAIL** iw6@columbia.edu

WOLOCH, NANCY
PERSONAL Born 05/04/1940, New York, NY, m, 1962, 2 children **DISCIPLINE** HISTORY **EDUCATION** Wellesley Coll, BA, 61; Columbia Univ, MA, 62; Indiana Univ, PhD, 68. **CAREER** Adj asst prof, Baruch Coll, CUNY, 77-79; adj asst prof, Columbia Univ, 85-87; adj asst prof, Barnard Coll, 88-. **HONORS AND AWARDS** NEH, 73-74, 99-00. **MEMBERSHIPS** AHA; OAH; ASA. **RESEARCH** US history; Women's hist; Am studies. **SELECTED PUBLICATIONS** Auth, Muller V Oregon: A Brief History with Documents, 96; auth, Early American Women: A Documentary History, 97; coauth, The American Century, 98, auth, Women and the American Experience, 00; auth, The Enduring Vision: A History the American People 00. **CONTACT ADDRESS** Dept Hist, Barnard Col, 3009 Broadway, New York, NY 10027. **EMAIL** nw49@columbia.edu

WOLOHOJIAN, STEPHAN S.
DISCIPLINE RENAISSANCE ART **EDUCATION** Rutgers Univ, BA, 84; Harvard, MA, 86; PhD, 95. **CAREER** Curator, Fogg Arts Mus, Harvard Univ, 99-. **RESEARCH** Amrogio Lorenzetti. **SELECTED PUBLICATIONS** Auth, "A Version of Raphael's Virgine and Child with Saint Jerome and Saint Francis in the Harvard Univ Art Museums," (in Festschrift for John Shearman, forthcoming; auth, "Francisco di Simone Ferrucci's Fogg Virgin and Child and the Martini Chapel in S. Giobbe, Venice," (in Burlington Magazine, 139, 97). **CONTACT ADDRESS** Fogg Art Museum, Harvard Univ, 32 Quincy St., Cambridge, MA 02138. **EMAIL** wolohoj@fas.harvard.edu

WOLPER, ETHEL SARA
DISCIPLINE HISTORY OF THE MIDDLE EAST, HISTORY OF ISLAM **EDUCATION** UCLA, PhD. **CAREER** Asst prof, Univ NH, 96-. **HONORS AND AWARDS** Mellow fel in Near Eastern Lit and Islamic Art Hist; Cornell Univ fel; Ittleson fel, Nat Gallery of Art; AAUW fel. **RESEARCH** Dervish lodges in pre-Ottoman Anatolia. **SELECTED PUBLICATIONS** Auth, "Religious Conversion and Social Transformation," Al 'Usur al-Wusta (94); auth, "The Politics of Patronage: Political Change and the Construction of Dervish Lodges in Silvas," Mugarnas (95); auth, "Portal Patterns in Seljuk Anatolia," in Studies in honor of Aptullah Kuran (99). **CONTACT ADDRESS** Univ of New Hampshire, Durham, Durham, NH 03824. **EMAIL** esw@hopper.unh.edu

WOLTER, JOHN A.
PERSONAL Born 07/25/1925, St. Paul, MN, m, 1956, 4 children **DISCIPLINE** GEOGRAPHY **EDUCATION** Univ Minn, BA, 56, MA, 65, PhD, 75 **CAREER** Map Libr and Lectr, 61-64, Asst to Dir Libraries, Univ Minn Libr, 64-65; Asst Prof, Univ Wi Wis-River Falls, 66-68, Actg Dept Chair, 68; Asst Chief to Division Chief, Geog & Map Division, Libr Congress, 68-91. **HONORS AND AWARDS** Awd for Distinguished Service, Libr Congress, 92. **MEMBERSHIPS** NMex Geog Soc; Asn Am Cartog; Am Libr Asn; Am Congress Surveying and Mapping; Soc Nautical Res; Hakluyt Soc; Int Soc Hist Cartog; Wash Map Soc; N Am Soc Oceanic Hist; Explorer's Club. **RESEARCH** History of cartography and nautical science. **SELECTED PUBLICATIONS** Auth, Johann Georg Kohl in America, Progress of Discovery: Johann Georg Kohl. Auf Den Spuren Der Entdecker, Akademische Druck-und Verlaganstalt, 93; coauth, Progress of Discovery: Johann George Kohl. Auf Den Spuren Der Entdecker, Akademische Druck-und Verlaganstalt, 93; co-ed, Images of the World: The Atlas Through History, McGraw Hill/Libr Congress, 97. **CONTACT ADDRESS** 5430 Ring Dove Ln., Columbia, MD 21044-1716.

WOLTERS, OLIVER WILLIAM
PERSONAL Born 06/08/1915, Reading, England, m, 1955, 2 children **DISCIPLINE** HISTORY OF SOUTHEAST ASIA **EDUCATION** Oxford Univ, BA, 37, MA, 45; Univ London, PhD, 62. **CAREER** Malayan Civil Serv, 37-57; lectr hist, Sch Orient & African Studies, Univ London, 57-63; prof, 63-75, chmn dept Asian studies, 70-72, Goldwin Smith Prof Southeast Asian Hist, 75-, Cornell Univ; trustee, Breezewood Found, Baltimore, 64-. **HONORS AND AWARDS** Distinguished Scholarship Awd, Asn for Asian Stud, 90; Guggenheim Fel, 72-73. **MEMBERSHIPS** Asn Asian Studies. **RESEARCH** Earlier Southeast Asian history with a special interest in earlier Vietnamese history. **SELECTED PUBLICATIONS** Auth, Early Indonesian Commerce, 67; auth, The Fall of Srivijaya in Malay History, 70; art, Assertions of Cultural Well-being in 14th century Vietnam, J Southeast Asian Studies, 79-80; art, Studying Srivijaya, J Malaysian Branch Royal Asiatic Soc, 80; auth, Two Essays on Dai-Viet in the Fourteenth Century, 88; auth, History, Culture, and Region in Southeast Asian Perspectives, rev ed, 99. **CONTACT ADDRESS** Southeast Asia Program, Cornell Univ, 180 Uris Hall, Ithaca, NY 14853.

WOLTERS, RAYMOND
PERSONAL Born 07/25/1938, Kansas City, MO, m, 1962, 3 children **DISCIPLINE** HISTORY **EDUCATION** Stanford Univ, BA, 60; Univ Calif, Berkeley, MA, 62; PhD, 67. **CAREER** Instr to prof, Univ Del, 65-, Thomas Muncy Keith Prof of Hist, 96-. **HONORS AND AWARDS** Silver Gavel Awd, Am Bar Asn, 85; Grant-in-Aid: Am Coun Learned Socs (70), Am Philos Soc (74), Del Humanities Forum (85), Crystal Trust (96), Pew Charitable Trust (99); Fel, Earhart Found, 89-90. **MEMBERSHIPS** Am Hist Asn, Org Am Hists, Southern Hist Asn. **SELECTED PUBLICATIONS** Auth, Negroes and the Great Depression: The Problem of Economic Recovery, Westport: Greenwood Press (70); auth, The New Negro on Campus: Black College Rebellions of the 1920's, Princeton: Princeton Univ Press (75); auth, The Burden of Brown: Thirty Years of School Desegregation, Knoxville: Univ Tenn Press (84); auth, Right Turn: William Bradford Reynolds, The Reagan Administration and Black Civil Rights, New Brunswick: Transaction Pubs (96); auth, Du Bois and His Rivals (in progress). **CONTACT ADDRESS** Dept Hist, Univ of Delaware, Newark, DE 19716-2555. **EMAIL** Wolters@udel.edu

WOOD, CAROLYN B.
DISCIPLINE ART HISTORY **EDUCATION** Univ NC, Chapel Hill, PhD. **CAREER** Educr for univ audiences, Univ NC, Chapel Hill. **RESEARCH** Baroque art. **SELECTED PUBLICATIONS** Coed, The Craft of Art: Originality and Industry in the Italian Renaissance and Baroque Workshop, Univ GA Press, 95. **CONTACT ADDRESS** Univ of No Carolina, Chapel Hill, Chapel Hill, NC 27599.

WOOD, CHARLES B., III
PERSONAL Born 09/29/1936, Hartford, CT, m, 1990, 2 children **DISCIPLINE** HISTORY OF ART AND ARCHITECTURE **EDUCATION** Univ Penn, MA, 65. **CAREER** Antiquarian bookseller, 67-, Charles B Wood III Inc. **MEMBERSHIPS** AAS; SAH. **RESEARCH** History of the Architectural Book. **SELECTED PUBLICATIONS** Collaborator of, 100 Rare Book Catalogues, 67-; auth, The New Pattern Books and the Role of the Agricultural Press, in: Prophet with Honor, The Career of Andrew Jackson Downing, eds, George B Tatum, Elizabeth MacDougal, Dum Barton Oaks, 89. **CONTACT ADDRESS** Box 2369, Cambridge, MA 02238. **EMAIL** cbw@world.std.com

WOOD, CHARLES TUTTLE
PERSONAL Born 10/29/1933, St. Paul, MN, m, 1955, 4 children **DISCIPLINE** HISTORY **EDUCATION** Harvard Univ, AB, 55, AM, 57, PhD, 62. **CAREER** Instr hist, Harvard Univ, 61-64; from asst prof to assoc prof, 64-71, actg chmn dept, 71-72, chmn prog comp lit, 77, Prof hist, 71-80, Chmn Dept, 76-89, Daniel Webster prof Hist, 80-96, Emeritus, 96, Dartmouth Col. **HONORS AND AWARDS** ACLS fel, 80-81; Am Bar Fdn fel,

81-82; Medieval Acad Am fel, 84-; John Simon Guggenheim fel, 86-87. **MEMBERSHIPS** AHA; Am Soc Legal Hist; Int Comn for Hist of Rep & Parliamentary Inst; Mediaeval Acad Am; Conf Brit Studies. **RESEARCH** Medieval history, especially England and France. **SELECTED PUBLICATIONS** Auth, French apanages and the Capetian monarchy 1224-1328, Harvard Univ, 66; The age of chivalry: Manners and morals 1000-1450, Weidenfeld & Nicolson, 70; ed, Philip the Fair and Boniface VIII: State vs Papacy, 2nd ed, Krieger, 76; auth, Joan of Arc and Richard III, Oxford, 88; co-ed, The Trial of Charles I, UPNE, 89; co-ed, Fresh P.C. Verdicts on Joan of Arc, Garland, 96; and various articles. **CONTACT ADDRESS** 7 N Balch St, Hanover, NH 03755. **EMAIL** charles.t.wood@dartmouth.edu

WOOD, CURTIS W.
PERSONAL Born 08/28/1941, High Point, NC, m, 1967, 2 children **DISCIPLINE** BRITISH HISTORY **EDUCATION** Univ NC, PhD. **CAREER** Hist Dept, Western Carolina Univ **HONORS AND AWARDS** Sossomon Endowed Chair, Dept of Hist, 98-00. **MEMBERSHIPS** Hist Soc of Ncar. **RESEARCH** Scotch-Irish migration; antebellum appalachia. **SELECTED PUBLICATIONS** Auth, Ulster and North America: Transatlantic Perspectives on the Scotch-Irish, 97; auth, From Ulster to Carolina: The Migration of the Scotch-Irish to Southwestern North Carolina, 98. **CONTACT ADDRESS** Western Carolina Univ, Cullowhee, NC 28723. **EMAIL** woodcw@wcu.edu

WOOD, FORREST GLEN
PERSONAL Born 03/15/1931, Oak Park, IL, m, 1978, 2 children **DISCIPLINE** AMERICAN NEGRO AND ECONOMIC HISTORY **EDUCATION** Sacramento State Col, AB, 57, MA, 58; Univ Calif, Berkeley, PhD(hist), 63. **CAREER** Asst prof hist, Bakersfield Ctr, 63-70, found res grant, 68, assoc prof, 70-80, Prof Hist, Calif State Col, Bakersfield, 80-, Vis prof Univ Iowa, summer 68 & Univ Calif, Santa Cruz, 71; Nat Endowment for Humanities, Brown, 76, Harvard, 81; consult, Nat Endowment for Humanities, 77-79. **MEMBERSHIPS** AHA; Orgn Am Historians; Southern Hist Asn; Asn Studies Negro Life & Cult. **RESEARCH** History of racism in America; Negro history; Civil War and Reconstruction. **SELECTED PUBLICATIONS** Auth, On revising reconstruction history, J Negro Hist, 4/66; Black Scare: The Racist Response to Emancipation and Reconstruction, Univ Calif, 68; Aspects of anti-Negro prejudice in mid-19th century America, Proc Afro-Am Conf, 69; On revising reconstruction history, White Power & Black Community, 69; The Era of Reconstruction, 1863-1877, Thomas Y Crowell, 75. **CONTACT ADDRESS** Dept of Hist, California State Univ, Bakersfield, Bakersfield, CA 93309.

WOOD, GORDON STEWART
PERSONAL Born 11/27/1933, Concord, MA, m, 1956, 3 children **DISCIPLINE** EARLY AMERICAN HISTORY **EDUCATION** Tufts Univ, AB, 55; Harvard Univ, AM, 59, PhD, 64. **CAREER** Asst prof early Am hist, Harvard Univ, 66-67; assoc prof, Univ Mich, 67-69; prof hist, Brown Univ, 69-; fel, Inst Early Am Hist & Cult, Williamsburg, Va, 64-66; mem educ bd, J Am Hist, 71-74; Guggenheim fel, 80-81; Pitt prof, Cambridge Univ, 82-83. **HONORS AND AWARDS** Bancroft Prize, 70; John H Dunning Prize, AHA, 70; Pulitzer Prize, 93. **MEMBERSHIPS** AHA; Orgn Am Hist; Soc Am Historians; Am Antiquarian Soc; Am Academy of Arts and Sciences; Am Philosophical Society. **RESEARCH** Early American history. **SELECTED PUBLICATIONS** Auth, The Creation of the American Republic, 1776-1787, Univ NC, 69; ed, Rising Glory of America, 1760-1820, Braziller, 71; coauth, The Great Republic, 77 & 81; auth, The Radicalism of the American Revolution. **CONTACT ADDRESS** Dept of History, Brown Univ, Providence, RI 02912. **EMAIL** GORDON_WOOD@BROWN.EDU

WOOD, JAMES BRIAN
PERSONAL Born 03/13/1946, Sandersville, GA, m, 1968, 3 children **DISCIPLINE** EARLY MODERN EUROPEAN HISTORY, MILITARY HISTORY **EDUCATION** Eckerd Col, BA, 68; Emory Univ, PhD(hist), 73. **CAREER** Asst prof, 73-80, assoc prof, 80-85, prof hist, Williams Col, 85-, chair, 94-98. **HONORS AND AWARDS** Nancy Roelker Prize, 84; Baxter Prof Hist, 94-97; Wilmott Family Third Century Prof Hist, 97-; Soc for Military Hist, Distinguished Book Awd, 98. **RESEARCH** Early modern French nobility; French wars of religion; French social and economic history; military history. **SELECTED PUBLICATIONS** Auth, La structure sociale de la Noblesse dans le bailliage de Caen et ses modifications (1463-1666), Annales de Normandie, 72; The decline of the nobility in sixteenth and early seventeenth century France: Myth or reality?, J Mod Hist, 76; Demographic pressure and social mobility among the nobility of early modern France, 16th Century J, 77; Endogamy and mesalliance: The marriage patterns of the nobility of the election of Bayeaux, 1430-1669, Fr Hist Studies, 78; The Nobility of the Election of Bayeaux, 1463-1666: Social Continuity and Change Among the Provincial Nobility of Early Modern France, Princeton Univ Press, 80; the Impact of Wars of Religion: A View of France in 1581, 16th Century Jour, 84; The Royal Army During the Early Wars of Religion, In: Society and Institutions in Early Modern France, Univ Ga Press, 91; The King's Army: Warfare, Soldiers, and Society during the Wars of Religion in France, 1562-76, Cambridge Univ Press, 96. **CONTACT ADDRESS** Dept of Hist, Williams Col, 880 Main St, Williamstown, MA 01267-2600. **EMAIL** james.b.wood@williams.edu

WOOD, PETER H.
PERSONAL Born 05/01/1943, St. Louis, MO **DISCIPLINE** HISTORY **EDUCATION** Harvard Univ, PhD, 72. **CAREER** Prof, 75-, Duke Univ. **HONORS AND AWARDS** Albert J. Beveridge Awd, 74; James Harvey Robinson Prize, 84. **MEMBERSHIPS** Am Gourd Soc. **RESEARCH** Early Am hist. **SELECTED PUBLICATIONS** Auth, Black Majority: Negroes in Colonial South Carolina from 1670 through the Stono Rebellion, 74; Strange New Land: African Americans 1617-1776, 96; co-auth, Natives and Newcomers: The Way We Lived in North Carolina before 1770, 83; Winslow Homer's Images of Blacks: The Civil War and Reconstruction Years, 88; co-ed, Powhatan's Mantle: Indian's in the Colonial Southeast, 89. **CONTACT ADDRESS** Dept of Hist, Duke Univ, 208 Carr Bldg, Durham, NC 27708. **EMAIL** pwood@duke.edu

WOOD, WALTER KIRK
PERSONAL m, 2 children **DISCIPLINE** HISTORY **EDUCATION** Frederick Col, BA, 68; Va Polytech Inst, MA, 70; Univ SC, PhD, 78. **CAREER** Assoc dir grad stud, Col Bus, Univ SC, 79-86; dead grad stud, 86-89, PROF HIST, 95-, ALA STATE UNIV. **HONORS AND AWARDS** Newcomen Society Awd for Economic History, Univ of South Carolina, 73; Nominee for Amoco Teacher of the Year Awd for Graduate Asst, 75; USDE, Patricia Harris Minority Grant , 87-89; Marguerite E Wilbur Foundation grant. **RESEARCH** American Revolution, South, Civil War, Historiography, American Myths. **SELECTED PUBLICATIONS** Auth, A Northern Daughter and A Southern Wife: The Civil War Letters and Reminiscences of Katherine H. Chumming, 11860-1865, Augusta, GA, Richmond County Historical Society, 76; auth," U B Phillips Historian: A Further Note on His Methodology and Use of Sources, "Southern Studies, XX (82): 146-162; auth, " Dear Mr Snowden: U B Phillips Letters to Prof Yates Snowden of South Carolina College 1904-1932," South Carolina Historical Magazine, 85 (84): 294-304; auth, " The Central Themes of Southern History: Republicanism, Not Slavery, Race, or Romanticism," Continuity: A Journal of History, 9, (84)L 33-71; auth, U B Phillips, " biographical-historiographical sketch in ibid; auth, " John C Calhoun," biog Sketch, Encyclopedia of the American Right; auth, Ulrich Bonnell Phillips: A Southern Historian and His Critics, Westport, CT, 90; auth, " Alexis De TocQueville and the Myth of Democracy in America," Southern Studies, New Series, V 94, 1-18, (98); auth, Frank L Owsley and the Search for Southern Identity, 1865-1965." ibid, VI 95, (99). **CONTACT ADDRESS** 300 Cheekwood Ln, Montgomery, AL 36116. **EMAIL** Kirkmyth@aol.com

WOODARD, KOMAZI
PERSONAL Born 06/07/1949, Newark, NJ, d, 5 children **DISCIPLINE** AMERICAN HISTORY **EDUCATION** Dickinson Col, BA, 71; Univ Pa, MA, 88, PhD, 91. **CAREER** Ed, Main Trend, New York City, 74-84; managing ed, Children's Express, New York City, 84-86; asst dir, African Am Studies Summer Inst, Univ Pa, 87; res consult, Pew Charitable Trusts & Delaware Valley Community Reinvestment Fund, 88; consult, Soc Sci Res Coun, Res on the Urban Underclass, 88; lectr, Rutgers Univ, 88; lectr, Col of St Elizabeth, Convent, NJ, 89; res consult, MacArthur Found Proj on Urban Poverty, Communities and Families, Univ of Pa, Philadelphia, 89; res assoc, Center of Urban Affairs & Policy Res and at African Am Studies Dept, Northwestern Univ, 91; Fac, Urban Studies, Eugene Lang Col, New Sch Univ, 93-; ed adv bd, The New press, New York City, 97-; reviewer, Am Coun of Learned Socs, New York City, 99-; Prof, Am Hist, Sarah Lawrence Col, 89-. **HONORS AND AWARDS** Res grant, NJ Hist Commission, 85; Martin Luther King, Jr Leadership Awd, 88; Fontaine Fel, Univ of Pa, 86-89; W. W. Smith Fel, Univ of Pa, 89; Burnham Fel, Univ of Pa, 90; Post-Doctoral Fel, Northwestern Univ, 91; Nominee, Allan Nevins Prize, 92; Simpson Res Grant, 94; Hewlett-Mellon Res Grant, 94; Flik Int Travel Grant, 95; listed in Who's Who in the World, Who's Who in America, Dictionary of Int Biography, Who's Who in the East. **MEMBERSHIPS** African Heritage Studies Asn, Am Hist Asn, Am Coun of Learned Socs, Am Studies Asn, Nat Coun on Black Studies, Org of Am Hists, Schomburg Res Center. **RESEARCH** Oral history; ethnography; urban and ethnic history, urban studies, social, cultural and intellectual history; radicalism; civil rights, Black power, Black nationalism, and Pan-Africanism. **SELECTED PUBLICATIONS** Auth, "The Making of the New Ark: Amiri Baraka, the Congress of African People, the Modern Black Convention Movement, 1966-1976," PhD diss, Univ Pa, UMI (91); auth, "The Leadership of Malcolm X," Silver Bullets, Sarah Lawrence Col (95); auth, "Black Crisis Myths," Dollars & Sense, No 226 (Nov/Dec 99); auth, A Nation Within a Nation: Amiri Baraka (LeRoi Jones) and Black Power Politics, Chapel Hill: Univ NC Press (99); auth, "The Influence of Malcolm X on Amiri Baraka," Encyclopedia of Malcolm X (forthcoming); auth, "The Black Arts Movement" and "The Black Convention Movement, Modern," Encyclopedia of Civil Rights in the United States, NY: Macmillan Reference (forthcoming). **CONTACT ADDRESS** Dept Am Hist, Sarah Lawrence Col, 1 Mead Way, Bronxville, NY 10708-5931.

WOODBRIDGE, JOHN M.
PERSONAL Born 01/26/1929, New York, NY, m, 1975, 3 children **DISCIPLINE** ENGLISH AND ARCHITECTURE **EDUCATION** Amherst Col, AB, 51; Princeton Univ, MFA, archit, 56. **CAREER** Archit, Princeton Univ Archaeol expedition to Morgantina, Sicily, 56; Holden Egan Wilson & Corser, NY and Wash DC, 56-57; archit, John Funk, San Francisco, 57-58; John Lyon Reid and Partners, San Francisco, 57-58; assoc partner, Skidmore Owings & Merrill, 59-73; pres adv coun on Penn Ave, chief of design, 63-64, staff dir, 65-66, Pennsylvania Ave Development Corp, exec dir, 73-77; vpres, Braccia Joe & Woodbridge, 77-80; cons, Stoller Partners, Berkeley, 80-82; adjunct partner, Sprankle Lynd & Sprague, 82-91. **HONORS AND AWARDS** Phi Beta Kappa, 50; AIA Student Medal, 56; fel, Amer Inst of Archit, 74; Fed Design Achievement Awd, 88. **MEMBERSHIPS** AIA. **RESEARCH** Spanish colonial architectural history especially Mexico; Architectural history in Europe and U.S. **SELECTED PUBLICATIONS** Coauth,with Sally B. Woodbridge, San Francisco Architecture, San Francisco, Chronicle Books, 92; with Sally B. Woodbridge, Architecture San Francisco, San Francisco, 101 Prod, 82; with David Gebhard, Roger Montgomery, Robert Winter and Sally B. Woodbridge, A Guide to the Architecture of San Francisco and Northern California, Salt Lake City, Peregrine Smith, 73; with Sally B. Woodbridge and Philip Thiel, Buildings of the Bay Area, NY, Grove Press, 60; auth, The Bay Area Style, Casabella 232, Oct 59; For the Cathedral of St. John the Divine, Relig Bldgs for Today, NY, F. W. Dodge, 57. **CONTACT ADDRESS** 19772 - 8th St. E, Sonoma, CA 95476. **EMAIL** jwoodbridge@peoplepo.com

WOODMAN, HAROLD DAVID
PERSONAL Born 04/21/1928, Chicago, IL, w, 1954, 2 children **DISCIPLINE** UNITED STATES ECONOMIC HISTORY **EDUCATION** Roosevelt Univ, BA, 57; Univ Chicago, MA, 59, PhD(hist), 64. **CAREER** Lectr hist, Roosevelt Univ, 62-63; from asst prof to prof, Univ Mo-Columbia, 63-71; Prof Hist, Purdue Univ, West Lafayette, 71-97, Soc Sci Res Coun fac fel, 69-70; fel, Woodrow Wilson Int Ctr Scholars, Washington, DC, 77; Prof Emer, 97-. **HONORS AND AWARDS** Everett E Edwards Awd, Agr Hist Soc, 63; Ramsdell Awd, South Hist Asn, 65; Otto Wirth Awd, Roosevelt Univ, 90. **MEMBERSHIPS** Econ Hist Asn; Orgn Am Historians; Southern Hist Asn; Agr Hist Soc. **RESEARCH** United States economic history of the 19th century; history of the American South. **SELECTED PUBLICATIONS** Auth, The decline of cotton factorage after the Civil War, Am Hist Rev, 7/66; Slavery and the Southern Economy, Harcourt, 67; King Cotton and His Retainers, Univ Ky, 68; Economic history and economic theory, J Interdisciplinary Hist, autumn 73; ed, The Legacy of the American Civil War, Wiley, 73; auth, Imperialism and economic development, Res Econ Hist II, 77; Sequel to slavery, J Southern Hist, 77; Post-Civil War southern agriculture and the law, Agr Hist, 79; auth, New South-New Law, Louisiana State Univ Press, 95. **CONTACT ADDRESS** Dept of Hist, Purdue Univ, West Lafayette, West Lafayette, IN 47907. **EMAIL** hwoodman@sla.purdue.edu

WOODMAN, TAYLOR
DISCIPLINE ART HISTORY **EDUCATION** Univ Chicago, PhD, 97. **CAREER** Asst prof, Univ IL at Chicago. **RESEARCH** Southeast Asian art; Islamic art. **SELECTED PUBLICATIONS** Auth, Bibliography of South and Southeast Asian Art and Archaeology 1989-1991. **CONTACT ADDRESS** Art Hist Dept, Univ of Illinois, Chicago, S Halsted St, PO Box 705, Chicago, IL 60607. **EMAIL** woodman@uic.edu

WOODRUFF, NAN ELIZABETH
PERSONAL Born 08/25/1949, Anniston, AL **DISCIPLINE** HISTORY **EDUCATION** Jacksonville State Univ, BA, 71; Univ Ark, MA, 73; Univ Tenn, PhD, 77. **CAREER** Asst ed, Booker T. Washington Papers, Univ Md, 77-78; asst prof, Col of Charleston, 79-88; asst prof, Pa State Univ, 88-92, assoc prof, 92-. **HONORS AND AWARDS** Smithsonian Inst Fel, 89-90; Am Coun for Learned Socs Fels, 86-87; Am Philos Soc, 82, 85, 87. **MEMBERSHIPS** Am Hist Asn, Org of Am Hists, Southern Hist Soc, Agricultural Hist Soc. **RESEARCH** Southern and African Americans. **SELECTED PUBLICATIONS** Auth, "The Failure of Relief in the Arkansas Drought of 1930-31," Ark Hist Quart, 39 (fall 81): 301-13; auth, As Rare as Rain: Federal Relief in the Great Southern Drought of 1930-31, Univ Ill (85); auth, "Pick or Fight: The Emergency Farm Labor Program and the Struggle Over Farm Wages in the Mississippi and Arkansas Deltas During World War II," Agricultural Hist, 64 (spring 90): 74-85; auth, "Agriculture," in Elliot J. Gorn, Mary Kupiec Cayton, and Peter Williams, Encyclopedia of American Social History, Vol 2, Charles Schribners American Civilization Series, New York (93): 1393-1406; auth, "African American Struggles for Citizenship in the Arkansas and Mississippi Deltas in the Age of Jim Crow," Radical Hist Rev, 55 (winter 93): 33-52; auth, "Mississippi Delta Planters and Debates over Mechanization, Labor, and Civil Rights in the 1940's," J of Southern Hist, No 2 (May 94): 263-284; auth, State, Labor, and Citizenship in the 'American Congo': The Arkansas and Mississippi Deltas in Depression and Wars, 1914-1950 (in progress). **CONTACT ADDRESS** Dept Hist, Pennsylvania State Univ, Univ Park, 108 Weaver Blvd, University Park, PA 16802-5500. **EMAIL** new7@psu.edu

WOODS, ALAN LAMBERT
PERSONAL Born 11/23/1942, Philadelphia, PA, m, 1967, 1 child **DISCIPLINE** THEATRE HISTORY **EDUCATION** Columbia Univ, AB, 64; Univ Southern Calif, MA, 69, PhD(theatre), 72. **CAREER** Lectr drama, Univ Southern Calif, 68-71; instr theatre, Long Beach City Col, 71-72; asst prof to assoc prof Theatre, Ohio State Univ, 72-, Lectr theatre, Calif State Univ, Los Angeles, 70; ed, Theatre Studies, 72-77; coordr res panel Comt Instnl Coop, 73-; lectr, Am Asn Health, Phys Educ & Recreation, 74; co-ed, Educ Theatre J, Univ Col Theatre Asn, 78-80; mem, res comn Am Theatre Asn, 78 & exec comt, Am Soc Theatre Res, 76-78, 89-92; visiting prof, Ind Univ, 78-79; dir, Lawrence and Lee Theatre Res Inst, 79-; pres, Ohio Theatre Alliance, 90-91. **HONORS AND AWARDS** Fel, Col of the Am Theatre, 96. **MEMBERSHIPS** Am Theatre Asn; Am Soc Theatre Res. **RESEARCH** Ancient theatre; 19th century popular theatre; theatre historiography. **SELECTED PUBLICATIONS** Coauth, A note on the symmetry of Delphi, Theatre Surv, 5/72; auth, Popular theatre in Los Angeles, Players, 5/73; A quantification approach to popular American theatre, Res in Educ, 1/74; James J Corbett, theatrical star, J Sports Hist, 76; Theatre historiography, Ohio Speech J, 76; Reconstructions of performances, Copenhagen, Royal Libr, 76; Frederick B Warde, tragedian, Educ Theatre J, 77; The Ohio Theatre, 80; Selected Plays of Jerome Lawrence and Robert E. Lee, Ohio State Univ Press, 95. **CONTACT ADDRESS** Dept of Theatre, Ohio State Univ, Columbus, 1089 Drake Union, 1849 Cannon Dr, Columbus, OH 43210-1266. **EMAIL** woods.1@osu.edu

WOODS, DANIEL
DISCIPLINE HISTORY **EDUCATION** Emmanuel Col, AA; Roanoke Col, BA; Univ Ga, MA; Univ Miss, PhD. **CAREER** Assoc prof. **RESEARCH** Religion in American life. **SELECTED PUBLICATIONS** Auth, rev of The Apostle, The Jour Southern Rel, 98. **CONTACT ADDRESS** Dept of Hist, Ferrum Col, PO Box 1000, Ferrum, VA 24088-9000. **EMAIL** dgwoods@ferrum.edu

WOODS, JOSEPH MICHAEL
PERSONAL Born 05/19/1927, Wilmington, DE **DISCIPLINE** MODERN BRITISH AND IRISH HISTORY **EDUCATION** Univ Del, BA, 48; Harvard Univ, MA, 49, PhD(hist), 67. **CAREER** Instr, Mass Inst Technol, 63-65; asst prof, Univ NH, 65-66; asst prof, Northeastern Univ, 67-68; Assoc Prof Hist, York Univ, 68-, Vis scholar, Menninger Found, Topeka, Kans, 72-73. **MEMBERSHIPS** Am Comt Irish Studies. **RESEARCH** Charles Stewart Parnell; psychohistory; English social history. **SELECTED PUBLICATIONS** Auth, Some considerations on psychohistory, The Historian, 8/74; Toward a psychoanalytic interpretation of Charles Stewart Parnell, Bull Menninger Clinic, 11/78. **CONTACT ADDRESS** York Univ, 20 Fashion Roseway Ste 518W, Willowdale, ON, Canada M2N 6B5.

WOODS, RANDALL
PERSONAL Born 10/10/1944, Galveston, TX, m, 1966, 2 children **DISCIPLINE** HISTORY **EDUCATION** Univ of Tex, Austin, BA, 67; MA, 69; PhD, 72. **CAREER** From instr to Cooper Distinguished Prof of Hist, Univ of Ark, 71-. **HONORS AND AWARDS** Woodrow Wilson Fel; NEH Sr Fel, Alumni Distinguished Teaching and Res Awd, Robert H. Ferrell Awd. **MEMBERSHIPS** AHA, OAH, Southern Hist Asn, Hist Soc, SHAFR. **RESEARCH** Twentieth-Century American History. **SELECTED PUBLICATIONS** Auth, John Lewis Waller and the Promise of American Life, Univ of Kans Press, 80; auth, A Changing of the Guard, Chapel Hill, 90; auth, The Dawning of the Cold War, Univ of Ga Press, 91; auth, Fulbright: A Biography, Cambridge, 95. **CONTACT ADDRESS** Dept Hist, Univ of Arkansas, Fayetteville, 416 Old Main, Fayetteville, AR 72701-1201. **EMAIL** rwoods@comp.uark.edu

WOODS, ROBERT L.
PERSONAL Born 02/17/1945, Pasadena, CA, m, 1975, 1 child **DISCIPLINE** HISTORY **EDUCATION** Pomona Col, BA, 67; UCLA, PhD, 74. **CAREER** Asst Prof to Prof, Pomona Col, 74-; Prof hist, 98-. **HONORS AND AWARDS** Fel in Legal Hist, Am Bar Asn, 83; Fel, Am Coun of Learned Soc, 96-97. **MEMBERSHIPS** Conf on Brit Studies, 16th Century Studies Conf, Renaissance Soc of Am, Am Soc for Legal Hist, Selden Soc, Past and Present Soc. **RESEARCH** English legal history in 15th and 16th centuries, transformation of civil culture, English politics and society from the 15th century to the Reformation. **SELECTED PUBLICATIONS** Auth, "Programmers, Computers, and Computer Languages: Some Implications for History," Computers & the Humanities 16 (82): 229-243; auth, "Individuals in the Rioting Crowd . . . ," J of Interdisciplinary Hist XIV-1 (83): 1-24; auth, "Charles II and the Politics of Sex and Scandal," in State, Sovereigns, & Society, ed. C. Carlton, R. Woods, M. Robertson, J. Block (Stoud: Allan Sutton, 97), 119-136. **CONTACT ADDRESS** Dept Hist, Pomona Col, 333 N Col Way, Claremont, CA 91711-4429. **EMAIL** Rwoods@Pomona.Edu

WOODWARD, DAVID
PERSONAL Born 08/29/1942, Leamington Spa, United Kingdom, m, 1966, 3 children **DISCIPLINE** GEOGRAPHY, CARTOGRAPHY **EDUCATION** Univ Wales, BA, 64; Univ Wisc, MA, 67; PhD, 70. **CAREER** Map Curator, Newberry Lib, 69-74; cen dir, 74-80; assoc prof, Univ Wisc, 80-81; Cart Lab Dir, 83-86; prof, 81-; IRH, Sr Mem, 97-. **HONORS AND AWARDS** Guggenheim Fel; Brit Acad Exch Fel; Bogliasco Fel; RV Tooley Awd; Corres Fel Brit Acad; James Henry Breasted Prize; Co-Found, Chicago Map Soc. **MEMBERSHIPS** AAG; BCS Fel; ICA; NACTS; CMS; WMS; NEMO; ISHC; IMCS; TMS; Philip Lee Philips Soc; APHA; PHSL; SHD; Hakluyt Soc. **RESEARCH** Renaissance Italian Cartography, Medieval Cartography, Maps and the Humanities, Maps as Material Cultural, Physical Analysis of Maps and Prints. **SELECTED PUBLICATIONS** Ed, Five Centuries of Map Printing, Univ of Chicago Press, 75; auth, The All-American Map, Wax-Engraving and its Influence on Cartography, Univ of Chicago Press, 77; ed, Art and Cartography: Six Historical Essays, Chicago: Univ of Chicago Press, 87; auth, Cartography in Prehistoric, Ancient, and Medieval Europe and the Mediterranean, Chicago: Univ of Chicago Press, 87; auth, The Maps and Prints of Paolo Forlani: A Descriptive Bibliography, Hermon Dunlap Smith Center for the History of Cartography Special Publication, No 4, Chicago: The Newberry Library, 90; auth, Cartography in the Traditional Islamic and South Asian Societies, Chicago, Univ of Chicago Press, 92; auth, Cartography in the Traditional East and Southeast Asian Societies, Chicago: Univ of Chicago Press, 94; auth, Maps as Prints in the Italian Renaissance, London: British Library, 96; auth, Catalogue of Watermarks in Italian Maps, ca. 1540-1600, Florence: Leo S. Olschki, 96; auth, Cartography in the Traditional African, American, Artic, Australian, and Pacific Societies, Chicago: Univ of Chicago Press, 98. **CONTACT ADDRESS** Dept Geography, Univ of Wisconsin, Madison, 550 N Park St, Madison, WI 53706-1491. **EMAIL** dawoodwa@facstaff.wisc.edu

WOODWARD, DAVID REID
PERSONAL Born 10/09/1939, Clarksville, TN, m, 1966, 1 child **DISCIPLINE** MODERN EUROPEAN & RUSSIAN HISTORY **EDUCATION** Austin Peay State Univ, BA, 61; Univ GA, MA, 63, PhD, 65. **CAREER** Asst prof hist, 65-70, Tex A&M Univ; assoc prof, 70-73, prof hist, 73-, Marshall Univ. **HONORS AND AWARDS** Research Awd Soc Sci, 76, 86, 89, tchng awards, 93, 99, Marshall Univ. **MEMBERSHIPS** N Amer Conf Brit Studies; Western Front Assn; Army Records Soc; Soc for Mil Hist; fel, Royal Hist Soc. **RESEARCH** Military and diplomatic history of World War I, British and US. **SELECTED PUBLICATIONS** Auth, Trail by Friendship: Anglo-American Relations 1917-1918, Univ Kentucky Press, 93; auth, Field Marshal Sir William Robertson: Chief of the Imperial General Staff in the Great War, Praeger, 98; ed, The Military Correspondence of Field-Marshal Sir William Robertson, Army Records Soc, 89; co-ed, America and World War I: A Selected Annotated Bibliography of English-Language Sources, Garland, 85; auth, Britain in a Continental War: Civil-Military Debate Over the Strategical Direction of the Great War of 1914-1918, Albion, 80; auth, Did Lloyd George Starve the British Army of Men Prior to the German March 21st Offensive, Hist J, 84. **CONTACT ADDRESS** Dept of History, Marshall Univ, 400 Hal Greer Blvd, Huntington, WV 25755. **EMAIL** woodwadr@marshall.edu

WOODWARD, RALPH L.
PERSONAL Born 12/02/1934, New London, CT, m, 1996, 3 children **DISCIPLINE** HISTORY **EDUCATION** Cent Col Mo, AB, 55; Tulane Univ, MA, 59, PhD, 62. **CAREER** Asst Prof Hist, Univ Witchita, 61-62; Asst Prof Hist, Univ SW La, 62-63; Asst to Assoc Prof of Hist, Univ NC, 63-70; Prof Hist, Tulane Univ, 70-99; Neville G. Penrose Prof of Latin American Studies and Prof of History, Texas Christian Univ, 99-. **HONORS AND AWARDS** Alfred B Thomas Book Awd, 95; La Humanist of the Yr, 96; Waldo G Leland Awd, 97. **MEMBERSHIPS** Am Hist Asn; Conf on Latin Am Hist; SE Coun on Latin Am Stud; La Hist Asn. **RESEARCH** Latin Am econ hist; Cent Am. **SELECTED PUBLICATIONS** Auth, Rafael Carrera and the Emergence of the Republic of Guatemala, 1821-1871, Univ Ga Press, 93, Spanish translation, 00; Asn ed, Encyclopedia of Latin American History and Culture, 5 vols, Charles Scribner's Sons, 96; auth, Central America, A Nation Divided, 3rd ed, Oxford Univ Press, 99. **CONTACT ADDRESS** TCU Box 297260, Fort Worth, TX 76129. **EMAIL** r.woodward@tcu.edu

WOOLEY, WESLEY THEODORE
PERSONAL Born 01/18/1942, Champaign, IL, m, 1964, 2 children **DISCIPLINE** AMERICAN HISTORY **EDUCATION** Univ Ill, Urbana, BA, 63; Univ Chicago, MA, 64, PhD(hist), 71. **CAREER** NDEA fel, 66-68; instr, 68-71, Prof Hist, Univ Victoria, 71-. **MEMBERSHIPS** AHA; Orgn Am Historians; Soc Hist Am Foreign Rels. **RESEARCH** Am diplomatic history, Am peace movements. **SELECTED PUBLICATIONS** Auth, "Learning to Fear the Bomb," in J. Mas and R. Stewart, Toward a World of Peace, Univ of the South Pacific, 86; auth, Alternatives to Anarchy: American Supra-nationalism since World War II, Indiana Univ Press, 88; auth, "Beyond the Nation-State System: Supra-nationalism and the American Peace Movement," Peace Research, 90; auth, "Finding a Usable Post: The Success of American World Federalism in the 1940s," Peace & Change, 99. **CONTACT ADDRESS** Dept Hist, Univ of Victoria, PO Box 3045, Victoria, BC, Canada V8W 3P4. **EMAIL** wtwooley@uvic.ca

WOOLLEY, PETER J.
PERSONAL Born 02/23/1960, New York, NY, m, 1994 **DISCIPLINE** COMPARATIVE POLITICS, HISTORY **EDUCATION** St. Joseph's Univ, BA, 81; Univ Pittsburgh, MA, 83, PhD, 89. **CAREER** Book review editor, Journal of Conflict Studies, 97-; Chair, Dept of Social Sciences and History, Prof of Comparative Politics, Fairleigh Dickinson Univ, Madison, NJ, 98-. **HONORS AND AWARDS** Edwin Miller History Prize, US Naval War College. **MEMBERSHIPS** APSA. **RESEARCH** Japanese defense policy, maritime powers and decline. **SELECTED PUBLICATIONS** Auth, Geography and the Limits of US Military Intervention, in Conflict Quart, vol XI, no 4, fall 91; Japan's Security Policies: Into the Twenty-First Century, Jour East and West Studies, vol 22, no 2, Oct 92; Low-Level Military Conflict and the Future of Japan's Armed Forces, Conflict Quart, vol XIII, no 4, fall 93; Geography Revisited: Expectations of US Military Intervention in the Post-Cold War Era, in Peacemaking, Peacekeeping and Coalition Warfare, Fariborz L. Mokhtari, ed, Nat Defense Univ Press, 94; The Role of War and Strategy in the Transformation and Decline of Great Powers, Naval War Col Rev, Vol XLIX, no 1, winter 96; with Cdr. Mark S. Woolley, USN, The Kata of Japan's Naval Forces, Naval War Col Rev, Vol XLIX, no 2, spring 96; Japan's Minesweeping Decision 1991: An Organizational Response, Asian Survey, Vol XXXVI, no 8, Aug 96, reprinted in Edward R. Beauchamp, ed, Dimensions of Contemporary Japan, Vol II, Garland Pub, 99; Japan's Sealane Defense Revisited, Strategic Rev, Vol XXIV, no IV, fall 96; Arguing From the Same Premises: the Ideology is Intact, American Politics: Core Argument and Current Controversy, P. J. Woolley and A. R. Papa, eds, Prentice Hall Pubs, 98; In Defense of Pacific Rim Democracies: the US-Japan Alliance, Aiding Democracies Under Seige, Gabriel Marcela and Anthony Joes, eds, Praeger Pubs, 99; Japan's Navy: Politics and Paradox, 1971-2000, Lynne-Reinner Pubs, 00. **CONTACT ADDRESS** Dept of Social Sciences and History, Fairleigh Dickinson Univ, Florham-Madison, Madison, NJ 07940. **EMAIL** Woolley@alpha.fdu.edu

WOOSTER, RALPH ANCIL
PERSONAL Born 11/09/1928, Baytown, TX, m, 1947, 1 child **DISCIPLINE** HISTORY **EDUCATION** Univ Houston, BA & MA, 50; Univ Tex, PhD(Hist), 54. **CAREER** Head dept Hist, 66-70, from instr to prof, 55-72, Regents prof Am Hist, Lamar Univ, 72-, dean Fac & Grad Studies, 76-91. **HONORS AND AWARDS** Phi Kappa Phi Teaching Awd; Ralph Steen Awd; Piper Professor Awd. **MEMBERSHIPS** AHA; Orgn Am Historians; Southern Hist Asn; Texas State Hist Assoc. **RESEARCH** Secession movement in the United States; American Civil War; state and local government in Old South. **SELECTED PUBLICATIONS** Auth, Analysis of membership of secession conventions in Lower South, J Southern Hist, 8/58; Secession of the Lower South, Civil War Hist, 6/61; Secession Conventions of the South, Princeton Univ, 62; The People In Power, Univ Tenn, 69; Early Texas statehood, Southwestern Hist Quart, 10/72; coauth, Texas and Texans, Steck-Vaughn, 72; auth, Politicians, Planters and Plain Folk, Univ Tenn, 75; co-ed, Texas Vistas, Tex State Hist Asn, 80; Texas and Texans in the Civil War, Eakin Press, 95; ed, Lone Star Blue & Gray, Tex State Hist Assoc, 95; auth, "Civil War Texas, Tex State Hist Assoc," 99; auth, "Lone Star Generals in Gray," Eakin Press, 00. **CONTACT ADDRESS** Dept of History, Lamar Univ, Beaumont, PO Box 10048, Beaumont, TX 77710-0048.

WOOSTER, ROBERT
PERSONAL Born 08/27/1956, Beaumont, TX, m, 1993 **DISCIPLINE** HISTORY **EDUCATION** Univ TX, Austin, PhD 85. **CAREER** TX A M Univ, prof hist, 86-, ch dept of hum, 97. **HONORS AND AWARDS** Civ Depu Dir, USMA rotc Mili Hist Fell; Piper Prof; Vis Schol TX ST Hist Assn. **MEMBERSHIPS** OAH; TSHA; SMH. **RESEARCH** 19th Century Military Hist; West. **SELECTED PUBLICATIONS** Fort Davis: Out Post on the Texas Frontire, TX State Hist Assn, 94; The Civil War 100, Carol Pub, 98; Nelson A Miles and the Twilight of the Frontier Army, Univ Nebraska Press, 93; The Military and the United States Indian Policy, 1865-1903, Yale Univ Press, 88. **CONTACT ADDRESS** Dept of Hist, Texas A&M Univ, Corpus Christi, 6300 Ocean Dr, Corpus Christi, TX 78412. **EMAIL** rwooster@falcon.tamucc.edu

WORCESTER, DONALD EMMET
PERSONAL Born 04/29/1915, Tempe, AZ **DISCIPLINE** LATIN AMERICAN HISTORY **EDUCATION** Bard Col, AB, 39; Univ Calif, AM, 40, PhD, 47. **CAREER** From asst prof to prof hist & head dept, Univ Fla, 47-59; prof, 63-71, chmn dept, 63-71, Lorin A Boswell prof hist, 71-80, Ida & Cecil Green Emer Prof, Tex Christian Univ, 81-, Vis prof, Univ Madrid, 56-57; managing ed, Hisp Am Hist Rev, 60-65. **HONORS AND AWARDS** Southwest Bk Awd, 79; Western Writers Am Spur Awd, 75 & 79. **MEMBERSHIPS** AHA; Paraguayan Inst Hist Res; Western Writers Am (vpres, 72-73, pres, 73-74); Western Hist Asn (pres, 74-75); Westerners Int (pres, 78-79). **RESEARCH** Brazilian history; Latin American colonial institutions; plains Indians. **SELECTED PUBLICATIONS** Auth, Chisholm, Jesse, NMex Hist Rev, Vol 0068, 93; Parker, Quanah, Comanche Chief, J Amer Hist, Vol 0081, 94; Buffalo Soldiers, Braves, and the Brass, J Amer Hist, Vol 0081, 94; Apache Reservation, Pac Hist Rev, Vol 0063, 94; North American Cattle Ranching Frontiers, Western Hist Quart, Vol 0025,

94; The Jumanos, Amer Indian Culture and Res J, Vol 0019, 95; Spanish Expeditions Into Texas, 1689-1768, Amer Indian Culture and Res J, Vol 0020, 96. **CONTACT ADDRESS** Texas Christian Univ, 9321 Bearcreek Rd, Aledo, TX 76008-4004.

WORKS, JOHN A.
PERSONAL Born 08/25/1944, St. Paul, MN **DISCIPLINE** HISTORY **EDUCATION** Yale Univ, BA, 66; Wi Univ, MA, 68, PhD, 72. **CAREER** Lectr, Northeast Col of Arts & Sci Maiduguri, Nigeria, 72-75; lectr, Univ of Maiduguri, Nigeria, 75-77; asst lectr to assoc prof, Univ Mo St. Louis, 77-; assoc porf, 77-99; assoc prof emer, 99-. **MEMBERSHIPS** African Stud Assoc; Societe des Africanistes. **RESEARCH** W Africa; Islam, Christianity, Hausa States; Chad. **SELECTED PUBLICATIONS** Auth, Pilgrims in a Strange Land, Columbia Univ Press, 76; The Muslim Maha of Wadai, in Islamic Peoples, Greenwood Press, 83. **CONTACT ADDRESS** Dept of History, Univ of Missouri, St. Louis, Lucas Hall, Saint Louis, MO 63121. **EMAIL** HISTORYWORKS@umsl.edu

WOROBEC, CHRISTINE D.
PERSONAL Born 07/30/1955, Toronto, ON, Canada, m, 1988, 2 children **DISCIPLINE** HISTORY **EDUCATION** Univ Toronto, BA, 77; MA, 78; PhD, 84. **CAREER** Asst prof to assoc prof, Kent State Univ, 84-99; assoc prof, Northern IL Univ, 99-. **HONORS AND AWARDS** Kennan Inst for Adv Russ Studies Fel, 85; NEH Grants, 88, 92; 93, 96; Heldt Prize, 91; OH Acad of Hist Pub Awd, 92; Amos Simpson Awd, 97. **MEMBERSHIPS** Am Assoc for the Advan of Slavic Studies; AHA; Assoc for Women in Slavic Studies; Can Assoc of Slavists; Am Assoc for Ukranian Studies. **RESEARCH** Imperial Russian - social history, Ukrainian and Russian peasants, popular Orthodoxy, and women. **SELECTED PUBLICATIONS** Auth, "Temptress or Virgin? The Precarious Sexual Position of Women in Post-Emancipation Ukrainian Peasant Society", Slavic Rev 49.2 (90): 227-238; coauth, Ukrainians in North America: A Select Bibliography, Univ of Minn, Immigration Hist Res Center, 81; coed, Russia's Women: Accommodation, Resistance, Transformation, Univ of Calif Pr, (Berkeley), 91; auth, "Victims or Actors? Russian Peasant Women and Patriarchy", Peasant Economy, Culture, and Politics of European Russian, 1800-1921, eds Esther Kingston-Mann and Timothy Mixter, Princeton Univ Pr, (91): 177-206; auth, Peasant Russia: Family and Community in the Post-Emancipation Period, Princeton Univ Pr, 91; auth, "Death Ritual Among Russian and Ukrainian Peasants: Linkages between the Living and the Dead", Cultures in Flux: Lower Class Values, Practices, and Resistance in Late Imperial Russian, eds Stephen P. Frank and Mark D. Steinberg, Princeton Univ Pr, (94): 11-33; auth, Possessed: Women, Witches, and Demons in Imperial Russia, Northern Il Univ Pr, (forthcoming); auth, "An Epidemic of Possession in a Moscow Rural Parish in 1909", The Human Tradition in Modern Russia, ed William B. Husband, Scholarly Res, (forthcoming). **CONTACT ADDRESS** Dept Hist, No Illinois Univ, 1425 W Lincoln Hwy, Dekalb, IL 60115-2828. **EMAIL** worobec@niu.edu

WORRALL, ARTHUR JOHN
PERSONAL Born 08/22/1933, Havelock, ON, Canada, m, 1967, 3 children **DISCIPLINE** UNITED STATES COLONIAL HISTORY **EDUCATION** Univ the South, BA, 55; Ind Univ, MA, 64, PhD(hist), 69. **CAREER** From instr to asst prof, 67-77, Assoc Prof Hist, Colo State Univ, 77-82, prof 82-. **MEMBERSHIPS** AHA; Orgn Am Historians; Friends Hist Asn; Am Soc Church Hist. **RESEARCH** Quaker history. **SELECTED PUBLICATIONS** Auth, Quakers in the Colonial Northeast, (Hanover, NH), 82; auth, Quaker Crosscurrents, (Syracuse), 95. **CONTACT ADDRESS** Dept of Hist, Colorado State Univ, Fort Collins, CO 80523. **EMAIL** aworrall@lamar.colostate.edu

WORRALL, JANET EVELYN
PERSONAL Born 12/16/1940, Minneapolis, MN, m, 1967, 3 children **DISCIPLINE** LATIN AMERICAN HISTORY, AMERICAN IMMIGRATION HISTORY **EDUCATION** Hamline Univ, BA, 64; Ind Univ, MA, 66, PhD(hist), 72. **CAREER** From instr to asst prof, 68-78, Assoc Prof Hist, Univ Northern Colo, 78-; assoc prof, 78-85; prof 85-. **MEMBERSHIPS** Conf Latin Am Hist; Immigration Hist Soc; Am Ital Hist Asn. **RESEARCH** Peru; immigration to North and South America. **SELECTED PUBLICATIONS** Auth, La Inmigracion Italiana al Peru: 1860-1914, Instituto Italiano de Cultura, Lima, Peru, 90; auth, Italian Prisoners of War in the U.S. 1943-45, Italian Americans in Transition, American Italian Historical Association, 90, Chapter 23; auth, Prisoners on the Home Front: Community Reactions to German and Italian POWs in Northern Colorado, 194346, Colorado Heritage, 90, 1, 34-47; auth, Reflections on Italian Prisoners of War: Fort Wadsworth, 1943-46, Italiana Americana, 10 spring/Summer 92: 147-155; auth, Work and Community: Italians in Denver, Colorado 1900-1940, Xth Intl Oral History Conference Proceedings, Vol. I. Rio de Janeiro, Brazil: 98; **CONTACT ADDRESS** Univ of No Colorado, Greeley, CO 80639. **EMAIL** jworrall@bentley.unco.edu

WORSFOLD, VICTOR
DISCIPLINE HISTORY **EDUCATION** Harvard Univ, PhD, 75. **CAREER** Assoc prof. **RESEARCH** Ethics; social and political philosophy; philosophy of education. **SELECTED PUBLICATIONS** Auth, Billy Budd: a humanities approach to professional ethics, 94; Tolerance: an antidote to political correctness, 93; MacIntyre and Bloom: Two Complementary Communitarians, Ill State Univ, 92; The Possibility of Liberal Education: MacIntyrean Skepticism, 90; Isreal Scheffler's Ethics: Theory and Practice, Studies Philos Edu, 96; Teaching Democracy Democratically, Edu Theory, 97. **CONTACT ADDRESS** Dept of History, Univ of Texas, Dallas, Richardson, TX 75083-0688. **EMAIL** worsfold@utdallas.edu

WORTHEN, THOMAS
DISCIPLINE ART HISTORY **EDUCATION** Univ IA, PhD. **CAREER** Assoc prof, Drake Univ. **RESEARCH** Europ art and archit; Italian Renaissance. **SELECTED PUBLICATIONS** Auth, articles in The Art Bulletin on Poussin and Tintoretto. **CONTACT ADDRESS** Drake Univ, University Ave, PO Box 2507, Des Moines, IA 50311-4505.

WORTHINGTON, IAN
PERSONAL Born 03/19/1958, Lytham Lanes, United Kingdom, m, 1996, 1 child **DISCIPLINE** CLASSICS, ANCIENT HISTORY **EDUCATION** Univ Hull, BA, 79; Univ Durham, MA, 81; Monash Univ, PhD, 87. **CAREER** Lectr, Univ New England, 88-92; sr lectr, Univ Tasmania, 93-97; prof, Univ Mo Columbia, 98-. **RESEARCH** Greek History, Alexander the Great, Greek Oratory. **SELECTED PUBLICATIONS** Auth, "[Plutarch], X.Or. 848e: A Loeb Mistranslation and Its Effect on Hyperides' Entry Into Athenian Political Life," Electronic Antiquity 3.2 (95); ed, Voice Into Text. Orality and Literacy in Ancient Greece, Brill, 96; rev, of "Theopompus of Chios, History and Rhetoric in the Fourth Century BC," by M. Flower, Classical Rev 46 (96): 179; rev, of "Faces of Power. Alexander's Image and Hellenistic Politics," by A. Stewart, Classical J 91 (96): 210-211; auth, "Alexander the Great and the 'Interests of Historical Accuracy': A Reply," Ancient Hist Bull 13.4 (99): 121-127; auth, "How 'Great' was Alexander?," Ancient Hist Bull 13.2 (99): 39-55; auth, Greek Orators Volume 2: Dinarchus and Hyperides, Aris & Phillips, 99; rev, of "Thucydides and Ancient Simplicity," by G. Crane, Classical Rev 49 (99): 368-369; **CONTACT ADDRESS** Dept Hist, Univ of Missouri, Columbia, 101 Read Hall, Columbia, MO 65211-7500. **EMAIL** worthingtoni@missouri.edu

WORTHY, BARBARA ANN
PERSONAL Born 11/01/1942, Thomaston, GA, s **DISCIPLINE** HISTORY **EDUCATION** Morris Brown Coll, Atlanta GA, BA, 1964; Atlanta Univ, Atlanta GA, MA, 1970; Tulane Univ, New Orleans LA, PhD, 1983. **CAREER** Camilla High School, Camilla GA, social science teacher, 64-69; Southern Univ at New Orleans LA, history teacher, 70-, social sciences dept chair, currently. **HONORS AND AWARDS** Overdyke History Awd, North Louisiana Historical Assn, 1981; one of 14 participants selected from six institutions of higher educ in Louisiana to participate in six-week Intl Curriculum Seminar in Kenya & Tanzania, East Africa, summer, 1985. **MEMBERSHIPS** Mem, Southern Historical Assn, 1983-; mem, Assn for Study of Afro-Amer Life & History, 1984-85; mem, Friends of Amistad, 1986-; bd of dir, Soc for the Study of Afro-LA & History, 1988-; mem, New Orleans League of Women Voters, 1988-; mem, Delta Sigma Theta. **CONTACT ADDRESS** History Department, So Univ, New Orleans, 6400 Press Drive, New Orleans, LA 70126.

WORTMAN, RICHARD
PERSONAL Born 03/24/1938, New York, NY, m, 1960, 1 child **DISCIPLINE** RUSSIAN HISTORY **EDUCATION** Cornell Col, BA, 58; Univ Chicago, PhD, 64. **CAREER** Prof. **SELECTED PUBLICATIONS** Auth, The Crisis of Russian Populism, 67; The Development of a Russian Legal Consciousness, 76; Scenarios of Power: Myth and Ceremony in Russian Monarchy, Vol 1, (95), Vol 2, (00). **CONTACT ADDRESS** Columbia Univ, 420 W 118 St, New York, NY 10027. **EMAIL** ysn3@columbia.edu

WORTMAN, ROY THEODORE
PERSONAL Born 11/23/1940, New York, NY, m, 1967, 2 children **DISCIPLINE** NORTH AMERICAN INDIAN HISTORY, AMERICAN SOCIAL HISTORY **EDUCATION** Colo State Univ, AB, 62; Univ Colo, Boulder, MA, 65; Ohio State Univ, PhD(hist), 71. **CAREER** Woodrow Wilson Found Teaching Fel and Instr, Cent State Univ, Ohio, 65-66; teaching assoc, Ohio State Univ, 67-71, res asst, Child & State Proj, 69-70; from asst prof to assoc prof, 71-87, Prof Hist, Kenyon Col, 87-; Fel, Newberry Library Program in the Humanities, 86; vis res prof, Saskatchewan Indian Federated Col, 92; Fulbright Sr Scholar, Saskatchewan Indian Federated Col, 99-00. **HONORS AND AWARDS** Jr and Sr Schol, Colo State Univ; Doctoral Dissertation Travel Grant, The Ohio State Univ, 70; Citation for Research and Service, Ohio Farmer's Union, 83; Lyndon Baines Johnson-Moody Found Presidential Library Grant, 85; Newberry Library Fac Fel in the Humanities, 86; NEH Fel, 89-90; Occassional Fel, Univ Chicago, Midwest Fac Seminar for independent study for N Am Urban Indian history, 90; Fel, Canadian Plains Res Ctr, 92; Smithsonian Short-Term Fel, 98; Fulbright Fel, 99-00; Kenyon Trustees Tchg Excel Awd, 00. **RESEARCH** Social history; North American Indian history. **SELECTED PUBLICATIONS** Ed, A volunteer wobbly hunter, Hist Musings, fall 71; auth, The Akron Rubber Strike of 1912, In: At the Point of Production: The Local History of the IWW, Greenwood Press, 81; Let the Hunter Speak: Ken Eyster as Hunter, Craftsman, and Unreconstructed Jeffersonian, Cynegeticus, 1/82; Progress and Parity: The Ohio Farmer's Union, 1910-1982, Ohio Farmer's Union, 83; From Syndicalism to Trade Unionism: The IWW in Ohio, 1913-1950, Garland Press, 85; Populism's Stepchildren: The National Farmers Union and Agriculture's Welfare in the Twentieth Century, In: For the General Welfare (co-ed), Peter Lang Publ, 89; auth, "Coughlin in the Countryside", US Cath Hist (95); Gray (Salter), John Hunter, In: Encyclopedia of Native American Civil Rights, Greenwood Press, 97. **CONTACT ADDRESS** Dept of Hist, Kenyon Col, Seitz House, Gambier, OH 43022-9623. **EMAIL** wortman@kenyon.edu

WOSH, PETER J.
PERSONAL Born 11/15/1954, NJ, m **DISCIPLINE** HISTORY **EDUCATION** Rutgers Univ, BA, 76; NYork Univ, MA, 79; PhD, 88. **CAREER** Adj Prof to Dir Archives Prog, NYork Univ, 93-. **HONORS AND AWARDS** Sister m. Claude Lane Awd, Soc of Am Archivists, 93; Arline Custer Awd, Mid-Atlantic Reg Archives, 85; Grant, Louisville Inst, 94; Grant, NY Metropolitan Ref and Res Libraries, 93. **MEMBERSHIPS** Soc of Am Archivists; NY Theol Librarians Asn; NJ State Hist Records Adv Board; Org of Am Hist; Am Hist Asn; Asn for Res on Nonprofit and Voluntary Asn. **SELECTED PUBLICATIONS** Auth, Portraits: An American Bible Society Catalog, New York, 90; ed, Scriptures of the World, New York, 91; coauth, "Smaller Archives and Professional Development: Some New York Stories," American Archivist, 92; auth, "American Bible Society Record," in Popular Religious Magazines of the United States, Greenwood Press, 94; auth, Spreading the word: The bible business in Nineteenth Century America, Cornell Univ Press, 94; auth, "From 'Colored Mission' to community Institution: St. Mark's Episcopal Church in Plainfield, 1903-1991," New Jersey History, (94): 17-38; auth, "A 'Special collection' in Nineteenth-Century New York: The American Bible Society and Its Library," Libraries & culture, (97): 324-336; auth, "Going Postal," American Archivist, (98): 220-239; auth, "Turing Pro: reflections on the Career of J. Franklin Jameson," Provenance XV, (97): 87-102; auth, Protestants At Play: Religion, Recreation, and Resorts in Modern America, Cornell Univ Press, forthcoming. **CONTACT ADDRESS** Dept Hist, New York Univ, 93 Washington Square S, New York, NY 10012-1098. **EMAIL** pw1@is.nyu.edu

WOSK, JULIE
PERSONAL Born 06/05/1944, Chicago, IL, m, 2000 **DISCIPLINE** ENGLISH, ART HISTORY **EDUCATION** Wash Univ, St Louis, BA, 66; Harvard Univ, MAT, 67; Univ Wis, PhD, 74. **CAREER** Prof, SUNY Maritime Col, 75-. **HONORS AND AWARDS** Phi Beta Kappa; Mortar Board; NEH Fel in Art Hist; Sloan Found Grant. **MEMBERSHIPS** Soc for the Hist of Technol, Col Art Asn, Int Comt for the Hist of Technol, Soc for Lit and Sci. **RESEARCH** Art and technology; literature and technology; representations of women and machines; society for literature and science. **SELECTED PUBLICATIONS** Auth, Breaking Frame: Technology and the Visual Arts in the Nineteenth Century, Rutgers Univ Press (92); auth, "Manhole Covers and the Myths of Am," Design Book Rev (MIT Press) (winter/spring 95); auth, "Brunel Meets Brubelleschi," Am Heritage of Invention and Technology (summer 95); auth, "Mutant Materials in Contemporary Design," Design Issues (spring 96); auth, Women and the Machine: Representations from the Spinning Wheel to the electronic Age, Oxford Univ Press (2001). **CONTACT ADDRESS** Dept Humanities, SUNY, Maritime Col, 6 Pennyfield Ave, Bronx, NY 10465-4127.

WOZNIAK, JUDITH
PERSONAL Born 12/23/1948, NJ, d **DISCIPLINE** HISTORY **EDUCATION** Caldwell Col, BA, 70; Seton Hall Univ, MA, 71; Luth Theol Sem Phil, MDiv, 88; SUNY-Buffalo, PhD, 95. **CAREER** Lectr, Cleveland State Univ, 94- ; pastor, St Paul Luth Church, Ravinna, OH, 99- . **MEMBERSHIPS** AHA **RESEARCH** Renaissance, Reformation, Old regime France, Church state & culture. **SELECTED PUBLICATIONS** Auth, A Time for Peace: The Ecclesiastes of Erasmus, Univ Press of S, (96). **CONTACT ADDRESS** Dept Hist, Cleveland State Univ, 1983 E 2 St, Cleveland, OH 44115-2403. **EMAIL** JWOZN26928@aol.com

WOZNIUK, VLADIMIR
PERSONAL Born Munich, Germany **DISCIPLINE** HISTORY **EDUCATION** Univ Conn, BA, 75; Univ Va, MA, 80; PhD, 84; Yale Univ, MA, 82. **CAREER** Asst Prof, Lafayette Col, 86-90; Prof, Western New England Col, 90-. **HONORS AND AWARDS** Thomas Jefferson Found Fel, 79-80; Inst for Study of World Polit Fel, 82-83. **SELECTED PUBLICATIONS** Rev, "Democracy from Scratch: Opposition and Regime in the New Russian Revolution," by Steven M Fish, Perspectives on Polit Sci, 25 (96): 162; auth, "In Search of Ideology: The Politics of Religion and Nationalism in the New Russia," Nationalities Papers, 25 (97): 195-210; auth, "The Wisdom of Solomon as Political Theology," J of Church and State, 39 (97): 657-680; auth, "Vladimir S Soloviev and the Politics of Human Rights," J of Church and State, 41 (99): 33-50;

auth, Politics, Law and Morality: Essays by V S Soloviev, Yale Univ Pr (New Haven, CT), 00. **CONTACT ADDRESS** Dept Hist, Western New England Col, 1215 Wilbraham Rd, Springfield, MA 01119. **EMAIL** vwozniuk@wnec.edu

WRESZIN, MICHAEL
PERSONAL Born 10/09/1926, Glen Ridge, NJ, m, 1951, 2 children **DISCIPLINE** MODERN AMERICAN HISTORY **EDUCATION** Syracuse Univ, BA, 51; Colgate Univ, MA, 55; Brown Univ, PhD(hist), 61. **CAREER** Instr Am hist, Wayne State Univ, 59-62; asst prof, Brown Univ, 62-64; instr, 62-63, asst prof, 64-66, assoc prof, 66-80, Prof Am Hist, Queens Col, NY, 80-. **MEMBERSHIPS** AHA; Orgn Am Historians; Am Studies Asn. **RESEARCH** American political history of the twentieth century; American intellectual history. **SELECTED PUBLICATIONS** Auth, Letters + Response to Phillips,William Comments on my Biography of Macdonald, Dwight, Partisan Rev, Vol 0062, 95; The Lively Arts, Amer Hist Rev, Vol 0102, 97. **CONTACT ADDRESS** Dept of Hist, Queens Col, CUNY, 6530 Kissena Blvd, Flushing, NY 11367-1597. **EMAIL** mwreszin@aol.com

WRIGHT, DONALD R.
PERSONAL Born 08/03/1944, Richmond, Indiana, w, 2 children **DISCIPLINE** HISTORY **EDUCATION** DePauw Univ, BA; Univ Ind, MA, PhD. **CAREER** Prof. **HONORS AND AWARDS** Excellence Tchg Awd, 89; Distinguished Teaching Professor, 90; NEH Fellowship, 82; Fulbright-Hzys Fellowship, 74. **MEMBERSHIPS** African Historical Assn; African Studies Assn; Mande Studies Assn. **RESEARCH** Senegzmbiz; African Diaspora; Atlantic World. **SELECTED PUBLICATIONS** Auth, The World and a Very Small Place in Africa, 97; African Americans in the Early Republic, 93; African Americans in the Colonial Era 2nd ed, 00, 89. **CONTACT ADDRESS** Dept of History, SUNY, Col at Cortland, PO Box 2000, Cortland, NY 13045-0900. **EMAIL** wrightd@syncorua.cortland.edu

WRIGHT, GEORGIA SOMMERS
PERSONAL m, 1967, 1 child **DISCIPLINE** ART HISTORY **EDUCATION** Swarthmore Col, BA 59; Columbia Univ, MA 61, PhD 66. **CAREER** Limestone Sculpture Provenance Project, co-dir 95-; Amer Univ, Paris, vis prof 90; Stanford Univ, vis prof 86-88; Mills College, asst prof 68-76; Univ Cal, Davis, vis lect 67-68; Univ Cal, Berk, vis lect 66-67. **HONORS AND AWARDS** Chevalier dans l'Order des Palmes Academiques. **MEMBERSHIPS** HIS; ICMA; NCIS **RESEARCH** Gothic sculpture **SELECTED PUBLICATIONS** Auth, Three articles in press for Dictionary of Art, MacMillan; Videos, Light On the Stones: The Medieval Church of Vezelay, 91, Three English Cathedrals: Norwich, Lincoln, Wells, 94, Medieval Sculpture and Nuclear Science, 96; Gothic Sculpture, Dictionary of the Middle Ages, Scribner, 90. **CONTACT ADDRESS** 105 Vicente Rd, Berkeley, CA 94705. **EMAIL** wrightga@msn.com

WRIGHT, GWENDOLYN
PERSONAL Born Chicago, IL, m, 1982, 2 children **DISCIPLINE** UNITED STATES HISTORY; ARCHITECTURAL AND URBAN HISTORY **EDUCATION** NYork Univ, BA, 69; Univ Ca, PhD, 80. **CAREER** Prof. **HONORS AND AWARDS** Getty fel; Stanford Humanities Inst Fel; NEH fel. **MEMBERSHIPS** OAH; CAA; Soc of Am Historians; Soc of Architectural Historians. **RESEARCH** Urban culture; transnational influences housing. **SELECTED PUBLICATIONS** Auth, Moralism and the Model Home: Domestic Architecture and Cultural Conflict in Chicago 1873-1913, 80; Building the Dream: A Social History of American Housing, 81; The History of History in American Schools of Architecture 1865-1975, 91; The Politics of Design in French Colonial Urbanism, 91. **CONTACT ADDRESS** Dept of History, Columbia Col, New York, 2960 Broadway, New York, NY 10027-6902. **EMAIL** gw8@columbia.edu

WRIGHT, HARRISON MORRIS
PERSONAL Born 10/06/1928, Philadelphia, PA, m, 1957, 5 children **DISCIPLINE** AFRICAN HISTORY **EDUCATION** Harvard Univ, AB, 50, MA, 53, PhD(hist), 57. **CAREER** From instr to assoc prof, 57-68, chmn dept, 68-79, prof hist, 68-79, Provost, 79-84, Acting Pres, 82, Isaac H. Clothier Prof of Hist & Int Rel, 87- , emeritus, 93- , Swarthmore Col; Ford Foreign Area training fel, England & Ghana, 61-62; Am Philos Soc res grant, S Africa, 66-67. **MEMBERSHIPS** AHA; Conf Brit Studies; African Studies Asn; Newport Hist Soc; Bd of Dir, Newport Hist Soc, 73-89; Bd of Counc, Hist Soc of Penn, 84-91, chemn, 89-91, emeritus, 91- ; Bd of Trustees, RI Hist Soc, 98- . **RESEARCH** South Africa; British Empire. **SELECTED PUBLICATIONS** Auth, New Zealand, 1769-1840: Early Years of Western Contact, Harvard Univ, 59; ed, The New Imperialism, Analysis of Late Nineteenth Century Expansion, Heath, 61, 2nd ed, 76; auth & contribr, British West Africa, Duke Univ, 66; auth, Imperialism: The Word and Its Meaning, Social Res, winter 67; ed, Sir James Rose Innes: Selected Correspondence, 1884-1902, Van Riebeeck Soc, 72; auth, The Burden of the President: Liberal-Radical Controversy Over Southern African History, D Philip & Collings, 77; The Burden of the Present and its Critics, Social Dynamics, 6/80. **CONTACT ADDRESS** PO Box 209, Jamestown, RI 02835.

WRIGHT, JAMES EDWARD
PERSONAL Born 08/16/1939, Madison, WI, m, 1984, 3 children **DISCIPLINE** AMERICAN HISTORY **EDUCATION** Univ Wis-Platteville, BS, 64; Univ Wis-Madison MS, 66, PhD, 69. **CAREER** Asst prof, 69-72, assoc prof, 74-80, prof hist, Dartmouth Col, 80-, assoc dean fac, 81-85; dean of fac, 89-97; provost, 97-98; pres, 98-. **HONORS AND AWARDS** Soc Sci Res Coun grant, 70-71; Guggenheim fel, 73-74; sr historian, Great Plains Hist Proj, Univ Mid-Am, 76-78; Charles Warren fel, Harvard Univ, 80-81. **MEMBERSHIPS** Orgn Am Historians; Western Hist Assn; Soc Sci Hist Assn. **RESEARCH** American political history; frontier movement; United States, 1877-1914. **SELECTED PUBLICATIONS** Auth, The Galena Lead District, State Hist Soc Wis, 67; co-ed, The West of the American People, Peacock, 70; auth, The Ethnocultural Model of Voting, Am Behav Sci, 6/73; The Politics of Populism, Yale Univ, 74; auth & co-ed, Great Plains Experience: Readings in the History of a Region, Univ Mid-Am, 78; auth, The Progressive Yankees: Republican Reformers in New Hampshire, 1906-1916, University Press New England, 87. **CONTACT ADDRESS** Dartmouth Col, Parkhurst Hall, Hanover, NH 03755-3529. **EMAIL** james.wright@dartmouth.edu

WRIGHT, JOHN ROBERT
PERSONAL Born 10/20/1936, Carbondale, IL, s **DISCIPLINE** PATRISTIC & MEDIEVAL CHURCH HISTORY **EDUCATION** Univ of the South, BA, 58; Emory Univ, MA, 59; Gen Theol Sem, MDiv, 63; Oxford Univ, DPhil, 67. **CAREER** Instr church hist, Episcopal Theol Sch, MA, 66-68; asst prof ecclesiastical hist, 68-72, prof church hist, Gen Theol Sem, 72-, res assoc, Pontifical Inst Mediaeval Studies, Toronto, 76 & 81; mem, Comn Faith & Order, World Coun Churches & Standing Ecumenical Comn of Episcopal Church, 77-; mem, Anglican/Roman Cath Consult in US, 70-; res scholar, Huntington Libr, 77; Canon Theologian to the Bishop of New York; Theological Consultant to Ecumenical Office of the Episcopal Church. **HONORS AND AWARDS** Honorary DD Episcopal Theological Seminary of the Southwest, Austin, TX; Honorary DD, Trinity Lutheran Seminary, Columbus, OH; Honorary D. Cn.L. The University of the South, Sewanee, TN; Patriarchal crosses of distinction from the Ecumenical Patriarch of Constantinople, the Russian Orthodox Patriarch of Moscow, the Armenian Patriarch of Jerusalem, and the Syrian Orthodox Patriarch of Antioch, also from the Catholics of the Malankara Orthodox Church of India; Life Fellow of the Royal Historical Society, London; Chaplain of the Royal Order of St. John of Jerusalem. **MEMBERSHIPS** AHA; Mediaeval Acad Am; Am Soc Church Hist; Church Hist Soc; Royal Historical Society; Anglican Society (Pres.); North American Academy of Ecumenists (Pres.) **RESEARCH** Fourteenth century church-state and Anglo-Papal relations; Walter Reynolds, Archbishop of Canterbury 1314-1327; Lambert of Auxerre, mid-thirteenth century Dominican commentator on Aristotle. **SELECTED PUBLICATIONS** Ed, Handbook of American Orthodoxy, Forward Movement, 72; co-ed, Episcopalians and Roman Catholics: Can They Ever Get Together?, Dimension, 72; coauth, A Pope for All Christians?, Paulist, 76 & SPCK, 77; auth, A Communion of Communions: One Eucharistic Fellowship, Seabury, 79; The Church and The English Crown 1305-1334, Pontifical Inst Mediaeval Studies, Toronto, 80; The Canterbury Statement and the Five Priesthoods, One in Christ, Vol 11: 3 & Anglican Theol Rev, Vol 57: 4; Anglicans and the Papacy, J Ecumenical Studies, Vol 13: 3; The Accounts of the Constables of Bordeaux 1381-1390, with Particular Notes on their Ecclesiastical and Liturgical Significance, Mediaeval Studies, 42: 238-307; An Anglican Commentary on Selected Documents of Vatican II, Ecumenical Trends, Vol 9: 8 & 9; Quadrilateral at One Hundred, Mowbray, 88; Prayer Book Spirituality, Church Publishing, 89; The Anglican Tradition, SPCK/Fortress, 91; Readings for the Daily Office from the Early Church, Church Publishing, 91; They Still Speak: Readings for the Lesser Feasts, Church Publishing, 93. **CONTACT ADDRESS** General Theol Sem, 175 9th Ave, New York, NY 10011-4924. **EMAIL** wright@gts.edu

WRIGHT, MARCIA
DISCIPLINE EASTERN AND SOUTHERN AFRICAN HISTORY **EDUCATION** Wellesley, BA, 57; PhD, 66; Yale, MA, 58; London, PhD, 66. **CAREER** Hist, Columbia Univ. **SELECTED PUBLICATIONS** Coed, African Women and the Law: Historical Perspectives, 82; auth, German Missions in Tanganyika, 1891-1941, 71; Strategies of Slaves & Women: Life-Stories from East/Central Africa, 93; auth, Maji Maji Prophecy and Historiography, 94; auth, An Old Nationalist in New Nationalist Times, Zambia: 1948-1963, 97; auth, Historical Instrustors, Zuler Woman, 3rd ed, 99. **CONTACT ADDRESS** Columbia Univ, 1180 Amsterdam, New York, NY 10027-6902.

WRIGHT, SCOTT KENNETH
PERSONAL Born 10/12/1942, St. Paul, MN, m, 1967, 4 children **DISCIPLINE** AMERICAN HISTORY **EDUCATION** Univ Minn, BA, 63, MA, 68, PhD(Am studies), 73. **CAREER** Acquisitions librn, 68-71, assoc dir & ref librn, 71-74, libr dir, 74-80, asst prof hist, col St Thomas, 78-, Fulbright lectr, Kyushu Univ & Seinan Gakuin Univ, Fukuoka, Japan, 79-80. **MEMBERSHIPS** Orgn Am Historians; Am Studies Asn; Popular Cult Asn. **RESEARCH** American popular culture. **SELECTED PUBLICATIONS** Coauth, Slide & sound projects in history, AV Instr, 11/73; auth, The role of Indiana in the works of George Barr McCutcheon, Ind English, fall 80; contribr, A Bibliographic Guide to Midwestern Literature, Univ Iowa, 81. **CONTACT ADDRESS** Hist Dept, Univ of St. Thomas, Minnesota, 2115 Summit Ave, Saint Paul, MN 55105-1096. **EMAIL** skwright@stthomas.edu

WRIGHT, THEODORE P., JR.
PERSONAL Born 04/12/1926, Port Washington, NY, m, 1967, 3 children **DISCIPLINE** ASIAN STUDIES, POLITICAL SCIENCE **EDUCATION** Swarthmore Col, BA, 49; Yale Univ, MA, 51, PhD, 57. **CAREER** Instr, Asst Prof, Assoc Prof, Bates Col, 55-65; Assoc Prof, Prof, Emeritus Prof, State Univ of NY at Albany, 65-95. **HONORS AND AWARDS** Phi Beta Kappa, Fulbright Awds, 61, 63-64, 83-84, 90-91; Am Inst of Indian Stud Awd, 69-70; ACLS/Soc Sci Res Counc Awd, 74-75. **MEMBERSHIPS** Asn for Asian Stud; NY Conf on Asian Stud; American Council for the Study of Islamic Societies; Colombia Univ Fac Seminar on S Asia; Harvard Univ Fac Seminar on S Asia; S Asian Muslim Stud Asn (pres). **RESEARCH** Politics of Muslim minority in India and of Muhajirin in Pakistan. **SELECTED PUBLICATIONS** Auth, American Support of Free Elections Abroad, 64; auth, US Perception of Islam in the Post Cold War Era: the Case of Pakistan, Pakistan J of Am Stud, 11:2, 28-39, 93; auth, Can there be a melting pot in Pakistan? Interprovincial marriage and national integration, Contemp S Asia, 3:2, 131-44, 94; auth, Impact of the Iraqi Aggression on Kuwait on South Asian Muslims, Int Conf on the Effects of the Iraqi Aggression on the State of Kuwait, Vol 1, 187-200, 96; authm, A New Demand for Muslim Reservations in India, Asian Survey, XXXVII, 9, 852-858, 9/97; auth, The BJV/Shiv Sena Coalition and the Muslim Minority in Maharashtra: the Interface of Foreign and Domestic Conflict, J of S Asian & Mid-E Stud, XXI, 2, 41-50, 98; auth, The Indian State and its Muslim Minority: from Dependence to Self-Reliance?, India: Fifty Years of Democracy & Development, APH Pubs, 313-339, 98. **CONTACT ADDRESS** 27 Vandenburg Ln, Latham, NY 12110. **EMAIL** wright15@juno.com

WRIGHT, THOMAS C.
DISCIPLINE HISTORY **EDUCATION** Univ Calif Berkeley, PhD, 71. **CAREER** Prof, Univ Nev Las Vegas. **RESEARCH** Latin American history. **SELECTED PUBLICATIONS** Auth, Latin America in the Era of the Cuban Revolution, Univ NY, 91; Landowners and Reform in Chile: The Sociedad Nacional de Agricultura, 1919-1940, Urbana, 82; co-auth, Flight from Chile: Voices of Exile, Albuquerque, 98; co-ed, Food, Politics, and Society in Latin America, Lincoln, 85. **CONTACT ADDRESS** History Dept, Univ of Nevada, Las Vegas, 4505 Md Pky, Las Vegas, NV 89154.

WRIGHT, WILLIAM JOHN
PERSONAL Born 04/07/1942, Chicago, IL, m, 1964, 2 children **DISCIPLINE** HISTORY **EDUCATION** Stetson Univ, BA, 64, MA, 65; Ohio State Univ, PhD(hist), 69. **CAREER** Asst prof, 69-75, Assoc Prof Hist, Univ Tenn, Chattanooga, 75-, Nat Endowment for Humanities fel, 79-80. **MEMBERSHIPS** Am Soc Reformation; Sixteenth Cent Studies Conf. **RESEARCH** Early modern European History. **SELECTED PUBLICATIONS** Auth, Capitalism, The State, and the Lutheran Reformation -- Athens O.: Ohio Univ Press, 88; auth, Economy Without a House--Economics of the Poor in Nuremberg in the Late 1400s--German, Amer Hist Rev, Vol 0100, 95; Ludwig-Iv, Landgrave of Hessen-Marburg 1537-1604--Land Division and Lutheranism in Hesse-German, Amer Hist Rev, Vol 0098, 93; Commerce and Cliques--Merchants of Cologne Trading in 16th-Century England--German, Amer Hist Rev, Vol 0097, 92; Between Fasting and Feasting--Hospital-Care in Munster 1540-1650, Amer Hist Rev, Vol 0101, 96. **CONTACT ADDRESS** Dept of Hist, Univ of Tennessee, Chattanooga, Chattanooga, TN 37401.

WROBEL, DAVID M.
PERSONAL Born 06/24/1964, London, England **DISCIPLINE** HISTORY **EDUCATION** Univ Kent-Canterbury, BA, 85; Ohio Univ, MA, 87, PhD, 91. **CAREER** Vis instr to vis asst prof hist, Col Wooster, 90-92; vis asst prof hist, Hartwick Col, 92-94; asst prof to assoc prof hist, Widener Univ, 94-. **HONORS AND AWARDS** Caillouette Fellow, Huntington Library, Summer 97; Newberry Library Fellow, 96; Am Phil Soc fellowship, 94; Mayer Fund Fellow, Huntington Library, 93. **MEMBERSHIPS** Am Hist Asn, West Hist Asn, SW Soc Sci Asn, Phi Alpha Theta Hist Honors Soc **RESEARCH** Am cult intellectual hist. **SELECTED PUBLICATIONS** Auth, The End of American Exceptionalism: Frontier Anxiety from the Old West to the New Deal, Univ Press Kans, 93; co-ed, Many Wests: Essays on Regional Consciousness, Univ Press Kans, 97; auth, "The View from Philadelphia," in Pacific Hist Rev, Aug 98; auth, "Beyond the Frontier-Region Dichotomy," in Pacific Hist Rev, Aug 96; auth, "Early Reflections on Teaching Western History," in Magazine of Hist, Fall 94; auth, "Frederick Jackson Turner," in Dictionary of Literary Biography, Nineteenth Century Western Writers, Bruccoli, Clark, 98; auth, "Arid Lands Thesis," "Frontier Thesis," "Historiography, Western," "New Western History," Safety Valve Theory," "Frederick Jackson Turner," and "West as Region School," in The Encyclopedia of the West, Macmillan, 96; auth, "Don Laughlin," in Introduction

to Casino Management, Kendall/Hunt, 95. **CONTACT ADDRESS** History Dept, Widener Univ, Pennsylvania, 1 Univ Pl, Chester, PA 19013. **EMAIL** david.m.wrobel@widener.edu

WU, PEI-YI

PERSONAL Born 12/03/1927, Nanking, China **DISCIPLINE** CHINESE LITERATURE, INTELLECTUAL HISTORY **EDUCATION** Nat Cent Univ, Nanking, AB, 50; Boston Univ, MA, 52; Columbia Univ, PhD(Chinese lit), 69. **CAREER** Ibstr Chinese, Army Lang Sch, 53-58; res linguist, Univ Calif, Berkeley, 58-59; preceptor, Columbia Univ, 62-63; instr, 63-66, lectr, 66-67; vis assoc prof, 67-69, Assoc Prof Chinese, Queens Col, 69-, Mem univ fac senate, City Univ New York, 71-74; VIS Assoc Prof, Columbia Univ, 72-; Nat Endowment for Humanities fel, 74. **MEMBERSHIPS** Am Orient Soc; Asn Asian Studies. **RESEARCH** Chinese autobiography and myth. **SELECTED PUBLICATIONS** Auth, Memories of Kai-Feng--Meng,Yuan-Lao Description of the City in Tung-Ching Meng Hua Lu, New Lit Hist, Vol 0025, 94. **CONTACT ADDRESS** Dept of Class & Orient Lang, Queens Col, CUNY, 6530 Kissena Blvd, Flushing, NY 11367.

WUNDER, JOHN R.

PERSONAL Born 01/07/1945, Vinton, IA, m, 1969, 2 children **DISCIPLINE** HISTORY **EDUCATION** Univ Iowa, BA, 67; MA, 70; JD, 70; Univ Wash, PhD, 74. **CAREER** Vis asst prof, Lewis & Clark Col, 74; asst prof, Case Western Reserve Univ, 74-78; vis assoc prof, Columbia Univ, 76; from asst to assoc prof, Tex Tech Univ, 78-84; dir, Ethnic Studies Prog, Tex Tech Univ, 80-82; prof & head of dept of hist, Clemson Univ, 84-88; acting head, dept of philos and relig, Clemson Univ, 86-87; dir, prof of hist, Univ of Nebr Lincoln, 88-; Center for Great Plains Studies, Univ of Nebr Lincoln, 88-97; assoc dean, col of arts and sci, Univ of Nebr Lincoln, 90-93; Bicentennial Chair, Renvall Inst, Univ of Helsinki, 95-96 vis fel, Australian Nat Univ, 97. **HONORS AND AWARDS** Annis Chaikin Sorensen Awd for Teaching Excellence, Univ of Nebr, 94; best book prize, Phi Alpha theta, 95; Bicentennial Chair Fulbright Prof, Univ of Helsinki, 95-96; Fel in Residence, Humanities Res Center, Australian Nat Univ, 97. **MEMBERSHIPS** Am Hist Asn, Orgn of Am Historians, Western Hist Asn, Am Soc for Legal Hist, Fulbright Alumni Asn, Nebr State Hist Soc. **RESEARCH** History of the American West, Native American history, American legal history, history of race and law, comparative world history, history of indigenous peoples. **SELECTED PUBLICATIONS** Auth, native Americans and the Law: Contemporary and Historical Perspectives on American Indian Rights, Freedomes, and Sovereignty (6 vols), Garland Press, 96; auth, Law and the Great Plains: Essays on the Legal History of the Heartland, Greenwood Press, 96; co-ed, Americans View Their Dust Bowl Experience, Univ Press of Colo, 99; coauth, "Of Lethal Places and Lethal Essays," Am Hist Rev 104 (99): 1229-1234. **CONTACT ADDRESS** Dept Hist, Univ of Nebraska, Lincoln, 612 Oldfather Hall, Lincoln, NE 68588-0327. **EMAIL** jwunder@unlserve.unl.edu

WUNDERLI, RICHARD M.

PERSONAL Born 11/15/1940, Salt Lake City, UT, m, 1967, 1 child **DISCIPLINE** HISTORY **EDUCATION** Univ Utah, BA 64, MA 66; Univ Cal Berk, PhD 75. **CAREER** Univ Colo, asst prof, assoc prof, prof, 76-, ch of dept, 84-90, 93-96. **HONORS AND AWARDS** Outstanding Teacher; 1st Annual Bk Awd for U of Colo. **MEMBERSHIPS** MAA **RESEARCH** Medieval History **SELECTED PUBLICATIONS** Auth, London Church Courts and Society on the Eve of Reformation, Cambridge MA, 81; Peasant Fires, Bloomington IN, 92; many articles. **CONTACT ADDRESS** Dept of History, PO Box 7150, Colorado Springs, CO 80933-7150. **EMAIL** rwunderl@mail.uccs.edu

WUNSCH, JAMES STEVENSON

PERSONAL Born 09/27/1946, Detroit, MI, m, 1983, 3 children **DISCIPLINE** POLITICAL SCIENCE, AFRICAN STUDIES **EDUCATION** Duke Univ, Hist, BA, 68; Ind Univ, Polit Sci, MA, 70, African Stud/Polit Sci, PhD, 74. **CAREER** Assoc instr, Polit Sci, Ind Univ, 69-70; res fel, Inst African Stud, Univ Ghana, 71-72; fac, Creighton Univ, 73; to asst prof 73-78; to assoc prof 78-86; to prof 81-; vis sch, Univ Mich, 74; assoc investr, Nat Inst Mental Health Res Proj, 75-76; eval spec, US Dept Agric, Off Int Prog, 78-79; soc sci anal, Off Rural Develop & Develop Admin, US Agency Int Develop, 78-80; assoc investr, Nat Sci Found, 86; sr fel, Ind Univ, 85-86; vis assoc prof, Polit Sci, Ind Univ, 85-86; chr, Dept Polit Sci, Creighton Univ, 83-92; act ch, Creighton Univ, 96-97; act dir, Dept Polit Sci & Int Stud, Creighton Univ, 96-97; chr, Polit Sci/Int Stud, Creighton Univ, 97-; dir, African Stud Prog, Creighton Univ, 98-. **HONORS AND AWARDS** Phi Beta Kappa, Duke Univ; Fulbright Fel, Ghana, 71-72; Council on For Rel Fel, 78-79; NEH Fel, 78, 82; Senior Fel, Am Philo Soc, 00-01. **MEMBERSHIPS** Am Polit Sci Asn; Midwest Polit Sci Asn; African Stud Asn; Policy Stud Org **SELECTED PUBLICATIONS** "Review Essay: Public Administration and Local Government," African Stud Rev, 97; coauth, "Regime Transformation from Below: Decentralization, Local Governance and Democratic Reform in Nigeria," Studies in Comp Develop, Winter, 96; coauth, "Decentralization, Local Government and Primary Health Care in Nigeria: An Analytical Study," Jour of African Policy Stud, 95; coauth, The Failure of the Centralized State: Institutions and Self Governance in Africa, Inst Contemp Stud, 95; "African Political Reforms and International Assistance: What Can and Should Be Done?", Africa: Develop & Publ Policy, Macmillan Press, 94. **CONTACT ADDRESS** Dept Polit Sci, Creighton Univ, Omaha, NE 68178. **EMAIL** jwunsch@creighton.edu

WYATT, DAVID KENT

PERSONAL Born 09/21/1937, Fitchburg, MA, m, 1959, 3 children **DISCIPLINE** SOUTHEAST ASIAN HISTORY **EDUCATION** Harvard Univ, AB, 59; Boston Univ, MA, 60; Cornell Univ, PhD(hist), 66. **CAREER** Lectr Southeast Asian hist, Sch Oriental & African Studies, Univ London, 64-68; asst prof hist, Univ Mich, Ann Arbor, 68-69; assoc prof, 69-76, prof hist, Cornell Univ, 76-; Vis Fulbright lectr hist, Univ Malaya, 66-67; sr fel, Nat Endowment Humanities, 75-76; dir, Cornell Univ Southeast Asia Prog, 76-79; ch, Dept of Hist, 83-87. **HONORS AND AWARDS** Elected honorary member, Siam Society, 97; pres, Assn Asian Studies, 93-94. **MEMBERSHIPS** Siam Soc; Asn Asian Studies; Malayan Br Royal Asiatic Soc. **RESEARCH** History of Thailand and Laos. **SELECTED PUBLICATIONS** Auth, The Politics of Reform in Thailand, Yale Univ, 69; coauth, Hikayat Patani: The Story of Patani, Martinus Nijhoff, 70; In Search of Southeast Asia: A Modern History, Praeger, 70, 2nd ed, U of Hawaii Press, 88; auth, The Crystal Sands: The Chronicles of Nagara Sri Dharrmaraja, Cornell Univ, 75; ed, The Short History of the Kings of Siam, by Jeremias van Vliet (1640), Siam Soc, Bangkok, 75; Studies in Thai History, Silkworm Bks, 94; auth, Studies in Thai History, Silkworm Books, 95; The Chiang Mai Chronicle, Silkworm, 95; coauth, The Chiang Mai Chronicle, 2nd ed, Silkworm Press, 98; auth, The Royal Chronicles of the Kings of Ayutthaya, 00. **CONTACT ADDRESS** Dept of History, Cornell Univ, Mcgraw Hall, Ithaca, NY 14853-4601. **EMAIL** dkw4@cornell.edu

WYATT, DON

PERSONAL Born 04/12/1953, Alton, IL, m, 1991, 2 children **DISCIPLINE** HISTORY **EDUCATION** Beloit Col, AB, 75; Harvard Univ, MA, 78; PhD, 84. **CAREER** Vis Lecturer, Clark Univ, 84; Vis Asst Prof, Wheaton Col, 85; Lecturer, Harvard Univ, 85-86; Asst Prof to Prof, Middlebury Col, 87-. **HONORS AND AWARDS** Marquis Who's Who in Am, marquis Who's Who in the World. **MEMBERSHIPS** Am Hist Asn, Asn for Asian Studies, Conf on Asian Hist, Intl Soc for Intellectual Hist, N England Hist Asn, Phi Beta Kappa, Vt Hist Soc, World Hist Asn. **RESEARCH** Chinese intellectual history and geography; Chinese philosophy; Philosophy of history. **SELECTED PUBLICATIONS** Auth, "The Invention of the Northern Song," in Political Frontiers, Ethnic Boundaries, and Human Geographies in Chinese History, Curzon Press, forthcoming; co-ed, "Political Frontiers, Ethnic Boundaries, and Human Geographies in Chinese History, Curzon Press, forthcoming; auth, "Bonds of Certain Consequence: The Personal Responses to Concubinage of Wang Anshi and Sima Guang," in Presence and presentation: Women in the Chinese Literati Tradition, St Martin's Press, 99; auth, The Recluse of Loyang: Shao Yung and the Moral Evolution of Early Sung Thought, Univ Hawaii Press, 96; auth, "Historicism, Contextualization, and the Western Reception of Master Shao," Intellectual News: Review of the International Society for Intellectual History, (99): 26-36; auth, "Ma Huan," in The Encyclopedia of Historians and Historical Writing, Fitzroy Dearborn Pub, 99; auth, "Kong-Zi (Confucius)," in The Encyclopedia of Historians and Historical Writing, Fitzroy Dearborn Pub, 99; rev, of "Confucian Moral Self Cultivation," by Philip J. Ivanhoe, China Review International, (99): 174-179. **CONTACT ADDRESS** Dept Hist, Middlebury Col, Middlebury, VT 05753-6200. **EMAIL** wyatt@middlebury.edu

WYATT-BROWN, BERTRAM

PERSONAL Born 03/09/1932, Harrisburg, PA, m, 1962, 1 child **DISCIPLINE** HISTORY **EDUCATION** Univ of the South, BA, 53; Cambridge Univ, BA, 57; MA, 61; Johns Hopkins Univ, PhD, 63. **CAREER** Asst Prof, Colo State Univ, 62-64; Asst Prof, Univ Colo, 64-66; Asst to Prof, Case Western Reserve Univ, 66-83; Vis Assoc Prof, Univ Wisc, 69-70; Prof, Univ Fla, 83-. **HONORS AND AWARDS** PBK, 52; Danforth Foundation Fel, 53-62; Ramsdell Prize, 71; Guggenheim Fel, 74-75; Davis Ctr Fel, 77-78; Finalist Pulitzer, 83; Finalist am Book Awd, 83; DDL, Univ of South, 85; Nat Endowment for the Humanities, 85-86; Nat Hum Ctr Fel, 89-90, 98-99. **MEMBERSHIPS** southern Hist Asn, Tucker Soc, Soc for Historians of Early Republic, Org Am Historians. **RESEARCH** southern cultural and social history, chiefly 19th century. **SELECTED PUBLICATIONS** Ed, The American People in the Antebellum South, Pendulum Press, 73; auth, southern Honor: Ethics and Behavior in the Old South, oxford Univ press, 82; auth, Yankee Saints and southern Sinners, Louisiana State Univ Press, 85; auth, The House of Percy: Honor, Melancholy and Imagination in a southern Family, Oxford Univ Press, 94; auth, the Literary Percys: Family History, Gender and Legend, Univ of Ga Press, 94; auth, Lewis Tappan and Evangelical War against slavery, Louisiana State Univ press, 97; auth, the shaping of southern Culture: Honor, Grace, and War, 1760s-1890s, Univ of NC Press, 00; auth, hearts of darkness: The Evolution of Southern Literary Alienation, Louisiana State Univ Press, forthcoming. **CONTACT ADDRESS** Dept History, Univ of Florida, PO Box 117320, Gainesville, FL 32611-7320. **EMAIL** bwyattb@history.ufl.edu

WYMAN, DAVID S.

PERSONAL Born 03/06/1929, Weymouth, MA, m, 1950, 2 children **DISCIPLINE** RECENT AMERICAN HISTORY **EDUCATION** Boston Univ, AB, 51; Plymouth State Col, MEd, 61; Harvard Univ, AM, 62, PhD(hist), 66. **CAREER** Teacher, Elem Sch, NH, 57-60 & High Sch, NH, 60-61; from asst prof to assoc prof, 66-75, Prof Hist, Univ Mass, Amherst, 75-, Soc Sci Res Coun fac res grant, 69-70; res fel, Charles Warren Ctr, Harvard Univ, 69-70; Am Coun Learned Soc grant-in-aid, 69-70; spec adv, US Holocaust Mem Coun, 81- **MEMBERSHIPS** Orgn Am Historians; AAUP. **RESEARCH** American refugee policy, 1930's and 1940's; American society, 1930-1945; the Jewish holocaust, 1933-1945. **SELECTED PUBLICATIONS** Auth, The Bombing of Auschwitz Re-Examined, Jour Military Hist, Vol 0061, 97; The Bombing of Auschwitz Revisited, Holocaust and Genocide Stud, Vol 0011, 97. **CONTACT ADDRESS** Dept of Hist, Univ of Massachusetts, Amherst, Amherst, MA 01002.

WYNAR, LUBOMYR ROMAN

PERSONAL Born 01/02/1932, Lviw, Ukraine, m, 1962 **DISCIPLINE** HISTORY **EDUCATION** Ukrainian Free Univ, Munich, MA, 55, PhD, 57; Western Reserve Univ, MS, 59. **CAREER** Instr bibliog, Case Inst Technol, 59-62; asst prof bibliog & head soc sci libr, Univ Colo, 62-65; head info & ref serv, Bowling Green State Univ, 65-67, assoc prof bibliog, dir, Res Ctr & assoc dir, Univ Libr, 67-69; Prof Hist Libr Sci, Kent State Univ, 69-, Dir Ethnic Studies, Ctr Study Ethnic Publ, 72-, Libr consult, Educ Res Coun Cleveland, 61-62; res assoc Soviet affairs, John Carroll Univ, 62-; Çoun Res & Creative Work grant, Univ Colo, 63; managing ed, Bio-Bibliog Ser & ed Soc Sci Ref Ser, Univ Colo, 63-65; chief ed, Ukrainian Historian, 64-; res grant, Comt Fac Res, Bowling Green State Univ, 66 & 68 & US Off Educ, Ethnic Heritage Studies, 77-; chmn, comt Slavic mat US & Can Libr, 68-, res rev comt, Ethnic Studies, Cleveland State Univ, 73-75 & Historiographical Comn, Ukrainian Hist Asn, 75- **MEMBERSHIPS** Am Asn Advan Slavic Studies; Am Libr Asn; Shevchenko Sci Soc (secy, 61); Ukrainian Hist Asn (secy, 65-68, pres, 81-); Asn Study of Nationalities (vpres, 77-). **RESEARCH** Slavic history, 16th to the 18th century; bibliography; history of Ukraine. **SELECTED PUBLICATIONS** Auth, To The Editor--Prymak,Thomas Review of Hrushevskyi,M. Na Porozi Novoi Ukrainy, Slavic Rev, Vol 0053, 94. **CONTACT ADDRESS** Sch of Libr Sci, Kent State Univ, Kent, OH 44242.

WYNES, CHARLES ELDRIDGE

PERSONAL Born 08/11/1929, Rectortown, VA **DISCIPLINE** UNITED STATES HISTORY **EDUCATION** James Madison Univ, BS, 52; Univ Va, MA, 57, PhD, 60. **CAREER** From instr to asst prof, Tex A&M Univ, 58-62; from asst prof to assoc prof, 62-70, dir grad studies, 66-68, asst dean arts & sci, 68-71, Prof Hist to Prof Emer, Univ GA, 70-; Vis scholar, James Madison Univ, 80. **MEMBERSHIPS** Southern Hist Asn. **RESEARCH** The South since 1865; American Negro history; Georgia history. **SELECTED PUBLICATIONS** Auth, Race Relations in Virginia, 1870-1902, 61 & ed, Southern Sketches from Virginia, 1881-1901, 64, Univ Va Press; ed, The Negro in the South Since 1865, Univ Ala, 65, Harper, 68 & Forgotten Voices, La State Univ, 67; auth, Fanny Kembless South Revisited, La Studies, fall 73; James Wormley of the Wormley Hotel agreement, Centennial Rev, winter 75; Ephraim Bowman, private, CAA, Southern Studies, spring 77; coauth, A History of Georgia, Univ Ga, 77. **CONTACT ADDRESS** Dept of Hist, Univ of Georgia, 202 LeConte Hall, Athens, GA 30602-1602.

WYSS, HILARY W.

PERSONAL Born 02/04/1965, New York, NY, m **DISCIPLINE** AMERICAN LITERATURE, AMERICAN STUDIES **EDUCATION** Hamil Col, BA, 86; Univ NCar, MA, 91; PhD, 98. **CAREER** Asst prof, Aub Col, 98-. **HONORS AND AWARDS** Phi Beta Kappa; Teach Fel, Princeton; Sr Teach Fel, UNC; Diss Res Fel, UNC; Ruth, Lincoln Ekstrom Fel; Holman Diss Awd; Fac Ment Gnt; Comp Res Gnt. **MEMBERSHIPS** MLA; SEA; ASA. **RESEARCH** Colonial Native American writing. **SELECTED PUBLICATIONS** Rev of, "The Indian Captivity Narrative 1550-1900, by Kathryn Zabelle Derounian-Stodola and James Levernier, Ear Am Lit 29 (94); auth, " 'Things That Do Accompany Salvation': Colonialism, Conversion, and Cultural Exchange," in Experience Mayhew's Indian Converts, Ear Am Lit (98); auth, "William Apess, Mary Jemison, and Narratives of Racial Identity," Am Ind Quart 23 (99); auth, Writing Indians: Literacy, Christianity, and Narrative Community in Early America, Univ Mass Press, forthcoming. **CONTACT ADDRESS** Dept English, Auburn Univ, 9030 Haley Center, Montgomery, AL 36849-2900. **EMAIL** wysshil@mail.auburn.edu

X

XING, JUN
PERSONAL Born 02/12/1955, Beijing, China, m, 1984, 3 children **DISCIPLINE** HISTORY **EDUCATION** Univ Minnesota, Twin Cities, PhD, 93; Beijing Univ International Studies, MA. 82. **CAREER** Dir, Center for Applied Studies in American Ethnicity, Colorado State Univ, 99-; Assoc Prof, Dept of History, Colorado State Univ, 99-. **HONORS AND AWARDS** Colorado Endowment for the Humanities Grant, 99; Virginia Foundation for the Humanities Fel, 94; Andrew Mellon Fel, 93. **MEMBERSHIPS** Amer Studies Assoc; National Assoc for Ethnic Studies; Asian Amer Studies Assoc. **RESEARCH** Popular Culture; Cultural Relations between U.S. and East Asia; Asian Amer Studies. **SELECTED PUBLICATIONS** Auth, "Asian America through the Lens: History, Representations and Identity, AltiMira Press, 98; auth, "Baptized in the Fire of Revolution: the American Social Gospel and the YMCA in China," Lehigh Univ Press, 96. **CONTACT ADDRESS** Dept History 1776, Colorado State Univ, Fort Collins, CO 80523-0001. **EMAIL** jxing@vines.colostate.edu

XIONG, VICTOR
DISCIPLINE ASIAN HISTORY **EDUCATION** Austra Nat Univ, PhD, 89. **CAREER** Vis instr, Univ Iowa, 87; asst prof, assoc prof, West Mich Univ, 89-. **MEMBERSHIPS** AAS; UCA. **RESEARCH** Sui-Tang China **SELECTED PUBLICATIONS** Auth, Sui-Tang Chang'an, Cen Asia Stud (Ann Arbor), 00. **CONTACT ADDRESS** Dept History, Western Michigan Univ, 1201 Oliver St, Kalamazoo, MI 49008-3804. **EMAIL** xiong@wmich.edu

XU, GUANGQIN
PERSONAL Born 11/01/1951, Guangzhou, China, m, 1985, 2 children **DISCIPLINE** HISTORY **EDUCATION** Zhongshan Univ, BA, 83; MA, 86; Univ Md, PhD, 93. **CAREER** Res asst, Univ of Md Col Park, 93-95; asst prof, NW Ark Community Col, 95-. **HONORS AND AWARDS** Outstanding Fac, NW Ark Comm Col, 97. **MEMBERSHIPS** Chinese Hist in the U.S. **RESEARCH** Relations of Sino-US History, Modern Chinese History. **SELECTED PUBLICATIONS** Auth, "The Chinese Anti-American Nationalism in the 1990's", Asian Perspective, 98; auth, The Ideological and Political Impact of U.S. Fulbrighters on China Students: 1970-1980", Asian Affairs; auth, "American-Brit aircraft competition in South China", Modern Asian Studies, 00. **CONTACT ADDRESS** Dept Soc and Behav Sci, Northwest Arkansas Comm Col, 1 College Dr, Bentonville, AR 72712-5091. **EMAIL** gxu@nwacc.cc.ar.us

Y

YAMAMOTO, MASAHIRO
PERSONAL Born 12/22/1959, Japan, s **DISCIPLINE** ASIAN STUDIES **EDUCATION** Univ Ala, PhD, 98. **CAREER** Vis Asst Prof, Randolph Macon Col, 98-. **MEMBERSHIPS** Soc for Military Hist, Assoc for Asian Studies. **RESEARCH** Military history, Japanese history. **SELECTED PUBLICATIONS** Auth, Nanking: Anatomy of an Atrocity, Praeger Publ, 00. **CONTACT ADDRESS** Dept Asian Studies, Randolph-Macon Col, 200 Henry St, PO Box 5005, Ashland, VA 23005. **EMAIL** myamamot@rmc.edu

YAMAMOTO, TRAISE
PERSONAL Born 08/06/1961, San Jose, CA, 2 children **DISCIPLINE** ASIAN AMERICAN LITERATURE AND CULTURE **EDUCATION** San Jose State Univ, BA; Univ Wash, MFA, MA, PhD. **CAREER** Prof, Univ Calif, Riverside, 94-. **HONORS AND AWARDS** Exec bd, Assn Asian Amer Stud; assoc dir, Ctr Asian Pacific Am. **RESEARCH** Poetry, race and gender theory, autobiography studies, and British and American Modernism. **SELECTED PUBLICATIONS** Auth, Between the Lines; "Different Silences: The Poetics and Politics of Location," The Intimate Critique, Duke Univ Press, 93; auth, Masking Selves, Making Subjects: Japanese American Women, Identity, and the Body, Univ of CA Press, 99. **CONTACT ADDRESS** Dept of Eng, Univ of California, Riverside, Riverside, CA 92521-0323. **EMAIL** traise.yamamoto@ucr.edu

YAMASHITA, SAMUEL HIDEO
PERSONAL Born 11/27/1946, Honolulu, HI, m, 1969 **DISCIPLINE** HISTORY, JAPANESE HISTORY **EDUCATION** Mid-Pacific Inst (col prep diploma), 64; Macalester Col, BA (Hist), 68; Univ MI, MA (Hist), 71, PhD (Hist, Japanese Hist), 81. **CAREER** Instr, Hobart & William Smith Colleges, 77-81, asst prof, 81-82; postdoctoral fel, Reischauer Inst of Japanese Studies, Harvard Univ, 82-83; sr tutor in Asian Studies, Harvard Univ, 82-83; asst prof, 83-88, assoc prof, 88-98, Prof, Pomona Col, 98-00; Prof, Henry E Sheffield, 00-. **HONORS AND AWARDS** Woodrow Wilson fel, 68; Rackham Prize fel, 71-72; Ford Found-Social Science Res Coun Foreign Area fel, 73-75; Wig Distinguished Prof Awd, Pomona Col, 86, 90, 95; Japan Found Prof fel, 91; Henry E. Sheffield Prof of Hist, 99; Associated Kyoto Progrm Fac Fel, 95, 98. **MEMBERSHIPS** Asn for Asian Studies, 70-. **RESEARCH** Japanese intellectual hist. **SELECTED PUBLICATIONS** Cotransl, The Four-Seven Debate: An Annotated Translation of the Most Famous Controversy in Korean Neo-Confucian Thought, SUNY Press, 93; auth, Master Sorai's Responsals: An Annotated Translation of Sorai sensei tomonsho, Univ HI Press, 94; Confucianism and the Modern Japanese State, 1904-1945, in Tu Wei-ming, ed, Confucian Traditions in East Asian Modernity: Moral Education and Economy and Culture in Japan and the Four Mini-Dragons, Harvard Univ Press, 96; Reading the New Tokugawa Intellectual Histories, J of Japanese Studies 22, winter 96; auth, "Asian Studies at American Private Colleges, 1808-1990," in Asia in the Undergraduate Curriculum: A Case for Asian Studies in Liberal Arts Education, ed. Suzanne Barnett and Van Symonds (M.E. Sharpe, 00). **CONTACT ADDRESS** Dept of Hist, Pomona Col, Claremont, CA 91711. **EMAIL** syamashita@pomona.edu

YAMAUCHI, EDWIN MASAO
PERSONAL Born 02/01/1937, Hilo, HI, m, 1962, 2 children **DISCIPLINE** ANCIENT HISTORY, SEMITIC LANGUAGES **EDUCATION** Shelton Col, BA, 60; Brandeis Univ, MA, 62, PhD(Mediter studies), 64. **CAREER** Asst prof ancient hist, Rutgers Univ, New Brunswick, 64-69; assoc prof, 69-73, dir grad studies, Hist Dept, 78-82, prof Hist, Miami Univ, 73-, Nat Endowment for Humanities fel, 68; Am Philos Soc grant, 70; consult ed hist, J Am Sci Affiliation, 70-; sr ed, Christianity Today, 92-94. **MEMBERSHIPS** Am Sci Affil (pres, 83); Archaeol Inst Am; Conf Faith & Hist (pres, 74-76); Near E Archaeol Soc (vpres, 78); Inst Bibl Res (pres, 87-89). **RESEARCH** Gnosticism; ancient magic; Old and New Testaments. **SELECTED PUBLICATIONS** Pre-Christian Gnosticism, Tyndale Press, London & Eerdmans, 73; The Archaeology of New Testament Cities in Western Asia Minor, Baker Bk, 80; The Scriptures and Archaeology, Western Conserv Baptist Sem, 80; World of the New Testament, Harper & Row, 81; Foes from the Northern Frontier, Baker Bk, 82; coeditor, Chronos, Kairos, Christos, Eisenbrauns, 89; Persia and the Bible, Baker Bk, 90; coauth, The Two Kingdoms, Moody, 93; coed, Peoples of the Old Testament World, Baker, 94; ed, Africa and Africans in Antiquity, Mich State Univ Pr, 00. **CONTACT ADDRESS** Dept of History, Miami Univ, 500 E High St, Oxford, OH 45056-1602. **EMAIL** Yamauce@muohio.edu

YANG, SUNG CHUL
DISCIPLINE DIPLOMACY **EDUCATION** Univ of Ky, PhD, 70. **CAREER** Prof, Univ Ky, prof, Kyunghee Univ. **MEMBERSHIPS** Korean Asn of Int Studies. **RESEARCH** Korea (North), Korea (South), politics (domestic issues), government. **SELECTED PUBLICATIONS** Auth, Korea and Two Regimes, Schenkman, 81; coauth, A Journey to North Korea, Univ of Calif-Berkeley, 83; auth, The North and South Korea Political Systems: A Comparative Analysis, Westview Pr, 94; auth, The Korean Governments 1948-1993 (in Korean), Pakyong-sa, Seoul, 94. **CONTACT ADDRESS** Kyung Hee Univ, Seoul, Korea.

YANG, WINSTON L.
PERSONAL Born 06/01/1935, Nanking, China, m, 1964, 2 children **DISCIPLINE** ASIAN STUDIES **EDUCATION** National Taiwan Univ, BA, 58; Stanford Univ, PhD, 70. **CAREER** Prof and Chair, Dept of Asian Stud, Seton Hall Univ, 84- . **HONORS AND AWARDS** Royal Asiatic Soc of Gt Brit and Ireland. **MEMBERSHIPS** Asn for Asian Stud. **RESEARCH** Modern China and Taiwan. **SELECTED PUBLICATIONS** Auth, Tianammon: China's Struggle for Democracy, Univ Maryland, 90; auth, The Political Journey of Lian Chan, Business Weekly, 96. **CONTACT ADDRESS** 3 Waldeck Ct, West Orange, NJ 07052. **EMAIL** wyanga@aol.com

YANG, ZONGSUI
DISCIPLINE HISTORY **EDUCATION** West China Union Univ, BA, 51. **CAREER** Vis prof History, Harvard; assoc prof History, Sichuan Univ, China. **RESEARCH** Boston Tea Party, Chinese translation. **CONTACT ADDRESS** 2300 Hampstead Ave, #2, Richmond, VA 23230-2337.

YANNI, CARLA
PERSONAL Born 09/18/1965, Allentown, PA **DISCIPLINE** ART HISTORY, ARCHITECTURAL HISTORY **EDUCATION** Wesleyan Univ, BA (high honors), 87; Univ Pa, PhD, 94. **CAREER** Univ New Mexico, Albuquerque, asst prof, 94-97; Rutgers Univ, asst prof, 97-. **HONORS AND AWARDS** Rosann Berry Awd, 91, Founders' Awd, 96, Soc of Archit Historians. **MEMBERSHIPS** Coll Art Assn; Soc of Archit Historians. **RESEARCH** Archit and science; museum archit. **SELECTED PUBLICATIONS** Auth, "Divine Display or Secular Science: Defining Nature at the Natural History Museum in London," Journ of the Soc of Archit History, 97; "On Nature and Nomenclature: William Whewell and the Production of Knowledge in Victorian Britain," Archit History, 97; auth, Nature's Museums: Victorian Science and the Architecture of Display, Johns Hopkins Univ Press, 00. **CONTACT ADDRESS** Art History Dept., Rutgers, The State Univ of New Jersey, New Brunswick, Voorhees Hall, New Brunswick, NJ 08903. **EMAIL** cyanni@rci.rutgers.edu

YARBOROUGH, RICHARD A.
PERSONAL Born 05/24/1951, Philadelphia, PA, d **DISCIPLINE** AFRICAN-AMERICAN STUDIES **EDUCATION** Mich State Univ, E Lansing MI, BA, 1973; Stanford Univ, Stanford CA, PhD, 1980. **CAREER** Univ of California, Los Angeles CA, asst prof 1979-86, assoc prof 1986-. **HONORS AND AWARDS** US Presidential Scholar, 1969; Alumni Dist Scholar's Awd, MI State Univ, 1969-73; Whiting Fellowship in Humanities, Stanford Univ, 1977-78; Natl Endowment for the Humanities fellowship, 1984-85; Dist Teaching Awd, UCLA, 1987; Ford Foundation postdoctoral fellowship, 1988-89; City of Los Angeles Commendation, 1990. **MEMBERSHIPS** Faculty res assoc, UCLA Center for African-Amer Studies, 1979-; mem, 1987-92, chair 1989-90, exec comm of Div of Black Amer Literature & Culture, Modern Lang Assn; bd of editorial advisors, American Quarterly, 1987-91; mem, Natl Council, Amer Studies Assn, 1988-91; member, editorial board, African American Review, 1989-; California Council for the Humanities, 1992-96. **SELECTED PUBLICATIONS** Assoc gen editor, The Heath Anthology of American Literature, 2nd ed, D C Heath, 1994, 3rd ed, Houghton Mifflin, 1998; general editor, "Library of Black Literature," Northeastern Univ Press, 1988-; coeditor, Norton Anthology of Afro-American Literature, 1996; author of scholarly essays in numerous journals & books. **CONTACT ADDRESS** Professor/Research/Writer, Univ of California, Los Angeles, 2225 Rolfe Hall, Box 951530, Los Angeles, CA 90095-1530.

YASKO, RICHARD ANTHONY
PERSONAL Born 01/22/1931, Racine, WI, m, 1963, 3 children **DISCIPLINE** HISTORY & JAPANESE STUDIES **EDUCATION** Dominican Col, BA, 63; Univ Chicago, MA, 65, PhD, 73. **CAREER** Vis lectr Japan hist, Univ MD, College Park, 72-73; asst prof hist, Sam Houston State Univ, 73-75; Assoc Prof Hist, 76-83, prof hist Univ WI-Whitewater, 84-, Fulbright Res Scholar, Tokyo Univ, 68-70. **HONORS AND AWARDS** Excellence in Teaching in the Hum, 93; Col of Letters & Sci Teaching Awd, 94. **MEMBERSHIPS** Asn Asian Studies; Western Soc Sci Asn. **RESEARCH** Prewar Showa polit hist; G.I.s in post-occupation Japan. **SELECTED PUBLICATIONS** Auth, Hiranuma Kiichiro and the New Structure Movement, 1940-1941, Asian Forum 6/73; Bribery Cases and the Rise of the Justice Ministry, In: Late Meiji Early Taisho Japan, Law in Japan, 79. **CONTACT ADDRESS** Dept of Hist, Univ of Wisconsin, Whitewater, 800 W Main, Whitewater, WI 53190-1790. **EMAIL** yasko@ticon.net

YATES, GAYLE GRAHAM
PERSONAL m, 2 children **DISCIPLINE** INTERDISCIPLINARY AMERICAN STUDIES **EDUCATION** Univ Minn, PhD, 73. **CAREER** Prof, ch, Women's Stud, Univ Minn, Twin Cities; vis instr, Univ Munich & Univ Amsterdam. **SELECTED PUBLICATIONS** Auth, What Women Want: The Ideas of the Movement, Harvard, 75; Mississippi Mind: A Personal Cultural History of an American State, Tenn, 90; ed, Harriet Martineau on Women, Rutgers, 85. **CONTACT ADDRESS** Univ of Minnesota, Twin Cities, 72 Pleasant St. SE, 104 Scott Hall, Minneapolis, MN 55455. **EMAIL** graha001@maroon.tc.umn.edu

YATES, ROBIN D. S.
DISCIPLINE EAST ASIAN STUDIES **EDUCATION** Harvard Univ, PhD. **CAREER** Prof dept of hist and east asian stud, McGill Univ. **RESEARCH** Early and traditional Chinese history; historical theory; archaeology of China; newly discovered ancient texts; Chinese science and technology; traditional popular culture; Chinese poetry. **SELECTED PUBLICATIONS** Auth, "An Introduction to and a Partial Reconsturction of the Yin Yang Texts form Yinqueshan: Notes on their Signifcance in Relation to HuangLao Daoism," ealry China 19, (94): 1-70; auth, "Boody, Space, Time, and Bureaucracy: Boundary Creation and Control Mechanisms in Early China," in John Hay, ed., Boundaries in Chinese Culture, Reaktion Books, (94): 56-80. **CONTACT ADDRESS** East Asian Studies Dept, McGill Univ, 845 Sherbrooke St, Montreal, QC, Canada H3A 2T5. **EMAIL** ryates@leacock.lan.mcgill.ca

YEANDLE, LAETITIA
PERSONAL Born 07/11/1930, Hong Kong, m, 1966 **DISCIPLINE** ENGLISH HISTORY **EDUCATION** Trinity Col, Dublin, BA, 53; Univ Col, London, dipl arch admin, 56. **CAREER** Asst archivist, Shropshire Rec Off, 55-57; manuscript cataloguer, 57-70, Cur Manuscripts, Folger Shakespeare Libr, 70-, Fel, Folger Libr-Brit Acad Exchange Prog, 75; Brit Acad Exchange Prog fel, Folger Libr, 75. **MEMBERSHIPS** Brit Rec Asn; Soc Textual Scholar; Soc Am Archivists. **RESEARCH** Textual editing and criticism; Tudor and Stuart history. **SELECTED PUBLICATIONS** Coauth, Elizabethan handwriting, WW Norton & Co, Inc (New York), 66, Faber and Faber Ltd (London), 68; coauth, English handwriting, 1400-1650: An introductory manual, Medieval and Renaissance Texts and Stud (Binghamton, New York), 92; co-ed, The Works of Richard Hooker, Vol 5, Belknap Press, Harvard Univ Press (Cambridge, MA), 90; co-ed, The Journal of John Winthrop 1630-1649, Belknap Press, Harvard Univ Press (Cambridge, MA), 96; coauth, "The Loseley Collegetion of Manuscripts at the Folger Shakespeare Library," Shakespeare Quart, Vol 0038 (87); coauth, "Books of Sir Edward Dering of Kent (1598-1644)," in

Private Libraries in Renaissance England, eds R.J. Fehrenbach and E.S. Leedham-Green), Medieval and Renaissance Texts and Studies (Binghamton, New York), 92; and several articles and reviews. **CONTACT ADDRESS** Folger Shakespeare Libr, 201 E Capitol St, Washington, DC 20003.

YEGUL, FIKRET KUTLU

PERSONAL Born 10/27/1941, Turkey **DISCIPLINE** HISTORY OF ART AND ARCHITECTURE **EDUCATION** Mid East Tech Univ, Ankara, Turkey, BArch, 64; Yale Univ, BArch, 65; Univ Pa, MArch, 66; Harvard Univ, PhD(art hist), 75. **CAREER** Asst prof, Wellesley Col, 75-76; Asst Prof Greek & Roman Art, Univ Calif, Santa Barbara, 76-, Mem excavation, Sardis Archaeol Excavation, Harvard Univ, 63-; Am Coun Learned Soc grant, 79-80; res fel, Am Res Inst, Turkey, 80-81. **MEMBERSHIPS** Am Inst Archaeol. **RESEARCH** Roman architecture, particularly bathing and the baths in classical antiquity; Greek architecture; Islamic architecture, particularly of the Mamluk Period in Cairo. **SELECTED PUBLICATIONS** Auth, Early Byzantine capitals from Sardis, Dumbarton Oaks Papers, Vol XXVIII, 74; The marble court of Sardis and historical reconstruction, J Field Archaeol, Vol XXXII, 76; The small city bath and a reconstruction study of Lucian's baths of Hippias, Archeol Class, Vol XXXI, 79; A study in architectural iconography: Kaisersaal and the imperial cult, Art Bull, Vol LXIV, 82. **CONTACT ADDRESS** Art Hist Dept, Univ of California, Santa Barbara, 552 University Rd, Santa Barbara, CA 93106-0001.

YEH, WEN-HSIN

PERSONAL m, 1 child **DISCIPLINE** EAST ASIAN HISTORY **EDUCATION** Univ Calif, Berkeley, PhD, 84. **CAREER** Asst prof to Prof, Dept Hist, Univ Calif, Berkeley, 87-. **HONORS AND AWARDS** Mellon fel. **MEMBERSHIPS** AHA, AAS. **RESEARCH** Modern China; hist; 20th century. **SELECTED PUBLICATIONS** Auth, The Alienated Academy: Culture and Politics in Republican China, 1919-37, Harvard, 90; Provincial Passages: Culture, Space, and the Origin of Chinese Communism, Calif Univ Press, 96. **CONTACT ADDRESS** Dept Hist, Univ of California, Berkeley, Berkeley, CA 94720-2550. **EMAIL** sha@socrates.berkeley.edu

YELLIN, JEAN FAGAN

PERSONAL Born 09/19/1930, Lansing, MI, m, 1948, 3 children **DISCIPLINE** AMERICAN LITERATURE AND STUDIES **EDUCATION** Roosevelt Univ, BA, 51; Univ Ill, Urbana, MA, 63, PhD(English), 69. **CAREER** Asst prof, 68-74, assoc prof, 74-80, Prof to distinguished prof emer, English & Dir, New York City Humanities Prog, Pace Univ, 80-. **HONORS AND AWARDS** Nat Endowment for Humanities younger humanist fel, 74-75; guest lectr, Univ Heidelberg, Sorbonne Nouvelle, Univ East Anglia, Univ Sussex, 75, 76; Nat Humanities Inst, Yale Univ, fel, 76-77; fels, Nat Endowment for Humanities, 78, Smithsonian Inst, Nat Collection of Fine Arts, 78-79 & Am Asn Univ Women, 81-82; proj dir, Nat Endowmnet for Humanities demonstration grant, Pace Univ, 79-81. **MEMBERSHIPS** MLA; Am Studies Asn; Asn Studies Afro-Am Life & Hist; Nat Women's Studies Asn. **RESEARCH** American literature and culture; women's studies; radical literature. **SELECTED PUBLICATIONS** Auth, Jacobs, Harriet Family History, Amer Lit, Vol 0066, 94; Written By Herself--Literary Production by African-American Women, 1746-1892, African Amer Rev, Vol 0030, 96. **CONTACT ADDRESS** 38 Lakeside Dr, New Rochelle, NY 10801.

YELLIN, VICTOR FELL

PERSONAL Born 12/14/1924, Boston, MA, m, 1948, 1 child **DISCIPLINE** MUSIC HISTORY, COMPOSITION **EDUCATION** Harvard Univ, AB, 49, AM, 52, PhD, 57. **CAREER** Asst prof music, NY Univ, 56-58; Williams Col, 58-60; assoc prof, OH State Univ, 60-61; assoc prof, 61-68, master, Weinstein Hall, 65-71, prof music hist, NY Univ , 68. **HONORS AND AWARDS** MacDowell Colony, Peterborough, NH, 69; Nat Endowment for Hum fel, 78. **MEMBERSHIPS** Am Musicol Soc; Sonneck Soc for Am Music; Redwood Libr, Redwood, Newport, RI. **RESEARCH** Hist of Am music; Early romantic opera; Chromatic harmony. **SELECTED PUBLICATIONS** Auth, When Is a Symphony Not a Symphony: The Symphonies of William Boyce, Musical Am, 2/53; Some Specific Advice to Young Opera Composers, Muiscal Am, 2/54; Opera's American History, Music Jour, 3/61; he Conflic of Generations in American Music (A Yankee View), Arts and Sci, NY Univ, winter 62; The Pronunciation of Recitative, Am Sppech, 12/68; Musical Activity in Virginia before 1620, J Am Musicol Soc, 69; The Operas of Virgil Thomson, In: Virgil Thomson American Music since 1910, Holt, 71; Ives' The Celestial Country, Music Quart 7/74; George Whitefield Chadwick, American Musical Realist, Musical Quart, 1/75; Restoration, Rayner Taylor's The Aethiop, recording, New World Records, 6/78; Rayner Taylor, Am Music, fall 83; Rayner Taylor's Music for the Aethiop I, Am Music, fall 86; Rayner Taylor's Music for the Aethiop II, Am Music, spring 87; Chadwick, Yankee Cmposer, Smithsonian, 90; Prosodic Syncopation, In: A Celebration of American Music: Words and Music in Honor of H. Wiley Hitchcock (Richard Crawford, ed), Univ Mich, 90; Sullivan and Thomson, Gilbert and Stein, Jour of Musicol, fall 93; Bristow's Divorce, Am Music, fall 94; The Aethiop (1813) Orch Score Restoration, In: Nineteenth-Century American Musical Theater (Deane L Root, ed), vol 2, Garland, 94; Mrs Belmont Matthew Perry, and the Japanese Minstrels, Am Music, fall 96; The Omnibus Idea, Harmonie Park Press, 98; Compositions, Passacaglia for Strings, 52; Ballet, The Bear that Wasn't, 52; Sonata for Violin and Piano, 53; Opera, Abaylar, 65; Sonata for Violoncello and Piano, 79; Song Cycle Teasdale, Dark of the Moon, 84; Variations on Bye Bye Blues for Violoncello or violin and piano, 88. **CONTACT ADDRESS** Dept of Music, New York Univ, 24 Waverly Pl, New York, NY 10003-6757.

YELTON, DAVID K.

PERSONAL Born 05/23/1960, Rutherfordton, NC, m, 1984, 3 children **DISCIPLINE** HISTORY **EDUCATION** Appalachian State Univ, BA, 82; UNC, MA, 85; PhD, 90. **CAREER** Asst prof, Gardner Webb Univ, 90-. **HONORS AND AWARDS** German Acad Exchange Service Short Term Res Grant, 88; Gardner Webb Univ Fac Sabbatical, 96. **MEMBERSHIPS** AHA, WWII Studies Asn, Soc for Mil Hist. **RESEARCH** Third Reich, second world war. **SELECTED PUBLICATIONS** Auth, "British Public Opinion: the Home Guard and the Defense of Great Britain," J of Mil Hist 58(3) (94): 461-480; auth, "Artois, Second Battle of," "Artois, Third Battle of," "Champagne, First Battle of," The European Powers in the First World War: An Encycl, Garland, 96; auth, "Bridge at Remagen," "British Home Guard," "Rhineland Campaign" and "Volkssturm," Encycl of World War II in Europe, Garland, 98; auth, "Ein Volk Steht Auf: The German Volkssturm and Nazi Strategy, 1944-1945," J of Mil Hist 58(3) (forthcoming). **CONTACT ADDRESS** Dept Soc Sci, Gardner-Webb Univ, PO Box 7204, Boiling Springs, NC 28017. **EMAIL** dyelton@gardner-webb.edu

YERUSHALMI, YOSEF HAYIM

PERSONAL Born 05/20/1932, New York City, NY, m, 1 child **DISCIPLINE** MEDIEVAL, MODERN JEWISH HISTORY, HISTORY OF PSYCHOANALYSIS **EDUCATION** Yeshiva Univ, BA, 53; Jewish Theological Seminary, MHL, 57; Columbia, PhD, 66. **CAREER** Preceptor in Hebrew, Columbia Univ, 62-65; Instr in Hebraic Studies, Rutgers Univ, 63-66; Asst prof of Hebrew and Jewish Hist, Harvard Univ, 66-70, prof of Hebrew and of Jewish Hist, 70-79, Jacob E. Safra prof of Jewish hist and Sephardic Civilization, Harvard Univ, 79-80, Chairman, Dept of Near Eastern Languages and Civilizations, 78-80, Salo Wittmayer Baron prof of Jewish Hist, Cult, Soc and dir, Ctr for Israel and Jewish Studies, Columbia Univ, 80-. **HONORS AND AWARDS** Fel of the Ctr for Israel and Jewish Studies, Columbia Univ, 61-62, president's fel, 62-64, Kent fel, 63; Traveling Fel, Nat Foun for Jewish Cult, 64; Ansley Award, Columbia Univ Press, 66; Fel of the Am Acad for Jewish Res, 72; Newman Medal for Distinguished Achievement, the City Univ of New York, 75; fel, Nat Endowment for the Humanities, 76-77; Rockefeller Fel in the Humanities, 83-84; Corres[p-mdomg mem, Portuguese Acad of Hist, Lisbon, 85; Fel of the Am Acad of Arts and Sciences, 86; Gold Medal, Portuguese Acad of Hist, Lisbon, 89; Guggenheim fel, 89-90; Award of the New York Psychoanalytic Inst for distinguished contributions to applied psychoanalysis, 91; Medal of the Nat Found for Jewish Culture for achievement in hist; fel of the Carl Friedrich von Siemens Stiftung, Munich, 96-97; Festschrift: Jewish History and Jewish Memory: Essays in Honor of Yosef Hayim Yerushalmi, ed. E. Carlebach, J. Efron, D. Myers, Hanover and London, Brandeis Univ Press, 98. **SELECTED PUBLICATIONS** Auth, From Spanish Court to Italian Ghetto, 71; Haggadah and History, 75; The Lisbon Massacre of 1506, 76; Zakhor: Jewish History and Jewish Memory, 82; A Jewish Classic in the Portuguese Language, 89; Freud's Moses, 91; Ein Feld in Anathoth, 93; Diener von Koenigen und nicht Diener von Dienern, 95; auth, sefardica: Essays sur l'histoire des juifs, des marranes, et des Nouveaux Chretiens, Dorigine Hispano-Portugaise, 98. **CONTACT ADDRESS** Dept of Hist, Columbia Univ, 1180 Amsterdam Ave, Fayerweather Hall, Rm 511, New York, NY 10027-6902. **EMAIL** yhy1@columbia.edu

YERXA, DONALD A.

PERSONAL Born 07/19/1950, Portland, ME, m, 1970 **DISCIPLINE** AMERICAN HISTORY & HISTORICAL METHODOLOGY **EDUCATION** Eastern Nazarene Col, BA; Univ ME, MA, PhD. **CAREER** Ch, dept hist, Eastern Nazarene Col, Contributing Ed, Books & Culture, Asst Dir, The Historical Soc. **MEMBERSHIPS** Am Hist Assoc; Am Sci Affil; Colonial Soc of Mass; Conf on Faith and Hist; Nat Asn of Scholars; Orgn of Am Historians; New England Hist Asn; Soc of Mil Historians; The Hist Soc. **RESEARCH** Historical Metrodology; Darwinism and American History. **SELECTED PUBLICATIONS** Auth, Admirals and Empire: The US Navy and the Caribbean, 1898-1945. **CONTACT ADDRESS** Eastern Nazarene Col, 23 East Elm Ave, Quincy, MA 02170-2999. **EMAIL** yerxad@enc.edu

YETMAN, NORMAN ROGER

PERSONAL Born 01/10/1938, New York, NY, m, 1964, 2 children **DISCIPLINE** AMERICAN STUDIES, SOCIOLOGY **EDUCATION** Univ Redlands, BA, 60; Univ Pa, MA, 61, PhD(Am Civilization), 69. **CAREER** Instr sociol, Univ Redlands, 62-63; from asst prof to prof Am studies & sociol, 66-77; Chancellors Club Teaching Prof of Am Stud and Sociol, 92-, chmn Am studies, 73-81, 93-96, 00-, chair, Sociol, 86-89, Univ Kansas; Danforth assoc; Inst Southern Hist, Johns Hopkins Univ, sr res fel, 72-73; eval consult, Nat Endowment for Humanities, 75-76; Am spec, Dept State, 77, 82, 98; Fulbright prof, Odense Univ & Univ Copenhagen, 81-82. **MEMBERSHIPS** Am Sociol Asn; Orgn Am Historians; Am Studies Asn. **RESEARCH** Racial and ethnic relations; sociology of slavery; sociology of sport. **SELECTED PUBLICATIONS** Ed, Life Under the Peculiar Institution, 70 & Voices From Slavery, 70, Holt, reprint ed, Dover, 00; ed, Majority and Minority, Allyn & Bacon, 71, 75, 82, 85, 91, 99; coauth, Black Americans in sports, Civil Rights Digest, 72, 77; Family planning services and the distribution of Black Americans, Social Problems, 6/74; auth, The rise and fall of time on the cross, Rev Am Hist, spring 76; The Irish experience in America, In: Irish History and Culture, 76; coauth, Sociology: Experiencing a Changing Societies, Allyn & Bacon, 97. **CONTACT ADDRESS** American Studies Prog, Univ of Kansas, Lawrence, Lawrence, KS 66045-2117. **EMAIL** norm@falcon.cc.ukans.edu

YICK, JOSEPH KONG SANG

DISCIPLINE HISTORY **EDUCATION** Univ Tex, Austin, BA, 76; Univ Calif, Santa Barbara, MA, 78, PhD, 88. **CAREER** Asst lectr, Hong Kong Baptist Col, 79-83; inst, Santa Barbara City Col, 84-87; asst prof, Auburn Univ, Montgomery, 88- 89; asst, 89-95, ASSOC PROF HIST, 95-00, prof hist, 00-, SOUTHWEST TEX STATE UNIV. **CONTACT ADDRESS** Dept of History, Southwest Texas State Univ, San Marcos, TX 78666. **EMAIL** jy02@swt.edu

YIN, XIAO-HUANG

DISCIPLINE US-CHINA RELATIONS, ASIAN AMERICAN STUDIES **EDUCATION** Nanjing Univ, BA, 80; Harvard Univ, AM, 87; PhD, 91. **CAREER** Asst prof, Occidental Col, 91-96; vis assoc prof, Harvard Univ, 96-98; assoc prof, Occidental Univ, 98-. **HONORS AND AWARDS** Haynes Found Grant, 97-98. **MEMBERSHIPS** AHA; AAA; ASA; AAS. **RESEARCH** US-China relations; Asian American studies; immigration and transnationalism. **SELECTED PUBLICATIONS** Auth, Chinese American Literature since the 1850s, Univ Ill Press, 00; auth, "Redefining Chinese American Sensibility: A Sociohistorical Study of Chinese Language Press in the United States," in Not English Only: Redefining "American" in American Studies, ed. Orm Overland (Amsterdam: VU Univ Press, 00): 302-34; auth, "The Growing Influence of Chinese Americans on US-China Relations," in The Outlook for U.S. China Relations, eds. Peter Koehn, Joseph Cheng., (Hong Kong: Chinese Univ of Hong Kong Press, 99): 331-49; auth, "Worlds of Difference: the Significance of Chinese Language Writing in America," in Multilingual America: Transnationalism, Ethnicity, and the Languages of America, ed. Wenner Sollors (NY UP, 98): 176-90; coauth, "Chinese Americans: A Rising Factor in U.S.-China Relations," J American-East Asian Relations 6 (97): 35-57; co-transl of, The Rise to Power of the Chinese Communist Party: Documents and Analysis, ed. AJ Saich (Armonk, NY: M.E. Sharpe, 96); auth, "China's Gilded Age," Atlantic Monthly 273 (94): 42-53; auth, "The Voice of a 'Cultivated Asian,'" in Origins and Destinations: 41 Essays on Chinese America, eds. Munson A Kwok, Ella Yee Quan (Asian American Studies Center, UCLA, 94): 337-45; auth, "Progress and Problems: American Studies in China during the Post-Mao Era," in As Others Read Us: International Perspectives on American Studies, ed. Huck Gutman (Univ Mass Press, 91): 49-64; auth, "Asian Americans: A Divided Community," LA Times (May 7, 00); auth, "Asian American Studies Must Go Beyond America to Succeed," LA Times (July 13, 97); auth, "Hong Kong's Protectors Are in China, Not Washington," LA Times (Feb 2, 97); auth, "Economic Success May Soon Force China to Deal with Internal Woes," LA Times (Aug 25, 96). **CONTACT ADDRESS** Dept American Studies, Occidental Col, 1600 Campus Rd, Los Angeles, CA 90041-3314. **EMAIL** emyin@oxy.edu

YIP, CHRISTOPHER

PERSONAL m, 1 child **DISCIPLINE** ARCHITECTURE; ARCHITECTURAL HISTORY **EDUCATION** Univ of CA, Berkeley, BA, 71, MA, June 77, PhD, Dec 85. **CAREER** Asst prof, Univ of Colorado, 82-87; Assoc Prof, 88-94, Prof, Sept 94-present, CA Polytechnic State Univ,; Assoc prof, Univ of Hawaii at Manoa, 94-96. **HONORS AND AWARDS** John K. Branner Travelling Fel, 75-76; Newhouse Found Scholar, Newhouse Found, 78-79; Regent Fel, regents of the Univ CA, 79-80. **MEMBERSHIPS** Soc of Architectural Historians; Vernacular Architecture Forum **RESEARCH** Asian Amer environments; Colonial urbanism and architecture in Asia; Asia Pacific architecture **SELECTED PUBLICATIONS** Auth, Asian American and African American Environments, with Bradford Grant in Sherry Ahrentzen & Janetta McCoy, eds., Doing Diversity: A Compendium of Architectural Courses Addressing Diversity Issues in Architecture, 96; The Creation of Periodic Street Markets as a Means of Social and Ecological Betterment, in the Proceedings of the Second International Symnposium on Asia Pacific Aritecture: The Making of Public Places, 97; A Chinatown of Gold Mountain: The Chinese in Locke, California, in Images of an American Land: Vernacular Architecture in the Western United States, Thomas Carter, ed, 97; Association Building, in Encyclopedia of Vernacular Architecture of the World, 97; Chinese American Temples, in Encyclopedia of

Vernacular Architecture of the World, 97; Chinese American, in Encyclopedia of Vernacular Architecture of the World, 97. **CONTACT ADDRESS** Architecture Dept, California Polytech State Univ, San Luis Obispo, 1151 Ella St, San Luis Obispo, CA 93407. **EMAIL** cyip@calpoly.edu

YIP, KA-CHE
PERSONAL Born Hong Kong, China **DISCIPLINE** HISTORY **EDUCATION** Univ Hong Kong, BA, 65; Columbia Univ, MA, 67, E Asian Inst Cert, 68, PhD, 70. **CAREER** Prof, Univ MD Baltimore County. **HONORS AND AWARDS** Presidential Teaching Prof. **MEMBERSHIPS** Hist Soc for 20th Century China. **RESEARCH** Mod Chinese hist. **SELECTED PUBLICATIONS** Auth, Religion, Nationalism and Chinese Students: the Anti-Christian Movement of 1922-1927; Health and National Reconstruction in Nationalist China. **CONTACT ADDRESS** Dept of Hist, Univ of Maryland, Baltimore County, 1000 Hilltop Circle, Baltimore, MD 21250. **EMAIL** yip@umbc.edu

YODER, JOHN
PERSONAL Born 02/12/1942, Iowa City, IA, m, 1966, 2 children **DISCIPLINE** INTERNATIONAL POLITICS AND PEACE STUDIES, AFRICAN STUDIES; AFRICAN HISTORY AND POLITICS **EDUCATION** Mennonite Sem, Mdiv; Northwestern Univ, PhD. **CAREER** Prof. **HONORS AND AWARDS** Fulbright grant, 87-88; Fulbright grant, 98; Pew Evangelical Scholars Prog grant, 97, 99; fulbright nat selection comm for africa. **RESEARCH** Relationship between the political values of ordinary citizens and the collapse of the Liberian state. **SELECTED PUBLICATIONS** Publ, articles on Dahomey, Uganda, Zaire, and colonial America; ed, Zaire, Dictionary of African Biography, Reference Publ, 79; auth, The Kanyok of Zaire, Cambridge, 92. **CONTACT ADDRESS** Dept of Hist, Whitworth Col, 300 West Hawthorne Rd, Spokane, WA 99251. **EMAIL** johnyoder@whitworth.edu

YODER, R. PAUL
DISCIPLINE LITERARY HISTORY FROM MILTON TO KEATS **EDUCATION** Duke Univ, PhD. **CAREER** English and Lit, Univ Ark **SELECTED PUBLICATIONS** Auth, Milton's The Passion, Milton Studies; William Blake, Hanoverian Britain, 1714-1834; Coed, Critical Essays on Alexander Pope; Approaches to Teaching Alexander Pope; Wordsworth Reimagines Thomas Gray, Criticism. **CONTACT ADDRESS** Univ of Arkansas, Little Rock, 2801 S University Ave., Little Rock, AR 72204-1099. **EMAIL** rpyoder@ualr.edu

YOON, WON Z.
PERSONAL Born 10/15/1932, Pyongyang, Korea, m, 1957, 3 children **DISCIPLINE** EAST ASIAN & SOUTHEAST ASIAN STUDIES **EDUCATION** Friends Univ, BA, 59; Wichita State Univ, MA, 61; NYork Univ, PhD(Hist), 71. **CAREER** Asst prof Hist, State Univ NY Col Geneseo, 63-71; coordr, vis Asian prof proj, 67, assoc prof, 71-74, prof Hist, Siena Col, 74-, vis fel, inst SE Asian Studies, Singapore, 78. **MEMBERSHIPS** Asn Asian Studies; AAUP. **RESEARCH** Japanese military administration in Burma, 1942-43; Japan's occupation of Burma, 1941-45. **SELECTED PUBLICATIONS** Transl, Burma: Japanese Military Administration, Selected Documents, 1941-1945, Univ Pa Press, 71; auth, Japan's scheme for the liberation of Burma and the role of the Minami Kikan and the Thirty Comrades, Ohio Univ, 73; Military Expediency--A Determining Factor in the Japanese Policy Regarding Burmese Independence, 78. **CONTACT ADDRESS** Dept of History, Siena Col, 515 Loudonville Rd, Loudonville, NY 12211-1462. **EMAIL** yoon@siena.edu

YORK, NEIL L.
PERSONAL Born 04/21/1951, San Luis Obispo, CA, m, 1981, 2 children **DISCIPLINE** HISTORY, AMERICAN STUDIES **EDUCATION** Brigham Young Univ, BA, 73; MA, 75; Univ Calif, Santa Barbara, PhD, 78. **CAREER** Instr, 77-79; asst prof, 79-84; assoc prof, 84-94; prof, 84-, BYU. **MEMBERSHIPS** OIEAHC; CSM; Phi Kappa Phi. **RESEARCH** American revolution; American constitutional; technology and society. **SELECTED PUBLICATIONS** Auth, Mechanical Metamorphosis: Technological Change in Revolutionary America (85); auth, Neither Kingdom Nor Nations: The Irish Quest for Constitutional Rights, 1698-1800 (94); auth, "Jack the Painter," The Arsonist as Revolutionary (00); auth, Fiction as Fact: The Horse Soldiers and Popular Memory (forthcoming); auth, Maxims for a Patriot: Josiah Quincy Jr. and His Commonplace Book (forthcoming). **CONTACT ADDRESS** Dept History, Brigham Young Univ, PO Box 24446, Provo, UT 84602-4446. **EMAIL** neil_york@byu.edu

YOST, ROBINSON M.
PERSONAL Born 05/06/1967, Ithaca, NY, m, 1998 **DISCIPLINE** HISTORY OF SCIENCE **EDUCATION** Centenary Col Louisiana, BA, 89; Iowa State Univ, MA, 94; PhD, 97. **CAREER** Lectr, teach asst, Iowa State Univ, 91-98; adj instr, William Pa Col, 99; instr, John Hopkins Univ, 99-00; adj instr, des Moines Area CC, 98-. **HONORS AND AWARDS** Res Excel Awd; Linda Hall Lib Res Fel; Who's Who Am Teach; Dean's Schl; Phi Alpha Theta. **MEMBERSHIPS** HSS. **RESEARCH** History of science; Victorian science; Darwinism; history of physics and astronomy. **SELECTED PUBLICATIONS** Auth, "Pondering the Imponderable: John Robison and Magnetic Theory in Britain, 1775-1805," Annals of Sci 56 (99): 143-174. **CONTACT ADDRESS** Dept Social, Behavioral Sci, Des Moines Area Comm Col, 2006 Ankeny Blvd, Ankeny, IA 50021. **EMAIL** rmyost@yahoo.com

YOUNG, ALFRED
PERSONAL Born 02/21/1946, New Orleans, LA, m **DISCIPLINE** HISTORY **EDUCATION** Louisiana State Univ, New Orleans, LA, BA 1970; Syracuse Univ, MA 1972, PhD 1977. **CAREER** History and African-American Studies, visiting professor, 95-97; Syracuse Univ, lecturer Afro-Amer studies 1971, instr history 1971-72, asst prof history 1972-82, assoc prof history 1982-88; SUNY Oswego; Colgate Univ, Hamilton, NY, A Lindsay O'Connor Chair, 88-89; Georgia Southern Univ, assoc profr, 89-94, Prof of History, 94-, director African and African-American studies program, 91. **HONORS AND AWARDS** Afro-Amer Fellowship Syracuse Univ 1970-72; Natl Fellowship Fund Fellow 1975-76 1976-77; Outstanding Young Men of Amer Awd 1979; summer research grant NY State Afro-Amer Institute 1987; certificate of appreciation Howard Univ Model OAU, 1989; numerous publs including "The Historical Origin & Significance of the Afro-Amer History Month Observance" Negro History Bulletin 1982; selected papers presented including US Department of Education Title IV, Grant 1991-93; The National Council for Black Studies Inc, Certificate of Outstanding Service Awd, 1994-96. **MEMBERSHIPS** Keeper of finance, 1980-85, chapter historian, 1988-89, Omega Psi Phi Frat Inc Chi Pi chapter; adjunct prof history, Syracuse Univ/Univ College Auburn Correctional Facility prog, 1981-89; consultant, faculty advisor, National Model OAU, Howard Univ, 1982--; bd mem, Friends of Syracuse Univ Alumni Organization, 1987-; board of directors, National Council for Black Studies, 1992-; Academic Council of the University Systems of Georgia Regents' Global Center, 1992-. **SELECTED PUBLICATIONS** Contributor to Historical Dictionary of Civil Rights in the United States, 1992; Contributing Editor, African Homefront; "Internationalizing the Curriculum: Africa and the Caribbean," International Studies Association Conference, Acapulco, Mexico, 1993; "Dr, Carter G Woodson's Legacy of Academic Excellence & Social Responsibility," Morehouse College Black History Month Lecture, February 1, 1996; Booker T Washington's Ideas on Black Economic Development: the Tuskegee Experiment," Southern Conference on African-American Studies Inc, Baton Rouge, February 1995; "The African-American Response to Post-Reconstruction Conditions in the South, Birmingham, Alabama, February, 1993. **CONTACT ADDRESS** History Dept, Georgia So Univ, PO Box 8054, Statesboro, GA 30460.

YOUNG, ALFRED F.
PERSONAL Born 01/17/1925, New York, NY, m, 1952, 3 children **DISCIPLINE** AMERICAN HISTORY **EDUCATION** Queen's Col, NYork, BA, 46; Columbia Univ, MA, 47; Northwestern Univ, PhD(hist), 58. **CAREER** Instr hist, Wesleyan Univ, 52-53; instr, Univ Conn, 55-56; from asst prof to assoc prof, Paterson State Col, 56-64; assoc prof, 64-68, Prof Hist, Northern Ill Univ, 68-, Am Philos Soc res grant, 59 & 61; Dixon Ryan Fox Fund res grant, NY Hist Asn, 61; consult, Bobbs Merrill Publ, 66-75; fels, Guggenheim, 69-70 & Nat Endowment for Humanities-Newberry Libr, 77-78; chmn, Newberry Libr Comt on Fels, 78- **HONORS AND AWARDS** Inst Early Am Hist Jamestown Prize, 67; Best article prize, Soc Daughters Colonial Wars, 81. **MEMBERSHIPS** AHA; Orgn Am Historians; Inst Early Am Hist; Am Antiquarian Soc. **RESEARCH** Early America; social-political movements; pre-industrial labor. **SELECTED PUBLICATIONS CONTACT ADDRESS** No Illinois Univ, 215 Forest Ave, Oak Park, IL 60302.

YOUNG, CHARLES ROBERT
PERSONAL Born 10/12/1927, Howard, KS, m, 1946, 2 children **DISCIPLINE** HISTORY **EDUCATION** Univ Kans, AB, 49, MA, 50; Cornell Univ, PhD(hist), 54. **CAREER** From instr to assoc prof, 54-70, Prof Hist, Duke Univ, 70-, Assoc Dean, Grad Sch, 78- **MEMBERSHIPS** AHA; Mediaeval Acad Am; Conf Brit Studies; Southern Hist Asn. **RESEARCH** Mediaeval institutions. **SELECTED PUBLICATIONS** Auth, The English Borough and Royal Administration 1130-1307, 61 & Hubert Walter, Lord of Canterbury and Lord of England, 68, Duke Univ; ed, The Twelfth-Century Renaissance, Holt, 69; English Royal Forests under the Angevin Kings, J Brit Studies, 11/72; The Forest Eyre in England during the thirteenth century, Am J Legal Hist, Vol 23, 74; The Royal Forests of Medieval England, Univ Pa, 79; Hugh de Neville, Medieval Prosopography, 2/81. **CONTACT ADDRESS** Duke Univ, 102 W Duke Bldg, Durham, NC 27708.

YOUNG, CYNTHIA A.
PERSONAL Born 10/16/1969, Cleveland, OH **DISCIPLINE** AFRICANA STUDIES, COMPARATIVE LITERATURE **EDUCATION** Columbia Univ, BA, 91; Yale Univ, PhD, 99. **CAREER** Asst Prof, SUNY Binghamton, 98-. **CONTACT ADDRESS** Dept Comp Lit, SUNY, Binghamton, PO Box 6000, Binghamton, NY 13902-6000. **EMAIL** cyoung@binghamton.edu

YOUNG, JAMES A.
PERSONAL Born 07/08/1941, Toledo, OH, m, 1988, 2 children **DISCIPLINE** HISTORY, COMMUNICATION **EDUCATION** Ohio Univ, BA, 63; Univ Toledo, MA, 66; Case Western Res, PhD, 71. **CAREER** Instr, Cleveland State Univ, 67-68; asst prof, Edinboro Univ, 69-86; adj fac, Union Lead Acad, 80-95; dir, Penn Soc Serv Union, 86-95; dir Disloc Worler Cen, 95-96; div chmn, Cen Penn Col, 97-. **HONORS AND AWARDS** CWRU Fel, 69; NEH Fel, 80; NDEA Fel, 68; Emeritus, Edinboro Univ. **MEMBERSHIPS** MLA;' AHA; ASA; SIHS; Penn Labor Hist Soc; ITA. **RESEARCH** American labor and social history; history of ideas; European labor and left history; global communications. **SELECTED PUBLICATIONS** Auth, Workin' on the Railroad: Multimedia Interactive Presentation Project, 01; auth, "W.H. Auden and D. H. Lawrence: A Journey in Ideas," in W. H. Auden: A Legacy, ed. David G. Izzo (01); auth of biographies of 'Clarence Darrow,' 'Agnes Smedley,' 'Norman Thomas,' 'George Seldes,' and 'Joseph Freeman,' in Advocates and Activists Who Shaped the 20th Century (01, 02). **CONTACT ADDRESS** 2038 Susquehanna St, Harrisburg, PA 17102-2120. **EMAIL** jimyoung@centralpenn.edu

YOUNG, JAMES HARVEY
PERSONAL Born 09/08/1915, Brooklyn, NY, m, 1940, 2 children **DISCIPLINE** HISTORY **EDUCATION** Knox Col, AB, 37; Univ IL, AM, 38, PhD, 41. **CAREER** From instr to assoc prof, 41-58, prof hist, 58-80, Vis assoc prof, Columbia Univ, 49-50; Ford fel, 54-55; Soc Sci res fel, 60-61; US Pub Health Serv grant, 60-65; mem nat adv food & drug coun, Food & Drug Admin, 64-67; Guggenheim Mem Found fel, 66-67; Nat Libr Med grant, 67-72; mem consumers task force, White House Conf Food, Nutrit & Health, 69; mem Hist Life Soc Study Sect, Nat Insts Health, 70-73 & 79-80, chmn, 72-73; consult-panelist, Nat Endowment for Humanities, 70-; res app hist, Intergovt Exchange Act, US Food & Drug Admin, 77-81. Candler prof Am soc hist, Emory Univ, 80-84. **HONORS AND AWARDS** Edward Kremers Awd, Am Inst Hist Pharmacy, 62; Logan Clendening lectr, Sch Med, Univ KS, 73; Radbill lectr, Col Physicians, Philadelphia, 78; Garrison lectr, Am Asn Hist Med, 79; Beaumont lectr, Sch Med, Yale Univ, 80; dhl, knox col, 71; dsc, rush univ, chicago, 76. **MEMBERSHIPS** AHA; Orgn Am Historians; Am Inst Hist Pharmacy; Am Asn Hist Med; Southern Hist Asn (pres 81-82). **RESEARCH** Am soc hist; hist of Am advert; Am med hist, espec hist of food and drug regulation. **SELECTED PUBLICATIONS** Auth, The Toadstool Millionaires, Princeton Univ, 61; co-ed, Truth Myth and Symbol, Prentice-Hall, 62; auth, Social history of American drug legislation, In: Drugs in Our Society, Johns Hopkins Univ, 64; The Medical Messiahs, Princeton Univ, 67; Quacksalber, Lempp, Schwabisch Gmund, 72; American Self-Dosage Medicines: An Historical Perspective, Coronado, 74; Botulism and the ripe olive scare of 1919-1920, Bull Hist Med, 76, co-ed, Disease and Distinctiveness in the American South, Univ of TN, 88; Pure Food, Princeton Univ, 89; American Health Quackery, Princeton Univ, 92. **CONTACT ADDRESS** Dept of History, Emory Univ, Atlanta, GA 30322. **EMAIL** jyoun02@emory.edu

YOUNG, JORDAN MARTEN
PERSONAL Born 09/25/1920, New York, NY, m, 1952, 1 child **DISCIPLINE** HISTORY **EDUCATION** Univ Calif, Berkeley, BA, 47, MA, 48; Princeton Univ, PhD, 53. **CAREER** Investment banker, Chase Bank, Rio de Janeiro, 53-55; gen mgr, Consolidated Industs, Venezuela, 55-56; Prof Hist, Pace Univ, 56-; Vis prof, Grad Sch, NY Univ, 59-65; vis prof, City Col NY, 64-67; Fulbright travel & res grant, Brazil, 66-67; vis prof, NY Univ, 67-68; exec dir, Inst Brazilian Am Bus Studies, World Trade Inst, Pace Univ. **MEMBERSHIPS** AHA; Int Studies Asn; Inter-Future; Americus Found (vpres); Brazilian Childrens Fund - Sloan Kettering Hosp (chmn). **RESEARCH** Contemporary political history of Latin America, especially Brazil and Chile. **SELECTED PUBLICATIONS** Auth, Brazil the 1930 Revolution, Rutgers Univ, 67; coauth, Political Forces in Latin America, Wadsworth, 68; contribr, Conflict & Continuity of a civilian cycle, Facts on File, 72; Brazil, An Emerging World Power, Krieger, 82. **CONTACT ADDRESS** Dept of Soc Sci, Pace Univ, New York, 1 Pace Plaza, New York, NY 10038-1598. **EMAIL** JordanYong@aol.com

YOUNG, KENNETH RAY
PERSONAL Born 11/06/1939, Lawton, OK **DISCIPLINE** ASIAN HISTORY **EDUCATION** Calif State Univ, Los Angeles, BA, 64, MA, 65; NYork Univ, PhD, 70. **CAREER** Assoc prof, 66-78, Prof Hist, Western Conn State Col, 78-97, Prof Emer, 97-; NEH fel int affairs, 76; Fulbright scholar, Phillippines, 79. **MEMBERSHIPS** Asn Asian Studies. **RESEARCH** American diplomacy in Asia; Southeast Asian history; American diplomacy in Asia. **SELECTED PUBLICATIONS** Auth, The Asia Pacific conference, Asia Forum, 71; And then there was one: Yung Wing at Yale, Conn Hist Soc Bull, 71; coauth, Harbinger to Nixon: Du Bois in China, Negro Hist Bull, 72; Adoniram Judson: The forgotten man, Commission, 74; The Stilwell controversy, Mil Affairs, 75; Guerill a warfare: Balangiga revisited, 77 & Atrocities and war crimes, 78, Leyte-Samar Studies; The General's General: Life & Times of General Arthur McArthur, Father of Douglas, Westview Press, 94, Harper Collins, 96. **CONTACT ADDRESS** Dept of Hist, Western Connecticut State Univ, 181 White St, Danbury, CT 06810-6826.

YOUNG, M. JANE
DISCIPLINE AMERICAN STUDIES **EDUCATION** Univ Pa, PhD, 82. **CAREER** Prof, Regents' lctr, Col of Arts and Sci, Univ NMex. **HONORS AND AWARDS** Fac Scholar Awd, Univ NMex, 90. **MEMBERSHIPS** Am Anthropol Asn; Am Asn for State and Local Hist; Am Folklore Soc; Am Stud Asn; Nat Women's Stud Asn. **RESEARCH** Material culture and ethnoaesthetics; archeol and ethnoastronomy, gender stud, and landscape stud. **SELECTED PUBLICATIONS** Auth, Signs from the Ancestors: Zuni Cultural Symbolism and Perceptions of Rock Art, 88; coed, Feminist Theory and the Study of Folklore, 93. **CONTACT ADDRESS** Univ of New Mexico, Albuquerque, Albuquerque, NM 87131. **EMAIL** mjyoung@unm.edu

YOUNG, MARY ELIZABETH
PERSONAL Born 12/16/1929, Utica, NY **DISCIPLINE** AMERICAN HISTORY **EDUCATION** Cornell Univ, PhD, 55. **CAREER** From instr to prof hist, Ohio State Univ, 55-73; prof hist, Univ Rochester, 73-, Robert Schalkenbach Found grant, 52-53; Soc Sci Res Coun fac res grant, 69; consult, Am Indian Policy Rev Comn, US Cong, 77. **HONORS AND AWARDS** Louis Pelzer Awd, Ms Valley Hist Asn, 55; Am Studies Asn Awd, 81; Ray Allen Billington Awd, W Hist Asn, 82. **MEMBERSHIPS** AHA; Orgn Am Historians; Soc Historians Early Am Repub. **RESEARCH** Violent and non-violent conflict resolution on the Indian frontier. **SELECTED PUBLICATIONS** Auth, Redskins, Ruffleshirts and Rednecks: Indian Land Allotments in Alabama and Mississippi, 1830-1860, Univ Okla, 61; co-ed & contribr, The Frontier in American Development, Cornell Univ, 69; auth, The West and American Cultural Identity, Western Hist Quart, 70; The Indian Question Revisited, Marxist Perspectives, 2/78; Friends of the Indian, Mary Baldwin Col, 80; auth, "The Cherokee Nation: Mirror of the Republic," American Quarterly, (81); auth, "Pagans, Christians, and Backsliders, All: A Secular View of the Metaphysic of Indian-White Relations," in Calvin Martin, ed., The American Indian and the Problem of History, (87); auth, "Tribal Reorganization in the Southeast, 1800-1840," in the Struggle for Political Autonomy, (89); auth, "Racism in Red and Black: Indians and Other Free People of Color in Georgia Law, Politics, and Removal Policy," Georgia Historical Quarterly, (89); auth, "The Exercise of Sovereignty in Cherokee Georgia," Journal of the Early Republic, (90); auth, "The Dark and Bloody but Endlessly Inventive Middle Ground of Indian Frontier Historiography," Journal of the Early Republic, (93); auth, "Why Was There No Cherokee War?" (forthcoming in collected volume, University of Oklahoma Press); auth, "Conflict Resolution on the Indian Frontier," Journal fo the Early Republic, (96). **CONTACT ADDRESS** Dept Hist, Univ of Rochester, 454 Rush Rhees Library, Rochester, NY 14627-0055. **EMAIL** yngm@mail.rochester.edu

YOUNG, MICHAEL B.
PERSONAL Born 12/07/1943, York, PA, m, 1968, 1 child **DISCIPLINE** HISTORY **EDUCATION** Moravian Col, BA, 65; Harvard Univ, MA, 66; PhD, 71. **CAREER** From asst prof to full prof, Ill Wesleyan Univ, 70-. **HONORS AND AWARDS** Woodrow Wilson Fel; Fulbright Fel; APS Grants; Teach of the Year Awd. **MEMBERSHIPS** AHA; NACBS; RHS. **RESEARCH** Early Stuart England; Parliament; Homosexuality. **SELECTED PUBLICATIONS** Auth, Servility and Service, RHS, 86; auth, Charles I, Macmillan/St Martin's, 97; auth, King James and the History of Homosexuality, Macmillan/NYork Univ Pr, 00. **CONTACT ADDRESS** Dept History, Illinois Wesleyan Univ, PO Box 2900, Bloomington, IL 61702-2900. **EMAIL** myoung@titan.iwu.edu

YOUNG, OTIS E.
PERSONAL Born 10/10/1925, South Bend, IN, m, 1950 **DISCIPLINE** HISTORY **EDUCATION** Ind Univ, AB, 48, MA, 49, PhD(hist), 52. **CAREER** Instr soc sci, Alpena Community Col, 52-54, asst prof hist, Bradley Univ, 54-63; assoc prof, 63-69, Prof Hist, Ariz State Univ, 69-, Howard vis scholar, Ohio State Univ, 59-60; consult, Mining Mus, Ariz Hist Soc, 77- & Western Mus Mining Indust, 80- **RESEARCH** United States western and military history; Appalachian metal mining frontier, 1640-1870. **SELECTED PUBLICATIONS** Auth, Roaring Days--Rosslands Mines and the History of British-Columbia, Pacific Hist Rev, Vol 0065, 96; Bisbee--Urban Outpost on the Frontier, Pacific Hist Rev, Vol 0063, 94; Islands in the Desert--A History of the Uplands of Southeastern Arizona, Pacific Hist Rev, Vol 0065, 96. **CONTACT ADDRESS** Dept of Hist, Arizona State Univ, Tempe, AZ 85281.

YOUNG, ROBERT
PERSONAL Born 02/19/1959, Wilkes-Barre, PA, m, 1985 **DISCIPLINE** HISTORY **EDUCATION** King's Col, Wilkes-Barre, Pa, BS, 81; SUNY Binghamton, MA, 84; Univ Md, Col Park, PhD, 93. **CAREER** Asst Prof, Caroll Community Col Westminster Md. **MEMBERSHIPS** AHA, SHA, SHAFR, OAH. **RESEARCH** American regional history, Politics, Foreign Affairs. **SELECTED PUBLICATIONS** Auth, Senator James Murray Mason: Defender of the Old South, Univ of Tenn Press, 98. **CONTACT ADDRESS** Dept Humanities and Soc Sci, Carroll Comm Col, 1601 Washington Rd, Westminster, MD 21157-6944. **EMAIL** osnfeel@erols.com

YOUNG, ROBERT JOHN
PERSONAL Born 04/27/1942, Moose Jaw, SK, Canada, m, 1965, 3 children **DISCIPLINE** HISTORY **EDUCATION** Univ Sask, BA, 64, MA, 65; Univ London, PhD(hist), 69. **CAREER** Asst prof, 68-74, assoc prof, 74-81, Prof Hist, Univ Winnipeg, 81-, Leave fel hist, Can Coun, 74-75, Soc Sci & Humanities Res Coun Can, 81-82. **MEMBERSHIPS** Soc French Hist Studies; Western Soc for French Hist; Can Hist Asn. **RESEARCH** French foreign policy and military planning 1919-1940. **SELECTED PUBLICATIONS** Auth, Anglo-American Policy Towards the Free French, Intl Hist Rev, Vol 0019, 97; In the Eye of the Beholder, the Cultural Representation of France and Germany by the New-York-Times, 1939-1940, Hist Reflections-Reflexions Historiques, Vol 0022, 96; Transforming Paris--The Life and Labors of Baron-Haussmenn, Urban Hist Rev-Rev d Hist Urbaine, Vol 0025, 97; Shanghai on the Metro--Spies, Intrigue and the French Between the Wars, Intl Hist Rev, Vol 0017, 95; The Beast in the Boudoir, Petkeeping in 19th-Century Paris, Urban Hist Rev-Rev d Hist Urbaine, Vol 0024, 96; The Republic in Danger--Gamelin,Maurice and the Politics of French Defense, 1933-1940, Intl Hist Rev, Vol 0016, 94; Arming Against Hitler--France and the Limits of Military Planning, Jour Military Hist, Vol 0061, 97; France and the German Presence, 1940-1944--French, Intl Hist Rev, Vol 0018, 96; Lost Comrades--Socialists of the Front-Generation, 1918-1945, Intl Hist Rev, Vol 0015, 93; Daladier, Edouard 1884-1970, Amer Hist Rev, Vol 0099, 94. **CONTACT ADDRESS** Dept of Hist, Univ of Winnipeg, 515 Portage Ave, Winnipeg, MB, Canada R3B 2E9. **EMAIL** robert.young@uwinnipeg.ca

YOUNG, WILLIAM H.
PERSONAL Born 03/16/1939, Schenectady, NY, m, 1962 **DISCIPLINE** AMERICAN STUDIES **EDUCATION** Col of William and Mary, AB, 62; Duke Univ, MA, 64; Emory Univ, PhD, 69. **CAREER** Prof, Lynchburg Col, 74-; Dir Am Studies Prog, Lynchburg Col, 69-94; Chair English Dept, Lynchburg Col, 76-78, 83-86. **MEMBERSHIPS** SAH, PCA, ASA, VAF. **RESEARCH** American Architecture. **SELECTED PUBLICATIONS** Auth, "In My Adobe Hacienda: Spanish Revival Styles in Lynchburg Architecture," Lynch's Ferry 8-2 (Fall/Winter 95-96): 42-47; auth, "From a Princely Palace to a Cottage in the Cotswalds: Tudor Architecture in Lynchburg," Lynch's Ferry 9-1 (Spring/Summer 96): 24-29; auth, "From Stoops . . . To Porches . . .to Decks . . . The Evolution of 'Outdoor Rooms' in Lynchburg Architecture," Lynch's Ferry, 9-2 (Fall/Winter 96-97): 30-35; auth, "An Architecture of Confidence and Nostalgia: Georgian Revival in Lynchburg," Lynch's Ferry 10-1 (Spring/Summer 97): 42-47; auth, "Temples of Commerce and Domesticity: The Greek Revival in Lynchburg," Lynch's Ferry 10-2 (Fall/Winter 97-98): 42-47; auth, "So Old . . . So New: Reflections of Colonial Architecture in Lynchburg," Lynch's Ferry, 11-1 (Spring/Summer 98): 24-29; auth, articles on Warren 'Baby' Dodds and Walter Page, in American Natioanl Biography (NY: Oxford Univ Press, 98); auth, articles on Michael Feldman, Casey Kasem, and Jazz Radio Formats, in Historical Dictionary of American Radio (Westport, CT: Greenwood Publ Group, 98); auth, "The Round Arch Style: Romanesque Acrhitecture in Lynchburg," Lynch's Ferry 13-2 (in press); coauth, Bert: A Memoir of Bertram F. Dodson, Sr., Warwick House Publ (Lynchburg, VA), in press. **CONTACT ADDRESS** Dept Commun, Lynchburg Col, 1501 Lakeside Dr, Lynchburg, VA 24501-3113. **EMAIL** young@acavax.lynchburg.edu

YOUNG, WILLIAM ROBERT
PERSONAL Born 06/02/1947, Toronto, ON, Canada **DISCIPLINE** HISTORY **EDUCATION** York Univ, BA Hons, 69; Univ BC, Vancouver, MA, 72, PhD, 78. **CAREER** Course dir hist, York Univ, 77-78; officer, Fed Provincial Rels Office, 77-78; Vis asst prof Hist, Simon Fraser Univ, 78-. **MEMBERSHIPS** Can Hist Asn. **RESEARCH** Canadian society during World War II. **SELECTED PUBLICATIONS** Auth, Conscription, rural depopulation and the farmers of Ontario, 1917-1919, Can Hist Rev, 9/72; coauth, Development of Canadian Consular Operations in the United States, 1940-1972, Dept of External Affairs, 73. **CONTACT ADDRESS** 5-171 MacLaren St, Ottawa, ON, Canada K2P 0K8.

YOUNG, ZENAIDA ISABEL
PERSONAL Born Panama City, Panama, 2 children **DISCIPLINE** INTERIOR DESIGN **EDUCATION** Fla St Univ, MS, 87. **CAREER** Sr designer, 89-91, Design Firm Inc, FL; Interior Design, 91-, Espinosa-Young Design Group, FL; Interior Design Dept Chair, 93-, Palm Beach Com Col. **MEMBERSHIPS** IDEC **RESEARCH** Sustainable Design, indoor air quality. **CONTACT ADDRESS** Division of Humanities, Palm Beach Community College, 4200 Congress Ave, Lake Worth, FL 33461. **EMAIL** youngz@pbcc.cc.fl.us

YOUNGBLOOD, DENISE J.
DISCIPLINE HISTORY **EDUCATION** Wright State Univ, BA, 74; Stanford Univ, MA, 75; PhD, 80. **CAREER** Vis Instr, Ciry Col of San Jose, 80; Ed Asst, Russian Rev, 80-82; Slavic Bibliog Asst, Stanford Univ Libr, 80-82; Asst to the Exec Dir, Am Asn for the Advancement of Slavi Studies, 82-88; From Vis Asst Prof to Assoc Prof, Middlebury Col, 92, 95; From Asst Prof to Prof, Dept Chair, Univ of Vt, 88-. **HONORS AND AWARDS** Int Res and Exchanges Bd Fel for Dissertation Res in the USSR, 78-79; Nat Coun of Soviet and E Europ Res grant, 83-84; Nat Endowment for the Humanities Travel to Collections Grant, 89; Am Coun of Learned Soc Travel Grant, 90; Am Coun of Learned Soc Grant-in-Aid, 90; Kroepsch-Maurice Awd for Excellence in Teaching, Univ of Vt, 93; Heldt Prize for the Best Book by a Woman in Slavic Studies, Asn for Women in Slavis Studies, 93; Summer Res Grant, Univ of Vt, 90, 94; Russian and E Europ Summer Res Inst Grant, Univ of Ill, 93, 94, 95; Presidential Fel, Salzburg Sem, 94; Kennan Inst for Advanced Russian Studies Short-Term Grant, 94; Int Res and Exchanges Bd Short-Term Grant, 95. **SELECTED PUBLICATIONS** Auth, Soviet Cinema in the Silent Era, 1918-1935, Studies in Cinema 35, UMI Res Press (Ann Arbor), 85, Univ of Tex Austin (Austin), 91, in Cinema Century vol 1 First 50 years (Dubuque, IA: Kendall/Hunt, 94); auth, "Cinema as Social Criticism: The Early Films of Fridrikh Ermler," in The Red Screen, ed. Anna Lawton (London: Routledge, 92), 66-89; auth, "'We DonÛt Know What to Laugh at': Comedy and Satire in Soviet Cinema (From the Miracle Worker to 'St. Jorger's Feast Day'," in Inside Soviet Film Satire: Laughter with a Lash, ed. Andrew S. Horton (NY: Cambridge Univ Press, 93), 36-47; auth, Movies for the Masses: Popular Cinema and Soviet Society in the 1920s, Cambridge Univ Press (Cambridge), 92, 93; auth, "'Repentance': Stalinist Terror and the Realism of Surrealism," in Revisioning History: Film and the Construction of a New Past, ed. Robert A. Rosenstone (Princeton, NJ: Princeton Univ Press, 95), 139-154; auth, "The Russians at the Movies," in Reemerging Russia: Search for Identity, ed. Max J. Okenfuss and Cheryl D. Roberts (St. Louis, MO: The Oasis Inst, 95), 21-42; auth, "'Andrei Rublev': The medieval Epic as Post-Utopian History," in The Persistence of History: Cinema, Televison and the Modern Event, ed. Vivian Sobchack (NY" Routledge, 96), 127-143; auth, "Post-Stalinist Cinema and the Myth of World War II: Tarkovskii's 'Ivan's Childhood' and Kilmov's 'Come and See'," in World War II, Film, and History, ed. John Whiteclay Chambers II and David Culbert (NY: Oxford Univ Press, 96), 85-96; auth, "A War Forgotten: The Great War in Russian and Soviet Cinema," in The First World War and Popular Cinema, 1914 to the Present, ed. Michael Paris (Edinburgh: Edinburgh Univ Press, 99), 172-191; auth, The Magic Mirror: Movie Making in Russia, 1908-1918, Wis Studies in Film, Univ of Wis Press (Madison), 99. **CONTACT ADDRESS** Hist Dept, Univ of Vermont, Wheeler House, Burlington, VT 05405-0164. **EMAIL** denise.youngblood@uvm.edu

YOUNGER, JOHN GRIMES
PERSONAL Born 09/01/1945, Columbus, OH **DISCIPLINE** PREHISTORIC GREEK ARCHEOLOGY **EDUCATION** Stanford Univ, BA, 67; Univ Cincinnati, MA, 69, PhD(classics), 73. **CAREER** Instr classics, Campion High Sch, Athens, Greece, 73-74; asst prof, 74-79, Assoc Prof Classics, Duke Univ, 79-. **MEMBERSHIPS** Archaeol Inst Am; assoc Brit Sch Archaeol. **RESEARCH** Engraved sealstones and finger rings of the Greek Late Bronze Age; prehistoric Greek art; Hellenistic and late Roman sculpture. **SELECTED PUBLICATIONS** Auth, A Glyptic sktch from Isopata, HM 908, Kadmos, 73; contribr, Die kretisch-mykenische Glyptik und ihre gegenwartige Probleme, 74 & Corpus der minoischen-mykenischen Siegel (Vol V), 75; auth, Bronze Age representations of Aegean bull-leaping, 76 & The Mycenae-Vapheio Lion workshop, 78, & The lapidary's workshop at Knossoss, 79 Annals of the British School of Archaeology, Am J Archaeol; Non-sphragistic uses of Minoan-Mycenaean sealstones and rings, Kadmos, 78; contribr, Papers in Cycladic prehistory, 79 & Corpus der minoischen-my kenischen, Siegel (Beiheft I). **CONTACT ADDRESS** Dept of Class Studies, Duke Univ, Durham, NC 27706.

YOX, ANDREW
PERSONAL Born 02/22/1955, Buffalo, NY, m, 1989, 3 children **DISCIPLINE** AMERICAN CULTURAL HISTORY **EDUCATION** Valparaiso Univ, BA, 77; Univ Chicago, MA, 78; Univ Chicago, PhD, 83. **CAREER** Part time lectr, Ball State Univ, 84-85; Vis Asst Prof, Southwest Tex State Univ, 85-89; Lectr, Univ Tex, 89-94; Assoc Prof, Northeast Tex Community Col, 94-. **HONORS AND AWARDS** Postdoctoral Fel, Ball State Univ, 85-86; Grant, Tex Commt for Humanities, 94; Who's Who Among America's Teachers, 00. **MEMBERSHIPS** Immigration and Ethnic Hist Soc. **RESEARCH** Rise and fall of the German-American community, art and the American community 1800-2000, history of popular theology. **SELECTED PUBLICATIONS** Auth, "Ethnic Loyalties of the Alsatians in Buffalo," Yearbk of German-Am Studies (85): 106-123; auth, "Bonds of Community: Buffalo's German Element 1853-1871," NY Hist (85): 141-163; auth, "When Women Dominated the Arts of Middletown U S A," in Proceedings of the 1986 Meeting of the Am Hist Asn (Ann Arbor: Univ Microfilms, 87), 1-15; auth, "Teaching the American History Survey," Perspectives: Am Hist Asn Newsletter (89): 24; auth, "An American Renaissance: Art and Community in the 1930s," Mid-Am (90): 107-118; auth, "The Parochial Context of Trusteeism: Buffalo's Saint Louis Church 1828-1855," The Cath Hist Rev (90): 712-733; auth, "The Fall of the German-American Community: Buffalo 1914-1919," in Immigration to NY (Philadelphia: Assoc UP, 91), 126-147. **CONTACT ADDRESS** Dept Soc Sci, Northeast Texas Comm Col, PO Box 1307, Mount Pleasant, TX 75456-9991. **EMAIL** ayox@ntcc.cc.tx.us

YU, HENRY
PERSONAL Born 03/12/1967, Vancouver, BC, Canada, m **DISCIPLINE** HISTORY **EDUCATION** Univ BC, BA, 89; Princeton Univ, MA, 92; PhD, 94. **CAREER** Asst prof, UCLA, 94-; vis asst prof, Yale Univ, 97. **HONORS AND AWARDS** Dissertation Fel, Soc Sci Humanities Res Coun of Canada, 92-94; Princeton Soc of Fel, 94; Fel, Univ Calif Humanities Res Inst, 96; Fel, Wesleyan Univ Humanities Ctr, 97. **MEMBERSHIPS** Am Hist Asn; Org of Am Hist; Asn of Asian Am Studies; Am Studies Asn. **RESEARCH** U.S. cultural and intellectual history; Asian American history; Race relations; U.S. immigration; Global migration; Ethnic and whiteness studies. **SELECTED PUBLICATIONS** Auth, "Constructing the 'Oriental Problem' in American Thought, 1920-1960," in Multicultural Education, Transformative Knowledge and Action: Historical and Contemporary Perspectives, New York, 96; auth, "Orientalizing the Pacific Rim: The Production of Exotic Knowledge by American Missionaries and Sociologists in the 1920's," J of Am-E Asian Relations, 96; auth, "The 'Oriental Problem' in America: Linking the Identities of Chinese and Japanese American Intellectuals," in Claiming America: constructing Chinese American Identities During the Exclusion Era," Temple Univ Press, 98; auth, "Mixing Bodies and Cultures: The Meaning of America's Fascination with Sex Between 'Orientals' and Whites," in Sex, Love, Race: Crossing boundaries in North American History, NY Univ Press, 98; auth, "How Tiger Woods Lost His Stripes: Post-National American Studies as a History of Race, Migration and the Commodification of Culture," in Post-National American Studies, Univ Calif Press, 00; auth, "On a stage Built by Others: Creating an Intellectual History of Asian Americans," in History and Historians in the Making, 00; auth, Thinking Orientals: Migration, Contact and Exoticism in Modern America, Oxford Univ Press, 01. **CONTACT ADDRESS** Dept Hist, Univ of California, Los Angeles, 6265 Bunche, Box 951473, Los Angeles, CA 90095-1473. **EMAIL** henryyu@ucla.edu

YUAN, TSING
PERSONAL Born 07/21/1937, Peking, China, m, 1972 **DISCIPLINE** ASIAN HISTORY **EDUCATION** George Washington Univ, BA, 60, MA, 62; Univ Pa, PhD(hist), 69. **CAREER** From lectr to asst prof hist, Swarthmore Col, 66-72; asst prof, 72-76, Assoc Prof Hist, Wright State Univ, 76-, Am Philos Soc fel, 70-71; Am Coun Learned Soc fel, 70-71; assoc, Univ Sem Traditional China, Columbia Univ, 70-; fel, Harvard E Asian Res Crt, 71-72; vis assoc prof hist, Ohio State Univ, 76. **MEMBERSHIPS** AHA; Asn Asian Studies. **RESEARCH** Ming history; economic and social history; agricultural history. **SELECTED PUBLICATIONS** Auth, Yakub Beg (1820-1877) and the Moslem rebellion in Chinese Turkestan, Cent Asiatic J, 61; The Japanese intervention in Shantung during World War I, In: China and Japan Since World War I: The Search for Balance, Clio, 77; Urban riots and disturbances during late Ming and eary Ch'ing, In: From Ming to Ch'ing, Yale Univ (in press). **CONTACT ADDRESS** Dept of Hist, Wright State Univ, Dayton, Dayton, OH 45431.

YUNGBLUT, LAURA HUNT
PERSONAL Born 01/12/1961, Alexander City, AL, m, 1994, 1 child **DISCIPLINE** HISTORY **EDUCATION** Western Carolina Univ, BA, 83; Univ Cincinnati, MA, 85, PhD, 93; Univ Ky, MS, 90. **CAREER** Assoc Prof, Univ Dayton. **RESEARCH** Early Modern England, Medieval Europe. **SELECTED PUBLICATIONS** Auth, Strangers Settled Here Amongst Us: Policy, Perception and the Presence of Aliens in Elizabethan England, London : Routledge, 96. **CONTACT ADDRESS** Dept of Hist, Univ of Dayton, 300 College Park, Dayton, OH 45469-1540. **EMAIL** yungblut@udayton.edu

Z

ZABEL, CRAIG
PERSONAL Born 02/14/1955, Chicago, IL, m, 1980, 1 child **DISCIPLINE** AMERICAN, MODERN EUROPEAN, AND RUSSIAN ARCHITECTURE **EDUCATION** Univ Wis, BA; Univ Ill Urbana-Champaign, MA, PhD. **CAREER** Assoc prof, Pa State Univ, 85-; Dept Hd, Art History, Penn State Univ. **HONORS AND AWARDS** Col Arts & Archit Fac Awd for Outstanding Tchg; interim hd & grad off, dept history. **RESEARCH** Am architecture during the 1930s and 1940s. **SELECTED PUBLICATIONS** Areas: bank architecture, Prairie School architects (particularly George G. Elmslie), American public architecture, and contemporary architecture; contrib, The Midwest in American Architecture, Univ Ill Press. **CONTACT ADDRESS** Pennsylvania State Univ, Univ Park, 229 Arts Bldg, University Park, PA 16802. **EMAIL** cxz3@psu.edu

ZABEL, JAMES ALLEN
PERSONAL Born 08/07/1945, Lincoln, NE, m, 1966, 2 children **DISCIPLINE** HISTORY **EDUCATION** Grinnell Col, BA, 67; Univ Chicago, MA, 68, PhD(hist), 71. **CAREER** Prof Hist, Sch Ozarks, 71-, Chmn Dept, 80-, Danforth assoc, Danforth Found, 78- **MEMBERSHIPS** AHA; AAUP; Western Asn Ger Studies. **RESEARCH** Churches in modern Germany. **SELECTED PUBLICATIONS** Auth, Nazism and the Pastors, Scholars, 76. **CONTACT ADDRESS** Dept of Hist, Sch of the Ozarks, Point Lookout, MO 65726.

ZACEK, JOSEPH FREDERICK
PERSONAL Born 12/18/1930, Berwyn, IL, m, 1979, 3 children **DISCIPLINE** MODERN EUROPEAN HISTORY **EDUCATION** Univ IL, AB, 52, MA, 53, PhD, 62; Columbia Univ, cert, Inst ECent Europe, 62; Columbia Univ, Ford Foundation, Foreign Aera Training Fellow, 60-62. **CAREER** Res asst Europ hist, Univ Ill, 57-58, teaching asst Europ & Russ hist, 59-60; asst prof hist, Occidental Col, 62-65 & Univ Calif, Los Angeles, 65-68; assoc prof, 68-71, dir, SUNY at Albany, 68-77, 91-92; chmn dept, 74-77, Prof History, SUNY, Albany, 71-, Vis asst prof hist, Univ Calif, Los Angeles, 63-65; **HONORS AND AWARDS** Duke Found grant, 67-68; State Univ NY res grants, 69-71; Nat Sci Found res grant, 72; Int Res & Exchanges Bd fel, Czech, 73; State Univ NY Res Found grants, 74, 75, 00; mem, Nat Bd Consult, Nat Endowment for Humanities, 75-; Rockefeller Found sabbatical res grant, 77-78; vis scholar East Europ hist, Inst ECent Europe, Columbia Univ, 77-78; mem, Columbia Univ Sem Hist Legal & Polit Thought; mem nat screening comt, East Europ exchanges, Int Res & Exchanges Bd, 78-81; Vis Scholar, Russian & E European Ctr, Univ Il, 87; Phi Beta Kappa, 52; Fel Russian Res Ctr, Harvard Univ, 86-91; Who's Who in Am, 90-; Comenius Medal, Govt Czech & Slovak Fed Repub, 92; Medal Comenius Pedag Inst, 92; Josef Hlavka Medal, Czech Acad Sci, 92. **MEMBERSHIPS** AHA; Am Asn Advan Slavic Studies; Czechoslovak Hist Conf; Slovak Studies Asn; Consortium on Revolutionary Europ; Asn for Study Ethnicity & Nat. **RESEARCH** History of East Central Europe; Czechs and Slovaks; East European immigration in United States. **SELECTED PUBLICATIONS** Contribr, Nationalism in Eastern Europe, Univ Wash, 69,94; auth, The Historian as Scholar and Nationalist: Palacky, Mouton, The Hague, 70; auth, Palacky's Politics: The Second Phase, Can Slavic Studies, 71; The French Revolution, Napoleon & the Czechs, Proc Consortium Revolutionary Europe, 80; ed and contribr, Frantisek Palacky, 1798-1876: A Centennial Appreciation, East Europ Quart, 81; ed and contribr, the Enlightenment and the National Revivals in Eastern Europe, Canadian Review of Studies in Nationalism, 83; ed and contribr, The Intimate Palacky, Nationalities Papers, 84; contribr, Reappraising the Munich Pact: Continental Perspectives, Johns Hopkins Univ, 92; auth, Czech National Consciousness in the Baroque Era, in the History of European Ideas, 93; contribr, Encyclopedia of Eastern Europe, Garland, 00. **CONTACT ADDRESS** Dept Hist, SUNY, Albany, 1400 Washington Ave, Albany, NY 12222-1000.

ZAGARRI, ROSEMARIE
PERSONAL Born 04/08/1957, St. Louis, MO, m, 1 child **DISCIPLINE** HISTORY **EDUCATION** Northwestern Univ, BA, 77; Yale Univ, MA, 78; MPhil, 80; PhD, 84. **CAREER** Asst prof, WV Univ, 84-87; asst prof, The Catholic Univ of Am, 87-91, assoc prof, 91-94; assoc prof, George Mason Univ, 94-97, prof, 97-. **HONORS AND AWARDS** Summa cum laude; departmental honors in Am Culture major; Phi Beta Kappa; Fulbright Fellowship, 93; Articles Prize, Am Soc for 18th Century Studies, 93; Nat Endowment for the Humanities, res fellowship, 97-98. **MEMBERSHIPS** Am Hist Asn; Soc for the Hist of the Early Am Republic; Eighteenth-Century Studies Asn. **RESEARCH** Colonial and revolutionary America, early Republic, women's history. **SELECTED PUBLICATIONS** Auth, The Politics of Size: Representation in the United States, 1776-1850, Ithaca, NY: Cornell Univ Press (87); ed, with intro, David Humphreys' "Life of General Washington" with George Washington's "Remarks," Athens, GA: The Univ GA Press (91); auth, A Woman's Dilema: Mercy Otis Warren and the American Revolution, Wheeling, IL: Harlan Davidson, Inc. (95). **CONTACT ADDRESS** Dept Hist, George Mason Univ, Fairfax, 4400 Univ Dr., Fairfax, VA 22030-4422. **EMAIL** rzagarri@gmu.edu

ZAGORIN, PEREZ
PERSONAL Born 05/29/1920, Chicago, IL, m, 1947, 1 child **DISCIPLINE** HISTORY **EDUCATION** Univ Chicago, AB, 41; Harvard Univ, MA, 47, PhD, 52. **CAREER** Instr hist, mherst Col, 47-49; lectr, Vassar Col, 51-53; from asst prof to assoc prof, to prof, McGill Univ, 55-65; Amundsen vis prof, 64; vis prof, Johns Hopkins Univ, 64-65; prof, Univ of Rochesrer, 65-90; Joseph C. Wilson Prof Hist, Univ Rochester, 82-90, Joseph C. Wilson Prof Hist, Emer, 90-. **HONORS AND AWARDS** Fulbright Fel, 49; Sheldon Travelling Fel, Harvard Univ, 49-50; Sr Fel, The Canada Coun, 58-59; Fac Res Fel, Soc Sci Res Coun, 59-60, 60-61; Sr Fel, Folger Shakespeare Libr, 64-65; Sr Fel, Nat Humanities Ctr, 78-79; Fel, J.S. Guggenheim Memorial Found, 83-84; Fel, Ctr for Advanced Study in The Behavioral Sciences, 83-84; Fel, Nat Endowment for the Humanities, 83-84; Mellon Fel, 83-84; Fel, Shannon Ctr for Advanced Studies, Univ of Va, 95-; Fel, Am Acad of Arts and Sciences; Fel, Royal Historical Soc, Great Britain. **MEMBERSHIPS** AHA; Renaissance Soc Am; Conf Brit Studies; fel Am Acad Arts & Sci; fel Royal Hist Soc. **RESEARCH** Early modern European and British history; history of political thought. **SELECTED PUBLICATIONS** Auth, A History of Political Thought in The English Revolution Routledge & Kegan Paul, 54, new eds. 66, Thoemmes Press, 97; auth, The English Revolution: Politics, Events, Ideas, Ashgate, 98; auth, Francis Bacon, Princeton Univ Press, 98, reissued in paperback ed. 99; auth, "History, The Referent, And Narrative: Reflections on Postmodernism Now," History and Theory, 1 (99): 1-24; auth, "Two books on Thomas Hobbes," J, of The History of Ideas 2 (99): 361-71; auth, "Hobbes Without Grotius," Histyory of Political Thought 1 (00): 16-40; auth, "Rejoinder to A Postmodernist, History and Theory 2 (00): 201-209; auth, "The Joys of Schadenfreude," Virginia Quarterly Review 3 (00): 446-50; auth, "Francis Bacon's Concept of Objectivity and The Idols of The Mind," British J For The Hist of Sci (01); auth, "Thomas Carlyle And Oliver Cromwell," History and Ideologues: Essays in Honor of Donald Kelley, Universoty of Rochester Press (01). **CONTACT ADDRESS** 2990 Beaumont Farm Rd., Charlottesville, VA 22901. **EMAIL** pz3p@virginia.edu

ZAHNISER, A. H. MATHIAS
PERSONAL Born 01/01/1938, Washington, DC, m, 1959, 3 children **DISCIPLINE** ISLAMIC STUDIES **EDUCATION** Greenville Col, IL, BA, 60; Am Univ, MA, 62; Asbury Theol Sem, M Div, 65; Johns Hopkins Univ, PhD, 73. **CAREER** Asst to assoc prof, relig stud, 71-78, Cent Mich Univ; prof, 78-83 Greenville Col; assoc prof, 83-86, Mission Asbury Theol Sem; John Wesley Beeson Prof Of Christian Mission, 86-, Asbury Theol Sem; Emeritus Prof, Asbury Theol Sem, 00-. **HONORS AND AWARDS** Univ Achievement Awd, Cent Mich Univ, 73. **MEMBERSHIPS** Am Soc of Missiology; AAR. **RESEARCH** Literary analysis of the Quran; use of symbols and ritual in Christian nurture and formation. **SELECTED PUBLICATIONS** Auth, Symbol and Ceremony: Making Disciples Across Cultures, MARC Pubs, 97; auth, Ritual Process and Christian Discipling: Contextualizing a Buddhist Rite of Passage, Missiology, XIX, no 1, 91; auth, The Word of God and the Apostleship of Isa: A Narrative Analysis of Al Imran, J of Semitic Studies, XXXVIII, no 1, 91; auth, Close Encounters of the Venerable Kind: Christian Dialogical Proclamation Among Muslims, Asbury Theol J, XLIX, no 1, 94; auth, Sura as Guidance and Exhortation: The Composition of Surat al-Nisa, Humanism, Culture, and Language in the Near East: Studies in Honor of Georg Krotkoff, Eisenbrauns, 97; co-ed, Humanism, Culture, and Language in the Near East: Studies in Honor of Georg Krotkoff, Eisenbrauns, 97. **CONTACT ADDRESS** Asbury Theol Sem, Wilmore, KY 40390. **EMAIL** mathias_zahniser@asburyseminary.edu

ZAHNISER, MARVIN RALPH
PERSONAL Born 06/29/1934, New Kensington, PA, m, 1956, 3 children **DISCIPLINE** AMERICAN HISTORY **EDUCATION** Greenville Col, AB, 56; Univ Mich, MA, 57; Univ Calif, Santa Barbara, PhD(hist), 63. **CAREER** Vis asst prof hist, Univ Wash, 63-64; vis asst prof, Univ Iowa, 64-65; from asst prof to assoc prof, 65-73, asst vprovost arts & sci, 72-73, chmn dept, 73-77, Prof Hist, Ohio State Univ, 73-, Chmn Dept, 81-, Mershon fel, Mershon Ctr Educ Nat Security, 66; vis assoc prof hist, Univ Calif, Santa Barbara, 68. **MEMBERSHIPS** AHA; Orgn Am Historians; Soc Historians of Am Foreign Rels (exec sectreas, 81-); Conf Faith & Hist (vpres, 76-78, pres, 78-80). **RESEARCH** American early national era, especially foreign policy; history of French-American relations, 1775-1975. **SELECTED PUBLICATIONS** Auth, Edward Rutledge, 4/63 & The first Pinckney mission to France, 10/65, SC Hist Mag; Charles Cotesworth Pinckney: Founding Father, Inst Early Am Hist & Cult, 67 & coed, The Letter Book of Eliza Lucas Pinckney, 72, Univ NC; auth, Uncertain Friendship: American-French Diplomatic Relations Through the Cold War, Wiley, 75; The continental system, In: Encyclopaedia of American Foreign Policy, Scribner's, 78; ed, John W Bricker reflects upon the fight for the Bricker Amendment, Ohio Hist, 4/78. **CONTACT ADDRESS** Dept of Hist, Ohio State Univ, Columbus, Columbus, OH 43210.

ZALESCH, SAUL E.
PERSONAL Born 01/07/1952, Baltimore, MD, s **DISCIPLINE** ART HISTORY **EDUCATION** Univ Del, PhD, 92. **CAREER** Assoc prof, La Tech Univ, 94- . **HONORS AND AWARDS** Henry R. Luce Found Fel, 86; Nat Mus of Am Art/Smithsonian Inst, pre-doctoral fel, 88; NEH postdoctoral fel at the Winterthur Mus, 93. **MEMBERSHIPS** Col Art Asn; Southeastern Col Art Conf; Asn of Hist of Am Art; Asn Hist of 19th Century Art. **RESEARCH** Mass-produced secular and religious art of the late 19th century; collecting. **SELECTED PUBLICATIONS** Auth, Against the Current: Anti-Modern Images in the Work of Winslow Homer, Am Art Rev, 93; auth, Competition and Conflict in the New York Art World 1874-1879, Winterthur Portfolio, 94; auth, What the Four Million Bought: Cheap Oil Paintings of the 1880s, Am Quart, 96; auth, The Religious Art of Benziger Brothers, American Art, 99. **CONTACT ADDRESS** School of Art, Louisiana Tech Univ, PO Box 3175, Ruston, LA 71272-0001. **EMAIL** szalesch@art.latech.edu

ZALLER, ROBERT
PERSONAL Born 03/19/1940, Brooklyn, NY, m, 1968, 1 child **DISCIPLINE** HISTORY **EDUCATION** Queens Col, BA, 60; Washington Univ, MA, 63; PhD, 68. **CAREER** Visiting Asst prof, Univ Calif, 68-69; Asst prof to prof, Univ Miami, 72-87; Prof, Drexel Univ, 87-. **HONORS AND AWARDS** Phi Beta Kappa; Phi Alpha Theta Prize, 72; Robinson Jeffers Tor House Foundation Awd, 84; John Simon Guggenheim Fel, 86; Fel, Royal Hist Soc, 91. **MEMBERSHIPS** am Hist Asn; Carolinas Symposium on British Studies; Hist of Early Modern Europe; N Am Conf on British Studies; Robinson Jeffers Asn. **RE-**

SEARCH Tudor-Stuart England; early Modern Europe; Modern literature and film. SELECTED PUBLICATIONS Ed, Centennial Essays for Robinson Jeffers, Univ Delaware press, 91; co-auth, Civilizations of the West: the Human Adventure, HarperCollins, 92; co-auth, Civilizations of the West: the Human Adventure 2nd ed, HarperCollins, 97; trans, The Scorpion (and other stories), Pella, 98. CONTACT ADDRESS Dept Hist & Govt, Drexel Univ, 3141 Chestnut St, Philadelphia, PA 19104-2816. EMAIL zallerrm@drexel.edu

ZANGRANDO, JOANNA SCHNEIDER

PERSONAL Born Hastings, MN, d, 1969, 2 children **DISCIPLINE** AMERICAN SOCIAL & CULTURAL HISTORY **EDUCATION** Wayne State Univ, BA, 61, MA, 63; George Washington Univ, PhD, 74. **CAREER** Hist researcher, US Atomic Energy Comn, MD, 64-66; legis asst, US Off Educ, 66-67; lectr hist, Albertus Magnus Col, 70; instr, Univ Hartford, 70-71; lectr, Univ Akron, 71-72; NEH Mus consult, Am hist & civilization prog community mus, Nat Am Studies Fac, 72-74; vis asst prof Am studies, George Washington Univ, 74-76; asst prof, 76-80, assoc prof Am Studies, 80-88, Full Prof, 89-, Chair, Am Studies Dept, 87-99, Dir, Liberal Studies Prog, 84-87, 98-, Skidmore Col; F D Roosevelt Libr res grant, 74-75; panel mem pub progs & res, fels, and seminars, general progs, Higher Ed Curriculum Devel and Focus Grants, preservation, NEH, 76-; mem bd rev for grant proposals, Eleanor Roosevelt Inst, FDR Libr, 77-81; dir, Skidmore Col London Study Abroad Prog & vis prof, 83, 90, 95; Scholar in Residence, NYU, 98. **HONORS AND AWARDS** Endowed Chair: Douglas Professor of American Culture, History, Literary & Interdisciplinary. **MEMBERSHIPS** AHA; Orgn Am Historians; Am Studies Asn; Am Asn State & Local Hist; Conf Group Women's History. **RESEARCH** American culture, technology and aesthetics; women's studies and women labor union organizers, 1930's to 1950's; American material culture and museum studies; women reformers; civil rights. **SELECTED PUBLICATIONS** Coauth, Black protest: A rejection of the American dream, J Black Studies, 12/70; Law, the American value system, and the black community, Rutgers-Camden Law J, spring 71; Black history in the college curriculum, In: New Perspectives on Black Studies, Univ Ill Press, 71; auth, Women and archives: An historian views the liberation of Clio, Am Archivist, 4/73; coauth, The object as subject: The role of museums and material culture collections in American studies, Am Quart, 8/74; contribr, For the duration: Working women and World War II, In: FDR's America, Forum Press, 76; auth, Women's studies: closer to reality, In: American Studies, Topics and Sources, Greenwood, 76; Women's Studies in the U. S., in Sources in Am Studies, Greenwood, 83; coauth, Eleanor Roosevelt & Black Civil Rights, in Joan Hoff and Marjorie Lightman, eds, Without Precedent. The Life and Career of Eleanor Roosevelt, IN Press, 84; book rev, Planning a New Liberal Studies Curriculum, George Mason Univ Conference on Non-Traditional Interdisc Progs, Proceedings, 86; coed, Charlotte Perkins Gilman: The Mixed Legacy, U of Delaware Press, 00. **CONTACT ADDRESS** Am Studies Dept, Skidmore Col, 815 N Broadway, Saratoga Springs, NY 12866-1698. **EMAIL** jzangran@skidmore.edu

ZANGRANDO, ROBERT LEWIS

PERSONAL Born 05/16/1932, Albany, NY, m, 1996, 2 children **DISCIPLINE** UNITED STATES HISTORY **EDUCATION** Union Col, NYork, BA, 58; Univ Pa, MA, 60, PhD(hist), 63. **CAREER** Asst prof hist, Rutgers Univ, Camden, 63-65, acting chmn dept, 64-65; asst exec secy, Am Hist Asn & dir, Serv Ctr for Teachers of Hist, 65-69; lectr hist dept, ed hist publications, Yale Univ, 69-71; assoc prof, 71-81, Prof Hist, Univ Akron, 81-94; prof emeritus, 94-; Prog coordr, State of NJ Off Econ Opportunity, 65; mem exec bd, Soc Educ, 65-69; Am Coun Learned Soc grant-in-aid, 69; Eleanor Roosevelt Found grant-in-aid, 74; Harry S.Truman Library Institute grant-in-aid, 83; consult, Nat Am Studis Fac, 74-78. **MEMBERSHIPS** AHA; Orgn Am Historians; Coord Council Women in Hist. **RESEARCH** Afro-American history and studies; 20th century US history; history of women in the US. **SELECTED PUBLICATIONS** Auth, "The Organized Negro: The NAACP and Civil Rights," in The Black Experience in America, Univ Tex, 70; coauth, Black Protest, A Rejection of the American Dream, J Black Studies, 70; auth, Law, the American Value System and the Black Community, Rutgers-Camden Law J, 71; auth, Black Outreach: Afro-Americans' Efforts to Attract Support Abroad, Phylon, 76; auth, The NAACP Crusade Against Lynching, 1909-1950, Temple Univ Press, 80; auth, "Manuscript Sources of Twentieth-Century Civil Rights Research," Jour of American History, 87; auth, "Historians' procedures for Handling Plagarism," Publishing Research Quarterly, 991-92; coauth, "Eleanor Roosevelt and Black Civil Rights," Without Precedent: The Life and Career of Eleanor Roosevelt, Indiana University Press, 84; coed, Civil Rights and African Americans, Northwestern University Press, 91. **CONTACT ADDRESS** Dept of hist, Univ of Akron, Akron, OH 44325-1902.

ZBORAY, MARY SARACINO

PERSONAL Born 10/24/1953, Bridgeport, CT, m, 1984 **DISCIPLINE** AMERICAN STUDIES **EDUCATION** Univ Bridgeport, BA, 75, MA 80. **CAREER** Hist, Georgia St Univ. **HONORS AND AWARDS** Summa cum Laude; Charles A Dana scholar, 72-73, 73-74; Smithsonian Fel, 82-83; Hon Vis Fel, Radcliffe Col, 98-99. **MEMBERSHIPS** Am Stud Asn; Am Hist Asn; Am Textile His Mus; Conn Hist Soc; Maine Hist Soc; MLA; New England Hist Geneal Soc; NH Hist Soc; Org Am Historians. **RESEARCH** United States cultural history. **SELECTED PUBLICATIONS** Auth, "Political News and Female Readership in Antebellum Boston and Its Region," Journalism Hist, 96; "Books, Reading and the World of Goods in Antebellum New England," Am Q, 96; "The Boston Book Trades, 1789-1850," Entrepreneurs, ed by Conrad Edick Wright, Mass Hist Soc, 97; "Whig Women, Politics, and Culture in the Campaign of 1840," J of the Early Republic, 97; "Reading and Everyday Life in Antebellum Boston," Libr & Culture, 97; "Have You Read..," Nineteenth-Century Lit, 97; "The Romance of Fisherwomen in Antebellum New England," Am Stud, 98; "The Mysteries of New England," Nineteenth-Century Contexts, 99; "Transcendentalism in Print," The Transient and the Permanent, ed Charles Capper, Mass Hist Soc, 99. **CONTACT ADDRESS** Dept of History, Georgia State Univ, University Plz, Atlanta, GA 30303. **EMAIL** hisrjz@mwa.org

ZBORAY, RONALD J.

PERSONAL Born 06/23/1953, Bridgeport, CT, m, 1984 **DISCIPLINE** HISTORY **EDUCATION** Univ Bridgeport, BA, 75; NYork Univ, MA, 77, PhD, 84. **CAREER** Assoc spec, microfilm ed, Emma Goldman Papers, Univ of Calif, Berkeley, 84-89; asst prof, History, Univ Texas at Arlington, 89-92; asst prof, Ga State Univ, 92-96, assoc prof, 96 - . **HONORS AND AWARDS** Summa cum Laude, 75; Louis M Lerner scholar, NYU, 76; NYU scholarship, 76-77; Humanist-in Museum, NY Inst for the Hum, 83; hon mention, Carl Bode Awd Comm, Am Culture Asn, 87; fel NEH, Am Antiq Soc, 91; Dale Somers Mem Awd, Georgia St Univ, 93; fel Mass Hist Soc, 94; Outstanding Jr Fac Awd, Georgia State Univ, 96; Cathy Covert Prize in Mass Commun Hist, 97; NEH fel, 98; hon vis fel, Schlesinger Lib, Radcliffe Col, 98-99; Elected to membership Texas Inst of Letters, 00. **MEMBERSHIPS** Am Asn of Univ Prof; Am Hist Asn; Am Mus of Textile Hist; Am Stud Asn; Andover Hist Soc; Asn of Georgia State Univ Hist; MLA; Am Lit Gp; New England Hist Geneal Soc; Org of Am Hist; Peabody Essex Mus; Soc for the Hist of the Early Am Republic, SC Hist Soc; Vt Hist Soc. **RESEARCH** United States cultural history. **SELECTED PUBLICATIONS** Ed, The Emma Goldman Papers: A Microfilm Edition, Chadwyck-Healey, 90; auth, A Fictive People: Antebellum Economic Development and the American Reading Public, Oxford, 93; auth, Technology and the Character of Community Life in Antebellum America: The Role of Story Papers, in Communication and Change in American Religious History, Eerdmans, 93; auth, Books, in Handbook on Mass Media in the United States: The Industry and Its Audiences, Greenwood, 94; auth, Editorial Prinicples and Procedures, in Emma Goldman: A Guide to Her Life and Documentary Sources, Chadwyck-Healey, 95; coauth, Political News and Female Readership in Antebellum Boston and Its Region, in Jour Hist, 96; coauth, Books, Reading, and the World of Goods in Antebellum New England, in Am Q, 96; coauth, The Boston Book Trades, 1789-1850: A Statistical and Geographical Analysis, in Entrepreneurs: The Boston Business Community, Mass Hist Soc, 97; coauth, Reading and Everyday Life in Antebellum Boston: The Diary of Daniel F.and Mary G. Child, in Libs and Culture, 97; coauth, Whig Women, Politics, and Culture in the Campaign of 1840: Three Perspectives from Massachusetts, in J of the Early Republic, 97; coauth, Have You Read..?: Real Readers and Their Responses in Antebellum Boston and Its Region, in Nineteenth-Century Lit, 97; coauth, The Romance of Fisherwomen in Antebellum New England, in Am Stud, 98; auth, Transcendentalism in Print: Production, Dissemination, and Common Reception," in Transient and Permanent: The Transcendentalist Movement and Its Contexts, Boston: Massachusetts Historical Society, 99, 310-381; auth, "A Handbook for the Study of Book History in the United States," Washington, D.C.: Library of Congress, 00; auth, "The Mysteries of New England: Eugene Sue's Imitators, 1844," Nineteenth-Century Contexts," 00, 457-492; auth, "Gender Slurs in Boston's Partisan Press During the 1840s," Journal of American Studies," 00, 413-446. **CONTACT ADDRESS** Dept of History, Georgia State Univ, University Plz, P O Box 4117, Atlanta, GA 30302-4117. **EMAIL** hisrjz@panther.gsu.edu

ZEIDEL, ROBERT F.

DISCIPLINE HISTORY **EDUCATION** Marquette Univ, PhD, 86 **CAREER** Sr. Lectr, Univ Wisconsin-Stout **MEMBERSHIPS** Amer Historical Assoc; OHA **RESEARCH** Immigration history **CONTACT ADDRESS** Social Science Dept, Univ of Wisconsin, Stout, Menomonie, WI 54751. **EMAIL** zeidelr@uwstout.edu

ZEIGLER, DONALD J.

PERSONAL Born 11/26/1951, Harrisburg, m, 1973, 2 children **DISCIPLINE** GEOGRAPHY **EDUCATION** Shippensburg Univ Penn, BS, 72; Univ RI, MA, 76; Mich State Univ, PhD, 80. **CAREER** Asst prof to prof, Old Dominion Univ, 80-; vis assoc prof, Univ Calif, 88; vis prof, Univ NC, 97. **HONORS AND AWARDS** Jesse S Heiges Distinguished Alum Awd, Penn, 99; Soc Sci Asn Scholar Awd in Geog. VA, 88; Gamma Theta Upsilon, Kappa Delta Pi, Phi Kappa Phi. **MEMBERSHIPS** Nat Coun for Geog Educ, Asn of Am Geogr, Am Geog Soc, N Am Cartographic Info Soc, VA Geog Soc. **RESEARCH** Cultural and political geography of the Middle East, Natural and technological hazards, Political cartography. **SELECTED PUBLICATIONS** Auth, Technological Hazards, Association of American Geographers, 83; co-ed, The Social Sciences and International Education, Kendall/Hunt, 89; auth, "Disaster Management: Post Chernobyl Perspectives on Nuclear Power," Environment and Planning C: Government and Policy, (88); ed, Virginia Geographer (1986-present). **CONTACT ADDRESS** Dept Polit Sci & Geog, Old Dominion Univ, Norfolk, VA 23529. **EMAIL** dzeigler@odu.edu

ZELIN, MADELEINE

DISCIPLINE MODERN CHINESE HISTORY **EDUCATION** Cornell Univ, BA, 70; Berkeley, PhD, 79. **CAREER** Prof, Columbia Univ, 79-; dir, E Asian Nat Resource Ct. **RESEARCH** Modern Chinese social and economic hist, Chinese economic development, Business and legal hist. **SELECTED PUBLICATIONS** Auth, The Magistrate's Tael, Rationalizing Fiscal Reform in Eighteenth Century Ch'ing China, 84; Rainbow, 92. **CONTACT ADDRESS** Dept of Hist, Columbia Univ, 2960 Broadway, New York, NY 10027-6902. **EMAIL** mhz1@columbia.edu

ZELINSKI, WILBUR

PERSONAL Born 12/21/1921, Chicago, IL, w, 1944, 2 children **DISCIPLINE** GEOGRAPHY **EDUCATION** Univ Cal, Berkeley, BA, 44; Univ Wis, MS, 46; Univ Cal, PhD, 53. **CAREER** Asst prof, Univ Georgia, 48-52; proj assoc, Univ Wis, 52-54; res anal, Chesapeake/Ohio RR, 54-59; prof, S Ill Univ, 59-63; prof, Pa State, 63-85; prof emer, 87-. **HONORS AND AWARDS** Merit Awd, AAG; Pres, AAG, 72-73; Guggenheim Fel; Mst Mentor Awd, NCGE; John Brinkerkoff Jackson Prize; Woodrow Wilson Gst Schl. **MEMBERSHIPS** AAG; AGS; Asn Gravestone Studies. **RESEARCH** Cultural, social and population geography of North America. **SELECTED PUBLICATIONS** Auth, Nation into State: The Shifting Symbolic Foundations of American Nationalism, Univ N Carolina Press, 88; auth, The Atlas of Pennsylvania, Temple Univ Press, 89; auth, The Emergency Evacuation of Cities, Rowman & Littlefield, 91; auth, The Cultural Geography of the United States, Prentice-Hall, 92; auth, Exploring the Beloved Country: Geographic Forays Into American Society And Culture, Univ Iowa Press, 94; auth, "Heterolocalism: An Alternative Model of the Sociospatial Behavior of Immigrant Ethnic Communities," Intl J Pop Geog 4 (98): 1-18; auth, "The World and Its Identity Crisis," in Textures of Place, Univ Minn Press, forthcoming). **CONTACT ADDRESS** Dept Geography, Pennsylvania State Univ, Univ Park, 302 Walker Bldg, University Park, PA 16802.

ZELLER, SUZANNE

DISCIPLINE INTELLECTUAL IMPACT OF SCIENCE IN CANADA **EDUCATION** Univ Windsor, BA, MA; Toronto, PhD. **CAREER** Prof. **RESEARCH** Intellectual impact of science in Canada; science in Victorian and modern culture and society; changing hist perceptions of the natural environment and the physical world; and the hist of scientific exploration and research. **SELECTED PUBLICATIONS** Auth, Inventing Canada: Early Victorian Science and the Idea of a Transcontinental Nation, U of Toronto P, 87; auth, "Mapping the Canadian Mind: Reports of the Geological Survey of Canada, 1842-1863," Canadian Literature, 131, (91): 156-67; auth, "Wiliam Brodie (1831-1909)," "J.B. Cherriman (1823-1908)," "G.M. Dawson (1849-1901)," and "D.P. Penhallow (1854-1910)," in Dictionary of Canadian Biography, (Toronto: Univ of Toronto Press, 94); Land of Promise, Promised Land: The Culture of Victorian Science in Canada, 96; auth, "Nature's Gullivers and Crusoes: The Scientific Exploration of British North America, 1800-1870," in North American Exploration, 3 vols., ed., John L. Allen, vol 3: A Continent Comprehended (Lincoln, Nebraska: Univ of Nebraska Press, 97): 190-243; auth, "Classical Codes: Biogeographical Assessments of Environment in Victorian Canada," Journal of Historical Geography, 98; auth, "Environment, Culture, and the Reception of Darwin in Canada, 1859-1909," in Responding to Darwin: Place, Race, Class, and Gender, ed., Ron Numbers and John Stenhouse, (Cambridge, England: Cambridge Univ Press, (forthcoming, 98); auth, "Merchants of Light: The Culture of Science in Sir Daniel Wilson's Ontario," in Daniel Wilson, ed. Elizabeth Huse, (Toronto: Univ of Toronto Press, (forthcoming, 98). **CONTACT ADDRESS** Dept of History, Wilfrid Laurier Univ, 75 University Ave W, Waterloo, ON, Canada N2L 3C5. **EMAIL** szeller@mach1.wlu.ca

ZELNIK, REGINALD ELY

PERSONAL Born 05/08/1936, New York, NY, m, 1956, 2 children **DISCIPLINE** MODERN RUSSIAN HISTORY **EDUCATION** Princeton Univ, AB, 56; Stanford Univ, MA, 61, PhD(Hist), 66. **CAREER** Lectr Hist, Ind Univ, Bloomington, 63-64; from asst prof to assoc prof, 64-76, chmn, Ctr Slavic & East Europ Studies, 77-80, prof Hist, Univ Calif, Berkeley, 76-, sr fel, Russ Inst, Columbia Univ, 68-69; Guggenheim Found fel, 71-72; Int Res & Exchanges Bd/Am Coun Learned Soc grant, inst Hist, Moscow, 72; fel, Hist Comn of Berlin, 76; chmn, Dept of Hist, UC Berkeley, 94-97. **HONORS AND AWARDS** AHA's Nancy Lyman Roelker Mentorship Awd; BABRA award for translation of a Radical Worker in Tsarist Russia. **MEMBERSHIPS** AHA; Am Asn Advan Slavic Studies. **RESEARCH** Russian labor history; comparative European labor history. **SELECTED PUBLICATIONS** Auth, The Sunday-school movement in Russia: 1859-1862, J Mod Hist, 6/65; coauth, The Politics of Escalation in Vietnam, Beacon, 66; auth, Labor and Society in Tsarist Russia: The Factory Workers of St Petersburg, 1855-1870, Stanford Univ, 71; Populists and workers, Soviet Studies, 72; Russian workers and the revolutionary movement, J Social Hist, Winter 72; Russian Rebels: An introduction to the memoirs of the Russian worker, Semen Kanatchiav and Matvei Fisher, Russ Rev, 7-10/76; Passivity and protest in Germany and Russia: Barrington Moore's conception of working-class responses to injustice, J Social Hist, 3/82; transl, A Radical Worker in Tsarist Russia: The Autobiography of Semen Ivanovich Kanatchikov, Stanford Univ, 86; Law Disorder on the Narova River: The Kreenholm Strike of 1872, Univ of Calif Press, 95; ed, Workers and intelligentsia in Late Imperial Russia: Realities, Representations, Reflections, Univ of CA's IAS, 99. **CONTACT ADDRESS** Dept of History, Univ of California, Berkeley, 3229 Dwinelle Hall, Berkeley, CA 94720-2551. **EMAIL** zelnik@socrates.berkeley.edu

ZEMAN, JAROLD K.
PERSONAL Born 02/27/1926, Czechoslovakia **DISCIPLINE** CHURCH HISTORY **EDUCATION** Knox Col, Univ Toronto, BD, 52; Univ Zurich, DTheol, 66; McMaster Univ, DD, 85; Acadia Univ, DD, 94. **CAREER** Dir, Cont Theol Educ, 70-81, 85-91, dir confs, 81-85, Prof Church History, Acadia Univ & Acadia Divinity Col, 68-91; dir, Acadia Ctr Baptist Anabaptist Stud, Acadia Univ, 91-97. **MEMBERSHIPS** Pres, Baptist Fed Can, 79-82; mem, Rel Adv Comt CBC, 79-84; mem, Can Soc Ch Hist; Am Soc Ch Hist; Am Acad Relig. **SELECTED PUBLICATIONS** Auth, God's Mission and Ours, 63; auth, The Whole World at Our Door, 64; auth, Historical Topography of Moravian Anabaptism, 67; auth, The Anabaptists and the Czech Brethren, 69; auth, Baptists in Canada and Co-operative Christianity, 72; auth, The Hussite Movement and the Reformation, 77; auth, Baptist Roots and Identity, 78; auth, Renewal of Church and Society in the Hussite Reformation, 84; coauth, Baptists in Canada 1760-1990: A Bibliography, 89; ed, Baptists in Canada, 80. **CONTACT ADDRESS** PO Box 164, Wolfville, NS, Canada BOP 1XO.

ZEMANS, JOYCE P.
PERSONAL Born 04/21/1940, Toronto, ON, Canada **DISCIPLINE** ART HISTORY **EDUCATION** Univ Toronto, BA, 62, MA, 66. **CAREER** Ch, dept lib arts stud, Ont Col Art, 66-75; dir, Can Coun, 89-92; ch, dept visual arts, 75-81, assoc prof art hist, 75-95, dean, fine arts, 85-88, prof Art History, York Univ, 95-, Robarts ch can stud, 95-96. **MEMBERSHIPS** Can Asn Fine Arts Deans; Int Coun Fine Arts Deans; Univ Art Asn Can Adv; bd mem, J Can Art Hist; bd mem, Art Gallery York Univ; bd mem, Laidlaw Foundation (pres, 96-). **RESEARCH** Canadian art; concerns of the artist working in the early twentieth century in Canada and the United States; the work of women artists of this period. **SELECTED PUBLICATIONS** Auth, New Perspectives on Modernism in Canada: Kathleen Munn and Edna Tacon, Toronto, The Art Gallery of York Univ, 88; auth, "The Essential Role of National Cultural Institutions," in Beyond Quebec: Taking Stock of Canada, (McGill-Queens Univ Press, 95): 138-162; auth, "Establishing the Canon: The Early History of Reproductions at the National Gallery of Canada,' in The Jouranl of Canadian Art History, (95); auth, "The Contemporary Role of National Cultural Instiututions," in Beyound Quebec: Taking Stock of Canada, (McGill-Queen's Press, 95, 97): 138-162; auth, "Where is Here," Canadian Cultural Policy in A Globalized World, Toronto, Robarts Centre for Canadian Studies, York Univ, 96; auth, "Envisioning Nation: Nationhood, Identity and the Sampson-Matthews Silkscreen Project," The Journal of Canadian Art History, Vol. XIX/1, (98): 6-40; auth, Comparing Cultural Policy: A Study of Japan and the United States, Walnut Creek, CA, AltaMira Press, 99; auth, "A Tale of Three Women: Kathleen Munn, Joyce Wieland and Vera Frenkel: The Status of Canadian Women Artists at the Turn of the Century," RACAR, (00); **CONTACT ADDRESS** Faculty of Fine Arts, York Univ, 4700 Keele St, Toronto, ON, Canada M3J 1P3. **EMAIL** jzemans@yorku.ca

ZEMEL, CAROL
DISCIPLINE ART HISTORY **EDUCATION** Columbia Univ, PhD. **CAREER** Fac, SUNY Buffalo. **HONORS AND AWARDS** Grant, NEH; Millard Meiss grant; Col Art Assoc. **RESEARCH** 19th- and 20th-century art; feminism; art criticism. **SELECTED PUBLICATIONS** Auth, Van Gogh's Progress: Utopian Modernity in Late Nineteenth Century Art, Univ Calif, 97; The Formation of a Legend, van Gogh Criticism 1890-1900, UMI Res, 80. **CONTACT ADDRESS** Dept Art, SUNY, Buffalo, 202 Center for the Arts, Buffalo, NY 14260-6010.

ZHU, LIPING
PERSONAL Born 05/30/1957, Shanghai, China, m, 1995, 1 child **DISCIPLINE** HISTORY **EDUCATION** E China Normal Univ, BA, 82; Wichita State Univ, MA, 86; Univ NMex, PhD, 94. **CAREER** Asst prof, Eastern Wash Univ, 96-. **HONORS AND AWARDS** Vivian A. Paladin Awd, Mont Hist Soc, 96. **MEMBERSHIPS** Western Hist Asn, Orgn of Am Historians, Mining Hist Asn. **RESEARCH** Chinese on the American Frontier, Ethnic Groups in the American West. **SELECTED PUBLICATIONS** Auth, A Chinaman's Chance: The Chinese on the Rocky Mountain Mining Frontier, Univ Press of Colo, 97. **CONTACT ADDRESS** Dept Hist, Eastern Washington Univ, M/S 27, Cheney, WA 99004. **EMAIL** lzhu@ewu.edu

ZHUK, SERGEI I.
PERSONAL Born 12/18/1958, Vatutino, Cherkassy region, Ukraine, m, 1981, 1 child **DISCIPLINE** AMERICAN HISTORY **EDUCATION** Dniepropetrovsk Univ, Ukraine, Dipl of Hist, 81, DHist Sci, 96; Moscow Inst of Hist, Hist Sci, 87. **CAREER** Prof American History, Dneipropetrovsk Univ, Ukraine. **HONORS AND AWARDS** Fulbright grant, 95-99; John Carter Brown Library; Americna Autiquarian Society; Newberry Library. **RESEARCH** Quakers' attitudes toward sectarian religious groups in the 17th and 18th centuries. **SELECTED PUBLICATIONS** Auth, From 'Inner Light' to 'New Canaan': The Quaker Society of the 'Middle' Colonies, Dniepropetrovsk Univ, 95; Levelling of the Extemes, In: Images of America, Free Univ of Brussels, 97. **CONTACT ADDRESS** Dept of History, Johns Hopkins Univ, Baltimore, 3400 N Charles St., Baltimore, MD 21218. **EMAIL** siz1@jhunix.hef.jhu.edu.

ZIEFLE, HELMUT W.
PERSONAL Born 04/02/1939, Heilbronn, Germany, m, 1965, 2 children **DISCIPLINE** GERMAN LITERATURE, MODERN GERMAN HISTORY **EDUCATION** SUNY, BA, 64, MA, 66; Univ ILL, PhD, 73. **CAREER** Tchr, German, 65-67, Bethlehem Cent High Schl; instr, 67-72, asst prof, 72-77, assoc prof, 77-82, prof, 82-, Wheaton Col. **MEMBERSHIPS** Am Asn of Teachers of German; Illinois Foreign Lang Teachers Asn; Illinois Council on the Teaching of Foreign Langs, 88-89; Modern Lang Asn, 97-98; North Am Asn of Christian Foreign Lang & Lit Fac; Delta Phi Alpha. **RESEARCH** Hermann Hesse, German theology, German hist. **SELECTED PUBLICATIONS** Auth, Sibylle Schwarz: Leben und Werk (Life and Work), Studien zur Anglistik und Komparatistik, Vol 35, Bonn: Bovier, 75; auth, Edited, Sibylle Schwarz Deutsche Poetische Gedichte, Sibylle Schwarz German Poetic Poems, Mittlere Deutsche Literatur, vol 25, Bern: Lang, 80; auth, Una Mujer Contra el Reich, Mexico: ediciones las americas, 89; auth, Glenn Ellyn: Advanced Memory Res, Beginning German Language Course, 83; auth, Glenn Ellyn: Advanced Memory Res, Advanced German Language Course, 83; auth, Theological German: A Reader, Grand Rapids, Baker Book House, 86; auth, Dictionary of Modern Theological German, Grand Rapids, Baker Book House, 92; auth, Theological German: A Reader, Grand Rapids, Baker Book House, 93; auth, edited and commentated, Hermann Hesse und das Christentum, Wuppertal and Zurich: Brockhaus, 94; auth, Modern Theological German: A Reader and Dictionary, Grand Rapids: Baker Book House, 97. **CONTACT ADDRESS** Wheaton Col, Illinois, 501 College Ave, Wheaton, IL 60187. **EMAIL** helmut.w.ziefle@wheaton.edu

ZIEGER, R. H.
PERSONAL Born 08/02/1938, Englewood, NJ, m, 1962, 1 child **DISCIPLINE** HISTORY **EDUCATION** Montclair State College, BA, 60; Univ Wyoming, MA, 61; Univ Maryland, PhD, 65. **CAREER** Prof, Dist Prof, 86 to 00-, Univ FL; Prof, 77-86, Wayne State Univ; Assoc Prof, 73-77, Kansas State Univ; Asst, Assoc Prof, 64-73, Univ Wisc SP. **HONORS AND AWARDS** Philip A Taft Awd for Best Book, 85 and 96; Norman Wilinsky Grad Teach Awd; U of FL TIP; U of FL Profess Excell Awd; John Mahon UG Teaching Awd. **MEMBERSHIPS** OAH; UFF; AHA; SHA; HAC. **RESEARCH** Modern US History; US Labor History. **SELECTED PUBLICATIONS** Auth, Americans Great War: American People in World War I, Rowman & Littlefield, 00; ed, Southern Labor in Transition, Univ Tenn Press, 97; auth, The CIO, 1935-1955, Univ of NC Press, 95, awd for best bk in labor hist; Auth, The Quest for Ntl Goals 1957-1981, in: The Carter Presidency: Policy Choices in the Post-New Deal Era, ed, Gary M Fink, Hugh Davis Graham, Univ Press of Kansas, 97; From Primordial Folk to Redundant Workers: Southern Textile Workers and Social Observers, 1920-1990, in: S Lab in Transition 1940-1995, ed, RH Zieger, U of Tenn Press. **CONTACT ADDRESS** Dept of History, Univ of Florida, Box 117320, Gainesville, FL 32611. **EMAIL** zieger@ufl.edu

ZIEGLER, PAUL R.
PERSONAL Born 05/18/1938, Orange, NJ, m, 4 children **DISCIPLINE** HISTORY **EDUCATION** Fairfield Univ, AB, 60; Fordham Univ, MA, 63; PhD, 75. **CAREER** Instr, Fordham Univ, 64-65; From Inst to Prof, Assumption Col, 67-. **HONORS AND AWARDS** Nat Endowment Humanities, 78; Danforth Assoc., 79-85; Nat Endowment Humanities, 91. **MEMBERSHIPS** Conf of Brit Studies. **RESEARCH** English political party system. **SELECTED PUBLICATIONS** Auth, "The New World and Christian Humanism: Three Views," Proceedings of the PMR Conf, vol 8 (83): 89-95; coauth, Joseph Hume: The People's M P, Am Philos Soc Pr, 85; auth, "The Use of Primary Sources in Western Public Culture," Resources in Educ (89); coauth, "Lost at Sea: A Proposal for Countering Information Overload in Introductory Courses," Perspectives: Newsletter of the Am Hist Assoc. (91); coauth, "The Assignment Driven Course: A Task Specific Approach to Teaching," J on Excellence in Cool Teaching 2 (91): 25-33; auth, "Archibald Prentice (1792-1850)," New Dict of Nat Biog (forthcoming); auth, Lord Palmerston: A Public Life, Macmillan Ltd (forthcoming). **CONTACT ADDRESS** Dept Hist, Assumption Col, Worcester, MA 01615-0005. **EMAIL** pziegler@eve.assumption.edu

ZIEMKE, EARL FREDERICK
PERSONAL Born 12/16/1922, WI, m, 1949, 1 child **DISCIPLINE** HISTORY **EDUCATION** Wis State Col, BS, 48; Univ Wis, MA, 49, PhD, 51. **CAREER** Researcher, Bur Applied Social Res, Columbia Univ, 51-55; historian, Off of Chief Mil Hist, US Dept Army, 55-67; prof hist, 67-77, Res Prof Hist, Univ GA, 77-93, ret 93. **MEMBERSHIPS** AHA **RESEARCH** Germany; Russia **SELECTED PUBLICATIONS** Coauth, Command Decisions, Harcourt, 59; auth, The German Northern Theatre of Operations, US Govt Printing Off, 60; coauth, Concise History of World War II, Praeger, 65; auth, Stalingrad to Berlin, US Govt Printing Off, 68; Battle for Berlin, Ballantine, 69; US Army in the Occupation of Germany, Govt Printing Off, 76; auth, Moscow to Stalingrad, Govt Printing Off, 86. **CONTACT ADDRESS** 400 Brookwood Dr, Athens, GA 30605.

ZIEWACZ, LAWRENCE E.
PERSONAL Born 12/23/1942, Sault Ste Marie, MI, m, 1968, 2 children **DISCIPLINE** AMERICAN HISTORY **EDUCATION** Mich State Univ, BA, 65, MA, 66, PhD(US hist), 71. **CAREER** Instr US hist, Lansing Community Col, 68-70 & Edinboro State Col, 70-71; Assoc Prof Am Thought & Lang, Mich State Univ, 71-, Reviewer, Nat En dowment for Humanities, 78-82. **MEMBERSHIPS** Orgn Am Historians; Soc Hist Educ; Popular Cult Asn; Soc Study Midwestern Lit & Cult. **RESEARCH** Michigan history; sports history; United States political and social history. **SELECTED PUBLICATIONS** Auth, The eighty-first ballot: The senatorial struggle of 1883, Mich Hist, fall 72; coauth, The election of 1882: A republican analysis, J Great Lakes Hist Conf, 76; The athletic revolution reconsidered: An examination of literature of athletic protest, Sport Sociol Bull, fall 77; The progress of woman suffrage in 19th century Michigan, J Great Lakes Hist Conf, 79; auth, The Old Northwest and Gilded Age politics: An analysis, Midwestern Miscellany, Vol VIII, 80; coauth, Michigan: A History of the Great Lakes States, Forum Press, 81; Violence in sports, In: Sports in Modern America, River City Publ, 81; Sports in the Twenties, In: The Evolution of Mass Culture in America, 82. **CONTACT ADDRESS** Dept of Am Thought & Lang, Michigan State Univ, 229 Bessey Hall, East Lansing, MI 48824-1033. **EMAIL** ziewacz@pilot.msu.edu

ZILFI, MADELINE CAROL
PERSONAL Born Norwood, MA, m, 1979, 1 child **DISCIPLINE** MIDDLE EAST, OTTOMAN EMPIRE, ISLAM, GENDER ISSUES **EDUCATION** Mt Holyoke Col, AB, 64; Univ Chicago, MA, 71, PhD(hist), 76. **CAREER** Asst prof Hist, Univ MD, Col Park, 76- **HONORS AND AWARDS** Recipent of grants and awards from Fulbright, the Social Sci Res Coun, and the Am Res Institute in Turkey as well as the University's Graduate Res Bd. **MEMBERSHIPS** AHA; Mid East Studies Asn; Turkish Studies Asn; Mid East Inst. **RESEARCH** Ottoman institutional history; Islamic law; Islamic fundamentalism. **SELECTED PUBLICATIONS** Auth, "The Kadizadelis: Discordant Revivalism in Seventh-Cenury Istanbul," Journal of Near Eastern Studies 45, 86; auth, The Politics of Piety: The Ottoman Ulema in the Post-Classical Age; ed, Women in the Ottaman Empire: Middle Eastern Women in the Early Modern Era, 97; auth, "We Don't Get Along: Women and Hul Divorce in the Eighteenth Century," 97. **CONTACT ADDRESS** Dept of Hist, Univ of Maryland, Col Park, College Park, MD 20742-0001. **EMAIL** mz11@umail.umd.edu

ZILVERSMIT, ARTHUR
PERSONAL Born 07/05/1932, The Hague, Netherlands, m, 1955, 2 children **DISCIPLINE** AMERICAN HISTORY **EDUCATION** Cornell Univ, BA, 54; Harvard Univ, MA, 55; Univ CA, Berkeley, PhD, 62. **CAREER** From instr to asst prof, Am hist, Williams Col, 61-66; from asst prof to assoc prof, 66-73, prof hist, Lake Forest Col, 73-, Dir Grad Prog Lib Studies, 76-90, Dir Continuing Educ, 77-90, Vis fel, Shelby Cullom Davis Ctr Hist Studies, Princeton Univ, 72-73. **MEMBERSHIPS** AHA; Orgn Am Historians; Am Studies Asn; Hist Educ Soc. **RESEARCH** Hist of Am educ; African-Am hist. **SELECTED PUBLICATIONS** Auth, The First Emancipation, Univ Chicago, 67; Mumbet, Quok Walker and the Abolition of Slavery in Massachusetts, William & Mary Quart, 68; contribr, The Abolitionists: From Patience to Militance, In: The Black Experience in America, Univ TX, 70; auth, Liberty and Property: New Jersey and the Abolition of Slavery, NJ Hist, winter 70; ed, Lincoln on Black and White: A Documentary History, Wadsworth, 71; contribr, The Failure of Progressive Education, In: Schooling and Society, Johns Hopkins Univ, 76; Lincoln and the Problem of Race: A Decade of Interpretations, In: Papers of the Abraham Lincoln Association, 81; Changing Schools: Progressive Education Theory and Practice, 1930-1960, Univ Chicago, 93; auth, "Closing the Door on Open Education: Butterfield School," in Susan Semel and Alan Sadovnik, eds. "Schools of Tomorrow," Schools of Today (NY: Peter Lang, 99); auth, "Douglass' 'Perplexing Difficulty'," in Approaches to the Teaching of Narrative of Frederick Douglass, James Hall ed. (NT Modern Lang

Assoc, 99). **CONTACT ADDRESS** Dept of Hist, Lake Forest Col, 555 N Sheridan Rd, Lake Forest, IL 60045-2399. **EMAIL** zilversmit@lfc.edu

ZIMMER, LOUIS BERNARD
PERSONAL Born 01/16/1931, New Rochelle, NY, m, 1954, 2 children **DISCIPLINE** EUROPEAN HISTORY, HISTORY OF IDEAS **EDUCATION** State Univ NYork Col Cortland, BS, 53; NYork Univ, MA, 59, PhD(English intellectual hist), 70. **CAREER** Teacher, Hackensack High Sch, 59-62; asst prof social studies, 62-64, assoc prof hist, 64-80, prof hist, 80-92, prof emer, hist, Montclair State Col, 92- . **HONORS AND AWARDS** Founders' Day Awd, NY Univ, 70. **MEMBERSHIPS** AHA; Am Soc Eighteenth Century Studies. **RESEARCH** English and European intellectual history; modern European history. **SELECTED PUBLICATIONS** Auth, "John Stuart Mill and Democracy," in The Mill News Letter, 76; auth, "The Negative Argument in John Stuart Mills 'Utilitarianism'," in J of Brit Studies, 77; auth, "Mill's 'On Liberty' and Burke's 'Reflections': A Study in the Contrast of Opposites," in The Mill News Letter, 82; auth, "Voltaire and Derrida," in Va Q Rev, 88; auth, "J.S. Mill and that special passage in the Essay 'On Liberty'" in Meta Philos, 89; auth, "J.S. Mill and Bentham on Liberty," in The Hist, 90. **CONTACT ADDRESS** Montclair State Univ, 127 Buckingham Rd, Upper Montclair, NJ 07043.

ZIMMERMAN, JAMES A.
PERSONAL Born 05/12/1933, Peoria, IL, m, 1956, 4 children **DISCIPLINE** HISTORY **EDUCATION** Ill State Univ, BS, 55; Univ Ill, PhD, 72. **CAREER** Asst prof, Mankato State Univ, 70-73; asst prof to prof, Tri State Univ, 73-; Dean, 81-84. **HONORS AND AWARDS** Gerald r. Moore Outstanding Prof. **MEMBERSHIPS** Org of Am Hist; Soc for Hist of Am For Rel; Ind Org of Hist. **RESEARCH** Public opinion and U.S. Foreign Policy. **SELECTED PUBLICATIONS** Auth, Who Were the Anti-Imperialists and Expansionists of 1898 and 1899: A Chicago Perspective, Pacific Hist Rev, 77. **CONTACT ADDRESS** Dept Humanities and Soc Sci, Tri-State Univ, 1 University Ave, Angola, IN 46703-1764. **EMAIL** zimmermanj@tristate.edu

ZIMMERMAN, JOSH
PERSONAL Born Minneapolis, MN, m, 1999, 1 child **DISCIPLINE** HISTORY **EDUCATION** Univ Calif Santa Cruz, BA, 89; UCLA, MA, 93; Brandeis Univ, PhD, 98. **CAREER** Asst Prof, Yeshiva Univ, 98-. **HONORS AND AWARDS** Postdoc Fel, Hebrew Univ, 97-98; Dessertation Fel, 96-97. **MEMBERSHIPS** AHA; AJS. **RESEARCH** Eastern Europe; East European Jewry, modern period. **SELECTED PUBLICATIONS** Auth, "Jozef Pilsudski and the Jewish Question, 1892-1905," East European Jewish Affairs, (98): 87-107; auth, "The Influence of the Polish Question on the Bond's National Program, 1897-1905," in Jewish Politics in Eastern Europe, (London: Macmillan, 00). **CONTACT ADDRESS** Dept Hist, Yeshiva Univ, 500 W 185th St, New York, NY 10033-3201. **EMAIL** zimmerm@ymail.yu.edu

ZIMMERMAN, LORETTA ELLEN
PERSONAL Born 09/14/1935, Metairie, LA, m, 1977 **DISCIPLINE** AMERICAN HISTORY **EDUCATION** Newcomb Col, BA, 57; Tulane Univ, MA, 61, PhD(hist), 64. **CAREER** Asst prof hist, Williams Wood Col, 64-65; vis prof, Augustana Col, 65-66; asst prof, Univ TX, Arlington, 66-67; assoc prof , 67-85, Prof Hist, Univ Portland, 86-, former dir Peace Studies prog. **HONORS AND AWARDS** Culligan Awd-Best Teacher/ Faculty Leadership. **MEMBERSHIPS** Phi Alpha Delta, Alpha Lambda Delta, Kappa Delta Pi, Phi Beta Kappa. **RESEARCH** History of American feminism; history of American reformism; European and American intellectual history. **SELECTED PUBLICATIONS** Auth, five articles, In: Notable American Women 1607-1950, Belknap, 71; Woman Suffrage, a Feminist Movement, 1848-1910, spring 72 & Mary Beard: an Activist of the Progressive Era, spring 74, Review; coauth, A History of the United States with Topics, vols I and II, with Jerry R. Baydo and John Boon, Gregory Press, 94-96; coauth, Readings for a History of the United States with Topics, vol II, with Jerry R. Baydo and John Boon, Gregory Press, 94-96; coauth, A Student Workbook for History of the United States with Topics, with Jerry R. Baydo and John Boon, Gregory Press, 94-96; author of a series of articles on culture for Salem Press. **CONTACT ADDRESS** Fac of Hist, Univ of Portland, 5000 N Willamette, Portland, OR 97203-5798. **EMAIL** Zummerma@vofport.edu

ZIMMERMANN, THOMAS C. PRICE
PERSONAL Born 08/22/1934, Bryn Mawr, PA, m, 1981 **DISCIPLINE** RENAISSANCE HISTORY **EDUCATION** Williams Col, BA, 56; Oxford Univ, BA, 58, MA, 64; Harvard Univ, AM, 60, PhD(hist), 64. **CAREER** From asst prof to prof hist & humanities, Reed Col, 64-77, chemn dept hist, 73-75; prof hist, vpres acad affairs & dean fac, Davidson Col, 77-86, Charles A Dana prof of hist, 86-; mem region XIV selection comt, Woodrow Wilson Nat Fel Found, 67-70; fel, Harvard Int Ctr Renaissance Studies, Villa I Tatti, Florence, Italy, 70-71; mem Ore comt humanities, Nat Endowment for Humanities, 71-77; Am Coun Learned Soc fel, 75-76; mem, Board of Advisors, Lowell Observatory, 88-93; mem, Rome Prize Jury, Am Acad in Rom, 93; Prof of History Emeritus, 99. **HONORS AND AWARDS** Danforth Fel, 56-62; Fulbright Fel, Italy, 62-64; Am Hist Assoc Marraro Prize, 97; President's Book Prize, Am Assoc for Italian Studies, 97. **MEMBERSHIPS** AHA; Renaissance Soc Am; Soc Italian Hist Studies; Phi Beta Kappa; 16th Century Studies Conf. **RESEARCH** Sixteenth century Italian history. **SELECTED PUBLICATIONS** Auth, A note on Clement VII and the divorce of Henry VIII, Eng Hist Rev, 7/67; Girolamo Savonarola: a study in mazeway resynthesis, Soundings, J Interdisciplinary Studies, spring 68; Confession and autobiography in the early Renaissance, In: Renaissance Studies in Honor of Hans Baron, Northern Ill Univ, 71; Paolo Giovio and the evolution of Renaissance art criticism, In: Essays in Honour of P O Kristeller, Manchester Univ, 76; For Paolo Giovio: The Historian and the Crisis of 16th Century Italy, Princeton Univ Press, 95. **CONTACT ADDRESS** Davidson Col, 16101 McAuley Rd., Huntersville, NC 28078.

ZINN, GROVER A.
PERSONAL Born 06/18/1937, El Dorado, AR, m, 1962, 2 children **DISCIPLINE** EUROPEAN CHRISTIAN HISTORY **EDUCATION** Rice Inst, BA, 59; Duke Univ, BD, 62; PhD, 69. **CAREER** William H. Danforth prof, 66. **HONORS AND AWARDS** NEH Younger Humanist Fellowship and Research States, Oberlin College, 72-73; Research State, Oberlin College, 97-98. **RESEARCH** Medieval Christian thought, mysticism, iconography. **SELECTED PUBLICATIONS** Auth, Richard of St. Victor: The Twelve Patriarchs, The Mystical Ark; Book Three of the Trinity; Medieval France: An Encyclopedia. **CONTACT ADDRESS** Dept of Relig, Oberlin Col, Oberlin, OH 44074. **EMAIL** grover.zinn@oberlin.edu

ZIPES, JACK
DISCIPLINE GERMAN AND EUROPEAN STUDIES **EDUCATION** Dartmouth Col, BA, 59; Columbia Univ, MA, 61; Univ Munich, 62; Univ Tubingen, 63; Columbia Univ, PhD, 65. **CAREER** Admin asst, Columbia Univ, 64-65; instr, Amerika-Institut, Univ of Munich, 66-67; asst prof, New York Univ, 67-72; assoc to full prof, Univ Wisc-Milwaukee, 72-86; prof, Univ of Fla, 86-89; prof, Univ of Minn, 89-, Dir of Grad Studies, 90-, acting chair, Scandinavian Studies Dept, 91-94, Chair, Dept of German, Dutch, and Scandinavian, 94-98, Dir, Center for German and European Studies, 98-. **HONORS AND AWARDS** Fulbright Fel grant, 81-82; John Simon Guggenheim Fel, 88-89; Univ of Minn Grad Sch Grant-in-Aid, 90-91, 92-93, 96-97, 97-98; Distinguished Scholar Awd, Int Asn for the Fantastic in the Arts, 92; Thomas D. Clark Lectureship, Univ Ky, 93; Scholar of Col, Univ of Minn, 97-2000; NEH grant, 98-99; Anne Devereaux Jordan Awd, Children's Lit Asn, 99; Int Brothers Grimm Awd, Int Inst for Children's Lit in Osaka, Japan, 99. **MEMBERSHIPS** Modern Lang Asn, Am Asn of Teachers of German, Children's Lit Asn, Am Folklore Asn, Europaische Marchengesellschaft, Bruder Grimm-Gesellschaft, Int Res Soc for Children's Lit, Am Section of PEN. **SELECTED PUBLICATIONS** Transl, The Fairy Tales of Herman Hesse, NY: Bantam (95); auth, Happily Ever After: Fairy Tales, Children, and the Culture Industry, NY: Routledge (97); co-ed with Sander Gilman, Yale companion of Jewish Writing and Thought in German Culture, 1066-1966, New Haven: Yale Univ Press (97); ed with intro, The Wonderful World of Oz: The Wizard of Oz, The Emerald City of Oz, Glinda of Oz, NY: Penguin (98); auth, When Dreams Came True: Classical Fairy Tales and Their Tradition, NY: Routledge (99); adapted from Richard F. Burton's unexpurgated transl, annotated, with afterword, The Arabian Nights: More Marvels and Wonders of the Thousand and One Nights, vol 2, NY: New Am Library, Signet Classic (99); auth, "George Tabori and the Jewish Question," Theater 29.2 (99): 98-107; auth, "Contested Jews: The Image of Jewishness in Contemporary German Literature," South Central Rev, 16 (summer-fall 99): 3-15; rev of William Crisman, The Crises of "Language and Dead Signs" in Ludwig Tieck's Prose Fiction in Studies in Romanticism, 38 (spring 99): 115-16; auth, The Oxford Companion to Fairy Tales: The Western Fairy Tale Tradition from Medieval to Modern, Oxford Univ Press (forthcoming). **CONTACT ADDRESS** Dept of German, Scandinavian and Dutch, Univ of Minnesota, Twin Cities, Minneapolis, MN 55455. **EMAIL** zipes001@umn.edu

ZIRINSKY, MICHAEL PAUL
PERSONAL Born 11/25/1942, Brooklyn, NY, m, 1965 **DISCIPLINE** HISTORY, GOVERNMENT **EDUCATION** Oberlin Col, AB, 64; Am Univ, MA, 68; Univ NC, Chapel Hill, PhD(hist), 76. **CAREER** Instr hist, Randolph Macon Col, 65-67; asst prof, 73-79, Prof, 79-86; assoc prof, 79-86, prof, 86-, Boise State Univ. **MEMBERSHIPS** AHA; Mid East Inst; Brit Soc M.E. Studies; Mid East Studies Asn; Society for Iranian Studies. **RESEARCH** Modern Middle Eastern history (20th century); 20th century Iran. **SELECTED PUBLICATIONS** Auth, American Presbyterian Missionaries at Urmia during the Great War, Persia and the Great War, Okiver Bast, ed, Tehran: Institut Francais de Recherche en Iran, in press; auth," Blood, Power, and Hypocrisy: The Murder of Robert Imbrie and American Relations with Pahlavi Iran, 1924," International Journal of Middle East Studies 18 (86): 275-292; auth, "Presbyterian Missionaries and American Relations with Pahlavi Iran," The Iranian Journal of International Affairs, (89): 71-86; auth, "Harbingers of Change: Presbyterian Women in Iran," 1883-1949, American Presbyterians: Journal of Presbyterian History 70:3 (92):173-86; auth, "Imperial Power and Dictatorship: Britain and the Rise of Reza Shah, 1921-1926," International Journal of Middle East Studies 24 (92): 639-94; auth, "Presbyterian Missionary Women in Late Nineteenth and Early Twentieth Century Iran," translated into Persian by Manijeh Badiozamani, Nimeye-Diagar: Persian Language Feminist Journal 17 (93): 38-63; auth, "A Panacea for the Ills of the Country: American Presbyterian Education in Inter-War Iran," Iranian Studies vol 26, (93):: 119-137; auth, "Render Therefore unto Caesar That Which is Caesar's: American Presbyterian Educators and Reza Shah," Iranian Studies, vol 26 (93): 337-56; auth, "The Rise of Reza Khan, in John Foran, ed Social Movements in Iran: Historical and Theoretical Perspectives (Minneapolis: Univ of MN Press, 94), 44-77; auth, A Panacea for the Ills of the Country, American Presbyterian Education in Interwar Iran, Amer Presbyterians-Jour Presbyterian Hist, Vol 0072, 94; auth, "The Presbyterian Who Introduced Soccer to Iran," Presbyterian Outlook, 98. **CONTACT ADDRESS** Dept of Hist, Boise State Univ, Boise, ID 83725. **EMAIL** mzirins@boisestate.edu

ZIRKEL, PATRICIA MCCORMICK
PERSONAL Born 11/02/1943, m, 1968, 1 child **DISCIPLINE** HISTORICAL THEOLOGY **EDUCATION** St Thomas Aquinas Col, Sparkill, NYork, BS Ed, 66; St John's Univ, MA, 78; Fordham Univ, PhD, 89. **CAREER** Assoc prof, Coll. Of Professional Studies, St John's Univ, 90-. **HONORS AND AWARDS** Faculty Merit award, 97, 98. **MEMBERSHIPS** Am Academy of Relig; Am Asn of Univ Profs; Col Theol Soc. **RESEARCH** Christian theol-Medieval Europe; Christian Liturgy; Theodicy-Holocaust Studies. **SELECTED PUBLICATIONS** Auth, The Ninth Century Eucharistic Controversy: A Context for the Beginnnings of Eucharistic Doctrine in the West, Worship, vol 68, no 1, Jan 94; Why Should It Be Neccessary That Christ Be Immolated Daily?, Paschasius Radbertus on Daily Eucharist, Am Benedictine Rev, Sept 96; The Body of Christ and the Future of Liturgy, Anglican Theol Rev., vol. 81, no. 3, Summer 99. **CONTACT ADDRESS** St. John's Univ, 8000 Utopia Pkwy, Jamaica, NY 11439. **EMAIL** zirkelp@stjohns.edu

ZNAYENKO, MYROSLAVA
DISCIPLINE SLAVIC STUDIES **EDUCATION** Univ Cal, BA, ; Yale Univ, MA; Colum Univ, MS; PhD, 73. **CAREER** Adj prof, Columbia Univ; assoc prof, Rutgers Univ. **MEMBERSHIPS** AAASS; ATSAEL; MLA; CS; SSS; UAAS; AN; AUS. **RESEARCH** Slavic mythology; Ukrainian literature. **SELECTED PUBLICATIONS** Auth, The Gods of Ancient Slavs, 80; auth, :Beauty and Saddness in a Strange Episode," in Depictions, Slavic Studies in the Narrative and Visual Arts in Honor of William E Harkins (Ardis, 00). **CONTACT ADDRESS** Dept Foreign Language, Rutgers, The State Univ of New Jersey, Newark, 180 University Ave, Newark, NJ 07102-1803 07102-1803. **EMAIL** Znayenko@andromeda.rutgers.edu

ZONDERMAN, DAVID A.
PERSONAL Born 10/04/1958, Boston, MA, m, 1983, 2 children **DISCIPLINE** HISTORY **EDUCATION** Amherst, BA, 80; Yale Univ, MA, 82, MPhilos, 83, PhD, 86. **CAREER** Assoc prof History, NC State Univ. **RESEARCH** Working class Activists and middle class reformers in 19th century Boston and New York **SELECTED PUBLICATIONS** Auth, Aspirations and Anxieties: New England Workers and the Mechanized Factory System, 1815-1850, Oxford Univ, 92; Foreign Pioneers: Immigrants and the Mechanized Factory System in Antebellum New England, In: Work, Recreation and Cutlure: Essays in American Labor History, Garland Publ, 96. **CONTACT ADDRESS** Dept of History, No Carolina State Univ, Box 8108, Raleigh, NC 27695. **EMAIL** zonderman@social.chass.ncsu.edu.

ZOPHY, JONATHAN W.
PERSONAL Born 09/05/1945, Milwaukee, WI **DISCIPLINE** HISTORY **EDUCATION** Mich State Univ, BA, 67; Ohio State Univ, MA, 68; PhD, 72. **CAREER** Asst prof, Lane Col, 72-73; asst prof, Carth Col, 73-87; assoc prof, Univ W Fla, 87-88; assoc, prof, Univ Hous, 88-. **HONORS AND AWARDS** Pres Dist Awd, 99; CRR Fel, Univ Tor, 98; SCSC Fel, 99; Outstand Teach Awd, 93; NDEA Fel, 71. **MEMBERSHIPS** AHA; SRR; SCSC. **RESEARCH** German Reformation; college teaching; social history. **SELECTED PUBLICATIONS** Auth, The Holy Roman Empire, Greenwood, 86; auth, Patriarchal Politics and Christoph Kress of Nuremberg, Mellon, 92; auth, A Short History of Reformation Europe, Prentice Hall, 97; auth, A Short History of Renaissance Europe, Prentice Hall, 97; auth, A Short History of Renaissance and Reformation Europe, Prentice Hall, 99, 2nd ed. **CONTACT ADDRESS** Dept Humanities, Univ of Houston, 2700 Bay Area Blvd, Box 901, Houston, TX 77058-1002. **EMAIL** zophy@cl.uh.edu

ZUBER, RICHARD LEE
PERSONAL Born 04/04/1932, Allendale, FL, d, 1954, 2 children **DISCIPLINE** AMERICAN HISTORY **EDUCATION** Appalachian State Teachers Col, BS, 54; Emory Univ, MA, 57; Duke Univ, PhD, 61. **CAREER** Asst prof hist, The Citadel, 60-62; from asst prof to prof, Wake Forest Univ, 62-00; chmn dept, Wake Forest Univ, 75-83. **HONORS AND AWARDS** Awd of Merit, Am Assn State & Local Hist, 66; Coop Prog Humanities fel, Univ NC, 67-68. **MEMBERSHIPS** Orgn Am Historians. **RESEARCH** Reconstruction period **SELECTED PUBLICA-**

TIONS Auth, Jonathan Worth: A Biography of a Southern Unionist, Univ NC, 65; auth, North Carolina During Reconstruction, NC Dept Arch & Hist; auth, The Prophetic Persona: Jeremiah and the Language of the Self, Sheffield, 84; auth, Conscientious Objectors in the Confederacy: The Quakers of North Carolina, Quaker Hist, 78; auth, Jonathan Worth, American National Biog, Oxford University Press, 98. **CONTACT ADDRESS** Dept of History, Wake Forest Univ, PO Box 7806, Winston-Salem, NC 27109-7806.

ZUCK, LOWELL H.
PERSONAL Born 06/24/1926, Ephrata, PA, m, 1950, 1 child **DISCIPLINE** CHURCH HISTORY **EDUCATION** Elizabethtown Col, BA, 47; Bethany Bibl Sem, BD, 50; Yale Univ, STM, 51, MA, 52, PhD(Reformation church hist), 55. **CAREER** Vis prof philos & relig, Col Idaho, 54-55; from asst prof to assoc prof, 55-62, PROF CHURCH HIST, EDEN THEOL SEM, 62-, Teacher univ col, Washington Univ, 57-; Am Asn Theol Schs grants, 64-65 & 75-76; Am Philos Soc grant, 80; Nat Endowment for Humanities summer seminar, Johns Hopkins Univ, 82. **HONORS AND AWARDS** Fulbright Scholar Lecturer: Religious Studies, Romania, 1st sem. 00-01. **MEMBERSHIPS** AHA; Am Soc Church Hist; Am Soc Reformation Res (treas, 69-78); 16th Century Studies Conf (treas, 69-71, pres, 71-72). **RESEARCH** Anabaptist research; Reformation church history; Puritan church history. **SELECTED PUBLICATIONS** "Consolidation & Expansion", Vol. IV of "Living Theological Heritage of the United Church of Christ" (Cleveland: Pilgrim, 1999, 666pp.) "Socially Responsible Believers", 1986, "European Roots of the United Church of Christ", 1976, "Christianity and Revolution," 300 pp. Sourcebook, 1975; Auth, From Reformation Orthodoxy to the Enlightenment--Geneva 1670-1737--French, Church Hist, Vol 0063, 94; Ingdoms--The Church and Culture Through the Ages, Sixteenth Century Jour, Vol 0025, 94; Sin and the Calvinists--Morals Control and the Consistory in the Reformed Tradition, Church Hist, Vol 0065, 96; Hochstift and Reformation--Studies in the History of the Imperial Church Between 1517 and 1648--German, Sixteenth Century Jour, Vol 0027, 96; Calvinism in Europe, 1540-1620, Church Hist, Vol 0065, 96; Adultery and Divorce in Calvin, John Geneva, Church Hist, Vol 0065, 96; Poverty and Deviance in Early-Modern Europe, Sixteenth Century Jour, Vol 0027, 96; A Short History of Renaissance and Reformation Europe--Dances Over Fire and Water, Sixteenth Century Jour, Vol 0027, 96; The Oxford Encyclopedia of the Reformation, 4 Vols, Sixteenth Century Jour, Vol 0028, 97; Documents on the Continental Reformation, Sixteenth Century Jour, Vol 0028, 97. **CONTACT ADDRESS** Eden Theol Sem, 475 E Lockwood Ave, Saint Louis, MO 63119. **EMAIL** lzuck@eden.edu

ZUCKER, ALFRED JOHN
PERSONAL Born 09/25/1940, Hartford, CT, m, 1966, 6 children **DISCIPLINE** ENGLISH, HISTORY **EDUCATION** Valley Col Los Angeles, AA, 60; Univ Calif at Los Angeles, AB English, 62; AB Speech, 62; MA Speech, 63; CSULA, MA English, 67, CSULB, MA Hist, 99, Univ Calif at Los Angeles, PhD, 67. **CAREER** Lectr, Los Angeles City Col, 62-68; Lectr, CSULA, 66-68; Prof, Chemn of English Dept, Chemn of the Humanities Div, Acad Senate Pres, Los Angeles Southwest Col, 68-88; Prof, Chemn English Dept, Los Angeles Valley Col, 88-. **HONORS AND AWARDS** Les Savants, Tau Alpha Epsilon, Phi Theta Kappa, Phi Kappa Phi, Phi Delta Kappa, Phi Beta Kappa. **MEMBERSHIPS** Emily Dickinson Soc. **RESEARCH** 19th Century American Literature, 19th Century American History. **CONTACT ADDRESS** English Dept, Los Angeles Valley Col, PO Box 3308, Palos Verdes, CA 90274.

ZUCKERMAN, BRUCE
PERSONAL Born 07/31/1947, Los Angeles, CA, m, 1975, 3 children **DISCIPLINE** NEAR EASTERN STUDIES **EDUCATION** Princeton Univ, BA, 69; Yale Univ, PhD, 80. **CAREER** Dir, Univ So Calif Archaeol Res Col, 81- ; dir, West Semitic Res Proj, 83- , assoc prof, relig, 88- , Univ So Calif, 83- . **MEMBERSHIPS** Am Oriental Soc; Am Res Ctr in Egypt; Nat Asn of Prof of Hebrew; Soc of Bibl Lit. **RESEARCH** Bible; Ancient Near East; Northwest Semitic epigraphy and philology. **SELECTED PUBLICATIONS** Co-ed, Facsimile Edition of the Leningrad Codex; auth, Job the Silent: A Study in Historical Counterpoint. **CONTACT ADDRESS** School of Religion, Univ of So California, Los Angeles, CA 90089-0355. **EMAIL** bzuckerm@bcf.usc.edu

ZUCKERMAN, MICHAEL
PERSONAL Born 04/24/1939, Philadelphia, PA, m, 1986, 5 children **DISCIPLINE** AMERICAN STUDIES **EDUCATION** Univ Pa, BA, 61; Harvard Univ, PhD, 67. **CAREER** Prof, Univ Penn, 65- . **HONORS AND AWARDS** SSRC fel; NEH fel; Guggenheim fel; ACLS fel; Rockefeller fel; Fulbright fel; Netherlands Inst for Advan Study fel. **RESEARCH** Early American history; American character; American community life; American family and identity. **SELECTED PUBLICATIONS** Auth, The Place of Religion in Urban and Community Studies, Relig and Amer Cult, 96; Ideology and Utopia: Philosophical Fantasies of Historical Knowledge, Amer Studies, 96; Cities in the Wilderness: Derelicts of Development, Trends, 97; The Dodo and the Phoenix: A Fable of American Exceptionalism in American Exceptionalism? US Working-Class Formation in an International Context, 97; Tocqueville, Turner, and Turds: Four Stories of Manners in Early America, Jour of Amer Hist, 98. **CONTACT ADDRESS** Dept of History, Univ of Pennsylvania, Philadelphia, PA 19104. **EMAIL** mzuckerm@history.upenn.edu

ZUKOWSKY, JOHN
DISCIPLINE ART HISTORY **EDUCATION** NYork State Univ, PhD. **CAREER** Archit cur, Art Inst Chicago; adj prof, Univ of Ill, Chicago. **SELECTED PUBLICATIONS** Ed, Chicago Architecture and Design 1923-1993; Chicago Architecture, 1872-1922; Karl Friedrich Schinkel 1781-1841. **CONTACT ADDRESS** Art Hist Dept, Univ of Illinois, Chicago, 935 W Harrison, Mail Stop 201, Chicago, IL 60607.

ZUNZ, OLIVIER
PERSONAL Born 07/19/1946, Paris, France, m, 1970, 2 children **DISCIPLINE** HISTORY **EDUCATION** Univ Paris, BA, 69; PhD, 77; Univ Paris-Sorbonne, PhD, 82. **CAREER** Vis appointments, Ecole des hautes Etudes en Sciences Sociales, Paris, 85-96; Vis prof, Col de France, 97; Asst Prof to Prof, Univ Va, 78-; vis Prof, Ecole Normale Superieure, 99-. **HONORS AND AWARDS** Res grants, Center National de la Recherche Scientifique, 76-78; John Simon Guggenheim Memorial Foundation, 86-87; NEH; Nat Sci Foundation; Russell Sage Foundation; Soc Sci Res Council, Univ Va, 92-93. **SELECTED PUBLICATIONS** Auth, The Changing Face of Inequality: Urbanization, Industrial Development, and Immigrants in Detroit, 1880-1920, Univ Chicago Press, 82; auth, Making America Corporate, 1870-1920, Univ Chicago Press, 90; auth, Why the American Century?, Univ Chicago Press, 98; ed, Reliving the Past: The Worlds of Social History, Univ NC Press, 85; co-ed, The Landscape of Modernity: Essays on New York City, 1900-1940, New York, 92; auth, "American History and the Changing Meaning of Assimilation," Journal of American Ethnic History, (85): 53-84; auth, "Producers, Brokers, and Users of Knowledge: The Institutional matrix," in Modernist Impulses in the Human Sciences, Johns Hopkins Univ Press, (94); 290-307; auth, "Exporting American Individualism," National Institute for research Advancement Research Output, (94): 9-18; auth, "Class," Encyclopedia of the United States in the Twentieth Century, Charles Scribner's Sons, (96): 195-220; auth, "History by Affirmation: The End of Democracy," in Reviews in American History (96); 299-303. **CONTACT ADDRESS** Dept History, Univ of Virginia, 0 Randall Hall, Charlottesville, VA 22903-3244. **EMAIL** oz@virginia.edu

ZUPKO, RONALD EDWARD
PERSONAL Born 08/05/1938, Youngstown, OH, m, 1974 **DISCIPLINE** MEDIEVAL ECONOMIC AND SOCIAL HISTORY **EDUCATION** Youngstown State Univ, BA, 60; Univ Chicago, MA, 62; Univ Wis, PhD(medieval hist), 66. **CAREER** Teaching asst, Dept Integrated Lib Studies, Univ Wis, 64-66; from asst prof to prof medieval hist, Marquette Univ, 66-; asst chemn, dept hist, Marquette Univ, 69-76; assoc mem, Inst Advan Studies, Princeton, 77-; consult, field reader & evaluator, Metric Educ Prog, US Off Educ, Washington, DC, 77- **HONORS AND AWARDS** Am Philos Soc res grants, 72, 73 & 80-81; NSF fel in res, 72-73; Teaching Excellence Awd, Marquette Univ, 77. **MEMBERSHIPS** Medieval Acad Am; Mid-West Medieval Asn; Am Econ Asn; Repetoire Int Medievistes; Am Econ Assoc. **RESEARCH** Medieval English history; medieval English weights and measures, including officials, legislation and all other aspects; medieval economic and social history. **SELECTED PUBLICATIONS** Auth, Revolution in Measurement: Western European Weights and Measures Since the Age of Science, The Am Philos Soc Memoirs 86 (Philedelphia), 90. **CONTACT ADDRESS** Dept of Hist, Marquette Univ, Coughlin Hall, Milwaukee, WI 53233. **EMAIL** ronald.zupko@marquette.edu

Geographic Index

COLORADO

CONNECTICUT

Hartford
Bijlefeld, Willem A.
Greenberg, Cheryl
Kassow, Samuel D.
Lang, Berel
Maciuika, Benedict Vytenis
Macro, Anthony David
Sloan, Edward William

Mashantucket
Newport, William H. A.

Middlebury
Bedford, Steven M.

Middletown
Buel, Richard (Van Wyck)
Butler, Jeffrey Ernest
Elphick, Richard
Gillmor, Charles Stewart
Greene, Nathanael
Hill, Patricia
Horgan, Paul
Kerr-Ritchie, Jeffrey R.
Long, Jerome Herbert
Meyer, Donald
Pomper, Philip
Slotkin, Richard S.
Vann, Richard T.

New Britain
Shen, Xiaoping
Snaden, James N.

New Haven
Adams, Marilyn M.
Amanat, Abbas
Ausmus, Harry Jack
Bartlett, Beatrice S.
Butler, Jon
Carby, Hazel V.
Cott, Nancy Falik
Davis, David Brion
de Bretteville, Sheila Levrant
Faragher, John Mack
Feinberg, Harvey Michael
Foos, Paul W.
Foster, Benjamin Read
Foster, Karen Polinger
Freeman, Joanne B.
Gaddis, John Lewis
Griffith, Ezra
Hersey, George Leonard
Imholt, Robert Joseph
Jansson, Maija
Kazemzadeh, Firuz
Lamar, Howard Roberts
Lee, Ta-ling
Macmullen, Ramsay
Matthews, John F.
Merriman, John M.
Minkema, Kenneth P.
Patterson, Robert Leyburne
Pelikan, Jaroslav J.
Perlis, Vivian
Pollitt, Jerome J.
Prown, Jules D.
Sanneh, Lamin
Schwartz, Stuart
Spence, Jonathan Dermot
Stoll, Steven
Stout, Harry S.
Thomas, Gerald Eustis
Thompson, Robert Farris
Trachtenberg, Alan
Turner, Frank Miller
Turner, Henry Ashby, Jr.
Waldstreicher, David L.
Wandycz, Piotr Stefan
Weinstein, Stanley
Winks, Robin William Evert
Winroth, Anders

New Heaven
Hayden, Dolores

New London
Ankeny, Rachel A.
Burlingame, Michael A.
Despalatovic, Elinor Murray
Forster, Marc R.
Lesser, Jeffrey
Paxton, Frederick S.
Taranow, Gerda
Wilson, Lisa H.

North Haven
Katsaros, Thomas

Northampton
Aldrich, Mark

Simsbury
Frost, James Arthur

Stamford
Babson, Jane F.

Storrs
Asher, Robert
Brown, Richard D.
Clifford, John Garry
Collier, Christopher
Coons, Ronald E.
Costigliola, Frank Charles
Curry, Richard Orr
Dayton, Cornelia H.
Dickerman, Edmund H.
Halvorson, Peter L.
Hoglund, A. William
Lewis, T.
Lougee, Robert Wayne
Moynihan, Ruth Barnes
Paterson, Thomas Graham
Stave, Bruce M.
Ward, Allen M.

Stratford
Fritz, Robert B.

Waterbury
Meyer, Judith

West Hartford
Auten, Arthur
Breit, Peter K.
Canning, Paul
Goodheart, Lawrence
Lacey, Barbara E.

West Haven
Glen, Robert Allan

Westport
Fraser, J(ulius) T(homas)
Millar, Steven

Willimantic
Dawson, Anne
Lacey, James
Lynch, Catherine
Pocock, Emil

Wilton
Stoetzer, O. Carlos

DELAWARE

Dover
Flayhart, William H., III

Georgetown
Williams, William Henry

Newark
Allmendinger, David F.
Athanassoglou-Kallmyer, Nina Maria
Bernstein, John Andrew
Boylan, Anne M.
Byrne, John M.
Callahan, Daniel Francis
Callahan, Raymond Aloysius
Chapman, H. Perry
Craven, Wayne
Crawford, John S.
Curtis, James C.
Duggan, Lawrence Gerald
Ferguson, Eugene S.
Geiger, Reed G.
Gibson, Ann Eden
Haber, Carole
Herman, Bernard L.
Heyrman, Christine L.
Hoffecker, Carol E.
Homer, William I.
Lopata, Roy Haywood
Martin, Ronald Edward
May, Gary
Meyer, Donald Harvey
Munroe, John Andrew
Ness, Lawrence
Newton, James E.
Pellecchia, Linda
Pong, David
Postle, Martin J.
Reedy, Chandra L.
Sidebotham, Steven Edward
Stillman, Damie
Stone, David M.
Tolles, Bryant F.
Wolters, Raymond

Wilmington
Finkelstein, Rona G.
Porter, Glenn

Winterthur
Smith, James Morton

DISTRICT OF COLUMBIA

Washington
Abel, Elie
Adams, Russell Lee
Andrews, Avery D.
Apostolos-Cappadona, Diane
Atkin, Muriel Ann
Baker, Richard Allan
Becker, William Henry
Beisner, Robert L.
Bell, William Gardner
Bergen, Barry
Berkowitz, Edward D.
Billington, James H.
Birch, Bruce Charles
Bishop, Donald M.
Blakely, Allison
Bloomfield, Maxwell H.
Boorstin, Daniel Joseph
Borelli, John
Boswell, Jackson Campbell
Bowling, Kenneth R.
Breitman, Richard D.
Brown, Dorothy M.
Campbell, Ted A.
Cenkner, William
Cheru, Fantu
Clarke, Duncan
Cline, Catherine Ann
Coll, Blanche D.
Crawford, Michael John
Crew, Spencer R.
Crouch, Tom Day
Cruz, Jo Ann Hoeppner Moran
Curran, Robert Emmott
Daniel, Pete
Davis, Audrey Blyman
Davison, Roderic Hollett
De Leon, David
Delio, Ilia
Dennis, George Thomas
Dudley, William Sheldon
Eisenstein, Elizabeth Lewisohn
England, James Merton
Eno, Robert Bryan
Esposito, John L.
Eyck, F. Gunther
Fern, Alan M.
Finan, John J.
Fisk, Deborah Payne
Forman, P.
French, Valerie
Garrard, Mary
Gephart, Ronald Michael
Gowans, Alan
Greenough, Sarah
Gribbin, William James
Griffith, Robert
Grimsted, David Allen
Gundersheimer, W. L.
Hallion, Richard Paul
Harris, Joseph E.
Harrison, Cynthia
Hartgrove, Joseph Dane
Hassing, Richard F.
Haynes, John Earl
Heffron, Paul Thayer
Helms, John Douglas
Henning, Randall
Herber, Charles Joseph
Hill, Bennett David
Hill, Peter Proal
Hirschmann, David
Horn, John Stephen
Horton, James O.
Hunt, Richard Allen
Jacks, Philip
Jaffe, Lorna S.
Johnson, Ronald Maberry
Kennedy, Dane Keith
Kim, Hyung Kook
Kinsella, David
Klaren, Peter Flindell
Klein, Ira N.
Kohler, Sue A.
Kraut, Alan M.
Kurland, Jordan Emil
Kuznick, Peter J.
Langer, Erick Detlef
LeMelle, Tilden J.
Lewis, Douglas
Liss, Peggy K.
Lubbers, Jeffrey S.
Lubrano, Linda L.
Lynch, John Edward
Lynn, Kenneth Schuyler
MacDonald, William L.
Mahony, Robert E. P.
Maisch, Christian
Mardin, Serif
Marty, Myron August
McCartin, Joseph A.
McNeill, John R.
Mergen, Bernard M.
Minnich, Nelson H.
Morris, Bonnie J.
Muller, Jerry Z.
Multhauf, Robert Phillip
Murray, Shoon
Nadell, Pamela
Needell, Allan A.
Nelson, Anna K.
Nordquist, Barbara K.
Nyang, Sulayman
O'Neill, James E.
Oppenheim, Janet
Palmer, Phyllis Marynick
Peloso, Vincent C.
Phillips, Ann
Pinkett, Harold Thomas
Poos, L. R.
Post, Robert C.
Rand, Harry
Reagon, Bernice Johnson
Riley, James Denson
Ritchie, Donald Arthur
Robinson, Lilien F.
Ross, Dorothy Rabin
Rothenberg, Marc
Ruedy, John D.
Sachar, Howard M.
Saperstein, Marc E.
Schneider, Robert A.
Schwoerer, Lois Green
Shahid, Irfan Arif
Sharoni, Simona
Sharrer, George Terry
Shedel, James P.
Spector, Ronald H.
Stephen, Elizabeth H.
Stephens, William Richard
Strong, Douglas M.
Talbot, Alice Mary
Taminiaux, Pierre S.
Teich, Albert Harris
Thornton, Richard C.
Trask, David F.
Trisco, Robert Frederick
Tucker, Nancy Bernkopf
Tushnet, Mark Victor
Viola, Herman Joseph
Vogt, George Leonard
Voll, John Obert
Walker, Robert Harris
Wetzell, Richard
Wheelock, Arthur K., Jr.
White, Charles Sidney John
White, Kevin
Williams, Joan C.
Wilmarth, Arthur E.
Wiser, Vivian
Witek, John W.
Yeandle, Laetitia

FLORIDA

Boca Raton
Breslow, Boyd
Brown, Sallie
Caputi, Jane
Curl, Donald Walter
Derfler, Leslie A.
Engle, Stephen D.
Ferrari, Roberto
Forage, Paul C.
Frazer, Heather
Ganson, Barbara
Kersey, Harry A.
Kollander, Patricia A.
Lowe, Benno P.
Marina, William F.
Rose, Mark
Tata, Robert J.
Taura, Graciella Cruz

Cape Coral
Magner, Lois

Coral Gables
Carlebach, Michael L.
Casebier, Allan
Graf, David Frank
Lohof, Bruce Alan
Muller, Peter O.

Deland
Croce, Paul Jerome
Favis, Roberta Smith
Hoogenboom, Hilde
Steeves, Paul David

Dunedin
Hyers, M. Conrad

Fort Lauderdale
Ryan, Thomas Joseph

Fort Pierce
Grego, Richard

Ft Lauderdale
Doan, James E.

Gainesville
Brundage, William F.
Bullivant, Keith
Bushnell, David
Colburn, David Richard
Dickison, Sheila Kathryn
Foltz, Richard
Formisano, Ronald P.
Funk, Arthur Layton
Geggus, D.
Giles, Geoffrey John
Gregory, Frederick
Hackett, David H.
Hatch, Robert A.
Isenberg, Sheldon Robert
McKeen, William
McMahon, Robert J.
Needell, Jeffrey D.
Paul, Harry W.
Pozzetta, George Enrico
Smocovitis, Vassiliki B.
Sommerville, Charles John
Sturgill, Claude C.
Thursby, Gene Robert
Todorova, M.
Turner, Eldon R.
Wyatt-Brown, Bertram
Zieger, R. H.

Hawthorne
Seelye, John D.

Jacksonville
Buettinger, Craig
Clifford, Dale Lothrop
Courtwright, David T.
Crooks, James Benedict
Leonard, Thomas M.
Oldakowski, Raymond K.
Pike, Fredrick B.
Qian, Wen-yuan
Thomas, Carl Eric

Kissimmee
Smith, Robert W.

Lake Worth
Slatery, William Patrick
Young, Zenaida Isabel

Lakeland
Denham, James M.
Mc Leod, Ann M.
Watson, Judge

Melbourne
Ritson, G. Joy
Taylor, Robert

Geographic Index

Brown, Richard Holbrook
Bruegmann, Robert
Buntrock, Dana
Burnell, Devin
Burton, J. D.
Cafferty, Pastora San Juan
Cardoza, Anthony L.
Civil, Miguel
Cohen, Sheldon S.
Cohn, Bernard Samuel
Craig, John Eldon
Daily, Jonathan
Danzer, Gerald
Dennis, David B.
Donner, Fred M.
Draznin, Yaffa Claire
Echols, James Kenneth
Edie, Carolyn A.
Elkins, James
Erenberg, Lewis
Erlebacher, Albert
Eslinger, Ellen T.
Fanning, Steve
Fasolt, Constantin
Fried, Richard M.
Gagliano, Joseph Anthony
Galush, William J.
Gariepy, Margo R.
Gebhard, Elizabeth Replogle
Geyer, M.
Ghazzal, Zouhair
Gilbert, Bentley Brinkerhoff
Gilfoyle, Timothy J.
Golb, Norman
Goldman, Jean
Gray, Hanna Holborn
Green, Jesse Dawes
Gross, Hanns
Gross-Diaz, Theresa
Groves, Nicholas
Gutek, Gerald Lee
Hales, Peter Bacon
Harrington, Ann M.
Harrington, Kevin
Hayes, Zachary Jerome
Hays, Jo N.
Headrick, Daniel Richard
Hellie, Richard
Helmholz, R. H.
Hendel, Kurt Karl
Hermansen, Marcia
Higgins, Hannah
Hirsch, Susan E.
Holli, Melvin G.
Hulse, Clark
John, Richard R.
Johnson, Paul B.
Johnson, Walker C.
Johnson-Odim, Cheryl
Jones, Peter D. A.
Jordan, David P.
Kaegi, Walter Emil
Kang, Soo Y.
Karamanski, Theodore J.
Karl, Barry D.
Kaufman, Suzanne
Khodarkovsky, Michael
Kirshner, Julius
Klein, R.
Knapp, Thomas A.
Krieger, Leonard
Kulczycki, John
Kuzdale, Ann E.
Levin, David J.
Levy, Richard S.
Macdonald, J. Fred
Mann, Arthur
Margolin, Victor
Mccaffrey, Lawrence John
McCullagh, Suzanne Folds
McGinn, Bernard John
McManamon, John
Mcneill, William Hardy
Mellon, Stanley
Messer, Robert Louis
Miller, David B.
Miller, Marion S.
Miller, Virginia E.
Misa, Thomas J.
Mooney-Melvin, Patricia
Moseley, Michael Edward
Moylan, Prudence A.
Najita, Tetsuo
Neary, Timothy B.
Nelson, Robert S.
Nolan, Janet
Novick, Peter
Nuzzo, Angelica
Nystrom, David P.
Ogorzaly, Michael
Olin, Margaret
Perelmuter, Hayim Goren
Perman, Michael
Pfeffer, Paula F.
Pinder, Kymberly
Pinney, Gloria Ferrari
Platt, Harold L.
Pollak, Martha
Power, Margaret
Ransby, Barbara
Reardon, John J.
Reiner, Erica
Reisch, George
Remini, Robert Vincent
Reynolds, Frank E.
Riess, Steve Allen
Roeder, George H., Jr.
Rosenwein, Barbara Herstein
Royster, Philip M.
Sack, James J.
Saller, Richard
Schelbert, Leo
Schmaus, Warren Stanley
Schroeder, Susan P.
Schultheiss, K.
Singleton, Gregory Holmes
Sloan, Thomas
Smith, Daniel Scott
Smith, Jonathan Zittell
Smith, Tom W.
Sochen, June
Sokol, David M.
Stafford, Barbara Maria
Stein, Leon
Stern, Robin
Tannenbaum, Rebecca J.
Tomlins, Christopher L.
Townsend, Richard
Vita, Steven
Walker, Sue Sheridan
Weiner, Lynn
Wente, Edward Frank
Williams, Daniel
Woodman, Taylor
Zukowsky, John

Danville
Cornelius, Janet Duitsman

De Kalb
Blomquist, Thomas W.
Dye, James Wayne
Foster, Stephen
George, Charles Hilles
Gildemeister, Glen A.
Kinser, Samuel
Meyer, Jerry D.
Moody, J. Carroll
Norris, James D.
Parot, Joseph John
Posadas, Barbara Mercedes
Resis, Albert
Schneider, Robert W.
Shesgreen, Sean Nicholas
Spencer, Elaine Glovka
Spencer, George W.
Wilson, Constance Maralyn

Decatur
Mittal, Sushil

Deerfield
Benson, Warren S.
Pointer, Steven R.

Dekalb
Atkins, E. Taylor
Kern, Stephen R.
Kyvig, David E.
Worobec, Christine D.

Edwardsville
Astour, Michael Czernichow
Chen, Ching-Chih
Haas, James M.
Nore, Ellen
Pearson, Samuel C.
Weingartner, James Joseph

Elsah
Helmer, Stephen
Sandford, George W.

Eureka
Rodriguez, Junius

Evanston
Binford, Henry C.
Breen, Timothy Hall
Clayson, S. Hollis
Davies, Carole Boyce
Davis, Whitney
Dillon, Diane
Fraser, Sarah
Heyck, Thomas William
Hindman, Sandra L.
Joravsky, David
Kalantzis, George
Kieckhefer, Richard
Lerner, Robert E.
Lowe, Eugene Y., Jr.
Maza, Sarah C.
Muir, Edward
Murphy, Larry G.
Okoye, Ikem
Perry, Edmund
Petry, Carl F.
Safford, Frank Robinson
Seymour, Jack L.
Sherry, Michael Stephen
Smith, Carl
Steinberg, Salme Harju
Stone-Richards, Michael
Van Zanten, David
Werckmeister, O. K.

Galesburg
Bailey, Stephen
Davis, Rodney
Gold, Penny Schine
Hane, Mikiso
Hord, Frederick Lee

Greenville
Huston, Richard P.

Grinnell
Sortor, M.

Homewood
Gerrish, Brian Albert

Jacksonville
Burnette, Rand
Davis, James Edward
Tracey, Donald Richard

Joliet
Cuvalo, Ante

Kankakee
Lowe, Stephen

Lake Forest
Beiriger, Eugene
Bronstein, Herbert
Ebner, Michael Howard
LeMahieu, Dan Lloyd
Schulze, Franz
Zilversmit, Arthur

Lincolnwood
Singer, David G.

Lombard
Weber, Timothy P.

Macomb
Armfield, Felix L.
Brown, Spencer Hunter
Burton, William Lester
Combs, William L.
Egler, David G.
Leonard, Virginia Waugh
Merrett, Christopher D.
Palmer, Scott W.
Sutton, Robert Paul
Watkins, Thomas H.
Werner, John M.
West, C. S'thembile

Maywood
Roeber, Anthony G.

Monmouth
Cordery, Simon
Cordery, Stacy A. Rozek
Urban, William Lawrence

Mountt Carmel
Owens, Patricia

Murphysboro
Lyons, Robin R.

Naperville
Mueller, Howard Ernest

Normal
Devinatz, Victor G.
Freed, John Beckmann
Holsinger, M. Paul
Homan, Gerlof Douwe
Jagodzinski, Cecile M.
Jelks, Edward Baker
Mai, James L.
Perez, Louis
Schapsmeier, Edward Lewis
Sessions, Kyle Cutler
Walker, Lawrence David

Oak Brook
Durnbaugh, Donald F.

Oak Park
Greenhouse, Wendy
Robinet, Harriette Gillem
Young, Alfred F.

Peoria
Bowers, William Lavalle
Guzman, Gregory G.
Smallwood, Arwin

Ridge
Doherty, Barbara

River Forest
Hays, Rosalind Conklin
Stadtwald, Kurt
Todd, Mary

Riverside
Martin, Marty
Marty, Martin Emil

Rock Island
Calder, Lendol
Mayer, Thomas F.
Symons, Van J.
Tredway, John Thomas

Rockford
Forslund, Catherine

Romeoville
Glueckert, Leopold
Lifka, Mary L.

Savoy
Tingley, Donald Fred

Springfield
Shiner, Larry
Taylor, Richard Stuart

Urbana
Accad, Evelyne
Barrett, James R.
Bernard, Paul Peter
Buckler, John
Burkhardt, Richard W.
Burton, Orville Vernon
Carringer, Robert L.
Cuno, Kenneth M.
Douglas, George Halsey
Fritzsche, Peter
Haboush, Ja-Hyun Kim
Hannon, Bruce M.
Hibbard, Caroline Marsh
Hitchins, Keith
Hoddeson, Lillian
Hoxie, Frederick E.
Irish, Sharon
Jaher, Frederic Cople
Jakle, John Allais
Johannsen, Robert W.
Kalipeni, Ezekiel
Koenker, Diane P.
Koslofsky, Craig
Leff, Mark H.
Love, Joseph L.
Lynn, John A.
Mckay, John Patrick
Michelson, Bruce
Mitchell, Richard E.
Nichols, Jalden
Pleck, Elizabeth
Porton, Gary Gilbert
Radding, Cynthia
Ratner, Lorman A. (Larry)
Reagan, Leslie J.
Solberg, Winton Udell
Spence, Clark Christian
Spence, Mary Lee
Stewart, Charles Cameron
Toby, Ronald P.
Violas, Paul Constantine
Walker, Juliet Elise Kirkpatrick

Western Springs
Fischer, Robert Harley

Wheaton
Blumhofer, Edith L.
Kay, Thomas O.
Lewis, James F.
Noll, Mark Allan
Ziefle, Helmut W.

Wilmette
Huppert, George
Smith, Lacey Baldwin

INDIANA

Anderson
Nelson, J. Douglas

Angola
Zimmerman, James A.

Bloomington
Alter, George
Bodnar, John Edward
Brooks, George E.
Brown, A. Peter
Burdick, Dakin
Burns, Sarah
Caldwell, L. K.
Capshew, James H.
Carmichael, Ann Grayton
Choksy, Jamsheed
Churchill, Frederick Barton
Cohen, William B.
Cole, Bruce
Facos, Michelle
Faries, Molly
Ferrell, Robert Hugh
Field, Arthur
Friedman, Lawrence Jacob
Gamber, Wendy
Gealt, Adelheid Medicus
Grant, Edward
Hudson, Herman C.
Ipsen, Carl
Irvine, B. J.
Jelavich, Barbara
Johnson, Owen V.
Kaplan, Herbert Harold
Katz, Irving
Kennedy, Janet
Kleinbauer, W. Eugene
Koertge, Noretta
Lloyd, Elisabeth A.
Lohmann, Christoph Karl
Madison, James H.
McGerr, M.
McNaughton, Patrick
Mehlinger, Howard Dean
Meli, Domenico Bertoloni
Meyerowitz, Joanne
Moore, John Clare
Nader, Helen
Nelson, Susan
Nordloh, David Joseph
Peterson, M. Jeanne
Pletcher, David Mitchell
Rabinowitch, Alexander
Ransel, David
Rasch, William
Remak, Henry Heymann Herman
Riley, James
Sheehan, Bernard W.
Sieber, Roy
Sorrenson, Richard J.
Strauss, Gerald
Wilson, George M.

Chesterton
Suellen, Hoy

Clarksville
Kramer, Carl Edward

IOWA

KANSAS

KENTUCKY

Edgewood
Borne, Lawrence Roger

Georgetown
Klotter, James

Grayson
Wineland, John D.

Highland Heights
Adams, Michael Charles

Lexington
Albisetti, James C.
Banning, Lance
Betts, Raymond Frederick
Cawelti, John George
Chassen-Lopez, Francie R.
Christianson, Eric Howard
Eastwood, Bruce Stansfield
Eller, Ronald
Freehling, William W.
Furlough, Ellen
Hargreaves, Mary Wilma Massey
Herring, George C.
Ireland, Robert
Jones, Paul Henry
Nugent, Donald Christopher
Olson, Robert W.
Perreiah, Alan Richard
Petrone, Karen
Popkin, Jeremy D.
Roland, Charles P.
Servlnikov, Sergio
Smith, Daniel B.
Smoot, Rick
Stanton, Edward F.
Starr-Lebeau, Gretchen D.
Warth, Robert Douglas
Withington, William Adriance

Louisville
Chancellor, James D.
Curry, Leonard Preston
Deering, Ronald F.
Henry, Gray
Hoyt-O'Connor, Paul E.
Kebric, Robert Barnett
Mackey, Thomas C.
McCarthy, Justin
McLeod, John
Morgan, William
Mulder, John Mark
Slavin, Arthur J.
Steeger, William P.
Webber, Randall C.
Weissbach, Lee Shai
Wills, Gregory A.

Morehead
Leroy, Perry Eugene
Sprague, Stuart Seely

Murray
Cartwright, Joseph Howard
Mulligan, William

Newport
Purvis, Thomas L.
Ramage, James A.
Vitz, Robert C.

Pikeville
Fitzgerald, Michael

Richmond
Appleton, Thomas H., Jr.
Ellis, William Elliott
Forderhase, Rudolph Eugene
Graybar, Lloyd Joseph
Hay, Melba Porter
Stebbins, Robert E.

Williamsburg
Carmical, Oline, Jr.

Wilmore
Arnold, Bill T.
Hamilton, Victor Paul
Kinghorn, Kenneth Cain
Zahniser, A. H. Mathias

LOUISIANA

Alexandria
Sanson, Jerry P.

Baton Rouge
Batinski, Emily E.
Becker, Robert Arthur
Burkett, Delbert Royce
Carleton, Mark Thomas
Cooper, William
Culbert, David H.
Di Maio, Irene S.
Djebar, Assia
Henderson, John B.
Holtman, Robert Barney
Kooi, Christine
Lindenfeld, David Frank
Loos, John Louis
Loveland, Anne C.
Martin, Benjamin F.
Owen, Thomas C.
Royster, Charles William
Schufreider, Gregory
Tolson, Arthur
Vincent, Charles
Warga, Richard G., Jr.

Bossier City
Tinsley, James R.

Eunice
Baltakis, Anthony

Grambling
Carter, Doris

Hammond
Kurtz, Michael L.
McGehee, R. V.
Nichols, C. Howard

Lafayette
Brasseaux, Carl A.
Conrad, Glenn Russell
Gentry, Judith Anne Fenner
Johnson, David C.
Reilly, Timothy F.
Richard, Carl
Schoonover, Thomas David

Lake Charles
Tarver, H. Michael
Watson, Thomas Davis

Monroe
Legan, Marshall Scott

Natchitoches
Le Breton, Marietta
Thomas, Jean D'Amato

New Orleans
Altman, Ida
Anderson, Nancy Fix
Bauer, Craig A.
Beck, Guy
Billings, William M.
Bischof, Gunter J., Jr.
Brown, Marilyn
Brumfield, William Craft
Brungardt, Maurice P.
Carter, Jane B.
Clark, Michael D.
Collin, Richard H.
Cook, Bernard Anthony
Desai, Gaurav Gajanan
Eskew, Harry Lee
Esthus, Raymond Arthur
Fann, Willerd Reese
Frey, Slyvia Rae
Gnuse, Robert
Goins, Richard Anthony
Greenleaf, Richard E.
Hall, Gwendolyn Midlo
Hirsch, Arnold Richard
Irwin, Robert McKee
James, Felix
Jenkins, A. Lawrence
Johnson, Jerah W.
Kehoe, Dennis P.
Kuczynski, Michael
Latner, Richard Barnett
Lazzerini, Edward James
Logsdon, Joseph
Malone, Bill Charles
Nair, Supryia M.
Reeves, William Dale
Sauder, Robert A.
Schafer, Judith
Schlunz, Thomas Paul
Stiebing, William H., Jr
Swift, Mary Grace
Tronzo, William
Tuttle, Richard J.
Verrett, Joyce M.
Vetrocq, Marcia E.
Weiss, Ellen B.
Worthy, Barbara Ann

Ruston
Attrep, Abraham M.
Bush, John M.
Cook, Philip C.
Daly, John P.
Graves, Steven
Ingram, Earl Glynn
Meade, Wade C.
Rea, Kenneth W.
Webre, Stephen
Zalesch, Saul E.

Saint Benedict
Nauman, Ann K.

Shreveport
Pederson, William David
Plummer, Marguerite R.
Thompson, Alan Smith

MAINE

Bangor
Baker, William Joseph

Brunswick
Helmreich, Ernst Christian
Levine, Daniel
Walter, John Christopher

Farmington
Condon, Richard Herrick
Flint, Allen Denis

Lewiston
Cole, John R.
Hochstadt, Steve
Leamon, James Shenstone

Orono
Babcock, Robert Harper
Blanke, Richard
Doty, Charles Stewart
Egenhofer, Max J.
Fries, Russell Inslee
Judd, Richard
Mooney, L. R.
Pease, Jane Hanna
Petrik, Paula E.
See, Scott W.
Smith, David Clayton
Smith, Laurence D.

Portland
Dietrich, Craig
Klooster, Willem
Sawyer, Dana

Strong
Decker, Leslie Edward

Waterville
Bassett, Charles Walker
Fleming, James Rodger
Leonard, Elizabeth D.
Prindle, Tamae K.
Taylor, Larissa Juliet
Weisbrot, Robert S.

Woolwich
Martin, Kenneth R.

York Beach
Davison, Nancy R.

MARYLAND

Annapolis
Abels, Richard
Carr, Lois Green
Coletta, Paolo E.
Culham, Phyllis
DeCredico, Mary A.
Good, Jane E.
Hagan, Kenneth James
Symonds, Craig Lee

Baltimore
Albrecht, Catherine
Arnold, Joseph L.
Baker, Jean Harvey
Baldwin, John Wesley
Bardaglio, Peter W.
Bell, John D.
Blumberg, Arnold
Boehling, Rebecca
Breihan, John R.
Brieger, Gert Henry
Browne, Gary Lawson
Burke, Colin B.
Chapelle, Suzanne E. G.
Chikeka, Charles
Cohen, Warren I.
Cooper, Jerrold Stephen
Cripps, Thomas
Curtin, Philip De Armond
Dombrowski, Nicole
Donaghy, Thomas J.
Elfenbein, Jessica
Fee, Elizabeth
Forster, Robert
Freedman, Robert Owen
Galambos, Louis Paul
Gardner, Bettye J.
Geiger, Mary Virginia
Gittlen, Barry M.
Goedicke, Hans
Goldthwaite, Richard A.
Gorman, Michael J.
Greene, Jack P.
Grubb, James S.
Ham, Debra Newman
Herbert, Sandra Swanson
Higham, John
Hirschmann, Edwin A.
Hopkins, Fred
Irwin, John Thomas
Jacklin, Thomas M.
Jeffrey, Julie Roy
Jeffries, John W.
Kagan, Richard Lauren
Kargon, Robert
Kars, Marjoleine
Kessler, Herbert Leon
King-Hammond, Leslie
Knight, Franklin Willis
Larew, Karl G.
Legon, Ronald
Leonard, Angela
Lidtke, Vernon Leroy
McConnell, Roland Calhoun
Mitchell, Reid
Mruck, Armin Einhard
Mulcahey, Donald C.
Neverdon-Morton, Cynthia
Nwadike, Fellina
Papadakis, Aristeides
Pegram, Thomas R.
Phillips, Glenn Owen
Pineo, Ronn
Ranum, Orest
Ritschel, Daniel
Roller, Matthew B.
Russell-Wood, A. J. R.
Ryon, Roderick Naylor
Sawyer, Jeffrey K.
Scherer, Imgard S.
Shapiro, H. Alan
Soria, Regina
Spiegel, Gabrielle Michele
Spring, David
Stanton, Phoebe Baroody
Struever, Nancy Schermerhorn
Tatarewicz, Joseph N.
Terborg-Penn, Rosalyn M.
Vaporis, Constantine N.
Varga, Nicholas
Walker, Ernestein
Walker, Mack
Walters, Ronald Gordon
Webb, Robert Kiefer
Wexler, Victor G.
Yip, Ka-che
Zhuk, Sergei I.

Bethesda
Cassedy, James Higgins
Hewlett, Richard Greening
Sappol, Michael
Smith, Dale Cary
Waserman, Manfred

Betterton
Kohl, Benjamin Gibbs

Bowie
Miller, M. Sammye

Burtonsville
Rothfeld, Anne

Catonsville
Loerke, William

Chestertown
Janson-La Palme, Bayly
Tatum, Nancy R.

Chevy Chase
Patterson, David Sands
Timbie, Janet Ann

College Park
Albert, Peter J.
Bedos-Rezak, Brigitte
Belz, Herman Julius
Berlin, Adele
Berlin, Ira
Bradbury, Miles L.
Brush, Stephen George
Caughey, John L.
Colantuono, Anthony
Cole, Wayne S.
Darden, Lindley
Denny, Don William
Eckstein, Arthur M.
Evans, Emory Gibbons
Finkelstein, Barbara
Flack, James
Friedel, Robert D.
Gerstel, Sharon E. J.
Gilbert, James B.
Gullickson, Gay Linda
Harlan, Louis R.
Harris, James F.
Henretta, James A.
Jashemski, Wilhelmina F.
Jenkins, Virginia Scott
Kornbluth, Genevra
Lounsbury, Myron
Lyons, Clare A.
Matossian, Mary Kilbourne
Olson, Alison Gilbert
Olson, Keith Waldemar
Pressly, William L.
Price, Richard
Promey, Sally M.
Ridgway, Whitman Hawley
Sies, Mary Corbin
Sullivan, Denis
Sumida, Jon T.
Vann, Robert Lindley
Walters, Ronald
Warren, Donald R.
Warren, J. Benedict
Weart, Spencer R.
Zilfi, Madeline Carol

Columbia
Ligon, Doris Hillian
Mitchell, Helen Buss
Wolter, John A.

Emmitsburg
Johnson, Curtis
Kalas, Robert
Krysiek, James Stephen
Rupp, Teresa
Whitman, T. Stephen

Fort Washington
Demolen, Richard Lee
Gustafson, Milton Odell

Frederick
Keeler, Mary Frear

Frostburg
Clulee, Nicholas H.
Rhodes, Randall
Saku, James C.
Wiseman, John Bailes

Kensington
Cline, Eric

Geehr, Richard Stockwell
Jick, Leon Allen
Jones, Jacqueline
Keller, Morton
Reinharz, Jehuda
Sarna, Jonathan D.
Todd, Ian Alexander
Whitfield, Stephen Jack

Wayland
Lane, Evelyn Staudinger
Walker, Robert Miller

Wellesley
Cohen, Paul Andrew
Cudjoe, Selwyn Reginald
Edelstein, Arthur
Fontijn-Harris, Claire
Johnson, Roger A.
Malino, Frances
Martin, Tony
O'Gorman, James F.
Rollins, Judith
Steady, Filomina
Thrasher, William

Wellesley Hills
Auerbach, Jerold

Wenham
Askew, Thomas A.
Howard, Thomas A.

West Harwich
Berry, J. Duncan

Westfield
Kaufman, Martin
Shannon, Catherine Barbara

Weston
Grad, Bonnie L.
Laska, Vera
Meade, Catherine M.
Wasson, Ellis Archer
Wintle, Thomas

Williamstown
Beaver, Donald de Blasiis
Dew, Charles Burgess
Frost, Peter K.
Hedreen, Guy
Holly, Michael Ann
Kohut, Thomas A.
Kubler, Cornelius C.
Oakley, Francis Christopher
Park, David Allen
Rudolph, Frederick
Stoddard, Whitney S.
Tracy, Patricia Juneau
Wagner, William Gilson
Wood, James Brian

Winchester
Meister, Maureen

Worcester
Attreed, Lorraine C.
Barnhill, Georgia Brady
Billias, George Athan
Borg, Daniel Raymond
Bullock, Steven C.
Burkett, Randall Keith
Cary, Noel D.
Dunn, Patrick Peter
Dykstra, Robert R.
Flynn, James Thomas
Hansen, Peter H.
Hench, John Bixler
Kealey, Edward J.
Kom, Ambroise
Kuzniewski, Anthony Joseph
Lapomarda, Vincent Anthony
Little, Douglas James
Lucas, Paul
Manfra, Jo Ann
Mcbride, Theresa Marie
Mcclymer, John Francis
McCorison, Marcus Allen
Moynihan, Kenneth J.
Pontius, Robert Gilmore, Jr.
Powers, James Francis
Ropp, Paul
Shary, Timothy
Shea, Emmett A.
Sokal, Michael Mark
Turner, B. L., II
Ziegler, Paul R.

MICHIGAN

Adrian
Fechner, Roger J.

Albion
Cocks, Geoffrey C.
Horstman, Allen

Allendale
Goode, James
Morison, William S.
Niemeyer, Glenn Alan

Alma
Massanari, Ronald Lee

Ann Arbor
Becker, Marvin Burton
Beckman, Gary M.
Chang, Chun-Shu
Cole, Juan R.
Cotera, Maria E.
Eadie, John W.
Eby, Cecil Degrotte
Eley, Geoff
Endelman, Todd Michael
Fine, Sidney
Frier, Bruce W.
George, Emery Edward
Goldstein, Laurence Alan
Green, Thomas Andrew
Grew, Raymond
Karlsen, Carol F.
King, John O.
Kirkpatrick, Diane Marie
Kivelson, Valerie
Knysh, Alexander D.
Krahmalkov, Charles R.
Lewis, David Lanier
Lindner, Rudi Paul
Marzolf, Marion Tuttle
Pedley, John Griffiths
Perkins, Bradford
Pernick, Martin Steven
Scott, Rebecca Jarvis
Smith, Richard Candida
Smith-Rosenberg, Carroll
Spector, Scott
Spink, Walter M.
Starr, Chester G.
Steneck, Nicholas H.
Suny, Ronald Grigor
Taylor, Dorceta E.
Trautmann, Thomas Roger
Vinovskis, Maris A.
Wald, Alan Maynard
Warner, Robert Mark

Berrien Springs
Bacchiocchi, Samuele
Geraty, Lawrence Thomas
Merling, David

Beulah
Tanner, Helen Hornbeck

Big Rapids
Mehler, Barry Alan

Dearborn
Friedman, Hal M.
Kamachi, Noriko
Papazian, Dennis Richard

Detroit
Ambler, Effie
Bonner, Thomas Neville
DeWindt, Anne R.
DeWindt, Edwin B.
Faue, Elizabeth V.
Finkenbine, Roy E.
Gilb, Corinne Lathrop
Goldman, Bernard
Gossman, Norbert Joseph
Guberti-Bassett, Sarah
Gutmann, Joseph
Haase, Donald P.
Johnson, Christopher Howard
Kruman, Marc Wayne
Lowe, William J.
Mason, Philip P.
Meisse, Tom
Moore, Marian J.
Nawrocki, Dennis Alan
Peck, William Henry
Raucher, Alan R.
Scott, Samuel Francis
Shapiro, Stanley
Small, Melvin
Staudenmaier, John M.
Stever, Sarah S.
Sumner, Gregory D.
Taylor, Cledie Collins
Uhr, Horst
Wise, Edward Martin

East Lansing
Barrows, Floyd Dell
Byron, Kristine Ann
Donakowski, Conrad L.
Dulai, Surjit Singh
Fisher, Alan Washburn
Flanagan, Maureen Anne
Graham, W. Fred
Haltman, Kenneth
Hudson, Robert Vernon
Huzar, Eleanor Goltz
Konvitz, Josef Wolf
Korth, Philip Alan
Lammers, Donald N.
Laurence, Richard Robert
Levine, Peter D.
Lunde, Erik Sheldon
Marcus, Harold G.
Matthews, Roy T.
Miller, Douglas T.
Noverr, Douglas Arthur
Platt, Franklin Dewitt
Pollack, Norman
Robinson, David W.
Schoenl, William J.
Seadle, Michael S.
Soltow, James Harold
Sowards, Steven W.
Stewart, Gordon Thomas
Sweet, Paul Robinson
Thomas, Samuel Joseph
Varg, Paul Albert
Ziewacz, Lawrence E.

Grand Rapids
Bolt, Robert
Brinks, Herbert John
Carlson, Lewis H.
Carpenter, Joel A.
De Vries, Bert
Romanowski, William D.
Scheifele, Eleanor L.
Van Liere, Frans

Hillsdale
Brown, Kendall Walker
Gilbert, Arlan Kemmerer

Holland
Cohen, William
Kennedy, James C.
Wagenaar, Larry

Houghton
Gill, Glenda E.
Reynolds, Terry S.
Seely, Bruce E.

Kalamazoo
Breisach, Ernst Adolf
Brown, Alan S.
Carlson, Andrew
Dooley, Howard John
Earhart, Harry Byron
Elder, Ellen Rozanne
Falk, Nancy Ellen
He, Chansheng
Jones, Leander Corbin
Joslin, Katherine
Maier, Paul Luther
Saillant, John D.
Strauss, David
Szarmach, Paul E.
Wickstrom, John B.
Wilson, B.
Xiong, Victor

Marquette
Dreisbach, Donald Fred
Magnaghi, Russell Mario
Whitehouse, Eugene Alan

Mount Pleasant
Blackburn, George Mccoy
Hall, Mitchell K.
Hall, Timothy D.
Johnson, Eric A.
Macleod, David
Purcell, Sarah

Pontiac
Cohassey, John F.

Rochester
Barnard, Virgil John
Dykes, DeWitt S., Jr.
Eberwein, Jane Donahue
Osthaus, Carl Richard
Strauss, Wallace Patrick
Tucker, Richard Philip

Southfield
Stern, Marvin

University Center
Braddock, Robert Cook
Jezierski, John V.
Renna, Thomas Julius

Ypsilanti
Boyer, Lee R.
Cassar, George H.
Citino, Robert M.
Delph, Ronald
Duley, Margot I.
Gimelli, Louis B.
Goff, Richard D.
Graves, Pamela
Hafter, Daryl Maslow
Higbee, Mark
Holoka, James P.
Homel, Michael W.
King, H. Roger
Ligibel, Theodore J.
Long, Roger D.
McNally, Michael
Moss, Walter Gerald
Nelson, Gersham
Ojala, Carl F.
Perry, Robert Lee
Terry, Janice J.
Upshur, Jiu-Hwa Lo
Vinyard, JoEllen

MINNESOTA

Archives Collegeville
Tegeder, Vincent George

Baxter
Bianchi, Robert S.

Bemidji
Spreng, Ronald
Thomaidis, Spero T.

Collegeville
Forman, Mary

Duluth
Craig, Robert
Evans, John Whitney
Fetzer, James Henry
Fischer, Roger Adrian
Graham, William C.
Gustafson, David
Storch, Neil T.
Trolander, Judith Ann

Mankato
Croce, Lewis Henry
Friend, Donald A.
Larson, Bruce Llewellyn
Lass, William Edward
Lopez, Jose Javier
Postma, Johannes
Wicker, Nancy L.

Minneapolis
Akehurst, F. R. P.
Allman, Jean M.
Altholz, Josef L.
Bachrach, Bernard S.
Bashiri, Iraj
Berlin, Andrea Michelle
Berman, Hyman
Brauer, Kinley
Chambers, Sarah
Clark, Anna
Clayton, Tom
Cooper, Frederick A.
Evans, John Karl
Evans, Sara M.
Farah, Caesar E.
Farmer, Edward
Good, David F.
Green, George D.
Howe, John R.
Isaacman, Allen
Isett, Christopher
Kelly, Thomas
Kieft, David
Kohlstedt, Sally Gregory
Kopf, David
Layton, Edwin Thomas
Levinson, Bernard M.
Malandra, William
Marshall, Byron K.
May, Elaine Tyler
May, Lary L.
Maynes, Mary Jo
McCaa, Robert
McNally, Sheila
Menard, Russell R.
Merritt, Raymond Harland
Miller, Carol
Munholland, John Kim
Myers, Samuel L., Jr.
Nagar, Richa
Noble, David Watson
Noonan, Thomas S.
Norling, Lisa A.
O'Brien, Jean
Pankake, Marcia J.
Phillips, Carla Rahn
Phillips, William D., Jr
Prell, Riv-Ellen
Rabinowitz, Paula
Reyerson, Kathryn L.
Ruggles, Steven
Samaha, Joel
Samatar, Abdi I.
Seidel, Robert H.
Spear, Allan H.
Stuewer, Roger H.
Taylor, David Vassar
Teraoka, Arlene
Thayer, John A.
Toure, Diala
Tracy, James
Tyler May, Elaine
Urness, Carol
Valdes, Dennis N.
Vecoli, Rudolph John
Waltner, Ann
Wang, Liping
Welke, Barbara Y.
Winters, Donald
Yates, Gayle Graham
Zipes, Jack

Moorhead
Aageson, James W.
Harris, Paul
Johnson, Leroy Ronald
Lintelman, Joy

Morris
Ahern, Wilbert H.
Guyotte, Roland L.
Hinds, Harold E., Jr
Underwood, Ted Leroy

New Ulm
Thompson, Glen L.

Northfield
Blake, Stephen
Bonner, Robert Elliott
Carrington, Laurel
Clark, Clifford E., Jr.
Crouter, Richard E.
DeLaney, Jeane
Entenmann, Robert
Fritz, Henry Eugene
Jeffrey, Kirk
Krey, Gary De
Kutulas, Judy
Lovoll, Odd Sverre
Lund, Eric
Ottaway, Susannah R.
Prowe, Diethelm Manfred-Hartmut
Rader, Rosemary
Rippley, La Vern J.
Wilkie, Nancy C.
Williams, Harry M.

Saint Cloud
Gower, Calvin William
Hofsommer, Don L.
Tripp, Luke S.

Saint Joseph
Grabowska, James A.

Wheeler, Douglas L.
Wolper, Ethel Sara

Exeter
Bedford, Henry F.
Cole, Donald Barnard

Hanover
Allan, Sarah K. M.
Cohen, Ada
Corrigan, Kathleen
Daniell, Jere
Doenges, Norman Arthur
Ermarth, Hans Michael
Garthwaite, Gene Ralph
Heck, Marlene
Hockley, Allen
Jordan, Jim
Kelley, Mary
Kenseth, Joy
Major, John Stephen
McGrath, Robert
Ohnuma, Reiko
Penner, Hans Henry
Randolph, Adrian W. B.
Rosenthal, Angela H.
Shewmaker, Kenneth Earl
Spitzer, Leo
Wood, Charles Tuttle
Wright, James Edward

Manchester
Cassidy, James G.
Constance, Joseph
Foster, Anne L.
Huff, Peter A.
Mason, Francis M.
Pajakowski, Philip E.
Piotrowski, Thaddeus M.
Resch, John P.
Shannon, Sylvia C.

Nashua
Kaloudis, George

New London
Freeberg, E.

Newmarket
Dorsey, Kurk

Portsmouth
Hilson, Arthur Lee

Rindge
Lupinin, Nickolas

Rye
Winslow, Richard E., III

NEW JERSEY

Caldwell
Mullaney, Marie

Camden
Carlisle, Rodney
Dorwart, Jeffrey M.
Hull, N. E. H.
Lees, Andrew
Scranton, Philip

Cranford
Hogan, Lawrence Daniel

Elizabeth
Lupia, John N.
Siegel, Adrienne

Englewood
Hertzberg, Arthur

Ewing
Dickinson, Gloria Harper
Kamber, Richard

Glassboro
Adelson, Fred B.
Applebaum, David
Grupenhoff, Richard
Hewsen, Robert
Hunter, Gary
Kress, Lee Bruce
Porterfield, Richard Maurice
Wang, Q. Edward
Wiltenburg, Joy

Highland Park
Necheles-Jansyn, Ruth F.

Hoboken
Clark, Geoffrey W.
Laccetti, Silvio R.
Prisco, Salvatore

Jersey City
Carter, Guy C.
Palmegiano, Eugenia M.
Schmidt, William John

Lawrenceville
Brown, Jerry Wayne
Long, John Wendell
Richardson, Charles O.

Lincroft
Trimble, Richard M.

Livingston
Caban, Pedro

Lodi
Karetzky, Stephen

Madison
Bull, Robert Jehu
Christensen, Michael
Dayton, Donald Wilber
Fishburn, Janet Forsythe
Marchione, Margherita Frances
McTague, Robert
Rose, Jonathan
Selinger, Suzanne
Woolley, Peter J.

Mahwah
Davis, Henry Vance
Leontovich, Olga
Padovano, Anthony
Rice, Stephen P.
Ross, Ellen

Montclair
Cray, Robert
Olenik, John Kenneth
Pastor, Peter
Schwartz, Joel

New Brunswick
Adas, Michael Peter
Baigell, Matthew
Baily, Samuel Longstreth
Becker, Seymour
Bell, Rudolph Mark
Bowden, Henry Warner
Brett-Smith, Sarah
Butler, Kim D.
Cargill, Jack
Chambers, John W., II
Coakley, John
Cobble, Dorothy Sue
Eidelberg, Martin
Ellis, Edward Earle
Figueira, Thomas J.
Garrison, Lora Dee
Gasster, Michael
Gillespie, Angus K.
Gillette, William
Gillis, John R.
Goffen, Rona
Grob, Gerald N.
Hartman, Mary Susan
Held, Joseph
Howard, Angela
Jeffrey, Thomas Edward
Kelley, Donald R.
Kenfield, John F., III
Lears, T. J. Jackson
Lee, Maurice D., Jr
Lewis, David Levering
Lutz, Jessie Gregory
Marder, Tod A.
Marter, Joan
Mccormick, Richard P.
McHam, Sarah Blake
McLachlan, Elizabeth Parker
Morrison, Karl F.
O'Neill, William L.
Puglisi, Catherine
Reed, James Wesley
Rockland, Michael Aaron
Saretzky, Gary D.
Slaughter, Thomas Paul
Small, Jocelyn Penny
Smalls, James
Spector, Jack
St Clair Harvey, Archer
Stauffer, George B.
Stephens, Thomas M.
Stoianovich, Traian
Tarbell, Roberta K.
Tu, Ching-I
Turshen, Meredeth
Wasserman, Mark
Westermann, Mariet
Yanni, Carla

Newark
Basch, Norma
Dain, Norman
Diner, Steven J.
Franklin, H. Bruce
Kimball, Warren
Lewis, Jan Ellen
O'Connor, John E.
Russell, Frederick
Stieglitz, Robert R.
Wagenheim, Olga
Znayenko, Myroslava

Newton
Cifelli, Edward M.

North Brunswick
Conolly-Smith, Peter

Paramus
Dolce, Philip Charles
Lenk, Richard William

Paterson
Collins, Elliott

Piscataway
Martinez-Fernandez, Luis

Pomona
Constantelos, Demetrios J.
Hayse, Michael
Lubenow, William Cornelius

Princeton
Bagley, Robert W.
Burke, Martin J.
Challener, Richard Delo
Champlin, Edward James
Clagett, Marshall
Coffin, David Robbins
Feldherr, Andrew
Frantz, Mary Alison
Geison, Gerald Lynn
Grafton, Anthony T.
Isaac, Ephraim
James, Harold
Jordan, William C.
Katz, Stanley Nider
Kaufmann, Thomas DaCosta
Link, Arthur S.
MacLennan, Robert S.
Mahoney, Michael Sean
Makino, Yasuko
Mayer, Arno Joseph
Mcpherson, James Munro
Mills, Kenneth R.
Modarressi, Hossein
Moffett, Samuel Hugh
Moorhead, James Howell
Morgan, Ann Lee
Murrin, John Matthew
Naquin, Susan
Ober, Josiah
Painter, Nell Irvine
Paret, Peter
Pemberton, Gayle R.
Peterson, Willard James
Rabb, Theodore K.
Tignor, Robert L.
Trentmann, Frank
Tull, Herman
Udovitch, Abraham L.
Ufford, Lettia W.
Waswo, Ann
Wilson, John Frederick

Randolph
Citron, Henry
Heller, Rita

Ridge
Keller, William

Short Hills
Feyerick, Ada
Steffensen-Bruce, Ingrid A.

South Orange
Chu, Petra
Leab, Daniel Josef
Mahoney, Joseph F.
Murzaku, Ines A.
Nardone, Richard Morton
Pastor, Leslie P.

Teaneck
Roberts, William
Torodash, Martin
Wiener, Joel H.

Tenafly
Rudy, Willis

Trenton
Gowaskie, Joseph M.
Levin, David S.
McFeely, Eliza

Union
Klein, Dennis B.
Rice, Arnold Sanford

Upper Montclair
Fabend, Firth Haring
Zimmer, Louis Bernard

Wayne
Bowles, Suzanne
Cho, Joanne M.
Cook, Theodore F., Jr.
Edelstein, Melvin A.
Finnegan, Terence Robert
Gonzalez, Evelyn
Gruber, Carlos S.
Livingston, John W.
Meaders, Daniel
Nalle, Sara Tilghman
O'Donnell, Krista E.
Robb, George
Tirado, Isabel A.
Williams, Bruce

West Long Branch
Greenberg, Brian
Pearson, Thomas Spencer
Stunkel, Kenneth Reagan

West New York
Cordasco, Francesco

West Orange
Osborne, John Walter
Shapiro, Edward S.
Yang, Winston L.

Westfield
Johnson, James Pearce

NEW MEXICO

Albuquerque
Baackmann, Susanne
Bailey, Beth
Berthold, Richard M.
Bieber, Judy
Connell-Szasz, Margaret
Cutter, Donald C.
Etulain, Richard W.
Feller, Daniel
Furman, Necah Stewart
Gallacher, Patrick
Hall, Linda
Hanson, Carl Aaron
Jameson, Elizabeth
Kern, Robert
Kukla, Rebecca
McClelland, Charles E.
Mead, Christopher Curtis
Melendez, Gabriel
Nash, Gerald David
Norwood, Vera
Okunor, Shiame
Orozco, Cynthia E.
Penhall, Michele M.
Porter, Jonathan
Pugach, Noel H.
Rabinowitz, Howard
Risso, Patricia
Robbins, Richard G.
Salvaggio, Ruth
Schmitter, Amy
Sullivan, Donald David
Szabo, Joyce
Szasz, Ferenc
Szasz, Margaret Connell
Tenenbaum, Sergio
Wilson, Christopher M.
Young, M. Jane

Las Cruces
Billington, Monroe
Blum, Albert A.
Eamon, William
Jacobs, Margaret D.
Jensen, Joan Maria
Malamud, Margaret
Matray, James Irving
Newman, Edgar Leon
Schlauch, Wolfgang T.

Portales
Walker, Forrest A.

Santa Fe
deBuys, William Eno
Garrett, Clarke W.
Keen, Benjamin
Lehmberg, Stanford E.
Utley, Robert Marshall

NEW YORK

Albany
Ballard, Allen Butler, Jr.
Barker, Thomas M.
Barker-Benfield, Graham John
Berger, Iris B.
Birn, Donald S.
Dressler, Rachel
Faul, Karene Tarquin
Hahner, June Edith
Haynes, Keith A.
Levesque, George August
Nagy-Zekmi, Silvia
Overbeck, John Clarence
Reedy, William T.
Refai, Shahid
Roberts, Warren Errol
Sarfoh, Kwabwo A.
Steen, Ivan David
Wesser, Robert F.
White, Dan Seligsberger
Withington, Ann F.
Wittner, Lawrence Stephen
Zacek, Joseph Frederick

Alfred
Campbell, Stuart Lorin
Ostrower, Gary Bert

Amherst
Quinan, Jack

Annandale
Botstein, Leon
Lytle, Mark Hamilton

Aurora
Bellinzoni, Arthur J.
Farnsworth, Beatrice

Barrytown
Mickler, Michael L.
Tsirpanlis, Constantine Nicholas

Bayside
Parmet, Herbert S.
Polak, Emil J.

Binghamton
Abou-El-Haj, Barbara
Abou-El-Haj, Rifaat Ali
Bernbeck, Reinhard W.
Burroughs, Charles
Dublin, Thomas
Dubofsky, Melvyn
Elbert, Sarah
Harcave, Sidney Samuel
Kadish, Gerald E.
King, Anthony D.
Mazrui, Ali Al'Amin
Nzegwu, Nkiru
O'Neil, Patrick M.
Oggins, Robin S.

Kupperman, Karen
Lagemann, Ellen Condliffe
Landau, Sarah Bradford
Lemay, Richard
Lerner, Barron H.
Levy, Darline G.
Libo, Kenneth Harold
Lienhard, Joseph T.
Lindo-Fuentes, Hector
Lippman, Edward
London, Herbert
Lotz, David Walter
Lufrano, Richard
Lynch, Hollis R.
Malefakis, Edward Emanuel
Marable, Manning
Marme, Michael
Marrin, Albert
Mattingly, Paul Havey
Matynia, Elzbieta
Maxwell, Kenneth R.
Mbodj, Mohamed
McCarthy, John P.
McCaughey, Robert Anthony
McGuckin, John A.
Mckitrick, Eric Louis
Muller, Priscilla Elkow
Mullin, Robert Bruce
Mundy, John Hine
Murphy, Kevin D.
Muscarella, Oscar White
Musto, Ronald G.
Naison, Mark
Nathan, Andrew J.
Newman, Judith H.
Nolan, Mary
Okihiro, Gary Y.
Oliva, L. Jay
Olugebefola, Ademola
Paca, Barbara
Page, Stanley W.
Panella, Robert J.
Patriarca, Silvana
Paulovskaya, Marianna
Paxton, Robert Owen
Peirce, Sarah
Perry, Marilyn
Pessen, Edward
Peters, Julie
Petrusewitz, Marta
Pflugfelder, Gregory
Piccato, Pablo
Pike, Ruth
Po-Chia Hsia, Ronnie
Pomeroy, Sarah B.
Preston, George Nelson
Prince, Carl E.
Purcell, E. A.
Raeff, Marc
Ragan, Bryant T., Jr.
Rajagopal, Arvind
Randall, Francis Ballard
Reff, Theodore Franklin
Riley, Terence
Rives, James
Romm, James S.
Rosand, David
Rosenberg, Rosalind Navin
Rosenblum, Robert
Rosner, David
Rothman, David
Sachs, William L.
Sandler, Lucy Freeman
Scaglia, Gustina
Schama, Simon
Schorsch, Ismar
Schrecker, Ellen
Schwartz, Shuly Rubin
Scott, Daryl
Segal, Alan Franklin
Shenton, James
Shneidman, J. Lee
Siegel, Jerrold
Silverman, Kenneth Eugene
Sims, Lowery Stokes
Sklar, Robert Anthony
Sloan, Herbert
Smit, J. W.
Smith, Henry
Smith, Joanna S.
Smith, Neil
Stahl, Alan Michael
Staley, Allen
Stanislawski, Michael
Stephanson, Anders
Stern, Fritz
Strozier, Charles B.
Struve, Walter
Swerdlow, Amy
Tarr, Zoltan
Tholfsen, Trygve Rainone
Tiersten, Lisa
Tilly, Louise A.
Trumbach, Randolph
Tsin, Michael
Twombly, Robert C.
Unger, Irwin
Valenze, Deborah
Valkenier, Elizabeth Kridl
van de Mieroop, Marc
van der Mieroop, Marc
Vaughan, Alden T.
Von Hagen, Mark L.
Waldman, Martin
Walkowitz, Daniel Jay
Walton, Guy E.
Ward, John William
Watkins-Owens, Irma
Weisberger, Bernard A.
Wemple, Suzanne Fonay
Wertheimer, Jack
Weston, Corinne Comstock
Whelan, Stephen T.
White, Donald Wallace
Whittaker, Cynthia Hyla
Woloch, Isser
Woloch, Nancy
Wortman, Richard
Wosh, Peter J.
Wright, Gwendolyn
Wright, John Robert
Wright, Marcia
Yellin, Victor Fell
Yerushalmi, Yosef Hayim
Young, Jordan Marten
Zelin, Madeleine
Zimmerman, Josh

New York City
Berkin, Carol Ruth

Niagara
Carpenter, Gerald

Nyack
Weir, David A.

Oneonta
Jackson, Robert H.
Morgan, Eileen M.

Oswego
Cheng, Weikun
Conrad, David C.
Deal, J. Douglas
Forbes, Geraldine May
Kulikowski, Mark
Loveridge-Sanbonmatsu, Joan
Peterson, Luther D.
Powell, Thomas F.
Thurber, Tim
Wellman, Judith

Patchogue
Armus, Seth

Pittsford
France, Jean R.

Plattsburgh
Abu-Ghazaleh, Adnan M.
Lindgren, James
Myers, John L.

Port Jefferson
Rosenthal, Naomi

Potsdam
Johnson, Arthur L.

Poughkeepsie
Adams, Nicholas
Blumenfeld, Rodica
Cohen, Miriam J.
Edwards, Rebecca
Fergusson, Frances D.
Rappaport, Rhoda
Rossi, Monica
Schneider, Jeffrey A.
Wohl, Anthony Stephen

Purchase
Thormann, Gerard Charles

Queensbury
Bailey, Charles E.

Rochester
Beaumont, Daniel E.
Berlo, Janet Catherine
Bond, Gerald Albert
Chiarenza, Carl
Crimp, Douglas
Dohanian, Diran Kavork
Doolittle, James
Engerman, Stanley Lewis
French, Henry P., Jr
Genovese, Eugene D.
Gordon, Lynn Dorothy
Gupta, Brijen Kishore
Hauser, William Barry
Kaeuper, Richard William
Kneeland, Timothy W.
Kollar, Nathan Rudolph
Lansky, Lewis
Lemke, Werner Erich
Meerbote, Ralf
More, Ellen Singer
Seiberling, Grace
Seidel, Robert Neal
Walsh, David A.
Waters, John J.
Wolff, Janet
Young, Mary Elizabeth

Saint Bonaventure
Eckert, Edward K.
Horowitz, Joel

Saratoga Springs
Clapper, Michael
Kuroda, Tadahisa
Lee, Patricia-Ann
Lynn, Mary Constance
Walker, Renee B.
Zangrando, Joanna Schneider

Schenectady
Finkelstein, Joseph
Jonas, Manfred
Khan, Yoshmitsu
Wells, Robert Vale

Selden
Becker, Lloyd George

Shoreham
Brinkman, John T.

Southampton
Baker, Donald G.
Strong, John A.

Staten Island
Anderson, Robert Mapes
Binder, Frederick Melvin
Brennan, John James
Cooper, Sandi E.
Frank, Sam Hager
Stearns, Stephen

Stone Ridge
Corrales, Edwin

Stony Brook
Barnhart, Michael
Bottigheimer, Karl S.
Burner, David B.
Charnon-Deutsch, Lou
Cowan, Ruth Schwartz
Gootenberg, Paul
Guilmain, Jacques
Kuisel, Richard F.
Landsman, Ned C.
Lebovics, Herman
Lemay, Helen Rodnite
Miller, Wilbur R.
Rubin, James Henry
Tomes, Nancy Jane
Weinstein, Fred

Syracuse
Bennett, David Harry
Blaszak, Barbara J.
Dixon, Laurinda S.
Donegan, Jane Bauer
Field, Daniel
Gregory, Robert G.
Griffith, Daniel A.
Hovendick, Kelly B.
Judge, Edward H.
Ketcham, Ralph Louis
Langdon, John W.
MacDonald, Mary N.
MacKillop, James J.
Marsh, Peter T.
Milac, Metod M.
Miller, Patricia Cox
Monmonier, Mark
Powell, James Matthew
Sharp, James Roger
Tatham, David Frederic
Telesca, William John
Thompson, Margaret Susan
Webb, Stephen Saunders
Wiecek, William Michael
Wiggins, James Bryan

Tonawanda
Tucker, Melvin Jay

Troy
Apena, Igho Adeline
Crouch, Dora Polk
Spector, Sherman David

Uniondale
Naylor, Natalie A.

Verbank
Salzman, Neil

Vestal
Africa, Thomas Wilson
Thomasson, Gordon C.

Watertown
Overacker, Ingrid

West Nyack
Olin, John C.

West Point
Doughty, Robert
Johnson, James M.
McDonald, Robert M. S.
Rogers, Clifford J.

White Plains
Serels, M. Mitchell
Slater, Peter Gregg

NORTH CAROLINA

Asheville
Dvorsky-Rohner, Dorothy
Walker, Philip Alfred

Boiling Springs
Ellington, Donna S.
Strokanov, Alexandre
Yelton, David K.

Boone
Hanft, Sheldon
Kinsey, Winston Lee
Moore, Michael J.
Simon, Stephen Joseph
Specht, Neva Jean
Wade, Michael G.
Williams, John Alexander

Brevard
Brown, Margaret T.

Buies Creek
Faulkner, Ronnie
Johnson, Lloyd
Martin, James I.

Chapel Hill
Barney, William Lesko
Baron, Samuel Haskell
Baxter, Stephen Bartow
Bennett, Judith M.
Boren, Henry C.
Bremer, William Walling
Brooks, E. Willis
Broughton, Thomas Robert Shannon
Browning, C. R.
Bullard, Melissa Meriam
Filene, Peter Gabriel
Folda, Jaroslav, III
Greenland, David E.
Grendler, Paul F.
Gura, Philip F.
Haar, James
Haggis, Donald
Hall, Jacquelyn Dowd
Harris, Michael D.
Headley, John M.
Henry, Eric Putnam
Higginbotham, R. Don
Hunt, Michael H.
Jones, Houston Gwynne
Kasson, John Franklin
Kohn, Richard Henry
Lee, Sherman E.
Lotchin, Roger W.
Marks, Arthur S.
Mathews, Donald G.
Matilsky, Barbara C.
Mavor, Carol
Mcvaugh, Michael Rogers
Miller, Marla R.
Orth, John Victor
Pfaff, Richard W.
Riggs, Timothy A.
Semonche, John Erwin
Shaw, Donald Lewis
Sheriff, Mary D.
Smither, Howard Elbert
Soloway, Richard Allen
Sturgeon, Mary C.
Tindall, George Brown
Verkerk, Dorothy Hoogland
Watson, Harry L.
Weaver, Garrett F.
Williamson, Joel R.
Wittig, Joseph Sylvester
Wood, Carolyn B.

Charlotte
Dupre, Dan
Escott, Paul David
Gabaccia, Donna
Gaide, Tanure
Goldfield, David
Govan, Sandra Yvonne
Heath, Kingston W.
Lansen, Oscar
Laurent, Jane Katherine
MacKinnon, Aran S.
Patterson, Karl David
Swanson, Randy

Cullowhee
Anderson, William L.
Blethen, H. Tyler
Dorondo, David R.
Graham, Gael N.
Lovin, Clifford R.
Philyaw, Scott L.
Schwartz, Gerald
Walton, Brian G.
Wood, Curtis W.

Dallas
Manikas, William T.

Davidson
Berkey, Jonathan P.
Edmondson, Clifton Earl
Krentz, Peter Martin
Levering, Ralph Brooks
Ligo, Larry L.
Serebrennikov, Nina Eugenia
Smith, C. Shaw, Jr.
Wertheimer, John

Durham
Antliff, Mark
Biddle, Tami Davis
Bruzelius, Caroline
Cell, John W.
Dirlik, Arif
Durden, Robert Franklin
Ferguson, Arthus Bowles
Gavins, Raymond
Goranson, Stephen
Heitzenrater, Richard
Herrup, Cynthia
Humphreys, Margaret
Jacobs, Sylvia M.
Jones, Barney Lee
Jones, Beverly Washington
Keefe, Susan Ann
Keyssar, Alexander
Koonz, Claudia
Kuniholm, Bruce Robellet
Leighten, Patricia
Lerner, Warren
Mauskopf, Seymour Harold
Mezzatesta, Michael P.
Miller, Martin Alan
Natavar, Mekhala D.

Oberlin
Colish, Marcia L.
Gouma-Peterson, Thalia
Hogan, Heather
Kornblith, Gary J.
Logan, Wendell
Soucy, Robert J.
Tregouet, Annie D.
Zinn, Grover A.

Oxford
Baird, Jay Warren
Coakley, Thomas M.
Ellison, Curtis William
Fahey, David Michael
Fryer, Judith
Goldy, Charlotte Newman
Jackson, W. Sherman
Kane, Stanley G.
Kimball, Jeffrey P.
Kirby, Jack Temple
O'Brien, Michael
Runyon, Randolph Paul
Sanabria, Sergio Luis
Smith, Dwight L.
Southard, Edna Carter
Swanson, Maynard William
Thurston, Robert
White, John Hoxland
Winkler, Allan M.
Yamauchi, Edwin Masao

Painesville
McQuaid, Kim

Pepper Pike
Pina, Leslie

Pickerington
Evans, Roger S.

Rio Grande
Barton, Marcella Biro
Tribe, Ivan Mathews

Springfield
Celms, Peter
Chatfield, E. Charles
Dickson, Charles Ellis
Hayden, Albert A.
Huffman, James Lamar
Lenz, Ralph D.
O'Connor, Joseph E.
Ortquist, Richard Theodore
Taylor, Thomas Templeton

Stow
Knepper, George W.

Tiffin
Bowlus, Bruce
Owens, Richard H.

Toledo
Aryeetey-Attoh, Samuel
Bourguignon, Henry J.
Cave, Alfred A.
Glaab, Charles Nelson
Hoover, William Davis
Lora, Ronald Gene
Messer-Kruse, Timothy
Smith, Robert Freeman
Wilcox, Larry Dean

University Heights
Duncan, Russell
Robson, David
Shockey, Gary C.

Westerville
MacLean, Elizabeth

Wilberforce
Bell, Leland V.

Wilmington
Gara, Larry

Wooster
Calhoun, Daniel Fairchild
Gates, John Morgan
Gedalecia, David
Hettinger, Madonna
Hickey, Damon
Hodges, James A.
Holliday, Vivian Loyrea
Hondros, John L.
Hults, Linda
Jefferson, Alphine W.
Lewis, Arnold
Taylor, Karen

Worthington
Bremner, Robert Hamlett
Ness, Gary Clifford

Yellow Springs
Davis, Barbara Beckerman
Fogarty, Robert Stephen
Whelchel, Marianne

Youngstown
Berger, Martin Edgar
Blue, Frederick J.
Friedman, Saul S.
Satre, Lowell Joseph

OKLAHOMA

Ada
Boeger, Palmer Henry
Joyce, Davis D.

Bartlesville
Wimberly, Dan

Chickasha
Meredith, Howard

Durant
Emge, Steven W.

Edmond
Baker, James Franklin
Baughman, T. H.
Faulk, Odie B.
Jackson, Joe C.
Kremm, Diane Neal
Li, Bing

Langston
Sagini, Meshack

Lawton
Blodgett, Ralph Edward
Stegmaier, Mark Joseph

Norman
Brown, Sidney DeVere
Cohen, Gary Bennett
Fears, J. Rufus
Gilje, Paul Arn
Glad, Paul Wilbur
Hagan, William Thomas
Hassrick, Peter H.
Hurtado, A. L.
Kamoche, Jidlaph Gitau
Kidwell, Clara Sue
Koshkin-Youritzin, Victor
Levy, David W.
Mical, Thomas
Miller, David H.
Morgan, H. Wayne
Nitzova, Petya
Norwood, Stephen H.
Savage, William W., Jr.
Shalhope, Robert E.
Stillman, Norman (Noam) Arthur
Taylor, Kenneth Lapham

Oklahoma City
Franks, Kenny Arthur
May, Jude Thomas
Smith, Dennis P.

Shawnee
Hall, Larry Joe

Stillwater
Bays, Brad A.
Byrnes, Joseph Francis
Converse, Hyla Stuntz
Cordova, Carlos E.
Jewsbury, George Frederick
Rohrs, Richard Carlton
Sirhandi, Marcella
Smallwood, James Milton
Smith, Michael Myrle
Stout, Joseph A.
Wikle, Thomas A.

Tahlequah
Corbett, William P.
Owen, Christopher H.

Tinker AFB
Barnhill, John Herschel

Tulsa
Bradley, Joseph C.
Buckley, Thomas Hugh
Epstein, David M.
Odell, George H.
Rutland, Robert Allen
Tabbernee, William

Weatherford
Hayden, John K.
Nadel, Stanley

OREGON

Ashland
Jones, Gregory

Corvallis
Chamberlain, Gordon Blanding
Farber, Paul L.
Ferngren, Gary Burt
Mcclintock, Thomas Coshow
Nye, Mary Jo
Nye, Robert Allen
Ramsey, Jeff
Robbins, William Grover
Rubert, Steven

Eugene
Bingham, Edwin Ralph
Birn, Raymond
Connolly, Thomas J.
Dumond, D. E.
Esherick, Joseph Wharton
Holbo, Paul S.
Jaegers, Marvin
Mate, Mavis
Mohr, James C.
Murphy, Alexander B.
Pomeroy, Earl
Pope, Daniel
Wade, Louise Carroll

Gresham
Alexander, Ralph H.

Klamath Falls
Clark, Mark

La Grande
Patterson, Joby

Monmouth
Cotroneo, Ross Ralph
Rector, John L.
Sil, Narasingha P.

Newberg
Beebe, Ralph Kenneth
Nash, Lee

Pendleton
Grover, Dorys Crow

Portland
Abbott, Carl
Beckham, Stephen Dow
Brown, John E.
Burke, Bernard V.
Butler, Leslie
Covert, James Thayne
Danner, Dan Gordon
Dmytryshyn, Basil
Dodds, Gordon B.
Heath, Jim Frank
Heying, Charles
Horowitz, David A.
Johnson, David Alan
Kristof, Jane
Lang, William
Leguin, Charles A.
Mandaville, Jon Elliott
Morris, Thomas Dean
Nash, Anedith
Nunn, Frederick Mckinley
Sacks, David Harris
Savage, David William
Segel, Edward Barton
Taylor, Sue
Weikel, Ann
West, Franklin Carl
Wheeler, Rachel
Zimmerman, Loretta Ellen

Salem
Lucas, Robert Harold

Spray
Fussner, Frank Smith

PENNSYLVANIA

Abington
August, Andrew
Isser, Natalie K.

Allentown
Malsberger, John William
Reed, John Julius
Shaw, Barton Carr
Wilson, Daniel Joseph

Altoona
Black, Brian C.
Wolfe, Michael

Ardmore
Bober, Phyllis Pray

Bala-Cynwyd
Keefe, Thomas M.
Murphey, Murray Griffin

Barracks Carlisle
Deutsch, Harold Charles

Beaver Falls
Wollman, David Harris

Bethelem
Saeger, James Schofield

Bethlehem
Baylor, Michael G.
Beidler, Peter Grant
Cooper, Gail
Cutcliffe, Stephen Hosmer
Girardot, Norman J.
Goldman, Steven
Jitendra, Asha K.
Kohls, Winfred A.
Loengard, Janet Senderowitz
Peters, Tom F.
Phillips, C. Robert, III
Radycki, Diane
Remer, Rosalind
Scott, William R.
Shade, William G.
Simon, Roger David
Smith, John K., Jr.
Soderlund, Jean
Stinson, Robert William

Bloomsburg
Fuller, Lawrence Benedict
Hickey, Michael C.
Smiley, Ralph

Bradford
Frederick, Richard G.

Bryn Mawr
Brand, Charles Macy
Cast, David Jesse Dale
Cohen, Jeffrey A.
Dudden, Arthur Power
Lane, Barbara Miller
Mellink, Machteld Johanna
Ridgway, Brunilde Sismondo
Salmon, John Hearsey Mcmillan
Silvera, Alain

Butler
Weisberger, William

California
Folmar, John Kent

Camp Hill
Wolf, George D.

Carlisle
Crane, Conrad Charles
Emery, Ted
Jarvis, Charles Austin
Richter, Daniel K.
Rogers, Kim L.
Schiffman, Joseph
Shrader, Charles R.
Weinberger, Stephen
Weissman, Neil Bruce

Chambersburg
Buck, Harry Merwyn

Chester
Wrobel, David M.

Clarion
Frakes, Robert
Piott, Steven L.

Collegeville
Akin, William Ernest
Clark, Hugh R.
Hemphill, C. Dallett
King, Richard D.
Procko, Bohdan P.
Visser, Derk

Coopersburg
Eckardt, Alice Lyons

Doylestown
Wiseman, Mary Bittner

East Stroudsburg
Donaghay, Marie
Henwood, James N. J.
Jarvis, Joseph Anthony

Easton
Cooke, Jacob Ernest
Fix, Andrew C.
Mattison, Robert S.

Edinboro
Girgis, Monir Saad
Hoffman, Donald Stone

Elizabethtown
Eller, David B.
Winpenny, Thomas R.

Elkins Park
Davidson, Abraham A.

Ellwood City
Lambert, Lynda J.

Erie
Frankforter, Albertus Daniel
Loss, Archie Krug

Gettysburg
Birkner, Michael J.
Gritsch, Eric W.
Shannon, Timothy J.
Trevelyan, Amelia M.

Glenside
Haywood, Geoffrey

Grantham
Davis, Edward B.
Lagrand, James B.

Greensburg
Spurlock, John C.

Grove City
Kemeny, P

Gwynedd Valley
Duclow, Donald F.

Harrisburg
Waddell, Louis Morton
Young, James A.

Haverford
Bronner, Edwin Blaine
Dillon, Clarissa F.
Eiteljorg, Harrison, II
Gerstein, Linda Groves
Lane, Roger
Lapsansky, Emma J.

PUERTO RICO

RHODE ISLAND

SOUTH CAROLINA

Clark, Malcolm Cameron
Gordon, John W.
Heisser, David C. R.
Moore, Winfred B., Jr.
Reynolds, Clark G.

Clemson
Burnett, G. Wesley
Mckale, Donald Marshall
McKate, Donald M.

Columbia
Augustinos, Gerasimos
Basil, John Duryea
Beardsley, Edward Henry
Becker, Peter Wolfgang
Beltman, Brian W.
Carter, Jeffrey D. R.
Clements, Kendrick A.
Connelly, Owen S.
Duffy, John Joseph
Edgar, Walter B.
Farley, Benjamin Wirt
Greenspan, Ezra
Gregg, Edward
Herzstein, Robert Edwin
Janiskee, Robert L.
Johanson, Herbert A.
Johnson, Herbert A.
Kross, Jessica
Layman, Richard
Lesesne, Henry H.
Maney, Patrick J.
Mathisen, Ralph Whitney
Minghi, Julian M.
Moore, Robert Joseph
Patterson, Robert Benjamin
Perkins, Kenneth J. Ames
Scardaville, Michael Charles
Stroup, Rodger Emerson
Synnott, Marcia G.
Terrill, Tom E.
Weir, Robert Mccolloch

Conway
Nance, Brian K.

Cullowhee
Lewis, James A.

Greenville
Abrams, Douglas Carl
Beale, David Otis
Ching, Erik K.
Hayner, Linda K.
Lawson, Darren P.
Matzko, John A.

Greenwood
Brennan, Pat

Hartsville
Lay, Shawn

Newberry
Wilson, James Hugh

Orangeburg
Harrold, Stanley
Hine, William Cassidy
Jones, Marcus E.
Michaux, Henry G.

Rock Hill
Haynes, Edward S.
Morgan, Thomas Sellers
Silverman, Jason H.
Viault, Birdsall Scrymser
Webb, Ross Allan

Spartanburg
Dunn, Joe Pender
Holcombe, Lee
Racine, Philip N.
Walker, Melissa

SOUTH DAKOTA

Aberdeen
King, Walter Joseph

Brookings
Funchion, Michael Francis
Miller, John E.
Napton, Darrell E.
Sweeney, Jerry K.

Huron
Meyer, Kenneth John

Sioux Falls
Olson, Gary Duane

Vermillion
Bucklin, Steve
Hilderbrand, Robert Clinton
Hoover, Herbert Theodore
Lee, Roy Alton
Lehmann, Clayton M.
Moyer, Ronald L.
Sebesta, Judith Lynn
Wolff, Gerald W.

Yankton
Kessler, Ann Verona

TENNESSEE

Athens
Dunn, Durwood
McDonald, William

Bristol
Wade, William Junius

Chattanooga
Froide, Amy
Giffin, Phillip E.
Ingle, Homer Larry
McClay, Wilfred M.
Rice, Richard
Russell, James M.
Townsend, Gavin
Ward, James A.
Wright, William John

Clarksville
Butts, Michele T.
Gildric, Richard P.
Muir, Malcolm, Jr
Pesely, George E.

Cleveland
Hoffman, Daniel

Cookeville
Lindenmeyer, Kriste A.
Reagan, Patrick
Schrader, William C.
Webb, George Ernest

Dayton
Ketchersid, William L.

Greenville
Sexton, Donal J.

Hermitage
Albin, Thomas R.
Moser, Harold Dean

Jackson
Carls, Stephen
David, Arthur LaCurtiss
Dockery, David S.
Lindley, Terry
Patterson, James A.

Johnson City
Baxter, Colin Frank
Day, Ronnie
Drinkard-Hawkshawe, Dorothy
Essin, Emmett M.
Fritz, Stephen G.

Knoxville
Ash, Stephen V.
Banker, Mark T.
Bast, Robert
Becker, Susan D.
Bergeron, Paul H.
Bing, J. Daniel
Bohstedt, John
Bradley, Owen
Brady, Patrick S.
Breslaw, Elaine
Brummett, Palmira
Burman, Thomas
Diacon, Todd
Farris, W. Wayne
Finger, John R.
Haas, Arthur G.
Habel, Dorothy Metzger
Hao, Yen-Ping
Higgs, Catherine
Hiles, Timothy
Hoeng, Peter
Klein, Milton M.
Maland, Charles J.
Martinson, Fred
Moffat, Frederick
Neff, Amy
Norrell, Robert J.
Peek, Marvin E.
Piehler, G. Kurt
Schroeder-Lein, Glenna R.
Wheeler, William Bruce

Martin
Carls, Alice-Catherine
Downing, Marvin Lee
Jones, Kenneth Paul
Maness, Lonnie E.

Memphis
Brown, Walter R.
Caffrey, Margaret M.
Crouse, Maurice A.
Fickle, James Edward
Garceau, Dee
Hatfield, Douglas Wilford
Hawes, Joseph
Huebner, Timothy
Hurley, Forrest Jack
Joiner, Burnett
Purtle, Carol Jean
Skeen, C. Edward
Tucker, David Milton
White, Lonnie Joe
Wilson, Major L.

Milligan College
Farmer, Craig S.

Murfreesboro
Anton, Harley F.
Brookshire, Jerry
Conard, Rebecca
Ferris, Norman B.
Huhta, James Kenneth
Rowe, D. L.
Staples, A.
West, Carroll V.

Nashville
Allen, Jack
Bisson, Douglas R.
Carlton, David L.
Conkin, Paul K.
Crawford, Katherine B.
Doyle, Don H.
Eakin, Marshall C.
Elliott, Derek W.
Epstein, James A.
Fryd, Vivien G.
Graham, Hugh Davis
Grantham, Dewey Wesley
Headrick, Annabeth
Helguera, J. Leon
Howell, Sarah McCanless
Isherwood, Robert M.
Johnson, Timothy D.
Lovett, Bobby L.
Luis, William
Mcseveney, Samuel Thompson
Quirin, James
Sasson, Jack Murad
Smith, Helmut
Todd, Margo
Voegeli, Victor Jacque
Winters, Donald Lee

Prospect
Trimble, Stanley W.

Sewanee
Patterson, William Brown
Perry, Charles R.

TEXAS

Abilene
Ferguson, Everett
Foster, Douglas A.
Madden, Paul
Shanafelt, Gary
Taylor, Ira Donathan

Aledo
Worcester, Donald Emmet

Alpine
Elam, Earl Henry

Amarillo
Sapper, Neil Gary

Arlington
Buisseret, David
Carroll, Bret E.
Green, George N.
Kyle, Donald G.
Maizlish, Stephen E.
Morris, Christopher
Palmer, Stanley Howard
Philp, Kenneth
Reinhartz, Dennis Paul
Richmond, Douglas Wertz
Rodnitzky, Jerome L.
Roemer, Kenneth M.
Stark, Gary Duane

Austin
Abboud, Peter Fouad
Abzug, Robert H.
Alofsin, Anthony
Baltzer, Rebecca
Barker, Nancy Nichols
Bertelsen, Lance
Bowman, Shearer Davis
Braisted, William Reynolds
Brandimarte, Cynthia A.
Brown, Norman D.
Burnham, Patricia
Carleton, Don E.
Carter, Joseph Coleman
Castiglione, Caroline F.
Charlesworth, Michael
Clarke, John R.
Crew, David F.
Davis, Donald G., Jr.
Dewar, Mary
Dietz, Hanns-Bertold
Divine, Robert Alexander
Dulles, John W. F.
Edlund-Berry, Ingrid E. M.
Falola, Toyin
Fisher, James T.
Foley, Neil
Fontanella, Lee
Forgie, George Barnard
Frazier, Alison
Goetzmann, William Harry
Gould, Lewis Ludlow
Graham, Richard
Grieder, Terence
Gutmann, Myron P.
Hall, Michael G.
Harzer, Edeltraud
Henderson, Linda
Hoberman, Louisa Schell
Holz, Robert K.
Hunt, Bruce J.
Kroll, John Hennig
Kruppa, Patricia Stallings
Lariviere, Richard Wilfred
Leoshko, Janice
Levack, Brian Paul
Meacham, Standish
Meikle, Jeffrey L.
Meisel, Janet Anne
Minault, Gail
Olasky, Marvin N.
Pells, Richard Henry
Rather, Susan
Reynolds, Ann
Rhoads, Edward J. M.
Segre, Claudio Giuseppe
Shelmerdine, Cynthia Wright
Shiff, Richard
Shirazi, Faegheh S.
Sidbury, James
Slawek, Stephen
Smith, Jeffrey Chipps
Stoff, Michael B.
Stott, William Merrell
Teorio-Trillo, Mauricio
Tusa, Michael
White, Philip Lloyd

Azle
Pate, J'Nell

Baytown
Maroney, James C.

Beaumont
Carroll, John M.
Fritze, Ronald H.
Wooster, Ralph Ancil

Brenham
Dietrich, Wilfred O.

Brownsville
Adams, William
Joseph, Harriet D.
Kearney, Milo

Brownwood
Mangrum, Robert G.

Bryan
Reagan, Rhonda

Canyon
Culley, John Joel
Nall, Garry Lynn

Cedar Park
Tijerina, Andres

College Station
Adams, Ralph James Quincy
Anderson, Terry Howard
Bass, George Fletcher
Baum, Dale
Beaumont, Roger A.
Black, Shirley Jean
Bornstein, Daniel E.
Bradford, James Chapin
Canup, John
Coopersmith, Jonathan C.
Dawson, Joseph G., III
Dethloff, Henry Clay
Kosztolnyik, Zoltan Joseph Desiderius
Kramer, Arnold Paul
Lenihan, John H.
Nance, Joseph Milton
Reese, Roger R.
Rosenheim, James Morton
Schmidt, Henry Conrad
Stranges, Anthony N.
Unterberger, Betty Miller
Vandiver, Frank Everson
Wang, Di

Commerce
Mc Farland, Keith D.
Reynolds, Donald E.
Sarantakes, Nick

Corpus Christi
Delaney, Norman
Lessoff, Alan H.
Wooster, Robert

Dallas
Babcock, William Summer
Chavez, John R.
Cordell, Dennis Dale
Countryman, Edward
Cox, Gary D.
Davis, Ronald Leroy
Early, James
McKnight, Joseph Webb
Mears, John A.
Niewyk, Donald Lee
Smith, Sherry L.
Trickel, John
Weber, David J.
Williams, Michael
Williams, Richard Hal
Winship, Peter

Denton
Campbell, Randolph B.
Cantrell, Gregg
Chipman, Donald Eugene
DeMoss, Dorothy Dell
Golden, Richard Martin
Hurley, Alfred Francis
Kamman, William
La Forte, Robert Sherman
Lowe, Richard Grady
Lowery, Bullitt
Lowry, Bullitt
Marcello, Ronald E.
Odom, Edwin Dale
Pickens, Donald Kenneth

UTAH

VERMONT

VIRGINIA

Sedgwick, Alexander
Simon, Roland Henri
Thomas, Mark
Twohig, Dorothy Ann
Wagner, Roy
Wells, Camille
White, G. Edward
Wilson, Richard Guy
Zagorin, Perez
Zunz, Olivier

Danville
Hayes, Jack

Fairfax
Brunette, Peter
Censer, Jack R.
Censer, Jane Turner
Deshmukh, Marion Fishel
Fuchs, Cynthia
Pfund, Peter H.
Rosenzweig, Roy A.
Smith, Paul
Stearns, Peter N.
Zagarri, Rosemarie

Farmville
Millar, Gilbert J.
Strait, John B.

Ferrum
Woods, Daniel

Fredericksburg
Bourdon, Roger J.
Krick, Robert Kenneth

Fredricksburg
Ryang, Key S.

Front Royal
Carroll, Warren Hasty

Hampden-Sydney
Arieti, James Alexander
Heinemann, Ronald

Hampton
Porter, Michael LeRoy
Whittenburg, Carolyn

Harrisonburg
Bland, Sidney Roderick
Congdon, Lee W.
Galgano, Michael J.
Hyser, Raymond M.
Riley, Philip Ferdinand

Lawrenceville
Kamau, Mosi

Lexington
Bausum, Henry S.
Davis, Thomas Webster
Davis, Winston
Fay, Mary Ann
Hays, Willard Murrell
Koeniger, A. Cash
McCleskey, Turk
Pierpaoli, Paul G.
Sheldon, Rose Mary
Thomas, Donald E.
Tucker, Spencer C.
Vandervort, Bruce

Lynchburg
Hostetler, Theodore J.
Huston, James Alvin
Matheny, William Edward
Potter, Dorothy T.
Vanauken, Sheldon
Young, William H.

McLean
Garen, Sally

Newport News
Eastman, John Robert
Kleber, Brooks Edward
Morris, James M.
Sishagne, Shumet

Norfolk
Bogger, Tommy L.
Boyd, Carl
Graf, Daniel William
Greene, Douglas G.
Kuehl, John William
Lawes, Carolyn J.
Perez-Lopez, Rene
Slane, Andrea
Wilson, Harold Stacy
Zeigler, Donald J.

Petersburg
Blouet, Olwyn
Toppin, Edgar Allan

Portsmouth
Paquette, William A.

Radford
Arbury, Steve
Hepburn, Sharon Roger
Ioffe, Grigory
Killen, Linda
Mcclellan, Charles W.

Richmond
Addiss, Stephen L.
Bendersky, Joseph William
Bolt, Ernest C., Jr.
Briceland, Alan Vance
Bryson, William Hamilton
Chestnut, Paul Ivar
Daniel, Wilbon Harrison
Engel, Arthur Jason
Hinson, E. Glenn
Kenzer, Robert C.
Lankford, Nelson Douglas
Leary, David E.
Moore, James Tice
Rilling, John R.
Schwarz, Philip James
Smylie, James Hutchinson
Tarter, Brent
Urofsky, Melvin Irving
Ward, Harry M.
Watts, Sydney
West, Hugh A.
Yang, Zongsui

Roanoke
Sargent, James E.

Salem
Selby, John G.

Springfield
Gawalt, Gerard Wilfred

Staunton
Cole, Mary Hill
Keller, Kenneth Wayne
Menk, Patricia Holbert

Sweet Briar
Berg, Gerald Michael
Moran, Diane D.
Richards, Michael Dulany
Witcombe, Christopher L. C. E.

Virginia Beach
Prosser, Peter E.
Synan, Vinson

Williamsburg
Abdalla, Ismail H.
Armbrecht, Thomas J. D.
Axtell, James Lewis
Carson, Barbara
Crapol, Edward P.
Donaldson, Scott
Ely, Melvin Patrick
Esler, Anthony J.
Ewell, Judith
Finn, Thomas M.
Funigiello, Philip J.
Gross, Robert A.
Hobson, Charles Frederic
Hoffman, Ronald
Jarvis, Michael J.
Lounsbury, Carl
Matthews, J. Rosser
McGiffert, Michael
Millar, John F.
Morgan, Phillip D.
Oakley, John H.
Preston, Katherine K.
Scholnick, Robert James
Selby, John Edward
Sheppard, Thomas Frederick
Sheriff, Carol
Sherman, Richard B.
Tate, Thad W.
Teute, Fredrika J.
Wallach, Alan
Whittenburg, James Penn

Winchester
Hofstra, Warren R.

Woodbridge
Gallick, Rosemary
Noone, Timothy

WASHINGTON

Aberdeen
Murrell, Gary J.

Bellevue
Torrey, Glenn E.

Bellingham
Buckland, Roscoe Lawrence
Danysk, Cecilia
Delorme, Roland L.
Janson, Carol
Kaplan, Edward Harold
Onorato, Michael P.
Ritter, Harry R.
Smeins, Linda
Stoever, William K. B.
Whisenhunt, Donald W.

Centralia
Vosper, Jim M.

Cheney
Green, Michael Knight
Kieswetter, James Kay
Lauritsen, Frederick Michael
Seedorf, Martin F.
Zhu, Liping

Edmonds
Lewarne, Charles Pierce

Ellenberg
McIntyre, Jerilyn S.

Ellensburg
Lowther, Lawrence Leland
Newman, Gerald Gordon

Pullman
Armitage, Susan
Ashby, LeRoy
Bennett, Edward Moore
Blackwell, Frederick Warn
Clanton, Orval Gene
Coon, David L.
Fowler, Shelli
Frykman, George Axel
Gough, Jerry B.
Harris, Laurilyn J.
Hirt, Paul W.
Hume, Richard L.
Kale, Steven D.
Kawamura, Noriko
Kennedy, Thomas L.
Kicza, John Edward
Kuhlman, Erika
Lipe, William David
Meyer, Kathryn E.
Peabody, Susan
Peterson, Jacqueline
Reed, T. V.
Schlesinger, Roger
Streets, Heather
Sun, Raymond
Svingen, Orlan J.
Tolmacheva, Marina
Trafzer, Clifford Earl
Watrous, Mary A.
Williams, Richard S.

Seattle
Alden, Dauril
Bacharach, Jere L.
Benson, Keith Rodney
Burnstein, Daniel
Butow, Robert J. C.
Clausen, Meredith L.
Conlon, Frank Fowler
Ellison, Herbert J.
Ferrill, Arther L.
Freeze, Karen J.
Hankins, Thomas Leroy
Johnson, Richard Rigby
Jones, Edward Louis
Leiren, Terje Ivan
Miller, Jacquelyn C.
Nutting, Maureen M.
Ochsner, Jeffrey Karl
Palais, James Bernard
Pauwels, Heidi
Pease, Otis Arnold
Rorabaugh, William J.
Salomon, Richard
Scalise, Charles J.
Sutton, Sharon Egretta
Taylor, Quintard, Jr.
Taylor, Tom
Thaden, Edward C.
Thomas, Carol G.
Ullman, Joan Connelly
Waugh, Daniel Clarke

Spokane
Carriker, Robert C.
Hunt, James
Migliazzo, Arlin C.
Sanford, Daniel
Schlatter, Fredric William
Soden, Dale
Stackleberg, J. Roderick
Yoder, John

Tacoma
Allen, Michael
Barnett, Suzanne Wilson
Carp, E. Wayne
Cooney, Terry Arnold
Honey, Michael
Orlin, Eric
Potts, David B.
Reigstad, Ruth
Smith, David Fredrick

Walla Walla
Breit, Frederick Joseph
Mesteller, Jean C.

Yakima
Newbill, James

WEST VIRGINIA

Charleston
Casdorph, Paul Douglas

Fairmont
Boggess, Jennifer H.
Pudsell, F. David

Huntington
Burgueno, Maria C.
Palmer, William
Riddel, Frank Stephen
Spindel, Donna Jane
Woodward, David Reid

Institute
Sharma, R. N.

Montgomery
Alexander, Ronald R.
Bradford, Richard Headlee
Long, Ronald Wilson

Morgantown
Bagby, Wesley Marvin
Maxon, Robert Mead
Mccluskey, Stephen C.
Roinila, Mika
Vehse, Charles T.
Walken, Chrisopher

Parkersburg
Allen, Bernard Lee

Salem
Florian, Robert Bruce

Shepherdstown
Hanak, Walter Karl
Henriksson, Anders H.
Holland, James C.
Stealey, John E.

Wheeling
Laker, Joseph Alphonse
Wack, John Theodore

WISCONSIN

Appleton
Chaney, William Albert
Cohen, Paul M.
Lawton, Carol
Podair, Jerald E.

Beloit
Hodge, Robert White

De Pere
Patterson, Wayne Kief

Eau Claire
Gross, Rita M.
Lauber, Jack M.
Oberly, James W.

Elkhart Lake
Lydolph, Paul E.

Glendale
Schmidt, Martin Edward

Green Bay
Aldrete, Gregory S.
Kaye, Harvey Jordan
Lockard, Craig Alan
Salisbury, Joyce E.

Hales Corners
McNally, Vincent J.

Kenosha
Bailey, John Wendell
Buenker, John D.
Egerton, Frank N.
Gellott, Laura S.
Greenfield, Gerald M.
Kummings, Donald D.
Mclean, Andrew Miller
Meyer, Stephen
Noer, Thomas John
Reeves, Thomas C.
Schunk, Thom

La Crosse
Chavalas, Mark W.
Jenson, Carol Elizabeth
Pemberton, William Erwin
Pinnell, Richard

Ladysmith
Lewis, Thomas T.

Madison
Archdeacon, Thomas John
Barker, John W.
Bender, Todd K.
Bogue, Allan G.
Boyer, Paul S.
Buhnemann, Gudrun
Chamberlain, Michael
Clover, Frank M.
Coffman, Edward M.
Cook, Harold J.
Courtenay, William James
Coutenay, Lynn
Fox, Michael
Friedman, Edward
Frykenberg, Robert E.
Ham, F. Gerald
Hamalainen, Pekka Kalevi
Hamerow, Theodore Stephen
Hemand, Jost
Hilts, Victor L.
Hollingsworth, Joseph Rogers
Kaminski, John Paul
Kingdon, Robert McCune
Knipe, David Maclay
Kutler, Stanley I.
Leary, James Patrick
Leavitt, Judith Walzer
Lee, Jean B.
Lin, Yu-sheng
Lindberg, David C.
Lindstrom, Diana
Lovejoy, David Sherman
Malone, Barbara S. (Bobbie)
Marks, Elaine
Mazzaoui, Maureen Fennell
Michels, Anthony
Mosse, George L.
Naess, Harald S.
Numbers, Ronald L.
O'Keefe, J. Paul

Geographic Index

Laird, Walter Roy
Lamirande, Emilien
Lipsett-Rivera, Sonya
Marshall, Dominique
McDowall, Duncan L.
McKillop, A. B.
McMullin, Stan
Merkley, Paul C.
Muise, D. A.
Neatby, H. Blair
Page, James E.
Pauli, Lori
Phillips, Roderick
Routledge, Marie I.
Shepherd, John
Spry, Irene
Swinton, George
Szabo, Franz A. J.
Theriault, Michel
Thomas, Diana
Tovell, Rosemarie
von Baeyer, Edwinna L.
Walker, Pamela J.
Wallot, Jean-Pierre
Watelet, Hubert
Wise, Sydney F.
Young, William Robert

Peterborough
Grant, Shelagh D.
Hodgins, Bruce W.
Jones, Elwood Hugh
Symons, T. H. B.

Saint Catharines
Anderson, Mark
Arthur, Alan
Drake, Fred
Hanyan, Craig
McLeod, Jane
Patrias, Carmela
Sainsbury, John
Taylor, Robert R.
Turner, Wes

Saint Catherines
Dirks, Patricia

Sudbury
Ambrose, Linda M.
Best, Henry
Bray, R. Matthew
Burke, Sara Z.
Lemieux, Germain
Liedl, Janice
Mount, Graeme S.
Wallace, Carl M.

Thunder Bay
Vervoort, Patricia

Toronto
Abbott, Elizabeth
Arciszewska, Barbara
Armstrong, Joe C. W.
Armstrong, Pat
Barnes, Timothy David
Bartlett, Kenneth Roy
Beckwith, John
Bedford, Harold
Benn, Carl E.
Blanchard, Peter
Bliss, John W. M.
Bothwell, Robert S.
Breton, Raymond J.
Brock, Peter de Beauvoir
Brown, R. Craig
Burnett, David G.
Callahan, William James
Careless, James M. S.
Clarke, Ernest George
Cohen, Judith
Collie, Michael J.
Davis, Natalie Zemon
Edmondson, Jonathan C.
Endicott, Stephen L.
Ernst, Joseph Albert
Estes, James Martin
Fernie, J. Donald
Finlayson, Michael G.
Fleming, Patricia L.
French, Goldwin S.
Gentles, Ian
Gervers, Michael
Goffart, Walter A.
Golombek, Lisa
Granatstein, Jack L.
Grayson, Albert K.
Greer, Allan R.
Gwyn, Alexandra
Harrison, Timothy P.
Hillgarth, Jocelyn Nigel
Howarth, Thomas
Hughes, Andrew
Iacovetta, Franca
Ingham, John Norman
Israel, Milton
Johnson, Robert E.
Johnson, William M.
Keep, John L. H.
Klein, Martin A.
Kolko, Gabriel
Kornberg, Jacques
Lachan, Katharine
Legge, Elizabeth
Lightman, Bernard V.
Lovejoy, Paul E.
Mason, Steve
Mcintire, Carl Thomas
Mertins, Detlef
Monet, Jacques
Moore, Christopher H.
Mowat, Farley
Nigosian, Solomon Alexander
Normore, Calvin Gerard
Ouellet, Fernand
Pierson, Ruth
Powicke, Michael Rhys
Rix, Brenda
Robson, Ann W.
Rutherford, Paul F. W.
Sadlier, Rosemary
Saywell, John T.
Shaw, Joseph Winterbotham
Silcox, David P.
Swinton, Katherine E.
Thornton, Archibald Paton
Tushingham, Arlotte Douglas
Waddams, Stephen M.
Webster, Donald B.
Webster, Jill
Weinrib, Ernest Joseph
Welsh-Ovcharov, Bogomila M.
Wilson, Ian E.
Winsor, Mary Pickard
Zemans, Joyce P.

Waterloo
Boire, Gary
Comacchio, Cynthia
Copp, John T.
Cornell, Paul G.
Cristi, Renato
Forsyth, Phyllis
Freed, Joann
Harrigan, Patrick Joseph
Klaassen, Walter
Lorimer, Douglas
Lorimer, Joyce
MacGillivray, Royce C.
McLaughlin, Ken
Mitchinson, Wendy
Packull, Werner O.
Rummel, Erika
Schaus, Gerald
Sibalis, Michael
Simpson, Chris
Snyder, Arnold C.
Stortz, Gerry
Wahl, Jim
Zeller, Suzanne

Whitby
Murray, Joan

Willowdale
Woods, Joseph Michael

Windsor
Bird, Harold Wesley
Klein, Owen
McCrone, Kathleen E.
Murray, Jacqueline
Tucker, Bruce

Woodville
Fleming, Rae B.

PRINCE EDWARD ISLAND

Charlottetown
Bolger, Francis W. P.
Cregier, Don Mesick
Robb, Stewart A.

QUEBEC

Aylmer
Trudel, Marcel

Downtown
Lusignan, Serge

Hull
McGhee, Robert J.
Russell, Hilary A.

Laval
Roberge, Rene-Michel

Montreal
Anctil, Pierre
Asselin, Olivier
Bates, Donald G.
Bayley, C. C.
Beaudoin-Ross, Jacqueline
Belisle, Jean
Bode, Frederick August
Boker, Hans J.
Carr, Graham
Chalk, Frank
Chausse, Gilles
Cote, Joanne
Culter, Suzanne
Dean, Kenneth
Decarie, Graeme
Domaradzki, Theodore F.
Dunlop, Anne
Durocher, Rene
Fahmy-Eid, Nadia
Fick, Carolyn E.
Fong, Grace
Foss, Brian
Galavaris, George
Galvaris, George
Glen, Thomas L.
Hill, John
Hoffman, Peter C. W.
Hould, Claudette
Hubbard, William H.
Hudson, Robert
Ingram, Norman
Kirby, Torrance W.
LaMarre, Thomas
Larouche, Michel
Lehuu, Isabel
Lemieux, Lucien
Lesser, Gloria
McSheffrey, Shannon
Merken, Kathleen
Miller, Carman I.
Morton, Desmond D. P.
Nish, Cameron
Orr, Leslie
Pedersen, Diana
Robert, Jean-Claude
Robinson, Ira
Rudin, Ronald
Sanders, Lionel
Schade, Rosemarie
Scheinberg, Stephen
Schoenauer, Norbert
Shlosser, Franziska E.
Shubert, Howard
Singer, Martin
Tittler, Robert
van Nus, Walter
Vipond, Mary
Vogel, Robert
Yates, Robin D. S.

Outremont
Potvin, Gilles E. J.

Quebec
Valois, Raynald

Saint-Jerome
Toupin, Robert

St-Joseph-de-la-rive
des Gagniers, Jean

Ste. Foy
Auger, Reginald
Dumont, Micheline
Fortin, Michel

SASKATCHEWAN

Regina
Bismanis, Maija

Saskatoon
Bietenholz, Peter Gerard
Fairbairn, Brett T.
Hayden, James Michael
Miller, James R.
Miquelon, Dale B.
Porter, John R.

OTHER COUNTRIES

AUSTRALIA
Rothenberg, Gunther Eric

ENGLAND
Heilbron, John L.
Betz, Mark W.
Martines, Lauro
Pagel, Ulrich

SCOTLAND
Graham, Joyce